CANADIAN ALMANAC & DIRECTORY

RÉPERTOIRE ET ALMANACH CANADIEN

2013

Additional Publications

For more detailed information or to place an order, see the back of the book.

ASSOCIATIONS CANADA 2012

Le répertoire des associations du Canada 2012
2104 pages, 8 1/2 x 11, Hardcover
33rd edition, February 2012
ISBN 978-1-59237-919-4
ISSN 1186-9798

Nearly 20,000 entries profile Canadian and international organizations active in Canada. Over 2,000 subject classifications index activities, professions and interests served by associations. Includes listings of NGOs, institutes, coalitions, social agencies, federations, foundations, trade unions, fraternal orders, political parties. Fully indexed by subject, geographic location, electronic addresses, executive name, acronym, mailing list availability, conferences and publications.

CANADIAN PARLIAMENTARY GUIDE 2012

Guide parlementaire canadien
1224 pages, 6 x 9, Hardcover
ISBN 978-1-59237-920-0
ISSN 0315-6168

Published annually since before Confederation, this indispensable guide to government in Canada provides information on Federal and Provincial governments, with biographical sketches of government members, descriptions of government institutions, and historical text and charts. With significant bilingual sections, the Guide covers elections from Confederation to the present, including the most recent provincial elections.

CANADIAN ENVIRONMENTAL RESOURCE GUIDE 2012-2013

Guide des ressources environnementales canadiennes
1590 pages, 8 1/2 x 11, Softcover
17th edition, July 2012
ISBN 978-1-59237-923-1
ISSN 1187-1202

Canada's most complete and ONLY national listing of environmental Associations and Organizations, Governmental Regulators and Purchasing Groups, Product and Service Companies, Special Libraries, and more! All indexed and categorized for quick and easy reference. Also included are companies registered by ISO 9001, 9002, 9003 and 14001.

FINANCIAL SERVICES CANADA 2012-2013

Services financiers au Canada
1612 pages, 8 1/2 x 11, Softcover
14th edition, May 2012
ISBN 978-1-59237-921-7

This directory of Canadian financial institutions and organizations includes banks and depository institutions, non-depository institutions, investment management firms, financial planners, insurance companies, accountants, major law firms, government and regulatory agencies, and associations. Fully indexed.

GOVERNMENTS CANADA 2012

Gouvernements du Canada
954 pages, 8 1/2 x 11, Softcover
ISBN 978-1-59237-986-6
ISSN 1493-3918
Governments Canada provides a solution to finding the departments and people that you are searching for within our federal and provincial political system.

LIBRARIES CANADA 2012-2013

Bibliothèques Canada
950 pages, 8 1/2 x 11, Softcover
27th edition, August 2012
ISBN 978-1-59237-922-4
ISSN 1191-1603

Offers comprehensive information on Canadian libraries, resource centres, business information centres, professional associations, regional library systems, archives, library schools, government libraries, and library technical programs.

CANADIAN ALMANAC & DIRECTORY

RÉPERTOIRE ET ALMANACH CANADIEN

2013

166th YEAR

Grey House Publishing Canada
PUBLISHER: Leslie Mackenzie
GENERAL MANAGER: Bryon Moore
MANAGING EDITOR: Tannys Williams
ASSOCIATE EDITORS: Jodelle Faye de Jesus, Janet Hawtin, Jill McCullough, Stuart Paterson
OPERATIONS & MARKETING COORDINATOR: Caitlin Beatty

Grey House Publishing
EDITORIAL DIRECTOR: Laura Mars
MARKETING DIRECTOR: Jessica Moody
PRODUCTION MANAGER & COMPOSITION: Kristen Thatcher

CONTRIBUTOR: Maj. (Ret.) Richard K. Malott, C.D., M.Sc., B.A., F.R.P.S.C., F.R.P.S.L., A.H.F. (British & Commonwealth Honours)

Grey House Publishing Canada
555 Richmond Street West, Suite 301
Toronto, ON M5V 3B1
866-433-4739
FAX 416-644-1904
www.greyhouse.ca
e-mail: info@greyhouse.ca

Printed in Canada by Webcom Inc.

166th edition published 2012
ISBN: 978-1-59237-988-0
ISSN: 0068-8193
Cataloguing in Publication data is available from Library and Archives Canada

Introduction

First published 166 years ago as *Canadian Mercantile Almanac for 1847,* the *Canadian Almanac & Directory* is now published by Grey House Publishing Canada. The 2013 edition of this significant work includes over 44,000 entries covering hundreds of topics, making this the number one reference for collected facts and figures about Canada.

The *Almanac* continues to be widely used by business professionals, government officials, information specialists, researchers, publishers, and anyone needing current, accessible information on all topics relevant to those who live and work in Canada. This latest edition provides the most comprehensive picture of Canada, from physical attributes to economic and business summaries to leisure and recreation. It combines textual material, charts, colour photographs and directory listings. This 2013 edition includes hundreds more listings and thousands more details than its predecessor. The comprehensiveness and currency of data is unparalleled.

Each of the 17 sections in this year's *Almanac* includes a detailed Table of Contents, outlining hundreds of subcategories. A *Topical Table of Contents* on the following pages and a comprehensive *Entry Name Index* at the end of the work make navigation of the massive amount of material easier than ever before.

Section 1: Almanac comprises 10 major categories, including History, Geography, Science, Awards & Regulations, Economics, Vital Statistics and more. Readers will find articles, colour maps and photographs, charts and tables for a fact-filled snapshot of Canada. This resource section, invaluable for residents, politicians, and the business community, includes a detailed Table of Contents for easy access.

DIRECTORY SECTIONS

Section 2: Arts & Culture includes nine categories: Aquaria, Art Galleries, Botanical Gardens, Museums, National Parks, Observatories, Performing Arts, Science Centres and Zoos. Categories are arranged by province and city. All listings include address, phone, fax, website, email, key executives and a brief description.

Section 3: Associations lists thousands of associations and organizations arranged in 113 topics from Accounting to Writers. Each listing includes valuable descriptions and current contact information. An Association Name Index precedes the listings.

Section 4: Broadcasting begins with Canada's Major Broadcasting Companies, then lists, by Province, all Radio and Television Stations, as well as Cable Companies and Specialty Broadcasters.

Section 5: Business & Finance combines Accounting, Banking, Insurance, and Canada's Major Companies and Stock Exchanges. It includes a separate section for Major Accounting Firms with company descriptions.

Section 6: Education is arranged by Province, and includes Government Agencies, Districts, Specialized and Independent Schools, University and Technical facilities, many with valuable descriptions.

Section 7: Federal Government begins with a Quick Reference Guide to help you find your way around government agencies. The Guide is followed by Federal and Provincial listings, plus information on The Royal Family and Foreign Diplomatic Representation.

Section 8: Municipal Government details all County and Municipal Districts and segregated Major Municipalities. All profiles include date of incorporation, square miles, and population figures. Also included are District Maps for all Provinces.

Section 9: Judicial Government provides thorough coverage for Courts in Canada, including Federal and Provincial. Listings are categorized by type of Court and City within each Province, and include presiding judges.

Section 10: Hospitals and Health Care Facilities is an overview of available facilities by Province. Government agencies, hospitals, community health centres, retirement care and mental health facilities, are all arranged alphabetically by city for easy access.

Originairement publié sous le nom « Canadian Mercantile Almanac for 1847 » il y a 166 ans, le *Répertoire et Almanach Canadien* est maintenant publié par Grey House Publishing Canada. L'édition 2013 comprend plus de 44 000 entrées couvrant des centaines de sujets, faisant de ce répertoire l'*Almanach* le plus complet jamais publié sur les faits et données concernant le Canada.

Le *Répertoire et Almanach Canadien* continu d'être largement consulté par les éditeurs, les gens d'affaires, les bureaux gouvernementaux, les spécialistes de l'information, les chercheurs et par tous ceux qui ont besoin d'une information à jour et facilement accessible sur tous les sujets imaginables concernant le travail et la vie au Canada. La présente édition brosse le tableau le mieux documenté qui soit du Canada en un seul volume, comprenant ses attributs physiques et économiques en passant par les activités commerciales, les divertissements et les loisirs qu'on y pratique. Il constitue un amalgame exceptionnel de textes, de chartes, de photographies couleur et de listes de répertoire. Cette édition comprend un plus grand nombre de données, de profils détaillés et des quantités de mises à jour.

En plus d'offrir un contenu plus riche en information, l'*Almanach* est restructuré de manière à faciliter la recherche. Des tables des matières détaillées pour chacune des 17 sections, une *Table des matières par sujets,* et un *Index par nom* détaillé, rendent la consultation de ces données imposantes plus aisée et accessible que jamais.

La section 1 : Almanach s'étend maintenant sur 10 catégories, dont Histoire, Géographie, Science, Prix et citations, Économies et Mensurations. Il contient plus d'articles, de cartes et de photographies couleur, de chartes et de tableaux qui offrent un portrait juste et à jour des faits et données importants sur le Canada. Elle constitue une source unique de renseignements pour tous les citoyens, les politiciens et les communautés d'affaires. Les tables des matières détaillées de chacune des catégories rendent maintenant la consultation plus facile.

RÉPERTOIRES

La section 2 : Arts et Culture comprend neuf matières principales, des galeries d'art aux parcs zoologiques. Les renseignements y sont regroupés par province et par ville. Chaque entrée comprend des données d'identification, dont l'adresse, numéros de téléphone et télécopieur, site Internet, courriel, cadres, ainsi qu'une brève description.

La section 3 : Associations répertorie des milliers d'associations et d'organismes regroupés sous 113 catégories. Chaque entrée comprend des données d'identification, dont celles de contacts. Un index par nom au début des catégories facilite la recherche.

La section 4 : Radiodiffusion et télédiffusion présente une liste des principales sociétés de radiodiffusion et télédiffusion au pays suivie des listes, par province, des stations de radio et de télévision ainsi que des entreprises de distribution par câble et des émetteurs spécialisés.

La section 5 : Affaires et finance comprend de l'information sur les cabinets comptables, les banques, les compagnies d'assurances, les plus grandes sociétés canadiennes et les bourses. Comprend aussi une liste des principaux cabinets de comptables et une description des sociétés répertoriées.

La section 6 : Éducation est divisée par province et donne des renseignements sur les agences gouvernementales, les commissions scolaires, les écoles privées et spécialisées, les institutions universitaires, collégiales et techniques. Vous y trouverez également plusieurs autres renseignements d'intérêts en matière d'éducation.

La section 7 : Gouvernement fédéral commence par un Guide de références rapide qui vous aidera à trouver votre chemin parmi la multitude d'agences gouvernementales répertoriées, suivi de leurs listes au niveau du pays et des provinces. Cette section comprend également les plus récents résultats d'élection de l'année 2008. Vous y trouverez de plus de l'information sur la Famille royale et les délégations diplomatiques à l'étranger.

La section 8 : Gouvernement municipal fournit de l'information sur les comtés, les municipalités régionales de comté et les principales villes canadiennes. Chaque profil a été revu pour y incorporer la date d'incorporation, la superficie et la population approximative. Vous trouverez aussi des cartes de comtés de chaque province.

Section 11: Law Firms includes a separate section of Major Law Firms with descriptions and Senior Partners. Following the Majors are law firms arranged by Province.

Section 12: Libraries begins with Canada's main Library/Archive and Government Departments for Libraries. Provincial listings follow, with Regional Systems listed first, then Public Libraries and Archives.

Section 13: Publishing includes Publishers—Book, Magazine, Newspapers—and Newspapers by Province. Magazine listings are arranged in six major categories, preceded by a Magazine Name Index for easy searching. Details include frequency and circulation figures.

Section 14: Religion starts off with broad information on religious groups, then lists Associations, arranged alphabetically by 18 denominations.

Section 15: Sports provides Associations for 88, plus detailed League and Team listings for Baseball, Basketball, Football, Hockey, Lacrosse and Soccer. You'll also find the major sports venues in Canada, both stadiums and racetracks.

Section 16: Transportation offers comprehensive listings for major transportation modes, plus industry Associations, Government Agencies and Port Authorities.

Section 17: Utilities includes Associations, Government Agencies and Provincial Utility Companies.

In addition, this edition of the *Canadian Almanac & Directory* includes a **Topical Table of Contents** in the front of the book, and a comprehensive **Entry Index** in the back of the book. These documents, used together with the three indexes in the body of the work, and the tables of contents for each individual section, make easy work of finding exactly what you are looking for.

The *Canadian Almanac & Directory 2013* is also available as part of **Grey House Publishing Canada's Canada Information Resource Center (CIRC)** on the web (www.greyhouse.ca) where subscribers have full access to this rich database right at their computer. Trial subscriptions are available to the CIRC database by calling 866-433-4739.

We acknowledge the valuable contributions of those individuals and organizations that have responded to our information gathering process. Their help and responses to our phone calls, faxes and questionnaires are greatly appreciated.

Every effort has been made to assure the accuracy of the information included in this edition of the *Canadian Almanac & Directory*. Do not hesitate to contact the editorial offices in Toronto with comments, or if revisions are necessary.

La section 9 : Gouvernement - Juridique dresse la liste de tous les tribunaux judiciaires au Canada, tant fédéraux que provinciaux. Les renseignements y sont regroupés par genre de tribunal et par ville, au niveau de chaque province. On y trouve également le nom des juges actuellement en fonction.

La section 10 : Hôpitaux et soins de santé donne une vue d'ensemble des établissements de santé par province. Pour simplifier la consultation, les agences gouvernementales, les hôpitaux, les centres de santé communautaire, les centres de santé mentale et les établissements de soins de longues durées pour personnes âgées sont regroupés par ville, en ordre alphabétique.

La section 11 : Bureaux d'avocats inclue une sous-section détaillant les principaux cabinets d'avocats au Canada et donnant une brève description de ceux-ci et de leurs principaux associés. Vient ensuite, la liste des bureaux d'avocats regroupés par province.

La section 12 : Bibliothèque présente en premier lieu les principales bibliothèques au Canada et les bibliothèques gouvernementales et d'archives. On y trouve ensuite des renseignements sur les bibliothèques, par province, où sont décrits les systèmes régionaux, suivis des principales bibliothèques publiques et d'archives.

La section 13 : Édition fournit de l'information, détaillé par province, sur les éditeurs des livres, magazines et journaux, ainsi que les quotidiens et autres journaux. La nomenclature des magazines est présentée en six catégories précédées d'un index par nom pour faciliter la recherche. Plusieurs données ont été ajoutées dont celles concernant la fréquence de publication et le tirage.

La section 14 : Religion fournit une vaste quantité d'informations sur les groupements religieux, suivie de celles sur les dix-huit principales confessions.

La section 15 : Sports fournit des principales informations sur 88 associations et des catégories de sportset des données sur les ligues et équipes de baseball, basketball, football, hockey, lacrosse et soccer. Vous y trouverez aussi des renseignements sur les majeures installations sportives du Canada comprenant les stades et les pistes de course.

La section 16 : Transport donne une liste détaillée des principaux modes de transport et organismes œuvrant dans le domaine au pays, ainsi qu'une liste des associations de l'industrie, des agences gouvernementales et des autorités portuaires.

La section 17 : Services publics regroupe sous un même chapitre les associations, les agences gouvernementales et les entreprises œuvrant dans les services publics de chaque province.

De plus, la présente édition du *Répertoire et Almanach Canadien* profite d'une **Table des matières par sujets** au début du volume, et un **Index par nom** à la fin du volume, avec référence au numéro de la page où se trouve l'information. Ces index, qui s'ajoute aux trois autres index contenus dans le répertoire, ont été incorporés pour faciliter davantage votre consultation.

Le *Répertoire et Almanach Canadien 2013* fait partie des vaste données électroniques du **Canada Information Resource Centre (CIRC) de Grey House Publishing Canada** (www.greyhouse.ca) auquel les abonnés peuvent avoir accès de leur ordinateur personnel. Vous pouvez obtenir un abonnement d'essai aux données du CIRC en composant le 866 433-4739.

Nous tenons à souligner la précieuse contribution des personnes et des organismes qui ont collaboré tout au long de l'année à notre procédé de cueillette d'information; votre aide, vos réponses à notre questionnaire dans les délais impartis, nos appels téléphoniques et nos envois par télécopieur sont grandement appréciés.

Nous avons mis tous les efforts pour nous assurer de l'exactitude de l'information contenue dans cette édition du *Répertoire et Almanach Canadien.* N'hésitez pas à communiquer avec le bureau de la rédaction pour faire part de vos commentaires ou si des modifications s'avèrent nécessaires.

Table of Contents

Table des matières

Topical Table of Contents

Hospitals & Health Care Facilities

Legal

Religion

Science

Sports & Recreation

Tourism

Transportation

Utilities

Table des Matières par Sujets

SECTION 1

ALMANAC

History

History of Canada

Over the past 400 years, Canada has evolved from a sparsely populated trading post to the tenth-richest sovereign power in the world. It stands alone as the only country to separate from its colonial power through peaceful means.

The political boundary of what is now known as Canada recorded thousands of years of history before European colonization, but was one of the last places on Earth to host human habitation. While modern *Homo sapiens* emerged from the eastern region of Africa 200,000 years ago, most scientists agree that it took another 175,000 years for humans to find their way across the ice bridge that once joined Alaska and Eastern Siberia. The land that now constitutes Canada has seen the longest period of human habitation in the New World: from the original migration 25,000 years ago came all the indigenous cultures of North and South America including the Arctic Inuit, Blackfoot, Cree, Algonquin, Dene, and Iroquois League of Five Nations. Estimates put the number of native peoples in the United States and Canada before European contact at about two million.

Columbus may have been given credit for the "discovery" of America in 1492, but proof exists that Vikings voyaged to Greenland and further west as early as 982 A.D. Archeological evidence points to Norse settlements in Newfoundland at L'Anse aux Meadows dating back to approximately 1000 A.D., making Canada the actual site of the European discovery of North America. The Vikings, however, were not concerned with permanent colonization, only Canadian natural resources. By the time Christopher Columbus arrived, the Norse settlements had been abandoned.

With Christopher Columbus came the European fervour of colonizing the New World. Seeking a way to circumvent the long land trade routes to Asian goods by crossing the Atlantic to what he thought was India, Columbus inadvertently began the Age of Discovery. European powers established colonies, seeking spice, gold, slaves, and new crops, as well as the promotion of Christianity among the native peoples. The earlier colonies, mostly Spanish and Portuguese, were concentrated in South America, Central America, and the Caribbean. England and France, however, turned their attention north. John Cabot, an Italian-born English explorer, is credited as being the first European explorer after the Vikings to set foot in North America. Although this exploration occurred only five years after Columbus's discoveries, it was not until 1605 that permanent settlements were established. Many explorers, including Henry Hudson, still attempted to find the Northwest Passage, a reputed waterway through the New World to Asia. The reasons for this 100-year gap have more to do with European affairs than those of the New World.

Two events slowed the colonization of North America: religious unrest and war in Europe. In 1517, Martin Luther distributed his list of 95 grievances against the Catholic Church by means of a new invention, the printing press. Thus began the Protestant Reformation. This schism was to have far-reaching consequences across all of European history, but in the short term, it created rancorous religious strife. Most of Europe turned inward to deal with unrest and religious crisis. Escalating political conflicts enveloped most of Western Europe for decades, drawing resources away from colonization efforts. The French Wars of Religion, the Italian Wars, and popular uprisings combined with new religious uprisings to turn the attention of Europe away from the New World for more than a century.

France looked to North America as the best possible source of wealth and power and as a relief from war debt. When French explorer Jacques Cartier sailed up the St. Lawrence River in 1534, he claimed the territory for France, and gave it the name it still bears today: Canada. Once fur traders arrived in Eastern Canada in the 1500s, France monopolized the fur trade. While the French made an effort to establish friendly trading relations with the native population, the Iroquois in particular proved openly hostile. Conflicts with local tribes soon convinced the crown that if traders were to make a profit in Canada, a permanent military and civilian presence was essential. King Henry IV sent his royal "hydrographer," Samuel de Champlain to map the region.

In 1605, after exploring the coast of North America as far south as Cape Cod, Champlain established the first permanent French settlement at Port Royal, and in 1608 he founded Quebec City. New France, as it was then called, grew slowly, mainly due to disinterest from the mainland and war with the Iroquois. The settlers survived attacks from native peoples through their alliance with the Algonquin, Montagnais, and Huron peoples. These alliances not only secured their survival, but greatly increased France's control of the fur trade. Europeans had little experience in the thick wilderness of the area, an expertise that the native peoples supplied.

Once again religious tensions in Europe interfered with Canada's settlement and growth. By the mid-seventeenth century, while England's American and Caribbean colonies grew self-sufficient, New France remained underpopulated. The struggling colony drained France's resources. The French crown decided to take action by creating land incentives for emigrants to New France. Only one caveat stood in the way: all settlers must be Roman Catholic, or convert to Roman Catholicism before leaving Europe. This change of policy, undertaken at the urging of the fanatical Catholic Cardinal Richelieu, closest advisor to King Louis XIII, created friction. Previously, French Protestants, especially the persecuted sect known as Huguenots, had fled to New France to escape religious persecution. Cardinal Richelieu's new edict would have a lasting impact on the religious and political makeup of modern Canada.

In the late seventeenth century, English and French colonies in the New World began to take a stronger foothold. Both nations finally saw a large-scale financial return on their investments, but a war in Europe again infringed on Canada's nascent growth. New France, already in the middle of brutal intertribal warfare with the Algonquins, conflicted with the Iroquois confederacy opposing them. With the War of the Grand Alliance in 1688, which pitted France against almost all of continental Europe, the Iroquois began to receive English weapons as part of government policy. This escalation by the English heightened the already bloody warfare. English armies and their Iroquois allies captured Port Royal, but were turned back from Quebec City, due mainly to a decimation of forces by disease. The war eventually petered out, and a peace was signed in 1697. The Iroquois, however, continued the fight without British help, and eventually suffered a series of major defeats, forcing them to sue for peace four years later.

New France, and thereby Canada, seemed securely in the mother country's domain following the end of the War of the Grand Alliance. However, France's control of the region was not to last. Queen Anne's War, which began only a year after the French peace with the Iroquois, lead England to claim Nova Scotia and Newfoundland, as well as the rights to the land surrounding Hudson Bay. Fighting broke out again three decades later in 1744, in a battle known as King George's War, but neither side was able to enlarge their colonial positions.

By 1754 the long-standing animosity between the English and French seeped into the New World, culminating in the Seven Years War, known in the Americas as the French and Indian War. The causes of the conflict were threefold. The lucrative fur trade, rich fishing grounds, ample lumber, and mineral deposits all promised great wealth to whoever controlled Canada. Secondly, the fiercely anti-Catholic British felt that the Protestant French were heretics, a feeling that was reciprocated by the French. Thirdly, possession of colonies overseas could be used as diplomatic bargaining chips should the war in Europe go badly.

The Seven Years War was the first worldwide war, fought on five continents: North America, South America, Africa, Europe and Asia. More than a million died, and the war resulted in a complete change in the power structure of the New World. Britain gained all of France's colonial possessions in North America, and Canada became a British colony. However, 150 years of French colonization didn't disappear overnight. Even today, French-English relations in Canada can be contentious.

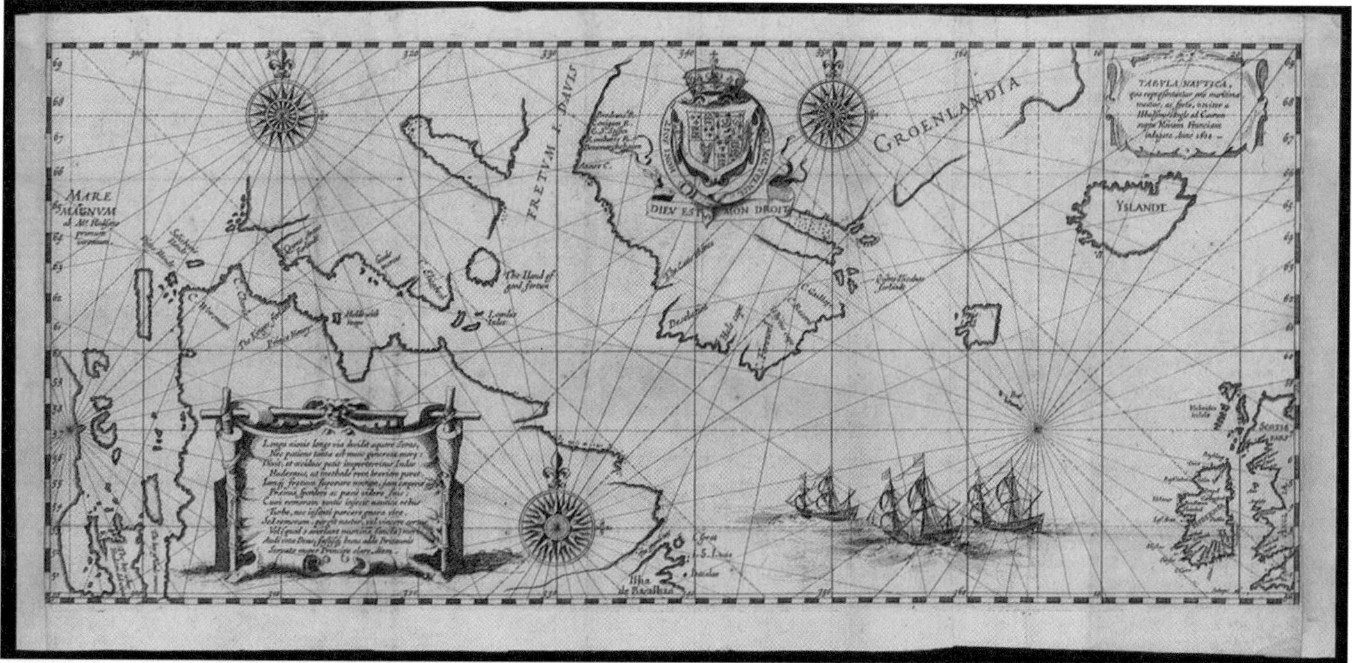

Henry Hudson arrived in Arctic waters in 1610 determined to find the Northwest Passage. He explored Hudson Bay and the mouth of the Bay. His crew mutinied and abandoned him in 1611 and returned to Europe. This map by Dutch cartographer Gerritsz is based on Hudson's discoveries.

Champlain's Map 1632

The British, upon taking control of Canada in 1764, left intact the religious and economic systems already in place, to the relief of the Catholic French colonists. The Quebec Act of 1774 allowed a separate system of French law to continue in Quebec. The British now controlled the entire eastern half of North America, from the eastern seaboard to the Mississippi River. However, George III's mistreatment of the American colonies would soon cause a shift in the balance of power in the New World.

As a base for the British forces, a refuge for fleeing Americans loyal to the British crown, and a source of militia for both the British and American armies, Canada played a large role in the American Revolution. The American army originally attempted to convince Canada to join their revolution but Canadians had just finished rebuilding after the Seven Years War and most did not want no take part in another feud. On June 27, 1775, American troops attacked Quebec and Montreal was taken without a fight. The attack on Quebec City was eventually defeated and in 1776, the American troops evacuated Montreal.

When America gained independence from Britain in 1783, citizens loyal to the British Empire were exiled. Over 35,000 of these loyalists flooded into Nova Scotia. This massive influx prompted the British government to divide Nova Scotia, creating the new colony of New Brunswick. Soon, the loyalists in Quebec were also making demands for their own colony, while the French Canadians were equally determined to have their own elected assembly. In 1791, Quebec was divided into Upper Canada and Lower Canada in order to meet the distinct needs of the English loyalists and the French Canadians.

Tensions between Britain and America remained high in the proceeding decades, and once again a conflict erupted that ensnared Canada. The United States declared war on Britain in 1812 over the arming and supplying of hostile Native American tribes and the forced conscription of American sailors into the British Navy. Canada became one of the primary battlegrounds in this conflict, with the United States planning to seize Canada and use it as leverage against the British. America expected support from the people of Canada, who they assumed were unhappy under English colonial rule. However, many Canadians at that time were children of British loyalists who fled America and saw the United States as invaders and occupiers.

The American army suffered a loss early in the war when they were soundly defeated by General Isaac Brock and his force of Indian allies and local military men at the Battle of Queenston Heights. But the American army did go on to occupy and loot many cities, including York (now Toronto) and Newark (now Niagara-on-the-Lake), eventually controlling much of present day Ontario and Quebec. Ultimately, the American army was driven back, and although the war ended with no real victor, the fact that an attempted American takeover had been thwarted gave Canadians confidence and stimulated national pride.

While Canadians rejected the idea of American invaders on their soil, the political example of the United States resonated throughout the country. Rebellions broke out against the British in 1837. Canadians, angry over the unfair distribution of wealth derived from Canada's natural resources, balked against not being represented in the British government. Based on the opinion of the British that friction between the French and English people was causing conflict in Canada, all of the Canadian colonies were merged together into the United Province of Canada in 1840. In 1849 the United States and the British Empire agreed that the 49th north parallel would be the boundary between the two nations, and the British extended Canada to the western seaboard, encompassing British Columbia.

Canadian independence had been debated in Britain and in Canada almost since the American Revolution. Some advocated violent revolution and total Canadian independence. Others wanted a slower, more gradual autonomy. On July 1st, 1867, the British parliament passed the British North America Act, which established The Dominion of Canada as a separate and self-governing colony. While it was not completely severed from England, especially in matters of foreign policy, domestically, Canada was allowed free reign.

During the next decades, Canada continued to expand westward. With the purchase of two huge northern territories, The North-Western Territory and Rupert's Land, from the Hudson Bay Company, the country more than doubled its size. The sections of Canada west of Ontario housed a large population of French-speaking, Catholic Métis, the children of indigenous people and white settlers. After the sale of Rupert's Land, many settlers from Ontario flooded into the region hoping to claim land. The Métis became worried that this influx of mostly English Protestant settlers would threaten their rights to language, religion and land. The Métis leader Louis Riel organized the Red River Resistance in 1869 in order to ensure that these rights were guaranteed. The revolt led to the creation of Manitoba, a province with strong laws protecting the Métis, French-speaking people and Catholics. By 1905, the founding provinces of Upper and Lower Canada, New Brunswick, and Nova Scotia were soon joined by British Columbia, Saskatchewan, Prince Edward Island, and Alberta.

The construction of a transcontinental railroad, completed in 1885, spurred Canada's expansion. While the railroad enabled additional settlers to move west into the new provinces, it also pushed the Native people aside. Again rebellion flared, resulting in more bloodshed. The sentiment that the Canadian government didn't heed the concerns of French-speaking Catholic citizens caused a political crisis resulting in the resignation of prime minister Mackenzie Bowell in 1896, when the government tried to ban French as an official language of Manitoba, contrary to the laws of the province.

Both Canada and the United States shared a period of western expansion in the late nineteenth century, based on the prominence of the railroad, the promise of free land and the discovery of mineral deposits. These factors, joined with a large influx of European immigrants, led to Canada becoming the fastest-growing economy in the world between 1896 and 1911. During that time, the Canadian government created the Yukon Territory, a land mass about the size of Germany, Austria and Switzerland combined, then populated by only 8,500 people.

On the verge of the twentieth century, Canada faced the first serious conflict with its colonial power. When Britain entered the Boer War in 1899, most English-speaking Canadians supported bringing South Africa into the fold of the British Empire. French Canadians, however, had little interest in British imperialism, seeing themselves as a separate concern, only nominally part of the Empire. As a compromise, volunteers were allowed to serve in the Boer War, but the Canadian Army stayed uninvolved. The view of French Canada as a separate entity, exacerbated by rebellion and anti-French laws of the past decades, would continue to play out in Canadian politics in years to come.

Arctic regions 1953

Although many French Canadians wanted out from under the British Empire's yoke, the country was still obligated to fall in line with British foreign policy. With the assassination of Archduke Ferdinand on June 28, 1914, Canada was swept into the chaotic system of alliances that created World War I. When Britain declared war on the central powers on August 4th, Canadian troops were called into action. Like most of the allied powers, internal disputes were put aside and support for the war remained high, even among French Canadians. After suffering more than 200,000 dead and wounded casualties out of a population of seven million, support for the war began to wane. By the time the government attempted to introduce conscription in 1917, many Canadians, especially in French Canada, were fiercely anti-war. Despite the popular sentiment, World War I greatly increased the sense of Canadian nationalism and identity, fed by the country's significant role in the largest war mankind had ever known. Massive Canadian casualties in what many Canadians saw as a "British" war also created additional animosity towards the Empire.

World War I radically changed Canada's political landscape. Soldiers returned home from the horrors of the conflict with altered political ideologies. Socialism, communism, trade unionism and other left-wing progressive movements gained traction in the years immediately after the war, as the influx of soldiers returning home caused high unemployment and wage cuts. The Winnipeg General Strike of 1919, the largest of a wave of strikes that swept the country, was violently crushed by police, killing one man and wounding 30. When women's suffrage was enacted nationwide in 1918, the ruling Conservative Party collapsed, partly because of their actions during the strike. The Liberal Party, upon assuming control of the government, enacted many of the original strike committee's demands, including the right to form unions without government permission. Progressive and socialist parties formed in subsequent years, including the Progressive Party of Canada and the Cooperative Commonwealth Federation.

In 1931, the British Parliament passed the Statute of Westminster, establishing all the colonies and dominions of the British Empire, including Canada, Australia, New Zealand, and Ireland as separate legislative entities. This act allowed these countries to write their own constitutions and removed the power of the British Government to legislate in these areas, effectively making them independent, while still being contained in a worldwide British Commonwealth.

When the American Stock Market crashed on Black Tuesday in 1929 kicking off the Great Depression, the Canadian economy soon felt the effects. By 1933, the Canadian gross national product had dropped 40 percent. Manufacturing and farming suffered the most, with the price of wheat, Canada's main export, cut in half. At its worst point in 1933, 30 percent of Canadians were out of work. Newfoundland, deciding that Canadian government policy was the cause of the economic difficulty, voted to leave the Canadian federation and rejoin the British Empire.

When both the Liberal and Conservative parties were unable to produce any solutions to the crisis, many Canadians began to turn to third parties, such as the socialist Cooperative Commonwealth Federation and the Social Credit Party of Canada. After the Conservative government of R.B. Bennett put unemployed men into work camps to offset the great cost of supporting a huge welfare system, the Workers' Unity League put together a massive protest called the "On to Ottawa Trek" in order to call for improved conditions and benefits. Bennett's attempt to repress the Trek resulted in the Regina Riot, and contributed to his defeat in the 1935 election. The new Liberal government did away with the camps and instituted social programs to help lessen the effects of the Depression, but Canada was still severely affected. Almost one-fifth of the population was surviving on government payouts and social support systems. Even after a resurgent boom in Canada's economy, brought on by World War II, these systems remained in place, and continued to evolve.

World War II officially began on September 1, 1939. Canada did not immediately enter the war upon the British declaration as it had in World War I. With its growing independence from England, Canada decided to declare war on its own nine days later. While the Japanese and Nazi onslaught was still in full effect, Canadian supplies and war material were instrumental in keeping Britain from succumbing to German invasion. Once the Allies were in a position to counterattack, Canadian troops were deployed all over the world, and served valiantly in some of the major battles, including the invasion of Sicily and Italy in 1943, the allied landing at Normandy in 1944, the liberation of the Netherlands, and the drive across France and Germany to end the war. However, Canada endured its own share of loss. A predominantly Canadian raid, at Dieppe, France, resulted in more than 3,000 dead, wounded or captured and German U-boats, which prowled Canadian waters, sank many supply ships. In the end, Canada suffered a total of 42,000 casualties.

When the Japanese bombed Pearl Harbor on December 7, 1941, the 22,000 Japanese Canadians then living in British Columbia took the brunt of the resulting pain and anger. The anti-Asian sentiment in the province was further fueled when thousands of Canadians were killed or captured in the Japanese invasion of Hong Kong. In 1942, all people of Japanese descent were sent to internment camps, and after the war, all Japanese

Canadians were deported from British Columbia. It was not until 1949 that they became free to live anywhere in Canada. Japanese Canadians were finally compensated in 1988 for the wrongs that they had suffered during the war.

At the close of World War II, Canada and the United States alone benefited from never having seen fighting on their home soil. Each country was, therefore, in a unique economic position. Due to a revitalized manufacturing sector, the discovery of oil in Alberta, and as the main trading partner to the economic superpower on their southern border, the Canadian economy exploded. This newfound wealth was put into a radical new program of social support. Based upon the centralized welfare state of the late 1930s and early 1940s, as well as many of the policies of the socialist Cooperative Commonwealth Federation, Canadians enjoyed hospital insurance, old-age pensions, veterans' pensions, and family allowance. These progressive social policies convinced Newfoundland to rejoin Canada in a 1949 referendum.

Canada cemented its position in the Cold War with its founding membership in NATO in 1949. The country's fortunes were firmly rooted with the United States. Canada participated in the Korean War, and Canadian troops were stationed in West Germany, on the border of the communist Eastern Bloc. Canada's voting record in the United Nations was not always aligned with the United States, but there is no question that Canada was an American ally pitted against the Soviet Union.

Canada's treatment of its Native peoples has a sad history. As far back as the late 1800s, when the buffalo were hunted almost to extinction and the expansion of the railroad brought more settlers to native territories, First Nations people were treated as second-class citizens. Starvation, assimilation and a crushed rebellion largely put an end to the native resistance movement, but it gained strength again after World War II. Decolonialization and a newfound spirit of democracy was being put forth by the Western powers in their opposition to Soviet tyranny, yet most First Nations people could not vote as late as 1950. In order to vote, First Nations people had to gain suffrage by renouncing their status as "Indians." It was not until 1960 (1969 in Quebec) that all First Nations people were allowed to vote freely.

As Canada entered the 1960s, the government faced growing radicalism and organization among its populace. Quebec nationalism had been growing ever since the British took Canada from the French in 1764. French Canadians saw themselves as a separate nation, and frequently found themselves disagreeing with the policies of the Canadian government. The more radical French Canadian factions felt they were being oppressed, and that their language and culture were under attack. Inspired by revolutions around the world, nationalist and left-wing terrorism began to rise, Canada was not unaffected. The Front de Libération du Québec (FLQ), committed more than 200 bombings, and killed five people in pursuit of an independent Quebec. While violence was rejected by a majority of the population, a genuine desire for independence fueled Québécois protests. When Pierre Elliott Trudeau was elected prime minister in 1968, he declared martial law in Quebec, arresting most members of the FLQ.

While the crisis in Quebec worsened throughout the 1970s, the United States became involved in one of the most controversial conflicts in modern history: the war in Indochina. The Vietnam War resulted in over 1,500,000 dead, and radicalized an entire generation. Canada was no exception. Young people throughout the country protested against what they saw as American imperialism. The Canadian government refused to participate in the war, and granted citizenship to as many as 125,000 American draft dodgers over the course of the conflict. This led to serious friction between the governments of Canada and the US. To this day Vietnam and Canada have a close relationship, and hundreds of thousands of Vietnamese have immigrated to Canada's west coast. The period of the Vietnam War also saw the rise of the New Democratic Party (NDP), the successor to the socialist Cooperative Commonwealth Federation. Since its beginning in 1962, the NDP has altered the balance of Canadian politics, regularly receiving between 10 and 20 percent of the national vote, and often having the ability to form a majority coalition by grouping itself with the winning party. In the 2011 federal election, the NDP had its best result, winning 30 percent of the vote and the role of official opposition for the first time. It has fought for the continuation of Canada's welfare state, a humanitarian foreign policy, and native rights.

Young people across Canada became increasingly involved in politics as a result of the Vietnam War, and this new political awareness allowed the question of Quebec sovereignty to be addressed. The Parti Québécois was formed in 1968 and elected to govern Quebec in 1976, making French the official language of the province in 1977. Finally, the party made good on its biggest promise and introduced a referendum to decide Quebec's fate. The actual referendum simply said that Quebec would "negotiate a new agreement with the rest of Canada, based on the equality of nations; this agreement would enable Quebec to acquire the exclusive power to make its laws, levy its taxes and establish relations abroad - in other words, sovereignty." The fact that the referendum did not advocate full independence, in combination with a full-out public relations assault from the federal government, doomed the referendum.

While Canada became a sovereign entity in 1867, and had its independence increased in 1931, it was not technically a separate nation. Canada could not make amendments to its own constitution and the power of Canada to act directly against the wishes of the British government was in question. In 1982, Trudeau finally sealed Canada's status as its own unique nation by signing the Canada Act and the Charter of Rights and Freedoms. Although still a member of the British Commonwealth, Canada was now free from control by the British parliament.

With Canada's complete independence from Britain, the question of trade with the United States became central to the Canadian economy. The Canada-United States Free Trade Agreement drafted in 1988 set the model for the subsequent North American Free Trade Agreement and Central American Free Trade Agreement. The criticism of the agreement, as well as later free trade agreements, was that by eliminating trade barriers, Canadian consumers and labour unions would be at the mercy of more powerful US corporations. The agreement was a decisive issue in the 1988 elections, with the Liberal Party and NDP in opposition, and the ruling Progressive Conservatives attempting to pass it. A 57 percent majority voted against the Progressive Conservatives, but because they received the most votes for one single party, they were rewarded with the most seats in parliament, and passed the free trade agreement.

The Parti Québécois, after failing in its referendum of 1980, had formed a national party, the Bloc Québécois, and doggedly pursued its agenda of an independent Quebec. A second referendum, called in 1995, created an even bigger debate than the referendum of 1980, with massive media campaigns on both sides of the issue. When the vote finally came up, it failed by a slim 54,000 votes, but the issue illustrated a true divide in Quebec. Considering that 86,000 ballots were thrown out as invalid, the question of Quebec independence failed by a razor-thin margin, and the probability of it arising again in the future is still possible.

In 1990, in a small town called Oka, west of Montreal, a First Nations revolt led to the intervention of the Canadian Army and three deaths. While this was far from the first violent conflict between First Nations people and the Canadian government, it has marked a new era of militant native resistance. With more than one million people of Aboriginal descent living in Canada, many native organizations have called for more indigenous control over resources in their lands, resulting in violent conflicts between First Nations people and corporations attempting to mine, fish, or harvest lumber. One effect of these protests was the creation of a new territory, Nunavut, in the far north of Canada in 1999. While the population is less than 30,000, more than 85 percent of its inhabitants claim Inuit status, and the territory has adopted many laws securing their rights and claims to land and resources.

Today, Canada continues to deal with its internal relations with French-speaking Canadians and First Nations peoples. As a unified country, it also faces other issues such as participation in peacekeeping missions, drug decriminalization, immigration, global warming, and control over Arctic seaways.

Histoire du Canada

Au cours des 400 dernières années, le Canada est passé de simple poste de traite peu peuplé au dixième état souverain le plus riche au monde. Il s'agit de plus du seul pays à s'être séparé pacifiquement de sa puissance coloniale.

Malgré que le grand territoire composant aujourd'hui le Canada avait déjà une histoire vieille de plusieurs millénaires au début de la colonisation européenne, il a néanmoins été un des derniers endroits au monde à accueillir des populations humaines. Alors que l'*Homo Sapiens* moderne aurait émergé dans l'est de l'Afrique il y a 200 000 ans, la majorité des scientifiques conviennent qu'il aura fallu 175 000 années de plus pour que les hommes traversent le pont de glace reliant jadis l'Alaska et l'est de la Sibérie. Sur ce nouveau continent, c'est l'espace que délimitent les frontières canadiennes actuelles qui est habité depuis le plus longtemps; la migration originale qui a eu lieu il y a 25 000 ans est la source des cultures indigènes d'Amérique du Nord et du Sud, incluant les Inuits de l'Arctique, les Pieds-Noirs, les Cris, les Algonquins, les Dénés et la Ligue iroquoise des Cinq-Nations. On estime à environ deux millions le nombre d'Autochtones vivant aux États-Unis et au Canada avant l'arrivée des Européens dans le Nouveau Monde.

Christophe Colomb est peut-être celui à qui l'on attribue la « découverte » de l'Amérique en 1492, mais l'on sait aujourd'hui avec certitudes que les Vikings ont atteint et dépassé le Groenland en 982 apr. J.-C. Des traces archéologiques qui dateraient d'environ 1000 ans indiquent la présence à cette époque de peuples norois à L'Anse aux Meadows, à Terre-Neuve, ce qui ferait du Canada le véritable lieu de découverte de l'Amérique du Nord par les Européens. Les Vikings ne visaient pas toutefois à établir une colonisation permanente, mais étaient plutôt intéressés aux ressources naturelles du Canada. Quand Christophe Colomb foula le sol américain pour la première fois, les installations qui y avaient été construites par les peuples norois étaient abandonnées depuis longtemps déjà.

Le voyage de Christophe Colomb déclencha en Europe une course à la colonisation du Nouveau Monde. En traversant l'Atlantique vers ce qu'il croyait être l'Inde pour trouver une voie alternative aux longues routes de commerce terrestres menant à l'Asie et à ses produits, Christophe Colomb donna sans le vouloir le coup d'envoi à l'Ère des grandes découvertes. Les puissances européennes établirent des colonies à la recherche d'épices, d'or, d'esclaves et de nouvelles cultures, ainsi que pour convertir les peuples autochtones au christianisme. Les premières colonies, principalement espagnoles et portugaises, étaient concentrées en Amérique du Sud, en Amérique Centrale et dans les Caraïbes. L'Angleterre et la France ont plutôt tourné leurs efforts vers le Nord. Jean Cabot, un explorateur anglais d'origine italienne, est considéré comme le premier explorateur européen à avoir mis le pied en Amérique du Nord après les Vikings. Bien que cette exploration eut lieu seulement cinq années après les découvertes de Christophe Colomb, il faudra attendre jusqu'en 1605 pour que des installations permanentes soient établies. À cette époque, beaucoup d'explorateurs, dont Henry Hudson, tentaient encore de trouver le passage du Nord-Ouest, la fameuse voie navigable qui devait relier le Nouveau Monde à l'Asie. Si plus de cent ans se sont écoulés avant ces premières installations permanentes, c'est davantage en raison d'événements se déroulant en Europe que de facteurs attribuables au Nouveau Monde.

Deux événements sont venus ralentir la colonisation de l'Amérique du Nord : l'agitation religieuse et la guerre en Europe. En 1517, Martin Luther diffusa sa liste de 95 griefs contre l'Église catholique en utilisant une invention toute nouvelle, la presse à imprimer. Ainsi débuta la réforme protestante. Ce schisme détournera de façon importante le cours de l'Histoire en Europe, mais à court terme, il suscita surtout un conflit religieux tumultueux. Presque toute l'Europe connut un repli sur soi pour faire face à cette agitation ainsi qu'à cette crise religieuse. Des conflits politiques croissants secouèrent la majeure partie de l'Europe de l'Ouest durant des décennies, accaparant les ressources qui auraient dû être attribuées aux efforts de colonisation. Les guerres de religion en France, les guerres en Italie et les révoltes populaires combinées aux soulèvements religieux ont détourné l'attention de l'Europe du Nouveau Monde pendant plus d'un siècle.

La France voyait l'Amérique du Nord comme la meilleure source de richesse et de puissance possible et souhaitait, en exploitant ces contrées, arriver à alléger ses dettes de guerre. Quand l'explorateur français Jacques Cartier navigua sur le fleuve Saint-Laurent en 1534, il revendiqua le territoire au nom de la France et lui donna le nom qu'il porte encore aujourd'hui : le Canada. Après que les commerçants de fourrure se furent implantés dans l'Est du Canada, la France monopolisa le commerce de la fourrure. Bien que les Français tentèrent d'établir des relations commerciales amicales avec les peuples autochtones, certains d'entre eux, dont les Iroquois, se révélèrent particulièrement hostiles. Les conflits avec les tribus locales ont rapidement fait de convaincre la Couronne que pour assurer la rentabilité du commerce au Canada, une présence militaire et civile permanente était essentielle. Le roi Henri IV dépêcha donc sur place son « hydrographe » Samuel de Champlain pour cartographier la région.

En 1605, après avoir exploré la côte de l'Amérique du Nord jusqu'à Cape Cod, Champlain établira un premier peuplement français à Port-Royal et fondera ensuite la ville de Québec en 1608. La Nouvelle-France, comme on l'appelait à l'époque, se développa lentement, principalement en raison du manque d'intérêt de la mère patrie et de la guerre avec les Iroquois. Les colons survécurent aux attaques des Autochtones grâce à leurs alliances avec les Algonquins, les Montagnais et les Hurons. En plus de garantir la survie des colons, ces alliances permirent à la France d'affermir son contrôle du commerce des fourrures. Les Européens n'avaient aucune notion du milieu sauvage de la région, connaissances que les Autochtones leur procureront.

Une fois de plus, des tensions religieuses en Europe vinrent interférer avec le développement des établissements au Canada. Vers le milieu du dix-septième siècle, alors que les colonies anglaises en Amérique et dans les Caraïbes devenaient autosuffisantes, la Nouvelle-France demeurait sous-peuplée. Cette colonie éprouvait des difficultés et épuisait les ressources de la France. La monarchie française décida de prendre les choses en mains en offrant des primes à ceux qui décideraient d'émigrer en Nouvelle-France. Une seule condition s'imposait : tous les colons en partance devaient être catholiques ou se convertir au catholicisme avant de quitter l'Europe. Ce changement de politique, imposé à la demande du fervent cardinal Richelieu, le conseiller le plus proche du roi Louis XIII, créera de nombreuses frictions. Auparavant, les protestants français, particulièrement la secte persécutée connue sous le nom de Huguenots, s'exilaient souvent en Nouvelle-France pour fuir les persécutions religieuses. Ce nouveau décret du cardinal Richelieu aura un effet durable sur la composition politique et religieuse du Canada moderne.

Vers la fin du dix-septième siècle, les assises des colonies anglaises et françaises du Nouveau Monde commençaient enfin à gagner en solidité. Les deux nations avaient remporté leur mise et leurs colonies dégageaient un bon profit, mais une guerre en Europe devait venir gêner une fois de plus la croissance balbutiante du Canada. La Nouvelle-France, déjà au cœur d'une brutale guerre intertribale avec les Algonquins, entra en conflit avec la confédération iroquoise qui s'opposait à elle. Avec la guerre de Neuf Ans, qui débuta en 1688 et vit la France entrer en conflit avec presque tout le reste de l'Europe, les Iroquois commencèrent à recevoir des armes de la part des Anglais, en accord aux politiques de leur gouvernement. Cette escalade de violence des Anglais envenima cette guerre déjà sanglante. L'armée anglaise et ses alliés iroquois capturèrent Port-Royal, mais furent repoussés de Québec, principalement en raison des maladies qui décimaient les forces. La guerre finit par s'essouffler sur le Continent, et un traité de paix fut signé en 1697. Les Iroquois continueront cependant à se battre sans les Britanniques, mais subiront finalement d'importantes défaites qui les forceront à établir la paix quatre ans plus tard.

La Nouvelle-France (et le Canada par le fait même) semblait bien acquise à la mère patrie à la suite de la conclusion de la guerre de Neuf Ans. Toutefois, le contrôle de la région par la France ne durera pas longtemps. La guerre de Succession d'Espagne, qui commencera un an seulement après la signature du traité de paix entre la France et les Iroquois, permettra à l'Angleterre de prendre possession de la Nouvelle-Écosse et de Terre-Neuve, ainsi que des droits sur la région entourant la baie d'Hudson. Un nouveau conflit, nommé la guerre du roi George, débutera trois décennies plus tard, soit en 1744, mais aucun des deux belligérants ne réussira à élargir alors ses positions coloniales.

En 1754, l'animosité de longue date entre les Anglais et les Français gagnera le Nouveau Monde, avec comme point culminant la guerre de Sept Ans, appelée aussi en Amérique guerre franco-indienne. Trois causes principales étaient à la base de ce conflit. D'abord, le lucratif commerce de la fourrure, l'abondance des poissons, la richesse des forêts et les gisements de minerais étaient tous des sources de fortune pour quiconque contrôlerait le Canada. Ensuite, les Anglais, anticatholiques invétérés, croyaient que les Français étaient des hérétiques, un sentiment qui était d'ailleurs réciproque! Enfin, le contrôle des colonies outre-mer pourrait servir comme monnaie d'échange diplomatique si la guerre en Europe devait se détériorer.

La guerre de Sept Ans fut la première guerre à l'échelle mondiale et qui fit rage sur cinq continents : l'Amérique du Nord, l'Amérique du Sud, l'Afrique, l'Europe et l'Asie. Plus d'un million de personnes perdront la vie et la conclusion de cette guerre changera totalement le partage du pouvoir dans le Nouveau Monde. La Grande-Bretagne obtiendra le contrôle de toutes les colonies françaises en Amérique du Nord, faisant ainsi du Canada une colonie britannique. Toutefois, 150 années de colonisation française ne pouvaient disparaître du jour au lendemain. Encore aujourd'hui, les relations entre Anglais et Français au Canada connaissent leurs tensions et contrariétés.

Les Britanniques, suite à leur prise de contrôle du Canada en 1764, ne touchèrent pas aux systèmes religieux et économiques en place, au grand soulagement des colons catholiques français. L'Acte de Québec de 1774 permit qu'un système indépendant de lois françaises continue au Québec. Les Britanniques contrôlaient maintenant complètement la portion est de l'Amérique du Nord, depuis la rive est du fleuve Mississippi jusqu'à la côte Atlantique. Le mauvais traitement réservé aux colonies américaines par George III viendrait cependant bientôt modifier de nouveau l'équilibre du pouvoir dans le Nouveau Monde.

À titre de base pour les forces britanniques, de refuge pour les Américains loyaux à la monarchie britannique qui étaient en fuite et de source de milice pour les armées britanniques et américaines, le Canada joua un rôle important dans la guerre de l'Indépendance américaine. L'armée américaine tenta à l'origine de convaincre le Canada de prendre part à sa révolution, mais les Canadiens se relevaient à peine de la guerre de Sept Ans, et la majorité d'entre eux ne voulaient pas d'un autre conflit. Le 27 juin 1775, les troupes américaines attaquèrent Québec. Montréal fut pris sans résistance, mais l'attaque sur la ville de Québec se solda par une défaite, et en 1776, les troupes américaines évacuèrent Montréal.

Lorsque l'Amérique gagna son indépendance de la Grande-Bretagne en 1783, les citoyens loyaux à l'Empire britannique durent s'exiler. Plus de 35 000 d'entre eux se rendirent en Nouvelle-Écosse. Cet important mouvement de masse força le gouvernement britannique à diviser la Nouvelle-Écosse, créant ainsi la nouvelle colonie du Nouveau-Brunswick. Peu de temps après, les loyalistes établis au Québec commencèrent à présenter des demandes pour obtenir leur propre colonie, alors que les Canadiens français étaient aussi déterminés à avoir leur propre assemblée d'élus. En 1791, le Québec fut divisé en deux parties, le Haut-Canada et le Bas-Canada, afin de répondre aux exigences des loyalistes anglais et des Canadiens français.

Au cours des décennies qui suivirent, les tensions entre la Grande-Bretagne et l'Amérique demeurèrent vives, et encore une fois, un conflit déchira le Canada. Les États-Unis déclarèrent la guerre à la Grande-Bretagne en 1812 en raison de l'approvisionnement en armes des tribus amérindiennes hostiles et du service militaire obligatoire des marins américains à la marine britannique. Le Canada fut un des champs de bataille principaux de ce conflit puisque les États-Unis avaient planifié s'emparer du Canada et l'utiliser comme monnaie d'échange pour négocier avec les Britanniques. Les Américains s'attendaient à gagner le soutien des Canadiens qu'ils croyaient malheureux sous le contrôle colonial des Anglais. Toutefois, beaucoup de Canadiens, descendants de loyalistes britanniques qui avaient fui l'Amérique, percevaient les États-Unis comme des envahisseurs et des occupants.

L'armée américaine subit une défaite tôt dans le conflit lorsqu'elle fut battue par le général Isaac Brock et ses forces d'alliés indiens et de militaires locaux lors de la bataille de Queenston Heights. L'armée américaine en arriva quand même occuper et à piller un grand nombre de villes, incluant York (aujourd'hui Toronto) et Newark (aujourd'hui Niagra-on-the-Lake), jusqu'à contrôler à un certain moment presque tout le territoire correspondant à l'Ontario et au Québec d'aujourd'hui, mais en fin de compte, l'armée américaine fut repoussée, et bien que la guerre finit sans réel vainqueur, le fait qu'une prise de contrôle américaine fut empêchée donna aux Canadiens un regain de confiance et devint source de fierté nationale.

Même si les Canadiens rejetaient l'idée d'un envahisseur américain sur leur sol, l'exemple politique des États-Unis laissait sa marque à travers le pays. Des rébellions éclatèrent contre les Britanniques en 1837. Les Canadiens, insatisfaits de la distribution inéquitable des richesses tirées des ressources naturelles du Canada, s'insurgeaient de ne pas être représentés au sein du gouvernement britannique. Puisque les Britanniques considéraient que les frictions entre les Français et les Anglais étaient la source des conflits qu'ils vivaient avec le Canada, toutes les colonies canadiennes furent réunies en 1840 sous le nom de la Province du Canada, aussi appelée le Canada-Uni. En 1849, les États-Unis et l'Empire britannique se mirent d'accord pour que le 49e parallèle nord serve de frontière entre les deux nations, et les Britanniques étendirent le Canada jusqu'au au littoral ouest, annexant ainsi la Colombie-Britannique.

C'est pratiquement depuis la guerre d'Indépendance américaine que l'indépendance du Canada fait l'objet de débats en Grande-Bretagne comme au Canada. Certains prônaient une révolution violente et une indépendance canadienne totale. D'autres désiraient suivre un processus vers l'autonomie plus lent et graduel. Le 1er juillet 1867, le Parlement britannique édicta l'Acte de l'Amérique du Nord britannique, qui établit le Dominion du Canada comme une colonie distincte et dotée d'un gouvernement autonome. Sans être complètement détaché de l'Angleterre, particulièrement en ce qui a trait à la politique étrangère, sur le plan de la politique intérieure, le Canada gagnait pleine liberté et souveraineté.

Au cours des décennies suivantes, le Canada continua son expansion vers l'Ouest. Grâce à l'achat de deux énormes territoires au nord, les Territoires du Nord-Ouest et la Terre de Rupert, acquis de la Compagnie de la Baie d'Hudson, le pays doubla pratiquement sa superficie. Beaucoup de francophones et de Métis catholiques, les enfants d'Autochtones et de pionniers, vivaient à l'ouest de l'Ontario. Après la vente de la Terre de Rupert, plusieurs colons ontariens affluèrent dans cette région en espérant réclamer ces terres. Les Métis se mirent à craindre que cette arrivée massive de protestants anglais mette en péril leurs droits linguistiques, religieux et territoriaux. Le chef Métis Louis Riel organisa la Rébellion de la rivière Rouge en 1869 dans le but de garantir la protection de ces droits. Cette révolte mena à la création du Manitoba, une province qui mit en place des lois rigoureuses protégeant les Métis, les francophones et les catholiques. En 1905, la Colombie-Britannique, la Saskatchewan, l'Île-du-Prince-Édouard et l'Alberta furent coup sur coup jointes aux provinces fondatrices du Haut et du Bas-Canada, au Nouveau-Brunswick et à la Nouvelle-Écosse.

La construction d'un chemin de fer transcontinental, complété en 1885, stimula l'expansion du Canada. Ce chemin de fer incita de nouveaux colons à déménager dans l'Ouest pour s'établir dans les nouvelles provinces, mais ces nouveaux arrivants voulurent chasser les Autochtones de leurs terres, ce qui, une fois de plus, fit éclater des rébellions qui finirent en bains de sang. Le sentiment que le gouvernement canadien n'écoutait pas les préoccupations des catholiques francophones engendra une crise politique qui entraîna la démission du premier ministre Mackenzie Bowell en 1896 lorsque le gouvernement tenta de retirer au français son statut de langue officielle au Manitoba, ce qui allait à l'encontre des lois de la province.

Le Canada et les États-Unis connurent une période d'expansion vers l'ouest à la fin du dix-neuvième siècle grâce au développement du chemin de fer, à l'attrait qu'exerçaient ses contrées vierges et à la découverte de gisements de minerais. Ces facteurs, additionnés de l'arrivée massive d'immigrants en provenance d'Europe, permirent au Canada d'être le pays présentant la croissance économique la plus forte entre 1896 et 1911. Durant cette période, le gouvernement canadien créa le Yukon, un territoire dont la superficie se compare à celle de l'Allemagne, l'Autriche et la Suisse combinées, et dont la population se chiffrait à seulement 8 500 habitants à ce moment.

À l'aube du vingtième siècle, le Canada connut son premier conflit d'importance avec sa puissance coloniale. Lorsque la Grande-Bretagne entra dans la Guerre des Boers en 1889, la majorité des Anglo-canadiens appuyaient l'annexion de l'Afrique du Sud à l'Empire britannique. Les Canadiens français, toutefois, ne s'intéressaient pas vraiment à l'impérialisme britannique, car ils se considéraient comme un cas à part et considéraient qu'ils faisaient partie de l'Empire britannique uniquement pour la forme. En guise de compromis, tous ceux se portant volontaires purent servir dans la Guerre des Boers, mais l'Armée canadienne comme telle ne s'impliqua pas dans ce conflit. Cette vision du Canada français comme une entité à part, vision exacerbée par les rébellions et par les lois anti-françaises des décennies précédentes, continuera de se manifester dans la politique du Canada des années à venir.

Bien qu'un grand nombre de Canadiens français désirait se départir du joug de l'Empire britannique, le pays devait tout de même se plier à la politique étrangère britannique. Avec l'assassinat de l'Archiduc Ferdinand le 28 juin 1914, le Canada fut pris dans le chaotique système d'alliances que suscita la Première Guerre mondiale. Lorsque la Grande-Bretagne déclara la guerre aux puissances centrales le 4 août, les troupes canadiennes furent appelées en renfort. Comme pour la majorité des puissances alliées, les disputes internes furent temporairement mises de côté, et l'appui à la guerre demeura massif, même chez les Canadiens français. Après plus de 200 000 morts et blessés de guerre, sur une population de 7 millions d'habitants, l'effort de guerre commença à s'essouffler. Au moment où le gouvernement tenta d'introduire le service obligatoire en 1917, beaucoup de Canadiens, et principalement des Canadiens français, s'opposèrent farouchement à la guerre. Malgré l'opinion populaire, la Première Guerre mondiale contribua à alimenter le sentiment de nationalisme et d'identité canadienne, surtout grâce au rôle important que joua le Canada dans la guerre la plus importante de l'histoire de l'humanité. Les très nombreuses victimes canadiennes occasionnées par ce conflit que plusieurs considéraient comme une guerre « britannique » vint aussi augmenter le ressentiment accumulé envers l'Empire.

La Première Guerre mondiale changea radicalement le visage politique du Canada. Après les horreurs vécues pendant ce conflit, les soldats rentrèrent chez eux avec de nouvelles idéologies politiques. Le socialisme, le communisme, le syndicalisme et d'autres courants progressistes de gauche gagnèrent en popularité dans les années suivant la guerre, tandis que le retour massif des soldats faisait augmenter le taux de chômage et diminuer les salaires. La grève générale de Winnipeg de 1919, la plus importante d'une série de grèves qui paralysèrent le pays, fut brutalement mise fin par la police, au prix d'un mort et de 30 blessés. Lorsque le Canada accorda le droit de vote aux femmes en 1918, le Parti conservateur en place s'effondra, en partie en raison de ses actions durant la grève. Le Parti libéral, en prenant le contrôle du gouvernement, acquiesça à une bonne partie des demandes originales du comité de grève, incluant le droit de former des syndicats sans la permission du gouvernement. Des partis progressistes et socialistes se formèrent les années suivantes, incluant le Parti progressiste du Canada et la Fédération du Commonwealth coopératif.

En 1931, le Parlement britannique promulgua le Statut de Westminster, qui donna le statut d'entité législative indépendante à toutes les colonies et à tous les dominions de l'Empire britannique, incluant le Canada, l'Australie, la Nouvelle-Zélande et l'Irlande. Cet acte permit à ces pays de rédiger leur propre constitution et supprima le pouvoir législatif qu'avait le gouvernement britannique dans ces régions, assurant ainsi l'indépendance de celles-ci tout en les incluant dans un Commonwealth britannique à l'échelle mondiale.

Lorsque le marché boursier américain connut son krach lors du mardi noir de 1929, événement qui marqua le début de la Grande dépression, l'économie canadienne ne tarda pas à en ressentir les effets. En 1933, le produit national brut canadien connut une baisse de 40 %. Les secteurs manufacturiers et agricoles furent le plus durement touchés, et le prix de blé, le principal produit d'exportation du Canada, chuta de moitié. Au creux de la vague, 30 % des Canadiens étaient sans emploi. Terre-Neuve, affirmant que les politiques du gouvernement canadien étaient la cause de ce creux économique, vota de quitter la Fédération canadienne pour rejoindre l'Empire britannique.

Après que les partis Libéral et Conservateur se soient montrés incapables de trouver des solutions à cette crise, beaucoup de Canadiens se tournèrent vers d'autres partis, comme la Fédération du Commonwealth coopératif et le Parti Crédit Social du Canada. Après que le gouvernement conservateur de R. B. Bennet ait placé des chômeurs dans des camps de travail pour pallier au coût élevé du système d'aide sociale, la Ligue d'unité ouvrière (LUO) organisa une importante manifestation appelée la « Marche sur Ottawa » dans le but d'obtenir des améliorations aux conditions et avantages dans les camps. La tentative de Bennett pour arrêter cette marche provoquera l'émeute de Regina et contribua en fin de compte à sa défaite aux élections de 1935. Le nouveau gouvernement libéral élimina les camps et institua des programmes sociaux pour diminuer les effets de la Dépression, mais ceci n'empêcha pas le Canada d'être fortement touché par cette dernière. Environ un cinquième de la population dépendait des allocations du gouvernement et du soutien des programmes sociaux. Même après le boom de l'économie canadienne causé par la Seconde Guerre mondiale, ces programmes restèrent en place et continuèrent d'évoluer.

La Seconde Guerre mondiale débuta le 1er septembre 1939. Puisque le Canada était de plus en plus indépendant de l'Angleterre, le pays n'entra pas en guerre immédiatement après la déclaration de la Grande-Bretagne comme il l'avait fait lors de la Première Guerre mondiale, mais décida plutôt de déclarer d'elle-même la guerre neuf jours plus tard. Alors que le massacre japonais et nazi était toujours à son comble, le ravitaillement et le matériel de guerre des Canadiens s'avérèrent d'une importance capitale pour permettre à la Grande-Bretagne de résister à l'invasion allemande. Une fois que les Alliés furent en position de contre-attaquer, les troupes canadiennes furent déployées partout dans le monde, et servirent vaillamment dans plusieurs batailles importantes, incluant l'invasion de la Sicile et de l'Italie en 1943, le débarquement allié en Normandie en 1944, la libération des Pays-Bas et la traversée de la France et de l'Allemagne pour mettre fin à la guerre. Un raid majoritairement canadien à Dieppe en France se solda par 3 000 morts, blessés et captifs, et les sous-marins allemands qui infestaient les eaux canadiennes coulèrent un grand nombre de navires de ravitaillement. En tout et partout, la Seconde Guerre mondiale entraînera la mort de 42 000 canadiens.

Lorsque les Japonais bombardèrent Pearl Harbor le 7 décembre 1941, les 22 000 Canadiens d'origine japonaise vivant alors en Colombie-Britannique durent composer avec les conséquences de la douleur et de la colère qui s'ensuivirent. Le sentiment anti-asiatique dans la province fut davantage attisé lorsque des milliers de Canadiens furent tués ou capturés durant l'invasion de Hong Kong par les Japonais. En 1942, toutes les personnes de descendance japonaise furent envoyées dans des camps d'internement, et après la fin de la guerre, tous les Canadiens d'origine japonaise furent déportés de la Colombie-Britannique. Ce n'est qu'en 1949 qu'ils furent libres de vivre n'importe où au Canada. En 1988, les Canadiens d'origine japonaise furent finalement indemnisés pour le tort qu'ils ont dû subir durant la guerre.

À la conclusion de la Seconde Guerre mondiale, le Canada et les États-Unis étaient les deux seuls pays à n'avoir pas eu de combats liés à cette guerre sur leur territoire. Cela permit à ces deux pays de profiter d'un contexte économique unique. Grâce à un secteur manufacturier en pleine relance, à la découverte de pétrole en Alberta et à sa position de partenaire commercial principal de la superpuissance économique juste au sud de la frontière, le Canada vit son économie exploser. Cette nouvelle prospérité favorisa la création d'un programme d'aide sociale radicalement amélioré. Grâce à l'aide sociale centralisée de la fin des années 1930 et du début des années 1940 ainsi qu'aux nombreuses politiques sociales de la Fédération du Commonwealth coopératif, les Canadiens profiteront de l'assurance-hospitalisation, d'un régime de pensions et des allocations familiales. Ces politiques sociales progressistes convainquirent Terre-Neuve de rejoindre le Canada suite à un référendum en 1949.

Le Canada consolida sa position lors de la Guerre froide grâce à son statut de membre fondateur de l'OTAN en 1949. L'économie du pays était directement liée à celle des États-Unis. Le Canada participa à la guerre de Corée, et ses troupes furent postées en Allemagne de l'Ouest, à la frontière du bloc communiste. Le vote canadien aux Nations Unies ne fut pas toujours identique à celui des États-Unis, mais il n'y avait aucun doute que le Canada était un allié des Américains dans sa guerre contre l'Union soviétique.

Le traitement que le Canada réserva à ses peuples autochtones au fil du temps présente une histoire peu reluisante. Si l'on recule à la fin des années 1800, lorsque le bison fut chassé au point d'être presque totalement exterminé et que les chemins de fer amenèrent davantage de colons dans les territoires autochtones, les membres des Premières nations furent traités comme des citoyens de second ordre. La famine, l'assimilation et une rébellion avortée mirent fin à la résistance autochtone, mais celle-ci reprit vigueur après la Seconde Guerre mondiale. La décolonisation et un esprit de démocratie renouvelé étaient mis de l'avant par les puissances occidentales dans leur lutte contre la tyrannie soviétique, mais la majorité des Premières nations n'obtinrent quand même le droit de vote qu'à la fin des années 1950. Pour pouvoir voter, les gens des Premières nations devaient renoncer à leur statut « d'Indien ». Ce n'est qu'en 1960 (1969 au Québec) que les gens des Premières nations obtinrent le droit de voter librement.

Au début des années 1960, le gouvernement canadien dut faire face à une croissance marquée du radicalisme et d'organisations populaires. Le mouvement nationaliste québécois n'avait cessé de prendre de l'ampleur depuis que les Britanniques avaient pris le contrôle du Canada aux dépens des Français en 1764. Les Canadiens français se considéraient comme une nation distincte, et étaient souvent en désaccord avec les politiques gouvernementales canadiennes. Les factions canadiennes-françaises les plus radicales avaient le sentiment d'être opprimées, et que leur langue et leur culture étaient menacées. Inspirés par les révolutions se déroulant partout dans le monde, les groupes de gauche nationalistes ou terroristes se multiplièrent, et le Canada ne fut pas épargné. Le Front de Libération du Québec commit plus de 200 attentats à la bombe, tuant ainsi cinq personnes dans sa quête d'un Québec indépendant. Bien que les actes de violence furent majoritairement condamnés par la population, un profond désir d'indépendance alimentait les protestations des Québécois. Lorsque Pierre Elliott Trudeau fut élu Premier ministre en 1968, il mit le Québec sous la loi martiale et procéda à l'arrestation de plusieurs membres du FLQ.

Pendant que la crise au Québec s'aggravait durant les années 1970, les États-Unis s'engagèrent dans un des conflits les plus controversés de l'histoire moderne : la guerre en Indochine. La guerre du Vietnam entraîna la mort de 1 500 000 personnes et radicalisa une génération entière. Le Canada ne fit pas exception. Les jeunes de tout le pays protestèrent contre ce qu'ils considéraient être l'impérialisme américain. Le gouvernement canadien refusa de participer à cette guerre, et accorda la citoyenneté à plus de 125 000 Américains réfractaires tout au long du conflit. Ceci mena à d'importantes frictions entre les gouvernements canadien et américain. Aujourd'hui encore, le Vietnam et le Canada jouissent d'une relation privilégiée, et des centaines de milliers de Vietnamiens ont immigré sur la côte Ouest du Canada. La guerre du Vietnam coïncida aussi avec l'ascension du Nouveau Parti Démocratique, le successeur de la Fédération du Commonwealth coopératif. Depuis ses débuts en 1962, le NPD changea le visage de la politique canadienne en obtenant régulièrement entre 10 et 20 % des votes et en formant une coalition majoritaire avec le parti vainqueur. Lors des élections fédérales de 2011, le NPD a obtenu son meilleur résultat à ce jour, en récoltant 30 % des voix et le rôle de l'opposition officielle pour la première fois. Il a combattu pour la sauvegarde du programme d'aide sociale du Canada, pour une politique étrangère humanitaire ainsi que pour les droits des Autochtones.

Les jeunes de tous les coins du Canada devinrent de plus en plus impliqués en politique après la guerre du Vietnam, et ce nouvel intérêt marqué pour la politique permit d'aborder la question de la souveraineté du Québec. Le Parti québécois fut formé en 1968, remporta les élections au Québec en 1976 et fit du français la langue officielle de la province en 1977. Finalement, le parti tint sa promesse et instaura un référendum pour décider de l'avenir du Québec. Ce référendum stipulait simplement que le Québec « négocierait une nouvelle entente avec le reste du Canada, entente fondée sur l'égalité des peuples, en vertu de laquelle le Québec aurait obtenu le pouvoir exclusif de faire ses lois, autrement dit, la souveraineté ». Le fait que le référendum ne garantissait pas une indépendance complète, combiné à un assaut du service des relations publiques du gouvernement, fit échouer le référendum.

Bien que le Canada devint une entité souveraine en 1867, et que son indépendance s'est accrue en 1931, techniquement, le pays n'était pas encore tout à fait une nation souveraine. Le Canada n'était pas en mesure d'apporter des amendements à sa propre constitution, et la capacité du Canada d'agir à l'encontre des désirs du gouvernement britannique était encore mise en doute. En 1982, Trudeau confirma le statut de nation souveraine du Canada en signant la loi constitutionnelle et la Charte canadienne des droits et libertés. Bien qu'il était encore membre du Commonwealth britannique, le Canada n'était plus sous le contrôle du parlement britannique.

Suite à l'indépendance complète du Canada par rapport à la Grande-Bretagne, la question du commerce avec les États-Unis devint la principale préoccupation de l'économie canadienne. L'Accord de libre-échange Canada-États-Unis rédigé en 1988 devint un modèle pour l'Accord de libre-échange nord-américain et l'Accord de libre-échange de l'Amérique centrale. Cet accord, de même que les accords de libre-échange subséquents, fut critiqué, car on considérait qu'éliminer les barrières commerciales ferait en sorte que les consommateurs canadiens seraient à la merci des puissantes corporations américaines. Cet accord fut au centre des élections de 1988 : le Parti libéral et le NPD s'y opposaient, alors que les progressistes conservateurs tentaient de le faire passer. Une majorité de 57 % vota contre les progressistes conservateurs, mais puisqu'ils reçurent néanmoins le plus grand nombre de votes pour un unique parti, ils obtinrent une majorité de sièges au parlement et conclurent l'accord de libre-échange.

Le Parti Québécois, suite à l'échec du référendum de 1980, forma un parti politique canadien, le Bloc Québécois, et poursuivit avec acharnement son échéancier pour un Québec indépendant. Un deuxième référendum, en 1995, occasionna un débat encore plus virulent que celui du référendum de 1980, avec des campagnes médiatiques massives de part et d'autres des deux camps. Le jour du scrutin, le référendum échoua par une mince marge de 54 000 votes, un résultat qui mit au jour la division du Québec sur cette question. Considérant que 86 000 bulletins avaient été rejetés comme invalides, le résultat sur la question de l'indépendance du Québec a été si près de la ligne décisive qu'il ne serait pas surprenant qu'un autre referendum ait lieu dans le futur.

En 1990, une révolte amérindienne dans une petite ville baptisée Oka, à l'ouest de Montréal, a mené à l'intervention de l'armée canadienne. Trois personnes moururent au cours de cette crise. Bien qu'il y ait précédemment eu de nombreux conflits violents entre les membres des Premières nations et le gouvernement du Canada, la situation à Oka marqua le début d'une nouvelle ère de résistance active des Autochtones. Comme le Canada compte plus d'un million d'habitants de descendance amérindienne, de nombreuses organisations autochtones ont réclamé un meilleur contrôle des ressources sur leurs terres, ce qui a causé des conflits violents entre les membres des Premières nations et les sociétés exploitant les ressources minières, maritimes ou forestières sur leurs territoires. L'une des conséquences de ces manifestations fut la création d'un nouveau territoire, le Nunavut en 1999, dans les régions de l'extrême nord du pays. Bien que ce territoire compte moins de 30 000 habitants, près de 85 % de sa population y possède le statut d'Inuit, et le territoire a été en mesure d'adopter de nombreuses lois assurant les droits des Inuits et donnant corps à leurs revendications concernant le territoire et ses ressources.

Aujourd'hui, le Canada doit continuer à gérer ses relations avec le Québec et les membres des Premières nations tout en faisant face à d'autres enjeux, comme la dépénalisation des drogues, l'immigration, sa participation aux missions de maintien de la paix, le réchauffement de la planète et le contrôle des bras de mer de l'Arctique.

National Anthem: O Canada

From "Chapter 5, Statutes of Canada 1980; proclaimed July 1, 1980." Composed by Calixa Lavallée; French lyrics written by Judge Adolphe-Basile Routhier; English lyrics written by Robert Stanley Weir (with some changes incorporated in 1967).

O Canada! Our home and native land!
True patriot love in all thy sons command.
With glowing hearts we see thee rise,
The True North strong and free!
From far and wide, O Canada, We stand on guard for thee.
God keep our land glorious and free!
O Canada, we stand on guard for thee.
O Canada, we stand on guard for thee.

O Canada! Terre de nos aïeux!
Ton front est ceint de fleurons glorieux!
Car ton bras sait porter l'épée, Il sait porter la croix!
Ton histoire est une épopée Des plus brillants exploits.
Et ta valeur, de foi trempée,
Protégera nos foyers et nos droits,
Protégera nos foyers et nos droits.

Emblems of Canada

The Beaver
Recognized as a symbol of Canada's sovereignty. Official status as an emblem of Canada as of May 24, 1975.
Maple Tree
Arboreal emblem of Canada, proclaimed April 25, 1996.
Official Colours
Red and white, as proclaimed in 1921.
Official Sports
Hockey (winter); Lacrosse (summer).

Full-colour images of Canadian and provincial flags, coats of arms, floral emblems, and selected honours start on page A-12.

Fathers of Confederation

Three conferences helped to pave the way for Confederation - those held at Charlottetown (September, 1864), Québec City (October, 1864) and London (December, 1866). As all the delegates who were at the Charlottetown conferences were also in attendance at Québec, the following list includes the names of all those who attended one or more of the three conferences.

*Hewitt Bernard was John A. Macdonald's private secretary. He served as secretary of both the Québec and London conferences.

DELEGATES TO THE CONFEDERATION CONFERENCES, 1864-1866

LEGEND:

Charlottetown, 1 September, 1864	C
Québec, 10 October, 1864	Q
London, 4 December, 1866	L

CANADA

John A. Macdonald	C Q L
George E. Cartier	C Q L
Alexander T. Galt	C Q L
William McDougall	C Q L
Hector L. Langevin	C Q L
George Brown	C Q
Thomas D'Arcy McGee	C Q
Alexander Campbell	C Q
Sir Etienne P. Taché	Q
Oliver Mowat	Q
J.C. Chapais	Q
James Cockburn	Q
W.P. Howland	L
*Hewitt Bernard	

NOVA SCOTIA

Charles Tupper	C Q L
William A. Henry	C Q L
Jonathan McCully	C Q L
Adams G. Archibald	C Q L
Robert B. Dickey	Q
J.W. Ritchie	L

NEW BRUNSWICK

Samuel L. Tilley	C Q L
J.M. Johnson	C Q L
William H. Steeves	C Q
E.B. Chandler	C Q
John Hamilton Gray	C Q
Peter Mitchell	Q L
Charles Fisher	Q L
R.D. Wilmot	L

PRINCE EDWARD ISLAND

John Hamilton Gray	C Q
Edward Palmer	C Q
William H. Pope	C Q
A.A. Macdonald	C Q
George Coles	C Q
T.H. Haviland	Q
Edward Whelan	Q

NEWFOUNDLAND

F.B.T. Carter	Q
Ambrose Shea	Q

PARTICIPANTS TO THE FIRST MINISTERS' CONSTITUTIONAL CONFERENCE ON PATRIATION OF THE CONSTITUTION

(Held in Ottawa from September 2 to 5, 1981)

- The Right Honourable Pierre Elliott Trudeau, P.C., Q.C., M.P., Prime Minister of Canada;
- The Honourable William G. Davis, Q.C., Premier of Ontario;
- The Honourable René Lévesque, Premier of Québec;
- The Honourable John M. Buchanan, Q.C., Premier of Nova Scotia;
- The Honourable Richard B. Hatfield, Premier of New Brunswick;
- The Honourable Sterling R. Lyon, Q.C., Premier of Manitoba;
- The Honourable W.R. Bennett, Premier of British Columbia;
- The Honourable J. Angus MacLean, P.C., D.F.C., C.D., Premier of Prince Edward Island;
- The Honourable Allan Blakeney, Q.C., Premier of Saskatchewan;
- The Honourable Peter Lougheed, Q.C., Premier of Alberta;
- The Honourable Brian Peckford, Premier of Newfoundland.

Timeline of Canadian History

- 12000 BC: Migration of natives across the Bering land bridge
- 2000 BC: Inuit arrive in North America
- 1000: Leif Erickson lands on Baffin Island
- 1497: John Cabot reaches Newfoundland
- 1534-1541: Jacque Cartier explores North America
- 1576-1578: Martin Frobisher searches for the Northwest Passage
- 1583: Humphrey Gilbert claims Newfoundland for England
- 1603: Samuel de Champlain's first voyage to New France. The fur trading monopoly Canada & Arcadia Company is formed.
- 1608: Champlain founds Quebec.
- 1609: The Battle of Ticonderoga. France allies with the Hurons to fight the Iroquois.
- 1610: Henry Hudson looks for the Northwest Passage. First European settlement in Newfoundland.
- 1629: Champlain surrenders New France to Great Britain.
- 1641: Village of Ville Marie (Montreal) is formed.
- 1649: The Iroquois destroy the missionary settlement of Huronia.
- 1663: France regains control of New France.
- 1670: Charles II forms the Hudson Bay Company. Fur trade attracts settlers to the Great Lakes area.
- 1682: LaSalle claims Louisiana for France.
- 1701: Peace is declared between native tribes and France.
- 1713: Nova Scotia's Acadian French population forced to swear allegiance to England.
- 1755-6: England deports the Acadians. Seven Years War begins.
- 1763: Seven Years War ends.
- 1766: Pontiac signs peace treaty with Great Britain.
- 1774: America's 13 Colonies urge Canada to join them against the English.
- 1776: American Loyalists flee to Canada.
- 1778: James Cook arrives on Vancouver Island.
- 1784: British divide Nova Scotia and create New Brunswick.
- 1791: King George II divides Quebec into Lower and Upper Canada.
- 1793: Alexander Mackenzie crosses the continent and reaches the Pacific Ocean.
- 1812: The War of 1812 begins when America declares war against Great Britain.
- 1814: The War of 1812 ends.
- 1834: The Patriotes of Lower Canada draw up a list of 92 grievances and deliver them to the government in England.
- 1841: United Canada created.
- 1849: The burning of Parliament in Montreal.
- 1858: Queen Victoria creates British Columbia. The gold rush begins.
- 1867: New Brunswick, Nova Scotia, and the Province of Canada were proclaimed the Dominion of Canada, with John A. Macdonald its first prime minister.
- 1885: Canadian Pacific Railway completed.
- 1896: Canada opens doors to European immigration.
- 1897-1899: Klondike gold rush. Canada enters Boer War.
- 1907: Chinese in Canada encounter violence.
- 1909: Coal miners strike in Cape Breton.
- 1914: Canada enters World War I.
- 1918: Spanish influenza kills millions. World War I ends. Women win vote.
- 1920: Bootlegging flourishes after America declares Prohibition.
- 1929: U.S. stock market crashes. Drought hits prairies.
- 1931: Ottawa outlaws Communist agitation. Socialist Party of Canada created.
- 1933: Unemployment crisis worsens.
- 1938: Canada rejects Jewish refugees escaping Nazi Germany.
- 1939: Canada enters World War II.
- 1945: World War II ends.
- 1947: First major oil find in Alberta.
- 1949: Newfoundland joins Canada.
- 1952: CBC television launched.
- 1956: Suez Canal crisis.
- 1960: Quebec's Quiet Revolution begins.
- 1965: New Maple Leaf flag raised.
- 1967: Expo in Montreal.
- 1970: Alberta aboriginals begin new era of native protests. British trade commissioner kidnapped by radical Quebec separatist group Front de Libération du Québec.
- 1971: Greenpeace begins in Vancouver.
- 1982: Trudeau brings home Canadian constitution.
- 1989: Free Trade with the US begins.
- 1999: New province of Nunavut separated from the Northwest Territories.
- 2001: Canada's border with the United States is on high alert in the aftermath of the September 11 Terrorist Attacks in the USA.
- 2003: Health Canada announces 17 suspected SARS cases in Canada
- 2007: Canada Census data is released; the population of Canada in 2006 was 31,612,897
- 2007: Canadian dollar reaches parity with US greenback
- 2009: The 40th Canadian Parliament reopens, January 26, 2009, for its second session after a two-month prorogation.
- 2011: 41st Canadian federal election, May 2, 2011. Prime Minister Stephen Harper's Conservative Party wins a majority. New Democratic Party attains status of official opposition for the first time, led by Jack Layton.
- 2012: The Conservative budget causes major cuts to public services and raises the age of retirement to 67.

Chronologie de l'histoire du Canada

- 12 000 av. J.-C. : Des peuples en migration traversent le pont continental de Béring.
- 2000 av. J.-C. : Arrivée des Inuits en Amérique du Nord.
- 1000 apr. J.-C. : Leif Erickson débarque sur l'Île de Baffin.
- 1497 : Jean Cabot atteint Terre-Neuve.
- 1534-1541 : Jacques Cartier explore l'Amérique du Nord.
- 1576-1578 : Martin Frobisher recherche le passage du Nord-Ouest.
- 1583 : Humphrey Gilbert revendique Terre-Neuve au nom de l'Angleterre.
- 1603 : Premier voyage de Samuel de Champlain en Nouvelle-France. La Canada & Arcadia Company, qui allait posséder le monopole du commerce des fourrures, voit le jour.
- 1608 : Champlain fonde la ville de Québec.
- 1609 : Bataille de Ticonderoga. La France s'allie aux Hurons pour combattre les Iroquois.
- 1610 : Henry Hudson recherche le passage du Nord-Ouest. Une première colonie européenne en Amérique du Nord est établie à Terre-Neuve.
- 1629 : Champlain cède la Nouvelle-France à la Grande-Bretagne.
- 1641 : Fondation du village de Ville-Marie (Montréal).
- 1649 : Les Iroquois détruisent la mission de Huronie.
- 1663 : La France reprend le contrôle de la Nouvelle-France.
- 1670 : Le roi Charles II forme la Compagnie de la Baie d'Hudson. Le commerce des fourrures attire des colons vers la région des Grands Lacs.
- 1682 : LaSalle revendique la Louisiane au nom de la France.
- 1701 : La paix est déclarée entre les tribus amérindiennes et la France.
- 1713 : La population acadienne francophone de la Nouvelle-Écosse est forcée de prêter serment d'allégeance à l'Angleterre.
- 1755-6 : L'Angleterre ordonne la déportation des Acadiens. Début de la guerre de Sept Ans.
- 1763 : Fin de la guerre de Sept Ans.
- 1766 : Pontiac signe un traité de paix avec la Grande-Bretagne.
- 1774 : Les 13 Colonies américaines recommandent vivement au Canada de se joindre à leur combat contre l'Angleterre.
- 1776 : Les loyalistes américains en fuite se réfugient au Canada.
- 1778 : James Cook découvre l'île de Vancouver.
- 1784 : L'Angleterre divise le territoire de la Nouvelle-Écosse et crée le Nouveau-Brunswick.
- 1791 : Le roi George II divise le Québec en deux parties : le Bas-Canada et le Haut-Canada.
- 1793 : Alexander Mackenzie traverse le continent et atteint l'océan Pacifique.
- 1812 : Les États-Unis déclarent la guerre à la Grande-Bretagne et déclenchent la guerre de 1812.
- 1814 : Fin de la guerre de 1812.
- 1834 : Les Patriotes du Bas-Canada dressent une liste de 92 griefs; elle est ensuite envoyée au gouvernement de l'Angleterre.
- 1841 : Création du Canada-Uni.
- 1849 : Incendie du Parlement à Montréal.
- 1858 : La reine Victoria crée la Colombie-Britannique. Début de la ruée vers l'or.
- 1867 : Le Nouveau-Brunswick, la Nouvelle-Écosse et la province du Canada deviennent le Dominion du Canada, et John A. Macdonald devient le premier Premier ministre du nouveau pays.
- 1885 : Le chemin de fer du Canadien Pacifique est complété.
- 1896 : Le Canada ouvre ses portes aux immigrants européens.
- 1897-1899 : Ruée vers l'or du Klondike. Participation du Canada à la guerre des Boers.
- 1907 : La population chinoise du Canada est victime d'actes de violence.
- 1909 : Grève du charbon au Cap-Breton.
- 1914 : Début de la participation du Canada à la Première Guerre mondiale.
- 1918 : La grippe espagnole fait des millions de victimes. Fin de la Première Guerre mondiale. Les femmes obtiennent le droit de vote.
- 1920 : Le commerce clandestin d'alcool devient florissant avec le début de la Prohibition aux États-Unis.
- 1929 : Aux États-Unis, le marché s'effondre. La sécheresse fait rage dans les Prairies.
- 1931 : Ottawa déclare l'agitation communiste illégale. Le Parti socialiste du Canada voit le jour.
- 1933 : La crise du chômage s'intensifie.
- 1938 : Le Canada refuse d'accueillir des réfugiés juifs ayant fui l'Allemagne nazie.
- 1939 : Début de la participation du Canada à la Deuxième Guerre mondiale.
- 1945 : Fin de la Deuxième Guerre mondiale.
- 1947 : Découverte d'un premier gisement de pétrole important en Alberta.
- 1949 : Terre-Neuve se joint au Canada.
- 1952 : Lancement de la télévision de Radio-Canada.
- 1956 : Crise du Canal de Suez.
- 1960 : Début de la Révolution tranquille au Québec.
- 1965 : Le nouveau drapeau unifolié est hissé pour la première fois.
- 1967 : L'Expo 67 bat son plein à Montréal.
- 1970 : Les Autochtones d'Alberta entament lune nouvelle ère de revendications autochtones. Un délégué commercial britannique est kidnappé par le Front de Libération du Québec, un groupe séparatiste radical.
- 1971 : Fondation de l'organisme Greenpeace à Vancouver.
- 1982 : Trudeau rapatrie la Constitution canadienne.
- 1989 : Début du libre-échange avec les États-Unis.
- 1999 : La nouvelle province du Nunavut se sépare des Territoires-du-Nord-Ouest.
- 2001 : La frontière du Canada et des États-Unis est sur un pied d'alerte par suite des attaques terroristes du 11 septembre chez nos voisins du sud.
- 2003 : Santé Canada annonce 17 cas soupçonnés de grippe aviaire au Canada.
- 2007 : Les données du recensement de Statistique Canada sont rendues publiques; en 2006, la population du Canada atteignait 31 612 897 habitants.
- 2007 : Le dollar canadien atteint la même valeur que celle du dollar américain.
- 2011 : 41e élection fédérale, le 2 mai 2011. Le parti conservateur du premier ministre Stephen Harper remporte la majorité. Le nouveau parti démocratique, dirigé par Jack Layton, obtient le statut de l'opposition officielle pour la première fois dans son histoire.
- 2012 : Le budget du gouvernement conservateur entraîne des coupes importantes dans les services publics et fait passer l'âge de la retraite à 67 ans.

THE ROYAL ARMS OF CANADA BY PROCLAMATION OF KING GEORGE V IN 1921

The Royal Arms of Canada were established by proclamation of King George V on 21 November, 1921. On the advice of the Prime Minister of Canada, Her Majesty the Queen approved, on 12 July, 1994, that the arms be augmented with a ribbon bearing the motto of the Order of Canada, DESIDERANTES MELIOREM PATRIAM - "They desire a better country".

This coat of arms was developed by a special committee appointed by Order in Council and is substantially based on a version of the Royal Arms of the United Kingdom, featuring the historic arms of England and Scotland. To this were added the old arms of Royal France and the historic emblem of Ireland, the harp of Tara, thus honouring many of the founding European peoples of modern Canada. To mark these arms as Canadian, the three red maple leaves on a field of white were added.

The supporters, and the crest, above the helmet, are also versions of elements of the Royal Arms of the United Kingdom, including the lion of England and unicorn of Scotland. The lion holds the Union Jack and the unicorn, the banner of Royal France. The crowned lion holding the maple leaf, which is the The Royal Crest of Canada, has, since 1981, also been the official symbol of the Governor General of Canada, the Sovereign's representative.

At the base of the Royal Arms are the floral emblems of the founding nations of Canada, the English Rose, the Scottish Thistle, the French Lily and the Irish Shamrock.

The motto - A MARI USQUE AD MARE - "From sea to sea" - is an extract from the Latin version of verse 8 of the 72nd Psalm - "He shall have dominion also from sea to sea, and from the river unto the ends of the earth."

THE NATIONAL FLAG

The National Flag of Canada, otherwise known as the Canadian Flag, was approved by Parliament and proclaimed by Her Majesty Queen Elizabeth II to be in force as of February 15, 1965. It is described as a red flag of the proportions two by length and one by width, containing in its centre a white square the width of the flag, bearing a single red maple leaf. Red and white are the official colours of Canada, as approved by the proclamation of King George V appointing Arms for Canada in 1921. The Flag is flown on land at all federal government buildings, airports, and military bases within and outside Canada, and may appropriately be flown or displayed by individuals and organizations. The Flag is the proper national colours for all Canadian ships and boats; and it is the flag flown on Canadian Naval vessels.

The Flag is flown daily from sunrise to sunset. However, it is not contrary to etiquette to have the Flag flying at night. No flag, banner or pennant should be flown or displayed above the Canadian Flag. Flags flown together should be approximately the same size and flown from separate staffs at the same height. When flown on a speaker's platform, it should be to the right of the speaker. When used in the body of an auditorium; it should be to the right of the audience. When two or more than three flags are flown together, the Flag should be on the left as seen by spectators in front of the flags. When three flags are flown together, the Canadian Flag should occupy the central position.

A complete set of rules for flying the Canadian Flag can be obtained from the Department of Canadian Heritage.

THE ROYAL UNION FLAG

The Royal Union Flag, generally known as the Union Jack, was approved by Parliament on December 18, 1964 for continued use in Canada as a symbol of Canada's membership in the Commonwealth of Nations and of her allegiance to the Crown. It will, where physical arrangements make it possible, be flown along with the National Flag at federal buildings, airports, and military bases and establishments within Canada on the date of the official observance of the Queen's birthday, the Anniversary of the Statute of Westminster (December 11th), Commonwealth Day (second Monday in March), and on the occasions of Royal visits and certain Commonwealth gatherings in Canada.

QUEEN'S PERSONAL CANADIAN FLAG

In 1962, Her Majesty The Queen adopted a personal flag specifically for use in Canada. The design comprises the Arms of Canada with The Queen's own device in the centre. The device - the initial "E" surmounted by the St. Edward's Crown within a chaplet of roses - is gold on a blue background.

When the Queen is in Canada, this flag is flown, day and night, at any building in which She is in residence. Generally, the flag is also flown behind the saluting base when She conducts troop inspections, on all vehicles in which She travels, and on Her Majesty's Canadian ships (HMCS) when the Queen is aboard.

FLAG OF THE GOVERNOR GENERAL

The Governor General's standard is a blue flag with the crest of the Arms of Canada in its centre. A symbol of the Sovereignty of Canada, the crest is made of a gold lion passant imperially crowned, on a wreath of the official colours of Canada, holding in its right paw a red maple leaf. The standard was approved by Her Majesty The Queen on February 23, 1981. The Governor General's personal standard flies whenever the incumbent is in residence, and takes precedence over all other flags in Canada, except The Queen's.

CANADIAN ARMED FORCES BADGE

The Canadian Armed Forces Badge was sanctioned by Her Majesty Queen Elizabeth II in May 1967. The description is as follows:

Within a wreath of 10 stylized maple leaves Red, a cartouche medium Blue edge Gold, charged with a foul anchor Gold, surmounted by Crusader's Swords in Saltire Silver and blue, pommelled and hilted Gold; and in front an eagle volant affront head to the sinister Gold, the whole ensigned with a Royal Crown proper.

The Canadian Forces Badge replaces the badges of the Royal Canadian Navy, the Canadian Army, and the Royal Canadian Air Force.

ALBERTA

The Arms of the Province of Alberta were granted by Royal Warrant on May 30, 1907. On July 30th, 1980, the Arms were augmented as follows: Crest: Upon a Helm with a Wreath Argent and Gules a Beaver couchant upholding on its back the Royal Crown both proper; Supporters: On the dexter side a Lion Or armed and langued Gules and on the sinister side a Pronghorn Antelope (Antilocapra americana) proper; the Compartment comprising a grassy mount with the Floral Emblem of the said Province of Alberta the Wild Rose (Rosa acicularis) growing therefrom proper; Motto: FORTIS ET LIBER (Strong and Free) to be borne and used together with the Arms upon Seals, Shields, Banners, Flags or otherwise according to the Laws of Arms.

In 1958, the Government of Alberta authorized the design and use of an official flag. A flag bearing the Armorial Ensign on a royal ultramarine blue background was adopted and the Flag Act proclaimed June 1st 1968. Proportions of the flag are two by length and one by width with the Armorial Ensign seven-elevenths of the width of the flag carried in the centre. The flag may be used by citizens of the Province and others in a manner befitting its dignity and importance but no other banner or flag that includes the Armorial Ensign may be assumed or used.

Floral Emblem: Wild Rose (Rosa Acicularis). Chosen in the Floral Emblem Act of 1930.

Provincial Bird: Great horned owl (budo virginianus). Adopted May 3, 1977.

BRITISH COLUMBIA

The shield of British Columbia was granted by Royal Warrant on March 31, 1906. On October 15th, 1987, the shield was augmented by Her Majesty Queen Elizabeth II. The crest and supporters have become part of the provincial Arms through usage. The heraldic description is as follows: Crest: Upon a Helm with a Wreath Argent and Gules the Royal Crest of general purpose of Our Royal Predecessor Queen Victoria differenced for Us and Our Successors in right of British Columbia with the Lion thereof garlanded about the neck with the Provincial Flower that is to say the Pacific Dogwood (Cornus nuttallii) with leaves all proper Mantled Gules doubled Argent; Supporters: On the dexter side a Wapiti Stag (Cervus canadensis) proper and on the sinister side a Bighorn Sheep Ram (Oviscanadensis) Argent armed and unguled Or; Compartment: Beneath the Shield a Scroll entwined with Pacific Dogwood flowers slipped and leaved proper inscribed with the Motto assigned by the said Warrant of Our Royal Predecessor King Edward VII that is to say SPLENDOR SINE OCCASU, (splendour without diminishment).

The flag of British Columbia was authorized by an Order-in-Council of June 27, 1960. The Union Jack symbolizes the province's origins as a British colony, and the crown at its centre represents the sovereign power linking the nations of the Commonwealth. The sun sets over the Pacific Ocean. The original design of the flag was located in 1960 by Hon. W.A.C. Bennett at the College of Arms in London.

Floral emblem: Pacific Dogwood (Cornus Nuttallii, Audubon). Adopted under the Floral Emblem Act, 1956.

Provincial Bird: Steller's jay. Adopted November 19, 1987.

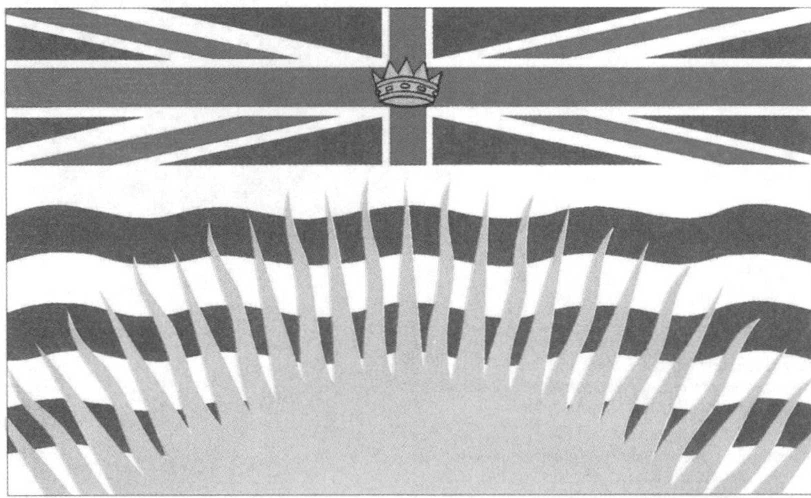

MANITOBA

The Arms of the Province of Manitoba were granted by Royal Warrant on May 10, 1905, augmented by warrant of the Governor General on October 23, 1992. The description is as follows: above the familiar shield of 1905 is a helmet and mantling; above the helmet is the Crest, including the beaver holding a prairie crocus, the province's floral emblem. On the beaver's back is the royal crown. The left supporter is a unicorn wearing a collar bearing a decorative frieze of maple leaves, the collar representing Manitoba's position as Canada's "keystone" province. Hanging from the collar is a wheel of a Red River cart. The right supporter is a white horse, and its collar of bead and bone honours First Peoples. The supporters and the shield rest on a compartment representing the province's rivers and lakes, grain fields and forests, composed of the provincial tree, the white spruce, and seven prairie crocuses. At the base is a Latin translation of the phrase "Glorious and Free."

The flag of the Province of Manitoba was adopted under The Provincial Flag Act, assented to May 11, 1965, and proclaimed into force on May 12, 1966. It incorporates parts of the Royal Armorial Ensigns, namely the Union and Red Ensign; the badge in the fly of the flag is the shield of the arms of the province.

Description: A flag of the proportions two by length and one by width with the Union Jack occupying the upper quarter next the staff and with the shield of the armorial bearings of the province centered in the half farthest from the staff.

Floral Emblem: Pasque Flower, known locally as Prairie Crocus (Anemone Patens). Adopted 1906.

Provincial Bird: Great gray owl. Adopted July 16, 1987.

NEW BRUNSWICK

The Arms of New Brunswick were granted by Royal Warrant on May 26, 1868. The motto SPEM REDUXIT (hope restored) was added by Order-in-Council in 1966. The description is as follows: The upper third of the shield is red and features a gold lion, symbolizing New Brunswick's ties to Britain. The lion is also found in the arms of the Duchy of Brunswick in Germany, the ancestral home of King George III. The lower part of the shield displays an ancient galley with oars in action. It could be interpreted as a reference to the importance of both shipbuilding and seafaring to New Brunswick in those days. It is also based on the design of the province's original great seal which featured a sailing ship on water. The shield is supported by two white-tailed deer wearing collars of Indian wampum. From one is suspended the Royal Union Flag (the Union Jack), from the other the fleur-de-lis to indicate the province's British and French background. The crest consists of an Atlantic Salmon leaping from a coronet of gold maple leaves and bearing St. Edward's Crown on its back. The base, or compartment, is a grassy mound with fiddleheads as well as purple violets, the provincial floral emblem. The motto "Spem Reduxit" is taken from the first great seal of the province and means "Hope restored.".

The flag of New Brunswick, adopted by Proclamation on February 24, 1965, is based on the Arms of the province. The chief and charge occupy the upper one-third of the flag, and the remainder of the armorial bearings occupy the lower two-thirds. The proportion is four by length and two and one half by width.

Floral Emblem: Purple Violet (Viola Cuculata). Adopted by Order-in-Council, December 1, 1936, at the request of the New Brunswick Women's Institute.

Provincial Bird: Black-capped chickadee. Adopted August 1983.

NEWFOUNDLAND & LABRADOR

The Arms of Newfoundland were granted by Royal Letters Patent dated January 1, 1637, by King Charles I. The heraldic description is as follows: Gules, a Cross Argent, in the first and fourth quarters a Lion passant guardant crowned Or, in the second and third quarters an Unicorn passant Argent armed and crined Or, gorged with a Coronet and a Chain affixed thereto reflexed of the last. Crest: on a wreath Or and Gules a Moose passant proper. Supporters: two Savages of the clime armed and apparelled according to their guise when they go to war. The motto reads QUAERITE PRIMEREGNUM DEI (seek ye first the kingdom of God).

The official flag of Newfoundland, adopted in 1980, has primary colours of Red, Gold and Blue, against a White background. The Blue section on the left represents Newfoundland's Commonwealth heritage and the Red and Gold section on the right represents the hopes for the future with the arrow pointing the way. The two triangles represent the mainland and island parts of the province.

Floral Emblem: Pitcher Plant (Sarracenia Purpurea). Adopted June 1954.

Provincial Bird: Atlantic puffin. Adopted 1992.

NORTHWEST TERRITORIES

The Arms of the Northwest Territories were approved by Her Majesty Queen Elizabeth II on February 24, 1956. The crest consists of two gold narwhals guarding a compass rose, symbolic of the magnetic north pole. The white upper third of the shield represents the polar ice pack and is crossed by a wavy blue line portraying the Northwest Passage. The tree line is reflected by a diagonal line separating the red and green segments of the lower portion of the shield: the green symbolizing the forested areas south of the tree line, and the red standing for the barren lands north of it. The important bases of northern wealth, minerals and fur, are represented by gold billets in the green portion and the mask of a white fox in the red.

The official flag of the Northwest Territories was adopted by the Territorial Council on January 1, 1969. Blue panels at either side of the flag represent the lakes and waters of the Territories. The white centre panel, equal in width to the two blue panels combined, symbolizes the ice and snow of the North. In the centre of the white portion is the shield from the Arms of the Territories.

Floral Emblem: Mountain Avens (Dryas Integrifolia). Adopted by the Council on June 7, 1957.

Territorial Bird: Gyrfalcon. Adopted June 1990.

NOVA SCOTIA

The Arms of the Province of Nova Scotia were granted to the Royal Province in 1625 by King Charles I. The complete Armorial Achievement includes the Arms, surmounted by a royal helm with a blue and silver scroll or mantling representing the Royal cloak. Above is the crest of heraldic symbols: two joined hands, one armoured and the other bare, supporting a spray of laurel for peace and thistle for Scotland. On the left is the mythical royal unicorn and on the right a 17th century representation of the North American Indian. The motto reads MUNIT HAEC ET ALTERA VINCIT (one defends and the other conquers). Entwined with the thistle of Scotland at the base is the mayflower, added in 1929, as the floral emblem of Nova Scotia.

The flag of the Province of Nova Scotia is a blue St. Andrew's Cross on a white field, with the Royal Arms of Scotland mounted thereon. The width of the flag is three-quarters of the length.

The flag was originally authorized by Charles I in 1625. In 1929, on petition of Nova Scotia, a Royal Warrant of King George V was issued, revoking the modern Arms and ordering that the original Arms granted by Charles I be borne upon (seals) shields, banners, and otherwise according to the laws of Arms.

Floral Emblem: Trailing Arbutus, also known as Mayflower (Epigaea Repens). Adopted April 1901.

Provincial Bird: Osprey. Adopted Spring, 1994.

NUNAVUT

The dominant colours blue and gold are the ones preferred by the Nunavut Implementation Commissioners to symbolize the riches of the land, sea and sky.

Red is a reference to Canada. In the base of the shield, the inuksuk symbolizes the stone monuments which guide the people on the land and mark sacred and other special places. The qulliq, or Inuit stone lamp, represents light and the warmth of family and the community. Above, the concave arc of five gold circles refers to the life-giving properties of the sun arching above and below the horizon, the unique part of the Nunavut year. The star is the Niqirtsuituq, the North Star and the traditional guide for navigation and more broadly, forever remains unchanged as the leadership of the elders in the community.

In the crest, the iglu represents the traditional life of the people and the means of survival. It also symbolizes the assembled members of the Legislature meeting together for the good of Nunavut; with the Royal Crown symbolizing public government for all the people of Nunavut and the equivalent status of Nunavut with other territories and provinces in Canadian Confederation. The tuktu (caribou) and qilalugaq tugaalik (narwhal) refer to land and sea animals which are part of the rich natural heritage of Nunavut and provide sustenance for people. The compartment at the base is composed of land and sea and features three important species of Arctic wild flowers.

Floral Emblem: Purple Saxifrage (Saxifraga oppositifolia). Adopted May 1, 2000.

Territorial Bird: Rock Ptarmigan.

ONTARIO

The Arms of the Province of Ontario were granted by Royal Warrants on May 26, 1868 (shield), and February 27, 1909 (crest and supporters). The heraldic description is as follows: Vert, a Sprig of three leaves of Maple slipped Or on a Chief Argent the Cross of St. George. Crest: upon a wreath Vert and Or a Bear passant Sable. The supporters are on the dexter side, a Moose, and on the sinister side a Canadian Deer, both proper. The motto reads: UT INCEPIT FIDELIS SIC PERMANET (loyal in the beginning, so it remained).

The flag of the Province of Ontario was adopted under the Flag Act of May 21, 1965. It incorporates parts of the Royal Armorial Ensigns, namely the Union and Red Ensign; the badge in the fly of the flag is the shield of the Arms of the province. The flag is of the proportions two by length and one by width, with the Union Jack occupying the upper quarter next the staff and the shield of the armorial hearings of the province centered in the half farthest from the staff.

Floral Emblem: White Trillium (Trillium Grandiflorum). Adopted March 25, 1937.

Provincial Bird: Common loon. Adopted June 23, 1994.

PRINCE EDWARD ISLAND

The Arms of the Province of Prince Edward Island were granted by Royal Warrant, May 30, 1905. The heraldic description is as follows: Argent on an Island Vert, to the sinister an Oak Tree fructed, to the dexter thereof three Oak saplings sprouting all proper, on a Chief Gules a Lion passant guardant Or. The motto reads: PARVA SUB INGENTI (the small under the protection of the great).

The flag of the Province of Prince Edward Island was authorized by an Act of the Legislative Assembly, March 24, 1964. The design of the flag is that part of the Arms contained within the shield, but is of rectangular shape, with a fringe of alternating red and white. The chief and charge of the Arms occupies the upper one-third of the flag, and the remainder of the Arms occupies the lower two-thirds. The proportions of the flag are six, four and one-quarter in relation to the fly, the hoist and the depth of the fringe.

Floral Emblem: Lady's Slipper (Cypripedium Acaule). Designated as the province's floral emblem by the Legislative Assembly in 1947. A more precise botanical name was included in an amendment to the Floral Emblem Act in 1965.

Provincial Bird: Blue Jay (cyanocitta cristata) was designated as avian emblem by the Provincial Emblems Acts, May 13, 1977.

QUÉBEC

The Arms of the Province of Québec were granted by Queen Victoria, May 26, 1868, and revised by a Provincial Order-in-Council on December 9, 1939. The heraldic description is as follows: Tierced in fess: Azure, three Fleurs-de-lis Or; Gules, a Lion passant guardant Or armed and langued Azure; Or, a Sugar Maple sprig with three leaves Vert veined Or. Surmounted with the Royal Crown. Below the shield a scroll Argent, surrounded by a bordure Azure, inscribed with the motto JE ME SOUVIENS (I remember) Azure.

The official flag of the Province of Québec was adopted by a Provincial Order-in-Council of January 21, 1948. It is a white cross on a sky blue ground, with the fleur-de-lis in an upright position on the blue ground in each of the four quarters. The proportion is six units wide by four units deep.

Floral Emblem: Iris Versicolor. Adopted November 5, 1999.

Provincial Bird: Snowy owl. Adopted December 17, 1987.

SASKATCHEWAN

The complete armorial bearings of the Province of Saskatchewan were granted by Royal Warrant on September 16, 1986, through augmentation of the original shield of arms granted by King Edward VII on August 25, 1906. The heraldic description is as follows: Shield: Vert three Garbs in fesse Or, on a Chief of the last a Lion passant guardant Gules. Crest: Upon a Helm with a Wreath Argent and Gules a Beaver upholding with its back Our Royal Crown and holding in the dexter fore-claws a Western Red Lily (Lilium philadelphicumandinum) slipped all proper Mantled Gules doubled Argent. Supporters: On the dexter side a Lion Or gorged with a Collar of Prairie Indian beadwork proper and dependent therefrom a six-pointed Mullet faceted Argent fimbriated and garnished Or charged with a Maple Leaf Gules and on the sinister side a White tailed deer (Odocoileus virginianus) proper gorged with a like Collar and dependent therefrom a like Mullet charged with a Western Red Lily slipped and leaved proper. Motto: Beneath the Shield a Scroll entwined with Western Red Lilies slipped and leaved proper inscribed with the motto MULTIS E GENTIBUS VIRES (From many peoples strength).

The official flag was dedicated on September 22, 1969, and features the Arms of the province in the upper quarter nearest the staff, with the Western Red Lily, in the half farthest from the staff. The upper green portion represents forests, while the gold symbolizes prairie wheat fields. The basic design was adopted from the prize-winning entry of Anthony Drake of Hodgeville from a province-wide flag design competition.

Floral Emblem: Western Red Lily (Lilium philadelphicum var. andinum). Adopted April 8, 1941.

Provincial Bird: Prairie sharp-tailed grouse. Adopted March 30, 1945.

YUKON

The Arms of the Yukon, granted by Queen Elizabeth II on February 24, 1956, have the following explanation: The wavy white and blue vertical stripe represents the Yukon River and refers also to the rivers and creeks where gold was discovered. The red spire-like forms represent the mountainous country, and the gold discs the mineral resources. The St. George's Cross is in reference to the early explorers and fur traders from Great Britain, and the roundel in vair in the centre of the cross is a symbol for the fur trade. The crest displays a Malamute dog, an animal which has played an important part in the early history of the Yukon.

The Yukon flag, designed by Lynn Lambert, a Haines Junction student, was adopted by Council in 1967. It is divided into thirds: green for forests, white for snow, and blue for water.

The flag consists of three vertical panels, the centre panel being one and one-half times the width of each of the other two panels. The panel adjacent to the mast is coloured green, the centre panel is coloured white and has the Yukon Crest disposed above a symbolic representation of the floral emblem of the territory, epilobium angustifolium, (fireweed), and the panel on the fly is coloured blue. The stem and leaves of the floral emblem are coloured green, and the flowers thereof are coloured red. The Yukon Crest is coloured red and blue, with the Malamute dog coloured black.

Floral Emblem: Fireweed (Epilobium Angustifolium). Adopted November 16, 1957.

Territorial Bird: Common raven. Adopted October 28, 1985.

Geography

Land and Freshwater Areas

(in square kilometres)

Provinces and Territories	Land	Water	Total Area	Percentage of Canadian Total
Newfoundland and Labrador	373,872	31,340	405,212	4.06
Prince Edward Island	5,660	Not Available	5,660	0.06
Nova Scotia	53,338	1,946	55,284	0.55
New Brunswick	71,450	1,458	72,908	0.73
Quebec	1,365,128	176,928	1,542,056	15.44
Ontario	917,741	158,654	1,076,395	10.78
Manitoba	553,556	94,241	647,797	6.49
Saskatchewan	591,670	59,366	651,036	6.52
Alberta	642,317	19,531	661,848	6.63
British Columbia	925,186	19,549	944,735	9.46
Yukon Territory	474,391	8,052	482,443	4.83
Northwest Territories	1,183,085	163,021	1,346,106	13.48
Nunavut	1,936,113	157,077	2,093,190	20.96
Canada	9,093,507	891,163	9,984,670	100

Reproduced with the permission of Natural Resources Canada, 2012.

Largest Lakes Wholly or Partially in Canada

Name	Provinces and Territories	Area (square kilometres)
Superior	Ontario (and United States)	82,101 (total); 28,748 in Canada
Huron	Ontario (and United States)	59,569 (total); 36,000 in Canada
Great Bear	Northwest Territories	30,764
Great Slave	Northwest Territories	27,048
Erie	Ontario (and United States)	25,666 (total); 12,768 in Canada
Winnipeg	Manitoba	23,760
Ontario	Ontario (and United States)	19,554 (total); 10,334 in Canada

Reproduced with the permission of Natural Resources Canada, 2012.

Number of Lakes by Region (size classes are in square kilometres)

Region	3 to 99	100 to 199	200 to 399	400 to 999	1,000 to 2,499	2,500 to 9,999	10,000 to 36,000	Total
Atlantic Provinces[1]	1,761	19	5	4	1	2	0	1,792
Quebec	8,182	49	27	12	5	0	0	8,275
Ontario	3,837	34	12	9	1	2	4	3,899
Prairie Provinces[2]	5,245	65	39	18	8	5	1	5,381
British Columbia	838	6	12	4	1	0	0	861
Territories[3]	11,328	108	60	35	8	3	2	11,544
Canada	31,191	281	155	82	24	12	7	31,752

[1]Atlantic Provinces: Newfoundland and Labrador, Prince Edward Island, Nova Scotia, New Brunswick

[2]Prairie Provinces: Manitoba, Saskatchewan, Alberta

[3]Territories: Yukon Territory, Northwest Territories, Nunavut

Reproduced with the permission of Natural Resources Canada, 2012.

Longest Rivers in Canada

Rank	Name (at outflow)	Length (kilometres)	Outflow	Component Parts
1	Mackenzie	4,241	Beaufort Sea	Mackenzie - Slave - Peace - Findlay
2	Yukon	3,185 (1,143 kilometres in Canada)	Bering Sea	Yukon
3	St. Lawrence	3,058 (small part wholly in U.S.)	Gulf of St. Lawrence	St. Lawrence - Niagara - Detroit - St. Clair - St. Marys - St. Louis
4	Nelson	2,575	Hudson Bay	Nelson - Saskatchewan - South Saskatchewan - Bow
5	Columbia	2,000 (801 kilometres in Canada)	Pacific Ocean	Columbia
6	Churchill	1,609	Hudson Bay	Churchill [of Manitoba and Saskatchewan]
7	Fraser	1,370	Pacific Ocean	Fraser
8	North	1,287	Saskatchewan River	North Saskatchewan
9	Ottawa	1,271	St. Lawrence River	Ottawa
10	Athabasca	1,231	Slave River	Athabasca
11	Liard	1,115	Mackenzie River	Liard
12	Assiniboine	1,070	Red River (part of Nelson River drainage basin)	Assiniboine

Reproduced with the permission of Natural Resources Canada, 2012.

Largest Islands of Canada

Rank	Name	Provinces and Territories	Area (square kilometres)
1	Baffin (5th largest in the world)	Nunavut	507,451
2	Victoria	Nunavut and Northwest	217,291
3	Ellesmere	Nunavut	196,236
4	Island of Newfoundland	Newfoundland and Labrador	108,860
5	Banks	Northwest Territories	70,028
6	Devon	Nunavut	55,247
7	Axel Heiberg	Nunavut	43,178
8	Melville	Northwest Territories and	42,149
9	Southampton	Nunavut	41,214
10	Prince of Wales	Nunavut	33,339
11	Vancouver	British Columbia	31,285

Reproduced with the permission of Natural Resources Canada, 2012.

Selected Waterfalls in Canada

Name of Waterfall	Vertical Drop (metres)	Location
Della Falls	440	Della Lake, BC
Takakkaw Falls	254	Daly Glacier, BC
Hunlen Falls	253	Atnarko River, BC
Panther Falls	183	Nigel Creek, AB
Helmcken Falls	137	Murtle River, BC
Bridal Veil Falls	122	Bridal Creek, BC
Virginia Falls	90	South Nahanni River, NT
Chute Montmorency	84	Rivière Montmorency, QC
Twin Falls	80	Yoho National Park, BC
Chute Ouiatchouan	79	Rivière Ouiatchouan, QC
Brandywine Falls	61	Brandywine Creek, BC
Niagara Falls (American Falls)	59	(Niagara River, USA)
Niagara Falls (Horseshoe Falls)	57	Niagara River, ON
Wilberforce Falls	49	Hood River, NU
Dog Falls	47	Kaministiquia River, ON
Kakabeka Falls	47	Kaministiquia River, ON
Chute de Shawinigan	46	Rivière Saint-Maurice, QC
Grand Falls	43	Exploits River, NL
Parry Falls	40	Lockhart River, NT
Wawaitin Falls	38	Mattagami River, ON
Elizabeth Falls	34	Fond du Lac River, SK
Aubrey Falls	33	Mississagi River, ON
Alexandra Falls	32	Hay River, NT
Thomas Falls	31	Unknown River, NL
Marengo Falls	30	Marengo Creek, NT
Barrow Falls	27	Barrow River, NU
Pigeon Falls	27	Pigeon River, ON
Scott Falls	27	Unknown River, NL
Tyrrell Falls	26	Lockhart River, NT
High Falls	24	Onaping River, ON
Schist Falls	24	Pukaskwa River, ON
Smoky Falls	24	Mattagami River, ON
Christopher Falls	23	Opasatika River, ON
Chute du Calcaire	22	Rivière Caniapiscau, QC
Chute au Granite	21	Rivière Caniapiscau, QC
Partridge Falls	21	Pigeon River, ON
Steephill Falls	21	Magpie River, ON
Louise Falls	20	Hay River, NT
Muhigan Falls	19	Muhigan River, MB
Big Beaver Falls	18	Kapuskasing River, ON
Chutes aux Schistes	18	Rivière Caniapiscau, QC
Twin Falls	18	Abitibi River, ON
Lady Evelyn Falls	17	Kakisa River, NT
Muskrat Falls	15	Churchill River, NL
Taskinigup Falls	15	Burntwood River, MB
Kazan Falls	14	Kazan River, NU
Rideau Falls	12	Rideau River, ON

Reproduced with the permission of Natural Resources Canada, 2012.

Highest Points by Province and Territory

Provinces and Territories	Name of Highest Point	Height (metres)
British Columbia	Fairweather Mountain (on Alaska-British Columbia border)	4,663
Alberta	Mount Columbia (on Alberta-British Columbia border	3,747
Saskatchewan	Cypress Hills	1,392
Manitoba	Baldy Mountain	832
Ontario	Ishpatina Ridge	693
Quebec	Mont D'Iberville (on Quebec-Newfoundland and Labrador boundary; known as Mount Caubvick in Newfoundland and Labrador)	1,652
New Brunswick	Mount Carleton	817
Nova Scotia	White Hill	532
Prince Edward Island	Unnamed hill at 46 degrees 20 minutes North, 63 degrees 25 minutes West	142
Newfoundland and Labrador	Mount Caubvick (on Newfoundland and Labrador -Quebec boundary; known as Mont D'Iberville in Quebec)	1,652
Yukon Territory	Mount Logan (highest point in Canada)	5,959
Northwest Territories	Unnamed peak at 61 degrees 52 minutes North, 127 degrees 42 minutes West	2,773
Nunavut	Barbeau Peak (on Ellesmere Island)	2,616

Reproduced with the permission of Natural Resources Canada, 2012.

SYMBOLS OF CANADA

Provinces and Territories	Floral Emblem	Tree	Bird
Alberta	Wild Rose	Lodgepole Pine	Great Horned Owl
British Columbia	Pacific Dogwood	Western Red Cedar	Steller's Jay
Manitoba	Prairie Crocus	White Spruce	Great Gray Owl
New Brunswick	Purple Violet	Balsam Fir	Black-capped Chickadee
Newfoundland and Labrador	Pitcher Plant	Black Spruce	Atlantic Puffin
Northwest Territories	Mountain Avens	Tamarack	Gyrfalcon
Nova Scotia	Mayflower	Red Spruce	Osprey
Nunavut	Purple Saxifrage	Rock Ptarmigan	
Ontario	White Trillium	Eastern White Pine	Loon
Prince Edward Island	Lady's Slipper	Red Oak	Blue Jay
Quebec	Blue Iris Versicolor	Yellow Birch	Snowy Owl
Saskatchewan	Western Red Lily	Paper Birch	Sharp-tailed Grouse
Yukon	Fireweed	Subalpine Fir	Common Raven

Banff, Alberta

Beaver Creek, Yukon

Niagara Falls, Ontario

Ice Hotel in Québec

Nova Scotia

Iceberg in Newfoundland

New Brunswick

Lighthouse on Prince Edward Island

Hans Pfaff/Nunavut Tourism

Walruses in Nunavut

Northwest Territories

Reproduced with the permission of Natural Resources Canada

CANADA
Relief
in metres / en mètres
5 959 Mt Logan
5 000
4 000
3 000
2 000
1 500
1 000
700
500
300
200
100
0 Sea level / Niveau de la mer
ARCTIC OCEAN
OCÉAN ARCTIQUE
Queen Elizabeth Islands
Îles de la Reine-Élisabeth
Ellesmere Island
Île d'Ellesmere
Victoria Island
Baffin Island
Île de Baffin
Hudson Bay
Baie d'Hudson
NUNAVUT
NORTHWEST TERRITORIES
TERRITOIRES DU NORD-OUEST
YUKON
ALASKA
USA / É-U d'A
BRITISH COLUMBIA
COLOMBIE-BRITANNIQUE
ALBERTA
SASKATCHEWAN
MANITOBA
ONTARIO
QUÉBEC
QUEBEC
NEWFOUNDLAND AND LABRADOR
TERRE-NEUVE-ET-LABRADOR
Saint-Pierre et Miquelon (France)
NOVA SCOTIA
NOUVELLE-ÉCOSSE
P E I
Î-P-É
NB
N-B
ATLANTIC OCEAN
OCÉAN ATLANTIQUE
PACIFIC OCEAN
OCÉAN PACIFIQUE
United States of America
États-Unis d'Amérique
Scale / Échelle
km 200 0 200 400 600 km
atlas.gc.ca
P E I = PRINCE EDWARD ISLAND
Î-P-É = ÎLE-DU-PRINCE-ÉDOUARD
N B = NEW BRUNSWICK
N-B = NOUVEAU-BRUNSWICK

AVERAGE TEMPERATURE & PRECIPITATION

	Average daily temperature		Average precipitation
	January	July	Annual
	°C		mm
St. John's	-4.8	15.4	1,513.70
Charlottetown	-8	18.5	1,173.30
Halifax	-6	18.6	1,452.20
Fredericton	-9.8	19.3	1,143.30
Québec	-12.8	19.2	1,230.30
Ottawa	-10.8	20.9	943.5
Toronto	-6.3	20.8	792.7
Winnipeg	-17.8	19.5	513.7
Regina	-16.2	18.8	388.1
Edmonton	-13.5	15.9	482.7
Victoria	3.8	16.4	883.3
Whitehorse	-17.7	14.1	267.4
Yellowknife	-26.8	16.8	280.7
Iqaluit	-26.6	7.7	412

Source: Environment Canada, *Canadian Climate Normals or Averages 1971-2000.*

KILOMETRES

MILES

	BANFF	BRANDON	CALGARY	CHARLOTTETOWN	CHICOUTIMI	CORNER BROOK	DAWSON CREEK	EDMONTON	FLIN FLON	FORT SMITH	FREDERICTON	GANDER	GASPÉ	HALIFAX	HAMILTON	JASPER	KENORA	LETHBRIDGE	LONDON	MONCTON	MONTRÉAL	NIAGARA FALLS	NORTH BAY	OTTAWA	PORT AUX BASQUES	PRINCE ALBERT	PRINCE GEORGE	PRINCE RUPERT	QUÉBEC	REGINA	RIVIÈRE-DU-LOUP	ROUYN	SAINT JOHN	ST. JOHN'S	SASKATOON	SAULT STE. MARIE	SEPT-ÎLES	SHERBROOKE	SUMMERSIDE	SYDNEY	THE PAS	THUNDER BAY	TORONTO	VANCOUVER	VICTORIA	WHITEHORSE	WINDSOR	WINNIPEG	YARMOUTH	YELLOWKNIFE
BANFF	•	782	80	3147	2702	3484	633	266	846	1094	2924	3725	2997	3225	2256	178	1037	216	2327	3047	2406	2299	2059	2288	3356	567	393	853	2574	555	2687	1960	2990	3932	465	1794	2980	2503	3131	3356	920	1354	2214	577	618	1562	2457	910	3055	1205
BRANDON	1259	•	702	2392	1920	2714	1082	715	451	1543	2142	2943	2215	2447	1474	944	255	622	1545	2292	1624	1517	1277	1506	2574	454	1159	1619	1792	227	1905	1178	2208	3152	387	1012	2198	1721	2349	2574	357	572	1432	1359	1400	2011	1677	128	2273	1654
CALGARY	129	1130	•	3055	2622	3404	553	186	766	1011	2832	3633	2917	3133	2176	258	957	136	2247	2955	2326	2219	1979	2208	3264	487	473	933	2494	475	2607	1880	2898	3842	385	1714	2900	2423	3051	3264	840	1274	2134	657	698	1482	2377	830	2963	1125
CHARLOTTETOWN	5065	3850	4917	•	552	368	3442	3075	2787	3903	223	597	516	144	1143	3304	2105	3014	1184	100	736	1147	1083	854	228	2814	3519	3979	587	2587	460	1136	192	804	2747	1348	531	706	39	228	2749	1788	1071	3719	3760	4371	1303	2232	257	4014
CHICOUTIMI	4348	3090	4220	888	•	901	3002	2635	2347	3463	329	1130	402	544	673	2864	1665	2542	744	452	296	716	643	414	761	2374	3079	3539	128	2147	92	696	383	1357	2307	908	385	261	536	761	2277	1348	631	3279	3320	3931	858	1792	460	3574
CORNER BROOK	5607	4368	5478	592	1450	•	3791	3424	3136	4252	572	229	865	402	1462	3653	2454	3336	1534	449	1085	1500	1432	1203	140	3163	3868	4328	936	2936	809	1485	541	436	3096	1697	911	1055	407	140	3071	2137	1420	4068	4109	4720	1652	2581	566	4363
DAWSON CREEK	1019	1741	890	5539	4831	6101	•	367	1020	640	3224	4020	3297	3525	2556	467	1337	689	2627	3342	2706	2599	2359	2588	3651	741	252	712	2874	855	2987	2260	3290	4227	695	2094	3280	2803	3426	3651	1013	1654	2514	747	788	929	2731	1210	3343	751
EDMONTON	428	1151	299	4949	4241	5510	591	•	653	828	2857	3653	2930	3158	2189	299	970	322	2260	2975	2339	2232	1992	2221	3284	374	444	904	2507	488	2620	1893	2923	3860	328	1727	2913	2436	3059	3284	646	1287	2147	773	814	1296	2364	843	2988	939
FLIN FLON	1362	668	1233	4485	3777	5047	1642	1051	•	1481	2569	3365	2642	2870	1901	882	682	862	1972	2687	2051	1944	1704	1933	2996	279	1097	1557	2219	467	2332	1605	2635	3572	381	1439	2625	2148	2771	2996	94	999	1859	1423	1464	1949	2086	555	2700	1592
FORT SMITH	1761	2483	1627	6281	5573	6843	1030	1333	2383	•	3685	4480	3758	3986	3017	995	1798	1150	3083	3803	3167	3055	2820	3049	4112	1202	892	1352	3335	1316	3448	2721	3751	4692	1156	2555	3741	3264	3887	4112	1474	2115	2975	1387	1428	1569	3192	1671	3816	443
FREDERICTON	4706	3447	4558	359	529	921	5189	4598	4134	5930	•	801	435	215	895	3086	1887	2764	966	123	518	938	865	636	432	2596	3301	3761	364	2369	237	918	66	1008	2529	1130	481	483	207	432	2499	1570	853	3501	3542	4153	1080	2014	131	3796
GANDER	5995	4736	5847	961	1819	369	6470	5879	5415	7210	1289	•	1094	631	1691	3882	2683	3560	1762	678	1314	1734	1661	1432	369	3392	4097	4557	1165	3165	1038	1714	770	207	3325	1926	1140	1284	636	369	3300	2366	1649	4297	4338	4949	1881	2810	795	4592
GASPÉ	4823	3565	4694	830	647	1392	5306	4715	4252	6048	700	1761	•	587	968	3159	1960	2837	1039	416	591	1011	938	709	725	2669	3374	3834	437	2442	310	991	501	1301	2602	1203	299	556	500	725	2572	1643	926	3574	3615	4226	1153	2087	566	3869
HALIFAX	5190	3938	5042	232	875	647	5673	5082	4619	6415	346	1015	945	•	1196	3387	2188	3065	1267	171	819	1239	1166	937	262	2897	3602	4062	567	2670	452	1219	149	838	2830	1431	628	698	188	262	2800	1871	1154	3802	3843	4454	1381	2315	217	4097
HAMILTON	3631	2372	3502	1839	1083	2353	4114	3523	3059	4855	1440	2721	1558	1925	•	2418	1219	2096	84	1013	377	43	250	290	1322	1928	2633	3093	545	1701	658	431	961	1898	1861	462	951	474	1097	1322	1831	902	42	2833	2874	3485	198	1346	1026	3128
JASPER	286	1519	415	5317	4609	5879	752	369	1419	1601	4966	6247	5084	5451	3891	•	1199	394	2489	3204	2568	2461	2221	2450	3513	603	215	675	2736	717	2849	2122	3152	4089	557	1956	3142	2665	3288	3513	875	1516	2376	544	585	1396	2635	1072	3217	1106
KENORA	1669	410	1510	3388	2680	3949	2152	1561	1098	2894	3037	4318	3154	3521	1962	1930	•	877	1290	2005	1369	1262	1022	1251	2314	709	1414	1874	1537	482	1650	923	1953	2890	642	757	1943	1466	2089	2314	612	317	1177	1614	1655	2266	1404	127	2018	1909
LETHBRIDGE	384	1001	219	4851	4091	5369	1109	518	1387	1851	4448	5729	4566	4933	3373	634	1411	•	2167	2882	2246	2139	1899	2128	3191	623	609	1069	2414	395	2527	1800	2830	2767	412	1626	2820	2343	2966	3191	768	1194	2054	710	751	1618	2297	750	2902	1261
LONDON	3745	2486	3616	1905	1197	2469	4228	3637	3174	4962	1555	2836	1672	2039	135	4006	2076	3487	•	1084	448	126	321	361	1393	2009	2704	3164	616	1772	729	502	1032	1969	1932	533	1022	545	1166	1393	1902	973	113	2904	2945	3548	126	1417	1097	3199
MONCTON	4904	3689	4756	161	727	723	5378	4788	4324	6120	198	1091	669	275	1630	5156	3227	4638	1745	•	636	1056	983	754	309	2714	3419	3879	487	2487	360	1036	92	885	2647	1248	462	606	84	309	2649	1688	971	3619	3660	4271	1203	2132	157	3914
MONTRÉAL	3872	2614	3743	1184	476	1746	4355	3764	3301	5097	834	2115	951	1318	607	4133	2203	3615	721	1024	•	420	347	118	945	2078	2783	3243	168	1851	281	400	584	1521	2011	612	574	97	720	945	1981	1052	335	2983	3024	3635	562	1496	649	3278
NIAGARA FALLS	3700	2441	3571	1846	1152	2414	4183	3592	3129	4917	1510	2791	1627	1994	69	3961	2031	3442	203	1699	676	•	293	333	1365	1971	2676	3136	588	1744	701	474	1004	1941	1904	505	983	517	1140	1365	1874	945	85	2876	2917	3528	241	1389	1069	3171
NORTH BAY	3314	2055	3185	1743	1035	2305	3796	3206	2742	4538	1392	2673	1510	1876	402	3574	1645	3056	517	1582	558	472	•	229	1292	1731	2436	2896	515	1504	628	181	931	1868	1664	265	921	444	1067	1292	1634	705	208	2636	2677	3280	435	1149	996	2931
OTTAWA	3682	2424	3553	1374	666	1936	4165	3574	3111	4907	1024	2305	1141	1508	467	3943	2013	3425	581	1213	190	536	369	•	1063	1960	2665	3125	286	1733	399	343	702	1639	1893	494	692	215	838	1063	1863	934	248	2865	2906	3517	475	1378	767	3160
PORT AUX BASQUES	5401	4142	5253	367	1225	225	5876	5285	4822	6618	695	594	1167	422	2128	5654	3724	5135	2242	497	1521	2197	2079	1711	•	3023	3728	4188	796	2796	669	1345	401	576	2956	1557	771	915	267	129	2931	1997	1280	3928	3969	4580	1512	2441	426	4223
PRINCE ALBERT	912	731	784	4529	3821	5090	1193	602	449	1934	4178	5459	4295	4662	3103	970	1141	1003	3233	4368	3344	3172	2786	3154	4865	•	818	1278	2246	227	2359	1632	2662	3599	102	1466	2652	2175	2798	3023	272	1026	1896	1144	1185	1670	2082	582	2727	1313
PRINCE GEORGE	632	1865	761	5663	4955	6225	406	715	1765	1436	5312	6593	5430	5797	4237	346	2276	980	4352	5502	4479	4307	3920	4289	6000	1316	•	460	2951	932	3064	2337	3367	4304	772	2163	3357	2880	3503	3728	1090	1731	2591	495	536	1181	2850	1287	3432	1003
PRINCE RUPERT	1373	2606	1502	6404	5695	6965	1146	1455	2506	2176	6053	7334	6170	6537	4978	1086	3016	1720	5092	6243	5219	5047	4661	5029	6740	2057	740	•	3411	1392	3524	2797	3827	4764	1232	2623	3817	3340	3963	4188	1550	2191	3051	955	996	1641	3310	1747	3892	1463
QUÉBEC	4142	2884	4014	945	206	1506	4625	4035	3571	5367	586	1875	703	912	877	4403	2474	3885	991	784	270	946	829	460	1281	3615	4749	5489	•	2019	127	568	418	1372	2179	780	406	133	571	796	2149	1220	503	3151	3192	3803	730	1664	495	3446
REGINA	893	365	764	4163	3455	4725	1376	785	752	2118	3813	5094	3930	4297	2737	1154	776	636	2852	4002	2979	2807	2420	2789	4500	365	1500	2240	3249	•	2132	1405	2435	3372	160	1231	2425	1948	2571	2796	373	799	1659	1132	1173	1784	1902	355	2507	1427
RIVIÈRE-DU-LOUP	4324	3066	4196	740	148	1302	4807	4216	3753	5549	381	1670	499	727	1059	4585	2655	4067	1173	579	452	1128	1011	642	1077	3796	4931	5671	204	3431	•	681	303	1245	2292	893	231	246	444	669	2262	1333	616	3264	3305	3916	843	1777	368	3559
ROUYN	3154	1896	3026	1828	1120	2390	3637	3046	2583	4379	1477	2758	1595	1962	694	3415	1485	2897	808	1667	644	763	291	552	2165	2626	3761	4501	914	2261	1096	•	984	1921	1565	446	974	497	1120	1345	1535	606	389	2537	2578	3189	616	1050	1049	2832
SAINT JOHN	4812	3553	4664	309	616	871	5295	4704	4241	6037	106	1239	806	240	1547	5073	3143	4554	1661	148	940	1616	1498	1130	645	4284	5419	6159	673	3919	488	1584	•	977	2595	1196	547	537	176	401	2565	1636	919	3567	3608	4219	1146	2080	65	3862
ST. JOHN'S	6328	5073	6183	1294	2184	702	6803	6212	5749	7551	1622	333	2094	1349	3055	6581	4651	4453	3169	1424	2448	3124	3006	2638	927	5792	6927	7667	2208	5427	2004	3092	1572	•	3532	2133	1347	1491	843	576	3507	2573	1856	4504	4545	5156	2088	3017	1012	4799
SASKATOON	748	623	620	4421	3713	4983	1118	528	613	1860	4070	5351	4188	4554	2995	896	1033	663	3109	4260	3236	3064	2678	3046	4757	164	1242	1983	3507	257	3689	2519	4176	5684	•	1391	2585	2108	2731	2956	346	959	1819	1042	1083	1624	2036	515	2660	1267
SAULT STE. MARIE	2887	1629	2758	2169	1461	2731	3370	2779	2360	4112	1819	3100	1936	2303	744	3148	1218	2617	858	2008	985	813	426	795	2506	2359	3481	4221	1255	1981	1437	718	1925	3422	2239	•	1186	709	1332	1557	1369	440	420	2363	2404	3015	647	884	1261	2666
SEPT-ÎLES	4796	3537	4667	855	620	1466	5279	4688	4225	6021	774	1835	481	1011	1530	5057	3127	4538	1645	744	924	1582	1482	1114	1241	4268	5403	6143	653	3903	372	1568	880	2168	4160	1909	•	539	515	771	2555	1626	909	3557	3598	4209	1136	2070	612	3852
SHERBROOKE	4028	2770	3899	1136	420	1698	4511	3920	3457	5253	777	2066	895	1123	763	4289	2359	3771	877	975	156	832	715	346	1473	3500	4635	5375	214	3135	396	800	864	2400	3392	1141	867	•	690	915	2078	1149	432	3080	3121	3732	659	1593	614	3375
SUMMERSIDE	5039	3780	4910	63	863	655	5514	4923	4459	6256	333	1024	805	303	1765	5292	3362	4773	1876	135	1159	1835	1717	1349	430	4503	5638	6378	919	4138	715	1802	283	1357	4395	2144	829	1110	•	267	2706	1772	1053	3703	3744	4355	1287	2216	241	3998
SYDNEY	5401	4142	5253	367	1225	225	5876	5285	4822	6618	695	594	1167	422	2128	5654	3724	5135	2242	497	1521	2197	2079	1711	207	4865	6000	6740	1281	4500	1077	2165	645	927	4757	2506	1241	1473	430	•	2931	1997	1280	3928	3969	4580	1512	2441	426	4223
THE PAS	1481	575	1352	4424	3664	4942	1630	1040	151	2372	4022	5311	4139	4506	2947	1408	985	1236	3061	4263	3188	3016	2630	2998	4717	438	1754	2494	3458	600	3640	2470	4128	5644	557	2203	4112	3344	4355	4717	•	929	1789	1388	1429	1942	2008	485	2630	1585
THUNDER BAY	2179	921	2050	2878	2169	3439	2662	2071	1608	3404	2527	3808	2644	3011	1452	2440	510	1922	1566	2717	1693	1521	1135	1503	3214	1651	2786	3526	1963	1286	2145	975	2633	4141	1543	708	2617	1849	2852	3214	1495	•	860	1931	1972	2583	1087	444	741	2226
TORONTO	3563	2305	3434	1724	1015	2285	4046	3455	2992	4788	1373	2654	1490	1857	68	3824	1894	3306	182	1563	539	137	335	399	2060	3051	4170	4910	810	2670	991	626	1479	2987	2927	676	1463	695	1695	2060	2879	1384	•	2791	2832	3435	227	1304	984	3086
VANCOUVER	929	2187	1057	5985	5277	6547	1202	1244	2290	2232	5634	6915	5752	6119	4559	875	2597	1143	4674	5824	4801	4628	4242	4611	6322	1841	797	1537	5071	1822	5253	4083	5741	7248	1677	3803	5724	4957	5959	6322	2234	3108	4492	•	41	1676	3034	1487	3632	1498
VICTORIA	995	2253	1123	6051	5343	6613	1268	1310	2356	2298	5700	6981	5818	6185	4625	941	2663	1209	4740	5890	4867	4694	4308	4677	6387	1907	863	1603	5137	1818	5319	4149	5807	7314	1743	3869	5790	5023	6025	6387	2300	3174	4558	66	•	1717	3053	1528	3673	1539
WHITEHORSE	2514	3236	2385	7034	6326	7596	1495	2086	3137	2525	6684	7965	6801	7168	5609	2247	3647	2604	5710	6874	5850	5678	5279	5660	7371	2688	1901	2641	6120	2871	6302	5132	6790	8298	2614	4852	6774	6006	7009	7371	3125	4157	5528	2697	2763	•	3660	2190	4284	1680
WIINDSOR	3954	2699	3825	2097	1381	2659	4395	3804	3357	5137	1738	3027	1856	2223	319	4241	2260	3697	203	1936	904	388	700	764	2433	3351	4587	5327	1175	3061	1357	991	1844	3360	3277	1041	1828	1061	2071	2433	3232	1749	365	4883	4913	5890	•	1547	1211	3303
WINNIPEG	1465	206	1336	3592	2884	4154	1947	1357	893	2689	3241	4522	3359	3726	2166	1725	204	1207	2280	3431	2408	2235	1849	2218	3928	937	2071	2812	2678	571	2860	1690	3347	4855	829	1423	3331	2564	3566	3928	781	715	2099	2393	2459	3524	2490	•	2145	1782
YARMOUTH	4917	3658	4768	414	740	911	5380	4809	4345	6141	211	1279	911	349	1651	5177	3248	4670	1765	253	1044	1720	1603	1234	686	4389	5523	6264	797	4035	592	1688	105	1629	4281	2029	985	988	388	686	4233	1193	1584	5845	5911	6894	1949	3452	•	3927
YELLOWKNIFE	1939	2662	1811	6460	5752	7022	1209	1511	2562	713	6109	7390	6227	6593	5034	1780	3072	2029	5148	6299	5275	5103	4717	5086	6796	2113	1614	2354	5546	2297	5728	4558	6215	7723	2039	4291	6199	5432	6418	6796	2551	3582	4966	2411	2477	2704	5316	2868	6320	•

Source: National Atlas Service, Natural Resources Canada

Science

Astronomical Calculations

ASTRONOMY IN CANADA

Astronomical research in Canada is carried out in universities, supported by the Natural Sciences and Engineering Research Council (NSERC) of Canada, and by the Canada Foundation for Innovation (CFI), and also in the National Research Council (NRC) — specifically by the Herzberg Institute of Astrophysics (HIA), which operates the following observatories: The Dominion Astrophysical Observatory (DAO) at Victoria, with optical telescopes of 1.8m and 1.2m aperture; and the Dominion Radio Astrophysical Observatory (DRAO) near Penticton, which has a 26m paraboloid and a 7-element array of 9m antennae. The National Research Council also maintains Canada's Time Service in its Institute of National Measurement Standards. The Canadian Astronomy Data Centre (CADC) is housed within HIA.

A number of Canadian universities offer graduate education in astronomy: Victoria, British Columbia (Vancouver), Alberta (Edmonton), Calgary, Saskatchewan (Saskatoon), Manitoba (Winnipeg), Western Ontario (London), Waterloo, McMaster (Hamilton), York (Toronto), Toronto, Queen's (Kingston), Montréal, McGill (Montréal), Laval (Québec), and St. Mary's (Halifax). Most of these have some local facilities for observational and theoretical studies, and all of them have access to national facilities in Canada and elsewhere. Among the major observatories operated by Canadian universities are: a 1.8m infrared telescope opened in 1987 by the University of Calgary; a 1.2m telescope at the University of Western Ontario; a 0.6m telescope now located in, and shared with, Argentina with access through the University of Toronto; and a 1.5m telescope at the Mont Mégantic Observatory operated by the University of Montréal, and Laval University. There is also a Canadian Institute for Theoretical Astrophysics hosted by the University of Toronto. Canadian astronomers have recently established the Association of Canadian Universities for Research in Astronomy (ACURA) to co-ordinate universities' participation in astronomy, especially in the development of large-scale facilities.

Through the National Research Council, Canadian astronomers also have access to excellent international facilities. One of these is the 3.6m Canada-France-Hawaii optical telescope atop Mauna Kea on the island of Hawaii, at an elevation of nearly 4200m. This telescope is shared, both as to cost and operation, by Canada, France, and the state of Hawaii. Canadian astronomers also share (with the Netherlands and the UK) in the operation of the James Clerk Maxwell telescope, a sophisticated millimetre-wave radio telescope at the same site. Canada also is a partner, along with several other countries, in the twin Gemini 8m telescopes, which are in operation in Hawaii and in Chile. Balloon-borne telescopes, Canada's first astronomical satellite MOST (Microvariability and Oscillations of STars), and participation in other space astronomy missions are funded through the Canadian Space Agency, and Canada is a partner in the James Webb Space Telescope, the planned successor to the Hubble Space Telescope. Canada is also a partner in the North American Program in Radio Astronomy, including the Atacama Large Millimetre Array, under contruction high in the Atacama Desert in Chile.

Astronomical education and outreach are carried out in a wide variety of settings. In the formal education system, astronomy is part of the elementary and secondary school science curriculum in most provinces, and is taught in most universities, most commonly in the form of introductory astronomy courses for non-majors. Canada's planetariums, science centres, and public observatories play a major role in communicating the nature and excitement of astronomy, as do science journalists, and the many professional and amateur astronomers who give public lectures, and organize open houses and star parties.

OBSERVATORIES

Observatories are open to the public as follows:

NEW Burke-Gaffney Observatory: St. Mary's University, Halifax NS B3H 3C3 - 902/420-5828; Info line: 902/496-8257; Fax: 902/496-8218; URL: www.smu.ca/academic/science/ap/bgo.html

Free public tours are held, weather permitting, on the 1st and 3rd Saturday of each month, except from June through September when they are held every Saturday. Tours begin at 7pm between November 1 and March 30 and at either 9pm or 10pm (depending on when it gets dark) between April 1 and October 31. On clear evenings, the 40-cm telescope is used to view the planets, the Moon, or other interesting celestial objects.

There will be no tour on cloudy or rainy nights. The decision to hold or cancel a tour is usually made by 6pm on Saturday. Always call the information line after 6pm to find out if the tour is on or off.

Groups wishing special tours can be accommodated on Monday evenings by reservation.

Canada Science & Technology Museum, Helen Sawyer Hogg Observatory: 1867 St. Laurent Blvd., Ottawa ON K1G 5A3 - 613/991-3044; Email: cts@technomuses.ca; URL: www.sciencetech.technomuses.ca

38-cm refractor (from the former Dominion Observatory). See website for details and special programs.

Canada-France-Hawaii Telescope: #65, 1238 Mamalahoa Hwy., Kamuela HI, 96743 - 808/885-7944; Fax: 808/885-7288; E-mail: outreach@cfht.hawaii.edu; URL: www.cfht.hawaii.edu

By appointment only.

Climenhaga Observatory: Dept. of Physics & Astronomy, University of Victoria, PO Box 3055, Station CSC, Victoria BC V8W 3P6 - 250/721-7700; Fax: 250/721-7715; URL: astrowww.phys.uvic.ca/events/

Daytime tours are open from the beginning of April until the end of June. The tour includes an entertaining educational presentation, a look through the big, fully automated telescope in the Climenhaga Observatory and weather permitting, an opportunity to search for sunspots using the smaller telescopes on the roof. The tours are free but space is limited. Interested parties are encouraged to book in advance.

Night time viewing sessions are open on Wednesdays from 8 p.m. (or sunset) until 10 p.m.

Gordon MacMillan Southam Observatory: H.R. MacMillan Space Centre, 1100 Chestnut St., Vancouver BC V6J 3J9 - 604/738-7827; Fax: 604/736-5665; E-mail: info@spacecentre.ca; URL: www.spacecentre.ca

Open Friday and Saturday starting at 8:30 p.m. To confirm observatory openings, please call 604/738-2855, or guest services at 604/738-7827 ext. 240 after 8:00 p.m. Admission is by donation.

Hume Cronyn Memorial Observatory: Dept. of Physics & Astronomy, University of Western Ontario, London ON N6A 3K7 - 519/661-2111, ext. 86708; URL: www.astro.uwo.ca/~dfgray/pub-nit.html

Public Nights run from late October through mid-December and mid-January through early April. This activity is oriented toward groups, and reservations must be made in advance.

Open House is run every Saturday evening during the months of June, July, and August. No reservations needed. Start time is 20:30 (8:30 p.m.). Closing time is 23:00 (11:00 p.m.).

National Research Council Canada, Centre of the Universe: Visitor Centre, 5071 West Saanich Rd., Victoria BC V9E 2E7 - 250/363-8262; Fax: 250/363-8290; E-mail: cu@nrc.gc.ca; URL: www.nrc-cnrc.gc.ca/eng/services/hia/centre-universe.html

Open for elementary, middle or high school class, or college or university students, for an exclusive daytime program for fall, winter and spring.

Open Tuesday to Saturday from 3:30 p.m. to 11:15 p.m. (last admission at 10:15 p.m.) during the summer, and 1:00 p.m. to 4:30 p.m. in September. See webpages for admission details.

National Research Council Canada, Dominion Astrophysical Observatory: 5071 West Saanich Rd., Victoria BC V9E 2E7 - 250/363-0001; Fax: 250/363-0045; E-mail: HIA-WWW@nrc-cnrc.gc.ca; URL: www.nrc-cnrc.gc.ca/eng/facilities/hia/astrophysical-observatory. html

Open every evening from April 1 up to and including October 31 to demonstrate the operation the research telescope, regardless of the weather, and to offer a viewing of celestial objects, weather permitting. See website for details.

National Research Council Canada, Dominion Radio Astrophysical Observatory: 717 White Lake Road, PO Box 248, Penticton BC V2A 6J9 - 250/493-2300; Fax: 250/497-2355; E-mail: HIA-WWW@nrc-cnrc.gc.ca; URL: www.nrc-cnrc.gc.ca/eng/facilities/hia/radio-astrophysical.html

The Observatory grounds and Visitors' Centre are open year-round for self-guided tours between 10 a.m. and 5 p.m., Monday to Friday (except statutory holidays). The grounds are also open on weekends from Easter until Thanksgiving, between 10 a.m. and 5 p.m., with staff on duty in the Visitors' Centre. Guided tours led by Observatory staff are offered on Sundays in July and August, from 2 p.m. until 5 p.m. Tours typically take about 1 hour.

Observatoire Astronomique Du Mont Mégantic: 189 route du Parc, Notre-Dame-des-Bois QC J0B 2E0 - 819/888-2941; Fax 819/888-2943; E-mail: parc.mont-megantic@sepaq.com; URL: www.astro.umontreal.ca/omm/

The observatory hosts "Festival d'Astronomie Populaire du mont Mégantic" on the weekends in July. For other times of the year, visits including interactive exhibitions, high definition multimedia show, and tours of the observatories can be arranged through AstroLab du Mont Mégantic. See website for details on dates & times.

Rothney Astrophysical Observatory: Dept. of Physics & Astronomy, University of Calgary, 2500 University Dr. NW, Calgary AB T2N 1N4 - 403/931-2366; E-mail: rao@phas.ucalgary.ca; URL: www.ucalgary.ca/rao/

Day and evening programs are available for school groups which involve a grade appropriate presentation, tour of the observatory and skyviewing. Programs run from 7:00 pm to 9:00 pm. Free drop-in visits to the Interpretive Centre are available Monday, Tuesday, and Wednesday from noon - 4pm. Private tours are available on other evenings during the year. School group tours are also available. See website for details.

Telus World of Science - Edmonton Observatory: 11211 - 142 St., Edmonton AB T5M 4A1 - 780/452-9100; Fax: 780/455-5882; URL: www.edmontonscience.com/pages/PlanVisit/Observatory.aspx

Summer hours (July to Labour Day weekend) 1:00 p.m. - 5:00 p.m. and 6:30 p.m. - 10 p.m. 7 days a week. Fall/Winter/Spring hours (After Labour Day to the following summer) Saturdays, Sundays & holidays 1:00 p.m. - 4:00 p.m., and Fridays, Saturdays & Sundays 7:00 p.m. - 10:00 p.m. Open weather permitting.

University of Alberta Observatory: Dept. of Physics, University of Alberta, Edmonton AB T6G 2J1 - 780/492-5286; Email: stars@ualberta.ca; URL: www.ualberta.ca/stars

Open to the public Thursday nights from September through April (closed for final exams and winter holidays), weather permitting. School groups, youth groups and other groups can book a private visit free of charge. See website for exact hours and details.

University of Saskatchewan Observatory: Dept. of Physics & Engineering Physics, University of Saskatchewan, 116 Science Place, Saskatoon SK S7N 5E2 - 306/966-6396; URL: physics.usask.ca/observatory/

Saturday evening programs year round; times vary. Tours for school and community groups are arranged for Friday evenings (October - March). Special tours may be arranged during the summer months.

PLANETARY FACT SHEET

	MERCURY	VENUS	EARTH	MOON	MARS	JUPITER	SATURN	URANUS	NEPTUNE	PLUTO
Mass **(10^{24}kg)**	0.33	4.87	5.97	0.073	0.642	1899	568	86.8	102	0.0125
Diameter **(km)**	4879	12,104	12,756	3475	6792	142,984	120,536	51,118	49,528	2390
Density **(kg/m^3)**	5427	5243	5515	3340	3933	1326	687	1270	1638	1750
Gravity **(m/s^2)**	3.7	8.9	9.8	1.6	3.7	23.1	9	8.7	11	0.6
Escape Velocity **(km/s)**	4.3	10.4	11.2	2.4	5	59.5	35.5	21.3	23.5	1.1
Rotation Period **(hours)**	1407.6	-5832.5	23.9	655.7	24.6	9.9	10.7	-17.2	16.1	-153.3
Length of Day **(hours)**	4222.6	2802	24	708.7	24.7	9.9	10.7	17.2	16.1	153.3
Distance from Sun **(10^6km)**	57.9	108.2	149.6	0.384*	227.9	778.6	1433.5	2872.5	4495.1	5870
Perihelion **(10^6 km)**	46	107.5	147.1	0.363*	206.6	740.5	1352.6	2741.3	4444.5	4435
Aphelion **(10^6 km)**	69.8	108.9	152.1	0.406*	249.2	816.6	1514.5	3003.6	4545.7	7304.3
Orbital Period **(days)**	88	224.7	365.2	27.3	687	4331	10,747	30,589	59,800	90,588
Orbital Velocity **(km/s)**	47.9	35	29.8	1	24.1	13.1	9.7	6.8	5.4	4.7
Orbital Inclination **(degrees)**	7	3.4	0	5.1	1.9	1.3	2.5	0.8	1.8	17.2
Orbital Eccentricity	0.205	0.007	0.017	0.055	0.094	0.049	0.057	0.046	0.011	0.244
Axial Tilt **(degrees)**	0.01	177.4	23.4	6.7	25.2	3.1	26.7	97.8	28.3	122.5
Mean Temperature **(C)**	167	464	15	-20	-65	-110	-140	-195	-200	-225
Surface Pressure **(bars)**	0	92	1	0	0.01	Unknown*	Unknown*	Unknown*	Unknown*	0
Number of Moons	0	0	1	0	2	67	62	27	13	5
Ring System?	No	No	No	No	No	Yes	Yes	Yes	Yes	No
Global Magnetic Field?	Yes	No	Yes	No	No	Yes	Yes	Yes	Yes	Unknown
	MERCURY	VENUS	EARTH	MOON	MARS	JUPITER	SATURN	URANUS	NEPTUNE	PLUTO

NSSDC/NASA

University of Toronto, St. George Campus Observatory: Dept. of Astronomy & Astrophysics, University of Toronto, 50 St. George Street, Toronto ON M5S 3H4 - 416/978-2016; URL: www1.astro.utoronto.ca/~gasa/public_talk/iWeb/index.php

Free tours are offered on the first Thursday of every month (excluding January). Tours start at 8 p.m. during winter months and 9 p.m. during summer months. Extra public tours may also be arranged. See website for details.

York University Observatory: 4700 Keele St., Toronto ON M3J 1P3 - 416/736-2100, ext. 77773 (voice mail); Email: pdelaney@yorku.ca; URL: www.physics.yorku.ca/observatory/

The observatory is open for online viewing Monday nights and public (in-person) viewing on Wednesday nights at the following times: October - March 7:30 p.m. - 9:30 p.m., and April - September 9:00 p.m. - 11:00 p.m. See website for further details.

PLANETARIUMS

A selection of planetaria with URL, phone number & related information:

ASTROLab du parc national du Mont-Mégantic: 189 route du Parc, Notre-Dame-des-Bois, QC J0B 2E0 - 819/888-2941; Toll Free: 1-800-665-6527; URL: www.astrolab-parc-national-mont-megantic.org

Cosmic Rhythms multimedia show; on-site lodging.

Doran Planetarium: Laurentian University, 935 Ramsey Lake Rd., Sudbury ON P3E 2C6 - 705/675-1151, ext. 2227, Fax: 705/675-4868; URL: www.oldwebsite.laurentian.ca/physics/planetarium/Planetarium.html

Largest planetarium in northern Ontario; programs.

The Lockhart Planetarium: 500 Dysart Rd., Winnipeg MB R3T 2M8 - 204/474-9785; URL: umanitoba.ca/faculties/science/astronomy/lockhart/

Dome seats 60; open year-round for public groups.

W.J. McCallion Planetarium: Dept. of Physics & Astronomy, McMaster University, 1280 Main St. West, Hamilton ON L8S 4M1 - 905/525-9140, ext. 27777; Fax: 905/546-1252; URL: physwww.physics.mcmaster.ca/planetarium

Planetarium has long history of support from RASC Hamilton Centre; first in Ontario open to the public. Public shows are Wednesdays (subject to change on occasion). See website for details.

MacMillan Planetarium: 1100 Chestnut St., Vancouver BC V6J 3J9. - 604/738-7827, Fax: 604/736-5665; URL: www.spacecentre.ca

Special laser shows in summer, numerous programs for school groups of all ages, teacher packages online.

Ontario Science Centre - CA Technologies Planetarium: 770 Don Mills Road, North York ON M3C 1T3 - 416/696-1000; URL: www.ontariosciencecentre.ca

Toronto's only public permanent planetarium. See website for details.

Planétarium de Montréal: 1000, rue St-Jacques Ouest, Montréal QC H3C 1G7 - 514/872-4530; Fax: 514/872-8102; E-mail: info@planetarium.montreal.qc.ca; URL: www.planetarium.montreal.qc.ca

Programs, activity sheets, classroom kits, advanced workshop for teachers & educators.

PLANETARY CONFIGURATIONS, 2013

Date		GMT (h:m)	Event
Jan	02	0:59	Earth at Perihelion: 0.98329
	04	03:00	Mercury at Aphelion
	07	01:28	Saturn 3.7°N of Moon
	10	11:36	Venus 2.8°S of Moon
	18	09	Mercury at Superior Conjunction
	22	02:57	Jupiter 0.5°N of Moon: Occn.
	24	12	Mars at Perihelion
Feb	03	09:55	Saturn 3.5°N of Moon
	08	16	Mercury-Mars: 0.3°
	06	21	Mercury at Greatest Elong: 18.1°E
	17	02	Mercury at Perihelion
	18	11:31	Jupiter 0.9°N of Moon: Occn.
	21	02	Venus at Aphelion
	21	07	Neptune-Sun Conjunction
Mar	02	15:21	Saturn 3.3°N of Moon
	04	13	Mercury at Inferior Conjunction
	18	01:16	Jupiter 1.5°N of Moon
	18	01:24	Jupiter-Aldebaran: 5.0°N
	28	17	Venus at Superior Conjunction
	29	00	Uranus-Sun Conjunction
	29	20:18	Saturn 3.3°N of Moon
	31	22	Mercury at Greatest Elong: 27.8°W
Apr	14	18:23	Jupiter 2.1°N of Moon
	18	00	Mars-Sun Conjunction
	26	02:28	Saturn 3.5°N of Moon
	28	08	Saturn at Opposition
May	11	21	Mercury at Superior Conjunction
	12	13:03	Jupiter 2.6°N of Moon
	16	02	Mercury at Perihelion
	23	09:55	Saturn 3.7°N of Moon
	27	06	Mercury-Jupiter: 2.4°
Jun	10	11:19	Venus 5.3°N of Moon
	12	17	Mercury at Greatest Elong: 24.3°E
	13	11	Venus at Perihelion
	19	15	Jupiter-Sun Conjunction
	19	17:45	Saturn 3.6°N of Moon
	20	07	Mercury-Venus: 1.9°
	22	04:49	Venus-Pollux: 5.1°S
	29	01	Mercury at Aphelion
Jul	03	15:26	Venus-Beehive: 0.1°N
	05	18:59	Earth at Aphelion: 1.01671
	09	19	Mercury at Inferior Conjunction
	17	01:19	Saturn 3.3°N of Moon
	22	09:30	Venus-Regulus: 1.0°N
	28	19	Mercury-Mars: 6.9°
	30	09	Mercury at Greatest Elong: 19.6°W
Aug	03	22:22	Jupiter 4.0°N of Moon
	10	02:19	Venus 5.1°N of Moon
	12	01	Mercury at Perihelion
	13	08:51	Saturn 2.8°N of Moon
	17	17:03	Mars-Pollux: 5.8°S
	24	21	Mercury at Superior Conjunction
	27	00	Neptune at Opposition
	31	16:38	Jupiter 4.5°N of Moon
Sep	06	00:37	Venus-Spica: 1.5°N
	08	10:00	Mars-Beehive: 0.5°S
	08	21:04	Venus 0.4°N of Moon: Occn.
	09	17:29	Saturn 2.3°N of Moon
	24	22:29	Mercury-Spica: 0.7°N
Oct	03	13	Uranus at Opposition
	03	19	Venus at Aphelion
	06	22:28	Mercury 2.8°S of Moon
	07	04:30	Saturn 1.9°N of Moon
	08	12:07	Venus 4.7°S of Moon
	08	13	Mercury-Saturn: 5.0°
	09	10	Mercury at Greatest Elong: 25.3°E
	15	03:51	Mars-Regulus: 0.9°N
	16	18:26	Venus-Antares: 1.5°N
Nov	01	09	Venus at Greatest Elong: 47.1°E
	01	20	Mercury at Inferior Conjunction
	06	11	Saturn-Sun Conjunction
	08	00	Mercury at Perihelion
	18	02	Mercury at Greatest Elong: 19.5°W
	26	05	Mercury-Saturn: 0.3°
Dec	01	10:13	Saturn 1.2°N of Moon: Occn.
	21	17:11	Winter Solstice
	22	00	Mercury at Aphelion
	26	02:45	Mars 4.6°N of Moon
	29	01:42	Saturn 0.9°N of Moon: Occn.
	29	06	Mercury at Superior Conjunction

Source: Planetary date courtesy of Fred Espenak, AstroPixels.com, Oct. 12, 2012.

Royal Ontario Museum: Outreach Services, ROM, Royal Ontario Museum, 100 Queens Park, Toronto ON M5S 2C6 - 416/586-5681; Fax: 416/586-5832; E-mail: outreach@rom.on.ca; URL: www.rom.on.ca

Portable Starlab dome available for any location in Ontario.

Science North: 100 Ramsey Lake Road, Sudbury ON P3E 5S9 - 705/522-3701 or toll-free 1-800-461-4898; Fax: 705/522-4954; E-mail: contactus@sciencenorth.ca; URL: sciencenorth.ca

Digital planetarium with feature films about astronomy and other space topics.

Telus World of Science - Calgary: PO Box 2100, Station M, #73, Calgary AB T2P 2M5 - 403/268-8300; Fax: 403/237-0186; E-mail: discover@calgaryscience.ca; URL: www.calgaryscience.ca

Join "Seymour Sky" at the Planetarium dome, several programs, multimedia shows & kits available.

Telus World of Science - Edmonton: 11211 - 142 St., Edmonton AB T5M 4A1 - 780/451-3344; Fax: 780/455-5882; URL: www.edmontonscience.com

Mobile planetarium available. Gift shop, IMAX theatre, science programs & computer lab; observatory operated by RASC volunteers.

University of Toronto: Dept. Of Astronomy & Astrophysics, University of Toronto, 50 St. George Street, Toronto ON M5S 3H4 - 416/978-2016; URL: www1.astro.utoronto.ca/~gasa/public_talk/iWeb/index.php

Portable Starlab dome. Free tours offered on the first Thursday of most months. Tours start at 8 p.m. during winter months and 9 p.m. during summer months. Extra public tours may be also arranged. See website for details.

Winnipeg Planetarium: 190 Rupert Ave., Winnipeg MB R3B 0N2 - 204/956-2830; Fax: 204/942-3679; E-mail: info@manitobamuseum.ca; URL: www.manitobamuseum.ca/main

Science centre, museum & planetarium in one site; mobile planetarium.

Many of Canada's professional astronomers, & most of Canada's enthusiastic amateur astronomers are members of the Royal Astronomical Society of Canada (see index) which has 27 Centres across Canada. An extensive list of astronomy clubs in Canada has been published online by SkyNews and can be found at www.skynewsmagazine.com/pages/clubs.html. Many of these clubs have programs for the general public.

ECLIPSES AND TRANSITS IN 2013

In 2013, there will be five eclipses, two solar, and three lunar.

1. A **partial eclipse** of the Moon on April 25, not visible from North America.
2. An **annular eclipse** of the Sun on May 10, not visible from North America.
3. A **penumbral eclipse** of the Moon on May 25, not visible from North America.
4. A **penumbral eclipse** of the Moon on October 18, visible from North America.
5. A **hybrid eclipse** of the Sun on November 3, partial visible from North America.

Source: NASA, eclipse.gsfc.nasa.gov/eclipse.html, Sept. 5, 2012.

METEORS, METEORITES, AND METEOR SHOWERS

A *meteor* or "shooting star" appears momentarily in the sky when a particle from beyond the earth enters the earth's atmosphere at a high velocity. Most visible meteors are caused by particles smaller than a grape or marble, and these small particles are completely vaporized in the atmosphere at a height of about 80 km. A spectacular meteor, known as a *fire-ball*, is caused by a larger body which may fall to the earth's surface in one or more pieces. Particles seen thus to fall, or subsequently found by analysis to be of this nature, are called meteorites.

Meteorites may be divided into two main classes—the irons, which are almost pure nickel-iron, and the stones. Any freshly-fallen meteorite is characterized by a dark, smooth crust caused by the fusion of the outer part.

Meteors may be observed on any clear, moonless night at an average rate of about five an hour. At times *meteor showers* occur, when meteors are seen with much greater frequency and appear to radiate from a particular part of the sky which is called the *radiant*. This is an effect of perspective, the radiant being the vanishing point of the parallel tracks of the meteors. Meteor showers usually repeat themselves annually, and in some cases have been associated with the orbits of comets. When the earth passes through or near the orbit of a comet it can intercept the small particles (meteoroids) which cause meteors. The principal meteor showers for the northern hemisphere are listed below. The information is based on that in the annual *Observer's Handbook* of the Royal Astronomical Society of Canada.

The study of meteors and meteorites adds to our knowledge of the nature and origin of the solar system and also to our knowledge of the earth's outer atmosphere.

MAPS OF THE NIGHT SKY

The maps on the next twelve pages cover the northern sky. Stars are shown down to a magnitude of 5, i.e. those which are readily apparent to the unaided eye on a reasonably dark night.

The maps are designed for 44°N latitude, but are useful for latitudes several degrees north or south of this. They show the hemisphere of sky visible to an observer at various times of the year. Because the aspect of the night sky changes continuously with both longitude and time, while time zones change discontinuously with both longitude and time of year, it is not possible to state simply when, in general, a particular observer will find that his or her sky fits exactly one of the twelve maps. The month indicated above each map is the time of year when the map will match the sky at 11 pm. On any particular night, successive maps will represent the sky as it appears every two hours. For example, at 2 am on a March night, the April map should be used. Just after dinner on a January night, the October map will be appropriate. The centre of each map is the zenith, the point directly overhead; the circumference is the horizon. To identify the stars, hold the map in front of you so that the part of the horizon which you are facing (west, for instance) is downward. (The four letters around the periphery of each map indicate compass directions.)

On the maps, stars forming the usual constellation patterns are linked by straight lines, constellation names being given in upper case letters. The names in lower case are those of first magnitude stars and Polaris, which is near the north celestial pole. Small clusters of dots indicate the positions of bright star clusters, nebulae or galaxies. Although a few of these are just visible to the naked eye, and most can be located with binoculars, a telesope is needed for good views of these objects. A dashed line appears on each of the twelve maps, which is the celestial equator. Coloured dots, each named, show the location of visual planets.

The twelve star charts on the following pages were prepared by Dirk Matussek and are copyright of AstroViewer, 2012.

REFERENCES

The tables and charts in the Canadian Almanac are intended for simple astronomical observations. To make more extensive observations the following are recommended: The Observer's Handbook (obtainable from the Royal Astronomical Society of Canada, 136 Dupont St., Toronto, ON M5R 1V2); Astronomical Phenomena (obtainable from The Superintendent of Documents, U.S. Government Printing Office, Washington, D.C.).
See also "Suggestions for Further Reading."

2013 Meteor Showers

A. **Meteor outbursts** are unusual showers (often of short duration) from the crossing of relatively recent comet ejecta. Dates are for the year 2013.
June 11, 08:28 UT, γ-Delphinids

B. **Annual meteor showers liable to have geophysical effects:**
Dates (based on UT in year 2013) are:

Dates	Peak Time (UT)	Name
Dec 28-Jan 12	Jan 03 13h25m	Quadrantids (QUA)
Apr 16-Apr 25	Apr 22 11h40m	Lyrids (LYR)
Apr 19-May 28	May 06 01h15m	η-Aquariids (ETA)
May 22-Jul 02	Jun 07 12h	Daytime Arietids (Ari)
May 20-Jul 05	Jun 09 11h	Daytime ζ-Perseids (Zeta Per)
Jun 05-Jul 17	Jun 28 10h	Daytime β-Taurids (Beta Tau)
Jul 12-Aug 23	Jul 30	Southern δ-Aquariids (SDA)
Jul 17-Aug 24	Aug 12 18h15m to 20h45m	Perseids (PER)
Sep 09-Oct 09	Sep 27 11h	Daytime Sextantids (Sex)
Oct 02-Nov 07	Oct 21	Orionids (ORI)
Nov 06-Nov 30	Nov 17 15h55m	Leonids (LEO)
Dec 07-Dec 17	Dec 13 13h15m - Dec 14 10h30m	Geminids (GEM)
Dec 17-Dec 26	Dec 22 14h15m	Ursids (URS)

C. **Annual meteor showers which may have geophysical effects:**
Dates (based on UT in year 2013) are:

Dates	Peak Time (UT)	Name
Apr 15-Apr 28	April 23 16h45m	η-Puppids(PPU)
Jun 22-Jul 02	June 27 09h15m	June Bootids (JBO)
Aug 28-Sep 05	Sep 1 01h35m	α-Aurigids (AUR)
Sep 05-Sep 21	Sep 9 14h50m - 15h30m	September ε-Perseids(SPE)
Oct 06-Oct 10	Oct 8 17h25m	Draconids (DRA)
Nov 15-Nov 25	Nov 21 16h15m	α-Monocerotids (AMO)

Source: www.ises-spaceweather.org (Dates selected from the International Meteor Organization Shower Calendar 2013. Peak times provided by A. McBeath.)

Sky Map

Toronto - Jan. 15, 2013 11:00 PM EST

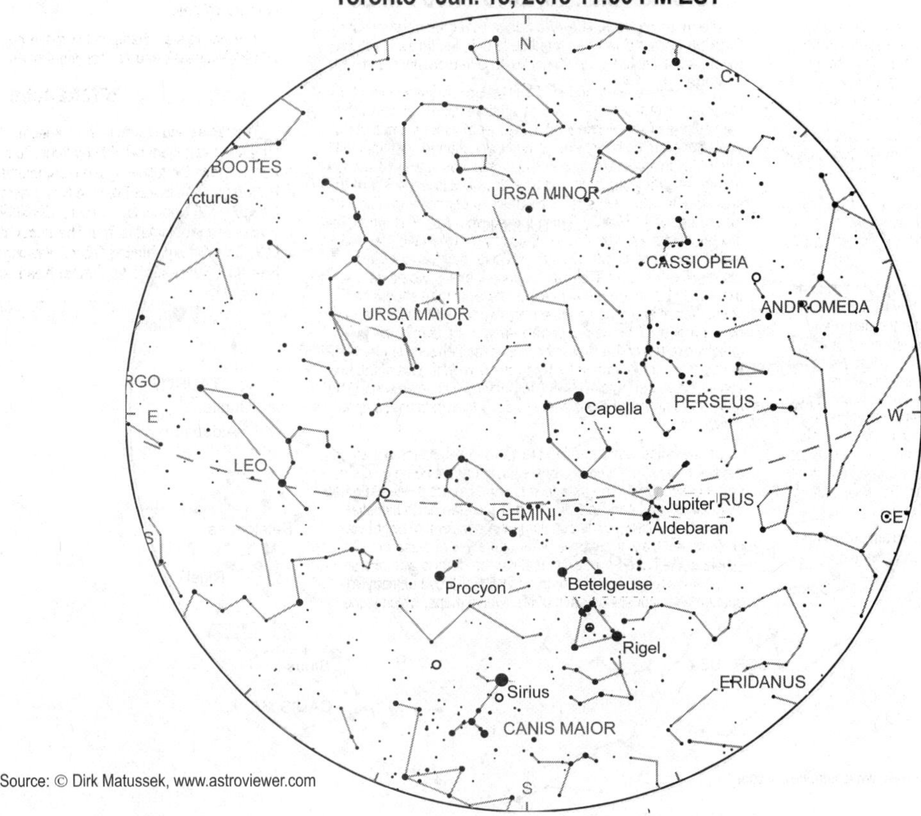

Source: © Dirk Matussek, www.astroviewer.com

Sky Map

Toronto - Feb. 15, 2013 11:00 PM EST

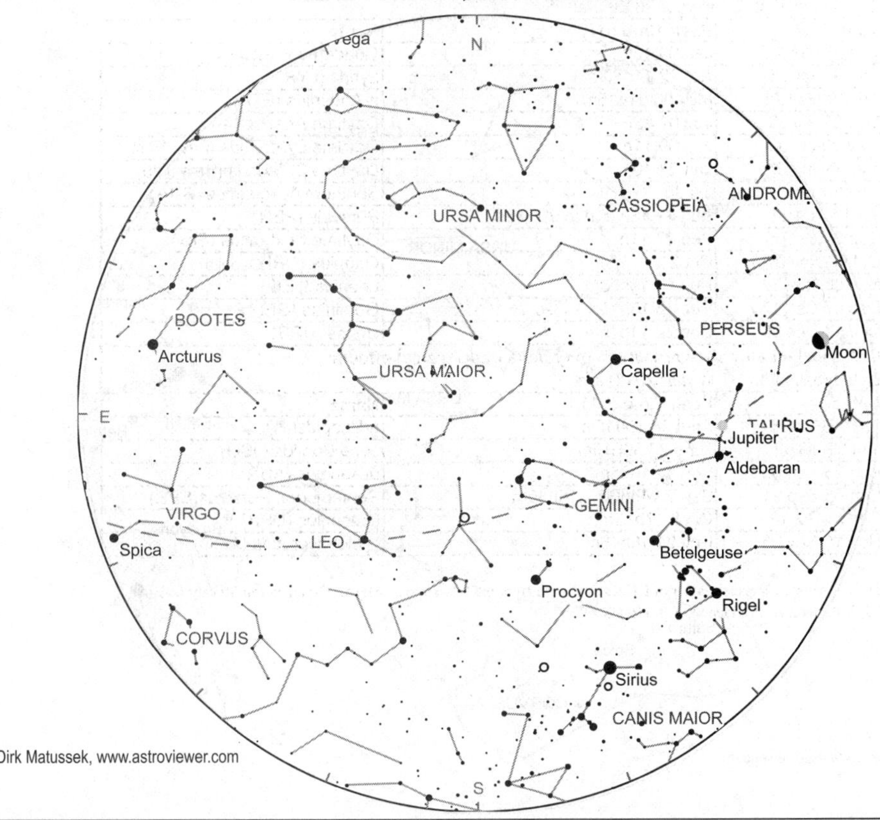

Source: © Dirk Matussek, www.astroviewer.com

Sky Map

Toronto - Mar. 15, 2013 11:00 PM EST

Source: © Dirk Matussek, www.astroviewer.com

Sky Map

Toronto - Apr. 15, 2013 11:00 PM EST

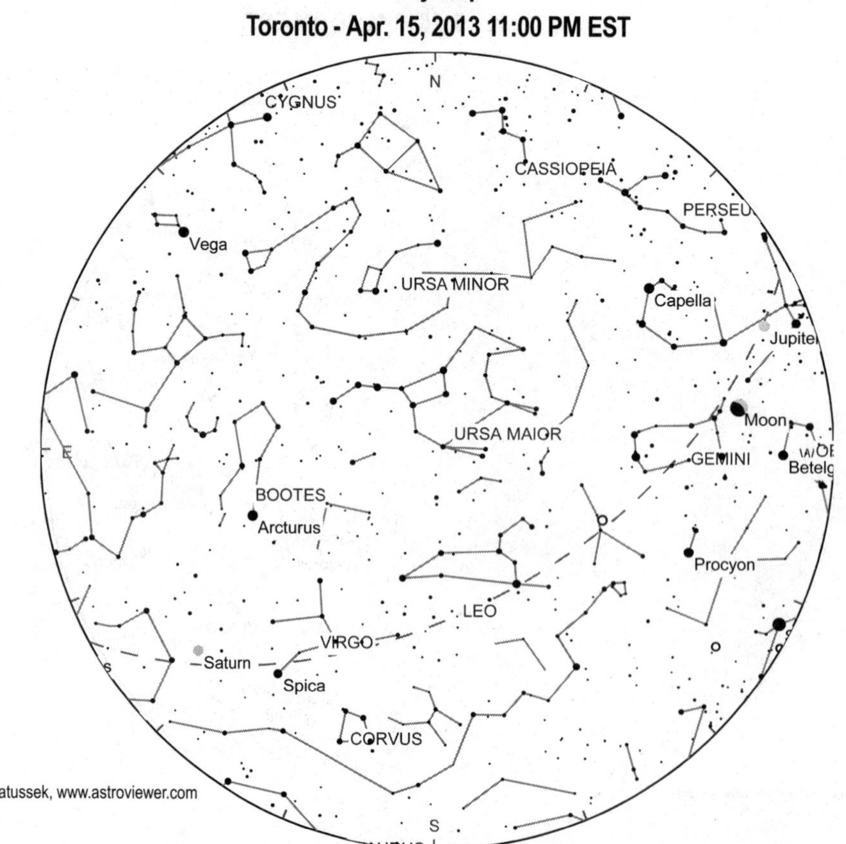

Source: © Dirk Matussek, www.astroviewer.com

Sky Map

Toronto - May 15, 2013 11:00 PM EST

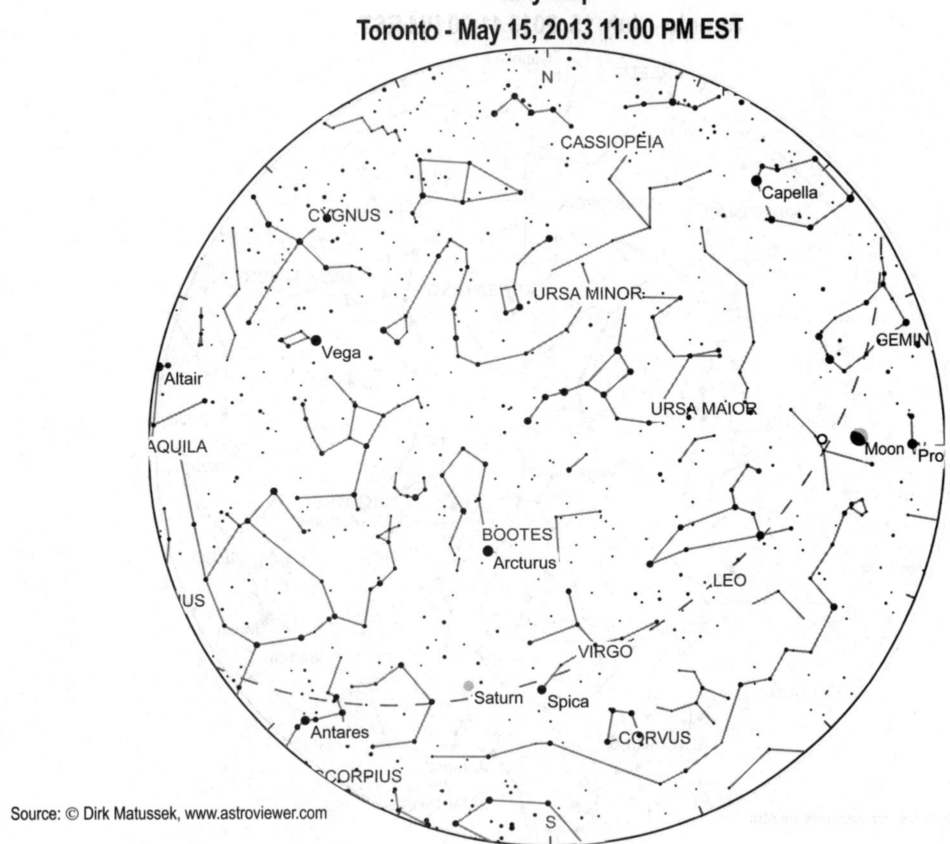

Source: © Dirk Matussek, www.astroviewer.com

Sky Map

Toronto - June 15, 2013 11:00 PM EST

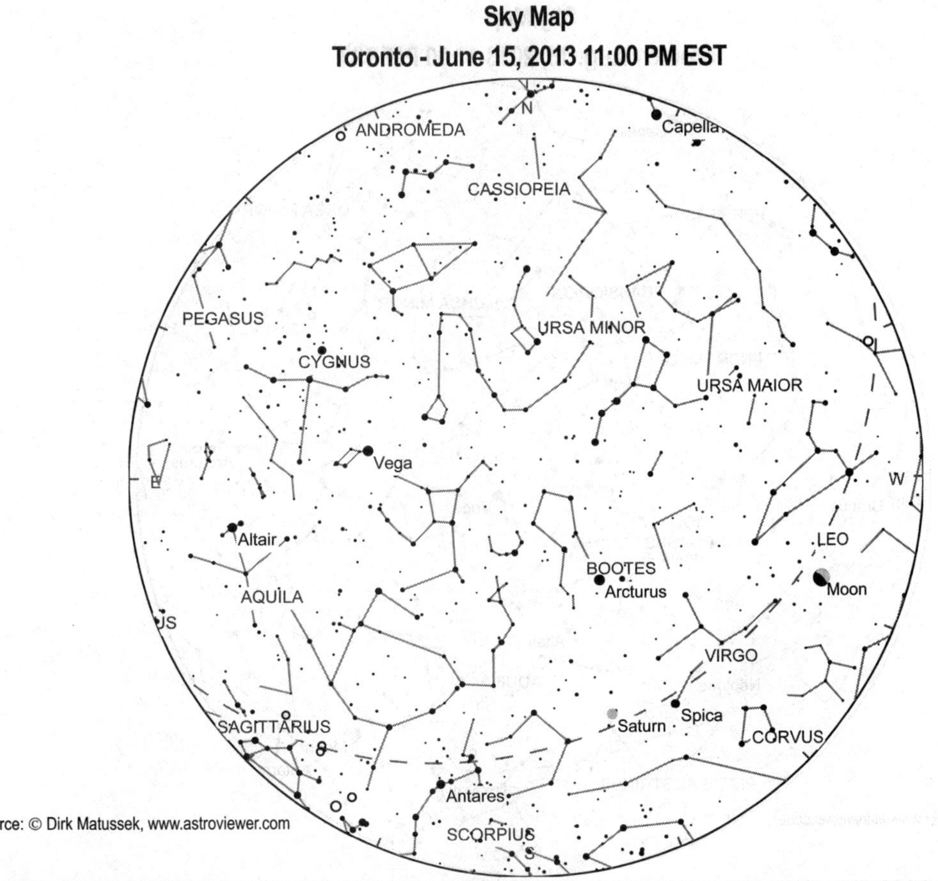

Source: © Dirk Matussek, www.astroviewer.com

Sky Map

Toronto - July 15, 2013 11:00 PM EST

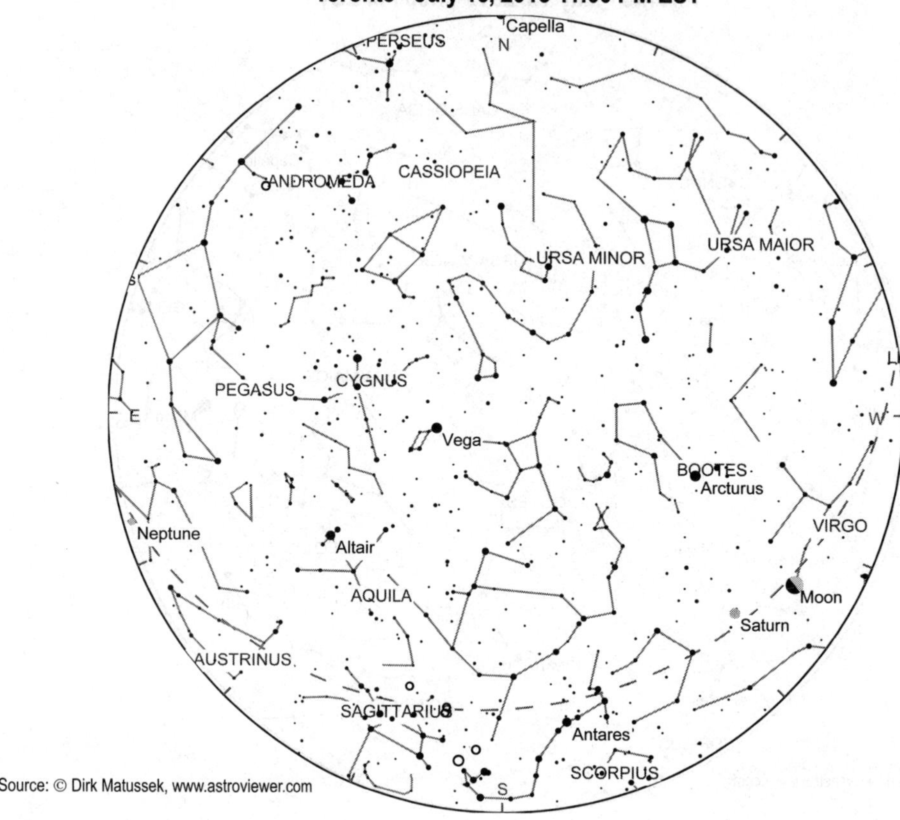

Source: © Dirk Matussek, www.astroviewer.com

Sky Map

Toronto - Aug. 15, 2013 11:00 PM EST

N
Capella
PERSEUS
URSA MAIOR
CASSIOPEIA
URSA MINOR
ANDROMEDA
BOOTES
Arcturus
E
W
CETUS
Uranus
CYGNUS
Vega
PEGASUS
Altair
Neptune
AQUILA
Moon
Antares
PISCIS AUSTRINUS
SAGITTARIUS
S

Source: © Dirk Matussek, www.astroviewer.com

Sky Map

Toronto - Sept. 15, 2013 11:00 PM EST

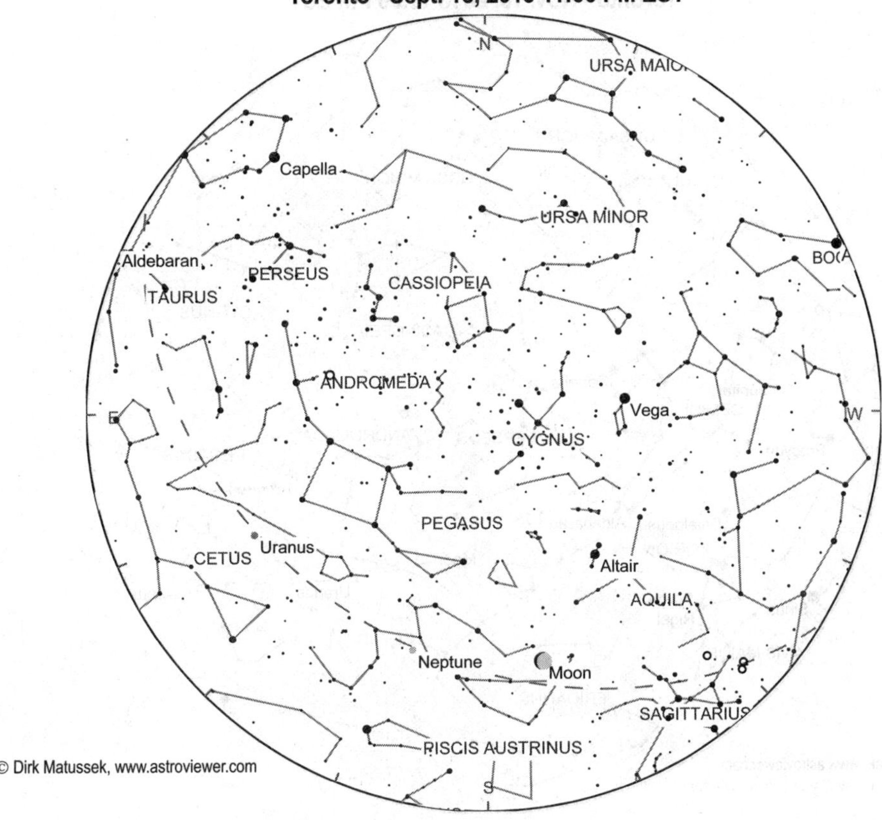

Source: © Dirk Matussek, www.astroviewer.com

Sky Map

Toronto - Oct. 15, 2013 11:00 PM EST

URSA MAIOR
upiter
GEMINI
URSA MINOR
Capella
CASSIOPEIA
Vega
Betelgeuse
PERSEUS
ORION
Aldebaran
E
TAURUS
ANDROMEDA
CYGNUS
W
gel
Altair
PEGASUS
AQUILA
Uranus
ERIDANUS
CETUS
Moon
Neptune
PISCIS AUSTRIN
S

Source: © Dirk Matussek, www.astroviewer.com

Sky Map
Toronto - Nov. 15, 2013 11:00 PM EST

Source: © Dirk Matussek, www.astroviewer.com

Sky Map
Toronto - Dec. 15, 2013 11:00 PM EST

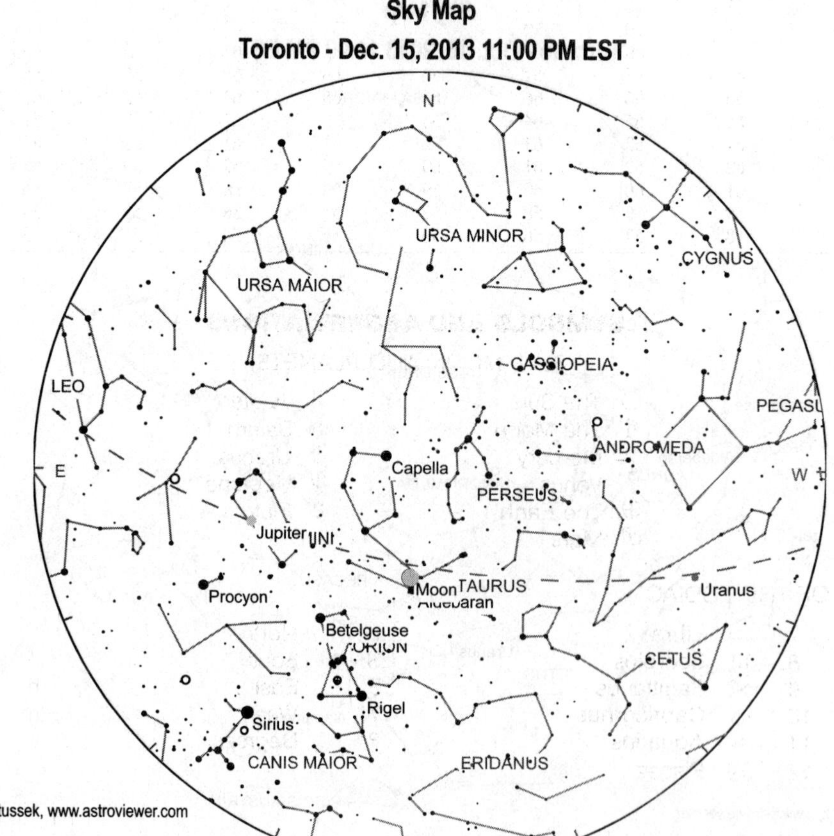

Source: © Dirk Matussek, www.astroviewer.com

AZIMUTHS OF THE POINTS OF RISING AND SETTING OF THE SUN FOR LATITUDES 43°N TO 52°N

In Degrees East of North for Rising and West of North for Setting

			43 N	44 N	45 N	46 N	47 N	48 N	49 N	50 N	51 N	52 N
Jan. 2	and	Dec. 11	122	123	124	124	125	126	127	127	128	129
Jan. 10	and	Dec. 3	121	121	122	123	123	124	125	126	127	127
Jan. 16	and	Nov. 27	119	120	120	121	122	122	123	124	125	126
Jan. 21	and	Nov. 22	118	118	119	120	120	121	121	122	123	124
Jan. 25	and	Nov. 17	116	117	117	118	119	119	120	120	121	122
Jan. 29	and	Nov. 14	115	115	116	116	117	118	118	119	119	120
Feb. 2	and	Nov. 10	114	114	114	115	115	116	116	117	118	118
Feb. 5	and	Nov. 6	112	113	113	113	114	114	115	115	116	116
Feb. 9	and	Nov. 3	111	111	111	112	112	113	113	114	114	115
Feb. 12	and	Oct. 31	109	110	110	110	111	111	112	112	113	113
Feb. 15	and	Oct. 28	108	108	109	109	109	110	110	110	111	111
Feb. 18	and	Oct. 25	107	107	107	107	108	108	108	109	109	110
Feb. 20	and	Oct. 22	105	105	106	106	106	106	107	107	108	108
Feb. 23	and	Oct. 19	104	104	104	104	105	105	105	106	106	106
Feb. 26	and	Oct. 17	102	103	103	103	103	104	104	104	104	105
Mar. 1	and	Oct. 14	101	101	101	102	102	102	102	102	103	103
Mar. 3	and	Oct. 11	100	100	100	100	100	100	101	101	101	101
Mar. 6	and	Oct. 9	98	98	98	99	99	99	99	99	100	100
Mar. 8	and	Oct. 6	97	97	97	97	97	97	98	98	98	98
Mar. 11	and	Oct. 4	95	96	96	96	96	96	96	96	96	96
Mar. 13	and	Oct. 1	94	94	94	94	94	94	95	95	95	95
Mar. 16	and	Sept. 28	93	93	93	93	93	93	93	93	93	93
Mar. 18	and	Sept. 26	91	91	91	91	91	92	92	92	92	92
Mar. 21	and	Sept. 23	90	90	90	90	90	90	90	90	90	90
Mar. 23	and	Sept. 21	89	89	89	89	89	88	88	88	88	88
Mar. 26	and	Sept. 18	87	87	87	87	87	87	87	87	87	87
Mar. 28	and	Sept. 16	86	86	86	86	86	86	85	85	85	85
Mar. 31	and	Sept. 13	85	84	84	84	84	84	84	84	84	84
Apr. 3	and	Sept. 10	83	83	83	83	83	83	82	82	82	82
Apr. 5	and	Sept. 8	82	82	82	81	81	81	81	81	80	80
Apr. 8	and	Sept. 5	80	80	80	80	80	80	79	79	79	79
Apr. 11	and	Sept. 2	79	79	79	78	78	78	78	78	77	77
Apr. 13	and	Aug. 30	78	77	77	77	77	76	76	76	76	75
Apr. 16	and	Aug. 28	76	76	76	76	75	75	75	74	74	74
Apr. 19	and	Aug. 25	75	75	74	74	74	73	73	73	72	72
Apr. 22	and	Aug. 22	73	73	73	73	72	72	72	71	71	70
Apr. 25	and	Aug. 19	72	72	71	71	71	70	70	70	69	69
Apr. 28	and	Aug. 16	71	70	70	70	69	69	68	68	67	67
May 1	and	Aug. 12	69	69	69	68	68	67	67	66	66	65
May 5	and	Aug. 9	68	67	67	67	66	66	65	65	64	63
May 8	and	Aug. 5	66	66	66	65	65	64	64	63	62	62
May 12	and	Aug. 2	65	65	64	64	63	62	62	61	61	60
May 16	and	July 28	64	63	63	62	61	61	60	60	59	58
May 21	and	June 24	62	62	61	60	60	59	59	58	57	56
May 26	and	June 19	61	60	60	59	58	58	57	56	55	54
June 1	and	July 12	59	59	58	57	57	56	55	54	53	53
June 10	and	July 3	58	57	56	56	55	54	53	53	52	51

SYMBOLS AND ABBREVIATIONS

SUN, MOON AND PLANETS

☉	The Sun	♃	Jupiter
☾	The Moon	♄	Saturn
☿	Mercury	♅	Uranus
♀	Venus	♆	Neptune
⊕	The Earth	♇	Pluto
♂	Mars		

SIGNS OF THE ZODIAC

1.	♈	Aries	7.	♎	Libra	N.	North	′	Minutes of Arc
2.	♉	Taurus	8.	♏	Scorpius	S.	South	″	Seconds of Arc
3.	♊	Gemini	9.	♐	Sagittarius	E.	East	h	Hours
4.	♋	Cancer	10.	♑	Capricornus	W.	West	m	Minutes of Time
5.	♌	Leo	11.	♒	Aquarius	°	Degrees	s	Seconds of Time
6.	♍	Virgo	12.	♓	Pisces				

AZIMUTH OF THE SUN AT RISING AND SETTING

Only twice a year, namely about March 21 and September 23, does the sun rise and set more or less exactly in the east and west respectively. It is of interest and sometimes of value to know the position of Sunrise and Sunset at other times. The table above tabulates these in degrees east of north and west of north for Sunrise and Sunset respectively for a selection of latitudes and dates. For latitudes and dates other than those tabulated take simple proportions. See table on page A-40.

SUGGESTIONS FOR FURTHER READING

There are many excellent astronomy books and materials. Here are some; the books are ones with a Canadian flavour.

Astronomical Society of the Pacific, 390 Ashton Ave., San Francisco CA USA 94112; URL: www.astrosociety.org. Excellent source of astronomical teaching resources, and other useful material; catalogue available. Also publish a free quarterly teachers' newsletter (available on-line).

Astronomy, PO Box 1612, Waukesha WI USA 53187; URL: www.astronomy.com. Popular non-technical monthly magazine for general astronomy readers.

The Backyard Astronomer's Guide, by Terence Dickinson & Alan Dyer. 2nd edition, Camden House Publishing, 2002. The best guide to equipment & techniques.

The Beginner's Observing Guide, by Leo Enright. Royal Astronomical Society of Canada, 136 Dupont St., Toronto ON M5R 1V2. A simple but serious introduction to the night sky. (5th edition: 2005-2010)

The Cold Light of Dawn, by Richard Jarrell. University of Toronto Press, 1988. An authoritative and comprehensive history of Canadian astronomy.

Exploring the Night Sky, by Terence Dickinson. Camden House Publishing, 1987. An award-winning guide, especially for young people.

Looking Up, by Peter Broughton. Dundurn Press, 1993. A history of the Royal Astronomical Society of Canada, illustrated.

Nightwatch, by Terence Dickinson. Camden House Publishing, (3rd revised edition, 1998). Excellent introduction to the night sky.

Observer's Handbook, edited by Patrick Kelly. Royal Astronomical Society of Canada, 136 Dupont St., Toronto ON M5R 1V2. Annual guide to sky phenomena & other astronomical information.

Sky Atlas 2000.0, by Wil Tirion. Sky Publishing. A popular sky atlas for amateur astronomers.

Sky & Telescope, PO Box 9111, Belmont MA USA 02178-9111; URL: skyandtelescope.com. A popular monthly magazine for amateur astronomers.

SkyNews. PO Box 1613, Belleville, ON K8N 9Z9; URL: www.skynews.ca. General astronomy from a Canadian perspective.

SkyWays, by Mary Lou Whitehorne. Royal Astronomical Society of Canada, 2003 (also available in French). A guide for Canadian schoolteachers.

Summer Stargazing, by Terence Dickinson. Firefly Books, 1996. A practical, user-friendly guide.

The Universe and Beyond, by Terence Dickinson, 4th Edition, Firefly Books, 2004. Excellent general book on Astronomy.

The Universe at your Fingertips, and More Universe at Your Fingertips, edited by Andrew Fraknoi et al. Astronomical Society of the Pacific, 390 Ashton Avenue, San Francisco CA USA 94112. An excellent collection of teaching activities & resources.

The Universe on a T-Shirt, by Dan Falk, Arcade Publishing, 2005 (paperback). An excellent short introduction to our understanding of the universe.

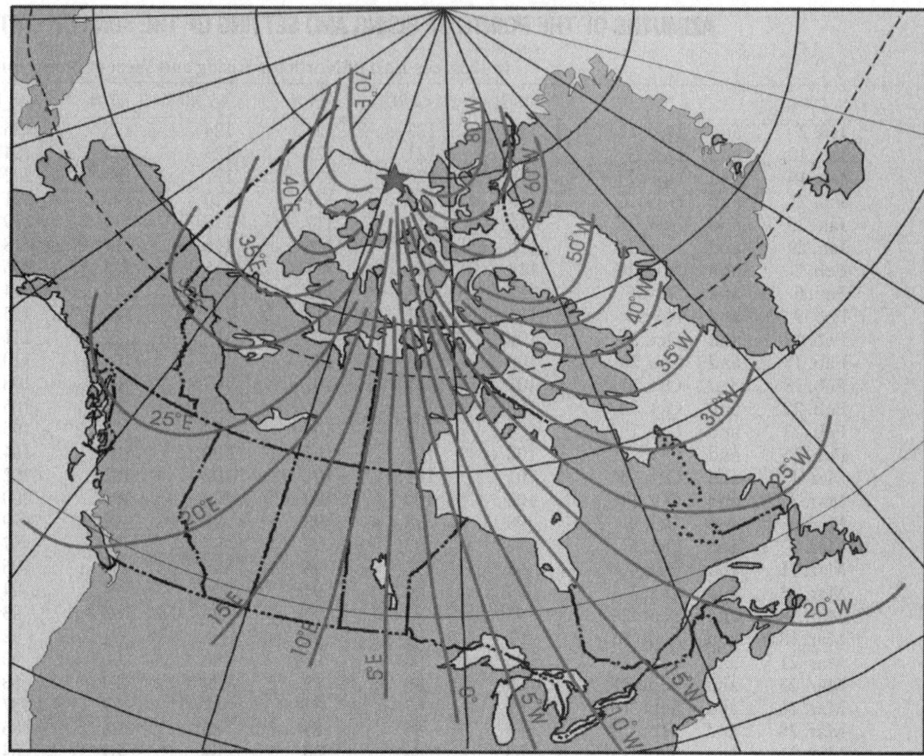

Reproduced with the permission of Natural Resources Canada 2012, courtesy of the Geological Survey of Canada.

CANADIAN ASTRONOMY WEBSITES

Most astronomical institutions and many of the branches of the Royal Astronomical Society of Canada have websites. They can be accessed from the following key sites:

- Canadian Astronomical Society: www.casca.ca
- Canadian Astronomy Education Website: www.cascaeducation.ca
- Canadian Space Agency: www.space.gc.ca
- Department of Astronomy and Astrophysics, University of Toronto: www.astro.utoronto.ca/home.html
- Herzberg Institute of Astrophysics: www.hia-iha.nrc-cnrc.gc.ca
- National Research Council Astronomy and Space Education: www.nrc-cnrc.gc.ca/education/skies/canadianskies_e.html
- Royal Astronomical Society of Canada: www.rasc.ca. Local branches of the RASC can be accessed through this site.

CHART OF MAGNETIC DECLINATION

A compass needle, even when unaffected by extraneous magnetic fields, does not in general point due north. The amount and direction by which its direction differs from true north is called magnetic declination or variation. The declination varies with the position of the observer and also varies slowly with time. The above chart gives the values of declination over Canada as of 2000. The chart is © Natural Resources Canada, and was kindly provided by Dr. Larry Newitt, National Geomagnetism Program, Geological Survey of Canada, Natural Resources Canada.

Example: What is the direction of the compass needle at the southern tip of Lake Manitoba?

That location is on the 5° east line; the declination is 5° east; the compass needle points 5° east of the true north.

For more information, see: http://gsc.nrcan.gc.ca/geomag; on the page http://geomag.nrcan.gc.ca/apps/mdcal-eng.php, you can do an online calculation of the magnetic declination for any place at any time.

NOTES ON THE ASTRONOMICAL TABLES

The purpose of the following notes is to explain the tables on pages A-42 to A-47 and to illustrate how they may be used for places other than those specified.

These tables give Standard Times of Sunrise and Sunset and Moonrise and Moonset for Ottawa, Toronto, Winnipeg and Vancouver. When Daylight Saving Time is in effect, of course, one hour must be added to the listed times. The calculations are for the upper limb (edge) of the sun and for the astronomical (sea) horizon. Accordingly, the actual observation of Sunrise or Sunset will differ from the tabulated value if the observer is below or above the level of his visible horizon at the point of Sunrise or Sunset.

To obtain the approximate times of Sunrise, Sunset, Moonrise and Moonset for other Canadian cities and towns proceed as indicated in the table on page A-52. The errors for Sunrise and Sunset by this approximate method will seldom exceed 10 minutes in winter and summer or 4 minutes in spring and fall, and for Moonrise and Moonset they will seldom exceed 15 minutes.

The tables have been calculated using the U.S.Naval Observatory website: aa.usno.navy.mil.

Rise & Set for the Sun for 2013
Ottawa

	Jan		Feb		Mar		Apr		May		June		July		Aug		Sept		Oct		Nov		Dec	
Day	Rise	Set	Rise	Set	Rise	Set	Rise	Set	Rise	Set	Rise	Set	Rise	Set	Rise	Set	Rise	Set	Rise	Set	Rise	Set	Rise	Set
	h m	h m	h m	h m	h m	h m	h m	h m	h m	h m	h m	h m	h m	h m	h m	h m	h m	h m	h m	h m	h m	h m	h m	h m
1	738	1629	719	1708	637	1748	540	1828	449	1906	416	1940	417	1950	446	1926	522	1837	558	1740	639	1648	718	1620
2	738	1630	718	1710	636	1749	538	1829	448	1907	416	1941	418	1950	447	1925	523	1835	600	1738	640	1646	719	1619
3	738	1631	717	1711	634	1750	537	1831	446	1908	415	1941	418	1950	448	1924	525	1833	601	1736	642	1645	720	1619
4	738	1632	716	1713	632	1752	535	1832	445	1910	415	1942	419	1950	449	1922	526	1831	602	1734	643	1644	722	1619
5	738	1633	715	1714	630	1753	533	1833	443	1911	415	1943	420	1949	450	1921	527	1829	603	1733	644	1642	723	1619
6	738	1634	713	1715	629	1755	531	1834	442	1912	414	1944	420	1949	451	1920	528	1827	605	1731	646	1641	724	1619
7	738	1635	712	1717	627	1756	529	1836	441	1913	414	1944	421	1948	453	1918	529	1826	606	1729	647	1640	725	1618
8	737	1637	711	1718	625	1757	527	1837	439	1914	414	1945	422	1948	454	1917	531	1824	607	1727	648	1639	726	1618
9	737	1638	709	1720	623	1758	526	1838	438	1916	413	1946	423	1947	455	1915	532	1822	608	1725	650	1637	727	1618
10	737	1639	708	1721	621	1800	524	1839	437	1917	413	1946	424	1947	456	1914	533	1820	610	1723	651	1636	727	1618
11	736	1640	706	1723	619	1801	522	1841	435	1918	413	1947	424	1946	457	1912	534	1818	611	1722	653	1635	728	1618
12	736	1641	705	1724	618	1802	520	1842	434	1919	413	1947	425	1946	458	1911	535	1816	612	1720	654	1634	729	1618
13	736	1643	703	1726	616	1804	518	1843	433	1920	413	1948	426	1945	500	1909	537	1814	613	1718	655	1633	730	1619
14	735	1644	702	1727	614	1805	517	1845	432	1921	413	1948	427	1944	501	1908	538	1812	615	1716	657	1632	731	1619
15	735	1645	700	1728	612	1806	515	1846	431	1923	413	1949	428	1944	502	1906	539	1810	616	1715	658	1631	732	1619
16	734	1646	659	1730	610	1808	513	1847	430	1924	413	1949	429	1943	503	1904	540	1808	617	1713	659	1630	732	1619
17	733	1648	657	1731	608	1809	511	1848	429	1925	413	1949	430	1942	504	1903	541	1807	619	1711	701	1629	733	1620
18	733	1649	656	1733	606	1810	510	1850	428	1926	413	1950	431	1941	506	1901	543	1805	620	1710	702	1628	734	1620
19	732	1650	654	1734	605	1811	508	1851	427	1927	413	1950	432	1940	507	1859	544	1803	621	1708	703	1627	734	1620
20	731	1652	653	1735	603	1813	506	1852	426	1928	413	1950	433	1940	508	1858	545	1801	623	1706	705	1626	735	1621
21	730	1653	651	1737	601	1814	505	1853	425	1929	413	1950	434	1939	509	1856	546	1759	624	1705	706	1626	735	1621
22	730	1654	649	1738	559	1815	503	1855	424	1930	414	1951	435	1938	510	1854	547	1757	625	1703	707	1625	736	1622
23	729	1656	648	1740	557	1817	501	1856	423	1931	414	1951	436	1937	512	1853	549	1755	627	1701	709	1624	736	1622
24	728	1657	646	1741	555	1818	500	1857	422	1932	414	1951	437	1936	513	1851	550	1753	628	1700	710	1623	737	1623
25	727	1658	644	1742	553	1819	458	1858	421	1933	415	1951	438	1935	514	1849	551	1751	629	1658	711	1623	737	1624
26	726	1700	643	1744	551	1820	457	1900	420	1934	415	1951	439	1933	515	1847	552	1749	631	1657	712	1622	737	1624
27	725	1701	641	1745	550	1822	455	1901	420	1935	415	1951	440	1932	516	1846	553	1748	632	1655	713	1622	738	1625
28	724	1703	639	1746	548	1823	454	1902	419	1936	416	1951	441	1931	517	1844	555	1746	633	1654	715	1621	738	1626
29	723	1704			546	1824	452	1903	418	1937	416	1951	442	1930	519	1842	556	1744	635	1652	716	1621	738	1627
30	722	1705			544	1826	451	1905	418	1938	417	1950	443	1929	520	1840	557	1742	636	1651	717	1620	738	1627
31	721	1707			542	1827			417	1939			445	1927	521	1838			637	1649			738	1628

Note: Blank space in the table indicates that a rising or setting did not occur during that 24-hour interval

Location: W075 00, N45 00

Zone: 5h West of Greenwich

Astronomical Applications Dept., U.S. Naval Observatory,

Washington, DC 20392-5420

Rise & Set for the Moon for 2013

Ottawa

	Jan		Feb		Mar		Apr		May		June		July		Aug		Sept		Oct		Nov		Dec	
Day	Rise	Set	Rise	Set	Rise	Set	Rise	Set	Rise	Set	Rise	Set	Rise	Set	Rise	Set	Rise	Set	Rise	Set	Rise	Set	Rise	Set
	h m	h m	h m	h m	h m	h m	h m	h m	h m	h m	h m	h m	h m	h m	h m	h m	h m	h m	h m	h m	h m	h m	h m	h m
1	2111	938	2332	934	2233	810		913	15	1025	29	1250		1354	19	1535	136	1618	223	1548	424	1542	530	1531
2	2216	1005		1007	2343	847	43	1016	53	1135	56	1356	27	1455	104	1623	234	1650	326	1616	533	1617	640	1622
3	2323	1031	42	1045		930	133	1124	126	1244	124	1459	101	1554	154	1706	334	1720	430	1644	644	1657	746	1722
4		1059	152	1130	50	1020	215	1233	156	1352	153	1601	138	1649	247	1744	436	1748	536	1714	754	1743	846	1829
5	32	1129	258	1223	152	1118	251	1343	224	1458	224	1702	220	1740	344	1819	539	1816	643	1746	901	1838	937	1942
6	143	1204	400	1325	247	1222	323	1452	252	1603	259	1759	307	1826	443	1849	644	1844	752	1822	1003	1940	1021	2055
7	255	1246	454	1434	335	1332	353	1600	320	1706	338	1853	358	1907	544	1918	749	1913	902	1903	1056	2047	1059	2208
8	406	1336	540	1547	415	1443	421	1707	350	1808	422	1943	453	1944	646	1945	856	1945	1009	1951	1143	2157	1132	2319
9	514	1436	619	1701	451	1554	449	1812	422	1908	511	2027	551	2016	749	2012	1004	2022	1112	2047	1222	2308	1203	
10	614	1544	653	1814	522	1705	518	1916	459	2005	603	2107	651	2046	853	2039	1112	2104	1209	2149	1257		1232	28
11	705	1658	724	1925	551	1814	549	2018	540	2058	659	2141	751	2113	958	2109	1217	2154	1259	2256	1328	19	1301	134
12	749	1813	752	2034	620	1921	623	2117	625	2146	758	2213	853	2140	1105	2142	1318	2251	1343		1358	128	1332	240
13	825	1927	820	2140	648	2027	701	2213	716	2228	857	2241	956	2206	1212	2220	1413	2355	1421	6	1428	236	1406	343
14	857	2039	849	2244	718	2130	744	2304	810	2306	959	2308	1100	2234	1320	2305	1502		1454	117	1458	342	1443	444
15	925	2147	919	2346	750	2231	831	2350	907	2339	1101	2335	1206	2305	1425	2358	1544	105	1525	228	1530	447	1524	542
16	953	2254	952		825	2329	923		1006		1205		1315	2340	1526		1621	217	1556	337	1605	551	1610	636
17	1020	2357	1028	45	905		1018	31	1107	10	1312	2	1424		1620	59	1655	330	1626	446	1644	652	1700	725
18	1048		1109	141	949	23	1117	107	1209	38	1421	31	1533	21	1708	208	1726	443	1657	554	1728	749	1754	808
19	1118	59	1156	232	1039	112	1217	139	1314	105	1532	105	1640	111	1749	322	1756	554	1731	700	1815	841	1850	847
20	1152	159	1247	319	1132	156	1320	209	1421	133	1644	144	1740	210	1825	437	1827	704	1808	803	1907	928	1947	921
21	1230	257	1343	401	1230	235	1425	238	1531	202	1755	230	1832	317	1858	552	1900	811	1849	903	2002	1010	2046	951
22	1313	351	1443	439	1330	310	1533	305	1643	234	1900	326	1917	431	1928	705	1935	916	1934	958	2058	1046	2145	1019
23	1402	440	1545	513	1433	341	1643	334	1757	310	1957	431	1956	547	1959	816	2013	1018	2023	1048	2157	1119	2246	1046
24	1456	525	1650	543	1538	411	1755	405	1910	354	2045	544	2029	703	2029	924	2055	1116	2116	1133	2256	1149	2347	1112
25	1554	606	1756	612	1645	439	1909	440	2018	446	2125	659	2100	817	2102	1030	2142	1208	2212	1212	2356	1216		1140
26	1655	641	1903	640	1755	508	2023	520	2118	548	2200	814	2130	928	2138	1133	2232	1256	2309	1247		1243	51	1209
27	1758	713	2012	708	1906	537	2132	608	2209	656	2231	927	2159	1036	2217	1232	2326	1338		1319	59	1310	157	1242
28	1903	742	2122	737	2018	609	2235	703	2252	809	2300	1038	2230	1142	2301	1327		1416	9	1348	203	1339	305	1320
29	2008	810			2131	646	2329	806	2328	922	2328	1146	2303	1245	2348	1417	23	1449	110	1416	310	1411	414	1405
30	2115	837			2241	728		914		1034	2357	1251	2339	1346		1502	122	1520	212	1443	419	1447	522	1500
31	2223	904			2346	817			0	1143				1442	40	1542			317	1512			626	1604

Note: Blank space in the table indicates that a rising or setting did not occur during that 24-hour interval

Location: W075 00, N45 00

Zone: 5h West of Greenwich

Astronomical Applications Dept.

Washington, DC 20392-5420

Rise & Set for the Sun for 2013
Toronto

	Jan		Feb		Mar		Apr		May		June		July		Aug		Sept		Oct		Nov		Dec	
Day	Rise	Set	Rise	Set	Rise	Set	Rise	Set	Rise	Set	Rise	Set	Rise	Set	Rise	Set	Rise	Set	Rise	Set	Rise	Set	Rise	Set
	h m	h m	h m	h m	h m	h m	h m	h m	h m	h m	h m	h m	h m	h m	h m	h m	h m	h m	h m	h m	h m	h m	h m	h m
1	747	1652	731	1729	652	1806	558	1843	510	1917	440	1949	441	1959	507	1937	541	1850	614	1757	651	1708	728	1642
2	747	1653	730	1730	650	1807	556	1844	508	1918	439	1949	441	1959	508	1936	542	1849	615	1755	652	1706	729	1642
3	747	1654	729	1732	648	1808	554	1845	507	1920	439	1950	442	1958	509	1934	543	1847	616	1753	653	1705	730	1642
4	747	1655	727	1733	647	1809	552	1846	505	1921	415	1951	443	1958	510	1933	544	1845	617	1752	655	1704	731	1642
5	747	1656	726	1734	645	1811	551	1847	504	1922	438	1952	443	1958	511	1932	545	1843	618	1750	656	1703	732	1641
6	747	1657	725	1736	643	1812	549	1848	503	1923	438	1952	444	1957	512	1931	546	1842	619	1748	657	1702	733	1641
7	747	1658	724	1737	642	1813	547	1850	502	1924	437	1953	445	1957	513	1929	547	1840	620	1746	659	1700	734	1641
8	747	1659	723	1738	640	1814	546	1851	500	1925	437	1953	445	1957	515	1928	548	1838	622	1745	700	1659	735	1641
9	747	1700	721	1740	638	1815	544	1852	459	1926	437	1954	446	1956	516	1927	549	1836	623	1743	701	1658	736	1641
10	746	1701	720	1741	636	1817	542	1853	458	1927	437	1955	447	1956	517	1925	550	1834	624	1741	702	1657	737	1641
11	746	1702	719	1742	635	1818	540	1854	457	1928	437	1955	447	1955	518	1924	552	1833	625	1740	704	1656	737	1641
12	746	1704	717	1744	633	1819	539	1855	456	1930	436	1956	448	1955	519	1922	553	1831	626	1738	705	1655	738	1641
13	745	1705	716	1745	631	1820	537	1856	455	1931	436	1956	449	1954	520	1921	554	1829	627	1736	706	1654	739	1642
14	745	1706	715	1746	629	1821	535	1858	454	1932	436	1957	450	1954	521	1919	555	1827	629	1735	707	1653	740	1642
15	744	1707	713	1748	628	1823	534	1859	453	1933	436	1957	451	1953	522	1918	556	1825	630	1733	709	1652	740	1642
16	744	1708	712	1749	626	1824	532	1900	452	1934	436	1957	452	1952	523	1916	557	1824	631	1731	710	1651	741	1642
17	743	1710	710	1750	624	1825	531	1901	451	1935	436	1958	452	1951	524	1915	558	1822	632	1730	711	1650	742	1643
18	743	1711	709	1752	622	1826	529	1902	450	1936	437	1958	453	1951	525	1913	559	1820	633	1728	712	1650	742	1643
19	742	1712	707	1753	621	1827	527	1903	449	1937	437	1958	454	1950	527	1912	600	1818	635	1727	714	1649	743	1644
20	741	1713	706	1754	619	1829	526	1905	448	1938	437	1959	455	1949	528	1910	601	1816	636	1725	715	1648	744	1644
21	741	1715	704	1755	617	1830	524	1906	447	1939	437	1959	456	1948	529	1909	602	1815	637	1723	716	1647	744	1644
22	740	1716	703	1757	615	1831	523	1907	446	1940	437	1959	457	1947	530	1907	604	1813	638	1722	717	1647	745	1645
23	739	1717	701	1758	614	1832	521	1908	445	1941	438	1959	458	1946	531	1905	605	1811	640	1720	719	1646	745	1646
24	738	1718	700	1759	612	1833	520	1909	445	1942	438	1959	459	1945	532	1904	606	1809	641	1719	720	1645	745	1646
25	738	1720	658	1801	610	1834	518	1910	444	1943	438	1959	500	1944	533	1902	607	1807	642	1717	721	1645	746	1647
26	737	1721	656	1802	608	1836	517	1912	443	1944	439	1959	501	1943	534	1900	608	1806	643	1716	722	1644	746	1647
27	736	1722	655	1803	606	1837	515	1913	442	1944	439	1959	502	1942	535	1859	609	1804	645	1715	723	1644	746	1648
28	735	1724	653	1804	605	1838	514	1914	442	1945	439	1959	503	1941	536	1857	610	1802	646	1713	724	1643	747	1649
29	734	1725			603	1839	512	1915	441	1946	440	1959	504	1940	537	1855	611	1800	647	1712	726	1643	747	1650
30	733	1726			601	1840	511	1916	441	1947	440	1959	505	1939	539	1854	612	1759	648	1710	727	1643	747	1650
31	732	1728			559	1841			440	1948			506	1938	540	1852			650	1709			747	1651

Note: Blank space in the table indicates that a rising or setting did not occur during that 24-hour interval

Location: W079 00, N43 00

Zone: 5h West of Greenwich

Astronomical Applications Dept., U.S. Naval Observatory

Washington, DC 20392-5420

Rise & Set for the Moon for 2013

Toronto

Day	Jan Rise	Jan Set	Feb Rise	Feb Set	Mar Rise	Mar Set	Apr Rise	Apr Set	May Rise	May Set	June Rise	June Set
	h m	h m	h m	h m	h m	h m	h m	h m	h m	h m	h m	h m
1	2129	952	2345	953	2245	830		936	26	1046	45	1307
2	2233	1020		1027	2354	908	54	1039	106	1155	113	1411
3	2338	1048	54	1106		952	144	1146	140	1303	142	1513
4		1117	203	1152	101	1043	227	1254	211	1409	213	1614
5	46	1149	309	1246	202	1141	304	1403	241	1514	245	1713
6	155	1225	410	1348	258	1245	338	1511	309	1617	321	1810
7	306	1308	504	1457	346	1353	408	1617	339	1720	401	1904
8	417	1359	551	1608	428	1503	437	1722	410	1821	445	1953
9	524	1459	632	1721	504	1613	507	1826	444	1920	533	2038
10	624	1607	707	1833	537	1723	537	1929	521	2016	626	2118
11	716	1720	739	1942	607	1830	609	2030	602	2108	721	2153
12	801	1834	809	2049	637	1936	644	2128	648	2156	818	2225
13	838	1947	838	2154	707	2040	723	2224	738	2239	917	2255
14	911	2057	908	2257	738	2143	806	2314	832	2317	1017	2323
15	941	2204	939	2358	811	2243	854		928	2352	1118	2351
16	1010	2309	1013		847	2340	945	0	1026		1221	
17	1038		1050	56	928		1040	41	1126	23	1326	19
18	1108	11	1132	151	1012	33	1138	118	1227	52	1434	50
19	1139	112	1219	243	1101	122	1238	152	1331	121	1544	125
20	1214	211	1310	330	1155	206	1339	223	1436	149	1656	205
21	1253	307	1405	412	1251	246	1443	252	1545	220	1805	253
22	1336	401	1504	450	1351	322	1549	322	1656	253	1910	349
23	1425	451	1605	525	1453	354	1658	352	1809	331	2007	454
24	1518	536	1709	557	1557	425	1809	424	1921	416	2056	606
25	1616	616	1814	627	1702	455	1922	500	2028	509	2138	720
26	1716	653	1920	656	1810	524	2034	542	2129	611	2214	834
27	1818	726	2027	725	1920	555	2143	630	2220	719	2246	946
28	1921	756	2136	756	2031	629	2245	726	2304	830	2317	1055
29	2025	825			2142	706	2340	829	2341	942	2346	1201
30	2131	853			2251	750		937		1053		1305
31	2237	922			2356	839			14	1201		

Day	July Rise	July Set	Aug Rise	Aug Set	Sept Rise	Sept Set	Oct Rise	Oct Set	Nov Rise	Nov Set	Dec Rise	Dec Set
	h m	h m	h m	h m	h m	h m	h m	h m	h m	h m	h m	h m
1	16	1407	42	1545	158	1630	242	1603	439	1601	542	1552
2	48	1507	127	1633	255	1703	344	1632	546	1637	651	1644
3	122	1605	216	1717	354	1734	446	1701	656	1718	757	1745
4	200	1659	310	1756	455	1803	551	1732	805	1806	857	1852
5	243	1750	406	1831	557	1832	658	1805	912	1901	949	2003
6	330	1836	504	1903	700	1901	805	1842	1013	2002	1034	2116
7	421	1918	604	1932	804	1932	913	1925	1107	2109	1112	2227
8	515	1955	704	2000	910	2005	1020	2014	1154	2219	1147	2337
9	612	2029	806	2028	1017	2043	1123	2110	1235	2328	1219	
10	711	2059	909	2057	1123	2126	1220	2211	1311		1249	44
11	810	2128	1013	2128	1228	2217	1311	2318	1344	37	1320	149
12	911	2156	1118	2202	1329	2314	1355		1415	145	1352	253
13	1012	2223	1224	2241	1424		1434	27	1445	251	1427	356
14	1116	2252	1331	2327	1513	18	1509	136	1517	357	1505	456
15	1220	2324	1436		1556	126	1541	246	1550	501	1546	553
16	1327		1536	21	1635	238	1612	354	1626	603	1632	646
17	1436	1	1631	122	1709	349	1644	502	1706	703	1722	735
18	1544	43	1719	230	1742	500	1717	608	1750	800	1816	819
19	1650	133	1802	343	1814	610	1752	713	1838	852	1911	858
20	1750	233	1839	457	1846	718	1829	815	1929	939	2008	933
21	1844	340	1913	610	1920	825	1911	914	2023	1021	2105	1004
22	1929	453	1945	722	1956	929	1957	1009	2119	1058	2204	1034
23	2009	608	2017	831	2035	1030	2046	1059	2217	1132	2303	1101
24	2044	723	2049	939	2118	1127	2138	1144	2315	1202		1129
25	2116	835	2123	1043	2204	1219	2233	1224		1231	3	1157
26	2147	944	2159	1145	2255	1306	2330	1259	14	1259	106	1228
27	2218	1051	2239	1243	2348	1349		1332	115	1327	210	1302
28	2250	1156	2323	1338		1427	28	1402	218	1357	317	1341
29	2324	1258		1428	44	1502	128	1431	324	1430	426	1428
30		1357	11	1513	142	1533	230	1459	432	1508	533	1523
31	1	1453	103	1553			333	1529			637	1626

Note: Blank space in the table indicates that a rising or setting did not occur during that 24-hour interval

Location: W079 00, N43 00

Zone: 5h West of Greenwich

Astronomical Applications Dept.

Washington, DC 20392-5420

Rise & Set for the Sun for 2013
Winnipeg

	Jan		Feb		Mar		Apr		May		June		July		Aug		Sept		Oct		Nov		Dec	
Day	Rise	Set	Rise	Set	Rise	Set	Rise	Set	Rise	Set	Rise	Set	Rise	Set	Rise	Set	Rise	Set	Rise	Set	Rise	Set	Rise	Set
	h m	h m	h m	h m	h m	h m	h m	h m	h m	h m	h m	h m	h m	h m	h m	h m	h m	h m	h m	h m	h m	h m	h m	h m
1	822	1642	758	1726	709	1812	605	1859	507	1944	428	2024	428	2035	501	2006	545	1910	628	1806	716	1707	801	1633
2	822	1643	757	1727	707	1813	603	1901	505	1946	428	2025	429	2035	503	2005	546	1908	630	1804	717	1705	802	1633
3	822	1644	755	1729	705	1815	601	1902	503	1947	427	2026	429	2035	504	2003	548	1906	631	1802	719	1704	804	1632
4	822	1645	754	1731	703	1817	559	1904	502	1949	415	2027	430	2034	505	2002	549	1904	632	1800	721	1702	805	1632
5	821	1646	752	1732	701	1818	557	1905	500	1950	426	2028	431	2034	507	2000	551	1901	634	1758	722	1700	806	1631
6	821	1647	751	1734	659	1820	555	1907	458	1952	425	2028	432	2033	508	1959	552	1859	635	1756	724	1659	807	1631
7	821	1648	749	1736	657	1821	552	1908	457	1953	425	2029	433	2033	509	1957	554	1857	637	1754	725	1657	808	1631
8	820	1650	748	1737	655	1823	550	1910	455	1954	425	2030	433	2032	511	1955	555	1855	638	1752	727	1656	809	1631
9	820	1651	746	1739	653	1824	548	1911	454	1956	424	2031	434	2032	512	1954	556	1853	640	1750	729	1655	810	1631
10	820	1652	744	1741	651	1826	546	1913	452	1957	424	2031	435	2031	514	1952	558	1851	641	1748	730	1653	811	1631
11	819	1654	743	1742	649	1828	544	1914	451	1959	424	2032	436	2030	515	1950	559	1849	643	1746	732	1652	812	1631
12	818	1655	741	1744	647	1829	542	1916	450	2000	424	2033	437	2030	517	1948	601	1847	644	1744	733	1651	813	1631
13	818	1656	739	1746	645	1831	540	1918	448	2001	423	2033	438	2029	518	1947	602	1845	646	1742	735	1649	814	1631
14	817	1658	738	1747	643	1832	538	1919	447	2003	423	2034	439	2028	519	1945	603	1842	648	1740	736	1648	815	1631
15	816	1659	736	1749	641	1834	536	1921	445	2004	423	2034	440	2027	521	1943	605	1840	649	1738	738	1647	816	1631
16	816	1701	734	1751	639	1835	534	1922	444	2005	423	2035	441	2026	522	1941	606	1838	651	1736	740	1646	816	1631
17	815	1702	732	1752	637	1837	532	1924	443	2007	423	2035	443	2025	524	1939	608	1836	652	1734	741	1645	817	1631
18	814	1704	730	1754	634	1838	530	1925	442	2008	423	2035	444	2024	525	1937	609	1834	654	1732	743	1643	818	1632
19	813	1705	729	1756	632	1840	529	1927	440	2009	423	2036	445	2023	526	1936	611	1832	655	1730	744	1642	818	1632
20	812	1707	727	1757	630	1841	527	1928	439	2011	424	2036	446	2022	528	1934	612	1830	657	1728	746	1641	819	1633
21	811	1708	725	1759	628	1843	525	1930	438	2012	424	2036	447	2021	529	1932	613	1827	658	1726	747	1640	819	1633
22	810	1710	723	1801	626	1844	523	1931	437	2013	424	2036	448	2020	531	1930	615	1825	700	1724	749	1639	820	1634
23	809	1711	721	1802	624	1846	521	1932	436	2014	424	2036	450	2019	532	1928	616	1823	701	1722	750	1639	820	1634
24	808	1713	719	1804	622	1847	519	1934	435	2015	425	2036	451	2017	534	1926	618	1821	703	1720	752	1638	821	1635
25	807	1714	717	1805	620	1849	517	1935	434	2017	425	2036	452	2016	535	1924	619	1819	705	1719	753	1637	821	1636
26	806	1716	715	1807	618	1850	515	1937	433	2018	425	2036	453	2015	536	1922	621	1817	706	1717	754	1636	821	1636
27	805	1718	713	1809	615	1852	514	1938	432	2019	426	2036	455	2013	538	1920	622	1815	708	1715	756	1635	822	1637
28	803	1719	711	1810	613	1853	512	1940	431	2020	426	2036	456	2012	539	1918	624	1812	709	1713	757	1635	822	1638
29	802	1721			611	1855	510	1941	430	2021	427	2036	457	2011	541	1916	625	1810	711	1712	758	1634	822	1639
30	801	1723			609	1856	508	1943	430	2022	428	2036	459	2009	542	1914	627	1808	713	1710	800	1634	822	1640
31	759	1724			607	1858			429	2023			500	2008	544	1912			714	1708			822	1641

Note: Blank space in the table indicates that a rising or setting did not occur during that 24-hour interval

Location: W097 00, N49 00

Zone: 6h West of Greenwich

Astronomical Applications Dept., U.S. Naval Observatory

Washington, DC 20392-5420

Rise & Set for the Moon for 2013

Winnipeg

Day	Jan		Feb		Mar		Apr		May		June		July		Aug		Sept		Oct		Nov		Dec	
	Rise	Set	Rise	Set	Rise	Set	Rise	Set	Rise	Set	Rise	Set	Rise	Set	Rise	Set	Rise	Set	Rise	Set	Rise	Set	Rise	Set
	h m	h m	h m	h m	h m	h m	h m	h m	h m	h m	h m	h m	h m	h m	h m	h m	h m	h m	h m	h m	h m	h m	h m	h m
1	2140	1012		957	2315	832	32	930	56	1047	59	1323	20	1434	36	1620	156	1658	249	1622	501	1607	613	1549
2	2248	1036	12	1028		906	129	1034	132	1200	124	1431	48	1537	121	1708	256	1728	355	1647	613	1639	725	1640
3	2358	1059	125	1103	28	947	216	1144	202	1312	149	1538	120	1638	211	1750	359	1755	502	1713	726	1716	832	1740
4		1124	237	1147	136	1037	256	1256	229	1423	215	1642	156	1734	306	1826	504	1821	611	1739	838	1802	931	1849
5	110	1152	345	1240	238	1135	329	1409	254	1532	245	1745	237	1825	405	1858	610	1846	721	1809	947	1856	1020	2003
6	224	1224	446	1343	332	1241	358	1521	318	1639	317	1844	324	1910	507	1926	717	1911	833	1842	1048	1958	1101	2120
7	339	1304	538	1453	417	1353	424	1632	344	1745	355	1939	416	1950	610	1952	826	1938	945	1922	1140	2107	1135	2235
8	453	1353	622	1609	455	1507	449	1741	411	1850	439	2028	513	2025	714	2017	936	2007	1054	2009	1224	2220	1205	2349
9	601	1453	658	1726	527	1621	514	1849	442	1952	528	2111	613	2055	820	2041	1046	2042	1158	2104	1301	2334	1233	
10	700	1602	728	1842	556	1735	541	1956	517	2050	622	2149	715	2122	927	2106	1156	2123	1254	2208	1332		1259	101
11	749	1718	756	1956	622	1847	610	2100	557	2143	719	2222	818	2147	1035	2133	1302	2211	1342	2317	1401	47	1326	210
12	829	1837	821	2108	647	1957	642	2201	642	2230	820	2250	922	2210	1145	2203	1404	2309	1423		1427	159	1355	318
13	902	1954	846	2217	713	2105	719	2258	733	2312	922	2316	1028	2234	1255	2239	1458		1458	29	1454	310	1426	424
14	930	2109	912	2324	740	2211	801	2349	828	2347	1026	2340	1135	2300	1405	2323	1544	15	1529	143	1522	419	1501	527
15	956	2220	940		810	2314	848		927		1131		1245	2328	1511		1623	126	1557	257	1552	527	1542	626
16	1020	2329	1010	28	844		941	34	1029	19	1239	4	1356		1612	15	1657	241	1624	410	1625	633	1627	720
17	1044		1045	129	922	14	1038	113	1132	46	1348	29	1508	0	1704	117	1728	358	1651	521	1702	735	1718	809
18	1110	36	1126	226	1006	108	1138	148	1238	112	1500	56	1619	40	1749	228	1756	513	1720	632	1745	833	1813	851
19	1138	141	1212	318	1056	157	1242	218	1346	136	1615	126	1726	128	1827	344	1824	627	1752	740	1833	926	1911	928
20	1210	243	1304	404	1151	239	1348	245	1456	201	1730	203	1825	227	1900	503	1852	740	1827	846	1925	1012	2010	1000
21	1247	342	1402	445	1250	317	1456	310	1609	227	1841	248	1915	336	1929	621	1922	850	1907	947	2021	1052	2112	1028
22	1329	436	1504	520	1353	349	1606	336	1725	257	1946	343	1957	452	1957	737	1954	958	1952	1043	2120	1127	2213	1054
23	1418	526	1609	551	1459	419	1720	402	1841	331	2041	449	2032	612	2024	851	2031	1101	2041	1133	2221	1157	2316	1118
24	1514	610	1716	619	1607	445	1835	430	1956	413	2126	604	2103	731	2053	1002	2113	1200	2135	1216	2322	1224		1142
25	1613	648	1826	645	1717	511	1952	502	2104	504	2203	722	2130	848	2123	1110	2159	1253	2232	1254		1249	21	1206
26	1717	722	1936	710	1830	536	2108	540	2203	605	2235	840	2157	1002	2157	1215	2250	1340	2332	1327	26	1314	128	1233
27	1823	751	2048	735	1944	603	2219	625	2252	715	2303	956	2224	1113	2235	1316	2346	1421		1356	131	1338	236	1303
28	1930	817	2202	802	2059	633	2321	720	2332	830	2328	1110	2252	1221	2318	1412		1456	34	1422	238	1405	347	1340
29	2039	842			2215	706		824		946	2354	1220	2322	1327		1502	45	1528	138	1448	348	1434	459	1424
30	2149	906			2326	746	13	934	5	1101		1328	2357	1429	6	1546	146	1556	243	1513	500	1508	608	1518
31	2300	931				834			33	1213				1527	59	1625			351	1539			712	1622

Note: Blank space in the table indicates that a rising or setting did not occur during that 24-hour interval
Location: W097 00, N43 00
Zone: 6h West of Greenwich
Astronomical Applications Dept.
Washington, DC 20392-5420

Rise & Set for the Sun for 2013
Vancouver

	Jan		Feb		Mar		Apr		May		June		July		Aug		Sept		Oct		Nov		Dec	
Day	Rise	Set	Rise	Set	Rise	Set	Rise	Set	Rise	Set	Rise	Set	Rise	Set	Rise	Set	Rise	Set	Rise	Set	Rise	Set	Rise	Set
	h m	h m	h m	h m	h m	h m	h m	h m	h m	h m	h m	h m	h m	h m	h m	h m	h m	h m	h m	h m	h m	h m	h m	h m
1	806	1626	742	1710	653	1756	549	1844	451	1928	412	2008	412	2019	445	1950	529	1854	612	1750	700	1651	745	1617
2	806	1627	741	1712	651	1758	547	1845	449	1930	412	2009	413	2019	447	1949	531	1852	614	1748	701	1649	746	1617
3	806	1628	739	1713	649	1759	545	1847	447	1931	411	2010	414	2019	448	1947	532	1849	615	1746	703	1647	748	1616
4	806	1629	738	1715	647	1801	543	1848	446	1933	415	2011	414	2018	449	1946	533	1847	617	1744	705	1646	749	1616
5	805	1630	736	1717	645	1802	540	1850	444	1934	410	2012	415	2018	451	1944	535	1845	618	1742	706	1644	750	1615
6	805	1631	735	1718	643	1804	538	1851	442	1936	409	2013	416	2017	452	1943	536	1843	620	1740	708	1643	751	1615
7	805	1633	733	1720	641	1805	536	1853	441	1937	409	2013	417	2017	454	1941	538	1841	621	1738	709	1641	752	1615
8	804	1634	731	1722	639	1807	534	1854	439	1939	409	2014	418	2016	455	1939	539	1839	623	1735	711	1640	753	1615
9	804	1635	730	1723	637	1809	532	1856	438	1940	408	2015	418	2016	456	1938	540	1837	624	1733	713	1639	754	1615
10	803	1636	728	1725	635	1810	530	1857	436	1941	408	2015	419	2015	458	1936	542	1835	626	1731	714	1637	755	1615
11	803	1638	727	1727	633	1812	528	1859	435	1943	408	2016	420	2014	459	1934	543	1833	627	1729	716	1636	756	1615
12	802	1639	725	1728	631	1813	526	1900	433	1944	408	2017	421	2013	501	1932	545	1830	629	1727	717	1634	757	1615
13	802	1640	723	1730	629	1815	524	1902	432	1946	407	2017	422	2013	502	1931	546	1828	630	1725	719	1633	758	1615
14	801	1642	721	1732	627	1816	522	1903	431	1947	407	2018	423	2012	503	1929	548	1826	632	1723	721	1632	759	1615
15	800	1643	720	1733	625	1818	520	1905	429	1948	407	2018	424	2011	505	1927	549	1824	633	1721	722	1631	800	1615
16	800	1645	718	1735	622	1819	518	1906	428	1950	407	2019	426	2010	506	1925	550	1822	635	1719	724	1630	800	1615
17	759	1646	716	1737	620	1821	516	1908	427	1951	407	2019	427	2009	508	1923	552	1820	636	1717	725	1628	801	1615
18	758	1648	714	1738	618	1822	514	1909	425	1952	407	2019	428	2008	509	1921	553	1818	638	1716	727	1627	802	1616
19	757	1649	712	1740	616	1824	512	1911	424	1953	407	2020	429	2007	511	1919	555	1815	639	1714	728	1626	802	1616
20	756	1651	711	1741	614	1825	510	1912	423	1955	408	2020	430	2006	512	1918	556	1813	641	1712	730	1625	803	1617
21	755	1652	709	1743	612	1827	509	1914	422	1956	408	2020	431	2005	513	1916	558	1811	642	1710	731	1624	804	1617
22	754	1654	707	1745	610	1829	507	1915	421	1957	408	2020	432	2004	515	1914	559	1809	644	1708	733	1623	804	1618
23	753	1655	705	1746	608	1830	505	1917	420	1958	408	2020	434	2002	516	1912	600	1807	646	1706	734	1622	804	1618
24	752	1657	703	1748	606	1832	503	1918	419	2000	409	2020	435	2001	518	1910	602	1805	647	1704	736	1622	805	1619
25	751	1659	701	1750	603	1833	501	1920	418	2001	409	2020	436	2000	519	1908	603	1803	649	1703	737	1621	805	1620
26	750	1700	659	1751	601	1835	459	1921	417	2002	409	2020	437	1959	521	1906	605	1801	650	1701	738	1620	805	1620
27	749	1702	657	1753	559	1836	458	1923	416	2003	410	2020	439	1957	522	1904	606	1758	652	1659	740	1619	806	1621
28	747	1703	655	1754	557	1838	456	1924	415	2004	410	2020	440	1956	523	1902	608	1756	654	1657	741	1619	806	1622
29	746	1705			555	1839	454	1925	414	2005	411	2020	441	1955	525	1900	609	1754	655	1656	743	1618	806	1623
30	745	1707			553	1841	452	1927	414	2006	412	2020	443	1953	526	1858	611	1752	657	1654	744	1618	806	1624
31	743	1708			551	1842			413	2007			444	1952	528	1856			658	1652			806	1625

Note: Blank space in the table indicates that a rising or setting did not occur during that 24-hour interval

Location: W123 00, N49 00

Zone: 8h West of Greenwich

Astronomical Applications Dept., U.S. Naval Observatory

Washington, DC 20392-5420

Rise & Set for the Moon for 2013

Vancouver

	Jan		Feb		Mar		Apr		May		June		July		Aug		Sept		Oct		Nov		Dec	
Day	Rise	Set	Rise	Set	Rise	Set	Rise	Set	Rise	Set	Rise	Set	Rise	Set	Rise	Set	Rise	Set	Rise	Set	Rise	Set	Rise	Set
	h m	h m	h m	h m	h m	h m	h m	h m	h m	h m	h m	h m	h m	h m	h m	h m	h m	h m	h m	h m	h m	h m	h m	h m
1	2129	958		943	2305	818	20	919	43	1036	45	1312	6	1423	23	1608	144	1645	238	1608	450	1553	603	1537
2	2237	1021	2	1014		853	116	1023	118	1150	109	1420	35	1526	108	1655	245	1714	343	1633	602	1625	714	1628
3	2347	1045	115	1050	17	935	203	1133	148	1302	135	1526	106	1626	159	1736	348	1741	451	1659	715	1703	821	1729
4		1110	226	1134	125	1025	242	1246	214	1412	201	1631	143	1722	254	1812	452	1807	600	1725	828	1749	918	1838
5	59	1138	334	1228	227	1123	315	1358	239	1521	231	1733	224	1812	353	1844	558	1831	711	1755	935	1844	1007	1953
6	214	1211	434	1331	320	1230	344	1510	304	1628	304	1832	311	1858	455	1912	706	1857	823	1829	1036	1947	1047	2109
7	329	1251	526	1443	404	1342	410	1621	330	1734	342	1926	404	1937	558	1938	815	1924	934	1909	1127	2056	1121	2225
8	442	1341	608	1559	442	1456	435	1730	357	1838	426	2015	501	2011	703	2002	925	1954	1043	1957	1211	2209	1151	2338
9	549	1441	644	1716	513	1610	500	1838	428	1940	515	2058	601	2041	809	2027	1035	2029	1146	2053	1247	2323	1219	
10	648	1552	715	1832	542	1724	527	1945	504	2038	610	2135	703	2108	916	2052	1145	2110	1242	2157	1318		1245	50
11	736	1708	742	1946	608	1836	556	2049	544	2131	708	2208	807	2132	1024	2119	1251	2159	1329	2306	1347	36	1312	159
12	815	1826	807	2057	633	1946	628	2150	630	2218	808	2236	911	2156	1134	2150	1352	2257	1410		1413	148	1341	307
13	848	1944	832	2206	659	2054	705	2246	721	2258	911	2302	1017	2220	1244	2226	1445		1444	19	1440	259	1413	412
14	916	2058	858	2313	726	2200	748	2337	817	2334	1015	2326	1124	2245	1354	2310	1531	4	1515	133	1508	408	1448	515
15	942	2210	926		756	2303	836		916		1120	2350	1234	2314	1500		1610	116	1543	246	1538	516	1529	614
16	1006	2318	957	17	830		929	21	1017	5	1227		1345	2347	1600	3	1644	231	1610	359	1611	621	1615	708
17	1030		1032	117	909	2	1026	100	1121	32	1337	15	1457		1652	106	1714	347	1637	510	1649	724	1706	756
18	1056	25	1113	214	953	56	1127	134	1227	58	1450	42	1608	27	1736	218	1742	503	1706	621	1732	821	1801	838
19	1124	129	1200	306	1043	144	1230	204	1335	122	1604	113	1715	116	1814	334	1810	617	1738	729	1820	914	1859	914
20	1156	231	1252	351	1139	226	1336	231	1445	147	1719	150	1813	216	1846	452	1838	729	1814	834	1913	959	1959	946
21	1234	330	1350	432	1238	303	1445	256	1558	213	1830	236	1903	325	1915	610	1908	839	1854	935	2010	1039	2100	1014
22	1317	424	1453	507	1342	336	1555	321	1714	243	1934	332	1944	442	1943	726	1941	947	1939	1031	2108	1113	2202	1040
23	1406	513	1558	538	1448	405	1709	347	1831	318	2028	439	2019	601	2010	840	2018	1050	2029	1120	2209	1143	2305	1104
24	1502	557	1705	605	1556	431	1825	416	1945	400	2113	553	2049	720	2039	951	2100	1148	2123	1203	2311	1210		1127
25	1602	635	1815	631	1706	457	1942	448	2053	452	2150	711	2116	837	2109	1059	2147	1241	2221	1241		1235	10	1152
26	1706	708	1925	656	1819	522	2057	527	2151	554	2221	830	2143	951	2143	1204	2238	1327	2321	1313	14	1259	116	1219
27	1812	737	2038	721	1933	549	2207	613	2239	704	2248	946	2209	1102	2222	1304	2334	1408		1342	120	1324	225	1250
28	1919	803	2151	748	2049	619	2309	709	2318	819	2314	1059	2238	1210	2305	1400		1443	23	1408	227	1351	336	1327
29	2028	828			2204	653		813	2351	935	2340	1209	2309	1315	2353	1449	33	1514	126	1433	337	1420	448	1411
30	2138	852			2315	733	1	923		1050		1317	2344	1417		1533	134	1542	232	1458	449	1455	557	1506
31	2249	916				822			19	1202				1515	47	1611			340	1524			700	1611

Note: Blank space in the table indicates that a rising or setting did not occur during that 24-hour interval
Location: W123 00, N49 00
Zone: 8h West of Greenwich
Astronomical Applications Dept.
Washington, DC 20392-5420

TABLE FOR FINDING APPROXIMATE STANDARD TIME OF SUNRISE, SUNSET, MOONRISE, MOONSET, FOR CANADIAN CITIES AND TOWNS

PLACE	Time Zone	FOR SUNRISE OR SUNSET Take value for	and apply correction	FOR MOONRISE OR MOONSET Take value for	and apply correction
Brandon	C	Winnipeg	+11*m*	50	+40*m*
Brantford	E	Toronto	+ 4	45	+21
Calgary	M	Winnipeg	+ 8	50	+36
Charlottetown	A	Ottawa	+10	45	+13
Cornwall	E	Ottawa	- 4	45	- 1
Edmonton	M	Winnipeg	+ 6	50	+34
Fredericton	A	Ottawa	+24	45	+27
Gander	N	Vancouver	- 4	50	+ 8
Glace Bay	A	Ottawa	- 3	45	0
Goose Bay	A	Winnipeg	-26	50	- 2
Granby	E	Ottawa	-12	45	- 9
Guelph	E	Toronto	+ 3	45	+21
Halifax	A	Ottawa	+11	45	+14
Hamilton	E	Toronto	+ 2	45	+21
Hull	E	Ottawa	0	45	+ 3
Kapuskasing	E	Vancouver	+17	50	+30
Kingston	E	Toronto	-12	45	+ 6
Kitchener	E	Toronto	+ 4	45	+22
London	E	Toronto	+ 8	45	+25
Medicine Hat	M	Winnipeg	- 4	50	+22
Moncton	A	Ottawa	+16	45	+19
Montréal	E	Ottawa	- 9	45	- 6
Moosonee	E	Winnipeg	- 6	50	+23
Moose Jaw	C	Winnipeg	+34	50	+62
Niagara Falls	E	Toronto	- 1	45	+16
North Bay	E	Ottawa	+14	45	+18
Ottawa	E	Ottawa	0	45	+ 3
Owen Sound	E	Ottawa	+21	45	+24
Penticton	P	Vancouver	-14	50	- 2
Peterborough	E	Toronto	- 4	45	+13
Prince Albert	C	Winnipeg	+36	50	+64
Prince Rupert	P	Winnipeg	+12	50	+40
Québec	E	Ottawa	-18	45	-15
Regina	C	Winnipeg	+30	50	+58
St. Catharines	E	Toronto	0	45	+17
St. Hyacinthe	E	Ottawa	-11	45	- 8
Saint John, NB	A	Ottawa	+22	45	+24
St. John's, NL	N	Vancouver	-11	50	+ 1
Sarnia	E	Toronto	+12	45	+30
Saskatoon	C	Winnipeg	+38	50	+66
Sault Ste. Marie	E	Ottawa	+34	45	+37
Shawinigan	E	Ottawa	-12	45	- 9
Sherbrooke	E	Ottawa	-14	45	-12
Stratford	E	Toronto	+ 6	45	+24
Sudbury	E	Ottawa	+21	45	+24
Sydney	A	Ottawa	- 2	45	+ 1
The Pas	C	Winnipeg	+16	50	+44
Trois-Rivières	E	Ottawa	-12	45	- 9
Thunder Bay	E	Vancouver	+44	50	+57
Timmins	E	Vancouver	+13	50	+25
Toronto	E	Toronto	0	45	+18
Trail	P	Vancouver	-22	50	-10
Truro	A	Ottawa	+10	45	+13
Vancouver	P	Vancouver	0	50	+12
Victoria	P	Vancouver	+2	50	+14
Windsor	E	Toronto	+14	45	+32
Winnipeg	C	Winnipeg	0	50	+28

PROMINENT CANADIAN SCIENTISTS

John F. Allen

Working with Pyotr Leonidovich Kapitsa and Don Misener, Allen discovered the superfluid phase of matter in 1937 at the Royal Society Mond Laboratory in Cambridge, England. A state achieved by a few liquids, such as helium, at extreme temperature where they become able to flow without friction, superfluids are used in high-precision devices, such as gyroscopes, which allow the measurement of some theoretically predicted gravitational effects. Allen along with Harry Jones also discovered the "fountain effect," in which superfluid helium flows up a tube and shoots into the air upon being exposed to a small heat source (the heat source in the original experiment was a flashlight that they were using to look at the apparatus). Allen was born in Winnipeg in 1908 and was professor of physics at St Andrews University, Scotland, from 1947 to 1978, and then emeritus professor until his death in 2001.

Sidney Altman

Born in 1939 in Montreal, the molecular biologist received a Nobel Prize in Chemistry in 1989 for his work with Thomas R. Cech on the catalytic properties of RNA. Their discovery, that ribonucleic acid in living cells is not only a molecule of heredity but also can function as a biocatalyst, affects fundamental aspects of the molecular basis of life. Virtually all chemical reactions taking place in a living cell require catalysts. Such biocatalysts are called enzymes and are determined by hereditary genes. Until the findings of Altman and Cech became known, all enzymes were considered to be proteins. The discovery of catalytic RNA will provide a new tool for gene technology, with potential to create defenses against viral infections. Altman is currently the Sterling Professor of Molecular, Cellular, and Developmental Biology and Professor of Chemistry at Yale University.

Frederick G. Banting

A doctor of orthopedic medicine and a decorated World War I veteran, Banting received a Nobel Prize in Medicine in 1923 for his discovery of insulin, a hormone that controls the metabolism of sugar. Early in his medical career, Banting became interested in diabetes, caused by a lack of insulin secreted by the pancreas. Before Banting's work, attempts to supply the missing insulin by feeding patients with fresh pancreas, or extracts of it, had failed. While working with his assistant Charles Best, Banting discovered how to extract insulin from the pancreas before it destroyed itself, thus birthing the first treatment for diabetes sufferers. The Banting and Best Diabetes Centre at the University of Toronto continues the work of the two doctors. The cause of diabetes remains a mystery. Banting was killed in an airplane disaster in 1941 in Newfoundland.

Alexander Graham Bell

A Naturalized U.S. citizen, Bell proved himself a Canadian at heart. While he spent winters in the U.S., Bell spent his summers on scientific research in his home in Baddeck, Cape Breton Island. His work with hearing & speech in 1875 birthed his idea of the telephone, which he developed & patented in1876. Bell experimented with the first long distance telephone call between Brantford & Paris, ON, in addition to other scientific experiments on the genetics of sheep breeding, his Silver Draft aircraft, & his hydrofoil speed boat, among others. Bell died of diabetes in 1922, and his grave lies on the summit of Cape Breton's Beinn Bhreagh Mountain overlooking the Bras D'or Lakes of Nova Scotia.

Williard S. Boyle

Boyle's family moved from Nova Scotia to Québec when he was a child. Boyle was homeschooled by his mother until secondary school when he enrolled in Lower Canada College, a Montreal private school. Upon graduation, Boyle joined the Royal Canadian Navy to fight in World War II; however, he became sea-sick & transferred to the Fleet Air Arm of the navy where he completed pilot training. He earned his doctorate in Physics from McGill University in 1950.

Three years later, Boyle joined Bell Laboratories where he contributed to the branch of Solid State Physics or Condensed Matter Physics. His inventions & innovations include the first continuously operating ruby laser & semiconductor lasers. Boyle went on to receive various awards, including his addition into the Science & Engineering Hall of Fame in 2005. In 2009, he received the Nobel Prize in Physics for co-inventing the Charge Coupled Device (CCD), a circuit used in many camcorders & digital cameras as imaging devices & which revolutionized astronomy when used in large telescopes. In 2010, he was recognized as a Companion of the Order of Canada for his lifetime achievements.

Boyle passed away in Wallace, Nova Scotia, in May 2011.

Bertram Brockhouse

Brockhouse was born in 1918 to homesteaders in Alberta and attended a one-room schoolhouse in Vancouver. During the Depression, the impoverished Brockhouses moved to Chicago, where, to help out with family finances, Brockhouse learned how to repair radios, and became involved in the socialist democratic movement. During World War II, he served six years in the Royal Canadian Navy repairing submarine-tracking equipment. At the war's end he attended the University of British Columbia, where he studied physics and mathematics, and received a PhD from the University of Toronto in the budding field of nuclear physics. In 1994 Brockhouse and Clifford G. Shull received a Nobel Prize in Physics for their contributions to the development of neutron scattering techniques for studies of condensed matter. Neutron scattering techniques are used in widely differing areas such as the study of the new ceramic superconductors, catalytic exhaust cleaning, elastic properties of polymers and virus structure.

Elizabeth Cannon

Born in Charlottetown, PEI, Cannon went to work for Nortech Surveys in Calgary where she utilized her BSc in Geomatics Engineering from the University of Calgary. During the halcyon days of the Global Positioning System (GPS) when it was largely used only by the US military, Cannon worked with the seismic surveying & geomatics company to develop new GPS methodologies. She returned to the University of Calgary to further her study in Geomatics, the science of production & management of spatial information, and won the 1988 Institute of Nagivation (ION) in a student paper competition.

She received her PhD in Geomatics Engineering and has since become a President and Vice-Chancellor of the University of Calgary. Currently, she researches the use of the GPS with aircraft positioning and altitude, precision farming, and improvements in precise positioning. She received the Calgary YWCA Women of Distinction Award in 1993, was named one of Canada's Top 40 Under 40 in 1998 and is a Fellow of the Canadian Academy of Engineering and the Royal Society of Canada..

John Herbert Chapman

For nearly two decades, Chapman served as scientist, superintendent and deputy chief superintendent in the Ottawa-based Defense Research Telecommunications Establishment, and then as assistant deputy minister for research in the Canadian Department of Communications. In 1966, a government study group appointed Chapman chairman; his report resulted in the redirection of the Canadian space program from scientific to application satellites. He also cooperated with NASA and the European Space Agency to design, develop and establish the Hermes Communications Technology Satellite. These initiatives shaped the Canadian space program. He passed away in Vancouver, B.C., in 1979, the same year he received a posthumous McNaughton Award to add to a list of awards he earned throughout his life.

H.S.M. Coxeter

Coxeter was born and educated in England. Shortly after finishing his doctoral studies at Cambridge University, he spent two years as a research visitor at Princeton University. In 1936 he joined the Faculty of the University of Toronto, where he remained as a mathematics professor until his death in 2003. Coxeter's work was mainly in geometry. In particular he made contributions of major importance in the theory of non-euclidean geometry, group theory, combinatorics, and polytopes or complicated geometric shapes of any number of dimensions that cannot be constructed in the real world but can be described mathematically and can sometimes be drawn. Much of Coxeter's time was devoted to group theory, or ways of measuring symmetry. This concerns the geometry of, for instance, kaleidoscopes and reflections in different planes, now known as Coxeter groups. Coxeter met the artist M.C. Escher, the master of depicting impossible reality, in 1954 and the two became lifelong friends. Coxeter also influenced Buckminster Fuller who used Coxeter's mathematical concepts of symmetry in his architecture. He attributed his long and productive life to vegetarianism and physical fitness.

J.C. Fields

John Charles Fields was born in Hamilton, Ontario, then Upper Canada, in 1863. He graduated with a degree in mathematics from the University of Toronto and was awarded a PhD from Johns Hopkins University in 1887. Dissatisfied with the state of mathematics in North America, Fields left for Europe, where he met the greatest mathematicians of the time, and changed his mathematical interests to algebraic functions. Fields worked tirelessly to raise the stature of mathematics within academic and public circles. He successfully lobbied the Ontario Legislature for an annual research grant of $75,000 for the university and helped establish the National Research Council of Canada, and the Ontario Research Foundation. Fields is best known for establishing what is now known as the Fields Medal, the premier award in mathematics, often called the Nobel Prize in Mathematics. It is awarded every four years to two to four mathematicians, under the age of 40, who have made important contributions to the field.

Sir Sandford Fleming

Fleming was born in Scotland in 1827, and at the age of 17, he emigrated to Ontario, where he was employed as a surveyor and map maker. In 1851 Fleming designed Canada's first postage stamp, which would do much to publicize the beaver as a distinctly Canadian emblem. In 1855 he became the chief engineer of the Northern Railway of Canada, where he instituted the construction of iron bridges instead of wood for safety reasons. Over the next few years he led a team of surveyors and engineers to investigate the first coast-to-coast railway line. Fleming was present in 1885 when the last spike was driven in Craigellachie, British Columbia. After missing a train in 1876 in Ireland because the printed schedule listed p.m. instead of a.m., he proposed Universal Time, a single 24-hour clock for the entire world, located in Greenwich, England, the center of the Earth and not linked to any surface meridian. He urged that standard time zones be used locally, but they were to be subordinate to his single world time. By 1929 all of the major countries of the world had accepted time zones. Fleming was knighted by Queen Victoria In 1897.

John Kenneth Galbraith

The economist's first major book, published in 1952, was American Capitalism: The Concept of Countervailing Power. In it he argued that giant firms had replaced small ones to the point where the competitive model no longer applied to much of the American economy. But, he argued, the muscle of large firms was offset by the power of large unions, so that consumers were protected by competing centres of power.

In his best-selling 1958 book The Affluent Society, Galbraith contrasted the affluence of the private sector with the squalor of the public sector. Galbraith's main argument is that as society becomes relatively more affluent, so private business must "create" consumer wants through advertising, and while this generates artificial affluence through the production of commercial goods and services, the "public sector" becomes neglected as a result. He proposed significant investment in parks, transportation, education, and other public amenities - what we now call infrastructure - to ameliorate these differences and postpone depression and revolution indefinitely.

Although born in Canada, Galbraith spent most of his life in the United States, namely as a professor at Harvard University. He was active in politics, serving four US presidents and was the US Ambassador to India under Kennedy. He was awarded the Order of Canada in 1997 and two Presidential Medals of Freedom. He died in 2006 at the age of 97.

Biruté Galdikas

Galdikas was born in 1946 in Germany en route to Canada from Lithuania. She grew up in Toronto where she frequented High Park, a home to the wild animals she spent hours observing. She moved to California to complete her undergraduate, Masters & PhD in Anthropology in UCLA & since then has received the PETA Humanitarian Award in 1990, the United Nations Global 500 Award in 1993 and many others. She co-founded and heads the Orangutan Foundation International and is recognized as the world's foremost authority on orangutans and the apes' anthropological connection with humans.

Galdikas is currently a Professor of Anthropology at Simon Fraser University and splits her time between her three homes in Deep Cove, BC; Los Angeles, CA; & Borneo.

William Francis Giauque

Born to American parents on the Canadian side of Niagara Falls, Giauque began his career at the Hooker Electro-Chemical Company in Niagara Falls, NY, as a chemical engineer. Soon after, he received a Ph.D. degree in chemistry with a minor in physics from the University of California, where he became a professor of chemistry in 1934. His principal objective was to demonstrate through a variety of accurate tests that the third law of thermodynamics is a basic natural law. In 1927 he proposed a new method of achieving extremely low temperatures using a process called adiabatic demagnetization. By 1933 he had a working apparatus that obtained a temperature within one-tenth of a degree of absolute zero. In the course of his low-temperature studies of oxygen, Giauque discovered with Herrick L. Johnston the oxygen isotopes of mass 17 and 18 in the Earth's atmosphere. He received the Nobel Prize in Chemistry in 1949.

James Gosling

The father of Java programming language was born in 1955 near Calgary, where he attended university. He received his PhD in Computer Science from Carnegie Mellon University. While at the college he built a multi-processor version of Unix, as well as several compilers and computer mail systems.

From 1984 to 2010, Gosling served Sun Microsystems as Vice President and Fellow. After spending six months at Google, Gosling moved to Liquid Robotics in August 2011, where he is chief software architect in the creation of robots that can explore the bottom of the ocean.

In February 2007, he was named an officer of the Order of Canada.

Gerhard Herzberg

Physicist Herzberg was born in Hamburg, Germany in 1904 but was forced to flee Nazi Germany in 1935, when he settled at the University of Saskatchewan. Herzberg's main contributions have enriched the fields of atomic and molecular spectroscopy for which he won a Nobel Prize in Chemistry in 1971. He and his associates determined the makeup of a large number of diatomic and polyatomic molecules, including the structures of many free radicals difficult to determine in any other way. Herzberg has also applied spectroscopic studies to the identification of certain molecules in planetary atmospheres, in comets, and in interstellar space. Herzberg was elected a Fellow of the Royal Society of Canada in 1939 and of the Royal Society of London in 1951. Herzberg died in 1999.

David Hubel

Hubel, along with Torsten Wiesel, greatly expanded the scientific knowledge of sensory processing, describing how signals from the eye are processed by the brain to generate edge detectors, motion detectors, stereoscopic depth detectors and color detectors, the building blocks of the visual scene. These studies opened the door for the understanding and treatment of childhood cataracts and strabismus. For their work the team was awarded the 1981 Nobel Prize in Physiology or Medicine. Hubel was born to American parents in Windsor, but spent his formative years in Montreal.

Harold Elford Johns

Johns was born in China but grew up in Ontario, where he earned his MA and PhD from the University of Toronto. He was a biophysicist and professor who helped develop the Medical Biophysics Department of the University of Toronto. He invented the cobalt bomb, a nuclear device that birthed the cobalt-60 therapy, which treats cancers located deep within the body that otherwise cannot be reached by other therapies. It has since saved more than 7 million cancer patients. Johns received the 1973 Gairdner International Award and the 1985 W.B. Lewis Award from the Canadian Nuclear Society.

Cecilia Krieger

Krieger was born in Poland but emigrated from Vienna to Toronto in 1920 to escape the persecution of Jews in Europe. Krieger taught at the University of Toronto for three decades after becoming the first woman to earn a Doctorate in Mathematics in Canada in 1930. In honour of Krieger & another woman mathematician, Evelyn Nelson, the Canadian Mathematical Society awarded the CMS Krieger-Nelson Prize Lectureship for Distinguished Research by Women.

Fernand Labrie

Labrie earned his M.D. in 1962 and Ph.D. in endocrinology in 1966 from the University of Laval. He left his Québec home to study in England with two-time Nobel Prize winner in medicine, Frederick Sanger, and returned in 1969 to found the Laboratory of Molecular Endocrinology at his alma mater. Labrie discovered that castrating hormones from the testes by adding a hormone called GNrH in prostate cancer patients eliminates the need for surgical castration. Next, he discovered that blocking male hormones from the adrenal glands prevents cancer from spreading, thus prolonging life of prostate cancer patients. Labrie also developed medication to prevent the binding of estrogens in the breast and uterus once he discovered that adding estrogen in women was linked to uterine and breast cancer.

Labrie resides in Québec and works as Director of the Laboratory of Molecular Endocrinology. Among other awards, He was appointed Fellow of the Royal Society of Canada in 1979 and Officer of the Order of Canada in 1981, and earned the Queen's Golden Jubilee Medal in 2002 and King Faisal International Prize in 2007.

Rudolph Marcus

Born in Montreal in 1923, Marcus received the 1992 Nobel Prize in Chemistry for his theory of electron transfer. The Marcus theory, named after him, provides a thermodynamic and kinetic framework for describing one electron outer-sphere electron transfer. The Marcus theory describes, and makes predictions concerning, such widely differing phenomena as the fixation of light energy by green plants, photochemical production of fuel, chemiluminescence (cold light), the conductivity of electrically conducting polymers, corrosion, the methodology of electrochemical synthesis and analysis, and more.

Marcus developed his theory for what is perhaps the simplest chemical elementary process, the transfer of an electron between two molecules. No chemical bonds are broken in such a reaction, but changes take place in the molecular structure of the reacting molecules and their nearest neighbors. This molecular change enables the electrons to jump between the molecules. He is currently a professor at Caltech and is a member of the International Academy of Quantum Molecular Science.

Sir William Osler

Osler, often dubbed the father of modern medicine, grew up in Ontario, the son of an Anglican minister. After two years at the Toronto School of Medicine, Osler obtained his medical degree in 1872 from McGill University. Upon his death, Osler willed his library to the Montreal university where it forms the nucleus of McGill's Osler Library of the History of Medicine, which opened in 1929. Osler's greatest contribution to medicine was to insist that students learned from seeing and talking to patients and the establishment of the medical residency program. In 1889, Osler accepted the position of Physician-in-Chief at the recently founded Johns Hopkins Hospital in Baltimore where he refined the residency program. He died, at the age of 70, in 1919, during the Spanish influenza epidemic.

Wilder Penfield

The American-born Canadian neurosurgeon studied at Princeton before becoming a Rhodes Scholar at Oxford University where he studied neuropathology, the scientific study of diseases of the nervous system. With his colleague, Herbert Jasper, he invented what is now called the Montreal procedure for treating patients with severe epilepsy by destroying nerve cells in the brain where the seizures originated. Before operating, he stimulated the brain with electrical probes while the patients were conscious on the operating table and observed their responses. In this way he could more accurately target the areas of the brain responsible, reducing the side-effects of the surgery. His technique enabled him to map the sensory and motor parts of the brain, thus showing their connection to the various limbs and organs of the body. After studying epilepsy in New York, Penfield moved to Montreal where he taught at at McGill University and the Royal Victoria hospital, becoming the city's first neurosurgeon. He eventually became the director of the Montreal Neurological Institute and the associated Montreal Neurological Hospital, which was established with funding from the Rockefeller Foundation. In 1967 he was made a Companion of the Order of Canada. In 1994 he was inducted into the Canadian Medical Hall of Fame.

John Polanyi

After completing his undergraduate education at Manchester University, Polanyi moved to Canada in 1952 at the age of 23 to work for the for the National Research Council of Canada before moving to the University of Toronto, where he remains to this day. In 1986 Polanyi shared a Nobel Prize in Chemistry with Dudley R. Herschbach and Yuan T. Lee for their research in reaction dynamics, offering much more understanding into how energy disposal in chemical reactions takes place. Polanyi developed the method of infrared chemiluminescence, in which the extremely weak infrared emission from a newly formed molecule is measured and analyzed.

Arthur Schawlow

Schawlow grew up in Canada in a deeply religious family and studied at the University of Toronto. After World War II, he studied at Columbia University, spent a decade at Bell Labs, then left to become a professor at Stanford, where he remained as professor emeritus until his retirement in 1996. While at Stanford, he teamed up with Robert Hofstadter, who, like Schawlow, had an autistic child, to help each other find solutions to the condition. Later Schawlow spearheaded an institution to care for people with autism in Paradise, CA, named the Arthur Schawlow Center. Although his research focused on optics, in particular, lasers and their use in spectroscopy, he also pursued investigations in the areas of superconductivity and nuclear resonance. He and Nicolaas Bloembergen shared the 1981 Nobel Prize in Physics by using lasers to study the interactions of electromagnetic radiation with matter.

Myron Scholes

The 1997 winner of the Nobel Memorial Prize in Economics began his early years in Timmins. After the family moved to Hamilton, Scholes attended McMaster University and earned an MBA and PhD from the University of Chicago. He eventually put his name to the Black-Scholes model, which provides the fundamental conceptual framework for valuing options, such as calls or puts, and has become the standard in financial markets globally. All did not go well for Scholes, however. In 2005, Scholes was implicated in the case of Long-Term Capital Holdings v. United States, where he attempted to invest funds from his company, Long-Term Capital Holdings, in an illegal tax shelter in order to avoid having to pay taxes on profits from company investments. It was found that Scholes and his partners were not eligible for US$106 million in tax deductions they had claimed. They were fined more than US$40 million by the IRS. Scholes now runs the hedge fund Platinum Grove Asset Management and is the chairman of the Board of Economic Advisors for Stamos Partners. He was awarded the 2011 CME Group Fred Arditti Innovation Award for his co-creation of the Black-Scholes options pricing model.

Michael Smith

Born in 1932 in Blackpool, England, Smith attended the University of Manchester and soon after receiving his PhD accepted a fellowship in Vancouver to work on the synthesis of biologically important organo-phosphates. The 1992 Nobel Prize winner in chemistry didn't keep the money he was granted from the award. He gave half of it to researchers working on the genetics of schizophrenia and shared the other half between Science World BC and the Society for Canadian Women in Science and Technology. Smith could afford to be generous. He had made a small fortune in 1988 when he sold his share of Zymogenetics Incorporated, a Seattle-based biotechnology company that he co-founded in 1981.

Andrew Michael Spence

For his work on the dynamics of information flows and market development, Spence and his colleagues George A. Akerlof and Joseph E. Stiglitz, received the 2001 Nobel Memorial Prize in Economics. In his Job-Market Signaling model, employees convey their respective skills to employers by acquiring a certain degree of education, which is costly to them. Employers will pay higher wages to more educated employees, because they know that the proportion of employees with high abilities is higher among the educated ones, as it is less costly for them to acquire education than it is for employees with low abilities. For the model to work, it is not even necessary for education to have any intrinsic value if it can convey information about the sender (employee) to the recipient (employer) and if the signal is costly. Spence is currently a professor at the NYU Stern School of Business. He grew up in Canada, during and after the war, before leaving for college in the United States.

Henry Taube

For his work on the mechanisms of electron transfer reactions, especially in metal complexes, Taube won the 1983 Nobel Prize in Chemistry. Born in Saskatchewan, Taube has published more than 350 articles and a book as a result of his research. A member of the Stanford University faculty since 1962, Taube was "one of the most creative contemporary workers in inorganic chemistry," according to the Nobel committee who rewarded him for his insights into how electrons are transferred from one molecule to another during chemical reactions. Taube maintained a lifelong interest in oxidation-reduction or redox reactions, in which electrons are lost and gained during a chemical reaction. He died in 2005 at the age of 89 at his home on the Stanford campus.

Richard E. Taylor

Born in 1929 in Medicine Hat, Alberta, Taylor received the 1990 Nobel Prize in Physics for his pioneering investigations concerning deep inelastic scattering of electrons on protons and bound neutrons, which have been of essential importance for the development of the quark model in particle physics. He shared the prize with Jerome Friedman and Henry Kendall. Taylor received his undergraduate degree from the University of Alberta and his PhD from Stanford, where he is a professor emeritus.

William Vickrey

Vickrey was born in Victoria, British Columbia, in 1914. His elementary and secondary education was in Europe and the United States, with graduation from Phillips Andover Academy in 1931. He received a B.S. in mathematics from Yale in 1935, followed by graduate work in economics at Columbia University from 1935 to 1937. A conscientious objector during World War II, he spent part of his alternate service designing a new inheritance tax for Puerto Rico. In 1946 he began his teaching career at Columbia University as a lecturer in economics. An essential part of Vickrey's research focused on the properties of different types of auctions, and how they can best be designed to generate economic efficiency. His work provided the basis for a field of research which has also been extended to practical applications such as auctions of treasury bonds and band spectrum licenses. He received the 1996 Nobel Prize in Economics for his endeavors.

John Tuzo Wilson

The Ottawa-born geologist achieved world-wide acclaim for his contributions to study of plate tectonics. Plate tectonics is the idea that the rigid outer layers of the Earth are broken up into numerous pieces that move independently over the weaker soft zone of the upper mantle. Wilson maintained that the Hawaiian Islands were created as a tectonic plate, extending across much of the Pacific Ocean, shifted slowly over a fixed hotspot, spawning a long series of volcanoes. He also conceived of the transform fault, a major plate boundary where two plates move past each other horizontally, such as the San Andreas Fault. The Wilson cycle of seabed expansion and contraction bears his name. He died in 1993 in Toronto.

CANADA'S ENERGY SOURCES

Canada is endowed with an abundant variety of energy resources. It ranks among top countries in the world for production of oil, natural gas, uranium and coal. Most of the country's energy is derived from hydrocarbons-coal, natural gas, and oil. These are used both as direct fuels and in the production of electricity. The only significant non-hydrocarbon energy sources are hydroelectricity and nuclear power. Canadians are the second-highest per capita consumers of energy in the world, doubling Japan and most of Europe. How will Canada cope with future energy needs and consumption?

Oil and Gas

Canada faces the same oil industry challenges as the rest of the world: recent crude oil prices have been high and volatile, and geopolitical uncertainty continues to be a threat to supply around the globe. The impact of severe weather on refining and production has resulted in higher crude oil and gasoline prices. Based on Canada's production rate, they have 10 years or less of proven reserves. This does not mean that Canada will run out of oil in 10 years. It means this is the size of its resource based on the oil pools today, production rates, and the portion that is recoverable using existing technology.

Canadian oil sands—a mixture of sand or clay, water, and extremely heavy crude oil—are estimated to contain 1.7 trillion barrels of oil, and based on today's technology, it's believed that 178 billion barrels can be recovered. To put this in perspective, the size of the recoverable resources ranks second only to Saudi Arabia. The oil sands currently account for approximately one-third of the 3.3 million barrels of oil produced per day in Canada. Conventional oil production in the Western Canada Sedimentary Basin peaked in 1973, but it still accounts for a significant portion of oil supply. There is call to slow the pace of oil sands development in order to allow for better understanding and assessment of the risks to the environment. This could mean temporarily halting further approvals of projects.

Natural Gas

Over the past decade, there has been a trend on the part of large energy consumers and the general public toward increased use of natural gas as the fuel of choice. This has been particularly noteworthy in the electricity generation industry. Canadian production of natural gas has probably already peaked, and will gradually decline as wells mature and become exhausted faster than new discoveries are made. In 2007, Canadian Liquefied Natural Gas production declined, but those deficiencies were offset by higher US imports. Drilling activity was weaker than it had been at the same time in each of the past three years. Annual increases in drilling activity and connection of new gas wells are necessary to maintain stable Canadian gas deliverability, because the productivity of new gas wells in the Western Canada Sedimentary Basin has lessened. In 2006, natural gas prices fell below the fuel oil range and competed with coal in the power generation market.

With North American natural gas supply expected to lag future increases in demand, imports of LNG from offshore sources are viewed as the largest source of additional natural gas to the continent. Over 40 import terminal projects have been proposed for North America and development of significant LNG trade could have implications for North American natural gas supply, demand and prices.

Canada will continue to research and develop gas hydrates, a form of natural gas found in the molecular structure of ice, in Northern provinces and offshore on both coasts. Canadian resource estimates are impressive: 1,500 to 28,000 trillion cubic feet of gas in place contained in hydrates, with 311 trillion cubic feet in the Beaufort/Mackenzie Delta region. Both the Pacific and Atlantic margins have confirmed gas hydrates deposits. If there was a system available to transport these deposits, hydrates would be as economical as gas. However, costs are not competitive with conventional gas at this time. Additional testing and modeling is required to ensure results. Plans are to have a full scale production test in about five years and first production by 2020.

Compressed natural gas seems to be a viable transportation option for stranded natural gas offshore Newfoundland, with possible development to occur by 2014 or later. Development still has a number of hurdles to overcome, including safety issues for the delivery to Boston or New York harbours.

Electricity and Coal

The size of Canada's coal resource dwarfs all other energy forms, even the oil sands. Based on current production rates, Canada has a 1,000-year reserve of coal. Currently about 60 percent of Canada's electricity comes from hydro projects, 18 percent from coal combustion, 13 percent from nuclear, 5 percent from natural gas, and the balance from oil and renewables. Coal-based generation became unpopular during the 1980s and 1990s because of its carbon emissions. Canada must develop ways to use coal in a manner that is environmentally acceptable. Until a few years ago, there were two ways to address the challenge of greenhouse gas management: to produce and use energy more efficiently or, to rely increasingly on low-carbon and carbon-free fuels. Unfortunately, energy efficiency and the use of alternative energy may not be enough to stabilize global concentrations of carbon dioxide. Carbon sequestration offers a third option that could, in tandem with the continued development of clean coal generation technologies, prove affordable, effective and environmentally safe.

Canadian metallurgical coal (coal consumed in making steel) is experiencing a comeback in Alberta and British Columbia, and opportunities for Canadian metallurgical coal are driven by demand in China, India and Brazil. Canadian steam coal (all non-metallurgical coal) production remains consistent with some export growth. Steam coal consumption is at risk in Ontario with projected plant shutdowns. Steam coal production remains strong in Alberta, Saskatchewan, New Brunswick and Nova Scotia. The government is to build and operate a full-scale clean coal demonstration plant by 2014.

A number of provinces have introduced or are in the process of introducing plans to address electricity needs by way of new generation and transmission projects. For example, British Columbia Transmission Corp. introduced a $3.2-billion 10-year transmission plan, Alberta Electric System Operator began a $3.5 billion 10-year transmission plan, Saskatchewan agreed to address its aging fleet of coal-fired generators, and the Ontario Power Authority moved on its Power System Plan.

Nuclear Energy

Ontario dominates Canada's nuclear industry, containing most of the country's nuclear power generating capacity. Ontario has 16 operating reactors—with another in the planning stage—providing about half of the province's electricity, plus two reactors undergoing refurbishment. Quebec and New Brunswick each have one reactor. Overall, nuclear power provides about 15.5 percent of Canada's electricity. The cost of nuclear power generation has been dropping over the last decade. This is because declining fuel (including enrichment), operating and maintenance costs, while the plant concerned has been paid for, or at least is being paid off. In general the construction costs of nuclear power plants are significantly higher than for coal- or gas-fired plants because of the need to use special materials, and to incorporate sophisticated safety features and back-up control equipment. These contribute much of the nuclear generation cost, but once the plant is built the cost variables are minor. Canada's nuclear plants, however, are quickly reaching the end of their operating lifespans and are entering the long and costly decommissioning phase.

Canada is one of the world's largest producers of uranium with about one third of world production coming from Saskatchewan mines. The country exports uranium and radioisotopes for medical and industrial purposes. These exports are subject to stringent nuclear non-proliferation policies.

Canada's used reactor fuel is now stored on an interim basis at licensed facilities located where the waste is produced. Like many other countries with nuclear power programs, Canada has yet to decide what to do with this used fuel over the long term. On site storage options are expected to perform well over the near term; however, existing reactor sites were not chosen for their suitability as permanent storage sites. Furthermore, the communities hosting the nuclear reactors have a reasonable expectation that used nuclear fuel will eventually be moved.

Alternative and Renewable Energy

Canadian energy development strategies traditionally focused on low-cost electric power, crude oil, and accessible energy resources. These strategies led to a strong energy industry that has contributed to Canadian prosperity. But today, the world's appetite for cheap energy is counterbalanced by climate change concerns and greenhouse gas emission restrictions. Canada has the potential to become a global leader in renewable energy given its abundant renewable energy resources such as solar, wind, earth, wave, water, tide and biomass. With its large forest and agricultural land base relative to its population, Canada is uniquely positioned to be a world leader in the production and use of biofuels derived from lignocellulose (forestry) biomass. However, renewable energy sources account for less than one percent of the total energy supply today. Utilization of these alternate sources will expand, but they will not become more than small, specialized niche contributors to Canada's energy supply for the foreseeable future.

A study by the Pembina Institute, a sustainable-energy think tank, concluded that smart, targeted investments in a diverse array of energy efficiency and renewable energy solutions over the next 20 years will achieve major cuts in greenhouse gas emissions, accelerate the closure of highly-polluting coal plants and avoid the need for new nuclear investments.

THE CALENDAR

The calendar is a method of identifying the passage of time and thereby regulating our civil life and religious observances.

Days, months and years are based on astronomical periods. The day is the time it takes the earth to make one revolution on its axis, the month is associated with the period of orbiting of the moon around the earth, while the year has to do with the orbiting of the earth around the sun.

Many religious ideas and observances have been connected with the changes of the moon, and in ancient times the calendar took account of the moon rather than the seasons. From new moon to new moon is 29.530 days, and from one spring equinox to the next is 365.24219 days. Since the two are incommensurable, the modern calendar disregards the moon, except insofar as our months are roughly equal to a lunation.

The Week

The division of the week is found only among Aryan nations and in nations and regions into which they have penetrated. The day is, for convenience, divided into 24 equal parts and is the period of a single rotation of the earth upon its own axis.

A solar or astronomical day commences at midnight, and is divided into two equal portions of 12 hours each - those before noon being termed (A.M.) those after noon (P.M.).

The Chinese week consists of 5 days, which are named after iron, wood, water, feathers and earth; they divide the day into 12 parts of 2 hours each.

The Anglo-Saxons named the days of the week after the following deities: Sunday, the Sun; Monday, the Moon; Tuesday, Tuesco (God of War); Wednesday, Woden (God of Storms); Thursday, Thor (God of Thunder); Friday, Freya (Goddess of Love); Saturday, Saturn (God of Time).

The word *week* is from Wikon (German); it means change, succession.

PERPETUAL CALENDAR

(Table for Determining the Weekday of a Given Date)

In the YEAR table, locate the first two figures of the given year (lower left) and the last two figures (upper right) and take the number at the intersection.

With that number, enter the MONTH table, and take the number at the intersection with the given month. Note the special columns for January and February in the case of a bissextile (leap) year.

With that number, enter the DAY OF THE MONTH table. The weekday is found at the intersection with the given day of the month.

Example: 1970 March 7

YEAR											
					00	01	02	03	—	04	05
					06	07	—	08	09	10	11
					—	12	13	14	15	—	16
					17	18	19	—	20	21	22
					23	—	24	25	26	27	—
					28	29	30	31	—	32	33
					34	35	—	36	37	38	39
					—	40	41	42	43	—	44
					45	46	47	—	48	49	50
					51	—	52	53	54	55	—
					56	57	58	59	—	60	61
					62	63	—	64	65	66	67
					—	68	69	70	71	—	72
					73	74	75	—	76	77	78
					79	—	80	81	82	83	—
					84	85	86	87	—	88	89
					90	91	—	92	93	94	95
					—	96	97	98	99		
0	7	14	17	21	6	0	1	2	3	4	5
1	8	15 *J*			5	6	0	1	2	3	4
2	9		18	22	4	5	6	0	1	2	3
3	10				3	4	5	6	0	1	2
4	11	15 *G*	19	23	2	3	4	5	6	0	1
5	12	16	20	24	1	2	3	4	5	6	0
6	13				0	1	2	3	4	5	6

J: until 1582 October 4 inclusively (Julian Calendar)
G: from 1582 October 15 onwards (Gregorian Calendar)
Example: In the first table, we find 5 at the intersection of 19 and 70.

MONTH	May	Feb. (*B*) Aug.	Feb. March Nov.	June	Sept. Dec.	Jan. (*B*) April July	Jan. Oct.
1	2	3	4	5	6	0	1
2	3	4	5	6	0	1	2
3	4	5	6	0	1	2	3
4	5	6	0	1	2	3	4
5	6	0	1	2	3	4	5
6	0	1	2	3	4	5	6
0	1	2	3	4	5	6	0

(*B*) = Bissextile (leap) year
Example: In the second table, we find 1 at the intersection of 5 and March.

DAY OF MONTH	1 8 15 22 29	2 9 16 23 30	3 10 17 24 31	4 11 18 25	5 12 19 26	6 13 20 27	7 14 21 28
1	Sun.	Mon.	Tue.	Wed.	Thur.	Fri.	Sat.
2	Mon.	Tue.	Wed.	Thur.	Fri.	Sat.	Sun.
3	Tue.	Wed.	Thur.	Fri.	Sat.	Sun.	Mon.
4	Wed.	Thur.	Fri.	Sat.	Sun.	Mon.	Tue.
5	Thur.	Fri.	Sat.	Sun.	Mon.	Tue.	Wed.
6	Fri.	Sat.	Sun.	Mon.	Tue.	Wed.	Thu.
0	Sat.	Sun.	Mon.	Tue.	Wed.	Thu.	Fri.

Example: In the third table, we find *Saturday* at the intersection of 1 and 7.

FIXED AND MOVABLE FESTIVALS AND ANNIVERSARIES

(Gregorian Calendar)

	2013			2014			2015			2016			2017		
JANUARY begins on	Tue.			Wed.			Thu.			Sat.			Sun.		
New Year's Day	Tu	Jan.	1	We	Jan.	1	Th	Jan.	1	Fr	Jan.	1	Su	Jan.	1
Circumcision	Tu	Jan.	1	We	Jan.	1	Th	Jan.	1	Fr	Jan.	1	Su	Jan.	1
Gantan-sai (Shinto New Year)	Tu	Jan.	1	We	Jan.	1	Th	Jan.	1	Fr	Jan.	1	Su	Jan.	1
Mary Mother of God	Tu	Jan.	1	We	Jan.	1	Th	Jan.	1	Fr	Jan.	1	Su	Jan.	1
Twelfth Night	Sa	Jan.	5	Su	Jan.	5	Mo	Jan.	5	Tu	Jan.	5	Th	Jan.	5
Epiphany	Su	Jan.	6	Mo	Jan.	6	Tu	Jan.	6	We	Jan.	6	F	Jan.	6
Maghi	Su	Jan.	13	Mo	Jan.	13	Tu	Jan.	13	We	Jan.	13	F	Jan.	13
New Year's Day (Orthodox Christian)	Mo	Jan.	14	Tu	Jan.	14	We	Jan.	14	Th	Jan.	14	S	Jan.	14
Lunar New Year (Chinese, etc.)	Su	Feb.	10	Su	Feb.	10	Fr	Jan.	31	Mo	Feb.	8	S	Jan.	28
FEBRUARY begins on	Fri.			Sat.			Sun.			Mon.			Wed.		
Mawlid an Nabi	Th	Jan.	24	Mo	Jan.	13	Sa	Jan.	3	We	Dec.	14	Fr	Dec.	12
							Fr	Dec.	23						
Tu B'shvat	Sa	Jan.	26	Th	Jan.	16	We	Feb.	4	Mo	Jan.	25	Sa	Feb.	11
St. Valentine's Day	Th	Feb.	14	Fr	Feb.	14	Sa	Feb.	14	Su	Feb.	14	Tu	Feb.	14
Nirvana	Fr	Feb.	15	Sa	Feb.	15	Su	Feb.	15	Mo	Feb.	15	We	Feb	15
MARCH begins on	Fri.			Sat.			Sun.			Tue.			Wed.		
Ash Wednesday	We	Feb.	13	We	Mar.	5	We	Feb.	25	Su	Feb.	10	We	Mar.	1
First Sunday of Lent	Su	Feb.	17	Su	Mar.	9	Su	Mar.	1	We	Feb.	14	Su	Mar.	5
St. David	Fr	Mar.	1	Sa	Mar.	1	Su	Mar.	1	Tu	Mar.	1	We	Mar	1
World Day of Prayer	Fr	Mar.	1	Fr	Mar.	7	Fr	Mar.	6	Fr	Mar.	4	Fr	Mar	3
Purim	Su	Feb.	24	Su	Mar.	16	Th	Mar.	5	Th	Mar.	24	Su	Mar	12
Daylight Savings Time begins**	Su	Mar.	10	Su	Mar.	9	Su	Mar.	8	Su	Mar.	13	Su	Mar	12
St. Patrick	Su	Mar.	17	Mo	Mar.	17	Tu	Mar.	17	Th	Mar.	17	Fr	Mar	17
St. Joseph (Patron Saint of Canada)	Tu	Mar.	19	We	Mar.	19	Th	Mar.	19	Sa	Mar.	19	Su	Mar	19
Naw Ruz (Baha'i New Year)	Th	Mar.	21	Fr	Mar.	21	Sa	Mar.	21	Mo	Mar.	21	Tu	Mar	21
Norouz (Persian/Zoroastrian New Year)	Th	Mar.	21	Fr	Mar.	21	Sa	Mar.	21	Mo	Mar.	21	Tu	Mar	21
Hindu New Year***	Th	Apr.	11	Mo	Mar.	31	Sa	Mar.	21	Fr	Apr.	8	Tu	Mar	28
Annunciation	Mo	Mar.	25	Tu	Mar.	25	We	Mar.	25	Fr	Mar.	25	Sa	Mar	25
Passion Sunday	Su	Mar.	17	Su	Apr.	6	Su	Mar.	22	Su	Mar.	13	Su	Apr.	2
Khordad Sal (Birth of Prophet Zaranhushtra)	Th	Mar.	28	Fr	Mar.	28	Sa	Mar.	28	Mo	Mar.	28	Tu	Mar	28
APRIL begins on	Mon.			Tue.			Wed.			Fri.			Sat.		
Palm Sunday	Su	Mar.	24	Su	Apr.	13	Su	Mar.	29	Su	Mar.	20	Su	Apr.	2
Good Friday	Fr	Mar.	29	Fr	Apr.	18	Fr	Apr.	3	Fr	Mar.	25	Fr	Apr.	14
First Day of Passover (Pesach)	Tu	Mar.	26	Tu	Apr.	15	Sa	Apr.	4	Sa	Apr.	23	Tu	Apr	11
Easter Sunday	Su	Mar.	31	Su	Apr.	20	Su	Apr.	5	Su	Mar.	27	Su	Apr	16
Baisakhi	Sa	Apr.	13	Mo	Apr.	14	Tu	Apr.	14	Th	Apr.	14	Fr	Apr	14
Yom HaSho'ah	Su	Apr.	7	Su	Apr.	27	Th	Apr.	16	Th	May	5	Su	Apr	23
First Day of Ridvan	Su	Apr.	21	Mo	Apr.	21	Tu	Apr.	21	Th	Apr.	21	Fr	Apr	21
St. George	Tu	Apr.	23	We	Apr.	23	Th	Apr.	23	Sa	Apr.	23	Su	Apr	23
St. James	Tu	Apr.	30	We	Apr.	30	Th	Apr.	30	Sa	Apr.	30	Su	Apr	30
MAY begins on	Wed.			Thu.			Fri.			Sun.			Mon.		
Buddha Day (Visakha Puja)	Fr	May	24	We	May	14	Mo	May	4	Su	May	15	We	May	10
Rogation Sunday	Su	May	5	Su	May	25	Su	May	10	Su	May	1	Su	May	21
Mother's Day	Su	May	12	Su	May	11	Su	May	10	Su	May	8	Su	May	14
Ascension Thursday	Th	May	9	Th	May	29	Th	May	7	Th	May	5	Th	May	25
Ascension Sunday	Su	May	12	Su	June	1	Su	May	10	Su	May	8	Su	May	28
Victoria Day	Mo	May	20	Mo	May	19	Mo	May	18	Mo	May	23	Mo	May	22
Pentecost (Shavuoth)	We	May	15	We	June	4	Su	May	24	Su	June	12	We	May	31
Pentecost (Whit Sunday)	Su	May	19	Su	June	8	Su	May	24	Su	May	15	Su	Jun.	4
Ascension of Baha'u'llah	We	May	29	Th	May	29	Fr	May	29	Su	May	29	Mo	May	29
JUNE begins on	Sat.			Sun.			Mon.			Wed.			Thu.		
Trinity Sunday	Su	May	26	Su	June	15	Su	May	31	Su	May	22	Su	June	11
Corpus Christi (Thursday)	Th	May	30	Th	June	19	Th	June	4	Th	May	26	Th	June	15
Corpus Christi (Sunday)	Su	June	2	Su	June	22	Su	June	7	Su	May	29	Su	June	18
Sacred Heart of Jesus	Su	June	23	Mo	June	23	Fr	June	19	Fr	June	3	Fr	June	23
Father's Day	Su	June	16	Su	June	15	Su	June	21	Su	June	19	Su	June	18
First Nations Day	Fr	June	21	Sa	June	21	Su	June	21	Tu	June	21	We	June	21
St-Jean-Baptiste	Mo	June	24	Tu	June	24	We	June	24	Fr	June	24	Mo	June	24
St. Peter and St. Paul	Sa	June	29	Su	June	29	Mo	June	29	We	June	29	Th	June	29
JULY begins on	Mon.			Tue.			Wed.			Fri.			Sat.		
Canada Day	Mo	July	1	Tu	July	1	We	July	1	Fr	July	1	Sa	July	1
Martyrdom of the Bab	Tu	July	9	We	July	9	Th	July	9	Sa	July	9	Su	July	9
St. Benedict Day	Th	July	11	Fr	July	11	Sa	July	11	Mo	July	11	Tu	July	11
Pioneer Day	We	July	14	Th	July	24	Fr	July	24	Su	July	24	Mo	July	24
AUGUST begins on	Thu.			Fri.			Sat.			Mon.			Tue.		
Lammas	Th	Aug.	1	We	Aug.	1	Sa	Aug.	1	Mo	Aug.	1	Tu	Aug.	1
Transfiguration	Th	Aug.	6	Fr	Aug.	6	Th	Aug.	6	Sa	Aug.	6	Su	Aug.	6
Assumption	Th	Aug.	15	Fr	Aug.	15	Sa	Aug.	15	Mo	Aug.	15	Tu	Aug.	15
Eid al Fitr (Ramadan ends)	Th	Aug.	8	Tu	July	29	Sa	July	18	Th	July	7	Mo	Sept.	4
First Day of Ramadan*	Th	July	9	Sa	June	28	Th	June	18	Mo	June	6	Sa	May	27
Tisha B'Av	Th	July	16	Tu	Aug.	5	Su	July	26	Su	Aug.	14	Tu	Aug.	1

SEPTEMBER begins on	Sun.			Mon.			Tue.			Thu.			Fri.		
Labour Day	Mo	Sept.	2	Mo	Sept.	1	Mo	Sept.	7	Mo	Sept.	5	Mo	Sept.	4
Hebrew New Year (Rosh Hashanah)	Tu	Sept.	5	Th	Sept.	25	Fr	Sept.	4	Mo	Oct.	3	Th	Sept.	21-22
Day of Atonement (Yom Kippur)	Sa	Sept.	14	Sa	Oct.	4	We	Sept.	23	We	Oct.	12	Sa	Sept.	30
St. Michael	Su	Sept.	29	Mo	Sept.	29	Tu	Sept.	29	Th	Sept.	29	Fr	Sept.	29
OCTOBER begins on	Tue.			Wed.			Thu.			Sat.			Sun.		
First Day of Feast of Tabernacles (Sukkoth)	Th	Sept.	19	Th	Oct.	9	Mo	Sept.	28	Mo	Oct.	17	Th	Oct.	5
St. Francis	Fr	Oct.	4	Sa	Oct.	4	Su	Oct.	4	Tu	Oct.	4	We	Oct.	4
Shemini Atzeret	Th	Sept.	26	Th	Oct.	16	Tu	Oct.	13	Mo	Oct.	24	Th	Oct.	12
Thanksgiving	Mo	Oct.	7	Mo	Oct.	13	Mo	Oct.	12	Mo	Oct.	10	Mo	Oct.	9
Simhat Torah	Fr	Sept.	27	Fr	Oct	17	We	Oct.	14	Tu	Oct.	25	Fr	Oct.	13
Birth of the B'ab	Su	Oct.	20	Mo	Oct	20	Tu	Oct.	20	Th	Oct.	20	Fr	Oct.	20
Reformation Day	Su	Oct.	27	Mo	Oct	27	Su	Oct.	25	Mo	Oct.	31	Su	Oct.	29
Daylight Savings Time ends**	Su	Oct.	27	Su	Oct	26	Su	Oct.	25	Su	Oct.	30	Su	Nov.	5
Mulvian Bridge Day	Su	Oct.	28	Tu	Oct	28	We	Oct.	28	Fr	Oct.	28	Sa	Oct.	28
All Hallows Eve	Mo	Oct.	31	Fr	Oct	31	Sa	Oct.	31	Mo	Oct.	31	Tu	Oct.	31
NOVEMBER begins on	Fri.			Sat.			Sun.			Tue.			Wed.		
All Saints' Day	Fr	Nov.	1	Sa	Nov.	1	Su	Nov.	1	Tu	Nov.	1	We	Nov.	1
All Souls' Day	Sa	Nov.	2	Su	Nov.	2	Mo	Nov.	2	We	Nov.	2	Th	Nov.	2
Remembrance Day	Mo	Nov.	11	Tu	Nov.	11	We	Nov.	11	Fr	Nov.	11	Sa	Nov.	11
Birth of Baha'u'llah	Tu	Nov.	12	We	Nov.	12	Th	Nov.	12	Sa	Nov.	12	Su	Nov.	12
Diwali	Su	Nov.	3	Th	Oct.	23	We	Nov.	11	Su	Oct.	30	Th	Oct.	19
Islamic New Year	Tu	Nov.	5	Sa	Oct.	25	We	Oct.	14	Sa	Oct.	2	W	Sept.	20
Day of Covenant	Tu	Nov.	26	We	Nov.	26	Th	Nov.	26	Sa	Nov.	26	Su	Nov.	26
St. Andrew's Day	Sa	Nov.	30	Su	Nov.	30	Mo	Nov.	30	We	Nov.	30	Th	Nov.	30
DECEMBER begins on	Sun.			Mon.			Tue.			Thu.			Fri.		
First Sunday in Advent	Su	Dec.	1	Su	Nov.	30	Su	Nov.	29	Su	Nov.	27	Su	Dec.	3
Bodhi Day	Su	Dec.	8	Mo	Dec.	8	Tu	Dec.	8	Th	Dec.	8	Fr	Dec.	8
First Day in Hanukkah	Th	Nov.	28	We	Dec.	17	Mo	Dec.	7	Su	Dec.	25	We	Dec.	13
Feast Day (Our Lady of Guadalupe)	Th	Dec.	12	Fr	Dec.	12	Sa	Dec.	12	Mo	Dec.	12	Tu	Dec.	12
Christmas Day	We	Dec.	25	Th	Dec.	25	Fr	Dec.	25	Su	Dec.	25	Mo	Dec.	25
Kwanzaa begins on	Th	Dec.	26	Fr	Dec.	26	Sa	Dec.	26	Mo	Dec.	26	Tu	Dec.	26
Zarathosht Diso (Death of Prophet Zarathushtra)	Th	Dec.	26	Fr	Dec.	26	Sa	Dec.	26	Mo	Dec.	26	Tu	Dec.	26
Last Day of Year	Tue.			Wed.			Thu.			Sat.			Sun.		

*These are tabular dates; the festival begins at sunset on the day before. According to Islamic custom, the date is actually set by the direct observation of the new crescent moon. **Alberta, British Columbia, Manitoba, New Brunswick, Newfoundland, Northwest Territories, Nova Scotia, Nunavut, Ontario, Prince Edward Island, Quebec and Yukon start Daylight Saving Time on the second Sunday in March and return to standard time on the first Sunday in November. Newfoundland, Nunavut and Yukon start Daylight Saving Time on the first Sunday in April and return to standard time on the last Sunday in October. Saskatchewan doesn't observe Daylight Saving Time. *** Different branches of Hinduism celebrate the new year at different times Jewish holidays begin at sunset the previous evening.

STANDARD HOLIDAYS in Canada include the following: New Year's Day, Good Friday, Victoria Day, Canada Day, Labour Day, Thanksgiving Day, Remembrance Day, Christmas Day, Boxing Day and any other day so proclaimed by the Governor General of Canada, or the Lieutenants Governor of the Provinces. Additionally, Provincial Holidays include: ALBERTA: Alberta Family Day (3rd Monday in February), Heritage Day (1st Monday in August); British Columbia Day (1st Monday in August); MANITOBA: Louis Riel Day (3rd Monday in February), Civic Holiday (1st Monday in August); NEW BRUNSWICK: New Brunswick Day (1st Monday in August); NEWFOUNDLAND: Regatta Day/Civic Holiday (by municipal orders); following celebrated on nearest Monday: St. Patrick's Day (Mar. 17), St. George's Day (Apr. 23), Discovery Day (June 24), Orangemen's Day (July 12); NORTHWEST TERRITORIES: National Aboriginal Day (June 21), Civic Holiday (1st Monday in August); NOVA SCOTIA: Natal Day (1st Monday in August, varies in Halifax); NUNAVUT: Nunavut Day (July 9), 1st Monday in August (1st Monday in August); ONTARIO: Family Day (3rd Monday in February); PRINCE EDWARD ISLAND: Natal Day (by proclamation, usually 1st Monday in August); QUEBEC: National Day (Fête nationale du Québec) (June 24); SASKATCHEWAN: Family Day (3rd Monday in February), Civic Holiday (1st Monday in August); YUKON: Discovery Day (3rd Monday in August)

The Julian Calendar

When Julius Caesar came to power, the Roman Calendar was hopelessly confused. With the advice of the Alexandrian astronomer Sosigenes, Julius Caesar established the Julian Calendar. The length of the year was taken as 365 1/4 days, and in order to account for the 1/4 day, an extra day was added every fourth year. From 45 B.C. each month has had its present number of days. In the old Roman Calendar which was based on the moon an extra month was inserted to straighten out the difference between 12 lunations 354.37 days, and 355 days, which they called a year. This was inserted when necessary after February 23rd. In the Julian Calendar the extra day was added by repeating the sixth day before the Kalends (1st) of March, whence comes our word bissextile for leap year.

No very significant change was made until the reform by Pope Gregory XIII in A.D. 1582.

The Julian Calendar is known as the "Old Style" whereas the calendar as improved by Pope Gregory is known as the "New Style". The difference between the two is now 13 days.

The Gregorian Calendar

Because the Solar Year is 11 minutes, 12 seconds less than the Julian Year of 365 1/4 days, it followed in course of years that the Julian Calendar became inaccurate by several days, and in 1582 this difference amounted to 10 days. Pope Gregory XIII, at the suggestion of Aloysius Lilus, an astronomer of Naples, determined to rectify this, and devised the Calendar now known as the Gregorian Calendar. He dropped or cancelled these 10 days—October 5th being called October 15th—and made centurial years leap years only once in 4 centuries; so that whilst 1700, 1800 and 1900 were to be ordinary years, 2000 would be a leap year. This modification brought the Gregorian year into such close exactitude with the solar year that there is only a difference of 26 seconds, which amounts to a day in 3,323 years. This is the "New Style". The Gregorian Calendar was adopted in Italy, France, Spain, Portugal and Poland in 1582, by most of the German Roman Catholic states, Holland and Flanders in 1583, Hungary in 1587. The adoption in Switzerland began in 1584 and was not completed till 1812. The German and Dutch Protestant states generally, along with Denmark, adopted it in 1700, British dominions in 1752, Sweden in 1753, Japan in 1873, China in 1912, Bulgaria in 1915, Soviet Russia in 1918, Yugoslavia in 1919, Romania and Greece in 1924, Turkey in 1927. The rules for Easter have not, however, been adopted by those oriental churches that are not subject to the Papacy.

The difference between the two "Styles" will remain 13 days until A.D. 2100.

The Jewish Calendar

The Jewish Calendar from the institution of the Mosaic Law downward was a lunar one, consisting of 12 months. The cycles of religious feasts commencing with the Passover depended not only on the month but on the moon; the 14th of the month of Abid or Nisan was coincident with the full moon; and the new moons themselves were the occasions of regular festivals; the commencement of the month was generally determined by observations of the new moon, but 12 lunar months would make but 354 1/2 days, the years would be short 12 days of the true year and it was necessary that an additional month, Veader, be inserted about every third year.

The modern Jewish Calendar is based on fixed rules and not on observation. A common year may contain 353, 354 or 355 days and the leap year 383, 384 or 385 days. The intercalary month always contains 30 days and is inserted before the month Adar, the name and place of which it takes, Adar itself called second Adar or Veadar. Tishri 1 is the Jewish New Year and it cannot be a Sunday, Wednesday or Friday. Tishri 1 is not necessarily the day of new moon but is governed by a mean new moon which is calculated from the value of a mean lunation. It is complicated as compared with the Gregorian Calendar. The intercalary month is introduced seven times in every 19 years.

The identification of the Jewish months with our own cannot be effected with precision on account of the variations existing between the lunar and solar month.

The Muslim Calendar

The Muslim Calendar is called also the calendar of Hegira (i.e. Migration) and is attributed to the primary migration of Mohammed, the Prophet of Islam, on July 16, 622 A.D. from Mecca, his native city in the land of Hejaz, Arabia, to the city of Medina in the north of the same land. In Medina the Prophet and Founder of the Islamic Faith died and was buried.

Each year consists of 12 lunar months and, since no intercalation is made, the months go round the seasons in between 32 and 33 years.

Far Eastern Calendars

The ancient Chinese calendar is a lunar calendar, divided into 12 months of either 29 or 30 days. It is synchronized with the solar calendar by the addition of extra months as required. The four-day Chinese New Year (Hsin Nien) begins at the first new moon over China after the sun enters Aquarius, and may fall between January 21 and February 19. The calendar runs on a 60-year cycle, and each year has both a number and a name: 2013 (Snake), 2014 (Horse), 2015 (Ram), 2016 (Monkey) and 2017 (Rooster). The three-day Vietnamese New Year (Tet) and the three-to-four-day Korean festival Suhl are set by the same new moon. The Japanese calendar uses the Gregorian date of new year, but with a different epoch.

The Hindu Calendar

The Hindu calendar contains both lunar and solar elements, and is therefore complex. Each lunar month is divided into two halves: the dark half (full moon to new moon) and the bright half (new moon to full moon). For some Hindus (primarily South Indian), the lunar month begins on the day following the new moon; for others (primarily North Indian), it begins on the day following the full moon. Likewise, the calculation of the date of New Year varies. There are some holidays which are set by the solar calendar, as well as several which are set by the lunar calendar.

The Indian Calendar

Various religious groups in India have their own calendars (see The Muslim Calendar, and The Hindu Calendar, above). The Indian civil calendar sets the New Year on March 22 in a common year, and on March 21 in a leap year. The years are reckoned according to the native Saka historical era.

The Zoroastrian Calendar

The Zoroastrian calendar is solar, and consists of 12 months of 30 days; five additional days called "gatha" bring the total days in a year to 365. The calculation of the date of the New Year varies among the various Zoroastrian groups.

The Baha'i Calendar

The Baha'i calendar is astronomically fixed, commencing at the vernal equinox. The calendar is solar, and consists of 19 months of 19 days, with the addition of four or five days to bring the total to 365 or 366.

US Civil Calendar 2013

New Year's Day	Tues. Jan. 1
Martin Luther King Day	Mon. Jan. 21
Presidents' Day	Mon. Feb. 18
Memorial Day	Mon. May 27
Independence Day	Thurs. July 4
Labor Day	Mon. Sept. 2
Columbus Day	Mon. Oct. 14
Election Day	Tue. Nov. 5
Veterans' Day	Mon. Nov. 11
Thanksgiving Day	Thu. Nov. 28

United Kingdom Civil Calendar 2013

St. David (Wales)	Fri. Mar. 1
Commonwealth Day	Mon. Mar. 11
St. Patrick (Ireland)	Sun. Mar. 17
Birthday of Queen Elizabeth II	Sun. Apr. 21
St. George (England)	Tues. Apr. 23
Queen's Diamond Jubilee (Coronation Day)	Tues. June 5
Remembrance Sunday	Sun. Nov. 11
St. Andrew (Scotland)	Sat. Nov. 30

For Canadian holidays and festivals, please see page A-58.

THE SEASONS 2013

Eastern Standard Time

- Spring begins March 20th 7h 02 m
- Summer begins June 21th 1 h 04 m
- Autumn begins Sept. 22nd 16 h 44 m
- Winter begins Dec. 21st 13 h 11 m

Eastern Standard Time applies in Ontario and Québec. Newfoundland time is 1 1/2 hours later than Eastern Standard time; in the Maritime Provinces, on Atlantic time, time is 1 hour later; in Manitoba and Saskatchewan, on Central time, time is 1 hour earlier; in Alberta and the western half of Saskatchewan, on Mountain time, time is 2 hours earlier; in B.C., on Pacific time, time is 3 hours earlier.

EPOCHS 2013

- The year 7522 of the Byzantine era begins on Sun., Sep. 1, 2013.
- The year 5774 of the Hebrew era begins at sunset on Thurs., Sep. 5, 2013.
- The New Year of the Chinese (ren chen) era begins on Sun., Jan. 28, 2013.
- The year 2766 of the Roman era begins on Sun., Apr. 21, 2013.
- The year 2762 of the Nabonassar era begins on Sat., Apr. 20, 2013.
- The year 2673 of the Japanese era begins on Tues., Jan. 1, 2013.
- The year 2325 of the Grecian (Seleucidae) era begins on Sat., Sep. 14, 2013 (or Sun., Oct. 14, 2013).
- The year 1935 of the Indian (Saka) era begins on Fri., Mar. 22, 2013.
- The year 1730 of the Diocletian era begins on Tues., Aug. 29, 2013.
- The year 1435 of the Islamic era (Hegira) begins at sunset on Sun., Nov. 13, 2013.
- January 1, 2013, of the Julian Calendar corresponds to Jan. 14, 2013, of the Gregorian Calendar.
- The 62nd year of the reign of Queen Elizabeth II begins on Weds., Feb. 6, 2013.
- The 147th year of the Dominion of Canada begins Mon., July 1, 2013.
- The 238th year of the Independence of the United States of America begins Thurs., July 4, 2013.
- The Julian Day 2,456,293 begins at Greenwich noon Jan. 1, 2013, Gregorian Calendar.

STANDARD TIME

Owing to the great breadth of Canada the difference in solar time in various parts of the country is adjusted by the creation of Standard Time Zones, one hour in width, fixed between arbitrary lines running approximately north and south, 15° of longitude apart, the time observed in each zone being an exact, except for Newfoundland, number of hours slow from Greenwich. Example: When it is 8 a.m. by Pacific Time it is 12 noon by Atlantic Time and 4 p.m. at Greenwich.

There are six zones divided as follows, reckoning from Greenwich:

- *Newfoundland Standard Time:* Newfoundland, excluding most of Labrador, 3 1/2 hours slow.
- *Atlantic Standard Time/60th Meridian Time:* most of Labrador, New Brunswick, Nova Scotia, Prince Edward Island, and those parts of Québec and Northwest Territories east of the 63rd Meridian, 4 hours slow.
- *Eastern Standard Time/75th Meridian Time:* Québec west of the 63rd Meridian and Ontario as far west as the 90th Meridian; Northwest Territories between the 68th and 85th Meridian, 5 hours slow.
- *Central Standard Time/90th Meridian Time:* Ontario west of the 90th Meridian, Manitoba, Saskatchewan and Northwest Territories between the 85th and 102nd Meridian, 6 hours slow.
- *Mountain Standard Time/105th Meridian Time:* Throughout Alberta and in Northwest Territories west of the 102nd Meridian, 7 hours slow.
- *Pacific Standard Time/120th Meridian Time:* Throughout most of British Columbia and in the Yukon, 8 hours slow.

Railways and airways make up their schedules according to Standard Time in winter and Daylight Saving Time in summer. Solar time around the globe varies four minutes with each degree of longitude.

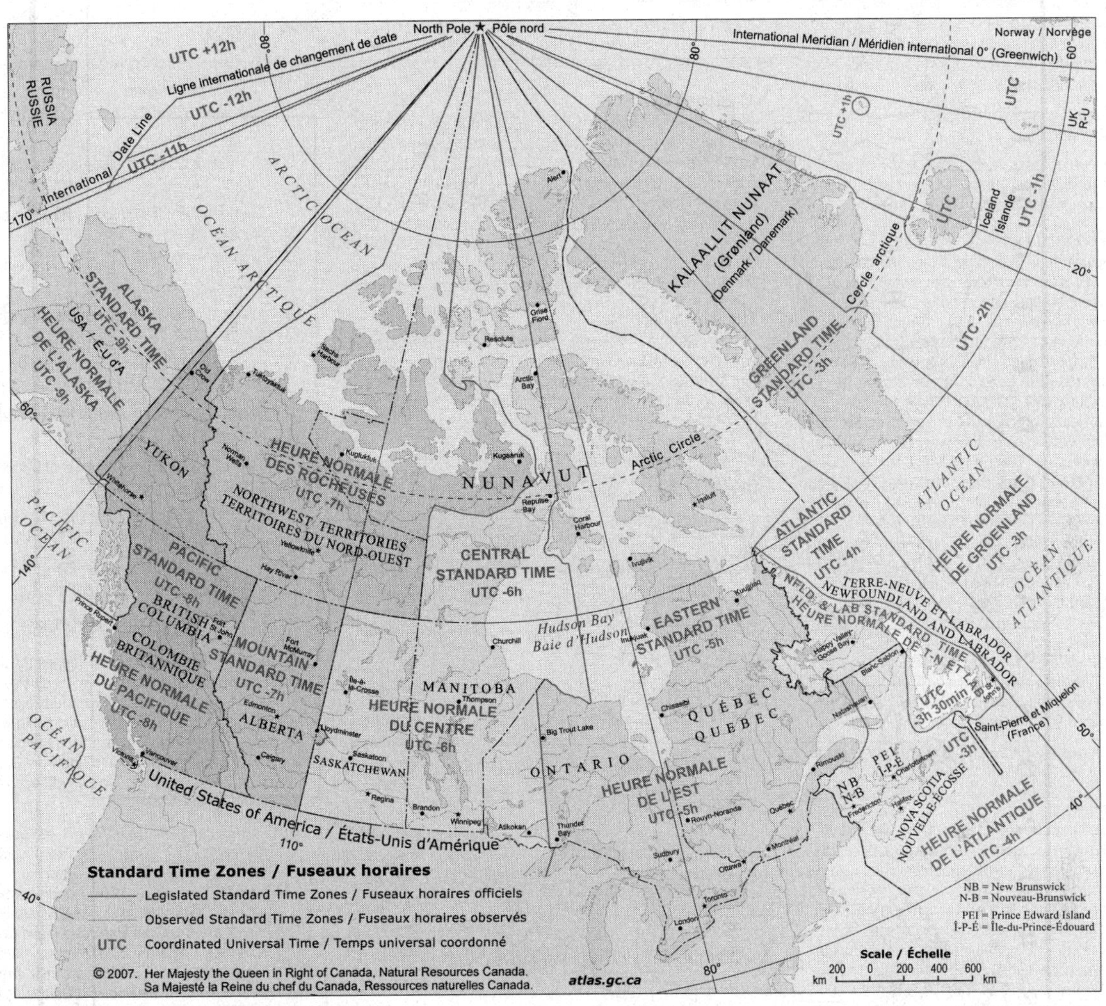

Reproduced with the permission of Natural Resources Canada, 2012.

WORLD MAP OF TIME ZONES

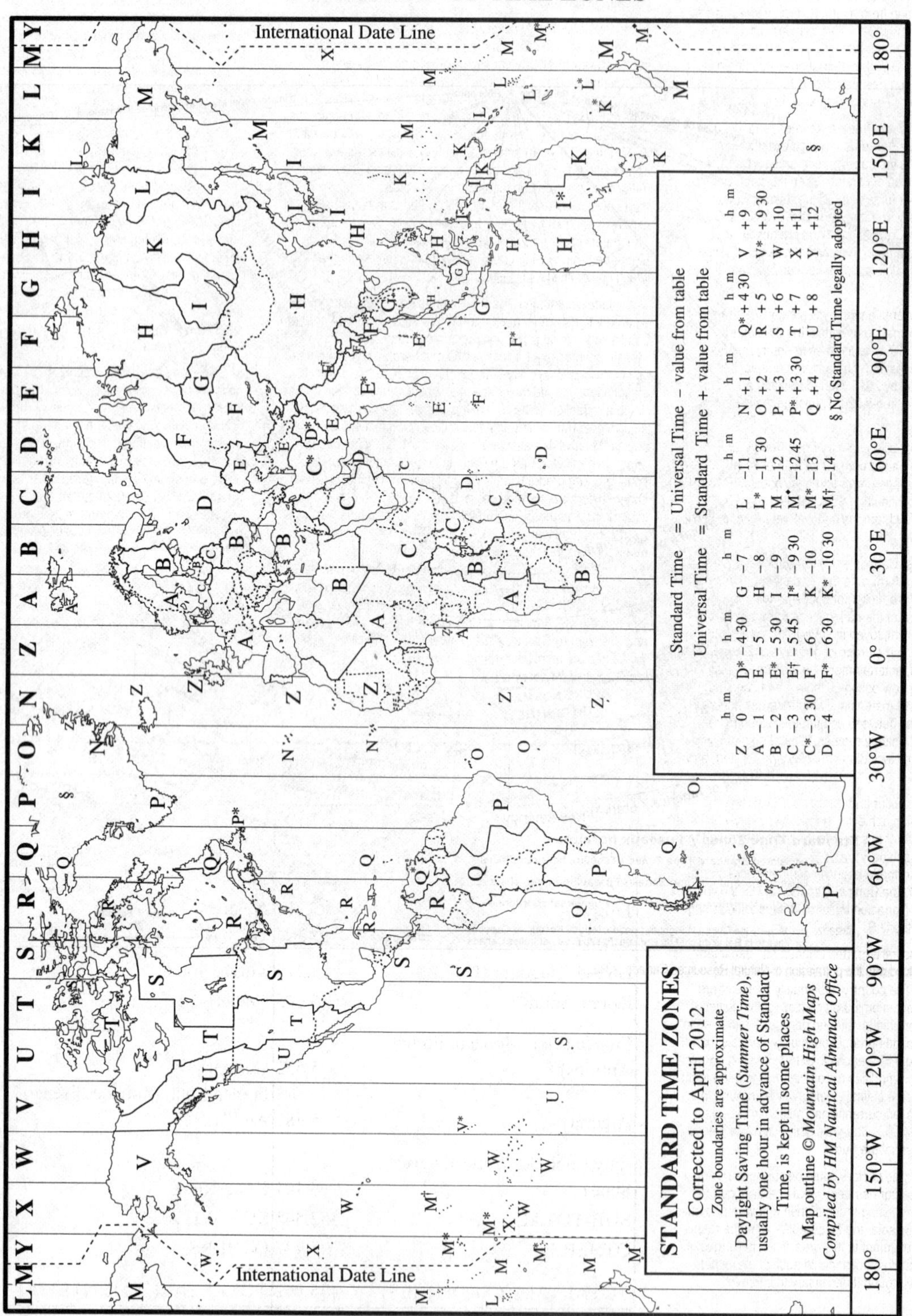
LMY X W V U T S R Q P O N Z A B C D E F G H I K L MY
International Date Line
STANDARD TIME ZONES
Corrected to April 2012
Zone boundaries are approximate
Daylight Saving Time (Summer Time), usually one hour in advance of Standard Time, is kept in some places
Map outline © Mountain High Maps
Compiled by HM Nautical Almanac Office
Standard Time = Universal Time – value from table
Universal Time = Standard Time + value from table
Z 0; A –1; B –2; C –3; C* –3 30; D –4
D* –4 30; E –5; E* –5 30; E† –5 45; F –6; F* –6 30
G –7; H –8; I –9; I* –9 30; K –10; K* –10 30
L –11; L* –11 30; M –12; M• –12 45; M* –13; M† –14
N +1; O +2; P +3; P* +3 30; Q +4
Q* +4 30; R +5; S +6; T +7; U +8
V +9; V* +9 30; W +10; X +11; Y +12
§ No Standard Time legally adopted
180° 150°W 120°W 90°W 60°W 30°W 0° 30°E 60°E 90°E 120°E 150°E 180°

Economics & Finance

Canada's Economy

Since World War II, the growth of Canada's manufacturing, mining and service sectors has transformed the economy of the world's second-largest nation from a largely rural model into one that is primarily industrial and urban. This transformation has been so progressive that Canada has long enjoyed top-level economic status within the G-7, the international grouping of seven leading industrial countries that also includes the United States, the United Kingdom, France, Germany, Italy and Japan.

The 1989 U.S.-Canada Free Trade Agreement and the 1994 North American Free Trade Agreement (which also includes Mexico) spurred a dramatic increase in trade and economic integration of the North American continent. Given its significant natural resources, skilled labor force and modern plants, Canada has benefited tremendously from the free-trade initiatives. Currently, some 79 percent of Canadian exports are absorbed by Canada's principal trading partner, making it the largest foreign supplier of energy, including oil, gas, uranium and electric power, to the U.S.

In general, Canada's overall economy is steady. After the recession, the economy returned to growth in the third quarter of 2009. Canada is the only G-7 country to have nearly recouped the loss incurred in the recession. The government plans to return to a budgetary surplus by 2015. Canada posted a 7.3 percent unemployment rate in August 2012, unchanged in six months.

However, like any other allied country from World War II, Canada will soon see the baby-boom generation pass into retirement, causing the working-age proportion of its population to diminish. As well, there is continuing public debate regarding the rising cost of Canada's world-famous and well-regarded, publicly funded healthcare system.

In the last few decades, Canada's economic model has moved away from being natural-resource dependant to being service-based. While the production of goods remains significant, accounting for a third of the national economy, three out of four citizens are currently employed in service industries. Maintaining the transportation and storage of goods, along with servicing restaurants, shops, entertainment, healthcare, education, defense and government now occupies more Canadians than the actual manufacturing of materials. Canada's gross domestic product, being the balance between consumers' expenditures and income, has shown healthy progress, illustrating a growing demand for big-ticket items including houses, cars, furniture and electronics.

In 2007, the Canadian dollar had reached a 31-year high against the American dollar, achieving one-to-one parity with its neighbour's currency. Later that same year, Bloomberg reported that the dollar was approaching $1.10 U.S., the currency's all-time high since the information-service company began monitoring it in February 1971 (the Bank of Canada only let the currency float in 1970). The Canadian dollar continues to be strong, starying near parity with the U.S.

As a major international oil exporter, Canada has benefited from soaring crude prices, more than offsetting its declining conventional oil production. The country has equally profited from the export of nickel, copper, aluminum and zinc, commodities that all sit at or near record highs. Mineral prices are expected to remain elevated and oil sands production is projected to expand dramatically in coming years to reach close to 3.5 million barrels per day by 2015. With commodities accounting for 35 percent of Canada's exports, the loonie is finally being viewed around the world as a commodity-based currency and has been bid up accordingly. Since January 2002, Canada's dollar-coin has gained more than 40 percent against the buck.

Certainly, some economic sectors could be stronger. Performance in the high-tech sector has been weak, partially due to Canadian companies purchasing much of their software and machinery from the U.S. That said, the favourable exchange rate is expected to lead to improvement in this area. The challenges of adjusting to a higher Canadian dollar could additionally benefit other exporters, who have found it necessary to improve efficiency.

A decline in the American housing market has caused lumber prices to tumble, hurting British Columbia's forestry industry. However, strong domestic housing starts have boosted the overall production of lumber and other timber products, increasing forestry exports despite U.S. softwood lumber tariffs. (Every one-cent increase in the value of the loonie against the U.S. dollar translates to a loss of more than $150 million in annual revenue for the pulp, paper and forest industry.) Non-residential construction activity will increase 3% between now and 2014, reflecting multi-billion dollar investments in projects in Canada's energy patch as well as increased investment in commercial building construction.

In May 2003, the discovery of Bovine Spongiform Encephalopathy (BSE), commonly known as mad-cow disease, in one cow from Alberta caused severe harm to Canada's beef-export market. Compounded by the advent of Severe Acute Respiratory Syndrome (SARS) in the late summer of that same year, Canada's growth forecast dampened from 3.4 percent to 2.3 percent, but the current outlook is improving. In September 2007, the U.S. Department of Agriculture (USDA) agreed to expand cattle trade with Canada, additionally urging beef-importing nations to eliminate unnecessary barriers erected after the mad-cow scare. More trade with the United States will help export-dependent Canadian ranchers recover from trade bans. The impact of the stronger Canadian dollar will also result in higher beef-processing costs relative to competitors in the U.S., which could offset more gains.

Canada's commercial ocean fisheries have experienced overall production decline, due in part to the 2003 closure of northern cod fishing grounds. The volume of production has been adversely affected by an average rate of 4 percent a year as a result of dwindling resources and problems caused by over-exploitation of some major species. West Coast over-fishing has led to a reduction in the size of the salmon fleet, as well as extensive government intervention in the fishing industry on both coasts. Meanwhile aquaculture, or fish farming, continues to thrive. In particular, Eastern Canada boasts extensive operations, growing predominantly Atlantic salmon and mussels. Other key species include bay and sea scallops, brook trout, oysters, bay quahogs, sea urchins, arctic char, haddock and bar clams, and significant progress has been made in the development of new species such as halibut, sturgeon, abalone and cod. That said, almost every province and territory in Canada, including the Yukon, runs commercial freshwater aquaculture operations, mostly raising rainbow and brook trout. Ontario and Québec are the dominant producers of freshwater fish in Canada, followed by Saskatchewan, Alberta and New Brunswick. As the Canadian freshwater aquaculture industry is young, it is also ideally poised for growth.

Always historically strong, the Canadian stock market has continued to thrive. The Toronto Stock Exchange (TSX) is the country's largest and the world's sixth largest by market capitalization. In addition, the TSX Group is the international leader in the oil and gas sector, boasting more oil and gas sector listings on the Toronto Stock Exchange and TSX Venture Exchange than any other exchange in the world (in 2012, 401 oil and gas companies were listed, with a total market capitalization of $352 billion). Oil and gas companies continue to raise equity on Canadian exchanges with $10.1 billion raised in 2011.

Sourcing from China continues to offer an economically viable solution for Canadian companies. This option to reduce costs while growing wealth in major Chinese cities creates vast new opportunities for Canadian firms, particularly exporters of services. With a small domestic market, the steady expansion of multilateral trade is critical to the structure of the country's economy and the continued prosperity of its citizens. The rapid and ongoing industrialization of China has boosted the world price of Canadian oil, gas, mineral, metal and farm-product exports. Canadian exports to China in 2010 accounted for 3.3 percent of our total, up from 1.8 percent in 2006. However, Canadian sales to Japan have lagged. In 1996, Japan received 4.1 percent of Canada's exports, but only 2.3 percent in 2010.

Since the early 1990s, the focus of Canadian monetary policy on low, stable and predictable inflation has helped to both anchor inflation expectations and reduce the ups and downs in economic activity. Canadians have been able to make spending, saving and investment decisions with greater certainty, knowing that their central bank will hold the line on future inflation and that the economy will be more stable. Low interest rates and greater confidence about the future have encouraged Canadian firms to undertake important restructuring initiatives, stepping up to meet the challenges of sweeping worldwide technological change and intensely competitive global markets.

Principal Trading Partners in 2011

Imports (millions $)		Exports (millions $)	
United States (U.S.)	220,895	United States (U.S.)	329,800
China	48,153	United Kingdom (U.K.)	18,791
Mexico	24,573	China	16,810
Japan	13,058	Japan	10,671
Germany	12,789	Mexico	5,476
United Kingdom (U.K.)	10,329	Korea, South	5,098
Korea, South	6,605	Netherlands	4,807
France (incl. Monaco, French Antilles)	5,552	Germany	3,955
Algeria	5,485	France (incl. Monaco, French Antilles)	3,081
Italy (includes Vatican City State)	5,107	Hong Kong	2,967
SUB-TOTAL	352,545	SUB-TOTAL	401,455
OTHERS	93,447	OTHERS	46,046
TOTAL (ALL COUNTRIES)	445,992	TOTAL (ALL COUNTRIES)	447,501

Source: "International Trade data," based on Statistics Canada's International Trade Division, retrieved on Industry Canada's web site: http://www.ic.gc.ca/sc_mrkti/tdst/tdo/tdo.php#tag

AVERAGE EARNINGS[1] OF MEN & WOMEN IN CANADA, 1995-2010

Work Activity Earnings Date	All Earners: Average earnings, females (dollars)	All Earners: Average earnings, males (dollars)	All Earners: Female-to-male average earnings ratio (percent)	All Earners: Median earnings, females (dollars)	All Earners: Median earnings, males (dollars)	All Earners: Female-to-male median earnings ratio (percent)	Full-Year Full-Time Workers: Average earnings, females (dollars)	Full-Year Full-Time Workers: Average earnings, males (dollars)	Full-Year Full-Time Workers: Female-to-male average earnings ratio (percent)	Full-Year Full-Time Workers: Median earnings, females (dollars)	Full-Year Full-Time Workers: Median earnings, males (dollars)	Full-Year Full-Time Workers: Female-to-male median earnings ratio (percent)
1995	25,800	40,100	64.2	20,100	34,600	58	39,100	53,600	73	35,900	49,000	73.3
1996	26,000	40,900	63.6	20,200	34,300	58.8	39,400	54,100	72.8	35,700	48,500	73.6
1997	25,900	42,000	61.8	20,600	34,800	59.1	39,000	55,800	70	36,100	49,100	73.5
1998	27,100	43,200	62.8	21,200	35,000	60.7	41,300	57,500	71.9	37,100	50,000	74.1
1999	27,500	43,900	62.6	21,500	35,900	59.8	39,700	58,100	68.4	35,500	50,200	70.8
2000	28,000	45,400	61.7	21,600	36,400	59.4	41,000	58,100	70.6	35,800	49,900	71.7
2001	28,200	45,300	62.1	21,800	35,600	61.2	41,400	59,300	69.9	36,300	49,900	72.7
2002	28,500	45,400	62.8	21,500	35,200	61	41,700	59,400	70.2	36,700	49,900	73.6
2003	28,100	44,700	62.9	21,700	35,100	61.7	41,500	59,200	70.2	36,500	50,200	72.7
2004	28,500	44,900	63.5	21,700	35,100	61.7	42,800	61,100	70.1	37,100	50,300	73.7
2005	29,200	45,600	64	22,000	35,600	61.8	42,700	60,600	70.5	36,500	49,600	73.6
2006	29,600	45,800	64.7	22,400	35,400	63.3	44,100	61,300	71.9	38,100	50,500	75.5
2007	30,400	46,500	65.5	23,000	35,900	64.1	44,900	63,100	71.2	38,500	51,900	74.2
2008	30,800	47,900	64.3	23,200	37,000	62.8	45,500	64,000	71.1	39,400	51,800	76
2009	31,600	46,100	68.6	23,700	35,100	67.6	47,300	63,500	74.4	40,700	52,000	78.2
2010	31,700	46,500	68.1	23,900	35,000	68.2	47,300	64,200	73.6	40,900	52,700	77.6

[1]2010 Constant Dollars

Source: Adapted from Statistics Canada's CANSIM database http://www5.statcan.gc.ca/cansim/home-accueil?lang=eng, Table 202-0102, July 2011 (accessed: October 12, 2012)

HOUSEHOLD SPENDING	
Annual (dollars)[1]	
Household expenditures, summary-level categories	**2010**
Total expenditure	70,574
Total current consumption	53,016
Food expenditures[2]	7,443
Shelter	14,997
Household operation[3]	3,773
Household furnishings and equipment	1,923
Clothing and accessories[4]	3,452
Transportation	10,999
Health care	2,194
Personal care	894
Recreation	3,539
Education	1,151
Reading materials and other printed matter	192
Tobacco products and alcoholic beverages	1,149
Games of chance	141
Miscellaneous expenditures	1,167
Income taxes	11,936
Personal insurance payments and pension contributions	4,013
Gifts of money, alimony and contributions to charity	1,609

Footnotes:

[1]This table replaces CANSIM tables 203-0001 to 203-0018 which have been terminated with the release of the 2009 data due to changes in the methodology of this survey.

[2]Does not include day board paid to other private households, which is now included in childcare expenses in household operation.

[3]Includes child care expenses, domestic and other custodial services, pet expenses, household cleaning supplies, paper, plastic and foil household supplies, garden supplies and services and other household supplies.

[4]Includes clothing gifts to non-household members, clothing material (excluding household textiles), laundry and dry-cleaning services, laundromats and self-service dry cleaning and other clothing services.

Source: Adapted from Statistics Canada's CANSIM database http://www5.statcan.gc.ca/cansim/home-accueil?lang=eng, Table 203-0001, July 2011. (Accessed October 12, 2012)

AVERAGE AFTER-TAX INCOME, 2000-2010

	2000	2001	2002	2003	2004	2005	2006	2007	2008	2009	2010
Canada	65,800	68,500	68,500	68,000	69,600	70,500	72,300	75,300	76,300	76,400	76,600
Newfoundland and Labrador	51,600	52,400	53,000	53,000	53,400	54,800	57,300	62,600	65,100	65,500	67,800
Prince Edward Island	53,900	55,100	56,600	56,300	57,400	58,000	60,200	61,300	63,500	64,100	63,600
Nova Scotia	56,500	58,500	59,000	57,000	58,700	61,800	63,100	63,800	63,100	65,900	65,500
New Brunswick	55,300	56,500	56,400	56,500	57,700	56,900	58,700	61,000	61,300	64,200	64,700
Quebec	57,700	60,400	60,700	60,000	61,900	62,000	63,300	65,000	66,000	67,200	66,800
Ontario	74,900	76,500	76,100	75,500	76,600	76,600	77,400	80,200	80,500	79,800	80,400
Manitoba	58,400	61,200	63,100	61,300	63,200	64,500	66,400	70,200	71,200	71,400	71,800
Saskatchewan	56,600	60,100	60,100	60,800	61,200	64,400	67,400	70,400	75,200	78,300	77,500
Alberta	70,200	75,300	73,500	75,000	77,300	79,800	85,300	90,200	91,400	91,700	90,700
British Columbia	62,100	66,100	67,400	65,800	67,900	70,800	73,000	77,200	79,100	77,800	78,200

Footnotes

[1]Average total income, economic families, 2 persons or more, 2010 constant dollars

Source: Adapted from Statistics Canada's CANSIM database http://www5.statcan.gc.ca/cansim/home-accueil?lang=eng, Table 202-0202 (Accessed: October 12, 2012)

CURRENT AND FORTHCOMING MINIMUM HOURLY WAGE RATES FOR EXPERIENCED ADULT WORKERS IN CANADA			
Jurisdiction	**Effective Date**	**Wage**	**Note**
Federal [1]	18-Dec-96		The minimum wage rate applicable in regard to employees under federal jurisdiction is the general adult minimum rate of the province or territory where the employee is usually employed
Alberta	1-Sep-11	$9.40	
Alberta	1-Sep-12	$9.75	
British Columbia	1-May-12	$10.25	
Manitoba	1-Oct-11	$10.00	
Manitoba	1-Oct-12	$10.25	
New Brunswick	1-Apr-12	$10.00	
Newfoundland and Labrador	1-Jul-10	$10.00	
Northwest Territories	1-Apr-11	$10.00	
Nova Scotia [2]	1-Apr-12	$10.15	On April 1 of each year, this rate is to increase to reflect changes in Statistics Canada's Low Income Cut-Off figures for the previous year.
Nunavut	1-Jan-11	$11.00	
Ontario	31-Mar-10	$10.25	
Prince Edward Island	1-Apr-12	$10.00	
Quebec	1-May-12	$9.90	
Saskatchewan	1-Sep-11	$9.50	
Yukon	1-May-12	$10.30	On April 1 of each year, this rate increases by an amount corresponding to the annual increase for the preceding year in the Consumer Price Index for the city of Whitehorse.

Note: In most jurisdictions, these rates also apply to young workers. More information is available on special rates for young workers under "Current And Forthcoming Minimum Wage Rates in Canada for Young Workers and Specific Occupations."

Footnotes:

[1] The federal jurisdiction includes labour market sectors coming under federal authority by virtue of the Constitution, such as international and interprovincial transportation, telecommunication and banking.

[2] There is a special minimum wage rate for inexperienced employees. See "Current and Forthcoming Minimum Wage Rates in Canada for Young Workers and Specific Occupations".

Source: Reproduced with the permission of the Minister of Public Works and Government Services Canada, 2012.

CONSUMER PRICE INDEX, CANADA, MONTHLY										
2009 BASKET, 2002=100										
Date	**All-Items CPI**	**Food**	**Shelter**	**Household Operations, Furnishings and Equipment**	**Clothing and Footwear**	**Transportation**	**Gasoline**	**Health and Personal Care**	**Recreation, Education and Reading**	**Alcoholic Beverages and Tobacco Products**
Jan. 2000	93.5	92.1	93.7	95.5	99.2	94.7	93.3	96.1	93.8	77.8
Jan. 2001	96.3	95.3	97.5	97.1	99.6	97.5	103.1	97.9	96.1	80.2
Jan. 2002	97.6	99.7	99.3	99.2	97.2	94.4	86.7	98.9	96.8	90.8
Jan. 2003	102	101.6	102.1	100.1	96.6	105.5	108.4	100.5	99.3	106.8
Jan. 2004	103.3	102.8	104.3	100.9	97.2	105.8	105.8	102	99.1	113.9
Jan. 2005	105.3	105.4	107.5	101.3	95.1	108.8	114.9	103	99.3	117.4
Jan. 2006	108.2	108.4	111.8	102.3	94.2	114.7	136.9	105	99.1	120
Jan. 2007	109.4	110.9	114.8	102.4	94.2	113.3	126.4	106.3	99.2	124.2
Jan. 2008	111.8	112.4	119.2	103.3	92.2	117.6	152.8	107.5	99.6	126.4
Jan. 2009	113	120.6	123.1	105.7	91.8	108.8	116.9	110.4	99.7	129.2
Jan. 2010	115.1	122.3	121.8	107.9	90.1	117.2	144.8	113.8	101.1	131.1
Jan. 2011	117.8	124.9	124.5	109.6	87.9	122.8	163.6	115.8	102.7	135.2
Jan. 2012	120.7	130.2	127.1	112.2	89.3	127.4	174.7	118.1	102.6	136.3
Aug. 2012	121.8	131.7	127.4	112.7	89.5	127.5	184.9	119.8	107.6	137.8

Source: Adapted from Statistics Canada's CANSIM database http://www5.statcan.gc.ca/cansim/home-accueil?lang=eng, Tables 326-0020 and 326-0021 July 2011. (Accessed October 12, 2012)

NEW HOUSING PRICE INDEXES, MONTHLY						
2007=100						
	Canada Total (house and land)	Atlantic Region Total (house and land)	Québec Total (house and land)	Ontario Total (house and land)	Prairie Region Total (house and land)	British Columbia Total (house and land)
Jan. 1995	66.7	78.8	65.3	70.4	40.4	94.4
Jan. 1996	65.4	79.1	65.4	69.9	40.3	88
Jan. 1997	65	78.7	65.5	69.9	41.7	83.9
Jan. 1998	65.8	76.6	65.5	72	44	80.7
Jan. 1999	66.1	77.7	65.8	73.3	45.9	76.3
Jan. 2000	67.3	79.1	68	75	47.3	74.9
Jan. 2001	69	80.9	70.9	77.5	48	74.3
Jan. 2002	71	82.5	73.7	79.5	49.7	76.2
Jan. 2003	74.6	85.7	80.4	83.1	52.9	78
Jan. 2004	78.4	88.1	85	87.2	55.6	82.4
Jan. 2005	82.4	91.2	90.3	91.9	58.2	85.7
Jan. 2006	87.9	95.1	93.8	95.9	67.7	90.8
Jan. 2007	96.8	97.4	97.8	98.7	92.7	96.5
Jan. 2008	103	104.4	102.5	102.4	104.5	102.3
Jan. 2009	102.2	114.2	106.8	103.9	97.6	98.9
Jan. 2010	102.3	117	109.7	105.4	94.7	97.3
Jan. 2011	104.2	120.9	113.6	107.4	95.9	97.3
Jan. 2012	106.7	121.2	115.7	112.3	97	97.1
Aug. 2012	108.3	122.6	116.7	114.9	98.3	96.8

Source: Adapted from Statistics Canada's CANSIM database http://www5.statcan.gc.ca/cansim/home-accueil?lang=eng, Table 327-0046, July 2011. (Accessed October 12, 2012)

Individuals Using the Internet from Any Location	
	2010 (%)
Canada	80
Newfoundland and Labrador	73
Prince Edward Island	75
Nova Scotia	79
New Brunswick	70
Quebec	76
Ontario	81
Manitoba	79
Saskatchewan	80
Alberta	84
British Columbia	86

Source: Adapted from Statistics Canada's Survey of Household Survey, table 62F0041, 2009

COUNTRIES VISITED BY CANADIANS, 2010		
One or More Nights		
	Country Visits	Spending in Country ($ Less Fares)
United States	19,964,000	14,602,578,300
Mexico	1,354,100	1,426,611,800
Cuba	1,010,200	748,272,500
United Kingdom	880,200	1,010,506,100
Dominican Republic	753,300	663,813,900
France	739,700	913,736,500
Italy	375,800	483,105,800
Germany	328,600	276,466,000
Mainland China	300,000	506,039,800
Netherlands	225,000	167,944,000
Spain	216,600	272,027,300
Hong Kong	183,300	196,192,600
Jamaica	166,100	171,068,800
Republic of Ireland	160,400	191,460,700
Switzerland	143,500	110,989,300

Source: Statistics Canada, http://www40.statcan.gc.ca/l01/cst01/arts37a-eng.htm, August 2011.

Labour Force Survey Estimates (LFS)							
Thousands, Annual Averages 1995-2011							
	Population 15+	Labour force	Employment	Unemployment	Unemployment rate	Participation rate (rate)	Employment rate
1995	22,660	14,689	13,295	1,394	9.5	64.8	58.7
1996	22,960	14,849	13,420	1,428	9.6	64.7	58.5
1997	23,247	15,081	13,708	1,372	9.1	64.9	59
1998	23,516	15,315	14,047	1,268	8.3	65.1	59.7
1999	23,781	15,584	14,402	1,182	7.6	65.5	60.6
2000	24,090	15,842	14,760	1,082	6.8	65.8	61.3
2001	24,439	16,105	14,941	1,164	7.2	65.9	61.1
2002	24,786	16,569	15,298	1,271	7.7	66.8	61.7
2003	25,099	16,948	15,663	1,285	7.6	67.5	62.4
2004	25,431	17,154	15,922	1,233	7.2	67.5	62.6
2005	25,780	17,294	16,125	1,169	6.8	67.1	62.5
2006	26,146	17,517	16,410	1,107	6.3	67	62.8
2007	26,520	17,884	16,806	1,079	6	67.4	63.4
2008	26,907	18,204	17,087	1,117	6.1	67.7	63.5
2009	27,298	18,329	16,813	1,516	8.3	67.1	61.6
2010	27,659	18,525	17,041	1,484	8	67	61.6
2011	27,987	18,699	17,306	1,393	7.4	66.8	61.8

Source: Adapted from Statistics Canada's CANSIM database http://www5.statcan.gc.ca/cansim/home-accueil?lang=eng, Table 282-0002, August 2011 (Accessed: October 12, 2012)

Labour Force Survey Estimates (LFS), Employment Rate By Age Group									
	15 Years and Over	15 to 24 Years	25 Years and Over	25 to 44 Years	45 Years and Over	25 to 54 Years	55 Years and Over	55 to 64 Years	65 Years and Over
1995	58.7	53.8	59.7	76.8	42.3	76.2	22	43.2	5.9
1996	58.5	52.7	59.6	76.9	42.4	76.2	22	43.5	5.9
1997	59	51.5	60.5	78.1	43.4	77.3	22.6	44.5	6.1
1998	59.7	52.4	61.2	79.3	44.2	78.4	23.1	45.3	6.3
1999	60.6	54.5	61.8	80.1	45.1	79.2	23.7	46.8	6
2000	61.3	56.2	62.3	80.8	45.9	79.9	24.3	48.1	5.9
2001	61.1	56.3	62.1	80.6	46.2	79.8	24.6	48.2	5.9
2002	61.7	57.4	62.6	80.8	47.5	80.3	26.2	50.1	6.5
2003	62.4	58.1	63.3	81.2	48.9	80.8	28.2	53	7.2
2004	62.6	57.9	63.6	81.7	49.5	81.3	29	53.9	7.5
2005	62.5	57.7	63.5	81.8	49.8	81.3	29.9	54.7	7.9
2006	62.8	58.5	63.6	82	50.3	81.6	30.5	55.5	7.9
2007	63.4	59.5	64.1	82.6	51.1	82.2	31.7	57	8.6
2008	63.5	59.7	64.3	82.6	51.7	82.3	32.6	57.5	9.8
2009	61.6	55.5	62.8	80.4	51	80.3	32.8	57.6	10
2010	61.6	55	62.9	80.5	51.3	80.5	33.7	58.3	10.9
2011	61.8	55.4	63.1	81	51.5	81	34.1	58.7	11.3

Source: Adapted from Statistics Canada's CANSIM database http://www5.statcan.gc.ca/cansim/home-accueil?lang=eng, Tables 282-0004 and 282-0051, August 2011 (Accessed: October 12, 2012)

Labour Force Survey Estimates (LFS), Annual Averages In Thousands, 2002-2011										
National Occupational Classification for Statistics (NOC-S)	2002	2003	2004	2005	2006	2007	2008	2009	2010	2011
Total, all occupations (10)	15,298	15,663	15,922	16,125	16,410	16,806	17,087	16,813	17,041	17,306
Management occupations [A]	1,354	1,368	1,442	1,449	1,503	1,498	1,565	1,533	1,525	1,477
Senior management occupations [A0]	70	80	105	91	92	85	78	82	77	78
Other management occupations [A1-A3]	1,283	1,288	1,337	1,359	1,411	1,413	1,488	1,450	1,448	1,399
Business, finance and administrative occupations [B]	2,727	2,794	2,888	2,888	2,969	3,025	3,121	3,045	3,060	3,122
Professional occupations in business and finance [B0]	458	448	467	478	497	522	537	568	575	582
Financial, secretarial and administrative occupations [B1-B3]	745	769	782	792	797	812	884	830	851	836
Clerical occupations, including supervisors [B4-B5]	1,524	1,577	1,639	1,618	1,676	1,691	1,700	1,648	1,635	1,704
Natural and applied sciences and related occupations [C]	1,037	1,036	1,047	1,103	1,128	1,180	1,204	1,188	1,256	1,272
Health occupations [D]	872	891	924	952	984	999	1,042	1,063	1,094	1,163
Professional occupations in health, nurse supervisors and registered nurses [D0-D1]	432	428	443	451	463	479	494	501	498	528
Technical, assisting and related occupations in health [D2-D3]	441	463	481	501	521	520	547	562	596	635
Occupations in social science, education, government service and religion [E]	1,235	1,263	1,243	1,338	1,397	1,434	1,483	1,554	1,611	1,593
Occupations in social science, government service and religion [E0 E2]	651	664	646	698	724	749	795	851	895	892
Teachers and professors [E1 E130] (12)	584	600	597	640	673	685	688	703	716	701
Occupations in art, culture, recreation and sport [F]	438	467	467	496	486	507	530	544	552	576
Sales and service occupations [G] (11)	3,722	3,822	3,840	3,842	3,895	4,101	4,097	4,104	4,142	4,171
Wholesale, technical, insurance, real estate sales specialists, and retail, wholesale and grain buyers [G1]	477	512	498	529	530	560	537	570	569	556
Retail salespersons, sales clerks, cashiers, including retail trade supervisors [G011 G2-G3]	977	1,003	1,018	1,021	1,025	1,072	1,062	1,063	1,079	1,063
Chefs and cooks, and occupations in food and beverage service, including supervisors [G012 G4-G5]	513	515	529	498	520	558	546	526	533	544
Occupation in protective services [G6]	224	229	235	223	221	236	243	251	256	264
Childcare and home support workers [G8]	189	197	202	186	193	213	211	219	220	209
Sales and service occupations n.e.c., including occupations in travel and accommodation, attendants in recreation and sport as well as supervisors [G013-G016 G7 G9]	1,343	1,366	1,358	1,384	1,407	1,461	1,497	1,474	1,485	1,536
Trades, transport and equipment operators and related occupations [H]	2,249	2,328	2,374	2,396	2,446	2,515	2,609	2,464	2,485	2,587
Contractors and supervisors in trades and transportation [H0]	220	217	237	244	245	248	271	268	259	268
Construction trades [H1]	317	328	323	344	360	376	405	381	396	396
Other trades occupations [H2-H5]	848	867	877	886	883	908	950	878	881	919
Transport and equipment operators [H6-H7]	585	603	608	590	615	634	624	612	618	649
Trades helpers, construction, and transportation labourers and related occupations [H8]	279	313	329	331	344	349	359	325	332	356
Occupations unique to primary industry [I]	526	545	557	576	584	578	543	531	527	530
Occupations unique to processing, manufacturing and utilities [J]	1,138	1,149	1,141	1,085	1,018	969	896	787	788	816
Machine operators and assemblers in manufacturing, including supervisors [J0-J2]	946	947	938	876	816	777	726	644	647	657
Labourers in processing, manufacturing and utilities [J3]	193	201	203	209	202	192	170	144	142	160

Source: Adapted from Statistics Canada's CANSIM database http://www5.statcan.gc.ca/cansim/home-acceuil?lang=eng, Table 282-0010. (Accessed October 2012)

GROWTH STATISTICS: MAJOR CANADIAN AIRLINES

Monthly (Data in Thousands)

	Passengers	Passenger Kilometres	Kilograms of Goods	Goods (tonne-kilometres)	Turbo Fuel Consumed (Litres)
Jan-95	1,520	3,634,871	27,841	119,215	269,301
Jan-96	1,688	4,018,453	30,045	136,019	287,673
Jan-97	1,818	4,368,201	31,504	144,036	295,153
Jan-98	1,785	4,597,429	34,253	152,452	306,313
Jan-99	1,730	4,692,697	31,047	133,200	189,790
Jan-00	1,705	4,570,249	34,569	156,250	329,249
Jan-01	1,834	5,265,411	29,191	133,318	297,278
Jan-02	1,810	5,216,405	25,284	117,616	277,532
Jan-03	1,687	5,059,160	24,588	122,199	270,713
Jan-04[1]	2,030	5,802,782	22,166	104,955	299,639
Jan-05	2,453	6,475,007	20,386	99,715	314,968
Jan-06	2,592	6,826,667	19,704	102,057	315,785
Jan-07	2,741	7,218,539	18,479	93,778	331,293
Jan-08	2,982	7,650,906	16,658	88,530	350,007
Jan-09	2,889	7,360,628	12,836	72,733	327,227
Jan-10	3,016	7,810,857	18,312	113,377	343,768
Jan-11	3,150	8,518,349	19,262	118,295	371,191
Jan-12	3,346	8,966,432	19,319	119,065	389,576
Jul-12	3,968	10,900,331	21,794	136,486	435,642

Footnotes:

[1]As of January 2004, major airline data includes both WestJet and Air Canada.

Source: Statistics Canada. Table 4001-0001 - Operating and financial statistics of major Canadian airlines, monthly (Accessed October 15, 2012)

GROWTH STATISTICS: AGRICULTURE					
FARM CASH RECEIPTS, ANNUAL (DOLLARS x 1,000)					
	Population	Wheat (harvested hectares)	Total Farm Cash Receipts ($)	Total Crops Receipts ($)	Total Receipts From Livestock and Livestock Products ($)
1995	29,302,311	11,122,700	27,123,321	13,114,105	12,703,800
1996	29,610,218	12,262,500	29,075,327	14,016,229	13,857,294
1997	29,905,948	11,416,000	29,835,513	14,093,889	14,632,865
1998	30,155,173	10,679,700	29,505,263	13,642,036	14,441,683
1999	30,401,286	10,380,800	30,256,780	13,121,182	15,159,564
2000	30,685,730	10,854,800	32,879,399	12,969,706	17,100,989
2001	31,019,020	10,605,500	36,243,327	13,504,866	18,972,521
2002	31,353,656	8,710,500	35,970,624	14,411,906	18,129,777
2003	31,639,670	10,214,500	34,244,827	13,312,062	16,084,649
2004	31,940,676	9,388,900	36,338,224	14,420,425	17,055,534
2005	32,245,209	9,403,800	36,798,456	13,488,871	18,386,163
2006	32,576,074	9,681,800	37,016,513	14,704,878	17,777,961
2007	32,927,517	8,636,300	40,846,861	18,433,199	18,320,755
2008	33,317,662	10,031,700	46,093,917	23,023,963	18,937,713
2009	33,726,915	9,638,200	44,599,139	23,201,510	18,106,591
2010	34,126,547	8,268,700	44,463,363	22,407,168	18,922,497
2011	34,483,975	8,543,600	49,724,275	25,700,552	20,538,730

Source: Adapted from the Statistics Canada publication 22-002-XIB, and CANSIM database http://www5.statcan.gc.ca/cansim/home-accueil?lang=eng, Tables 002-0001, 051-0001 and 304-0014, August 2011. (Accessed October 12, 2012)

GROWTH STATISTICS: MONTHLY PRODUCTION OF SELECTED MINERALS/METALS			
	Total, Cement Products (metric tonnes)	Pig Iron (metric tonnes)	Crude oil and Natural Gas (000,000 cubic metres)
Jan, 2004	618,671.0	710,783	19,243.9
Jan, 2005	692,449.0	714,223	19,405.4
Jan, 2006	755,813.0	706,407	19,248.1
Jan, 2007	959,157.0	753,155	19,214.7
Jan, 2008	690,061.0	860,637	18,875.5
Jan, 2009	470,647.0	518,216	18,544.7
Jan, 2010	621,283.0	637,168	17,416.0
Jan, 2011	562,327.0	579,775	17,731.6
Jan, 2012	537,963.0	676,713	16,436.4
July, 2012	1,318,614.0	652,898	13,750.3

Source: Adapted from Statistics Canada. Tables 303-0060, 131-0001, and 303-0048; retrieved from CANSIM database http://www5.statcan.gc.ca/cansim/a01?lang=eng. (Accessed October 15, 2012)

GROWTH STATISTICS: IMPORTS AND EXPORTS						
			Imports			
	Total Imports (millions of Cdn $)	Total Exports (millions of Cdn $)	Sugar (millions of Cdn $)	Rubber and Articles Thereof (millions of Cdn $)	Raw Cotton (thousands of Cdn $)	Mineral Fuels, Oils, Waxes, & Bituminous Substances (millions of Cdn $)
2002	348,957	396,382	798	5,386	805,103	17,156
2003	336,141	381,172	821	4,905	659,015	21,202
2004	355,886	412,290	743	5,245	566,654	25,243
2005	380,858	436,351	791	5,483	425,262	34,999
2006	397,044	440,365	908	5,558	314,500	36,298
2007	407,301	450,321	829	5,511	247,412	37,974
2008	433,999	483,488	918	5,749	188,593	53,743
2009	365,359	359,754	1,008	5,465	150,661	34,372
2010	403,750	399,300	1,098	5,961	161,157	40,739
2011	445,992	447,501	13,449	7,077	170,858	52,690

Source: "International Trade data", based on Statistics Canada's International Trade Division, retrieved on Industry Canada's website: http://www.ic.gc.ca/sc_mrkti/tdst/tdo/tdo.php?lang=30&headFootDir=/sc_mrkti/tdst/headfoot&productType=HS6&cacheTime=962115865#tag. (accessed: October 15, 2012)

GROWTH STATISTICS: FINANCIAL
FEDERAL FINANCE, Quarterly ($ millions)

	Revenue	Total expenditure	Net worth	Net financial worth
Q1 2000	110,204	112,009	-367,187	-765,578
Q2 2000	119,113	106,344	-346,598	-748,892
Q3 2000	119,989	107,541	-329,569	-736,987
Q4 2000	119,363	111,070	-329,144	-742,020
Q1 2001	116,004	119,204	-342,830	-756,940
Q2 2001	122,367	111,701	-313,142	-729,113
Q3 2001	114,633	112,274	-311,634	-730,878
Q4 2001	114,399	116,932	-317,432	-739,436
Q1 2002	112,129	121,525	-327,941	-753,391
Q2 2002	118,322	113,842	-324,712	-753,737
Q3 2002	118,715	116,027	-330,648	-764,457
Q4 2002	121,284	120,144	-326,372	-763,601
Q1 2003	120,880	127,325	-315,512	-756,377
Q2 2003	121,693	120,718	-317,781	-762,942
Q3 2003	125,575	122,565	-295,583	-745,764
Q4 2003	125,918	124,482	-272,427	-726,859
Q1 2004	126,906	132,110	-260,203	-720,121
Q2 2004	130,139	125,160	-233,006	-699,546
Q3 2004	133,632	125,967	-223,358	-697,938
Q4 2004	133,295	129,589	-212,509	-694,313
Q1 2005	135,942	136,001	-211,919	-690,911
Q2 2005	139,507	132,644	-216,299	-701,555
Q3 2005	141,141	133,041	-185,844	-679,713
Q4 2005	143,192	136,848	-169,527	-671,543
Q1 2006	145,715	147,120	-144,349	-655,583
Q2 2006	148,042	139,311	-126,786	-649,122
Q3 2006	148,881	139,957	-105,800	-641,113
Q4 2006	151,646	144,116	-80,193	-627,263
Q1 2007	151,950	150,440	-55,324	-614,494
Q2 2007	158,543	148,086	-15,862	-586,999
Q3 2007	155,521	149,244	-1,231	-585,093
Q4 2007	156,014	152,707	995	-594,732
Q1 2008	157,311	162,806	-4,745	-614,629
Q2 2008	160,095	156,654	21,660	-603,806
Q3 2008	161,400	157,600	11,639	-633,071
Q4 2008	153,863	161,926	-6,722	-669,102
Q1 2009	148,999	170,847	-24,354	-689,897
Q2 2009	146,465	165,361	-19,607	-690,129
Q3 2009	150,226	167,949	-31,112	-711,108
Q4 2009	156,759	173,016	-40,290	-730,771
Q1 2010	160,258	180,341	-35,308	-727,799
Q2 2010	152,062	174,420	-65,405	-765,049
Q3 2010	154,225	177,335	-73,052	-786,799
Q4 2010	158,497	183,190	-80,466	-797,376
Q1 2011	161,994	188,372	-74,649	-804,609
Q2 2011	164,175	180,634	-98,497	-842,675
Q3 2011	165,839	181,953	-132,700	-893,863
Q4 2011	167,538	184,205	-145,618	-920,283
Q1 2012	170,071	189,644	-125,251	-919,941

Source: Adapted from Statistics Canada's CANSIM database http://www5.statcan.gc.ca/cansim/home-accueil?lang=eng, Table 385-0032, August 2011. (Accessed October 15, 2012)

GROWTH STATISTICS: FINANCIAL
BALANCE OF INTERNATIONAL PAYMENTS $ millions

	Canadian Direct Investment Abroad (All Countries, $000,000)							Foreign Direct Investment in Canada (All Countries, $000,000)						
Year	All Industries	Wood and paper	Energy and metallic minerals	Machinery and Transportation Equipment	Finance and Insurance	Services and Retailing	Other Industries	All Industries	Wood and paper	Energy and metallic minerals	Machinery and Transportation Equipment	Finance and Insurance	Services and Retailing	Other Industries
1995	-15,732	-1,171	-5,669	-431	-817	-1,321	-6,322	12,703	647	-441	1,802	1,086	2,032	7,577
1996	-17,858	782	-9,125	-1,230	-3,813	-2,317	-2,155	13,137	15	3,249	729	2,443	2,659	4,040
1997	-31,937	-1,130	-8,728	-2,046	-8,320	-3,859	-7,853	15,958	282	3,566	2,304	4,054	1,606	4,146
1998	-50,957	-440	-4,915	-2,988	-13,287	-7,718	-21,610	33,828	2,847	9,104	2,185	5,931	2,796	10,965
1999	-25,625	-258	-5,964	-1,999	-11,809	-1,237	-4,357	36,762	2,280	4,362	1,447	12,633	3,033	13,008
2000	-66,352	82	-9,982	-12,532	-7,278	-3,033	-33,610	99,198	4,286	13,492	13,717	4,122	1,804	61,776
2001	-55,800	-2,469	-10,740	-5,161	-27,838	-3,566	-6,027	42,844	442	23,940	4,640	3,598	529	9,694
2002	-42,015	-555	-8,665	-3,913	-26,669	-1,592	-621	34,769	889	16,207	6,131	1,599	3,722	6,220
2003	-32,118	-647	-14,379	-2,670	-8,764	-971	-4,686	10,483	-45	2,782	-1,227	4,229	958	3,785
2004	-56,395	1,330	-16,118	-5,473	-24,627	-8,672	-2,835	-579	-1,010	3,392	-2,470	-6,212	1,569	4,151
2005	-33,370	-352	-11,133	234	-23,377	-1,532	2,789	31,132	62	22,157	-4,297	4,734	3,538	4,938
2006	-52,423	-2,498	-6,745	667	-34,098	-5,643	-4,104	68,395	850	45,166	5,477	-4,046	4,258	16,690
2007	-62,003	-1,177	-16,306	-120	-33,633	-1,198	-9,570	123,148	3,241	69,236	7,060	22,758	7,985	12,869
2008	-85,143	-437	-21,263	1,064	-53,212	-2,382	-8,913	61,010	-1,392	38,120	-1,619	6,938	4,995	13,969
2009	-47,627	-692	-3,815	-477	-29,176	-1,100	-12,368	24,469	-473	11,464	1,523	3,459	2,861	5,634
2010	-39,749	-2,852	-7,273	311	-26,891	-2,848	-196	24,119	662	11,627	255	5,217	2,875	3,483
2011	-49,050	-869	-8,027	-742	-26,466	-5,489	-7,457	40,503	289	22,133	4,305	2,104	1,984	9,688

Source: Adapted from Statistics Canada's CANSIM database http://www5.statcan.gc.ca/cansim/home-accueil?lang=eng, Table 376-0014, August 2011 (Accessed October 15, 2012)

MANUFACTURING SALES BY SUBSECTOR, CANADA MONTHLY
$ thousands

	Jan. 2007	Jan. 2008	Jan. 2009	Jan. 2010	Jan. 2011	Jan. 2012	Aug. 2012
All Manufacturing Industries	47,700,458	45,322,947	37,364,430	39,243,404	43,646,911	46,182,905	45,372,750
Food	5,531,602	5,679,455	6,032,910	5,916,359	6,287,303	6,438,639	7,157,478
Beverage and tobacco product	702,702	633,261	669,408	620,939	640,644	648,916	1,165,161
Textile mills	168,251	150,660	133,085	127,055	126,781	135,266	150,680
Textile product mills	187,611	170,288	133,054	124,621	121,111	126,801	147,002
Clothing	293,109	220,921	173,427	153,853	161,406	158,849	144,680
Leather and allied product	27,776	29,153	27,970	26,401	26,967	29,303	29,761
Paper	2,568,786	2,336,836	2,155,445	2,062,696	2,159,462	2,048,792	1,994,540
Printing and related support activities	763,145	793,097	734,206	661,921	619,852	630,916	654,621
Petroleum and coal product	4,673,420	6,236,648	4,472,178	5,636,940	6,307,216	6,922,656	5,855,846
Chemical	4,034,534	3,851,761	3,418,334	3,486,370	3,831,258	3,987,140	3,703,910
Plastics and rubber products	2,001,451	1,857,834	1,410,335	1,462,156	1,587,990	1,791,232	1,900,123
Wood product	1,977,911	1,599,776	1,217,775	1,245,417	1,387,889	1,353,710	1,783,057
Non-metallic mineral product	881,584	802,916	633,742	679,231	731,441	698,279	1,326,435
Primary metal	4,450,909	4,188,973	2,912,601	3,100,641	3,838,863	4,027,297	3,745,681
Fabricated metal product	2,697,128	2,695,722	2,330,062	2,096,374	2,336,351	2,681,913	2,869,967
Machinery	2,525,036	2,494,385	2,284,885	1,972,557	2,454,532	2,830,540	3,009,520
Computer and electronic product	1,423,423	1,280,566	1,211,391	1,139,423	1,132,666	1,048,993	1,080,926
Electrical equipment, appliance and component	862,945	810,628	759,051	715,981	791,422	803,739	801,169
Transportation equipment	10,183,159	7,832,687	5,118,003	6,551,724	7,608,033	8,249,415	6,119,584
Furniture and related product	1,050,058	988,661	778,064	761,996	771,305	798,889	927,853
Miscellaneous	695,918	668,719	758,504	700,749	724,421	771,622	804,755

Source: Statistics Canada, http://www40.statcan.ca/l01/cst01/MANUF11-eng.htm, August 2011 (Accessed October 15, 2012)

IMPORTS AND EXPORTS FOR CANADA, 2011

	Exports ($)	Imports ($)		Exports ($)	Imports ($)		Exports ($)	Imports ($)
Afghanistan	57,591,008	1,603,697	France (incl. Monaco, Fr. Ant.)	3,080,793,524	5,551,688,769	Nigeria	227,091,939	2,491,719,513
Albania	60,815,502	6,254,311	French Polynesia	12,156,328	828,381	Niue	65,561	25,916
Algeria	248,235,844	5,485,089,122	French Southern Territories	69,348	17	Norfolk Island	0	35,436
American Samoa	1,224,060	567,699	Gabon	20,471,500	3,484,219	Norway	2,791,783,524	4,344,131,842
Andorra	106,665	458,976	Gambia	812,099	64,627	Oman (Muscat)	113,645,535	19,258,806
Angola	123,188,686	2,443,863,105	Georgia	22,630,254	111,935,419	Pakistan	689,317,256	260,703,668
Anguilla	2,422,089	271,087	Germany	3,955,032,843	12,789,026,414	Panama	111,222,796	124,125,000
Antartica	954,761	644,345	Ghana	266,371,414	55,453,172	Papua New Guinea	46,448,467	1,622,392
Antigua and Barbuda	10,235,488	414,390	Gibraltar	94,436,151	1,676,531	Paraguay	13,737,378	6,299,802
Argentina	495,296,016	2,358,757,983	Greece	88,144,197	168,159,996	Peru	516,425,420	4,402,672,597
Armenia	16,766,672	67,366,959	Greenland	15,801,332	770,122	Philippines	554,693,616	915,931,585
Aruba Island	6,883,637	5,529,411	Grenada	4,750,442	1,718,032	Pitcairn Island	54,158	56,937
Australia	1,897,952,440	1,767,113,535	Guam (U.S.)	2,122,404	181,012	Poland	251,579,839	1,439,243,039
Austria	390,857,100	1,278,458,539	Guatemala	109,636,340	403,981,259	Portugal	225,363,038	357,571,977
Azerbaijan	13,446,591	434,988,380	Guinea	27,096,051	58,057,706	Qatar	161,648,135	397,898,533
Bahamas	131,029,501	21,880,776	Guinea-Bissau	236,731	2,580	Romania	74,483,455	328,923,248
Bahrain	72,549,821	4,276,234	Guyana	37,749,985	394,656,856	Russia	1,496,940,889	1,286,338,595
Bangladesh	551,787,481	1,061,292,263	Haiti	37,728,858	25,743,928	Rwanda	1,795,286	1,114,418
Barbados	49,556,575	6,919,737	Heard/McDonald Island	0	12,854	Saint Lucia	9,430,402	272,278
Belarus (Byelorussia)	2,160,660	35,634,925	Honduras	49,185,206	186,059,148	Samoa (Western)	812,428	12,372
Belgium	2,388,497,670	1,666,264,856	Hong Kong	2,966,584,488	318,448,157	São Tomé and Principe	147,238	155,561
Belize	6,112,774	7,515,366	Hungary	367,757,284	357,747,791	Saudi Arabia	860,005,068	2,736,463,835
Benin	14,079,767	22,981	Iceland	52,461,800	42,015,350	Senegal	28,171,271	934,873
Bermuda	79,226,569	975,769	India	2,628,585,061	2,533,472,103	Serbia	9,483,078	15,017,500
Bhutan	562,397	47,262	Indonesia	1,644,643,450	1,428,759,812	Seychelles	6,841,721	580,374
Bolivia	16,435,452	237,794,899	Iran	127,257,527	34,486,526	Sierra Leone	11,500,840	4,900,409
Bosnia-Hercegovina	4,384,470	11,488,422	Iraq	185,875,952	2,464,505,912	Singapore	804,358,079	1,555,287,241
Botswana	4,791,816	135,320	Ireland	371,059,030	1,228,465,064	Slovakia	130,618,279	251,027,864
Bouvet Island	0	3,717	Israel	399,907,760	982,370,509	Slovenia	13,619,319	101,996,299
Brazil	2,840,773,482	3,880,041,627	Italy (includes Vatican City State)	1,968,547,885	5,106,760,051	Solomon Islands	324,666	184,977
British Indian Ocean Territories	20,491	67,727	Jamaica	112,148,400	275,412,173	Somalia	1,158,781	61,785
British Virgin Islands	48,346,362	820,635	Japan	10,670,582,514	13,057,675,788	South Africa	683,007,856	925,239,365
Brunei Darussalam	3,686,486	8,131,105	Jordan	70,145,780	18,728,359	Spain	977,246,579	1,748,031,066
Bulgaria	190,509,452	150,843,834	Kazakhstan	152,526,152	2,854,466,185	Sri Lanka	302,969,277	161,955,548
Burkina Faso	50,204,934	5,235,062	Kenya	83,299,680	22,463,454	St. Helena	66,459	111,858
Burma (Myanmar)	814,651	62,652	Kiribati (includes Tuvalu)	133,063	72,511	St. Kitts-Nevis	5,989,908	9,165,976
Burundi	1,096,154	359,224	Korea, North	5,302,597	71,713	St.Pierre-Miquelon	21,582,275	1,936,385
Cambodia (Kampuchea)	11,420,243	522,111,755	Korea, South	5,098,434,553	6,604,750,944	St.Vincent-Grenadines	7,505,643	259,172
Cameroon	27,142,424	7,539,529	Kuwait	129,463,333	56,700,173	Sudan	137,743,934	117,109,356
Cape Verde	1,823,248	101,781	Kyrgyzstan	13,733,084	180,103	Surinam	14,662,228	253,418,877
Cayman Islands	8,468,356	777,972	Laos	7,065,305	6,587,485	Swaziland	1,451,486	1,823,877
Central African Republic	309,421	591,698	Latvia	49,529,785	27,616,512	Sweden	484,831,944	2,259,637,412
Chad	2,927,047	435,521	Lebanon	90,047,507	17,381,457	Switzerland	1,141,382,200	3,163,257,143
Chile	818,777,273	1,910,734,928	Lesotho	87,652	11,857,960	Syria	52,696,478	38,943,128
China	16,809,661,570	48,152,674,921	Liberia	15,592,550	33,752,797	Taiwan	1,746,489,657	4,930,299,933
Christmas Island	488,797	104,240	Libya	51,279,373	5,095,598	Tajikistan	3,638,581	3,965
Cocos (Keeling) Islands	302,893	18,544	Lithuania	57,931,377	603,334,956	Tanzania	61,461,920	5,342,888
Colombia	760,888,169	799,773,636	Luxembourg	88,835,055	114,672,802	Thailand	839,166,173	2,674,510,935
Comoros	431,264	150,972	Macau (Macao)	3,717,238	8,671,511	Togo	15,485,380	12,852,640
Congo (Brazzaville)	26,202,940	4,041,790	Macedonia	17,540,791	8,391,571	Tonga	198,749	19,193
Congo (former Zaire)	19,056,027	1,017,668	Madagascar	23,907,912	63,525,957	Trinidad and Tobago	341,661,370	388,960,604
Cook Islands	238,080	169,584	Malawi	4,612,159	123,719,381	Tunisia	101,898,495	53,033,302
Costa Rica	160,755,858	475,761,469	Malaysia	761,727,886	2,138,824,065	Turkey	1,271,493,189	1,122,316,998
Côte-D'Ivoire (Ivory Coast)	20,440,072	629,436,562	Maldives	6,062,447	185,208	Turkmenistan	16,747,947	716,366
Croatia	36,014,612	26,966,621	Mali	26,271,370	878,050	Turks and Caicos Islands	2,437,401	118,643
Cuba	462,409,273	702,599,376	Malta	54,087,606	25,682,703	U.S. Minor Outlying Islands	12,471,344	3,342,532
Cyprus	12,408,475	2,952,383	Mauritania	16,035,675	114,860	Uganda	11,486,643	3,347,021
Czech Republic	120,998,001	372,916,058	Mauritius	5,263,445	9,722,682	Ukraine	150,190,919	136,348,202
Denmark	273,135,029	1,444,678,150	Mexico	5,476,487,629	24,572,828,961	United Arab Emirates	1,358,222,045	900,924,240
Djibouti	1,667,759	14,659	Moldova	1,195,535	2,052,242	United Kingdom (U.K.)	18,791,399,802	10,328,550,280
Dominica	4,037,937	288,853	Mongolia	91,319,653	242,177,665	United States (U.S.)	329,799,505,820	220,895,498,794
Dominican Republic	148,768,143	148,512,831	Montenegro	1,724,167	636,647	Uruguay	115,793,725	40,924,895
East Timor	257,505	389,131	Montserrat	325,005	290,786	Uzbekistan	7,350,607	1,882,196
Ecuador	281,316,351	224,630,389	Morocco	299,794,541	119,110,335	Vanuatu (New Hebrides)	1,824,569	55,092
Egypt	711,330,988	449,832,164	Mozambique	13,542,427	3,654,444	Venezuela	607,316,914	739,241,096
El Salvador	36,205,693	129,441,454	Namibia	7,884,980	230,324,161	Vietnam	335,313,317	1,332,142,729
Equatorial Guinea	11,443,420	629,176,114	Nauru	0	41,816	Wallis and Futuna Islands	44,000	4,876
Eritrea	4,700,718	321,146,425	Nepal	6,338,701	15,728,305	Western Sahara	4,332	0
Estonia	104,839,931	90,287,331	Netherlands	4,806,872,317	2,559,321,008	Yemen	10,828,728	110,325
Ethiopia	20,485,335	17,456,146	Netherlands Antilles	132,186,717	23,843,412	Zambia (Zambi)	32,670,510	1,413,349
Faeroe Islands	542,698	8,019,755	New Caledonia	8,342,468	169,612	Zimbabwe	9,162,219	6,898,250
Falkland Islands	111,523	365,420	New Zealand	381,964,416	550,176,181			
Fiji	7,908,063	4,545,620	Nicaragua	37,313,185	333,663,991			
Finland	754,253,310	1,699,782,040	Niger	9,501,641	1,241,506	**TOTAL (All Countries)**	**447,501,002,970**	**445,991,537,386**

Source: "International Trade data," based on Statistics Canada's International Trade Division, retrieved on Industry Canada's website: http://www.ic.gc.ca/sc_mrkti/tdst/tdo/tdo.php?lang=30&headFootDir=/sc_mrkti/tdst/headfoot&productType=HS6&cacheTime=962115865#tag, accessed October 2012.

Exhibitions, Shows & Events

The following list includes Consumer & Trade Shows, Public Events, Conferences & Festivals arranged by category of interest. The addresses given are the addresses of associations/sponsors. Focus is on events of an ongoing annual or biennial nature. The lists are not complete but are fairly representative of shows held throughout Canada. Users are cautioned that dates or venues may vary.

ABORIGINAL *See* MULTICULTURAL

AGRICULTURE *See* FARM BUSINESS/AGRICULTURE

AIR SHOWS/AVIATION

15 Wing Armed Forces Day, also known as Snowbirds Demonstration, 15 Wing, PO Box 5000, Moose Jaw, SK S6H 7Z8 - 306-694-2222; Fax: 306-694-2880; Email: snowbird.team@sasktel.net; URL: www.airforce.forces.gc.ca/15wing - Show Organizer, Ms. Marg Fowler – Supply Manual - Aug., Moose Jaw SK

Abbotsford International Airshow, Abbotsford International Airshow Society, #4, 1276 Tower St., Abbotsford, BC V2T 6H5 - 604-852-8511; Fax: 604-852-6093; Email: info@abbotsfordairshow.com; media@abbotsford airshow.com; URL: www.abbotsfordairshow.com - Large static display. Six hour flying show - Aug., Abbotsford International Airport, BC

Alberta International Airshow, Lethbridge International Airshow Association, PO Box 1315, Stn. Main, Lethbridge, AB T1K 4K1 - 403-380-4245; Toll Free (Ticketing Support): 1-888-695-0888; Email: office@liasa.ca; URL: www.albertaairshow.com - July, Lethbridge International Airport, AB

Atlantic Canada International Air Show, Nova Scotia International Air Show Association (NSIASA), PO Box 218, Shearwater, NS B0J 3A0 - 902-465-2725; Fax: 902-484-3222; Email: info@nsairshow.ca; URL: www.airshowatlantic.ca - Executive Director, Colin Stephenson, Email: colin@nsairshow.ca - Aerial displays, including military & civilian aircraft. Ground displays - Sept., Halifax Stanfield International Airport, Halifax, NS

Borden Canadian Forces Day & Airshow, CFSTG/Base Borden Public Affairs Officer, Canadian Forces Base Borden, PO Box 1000 Stn. Main, 400 Cambrai Rd. Borden, ON L0M 1C0 - 705-423-3162; URL: www.airforce.forces.gc.ca/16wing - Military & civilian air demonstration & acrobatic teams. Ground displays - June, Canadian Forces Base Borden, Borden, ON

Canada Remembers Airshow, Saskatchewan Place, #101, 3515 Thatcher Ave., Saskatoon, SK S7R 1C4 - 306-975-2907; Email: b.swid@creditunioncentre.com; Annual. Parade of Veterans. Active & static displays - Aug., Saskatoon, SK

Canadian International Airshow, Press Bldg., Exhibition Place, 210 Princes' Blvd., Toronto, ON M6K 3C3 - 416-263-3650; Fax: 416-263-3654 ; URL: www.cias.org - Annually, three days of the Labour Day Weekend. Best viewed from Canadian National Exhibition grounds - Sept., Over Lake Ontario, Toronto, ON

Festival of Flight, Festival of Flight Staff, Parks, Recreation & Tourism, Town of Gander, 100 Elizabeth Dr., Gander, NL A1V 1G7 - 709-651-5958; URL: www.gandercanada.com - Director, Parks, Recreation & Tourism, Kevin Waterman - Annual. A celebration of Gander's aviation history - 1st weekend in Aug.

Friendship Festival Air Show, Friendship Festival International Air Show, PO Box 1241, Fort Erie ON L2A 5Y2 - 905-871-6454; Fax: 905-871-1266; Tollfree: 1-888-333-1987; Email: flo@friendshipfestival.com; URL: www.friendshipfestival.com - Annual - July

Yukon Sourdough Rendezvous Airshow, Yukon Sourdough Rendezvous Society, PO Box 31721, Whitehorse YT Y1A 6L3 - 867-393-4467; Fax: 867-668-6755; URL: www.yukonrendezvous.com - Vice-President, Public Relations, Anna Barron - Annual. Aerial & static displays - Feb., Whitehorse Airport, Whitehorse, YT

ANTIQUES

The Toronto Toy, Doll, & Train Collectors' Show, PO Box 217, Grimsby, ON L3M 4G3 - 905-945-2775; Fax: 905-945-0197; Email: info@antiquetoys.ca; URL: www.antiquetoys.ca - Doug Jarvis, Email: dougjarvis@sympatico.ca - Annual antique & collectible childhood memorabilia - Nov., Mississauga, ON

APPAREL *See* FASHION

ARCHITECTURE *See* CONSTRUCTION

ART/ARTS

***See Also* First Night; Crafts; Music; Events**

Arnold Mikelson Festival of Arts, Arnold Mikelson Mind and Matter Gallery, 13743 - 16 Ave., Surrey, BC V4A 1P7 - 604-536-6460; URL: www.mindandmatterart.com - Mary Mikelson - Featuring new & established artists offering their exhibits for sale - July

Banff Summer Arts Festival, The Banff Centre, PO Box 1020, Banff AB T1L 1H5 - 403-762-6301; Fax: 403-762-6483; Tollfree: 1-800-413-8368; Email: box_office@banffcentre.ca; URL: www.banffcentre.ca - President & CEO, Mary E. Hofstetter

Bard on the Beach Shakespeare Festival, #301, 601 Cambie St., Vancouver, BC V6B 2P1 - 604-737-0625; Box Office: 604-739-0559; Fax: 604-737-0425; Tollfree: 1-877-739-0559; Email: info@bardonthebeach.org; URL: www.bardonthebeach.org - Artistic Director, Christopher Gaze; General Manager, Robert Barr - May - Sept., Vanier Park waterfront, Vancouver, BC

Blyth Festival, 423 Queen St., PO Box 10, Blyth, ON N0M 1H0 - 519-523-9300; Fax: 519-523-9804; Tollfree: 1-877-862-5984; Email: info@blythfestival.com; URL: www.blythfestival.com - Artistic Director, Eric Coates, Email: ecoates@blythfestival.com - June - Sept., Blyth Memorial Community Hall, Blyth, ON

Charlottetown Festival, Confederation Centre of the Arts, 145 Richmond St., Charlottetown PE C1A 1J1 - 902-628-1864; Fax: 902-566-4648; Tollfree: 1-800-565-0278; Email: info@confederationcentre.com; URL: www.confederationcentre.com - CEO, Jessie Inman, Email: jinman@confederationcentre; Artistic Director, Anne Allan, Email: aallan@confederationcentre.com - Annual. Musical & dramatic entertainment - June - Sept.

Festival Antigonish, Bauer Theatre, St. Francis Xavier University, PO Box 5000, Antigonish NS B2G 2W5 - 902-867-3333; Email: boxoffice@festivalantigonish.com; URL: www.festivalantigonish.com - Theatre Manager, Tina Dickieson; Artistic Producer Ed Thomason - July - Sept., Bauer Theatre, Antigonish, NS

Festival by the Sea, PO Box 6157, Saint John NB E2L 4R6 - 506-632-0086; Fax: 506-642-4644; URL: www.festivalofthesea.ca; Chair, Sherry Gambin-Walsh, Vice Chair, Bob Gillard - Annually, Performing arts - Aug.

Fringe Theatre Event, Fringe Theatre Festival, 10330 - 84 Ave., Edmonton AB T6E 2G9 - 780-448-9000; Fax: 780-431-1893; Email: fta@fringetheatreadventures. ca; URL: www.fringetheatreadventures.ca - Executive Director, Julian Mayne, Office Manager, Geralder Osborn - Aug.

Lunenburg Street Festival & Artwalk, 902-634-8511 - Contact, Robert Black - Annual - Features over 100 Nova Scotian crafters - July, Community Center Grounds, Lunenburg, NS

Manitoba Holiday Festival of the Arts, Margaret Laurence Home, PO Box 147, Neepawa, MB R0J 1H0 - 204-476-2927; Fax: 204-476-2927; Email: mhfa@mts.net; URL: www.mts.net/~mhfa - Administrator, Greg Heschuk - Annual. Programs for children, youth, & adults - July, Neepawa, MB

Nova Scotia Folk Art Festival - 902-640-2113; Email: info@nsfolkartfestival.com; URL: www.nsfolkartfestival.com - Contact, Nancy Wilson - Annual. Juried event, featuring an exhibition, workshops, speaker's corner, & sale of work by Nova Scotia folk artists - Aug., Lunenburg War Memorial Arena, Lunenburg, NS

Open Ears Festival of Music & Sound, c/o Kitchener-Waterloo Symphony, 101 Queen St. North, Kitchener, ON N2H 6P7 - 519- 579-8564; Fax: 519-743-6773; Toll Free: 1-888-363-3591; Email: info@openears.ca; URL: www.openears.ca - Musical performances, music in alternative venues, sound poetry, sound installations, & conference activity - April / May, Kitchener, ON

Ottawa Fringe Theatre, Ottawa Fringe Festival, #100, 2 Daly Ave., Ottawa ON K1N 6E2 - 613-232-6162; Email: admin@ottawafringe.com; URL: www.ottawafringe.com

PotashCorp Fringe Theatre Festival, #9, 2404 Thayer Ave., Saskatoon, SK S7L 6B4 - 306-664-2239; Fax: 306-653-7701; URL: www.25thstreettheatre.org - Annual - July / Aug., 6 venues, Saskatoon, SK

Shakespeare by the Sea, 5799 Charles St., Halifax NS B3K 1K7 - 902-422-0295; Fax: 902-422-4250; Email: info@shakespearebythesea.ca; URL: www.shakespearebythesea.ca - General Manager, Elizabeth Murphy Shakespeare by the Sea Festival, 11 Bavidge St., St. John's NL A1A 5B9 - 709-691-7287; Email: sbts@nfld.com; URL: www.nfld.com/~sbts

Shakespeare in High Park, The Canadian Stage Company, 26 Berkeley St., Toronto, ON M5A 2W3 - 416-367-8243; Box Office: 416-368-3110; Fax: 416-367-1768; Email: general@canstage.com ; boxoffice@canstage.com; URL: www.canstage.com - Director, Production, Alistair Hepburn; Artistic Producer, Martin Bragg, July 1 - Labour Day, High Park, Toronto, ON

Shakespeare on the Saskatchewan Festival, PO Box 1646, Stn Main, Saskatoon SK S7K 3R8 - 306-653-2300; Fax: 306-653-2357; Email: shakespeare@sasktel.net; URL: www.shakespeareonthesaskatchewan.com - Executive & Artistic Director, Mark von Eschen, July/Aug.

Summerworks, 54 Wolseley St, 2nd Fl., PO Box 12, Stn C, Toronto ON M6J 3M7 - 416-410-1048; Email: info@summerworks.ca; URL: www.summerworks.ca - Artistic Producer, Kimahli Powell, Artistic Producer, Keira Loughran

Toronto Outdoor Art Exhibition (TOAE), #264, 401 Richmond St. West, Toronto, ON M5V 3A8 - 416-408-2754; Fax: 416-408-2202; Email: toae@torontooutdoorart.org; URL: www.torontooutdoorart.org - Executive Director, Kelly Rintoul, Email: kelly@torontooutdoorart.org - Canada's largest outdoor art exhibition, held annually. Award program for participating artists - July, Nathan Phillips Square, Toronto ON

Vancouver Fringe Festival, 1398 Cartwright Street, Vancouver BC V6H 3R8 - 604-257-0350; Fax: 604-253-1924; Email: administration@vancouverfringe.com; URL: www.vancouverfringe.com - Executive Director, David Jordan - Annual - Sept.

Winnipeg Fringe Theatre Festival, Manitoba Theatre Centre, 174 Market Ave., Winnipeg MB R3B 0P8 - 204-956-1340; Fax: 204-947- 3741; Email: info@winnipegfringe.com; URL: www.winnipegfringe.com - Executive Producer, Bertram Schneider - Annual, July

World Stage, Harbourfront Centre, 235 Queens Quay West, Toronto ON M5J 2G8 - 416-973-4600; Fax: 416-973- 6055; Email: info@harbourfrontcentre.com; URL: www.harbourfrontcentre.com/worldstage - CEO, William J.S. Boyle - International theatre festival - April - Harbourfront Centre, Toronto ON

York Shakespeare Festival, Resurgence Theatre Company, 211 Main Street South, Newmarket ON L3Y 3Y9 - 905-953-2838; Email: info@resurgence.on.ca; URL: www.resurgence.on.ca - General Manager, Anthony Leo

AUTOMOTIVE

Air Canada Grand Prix, Grand Prix of Canada, 222, Circuit Gilles-Villeneuve, Montréal QC H3C 6A1 - 514-350-0000; Fax: 514-350-0007; URL: www.circuitgillesvilleneuve.ca - Vice-Présidente, Services corporatifs, Marie-Josée Labbé, - Annual international auto racing event - June - Gilles-Villeneuve Circuit, Montréal QC

Annual RV Camping & Leisure Show, Recreation Vehicle Dealers Association of Manitoba, 69 Morin Rd., St Francois Xavier MB R4L 1A8 - 204-864-2112; Fax: 204-864-2232; Email: rvdamb@mts.net; URL: www.manitobarvda.com - RV Show Manager, Coralee Dolyniuk - Annual consumer show - March, Winnipeg MB

Atlantic Truck Show, Master Promotions Ltd., PO Box 565, 48 Broad St., Saint John NB E2L 3Z8 - 506-658-0018; Fax: 506-658-0750; Tollfree: 1-888-454-7469; Email: info@mpltd.ca; URL: www.masterpromotions.ca - Annual - Show Manager, Mark Cusack, June - Coliseum, Moncton NB

CamExpo Québec, Newcom Business Media, 451 Attwell Dr., Toronto ON M9W 5C4 - 416-877-1919; Fax: 416-614-8861; URL: www.camexpo.ca - President, Roger Desrosiers - Biennial trade & consumer show - Nov.

Canadian International Motorcycle & Powersports Super Show, Bar Hodgson Productions Ltd., 8780 Baldwin St., Ashburn ON L0B 1A0 - 905-655-5403; Fax: 905-655- 3812; URL: www.supershowevents. com - President, Bar Hodgson - Annual consumer & trade show - Jan. - International Centre, Toronto ON

Edmonton Motor Show, Edmonton Motor Dealers' Association, 10310 - 39A Ave. NW, Edmonton AB T6H 5X9 - 780-423-2401; Fax: 780-423-2413; Email: contactemda@emdacars.com; URL: www.emdacars.com - Executive Manager, Robert Vilas - Annual consumer show

Halifax RV Show, Master Promotions Ltd., PO Box 565, Saint John NB E2L 3Z8 - 506-658-0018; Fax: 506-658- 0750; Tollfree: 1-888-454-7469; Email: info@masterpromotions. ca; URL: www.masterpromotions.ca - Annual consumer show - Show Manager, Scott Sprague, Feb., Halifax NS

Honda Indy Toronto, #300A, 370 Queens Quay West, Toronto ON M5V 3J3 - 416-588-7223; URL: www.hondaindytoronto.com - Contact, Jeff Atkinson - Annual - July, Toronto ON

Moncton RV Show, Master Promotions Ltd., PO Box 565, Saint John NB E2L 3Z8 - 506-658-0018; Fax: 506-658- 0750;

Tollfree: 1-888-454-7469; Email: info@masterpromotions. ca; URL: www.masterpromotions.ca - Annual consumer show - Show Manager, Scott Sprague, Feb., Moncton NB

Montréal International Auto Show, 2335, rue Guénette, Saint-Laurent QC H4R 2E9 - URL: www.salonautomontreal.com - Executive Director, Francine St-Laurent - Annual consumer show. New cars, light trucks, accessories - Jan. - Palais des Congrès, Montréal QC

Performance World Custom Car & Truck Show, Pro-Sho Inc., 6900 Airport Rd Toronto, ON L4V 1E8 - 416-229- 9919; Fax: 416-223-2826; Tollfree: 1-877-950-1500; Email: prosho@meteorshows.com; URL: www.performanceworldcarshow.com; www.llhashows. com - Annual consumer show - Contact, Larry King, March

RV Exposition & Sale, Recreation Vehicle Dealers Association of Alberta, #101, 10561 - 172 St. NW., Edmonton AB T5S 1P1 - Tollfree: 1-888-858-8787; Email: rvda@rvda-alberta. org; URL: www.rvda-alberta.org - Executive Vice-President, Dan Merkowsky - Annual consumer show held in Calgary, Edmonton & Red Deer

Salon de la Moto de Montréal/de Québec, ExpoMAX Canada Inc.; Executive Vice- President, Roger Saint-Laurent - Annual consumer show - Feb.

Toronto International Spring Bike Show, Bar Hodgson Productions Inc., 8780 Baldwin St., Ashburn ON L0B 1A0 - 905-655-5403; Fax: 905-655-3812; Email: info@supershow events. com; URL: www.bicycleshowtoronto.com - President, Bar Hodgson, April - International Centre, Toronto ON

Vancouver International RV Show, Recreation Vehicle Dealers Association of British Columbia, #201, 17700 - 56th Ave., Surrey BC V3S 1C7 - 604-575-3868; Fax: 604-575-3869; Email: admin@rvda.bc.ca; URL: www.rvda.bc.ca - Annual consumer show - Show Manager, Cathy James, March, Vancouver BC

BLUEGRASS *See* MUSIC

BOATING

Classic Boat Festival, Victoria BC - Email: registration@classicboatfestival.ca; URL: www.classic boatfestival.ca - Communications Manager, Michael Sampson - Annually, Labour Day weekend, Victoria BC

Sudbury Sportsman Show, DAC Marketing Ltd., PO Box 2837, Stn A, Sudbury ON P3A 5J3 - 705-673- 5588; Fax: 705-525-0626; URL: www.dacshows.com, Mar., Sudbury ON

Toronto International Boat Show, National Marine Manufacturers Association, 8, 14 McEwan Dr. West, Bolton ON L7E 1H1 - 905-951-0009; Fax: 905-951-0018; URL: www.torontoboatshow.com - Show Manager, Linda Waddell, Jan. - National Trade Centre, Exhibition Place, Toronto ON

Victoria Boat & Fishing Show, Canwest Shows Inc., #218, 7710 – 5 St. East, Calgary AB T2H 2L9 - Fax: 403-246-3856; Toll-Free: 1-800-626-1538; Email: info@canwestshows.com; URL: www.canwestshows.com - Show Director, Kevin Blackburn - Annual consumer show - Feb. - Pearkes Recreation Centre, Victoria BC

BOOKS

International Festival of Authors, 235 Queen's Quay West, Toronto ON M5J 2G8 - 416-973-4760; Fax: 416-954- 4323; Email: readings@harbourfrontcentre.com URL: www.readings.org - Director, Geoffrey E. Taylor - Interviews & readings by novelists, poets, playwrights & biographers - Oct. - Harbourfront Centre, Toronto ON

Montréal Book Fair/Salon du livre de Montréal, Salon du livre de Montréal, #403, 480, boul St-Laurent, Montréal QC H2Y 3Y7 - 514-845-2365; Fax: 514-845-7119; Email: slm.info@ videotron.ca; URL: www.salondulivredemontreal.com - Directrice Générale, Francine Bois - Annual consumer show - Nov., Montréal QC

Salon international du Livre de Québec, 26, rue Saint- Pierre, Québec QC G1K 8A3 - 418-692-0010; Fax: 418-692-0029; Email: info@silq.org; URL: www.silq.org - Annual consumer show - avril, Québec QC

The Word on the Street, The Word on the Street Book & Magazine Fair, #142, 67 Mowat Ave., Toronto ON M6K 3E3 - 416-504-7241; Fax: 416-504-7656; Email: toronto@theword onthestreet.ca; URL: www.thewordonthestreet.ca - Festival Director, Nicola Dufficy - Annual celebration of literacy & the printed word; held in Toronto, Halifax, Calgary & Vancouver - Sept.

BRIDAL

Canada's Bridal Show, #10, 136 Winges Rd., 2nd Fl., Woodbridge ON L4L 6C4 - 905-264-7000; Fax: 905-264-7300; URL: www.canadasbridalshow.com - Lorie Sansone - Annual consumer show. Bridal fashion shows, gifts, florists, photography, entertainment, travel - Jan. & Oct., Toronto ON

Le Salon de la Mariée, Sheldon Kagan International Ltd., 35, McConnell, Dorval QC H9S 5L9 - 514-631-2160; Fax: 514-631-4430; Tollfree: 1-888-524-2648; Email: info@sheldonkagan.com; URL: www.sheldonkagan.com - President, Sheldon Kagan - Annual consumer show - Nov. - Palais des Congrès, Montréal QC

The Total Wedding Show, Ten Star Productions Inc., 155 Castle Cres., Oakville ON L6J 5H4 - 905-845-2644; Fax: 905-845-8050; Email: info@totalweddingshow. com; URL: www.totalweddingshow.com - Katherine Griggs - Annual consumer show - Jan. - International Centre, Mississauga ON

Wedding Dreams Bridal Show, Grand River Shows, 160 King St. East, Kitchener ON N2G 4E5 - 519-895-5239; Fax: 519-894-3912; Tollfree: 1-800-667-0833; Email: shows@grandrivershows.com - Contact, Simon G. Dowrick - Consumer show. Fashion shows, wedding exhibits; Jan. & Oct.

Wedding Wishes, Thunder Bay Chamber of Commerce Trade Show, #102, 200 Syndicate Ave. South, Thunder Bay ON P7E 1C9 - 807-624-2621; Fax: 807-622-7752; Email: nancy@tb-chamber.on.ca; URL: www.tbchamber. on.ca - Show Manager, Nancy Milani - Annual consumer show - Nov., Thunder Bay ON

BUSINESS

Business Awards Gala, Thunder Bay Chamber of Commerce, #102, 200 Syndicate Ave. South, Thunder Bay ON P7E 1C9 - 807-624-2621; Fax: 807-622-7752; Email: nancy@tbchamber. on.ca; URL: www.tb-chamber.on.ca - Show Manager, Nancy Milani - Annual trade & consumer show - May

Business Expo, Greater Nanaimo Chamber of Commerce, 2133 Bowen Rd., Nanaimo BC V9S 1H8 - 250-756-1191; Fax: 250-756-1584; Email: info@nanaimochamber. bc.ca; URL: www.nanaimochamber.bc.ca - Executive Director, S.D. (Lee) Mason, President, Rick Thurmeier, Oct. - Woodgrove Mall

CARS *See* AUTOMOTIVE

CHEMISTRY

Canadian Society of Clinical Chemists Conference, Events & Management Plus Inc., #310, 4 Cataraqui St., Kingston ON K7K 1Z7 - 613-531-8899; Fax: 866-303-0626; Tollfree: 1-866-560-3838; Email: office@cscc.ca; URL: www.cscc.ca - Owner, E. Hooper, June, Hamilton ON

CHILDREN

Calgary International Children's Festival, EPCOR Centre for the Performing Arts, 205 - 8th Ave. SE, Calgary AB T2G 0K9 - 403-294-7414; Fax: 403-294-7425; Email: admin@calgarychildfest.org; URL: www.calgarychildfest.org - Producer, JoAnne James - Annual - May, Calgary AB

International Children's Festival, #201, One Forks Market Rd.., Winnipeg MB R3C 4L9 - 204-958- 4730; Fax: 204-943-7915; Tollfree: 1-800-527-1515; Email: kidsfest@kidsfest.ca; URL: www.kidsfest.ca - Neal Rempel - Annual - June, Winnipeg MB

Northern Alberta International Children's Festival, 5 St. Anne St., St. Albert AB T8N 3Z9 - URL: www.childfest.com - Festival Manager, Paul Moulton - June, St. Albert AB

PotashCorp Children's Festival of Saskatchewan, 706 – 601 Spadina Cres. East, Saskatoon SK S7K 3G8 - 306-664-3378; Fax: 306-664-2344; Email: admin.childfest@sasktel.net; URL: www.potashcorpchildrensfestival.com - Artistic Director, Cass Cozens - Annually, June. Four-day international festival of the performing arts for children

CHRISTMAS CRAFTS *See* CRAFTS

COMMUNICATIONS

CTCA Conference, Canadian Telecommunications Consultants Association, #310, 2175 Sheppard Ave., Toronto ON M2J 1W8 - 416-495-7761; Fax: 416-491-1670; Tollfree: 1-800-463-2569; Email: office@ ctca.ca; URL: www.ctca.ca - Contact, Cheryl Mottershead, 905-451-9819

COMPUTERS

Canada's National Manufacturing Event, Canadian Manufacturing Technology Show, 690 Airport Rd. Mississauga ON - Tollfree: 888-322-7333; Email: bkiller@sme.org; URL: cmts.ca - Customer Service Manager, Bruce Killer - Annual trade show alternating between Toronto & Montréal

Computer Fest, Show Fest Productions Inc., #5, 60 St. Clair Ave. West Toronto, ON M4V 1M7 - 416-925-4533 - Consumer show Feb. (Toronto), Apr. (Mississauga), Sept. (Toronto), Nov. (Mississauga). Computers & internet products, services, seminars, demonstrations & information for home, business & education

Exposition industrielle et commerciale, Chambre de Commerce de Sept-Iles, #237, 700, boul Laure, Sept-Iles QC G4R 1Y1 - 418-968-3488; Fax: 418-968-3432; Email: ccsi@globetrotter.net - Directrice générale, Ginette Lehoux - Computer & small business consumer show

InfoSecurity Canada, #1, 3761 Victoria Park Ave., Toronto ON M1W 3S2 - 416-491-7565; Fax: 416-491-5088; URL: infosecuritycanada.com - John Lewinski - Annual trade show - June, Toronto ON

CONSTRUCTION & BUILDING PRODUCTS

Atlantic Building Trade Show, Atlantic Building Supply Dealers Association, 70 Englehart St., Dieppe NB E1A 8H3 - 506-858-0700; Fax: 506-859-0064; Tollfree: 1-800-561-7114; Email: absda@nbnet.nb.ca; URL: www.absda.ca - President, Don Sherwood, Chair, David Pritchett - Annual trade show - March

Construct Canada, 100, Alcorn Ave., Toronto ON M4V 3A9 - 416-512-1215; Fax: 416-512-1993; Tollfree: 1-800-660-7083; Email: jacqui@yorkcom.to; URL: www.constructcanada.com - Principal, Jacqui Peake - Annual trade show. Products, technologies & systems for the design & construction of all building types - Dec. - Metro Toronto Convention Centre, Toronto ON

Homebuilder & Renovation Expo, 100 Alcorn Ave., Toronto ON M4V 3A9 - 416-512-1215; Fax: 416-512-1993; Tollfree: 1-800-660- 7083; Email: jacqui@yorkcom.to; URL: www.homebuilderexpo.ca - Principal, Jacqui Peake - Annual trade show - Dec. - Metro Toronto Convention Centre, Toronto ON

CRAFTS

Art Market, Art Market Productions, PO Box 190, Barriere BC V0E 1E0 - 250-672-2411; Fax: 250-672-9517; Tollfree: 1-877-929-9933; Email: info@artmarketcraftsale. com; URL: www.artmarketcraftsale.com - Marlene Loney - Annual consumer show; art & craft sale - Nov., Calgary AB

Atlantic Craft Trade Show, Nova Scotia Business Inc., PO Box 3, 1574 Argyle St., Halifax NS B3J 2B3 - 902-492-2773; Fax: 902-429-9059; Email: acts@craftalliance.ca; URL: www.actshow.ca - Show Manager, Bernard Burton - Annual trade show. Juried craft & giftware products

Bazaart, MacKenzie Art Gallery, 3475 Albert St., Regina SK S4S 6X6 - 306-584-4250; Fax: 306-569-8191; Email: mackenzie@ uregina.ca; URL: www.mackenzieartgallery-bazaart.ca - Juried outdoor art show & sale; complete range of crafts - June

Christmas at the Forum Crafts Festival, PO Box 34, Annapolis Royal NS B0S 1A0; Tollfree: 1-866- 995-7469; Email: dmsshows@hotmail.com; URL: www.forumcrafts.com - Coordinator, Jason Susnick - Annual consumer show - Nov., Halifax NS

Creative Stitches & Crafting Alive, Canwest Shows Inc., 7 Panorama Bay SW, Calgary AB T3Z 3L6 - 403-686- 9699; Fax: 403-246-3856; Email: info@canwestshows. com; URL: www.canwestshows.com - General Manager, Terra Connors - Annual consumer show in Calgary (Sept.) & Edmonton (April)

One of a Kind Christmas Canadian Craft Show & Sale, The Canadian Craft Show Ltd., #300, 717 Church St., Toronto ON M4W 2M4 - 416-960-3680; Fax: 416-923- 5624; Email: info@oneofakindshow.com; URL: www.oneofakindshow.com - Show Director, Patti Stewart - Annual consumer show - Nov./Dec. - National Trade Centre, Exhibition Place, Toronto ON

One of a Kind Springtime Canadian Craft Show & Sale, The Canadian Craft Show Ltd., #300, 717 Church St., Toronto ON M4W 2M4 - 416-960-3680; Fax: 416-923- 5624; Email: info@oneofakindshow.com; URL: www.oneofakindshow.com - Show Director, Patti Stewart - Annual consumer show - March/April - Automotive Building, Exhibition Place, Toronto ON

Originals Ottawa Christmas Craft Show, Signatures Craft Shows Ltd., #810, 325 Dalhousie St., Ottawa ON K1N 7G2 - 613-241-5777; Fax: 613-241-5678; Tollfree: 1-800- 773-4444; Email: inf@signatures.ca; URL: www.signatures.ca, Dec.

Pine Tree Potters Sale, 15145 Yonge St., Aurora ON L4G 6S6 - 905-727-1278 - May & Nov.

Saskatchewan Handcraft Festival, Saskatchewan Craft Council, 813 Broadway Ave., Saskatoon SK S7N 1B5 - 306-653-3616; Fax: 306-244-2711; Tollfree: 1-866- 653-3616; Email: saskcraftcouncil@shaw.ca; URL: www.saskcraftcouncil.org - Chair, Paula Cooley, Executive Director, Glenn Saganace, July, Battleford SK

Signatures Ottawa, Signatures Craft Shows Ltd., #810, 325 Dalhousie St., Ottawa ON K1N 7G2 - 613-241-5777; Fax: 613-241-5678; Tollfree: 1-800-773-4444; Email: inf@signatures.ca; URL: www.signatures.ca - Annual consumer show - Nov., Ottawa ON

Signatures Toronto, Signatures Craft Shows Ltd., #810, 325 Dalhousie St., Ottawa ON K1N 7G2 - 613-241-5777; Fax: 613-241-5678; Tollfree: 1-800-773-4444; Email: inf@signatures.ca; URL: www.signatures.ca - Annual consumer show - Nov., Toronto ON

Signatures Winnipeg, Signatures Craft Shows Ltd., #810, 325 Dalhousie St., Ottawa ON K1N 7G2 - 613-241- 5777; Fax: 613-241-5678; Tollfree: 1-800-773-4444; Email: inf@signatures.ca; URL: www.signatures.ca - Annual consumer show - Nov., Winnipeg MB

Sundog Handcraft Fair, PO Box 7183, Saskatoon SK S7K 4J1 - 306-384-7364; Fax: 306-384-7364; Email: sundoghand craftfaire@sasktel.net - Coordinator, Diane Boyko-Banda - Juried three-day craft market plus continuous stage acts & gourmet food court. Annually, first weekend of Dec.

Victoria Park Arts/Crafts Fair, PO Box 1394, Moncton NB E1C 8T6 - 506-386-1200; Fax: 506-857-0279; Email: oscar@nb.aibn.com; URL: www.victoriaparkcrafts. com - Annually - Aug.

Wintergreen Fine Craft Market, Saskatchewan Craft Council, 813 Broadway Ave., Saskatoon SK S7N 1B5 - 306-653-3616; Fax: 306-244-2711; Tollfree: 1-866-653-3616; Email: saskcraftcouncil@shaw.ca; URL: www.saskcraftcouncil.org - Chair, Paula Cooley, Executive Director, Glenn Saganace - Annual. Threeday Christmas craft market - Nov., Regina SK

DANCE *See* MUSIC

DECORATING *See* HOME SHOWS

ELECTRICAL/ELECTRONICS

Eptech, LVP Media Inc., #27, 1200 Aerowood Dr., Mississauga ON L4W 2S7 - 905-624-8100; Fax: 905-624- 1760; Email: info@ept.ca; URL: www.ept.ca - Trade show held in various locations. Electronic components, systems

La Salon de la Technologie Electronique au Québec/Quebec Electronics Technology Show, Reed Exhibition Companies Inc., #1, 3761 Victoria Park Ave., Toronto ON M1W 3S2 - 416-491-7565; Fax: 416-491-5088; Email: canada@ reedexpo.com; URL: www.reedexpo.com - John Lewinski - Biennial trade show

ENERGY

Enercom, The MEARIE Group, #1100, 3700 Steeles Ave. West, Vaughan ON L4L 8K8 - 416-512-1215; Fax: 416-512- 1993; Tollfree: 1-800-660-7083; Email: jacqui@ yorkcom.to; URL: enercom.to - Principal, Jacqui Peake - Annual conference & exposition focusing on major trends & emerging issues in the procurement, production & distribution of electricity, gas, oil & renewable energy - March - Metro Toronto Convention Centre, Toronto ON

ENVIRONMENT

National Conference on Drinking Water, Canadian Water & Wastewater Association, #11, 1010 Polytek Rd., Ottawa ON K1J 9H9 - 613-747-0524; Fax: 613-747-0523; Email: admin@cwwa.ca; URL: www.cwwa.ca - Executive Director, T. Duncan Ellison - Biennial - April, 2008, Québec QC

ETHNIC *See* MULTICULTURAL

EVENTS

***See Also* specific categories for events such as Winter Carnivals, Music Festivals, Rodeos, Exhibitions, etc.**

Ashkenaz: A Festival of New Yiddish Culture, #303, 455 Spadina Ave., Toronto ON M5S 2G8 - 416-979-9901; Email: info@ashkenazfestival.com; URL: www.ashkenazfestival.com - President, Judy Wolfe - Bienniel; Aug./Sept.

Atlantic Canada Bicycle Rally, c/o Atlantic Canada Cycling, PO Box 1555, Stn M, Halifax NS B3J 2Y3 - 902-423-2453; Fax: 902-423-2452; Email: acbr@atlanticcanadacycling. com; URL: www.atlanticcanadacycling.com - Largest bicycle event in Atlantic Canada - Aug.

Billy Barker Days, PO Box 4441, Quesnel BC V2J 3J4 - 250-992-5083; Email: office@billbarkerdays; URL: www.billybarkerdays.ca, July Blossom Festival, PO Box 329, Creston BC V0B 1G0 - 250-428-2266; Fax: 250-428-3320 - Contact, Bernice Hamilton - May, long weekend

The Canadian Tulip Festival, Canadian Tulip Festival, #106, 112 Nelson St., Ottawa ON K1N 7R5 - 613-567- 5757; Fax: 613-567-6216; Tollfree: 1-800-668-8547; Email: info@tulipfestival.ca; URL: www.tulipfestival.ca - Executive Director, BemoOt Hubert, May

Canmore Highland Games, Three Sisters Scottish Festival Society, PO Box 8102, Canmore AB T1W 2T8 - 403-678-9454; Fax: 403-678-3385; Email: canmorehighlandgames@telus.net; URL: www.canmorehighlandgames.ca - Annually, Labour Day Sunday - Sept., Canmore AB

CHIN International Picnic, Exhibition Place, Toronto ON M6K 3C3 - 416-531-9991; Fax: 416-531-5274; Email: info@chinradio.com; URL: www.scotiabankchinpicnic.com - June/July

Chocolate Fest, Chocolate Festival, PO Box 5002, St. Stephen NB E3L 2X5 - 506-465-5616; Fax: 506-465- 5610; Email: info@chocolate-fest.ca; URL: www.chocolate-fest.ca - Coordinator, Roxanne Grant - Annual - Aug

Discovery Days Celebrations, Discovery Days Festival, PO Box 389, Dawson YT Y0B 1G0 - 867-993-5575; Fax: 867-993-6415; Email: kva@dawsoncity.net; URL: www.dawsoncity.ca - Aug.

Feast of St. Louis, 259 Park Service Rd., Louisbourg NS B1C 2L2 - 902-733-2280; Fax: 902-733-2362; Email: louisbourg.info@pc.gc.ca - Manager, Heritage Presentation, Anne O'Neill, Superintendent, Carol Whitfield - Eighteenth-century celebrations in honour of St. Louis - August, Louisbourg NS

Festival des peches et de l'aquaculture du Nouveau Brunswick, #200, 1 av Hotel de Ville, Shippagan NB E8S 1M1 - 506-336-8726; Fax: 506-336-3901; Email: festival@shippagan.com

Icelandic Festival of Manitoba, #107, 94 - 1st Ave., Gimli MB R0C 1B0 - 204-642-7417; Fax: 204-642-9382; Email: icefest@mts.net; URL: www.icelandicfestival.com, Aug., Gimli MB

Just for Laughs Festival, 2101, boul Saint-Laurent, Montréal QC H2X 2T5 - 514-845-3155; Fax: 514-845-4140; Tollfree: 1-888-244-3155; Email: info@hahaha.com; URL: www.hahaha.com, July

Kitchener-Waterloo Oktoberfest, 17 Benton St., PO Box 1053, Kitchener ON N2G 4G1 - 519-570-4267; Fax: 519-742-3072; Tollfree: 1-888-294-4267; Email: info@oktoberfest.ca; URL: www.oktoberfest.ca - Executive Director, Larry Blundell - Annually, October. Bavarian festival: foods, entertainment, parades

Labrador Straits Bakeapple Folk Festival, PO Box 112, Forteau NL A0K 2P0 - 709-931-2013; Email: info@labradorcoastal drive.com - Director, Marketing, Bonnie Goudie - Annually, Aug.

Little Lake Musicfest, 610 Parkhill Rd., Peterborough ON K9J 6N6 - 705-755-1111; Fax: 705-755-0188; Email: info@festivaloflights.ca; URL: www.festivaloflights.ca - Special Events Coordinator, Emily Martin, General Manager, Kathy Kirkland - June to Aug. every Wednesday & Saturday evening at Del Crary Park

Manitoba Sunflower Festival, PO Box 1630, Altona MB R0G 0B0 - 204-324-9005; Fax: 204-324-1550; Email: info@townofaltona.com; URL: altona.ca - Annual, last weekend of July

Northern Manitoba Trappers' Festival, Inc., PO Box 475, The Pas MB R9A 1K6 - 204-623-2912; Fax: 204-623- 1974; URL: www.trappersfestival.com - Annually, Feb.; world championship sled dog race

Northwest Territorial Days, PO Box 668, North Battleford SK S9A 2Y9 - 306-445-2024; Fax: 306-445-3352; Email: b.agsociety@sasktel.net; URL: www.agsociety.com - Aug.

Nova Scotia Gaelic Mod, F,is A' MhThe Gaelic Mod, PO Box 80, Englishtown NS B0C 1H0 - 902-295-3411; Fax: 902-295-2912; Email: hector@gaeliccollege.edu; URL: www.gaeliccollege.edu - One-day festival - Aug. - Gaelic College, St. Ann's NS Nova Scotia International Tattoo, 1586 Queen St., Halifax NS B3J 2V1 - 902-420-1114; Fax: 902-423-6629; Tollfree: 1-800-563-1114; Email: info@nstattoo.ca; URL: www.nstattoo.ca - Ian Fraser - Annually, June/July

Penticton Peach Festival, #113, 437 Martin St., S343, Penticton BC V2A 5L1 - 250-492-9830; Fax: 250-492- 7980; Email: info@peachfest.com; URL: www.peachfest.com - Aug.

Pictou Lobster Carnival, PO Box 1480, Pictou NS B0K 1H0 - 902-485-5150; Fax: 902-485-4915; Email: picoulobstercarnival@hotmail.com; URL: pictoulobstercarnival.ca - Annual - July

Québec City Summer Festival, 226, rue St-Joseph est, Québec QC G1K 3A9 - 418-523-4540; Fax: 418-523- 0194; Tollfree: 1-888-992-5200; Email: infofestival@ infofestival.com; URL: www.infofestival.com - Entertainment in the streets & parks of Old Québec, July

Royal St. John's Regatta, PO Box 214, St. John's NL A1C 5J9 - 709-579-8921; Fax: 709-576-3315; Email: stjohnsregatta@nf.aibn.com; URL: www.stjohnsregatta.org - North America's oldest continuing sporting event - Aug., St. John's NL

Sam Steele Days, PO Box 115, Cranbrook BC V1C 4H6 - 250-426-4161; Fax: 250-426-3873; Tollfree: 1-800- 222-6174; Email: info@samsteeledays.org; URL: www.samsteeledays.org, June

Shediac Lobster Festival, 231A Belliveau Ave., Shediac NB E4P 1H4 - 506-532-1122; Fax: 506-532-7986; Tollfree: 1-888-707-1755; Email: lobsterf@ nbnet.nb.ca; URL: www.lobsterfestival.nb.ca - Guy Lavine - Annually, first week of July

Steinbach Pioneer Days, c/o Mennonite Heritage Village, 231, PTH 12 North, Steinbach MB R0A 2A0 - 204-326- 9661

Storytelling Festival, The Storytellers School of Toronto, 43 Queens Park Cres. East, Toronto ON M5S 2C3 - 416-656-2445; Fax: 416-656-8510; Email: admin@storytelling toronto.org; URL: www.torontostorytellingfestival.ca - President, Michael Lobraico, Managing Director, Catherine Melville - Held annually, April

Summerside Lobster Carnival, PO Box 1295, Summerside PE C1N 4K2 - 902-436-4925; Fax: 902-436-0129; URL: www.summersidelobstercarnival.ca, July

Trinity Conception Fair, c/o Harbour Grace Stadium, PO Box 365, Harbour Grace NL A0A 2M0 - 709-596-6201; Fax: 709-596-6261; Tollfree: 1-800-596-3233; Email: hgrecdept@nf.aibn.com - Fair Manager, Kevin Bennett - Annually, Sept.

Welland Rose Festival, 800 Niagara St. North, PO Box 23031, Welland ON L3C 5Z4 - 905-735-8696; Fax: 905-735-4832; URL: www.wellandrosefestival.on.ca - Director, Shane Sargant - Annually, June. Rose show, lobsterfest, sporting events, juried art show, seniors' events, day in the park, day-on-the-island, craft show, fishing derby, children's events, grand parade

Winnipeg Oktoberfest, Winnipeg Convention Centre, 375 York Ave., 3rd Fl., Winnipeg MB R3C 3J3 - 204-957- 4535; Fax: 204-943-0310; Email: oktoberfest@ wcc.mb.ca; URL: www.amm.mb.ca, Sept.

World's Invitational Class "A" Gold Panning Championships, Taylor Gold Panning Society, District of Taylor, PO Box 300, Taylor BC V0C 2K0 - 250-789-3004; Fax: 250-789-9076; URL: www.districtoftaylor.com - Director, Community Services, Natalie Poole-Moffat - Annually, Aug. long weekend Yukon Gold-Panning Championships, Klondike Visitors Association, PO Box 389, Dawson YT Y0B 1G0 - 867-993-5575; Fax: 867-993-6415; Email: kva@ dawson.net; URL: www.dawsoncity.org - On Canada Day - July, Dawson City YT

Yukon River World Championship Bathtub Race, Yukon Sourdough Rendezvous Society, PO Box 31721, Whitehorse YT Y1A 6L3 - 867-393-4467; Fax: 867-668-6755; Email: ysr@polarcom. com; URL: www.yukonrendezvous.com - Executive Director, Harold Sher, President, Marj Eschak - Longest & hardest bathtub race. Two days, 486 miles, Yukon River - Aug.

Yukon Sourdough Rendezvous, Yukon Sourdough Rendezvous Society, PO Box 31721, Whitehorse YT Y1A 6L3 - 867-393-4467; Fax: 867-668-6755; Email: ysr@polarcom.com; URL: www.yukonrendezvous.com - Executive Director, Harold Sher, President, Marj Eschak - Annually. Celebrates the gold rush times. Mad trapper, flour packing, tug-a-truck contests, fiddle show, lip sync & queen contests - Feb.

EXHIBITIONS

***See Also* Farm Business/Agriculture, Rodeos**

Buffalo Days Exhibition, Regina Exhibition Park, PO Box 167, Regina SK S4P 2Z6 - 306-781-9200; Fax: 306-565-3443; Tollfree: 1-888-734-3975; Email: info@reginaexhibition. com - Marketing Manager, Tom Mullin, General Manager, Douglas Cressman, July

Canadian Lakehead Exhibition, 425 Northern Ave., Thunder Bay ON P7C 2V7 - 807-622-6473; Fax: 807-623-5540; Email: info@cle.on.ca; URL: www.cle.on.ca - Administrative Clerk, Dulcie Prystanski - Annually, Aug.

Canadian National Exhibition, Canadian National Exhibition Association, Exhibition Place, Toronto ON M6K 3C3 - 416-263-3800; Fax: 416-263-3838; Email: info@theex.com; URL: www.theex.com - Annual public show

Edmonton's Klondike Days Exposition, PO Box 1480, Edmonton AB T5J 2N5 - 780-471-7210; Fax: 780-471- 8176; Tollfree: 1-888-800-7275; Email: info@northlands. com; URL: www.capitalex.ca - Annual consumer show

Expo Québec, ExpoCity, 250, boul Wilfrid-Hamel, Québec QC G1L 5A7 - 418-691-7110; Fax: 418-691-7249; Email: info@expocite.com; URL: www.expoquebec.com - General

Manager, Mark Sparrow - Annual exhibition. Industrial, agricultural, food - Aug. - City Fairgrounds, Québec QC

Fredericton Exhibition, PO Box 235, Stn A, Fredericton NB E3B 4Y9 - 506-458-9819; Fax: 506-458-9294; Email: frex@nb.net.nb.ca; URL: www.frex.ca - Annual, begins on Labour Day - Sept.

Interior Provincial Exhibition & Stampede, PO Box 490, Armstrong BC V0E 1B0 - 250-546-9406; Fax: 250-546-6181; Email: ipeandstampede@ telus.net; URL: www.armstrongipe.com - General Manager, Ken Mather - Annual consumer agricultural fair & show, Aug.-Sept. - Aug.

Lindsay Central Exhibition, 354 Angeline St. South, Lindsay ON K9V 4W9 - 705-324-5551; Fax: 705-324-8111; Email: info@ lindsayex.com; URL: www.lindsayex.com - Manager, Tom Saunders - Annual consumer agricultural fair & show - Sept.

Markham Agricultural Fair, 10801 McCowan Rd., Markham ON L3P 3J3 - 905-642-3247; Fax: 905-640- 8458; Tollfree: 1-800-450-3557; Email: office@ markhamfair.ca; URL: www.markhamfair.ca - Annual consumer show - Sept./Oct.

Medicine Hat Exhibition & Stampede Co., 2055 - 21st Ave. SE, PO Box 1298, Medicine Hat AB T1A 7N1 - 403-527- 1234; Fax: 403-529-6553; Email: mhstampede@mhstampede. com; URL: www.mhstampede.com/- General Manager, Jim MacArthur - Annual consumer show - July

New Atlantic National Exhibition, PO Box 284, Saint John NB E2L 3Y2 - 506-633-2020; Fax: 506-636-6958 - Annual - Aug.

Niagara Regional Exhibition, 1100 Niagara St. North, Welland ON L3C 1M6 - 905-735-6413; Fax: 905-735- 2317; Email: nreoffice@nre.ca; URL: www.niagararegionalexhibition.ca - Annual consumer agricultural fair & show, Sept. - Sept.

Nova Scotia Provincial Exhibition, PO Box 192, Truro NS B2N 5C5 - 902-893-9222; Fax: 902-897-0069; Email: nspe@eastlink.ca; URL:www.nspe.ca - David Coombes - Agricultural exhibition - August, Bible Hill NS

Pacific National Exhibition, 2901 East Hastings St., Stn Hastings Park, Vancouver BC V5K 5J1 - 604-253- 2311; Fax: 604-251-7768; Email: info@pne.ca; URL: www.pne.ca - President & CEO, Michael McDaniel - Annual event; agricultural competitions, parade

Paris Fall Fair, PO Box 124, Paris ON N3L 3E7 - 519-442- 2823; Fax: 519-442-5121; Email: parisfair@ on.aibn.com; URL: www.parisfair.com - Manager, Harry Emmott - Annual Labour Day weekend consumer show

Prince Albert Exhibition, Prince Albert Exhibition Association, PO Box 1538, Prince Albert SK S6V 5T1 - 306-764-1711; Fax: 306-764-5246; URL: www.paexhibition.com - Manager, Dave Young - Annual

Red River Exhibition, Red River Exhibition Association, Red River Exhibition Park, 3977 Portage Ave., Winnipeg MB R3K 2E8 - 204-888-6990; Fax: 204-888- 6992; Email: info@redriverex.com; URL: www.redriverex.com - Manitoba's largest fair & single-site entertainment event. Annually, 10 days, last two weeks in June

Thresherman's Reunion & Stampede, Central Canada's Fiddle Festival, PO Box 10, High Bluff MB R0H 0C0 - 204-637-2354; Fax: 204-637-2395; Email: info@agmuseum. mb.ca; URL: www.ag-museum.mb.ca - Contact, Sandra Head - Annual

Western Nova Scotia Exhibition, PO Box 425, Yarmouth NS B5A 4B3 - 902-742-8222; Fax: 902-742-5229; Email: frank@swsda.com; URL: yarmouthexhibition.com/index.html - Frank Anderson - Six-day agricultural fair & talent competition - July or Aug., Yarmouth NS

FARM BUSINESS/AGRICULTURE

See Also **Exhibitions, Rodeos**

Agribition Show & Rodeo, Canadian Western Agribition Show & Rodeo, c/o Public Relations Office, Canadian Western Agribition, PO Box 3535, Regina SK S4P 3J8 - 306-565-0565; Fax: 306-757-9963; Email: info@agribition. com; URL: www.agribition.com - General Manager, Leon Brin - Annually, Nov.

CAAR Convention, Canadian Association of Agri-Retailers, #107, 1090 Waverley St., Winnipeg MB R3T 0P4 - 204-989-9300; Fax: 204-989-9306; Tollfree: 1-800-463-9323; Email: info@caar.org; URL: www.caar.org - Executive Director, Jacqueline Ryrie, President, Bob Evans

Canadian National Hereford Show, c/o Canadian Hereford Association, 5160 Skyline Way NE, Calgary AB T2E 6V1 - 403-275-2662; Fax: 403-295-1333; Email: herefords@ hereford.ca; URL: www.hereford.ca, Nov., Regina SK

Maritime Fall Fair, 200 Prospect Rd., Goodwood NS B3T 1P2 - 902-876-8221; Fax: 902-876-8551; URL: www.maritimefallfair.com - Annual consumer exhibition, Oct., over the Thanksgiving weekend

Norfolk County Fair & Horse Show, Norfolk County Agricultural Society, 172 South Dr., Simcoe ON N3Y 1G6 - 519-426-7280; Fax: 519-426-7286; URL: norfolkcountryfair.com - General Manager, Karen Matthews, Email: kmatthews@norfolkcountyfair.com - Annual consumer show

Northlands Farmfair, Farmfair International, PO Box 1480, Edmonton AB T5J 2N5 - 780-471-7210; Fax: 780-471- 8169; Tollfree: 1-888-800-7275; URL: www.farmfair.ca - Annually, Nov.

Poultry Industry Conference & Exhibition, Western Fair Association, 900 King St., PO Box 7550, London ON N5Y 5P8 - 519-438-7203; Fax: 519-679-3124; Tollfree: 1-800-619-4629; Email: gmcrae@westernfair. com; URL: www.westernfair.com - General Manager, Gary McRae - Annual trade show

Royal Agricultural Winter Fair, Royal Agricultural Winter Fair Association, The Coliseum, National Trade Centre, Exhibition Place, Toronto ON M6K 3C3 - 416-263- 3400; Fax: 416-263-3488; Email: information@royalfair. org; URL: www.royalfair.org - Annual consumer show. World's largest agricultural fair & equestrian event - Nov., Toronto ON

Salon de l'Agriculture, #120, 2200, rue Pratte, Saint-Hyacinthe QC J2S 4B6 - 450-771-1226; Fax: 450-771- 6073; Email: info@salonagr.qc.ca; URL: salondelagriculture.com - Annual trade show. Agricultural products - Jan., St-Hyacinthe QC

Western Canada Farm Progress Show, PO Box 167, Regina SK S4P 2Z6 - 306-781-9200; Fax: 306-781-9396; Tollfree: 1-888-734-3975; Email: wcfps@reginaexhibition. com; URL: www.myfarmshow.com - Show Manager, Rob O'Connor, Vice-President, Major Event Development, Darrell Komick - Annual consumer & trade show - June - Regina Exhibition Park, Regina SK

Western Fair, Western Fair Association, 900 King St., PO Box 7550, London ON N5Y 5P8 - 519-438-7203; Fax: 519-679-3124; Tollfree: 1-800-619-4629; Email: gmcrae@westernfair.com; URL: www.westernfair.com - General Manager, Gary McRae - Annual consumer show

FESTIVALS *See* EVENTS

FILM & VIDEO FESTIVALS & SPECIAL EVENTS

Alberta Film & Television Awards, Alberta Motion Picture Industries Association, #401, 11456 Jasper Ave., Edmonton AB T5K 0M1 - 780-944-0707; Fax: 780-426- 3057; Email: info@ampia.org; URL: www.ampia.org - President, Connie Edwards, Executive Director, Richard Horne, Feb.

Le Carrousel international du film de Rimouski, #105, 143 rue St-Germain ouest, Rimouski QC G5L 4B6 - 418-722-0103; Fax: 418-724-9504; Email: cifr@carrousel.qc.ca; URL: www.carrousel.qc.ca - Kathleen Aubry - Films for children. Competition, workshops - Sept., Rimouski QC

Cinéfest - The Sudbury International Film Festival, #103, 40 Larch St., Sudbury ON P3E 5M7 - 705-688-1234; Fax: 705-688-1351; Tollfree: 1-877-212-3222; Email: cinefest@vianet.on.ca; URL: www.cinefest.com - Executive Director, Tammy Frick - Full-length feature festival with over 100 Canadian & international films, animations, shorts, Midnight Madness, documentary & children's film series - Sept., Sudbury ON

Festival du cinéma international en Abitibi-Témiscamingue, 215, av Mercier, Rouyn-Noranda QC J9X 5W8 - 819-762-6212; Fax: 819-762-6762; Email: info@festivalcinema. ca; URL: www.lino. com/festivalcinema - Executive Director, Jacques Matte - Features, mediumlength & short films. Competition; regional jury award for short or medium-length film; people's choice award for feature & animation - Oct., Rouyn-Noranda QC

Festival du film étudiant canadien/Canadian Student Film Festival, Festival du film ,tudiant canadien, 1432, rue de Bleury, Montréal QC H3A 2J1 - 514-848-7186; Fax: 514-848-3886; Email: info@ffm-montreal.org - Films & videos by Canadian students. Film competition - Aug., Montréal QC

Festival du nouveau cinéma, 3805, boul. Saint-Laurent, Montréal QC H2W 1X9 - 514-282-0004; Fax: 514-282-6664; Email: info@nouveaucinema.ca - Directeur général, Nicolas Girard Deltruc - New trends in new cinema, video & new media; non-competitive; people's choice award

Film Studies Association of Canada Conference, Film Studies Association of Canada, c/o Global Studies, Wilfrid Laurier Univ., Dr. Alvin Woods Bldg., 75 University Ave. West, Room 3-205, Waterloo ON N2L 3C5; Email: gekoff@contact.net; URL: www.filmstudies.ca - President, Brenda Austin-Smith, Vice-President, Janina Falkowska, Secretary, Christina Stojanowa - May/June annually, held at a different university each year

Flicks: Saskatchewan International Children's Film Festival, Flicks International Children's Film Festival, 715 Broadway Ave., Saskatoon SK S7K 1B3 - 306-956-3456; Fax: 306-664-2344; Email: flicksfilmfestival@sasktel.net; URL: www.flicksfilmfest. org - Artistic Director, Cass Cozens - Annually in March, three day international film festival for children

Images Festival of Independent Film & Video, #448, 401 Richmond St. West, Toronto ON M5V 3A8 - 416-971- 8405; Fax: 416-971-7412; Email: images@imagesfestival. com; URL: www.imagesfestival.com/- Executive Director, Peter Chevrier - Annual. Independent films & videos. Workshops - April, Toronto ON

Les Journées africaines et créoles, Vues d'Afrique, #3100, 100, rue Sherbrooke est, Montréal QC H2X 1C3 - 514-284-3322; Fax: 514-845-0631; Email: info@vuesdafrique. org; URL: www.vuesdafrique.org - Gérard Le Chêne - Competition. Films by & about African & Creole peoples - April, Montréal QC

Les Rendez-vous du cinéma québécois, 1000, rue Fullum, Montréal QC H2K 3L7 - 514-526-9635; Fax: 514-526- 1955; Email: info@rvcq.com; URL: www.rvcq.com - Président, Denis Chouinard - Restrospective of recent Québec productions - Feb., Montréal QC

Ottawa International Animation Festival, #120, 2 Daly Ave., Ottawa ON K1N 6E2 - 613-232-8769; Fax: 613-232-6315; Email: info@animationfestival.ca; URL: www.awn.com/ottawa - Annual. Animation films & videos. Television animation conference. Workshops & panels - Sept., Ottawa ON

St. John's International Women's Film & Video Festival, PO Box 984, St. John's NL A1C 5M3 - 709-754-3141; Fax: 709-754-3143; Email: womensfilmfest@nfld.net; URL: www.womensfilmfestival.com - Festival Director, Katie Nicholson - Women's films & videos. Workshops & panels - Oct., St. John's NL Toronto International Film Festival,

Toronto International Film Festival Group, TIFF Bell Lightbox, Reitman Square, 350 King Street West, Toronto ON M5V 3X5 - 416-934-3200; Email:proffice@tiff.net; URL: tiff.net - Features & theatrical shorts. Competition. Awards for excellence in Canadian production. People's choice & film critics awards. Symposium, workshops, sales office - Sept., Toronto ON

Vancouver International Film Festival, 1181 Seymour St., Vancouver BC V6B 3M7 - 604-685-0260; Fax: 604-688-8221; Email: viff@viff.org; URL: www.viff.org - Festival Director, Alan Franey - Features, mediumlength & short films. Competition; juried awards for best western Canadian feature film, best young western Canadian director of a short film, best documentary feature & best film by a new director from Pacific Asia; people's choice award for most popular international film & for most popular Canadian film. Trade forum - Sept./Oct., Vancouver BC World Film Festival, Montréal

World Film Festival, 1432, rue de Bleury, Montréal QC H3A 2J1 - 514-848-3883; Fax: 514-848-3886; Email: info@ffm-montreal.org; URL: www.ffm-montreal.org/- Features, mediumlength & short films. Competition, symposium, markets - Aug., Montréal QC

FIRST NIGHT CELEBRATIONS

First Night Whistler, 4010 Whistler Way, Whistler BC V0N 1B4 - 604-932-3928; Fax: 604-932-7231; URL: www.whistler.com

FISHING/AQUACULTURE

Adams River Sockeye Salmon Run, PO Box 1563, Chase BC V0E 1M0 - 250-679-8315; URL: www.salmonsociety.com - Oct.

Eastern Canada Fisheries Exposition, Master Promotions Ltd., PO Box 565, Saint John NB E2L 3Z8 - 506-658- 0018; Fax: 506-658-0750; Tollfree: 1-888-454-7469; Email: info@masterpromotions.ca; URL: www.masterpromotions.ca - Annual commercial fishing show - Show Manager, Jeff Lacey, Feb - Mariner's Centre, Yarmouth NS

Flin Flon Trout Festival, PO Box 751, Flin Flon MB R8A 1N6 - 204-687-5166; URL: www.flinflontroutfestival.com - June, Flin Flon MB

Nipawin Pike Festival, PO Box 863, Nipawin SK S0E 1E0 - 306-862-9866; Fax: 306-862-3076; Tollfree: 1-877-647-2946; Email: events@ nipawin.com; URL: www.nipawinpikefestival.com - June - Sept.

North Atlantic Fish/Workboat Show, Master Promotions Ltd., PO Box 565, Saint John NB E2L 3Z8 - 506-658- 0018; Fax: 506-658-0750; Tollfree: 1-888-454-7469; Email: info@masterpromotions.ca; URL: www.masterpromotions.ca - Bienniel commercial fishing/boat show - Show Manager, Sydney Peacock, Nov., Vancouver BC

Salmon Festival, PO Box 24, Campbellton NB E3N 3G1 - 506-759-7997; Fax: 506-759-7403; Tollfree: 1-888- 813-4433; Email: tourism@campbellton.org; URL: www.campbellton.org - Contact, Gilbert Cyr, Email: gilbert.cyr@campbellton.org - June

FLOWERS/LANDSCAPING/GARDENING

Hamilton & Burlington Rose Society Show, Royal Botanical Gardens, 3041 Silverthorn Dr. Oakville, ON L6L 5N4 -

905-527-1158; Fax: 905-577-0375, June Hamilton Orchid Show, Royal Botanical Gardens, 680 Plains Rd. West, Burlington ON L7T 4H4 - 905-527- 1158; Fax: 905-577-0375, March

Ikenobo Ikebana Japanese Flower Show, Royal Botanical Gardens, 680 Plains Rd. West, Burlington ON L7T 4H4 - 905-527-1158; Fax: 905-577-0375, Sept.

FOOD & BEVERAGE

***See Also* Hospitality Industry**

Natural Health Products Week, Canadian Health Food Association, #302, 235 Yorkland Blvd. Toronto ON M2J 4Y8 - 416-497-6939; Fax: 905-479- 1516; Tollfree: 1-800-661-4510, fax 1-888-2927; Email: admin@chfa.ca; URL: www.chfa.ca - Organic & natural products; homeopathy, food supplements & herbs. April & Oct.

The Good Food Festival & Market, 117 Evelyn Ave., Toronto ON M6J 4G7 - 416-766-2084; Fax: 416-762-9942; Email: info@goodfoodfestival.net; URL: www.goodfoodfestival.net - General Manager, Lynda Chubak - Annual consumer festival - April - International Centre, Hall 5, Mississauga ON

Gourmet Food & Wine Expo, Town Media, 1074 Cooke Blvd., Burlington ON L7T 4A8 - 905-634-8003; Fax: 905-634-7661; URL: www.foodandwineshow.ca - Consumer show - Nov. - Metro Toronto Convention Centre, Toronto ON

Ottawa Wine & Food Show, Player Expositions International, 255 Clemow Ave., Ottawa ON K1S 2B5 - 613-567-6408; Fax: 613-567-2718; Email: rplayer@sympatico. ca; URL: www.playerexpo.com - Show Organizer, Halina Player - Annual trade & consumer show - Oct./Nov.

Salon des vins et spiritueux de Montréal, AFLD Consultants Inc., 3565, rue Edgar Leduc, Lachine QC H8T 3L5 - 514-639-6806; Fax: 514-639-6629; Email: afld@ videotron.ca - Show Manager, Lucie Desharnais, CDE - Biennial trade & public show

Super Salon de l'alimentation, SIAL Montréal - Salon international de l'alimentation, #1100, 300, rue Léo Pariseau, CP 159, Montréal QC H2W 2M9 - 514-289-9669; Fax: 514-289-1034; Tollfree: 1-800- 281-7425; Email: info@sialmontreal.ca; URL: www.sial-montreal.com/- Directeur général, Alain Bellefeuille - Annual trade show for the food retail industry including food & beverage products & store equipment - April

Toronto Wine & Cheese Show, Premier Publications & Shows, 467 Speers Rd., Oakville ON L6K 3S4; Fax: 905-337-5570; Tollfree: 1-800-265-3673; URL: www.towineandcheese.com - Marti Milks, 905-815-0017, ext.426, Email: marti.milks@ sympatico.ca, Brad Dean, 416-365-1500, ext.41, Email: bdean@travelweek. ca, Christine Wong, 905-815-0017, ext.447, Email: cwong@metroland.com - Annual consumer show - March - International Centre, Toronto ON

FOREST INDUSTRY

BC Log Home, Timber Frame & Country Living Show, Master Promotions Ltd., PO Box 565, Saint John NB E2L 3Z8 - 506-658-0018; Fax: 506-658-0750; Tollfree: 1-888-454-7469; Email: info@masterpromotions. ca; URL: www.masterpromotions.ca - Marketing & Operations Manager, Jennifer Allaby, President, Wendell Howes - Biennial logging & forestry show - Sept.

DEMO International, Master Promotions Ltd., PO Box 565, 48 Broad St., Saint John NB E2L 3Z8 - 506-658-0018; Fax: 506-658- 0750; Tollfree: 1-888-454-7469; Email: info@masterpromotions. ca; URL: www.masterpromotions.ca - Active demonstrations of all types of industrial woodlands equipment. Harvesting, silviculture, transportation & handling, Sept. - Show Manager, Mark Cusack, Sept. - Laval University, Laval QC

Forest Expo, 850 River Rd., Prince George BC V2L 5S8 - 250-563-8833; Fax: 250-563-3697; Email: info@forestexpo. bc.ca; URL: www.forestexpo.bc.ca - General Manager, Trudy Swaan - Biennial - June 5-7, 2008, Prince George BC

FUNERALS

Canadian Funeral Trade Show, PO Box 97507, Toronto ON M1C 4Z1 - 416-281-5460; Fax: 416-282-9095; Email: info@canadianfuneraltradeassociation.com; URL: www.thecfta.org - Executive Director, Brenda Broughton - Annual trade show - June

FURNITURE *See* HOME SHOWS

GARDENING *See* FLOWERS

GIFTS & JEWELLERY

Expo Prestige, Corporation des bijoutiers du Québec, 868, rue Brisette, Sainte-Julie QC J3E 2B1 - 514-485-3333; Fax: 450-649-8984; Email: info@cbq.qc.ca; URL: www.cbq.qc.ca - Président, André Marchand, Directrice générale, Lise Petitpas, août - Palais des Congrès, Montréal QC

Jewellery World Expo, Reed Exhibition Companies Inc., #1, 3761 Victoria Park Ave., Toronto ON M1W 3S2 - 416-491-7565; Fax: 416-491-5088; Email: canada@ reedexpo.com; URL: www.reedexpo.com - John Lewinski - Annual trade show - Aug., Toronto ON

Montréal Gift Show/Le Salon du Cadeau - Montréal, dmg World Media, 180 Duncan Mills Rd., 4th Fl., Toronto ON M3B 1Z6 - 416-385-1880; Fax: 416-385-1855; Tollfree: 1-888-823-7469; URL: www.dmgworldmedia.com - Show Manager, Glen Chiasson - Annual trade show. Giftware, stationery, kitchenware, luggage & leathergoods, pottery, china, glass, jewellery - March, Montréal QC

North Bay Gift Show, North Bay & District Chamber of Commerce, 1375 Seymour St., PO Box 747, North Bay ON P1B 8J8 - 705-472-8480; Fax: 705-472-8027; Tollfree: 1-888-249-8998; Email: nbcc@northbaychamber. com; URL: www.northbay chamber.com - Manager, Patti Alcorn-Carr - Annual trade show. Giftware, fashion, food services & furniture - April - West Ferris Community Centre, North Bay ON

Toronto International Gift Fair, dmg World Media, 180 Duncan Mills Rd., 4th Fl., Toronto ON M3B 1Z6 - 416-385-1880; Fax: 416-385-1855; Tollfree: 1-888-823- 7469; URL: www.dmgworldmedia.com - Show Manager, Glen Chiasson

Vancouver Spring/Fall Gift Show, dmg World Media (Canada) Inc., #402, 4601 Canada Way, Burnaby BC V5G 4X7 - 604-433-5121; Fax: 604-434-6853; Tollfree: 1-800-633-8332; URL: www.vancouvergiftexpo.com - Exec. Vice-President, Gifts Sector, Fred Barnes - Annual trade show. Giftwares, housewares, luggage & leathergoods, jewellery. March & Sept.

GRAPHIC ARTS

Print World Trade Show, #8, 1606 Sedlescomb Dr., Mississauga ON L4X 1M6 - 905-625-7070; Fax: 905-625- 4856; Tollfree: 1-800-331-7408 - Biennial trade show - Nov. - Exhibition Place, Toronto ON

HAIRDRESSING

Allied Beauty Show, Allied Beauty Association, #46/47, 450 Matheson Blvd. East, Mississauga ON L4Z 1R5 - 905-568-0158; Fax: 905-568-1581; Email: abacan@idirect. com; URL: www.abacanada.com - Executive Director, Marc Speir - Held in various locations

HEATING, PLUMBING & AIR CONDITIONING

***See Also* Hardware**

CIPHEX, CIPH, #330, 295 The West Mall, Toronto ON M9C 4Z4 - 416-695-0447; Fax: 416-695-0450; Tollfree: 1-800-639-2474; Email: info@ciph.com; URL: www.ciph.com - Elizabeth McCullugh - Biennial trade show. Plumbing, heating, cooling & piping exhibits & conference (Calgary, Toronto & Montreal)

CMX, Shield Associates Ltd., 25 Bradgate Rd., Toronto ON M3B 1J6 - 416-444-5225; Fax: 416-444-8268; Tollfree: 1-800-282-0003; Email: sal@salshow.com; URL: www.cmxshow.com; www.windoorshow.com - Show Coordinator, Patrick Shield - Biennial trade show. Heating, ventilation, plumbing, air conditioning, ventilation & refrigeration - March

HOBBIES

***See Also* Crafts**

Gem, Mineral & Fossil Show, Calgary Rock & Lapidary Club, 110 Lissington Dr. SW, Calgary AB T3E 5E3 - 403-287-1570; Email: martintm@telus.net; URL: www.crlc.ca - Director, Public Relations, Trudy Martin - Annual

Toronto Model Railway Show, 2938 Dundas St. West, PO Box 70618, Toronto ON M6P 4E7 - 416-249-4563; URL: www.modelrailroadclub.com - Show Co-ordinator, Jack Bell - Annual consumer show held 3rd weekend of March

HOME ENTERTAINMENT *See* ELECTRICAL/ELECTRONICS

HOME SHOWS

Atlantic National Home Show, Master Promotions Ltd., PO Box 565, Saint John NB E2L 3Z8 - 506-658-0018; Fax: 506-658-0750; Tollfree: 1-888-454-7469; Email: info@masterpromotions.ca; URL: www.masterpromotions.ca - Annual consumer show - Show Manager, Brian McKiel, March, Saint John NB

Bridgewater Home & Leisure Show, Master Promotions Ltd., PO Box 565, Saint John NB E2L 3Z8 - 506-658- 0018; Fax: 506-658-0750; Tollfree: 1-888-454-7469; Email: info@masterpromotions.ca; URL: www.masterpromotions.ca - Annual consumer show. Home products, services & leisure products - Show Manager, Brian McKeil, April - Bridgewater Arena, Bridgewater NS

Burlington Fall Lifestyle Home Show, Jenkins Show Productions, 1076 Skyvalley Cres., Oakville ON L6M 3L2 - 905-827-4632; Fax: 905-827-8139; Tollfree: 1-800- 465-1073; Email: djenkins2@cogeco.ca; URL: www.jenkinsshow.com - President, Dave Jenkins - Annual consumer show - Sept., Burlington ON

Burlington Lifestyle Home Show, Jenkins Show Productions, 1076 Skyvalley Cres., Oakville ON L6M 3L2 - 905-827-4632; Fax: 905-827-8139; Tollfree: 1-800- 465-1073; Email: djenkins2@cogeco.ca; URL: www.jenkinsshow.com - President, Dave Jenkins - Annual consumer show - April, Burlington ON

Calgary Home & Interior Design Show, dmg World Media, #605, 999 - 8 St. SW, Calgary AB T2R 1N7 - 403-209- 3555; Fax: 403-245-8649; Tollfree: 1-888-799-2545; URL: www.dmgworldmedia.com - Annual consumer show - Show Manager, Lisa Macintosh, Sept. - Stampede Park, Calgary AB

Canadian Spa & Pool Conference & Expo, Pool & Hot Tub Council of Canada, #10B, 242 Applewood Cres., Vaughan ON L4K 4E5 - 905-761-7920; Fax: 905-761- 8837; Tollfree: 1-800-879-7066; Email: office@poolcouncil. ca; URL: www.poolcouncil.ca - Executive Director, Ken Tomihiro - Annual trade & consumer show - Dec. - Scotiabank Convention Centre, Niagara ON

Colchester County Home Show, Master Promotions Ltd., PO Box 565, Saint John NB E2L 3Z8 - 506-658-0018; Fax: 506-658-0750; Tollfree: 1-888-454-7469; Email: info@mpltd.ca; URL: www.masterpromotions.ca - Annual consumer show - Show Manager, Scott Sprague, April - Legion Stadium, Truro NS

Edmonton Home & Interior Design Show, #605, 999 - 8 St. SW, Calgary AB T2R 1N7 - 403-209-3555; Fax: 403-245-8649; Tollfree: 1-888- 799-2545; URL: www.ehids.com - Annual consumer show - Show Manager, Lisa Macintosh, Sept. - Northlands AgriCom, Edmonton AB

Expo Habitat de St-Hyacinthe, DBC Communications Inc., 655, av Ste-Anne, Saint-Hyacinthe QC J2S 5G4 - 450-773-3976; Fax: 450-773-3115 - Personne ressource, Pierre Charbonneau - Annual consumer show. Home construction & renovation products & services - April - Pavillion de Pionnieres, St-Hyacinthe QC

Fall Home Show, 195 Princes Blvd., Toronto ON M6K 3C3 - 416-385-1880; Fax: 416-385-1855; Tollfree: 1-888-823-7469; URL: www.fallhomeshow.com - Show Manager, Glen Chiasson

Fredericton Lifestyles Show, Master Promotions Ltd., PO Box 565, Saint John NB E2L 3Z8 - 506-658-0018; Fax: 506-658-0750; Tollfree: 1-888-454-7469; Email: info@mpltd.ca; URL: www.masterpromotions.ca - Annual consumer show - Show Manager, Brian McKeil, March - Capital Exhibit Centre, Fredericton NB

Home, Garden & Leisure Show, Medicine Hat & District Chamber of Commerce, 413 - 6th Ave. SE, Medicine Hat AB T1A 2S7 - 403-527-5214; Fax: 403-527-5182; Email: mhchamber@monarch.net; URL: www.medicinehatchamber. com - President, Jason Mutschler, Executive Director, Mary Lou Hansen - Consumer show - October - Cypress Centre, Stampede Park, Medicine Hat AB

International Home & Garden Show, Showcase Marketing Ltd., #410, 1110 Sheppard Ave. East, Toronto ON M2K 2W2 - 416-512-1305; Email: homeshow@idirect. com - Paul Newdick - Annual consumer show - March - International Centre, Toronto ON

International Home Show, Showcase Marketing Ltd., #410, 1110 Sheppard Ave. East, Toronto ON M2K 2W2 - 416-512-1305; Email: homeshow@idirect.com - Paul Newdick - Annual consumer show - Oct. - International Centre, Toronto ON

London Spring Home & Garden Show, London Show Productions, 2326 Fanshawe Park Rd. East, London ON N5X 4A2 - 519-455-5888; Fax: 519-455-7780 - Consumer show - April, London ON

Lifestyle Fall Home Show, Jenkins Show Productions, 1076 Skyvalley Cres., Oakville ON L6M 3L2 - 905-827-4632; Fax: 905-827-8139; Tollfree: 1-800-465-1073; Email: djenkins2@cogeco.ca; URL: www.jenkinsshow.com - President, Dave Jenkins - Shows at shopping centres throughout Ontario in Feb., Mar., June, Oct., Nov.

Miramichi Lifestyles Show, Master Promotions Ltd., PO Box 565, Saint John NB E2L 3Z8 - 506-658-0018; Fax: 506-658-0750;

Tollfree: 1-888-454-7469; Email: info@mpltd.ca; URL: www.masterpromotions.ca - Annual consumer show - Show Manager, Brian McKeil, April - Miramichi Civic Centre, Miramichi NB

Moncton Kiwanis Lifestyles Show, Master Promotions Ltd., PO Box 565, Saint John NB E2L 3Z8 - 506-658- 0018; Fax: 506-658-0750; Tollfree: 1-888-454-7469; Email: info@masterpromotions.ca; URL: www.masterpromotions.ca - Annual consumer show - Show manager, Brian McKiel, April, Moncton NB

Montréal National Home Show, 180 Duncan Mills Rd., 4th Fl., Toronto ON M3B 1Z6 - 416-385-1880; Fax: 416-385-1855; Tollfree: 1-888-823- 7469; URL: www.salonnationalhabitation.com - Show Manager, Glen Chiasson

National Home Show, dmg World Media, 100 Princes' Blvd. Toronto, ON M6K 3C3 - 416-385- 1880; Fax: 416-385-1855; Tollfree: 1-888-823-7469; URL: www.nationalhomeshow.com - Show Manager, Glen Chiasson - Annual consumer show - April - Coliseum Bldg., Exhibition Place, Toronto ON

Niagara Lifestyle Home Show, Jenkins Show Productions, 1076 Skyvalley Cres., Oakville ON L6M 3L2 - 905-827-4632; Fax: 905-827-8139; Tollfree: 1-800-465- 1073; Email: djenkins2@cogeco.ca; URL: www.jenkinsshow.com - President, Dave Jenkins - Annual consumer show - April - Garden City/Rex Stimers Arena, St Catharines ON

Nova Scotia Fall Ideal Home Show, Master Promotions Ltd., PO Box 565, Saint John NB E2L 3Z8 - 506-658- 0018; Fax: 506-658-0750; Tollfree: 1-888-454-7469; Email: info@mpltd.ca; URL: www.masterpromotions.ca - Annual consumer show - Show Manager, Bev Campbell, Oct., Halifax NS

Nova Scotia Spring Ideal Home Show, Master Promotions Ltd., PO Box 565, Saint John NB E2L 3Z8 - 506-658- 0018; Fax: 506-658-0750; Tollfree: 1-888-454-7469; Email: info@mpltd.ca; URL: www.masterpromotions.ca - Annual consumer show - Show Manager, Bev Campbell, April, Halifax NS

Oakville Lifestyle Home Show, Jenkins Show Productions, 1076 Skyvalley Cres., Oakville ON L6M 3L2 - 905-827-4632; Fax: 905-827-8139; Tollfree: 1-800-465- 1073; Email: djenkins2@cogeco.ca; URL: www.jenkinsshow.com - President, Dave Jenkins - Annual consumer show - April - Glen Abbey Recreation Centre, Oakville ON

Ottawa Home & Garden Show, dmg World Media, 4899 Uplands Dr., Ottawa ON K1V 2N6 - 613-241-2888; Fax: 613-241-4827; Tollfree: 1-877-241-0007; URL: www.ottawahomeshows.com - Show Manager, Chantale Boisvert - Annual consumer show. March & Sept.

PEI Provincial Home Show, Master Promotions Ltd., PO Box 565, Saint John NB E2L 3Z8 - 506-658-0018; Fax: 506-658-0750; Tollfree: 1-888-454-7469; Email: info@mpltd.ca; URL: www.masterpromotions.ca - Annual consumer show - Show Manager, Brian McKeil, March, Charlottetown PE

Red Deer Home Ideas, Home Ideas & Lifestyles, #10, 7895 - 49 Ave., Red Deer AB T4P 2B4 - 403-346-5321; Fax: 403-342-1301; Email: admin@cahb.ca; URL: www.cahba.ca - Contact, Joan Butler - Annual, Feb./March

Showcase, Medicine Hat & District Chamber of Commerce, 413 - 6th Ave. SE, Medicine Hat AB T1A 2S7 - 403-527-5214; Fax: 403-527-5182; Email: mhchamber@monarch.net; URL: www.medicinehatchamber.com - President, Jason Mutschler, Executive Director, Mary Lou Hansen - Annual consumer show - Nov.

Success With Gardening, Showcase Marketing Ltd., #410, 1110 Sheppard Ave. East, Toronto ON M2K 2W2 - 416-512-1305; Email: homeshow@idirect.com; URL: www.home-show.net/successfulgardening - Paul Newdick - Annual consumer show - Mar. - International Centre, Toronto ON

Sudbury Spring Home Show, DAC Marketing Ltd., PO Box 2837, Stn A, Sudbury ON P3A 5J3 - 705-673-5588; Fax: 705-525-0626; Email: dac@vianet.on.ca; URL: www.dacshows.com, March, Sudbury ON

Vancouver Home & Interior Design Show, dmg World Media (Canada) Inc., #402, 4601 Canada Way, Burnaby BC V5G 4X7 - 604-433-5121; Fax: 604-434-6853; Tollfree: 1-800-633-8332; URL: www.vancouverhomeanddesignshow.com - Annual consumer show - Show Manager, Trish Almeida, Oct.

Western Canada Kitchen, Bath & Renovation Show, Manitoba Home Builders' Association, #1, 1420 Clarence Ave., Winnipeg MB R3T 1T6 - 204-925-2560; Fax: 204-925-2567; Email: mbhomebd@mb.sympatico. ca; URL: www.homebuilders.mb.ca - Show Manager, Danita Brisson - Annual consumer show

Windsor Home & Leisure Show, 20/20 Show Productions Inc., 136 Thames St., Chatham ON N7L 2Y8 - 519-351- 8344; Fax: 519-351-8345; Tollfree: 1-866-640-9663; Email: stuart@exposition.com; URL: www.windsorhomeshow.com - Stuart Galloway - Annual - Feb. - University of Windsor, Windsor ON

Yarmouth Lifestyles Show, Master Promotions Ltd., PO Box 565, Saint John NB E2L 3Z8 - 506-658-0018; Fax: 506-658-0750; Tollfree: 1-888-454-7469; Email: info@mpltd.ca; URL: www.masterpromotions.ca - Marketing & Operations Manager, Jennifer Allaby, President, Wendell Howes, April, Yarmouth NS

HORSES

The Masters Show Jumping Tournament, Spruce Meadows, RR#9, Calgary AB T2J 5G5 - 403-974-4200; Fax: 403-974-4270; Email: information@sprucemeadows.com; URL: www.sprucemeadows.com - Annual tournament. Includes consumer/trade show Equi-Fair, & the Festival of Nations - Sept.

North American Tournament, RR#9, Calgary AB T2J 5G5 - 403-974-4249; Fax: 403-947-4266; Email: jack.hugill@ sprucemeadows.com; URL: www.sprucemeadows.com - Coordinator, Sales, Jack Hugill - Annual. Showcased through Sun Life Financials at Fort Meadows - July

Royal Red Arabian Horse Show, PO Box 167, Regina SK S4P 2Z6 - 306-781-9200; Fax: 306-781-9396; Email: roconnor@reginaexhibition.com - Facility Contact, Rob O'Connor - Annual - Aug.

HORTICULTURE *See* FLOWERS

HOSPITALITY INDUSTRY (HOTEL, MOTEL, RESTAURANT)

***See Also* Food & Beverage**

ApEx, Canadian Restaurant & Foodservices Association, 316 Bloor St. West, Toronto ON M5S 1W5 - 416-923- 8416; Fax: 416-923-1450; Tollfree: 1-800-387-5649; Email: info@crfa.ca; URL: www.crfa.ca - President, Douglas C. Needham, Senior Exec. Vice-President, David Harris - Annual trade show - April

CRFA Show, Canadian Restaurant & Foodservices Association, 316 Bloor St. West, Toronto ON M5S 1W5 - 416-923- 8416; Fax: 416-923-1450; Tollfree: 1-800-387-5649; Email: info@crfa.ca; URL: www.crfa.ca - President, Douglas C. Needham, Senior Exec. Vice-President, David Harris - Annual trade show

Grocery Innovations Canada, Canadian Federation of Independent Grocers, #902, 2235 Sheppard Ave. East, Toronto ON M2J 5B5 - 416-492-2311; Fax: 416-492-2347; Tollfree: 1-800-661-2344; Email: info@cfig.ca; URL: www.cfig.ca - President, John F.T. Scott, Chair, Mike Coleman, Vice-President, Gary Sanos - Annual trade show - Oct.

INDUSTRIAL

Salon industriel de L'Estrie, Les Promotions André Pageau Inc., 1627, boul Bastien, Québec QC G2K 1H1 - 418-623-3383; Fax: 418-623-5033; Tollfree: 1-800-387- 3383; Email: info@promoapageau.com; URL: www.promoapageau.com - Pr,sident, Andr, Pageau, Sept., St-Hyacinthe QC

Salon Industriel de Québec, Les Promotions Andr, Pageau Inc., 1627, boul Bastien, Québec QC G2K 1H1 - 418-623-3383; Fax: 418-623-5033; Tollfree: 1-800-387- 3383; Email: info@promoapageau.com; URL: www.promoapageau.com - Président, André Pageau - Biennial trade show - Oct., Québec QC Salon Industriel du Saguenay/Lac-St-Jean, Les Promotions André Pageau Inc., 1627, boul Bastien, Québec QC G2K 1H1 - 418-623-3383; Fax: 418-623-5033; Tollfree: 1-800-387-3383; Email: info@promoapageau. com; URL: www.promoapageau.com - Président, André Pageau - Biennial - May, Chicoutimi QC

Weld Expo Canada, 650 Dixon Rd., Toronto ON M9W 1J1 - 416-491-7565; Fax: 416-491-5088 - John Lewinski - Biennial trade show - Oct.

Western Manufacturing Technology Show - Edmonton, Reed Exhibition Companies Inc., #1, 3761 Victoria Park Ave., Toronto ON M1W 3S2 - 416-491-7565; Fax: 416-491-5088; Email: canada@reedexpo.com; URL: www.reedexpo.com - John Lewinski - Biennial trade show - June, Edmonton AB

Western Manufacturing Technology Show - Vancouver, Reed Exhibition Companies Inc., #1, 3761 Victoria Park Ave., Toronto ON M1W 3S2 - 416-491-7565; Fax: 416-491-5088; Email: canada@reedexpo.com; URL: www.reedexpo.com - John Lewinski - Biennial trade show - June, Abbotsford BC

JEWELLERY *See* GIFTS

LANDSCAPING *See* FLOWERS

LEGAL

Canadian Association of Law Libraries, Events & Management Plus Inc., #310, 4 Cataraqui St., Kingston ON K7K 1Z7 - 613-531-9210; Fax: 613-531-0626; Tollfree: 1-866-560-3838; Email: office@ eventsmgt.com; URL: www.callacbd.ca - Owner, E. Hooper, May

LEISURE *See* SPORTS & RECREATION

MACHINERY & MANUFACTURING

***See Also* Industrial**

Atlantic Heavy Equipment Show, Master Promotions Ltd., PO Box 565, Saint John NB E2L 3Z8 - 506-658-0018; Fax: 506-658-0750; Tollfree: 1-888-454-7469; Email: info@mpltd.ca; URL: www.masterpromotions.ca - Biennial

Canadian Manufacturing Week, #1, 3761 Victoria Park Ave., Toronto ON M1W 3S2 - 416-491-7565; Fax: 416-491-5088; Email: canada@reedexpo.com; URL: www.reedexpo.com - John Lewinski - Biennial trade show - Sept., Mississauga ON

National Heavy Equipment Show, Master Promotions Ltd., PO Box 565, Saint John NB E2L 3Z8 - 506-658-0018; Fax: 506-658-0750; Tollfree: 1-888-454-7469; Email: info@mpltd.ca; URL: www.masterpromotions.ca - Biennial - Show Manager, Mark Cusack, March - International Centre, Toronto ON

Toronto ISA Show, dmg World Media, 180 Duncan Mills Rd., 4th Fl., Toronto ON M3B 1Z6 - 416-385-1880; Fax: 416-385-1855; Tollfree: 1-888-823-7469; URL: www.dmgworldmedia.com - Show Manager, Glen Chiasson

MAGAZINES

Magazines, Print World, #8, 1606 Sedlescomb Dr., Mississauga ON L4X 1M6 - 905-625-7070; Fax: 905-625- 4856; Tollfree: 1-800-331-7408 - Annual conference & trade show for publishing professionals - June, Toronto ON

MARKETING *See* ADVERTISING

MATERIALS HANDLING *See* LOGISTICS

MEDICAL

Canadian Congress of Neurological Sciences, Venue West Conference Services Ltd., #645, 375 Water St., Vancouver BC V6B 5C6 - 604-681-5226; Fax: 604-681- 2503; Email: congress@venuewest.com; URL: www.venuewest.com

COS Annual Meeting & Exhibition, Canadian Ophthalmological Society, #610, 1525 Carling Ave., Ottawa ON K1Z 8R9 - 613-729-6779; Fax: 613-729-7209; Email: cos@eyesite.ca; URL: www.eyesite.ca - Executive Director, Hubert Drouin, June

Mayfest, The Canadian Hearing Society, 271 Spadina Rd., Toronto ON M5R 2V3 - 416-928-2500; Fax: 416-928- 2506; Tollfree: 1-877-347-3427; Email: info@chs.ca; URL: www.chs.ca - Executive Assistant, Mary Lumgair, President/CEO, Kelly Duffin, Vice-President, Regional Operations, Maribeth Meijer, President, Access, Counselling & Training, Katherine Hum-Antonopoulus, Vice-President Finance/CFO, Fred Enzel, Director, Human Resources, Lisa Smecca, Director, Marketing Communications, Susan Main, Director, External Affairs & Employment Development, Gary Malkowski - Latest innovations & access for deaf, deafened & hard of hearing people - May, Toronto ON

MINING & MINERALS

CIM Conference & Exhibition, Canadian Institute of Mining, Metallurgy & Petroleum, #855, 3400, boul de Maisonneuve ouest, Montréal QC H3Z 3B8 - 514-939- 2710; Fax: 514-939-2714; Email: cim@cim.org; URL: www.cim.org - Executive Director, Jean Vavrek - Annual consumers show. Mining industry, equipment & services - April-May - Palais des congrSs de Montréal, Montréal QC

Mines & Minerals Symposia, Ministry of Northern Development & Mines, 933 Ramsey Lake Rd., 6th Fl., Sudbury ON P3E 6B5 - 705-670-5838; Fax: 705-670-5807; URL: www.mndm.gov.on.ca/mndm/mines/- Annual trade show & seminar in April (Northern Ontario) & Dec. (Toronto)

MOTORCYCLES *See* AUTOMOTIVE

MULTICULTURAL

Canada's National Ukrainian Festival, 1550 Main St. South, PO Box 368, Dauphin MB R7N 2V2 - 204-622-4600; Fax: 204-622-4606; Tollfree: 1-877-474-2683; Email:

cnuf@mymts.net; URL: www.cnuf.ca - Annual. Three days of song, dance, music, costume, cuisine, culture - Aug.

Celebration Multicultural Festival, Multicultural Association of Nova Scotia, 1113 Marginal Rd., Halifax NS B3H 4P7 - 902-423-6534; Fax: 902-422-0881; Email: admin@mans.ns.ca; URL: www.multifest.ca - Executive Director, Alexandra McCallum, President, Dr. Bridglal Pachai - Annual festival - June, Dartmouth NS

Le Festival de l'Escaouette, a/s Les Trois Pignons, CP 522, D'Escousse NS B0E 1K0 - 902-224-2612; Fax: 902-224-1579; Email: lestroispignons@ns.sympatico. ca; URL: www.lestroispignons.com - Assistant Manager, Daniel Aucoin - Annually. Acadian folklore, traditions, culture - Aug.

Foire Brayonne, CP 218, Edmundston NB E3V 3K8 - 506-739-6608; Fax: 506-739-9578; Email: info@ foirebrayonne.com; URL: www.foirebrayonne.com - July/Aug. Brayon heritage festival

Folkfest, #303, 506 - 25th St. East, Saskatoon SK S7K 4A7 - 306-931-0100; Fax: 306-665-3421; Email: info@ saskatoonfolkfest.com; URL: www.saskatoonfolkfest.ca- Coordinator, Deneen Gudjonson, Terri Rau - Annual. Three days. Twenty or more ethnic pavilions - Aug.

Folklorama - Canada's Cultural Celebration, 183 Kennedy St., 2nd Fl., Winnipeg MB R3C 1S6 - 204-982-6210; Fax: 204-943-1956; Tollfree: 1-800-665-0234; Email: folkarts@ folklorama.ca; URL: www.folklorama.ca - Executive Director, Ron Gauthier, Email: gauthierr@folklorama. ca - Annual. Fourteen days. More than forty ethnic pavilions - Aug.

Manitoba Highland Gathering, PO Box 59, Selkirk MB R1A 2B1 - 204-269-1304; Fax: 204-269-1304; Email: ccox@mts.net - Treasurer, John Cox - Annual - July

MOSAIC - Regina's Annual Festival of Cultures, Regina Multicultural Council, 2054 Broad St., Regina SK S4P 1Y3 - 306-757-5990; Fax: 306-352-1977; Email: rmc.pa@sasktel.net; URL: www.reginamulticulturalcouncil.ca/mosaic.htm - Executive Director, Vivian Molnar - Annual. First weekend in June. Twenty ethno-cultural pavilions

Vesna Festival, PO Box 1592, Saskatoon SK S7K 3R3 - 306-657-4412; Fax: 306-657-4410; Email: mail@vesnafestival.com; URL: www.vesnafestival.com - Annual Spring celebration. Two days of entertainment, dancing, cultural demonstrations & displays. The World's Largest Ukrainian Cabaret - May

MUSIC

Beaches International Jazz Festival, 1798 Queen St. East, Toronto ON M4L 1G8 - 416-698-2152; Fax: 416-698- 2064; Email: infobeachesjazz@rogers.com; URL: www.beachesjazz.com - Executive Producer, Lido Chilelli, July, Toronto ON

Big Valley Jamboree, 4238 -37th St., Camrose AB T4V 4L6 - 780-672-0224; Fax: 780-672-9530; Tollfree: 1-888-404-1234; Email: bvj@bigvalleyjamboree. com; URL: www.bigvalleyjamboree.com - Country music - Aug.

Brandon Folk Music & Arts Festival, PO Box 22091, Brandon MB R7A 6Y9 - 204-727-3928; Fax: 204-571- 9243; Email: info@brandonfolkfestival.com; URL: www.brandonfolkfestival.com - Music Director, Jody Weger - Annually, last weekend in July

Canada Dance Festival, Canada Dance Festival Society, PO Box 1376, Stn B, Ottawa ON K1P 5R4 - 613-947-7000, ext.576; Fax: 613-943-1399; Email: cdffdc@nac-cna.ca; URL: www.canadadance.ca - Artistic Producer, Brian H. Webb, Email: webb@shaw.ca, Chair, Myrna Barwin

Canadian Open Old Time Fiddler's Contest, Canadian Open Old Time Fiddle Championship, Sports Complex, c/o, PO Box 27, Shelburne ON L0N 1S0 - 519-925- 3551; Fax: 519-925-1105; Email: cindy.sabo@sympatico. ca; URL: www.shelburnefiddlecontest.on.ca/, Aug.

Dawson City Music Festival, PO Box 456, Dawson YT Y0B 1G0 - 867-993-5584; Fax: 867-993-5510; Email: info@dcmf.com; URL: www.dcmf.com - Producer, Dylan Griffith - Annually, second last weekend in July

Dockside Ceilidh, 89 King St., North Sydney NS B2A 2T3 - 902-794-3772; Fax: 902-539-7210; Email: 7batherson@ns.sympatico.ca - President, Northside Highland Dancers' Association, Kay Batherson, Secretary, Sheila Hall, Treasurer, Jeannie Niesten - Daily, July-Sept. Cultural music & entertainment at Marine Atlantic Ferry Terminal

Downtown Oakville Jazz Festival,Downtown Oakville BIA, 146 Lakeshore Rd. East, Oakville ON L6J 1H4 - 905-844-4520; Fax: 905-844-1154; Email: production@oakvilledowntown.com; URL: www.oakvillejazz.com, Aug., Oakville ON

Edgefest, Edge 102, #1600, 1 Dundas St. West, Toronto ON M5T 1Z3 - 416-408-3343; Fax: 416-408-3300; URL: www.edge.ca/edgefest, July

Elora Festival & Singers, 33 Henderson St., 33 Henderson St., Elora ON N0B 1S0 - 519-846-0331; Fax: 519-846-5947; Tollfree: 1-800-265-8977; Email: info@elorafestival. com; URL: www.elorafestival.com - Artistic Director, Noel Edison - July - Aug. Choral & contemporary Canadian & international music

Enbridge Symphony Under the Sky, Edmonton Symphony Orchestra, 99 St., Edmonton AB T5J 4B2 - 780-428-1108; Fax: 780-425-0167; Tollfree: 1-800- 563-5081; Email: box.office@winspearcentre.com; URL: www.edmonton symphony.com - Managing Director, Elaine Calder, Music Director, Bill Eddins - Aug.-Sept.

Festival de Lanaudière, 1500, boul Base-de-Roc, Joliette QC J6E 3Z1 - 450-759-7636; Fax: 450-759-3082; Email: festival@lanaudiere.org; URL: www.lanaudiere.org - Annually June-Aug.; biggest mostly classical festival in Canada

Festival International de Jazz de Montréal, 305, rue Ste-Catherine oust, Montréal QC H2X 2A3 - 514-523-3378; Fax: 514-525-8033; Tollfree: 1-888-515-0515; URL: www.montrealjazzfest.com - Senior Director, Communications & Advertising, Nathalie Carriere - Annual. Over 2,000 musicians & 450 shows - July, Montréal QC

Festival International de Musique Actuelle de Victoriaville, CP 460, 82, rue Notre-Dame est, Victoriaville QC G6P 6T3 - 819-752-7912; Fax: 819-758-4370; Email: info@ fimav.qc.ca; URL: www.fimav.qc.ca - 25 concerts in 5 days, musicians from 12 different countries - May

Le Festival International du Domaine Forget, Le Festival International de Domaine Forget, 5, rang Saint-Antoine, Saint-Irénée QC G0T 1V0 - 418-452-8111; Fax: 418-452-3503; Tollfree: 1-888-336-7438; Email: info@domaineforget.com; URL: www.domaineforget.com - June-Aug.

Festival International Nuits d'Afrique de Montréal, 4374, boul St-Laurent, 1 étage, Montréal QC H2W 1Z5 - 514-499-9239, 9520; Fax: 514-499-9215; Email: info@festivalnuitsdafrique. com; URL: www.festivalnuitsdafrique.com, juil.

Festival of the Sound - 705-746-2410; Fax: 705-746- 5639; Tollfree: 1-866-364-0061; Email: info@festivalofthesound. on.ca; URL: www.festivalofthesound.on.ca - July-Aug.

FFIDA Fringe Festival of Independent Dance Artists, FFIDA - 416-214-5854; Email: info@ffida.org; URL: www.ffida.org - Artistic Director, Michael Menegon

Folk on the Rocks, PO Box 326, Yellowknife NT X1A 2N3 - 867-920-7806; Fax: 867-873-6535; Email: info@ folkonthe rocks.com; URL: www.folkontherocks.com - Annual. Two days. Inuit, Dene, other northern & southern folk groups - July

Guelph Jazz Festival, 123 Woolwich St., 2nd Fl., Guelph ON N1H 3V1 - 519-763-4952; Fax: 519-763-3155; Email: info@guelphjazzfestival.com; URL: www.guelphjazz festival.com, Sept., Guelph ON

Halifax Jazz Festival, PO Box 33043, Halifax NS B3L 4T6 - 902-492-2225; Fax: 902-425-7946; Tollfree: 1-800- 567-5277; Email: info@jazzeast.com; URL: www.jazzeast.com - Manager, Operations, Geoff Barnes - July

Harvest Jazz & Blues Festival, 81 Regent St., Fredericton NB E3B 3W3 - 506-454-2583; Fax: 506-457-1815; Tollfree: 1-888-622-5837; Email: info@harvestjazzandblues. com; URL: www.harvestjazzandblues.com, Sept.

International Festival of Baroque Music, International Baroque Music Festival, #2, 28, rue de l'H"pital, Lameque NB E8T 1C3 - 506-344-5846; Fax: 506-344-5741; Tollfree: 1-800-320-2276; Email: baroque@ nbnet.nb.ca; URL: www.festivalbaroque.com - Executive Director, Claire Guimond - Early music festival with five productions, last week of July (Northeastern New Brunswick, on Lameque Island)

JazzFest International, Victoria Jazz Society, #250, 727 Johnson St., PO Box 8542, Victoria BC V8W 3S2 - 250-388-4423; Fax: 250-388-4407; Tollfree: 1-888-671- 2112; Email: vicjazz@pacificcoast.net; URL: jazzvictoria.ca/jazz-fest

Kinsmen International Band & Choral Festival, Moose Jaw Kinsmen Club, PO Box 883, Moose Jaw SK S6H 4P5 - 306-692-1291; Fax: 306-692-2091; Email: bl.mcdonald@ sasktel.net; URL: www.mjkinsmenfestival.com - Bill McDonald - 3,000 musicians, evening concerts. Annual - May, Moose Jaw SK

Kiwanis Music Festival of Greater Toronto, #A, 1422 Bayview Ave. Toronto, ON M4G 3A7 - 416-487-5885; Fax: 416-487-5784; Email: kiwanismusic@bellnet.ca; URL: kiwanismusictoronto.org - Festival Coordinator, Pam Allen, General Manager, Pam Allen, Feb., Toronto ON

L'OFF Festival de Jazz, L'OFF Festival de Jazz de Montréal, 5101, rue St-Denis, CP 60150, Montréal QC H2J 4E1 - 514-524-0831; Email: info@lofffestivaldejazz. com; URL: www.lofffestivaldejazz.com

Mariposa Folk Festival, Mariposa Folk Foundation, PO Box 383, Orillia ON L3V 6J8 - 705-329-2333; Fax: 705-329-4099; Email: info@mariposafolk. com; URL: www.mariposafolkfestival.com - President, Chris Lusty

Maritime Fiddle Fest, Maritime Fiddle Festival, #600, 73 Tacoma Dr., Dartmouth NS B2W 4Y3 - 902-434- 5466; Fax: 902-434-5466; Email: info@maritimefiddlefestival.ca; URL: maritimefiddlefestival.ca - Hon. Chair, James Delaney, Co-Chair, Betty Ann Chennell, 902-835-5988, Co-Chair, Doug Morash, 902-435-4168, Email: rdouglas@ns.sympatico.ca, July

Markham Jazz Festival, #281, 4261 A-145, Hwy.#7, Unionville ON L3R 9W6 - 905-471-5299; Fax: 905-471- 7764; Email: contactus@markhamjazzfestival.com; URL: www.markhamjazzfestival.com, Aug., Markham ON

Miramichi Folk Song Festival, PO Box 13, Miramichi NB E1V 3M2 - 506-623-2150; Fax: 506-623-2261; Email: bb2@nb.sympatico.ca; URL: www.miramichifolksongfestival.com/- Susan Butler - Aug.

Newfoundland & Labrador Folk Festival, #204, 223 Duckworth St. St. John's, NL A1C 6N1 - 709-576-8508; Fax: 709-757-8500; Tollfree: 1-866-576-8508; Email: office@nlfolk.com; URL: www.nlfolk.com - Contact, Erin McArthur - Traditional Newfoundland & Labrador music & dance - Aug.

Northern Lights Festival Boréal, Northern Lights Festival Boréal, #3, 19 Grey St., Sudbury ON P3E 3L2 - 705-674- 5512; Fax: 705-222-9574; URL: www.nlfbsudbury.com - July

Nova Scotia Bluegrass Oldtime Music Festival, Annual Nova Scotia Bluegrass/Oldtime Music Festival, 1455 Hwy. 2, Lantz NS B2S 2A2 - 902-883-7189; Email: jerry@rushcomm.ca - Correspondent, Jerry Murphy - Annually, last weekend in July

Nova Scotia Kiwanis Music Festival, 107, 5657 Spring Garden Rd., Halifax NS B3J 3R4 - 902-423-6147; Fax: 902-423-8668; URL: www.hfxmusicfest.com - Executive Director, Nancy Keating, Chair, Art Hood - Adjudicated music festival & closing concert - Feb., Halifax NS

Old Time Fiddle & Step Dancing Championships, PO Box 1329, Deep River ON K0J 1P0 - 613-584-3962 - Labour Day weekend, annually

Orford Festival, 3165, ch. du Parc Orford, Orford QC J1X 7A2 - 819-843-9871; Fax: 819-843-7274; Tollfree: 1-800-567-6155; Email: centre@arts-orford. org; URL: www.arts-orford.org - June-Aug. Ottawa Bluesfest,

Ottawa BluesFest, 265 Catherine St., Ottawa ON K1R 7S5 - 613-247-1188; Fax: 613-247-2220; Tollfree: 1-866-258-3748; URL: ottawabluesfest.ca - Executive Director, Mark Monahan - Annual blues music & gospel festival - July

Ottawa Folk Festival, 265 Catherine St., 2nd Fl., Ottawa ON K1R 7S5 - 613-230-8234; Fax: 613-230-7887; Email: festival@ottawafolk.ca; URL: www.ottawafolk.ca, Aug.

Ottawa International Chamber Music Festival, Ottawa Chamber Music Society, #201, 4 Florence St., Ottawa ON K1N 1A3 - 613-234-8008; Fax: 613-234-7692; Email: info@chamberfest. com; URL: www.chamberfest.com, July-Aug.

Ottawa Jazz Festival, #602, 294 Albert St., Ottawa ON K1P 6E6 - 613-241-2633; Fax: 613-241-5774; Email: info@ottawajazzfestival.com; URL: www.ottawajazzfestival.com - Manager, Programming, Jacques Emond - June-July

Regina Folk Festival, #101, 1855 Scarth St., PO Box 1203, Regina SK S4P 3B4 - 306-757-0308; Fax: 306-757- 7688; Email: info@reginafolkfestival.com; URL: www.reginafolk festival.com - Artistic Director, Sandra Butel - Annual three day folk-based music festival - Aug.

Scotia Festival of Music, 6181 Lady Hammond Rd., Halifax NS B3K 2R9 - 902-429-9467; Fax: 902-425-6785; Email: admin@scotiafestival.ns.ca; URL: www.scotiafestival.ns.ca - Contact, Christopher Wilcox - Annually, May. Chamber music

Stan Rogers Folk Festival, PO Box 46, Canso NS B0H 1H0 - 902-366-2475; Fax: 902-366-2978; Tollfree: 1-888- 554-7826; Email: queries@stanfest.com; URL: www.stanfest.com - Artistic Director, Troy Greencorn

Summerfolk Music & Crafts Festival, Georgian Bay Folk Society, PO Box 521, Owen Sound ON N4K 5R1 - 519-371-2995; Fax: 519-371-2973; Email: gbfs@bmts.com; URL: www.summerfolk.org - President, David McLeish

TD Toronto Jazz Festival, Toronto Downtown Jazz, 82 Bleecker St., Toronto ON M4X 1L8 - 416-928- 2033; Fax: 416-928-0533; URL: www.torontojazz.com - Artistic Director, Josh Grossman

TD Vancouver International Jazz Festival, Vancouver International Jazz Festival/Coastal Jazz & Blues Society, 295 West, 7th Ave. 2nd Fl., Vancouver BC V5Y 1L9 - 604-872-5200; Fax: 604-872-5250; Tollfree: 1-888-438-5200; Email: cjbs@coastaljazz.ca; URL: www.coastaljazz.ca - Executive

Director, Robert Kerr, Artistic Director, Ken Pickering - June-July
Vancouver Chamber Music Festival, Vancouver Recital Society, #304, 873 Beatty St., Vancouver BC V6B 2M6 - 604-602-0363; Fax: 604-602-0364; URL: www.vanrecital.com - Artistic Director, Leila Getz, July
Vancouver Folk Music Festival, #1114, 207 West Hastings St., Vancouver BC V6B 1H7 - 604-602-9798; Fax: 604-602-9790; Tollfree: 1-800-883-3655; Email: info@ thefestival.bc.ca; URL: www.thefestival.bc.ca - Artistic Director, Dugg Simpson - Annual festival - July, Vancouver BC
Vancouver Island Music Fest, PO Box 338, Courtenay BC V9N 7P2 - 250-336-7981; Email: dougcox@shaw.ca; URL: www.islandmusicfest.com - Artistic Director, Doug Cox, July
Winnipeg Folk Festival, #203, 211 Bannatyne Ave., Winnipeg MB R3B 3P2 - 204-231-0096; Fax: 204-231- 0076; Email: info@winnipegfolkfestival.ca; URL: www.winnipegfolkfestival.ca - Annually, July
Winnipeg Jazz Festival, #007, 100 Arthur St., Winnipeg MB R3B 1H3 - 204-989-1656; URL: www.jazzwinnipeg.com, June

OKTOBERFESTS *See* EVENTS

PACKAGING

Pacex International, Packaging Association of Canada, #E330, 2255 Sheppard Ave. East, Toronto ON M2J 4Y1 - 416-490-7860; Fax: 416-490-7844; Email: info@ pac.ca; URL: www.pac.ca - President/CEO, Alan M. Robinson, Chair, Sylvia MacVey - Biennial trade show - May - National Trade Centre, Exhibition Place, Toronto ON

PARENTS *See* CHILDREN

PETROLEUM

Atlantic Canada Petroleum Show, dmg events, #302, 1333 – 8 St., Calgary AB T2R 1M6 - 403-209-3555; Fax: 403-245-8649; Tollfree: 1-888- 799-2545; URL: atlanticcanadapetroleumshow.com - Pat Atkinson
Go-Expo Show, #605, 999 - 8 St. SW, Calgary AB T2R 1N7 - 403-209-3555; Fax: 403-245- 8649; Tollfree: 1-888-799-2545; URL: www.gasandoilexpo.com - Pat Atkinson - Biennial trade show. Petroleum & natural gas products, services & technology; exploration, production, transmission, processing, marketing

PETS

PetExpo Calgary, Canwest Shows Inc., #218, 7710 – 5 St. SE, Calgary AB T2H 2L9 - 403-242-0859; Fax: 403-246-3856; Email: info@canwestshows.com; URL: www.canwestshows.com - General Manager, Terra Connors - Annual consumer trade show - Sept. - Stampede Park, Calgary AB
Vancouver PetExpo, Canwest Shows Inc., 7 Panorama Bay SW, Calgary AB T3Z 3L6 - 403-686-9699; Fax: 403-246-3856; Email: info@canwestshows.com; URL: www.canwestshows.com - General Manager, Terra Connors - Annual consumer trade show - March - Vancouver Convention & Exhibition Centre, Vancouver BC

PLASTICS & RUBBER

Expoplast, Canadian Plastics Industry Association, #125, 5955 Airport Rd., Mississauga ON L4V 1R9 - 905-678- 7748; Fax: 905-678-0774; Email: national@cpia.ca; URL: www.plastics.ca - President & CEO, Serge Lavoie, Show Director, Sally Damstra - Triennial international trade show: plastics machinery, raw materials suppliers, mold makers, processors, fabricators, auxiliary equipment
Plast-Ex, Canadian Plastics Industry Association, #712, 5915 Airport Rd., Mississauga ON L4V 1T1 - 905-678- 7748; Fax: 905-678-0774; Email: national@cpia.ca; URL: www.canontradeshows.com - Triennial international trade show: plastics machinery, raw materials suppliers, mold makers, processors, fabricators, auxiliary equipment - Show Director: Sally Damstra, May - International Centre, Toronto ON

PSYCHIC PHENOMENA

ESP Psychic Expo, Impact Event Management, 358 Danforth Ave., PO Box 65060, Toronto ON M4K 3Z2 - 416-461-5306; Fax: 416-461-8460; Email: impactevent@ sympatico.ca - Donald Nausbaum - Annual consumer show. Psychics, astrologers, natural healing, crystals, books, tapes, computers - Feb. - International Centre, Toronto ON
Toronto Psychic Expo, Impact Event Management, 358 Danforth Ave., PO Box 65060, Toronto ON M4K 3Z2 - 416-461-5306; Fax: 416-461-8460; Email: impactevent@sympatico.ca - Donald Nausbaum - Consumer show. Psychics, astrologers, tarot card readers, holistic health, computers - Oct. - Exhibition Place, Toronto ON

REAL ESTATE

Leadership Summit, National Association of Realtors, Minto Place, The Canada Bldg., #1600, 344 Slater St., Ottawa ON K1R 7Y3 - 613-237-7111; Fax: 613-234-2567; Tollfree: 1-800-842-2732; Email: info@ crea.ca; URL: www.realtor.org - Annual trade show - Coordinator, Sherry Watson, March
Property Management Today, Master Promotions Ltd., PO Box 565, Saint John NB E2L 3Z8 - 506-658-0018; Fax: 506-658-0750; Tollfree: 1-888-454-7469; Email: info@mpltd.ca; URL: www.masterpromotions.ca - Annual trade show - Show Manager, Brian McKiel, Oct. - Trade & Convention Centre, Saint John NB

RECREATIONAL VEHICLES *See* AUTOMOTIVE

RODEOS

***See Also* Exhibitions, Farm Business/Agriculture**

Calgary Exhibition & Stampede, PO Box 1060, Stn M, Calgary AB T2P 2K8 - 403-261-0101; Fax: 403-265-7197; Tollfree: 1-800-661-1260; URL: www.calgarystampede.com - COO, Vern Kimball, Senior Manager, Corporate Communications, Lindsey Galloway - Annual city-wide festival; agricultural exhibits
CCA Finals Rodeo, RR#4, Site 412, PO Box 1027, Saskatoon SK S7K 3J8 - 306-931-2700; Fax: 306-931-4480; Email: canadiancowboy@yourlink.ca; URL: www.canadiancowboys.sk.ca - Office Coordinator, Charlene Symington - Annually, Oct. Four days
Williams Lake Stampede, Williams Lake Stampede Association, PO Box 4076, Williams Lake BC V2G 2V2 - 250-392-6585; Fax: 250-398-7701; Tollfree: 1-800- 717-6336; Email: info@williamslakestampede.com; URL: www.williamslakestampede.com - President, Bob Breitkreutz, July

RVS *See* AUTOMOTIVE; SPORTS & RECREATION

SEWING *See* CRAFTS

SEX

The Everything to Do with Sex Show, SX Marketing Inc., #203, 2700 Steeles Ave. West, Concord ON L4K 3C8 - 905-738-8884; Fax: 905-738-7848; URL: everythingtodowithsex.com - General Manager, Terra Connors

SPORTS & RECREATION

***See Also* Boating; Automotive, for combined auto/RV shows**

24 Hours of Adrenalin, #4, 160 Gibson Dr., Markham ON L3R 1K1 - 416-640-0824; Fax: 416-640-0825; Email: info@twenty4sports.com; URL: www.24hoursofadrenalin.com - Team & solo mountain biking events that take place in Alberta, Ontario & BC in June, July & Aug.
Atlantic Outdoor Sports & RV Show, 2047 Langille Dr., Coldbrook NS B4R 1C3 - 902-679-7177; Fax: 902-678-4436; Email: info@darwineventgroup.com; URL: www.sportsandrvshow.com - Manager, Darrelyn Hubley - Annual consumer show. Trailer & motor homes, 4x4s, tent trailers, boats, motors, hunting, fishing & camping, tourism & sporting goods - March, Halifax NS
Bicycle Fall Blowout Sale, #1801, One Yonge St., Toronto ON M5E 1W7 - 416-363-1292; Fax: 416-369-0515; Email: josie@telsec.net; URL: www.bicycleshowtoronto.com - Marketing & Sales Manager, Josie Graziosi - Annual; fall - Oct., Toronto ON
Canadian Power Toboggan Championship, PO Box 22, Beausejour MB R0E 0C0 - 204-268-2049; Fax: 204-268-4209; URL: www.cptcracing.com/- Annual - March
Country Living Show, Square Feet Northwest Event Management Inc., PO Box 82550, Stn N, Burnaby BC V5C 5Z1 - 604-683-4766; Fax: 604-688-0270; Tollfree: 1-877-888-7111; Email: mgmt@sqftevent.com; URL: www.countryliving.com - Blaine Woit - Annual consumer show - March - Tradex, Abbotsford BC
Ironman Canada Triathlon Championship, 416 Westminster Ave. West, Penticton BC V2A 1K5 - 250-490-8787; Fax: 250-490-8788; Email: ironman@vip.net; URL: www.ironman.ca - Race Director, Dave Bullock - Annual four-day trade expo staged as part of the events prior to the Ironman race - Aug.
London Boat, Fishing & Leisure Show, Western Fair Association, 2104 Garrison Gate, Sarnia ON N7H 1H7 - 519-438-7203; Fax: 519-679-3124; Tollfree: 1-800-619- 4629; Email: don.chamberlain@cogeco.ca; URL: www.boatcottagefishingshow.com - General Manager, Gary McRae - Annual consumer show
Motorhead Snowmobile, Watercraft & ATV Show, Marketer Shows Inc., #4, 1195 Stellar Dr., Newmarket ON L3Y 7B8 - 905-898-8585; Fax: 905-898-8071; Tollfree: 1-888-661-7469; Email: rkehoe@bellnet.ca - Richard Kehoe - Annual consumer show - March - Toronto International Centre, Toronto ON
National Outfitter's Hunting & Fishing Show, Mobilvision Inc., 9200, boul Henri-Bourassa ouest, Montréal QC H4S 1L5 - 514-334-7277; Fax: 514-334-1180; Tollfree: 1-800-668-3976; Email: mobilvision@pourvoirie. net; URL: www.pourvoirie.net - Président, Jacques Forest, Feb. - Montréal Congress Centre
Salon Camping, Plein Air, Chasse et Pêche de Montréal/Montréal Sportsmen's Show, Canadian National Sportsmen's Shows (1989) Ltd., #222, 980, St-Antoine ouest, Montréal QC H3C 1A8 - 514-866-5409; Fax: 514-866-4092; URL: www.sportshows.ca - Regional Manager, Francine St-Laurent - Annual consumer show: camping, fishing, hunting, RVs, tourism
Supertrax International Snowmobilers Show, Marketer Shows Inc., 78 Main St. South, Newmarket ON L3Y 3Y6 - 905-898-8585; Fax: 905-898-8071; Tollfree: 1-888-661-7469; Email: rkehoe@bellnet.ca; URL: www.supertraxmag.com - Richard Kehoe - Annual consumer show - Oct. - Toronto International Centre, Toronto ON
Toronto Ski & Snowboard Show, Canadian National Sportsmen's Shows (1989) Ltd., 30 Village Centre Pl., Mississauga ON L4Z 1V9 - 905-361-2677; Fax: 905-361-2679; URL: www.torontoskishow.ca - Annual consumer show - Show Manager, Harley Austin, Oct. - National Trade Centre, Exhibition Place, Toronto ON
Toronto Sportsmen's Show, Canadian National Sportsmen's Shows (1989) Ltd., 30 Village Centre Pl., Mississauga ON L4Z 1V9 - 905-361-2677; Fax: 905-361-2679; URL: www.torontosportshow.ca - Annual consumer show - Show Manager, Harley Austin, March - National Trade Centre, Exhibition Place, Toronto ON
The Toronto Golf & Travel Show, Premier Consumer Shows, #4, 447 Speers Rd., Oakville ON L6K 3S7 - 905-842-6591; Fax: 905-842-6843; Tollfree: 1-800-693-7986; URL: www.torontogolfshow.com - Show Manager, Jane Hills - Annual consumer show - March

STAMPEDES *See* RODEOS

THEATRE *See* ARTS

TOYS & GAMES

The Toronto Christmas Train Show, Toronto Show Promotions, PO Box 217, Grimsby ON L3M 4G3 - 905-945- 2775; Fax: 905-945-0197; Email: info@antiquetoys.ca; URL: www.antiquetoys.ca - Doug Jarvis - Annual; operating train layouts, memorabilia - Nov., Mississauga ON

TRANSPORTATION

***See Also* Automotive**

Annual Convention & Trade Show, Ontario School Bus Association, #304, 1 Eva Rd., Toronto ON M9C 4Z5 - 416-695-9965; Fax: 416-695-9977; Email: info@ osba.on.ca; URL: www.osba.on.ca - Coordinator of Communications, Jackie Laurie, Executive Director, Richard Donaldson - Annual conference & trade show. Safety, fuel economy, buses & accessories, computers

TRAVEL & TOURISM

Canadian Meetings & Incentive Travel Symposium & Trade Show, 1 Mount Pleasant Rd., Toronto ON M4Y 2Y5 - 416-764-1635; Fax: 416-764-1419; URL: www.meetingscanada.com - Annual trade show & conference - Aug.
The Travel & Vacation Show, 255 Clemow Ave., Ottawa ON K1S 2B5 - 613-567-6408; Fax: 613-567-2718; Email: rplayer@sympatico. ca; URL: www.travelandvacationshows.ca - Show Organizer, Halina Player - Annual consumer & trade show - May - Lansdowne Park, Ottawa ON

TRUCKS *See* AUTOMOTIVE

TVS, STEREOS *See* ELECTRICAL/ELECTRONICS

VIDEO *See* COMMUNICATIONS

WINTER CARNIVALS

Banff/Lake Louise Winter Festival, PO Box 1298, Banff AB T0L 0C0 - 403-762-8421; Fax: 403-762-8163; Email: info@banfflakelouise.com; URL: www.banfflakelouise.com, Feb.

Carnaval de Québec M. Christie/Mr. Christie's Québec Winter Carnival, Carnaval de Québec, 205, boul des Cèdres, Québec QC G1L 1N8 - 418-626-3716; Fax: 418-626- 7252; Tollfree: 1-866-422-7628; Email: comm@carnaval. qc.ca; URL: www.carnaval.qc.ca - Directeur général, Jean Pelletier, Directeur du marketing et des communications, Annick Marchand - 17 days, major winter event

Carnaval-Souvenir de Chicoutimi, 49, rue Lafontaine, CP 567, Chicoutimi QC G7H 5C8 - 418-543-4438; Fax: 418-543-4884; Tollfree: 1-877-543-4439; Email: info@carnavalsouvenir.qc.ca; URL: www.cslaval.qc.ca - Ten days, major winter event - Feb.

Charlottetown Winter Carnival, PO Box 98, Charlottetown PE C1A 7K2 - 902-892-5708, Feb.

Conception Bay South Winterfest, Conception Bay South NL - 709-834-6534, 834-6548, 682-0453; Fax: 709-834-8337, Feb.

Corner Brook Winter Carnival, PO Box 886, Corner Brook NL A2H 6H6 - 709-632-5343; Fax: 709-632-5344; Email: cbwc@nf.aibn.com; URL: www.cornerbrookwinercarnival.ca - General Manager, Shirley M. Brake - Annually, 10 days - Feb.

Elliot Lake Winterfest, Lester B. Pearson Civic Centre, Hwy.#108, Elliot Lake ON P5A 2T1 - 705-848-2084; Fax: 705-848-7121 - Donna Hennessy, Feb.

Fête des Neiges, Parc Jean-Drapeau, 1, circuit Gilles-Villeneuve, Montréal QC H3C 1A9 - 514-872-6120; Fax: 514-872-6779; Email: webmaster@fetedesneiges. com; URL: www.parcjeandrapeau.com - Marcel Caron - 6 day major winter event. Sports, cultural, ice sculptures - Jan.

Hamilton Winterfest, Culture & Recreation Division, Public Health & Community Services, #305, 77 James St. North, Hamilton ON L8R 2K3 - 905-546-2424, ext.2747; Fax: 905-546-2338; URL: hamiltonwinterfest.ca - Special Events Coordinator, Jim Moore, Feb.

Jasper in January, PO Box 98, Jasper AB T0E 1E0 - 780-852-3858; Fax: 780-852-4932; URL: www.jasperinjanuary.com, Jan.

Kapuskasing Winter Carnival, 88 Riverside Dr., Kapuskasing ON P5N 1B3 - 705-335-2341; URL: kapuskasing.com - Feb. & March

Kirkland Lake Winter Carnival, Kirkland Lake Festivals Committee, PO Box 277, Kirkland Lake ON P2N 3H7, March

Mount Pearl Frosty Festival, PO Box 898, Mount Pearl NL A1N 3C8 - 709-748-1008; Fax: 709-748-1150; Email: smoothsaleing@nl.rogers.com; URL: www.frostyfestival.ca - Contact, Karen Bowering, Feb.

Prince Albert Winter Festival, 1211 - 1 Ave. West, Prince Albert SK S6V 4T8 - 306-764-7595; Fax: 306-763- 3311; Email: pa.winterfestival@sasktel.net; URL: www.panow.com - Jane Smith, Feb.

Riverview Winter Carnival, 30 Honour House Court, Riverview NB E1B 3Y9 - 506-387-2028; Fax: 506-387- 7455 - Gina McNeil, Feb.

Vernon Winter Carnival, 3401 - 35th Ave., Vernon BC V1T 2T5 - 250-545-2236; Fax: 250-545-0006; Email: carnival@junction.net; URL: www.vernonwintercarnival.com - Chairman, Donna Hall, Feb.

Winterlude, #202, 40 Elgin St., Ottawa ON K1P 1C7 - 613-239-5555; Fax: 613-239-5063; Tollfree: 1-800-704- 8227; Email: info@ncc-ccn.ca; URL: www.canadascapital.gc.ca - Sr. Program Manager, Thérèse St-Onge, 613-239-5278 - Major winter festival, first three weekends of February. Skating on Rideau Canal, international ice & snow sculpture competitions, musical & figure skating shows, North America's largest winter playground for kids, various sporting & social events, fireworks, stage performances & buskers - Feb.

Winterlude, PO Box 439, Grand Falls-Windsor NL A2A 2J8 - 709-489-0450; Fax: 709-489-0454; URL: www.grandfallswindsor.com/centennial/events - Contact, Dave Nichols, Feb.

WOMEN

Calgary Woman's Show, The Calgary Woman's Show Ltd., #224, 1982 Kensington Rd. NW, Calgary AB T2N 3R5 - 403-270-7274; Fax: 403-270-3037; Email: calgary.woman.show@home.com; URL: www.calgarywomansshow.com - President, Judy Markle - Semi-annual consumer show in April & Oct.; Products & services.

Women's Conferences, PO Box 25125, London ON N6C 6A9 - 519-668-5677; Fax: 519-668-6883; Email: dianvail@execulink.com - Contact, Diann Vail - Bi-annual conference, spring & fall for business professional & corporate women

World of Women, #37471 Hwy. 2 South, Red Deer, AB T4E 1B3 - 403-887-0111; Fax: 403-887-0133; Email: ptkennedy@shaw.ca; URL: www.worldofwomenshow.com - Event Marketing, Sherall Kennedy, Sept.

WOOD/WOODWORKING

Chatham Woodworking Show, Cryderman Productions Inc., 136 Thames St., Chatham ON N7L 2Y8 - 519-351- 8344; Fax: 519-351-8345; Tollfree: 1-866-640-9663; Email: john@crydermanproductions.com; URL: www.crydermanproductions.com - John Cryderman - Annual - Jan. - Kinsmen Auditorium

Salon Industriel du Bois Ouvre, #1, 3761 Victoria Park Ave., Toronto ON M1W 3S2 - 416-491-7565; Fax: 416-491-5088; Email: canada@reed expo.com; URL: www.sibo.ca - John Lewinski - Biennial trade show - Sept., Montréal QC

Woodworking Show, 7 Panorama Bay SW, Calgary AB T3Z 3L6 - 403-686-9699; Fax: 403-246-3856; Email: info@canwestshows.com; URL: thewoodworkingshows.com - General Manager, Terra Connors - Annual consumer show - Oct.

Awards & Honours

Canadian Awards

(Including Scholarships, Grants, Bursaries)

Awards are listed under the following categories:

ADVERTISING & PUBLIC RELATIONS

The Advertising & Design Club of Canada

#318, 160 Pears Ave., Toronto ON M5R 3P8
416-423-4113; Fax: 416-423-3362
Email: info@theadcc.ca; URL: www.theadcc.ca

The Advertising & Design Club of Canada Awards
Main categories of awards are: Advertising Print, Advertising Broadcast, Advertising Multiple Media, Graphic Design, Editorial Design & Interactive Design; winners receive gold, silver or merit awards

Canadian Marketing Association / Association canadienne du marketing

#607, One Concorde Gate, Toronto ON M3C 3N6
416-391-2362; Fax: 416-441-4062
Email: info@the-cma.org; URL: www.the-cma.org

CMA Awards
Celebrating the art and science of marketing, CMA has restructured its judging breakdown to 40%-Results, 40%-Creative, 20%-Production. Entries can be submitted under type of business, type of program or specialty, representing particularly innovative solutions. CMA also offers Student Awards to post secondary students enrolled in direct marketing, marketing or business programs.

Institute of Communication Agencies & Advertising / Institut des communications et de la publicité

#500, 2300 Yonge St., Toronto ON M4P 1E4
416-764-1608; Fax: 416-482-1856
Email: ica@ica-ad.com; URL: icacanada.ca

CASSIES Awards
Established 1993; CASSIES (Canadian Advertising Success Stories) are open to all channels of marketing communications. Eligible submissions must show impressive business results and convincingly prove results were a result of the advertising.

Marketing Magazine

1 Mount Pleasant Rd., 7th floor Toronto ON M4Y 2Y5
416-764-2000; Fax: 416-764-1519
URL: www.marketingmag.ca

The Marketing Awards
Annual advertising awards offering 40 Gold Awards in the following categories: social media, branded content, experiential & event marketing, television/cinema, radio, magazine, newspaper, transit, business press, direct mail, outdoor, point-of-purchase/interior store design, multimedia campaign, non-traditional & public service. Silver Awards, Bronze Awards, & Certificates of Excellence are also awarded. Entries must have run in the previous year & must have been conceived & created by people working in English in the Canadian advertising business

Publicité Club de Montréal

#200, 4316, boulevard St.-Laurent, Montréal QC H2W 1Z3
514-499-1391; Fax: 514-842-4886
Email: info@amm-pcm.ca; URL: www.pcm.qc.ca
Le Concourse Stratégics vise à mettre en valeur les réalisations des professionnels de l'industrie des communications et du marketing au Québec. Un jury selectionne une finalist pour chacune des cinq catégories du concours: Innovation, Créativité, Audace, Impacte et Efficience.

AGRICULTURE & FARMING

Canadian Society of Animal Science / Société canadienne de science animale

c/o Agriculture & Agri-Food Canada Research Station, PO Box 90, Lennoxville QC J1M 1Z3
819-565-9171; Fax: 819-564-5507
Email: info@csas.net; URL: www.csas.net
CSAS offers five prestigious awards:

Fellowship Award
Awarded to members who have made an outstanding contribution in any field of animal contribution

Award for Excellence in Nutrition and Meat Sciences

Award for Technical Innovation in Enhancing Production of Safe Affordable Food

Young Scientist Award

Animal Indutries Award in Extension & Public Service

International Development Research Centre / Centre de recherches pour le développement international

PO Box 8500, Ottawa ON K1G 3H9
613-236-6163; Fax: 613-238-7230
Email: info@idrc.ca; URL: www.idrc.ca
IRDC has five special awards awarded at the discretion of its Board of Governors. They include:

IDRC Challenge Fund

Think Tank Initiative

Agriculture & Food Security

Provincial Exhibition of Manitoba

#3, 1175 - 18 St., Brandon MB R7A 7C5
204-726-3590; Fax: 204-725-0202; Toll Free: 1-877-729-0001
Email: info@brandonfairs.com; URL: www.brandonfairs.com

Royal Manitoba Winter Fair Awards
Prizes given in various categories for best of show for agricultural products, animals & crops; several equestrian events offer prizes for best in competition

Royal Agricultural Winter Fair Association / Foire agricole royale d'hiver

The Ricoh Coliseum, Direct Energy Centre
Exhibition Place, Toronto ON M6K 3C3
416-263-3400; Fax: 416-263-3488
Email: info@royalfair.org; URL: www.royalfair.org

Agricultural Awards
Grand Champion is the highest honour in the following categories: dairy, beef, sheep, goats, swine, market livestock, field crops, vegetables, honey & maple, poultry, jams/jellies/pickles, dairy products, square dancing, fiddling, fleece wool, rabbits, & eight youth activities

Breeding Horse Awards
17 sections award prizes in this category

Performance Horse Awards
35 divisions & classes offer prizes; Leading International Rider is the highest honour in the horse show

BROADCASTING & FILM

Academy of Canadian Cinema & Television / Académie canadienne du cinéma et de la télévision

172 King St. East, Toronto ON M5A 1J3
416-366-2227; Fax: 416-366-8454; Toll Free: 1-800-644-5194
Email: info@academy.ca; URL: www.academy.ca

Canadian Screen Awards

Gemini Awards
The nationally telecast awards for excellence & achievement in Canadian English-language television production are awarded annually & presented to winners in more than 80 categories covering Best Program, Best Performance & Best Craft, as well as special awards following nomination & voting by a peer group

Genie Awards
The nationally telecast Genie Awards celebrate excellence in Canadian cinema. The annual awards cover 21 categories from Best Picture to Best Sound, as well as the Golden Reel award for the top Canadian box office gross. Special achievement awards are voted by members of the Academy.

Prix Gémeaux
For excellence & achievement in French-language television production; held annually & presented in 70 categories covering Programs, Performance & Crafts; nominations & voting by peer groups composed of academy members

Alberta Motion Picture Industries Association

#318, 8944 - 182 Street NW, Edmonton AB T5T 2E3
780-944-0707; Fax: 780-426-3057
URL: www.ampia.org

Alberta Film & Television Awards
Awarded annually, the "Rosie Awards", are presented to producers and craftpeople, who reside in Alberta, in recognition of their outstanding film & television works. Awards are given in 22 class categories (ie. Best Documentary, Best Drama, Best Movie, Best Musical etc.) and 22 craft categories (ie. Best Director; Best Screenwriter, Cinematography etc.)

David Billington Awards
Awarded to a special individual in recognition of their incomparable dedication and contribution to the growth of Alberta's film and television industry.

Banff World Television Festival

c/o Achilles Media Ltd., #202, 102 Boulder Cres., Canmore AB T1W 1L2
403-678-1216; Fax: 403-678-3357
Email: info@achillesmedia.com; URL: www.bwtvf.com

Banff Rockie Awards
Annual television awards for: made-for-TV-movies; mini-series; continuing series; short dramas; comedies; social & political documentaries; original webcasts; popular science programs & natural history; arts documentaries; performance specials; animation; sports; children's programs; history & biography programs; & information programs. Also a grand prize winner, two special jury awards & best HDTV program. All entries must be made for television & either in English or French

Canadian Association of Broadcasters / Association canadienne des radiodiffuseurs

PO Box 627, Stn B, Ottawa ON K1P 5S2
613-233-4035; Fax: 613-233-6961
Email: cab@cab-acr.ca; URL: www.cab-acr.ca

Astral Media Scholarship
Established in 1975 by Astral Media with the association; awarded annually to French Canadian students who are members of a of visible minority or who are Aboriginals with broadcasting experience who are enrolled in, or wish to begin or complete a program of studies in communications at the university level
$5,000

BBM Scholarship
Established in 1986; awarded annually to a student in a graduate study program, or final year of an Honours degree with the intention of entering a graduate program at a Canadian university or post-secondary institution, who has demonstrated achievement in & knowledge of statistical &/or quantitative research methodology
$4,000

Jim Allard Broadcast Journalism Scholarship
Established 1983; awarded annually to an aspiring broadcaster enrolled in a broadcast journalism program at a Canadian college or university, who best combines academic achievement with natural talent
$2,500

Ruth Hancock Memorial Scholarships
Award established jointly in 1975 by the association, the Broadcast Executives Society & Canadian Association of Broadcast Representatives; presented annually to three Canadian students enrolled in recognized communications courses
$1,500 (x3)

Canadian Ethnic Media Association

24 Tarlton Rd., Toronto ON M5P 2M4
416-260-3625; Fax: 416-260-3810
Email: canscene@rogers.com; URL: www.canadianethnicmedia.com

Awards of Achievement
Up to nine plaques are offered annually to jounalists in print, radio, & television; awards are given to journalists for excellence in their field; competition is open to all journalists, in any language, whether or not they are members of the Club; a single award is

also given to writers of a published work of fact, fiction or poetry in book form

Sierhey Khmara Ziniak Award
In honour of the Club's founder, award is presented to a single person, based on a body or work celebrating Canada's diversity

Canadian Media Production Association (CMPA)
601 Bank St., 2nd Fl., Ottawa ON K1S 3T4
613-233-1444; Fax: 613-233-0073; Toll Free: 1-800-656-7440
Email: ottawa@cmpa.ca; URL: www.cmpa.ca

CMPA Producer's Award
Awarded to an independent producer of a Canadian feature being screened at the Toronto International Film Festival

Canadian Society of Cinematographers
#131, 3007 Kingston Rd., Toronto ON M1M 1P1
416-266-0591; Fax: 416-266-3996
Email: admin@csc.ca; URL: www.csc.ca

Canadian Society of Cinematography Awards
16 Awards given annually for various genres and contributions.

Media Communications Association International - Toronto Chapter
PO Box 5822, Stn A, Toronto ON M5W 1P2
416-910-4776
Email: execdirect@mca-i.org; URL: www.mca-i.org

The Chuck Webb Award
This award recognizes and honours individuals who have demonstrated the highest level of involvement in, dedication and commmitment to the Association without regard for personal profit of gain. Candidates are nominated by the Board of Directors.

The Board of Directors Award
This award recognizes and honours members who have demonstrated outstanding service to the Association on a regional or national level. Candidates are nominated by the Board of Directors.

The President's Award
This prestigious recognition is not given annually, but allows the President to recognize individuals who have been of particular significance during his or her term.

Shining Star Award
This award was developed to recognize the special volunteers who give freely of their time and talents to the Association. The International Shining Star award recognizes chapter leaders who standout above all other member with their significant contributions to the chapter. The Chapter Shining Star recognizes chapter members who have gone above and beyond for the chapter.

G. Warren Scholarship Award
Presented annually, this $500 scholarship program was developed in memory of G. Warren. The only requirement is that the student will be returning for at least one more term of school

Toronto International Film Festival Group
2 Carlton St., Suite 1600., Toronto ON M5B 1J3
416-967-7371; Fax: 416-967-9477
Email: customerrelations@tiffg.ca; URL: www.tiffg.ca

Award for Best Canadian Short Film
CityTV Award for Best Canadian First Feature Film
Established by CityTV; awarded to a Canadian filmmaker whose first feature film is considered exemplary; award acknowledges the fresh new talent emerging within Canadian cinema
$15,000

Blackberry People's Choice Award
Sponsored by Blackberry & voted best film of the festival by festival audiences

FIPRESCI Prize
Selected by an international FIPRESCI jury, awarded to a feature film by an emerging filmmaker having its world premiere at the festival

Toronto-City Award for Best Canadian Feature Film
Jointly sponsored by the City of Toronto & CityTV; awarded to the Best Canadian Feature Film
$25,000

Youth Media Alliance/L'Alliance Médias Jeunesse
#106, 1400, boul René-Lévesque est, Montréal QC H2L 2M2
514-597-5417; Fax: 514-597-5205
Email: alliance@ymamj.org; URL: www.ymamj.org

The Award of Excellence
The Alliance for Children & Television has been recognizing the importance of quality television for Canadian children for over 30 years. This award is presented to a person or team for their exceptional work on a children's television show produced in Canada, which stands out for its excellence.

Award of Excellence for best digital production

Award of Excellence for best convergent project

Outstanding Achievement Award

Emerging Talent Award

Parents' Choice Award

Kids' Choice Award

BUSINESS & TRADE

Business Development Bank of Canada (BDC)
5, Place Ville-Marie, Suite 400, Montréal QC H3B 5E7
Fax: 1-877-329-9232; Toll Free: 1-877-232-2269
Email: yea@bdc.ca; URL: www.bdc.ca

BDC Young Entrepreneur Award
Introduced in 2003, this award is offered to an entrepreneur who received the a Young Entrepreneur Award between 1988 and 2002 and whose business has since undergone sustained growth.

Laurentian Bank Export Achievement Award
This award is presented to the entrepreneurs to have most distinguished himself in the area of exports.

Bell Creative Mind Award
This award is presented to a company, in recognition of it's original approach and initiative that allows it to successfully differentiate itself from its competitors.

The Caldwell Partners
165 Avenue Rd., Toronto ON M5R 3S4
416-920-7702; Fax: 416-922-8646
Email: leaders@caldwell.ca; URL: www.caldwell.ca

Canada's Outstanding CEO of the Year
Sponsored by The Caldwell Partners, this annual award takes into consideration the candidate's leadership, innovation, business achievements, corporate performance, social responsibility, sense of vision & global competitiveness

Canada's Top 40 Under 40
Established & managed by The Caldwell Partners, celebrates Canadian leaders who have demonstrated remarkable success before the age of 40.

Canada's CFO of the Year
Founded in 2003 and sponsored by Financial Executives International, PricewaterhouseCoopers LLP and in association with The Caldwell Partners International, this annual award is designed to recognize the very highest level of financial leadership in the country. Winners are chosen by a distinguished panel of business leaders.

Certified General Accountants Association of Canada
#800, 1188 West Georgia St., Vancouver BC V6E 4A2
604-669-3555; Fax: 604-689-5845; Toll Free: 1-800-663-1529
Email: public@cga-canada.org; URL: www.ww.cga-canada.org

Awards of Excellence

ENCON Group Inc. Insurance Public Practice Award

Porter Hétu International Award

Fellowship Award
This annual award was designed to recognize members who provide exemplary service to the Association, the profession or the public, or achiever prominence through a variety of means. Only members in good standing, who have been admitted into membership at least two year prior are eligible.

John Leslie Award
Given to a member who has achieved national recognition for exceptional service to business, the community, politics, & the arts, or who has overcome physical adversity

Top Ten Recognition Award

The Conference Board of Canada
255 Smyth Rd., Ottawa ON K1H 8M7
613-526-3280; Fax: 613-526-4857; Toll Free: 1-866-711-2262
Email: infoserv@conferenceboard.ca; URL: www.conferenceboard.ca

National Awards for Excellence in Business-Education Partnership
Awarded to partnerships that have a demonstrated record of success in promoting the importance of science, technology &/or mathematics; linking education & the world of work, promoting teacher development, encouraging students to stay in school, expanding vocational &/or apprenticeship training
- Mary Ann McLaughlin

Global Best Award

Honorary Associate Award

Ernst & Young Entrepreneur of the Year Award
Ernst & Young Tower, TD Centre, 222 Bay St., PO Box 251, Toronto ON M5K 1J7
416-943-3785; Fax: 416-943-2207; Toll Free: 1-888-946-3694
Email: linda.moss@ca.ey.com; URL: www.eoy.ca

Ernst & Young Entrepreneur of the Year Award
Best entrepreneurs in 5 regions nationwide (Pacific Canada, The Prairies, Ontario, Québec, Atlantic Canada); other awards include Master Entrepreneur, Emerging Entrepreneur, Turnaround Entrepreneur, Young Entrepreneur, Supporter of Entrepreneurship. Awarded annually

Heritage Canada Foundation / Fondation Héritage Canada
5 Blackburn Ave., Ottawa ON K1N 8A2
613-237-1066; Fax: 613-237-5987
Email: heritagecanada@heritagecanada.org; URL: www.heritagecanada.org

The Prince of Wales Prize for Municipal Heritage Leadership
Established in 1999, The Prince of Wales agreed to lend his title to this annual award in recognition of the government of a municipality, which has demonstrated a strong and sustained commitment to the conservation of its historic places.

Gabrielle Léger Award for Lifetime Achievement in Heritage Conservation
Founded in 1978, this annual award is Canada's premier honour of individual achievement in heritage conservation

The Journalism Award
Presented annually to a journalist whose work has brought profile to Canadian communities' historic places.

Corporate Price
This annual award recognizes Canadian corporations, which have invested in the conservation of historic property of the purposes of restoration, rehabilitation, or reuse.

Achievement Awards
These awards honour individuals or groups for their achievement in heritage advocacy and volunteerism, and for projects that demonstrate a community's commitment to heritage conservation.

National Quality Institute / Institut national de la qualité
#307, 2275 Lakeshore West Blvd., Toronto ON M8V 3Y3
416-251-7600; Fax: 416-251-9131; Toll Free: 1-800-263-9648
Email: info@nqi.ca; URL: www.nqi.ca

Canada Awards for Excellence
Previously called the Canada Awards for Business Excellence & established by the Government of Canada in 1984, the awards recognize outstanding continuous achievement in seven key areas: Leadership, Customer Focus, Planning for Improvement, People Focus, Process Optimization, Supplier Focus & Organizational Performance

Skills/Compétences Canada
#205, 260, boul Saint Raymond, Gatineau QC J9A 3G7
819-771-7545; Fax: 819-771-5575; Toll Free: 1-877-754-5226
Email: skillscanada@skillscanada.com; URL: www.skillscanada.com

Canadian Skills National Competition
Awarded annually; is an olympic-style skills competition in over 40 skilled trades, technology & leadership contests, representing 6 industry sectors, designed to test skills required in technology & trade occupations; allows students access to newest technologies & communicate with industry experts who serve as mentors Students compete at the local, regional & provincial levels to win the right to represent their province at the national level
Gold, silver & bronze medals

Transportation Association of Canada
Crowchild Square, #201, 5403 Crowchild Trail NW
Calgary AB T3B 4Z1
403-247-4115; Fax: 403-541-0915
Email: ntwsnt@igs.net

Transportation Person of the Year
This award is given annually to an individual who has assumed a leadership role that has contributed to significant improvements or advancements in the transportation industry in Canada.

Award of Achievement
Established 1987; awarded to those who have brought about positive & measurable developments of significant & lasting benefit to transportation in Canada

Award of Excellence
Established 1975; for an outstanding contribution to the betterment of the transportation industry

Award of Academic Merit

Citation for Lifetime Achievement in Transportation Policy & Decision-Making

University of Alberta
School of Business, 3-23 Business Bldg.
Edmonton AB T6G 2R6
780-492-7676; Fax: 780-492-3325
URL: www.business.ualberta.ca

Canadian Business Leader Award
Annual award recognizes distinguished professional achievements & contributions to the community

CITIZENSHIP & BRAVERY

Alberta Order of Excellence
Executive Secretary, Alberta Order of Excellence Council
c/o Policy Coordination Office
Executive Council
1201 Legislature Annex
9718 - 107 Street., Edmonton AB T5K 1E4
780-427-7243; Fax: 780-427-0305
Email: aoe@gov.ab.ca; URL: www.lieutenantgovernor.ab.ca/aoe/

Alberta Order of Excellence
Established in 1979, the award recognizes those persons who have rendered service of the greatest distinction & of singular excellence for or on behalf of Albertans.

Bridgestone/Firestone Canada Inc.
#400, 5770 Hurontario St., Mississauga ON L5R 3G5
905-890-1990; Fax: 905-890-1991; Toll Free: 1-800-267-1318
URL: www.truckhero.ca

National Truck Hero Award
Established 1956; endorsed by the Canada Safety Council, the Traffic Injury Research Foundation & the trucking industry; designed to promote highway safety by focusing public attention on acts of bravery performed by professional Canadian truck drivers in the course of their daily work

The Canadian Council of Christians & Jews / Conseil canadien des chrétiens et des juifs
4211 Yonge St., PO Box 17, Toronto ON M2P 2A9
416-597-9693; Fax: 416-597-9775; Toll Free: 1-800-663-1848
Email: info@cccj.ca; URL: www.cccj.ca

Human Relations Award
This prestigious annual award recognizes outstanding contributions to Canadian society crossing cultural, religious, racial and ethnic lines.

Good Servant Medal
Created to commemorate the retirement of Richard D. Jones, O.C., LL.D., after 30 years of continuous service to CCCJ, as founder & principal officer, 1947-1977; recognizes individuals who have rendered extraordinary service to their community beyond the call of duty without seeking public recognition

Discovering Diversity Award
Established in 2004, this award is given to a student and his/her school who have made an outstanding effort to build community understanding and respect for others or different faiths and ethnic backgrounds.

The Canadian Council of the Blind / Le Conseil canadien des aveugles
#100, 20 James St., Ottawa ON K2P 0T6
613-567-0311; Fax: 613-567-2728; Toll Free: 1-877-304-0968
Email: ccb@ccbnational.net; URL: ccbnational.net

Award of Merit
This award is bestowed in recognition of service to Canadians who are blind and vision impaired.

Book of Fame Citation
The Book of Fame was donated to the Council in 1958 by the disbanded Comrades Club of Toronto; it contains the names & citations of outstanding blind Canadians selected yearly by the eight divisions & the National Board of Directors of the Council; each recipient of a citation is presented with a framed photograph of the appropriate page in the book

Canadian Decorations for Bravery
c/o The Chancellory, Rideau Hall, One Sussex Drive
Ottawa ON K1A 0A1
613-991-0895; Fax: 613-991-1681; Toll Free: 1-800-465-6890
URL: www.gg.ca/honours/decorations/bra/bd-info_e.asp

Canadian Decorations for Bravery
Presented by the Governor General, Bravery decorations recognize people who have risked their lives to save or protect others; Three levels - the Cross of Valour, the Star of Courage & the Medal of Bravery - reflect the varying degrees of risk involved in any act of bravery

The Duke of Edinburgh's Award
#415, 207 Queen's Quay West, PO Box 124
Toronto ON M5J 1A7
416-203-0674; Fax: 416-203-0676
Email: sanderson@dukeofed.org; URL: www.dukeofed.org

Young Canadians Challenge
Established in Canada in 1963 with His Royal Highness Prince Philip as Patron, the award recognizes personal achievement in a voluntary program of activities by young people in the age range of 14-25.
Open to all Canadian youth; young people participate independently or through youth groups, clubs, schools, etc.; program is operated throughout Canada, with divisional offices located in each of the ten provinces.
Award is in the form of a pin & an inscribed certificate representing Gold, Silver, & Bronze levels; Gold awards are presented by Her Excellency The Governor General of Canada, or a member of the Royal Family, at national awards ceremonies

Indspire
#450, 215 Spadina Ave., Toronto ON M5T 2C7
416-926-0775; Fax: 416-926-7554; Toll Free: 1-855-463-7747
Email: info@naaf.ca; URL: www.indspire.ca

Indspire Awards
Established in 1993, the awards recognize the outstanding career achievemennts of First Nations, Inuit & Métis people, in diverse occupations.

Ontario Ministry of Citizenship & Immigration
Ontario Honours & Awards
400 University Ave. West, 6th Fl., Toronto ON M7A 2R9
416-327-2422; Fax: 416-314-4965; Toll Free: 1-800-267-7329

June Callwood Outstanding Achievement Award
Created in 2007 to commemorate the life of June Callwood CC, O.Ont, LL.D, a Canadian journalist whose life was marked by a strong concern for social justice, especially on issues affecting children and women. This annual award is given to 20 individual volunteers, volunteer groups, businesses and other organizations in recognition of their outstanding contributions to their communities ad the province.

Lieutenant Governor's Community Volunteer Award
This award honours one graduating student from each of Ontario's post secondary schools who not only completed the number of volunteer hours required to graduate, but have gone above and byond.

Ontario Medal for Good Citizenship
This award recognizes residents of Ontario for outstanding achievement, whose lives serve as an example to all Ontarians. They are individuals who have made their communities better places to live.

Ontario Medal for Young Volunteers
Recognizes the outstanding achievements of 10 young volunteers, 15-24 who have made a difference to their communities

The Lincoln M. Alexander Award
Recognizes young people who have demonstrated exemplary leadership in eliminating racial discrimination; 3 student awards & 1 community award are offered yearly

The Ontario Medal for Firefighters Bravery
Established 1976 to recognize acts of superlative courage & bravery performed in the line of duty by members of Ontario's firefighting forces

The Ontario Medal for Good Citizenship
Established 1973 to recognize people who, through exceptional long-term efforts have made outstanding contributions to the well being of their communities

The Ontario Medal for Police Bravery
Established 1975 to recognize acts of superlative courage & bravery performed in the line of duty by members of Ontario's police forces

The Order of Ontario
Established 1986 to recognize those men & women who have rendered service of the greatest distinction & of singular excellence in all fields of endeavour benefiting society in Ontario & elsewhere

The Order of British Columbia
Honours & Awards Secretariat, PO Box 9422, Stn Prov Govt, Victoria BC V8W 9V1
250-387-1616; Fax: 250-356-2814
Email: protocol@gov.bc.ca; URL: www.protocol.gov.bc.ca

The Order of British Columbia
Established in 1989 to recognize individuals who have served with the greatest distinction & excelled in any field of endeavour benefiting the people of British Columbia or elsewhere.

Order of New Brunswick / Ordre du Nouveau-Brunswick
Intergovernmental & International Relations,
Office of Protocol
#274, 670 King St., PO Box 6000, Fredericton NB E3B 5H1
506-453-2671; Fax: 506-453-2995
URL: www.gnb.ca/lg/ONB/index-e.asp

Order of New Brunswick
Established in December, 2000 to recognize individuals who have demonstrated excellence & achievement & who have made outstanding contributions to the social, cultural or economic well-being of New Brunswick & its residents. Maximum of 10 recipients annually

The Order of Prince Edward Island
Legislative Assembly, Province House, PO Box 2000, Charlottetown PE C1A 7N8
902-368-5970; Fax: 902-368-5175
Email: chmackay@gov.pe.ca; URL: www.assembly.pe.ca

The Order of Prince Edward Island
Highest provincial honour that can be bestowed on a resident of the province; it is awarded in public recognition of individual Islanders whose efforts & accomplishments have been exemplary An enameled medallion, which incorporates the Provincial emblem against a blue background worn with a ribbon of rust, green & white. Recipients receive a stylized lapel pin & miniature medal, an official certificate & are entitled to use O.P.E.I. after their names

The Saskatchewan Order of Merit
Saskatchewan Honours & Awards Program
Office of Protocol & Honours
#1530 - 1855 Victoria Ave., Regina SK S4P 3T2
306-787-8965; Fax: 306-787-1269; Toll Free: 1-877-427-5505
Email: honours@gr.gov.sk.ca; URL: www.gr.gov.sk.ca/Protocol/Honours/SOM.htm

The Saskatchewan Order of Merit
This is a prestigious recognizes of excellence, achievement and contributions to the social, cultural and economic well-being of the province and its residence.

Secrétariat de l'Ordre national du Québec
Ministère du Conseil exécutif, #3.221, 875, Grande Allée Est, Québec QC G1R 4Y8
418-643-8895; Fax: 418-646-4307
Email: ordre-national@mce.gouv.qc.ca; URL: www.ordre-national.gouv.qc.ca/index.htm

Ordre national du Québec
L'Ordre national du Québec est la plus haute distinction décernée par le gouvernement du Québec. Il a été institué par la Loi sur l'Ordre national du Québec (L.R.Q., c. 0-7.01) sanctionnée le 20 juin 1984 par le Parlement de Québec. L'Ordre national du Québec est composé de personnes à qui le gouvernement a conféré le titre de Grand Officier (G.O.) ou d'Officier (O.Q.) ou de Chevalier de l'Ordre national du Québec (C.Q.). La loi prévoit qu'une nomination puisse être faite à titre posthume. Elle accorde aussi au premier ministre du Québec le privilège exclusif de procéder à des nominations étrangères

Société Saint-Jean-Baptiste de Montréal
82, rue Sherbrooke Ouest, Montréal QC H2X 1X3
514-843-8851; Fax: 514-844-6369
Email: mbeaulieu@ssjb.com; URL: www.ssjb.com

Prix Bene Merenti De Patria
Créée en 1923, cette médaille souligne les mérites d'un compatriote ayant rendu des services exceptionnels à la patrie.

La maquette est l'oeuvre d'un artiste qui a préparé les chars allégoriques de nos grands défilés pendant de nombreuses années
Médaille d'argent

Prix Patriote de l'année
Décerné à une personnalité qui s'est distinguée dans la défense des intérêts du Québec et de la démocratie des peuples, en mémoire des Patriotes des années 1830; créé en 1975

St. John Ambulance / Ambulance Saint-Jean
#400, 1900 City Park Dr., Ottawa ON K1J 1A3
613-236-7461; Fax: 613-236-2425
Email: nhq@sja.ca; URL: www.sja.ca

Life-saving Awards of the Order of St. John
Instituted in 1874, recognizes those who risk their lives in unselfish acts of bravery & heroism when saving or attempting to save a life.

United Nations Association in Canada / Association canadienne pour les Nations-Unies
#300, 309 Cooper St., Ottawa ON K2P 0G5
613-232-5751; Fax: 613-563-2455
Email: info@unac.org; URL: www.unac.org

Pearson Peace Medal
Awarded to a Canadian who has contributed significantly to humanitarian causes

CULTURE, VISUAL ARTS & ARCHITECTURE

The Canada Council for the Arts / Conseil des Arts du Canada
350 Albert St., PO Box 1047, Ottawa ON K1P 5V8
613-566-4414; Fax: 613-566-4390; Toll Free: 1-800-263-5588
Email: info@canadacouncil.ca; URL: www.canadacouncil.ca

Bell Canada Award in Video Art
$10,000 awarded annually to a Canadian video artist who has made an exceptional contribution to the advancement of video art in Canada through his/her video tapes or video installations; candidates are nominated by three professional curators &/or critics who are specialists in Canadian video art; the winner is selected by the committee of professional video artists

Duke & Duchess of York Prize in Photography
Endowed by the Government of Canada in 1986 on the occasion of Prince Andrew's marriage; $8,000 prize awarded annually to the best candidate in the competition for the Grants to Professional Artists in visual arts; prize is given in addition to the arts grant received

Governor General's Medals in Architecture
Awarded every two years; recognizes excellence in the art of architecture in completed projects; Canada Council adminsters the jurying of the awards & contributes $20,000 to the Royal Architectural Institute of Canada towards the publication of a book/catalogue on the winning projects

Governor-General's Awards for Visual & Media Arts
Six $15,000 prizes awarded annually for distinguished career achievement in visual & media arts, plus one $15,0000 prize for distinguished contributions to the visual & media arts through voluntarism, philanthropy, board governance or community outreach activities.
Nominees must be Canadian Citizens or permanent residents of Canada, & they may not apply for an award. They must be nominated by specialist in the field. To be nominated for one of the six awards in the artistic category, candidates must have created an outstanding, distinguished body of work in visual or media arts & have made a substantial contribution to the development of visual or media arts in Canada over a significant period of time. A peer assessment committee selects the winners

J.B.C. Watkins Award
A bequest from the estate of the late John B.C . Watkins, provides special fellowships of $5,000 to Canadian artists in any field, who are graduates of a Canadian university or post-secondary art institution or training school. Preference is given to those who wish to carry out their post-graduate studies in Denmark, Norway, Sweden or Iceland, but applications are accepted for studies in any country other than Canada. Post-graduate schools include post-secondary institutions or training schools, whether or not these are degree-granting institutions; fellowships are normally awarded in music, visual arts (architecture only), theatre & media arts

Joseph S. Stauffer Prizes
Each year the Canada Council designates up to three Canadians who have been awarded an arts grant in the fields of music, visual arts or literature as winners; the prizes, which provide an additional $5,000 each, honour the memory of the benefactor whose bequest to the Canada Council enables it to "encourage young Canadians of outstanding promise or potential"
Molson Prizes.
Two prizes of $50,000 each are awarded annully to distinguished Canadians, one in the arts and the other in the social sciences and humanities.

Petro-Canada Award in New Media
Endowed by Petro-Canada in 1987 to celebrate the centenary of engineering in Canada, $10,000 awarded approximately every three years to a professional Canadian artist. The recipient must demonstrate outstanding & innovative use of new technology in the media arts. Candidates are nominated by a committee of three professional curators &/or critics who are specialists in new media & audio arts; winner is selected by a committee of professional new media & audio artists

Prix de Rome in Architecture
Established 1987; designed to recognize the work of a Canadians actively engaged in the field of contemporary architecture whose career is well under way & whose personal work shows exceptional talent. Winner is chosen by a peer asessment committee convened by the Canada Council for the Arts

Ronald J. Thom Award for Early Design Achievement
$10,000 awarded every two years to a Canadian in the early stages of his/her career in architecture who must demonstrate both outstanding creative talent & exceptional potential in architectural design.
Sensitivity to architecture's allied arts, crafts & professions in the context of the integrated building environment must be evident in all work. Winner is chosen by the peer assessment committee for the Creation/Production Grants to Professional Artists in architecture

Saidye Bronfman Awards
Funded by the Samuel & Saidye Bronfman Family Foundation, $25,000 prize is awarded annually to an exceptional craftsperson for excellence in the fine crafts; in addition to the cash award, works by the recipient are acquired by the Canadian Museum of Civilization.
Candidates must be nominated by the national or provincial crafts council, a previous recipient of the awards, a member association of the Canadian Craft Council or a single media guild. Laureates are chosen by a peer assessment committee of distinguished craftspersons & experts in the fine crafts

Victor Martyn Lynch-Staunton Awards
Each year the Canada Council designates several Canadian artists who have been awarded grants in music & visual arts as holders of Victor Martyn Lynch-Staunton Awards; this designation is made to honour the memory of the benefactor whose bequest to the Council enables it to increase the number of grants available to senior or established artists; the awards provide each recipient with $4,000 in addition to the arts grant, which is also provided by the income from this bequest

York Wilson Endowment Awards
$30,000 awarded annually; enables Canadian art museums & public art galleries to purchase original works by living, contemporary Canadian painters & sculptors; awarded through a Canada Council for the Arts competition, to an eligible Canadian institution to allow it to purchase an original artwork that would significantly enhance its collection of contemporaray Canadian painting or sculpture. Winner is chosen by a peer assessment committee of Canadian curators of contemporary art or other appropriate peers

Canadian Conference of the Arts / Conférence canadienne des arts
#804, 130 Albert St., Ottawa ON K1P 5G4
613-238-3561; Fax: 613-238-4849
Email: info@ccarts.ca; URL: www.ccarts.ca

Diplôme d'honneur
Established in 1954; presented annually to Canadians who have contributed outstanding service to the arts; recipients have included Vincent Massey, Wilfrid Pelletier, Maureen Forrester, Floyd Chalmers, Gabrielle Roy, Glenn Gould, Alfred Pellan, Bill Reid, Antonine Maillet

Canadian Historical Association / Société historique du Canada
395 Wellington St., Ottawa ON K1A 0N3
613-233-7885; Fax: 613-567-3110
Email: cha-shc@lac-bac.bc.ca; URL: www.cha-shc.ca

Albert B. Corey Prize
Established 1966 & jointly sponsored by the CHA & the American Historical Association; awarded every two years to the best book dealing with the history of Canadian-American relations or the history of both countries
$1,000

The Wallace K. Ferguson Prize
Established 1979; awarded annually for outstanding work in a field of history other than Canadian
$1,000

The City of Toronto
Chief Administrator's Office, City Hall, 100 Queen St. West, 11th Fl., East Tower, Toronto ON M5H 2N2
416-392-8592; Fax: 416-696-3645

Architecture & Urban Design Awards
Awarded every two years, this award recognizes and celebrates design excellence and in turn elevates public awareness of the vital role that design plays in Toronto

Fondation Émile-Nelligan
261, rue Bloomfield, Outremont QC H2V 3R6
514-278-4657; Fax: 514-271-6369
Email: info@fondation-nelligan.org; URL: www.fondation-nelligan.org

Prix Émile-Nelligan
Ce prix annuel date de 1979, année de la création de la Fontation Émile-Nelligan. C'est un prix de poésie décerné à des poètes de 35 ans ou moins, pour un recueil publié au cours de l'année.
7 500$

Prix Ozias-Leduc
Prix triennal en arts visuels (peinture, sculpture, gravure, installations, 'land art'). Décerné à un artiste citoyen du Canada né au Québec ou à un artiste citoyen du Canada ayant sa résidence principale au Québec depuis au moins dix ans
25 000$

Prix Gilles-Corbeil
Le prix Gilles-Corbeil est un prix de littérature. C'est un prix triennal et is al été décerné pour la première fois en 1990.
100 000$

Prix Serge-Garant
Le prix Serge-Garant est un prix de compostiion musicale. C'est un prix triennal qui a été décerné pour le première fois en 1991.
25 000$

The Gershon Iskowitz Foundation
#302, 862 Richmond St. West, Toronto ON M6J 1C9
416-351-0216; Fax: 416-351-0217

Gershon Iskowitz Prize
$25,000 to recognize achievements in visual art

Heritage Canada Foundation / Fondation Héritage Canada
5 Blackburn Ave., Ottawa ON K1N 8A2
613-237-1066; Fax: 613-237-5987
Email: heritagecanada@heritagecanada.org; URL: www.heritagecanada.org

Achievement Awards
Established 1989, these awards honour individuals or groups for their achievement in heritage advocacy and volunteerism, and for projects that demonstrate a community's commitment to heritage conservation. Local Heritage organizations are encouraged to submit nominations within prescribed criteria and eligibility rules. Each award is given jointly by the Heritage Canada Foundation and the heritage organization making the nomination. In this way, the Heritage Canada Foundation also recognizes the nominating organizations for their dedication and commitment to excellence in heritage conservation.

Gabrielle Léger Award
Recognizes outstanding work in architectural conservation in Canada; this is an annual national award to an individual who has contributed outstanding community service in the cause of heritage conservation

Lieutenant Governor's Award
Established 1979 to recognize outstanding work in architectural conservation on a provincial level by an individual or group
It must be demonstrated that the applicant's continuous efforts in the field of heritage conservation have benefited the province where the foundation's annual meeting is being held; applicants must be sponsored by an organized heritage group &/or elected officials at any level of government

Prince of Wales Prize
Established in 1999, awarded annually to a municipal government which has shown exemplary commitment to heritage preservation within its jurisdiction

Ontario Arts Council / Conseil des arts de l'Ontario
151 Bloor St. West, 5th Fl., Toronto ON M5S 1T6
416-961-1660; Fax: 416-961-7796; Toll Free: 1-800-387-0058
Email: info@arts.on.ca; URL: www.arts.on.ca
The Ontario Arts Council provides a variety of Funds and Scholarships for different studies and careers in the arts. For more information visit their website.

PEI Council of the Arts
115 Richmond St., Charlottetown PE C1A 1H7
902-368-6176; Fax: 902-368-4418 Toll Free: 1-888-734-2784
Email: info@peiartscouncil.com; URL: www.peica.ca

Father Adrien Arsenault Senior Arts Awards
The Price Edward Island Council of the Arts recognizes the achievements of artists on Prince Edward Island through a program of annual and bi-annual awards and prizes.

Island Literary Awards
These awards are given annually to Prince Edward Island's writers. Awards are made to all levels of the discipline from students, through senior memebers of the writing community.

Québec Ministère de la culture et des communications
225, Grande Allée est, Québec QC G1R 5G5
418-380-2300; Fax: 418-080-2364
Email: DC@mcc.gouv.qc.ca; URL: www.mcc.gouv.qc.ca

Les Prix du Québec:

Prix d'excellence en architecture
Ce prix souligne, depuis 1978, la contribution essentielle des architectes québecois au cadre bâti. Les prix accordés par l'Order des architectres du Québec permettent d'identifier et de valoriser les meilleures réalisations architecturales au Québec et ailleurs dans le monde.

Prix Paul-Émile-Borduas
Accordée à un artisan ou un artiste pour l'ensemble de son oeuvre dans le domaine des arts visuels, des métiers d'art, de l'architecture et du design

Royal Architectural Institute of Canada / Institut royal d'architecture du Canada
#330, 55 Murray St., Ottawa ON K1N 5M3
613-241-3600; Fax: 613-241-5750
Email: info@raic.org; URL: www.raic.org

College of Fellows Centennial Fund for Intern/Intern Architect

Canada Green Building Council Scholarship for Sustainable Design & Research

André Francou Legacy

Bernard Jodoin Scholarships

RAIC Foundation Bursary

Ernest Wilby Memorial Scholarship

The Royal Society of Canada / La Société royale du Canada
170 Waller St., Ottawa ON K1N 9B9
613-991-6990; Fax: 613-991-6996
Email: info@rsc.ca; URL: www.rsc.ca

Centenary Medal
Established 1982; awarded at irregular intervals in recognition of outstanding contributions to the object of the society & to recognize links to international organizations

Sir John William Dawson Medal
Established 1985; awarded for important & sustained contributions by one individual in at least two different fields in the general areas of interest of the Society or in a broad domain that transcends the usual disciplinary boundaries
$2,500 & a silver medal

The J.B. Tyrrell Historical Medal
Established 1927; awarded at least every two years for outstanding work in the history of Canada

Sobey Art Foundation
c/o Art Gallery of Nova Scotia
1723 Hollis Street, PO Box 2262, Halifax NS B3J 3C8
902-424.5169;
Email: fillmose@gov.ns.ca URL: www.sobeyartaward.ca

Sobey Art Award
Awarded every year to an artist 39 years old or younger who has shown their work in a public or commercial art gallery in Canada in the past 18 monthe.
$50 000

Social Sciences & Humanities Research Council of Canada
350 Albert St., PO Box 1610, Ottawa ON K1P 6G4
613-992-0691; Fax: 613-992-1787
Email: info@sshrc.ca; URL: www.sshrc.ca

Doctoral Fellowships
Must have completed one year of doctoral study or a master's degree leading to a Ph.D. or equivalent; disciplines include: Geography, Health Studies, Applied Health Studies & Environmental Studies
Approx. $38,000 per year

Postdoctoral Fellowships
To support a core of the most promising new scholars in the social sciences & humanities & to assist them in establishing a research base at an important time in their research career; provides stipendiary support to non-tenured PhD graduates who are undertaking new research, publishing research findings, developing & expanding personal research networks, broadening teaching experience & preparing to become competitive in national research competitions.
Approximately $38,000 per year (for a maximum of two years) plus a $5,000 accountable research allowance

The Bora Laskin National Fellowship in Human Rights Research
To support interdisciplinary or multidisciplinary research & the development of expertise in the field of human rights, with emphasis on Canadian human rights issues
$45,000 stipend plus $10,000 for research & research-related travel expenses

The Jules & Gabrielle Léger Fellowship
Awarded to promote research & writing on the historical contribution of the Crown & its representatives, federal & provincial, to the political, constitutional, cultural, intellectual & social life of the country.
Award is for $40,000, plus $10,000 for research & research -travel expenses

Salon international du livre de Quebec
26, rue Saint-Pierre, Québec QC G1K 8A3
418-692-0010; Fax: 418-692-0029
Email: info@silq.ca; URL: www.silq.ca

Prix littéraires de la Ville de Québec et Salon international du livre de Québec

Toronto Arts Council Foundation
141 Bathurst St., Toronto ON M5V 2R2
416-392-6800; Fax: 416-392-6920
Email: mail@torontoartscouncil.org; URL: www.torontoartscouncil.org

Margo Bindhardt Award
$10,000 cash prize presented every second year to Toronto artist or administrator whose leadership & vision, whether through their creative work or cultural activism, have had a significant impact on the arts in Toronto & for whom the cash prize will make a difference

Muriel Sherrin Award
$10,000 cash prize presented to an artist or creator who has made a contribution to the cultural life ot Toronto through outstanding achievement in music. The recipient will also have participated in international initiatives, including touring, study abroad & artist exchanges. Awarded every second year

Rita Davies Award
$5,000 cash prize presented to a Toronto artist, volunteer or administrator who has demonstrated creative leadership in the development of arts & culture in Toronto. Awarded every second year

William Kilbourn Award
$5,000 cash prize presented to an individual performer, teacher, administrator or creator in any arts discipline, including architecture & design, whose work is a celebration of life through the arts in Toronto. Awarded every second year

Ville de Montréal
Service du développement culturel
5650, d'Iberville, 4e étage, Montréal QC H2G 3E4
514-872-1156
URL: www.ville.montreal.qc.ca/culture/culture.htm

Prix François-Houdé
La Ville de Montréal, en collaboration avec le Conseil des métiers d'art du Québec décerne annuellement ce Prix afin de promouvoir l'excellence de la nouvelle création montréalaise en métiers d'art et de favoriser la diffusion d'oeuvres des jeunes artisans créateurs. Bourse de 3000$ et 2 500$ pour organiser une exposition

Prix Louis-Comtois
La Ville de Montréal, en collaboration avec l'Association des galeries d'art contemporain, décerne annuellement ce Prix qui vient apppuyer et promouvoir le travail d'un artiste en mi-carrière qui s'est distingué dans le domaine de l'art contemporain à Montréal depuis les 15 dernières années. Bourse 5000$ et 2 500$ pour organiser une exposition solo

Prix Pierre-Ayot
La Ville de Montréal, en collaboration avec l'Association des galeries d'art contemporain, décerne annuellement ce Prix qui souligne la facture exceptionnelle et l'apport original de la production des jeunes artistes en peinture, en estampe, en dessin, en illustration, en photographie ou tout autre médium. Bourse 3000$ et 2 500$ pour organiser une exposition solo

EDUCATIONAL

Alberta Scholarship Programs
PO Box 28000, Stn Main, Edmonton AB T5J 4R4
780-427-8640; Fax: 780-427-1288
Email: scholarships@gov.ab.ca; URL: www.alis.gov.ab.ca/scholarships/main.asp

Alberta Scholarships Program
32 scholarships & awards are available in various fields of study

Association of Universities & Colleges of Canada / Association des universités et collèges du Canada
#600, 350 Albert St., Ottawa ON K1R 1B1
613-563-1236; Fax: 613-563-9745
Email: awards@aucc.ca; URL: www.aucc.ca

AUCC Scholarship for Students with Disabilities
Scholarships open to students entering full-time studies leading to a first undergraduate degree
Up to ten $5,000

Bowater Maritimes Scholarship Program
Scholarships open to grade 12 New Brunswick students
Three $1,500 for undergraduate studies

CATSA - Brian Flemming Research Fellowship and Security Award
Scholarship open to doctoral or post-doctoral research relating to tactical and strategic issues of Canadian aviation security screening
$15,000

C.D. Howe Memorial Foundation Engineering Awards
(One male, one female) for students who have completed the first year of an engineering program
Two $7,500 scholarships

C.D. Howe Scholarship Program
Scholarships open to all disciplines but for students from Thunder Bay or the following school boards: Lakehead, Lakehead District R.C., Lake Superior, North of Superior District R.C., Geraldton, Geraldton District R.C., Nipigon-Red Rock, & Hornepayne
Two $5,500

Cable Telecommunications Research Fellowship (Canadian Cable Telecommunications Association)
Scholarship awarded annually to students pursuing a master's degree in any discipline directly related to the development & delivery of cable in Canada
$5,000

CIBC Youthvision Scholarship
Must be enrolled in Big Brothers/Big Sisters of Canada
30 scholarships: $4,000 or actual tuition fees, plus paid summer employment with YMCA Canada

Conocophillips Canada Centennial Scholarship
Scholarship program encourages individuals with academic excellence and demonstrated leadership.
Three scholarships of up to $10,000 per year for a maximum of 2 consecutive years

Department of National Defence Security & Defence Forum
Eight $8,000 (master's), four $16,000 (doctorate) scholarships & two $35,000 (post-doctoral) fellowships in studies relating to current & future Canadian natural security & defence issues. Three internships of up to 12 months worth $32,000 to help recent MA graduates obtain work experience in security & defence studies

by working in this field in the non-governmental or private sectors.

Fessenden-Trott Awards
Scholarships open to all disciplines; restricted to Ontario in 2005
Four $9,000

Frank Knox Memorial Fellowship Program
Awards, plus tuition fees & health insurance for Canadian citizens or permanent residents who have graduated from a AUCC member institution before Sept. 2005 & wish to study at Harvard in the following disciplines: arts & sciences (including engineering), business administration, design, divinity studies, education, law, public administration, medicine, dental medicine & public health; applications for students currently studying in the US will not be considered
Up to three US$18,500

Mattinson Endowment Fund Scholarship for Disabled Students
For undergraduate study, all disciplines
$2,500

Programme canadien de bourses de la Francophonie
Scholarship based on merit for especially deserving and motivated applicants, funded by the Canadian International Development Agency. Awarded by competition for professional training in leading-edge technologies at the college level (certificate or diploma) or for undergraduate, master's or doctoral studies at a university

Public Safety & Emergency Preparedeness Canada Research Fellowship in Honour of Stuart Nesbitt White
For research in the area of disaster/emergency research & planning; preference is given to applicants who hold a Master's degree & who are planning research in the following fields: Urban & Regional Planning, Economics, Earth Sciences, Risk Analysis & Management, Systems Science, Social Sciences, Business Administration & Health Administration
Eight up to $19,250

Queen Elizabeth Silver Jubilee Endowment Fund for Study in a Second Official Language Award Program
Scholarships open to all disciplines, except translations, for students studying in their second language
Three $5,000 (plus travel costs)

TD Canada Trust Scholarships Community Leadership
All disciplines, undergraduate degrees
Valued at up to $70,000, including a year's tuition, living expenses, an offer of paid summer employment, mentorship opportunities, & invitations to networking events.

BC Ministry of Advanced Education
PO Box 9173, Stn Prov Govt, Victoria BC V8W 9H7
250-387-6100; Fax: 250-356-9455; Toll Free: 1-800-561-1818
URL: www.bcsap.bc.ca

Governor General's Academic Medal Award
Awards medals to college & university students achieving the highest academic standing upon graduation

Irving K. Barber Transfer Scholarship
Up to 150 scholarships worth $5,000 annually; open to students who have completed two years at a BC community college, university college or institute & must transfer to a public degree-granting institution in BC in order to complete their degrees

Lieutenant Governor's Silver Medal Award
Honours students registered in a vocational or career program of less than two years duration, who have excelled academically, & have contributed to the life of the college or institute or their community

Premier's Excellence Award
Recognizes the top all-around graduating secondary students, from the 15 college regions in BC, who are proceeding to full-time post secondary education in BC

United World College Scholarships
Valued at approximately $60,000, the award covers full tuition & residence for two years at the Lester B. Pearson College of the Pacific; the International Baccalaureate allows students to finish their final year of high school & earn credit towards the first year of university

Black Business & Professional Association
#210, 675 King St. West, Toronto ON M5V 1M9
416-504-4097; Fax: 416-504-7343
Email: bbpa@bellnet.ca; URL: www.bbpa.org

Harry Jerome Scholarships
Scholarship celebrates excellence in achievement in the Black community. Award recipients are selected from among Canada-wide nominees recommended by business and professional colleagues, teachers, relatives and friends.
Five $2,000 annual awards

The Canada Council for the Arts / Conseil des Arts du Canada
350 Albert St., PO Box 1047, Ottawa ON K1P 5V8
613-566-4414; Fax: 613-566-4390; Toll Free: 1-800-263-5588
Email: info@canadacouncil.ca; URL: www.canadacouncil.ca

Coburn Fellowships
Up to three $20,000 fellowships are awarded annually to a Canadian student (at Victoria University or the University of Toronto) & an Israeli student, in the fields of fine arts or humanities, to study on a reciprocal basis; they are intended to cover travel expenses, tuition & accommodation costs for a year; winners are chosen by Victoria University

John G. Diefenbaker Award
Funded by the Government of Canada, this annual award honours the memory of former Prime Minister John G. Diefenbaker; it enables a German scholar to spend up to 12 months in Canada to pursue research in any of the disciplines in the social sciences & humanities; candidates must be nominated by university departments or research institutes in Canada. Value of full award is $75,000; in addition, the Social Sciences & Humanities Research Council of Canada provides a travel allowance of up to $20,000

Canadian Association of University Business Officers / Association canadienne du personnel administratif universitaire
#320, 350 Albert St., Ottawa ON K1R 1B1
613-230-6760; Fax: 613-563-7739
Email: cworkman@caubo.ca; URL: www.caubo.ca

CAUBO Quality & Productivity Awards
Designed to recognize, reward & share university achievements in improving the quality & reducing the cost of higher education programs & services; National & Regional categories
Awards evaluated on portability, originality, quality impact, productivity impact, & involvement
National: first prize $10,000; second prize $5,000; third prize $3,000

Canadian Mathematical Society / Société mathématique du Canada
#209, 1725 St. Laurent Blvd., Ottawa ON K1G 3V4
613-733-2662; Fax: 613-33-8994
Email: office@cms.math.ca; URL: www.cms.math.ca

Canadian Mathematical Olympiad
Annual mathematics competition established to provide an opportunity for students to perform well on the Canadian Open Mathematics Challenge & to complete on a national basis.
Fifteen cash prizes

Canadian Merit Scholarship Foundation
#502 - 460 Richmond Street West St., Toronto ON M5V 1Y1
416-646-2120; Fax: 416-646-0846; Toll Free: 1-866-544-2673
URL: www.cmsf.ca

Loran Finalist Award
Given to every finalist who is selected for & attends, National Selections
$2,500 awarded to outstanding students from across the country as one-time entrance awards to be used at any accredited Canadian university

Loran Provincial Award
One-time entrance award tenable at any accredited university in Canada at which the recipient gains admission & enrolls in a full-time program of study
$1,500

National Award
Up to $8,000 per year plus a tuition stipend, for up to four years of full-time undergraduate study at any one of our participating Canadian universities

Regional Award
One-time entrance award tenable at any accredited university in Canada at which the recipient gains admission & enrolls in a full-time program of study
$1,500

Canadian Sociology & Anthropology Association / Société canadienne de sociologie et d'anthropologie
Université Concordia University SB-323
1455, De Maisonneuve Ouest, Montréal QC H3G 1M8
514-848-8780; Fax: 514-848-8780
Email: info@csaa.ca; URL: www.csaa.ca

John Porter Memorial Award
Recognizes outstanding published scholarly contributions within the "John Porter Tradition" to the advancement of sociological and/or anthropological knowledge in Canada
Outstanding Contribution Award
Given to recognize the work of eminent sociologists & anthropologists

Best Student Paper Award
Recognizes the best paper among those received for adjudication, written by a graduate student

CIDA Awards Program
Canadian Bureau for International Education
#1550, 220 Laurier Ave. West, Ottawa ON K1P 5Z9
613-237-4820; Fax: 613-237-1073
Email: info@cbie.ca; URL: www.cbie.ca

Awards for Canadians
A program funded by CIDA & managed by the Canadian Bureau for International Education; CIDA wishes to increase the number of Canadian professionals capable of working in the international arena by providing funding up to $15,000 for short-term, overseas work experiences
Must possess a university degree, college diploma or professional designation, have substantial work experience, two years of which have involved using specific skills necessary to undertake the proposed project. For information on fields of specialization & eligible countries, contact CIDA Communications Branch, 200 Promenade du Portage, Hull PQ K1A 0G4; 819-997-5006; Fax: 819-953-6088. Other information & applications should be sent to the CBIE at the above address

Foundation for Educational Exchange Between Canada & the United States of America
#2015, 350 Albert St., Ottawa ON K1R 1A4
613-688-5540; Fax: 613-237-2029
Email: info@fulbright.ca; URL: www.fulbright.ca

Fulbright Canada – Awards for Canadian Scholars
To expand research, teaching & study opportunities for Canadian & American faculty & students engaged in the study of Canada, the United States & the relationship between the two countries; based on academic excellence & the merit of the applicant's proposed project, awards given annually for study in a number of different fields including conservation, ecology, environmental management, resource analysis & environmental policy. Applicants must relocate from the U.S. to Canada, or Canada to the U.S.
$15,000 US for graduate students; $25,000 US for faculty

International Development Research Centre / Centre de recherches pour le développement international
250 Albert St., Ottawa ON K1G 3H9
613-236-6163; Fax: 613-238-7230
Email: info@idrc.ca; URL: www.idrc.ca

Canadian Window on International Development Awards
Award offered for doctoral research that explores the relationship between Canadian aid, trade, immigration & diplomatic policy, & international development & the alleviation of global policy
Applicants must hold Canadian citizenship or permanent residency status; be registered at a Canadian university; be conducting the proposed research for a doctoral dissertation & have completed course work & passed comprehensive examinations by the time of the award tenure
$20,000 per year - Centre Training & Awards Unit, 613-236-6163 ext 2098; Fax: 613-563-0815; Email: cta@idrc.ca

Centre Internships
These awards provide exposure to research for international development through program work & research under the guidance of IDRD program staff. Internships will be considered for a program of work & research responding to IDRC's current Program Initiatives
The program is aimed at candidates who, through demonstrated achievements in academic studies, work or research, have shown interest in the creation & utilization of knowledge from an international perspective. Candidates can be both Canadians (or permanent residents) or citizens of developing countries, & will have had some training at the master's level. Candidates need not be affiliated with an institution. They may participate in internships as part of an academic requirement
Stipend $2,500 - $28,000 per year - Centre Training & Awards Unit, 613-236-6163 ext 2098; Fax: 613-563-0815; Email cta@idrc.ca

The Japan Foundation, Toronto / Kokosai Koryu Kikin Toronto Nihon Bunka Centre
#213, 131 Bloor St. West, Toronto ON M5S 1R1
416-966-1600; Fax: 416-966-9773

Email: info@jftor.org; URL: www.jftor.org

The Japan Foundation Fellowships
Scholars, researchers, artists & other professionals are provided an opportunity to conduct research or pursue projects in Japan. Term of award is from two to 14 months, depending on category; annual application deadline is Dec. 1 for funding year beginning the following April 1

The Japan Foundation Scholarships & Programs
The Foundation offers a wide range of programs in more than 180 countries, including the following: exchange of persons (fellowships); support for Japanese-language instruction; support for Japanese studies; support for arts-related exchange; support for media exchange

Northern Enterprise Fund Inc.
PO Box 220, Beauval SK S0M 0G0
306-288-2258; Fax: 306-288-4667; Toll Free: 1-800-864-3022
Email: info@nefi.ca; URL: www.nefi.ca

Northern Spirit Scholarship Program
To promote entrepreneurial spirit in Northern Saskatchewan by providing scholarships to students enrolled in courses related to business or based on occupational shortages in the north
Ten $2,500 scholarships are awarded to full-time students who are permanent northern residents of the Northern Administration District; priority will be given to applicants showing intention of returning to, or remaining in the north; with an academic record of 70% average in most recent year completed

Ontario Council on Graduate Studies / Conseil ontarien des études supérieures
#1100, 180 Dundas St. West, Toronto ON M5G 1Z8
416-979-2165; Fax: 416-595-7392
Email: kpanesar@cou.on.ca/; URL: ocgs.cou.on.ca/

John Charles Polanyi Prizes
In honour of the achievement of John Charles Polanyi, co-recipient of the 1986 Nobel Prize in Chemistry, the Government of Ontario has established a fund to provide annually up to five prizes to persons continuing to post-doctoral studies at an Ontario university; prizes available in the areas of Physics, Chemistry, Physiology or Medicine, Literature & Economic Science
$15,000

Ordre des conseillers en ressources humaines et en relations industrielles agrées du Québec
#1400, 1200, av McGill College, Montréal QC H3B 4G7
514-879-1636; Fax: 514-879-1722; Toll Free: 1 (800) 214-1609
Email: info@orhri.org; URL: www.orhri.org

EXCALIBUR: Le tournoi universitaire canadien en ressources humaines
Promouvoir un enseignement de la gestion des ressources humaines dans les universités canadiennes préparant les étudiants au marché du travail
3 000$; 2 250$; 1 500$

The Royal Society of Canada / La Société royale du Canada
170 Waller St., Ottawa ON K1N 9B9
613-991-6990; Fax: 613-991-6996
Email: info@rsc.ca; URL: www.rsc.ca

Innis-Gérin Medal
Established 1966; awarded every two years for a distinguished & sustained contribution to the literature of the social sciences including human geography & social psychology

Pierre Chauveau Medal
Established 1951; awarded every two years (since 1966) for a distinguished contribution to knowledge in the humanities other than Canadian literature & Canadian history

Social Sciences & Humanities Research Council of Canada
350 Albert St., PO Box 1610, Ottawa ON K1P 6G4
613-992-0691; Fax: 613-992-1787
Email: info@sshrc.ca; URL: www.sshrc.ca

The Thérèse F.-Casgrain Fellowship
$40,000 stipend awarded every second year (2004, 2006, etc.) to support research on women & social change in Canada

Yukon Government
PO Box 2703, Whitehorse YT Y1A 2C6
867-667-5811; Fax: 867-393-6339
Email: information@gov.yk.ca

Excellence in Education Award
Awarded to individuals or groups that have demonstrated innovation, superior dedication or outstanding service to public school education in the Yukon; winners receive a specially commissioned artwork created by Ted Harrison

ENVIRONMENTAL

Alberta Emerald Foundation
#205, 3132 Parsons Rd NW, Edmonton, AB T6N 1L6
780-413-9629; Fax: 780-439-2369; Toll Free: 1-800-219-8329
Email: info@emeraldawards.com; URL: emeraldfoundation.ca

Emerald Awards
Awarded to Albertans who have made a significant contribution to the protection or enhancement of the environment
Nominations are open to individual, not-for-profit organizations, business & industry, communities & government, educational institutions & volunteer organizations excelling in environmental achievements

Alberta Environment & Sustainable Resource Development
Fish & Wildlife Division
Information Centre, Main Floor, 9920 - 108 St. Edmonton AB T5K 2M4
780-944-0313; Fax: 780-427-4407
URL: www.srd.alberta.ca

Order of the Bighorn Awards
Fish & wildlife conservation awards presented every other year, to individuals, organizations & corporations for their outstanding contributions to fish & wildlife conservation in Alberta - Program Manager, Dave England

Association of Universities & Colleges of Canada / Association des universités et collèges du Canada
#600, 350 Albert St., Ottawa ON K1R 1B1
613-563-1236; Fax: 613-563-9745
Email: info@aucc.ca; URL: www.aucc.ca

Cement Association of Canada Environmental Scholarship Program
Open to students in Alberta, British Columbia, Newfoundland, Nova Scotia, Ontario & Quebec who have fully completed the two years of course work in an environmental science or environmental engineering program that is required to continue a third year of their eligible program
Six $2,000

Atlantic Salmon Federation / Fédération du saumon atlantique
PO Box 5200, 15 Rankine Mill Road, Chamcook NB E5B 3A9
506-529-4581; Fax: 506-529-1070; Toll Free: 1-800-565-5666
URL: www.asf.ca

Affiliate of the Year
Recognizes outstanding leadership & achievement in Atlantic salmon conservation within the federation's affiliate structure
Engraved plaque & a cheque for $500 to be used toward its conservation programs - Muriel Ferguson, Manager, Public Information

Olin Fellowship
Fellowships offered annually to individuals seeking to improve their knowledge or skills in fields dealing with current problems in biology, management, or conservation of Atlantic salmon & its habitat; the fellowship may be applied toward a wide range of endeavours such as salmon management, graduate study, & research.
Applicants need not be enrolled in a degree program, but must be legal residents of the US or Canada
$1,000-$3,000 - Ellen Merrill

Roll of Honour
Presented annually to individuals who exhibit outstanding commitment to salmon conservation at the grassroots level
ASF member in good standing - Muriel Ferguson, Manager, Public Information

T.B. (Happy) Fraser Award
Presented annually to an individual who has made outstanding long-term contributions to Atlantic salmon conservation in Canada. The award reflects efforts on a regional or national level - Muriel Ferguson, Manager, Public Information

BC Ministry of Environment
PO Box 5200, Stn Prov Govt, Victoria BC V8W 9M1
250-387-9422
URL: www.gov.bc.ca

Minister's Environmental Awards
Awarded for identifying, reducing, solving or avoiding an environmental problem; demonstrating consistently responsible environmental management practices; &/or promoting public awareness, understanding & active concern for the enhancement & protection of the environment
Categories include individual citizen, youth, government, community or non-profit organization, business, industry or labour, environmental educator, scientist or innovator, environmental steward by nomination

Canadian Land Reclamation Association / Association canadienne de réhabilitation des sites dégradés
PO Box 61047, RPO Kensington, Calgary AB T2N 4S6
403-289-9435; Fax: 403-289-9435
Email: clra@telusplanet.net; URL: www.clra.ca

Dr. Edward M. Watkin Award
Presented annually to an association member in recognition of outstanding contribution to the field of reclamation, through research, field work, teaching or innovation, or distinguished service to the association through active participation & leadership

The Noranda Land Reclamation Award
Presented annually by the association on behalf of Noranda Mines Inc. in recognition of superior research or field work in reclamation; not restricted to members

Canadian Wildlife Federation / Fédération canadienne de la faune
350 Michael Cowpland Dr., Kanata ON K2M 2W1
613-599-9594; Fax: 613-599-4428; Toll Free: 1-800-563-9453
Email: info@cwf-fcf.org; URL: www.cwf-fcf.org

Canadian Conservation Achievement Awards Program:

Roderick Haig-Brown Memorial Award
Awarded annually to an individual who has made a significant contribution to furthering the sport of angling &/or conservation & wise use of Canada's recreational fisheries resources

Roland Michener Conservation Award
A trophy is given annually in recognition of an individual's outstanding achievement in the field of conservation in Canada

Stan Hodgkiss Outdoorsman of the Year Award
Presented annually to an outdoorsperson who has demonstrated an active commitment to conservation in Canada

Centre for Environment
University of Toronto, #1016, 33 Wilcocks St.
Toronto ON M5S 3E8
416-978-7077; Fax: 416-978-3884
Email: centre.environment@utoronto.ca; URL: www.environment.utoronto.ca/

Adaptation & Impacts Research Group (AIRG) Annual Prize
Awarded to a qualified graduate student for the best research paper addressing one or more of AIRG's research directions. This includes impacts of, & adaptation to, climate change/variability & extreme events; atmospheric natural hazards/disasters & societal adjustment; & integrated assessment of multiple atmospheric issues (climate change, stratospheric ozone depletion, acidic deposition & air quality), particularly in terms of their cumulative effects on human health

Energy Probe Research Foundation
225 Brunswick Ave., Toronto ON M5S 2M6
416-964-9223; Fax: 416-964-8239
Email: webadmin@eprf.ca; URL: www.eprf.ca/eprf/index.html

The Margaret Laurence Fund
Grants & scholarships are made to foster an understanding of peace & the environment upon which the fate of the planet rests
Recipients of the grants & scholarships are limited to students, authors, researchers, & publishers, working with the foundation in collaborative projects approved by the directors

International Development Research Centre / Centre de recherches pour le développement international
250 Albert St., Ottawa ON K1P 6M1
613-236-6163; Fax: 613-238-7230
Email: info@idrc.ca; URL: www.idrc.ca

Ecosystem Approaches to Human Health Training Awards
Supports research that focuses on ecosystem management interventions leading to the improvement of human health & well-being while simultaneously maintaining or improving the condition of the ecosystem as a whole. Awards will be granted for training & research linked to the Ecosystem Approaches to Human Health Program Initiatives of the Centre. Priority will be give to proposals for research on ecosystems that are stressed through agriculture, urbanization or mining activities.
Citizens of developing countries &/or Canadian citizens or landed immigrants students currently enrolled in a graduate

programme at a recognized university in Canada or in a developing country. Relevant language proficiency for site of study
Up to 6 awards for a maximum of $15,000 - Centre Training & Awards Unit, 613-236-6163 ext 2098; Fax: 563-0815; Email: info@idrc.ca

IDRC Doctoral Research Awards (IDRA)
Supports the field research of Canadian graduate students enrolled in a Canadian university for doctoral research on a topic of relevance to sustainable & equitable development
Applicants must hold Canadian citizenship or permanent residency status; be registered at a Canadian university; research proposal is for a doctoral thesis; provide evidence of affiliation with an institution or organization in the region in which the research will take place; have completed course work & passed comprehensive examinations by the time of award tenure
Maximum of $20,000 per year - Centre Training & Awards Unit, 613-236-6163 ext 2098; Fax: 613-563-0815; Email: cta@irdc.ca

John G. Bene Fellowship: Community Forestry, Trees & People
Contributes to the expenses of Canadian graduate students undertaking field research in social forestry in a developing country
Applicants must be Canadian citizens or hold permanent residency status; be registered in a Canadian university at the master's or doctoral level; have an academic background that combines forestry or agroforestry with social sciences. Applicants from interdisciplinary programs (e.g. environmental studies) may also be eligible, provided their programs contain the specified elements
$15,000 per year - Centre Training & Awards Unit, 613-236-6163 ext. 2098; Fax: 613-563-0815; Emails cta@irdc.ca

Newfoundland & Labrador Department of Environment & Conservation
Confederation Bldg., West Block, 4th Fl., PO Box 8700, St. John's NL A1B 4J6
709-729-2664; Fax: 709-729-6639
Email: info@gov.nl.ca; URL: www.env.gov.nl.ca/env/

The Newfoundland & Labrador Environmental Awards Program
Established in partnership with the Newfoundland & Labrador Women's Institutes Multi-Materials Stewardship Board & the Dept. of Environment to create public awareness for the proactive environmental actions being taken by Newfoundlanders & Labradorians; the object is to demonstrate the contributions people are making to create a healthier environment & through their efforts, encourage others to do the same; awards are given in seven categories: individual, citizen's group or organization, educator, youth, school, business, & municipal - Newfoundland & Labrador Women's Institutes, Executive Director, Sylvia Manning, 709-753-8780; email nlwi@nfld.com

Recycling Council of Ontario / Conseil du recyclage de l'Ontario
#225 - 215 Spadina Av., Toronto ON M5T 2C7
416-657-2797; Fax: 416-960-8053
Email: rco@rco.on.ca; URL: www.rco.on.ca

Ontario Waste Minimization Awards
A series of awards for outstanding achievement in recycling: includes 3Rs initiatives in commercial, industrial & institutional settings; Outstanding Municipal, Non-profit Organization, Recycling Program Operator; Outstanding School Program, & Media Contribution Award - Tracy Sakamoto

The Royal Society of Canada / La Société royale du Canada
170 Waller St., Ottawa ON K1N 9B9
613-991-6990; Fax: 613-991-6996
Email: info@rsc.ca; URL: www.rsc.ca

Miroslaw Romanowski Medal
Established in 1994; awarded every year in recognition of significant contributions to the resolution of scientific aspects of environmental problems or for important improvements to the quality of an eco-system in all aspects, terrestrial, atmospheric & aqueous brought about by scientific means.
$3,000 & a medal - Geneviève Gouin, Awards Coordinator, 613-991-5760

HEALTH & MEDICAL

Canadian Association of Medical Radiation Technologists / Association canadienne des technologues en radiation médicale
#100, 85 Albert St., Ottawa ON K1P 6A4
613-234-0012; Fax: 613-234-1097; Toll Free: 1-800-463-9729
URL: www.camrt.ca

CAMRT Awards
Administers awards for students & registered technologists including: Dr. M. Mallett Student Award, Dr. Petrie Memorial Award, George Reason Memorial Cup, E.I. Hood Award, CAMRT Student Achievement Award, Philips Rose Bowl, PACS Technology Award

Canadian Association on Gerontology / Association canadienne de gérontologie
#328, 263 McCaul St., Toronto ON M5T 1W7
416-978-7977; Fax: 416-978-4771; Toll Free: 855-224-2240
Email: contact@cagacg.ca; URL: www.cagacg.ca

CAG Award for Contribution to Gerontology
To recognize an individual who has recently made an outstanding contribution to the field of aging
Certificate

Canadian Federation for Sexual Health / Fédération canadienne pour la santé sexuelle
#403, 2197 Riverside Dr., Ottawa ON K1H 7X3
613-241-4474; Fax: 613-241-7550
Email: admin@cfsh.ca; URL: www.cfsh.ca

John & Lois Lamont Graduate Scholarship
Established 2004; awarded to a full-time graduate student in the field of sexual & reproductive health
$2,600

Phyllis P. Harris Undergraduate Scholarship
Endowed in the memory of Phyllis P. Harris, who for over thirty years was an inspiring presence in the world of family planning. This scholarship is awarded to a volunteer or individual currently enrolled in undergraduate studies in the general field of human sexuality, family planning or population including: biology, education, history, medicine, political science, psychology.
$2,600

Canadian Institutes of Health Research
160 Elgin St., 9th Floor; Address Locator 4809A, Ottawa ON K1A 0W9
613-941-2672; Fax: 613-954-1800; Toll Free: 1-888-603-4178
Email: info@cihr-irsc.gc.ca; URL: www.cihr-irsc.gc.ca

Michael Smith Prize in Health Research
A medal plus $50,000 research grant awarded annually to an outstanding Canadian researcher who has demonstrated innovation, creativity & dedication to health research

Canadian Nurses Association / Association des infirmières et infirmiers du Canada
50 Driveway, Ottawa ON K2P 1E2
613-237-2133; Fax: 613-237-3520; Toll Free: 1-800-361-8404
Email: info@cna-aiic.ca; URL: www.cna-aiic.ca

Jeanne Mance Awards
Established in 1971, this award is named after one of Canada's most inspirational nurses. Awarded every other year, Nurses nominated for this have have made significant and innovative contributions to the health of Canadians.

Canadian Orthopaedic Foundation / Fondation orthopédique du Canada
PO Box 7029, Innisfil ON L9S 1A8
416-410-2341; Toll Free: 1-800-461-3639
Email: mailbox@canorth.org; URL: www.canorth.org

I. Edouard Samson Award
Medal & $15,000 awarded for outstanding orthopaedic research by a young investigator; paper presented at the annual meeting of the Canadian Orthopaedic Research Society

Canadian Society for Medical Laboratory Science / Société canadienne de science de laboratoire médical
PO Box 2830, Stn LCD 1, Hamilton ON L8N 3N8
905-528-8642; Fax: 905-528-4968; Toll Free: 1-800-263-8277
Email: michellee@csmls.org; URL: www.csmls.org

CSMLS Student Scholarship Program
Awarded to the best students who are enrolled in general medical laboratory technology, cytotechnology, or cytogenetics studies
Five scholarships of $500 each

E.V. Booth Scholarship Award
Awarded to certified medical laboratory technologists who are enrolled in studies leading to a degree in medical laboratory science
Two awards of $500

Canadian Veterinary Medical Association / Association canadienne des médecins vétérinaires
339 Booth St., Ottawa ON K1R 7K1
613-236-1162; Fax: 613-236-9681; Toll Free: 1-800-567-2862
Email: admin@cvma-acmv.org; URL: www.canadianveterinarians.net; www.veterinairesaucanada.net

The CVMA Humane Award
Established 1986 to encourage care & well-being of animals; awarded to an individual (veterinarian or non-veterinarian) whose work is judged to have contributed significantly to the welfare & well-being of animals; $1,000 & a plaque awarded

The Schering-Plough Veterinary Award
Established 1985 to enhance progress in large animal medicine & surgery; award made to a veterinarian whose work in large animal practice, clinical research or basic sciences is judged to have contributed significantly to the advancement of large animal medicine, surgery & theriogenology, including herd health management; $1,000 & a plaque awarded

The Small Animal Practitioner Award
Established 1987 to encourage progress in the field of small animal medicine & surgery; awarded to a veterinarian whose work in small animal practice, clinical research or basic sciences is judged to have contributed significantly to the advancement of small animal medicine, surgery, or the management of small animal practice, including the advancement of the public's knowledge of the responsibilities of pet ownership; $1,000 & a plaque awarded

Catholic Health Association of Canada / Association catholique canadienne de la santé
1247 Kilborn Pl., Ottawa ON K1H 6K9
613-731-7148; Fax: 613-731-7797
Email: info@chac.ca; URL: www.chac.ca

Performance Citation Award
Established 1981; awarded annually to an individual who makes an outstanding contribution to health care in a Christian context, who exhibits exemplary leadership of a national effort at building the Christian community & unselfish dedication to others

College of Family Physicians of Canada / Collège des médecins de famille du Canada
2630 Skymark Ave., Mississauga ON L4W 5A4
905-629-0900; Fax: 905-629-0893; Toll Free: 800/387-6197
Email: info@cfpc.ca; URL: www.cfpc.ca

AMS-Mimi Divinsky Awards for History & Narrative in Family Medicine

Awards of Excellence

Bob Robertson Award

Bruce Halliday Award for Care of the Disabled

Early Career Development Awards

Family Physician of the Year Award/Reg L. Perkin Award

Geeta Gupta Equity & Diversity Award

Irwin Bean Award

Lifetime Achievement Awards in Family Medicine Research

Epilepsy Canada / Épilepsie Canada
#1510, 130 Albert St., Ottawa ON K1P 5G4
Toll Free: 1-877-734-0873
Email: epilepsy@epilepsy.ca; URL: www.epilepsy.ca

Epilepsy Canada Research Fellowships
To develop expertise in clinical or basic epilepsy research & to enhance the quality of care for epilepsy patients in Canada; awarded annually to a Ph.D. or M.D. for clinical research at a Canadian institution; designed as a training program & not intended for those holding faculty appointments

The Royal College of Physicians & Surgeons of Canada / Le Collège royal des médecins et chirurgiens du Canada
774 Echo Dr., Ottawa ON K1S 5N8
613-730-8177; Fax: 613-730-8830; Toll Free: 1-800-668-3740
Email: infos@rcpsc.edu; URL: medical.org
The Office of Fellowship Affairs administers an annual competition for five Fellowship grants, three Awards that recognize original research, and three faculty development projects.

The Royal Society of Canada / La Société royale du Canada
170 Waller St., Ottawa ON K1N 9B9
613-991-6990; Fax: 613-991-6996
Email: info@rsc.ca; URL: www.rsc.ca

Jason A. Hannah Medal
Established 1976; awarded annually for an important publication in the history of medicine

$1,500 & a bronze medal

The McLaughlin Medal
Awarded annually for important research of sustained excellence in any branch of medical science
$2,500 & a medal

JOURNALISM

Atlantic Journalism Awards
46 Swanton Dr., Dartmouth NS B3W 2C5
902-425-2727; Fax: 902-462-1892
Email: office@ajas.ca; URL: ajas.ca

Atlantic Journalism Awards
Originally a program of the University of King's College School of Journalism established in 1981, is now a non-profit organization to recognize excellence & achievement in work by Atlantic Canadian journalists; covers work in English or French; 23 award categories featuring work published or broadcast in the news media of Atlantic Canada.
Winners in individual categories will receive framed certificate presented at the Awards dinner.

Journalistic Achievement Award
An award which recognizes outstanding work in Atlantic Canada by an individual journalist, team of journalists, or a media organization, presented at the Awards dinner

Canadian Association of Journalists / L'Association canadienne des journalistes
c/o Algonquin College, #B224, 1385 Woodroffe Ave.,
Ottawa ON K2G 1V8
613-526-8061; Fax: 613-521-3904
Email: canadianjour@magma.ca; URL: www.caj.ca

The CAJ Awards
Awards presented for the top investigative report published or broadcast in the following media: Newspaper/Newswire (open category), Newspaper (circulation under 25,000), Magazine, TV, Radio, Faith & Spirituality, Photojournalism, Computer assisting reporting & the Don McGillivray award for Best Investigative Report
$1,000 - John Dickins

Canadian Business Press / La Presse spécialisée du Canada
#346, 4195 Dundas St. West, Toronto ON M8X 1Y4
416-239-1022; Fax: 416-239-1076
Email: admin@cbp.ca; URL: www.cbp.ca; www.krwawards.ca

Kenneth R. Wilson Awards
Recognize excellence in writing & graphic design (17 categories) in specialized business/professional publications; open to all business publications, regardless of CBP membership, that are published in English &/or French; all awards, except the Harvey Southam Editorial Career Award, require an entry fee - krwawards@cbp.ca

Newspapers Canada
#200, 890 Yonge St., Toronto ON M4W 3P4
416-923-3567; Fax: 416-923-7206; Toll Free: 1-877-305-2262
Email: info@newspaperscanada.ca; URL:
www.newspaperscanada.ca

National Newspaper Awards/Concours canadien de journalisme
Awards are presented annually in early spring in 16 categories: Spot News Reporting, Enterprise Reporting, Special Project, Layout & Design, Critical Writing, Sports Writing, Feature Writing, Cartooning, Columns, Business Reporting, International Reporting, Spot News Photography, Feature Photography, Sports Photography, Editorial Writing, Local Reporting.
Eligible are those employed by or freelance for daily newspapers or wire services in French or English; awards are governed by an independent board of governors consisting of newspaper & public representatives.
Winners receive $2,500 plus certificates; two runners-up in each category receive citations of merit & $250

Canadian Community Newspaper Awards

EXTRA Awards

Great Idea Awards

Geoff Penny Awards

Canadian Science Writers' Association / Association canadienne des rédacteurs scientifiques
PO Box 75, Stn A, Toronto ON M5W 1A2
Toll Free: 1-800-796-8595
Email: office@sciencewriters.ca; URL: www.sciencewriters.ca

Science in Society Journalism Awards
Open to Canadian journalists in all media for work appearing in the previous calendar year; 14 categories include newspapers, magazines, trade publications, radio, television, children's books & general books; awards total $14,000

L'Oreal Excellence In Science Journalism Award

Heritage Canada Foundation / Fondation Héritage Canada
190, av Bronson, Ottawa ON K1R 6H4
613-237-1066; Fax: 613-237-5987; Toll Free: 1-866-964-1066
Email: heritagecanada@heritagecanada.org; URL:
www.heritagecanada.org

The Heritage Canada Journalism Prize
Awarded annually to a journalist, working in either the print or electronic media, whose coverage of heritage issues is judged to be outstanding

National Magazine Awards Foundation / Fondation nationale des prix du magazine canadien
#700, 425 Adelaide St. West, Toronto ON M5V 3C1
416-828-9011; Fax: 416-504-0437
Email: staff@magazine-awards.com; URL: www.magazine-awards.com

National Magazine Awards
Awards are presented annually in 26 categories including Personal Journalism, Arts & Entertainment, Humour, Business, Science, Health & Medicine, Sports & Recreation, Fiction, Poetry, Travel, Magazine Illustration, Photojournalism, Art Direction, Magazine Covers, & Photography; all above awards go to individual magazine writers, photographers, illustrators, or art directors; Magazine of the Year recognizes continual overall excellence, The President's Medal is awarded to an article from the text categories & offers a prize of $3,000; The Foundation Award for Outstanding Achievement was introduced in 1990 & recognizes an individual's innovation & creativity through career-long contributions to the magazine industry
Awards are gold or silver scrolls with $1,500 & $500 cash prizes respectively; President's Medal $3,000

Ontario Newspaper Awards
c/o The Record, 160 King St. East, Kitchener ON N2G 4E5
519-894-2231
Email: lwilson@therecord.com
Celebrated annually and available in a variety of journalism categories such as: Novice Reporting; Sports Writing; Sports Photography, Humour Writing.

Société Saint-Jean-Baptiste de Montréal
82, rue Sherbrooke Ouest, Montréal QC H2X 1X3
514-843-8851; Fax: 514-844-6369
Email: mbeaulieu@ssjb.com; URL: www.ssjb.com

Prix Olivar-Asselin
Established 1955; $1,500 & a medal awarded annually to a French Canadian in recognition of outstanding achievement in journalism in serving the higher interests of the French Canadian people

Western Magazine Awards Foundation
857 Prairie Ave., Port Coquitlam, BC V3B 1R9
604-669-3717
URL: www.westernmagazineawards.ca

The Western Magazine Awards
Editorial excellence in western Canadian magazine writing, photography, illustration & art direction

LEGAL, GOVERNMENTAL, PUBLIC ADMINISTRATION

Alberta Solicitor General and Public Security
Communications, 10365 - 97 St., 10th Fl., Edmonton AB T5J 3W7
780-427-3441; Fax: 780-427-1903
URL: www.solgen.gov.ab.ca/crime_prev/awards.aspx

Crime Prevention Awards
Awards highlight the activities & accomplishments of special Albertans who prove that preventing crime is everyone's responsibility; awards are presented to an individual, for youth leadership, business, community program or organization & police member for efforts beyond regular duties

Canadian Society of Association Executives / Société canadienne des directeurs d'association
#1100, 10 King St. East, Toronto ON M5C 1C3
416-363-3555; Fax: 416-363-3630; Toll Free: 1-800-461-3608
Email: csae@csae.com; URL: www.csae.com

Pinnacle Award
Recognizes the association executive who has demonstrated exceptional & outstanding leadership qualities within their organization, has contributed to other voluntary organizations & the community at large, to CSAE at local & national levels

Institute of Public Administration of Canada / Institut d'administration publique du Canada
#401, 1075 Bay St., Toronto ON M5S 2B1
416-924-8787; Fax: 416-924-4992
URL: www.ipac.ca

IPAC Award for Innovative Management
Awarded in recognition of outstanding organizational achievement in the public sector

Vanier Medal
A gold medal is awarded annually as a mark of distinction & exceptional achievement to a person who has shown outstanding leadership in public administration in Canada

Justice Canada
Legal Studies for Aboriginal People Program, c/o Indspire, P.O. Box 759, 50 Generations Dr., Six Nations of the Grand River, Ohsweken, Ontario N0A 1M0
Toll Free: 1-855-463-7747
URL: www.justice.gc.ca/eng/pi/pb-dgp/prog/lsap-aeda.html; www.indspire.ca

Legal Studies for Aboriginal People Program
A scholarship program to encourage Métis & Non-Status Indians to enter the legal profession by providing financial assistance through a pre-law orientation course & an annual scholarship program for a maximum of 3 years
Open to Aboriginal People (Métis & Non-Status Indians)

The Professional Institute of the Public Service of Canada / Institut professionnel de la fonction publique du Canada
250 Tremblay Rd., Ottawa ON K1G 3J8
613-228-6310; Fax: 613-228-9048; Toll Free: 1-800-267-0446
URL: www.pipsc.ca

Gold Medal Awards
Established 1937; the gold medals are presented biennially.
Those eligible are scientific, professional, or technical workers or groups of workers employed by the federal, provincial, or municipal government services of Canada who have made a contribution of outstanding importance to national or world well-being in either pure or applied science or in some field outside pure or applied science

LITERARY ARTS, BOOKS & LIBRARIES

Book Publishers Association of Alberta
10523 - 100 Ave., Edmonton AB T5J 0A8
780-424-5060; Fax: 780-424-7943
Email: info@bookpublishers.ab.ca; URL:
www.bookpublishers.ab.ca

Alberta Book Pubishing Awards
To recognize outstanding achievements in Alberta publishing; nine awards are given - Alberta Publisher of the Year, Alberta Trade Book of the Year, Alberta Book Design Award, Alberta Book Cover Design Award, Alberta Educational Book of the Year, Alberta Childrens' Book of the Year, Alberta Book Illustration Award, Alberta Scholarly Book, Alberta Emerging Publisher of the Year.
Stone carvings by Brian Clark are presented & kept by the winner in the award year & exchanged for plaques the following year.

Lois Hole Award for Editorial Excellence
Established in honour of Lois Hole's dedication to books, libraries, literacy and respect for editors.

Alberta Book Publishing Achievement Award
Established to recognize long-standing contributions made to Alberta book publishing.

British Columbia Historical Federation
PO Box 5254, Stn B, Victoria BC V8R 6N4
604-277-2627; Fax: 604-277-2657
Email: info@bchistory.ca; URL: www.bchistory.ca

W. Kaye Lamb Award for the Best Student Essays
Awarded for essays written by students at BC colleges or universities on a topic related to BC history

Writing Awards
Established 1983; Lieutenant-Governor's Medal for Historical Writing, three Certificates of Merit, & cash awards given annually to authors of best books on any facet of BC history

The Canada Council for the Arts / Conseil des Arts du Canada

350 Albert St., PO Box 1047, Ottawa ON K1P 5V8
613-566-4414; Fax: 613-566-4390; Toll Free: 1-800-263-5588
Email: info@canadacouncil.ca; URL: www.canadacouncil.ca

Canada-Japan Literary Awards
Two awards valued at $10,000 awarded every two years in recognition of literary excellence by Canadian writers writing about Japan, Japanese themes or themes that promote mutual understanding between Japan & Canada, or by Canadian translators of such books from Japanese into English or French

CBC Literary Awards
A joint presentation of CBC, enRoute magazine & the Canada Council for the Arts; two prizes of $6,000 & $4,000 given in each of three categories in English & French: poetry, travel literature & short fiction. CBC selects the jury & administers the adjudication process, enRoute publishes the winning entries & the Canada Council provides the cash prizes to the six winners in French & English

The Governor General's Literary Awards
$15,000 each awarded annually to the best English-language & best French-language work in each of the following categories: children's literature (text & illustration), drama, fiction, poetry, literary non-fiction, & translation.
Books must be by Canadian authors, illustrators & translators, published in Canada or abroad. In the case of translation, the original work must also be a Canadian-authored title. Peer assessment committees select the winning titles from the books formally nominated by publishers.

Canadian Association for School Libraries

c/o Canadian Library Association, 328 Frank St., Ottawa ON K2P 0X8
613-232-9625; Fax: 613-563-9895
URL: www.cla.ca/AM/Template.cfm?Section=CASL2

The Angela Thacker Memorial Award
Established in memory of Angela Thacker, teacher-librarian, library coordinator, this award honours teacher-librarians who have made contributions to the profession through publications, productions or professional development activities that deal with topics relevant to teacher-librarianship and/or information literacy.

Chancellor Group Conference Grant
The grant provides $500 support attendance of new teacher-librarians at the next conference of the Canadian Library Association.

Canadian Association of Children's Librarians

c/o Canadian Library Association, 328 Frank St., Ottawa ON K2P 0X8
613-232-9625; Fax: 613-563-9895
Email: info@cla.ca; URL: www.cla.ca/divisions/capl/cacl.htm

Amelia Frances Howard-Gibbon Illustrators Medal
Established 1971; a silver medal awarded annually for outstanding illustrations in a children's book published in Canada; the illustrator must be a Canadian or a Canadian resident - Brenda Shield

Book of the Year for Children Award
A silver medal awarded annually for the outstanding children's book published during the calendar year; book must have been written by a Canadian or a resident of Canada - Brenda Shield

Canadian Association of College & University Libraries

c/o Canadian Library Association, 328 Frank St., Ottawa ON K2P 0X8
613-232-9625; Fax: 613-563-9895
Email: info@cla.ca; URL: www.cla.ca/AM/Template.cfm?Section=CACUL

Robert H. Blackburn Distinguished Paper Award
This award recognizes notable research by CLA members.

Canadian Association of Public Libraries

c/o Canadian Library Association, 328 Frank St., Ottawa ON K2P 0X8
613-232-9625; Fax: 613-563-9895
Email: info@cla.ca; URL: www.cla.ca/divisions/capl/

CAPL/Brodart Outstanding Public Library Service Award
The Canadian Association of Public Libraries, in partnership with Brodart, is please to offer this prestigious award offered annually for outstanding service in the field of Canadian public librarianship.

Canadian Authors Association

74 Mississauga St. East, Orillia ON L3V 1V5
705-653-0323; Toll Free: 1-866-216-6222
Email: admin@canauthors.org; URL: www.canauthors.org

CAA Award for Fiction
$2,500 & a silver medal

CAA Carol Bolt Award
$1,000 & a silver medal

CAA Jack Chalmers Poetry Award
$1,000 & a silver medal

Lela Common Award for Canadian History
$2,500 & a silver medal

The Canadian Children's Book Centre

#217, 40 Orchard View Blvd., Toronto ON M4R 1B9
416-975-0010; Fax: 416-975-8970
Email: info@bookcentre.ca; URL: www.bookcentre.ca

The Geoffrey Bilson Award for Historical Fiction
Rewards excellence in outstanding work of historical fiction for young people by a Canadian author, published in previous calendar year; judges are: a writer, bookseller, children's books specialist, historian, librarian
$1,000

The Norma Fleck Award for Non-Fiction
Rewards excellence in outstanding work of non-fiction for young people by a Canadian author, published in previous calendar year; jury members include a teacher, a librarian, a reviewer & a bookseller
$10,000

Canadian Historical Association / Société historique du Canada

395 Wellington St., Ottawa ON K1A 0N3
613-233-7885; Fax: 613-567-3110
Email: cha-shc@lac-bac.gc.ca; URL: www.cha-shc.ca
24 Awards available for outstanding nonfiction publications in the field of history.
Prizes also available for High School and University levels as well as Research Work and Popular Work.

Canadian Library Association

328 Frank St., Ottawa ON K2P 0X8
613-232-9625; Fax: 613-563-9895
Email: info@cla.ca; URL: www.cla.ca

Dafoe Scholarship
$5,000 awarded annually to a student entering an accredited Canadian library school

H.W. Wilson Scholarship
$2,500 presented annually to a student entering an accredited Canadian library school

World Book Scholarship in Library Science & Information Studies
$2,500 scholarship given annually to be used for a program of study or series of courses either leading to a further library degree or related library work in which the candidate is currently engaged

Young Adult Canadian Book Award
Presented to recognize the best English-language fiction for young adults by a Canadian author

Canadian Library Trustees Association

c/o Canadian Library Association, 328 Frank St., Ottawa ON K2P 0X8
613-232-9625; Fax: 613-563-9895
Email: info@cla.ca; URL: www.cla.ca/AM/Template.cfm?Section=CLTA

Stan Heath Achievement in Literacy Award
Through this award, CLTA endorses the initiatives of the public library systems, which have structured literacy programs as a component of library services to the community

Merit Award for Distinguished Service as a Public Library Trustee
The CLTA Merit Award is presented annually to a library trustee who has demonstrated outstanding leadership in the advancement of trusteeship and public library service in Canada.

CBC Literary Awards/Prix Littéraires Radio-Canada

CBC Radio, PO Box 6000, Montréal QC H3C 3A8
Toll Free: 1-877-888-6788
URL: www.radio-canada.ca/prixlitteraires/

CBC Literary Awards/Prix Littéraires Radio-Canada
The only literary competition that celebrates original, unpublished works, in Canada's two official languages. Prizes are available in three categories: short story, poetry and creative nonfiction. Winning entries are published in Air Canada's enRoute magazine.

Corporation des bibliothécaires professionnels du Québec / Corporation of Professional Librarians of Québec

#103, 353, rue St. Nicolas, Montréal QC H2Y 2P1
514-845-3327; Fax: 514-845-1618
Email: info@cbpq.qc.ca; URL: www.cbpq.qc.ca

Annuel de la CBPQ - Bibliothécaire de l'année
Stimuler et reconnaître l'excellence parmi les membres; attirer l'attention des médias sur les récipiendaires de cette distinction honorifique et sur la nature des réalisations primées; orienter des perceptions; le prix comporte les volets suivants: distinction honorifique, remise d'une épinglette en or, publicité entourant l'événement

The Crime Writers of Canada

3007 Kingston Rd., PO Box 113, Toronto ON M1M 1P1
416-597-9938
Email: info@crimewriterscanada.com; URL: www.crimewriterscanada.com

The Arthur Ellis Awards
Established 1984; awarded annually in the following categories: best crime novel (by a previously published novelist), best crime non-fiction, best first crime novel (by a previously unpublished novelist), best crime short story, best juvenile crime book, & best crime writing in French

Donner Canadian Foundation

400 Logan Ave., Toronto ON M4M 2N9
416-368-8253; 368-3763; Fax: 416-363-1448
Email: meisnerpublicity@sympatico.ca; URL: www.donnerbookprize.com

The Donner Prize
Award of $35,000 for the best book on Canadian public policy; five runners-up prizes of $5,000 each

Fondation Émile-Nelligan

261, rue Bloomfield, Outremont QC H2V 3R6
514-278-4657; Fax: 514-271-6369
Email: info@fondation-nelligan.org; URL: www.fondation-nelligan.org

Prix Émile-Nelligan
Prix annuel. Il s'agit d'un prix de poésie décerné à un poète de moins de 35 ans, pour un recueil publié au cours de l'année
7 500$ et une médaille en bronze frappée à l'effigie d'Émile Nelligan

Prix Gilles-Corbeil
Prix triennal en littérature (poésie, roman, nouvelles, récits, théâtre ou essai littéraire). Décerné à un écrivain citoyen du Canada ou des États-Unis, pour une oeuvre écrite en langue française
100 000$

Fondation Les Forges

1497, rue Laviolette, CP 335, Trois-Rivières QC G9A 5G4
819-379-9813; Fax: 819-376-0774
Email: info@fiptr.com; URL: www.fiptr.com

Grand Prix Quebecor du Festival International de la Poésie
Le Festival International de la Poésie remet une bourse de 5 000 $ au lauréat lors de l'ouverture officielle du festival; le candidat doit: être de citoyenneté canadienne et avoir déjà publié trois ouvrages de poésie chez un éditeur reconnu

Prix Félix-Antoine-Savard de poésie
Décerné annuellement lors des cérémonies d'ouverture du Festival International de la Poésie; vise à honorer, tout en les respectant, la mémoire, l'esprit et l'oeuvre poétique de cet écrivain; une bourse de 250$ y est rattachée et le contenant de 100 feuilles de papier Saint-Gilles sont remis à St-Joseph-de-la-Rive, le jour de l'Action de Grâce
Prix Félix-Leclerc de poésie
Créé en octobre 1997, à l'occasion du 10e anniversaire de la mort du poète; décerné tous les 2 ans lors des cérémonies d'ouverture du Festival International de la Poésie; prix de 1000$
Prix Piché de poésie

Les bourses sont offertes par le Festival International de la Poésie; 1er prix, 2 000 $, 2e prix, 500 $; le candidat doit être de citoyenneté canadienne et n'avoir jamais publié d'ouvrage de poésie chez un éditeur reconnu

The Griffin Trust for Excellence in Poetry

363 Parkridge Cres., Oakville ON L6M 1A8
905-565-5993
Email: info@griffinpoetryprize.com; URL: www.griffinpoetryprize.com

The Griffin Prize
Established in 2000, two prizes of $50,000 each awarded annually for collections of poetry published in English during the preceding year; one will go to a living Canadian poet; the other to a living poet or translator from any other country which may include Canada

International Board on Books for Young People - Canadian Section / Union internationale pour les livres de jeunesse

c/o Canadian Children's Book Centre, #101, 40 Orchard View Blvd., Toronto ON M4R 1B9
416-975-0010; Fax: 416-975-8970
Email: info@ibby-canada.org; URL: www.ibby-canada.org

Claude Aubry Award
Awarded biennially for distinguished contributions to Canadian children's literature by a librarian, teacher, author, illustrator, publisher, bookseller, or editor
$1,000

Elizabeth Mrazik-Cleaver Award
Awarded for distinguished Canadian picture book illustration; submissions to Children's Literature Service, National Library of Canada, 395 Wellington St., Ottawa, ON K1A 0N4
$1,000

Frances E. Russell Award
Awarded to initiate & encourage research in children's literature in Canada
$1,000

The League of Canadian Poets

#608, 920 Yonge St., Toronto ON M4W 3C7
416-504-1657; Fax: 416-504-0096
Email: info@poets.ca; URL: www.poets.ca

Gerald Lampert Memorial Award
Established 1979; awarded annually for excellence in a first book of poetry, written by a Canadian citizen or landed immigrant, & published in the preceding year
$1,000

Pat Lowther Memorial Award
$1,000 awarded annually for excellence in a book of poetry, written by a Canadian female citizen or landed immigrant, & published in the preceding year

The Lionel Gelber Prize

c/o Prize Administrator, Munk Centre for International Studies, University of Toronto, 1 Devonshire Pl., Toronto ON M5S 3K7
416-946-8901; Fax: 416-946-9815
Email: gelberprize.munk@utoronto.ca; URL: www.utoronto.ca/mcis/gelber

The Lionel Gelber Prize
This $15,000 prize is the largest of its kind in the world; a legacy of Lionel Gelber, international writer who died in 1989 & who was much acclaimed for his service to Canada; the prize is "designed to stimulate authors of any nationality who write about international relations, & to encourage the audience for these books to grow"
Books published in English or English translation, must be copyrighted in the year in which the prize is awarded; books must be published or distributed in Canada; submissions by publishers only

Literary Translators' Association of Canada / Association des traducteurs et traductrices littéraires du Canada

Concordia University LB 631, 1455, boul de Maisonneuve ouest, Montréal QC H3G 1M8
514-848-2424, ext. 8702; Fax: 514-848-4514
Email: info@attlc-ltac.org; URL: www.attlc-ltac.org

John Glassco Translation Prize
Awarded annually for a translator's first work in book-length literary translation into French or English, published in Canada during the previous calendar year
$1,000 & one year's membership in the association

Manitoba Writers' Guild Inc.

#206, 100 Arthur St., Winnipeg MB R3B 1H3
204-942-6134; Fax: 204-942-5754; Toll Free: 1-888-637-5802
Email: info@mbwriter.mb.ca; URL: www.mbwriter.mb.ca/book-awards

Alexander Kennedy Isbister Award for Non-Fiction
Presented to the Manitoba writer whose book is judged the best book of adult non-fiction written in English
$3,500

Carol Shields City of Winnipeg Award
To honour books that evoke the special caracter of & contribute to the appreciation & understanding of the City of Winnipeg
$5,000

Eileen McTavish Sykes Award for Best First Book
Awarded annually to a Manitoba author whose first professionally published book is deemed the best written
Must have been written in the previous year
$2,000

John Hirsch Award for Most Promising Manitoba Writer
Awarded annually to the most promising Manitoba writer working in poetry, fiction, creative non-fiction or drama
$2,500

Le Prix littéraire Rue des Chambeault
Biennial award presented to the author whose published book or play is judged to be the best French language work by a Manitoba author
$3,500

Manitoba Book Design of the Year Awards
For the best overall design in Manitoba book publishing in two categories: book design & best illustration

Margaret Laurence Award for Fiction
Presented to the Manitoba writer whose book is judged the best book of adult fiction written in English
$3,500

Mary Scorer Award for Best Book by a Manitoba Publisher
Awarded to the best book published by a Manitoba publisher & written for the trade, bookstore, educational, academic or scholarly market
$1,000

McNally Robinson Book for Young People Awards
Awarded annually to the writer whose young person's book is judged the best written by a Manitoba author; two categories: children's & young adult
$2,500

McNally Robinson Book of the Year
To the Manitoba author judged to have written the best book in the calendar year
$5,000

McClelland & Stewart

c/o McClelland & Stewart Ltd., #900 - 481 University Ave., Toronto ON M5G 2E9
416-598-1114; Fax: 416-598-7764
Email: journeyprize@mcclelland.com; URL: www.mcclelland.com/jpa

The Writers' Trust of Canada/McClelland & Stewart Journey Prize
$10,000 awarded annually to a new & developing writer of distinction for a short story published in a Canadian literary journal. The shortlisted stories are selected from journal submissions & published annually by McClelland & Stewart as The Journey Prize Anthology. M&S presents its own award of $2,000 to the literary journal that originally published the winning story.
Only submissions from Canadian literary journals are accepted. Stories must have had original publication in the nominating journal during the previous year.

The Municipal Chapter of Toronto IODE

#205, 40 St. Clair Ave. East, Toronto ON M4T 1M9
Phone: 416-925-5078; Fax: 416-925-5127
Email: iodetoronto@bellnet.ca

IODE Book Award
Established in 1975; an inscribed scroll & not less than $1,000 awarded annually to the author or illustrator of the best children's book written or illustrated by a Canadian resident in Toronto or surrounding area & published by a Canadian publisher within the preceding 12 months

The National Chapter of Canada IODE

#254, 40 Orchard View Blvd., Toronto ON M4R 1B9
416-487-4416; Fax: 416-487-4417; Toll Free: 1-866-827-7428
Email: iodecanada@bellnet.ca

The National Chapter of Canada IODE Violet Downey Book Award
Awarded annually for the best English-language book, containing at least 500 words of text, preferably with Canadian content, in any category suitable for children aged 13 & under
$3,000

Nova Scotia Library Association

c/o Nova Scotia Provincial Library, 3770 Kempt Rd., Halifax NS B3K 4X8
902-742-2486; Fax: 902-742-6920
Email: mlandry@nsme.library.ns.ca; URL: www.nsla.ns.ca

Ann Connor Brimer Award
Awarded to the author of fiction or non-fiction books published in Canada currently in print & intended for children up to the age of 15; writer must be residing in Atlantic Canada
$1,000 - Heather Mackenzie, Halifax Regional Library, 5381 Spring Garden Rd., Halifax NS B3J 1E9; Email: mahm1@nsh.library.ns.ca

Norman Horrocks Award for Library Leadership
Honours leadership in the Nova Scotia Library community & is awarded for distinguished contributions to the promotion & development of library service in Nova Scotia - Trudy Amirault, Western Counties Regional Library, 405 Main St., Yarmouth NS B5A 1G3, Email: tamiraul@nsy.library.ns.ca

Ontario Arts Council / Conseil des arts de l'Ontario

151 Bloor St. West, 5th Fl., Toronto ON M5S 1T6
416-961-1660; Fax: 416-961-7796; Toll Free: 1-800-387-0058
Email: info@arts.on.ca; URL: www.arts.on.ca

Ruth Schwartz Children's Book Award
Two awards presented annually; $3,000 for best picture book & $2,000 for best young adult/middle reader book; in conjunction with the Canadian Booksellers Association

Ontario Library Association

50 Wellington St. East, Suite 201, Toronto, ON M5E 1C8
416-363-3388; Fax: 416-941-9581
Email: info@accessola.com; URL: www.accessola.com

Blue Spruce(tm) Award Program
The Blue Spruce Award(tm) is a provincial primary reading program which brings recently published Canadian children's picture books to Ontario children ages 4 to 7 in kindergarten through to grade two. Award given out in May every year.

Silver Birch(r) Fiction, Non-Fiction And Express Award Program
The Silver Birch Award(r) is given by Grade 3, 4, 5 and 6 students in a spectacular ceremony held annually in May before fifteen hundred of their peers. The children choose winners in Fiction, Non-Fiction and Express when they cast their ballots on the province-wide Voting Day earlier in the same month. It is the most democratic and unbiased process possible when the children make their choice. The program is administered by the Ontario Library Association and run by teacher-librarians and teachers in schools and by children's librarians in public libraries. But the choice belongs to the children. And, in their tens of thousands, they know what they are doing.

Red Maple(tm) Award Program
The Red Maple Award(tm) reading program is offered for the enjoyment of students in Grades 7 and 8. The program, like the Association's Silver Birch Awards(tm) reading program, gives students who have read a minimum number of nominated titles the opportunity to vote with a large group of their peers for the nominated title that they feel should win the Red Maple Award(tm) each year.

White Pine(tm) Award Program
The White Pine Award(tm) reading program offers high school-aged teens at all grade levels the opportunity to read the best of Canada's recent young adult fiction titles. All of these 10 books for Young Adults on this list are accessible and will allow all readers to be successful participants/voters. As in all of the independent reading programs, a reader only needs to read 5 books out of a list of 10 to qualify to vote. Based on student voting across the province, the most popular book is then selected and author is honoured with the White Pine Award(tm).

The Evergreen(r) Award Program
The Evergreen Award(tm) is OLA's newest addition to the Forest of Reading(r). It was introduced at Super Conference 2005 for adults of any age. It gives adult library patrons the opportunity to vote for a work of Canadian fiction or non-fiction that they have liked the most.

Ontario Media Development Corporation

c/o OMDC, North Tower, #501, 175 Bloor St. East, Toronto ON M4W 3R8
416-314-6858; Fax: 416-314-6876
Email: reception@omdc.on.ca; URL: www.omdc.on.ca

Trillium Book Award for Poetry
Awarded in both English & French
$10,000

Trillium Book Award/Prix Trillium
Awarded annually to an Ontario author of a book of excellence; the winning book must have been published within the preceding 12 months; books in English or French in any genre are eligible; winner receives $12,000 & the publisher receives $2,500

PEI Writers' Guild

81 Prince St, Charlottetown PEI C1A 4R3
Email: peiwritersguild@gmail.com; URL: www.peiwritersguild.com/island-literary-awards-2

Cox & Palmer Island Literary Awards
Established in 1987 in recognition of Island writers in six categories: Short Story, Poetry, Children's Literature, Feature Article, Creative Writing for Children, Playwriting; an additional award is made "for distinguished contribution to the literary arts"
$500, $200 & $100

Periodical Marketers of Canada

South Tower, #1007, 175 Bloor St. East, Toronto ON M4W 3R8
416-968-7311; Fax: 416-968-6281

Canadian Letters Awards
Established 1996; recognizes an individual who has made an outstanding contribution to writing, publishing, teaching or literary administration; award consists of a statuette & a $5,000 donation to the charitable literary organization or educational institution of the winner's choice

Phoenix Community Works Foundation

316 Dupont St., Toronto ON M5R 1V9
416-964-7919; Fax: 416-964-8516
Email: info@pcwf.ca; URL: www.pcwf.ca

The Chap-Book Award
Awarded for the best poetry chap-book in English, published in Canada; entries must be from 10-48 pages in length
$1,000

PriceWaterhouseCoopers

Royal Trust Tower, #3000, 77 King St. West, Toronto ON M5K 1G8
416-869-1130; Fax: 416-941-8345
URL: www.pwcglobal.com/ca/eng/about/events/nbba.html

National Business Book Award
URL: nbbaward.com. Established 1985; annual prize of $20,000 awarded to author of book containing key material on business in Canada - Mary Ann Freedman

Prism International

Creative Writing Program, UBC, Buch. E462 - 1866 Main Mall, Vancouver BC V6T 1Z1
604-822-2514; Fax: 604-822-3616
Email: prism@interchange.ubc.ca; URL: prism.arts.ubc.ca

Earle Birney Prize for Poetry
Awarded annually to an outstanding poetry contributor published in Prism International
$500

Literary Non-Fiction Contest
$1,500

Prism Short Fiction Contest
$3,000 in prizes for annual short fiction contest

Prix Aurora Awards

#501, 88 Bruce St., Kitchener ON N2B 1Y8
Email: prix.aurora.awards@gmail.com; URL: www.prixaurorawards.ca

Prix Aurora Awards
Awards presented annually for the best in Canadian Science Fiction & Fantasy; 10 categories: six professional awards (three English & three French), three fan awards & the artistic achievement award

Québec Ministère de la culture et des communications

225, Grande Allée est, Québec QC G1R 5G5
418-380-2300; Fax: 418-080-2364
Email: DC@mcc.gouv.qc.ca; URL: www.mcc.gouv.qc.ca

Les Prix du Québec
Founded in 1977, these awards are given annually by the Government of Quebec to individuals for cultural and scientific achievements. There are six awards in the cultural field.

Québec Ministère des Relations internationales

Édifice Hector-Fabre, 525, boul René-Lévesque est, Québec QC G1R 5R9
418-649-2300; Fax: 418-649-2656
Email: francine.marcotte@mri.gouv.qc.ca; URL: www.mri.gouv.qc.ca

Prix Québec Wallonie-Bruxelles de littérature de jeunesse
Créé en 1978; vise à encourager le développement de la littérature de jeunesse de langue fran‡aise et à faire la promotion des lauréats. Décerné conjointement par le ministère des Relations internationales et ministère de la Culture et des Communications

Québec Writers' Federation / Fédération des Écrivaines et Écrivains du Québec

1200 Atwater av., Montréal QC H3Z 1X4
514-933-0878; Fax: 514-933-0878
Email: info@qwf.org; URL: www.qwf.org

QWF Literary Awards
Established 1988; awards five annual prizes of $2,000 each to honour literary excellence: The A.M. Klein poetry prize, The Hugh MacLennan fiction prize, Mavis Gallant prize for non-fiction, The McAuslan First Book Award & Translation award Books can be submitted for prizes in five categories by publishers or authors; four copies, accompanied by entry form & $10 registration fee per submission; authors must have lived in Québec three of the past five years

The Royal Society of Canada / La Société royale du Canada

170 Waller St., Ottawa ON K1N 9B9
613-991-6990; Fax: 613-991-6996
Email: info@rsc.ca; URL: www.rsc.ca

Lorne Pierce Medal
Established 1926; awarded every two years for an achievement of special significance & conspicuous merit in imaginative or critical literature written in either English or French, preferably dealing with a Canadian subject

Salon International du livre de Québec

#801, 407, boul St-Laurent, Montréal QC H2Y 2Y5
418-692-0010; Fax: 418-692-0029
Email: info@silq.org; URL: www.silq.org

Prix des libraires du Québec
Ce prix fut créé en 1994 par l'Association des libraires du Québec et le Salon international du livre de Québec; il souligne l'excellence d'un roman québécois par sa qualité d'écriture et son originalité; une bourse de 2 000 $ est offerte en 2005 par le Conseil des Arts et des Lettres du Québec

Saskatchewan Book Awards

#205B, 2314 - 11th Ave., Regina SK S4P 0K1
306-569-1585; Fax: 306-569-4187
Email: director@bookawards.sk.ca; URL: www.bookawards.sk.ca

Anne Szumigalski Poetry Award
$2,000 awarded for the best book of poetry by a Saskatchewan author; sponsored by the Saskatchewan Arts Board

Award for Publishing
A commemorative plaque for the publisher & a certificate for the author presented to the best book published in Saskatchewan; judged on overall quality of design, production, content & significance; sponsored by Saskatchewan Culture, Youth & Recreation

Book of the Year Award
$2,000 awarded for the best book (any genre) by a Saskatchewan author

Brenda MacDonald Riches First Book Award
$2,000 for the best first book by a Saskatchewan writer; sponsored by Agrium Inc.

Children's Literature Award
$2,000 awarded for the best book of children's literature by a Saskatchewan author; sponsored by SaskEnergy

Fiction Award
$2,000 awarded for the best book of fiction (novel or short fiction) by a Saskatchewan author; sponsored by SaskPower

First Peoples Publishing Award
Commemorative certificate for the publisher & for the writer of the best book with First Nations, Metis, or non-status Indian content written, or in the case of an anthology, edited by a person of First Nations, Metis, or non-status Indian descent; based on the quality of publisher's craft, editing, & literary or artistic value; sponsored by the University of Saskatchewan

Non-Fiction Award
$2,000 award awarded for the best book of non-fiction by a Saskatchewan author; sponsored by the University of Saskatchewan

Prix du livre français
$2,000 awarded biennially for the best book written in French by a Saskatchewan author; sponsored by Fondation fransaskoise

Publishing in Education Award
Commemorative plaque for the publisher & certificates for the writer or editor & publisher of the best book produced as an educational resource, judged on the quality of the publisher's craft, editing & its value to educators at primary, secondary or post secondary levels; sponsored by the University of Regina Bookstore

Regina Book Award
$2,000 to the author of the best book by a Regina writer; sponsored by the City of Regina & Regina Public Library

Saskatoon Book Award
$2,000 awarded to the best book written by a Saskatoon author; sponsored jointly by the Saskatoon Public Library & the City of Saskatoon

Scholarly Writing Award
$2,000 awarded for the book making the best contribution to scholarship by a Saskatchewan author; sponsored by Luther College

Saskatchewan Library Association

#15, 2010 - 7th Ave., Regina SK S4R 1C2
306-780-9413; Fax: 306-780-9447
Email: slaexdir@sasktel.net; URL: www.lib.sk.ca/sla/

The Mary Donaldson Award of Merit
Awarded for excellence to a student studying at a library education institution in Saskatchewan

The SLA Frances Morrison Award
Awarded for outstanding service to libraries

Saskatchewan Writers Guild Inc.

#205, 2314 - 11th Ave., Regina SK S4P 0K1
306-757-6310; Fax: 306-565-8554; Toll Free: 1-800-667-6788
Email: swg@sasktel.net; URL: www.skwriter.com

City of Regina Writing Award
To a Regina writer to reward merit & enable a writer to work on a specific writing project; funded by the City of Regina Arts Commission & administered by the SWG
$4,000

The Scotiabank Giller Prize

c/o Elana Rabinovitch, 576 Davenport Rd., Toronto ON M5R 1K9
416-934-0755
Email: contact@scotiabankgillerprize.ca; URL: www.scotiabankgillerprize.ca/

The Giller Prize
$25,000 award to the author of the best Canadian novel or collection of short stories published in English

Stephen Leacock Association Inc.

PO Box 854, Orillia ON L3V 6K8
705-835-7061; Fax: 705-835-7062
Email: info@leacock.ca; URL: www.leacock.ca

Stephen Leacock Memorial Medal for Humour
Established 1946 to encourage the writing & publishing of humorous works in Canada; given annually for the best Canadian book of humour published in the preceding year
Winner receives the medal & a cash award of $10,000 donated by TD Canada Trust

The Order of Mariposa
Awarded occasionally to someone who has contributed significantly to humour in Canada, in other than the written word

University of British Columbia

President's Office, 6328 Memorial Rd., Vancouver BC V6T 1Z2
604-822-4439; Fax: 604-822-6906
Email: jflick@interchange.ubc.ca

Medal for Canadian Biography
Established 1952; awarded annually for the best biography written either about or by a Canadian & published in the preceding year - Jane Flick

Ville de Montréal
Service du développement culturel
5650, d'Iberville, 4e étage, Montréal QC H2G 3E4
514-872-1156
URL: www.ville.montreal.qc.ca/culture/culture.htm

Grand Prix du livre de Montréal
Le prix est offert par la Ville de Montréal à l'auteur ou aux co-auteurs d'un ouvrage de langue française ou anglaise, pour la facture exceptionnelle et l'apport original de cette publication; le prix consiste en une bourse de 15 000 $, ount admissibles un auteur ou un éditeur qui habite sur le territoire de la Ville de Montréal

West Coast Book Prize Society
#902, 207 West Hastings St., Vancouver BC V6B 1H7
604-687-2405; Fax: 604-669-3701
Email: info@bcbookprizes.ca; URL: www.bcbookprizes.ca

BC Book Prizes:
Established 1985; awards of $2,000 presented to winners in each of six categories; the book may have been published anywhere in the world; $25 fee per entry:

Dorothy Livesay Poetry Prize
Awarded to the author of the best work of poetry; the writer must have lived in BC for three of the preceding five years

Lieutenant Governor's Award of Literary Excellence

The Bill Duthie Booksellers' Choice Prize
Awarded for the best book in terms of public appeal, initiative, design, production & content; the book must have been published in BC
The Christie Harris Illustrated Children's Literature Prize

The Ethel Wilson Fiction Prize
Awarded to the author of the best work of fiction; the writer must have lived in BC for three of the preceding five years

The Hubert Evans Non-Fiction Prize
Awarded to the author of the best original non-fiction literary work (philosophy, belles lettres, biography, history, etc.); the writer must have lived in BC for three of the preceding five years

The Haig-Brown Regional Prize
Awarded to the author of the book that contributes most to the enjoyment & understanding of BC; the book may deal with any aspect of the province & should epitomize the BC experience

The Sheila A. Egoff Children's Literature Prize
Awarded to the author of the best book for young people aged 16 & under; the author or illustrator must have lived in BC for three of the preceding five years

Writers Guild of Alberta
11759 Groat Rd., Edmonton AB T5M 3K6
780-422-8174; Fax: 780-422-2663; Toll Free: 1-800-665-5354
Email: mail@writersguild.ab.ca; URL: www.writersguild.ab.ca

Annual Awards Program
Established 1982 to recognize excellence in writing by Alberta authors; published books may be entered in any of the following categories: Children's Literature (any genre), Drama, Novel, Non-Fiction, Poetry, Short Fiction, Best First Book; winners receive $1000 cash award

Writers' Federation of Nova Scotia
1113 Marginal Rd., Halifax NS B3H 4P7
902-423-8116; Fax: 902-422-0881
Email: talk@writers.ns.ca; URL: www.writers.ns.ca

Atlantic Poetry Prize
$2,000

Evelyn Richardson Memorial Literary Trust Award
Award was established in 1978 to recognize outstanding work in non-fiction by a Nova Scotian writer (native or resident)
$2,000

Thomas H. Raddall Atlantic Fiction Prize
Honours the best fiction writing by an Atlantic Canadian writer
$10,000

The Writers' Trust of Canada
#200, 90 Richmond St. East, Toronto ON M5C 1P1
416-504-8222; Fax: 416-504-9090
Email: info@writerstrust.com; URL: www.writerstrust.com

The Bronwen Wallace Memorial Award
Awarded annually to a Canadian writer under the age of 35 who is not yet published in book form; award alternates each year between poetry & short fiction
$1,000

McClelland & Stewart Journey Prize
Awarded annually to a new & developing writer
$10,000

The Marian Engel Award
Established 1986; awarded annually to a female Canadian writer, for a body of work & in hope of future contributions
$15,000

Matt Cohen Award
For a lifetime of distinguished work by a Canadian writer, working in either poetry or prose, writing in either French or English who has dedicated their life to writing as a primary pursuit
$20,000

Rogers Writers' Trust Fiction Prize
Annually to the author of the work of fiction published in the previous year that in the opinion of the judges, shows the best literary merit
$15,000

Nereus Writers' Trust Non-Fiction Prize
Awarded annually to the author of the work of non-fiction published in the previous year that, in the opinion of the judges, shows the best literary merit
$15,000

The Writers Trust of Canada's Shaughnessy Cohen Award for Political Writing
Sponsored by CTV awarded to a non-fiction book of outstanding literary merit that enlarges our understanding of contemporary Canadian political & social issues
$10,000

Vicky Metcalf Prize for Children's Literature
Awarded annually to an author of children's literature, either fiction, non-fiction, picture books or poetry, not for a single book, but for a body of work, unless, in the opinion of the jury, there is no author worthy of the award that year
$15,000

The Writers' Union of Canada
#200, 90 Richmond St. East, Toronto ON M5C 1P1
416-703-8982; Fax: 416-504-9090
Email: info@writersunion.ca; URL: www.writersunion.ca

Danuta Gleed Literary Award
Awarded to a Canadian writer for the best first collection of published short stories in the English language
$10,000

Postcard Story Competition
$500

Short Prose Competition for Developing Writers
$2,500

Writing for Children Competition
$1,500

PERFORMING ARTS

Alberta Scholarship Programs
PO Box 28000, Stn Main, Edmonton AB T5J 4R4
780-427-8640; Fax: 780-427-1288
Email: scholarships@gov.ab.ca; URL: www.alis.gov.ab.ca/scholarships/main.asp

Arts Graduate Scholarships
Five awards of $5,000 at graduate level for study in music, drama, dance & the visual arts & up to $50,000 is available to assist Alberta artists to further their training through non-academic short-term courses & internship or apprenticeship programs

Association québécoise de l'industrie du disque, du spectacle et de la vidéo
6420, rue Saint-Denis, Montréal QC H2S 2R7
514-842-5147; Fax: 514-842-7762
Email: info@adisq.com; URL: www.adisq.com

Les Prix ADISQ
The event honours the best musical achievement produced in Québec during the past year

The Banff Centre
PO Box 1020, Banff AB T1L 1H5
403-762-6180; Fax: 403-762-6345
Email: arts_info@banffcentre.ca; URL: www.banffcentre.ca

The Clifford E. Lee Choreography Award
Established 1978; awarded annually in recognition of outstanding Canadian choreography & jointly sponsored by the Banff Centre & the Edmonton-based Clifford E. Lee Foundation. Winner receives a $5,000 cash prize & a commission to mount a new work for premiere at the Banff Festival of the Arts - George Ross.

The Canada Council for the Arts / Conseil des Arts du Canada
350 Albert St., PO Box 1047, Ottawa ON K1P 5V8
613-566-4414; Fax: 613-566-4390; Toll Free: 1-800-263-5588
Email: info@canadacouncil.ca; URL: www.canadacouncil.ca

Bernard Diamant Prize
Offers professional Canadian classical singers under 35 an opportunity to pursue their career through further studies. $5,000 awarded in addition to the regular grant to an outstanding young classical singer in the annual competition for Grants to Professional Musicians

Canada Council for the Arts Grand Prize for the CBC Young Composers Competition
$10,000 grand prize awarded every two years to the winner of the CBC Young Composers Competition

Canada Council for the Arts/CBC First Prizes for the CBC Radio National Young Performers Competition
Every two years; two first prizes of $15,000 is awarded to the winners of each of the two categories

Canada Council Musical Instrument Bank
Created in 1987 as a means of acquiring exceptional instruments to be loaned to established Canadian musicians or gifted young musicians who are about to embark on an international solo career, following a national jured competition; collection includes the 1827 McConnel Nicolaus Gagliano cello & the 1717 Windsor-Weinstein Stradivarius violin

Eckhardt-Gramatté National Music Competition
Provides assistance in the amount of $9,000 towards the cost of administering the competiton

Healey Willan Prize
$5,000 awarded every two years to the Canadian amateur choir that gives the best performance in terms of musicianship, technique & program in the CBC National Radio Competition for Amateur Choirs

Jacqueline Lemieux Prize
$6,000 awarded annually to the most talented Canadian candidate in the Grants to Dance Professionals competition

Japan-Canada Fund
Supports performance, exhibitions, distribution networks, etc. of Japanese performing artists, media artists, visual artists through established, professional Canadian presenters, as well as for the translations of Canadian & Japanese literary works

Jean-Marie Beaudet Award in Orchestra Conducting
$1,000 awarded annually to a young Canadian conductor, is adjudicated by a committee of music professionals convened by the Canada Council

John Hirsh Prize
$6,000 awarded to a new & developing theatre director who has demonstrated great potential for future excellence & exciting artistic vision; awarded every two years, one in each of the Anglophone & Francophone theatre communites; nominations are made by the professional theatre community & the winners are chosen by a peer assessment committee for the Canada Council Grants to Theatre Artists program

Jules Léger Prize for New Chamber Music
Established in 1978; annual $7,500 prize designed to encourage Canadian composers to write for chamber music groups & to foster the performance of Canadian chamber music by these groups; the Canadian Music Centre administers the award, the Canada Council funds the award & selects the assessment committee of musicians to study the submitted scores; the CBC Radio Two & La Chaîne culturelle de Radio-Canada broadcasts the winning work on the English- & French-language stereo networks

Robert Fleming Prizes
The annual $2,000 prize in memory of Robert Fleming is intended to encourage the career development of young composers & is awarded to the most talented Canadian music composer in the competition for Canada Council Grants to Professional Musicians in classical music

Sylva Gelber Foundation Award
Established 1981; $15,000 awarded annually to the most talented Canadian artist under the age of 30 in the "Grants to Musicians" competition for performers in classical music

Virginia Parker Award
Approximately $25,000 awarded annually to a young Canadian classical musician, instrumentalist, or conductor who has re-

ceived at least one Canada Council grant awarded by a peer assessment committee; the prize is intended to assist a young performer in furthering his/her career

Peter Dwyer Scholarships
Annual scholarships totalling $20,000 awarded to the most promising Canadian students at the National Ballet School & the National Theatre School; each school is awarded $10,000 & chooses the winner on behalf of the Canada Council

Walter Carsen Prize for Excellence in the Performing Arts
Awarded annually, $50,000 prize recognizes the highest level of artistic excellence & distinguished career in the performing arts; awarded to a Canadian artist who is actively performing or who has spent the major part of his/her career in Canada in dance, theatre, or music - in creation or interpretation; prize will be presented on a four-year cycle - dance, theatre, dance, music

Canadian Academy of Recording Arts & Sciences / Académie canadienne des arts et des sciences de l'enregistrement

345 Adelaide Street West, 2nd Floor, Toronto ON M5V 1R5
416-485-3135, ext. 227; Fax: 416-485-4978; Toll Free: 1-888-440-5866
Email: info@carasonline.ca; URL: www.carasonline.ca; www.junoawards.ca

Juno Awards
Annual awards for: Canadian Hall of Fame Award, Walt Grealis Special Achievement Award, Juno Fan Choice (presented by Doritos), Single of the Year, International Album of the Year, Francophone Album of the Year, Artist of the Year, Group of the Year, Instrumental Album of the Year, New Artist of the Year (sponsored by FACTOR & Canada's Private Radio Broadcasters), New Group of the Year (sponsored by FACTOR & Canada's Private Radio Broadcasters), Songwriter of the Year, Country Recording of the Year, Rap Recording of the Year, Pop Album of the Year, Rock Album of the Year, Vocal Jazz Album of the Year, Contemporary Jazz Album of the Year, Traditional Jazz Album of the Year, Children's Album of the Year, Classical Album of the Year: Solo or Chamber Ensemble, Classical Album of the Year: Large Ensemble or Soloist(s) with Large Ensemble Accompaniment, Classical Album of the Year: Vocal or Choral Performance, Classical Composition of the Year, Alternative Album of the Year, Dance Recording of the Year,
Also: Reggae Recording of the Year, Roots & Traditional Album of the Year-Solo, Roots & Traditional Album of the Year-Group, Blues Album of the Year, Jack Richardson Producer of the Year, Recording Engineer of the Year, Album Design of the Year (sponsored by Ever-Reddy Packaging Ltd.), Video of the Year, Music DVD of the Year

Canadian Broadcasting Corporation

CBC Radio Music, PO Box 500, Stn A, Toronto ON M5W 1E6
416-205-3311; Fax: 416-205-6040
URL: www.radio.cbc.ca

National Radio Competition for Amateur Choirs
Established 1975; in partnership with the Association of Canadian Choral Communities; awarded biennially; prizes offered in following categories: Children's, Youth, Large, Adult Mixed Chamber, Adult Equal Voice, Church, Traditional & Ethno-Cultural, & Contemporary Choral Music.
Eight first prizes of $3,000 each; eight 2nd prizes of $2,000 each; $1,000 for best performance of a Canadian work.

National Radio Competition for Young Composers
Established 1973; competition sponsored every two years by CBC & the Canada Council; entrants must be Canadian citizens or landed immigrants, 30 years of age or under, & must not be employees of the CBC.
Up to 10 prizes are given: three 1st prizes of $5,000 each; three 2nd prizes of $4,000 each; three 3rd prizes; a $5,000 Grand Prize; a performance of the winning works is given on CBC English & French radio networks.

National Radio Competition for Young Performers
Established 1960; competition sponsored every two years by CBC/Radio-Canada & the Canada Council for the Arts; entrants must be Canadian citizens or landed immigrants, 30 years of age or under (32 for singers); categories rotate among strings, piano, voice, winds & brass; finals of competiton heard live on CBC Radio Two & La Chaîne culturelle.
First prize $15,000; 2nd prize $10,000; 3rd prize $5,000; prizes also include recital & concert engagements across Canada - URL: www.cbc.ca/ypc.

Canadian Country Music Association / Association de la musique country canadienne

#200, 120 Adelaide St. East, Toronto ON M5C 1K9
416-947-1331; Fax: 416-947-5924
Email: country@ccma.org; URL: www.ccma.org

Music Awards
Awards in 10 categories are presented annually to outstanding performers; 35 citations honour individuals & organizations which, have made a significant contribution to country music

Canadian Theatre Critics Association / Association des critiques de théâtre du Canada

#700, 250 Dundas St. West, Toronto ON M5T 2Z5
416-782-0966; Fax: 416-782-0366
Email: aruprech@ccs.carleton.ca; URL: www.canadiantheatrecritics.ca

The Herbert Whittaker/Drama Bench Award for Outstanding Contribution to Canadian Theatre
Presented annually to Canadian citizen or permanent resident working in any theatrical discipline who has demonstrated distinguished contribution in playwriting, performance, direction or design; named after Herbert Whittaker Founding Chairman of the Canadian Theatre Critics Assoc.

Council for Business & the Arts in Canada / Conseil pour le monde des affaires et des arts du Canada

#903, 165 University Ave., Toronto ON M5H 3B8
416-869-3016; Fax: 416-869-0435
Email: info@businessforarts.org; URL: www.businessforarts.org

Edmund C. Bovey Award
To recognize individual members of the business community who contribute leadership, time, money & expertise to the arts
A sculpture to the winner & $20,000 distributed to the arts in a way specified by the winner

Dance Ontario Association / Association Ontario Danse

Case Goods Bldg., #304, 15 Case Goods Lane,, Toronto ON M5A 3C4
416-204-1083; Fax: 416-204-1085
Email: contact@danceontario.ca; URL: www.danceontario.ca

Dance Ontario Award
Recognizes a lifetime commitment to dance - Peter Ryan

Dancer Transition Resource Centre / Centre de ressources et transition pour danseurs

The Lynda Hamilton Centre, #500, 250 The Esplanade, Toronto ON M5A 1J2
416-595-5655; Fax: 416-595-0009; Toll Free: 1-800-667-0851
Email: nationaloffice@dtrc.ca; URL: www.dtrc.ca

Anne M. Delicaet Bursary
To help fund tuition, books &/or supplies for applicant in their third year of full-time retraining/grants received from the DTRC
Award amount is discretionary

Karen Kain Award
Given to a dancer entering a second or subsequent year of full-time retraining
Award is discretionary

Lynda Hamilton Award
Awarded annually to a dancer in transition who has completed two years of study & requires a third to complete or continue the proposed course of study
$18,000 subsistence & $4,000 for tuition & supplies

Peter F. Bronfman Scholarship of Merit
It is earmarked for a second or third year of retraining & subsistence & may be only awarded for the full amount
$18,000 subsistence & $4,000 for tuition & supplies

Zella Wolofsky/Doug Wright Bursary
Awarded to a dancer with a degree from a recognized university & who is in second or subsequent year of professional program or doing graduate studies or second degree
$2,000 for any purpose

East Coast Music Association / Association de la musique de la côte est

PO Box 31237, Halifax NS B3K 5Y1
902-892-9040; Fax: 902-892-9041
Email: ecma@ecma.ca; URL: www.ecma.ca

East Coast Music Awards
General Categories: Male Artist of the Year, Female Artist of the Year, Group of the Year, Songwriter of the Year, Single of the Year, Video of the Year, Album of the Year, New Artist(s) of the Year, Entertainer of the Year; Genre Specific Categories: Country Recording of the Year, Pop Recording of the Year, Rock Recording of the Year, Instrumental Recording of the Year, Alternative Recording of the Year, Jazz Recording of the Year, Blues Recording of the Year, Gospel Recording of the Year, Children's Recording of the Year, Bluegrass Recording of the Year, Urban Recording of the Year, Classical Recording of the Year, Roots/Traditional Recording of the Year, Folk Recording of the Year; Cultural Categories: Francophone Recording of the Year, Aboriginal Recording of the Year, African-Canadian Recording of the Year

Elinore & Lou Siminovitch Prize in Theatre

c/o BMO Financial Group, 55 Bloor St. West, 4th Fl., Toronto ON M4W 3N5
(416) 9927-2771
Email: andrew.soren@bmo.com; URL: www.siminovitchprize.com

Elinore & Lou Siminovitch Prize
Awarded annually; honours a director, playwright, or designer who in mid-career has made a significant contribution through a body of work to the theatre in Canada; direction, playwriting & design will be honoured on a three year cycle.
$100,000; the winner will receive an immediate cash prize of $75,000, in addition the honoured artist will be invited to designate $25,000 to a protegé of his/her choice who is involved in direction, playwriting or design in theatre in Canada or to an institution (theatre or educational facility) that contributes to better & more successful theatre in Canada

Fondation Émile-Nelligan

261, rue Bloomfield, Outremont QC H2V 3R6
514-278-4657; Fax: 514-278-1943
Email: info@fondation-nelligan.org; URL: www.fondation-nelligan.org

Prix Émile-Nelligan

Governor General's Performing Arts Awards Foundation

#113, 24 York St., Ottawa ON K1N 1K2
613-241-5297; Fax: 613-241-4677
URL: www.bce.ca/ggawards

Governor General's Performing Arts Awards
Established in 1992; honours six performing artists for their lifetime achievement & contribution to the cultural enrichment of Canada; each recipient is awarded $15,000 & a commemorative medal

Ramon John Hnatyshyn Award for Voluntarism in the Performing Arts
Recognizes outstanding service to the performing arts; the recipient is presented with a specially commissioned artwork by Canadian glass artist Naoko Takenouchi

Ontario Arts Council / Conseil des arts de l'Ontario

151 Bloor St. West, 5th Fl., Toronto ON M5S 1T6
416-969-7422; Fax: 416-961-7796;
Toll Free: 1-800-387-0058 ext. 7422
Email: mwarren@arts.on.ca; URL: www.arts.on.ca

John Adaskin Memorial Fund
Established in memorial of the Canadian Music Centre's first executive secretary; supports a project that encourages the promotion & development of Canadian music in the school system

Colleen Peterson Songwriting Award
Established in 2003, in honour of Colleen Peterson's contribution to Canadian folk and country music. This annual award was designed to support and promote the work of an emerging professional singer/songwriter in the genres of roots, traditional, folk and country music
$1,000

Heinz Unger Award for Conducting
Awarded every two years; Established 1968 & awarded biennially to honour the memory of the York Concert Society music director; administered by the Music Office of the Ontario Arts Council in cooperation with the Association of Canadian Orchestras
Up to $9,000

John Hirsch Director's Award
Established by a bequest to the Ontario Arts Council from the late John Hirsch; presented every three years to a promising theatre director in Ontario
$5,000

Leslie Bell Scholarship for Choral Conducting
Established 1973; awarded biennially in competition; the purpose of the award is to help young emerging choral conductors in Ontario further their studies in the choral music field either in Canada or abroad; competition organized by the Ontario Choral Federation
Up to $2,000

Pauline McGibbon Award
Annual award alternates between designers, directors & production crafts persons

$7,000

Premier's Award for Excellence in the Arts
Established in 2006, the Government of Ontario created this award to recognize outstanding achievement in the professional arts by an individual and a group.
Up to $50,000

The Vida Peene Fund
Provides assistance to projects which benefit the orchestra community as a whole

Tim Sims Encouragement Fund Award
Established in 1995; to be awarded annually to a promising young comedic performer or troupe
$1,000

Québec Ministère de la culture, des communications et de la condition féminine
Direction générale du secrétariat et des sociétés d'Etat
225, Grande Allée est, Québec QC G1R 5G5
418-380-2358 ext. 7220; Fax: 418-080-2364
Email: claude.janelle@mcc.gouv.qc.ca; URL: www.prixduquebec.gouv.qc.ca

Prix Denise-Pelletier
Prix réservé aux domaines de la chanson, de la musique, de l'art lyrique, du théâtre et de la danse

Québec Ministère des Relations internationales
Édifice Hector-Fabre, 525, boul René-Lévesque est, Québec QC G1R 5R9
418-649-2300; Fax: 418-649-2656
URL: www.mri.gouv.qc.ca

Prix de musique contemporaine Québec-Flandre
Créé en 1988; récompense les compositeurs flamands et interprètes québecois; décerné aux deux ans et en alternance, ce prix est constitué d'une bourse pour le compositeur et l'exécution de l'ouvre devant le public de l'autre communauté

Prix Rapsat-Lelièvre du disque de chanson
Initialement connu sous le nom Prix Québec/Wallonie-Bruxelles du disque de chanson; vise à encourager le développement et la promotion de la langue française, à stimuler la production et la diffusion de disques francophones

Société Saint-Jean-Baptiste de Montréal
82, rue Sherbrooke ouest, Montréal QC H2X 1X3
514-843-8851; Fax: 514-844-6369
Email: mbeaulieu@ssjb.com; URL: www.ssjb.com

Prix Calixa-Lavallée
Established 1959; $1,500 & a medal awarded annually to a French Canadian in recognition of outstanding achievement in music in serving the higher interests of the French Canadian people

Toronto Alliance for the Performing Arts
#210, 215 Spadina Ave., Toronto ON M5T 2C7
416-536-6468; Fax: 416-536-3463; Toll Free: 1-800-541-0499
URL: www.tapa.ca

Dora Mavor Moore Awards
Established 1979; celebrating excellence in Toronto theatre, 33 awards in large, medium & small theatre divisions, Theatre for Young Audiences & New Choreography

Western Canadian Music Alliance
#340, 955 Portage Ave., Winnipeg MB R3M 0Y1
204-943-8485; Fax: 204-453-1594
Email: info@breakoutwest.ca; URL: www.breakoutwest.ca

Prairie Music Awards
Annual Awards in the following categories: Recording Engineer of the Year, Record Producer of the Year, Recording Studio of the Year, Record Company of the Year, Publishing Company of the Year, Best Compilation Album of the Year, Best Album Design of the Year, Best Music Score of the Year, Best Music Video, Best Booking Agent, Manager of the Year, & Musician of the Year; also Annual Awards for Prairie artists in the following categories: People's Choice Award, Female/Male Recording Artist of the Year, Group Recording of the Year, Most Promising Artist, Best Pop/Light Rock, Best Rock/Heavy Metal, Best Alternative, Best Country, Best Blues/R&B/Soul, Best Roots/Traditional/Ethnic, Best Rap/Dance/Rhythm, Best Jazz, Best Classical Performance

PUBLIC AFFAIRS

B'nai Brith Canada
15 Hove St., Toronto ON M3H 4Y8
416-633-6224; Fax: 416-630-2159
Email: bnb@bnaibrith.ca; URL: www.bnaibrith.ca

Award of Merit & Humanitarian Awards
Established 1981; presented annually at gala events in major communities across Canada
Selection of honourees based on outstanding achievement in their chosen fields as well as personal commitment to the overall betterment of Canadian society - Sharon Anisman

Canadian Association on Gerontology / Association canadienne de gérontologie
#328 McCaul St., Toronto ON M5T 1W7
416-978-7977; Fax: 416-978-4771
Email: contact@cagacg.ca; URL: www.cagacg.ca

The CAG Donald Menzies Bursary
To support post-baccalaureate students registered in a program of study focused on aging or the aged
$1,500

The CAG Margery Boyce Bursary
To support post-baccalaureate students who have made a significant contribution to their community through volunteer activities with or on behalf of seniors & who are registered in a program of study focused on aging or the aged
$500

The Canadian Council of Christians & Jews / Conseil canadien des chrétiens et des juifs
4211 Yonge St., PO Box 17, Toronto ON M2P 2A9
416-597-9693; Fax: 416-597-9775; Toll Free: 1-800-663-1848
Email: info@cccj.ca; URL: www.cccj.ca

Human Relations Award
Made to outstanding Canadians who have made a significant contribution towards bringing people together regardless of race, religion, or social status, in an atmosphere of understanding & respect; the award is made annually & is approved by a National Nominating Committee from the Board of Directors of CCCJ

Canadian Council of Professional Engineers / Conseil canadien des ingénieurs
#1100, 180 Elgin St., Ottawa ON K2P 2K3
613-232-2474; Fax: 613-230-5759
Email: info@engineerscanada.ca; URL: www.engineerscanada.ca

Meritorious Service Award for Community Service
Awarded for exemplary voluntary contribution to a community organization or humanitarian endeavour

Canadian Federation for Sexual Health / Fédération canadienne pour la santé sexuelle
#403, 2197 Riverside Dr., Ottawa ON K1H 7X3
613-241-4474; Fax: 613-241-7550
Email: admin@cfsh.ca; URL: www.cfsh.ca

Phyllis P. Harris Scholarship
For students who have worked or volunteered in the general field of human sexuality who intend to work for a degree in the field of family planning or population issues
$2,500 towards full-time study at a Canadian university

The City of Toronto
Diversity Management and Community Engagement, Strategic and Corporate Policy/Healthy City Office, Manager's Office, City Hall, 100 Queen St. West, 11th Fl., East Tower, Toronto ON M5H 2N2
416-392-8592; Fax: 416-696-3645
Email: diversity@toronto.ca; URL: www.toronto.ca/civicawards/

Aboriginal Affairs Award
Est. 2003, given to a person(s) or organization whose volunteer efforts have made or are making a significant or ongoing contribution to the well-being & advancement of the Aboriginal community in Toronto

Access Award for Disability Issues
Established 1982; honours people or organizations that have made or are making a significant or ongoing contribution, beyond legislated requirements, to the well-being & advancement of people with disabilities; the award honours those who are sensitive to the access needs of persons with disabilities when planning structures or programs (this could include consideration of access requirements in the design of new or renovated buildings, a job creation campaign, a transportation system, recreational program, etc.)

Constance E. Hamilton Award on the Status of Women
This award commemorates the Privy Council of Great Britain granting women status as persons in 1929; award is named after the first woman member of City Council; recipients are persons who have made a significant contribution to securing equitable treatment for Toronto women

Pride Award for Lesbian Gay Bisexual Transgender Transsexual Two Spirited Issues
Est. 2003, the Pride Award honours individuals &/or organizations that have made or are making a significant or ongoing contribution to the well-being & advancement of these communities in Toronto

William P. Hubbard Race Relations Award
Named for Toronto's first visible minority Member of Council & Acting Mayor, this award honours persons with outstanding achievement & commitment to this field in Toronto; award was presented for the first time in 1990

Ethics in Action Awards
c/o VanCity, 183 Terminal Ave., PO Box 2120, Stn Terminal, Vancouver BC V6B 5R8
604-877-7000; Toll Free: 1-800-826-2489
Email: eia@ethicsinaction.com; URL: www.ethicsinaction.com

Ethics in Action Awards
Awards recognize businesses & individuals in business, whose actions & decisions have made a positive impact on our communities

Ontario Ministry of Citizenship & Immigration
Ontario Honours & Awards
Secretariat Ministry of Citizenship and Immigration, 400 University Ave., 4th Fl., Toronto ON M7A 2R9
416-314-7526; Fax: 416-314-7743
Email: ontariohonoursandawards@ontario.ca; URL: www.citizenship.gov.on.ca/english/honours

Ontario Senior Achievement Award
Presented annually to Ontario residents who have made a significant contribution to their communities after reaching 65 years of age; nominations may be made by any individual or organization

Status of Women Canada
123 Slater St., Ottawa ON K1P 1H9
613-995-7835; Fax: 613-943-2386
URL: www.swc-cfc.gc.ca

Governor General's Award in Commemoration of Persons Case
Established 1979 to celebrate the 50th anniversary of the "Persons Case" which resulted in women being declared eligible for appointment to the Senate; annual awards recognize contributions by individuals toward promoting the equality of women in Canada

SCIENTIFIC, ENGINEERING, TECHNICAL

Association of Universities & Colleges of Canada / Association des universités et collèges du Canada
#600, 350 Albert St., Ottawa ON K1R 1B1
613-563-1236; Fax: 613-563-9745
Email: awards@aucc.ca; URL: www.aucc.ca

Fairfax Financial Holdings Limited Scholarship Program
Undergraduate students of all disciplines
36 university undergraduate scholarships of $5,000; 24 college diploma scholarships of $3,500

BC Innovation Council
1188 West Georgia St., 9th Fl., Vancouver BC V6E 4A2
604-438-2752; Fax: 604-438-6564; Toll Free: 1-800-665-7222
Email: info@bcinnovationcouncil.com; URL: www.bcinnovationcouncil.com

BC Innovation Council Awards
Up to six gold medals awarded each year for outstanding achievements by BC scientists, engineers, industrial innovators & science communicators. The awards are: BC Science & Technology Champion of the Year, Young Innovator Award, Frontiers in Research, Cecil Green Award for Technology Entrepreneurship, Chairman's Award for Career Achievement, Lieutenant Govenor's Technology Innovation Award & Eve Savory Award for Science Communication

The Canada Council for the Arts / Conseil des Arts du Canada
350 Albert St., PO Box 1047, Ottawa ON K1P 5V8
613-566-4414; Fax: 613-566-4390; Toll Free: 1-800-263-5588
Email: info@canadacouncil.ca; URL: www.canadacouncil.ca

Killam Prizes
Up to five prizes of $100,000 each are given annually to eminent Canadian scholars in recognition of a distinguished career achievement in the natural sciences, health sciences, engineer-

ing, social sciences & humanities. Candidates must be nominated by three experts in their field. Chosen by Killam Selection

Killam Research Fellowships
Fellowships offered on a competitive basis to support specific research projects by distinguished Canadian researchers in any of the following broad fields: humanities, social sciences, natural sciences, health sciences, engineering & studies linking any of the disciplines within these broad fields; provide release time to individual scholars, normally full professors in Canadian universitites, who wish to pursue individual research; provides two years of teaching replacement to a maximum of $53,000 per year, plus the cost of fringe benefits of the Fellow, based on actual salary for the year before the tenure of the award; application must be made by individuals, not by institutions, universities or organizations

Canadian Aeronautics & Space Institute / Institut aéronautique et spatial du Canada

#104, 350 Terry Fox Drive., Kanata ON K2K 2W5
613-591-8787; Fax: 613-591-7291
Email: casi@casi.ca; URL: www.casi.ca

C.D. Howe Award
Established 1966; a silver plaque presented annually for achievement in the fields of planning, policy making & overall leadership in Canadian aeronautics & space activities

McCurdy Award
Established 1954; a silver medal & trophy presented annually for outstanding achievement in art, science & engineering relating to aeronautics & space

Romeo Vachon Award
Established 1969; bronze plaque awarded annually for outstanding contribution of a practical nature to the art, science, & engineering of aeronautics & space in Canada

Trans-Canada (McKee) Trophy
Canada's oldest aviation award established 1927; presented annually except when no qualified recipient is nominated for outstanding achievement in the field of air operations

Canadian Council of Professional Engineers / Conseil canadien des ingénieurs

#1100, 180 Elgin St., Ottawa ON K2P 2K3
613-232-2474; Fax: 613-230-5759

Email: info@engineerscanada.ca; URL: www.engineerscanada.ca
Gold Medal Award
Awarded for exceptional individual achievement & distinction in a field of engineering

Medal for Distinction in Engineering Education
Awarded for exemplary contribution to engineering teaching at a Canadian University

The Young Engineer Achievement Award
Awarded for outstanding contribution in a field of engineering by an engineer 35 years of age or younger

Canadian Institute of Forestry / Institut forestier du Canada

#504, 151 Slater St., Ottawa ON K1P 5H3
613-234-2242; Fax: 613-234-6181
Email: cif@cif-ifc.org; URL: www.cif-ifc.org

Canadian Forest Management Group Achievement Award
Established 1998; to recognize outstanding achievement by teams in groups of Natural Resource managers, researchers and NGO groups in forest resources related activities in Canada.

Canadian Forestry Achievement Award
Established 1966 & presented annually in recognition of superior accomplishments in forestry research &/or in recognition of outstanding administrative leadership in management, education, research & affairs of professional & scientific societies

Canadian Forestry Scientific Achievement Award
Established 1980; presented annually in recognition of superior accomplishments in scientific forestry

International Forestry Achievement Award
Established 1980; presented in recognition of outstanding achievement in international forestry

James M. Kitz Award
Awarded to a person who has made outstanding contributions to the practice of forestry, including: superior personal accomplishments; outstanding leadership in education, management research or professional association work; promotion of forestry to various audiences
Open to anyone involved in forestry

Canadian Institute of Mining, Metallurgy & Petroleum / Institut canadien des mines, de la métallurgie et du pétrole

#855, 3400, boul de Maisonneuve ouest, Montréal QC H3Z 3B8
514-939-2710; Fax: 514-939-2714
Email: cim@cim.org; URL: www.cim.org

CIM Awards
The institute administers 26 awards recognizing achievement in mining, metallurgy & petroleum industries

CANARIE Inc.: Canada's Advanced Internet Development Organization

110 O'Connor St., Ottawa ON K1P 1H1
613-943-5454; Fax: 613-943-5443
Email: info@canarie.ca; URL: www.canarie.ca

IWAY Awards
The Canarie IWAY Awards honors individuals or group & organizations who have made outstanding contributions to Canada's information society; focuses on R&D, advancements in internet technology providing cultural, social & economic benefits; five categories: New Technology Development; Application of Technology; Public Leadership; Community Service; Adaptive Technologies; Judges Award

The Chemical Institute of Canada / Institut de chimie du Canada

#550, 130 Slater St., Ottawa ON K1P 6E2
613-232-6252; Fax: 613-232-5862; Toll Free: 1-888-542-2242
Email: info@cheminst.ca; URL: www.cheminst.ca

Chemical Institute of Canada Awards
The institute administers several awards & scholarships in chemistry, chemical engineering, & macromolecular science or engineering

E.W.R. Steacie Memorial Fund / Fondation E.W.R. Steacie

100 Sussex Dr., Ottawa ON K1A 0R6
613-993-1212; Fax: 613-954-5242
Email: PrixSteaciePrize.SIMS@nrc-cnrc.gc.ca; URL: www.steacieprize.ca/index_e.html

The Steacie Prize
Canada's most prestigious award for young scientists & engineers; named to honour the memory of Edgar William Richard Steacie, a physical chemist & former President of the National Research Council of Canada; established 1963; awarded annually to a young scientist or engineer up to 40 years of age for outstanding scientific work in a Canadian context; winner receives a certificate & $10,000
$15,000

The Engineering Institute of Canada / Institut canadien des ingénieurs

1295 Hwy. 2 East, Kingston ON K7L 4V1
613-547-5989; Fax: 613-547-0195
Email: jplant1@cogeco.ca; URL: www.eic-ici.ca

The Sir John Kennedy Medal
Established in 1927 in commemoration of the great services rendered in the field of engineering by Sir John Kennedy, a past president of the EIC; medal is awarded every two years by the council in recognition of outstanding merit in the profession or of noteworthy contributions to the science of engineering or to the benefit of the institute

Ernest C. Manning Awards Foundation

#267, 3553 – 31st St. NW, Calgary AB T2L 2K7
403-645-8277; Fax: 403-645-8320
Email: manning@encana.com; URL: www.manningawards.ca

The Manning Awards
Given annually to Canadian innovators who have conceived & developed new concepts, procedures, processes or products of benefit to Canada; awards may be in any area of activity.
One $100,000 Principal Award; one $25,000 Award of Distinction; two $10,000 Innovation prizes, & four $4,000 Young Canadian Innovation Awards.

Natural Sciences & Engineering Research Council of Canada / Conseil de recherches en sciences naturelles et en génie

350 Albert St., Ottawa ON K1A 1H5
613-995-5992; Fax: 613-992-5337
URL: www.nserc.ca

Gerhard Herzberg Gold Medal for Science & Engineering
Awarded annually to an individual who has made outstanding & sustained contributions to Canadian research in natural sciences & engineering; the gold medal will be awarded for any activity of exceptional importance & impact that leads to the enhancement of the research enterprise in Canada - such activities may include contributions to knowledge, the application of existing knowledge, to the novel solution of practical problems, the promotion or management of research activity, the leadership in the transfer of knowledge.
The accomplishments for which the award is given must have been carried out in Canada & achieved over a substantial period of time; persons from any sector (academic, business & industry, or government) are eligible; current members of council are not eligible; awardee's performance in relation to the cited achievement must demonstrate an unusually high degree of ability & the application of such qualities as expertise, creativity, imagination, leadership, perseverance & dedication.

The E.W.R. Steacie Memorial Fellowships
Awarded to enhance the career development of outstanding & highly promising scientists & engineers who are staff members of Canadian universities; successful fellows are relieved of any teaching & administrative duties, enabling them to devote all their time & energy to research; up to four fellowships are awarded annually for a one or two-year period; fellowships are held at a Canadian university or affiliated research institution
Set at $90,000 to be paid to the university by NSERC to cover the cost of replacing the Steacie Fellow's teaching & administrative responsibilities

Prix Galien Canada

#240, 1100, Avenue des Canadiens-de-Montréal, Montréal QC H3B 2S2
514-216-2513
Email: info@prix-galien-canada.com; URL: eng.prix-galien-canada.com

Belleau-Nickerson Prize
Awarded in recognition of a drug that has been on the market for the past 10 years anywhere in the world & for at least three years in Canada

MacLean Hunter Health Fellowship
Awarded to a deserving young Canadian researcher
$15,000

Prix Galien - Innovative Drug
Awarded to a company that has developed & marketed a drug that has made the most significant contribution to the well-being of the general public, in terms of efficacy, safety & innovation

Prix Galien - Research
Awarded to a scientist who is known for his/her contribution to pharmaceutical research in Canada

Québec Ministère du Développement économique, de l'Innovation et de l'Exportation

710, place D'Youville, 3e étage, Québec QC G1R 4Y4
418-691-5950; Fax: 418-644-0118; Toll Free: 1-866-463-6642
URL: www.mdeie.gouv.qc.ca/

Prix Armand-Frappier
Décerné pour la création ou le développement d'institutions de recherche, ou pour l'administration et la promotion de recherche

Prix Lionel-Boulet
Décerné au chercheur qui s'est distingué par ses inventions, ses innovations scientifiques et technologiques, son leadership dans le développement scientifique et sa contribution à la croissance économique du Québec

Prix Marie-Victorin
Décerné aux chercheurs de sciences exactes et naturelles, les sciences de l'ingénierie et technologiques ainsi que les sciences agricoles

Prix Wilder-Penfield
Décerné aux scientifiques dont l'objet de recherche appartient au domaine biomédical

Royal Astronomical Society of Canada / Société royale d'astronomie du Canada

282 Somerset West, Ottawa ON K2P 0J6
613-991-6990; Fax: 613-991-6996
Email: nationaloffice100000@rsc-src.ca; URL: rsc-src.ca

Chant Medal
Established 1940 in appreciation of the great work of the late Prof. C.A. Chant in furthering the interests of astronomy in Canada; silver medal is awarded no more than once a year to an amateur astronomer resident in Canada on the basis of the value of the work which he/she has carried out in astronomy & closely allied fields of original investigation

Ken Chilton Prize
Established 1977; plaque awarded annually to an amateur astronomer resident in Canada, in recognition of a significant piece of work carried out or published during the year

Simon Newcomb Award
Established 1978; trophy awarded annually for the best article on astronomy, astrophysics or space sciences submitted by a member of the society during the year

The Plaskett Medal
Presented jointly with CASCA for an outstanding doctoral thesis

The Royal Canadian Geographical Society / Société géographique royale du Canada
39 McArthur Ave., Vanier ON K1L 8L7
613-745-4629; Fax: 613-744-0947; Toll Free: 1-800-267-0824
Email: rcgs@rcgs.org; URL: www.rcgs.org

The Gold Medal
Established 1972; to recognize a particular achievement of one or more individuals in the field of geography, or a significant national or international event - Coordinator, Society Programs, Carolyn Milano

The Massey Medal
Established 1959; awarded annually for outstanding personal achievement in the exploration, development, or description of the geography of Canada

The Royal Society of Canada / La Société royale du Canada
170 Waller St., Ottawa ON K1N 9B9
613-991-6990; Fax: 613-991-6996
Email: info@rsc.ca; URL: www.rsc-src.ca

Bancroft Award
Established 1968; awarded every two years for publication, instruction & research in the earth sciences that have conspicuously contributed to public understanding & appreciation of the subject
$2,500 & a presentation scroll - Geneviève Gouin, Awards Coordinator, 613-991-5760

John L. Synge Award
Established 1986; awarded at irregular intervals for outstanding research in any of the branches of mathematics
$2,500 & a diploma

Rutherford Memorial Medals: Chemistry & Physics
Established 1980; awarded annually for outstanding research, one in chemistry, one in physics
Two medals & $2,500 each

The Flavelle Medal
Established 1924; awarded every two years (since 1966) for an outstanding contribution to biological science during the preceding 10 years or for significant additions to a previous outstanding contribution to biological science

The Henry Marshall Tory Medal
Established 1941; awarded every two years (since 1947) for outstanding research in a branch of astronomy, chemistry, mathematics, physics, or an allied science

The McNeil Medal
Awarded to encourage communication of science to students & the public
$1,500 bursary & a medal

Willet G. Miller Medal
Established 1943; awarded every two years for outstanding research in any branch of the earth sciences - Geneviève Gouin, Awards Coordinator, 613-991-5760

Society of Chemical Industry - Canada International Group
14/15 Belgrave Sq., London UK SW1X 8PS
Email: awards@soci.org; URL: www.soci.org

Canada Medal Award
Established 1939; awarded every two years for outstanding services in the Canadian chemical industry; recipient delivers an address at a meeting of the society

International Award
Established 1976; award is presented in recognition of outstanding service in the chemical industry in the international sphere, preferably to Canadians or persons who have contributed measurably to the Canadian chemical scene

LeSueur Memorial Award
Established 1955 to commemorate Ernest A. Le Sueur; award is presented in recognition of outstanding innovation in the Canadian chemical industry

Julia Levy Award

Kalev Pugi Award

Merit Awards

Purvis Memorial Award

SPORTS & RECREATION

Physical & Health Education Canada
#301, 2197 Riverside Dr., Ottawa ON K1H 7X3
613-523-1348; Fax: 613-523-1206; Toll Free: 1-800-663-8708
Email: info@phecanada.ca; URL: www.phecanada.ca

R. Tait McKenzie Award of Honour
Instituted at the Montreal Convention in 1948, this is the most prestigious award presented by CAHPERD; named after the distinguished Canadian physician, sculptor & physical educator, Dr. Robert Tait McKenzie; candidate shall have performed distinguished, meritorious service as a recognized leader regionally & nationally in his/her field

Canadian Association for the Advancement of Women & Sport & Physical Activity / Association canadienne pour l'avancement des femmes du sport et de l'activité physique
#N202, 801 King Edward Ave., Ottawa ON K1N 6N5
613-562-5667; Fax: 613-562-5668
Email: caaws@caaws.ca; URL: www.caaws.ca

Breakthrough Awards
Presented annually to outstanding nominees who have used innovative ideas & alternative approaches to encourage & enable more girls & women to participate/lead/coach in sport & physical activity - Karin Lofstrom

CAAWS/Nike Girls@Play MVP Grant
Monthly grant awarded to a female athlete, coach, official or sport/recreation organization to help make their sporting goals & dreams - URL: www.caaws.ca/girlsatplay/grants/index.htm

Girls@Play Nike Youth Award

Stacey Levitt Women & Sport Scholarships
Awarded each year on behalf of the Levitt family & in memory of Stacey Levitt, who was killed while jogging in 1995 after being hit by a car.
$500 & a copy of "I am a Rose," a collection of poetry written by Stacey is given to a young woman, a girl's team or a sport organization that exemplifies Stacey's ideals & qualities.

Canadian Curling Association / Association canadienne de curling
1660 Vimont Ct., Cumberland ON K4A 4J4
613-834-2076; Fax: 613-834-0716; Toll Free: 1-800-550-2875
Email: info@curling.ca; URL: www.curling.ca

Award of Achievement
Commemorative plaque presented in recognition of individuals who have contributed significantly to any aspect of Canadian curling operations

Ray Kingsmith Award
Awarded to an individual who parallels the level of involvement & commitment exemplified by Ray Kingsmith

Volunteer of the Year Award
Based on contributions from the previous curling season; national volunteer of the year receives an all-expense paid weekend trip to Nokia Brier or Scott Tournament of Hearts, where they will be recognized during a playoff game

Ontario Ministry of Tourism & Recreation
Ontario Sport Awards
900 Bay St., 9th Fl., Toronto ON M7A 2R9
416-326-9326
URL: www.tourism.gov.on.ca/english/sportdiv/sport/sports-awards.htm

Ontario Sports Awards
Awards for Athlete of the Year (Male & Female), Coach of the Year (Male & Female), Athlete with a Disability of the Year (Male & Female), Team of the Year, Special Achievement Award for Volunteers, Corporate Sport Citation

Swimming/Natation Canada
#700, 2197 Riverside Dr., Ottawa ON K1H 7X3
613-260-1348; Fax: 613-260-0804
Email: natloffice@swimming.ca; URL: www.swimming.ca

Administrator of the Year Award
Annual award presented to a volunteer, who has demonstrated outstanding commitment to the organization

Club of the Year Award
Awards presented annually to three clubs

Coach of the Year
Annual awards recognize coaches of swimmers in the following categories: 1) able-bodied athletes; 2) athletes with a disability, & 3) long distance competitors; each winner receives a plaque & gift

Dr. Jeno Tihanyi Memorial Bursary

Female/Male Swimmer of the Year
Annual awards recognize best international swimmers in the following categories: 1) able-bodied athletes, 2) athletes with a disability, & 3) long distance competitors; each winner receives a plaque & gift

Official of the Year Award
Annual award recognizes outstanding service to Canadian swimming

Victor Davis Memorial Award
Annual awards from the Victor Davis Memorial Fund assist young Canadian swimmers to continue their training, education & pursuit of excellence at the international level of competition; recipients are determined by the Victor Davis Memorial Fund Awards Committee

Canadian Honours System

For some years after Confederation, awards were made of a few hereditary honours and some knighthoods and companionships in orders of chivalry, and this policy continued until the end of the First World War.

From 1919 until 1933 no titular honours were granted. There was a brief revival of the defunct honours policy during the Conservative administration of R.B. Bennett, and several distinctions were awarded from 1934 to 1935, but the prohibition was reinstated with the return of the Liberals to office in 1935. Consequently, at the outset of the Second World War, Canadians in the armed services were not entitled to receive awards in the order of chivalry for which other Commonwealth personnel were eligible. A parliamentary committee appointed in 1943 recommended that the ban on nontitular honours be lifted, clearing the way for members of the military and civilians to receive recognition for wartime services.

The hundredth anniversary of Confederation, July 1st, 1967, was the occasion on which the Order of Canada was created as the first component of a distinctly Canadian honours system. More information concerning Orders, Decorations and Medals (as well as various Governor General's awards) may be obtained by writing to: Public Information Directorate, Government House, 1 Sussex Dr., Ottawa ON K1A 0A1.

HERALDRY

Coats-of-arms, flags, badges and other heraldic devices are marks of honour and symbols of identity, authority and, in some cases, sovereignty. Each is granted by the Crown under an exercise of the Sovereign's prerogative to create heraldic honours.

Until June 4, 1988, Canadian corporations and individuals wishing to bear lawful arms petitioned the Sovereign's traditional heraldic officers in London and Edinburgh. On that date, by Royal Letters Patent, the Queen transferred the exercise of her heraldic prerogative, as Queen of Canada, to the Governor General who now heads a new office, the Canadian Heraldic Authority. With the act, heraldry, which has a long history in Canada, has been fully repatriated.

These vice-regal responsibilities are administered by Canadian officers of arms appointed by commission under the Governor General's privy seal: the Herald Chancellor (the Secretary to the Governor General), the Deputy Herald Chancellor (the Deputy Secretary, Chancellery) and the Chief Herald of Canada (Director, Heraldry). He is assisted by three officers of arms: Saint-Laurent, Athabaska, and Fraser heralds, and one officer of arms extraordinary, Dauphin Herald.

New heraldic emblems are granted, and existing ones registered, by the Chief Herald upon receipt of an enabling Warrant from the Herald Chancellor or the Deputy Herald Chancellor acting on behalf of the Governor General. Grants and registrations are made by Letters Patent, documents that set out the Governor General's heraldic responsibilities, describe the emblem granted, and feature a representation of the Governor General's personal arms. To ensure a lasting record, the newly granted and registered emblems are entered in Canada's national armorial, the Public Register of Arms, Flags and Badges of Canada.

Since the Authority was created, hundreds of petitions have been received from every part of the country, most for new grants of arms.

Canadian Honours List

ORDER OF CANADA

As mentioned above, the Order of Canada was created July 1, 1967. Her Majesty The Queen is Sovereign of the Order of Canada and the Governor General is, by virtue of that office, Chancellor and Principal Companion. He/She is assisted in the administration of the Order by an Advisory Council which comprises of:

a) the Chief Justice of Canada (Chair)
b) the Clerk of the Privy Council
c) the Deputy Minister, Canadian Heritage
d) the Chair of the Canada Council
e) the President of the Royal Society of Canada
f) the Chair of the Board of the Association of Universities and Colleges of Canada
g) not more than five other members, when considered appropriate by the Governor General, can be appointed for three-year terms.

The Secretary to the Governor General is, by his/her office, Secretary General of the Order.

The Order of Canada is designed to honour Canadian citizens for outstanding achievement and service to the country or to humanity at large and also for distinguished service in particular localities and fields of activity. The Order comprises three levels of membership: Companion, Officer, and Member. Up to 15 Companions may be appointed annually, but the total number of living Companions may not exceed 165. Up to 64 Officers and 136 Members may be appointed annually with no over-all limit.

The Order includes no titles of honour and confers no special privileges, hereditary or otherwise. Awards are made solely on the basis of merit. Members of the Order are entitled to place after their names the letters "C.C." for Companions, "O.C." for Officers, and "C.M." for Members.

Any person or organization may make nominations for appointment to the Order by writing to the Chancellery, Rideau Hall, Ottawa. The Advisory Council submits to the Governor General lists of those nominees who, in the opinion of the Council, are of greatest merit. Appointments to the Order are made by the Sovereign of the Order on the recommendation of the Governor General as Chancellor of the Order, under an instrument sealed with the Seal of the Order.

Non-Canadians whom the Government desires to honour may be accorded honourary membership in the Order.

Companions of the Order of Canada/
Compagnons de l'Ordre du Canada (C.C.)
(Announced June 29, 2012)
The Honourable Ian Corneil Binnie, C.C., Toronto, ON
Natalie Zemon Davis, C.C., Toronto, ON
Yannick Nézet-Séguin, C.C., Montréal, QC

(Invested May 25, 2012)
The Right Honourable Paul Martin, P.C., C.C., Montréal, QC

(Invested November 4, 2011)
Robert Lepage, C.C., O.Q., Québec, QC*
** Indicates a promotion within the Order.*

Officers of the Order of Canada/
Officiers de l'Ordre du Canada (O.C.)
(Announced June 29, 2012)
Robert G. Bertram, O.C., Aurora, ON
Jean Bissonnette, O.C., Montréal, QC
Francine Décary, O.C., O.Q., Montréal, QC
Elizabeth Dowdeswell, O.C., Toronto, ON
Angèle Dubeau, O.C., C.Q., Westmount QC*
Chantal St-Cyr Hébert, O.C., Montréal, QC
Paul F. Hoffman, O.C., Victoria, B.C.
Prabhat Jha, O.C., Toronto, ON
Ralph Kein, O.C., A.O.E., Calgary, AB
Maryse Lassonde, O.C., C.Q.
John Last, O.C., Ottawa, ON
Jean-François Lépine, O.C., Ville Mont-Royal, QC
Hadi-Khan Mahabadi, O.C., Mississauga, ON
Ermanno Mauro, O.C., Mississauga, QC
Marianne McKenna, O.C., Toronto, ON
Craig Oliver, O.C., Ottawa, ON
The Honourable P. Michael Pitfield, P.C., O.C., C.V.O., Ottawa, ON
Sharon Pollock, O.C., Calgary, AB
John Brian Patrick "Pat" Quinn, O.C., West Vancouver, B.C.
The Honourable John D. Richard, O.C., Ottawa, ON
Cecil H. Rorabeck, O.C., London, ON
Louise Roy, O.C., O.Q., Montréal, QC
Gordon Semenoff, O.C., Surrey, B.C.
Gilles Tremblay, O.C., O.Q., Montréal, QC
The Honourable Marilyn Trenholme Counsell, O.C., O.N.B., Sackville, N.B.

(Invested June 11, 2012)
Yuli Turovsky, O.C., C.Q., Montréal, QC

(Invested May 25, 2012)
André Bandrauk, O.C., Hatley, QC
General Maurice Baril, O.C., C.M.M., M.S.M., C.D. (Ret'd), Ottawa, ON
The Honourable James Bartleman, O.C., O.Ont, Perth, ON
Aldo Albert Daniel Bensadoun, O.C., Montréal, QC
William Scott Bowman, O.C., Montréal, QC & Sarasota, FL, U.S.A.
Nicole Brossard, O.C., Montréal, QC
Alain Dubuc, O.C., Montréal, QC
Gwynne Dyer, O.C., St. John's, NL & London, England
Robert R. Fowler, O.C., Ottawa, ON
Donald Fraser, O.C., Toronto, ON
Dom Laurence Freeman, O.C., Montréal, QC & London, England
Hugh Arthur Krentz, O.C., Calgary, AB
Bruce Kuwabara, O.C., Toronto, ON
R.Petter MacKinnon, O.C., Saskatoon, SK
John Mighton, O.C., Toronto, ON
David W. Scott, O.C., Ottawa, ON
Peter Alexander Singer, O.C., Toronto, ON
Jeffrey Skoll, O.C., Toronto, ON & Beverly Hills, CA, U.S.A.
Annette Verschuren, O.C., TOronto, ON
Brian Williams, O.C., Willowdale, ON
Alvin Zipursky, O.C., Toronto, ON

(Announced December 30, 2011)
General Maurice Baril, O.C., C.M.M., M.S.M., C.D. (ret'd), Ottawa, ON
The Honourable James Karl Bartleman, O.C., O.Ont., Perth, ON
Aldo Albert Daniel Bensadoun, O.C., Montréal, QC
Lieutenant-General Joseph Jacques Charles Bouchard, O.C., C.M.M., M.S.C., C.D., Ottawa, ON
William Scott Bowman, O.C., Montréal, OC and Sarasota, FL, U.S.A.
Alain Dubuc, O.C., Montréal, QC
Robert R. Fowler, O.C., Ottawa, ON
Donald A.S. Fraser, O.C., Toronto, ON
Gordon Guyatt, O.C., Dundas, ON
General Rick J. Hillier, O.C., C.M.M., M.S.C., C.D. (Ret'd), Ottawa, ON
P. Thomas (Tom) Jenkins, O.C., Waterloo, ON
Hugh A. Krentz, O.C., Calgary, AB
Bruce Kuwabara, O.C., Toronto, ON
The Honourable Kevin G. Lynch, P.C., O.C., Ottawa, ON
R. Peter MacKinnon, O.C., Saskatoon, SK
James McEwen, O.C., Vancouver, B.C.
Stuart McLean, O.C., Toronto, ON
Jean-Jacques Nattiez, O.C., C.Q., Montréal, QC
Charles Pachter, O.C., Toronto, ON*
Catherine Robbin, O.C., Tottenham, ON
Seymour Schulich, O.C., Willowdale, ON*
David W. Scott, O.C., Ottawa, ON
Jeffrey Skoll, O.C., Toronto, ON, and Beverly Hills, CA, U.S.A.
Calvin Ralph Stiller, O.C., O.Ont., Arva, ON*
Yuli Turovsky, O.C., C.Q., Montréal, QC
Brian Williams, O.C., Willowdale, ON
Tim Wynne-Jones, O.C., Perth, ON
Alvin Zipursky, O.C., Toronto, ON
** Indicates a promotion within the Order.*

(Invested November 4, 2011)
William J. Buyers, O.C., Deep River, ON
The Hon. Herménégilde Chiasson, O.C., O.N.B., Grand-Barachois, NB
Lorna Crozier, O.C., Saanich, BC
Richard (Rick) L. George, O.C., Calgary, AB
Alain Lefèvre, O.C., C.Q., Montréal, QC
Bob McDonald, O.C., Toronto, ON
Maureen O'Neil, O.C., Ottawa, ON
Viola Robinson, O.C., O.N.S., Yarmouth, NS
Maureen Sabia, O.C., Toronto, ON
Hayley Wickenheiser, O.C., Calgary, AB

(Invested September 14, 2011)
Richard B. Baltzan, O.C., Saskatoon, SK
James A. Dosman, O.C., S.O.M., Saskatoon, SK
René Dussault, O.C., O.Q., Québec, QC
Angela Enright, O.C., Victoria, BC
John Furlong, O.C., Vancouver, BC
Clément Gosselin, O.C., Québec, QC
R. Brian Haynes, O.C., Dundas, ON
Linda Hutcheon, O.C., Toronto, ON
Anthony Lang, O.C., Toronto, ON
Terence Macartney-Filgate, O.C., Toronto, ON
James Orbinski, O.C., O.Ont., M.S.C., Toronto, ON
Julie Payette, O.C., C.Q., Montréal, QC
Shelagh Rogers, O.C., Vancouver, BC

Honorary Officer of the Order of Canada/
Officier honorifique de l'Ordre du Canada
None awarded since last edition.

Honorary Member of the Order of Canada/
Membre honorifique de l'Ordre du Canada
None awarded since last edition.

Members of the Order of Canada/
Membres de l'Ordre du Canada (C.M.)
(Announced June 29, 2012)
Carolyn Acker, C.M., Toronto, ON
Dyane Adam, C.M., Saint-François-de-l'Île-d'Orléans, QC
Patsy Anderson, C.N., Toronto, ON
Allan Gordon Bell, C.M., Cochrane, AB
Rabbi Arthur Norman Bielfeld, C.M., Toronto, ON
Roger Bland, C.M., Edmonton, AB
Robert B. Bourne, C.M., London, ON
Pierre Bruneau, C.M., O.Q., Montréal, QC
John Buhler, C.M., Winnipeg, MB
Silver Donald Cameron, C.M., Halifax, N.S.
Stephen Chatman, C.M., Vancouver, B.C.
Guy Corneau, C.M., Montréal, QC
Franklin Delaney, C.M., Beaconsfield, QC
Wadih M.Fares, C.M., Halifax, N.S.
Anthony (Tony) Fields, C.M., Edmonton, AB
Allan Gotlib, C.M., Thornhill, ON
Michel Goulet, C.M., Montréal, QC
Alia Hogben, C.M., Gananoque, ON
Greg Hollingshead, C.M., Edmonton, AB
Nancy Kilgour, C.M., Calgary, AB
Henry Kloppenburg, C.M., Saskatoon, SK
Merril Knudtson, C.M., Calgary, AB
The Honourable Frances Lankin, P.C., C.M., Restoule, ON
Louis LaPierre, C.M., Moncton, N.B.
William Laskin, C.M., Toronto, ON
Monique F. Leroux, C.M., Montréal, QC
Guy Maddin, C.M., O.M., Winnipeg, MB
Salem Masry, C.M., Fredericton, N.B.
Kenneth Maybee, C.M., O.M.M., New Maryland, N.B.
Des McAnuff, C.M., Stratford, ON
Elizabeth McWeeny, C.M., Thunder Bay, ON
Lois Mitchell, C.M., Calgary, AB
Bernice Morgan, C.M., St. John's, NL
Narian Packham, C.M., Toronto, ON
Gordon Rawlinson, C.M., Calgary, AB, and Prince Albert, SK
Jean-Guy Rioux, C.M., Pointe-Brûlée, N.B.
Michèle Rouleau, C.M., C.Q., Montréal, QC
Marie Saint Pierre, C.M., C.Q., Montréal, QC
Emanuele (Lino) Saputo, C.M., O.Q., Senneville, QC
Steven Schipper, C.M., Winnipeg, MB
Cyril Simard, C.M., O.Q., Québec, QC
Laure Waridel, C.M., Montréal, QC

(Invested May 25, 2012)
Archibald Alexander Alleyne, C.M., Toronto, ON
Hans-Ludwig Blohm, C.M., Ottawa, ON
Lawrence S. Bloomberg, C.M., O.Ont., Toronto, ON
The Honourable Benoît Couchard, P.C., C.M., Roberval, QC
Ronald Caplan, C.M., Sydney, NS
Jean Deslauriers, C.M., Saint-Laurent-de-l'île d'Orléans, QC
Joella Foulds, C.M., Southside Boularderie, NS
John H.V. Gilbert, C.M., Vancouver, BC
The Honourable Mary M. Hetherington, C.M., Calgary, AB
Paul Valdemar (Valdy) Horsdal, C.M.
Denis Losier, C.M., Moncton, N.B.
Pierre Nepveu, C.M., Montréal, QC
David Northcott, C.M., O.M., Winnipeg, MB
Eric Peterson, C.M., Toronto, ON
F. Thomas Stanfield, C.M., Truro, NS
Anita Stewart, C.M., Elora, ON
Donald J.Taylor, C.M., Calgary, AB
R.H. (Robert Holmes) Thomson, C.M., Toronto, ON
Maïr Verthuy, C.M., Montréal, QC
Bernard Zinman, C.M., Toronto, ON

(Invested January 19, 2012)
Nigel Rusted, C.M., O.N.L., St. John's, N.L.

(Announced December 30, 2011)
Miriam Adams, C.M., Toronto, ON
Archibald (Archie) Alleyne, C.M., Toronto, ON
Cheryl Bartlett, C.M., Sydney, N.S.

Hans-Ludwig Blohm, C.M., Ottawa, ON
Margaret Bloodworth, C.M., Ottawa, ON
Lawrence S. Bloomberg, C.M., O.Ont., Toronto, ON
Benôit Bouchard, C.M., Roberval, QC
France Chrétien Desmarais, C.M., Westmount, QC
Jocelyne Côté-O'Hara, C.M., TOronto, ON
Thomas (Tom) Dawe, C.M., Conception Bary South, N.L.
Jean Deslauriers, C.M., Saint-Laurent-de-l'île d'Orléans, QC
Daphne E. Dumont, C.M., Charlottetown, P.E.I.
John T. Ferguson, C.M., Edmonton, AB
Mary Ferguson-Paré, C.M., Lakefield, ON
Joella Foulds, C.M., Southside Boularderie, NS
Mary Margaret Hetherington, C.M., Calgary, AB
Noel Pattison James, C.M., Kingston, ON
Ana Paula Lopes, C.M., Toronto, ON
Denis Losier, C.M., Moncton, N.B.
Leslie (Les) Manning, C.M., Medicine Hat, AB
Michael Meaney, C.M., C.Q., Beaconsfield, QC
David Northcott, C.M., O.M., Winnipeg, MB
Ratna Omidvar, C.M., O.Ont, TOronto, ON
Aaju Peter, C.M., Iqaluit, NU
Samuel Pierre, C.M., C.Q., Saint-Laurent, QC
Sean Riley, C.M., Antigonish, N.S.
Pierrette Robitaille, C.M., Longueuil, QC
Kathleen (Kathy) Sendall, C.M., Calgary, AB
Louise Sicuro, C.M., Montréal, QC
Margaret Spoelstra, C.M., Toronto, ON
Anita Stewart, C.M., Elora, ON
Claude St-Laurent, C.M., Saint-Lambert, QC
Garnette Sutherland, C.M., Calgary, AB
Donald J.Taylor, C.M., Bragg Creek, AB
Maïr Verthuy, C.M., Montréal, QC
Bernard Zinman, C.M., Toronto, ON

(Invested November 4, 2011)
Arnold Aberman, C.M., Toronto, ON
Patricia Aldana, C.M., Toronto, ON
Shirley Bear, C.M., Tobique, Maliseet Reserve, NB
Jeanne Besner, C.M., Calgary, AB
Anita Best, C.M., Norris Point, NL
John M. W. Bradford, C.M., Brockville, ON
Anthony & Elizabeth Comper, C.M., Toronto, ON
Joan Donald, C.M., Red Deer, AB
Mary Lou Fallis, C.M., Toronto, ON
Jean-Claude Fouron, C.M., O.Q., Montréal, QC
Marie Gignac, C.M., Québec, QC
Monique Giroux, C.M., Montréal, QC
Dorothy Griffiths, C.M., O. Ont., Welland, ON
Michael Hayden, C.M., O.B.C., Vancouver, BC
Frederic Langford Rowell Jackman, C.M., O. Ont., Toronto, ON
Patrick Jarvis, C.M., Calgary, AB
Eugene Levy, C.M., Toronto, ON
Trevor Linden, C.M., O.B.C., Vancouver, BC
Robert Y. McMurtry, C.M., Picton, ON
Alvaro Morales, C.M., Kingston, ON
Gwyn Morgan, C.M., Calgary, AB, & North Saanich, BC
Larry Nelson, C.M., Moncton, NB
Nino Ricci, C.M., Toronto, ON
David William Shannon, C.M., O. Ont., Thudner Bay, ON
Tricia Smith, C.M., Vancouver BC
David Staines, C.M., O. Ont., Ottawa, ON
Robert H. Taylor, C.M., Vancouver, BC

(Invested September 14, 2011)
Marthe Asselin-Vaillancourt, C.M., C.Q., Saguenay, QC
Robert Bourdeau, C.M., Ottawa, ON
The Honourable Patricia Carney, P.C., C.M., Saturna Island, BC
Marc Chouinard, C.M., Memramcook, NB
Paul D. Copeland, C.M., Toronto, ON
Ollie Currie, C.M., Edmonton, AB
Vera Elizabeth Dewar, C.M., Stratford, PEI
Pierre Fréchette, C.M., C.Q., Québec, QC
David Halliday, C.M., Maple Ridge, BC
Robert D. Hare, C.M., Surrey, BC
Hanny Hassan, C.M., London, ON
Ellis Jacob, C.M., Toronto, ON
Gilles Julien, C.M., Montréal, QC
Ruth E. Kajander, C.M., Thunder Bay, ON
Josef Kates, C.M., North York, ON
Jamie Kennedy, C.M., Toronto, ON
Jeffrey C. Lozon, C.M., Toronto, ON
Pierre Maranda, C.M., Québec, QC
John McLaughlin, C.M., O.N.B., Fredericton, NB
Rudolph (Rudy) North, C.M., Vancouver, BC
Gilles G. Patry, C.M.,O.Ont., Ottawa, ON
Shirley Post, C.M., Peterborough, ON
Terrence Punch, C.M., Halifax, NS
Charlene M. T. Robertson, C.M., Edmonton, AB
Bernard Saladin d'Anglure, C.M., Québec, QC
Jennifer Simons, C.M., Vancouver, BC
Ann Southam, C.M. (*deceased*), Toronto, ON
Beth Symes, C.M., Toronto, ON
Louis Taillefer, C.M., Sherbrooke, QC
Robert C. P. Westbury, C.M., Edmonton, AB
Edwina Wetzel, C.M., Conne River, NL
Christopher Wiseman, C.M., Calgary, AB

ORDER OF MILITARY MERIT

The Order of Military Merit was created on July 1, 1972 to recognize meritorious service and devotion to duty by members of the Canadian Forces. The Order has three grades of membership: Commander (C.M.M.), Officer (O.M.M.) and Member (M.M.M.). The annual number of appointments is limited to one-tenth of one percent of the number of persons in the Canadian Forces in the preceding year.

Commanders of the Order of Military Merit/ Commandeurs de l'Ordre du mérite militaire (C.M.M.) (Invested June 8, 2012)
Major-General Yvan Blondin, C.M.M., C.D., Ottawa, ON*
Major-General Alan John Howard, C.M.M., M.S.M., C.D., Ottawa, ON
Major-General Ian Poulter, C.M.M., C.D., Ottawa, ON*
Major-General Walter Semianiw, C.M.M., M.S.C., C.D., Ottawa, ON*
** Indicates a promotion within the Order.*

(Invested March 2, 2012)
Major-General Robert Bertrand, C.M.M., C.D., Ottawa, ON
Rear-Admiral Adnrew Smith, C.M.M., C.D., Ottawa, ON*
** Indicates a promotion within the Order.*

(Announced December 19, 2011)
Major-General Joseph Rousseau, C.M.M., C.D., Ottawa, ON

(Invested December 2, 2011)
Rear-Admiral Nigel Greenwood, C.M.M., C.D., Joint Task Force Pacific Headquarters, Victoria, BC*
Major-General Mark McQuillan, C.M.M., C.D., Canadian Operational Support Command Headquarters, Ottawa, ON
Major-General Guy Thibault, C.M.M., C.D., Office of the Assistant Deputy Minister (Information Management), Ottawa, ON
** Indicates a promotion within the Order.*

Officers of the the Order of Military Merit/ Officiers de l'Ordre du mérite militaire (O.M.M.) (Invested June 8, 2012)
Lieutenant-Colonel Sean Boyle, O.M.M., C.D., Doha, Qatar
Brigadier-General Paul Bury, O.M.M., C.D., Edmonton, AB
Colonel Jamieson Cade, O.M.M., M.S.M., C.D., Kingston, ON
Lieutenant-Commander Luke Charbonneau, O.M.M., C.D., Hornell Heights, ON
Major Marjorie Coakwell, O.M.M., C.D., Ottawa, ON
Colonel Martin Girard, O.M.M., M.S.M., C.D., Ottawa, ON
Colonel Hercule Gosselin, O.M.M., C.D., Courcelette, QC
Colonel Guy Maillet, O.M.M., C.D., RIchelain, QC
Lieutenant-Colonel Darlene Quinn, O.M.M., C.D., Victoria, BC

(Invested March 2, 2012)
Captain Gilles Couturier, O.M.M., C.D., Ottawa, ON
Lieutenant-Commander Cindy Galt, O.M.M., C.D., Kensington, PEI
Commander Stephen Irwin, O.M.M., C.D., Victoria, BC
Colonel Omer Lavoie, O.M.M., M.S.C., C.D., Edmonton, AB
Lieutenant-Colonel John Pumphrey, O.M.M., C.D., Ottawa, ON
Lieutenant-Colonel Gilles Sansterre, O.M.M., C.D., Ottawa, ON
Colonel James Simms, O.M.M., C.D., Oromocto, NB
Colonel Sylvain Sirois, O.M.M., C.D., Ottawa, ON
Brigadier-General Anthony Stack, O.M.M., C.D., Halifax, NS

(Announced December 19, 2011)
Colonel Donald Kirby Abbott, O.M.M., C.D., Belleville, ON
Captain (N) Marie Courchesne, O.M.M., C.D., Ottawa, ON
Lieutenant-Colonel Daniel Farris, O.M.M., C.D., Ottawa, ON
Major Michael Fawcett, O.M.M., C.D., Kingston, ON
Colonel Gregory Loos, O.M.M., MSC, C.D., Ottawa, ON
Lieutenant-Colonel Telah Morrison, O.M.M., C.D., Ottawa, ON
Colonel Pierre Ruel, O.M.M., C.D., Colorado Springs, CO, U.S.A.
Major Raymond Stockermans, O.M.M., C.D., Astra, ON

(Invested December 2, 2011)
Lieutenant-Colonel Allan Bratland, O.M.M., C.D., Winnipeg, MB
Major James Burton, O.M.M., C.D., Hornell Heights, ON
Colonel André Corbould, O.M.M., C.D., Edmonton, AB
Commander Anthony Evans, O.M.M., C.D., Victoria, BC
Commander Robert Lewis-Manning, O.M.M., C.D., Victoria, BC
Lieutenant-Colonel Shawn McKinstry, O.M.M., C.D., Washington D.C., U.S.A.
Colonel Dean Milner, O.M.M., C.D., Petawawa, ON
Lieutenant-Colonel Homer Tien, O.M.M., C.D., Petawawa, ON

Members of the Order of Military Merit/ Membres de l'Ordre du mérite militaire (M.M.M.) (Invested June 8, 2012)
Warrant Officer Patrick Bowers, M.M.M., C.D., Halfiax, NS
Chief Warrant Officer Marcel Chiasson, M.M.M., C.D., Canadian Defence Academy Headquarters, Kingston, ON
Petty Officer 2nd Class Yves Clément, M.M.M., M.S.M., C.D. Halifax, NS
Chief Warrant Officer Bernard Curtis, M.M.M., C.D., Sydney, NS
Master Warrant Officer Trent Doucette M.M.M., C.D., Astra, ,ON
Chief Petty Officer 1st Class Walter Dubeau, M.M.M., C.D., Ottawa, ON
Chief Warrant Officer Joseph Dulong, M.M.M., C.D., Halifax, NS
Chief Wawrrant Officer Karl Ellis, M.M.M., C.D., , Meaford, ON
Lieutenant (N) Linda Forward, M.M.M., C.D., Shilo, MB
Chief Petty Officer 2nd Class Michael Garuk, M.M.M., C.D., Ottawa, ON
Chief Petty Officer 2nd Class Janet Graham-Smith, M.M.M., C.D., Victoria, BC
Chief Petty Officer 2nd Class Christopher Koblun, M.M.M., C.D., Victoria, BC
Chief Warrant Officer Robert Lamothe, M.M.M., C.D., Ottawa, ON
Chief Warrant Officer Guy Martin, M.M.M., C.D., Richelain, QC
Warrant Officer Deryk McGougan, M.M.M., C.D., Edmonton, AB
Master Warrant Officer Stephen McNabb, M.M.M., C.D., Petawawa, ON
Captain Nathalie Mercer, M.M.M., C.D., Kingston, ON
Master Warrant Officer Steven Merry, M.M.M., C.D., Edmonton, AB
Petty Officer 1st Class Dion Randell, M.M.M., C.D., Halifax, NS
Chief Warrant Officer William Richards, M.M.M., M.S.M., C.D., Petawawa, ON
Chief Warrant Officer Patrice Rioux, M.M.M., C.D., Alouette, QC
Chief Warrant Officer Jean-Oaul Savoie, M.M.M., C.D., Saint John, NB
Sergeant Karen Squires, M.M.M., C.D., St. John's NL
Chief Warrant Officer Guy St-Jean, M.M.M., C.D., Winnipeg, MB
Master Warrant Officer Suzie Thibault, M.M.M., C.D., Courcelette, QC
Master Warrant Officer James Warwick, M.M.M., C.D., Borden, ON
Chief Warrant Officer Kevin West, M.M.M., C.D., Afghanistan
Warrant Officer Alfred Willston, M.M.M., C.D., Denwood AB
Warrant Officer Troy Zuorro, M.M.M., C.D., Winnipeg, MB

(Invested March 2, 2012)
Warrant Officer Barbara Bajema, M.M.M., C.D., Kingston, ON
Chief Warrant Officer Wayne Bartlett, M.M.M., M.S.C., C.D., Petawawa, ON
Chief Warrant Officer Denis Bédard, M.M.M., C.D., Québec, QC
Sergeant Jeanette Botari, M.M.M., C.D., Québec, QC
Chief Warrant Officer Bernard Caron, M.M.M., C.D., Borden, ON
Warrant Officer Robert Clarkre, M.M.M., C.D., Edmonton, AB
Petty Officer 1st Class Ronald Crawford, M.M.M., C.D., Victoria, BC
Master Warrant Officer Yves Demers, M.M.M., C.D., Courcelette, QC
Chief Petty Officer 1st Class Leonard Denning, M.M.M., C.D., Victoria, BC
Chief Petty Officer 2nd Class Harry Fong, M.M.M., C.D., Vancouver BC
Lieutenant Wayne Forster, M.M.M., C.D., Ottawa, ON
Corporal Glenn Gray, M.M.M., C.D., Ottawa, ON
Chief Petty Officer 1st Class David Hart, M.M.M., C.D., Victoria, BC
Chief Warrant Officer Pierre Léger, M.M.M., C.D., Ottawa, ON
Chief Warrant Officer Norman McLanaghan, M.M.M., C.D., Kingston, ON
Chief Warrant Officer Bradley Montgomery, M.M.M., M.S.M., C.D., Oromocto, NB
Major Marc Moo Sang, M.M.M., C.D., Ottawa, ON
Sergeant Peter Moon, M.M.M., C.D., Borden ON
Petty Officer 1st Class Derrick Nearing, M.M.M., C.D., Petawawa, ON
Warrant Officer Gordon Nichl, M.M.M., C.D., Winnipeg, MB
Master Warrant Officer Keith Olstad, M.M.M., C.D., Petawawa, ON
Captain Tony Pépin, M.M.M., C.D., Astra, ON
Chief Petty Officer, 1st Class Barry Petten, M.M.M., C.D., Victoria, BC
Master Warrant Officer Bryan Pierce, C.V., M.M.M., M.S.M., C.D., Winnipeg, MB
Chief Warrant Officer Gérard Poitras, M.M.M., M.S.M., C.D., Shearwater, NS
Chief Petty Officer 2nd Class Mario Richard, M.M.M., C.D., Ottawa, ON

Captain Réjean Richard, M.M.M., C.D., Kingston, ON
Warrant Officer Wayde Simpson, M.M.M., M.B., C.D., Astra, ON
Captain Leo Snook, M.M.M., C.D., Oromocto, NB
Master Warrant Officer Sandra Spragg, M.M.M., C.D., Astra, ON
Warrant Officer Cameron Stevens, M.M.M., C.D., Montréal, QC
Chief Warrant Officer Shawn Stevens, M.M.M., M.S.C., M.S.M., C.D., Edmonton, AB
Master Warrant Officer Stéphane Val e, M.M.M., C.D., Courcelette, QC
Captain Grant Whittla, M.M.M., C.D., Victoria, BC

(Announced December 19, 2011)
Master Warrant Officer Jorg Adler, M.M.M., C.D., Belleville, ON
Chief Warrant Officer Haley Bransfield, M.M.M., C.D., Edmonton, AB
Chief Warrant Officer Joseph Chouinard, M.M.M., C.D., Oromocto, NB
Warrant Officer Robert Clarke, M.M.M., C.D., Edmonton, AB
Warrant Officer Peter Dingle, M.M.M., C.D., Kentville, NS
Master Warrant Officer Shane Holwell, M.M.M., C.D., Victoria, BC
Chief Warrant Officer Joseph Jetté, M.M.M., C.D., Kingston, ON
Master Warrant Officer Serge Laforge, M.M.M., C.D., Winnipeg, MB
Lieutenant Horace Lane, M.M.M., C.D., Gander, NL
Master Warrant Officer Joseph Lavoie, M.M.M., C.D., Richelain, QC
Chief Warrant Officer Joseph Leger, M.M.M., C.D., Ottawa, ON
Warrant Officer Wayne Lundrigan, M.M.M., C.D., Shilo, MB
Chief Warrant Officer Dianne Maidment, M.M.M., C.D., Borden, ON
Master Warrant Officer Joseph Marcil, M.M.M., C.D., Courcelette, QC
Chief Warrant Officer Deborah Matthews, M.M.M., C.D., Moose Jaw, SK
Chief Warrant Officer Robert McCann, M.M.M., C.D., Belleville, ON
Warrant Officer Patricia Mears, M.M.M., C.D., Lazo, BC
Chief Warrant Officer Joseph Morin, M.M.M., C.D., Kingston, ON
Chief Warrant Officer Daniel Moyer, M.M.M., C.D., Washington, D.C., U.S.A
Chief Warrant Officer Derek John Munroe, M.M.M., C.D., Oshawa, ON
Warrant Officer Gordon Nichol, M.M.M., C.D., Dundurn, SK
Petty Officer 1st Class Linda Parrish, M.M.M., C.D., Victoria, BC
Master Warrant Officer Paul Pinel, M.M.M., C.D., Shilo, MB
Petty Officer 1st Class David Poole, M.M.M., M.S.M., C.D., Shearwater, NS
Master Warrant Officer Joseph Richer, M.M.M., C.D., Courcelette, QC
Master Warrant Officer Joseph Rodrigue, M.M.M., C.D., Courcelette, QC
Warrant Officer Joseph Roux, M.M.M., C.D., Courcelette, QC
Master Warrant Officer Joseph Saint-Pierre, M.M.M., C.D., Courcelette, QC
Sergeant Harold Smallbones, M.M.M., C.D., Medicine Hat, AB
Sergeant Karen Squires, M.M.M., C.D., St. John's, NL
Chief Warrant Officer Robert Unger, M.M.M., C.D., Montréal, QC
Captain Jonathan Utton, M.M.M., C.D., Ottawa, ON
Master Warrant Officer Joseph Vallée, M.M.M., C.D., Courcelette, QC
Chief Warrant Officer Chadley Wagar, M.M.M., C.D., Courcelette, QC
Chief Warrant Officer Christopher Waugh, M.M.M., C.D., Shilo, MB
Warrant Officer Alfred Williston, M.M.M., C.D., Kingston, ON
Warrant Officer Alan Wilson, M.M.M., C.D., Halifax, NS
Chief Petty Officer 1st Class Stephen Wood, M.M.M., C.D., Halifax, NS
Warrant Officer Joseph Yargeau, M.M.M., C.D., Denwood, AB

(Invested December 2, 2011)
Sergeant Jorgan Aitaok Jr., M.M.M., Yellowknife, NT
Master Warrant Officer Jeffrey Aman, M.M.M., C.D., Petawawa, ON
Chief Warrant Officer Mark Arden, M.M.M., C.D., Vancouver, BC
Sergeant Alain Barriault, M.M.M., C.D., Courcelette, QC
Master Warrant Officer Robert Bartlett, M.M.M., C.D., Oromocto, NB
Petty Officer 1st Class Stephen Beastall, M.M.M., C.D., London, ON
Chief Warrant Officer Gerard Brennan, M.M.M., C.D., Halifax, NS
Major Patrick Brizay, M.M.M., C.D., Petawawa, ON
Master Warrant Officer Kirby Burgess, M.M.M., C.D., Oromocto, NB
Chief Warrant Officer Michael Clough, M.M.M., C.D., Edmonton, AB
Warrant Officer William Doupe, M.M.M., C.D., Petawawa, ON
Chief Petty Officer 1st Class Michael Feltham, M.M.M., C.D., Halifax, NS
Lieutenant (N) Corey Gleason, M.M.M., C.D., Victoria, BC
Chief Warrant Officer Gilles Godbout, M.M.M., C.D., Courcelette, QC
Warrant Officer Kelly Grant, M.M.M., C.D., Oromocto, NB
Chief Warrant Officer Éric Gravel, M.M.M., C.D., Courcelette, QC
Chief Warrant Officer Alain Grenier, M.M.M., C.D., Courcelette, QC
Captain John Hill, M.M.M., C.D., Oromocto, NB
Warrant Officer Murray Hiltz, M.M.M., C.D., Greenwood, NS
Warrant Officer Lewis Johnstone, M.M.M., C.D., Shilo, MB
Warrant Officer Ronald Leblanc, M.M.M., C.D., Vancouver, BC
Petty Officer 2nd Class James Leith, M.M.M., S.C., M.S.M., C.D., Shearwater, NS
Master Warrant Officer Donald MacIntyre, M.M.M., C.D., Shearwater, NS
Warrant Officer Patricia MacWilliams, M.M.M., C.D., Edmonton, AB
Major Wendy McKenzie, M.M.M., C.D., Vancouver, BC
Warrant Officer David McLaughlin, M.M.M., C.D., Borden, ON
Chief Warrant Officer Steven Milton, M.M.M., C.D., Halifax, NS
Captain William Moore, M.M.M., C.D., Charlottetown, PE
Master Warrant Officer Roy Pugh, M.M.M., C.D., Halifax, NS
Chief Warrant Officer Christopher Rusk, M.M.M., C.D., Petawawa, ON
Chief Petty Officer 2nd Class Angela Schenkers, M.M.M., C.D., Victoria, BC
Warrant Officer Sylvie Seaward, M.M.M., C.D., Shilo, MB
Petty Officer 1st Class Cavel Shebib, M.M.M., C.D., Halifax, NS
Sergeant Yan St-Pierre, M.M.M., C.D., Courcelette, QC
Master Warrant Officer Keith Thibault, M.M.M., C.D., Cold Lake, AB
Chief Warrant Officer David Tofts, M.M.M., C.D., Courcelette, QC
Master Warrant Officer Pierre Tremblay, M.M.M., C.D., Courcelette, QC
Chief Petty Officer 2nd Class Charles Trombley, M.M.M., C.D., Shearwater, NS

ORDER OF MERIT OF THE POLICE FORCES

In October 2000, Her Majesty The Queen approved the creation of the Order as a means of recognizing conspicuous merit and exceptional service by members and employees of the Canadian police forces whose contributions extend beyond protection of the community. There are three levels of membership - Commander, Officer and Member - that reflect long-term, outstanding service in varying degrees of responsibility. Each level has corresponding nominal letters: C.O.M., O.O.M. and M.O.M.

Commander of the Order of Merit of the Police Forces/ Commandeur de l'Ordre du mérite des corps policiers (C.O.M.)

(Invested May 9, 2012)
Chief William Sterling Blair, C.O.M., Toronto Police Service, ON

Officers of the the Order of Merit of the Police Forces/ Officiers de l'Ordre du mérite des corps policiers (O.O.M.)

(Invested May 9, 2012)
Assistant Commissioner Roger L. Brown, O.O.M., Royal Canadian Mounted Police, Regina, SK
Chief COnstable Michael Robert Chadwick, O.O.M., Saanich Police Department, BC
Superintendent Mario Di Tommaso, O.O.M., Toronto Police Service, ON
Director General Robert C. Fahlman, O.O.M., Royal Canadian Mounted Police, Ottawa, ON
Chief Robert Philip Johnston, O.O.M., Royal Newfoundland Constabulary, NL
Deputy Chief Constable Douglas A. LePard, O.O.M., Vancouver Police Department, BC*
Chief Thomas Mathew McKenzie, O.O.M., Lethbridge Regional Police Service, AB
Chief Stephen J. Tanner, O.O.M., Kingston Police, ON
Chief Matthew A. Torigian, O.O.M., Waterloo Regional Police Service, ON
** Indicates promotion within the Order.*

Members of the the Order of Merit of the Police Forces/ Membres de l'Ordre du mérite des corps policiers (M.O.M.)

(Invested September 19, 2012)
Inspector William (Bill) A. Renton, M.O.M., Woodstock, ON
Superintendent John Schmidt, M.O.M., London, ON

(Invested May 9, 2012)
Sergeant Jocelyn April, M.O.M., Sûreté du Québec, Montréal, QC
Alexandre Beaudoin, M.O.M., Sûreté du Québec, Montréal, QC
Maître Francis Brabant, M.O.M., Sûreté du Québec, Montréal, QC
Staff Sergeant Patrick Adrian Cahill, M.O.M., Royal Canadian Mounted Police, Placentia, NL
Sergeant François Caron, M.O.M., Sûreté du Québec, Montréal, QC
Assistant Director General François Charpentier, M.O.M., Sûreté du Québec, Montréal, QC
Superintendent Deborah A. Clark, M.O.M., Hamilton Police Service, ON
Deputy Chief Andrew M. Fletcher, M.O.M., Halton Regional Police Service, ON
Chief Inspector Yves Guay, M.O.M., Sûreté du Québec, Cap-de-la-Madeleine, QC
Sergeant Michael J. MacDonal, M.O.M., Royal Canadian Mounted Police, Milton, ON
Constable Linda A. Malcolm, M.O.M., Vancouver Police Department, BC
Sergeant Michael A. Novakowski, M.O.M., Abbotsford Police Department, BC
Inspector Trent Rolfe, M.O.M., Royal Canadian Mounted Police, Surrey, BC
Sergeant Daniel Patrick Russell, M.O.M., Royal Canadian Mounted Police, London, ON
Inspector Sean Ryan, M.O.M., Royal Newfoundland Constabulary, NL
Detective Constable Jonathan P.R. Sheldan, M.O.M., Victoria Police Department, BC
Superintendent William Stewart, M.O.M., Hamilton Police Service, ON
Chief Superintendent Richard Bruce Taylor, M.O.M., Royal Canadian Mounted Police, Edmonton, AB
Deputy Chief S. Brent Thomlison, M.O.M., Waterloo Regional Police Service, ON
Inspector Scott A. Thompson, M.O.M., Vancouver Police Department, BC
Inspector Richard Wayne Votour, M.O.M., Royal Canadian Mounted Police, Fredericton, NB
Deputy Chief Alan Williams, M.O.M., North Bay Police Service, ON

(Invested September 20, 2011)
Director Marc Parent, M.O.M., Service de police de la Ville de Montréal, QC
Assistant Director Mario Plante, M.O.M.,Service de police de la Ville de Montréal, QC

MILITARY VALOUR DECORATIONS/DÉCORATIONS DE LA VAILLANCE MILITAIRE

Military Valour Decorations are national honours awarded to recognize acts of valour, self-sacrifice or devotion to duty in the presence of the enemy. The decorations were approved by Her Majesty Queen Elizabeth II in 1993. They consist of the Victoria Cross, the Star of Military Valour and the Medal of Military Valour.

Victoria Cross/La Croix de Victoria (C.V.)

None awarded since last edition.

Star of Military Valour/Étoile de la vaillance militaire (É.V.M.)

(Invested September 19, 2012)
Corporal Jean-François Roger Donald Belzil, S.M.V., Montréal, QC

(Announced September 8, 2011)
Master Corporal Paul D. Rachynski, M.M.V., Edmonton and Bonnyville, AB

Medal of Military Valour/ Médaille de la vaillance militaire (M.V.M)

(Invested September 19, 2012)
Corporal Marc-André Cousineau, M.M.V., Greenfield Park, QC
Sergeant Joseph André Steve Poulin, M.M.V., C.D. Québec, QC
Corporal Marco Tremblay, M.M.V., Jonquière, QC

(Invested June 20, 2012)
Corporal Brian Bélanger, M.M.V., Montréal, QC
Captain Ashley Collette, M.M.V., Yarmouth, N.S.
Staff Sergeant Adam Hever, M.M.V., Peabody, MA, U.S.A.
Corporal Eric Monnin, M.M.V., Cornwall, ON
Master Corporal Charles St-Pierre, M.M.V., Saint-Quentin, N.B.

(Invested January 26, 2012)
Captain William Todd Fielding, M.M.V., C.D., Niagara Falls, ON
Master Corporal Adam Holmes, M.M.V., Kapuskasing, ON
Master Corporal Gilles-Remi Mikkelson, M.M.V., Bella Colla, BC
Private Philip Millar, M.M.V., Lower Sackville, NS
Master Corporal Paul Douglas Mitchell, M.M.V., Weymouth, NS
Private John Nelson, M.M.V., Wiseton, SK
Sergeant Graham Marc Verrier, M.M.V., C.D., Winnipeg, MB

(Invested December 13, 2011)

Private Tony Harris, M.M.V., Penfield, NB
Warrant Officer Michael Jackson, M.M.V., C.D., Abbotsford, BC
Captain Michael MacKillop, M.M.V., C.D., Calgary, AB

(Invested September 20, 2011)
Lieutenant Guillaume Caron, M.M.V., C.D., Rimouski, QC
Corporal Bradley Casey, M.M.V., Pugwash, NS
Sergeant Marc-André Rousseau, M.M.V., La Sarre, QC

CANADIAN BRAVERY DECORATIONS/DÉCORATIONS CANADIENNES POUR ACTES DE BRAVOURE

The Decorations for Bravery, consisting of the Cross of Valour, the Star of Courage, and the Medal of Bravery, were instituted and created on May 10, 1972. They may be awarded to Canadian citizens or to non-Canadians who have performed an act of bravery in Canada, or outside Canada if the act was in Canada's interest. The Decorations for Bravery may be awarded posthumously.

The Cross of Valour is awarded for acts of the most conspicuous courage in circumstances of extreme peril. The Star of Courage is awarded for acts of conspicuous courage in circumstances of great peril. The Medal of Bravery is awarded for acts of bravery in hazardous circumstances.

Cross of Valour/Croix de Valeur (C.V.)
None awarded since last edition.

Star of Courage/Étoile du courage (S.C.)
(Invested September 19, 2012)
Simon Bernier, S.C., Chambly, QC
Marcel Bouffard, S.C., Delson, QC

(Invested April 20, 2012)
Marc Fortier, S.C. (posthumous), Amos, QC
Corporal Winston William Matheson, S.C., C.D., Enfield, NS

(Invested February 24, 2012)
Constable David Edgar, S.C., Barrie, ON
Constable Clayton Speers, S.C., Stayner, ON
Kenneth Franklin Lehman, S.C., Espanola, ON

(Invested October 28, 2011)
Angela Jeannette Stirk, S.C., Norland & Oro-Medonte, ON
Fontella Twoyoungmen, S.C. (posthumous), Morley, AB

(Invested September 20, 2011)
Private Adam J. P. Fraser, S.C., St-Jean-sur-Richelieu & Courcelette, QC
Corporal Déri J. G. Langevin, S.C., Chicoutimi & Québec, QC
Corporal Marc-André Poirier, S.C., Amos & Québec, QC

(Announced September 8, 2011)
Private Adam J. P. Fraser, S.C., Saint-Jean-sur-Richelieu and Courcelette, QC
Corporal Déri J. G. Langevin, S.C., Chicoutimi and Québec, QC
Corporal Marc-André Poirier, S.C., Amos and Québec, QC

Medal of Bravery/Médaille de la bravoure (M.B.)
(Invested September 19, 2012)
Réal April, M.B., Saint-François and Saint-Simon-de-Rimouski, QC
Éric Beaulieu, M.B., Les Escoumins, QC
François Bergeron, M.B., Québec and Saint-Augustin-de-Desmaures, QC
Alexandre Yves Duperré, M.B., Baie-Comeau and Saguenay, QC
Sébastien Gilbert, M.B., Grenville-sur-la-Rouge, QC
Patrick Grondin, M.B., Lévis, QC
Jules Groulx-Swennen, M.B., Bedford, QC
Gisèle Huot, M.B. (posthumous), Saint-Canut and Rimouski, QC
Constable Guillaume Jacques, M.B., Montréal, QC
Raphaëlle Jetté, M.B., Saint-Jérôme and Farnham, QC
Sergeant François Paquette, M.B., Montréal and LaSalle, QC
Constable Simon Rivard, M.B., Saint-Jean-sur-Richelieu and Carignan, QC

(Invested May 29, 2012)
Jubal Daley, M.B., Negril, Jamaica

(Invested April 20, 2012)
Constable Mansoor Ahmad, M.B., Richmond Hill, ON
Lauchlin Henry Alexander Armstrong, M.B., Port Hawkesbury, NS
Lieutenant André D. Bard, M.B., C.D., Esquimalt, BC
Tyler Bell-Morena, M.B., Brantford, ON
Paul Bergeron, M.B., Hemmingford, QC
Darren Jason Bieber, M.B., Weyburn, SK
Constable Michael Allan Biron, M.B., Cornwall, ON
Freddy Borau, M.B., Montréal, QC
James Joseph Bourgeois, M.B., Prince Rupert, BC
Yves Ducharme, M.B., Hemmingford, QC
Richard Dufresne, M.B., Mississauga, ON
Constrable Michel Durocher, M.B., Salaberry-de-Valleyfield, QC
Sergeant Kent James Gulliford, M.B., M.S.M., C.D., Kamloops, BC and Gander, NL
Michael John Hancock, M.B., (posthumous), Kitchener, ON
Ernest John Herrfort, M.B., Listowel, ON
Mark Arthur Janke, M.B., Elbow, SK
Kevin Jelley-Kasper, M.B., Toronto, ON
Chad Khadr, M.B., Gatineau, QC
Corporal Tamer Khadr, M.B., Ottawa, ON
Gunter Lambeets, M.B., Hemmingford, QC
Tyler ROss Laton, M.B., Airdrie, AB
Daniel Magny, M.B., Sainte-Geneviève-de-Batiscan, QC
Dawn Rene Manning, M.B., Rossland, BC
Michel Masse, M.B., Verdun and Salaberry-de-Valleyfield, QC
Jeff Sean McCarthy, M.B., Regina, SK
Jeremy Francis Michelin, M.B., North West River, NL
Leading Seaman Patrick S. Moulden, M.B., C.D., Hamilton, ON and Victoria, BC
Constable David Paul Murtha, M.B., Lindsay, ON
Jason William Phillips, M.B., Kincardine, ON
Wayne Pruden, M.B., Trenton, ON
Master Corporal Daniel Edward Gilles Rochette, M.B., C.D., Sudbury and Napanee, ON
George Cosmin Rusu, M.B., Ottawa, ON
Yves Soumillon, M.B., Cornwall, ON
David Wilbert Townsend, M.B., Fergus, ON
Ronald Earl Walton, M.B., Elmira, ON
Constable Daryl Whitten, M.B., Peterborough, ON

(Invested February 24, 2012)
Paul George Akehurst, M.B., Ottawa, ON
Constable Andrew Curtis Ashton, M.B., Morinville & Fort McMurray, AB
Michel Bérub , M.B., La Tuque, QC
Corporal Joseph Landre Mickal Couture, M.B., Magog & Québec, QC
Constable Scott Dargie, M.B., Oshawa, ON
Steve Degrace, M.B., Beresford, NB
Leading Seaman David J.S. Denman, M.B., Shearwater, NS
Constable Karen Mary Desaulniers, M.B., Ottawa, ON
Constable Patrick Duerden, M.B., Oakville & Milton, ON
Chief Warrant Officer Anthony Eric Fequet, M.B., C.D. (Retired), Bonne-Esp rance, QC & Amherstview, ON
Sergeant Lorraine Fequet, M.B., C.D., Ottawa & Amherstview, ON
Constable Avery Curt Flangan, M.B., Ottawa, ON
Warrant Officer Marc Joseph Fortin, M.B.,C.D., (Retired), Notre-Dame-d'Hébertville & Gatineau, QC
Monique Gagnon, M.B., Petit-Rocher, NB
Kevin Gooding, M.B., Stoney Creek, ON
Donald George Gough, M.B., Summerland, BC
Jewel James, M.B., Kirkland Lake & Swastika, ON
Bernard Keetash, M.B., Mishkeegogamang, ON
Richard Kelly, M.B., (Posthumous), Oshawa, ON
Lana Mae Krieser, M.B., Brandon, MB
Jonathan Yvan Leblond, M.B., Embrun, ON
Constable George J. MacNeil, M.B., Kenora, ON
William Edward Lance Matthews, M.B., Mansfield, ON
Constable Kris Miclash, M.B., Kenora, ON
Ross P. Moore, M.B., Dwight, ON
Tina Maryann Moores, M.B., (Posthumous), Grand Falls-Windsor, NL
Peter Nesbeth, M.B., Ottawa, ON
Constable Allen George Percival, M.B., Ottawa, ON
Sergeant John K. Potts, M.B., Hastings & Larder Lake, ON
Lindsy RIchardson, M.B., Ottawa, ON
Madden Sarver, M.B., 100 Mile House, BC
Major Ryan Denis Smid, M.B., C.D., Edmonton AB
Elaine Kathryne Spray, M.B., (Posthumous), Lundar, MB
Jakki Spray, M.B., Lundar, MB
Constable Michelle L. Stinson, M.B., La Ronge, SK & Kirkland Lake, ON
Chance William Gene Stewart, M.B., Vancouver, BC
Colleen Taylor, M.B., Ottawa, ON
Frank William Taylor, M.B., Ladysmith, BC
Kevin Thomas, M.B., Oshawa, ON
Philbert Truong, M.B., (Posthumous), Victoria, BC

(Invested October 28, 2011)
Michael Lee Anderson, M.B., Vancouver, BC
Brent Michael Blackmore, M.B., Nanaimo, BC
Constable Nicholas Bell, M.B., West Vancouver, BC
Robert C. Bombardir, M.B., Powell River, BC
Maxime Bondu, M.B., Charlemagne & Notre-Dame-de-Pontmain, QC
Darryl Fabian Boone, M.B., Marion Bridge, NS
Dale Brady, M.B., Valemount, BC
Kingsley Cheung, M.B., Williams Lake, BC
Darren Coogan, M.B., Orangeville, ON
Sergeant Delkie Curtis, M.B., Cobourg, ON
Jewel Denison, M.B., Kingston, ON
Denis Diotte, M.B., Lac-des-Îles & Notre-Dame-de-Pontmain, QC
Ratko Ray Djuric, M.B., Prince George & Bear Lake, BC
Brian Dean Fowlow, M.B., Happy Valley-Goose Bay, NL
Dennis William Robert Fowlow, M.B., Buchans, NL
Bonnie Gamble, M.B., Calgary, AB
Gordon Gamble, M.B., Calgary, AB
Krista Dorothy Girvan, M.B., Edmonton, AB & Riverview, NB
Jeremy Hodder, M.B., Stoneville, NL & Girouxville, AB
Justin Kenneth Darwin Ilnicki, M.B., Williams Lake, BC
Matthew Michael Jackson, M.B., Kelowna, BC
Tara Michelle Josey, M.B., Ottawa, ON
Tamsen Laine Lahnalampi, M.B., Onaping & Ottawa, ON
Nadine Anik Leduc, M.B., Ottawa, ON
Kevin Joseph Leski, M.B., Langley & Squamish, BC
Tyler Norman David Lockerby, M.B., Kelowna, BC
André J. Maillet, M.B., Bouctouche & Saint-Thomas-de-Kent, NB
J. Robert Maillet, M.B., Bouctouche & Saint-Thomas-de-Kent, NB
RCMP Constable Shane Douglas Nicoll, M.B., Terrace & Surrey, BC
Barry Ryder Nilsen, M.B., Bear Lake, BC & Kelvington, SK
Patrick Robert O'Connor, M.B., Calgary, AB
Steven C. Reynolds, M.B., Milton, ON
Sharon Yvonne Rider, M.B., Kincardine, ON
Timothy Andrew Rider, M.B., Kincardine, ON
Vince P. Sharpe, M.B., Inuvik, NT
Sergeant Roger Thomas, M.B., Cobourg, ON
Pazia Toyne, M.B., Lorette, MB
Major Frank Wagener, M.B., Wilnsdorf, Germany & Gilbert, AZ, U.S.A.
Michael Braden Walker, M.B., Toronto, ON
Glen William Watts, M.B., Nanaimo, BC
Russell Ryan Werner, M.B., Powell River, BC
Sheldon Steven Willier, M.B., Rocky Mountain House, AB

(Announced October 19, 2011)
Ian Joseph Wheeler, M.B., C.D., St. John's, NL

(Invested September 20, 2011)
Lieutenant-Colonel Douglas Wynn Baird, M.B., C.D., Aylesford, NS
Leading Seaman Cory K. Bond, M.B., La Poile, NL & Beaverbank, NS
Sergeant André Coallier, MB, Montréal, QC
Archie L. Coughlin, M.B., Kensington, PE
Lieutenant (N) Christopher Michael Devita, M.B., C.D., Bedford, NS & Richmond Hill, ON
Constable Karine Giroux, M.B., Montréal, QC
Geneviève Otis-Leduc, M.B., Montréal, QC
Alexandre Phaneuf, M.B., Laval, QC
Constable David Pilote, M.B., Montréal, QC
Jean-François Renault, M.B., Mirabel, QC
Tyler Glenn Sampson, M.B. (posthumous), Halifax, NS
Constable Daniel Tétreault, M.B., Montréal, QC

MERITORIOUS SERVICE DECORATIONS/DÉCORATIONS POUR SERVICE MÉRITOIRE

Approved by Her Majesty the Queen on July 10, 1991, the Meritorious Service Decorations were created to honour Canadians & foreigners (military) for commendable actions performed on or after June 11, 1984.

The Meritorious Service Cross (Military Division) is awarded for the performance of a military deed or a military activity in an outstandingly professional manner or of a rare high standard that brings considerable benefit or great honour to the Canadian Forces.

The Meritorious Service Medal (Military Division) is awarded for the performance of a military deed or a military activity in a highly professional manner or of a very high standard that brings benefit or honour to the Canadian Forces.

Meritorious Service Cross/M.S.C. (Military)/
La Croix du service méritoire (militaire)
(Invested June 20, 2012)
Brigadier-General Craig Randall King, O.M.M., M.S.C., C.D., M.B.E., Winnipeg, MB
Major-General Michael James Ward, M.S.C., C.D., Pembroke, ON

(Invested January 26, 2012)
Colonel Christian Drouin, M.S.C., C.D., Montréal, QC
Colonel Simon Charles Hetherington, M.S.C., C.D., Oakville, ON
Chief Warrant Officer Joseph Simon Armand Vinet, M.M.M., M.S.C., C.D., Longueuil, QC
Lieutenant-Colonel Jerome Francis Walsh, , M.S.C., C.D., Ottawa, ON

(Invested December 13, 2011)

ORDER OF CANADA

Companions of the Order of Canada

Members of the Order of Canada

Officers of the Order of Canada

ORDER OF MILITARY MERIT

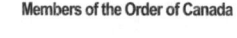

Officers of the Order of Military Merit

Commanders of the Order of Military Merit

Members of the Order of Military Merit

Sergeant Michael Smith, M.S.C., C.D., Sainte-Thérèse-de-Blainville, QC
Chief Warrant Officer Shawn Stevens, M.S.C., M.S.M., C.D., Port Arthur, ON
Lieutenant-Colonel Gilbert Thibault, M.S.C., C.D., Gaspé, QC
Lieutenant-Colonel Carl Turenne, M.S.C., C.D., Kingston, ON
Brigadier-General Jonathan Vance, O.M.M., M.S.C., C.D., Tweed, ON

(Announced December 7, 2011)
Admiral Michael Mullen, M.S.C. (United States Navy), Los Angeles, CA, U.S.A.

(Invested November 24, 2011)
Lieutenant-General Joseph Jacques Charles Bouchard, C.M.M., M.S.C., C.D., Chicoutimi, QC

(Invested September 20, 2011)
Chief Warrant Officer Jules Joseph Moreau, M.M.M., M.S.C., C.D., Saint-Pamphile, QC
Lieutenant-Colonel Jocelyn J. J. M. J. Paul, M.S.C., C.D., Wendake Indian Reserve, QC

Meritorious Service Medal M.S.M. (Military)/
La Médaille du service méritoire (militaire)
(Invested June 20, 2012)
Major Derek John Adams, M.S.M., C.D., Ottawa, ON
Lieutenant-Colonel Ronald Allan Allison, M.S.M., C.D., Miramichi, N.B.
Master Warrant Officer Raymond Joseph Brodeur, M.S.M., C.D., Lafleche, SK
Lieutenant-Colonel Malcolm David Bruce, M.S.M., C.D., Montréal, QC
Sergeant Yannick Campbell, M.S.M., C.D., Québec, QC
Major General Raymond Carpenter, M.S.M., (United States Army National Guard), Rapid City, SD, U.S.A.
Master Warrant Officer Joseph Guy Alain Richmond Champagne, M.S.M., C.D., Valleyfield, QC
Major Michael James Cole, M.S.M., C.D., London, ON
Colonel Ian Robert Creighton, M.S.M., C.D., Whyalla, South Australia
Sergeant Gordon Percy Cullen, M.S.M., C.D., St. James, MB
Major Austin Matthew Douglas, M.S.M., C.D., Montréal, QC
Sergeant Scott William Duffy, M.S.M., C.D., Brampton, ON
Warrant Officer Marc Charles Joseph Filiatrault, M.S.M., C.D., Verner, ON
Corporal Joy Francis, M.S.M., Burlington, ON
Major Douglas Andrew Grant, M.S.M., C.D., Toronto, ON
Major Steve Jourdain, M.S.M., C.D., Shawinigan, QC
Lieutenant-Colonel Scott Gerard Long, M.S.M., C.D., St. John's, NL
Lieutenant-Colonel David Williams Lowthian, M.S.M., C.D., Ottawa, ON
Captain Vincent Lussier, M.S.M., Ottawa, ON
Honorary Lieutenant-Colonel James William Martin, M.S.M., C.D., London, ON
Colonel John Gerard Milne, M.S.M., C.D., Stittsville, ON & Calgary, AB
Major Jeffrey Karl Monaghan, M.S.M., C.D., Regina, SK
Chief Warrant Officer Kirk Newhook, M.S.M., C.D., Winnipeg, MB
Lieutenant-Colonel Paul James Peyton, M.S.M., C.D., Happy Valley-Goose Bay, N.L.
Master Warrant Officer Dean Edward Poffley, M.S.M., C.D., Kingston, ON
Lieutenant-Colonel Joseph Raynald Yan Poirier, M.S.M., C.D., Hauterive, QC
Master Corporal Jeffrey Quesnelle, M.S.M., Penetanguishene, ON
Corporal Corey Sagstuen, M.S.M., C.D., Edmonton, AB
Corporal John Tommy Salois, M.S.M., Greenfield Park, QC
Captain Mark Savard, M.S.M., Montréal, QC
Sergeant Michel Simoneau, M.S.M., C.D., St-Georges-de-Beauce, QC
Chief Warrant Officer Kevin Peter Sinden, M.S.M., C.D., Thunder Bay, ON
Lieutenant-General Jack Calvin Stultz, M.S.M., (US Army Reserve), Leaksville, NC, U.S.A.
Najor Eleanor Frances Taylor, M.S.M., C.D., Antigonish, N.S.
Lieutenant Chad Thain, M.S.M., New Westminster, BC

(Invested January 26, 2012)
Colonel David Edward Barr, M.S.M., C.D., Victoria, BC
Major Annie Bouchard, M.S.M., C.D., Roberval, QC
Master Corporal Danny Denis Boyd, M.S.M., C.D., La Tuque, QC
Colonel Shane Anthony Brennan, M.S.M., C.D., Ottawa, ON
Corporal Bobby Brown, M.S.M., Holland Centre, ON
Lieutenant-Colonel Kenneth Freeman Butterworth, M.S.M., C.D., Glace Bay, NS
Colonel James Roy Forestell, M.S.M., C.D., Campbellford, ON
Warrant Officer Joseph Jacques Friolet, M.S.M., C.D., Bathurst, NB
Colonel Raymond Marc Gagné, M.S.M., C.D., St-Gilles de Lothbinière, QC
Lieutenant-Commander Louis Christian Haché, M.S.M., C.D., Petit-Rocher, NB & Middle Sackville, NS
Captain (N) Richard Philip Harrison, O.M.M., M.S.M., C.D., Victoria, BC
Colonel Jeffrey Holachek, M.S.M. (United States Army), Cleveland, Ohio, U.S.A.,
Major Patrick John Koch, M.S.M., C.D., White Rock, BC
Lieutenant-Colonel Thomas Frederick McGrath, O.M.M., M.S.M., C.D., St. John's, NL
Sergeant Charles Andrew McLean, M.M.M., M.S.M., C.D., Ottawa, ON
Captain (N) John Frederick Newton, O.M.M., M.S.M., C.D., Halifax, NS
Captain James Alan O'Neill, M.S.M., C.D., Hamilton, ON
Warrant Officer George Nelson Parrott, M.S.M., C.D., Duncan, BC
Lieutenant-Colonel Michael Brian Patrick, M.S.M., C.D., Kitchener, ON
Captain (N) Kenneth John Pickford, M.S.M., C.D., Ottawa, ON & Halifax, NS

CANADIAN BRAVERY DECORATIONS

Star of Courage

Cross of Valor

Medal of Bravery

MERITORIOUS SERVICE DECORATIONS

Meritorious Service Cross
Obverse (Military Version)

Meritorious Service Medal
Reverse (Civil Version)

Major Derek Prohar, M.M.V., M.S.M., Avonlea, SK
Major Liam Wade Rutland, M.S.M., C.D., Pembroke, ON
Lieutenant-Colonel Andrew Scheidl, M.S.M., C.D., Ottawa, ON
Captain Robert Scott, M.S.M., Prince Albert, SK
Major Donald James Senft, M.S.M., C.D., Kelowna, BC
Lieutenant-Colonel Jeffery Douglas Smyth, M.S.M., C.D., Chatham, ON
Lieutenant-Colonel Michael Whited, Jr., M.S.M. (United States Army), Colorado Springs, Colorado, U.S.A.
Brigadier-General Gregory Achilles Young, O.M.M., M.S.M., C.D., Windsor, ON

(Invested December 13, 2011)
Major Emanuel Jeannot Boucher, M.S.M., C.D., Granby, QC
Lieutenant-Colonel Marie Carignan, M.S.M., C.D., Asbestos, QC
Captain Breen Carson, M.S.M., Toronto, ON
Major-General Mart C. de Kruif, M.S.M. (Royal Netherlands Army), Apeldoorn, Netherlands
Corporal Eric Dionne, M.S.M., Boucherville, QC
Major Michael Kaiser, M.S.M., C.D., Windsor, ON
Sergeant William Kelland, M.S.M., C.D., St. John's, NL
Captain Enno Kerckhoff, M.S.M., C.D., Huntsville, ON
Master Warrant Officer René Kiens, M.S.M., C.D., Oakville, ON
Major Steven MacBeth, M.S.M., C.D., Whitby, ON
Major Joshua Major, M.S.M., C.D., North Bay, ON
Master Warrant Officer Kevin Mathers, M.S.M., C.D., Barrie, ON
Captain James McKay, M.S.M., Brantford, ON
Captain Andrew Mercer, M.S.M., C.D., Toronto, ON
Honorary Colonel Stanley Milner, O.C., A.O.E., M.S.M., C.D., Edmonton, AB
Warrant Officer Keith Mitchell, C.V., M.S.M., C.D., Lasalle, QC
Major Lee Mossop, M.S.M., C.D., Saskatoon, SK
Lieutenant-Colonel David Murphy, M.S.M., C.D., Vancouver, BC
Major Wayne Niven, M.S.M., C.D., New Westminster, BC
Lieutenant Andrew Nuttall, M.S.M. (Posthumous), Victoria, BC
Warrant Officer Steeve Ouellet, M.S.M., C.D., Rivière-du-Loup, QC
Sergeant David Pawulski, S.C., M.S.M., C.D., Calgary, AB
Corporal Emelie Pilon, M.S.M., Mississauga, ON
Colonel John Ploughman, M.S.M., C.D., St. John's, NL
Chief Warrant Officer Joseph Robichaud, M.S.M., C.D., Rexton, NB
Colonel Marie Savard, M.S.M., C.D., Chicoutimi, QC
Major Paul Scannell, M.S.M. (British Army), Ruislip, UK
Honorary Colonel Gary Solar, M.S.M., C.D., Winnipeg, MB
Master Corporal Jeffrey Spence, M.S.M., C.D., Kamloops, BC
Chief Warrant Officer Andrew Stapleford, M.S.M., C.D., Halifax, NS
Lieutenant-Colonel Ann-Marie Tardif, M.S.M., C.D., Plessisville, QC
Lieutenant-Colonel John Tringali, M.S.M. (United States Air Force), Charleston, SC, U.S.A.
Captain Kristian Udesen, M.S.M., Kamloops, BC
Major Joseph Verret, M.S.M., C.D., Ottawa, ON
Commander Steven Waddell, M.S.M., C.D., Temagami, ON
Sergeant Austin Williams, M.S.M., Lillooet, BC
Brigadier-General Paul Wynnyk, O.M.M., M.S.M., C.D., Sherwood Park & Breton, AB

(Announced December 7, 2011)
Lieutenant-Colonel David Bruce Cochrane, M.S.M., C.D., Tweed, ON
Major Jay Lyman Indewey, M.S.M., C.D., Georgetown, PE

(Invested September 20, 2011)
Corporal François-Jonathan Gilles Michel Hébert, M.S.M., **Montréal, QC**
Major Joseph Serge Raynald Morin, M.S.M., C.D., Lac Mégantic,QC
Major Yannick Pépin, M.S.M., C.D. (posthumous), Warwick, QC
Sergeant Joseph François Colin Piché, M.S.M., C.D., St-Basile-de-Portneuf, QC
Chief Warrant Officer Joseph Gérard Gilbert Poirier, M.M.M., M.S.M., C.D., Verdun, QC
Chief Warrant Officer Ernest Gérard Joseph Poitras, M.S.M., C.D., Tracadie, NB

GENERAL SERVICE AWARDS

Rather than creating a new honour for each new Canadian Forces operation as it arises, in July of 2004, Her Majesty the Queen approved the creation of the following:

The General Campaign Star (G.C.S.) recognizes military service in a theatre of operations in the presence of an armed enemy.

The General Service Medal (G.S.M.) acknowledges civilian and military service in direct support of operations in the presence of an armed enemy.

General Campaign Star/Étoile de campagne générale (G.C.S.)
None awarded since last edition.

General Service Medal/Médaille du service général
(G.S.M.)None awarded since last edition.

British & Commonwealth Honours

In earlier times Canadians could receive hereditary titles, knighthoods and other such honours under the British system of honours, and this is still the case with Canadians who pursue careers in the United Kingdom. Furthermore, the Canadian military system of decorations was based on the British system and many Canadians hold British honours as a result of service in Canadian, British or other Commonwealth forces. While Canada has developed its own honours system, honours are still from time to time granted by the Sovereign to Canadians for, among other things, service to the Commonwealth.

VICTORIA CROSS (V.C.)

The Victoria Cross was founded by Queen Victoria at the close of the Crimean War in 1856, but made retroactive to 1854. It is described as a Maltese cross, made of gun metal, with a Royal Crest in the centre and underneath it an escroll bearing the inscription "For Valour". It is awarded, irrespective of rank, to members of any branch of Her Majesty's services, either in the British Forces or those of any Commonwealth realm, dominion, colony or dependency, the Mercantile Marine, nurses or staffs of hospitals, or to civilians of either sex while serving in either regular or temporary capacity during naval, military, or air force operations. It is awarded only "for most conspicuous bravery or some daring or pre-eminent act of valour or self-sacrifice or extreme devotion to duty in the presence of the enemy." For additional conduct of similar bravery, a Bar is added. The ribbon was formerly red for the Army and blue for the Navy, but it is now red (a dull crimson) for all services. Since June 17th, 1943, the financial responsibility for a stipend to Canadian recipients has been assumed by the Canadian Government. Ninetysix V.C.s have been awarded to Canadians or to foreigners serving in Canadian forces.

GEORGE CROSS (G.C.)

Arthur Richard Cecil Butson, G.C., O.M.M., C.St.J., C.D., M.A., M.D., F.R.C.S. (Eng.), F.R.C.S.C.C. In 1940, King George VI instituted the George Cross for civilians and members of the services alike, male or female, who performed "acts of the greatest heroism or of the most conspicuous courage in circumstances of extreme danger." This decoration - the second highest Commonwealth award for bravery - is a plain silver cross bearing in the centre a representation of Saint George slaying the dragon and the words: "For Gallantry". The ribbon is garter blue. Eleven Canadians, and a Bermudian serving in the Canadian Forces, have won the G.C. Not all were members of the armed forces.

ALBERT MEDAL (A.M.)

Ernest Alfred Wooding, A.M., R.C.N.V.R. Queen Elizabeth II requested that all living Albert Medal recipients convert their Albert Medal to a George Cross. For some reason Mr. Wooding did not convert his Albert Medal.

ROYAL HONOURS (COMMONWEALTH)

The Order of Baronets, the lowest Hereditary rank, was instituted in 1611; a Baronet is designated "Sir John Smith, Baronet." The abbreviation Bt. is used in Court Circulars and has been generally adopted in lieu of "Bart." Taking precedence to Baronets are members of The Most Honourable Privy Council, who are addressed "Right Honourable."

The Most Noble Order of the Garter, instituted 1349. - K.G.

The Most Ancient and Most Noble Order of the Thistle, instituted 1687. - K.T.

The Most Honourable Order of the Bath, instituted in 1399, and revived in 1725, is divided into three classes - Knights Grand Cross, G.C.B.; Knights Commanders, K.C.B.; and Companions, C.B.

The Order of Merit, O.M., carries no title.

The Most Distinguished Order of St. Michael and St. George, instituted in 1818, has three classes - Knights Grand Cross, G.C.M.G.; Knights Commanders, K.C.M.G.; Companions, C.M.G.

The Most Eminent Order of the Indian Empire instituted 1877, has three classes - Knights Grand Commanders, G.C.I.E.; Knights Commanders, K.C.I.E.; Companions, C.I.E. (This Order has not been conferred since 1947.)

The Royal Victorian Order, instituted in 1896, has five classes - Knights Grand Cross, G.C.V.O.; Knights Commanders, K.C.V.O.; Commanders, C.V.O., Lieutenants, L.V.O.; Members 4th and 5th classes - M.V.O. Ribbon, blue with red and white edges.

The Most Excellent Order of the British Empire, instituted in 1917, has five classes - Knights (or Dames) Grand Cross, G.B.E.; Knights Commanders, K.B.E.; Dames Commanders, D.B.E.; Commanders, C.B.E.; Officers, O.B.E.; and Members, M.B.E. Ribbon (Military) rose pink, pearl grey edging, vertical pearl stripe in centre; (Civil) rose pink, pearl grey edging, and no central vertical stripe.

Knights Bachelors are gentlemen unconnected with any order who have received the honour of Knighthood, and are entitled to the prefix "Sir". They rank immediately after Knights Commanders of the British Empire.

The Companions of Honour, C.H., instituted in 1917 rank immediately after Knights (Dames) Grand Cross of the Order of the British Empire. Membership is limited and carries no title.

In all Orders of Knighthood the Knights Grand Cross and the Knights Commanders have the prefix "Sir" with the initials of their class following the name. Companions and Members bear no title, but have the letters C.B., C.M.G., L.V.O., M.V.O., as the case may be, attached to their names.

The Garter, the Thistle, The Order of Merit and the Royal Victorian Order are all in the personal bestowal of the Sovereign. Appointments to the other Orders are made by Her Majesty on recommendation of the Prime Ministers of Commonwealth countries who wish to secure such appointments. Premiers of individual Australian states may also make recommendations.

MARQUESS

The Most Hon. the Marquess of Exeter, Michael Anthony Cecil, 8th Marquess

The Most Hon. the Marquess of Ely, Charles John Tottenham, 9th Marquess

EARLS

The Right Hon. the Earl of Egmont, Thomas Frederick Gerald Perceval, 12th Earl and 16th Baronet

The Right Hon. the Earl Grey, Richard Fleming George Charles Grey, 6th Earl

The Right Hon. the Earl of Orkney, Peter St. John, 9th Earl

The Right Hon. the Earl Winterton, Donald David Turnour, 8th Earl

VISCOUNTS

The Right Hon. the Viscount Charlemont, John Dodd Caulfield, 15th Viscount

The Right Hon. the Viscount Galway, L.Cdr. George Rupert Monckton, R.C.N. (Ret'd), 12th Viscount

The Right Hon. the Viscount Hardinge, Andrew Hartland Hardinge, 7th Viscount

OLD CANADIAN TITLE

The title of Baron de Longueuil existed prior to the Treaty of Paris (1763), and was duly recognized by Queen Victoria pursuant to that treaty.

BARONS

The Right Hon. the Lord Beaverbrook, Maxwell William Henry Aitken, 3rd Baron and 3rd Baronet

The Right Hon. the Lord Cullen of Ashbourne, Edmund Willoughby Marsham Cokayne, 3rd Baron

The Right Hon. the Lord Lucas of Chilworth, Simon William Lucas, 3rd Baron

The Right Hon. the Lord Martonmere, John Stephen Robinson, 2nd Baron

The Right Hon. the Lord Morris, Thomas Anthony Salmon Morris, 4th Baron

The Right Hon. the Lord Rodney, John George Brydges Rodney, 11th Baron and 11th Baronet

The Right Hon. the Lord Sanford, James John Mowbray Edmonton Sanford, 3rd Baron

The Right Hon. The Lord Shaughnessy, Charles George Patrick Shaughnessy, 5th Baron

The Right Hon. the Lord Strathcona and Mount Royal, Hon. Col. Donald Euan Palmer Howard, 4th Baron

The Right Hon. the Lord Thomson of Fleet David Kenneth Roy Thomson, 3rd Baron

BARONETS

Sir Richard Aylmer (16th Bt.)
Sir Christopher Hilaro Barlow (7th Bt.)
Sir James Barlow (4th Bt.)
Sir Benjamin Barrington (8th Bt.)
Sir James Bates (7th Bt)
Sir John Irving Bell, (1st Bt.)
Sir Alexander Boyd (3rd Bt.)
Sir Theodore Brinckman (6th Bt.)
Sir James Brunton (4th Bt.)
Sir Peter Burbidge (6th Bt.)
Sir Michael Butler (3rd Bt.)
Sir Robert Cave-Brown-Cave (16th Bt.)
Sir Bruce Chaytor (9th Bt.)
Sir Robin Chetwynd (9th Bt.)
Sir John Davis (3rd Bt.)
Sir David Hart Dyke (10th Bt.)
The Revd. Sir Christopher Gibson, Bt., C.P. (4th Bt.)
Sir James Grant-Suttie (9th Bt.)
Sir Philip Grotrian (3rd Bt.)
Sir Charles Gunning C.D., (8th Bt.)
Sir Wayne King (8th Bt,)
Sir Charles Knowles (7th Bt.)
Sir Colpoys Johnson (8th Bt.)
Sir Peter Lambert (10th Bt.)
Sir Richard Latham (3rd Bt.)
Sir John Leeds (9th Bt.)
Sir Ian McGregor (8th Bt.)
Sir Roderick McQuhae MacKenzie (12th Bt.)
Sir Allan Morris (11th Bt.)
Sir Christopher Oakes (3rd Bt.)
Sir Mathew Philipson-Stow (6th Bt.)
Sir James Piers (11 Bt.)
Sir Francis Price, Bt. (7th Bt.)
Sir Christopher Robinson (8th Bt.)
Sir John James Michael Laud Robinson (11th Bt.)
Sir Julian Rose (5th Bt.)
Sir James Rugge-Price (10th Bt.)
Sir John Samuel (5th Bt.)
Sir Adrian Sharp (4th Bt.)
Sir Richard Simeon (8th Bt.)
The Rev. Sir Michael Stonhouse (19th Bt.)
Sir Adrian Stott (4th Bt.)
Sir John Stracey (9th Bt.)
Sir Philip Stuart (9th Bt.)
Sir Richard Sullivan (9th Bt.)
Sir Robert Synge (8th Bt.)
Sir Rodney Touche (2nd Bt.)
Sir Charles Hibbert Tupper (6th Bt.)
Sir Gerald Walsham (6th Bt.)
Sir Christopher Wells, M.D. (3rd Bt.)
Sir Donald Williams (10th Bt.)

Knight Grand Cross of the Most Honourable Order of the Bath (G.C.B.)

Air Chief Marshal Sir David Evans, G.C.B., C.B.E.

The Order of Merit (O.M.)

The Right Honourable Jean Chrétien, PC, OM, CC.

Knight Grand Cross or Dame Grand Cross of the Most Excellent Order of the British Empire (G.B.E.)

Member of the Order of the Companions of Honour (C.H.)

General John de Chastelaine, O.C., C.M.M., C.H., E.D.
Dr. Anthony Pawson, C.H., O.C., O.Ont.

Knight Commander of the Most Distinguished Order of St. Michael and St. George (K.C.M.G.)

Knight Commander of the Royal Victorian Order (K.C.V.O.)

Sir Conrad Swan, K.C.V.O.

Knight Commander of the Most Excellent Order of the British Empire (K.B.E.)

Knight Commander or Dame Commander of the Most Excellent Order of the British Empire (K.B.E. or D.B.E.)

Dame Clara Furse, D.B.E.

KNIGHT BACHELOR

Sir George Bain
Sir Graham Day
Sir John Reginald Gorman, C.V.O., C.B.E., M.C
Sir Terence Matthews, O.B.E.
Sir Christopher Ondaatje, C.B.E.
Sir Neil Shaw

Companion of the Most Honourable Order of the Bath (C.B.)

Air Vice-Marshal George Brookes, C.B., O.B.E.

Companion of the Most Distinguished Order of St. Michael and St. George (C.M.G.)

H.J. Carmichael, C.M.G.
Edmond Cloutier, C.M.G., B.A., L.Ph.
Donovan Bartley Finn, C.M.G., M.Sc., Ph.D., F.R.S.C., F.C.I.C.
George H. McIvor, C.M.G.
Hector Brown McKinnon, C.C., C.M.G.
William Andrew O'Neil, C.M.G.
Alexander Ross, C.M.G.
Joseph Emile St. Laurent, C.M.G.
Ivor Otterbein Smith, C.M.G., O.B.E.

Companion of the Most Eminent Order of the Indian Empire (C.I.E.)

Maj. Frederick Wernham Gerrard, C.I.E.
Capt. John Ryland, C.I.E., R.C.N.
Maj. Frederick Augustus Berrill Sheppard, C.I.E., O.B.E.

Commander of the Royal Victorian Order (C.V.O.)

Leopold Henry Amyot, C.V.O.
Dr. Michael Jackson, C.V.O., C.D.

The Hon. David C. Lam, C.V.O., C.M., K.St.J., O.B.C., B.A.(Econ.), M.B.A., L.L.D., D.Mil.Sc., D.H.L., D.H.
Veronica Jane Langton, C.V.O.
Judith A. LaRocque, C.V.O.
Kevin Stewart MacLeod, C.V.O.
Cdr. G.J. Manson, C.V.O., C.D., R.C.N.
John Crosbie Perlin, C.V.O.
Peter Michael Pitfield, C.V.O., P.C., Q.C.
M.Gen. Roy A. Reid, C.V.O., C.M., M.C., C.D.
L.Cdr. Lawrence James Wallace, C.V.O., O.C., O.B.C., R.C.N.V.R.

Commander of the Order of the British Empire (C.B.E.)
William Eric Adams, C.B.E.
James Pomeroy Anderson, C.B.E.
Brig. Gerald Gardiner Anglin, C.B.E., M.C., E.D.
Brig. Walter A. Bean, C.B.E., E.D., C.D.
Brig. John Arthur Watson Bennett, C.B.E., C.D.
Brig. John Francis Bingham, C.B.E.
Brig. Dudley Kingdon Black, C.B.E., D.S.O.
George Herbert Bowler, C.B.E.
Garrett Brownrigg, C.B.E.
John Burke, C.B.E.
Alfred Charpentier, C.B.E.
Howard Brown Chase, C.B.E.
Brig. Frederick Graham Coleman, C.B.E.
Air Commodore Barbara Cooper, C.B.E., R.A.F.
Brig. J. A. de Lalanne, C.B.E., M.C., E.D.
Conrad Trelawny Fitz-Gerald, C.B.E., M.D.
Charles Gavsie, C.B.E., Q.C.
Gerald Godsoe, C.B.E., Q.C.
Joseph Ernest Gregoire, C.B.E.
Frank Sydney Grisdale, C.B.E.
Raymond Gushue, O.C., C.B.E., Q.C.
Wallace Bruce Haughan, C.B.E.
Brig. Robert James Henderson, C.B.E.
Harold Ferguson Hodgson, C.B.E.
Sandra Horley, C.B.E.
Capt. Francis Deschamps Howie, C.B.E., D.S.O., R.N.
Alexander George Irvine, C.B.E.
Lester Millman Keachie, C.B.E., Q.C.
Capt. Thomas Douglas Kelly, C.B.E., R.C.N.R.
Allan Collingwood Travers Lewis, C.B.E., Q.C.
Col. Edward Raymond Lewis, C.B.E.
Wilfrid Bennett Lewis, C.O., C.B.E., Ph.D
Gordon Clapp Lindsay, C.B.E.
John Struthers McNeil, C.B.E.
E.J. Mackie, C.B.E.
Raymond Charles Manning, C.B.E.
Walter Melvill Marshall, C.B.E.
James Matson, C.B.E.
Ronald Henry Moray Mavor, C.B.E.
Air Vice-Marshal Walter Alyn Orr, C.B.E., C.D., R.C.A.F.
Luke William Pearsall, C.B.E.
M.Gen. Matthew Howard Somers Penhale, C.B.E., C.D.
Cyril Horace Frederick Pierrepont, C.B.E., E.D.
M.Gen. Norman Elliott Rodger, C.B.E.
James Joseph Alexander Ross, C.B.E., C.D.
T.H. Savage, C.B.E.
Lynn Seymour, C.B.E.
Air Vice-Marshal Douglas McCully Smith, C.B.E., C.D.
Brig. Gerald Lucian Morgan Smith, C.B.E., C.D.
George Spence, C.B.E., LL.D.
William Leonard O'Brien Stallard, C.B.E.
Basil Otto Stevenson, C.B.E.
Air Cdre. Stanley Gibson Tackaberry, C.B.E.
Kenneth Wiffin Taylor, O.C., C.B.E.
George Gamlin Thomas, C.B.E.
Lyman Trumbull, C.B.E.
M.Gen. Arthur Egbert Wrinch, C.B.E., C.D.
Henry Wrong, C.B.E.

IMPERIAL SERVICE ORDER (I.S.O.)
George Clayton Anderson
Robert Albert Andison
Arthur Barnstead
Avila Bedard
Peter Cooligan
Henri Fortier
Frank Henry French
Arthur Leigh Jolliffe
Edward Jost
Louis MacMillan
Walter Clifton Ronson
David John Scott
Ivan Vallee

ROYAL VICTORIAN CHAIN
Bestows no precedence; currently not held by anyone.

QUEEN ELIZABETH II'S DIAMOND JUBILEE MEDAL

(Invested September 7, 2012)
The Honourable Ed Broadbent, P.C., C.C.
Vernon Douglas Burrows, C.M.
Hugh Clifford Chadderton, C.C., O.Ont.
Young Sup Chung, C.M., C.Q.
Dr. Adolfo de Bold O.C.
Claudette Gravelle, C.M.
Jean-Marc Hamel, O.C.
Charles Richard Harington, O.C.
Sultan Jessa, C.M.
Huguette Labelle, O.C., O. Ont.
Norma Lamont
George F. MacDonald, C.M.
Joy Harvie Maclaren, C.M.
John McGowan
Rick Mercer
Rose Eleanor Milne, C.M.
Frank O'Dea, O.C.
Sandra Oh
Christie Paquet and Stan Witten
The Honourable Landon Pearson, O.C.
His Grace Joseph-Aurèle Plourde, O.C.
Shirley Post, C.M.
Luke and Stephanie Richardson, Morgan Richardson
Dr. William George Schneider, O.C.
Jérôme Tremblay

(Invested February 6, 2012)
Tomas Avendano
Michael Ball
Maureen Basnicki
Wanda Bedard
Teresa Berezowski
Michel G. Bergeron
Alexandre Bilodeau
Lieutenant-Colonel John R. Bishop, C.D., (Ret'd)
Pierre Boileau
Major-General Lionel Bourgeois, C.M.M., C.D. (Ret'd)
Melvin James Boutilier, C.M., O.N.S.
David A. Chalack
Clément Chartier
Joël Chéruet
Lieutenant (N) James W. Clute, C.D.
Gail Cyr
Priscilla de Viliers, M.S.M.
Corporal Ryan Doherty
Budhendranauth Doobay, O.Ont.
Barney Ellis-Perry
Alex Forrest
Darrell Fox
Bruce Gitelman
Bryden Hutt
Master Corporal Deven Thomas Iles
Johnny Issaluk
Roberta L. Jamieson, C.M.
Major Gordon Jenkins, C.D. (Ret'd)
William Matthew Raistlen Jones
Melpa Kamateros
Chil-Yong Kang
Captain Ray Kokkonen, C.D. (Ret'd)
Veronica (Vonnie) Lavers
Huguette Lépine
Captain Simon J. Mailloux
Shawnee Main
Captain E. Maria Mangnall-Schonert, C.D.
Patricia McDermott
Peter P.M. Meincke
Bryna Monson
Leslie Natynczyk
Paul Nguyen
ConstableAnne O'Shaughnessy
Master Warrant Officer Jean-Claude Parent, C.D.
Linda Patterson
Tom Quinn
Brigadier-General Bob Robert, C.D. (Ret'd)
Ronald Schlegel
Rachel Scott-Mignon
Maureen Shaw
Master Seaman Christopher Mark Switzer
Hannah Catherine Taylor
Travis Toews
Patricia (Pat) Varga
Kathryn Laura Whitfield
W. Brett Wilson, C.M.
Sergeant Angela Wintonyk, C.D.
Pauline Wong
Lauren Woolstencroft
Xinsheng (Simon) Zhong

Order of Precedence for Orders, Decorations and Medals

The following is the approved order of predecence as of April 2, 1998. The asterisk indicates honours added since that date.

SEQUENCE 1
1. The sequence for wearing the insignia of Canadian orders, decorations and medals, and the post-nominal letters associated with such orders, decorations and medals are the following:
Victoria Cross (V.C.)
Cross of Valour (C.V.)

NATIONAL ORDERS
Companion of the Order of Canada (C.C.)
Officer of the Order of Canada (O.C.)
Member of the Order of Canada (C.M.)
Commander of the Order of Military Merit (C.M.M.)
*Commander of the Order of Merit of the Police Forces (C.O.M.)
Commander of the Royal Victorian Order (C.V.O.)
Officer of the Order of Military Merit (O.M.M.)
*Officer of the Order of Merit of the Police Forces (O.O.M.)
Lieutenant of the Royal Victorian Order (L.V.O.)
Member of the Order of Military Merit (M.M.M.)
*Member of the Order of Merit of the Police Forces (M.O.M.)
Member of the Royal Victorian Order (M.V.O.)
The Most Venerable Order of the Hospital of St. John of Jerusalem (all grades) (post-nominal letters only for internal use by the Order of St. John)

PROVINCIAL ORDERS
*Ordre national du Québec (G.O.Q., O.Q., C.Q.)
Saskatchewan Order of Merit (S.O.M.)
Order of Ontario (O.Ont.)
Order of British Columbia (O.B.C.)
Alberta Order of Excellence (A.O.E.)
Order of Prince Edward Island (O.P.E.I.)
Order of Manitoba (O.M.)
Order of New Brunswick (O.N.B.)
Order of Nova Scotia (O.N.S.)
Order of Newfoundland & Labrador (O.N.L.)

DECORATIONS
Star of Military Valour (S.M.V.)
Star of Courage (S.C)
Meritorious Service Cross (M.S.C.)
Medal of Military Valour (M.M.V.)
Medal of Bravery (M.B.)
Meritorious Service Medal (M.S.M.)
Royal Victorian Medal (R.V.M.)

WAR AND OPERATIONAL SERVICE MEDALS
Korea Medal
Canadian Volunteer Service Medal for Korea
Gulf and Kuwait Medal
Somalia Medal
*South-West Asia Service Medal
*General Campaign Star
*General Service Medal

SPECIAL SERVICE MEDALS (S.S.M.)
S.S.M. with bars for:
Pakistan (1989-1990)
Alert
Humanitas
NATO/OTAN
Peace/Paix
*Ranger
*Canadian Peacekeeping Service Medal (C.P.S.M.)

UNITED NATIONS MEDALS
Service (Korea) (1950-1954)
Emergency Force (Egypt/Sinai) (1956-67)
Truce Supervision Organization in Palestine (1948-) and Observer Group in Lebanon (1958)
Military Observation Group in India and Pakistan (1948-)
Operation in Congo (1960-64)
Temporary Executive Authority in West New Guinea (1962-63)
Yemen Observation Mission (1963-64)
Force in Cyprus (1964-)
India/Pakistan Observation Misison (1965-66)
Emergency Force Middle East (1973-79)
Disengagement Observation Force Golan Heights (1974-)
Interim Force in Lebanon (1978-)
Military Observation Group in Iran/Iraq (1988-91)
Transition Assistance Group (Namibia) (1989-90)
Observer Group in Central America (1989-92)
Iraq/Kuwait Observer Mission (1991-)
Angola Verification Mission (1988-97)

Mission for the Referendum in Western Sahara (1991-)
Observer Mission in El Salvador (1991-95)
Protection Force (Yugoslavia) (1992-95)
Advance Mission in Cambodia (1991-92)
Transitional Authority in Cambodia (1992-93)
Operation in Somalia (1992-93)
Operation in Mozambique (1992-94)
Observation Mission in Uganda/Rwanda (1993-94)
Assistance Mission in Rwanda (1993-96)
Mission in Haïti (1993-)
Verification of Human Rights and Compliance with the Comprehensive Agreement on Human Rights in Guatemala (1997-98)
*Mission in the Central African Republic (1998-2000)
*Preventive Deployment Force (Macedonia) (1995- 99)
*Mission in Bosnia and Herzegovina (1995-)
*Mission of Observers in Prevlaka (Croatia) (1996-)
*Interim Administration Mission in Kosovo (1999-)
*Observer Mission in Sierra Leone (1999-)
*Mission in East Timor and Transitional Administration in East Timor (1999-)
*Mission in the Democratic Republic of the Congo (1999-)
*Mission in Ethiopia and Eritrea (2000-)
Special Service (1995-)
*Headquarters

NATO MEDALS

*North Atlantic Treaty Organization (NATO) Medal for the Former Yugoslavia (1992-2002)
*NATO Medal for Kosovo (1999-)
*NATO Medal for the Former Yugoslav Republic of Macedonia (2001-02)
*Article 5 NATO Medal for Operation "Eagle Assist" (2001-02)
*Article 5 NATO Medal for Operation "Active Endeavour" (2001-)
*Non-Article 5 NATO Medal for Operations in the Balkans (2003-)

INTERNATIONAL MISSION MEDALS

International Commission for Supervision and Control (Indo-China) (1954-74)
International Commission for Control and Supervision (Vietnam) (1973)
Multinational Force and Observers (Sinai) (1982-)
European Community Monitor Mission (Yugoslavia) (1991-)
*International Force East Timor (1999-)
*European Security and Defence Policy Service Medal

COMMEMORATIVE MEDALS

Canadian Centennial Medal (1967)
Queen Elizabeth II's Silver Jubilee Medal (1977)
125th Anniversary of the Confederation of Canada Medal (1992)
*Queen Elizabeth II's Golden Jubilee Medal (2002)
*Queen Elizabeth II's Diamond Jubilee Medal (2012)

LONG SERVICE AND GOOD CONDUCT MEDALS

R.C.M.P. Long Service Medal
Canadian Forces Decoration (C.D.)

EXEMPLARY SERVICE MEDALS

Police Exemplary Service Medal
Corrections Exemplary Service Medal
Fire Services Exemplary Service Medal
Canadian Coast Guard Exemplary Service Medal
Emergency Medical Services Exemplary Service Medal
*Peace Officer Exemplary Service Medal

SPECIAL MEDAL

Queen's Medal for Champion Shot

OTHER DECORATIONS AND MEDALS

Ontario Medal for Good Citizenship (O.M.C.)
Ontario Medal for Police Bravery
Ontario Medal for Firefighters Bravery
Saskatchewan Volunteer Medal (S.V.M.)
Ontario Provincial Police Long Service and Good Conduct Medal
Service Medal of the Most Venerable Order of the Hospital of St. John of Jerusalem
Commissionaire Long Service Medal
*Newfoundland and Labrador Bravery Award
*Newfoundland and Labrador Volunteer Service Medal
*British Columbia Fire Services Long Service and Bravery Medals
*Commemorative Medal for the Centennial of Saskatchewan
*Alberta Centennial Medal

2. The Bar to the Special Service Medal is worn centred on the ribbon. If there is more than one Bar, they are spaced evenly on the ribbon with the most recent uppermost.

3. Commonwealth orders, decorations and medals, the award of which is approved by the Government of Canada, are worn after Canadian orders, decorations and medals listed in Section 1, the precedence in each category being set by the date of appointment or award.

4. Foreign orders, decorations and medals, the award of which is approved by the Government of Canada, are worn after those referred to in Sections 1 and 3, the precedence in each category being set by the date of appointment or award.

5. Notwithstanding Sections 1, 3 and 4, a person who, **prior to 1 June, 1972,** was a member of a British Order or the recipient of a British decoration or medal referred to in this section, may wear the insignia of the decoration or medal together with the insignia of any Canadian order, decoration or medal that the person is entitled to wear, the proper sequence being the following:
Victoria Cross (V.C.)
George Cross (G.C.)
Cross of Valour (C.V.)
Order of Merit (O.M.)
Order of the Companions of Honour (C.H.)
Companion of the Order of Canada (C.C.)
Officer of the Order of Canada (O.C.)
Member of the Order of Canada (C.M.)
Commander of the Order of Military Merit (C.M.M.)
*Commander of the Order of Merit of the Police Forces (C.O.M.)
Companion of the Order of the Bath (C.B.)
Companion of the Order of St. Michael and St. George (C.M.G.)
Commander of the Royal Victorian Order (C.V.O.)
Commander of the Order of the British Empire (C.B.E.)
Distinguished Service Order (D.S.O.)
Officer of the Order of Military Merit (O.M.M.)
*Officer of the Order of Merit of the Police Force (O.O.M.)
Lieutenant of the Royal Victorian Order (L.V.O.)
Officer of the Order of the British Empire (O.B.E.)
Imperial Service Order (I.S.O.)
Member of the Order of Military Merit (M.M.M.)
*Member of the Order of the Police Forces (M.O.M.)
Member of the Royal Victorian Order (M.V.O.)
Member of the Order of the British Empire (M.B.E.)
Member of the Royal Red Cross (R.R.C.)
Distinguished Service Cross (D.S.C.)
Military Cross (M.C.)
Distinguished Flying Cross (D.F.C.)
Air Force Cross (A.F.C.)
Star of Military Valour (S.M.V.)
Star of Courage (S.C.)
Meritorious Service Cross (M.S.C.)
Medal of Military Valour (M.M.V.)
Medal of Bravery (M.B.)
Meritorious Service Medal (M.S.M.)
Associate of the Royal Red Cross (A.R.R.C.)
The Most Venerable Order of St. John of Jerusalem (all grades) (post-nominal letters only for internal use by the Order of St. John)
Provincial Orders (order of precedence as set out in Section 1)
Distinguished Conduct Medal (D.C.M.)
Conspicuous Gallantry Medal (C.G.M.)
George Medal (G.M.)
Distinguished Service Medal (D.S.M.)
Military Medal (M.M.)
Distinguished Flying Medal (D.F.M.)
Air Force Medal (A.F.M.)
Queen's Gallantry Medal (Q.G.M.)
Royal Victorian Medal (R.V.M.)
British Empire Medal (B.E.M.)

WAR AND OPERATIONAL SERVICE MEDALS

Africa General Service Medal (1902-1956)
India General Service Medal (1908-1935)
Naval General Service Medal (1915-1962)
India General Service Medal (1936-39)
General Service Medal - Army and Air Force (1918- 1962)
General Service Medal (1962-)
1914 Star
1914-15 Star
British War Medal (1914-18)
Mercantile Marine War Medal (1914-18)
Victory Medal (1914-18)
Territorial Force War Medal (1914-19)
1939-45 Star
Atlantic Star
Air Crew Europe Star
Africa Star
Pacific Star
Burma Star
Italy Star
France and Germany Star
Defence Medal
Canadian Volunteer Service Medal
Newfoundland Second World War Volunteer Service Medal (see Section 6)
War Medal (1939-45)
Korea Medal
Canadian Volunteer Service Medal for Korea
Gulf and Kuwait Medal Somalia Medal
*South-West Asia Service Medal
*General Campaign Medal
*General Service Medal

SPECIAL SERVICE MEDALS

(The order of precedence is as set out for Special Service Medals in Section 1.)

UNITED NATIONS MEDALS

(The order of precedence is as set out for United Nations Medals in Section 1.)

INTERNATIONAL COMMISSION AND ORGANIZATION MEDALS

(The order of precedence is as set out for International Commission and Organization Medals in Section 1.)

POLAR MEDALS

(The order of precedence is by order of date awarded.)

COMMEMORATIVE MEDALS

King George V's Silver Jubilee Medal (1935)
King George VI's Coronation Medal (1937)
Queen Elizabeth II's Coronation Medal (1953)
Canadian Centennial Medal (1967)
Queen Elizabeth II's Silver Jubilee Medal (1977)
125th Anniversary of the Confederation of Canada Medal (1992)
*Queen Elizabeth II's Golden Jubilee Medal (2002)
*Queen Elizabeth II's Diamond Jubilee Medal (2012)

LONG SERVICE AND GOOD CONDUCT MEDALS

Army Long Service and Good Conduct Medal
Naval Long Service and Good Conduct Medal
Air Force Long Service and Good Conduct Medal
RCMP Long Service Medal
Canadian Forces Decoration (C.D.)
Volunteer Officer's Decoration (V.D.)
Volunteer Long Service Medal
Colonial Auxiliary Forces Officer's Decoration (V.D.)
Colonial Auxiliary Forces Long Service Medal
Efficiency Decoration (E.D.)
Efficiency Medal
Naval Volunteer Reserve Decoration (V.R.D.)
Naval Volunteer Reserve Long Service and Good Conduct Medal
Air Efficiency Award Canadian Forces Decoration (C.D.)

EXEMPLARY SERVICE MEDALS

(The order of precedence is as set out for Exemplary Service Medals in Section 1.)

SPECIAL MEDAL

Queen's Medal for Champion Shot

OTHER DECORATIONS AND MEDALS

(The order of precedence is as set out for Other Decorations and Medals in Section 1.)

6. The Newfoundland Volunteer War Service Medal has the same precedence as the Canadian Volunteer Service Medal.

7. The insignia of orders, decorations and medals not listed above, as well as foreign awards, the award of which has not been approved by the Government of Canada, shall not be mounted or worn in conjunction with orders, decorations and medals listed above.

8. The insignia of orders, decorations and medals shall not be worn by anyone other than the recipient of the orders, decorations or medals.

NOTE: Policy regarding the wearing on non-authorized awards Only the insignia of orders, decorations and medals officially awarded under the authority of the Crown or that the wearing of which has been authorized by the Crown may be worn. Only the actual recipient of an honour can wear its insignia; no family member or any person other than the original recipient may wear the insignia of an order, decoration or medal. Insignia that are purchased or otherwise acquired may be used for display purpose only and cannot be worn on the person in any form or manner.

Abbreviations Indicating Honours and Decorations

A.F.C. - Air Force Cross. Ribbon, wide diagonal stripes of white and red.
A.F.M. - Air Force Medal. Ribbon, narrow diagonal stripes of white and red.
A.M. - Albert Medal, gold (Sea). Ribbon, nine alternate narrow stripes of blue and white.
Albert Medal, gold (Land). Ribbon, nine alternate narrow stripes of red and white.
Albert Medal, bronze (Sea). Ribbon, blue ground with two wide stripes of white.
Albert Medal, bronze (Land). Ribbon, red ground with two wide stripes of white.
B.E.M. - British Empire Medal.
Bt. - Baronet
C.B. - Companion of the Most Honourable Order of the Bath.
C.B.E. - Commander of the Order of the British Empire.
C.C. - Companion of the Order of Canada.
C.D. - Canadian Forces Decoration.
C.G.M. - Conspicuous Gallantry Medal; Navy and Air Force. It carries a cash grant. The Navy Medal ribbon is white with dark blue edges; the Air Force ribbon is light blue with dark blue edges.
C.H. - Member of the Order of the Companions of Honour.
C.I.E. - Companion of the Most Eminent Order of the Indian Empire.
C.M. - Member of the Order of Canada.
C.M.G. - Companion of the Most Distinguished Order of St. Michael and St. George.
C.M.M. - Commander of the Order of Military Merit.
C.P.S.M. - Canadian Peacekeeping Service Medal.
C.S.I. - Companion of the Most Exalted Order of the Star of India.
C.V. - Cross of Valour.
C.V.O. - Commander of the Royal Victorian Order.
D.C.M. - Distinguished Conduct Medal. Ribbon, red ground, dark blue stripe in centre.
D.F.C. - Distinguished Flying Cross. Ribbon, wide diagonal stripes of violet and white.
D.F.M. - Distinguished Flying Medal. Ribbon, narrow diagonal stripes of white and violet.
D.S.C. - Distinguished Service Cross. Ribbon, three broad bands, dark blue, white, dark blue.
D.S.M. - Distinguished Service Medal.
D.S.O. - Companion of the Distinguished Service Order. Instituted 1886. Ribbon, dark red with dark blue stripe at each end.
E.D. - Canadian Efficiency Decoration for Officers of Military Auxiliary Forces.
E.M. - Edward Medal. Posthumous award.
E.M. - Efficiency Medal.
G.B.E. - Knight Grand Cross or Dame Grand Cross of the Most Excellent Order of the British Empire.
G.C. - George Cross.
G.C.B. - Knight Grand Cross of the Most Honourable Order of the Bath.
G.C.I.E. - Knight Grand Commander of the Most Eminent Order of the Indian Empire.
G.C.M.G. - Knight Grand Cross of the Most Distinguished Order of St. Michael and St. George.
G.C.S.I. - Knight Grand Commander of the Most Exalted Order of the Star of India.
G.C.V.O. - Knight Grand Cross of the Royal Victorian Order.
G.M. - George Medal.
I.S.M. - Imperial Service Medal.
I.S.O. - Companion of the Imperial Service Order. Instituted 1902.
K.B.E. - Knight Commander of the Most Excellent Order of the British Empire.
K.C.B. - Knight Commander of the Most Honourable Order of the Bath.
K.C.I.E. - Knight Commander of the Most Eminent Order of the Indian Empire.
K.C.M.G. - Knight Commander of the Most Distinguished Order of St. Michael and St. George.
K.C.S.I. - Knight Commander of the Most Exalted Order of the Star of India.
K.C.V.O. - Knight Commander of the Royal Victorian Order.
K.G. - Knight of the Most Noble Order of the Garter.
K.P. - Knight of the Most Illustrious Order of St. Patrick.
Kt. - Knight Bachelor.
K.T. - Knight of the Most Ancient and Most Noble Order of the Thistle.
L.V.O. - Lieutenant of the Royal Victorian Order.
M.B. - Medal of Bravery.
M.B.E. - Member of the Order of the British Empire.
M.C. - Military Cross. Instituted 1915. Ribbon, white with broad band of blue in centre.
M. du C. - Canada Medal.
M.M. - Military Medal.
M.M.M. - Member of the Order of Military Merit.
M.V.O. - Member of the Royal Victorian Order.
M.S.C. - Meritorous Service Cross.
M.S.M. - Meritorious Service Medal.
O.B.E. - Officer of the Order of the British Empire.
O.C. - Officer of the Order of Canada.
O.M. - Member of the Order of Merit.
O.M.M. - Officer of the Order of Military Merit.
P.C. - Privy Counsellor.
R.R.C. - Royal Red Cross. Instituted 1883. Ribbon, dark blue with narrow band of dark red at each end.
R.V.M. - Royal Victorian Medal.
S.C. - Star of Courage.
S.S.M. - Special Service Medal
U.E. - Unity of Empire. Descendants of United Empire Loyalists.
V.C. - Victoria Cross.
V.D. - Auxiliary Forces (Volunteer) Officers' Decoration.
V.R.D. - Naval Volunteer Reserve Decoration.

Government

Table of Precedence for Canada

1. The Governor General of Canada or the Administrator of the Government of Canada. (Notes 1, 2 & 2.1).
2. The Prime Minister of Canada. (Note 3).
3. The Chief Justice of Canada. (Note 4).
4. The Speaker of the Senate.
5. The Speaker of the House of Commons.
6. Ambassadors, High Commissioners, Ministers Plenipotentiary. (Note 5).
7. Members of the Canadian Ministry:
   a. Members of the Cabinet; and
   b. Secretaries of the State; with relative precedence within sub-categories (a) and (b) governed by the date of their appointment to the Queen's Privy Council for Canada.
8. The Leader of the Opposition. (Subject to Note 3).
9. The Lieutenant Governor of Ontario;
   The Lieutenant Governor of Québec;
   The Lieutenant Governor of Nova Scotia;
   The Lieutenant Governor of New Brunswick;
   The Lieutenant Governor of Manitoba;
   The Lieutenant Governor of British Columbia;
   The Lieutenant Governor of Prince Edward Island;
   The Lieutenant Governor of Saskatchewan;
   The Lieutenant Governor of Alberta;
   The Lieutenant Governor of Newfoundland
   (Note 6).
10. Members of the Queen's Privy Council for Canada, not of the Canadian Ministry, in accordance with the date of their appointment to the Privy Council.
11. Premiers of the Provinces of Canada in the same order as Lieutenant Governors. (Note 6).
12. The Commissioner of the Northwest Territories; The Commissioner of the Yukon Territory; The Commissioner of Nunavut
13. Government Leader of the Northwest Territories; The Government Leader of the Yukon Territory; The Government Leader of Nunavut
14. Representatives of faith communities. (Note 7).
15. Puisne Judges of the Supreme Court of Canada.
16. The Chief Justice and the Associate Chief Justice of the Federal Court of Canada.
17. (a) Chief Justices of the highest court of each Province and Territory; and
    (b) Chief Justices and Associate Chief Justices of the other superior courts of the Provinces and Territories; with precedence within sub-categories (a) and (b) governed by the date of appointment as Chief Justice.
18. (a) Judges of the Federal Court of Canada.
    (b) Puisne Judges of the superior courts of the Provinces and Territories.
    (c) the Chief Judge of the Tax Court of Canada;
    (d) the Associate Chief Judge of the Tax Court of Canada; and
    (e) Judges of the Tax Court of Canada; with precedence within each sub-category governed by date of appointment.
19. Senators of Canada.
20. Members of the House of Commons.
21. Consuls General of countries without diplomatic representation.
22. The Chief of the Defence Staff and the Commissioner of the Royal Canadian Mounted Police.
    (Note 8).
23. Speakers of Legislative Assemblies, within their Provinces and Territory.
24. Members of the Executive Councils, within their Provinces and Territory.
25. Judges of Provincial and Territorial Courts, within their Province and Territory.
26. Members of Legislative Assemblies, within their Provinces and Territory.

NOTES

1. The presence of the Sovereign in Canada does not impair or supersede the authority of the Governor General to perform the functions delegated to him under the Letters Patent constituting the office of the Governor General. The Governor General, under all circumstances, should be accorded precedence immediately after the Sovereign.
2. Precedence to be given immediately after the Chief Justice of Canada to former Governors General, with relative precedence among them governed by the date of their leaving office.

2.1 Precedence to be given immediately after the former Governors General to surviving spouses of deceased former Governors General (applicable only where the spouse was married to the Governor General during the latter's term of office), with relative precedence among them governed by the dates on which the deceased former Governor General left office.

3. Precedence to be given immediately after the surviving spouses of deceased former Governors General referred to in Note 2.1 to former Prime Ministers, with relative precedence among them governed by the dates of their first assumption of office.
4. Precedence to be given immediately after former Prime Ministers to former Chief Justices of Canada, with relative precedence among them governed by the dates of their appointment as Chief Justice of Canada.
5. Precedence among Ambassadors and High Commissioners, who rank equally, to be determined by the date of the presentation of their credentials. Precedence to be given to Chargés d'Affaires immediately after Ministers Plenipotentiary.
6. This provision does not apply to such ceremonies and occasions which are of a provincial nature.
7. The religious dignitaries will be senior Canadian representatives of faith communities having a significant presence in a relevant jurisdiction. The relevant precedence of the representatives of faith communities is to be governed by the date of their assumption in their present office, their representatives being given the same relative precedence.
8. This precedence to be given to the Chief of the Defence Staff and the Commissioner of the R.C.M.P. on occasions when they have official functions to perform, otherwise they are to have equal precedence with Deputy Ministers, with their relative position to be determined according to the respective dates of their appointments to office. The relative precedence of Deputy Ministers and other high officials of the public service of Canada is to be determined from time to time by the Minister of Canadian Heritage in consultation with the Prime Minister.

Table of Titles to Be Used in Canada

1. The Governor General of Canada to be styled "Right Honourable" for life and to be styled "His Excellency" and his wife "Her Excellency", or "Her Excellency" and her husband "His Excellency", as the case may be, while in office.
2. The Lieutenant Governor of a Province to be styled "Honourable" for life and to be styled "His Honour" and his wife "Her Honour", or "Her Honour" and her husband "His Honour", as the case may be, while in office.
3. The Prime Minister of Canada to be styled "Right Honourable" for life.
4. The Chief Justice of Canada to be styled "Right Honourable" for life.
5. Privy Councillors of Canada to be styled "Honourable" for life.
6. Senators of Canada to be styled "Honourable" for life.
7. The Speaker of the House of Commons to be styled "Honourable" while in office.
8. The Commissioner of a Territory to be styled "Honourable" while in office.
9. Puisne Judges of the Supreme Court of Canada and Judges of the Federal Courts and the Tax Court of Canada as well as the Judges of the undermentioned Courts in the Provinces and Territories:
   Ontario - Court of Appeal and the Ontario Court of Justice (General Division)
   Québec - The Court of Appeal and the Superior Court of Québec
   Nova Scotia - The Court of Appeal and the Supreme Court of Nova Scotia
   New Brunswick - The Court of Appeal and the Court of Queen's Bench of New Brunswick
   Manitoba - The Court of Appeal and the Court of Queen's Bench of Manitoba
   British Columbia - The Court of Appeal and the Supreme Court of British Columbia
   Prince Edward Island - The Supreme Court of Prince Edward Island

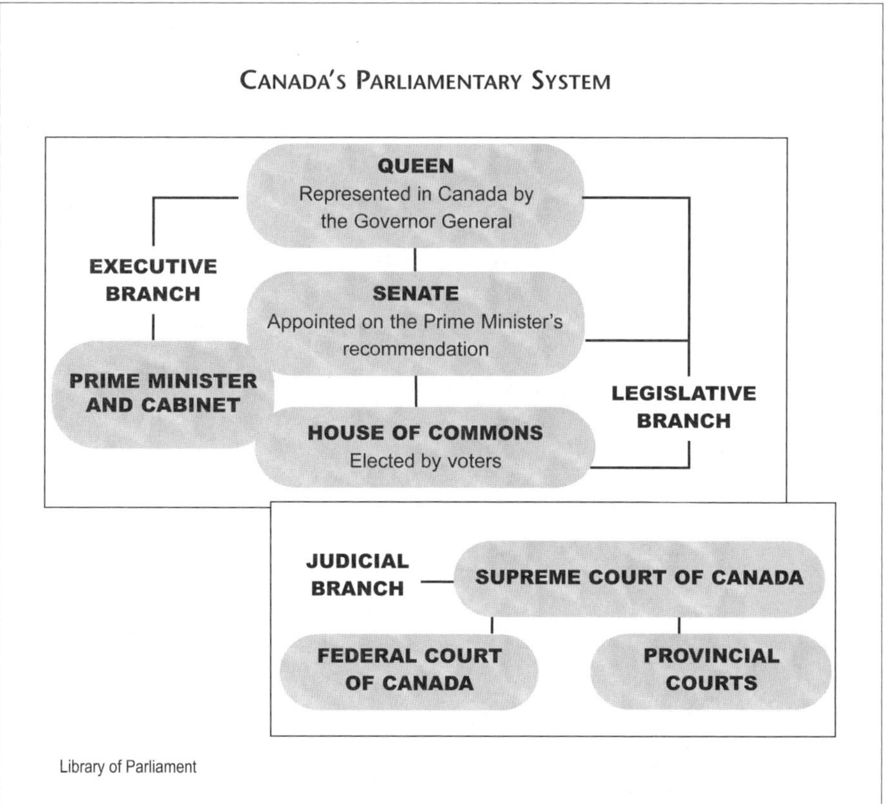

Parliament as a legislative body functions as an instrument of government within a broader structure that includes the Executive Branch and the Judicial Branch. In the Westminster-based model of parliamentary government, the Executive, comprised of the Prime Minister and the Cabinet, is incorporated into Parliament, while retaining a separate sphere of authority and autonomy. The Judiciary, consisting of the Supreme Court and all the other courts of the land, is the third branch of government that is also independent of either Parliament or the Executive.

Saskatchewan - The Court of Appeal and the Court of Queen's Bench of Saskatchewan
Alberta - The Court of Appeal and the Court of Queen's Bench of Alberta
Newfoundland - The Supreme Court of Newfoundland
Northwest Territories - The Supreme Court of Northwest Territories
Yukon Territory - The Supreme Court of Yukon
Nunavut Territory - The Nunavut Court of Justice
to be styled "The Honourable" while in office.

10. Presidents and Speakers of the Legislative Assemblies of the Provinces and Territories to be styled "Honourable" while in office.
11. Members of the Executive Councils of the Provinces and Territories to be styled "Honourable" while in office.
12. Judges of Provincial and Territorial Courts (appointed by the Provincial and Territorial Governments) to be styled "Honourable" while in office.
13. The following are eligible to be granted permission by the Governor General, in the name of Her Majesty The Queen, to retain the title of "Honourable" after they have ceased to hold office: (a) Speakers of the House of Commons; (b) Commissioners of Territories; (c) Judges designated in item 9.
14. The title "Right Honourable" is granted for life to the following eminent Canadians: The Right Honourable Martial Asselin The Right Honourable Ellen L. Fairclough The Right Honourable Francis Alvin George Hamilton The Right Honourable Donald F. Mazankowski The Right Honourable Robert Lorne Stanfield The Right Honourable Herb Eser Grey
15. Mayors of Area Municipalities to be styled "His Worship" or "Her Worship", as the case may be, while in office.
16. Visiting Heads of State to be styled:
    • "His Excellency The Honourable" or "Her Excellency The Honourable", as the case may be, if the President of the United States,
    • "His Excellency" or "Her Excellency" as the case may be, for all other visiting Heads of State.

GOVERNORS GENERAL OF CANADA SINCE CONFEDERATION
(WITH DATE APPOINTED)

The Viscount Monck,
G.C.M.G.
June 1, 1867

Lord Lisgar,
G.C.M.G.
Dec. 29, 1868

The Earl of Dufferin,
K.P., G.C.B., G.C.S.I., G.C.M.G., G.C.I.E
May 22, 1872

The Marquess of Lorne,
K.T., G.C.M.G., G.C.V.O.
Oct. 5, 1878

The Marquess of Lansdowne,
K.G., G.C.S.I., G.C.M.G., G.C.I.E.
Aug. 18, 1883

Lord Stanley of Preston,
K.G., G.C.B., G.C.V.O.
May 1, 1888

The Earl of Aberdeen,
K.T., G.C.M.G., G.C.V.O.
May 22, 1893

The Earl of Minto,
K.G., G.C.S.I., G.C.M.G., G.C.I.E.
July 30, 1898

The Earl Grey,
G.C.B., G.C.M.G., G.C.V.O.
Sept. 26, 1904

H.R.H. The Duke of Connaught,
K.G., K.T., K.P., G.M.B., G.C.S.I., G.C.M.G., G.C.I.E., G.C.V.O., G.B.E., T.D.
Mar. 21, 1911

The Duke of Devonshire,
K.G., G.C.M.G., G.C.V.O., T.D.
Aug.. 19, 1916

Lord Byng of Vimy,
G.C.B., G.C.M.G., M.V.O.
Aug. 2, 1921

The Viscount Willingdon of Ratton,
G.C.S.I., G.C.M.G., G.C.I.E., G.B.E.
Aug. 5, 1926

The Earl of Bessborough,
G.C.M.G.
Feb. 9, 1931

Baron Tweedsmuir of Elsfield, G.C.M.G., G.C.V.O., C.H.
Aug. 10, 1935

Major-General The Earl of Athlone, K.G., G.C.B., G.C.M.G., G.C.V.O., D.S.O.
Apr. 3, 1940

Field Marshal The Viscount Alexander of Tunis, K.G., G.C.B., O.M., G.C.M.G., C.S.I., D.S.O., M.C., A.D.C.
Aug. 1, 1945

The Rt. Hon. Vincent Massey, P.C., C.C., C.H.
Jan. 24, 1952

Major General The Rt. Hon. Georges-P. Vanier, D.S.O., M.C., C.D.
Aug. 1, 1959

The Rt. Hon. Roland Michener, P.C., C.C., C.M.M., C.D., Q.C.
Mar. 25, 1967

The Rt. Hon. Jules Léger P.C., C.C., C.M.M., C.D.
Oct. 5, 1973

The Rt. Hon. Edward Richard Schreyer, P.C., C.C., C.M.M., C.D.
Dec. 7, 1978

The Rt. Hon. Jeanne Sauvé, P.C., C.C., C.M.M., C.D.
Dec. 23, 1983

Photo Credit: Yousuf Karsh

The Rt. Hon. Ramon John Hnatyshyn, P.C., C.C., C.M.M., C.D., Q.C.
Oct. 6, 1989

Photo Credit: Rideau Hall

The Rt. Hon. Roméo LeBlanc, P.C., C.C., C.M.M., C.D.
Nov. 22, 1994

Photo Credit: Rideau Hall

Her Excellency, the Rt. Hon.
Adrienne Clarkson,
C.C., C.M.M., C.O.M., C.D.
Oct. 7, 1999

Photo Credit: Andrew MacNaughtan
© Her Majesty The Queen in Right of Canada represented by the Office of the Secretary to the Governor General (1999)

Her Excellency, the Rt. Hon.
Michaëlle Jean,
C.C., C.M.M., C.O.M., C.D.
Sept. 27, 2005

Photo Credit: Sgt Eric Jolin, Rideau Hall
© Her Majesty The Queen in Right of Canada represented by the Office of the Secretary to the Governor General (2006)

His Excellency, the Rt. Hon.
David Johnston,
C.C., C.M.M., C.O.M., C.D.
Oct. 1, 2010

Photo Credit: Sgt Serge Gouin, Rideau Hall
© Her Majesty The Queen in Right of Canada represented by the Office of the Secretary to the Governor General (2010)

CANADIAN PRIME MINISTERS

(WITH PARTY AFFILIATION AND TIME IN OFFICE)

Rt. Hon. Sir John A. Macdonald
(Conservative)
July 1, 1867 to Nov. 5, 1873
Oct. 17, 1878 to June 6, 1891

Photo credit: William James Topley/National Archives of Canada/PA-027013

Hon. Alexander MacKenzie
(Liberal)
Nov. 7, 1873 to Oct. 16, 1878

Photo credit: William James Topley/National Archives of Canada/PA-026308

Hon. Sir John J. Abbott
(Conservative)
June 16, 1891 to Nov. 24, 1892

Photo credit: William James Topley/National Archives of Canada/PA-033933

Rt. Hon. Sir John S. D. Thompson
(Conservative)
Dec. 5, 1892 to Dec. 12, 1894

Photo Credit: National Archives of Canada/C-000698

Hon. Sir Mackenzie Bowell
(Conservative)
Dec. 21, 1894 to April 27, 1896

Photo Credit: William James Topley/National Archives of Canada/PA-027159

Rt. Hon. Sir Charles Tupper
(Conservative)
May 1, 1896 to July 8, 1896

Photo Credit: National Archives of Canada/PA-027743

Rt. Hon. Sir Wilrid Laurier
(Liberal)
July 11, 1896 to Oct. 6, 1911

Photo Credit: William James Topley/National Archives of Canada/C-001971

Rt. Hon. Sir Robert L. Borden
Oct. 10, 1911 to Oct. 12, 1917
(Conservative Administration)
Oct. 12, 1917 to July 10, 1920
(Unionist Administration)

Photo Credit: William James Topley/National Archives of Canada/PA-028128

Rt. Hon. Arthur Meighen
July 10, 1920 to Dec. 29, 1921
(Unionist "National Liberal and Conservative Party")
June 29, 1926 to Sept. 25, 1926
(Conservative)

Photo Credit: William James Topley/National Archives of Canada/PA-026987

Rt. Hon. William Lyon Mackenzie King
(Liberal)
Dec. 29, 1921 to June 28, 1926
Sept. 25, 1926 to Aug. 6, 1930
Oct. 23, 1935 to Nov. 15, 1948

Photo Credit: National Archives of Canada/C-027645

Rt. Hon. Richard Bedford Bennett
(Conservative)
(Became Viscount Bennett, 1941)
Aug. 7, 1930 to Oct. 23, 1935

Photo Credit: National Archives of Canada/C-000687

Rt. Hon. Louis Stephen St. Laurent
(Liberal)
Nov. 15, 1948 to June 21, 1957
Photo Credit: National Archives of Canada/C-010461

Rt. Hon. John G. Diefenbaker
(Progressive Conservative)
June 21, 1957 to April 22, 1963
Photo Credit: Paul Horsdal/National Archives of Canada/PA-130070

Rt. Hon. Lester Bowles Pearson
(Liberal)
April 22, 1963 to April 20, 1968
Photo Credit: Ashley-Crippen Studio/National Archives of Canada/PA-126393

Rt. Hon. Pierre Elliott Trudeau
(Liberal)
April 20, 1968 to June 4, 1979
Mar. 3, 1980 to June 30, 1984
Photo Credit: National Archives of Canada/C-046600

Rt. Hon. Charles Joseph Clark
(Progressive Conservative)
June 4, 1979 to Mar. 3, 1980
Photo Credit: House of Commons, Ottawa

Rt. Hon. John Napier Turner
(Liberal)
June 30, 1984 to Sept. 17, 1984
Photo Credit: Jean-Marc Carisse

Rt. Hon. Martin Brian Mulroney
(Progressive Conservative)
Sept 17, 1984 to June 25, 1993
Photo Credit: Robert Cooper/National Archives of Canada/PA-152416

Rt. Hon. Kim Campbell
(Progressive Conservative)
June 25, 1993 to Nov. 4, 1993
Photo Credit: Courtesy of the Office of Rt. Hon. Kim Campbell

Rt. Hon. Jean Chrétien
(Liberal)
Nov. 4, 1993 to Dec. 11, 2003
Photo Credit: Jean-Marc Carisse

Rt. Hon. Paul Edgar Philippe Martin
(Liberal)
Dec. 12, 2003 to Feb. 6, 2006
Photo Credit: Dave Chan

Rt. Hon. Stephen Joseph Harper
(Conservative)
Feb. 6, 2006 to —
Photo Credit: Courtesy of The Office of the Prime Minister

PORTRAITS OF PRIME MINISTERS IN THE HOUSE OF COMMONS

Reproduced with the permission of the Curator, House of Commons

Sir John Alexander Macdonald
Credit: Henry Sandham
National Archives of Canada C-025743

Hon. Alexander Mackenzie
Credit: John Wycliffe Lowes Forster
National Archives of Canada C-116811

Hon. Sir John J. Abbott
Credit: Muli Tang
House of Commons Collection

Sir John Thompson
Credit: John Wycliffe Lowes Forster
National Archives of Canada C-116812

Hon. Sir Mackenzie Bowell
Credit: Joanne Tod
House of Commons Collection

Sir Charles Tupper
Credit: Victor A. Long
National Archives of Canada C-116813

Sir Wilfrid Laurier
Credit: John Wentworth Russell
National Archives of Canada C-116814

Sir Robert Borden
Credit: Kenneth Keith Forbes
National Archives of Canada C-116815

Rt. Hon. Arthur Meighen
Credit: George Ernest Fosbery
National Archives of Canada C-116816

Rt. Hon. William Lyon Mackenzie King
Credit: Frank O. Salisbury
National Archives of Canada C-116818

Rt. Hon. Richard Bedford Bennett
Credit: Kenneth Keith Forbes
National Archives of Canada C-116817

Rt. Hon. Louis St. Laurent
Credit: Audrey Watts McNaughton
National Archives of Canada C-116819

Rt. Hon. John G. Diefenbaker
Credit: Arthur Edward Cleeve Horne
National Archives of Canada C-116820

Rt. Hon. Lester Bowles Pearson
Credit: Hugh Seaforth MacKenzie
National Archives of Canada C-116821

Rt. Hon. Pierre Elliott Trudeau
Credit: Myfanwy Pavelic
House of Commons Collection

Rt. Hon. Charles Joseph Clark
Credit: Patrick Douglass Cox
House of Commons Collection

Rt. Hon. John Napier Turner
Credit: Brenda Bury
House of Commons Collection

Rt. Hon. Brian Mulroney
Credit: Igor Babailov
House of Commons Collection

Rt. Hon. Kim Campbell
Credit: David Goatley
House of Commons Collection

Rt. Hon. Jean Chrétien
Credit: Christian Nicholson
House of Commons Collection

Regulations & Abbreviations

Forms of Address

The following are reprinted with the permission of Canadian Heritage.

The Royal Family/La Famille Royale

THE QUEEN:

Her Majesty The Queen, Buckingham Palace, London SW1A 1AA United Kingdom
Salutation - Your Majesty:
Final Salutation - I remain Your Majesty's faithful and devoted servant,
In Conversation - "Your Majesty" first then "Ma'am"
Note: The Queen's full title is "Her Majesty Queen Elizabeth II, Queen of Canada" Normally one refers to "Her Majesty The Queen" or "The Queen"

LA REINE:

Sa Majesté la Reine, Palais de Buckingham, Londres SW1A 1AA Royaume-Uni
Appel - Majesté,
Salutation - Je prie Votre Majesté d'agréer l'expression de ma très haute considération.
Conversation - «Majesté»
Remarques: Le titre complet de la Reine est le suivant: «Sa Majesté la reine Ellizabeth II, Reine du Canada» On parle normalement de «Sa Majesté» ou de «la Reine»

THE PRINCE OF WALES:

His Royal Highness The Prince of Wales, St. James's Palace, London SW1A 1BS United Kingdom
Salutation - Your Royal Highness:
Final Salutation - Yours very truly,
In Conversation - "Your Royal Highness" first then "Sir"
Note: Should never be referred to as: "Charles, Prince of Wales" or Prince Charles.

LE PRINCE DE GALLES:

Son Altesse Royale le prince de Galles, Palais de St. James, Londres SW1A 1BS Royaume-Uni
Appel - Altesse Royale,
Saluation - Je prie Votre Altesse Royal d'agréer l'expression de ma très haute considération.
Conversation - «Altesse Royale»
Remarques: Il ne faut jamais dire: «Charles, prince de Galles» ou «le prince Charles»

Government/Gouvernement

GOVERNOR GENERAL OF CANADA:

His/Her Excellency the Right Honourable (full name), C.C., C.M.M., C.D., Governor General of Canada, Rideau Hall, 1 Sussex Dr., Ottawa ON K1A 0A1
Salutation - Excellency:
Final Salutation - Yours truly,
In Conversation - "Your Excellency" or "Excellency" first then "Sir" or "Madam"
Note: The Governor General may have other postnominal letters, such as P.C., Q.C.

GOVERNEUR GÉNÉRAL DU CANADA:

(homme) Son Excellence le très honorable (prénom et nom), C.C., C.M.M., C.O.M., C.D., Gouverneur général du Canada, Rideau Hall, 1, promenade Sussex, Ottawa ON K1A 0A1
(femme) Son Excellence la très honorable (prénom et nom), C.C., C.M.M., C.O.M., C.D., Gouverneure générale du Canada, Rideau Hall, 1, promenade Sussex, Ottawa ON K1A 0A1
Appel - (homme) Monsieur le Gouverneur général,
(femme) Madame la Gouverneure générale,
Saluation - (homme) Je vous prie d'agréer, Monsieur le Gouverneur général, l'expression de ma très haute considération.
(femme) Je vous prie d'agréer, Madame la Gouverneure générale, l'hommage de mon profond respect.
Remarques: D'autres initiales peuvent suivre le nom du gouverneur général, comme C.P. et C.R.

LIEUTENANT GOVERNOR OF A PROVINCE:

His/Her Honour the Honourable (full name) Lieutenant Governor of (Province), Address
Salutation - Your Honour or My dear Lieutenant Governor:
Final Salutation - Yours sincerely,
In Conversation - "Your Honour" first then "Sir" or "Madam" or "Mr./Mrs./Ms./Miss (name)"
Note: The Lieutenant Governor of a province has the title "Honourable" for life; the courtesy title "His/ Her Honour" is used only while in office.

LIEUTENANT-GOUVERNEUR

(homme) Son Honneur l'honorable (prénom et nom) Lieutenant-gouverneur de (province), Adresse
(femme) Son Honneur l'honorable (prénom et nom) Lieutenante-gouverneure de (province), Adresse
Appel - (homme) Monsieur le Lieutenant-Gouverneur,
(femme) Madame la Lieutenante-Gouverneure,
Salutation - (homme) Je vous prie d'agréer, Monsieur le Lieutenant-Gouverneur, l'expression de ma haute considération.
(femme) Je vous prie d'agréer, Madame la Lieutenante-Gouverneure, l'hommage de mes respectueux hommages.
Conversation - On commence par «Votre Honneur». On poursuit avec «Monsieur» ou «Madame»
Remarques: Le titre «honorable» est accordé à vie au lieutenant-gouverneur; le titre de courtoisie «Son Honneur» n'est utilisé que pendant la durée du mandat.

THE PRIME MINISTER OF CANADA:

The Right Honourable (full name), P.C., M.P., Prime Minister of Canada, Langevin Block, Ottawa, ON K1A 0A2
Salutation - Dear Prime Minister: or Prime Minister:
Final Salutation - Yours sincerely,
In Conversation - "Prime Minister" first then "Mr./ Mrs./Ms./Miss (name)"
Note: The term "Mr. Prime Minister" should not be used. The Prime Minister may have other post-nominal letters, such as Q.C.

PREMIER MINISTRE DU CANADA

(homme) Le très honorable (prénom et nom), C.P., député Premier Ministre du Canada, Édifice Langevin, Ottawa ON K1A 0A2
(femme) La très honorable (prénom et nom), C.P., députée Première Ministre du Canada, Édifice Langevin, Ottawa ON K1A 0A2
Appel - (homme) Monsieur le Premier Ministre,
(femme) Madame la Première Ministre,
Salutation -
(homme) Je vous prie d'agréer, Monsieur le Premier Ministre, l'expression de ma très haute considération.
(femme) Je vous prie d'agréer, Madame la Première Ministre, l'hommage de mon profond respect. Conversation -
(homme) On commence par «Monsieur le Premier Ministre». On poursuit avec «Monsieur»
(femme) On commence par «Madame la Première Ministre». On pousuit avec «Madame»
Remarques: D'autres initiales peuvent suivre le nom, comme C.R.

THE PREMIER OF A PROVINCE OF CANADA:

The Honourable (full name), M.L.A. or (M.P.P., M.N.A., or M.H.A.), Premier of (Province), Address
Salutation - Dear Premier:
Final Salutation - Yours sincerely,
In Conversation - "Premier" first then "Mr./Mrs./Ms./ Miss (name)"
Note: The title "Honourable" is used only while in office, unless he/she is a member of the Privy Council. The term "Mr./Madam Premier" should not be used.

LE PREMIER MINISTRE D'UNE PROVINCE

(homme) L'honorable (prénom et nom) M.A.L ou (M.A.N., M.P.P. ou M.C.A) Premier Ministre de (province), Adresse
(femme) L'honorable (prénom et nom) M.A.L ou (M.A.N., M.P.P. ou M.C.A) Première Ministre de (province), Adresse
Appel - (homme) Monsieur le Premier Ministre,
(femme) Madame la Première Ministre,
Salutation - (homme) Je vous prie d'agréer, Monsieur le Premier Ministre, l'expression de ma haute considération.
(femme) Je vous prie d'agréer, Madame la Première Ministre, l'hommage de mon profond respect.
Conversation - On commence par «Monsieur le Premier Ministre». On poursuit avec «Monsieur»
(femme) On commence par «Madame la Première Ministre». On poursuit avec «Madame»
Remarques: Les premiers ministres ne conservent pas le titre «honorable» après la fin de leur mandat, à moins qu'ils ne soient membres du Conseil privé.

COMMISSIONER OF A TERRITORY:

The Honourable (full name), Commissioner of (Territory), Address
Salutation - Commissioner (name):
Final Salutation - Yours sincerely,
In Conversation - "Sir" or "Madam" or "Mr./Mrs./ Ms./Miss (name)"

COMMISSAIRE DU TERRITOIRE

(homme/femme) L'honorable (prénom et nom) Commissaire du (territoire), Adresse
Appel - (homme) Monsieur le Commissaire,
(femme) Madame la Commissaire,
Salutation - Je vous prie d'agréer, Monsieur le Commissaire, l'expression de ma haute considération.
(femme) Je vous prie d'agréer, Madame la Commissaire, l'expression de mes respectueux hommages. Conversation -
(homme) «Monsieur»
(femme) «Madame»
Remarques: Le titre «honorable» n'est utilisé que pendant la durée de ses fonctions.

GOVERNMENT LEADER OF A TERRITORY:

The Honourable (full name), M.L.A., Government Leader of (Territory), Address
Salutation - Dear Mr./Mrs./Ms./Miss (name):
Final Salutation - Yours sincerely,
In Conversation - "Mr./Mrs./Ms./Miss (name)"
Note: The title "Honourable" is used only while in office, unless he/she is a member of the Privy Council. The term "Mr./Madam Leader" should not be used.

LE LEADER DU GOUVERNEMENT D'UN TERRITOIRE

(homme/femme) L'honorable (prénom et nom), M.A.L. Leader du gouvernement du (territoire), Adresse
Appel - (homme) Monsieur le leader du gouvernement,
(femme) Madame la leader du gouvernement,
Salutation - (homme) Je vous prie d'agréer, Monsieur le Leader du gouvernement, l'expression de ma haute consideration.
(femme) Je vous prie d'agréer, Madame la Leader du gouvernement, l'hommage de mon profond respect.
Conversation - On commence par «Monsieur le Leader du gouvernement». On poursuit avec «Monsieur»
(femme) On commence par «Madame la Leader du gouvernement». On poursuit avec «Madame»
Remarques: Les leaders ne conservent pas le titre «honorable» après la fin de leur mandat, à moins qu'ils ne soient membres du Conseil privé.

CABINET MINISTERS:

Member of the House of Commons: The Honourable (full name), P.C., M.P., Minister of ________, House of Commons, Ottawa ON K1A 0A6
Salutation - Dear Minister: or Dear Colleague: (between colleagues)
Final Salutation - Yours sincerely,
In Conversation - "Minister" first then "Mr./Mrs./ Ms./Miss (name)"
For a Senator: Senator the Honourable (full name), P.C., Minister of ________ , The Senate, Ottawa, ON K1A 0A4
Salutation - Dear Minister: or Dear Colleague: (between colleagues)
Final Salutation - Yours sincerely,
In Conversation - "Minister" first then "Mr./Mrs./ Ms./Miss (name)"

CONSEIL DES MINISTRES DU CANADA

(homme) L'honorable (prénom et nom), C.P. député Ministre de ________, Chambre de communes, Ottawa ON K1A 0A6
(femme) L'honorable (prénom et nom), C.P. députée Ministre de ________, Chambre de communes, Ottawa ON K1A 0A6
Appel - (homme) Monsieur le Ministre, ou Cher collègue, (Entre collègues)
(femme) Madame la Ministre, ou Chère collègue, (Entre collègues)
Salutation -
(homme) Je vous prie d'agréer, Monsieur le Ministre, l'expression de ma considération respectueuse.
(femme) Je vous prie d'agréer, Madame la Ministre, l'hommage de mon profond respect. Conversation -
(homme) On commence par «Monsieur le Ministre». On poursuit avec «Monsieur»
(femme) On commence par «Madame la Ministre». On poursuit avec «Madame»
Remarques: Les ministres fédéraux sont membres du Conseil privé de la Reine pour le Canada et conservent le titre «honorable» à vie. On place les initiales C.P. après leur nom.

SECRETARIES OF STATE:

The Honourable (full name), P.C., M.P., Secretary of State (Portfolio), House of Commons, Ottawa, ON K1A 0A6
Salutation - Dear Secretary of State: or Dear Colleague: (between colleagues)
Final Salutation - Yours sincerely,
In Conversation - "Secretary of State" first then "Mr./ Mrs./Ms./Miss (name)"
Note: Members of the Ministry are members of the Queen's Privy Council for Canada and retain the title "Honourable" for life, using the initials P.C. after their name. The term "Mr. Minister" or "Madame Minister" should not be used. The term "Mr. Secretary of State" or "Madame Secretary of State" should not be used.

SECRÉTAIRES D'ÉTAT

(homme) L'honorable (prénom et nom), C.P. député Secrétaire d'État (Portefeuille), Chambre des communes, Ottawa ON K1A 0A6

(femme) L'honorable (prénom et nom), C.P. députée Secrétaire d'État (Portefeuille), Chambre des communes, Ottawa ON K1A 0A6

Appel - (homme) Monsieur le Secrétaire d'État, ou Cher collègue, (Entre collègues)

(femme) Madame la Secrétaire d'État, ou Chère collègue, (Entre collègues)

Salutation - (homme) Je vous prie d'agréer, Monsieur le Secrétaire d'État, l'expression de ma considération respectueuse. Ou Je vous prie, cher collègue, de recevoir mes cordiales salutations. (Entre collègues)

(femme) Je vous prie d'agréer, Madame la Secrétaire d'État, l'hommage de mon profond respect. Ou Je vous prie, chère collègue, de recevoir mes cordiales salutations. (Entre collègues) Conversation -

(homme) On commence par ‹‹Monsieur le Secrétaire d'État››. On poursuit avec ‹‹Monsieur››

(femme) On commence par ‹‹Madame la Secrétaire d'État››. On poursuit avec ‹‹Madame››

Remarques: Les secrétaires d'État sont membres du Conseil privé de la Reine pour le Canada et conservent le titre ‹‹honorable›› à vie. On place les initiales C.P. aprés leur nom.

SPEAKER OF THE SENATE:

The Honourable (full name), Senator, Speaker of State, The Senate, Ottawa, ON K1A 0A4

Salutation - Dear Mr./Madam Speaker:

Final Salutation - Yours sincerely,

In Conversation - "Mr. Speaker" or "Madam Speaker"

Note: A senator who is a member of the Canadian Privy Council is addressed as "Senator the Honourable (name), P.C. " After a Senator retires, he/she retains the title "Honourable" but the salutation is "Dear Sir/ Madam" or "Dear Mr./Mrs./Ms./Miss (name)"

PRÉSIDENT OU PRÉSIDENTE DU SÉNAT

(homme) L'honorable (prénom et nom), sénateur Président du Sénat, Le Sénat, Ottawa ON K1A 0A4

(femme) L'honorable (prénom et nom), sénatrice Présidente du Sénat, Le Sénat, Ottawa ON K1A 0A4

Appel - (homme) Monsieur le Président,

(femme) Madame la Présidente,

Salutation - (homme) Je vous prie d'agréer, Monsieur le Président, l'expression de ma haute considération.

(femme) Je vous prie d'agréer, Madame la Présidente, l'hommage de mon profond respect. Conversation -

(homme) ‹‹Monsieur le Président››

(femme) ‹‹Madame la Présidente››

Remarques: Dans le cas d'un sénateur ou d'une sénatrice qui est membre du Conseil privé, la formule d'appel à utiliser est ‹‹L'honorable (nom), C.P., sénateur(trice)››. Après leur retraite, les sénateurs conservent le titre ‹‹honorable›› mais la formule d'appel devient: ‹‹Monsieur/Madame››.

SPEAKER OF THE HOUSE OF COMMONS:

The Honourable (full name), M.P., Speaker of the House of Commons, House of Commons, Ottawa, ON K1A 0A6

Salutation - Dear Mr./Madam Speaker:

Final Salutation - Yours sincerely,

In Conversation - "Mr. Speaker" or "Madam Speaker"

PRÉSIDENT OU PRÉSIDENTE DE LA CHAMBRE DES COMMUNES

(homme) L'honorable (prénom et nom) député Président de la Chambre des communes, Chambre des communes, Ottawa ON K1A 0A6

(femme) L'honorable (prénom et nom) députée Présidente de la Chambre des communes, Chambre des communes, Ottawa ON K1A 0A6

Appel - (homme) Monsieur le Président,

(femme) Madame la Présidente,

Salutation - (homme) Je vous prie d'agréer, Monsieur le Président, l'expression de ma haute considération.

(femme) Je vous prie d'agréer, Madame la Présidente, l'hommage de mon profond respect. Conversation -

(homme) ‹‹Monsieur le Président››

(femme) ‹‹Madame la Présidente››

SENATORS:

The Honourable (full name), Senator, The Senate, Ottawa, ON K1A 0A1

Salutation - Dear Senator (name):

Final Salutation - Yours sincerely,

In Conversation - "Senator (name)"

Note: A senator who is a member of the Queen's Privy Council is addressed as "Senator the Honourable (full name), P.C." After a Senator retires, he/she retains the title "Honourable" for life but the salutation is "Dear Sir/Madam" or "Dear Mr./Mrs./Ms./Miss (name)".

SÉNATEURS:

(homme) L'honorable (prénom et nom) sénateur, Le Sénat, Ottawa ON K1A 0A4

(femme) L'honorable (prénom et nom) sénatrice, Le Sénat, Ottawa ON K1A 0A4

Appel - (homme) Monsieur le Sénateur,

(femme) Madame la Sénatrice,

Salutation - (homme) Je vous prie d'agréer, Monsieur le Sénateur, l'expression de mes meilleurs sentiments.

(femme) Je vous prie d'agréer, Madame la Sénatrice, mes hommages respectueux. Conversation -

(homme) ‹‹Monsieur le Sénateur››. On poursuit avec ‹‹Monsieur››

(femme) ‹‹Madame la Sénatrice››. On poursuit avec ‹‹Madame››

Remarques: Après leur retraite, les sénateurs conservent le titre ‹‹honorable››, mais la formule d'appel devient: ‹‹Monsieur›› ou ‹‹Madame››.

MEMBERS OF THE HOUSE OF COMMONS:

Mr. John Smith, M.P. or The Honourable John Smith, P.C., M.P., House of Commons, Ottawa, ON K1A 0A6

Salutation - Dear Mr./Mrs./Ms./Miss (name):

Final Salutation - Yours sincerely,

In Conversation - "Mr./Mrs./Ms./Miss (name)"

Note: The members of the House of Commons who are members of the Queen's Privy Council retain the title "Honourable" for life and use the initials "P.C." after their name. M.P.: Member of the House of Commons P.C., M.P.: Member of the Privy Council and Member of the House of Commons

DÉPUTÉS FÉDÉRAUX

(homme) Monsieur (prénom et nom), député ou L'honorable (prénom et nom), C.P., député Chambre des communes, Ottawa ON K1A 0A6

(femme) Madame (prénom et nom), députée ou L'honorable (prénom et nom), C.P., députée Chambre des communes, Ottawa ON K1A 0A6

Appel - (homme) Monsieur le Député,

(femme) Madame la Députee,

Salutation - (homme) Je vous prie d'agréer, Monsieur le Député, l'expression de mes meilleurs sentiments.

(femme) Je vous prie d'agréer, Madame la Députée, mes respectueux hommages. Conversation -

(homme) On commence par ‹‹Monsieur le Député››. On poursuit avec ‹‹Monsieur››

(femme) On commence par ‹‹Madame la Députee››. On poursuit avec ‹‹Madame››

Remarques: Les députés qui sont membres du Conseil privé de la Reine pour le Canada ont le ‹‹honorable›› à vie et portent les initiales ‹‹C.P.›› après leur nom.

MEMBER OF THE PROVINCIAL/TERRITORIAL CABINET:

The Honourable (full name), M.L.A. or (M.P.P., M.N.A. or M.H.A.), Minister of ________, Address

Salutation - Dear Minister: or Dear Colleague: (between colleagues)

Final Salutation - Yours sincerely,

In Conversation - "Minister" first then "Mr./Mrs./ Ms./Miss (name)"

Note: A provincial/territorial cabinet minister does not retain the title "Honourable" after tenure of office unless he/she is a member of the Privy Council. M.L.A.: all provinces/territories except for: Ontario (M.P.P.); Québec (M.N.A.); Newfoundland (M.H.A.). The term "Mr./Madam Minister" should not be used.

MINISTRES PROVINCIAUX/TERRITORIAUX

(homme/femme) L'honorable (prénom et nom), M.A.L. ou (M.A.N., M.P.P. ou M.C.A.) Ministre de ________, Adresse

Appel - (homme) Monsieur le Ministre, ou Cher collègue, (Entre collègues)

(femme) Madame la Ministre, ou Chère collègue, (Entre collègues)

Salutation - (homme) Je vous prie d'agréer, Monsieur le Ministre, l'expression de ma considération respectueuse. Ou Je vous prie, cher collègue, de recevoir mes cordiales salutations. (Entre collègues)

(femme) Je vous prie d'agréer, Madame la Ministre, l'expression de ma considération respectueuse. Ou Je vous prie, chère collègue, de recevoir mes cordiales salutations. (Entre collègues) Conversation -

(homme) On commence par ‹‹Monsieur le Ministre››. On poursuit avec ‹‹Monsieur››

(femme) On commence par ‹‹Madame la Ministre››. On poursuit avec ‹‹Madame››

Remarques: Les ministres provinciaux/territoriaux ne conservent pas le titre ‹‹honorable›› après la fin de leur mandat à moins qu'ils ne soient membres du Conseil privè. M.A.L.: toutes les provinces et les territoires, sauf: - l'Ontario (M.P.P.) - le Québec (M.A.N.) - Terre- Neuve (M.C.A.)

MEMBER OF A PROVINCIAL/TERRITORIAL LEGISLATIVE ASSEMBLY:

Mr. John Smith, M.L.A. or (M.P.P., M.N.A., or M.H.A.)

Salutation - Dear Mr./Mrs./Ms./Miss (name),

Final Salutation - Yours sincerely,

In Conversation - "Mr./Mrs./Ms./Miss (name)"

Note: Members of the Queen's Privy Council retain the title "Honourable" for life and use the initials "P.C." after their name. M.L.A.: all provinces/territories except for: Ontario (M.P.P.); Quebec (M.N.A.); Newfoundland (M.H.A.) P.C., M.L.A.: Member of the Privy Council and Member of the Legislative Assembly

DÉPUTÉS PROVINCIAUX/TERRITORIAUX

(homme) Monsieur (prénom et nom), M.A.L. ou (M.P.P., M.A.N. ou M.C.A.), Adresse

(femme) Madame (prénom et nom), M.A.L. ou (M.P.P., M.A.N. ou M.C.A.), Adresse

Appel - (homme) Monsieur le Député,

(femme) Madame la Députee,

Salutation - (homme) Je vous prie d'agréer, Monsieur le Député, l'expression de mes meilleurs sentiments.

(femme) Je vous prie d'agréer, Madame la Députée, mes respectueux hommages. Conversation -

(homme) ‹‹Monsieur››

(femme) ‹‹Madame››

Remarques: Les membres du Conseil privé de la Reine conservent le titre ‹‹honorable›› à vie et placent les initiales C.P. après leur nom. M.A.L.: toutes les provinces et les territoires sauf: - l'Ontario (M.P.P.) - le Québec (M.A.N.), Terre-Neuve (M.C.A.) C.P., M.A.L.: Membre du Conseil privé et membre de l'Assemblée législative.

MAYOR OF A CITY OR TOWN:

His/Her Worship (full name), Mayor of (name), Address

Salutation - Dear Sir/Madam: or Dear Mr./Madam Mayor:

Final Salutation - Yours sincerely,

In Conversation - "Your Worship" first then "Mayor (name)"

MAIRE/MAIRESSE

(homme) Son Honneur monsieur (prénom et nom), Maire de (Ville), Adresse

(femme) Son Honneur madame (prénom et nom), Mairesse de (Ville), Adresse Appel - Monsieur le Maire,

(femme) Madame la Mairesse,

Salutation - (homme) Je vous prie d'agréer, Monsieur le Maire, l'expression de mes meilleurs sentiments.

(femme) Je vous prie d'agréer, Madame la Mairesse, mes hommages respectueux. Conversation -

(homme) On commence par ‹‹Votre Honneur››. On poursuit avec ‹‹Monsieur le Maire››

(femme) On commence par ‹‹Votre Honneur››. On poursuit avec ‹‹Madame la Mairesse››

JUDGES/JUGES

CHIEF JUSTICE: The Right Honourable (full name), P.C., Chief Justice of Canada, Supreme Court of Canada, Ottawa, ON K1A 0J1

Salutation - Dear Chief Justice:

Final Salutation - Yours sincerely,

In Conversation - "Mr./Madam Chief Justice" first then "Sir/Madam" or "Mr./Mrs./Ms./Miss (name)"

JUGE EN CHEF DU CANADA

(homme) Le très honorable (prenom et nom), C.P. Juge en chef du Canada, Cour suprême du Canada, Ottawa ON K1A 0J1

(femme) La très honorable (prenom et nom), C.P. Juge en chef du Canada, Cour suprême du Canada, Ottawa ON K1A 0J1

Appel - (homme) Monsieur le Juge en chef,

(femme) Madame la Juge en chef,

Salutation - (homme) Je vous prie d'agréer, Monsieur le Juge en chef, l'expression de ma très haute considération.

(femme) Je vous prie d'agréer, Madame la Juge en chef, l'hommage de mon profond respect. Conversation -

(homme) On commence par ‹‹Monsieur le Juge en chef››. On poursuit avec ‹‹Monsieur››

(femme) On commence par ‹‹Madame la Juge en chef››. On poursuit avec ‹‹Madame››

JUDGES OF SUPERIOR COURTS:

Supreme Court of Canada & Federal Court of Canada: The Honourable (full name), Judge of the ________ Court of Canada, Address.

Salutation - Dear Mr./Madam Justice (name):

Final Salutation - Yours sincerely,

In Conversation - "Mr./Madam Justice" Appeal Court, Superior Court, Court of the Queen's Bench: The Honourable (full name), Judge of ________, Address

Salutation - Dear Mr./Madam Justice (name):

Final Salutation - Yours sincerely,

In Conversation - "Mr./Madam Justice (name)"

JUGES DES COURS SUPÉRIEURES

Cour suprême, Cour fédérale et Cour de l'impôt: L'honorable (prénom et nom), Titre, Adresse
Appel - (homme) Monsieur le Juge,
(femme) Madame la Juge,
Salutation - (homme) Je vous prie d'agréer, Monsieur le Juge, l'expression de ma haute considération.
(femme) Je vous prie d'agréer, Madame la Juge l'hommage de mon profond respect. Conversation -
(homme) «Monsieur le Juge»
(femme) «Madame la Juge» Cour d'appel, Cour supérieure, Cour du Banc de la Reine, L'honorable (prénom et nom) Juge de ________, Adresse
Appel - (homme) Monsieur le Juge,
(femme) Madame la Juge,
Salutation -
(homme) Je vous prie d'agréer, Monsieur le Juge, l'expression de ma haute considération.
(femme) Je vous prie d'agréer, Madame la Juge, l'hommage de mon profond respect. Conversation -
(homme) «Monsieur le Juge»
(femme) «Madame la Juge»

JUDGES OF THE TAX COURT:

The Honourable (full name), Judge of the Tax Court of Canada, Address
Salutation - Dear Chief Judge/Judge (name):
Final Salutation - Yours sincerely,
In Conversation - "Chief Judge/Judge (name)"
Remarques: En français, voir ci-dessus.

CHIEF JUDGES/JUDGES OF PROVINCIAL/TERRITORIAL COURTS:

The Honourable (full name), Provincial/Territorial Court of ________ , Address
Salutation - Dear Chief Judge/Judge (name):
Final Salutation - Yours sincerely,
In Conversation - "Judge (name)"
Note: The titles to be used in Canada now recognize the title"Honourable" for provincially/territorially appointed judges. The courtesy title "His/Her Honour" is no longer appropriate given an official title has been granted.

JUGES EN CHEF/JUGES DES COURS PROVINCIALES/ TERRITORIALES

L'honorable (prénom et nom), Cour provinciale de ________, Adresse
Appel - (homme) Monsieur le Juge en chef/le Juge,
(femme) Madame la Juge en chef/la Juge,
Salutation -
(homme) Je vous prie d'agréer, Monsieur le Juge en chef/le Juge, l'expression de mon profond respect.
(femme) Je vous prie d'agréer, Madame la Juge en chef//la Juge, l'hommage de mon profond respect. Conversation -
(homme) «Monsieur le Juge en chef/ le Juge»
(femme) «Madame la Juge en chef/la Juge»
Remarques: Le tableau des titres pour le Canada reconnaît le titre «honorable» aux juges des cours provinciales/ territoriales; le titre de courtoisie «Son Honneur» n'est plus de mise maintenant qu'un titre officiel est utilisé.

Religion

Anglican Church of Canada/ Église anglicane du Canada

PRIMATE:

The Most Reverend (full name), Primate of the Anglican Church of Canada, Address
Salutation - Dear Archbishop (name):
Final Salutation - Yours sincerely,
In Conversation - "Archbishop"

PRIMAT:

Le révérendissime (prénom et nom), Primate de l'Église anglicane du Canada, Adresse Appel - Monsieur le Primat,
Salutation - Je vous prie d'agréer, Monsieur le Primat, l'expression de mes sentiments les plus respectueux.
Conversation - «Monsieur l'Archevêque»

ARCHBISHOP:

The Most Reverend (full name), D.D., Archbishop of (name of Diocese), Address
Salutation - Dear Archbishop (name):
Final Salutation - Yours very truly,
In Conversation - "Archbishop"
ARCHEVÊQUE:
Le révérendissime (prénom et nom), Archevêque de (nom du diocèse), Adresse Appel - Monsieur l'Archevêque,
Salutation - Je vous prie d'agréer, Monsieur l'Archevêque, l'expression de mes sentiments les plus respectueux.
Conversation - «Monsieur l'Archevêque»

BISHOP:

The Right Reverend (full name), Bishop of (name of Diocese), Address
Salutation - Dear Bishop (name):
Final Salutation - Yours very truly,
In Conversation - "Bishop (name)" or "Bishop"

ÉVÊQUE:

(homme) Le très révérend (prénom et nom), Évêque de (nom du diocèse), Adresse
(femme) La très révérende (prénom et nom), Évêque de (nom du diocèse), Adresse
Appel - (homme) Monsieur l'Évêque,
(femme) Madame l'Évêque,
Salutation - (homme) Je vous prie d'agréer, Monsieur l'Évêque, l'expression de mes sentiments les plus respectueux.
(femme) Je vous prie d'agréer, Madame l'Évêque, l'hommage de mon profond respect. Conversation -
(homme) «Monsieur l'Évêque»
(femme) «Madame l'Évêque»

ARCHDEACON:

The Venerable (full name), Archdeacon, Address
Salutation - Dear Archdeacon (name):
Final Salutation - Yours sincerely,
In Conversation - "Archdeacon (name)"

ARCHIDIACRE:

(homme) Le vénérable (prénom et nom), Archidiacre, Adresse
(femme) La vénérable (prénom et nom), Archidiacre, Adresse
Appel - (homme) Monsieur l'Archidiacre,
(femme) Madame l'Archidiacre,
Salutation - (homme) Je vous prie d'agréer, Monsieur l'Archidacre, l'expression de mes sentiments les plus respectueux.
(femme) Je vous prie d'agréer, Madame l'Archidacre, l'hommage de mon profond respect. Conversation -
(homme) «Monsieur l'Archidiacre»
(femme) «Madame l'Archidiacre»

DEAN:

The Very Reverend (full name), Dean of (name of Cathedral), Address
Salutation - Dear Dean (name):
Final Salutation - Yours sincerely,
In Conversation - "Dean (name)" or "Mr./Mrs./Ms./ Miss (name)"

DOYEN:

(homme) Le très révérend (prénom et nom), Doyen de (nom de la cathédrale), Adresse
(femme) La très révérende (prénom et nom), Doyenne de (nom de la cathédrale), Adresse
Appel - (homme) Monsieur le Doyen,
(femme) Madame la Doyenne,
Salutation - (homme) Je vous prie d'agréer, Monsieur le Doyen, l'expression de mes sentiments les plus respectueux.
(femme) Je vous prie d'agréer, Madame la Doyenne, l'hommage de mon profond respect. Conversation -
(homme) «Monsieur le Doyen» ou «Monsieur»
(femme) «Madame la Doyenne» ou «Madame»

CANON:

The Reverend Canon (full name), Address
Salutation - Dear Canon (name):
Final Salutation - Yours sincerely,
In Conversation - "Canon (name)"

CHANOINE:

(homme) Le chanoine, (prénom et nom), Adresse
(femme) La chanoinesse, (prénom et nom), Adresse
Appel - (homme) Monsieur le Chanoine,
(femme) Madame la Chanoinesse,
Salutation - (homme) Je vous prie d'agréer, Monsieur le Chanoine, l'expression de mes sentiments les plus respectueux.
(femme) Je vous prie d'agréer, Madame La Chanoinesse, l'hommage de mon profond respect. Conversation -
(homme) «Monsieur le Chanoine»
(femme) «Madame la Chanoinesse»

PRIEST:

The Reverend (full name), Address
Salutation - Dear Father (name) or Dear Mr. (name): or Dear Mrs./Ms./Miss (name)
Final Salutation - Yours sincerely,
In Conversation - "Father" or "Father (name) or "Mrs./Ms./Miss (name)"
Note: "Reverend" is an adjective which is never used without the full name.

PRÊTRE:

(homme) Le révérend père (prénom et nom), Adresse
(femme) La révérende (prénom et nom), Adresse
Appel - (homme) Monsieur le Curé, Monsieur l'Abbé,
(femme) Madame,
Salutation - (homme) Je vous prie d'agréer, Monsieur le Curé, l'expression de mes sentiments respectueux.
(femme) Je vous prie d'agréer, Madame, l'expression de mes sentiments respectueux. Conversation -
(homme) «Monsieur le Curé/Monsieur l'Abbé»
(femme) « Madame)»

RELIGIOUS:

(man) The Reverend Father (full name), Address
Salutation - Dear Father (name):
Final Salutation - Yours sincerely,
In Conversation - "Reverend Father" (woman) Reverend Mother (full name)/Reverend Sister (full name)
Salutation - Dear Reverend Mother/Sister:
Final Salutation - Yours sincerely,
In Conversation - "Reverend Mother (name)/Reverend Sister (name)"

RELIGIEUX/RELIGIEUSE:

(homme) Le révérend père (prénom et nom), Adresse
(femme) La révérende mère/ soeur (prénom et nom), Adresse
Appel - (homme) Révérend père/Mon père,
(femme) Révérende mère/Ma soeur
Salutation - (homme) Je vous prie d'agréer, Révérend père/Mon père, l'expression de mes sentiments les plus respectueux.
(femme) Je vous prie d'agréer, Révérende mère/ Ma soeur, l'hommage de mon profond respect. Conversation -
(homme) «Révérend père/Mon père»
(femme) «Révérende mère/Ma soeur»

Roman Catholic Church/Église catholique romaine

THE POPE:

His Holiness Pope Benedict XVI, Address
Salutation - Your Holiness:
Final Salutation - I have the honour to remain Your Holiness's obedient servant,
In Conversation - "Your Holiness"

LE PAPE:

Sa Sainteté le pape Benedict XVI, Adresse Appel - Très Saint-Père,
Salutation - Je vous prie d'agréer, Très Saint-Père, l'expression de mon profond respect et de ma très haute considération.
Conversation - «Votre Sainteté» ou «Très Saint- Père»

CARDINAL:

His Eminence John Cardinal Smith, Address
Salutation - Your Eminence: or Dear Cardinal (name):
Final Salutation - Yours very truly,
In Conversation - "Your Eminence"

CARDINAL:

Son Éminence le cardinal (prénom et nom), Adresse Appel - Monsieur le Cardinal,
Salutation - Je vous prie d'agréer, Monsieur le Cardinal, l'expression de mon profond respect.

Conversation - «Éminence»

ARCHBISHOP/BISHOP:
The Most Reverend (full name), Archbishop/Bishop of (name of Diocese). Address
Salutation - Dear Archbishop/Bishop (name):
Final Salutation - Yours very truly,
In Conversation - "Archbishop/Bishop"
Note: The Holy See accorded the courtesy title "His Excellency" to Roman Catholic Archbishops and Bishops; that title is not recognized by Canadian civil authorities.

ARCHEVÊQUE/ÉVÊQUE:

Monseigneur (prénom et nom), Archevêque ou Évêque de (nom du diocèse), Adresse Appel - Monseigneur,
Salutation - Je vous prie d'agréer, Monseigneur , l'expression de mes sentiments les plus respectueux.
Conversation - «Monseigneur»
Remarques: Le titre «Son Excellence» est utilisé par le Saint-Siège pour les archevêques et évêques catholiques; il n'est toutefois pas reconnu par les autorités civiles canadiennes.

ABBOT:

The Right Reverend (full name), Abbot of (name of ________), Address
Salutation - Right Reverend Father: or Dear Abbott (name):
Final Salutation - Yours sincerely,
In Conversation - "Father Abbott"

ABBÉ:

Le révérend père (prénom et nom), Adresse Appel - Monsieur l'Abbé,

Salutation - Je vous prie d'agréer, Monsieur l'Abbé, l'expression de mes sentiments les plus respectueux.
Conversation - «Monsieur l'Abbé»

CANON:
The Very Reverend (full name), Address
Salutation - Dear Canon (name):
Final Salutation - Yours sincerely,
In Conversation - "Canon (name)"

CHANOINE:
Le chanoine (prénom et nom), Adresse Appel - Monsieur le Chanoine,
Salutation - Je vous prie d'agréer, Monsieur le Chanoine, l'expression de mes sentiments respectueux.
Conversation - «Monsieur le Chanoine»

PRIEST
The Reverend (full name), Address
Salutation - Dear Father:
Final Salutation - Yours sincerely,
In Conversation - "Father" or "Father (name)"
Note: "Reverend" is an adjective which is never used without the full name.

PRÊTRE:
Le révérend père (prénom et nom), Adresse Appel - Monsieur le Curé/l'Abbé,
Salutation - Je vous prie d'agréer, Monsieur le Curé, l'expression de mes sentiments respectueux.
Conversation - «Monsieur le Curé/l'Abbé»

SULPICIAN:
Mr. (full name), Address
Salutation - Dear Mr. (name):
Final Salutation - Yours truly,
In Conversation - "Mr. (name)"

SULPICIEN:
Monsieur (prénom et nom), Adresse Appel - Monsieur,
Salutation - Je vous prie d'agréer, Monsieur, l'expression de mes sentiments respectueux.
Conversation - «Monsieur»

RELIGIOUS:
(man) The Reverend Father (full name), Address
Salutation - Dear Father (name):
Final Salutation - Yours sincerely,
In Conversation - "Reverend Father" (woman) Reverend Mother (full name)/Reverend Sister (full name)
Salutation - Dear Reverend Mother/Sister:
Final Salutation - Yours sincerely,
In Conversation - "Reverend Mother/Sister (name)"

RELIGIEUX/RELIGIEUSE:
(homme) Le révérend père (prénom et nom), Adresse
(femme) La révérende mère/soeur (prénom et nom), Adresse
Appel - (homme) Révérend père/Mon père,
(femme) Révérende mère/Ma soeur,
Salutation - (homme) Je vous prie d'agréer, Révérend père/Mon père, l'expression de mes sentiments respectueux.
(femme) Je vous prie d'agréer, Révérende mère/Ma soeur, l'hommage de mon profond respect. Conversation -
(homme) «Révérend père ou Mon père»
(femme) «Révérende mère/Ma soeur»

Other Religious Denominations/ Autres dénominations:

MODERATOR:
(United Church of Canada and Presbyterian Church in Canada) A present ordained Moderator: The Right Reverend (full name), Moderator of (name of Church), Address
Salutation - Dear Mr./Mrs./Ms./Miss (name):
Final Salutation - Yours sincerely,
In Conversation - "Mr./Mrs./Ms./Miss (name)" A past ordained Moderator: The Very Reverend (full name), Moderator of (name of Church), Address
Salutation - Dear Mr./Mrs./Ms./Miss (name):
Final Salutation - Yours sincerely,
In Conversation - "Mr./Mrs./Ms./Miss (name)"

MODÉRATEURS:
(Église unie du Canada et Église presbytérienne au Canada)
(homme) Le très révérend (prénom et nom), Modérateur de (nom de l'Église), Adresse
(femme) La très révérende (prénom et nom), Modératrice de (nom de l'Église), Adresse
Appel - (homme) Monsieur le Modérateur,
(femme) Madame la Modératrice,
Salutation - (homme) Je vous prie d'agréer, Monsieur le Modérateur, l'expression de mes sentiments respectueux.
(femme) Je vous prie d'agréer, Madame la Modératrice, l'hommage de mon profond respect. Conversation -
(homme) «Monsieur le Modérateur»
(femme) «Madame la Modératrice»

MINISTER:
The Reverend (full name), Address
Salutation - Dear Mr./Mrs./Ms./Miss (name):
Final Salutation - Yours sincerely,
In Conversation - "Mr./Mrs./Ms./Miss (name)"
Note: "Reverend" is an adjective which is never used without the full name.

MINISTRE:
(homme) Le révérend (prénom et nom), Adresse
(femme) La révérende (prénom et nom), Adresse
Appel - (homme) Monsieur le Pasteur,
(femme) Madame,
Salutation - (homme) Je vous prie d'agréer, Monsieur le Pasteur, l'expression de mes sentiments respectueux.
(femme) Je vous prie d'agréer, Madame, l'hommage de mon profond respect.
Conversation - (homme) «Monsieur le Pasteur»
(femme) «Madame»

RABBI:
Rabbi (full name), Address
Salutation - Dear Rabbi (name):
Final Salutation - Yours sincerely,
In Conversation - "Rabbi (name)"

RABBIN:
Le rabbin (prénom et nom), Adresse Appel - Monsieur le Rabbin,
Salutation - Je vous prie d'agréer, Monsieur le Rabbin, l'expression de mes sentiments respectueux.
Conversation - «Monsieur le Rabbin»

Diplomatic/Diplomates

AMBASSADORS/HIGH COMMISSIONERS of foreign countries in Canada:
His/Her Excellency (full name), Ambassador of Canada to _________ /High Commissioner for _________ , Address
Salutation - Dear Ambassador/High Commissioner:
Final Salutation - Yours sincerely,
In Conversation - "Your Excellency" or "Excellency"
Note: British High Commissioner and not High Commissioner for Britain

AMBASSADEURS/HAUTS-COMMISSAIRES de pays étrangers au Canada:
(homme) Son Excellence monsieur (prénom et nom), Ambassadeur de ________/Haut-Commissaire de ________, Adresse
(femme) Son Excellence madame (prénom et nom), Ambassadrice de ________/Haute-Commissaire de ________, Adresse
Appel - (homme) Monsieur/l'Ambassadeur/le Haut - Commissaire,
(femme) Madame l'Ambassadrice/la Haute-Commissaire,
Salutation - (homme) Je vous prie d'agréer, Monsieur l'Ambassadeur/le Haut-Commissaire, l'expression de ma haute considération.
(femme) Je vous prie d'agréer, Madame l'Ambassadrice/ la Haute-Commissaire, l'expression de mes respectueux hommages.
Conversation - «Excellence»

CANADIAN AMBASSADORS/HIGH COMMISSIONERS abroad:
Mr./Mrs. (full name), Ambassador of Canada to _________ /High Commissioner for Canada to _________ , Address
Salutation - Dear Ambassador/High Commissioner:
Final Salutation - Yours sincerely,
In Conversation - "Mr./Madam Ambassador/High Commissioner"
AMBASSADEURS DU CANADA/HAUTS-COMMISSAIRES à l'étranger
(homme) Monsieur (prénom et nom) Ambassadeur du Canada/Haute-commissaire du Canada au ________, Adresse
(femme) Madame (prénom et nom) l'Ambassadrice du Canada/Haute-commissaire du Canada au ________, Adresse
Appel - (homme) Monsieur l'Ambassadeur/le Haut-Commissaire,
(femme) Madame l'Ambassadrice/la Haute-Commissaire,
Salutation - (homme) Je vous prie d'agréer, Monsieur l'Ambassadeur/le Haut-commissaire, l'expression de ma haute considération.
(femme) Je vous prie d'agréer, Madame l'Ambassadrice/ la Haute-commissaire, l'expression de mes respectueux hommages.
Conversation - (homme) «Monsieur l'Ambassadeur/ le Haut-Commissaire»
(femme) «Madame l'Ambassadrice/la Haut-Commissaire»
Remarques: Si un ambassadeur du Canada ou un haut-commissaire du Canada se trouve au Canada ou à l'étranger, la formule à employer est simplement «Ambassadeur» ou «Haut-commissaire». Le titre «Excellence» n'est pas accordé par un citoyen canadien à un ambassadeur du Canada ou à un haut-commissaire du Canada, mais par le gouvernement et les citoyens du pays auprès duquel l'ambassadeur ou le haut-commissaire est accédité.

Armed Forces/Forces Armeés

OFFICER RANK:
Brigadier General/Major General/Lieutenant General/General (full name), Address
Salutation - Dear General:
Final Salutation - Yours sincerely,
In Conversation - "General (name)"
Colonel (full name), Address
Salutation - Dear Colonel:
Final Salutation - Yours sincerely,
In Conversation - "Colonel (name)"
Lieutenant Colonel (full name), Address
Salutation - Lieutenant Colonel:
Final Salutation - Yours sincerely,
In Conversation - "Lieutenant Colonel (name)"
Major (full name), Address
Salutation - Dear Major:
Final Salutation - Yours sincerely,
In Conversation - "Major (name)"
Captain (full name), Address
Salutation - Dear Captain:
Final Salutation - Yours sincerely,
In Conversation - "Captain (name)"
Lieutenant (full name), Address
Salutation - Dear Lieutenant:
Final Salutation - Yours sincerely,
In Conversation - "Lieutenant (name)"

AVEC GRADE:
(homme) Le brigadier-général/major-général/lieutenant- général (prénom et nom), Adresse
(femme) La brigadière-générale/majore-générale/lieutenante-générale (prénom et nom), Adresse
Appel - (homme) Général,
(femme) Générale,
Salutation - (homme) Je vous prie d'agréer, Général, l'expression de mes meilleurs sentiments.
(femme) Je vous prie d'agréer, Générale, l'expression de mes hommages respectueux.
Conversation - (homme) «Général»
(femme) «Générale»
(homme) Le colonel (prénom et nom), Adresse
(femme) La colonelle (prénom et nom), Adresse
Appel - (homme) Colonel,
(femme) Colonelle,
Salutation - (homme) Je vous prie d'agréer, Colonel, l'expression de mes meilleurs sentiments.
(femme) Je vous prie d'agréer, Colonelle, l'expression de mes hommages respectueux.
Conversation - (homme) «Colonel»
(femme) «Colonelle»
(homme) La lieutenant-colonel, (prénom et nom), Adresse
(femme) La lieutenante-colonelle, (prénom et nom), Adresse
Appel - (homme) Lieutenant-Colonel,
(femme) Lieutenante-Colonelle,
Salutation - (homme) Je vous prie d'agréer, Lieutenant- Colonel, l'expression de mes meilleurs sentiments.
(femme) Je vous prie d'agréer, Lieutenante-Colonelle, l'expression de mes meilleurs hommages respectueux.
Conversation - (homme) «Lieutenant-Colonel»
(femme) «Lieutenante-Colonelle»
(homme) Le major (prénom et nom), Adresse
(femme) La majore (prénom et nom), Adresse
Appel - (homme) Major,
(femme) Majore,
Salutation - (homme) Je vous prie d'agréer, Major, l'expression de mes meilleurs sentiments.
(femme) Je vous prie d'agréer, Majore, l'expression de mes hommages respectueux.
Conversation - (homme) «Major»
(femme) «Majore»
(homme) Le capitaine (prénom et nom), Adresse
(femme) La capitaine (prénom et nom), Adresse
Appel - Capitaine,
Salutation - (homme) Je vous prie d'agréer, Capitaine, l'expression de mes meilleurs sentiments.
(femme) Je vous prie d'agréer, Capitaine, l'expression de mes hommages respectueux.
Conversation - «Capitaine»
(homme) Le lieutenant (prénom et nom), Adresse

(femme) La lieutenante (prénom et nom), Adresse
Appel - (homme) Lieutenant,
(femme) Lieutenante,
Salutation - (homme) Je vous prie d'agréer, Lieutenant, l'expression de mes meilleurs sentiments.
(femme) Je vous prie d'agréer, Lieutenante, l'expression de mes hommages respectueux.
Conversation - (homme) ‹‹Lieutenant››
(femme) ‹‹Lieutenante››

NCO and other ranks:

Chief Warrant Officer (full name)
Salutation - Dear Chief Warrant (name)
Final Salutation - Yours sincerely,
In Conversation - "Mr./Mrs./Ms./Miss (name)"

Master Warrant Officer (full name)
Salutation - Dear Master Warrant (name):
Final Salutation - Yours sincerely,
In Conversation - "Mr./Mrs./Ms./Miss (name)"

Warrant Officer (full name)
Salutation - Dear Warrant (name):
Final Salutation - Yours sincerely,
In Conversation - "Mr./Mrs./Ms./Miss (name)"

Sergeant (full name)
Salutation - Dear Sergeant (name):
Final Salutation - Yours sincerely,
In Conversation - "Mr./Mrs./Ms./Miss (name)"

Corporal (full name)
Salutation - Dear Corporal (name):
Final Salutation - Yours sincerely,
In Conversation - "Mr./Mrs./Ms./Miss (name)"

Private (full name)
Salutation - Dear Private (name):
Final Salutation - Yours sincerely,
In Conversation - "Mr./Mrs./Ms./Miss (name)"

SOUS OFFICIERS ET AUTRES GRADES:

(homme) L'adjudant-chef (prénom et nom)
(femme) L'adjudante-chef (prénom et nom)
Appel - (homme) Adjudant-chef,
(femme) Adjudante-chef,
Salutation - (homme) Je vous prie d'agréer, Adjudant-chef, l'expression de mes meilleurs sentiments.
(femme) Je vous prie d'agréer, Adjudante-chef, l'expression de mes hommages respectueux.
Conversation - Le qualificatif du grade ‹‹Monsieur/ Madame/Mademoiselle››

(homme) L'adjudant-maître (prénom et nom)
(femme) L'adjudante-maîtresse (prénom et nom)
Appel - (homme) Adjudant-maître,
(femme) Adjudante-maîtresse,
Salutation - (homme) Je vous prie d'agréer, Adjudant-maître, l'expression de mes meilleurs hommages respectueux.
(femme) Je vous prie d'agréer, Adjudantemaîtresse, l'expression de mes hommages respectueux.
Conversation - Le qualificatif du grade ‹‹Monsieur/ Madame/Mademoiselle››

(homme) L'adjudant (prénom et nom)
(femme) L'adjudante (prénom et nom)
Appel - (homme) Adjudant,
(femme) Adjudante,
Salutation - (homme) Je vous prie d'agréer, Adjudant, l'expression de mes meilleurs sentiments.
(femme) Je vous prie d'agréer, Adjudante, l'expression de mes hommages respectueux.
Conversation - Le qualificatif du grade ‹‹Monsieur/ Madame/Mademoiselle››

(homme) Le sergent (prénom et nom)
(femme) La sergente (prénom et nom)
Appel - (homme) Sergent,
(femme) Sergente,
Salutation - (homme) Je vous prie d'agréer, Sergent, l'expression de mes meilleurs sentiments.
(femme) Je vous prie d'agréer, Sergente, l'expression de mes hommages respectueux.
Conversation - Le qualificatif du grade ‹‹Monsieur/ Madame/Mademoiselle››

(homme) Le caporal (prénom et nom)
(femme) La caporale (prénom et nom)
Appel - (homme) Caporal,
(femme) Caporale,
Salutation - (homme) Je vous prie d'agréer, Caporal, l'expression de mes meilleurs sentiments.
(femme) Je vous prie d'agréer, Caporale, l'expression de mes hommages respectueux.
Conversation - Le qualificatif du grade ‹‹Monsieur/ Madame/Mademoiselle››

(homme) Le soldat (prénom et nom)
(femme) La soldate (prénom et nom)
Appel - Monsieur/Madame/Mademoiselle,
Salutation - (homme) Je vous prie d'agréer, Monsieur, l'expression de mes meilleurs sentiments.
(femme) Je vous prie d'agréer, Madame/Mademoiselle, l'expression de mes hommages respectueux.
Conversation - Le qualificatif du grade ‹‹Monsieur/ Madame/Mademoiselle››

Foreign Dignitaries/Les Dignitaires Étrangers

AN EMPEROR:

His Imperial Majesty Akihito, Emperor of Japan, Address
Salutation - Your dignified Majesty:
Final Salutation - I have the honour to remain, Your Imperial Majesty's obedient servant,
In Conversation - "Your Majesty" first then "Sire"

EMPEREUR:

Sa Majesté Impériale (Nom) ________, Empereur du ________, Adresse Appel - Votre Majesté Impériale,
Salutation - Je prie Votre Majesté Impériale d'agréer l'hommage de mon profond respect et de ma très haute considération.
Conversation - On commence par ‹‹Majesté››. On poursuit avec ‹‹Sire››

A KING:

His Majesty Juan Carlos, King of Spain, Address
Salutation - Your Majesty/Sire:
Final Salutation - I have the honour to remain, Your Majesty's obedient servant,
In Conversation - "Your Majesty" first then "Sire"

UN ROI:

Sa Majesté (Nom) ________, Roi de ________, Adresse Appel - Majesté/Sire,
Salutation - Je prie Votre Majesté d'agréer l'hommage de mon profond respect et de ma très haute considération.
Conversation - On commence par ‹‹Majesté››. On poursuit avec ‹‹Sire››

A QUEEN:

Her Majesty Queen Sophia, Queen of Spain, Address
Salutation - Your Majesty/Madame:
Final Salutation - I have the honour to remain, Your Majesty's obedient servant,
In Conversation - "Your Majesty" first then "Ma'am"

UNE REINE:

Sa Majesté la reine (Nom) ________, Reine de ________, Adresse Appel - Majesté/Madame,
Salutation - Je vous prie d'agréer Madame, l'hommage de mon profond respect et de ma très haute considération.
Conversation - On commence par ‹‹Majesté››. On poursuit avec ‹‹Madame››

A PRESIDENT OF A REPUBLIC:

His/Her Excellency (full name), President of the Republic of (name), Address
Salutation - Excellency:
Final Salutation - Yours sincerely
In Conversation - "Excellency" first then "President" or "Sir/Madam"

UN PRÉSIDENT DE RÉPUBLIQUE:
(homme) Son Excellence monsieur (prénom et nom) Président de la République (nom), Adresse
(femme) Son Excellence madame (prénom et nom) Présidente de la République (nom), Adresse
Appel - (homme) Monsieur le Président,
(femme) Madame la Présidente,
Salutation - (homme) Je vous prie d'agréer Monsieur le Président, l'expression de ma très haute considération.
(femme) Je vous prie d'agréer Madame la Présidente, l'hommage de mon profond respect. Conversation -
(homme) On commence par ‹‹Excellence››. On poursuit avec ‹‹Monsieur le Président›› ou ‹‹Monsieur››
(femme) On commence par ‹‹Excellence››. On poursuit avec ‹‹Madame la Présidente›› ou ‹‹Madame››

THE PRESIDENT OF THE UNITED STATES:

The Honourable (full name), President of the United States, The White House, Washington, D.C.
Salutation - Dear Mr. President:
Final Salutation - Yours sincerely,
In Conversation - "Mr. President" first then "Sir"

PRÉSIDENT DES ÉTATS-UNIS D'AMÉRIQUE:

Son Excellence l'honorable (prénom et nom) Président de États-Unis d'Amérique, The White House, Washington D.C. Appel - Monsieur le Président,
Salutation - Je vous prie d'agréer Monsieur le Président, l'expression de ma très haute considération.
Conversation - On commence par ‹‹Monsieur le Président›› ou ‹‹Excellence››

A PRIME MINISTER:

His/Her Excellency (full name), Prime Minister of (name), Address
Salutation - Dear Prime Minister:
Final Salutation - Yours sincerely,
In Conversation - "Prime Minister" or "Excellency" first then "Sir/Madam" or "Mr./Mrs./Ms./Miss (name)"

PREMIER MINISTRE:

(homme) Son Excellence monsieur (prénom et nom) Premier Ministre de ________, Adresse
(femme) Son Excellence madame (prénom et nom) Première Ministre de ________, Adresse
Appel - (homme) Monsieur le Premier Ministre,
(femme) Madame la Première Ministre,
Salutation - (homme) Je vous prie d'agréer Monsieur le Premier Ministre, l'expression de ma haute considération.
(femme) Je vous prie d'agréer Madame la Première Ministre, l'hommage de mon profond respect. Conversation -
(homme) On commence par ‹‹Monsieur le Premier Ministre›› ou ‹‹Excellence››. On poursuit par ‹‹Monsieur››
(femme) On commence par ‹‹Madame la Première Ministre›› ou ‹‹Excellence››. On poursuit par ‹‹Madame››

Others/Autres

LAWYERS/NOTARIES:

Mr./Mrs./Ms./Miss (full name) or Mr./Mrs./Ms./Miss, Q.C.
Salutation - Dear Mr./Mrs./Ms./Miss (name):
Final Salutation - Yours sincerely,
In Conversation - "Mr./Mrs./Ms./Miss (name)"

AVOCATS/NOTAIRES:

Me (prénom et nom) Appel - Maître,
Salutation - Je vous prie d'agréer, Maître, l'expression de mes meilleurs sentiments.
Conversation - ‹‹Maître››

AIDE-DE-CAMP:

Military: (See Armed Forces) Civilian (according to their title), Mr./Mrs./Ms./Miss (full name)
Salutation - Dear Mr./Mrs./Ms./Miss (name):
Final Salutation - Yours sincerely,
In Conversation - "Mr./Mrs./Ms./Miss (name)"
Note: Post nominals "A. de C." have been authorized for Aides-de-camps to the Governor General and Lieutenant Governors. Militaire: (voir la rubrique ‹‹Forces armées››) Civil (selon le titre), Monsieur/Madame/Mademoiselle (prénom et nom) Appel - Monsieur/Madame/Mademoiselle,
Salutation - Je vous prie d'agréer, Monsieur/Madame/ Mademoiselle, l'expression de mes sentiments les meilleurs.
Conversation - ‹‹Monsieur/Madame/Mademoiselle›› Remarque: Les initiales ‹‹A. de C.›› sont autorisées pour les aides de camp du Governeur général et des lieutenants-gouverneurs.

NATIVE CITIZENS/AUTOCHTONES:

Indian Chiefs:

Chief (full name), Chief of (name), Address
Salutation - Chief (name):
Final Salutation - Yours sincerely,
In Conversation - "Chief (name)"

Chefs indiens:

Chef (prénom et nom), Chef de (nom), Adresse Appel - Chef,
Salutation - Je vous prie d'agréer, Chef, l'expression de mes sentiments les meilleurs.
Conversation - ‹‹Chef››

Band Councillors:

Mr./Mrs./Ms./Miss (full name):
Salutation - Mr./Mrs./Ms./Miss (name):
Final Salutation - Yours sincerely,
In Conversation - "Mr./Mrs./Ms./Miss (name)"

Conseillers de bandes:

Monsieur/Madame/Mademoiselle (prénom et nom), Adresse Appel - Monsieur/Madame/Mademoiselle,
Salutation - Je vous prie d'agréer, Monsieur/Madame/ Mademoiselle, l'expression de mes sentiments les meilleurs.
Conversation - ‹‹Monsieur/Madame/Mademoiselle››

Abbreviations

Indicating Academic, Ecclesiastical and other Degrees, membership in Societies and Institutions, military ranks, etc., appearing in the Canadian Almanac and Directory. For other lists of abbreviations, see Index.

AACCA .... Associate of Association of Certified Accountants & Corporate Accountants (British)
AACI .... Accredited Appraiser Canadian Institute
AAE .... Associate of Accountants' & Executives' Corp. of Canada
AAGO .... — of the American Guild of Organists
AASA............... — of the Alberta Society of Artists
AB .... Bachelor of Arts, American (Artium Baccalaureus)
AC .... "Advanced Certification" Canadian Association of Medical Radiation Technologists
ACA................ Associate of Institute of Chartered Accountants (Eng.)
ACAM .... Associate Certified Administrative Manager
ACCO .... — of Canadian College of Organists
AccSCRP............ — of Canadian Public Relations Society Inc.
ACD................ Archaeologiae Christianae Doctor
ACGI .... Associate of the City & Guilds of London Institute
ACIC .... — of Canadian Institute of Chemistry
ACInstM............. — of the Institute of Marketing
ACIS .... — of Chartered Institute of Secretaries (British)
ACSM .... — of Cambourne School of Mines
Adm. .... Admiral
Adm. A. Pl.Fin......... Administrateur agréé en planification financière
AFC .... Accredited Financial Counsellor
AFRAS (AFRAeS) ..... Fellow of the Royal Aeronautical Society
Ag de l'U (Paris)....... Honorary Professor of University of Paris (Agrégé de l'Université Paris)
Ag. de Phil. .... Professor of Philosophy (Agrégé en Philosophie Louvain)
AGSM .... Associate of the Guildhall School of Music (British)
AIC................. — of the Institute of Chemistry (British)
AICB .... Associate of the Institute of Canadian Bankers
AIIC .... — of the Insurance Institute of Canada
AKC................ — of King's College (London)
ALCM............... — of London (Canada) Conservatory of Music
ALS .... Commissioned Alberta Land Surveyor
AM................. Master of Arts (Artium Magister)
AMEIC.............. Associate Member of the Engineering Institute of Canada
AMICE.............. — Member of the Institution of Civil Engineers (British)
AMIEE .... — Member of the Institute of Electrical Engineers
AMIMechE........... — Member of the Institution of Mechanical Engineers (British)
A.Mus............... — of Music
APA .... — Member of the Institute of Accredited Public Accountants (British)
APHA............... — Member of the Public Health Association (British)
APR................ Accredited Member of the Canadian Public Relations Society
ARA................ Associate of the Royal Academy (honorary)
ARCD............... — of the Royal College of Dancing
ARCM .... — of the Royal College of Music
ARCO .... — of the Royal College of Organists (Canadian)
ARCS (A.R.C.Sc.) ..... — of the Royal College of Science
ARCT............... — of the Royal Conservatory of Music of Toronto
ARCVS .... — of the Royal College of Veterinary Surgeons
ARDIO.............. — of Registered Interior Designers of Ontario
ARDS............... — of the Royal Drawing Society (London, Eng.)
ARIBA .... — of the Royal Institute of British Architects
ARIC .... — of the Royal Institute of Chemistry
ARSH............... — of the Royal Society of Health
ARSM .... — of the Royal School of Mines
ARSM .... — of the Royal School of Music
AScT .... Applied Science Technologist
Assoc. Inst. M.M....... Associate of the Institute of Mining and Metallurgy (British)
ATCL .... — of Trinity College, London (Eng.)
ATCM............... — of the Toronto Conservatory of Music
A.Th. .... — in Theology
BA .... Bachelor of Arts
BAA .... — of Applied Arts
B.Acc. .... — of Accountancy
B.Adm. (B.Admin.) ..... — of Administration
B.Adm.Pub. .... — Baccalauréat spécialisé en administration publique
BAeE (BAeroE) .... Bachelor of Aeronautical Engineering
BAI................. — of Engineering (U. of Dublin)
BALS .... — of Arts in Library Science
BAO................ — of Obstetrics
B.Arch............... — in Architecture
BAS (B.A.Sc.) .... — of Applied Science
BASM............... — of Arts, Master of Science
B.A.Theo............. — of Arts in Theology
BBA................ — of Business Administration
BCD .... Bachelier en Chirurgie Dentale
BCE .... Bachelor of Civil Engineering
B.Ch. (ChB).......... — in Surgery (British)
BChE............... — in Chemical Engineering (American)
BCL .... — of Civil Law (or Canon Law)
B.Com. (B. Comm.) .... — of Commerce
B.Comp.Sc. .... — of Computer Science
BD .... — of Divinity
BDC .... Bachelier en droit canonique
B.Des. .... Bachelor of Design
BDS................ — of Dental Surgery (British)
BE (B.Eng.) .... — of Engineering
B.Ed. (BEAD)......... — of Education
BEDS............... — of Environmental Design Studies
BEE .... — of Electrical Engineering (American)
B. en Ph. .... Bachelier en Philosophie
B. en Sc. Com......... — en Science Commerciale
BES .... Bachelor of Environmental Sciences (or Studies)
B ès A .... Bachelier ès Arts
B ès L............... — ès Lettres
B. ès Sc. .... — ès Science
B. ès Sc. App. .... — ès Science Appliquée
BF .... Bachelor of Forestry (American)
BFA .... — of Fine Arts
B.Gen............... Brigadier-General
BHE (B.H.Ec.) .... Bachelor of Home Economics
B.H.Sc............... — of Household Science
BJ .... — of Journalism
BJC .... — in Canon Law
BL .... — in Literature (or of Laws)
BLA .... — of Landscape Architecture
B.Litt................ — of Literature (American & British)
BLS .... — of Library Science
BM .... — of Medicine
B.Mus............... — of Music
BMV .... Bachelier en Médecine Vetérinaire
BN .... Bachelor of Nursing
B.N.Sc............... — of Nursing Science
B. Paed. (Péd.) .... — of Pedagogy
BPA .... — of Public Administration
BPE .... — of Physical Education
B.Ph. (B.Phil.) .... — of Philosophy
BPHE................ — of Physical & Health Education
B.Ps. .... Baccalauréat en Psychologie
Br. .... Brother
BS .... Bachelor of Science (or of Surgery) (American)
BSA .... — of Science in Agriculture (or in Accounting, or in Administration)
B.Sc. .... — of Science
BScA .... Bachelier ès science appliquées
BScB .... — en Bibliothéconomie
B.Sc.(CE) .... Bachelor of Science in Civil Engineering
B.Sc.Com. .... — of Commercial Science
B.Sc.Dom. .... Baccalauréat en Sciences Domestiques
BScF (BSF) .... Bachelor of Science in Forestry
BScFE .... — of Science in Forestry Engineering
BScH .... Bachelier en Sciences Hospitalières
BScN .... Bachelor of Science in Nursing
B.Sc.(Nurs.) .... — of Science in Nursing
B.Sc.(Occ.Ther.) ...... — of Science in Occupational Therapy
B.Sc.(OT)............ — of Science in Occupational Therapy
B.Sc.Phm.(BSP) ...... — of Science in Pharmacy
B.Sc.Soc............. — of Social Science
BSCE............... — of Science in Civil Engineering
B.S.Ed.............. — of Science in Education
BSEE............... — of Science in Electrical Engineering
BSN .... — of Science in Nursing
BSS .... — of Social Sciences
BSW................ — of Social Work (or Welfare)
B.Tech............... — of Technology
B.Th. .... — of Theology
BTS .... — of Technological Science (Edinburgh)
B.V.Sc............... — of Veterinary Science
CA .... Chartered Accountant
C. Adm., F.P. .... Chartered Administrator in Financial Planning
CAAP .... Certified Advertising Agency Practitioner
CAE................ — Association Executive
CAE/c.a.é. .... Chartered Account Executive
CAM .... Certified Administrative Manager
CAP .... Certificat d'Aptitude Pedagogique
Capt. (or Capt.(N)) .... Captain (or Captain (Naval))
CBE .... Commander, Order of the British Empire
CBV .... Chartered Business Valuator

CC . . . . . . Chartered Cartographer
CC . . . . . . Companion, Order of Canada
CD . . . . . . Canadian Forces Decoration
Cdr. . . . . . . Commander
CE . . . . . . Civil Engineer
CEA . . . . . . Certified Environmental Administrator
CEA . . . . . . Certified Environmental Auditor
CEBS . . . . . . Certified Employee Benefit Specialist
Cer.E. . . . . . . Ceramic Engineer
Cert. Bus. Admin. . . . . . Doctor of Applied Science Diploma Business Administration
CES . . . . . . Certificat d'Études Secondaires (La Sorbonne)
CFA . . . . . . Chartered Financial Analyst
CFP . . . . . . Chartered Financial Planner
CGA . . . . . . Certified General Accountant
CHA . . . . . . Certified Housing Administrator
Chan. . . . . . . Chanoine (Canon)
Ch.E. . . . . . . Chartered Executive
CHE . . . . . . Certified Health Executive
Chem. Ing. . . . . . . Ingénieur Chimiste Diplomé (Swiss Fed. Inst. Technology)
CHFC . . . . . . Chartered Financial Consultant
CIF . . . . . . Canadian Institute of Forestry
CIM . . . . . . Certificate in Management
CIM . . . . . . Certified Industrial Manager
CIM . . . . . . Certified Investment Manager
CIS&P . . . . . . Canadian Inst. of Surveying & Photogrammetry
CLA . . . . . . Canadian Library Association
CLS . . . . . . Canada Land Surveyor
CLU . . . . . . Chartered Life Underwriter
CM . . . . . . Master in Medicine (British)
CM . . . . . . Member, Order of Canada
CMA . . . . . . Certified Management Accountant (or Canadian Medical Association or Canadian Management Association)
CMC . . . . . . Certified Management Consultant
CmdO . . . . . . Commissioned Officer
Cmdre. . . . . . . Commodore
CMM . . . . . . Certified Municipal Manager (Ontario)
CMM . . . . . . Commander, Order of Military Merit
COM . . . . . . Commander of the Order of Merit (Police Forces)
Col. . . . . . . Colonel
CPA . . . . . . Certified Public Accountant
CPC . . . . . . — Personnel Consultant
CPM . . . . . . Certificate in Personnel Management
CPPMA . . . . . . — in Public Personnel Management Association
CPPO . . . . . . Certified Public Purchasing Officer
CPP . . . . . . — Professional Purchaser
CR (c.r.) . . . . . . Conseiller de la Reine (Queen's Counsel)
CRA . . . . . . Canadian Residential Appraiser
CSC . . . . . . Canadian Securities Course
CSR . . . . . . Chartered Stenographic Reporter
CTC . . . . . . Certified Travel Counsellor
C.Tech. . . . . . . — Technician
CWO . . . . . . Chief Warrant Officer
DA . . . . . . Doctor of Arts (honorary)
DA . . . . . . — of Archaeology (Laval)
D.Arch. . . . . . . — of Architecture
D.A.Sc. . . . . . . — in Applied Sciences
DC . . . . . . — of Chiropractic
DCD . . . . . . Docteur en Chirurgie Dentale
D.Ch. . . . . . . Doctor of Surgery (British)
DChE . . . . . . — of Chemical Engineering (American)
DCL . . . . . . — of Civil Law (or Canon Law)
DD . . . . . . — of Divinity
DDC . . . . . . Doctorat Droit Canonique
D. de l'Un. . . . . . . — Docteur de l'Université
DDS . . . . . . Doctor of Dental Surgery (British)
DDT . . . . . . — of Drugless Therapy
D.Ed. . . . . . . — of Education
D.Eng. . . . . . . — of Engineering
D. en Méd. Vet. . . . . . . Docteur en Médecine Vetérinaire
D. en Ph. . . . . . . — en Philosophie
D ès L . . . . . . — ès Lettres (Doctor of Letters)
D. ès Sc. App. . . . . . . Doctor of Applied Science
DF . . . . . . — of Forestry (American)
DFA . . . . . . — of Fine Arts (often honorary)
D.F.Sc. . . . . . . — of Financial Science (Laval)
DIC . . . . . . Diploma of Membership of Imperial College of Science & Technology (British)
Dip. Bact. . . . . . . — in Bacteriology
Dip d'É . . . . . . Diplome d'Études
Dip de l'U (P) . . . . . . Diploma of the U. of Paris
Dip. d'É. Sup. or DipES . . Diplome d'Études Supérieures, Paris
Dip. Ing. . . . . . . Diploma in Engineering
Dipl. Bus. Admin. . . . . . Diploma Business Administration
D.Jour . . . . . . Doctor of Journalism
D. Lit. (D. Litt.) . . . . . . — of Letters (or Literature)
DLO . . . . . . Diploma in Laryngology & Otology
DLS . . . . . . Dominion Land Surveyor (or Doctor of Library Science)
DM . . . . . . Doctorat Médecine
DMD . . . . . . Doctor of Dental Medicine
D.Ms. . . . . . . — in Missionology
D.Mus. . . . . . . Doctorat en Musique
DMR (D or T) . . . . . . Diploma in Medical Radiology (Royal Coll. of Surgeons, London)
DMT . . . . . . — in Tropical Medicine
DMT & H (Eng.) . . . . . . — in Tropical Medicine & Hygiene
D.N.S (D.N.Sc.) . . . . . . Doctor of Nursing Science
DO . . . . . . — of Osteopathy
Doct.Arch. . . . . . . — of Christian Archaeology (Pontifical Institute, Rome)
D.Paed. (Péd.) . . . . . . — of Paedagogy
DPE . . . . . . Diploma in Physical Education
D.Ph. (D.Phil. or PhD) . . Doctor of Philosophy
D.P.Ec. . . . . . . — of Political Economy
DPH . . . . . . — (or Diploma) in Public Health
D.Ps. (D.Psy.) . . . . . . — of Psychologie
D.P.Sc. . . . . . . — of Political Science
D.Psych. . . . . . . — (or Diploma) in Psychiatry
DPT . . . . . . — of Physio-Therapy
Dr. . . . . . . Doctor
DR . . . . . . Doctor of Radiology
Dr.Com.Sc. . . . . . . — of Commercial Science
Dr de l'U (P) . . . . . . — of the U. of Paris
Dr. ès Lettres . . . . . . — of Letters (History of Literature)
Dr. jur. . . . . . . — of Law (Dr. Juris)
Dr. rer. pol. . . . . . . — of Political Economy (Dr. Rerum Politicarum) (Docteur des Sciences Politiques)
DSA (DScA) . . . . . . Docteur ès science appliqués
D.Sc. . . . . . . Doctor of Science
D.Sc.Mil. . . . . . . — of Military Science
DSL . . . . . . — of Sacred Letters
D.Sc.Com. . . . . . . — of Commercial Science
D.Sc.Fin. . . . . . . — of Financial Science
D.Sc.Nat. . . . . . . — in Natural Science
D.Sc.Soc. . . . . . . — of Social Science
D.Th. . . . . . . — of Theology
DVM (DMV) . . . . . . — of Veterinary Medicine
D.V.Sc. . . . . . . — of Veterinary Science
E.C.E. . . . . . . Early Childhood Educator
EdD . . . . . . Doctor of Education
EdM . . . . . . Master of Education (Harvard)
EE . . . . . . Electrical Engineer
EM . . . . . . Mining Engineer
ETCM . . . . . . Graduate of Eastern Townships Conservatory of Music
FAAO . . . . . . Fellow of the American Academy of Optometry
F.A.A.O.Dip. . . . . . . Diplomatic Fellow of the American Academy of Optometry
FACD . . . . . . Fellow of the American College of Dentists
FACO . . . . . . — of the American College of Organists
FACP . . . . . . — of the American College of Physicians
FACR . . . . . . — of the American College of Radiology
FACS . . . . . . — of the American College of Surgeons
FAE . . . . . . — of the Accountants' & Executives' Corp. of Canada
FAGS . . . . . . — of the American Geographical Society
FAIA . . . . . . — of the American Institute of Actuaries
. . . . . . — of the American Institute of Architects
FAIA . . . . . . Association of International Accountants
FAOU . . . . . . Fellow of the American Ornithologists Union
FAPHA . . . . . . — of the American Public Health Association
FAPS . . . . . . — of the American Physical Society
FAS . . . . . . — of the Actuarial Society
FBA . . . . . . — of the British Academy (honorary)
FBOA . . . . . . — of British Association of Optometrists
FCA . . . . . . — of the Institute of Chartered Accountants (British)
FCAM . . . . . . — of the Certified Administrative Manager
FCBA . . . . . . — of Canadian Bankers' Association
FCCA . . . . . . — of the Association of Certified Accountants
FCCO . . . . . . — of the Canadian College of Organists
FCCT . . . . . . — of the Canadian College of Teachers
FCCUI . . . . . . — of the Canadian Credit Union Institute
FCGI . . . . . . — of the City & Guilds of London Institute
FCI . . . . . . — of the Canadian Credit Institute
FCIC . . . . . . — of the Chemical Institute of Canada
FCII . . . . . . — of the Chartered Insurance Institute (British)

FCIS .... — of the Chartered Institute of Secretaries (British)
FCOG .... — of the College of Obstetricians & Gynaecologists (British)
FCAMRT .... — of Canadian Association of Medical Radiation Technologists
FCIA .... — of the Canadian Institute of Actuaries
FCMA .... — of the Society of Management Accountants of Canada
FCSI .... — of the Canadian Securities Institute
FCTC .... — of the Canadian Institute of Travel Counsellors
FCUIC .... — of the Credit Union Institute of Canada
FE .... Forest Engineer
FEIC .... Fellow of the Engineering Institute of Canada
FFA .... — of the Faculty of Actuaries (Scotland)
FFR .... — of the Faculty of Radiologists (British)
FGS .... — of the Geological Society (British)
FGSA .... — of the Geological Society of America
FIA .... — of the Institute of Actuaries (British)
FIC .... — of the Institute of Chemistry
FICB .... — of the Institute of Canadian Bankers
FICE .... — of the Institution of Civil Engineers
FIEE .... — of the Institution of Electrical Engineers
FIIC .... — of the Insurance Institute of Canada
FIL .... — of the Institute of Linguists (British)
FLA .... — of the Library Association (England)
FMA .... Financial Management Advisor
FMSA .... — of the Mineralogical Society of America
Fr. .... Father
FRAI .... Fellow of the Royal Anthropological Institute
FRAIC .... — of the Royal Architectural Institute of Canada
FRAM .... — of the Royal Academy of Music
FRAS .... — of the Royal Astronomical Society
FRCCO .... — of the Royal Canadian College of Organists
FRCM .... — of the Royal College of Music
FRCO .... — of the Royal College of Organists
FRCOG .... — of the Royal College of Obstetricians & Gynaecologists
FRCP .... — of the Royal College of Physicians of London
FRCP(C) .... — of the Royal College of Physicians of Canada
FRCP(E) .... — of the Royal College of Physicians of Edinburgh
FRCP(I) .... — of the Royal College of Physicians of Ireland
FRCP(Glas) .... — of the Royal College of Physicians of Glasgow
FRCS .... — of the Royal College of Surgeons of England
FRCS(C) .... — of the Royal College of Surgeons of Canada
FRCS(E) .... — of the Royal College of Surgeons of Edinburgh
FRCS(I) .... — of the Royal College of Surgeons of Ireland
FRCS(Glas) .... — of the Royal College of Surgeons of Glasgow
FRGS .... — of the Royal Geographical Society
FRHistS .... — of the Royal Historical Society
FRHortS .... — of the Royal Horticultural Society
FRIBA .... — of the Royal Institute of British Architects
FRIC .... — of the Royal Institute of Chemistry
FRICS .... — of the Royal Institution of Chartered Surveyors
FRMCM .... — of Royal Manchester College of Music
FRMS (FRMetS) ...... — of the Royal Meteorological Society
FRS .... — of the Royal Society (honorary)
FRSA .... — of the Royal Society of Arts
FRSC .... — of the Royal Society of Canada
FRSE .... — of the Royal Society of Edinburgh
FRSH .... — of the Royal Society of Health
FRSL .... — of the Royal Society of Literature
FSA .... — of the Society of Actuaries (or of Antiquaries) (honorary)
FSMAC .... — of the Society of Management Accountants of Canada
FSS .... — of the Royal Statistical Society
FTCL .... — of Trinity College of Music (London)
FZS .... — of the Zoological Society (British)
Gen. .... General
GJ .... Graduate Jeweller
HARCVS .... Honorary Associate of Royal College of Veterinary Surgeons
IA .... Investment Advisor
IC .... Investment Counsellor
IngETP .... Diplome de l'École Spéciale des Travaux Publiques
JCB .... Bachelor of Canon Law
JCD .... Doctor of Canon Law (or of Civil Law)
JCL .... Licentiate in Canon Law (Juris Canonici Licentiatus)
JD .... Doctor of Jurisprudence
JDS .... — of Jurisdical Science
Jr. .... Junior
JUL .... Licentiate of Law in Utroque (both Civil & Canon Law)
JurM .... Master of Jurisprudence
Jur. utr. Dr. .... Juris utriusque doctor, Equiv. to LL.D.
LAB .... Licentiate of the Assoc. Bd. of Royal Schools of Music (London, Eng.)
L.Cdr. .... Lieutenant-Commander
LCL .... Licentiate in Canon Law
LCMI .... — of the Cost & Management Institute
L.Col. .... Lieutenant-Colonel
LDC .... Licencié ès Droit Canonique
LDS .... Licentiate in Dental Surgery (British)
L ès L .... Licencié ès Lettres
L. ès Sc. .... — ès Sciences
L.Gen. .... Lieutenant-General
LGSM .... Licentiate of the Guildhall School of Music & Drama (London, Eng.)
LittD .... Doctor of Letters (or Literature)
LittL .... Licence ès Lettres
Litt.M. .... Master of Letters (or Literature)
LJC .... Licentiatus Juris Canonici
LL .... License in Civil Law
LLB .... Bachelor of Laws (Legum Baccalaureus)
LLD .... Doctor of Laws (usually honorary)
LLL .... Licence en droit
LLM .... Master of Law
L. Mus. .... Licentiate in Music
LMUS .... — in Music of the Univ. of Saskatchewan
L Mus TCL .... — in General Musicianship of Trinity College, London
L.Péd. .... Licence en Pédagogie
L.Ph. .... — en Philosophie
L.Psych. .... Licencié en Psychologie
LRAM .... Licentiate of the Royal Academy of Music (London)
LRCM .... — of the Royal College of Music (London)
LRCP .... — of the Royal College of Physicians
LRCS .... — of the Royal College of Surgeons
LRCT .... — of the Royal Conservatory of Toronto
LRE .... — in Religious Education
LRSM .... — of the Royal Schools of Music (London)
LS .... Land Surveyor
LSA .... Licentiate in Agricultural Science
L.Sc.Com. .... — in Commercial Science
LScO .... Licence en optométrie
L.S.Sc. .... Licentiate in Sacred Scriptures
L.Sc.Soc. .... Licence in Social Science
LST .... Licentiate in Sacred Theology
Lt. (or Lt(N)) .... Lieutenant (or Lieutenant (Naval))
LTCL .... Licentiate of Trinity College of Music (London)
LTCM .... — of the Toronto Conservatory of Music
L.Th .... Licentiate in Theology
M. .... Monsieur
MA .... Master of Arts
M.Acc. .... — of Accountancy
MACF .... Membre de l'Académie canadiennefrançaise
MAeE .... Master of Aeronautical Engineering
MAIEE .... Member of American Institute of Electrical Engineers
MAIME .... — of American Institute of Mining Engineers
Maj. .... Major
MALS .... Master of Arts in Library Science
MAP .... Maîtrise en administration publique
M.Arch. .... Master of Architecture
MAS .... — of Archival Studies
M.A.Sc. (MAS) .... — of Applied Science
MASCE .... Member of the American Society of Civil Engineers
MASME .... — of the American Society of Mechanical Engineers
MAust IM .... — of the Australian Institute of Mining & Metallurgy
MB .... Bachelor of Medicine (British)
MBA .... Master in Business Administration
MCE .... — of Civil Engineering
M.Ch. (ChM) .... — of Surgery (British)
MChE .... — of Chemical Engineering (American)
MCI .... Member of the Credit Institute
MCIC .... — of the Chemical Institute of Canada
MCIF .... — of the Canadian Institute of Forestry
MCIM .... — of the Canadian Institute of Mining
MCIMM .... — of the Canadian Institute of Mining & Metallurgy
MCInstM .... — of the Canadian Institute of Marketing
MCL .... Master of Civil Law
M.Com. .... — of Commerce
M.Comp. .... — of Canon Law
M.Comp.Sc. .... — of Computer Science
MD .... Doctor of Medicine
MDC .... Master of Canon Law
MDCM .... Doctor of Medicine & Master of Surgery
M.Des. .... Master of Design
M.Div. .... — of Divinity
MDS .... — of Dental Surgery (British)
MDV .... Doctor of Veterinary Medicine
Me .... Maître

ME .... Master of Mechanical Engineering
M.Ed. (M.A.Ed.) .... — of Education
MEDS .... — of Environmental Design Studies
MEE .... — of Electrical Engineering (American)
MEIC .... Member of the Engineering Institute of Canada
M.Eng. .... Master of Engineering
MF .... — of Forestry
MFA .... — of Fine Arts
M.Gen. .... Major-General
Mgr. .... Monsignor (or Manager or Monseigneur)
MHA .... Master of Health (or Hospital) Administration
MHE (M.H.Ec.) .... — of Home Economics
MICE .... Member of the Institution of Civil Engineers (British)
MICIA .... — of Industrial, Commercial & Institutional Accountants
MIEE .... — of the Institution of Electrical Engineers (British)
MIMM .... — of the Institute of Mining & Metallurgy (British)
MINA .... — of the Institute of Naval Architects
MIRE .... — of the Institute of Radio Engineers
M.I.St. .... Master of Information Studies
MJ .... — of Journalism
M.Litt. .... — of Letters (or Literature)
MLIS .... — of Library & Information Science
MLS .... — of Library Science (or Licentiate in Medieval Studies)
MM (M.Mus.) .... — of Music
MMM .... Member, Order of Military Merit
MOM .... Member of the Order of Merit (Police Forces)
MN (M.Nurs.) .... Master of Nursing
MP .... — of Planning
MP .... Member of Parliament
MPE .... Master of Physical Education
M.Ph. (M.Phil.) .... — of Philosophy
MPM .... — of Pest Management
MPP .... Member of Provincial Parliament
M.Ps. (M.Psy.) .... Master of Psychology
MRAIC .... Member of the Royal Architectural Institute of Canada
MRCOG .... — of the Royal College of Obstetricians & Gynaecologists
MRCP .... — of the Royal College of Physicians
MRCP(E) .... — of the Royal College of Physicians of Edinburgh
MRCP(I) .... — of the Royal College of Physicians of Ireland
MRCP(Glas) .... — of the Royal College of Physicians of Glasgow
MRCS .... — of the Royal College of Surgeons
MRCS(E) .... — of the Royal College of Surgeons of Edinburgh
MRCVS .... — of the Royal College of Veterinary Surgeons
MRM .... Master of Resource Management
MRSC .... Member of the Royal Society of Canada
MRSH .... — of the Royal Society of Health
MRST .... — of the Royal Society of Teachers
MS .... Master of Surgery (British)
MSA .... — of Science in Agriculture
M.Sc. .... — of Science
MScA .... — of Applied Science
MSCE .... — of Science in Civil Engineering
MScF .... — of Science in Forestry
M.Sc.(Med.) .... — of Science in Medicine
MScN (MSN) .... — of Science in Nursing
M.Sc.Phm. .... — of Science in Pharmacy
M.Sc.Soc. .... — in Social Sciences
M.S.Ed. .... — of Science in Education
M.S.Litt. .... — of Sacred Letters
MSPE .... McGill School of Physical Education
MSRC .... Membre Société Royale du Canada
MSS .... Master of Social Science
MSW .... — of Social Work
MTCI .... Member of Trust Companies Institute
M.U.Dr. .... Medecinae Universae Doctor (Prague) (Dentistry & Medicine)
MUP .... Master of Planning
MURP .... — of Urban & Rural Planning
Mus. Bac. (Mus.B.) .... Bachelor of Music
Mus. Doc. (Mus.D.) .... Doctor of Music
Mus. G. Paed. .... Musicae Graduatus Paedagogus (Graduate Teacher in Music)
MusM .... Master of Music
MV .... Médécin Vétérinaire
M.V.Sc. .... Master of Veterinary Science
NDA .... National Diploma in Agriculture (Royal Ag. Soc. of Engineering)
NDD .... National Diploma in Dairying (Scotland)
NP .... Notary Public
OA .... Officier d'Académie (France)
OC .... Order of Canada
OD .... Doctor of Optometry
OIP .... Officier de l'Instruction Publique
OLS .... Ontario Land Surveyor
OMM .... Officer, Order of Military Merit
OOM .... Officer of the Order of Merit (Police Forces)
OSA .... Ontario Society of Artists
PC .... Privy Councillor
PD .... Doctor of Parapsychology
PE .... Professional Engineer
P.Eng. .... Registered Professional Engineer
PFC .... Planificateur Financier Certifié
PFP .... Personal Financial Planner
PhB .... Bachelor of Philosophy
PhC .... Philosopher of Chiropractic
PhD .... Doctor of Philosophy
PhTD .... Physical Therapy Doctor
PhL .... Licentiate in Philosophy
PLS .... Professional Legal Secretary
P.Mgr. .... — Manager
PP .... — Purchaser
PPB .... — Public Buyer
Prof. .... Professor
PTIC .... Patent & Trade Mark Institute of Canada
QAA .... Qualified Administrative Assistant
QC .... Queen's Counsel
QLS .... Québec Land Surveyor
RA .... Royal Academy (honorary)
R.Adm. .... Rear-Admiral
RAM .... Royal Academy of Music (Budapest)
RAS .... Royal Aeronautical Society
RBA .... Royal Society of British Artists
RCA .... Royal Canadian Academy of Arts
RCAM .... Royal College & Academy of Music (Budapest)
RCM .... Royal Conservatory of Music (Leipzig)
RE .... Royal Engineers
REBC .... Registered Employee Benefits Consultant
Rev. .... Reverend
RFP .... Registered Financial Planner
RHU .... Registered Health Underwriter
RMS .... Royal Society of Miniature Painters
RMT .... Registered Music Teacher
RN .... — Nurse
ROI .... Royal Institute of Oil Painters
RP .... Member of the Royal Society of Portrait Painters
RP .... Révérend Père (Reverend Father)
RPA .... Registered Professional Accountant
R.P.Bio. .... — Professional Biologist
R.P.Dt. .... — Professional Dietitian
RPF .... — Professional Forester
RRL .... — Record Librarian
RSH .... Royal Society of Health
RSW .... Registered Specification Writer
RT .... — Technician of the Cdn. Association of Medical Radiation Technologists
SC .... Senior Counsel (Eire) equivalent of Q.C.
ScD .... Doctorat ès Sciences
ScL .... Licence ès Sciences
Sc Soc B .... Bachelier Science Sociale
Sc Soc D .... Doctor of Social Science
Sc Soc L .... License in Social Science
SFC .... Specialist in Financial Counselling
SJ .... Society of Jesus
SLS .... Saskatchewan Land Surveyor
S.Lt. .... Sub-Lieutenant
SM .... Master of Science
Sr. .... Senior
Sr. .... Sister
SSB .... Bachelier en Science Sacrée
SSC .... Sculptors' Society of Canada
SSL .... Licentiate in Sacred Scripture
STB (SThB) .... Bachelor of Sacred Theology
STD (SThD) .... Doctor of Sacred Theology
STL (SThL) .... Sacrae Theologiae Licentiatus (Licentiate in Sacred Theology)
STM .... Master of Sacred Theology
TCL .... Trinity College, London
TMMG .... Teacher, Massage & Medical Gymnastics
ThD .... Doctor of Theology
V.Adm. .... Vice-Admiral
VG .... Vicar-General
VS .... Veterinary Surgeon

Business & Shipping Abbreviations

As shipping terms vary in different countries, insurance or shipping agents should be consulted. For other lists of abbreviations, academic, etc., see Index.

a/c . . . . Account
Ad val. . . . . Ad valorem
avoir . . . . Avoirdupois
bbl. . . . . Barrel
B/L. . . . . Bill of Lading
b.m. . . . . Board Measure
B.O. . . . . Buyer's Option
B/P. . . . . Bills Payable
B/R. . . . . Bills Receivable
B/S. . . . . Bill of Sale
c. . . . . Hundred
C or Cent. . . . . . Centigrade
cf. . . . . Compare
C. and F. . . . . . . Cost & Freight
Cie . . . . Compagnie
c.i.f. . . . . Cost insurance & freight
C.L. . . . . Car Load (of freight)
Co. . . . . Company
C.O.D. . . . . Cash on Delivery
C. of F. . . . . Cost of Freight
Cr. . . . . Credit
C.W.O. . . . . Cash with Order
Cwt. . . . . Hundredweight
D/A. . . . . Documents Attached, also Deposit Account
Dis. (Disct.) . . . . Discount
Dl. (or Tl.) . . . . . . Double (or triple) first class
D.O.A. . . . . Deliver Documents on Acceptance of Draft
D.O.P. . . . . Deliver Documents on Payment of Draft
Dr. . . . . Debit
D.V. . . . . God willing (Deo volente)
e.g. . . . . For example (exempli gratia)
E.&.O.E. . . . . Errors & omissions excepted
Est. Wt. . . . . Estimated Weight
et seq. . . . . And the following (et sequens)
Ex. Div. . . . . Without Dividend
Ex-Warehouse . . Purchaser pays carriage charges & assumes risks from seller's warehouse
F. . . . . Fahrenheit
F.a.a. . . . . Free of Average (marine insurance)
F.A.S. . . . . Free Alongside (Seller assumes risks & delivers goods to alongside of steamer free of carriage charges)
F.O.B. . . . . Free on Board (Purchaser pays carriage charges & assumes risks from point specified)
F.P.A. . . . . Free of Particular Average (Insured can recover only for a total loss, subject to other conditions of the contract)
Franco. . . . . Pre-paid free of expense to point specified
G.A. . . . . General Average (All owners of cargo & vessel share in any loss arising from expense incurred to preserve ship & contents from greater loss)
gm. . . . . Grammes
gr. . . . . Grain; grains, or gross
ibid. . . . . In the same place (ibidem)
i.e. . . . . That is (id est)
Inc. . . . . Incorporated
Int. . . . . Interest
K.D. . . . . Knocked down
lb. (libra) . . . . Pound
L/C. . . . . Letter of Credit
L.C.L. . . . . Less than Car Load (of freight)
Limited; Ltd. . . . . Limited Liability (Shareholders are "limited" in liability to the amount of their subscribed stock in certain companies)
L.P. . . . . List Price
M. . . . . Thousand (Mille)
MS., MSS. . . . . . Manuscript(s)
N.E.S. (N.O.P.) . . Not Otherwise Provided For (Customs)
N.O.S. . . . . Not Otherwise Specified
N.S.F. . . . . Not Sufficient Funds (re cheques)
Nstd. . . . . Nested
O.K. . . . . Correct
op. cit. . . . . In the work quoted (opere citato)
O.R. . . . . At Owner's Risk
O.R.B. . . . . At Owner's Risk of Breakage
oz. . . . . Ounce
P.A. . . . . Particular Average (As used in Marine Insurance, means damage to the goods caused by perils insured against & named in the contract. This form is often written with a Franchise Clause, & means there will be no claim unless the loss exceeds the percentage named)
P/A. . . . . Power of Attorney
P & D. . . . . Pick Up & Deliver
pp. . . . . Pages
Pro forma . . . . . . As a Matter of Form
P.S. . . . . Postscript
q.v. . . . . Which see (quod vide)
R.R. . . . . Rural Route (Postal delivery)
S.B. . . . . Shipping Bill
s.s. . . . . Steamship
s/o . . . . Ship's Option, weight or measurement
S.U. . . . . Set Up (meaning article is complete)
T.B.L. . . . . Through Bill of Lading
Tare . . . . Weight of Container (Deducting tare from "gross weight" gives "net weight")
Ton . . . . 2,000 (short ton) or 2,240 (long ton) lbs. avoirdupois. A cubic ton in marine freight = 40 cubic feet
Ton wt/M. . . . . . . Ton, weight or measurement (ship's option)
vide . . . . See
viz . . . . Namely; to wit (videlicet)

Border Services, Customs Regulations for Canadians Returning from Abroad

Note: The Canada Border Services Agency (CBSA) operates as an agency under the Public Safety and Emergency Preparedness (PSEP) portfolio, and its mission is to ensure the security and prosperity of Canada by managing the access of people and goods to and from Canada. With a workforce of approximately 12,000 public servants, the Canada Border Services Agency (CBSA) provides services at 1,200 points across Canada and over 30 locations abroad. At over 100 land border crossings and nine international airports, it operates on a 24/7 basis. It administers more than 90 acts and regulations on behalf of other Government of Canada departments and agencies, and international agreements.

It integrates several key functions previously spread among three organizations: the Customs program from the Canada Customs Revenue Agency, the Intelligence, Interdiction and Enforcement program from Citizenship and Immigration Canada, and the Import Inspection at Ports of Entry program from the Canadian Food Inspection Agency.

If you have information about suspicious cross-border activity, please call the CBSA Border Watch tollfree line at 1-888-502-9060.

Canadians returning to Canada may bring any amount of goods into the country subject to duties and any provincial or territorial assessments, with the exception of restricted items. This applies even if you do not qualify for a personal exemption. The term duty can include Goods and Services. Duties represent duty, excise taxes and the Goods & Services Tax (GST) or Harmonized Sales Tax (HST). In addition to duties, provincial and territorial taxes (PST) are assessed if an agreement has been signed between the federal government and a province or territory whereby the federal government collects the PST, levies and fees on their behalf.

Goods included in personal exemptions must be for personal or household use, souvenirs or gifts. Goods brought in for commercial use, or on behalf of another person do not qualify and are subject to full duties.

On your return to Canada, you must declare to the Canada Border Services Agency (CBSA) all goods acquired (purchases, gifts, awards, prizes, and purchases made at Canadian or foreign duty-free shops and still in your possession) and repairs or modifications you made to your vehicle, vessel or aircraft while outside Canada.

Personal Exemptions

To qualify for personal exemptions you must be:

- Canadian resident returning from a trip abroad;
- former resident of Canada returning to live in Canada; or
- temporary resident of Canada.

Children and infants qualify for personal exemptions as long as the goods are for the use of the child or infant. The parent or guardian makes the customs declaration for the child.

Personal exemptions are applicable after the following minimum absences:

1. After an absence of 24 hours but less than 48 hours: up to a value of $50 (Canadian) in total (with the exception of tobacco products and alcoholic beverages) any number of times a year. If the value of the goods exceeds $50, you pay duties and PST on the full value (exemption cannot be claimed). The goods must accompany you on your return to Canada.

2. After an absence of 48 hours but less than seven days: up to $400 (Canadian) in total any number of times in a year. The goods must accompany you on your return to Canada.

3. After an absence of seven days or more: up to $750 (Canadian) any number of times in a year. You may have to make a written declaration. Goods you claim under this exemption may follow you by mail or other means, with the exception of alcoholic beverages and tobacco products. You require a Form E24, Personal Exemption Customs Declaration, which is to be completed at the time of arrival and can be obtained from a customs officer. To claim your goods when they arrive, present your copy of the E24 to the CBSA for clearance. Goods must be claimed within 40 days of their arrival in Canada; duties and taxes are then payable, along with a Canada Post Corporation processing fee. You may pay the duties and then apply to the CBSA for a refund (if the personal exemption applies) or refuse delivery; following a review that determines if the goods are eligible for free importation, the goods will be released to you without an assessment.

Persons residing outside Canada for part of the year are considered to be residents of Canada and are entitled to the above personal exemptions.

Exemptions cannot be transferred to another person or combined with another person's personal exemption. You cannot combine a 24-hour ($50) or 48- hour ($400) or the seven-day ($750) exemption when claiming an exemption, nor can you carry over an unused portion of an exemption for another period of absence.

Tobacco & Alcohol

Tobacco products and alcoholic beverages must accompany you in your hand or checked luggage and may be included in the 48-hour ($400) or the seven-day ($750) exemptions, but not in the 24-hour ($50) exemption. You must meet the age requirements set by the province or territory where you enter Canada. In addition the following conditions apply:

1. You may bring in up to 200 cigarettes, 50 cigars or cigarillos, 200 tobacco sticks **and** 200 grams of manufactured tobacco. Duties must be paid on anything above this allowance, plus any applicable provincial or territorial limits or assessments.

If you include cigarettes, tobacco sticks, or manufactured tobacco in your personal allowance, only a partial exemption will apply. You will have to pay a special duty on these products **unless** they are marked "CANADA DUTY-PAID — DROIT ACQUITTÉ." You will find Canadian-made products sold at a duty-free shop marked this way. You can speed up your clearance by having your tobacco products available for inspection when you arrive.

2. You may include up to 1.5 litres of wine, or 1.14 litres (40 ounces) of liquor, or a total of 1.14 litres (40 ounces), or 24 x 335 ml (12-ounce) cans or bottles (8.5 litres) of beer or ale. Wine coolers are classified as wine; beer coolers are classified as beer. Beer or wine that contains 0.5% alcohol by volume or less is not classified as an alcoholic beverage, so no quantity limits apply. You may bring in more than this allowance of alcohol anywhere in Canada (with the exception of the Northwest Territories and Nunavut) as long as the quantities are within the limits set by the province or territory. If bringing in more than the free allowance, you must pay customs and provincial/territorial assessments. For more information, check with the appropriate provincial/ territorial liquor control agency prior to leaving Canada.

Gifts

While abroad, you may send gifts duty- and tax-free to recipients in Canada. To qualify, the gift must be valued at $60 CAN or less and cannot be an alcoholic beverage, tobacco product, or advertising material. Gifts in excess of $60 CAN require duty payment by the recipient on the excess amount. Gifts that accompany you on your return to Canada must be included in your personal exemption, while gifts you send from abroad are not included. Some conditions apply - for additional information, contact the CBSA Border Information Service (BIS) at one of the numbers listed at the end of this section.

Prizes & Awards

In most cases, you pay regular duties on prizes or awards received outside Canada. Contact the BIS line for more information.

Paying Duties

Duties may be paid by cash or travellers' cheques. Personal cheques are also acceptable (for amounts of $2,500 or less and with proper identification); VISA, American Express and MasterCard are accepted at most border services locations and Debit Cards at many locations.

For information on duty rates for particular items, contact the BIS line.

Special Duty Rate

After any trip abroad of 48 hours or longer you are entitled to a special duty rate on goods worth up to $300 more than your personal exemption of $400 or $750. The goods must accompany you. The special duty rate does not apply to tobacco or alcoholic beverages. The special duty rate for goods not eligible under NAFTA, when combined with the GST, is about 14% or 22% when combined with the HST.

NAFTA Special Duty Rate

Goods qualify for a lower U.S. duty rate under NAFTA if they are:

- for personal use; and
- marked as made in the U.S. or Canada; or
- not marked or labelled to indicate they were made anywhere other than in the U.S. or Canada.

Your goods qualify for the lower Mexican duty rate in a similar way.

If you do not qualify for a personal exemption, or if you exceed your exemption limit, you will have to pay GST or HST over and above applicable duties or taxes on the portion not eligible under your exemption. The rates vary according to the goods, their country of origin, and the country from which you are importing them.

For information on goods eligible for the special duty rate under NAFTA, contact your nearest CBSA office and ask for a copy of Memorandum D11-4-13, Rules of Origin for Casual Goods Regulations.

Regular Duty Rates

If you do not qualify for a personal exemption, or you exceed your exemption limit, you will pay GST or HST over and above all duties, taxes, and assessments that apply on the portion not eligible under your exemption. The rates vary according to the goods, their country of origin, and the country from which you are importing them. You may also have to pay provincial sales tax if you live in a province where we have an agreement to collect the tax and you return from your trip through your province.

World Trade Organization (WTO) Agreement

The duty on a wide range of products originating in non-NAFTA countries has been eliminated or will be reduced to zero within the next few years. NAFTA goods also qualify for the WTO rate, so if the rate on the goods you are importing is lower under WTO than under NAFTA, the lower rate will automatically be applied.

Value for Duty/Foreign Sales Tax

Value for duty is the amount used to calculate duty and is generally the price you paid for the item. Foreign sales tax is included in the price and forms part of the value of the item.

Some foreign governments will refund sales tax to you if you export the items you bought. If this is the case, you do not include the amount of the foreign sales tax that was or will be refunded to you.

Declaration

When returning to Canada by commercial aircraft, a Canada Border Services Agency (CBSA) declaration card is distributed for completion before arrival. The cards are also used at some locations for people arriving by train, vessel or bus. If arriving by a private vehicle (e.g., automobile), you must make an oral declaration unless you are claiming goods that preceded or will follow your arrival in Canada as part of your $750 exemption. If this is the case, ask the border services officer for Form E24, Personal Exemption Customs Declaration. You will need your copy of this form to claim your goods. Otherwise, you may have to pay regular duty on them.

CBSA officers are legally entitled to examine luggage; you are responsible for opening, unpacking and repacking the luggage. Retain receipts of purchases and repairs made to verify length of stay and value of goods or repairs. Failure to declare or a false declaration may result in the seizure of goods. Penalties range from 25 to 80% of the value of the seized goods. Vehicles used to transport unlawfully imported goods may also be seized, with a penalty imposed before the vehicle can be returned. Commodities such as alcohol and tobacco are seized and not returned.

Currency and Monetary Instruments

If you are importing or exporting monetary instruments equal to or greater than CAN$10,000 (or its equivalent in a foreign currency), whether in cash or other monetary instruments, you must report it to the CBSA when you arrive or before you leave Canada. For more information, ask for a copy of the publication called "Crossing the Border with $10,000 or More?" or select "Publications and forms" on our Web site at www.cbsa.gc.ca.

Restrictions

Firearms: Contact the Canadian Firearms Program at:(613) 993 7267, Fax: (613) 993-0260, Website: www.rcmp-grc.gc.ca/cfp-pcaf.

Replica firearms are designed or intended to resemble a firearm with near precision. They are classified as prohibited devices and you cannot import them into Canada.

Mace or pepper spray that is used for the purpose of injuring, immobilizing or otherwise incapacitating any person is considered a prohibited weapon. You cannot import it into Canada. Aerosol or similar dispensers that contain substances capable of repelling or subduing animals are not considered weapons if the label of the container specifically indicates that they are for use against animals.

Explosives, fireworks, certain types of ammunition: You require written authorization and permits. Contact Chief Inspector of Explosives Regulatory Division, Natural Resources Canada, 1431 Merivale Rd., Ottawa ON K1A 0G1, 613/948-5200.

Vehicles: Vehicles must meet the requirements of the CBSA, Transport Canada and the Canadian Food Inspection Agency before they can be imported. Transport Canada defines a vehicle as any vehicle that is capable of being driven or drawn on roads, by any means other than muscular power exclusively, but does not run exclusively on rails. It considers trailers such as recreational, camping, boat, horse and stock trailers as vehicles, as well as woodchippers, generators and any other equipment mounted on rims and tires.

CBSA import restrictions apply to most used or second- hand vehicles that are not manufactured in the current year. Transport Canada requirements apply to vehicles that are less than fifteen years old. All imported vehicles less than fifteen years old must comply with Canadian federal safety and emission standards. The person importing the vehicle is responsible for ensuring it meets the Canadian safety standards.

If you have acquired a vehicle from the United States, you must contact the Transport Canada's Registrar of Imported Vehicle (RIV) before you import your vehicle, to ensure that it is admissible for importation and can be modified to meet the Canadian standards after you import it.

Registrar of Imported Vehicles: Telephone: 1-888- 848-8240 (toll free in Canada, the United States and Mexico); (416) 626-6812 (from all other countries), Fax: 1-888-346-8235, Website: www.riv.ca.

Import restrictions apply to most used or secondhand cars, generally from countries other than the United States. Under NAFTA, restrictions do not apply to vehicles imported from the U.S., however, not all vehicles that are manufactured for sale in the U.S. can be imported because they do not meet the Transport Canada requirements; special duty rates, as outlined above, apply. Excise tax and GST continue to apply in the usual way. Under NAFTA, customs restrictions continue to apply to vehicles imported from Mexico until 2009, when you will be able to import vehicles ten years or older. The age restriction will drop every second year until the restriction is dropped altogether in 2019.

In most instances, Canadian residents are not allowed to import vehicles into Canada that have been purchased or obtained in countries other than the United States. If you have acquired a vehicle from a country other than the United States, before importing it, contact: Transport Canada, Road Safety & Motor Vehicle Regulation, Place de Ville, Tower C, 330 Sparks St., 8th Fl., Ottawa ON K1A 0N5, 613/998-8616, or 1-800-333- 0371 (toll free from Canada and the U.S.); Fax: 613/998- 4831; Website: www.tc.gc.ca.

Your vehicle may be subject to provincial or territorial sales tax; contact your provincial or territorial department of motor vehicles for information. In addition, you may need to meet some requirements in the country which the vehicle is being exported.

Import Controls: Importations of certain goods are controlled. You may need a permit to import, even for personal and household use. For information, contact: Export & Import Controls Bureau, International Trade Canada (ITCan) , Tower C, 4th Floor, 125 Sussex Drive, Ottawa ON K1A 0G2, Website: www.international. gc.ca.

Meat, dairy products, wheat, barley, and their products: Complex requirements and restrictions exist; importation of certain meat and dairy products from certain U.S. states is allowed. All meat and meat products have to be identified as products of the United States. Limits exist for amounts or dollar value in certain foodstuffs you can import for personal use; if above those limits, duty ranges from 150 to 300% and you may also require an agricultural inspection certificate. For more information, contact the CBSA BIS line.

Agricultural products: Restrictions exist on live animals and animal products, meat and poultry products, dairy products, egg and egg products, honey and fresh fruits and vegetables, seeds and grains, animal feeds, plant and plant products, forestry products, soil and fertilizers, pest control products, biological products. For information on these products, refer to the Automated Import Reference System (AIRS) on the CFIA Website at www.inspection.gc.ca or call the CBSA BIS line.

Cultural property: Antiquities or cultural objects of significance in the country of origin cannot be imported into Canada. For information, contact Movable Cultural Property, Canadian Heritage, 15 Eddy St., 3rd Fl., Gatineau, QC K1A 0M5, 819/997-7761, Fax: 613/997- 7757.

Endangered species: Canada has signed an international agreement restricting the sale, trade or movement of endangered animals, birds, reptiles, fish, insects and certain forms of plant life; the restrictions also apply to their parts or products made from their parts. Before you bring back any of these products, you should contact CITES Administrator, Canadian Wildlife Service, Environment Canada, Ottawa ON K1A 0H3, 1-800-668-6767 (toll-free number in Canada), 819/ 997-1840 (local calls and from all other countries).

Appeals

If you disagree with the amount of duty and taxes that you had to pay, please ask to speak with the superintendent on duty. A consultation can often resolve the issue quickly and without cost. If you are still not satisfied, our officers can tell you how to make a formal appeal. If you do not declare goods, or if you falsely declare them, we can seize the goods. This means that you may lose the goods permanently, or that you may have to pay a penalty to get them back.

If you do not declare tobacco products and alcoholic beverages at the time of importation, we will seize them permanently.

Depending on the type of goods and the circumstances involved, we may impose a penalty that ranges from 25% to 80% of the value of the seized goods.

In addition, the *Customs Act* provides CBSA officers with the authority to seize all vehicles that were used unlawfully to import goods. When this happens, we impose a penalty you have to pay before we return the vehicle.

If goods have been seized and you disagree with the action taken, you must notify the CBSA in writing within 90 days of the seizure date of your intention to appeal. You should send your appeal to the CBSA Office where the seizure took place. You can find more information about this process on the front of your seizure receipt form.

In addition to the activities mentioned above, designated CBSA officers may arrest for a criminal offence under the *Criminal Code* or any other Act of Parliament. This includes the offences of impaired driving, outstanding arrest warrants, stolen property, and abductions/kidnappings. If you are arrested, you may be compelled to attend court in Canada. You should note that all persons arrested in Canada are protected by, and will be treated in accordance with, the *Canadian Charter of Rights and Freedoms.*

A record of infractions is kept in the CBSA computer system. If you have an infraction record, you may have to undergo a more detailed examination on future trips.

Precautions

Carry proper identification.

Traveling with Children

Border services officers are on alert for children who need protection. Children under the age of 18 are classified as minors and are subject to the same entry requirements as any other visitor to Canada.

We will conduct a more detailed examination of minors entering Canada without proper identification or those traveling in the company of adults other than their parents or legal guardian(s). This additional scrutiny helps ensure the safety of the children.

Minors traveling alone must have proof of citizenship and a letter from both parents detailing the length of stay, providing the parents' telephone number and authorizing the person waiting for them to take care of them while they are in Canada.

If you are traveling with minors, you must carry proper identification for each child such as a birth certificate, passport, citizenship card, permanent resident card or Certificate of Indian Status.

If you are a parent traveling alone with your child, it is recommended that you have a letter of authorization from your spouse. If you are divorced or separated, you should carry with you copies of the legal custody agreements for your children. If you are traveling with minors and you are not their parent/guardian, you should have written permission from the parent/guardian authorizing the trip. The letter should include addresses and telephone numbers of where the parents or guardian can be reached and identify a person who can confirm that the children are not being abducted or taken against their will.

If you are traveling with a group of vehicles, make sure you arrive at the border in the same vehicle as your children, to avoid any confusion.

"Identification of Articles for Temporary Exportation": CBSA offices offer a free identification program for valuables; a list of your valuables (excluding jewellery) and their serial numbers on a wallet-sized form will show border services officers that the items were previously purchased in Canada or that you lawfully imported them prior to your current time abroad. In the case of jewellery, carry an appraisal of the item(s) from a gemmologist, jeweller or insurance agent, together with a signed and dated photograph and a written declaration that the items in the photograph are those described in the appraisal report. If previously imported, carry a copy of the customs receipt.

If you take any item outside Canada and modify it, it is considered to be a new item and its full value will need to be declared. Similarly, under Canadian law, any repairs or modifications to a vehicle that increase its value, improve its condition or modify it while abroad may require that you pay duties on its full value on your return to Canada. This does not apply to incidental repairs to keep the car in operational condition while abroad, although you may be required to pay duties on the repairs and parts. A special provision is available that waives duties payable in such cases. Contact the CBSA for information.

Additional Information

If you have any other questions, contact the Border Information Service (BIS) line. This is a 24-hour telephone service that automatically answers all incoming calls and provides general border services information. If you call during regular business hours (8:00 a.m. to 4:00 p.m. local time, Monday to Friday, except holidays), you can speak directly to an agent by pressing "0" at any time.

English Enquiries: 1-800-461-9999 (toll-free in Canada)
French Enquiries: 1-800-959-2036 (toll-free in Canada)
Out-of-Canada callers can reach BIS by calling:

Western Sites
English: . . . . . . 204/983-3500 (long-distance charges will apply)
French . . . . . . : 204/983-3700 (long-distance charges will apply)

Eastern Sites
English: . . . . . . 506/636-5064 (long-distance charges will apply)
French . . . . . . : 506/636-5067 (long-distance charges will apply)

Website: . . . . www.cbsa-asfc.gc.ca

Election Regulations

According to the Canada Elections Act, and subject to certain exceptions, the general rule as to the franchise of electors at a federal election is that every person is qualified as an elector if such person

(a) is of the full age of 18 years on election day;

(b) is a Canadian citizen.

Among persons disqualified are certain officials charged with administering the elections, and, individuals who have lost their right to vote for a specified period for the commission of an election-related offence.

Writs for an election (general or by-election) are issued at least 36 days before the date fixed for election day.

Similar qualifications apply in the Provinces and Territories, although for provincial and territorial elections there is usually a residence requirement of either six or twelve months before the date of the issue of the writ of election. The age requirement is 18 years.

To contact election officers see Index, "Elections, Govt. Info. Sources".

Elections Canada - 613/993-2975; Toll Free: 1-800-463-6868; TTY: 1-800-361-8935; Fax: 1-888-524-1444; URL: www.elections.ca.

Liquor Regulations

For names of personnel of the various Liquor Control Boards see index "Liquor Board, Commission, or Control."

Alberta

- Ensure integrity, transparency, disclosure, public consultation & accountability in Alberta's gaming & liquor industries;
- Administer the Alberta Lottery Fund with full public disclosure & continue to support communities & charitable organizations;
- License, regulate & monitor liquor & gaming activities, as well as certain aspects of tobacco sales;
- Implement & account for specific lottery fund programs administered by Alberta Gaming;
- Develop & communicate provincial gaming & liquor policy;
- Responsible for the Department of Gaming, the Alberta Gaming & Liquor Commission (AGLC), the Alberta Gaming Research Council.

Alberta Gaming & Liquor Commission, 50 Corriveau Ave., St. Albert AB T8N 3T5 - 780/447-8600; Fax: 780/447-8918; Toll Free: 1-800-272-8876; URL: www.aglc.ca

British Columbia

The Liquor Control & Licensing Branch is responsible for issuing licences to:

- pubs, bars, lounges, stadiums, nightclubs & restaurants to sell liquor by the glass, & cold beer & wine stores to sell liquor by the bottle
- breweries, distilleries & wineries to manufacture liquor, &
- UBrews/UVins to sell their customers the ingredients, equipment & advice they need to make their own beer, wine cider or coolers

In addition, the branch:

- regulates both Serving It Right: The Responsible Beverage Service Program & Special Occasion Licences for the events such as community celebrations, weddings or banquets
- educates those who hold liquor licences (called licensees) about the laws & rules that may affect them inspects licensed establishments, &
- takes enforcement action when licensees do not follow the *Liquor Control & Licensing Act*, Regulations, &/or the specific terms & conditions of their licences British Columbia Liquor Control & Licensing

Branch, PO Box 9292, Stn Prov Govt, Victoria BC V8W 9J8; street address: 1019 Wharf St., 250/387-1254; Fax: 250/387-9184; Toll Free: 1-866-209-2111; Email: lclb.lclb@gems4.gov.bc.ca; URL: www.pssg.gov.bc.ca/lclb

Manitoba

Persons over the age of 18 years and who are not otherwise prohibited may purchase and consume spirits, wine and beer in premises licensed by the Liquor Control Commission. Further, those persons may purchase from a MLCC liquor mart, liquor vendor or specialty wine store for consumption in a residence.

Beer may also be purchased from beer vendor depots located in most hotels throughout the province.

Parents dining with their children may purchase alcoholic beverages for the latter, for consumption with meals, only in licensed restaurants, dining rooms, cocktail lounges or cabarets.

Beverage rooms and cocktail rooms must be vacated within 30 minutes after the hour at which sale of liquor must cease.

Manitoba Liquor Control Commission, 1555 Buffalo Place, PO Box 1023, Winnipeg MB R3C 2X1 - 204/ 284-2501; Fax: 204/453-5254; URL: www.liquormartsonline.com

New Brunswick

Intoxicating liquor is sold in sealed packages at Liquor Stores and agency stores. Where a permit and/or a license has been obtained, liquor may be sold by the glass in dining rooms, restaurants, taverns, cabarets, lounges, beverage rooms, and clubs. Age of majority is 19.

New Brunswick Liquor Corp., PO Box 20787, Fredericton NB E3B 5B8 - 506/452-6826; Fax: 506/462- 2024; Email: info@anbl.com; URL: www.anbl.com

Newfoundland & Labrador

The importation, manufacture, and sale of alcoholic beverages through Retail Liquor outlets is the responsibility of the Newfoundland Liquor Corp.

The Newfoundland Liquor Corporation is also responsible for the issuing of all licenses, including those to manufacture and to sell packaged beer, and enforcement of regulations including, but not limited, to the following:

- All liquor sold upon licensed premises shall be consumed thereon.
- All liquor served in licensed premises shall be dispensed from the original container in which the liquor is purchased from or under the authority of the Liquor Corp.
- The drinking age in Newfoundland is 19 years.

Nfld. Liquor Corp., PO Box 8750, Stn A, St. John's NL A1B 3V1 - 709/724-1100; Fax: 709/754-0321; URL: www.nlliquor.com

Northwest Territories

The *Northwest Territories Act*, Chapter 331 of the Revised Statutes of Canada, 1952, authorizes the Commissioner in Council of the Northwest Territories to make acts respecting intoxicants.

The Liquor Licensing Board, established under Part I of the *Liquor Act*, controls the conduct of licensees and operation of licensed premises; grants, renews and transfers licenses and, after a hearing, may cancel or suspend licenses. There are presently twelve types of licenses issued by the Board. Part I also provides for plebiscites to be held concerning new liquor license applications and also concerning restriction or prohibition in a community.

Part II of the *Liquor Act* establishes a Liquor Commission. The Minister responsible for this Part may designate his powers to the Liquor Commission to operate liquor stores and to purchase, sell and distribute liquor in the Northwest Territories. Through agency agreements, private contractors operate retail liquor stores on behalf of the Liquor Commission in Fort Simpson, Fort Smith, Hay River, Inuvik, Yellowknife, Norman Wells and liquor warehouses in Hay River and Yellowknife.

Northwest Territories Liquor Commission, #201, 31 Capital Dr., Hay River NT X0E 1G2 - 867/874-2100; Fax: 867/874-2180; URL: www.fin.gov.nt.ca/liquor

Northwest Territories Liquor Licensing Board, #210, 31 Capital Dr., Hay River NT X0E 1G2 - 867/874- 2906; Fax: 867/874-6011

Nova Scotia

All liquor is sold through Government Stores.

Generally local option vote applies.

Eating establishment liquor licenses, lounges, clubs and cabarets serve spirits, draught beer, bottled beer and wine.

The legal minimum drinking age is 19 years.

Nova Scotia Alcohol & Gaming Authority, PO Box 545, Alderney Gate, 40 Alderney Dr., Dartmouth NS B2Y 3Y8 - 902/424-6160; Fax: 902/424-4942; Toll Free: 1-877-565-0556; URL: www.mynslc.ca

Nova Scotia Liquor Corporation, PO Box 8720, Stn A, Halifax NS B3K 5M4 - 902/450-6752; Fax: 902/453-1153

Nunavut

Nunavut Liquor Management is a Branch of the Department of Finance within the Government of Nunavut. Nunavut Liquor Management has two sections, referred to as the Nunavut Liquor Commission and the Nunavut Liquor Licensing Board.

The Nunavut Liquor Commission is responsible for, as first receiver, the purchasing, storage and distribution of alcohol products within the Nunavut Territory.

The Nunavut Liquor Licensing Board deals with the issuance of liquor licenses, liquor permits, inspection and enforcement under the *Nunavut Liquor Act*.

Communities in Nunavut are empowered and are enabled to establish their own liquor controls through the *Nunavut Liquor Act*. They are prohibited, restricted (variety) and unrestricted (only Liquor Act applies). The age of majority in Nunavut is nineteen.

Nunavut Liquor Commission, Bag 002, Rankin Inlet, NU X0C 0G0 - 867/645-3148; 867/645-3327

Nunavut Liquor Licensing Board, Bag 002, Rankin Inlet, NU X0C 0G0 - 867/645-3302; 867/645-3327

Ontario

In accordance with the provisions of the *Liquor Control Act* of Ontario, the Liquor Control Board buys wine, spirits and beer from all over the world for distribution and sale to Ontario consumers and licensed establishments. To provide this service, the

LCBO operates five major regional storage and distribution centres which supply more than 600 retail liquor stores.

In the interests of consumer protection, the LCBO also regularly tests all alcoholic beverages sold in Ontario. This "quality control" testing ensures that all products carried by LCBO stores, Ontario winery stores and Brewers Retail outlets comply with the standards required under the Federal *Food & Drug Act* and Regulations.

The Alcohol and Gaming Commission of Ontario (AGCO) is a Provincial agency that was established on February 23, 1998 after legislation was tabled to merge the Liquor Licence Board of Ontario (LLBO) with the Gaming Control Commission (GCC). The AGCO is responsible for administering the *Liquor Licence Act*, the *Gaming Control Act*, 1992, and the *Wine Content Act*. The AGCO conducts hearings as required: to determine the eligibility for liquor licences or gaming registration; to determine the eligibility for, or the revocation of liquor licences in public interest cases; and, in disciplinary cases involving liquor licensees or gaming registrants.

Liquor-related responsibilities include: licensing of public places which serve beverage alcohol for on-premises consumption; licensing of Ontario liquor manufacturers and the sales representatives of foreign manufacturers; promoting moderation and the responsible use of beverage alcohol.

Gaming-related responsibilities include: regulating charitable and casino gambling in Ontario; ensuring that games of chance are conducted fairly in compliance with the *Gaming Control Act*, regulations, and the terms and conditions that are imposed with charity gaming licences; ensuring that the people and the companies involved in casino and charitable gaming satisfy high standards of honesty, integrity and financial responsibility; registering commercial suppliers and gaming assistants of charitable gaming events and administering the issuance of charity gaming licences in partnership with municipalities.

Alcohol and Gaming Commission of Ontario, 20 Dundas St. W., Toronto ON M5G 2N6; Enquiries: 416/326-8700, or 1-800-522-2876 (toll-free in Ontario); Fax: 416/326-5555 (liquor), 416/326-8711 (gaming); URL:www.agco.on.ca

Prince Edward Island

Beverage alcohol sealed packages may be purchased at Commission Stores throughout the Province by any person 19 or older who is not otherwise disqualified.

Spirits by the glass, and beer and wine by the open bottle or glass, may be purchased in dining rooms, lounges, clubs and military canteens licensed by the Commission.

Prince Edward Island Liquor Control Commission, 3 Garfield St., PO Box 967, Charlottetown, PE C1A 7M4 - 902/368-5710; Fax: 902/368-5735; URL: www.peilcc.ca

Québec

Spirits and wines are sold by Québec Liquor Corporation (Société des alcools du Québec) stores only.

Spirits, beer and wine may be sold to the public by restaurants, bars and clubs under permit for consumption on the premises. Taverns may sell beer and cider. Pubs may sell beer, draught wine and cider.

A licensed grocery store may sell beer and certain designated wines and the product must not be consumed on the premises.

Persons under the age of 18 years old cannot be admitted into bars, pubs and taverns and at no time may alcoholic beverages be sold to them in other establishments.

Régie des Alcools, des courses et des jeux, 1, rue Notre-Dame est, Montréal PQ H2Y 1B6 - 514/873- 3577; 560, boul Charest est, Québec PQ G1K 3J3 - 418/643-7667; URL: www.saq.com

Saskatchewan

The Saskatchewan Liquor & Gaming Authority, a Treasury Board Crown corporation, regulates liquor and gaming activities and conducts and manages gaming in the Saskatchewan Indian Gaming Authority Casinos and the Video Lottery Terminals throughout the province. It is responsible for the control, sale and distribution of liquor in the province, and also licenses and regulates bingos, raffles, casinos, and breakopen tickets.

The minimum drinking age is 19.

Saskatchewan Liquor & Gaming Authority, PO Box 5054, Regina SK S4P 3M3 -306/787-4213; Fax: 306/798-2252; www.saskliquor.com

Yukon Territory

The *Yukon Act*, Chapter Y-2 of the Revised Statutes of Canada, 1970, authorizes the Commissioner in Executive Council, Yukon Territory, to make acts respecting intoxicants.

By virtue of Chapter 105 cited as the *Liquor Act*, established the laws governing the importation, distributing, licensing and retailing of alcoholic beverages in Yukon.

The formation of the Yukon Liquor Corporation by means of amendments to the *Liquor Act* came into force on April 1st, 1977. The separation as a Corporate entity resulted in increased responsibility and full accountability in all areas except major government policy.

The five members of the Board of Directors are appointed by the Commissioner in executive council to hold office at pleasure.

The President and Chief Executive Officer of the Corporation, is charged with the general direction, supervision and control of the Corporation and the administration of the Act.

Yukon Liquor Corp., 9031 Quartz Road, Whitehorse YT Y1A 4P9 - 867/667-5245; Fax: 867/393-6306; URL: www.ylc.yk.ca

Legal Age of Consent to Sexual Activity

Age of Consent, under the *Tackling Violent Crime Act, 2008*:

Raises the age at which youths can consent to non-exploitative sexual activity from 14 to 16 years of age;

Maintains the existing age of protection of 18 years for exploitative sexual activity (i.e. sexual activity involving prostitution, pornography, or a relationship of trust, authority or dependency or that is otherwise exploitative); and

Includes a close-in-age exception which permits 14- and 15-year old youths to engage in consensual, non-exploitative sexual activity with a partner who is less than five years older. Another exception will be available for marriages and for pre-existing common-law relationships.

Marriage Regulations

Divorce Act in Canada

Divorce grounds in Canada, under the *Divorce Act, 1985:*

Breakdown of marriage, established by:
- Spouses intentionally living separate and apart at least one year with the idea that the marriage is over, or

Since the marriage, either spouse has:
- Committed adultery, or
- Treated the other spouse with physical or mental cruelty rendering continued cohabitation intolerable.

Alberta

Marriageable age:
- Without parental consent: 18 years
- With parental consent: 16 years
- A female, under the age of 16, may be married with parental consent & proof that she is the mother of a living child or proof that she is expecting a child.

Blood Test: not required
Waiting Period: None. Marriage Licence is valid immediately & is valid for 3 months (from date of issuance).
Licence fee: $40 + agent
Civic Marriage ceremony fee: uncapped

British Columbia

Marriageable age:
- Without parental consent: 19 years
- With parental consent: 16 to 18 years
- A court order of consent: under 16 years

Blood test: not required
Waiting period for licence: none
Marriage Licence: $100
Civil Marriage Ceremony: $80.25

Manitoba

Marriageable age:
- Without parental consent: 18 years
- With parental consent: 16 years (Persons under 16 years of age can be married only with the consent of a judge of the Family Court.)

Blood test: not required
Waiting period for licence: none
Waiting period after issuance of licence: 24 hours (This may be waived in exceptional circumstances by person performing ceremony.)
Licence fee: $90. Licence valid for 3 months (from date of issuance).

New Brunswick

Marriageable age:
- Without parental consent: 18 years
- With parental consent: under 18 years
- Under 16 years: a declaration of a Judge of the Court of Queen's Bench that the proposed marriage may take place is necessary.

Blood test: not required
Waiting period for licence: none
Licence fee: none
Vital Statistics, Dept. of Health & Wellness - 506/ 453-7411; Fax: 506/453-3245; URL: www.gov.nb.ca/en/ index.htm

Newfoundland & Labrador

Marriageable age:
- Greater than or equal to 19 years: without parental consent
- Greater than or equal to 18 years: without parental consent in certain circumstances
- Greater than or equal to 16 years and less than 19 years: with the applicable parental, guardian or Director of Child Welfare consent (Consent may be dispensed within exceptional cases.)
- Less than 16 years: where by reason of pregnancy a judge issues a licence

Blood test: not required
Licence fee: $50

Northwest Territories

Marriageable age:
- Without parental consent: 19 years
- Under the age of 19 years and declares via statutory declaration that:
  - (a) that no person has lawful custody of the minor; or
  - (b) that any person who has lawful custody of the minor not a resident of the Territories & that the minor has been a resident of the Territories for not less than 12 months immediately preceding the date of the declaration; or
  - (c) that any person who has lawful custody of the minor is unable to consent by reason of disability; or
  - (d) that the minor has, for not less than six months immediately preceding the date of the declaration, withdrawn from the charge of the persons who have lawful custody of the minor & that the minor has not returned to such charge
- With parental consent: 15 years, or under 15 years & pregnant

Blood test: not required
Waiting period for licence: none
Licence fee: $50

Nova Scotia

Marriageable age:
- Without parental consent: 19 years or over
- With parental consent, or if a widow, widower, or divorcee: 16 years
- With court order: under 16 years

Blood test: not required
Waiting period for licence: 5 days
Licence fee: $106.50

Nunavut

Marriageable age:
- Without parental consent: 19 years
- At least 18 years of age

Blood test: not required
Waiting period for licence: none
Licence fee: $25

Ontario

Marriageable age:
- Without parental consent: 18 years
- With parental consent: 16 years

Blood test: not required
Waiting period after issuance of licence: none
Licence fee: $75-$100
Fee for solemnization of marriage by judge or justice of the peace: $75
Purchased marriage licence must be used within 3 months.

Prince Edward Island

Marriageable age:
- Without parental consent: 18 years
- With parental consent: under 18 years

Other requirements: birth certificates and Social Insurance Numbers; in the case of a widow or widower, death certificate; in the case of a divorced person, certified copy of the Decree Absolute or Certificate of Divorce

Waiting period for licence: none
Licence fee: $100

Québec

Marriageable age:
- Minimum age: 16 years (ref.: art. 373, Code Civil du Québec)
- Moreover, a minor (under 18 years of age) must have the authorization of his or her parent(s) or tutor to get married.

Blood test: not required
Waiting period for licence: none
Fee for civil marriage: $186.89 (taxes included)

Saskatchewan

Marriageable age:
- Without parental consent: 18 years
- With parental consent: 16 to 18 years
- With parental and court consent: under 16 years

Blood test: not required
Licence fee: $50

Yukon Territory

Marriageable age:
- Without parental consent: 19 years (In the case of an 18 year old person who has lived apart from his parents/ guardians for at least 6 months & received no financial aid from them during that time, no consent is needed.)

A certificate of divorce or death must be produced if previously married
Blood test: not required
Waiting period for licence: none
Waiting period after issuance of licence: 24 hours
Licence fee: $20
Vital Statistics - Email: vital.statistics@gov.yk.ca; URL: www.hss.gov.yk.ca

Postal Information

Services and rates quoted are subject to change. For complete and up-to-date information you may: consult a local Canada Post retail outlet; call 1-800-267-1177, TTD 1-800-267-2797; or refer to the Canada Post website at www.canadapost.ca. For distribution services, call 1-888-550-6333, and for Postal Code information (fees apply) call 1-900-565-2633 (English) or 1-900-565- 2634 (French).

Communications Services

LETTERMAIL™ SERVICE RATES FOR DELIVERY IN CANADA

Includes letters, postcards, greeting cards and business correspondence.

Standard Lettermail™ service:

Up to 30 g	$0.61
Over 30 g to 50 g	$1.05

Medium Lettermail™ service (only available to consumers):

Up to 20g	$1.05
Over 20g to 50g	$1.22

Other Lettermail Incl. Non-Standard & Oversize:

Up to 100 g	$1.29
Over 100 g to 200 g	$2.10
Over 200 g to 300 g	$2.95
Over 300 g to 400 g	$3.40
Over 400 g to 500 g	$3.65

For cards and postcards, the maximum dimensions are 23.5 cm (length) x 12 cm (width). Oversize Letter Rates apply to all letters with any dimension greater than 24.5 cm (length) x 15 cm (width) x .5 mm (thickness), but not greater than 38 cm (length) x 27 cm (width) x 2 cm (thickness). For cards and postcards the maximum dimensions are 23.5 cm (length) x 12.0cm (width). Maximum weight for Standard and Medium Lettermail ™ service is 50 g and for Other Lettermail ™ service is 500g. Items with any dimension exceeding the maximum dimension for Oversize Lettermail ™ mailpieces or exceeding 500g must be paid at parcel rates. Incentive Rates are available under sales agreements for customers whose mailing meets volume and mail preparation requirements. For details, please contact a Canada Post representative. Canada Post is committed to consistently deliver Lettermail ™ mailpieces as follows: two business days within the same metropolitan area/community; three business days within the same province; four business days between provinces (some exceptions apply).

Distribution Services

PRIORITY™SERVICE

Priority ™ service is an overnight domestic courier service providing next business day noon delivery of your items for local and regional destinations and next business day noon to three day delivery nationally between major Canadian centres. This service comes with an on-time delivery guarantee, an acceptance scan, delivery confirmation, free insurance up to $100 and a no-charge signature-on-delivery option. Prepaid envelopes are available in two sizes and prepaid labels are available to business customers in 4 weight increments. For item delivery status or product information, customers can call 1-888-550-6333 or visit the website at www.canadapost.ca.

XPRESSPOST™ SERVICE

Xpresspost™ service is an affordable, simple to use delivery service for packages and documents which provides an on-time service guarantee and confirmation of delivery. Positioned right in the middle between Priority™ and Regular Post services in terms of price, service and features, Xpresspost™ service offers next business day locally and regionally, and 2 days national between most major urban centres. Customers can verify delivery of their items or obtain product information by calling 1- 888-550-6333, or by accessing the Internet.

EXPEDITED PARCEL™ SERVICE

Expedited Parcel™ service is the fastest ground service providing next business day local, 1-3 business day regional and 2-7 business day national delivery and a no-charge delivery confirmation/guarantee option. A full range of prepaid labels are also available to business customers.

REGULAR PARCEL™ SERVICE

Regular Parcel™ service is the most economical, domestic, ground parcel service. Service is 3 business days local, 4-6 business days regional and 5-10 business days national between most major urban centres.

ADVICE OF RECEIPT (USA/INTERNATIONAL ONLY)

The Advice of Receipt (AR) service provides mailers with the actual signature of the addressee. An Advice of Receipt card is purchased at the time of mailing. The addressee's signature is obtained on the AR card and returned to the sender, thus providing the mailer with a Delivery Confirmation.

To international and USA destinations, AR can be used only with Registered Mail and only at the time of mailing, for a fee of $1.75.

AIR STAGE SERVICE (LESS THAN 5 ITEMS)

Canada Post services many communities where the only access to the community is by air. These communities are called Air Stage Offices.

The casual mailer who sends the occasional letter and parcel to these isolated communities pays the normal rate outlined in the various rate charts for Lettermail™, Parcel Post, Xpresspost™ & Priority™ services.

Any customer (individual or business) who ships more than 5 parcels or more than 20 kg of parcels on any day or more than 20 parcels or more than 80 kg of parcels in any month is considered an Air Stage Service Shipper and must pay Air Stage Freight Service rates. These shippers must also sign an agreement with Canada Post in order to use this service. An infrequent mailer who meets the volume or weight criteria can use the Air Stage Freight Service rates providing the goods shipped are not for resale. There are various rate levels based on the type of goods shipped.

Air Stage Freight Service rates apply whether the mailer is a business or an individual. Appropriate Regular Post zoned parcel rates apply for all other shippers, and appropriate Priority™ or Xpresspost™ service rates apply.

CANADIAN FORCES MAIL SERVICE

Canadian Forces Mail is mail sent to or by Canadian Forces personnel, their dependents and the civilians attached to the Canadian Forces served through the Canadian Forces Post Office (CFPO) or the Fleet Mail Office (FMO).

The rate charged for domestic mail is applicable for mail sent to Canadian Forces personnel providing it is sent through a CFPO or an FMO.

All parcels must include an International Customs Declaration form (CP72) and are subject to customs inspection in the country of destination. Oversize parcels and parcels over 20 kg are not acceptable.

COLLECT ON DELIVERY (COD)

COD is a service for domestic mail for which an amount due to the sender, up to $1,000 where the amount to be collected is in cash and $25,000 where the amount to be collected is by cheque, is collected from the addressee before delivery and returned to the mailer. It is a service available to consumer and business mailers. COD is available for parcels only or items mailed at parcel rates. The amount collected from the addressee can include:

1. Amount representing the value of the item.
2. Service charge in the case of repairs.
3. Sales tax.
4. Postage.
5. COD fee & special service fees.

COD cannot be used to collect on items not ordered or requested by the addressee or to collect money owing on previous accounts. Insurance is available up to $5,000. Items sent COD must abide by Canada Post mail preparation requirements. The amount of the COD collected from the addressee will be forwarded to the sender by Postal Money Order when payment is made by cash or by cheque drawn up by the addressee payable to the sender.

DEFICIENT POSTAGE FEE

Unpaid or shortpaid mail is mail for which the postage or fees have not been paid or have been partially paid. Lettermail™ and Parcelmail items are returned to the sender for the collection of the postage.

When there is no return address on the item, the item is forwarded to the addressee for the collection of the postage plus an administrative charge. All postage due charges must be paid before delivery.

DO NOT FORWARD SERVICE

Do Not Forward is a service for Lettermail™ items, mailed in Canada for delivery in Canada. If mail that cannot be delivered as addressed because the addressee has filed a Change Of Address Notification, it will be returned to the sender rather than being forwarded to the addressee.

FRANKED MAIL

Canada Post provides free mailing privileges to the following:

1. Governor General or Secretary to the Governor General;
2. Speaker or Clerk of the Senate or House of Commons;
3. Parliamentary Librarian or Associate Parliamentary Librarian;
4. Members of the Senate;
5. Members of the House of Commons.

In addition, anyone mailing an item to the above in Canada receives free postage. As a general rule, only Lettermail™ items, Publications Mail™ items and addressed Admail™ mailpieces are acceptable. Parcels and add-on services are not acceptable as part of this service. As long as the letters M.P. appear on the mailing, it can be sent free of postage.

COLLECTION OF THE GST

The Goods & Service Tax (GST) is a value added consumption tax instituted by the Federal Government. By law, businesses must charge 5% on most goods and services provided.

Most postal services and products are subject to the GST, such as stamps, Advance Purchase Products, all add-on options (e.g., Insurance, Trace Mail, COD), optional Postal Box rentals, and postage meter fill-ups.

There are certain items sold by Canada Post that are not taxable such as Postal Money Orders, the fee on a Money Order and the exchange on a Money Order. Provincial governments are exempt from paying the GST.

Mail addressed to foreign destinations requiring total shipping charges of $5 or more (single item or a cumulative purchase) and products ordered from and shipped directly by Canada Post to a foreign destination, such as Philatelic and Retail products, are not subject to the GST. The 5% tax is calculated on the total taxable purchased and rounded up or down to the nearest cent.

HOLD MAIL

Canada Post Hold Mail service provides individuals with a convenient way to temporarily suspend mail delivery for a specified period of time while they are away from their home or business. The most convenient way to purchase a Hold Mail service is through a secure online application at canadapost.ca. The online registration feature offers self-service capabilities with immediate insight to all transaction details that are included in the automated confirmation email that is sent after the registration has been completed. Individuals can also purchase the Hold Mail service at their nearest Canada Post location.

The Hold Mails service's set-up fee includes two weeks of service for residential purchases, and one week of service for

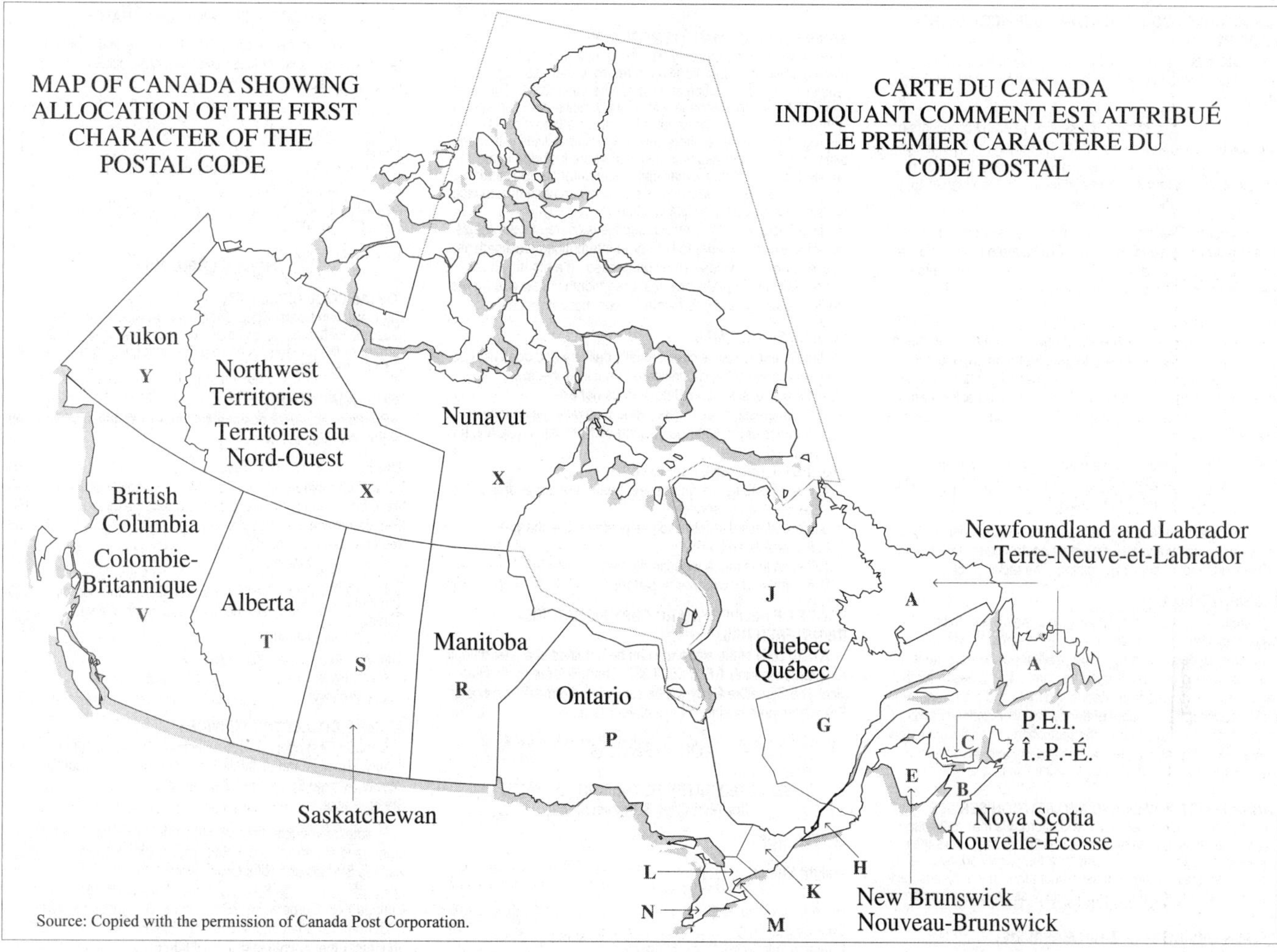

Source: Copied with the permission of Canada Post Corporation.

commercial purchases. Service can be extended in weekly increments with applicable fees.

HUNTING PERMITS

Prior to hunting season, hunting permits can be purchased from a postal outlet. The rules, regulations and fees pertaining to these permits are provided to the outlets by the Provincial and Federal bodies responsible for these permits. Unsold permits can be returned by the postal outlet to the depot from where they were originally ordered at the end of the hunting season for a refund.

INSURANCE

Insurance is available from Canada Post to provide compensation for the loss or damage of mailable items if the requirements are met. Coverage for up to $100 is included for Registered Mail™ services; however, Canada Post shall have no liability for loss or damage of Registered Mail™ items containing:

1. Bank notes, travellers' cheques & coins;
2. Stocks, bonds, coupons, & other securities negotiable by bearer;
3. Lottery tickets;
4. Jewellery;
5. Manufactured & non-manufactured precious metals, precious stones, gold bullion & gold dust;
6. Canceled or uncanceled postage stamps.

Additional coverage is available, for a fee, for domestic Registered Mail™ items up to $5,000.

To USA destinations, coverage for up to $60 is included for Registered Mail™ services, with the same exceptions as above.

KEY SERVICE™ SERVICES

Hotel, motel and automobile keys can be mailed without postage at any postal outlet in Canada for delivery in Canada if the keys have a tag clearly showing the complete address of the addressee. They can also be dropped in a street letter box.

LIBRARY BOOKS

Available to Public Libraries, University Libraries, and Libraries maintained by non-profit organizations for use by the general public in Canada to mail library books to their Canadian patrons. This service is for books only (not CDs, DVDs or other recordings). The library completes an "Application for Mail Privileges" form and be authorized by Canada Post to use this service. The maximum weight per shipment is 5 kg.

The maximum weight for sewn or bound books is 5 kg and 3 kg for books that are not sewn or bound. The rates are based on a per item cost plus weight and destination. Postage paid by the library at the time of mailing covers both the outgoing and the return postage.

LITERATURE FOR THE BLIND

Literature for the Blind is a service available free of charge from Canada Post allowing blind persons and recognized institutions for the blind to mail free of postage specific items used by blind persons.

Admissible items in Canada include items impressed in Braille or similar raised type, plates for printing literature for the blind, tapes and records posted by the blind in Canada for delivery in Canada and recording tapes, records and special writing paper intended solely for the use of the blind-when mailed by or addressed to a recognized institution for the blind.

The maximum weight in Canada is 7 kg. Add on services such as Registered (500 g), and Advice of Receipt (USA/International only), which should be endorsed "Braille Free" can be applied to Literature for the Blind at no charge.

This service is also available to the USA and to international destinations at no charge. The maximum weight is 7 kg. International Literature for the Blind items must bear a label or the words "CECOGRAMMES" or "CECOGRAMMES (LITERATURE FOR THE BLIND)" in the upper right-hand corner on the address side of the item (by means of marking, printing or labelling). All other forms of labelling must be approved by Canada Post.

MAILING LISTS

Some Canadians may object to receiving Addressed Admail™ mailpieces and would like their name removed from all mailing lists. Canadians are advised to contact the sender of the Addressed Admail™ mailpiece to request that his or her name be removed from their mailing list.

If any recipient of this type of mail wishes to have all Addressed Admail™ mailpieces stopped, the customer should write to the following addresses asking them to have their members delete his or her name from their mailing lists.

In Canada:
Canadian Direct Marketing Association
Do Not Mail Service
#607, 1 Concorde Gate, Don Mills ON M3C 3N6
416/391-2362; Fax: 416/441-4062

In the United States:
Direct Marketing Association
Mail Preference Service
PO Box 9008, Farmingdale NY 11735-9008, USA.
212/768-7277

PHILATELIC PRODUCTS

Canada Post offers stamp collectors, ranging from the person with a passing interest in stamps to a very serious collector, a complete range of philatelic products. Stamp collectors are concerned with product quality. It is for this reason that we have set up philatelic centres within specific postal outlets across the country. It is from these centres that the philatelist can more easily obtain the product and information required. There is also a National Philatelic Centre in Antigonish, Nova Scotia, from which any collector can get access to information and products by mail or by telephone.

POSTAL BOXES/CONTAINERS/BAG SERVICE/GENERAL DELIVERY

A postal box is a numbered compartment in a post office that is kept locked, and to which the boxholder and postal employee have access.

The container/bag service is a service whereby containers or bags are assigned to a customer for the delivery of mail, either because postal boxes are not available or because the size of the postal boxes cannot accommodate the volume of mail addressed to this particular customer.

The General Delivery service at post offices is offered to the travelling public, customers with no fixed address within the letter carrier delivery area, or to anyone who cannot receive their mail from the normal delivery modes.

MONEY ORDERS

A Money Order is a secured cashable document, guaranteed by Canada Post, which is used to transfer funds anywhere in Canada and to countries with whom Canada Post has an active agreement. The service guarantee offers a refund of lost or destroyed money orders upon enquiry from the purchaser. Some conditions apply.

Postal money orders can be purchased by consumers and businesses, and constitute a guaranteed payment. They can be used for financial or retail transactions.

Postal money orders may be purchased in Canadian or U.S funds.The maximum value of a single postal money order is $999.99 (Canadian and U.S. dollars). The fee is $6.50.

PROHIBITED MAIL

Prohibited Mail is defined as any mail which is prohibited by law or may contain products or substances that could harm postal employees or damage other mail or postal equipment. The mail service cannot be used for criminal activities or for the transportation of dangerous goods. Animals and plants are generally not acceptable except under certain well-defined conditions in Canada. Prohibitions and restrictions on mail sent to the USA and to international destinations exists and are wide-ranging.

CANADA POST MOVER AND REDIRECTION SERVICE

Canada Post provides a secure and affordable mail redirection service that allows all individuals across Canada to have their mail forwarded to their new home or a temporary address. All individuals with residential requests must allow at least 3 business days before services start, and 10 business days for commercial requests.

CHANGE OF ADDRESS (MOVER SERVICE)

When individuals are permanently moving (not planning to return to their old address), a Canada Post Change of Address mover service can be purchased to ensure that all their important mail follows them to their new address. The most convenient way to purchase a mover service is through a secure online application at canadapost.ca. The online registration feature offers self-service capabilities with immediate insight to all transaction details that are included in the automated confirmation email that is sent after the registration has been completed. Individuals can also purchase this service at their nearest Canada Post location.

By signing up online, individuals will gain immediate access to special offers and deals on moving-related products and services.

Mail can be redirected from any Canadian address to any other address in Canada, the USAand most international destinations. The service is available for a twelve-month period.

REDIRECTION OF MAIL (TEMPORARY)

If an individual is temporarily relocating their business or their place of residence and planning to return to their old address, a temporary mail redirection service can be purchased. The most convenient way to purchase a temporary mail redirection service is through a secure online application at canadapost.ca. The online registration feature offers self-service capabilities with immediate insight to all transaction details that are included in the automated confirmation email that is sent after the registration has been completed. Individuals can also purchase this service at their nearest Canada Post location.

The temporary mail redirection service is offered to individuals travelling within Canada, to U.S. or to International destinations. The temporary services can be purchased on a monthly basis and the initial set-up fee includes three months of service for residential requests, and one month for commercial requests.

UNDELIVERABLE MAIL

Undeliverable Mail is mail that fails delivery and does not bear a return address. Mail is considered undeliverable if:

1. the address is incomplete or does not exist
2. the addressee has moved without providing a change of address or the Change of Address Notification (COAN) has expired
3. it is refused by the addressee
4. it is refused by the addressee, bears a return address, & is refused by the sender
5. the addressee refuses to pay postage due charges
6. it is prohibited by law
7. it is an item found loose in the mail
8. it is an empty wrapper or carton.

PROOF OF DELIVERY/HARD COPY SIGNATURE - REGISTERED MAIL

A hard copy of the signature can be obtained at a later date, if required, by calling 1-888-550-6333. There is a fee for this service. The Signature Copy will be sent via Lettermail™ service or Fax within three business days of your request.

Other Services

SELECTED RATES TO THE UNITED STATES (its Territories & Possessions):

LETTER-POST

Weight Steps:

Up to & including 30 g	$ 1.05
Over 30 g to 50 g	1.29
Oversize letter rates (max. 500g)	
Up to & including 100 g	2.10
100 g to 200 g	3.70
Over 200 g to 500 g	7.40

Letter-post cannot be more than 27 cm (width) x 38 cm (length) x 2 cm (thickness) up to 90 cm length plus width plus thickness (longest side may not exceed 60 cm).

USA Incentive Letterpost offers Canadian mailers postage savings linked to volume, and quality of mail preparation. For information on USA Incentive Letter-Post rates, please contact Canada Post Customer Service at 866-757-5480.

REGISTERED MAIL SERVICE

Available for airmail Letter-post items. Fees to the USA- $14.50 plus the applicable postage.

SELECTED INTERNATIONAL RATES

All countries except the USA, its Territories and Possessions, Canadian Forces post offices and Fleet Mail Offices.

LETTER-POST

Weight Steps	Air Mail
Up to & including 30 g	$ 1.80
Over 30 g to 50 g	2.80
Other letter rates, including Oversize (max. 500g)	
Up to & including 100g	4.20
Over 100 g to 200 g	7.40
Over 200 g to 500 g	14.80

General Information

POSTAL CODE DIRECTORY

The Canadian Postal Code Directory is available for $199.95 (plus applicable taxes) and may be ordered no later than November of the previous year from the National Philatelic Centre at 1-800-565-4362.

PROVINCIAL SYMBOLS

Standard two-letter postal abbreviations for the provinces and territories are as follows:

Alberta	AB
British Columbia	BC
Manitoba	MB
New Brunswick	NB
Newfoundland & Labrador	NL
Northwest Territories	NT
Nova Scotia	NS
Nunavut	NU
Ontario	ON
Prince Edward Island	PE
Québec	QC
Saskatchewan	SK
Yukon Territory	YT

STAMP & COLLECTOR SERVICES

Canada Post offers a wide selection of postage stamps, stationery, supplies and philatelic products such as Official First Day Covers, Annual Souvenir Collections and Commemorative Stamp Packs.

Philatelic products are available at postal outlets and through authorized stamp sales agents across Canada. Customers may visit the Stamps and Gifts Online store (www.canadapost.ca/Stamps) or the National Philatelic Centre, Canada Post Corporation, 75 St. Ninian St., Antigonish NS B2G 2R8; from Canada and the USA call toll-free 1-800-565- 4362, and from other countries call 902/863-6550.

CUSTOMER SERVICE

Further information on Canada Post's products and services can be obtained through your local postal outlets, postal directory, your local customer service representative, or by calling one of the following numbers:

Toll Free (Canada) (8 a.m. to 6 p.m. local time)	1-800-267-1177
Outside of Canada	416/979-8822
Hearing Impaired with TTY-Teletyping	1-800-267-2797

Customers may also contact Canada Post via the Internet: www.canadapost.ca or mail: Canada Post Corporation, 2701 Riverside Dr., Ottawa ON K1A 0B1.

Vital Statistics

POPULATION COUNTS, FOR CANADA, PROVINCES AND TERRITORIES, 2011 AND 2006 CENSUSES

Geographic name	Population, 2011	Population, 2006	Population, % change	Population density per kilometre², 2011
Canada	33,476,688	31,612,897	5.9	3.73
Newfoundland and Labrador	514,536	505,469	1.8	1.39
Prince Edward Island	140,204	135,851	3.2	24.66
Nova Scotia	921,727	913,462	0.9	17.41
New Brunswick	751,171	729,997	2.9	10.52
Quebec	7,903,001	7,546,131	4.7	5.83
Ontario	12,851,821	12,160,282	5.7	14.14
Manitoba	1,208,268	1,148,401	5.2	2.19
Saskatchewan	1,033,381	968,157	6.7	1.76
Alberta	3,645,257	3,290,350	10.8	5.70
British Columbia	4,400,057	4,113,487	7	4.77
Yukon	33,897	30,372	11.6	0.07
Northwest Territories	41,462	41,464	0	0.04
Nunavut	31,906	29,474	8.3	0.02

Source: Adapted from the Statistics Canada publications *A National Overview: Population and Dwelling Counts, 2001 Census* Catalogue 93-360-XPB and *A National Overview: Population and Dwelling Counts, 2006 Census* Catalogue 92-200-XPB. Accessed October 15, 2012.

POPULATION OF CANADA, PROVINCES AND TERRITORIES, BY AGE GROUPS, 2011 CENSUS OF POPULATION

	Sex	Children: 0 to 14	Working-age population: 15 to 64 years	Seniors: 65 years and over	Seniors: 80 years and over	Total
Canada	Both sexes	5,607,345	22,924,290	4,945,055	1,347,580	33,476,690
	Females	2,736,240	11,579,935	2,746,280	848,200	17,062,460
	Males	2,871,100	11,344,355	2,198,775	499,385	16,414,230
Newfoundland and Labrador	Both sexes	76,630	355,800	82,110	18,630	514,540
	Females	37,370	182,020	44,580	11,720	263,970
	Males	39,260	173,780	37,525	6,910	250,570
Prince Edward Island	Both sexes	23,060	94,360	22,785	5,925	140,205
	Females	11,360	48,595	12,650	3,825	72,600
	Males	11,700	45,765	10,135	2,100	67,605
Nova Scotia	Both sexes	138,215	630,140	153,375	40,400	921,730
	Females	67,435	323,255	85,445	26,075	476,140
	Males	70,775	306,885	67,925	14,320	445,590
New Brunswick	Both sexes	113,575	513,960	123,630	32,795	751,170
	Females	55,625	260,740	68,365	21,025	384,735
	Males	57,950	253,220	55,270	11,770	366,440
Quebec	Both sexes	1,258,620	5,386,695	1,257,690	330,370	7,903,000
	Females	615,880	2,700,495	710,765	215,255	4,027,140
	Males	642,745	2,686,195	546,920	115,115	3,875,865
Ontario	Both sexes	2,180,775	8,792,725	1,878,325	517,910	12,851,820
	Females	1,063,260	4,480,195	1,045,220	323,370	6,588,685
	Males	1,117,510	4,312,525	833,105	194,545	6,263,140
Manitoba	Both sexes	231,160	804,655	172,450	52,210	1,208,270
	Females	112,540	404,005	97,170	33,470	613,715
	Males	118,620	400,650	75,285	18,745	594,550
Saskatchewan	Both sexes	197,860	681,815	153,710	49,430	1,033,380
	Females	96,850	339,575	85,405	30,830	521,830
	Males	101,015	342,240	68,300	18,600	511,555
Alberta	Both sexes	684,790	2,554,745	405,725	109,210	3,645,260
	Females	333,705	1,262,135	221,605	67,305	1,817,440
	Males	351,085	1,292,610	184,125	41,905	1,827,810
British Columbia	Both sexes	677,360	3,033,975	688,715	189,625	4,400,055
	Females	329,805	1,541,695	371,955	114,725	2,243,455
	Males	347,560	1,492,285	316,760	74,900	2,156,605
Yukon	Both sexes	5,865	24,940	3,090	530	33,895
	Females	2,845	12,545	1,450	285	16,840
	Males	3,015	12,400	1,640	240	17,055
Northwest Territories	Both sexes	9,010	30,055	2,395	440	41,460
	Females	4,475	14,750	1,180	255	20,400
	Males	4,535	15,310	1,220	185	21,060
Nunavut	Both sexes	10,425	20,420	1,060	115	31,905
	Females	5,090	9,930	495	70	15,510
	Males	5,335	10,490	565	45	16,395

Source: Adapted from the Statistics Canada publication *Age and sex - 2006 Census*, Catalogue 97-551-X, Issue 2006005

POPULATION OF CENSUS METROPOLITAN AREAS (2006, 2011)

Geographic name	Total (2011 counts)	Total (2006 counts)	Total (2006 to 2011 % change)
Canada	33,476,690	31,612,895	5.9
St. John's (N.L.)	196,965	181,110	8.8
Halifax (N.S.)	390,325	372,860	4.7
Saint John (N.B.)	127,765	122,390	4.4
Fredericton (N.B.)	94,270	86,225	9.3
Québec (Que.)	765,705	719,155	6.5
Trois-Rivières (Que.)	151,775	144,840	4.8
Montréal (Que.)	3,824,220	3,635,570	5.2
Ottawa - Gatineau (Ont.)	1,236,320	1,133,635	9.1
Kingston (Ont.)	159,560	152,355	4.7
Peterborough (Ont.)	118,975	116,570	2.1
Toronto (Ont.)	5,583,065	5,113,150	9.2
Hamilton (Ont.)	721,050	692,910	4.1
Guelph (Ont.)	141,100	133,700	5.5
London (Ont.)	474,790	457,720	3.7
Windsor (Ont.)	319,245	323,340	-1.3
Barrie (Ont.)	187,015	177,060	5.6
Thunder Bay (Ont.)	121,595	122,905	-1.1
Winnipeg (Man.)	730,015	694,665	5.1
Regina (Sask.)	210,560	194,970	8
Saskatoon (Sask.)	260,600	233,930	11.4
Calgary (Alta.)	1,214,840	1,079,310	12.6
Edmonton (Alta.)	1,159,870	1,034,945	12.1
Kelowna (B.C.)	179,840	162,275	10.8
Vancouver (B.C.)	2,313,325	2,116,580	9.3
Victoria (B.C.)	344,615	330,085	4.4

Source: Statistics Canada. 2012. Age and Sex 2011 counts for both sexes for Canada provinces and territories, Age and Sex Highlight Tables. 2011 Census. Statistics Canada Catalogue no. 98-311-XWE2011002. Ottawa. Released May 29, 2012

Population of Canada, Projections, 2015-2061

(in thousands)

	Projection Scenario								
Year	L: low-growth	M1: medium-growth, historical trends (1981 to 2008)	M2: medium-growth, 2006 to 2008 trends	M3: medium-growth, 1988 to 1996 trends	M4: medium-growth, 2001 to 2006 trends	H: high-growth	A1: replacement fertility	A2: zero immigration	A3: 1% immigration
2015	35,643.2	36,103.9	36,105.0	36,102.4	36,105.1	36,545.2	36,500.4	34,454.6	36,687.7
2016	35,912.8	36,493.8	36,495.3	36,491.9	36,495.4	37,057.1	36,990.3	34,538.5	37,186.7
2017	36,176.1	36,881.0	36,882.8	36,878.6	36,882.9	37,570.6	37,478.8	34,611.8	37,686.9
2018	36,432.5	37,264.8	37,266.9	37,261.8	37,267.0	38,084.8	37,965.0	34,674.1	38,187.7
2019	36,681.7	37,644.6	37,647.2	37,641.1	37,647.3	38,599.2	38,448.4	34,725.0	38,688.5
2020	36,928.1	38,025.1	38,028.0	38,021.0	38,028.1	39,118.2	38,933.2	34,769.4	39,193.7
2021	37,171.2	38,405.5	38,408.9	38,400.9	38,409.0	39,641.2	39,418.8	34,806.8	39,702.9
2022	37,410.6	38,785.5	38,789.2	38,780.3	38,789.3	40,167.4	39,904.6	34,837.1	40,215.3
2023	37,645.6	39,164.3	39,168.4	39,158.5	39,168.4	40,696.3	40,389.8	34,859.7	40,730.5
2024	37,875.9	39,541.3	39,545.7	39,535.0	39,545.8	41,227.1	40,873.7	34,874.2	41,247.7
2025	38,100.7	39,915.9	39,920.7	39,909.1	39,920.7	41,759.4	41,355.9	34,880.3	41,766.5
2026	38,319.6	40,287.7	40,292.8	40,280.4	40,292.7	42,292.6	41,835.7	34,877.5	42,286.2
2027	38,532.3	40,656.2	40,661.5	40,648.4	40,661.5	42,826.5	42,313.2	34,865.6	42,806.5
2028	38,738.3	41,021.1	41,026.8	41,012.8	41,026.6	43,360.9	42,788.1	34,844.5	43,327.3
2029	38,937.5	41,382.4	41,388.3	41,373.6	41,388.1	43,895.8	43,260.9	34,814.0	43,848.3
2030	39,129.6	41,740.0	41,746.1	41,730.7	41,745.9	44,431.3	43,732.1	34,774.2	44,369.6
2031	39,314.5	42,093.9	42,100.3	42,084.1	42,100.0	44,968.0	44,202.3	34,725.2	44,891.3
2032	39,492.5	42,444.6	42,451.1	42,434.2	42,450.8	45,506.4	44,672.6	34,667.4	45,413.8
2033	39,664.0	42,792.2	42,799.0	42,781.3	42,798.6	46,046.6	45,144.0	34,601.1	45,937.5
2034	39,829.3	43,137.3	43,144.4	43,125.8	43,143.9	46,589.4	45,617.6	34,526.6	46,462.9
2035	39,988.7	43,480.4	43,487.6	43,468.2	43,487.1	47,135.7	46,094.6	34,444.5	46,990.6
2036	40,142.4	43,821.7	43,829.3	43,808.9	43,828.7	47,686.0	46,576.1	34,355.3	47,521.0
2037	40,290.8	44,162.0	44,169.8	44,148.4	44,169.2	48,241.2	47,063.2	34,259.2	48,054.6
2038	40,434.6	44,501.4	44,509.5	44,487.0	44,508.9	48,801.5	47,557.0	34,156.7	48,592.1
2039	40,573.9	44,840.5	44,848.9	44,825.3	44,848.3	49,367.6	48,058.6	34,048.2	49,133.8
2040	40,708.9	45,179.6	45,188.3	45,163.4	45,187.6	49,940.2	48,568.9	33,933.9	49,680.3
2041	40,839.8	45,518.8	45,527.9	45,501.7	45,527.2	50,519.6	49,088.5	33,814.1	50,231.7
2042	40,966.6	45,858.5	45,868.0	45,840.3	45,867.2	51,106.4	49,617.9	33,688.8	50,788.4
2043	41,089.4	46,198.7	46,208.6	46,179.5	46,207.9	51,700.8	50,157.3	33,558.3	51,350.7
2044	41,208.5	46,539.6	46,550.0	46,519.3	46,549.2	52,302.8	50,706.7	33,422.6	51,918.7
2045	41,324.2	46,881.3	46,892.1	46,859.8	46,891.3	52,912.5	51,265.8	33,282.0	52,492.7
2046	41,436.5	47,224.0	47,235.2	47,201.1	47,234.4	53,529.9	51,834.0	33,136.6	53,072.7
2047	41,546.0	47,567.5	47,579.3	47,543.4	47,578.5	54,154.9	52,411.1	32,986.5	53,659.0
2048	41,652.9	47,912.3	47,924.5	47,886.8	47,923.7	54,787.3	52,996.3	32,832.0	54,251.7
2049	41,757.8	48,258.3	48,271.1	48,231.4	48,270.2	55,427.2	53,589.3	32,673.5	54,851.0
2050	41,860.9	48,605.9	48,619.2	48,577.6	48,618.3	56,074.4	54,189.5	32,511.3	55,457.2
2051	41,962.9	48,955.2	48,969.1	48,925.4	48,968.2	56,729.1	54,796.8	32,345.8	56,070.5
2052	42,064.1	49,306.6	49,320.9	49,275.2	49,320.0	57,391.3	55,410.7	32,177.6	56,691.1
2053	42,164.9	49,660.2	49,675.1	49,627.3	49,674.2	58,061.2	56,031.3	32,007.0	57,319.5
2054	42,265.7	50,016.5	50,032.0	49,982.0	50,031.0	58,739.1	56,658.8	31,834.8	57,955.9
2055	42,367.1	50,375.9	50,391.9	50,339.8	50,390.9	59,425.5	57,293.6	31,661.6	58,600.9
2056	42,469.4	50,738.9	50,755.5	50,701.1	50,754.4	60,121.0	57,936.0	31,487.9	59,254.8
2057	42,572.9	51,105.8	51,122.9	51,066.3	51,121.8	60,826.1	58,586.8	31,314.5	59,918.1
2058	42,677.8	51,477.1	51,494.8	51,435.8	51,493.5	61,541.5	59,246.5	31,141.9	60,591.2
2059	42,784.4	51,853.2	51,871.4	51,810.1	51,870.1	62,267.8	59,915.9	30,970.7	61,274.5
2060	42,892.8	52,234.3	52,253.1	52,189.4	52,251.7	63,005.7	60,595.9	30,801.4	61,968.4
2061	43,003.1	52,620.8	52,640.2	52,573.9	52,638.6	63,755.9	61,287.2	30,634.5	62,673.2

Source: Adapted from Statistics Canada's CANSIM database http://www5.statcan.gc.ca/cansim/home-accueil?lang=eng, Table 052-0005, August 2010.

VITAL STATISTICS COMPARED WITH MACROREGIONS & REGIONS 1995-2000

MACRO REGIONS AND REGIONS	BIRTH RATE 0/000	DEATH RATE 0/000
World	**22**	**9**
Africa	**38**	**14**
Eastern Africa	42	18
Middle Africa	45	15
Northern Africa	28	7
Southern Africa	28	12
Western Africa	40	15
Northern America	**14**	**8**
Latin America	**23**	**6**
Caribbean	21	8
Central America	27	5
South America	22	7
Asia	**22**	**8**
Eastern Asia	16	7
South Central Asia	27	9
South Eastern Asia	23	7
Western Asia	30	7
Europe	**10**	**11**
Eastern Europe	10	13
Northern Europe	12	11
Southern Europe	10	10
Western Europe	11	10
Oceania	**18**	**8**
Australia and New Zealand	14	8
Melanesia	31	9
Micronesia	36	5
Polynesia	25	5

Source: United Nations Statistical Yearbook, 45th issue, Perm. No. 2011-278

ESTIMATES OF BIRTHS, CANADA, PROVINCES AND TERRITORIES
Annual (persons)

	2007/2008	2008/2009	2009/2010	2010/2011	2011/2012
Canada	373,695	379,290	379,373	378,683	381,598
Newfoundland and Labrador	4,664	4,925	4,945	4,875	4,823
Prince Edward Island	1,447	1,471	1,407	1,412	1,420
Nova Scotia	9,114	8,930	9,096	8,875	8,848
New Brunswick	7,269	7,440	7,390	7,348	7,313
Quebec	85,649	88,676	88,433	88,589	88,500
Ontario	140,547	140,326	139,771	140,267	141,799
Manitoba	15,391	15,731	15,952	15,943	16,250
Saskatchewan	13,630	13,897	14,239	14,448	14,801
Alberta	49,949	51,308	51,522	51,175	52,243
British Columbia	44,142	44,690	44,641	43,835	43,677
Yukon	349	400	370	383	383
Northwest Territories	725	696	737	704	706
Nunavut	819	800	870	829	835

Footnotes:

[1]Period from July 1 to June 30.

[2] The number of births is final up to 2009/2010, updated for 2010/2011 and preliminary for 2011/2012.

[5] Preliminary and updated estimates of births were produced by Demography Division, Statistics Canada (See Definitions, data sources and methods record number 3601). Final data were produced by Health Statistics Division, Statistics Canada (See Definitions, data sources and methods record number 3231). However, the final estimates included in this table may differ from the data released by the Health Statistics Division, due to distribution of unknown

Source: Adapted from Statistics Canada's CANSIM database http://www5.statcan.gc.ca/cansim/home-accueil?lang=eng, Tables 102-4502, 102-4505, 102-0504, 102-0507, September 2011. (Accessed October 15, 2012)

Leading Causes of Death, Total Population, by Sex, Canada, 2009

		Males	Females
Malignant neoplasms	Rank of leading causes of death	1	1
	Number of deaths	37,452	33,673
	Mortality rate[1]	224	198
Diabetes mellitus	Rank of leading causes of death	6	7
	Number of deaths	3,616	3,307
	Mortality rate	22	20
Alzheimer's disease	Rank of leading causes of death	9	5
	Number of deaths	1,932	4,349
	Mortality rate	12	26
Diseases of heart	Rank of leading causes of death	2	2
	Number of deaths	25,950	23,321
	Mortality rate	155	137
Cerebrovascular diseases	Rank of leading causes of death	4	3
	Number of deaths	5,823	8,282
	Mortality rate	35	49
Influenza and pneumonia	Rank of leading causes of death	8	8
	Number of deaths	2,694	3,132
	Mortality rate	16	18
Chronic lower respiratory diseases	Rank of leading causes of death	5	4
	Number of deaths	5,525	5,334
	Mortality rate	33	31
Nephritis, nephrotic syndrome and nephrosis	Rank of leading causes of death	10	9
	Number of deaths	1,775	1,834
	Mortality rate	11	11
Accidents (unintentional injuries)	Rank of leading causes of death	3	6
	Number of deaths	6,045	4,205
	Mortality rate	36	25
Intentional self-harm (suicide)	Rank of leading causes of death	7	13
	Number of deaths	2,989	901
	Mortality rate	18	5
Assault (homicide)	Rank of leading causes of death	20	26
	Number of deaths	430	144
	Mortality rate	3	1

[1]per 100,000 population

Source: Adapted from Statistics Canada's CANSIM database http://www5.statcan.gc.ca/cansim/home-accueil?lang=eng, Table 102-0551, August 2011. (Accessed October 15, 2012)

IMMIGRANTS TO CANADA, BY CLASS, 1992 - 2010

Year	Economic	Family	Refugees	Others [1]	Total
1992	95,796	101,112	52,345	5,544	254,797
1993	105,653	112,647	30,600	7,751	256,651
1994	102,309	94,193	20,435	7,455	224,392
1995	106,626	77,386	28,093	761	212,866
1996	125,370	68,359	28,478	3,866	226,073
1997	128,350	59,979	24,308	3,400	216,037
1998	97,912	50,896	22,843	2,547	174,198
1999	109,249	55,274	24,397	1,031	189,951
2000	136,287	60,616	30,092	460	227,455
2001	155,718	66,795	27,919	207	250,639
2002	137,863	62,292	25,114	3,780	229,049
2003	121,047	65,120	25,983	9,199	221,349
2004	133,748	62,269	32,687	7,121	235,825
2005	156,312	63,367	35,776	6,786	262,241
2006	138,251	70,517	32,499	10,375	251,642
2007	131,245	66,242	27,954	11,313	236,754
2008	149,071	65,580	21,860	10,736	247,247
2009	153,492	65,206	22,846	10,628	252,172
2010 [2]	186,881	60,207	24,693	8,848	280,636
		%			
1992	37.6	39.7	20.5	2.2	100.0
1993	41.2	43.9	11.9	3.0	100.0
1994	45.6	42.0	9.1	3.3	100.0
1995	50.1	36.4	13.2	0.4	100.0
1996	55.5	30.2	12.6	1.7	100.0
1997	59.4	27.8	11.3	1.6	100.0
1998	56.2	29.2	13.1	1.5	100.0
1999	57.5	29.1	12.8	0.5	100.0
2000	59.9	26.6	13.2	0.2	100.0
2001	62.1	26.6	11.1	0.1	100.0
2002	60.2	27.2	11.0	1.7	100.0
2003	54.7	29.4	11.7	4.2	100.0
2004	56.7	26.4	13.9	3.0	100.0
2005	59.6	24.2	13.6	2.6	100.0
2006	54.9	28.0	12.9	4.1	100.0
2007	55.4	28.0	11.8	4.8	100.0
2008	60.3	26.5	8.8	4.3	100.0
2009	60.9	25.9	9.1	4.2	100.0
2010 [2]	66.6	21.5	8.8	3.2	100.0

[1] Includes defered removal order class, post determination refugee claimant class, temporary resident permit holders and humanitarian and compassionate/public policy cases.
[2] Observed data are preliminary

Source: Adapted from the Statistics Canada publication *Report on the demographic situation in Canada,* Catalogue 91-209-X, Issue 2011001, http://www.statcan.gc.ca/bsolc/olc-cel/olc-cel?catno=91-209-XWE&lang=eng

MOTHER TONGUE[1]
2006 CENSUS (TOP 25)

Language	Total Responses
English	18,232,200
French	6,970,405
Italian	476,905
Chinese, n.o.s.	467,235
German	466,655
Panjabi (Punjabi)	382,585
Cantonese	369,645
Spanish	362,120
Arabic	286,790
Tagalog (Pilipino, Filipino)	266,445
Portuguese	229,280
Polish	217,605
Mandarin	173,730
Urdu	156,420
Vietnamese	146,410
Ukrainian	141,805
Persian (Farsi)	138,075
Russian	136,235
Dutch	133,240
Korean	128,120
Greek	123,575
Tamil	122,020
Gujarati	86,285
Hindi	85,500
Cree	84,905

[1] Total Single and Multiple Responses

Source: Adapted from the Statistics Canada publication *Language, 2006 Census,* Catalogue 97-555-X, Issue 2006007.

Net Migration for Provinces and Territories, 1995-2012													
Year [1]	NL	PE	NS	NB	QC	ON	MB	SK	AB	BC	YK	NT	NU
1995/1996	-7,436	638	-1,245	-369	-12,626	-2,822	-3,566	-2,161	7,656	22,025	564	-554	-104
1996/1997	-8,134	136	-1,648	-1,263	-17,436	1,977	-5,873	-2,794	26,282	9,880	-54	-696	-377
1997/1998	-9,490	-416	-2,569	-3,192	-16,958	9,231	-5,276	-1,940	43,089	-10,029	-1,024	-1,316	-110
1998/1999	-5,695	193	201	-1,244	-13,065	16,706	-2,113	-4,333	25,191	-14,484	-747	-555	-55
1999/2000	-4,263	104	-270	-1,183	-12,146	22,369	-3,456	-7,947	22,674	-14,610	-691	-651	70
2000/2001	-4,493	165	-2,077	-1,530	-9,442	18,623	-4,323	-8,410	20,457	-8,286	-572	-160	48
2001/2002	-3,352	62	-898	-1,218	-4,350	5,354	-4,344	-8,820	26,235	-8,556	-221	84	24
2002/2003	-1,683	165	510	-843	-1,829	637	-2,875	-5,141	11,903	-1,037	149	242	-198
2003/2004	-2,027	144	-772	-760	-822	-6,935	-2,565	-4,521	10,606	7,865	27	-105	-135
2004/2005	-3,710	-139	-3,041	-2,074	-4,963	-11,172	-7,227	-9,515	34,423	8,214	53	-668	-181
2005/2006	-4,342	-639	-3,024	-3,487	-9,411	-17,501	-7,881	-7,083	45,795	8,800	-73	-954	-200
2006/2007	-4,067	-849	-4,126	-2,632	-12,865	-20,047	-5,500	1,549	33,809	15,005	101	-221	-157
2007/2008	-528	-291	-1,794	-908	-11,682	-14,750	-3,703	4,171	15,317	14,643	235	-420	-290
2008/2009	1,877	-536	-751	-237	-7,419	-15,601	-3,111	2,983	13,184	9,995	228	-577	-35
2009/2010	1,558	60	612	571	-3,258	-4,662	-2,412	2,153	-3,271	8,728	325	-351	-53
2010/2011	30	-210	-41	-158	-4,763	-4,007	-3,517	545	8,443	3,421	363	-179	73
2011/2012	-1,556	-1,252	-3,008	-2,182	-3,886	-8,091	-4,675	2,846	28,170	-4,648	265	-1,491	-492

Footnotes

[1]Period from July 1 to June 30

Source: Adapted from Statistics Canada's CANSIM database http://www5.statcan.gc.ca/cansim/home-accueil?lang=eng Table 051-0018, August 2011.

(accessed: October 15, 2012)

EDUCATION STATISTICS, CANADA				
	Total enrolment	University enrolment	College enrolment	Total post-secondary educators
2004/2005	1,629,852	1,021,500	608,352	38,572
2005/2006	1,655,697	1,050,057	605,637	39,615
2006/2007	1,678,587	1,066,764	611,823	40,567
2007/2008	1,714,902	1,072,899	642,000	41,306
2008/2009	1,744,554	1,114,701	629,853	41,954
2009/2010	1,905,516	1,203,894	701,622	44,423

Source: Adapted from Statistics Canada, 81C9996, Culture, Tourism and Education Statistics Division, various education surveys, 2008/2009. (Accessed October 15, 2012)

Incident-Based Crime Statistics, by Detailed Violations Annual						
	Statistics	2,007	2,008	2,009	2,010	2,011
Total, all violations	Actual incidents	2,534,730	2,485,207	2,448,805	2,379,667	2,277,258
Total, all violations	Rate per 100,000 population	7,697	7,459	7,260	6,973	6,604
Total, all Criminal Code violations (excluding traffic)	Actual incidents	2,271,754	2,204,643	2,172,960	2,094,875	1,984,916
Total, all Criminal Code violations (excluding traffic)	Rate per 100,000 population	6,899	6,617	6,442	6,139	5,756
Homicide (17,24)	Actual incidents	594	611	610	554	598
Homicide (17,24)	Rate per 100,000 population	2	2	2	2	2
Sexual assault, level 3, aggravated	Actual incidents	141	139	119	179	140
Sexual assault, level 3, aggravated	Rate per 100,000 population	0	0	0	1	0
Assault, level 3, aggravated	Actual incidents	3,481	3,593	3,619	3,481	3,486
Assault, level 3, aggravated	Rate per 100,000 population	11	11	11	10	10
Total firearms; use of, discharge, pointing	Actual incidents	1,642	1,479	1,736	2,017	1,936
Total firearms; use of, discharge, pointing	Rate per 100,000 population	5	4	5	6	6
Total robbery (18)	Actual incidents	34,182	32,372	32,463	30,478	29,746
Total robbery (18)	Rate per 100,000 population	104	97	96	89	86
Total forcible confinement or kidnapping (34)	Actual incidents	4,660	4,732	4,791	4,301	3,774
Total forcible confinement or kidnapping (34)	Rate per 100,000 population	14	14	14	13	11
Total theft of motor vehicle (46)	Actual incidents	145,714	125,568	107,992	92,506	82,411
Total theft of motor vehicle (46)	Rate per 100,000 population	443	377	320	271	239
Total theft over $5,000 (non-motor vehicle)	Actual incidents	17,430	16,758	15,795	15,649	15,153
Total theft over $5,000 (non-motor vehicle)	Rate per 100,000 population	53	50	47	46	44
Identity fraud (30)	Actual incidents	0	105	564	6,188	7,914
Identity fraud (30)	Rate per 100,000 population	0	0	2	18	23
Arson	Actual incidents	13,015	13,371	13,404	12,234	10,378
Arson	Rate per 100,000 population	40	40	40	36	30
Counterfeiting (19)	Actual incidents	719	1,028	818	815	620
Counterfeiting (19)	Rate per 100,000 population	2	3	2	2	2
Total impaired driving	Actual incidents	79,395	84,694	88,303	87,231	90,277
Total impaired driving	Rate per 100,000 population	241	254	262	256	262
Total, possession, other Controlled Drugs and Substances Act drugs	Actual incidents	9,310	9,091	8,224	9,761	10,332
Total, possession, other Controlled Drugs and Substances Act drugs	Rate per 100,000 population	28	27	24	29	30

Source: Adapted from the Statistics Canada publication, *Juristat*, Catalogue 85-002-XIE2011001, July 2011, http://www.statcan.gc.ca/bsolc/olccel/olccel?catno=85-002-XIE?lang=eng. (Accessed October 15, 2012)

Canadian Internet use, By Age Group and Internet Activity, 2010 (Percent)

	Internet Users				
	16 years and under	16 to 24 years	25 to 44 years	45 to 64 years	65 years and over
E-mail	93.5	96.8	95.6	90.3	89.7
Use instant messenger	47.2	73.4	52.3	33.5	24.3
Visit or interact with government websites	64.5	60.5	73.1	62.3	42.6
Search for medical or health-related information	64.1	58.7	68	63	62.8
Formal education, training or school work	36.7	74.3	39.2	21.4	7.7
Travel information or making travel arrangements	65.1	54.2	69.3	68	56.5
Search for employment	37.3	55		25.4	3.5
Electronic banking (paying bills, viewing statements, transferring funds between accounts)	68.3	65.7	80.1	62	45.2
Research investments	27.3	16.2	29.7	30.7	25.1
Read or watch the news	68	69.7	73.9	63.7	54.8
Research community events	53.9	50.1	61.4	51.2	38.4
Window shop or browse for information on goods or services	74.3	76.5	82.4	69.5	51.8
Sell goods or services (through auction sites)	19.3	17.4	24.2	17.2	9.8
Use social networking sites	58.1	91	70.2	36.7	19.9
Contribute content or participate in discussion groups (blogging, message boards, posting images)	19.2	33.1	22.5	11.2	7
Play online games	32.8	57.9	32.3	21.3	29.8
Obtain or save music (free or paid downloads)	45.6	76.9	52	28.9	18.3
Obtain or save software (free or paid downloads)	35.1	51.1	38.5	26.7	20.5
Listen to the radio online	36.6	41.7	44.9	29.4	17.4
Download or watch television online	32.6	54.7	39.8	18.4	11.4
Download or watch movies or video clips online	47.1	75.3	55.3	30.5	17.8
Make telephone calls online	23.8	27.7	28.5	17.9	18

Footnotes:

[1]Internet users are individuals who answered that they used the Internet for personal non business use from any location in the past twelve months.

[2]The Canadian Internet Use Survey was redesigned for 2010 and its findings should not be compared with those from previous surveys.

Source: Statistics Canada, http://www40.statcan.gc.ca/l01/cst01/comm24-eng.htm, August 2011. (Accessed October 15, 2012)

Weights & Measures

THE INTERNATIONAL SYSTEM OF UNITS (SI) (BASE & SUPPLEMENTARY UNITS)

With the permission of the Canadian Standards Association, material is reproduced from CSA Standard CAN/CSA-Z234.1-89 (Canadian Metric Practice Guide), which is copyrighted by CSA, 178 Rexdale Blvd., Etobicoke, ON M9W 1R3. While use of this material has been authorized, CSA shall not be responsible for the manner in which the information is presented, nor for any interpretations thereof.

BASE UNITS

The International System of Units includes two classes of units: seven base units, and derived units. The base units are seven precisely defined units used internationally for teaching and scientific research.

SI BASE UNITS

Quantity	Name	Symbol
length	metre	m
mass	kilogram	kg
time	second	s
electric current	ampere	A
thermodynamic temperature	kelvin	K
amount of substance	mole	mol
luminous intensity	candela	cd

SI PREFIXES

Multiplying Factor	Prefix	Symbol
1 000 000 000 000 000 000 = 10^{18}	exa	E
1 000 000 000 000 000 = 10^{15}	peta	P
1 000 000 000 000 = 10^{12}	tera	T
1 000 000 000 = 10^{9}	giga	G
1 000 000 = 10^{6}	mega	M
1 000 = 10^{3}	kilo	k
100 = 10^{2}	hecto	h
10 = 10^{1}	deca	da
0.1 = 10^{-1}	deci	d
0.01 = 10^{-2}	centi	c
0.001 = 10^{-3}	milli	m
0.000 001 = 10^{-6}	micro	µ
0.000 000 001 = 10^{-9}	nano	n
0.000 000 000 001 = 10^{-12}	pico	p
0.000 000 000 000 001 = 10^{-15}	femto	f
0.000 000 000 000 000 001 = 10^{-18}	atto	a

SI Prefixes and their symbols given in the above table are used to form names and symbols of decimal multiples or sub-multiples of SI units.

SI DERIVED UNITS WITH SPECIAL NAMES

Name	Symbol	Typical Form [1]	In Base Units	Quantity
becquerel	Bq	s^{-1}	s^{-1}	activity of radionuclides
coulomb	C	s•A	s•A	quantity of electricity, electric charge
degree Celsius	°C	K	K	Celsius Temperature [2]
farad	F	C/V	$m^{-2}•kg^{-1}•s^{4}•A^{2}$	electric capacitance
gray	Gy	J/kg	$m^{2}•s^{-2}$	absorbed dose of ionizing radiation
henry	H	Wb/A	$m^{2}•kg•s^{-2}•A^{-2}$	inductance
hertz	Hz	s^{-1}	s^{-1}	frequency [3]
joule	J	N•m	$m^{2}•kg•s^{-2}$	energy, work, quantity of heat
lumen	lm	cd•sr	cd	luminous flux
lux	lx	lm/m^{2}	$m^{-2}•cd$	illuminance
newton	N	$m•kg/s^{2}$	$m•kg•s^{-2}$	force
ohm		V/A	$m^{2}•kg•s^{-3}•A^{-2}$	electric resistance
pascal	Pa	N/m^{2}	$m^{-1}•kg•s^{-2}$	pressure, stress
radian	rad	m/m	$m•m^{-1} = 1$	plane angle
siemens	S	A/V	$m^{-2}•kg^{-1}•s^{3}•A^{2}$	electric conductance
sievert	Sv	J/kg	$m^{2}•s^{-2}$	dose equivalent of ionizing radiation
steradian	sr	m^{2}/m^{2}	$m^{2}•m^{-2} = 1$	solid angle
tesla	T	Wb/m^{2}	$kg•s^{-2}•A^{-1}$	magnetic flux density
volt	V	W/A	$m^{2}•kg•s^{-3}•A^{-1}$	electric potential, potential difference, electromotive force
watt	W	J/s	$m^{2}•kg•s^{-3}$	power, radiant flux
weber	Wb	V•s	$m^{2}•kg•s^{-2}•A^{-1}$	magnetic flux

1. The formulae for derived units are not necessarily unique. For example, the volt may be defined as one joule per coulomb.
2. The Celsius temperature scale (previously called Centigrade, but renamed to avoid confusion with "centigrade", associated with the centesimal system of angular measurement) is the commonly used scale, except for certain scientific and technological purposes where the thermodynamic temperature scale is preferred. Note the use of uppercase C for Celsius.
3. The SI unit of frequency, the hertz, is one cycle per second. The reciprocal of the frequency is the period. The hertz should not be used as a measure of discrete items per unit of time, e.g. 5 boxes per second on an assembly line would not be referred to as 5 hertz, but may be referred to in terms of the reciprocal second i.e. $5s^{-1}$.

EXAMPLE OF SI DERIVED UNITS WITHOUT SPECIAL NAMES

Name	Typical Form	In Base Units	Quantity
ampere per metre	A/m	$A \bullet m^{-1}$	magnetic field strength
ampere per square metre	A/m^2	$A \bullet m^{-2}$	current density
candela per square metre	cd/m^2	$cd \bullet m^{-2}$	luminance
coulomb per cubic metre	C/m^3	$m^{-3} \bullet s \bullet A$	electric charge density
coulomb per kilogram	C/kg	$A \bullet s \bullet kg^{-1}$	exposure
coulomb per square metre	C/m^2	$m^{-2} \bullet s \bullet A$	surface density of charge, flux density
cubic metre	m^3	m^3	volume
cubic metre per kilogram	m^3/kg	$m^3 \bullet kg^{-1}$	specific volume
farad per metre	F/m	$m^{-3} \bullet kg^{-1} \bullet s^4 \bullet A^2$	permittivity
gray per second	Gy/s	$m^2 \bullet s^{-3}$	absorbed dose rate
henry per metre	H/m	$m \bullet kg \bullet s^{-2} \bullet A^{-2}$	permeability
joule per cubic metre	J/m^3	$m^{-1} \bullet kg \bullet s^{-2}$	energy density
joule per kelvin	J/K	$m^2 \bullet kg \bullet s^{-2} \bullet K^{-1}$	heat capacity, entropy
joule per kilogram kelvin	$J/(kg \bullet K)$	$m^2 \bullet s^{-2} \bullet K^{-1}$	specific heat capacity, specific entropy
joule per kilogram	J/kg	$m^2 \bullet s^{-2}$	specific energy
joule per mole	J/mol	$m^2 \bullet kg \bullet s^{-2} \bullet mol^{-1}$	molar energy
joule per mole kelvin	$J/(mol \bullet K)$	$m^2 \bullet kg \bullet s^{-2} \bullet K^{-1} \bullet mol^{-1}$	molar entropy, molar heat capacity
kilogram per cubic metre	kg/m^3	$kg \bullet m^{-3}$	density, mass density
metre per second	m/s	$m \bullet s^{-1}$	speed - linear
metre per second squared	m/s^2	$m \bullet s^{-2}$	acceleration - linear
mole per cubic metre	mol/m^3	$mol \bullet m^{-3}$	concentration (of amount of substance)
newton metre	$N \bullet m$	$m^2 \bullet kg \bullet s^{-2}$	moment of force
newton per metre	N/m	$kg \bullet s^{-2}$	surface tension
pascal second	$Pa \bullet s$	$m^{-1} \bullet kg \bullet s^{-1}$	dynamic viscosity
radian per second	rad/s	s^{-1}	speed- angular
radian per second squared	rad/s^2	s^{-2}	acceleration- angular
reciprocal metre	m^{-1}	m^{-1}	wave number*
square metre	m^2	m^2	area
square metre per second	m^2/s	$m^2 \bullet s^{-1}$	kinematic viscosity
volt per metre	V/m	$m \bullet kg \bullet s^{-3} \bullet A^{-1}$	electric field strength
watt per metre kelvin	$W/(m \bullet K)$	$m \bullet kg \bullet s^{-3} \bullet K^{-1}$	thermal conductivity
watt per square metre	W/m^2	$kg \bullet s^{-3}$	heat flux density, irradiance
watt per square metre steradian	$W/(m^2 \bullet sr)$	$kg \bullet s^{-3}$	radiance
watt per steradian	W/sr	$m^2 \bullet kg \bullet s^{-3}$	radiant intensity

UNITS PERMITTED FOR USE WITH THE SI

Quantity	Name (UNIT)	Symbol (UNIT)	Definition [1]
time	minute	min	1 min = **60** s [2]
	hour	h	1 h = **3600** s [2]
	day	d	1 d = **86 400** s [2]
	year	a	
plane angle	degree	°	1° = (**/180**) rad [3]
	minute	’	1’ = (**/10 800**) rad [3]
	second	”	1” = (**/648 000**) rad [3]
	revolution	r	1 r = **2** rad [4]
area	hectare	ha	1 ha = **1** hm^2 = **10 000** m^2 [5]
volume	litre	L	1 L = **1** dm^3 [6]
mass	metric ton or tonne	t	1 t = **1000** kg [7] = **1** Mg
linear density	tex	tex	1 tex = **1 x 10^{-6}** kg/m [8]
energy	electronovolt	eV	* [9]
mass of atom	unified atomic mass unit	u	* [10]
length	astronomical unit parsec	pc	* [11, 12]

1. Conversion factors that are exact are shown in boldface.
2. These sysmbols are used only in the sense of duration of time & not for expressing the time of day.
3. No space is left between these symbols & the last digit of a number. The unit “degree”, with its decimal subdivisions, is used when the unit “radian” is not suitable.
4. The designations revolution per minute (r/min) and revolution per second (r/s) are widely used in connection with rotating machinery.
5. Because of the need for a unit similar to the acre, the hectare will continue to be recognized as a unit for use in surveying & agriculture.
6. The international symbol for litre is L or l. In order to avoid possible confusion with the number one, the “L” is preferred in Canada.
7. Care must be taken in the interpretation of the word “tonne” when it occurs in French text of Canadian origin, where the meaning may be a “ton of 2000 pounds”.
8. The tex is used only in the textile industry.
9. One electronvolt is the kinetic energy acquired by an electron in passing through a potential difference of 1V in vacuum.
10. The unified atomic mass unit is equal to the fraction 1/12 of the mass of an atom of the nuclide ^{12}C.
11. The astronomical symbol does not have an international symbol; abbreviations are used (e.g. AU in English, UA in French). The astronomical unit of distance is the length of the radius of the unperturbed circular orbit of a body of negligible mass moving around the sun with a sidereal angular velocity of 0.017 202 098 950 radian per day of 86 400 ephemeris seconds.
12. 1 parsec (pc) is the distance at which 1 astronomical unit subtends an angle of 1 second of arc.

CONVERSION OF UNITS TO THE INTERNATIONAL SYSTEM OF UNITS (SI)

Area

1 acre	=0.404 685 6 ha
1 arpent (French measure)*	=0.341 889 4 ha
1 circular mil	=506.7 x 10^{-6} or μm^2
1 legal subdivision (40 acres)	=0.161 874 2 km^2
1 perch (French measure)*	=34.188 94 m^2
1 rood (1210 square yards)	=0.101 171 4 ha
1 section (1 mile square, 640 acres)	=2.589 988 km^2
1 square foot	=929.030 4 cm^2
1 square foot (French measure)*	=1 055.214 cm^2
1 square inch	=645.16 mm^2
1 square mile	=2.589 988 km^2
1 square yard	=0.836 127 4 m^2
1 township (36 sections)	=93.239 57 km^2

* Measures formerly used to describe certain land in the Province of Québec

Energy

1 British thermal unit (Btu) (International Table)	= 1.055 056 kJ
1 British thermal unit (Btu) (mean)	= 1.055 87 kJ
1 British thermal unit (Btu) (thermochemical)	= 1.054 35 kJ
1 British thermal unit (Btu) (39° F)	= 1.059 67 kJ
1 British thermal unit (Btu) (59° F, 15° C)	= 1.054 80 kJ
1 British thermal unit (Btu) (60.5° F)	= 1.054 615 kJ
1 Calorie (dietetic)	= 4.185 5 kJ
1 calorie (International Table)	= 4.186 8 J
1 calorie (thermochemical)	= 4.184 J
1 calorie (15° C)	= 4.185 5 J
1 calorie (15° C)	= 4.185 8 J
1 electronovolt	= 0.160 217 7 aJ
1 erg	= 0.1 µJ
1 foot poundal	= 42.140 11 mJ
1 foot pound-force	= 1.355 818 J
1 horsepower hour	= 2.684 520 MJ
1 kilowatt hour	= 3.6 MJ
1 therm	= 105.506 MJ
1 ton (nuclear equivalent of TNT)	= 4.2 GJ
1 watt hour	= 3.6 kJ
1 watt second	= 1 J

Force

1 dyne	=10 µN
1 kilogram-force	= 9.806 65 N
1 kilopond	= 9.806 65 N
1 kip (thousand pounds force)	= 4.448 222 kN
1 ounce-force	= 0.278 013 9 N
1 poundal	= 0.138 255 0 N
1 pound-force	= 4.448 222 N

Length

1 angstrom	=0.1 nm
1 arpent (French measure)*	=58.471 31 m
1 astronomical unit	=149.597 870 Gm
1 chain (66 feet)	=20.116 8 m
1 ell (45 inches)	=1.143 m
1 fathom	=1.828 8 m
1 fermi	=1 fm
1 foot	=0.304 8 m
1 foot (French measure)*	=0.324 840 6 m
1 foot (US survey, limited usage)	=0.304 800 6 m
1 furlong	=0.201 168 km
1 inch	=25.4 mm
1 league (Intl. nautical)	=5.556 km
1 league (UK nautical)	=5.559 552 km
1 league (US)	=4.828 032 km
1 light year	=9.460 528 Pm
1 link (1/100 chain)	=0.201 168 m
1 microinch	=25.4 nm
1 micron	=1 µm
1 mil (0.001 inch)	=25.4 µm
1 mile	=1.609 344 km
1 mile (Intl. nautical)	=1.852 km
1 mile (UK nautical)	=1.853 184 km
1 mile (US nautical)	=1.852 km
1 parsec	=30.856 78 Pm
1 perch	=5.029 2 m
1 perch (French measure)*	=5.847 130 8 m
1 pica (printers)	=4.217 518 mm
1 point (printers)	=0.351 459 8 mm
1 pole	=5.029 2 m
1 rod	=5.029 2 m
1 yard	=0.914 4 m

Mass

1 carat	=200 mg
1 cental (100 lb)	=45.359 237 kg
1 coal tub (100 lb, Newfoundland)	=45.359 237 kg
1 drachm (apothecary)	=3.887 935 g
1 dram (apothecary, US)	=3.887 935 g
1 dram (avoirdupois)	=1.771 845 g
1 gamma	=1 µg
1 grain	=64.798 91 mg
1 hundredweight (100 lb)	=45.359 237 kg
1 hundredweight (long 112 lb, UK)	=50.802 35 kg
1 ounce (avoirdupois)	=28.349 523 g
1 ounce (troy or apothecary)	=31.103 476 8 g
1 metric carat	=200 mg
1 pennyweight	=1.555 174 g
1 pound (avoirdupois)	=0.453 592 37 kg
1 pound (troy or apothecary)	=373.241 721 6 g
1 quarter (28 lb, UK)	=12.700 58 kg
1 scruple (apothecary, 20 grains)	=1.295 978 g
1 slug	=14.593 90 kg
1 stone (14 lb, UK)	=6.350 293 kg
1 ton (2240 lb, UK)	=1.016 046 908 8 Mg
1 ton (short, 2000 lb)	=0.907 184 74 Mg
1 unified atomic mass	=1.660 540 x 10^{-27} kg

Power

1 Btu (IT) per hour	=0.293 071 1 W
1 Btu (thermochemical) per hour	=0.292 875 1 W
1 Btu (thermochemical) per minute	=17.572 50 W
1 Btu (thermochemical) per second	=1.054 350 kW
1 foot pound-force per hour	=0.376 616 1 mW

1 foot pound-force per second	=1.355 818 W
1 horsepower (boiler)	=9.809 50 kW
1 horsepower (electric)	=746 W
1 horsepower (metric, cheval vapeur)	=735.498 75 W
1 horsepower (water)	=746.043 W
1 horsepower (550 ft•lbf/s)	=745.699 9 W

Pressure or Stress (Force per Area)

1 atmosphere, standard	=101.325 kPa (=760 torr)
1 atmosphere, technical	=98.066 5 kPa (=1 kgf/cm^2)
1 bar	=100 kPa
1 foot of water (39.2° F, 4° C)	=2.988 98 kPa
1 inch of mercury (conventional 32° F)	=3.386 39 kPa
1 inch of mercury (60° F)	=3.376 85 kPa
1 inch of mercury (68° F, 20° C)	=3.374 11 kPa
1 inch of water (conventional)	=249.088 9 Pa
1 inch of water (39.2° F, 4° C)	=249.082 Pa
1 inch of water (60° F)	=248.843 Pa
1 inch of water (68° F, 20° C)	=248.641 Pa
1 ksi (1000 lbf/in^2)	=6.894 757 MPa
1 poundal /square foot	=1.488 164 Pa
1 pound-force/square foot	=47.880 26 Pa
1 pound-force/square inch (psi)	=6.894 757 kPa
1 ton-force/square inch	=13.789 514 MPa
1 ton-force (UK)/square inch	=15.444 3 MPa
1 torr	=133.322 4 Pa

Temperature

Celsius temperature	= temperature in kelvins - 273.15
Fahrenheit temperature	= 1.8 (Celsius temperature) + 32
Fahrenheit temperature	= 1.8 (temperature in kelvins) - 459.67
Rankine temperature	= 1.8 (temperature in kelvins)

Velocity (Speed)

1 foot per hour	=84.666 67 µm/s =304.8 mm/h
1 foot per minute	=5.08 mm/s =304.8 mm/min
1 foot per second	=304.8 mm/s
1 inch per minute	=25.4 mm/min
1 inch per second	=25.4 mm/s
1 knot (International)	=1.852 km/h =0.514 444 4 m/s
1 knot (UK)	=1.853 184 km/h
1 mile per hour	=0.447 04 m/s =1.609 344 km/h
1 mile per minute	=26.822 4 m/s

Volume

1 acre foot	=1233.482 m^3
1 barrel (oil, 42 US gallons)	=0.158 987 3 m^3
1 barrel (US dry, 7056 in^3)	=0.115 627 1 m^3
1 barrel (US dry, cranberries, 5826 in^3)	=95.471 03 dm^3
1 barrel (36 UK gallons)	=0.163 659 2 m^3
1 board foot [a]	=2.359 737 dm^3
1 bushel	=36.368 72 dm^3
1 bushel (US dry, 2150.42 in^3)	=35.239 07 dm^3
1 cord (128 ft^3, 4 ft x 4 ft x 8 ft, stacked wood)	=3.624 556 m^3
1 cubic foot	=28.316 85 dm^3
1 cubic inch	=16.387 064 cm^3
1 cubic yard	=0.764 554 9 m^3
1 cunit (100 ft^3, solid wood)	=2.831 685 m^3
1 cup	=250 cm^3
1 demiard	=0.284 130 6 dm^3
1 drop (1/100 teaspoon)	=0.05 cm^3
1 fluid dram	=3.551 633 cm^3
1 fluid dram (US measure)	=3.696 691 cm^3
1 fluid ounce	=28.413 062 cm^3
1 fluid ounce (US)	=29.573 53 cm^3
1 gallon	=4.546 09 dm^3
1 gallon (US)	=3.785 412 dm^3
1 gill	=0.142 065 dm^3
1 gill (US)	=0.118 294 dm^3
1 herring barrel	=145.474 9 dm^3
1 herring tub	=72.737 44 dm^3
1 hogshead	=245.488 9 dm^3
1 lambda	=1 mm^3
1 minim	=59.193 9 mm^3
1 minim (US)	=61.611 52 mm^3
1 peck	=9.092 180 dm^3
1 peck (US dry)	=8.809 768 dm^3
1 Petrograd standard (165 ft^3, sawn timber)	=4.672 280 m^3
1 pint	=0.568 261 2 dm^3
1 pint (US dry)	=0.550 610 5 dm^3
1 pint (US liquid)	=0.473 176 5 dm^3
1 quart	=1.136 522 dm^3
1 quart (US dry)	=1.101 221 dm^3
1 quart (US liquid)	=0.946 352 9 dm^3
1 salt cart	=490.977 7 dm^3
1 salt tub	=81.829 62 dm^3
1 sand barrel	=81.829 62 dm^3
1 tablespoon	=15 cm^3
1 teaspoon	=5 cm^3
1 ton (register)	=2.831 685 m^3

a. The board foot is nominally 1x12x12 = 144 in^3. However, the actual volume of wood is about 2/3 of the nominal quality.

b. This applies to stacked wood, comprising wood, bark, & arispace, to a total volume of 128 ft^3.

c. Also referred to as the "imperial gallon".

MEASURES HAVING FORMER HOUSEHOLD USAGE

1 cup (Canadian, 8 fluid ounces)	=227 cm^3
1 cup (US, 8 fluid ounces)	=236 cm^3
1 cup (UK, 10 fluid ounces)	=284 cm^3
1 tablespoon (Canadian, 1/2 fluid ounce)	=14.21 cm^3
1 tablespoon (UK, 5/8 fluid ounce)	=17.8 cm^3
1 tablespoon (US, 1/2 fluid ounce)	=14.8 cm^3
1 teaspoon (1/6 fluid ounce)	=4.74 cm^3
1 teaspoon (UK, 5/24 fluid ounce)	=5.92 cm^3
1 teaspoon (US, 1/6 fluid ounce)	=4.93 cm^3
*1 cm^3	=1 ml

SECTION 2
ARTS & CULTURE

Many of the following categories are also represented in Section 3: Associations.

Art Galleries

National Art Galleries

National Gallery of Canada (NGC) / Musée des beaux-arts du Canada (MBAC)
PO Box 427 A, 380 Sussex Dr., Ottawa, ON K1N 9N4
Tel: 613-990-1985; Fax: 613-993-4385
Toll-Free: 800-319-2787
info@gallery.ca
www.gallery.ca
Social Media: www.youtube.com/ngcmedia
twitter.com/gallerydotca
www.facebook.com/nat ionalgallerycanada
Other contact information: TTY: 613-990-0777
The permanent collection of the National Gallery comprises paintings, sculpture, prints & drawings, photographs, film & video art from the Canadian, European, American & Asian schools. Special exhibitions as well as permanent installations of the gallery's collections are on display. The gallery also sends its exhibitions on tour across the country & participates in international exhibitions. Ser
Michael J. Audain, Chair OC, OBC, LLD
Marc Mayer, Director/CEO
Paul Lang, Deputy Director/Chief Curator, Collections, Research & Education
David Baxter, Deputy Director, Administration & Finance
Karen Colby-Stothart, Deputy Director, Exhibitions & Installations
Stephen Gritt, Director, Conservation & Technical Research
Allen LeBlanc, Director, Institutional Advancement
Lynne Perron, Acting Director, Human Resources
Matthew Symonds, Director/Ministerial Liaison, Corporate Secretariat
Serge Thériault, Director, Publishing, New Media & Distribution
J. Drouin-Brisebois, Curator, Contemporary Art
C. Hill, Curator, Canadian Art
G. Hill, Curator, Indigenous Art
A. Thomas, Curator, Photographs
J. Franklin, Head, Library, Archives & Research Fellowship Programs
M. Richardson, Head, Education & Research Programs

Online Art Galleries

Yaneff.com
Tel: 905-584-9398Toll-Free: 888-304-7843
posters@yaneff.com
www.yaneff.com
www.facebook.com/pages/Yaneffcom/207 960699224765
Specializes in rare, 19th-century, 20th century & modern posters online
Chris Yaneff, Director R.C.A., R.GDC, F.GDC
Greg Yaneff, Director/Curator

Alberta

Provincial Art Galleries

Art Gallery of Alberta (AGA)
2 Sir Winston Churchill Sq., Edmonton, AB T5J 2C1
Tel: 780-422-6223; Fax: 780-426-3105
info@youraga.ca
www.youraga.ca
Social Media: www.youtube.com/user/ArtGalleryAlberta
twitter.com/yourAGA
www.faceboo k.com/artgalleryofalberta
Collections include: Canadian & international contemporary & historical paintings, sculpture, photography, video & graphic art. Research fields: Western Canadian art, historical & contemporary art; painting; sculpture; photography; graphics. Activities: Guided tours; lectures; films; gallery talks; art rental & sales gallery; studio art classes for children & adults; program workshops & seminars
Barry Zalmanowitz, Chair Q.C.
Catherine Crowston, Executive Director & Chief Curator
Rochelle Ball, Curatorial Administrator
Janis Galloway, Coordinator, Marketing

Local Art Galleries in Alberta

***Banff:* Walter Phillips Gallery (WPG)**
The Banff Centre, PO Box 1020 14, 107 Tunnel Mountain Dr., Banff, AB T1L 1H5
Tel: 403-762-6281; Fax: 403-762-6444
walter_phillipsgallery@banffcentre.ca
www.banffcentre.ca/WPG
Social Media: www.youtube.com/thebanffcentre
twitter.com/thebanffcentre
www.facebook.com/242702459137814
Contemporary, national & international fine arts; open year round

Jeff Melanson, President, Banff Centre
Sylvie Gilbert, Senior Curator

***Brocket:* Oldman River Cultural Centre**
PO Box 70, Brocket, AB T0K 0H0
Tel: 403-965-3939
Aboriginal history

***Calgary:* Art Gallery of Calgary**
117 - 8th Ave. SW, Calgary, AB T2P 1B4
Tel: 403-770-1350; Fax: 403-264-8077
info@artgallerycalgary.org
www.artgallerycalgary.org
Social Media: www.youtube.com/user/artgalleryofcalgary
twitter.com/TheAGC
www.facebo ok.com/147372308665188
Non-profit public gallery, exhibiting works by contemporary Canadian artists; travelling exhibitions & education programs
Brian Hearst, Managing Director, managingdirector@artgallerycalgary.org

***Calgary:* Illingworth Kerr Gallery (IKG)**
Alberta College of Art & Design, 1407 - 14 Ave. NW, Calgary, AB T2N 4R3
Tel: 403-284-7680; Fax: 403-289-6682
www.acad.ca/ikg.html
Contemporary art exhibitions, publications, lectures, screenings & related events
Wayne Baerwaldt, Director/Curator, 403-284-7632, wayne.baerwaldt@acad.ca
Tatiana Mellema, Assistant Curator, 403-284-7633, tatiana.mellema@acad.ca
Ann Thrale, Head Technician, ann.thrale@acad.ca

***Calgary:* Leighton Art Centre**
Box 9, Site 31, RR#8, Calgary, AB T2J 2T9
Tel: 403-931-3633; Fax: 403-931-3673
info@leightoncentre.org
www.leightoncentre.org
Year Founded: 1974 A.C. Leighton's paintings, as well as those by other prominent Alberta artists; programs for children & adults; open year round
Gervais Goodman, Chair
Tony Luppino, Executive Director, tluppino@leightoncentre.org
Karen Freeman, Director, Education Centre, karenf@leightoncentre.org

***Calgary:* Marion Nicoll Gallery**
Alberta College of Art & Design, 1407 - 14th Ave. NW, Calgary, AB T2N 4R3
Tel: 403-283-7655
mng.acadsa@acad.ca
marionnicollgallery.wordpress.com; www.acad.ca/mng.html
Student-run gallery for students attending the Alberta College of Art & Design.
Melinda Topilko, Coordinator, Marion Nicoll Gallery, 403-284-7674

***Edmonton:* Front Gallery**
12312 Jasper Ave., Edmonton, AB T5N 3K6
Tel: 780-488-2952
www.thefrontgallery.com
Also provides picture framing services.

***Edmonton:* Latitude 53**
10248 - 106 St., Edmonton, AB T5J 1H5
Tel: 780-423-5353; Fax: 780-424-9117
info@latitude53.org; admin@latitude53.org
www.latitude53.org
twitter.com/Latitude53
www.facebook.com/Latitude53
Contemporary artistic projects, experimental cultural development; performance art; literary projects; interdisciplinary art
Vieri Berretti, President, board@latitude53.org
Todd Janes, Executive Director, todd.janes@latitude53.org

***Edmonton:* West End Gallery**
12308 Jasper Ave., Edmonton, AB T5N 3K5
Tel: 780-488-4892Toll-Free: 855-488-4892
art@westendgalleryltd.com
www.westendgalleryltd.com
twitter.com/westen dgallery
www.facebook.com/pages/West-End-Gallery/185219480017
Year Founded: 1975 Fine art gallery representing Canadian paintings & sculpture; the largest representation of glass artists in Canada

***Victoria:* West End Gallery**
1203 Broad St., Victoria, BC V8W 2A4
Tel: 250-388-0009Toll-Free: 877-388-0009
Year Founded: 1994
Daniel Hudon, Co-Owner
Lana Hudon, Co-Owner

***Grande Prairie:* The Art Gallery of Grande Prairie**
#103, 9839 - 103 Ave., Grande Prairie, AB T8V 6M7
Tel: 780-532-8111; Fax: 780-539-9522
info@prariegallery.com
aggp.ca
Public art gallery. The gallery's collection currently stands at approximately 600 works of art, almost exclusively created in Alberta in the midto late 20th Century.
Robert Steven, Executive Director/Curator, rsteven@prairiegallery.com

***Lethbridge:* Southern Alberta Art Gallery (SAAG)**
601 - 3 Ave. South, Lethbridge, AB T1J 0H4
Tel: 403-327-8770; Fax: 403-328-3913
info@saag.ca
www.saag.ca
twitter.com/THESAAG
www.facebook.com/southe rnalbertaartgallery
Fosters the work of contemporary visual artists who challenge the boundaries of their discipline & advance their work in a larger public realm
Marilyn Smith, Director, msmith@saag.ca
Ryan Doherty, Curator, rdoherty@saag.ca

***Lethbridge:* University of Lethbridge Art Gallery**
W600, Centre for the Arts, 4401 University Dr., Lethbridge, AB T1K 3M4
Tel: 403-329-2666; Fax: 403-382-7115
www.uleth.ca/artgallery
Social Media: vimeo.com/ulethartgallery
twitter.com/ulethartgallery
www.facebook.com /201495055897
Josephine Mills, Director & Curator, josephine.mills@uleth.ca

***Okotoks:* Okotoks Art Gallery (OAG)**
Station Cultural Centre, 53 North Railway St., Okotoks, AB T1S 1K1
Tel: 403-938-3204; Fax: 403-938-8963
culturehistory@okotoks.ca
www.okotoks.ca/artgallery.aspx
Year Founded: 1981 The art gallery serves the Town of Okotoks & the Foothills region, promoting art & visual culture. Summer hours: M-F 10:00-5:00, Sa, Su 12:00-5:00; Fall & Winter hours: Tu-Sa 10:00-5:00

***St Albert:* Art Gallery of St. Albert (AGSA)**
19 Perron St., St Albert, AB T8N 1E5
Tel: 780-460-4310; Fax: 780-460-9537
ahfgallery@artsheritage.ca
artgalleryofstalbert.ca
twitter.com/artgall erystalb
www.facebook.com/ArtsAndHeritageStAlbert
Hours of operation: Tu, W, F, Sa 1:00-5:00, Th 10:00-8:00.
Frances Gagnon, Director, Arts, francesg@artsheritage.ca
Glenda Haughian, Education Curator, glendah@artsheritage.ca
Jenny Willson-McGrath, Exhibition Curator, Rental & Sales, jennyw@artsheritage.ca

British Columbia

Provincial Art Galleries

Vancouver Art Gallery
750 Hornby St., Vancouver, BC V6Z 2H7
Tel: 604-662-4700; Fax: 604-682-1086
customerservice@vanartgallery.bc.ca
www.vanartgallery.bc.ca
twitter.co m/VanArtGallery
www.facebook.com/VancouverArtGallery
Other contact information: Info Line: 604-662-4719
Largest gallery in western Canada; presents major exhibitions from contemporary art to historical masters; founded in 1931, has over 7,800 works in its collection, 41,400 sq. ft. of exhibition space & is located in the former provincial courthouse in downtown Vancouver; collection includes acclaimed Canadian artists such as Stan Douglas, Jeff Wall & Ian Wallace.
George Kelly, Chair
Kathleen Bartels, Director
Paul Larocque, Associate Director

Local Art Galleries in British Columbia

***Brackendale:* Brackendale Art Gallery Theatre Teahouse**
PO Box 100, 41950 Government Rd., Brackendale, BC V0N 1H0
Tel: 604-898-3333; Fax: 604-898-3333
info@brackendaleartgallery.com
www.brackendaleartgallery.com
www.faceb ook.com/139533814492
The gallery also serves food, holds concerts, presents theatre productions, hosts workshops with artists, & more. Hours of operation: Sa, Su, & holidays 12:00-10:00.

***Burnaby:* Burnaby Art Gallery**
6344 Deer Lake Ave., Burnaby, BC V5G 2J3
Tel: 604-297-4422; Fax: 604-205-7339
gallery@burnaby.ca
www.burnabyartgallery.ca
Services include educational programs for children, adults & seniors; community projects & exhibitions in libraries & recreational centres; school programs support the exhibitions & take works of art into the schools
Darrin Martens, Director/Curator, darrin.martens@burnaby.ca

***Burnaby:* The Simon Fraser University Gallery**
AQ 3004, Simon Fraser University, 8888 University Dr., Burnaby, BC V5A 1S6
Tel: 604-291-4266; Fax: 604-291-3029
gallery@sfu.ca
www.sfu.ca/gallery
Hosts six or seven exhibitions a year, both historical & contemporary, covering the full range of media; serves the SFU community directly by providing an occasional platform for student, staff & faculty work to be shown; The Gallery also administers the Teck Gallery at the SFU Vancouver Campus, a small space used to show work that deals with social & environmental issues
Bill Jeffries, Director/Curator, bill_jeffries@sfu.ca
Adriana Contreras, Coordinator, acontrea@sfu.ca

***Campbell River:* Campbell River Art Gallery**
***Parent:* Campbell River & District Public Art Gallery**
Tyee Plaza, 1235 Shopper's Row, Campbell River, BC V9W 2C7
Tel: 250-287-2261; Fax: 250-287-2268
contact@crartgallery.ca
www.crartgallery.ca
www.facebook.com/290415662 283
Contemporary work from both local & visiting artists; classes, lectures & workshops throughout the year; open Tue.-Sat., 12:00-5:00; May-Sept. Mon.-Sat., 10:00-5:00
Jeanette Taylor, Executive Director
Liz Larsen Stoneberger, Curator

***Castlegar:* Kootenay Gallery of Art, History & Science**
***Also known as:* Kootenay Gallery**
120 Heritage Way, Castlegar, BC V1N 4M5
Tel: 250-365-3337
kootenaygallery@telus.net
www.kootenaygallery.com
Exhibits on art, history & science, from international to local sources; offers workshops, performances, lectures & classes; gift shop
Kathy Howard, Chair
Valentine Field, Executive Director

***Courtenay:* Comox Valley Art Gallery**
580 Duncan Ave., Courtenay, BC V9N 2M7
Tel: 250-338-6211; Fax: 250-338-6287
admin@comoxvalleyartgallery.com
www.comoxvalleyartgallery.com
Social Media: www.youtube.com/user/CVArtGallery
twitter.com/C_V_A_G
www.facebook.com /184055261880
The Comox Valley Art Gallery features contemporary art by regional, national, & international artists. Open Th-Sa 10:00-5:00.
Roger Albert, President
Sharon Karsten, Administrator
Anh Le, Curator, curator@comoxvalleyartgallery.com

***Dawson Creek:* Dawson Creek Art Gallery**
***Parent:* South Peace Arts Society**
#101, 816 Alaska Ave., Dawson Creek, BC V1G 4T6
Tel: 250-782-2601; Fax: 250-782-8801
artadmin@dcartgallery.ca
www.dcartgallery.ca
Open year round
Ellen Corea, Curator, curator@dcartgallery.ca

***Golden:* Kicking Horse Culture: Art Gallery of Golden (AGOG)**
PO Box 228, 516 - 9th Ave. North, Golden, BC V0A 1A0
Tel: 250-344-6186
info@kickinghorseculture.ca
kickinghorseculture.ca/art-gallery-of-golden
Social Media: www.youtube.com/user/khcgdac
twitter.com/goldenculture
www/facebook.co m/groups/43898318129
Open M-Sa 10:00-6:00.
Bill Usher, Executive Director, director@kickinghorseculture.ca

***Grand Forks:* Grand Forks & District Art & Heritage Centre**
***Also known as:* Gallery 2**
PO Box 2140, 524 Central Ave., Grand Forks, BC V0H 1H0
Tel: 250-442-2211; Fax: 250-442-0099
www.gallery2grandforks.ca
Historical & contemporary works by established & emerging regional, national & international artists
Robert Morton, President
Ted Fogg, Director/Curator, gfag1@shaw.ca

***Hope:* John Weaver Sculpture Museum**
***Also known as:* John Weaver Fine Arts Ltd.**
PO Box 1723, 19225 Silverhope Rd., Hope, BC V0X 1L0
Tel: 604-869-5312
johnweaver@johnweaverfinearts.com
www.johnweaverfinearts.com
Other contact information: Alternate Phone: 604-869-7293
Year Founded: 1977 John Weaver's work of bronzes based on historical, anthropological, & charity-work themes can be viewed by those wishing to learn about bronze sculpture & by those who wish to be commissioners of work; collection of over 60 years of work
Sara M. Lesztak, Secretary

***Kamloops:* Kamloops Art Gallery**
#101, 465 Victoria St., Kamloops, BC V2C 2A9
Tel: 250-377-2400; Fax: 250-828-0662
kamloopsartgallery@kag.bc.ca
www.kag.bc.ca
twitter.com/artsinkamloops
www.facebook.com/KamloopsArtsGallery
Changing exhibits of contemporary & historical art; permanent collection of Canadian art
Jaimie Drew, President
Jann L.M. Bailey, Executive Director, jlmb@kag.bc.ca
Charo Neville, Curator, cneville@kag.bc.ca

***Kaslo:* Langham Cultural Centre**
***Parent:* The Langham Cultural Society**
PO Box 1000, Kaslo, BC V0G 1M0
Tel: 250-353-2661; Fax: 250-353-2671
langham@netidea.com
www.thelangham.ca
Year Founded: 1975 Art exhibits; theatre; music; workshops; The Japanese Canadian Museum. Open Mon.-Fri. 9:00-12:00
Alice Windsor, Executive Director

***Kelowna:* Kelowna Art Gallery**
1315 Water St., Kelowna, BC V1Y 9R3
Tel: 250-762-2226; Fax: 250-762-9875
info@kelownaartgallery.com
www.kelownaartgallery.com
Social Media: www.youtube.com/user/KelownaArt
twitter.com/kelownaart
www.facebook.com/KelownaArtGallery
Historical & contemporary fine art; extensive education programs; open year round
Leona Baxter, President
Nataley Nagy, Executive Director, nataley@kelownaartgallery.com
Liz Wylie, Curator, liz@kelownaartgallery.com

***Maple Ridge:* Maple Ridge Art Gallery Society**
11944 Haney Pl., Maple Ridge, BC V2X 6G1
Tel: 604-476-2787; Fax: 604-476-2187
info@mract.org
www.theactmapleridge.org
twitter.com/mapleridgeact
ww w.facebook.com/mapleridgeact
Exhibition of local, amateur & professional artists; art rental program for patrons
Lindy Sisson, Executive Director

***Nakusp:* Bonnington Arts Centre**
6th Ave. West & 4th St. North, Nakusp, BC V0G 1R0
Tel: 250-265-4234
Located in Nakusp Elementary School. Open Sept.-June.

***Nanaimo:* Nanaimo Art Gallery**
c/o Vancouver Island University, Nanaimo Campus, #330, 900 - 5th St., Nanaimo, BC V9R 5S5
Tel: 250-740-6350; Fax: 250-740-6475
info@nanaimogallery.ca
www.nanaimogallery.ca
Celebrating art on the west coast; art central & sales program; gift shop full of elegant & eclectic gifts; inspiring & thought provoking exhibitions
Ian Niamath, President
Julie Bevan, Executive/Artistic Director
Ellen McCluskey, Curator
Chris Kuderle, Administrative Director

***New Westminster:* Amelia Douglas Gallery**
PO Box 2503, New Westminster, BC V3L 5B2
Tel: 604-527-5723
www.douglas.bc.ca/artscomm
A non-profit organization run by members of the Arts Exhibition Committee at Douglas College; mandate is to feature new & established BC artists & to enhance the educational offerings of the College
Nassi Soofin, Arts Events Officer, soofin@douglascollege.ca

***North Vancouver:* Presentation House Museum Galleries**
333 Chesterfield Ave., North Vancouver, BC V7M 3G9
Tel: 604-986-1351; Fax: 604-986-5380
info@presentationhousegallery.org
presentationhousegallery.org
Celebrates & preserves North Vancouver's social, industrial & cultural history
Cheryl Stevens, Chair
Reid Shier, Director/Curator, rshier@presentationhousegallery.org
Helga Pakasaar, Curator, hpakasaar@presentationhousegallery.org

***North Vancouver:* Seymour Art Gallery**
4360 Gallant Ave., North Vancouver, BC V7G 1L2
Tel: 604-924-1378; Fax: 604-924-3786
info@seymourartgallery.com
seymourartgallery.com
twitter.com/seymourga llery
www.facebook.com/373276142313
Open year round
Alan Bell, President
Sarah Cavanaugh, Curator
Marina Van Den Berg, Gallery Administrator

***Osoyoos:* Osoyoos Art Gallery**
8713 Main St., Osoyoos, BC V0H 1V0
Tel: 250-495-2800
www.osoyoosarts.com/artgallery.html
Open year round
Sue Whittaker, President, Osoyoos & District Arts Council Bd. of Dir., 250-495-7664, swhit@persona.ca
Tony Brummet, Director, 250-495-7968
Sharon Leonard, Curator, 250-495-2019

***Penticton:* Penticton Art Gallery**
199 Marina Way, Penticton, BC V2A 1H3
Tel: 250-493-2928; Fax: 250-493-3992
agso@shawbiz.ca
www.pentictonartgallery.com
Year Founded: 1972 The Penticton Art Gallery offers in-house & touring exhibitions from local, regional & national sources.
Robert Doull, President
Paul Crawford, Director/Curator, curator@pentictonartgallery.com

***Port Alberni:* Rollin Art Centre**
***Also known as:* Community Arts Council of the Alberni Valley**
3061 - 8th Ave., Port Alberni, BC V9Y 2K5
Tel: 250-724-3412
communityarts@shawcable.com
www.portalberniarts.com/portalberniarts_rollinartcentre.html
www.faceboo k.com/CommunityArtsCouncilOfTheAlberniValley
Melissa Martin, Arts Administrator

***Prince George:* Two Rivers Gallery**
***Parent:* Prince George Regional Art Gallery Association**
Prince George Art Gallery Association, 725 Civic Plaza, Prince George, BC V2L 5T1
Tel: 250-614-7800; Fax: 250-563-3211
www.tworiversartgallery.com
www.facebook.com/tworiversart
The Two Rivers Gallery is a centre for visual art in Prince George & the central interior of British Columbia, Canada. It seeks to encourage lifelong learning through the arts, create an environment for artistic & cultural expression, & provide opportunities through participation & exhibition.
Peter L. Thompson, Managing Director
George Harris, Curator

***Qualicum Beach:* The Old School House Arts Centre (TOSH)**
PO Box 791, 122 Fern Rd. West, Qualicum Beach, BC V9K 1T2
Tel: 250-752-6133
qbtosh@shaw.ca
www.theoldschoolhouse.org
Twelve resident artists; 3 exhibition galleries; concert series; classrooms; gift shop
Greg Sabo, President

***Richmond:* Richmond Art Gallery**
7700 Minoru Gate, Richmond, BC V6Y 1R9
Tel: 604-247-8300; Fax: 604-247-8368
gallery@richmond.ca
www.richmondartgallery.org
Social Media: www.youtube.com/user/RichmondArtGallery
www.facebook.com/RichmondArtGall eryBC
Presents a diverse program of exhibitions, workshops, lectures & special events, as well as outreach programs which focus on contemporary art & art issues
Barry Magrill, President
Lynn Beavis, Director
Nan Capogna, Curator

***Smithers:* Smithers Art Gallery**
Central Park Bldg., PO Box 122, 1425 Main St., Smithers, BC V0J 2N0
Tel: 250-847-3898
info@smithersart.org
smithersart.org
Public gallery, admission by donation; monthly exhibition rotation; workshops & artcamps for young & old, all artisan levels & mediums; call for a current listing

***South Surrey:* Arnold Mikelson Mind & Matter Gallery**
13743 -16 Ave., South Surrey, BC V4A 1P7
Tel: 604-536-6460
www.mindandmatterart.com
www.facebook.com/129219007093865
Wood sculptures of the late Arnold Mikelson
Mary Mikelson, Owner/Director, mary@mindandmatterart.com

***Vancouver:* Bill Reid Foundation**
639 Hornby St., Vancouver, BC V6C 2G3
Tel: 604-682-3455; Fax: 604-682-3310
info@billreidfoundation.org
billreidfoundation.org
The foundation collects & preserves the works of Haida artist, goldsmith, & writer Bill Reid.

***Vancouver:* Charles H. Scott Gallery**
Emily Carr University of Art & Design, 1399 Johnston St., Granville Island, Vancouver, BC V6H 3R9
Tel: 604-844-3809; Fax: 604-844-3801
scottgal@ecuad.ca
chscott.ecuad.ca
A public art gallery specializing in contemporary art. Open seven days a week.
Greg Bellerby, Director/Curator
Cate Rimmer, Curator

***Vancouver:* Circle Craft Gallery**
#, 1666 Johnston St., Net Loft Granville Island, Vancouver, BC V6H 3S2
Tel: 604-669-8021; Fax: 604-669-8585
market@circlecraft.net; shop@circlecraft.net
www.circlecraft.net
Social Media: www.flickr.com/photos/circle_craft_coop
twitter.com/circlecraft
www.fa cebook.com/CircleCraft
Features over 200 works of BC artists
Ron Kong, Store Manager
Paul Yard, Show Producer

***Vancouver:* Contemporary Art Gallery (CAG)**
555 Nelson St., Vancouver, BC V6B 6R5
Tel: 604-681-2700; Fax: 604-683-2710
info@contemporaryartgallery.ca
www.contemporaryartgallery.ca
Social Media: www.youtube.com/user/TheCAGchannel
twitter.com/CAGVancouver
www.facebo ok.com/114252503695
Promotes knowledge & understanding of contemporary visual art through: exhibitions that address current issues in contemporary art; educational programs in the form of artist & curator talks, student tours, high school projects, public symposia; publications; visiting artist/curator programs; information & resource services; The City of Vancouver Art Collection of 3,000 works of art
Ross Hill, President
Nigel Prince, Executive Director
Jenifer Papararo, Curator

***Vancouver:* Gallery Gachet**
88 East Cordova St., Vancouver, BC V6A 1K3
Tel: 604-687-2468; Fax: 604-687-1196
contact@gachet.org
gachet.org
Social Media: www.flickr.com/photos/gallerygachet
twitter.com/gallerygachet
Gallery Gachet is an artist-run public gallery in Vancouver's Downtown Eastside. Open W-Su 12:00-6:00.

***Vancouver:* grunt gallery**
#116, 350 - East 2nd Ave., Vancouver, BC V5T 4R8
Tel: 604-875-9516; Fax: 604-877-0073
grunt@telus.net
grunt.ca
Social Media: www.youtube.com/user/gruntgallery1
twitter.com/gruntgallery
www.facebo ok.com/gruntgallery
Year Founded: 1984 Artist-run centre furthering contemporary art through exhibitions, performances, artist talks, publications, & other projects. Open Wed. - Sat., 12-6
Glenn Alteen, Program Director, glenn@grunt.ca
Meagan Kus, Operations Director, meagan@grunt.ca
Demian Petryshyn, Coordinator, Programming & Communications, demian@grunt.ca

***Vancouver:* Heffel Gallery Limited**
2247 Granville St., Vancouver, BC V6H 3G1
Tel: 604-732-6505; Fax: 604-732-4245
Toll-Free: 800-528-9608
mail@heffel.com
www.heffel.com
Social Media: www.youtube.com/user/HeffelAuctions
twitter.com/heffelauction
Fine art auction house.
David K.J. Heffel, President, david@heffel.com
David K.J. Heffel, Director, david@heffel.com
Lisa Christensen, Calgary Representative, lisa@heffel.com

***Vancouver:* Marion Scott Gallery/Kardosh Projects**
2423 Granville St., Vancouver, BC V6B 1B6
Tel: 604-685-1934; Fax: 604-685-1890
art@marionscottgallery.com
www.marionscottgallery.com
www.facebook.com /141219279227412
Established in 1975, & one of the leading galleries dealing with Canadian Inuit art
Judy Kardosh, Director, judy@marionscottgallery.com
Robert Kardosh, Director/Curator, robert@marionscottgallery.com

***Vancouver:* Morris & Helen Belkin Art Gallery**
University of British Columbia, 1825 Main Mall, Vancouver, BC V6T 1Z2
Tel: 604-822-2759; Fax: 604-822-6689
belkin@interchange.ubc.ca
belkin.ubc.ca
Social Media: www.youtube.com/user/belkinartgallery
www.facebook.com/BelkinArtGallery
Specializes in exhibiting contemporary work by national & international artists; programming includes exhibitions, artists' talks, publications & collaborative projects with other galleries/organizations; masters program in Critical Curatorial Studies; archival collections focus on Vancouver Canadian avant garde in 1960s-70s
Scott Watson, Director/Curator/Professor, Art History, Visual Art & Theory, scott.watson@ubc.ca

***Vancouver:* VIVO Media Arts Centre**
1965 Main St., Vancouver, BC V5T 3C1
Tel: 604-872-8337
info@vivomediaarts.com
vivomediaarts.com
Year Founded: 1973 VIVO is vancouver's oldest media arts access centre, specializing in video production, exhibition, & distribution. Open Tu-Sa 11:00-6:00, & M by appointment.
Crista Dahl, Chair
Emma Hendrix, General Manager, admin@vivomediaarts.com

***Vancouver:* Western Front**
303 East 8th Ave., Vancouver, BC V5T 1S1
Tel: 604-876-9343; Fax: 604-876-4099
front.bc.ca
twitter.com/western_front
www.facebook.com/164127636934501
Year Founded: 1973 An artist-run centre dedicated to contemporary art & new music. The centre is open Tu-Sa 12:00-5:00.
Carie Helm, President
Kate Armstrong, Interim Executive Director, katearmstrong@front.bc.ca
Jesse Birch, Curator, Exhibitions, jessebirch@front.bc.ca
D.B. Boyko, Curator/Director, New Music, newmusic@front.bc.ca
Sarah Todd, Curator, Media Arts, sarahtodd@front.bc.ca

***Vancouver:* Wickaninnish Gallery**
The Net Loft, #14, 1166 Johnston St., Vancouver, BC V6H 3S2
Tel: 604-681-1057
wickgallery@gmail.com; wickaninnish@telus.net
www.wickaninnishgallery.com
Year Founded: 1987 Native-owned art gallery & boutique
Patricia Rivard, Owner

***Vernon:* Vernon Public Art Gallery (VPAG)**
3228 - 31st Ave., Vernon, BC V1T 2H3
Tel: 250-545-3173; Fax: 250-545-9096
info@vernonpublicartgallery.com
www.vernonpublicartgallery.com
Social Media: www.youtube.com/user/artgalleryvernon
twitter.com/VernonAGallery
www.facebook.com/92358973285
Community programming; local, regional, national & international exhibitions; gift shop; art & video rentals; group tours
Marion Morrison, President
Dauna Grant, Executive Director, dauna@vernonpublicartgallery.com
Lobos Culen, Curator, curator@vernonpublicartgallery.com

***Victoria:* Art Gallery of Greater Victoria (AGGV)**
1040 Moss St., Victoria, BC V8V 4P1
Tel: 250-384-4171; Fax: 250-361-3995
aggv@aggv.bc.ca
aggv.ca
Social Media: www.youtube.com/user/ArtGalleryVictoriaBC
www.facebook.com/artgalleryvic toria
Canadiana 1860 to present; work of Emily Carr; extensive collection of Asian art
John Tupper, Director, jtupper@aggv.ca

***Victoria:* Open Space**
510 Fort St., 2nd Fl., Victoria, BC V8W 1E6
Tel: 250-383-8833
openspace@openspace.ca
www.openspace.ca
Social Media: www.flickr.com/groups/79807275@N00
www.facebook.com/openspace.victoria
Year Founded: 1972 An artist-run centre dedicated to exploring the boundaries of contemporary art & media in all forms. Hours of Operation: Tu-Sa 12:00-5:00.
Robert Randall, Chair
Helen Merzolf, Executive Director, director@openspace.ca
Peter Morin, Curator-in-Residence

***Victoria:* University of Victoria Art Collections**
630 Yates St., Victoria, BC V8W 1K9
Tel: 250-721-6562; Fax: 250-721-6607
legacy@uvic.ca
uvac.uvic.ca; legacygallery.ca
twitter.com/UVICGalleries
www.facebook.com/uvac.legacygallery
Now the University of Victoria's main gallery space; showcasing the Michael C. Williams Collection, as well as other holdings of the university

***Victoria:* Maltwood Prints & Drawings Gallery**
***Parent:* University of Victoria Art Collections**
McPherson Library, University of Victoria, PO Box 1800, Victoria, BC V8W 3H5
Tel: 250-472-5619
curator@uvic.ca
www.maltwood.uvic.ca
Social Media: www.flickr.com/people/maltwood
Named after the collection of fine, decorative & applied arts of English sculptress & antiquarian Katherine Emma Maltwood, F.R.S.A. (1878-1961); over 6,000 items representing the work of contemporary Western Canadian artists
Mary Jo Hughes, Director, artgallerydirector@uvic.ca
Caroline Riedel, Curator, curator@uvic.ca

***Wells:* Island Mountain Gallery**
PO Box 65, Wells, BC V0K 2R0
Tel: 250-994-3466; Fax: 250-994-3433
Toll-Free: 800-442-2787
info@imarts.com
www.imarts.com
Provides visual, literary & performing arts instruction; presents contemporary art exhibitions; concert venue in summer; also holds workshops
Yael Wand, President
Julie Fowler, Executive Director, media@imarts.com

***Williams Lake:* Station House Gallery & Gift Shop**
1 Mackenzie Ave. North, Williams Lake, BC V2G 1N4
Tel: 250-392-6113; Fax: 250-392-6184
www.stationhousegallery.com
www.facebook.com/stationhousegallery
Monthly exhibitions; gift shop
Kimberly McLennan, President
Diane Toop, Gallery Manager, manager@stationhousegallery.com

Manitoba

Provincial Art Galleries

The Winnipeg Art Gallery (WAG)
300 Memorial Blvd., Winnipeg, MB R3C 1V1
Tel: 204-786-6641; Fax: 204-788-4998
inquiries@wag.mb.ca
www.wag.mb.ca
Social Media: www.youtube.com/winnipegartgallery1
twitter.com/wag_ca
www.facebook.co m/201997979832748
Other contact information: Info Line: 204-789-1760
Founded in 1912, the WAG is Western Canada's oldest civic art gallery. With over 23,000 works in its collection, the WAG features 9 galleries of contemporary & historical works (fine arts, decorative arts & photography) by Manitoban, Canadian & international artists. A highlight is the Gort Collection of Northern Gothic & Renaissance paintings & altar panels.
Stephen Borys, Executive Director, executivedirector@wag.ca
Helen Delacretaz, Chief Curator/Curator, Decorative Arts, chief-curator@wag.ca

Local Art Galleries in Manitoba

Brandon: **The Art Gallery of Southwestern Manitoba (AGSM) / Le Musé D'art du Sud-ouest du Manitoba**
Also known as: **Art Gallery of Southwestern Manitoba**
#2, 710 Rosser Ave., Brandon, MB R7A 0K9
Tel: 204-727-1036; Fax: 204-726-8139
info@agsm.ca
www.agsm.ca
www.facebook.com/groups/artgalleryswm
Contemporary Manitoban art; approximately 16 exhibitions a year; open year round
Jeff Fawcett, Chair
Jennifer Woodbury, Executive Director, director@agsm.ca
Natalia Lebedinskaia, Curator, Contemporary Art, curator@agsm.ca

Flin Flon: **Northern Visual Arts Centre**
Also known as: **NorVa Centre**
177 Green St., Flin Flon, MB R8A 0G5
Tel: 204-686-4237
Gallery specializing in a variety of art forms, includign pottery & painting. Visitors can watch artists at work.
Sarah Trevor, Chair, 306-362-2530, saranjou@hotmail.com

Winnipeg: **aceartinc.**
290 McDermot Ave., 2nd Fl., Winnipeg, MB R3B 0T2
Tel: 204-944-9763
board@aceart.org
www.aceart.org
aceartinc. is an artist-run centre dedicated to the development, exhibition & dissemination of contemporary art by cultural producers; dedicated to cultural diversity
Joshua Ruth, President
Hannah G., Co-Director, hannah_g@aceart.org
Jamie Wright, Co-Director, jamie@aceart.org

Winnipeg: **Centre culturel franco-manitobain (CCFM)**
340, boul Provencher, Winnipeg, MB R2H 0G7
Tél: 204-233-8972; Téléc: 204-233-3324
www.ccfm.mb.ca
twitter.com/CCFManitobain
www.facebook.com/CCFManitobai n
Le Centre culturel franco-manitobain a un rôle de premier plan comme maison de la culture et carrefour de la vie culturelle et artistique en français à Winnipeg et au Manitoba/The Centre culturel franco-manitobain is the focal point of French cultural life in Winnipeg & Manitoba
Sylviane Lanthier, Directrice générale, direction@ccfm.mb.ca

Winnipeg: **Gallery One One One**
Also known as: **FitzGerald Study Centre**
School of Art, Fitzgerald Bldg., Main Fl., Fort Garry Campus, University of Manitoba, Winnipeg, MB R3T 2N2
Tel: 204-474-9322; Fax: 204-474-7605
gallery@cc.umanitoba.ca
www.umanitoba.ca/schools/art/content/galleryoneo neone
The gallery exhibits & collects contemporary & historical art, & includes the FitzGerald Study Collection, featuring papers, drawings & watercolours of L.L. Fitzgerald. Open year round.
Mary Reid, Director/Curator, reidm@cc.umanitoba.ca
Jenny Western, Coordinator, Art Collections, western@cc.umanitoba.ca
Robert Epp, Gallerist, eppr@ms.umanitoba.ca

Winnipeg: **Pavilion Gallery Museum**
Assiniboine Park, 55 Pavilion Cres., Winnipeg, MB R3P 2N6
Tel: 204-927-6070
www.assiniboinepark.ca/attractions/pavilion-gallery-museum.php
Year Founded: 1998 The gallery museum features a large collection of works by Ivan Eyre, Clarence Tillenius, & Walter J. Phillips, all renowned Manitoba artists. Open May-Sept.

Winnipeg: **School of Art Gallery**
255 ARTlab, School of Art, University of Manitoba, Winnipeg, MB R3T 2N2
Tel: 204-474-9322; Fax: 204-474-7605
umanitoba.ca/schools/art
Mary Reid, Gallery Director/Curator, mary.reid@ad.umanitoba.ca

Winnipeg: **University of Winnipeg Fine Art Collection & Gallery 1C03**
515 Portage Ave., Winnipeg, MB R3B 2E9
Tel: 204-786-9253; Fax: 204-774-4134
j.gibson@uwinnipeg.ca
www.uwinnipeg.ca/index/artgallery-index;
gallery1c03.blogspot.ca
www.facebook.com/23472162878
Year Founded: 1986 19th & 20th century paintings, drawings, prints, photographs & sculptures; open year round
Jennifer Gibson, Director/Curator, j.gibson@uwinnipeg.ca

New Brunswick

Provincial Art Galleries

Owens Art Gallery
c/o Mount Allison University, 61 York St., Sackville, NB E4L 1E1
Tel: 506-364-2574; Fax: 506-364-2575
owens@mta.ca
www.mta.ca/owens
www.facebook.com/pages/Owens-Art-Gallery /118900188982
Permanent collection of over 2500 works, dating from the 18th century; 30 exhibitions yearly
Gemey Kelly, Director/Curator, gkelly@mta.ca

Local Art Galleries in New Brunswick

Campbellton: **Galerie Restigouche Gallery**
PO Box 674, 39 Andrew St., Campbellton, NB E3N 3H1
Tel: 506-753-5750; Fax: 506-759-9601
www.grg.nb.ca

Edmundston: **Galerie Colline**
195, boul Hébert, Edmundston, NB E3V 2S8
Tel: 506-737-5051 Toll-Free: 800-363-8336
www.umoncton.ca/umce/galerie_colline
www.facebook.com/UdeMEdmundston
Year Founded: 1968 Trente ans d'expositions d'artistes amateurs et professionnels qui ont aidé à l'appréciation de l'art dans notre milieu.

Fredericton: **The Beaverbrook Art Gallery / La galerie d'art Beaverbrook**
PO Box 605, 703 Queen St., Fredericton, NB E3B 5A6
Tel: 506-458-8545; Fax: 506-459-7450
emailbag@beaverbrookartgallery.org
www.beaverbrookartgallery.org;
beaverbrookartgallery.wordpress.com
twitter.com/BeaverbrookAG
www.face book.com/BeaverbrookArtGallery
Other contact information: Alternate Phones: 506-458-8545; 506-458-2028
Year Founded: 1959 Atlantic Canadian art & historical British art; open year round
Bernard Riordon, Director/CEO O.C., 506-458-2030, briordon@beaverbrookartgallery.org
Terry Graff, Curator/Deputy Director, 506-458-2022, tgraff@beaverbrookartgallery.org

Fredericton: **Gallery Connexion**
Chestnut Complex, PO Box 696, 440 York St., Fredericton, NB E3B 5B4
Tel: 506-454-1433; Fax: 506-454-8681
connex@nbnet.nb.ca
galleryconnexion.ca
Artist-run centre, non-profit & non commercial; gallery exists for the purpose of exhibiting, supporting, & promoting the development & understanding of all forms of contemporary art practice of local, national & international significance
Mary Green, President
Julie Scriver, Art Director

Fredericton: **UNB Art Centre**
Memorial Hall, University of New Brunswick, PO Box 4400, 9 Bailey Dr., Fredericton, NB E3B 5A3
Tel: 506-453-4623; Fax: 506-453-5012
extend@unb.ca
www.unb.ca/cel/programs/creative/exhibition/index.html
Historical & contemporary exhibitions; interpretive programs; Atlantic art collection
Marie Maltais, Director

Moncton: **Atelier IMAGO**
140 Botsford St., Local 17, Moncton, NB E1C 4X5
Tel: 506-388-1431
atelierestampeimago@gmail.com
www.atelierimago.com
Artist-run not-for-profit printmaking studio

Moncton: **Galerie d'art Louise-et-Reuben-Cohen**
c/o Campus de Moncton, Université de Moncton, 18, av Antonine-Maillet, Moncton, NB E1A 3E9
Tél: 506-858-4088
galrc@umoncton.ca
www.umoncton.ca/umcm-ga
Fondée en: 1964 La Galerie a pour mission encourager la créativité des artistes acadiens/acadiennes, et collectioner et documenter les oeuvres d'art; centre de documentation; programmation.
Nisk Imbeault, Directeur-conservateur, 506-858-4687

Moncton: **Galerie Georges-Goguen SRC**
Also known as: **Mini Galerie Radio-Canada**
c/o Radio-Canada Acadie, CP 950, 250, av Université, Moncton, NB E1C 8N8
Tél: 506-382-8326
ghg@nbnet.nb.ca
www.radio-canada.ca/acadie
Primarily promotes the works of Atlantic artists
Georges Goguen

Moncton: **Galerie Sans Nom Coop Ltée (GSN)**
Also known as: **GSN Coopérative**
Centre Culturel Aberdeen, #13 & 16, 140 rue Botsford, Moncton, NB E1C 4X4
Tél: 506-854-5381; Téléc: 506-857-2064
info@galeriesansnom.org
galeriesansnom.org
twitter.com/GalerieSansNom; twitter.com/REFLUXfestival
www.facebook.com/123436297725404
Galerie Sans Nom (GSN) is a non-profit, artist-run centre involved in the promotion, production & exhibition of contemporary art. GSN is a venue for creative expression of the artistic community & acting as a vital communication vehicle, provides an impetus for innovation & creativity
Léo Goguen, Président
Amanda Dawn Christie, Directrice

Saint John: **Saint John Arts Centre (SJAC)**
20 Hazen Ave., Saint John, NB E2L 5A5
Tel: 506-633-4870; Fax: 506-674-1040
sjac@saintjohnartscentre.com
www.saintjohnartscentre.com
twitter.com/S JArtsCentre
www.facebook.com/114375408575288
First municipally funded art gallery in Atlantic Canada; features monthly exhibitions of local & regional art works
Andrew Kierstead, Executive Director, a.kierstead@saintjohnartscentre.com

St Andrews: **Sunbury Shores Arts & Nature Centre**
139 Water St., St Andrews, NB E5B 1A7
Tel: 506-529-3386
info@sunburyshores.org
www.sunburyshores.org
www.facebook.com/sunburyshores
Provides facilities for the study, practice & appreciation of the art, crafts & environmental sciences; stresses the aesthetic appreciation of nature & the importance of its use
Muriel Jarvis, President
James Steel, Executive Director

Newfoundland & Labrador

Provincial Art Galleries

The Rooms Provincial Art Gallery
The Rooms Corporation of Newfoundland & Labrador, PO Box 1800 C, 9 Bonaventure Ave., St. John's, NL A1C 5P9
Tel: 709-757-8040; Fax: 709-757-8041
information@therooms.ca
www.therooms.ca/artgallery
Regularly changing exhibitions of all media, chiefly contemporary Canadian, with some international, historic Canadian & Newfoundland folk art & traditional crafts; permanent collection of contemporary Canadian art in many media, with strong holdings of Newfoundland work; art slide library. Extensive public programming & special projects with emphasis on collaboration with professional artists.
Tom Foran, Chair
Sheila Perry, Director, sheilaperry@therooms.ca
Mireille Eagan, Curator, Canadian Art, mireilleeagan@therooms.ca
Bruce Johnson, Curator, brucejohnson@therooms.ca
Caroline Stone, Curator, carolinestone@therooms.ca

Local Art Galleries in Newfoundland & Labrador

Corner Brook: **Sir Wilfred Grenfell College Art Gallery (SWGC)**
Also known as: **Grenfell Campus Art Gallery**
Fine Arts Bldg., Memorial University of Newfoundland, University Dr., Corner Brook, NL A2H 6P9
Tel: 709-637-6209
www2.swgc.mun.ca/artgallery
www.facebook.com/GrenfellArtGallery
Contemporary art

St. John's: **Eastern Edge Art Gallery**
PO Box 2641 C, 72 Harbour Dr., St. John's, NL A1C 6K1
Tel: 709-739-1882; Fax: 709-739-1866
easternedgegallery@gmail.com
www.easternedge.ca
twitter.com/easternedg e
www.facebook.com/groups/2661000728

Year Founded: 1984 Not-for-profit, artist-run centre dedicated to exhibiting contemporary art in diverse media; exhibitions include work by Newfoundland artists & artists from the rest of Canada
Michael Waterman, Chair

Northwest Territories

Territorial Art Galleries

Gallery of the Midnight Sun
5005 Bryson Dr., Yellowknife, NT X1A 2A3
Tel: 867-873-8064; Fax: 867-873-8065

Year Founded: 1998 NWT's largest selection of Inuit & Dene arts & crafts
Lisa Seagrave, Contact

Nova Scotia

Provincial Art Galleries

Art Gallery of Nova Scotia Halifax (AGNS)
PO Box 2262, 1723 Hollis St., Halifax, NS B3J 3C8
Tel: 902-424-5280; Fax: 902-424-7359
infodesk@gov.ns.ca
www.artgalleryofnovascotia.ca/en/AGNS_Halifax
twitt er.com/ArtGalleryNS
www.facebook.com/89366582597
Housed in 1868 heritage building. The Gallery has over 13,000 peices in its permanent collection.
Jeffrey Spalding, Director/Chief Curator

Art Gallery of Nova Scotia Yarmouth (AGNS)
PO Box 246, 341 Main St., Yarmouth, NS B5A 4B2
Tel: 902-749-2248; Fax: 902-749-2255
agnsyarmouth@gov.ns.ca
www.artgalleryofnovascotia.ca/en/AGNS_Yarmouth
twitter.com/ArtGalleryNS
www.facebook.com/89366582597
Angela Collier, Gallery Coordinator, collieal@gov.ns.ca
David Diviney, Curator of Exhibitions, divinedm@gov.ns.ca

Local Art Galleries in Nova Scotia

***Chéticamp:* Les Trois Pignon**
c/o La Société St-Pierre, CP 430, 15584 Cabot Trail, Chéticamp, NS B0E 1H0
Tél: 902-224-2642; Téléc: 902-224-1579
lestroispignons@ns.sympatico.ca
www.lestroispignons.com
twitter.com/Le sTroisPignons
www.facebook.com/pages/Les-Trois-Pignons/249801311699866
Les tapisseries du Dr. Elizabeth LeFort ainsi que d'autres tapis historiques de la région; le musée d'antiquité à Marguerite Gallant est attaché sur la Galerie aussi que centre généalogique
Lisette Aucoin-Bourgeois, Executive Director, lisettebourgeois@ns.sympatico.ca

***Halifax:* Centre for Art Tapes**
#207, 5600 Sackville St., Halifax, NS B3J 2A1
Tel: 902-422-6822; Fax: 902-422-6823
www.centreforarttapes.ca
twitter.com/CentreforArtTap
www.facebook.com/ 159960707402522
An artist-run centre that facilitates & supports emerging, intermediate & established artists working with electronic media, such as video, audio & new media; strives to provide production facilities, ongoing programming & training to a diverse membership whose creative abilities contribute to social & artistic goals
Crystal Melville, Chair
Mireille Bourgeois, Director, cfat.operations@ns.sympatico.ca
Kristen Atkins, Coordinator, Communications, cfat.communication@ns.sympatico.ca

***Halifax:* Dalhousie Art Gallery (DAG)**
6101 University Ave., Halifax, NS B3H 1W8
Tel: 902-494-2403; Fax: 902-423-0591
art.gallery@dal.ca
www.artgallery.dal.ca
twitter.com/DalArtGallery
www.facebook.com/pages/Dalhousie-Art-Gallery/197088913670695
The Dalhousie Art Gallery is a public art gallery, an academic support unit within the educational & research context of Dalhousie University, & a cultural resource for the whole community.
Peter Dykuis, Director/Curator, peter.dykhuis@dal.ca

***Halifax:* Eye Level Gallery**
2128 Gottingen St., Halifax, NS B3K 3B3
Tel: 902-425-6412
www.eyelevelgallery.ca
Year Founded: 1974 Not-for-profit organization dedicated to presenting, developing, & promoting contemporary art. Open Tues-Sat., 12-5, or at random times when the lights are on.
Kate McKenna, Chair
Michael McCormack, Director, director@eyelevelgallery.ca

***Halifax:* MSVU Art Gallery, Mount Saint Vincent University**
166 Bedford Hwy., Halifax, NS B3M 2J6
Tel: 902-457-6160; Fax: 902-457-2447
info@msvuart.ca
msvuart.ca
twitter.com/msvuartgallery
www.facebook.com/pages/MSVU-Art-Gallery/177537538924695
Year Founded: 1971 Open daily except Mondays; exhibition program emphasizes women as cultural subjects & producers, new Nova Scotia artists, & themes relevant to the university's academic programs; admission free
Ingrid Jenkner, Director, director@msvuart.ca
David Dahms, Gallery Technician, david.dahms@msvuart.ca
Katie Belcher, Program Coordinator, 902-457-6291, katie.belcher@msvuart.ca

***Halifax:* Nova Scotia Centre for Craft & Design & Maray E. Black Gallery (NSCCD)**
#104, 1061 & 1096 Marginal Rd., Halifax, NS B3H 4P7
Tel: 902-424-2522; Fax: 902-492-2526
info@craft-design.ns.ca
www.craft-design.ns.ca
Develops & promotes crafts & design in Nova Scotia; includes the Mary E. Black Gallery, a craft showroom, an info. centre, & 5 studios; open year round

***Sydney:* Cape Breton Centre for Craft & Design (CBCC&D)**
PO Box 1686, 322 Charlotte St., Sydney, NS B1P 6T7
Tel: 902-539-7491; Fax: 902-539-4807
info@capebretoncraft.com
www.capebretoncraft.com
twitter.com/CapeBreto nCraft
www.facebook.com/capebretoncentreforcraftanddesign
Susan Charles, Director, director@craft-design.ns.ca

***Halifax:* Saint Mary's University Art Gallery**
923 Robie St., Halifax, NS B3H 3C3
Tel: 902-420-5445
gallery@smu.ca
www.smu.ca/administration/externalaffairs/artgallery
Contemporary visual arts by artists within & outside the region; lectures, publications & performing arts program; permanent collection of over 1,800 works
Robin Metcalfe, Director/Curator

***Lunenburg:* Lunenburg Art Gallery (LAG)**
PO Box 1418, 79-81 Pelham St., Lunenburg, NS B0J 2C0
Tel: 902-640-4044; Fax: 902-640-3035
lag@eastlink.ca
www.lunenburgartgallery.com
www.facebook.com/Lunenburg ArtGallery
Year Founded: 1972 The gallery promotes the works of local, provincial & international artists, sponsors workshops & raises funds; houses the Meldrum collection by the late Earl Bailly; month-long solo exhibitions & ongoing Members Gallery; open seasonally: Mar.-Oct., Tues-Sat 10-5 & Sun 1-5.
Garry Woodcock, President
Diana Dines, Treasurer
Jo McGee, Contact, Planning & Exhibition

***Pictou:* Hector Exhibit Centre & Archives**
PO Box 1210, 86 Haliburton Rd., Pictou, NS B0K 1H0
Tel: 902-485-4563; Fax: 902-485-5213
pcghs@gov.ns.ca
www.mccullochcentre.ca
twitter.com/HectorCentre
www. facebook.com/234152123269050
Genealogical & historical archives for Pictou County - census records, cemetery records, shipping lists, newspapers, etc.; local historical, cultural, genealogical & craft exhibits

***Sydney:* Cape Breton University Art Gallery**
PO Box 5300, 1250 Grand Lake Rd., Sydney, NS B1P 6L2
Tel: 902-563-1342; Fax: 902-563-1142
www.cbu.ca/art-gallery; capebretonartgallery.blogspot.ca
First & only full-time public art gallery on Cape Breton Island; acquires & presents art with emphasis on contemporary Canadian works & the artistic traditions of Cape Breton Island; offers educational & research facilities; a major cultural resource within the educational & research context of the university
Laura Schneider, Director/Curator, laura_schneider@cbu.ca
Graham Iddon, Technician, Gallery & Collections, graham_iddon@cbu.ca

***Wolfville:* Acadia University Art Gallery**
10 Highland Ave., Wolfville, NS B4P 2R6
Tel: 902-585-1373
artgallery@acadiau.ca
gallery.acadiau.ca
www.facebook.com/95064121286
The University Gallery serves both as a public gallery & as a teaching facility within Acadia's Faculty of Arts. Its purpose in the community & on the campus is to enrich visual experience through showcasing original works of historical or contemporary importance. The Gallery looks after Acadia's collection of art.
Laurie Dalton, Director/Curator

Ontario

Provincial Art Galleries

Art Gallery of Hamilton (AGH)
123 King St. West, Hamilton, ON L8P 4S8
Tel: 905-527-6610; Fax: 905-577-6940
larissa@artgalleryofhamilton.com
www.artgalleryofhamilton.com
Collection of 8,000 art objects; holds one of Canada's most comprehensive collections of Canadian historical, modernist & contemporary art; British, American & European works
Louise Dompierre, President/CEO

Art Gallery of Ontario (AGO) / Musée des beaux-arts de l'Ontario
317 Dundas St. West, Toronto, ON M5T 1G4
Tel: 416-979-6648; Fax: 416-204-2713
Toll-Free: 877-225-4246
ticketing@ago.net
www.ago.net
Social Media: www.youtube.com/user/ArtGalleryofOntario
twitter.com/agotoronto
www.fa cebook.com/AGOToronto
Visit the AGO, located in the heart of Toronto, for an experience of art that includes European Old Masters, Group of Seven, & Canadian & international contemporary works — plus the world's largest public collection of sculptures by Henry Moore.
Tony Gagliano, President
Matthew Teitelbaum, Director/CEO
Elizabeth Smith, Executive Director, Curatorial Affairs

Art Gallery of Windsor (AGW)
401 Riverside Dr. West, Windsor, ON N9A 7J1
Tel: 519-977-0013; Fax: 519-977-0776
email@artgalleryofwindsor.com
www.artgalleryofwindsor.com
twitter.com/ A_G_W
www.facebook.com/198575240184786
One of the larger, non-government run galleries in Ontario; focus is on Canadian art in an international context; permanent collection of 2,500 paintings & sculptures; resource centre & gift shop; closed Mon., Tue.
Sean White, President
Catharine M. Mastin, Director, cmastin@agw.ca
Srimoyeee Mitra, Curator, Contemporary Art, smitra@agw.ca

Government of Ontario Art Collection
c/o The Archives of Ontario, 134 Ian Macdonald Boul., Toronto, ON M7A 2C5
Tel: 416-327-1600; Fax: 416-327-1999
Toll-Free: 800-668-9933
reference@ontario.ca
www.archives.gov.on.ca/english/on -line-exhibits/art/index.aspx
The Government of Ontario's art collection is spread throughout ministry & government offices around Toronto, although many of the works are featured in the Legislative Building. In all, the collection comprises around 2,500 pieces.

McMichael Canadian Art Collection
10365 Islington Ave., Kleinburg, ON L0J 1C0
Tel: 905-893-1121; Fax: 905-893-0692
Toll-Free: 888-213-1121
info@mcmichael.com
www.mcmichael.com
Year Founded: 1965 The collection features works of art created by First Nations & Inuit artists, the artists of the Group of Seven & their contemporaries, & other artists who have contributed to the development of Canadian art. Comprehensive education program at kindergarten, elementary & secondary school levels; guided group tours by appt.; extension program & temporary exhibition program. Also programs for adults
Thomas Smart, Executive Director/CEO
Mary Benvenuto, CFO

Local Art Galleries in Ontario

***Bancroft:* The Art Gallery of Bancroft (AGB)**
PO Box 398, 10 Flint Ave., Bancroft, ON K0L 1C0
Tel: 613-332-1542
agb@nexicom.net
agb.weebly.com
Local & other Ontario artists; gift shop for area artists only; open year round

***Barrie:* MacLaren Art Centre**
37 Mulcaster St., Barrie, ON L4M 3M2
Tel: 705-721-9696; Fax: 705-735-6935
maclaren@maclarenart.com
www.maclarenart.com
twitter.com/MacLarenArt
www.facebook.com/127102583989513
Open Tue.-Fri. 10-5, Sat. 10-4
Carolyn Bell Farrell, Executive Director

***Bracebridge:* Chapel Gallery**
c/o Muskoka Arts & Crafts Inc., PO Box 376, 15 King St., Bracebridge, ON P1L 1T7
Tel: 705-645-5501; Fax: 705-645-0385
info@muskokaartsandcrafts.com
www.muskokaartsandcrafts.com/Chapel_Gallery/chapel_gallery.htm
www.facebook.com/home.php?sk=group_138164915233
Year Founded: 1989 Open Tue.-Sat.
Kelly Holinshead, President
Elene J. Freer, Curator/Coordinator

***Bracebridge:* Ziska Gallery Muskoka**
RR#1, Bracebridge, ON P1L 1W8
Tel: 705-645-2587
The beauty of nature in paintings & sculpture; open June to Oct.
Jack MacCallum, Curator

***Brampton:* Art Gallery of Peel**
Peel Heritage Complex, 9 Wellington St. East, Brampton, ON L6W 1Y1
Tel: 905-791-4055; Fax: 905-451-4931
www.peelregion.ca/heritage
Social Media: www.flickr.com/photos/peelheritage
www.facebook.com/visitPAMA
Located within a cluster of 19th century buildings; features the works of local artists in Peel & contemporary art from across Canada; collection of over 1,500 works consists of contemporary & historic Canadian works with a special emphasis on artists from Peel.
David Somers, Curator

***Brantford:* Glenhyrst Art Gallery of Brant**
20 Ava Rd., Brantford, ON N3T 5G9
Tel: 519-756-5932
info@glenhyrstartgallery.ca
www.glenhyrst.ca
twitter.com/Glenhyrst
www.facebook.com/376509061505
Permanent collection comprises contemporary works on paper & paintings by Robert Reginald Whale & his descendants; offers a rotating schedule of art exhibitions, an art rental & sales showroom, giftshop & a variety of classes & programmes
Stan Gorecki, President
Marcia Lea, Executive Director/Curator, director@glenhyrstartgallery.ca

***Bright's Grove:* Gallery in the Grove**
PO Box 339, 2618 Hamilton Rd. at Wildwood Park, Bright's Grove, ON N0N 1C0
Tel: 519-869-4643
info@galleryinthegrove.com
www.galleryinthegrove.com
www.facebook.com/178962708813607
Year Founded: 1980 The gallery is housed on the second floor of the historic Faethorne House, circa 1875. Open M-Th 11:00-5:00, Sa 11:00-3:00.
Joan Elliott, Chair
Sheila Brown, Contact, Exhibition Planning

***Brockville:* Marianne van Silfhout Gallery**
Brockville Campus, St. Lawrence College, 2288 Parkedale Ave., Brockville, ON K6V 5X3
Tel: 613-345-0660
gallery@sl.on.ca
www.stlawrencecollege.ca
Marje Fletcher, Gallery Curator

***Burlington:* Burlington Art Centre (BAC)**
1333 Lakeshore Rd., Burlington, ON L7S 1A9
Tel: 905-632-7796; Fax: 905-632-0278
www.thebac.ca
Social Media: www.linkedin.com/company/burlington-art-centre
*twitter.com/the_BAC_*
www.facebook.com/BurlingtonArtCentre
Exhibitions of regional & nationally recognized Canadian artists; a permanent collection of contemporary Canadian ceramic art & a gallery shop, art rental & sales & studios; open daily
Ian D. Ross, Executive Director MFA, rossi@thebac.ca
Jonathan Smith, Curator, Permanent Collection, smithj@thebac.ca

***Cambridge:* Cambridge Galleries**
Queen's Square, 1 North Square, Cambridge, ON N1S 2K6
Tel: 519-621-0460; Fax: 519-621-2080
galleriesinfo@cambridgegalleries.ca
www.cambridgegalleries.ca
twitter.com/CGalleries
www.facebook.com/pages/Cambridge-Galleries/335285275042
Exhibitions offered at 3 locations within Cambridge (as well as Hespeler & Clemens Mill libraries) reflect a range of local & international developments in contemporary & historical visual arts & architecture; collection of contemporary Canadian fibre art; studio courses for all ages; concerts; Canadian international film series

***Cambridge:* Design at Riverside**
7 Melville St. South, Cambridge, ON N1S 2H4
Tel: 519-621-0460; Fax: 519-623-3890

***Cambridge:* Preston Branch**
435 Kind St. East, Cambridge, ON N3H 3N1
Tel: 519-653-3632
Mary Misner, Gallery Director
Ivan Jurakic, Curator

***Chatham:* Thames Art Gallery (TAG)**
Chatham Cultural Centre, 75 William St. North, Chatham, ON N7M 4L4
Tel: 519-360-1998; Fax: 519-354-4170
CKccc@chatham-kent.ca
www.chatham-kent.ca/ccc
Historical & contemporary artwork by local, national & international artists; hosts 12-15 exhibitions a year; guided tours available with advanced bookings; art lectures & workshops for children & adults; open daily 1-5; admission by donation
Carl L. Lavoy, Curator

***Cobourg:* Art Gallery of Northumberland**
***Also known as:* AGN Cobourg**
55 King St. West, 3rd Fl., Cobourg, ON K9A 2M2
Tel: 416-372-0333; Fax: 416-372-1587
agn@eagle.ca
www.artgalleryofnorthumberland.com
Maintains a permanent collection of more than 600 works of art; changing exhibitions are displayed throughout the year; lectures; education trips; workshops & special events

***Port Hope:* Art Gallery of Northumberland**
***Also known as:* AGN Port Hope**
60 Walton St., Port Hope, ON L1A 1N1
Tel: 905-885-2115
Frankie Liberty, President
Dorette E. Carter, Director/Curator B.A., M.Ed.

***Cornwall:* Cornwall Regional Art Gallery (CRAG) / Galerie régionale des arts de Cornwall**
168 Pitt St., Cornwall, ON K6J 3P4
Tel: 613-938-7387
info@cornwallregionalartgallery.ca
www.cornwallregionalartgallery.ca
Social Media: www.youtube.com/user/theCRAGgallery
twitter.com/CRAG_gallery
www.facebook.com/cornwallregionalartgallery
Year Founded: 1982 Promotes and stimulates interest in and the study of the visual arts; advances knowledge and appreciation of the visual arts; provides improved opportunities for Canadian artistic talent; advances the development of the visualarts in Canada.
Sylvie Lizotte, Executive Director, 613-938-7387, info@cornwallregionalartgallery.ca

***Curve Lake Indian Reserve:* Whetung Ojibwa Centre**
Curve Lake Indian Reserve, ON K0L 1R0
Tel: 705-657-3661; Fax: 705-657-3412
mwhetung@whetung.com
www.whetung.com
www.facebook.com/WhetungOjibwaCentre
Craft centre & art gallery; authentic works by Indian artists from across Canada.
Michael Whetung, Owner

***Durham:* Durham Art Gallery**
PO Box 1021, 251 George St. East, Durham, ON N0G 1R0
Tel: 519-369-3692
info@durhamart.on.ca
www.durhamart.on.ca
www.facebook.com/Durham.Art.Gallery
Ilse Gassinger, Executive Director, igassinger@durhamart.on.ca

***Etobicoke:* The Art Gallery, Neilson Park Creative Centre**
56 Neilson Dr., Etobicoke, ON M9C 1V7
Tel: 416-622-5294; Fax: 416-622-0892
info@neilsonparkcreativecentre.com
www.neilsonparkcreativecentre.com
Provides a community focus for creative visual arts; variety of exhibitions with strong emphasis on local & contemporary artists
Kathleen Haushalter, President
Cathy Frank, Manager, Programs & Gallery
Cindy Sherman, Office Manager

***Grimsby:* Grimsby Public Art Gallery**
18 Carnegie Lane, Grimsby, ON L3M 1Y1
Tel: 905-945-3246; Fax: 905-945-1789
www.town.grimsby.on.ca/ArtGallery/Main;
grimsbypublicartgallery.blogspot.ca
twitter.com/thegpag
www.facebook.com/129646767112893
Permanent collection of 1,000+ works; contemporary exhibitions & programmes year round
Rhona Wenger, Director/Curator, rwenger@town.grimsby.on.ca

***Guelph:* Macdonald Stewart Art Centre (MSAC)**
358 Gordon St., Guelph, ON N1G 1Y1
Tel: 519-837-0010; Fax: 519-767-2661
www.uoguelph.ca/msac
twitter.com/MSAC
www.facebook.com/10806818998
Permanent collection of over 4,000 works; contemporary Inuit drawings & the Donald Forster Sculpture Park
Aidan Ware, Coordinator, aware@msac.ca

***Haileybury:* Temiskaming Art Gallery**
PO Box 1090, 325 Farr Dr., Haileybury, ON P0J 1K0
Tel: 705-672-3706
www.temiskamingartgallery.ca
twitter.com/TemisArtGallery
www.facebook.com/temiskamingartgallery
Public gallery; open year round
Felicity Wowk, President
Peter Greyson, Director/Curator

***Haliburton:* Rails End Gallery & Arts Centre**
PO Box 912, 23 York St., Haliburton, ON K0M 1S0
Tel: 705-457-2330
info@railsendgallery.com
www.railsendgallery.com
twitter.com/RailsEnd
www.facebook.com/railsend
Open year round
Laurie Jones, Executive Director

***Ingersoll:* Ingersoll Creative Arts Centre**
PO Box 384, 125 Centennial Lane, Ingersoll, ON N5C 3V3
Tel: 519-485-4691
creative.arts@on.aibn.com
creativeartscentre.com
www.facebook.com/304505136251524
The centre aims to provide members of the community with the opportunity for creative expression & development, specifically in the following areas: fine arts, pottery, quilting, rug hooking, & fibre arts. The centre also hosts exhibitions & a gallery. Office hours: M-F 9:00-12:00 & 1:00-4:00; Gallery hours: F-Su 2:00-4:00.
Heather MacIntosh, Contact

***Kingston:* Agnes Etherington Art Centre (AEAC) / Centre d'art Agnes Etherington**
Queen's University, University Ave. at Bader Lane, Kingston, ON K7L 3N6
Tel: 613-533-2190; Fax: 613-533-6765
aeac@queensu.ca; artgall@queensu.ca (Shop)
www.aeac.ca
twitter.com/aeartcentre
www.facebook.com/aeartcentre
Contemporary & historical art collections & exhibitions; gallery shop, art rental & sales gallery, facility rentals; open year round
Janet M. Brooke, Director, janet.brooke@queensu.ca
Jan Allen, Chief Curator/Curator, Contemporary Art, jan.allen@queensu.ca
Alicia Boutilier, Curator, Canadian Historical Art, alicia.boutilier@queensu.ca
David de Witt, Curator, European Art, david.dewitt@queensu.ca

***Kitchener:* Homer Watson House & Gallery**
1754 Old Mill Rd., Kitchener, ON N2P 1H7
Tel: 519-748-4377; Fax: 519-748-6808
programs@homerwatson.on.ca
www.homerwatson.on.ca
twitter.com/HomerWatson
www.facebook.com/HomerRWatson
Open Jan. - Dec.
Faith Hieblinger, Executive Director, curator@homerwatson.on.ca
Sandu Sindile, Curator, exhibitions@homerwatson.on.ca

Kitchener: **Kitchener-Waterloo Art Gallery (KWAG)**
101 Queen St. North, Kitchener, ON N2H 6P7
Tel: 519-579-5860; Fax: 519-578-0740
mail@kwag.on.ca
www.kwag.ca
Year Founded: 1956 Open year round; Monday - Wednesday: 9:30-5:00; Thursday: 9:30-9:00; Saturday: 10:00-5:00; Sunday 1:00-5:00.
Alf Bogusky, Director General
Caroline Oliver, Director, Development & Marketing

Leamington: **Leamington Art Centre**
72 Talbot St. West, Leamington, ON N8H 1M4
Tel: 519-326-2711
artcentr@mnsi.net
www.leamingtonartscentre.com
www.facebook.com/leamingtonartscentre
The Leamington Arts Centre, run by the South Essex Arts Association, is a charitable, not-for-profit organization. Its purpose is to serve the community through arts & culture. The Leamington Arts Centre includes a main gallery, which exhibits the work of local artists. Heinz Memorabilia explains the history of the Heinz Co.. The Centre also features the Marine Heritage Interpretive Centre, Signature Gifts, & several educational programs throughout the year for both adults & children.
Susan Dupont Baptista, President
Chad Riley, Gallery Director M.F.A.

Lindsay: **The Lindsay Gallery**
190 Kent St. West, 2nd Fl., Lindsay, ON K9V 2Y6
Tel: 705-324-1780; Fax: 705-324-9349
art@thelindsaygallery.com
www.thelindsaygallery.com
Not-for-profit gallery offering regular exhibitions, art classes & a boutique

London: **The Innuit Gallery**
201 Queens Ave., London, ON N6A 1J1
Tel: 519-672-7770; Fax: 519-672-7770
Toll-Free: 866-589-9990
art@innuitgallery.com
www.innuitgallery.com
twitter. com/innuitgallery
Contemporary Inuit art, including prints, paintings, drawings, sculpture, & jewellery
Howard Isaacs, Founder
Janet Evans, Partner

London: **McIntosh Gallery**
The University of Western Ontario, London, ON N6A 3K7
Tel: 519-661-3181
mcintoshgallery@uwo.ca
www.mcintoshgallery.ca
twitter.com/McIntoshGallery
www.facebook.com/Mc IntoshGallery
Exhibitions featuring local, national, & international artists working in various media; exhibitions change every 6 weeks & are accompanied by art-related videos, films & lectures; art collection & gallery's records, some artist archives & periodical library available as resources to students for research purposes; open 6 days/week
James Patten, Director/Chief Curator, jpatten2@uwo.ca
Catherine Elliot Shaw, Curator, celliots@uwo.ca
Brian Lambert, Collections Manager, blamber3@uwo.ca

Minden: **Agnes Jamieson Gallery**
Minden Hills Cultural Centre, PO Box 648, #174, 176 Bobcaygeon Rd. North, Minden, ON K0M 2K0
Tel: 705-286-3763
gallery@mindenhills.ca
www.mindenculturalcentre.com/gallery.php
Laurie Carmount, Curator

Mississauga: **Art Gallery of Mississauga (AGM)**
300 City Centre Dr., Mississauga, ON L5B 3C1
Tel: 905-896-5088
fred.troughton@mississauga.ca
www.artgalleryofmississauga.com;
artgalleryofmississauga.wordpress.com
twitter.com/artgallerymiss
www.facebook.com/ArtGalleryofMississauga
A public art gallery providing state of the art exhibitions by local, national & international artists; exhibits change every 7 weeks; admission is free; open Mon.-Fri. 9 am to 5 pm, weekends: noon to 4 pm
Arshad Mahmood, President
Robert Freeman, Executive Director, robert.freeman@mississauga.ca
Stuart Keeler, Curator/Director, Programmes, stuart.keeler@mississauga.ca

Mississauga: **Blackwood Gallery**
University of Toronto, 3359 Mississauga Rd. North, Mississauga, ON L5L 1C6
Tel: 905-828-3789; Fax: 905-569-4262
blackwood.gallery@utoronto.ca
www.blackwoodgallery.ca
Year Founded: 1992 Presents exhibitions of contemporary art in all media.
Carmen Victor, Curatorial Assistant
Christof Migone, Director/Curator

Mississauga: **Harbour Gallery**
1697 Lakeshore Rd. West, Mississauga, ON L5J 1J4
Tel: 905-822-5495
inforequest@harbourgallery.com
www.harbourgallery.com
Rotating collection of over 30 accredited Canadian artists in a variety of mediums.

Niagara-on-the-Lake: **RiverBrink Art Museum**
PO Box 266, 116 Queenston St., Niagara-on-the-Lake, ON L0S 1J0
Tel: 905-262-4510
riverbrink.org
twitter.com/RiverBrinkArt
www.facebook.com/riverbrink.artmuseum
Open Victoria Day - Thanksgiving
Linda Fritz, President/Treasurer
David Aurandt, Director/Curator
Debra Antoncic, Curator

North Bay: **W.K.P. Kennedy Gallery**
150 Main St. East, North Bay, ON P1B 1A8
Tel: 705-474-1944
info@kennedygallery.org
www.kennedygallery.org
A changing program of historical & contemporary visual art; free
Dermot Wilson, Director/Curator, dermot@kennedygallery.org

North Bay: **White Water Gallery**
PO Box 1491, 143 Main St. West, North Bay, ON P1B 8K6
Tel: 705-476-2444
info@whitewatergallery.com
whitewatergallery.com
Artist-run centre for contemporary art
Clayton Windatt, Programming Director & Executive Director

Oakville: **Oakville Galleries**
1306 Lakeshore Rd. East, Oakville, ON L6J 1L6
Tel: 905-844-4402; Fax: 905-844-7968
info@oakvillegalleries.com
www.oakvillegalleries.com
www.facebook.com/ OakvilleGalleries
Contemporary art gallery with 2 exhibition spaces: Oakville Galleries at Centennial Square, 120 Navy St. & Oakville Galleries in Gairloch Gardens, 1306 Lakeshore Rd. East
Matthew Hyland, Director, matthew@oakvillegalleries.com
Marnie Fleming, Curator, Contemporary Art, marnie@oakvillegalleries.com

Ohsweken: **Two Turtle Iroquois Fine Art Gallery**
c/o Arnold Jacobs, RR#1, Ohsweken, ON N0A 1M0
Tel: 519-751-2774
twoturtleartgallery@live.ca
www.twoturtlenativeart.com
Year Founded: 1985 Showcasing the art of the Hodenosaunee & Arnold Jacobs.
Arnold Aron Jacobs, Owner

Orillia: **Orillia Museum of Art & History (OMAH)**
30 Peter St. South, Orillia, ON L3V 5A9
Tel: 705-326-2159; Fax: 705-326-7828
info@orilliamuseum.org
www.orilliamuseum.org
www.facebook.com/22137864 7891108
Year Founded: 1999 Public art gallery & museum; gift shop; open Mon. - Sat.
Linda Whiston, Director/Curator

Oshawa: **The Robert McLaughlin Gallery**
Civic Centre, 72 Queen St., Oshawa, ON L1H 3Z3
Tel: 905-576-3000
communications@rmg.on.ca
www.rmg.on.ca
Social Media: www.youtube.com/RMGOshawa
twitter.com/theRMG
www.facebook.com/TheRMG
Permanent exhibitions include masterpieces of Canadian Art: Emily Carr, members of the Group of Seven, Painters Eleven
Gabrielle Peacock, CEO, gpeacock@rmg.on.ca
Michael Crunkhorn, President
Linda Jansma, Curator, ljansma@rmg.on.ca

Ottawa: **Artists' Centre d'Artistes Ottawa Inc.**
Also known as: **Gallery 101**
#1, 301 1/2 Bank St., Ottawa, ON K2P 1X7
Tel: 613-230-2799
office@g101.ca
www.g101.org
A non-profit artist operated centre dedicated to the professional presentation & circulation of visual & media arts; solo & curated group exhibitions by local Canadian & international contemporary artists
Laura Margita, Director/Curator

Ottawa: **Carleton University Art Gallery (CUAG)**
Carleton University, St. Patrick's Bldg., 1125 Colonel By Dr., Ottawa, ON K1S 5B6
Tel: 613-520-2120; Fax: 613-520-4409
cuag.carleton.ca
Social Media: www.youtube.com/CUArtGallery
twitter.com/CUArtGallery
www.faceboo k.com/carleton.university.art.gallery
27,000 works in contemporary Canadian art; European prints & drawings from the 16th to 19th centuries; Inuit prints & sculpture.
Sandra Dyck, Director, sandra_dyck@carleton.ca

Ottawa: **Exposure Gallery**
Thyme & Again, 1255 Wellington St. West, 2nd Fl., Ottawa, ON K1Y 3A6
Tel: 604-722-0093
exposuregallery@thymeandagain.ca
www.exposuregallery.info
www.facebook.com/ExposureGallery
Gallery specializing in fine art photography, located in the second floor studio of Thyme & Again catering & food shop. From 2011 onward the gallery will feature guest curators on a changing basis.
Patrick Gordon, Curator, curator@exposuregallery.info

Ottawa: **Heffel Gallery Ottawa**
451 Daly Ave., Ottawa, ON K1N 6H6
Tel: 613-230-6505; Fax: 613-230-8884
Toll-Free: 866-747-6505
www.heffel.com
Fine art auction house, headquartered in Vancouver, BC.
Andrew J.H. Gibbs, Ottawa Representative, andrew@heffel.com

Owen Sound: **Tom Thomson Art Gallery**
840 First Ave. West, Owen Sound, ON N4K 4K4
Tel: 519-376-1932
ttag@tomthomson.org; ttag@owensound.ca
www.tomthomson.org
Social Media: www.youtube.com/user/TomThomsonArtGallery
twitter.com/TheTomThomson
ww w.facebook.com/pages/Tom-Thomson-Art-Gallery/33138171071 4
Public art gallery featuring an extensive collection of Canadian art, historical & contemporary, with a focus on Thomson & the Group of Seven; full range of educational activities including lectures, workshops, & tours; gallery shop
Ted Renner, Chair
Virginia Eichhorn, Director/Curator, veichhorn@tomthomson.org

Peterborough: **Art Gallery of Peterborough**
250 Crescent St., Peterborough, ON K9J 2G1
Tel: 705-743-9179; Fax: 705-743-8168
gallery@agp.on.ca
www.agp.on.ca
www.facebook.com/139384686142024
Public art gallery with changing exhibitions
Cathy Wilson, President
Celeste Scopelites, Director, cscopelites@peterborough.ca
Carla Garnet, Curator, cgarnet@peterborough.ca

Peterborough: **Artspace**
PO Box 1748, #3, 378 Aylmer St. North, Peterborough, ON K9J 7X6
Tel: 705-748-3883
gallery@artspace-arc.org
www.artspace-arc.org
Social Media: artspaceptbo.tumblr.com; vimeo.com/artspacearc
www.facebook.com/ARTSPACEptbo
Committed to supporting the growth & development of contemporary artists & related-art practices; dedicated to artistic freedom & exploration
Fynn Leitch, Director, fynn@artspace-arc.org

Peterborough: **The Russell Gallery of Fine Art**
165 King St., Peterborough, ON K9J 2R8
Tel: 705-743-0151
www.russellgallery.com
Representing leading Canadian & international contemporary artists

***St Catharines:* Rodman Hall Art Centre**
109 St. Paul Cres., St Catharines, ON L2S 1M3
Tel: 905-684-2925; Fax: 905-682-4733
rodmanhall@brocku.ca
www.brocku.ca/rodmanhall/
Social Media: www.flickr.com/photos/rodmanhall
twitter.com/RodmanHall
www.facebook.c om/286652891904
Collection of about 1000 works of art, contemporary & historical, majority by Canadian artists; closed Mon.
Peter Partridge, Chair
Stuart Reid, Director/Curator, stuart.reid@brocku.ca
Marcie Bronson, Curator, Art/Registrar, mbronson2@brocku.ca

***St Thomas:* St Thomas-Elgin Public Art Centre**
301 Talbot St., St Thomas, ON N5P 1B5
Tel: 519-631-4040
info@stepac.ca
www.stepac.ca
twitter.com/STEPACDOTCA
www.facebook.com/111283576116
Promotion of visual arts by a permanent collection of over 800 artworks, exhibitions by current artists, & a variety of art education programs; volunteers & new members welcome; facility rental available; open Tue. - Sun.
Brent Shaw, President
Laura Woermke, Executive Director/Curator, lwoermke@stepac.ca
Katelyn Tippin, Administrative Assistant, ktippin@stepac.ca
Sherri Howard, Education Coordinator/Events Coordinator

***Sarnia:* Gallery Lambton**
Bayside Mall, 150 Christina St. North, Sarnia, ON N7T 7W5
Tel: 519-336-8127; Fax: 519-336-8128
www.lclmg.org
Exhibitions of contemporary art, featuring some of the best artists working in Ontario today, many with national & international reputations; collection contains paintings by the Group of Seven, & others, which are important to Canadian art history & are considered national treasures; wide range of changing exhibitions; tours for adults & school groups; education services; artist talks; films; pub
Lisa Daniels, Curator, lisa.daniels@county-lambton.on.ca

***Sault Ste Marie:* Art Gallery of Algoma**
10 East St., Sault Ste Marie, ON P6A 3C3
Tel: 705-949-9067; Fax: 705-949-6261
www.artgalleryofalgoma.com
www.facebook.com/groups/74480865690
Dedicated to cultivating & advancing the awareness of visual arts in Sault Ste Marie & the district of Algoma; open year round
Susan Hunter, President, susan.hunter@saultcollege.ca

***Scarborough:* Cedar Ridge Creative Centre**
225 Confederation Dr., Scarborough, ON M1G 1B2
Tel: 416-396-4026; Fax: 416-396-7044
crcc@toronto.ca
www.toronto.ca/culture/cedar_ridge/index.htm
An arts hub housed in a 1912 mansion. Art exhibitions are featured in the ground floor gallery from Sept.-June.

***Simcoe:* Norfolk Arts Centre**
Lynnwood Historic Site, 21 Lynnwood Ave., Simcoe, ON N3Y 4K8
Tel: 519-428-0540
norfolkartscentre@norfolkcounty.ca
www.norfolkartscentre.ca
www.facebook.com/NorfolkArtsCentre
Norfolk county's only arts centre, located in downtown Simcoe; programming includes exhibitions, kids studio, adult art workshops, Lynnwood's Film Simcoe, annual drive-thru art gallery exhibition
Deirdre Chisholm, Curator/Director

***Stouffville:* The Latcham Gallery**
PO Box 3, 6240 Main St., Stouffville, ON L4A 7Z4
Tel: 905-640-8954
info@latchamgallery.ca
www.latchamgallery.ca
Public art gallery
Roz Pritchard, Director
Chai Duncan, Curator

***Stratford:* Gallery Stratford**
54 Romeo St. South, Stratford, ON N5A 4S9
Tel: 519-271-5271; Fax: 519-271-1642
info@gallerystratford.on.ca
www.gallerystratford.on.ca
twitter.com/Gal leryStrtfrd
www.facebook.com/pages/Gallery-Stratford/28041706502
A non-profit, public art gallery open year round; contemporary, historical, local, national & international artists are highlighted annually in the heritage building; offers educational programs, workshops & fundraisers
Barbara Vallis, President
Zhe Gu, Executive Director, zgu@gallerystratford.on.ca

***Sudbury:* Art Gallery of Sudbury / Galerie d'art de Sudbury**
251 John St., Sudbury, ON P3E 1P9
Tel: 705-675-4871; Fax: 705-674-3065
gallery@artsudbury.org
www.artsudbury.org
Year Founded: 1967 Historical & contemporary Canadian art; open Tue.-Sat. 10-5, Sun. 12-5
Alan Nursall, Chair
Karen Tait-Peacock, Director, ktait@artsudbury.org

***Thunder Bay:* Thunder Bay Art Gallery**
***Also known as:* Thunder Bay National Exhibition Centre & Centre for Indian Art**
PO Box 10193 F, 1080 Keewatin St., Thunder Bay, ON P7B 6T7
Tel: 807-577-6427; Fax: 807-577-3781
info@theag.ca
www.theag.ca
Year Founded: 1967 Collection & exhibition of contemporary First Nations art, regional & international exhibits
Sharon Godwin, Executive Director, segodwin@theag.ca
Nadia Kurd, Curator, curator@theag.ca
Heidi Uhlig, President of the Board of Directors

***Toronto:* Academy of Spherical Arts**
38 Hanna Ave., Toronto, ON M6K 1X5
Tel: 416-532-2782; Fax: 416-532-3075
Toll-Free: 866-532-2782
jsorgente@sphericalarts.com
www.sphericalarts.com
Four room gallery displaying Canada's oldest collection of billiard tables, as well as billiard related accessories. Also hosts yearly art exhibitions for emerging Canadian artists, and includes Canadian art in its permanent collection.
Rick Williams, Founder

***Toronto:* Angell Gallery**
12 Ossington Ave., Toronto, ON M6J 2Y7
Tel: 416-530-0444
info@angellgallery.com
www.angellgallery.com
www.facebook.com/pages/Angell-Gallery/256380025273
Wed.-Sat. 12-5
Jamie Angell, Director/Owner
Gareth Brown-Jowett, Associate Director
Joey Chiu, Gallery Manager

***Toronto:* Annex Art Centre**
1073 Bathurst St., Toronto, ON M5R 3G8
Tel: 416-516-0110
info@annexartcentre.com
Art gallery & teaching studio located in Toronto's Annex, offering visual art & drama for kids, teens, & adults.

***Toronto:* Art Dialogue Gallery**
#501, 900 Yonge St., Toronto, ON M4W 3P5
Tel: 416-928-5904
Provides educated information & guidance in acquiring fine art; exhibitions & consultations for the display of artwork; lectures on various topics of contemporary art
Luciana Benzi, Director

***Toronto:* Art Gallery of York University (AGYU)**
Accolade East Bldg., 4700 Keele St., Toronto, ON M3J 1P3
Tel: 416-736-5169
agyu@yorku.ca
theagyuisoutthere.org/everywhere
Devoted to the presentation of innovative contemporary art; aims to situate Canadian art within an international context & to introduce Canadian audiences to important artists working abroad
Philip Monk, Director, pmonk@yorku.ca
Emelie Chhangur, Assistant Director/Curator, emelie@yorku.ca

***Toronto:* Art Metropole**
1490 Dundas St. West, Toronto, ON M6K 1T5
Tel: 416-703-4400; Fax: 416-703-4404
info@artmetropole.com
www.artmetropole.com; artmetropole.blogspot.ca
twitter.com/ArtMetropole
www.facebook.com/pages/Art-Metropole/3548841157 3
Year Founded: 1974 Specializes in contemporary art in multiple formats; offers artists' products for sale on premises & through web site as well as publishes, promotes, exhibits & distributes artists' products in various formats
Corinn Gerber, Director, corinn@artmetropole.com
Cheyanne Turions, Curator/Shop Manager, cheyanne@artmetropole.com

***Toronto:* The Bluffs Gallery**
***Parent:* Scarborough Arts**
Scarborough Arts, 1859 Kingston Rd., Toronto, ON M1N 1T3
Tel: 416-698-7322; Fax: 416-698-7972
info@scarborougharts.com
www.scarborougharts.com
Social Media: www.youtube.com/scarborougharts
twitter.com/scararts
www.facebook.com/ scarborougharts
Year Founded: 1979 The Bluffs Gallery is dedicated to the exhibition & sale of artwork by Scarborough Arts members. The Gallery offers solo & group exhibitions of all arts media, special events, workshops, & city-wide programs to promote the arts. Open Monday - Saturday; Closed on long weekends.
Daniel Broome, Chair
Tim Whalley, Executive Director, ed@scarborougharts.com

***Toronto:* Corkin Gallery**
7 Tank House Lane, Toronto, ON M5A 3C4
Tel: 416-979-1980; Fax: 416-979-7018
www.corkingallery.com
www.facebook.com/corkingallery
Eclectic works by contemporary artists in all media
Kimberly Fletcher, Director, director@corkingallery.com

***Toronto:* Creative Spirit Art Centre (CSAC)**
PO Box 16 P, 122 Wells St., Toronto, ON M5S 2S6
Tel: 416-588-8801; Fax: 416-588-8966
csac@creativespirit.on.ca
creativespirit.on.ca
Year Founded: 1992 Arts & Disabilities - Public Art Gallery/Studio, resource and information centre. Monthly exhibitions - Special area of collection of Art Brut, Outsider Art, Folk Art - Integrated exhibitions of Art produced by Artists with disabilities and Artists without disabilities. Closed August.
Ellen Anderson, Director

***Toronto:* Doris McCarthy Gallery (DMG)**
University of Toronto Scarborough, 1265 Military Trail, Toronto, ON M1C 1A4
Tel: 416-287-7007
dmg@utsc.utoronto.ca
www.utsc.utoronto.ca/~dmg
The gallery seeks to display works in all media forms by contemporary Canadian & international artists. Open W-F 10:00-4:00, Sa 12:00-5:00.
Ann MacDonald, Director/Curator, amacdonald@utsc.utoronto.ca

***Toronto:* Edward Day Gallery**
#200, 952 Queen St. West, Toronto, ON M6J 1G8
Tel: 416-921-6540
eddaygal.toronto@sympatico.ca
www.edwarddaygallery.com
Social Media: www.youtube.com/user/EdwardDayGallery
twitter.com/marysuerankin
www.fa
cebook.com/pages/Edward-Day-Gallery/187160541302483
Mary Sue Rankin, Director

***Toronto:* Gabor Mezei Studio**
587 Markham St., Toronto, ON M6G 2L7
Tel: 416-534-9800
Other contact information: Mobile: 416/319-0914
Small art gallery showing mainly the owner's work & a small selection of Canadian & international artists; approximately four exhibitions per year; by appt.
Gabor P. Mezei, Director/Curator

***Toronto:* Gallery Arcturus**
80 Gerrard St. East, Toronto, ON M5B 1G6
Tel: 416-977-1077; Fax: 416-977-1066
ob-art@arcturus.ca; info@arcturus.ca
www.arcturus.ca
Contemporary art gallery.
Eron Boyd, Gallery Manager
Cathy Stilo, Curator
Deborah Harris, Artist-in-Residence

***Toronto:* Gallery TPW**
***Also known as:* Toronto Photographers Workshop**
1256 Dundas St. West, Toronto, ON M6J 1X5
Tel: 416-645-1066; Fax: 416-645-1681
info@gallerytp.ca
gallerytpw.ca
Contemporary photography by Canadian & international artists.
Gary Hall, Executive Director, gary@gallerytpw.ca
Kim Simon, Programming Director, kim@gallerytpw.ca

***Toronto:* Glendon Gallery / Galerie Glendon**
Glendon College, York University, 2275 Bayview Ave., Toronto, ON M4N 3M6
Tel: 416-487-6721
gallery@glendon.yorku.ca
www.glendon.yorku.ca/gallery

University-affiliated public art gallery that focuses on contemporary Canadian art of merit with an added interest in francophone artistic expression; literature in French & English; guided tours & lectures
Martine Rheault, Coordinator, Cultural & Artistic Affairs
Marc Audette, Gallery Curator

Toronto: Heffel Gallery Inc.
13 Hazelton Ave., Toronto, ON M5R 2E1
Tel: 416-961-6505; Fax: 416-961-4245
Toll-Free: 866-961-6505
mail@heffel.com
www.heffel.com
Fine art auction house, headquartered in Vancouver, BC.
David K.J. Heffel, President, david@heffel.com
Judith Scolnick, Director, Toronto Office, judith@heffel.com

Toronto: Joseph D. Carrier Art Gallery
Columbus Centre, 901 Lawrence Ave. West, Toronto, ON M6A 1C3
Tel: 416-789-7011; Fax: 416-789-3951
www.villacharities.com/carrier
Year Founded: 1987 Third largest public art gallery in Toronto; features contemporary photography, painting, sculpture, & design.
Flavio Belli, Curator/Director

Toronto: The Justina M. Barnicke Gallery
Hart House, University of Toronto, 7 Hart House Circle, Toronto, ON M5S 3H3
Tel: 416-978-8398; Fax: 416-978-8387
www.jmbgallery.ca
www.facebook.com/265268153486093
Each year, 8-10 exhibitions are mounted featuring contemporary Canadian artists as well as historical exhibitions
Barbara Fischer, Executive Director/Chief Curator, barbara.fischer@utoronto.ca
Su-Ying Lee, Curator-in-Residence, suying.lee@utoronto.ca

Toronto: Knight Galleries International
472 Coldstream Ave., Toronto, ON M5N 1Y5
Tel: 416-923-0836
knight@knightgalleries.net
www.knightgall.com
The galleries specialize in contemporary international prints & paintings, as well as South African contemporary artwork & beadwork. There are two locations: Toronto, Canada, & Johannesburg, South Africa.
Julian Liknaitzky, President, 416-566-9027, julian@knightgalleries.net
Natalie Knight, Contact, The Art Source, Johannesburg, South Africa, 011-485-3606, Fax: 011-485-3614, nknight@icon.co.za

Toronto: Koffler Gallery/Koffler Centre of the Arts
4588 Bathurst St., Toronto, ON M2R 1W6
Tel: 416-636-1881
www.kofflerarts.org
The Koffler Gallery maintains a year-round exhibition program of contemporary art; programming emphasizes new work by mid-career & more senior Canadian artists, & within this context, work of special interest to the Jewish community
Tiana Koffler Boyman, Chair
Mona Filip, Curator, Koffler Gallery, mfilip@kofflerarts.org
Lori Starr, Executive Director, lstarr@kofflerarts.org

Toronto: The Market Gallery
South St. Lawrence Market, 95 Front St. East, Toronto, ON M5E 1C2
Tel: 416-392-7604; Fax: 416-392-0572
marketgallery@toronto.ca
www.toronto.ca/culture/the_market_gallery.htm
A focus on the art & history of Toronto
Pamela Wachna, Coordinator, Collections & Outreach, pwachna@toronto.ca

Toronto: Mercer Union, A Centre for Contemporary Visual Art
1286 Bloor St. West, Toronto, ON M6H 1N9
Tel: 416-536-1519; Fax: 416-536-2955
info@mercerunion.org
www.mercerunion.org
An artist-run centre dedicated to the existence of contemporary art; provides a forum for the production & exhibition of Canadian & international conceptually & aesthetically engaging art & related cultural practices; pursues primary concerns through critical activities that include exhibitions, lectures, screenings, performances, publications, events & special projects; non-profit, charitable organization.
York Lethbridge, Director, Operations & Development, york@mercerunion.org
Sarah Robayo Sheridan, Director, Exhibitions & Publications, sarah@mercerunion.org

Toronto: Museum of Contemporary Canadian Art
952 Queen St. West, Toronto, ON M6J 1G8
Tel: 416-395-0067; Fax: 416-395-7598
info@mocca.ca
www.mocca.ca
Social Media: www.youtube.com/moccatoronto
twitter.com/MOCCA_TO
www.facebook.com/431 05856701
Contemporary Canadian artists' works, including traditional & new media; six exhibitions a year showcase established & emerging artists from across Canada; exhibition based programming; open Tue.-Sun., 11-6; free admission; groups & tours by appt.
Julia Ouellette, Chair
David Liss, Artistic Director/Curator

Toronto: Odon Wagner Contemporary
198 Davenport Rd., Toronto, ON M5R 1J2
Tel: 416-962-0438; Fax: 416-962-1581
Toll-Free: 800-551-2465
info@odonwagnergallery.com
www.odonwagnergallery.com/o wc_home.php
Social Media: odonwagnercontemporary.tumblr.com
twitter.com/owgallery
www.facebook.com/odonwagnergallery
Specializes in paintings, sculpture, & prints by Canadian & international artists.
Nicholas Wagner, Contact, nicholas@odonwagnergallery.com

Toronto: Odon Wagner Gallery
196 Davenport Rd., Toronto, ON M5R 1J2
Tel: 416-962-0438; Fax: 416-962-1581
Toll-Free: 800-551-2465
info@odonwagnergallery.com
www.odonwagnergallery.com/o wg_home.php
twitter.com/owgallery
www.facebook.com/odonwagnergallery
Fine art gallery featuring masterpieces of past & present; sale & purchase of quality paintings, restoration, appraisal, consultation & framing services
Odon Wagner, Director, odon@odonwagnergallery.com

Toronto: Olga Korper Gallery Inc.
17 Morrow Ave., Toronto, ON M6R 2H9
Tel: 416-538-8220; Fax: 416-538-8772
info@olgakorpergallery.com
www.olgakorpergallery.com
Year Founded: 1973 The gallery exists to exhibit & promote Canadian & international contemporary art
Shelli Cassidy-McIntosh, Executive Director
Olga Korper, Director
Sasha Korper, Director

Toronto: A Space Gallery
#110, 401 Richmond St. West, Toronto, ON M5V 3A8
Tel: 416-979-9633
info@aspacegallery.org
www.aspacegallery.org
Year Founded: 1971 A Space has a thirty year history of multi-disciplinary artist-run activity. The organizations' mandate encompasses the investigation, presentation & interpretation of contemporary art forms, different disciplines & theories. A Space maintains a politically engaged issue oriented programming that is inclusive of a wide range of media, disciplines & views.
Rebecca McGowan, Executive Director
Vicky Moufwad-Paul, Artistic Director

Toronto: Susan Hobbs Gallery
137 Tecumseth St., Toronto, ON M6J 2H2
Tel: 416-504-3699; Fax: 416-504-8064
info@susanhobbs.com
www.susanhobbs.com
www.facebook.com/48701573223
Exhibition & sales of contemporary Canadian art; artists represented include Ian Carr-Harris, Magdalen Celestino, Robin Collyer, Max Dean, Brian Groombridge, Scott Lyall, Arnaud Maggs, Liz Magor, Sandra Meigs, Colette Whiten, Robert Wiens, Shirley Wiitasalo, & Kevin Yates
Susan Hobbs, Director

Toronto: University of Toronto Art Centre
University College, 15 King's College Circle, Toronto, ON M5S 3H7
Tel: 416-978-1838; Fax: 416-971-2059
www.utac.utoronto.ca
twitter.com/utac
www.facebook.com/UofTArtCentre
Year Founded: 1996 Housing galleries with selections from university collections as well as a schedule of changing exhibitions
Lyndsay Green, Chair
Dr. Niamh O'Laoghaire, Director, 416-946-7015, niamh.olaoghaire@utoronto.ca
Heather Darling Pigat, Collections Manager, 416-946-7090, heather.pigat@utoronto.ca

Toronto: Ydessa Hendeles Art Foundation (YHAF)
778 King St. West, Toronto, ON M4Y 2N6
Tel: 416-413-9400
Contemporary art collection; features work of international artists; works on display include paintings, photography, & multimedia projects.
Ydessa Hendeles, Owner

Toronto: York Quay Gallery
Harbourfront Centre, 235 Queen's Quay West, Toronto, ON M5J 2G8
Tel: 416-973-4600; Fax: 416-973-6055
info@harbourfrontcentre.com
www.harbourfrontcentre.com
Contemporary art at Toronto's Harbourfront Centre.

Toronto: YYZ Artists' Outlet
#140, 401 Richmond St. West, Toronto, ON M5V 3A8
Tel: 416-598-4546; Fax: 416-598-2282
yyz@yyzartistsoutlet.org
www.yyzartistsoutlet.org
twitter.com/YYZ_YYZB OOKS
www.facebook.com/yyzartistsoutlet
YYZ is dedicated to the support of work by contemporary artists working in all media, & to the provision of a venue for the exhibition of this work through on-going programs in both visual & time-based arts - video, film & performance.
Darryl Bank, Chair, bod@yyzartistsoutlet.org
Ana Barajas, Director, abarajas@yyzartistsoutlet.org

Waterloo: Canadian Clay & Glass Gallery / Galerie Canadienne de la Céramique et du Verre
25 Caroline St. North, Waterloo, ON N2L 2Y5
Tel: 519-746-1882; Fax: 519-746-6396
info@canadianclayandglass.ca
www.canadianclayandglass.ca
twitter.com/c dnclayandglass
www.facebook.com/190913524282373
Exhibits contemporary artworks executed in clay, glass, stained glass & enamel for public education & enjoyment
Armin Froelich, Chair
William D. Poole, Executive Director, director@canadianclayandglass.ca
Christian Bernard Singer, Curator, christian@canadianclayandglass.ca

Waterloo: Robert Langen Gallery
Wilfrid Laurier University, Waterloo, ON N2L 3C5
Tel: 519-884-1970
www.wlu.ca/homepage.php?grp_id=12554
twitter.com/Lauri erNews
www.facebook.com/LaurierNow
Year Founded: 1989 The University's visual arts centre; provides knowledge, stewardship, appreciation & enjoyment of Canadian art & culture to members of the Laurier community & the community at large
Deborah Currie, Manager, Academic Events, dcurrie@wlu.ca
Suzanne Luke, Curator/Art Gallery Coordinator, sluke@wlu.ca

Waterloo: University of Waterloo Art Gallery (UWAG)
University of Waterloo, 200 University Ave. West., ECH, Waterloo, ON N2L 3G1
Tel: 519-888-4567
uwag.uwaterloo.ca
Social Media: www.flickr.com/photos/56851697@N04
www.facebook.com/uwag.waterloo
Produces exhibitions of contemporary Canadian art in all media; holds a collection of contemporary Canadian art since 1960; open Tue. - Sat. during academic year at two sites: Modern Languages Building & the main gallery in East Campus Hall
Ivan Jurakic, Director/Curator, ijurakic@uwaterloo.ca

Whitby: The Station Gallery
1450 Henry St., Whitby, ON L1N 0A8
Tel: 905-668-4185; Fax: 905-668-1934
art@whitbystationgallery.com
www.whitbystationgallery.com
Social Media: www.linkedin.com/company/885487
twitter.com/stationgallery
www.facebook.com/stationgallery
The gallery's Permanent Collection exceeds 300 original prints, paintings, sculpture, & mixed media works.
Greg Murphy, Chair
Donna Raetsen-Kemp, CEO, raetsen-kempd@whitbystationgallery.com
Olexander Wlasenko, Curator, wlasenkoo@whitbystationgallery.com

Windsor: Artcite Inc.
109 University Ave. West, Windsor, ON N9A 5P4
Tel: 519-977-6564; Fax: 519-977-6564
info@artcite.ca
www.artcite.ca
Year Founded: 1982 Artcite is Windsor's only artist-run centre exclusively dedicated to presenting contemporary &

experimental art forms. The gallery is open W-Sa 12:00-5:00, or by appointment; the office is open Tu-Sa 12:00-5:00.
Samantha Therrien, President
Christine Burchnall, Administrative Coordinator, xtine@artcite.ca

Bernard Helling, Artistic Coordinator

Woodstock: **Woodstock Art Gallery (WAG)**
449 Dundas St., Woodstock, ON N4S 1C2
Tel: 519-539-6761; Fax: 519-539-2564
gallery@city.woodstock.on.ca
www.woodstockartgallery.ca
Features contemporary & historical exhibitions; wide range of classes & workshops for adults & children; focuses on local painter Florence Carlyle through an extensive permanent collection & family artifacts
Patricia Deadman, Acting Curator, pdeadman@city.woodstock.on.ca

Prince Edward Island

Provincial Art Galleries

Confederation Centre Art Gallery (CCAG) / Le Musée d'Art du Centre de la Confédération
145 Richmond St., Charlottetown, PE C1A 1J1
Tel: 902-628-6142; Fax: 902-566-4648
info@confederationcentre.com
www.confederationcentre.com
Social Media: www.youtube.com/confedcentre
twitter.com/confedboxoffice
www.facebook.com/ccoagallery
Critical inquiry into 200 years of Canadian art; 28 annual exhibitions; 15,000 work collection
Pan Wendt, Curator, curator@confederationcentre.com

Quebec

Provincial Art Galleries

Musée d'art contemporain de Montréal (MACM)
185, rue Ste-Catherine ouest, Montréal, QC H2X 3X5
Tél: 514-847-6226; Téléc: 514-847-6292
www.macm.org
Médias sociaux: www.youtube.com/macmvideos
twitter.com/macmtl
www.facebook.com/macmontreal
Collection of over 6,000 works dating from 1939 by artists from Québec, Canada & around the world; a specialized reference centre is available for research; various performances, lectures & educational programs are offered by the museum throughout the year; restaurant, boutique & bookstore
Alexandre Taillefer, Président
Paulette Gagnon, Directrice générale

Musée des beaux-arts de Montréal (MBAM) / Montreal Museum of Fine Arts (MMFA)
CP 3000 H, #1379, 1380, rue Sherbrooke ouest, Montréal, QC H3G 2T9
Tél: 514-285-2000Ligne sans frais: 800-899-6873
www.mbam.qc.ca
twitter.com/mbamtl
www.facebook.com/mbamtl
The Museum houses an encyclopaedic collection that includes Canadian Art, Contemporary Art, European Art, Decorative Arts, Ancient Cultures, & Mediterranean Archeology; since 2007 the museum has hosted the collection from the former Musée Marc-Aurèle Fortin; access to the permanent collection is free
Nathalie Bondil, Directrice/Conservatrice en chef, L'art européen

Hilliard T. Goldfarb, Conservateur en chef adjoint, Maîtres anciens
Monique Dénommée, Adjointe administrative, mdenommee@mbamtl.org

Musée national des beaux-arts du Québec
Parc des Champs-de-Bataille, Québec, QC G1R 5H3
Tél: 418-643-2150; Téléc: 418-646-3330
Ligne sans frais: 866-220-2150
info@mnba.qc.ca
www.mnba.qc.ca
Fondée en: 1933 The museum, situated on the Plains of Abraham, houses prestigious collections of 17th, 18th, & 19th century art, plus a collection of contemporary art. Various temporary exhibitions are also held. Open year round, the museum also features a library, a bookstore, & an educational service.
Esther Trépanier, Director

Local Art Galleries in Quebec

Alma: **Langage Plus**
CP 518, 555, rue Collard ouest, Alma, QC G8B 5W1
Tél: 418-668-6635; Téléc: 418-668-3263
info@langageplus.com
www.langageplus.com
Jean Briand, Président
Jocelyne Fortin, Directrice, direction@langageplus.com

Amos: **Centre d'exposition d'Amos**
222, 1e av est, Amos, QC J9T 1H3
Tel: 819-732-6070; Fax: 819-732-3242
www.ville.amos.qc.ca/fr/citoyen/centre_exposition
L'art actuel et traditionnel; les sciences et l'histoire
Marianne Trudel, Directrice

Aylmer: **Centre d'exposition l'Imagier**
9, rue Front, Aylmer, QC J9H 4W8
Tél: 819-684-1445; Téléc: 819-684-4058
info@limagier.qc.ca
www.limagier.qc.ca
www.facebook.com/Imagier
Véronique Guitard, Directrice par interim

Baie-Saint-Paul: **Musée d'art contemporain de Baie-Saint-Paul**
23, rue Ambroise-Fafand, Baie-Saint-Paul, QC G3Z 2J2
Tél: 418-435-3681; Téléc: 418-435-6269
info@macbsp.com
www.macbsp.com
Médias sociaux: www.youtube.com/user/MACBaieStPaul
Mathieu Simard, Président
Jacques Saint-Gelais Tremblay, Directeur général, j.s.tremblay@macbsp.com

Carleton: **Centre d'Artistes Vaste et Vague**
774, boul Perron est, Carleton, QC G0C 1J0
Tél: 418-364-3123; Téléc: 418-364-6822
communication@vasteetvague.ca
www.vasteetvague.ca
Centre de production et de diffusion en art actuel et contemporain Expositions, résidences d'artiste, atelier de production, production d'événements majeurs (Symposium)
Maryse Goudreau, Présidente
Guylaine Langlois, Directrice générale

Chicoutimi: **Espace Virtuel**
534, rue Jacques-Cartier est, Chicoutimi, QC G7H 1Z6
Tél: 418-698-3873; Téléc: 418-698-3874
Ligne sans frais: 877-998-3873
information@espacevirtuel.ca
espacevirtuel.ca/centre.html
www.facebook.com/groups/33544647534
Sébastien Harvey, Directeur, direction@espacevirtuel.ca

Drummondville: **Galerie d'art Desjardins**
175, rue Ringuet, Drummondville, QC J2C 2P7
Tél: 819-477-5518; Téléc: 819-477-5723
www.artsdrummondville.com
Médias sociaux: www.youtube.com/drspectacles
twitter.com/artsdrummond
www.facebook.com /maisondesarts
Open year round
Normand Blanchette, Directeur, nblanchette@artsdrummondville.com

Gatineau: **AXENÉO7**
80, rue Hanson, Gatineau, QC J8Y 3M5
Tél: 819-771-2122; Téléc: 819-771-0696
axeneo7@axeneo7.qc.ca
www.axeneo7.qc.ca
twitter.com/axeneo7
www.face book.com/AXENEO7
Fondée en: 1983
Jonathan Demers, Directeur, jonathan.demers@axeneo7.qc.ca

Gatineau: **Centre d'exposition Art-Image et espace Odyssée Maison de la Culture de Gatineau**
855, boul de la Gappe, Gatineau, QC J8T 8H9
Tél: 819-243-2325; Téléc: 819-243-2527
artimage@gatineau.ca
www.ville.gatineau.qc.ca/artimage
www.facebook.co m/artimageetespaceodyssee
To increase communication between the artistic fields & the general public
Marie Hélène Giguère, Coordonnatrice des espaces d'exposition

Gatineau: **Galerie Montcalm**
Maison du Citoyen, CP 1970 Hull, 25, rue Laurier, 1er étage, Gatineau, QC J8X 3Y9
Tél: 819-595-7488
galeriemontcalm1@gatineau.ca
www.gatineau.ca

Jonquière: **Centre national d'exposition (CNE)**
CP 605, 4160, rue du Vieux Pont, Jonquière, QC G7X 7W4
Tél: 418-546-2177; Téléc: 418-546-2180
info@centrenationalexposition.com
www.centrenationalexposition.com
Presents exhibitions of the works of professional artists & several travelling shows; demonstrates richness of the collections of Québec & other Canadian & international museums; guided tours, workshops, demonstrations & edukits available
Manon Guérin, Directrice

Laval: **Salle Alfred Pellan, Maison des arts de Laval**
1395, boul de la Concorde ouest, Laval, QC H7N 5W1
Tél: 450-662-4440; Téléc: 450-662-4428
sallealfredpellan@ville.laval.qc.ca
www.ville.laval.qc.ca
www.facebook .com/maisondesartsdelaval
Arts visuels à caractère contemporain
Ginette Beaunoyer, Contact

Lennoxville: **Foreman Art Gallery of Bishop's University / Galerie d'art Foreman de l'Université Bishop's**
Also known as: **Art Lab**
Bishop's University, 2600 College St., Lennoxville, QC J1M 1Z7
Tel: 819-822-9600; Fax: 819-822-9703
gallery@ubishops.ca
www.foreman.ubishops.ca; artlab.ubishops.ca
twitter.com/ForemanArtGal
www.facebook.com/foremanartgallery
To serve as a forum for the presentation & examination of the visual arts through the programming of contemporary & historical exhibitions as well as lecture series , workshops & films; open Tues. - Sat. 12-5, evenings when Centennial Theatre open; admission free
Vicky Chainey Gagnon, Director/Curator

Longueuil: **Plein sud, centre d'exposition en art actuel à Longueuil**
150, rue de Gentilly est, local D-0626, Longueuil, QC J4H 4A9
Tél: 450-679-2966; Téléc: 450-679-4480
plein-sud@plein-sud.org
www.plein-sud.org
Diffuse la production d'artistes professionnels dont les recherches s'inscrivent en art actuel; présente des expositions temporaires et offre des activités qui visent à familiariser le public avec les différentes avenues proposées par cet art
Monic Brassard, Présidente
Hélène Poirier, Directrice générale et artistique, hpoirier@plein-sud.org

Matane: **Galerie d'art de Matane**
#101, 520, av Saint-Jérôme, Matane, QC G4W 3B5
Tél: 418-566-6687
www.galerieartmatane.org
Présenter environ 8 expositions d'artistiques du Québec, du Canada et de l'étranger
Michel Hébert, Président
François Wells, Administrateur

Mont-Laurier: **Centre d'exposition Mont-Laurier**
CP 334, 385, rue Du Pont, Mont-Laurier, QC J9L 3N7
Tél: 819-623-2441; Téléc: 819-623-3007
ceml@lino.sympatico.ca
www.villemontlaurier.qc.ca
Le Centre d'exposition de Mont-Laurier est une institution muséale dont la mission est la diffusion, l'éducation et l'action culturelle en arts visuels et en patrimoine

Montréal: **Artothèque**
5720, rue St-André, Montréal, QC H2S 2K1
Tél: 514-278-8181; Téléc: 514-278-3044
www.artotheque.ca
www.facebook.com/artotheque.quisemporte

Montréal: **La Centrale (Galerie Powerhouse)**
4296, boul Saint-Laurent, Montréal, QC H2W 1Z3
Tél: 514-871-0268
galerie@lacentrale.org
www.lacentrale.org
twitter.com/lacentralemtl
www.facebook.com/25308401 1386087
Artist-run centre dedicated to the presentation of women's contemporary art
Virginie Jourdain, Coordonnatrice des expositions
Jen Leigh Fisher, Coordonnatrice artistique, programmation@lacentrale.org
Diane St-Antoine, Coordonnatrice administration, administration@lacentrale.org

***Montréal:* Centre international d'art contemporain de Montréal**
CP 760 Place du Parc, Montréal, QC H2X 4A6
Tél: 514-288-0811; Téléc: 514-288-5021
ciac@ciac.ca
www.ciac.ca
Centre international d'art contemporain de Montréal is an office for contemporary art producing exhibitions, La Biennale de Montréal, an electronic art magazine, publications, & events.
Claude Gosselin, Director

***Montréal:* Galerie de l'UQAM**
Université du Québec à Montréal, CP 8888 Centre-ville, 1400, rue Berri, Pavillon Judith-Jasmin, Local J-R 120, Montréal, QC H3C 3P8
Tél: 514-987-6150; Téléc: 514-987-6897
galerie@uqam.ca
www.galerie.uqam.ca
twitter.com/galeriedeluqam
www.f acebook.com/galerie.uqam
Louise Déry, Directrice

***Montréal:* Galerie Heffel Québec Ltée**
1840, rue Sherbrooke ouest, Montréal, QC H3H 1E4
Tél: 514-939-6505; Téléc: 514-939-1100
Ligne sans frais: 866-939-6505
mail@heffel.com
www.heffel.com
Fine art auction house, headquartered in Vancouver, BC.

***Montréal:* Leonard & Bina Ellen Art Gallery / Galerie Leonard et Bina Ellen**
Concordia University, 1455, boul de Maisonneuve ouest, Montréal, QC H3G 1M8
Tel: 514-848-2424; Fax: 514-848-4751
ellengal@alcor.concordia.ca
ellengallery.concordia.ca
twitter.com/elle ngallery
www.facebook.com/ellengallery
Committed to researching, collecting & interpreting Canadian art; programming centres on exhibitions that help advance knowledge in the visual arts; in keeping with Concordia's academic mission, the Gallery is committed to the enhancement of the University's educational programmes & cultural environment
Michèle Thériault, Director, michele.theriault@concordia.ca

***Montréal:* Segal Centre for Performing Arts**
5170, côte Sainte-Catherine, Montréal, QC H3W 1M7
Tel: 514-739-2301; Fax: 514-739-9340
info@segalcentre.org
www.segalcentre.org
Alvin Segal, President
Joel Segal, Vice-President
Bryna Wasserman, Artistic & Executive Director
Barry Taggart, Director, Finance & Operations
Michael Blumenstein, Secretary
Tasso Lagios, Treasurer

***Mont-Saint-Hilaire:* Musée des beaux-arts de Mont-Saint-Hilaire**
150, rue du Centre-Civique, Mont-Saint-Hilaire, QC J3H 5Z5
Tél: 450-536-3033; Téléc: 450-536-3032
www.mbamsh.qc.ca
Promotes work of local artists Ozias Leduc, Paul-Émile Borduas & Jordi Benet; works of contemporary artists
Marie-Andrée Leclerc, Directrice générale, maleclerc@mbamsh.qc.ca

***Pointe-Claire:* La Galerie d'art Stewart Hall Art Gallery**
Centre culturel de Pointe-Claire Stewart Hall, 176, ch Bord-du-Lac, Pointe-Claire, QC H9S 4J7
Tél: 514-630-1254; Téléc: 514-630-1285
millarj@ville.pointe-claire.qc.ca
www.ville.pointe-claire.qc.ca
Open year round; exhibitions from local, national & international sources; paintings, photographs, sculptures, graphics & theme exhibitions; free admission; wheelchair access
Joyce Millar, Directrice/Conservatrice, millarj@ville.pointe-claire.qc.ca

***Québec:* VU centre de diffusion et de production de la photographie**
***Also known as:* Centre VU**
523, Saint-Vallier est, Québec, QC G1K 3P9
Tél: 418-640-2558; Téléc: 418-640-2586
info@vuphoto.org
www.vuphoto.org
www.facebook.com/pages/VU-PHOTO/18771 4927147
VU se consacre à la promotion et au développement de la photographie d'auteur. Son mandat vise prioritairement le soutien aux activités de recherche et de création en photographie à travers des expositions, des résidences d'artistes, des publications et des événements spéciaux. VU offre un accès privilégié à une vaste gamme d'équipements de production en photographie argentique et numérique
Rodrigue Bélanger, Président
Pascale Bureau, Directrice générale, direction@vuphoto.org

***Rimouski:* Galerie Coup d'Oeuil**
CP 710, 22, rue Sainte-Marie, Rimouski, QC G5L 7C7
Tél: 418-724-3235; Téléc: 418-724-3139

***Rouyn-Noranda:* Centre d'exposition de Rouyn-Noranda inc.**
201, av Dallaire, local 154, Rouyn-Noranda, QC J9X 4T5
Tél: 819-762-6600; Téléc: 819-762-9425
info.cern@rouyn-noranda.ca
www.cern.ca
www.facebook.com/centredexposit ion.rouynnoranda
Noël Neveu, Président
Chantal Polard, Directrice générale, direction.cern@rouyn-noranda.ca

***Saint-Hyacinthe:* Expression, Centre d'exposition de Saint-Hyacinthe**
495, rue Saint-Simon, Saint-Hyacinthe, QC J2S 5C3
Tél: 450-773-4209; Téléc: 450-773-5270
expression@expression.qc.ca
www.expression.qc.ca
www.facebook.com/Expr essionCentreDexpositionDeSaintHyacinthe
Une institution muséale dont la mission est de promouvoir et de diffuser l'art contemporain et actuel. Depuis 1985, Expression présente au public, dans une salle magnifique et spacieuse, des expositions réputées pour leur qualité artistique. A ces expositions, s'ajoutent un service d'animation, des conférences et des publications. De plus, Expression insère ponctuellement des activités satellites
Marcel Blouin, Direction génerale et artistique

***Saint-Jean-Port-Joli:* Maison-musée Médard-Bourgault**
322, av de Gaspé ouest, Saint-Jean-Port-Joli, QC G0R 3G0
Tél: 418-598-3880
mmbcontact@gmail.com
medardbourgault.org

***Saint-Laurent:* Musée des maîtres et artisans du Québec (MMAQ)**
615, av Sainte-Croix, Saint-Laurent, QC H4L 3X6
Tél: 514-747-7367; Téléc: 514-747-8892
info@mmaq.qc.ca
www.mmaq.qc.ca; lenclume.wordpress.com
Médias sociaux: www.youtube.com/user/MuseeMAQ
twitter.com/museemaq
www.facebook.com/74228420780
Chefs d'oeuvres de grands maîtres et pièces exceptionnelles d'artisans anonymes présentent un panorama de la culture traditionnelle québécoise dans une église néo-gothique de 1867
Pierre Wilson, Directeur-conservateur, p.wilson@mmaq.qc.ca
Isolda Gavidia, Collection Archivist, i.gavidia@mmaq.qc.ca

***Saint-Léonard:* Galerie Port-Maurice**
8420, boul Lacordaire, Saint-Léonard, QC H1R 3G5
Tél: 514-328-8514
Fondée en: 1979 Crée en 1979; sensibilise la population aux différents courants contemporains d'arts visuels

***La Sarre:* Centre d'art Rotary**
195, rue Principale, La Sarre, QC J9Z 1Y3
Tél: 819-333-2294; Téléc: 819-333-2296
www.ville.lasarre.qc.ca/culture
www.facebook.com/centredartrotary.lasarr e
Lise Gaignard, Directrice des loisirs et de la culture, lgaignard@ville.lasarre.qc.ca

***Shawinigan:* Centre d'exposition Léo-Ayotte**
***Also known as:* Centre des Arts de Shawinigan**
c/o Corporation culturelle de Shawinigan, 2100, boul Des Hêtres, Shawinigan, QC G9N 8R8
Tél: 819-539-1888; Téléc: 819-539-2400
corporationculturelle@shawinigan.ca
www.cultureshawinigan.ca/CentreExpos ition.aspx?id=1
Louise Martin, Directrice générale et artistique, lmartin@shawinigan.ca
Clémence Bélanger, Muséologue, cbelanger@shawinigan.ca
Isabelle Gingras, Responsable des programmes éducatifs, igingras@shawinigan.ca

***Sherbrooke:* Galerie d'art du Centre culturel de l'Université de Sherbrooke**
2500, boul Université, Sherbrooke, QC J1K 2R1
Tél: 819-820-1000
galerie@ushebrooke.ca
www.centrecultureludes.ca
Suzanne Pressé, Coordonnatrice

***Sherbrooke:* Musée des beaux-arts de Sherbrooke**
241, rue Dufferin, Sherbrooke, QC J1H 4M3
Tél: 819-821-2115; Téléc: 819-821-4003
mbas@mbas.qc.ca
www.mbas.qc.ca
www.facebook.com/148126951901795
Plusieurs expositions temporaires ainsi que la collection du Musée, notamment les oeuvres de Frederick Simpson Coburn et la collection Luc LaRochelle
Cécile Gélinas, Directrice

***St-Georges:* Centre d'Art de St-Georges**
c/o Centre culturel Marie-Fitzbach, 250, 18e rue ouest, St-Georges, QC G5Y 4S9
Tél: 418-226-2238
Fondée en: 1992
Marie Tanguay, Chef de division, marie.tanguay@ville.saint-georges.qc.ca

***Trois-Rivières:* Galerie d'art du Parc et Manoir de Tonnancour**
CP 871, 864, rue des Ursulines, Trois-Rivières, QC G9A 5J9
Tél: 819-374-2355; Téléc: 819-374-1758
galerie@galeriedartduparc.qc.ca
www.galeriedartduparc.qc.ca
www.facebo ok.com/galeriedartduparc
Drawings, paintings, sculptures, stamps, photos, videos & mixed-media exhibitions; permanent exhibition on the history of the Manoir de Tonnancour

***Valcourt:* Centre culturel Yvonne L. Bombardier**
1002, av J.-A.-Bombardier, Valcourt, QC J0E 2L0
Tél: 450-532-3033
ccylb@fjab.qc.ca
www.centreculturelbombardier.com
www.facebook.com/CentreCulturelBombardi er

***Val-d'Or:* Centre d'exposition de Val d'Or**
600, 7e rue, Val-d'Or, QC J9P 3P3
Tél: 819-825-0942; Téléc: 819-825-3062
expovd@ville.valdor.qc.ca
www.expovd.ca
Ginette Vézina, Présidente
Carmelle Adam, Directrice, carmelle.adam@ville.valdor.qc.ca

***Verdun:* Centre culturel de Verdun**
5955, rue Bannantyne, Verdun, QC H4H 1H6
Tel: 514-765-7170; Fax: 514-765-7263
nancy.raymond@verdun.ca

Saskatchewan

Provincial Art Galleries

MacKenzie Art Gallery (MAG)
T.C. Douglas Bldg., 3475 Albert St., Regina, SK S4S 6X6
Tel: 306-584-4250; Fax: 306-569-8191
info@mackenzieartgallery.ca
www.mackenzieartgallery.sk.ca
Social Media: www.youtube.com/atthemag
twitter.com/AtTheMAG
www.facebook.com/MacKenzieArtGallery
Year Founded: 1953 Historical & contemporary Canadian, American & European works; special emphasis on western Canadian art; works on paper, contemporary photography, major touring exhibits; facilities include learning centre, studios, theatre, gift shop; sculpture court; outdoor sculpture garden; open daily year round
Jeremy Morgan, Executive Director, jeremy.morgan@mackenzieartgallery.ca
Timothy Long, Head Curator, timothy.long@mackenzieartgallery.ca

Mendel Art Gallery & Civic Conservatory (MAG)
PO Box 569, 950 Spadina Cres. East, Saskatoon, SK S7K 3L6
Tel: 306-975-7610; Fax: 306-975-7670
info@mendel.ca
www.mendel.ca
Social Media: www.youtube.com/user/MendelArtGallery
twitter.com/MendelGallery
www.fa cebook.com/mendelartgallery
Historical & contemporary Canadian & international art; 5 exhibition periods/year; open year-round; the Saskatoon Civic Conservatory is adjacent to the gallery
Jason Aebig, President/Chair
Angela Larson, Acting Executive Director/CEO, alarson@mendel.ca
Mark Heit, Greenhouse Supervisor, mark.heit@saskatoon.ca

Local Art Galleries in Saskatchewan

***Denare Beach:* Lakefront Gallery**
2025 Amisk Dr., Denare Beach, SK S0P 0B0

Original works & prints by Robert Russell; open daily 1:00-8:00 during the summer.

North Battleford: Allen Sapp Gallery
Also known as: Allen Sapp Gallery - The Gonor Collection
PO Box 460, 1 Railway Ave. East, North Battleford, SK S9A 2Y6
Tel: 306-445-1760; Fax: 306-445-1694
sapp@accesscomm.ca
www.allensapp.com
Cree art & interpretive centre; open year round
Robin Dyck, Acting Administrator

North Battleford: The Chapel Gallery
PO Box 460, 891 - 99 St., North Battleford, SK S9A 2Y6
Tel: 306-445-1757; Fax: 306-445-1009
chapelgallery@sasktel.net
www.chapelgallery.ca
Exhibition of local to international artists, permanent collection of the city of North Battleford
Michael Brukop, Curator

Prince Albert: Grace Campbell Gallery
c/o John M. Cuelenaere Public Library, 125 - 12 St. East, Prince Albert, SK S6V 1B7
Tel: 306-763-8496; Fax: 306-763-3816
library@jmcpl.ca
www.jmcpl.ca/about-the-library/grace-campbell-art-galle ry
twitter.com/JMCPLca
www.facebook.com/jmcpl.ca
Local, provincial & national exhibitions; no permanent collection
Alex Juorio, Library Director

Prince Albert: Mann Art Gallery
142 - 12th St. West, Prince Albert, SK S6V 3B5
Tel: 306-763-7080; Fax: 306-763-7838
info@mannartgallery.ca
mannartgallery.ca
www.facebook.com/mann.artgall ery
The gallery specializes in contemporary art, & seeks to promote artistic creation & appreciation in the region.
Griffith Aaron Baker, Director/Curator, curator@mannartgallery.ca

Regina: Art Gallery of Regina
Neil Balkwill Civic Arts Centre, PO Box 1790, 2420 Elphinstone St., Regina, SK S4P 3C8
Tel: 306-522-5940; Fax: 306-522-5944
agr@sasktel.net
www.artgalleryofregina.ca
www.facebook.com/groups/AGRg allery
Year Founded: 1974 The gallery focuses on contemporary art, especially works by Saskatchewan artists.
Karen Schoonover, Director/Curator

Regina: Dunlop Art Gallery
Regina Public Library, PO Box 2311, 2311 - 12th Ave., Regina, SK S4P 3Z5
Tel: 306-777-6040
www.dunlopartgallery.org
Permanent art collection of contemporary & historical significance by Saskatchewan artists; open year round

Regina: Sherwood Village Branch Gallery
6121 Rochdale Blvd., Regina, SK S4X 2R1
Tel: 306-777-6040; Fax: 306-949-7264
Open year round; closed Sundays July & Aug.
Dr. Curtis Collins, Director, ccollins@reginalibrary.ca
Wendy Peart, Curator, Education & Community Outreach, wpeart@reginalibrary.ca

Regina: McIntyre Gallery
2347 McIntyre St., Regina, SK S4P 2S3
Tel: 306-757-4323
mcintyre.gallery@sasktel.net
www.mcintyregallery.ca
Contemporary Saskatchewan art; open year round
Louise Durnford, Director/Owner

Saskatoon: A.K.A. Gallery
424 - 20th St. West, Saskatoon, SK S7M 0X4
Tel: 306-652-0044; Fax: 306-652-0044
info@akagallery.org
www.akagallery.org
Artist-run centre; membership open to all
Dagmara Genda, Director, director@akagallery.org
Bart Gazzola, Gallery Coordinator, communications@akagallery.org

Saskatoon: Gordon Snelgrove Art Gallery
191 Murray Bldg., University of Saskatchewan, 3 Campus Dr., Saskatoon, SK S7N 5A4
Tel: 306-966-4208; Fax: 306-966-4266
gary.young@usask.ca
www.usask.ca/snelgrove
The gallery, managed by the Univ. of Sask. department of Art & Art History, supports program & course instruction, student shows & exhibitions, & community outreach.
Gary Young, Coordinator

Saskatoon: St. Thomas More Art Gallery
St. Thomas More College, 1437 College Dr., Saskatoon, SK S7N 0W6
Tel: 306-966-8900; Fax: 306-966-8904
Toll-Free: 800-667-2019
lstark@stmcollege.ca
www.stmcollege.ca
Year Founded: 1964 Located on the 2nd floor of the College, next to the Library. Exhibitions from Sept. through April, featuring local & regional artists with a university level studio background or extensive formal training. Submissions accepted year round.
Linda Stark, Curator

Saskatoon: U of S Art Galleries
University of Saskatchewan, #12, College Bldg., 107 Administration Pl., Saskatoon, SK S7N 5A2
Tel: 306-966-4571; Fax: 306-978-8340
kag.cag@usask.ca
www.art.usask.ca; kagcag.tumblr.com
www.facebook.com/kenderdine.gallery
This central office administers the following university galleries: The University of Saskatchewan Permanent Art Collection (UAC); The Kenderdine Art Gallery (KAG); & The College Art Galleries 1 & 2 (CAG). Office open M-F 8:30-4:30, & Sa 11:00-4:00; Kenderdine Art Gallery open Tu-F 11:30-4:00; College Art Gallery open Tu-Sa 11:00-4:00.
Kent Archer, Director/Curator, kent.archer@usask.ca
Leah Taylor, Associate Curator, leah.taylor@usask.ca
Blair Barbeau, Gallery Technician, blair.barbeau@usask.ca

Watrous: Gallery on 3rd
PO Box 63, 102 - 3rd Ave. East, Watrous, SK S0K 4T0
Tel: 306-261-1728
The gallery features local artists, as well as traveling art shows. Open year-round, W-Sa 1:00-4:00.
Bryce Erickson, Contact, bryceerickson@me.com
Lynnette Wall, Contact, 306-946-3451

Weyburn: Allie Griffin Art Gallery (AGAG)
45 Bison Ave., Weyburn, SK S4H 1L8
Tel: 306-848-3278; Fax: 306-848-3271
weyburnartscouncil@live.ca
www.weyburnartscouncil.ca
Year Founded: 1964 Features touring exhibitions from the Mendel Art Gallery, the Mackenzie Art Gallery, the Saskatchewan Craft Council, the Saskatchewan Arts Board through OSAC, and many locally curated shows. The exhibitions feature the work of well-known as well as emerging Saskatchewan artists.
Marnie Bernard, Gallery Curator
Alice Neufeld, Arts Director

Weyburn: Signal Hill Arts Centre
424 - 10 Ave. South, Weyburn, SK S4H 2A1
Tel: 306-848-3278; Fax: 306-848-3271
aneufeld@weyburn.ca
Year Founded: 1985 The Signal Hill Arts Centre is located in a five storey multi-purpose civic heritage facility, which also houses a pottery studio, gallery, gift shop, kitchen, dance studio, an office, & meeting rooms.
Alice Neufeld, Arts & Cultural Director

Yorkton: Godfrey Dean Art Gallery
Yorkton Arts Council, 49 Smith St. East, Yorkton, SK S3N 0H4
Tel: 306-786-2992; Fax: 306-782-2767
gdag@sasktel.net
www.deangallery.ca
Year Founded: 1981 Devoted to the exhibition of visual art that reflects contemporary issues relevant to the Yorkton region; classes & special events programming.
Donald Stein, Director

Yukon Territory

Territorial Art Galleries

Yukon Arts Centre (YAC)
Yukon Place, PO Box 16, 300 College Dr., Whitehorse, YT Y1A 5X9
Tel: 867-667-8485; Fax: 867-393-6300
yukonartscentre.com
twitter.com/YukonArtsCentre
www.facebook.com/Yukon ArtsCentre
Yukon Arts Centre is the territory's premier venue for performing &d visual arts. The Gallery hosts 10-14 contemporary art exhibitions per year. Emphasis is to showcase work of professional Yukon artists & to bring exhibitions of national importance to the Yukon. The Theatre is a 428-seat proscenium theatre.
Joan Stanton, Chair
Al Cushing, Executive Director, ceo@yac.ca
Mary Bradshaw, Curator, Public Art Gallery, gallerydirector@yac.ca
Eric Epstein, Artistic Director, ad@yac.ca

Local Art Galleries in Yukon Territory

Pelly Crossing: Big Jonathan House
PO Box 40, Pelly Crossing, YT Y0B 1P0
Tel: 867-537-3150; Fax: 867-537-3902
Big Jonathan House is a cultural centre for the Selkirk First Nations people, featuring works by local artists, as well as locally made clothing, baskets, & traditional items. A video presentaion called "Fort Selkirk: Voices of the People" reveals the history of the region & its people. Open May-Sept., daily 9:00-7:00.

Aquaria

British Columbia

Local Aquaria in British Columbia

Sidney: Shaw Ocean Discovery Centre
Port Sidney Marina, 9811 Seaport Pl., Sidney, BC V8L 4X3
Tel: 250-655-7511; Fax: 778-426-0715
info@oceandiscovery.ca
www.oceandiscovery.ca
twitter.com/oceandiscover y
www.facebook.com/oceandiscovery
Year Founded: 2009 Dedicated to marine education, awareness & stewardship; open year round
Nancy Barbour, Chair
Angus Matthews, Executive Director

Vancouver: Vancouver Aquarium
PO Box 3232, Vancouver, BC V6B 3X8
Tel: 604-659-3400; Fax: 604-659-3515
Toll-Free: 800-931-1186
visitorexperience@vanaqua.org
www.vanaqua.org
Social Media: www.youtube.com/user/VancouverAquarium
twitter.com/vancouveraqua
www.facebook.com/vanaqua
Other contact information: Info Line: 604-659-3474
The largest aquarium in Canada & one of the five largest in North America; a self-sufficient, non-profit organization, the Aquarium is internationally recognized for display & interpretation excellence & was the first facility to incorporate professional Naturalists into the galleries to complement interpretive graphics; research projects extend world wide & it is internationally recognized for its success
Margot Spence, Chair
Dr. John Nightingale, President Ph.D., john.nightingale@vanaqua.org

New Brunswick

Local Aquaria in New Brunswick

St Andrews: Huntsman Marine Science Centre
1 Lower Campus Rd., St Andrews, NB E5B 2L7
Tel: 506-529-1200; Fax: 506-529-1212
huntsman@huntsmanmarine.ca
www.huntsmanmarine.ca; huntsmaneducation.blogspot.ca
www.facebook.com/HuntsmanMarineScienceCent re
Public aquarium/museum with local flora & fauna, & the Atlantic Reference Centre which houses a zoological & botanical museum reference collection; research & teaching in marine sciences & coastal biology; marine education courses for elementary, high school & university groups; aquaculture research & development facilities
William Robertson, Executive Director, brobertson@huntsmanmarine.ca

Shippagan: Aquarium et Centre marin du Nouveau-Brunswick (ACM)
100, rue Aquarium, Shippagan, NB E8S 1H9
Tél: 506-336-3013; Téléc: 506-336-3057
info@aquariumnb.ca
www.aquariumnb.ca
www.facebook.com/116268635055142
Aquarium publique qui expose un nombre impressionnant d'espèces de poissons qui vivent dans les eaux du golfe St-Laurent ainsi que dans les lacs et rivières de l'est du Canada. L'Attraction vedette est une famille de phoque communs; présentation audio-visuelle; bassin touchez-y; ouvert de mai á sept.; acceptons réservations de groups hors saison
Robert Rioux, Directeur

Newfoundland & Labrador

Local Aquaria in Newfoundland & Labrador

St. John's: **The Suncor Energy Fluvarium**
Nagle's Place, Box 5, St. John's, NL A1B 2Z2
Tel: 709-754-3474; Fax: 709-754-5947
info@fluvarium.ca
www.fluvarium.ca
Other contact information: Alternate Phone: 709-722-3825
Delivers an environmental education program to over 10,000 school children annually; houses interactive fresh water exhibits & nine underwater viewing windows into Nagle's Hill Brook
Jane Smith-Parsons, Executive Director

Ontario

Local Aquaria in Ontario

Niagara Falls: **Marineland of Canada Inc.**
Also known as: **Marineland Theme Park**
c/o Marineland, Marketing/Group Sales Dept., 8375 Stanley Ave., Niagara Falls, ON L2G 0C8
Tel: 905-356-9565
marketing@marineland.ca
www.marinelandcanada.com
Interactive marina & amusement park; facility for animal & marine mammal care, where guests can learn about animals through a mix of entertainment & education. Contains the largest whale habitat in the world. Open May - Oct.
John Holer, President/Owner

Prince Edward Island

Local Aquaria in Prince Edward Island

Stanley Bridge: **Stanley Bridge Marine Aquarium & Manor of Birds**
Rte. 6, Stanley Bridge, PE C0A 1E0
Tel: 902-886-3355
www.kata.pe.ca/attract/marine/marine.htm
The aquarium features live fish, the World of Butterflies display, & over 700 mounted birds. Also featured are the histories of Malpeque oysters, Irish moss, & shellfish industries. Carr's Oyster Bar & Restaurant is located on-site.

Quebec

Local Aquaria in Quebec

Sainte-Flavie: **Parc de la rivière Mitis (CISA)**
900, route de la Mer, Sainte-Flavie, QC G0J 2L0
Tél: 418-775-2969; Téléc: 418-775-9466
info@parcmitis.com
www.parcmitis.com
Le Parc de la riviére Mitis est situé à Saint-Flavie et se veut un site écotouriste qui améne les gens à porter un nouveau regard sur l'interprétation et la préservation du patrimonie naturel et culturel. Ouvert mi-juin - sept.

Sainte-Foy: **Aquarium du Québec**
1675, av des Hôtels, Sainte-Foy, QC G1W 4S3
Tel: 418-659-5264; Fax: 418-646-9238
Toll-Free: 866-659-5264
aquarium@sepaq.com
www.aquariumduquebec.com
www.face book.com/aquariumduquebec
Year Founded: 1959 16 hectare park encompassing aspects of the northern ecosystem and marine life. Observe and interact with over 10,000 fresh and salt-water fish specimens, reptiles, amphibians, invertebrates, as well as marine mammals, such as Atlantic and Pacific walruses, seals and polar bears. Winter Hours: M-Su 10:00-4:00; Summer Hours: 10:00-5:00
Manon Falardeau, Marketing Agent, 416-659-5266, falardeau.manon@sepaq.com

Saskatchewan

Local Aquaria in Saskatchewan

Fort Qu'appelle: **Fish Culture Station**
PO Box 190, Fort Qu'appelle, SK S0G 1S0
Tel: 306-332-3200; Fax: 306-332-3203

Botanical Gardens

Alberta

Local Botanical Gardens in Alberta

Brooks: **Golden Prairie Arboretum**
Alberta Agriculture, Food & Rural Development, 301 Horticulture Station Road East, Brooks, AB T1R 1E6
Tel: 403-362-1300; Fax: 403-362-1306
Collection of deciduous trees & shrubs
Nigel Seymour

Calgary: **University of Calgary Herbarium**
Dept. of Biological Sciences, 2500 University Dr. NW, Calgary, AB T2N 1N4
Tel: 403-220-5262; Fax: 403-289-9311
ccchinna@ucalgary.ca
www.ucalgary.ca/herbarium
Vascular plants
Dr. C.C. Chinnappa, Director, ccchinna@ucalgary.ca
Dr. Jana Vamosi, Director, Online Herbarium, jvamosi@ucalgary.ca

Edmonton: **Devonian Botanic Garden**
University of Alberta, Edmonton, AB T6G 2E1
Tel: 780-987-3054; Fax: 780-987-4141
www.devonian.ualberta.ca
twitter.com/DevonianGarden
www.facebook.com/D evonianBotanicGarden
Year Founded: 1953 80 acres of cultivated gardens & 110 acres of natural area; native & alpine plants, ecological reserves, Kurimoto Japanese Garden & Orchid House & a Butterly House; picnic area, patio cafe & gift shop; open daily, Apr.-Dec.
Lee Foote, Director, lee.foote@ualberta.ca
Ruby Swanson, Managing Director, ruby.swanson@ualberta.ca
Rene Belland, Curator/DataSystems Manager, Plant Herbarium, rbelland@ualberta.ca

Edmonton: **Muttart Conservatory**
9626 - 96A St., Edmonton, AB T6C 4L8
Tel: 780-442-5311
muttartquestions@edmonton.ca
www.edmonton.ca/muttart
www.facebook.com/muttart.conservatory1
Four pyramids house flora of different world climatic zones, including arid, temperate, & tropical; Show Pyramid features 6 different floral shows per year; species orchid greenhouse; outdoor trail gardens in summer; in Edmonton, call 311 to reach the Conservatory

Lethbridge: **Nikka Yuko Japanese Garden**
c/o Lethbridge & District Japanese Garden Society, PO Box 751, Lethbridge, AB T1J 3Z6
Tel: 403-328-3511; Fax: 403-328-0511
info@nikkayuko.com
www.nikkayuko.com
twitter.com/NikkaYuko
www.faceb ook.com/123765594310823
The Nikka Yuko Japanese Garden is a mature four acre garden providing a quiet, serene place for the appreciation of nature & discovery of inner peace. Includes dry rock garden, mountain & waterfall, streams & bridges, ponds and islands, flat prarie garden.

Trochu: **Trochu Arboretum & Gardens**
Also known as: **The Arboretum at Trochu**
PO Box 340, Trochu, AB T0M 2C0
Tel: 403-442-2111; Fax: 403-442-2528
trochumuseum@gmail.com
www.town.trochu.ab.ca/trochu-arboretum-gardens
Open Victoria Day to Thanksgiving
Bill Cunningham, Director/President

British Columbia

Local Botanical Gardens in British Columbia

Burnaby: **Simon Fraser University Arboretum**
Dept. of Biological Sciences, Simon Fraser University, 8888 University Dr., Burnaby, BC V5A 1S6
Tel: 604-291-4475
www.biology.sfu.ca
Felix Breden, Department Chair/Director, Dept. of Biological Sciences, biscchr@sfu.ca
Leslie Dodd, Curator/Greenhouse Technician

Kimberley: **Cominco Gardens**
340 Spokane St., Kimberley, BC V1A 2E8
Tel: 250-427-5160
kcds@kimberley.ca
Open May-Oct.

North Vancouver: **Park & Tilford Gardens**
Park & Tilford Centre, #440, 333 Brookbank Ave., North Vancouver, BC V7J 3S8
Tel: 604-984-8200
www.parkandtilford.ca
8 themed public gardens; free admission; open dawn to dusk

Rosedale: **Minter Gardens**
52892 Bunker Rd., Rosedale, BC V0X 1X0
Tel: 604-792-3799Toll-Free: 888-646-8377
mail@mintergardens.com
www.mintergardens.com
Year Founded: 1980 Open Apr. - mid-Oct.; located at 52892 Bunker Rd., Rosedale BC; take exit #135 of the Trans Canada Hwy #1
Brian Minter
Faye Minter

Surrey: **Surrey Art Gallery**
Surrey Arts Centre, 13750 - 88 Ave., Surrey, BC V3W 3L1
Tel: 604-501-5566; Fax: 604-501-5581
artgallery@surrey.ca
www.arts.surrey.ca
Promotes contemporary BC & Canadian artists; exhibitions & public programs encourage community appreciation of contemporary visual art; open year round

Vancouver: **Bloedel Conservatory**
Queen Elizabeth Park, c/o Van. Bd. of Parks & Recreation, 2099 Beach Ave., Vancouver, BC V6G 1Z4
Tel: 604-257-8584; Fax: 604-257-8427
vancouver.ca/parks-recreation-culture/bloedel-conservatory.aspx
Canada's largest single-structure tropical conservatory featuring over 500 species in simulated rain-forest, subtropic & desert environments; also features free-flying tropical birds & a Japanese Koi fish collection

Vancouver: **Dr. Sun Yat-Sen Classical Chinese Garden**
578 Carrall St., Vancouver, BC V6B 5K2
Tel: 604-662-3207; Fax: 604-682-4008
sunyatsen@telus.net
www.vancouverchinesegarden.com
Social Media: www.youtube.com/user/vanchinesegarden
twitter.com/vangarden
www.facebo ok.com/vancouverchinesegarden
The first authentic, full-scale, classical Chinese garden built outside China; museum, garden & cultural attraction
Shirley Chan, President
Kathy Gibler, Executive Director, director@vancouverchinesegarden.com

Vancouver: **Nitobe Memorial Garden**
c/o UBC Botanical Garden & Centre for Plant Research, 6804 Southwest Marine Dr., Vancouver, BC V6T 1Z4
Tel: 604-822-6038; Fax: 604-822-2016
garden.info@ubc.ca
www.botanicalgarden.ubc.ca/nitobe
twitter.com/UBCga rden
www.facebook.com/UBCgarden
Authentic Japanese tea & stroll garden; cherry blossoms; Japanese Irises, Japanese Maples; Koi; lanterns & much more
Patrick Lewis, Director, UBC Biodiversity Collections, patrick.lewis@ubc.ca
Douglas Justice, Associate Director/Curator, Collections, douglas.justice@ubc.ca
Andy Hill, Curator, Asian Garden, andy.hill@ubc.ca

Vancouver: **Queen Elizabeth Park & Arboretum**
c/o City of Vancouver, 453 West 12th Ave., Vancouver, BC V5Y 1V4
Tel: 604-257-8584
A 125 acre public park with extensive floral display gardens, naturalized area, arboretum, golf course, tennis courts, roller hockey rinks & basketball courts

Vancouver: **UBC Botanical Garden**
University of British Columbia, 6804 Southwest Marine Dr., Vancouver, BC V6T 1Z4
Tel: 604-822-3928; Fax: 604-822-2016
garden.info@ubc.ca
www.botanicalgarden.ubc.ca
twitter.com/UBCgarden
www.facebook.com/UBCgarden
Living museum of plants in 110 acres of BC coastal native forest; over 10,000 assorted trees, shrubs, flowers; divided into various components
Patrick Lewis, Director, UBC Biodiversity Collections, patrick.lewis@ubc.ca
Douglas Justice, Associate Director/Curator, Collections, douglas.justice@ubc.ca

Vancouver: **VanDusen Botanical Garden**
5251 Oak St., Vancouver, BC V6M 4H1
Tel: 604-257-8666; Fax: 604-257-8679
www.vandusengarden.org
www.facebook.com/210746535227
Other contact information: 24-Hour Information Line: 604-257-8335
22-hectare garden comprised of over 255,000 plants. Open year-round.
Harry Jongerden, Garden Director,
harry.jongerden@vancouver.ca

Victoria: **The Butchart Gardens Ltd.**
PO Box 4010, Victoria, BC V8X 3X4
Tel: 250-652-4422; Fax: 250-652-7751
Toll-Free: 866-652-4422
email@butchartgardens.com
www.butchartgardens.com
Other contact information: General Information Phone: 250-652-5256
55 acres of manicured gardens on a 130 acre private estate; open year-round

Victoria: **Horticulture Centre of the Pacific**
505 Quayle Rd., Victoria, BC V6E 2J7
Tel: 250-479-6162; Fax: 250-479-6047
gardeninfo@hcp.ca
hcp.ca
Social Media: www.youtube.com/hcpacific
twitter.com/hcpacific
www.facebook.com/HCPac ific
A nonprofit organization founded in 1979 as The Horticulture Centre of the Pacific or HCP, it manages 103 acres to demonstrate sound gardening practices using the diversity of plants that can be grown in this area, to preserve natural plant & animal habitat, & to provide a unique environment for preparing students for careers in horticulture. It relies on public funding, on local businesses, & on its own fundraising activities to support these activities.

Victoria: **Royal Roads Botanical Garden**
Also known as: **Hatley Park Gardens**
c/o Royal Roads University, 2005 Sooke Rd., Victoria, BC V9B 5Y2
Tel: 250-391-2666; Fax: 250-391-2620
Toll-Free: 866-241-0674
info@hatleypark.ca
www.hatleypark.ca
Native coastal forest & formal gardens
Bonnie Nelson, Director, Campus Services
Carol Louch, Administrative Assistant,
carol.louch@hatleypark.ca

Manitoba

Local Botanical Gardens in Manitoba

Boissevain: **International Peace Garden**
PO Box 419, Boissevain, MB R0K 0E0
Tel: 204-534-2510Toll-Free: 888-432-6733
kathy@peacegarden.com
www.peacegarden.com
www.facebook.com/12877310047 1418
2300-acre park located on the North Dakota & Manitoba boarders; tribute to peace & friendship between the people of Canada & the United States of America; maintains extensive gardens containing a wide variety of shrubs, perennials, & annual plants; souvenir shop, interpretative centre, picnic sites, hiking trails, International music camp, Royal Canadian Legion sports camp, & 9/11 Memorial Site.
Doug Hevenor, CEO

Leaf Rapids: **Leaf Rapids National Exhibition Centre**
Also known as: **Societé des Arts of Leaf Rapids, Inc.**
Town Centre Complex, PO Box 220, Leaf Rapids, MB R0B 1W0
Tel: 204-473-8682
Other contact information: Alternate Phone: 204-473-2436
The Exhibition Centre features traveling displays and local and regional artists exhibits. Each year, two to four live performances are offered for youth and adults.

Morden: **Morden Arboretum**
Morden Research Centre, Agriculture & Agri-Food Canada, PO Box 3001, 100 - 101, Rte. 100, Morden, MB R6M 1Y5
Tel: 204-822-4471; Fax: 204-983-4604
www.mordenmb.com/residents/researchstation.shtml
A federal government research centre; variety of programs including breeding & development of trees, shrubs, roses & herbaceous perennials; improvement & agronomic research programs carried out on linseed flax, field peas & dry edible beans
Scott Duguid, Director, scott.duguid@agr.gc.ca

Winnipeg: **Assiniboine Park**
55 Pavilion Cres., Winnipeg, MB R3P 2N6
Tel: 204-927-6000; Fax: 204-927-7200
Toll-Free: 877-927-6006
www.assiniboinepark.ca
Social Media: www.youtube.com/user/AssiniboinePark
twitter.com/assiniboinepark
www.f acebook.com/assiniboineparkzoo
Includes Assiniboine Park Zoo, Assiniboine Park Conservatory, Leo Mol Sculpture Garden, Pavillion Art Gallery, English & Formal Gardens, Assiniboine Forest Natural Area
Hartley Richardson, Chair
Margaret Redmond, President & CEO

Winnipeg: **Living Prairie Museum Interpretive Centre**
2795 Ness Ave., Winnipeg, MB R3J 3S4
Tel: 204-832-0167
www.winnipeg.ca/publicworks/naturalist/livingprairie
38-hectare preserve of original tall grass; interpretive centre; open Apr. 15 - Aug.; Sept - April by appt.

New Brunswick

Local Botanical Gardens in New Brunswick

Edmunston: **New Brunswick Botanical Garden / Jardin botanique du Nouveau-Brunswick**
PO Box 1629, 15 Main St., St. Jacques District, Edmunston, NB E7B 1A3
Tel: 506-737-4444
info@jardinNBgarden.com
jardinnbgarden.com
Social Media: www.youtube.com/user/JardinBotaniqueNB
twitter.com/jardinNBgarden
www. facebook.com/jardinNBgarden
7 hectares; over 50,000 plants.

Newfoundland & Labrador

Local Botanical Gardens in Newfoundland & Labrador

St. John's: **The Memorial University of Newfoundland Botanical Garden**
306 Mt. Scio Rd., St. John's, NL A1C 5S7
Tel: 709-737-8590
janec@mun.ca
www.mun.ca/botgarden
www.facebook.com/p ages/MUN-Botanical-Garden-Inc/280608787849
The Memorial University of Newfoundland Botanical Garden maintains cultivated gardens and natural habitats for public display and is a centre for botanical, horticultural and environmental research and education.

Nova Scotia

Local Botanical Gardens in Nova Scotia

Annapolis Royal: **Annapolis Royal Historic Gardens**
PO Box 278, 441 Saint George St., Annapolis Royal, NS B0S 1A0
Tel: 902-532-7018; Fax: 902-532-7445
admin@historicgardens.com
www.historicgardens.com
Social Media: www.youtube.com/historicgardens
twitter.com/Historicgardens
www.facebo ok.com/historic.gardens.7
Theme gardens, collections & displays reflect historical periods - Open May - Oct.

Halifax: **Halifax Public Gardens**
PO Box 36013, 5665 Spring Garden Rd., Halifax, NS B3J 3S9
info@halifaxpublicgardens.ca
www.halifaxpublicgardens.ca
www.facebo ok.com/128749280505802
Formal Victorian Garden, located at Summer St. & Spring Garden Rd.

Ontario

Local Botanical Gardens in Ontario

Burlington: **Centre for Canadian Historical Horticultural Studies (CCHHS)**
c/o Royal Botanical Gardens, 680 Plains Rd. West, Burlington, ON L7T 4H4
Tel: 905-527-1158; Fax: 905-577-0375
info@rbg.ca
Alex Henderson, Curator, Collections & Horticulturist

Burlington: **Royal Botanical Gardens (RBG)**
680 Plains Rd. West, Burlington, ON L7T 4H4
Tel: 905-527-1158; Fax: 905-577-0375
Toll-Free: 800-694-4769
info@rbg.ca
www.rbg.ca
Social Media: www.youtube.com/user/royalbotanicalgarden
twitter.com/RBGCanada
www.fa cebook.com/pages/Royal-Botanical-Gardens/1400384593746
A living museum which serves local, regional & global communities while developing & promoting public understanding of the relationship between the plant world, humanity & the rest of nature. 1,100 hectares of land: 120 cultivated hectares, while the rest remains a managed natural area including marshlands & walking trails.
Mark Runciman, CEO & Director, Capital Projects,
mrunciman@rbg.ca

Guelph: **The Arboretum**
University of Guelph, Guelph, ON N1G 2W1
Tel: 519-824-4120; Fax: 519-763-9598
arbor@uoguelph.ca
www.uoguelph.ca/arboretum
Social Media: www.flickr.com/photos/52649814@N05
twitter.com/ArborUofG
www.facebook. com/226671253176
Environmental education & research activities; plant collections; formal gardens; recreational workshops; dinner theatre; meeting & banquet facilities
Prof. Alan Watson, Director, awatson@uoguelph.ca
Ric Jordan, Manager, rjordan@uoguelph.ca

Kingsville: **Colasanti's Tropical Gardens**
1550 Rd. 3 East, Kingsville, ON N9Y 2E5
Tel: 519-326-3287; Fax: 519-322-2302
tropical@colasanti.com
www.colasanti.com
Year Founded: 1941 Colasanti's Tropical Gardens features over 3.5 acres of tropical greenhouses. It is open 363 days each year. Attractions include exotic plants, animals, indoor miniature golf, children's rides, an indoor playground, an arcade, a restaurant, plus home decor & collectables.
Joe Colasanti, Contact
Terry Colasanti

London: **Sherwood Fox Arboretum**
University of Western Ontario, Richmond St. North, London, ON N6A 5B7
Tel: 519-661-2111; Fax: 519-661-3935
arboretum@uwo.ca
www.uwo.ca/biology/arboretum
The arboretum includes the trees planted on the campus of the university
Dr. Jane Bowles, Director, jbowles@uwo.ca

Miller Lake: **Larkwhistle Garden**
191 Lindsay Rd. 40, Miller Lake, ON N0H 1Z0
Tel: 519-795-7763
larkwhistle@amtelecom.net

Niagara Falls: **Niagara Parks Botanical Gardens & School of Horticulture**
c/o Niagara Parks Commission, PO Box 150, Niagara Falls, ON L2E 6T2
Tel: 905-356-8554; Fax: 905-356-5488
schoolofhorticulture@niagaraparks.com
www.niagaraparks.com/school-of-hor ticulture
Includes the Niagara Parks Butterfly Conservatory
Tom Laviolette, Superintendent, Botanical Gardens & Butterfly Conservatory
Ruth Stoner, Librarian, School of Horticulture,
rstoner@niagaraparks.com

North Bay: **North Bay Heritage Gardeners**
Parent: **Heritage North Bay**
100 Ferguson St., North Bay, ON P1B 1W8
Tel: 705-472-4006
heritage.gardeners@heritagenorthbay.com
gardeners.heritagenorthbay.ca
The Nipissing Botanical Gardens is a committee of the Heritage Gardeners, whose mission is to identify, preserve, & create green space in the City of North Bay. Please see the Heritage Gardeners' website for a detailed map of heritage gardens around the city.
Monica McLaren, Coordinator

Ottawa: **Central Experimental Farm**
c/o CEF Information, Agriculture & Agri-Food Canada, K.W. Neatly Bldg., #1103, 960 Carling Ave., Ottawa, ON K1A 0C6
Tel: 613-759-1982; Fax: 613-759-6901
info@friendsofthefarm.ca; cef-fec@agr.gc.ca
www.friendsofthefarm.ca
The farm is a National Historic Site of Canada.
Chuck Craddock, President, Friends of the Farm

Ridgetown: **J.J. Neilson Arboretum**
120 Main St. East, Ridgetown, ON N0P 2C0
Tel: 519-674-1570; Fax: 519-674-1600
arboretu@ridgetownc.uoguelph.ca
www.ridgetownc.uoguelph.ca/aboutus/arbor etum.cfm
Year Founded: 1986 Includes upwards of 500 taxa., including Carolinian trees & shrubs, & collections of Viburnum & Dogwood, along with perennial & annual displays, & theme landscape areas. Free admission; open every day; staff available M-F 8:30-4:30.

Sault Ste Marie: **Great Lakes Forestry Centre Arboretum (GLFC)**
Canadian Forest Service, PO Box 490, 1219 Queen St. East, Sault Ste Marie, ON P6A 2E5
Tel: 705-949-9461; Fax: 705-541-5700
cfs.nrcan.gc.ca/centres/read/glfc
Two hectares of natural land & forest featuring a wide array of trees collected & labelled by species.

Thunder Bay: **Centennial Conservatory**
c/o City Parks Division, 111 Syndicate Ave. South, Thunder Bay, ON P7E 6S4
Tel: 807-622-7036; Fax: 807-622-7602
www.thunderbay.ca/parks
Four seasonal flower displays; cactus & tropical displays year round; open year round, 1-4 pm daily; free admission

Thunder Bay: **Soroptimist International Friendship Garden**
Parks Division, Victoriaville Civic Centre, 111 South Syndicate Ave., Thunder Bay, ON P7E 6S4
Tel: 807-625-3166; Fax: 807-625-3258

Soroptimist International Friendship Garden was created by Canadians of varied ethnic origins as a centennial gift to Canada & the community. Individual gardens have been planned, designed, constructed, & financed by the respective groups; Each group has created a garden typical of their culture & homeland.
Don Vezina, Coordinator, Parks Services,
dvezina@thunderbay.ca

Toronto: **Allan Gardens Conservatory**
19 Horticultural Ave., Toronto, ON M5A 2P2
Tel: 416-392-7288
Permanent plant collection of tropical & sub-tropical plants; seasonal plant displays; open daily 10-5
Chris Kennedy, Superintendent

Toronto: **Edwards Gardens**
777 Lawrence Ave. East, Toronto, ON M3C 1P2
Tel: 416-392-8188
parks@toronto.ca
www.toronto.ca/parks
Edwards Gardens is a former Estate garden turned public park, featuring a wide variety of plants & flowers, as well as rock gardens, a greenhouse, wooden arch bridges, a waterwheel, fountains, & walking trails. The Toronto Botanical Gardens (TBG) is also housed here.

Toronto: **Humber Arboretum & Centre for Urban Ecology**
205 Humber College Blvd., Toronto, ON M9W 5L7
Tel: 416-675-6622; Fax: 416-675-2755
arboretum@humber.ca
www.humberarboretum.on.ca
twitter.com/HumberArb
www.facebook.com/HumberArb
Other contact information: Centre for Urban Ecology Phone: 416-675-5009
Year Founded: 1977 100 hectares of ornamental gardens & green space on the west branch of the Humber River; also on-site is the educational Centre for Urban Ecology
Alexandra Link, Director

Toronto: **The Power Plant Contemporary Art Gallery at Harbourfront Centre**
Also known as: **The Power Plant**
231 Queens Quay West, Toronto, ON M5J 2G8
Tel: 416-973-4949; Fax: 416-973-4933
info@thepowerplant.org
www.thepowerplant.org
Social Media: vimeo.com/thepowerplant
www.facebook.com/ThePowerPlantContemporaryArtGal lery
Year Founded: 1987 Exclusively promotes Canadian contemporary art through exhibitions, publications & public programming.
Paul Marks, President
Gaëtane Verna, Director

Toronto: **Toronto Botanical Gardens (TBG)**
777 Lawrence Ave. East, Toronto, ON M3C 1P2
Tel: 416-397-1340; Fax: 416-397-1354
info@torontobotanicalgarden.ca
torontobotanicalgarden.ca
Social Media: www.youtube.com/user/tobotanical
twitter.com/TBG_Canada
www.facebook.com/TorontoBotanicalGarden
Other contact information: Reception: 416-397-1341
Located within the Edwards Gardens public park, the Toronto Botanical Gardens features 17 themed gardens on four acres of land. The TBG offers garden tours, day camps, field trips, a horticultural library, rental facilities, gift shop, & seasonal café.
Mary Fisher, President/Co-Chair
Aldona Satterthwaite, Executive Director, 416-397-1346,
director@torontobotanicalgarden.ca
Paul Zammit, Nancy Eaton Director, Horticulture, 416-397-1358,
horticulture@torontobotanicalgarden.ca
Sandra Pella, Head Gardener, 416-397-1316,
gardener@torontobotanicalgarden.ca

Toronto: **Toronto Sculpture Garden**
115 King St. East, Toronto, ON M5C 1G6
Tel: 416-515-9658
info@torontosculpturegarden.com
www.torontosculpturegarden.com
Semi-annual exhibitions of contemporary sculpture in a park.
Louis L. Odette, Founder
Rina Greer, Director

Windsor: **Fogolar Furlan Botanic Garden**
1800 E.C. Row, North Service Rd., Windsor, ON N8W 1Y3

Windsor: **Jackson Park**
c/o Parks & Forestry Dept., 2450 McDougall St., Windsor, ON N8X 3N6
Tel: 519-253-2300; Fax: 519-255-7990
parkrec@city.windsor.on.ca
www.city.windsor.on.ca
More than 10,000 plants, formal gardens, fountains, & sports park.

Prince Edward Island

Local Botanical Gardens in Prince Edward Island

Kensington: **Malpeque Gardens**
RR#1, Blue Heron Dr., Kensington, PE C0B 1M0

Open June 15 - Aug. 15
George MacKay

Quebec

Local Botanical Gardens in Quebec

Grand-Métis: **Jardin de Métis / Reford Gardens**
200, rte 132, Grand-Métis, QC G0J 1Z0
Tél: 418-775-2222; Téléc: 418-775-6201
info@jardinsdemetis.com; info@refordgardens.com
www.jardinsmetis.com; www.refordgardens.com
twitter.com/jardinsdemetis
www.facebook.com/Jard insdeMetis
3,000 species; native & exotic plants
Alexander Redford, Directeur,
alexander.reford@jardinsdemetis.com
Brigitte Bourdages, Agente de secrétariat,
brigitte.bourdages@jardinsdemetis.com

Montréal: **Jardin botanique de Montréal / Montréal Botanical Garden**
4101, rue Sherbrooke est, Montréal, QC H1X 2B2
Tel: 514-872-1400
www.ville.montreal.qc.ca/jardin
Collection of 22,000 plant species & varieties, 10 exhibition greenhouses & 30 thematic gardens from around the world; Insectarium; covers 75 hectares
Gilles Vincent, Directeur

Sainte-Anne-de-Bellevue: **Morgan Arboretum**
Macdonald Campus, McGill University, PO Box 186, 21 111, ch Lakeshore, Sainte-Anne-de-Bellevue, QC H9X 3V9
Tel: 514-398-7811; Fax: 514-398-7959
morgan.arboretum@mcgill.ca
www.morganarboretum.org
Year Founded: 1945 Situated at the western tip of the island of Montreal; trees grow in forests, experimental plantations & ornamental collections
Christina Idziak, Curator

Sainte-Foy: **Jardin botanique Roger-Van den Hende**
Université Laval, Pavillon de L'Envirotron, 2480 Hochelaga, Sainte-Foy, QC G1K 7P4
Tél: 418-656-3742; Téléc: 418-656-3515
jardin@fsaa.ulaval.ca
www.jardin.ulaval.ca
More than 4000 species & cultivars arranged in order of botanical family. Open April - Oct.; free admission
Hélène Corriveau, Responsable agronomique,
Helene.Corriveau@fsaa.ulaval.ca

Saskatchewan

Local Botanical Gardens in Saskatchewan

Estevan: **Shand Greenhouse**
PO Box 280, Estevan, SK S4A 2A3
Tel: 306-634-9771; Fax: 306-634-6682
Toll-Free: 866-778-7337
greenhouse@saskpower.com
www.saskpower.com/shandgreenh ouse
Greenhouse, shade houses, nursery, display area; uses by-products of energy generation from the Shand Power Station; open year round
Debbie Packet, Chair
Shelly Heidinger, Acting Manager

Indian Head: **Agri-Environment Services Branch Agroforestry Development Centre (AESB)**
PO Box 940, Hwys. 1 & 56, Indian Head, SK S0G 2K0
Fax: 306-695-2568
Toll-Free: 866-766-2284
agroforestry@agr.gc.ca
www.agr.ca/pfra/shelterbelt.htm
The AESB administers the Prairie Shelterbelt Program out of the Agroforestry Development Centre, supplying farmers with tree & shrub seedlings as well as technical services.

Saskatoon: **Patterson Garden Arboretum**
Dept. of Plant Sciences, University of Saskatchewan, 51 Campus Dr., Saskatoon, SK S7N 5A8
Tel: 306-966-5855; Fax: 306-966-5015
agbio.usask.ca/index.php?page=plant-sci
Year Founded: 1966 Patterson Garden Arboretum is one of the last remaining Prairie Regional Trials for Woody Ornamentals sites, dedicated to Dr. Cecil Patterson in 1969.
Dr. Bruce Coulman, Department Head
Jackie Bantle, Manager, Plant Sciences, 306-966-5864,
jackie.bantle@usask.ca
Alan Weninger, Manager, Plant Sciences, 306-978-8316

Swift Current: **Art Gallery of Swift Current (AGSC)**
411 Hebert St. East, Swift Current, SK S9H 1M5
Tel: 306-778-2736; Fax: 306-773-8769
www.artgalleryofswiftcurrent.org
www.facebook.com/107239462690065
Non-profit public art gallery & national standard art museum offering exhibitions of provincial, national & international artwork; provides access to & education in visual art culture for Southwest Saskatchewan
Kim Houghtaling, Director/Curator,
k.houghtaling@swiftcurrent.ca

Museums

National Museums

Canada Aviation Museum / Musée de l'aviation du Canada

PO Box 9724 T, 11 Aviation Pkwy., Ottawa, ON K1G 5A3
Tel: 613-993-2010; Fax: 613-990-3655
Toll-Free: 800-463-2038
aviation@technomuses.ca; member@technomuses.ca
www.aviation.technomuses.ca
Other contact information: TTY: 613-990-7530; Phone, Library & Archives: 613-993-2303
As a component of the Canada Science and Technology Museum Corporation, the Canada Aviation Museum collects, preserves, & displays aviation-related objects, from the pioneer era, through war & peace, & to the present time.
Denise Amyot, President & Chief Executive Officer, Canada Science & Technology Museum Corporation
Anthony P. Smyth, Director General, Canada Aviation Museum

Canada Science & Technology Museum Corporation (CSTMC/SMSTC) / Société du Musée des Sciences et de la technologie du Canad
PO Box 9724 T, 1867 St. Laurent Blvd., Ottawa, ON K1G 5A3
Tel: 613-991-3044; Fax: 613-990-3636
Toll-Free: 866-442-4416
info@technomuses.ca
www.sciencetech.technomuses.ca
Other contact information: TTY: 613-991-9207; E-mail, Library: library@technomuses.ca
Exhibits at the Canada Science & Technology Museum include astronomy, space, marine & land transportation, communications, computer technology, & domestic technology. The library of the Canada Science & Technology Museum contains material about the history & development of science & technology, with an emphasis upon Canada.
Denise Amyot, President & Chief Executive Officer
James Paul, Chair
Michèle Desloges, Corporate Secretariat, 613-990-6352

The Canadian Museum of Civilization Corporation (CMCC) / Société du Musée canadien des civilisations
100, rue Laurier, Gatineau, QC K1A 0M8
Tel: 819-776-7000; Fax: 819-776-8300
Toll-Free: 800-555-5621
web@civilization.ca
www.civilization.ca
The Canadian Museum of Civilization conducts research in Canadian studies & collects, preserves & displays objects which reflect Canada's cultural heritage. Its activities extend across the country through field research programs, publications & loans to various groups & institutions. Through permanent & changing exhibitions, public programs, film & theatre programs, the museum unfolds the storie
Victor Rabinovitch, President & CEO, victor.rabinovitch@civilization.ca
Chantal Schryer, Vice-President, Public Affairs & Publishing, chantal.schryer@civilization.ca

Canadian Museum of Contemporary Photography (CMCP / MCPC) / Musée canadien de la photographie contemporaine
PO Box 465 A, 380 Sussex Dr., Ottawa, ON K1N 9N6
Tel: 613-990-1985; Fax: 613-993-4385
Toll-Free: 800-319-2787
cmcp@gallery.ca
www.cmcp.gallery.ca
Other contact information: TTY: 613-990-0777
Year Founded: 1985 Affiliated with the National Gallery of Canada, the collection of the Canadian Museum of Contemporary Photography dates from the early 1960s to the present. Photographic works include prints, negatives, transparencies, books, filmstrips, video art, audio-visual presentations, mixed media works, assemblages, & installation pieces.
Martha Hanna, Director
Joanne Charette, Director, Public Affairs, 613-990-5050, Fax: 613-990-9824, jcharette@gallery.ca

Canadian Museum of Nature / Musée canadien de la nature
PO Box 3443 D, Ottawa, ON K1P 6P4
Tel: 613-566-4700; Fax: 613-364-4021
Toll-Free: 800-263-4433
questions@mus-nature.ca; cmnlib@mus-nature.ca
www.nature.ca
Other contact information: TTY: 613-566-4770; 1-866-600-8801
The natural sciences & natural history museum features specimens, such as fossils, horned dinosaurs, fish, freshwater mussels, tropical beetles, animals, lichens, plants, & minerals from Canada & around the world.
Joanne DiCosimo, President & Chief Executive Officer, 613-566-4733, Fax: 613-364-4020, jdicosimo@mus-nature.ca
Maureen Dougan, Vice-President & Chief Operating Officer, 613-566-4732, Fax: 613-364-4020, mdougan@mus-nature.ca
Roger Baird, Director, Collection Services, 613-364-4138, Fax: 613-364-4022, rbaird@mus-nature.ca
Kim Curran, Director, Development & Fundraising Services, 613-566-4790, Fax: 613-364-4021, kcurran@mus-nature.ca
Mark S. Graham, Director, Research, 613-566-4743, Fax: 613-364-4022, mgraham@mus-nature.ca
Denyse Jomphe, Director, Human Resources Management Services, 613-566-4294, Fax: 613-364-4028, djomphe@mus-nature.ca
Lynne Ladouceur, Director, Financial Management Services, 613-566-4253, Fax: 613-364-4025, lladouceur@mus-nature.ca
Marie Lasnier, Director, Community Services, 613-364-4101, Fax: 613-566-4746, mlasnier@mus-nature.ca
Jennifer Doubt, Chief Collection Manager, Botany, 613-364-4076, Fax: 613-364-4027, jdoubt@mus-nature.ca
Jean-Marc Gagnon, Chief Collection Manager, Invertebrates, 613-364-4066, Fax: 613-364-4027, jmgagnon@mus-nature.ca
Kamal Khidas, Chief Collection Manager, Vertebrates, 613-364-4098, Fax: 613-364-4027, kkhidas@mus-nature.ca
Kieran Shepherd, Chief Collection Manager, Earth Sciences, 613-364-4054, Fax: 613-364-4027, kshepherd@mus-nature.ca
Elizabeth McCrea, Manager, Communications Services, 613-566-4249, Fax: 613-364-4021, emccrea@mus-nature.ca

The Canadian War Museum (CWM) / Musée canadien de la guerre
1 Vimy Place, Ottawa, ON K1A 0M8
Tel: 819-776-8600; Fax: 819-776-8623
Toll-Free: 800-555-5621
info@warmuseum.ca
www.warmuseum.ca
Affiliated museum of the Canadian Museum of Civilization; war art; uniforms & accoutrements; medals; weapons & small arms; archives; the Hartland Molson library; vast collection of military vehicles & artillery
Dr. Victor Rabinovitch, President/CEO, mark.oneill@warmuseum.ca
Mark O'Neill, Director General, mark.oneill@warmuseum.ca
Chantal Schryer, Public Affairs & Publishing

Currency Museum of the Bank of Canada / Musée de la monnaie de la Banque du Canada
245 Sparks St., Ottawa, ON K1A 0G9
Tel: 613-782-8914; Fax: 613-782-7761
museum-musee@bank-banque-canada.ca
www.currencymuseum.ca; www.museedelamonnaie.ca
The most complete collection of Canadian notes & coins in the world, plus representative collections of world coins & paper money, including whales' teeth, glass pearls, elephant-hair bracelets, shells & copper axes
Paul S. Berry, Chief Curator
Henriette Riegel, Director, Visitor Services
Enrica Schwilden, Manager, Marketing & Communications

Alberta

Provincial Museums

Glenbow Museum, Art Gallery, Library & Archives
130 - 9 Ave. SE, Calgary, AB T2G 0P3
Tel: 403-268-4100; Fax: 403-265-9769
glenbow@glenbow.org
www.glenbow.org
Glenbow documents the settlement of western Canada with exhibits tracing the lives & traditions of native peoples, the development of the railway, ranching, farming & growing up in the West. A large art gallery highlights historical & contemporary art from Glenbow's own collections as well as from national & international collections.

Kristin Evenden, President & CEO
Lauchlan Currie, Chair

The Military Museums of Calgary (TMM)
***Also known as:* The Military Museums**
4520 Crowchild Trail SW, Calgary, AB T2T 5J4
Tel: 403-974-2850; Fax: 403-974-2858
tmmadmin@themilitarymuseums.ca
www.themilitarymuseums.ca
Other contact information: Commissionarie Phone: 403-974-2857
The Military Museums features the following museums, houses under one roof: Air Force Museum of Alberta; Army Museum of Alberta; Lord Strathcona's Horse (Royal Canadians) Museum; Princess Patricia's Canadian Light Infantry Museum & Archives; The Calgary Highlanders Regimental Museum & Archives; The King's Own Calgary Regiment (Royal Canadian Armoured Corps) Museum; & The University of Calgary Military Museums Library & Archives. The Military Museums also contains art & exhibit space, an Education Centre for students, & an Archival Reading Room.

Royal Alberta Museum
12845 - 102 Ave., Edmonton, AB T5N 0M6
Tel: 780-453-9100; Fax: 780-454-6629
www.royalalbertamuseum.ca
Social Media: www.youtube.com/user/royalalbertamuseum
twitter.com/RoyalAlberta
www.f acebook.com/RoyalAlbertaMuseum
Major collections & exhibits of Alberta's natural & human history, including habitat groups, geology, palaeontology, archaeology, & western Canadian history & the Syncrude Gallery of Aboriginal Culture; feature exhibitions, museum shop, café, films, lectures, live demonstrations & cultural performances; special programs for schools & other groups; & discovery room.
Chris Robinson, Acting Executive Director, 780-453-9168, chris.robinson@gov.ab.ca
Albert Finnamore, Director, Curatorial & Collections Preservation, 780-453-9177, Fax: 780-454-6629, albert.finnamore@gov.ab.ca
Chris Robinson, Director, Marketing, Communications & Education, 780-453-9168, chris.robinson@gov.ab.ca
Bruce Bolton, Director, Business Operations, 780-453-9130, Fax: 780-454-6629, bruce.bolton@gov.ab.ca
Tom Thurston, Director, Renewal Project, 780-453-9105, Fax: 780-454-9105, tom.thurston@gov.ab.ca

Royal Tyrrell Museum
PO Box 7500, Drumheller, AB T0J 0Y0
Tel: 403-823-7707; Fax: 403-823-7131
Toll-Free: 888-440-4240
tyrrell.info@gov.ab.ca
www.tyrrellmuseum.com
Year Founded: 1985 Located in Midland Provincial Park, on Hwy #838 in Drumheller, the internationally recognized Royal Tyrrell Museum is in the heart of one of the richest fossil localities in the world. The Museum is Canada's only museum dedicated exclusively to palaeontology & showcases Alberta's abundant & diverse fossil record, featuring more than 800 fossils & 35 dinosaur skeletons on display. Other highlights include dramatic dioramas, interactive exhibits, computer stations & mini-theatre, special events & programming, gift shop & cafeteria
Andrew Neuman, Executive Director M.Sc.

Local Museums in Alberta

***Airdrie:* Nose Creek Valley Museum**
1701 Main St. SW, Airdrie, AB T4B 1C5
Tel: 403-948-6685
ncvm@telus.net
www.nosecreekvalleymuseum.com
Nose Creek Valley Museum offers the history of Airdrie & the surrounding region. Visitors will learn about the geology & natural history of the area, the First Nations & pioneers, farming, antique automobiles, & military history. A Canadian Pacific caboose is also on display. The museum is open year-round.
Laurie Harvey, Curator

***Alberta Beach:* Alberta Beach & District Museum**
5000 - 47th Ave., Alberta Beach, AB T0E 0A0
Tel: 780-924-2140
abmuseum@xplornet.ca
www.albertabeachmuseum.com
History of the Lac Ste Anne area; open every day July & Aug., except Tuesdays

***Alberta Beach:* Garden Park Farm Museum**
PO Box 639, Alberta Beach, AB T0E 0A0
Tel: 780-924-3391
David Oselies

***Alix:* Alix Wagon Wheel Museum**
PO Box 245, Alix, AB T0C 0B0
Tel: 403-747-3119
alixwagonwheelmuseum@live.ca
alixwagonwheelmuseum.wordpress.com
Local history and artifacts; souvenir shop. Open year round, but by appointment from Oct. through May.
Eve Keates, Curator

***Alliance:* Alliance & District Museum**
***Parent:* Alliance & District Museum Society**
PO Box 101, Alliance, AB T0B 0A0
Tel: 780-879-2333
www.villageofalliance.ca/Attractions-Events.page
Local history; pioneer & farming artifacts; early log cabin & blacksmith shop on-site; doll collection; Norman Johnston room.

***Andrew:* Andrew & District Local History Museum**
PO Box 180, Andrew, AB T0B 0C0
Tel: 403-365-3687
Local artifacts & records; open year round

***Banff:* Banff Park Museum National Historic Site**
PO Box 900, Banff, AB T1L 1K2
Tel: 403-762-1558; Fax: 403-762-1565
banff.vrc@pc.gc.ca
www.pc.gc.ca/lhn-nhs/ab/banff/index_e.asp
Year Founded: 1895 The Banff Park Museum is a natural history museum. The collection is located in a 1903 building.

***Banff:* Buffalo Nations Luxton Museum**
PO Box 850, 1 Birch Ave., Banff, AB T1L 1A8
Tel: 403-762-2388
luxton@telusplanet.net
The Buffalo Nations Luxton Museum depicts the cultures & traditions of the First Nations people of the Plains. Artifacts date back over 100 years.
Joseph Yellowhorn, President
Roy Louis, Vice-President
Judy Bedford, Secretary
Gloria Buehler-Cowley, Treasurer

***Banff:* Luxton Home Museum**
***Parent:* Eleanor Historical Foundation**
PO Box 1480, 206 Beaver St., Banff, AB T1L 1B4
Tel: 403-762-2105
luxton@webarmour.ca
www.luxtonfoundation.org
The house was once owned by one of Banff's prominent pioneer families, the Luxtons. Now the museum holds a collection featuring native artifacts, antiques, costumes, & unique international items. Open year-round; Summer hours are 11:00-3:00.

***Banff:* Whyte Museum of the Canadian Rockies**
PO Box 160, 111 Bear St., Banff, AB T1L 1A3
Tel: 403-762-2291; Fax: 403-762-8919
info@whyte.org; archives@whyte.org
www.whyte.org
Other contact information: Phone, Archives: 403-762-2291, ext. 335
Visitors to the Whyte Museum discover the history, art, & social & cultural past of the Canadian Rockies. Guided tours are provided of the heritage gallery, the art gallery, heritage homes, the Luxton home & garden, & historic Banff. The Archives & Library, located at the museum, collects books, journals, maps, newspaper clippings, microforms, textual records, photographs, & audio-visual materials related to the Canadian Rockies.
Michale Lang, Executive Director & Chief Curator
Graeme Nunn, Chief Financial & Operating Officer & Executive Director, Whyte Foundation
Natalie Fedrau, Manager, Visitor Services
Elizabeth Kundert-Cameron, Manager, Archives & Library, Fax: 403-762-2339, archives@whyte.org
Craig Richards, Curator, Photography
Jennifer Rutkair, Archivist
Lena Goon, Reference Archivist
Catherine Hawkins, Coordinator, Education & Interpretation
Katie Daniel, Specialist, Marketing & Communications

***Barrhead:* Barrhead Centennial Museum & Visitor Information Center**
PO Box 4122, 5629 - 49th St., Barrhead, AB T7N 1A1
Tel: 780-674-5203
barrheadmuseum@lycos.ca
Year Founded: 1967 The Barrhead Centennial Museum is operated by the Barrhead & District Historical Society. Exhibits at the Barrhead Centennial Museum & Visitor Information Center include Barrhead settlers' furniture, pioneer farm equipment, & tools. The complete local newspaper is also available at the museum, plus a large collection of African artifacts. The museum is open from the Victoria Day weekend in May to the Labour Day weekend in September.

***Beaverlodge:* South Peace Centennial Museum**
PO Box 493, Beaverlodge, AB T0H 0C0
Tel: 780-354-8869; Fax: 780-354-8068
sitemanager@spcm.ca
www.spcm.ca
Pioneer equipment & buildings; open mid-May - Sept. 1
Lois Dueck, President

***Bellevue:* Bellevue Underground Mine Tours**
***Parent:* Crowsnest Pass Ecomuseum Trust Society**
21814 - 28th Ave., Bellevue, AB T0K 0E0
Tel: 403-564-4700; Fax: 403-564-4711
cpets@shaw.ca
www.bellevueundergroundmine.org
twitter.com/BellevueMine
Guided tours through a mine originally used from 1903-1961. Open May-Sept., daily 10:00-6:30.

***Bentley:* Bentley Museum**
PO Box 620, 4929 - 51st Ave., Bentley, AB T0C 0J0
Tel: 403-748-2455; Fax: 403-748-4537
bentleymuseum@shaw.ca
The museum depicts the lives of early settlers through exhibits housed in a 1924 farmhouse & separate agricultural buildings. Summer Hours: M-W & Sa 9:00-5:00, Su 2:00-5:00. Winter Hours: Open W morning, or by request.

***Big Valley:* Big Valley Creation Science Museum**
PO Box 340, Big Valley, AB T0J 0G0
Tel: 403-876-2100
info@bvcsm.com
www.bvcsm.com
Year Founded: 2008 The museum seeks to "refute the lie of evolution" through its exhibits, which include fossils & a large model of Noah's ark. Open M-Sa 11:00-5:00, Su 1:00-5:00.
Harry Nibourg, Owner

***Big Valley:* Big Valley Museum**
PO Box 342, 57 Railway Ave. South, Big Valley, AB T0J 0G0
Tel: 403-876-2593
allanjoh@telusplanet.net
The museum includes a number of sites: a garage featuring artifacts & antique vehicles & machinery; St. Edmund's Church; former Alberta Wheat Pool grain elevator; two antique railway baggage cars featuring thousands of artifacts; & a section of the CNR station, featuring local memorabilia. Open May-Sept., 10:00-6:00; open by request the rest of the year.

***Bowden:* Bowden Pioneer Museum**
PO Box 576, 2201 - 19th Ave., Bowden, AB T0M 0K0
Tel: 403-224-2122
bhs@shawbiz.ca
museum.anwc.net
Year Founded: 1967 Goverened by the Bowden Historical Society, the Bowden Pioneer Museum is located in the old Bowden curling rink. The museum contains the following artifacts & exhibits: The Bob Hoare Photography Exhibit; The Eastern Star Exhibit; The Irene M. Wood Avon Collection, The Women of Aspenland Lives & Works; a hardware & general store display; military artifacts; geological collections, decorative arts, such as musical instruments; fine arts of First Nations & European origins; & human hisotry artifacts, such as religious objects, household items, & sports equipment. The museum also conducts research services. It is open from the long weekend in May to September.

***Breton:* Breton & District Historical Museum**
Breton Elementary School, 4711 - 52st St., Breton, AB T0C 0P0
Tel: 780-696-2551
bretonmuse@yahoo.com
www.village.breton.ab.ca/history.html
The museum focuses on the history of black prisoners who emigrated to Canada during the early 1900s, becomming pioneers as they established their own community in central Alberta. Open July & Aug., daily 11:00-5:00; other times by appointment.

Allan Goddard, Contact

***Brooks:* Brooks & District Museum & Historical Society**
568 Sutherland Dr. East, Brooks, AB T1R 1C7
Tel: 403-362-5073; Fax: 403-362-5085
museum@xplornet.com
www.brooksmuseum.ca
Year Founded: 1974 Local history; open May-Sept., daily 9:00-5:00; weekly March-May.

***Brooks:* Brooks Aqueduct National & Provincial Historic Site**
c/o Eastern Irrigation District, PO Box 8, 550 Industrial Rd., Brooks, AB T1R 1B2
Tel: 403-653-5139
eid@eid.ab.ca
www.eidnet.org/local/aqueduct
Other contact information: Phone, Information Kiosk: 403-362-4451
The Brooks Aqueduct is located 8 km southeast of Brooks, Alberta. The structure was completed in 1914 by the irrigation division of the Canadian Pacific Railway. It has been preserved by the Government of Alberta, Environment Canada, the Prairie Farm Rehabilitation Administration, & the Eastern Irrigation District. The interpretive center at the aqueduct is open from May 15th to Labour Day.

***Brownvale:* Brownvale North Peace Agricultural Museum**
PO Box 186, Brownvale, AB T0H 0L0
Tel: 780-597-3934; Fax: 780-597-3950

The Brownvale North Peace Agricultural Museum features artifacts such as historic farm machinery, horse-powered equipment, & construction equipment. The museum is open during July & August.

***Calgary:* Aero Space Museum of Calgary**
4629 McCall Way NE, Calgary, AB T2E 8A5
Tel: 403-250-3752; Fax: 403-250-8399
info@asmac.ab.ca
www.asmac.ab.ca
With over 20 historical aircrafts on display, guests can explore Canadian achievements in aviation & space. Aircraft engines, extensive aviation library & interactive exhibits; educational programs & tours; gift shop; meeting/function room rentals. Open year round.
Steven Ogle, CEO
Jennifer Herrick, Executive Director
Sara Bateman, Marketing & Development
Anthony Worman, Curator

***Calgary:* Air Force Museum of Alberta (AFMA)**
***Parent:* The Military Museums of Calgary**
4520 Crowchild Trail SW, Calgary, AB T2T 5J4
Tel: 403-249-8818; Fax: 403-974-2858
tmmadmin@themilitarymuseums.ca
www.themilitarymuseums.ca/gallery-airforc e
The Air Force Museum of Alberta tells the story of Canada's Air Force through artifacts, models, interactive displays, & films.
Alison Mercer, Curator, alison@themilitarymuseums.ca

***Calgary:* Army Museum of Alberta (AMA)**
***Parent:* The Military Museums of Calgary**
4520 Crowchild Trail SW, Calgary, AB T2T 5J4
Tel: 403-974-2852; Fax: 403-974-2858
tmmadmin@themilitarymuseums.ca
www.themilitarymuseums.ca/gallery-army
The Army Museum of Alberta exhibits the province's army heritage from 1885 to the present. A major exhibit is The Fall of '44, which commemorates the efforts of Canadian troops during the last years of the Second World War.
Rory M. Cory, Senior Curator, seniorcurator@themilitarymuseums.ca

***Calgary:* Calgary Chinese Cultural Centre**
197 - First St. SW, Calgary, AB T2P 4M4
Tel: 403-262-5071; Fax: 403-232-6387
info@culturalcentre.ca
www.culturalcentre.ca
Year Founded: 1992 The Calgary Chinese Cultural Centre promotes Chinese heritage, history, & culture, as well as cultural diversity.
Victor Mah, Chair
Malcolm Chow, Vice-President
Samantha Yang, Executive Administrator
Tony Wong, Secretary
Leonard Chow-Wah, Treasurer

***Calgary:* The Calgary Highlanders Museum & Archives**
***Parent:* The Military Museums of Calgary**
4520 Crowchild Trail SW, Calgary, AB T2T 5J4
Tel: 403-974-2855; Fax: 403-974-2858
museum@calgaryhighlanders.com
www.calgaryhighlanders.com
A history & recollection of the Calgary Highlanders.
Captain Peter Boyle, Curator CD, AdeC
Sergeant Dennis Russell, Curator CD
Mike Henry, Archivist

***Calgary:* Canada's Sports Hall of Fame (CSHOF) / Panthéon des Sports Canadiens**
169 Canada Olympic Rd. SW, Calgary, AB T3B 6B7
Tel: 403-776-1040
info@cshof.ca
www.cshof.ca
twitter.com/CANsportshall
www.facebook.com/107867826839
Canada's Sports Hall of Fame tells the stories of Canadian amateur & professional athletes, as well as sport builders, who have made outstanding achievements thoughout sports history.
Colin MacDonald, Chair M.A., B.B.A.
Mario Siciliano, President & CEO, msiciliano@cshof.ca
Janice Smith, Director, Exhibits & Programs, jsmith@cshof.ca
Richard Clement, Manager, Galleries, rclement@cshof.ca

***Calgary:* Fort Calgary**
***Also known as:* Fort Calgary Historic Park**
PO Box 2100 M, #106, 750 - 9th Ave. SE, Calgary, AB T2P 2M5
Tel: 403-290-1875; Fax: 403-265-6534
info@fortcalgary.com
www.fortcalgary.com
40-acre park; interpretive centre; 1875 fort reconstruction project; guided tours; open year round
Sara Jane Gruetzner, Executive Director

***Calgary:* The Grain Academy**
Plus 15 Level, Roundup Centre, Stampede Park, PO Box 1060 M, Calgary, AB T2P 2K8
Tel: 403-263-4594; Fax: 403-233-9500
grainacademy@nucleus.com
www.grainacademymuseum.com
Year Founded: 1981 Grain elevator; grain transportation exhibit

***Calgary:* Heritage Park Historical Village**
1900 Heritage Dr. SW, Calgary, AB T2V 2X3
Tel: 403-268-8500; Fax: 403-268-8501
info@heritagepark.ab.ca
www.heritagepark.ca
www.facebook.com/pages/Her itage-Park/177397676028
Year Founded: 1964 Billed as a living history museum, the expansive site offers a wide range of exhibits and activities, most notably the exploration of a village of historical, "old west" buildings replete with antiques, artifacts and costumed guides. Gasoline Alley Museum focuses on the history of the automobile. There is a steam train, antique midway and Haskayne Mercantile Block of shops. Open May - Sept.
Ms Alida Visbach, President/CEO

***Calgary:* The King's Own Calgary Regiment (RCAC) Museum**
***Also known as:* Museum of the Regiments**
***Parent:* The Military Museums of Calgary**
4520 Crowchild Trail SW, Calgary, AB T2T 5J4
Tel: 403-974-2856; Fax: 403-974-2858
www.kingsown.ca

Depicts the history of the four regiments of Calgary; art gallery; open all year. Artifacts & pictures of regimental "family tree"; permanent displays of the 50th Battalion C.E.F. which deature The Deadly Sniper; Cpl. Henry Norwest; M.M. Vimy; Pte. John George Pattison V.C.; non-permanent active militial Dieppel The Prisoner of War Room; Sicily, Italy, including the Kingsmill Bridge & the Battle of Cassino. Special film & military documentaties in the Amoco Theatre.
Al Judson, Curator/Archivist, ajudson@ucalgary.ca

***Calgary:* Lord Strathcona's Horse (Royal Canadians) Regimental Museum**
***Parent:* The Military Museums of Calgary**
4520 Crowchild Trail SW, Calgary, AB T2T 5J4
Tel: 403-974-2854; Fax: 403-974-2858
museum@strathconas.ca; archives@strathconas.ca
www.strathconas.ca/strathcona-museum
Year Founded: 1990 Museum relates the history of the Regiment from 1900 to present. The collection holds many artifacts yet undisplayed. The Archives store photographs, records, documents & diaries and research is conducted for personal & professional institutions. Open year round.
Warrant Officer D.E. (Ted) MacLeod, Curator
Sergeant Todd Giberson, Collections Manager, 403-974-2886

***Calgary:* Lougheed House**
***Parent:* Lougheed House Conservation Society**
707 - 13th Ave. SW, Calgary, AB T2R 0K8
Tel: 403-244-6333; Fax: 403-244-6354
info@lougheedhouse.com
www.lougheedhouse.com; lougheedhouse.blogspot.ca
twitter.com/lougheedhouse
www.facebook.com/1 05991712783670
Lougheed House was built in 1891 & was originally known was Beaulieu, & is a National Historic Site. Visitors can tour the building, eat lunch in the on-site restaurant, & visit the gift shop. The house is open W-F 11:00-4:00, Sa & Su 10:00-4:00.
Ron Robertson, Chair
Blane Hogue, Executive Director, blanehogue@lougheedhouse.com
Ian Rogan, Curator, ianrogan@lougheedhouse.com
Cassandra Cummings, Archives, cassandra@lougheedhouse.com

***Calgary:* Naval Museum of Alberta**
***Parent:* The Military Museums of Calgary**
4520 Crowchild Trail SW, Calgary, AB T2T 5J4
Tel: 403-974-2807; Fax: 403-974-2858
tmmadmin@themilitarymuseums.ca
www.themilitarymuseums.ca/gallery-navy
Collection includes one each of the 3 naval aircraft (fighter planes) used by RCN; naval armament including guns, torpedos, anti-submarine equipment, clothing etc.
Bruce Connolly, Assistant Curator, bruceconnolly41@gmail.com

***Calgary:* The Nickle Arts Museum**
The University of Calgary, 2500 University Dr. NW, Calgary, AB T2N 1N4
Tel: 403-220-7234
nickle@ucalgary.ca
people.ucalgary.ca/~nickle/index.shtml
Founded in 1979 through a donation from Sam Nickle & a Province of Alberta grant; champions contemporary Canadian art, numismatics & Oriental carpets; changing exhibitions & programs. As of Aug. 2012 the museum is temporarily closed while they move their collection to the Taylor Family Digital Library. Please see the website for updates on the progress of the move.
John Wright, Director

***Calgary:* Olympic Hall of Fame & Museum**
c/o Canada Olympic Park, 88 Canada Olympic Rd. SW, Calgary, AB T3B 5R5
Tel: 403-247-5452
info@winsportcanada.ca; groups@winsportcanada.ca
www.winsportcanada.ca/cop
twitter.com/winspor tcanada
www.facebook.com/CanadaOlympicPark
Other contact information: Phone, School Department, Outdoor Education Programming: 403-202-6577
The Olympic Hall of Fame & Museum honours past & present Canadian Olympians & Paralympians. A large collection of Olympic artifacts is featured, such as Olympic torches. Visitors can test their skills with interactive simulators of Olympic sports, including alpine skiing. The Olympic Hall of Fame & Museum is open year-round.
Gordon Ritchie, Chair, WinSport Canada Board of Directors
Tracy Cobb, National Director, Communications & Fund Development, WinSport Canada, 403-247-5954, tracy.cobb@winsportcanada.ca

***Calgary:* Princess Patricia's Canadian Light Infantry Regimental Museum & Archives (PPCLI)**
***Parent:* The Military Museums of Calgary**
4520 Crowchild Trail SW, Calgary, AB T2T 5J4
Tel: 403-974-2860
www.ppcli.com
www.facebook.com/ppcli
Princess Patricia's Canadian Light Infantry Regimental Museum & Archives collects & preserves items that cover the dates from 1914, when Princess Patricia's Canadian Light Infantry was founded, to the present day. The Infantry is known for its service in both World Wars, Korea, & Afghanistan, & during other operations for the United Nations & NATO. Holdings include war journals, photographs, training manuals, cartographic materials, & audio-visual resources, especially related to the Princess Patricia's Canadian Light Infantry, & to the Canadian Army in general. The museum is open year-round.
Warrant Officer Jason Yardley, General Manager, gm.museum@ppcli.com
Sergeant George Goulet, Archivist

***Calgary:* Sarcee Tsuu T'ina People's Museum**
#135, 3700 Anderson Rd. SW, Calgary, AB T2W 3C4
Tel: 403-238-2677
Located on Sarcee (Tsuu T'ina) Reserve, the museum features artifacts such as headdresses from around 1938 & a model tipi.

***Calgary:* University of Calgary, Museum of Zoology**
Biological Sciences Bldg., 2500 University Dr., Calgary, AB T2N 1N4
Tel: 403-220-5261; Fax: 403-289-9311
www.bio.ucalgary.ca/facilities/museum.html
Teaching museum used for zoology & ecology courses; also services the Archaeology, Geology, & Art departments, as well as Inglewood Bird Sanctuary & the Alberta Science Centre.
Warren Fitch, Curator, fitch@ucalgary.ca

***Calgary:* Youthlink Calgary: Calgary Police Service Interpretive Centre**
133 - 6th Ave. SE, Calgary, AB T2G 4Z1
Tel: 403-206-4566
www.youthlinkcalgary.com
Interactive exhibits & programs educate youth about life, crime, & law enforcement.
Janet Pieschel, Executive Director, janet.pieschel@calgarypolice.ca
Gail Niinimaa, Administrator, 403-206-8927, gail.niinimaa@calgarypolice.ca
Lindsie Bruns, Technician, Historical Collections, 403-206-8691, lbruns@calgarypolice.ca
Colleen Acheson, Coordinator, Booking, 403-206-8950, colleen.acheson@calgarypolice.ca
Rachel Joo, Coordinator, Outreach Programs, 403-206-8691, rachel.joo@calgarypolice.ca

***Calgary:* YouthLink Calgary: The Calgary Police Interpretive Centre**
5111 - 47th St. NE, Calgary, AB T3J 3R2
www.youthlinkcalgary.com
twitter.com/YouthLinkCGY
www.facebook.com/YouthLinkCGY
The purpose of YouthLink is to education young people about the role of police in society, & the consequences of crime, through exhibits & programs. Open year-round; Sept.-June, W 2:30-5:00; July-Aug., M-F 10:00-4:00.
Janet Pieschel, Executive Director, janet.pieschel@calgarypolice.ca

***Camrose:* Camrose & District Centennial Museum**
PO Box 1622, Camrose, AB T4V 1X6
Tel: 780-672-3298
www.camrosemuseum.ca
Year Founded: 1967 Buildings on the museum grounds include a pioneer home, The Likeness School, the St. Dunstan's Church, a firehall, the local newspaper building, a blacksmith shop, the Mona Sparling Building, the Oldtimers Hut, & the R.C.M.P. Machine Building. The musuem is open from Victoria Day weekend to Labour Day weekend. Appointments may be arranged at other times of the year.

***Canmore:* Canmore Museum & Geoscience Centre**
Civic Centre, 902B - 7th Ave., Canmore, AB T1W 3K1
Tel: 403-678-2462; Fax: 403-678-2216
info@cmags.org
www.cmags.org
Other contact information: Phone, 1893 North West Mounted Police Barracks: 403-678-1955
The Canmore Museum & Geoscience Centre features historical artifacts, geological collections, & information about the heritage of Canmore & the surrounding mountainous area. The museum also operates the 1893 North West Mounted Police Barracks, which is situated on 609 Main Street.
V. Richard (Rick) Green, President
Ian Schofield, Vice-President, Heritage
Edward van Vliet, Director & Curator
Lindsay Walker, Coordinator, Earth Science
David Moore, Treasurer

***Cardston:* C.O. Card Pioneer Home & Museum**
PO Box 1830, 337 Main St., Cardston, AB T0K 0K0
Tel: 403-653-4322
Other contact information: Phone, Off Season: 403-653-3366
C.O. Card Home & Museum is a Provincial Historic Site. It features the log cabin built by Charles Ora Card, who was the founder of Cardston. The museum is open during July & August. During the off season, appointments may be arranged.

***Cardston:* Courthouse Museum**
89 - 3rd Ave. West, Cardston, AB T0K 0K0
Tel: 403-653-4322
Other contact information: Phone, Off Season: 403-653-3366
The Courthouse is a Provincial Historic Site, which was constructed in 1907 from local sandstone. Court artifacts are on display, including the witness stand, judge's bench, & orginal jail cells. The musuem is open during July & August. During the off season, appointments may be arranged.

***Cardston:* Remington Carriage Museum**
PO Box 1649, Cardston, AB T0K 0K0
Tel: 403-653-5139; Fax: 403-653-5160
info@remingtoncentre.com
www.remingtoncarriagemuseum.com
Year Founded: 1993 The Remington Carriage Museum features the largest collection of horse-drawn vehicles in North America, such as carriages, sleighs, & wagons. The facility also contains a working stable, a carriage factory, & a restoration shop. Educational programs are offered. The museum is open year-round.

***Caroline:* Caroline Wheels of Time Museum**
***Parent:* Community Historical Society of Caroline**
PO Box 535, Caroline, AB T0M 0M0
Tel: 403-722-3884
vlarsen@telusplanet.net
Year Founded: 1991 The museum operates five historic buildings, including a country store, a school, & a trapper's cabin. Open May-Sept., 12:00-6:00

***Carstairs:* Roulston Museum**
***Also known as:* Carstairs Museum**
***Parent:* Carstairs & District Historical Society**
PO Box 1067, Carstairs, AB T0M 0N0
Tel: 403-337-3710; Fax: 403-337-3343
Year Founded: 1988 Located at 1138 Nanton St. in Carstairs. Main collection housed in the hall of Knox Presbyterian Church (1901), a registered historic site; church records; pictures & artifacts of local life from early settlement to present; McCaig House (1901); archives; new library research room; new farm implement display building
Betty Ayers, Curator
Robert Disney, President

***Castor:* Castor & District Museum**
PO Box 864, Pacific Ave., Castor, AB T0C 0X0
Tel: 403-882-3271; Fax: 403-882-3297
wrightjm@telus.net
Year Founded: 1978 Local history, including a 1910 Alberta Pacific Grain Elevator & collection of restored railcars. Open March-Nov., Th, Sa & Su 2:00-4:00.

***Cereal:* Cereal Prairie Pioneer Museum**
PO Box 131, Cereal, AB T0J 0N0
Tel: 403-326-3899
Museum of artifacts from Pioneer days; pictures, papers & cards of the period; museum was once old CN Railway Station with living quarters; yard includes old jail house & restoration of old Cereal Town Office

***Claresholm:* Appaloosa Horse Club of Canada Museum & Archives**
***Parent:* ApHCC Museum & Archive Society**
PO Box 940, 4189 - 3rd St. SE, Claresholm, AB T0L 0T0
Tel: 403-625-3326; Fax: 403-625-2274
registry@appaloosa.ca
www.appaloosa.ca/museum.html
History of the Appaloosa horse
Donna Wyatt, President & Museum Liaison, dmwyatt@live.com

***Claresholm:* Claresholm Museum**
PO Box 1000, 5126 1st St. W., Claresholm, AB T0L 0T0
Tel: 403-625-3131; Fax: 403-625-3869
claresholmmuseum@gmail.com
www.town.claresholm.ab.ca
Year Founded: 1969 Local history museum in the old Sandstone Railway Station; Claresholm was home to Louise C. McKinney, a social activist for the cause of women's welfare and legal status, and the first woman parliamentarian in the British Empire; open daily May-Sept; admission by donation
Jo-Ann Peach, Collections Assistant

Cochrane: **Cochrane Ranche Historic Site**
PO Box 1522, Cochrane, AB T0L 0W0
Tel: 403-932-2902
www.cochrane.ca
Located off Hwy #22, north of downtown Cochrane, The Cochrane Ranche is Alberta's first large-scale livestock ranch, comprising approx. 136 acres; open May 15 - Labour Day; hiking & picnic areas open year round

Coleman: **Crowsnest Museum**
PO Box 306, 7701 - 18 Ave., Coleman, AB T0K 0M0
Tel: 403-563-5434; Fax: 403-563-5434
cnmuseum@shaw.ca
www.crowsnestmuseum.ca
Over 25,000 artifacts on display interpreting the history of the Crowsnest Pass & its people; themed galleries include pioneers, underground mining, general store/blacksmith shop, Legends of Prohibition, Gushul Studio. Veterans' exhibit, wildlife diorama; open year round
Wendy Zack, Manager, Operations

Crowsnest Pass: **The Frank Slide Interpretive Centre (FSIC)**
PO Box 959 Blairmore, Crowsnest Pass, AB T0K 0E0
Tel: 403-562-7388; Fax: 403-562-8635
info@frankslide.com
www.frankslide.com
Site of the 1903 rockslide avalanche; visual presentation "In the Mountain's Shadow" shown daily; open year-round.
Monica Field, Manager

Crowsnest Pass: **Leitch Collieries Provincial Historic Site**
c/o Frank Slide Interpretive Centre, PO Box 959 Blairmore, Crowsnest Pass, AB T0K 0E0
Tel: 403-562-7388; Fax: 403-562-8635
info@frankslide.com
www.history.alberta.ca/leitch/default.aspx
Other contact information: May-Sept. Phone: 403-564-4211
Ruin of coal mining operation; staffed May 15 - Labour Day; located off Hwy. #3 in Crowsnest Pass, AB.

Czar: **Prairie Panorama Museum**
PO Box 60, Czar, AB T0B 0Z0
Tel: 780-857-2155
Displays many historical artifacts; includes a school section

DeBolt: **DeBolt & District Pioneer Museum**
311 - 1st St. West, DeBolt, AB T0H 1B0
Tel: 780-957-3957; Fax: 780-957-2934
Year Founded: 1975 The museum comprises 8 heritage buildings with displays: in Hubert Memorial Park on Viriginia Ave., in the community church & Legion Hall; collections include the Bickell Fossil Collection. Open summer.
Fran Moore, Curator, franmoore@iwantwireless.ca

Delburne: **Anthony Henday Museum**
PO Box 374, 2517 - 20 St., Delburne, AB T0M 0V0
Tel: 403-749-2711
ahenday@xplornet.com
Other contact information: Alternate Phone: 403-749-2186
Housed in the former CNR train station; water tank tower, caboose, machine shed & pioneer cabin replica on site; depicts history of Delburne & district with emphasis on agriculture, households & coal mining. Open June M-F, 9:00-5:00. From July to Labour Day open daily 9:00-5:00.

Dewberry: **Dewberry Valley Museum**
PO Box 30, Centre St., Dewberry, AB T0B 1G0
Tel: 403-847-3053
History of the Dewberry Valley area, including prehistoric, fur trade, Riel Rebellion, & pioneer artifacts; also features a pioneer log cabin.

Didsbury: **Didsbury & District Museum**
PO Box 1175, 2118 - 21st Ave., Didsbury, AB T0M 0W0
Tel: 403-335-9295
ddhs@telusplanet.net
1906 building; local history; open year round; Tue.-Wed. 1-4:30; Sat. 1-5
Tyrone Patten, President
Joan Court, Secretary

Donalda: **Donalda & District Museum**
PO Box 179, Donalda, AB T0B 1H0
Tel: 403-883-2100; Fax: 403-883-2022
info@donaldamuseum.com
www.donaldamuseum.com
Over 850 lamps; Whitford Collection of Métis artifacts from the late 1800s; native tools; artifacts; open year round
Gail Kerr, Manager

Drayton Valley: **Drayton Valley & District Historical Society**
PO Box 5099, Drayton Valley, AB T7A 1R3
Tel: 780-542-5482
Local history; open Wed. & Sat. 1-4
Fred Cox, Vice-President
Vi Koehmstedt, President
Charlie Miner, Secretary

Drumheller: **Drumheller & District Museum**
PO Box 2135, 335 - 1st St., Drumheller, AB T0J 0Y0
Tel: 403-823-2593; Fax: 403-823-4737
Fossil remains; interpretive displays; Aboriginal artifacts & items of local historical interest

Drumheller: **Homestead Pioneer Museum**
PO Box 3154, 901 North Dinosaur Trail, Drumheller, AB T0J 0Y0
Tel: 403-823-2600; Fax: 403-823-5411
www.traveldrumheller.com/homestead-museum.html
Year Founded: 1965 Situated in the Canadian Badlands, the Homestead Pioneer Museum presents exhibits from the Drumheller Valley, including farm machinery & tools, vehicles, & a 1919 house. The museum is open from mid May to mid October.

East Coulee: **Atlas Coal Mine National Historic Site**
PO Box 521, 110 Century Ave., East Coulee, AB T0J 1B0
Tel: 403-822-2220; Fax: 403-822-2225
info@atlascoalmine.ab.ca
www.atlascoalmine.ab.ca
Social Media: www.youtube.com/user/atlascoalmine
www.facebook.com/184631621585939
Year Founded: 1989 Located in the Canadian Badlands, the Atlas Coal Mine National Historic Site offers tours & educational programs. Visitors can go underground, explore the last wooden tipple in Canada, see the blacksmith shop, & ride an authentic mine locomotive. The site is open from the beginning of May to mid-October.
Linda Digby, Executive Director

East Coulee: **East Coulee School Museum**
PO Box 539, East Coulee, AB T0J 1B0
Tel: 403-822-3970; Fax: 403-922-2111
info@ecsmuseum.ca
www.ecsmuseum.ca
Open year round
Heather Farquherson, Museum Administrator

Edmonton: **Alberta Aviation Museum**
11410 Kingsway Ave., Edmonton, AB T5G 0X4
Tel: 780-451-1175; Fax: 780-451-1607
info@albertaaviationmuseum.com
www.albertaaviationmuseum.com
Tells & interprets the story of aviation & its importance to Edmonton & Northern Alberta; displays & exhibits allow visitors to embrace the spirit of those involved in early aviation endeavours that helped Edmonton establish its title as "Gateway to the North". Flight simulators, aircraft restoration area, activities for children, guided tours, special events. Space rentals, with theatre projection & sound system, wireless Internet available. Open year round.
Jim Salzman, President

Edmonton: **Alberta Railway Museum**
24215 - 34th St., Edmonton, AB T5Y 6B4
Tel: 780-472-6229
www.railwaymuseum.ab.ca
Year Founded: 1968 The Alberta Railway Museum features over sixty railway cars & locomotives, interpretive displays, a Morse telegraph demonstration, tours, & train rides on selected long weekends. The museum is open on weekends only from Victoria Day (the long weekend in May) to Labour Day (the long weekend in September).
Herb Dixon, President, 780-718-0299

Edmonton: **Calgary & Edmonton (1891) Railway Museum**
10447 - 86th Ave., Edmonton, AB T6E 2M4
Tel: 780-433-9739
Visitors to the Calgary & Edmonton (1891) Railway Museum can see a replica railway station, which served the area from 1891 to 1907. Train & station artifacts are on display, including a working telegraph service. The museum is open from June to August. At other times, appointments may be arranged.

Edmonton: **College & Association of Registered Nurses of Alberta (CARNA) Museum & Archives**
CARNA Provincial Office, 11620 - 168 St., Edmonton, AB T5M 4A6
Tel: 780-451-0043; Fax: 780-452-3276
Toll-Free: 800-252-9392
carna@nurses.ab.ca
www.nurses.ab.ca/Carna/index.aspx?W ebStructureID=2690
The museum & archives are available for research purposes; permanent & temporary exhibits are maintained; collection includes a lamp used by Florence Nightingale during the Crimean War; databases can be searched online; open M-F 8:30-4:30.
Margaret Ward-Jack, Director, Communications, 780-453-0515, mwardjack@nurses.ab.ca

Edmonton: **College & Association of Registered Nurses Of Alberta Museum & Archives**
11620 - 168 St., Edmonton, AB T5M 4A6
Tel: 780-453-0534; Fax: 780-482-4459
Toll-Free: 800-252-9392
www.nurses.ab.ca
Items related to the founding & development of the AARN, as well as the early history of professional nursing in Alberta; Collection includes caps, pins, uniforms, yearbooks, original diplomas, & photographs from early days of nurses' education in Alberta to present; Scrapbooks, uniforms, & military medals (WWI & WWII) from the Nursing Sisters Association; Records of various nursing interest groups
Lorraine Mychajlunow, Curator & Archivist, 780-453-0534, lmychajlunow@nurses.ab.ca

Edmonton: **Edmonton Power Historical Foundation Museum (EPHF)**
PO Box 31121, 16504 - 95 St., Edmonton, AB T5Z 2P3
Tel: 780-471-4285
p.collis@shaw.ca
www.ephf.ca/museum
The museum seeks to relate Alberta's electrical power industry to the general public, including hands-on activities & games for kids. The website also features a Online Museum with pictures & descriptions of items from the physical collection. Open May 26, July 28 & 29, & Sept. 15; open to groups by appointment.

Edmonton: **Edmonton Public Schools Archives & Museum**
McKay Avenue School, 10425 - 99 Ave., Edmonton, AB T5K 0E5
Tel: 780-422-1970
archives@epsb.ca
archives.epsb.net
Located in historic McKay Ave. School, site of the first session of the Alberta Legislature; 1905 restored brick building & features the restored 1906 legislative Chamber; holdings include Edmonton Public School Board District #7 & individual school records from 1885 to present
Catherine Luck, Supervisor

Edmonton: **Edmonton Radial Railway Society**
PO Box 76057 Southgate, Edmonton, AB T6H 5Y7
Tel: 780-437-7721
info@edmonton-radial-railway.ab.ca
edmonton-radial-railway.ab.ca
Other contact information: Park Line: 780-496-1464
Vintage 3 km streetcar ride from Strathcona to downtown Edmonton along former CPR right of way & across the High Level Bridge; restored streetcar rides for visitors to Fort Edmonton Park

Edmonton: **Father Lacombe Chapel - Provincial Historic Site / La Chapelle du Père Lacombe**
Historic Sites & Museums Branch, Alberta Culture, 8820 - 112 St., Edmonton, AB T6G 2P8
Tel: 780-459-7663
father.lacombe@gov.ab.ca
www.history.alberta.ca/fatherlacombe
Alberta's oldest building; Located on St. Vital Ave., St. Albert; open May 15 - Labour Day
Charlene Garvey, Contact, 780-431-2300

Edmonton: **Fort Edmonton Park**
c/o City of Edmonton Community Services, PO Box 2359, Edmonton, AB T5J 2R7
Tel: 780-442-5311; Fax: 780-496-8797
attractions@edmonton.ca
www.fortedmontonpark.ca
Canada's largest living history park; a complete 1846 fur-trading fort & 1885, 1905 & 1920 costumed interpreters; steam train & street car; giftshops & restaurants; fully operational hotel on site
Roger Jevne, Director

Edmonton: **John Janzen Nature Centre**
PO Box 2359, Edmonton, AB T5J 2R7
Tel: 780-442-5311
attractions@edmonton.ca
www.edmonton.ca
www.facebook.com/JohnJanzenNatureCentre

Edmonton: **John Walter Museum**
10661 - 91A Ave., Edmonton, AB T5K 0B3
Tel: 780-496-8787; Fax: 780-496-4701
attractions@edmonton.caton.ca
www.edmonton.ca/johnwalter
Other contact information: E-mail, School Programs: cmsschoolbookings@edmonton.ca
The museum consists of houses from 1874, 1886, & 1901. A variety of group programs are available. John Walter Museum is open from mid March to mid December.

Edmonton: **The Loyal Edmonton Regiment Military Museum**

Prince of Wales Armouries, #118, 10440 - 108 Ave., Edmonton, AB T5H 3Z9

Tel: 780-421-9943; Fax: 780-421-9943
lermus1@telus.net
www.lermuseum.org

Military museum focusing on history of The Loyal Edmonton Regiment & other military service branches from Northern Alberta
David Haas, Curator

Edmonton: **Rutherford House Provincial Historic Site**
11153 Saskatchewan Dr., Edmonton, AB T6G 2S1

Tel: 780-427-3995; Fax: 780-422-4288
info@rutherfordhouse.ca
www.rutherfordhouse.ca

Home of Alberta's first premier; gift shop, tea room, tours & special events; open year round

Edmonton: **Stephansson House Provincial Historic Site**
8820 - 112 St., Edmonton, AB T6G 2P8

Tel: 780-427-3995; Fax: 780-422-4288
www.history.alberta.ca/stephansson
Other contact information: Summer Phone: 403-728-3929; Fax: 403-728-3928

Icelandic poet's pioneer home; open May 15 - Labour Day; located 7 km. north of Markerville off Hwy. 592 or 781
Olga Fowler, Contact, olga.fowler@gov.ab.ca

Edmonton: **The Telephone Historical Centre (THC)**
PO Box 188 Main, 10440 - 108 Ave., Edmonton, AB T5J 2J1

Tel: 780-433-1010; Fax: 780-426-1876
bertyeudall@hotmail.com
www.telephonehistoricalcentre.com

Open year round; Canada's largest independent telephone museum
Bert Yeudall, Executive Director

Edmonton: **Ukrainian Canadian Archives & Museum of Alberta**
9543 - 110 Ave., Edmonton, AB T5H 1H3

Tel: 780-424-7580; Fax: 780-420-0562
ucama@shaw.ca
www.ucama.ca

The Ukrainian Canadian Archives & Museum of Alberta is dedicated to preserving Ukrainian-Canadian history & culture. Collections include Ukrainian-Canadian military memorabilia such as uniforms, textiles made by Ukrainian pioneers in Alberta, as well as ecclesiastical artifacts. The museum is open year-round, from Tuesday to Friday.
Khrystyna Kohut, President
Michelle Tracy, Vice-President
Christina Scharabun, Secretary
Greg Borowetz, Contact

Edmonton: **Ukrainian Catholic Women's League of Canada Arts & Crafts Museum (UCWLC)**
10825 - 97th St., Edmonton, AB T5H 2M4

Tel: 780-424-7505
www.ucwlc.ca

Open by appt.
Gloria Leniuk, UCWLC National President, 306-692-1550, Fax: 306-694-5779, gloriajalen@sasktel.net

Edmonton: **Ukrainian Cultural Heritage Village**
8820 - 112 St. NW, Edmonton, AB T6G 2P8

Tel: 780-662-3640; Fax: 780-662-3273
uchv@gov.ab.ca
www.ukrainianvillage.ca

The provincial historic site presents Ukrainian settlement in east central Alberta between 1892 & 1930. The Ukrainian Cultural Heritage Village has over thiry historic buildings for visitors to explore, including a grain elevator, a budei (a sod hut), & three churches of Eastern Byzantine Rite. The village is open from the May long weekend to Labour Day. School groups may book a tour at other times of the year.
Arnold Grandt, Acting Director, Arnold.Grandt@gov.ab.ca
Becky Dahl, Curator, Becky.Dahl@gov.ab.ca
Shirley Hauck, Head, Special Events, Shirley.Hauck@gov.ab.ca
Pamela Trischuk, Head, Education & Interpretation Services, Pamela.Trischuk@gov.ab.ca
Radomir Bilash, Senior Historian & Project Manager, Alberta-Ukraine Genealogical Project, Radomir.Bilash@gov.ab.ca
Bruce McGregor, Coordinator, Historic Farm Program, Bruce.McGregor@gov.ab.ca

Edmonton: **University of Alberta Dental Museum**
Edmonton, AB T6G 2N8

Tel: 780-492-4468

Collection of antique dental instruments & furniture; natural history collection of animal skulls & fossil hominid models. Although the collection still exists, the museum is currently inactive, as the School of Dentistry moved to a location that could not accommodate the collection.
Dr. Loren Kline, Contact, lkline@ualberta.ca

Edmonton: **University of Alberta Museum of Paleontology**
University of Alberta - B-01 Earth Sciences Building, Edmonton, AB T6G 2E3

Tel: 780-492-3265; Fax: 780-492-2030
eas.inquiries@ualberta.ca
easweb.eas.ualberta.ca/page/Paleontology_Museu m
twitter.com/UofA_EAS
www.facebook.com/UofAEarthandAtmosphericScience sDepartment

The museum presents the history of life over the course of geological time, starting with PreCambrian stromatolites & ending with Pleistocene megafauna; open during business hours Mon.-Fri.
Martin Sharp, Chair, martin.sharp@ualberta.ca
Andrew Locock, Collections Manager, alocock@ualberta.ca

Edmonton: **University of Alberta Museum of Zoology (UAMZ)**
#Z1011, Biological Sciences Bldg., University of Alberta, Edmonton, AB T6G 2E9

Tel: 780-492-4622; Fax: 780-492-9234
www.biology.ualberta.ca/uamz.hp/uamz.html

Open year round

Edmonton: **University of Alberta Museums**
c/o Museums & Collections Services, University of Alberta, Ring House #1, Edmonton, AB T6G 2E1

Tel: 780-492-5834; Fax: 780-492-6185
museums@ualberta.ca
www.museums.ualberta.ca
twitter.com/UAlbertaMuseum s
www.facebook.com/ualbertamuseums

Museum services & expertise are provided to more than 35 teaching & research collections at the University; human history, fine art, natural & applied science collections, public programs, educational outreach & other community service programs offered
Janine Andrews, Executive Director, janine.andrews@ualberta.ca
Frannie Blondheim, Associate Director, frannie.blondheim@ualberta.ca
Helen Chimirri-Russell, Museums Advisor, helen.chimirri-russell@ualberta.ca
Jim Corrigan, Curator, Univ. of Alberta Art & Artifact Collection, jim.corrigan@ualberta.ca
Lisa Claypool, Curator, Mactaggart Art Collection, lisa.claypool@ualberta.ca

Edmonton: **University of Alberta Vascular Plant Herbarium (ALTA)**
Dept. of Biological Sciences, University of Alberta, B-414, Biological Sciences, Edmonton, AB T6G 2E1

Tel: 780-492-5834; Fax: 780-492-6185
vascularplant.museums.ualberta.ca

Jocelyn Hall, Curator, 780-492-8611, jocelyn.hall@ualberta.ca
Dorothy Fabijan, Assistant Curator, 780-492-5523, dorothy.fabijan@ualberta.ca

Edmonton: **Victoria School Archives & Museum**
10210 - 108 Ave., Edmonton, AB T5H 1A8

Tel: 780-426-3010
museum.victoria-school.ca/gallery
Other contact information: Alternate Phone: 780-498-8715

Artifacts that relate to the school from 1903 to present; student & teacher records from 1911; books, playbills, posters, uniforms, photos, sweaters; the museum's collection is temporarily in storage while staff search for a new home.
Jack Calkins, Director

Edson: **Galloway Station Museum**
5425A - 3 Ave., Edson, AB T7E 1L5

Tel: 780-723-5696

Forestry; coal mining; railway
Jean Hatlen

Edson: **Red Brick Arts Centre & Museum**
4818 - 7 Ave., Edson, AB T7E 1K8

Tel: 780-723-3582
echored@telus.net

Art gallery, theatre, school room museum, dance studio & gift shop
Betty Stitzenberger, President

Elk Point: **Fort George Museum**
PO Box 66, Elk Point, AB T0A 1A0

Tel: 780-645-6256; Fax: 780-645-4760

Historical & archaeological material of a local nature; located 13 km SE of Elk Point on Secondary Rd. #646

Etzikom: **Etzikom Museum & Historic Windmill Centre**
PO Box 585, Etzikom, AB T0K 0W0

Tel: 403-666-3737

Canadian national historic windmill centre; open May long weekend - Sept. long weekend Mon-Sat 10-5, Sun. 12-6
Harold Halvorson, President
June Mitzel, Curator

Evansburg: **Pembina Lobstick Historical Museum**
PO Box 85, Evansburg, AB T0E 0T0

Artifacts of local historical interest

Fairview: **RCMP Centennial Celebration Museum**
PO Box 1994, 10813 - 103 Ave., Fairview, AB T0H 1L0

Tel: 780-835-2632; Fax: 780-835-2632

Original barracks; also 2nd museum on a 10-acre site; open summer
Jean Bartlett, 780-835-4715
Robert Keddie, 780-835-2847
Marshall Rolling, 780-835-2392

Forestburg: **Forestburg & District Museum**
PO Box 46, 4707 - 50 St., Forestburg, AB T0B 1N0

Tel: 780-582-2165; Fax: 780-582-4203

Housed in former Masonic Hall; displays relevant to the area; open by appt.

Fort Chipewyan: **Fort Chipewyan Bicentennial Museum**
PO Box 203, Fort Chipewyan, AB T0P 1B0

Tel: 780-697-3844; Fax: 780-697-2389
fortchipmuseum@telus.net
www.woodbuffalo.ab.ca

Year Founded: 1991 The museum is a replica of the Hudson's Bay Store; local artifacts & archives; library reference collection; classes. Located on Mackenzie Ave. in Fort Chipewyan.
Oliver Glanfield, Chair
Maureen Clarke, Vice-Chair

Fort MacLeod: **The Fort Museum**
PO Box 776, 219 Jerry Potts Blvd., Fort MacLeod, AB T0L 0Z0

Tel: 403-553-4703; Fax: 403-553-3451
info@nwmpmuseum.com; sitemanager@fortmacleod.com
www.nwmpmuseum.com; thefortmuseum.tumblr.com
Social Media: www.flickr.com/photos/63129174@N04
twitter.com/thefortmuseum
www.faceb ook.com/106507912770906

Tells the story of the arrival of the NWMP into Western Canada, & the Natives & Pioneers of that time

Fort MacLeod: **Head-Smashed-In Buffalo Jump**
PO Box 1977, Fort MacLeod, AB T0L 0Z0

Tel: 403-553-2731; Fax: 403-553-3141
info@head-smashed-in.com
www.head-smashed-in.com

Year Founded: 1987 Designated a UNESCO World Heritage Site in 1981, this jump is a testimony to the hunting customs of native peoples, particularly the Blackfoot, for thousands of years. The Interpretive Centre, blending into a sandstone cliff, explores the lives of the Blackfoot peoples from the geography of the region to the family life and ceremonies. Open year round.
Terry Malone, Facility Manager

Fort McMurray: **Fort McMurray Oil Sands Discovery Centre**
515 MacKenzie Blvd., Fort McMurray, AB T9H 4X3

Tel: 780-743-7167; Fax: 780-791-0710
osdc@gov.ab.ca
www.oilsandsdiscovery.com

Open year round
Nancy Dodsworth, Facility Supervisor

Fort McMurray: **Heritage Park**
Parent: **Fort McMurray Historical Society**
1 Tolen Dr., Fort McMurray, AB T9H 1G7

Tel: 780-791-7575; Fax: 780-791-5180
heritage@fortmcmurrayhistory.com
www.fortmcmurrayhistory.com
twitter.c om/McMurrayHistory
www.facebook.com/260650299824

Year Founded: 1974 The park is a village of 17 historic buildings, including a trapper's cabin & a Catholic Mission, designed to celebratethe history of Ft. McMurray & the region. On site are 2 railway cars. Exhibits cover the logging, fishing & trapping industries. There is an extensive archive of photographs & historical documents.
Roseann Davidson, Executive Director, 780-791-7575

Fort Saskatchewan: **Fort Saskatchewan Museum & Historic Site**
10006 - 101 St., Fort Saskatchewan, AB T8L 1V9

Tel: 780-998-1783; Fax: 780-998-1783
museum@fortsask.ca
www.fortsask.ca
twitter.com/AuggieFtSk

Year Founded: 1971
Kris Nygren, Curator, 780-998-1783, knygren@fortsask.ca
Diane Yanch, Culture & Historic Precinct Supervisor, 780-992-6261, dyanch@fortsask.ca

Girouxville: **Musée Girouxville Museum**
Village of Girouxville, PO Box 276, 5015 - 50 St., Girouxville, AB T0H 1S0
Tel: 780-323-4252; Fax: 780-323-4110

Located in the heart of Girouxville, museum offers visitors a glimpse back into a time when pioneers first settled in the Smoky River Region; more than 6,000 pieces on display; collections includes: Religion, Native history, Natural history, Pioneer life, Hunting & Trapping, Transportation, Fur trade, Domestic history, Communications, Agriculture, Photography, Education, Geology & Palaeontology

Grande Prairie: **Grande Prairie Museum**
Pioneer Museum Society of Grande Prairie & District, Muskoseepi Park, Grande Prairie, AB T8V 3A8
Tel: 780-532-5482; Fax: 780-831-7371
info@grandeprairiemuseum.org
www.cityofgp.com
www.facebook.com/G.P.Mus eum
Dinosaur bones; arrowheads; wildlife exhibits; pioneer artifacts; heritage village; archives; open daily, closed on holidays
Heather Schultz, Program Director, hschultz@cityofgp.com

Grande Prairie: **The Heritage Discovery Centre (HDC)**
Centre 2000 Bldg., PO Box 687, 11330 - 106 St., Lower Level, Grande Prairie, AB T8V 7X9
Tel: 780-532-5790; Fax: 780-532-8039
www.cityofgp.com
Located at Centre 2000 in the Tourist Information Bldg.; includes a main exhibit gallery, a Rotary Learning Theatre, & the Kin Gallery. Also includes dinosaur exhibit, survivor games, mini-theatres, and hands-on display.

Grouard: **Native Cultural Arts Museum**
62 Mission St., Grouard, AB T0G 1C0
Tel: 780-751-3306; Fax: 780-751-3308
Toll-Free: 866-652-3456
myrel@northernlakescollege.ca
www.northernlakescollege .ca/content.aspx?id=2472
Year Founded: 1976 Cultural & arts collections of the Woodland Cree & Métis People of northern Alberta. Summer hours: June-Aug., M-F 10:00-4:00; Winter hours: Sept.-May, Tu-Th 10:00-4:00; closed in Jan.
Rachel Cripps, Coordinator, crippsr@northernlakescollege.ca

Hanna: **Hanna Museum & Pioneer Village**
Parent: **Hanna & District Historical Society**
PO Box 1528, Pioneer Trail, Hanna, AB T0J 1P0
Tel: 403-854-4244
www.hanna.ca
Historic buildings at the pioneer village include a ranch house, a one room schoolhouse, a store, a church, a hospital, a dental office, & a power mill. Archives are also available for research. The museum & pioneer village is open from June to August, & in May & September by appointment.
Vic Mohl, Secretary-Treasurer

High Prairie: **High Prairie & District Museum & Historical Society**
PO Box 1442, High Prairie, AB T0G 1E0
Tel: 780-523-2601; Fax: 780-523-2633
hpdmhs@telusplanet.net
www.highprairiemuseum.com
Year Founded: 1967 The museum preserves the history of High Prairie & surrounding area by conserving artifacts used by homesteaders from the early 1900s. Stories of the settlers are also archived. Programs offered to children include butter-making, bread-making and sewing lessons. Open year round, with summer & winter hrs.

High River: **Museum of the Highwood**
309B Macleod Trail SW, High River, AB T1V 1Z5
Tel: 403-652-7156; Fax: 403-652-2396
museumofthehighwood@highriver.ca
www.highriver.ca
Located in the historic sandstone Canadian Pacific Railway Station on 1st Street Southwest in High River, the Museum of the Highwood exhibits the history of the Highwood River basin. The museum features a family discovery room, which is a hands-on space with old fashioned games & toys. Programs & tours are available upon request.

Hines Creek: **End of Steel Heritage Society**
PO Box 686, Hines Creek, AB T0H 2A0
Tel: 403-494-3522
Former Northern Alberta Railway cars; homes & church circa. 1930; pioneering artifacts; trapper's cabin; community hall

Hinton: **Alberta Forest Service Museum**
1176 Switzer Dr., Hinton, AB T7V 1V3
Tel: 780-865-8200; Fax: 780-865-8266

Established to preserve a history of forestry in the province of Alberta; displays reflect work performed by the early rangers & provide an appreciation of their accomplishments achieved without benefit of modern transportation, tools & technology; "compact disk" guided tour; ranger headquarters cabin built in 1922; open daily; weekends by appt

Holden: **Holden Historical Society Museum**
PO Box 32, 4920 - 50 Holden Ave., Holden, AB T0B 2C0
Tel: 780-688-3593
holdenmuseum@gmail.com
The collection is of the local farming community with objects pertaining to pioneer life. Open Wed., Fri., & Sun. in summer, 2-4
Dave Maruszczka, President

Iddesleigh: **Rainy Hills Historical Society Pioneer Exhibits (RHHS)**
Parent: **Rainy Hills Historical Society**
PO Box 107, Iddesleigh, AB T0J 1T0
Tel: 403-898-2443
Community museum exhibiting homestead items including furnishings, clothing, farm equipment & photographs; also features a blacksmith shop, school room, general store, an old-time kitchen & the original Iddlesleigh Alberta Wheat Post Office building

Innisfail: **Innisfail & District Historical Village**
PO Box 6042, 5139 - 42 St., Innisfail, AB T4G 1S7
Tel: 403-227-2906; Fax: 403-227-2901
idhs@telus.net
www.innisfailhistory.ca
Promote the preservation, interpretation, enjoyment of the history of Innisfail & District; village is made up of seventeen buildings on two acres of land; farm machinary and picnic area.
Debbie Becker Matthie, Museum Manager

Irvine: **Prairie Memories Museum**
PO Box 215, Irvine, AB T0J 1V0
Tel: 403-834-3923
Local history; open June 30 - Sept.

Islay: **Morrison Museum of the Country School**
PO Box 4, Islay, AB T0B 2J0
Tel: 780-744-2271
Contains a collection of the artifacts to be found in a western Canadian country school of the 1930s & 1940s
Shirley Ronaghan, Contact
Mary Ternoster, Contact, 780-744-2260

Jasper: **Jasper Yellowhead Museum & Archives (JYHS)**
PO Box 42, 400 Pyramid Lake Rd., Jasper, AB T0E 1E0
Tel: 780-852-3013
webadministrator@jaspermuseum.org
www.jaspermuseum.org
www.facebook.com/pages/Jasper-Museum/12356174765713 6
Other contact information: Phone, Archives: 780-852-3240
The Jasper Yellowhead Museum & Archives collects, preserves, & exhibits artifacts & documents related to the human history of Jasper National Park & the Yellowhead corridor. Displays in the historical gallery tell the story of the fur trade, the railway, & early tourism. The area has been designated as part of a World Heritage Site. The Jasper Yellowhead Museum & Archives is open year-round. Visits to the archives are by appointment only.
B. Bell, President
Karen Byers, Manager, manager@jaspermuseum.org
J. Couture, Historian
Dee Dee Bartlett, Contact, Collections, collections@jaspermuseum.org
Val Delill, Contact, Exhibits, exhibits@jaspermuseum.org
Lucie Doucet, Contact, Gift Shop, giftshop@jaspermuseum.org
Meghan Power, Contact, Archives, archives@jaspermuseum.org

Kingman: **Kingman Regional School Museum & Tea House**
PO Box 97, 222 Main St., Kingman, AB T0B 2M0
Tel: 780-672-8220
Other contact information: Alternate Phone: 780-672-6969
Country school building from 1938; open year-round, M-F 2:00-4:00.

Leduc: **Dr. Woods House Museum**
4801 - 49 Ave., Leduc, AB T9E 6L6
Tel: 780-986-1517
Restored 1920s house with attached garage & medical wing

Lethbridge: **Fort Whoop-Up**
Also known as: **Fort Hamilton**
PO Box 1074, Lethbridge, AB T1J 4A2
Tel: 403-329-0444; Fax: 403-329-0645
info@fortwhoopup.ca
www.fortwhoopup.ca
Located in Indian Battle Park, west end of 3rd Ave. As an Interpretive Centre, "the Fort" has been reconstructed and interpreted to be the norotirious whiskey fort: as such is has electronic displays, historical sights, and sounds to pay tribute to and commentorate the legact of the NMMP, Aboriginal People, and pioneers that shaped Western Canada. Open year round
Doran Degenstein, Curator and Director, 403-329-0444

Lethbridge: **Galt Historic Railway Park**
c/o Great Canadian Plains Railway Society, PO Box 1013, Lethbridge, AB T1J 4A2
Tel: 403-756-2220
gcprs@telus.net
galtrailway.com
Exhibits include a variety of items related to rail travel in the late 1800s.
Ray Oldenburger, President, 403-756-3313

Lethbridge: **Sir Alexander Galt Museum & Archives**
910 - 4 Ave. South, Lethbridge, AB T1J 0P6
Tel: 403-320-3898; Fax: 403-329-4958
info@galtmuseum.com
www.galtmuseum.com
The human history of Lethbridge & southern Alberta in 5 galleries & an outdoor courtyard; free admission
Wendy Aitkens, Curator

Lloydminster: **Barr Colony Heritage Cultural Centre**
4420 - 50th Ave., Lloydminster, AB T9V 0W2
Tel: 306-825-5655; Fax: 306-825-9070
bchcc.ca
Other contact information: Phone, City of Lloydminster: 780-875-6184; Fax: 780-871-8345
Located at Highway 16 & 45th Avenue, the Barr Colony Heritage Cultural Centre consists of an antique museum, the Imhoff art collection, the OTS Heavy Oil Science Centre, & the Fuchs wildlife exhibit. The Richard Larsen Museum presents antiques of the Barr Colonists. Artifacts include funiture & agricultural equipment. Visitors can also see Lloydminster's first church, a log cabin, a filling station, & a 1906 schoolhouse. The centre is open year-round.
Barb McKeand, Manager, bmckeand@lloydminster.ca

Longview: **Bar U Ranch National Historic Site of Canada**
PO Box 168, Longview, AB T0L 1H0
Tel: 403-395-2212; Fax: 403-395-2331
Toll-Free: 888-773-8888
BarU.info@pc.gc.ca
www.pc.gc.ca/lhn-nhs/ab/baru/index_ e.asp
Other contact information: TTY: 1-866-787-6221
With 35 buildings & structures, the Bar U Ranch commemorates the history of ranching in Canada. The Ranch is open from late May to the end of September. Visits can be arranged during the off season.

Lougheed: **Iron Creek Museum**
PO Box 249, Lougheed, AB T0B 2V0
Tel: 780-386-3787
ironcreekmuseum@hotmail.com
Other contact information: Alternate Phone: 780-386-2337
Two one-room schoolhouses; church; blacksmith & shoe repair shop; log hall housing artifacts & farm machinery: located at 49 St. & 51 Ave., Lougheed, AB.

Magrath: **Magrath Museum**
PO Box 907, 37 North - 1st St. West, Magrath, AB T0K 1J0
Tel: 403-758-6618
www.magrathmuseum.ca
twitter.com/MagrathMuseum
www.facebook.com/146547325418743
Local history & pioneer artifacts; open May-Aug., M-F 9:00-5:00.

Mallaig: **Mallaig & District Museum**
PO Box 211, Mallaig, AB T0A 2K0
Tel: 780-726-2614; Fax: 780-635-3757
mallaigmuseum@hotmail.com
The museum's exhibits are housed in a replica 1920 log schoolhouse & a 1931 church. Open M-F 10:00-4:00.

Manning: **Battle River Pioneer Museum**
PO Box 574, Manning, AB T0H 2M0
Tel: 780-836-2180; Fax: 780-836-2180
www.manning.govoffice.com
Other contact information: Alternate Phone: 780-836-2374
Artifacts from pioneer life; 1,500 year-old arrowhead; albino moose; open May-Sept., daily 1:00-6:00; open 10:00 am in July & Aug.

Markerville: **Historic Markerville Creamery**
Parent: **Stephan G. Stephansson Icelandic Society**
c/o Stephan G. Stephansson Icelandic Society, PO Box 837, Markerville, AB T0M 1M0
Tel: 403-728-3006; Fax: 403-728-3225
Toll-Free: 877-728-3007
admin@historicmarkerville. com
www.historicmarkerville. com
www.facebook.com/Historic.Markerville
Creamery museum restored to 1930s profiles Icelandic settlement of central Alberta; "Kaffistofa" features Icelandic menu

Donna Nelson, President, 403-728-3438
Linda Nelson, Secretary, 403-728-3840
Brooke Henrikson, Manager

***Medicine Hat:* Esplanade Arts & Heritage Centre (MHM&AG)**
401 First St. SE, Medicine Hat, AB T1A 8W2
Tel: 403-502-8580; Fax: 403-502-8589
esplanade@medicinthat.ca
www.esplanade.ca
Museum: Permanent Gallery featuring the history of Medicine Hat & area using pieces from vast collection, including pioneer home funishings, Victorian period artifacts, archaeological artifacts, military, sporting & Native artifacts, business & industry equipment, clothing & more; Archives: database of manuscripts, extensive black & white photographic collection, genealogical information & more; A
Carol Beatty, Manager

***Medicine Hat:* Medicine Hat Clay Industries National Historic District**
***Also known as:* Medalta**
713 Medalta Ave. SE, Medicine Hat, AB T1A 3K9
Tel: 403-529-1070; Fax: 403-580-5868
Toll-Free: 866-526-2777
info@medalta.org
www.medalta.org
twitter.com/medalta
www.facebook.com/112945865394219
The 150-acre Historic Clay District preserves the history of the region's pottery industry. With working, circular kilns and original factory, it is living museum. The Medalta International Artists in Residence (MIAIR) program hosts contemporary ceramic artists. An interactive clay area and education programs are available for children.
Mr. Barry G. Finkelman, General Manager/Executive Director, barry@medalta.org

***Millet:* Millet & District Museum & Archives**
PO Box 178, 5120 - 50 St., Millet, AB T0C 1Z0
Tel: 780-387-5558; Fax: 780-387-5548
info@milletmuseum.ca
www.milletmuseum.ca
twitter.com/MilletMuseum
ww w.facebook.com/221092931274232
Year Founded: 1985 Exhibits incude archives on local history, home settings from 1900-1950 and portraits of over 200 local veterans of World Wars I, II. Building also houses the Millet Visitor Information Centre; open to the public Tues. - Sat. in summer
Tracey Leavitt, Executive Director/Curator

***Mirror:* Mirror & District Museum**
PO Box 246, 4910 - 53 St., Mirror, AB T0B 3C0
Tel: 403-788-3828
mmuseum@telus.net
Other contact information: Phone, Off season: 403-788-3094
Settler & railway artifacts are presented at the Mirror & District Museum. The museum if open from mid May to the beginning of September. Appointments may be arranged at other times.

***Morinville:* Musée Morinville Museum**
PO Box 3252, 10010 - 101 St., Morinville, AB T8R 1S2
Tel: 780-801-3290; Fax: 780-801-3291
morinvillemuseum@shaw.ca
museemorinvillemuseum.com
Local history; designated a Provincial Historic Site; open M-Sa 12:00-5:00.
Sheila Houle, President
Donna Garrett, Museum Attendant

***Mundare:* Basilian Fathers Museum**
PO Box 386, Mundare, AB T0B 3H0
Tel: 780-764-3887; Fax: 780-764-3825
curator@basilianmuseum.org
www.basilianmuseum.org
Ukrainian culture & religion
Karen Lemiski, Associate Director/Curator

***Nanton:* Bomber Command Museum of Canada**
PO Box 1051, Nanton, AB T0L 1R0
Tel: 403-646-2270; Fax: 403-646-2214
office@bombercommandmuseum.ca
www.bombercommandmuseum.ca
twitter.com/B CMofCanada
www.facebook.com/101722206538665
The Bomber Command Museum of Canada honours persons associated with Bomber Command during World War II. It also commemorates the operations of the British Commonwealth Air Training Plan. The Museum's library & archives may be contacted at the following e-mail address: library@bombercommandmuseum.ca. School & group visits may be organized by contacting the following e-mail address: visitorservices@bombercommandmuseum.ca.
Bob Evans, Curator, curator@bombercommandmuseum.ca
Robert Pedersen, President

***Nobleford:* Nobleford Area Museum**
PO Box 505, 225 Milnes St., Nobleford, AB T0L 1S0
Tel: 403-824-3909
The museum replicates the manufacturing process of the Noble Blade, invented by Charles Noble. Open July & Aug., M-F 10:00-4:00, or by appointment.

***Okotoks:* Okotoks Museum & Archives (OMA)**
Heritage House, 49 North Railway St., Okotoks, AB T1S 1K1
Tel: 403-938-8969; Fax: 403-938-8963
culture@okotoks.ca
www.okotoks.ca/artgallery.aspx; www.archivesonline.okotoks.ca
Year Founded: 2000 Local history; the online archives allows users to search the Archive's photographic collection. Summer hours: M-Sa 10:00-5:00, Su & holidays 12:00-5:00.

***Olds:* Mountain View Museum & Archives**
***Parent:* Olds Historical Society**
PO Box 3882, 5038 - 50th St., Olds, AB T4H 1P6
Tel: 403-556-8464
info@oldsmuseum.ca
www.oldsmuseum.ca
Year Founded: 1972 The Olds Historical Society preserves artifacts, textual documents, & photographs, which depict the history & heritage of Olds & its surrounding area. Items are displayed & research services are available at the Mountain View Museum & Archives, which is located in the 1920 Olds AGT building. The museum is open from Monday to Friday. Guided tours & educational programs are offered.
Michael Dougherty, Museum Manager, manager@oldsmuseum.ca
Jeffery Kearney, Archivist, archives@oldsmuseum.ca

***Onoway:* Onoway Museum**
***Parent:* Onoway & District Historical Guild**
c/o Onoway & District Historical Guild, PO Box 1368, 4708 Lac Sainte Anne Trail, Onoway, AB T0E 1V0
Tel: 780-967-1015
info1@onowaymuseum.ca
www.onowaymuseum.ca
www.facebook.com/OnowayMuseum
Other contact information: Appointment Phone: 780-967-5263
Year Founded: 2008 Housed in an old schoolhouse, the museum presents artifacts of local Onoway life from the communtiy's early years. Opening hours: Sept.-June, M, W, F 10:00-3:00; July & Aug. M-F 10:00-3:00.

***Oyen:* Crossroads Museum**
PO Box 563, 310 1st Avenue East, Oyen, AB T0J 2J0
Tel: 403-664-2330
Buildings include a period house (1918); cook car; blacksmith shop; tractor & truck building; a 120x40 Quonset; 1912 schoolhouse; former community hall; "teepee" type building containing archaelogical artifacts; season May-Aug.
Nellie Eaton, President

***Paradise Valley:* Climb Thru Time Museum**
Paradise Valley, AB
Tel: 780-745-2412
Other contact information: Alternate Phone: 780-745-2150
The museum is located inside the Paradise Valley grain elevator, & features objects & art portraying agricultural life in Western Canada.

***Patricia:* Dinosaur Provincial Park**
PO Box 60, Patricia, AB T0J 2K0
Tel: 403-378-4342
albertaparks.ca/dinosaur.aspx
Social Media: www.youtube.com/user/AlbertaParks
www.facebook.com/AlbertaParksDinosaur
Some of the most extensive dinosaur fossil fields in the world are found here; the area's badlands & cottonwood river habitat are the other significant features that resulted in the park's designation as a UNESCO World Heritage Site in 1979; also includes the Royal Tyrrell Museum of Palaeontology Field Station, located within the park.

***Peace River:* Peace River Museum, Archives, & Mackenzie Centre**
***Also known as:* Peace River Museum**
10302 - 99 St., Peace River, AB T8S 1K1
Tel: 780-624-4261; Fax: 780-624-2470
museum@peaceriver.net
www.peaceriver.ca/visitors/museum;
peacerivermuseum.blogspot.ca
Displays include: Sir Alexander Mackenzie, fur trade, town of Peace River
Laura Gloor, Director & Curator
Wendy Dyck, Archivist

***Picture Butte:* Prairie Acres Museum**
PO Box 768, 3A St. South, Secondary Hwy. 843, Picture Butte, AB T0K 1V0
Tel: 403-330-4117
Other contact information: Alternate Phone: 403-329-1201
The museum's collection includes antique automobiles, machinery, tractors, combines, & small antique items.

***Pincher Creek:* Heritage Acres Farm Museum**
PO Box 2496, Pincher Creek, AB T0K 1W0
Tel: 403-627-2082
heritageacres.org
The museum seeks to preserve & promote the agricultural history of Southern Alberta from 1880-1960. In its collection it has a grain elevator, antique cars, Doukhobor barn, church, model railway, log house, general store, sawmill, & school. Open May-Sept., 10:00-5:00.

***Pincher Creek:* Kootenai Brown Pioneer Village**
PO Box 1226, 1037 Bev McLachlin Dr., Pincher Creek, AB T0K 1W0
Tel: 403-627-3684
mail.kbpv@gmail.com
www.kootenaibrown.org
Year Founded: 1966 Open year round

***Plamondon:* Plamondon & District Museum**
c/o Emilie Chevigny, PO Box 119, Plamondon, AB T0A 2T0
Tel: 403-798-3193
www.plamondonalberta.ca
Operated by the Plamondon & District Museum Society, the Plamondon & District Museum features local cultural artifacts from early pioneers. The museum is open from June to August.
Bonita Marchand, Contact

***Ponoka:* Fort Ostell Museum**
***Parent:* Fort Ostell Museum Society**
5320 - 54 St., Ponoka, AB T4J 1L8
Tel: 403-783-5224
www.ponoka.org
Year Founded: 1967 Open May 24-Sept. 4, winter special occasions or by appt.

***Raymond:* Raymond Pioneer Museum**
***Parent:* Raymond & District Historical Society**
PO Box 1151, 10 Broadway, Raymond, AB T0K 2S0
Tel: 403-752-4799
peedywifie@shaw.ca
Other contact information: After-hours Phone: 403-752-4516
Year Founded: 1989 The museum's collection details the founding of the town of Raymond, mostly through photographs & text. Hours of operation: Summer, Tu-Sa 11:00-5:00; Winter, W 2:00-5:00; tours on request.

***Red Deer:* Alberta Sports Hall of Fame & Museum**
30 Riverview Park, Red Deer, AB T4N 1E3
Tel: 403-341-8614; Fax: 403-341-8619
postmaster@albertasportshalloffame.com
www.albertasportshalloffame.com
Year Founded: 1957 To preserve artifacts & archival material that are significant in Alberta's sporting history; 7 Honoured Members are inducted into the Sports Hall of Fame each year, plus 3 award recipients; interactive multisport virtual game system & a curriculum based education program; theatre; boardroom rental.
Donna Hately, Managing Director

***Red Deer:* Kerry Wood Nature Centre**
6300 - 45 Ave., Red Deer, AB T4N 3M4
Tel: 403-346-2010; Fax: 403-347-2550
general@waskasoopark.ca; director@waskasoopark.ca
www.waskasoopark.ca
Social Media: www.youtube.com/user/NatureCentre
twitter.com/naturecentre
www.faceboo k.com/groups/76141171395
Central Alberta's year-round home of entertaining & informative nature activities & exhibits; gateway to Gaetz Lakes Sanctuary; features art gallery, bookshop, A/V theatre, meeting rooms, children's Discovery Room & exhibits; extensive programs, courses, field trips for all ages; open daily except Christmas; admission by donation
Jim Robertson, Executive Director, jim.robertson@waskasoopark.ca

***Red Deer:* Norwegian Laft Hus Society & Museum**
4402 - 47th Ave., Red Deer, AB T4N 6T4
Tel: 403-347-2055
norwegianlafthus@gmail.com
www.norwegianlafthussociety.ca
Other contact information: Alternate Phones: 403-346-5952; 403-505-3780
Norwegian-style log house with a sod roof, located in downtown Red Deer. Open year-round; Winter hours: W 9:00-3:00; Summer hours: Tu, Th 10:00-4:00, W 9:00-4:00, F, Sa 12:00-4:00.

***Red Deer:* Red Deer Museum & Art Gallery**
4525 - 47A Ave., Red Deer, AB T4N 6Z6
Tel: 403-309-8405; Fax: 403-342-6644
museum@reddeer.ca
www.reddeermuseum.com
Year Founded: 1973 The Red Deer Museum & Art Gallery tells the story of the people, history, & culture of central Alberta, through its collections, exhibitions, & programs. The museum's

more than 85,000 objects include clothing & First Nations & Inuit art. A library on the site houses artifact books, catalogues, & other printed material.
Lorna Johnson, Executive Director BFA, M.ED, lorna.johnson@reddeer.ca
Michael Dawe, Curator, History, michael.dawe@reddeer.ca
Valerie Miller, Coordinator, Collections, valerie.miller@reddeer.ca
Lynn Norman, Coordinator, Communications & Marketing, lynn.norman@reddeer.ca

***Red Deer:* Sunnybrook Farm Museum**
4701 - 30th St., Red Deer, AB T4N 5H7
Tel: 403-340-3511; Fax: 403-340-3574
sbfs@shaw.ca
www.sunnybrookfarmmuseum.ca
The museum celebrates the early days of farming in Alberta, as the farm itself dates back to the turn of the century. Summer hours: May-Sept., daily 10:00-4:00; off-season hours: M-F 1:00-4:00, or by appointment.
Ian Warwick, Executive Director
Baukje Groothof, Coordinator, Interpretive Program

***Red Deer County:* Danish Canadian National Museum & Gardens**
PO Box 92, 35544 Range Rd. 31, Red Deer County, AB T0M 1V0
Tel: 403-728-0019; Fax: 403-728-0020
Toll-Free: 888-443-4114
manager@danishcanadians.com
www.danishcanadians.com
twitter.com/danishcanadians
www.facebook.com/101324959919
The museum's exhibits celebrate the contribution of Danish immigrants to Canada. The grounds also offer paths, hiking trails, picnic spots, & a man-made lake. Open May-Sept., M-Sa 10:00-5:30, Su 12:30-5:30.

***Redcliff:* Redcliff Historical & Museum Society**
***Also known as:* Redcliff Museum**
PO Box 758, 2 - 3rd St. NE, Redcliff, AB T0J 2P0
Tel: 403-548-6260
redcliff.museum@gmail.com
www.town.redcliff.ab.ca/museum.htm
Exhibits showing the commercial & recreational aspect of Redcliff citizens; extensive drug store, domestic, school, toy & organizational exhibits; history of past industries with manufactured artifacts; weekly newpaper on microfilm 1910-1939; open May-Aug., Tue.-Sat., Sun., Oct.-Apr. by appt.

***Rimbey:* PasKaPoo Historic Park & Smithson International Truck Museum**
***Parent:* Rimbey Historical Society**
PO Box 813, 5620 - 51st St., Rimbey, AB T0C 2J0
Tel: 403-843-2004
paskapoo@telus.net
www.paskapoopark.com
The park offers two museum buildings & ten historic buildings; included in the park is the Truck Museum, which features 19 refurbished International trucks, as well as farm machinery, a police car, an ambulance, vintage photographs, & more. The park is open May-Sept., 9:00-4:00; the museum is open year-round, 9:00-4:00.

***Rocky Mountain House:* Nordegg Heritage Museum/Brazeau Collieries Mine Site**
***Parent:* Nordegg Historical Society**
c/o Nordegg Historical Society, PO Box 550, Rocky Mountain House, AB T4T 1A4
Tel: 403-845-4444
administrator@nordegghistoricalsociety.org
www.nordegghistoricalsociety.org
Other contact information: Museum Phone: 403-721-2625
The museum holds artifacts pertaining to local history & coal mining at the Brazeau Collieries. The mine site, which is a both a Provincial & National Historic Site, is open for guided tours. The museum is open May-Sept., daily 9:00-5:00; the mine tour season is May-Sept.; site tours are held at 10:00 am, & technical tours are held at 1:00 pm, July-Aug.
Tom Clark, President
Joe Baker, Director, Planning & West Country
Misty Moore, Visitor Information Host

***Rocky Mountain House:* Rocky Mountain House National Historic Site of Canada**
Comp. 6, Site 127, RR#4, Rocky Mountain House, AB T4T 2A4
Tel: 403-845-2412; Fax: 403-845-5320
rocky.info@pc.gc.ca
www.pc.gc.ca/rockymountainhouse
Site of four fur trading posts dating back to 1799; Commemorates the fur trade & the role of Native peoples in the fur trade & western exploration (David Thompson); Over 500 acres; Hiking trails, displays, herd of bisons; Exhibits; 3/4 size playfort; Eight trailside listening stations; Heritage demonstrations & presentations; Open Victoria Day weekend - Labour Day

***Rosebud:* Rosebud Centennial & District Museum**
***Parent:* Rosebud Historical Society**
PO Box 601, Rosebud, AB T0J 2T0
Tel: 403-677-2601
rosebud.museum@gmail.com
www.rosebud.ca/museum_home.htm
Year Founded: 1967 A collection of pioneer tools, etc. that have been donated to the museum; open year round
George Comstock, President

***Rowley:* Yester-Year Artifacts Museum**
General Delivery, Rowley, AB T0J 2X0
Tel: 403-368-3757
www.starlandcounty.com/rowley.htm
Other contact information: Alternate Phone: 403-772-3901; 403-368-2355 (Tour Info)
Early settlers artifacts housed in original buildings

***St Albert:* Little White School**
2 Madonna Dr., St Albert, AB T8N 2M2
Tel: 780-459-4404; Fax: 780-459-1528
museum@artsheritage.ca
museeheritage.ca
Call ahead to book a visit.

***St Albert:* Musée Heritage Museum**
***Parent:* Arts & Heritage St. Albert**
St. Albert Place, 5 St. Anne St., St Albert, AB T8N 3Z9
Tel: 780-459-1528; Fax: 780-459-1232
museum@artsheritage.ca
museeheritage.ca; museeheritagemuseum.blogspot.ca
twitter.com/artsandheritage
www.facebo ok.com/ArtsAndHeritageStAlbert
The museum presents the history of St. Albert through various exhibits & programs, in an effort to preserve the community's history. It also manages St. Albert's Heritage Sites: Little White School, St. Albert Grain Elevator Park, & River Lot 24. Hours of operation: Tu-Sa 10:00-5:00, Su 1:00-5:00.
Ann Ramsden, Director, Heritage, annr@artsheritage.ca
Joanne White, Curator, joannew@artsheritage.ca
Rene Georgopalis, Archivist, reneg@artsheritage.ca

***St Albert:* Musée Héritage Museum & Archives**
***Also known as:* St. Albert Museum**
St. Albert Place, 5 Ste-Anne St., St Albert, AB T8N 3Z9
Tel: 780-459-1528; Fax: 780-459-1234
museum@artsheritage.ca
museeheritage.ca; museeheritagemuseum.blogspot.ca
twitter.com/artsandheritage
www.facebo ok.com/ArtsAndHeritageStAlbert
History of St. Albert & surrounding area
Ann Ramsden, Director, Heritage, annr@artsheritage.ca
Joanne White, Curator, joannew@artsheritage.ca
Rene Georgopalis, Archivist, reneg@artsheritage.ca

***St Albert:* St. Albert Grain Elevator Park**
4 Meadowview Dr., St Albert, AB T8N 2R9
Tel: 780-419-7354; Fax: 780-459-1528
museum@artsheritage.ca
museeheritage.ca
Open May-Sept., W-Su 10:00-6:00.

***St Paul:* Fort George & Buckingham House Provincial Historic Site (FGBH)**
#318, Provincial Bldg., 5025 - 49th Ave., St Paul, AB T0A 3A4
Tel: 403-645-6256
fort.george@gov.ab.ca
www.history.alberta.ca/fortgeorge/default.aspx
Other contact information: Summer Phone: 780-724-2611; Fax: 780-724-2611
Archaeological remains of 2 fur trade forts; interpretive centre & gift shop; open May 15 - Labour Day; located 13 km SE of Elk Point on Hwy. 646
Ross Stromberg, Contact, ross.stromberg@gov.ab.ca

***Saint-Paul:* Musée historique de Saint-Paul**
CP 1925, Saint-Paul, AB T0A 3A0
Tél: 780-645-4800; Téléc: 780-645-5959
Fondée en: 1984 Relever l'histoire de la communauté de Saint-Paul; expositions; cours d'histoire aux élèves; projets spécials.
Jeannette Létourneau, Trésorière

***St Paul:* Musée St. Paul Museum**
PO Box 410, 5409 - 50th Ave., St Paul, AB T0A 3A0
Tel: 780-645-5562
www.town.stpaul.ab.ca
The museum is located on the same site as People's Museum of St. Paul & District; open July & Aug, daily 10:00-4:00.

***St Paul:* People's Museum of St. Paul & District**
***Parent:* Peoples Museum Society of St. Paul & District**
PO Box 410, 5409 - 50th Ave., St Paul, AB T0A 3A0
Tel: 780-645-5562; Fax: 780-645-5273
www.town.stpaul.ab.ca
Local agricultural history; part of the same complex as Musée St. Paul Museum; open July & Aug, daily 10:00-4:00.

***St Paul:* Victoria Settlement Provincial Historic Site**
***Also known as:* Fort Victoria**
#318 Provincial Bldg., 5025 - 49th Ave., St Paul, AB T0A 3A4
Tel: 403-645-6256; Fax: 403-645-4760
www.history.alberta.ca/victoria
www.facebook.com/Vic.Settlement
Other contact information: Summer Phone/Fax: 780-656-2333
Located 10 km south of Smoky Lake on Hwy. 855, 6 km east along Victoria Trail; Hudson Bay Company post & settlement; open May 15-Labour Day
Ross Stromberg, Contact, ross.stromberg@gov.ab.ca

***Sangudo:* Lac Ste-Anne Historical Society Pioneer Museum**
PO Box 525, Rochfort Bridge, Sangudo, AB T0E 2A0
Tel: 403-785-2674
Ed Liss, President

***Seba Beach:* Seba Beach Heritage Museum**
General Delivery, Seba Beach, AB T0E 2B0
Tel: 403-420-6704
Summer resort themed artifacts, such as regatta trophies & photographs; historical material related to Seba Beach; located at Main Ave. & 101 St. North

***Sedgewick:* Sedgewick Archives, Gallery & Museum**
PO Box 538, Sedgewick, AB T0B 4C0
Tel: 780-384-3741
www.sedgewick.ca
Year Founded: 1989 Clothing, jewelry, books, photographs, tools; open Tues-Fri, 1:30-4:30; located in the historic Bank of Montreal building on Main St. in Sedgewick
Lorne Abre, President
Myrtle Matthews, Secretary

***Sherwood Park:* Strathcona County Museum & Archives**
913 Ash St., Sherwood Park, AB T8A 2G3
Tel: 780-467-8189
Social Media: www.youtube.com/user/strathconacountymuse
Local history; open year round

***Siksika:* Siksika Nation Museum**
PO Box 1730, Siksika, AB T0J 3W0
Tel: 403-734-5361; Fax: 403-264-9659

***Spirit River:* Spirit River & District Museum**
***Parent:* Spirit River Settlement Historical Society**
PO Box 221, 4403 - 48th St., Spirit River, AB T0H 3G0
Tel: 780-864-2180; Fax: 780-864-2199
contact@spiritrivermuseum.com
www.spiritrivermuseum.com
Local history; open May-Sept., M-Su 10:00-5:00; call for winter hours.

***Spruce View:* Dickson Store Museum**
PO Box 146, Spruce View, AB T0M 1V0
Tel: 403-728-3355; Fax: 403-728-3351
dsms@pentnet.net
www.dicksonstoremuseum.com;
dicksonstoremuseum.blogspot.ca
A general store circa the 1930s, staffed by costumed interpreters who recreate the store's operations for visitors. Open May-Sept., M-Sa 10:00-5:30, Su 12:30-5:30

***Stettler:* Stettler Town & Country Museum**
PO Box 2118, 6304 - 44th Ave., Stettler, AB T0C 2L0
Tel: 403-742-4534
stcmuse@telus.net
Other contact information: Alternate Phone: 403-742-2461
A village replica housing artifacts from the local & surrounding areas; includes a courthouse, schools, church, CN station, pioneer homes & barns, agricultural items as well as a local sports museum; also an original Estonian Grist mill & log cabin of the early twenties constructed by early Estonian pioneers; situated on 10 acres in SW Stettler; open daily May-Sept. or by appt.
Wilda V. Gibbon, Curator
Karen Wahlund, Assistant

***Stony Plain:* Multicultural Heritage Centre**
PO Box 2188, 5411 - 51 St., Stony Plain, AB T7Z 1X7
Tel: 780-963-2777; Fax: 780-963-0233
info@multicentre.org
multicentre.org
twitter.com/MultiCentre
www.fac ebook.com/143010392428737
The Heritage Centre includes restored buildings including a 1925 high school, a settler's cabin, & a homestead's kitchen. This

living history museum offers entertainment & weekend demos. Open M-Sa 10:00-6:00, Su 10:00-6:30
Judy Unterschultz, Executive Director, judyu@multicentre.org

Stony Plain: Stony Plain & Parkland Pioneer Museum Society
5120 - 43 Ave., Stony Plain, AB T7Z 1L5
Tel: 780-963-1234; Fax: 780-968-5564
pioneermuseum@telus.net
Open April 1 - Oct. 31

Strome: Sodbuster Archives Museum
5029 - 50th St., Strome, AB T0B 4H0
Tel: 780-376-3688
Shows the development of the West & of the Strome & district community from 1900 to the 1950s

Sundre: Sundre Pioneer Village Museum
PO Box 314, 211, 1st Ave. SW, Sundre, AB T0M 1X0
Tel: 403-638-3233
sundremuseum@telus.net
www.museum.sundre.com
Located at 130 Centre St. South; open May-Sept.
Darleen Smee, Secretary

Taber: Taber Irrigation Impact Museum
4702 - 50 St., Taber, AB T1G 2B6
Tel: 403-223-5708; Fax: 403-223-0529
tiimchin@telusplanet.net
Open year-round, closed in Aug.

Thorhild: Thorhild Museum
Parent: Thorhild & District Historical Society
c/o Thorhild & District Municipal Library, PO Box 658, Thorhild, AB T0A 3A0
Tel: 780-398-3502; Fax: 780-398-3504
www.thorhildlibrary.ab.ca/Museum
Local history; housed in the town library; open year-round.

Three Hills: Knee Hill Historical Museum
PO Box 653, 1301-2nd St.N, Three Hills, AB T0M 2A0
Tel: 403-443-2092; Fax: 403-443-7941
khsmuseum@gmail.com
www.threehills.ca
Pioneer Museum & tourist information centre.

Three Hills: Kneehill Historical Museum
PO Box 653, 1301 - 2nd St. North, Three Hills, AB T0M 2A0
Tel: 403-443-2092; Fax: 403-443-7941
khsmuseum@gmail.com
www.unlockthepast.ca/places/Kneehill-Historical-Muse um_8285
Local history; collection housed in three historic buildings; open May-Sept., M-Sa 9:00-4:30, Su 1:00-4:30.

Tofield: Beaverhill Lake Nature Centre & Tofield Museum
PO Box 30, 5020 - 48th Ave., Tofield, AB T0B 4J0
Tel: 780-662-3269
Year Founded: 1985 The Beaverhill Lake Nature Centre presents information about Beaverhill Lake & its wildlife. The lake is a federally recognized bird sanctuary. Located in the Beaverhill Lake Nature Centre facility is the Tofield Museum. The museum features the history of the community since 1882. The Tofield Museum is open from mid-April to Labour Day. Appointments may be arranged at other times of the year.

Trochu: Trochu & District Museum
Parent: Trochu & District Historical Society
PO Box 538, 315 Arena Ave., Trochu, AB T0M 2C0
Tel: 403-442-2220
trochumuseum@gmail.com
www.town.trochu.ab.ca/culture-tourism/trochu-museum
Displays on the early pioneers including a kitchen, blacksmith shop, general store, schools, coal mining & an extensive collection of WW I & II pictures & uniforms; open May to Aug.
Bill Cunningham, President, willcunningham@persona.ca
Agnes Cunningham, Secretary, 403-442-2529

Two Hills: Two Hills & District Historical Museum
PO Box 566, 5910 - 51 St, Two Hills, AB T0B 4K0
Tel: 403-657-2461
Houses 4,000 artifacts pertaining to the area; collection of steamers, automobiles, farm equipment, farm tools, early household artifacts, buildings, railways caboose, etc.

Valhalla Centre: Melsness Mercantile Café & Museum
Parent: Valhalla Heritage Society
PO Box 52, Valhalla Centre, AB T0H 3M0
Tel: 780-356-3535
vhs@gpnet.ca
www.valhallaheritagesociety.ca
Provincial historic site; museum displays, deli café, gift shop
Emily Loberg, President

Vegreville: Vegreville Regional Museum
PO Box 328, Vegreville, AB T9C 1R3
Tel: 780-632-7650
museum@digitalweb.net
www.vegreville.com
Located on the site of the solonetzic soils research station of Agriculture Canada, The Vegreville Regional Museum depicts the history of Vegreville & its agricultural & business development. A special collection is The Right Honourable Donald Mazankowski, P.C. Collection. Mazankowski was the former Deputy Prime Minister of Canada. The regional museum also houses the Vegreville & District Sports Hall of Fame. The museum is open year-round.

Vermilion: Vermilion Heritage Museum
5310 - 50 Ave., Vermilion, AB T9X 1L1
Tel: 780-853-6211
History of Vermilion, AB; located in the forme S.R.P. Cooper School.

Viking: Viking Historical Museum
PO Box 270, 5108 - 61st Ave., Viking, AB T0B 4N0
Tel: 780-336-3066
Displays various facets of pioneer life; includes 1907 school, 1903 log store, 1938 church & 1919 farm house; open summer; May 15 - Thanksgiving

Vulcan: Vulcan & District Museum
Parent: Vulcan & District Historical Society
PO Box 401, 232 Centre St., Vulcan, AB T0L 2B0
Tel: 403-485-2768
www.vdhs.vulcancountyhistory.com
The museum's collection emphasizes agriculture, communications, medical history & education. Open July & Aug., Tu-Sa 10:00-12:00, 12:45-4:30.

Wainwright: Wainwright & District Museum
Parent: Battle River Historical Society
PO Box 2994, 1018 - 2nd Ave., Wainwright, AB T9W 1S9
Tel: 780-842-3115
Year Founded: 1984 Open year round
Billie Patterson

Wainwright: Wainwright Rail Park
Parent: Wainwright Railway Preservation Society
c/o Wainwright Railway Preservation Society, PO Box 2972, 4th Ave. South, Wainwright, AB T9W 1S8
Tel: 780-842-3138
info@railpark.org
www.railpark.org
www.facebook.com/ 131026620265329
The Society collects & preserves items relating to Canadian National Railways in the Wainwright area. The park is open May-Sept., 10:00-4:00.

Wanham: Grizzly Bear Prairie Museum
PO Box 68, Wanham, AB T0H 3P0
Tel: 780-694-3933
jesather@telusplanet.net
Several buildings including 1920s log house, Presbyterian church & storage building; displays of agricultural machinery & artifacts used by the pioneers of the area; forestry tower; forestry cabin containing schoolroom, toolroom & pioneer kitchen displays; 1920 era hiproof barn; CNR rail display: building to store two handcars; two handcars; various tools related to work on CNR
Stan Sather

Warner: Devil's Coulee Dinosaur Heritage Museum
PO Box 156, 300 County Rd., Warner, AB T0K 2L0
Tel: 403-642-2118; Fax: 403-642-3660
dinoegg@telusplanet.net
www.devilscoulee.com
Dinosaur eggs; local fossils; local history

Westlock: Canadian Tractor Museum
Parent: Westlock & District Tractor Museum Foundation
PO Box 5414, 9704 - 96 Ave., Westlock, AB T7P 2P5
Tel: 780-349-3353
canadiantractormuseum@telus.net
www.canadiantractormuseum.ca
Year Founded: 1999 The museum features over 200 restored antique tractors, as well as steam engines. The museum is open May-Sept., daily 10:00-5:00.

Westlock: Westlock Pioneer Museum
Parent: Westlock & District Historical Society
c/o Westlock & District Historical Society, PO Box 5806, 10216 - 100 St., Westlock, AB T7P 2P6
Tel: 780-349-4849Toll-Free: 866-349-4445
info@westlock.ca; westlockmuseum@yahoo.ca
westlockmuseum.com
Social Media: www.youtube.com/user/westlockmusem/videos
www.facebook.com/137525636273005
Other contact information: Off-Season Phone (Town of Westlock): 780-349-4444

Year Founded: 1962 Local history; open May-Sept.; off-season by appointment.

Wetaskiwin: Alberta Central Railway Museum
RR#2, Wetaskiwin, AB T9A 1W9
Tel: 780-352-2257; Fax: 780-352-3202
abcentral@incentre.net
www.abcentralrailway.com
Collection of early heavy weight cars from the passenger era, as well as fright equipment, cabooses, freight cars, and a snowplow. They also house the second oldest standing grain elevator in Alberta built by the Alberta Grain Company in 1906. Located southeast of Westaskiwin. Open from Victoria Day until Labour Day.
W.G. Wilson, Operations Manager
Ellen Wilson, Customer Services Manager

Wetaskiwin: Canada's Aviation Hall of Fame / Panthéon de l'Aviation du Canada
PO Box 6360, Hwy. 13, Wetaskiwin, AB T9A 2G1
Tel: 780-361-1351
cahf@telusplanet.net
www.cahf.ca
Year Founded: 1973 Canada's Aviation Hall of Fame collects, preserves, & exhibits material related to individuals & organizations that have made outstanding contributions to aviation & aerospace in Canada.
John Holding, Chair
Brian Fowler, Chair, Operations
Rosella Bjornson, Secretary-Treasurer

Wetaskiwin: Reynolds-Alberta Museum
PO Box 6360, 6426 - 40th Ave., Wetaskiwin, AB T9A 2G1
Tel: 780-361-1351; Fax: 780-361-1239
Toll-Free: 800-661-4726
reynoldsalbertamuseum@gov.ab.ca
www.history.alberta.ca /reynolds
Social Media: www.youtube.com/user/ReynoldsABMuseum
twitter.com/friendsofram
www.facebook.com/pages/Reynolds-Alberta-Museum/ 7542224425
Year Founded: 1992 The museum houses more than 5,000 artifacts, around 100 of which are on display. The collections are organized by the following themes: Transportation, Aviation, Agriculture, & Industry. The core collection of 1,500 items was donated by the late Stan Reynolds between 1982 & 1986, & continued to donate items until his death in 2012.
Dale Quinn, Volunteer Coordinator, dale.quinn@gov.ab.ca

Wetaskiwin: Wetaskiwin & District Heritage Museum
5007 - 50th Ave., Wetaskiwin, AB T9A 0S3
Tel: 780-352-0227; Fax: 780-352-0226
wdhm@persona.ca
www.wetaskiwinmuseum.com
twitter.com/HeritageMuseum1
www.facebook.com/156610574404392
Year Founded: 1986 The Wetaskiwin & District Heritage Museum presents the history of Westaskiwin, Alberta & the surrounding area, from dinosaur fossils, to First Nations' history, to the war years. Visitors can also learn about life on a Hutterite colony. A resource library is part of the museum. The museum is open year-round.
Sylvia Larson, President/CEO
Robert W. Reader, Curator/Manager
Elizabeth Harrison, Manager, Collections

Willingdon: Historic Village & Pioneer Museum at Shandro
PO Box 102, Willingdon, AB T0B 4R0
Tel: 780-367-2452
Other contact information: Alternate Phone: 780-367-2445
Ukrainian architecture & artifacts; open summer, other seasons by appt.

British Columbia

Provincial Museums

Museum of Anthropology
University of British Columbia, 6393 Marine Dr. NW, Vancouver, BC V6T 1Z2
Tel: 604-827-5932; Fax: 604-822-2974
info@moa.ubc.ca
www.moa.ubc.ca
Social Media: www.youtube.com/MUSEUMofANTHROPOLOGY
twitter.com/MOA_UBC
www.facebook. com/261008030084
Art & objects from around the world, with emphasis on First Nations cultures of the Northwest Coast; displayed in architect Arthur Erickson's award-winning building overlooking Howe Sound
Dr. Anthony A. Shelton, Director, anthony.shelton@ubc.ca

Museum of Vancouver (MOV)
1100 Chestnut St., Vancouver, BC V6J 3J9
Tel: 604-736-4431
guestservices@museumofvancouver.ca
www.museumofvancouver.ca
twitter.com/museumofvan
The Museum of Vancouver offers permanent displays, exhibitions, & educational programs about the human, cultural, & natural history of the city of Vancouver & the surrounding area. The Local History Lab & the Archaeology Education Centre contribute to the museum's school programs. The museum is open year-round.
Nancy Noble, Chief Executive Officer, 604-730-5323, nnoble@museumofvancouver.ca
Amanda Gibbs, Director, Audience Engagement, 604-730-5317, agibbs@museumofvancouver.ca
Joan Seidl, Director, Collections & Exhibitions, 604-730-5316, jseidl@museumofvancouver.ca
Viviane Gosselin, Curator, Contemporary Issues, 604-730-5318, vgosselin@museumofvancouver.ca
Wendy Nichols, Curator, Collections, 604-730-5312, wnichols@museumofvancouver.ca
Genny Krikorian, Officer, Marketing, 604-730-5309, gkrikorian@museumofvancouver.ca
Jane Lougheed, Officer, Education Program, 604-730-5307, jlougheed@museumofvancouver.ca

Royal BC Museum Corp.
675 Belleville St., Victoria, BC V8W 9W2
Tel: 250-356-7226; Fax: 250-387-5674
Toll-Free: 888-447-7977
reception@royalbcmuseum.bc.ca
www.royalbcmuseum.bc.ca
Founded in 1886, the RBCM specializes in the natural & human history of British Columbia
Pauline Rafferty, CEO
Grant Hughes, Director, Curatorial Services
Cynthia Wrate, Director, Marketing & Communications
Angela Williams, Director, Visitor & Human Resource Services
Gary Mitchell, Director, Access & Information Management
Faye Zinck, CFO

Local Museums in British Columbia

***108 Mile Ranch:* 108 Mile House Heritage Site & Museum**
100 Mile & District Historical Society, Hwy. 97, Box 225, 108 Mile Ranch, BC V0K 2Z0
Tel: 250-791-5288; Fax: 250-791-1947
historical@bcinternet.net
www.historical.bc.ca
Original 105 Mile Roadhouse along the Cariboo Gold Rush Trail, 10 other historical buildings including the largest log barn in Canada (circa 1908), also mill equipment display
Marianne Rutledge, Director

***108 Mile Ranch:* 108 Mile Ranch Heritage Site**
***Parent:* 100 Mile & District Historical Society**
PO Box 225, 108 Mile Ranch, BC V0K 2Z0
Tel: 250-791-5288; Fax: 250-791-1947
historical@bcinternet.net
www.historical.bc.ca/main.html
The 108 Mile Ranch Heritage Site comprises 11 historical buildings dating from the Gold Rush era; largest log barn in Canada; open May long weekend to Labour Day
Tom Rutledge, President

***Abbotsford:* Matsqui-Sumas-Abbotsford Museum - Trethewey House**
***Also known as:* MSA Museum**
***Parent:* MSA Museum Society**
2313 Ware St., Abbotsford, BC V2S 3C6
Tel: 604-853-0313; Fax: 866-373-2771
www.msamuseum.ca
Social Media: www.flickr.com/photos/msamuseum
twitter.com/MSAMuseum
Trethewey House was built in 1920 by B.C. timber baron, J.O. Trethewey & has been restored to period style, incuding its gardens and grounds. Also on site are the Playhouse & the Carriage House with the museum offices. Exhibits include an extensive collection of historical photographs of the region, in addition to an array of artifacts from local home life & businesses, particularly the lumber industry. Tours are available.
Cindy Boury, President, MSA Museum Society

***Agassiz:* Agassiz-Harrison Museum & Visitor Information Centre**
PO Box 313, 7011 Pioneer Ave., Agassiz, BC V0M 1A0
Tel: 604-796-3545
agassizharrisonmuseum@shawbiz.ca
www.agassizharrisonmuseum.org
www.facebook.com/110299242344218
Year Founded: 1986 The museum presents local & Canadian Pacific Railway history, & is housed in a CPR station, circa 1893. Hours of operation: M-Sa 10:00-4:00, Su 1:00-4:00; May-Oct. M-F 8:30-4:00.
Joan Vogstad, President
Judy Pickard, Museum Staff Contact, jpickard.ahmuseum@shawbiz.ca

***Ainsworth Hot Springs:* Silver Ledge Hotel Museum**
PO Box 1314, Ainsworth Hot Springs, BC V0G 1A0
Tel: 403-243-6302; Fax: 403-243-3672
silverledge@shaw.ca
www.members.shaw.ca/silverledge
Photographic history of the first community in the west Kootenays & the Ainsworth Mining District housed in the Silver Ledge Hotel built in 1896
J.E Duff, President, 604/221-7605

***Alert Bay:* Alert Bay Library & Museum**
PO Box 440, 118 Fir St., Alert Bay, BC V0N 1A0
Tel: 250-974-5721; Fax: 250-974-5026
abplb@island.net
www.alertbay.bclibrary.ca; www.alertbay.ca
Ethnographic material; artifacts related to the fishing industry, local history; gift shop
Joyce Wilby, Head Librarian/Archivist

***Alert Bay:* U'mista Cultural Centre**
***Parent:* U'mista Cultural Society**
c/o U'mista Cultural Society, PO Box 253, #1 Front St., Alert Bay, BC V0N 1A0
Tel: 250-974-5403; Fax: 250-974-5499
Toll-Free: 800-690-8222
info@umista.org
www.umista.org
Kwakwaka'wakw masks depicting the Potlatch ceremony; traditional & contemporary arts & crafts

***Armstrong:* Armstrong Spallumcheen Museum & Arts Society**
PO Box 308, 3415 Pleasant Valley Rd., Armstrong, BC V0E 1B0
Tel: 250-546-8318
www.asmas.ca
Other contact information: asmas@telus.net
Year Founded: 1974 The Armstrong Spallumcheen Museum and Arts Society features a museum, archives, & an art gallery. Visitors are educated about the history of the local region. Genealogy & art workshops are conducted.

***Ashcroft:* Ashcroft Museum & Archives**
PO Box 129, Ashcroft, BC V0K 1A0
Tel: 250-453-9161; Fax: 250-453-9664
admin@village.ashcroft.bc.ca
www.village.ashcroft.bc.ca
Year Founded: 1935 History of the Southern Cariboo region, & the farming & ranching communities of Hat Creek Valley. Open 5 days a week, Apr.-Nov.; open 7 days a week July & Aug. Admission by donation. Located at the corner of Brink & Fourth streets in Ashcroft.
Kathy Paulos, Curator

***Atlin:* Atlin Historical Museum (AHS)**
***Also known as:* Atlin Historical Society**
PO Box 111, Atlin, BC V0W 1A0
Tel: 250-651-7522; Fax: 250-651-7522
heritage@atlin.net
Open May 15 - Labour Day. Closed on Mondays.

***Bamfield:* Bamfield Community Museum & Archive**
***Parent:* Bamfield Community School Association**
240 Nuthatch Rd., Bamfield, BC V0R 1B0
Tel: 250-728-1220; Fax: 250-728-1220
bcsa.ct@gmail.com
bamfieldcommunity.ca
Local history; collection built from community donations; open M-F 9:00-4:30.
Louis Druehl, Chair
Steve Clarke, Collection Volunteer
Heather Cooper, Cataloguing Volunteer

***Barkerville:* Barkerville Historic Town**
***Parent:* Barkerville Heritage Trust**
PO Box 19, Barkerville, BC V0K 1B0
Tel: 250-994-3332; Fax: 250-994-3435
Toll-Free: 888-994-3332
barkerville@barkerville.ca
www.barkerville.ca
twitte r.com/BarkervilleBC
Other contact information: Info Email: barkerville@gems8.gov.bc.ca
Restored Cariboo Gold Rush town; Blessing's Grave; Richfield Court House; open year round; peak season from early May to late Sept.
Sue Morhun, Chair
Dirk Van Stralen, Media Contact, dirk.vanstralen@barkerville.ca
Reuben Berlin, Manager, Operations

***Barriere:* North Thompson Museum**
***Parent:* Barriere & District Heritage Society**
PO Box 228, 352 Lilley Rd., Barriere, BC V0E 1E0
Tel: 250-672-5583; Fax: 250-672-9501
Year Founded: 1987 Local history; open seasonally.
Shirley Kristensen, Vice-President

***Bella Coola:* Bella Coola Museum**
PO Box 726, 269 Hwy. 20, Bella Coola, BC V0T 1C0
Tel: 250-799-5767
info@bellacoolamuseum.ca
www.bellacoolamuseum.ca
Other contact information: Phone, Archives: 250-982-2130
Year Founded: 1963 Owned & operated by the Bella Coola Valley Museum Society, the Bella Coola Valley Museum depicts the human history of the Bella Coola Valley. Exhibits present the history of the area from European contact to 1955. The museum's historic building is open from June to September. School presentations can be arranged at other times of the year. The British Columbia Central Coast Archives is open year-round, from Tuesday to Thursday.
Wendy Kingsley, Manager

***Bowen Island:* Bowen Island Museum & Archives**
PO Box 97, 1014 Miller Rd., Bowen Island, BC V0N 1G0
Tel: 604-947-2655
bihistorians@telus.net
bowenhistory.ca
Year Founded: 1967 Local history displayed through two exhibits & the archival collection. Open daily in the summer, Su-M 10:00-4:00, Tu-Sa 10:00-4:30, & by appointment.

***Bralorne:* Bralorne Pioneer Museum**
PO Box 40, 400 Hawkes Ave., Bralorne, BC V0K 1P0
Tel: 250-238-2349; Fax: 250-238-2349
bralornepioneermuseum@gmail.com
Year Founded: 1977 Bralorne Pioneer Museum depicts the history of a community which is known as the home of the Bralorne Mine, a productive gold mine during the gold mining era. Mining artifacts are part of the museum's collection, as well as general historical information about the local Bridge River Valley area. The museum is situated in the industrial education shop of the Bralorne High School. It is open during the summer & on weekends.

***Britannia Beach:* British Columbia Museum of Mining**
PO Box 188, Britannia Beach, BC V0N 1J0
Tel: 604-896-2233; Fax: 604-896-2260
Toll-Free: 800-896-4044
general@bcmuseumofmining.org
www.bcmuseumofmining.org
Year Founded: 1971 Governed by the Britannia Beach Historical Society, the British Columbia Museum of Mining preserves the material & social history of mining in British Columbia.
Mark Germyn, President, Britannia Beach Historical Society, mark@bcmuseumofmining.org
Kirsten Clausen, Executive Director, kclausen@bcmuseumofmining.org
Diane Mitchell, Curator, Education & Collections, diane@bcmuseumofmining.org
Henry Gottardi, Site Manager & Coordinator, Filming, henry@bcmuseumofmining.org
Carol Watts, Manager, Visitor Services, Retail Operations, & Tour Buses, carol@bcmuseumofmining.org
Katherine Flett, Director, Marketing, 604-924-5542
Robin MacDonald, Coordinator, Bookings & Communications, robin@bcmuseumofmining.org
Rory Odenbach, Coordinator, Programmes & Head Tour Guide, rory@bcmuseumofmining.org

***Burnaby:* Burnaby Village Museum & Carousel**
6501 Deer Lake Ave., Burnaby, BC V5G 3T6
Tel: 604-297-4565; Fax: 604-297-4557
bvm@burnaby.ca
www.burnabyvillagemuseum.ca
twitter.com/bbyvillage
ww w.facebook.com/BurnabyVillageMuseum
Other contact information: Phone, Schools: 604-297-4558; Phone, Rentals: 604-297-4552
The Burnaby Village Museum consists of heritage & replica buildings from the 1920s, such as a blacksmith shop, a general store, a print shop, a farmhouse, a restored interurban tram & a carousel.
Lisa Codd, Curator
Elisabeth Czerwinski, Conservator
Sanya Pleshakov, Coordinator, Museum Programs
Nancy Stagg, Coordinator, Marketing & Sponsorship

***Burnaby:* Canadiana Costume Society of British Columbia & Western Canada**
6501 Deer Lake Ave., Burnaby, BC V5G 3T6
Tel: 604-293-6520; Fax: 604-293-6525
www.canadianacostumesociety.ca

Year Founded: 1976 The Canadiana Costume Society of British Columbia & Western Canada collects, conserves, researches, & displays British Columbia's costume heritage. The collection dates from the late 1700s to the 1980s. The Society's members create displays & provide lectures.

***Burnaby:* Nikkei National Museum & Cultural Centre (NNMCC)**
6688 Southoaks Cres., Burnaby, BC V5E 4M7
Tel: 604-777-7000
info@nikkeiplace.org
centre.nikkeiplace.org
Social Media: www.youtube.com/user/nikkeimuse
twitter.com/nikkeimuse
www.facebook.co m/NNMCC
Year Founded: 2000 The complex houses a Japanese-Canadian cultural centre, the museum, a community centre, & a Japanese-Canadian garden. Centre hours: Tu-F 10:00-9:30, Sa 9:00-4:30; Museum hours: Tu-Sa 11:00-5:00.
Mitsuo Hayashi, Chair
Cathy Makihara, Co-President
Craig Natsuhara, Co-President
Miko Hoffman, Executive Director, mhoffman@nikkeiplace.org
Beth Carter, Director/Curator, bcarter@nikkeiplace.org

***Burnaby:* Simon Fraser University Museum of Archaeology & Ethnology**
c/o Dept. of Archaeology, Simon Fraser University, 8888 University Dr., Burnaby, BC V5A 1S6
Tel: 604-291-3325
www.sfu.museum
Major emphasis on the Pacific Northwest coast; open year round

Dr. Barbara J. Winter, Curator, bwinter@sfu.ca

***Burns Lake:* Lakes District Museum Society**
PO Box 266, Burns Lake, BC V0J 1E0
Tel: 250-692-7450
Year Founded: 1978 Artifacts, archival records, & historical reference material relation to the Lakes District of northwestern B.C., including Burns Lake, Palling, Francois Lake, Babine Lake, Ootsa Lake, & Tweedsmuir Provinvial Park. Includes interviews with early settlers (& descendants) in the Lakes District.

***Cache Creek:* Historic Hat Creek Ranch**
PO Box 878, Junction Hwy. 97-99, Cache Creek, BC V0K 1H0

Tel: 250-457-9722; Fax: 250-457-9311
Toll-Free: 800-782-0922
contact@hatcreekranch.com
www.hatcreekranch.com
Year Founded: 1984 Offering a blend of cultures, on site are an 1860 roadhouse with gold rush era artifacts and a traditional kekuli, or pit house, used as a winter home by people of the Shuswap Nation. Costumed guides explain the life of area's history & culture and visitors can experience firsthand a stagecoach ride. Other activities include gold panning and archery. There are a gift shop, food services, as well as cabins & campground facilities. Open daily, May to Sept.
Mr. Ken Mather, General Manager, kenm@hatcreekranch.com

***Campbell River:* Campbell River Maritime Heritage Centre**
***Parent:* Maritime Heritage Society**
PO Box 483, 621 Island Hwy., Campbell River, BC V9W 5C1
Tel: 250-286-3161; Fax: 250-286-3162
www.maritimeheritagecentre.ca
www.facebook.com/221432144123
Year Founded: 1998 The Maritime Heritage Centre seeks to educate visitors about the mhistory of the Campbell River area, & to preserve marine documents & artifacts. Open M-F 12:00-3:00.
Marv Everett, President
Vic Andersen, Director, Exhibits & Maintenance
Jim Best, Director, Education & Advertising & Promotion

***Campbell River:* Haig-Brown Heritage House**
***Parent:* Museum at Campbell River**
2250 Campbell River Rd., Campbell River, BC V9W 4N7
Tel: 250-286-6646; Fax: 250-286-0109
haig.brown@crmuseum.ca
www.haig-brown.bc.ca; haig-brownhouse.blogspot.ca
Operated by the Museum at Campbell River, the Haig-Brown House is a historic building that offers bed & breakfast accomodation, & can be rented for private functions.

***Campbell River:* Museum at Campbell River (MCR)**
***Also known as:* Campbell River Museum & Archives**
PO Box 70 A, 470 Island Hwy., Campbell River, BC V9W 4Z9
Tel: 250-287-3103; Fax: 250-286-0109
general.inquiries@crmuseum.ca
www.crmuseum.ca
Year Founded: 1958 Exhibits include First Nations ceremonial masks & regalia, coastal logging, fishing history & settler development; archives & research centre; gift shop
Lesia Davis, Executive Director, lesia.davis@crmuseum.ca

***Castlegar:* Castlegar & District Heritage Society**
400 - 13th Ave., Castlegar, BC V1N 1G2
Tel: 250-365-6440
www.stationmuseum.ca/museum/
The Society operates the CPR Museum, housed in a 99 year old station, & Zuckerberg Island park; newspaper archives; gift shop featuring local artisans; special events & programming.

***Chase:* Chase & District Museum & Archives Society**
PO Box 160, 400 Shuswap Ave., Chase, BC V0E 1M0
Tel: 250-679-8847
info@chasemuseum.ca
www.chasemuseum.ca
www.facebook.com/125651564125503
Year Founded: 1984 The museum at 1042 Shuswap Ave. is temporarily closed due to fire damage, but a temporary office has been set up at 400 Shuswap Ave. in the meantime.

***Chemainus:* Chemainus Valley Museum**
***Parent:* Chemainus Valley Historical Society**
c/o Chemainus Valley Historical Society, PO Box 172, 9799 Water Wheel Cres., Chemainus, BC V0R 1K0
Tel: 250-246-2445
www.chemainusvalleymuseum.ca
Local history; Hours of operation: summer, daily 9:00-4:00; winter, daily 10:00-3:00

***Chetwynd:* Little Prairie Heritage Museum**
***Parent:* Little Prairie Heritage Society**
PO Box 1777, Chetwynd, BC V0C 1J0
Tel: 250-788-3358
Open July & Aug.
Shirley Weeks, President

***Chilliwack:* Chilliwack Museum & Archives**
45820 Spadina Ave., Chilliwack, BC V2P 1T3
Tel: 604-795-5210; Fax: 604-795-5291
info@chiliwackmuseum.ca
www.chilliwackmuseum.ca
Year Founded: 1958 The Archives are located at 9291 Corbould St. in Chilliwack, phone 604-795-9255; newspapers, photographs, books, DVDs, maps relating to the flood history of Chilliwack; special exhibits; programming; gift shop; open year round. Hours: M-F 9:00-4:30
Ron Denman, Director
Brenda Paterson, Education Co-ordinator
Paul Ferguson, Manager, Heritage Collections

***Clearbrook:* Fraser Valley Antique Farm Machinery Association**
PO Box 2234, Clearbrook, BC V2T 3X8
Tel: 604-856-4571
johnbateman@telus.net
To collect & restore to working condition antique farm & household machinery; displays annually at Agrifair; visitors welcome to building any time of year; call for appt.
Phil Chapman, President

***Clinton:* Clinton Museum**
***Also known as:* South Cariboo Historical Museum**
***Parent:* South Cariboo Historical Museum Society**
PO Box 217, 1419 Cariboo Hwy., Clinton, BC V0K 1K0
Tel: 250-459-2442; Fax: 250-459-0058
clintonmuseum@telus.net
Other contact information: Clinton Village Office Phone: 250-459-2261
Open daily June - Sept.

***Comox:* Comox Archives & Museum Society**
1729 Comox Ave., Comox, BC V9M 3M2
Tel: 250-339-2885
comoxmuseum@shaw.ca
www.comoxmuseum.ca
Local history; open W-Sa 1:00-4:00.

***Comox:* Filberg Heritage Lodge & Park**
***Parent:* Filberg Heritage Lodge & Park Association**
c/o Filberg Heritage Lodge & Park Association, 61 Filberg Rd., Comox, BC V9M 2S7
Tel: 250-339-2715; Fax: 250-339-2750
filberg.com
www.facebook.com/FHLPA
The park features nine acres of landscaped grounds, on which sit a number of heritage buildings. Former Comox Logging Company President Robert Filberg once owned the land.
Mo MacKendrick, Chair
Eden Lindsay-Bodie, Administrator

***Coquitlam:* Mackin House Museum**
***Parent:* Coquitlam Heritage Society**
1116 Brunette Ave., Coquitlam, BC V3K 1G3
Tel: 604-516-6151
info@coquitlamheritage.ca
www.coquitlamheritage.ca
www.facebook.com/mackin.house
An historic house that serves as a museum, tourist information stop, & administrative offices for the Coquitlam Heritage Society. Open year-round, Tu-F 11:00-5:00, Sa 12:00-4:00.
Hazel Postma, Chair, postmah@douglas.bc.ca
Jill Cook, Executive Director, jcook@coquitlamheritage.ca
Sandra Martins, Collections Manager, collections@coquitlamheritage.ca

***Courtenay:* Courtenay & District Museum & Palaeontology Centre**
207 - 4th St., Courtenay, BC V9N 1G7
Tel: 250-334-0686; Fax: 250-338-0619
museum@island.net
www.courtenaymuseum.ca
Includes archives; open year round
Deborah Griffiths, Curator

***Cowichan Bay:* Cowichan Bay Maritime Centre**
***Parent:* Cowichan Wooden Boat Society**
PO Box 22, 1761 Cowichan Bay Rd., Cowichan Bay, BC V0R 1NO
Tel: 250-746-4955
cwbs@classicboats.org
www.classicboats.org
Exhibits housed in unique pods designed to reflect the surrounding landspace & reveal the rich maritime history of Cowichan Bay; offers classic wooden boat building programs & undertakes restoration projects; open daily
Dave Knott, President
Suzan Lagrove, Executive Director

***Cranbrook:* Aasland Museum Taxidermy**
2200 Kimberley Hwy. NE, Cranbrook, BC V1C 4H4
Tel: 250-426-3566
Small natural history museum displaying mounted birds & animals for the public; admission free; a lecture accompanies the visit if prior arrangements are made; school groups, handicapped, adult groups & individual visitors welcome; Mon.-Sat.
Odd Aasland, Director

***Cranbrook:* Canadian Museum of Rail Travel**
***Also known as:* The Cranbrook Archives, Museum & Landmark Foundation**
PO Box 400, 57 Van Horne St. South, Cranbrook, BC V1C 4H9
Tel: 250-489-3918; Fax: 250-489-5744
mail@trainsdeluxe.com
www.trainsdeluxe.com
The Canadian Museum of Rail Travel depicts the story of rail travel in Canada, through the collection, restoration, & display of historic rail equipment from various eras. The museum features a large historic railcar collection. Other sights at the museum include the Royal Alexandra Hall, which was the former cafe from the Canadian Pacific Railway's 1906 Royal Alexandra Hotel in Winnipeg, an 1898 railway freight shed, & a wooden railway water tower.
Garry W. Anderson, Executive Director
Brian Dees, Office Manager

***Creston:* Creston & District Museum**
***Also known as:* Stone House Museum**
219 Devon St., Creston, BC V0B 1G3
Tel: 250-428-9262
mail@creston.museum.bc.ca
www.creston.museum.bc.ca
twitter.com/CrestonMuseum
www.facebook.com/Cr estonMuseum
Guided tours, permanent & temporary exhibits; open spring, summer, fall; in winter by appt.
Ian Currie, President

***Crofton:* Old Crofton School Museum Society**
PO Box 49, 1507 Joan St., Crofton, BC V0R 1R0
Tel: 250-246-2456
History of old schools, Crofton & area; open June-Sept.
Pat Montgomery, President

***Cumberland:* Cumberland Museum & Archives**
***Also known as:* Cumberland & District Historical Society**
PO Box 258, 2680 Dunsmuir Ave., Cumberland, BC V0R 1S0
Tel: 250-336-2445; Fax: 250-336-2321
info@cumberland.museum.bc.ca
www.museum.bc.ca/cma
Open year round

***Dawson Creek:* Dawson Creek Station Museum**
***Parent:* South Peace Historical Society**
900 Alaska Ave., Dawson Creek, BC V1G 4T6
Tel: 250-782-9595; Fax: 250-782-9538
frontoffice@tourismdawsoncreek.com
www.pris.bc.ca/dcsm
Two galleries, the Northern Alberta Railway & the Natural History Gallery. Open year round
Dan Bastiansen, President, 250-782-5408, museum@pris.ca

Dawson Creek: **Walter Wright Pioneer Village & Sudeten Hall**
1901 Alaska Hwy., Dawson Creek, BC V1G 1P7
Tel: 250-782-7144
info@tourismdawsoncreek.com
www.dawsoncreek.ca/life/recreation/walter.asp
The Walter Wright Pioneer Village presents life in Dawson Creek, before the construction of the Alaska Highway. Historic buildings include the Pouce Coupe School, the W.O. Harper General Store, & the St. Paul's Anglican Church. The Sudeten Hall honours Germany's Sudeten people who arrived in the area in 1939.

Delta: **Delta Museum & Archives**
4858 Delta St., Delta, BC V4K 2T8
Tel: 604-946-9322; Fax: 604-946-5791
info@deltamuseum.ca
www.deltamuseum.ca
www.facebook.com/DeltaMuseumAnd ArchivesSociety
1912 heritage building; archives; exhibitions on pioneer homelife, village life, farming, fishing, duck decoys, First Nations archeology, basketry
Mark Sakai, Executive Director, msakai@deltamuseum.ca
Darryl MacKenzie, Curator, dmackenzie@deltamuseum.ca
Carol Ballard, Program Coordinator, cballard@deltamuseum.ca
Brenda Richmond, Archivist, brichmond@deltamuseum.ca

Denman Island: **Denman Island Museum**
PO Box 28, Denman Island, BC V0R 1T0
Tel: 250-335-0880
Collection houses NW Coast artifacts from the Salish; natural history specimens; European settlement items; photographs & maps

Duncan: **British Columbia Forest Discovery Centre**
2892 Drinkwater Rd., Duncan, BC V9L 6C2
Tel: 250-715-1113; Fax: 250-715-1170
info.bcfdc@shawlink.ca
www.discoveryforest.com
twitter.com/forestmuseu m
www.facebook.com/112291022115893
The BC Forest Discovery Centre is a 100-acre, open air museum, which features forest & marsh trails, logging artifacts, & heritage buildings.
Vicki Holman, Manager
Jennifer Manuel, Curator/Coordinator, Education Programs

Duncan: **Cowichan Valley Museum**
PO Box 1014, Duncan, BC V9L 3Y2
Tel: 250-746-6612
cvmuseum.archives@shaw.ca
www.cowichanvalleymuseum.bc.ca
Local history museum; includes archives; open year round

Duncan: **Fairbridge Chapel Heritage Society**
4791 Fairbridge Dr., Duncan, BC V9L 6N9
Tel: 250-746-7519
fairbridgechapel.com
Year Founded: 1987 The Society protects & maintains the Fairbridge Chapel, a provincial heritage site, & provides guided tours on request.
Karen Laurie, President
Ron Smith, Secretary-Treasurer, rgwsmiths@hotmail.com

Enderby: **Enderby & District Museum Society**
901 George St., Enderby, BC V0E 1V0
Tel: 250-838-7170; Fax: 250-838-9641
edms@jetstream.net
www.enderbymuseum.ca
www.facebook.com/enderbymuseum
Year Founded: 1973 Winter Hours: Tu-Su 12:00pm-4:00pm; Summer Hours: Tu-Sa 10:00am-4:00pm
Joan Cowan, Curator, 250-838-7171

Fernie: **Fernie & District Historical Society Museum**
PO Box 1527, 491 Victoria Ave., Fernie, BC V0B 1M0
Tel: 250-423-7016
www.ferniemuseum.com
Coal mining history museum; local history & early families research

Fort Langley: **British Columbia Farm Machinery & Agricultural Museum Association**
PO Box 279, 9131 King St., Fort Langley, BC V1M 2R6
Tel: 604-888-2273
bcfm@telus.net
www.bcfma.com
British Columbia Farm Machinery & Agricultural Museum Association presents the history of farming in British Columbia. Displays include horse drawn carriages & wagons, steam, gas & diesel powered grinders & tractors, an 1890s sawmill, a blacksmith shop, & British Columbia's first crop duster, the Tiger Moth airplane. The museum is open seven days a week from April 1st to Thanksgiving Day.

Fort Langley: **Fort Langley National Historic Site of Canada (FLNHSC) / Lieu historique national du Canada Fort-Langley**
PO Box 129, 23433 Mavis Ave., Fort Langley, BC V1M 2R5
Tel: 604-513-4777; Fax: 604-513-4798
fort.langley@pc.gc.ca
www.pc.gc.ca/lhn-nhs/bc/langley.aspx
www.faceboo k.com/FortLangleyNHS
Birthplace of British Columbia; 19th century Hudson's Bay Co. trading post; Open year round
Steve Langdon, Superintendent, Coastal BC Field Unit, Parks Canada

Fort Langley: **Langley Centennial Museum & National Exhibition Centre**
PO Box 800, 9135 King St., Fort Langley, BC V1M 2S2
Tel: 604-532-3536; Fax: 604-888-7291
information@langleymuseum.org
www.langleymuseum.org
Art, history & science exhibits; open year round
Peter Tulumello, Manager, Cultural Services, ptulumello@tol.ca
Jane Lemke, Interim Curator, jlemke@tol.ca

Fort Nelson: **Fort Nelson Heritage Museum**
PO Box 716, Fort Nelson, BC V0C 1R0
Tel: 250-774-3536
info@fortnelsonmuseum.ca
www.fortnelsonmuseum.ca
Artifacts related to the construction of the Alaska Highway; open mid-May - mid-Sept.
Marlin Brown, Curator

Fort St. James: **Fort St. James National Historic Site of Canada**
280 Kwah Rd. West, Fort St. James, BC V0J 1P0
Tel: 250-996-7191; Fax: 250-996-8566
bob_grill@pch.gc.ca
The Fort St James National Historic Site offers the largest collection of original wooden buildings, representing the fur trade in Canada. The following buildings are located at the site: Fur WareHouse (1888-1889); Fish cache (1889); Men's House (1884); Trade Store & Office (1884); Murray House (1883-1884); Dairy (1884); & Wharf & Tramway (1894-1914). The Historic Site is open daily from 9:00 to 5:00, from the long weekend in May to the end of September.
Alan Latourelle, Chief Officer

Fort St John: **Fort St. John-North Peace Museum**
9323 - 100 St., Fort St John, BC V1J 4N4
Tel: 250-787-0430
fsjnpmuseum@fsjmail.com; fsjmarchives@fsjmail.com
www.fsjmuseum.com
www.facebook.com/1027130598 06910
Hours: Open year round, M-Sa 9:00-5:00
Larry Evans, President
Heather Longworth, Curator

Fort Steele: **Fort Steele Heritage Town**
9851 Hwy. 93/95, Fort Steele, BC V0B 1N0
Tel: 250-417-6000; Fax: 250-489-2624
info@FortSteele.bc.ca
www.fortsteele.ca
twitter.com/fortsteele
www.f acebook.com/fortsteeleheritagetown
Other contact information: 24-Hour Info Line: 250-426-7352
Restored 1890s mining boom town of the East Kootenay; open year round with varying program levels each season, call for details
Nikki Bose, Assistant Curator, nikki.bose@fortsteele.bc.ca

Fraser Lake: **Fraser Lake Museum**
PO Box 430, Fraser Lake, BC V0J 1S0
Tel: 250-699-6257; Fax: 250-699-6469
village@fraserlake.ca
Open summer
Donna Ward, Clerk/Treas.

Gabriola Island: **Gabriola Museum**
Parent: **Gabriola Historical & Museum Society**
PO Box 213, 505 South Rd., Gabriola Island, BC V0R 1X0
Tel: 250-247-9987
info@gabriolamuseum.org
www.gabriolamuseum.org
Year Founded: 1996 Through its museum, the Historical Society presents the history of the island through displays, exhibits, lectures, presentations, & tours.
Connie Clifford, President
Janet Stobbs, Director/Archivist

Gibsons: **Sunshine Coast Museum & Archives**
PO Box 766, 716 Winn Rd., Gibsons, BC V0N 1V0
Tel: 604-886-8232; Fax: 604-886-8232
scm_a@dccnet.com
www.sunshinecoastmuseum.ca
Collection of historical documents & artifacts pertaining to the Sunshine Coast of BC; open year round; closed Sun. & Mon.

Golden: **Golden & District Museum**
Also known as: **Golden Museum & Archives**
PO Box 992, 1302 - 11 Ave., Golden, BC V0A 1H0
Tel: 250-344-5169; Fax: 250-344-5169
museum.golden@gmail.com
www.goldenbcmuseum.com
www.facebook.com/150197 378373720
Year Founded: 1974 Open May-Sept.
Colleen Palumbo, Executive Director

Grand Forks: **Boundary Museum**
Boundary Museum Society, PO Box 817, 6145 Reservoir Rd., Grand Forks, BC V0H 1H0
Tel: 250-442-3737; Fax: 250-442-3737
boundarymuse@shaw.ca
www.boundarymuseum.com
The Boundary Museum is situated in a former schoolhouse, which was built in 1929 by the Christian Communities of Universal Brotherhood Doukhobors. The grounds of the restored schoolhouse feature a fruit drying facility & a bread oven which were also built by the society.

Grand Forks: **Mountain View Doukhobor Museum**
PO Box 1235, 3655 Hardy Mountain Rd., Grand Forks, BC V0H 1H0
Tel: 250-442-8855

Granisle: **Granisle Museum & Information Centre**
PO Box 128, Babine Dr., Granisle, BC V0J 1W0
Tel: 250-697-2428; Fax: 250-697-2568
Other contact information: Alternate Phone: 250-847-5322
The log house museum contains artifacts from pioneer days & earlier. Open May-Sept., daily 9:00-5:00.

Greenwood: **Greenwood Museum & Visitor Centre**
PO Box 399, 214 South Copper St., Greenwood, BC V0H 1J0
Tel: 250-445-6355
www.greenwoodmuseum.com
Year Founded: 1967 Mining, forestry, ranching & the internment of Japanese Canadians; Greenwood was an internment camp during WW II

Groundbirch: **Bruce Groner Museum**
PO Box 124, Groundbirch, BC V0C 1T0
Open summer

Harrison Mills: **Kilby Historic Site**
PO Box 55, 215 Kilby Rd., Harrison Mills, BC V0M 1L0
Tel: 604-796-9576; Fax: 604-796-9592
info@kilby.ca
www.kilby.ca
Other contact information: Administration Phone: 604-796-0414
Open daily May-Sept. 11-5, then seasonal hours
Bev Kennedy, Curator, bkennedy@kilby.ca

Hazelton: **'Ksan Historical Village & Museum**
PO Box 326, Hazelton, BC V0J 1Y0
Tel: 250-842-5544; Fax: 250-842-6533
Toll-Free: 877-842-5518
ksan@ksan.org
www.ksan.org
Replica Gitxkan Indian Village; museum has approx. 600 items on display, including ceremonial artifacts, hunting and fishing tools, masks and shaman's regalia; open year round

Hazelton: **Hazelton Pioneer Museum & Archives**
PO Box 323, 4255 Government St., Hazelton, BC V0J 1Y0
Tel: 250-842-5961; Fax: 250-842-2176
hazlib@bulkley.net
hazelton.bclibrary.ca/services
The museum is located in the Hazelton District Public Library, & houses artifacts pertaining to local history.

Hope: **Hope Museum**
PO Box 370, 919 Water Ave., Hope, BC V0X 1L0
Tel: 604-869-7322; Fax: 604-869-2160
Toll-Free: 866-467-3842
destinationhope@telus.net
Open summer; off-season tours by request
Inge Wilson, Manager

Horsefly: **Jack Lynn Memorial Museum**
c/o Horsefly Historical Society, PO Box 11, Boswell St., Horsefly, BC V0L 1L0
Tel: 250-620-3440
Open daily July to Aug. anually; Sept. to June by appointment only; small museum run by volunteers; features artifacts, photos & paper archives, all relating to Horsefly

Hudson's Hope: **Hudson's Hope Museum & Historical Society**
PO Box 98, 9510 Beattie Dr., Hudson's Hope, BC V0C 1V0
Tel: 250-783-5735
hhmuseum@gmail.com; hhmuseum@pris.ca
www.hudsonshopemuseum.com
twitter.com/hhmuseum
www. facebook.com/124162084280248
Hudson's Bay Company store of 1942; archives; fossil collection; Aboriginal display; North West & Hudson's Bay Company artifacts; North West Mounted Police, trapping, coal mining, gold mining, pioneer, logging & World War memorabilia & photographic history of W.A.C. Bennett dam
Elinor Morrissey, Manager

Invermere: **Windermere Valley Museum & Archives**
PO Box 2315, 222 - 6th Ave., Invermere, BC V0A 1K0
Tel: 250-342-9769
wvmuseum@cyberlink.bc.ca
www.windermerevalleymuseum.ca
Open Mon. - Fri. June & Sept.; Tue.-Sat. July & Aug.; Oct. - May by appt.
Margaret Christensen, President
J.D. Jeffery, Curator

Kamloops: **Kamloops Museum & Archives**
207 Seymour St., Kamloops, BC V2C 2E7
Tel: 250-828-3576; Fax: 250-828-3760
museum@kamloops.ca
www.kamloops.ca/museum
Open year round

Kamloops: **Rocky Mountain Rangers Museum & Archives**
J.R. Vicars Armoury, PO Box 3250, 1221 McGill Rd., Kamloops, BC V2C 6K7
Tel: 250-851-4890; Fax: 250-851-4891

Kamloops: **Secwepemc Museum & Heritage Park (SCES)**
Parent: **Secwepemc Cultural Education Society**
#311, 355 Yellowhead Hwy., Kamloops, BC V2H 1H1
Tel: 250-828-9749; Fax: 250-372-8833
www.secwepemc.org/museum
Museum is located on 12 acres & exhibits artifacts, photographs & histories of the Secwepemc people; displays include canoes, hunting & fishing objects, clothing, games; the Heritage Park complements the Museum with outdoor displays & reconstructed winter pit houses. lean-tos, smoke house & traditional plant foods; trails, gardens; giftshop (seasonal); museum open year round
Daniel Saul, Museum Manager, dsaul@kib.ca

Kaslo: **Kaslo Village Hall**
PO Box 576, 312 - 4th St., Kaslo, BC V0G 1M0
Tel: 250-353-2311; Fax: 250-353-7767
village@netidea.com
www.kaslo.ca
One of only two wooden municipal buildings left in Canada still used as a seat of government; designated National Historic Site; open Mon. - Fri.
Rae Sawyer, CAO, kasloclerk@netidea.com

Kaslo: **S.S. Moyie National Historic Site**
Parent: **Kootenay Lake Historical Society**
PO Box 537, Kaslo, BC V0G 1M0
Tel: 250-353-2525
ssmoyie@klhs.bc.ca
www.klhs.bc.ca
www.facebook.com/s smoyie.sternwheeler
Moored in the town of Kaslo, this is the oldest intact passenger sternwheeler in the world; gift shop; operated by the Kootenay Lake Historical Society; open daily mid-May to mid-Oct.
Bill Yeo, President

Kelowna: **Benvoulin Heritage Park & Benvoulin Heritage Church**
c/o Central Okanagan Heritage Society, 1060 Cameron Ave., Kelowna, BC V1Y 8V3
Tel: 250-861-7188; Fax: 250-868-1392
cohs@telus.net
www.okheritagesociety.com
Located at 2279 Benvoulin Road in Kelowna, the Benvoulin Church was built in 1892 in the Gothic Revival style. The pioneer church was restored by the Central Okanagan Heritage Society, which owns & operates Benvoulin Heritage Park.
Janice Henry, Executive Director, Central Okanagan Heritage Society

Kelowna: **British Columbia Orchard Industry Museum**
Parent: **Kelowna Museums**
1304 Ellis St., Kelowna, BC V1Y 1Z8
Tel: 250-478-0347
orchard@kelownamuseums.ca
www.kelownamuseums.ca/museums/the-bc-orchard-industry-museum
Year Founded: 1989 The BC Orchard Industry Museum is located in the historic, restored Laurel Packinghouse. The museum features exhibits about the Okanagan Valley's orchard industry, including picking, processeing, packing, preserving, & marketing. The BC Wine Museum & VQA Wine Shop is also at this location. The museum is open year round.

Kelowna: **British Columbia Wine Museum & VQA Wine Shop**
Parent: **Kelowna Museums**
1304 Ellis St., Kelowna, BC V1Y 1Z8
Tel: 250-868-0441
wine@kelownamuseums.ca
www.kelownamuseums.ca/museums/the-bc-wine-museum-vqa-wine-shop
The museum aims to bring Okanagan wine heritage, as well as the broader history of BC wine, to the public. The VQA Wine Shop carries wine from over 90 BC wineries. The museum & shop are at the same location as the British Columbia Orchard Industry Museum. Open year round.
Andrea Taylor, Coordinator, Wine Shop, ataylor@kelownamuseums.ca
Roger Ward, Associate, Wine Shop, rward@kelownamuseums.ca

Kelowna: **Central Okanagan Heritage Society**
1060 Cameron Ave., Kelowna, BC V1Y 8V3
Tel: 250-861-7188; Fax: 250-868-0391
cohs@telus.net
www.okheritagesociety.com
Year Founded: 1982 The Society promotes & participates in the preservation of the Central Okanagan region's natural, cultural & horticultural heritage; operates the Guisachan Heritage Park, the Benvoulin Heritage Park, Brent's Grist Mill Park.
Janice Henry, Executive Director

Kelowna: **Central Okanagan Sports Hall of Fame & Museum**
Parent: **Kelowna Museums**
c/o Kelowna Museums, 470 Queensway Ave., Kelowna, BC V1Y 6S7
Tel: 250-763-2417
sportshall@kelownamuseums.ca
www.kelownamuseums.ca/museums/the-central-okanagan-sports-hall-of-fame
Located at the Capri Mall on Gordon Drive. Open year round.

Kelowna: **Father Pandosy Mission**
Box 22105, Capri PO, Kelowna, BC V1Y 9N9
Tel: 250-860-8369
www.okanaganhistoricalsociety.org/pandosy_mission.html
Oblate Mission, 1859
John Sugars, Contact

Kelowna: **Kelowna Museums**
Parent: **Kelowna Museums Society**
470 Queensway Ave., Kelowna, BC V1Y 6S7
Tel: 250-763-2417
info@kelownamuseums.ca
www.kelownamuseum.ca
Social Media: www.youtube.com/user/KelownaMuseums
twitter.com/kelownamuseums
www.facebook.com/pages/KelownaMuseums/260810793981037
Open Tue.-Sat. 10-5; admission by donation; this location also houses the Kelowna Public Archives.
Lesley Moore, Executive Director, lmoore@kelownamuseums.ca

Patti Kilback, Associate Director, Exhibitions & Public Programming, pkilback@kelownamuseums.ca
Debbie Rehm, Associate Director, Administraition & Operations, drehm@kelownamuseums.ca
Tracy Satin, Associate Director, Collections & Conservation, tsatin@kelownamuseums.ca
Donna Johnson, Archivist, archives@kelownamuseums.ca

Kelowna: **Okanagan Military Museum**
Parent: **Kelowna Museums**
1424 Ellis St., Kelowna, BC V1Y 2A5
Tel: 250-763-9292
military@kelownamuseums.ca
www.kelownamuseums.ca/museums/the-okanagan-military-museum
The museum is dedicated to preserving the military heritage of Okanagan Valley residents. The collection includes small arms, uniforms, insignia, badges, & equipment. Open year round.
Keith Boehmer, Curatorial Assistant

Kelowna: **Silver Lake Forestry Centre**
Also known as: **Silver Lake Camp**
Parent: **Silver Lake Forest Education Society**
c/o Kelowna Family Y, 375 Hartman Rd., Kelowna, BC V1X 2M9
Tel: 250-491-9622; Fax: 250-765-7962
silverlake@ymca-ywca.com
www.silverlakekidscamp.com/society.html
Other contact information: E-mail, Education Society: chair@silverlakekidscamp.com.
Year Founded: 1971 The Silver Lake Forestry Centre is owned & managed by the Silver Lake Forest Education Society. Year-round outdoor environmental education is available for youth, adults, & educators. The society is also engaged in the collection, restoration, & display of logging & forestry artifacts. In 2011 the Society partnered with the YMCA-YWCA of Okanagan to bring a summer camp to the Centre.

Keremeos: **Keremeos Museum**
Parent: **South Similkameen Museum Society**
PO Box 135, 604 - 6th Ave., Keremeos, BC V0X 1N0
Tel: 250-499-9295
ssimmuseumsoc@hotmail.ca
www.keremeosmuseum.ca
Restored gaol-house with B.C. provincial police displays, pioneer artifacts
Judy Chisholm, President
Francis Peck, Appointed Historian

Keremeos: **The Old Grist Mill & Gardens at Keremeos**
2691 Upper Bench Rd., Keremeos, BC V0X 1N4
Tel: 250-499-2888
info@oldmillgardens.ca
oldmillgardens.ca
Designated British Columbia Heritage Site; open May - Oct & by appt.
Jim Millar, Contact
Brenda Millar, Contact

Kimberley: **Kimberley Heritage Musuem**
105 Spokane St., Kimberley, BC V1A 2E5
Tel: 250-427-7510
kdhs@shawbiz.ca
kimberleyheritagemuseum.blogspot.ca
www.facebook.com/263618083650062
Year Founded: 1978 Early Kimberley History; Sullivan Mine display; open year round; admission by donation; archives available for research, by request, at a nominal fee
Marie Stang, Curator

Kitimat: **Kitimat Museum & Archives**
293 City Centre, Kitimat, BC V8C 1T6
Tel: 250-632-8950; Fax: 250-632-7429
kitimatmuseum@telus.net
www.kitimatmuseum.ca
www.facebook.com/pages/Kitimat-Museum-Archives/161440070544293
Year Founded: 1968 Natural history; homesteader & Haida histories; Kemano-Kitimat Project history; temporary exhibitions; giftshop. Hours: June-Aug. M-Sa 10:00-5:00; Sept.-May M-F 10:00-4:00, Sa 12:00-4:00
Louise Avery, Curator, 250-632-8951

Kitwanga: **Meanskinisht Village Historical Association, Cedarvale**
Also known as: **Meanskinisht Museum**
PO Box 183, Kitwanga, BC V0J 2A0
Tel: 250-849-5732
Houses the history & remnants of ancient village of Gitlusec, Meanskinisht village & Cedarvale; also looks after the graveyard (private); Cedarvale Museum open by appt.
Mary G. Dalen, Director

Ladysmith: **Black Nugget Museum**
PO Box 1449, 12 Gatacre St., Ladysmith, BC V0R 2E0
Tel: 250-245-4846
Formerly the Jones Hotel, the Black Nugget Museum depicts the history of Ladysmith, through antiques & memorabilia dating back to the late 1800s. The hotel's barroom & lobby have been restored. The museum is open during the summer, and at other times when requested by groups.
Kurt Guilbride, Owner

Lake Cowichan: **Kaatza Station Museum & Archives**
PO Box 135, Lake Cowichan, BC V0R 2G0
Tel: 250-749-6142; Fax: 250-749-3900
kaatzamuseum@shaw.ca
www.kaatzamuseum.ca
Open year round
Barbara Simkins, Curator/Manager

Langley: **Canadian Museum of Flight (CMF)**
Hangar 3, Langley Airport, 5333 - 216th St., Langley, BC V2Y 2N3
Tel: 604-532-0035; Fax: 604-532-0056
cmflight@telus.net
www.canadianflight.org
Year Founded: 1977 The Canadian Museum of Flight restores, preserves, & displays Canada's aviation heritage. The museum & restoration site features more than twenty-five aircraft, such as a World War II Handley Page Hampden & a T-33 Silver Star. The Millennium Kids Room ia a "hands-on" facility for young visitors.
Gord Wintrup, President
George Miller, Vice-President
Terry Brunner, General Manager, tbrunner@telus.net
Paul de Lange, Treasurer
Matt Offer, Secretary

Lazo: **Comox Air Force Museum (CAFM)**
PO Box 1000 Forces, 19 Wing Comox, Lazo, BC V0R 2K0
Tel: 250-339-8162
info@comoxairforcemuseum.ca
www.comoxairforcemuseum.ca
www.facebook.com/ComoxAirForceMuseum
History of CFB Comox & West Coast aviation
Capt. Barley, Executive Director
Lorraine Analy, Curator

Lillooet: **Lillooet District Historical Society & Museum**
PO Box 441, Lillooet, BC V0K 1V0
Tel: 250-256-4308
lillmuseum@cablelan.net
www.lillooetbc.com
Open May-Oct., Tue.-Sat., 10-4; daily July & Aug. 9-5
Joan Duguid, President
Susan H. Bell, Manager

Lytton: **Lytton Museum & Archives**
420 Fraser St., Lytton, BC V0K 1Z0
Tel: 250-455-2254; Fax: 250-455-2394
curator@lyttonmuseum.ca
www.botaniecreek.com/museum
Year Founded: 1995 Built by the Canadian National Railway as a residence in 1942, the museum is filled with local artifacts and archives, including pieces formally used at the C.N. station.
Mr. Richard Forrest, President, Lytton Museum and Archives Commission
Dorothy Dodge, Curator

Mackenzie: **Mackenzie & District Museum**
Parent: **Mackenzie & District Museum Society**
Ernie Bodin Centre, PO Box 340, 86 Centennial Dr., Mackenzie, BC V0J 2C0
Tel: 250-997-3021
museum@mackbc.com
www.mackenziemuseum.ca; www.settlerseffects.ca (Virtual Museum)
www.facebook.com/mackenziemuseum

Maple Ridge: **Haney House Museum**
Parent: **Maple Ridge Historical Society**
11612 - 224th St., Maple Ridge, BC V2X 5Z7
Tel: 604-463-1377
www.mapleridgemuseum.org
Year Founded: 1981 Haney House was the residence of pioneer Thomas Haney, who came to Maple Ridge, British Columbia in 1876. Guided tours are available year-round.

Maple Ridge: **Maple Ridge Museum & Archives**
Parent: **Maple Ridge Historical Society**
22520 - 116th Ave., Maple Ridge, BC V2X 0S4
Tel: 604-463-5311; Fax: 604-463-5317
mrmuseum@uniserve.com
www.mapleridgemuseum.org
www.facebook.com/106860 626035721
Open year round
Val Patenaude, Executive Director
Allison White, Curator

Mayne Island: **Mayne Island Museum**
Comp. 4, Site 1, RR#1, Mayne Island, BC V0N 2J0
Tel: 250-539-5286

McBride: **Valley Museum & Archives**
PO Box 775, 241 Dominion St., McBride, BC V0J 2E0
Tel: 250-569-2411
www.mcbridemuseum.ca; www.settlerseffects.ca (Virtual Museum)
Displays within McBride & District Public Library

Merritt: **Nicola Valley Museum & Archives**
PO Box 1262, 1675 Tutill Court, Merritt, BC V1K 1B8
Tel: 250-378-4145
www.nicolavalleymuseum.org
www.facebook.com/123292923631
Year Founded: 1976 The museum houses an extensive collection of artifacts & photographs of various aspects of Nicola Valley's history, including churches, the general hospital, rail travel & other transportation, Craigmont mine history, Judge Henry Castillou, ranching & mining displays; James Teit Gallery & First Nations displays; Merritt Model Railway club display; the Archives preserves the James Teit First Nations reference material, early newspapers, mining reports, cemetery information, early maps & hundreds of photopgraphs. Open year round.
Barbara Watson, Office Manager

Midway: **Kettle River Museum**
Parent: **Kettle River Museum Society**
PO Box 149, Midway, BC V0H 1M0
Tel: 250-449-2614
kettlerivermuseum@shaw.ca
Mile of Kettle Valley Railway; restored 1900s CPR Station; B.C. Provincial Police display
Tannis Killough, President

Mission: **Fraser River Heritage Park**
PO Box 3341, 7494 Mary St., Mission, BC V2V 4J5
Tel: 604-826-0277; Fax: 604-826-0333
mhadmin@direct.ca
www.heritagepark-mission.ca
Original site of St. Mary's Mission & Indian Residential School, founded in 1861; park features foundations of mission

Mission: **Mission District Historical Society & Museum**
33201 - 2nd Ave., Mission, BC V2V 1J9
Tel: 604-826-1011
info@missionmuseum.com
www.missionmuseum.com
www.facebook.com/missionmuseum
Year Founded: 1972 Permanent exhibits include Sto:lo First Nations display, the history of settlement with pioneers, rails, rivers, and items from business and home life, notably period 1920s rooms. Also featured are items from Mission's old Chinatown. Museum is housed in a 1907 B.C. Mills, prefabricated, Canadian Bank of Commerce Bldg. Gift shop offers books on Mission's history. There is a selection of school tours.
Hazel Godley, Manager

Mission: **Xá:ytem Longhouse Interpretive Centre**
Parent: **Sto:lo Heritage Trust Society**
c/o Sto:lo Heritage Trust Society, 35087 Lougheed Hwy., Mission, BC V2V 6T1
Tel: 604-820-9725
www.xaytem.ca
On the coast of British Columbia, Xá:ytem has been an important Salish spiritual site. Today, Xá:ytem is a National Historic Site, where visitors discover a traditional Salish cedar longhouse & two pit houses. The site is open year-round.

Naksup: **Arrow Lakes Historical Society**
PO Box 819, 92 - 7th Ave., Naksup, BC V0G 1R0
Tel: 250-265-0110
alhs1234@telus.net
www.alhs-archives.com
Other contact information: Appointment Phone: 250-265-3323
The society stores archival material for the Arrow Lakes & Trout Lake regions.

Nanaimo: **The Bastion**
c/o Nanaimo Museum, 100 Museum Way, Nanaimo, BC V9R 5J8
Tel: 250-735-1821
www.nanaimomuseum.ca
1853 Hudson's Bay Co. log fortification; located on the Pioneer Waterfront Plaza (Front St. & Bastion St.), across from the Coast Bastion Hotel.

Nanaimo: **Centennial Museum of the Nanaimo Regional General Hospital**
Nanaimo Regional General Hospital, 1200 Dufferin Cres., Nanaimo, BC V9S 2B7
Tel: 250-755-7637; Fax: 250-755-7947
www.viha.ca
Health care records & artifacts
Lynne Tourond, Manager, Volunteer Resources, lynne.tourond@viha.ca

Nanaimo: **Museum of Natural History**
Building 370, Vancouver Island University, Nanaimo Campus, 900 - 5th St., Nanaimo, BC V9R 5S5
Tel: 250-753-3245
www.viu.ca/museum
Year Founded: 1976 The museum supports student, faculty, & external research. It is open by appointment only.
Sarah Greenway, Contact, 250-753-3245, Sarah.Greenway@viu.ca

Nanaimo: **Nanaimo District Museum (NDM)**
Vancouver Island Conference Centre, 100 Cameron Rd., Nanaimo, BC V9R 5J8
Tel: 250-753-1821
www.nanaimomuseum.ca
www.facebook.com/NanaimoMuseum
Open year round
Debbie Trueman, General Manager, debbie@nanaimomuseum.ca
David Hill-Turner, Curator, david@nanaimomuseum.ca

Nanaimo: **Vancouver Island Military Museum**
Parent: **Vancouver Island Military Museum Society**
100 Cameron Rd., Nanaimo, BC V9R 0C8
Tel: 250-753-3814; Fax: 250-753-3815
oic@vimms.ca
www.vimms.ca
The museum is entirely staffed by volunteers, & seeks to collect, conserve, & display artifacts related to the Canadian armed forces.

Naramata: **Naramata Heritage Museum**
PO Box 95, 224 Robinson Ave., Naramata, BC V0H 1N0
Tel: 250-496-5866
contact@naramatamuseum.com
naramatamuseum.com
Local history; 3 permanent displays
Berte Berry, Chair

Nelson: **Touchstones Nelson: Museum of Art & History**
Also known as: **Nelson & District Museum, Archives, Art Gallery & Historical Soc.**
502 Vernon St., Nelson, BC V1L 4E7
Tel: 250-352-9813; Fax: 250-352-9810
info@touchstonesnelson.ca
www.touchstonesnelson.ca
www.facebook.com/62 908084663
Other contact information: E-Mail, Exhibitions: exhibitions@touchstonesnelson.ca
The museum displays the history & culture of Nelson, British Columbia. Archives & an art gallery are also part of the museum.

Best Leah, Executive Director, director@touchstonesnelson.ca
Rod Taylor, Co-Curator, rod@touchstonesnelson.ca
Deborah Thompson, Co-Curator, deborah@touchstonesnelson.ca
Alex Dudley, Manager, Visitor Services, shop@touchstonesnelson.ca
Laura Fortier, Archivist & Manager, Collections, collections@touchstonesnelson.ca

New Denver: **Sandon Historical Society Museum & Visitors' Centre**
Parent: **Sandon Historical Society**
PO Box 52, New Denver, BC V0G 1S0
Tel: 250-358-7920
www.sandonmuseum.ca
Historic museum & archives of Sandon & area; heritage photographs, artifacts, guided tours
Dan Nicholson, President, 250-358-7215

New Denver: **Silvery Slocan Historical Museum**
Parent: **Silvery Slocan Historical Society**
PO Box 301, 202 - 6th Ave., New Denver, BC V0G 1S0
Tel: 250-358-2201; Fax: 250-358-7251
office@newdenver.ca
Cultural & economic history of the Slocan Lake area; open July & Aug.
Stan Wilson, Contact, 250-358-2478

New Westminster: **Canadian Lacrosse Hall of Fame**
Parent: **Canadian Lacrosse Association**
c/o 302 Royal Ave., New Westminster, BC V3L 1H7
Tel: 604-527-4640; Fax: 604-527-4641
info@canadianlacrossehalloffame.com
www.lacrosse.ca; www.canadianlacrossehalloffame.com
Year Founded: 1965 Inductees to the Canadian Lacrosse Hall of Fame are featured in the following categories: builders, box players, field players, veteran players, & teams.

New Westminster: **New Westminster Museum & Archives**
302 Royal Ave., New Westminster, BC V3L 1H7
Tel: 604-527-4640; Fax: 604-527-4641
www.nwpr.bc.ca
The New Westminster Museum, with more than 30,000 items in its collection, depicts the history of British Columbia's first capital. The New Westminster Archives, which contains 13,000 archival items, preserves the documentary heritage of the city from its time as a Royal Engineers' settlement camp. Irving House is an 1865 colonial period house. Guided tours are given of the home.
Colin Stevens, Manager, cstevens@newwestcity.ca
Cynthia Bronaugh, Coordinator, Tour Groups, cbronaugh@city.new-westminster.bc.ca
Barry Dykes, Archivist, 604-527-4642, bdykes@newwestcity.ca

New Westminster: **The Royal Westminster Regiment Historical Society & Museum**
The Armouries, 530 Queens Ave., New Westminster, BC V3L 1K3
Tel: 604-526-5116
www.royal-westies-assn.ca/museum.html

Permanent collection of military artifacts & memorabilia from the experience of The Royal Westminster Regiment & its antecedents; open every Tue. & Thurs.
Terry Leith, President, president@royal-westies-assn.ca
B. Gen. Herb E. Hamm, Secretary C.D., (Ret'd), secretary@royal-westies-assn.ca
Lt.Col. B.V. Morgan, Curator (Ret'd)

New Westminster: **Samson V Maritime Museum**
c/o Royal Agricultural & Industrial Society of BC, PO Box 42516, #105, 1005 Columbia St., New Westminster, BC V3M 6H5
Tel: 604-522-6894; Fax: 604-522-6094
museum@newwestcity.ca
www.nwheritage.org/heritagesite/orgs/samson
A restored sternwheel snagpuller, moored on the Fraser River at the Westminster Quay Market; history of the vessel, educational programming
Valerie Francis, Manager

North Vancouver: **Deep Cove Heritage Society**
4360 Gallant Rd., North Vancouver, BC V7G 1L2
Tel: 604-929-5744; Fax: 604-929-9456
deepcoveheritage.com
The Society provides archival documents on Deep Cove's history, as well as an organized walking tour of the area, highlighting many historical sites that helped shape the community. Office hours: M, W 10:00-2:00, Su 11:00-4:00; also open by appointment.
Pat Morrice, President
Vickie Boughen, Coordinator

North Vancouver: **Lynn Canyon Ecology Centre**
3663 Park Rd., North Vancouver, BC V7J 3G3
Tel: 604-990-3755
ecocentre@dnv.org
www.dnv.org/ecology
twitter.com/ecologycentre
www.facebook.com/1301270 93705007
Open year round

North Vancouver: **North Vancouver Museum & Archives**
Community History Centre, 3203 Institute Rd., North Vancouver, BC V7K 3E5
Tel: 604-990-3700; Fax: 604-987-5688
nvmac@dnv.org
www.dnv.org/nvma
Celebrates & preserves North Vancouver's social, industrial & cultural history; WWII shipbuilding; P.G.E. Railway; logging; Archives Reading Room & Archives Collection
Nancy L. Kirkpatrick, Director

North Vancouver: **Pacific Great Eastern (PGE) Railway Station**
107 Carrie Cates Ct., North Vancouver, BC V7M 3J4
Restored station building with railway exhibits

Okanagan: **Lake Country Museum**
11255 Okanagan Centre Rd. West, Okanagan, BC V4V 2J7
Tel: 250-766-0111
lcmuseum@shaw.ca
www.lakecountrymuseum.com
Open Mid-May - Aug.
Dr. Duane Thomson, President, duane.thomson@shaw.ca
Shannon Jorgenson, Manager, slgca@shaw.ca
Dan Bruce, Curator, caballero@shaw.ca
Sonja MacCrimmon, Archivist, maceast@shaw.ca

Okanagan Falls: **Okanagan Falls Heritage House & Museum**
Also known as: **Bassett House**
Okanagan Falls Heritage & Museum Society, PO Box 323, 1145 Main St., Okanagan Falls, BC V0H 1R0
Tel: 250-497-7047
www3.telus.net/okmuseum
The Bassett House is a prefabricated house. Ordered from the T. Eaton & Company catalogue, the house was shipped by rail from the east, and then by sternwheeler, & horse-drawn wagon to Okanagan Falls. The pioneer Bassett family lived in the home from 1909.

Oliver: **Oliver & District Heritage Society Museum & Archives**
PO Box 847, 9726 - 350th Ave., Oliver, BC V0H 1T0
Tel: 250-498-4027; Fax: 250-498-4027
odhs@persona.ca
www.oliverheritage.ca
Year Founded: 1980 Local history; open M-Th 9:00-4:00.

Osoyoos: **Nk'Mip Desert Cultural Centre**
1000 Rancher Creek Rd., Osoyoos, BC V0H 1V6
Tel: 250-495-7901; Fax: 250-495-7912
Toll-Free: 888-495-8555
www.nkmipdesert.com
Social Media: www.flickr.com/photos/nkmipdesert
twitter.com/NkmipDesert
www.facebook .com/NkmipDCC
The centre houses indoor & outdoor cultural & nature exhibits, & provides guided desert trail walks by interpreters. Open March-April, Tu-Sa 9:30-4:00; May-June, daily 9:30-4:30.
Charlotte Stringam, Manager, cstringam@oib.ca

Osoyoos: **Osoyoos & District Museum & Archives**
Parent: **Osoyoos Museum Society**
PO Box 791, 19 Park Pl., Osoyoos, BC V0H 1V0
Tel: 250-495-2582
museum2@vip.net
osoyoosmuseum.ca
Year Founded: 1963 Local history; open Sept.-May, Tu-F 11:00-3:00; June, Tu-Sa 11:00-3:00; July & Aug., daily 10:00-4:00.
Mat Hassen, President
Kenneth Favrholdt, Curator, museum1@vip.net

Osoyoos: **Osoyoos Desert Society & Osoyoos Desert Centre**
PO Box 123, Osoyoos, BC V0H 1V0
Tel: 250-495-2470; Fax: 250-495-2474
mail@desert.org
www.desert.org
Year Founded: 1991 The Osoyoos Desert Society is a non-profit society that was founded in 1991 to conserve the biologically rich and diverse habitats of British Columbia's southern interior. The south Okanagan is home to one of the largest concentrations of rare and at-risk species in all of Canada. Through conservation and education, the society strives to generate public knowledge, respect and active concern for these fragile and endangered ecosystems. In 1998, as part of it's effort to conserve the Southern Okanagan's unique habitats, the Desert Society opened an interpretive facility - the Osoyoos Desert Centre. In addition to an interpetive centre with hands-on exhibits, the Desert Centre also features a 1.5 km elevated wooden walkway. Visitors are invited to explore Canada's desert while enjoying a guided or self-guided tour along the boardwalk. The Desert Centre, located 3 km north of Osoyoos off Highway 97, is open annually from April through October
Marlin Clapson, Treasurer
Leslie Plaskett, President

Parksville: **Craig Heritage Park Museum**
PO Box 1452, Parksville, BC V9P 2H4
Tel: 250-248-6966
parksvillemuseum@shaw.ca
www.parksvillemuseum.ca
Open mid-May - Sept. 30
J. Tryon, Museum Manager
P. Cardwell, Archives

Pemberton: **Pemberton & District Museum & Archives Society**
PO Box 267, 7455 Prospect St., Pemberton, BC V0N 2L0
Tel: 604-894-5504
www.pembertonmuseum.org
www.facebook.com/16321843708551l
Three heritage buildings decorated with artifacts depicting local history dating back to 1850s
George Henry, President
Niki Madigan, Curator

Penticton: **Penticton Museum**
785 Main St., Penticton, BC V2A 5E3
Tel: 250-490-2451; Fax: 250-490-2442
www.pentictonmuseum.com
Year Founded: 1954 The museum is open Tu-Sa 10:00-5:00; the archives are open Wed-F 1:00-4:00.
Peter Ord, Manager/Curator
Jeanne Boyle, Museum Assistant

Penticton: **S.S. Sicamous Inland Marine Museum**
Parent: **Historic Okanagan Lake Steamships**
1099 Lakeshore Dr. West, Penticton, BC V2A 7B3
Tel: 250-492-0403Toll-Free: 866-492-0403
info@sssicamous.ca
sssicamous.ca
The 1914 steamship that houses the museum is a Provincial Heritage site. The museum is in the process of restoring another steamship, the S.S. Naramata. Hours of Operation: M, Th 11:00-5:30, Tu 1:00-9:00, F 11:00-7:00, Sa & Su 10:00-5:30.

Pitt Meadows: **Pitt Meadows Museum**
12294 Harris Rd., Pitt Meadows, BC V3Y 2E9
Tel: 604-465-4322
pittmeadowsmuseum@telus.net
www.pittmeadows.bc.ca
twitter.com/PittMeadowsmuse
Year Founded: 1997 Located in an 1885 general store, which was later used as a post office & a residence, the Pitt Meadows Museum relates the pioneer & agricultural history of the Pitt Meadows community. An archives is also situated at the museum. The Hoffmann & Son machine shop & ditching business was donated to the Pitt Meadows Heritage & Museum Society. Hoffmann & Son Ltd. had been in business since the 1920s. The museum is open year-round.

Port Alberni: **Alberni Valley Museum**
4255 Wallace St., Port Alberni, BC V9Y 3Y6
Tel: 250-723-2181; Fax: 250-723-1035
info@alberniheritage.com
www.alberniheritage.com
History & culture of Alberni Valley & West Coast of Vancouver Island; exhibits include aboriginal artifacts, particularly the Nuu chah Nulth basketry; clothing and textiles; household implements and tools; agricultural equipment; local memorabilia; and 17,0000 historic photographs available for research purposes or reproduction on request. Open year round

Port Alberni: **McLean Mill National Historic Site**
Parent: **Alberni District Museum & Historical Society**
5633 Smith Rd., Comp. 14, Site 125, Port Alberni, BC V9Y 7L5
Tel: 250-723-1376
info@alberniheritage.com
www.alberniheritage.com/mclean-mill/welcome-mclean-steam-sawmill
www.fac ebook.com/106253281318
Year Founded: 1989 Operated by R.B. McLean & his three sons from 1926 to 1965, the site commemorates the history of logging & saw milling in British Columbia. As well as the steam sawmill, typical remote coastal lumber camp buildings are being restored. A resident troupe of interpretive actors called the Tin Pants Theatre Company perform original stage shows & offer guided tours. There is also a cafe & gift shop.
Mr. Neil Malbon, General Manager

Port Clements: **Port Clements Museum**
c/o Port Clements Museum Society, PO Box 417, 45 Bayview Dr., Port Clements, BC V0T 1R0
Tel: 250-557-4255
pcmuseum@island.net
www.portclementsmuseum.org
The Port Clements Museum contains artifacts of pioneer life on the Queen Charlotte Islands, including information & photographs about the logging, farming, fishing, & mining industries. The museum grounds display early machinery from the logging industry.

Port Coquitlam: **Port Coquitlam Heritage & Cultural Society**
Also known as: **PoCo Heritage**
2100 - 2253 Leigh Square, Port Coquitlam, BC V3C 3B8
Tel: 604-927-8403
pocoheritage1@gmail.com
www.pocoheritage.org
www.facebook.com/168106719902719
Year Founded: 1988 Members of the Society create exhibits & displays at the Display Centre, Port Coquitlam City Hal, & the Terry Fox Library, showcasing their collection of photographs, collectables, antiques, maps, & First Nations artifacts. The Society is opening a Heritage Centre in 2013.

Port Edward: **North Pacific Cannery Historic Site & Museum**
PO Box 1109, 1889 Skeena Dr., Port Edward, BC V0V 1G0
Tel: 250-628-3538; Fax: 250-628-3540
northpac@citytel.net
www.cannery.ca
National historic site; oldest & most complete cannery village in BC; guided tours, gift shop, café; open May-Sept.

Port Hardy: **Port Hardy Museum & Archives**
Parent: **Port Hardy Heritage Society**
c/o Port Hardy Heritage Society, PO Box 2126, 7110 Market St, Port Hardy, BC V0N 2P0
Tel: 250-949-8143
info@porthardymuseum.com
porthardymuseum.com
The Port Hardy Museum & Archives houses geological & First Nations displays, as well as exhibits of settlers' history. The story of the fishing & logging industries in Port Hardy, Port Alice, Cape Scott, & Quatsino is also depicted at the museum. The museum is open year-round.
Jane Hutton, Curator

Port McNeill: **Port McNeill Museum**
351 Shelley Cres., Port McNeill, BC V0N 2R0
Tel: 250-956-9898
Hornsby steam tractor located at Seven Hills Golf Course

Port Moody: **Port Moody Station Museum**
2734 Murray St., Port Moody, BC V3H 1X2
Tel: 604-939-1648
info@portmoodymuseum.org
www.portmoodymuseum.org
Social Media: www.flickr.com/photos/55316408@N00
twitter.com/pmmuseum
www.facebook.c om/169200448399
Year Founded: 1983 Exhibits & programs about the heritage of Port Moody & the surrounding area are presented at the Port Moody Station Museum. The museum is located in the Port Moody Station, which was built by the Canadian Pacific Railway

Company in 1905. The Port Moody Heritage Society is the owner & operator of the museum.
Robert Simons, President
Jim Millar, Manager, jim@portmoodymuseum.org
Rebecca Clarke, Coordinator, rebecca@portmoodymuseum.org
Deb Naso, Bookkeeper

***Pouce Coupe:* Pouce Coupe Museum**
PO Box 293, 5006 - 49th Ave., Pouce Coupe, BC V0C 2C0
Tel: 250-786-5555; Fax: 250-786-5555
www.poucecoupe.ca/museum
Other contact information: Winter Phone: 250-786-5794
Pioneer artifacts & archives
Joe Tremblay, President

***Powell River:* Powell River Historical Museum & Archives**
PO Box 42, 4798 Marine Ave., Powell River, BC V8A 4Z5
Tel: 604-485-2222; Fax: 604-485-2327
museum@powellrivermuseum.ca
www.powellrivermuseum.ca
Open year-round, exhibits at the Powell River Historical Museum & Archives include the local First Nation culture, logging at the Powell River Mill, & the war years.
Don Allan, President
Teedie Kagume, Coordinator
Debbie Dan, Curator
Frances Cudworth, Bookkeeper

***Powell River:* Townsite Heritage Society of Powell River**
6211 Walnut St., Powell River, BC V8A 4K2
Tel: 604-483-3901; Fax: 604-483-3991
thetownsite@shaw.ca
www.powellrivertownsite.com
Year Founded: 1992 The Society seeks to preserve local history through education, by providing workshops, restoration projects, guided tours, as well as hosting a research centre.
Peter Sansburn, Manager

***Prince George:* The Exploration Place at the Fraser-Fort George Regional Museum (FFGRM)**
PO Box 1779, 333 Becott Pl., Prince George, BC V2L 4V7
Tel: 250-562-1612; Fax: 250-562-6395
Toll-Free: 866-562-1612
info@theexplorationplace.com
www.theexplorationplace.c om
Children's gallery; hands-on Explorations Gallery of Science & Natural History; History Hall of regional development; photo archives; motion simulator ride; Nature Exchange; Sports Hall of Fame Gallery with interactive sports machine
Tracy Calogheros, Executive Director

***Prince George:* Huble Homestead/Giscome Portage Heritage Society**
#202, 1685 - 3rd Ave., Prince George, BC V2L 3G5
Tel: 250-564-7033; Fax: 250-564-7040
admin@hublehomestead.ca
www.hublehomestead.ca
www.facebook.com/hubleho mestead
A living heritage site with over one dozen historic buildings

***Prince George:* The Railway & Forestry Museum, Prince George & Region**
***Also known as:* Prince George Railway & Forestry Museum**
850 River Rd., Prince George, BC V2L 5S8
Tel: 250-563-7351; Fax: 250-563-3697
trains@pgrfm.bc.ca
www.pgrfm.bc.ca
1913 100-tonne steam wrecking crane; wooden 1903 Ruissell snowplow

***Prince Rupert:* Kwinitsa Station Railway Museum**
PO Box 669, Bill Murray Way, Prince Rupert, BC V8J 3S1
Tel: 250-624-3207; Fax: 250-627-8009
mnbc@citytel.net
www.museumofnorthernbc.com
Depicts the life of early station agents & linemen who worked the Grand Trunk Railway at the turn of the 20th century; located at the Prince Rupert waterfront next to Rotary Waterfront Park; June - Aug.

***Prince Rupert:* Museum of Northern British Columbia**
PO Box 669, 100 First Ave. West, Prince Rupert, BC V8J 3S1
Tel: 250-624-3207; Fax: 250-627-8009
www.museumofnorthernbc.com
Exhibits artifacts depicting 12,000 years of human & natural history of the Northwest Coast of BC
Robin R. Weber, Director
Susan Marsden, Registrar

***Prince Rupert:* Prince Rupert Fire Museum Society**
200 - 1st Ave. West, Prince Rupert, BC V8J 1A8
Tel: 250-624-2211; Fax: 250-624-3407
shirts@citytel.net
www.princerupertlibrary.ca/fire
Firefighting in Prince Rupert since 1908; restored 1925 fire engine; old fire alarm system

***Princeton:* Princeton & District Museum & Archives Society**
PO Box 281, 167 Vermilion Ave., Princeton, BC V0X 1W0
Tel: 250-295-7588; Fax: 250-295-3477
Year Founded: 1958 The museum's collection features fossils & mining artifacts, as well as Aboriginal, Chinese, & pioneer items. Archives collected include records of Princeton & surrounding area organizations, land assessment rolls, court information, photographs, historical newspapers, postcards, posters, & personal papers.

***Quathiaski Cove:* Nuyumbalees Cultural Centre**
***Parent:* Nuyumbalees Society**
PO Box 8, 34 WeWay Rd., Quathiaski Cove, BC V0P 1N0
Tel: 250-285-3733; Fax: 250-285-3753
info@nuyumbalees.com
www.nuyumbalees.com
twitter.com/Nuyumbalees
www .facebook.com/132765133452990
Year Founded: 2007 Potlatch collection of Kwakwaka'wakw (Kwagiulth) ceremonial artifacts
Donald Assu, President

***Queen Charlotte:* Gitwangak Battle Hill National Historic Site**
c/o Gwaii Haanas Field Unit, Parks Canada, PO Box 37, Queen Charlotte, BC V0T 1S0
Tel: 250-559-8818; Fax: 250-559-8366
gwaii.haanas@pc.gc.ca
www.pc.gc.ca/eng/lhn-nhs/bc/gitwangak/index.aspx
Other contact information: TTY: 250-559-8139
Commemorates the culture of the Tsimshian people & their history; located near an important native trade route between the Skeena & Nass Rivers; Battle Hill features archaeological evidence from the 1750-1835 period
Ernie Gladstone, Field Unit Superintendent, ernie.gladstone@pc.gc.ca

***Quesnel:* Cottonwood House Historic Site**
241 Kinchant St., Quesnel, BC V2J 2R3
Tel: 250-992-2071; Fax: 250-992-6830
cottonwoodhouse@sd28.bc.ca
www.cottonwoodhouse.com
twitter.com/cottonw oodh
www.facebook.com/cottonwood.house
Year Founded: 1963 A Provincial Historic Site that trains secondary & post-secondary students in the areas of tourism & agriculture. The house is open to the public, & visitors can explore the site, farm, & nearby trail system, as well as stay overnight in one of the site's cabin accommodations. Open May-Sept., daily 10:00-5:00.
Ed Coleman, Manager, Operations, edcoleman@sd28.bc.ca

***Quesnel:* Quesnel & District Museum & Archives (QDMA)**
705 Carson Ave., Quesnel, BC V2J 2B6
Tel: 250-992-9580
ehunter@city.quesnel.bc.ca
www.quesnelmuseum.ca
Artifacts & archival items include Chinese artifacts, pioneer items, medical instruments, World War II letters from service men & women, & photographs from Quesnel & the surrounding area. Quesnel & District Museum & Archives is open year-round.

Elizabeth Hunter, Manager, Museum & Heritage, ehunter@quesnel.ca

***Revelstoke:* Revelstoke Court House**
1123 - 2nd St. West, Revelstoke, BC V0E 2S0
Tel: 250-837-6981; Fax: 250-837-4669
Courthouse built in 1913; no tours & no collections

***Revelstoke:* Revelstoke Firefighters Museum**
227 West 4th St., Revelstoke, BC V0E 2S0
Tel: 250-837-2884; Fax: 250-837-4154
www.cityofrevelstoke.com
Other contact information: City Office Phone: 250-837-2161; Fax 250-837-4930
The museum exhibits artifacts depicting the history of firefighting in Revelstoke. Open by appointment.

***Revelstoke:* Revelstoke Museum & Archives**
PO Box 1908, 315 First St. West, Revelstoke, BC V0E 2S0
Tel: 250-837-3067; Fax: 250-837-3094
info@revelstokemuseum.ca
www.revelstokemuseum.ca; revelstokemuseum.blogspot.ca
www.facebook.com/pages/Revelstoke-Museum-Archives/144528853796
Year Founded: 1958 The Revelstoke Museum & Archives is situated in Revelstoke's former post office & customs building, where the history of Revelstoke & the surrounding district is presented. The museum organizes exhibits, programs, heritage walks, & cemetery tours. The archives, consisting of photographs, newspapers, assessment rolls, & records of local businesses & organizations, are housed on the second floor of the building. There, visitors will find a microform reader/printer to facilitate their research. Hours: M-Sa 10:00-5:00
Cathy English, Curator, curator@revelstokemuseum.ca

***Revelstoke:* Revelstoke Railway Museum (RRM)**
***Parent:* The Revelstoke Heritage Railway Society**
PO Box 3018, 719 Track St. West, Revelstoke, BC V0E 2S0
Tel: 250-837-6060; Fax: 250-837-3732
Toll-Free: 877-837-6060
railway@telus.net; finance.railway@telus.net
www.railwaymuseum.com
Other contact information: E-mail, Gift Shop: giftshop.railway@telus.net
Visitors to the Revelstoke Railway Museum will learn about the challenges of building the Canadian Pacific Railway through British Columbia. Displays include survey & railway tools, CPR china & silverware, a locomotive, a car, a CPR telegraph service office, & a CPR weight scale shack. The museum also collects & organizes photographic archives. The museum is open year-round.
Jennifer Dunkerson, Executive Director, director.railway@telus.net

***Revelstoke:* Rogers Pass National Historic Site**
***Also known as:* Rogers Pass Discovery Centre**
Mount Revelstoke & Glacier National Parks, PO Box 350, Revelstoke, BC V0E 2S0
Tel: 250-837-7500; Fax: 250-837-7536
Toll-Free: 866-787-6221
revglacier.reception@pc.gc.ca
www.pc.gc.ca/eng/lhn-nhs /bc/rogers/index.aspx
Natural & human history of Mount Revelstoke & Glacier National Park
Karen Tierney, Field Unit Superintendent

***Revelstoke:* Three Valley Gap Heritage Ghost Town**
PO Box 860, Revelstoke, BC V0E 2S0
Tel: 250-837-2109; Fax: 250-837-5220
Toll-Free: 888-667-2109
hello@3valley.com; 3valley@revelstoke.net
www.3valleyroundhouse.com
Guided tours of historic town of late 1800s; open mid April - mid Oct.

***Richmond:* 12 (Vancouver) Service Battalion Museum**
The Sherman Armoury, 5500 - No. 4 Rd., Richmond, BC V6X 3L5
Tel: 604-238-2320; Fax: 604-238-2302
12svcbnmuseum.org
Year Founded: 1990 An accredited Canadian Forces museum; military artifacts, with particular emphasis on the 12 Service Battalion & it's predecessor corps; small reference library of military-related materials; open Tue. & Thu. evenings

***Richmond:* Britannia Heritage Shipyard**
Britannia Heritage Shipyard Site Office, 5180 Westwater Dr., Richmond, BC V7E 6P3
Tel: 604-718-8050; Fax: 604-718-8040
britannia@richmond.ca
www.britannia-hss.ca
Britannia Heritage Shipyard is a National Historic Site, which depicts Canada's west coast marine history. It is an example of a village which served the fishing industry. Many buildings date back to 1885. The Britannia Heritage Shipyard Society works to preserve the history of commercial boat building in Steveston. The shipyard is open from the beginning of May to the end of September. From October to April, the shipyard is open on weekends.
Bryan Klassen, Site Supervisor, 604-718-8044
Brooke Lees, Coordinator, Heritage, 604-718-8043
Angela Soon, Coordinator, Special Projects, 604-718-8037

***Richmond:* Gulf of Georgia Cannery National Historic Site**
***Parent:* Gulf of Georgia Cannery Society**
12138 - 4th Ave., Richmond, BC V7E 3J1
Tel: 604-664-9009; Fax: 604-664-9008
gog.info@pc.gc.ca
www.gulfofgeorgiacannery.com
Social Media: www.flickr.com/groups/gulfofgeorgiacannery
twitter.com/gogcannery
www. facebook.com/GulfofGeorgiaCannery

Year Founded: 1986 History of the west coast fishing industry; open May-Oct..
Marie Fenwick, Executive Director, marie.fenwick@pc.gc.ca
Heidi Rampfl, Collections Manager, heidi.rampfl@pc.gc.ca

***Richmond:* Richmond Museum**
Richmond Cultural Centre, 7700 Minoru Gate, Richmond, BC V6Y 1R9
Tel: 604-247-8300; Fax: 604-247-8341
museum@richmond.ca
www.richmond.ca
The mission of the Richmond Musuem is to collect, research, document, preserve, exhibit, & interpret items of significance to the history of the community.
Connie Baxter, Supervisor, Museum & Heritage Services
Rebecca Forrest, Curator
Peter Harris, Coordinator, Exhibits & Programs
Emily So, Coordinator, Educational Programs
Bill Jones, Treasurer

***Richmond:* Steveston Museum**
3811 Moncton St., Richmond, BC V7E 3A7
Tel: 604-271-6868
www.steveston.bc.ca/online/museum.html
Year Founded: 1976 Housed in a 1905 bank building, currently a post office; summer music series on the museum grounds; music & craft programs; museum tours; walking tours of Steveston Village.

***Rose Prairie:* Doig River First Nation Cultural Centre**
c/o Band Office, Indian Reserve 206, PO Box 56, Rose Prairie, BC V0C 2H0
Tel: 250-827-3776; Fax: 250-827-3778
Toll-Free: 888-344-9997
reception@doigriverfn.com
doigriverfn.com
Year Founded: 2003 The centre houses a museum, administrative space, gathering space, health care offices, a gym, & rodeo grounds.

***Rossland:* Rossland Historical Museum**
***Parent:* Rossland Museum & Archives Association**
11 Hwy. 3B, Rossland, BC V0G 1Y0
Tel: 250-362-7722; Fax: 250-362-5379
Toll-Free: 888-448-7444
rosslandmuseum@netidea.com
www.rosslandmuseum.ca
Local pioneer & mining history; Western Canada Ski Hall of Fame; underground mine tour; open daily mid-May - mid-Sept.; in winter by appt.
Joyce Austin, Manager

***Saanichton:* Log Cabin Museum & Archives**
***Parent:* Saanich Pioneer Society**
c/o Saanich Pioneer Society, 7910 Polo Park Cres., Saanichton, BC V8M 2J4
Tel: 250-658-8347; Fax: 250-483-1471
info@saanichpioneersociety.org
www.saanichpioneersociety.org
Other contact information: Alternate Phone: 250-483-1468
Artifacts & archives from the early days of the Saanich Peninsula pioneer families; operates in the log cabin built for this purpose in 1933

***Saanichton:* Saanich Historical Artifacts Society (SHAS)**
7321 Lochside Dr., Saanichton, BC V8M 1W4
Tel: 250-652-5522
shas@shas.ca
shas.ca
Collects & preserves artifacts from Saanich's rural past, including household & industrial objects, working steam engines, tractors & other agricultural machinery; chapel, schoolhouse & other buildings on site; trails & picnic area; open year round
Dave Hopkins, President

***Salmo:* Salmo Museum**
PO Box 69, 100 - 4th St., Salmo, BC V0G 1Z0
Tel: 250-357-2200; Fax: 250-357-2596
salmomus@telus.net
www.salmovillage.ca
Local histories, photographs, mining/logging/farming artifacts; household objects & clothing; tours; educational programming; annual Heritage Tea & annual Dinner Evening; admission by donation; open May-Sept.

***Salmon Arm:* R.J. Haney Heritage Village & Museum (SAM)**
***Parent:* Salmon Arm Museum & Heritage Association**
PO Box 1642, 751 Hwy. 97B NE, Salmon Arm, BC V1E 4P7
Tel: 250-832-5243; Fax: 250-832-5291
hpark@sunlite.ca
www.salmonarmmuseum.org
Other contact information: Archives phone: 250/832-5289; Email: samha@sunlite.ca
40-acre parcel of land with a municipally designated heritage home; 10 relocated, replicated & restored buildings from the village depict thematic displays on the history of Salmon Arm; 2 km nature trail; majority of collection housed in Salmon Arm Museum; Ernie Doe Archives Room also on site, with 111 linear feet of records dating from turn of 20th century; Museum open May-Sept., W-Su, 10-5, May & Oct., M-F, 9-4. Archives open all year round, W & Th, 10-4.
Gary Cruikshank, General Manager
Colleen McLellan, Coordinator, Visitor Services

***Scotch Creek:* Shuswap Lake Provincial Park Nature House**

PO Box 24106, 4120 Squilax-Anglemont Rd., Scotch Creek, BC V0E 3L0
Tel: 250-955-0861
info@shuswaplakepark.com
shuswaplakepark.com
Natural history

***Sechelt:* Téms Swįya Museum**
PO Box 740, 5555 Hwy. 101, Sechelt, BC V0N 3A0
Tel: 604-885-2273; Fax: 604-885-3490

***Shawnigan Lake:* Shawnigan Lake Museum**
PO Box 331, 1775 Shawnigan-Mill Bay Rd., Shawnigan Lake, BC V0R 2W0
Tel: 250-743-8675
shawniganlakemuseum@shaw.ca
www.shawniganlakemuseum.com
twitter.com/shawniganmuseum
www.facebook.c om/145218715433
Local history, featuring information on the Kinsol Trestle, the Esquimalt-Nanaimo railway, & artist E.J. Hughes.

***Sicamous:* Sicamous & District Museum & Historical Society**
Finlayson Park, PO Box 944, Sicamous, BC V0E 2V0
Tel: 250-836-4456
Museum & archives; collects, preserves, records, exhibits & promotes information, of artifacts & archival, historical & cultural value associated with the Columbia Shuswap Regional District Electoral Area E; open July & Aug.; located in Finlayson Park

***Sidney:* A.N.A.F. Vets Sidney No. 302 Museum Unit**
9831 - 4th St., Sidney, BC V8L 3S3
Tel: 250-656-3777; Fax: 250-656-6410
info@unit302.ca
www.unit302.ca
Military artifacts
Shane Holwell, President, Unit 302

***Sidney:* British Columbia Aviation Museum**
1910 Norseman Rd., Sidney, BC V8L 5V5
Tel: 250-655-3300
inquiries@bcam.net
www.bcam.net
Located beside Victoria International Airport, the British Columbia Aviation Museum preserves & displays aircraft & aviation artifacts, with an emphasis on the history of aviation in British Columbia. Aircraft on display include the Avro Anson MK II, the Eastman E2 Sea Rover, & the Bristol Bolingbroke MK IV. The museum is open year-round.

***Sidney:* Sidney Museum & Archives**
***Parent:* Society of Saanich Peninsula Museums**
2423 Beacon Ave., L3, Sidney, BC V8L 1X5
Tel: 250-655-6355
info@sidneymuseum.ca
www.sidneymuseum.ca
twitter.com/sidneymuseum
www.facebook.com/SidneyMu seumArchives
Year Founded: 1971 The museum's collection features over 6,000 items related to the history of Sidney & North Saanich. Open daily 10:00-4:00.
Graham Debling, President
Peter Graham, Executive Director
Lynda Spence, Contact, Educational Programs, 250-656-4476

***Silverton:* Silverton Outdoor Mining Exhibit**
PO Box 69, Silverton, BC V0G 1S0
Tel: 250-358-2485; Fax: 250-358-2485

Open May - Sept.

***Skidegate:* Haida Heritage Centre at Kaay Llnagaay**
Second Beach Rd., Skidegate, BC VoT 1S1
Tel: 250-559-7885; Fax: 250-559-7886
info@haidaheritagecentre.com
www.haidaheritagecentre.com

***Skidegate:* Haida Gwaii Museum at Kaay Llnagaay**
***Parent:* Haida Heritage Centre at Kaay Llnagaay**
PO Box 1373, Skidegate, BC V0T 1S1
Tel: 250-559-4643
museum@haidagwaii.net
www.haidagwaiimuseum.ca
History collections of the Queen Charlotte Islands; open year round
Jason Alsop, CEO, jason.alsop@haidaheritagecentre.com

***Smithers:* Adams Igloo Wildlife Museum**
Hwy. 16 West, Smithers, BC V0J 2N2
Tel: 250-847-3188
Display of area wildlife, including bear & cougar.

***Smithers:* Bulkley Valley Museum**
***Also known as:* BV Museum**
PO Box 2615, 1425 Main St., Smithers, BC V0J 2N0
Tel: 250-847-5322; Fax: 250-847-5363
info@bvmuseum.com
www.bvmuseum.com
Year Founded: 1976 The Bulkley Valley Museum's collection showcases the social & technological development of the Bulkley Valley. Exhibits include the Bulkley Valley First Nations, the Grand Trunk Pacific Railway in Smithers, & the forestry & mining industries in the area. The museum, operated under the Bulkley Valley Historical & Museum Society, is open year-round.

***Sooke:* Sooke Region Museum, Gallery, Historic Cottage & Lighthouse**
PO Box 774, 2070 Phillips Rd., Sooke, BC V0S 1N0
Tel: 250-642-6351; Fax: 250-642-7089
Toll-Free: 866-888-4748
info@sookeregionmuseum.com
www.sookeregionmuseum.com
Extensive archive and significant collection of photographs from Sooke's past. Aritfacts include a restored steam engine yarder, blacksmith shop, and a rotating lighthouse light.
Elida Peers, Executive Director

***Squamish:* West Coast Railway Heritage Park**
***Parent:* West Coast Railway Association**
39645 Government Rd., Squamish, BC V8B 0B6
Tel: 604-898-9336Toll-Free: 800-722-1233
park@wcra.org; info@wcra.org; tours@wcra.org
www.wcra.org
twitter.com/WCRailway
www.facebook.com/groups/4968165255
Other contact information: E-mail, Archives: archives@wcra.org
The mission of the West Coast Railway Association is the collection & preservation of British Columbia's railway heritage. Visitors to the West Coast Railway Heritage Park have the opportunity to view authentic railway equipment, including seventy locomotives & cars. The site also features the 1914 Pacific Great Eastern carshop & a railway station, built to 1915 Pacific Great Eastern plans. The heritage park is open year-round.

***Stewart:* Stewart Historical Museum**
PO Box 402, 603 Columbia St., Stewart, BC V0T 1W0
Tel: 250-636-2568

***Summerland:* Kettle Valley Steam Railway (KVSR)**
***Parent:* Kettle Valley Railway Society**
PO Box 1288, 18404 Bathville Rd., Summerland, BC V0H 1Z0

Tel: 250-494-8422Toll-Free: 877-494-8424
reservation@kettlevalleyrail.org
www.kettlevalleyrail.org
www.facebook .com/194424890596120
The Kettle Valley Steam Railway operates on ten miles preserved historic land, & visitors can ride in a passenger coach or open-air car. Please see the website for schedule details.
Doug Clayton, President

***Summerland:* Summerland Museum & Heritage Society**
PO Box 1491, 9521 Wharton St., Summerland, BC V0H 1Z0
Tel: 250-494-9395; Fax: 250-494-9326
info@summerlandmuseum.org
www.summerlandmuseum.org
Collections & displays devoted to Summerland's history.

***Surrey:* Historic Stewart Farmhouse**
13723 Crescent Rd., Surrey, BC V4A 2W3
Tel: 604-592-6956; Fax: 604-591-4789
heritage@surrey.ca
www.surrey.ca/Living+in+Surrey/Heritage/default.htm
This restored Victorian farmhouse was originally built in 1894 and features a parlor, dining room and kitchen with working wood-burning stove. Also on site are a circa-1900 pole barn which used to house 6 draft horses and other animals, as well as a fully loaded hay wagon. A team of staff and volunteers tend the heritage gardens of period flowers, vegetables and herbs, and to the orchards with trees of apple, pear and plum. Tours and school programs are also available. Open mid-Feb. - mid-Dec.

***Surrey:* Surrey Museum**
17710 - 56A Ave., Surrey, BC V3S 5H8
Tel: 604-592-6956; Fax: 604-592-6957
www.surrey.ca
City Museum; Local history collections; Textile studio; open Tuesdays to Saturdays; admission free

Tahsis: **Tahsis Heritage Museum**
c/o Village of Tahsis Municipal Office, PO Box 219, Tahsis, BC V0P 1X0
Tel: 250-934-6344
reception@villageoftahsis.com
www.villageoftahsis.com/history-heritage.php
Year Founded: 2000 Local history; open seasonally, or by appointment in the off-season.

Telkwa: **Telkwa Museum**
PO Box 595, Telkwa, BC V0J 2X0
Tel: 250-846-9656
Open May - Sept.
Doug Boersema, Contact, 250-846-9642

Terrace: **Heritage Park Museum**
PO Box 512, 4702 Kerby Ave., Terrace, BC V8G 4B5
Tel: 250-635-4546
curator@heritageparkmuseum.com
heritageparkmuseum.com
Contains historic log buildings, depicting the history of the pioneers in the region; guided tours offered; open May - Aug.
Kelsey Wiebe, Curator

Trail: **Trail Museum**
Parent: **Trail Historical Society**
PO Box 405, 1051 Victoria St., Trail, BC V1R 4L7
Tel: 250-364-0829; Fax: 250-364-0830
history@trail.ca
www.trailhistory.com
Open June - Aug., or by appointment.

Valemount: **Valemount Museum & Archives**
Parent: **Valemount Historic Society**
1090 Main St., Valemount, BC V0E 2Z0
Tel: 250-566-4177; Fax: 250-566-4244
administrator@valemountmuseum.ca
www.valemountmuseum.ca
Year Founded: 1992 The Valemount Museum & Archives is housed in the original train station, where visitors learn about the history of the community. Exhibits include information about trapping, the railroad, early settlers, & the Japanese internment camps. The museum is open from May to September.

Van Anda: **Texada Island Historical Society, Museum & Archives**
PO Box 53, Van Anda, BC V0N 3K0
Tel: 604-486-7109
info@texadaheritagesociety.com
www.texadaheritagesociety.com
Local history; open July-Sept., Th-Su 11:00-3:00; open rest of the year W 10:00-12:00.
Ken Barton, President
Peter Stiles, Corresponding Secretary/Treasurer
Doug Paton, Curator, 604-486-7109

Vancouver: **15th Field Artillery Regiment Museum & Archives Society**
Bessborough Armoury, 2025 - 11th Ave. West, Vancouver, BC V6J 2C7
Tel: 604-666-4387; Fax: 604-666-4083
Equipment of artillery units from Vancouver area; open year round

Vancouver: **Artspeak Gallery**
233 Carrall St., Vancouver, BC V6B 2J2
Tel: 604-688-0051; Fax: 604-685-1912
info@artspeak.ca
artspeak.ca; ieartspeakgallerysociety.tumblr.com
www.facebook.com/ArtspeakGallery
Year Founded: 1986 A non-profit artist-run centre for contemporary art & writing.
Kim Nguyen, Director/Curator

Vancouver: **Beaty Biodiversity Museum**
University of British Columbia, 2212 Main Mall, Vancouver, BC V6T 1Z4
Tel: 604-827-4955; Fax: 604-827-5350
info@beatymuseum.ubc.ca
www.beatymuseum.ubc.ca
Social Media: www.youtube.com/user/beatymuseum
www.facebook.com/BeatyMuseum
Year Founded: 2010 The museum is divided into six different collections: Cowan Tetrapod Collection, The Herbarium, Spencer Entomological Collection, The Fish Museum, Marine Invertebrate Collection, & Fossil Collection.
Patrick Lewis, Director, UBC Biodiversity Collections, patrick.lewis@ubc.ca
Katie Teed, Senior Manager, Marketing & Communications, katie.teed@ubc.ca
Susana Leon, Administrator, susana.leon@ubc.ca

Vancouver: **British Columbia Golf Museum & Hall of Fame**
Parent: **BC Golf House Society**
University Golf Club, 2545 Blanca St., Vancouver, BC V6R 4N1
Tel: 604-222-4653
office@bcgolfhouse.com
www.bcgolfhouse.com
twitter.com/BCGolfHouse
www.facebook.com/BCGolfHou se
Year Founded: 1986 The BC Golf Museum & Hall of Fame collects, preserves, & displays the history of golf & golfers in British Columbia. A collection of golf clubs dates back to 1790. The reference library houses a collection of over 5,000 books, plus player biographies & tournament records. The museum is open year round.
Barrie McWha, Executive Director
Peter Young, Treasurer

Vancouver: **British Columbia Medical Association Medical Museum**
c/o British Columbia Medical Association Archives Department, #115, 1665 West Broadway, Vancouver, BC V6J 5A4
museum@bcma.bc.ca
www.bcmamedicalmuseum.org
Year Founded: 1962 The BCMA Medical Museum holdings include instruments & other equipment used by physicians in British Columbia throughout the past 150 years.

Vancouver: **British Columbia Sports Hall of Fame & Museum**
Gate A, BC Place Stadium, 777 Pacific Blvd. South, Vancouver, BC V6B 4Y8
Tel: 604-687-5520; Fax: 604-687-5510
sportsinfo@bcsportshalloffame.com
www.bcsportshalloffame.com
Social Media: www.youtube.com/user/BCSportsHallofFame
twitter.com/BCSportsHall
www.facebook.com/bcsportshall
The BC Sports Hall of Fame & Museum contains interactive displays about British Columbia's world-class athletes. In addition to its history galleries, the Hall of Fame & Museum features galleries devoted to Terry Fox & Rick Hansen, a Greg Moore gallery, & a participation gallery.
Sue Griffin, President & CEO, sue.griffin@bcsportshalloffame.com
Jason Beck, Curator, jason.beck@bcsportshalloffame.com
John Ormiston, Secretary-Treasurer

Vancouver: **Cowan Vertebrate Museum**
Dept. of Zoology, University of British Columbia, #4349, 6270 University Blvd., Vancouver, BC V6T 1Z4
Tel: 604-822-4665; Fax: 604-822-2416
vertmus@zoology.ubc.ca
www.zoology.ubc.ca/~vertmus
Natural history collection with bird, mammal & herpetological specimens; open year round, by appt.
Dr. D. Irwin, Director
Dr. R. Kenner, Curator

Vancouver: **Deeley Motorcycle Exhibition**
1875 Boundary Rd., Vancouver, BC V5M 3Y7
Tel: 604-293-2221; Fax: 604-909-6232
info@deeleymotorcycleexhibition.ca
www.deeleymotorcycleexhibition.ca
Display of over 250 classic & antique motorcycles; open year round Mon.-Fri., 10-4.

Vancouver: **Jewish Museum & Archives of British Columbia**
Peretz Centre for Secular Jewish Culture, 6184 Ash St., Vancouver, BC V5Z 3G9
Tel: 604-257-5199
info@jewishmuseum.ca; info@peretz-centre.org
www.jewishmuseum.ca; www.peretz-centre.org
www.flickr.com/photos/jewishmuseum
www.facebook.com/JewishBC
The museum's administrative offices are located at the Peretz Centre, & are open to researchers & volunteers by appointment only. Museum exhibits & displays are located in various venues throughout the year; please see the website for current listings. The museum also has a virtual component accessible through their website.
Mark Zlotnik, Acting President
Marcy Babins, Administrator
Jennifer Yuhasz, Archivist, archives@jewishmuseum.ca

Vancouver: **Old Hastings Mill Store Museum**
1575 Alma Rd., Vancouver, BC V6R 3P3
Tel: 604-734-1212; Fax: 604-876-9779
eandelockhart@shaw.ca
www.findfamilyfun.com/hastingsmill.htm
Year Founded: 1919 Oldest building in Vancouver owned by The Native Daughters of British Columbia Post No. 1; houses artifacts pertaining to the pioneers of the city and Native peoples; open Tue.-Sun., June 15 - Sept. 15, 1-4; weekends in winter months, closed Dec. & Jan.
Jacqui Underwood, Chief Factor
Elsie Lockhart, Corresponding Secretary

Vancouver: **The Pacific Museum of the Earth**
Dept. of Earth & Ocean Sciences, University of British Columbia, 6339 Stores Rd., Vancouver, BC V6T 1Z4
Tel: 604-822-6992; Fax: 604-228-6088
mparker@eos.ubc.ca
www.eos.ubc.ca/resources/museum
Includes mounted dinosaur, insects in amber, wide variety of fossils & minerals
Kirsten Parker, Curator

Vancouver: **Roedde House Museum**
Parent: **Roedde House Preservation Society**
1415 Barclay St., Vancouver, BC V6G 1J6
Tel: 604-684-7040; Fax: 604-684-7040
info@roeddehouse.org
www.roeddehouse.org
twitter.com/RoeddeHouse
www .facebook.com/RoeddeHouseMuseum
Year Founded: 1990 Roedde House is a late-Victorian home, built in 1893. Today, the house reflects the life of an immigrant, middle class family around 1900. The museum provides guided tours & educational & cultural programs. Hours: Seasonal hours may vary, contact for details. Open for Tea & Tour Su 1:00-4:00
Anthony Norfolk, President, anorfolk@uniserve.com
Philip Waddell, Vice President, phwad@hotmail.ca
Susan Erb, Secretary, dserb@shaw.ca
Nikhila Prakash, Treasurer, nikhilaprakash@hotmail.com
Benedicte Schoepflin, Museum Manager, 604-684-7040, info@roeddehouse.org

Vancouver: **St. Roch National Historic Site**
c/o Vancouver Maritime Museum, 1095 Ogden Ave., Vancouver, BC V6J 1A3
Tel: 604-257-8300; Fax: 604-737-2621
info@vancouvermaritimemuseum.com
www.vancouvermaritimemuseum.com
Arctic patrol vessel & 1944 RCMP memorabilia
Simon Robinson, Executive Director

Vancouver: **Seaforth Highlanders Regimental Museum**
Seaforth Armoury, 1650 Burrard St., Vancouver, BC V6J 3G4
Tel: 604-733-3836; Fax: 604-666-4078
seaforthmuseum@gmail.com
bcoy1cpb.pacdat.net/museum.htm
Year Founded: 1972 Artifacts pertaining to the Seaforth Highlanders of Canada & affiliated regiments
Colin Stevens, Curator

Vancouver: **Spencer Entomological Museum (SEM)**
Dept. of Zoology, University of British Columbia, 6270 University Blvd., Vancouver, BC V6T 1Z4
Tel: 604-822-3379; Fax: 604-822-2416
needham@zoology.ubc.ca
www.insecta.com
Largest collection of BC insects in the world containing 700,000 specimens; museum closed to public
Karen Needham, Curator
G.G.E. Scudder, Director

Vancouver: **Vancouver Holocaust Education Centre (VHEC)**
Parent: **Vancouver Holocaust Centre Society**
#50, 950 - 41st Ave. West, Vancouver, BC V5Z 2N7
Tel: 604-264-0499; Fax: 604-264-0497
info@vhec.org; library@vhec.org
www.vhec.org
www.facebook.com/140874547755
Year Founded: 1994 The Vancouver Holocaust Education Centre is a teaching museum which provides Holocaust based anti-racism education. It aims to promote human rights, genocide awareness, & social justice. The causes & consequences of discrimination, racism, & antisemitism are explored. The centre includes a museum collection, archives, a library, & a resource centre. The education centre is also engaged in a survivor testimony project. School programs & outreach speakers are available. Exhibits are not recommended for children under the age of ten. The education centre is open year-round.
Frieda Miller, Executive Director
Nina Krieger, Education Director
Shannon LaBelle, Librarian
Elizabeth Shaffer, Archivist
Gisella Levitt, Coordinator, Suvivivor Services
Marla Guralnick Pekarsky, Secretary
Robbie Waisman, Treasurer

Vancouver: **The Vancouver Maritime Museum Society (VMM)**
1905 Ogden Ave., Vancouver, BC V6J 1A3
Tel: 604-257-8300; Fax: 604-737-2621
info@vancouvermaritimemuseum.com
www.vancouvermaritimemuseum.com
Includes National Historic Site St. Roch, RCMP Schooner
Simon Robinson, Executive Director

Vancouver: **Vancouver Police Museum**
Parent: **Vancouver Police Historical Society**
240 Cordova St. East, Vancouver, BC V6A 1L3
Tel: 604-665-3346; Fax: 604-665-3585
info@vancouverpolicemuseum.ca
www.vancouverpolicemuseum.ca
twitter.com /policemuseum
www.facebook.com/PoliceMuseum
Year Founded: 1986 Located in the historic City Morgue & Coroner's Court in Vancouver, the Vancouver Police Museum presents a collection of artifacts, papers, photographs, & published materials related to the history of the Vancouver Police Department. The museum is open year-round.

Vanderhoof: **Vanderhoof Community Museum & O.K. Cafe**
Parent: **Nechako Valley Historical Society**
c/o Nechako Valley Historical Society, PO Box 1515, 478 - First St. West, Vanderhoof, BC V0J 3A0
Tel: 250-567-2991; Fax: 250-567-2331
www.vanderhoofchamber.com
Other contact information: Cafe Phone: 250-567-5262
1920's heritage village & community museum with restaurant café serving old-fashioned food
Ken Holden, President, 250-567-0213
Heather Stephens, Curator, curator@vanderhoofmuseum.ca

Vavenby: **Michif Métis Museum**
Parent: **Michif Historical & Cultural Preservation Society**
c/o Michif Historical & Cultural Preservation Society, PO Box 126, 337 Bernard Rd., Vavenby, BC V0E 3A0
Tel: 250-676-0096; Fax: 250-676-0069
metismuseum@yahoo.ca
www.michifmetismuseum.org
The museum seeks to preserve Michif Métis culture; it is the only museum in British Columbia of its kind.
Dale R. Haggerty, President/Curator

Vernon: **Greater Vernon Museum & Archives**
3009 - 32 Ave., Vernon, BC V1T 2L8
Tel: 250-542-3142; Fax: 250-542-5358
mail@vernonmuseum.ca
www.vernonmuseum.ca
Open year round
Ron Candy, Curator

Vernon: **O'Keefe Ranch**
Also known as: **Historic O'Keefe Ranch**
9380 Hwy. 97, Vernon, BC V1H 1W9
Tel: 250-542-7868
www.okeeferanch.ca
Year Founded: 1867 Founded in 1867, the O'Keefe Ranch operated when thousands of cattle grazed in the Okanagan, Thompson, & Cariboo regions. Today, Historic O'Keefe Ranch depicts the story of early ranching in British Columbia. The ranch offers an informative & entertaining school program. Each summer the ranch hosts a Cowboy Festival.

Victoria: **Canadian Forces Base Esquimalt Naval & Military Museum**
Canadian Forces Base Esquimalt, PO Box 17000 Forces, 1299 Naden Way, Victoria, BC V9A 7N2
Tel: 250-363-4312; Fax: 250-363-4252
info@navalandmilitarymuseum.org
www.navalandmilitarymuseum.org
Other contact information: Alternate Phone: 250-363-5655
The CFB Esquimalt Naval & Military Museum collects, preserves, & displays the history of naval presence on the Canadian west coast. In addition, the history of the military on southern Vancouver Island is also depicted. The musuem features an archive & research library. Reproductions of photographs in the archive are available.

Victoria: **The Canadian Scottish Regiment (Princess Mary's) Regimental Museum**
Bay Street Armoury, 715 Bay St., Victoria, BC V8T 1R1
Tel: 250-363-8753; Fax: 250-363-3593
csrmuse@islandnet.com
www.islandnet.com/~csrmuse
Items of historical significance to the regiment; located in the Bay Street Armoury, a National Historic Site built in 1915

Victoria: **Craigdarroch Castle**
1050 Joan Cres., Victoria, BC V8S 3L5
Tel: 250-592-5323; Fax: 250-592-1099
info@thecastle.ca
www.craigdarrochcastle.com
Historic house museum, built in 1890 by Robert Dunsmuir, wealthy coal baron; 39 rooms, 87 stairs to tower, lavish Victorian era furnishings, woodwork, stained glass
C. Williams, Executive Director

Victoria: **Craigflower Manor & Schoolhouse National Historic Sites of Canada**
Parent: **The Land Conservancy**
c/o The Land Conservancy, 301-1195 Esquimalt Rd., Victoria, BC V9A 3N6
Tel: 250-479-8053; Fax: 250-744-2251
blog.conservancy.bc.ca
Social Media: www.youtube.com/tlcadmin
twitter.com/tlc4bc
www.facebook.com/50839065407
Other contact information: Alternate Phone: 250-386-1606
The farm & schoolhouse are part of a Hudson's Bay Company complex built in 1853. Open May-Sept., daily 11:00-5:00.

Victoria: **Emily Carr House**
207 Government St., Victoria, BC V8V 2K8
Tel: 250-383-5843; Fax: 250-356-7796
ecarr@shaw.ca
www.emilycarr.com
Birthplace of Emily Carr; People's Gallery; open May-Oct. & Dec. or by appointment

Victoria: **Fort Rodd Hill & Fisgard Lighthouse National Historic Sites**
603 Fort Rodd Hill Rd., Victoria, BC V9C 2W8
Tel: 250-478-5849; Fax: 250-478-2816
fort.rodd@pc.gc.ca
www.fortroddhill.com
Turn of the century coastal defence gun batteries & first permanent lighthouse (1860) on Canada's west coast

Victoria: **Goldstream Regional Museum**
#2, 697 Goldstream Ave., Victoria, BC V9B 2X2
Tel: 250-474-6113
History of region; WWI & WWII displays; open year round

Victoria: **Hatley Park National Historic Site**
2005 Sooke Rd., Victoria, BC V9B 5Y2
Tel: 250-391-2666; Fax: 250-391-2620
Toll-Free: 866-241-0674
info@hatleypark.ca
www.hatleypark.ca
Year Founded: 1999 The museum is located in the basement of Hatley Castle & features two rooms of artifacts, photos, replicas & reconstructions, & local history.
Bonnie Nelson, Director, Campus Services
Carol Louch, Administrative Assistant, carol.louch@hatleypark.ca

Victoria: **Helmcken House**
Royal BC Museum, 675 Belleville St., Victoria, BC V8W 9W2
Tel: 250-356-7226; Fax: 250-387-5674
Toll-Free: 888-447-7977
reception@royalbcmuseum.bc.ca
www.royalbcmuseum.bc.ca
Home of Dr. John Sebastian Helmcken built in 1852; medical & domestic collections; managed by the Royal BC Museum
Pauline Rafferty, CEO

Victoria: **Lt. General Ashton Armoury Museum**
724 Vanalman Ave., Victoria, BC V8Z 3B5
Tel: 250-363-8346; Fax: 250-363-8326
Army service support
Lt.-Col. (Ret'd) Ted Leaker, Director

Victoria: **Maritime Museum of British Columbia**
28 Bastion Sq., Victoria, BC V8W 1H9
Tel: 250-385-4222; Fax: 250-382-2869
info@mmbc.bc.ca
www.mmbc.bc.ca
Year Founded: 1954 This extensive museum of 3 floors covers the history of marine navigation on the BC coast from First Nation cultures through to European explorers and territorial tussles. Interactive displays include a mock-up of a ship's deck complete with climbable crow's nest & ratlines. The 2nd floor offers model ships for viewing, while the 3rd floor houses a library. Open all year, with winter & summer hrs.
Shirley Vickers, Executive Director, 250-385-4222, svickers@mmbc.bc.ca

Victoria: **Metchosin School Museum**
Parent: **Metchosin Museum Society**
4475 Happy Valley Rd., Victoria, BC V9C 3Z3
Tel: 250-478-3451
metchosinmuseum.ca
Other contact information: Alternate Phone: 250-478-5447
Year Founded: 1972 School, household & agricultural exhibits/archives pertaining to the School and the area; operated by a society of volunteers; open April-Oct.

Victoria: **Museum & Archives of 5 (BC) Regiment, Royal Canadian Artillery**
The Armoury, #304, 715 Bay St., Victoria, BC V8T 1R1
Tel: 250-363-3814; Fax: 250-363-3512
info@5rcamuseum.ca; curator@5rcamuseum.ca
www.5rcamuseum.ca
Other contact information: E-mail, Archives: archivist@5rcamuseum.ca; Gifts: shop@5rcamuseum.ca
Year Founded: 1996 The Museum & Archives of 5 (BC) Regiment depicts the history of coast artillery & associated units. Displays date from 1861 to the present. Examples of artifacts include a rifled muzzle loading gun & a vintage cannon. An archives & reference library are also available for research. The museum is open year-round, two days each week. For visits outside regular hours, please call 250-363-8270.

Victoria: **Point Ellice House & Gardens**
Parent: **Point Ellice House Preservation Society**
2616 Pleasant St., Victoria, BC V8T 4V3
Tel: 250-380-6506; Fax: 250-381-2338
ellicehouse@gmail.com
www.pointellicehouse.ca
twitter.com/ElliceHouse
Point Ellice House was owned by Magistrate & Gold Commissioner Peter O'Reilly, starting in 1867. The home & garden are open from May to September.

Victoria: **Royal London Wax Museum**
470 Belleville St., Victoria, BC V8V 1W9
Tel: 250-388-4461
info@waxmuseum.bc.ca
www.waxmuseum.bc.ca
Houses over 300 wax sculptures; closed until further notice during relocation
Dr. Arne H. Lane, President
Ken H. Lane, CEO, khl@waxmuseum.bc.ca

Victoria: **St. Ann's Academy National Historic Site**
613 Pandora Ave., Victoria, BC V8W 1N8
Tel: 250-953-8829
stanns.academy@gov.bc.ca
www.stannsacademy.com
The restored 1920s-era building services as office space for BC's Ministry of Advanced Education, as well as housing an Interpretive Centre for visitors. Winter hours: Sept.-May, Tu-Su 1:00-4:00; Summer hours: May-Sept., daily 10:00-4:00.

Victoria: **Victoria Police Historical Society**
850 Caledonia Ave., Victoria, BC V8T 5J8
Tel: 250-995-7654; Fax: 250-995-7394
museum@police.victoria.bc.ca
History of the Victoria police, est. 1858; exhibits include 1921 "Commerce" Patrol Wagon, 1938 UL Harley Davidson motorcycle & sidecar, 1940 Dodge police car

Wells: **Wells Museum**
Parent: **Wells Historical Society**
PO Box 244, Wells, BC V0K 2R0
Tel: 250-994-3422
museum@wellsbc.come
www.wellsmuseum.ca
Wells Museum is located within the Island Mountain Mine office, which was built during the 1930s when Wells was established as a company town for the Cariboo Gold-Quartz Mine. The museum features displays about the mining history in the area. It is open from May to September.
William (W.G) (W.G) Quackenbush, Contact

West Vancouver: **Vancouver Naval Museum & Heritage Society**
PO Box 91399, 1200 Stanley Park, West Vancouver, BC V7V 3P1
Tel: 604-913-3363
susan_denwison@telus.net
Depicts the history of the Royal Canadian Navy since its inception: uniforms, medals & decorations, 3D artifacts, pictorial displays, including naval library & archives

West Vancouver: **West Vancouver Museum**
680 - 17th St., West Vancouver, BC V7V 3T2
Tel: 604-925-7295
www.westvancouvermuseum.ca
www.facebook.com/267457985520
The West Vancouver Museum offers exhibitions & educational programs to increase awareness of the history, culture, & art of the West Vancouver region & the country. The museum is open year-round.
Darrin Morrison, Curator, 604-925-7296, dmorrison@westvancouver.ca
Carol Howie, Coordinator, Collections, 604-925-7294, chowie@westvancouver.ca
Isaac Vanderhorst, Coordinator, Education, 604-925-7297, ivanderhorst@westvancouver.ca

Westbank: **Westbank Museum**
2376 Dobbin Rd., Westbank, BC V4T 2H9
Tel: 250-768-0110
info@westbankmuseum.com
www.westbankmuseum.com
Local history; also houses the West Kelowna Visitor Centre; open M-Su 9:00-6:00.

Whistler: **Whistler Museum & Archives**
4333 Main St., Whistler, BC V0N 1B4
Tel: 604-932-2019; Fax: 604-932-2077
info@whistlermuseum.org
www.whistlermuseum.org
twitter.com/WhistlerMus eum
www.facebook.com/WhistlerMuseum
Year Founded: 1986 The museum celebrates the history of the Whistler community. Open daily 11:00-5:00.

White Rock: **White Rock Museum & Archives**
14970 Marine Drive, White Rock, BC V4B 1C4
Tel: 604-541-2221; Fax: 604-541 2223
whiterockmuseum@telus.net
www.whiterock.museum.bc.ca
Located in the White Rock Train Station; collections include artifacts relating to the history & families of White Rock, documentation relating to the civic, political & business life of the community, objects relating to the Great Northern Railway & rail history of the area, and natural history objects of the locality.
Marilena Fluckiger, President
Sharon Oldaker, Executive Director, whiterockoffice@telus.net
Hugh Ellenwood, Archives Manager, whiterockarchives@telus.net

Williams Lake: **Museum of the Cariboo-Chilcotin**
113 - 4th Ave. North, Williams Lake, BC V2G 2C8
Tel: 250-392-7404; Fax: 250-392-7404
mccwl@uniserve.com
cowboy-museum.com
Displays focusing on the ranching & rodeo history of the Cariboo Chilcotin area; home of the BC Cowboy Hall of Fame; Shuswap First Nation, Chinese & Chilcotin materials; open June-Aug., Mon.-Sat. 10-4; Sept.-May, Tues.-Sat. 11-4
Pat Skoblanuik, Manager

Yale: **Historic Yale Museum**
Parent: **Yale & District Historical Society**
PO Box 74, 31187 Douglas St., Yale, BC V0K 2S0
Tel: 604-863-2324
info@historicyale.ca
historicyale.ca
www.facebook.co m/pages/Yale-Historic-Site/193966850649397
First Nations; Gold Rush; Railway Era

Ymir: **Ymir Arts & Museum Society**
PO Box 65, Ymir, BC V0G 2K0
Tel: 250-357-9262
ymirartsandmuseumsociety@hotmail.com
www.ymirbc.com/ya ms
The Ymir Arts & Museum Society preserves the Ymir Schoolhouse, where arts & culture in Ymir are promoted. Located in the West Kootenays of British Columbia, Ymir was an active mining town in the late 1800s.
Robyn Balaski, Arts & Museum Contact, rainspirit13@hotmail.com

Manitoba

Provincial Museums

The Manitoba Museum / Le Musée du Manitoba
190 Rupert Ave., Winnipeg, MB R3B 0N2
Tel: 204-956-2830; Fax: 204-942-3679
Toll-Free: 888-231-9739
info@manitobamuseum.ca
www.manitobamuseum.ca
Other contact information: Info Line: 204/943-3139
Nine permanent galleries & Alloway Hall which houses temporary & travelling exhibitions. Permanent galleries are: Orientation (in which the main theme of the Museum is explained), Earth History, Grasslands, Urban (a section of Winnipeg, reconstructed as it might have been in 1920), Nonsuch (a replica of the 17th-century Ketch), Arctic-Subarctic & Boreal Forest. The Hudson's Bay Company Gallery reflects the legacy of the Company & the people whose daily activities & legendary deed bring to life the drama & history of Canada's fur trade. The all new Parklands/mixed woods Gallery, representing the most natural & culturally diverse region of the province. The Planetarium provides educational & entertaining programs for the general public & school groups in the 287-seat Star Theatre; feature presentations touch all aspects of astronomy, science facts/science fiction, as well as present day space programs & technology
Claudette Leclerc, Chief Executive Officer
C. Ellis, Director, Operations
J. Schwersensky, Director, Marketing
Mike Jensen, Supervisor, Planetarium Programs

Local Museums in Manitoba

Alonsa: **Alex Robertson Museum**
PO Box 33, 6 Church Ave., Alonsa, MB R0H 0A0
Tel: 204-767-2101; Fax: 204-767-2044
alonsa@mts.net
Antique guns; pioneer tools & artifacts; 1939 fire engine; open year round

Anola: **Anola & District Museum**
PO Box 153, Anola, MB R0E 0A0
Tel: 204-866-2922
Open May - Sept., Sun. or by appt.
Jack Mavins, Treasurer

Arborg: **Arborg & District Multicultural Heritage Village**
PO Box 4007, Arborg, MB R0C 0A0
Tel: 204-376-5079
admhv@hotmail.ca
www.arborgheritagevillage.ca
A working museum & interpretive centre specializing in the multicultural history of rural life in the pre-1930s Interlake region. Structures from the former Winnipeg Beach Ukrainian Homestead are now housed here.
Pat Eyolfson, Association Contact

Ashern: **Ashern Pioneer Museum**
PO Box 642, 36 - 1st St. South, Ashern, MB R0C 0E0
Tel: 204-768-3147; Fax: 204-768-3051
Other contact information: Phone, appointments: 204-768-2394
The Ashern Museum features the following restored buildings: St Michael's Anglican Church, the CNR station, the Ashern Post Office, the Hoffman Log House, the Darwin School House, & Ashern's first Rural Municipality of Siglunes Office. Artifacts include a threshing machine, tractor, bailer, & plow. The museum is open from May to September. At other times, tours can be arranged.

Austin: **Manitoba Agricultural Museum**
PO Box 10, Austin, MB R0H 0C0
Tel: 204-637-2354; Fax: 204-637-2395
agmuseum@mts.net; info@ag-museum.mb.ca
www.ag-museum.mb.ca
Year Founded: 1953 Located 3 km south of Hwys. 1 & 34, the site boasts Canada's largest collection of vintage agricultural equipment from 1900 on. There is also a pioneer village with over 20 buildings from log cabins to mills & mansions. The Manitoba Amateur Radio Museum is also housed on site. Events include the annual Thresherman's Reunion & Stampede last week in July. Open daily 9:00-5:00, May 12 - Oct. 5.
Diane Nesbitt, Administrator

Austin: **Manitoba Amateur Radio Museum Inc. (MARM)**
PO Box 10, Austin, MB R0H 0C0
Tel: 204-728-2463; Fax: 204-728-2463
ve4arm@mts.net
www.marminc.ca
Located on the grounds of the Manitoba Agricultural Museum, Hwy. #34 in Austin; Canada's only amateur radio museum; home of amateur radio station VE4ARM/VE4MTR.
Dave Snydal, Curator, dsnydal@mts.net

Beausejour: **Pioneer Village Museum**
Parent: **Brokenhead-Beausejour Historical Society**
PO Box 310, 7th St. North, Beausejour, MB R0E 0C0
Tel: 204-268-1318
info@broken-beau-museum.com
broken-beau-museum.com
Other contact information: Alternate Phones: 204-268-3911; 204-265-3204
Open July & Aug.

Belmont: **Belmont & District Museum**
PO Box 69, 202 - 5th St., Belmont, MB R0K 0C0
Tel: 204-528-3300
Other contact information: Phone, Off-season: 204-537-2405; 204-537-2474
The Belmont & District Museum features a CNR caboose, plus displays of medical equipment, sports memorabilia, military uniforms, & printing equipment for the Belmont News. The museum is open during July & August, & by appointment at other times of the year.

Belmont: **Evergreen Firearms Museum Inc.**
PO Box 57, Belmont, MB R0K 0C0
Tel: 204-537-2647
www.museumsmanitoba.com/dir/western/95.html
Military & non-military historical firearms; open year round

Binscarth: **Binscarth & District Gordon Orr Memorial Museum**
PO Box 239, 162 - 2nd Ave., Binscarth, MB R0J 0G0
Tel: 204-532-2217; Fax: 204-532-2153
vilbins@mts.net
www.binscarthmb.com/museum.html
The Binscarth & District Gordon Orr Memorial Museum contains displays such as Native artifacts, a chapel, a general store, a school room, & large agricultural machinery. The museum is open during July & August.
Rita Wasslen, Contact

Birtle: **Birdtail Country Museum**
PO Box 508, 738 Main St., Birtle, MB R0M 0C0
Tel: 204-842-5342
Other contact information: Alternative Phone: 204-842-3363; 204-842-5350
The Birdtail Country Museum is housed in the former Union Bank Building in Birtle. It contains a variety of objects from pioneer days in the Birtle area. The museum also holds local newspapers on microfilm. Birdtail Country Museum is open from mid-May to the end of August.

Boissevain: **Beckoning Hills Museum**
PO Box 389, 425 Mill Rd. South, Boissevain, MB R0K 0E0
Tel: 204-534-6544
bhmuseum@mts.net
The Beckoning Hills Museum presents historical displays from Boissevain & the surrounding area. Exhibits include pioneer household items, agricultural tools & implements, native artifacts, & military items. The museum is open from June until September. Appointments can be arranged at other times of the year.

Boissevain: **Irvin Goodon International Wildlife Museum**
PO Box 368, 298 Mountain St., Boissevain, MB R0K 0E0
Tel: 204-534-6662
turtlemountain@mymts.net
www.boissevain.ca/goodonmuseum
The museum features over 300 mounted animals in natural scenes, with full descriptions of each creature. Open in the summer, M-F 8:30-6:00, Sa & Su 10:00-6:00.
Irvin Goodon, Director

Boissevain: **Moncur Gallery**
PO Box 1241, Civic Centre, Boissevain, MB R0K 0E0
Tel: 204-534-6478; Fax: 204-534-3710
info@moncurgallery.org
www.moncurgallery.org
Year Founded: 1984 Gallery showcases an extensive collection of ancient artifacts portraying the earliest history of the Turtle Mountain and surrounding prairie area in southwestern Manitoba. Exhibits include lifestyle artifacts of nomadic peoples which predate the written record, such as ceremonial items, food preparation utensils & tools. Open Tue.-Sat., 10:00-5:00.
Shannon Moncur, Chair
Phyllis Hallett, Secretary

Brandon: **B.J. Hales Museum of Natural History**
George T. Richardson Library, Lower Level, Brandon University, 270 - 18th St., Brandon, MB R7A 6A9
Tel: 204-727-7307; Fax: 204-728-7346
jacksonk@brandonu.ca
www2.brandonu.ca/bjhales
The B.J. Hales Museum of Natural History collects, preserves, & presents artifacts of the natural heritage of Manitoba. Collections include bird & mammal specimens & a geological display. The museum is open year-round, Monday to Friday.

Brandon: **Chapman Museum**
PO Box 43, RR#2, Brandon, MB R7A 5Y2
Tel: 204-728-7396
Village-type museum setting with 16 historic buildings, among them the Roseville Church, Harrow School, Pendennis Rail Station, Robinville School, and various shops; guided tours; special needs facilities & wheelchair access; picnic area; open during the summer, free admission or donations appreciated.
Albert T. Chapman, Director

Brandon: **Commonwealth Air Training Plan Museum**
PO Box 3, Group 520, RR#5, Brandon, MB R7A 5Y5
Tel: 204-727-2444; Fax: 204-725-2334
airmuseum@inetlink.ca
www.airmuseum.ca
Canada's only air museum dedicated to those who trained & fought for the British Commmonwealth during WW II; artifacts include photographs, uniforms & clothing, personal papers, logbooks, station magazines, tools, equipment, trade badges, & medals; display of training aircraft
Stephen Hayter, Executive Director
John McNarry, President

Brandon: **Daly House Museum & Steve Magnacca Research Centre**
122 - 18 St., Brandon, MB R7A 5A4
Tel: 204-727-1722; Fax: 204-727-1722
dalymuseum@wcgwave.ca
www.dalyhousemuseum.ca
twitter.com/DalyHouseMuse um
www.facebook.com/dalyhouse
Period home of the 1880s; 1903 grocery store; 1892 council chambers; open daily in the summer; Tue.-Sun. winter

Eileen Trott, Curator

***Brandon:* Manitoba Agricultural Hall of Fame**
1129 Queens Ave., Brandon, MB R7A 1L9
Tel: 204-728-3736; Fax: 204-726-6260
info@manitobaaghalloffame.com
www.manitobaaghalloffame.com
Recognizing those who improved agricultural & rural living; plaques are at the Keystone Centre in Brandon (1175 - 18th St.); open daily
Robert G. (Bob) Roehle, President
Allan Chambers, Treasurer
Patricia Bailey, Office Manager, info@manitobaaghalloffame.com

***Brandon:* XII Manitoba Dragoons/26 Field Regiment Museum**
Brandon Armoury, 1116 Victoria Ave., Brandon, MB R7A 1B2
Tel: 204-726-3498; Fax: 204-725-1766
sim.gordo@gmail.com
www.12mbdragoons.com
Year Founded: 1979 The museum has a wide range of military memorabilia and artifacts on display, including photos, uniforms and equipment; small research library; archival materials; regimental button collection; open Tuesdays throughout the year

Mr. Ed McArthur, Curator

***La Broquerie:* Musée Saint-Jachim**
PO Box 66, La Broquerie, MB R0A 0W0
Tel: 204-424-5232

***Carberry:* Carberry Plains Museum**
PO Box 1072, 520 - 4th Ave., Carberry, MB R0K 0H0
Tel: 204-834-6609
www.townofcarberry.ca
The Carberry Plains Museum reflects early prairie life, through its collections from former residents, including a First World War pilot & Ernest Thompson Seton, a well-known naturalist. The museum is open during July & August. Appointments may be made during June & September.
Rae Anderson, Contact, 204-834-2284

***Carberry:* The Seton Centre**
PO Box 508, 116 Main St., Carberry, MB R0K 0H0
Tel: 204-834-2509
etseton@mts.net
www.thesetoncentre.ca
www.facebook.com/TheSetonCentre
Materials by & about Ernest Thompson Seton, 1860-1946; open June - Sept. long weekend
Cheryl Orr, Chair, 204-834-2056

***Carberry:* Spruce Woods Provincial Heritage Park**
c/o Manitoba Conservation, PO Box 900, Carberry, MB R0K 0H0
Tel: 204-834-3223; Fax: 204-834-2614
www.manitobaparks.com
Northwest Co. fur-trading artifacts

***Carman:* Dufferin Historical Museum**
PO Box 1646, 44 King's Park Ed., Carman, MB R0G 0J0
Tel: 204-745-3597; Fax: 204-828-3698
www.cici.mb.ca/mmedia/dufferin.html
Other contact information: Off-season phone: 204/745-2443
An early 20th century home. Open Mid-June - September.
Shirley Snider, President

***Carman:* Heaman's Antique Autorama**
PO Box 105, Carman, MB R0G 0J0
Tel: 204-745-2981
Canadian & American automobiles dating back to 1902

***Cartwright:* Heritage Village Museums**
***Parent:* Cartwright/Roblin Historical Society**
PO Box 9, Cartwright, MB R0K 0L0
Tel: 204-529-2363
www.cartwrightroblin.ca/node/97
This is a collection of historic buildings representing village life in pioneer days. The Blacksmith Museum is a fully restored, functional smithy. Todds Shoe Repairs has authentic cobbling equipment. Badger Creek Museum conserves artifacts of rural family life. There are also a schoolhouse, post office and telephone office.

***Churchill:* Eskimo Museum**
PO Box 10, 242 La Verendrye Ave., Churchill, MB R0B 0E0
Tel: 204-675-2030; Fax: 204-675-2140
chhbay@mts.net
Open Mon.-Sat., year-round
Lorraine Brandson, Curator

***Churchill:* Manitoba North National Historic Sites**
Parks Canada Visitor Centre, PO Box 127, 1 Manteyo Seepee Meskanow, Churchill, MB R0B 0E0
Tel: 204-675-8863; Fax: 204-675-2026
mannorth.nhs@pc.gc.ca
www.pc.gc.ca/eng/lhn-nhs/mb/prince/index.aspx
Guided tours are offered to Prince of Wales Fort, Cape Merry Battery, Sloop Cove & York Factory by contacting the Parks Canada Visitor Centre in Churchill which houses exhibits introducing the history of the Hudson's Bay Company and the fur trade of the 1700s. Open year round.
Sheldon Kowalchuk, Contact, sheldon.kowalchuk@pc.gc.ca

***Cranberry Portage:* Cranberry Portage Heritage Museum Corp.**
PO Box 310, Cranberry Portage, MB R0B 0H0
Tel: 204-472-3684; Fax: 204-472-3220
cphmuseum@gmail.com
www.cpmuseum.ca
Year Founded: 2001 Local history.
Richard Gibbons, President, r.cgibbons@mymts.net
Mary-Ann Playford, Curator
Leonard Gluska, Building Acquisition & Preservation Officer, lgluska@mymts.net

***Crystal City:* Crystal City Community Printing Museum**
PO Box 302, 218 Broadway St. South, Crystal City, MB R0K 0N0
Tel: 204-873-2260; Fax: 204-873-3829
Newspaper print shop started by Thomas Greenway (7th premier of Manitoba) in 1881; tours on request
Elaine Horsburgh, Contact, 204-873-2116
Ruth Lewis, Contact, 204-873-2441, jrlewis@goinet.com
Bill Sandercock, Contact, 204-873-2659
Beverley Treble, Contact

***Darlingford:* Darlingford School Heritage Museum**
PO Box 98, 197 Bradburn St., Darlingford, MB R0G 0L0
Tel: 204-246-2015
School built in 1910; open by appointment
Robert Jordan

***Dauphin:* Cross of Freedom Historical Site & Museum**
***Also known as:* Trembowla Cross of Freedom**
121 - 7 Ave. SE, Dauphin, MB R7N 2E3
Tel: 204-638-9641; Fax: 204-638-9963
The history & culture of Ukrainian pioneers; Cross of Freedom site of first Ukrainian Catholic Divine Liturgy & first Ukrainian Catholic Church St. Michael's, the oldest such church in Canada & dedicated as an Heritage site building in 2000; monuments include a large granite cross, bronze bust of Rev. Nestor Dmytriw, a grotto & monument of the first Ukrainian Catholic Bishop in Canada, Bishop Nyky
Kay Slobodzian, Secretary
Stella Sapach, Treasurer
John Slobodzian, President

***Dauphin:* Dauphin Rail Museum**
101 - 1st Ave. NW, Dauphin, MB R7N 1G8
Tel: 204-638-5495
tourismdauphin.ca/to-do/attractions-and-activities/dauphin-rail-museum
The museum is housed in a CNR railway station circa 1912, & features artifacts, pictures, & archival material about the history of rail travel in Dauphin. Hours of Operation: Sept.-June, Sa 9:00-1:00; open afternoons in the summer; other times by appointment.

***Dauphin:* Fort Dauphin Museum**
PO Box 181, 140 Jackson Ave., Dauphin, MB R7N 2V1
Tel: 204-638-6630; Fax: 204-629-2327
fortdphn@mymts.net
fortdauphinmuseum.wordpress.com
www.facebook.com/pages/Fort-Dauphin-Museum/225124957503412
Fur trade history, pioneer history, local history, the Parkland Archaeological Laboratory; open mid-May - early Sept. & by appt. early Sept.-mid May

***Dauphin:* Trembowla Cross of Freedom Museum**
121 - 7th Ave. SE, Dauphin, MB R7N 2E3
Tel: 204-638-9641
Other contact information: Alternate Phone: 204-638-9047
History of early Ukrainian settlement in the Dauphin area. Open June-Aug., or by appointment.

***Dufresne:* Aunt Margaret's Museum of Childhood Inc.**
Trans-Canada Hwy., Dufresne, MB R0A 0J0
Tel: 204-422-8426
Aunt Margaret's Museum of Childhood includes a collection of antique furniture & artifacts.

***Dugald:* Cook's Creek Heritage Museum**
Group 2, Box 10, RR#2, Dugald, MB R0E 0K0
Tel: 204-444-4448; Fax: 204-444-4224
info@cchm.ca
www.cchm.ca
www.facebook.com/pages/CCHM/124965140914084
Other contact information: Off-Season Contact Liz: 204-444-3247
Open daily, except Wed. May-Aug. 11-5
Jane Burpee, President

***Elgin:* Elgin & District Historical Museum Inc.**
PO Box 102, Main St., Elgin, MB R0K 0T0
Tel: 204-769-2147; Fax: 204-769-2002
Year Founded: 1995 Local history; open by appointment only.

***Elkhorn:* Manitoba Antique Automobile Museum**
PO Box 477, Elkhorn, MB R0M 0N0
Tel: 204-845-2604; Fax: 204-845-2312
info@elkhorn.mb.ca
www.mbautomuseum.com
Year Founded: 1961 Donated to the community by local farmer, Isaac "Ike" Clarkson, the collection began with a hand-restored 1909 Hupmobile to a sizeable array of vintage automobiles. The site also includes exhibits of agricultural machinery and household articles. Open May - Sept., 9:00-6:00.
Agnes Wolfe, Curator
Roland Gagnon, Chair
Garth Mitchell, Sec.-Treas.

***Erickson:* Erickson Centennial Grounds**
c/o Town Office, PO Box 40, 45 Main St., Erickson, MB R0J 0P0
Tel: 204-636-2431; Fax: 204-636-2516
erikclan@mts.net
The Parsonage, built in 1897-98 & the Nedrob School feature period artifacts; open by appt.

***Eriksdale:* Eriksdale Museum**
PO Box 71, Eriksdale, MB R0C 0W0
Tel: 204-739-2621; Fax: 204-739-2073
dmysmith@mts.net
www.eriksdale.com
Open mid-May - Sept., excluding Thurs. & Sun.; Eriksdale Creamery Museum now open
Elaine Henrotte, Secretary
Donna Smith, Chair

***Ethelbert:* Ethelbert & District Museum**
35 Railway Ave. North, Ethelbert, MB R0L 0T0
Tel: 204-742-8860
ethelbertmuseum@gmail.com
ethelbertmuseum.googlepages.com
Other contact information: Alternate Phones: 204-742-3761; 204-742-3376; 204-742-3672
The museum's collections pertain to the pioneer history of the area, featuring a kitchen, sewing room, nursery, bedroom, & school room. Open July & Aug., all other times by appointment only.

***Flin Flon:* Flin Flon Station Museum**
CN Building, PO Box 160, Highway 10, Flin Flon, MB R8A 1M6
Tel: 204-687-2946; Fax: 204-687-4456
www.cityofflinflon.com
Household artifacts from the late 1920s; mining; open Victoria Day - Labour Day
Ron Dodds

***Foxwarren:* Foxwarren Historical Society Inc.**
PO Box 85, Foxwarren, MB R0J 0R0
Tel: 204-847-2185
foxmuseum@mts.net
Local history.
Garth Butler, President

***Gardenton:* Ukrainian Museum & Village Society**
***Also known as:* Gardenton Park**
Gardenton, MB R0A 0M0
Tel: 204-425-3501
Clothing, icons & many articles from the early settlers; an exhibit of churches & photos of early pioneer life; clay thatched roof house & a one-room school; picnic facilities; tours & meals upon request
Linda Shewchuk, President

***Gilbert Plains:* Gilbert Plains & District Historical Society**
PO Box 662, Gilbert Plains, MB R0L 0X0
Tel: 204-548-4448; Fax: 204-548-2564
rmofgilbertplains@mts.net
10 log buildings; Ukrainian artifacts; open July & Aug.
Susan Boyachek, Sec.-Treas.
Eugene Dedio, President
Jim Michaluk, Vice-President

Gimli: **New Iceland Heritage Museum**
The Waterfront Centre, #108, 94 - 1st Ave., Gimli, MB R0C 1B1
Tel: 204-642-4001; Fax: 204-642-9382
nihm@mts.net
www.nihm.ca
www.facebook.com/263641135716
The New Iceland Heritage Museum preserves & interprets the history of New Iceland & Lake Winnipeg & its fishing industry.
Tammy Axelsson, Executive Director

Gladstone: **Gladstone & District Museum**
PO Box 651, 49 - 6th St., Gladstone, MB R0J 0T0
Tel: 204-385-2551; Fax: 204-385-2391
Local pioneer artifacts

Glenboro: **Burrough of the Gleann Museum**
Parent: **Glenboro Community Development Corporation**
PO Box 385, 237 Broadway, Glenboro, MB R0K 0X0
Tel: 204-827-2444
www.glenboro.com/Tourism/museum.htm
Antiques & memorabilia related to the history of Glenboro. Open July & Aug., daily 9:00-4:00; other times by appointment.
Ernestine Sepke, Contact

Grandview: **The Watson Crossley Community Museum**
PO Box 396, RR#4, Grandview, MB R0L 0Y0
Tel: 204-546-2661; Fax: 204-546-2027
guards56@goinet.ca
Facility includes museum display of local area pioneer artifacts, shedded display of antique farm machinery, tractors & automobiles; also included is a pioneer homestead building (1896), pioneer house (1918), rural one-room schoolhouse & a pioneer Ukrainian Orthodox church; open June-Sept. & year round by appt.

Haines Junction: **Da Ku (Our House)**
PO Box 5310, 280 Alaksa Hwy., Haines Junction, MB Y0B 1L0
Tel: 867-634-3300; Fax: 867-634-2287
www.cafn.ca/centre.html
The centre is owned & operated by the Champagne & Aishihik First Nations, & features cultural displays, heritage resource centre, classroom space, language lab, & more.
Diane Strand, Manager, dstrand@cafn.ca

Hamiota: **Hamiota Pioneer Club Museum**
Hamiota Recreation Grounds, PO Box 279, 7th St. South, Hamiota, MB R0M 0T0
Tel: 204-764-2552
www.hamiota.com/hc_museum.html
Open by appointment & for special events.

Hartney: **Hart-Cam Museum**
PO Box 399, 310 Poplar St., Hartney, MB R0M 0X0
Tel: 204-858-2590; Fax: 204-858-2681
hartney@mts.net
www.hartney.ca
Artifacts from Aboriginal to post-settlement times
Pat Phillips, Contact, 204-858-2127
Eleanor Vandusen, Contact, 204-858-2064

Headingly: **Headingley Heritage Centre, Jim's Vintage Garages**
5353 Portage Ave., Headingly, MB R4H 1J9
Tel: 204-889-3132; Fax: 204-831-0816
dwhite@rmofheadingley.ca
www.rmofheadingley.ca
Year Founded: 2005 The museum's collection features automotive & petroleum industry memorabilia collected & donated to the Rural Municipality of Headingley by a couple of long-time residents. Hours of Operation: May-Sept., W-Sa 10:00-4:00, Su 12:00-4:00; Sept.-Apr. by appointment.

Inglis: **Inglis Grain Elevators National Historic Site**
Parent: **Inglis Area Heritage Committee**
PO Box 81, Inglis, MB R0J 0X0
Tel: 204-564-2243; Fax: 204-564-2617
iahc@mts.net
www.ingliselevators.com
www.facebook.com/219879914711288
The site represents the development of Canada's grain industry from 1900-1930. Open summer, M-F 10:00-6:00, Su 12:00-6:00; off-season by appointment only.

Inglis: **St. Elijah Pioneer Museum**
Inglis, MB R0J 0X0
Tel: 204-564-2228
info@stelijahpioneermuseum.ca
www.stelijahpioneermuseum.ca
twitter.com/stelijahmuseum
Designated provincial historic site
Barry Sawchuk, President

Killarney: **J.A.V. David Museum**
PO Box 584, 414 Williams Ave., Killarney, MB R0K 1G0
Tel: 204-523-7325
Other contact information: Off-Season Phone: 204-523-8836
Museum of artifacts, clothing & memorabilia associated with Killarney & area history
Mark Witherspoon, Chair

Lac du Bonnet: **Lac du Bonnet & District Historical Society**
PO Box 658, 578 Riverland, Lac du Bonnet, MB R0E 1A0
Tel: 204-345-2726
ldbhistorical.ca
Kathy Willis, President, kwillis@watersidewireless.net

Ladywood: **Atelier Ladywood Museum**
PO Box 14, RR#3, Ladywood, MB R0E 0C0
Tel: 204-265-3226
Atelier Ladywood Museum features the former H. Gabel's General Store, with items from the 1930s to the 1950s.

Lundar: **Lundar Museum Society**
PO Box 265, Lundar, MB R0C 1Y0
Tel: 204-739-0147
Other contact information: Off-Season Phone: 204-762-5281
Open mid-June - Sept.; located at Railway & Main St.
Harold Hallson, President

Lynn Lake: **Lynn Lake Mining Town Museum**
PO Box 847, 470 Cobalt Pl., Lynn Lake, MB R0B 0W0
Tel: 204-356-8302
Open May 24 - Aug. 31
Neil Campbell, Contact

McCreary: **Satterthwaite Log Cabin**
PO Box 251, McCreary, MB R0J 1B0
Tel: 204-835-2341
A restored 1800s log cabin that shows pioneer building methods, & offers visitors a recreated pioneer garden, memorial plaques, & a rest area. Open July-Sept. by appointment.

Melita: **Antler River Historical Society Museum**
PO Box 67, 71 Ash St., Melita, MB R0M 1L0
Tel: 204-522-3103
Other contact information: Alternate Phones: 204-522-3438; 204-522-3825
Year Founded: 1972 Local history
W.H. Critchlow, President

Miami: **Miami Museum**
PO Box 153, Miami, MB R0G 1H0
Tel: 204-435-2305; Fax: 204-435-2534
Fossils; souvenirs of WWI & WWII; wedding dresses from 1896-1900

Miniota: **Miniota Municipal Museum Inc.**
PO Box 189, Government Rd. Allowance (Hwy. 83), Miniota, MB R0M 1M0
Tel: 204-567-3690; Fax: 204-567-3807
Open May - Oct.; pioneer & Aboriginal artifacts
R. Moorehead, President
S. Moorehead, Secretary

Minnedosa: **Minnedosa Heritage Museum**
PO Box 2005, 100 Heritage Park Cres., Minnedosa, MB R0J 1E0
Tel: 204-867-3542
minnedosamuseum@gmail.com
www.minnedosa.com
Other contact information: Off-Season Phone: 204-867-2027
Local history includes Cadurcis House, Hunterville Church, Havelock School, McManus Trappers' Cabin, Munro Blacksmith Shop, Minnedosa Power House, Hopkins Log Barn & operating windmill & waterwheel; museum open July 1st - Sept. long weekend; group tours by appt.

Moosehorn: **Moosehorn Heritage Museum Inc.**
Station Bldg., PO Box 28, Railway Ave. & 1st St. North, Moosehorn, MB R0C 2E0
Tel: 204-768-3788
Local pioneer history; radar equipment
Esther Sveinson, Contact

Morden: **Canadian Fossil Discovery Centre**
111B Gilmour St., Morden, MB R6M 1N9
Tel: 204-822-3406; Fax: 204-272-3303
info@discoverfossils.com
www.discoverfossils.com
Social Media: www.youtube.com/cdnfossildiscovery
www.facebook.com/bruce.mosasaur
Housing an extensive collection of marine reptile fossils, the galleries of the Canadian Fossil Discovery Centre interpret life in the Western Interior Seaway during the cretaceous period. The museum is open year round.
Anita-Maria Janzic, Executive Director/Curator, curator@discoverfossils.com

Morden: **Manitoba Baseball Hall of Fame (MBHOF)**
111C Gilmour St., Morden, MB R6M 1M9
Tel: 204-822-4634; Fax: 204-822-1483
mbbhof@mts.net
www.mbhof.ca
Year Founded: 1997 The Hall of Fame also includes a museum where visitors can explore the history of baseball in Manitoba. Open daily 8:00-9:00.
Jack Callum, Chair, 204-889-0818
Joe Wiwchar, Administrative Manager, Museum, 204-822-4636

Morris: **Morris & District Centennial Museum Inc.**
PO Box 344, 350 Main St. South, Morris, MB R0G 1K0
Tel: 204-746-2169
Exhibits artifacts which depict pioneer life in the Red River Valley
Larry McCrady, Director

Neepawa: **Beautiful Plains Museum**
PO Box 1732, 91 Hamilton St. West, Neepawa, MB R0J 1H0
Tel: 204-476-3896
www.neepawa.ca/museum
Other contact information: Phone, September - May: 204-476-3232
The Beautiful Plains Museum features the following attractions: a military room; costume rooms; a medical hall; jewellery & general store displays; a post office exhibit; a local history room; office equipment; farm & home tools; information about local lodges; sports memorabilia; information about the local Ukranian Polish culture; & a chapel room, which depicts the history of religious settlement in the Neepawa area. The museum is house in the CNR station, which was built in 1902. Neepawa's Beautiful Plains Museum is open from Victoria Day to Labour Day.

Neepawa: **The Margaret Laurence Home**
PO Box 2099, 312 - 1st Ave., Neepawa, MB R0J 1H0
Tel: 204-476-3612
mlhome@mts.net
www.mts.net/~mlhome/
Birthplace of Margaret Laurence; includes research area, meeting room & modern artwork; open daily in summer, other times by appt.
Lane England

Notre Dame de Lourdes: **Pioneers & Chanoinesses Museum / Musée des Pionniers et des Chanoinessess**
PO Box 186, 55 Rogers St., Notre Dame de Lourdes, MB R0G 1M0
Tel: 204-248-2687
museend@mts.net
The first pioneers in Notre Dame de Lourdes arrived from Quebec in 1880, & soon after pioneers came from France & Switzerland. The Chanoinesses Regulieres des Cinq-Plaies du Sauveur came to Notre Dame de Lourdes from Lyon, France in 1895. The Pioneers & Chanoinesses Museum houses artifacts of the pioneers & Chanoinesses in the community. The museum is open year round.
Collette Lesage, Conatct, 204-248-7220

The Pas: **Charlebois Heritage Museum**
PO Box 270, 108 - 1st St. West, The Pas, MB R9A 1K4
Tel: 204-623-6152; Fax: 204-623-6121
archives@keepas.ca
History & information about Bishop Charlebois, housed in a chapel built in 1897. Open M-F 1:00-5:00.

The Pas: **The Sam Waller Museum**
PO Box 185, 306 Fischer Ave., The Pas, MB R9A 1K4
Tel: 204-623-3802; Fax: 204-623-5506
samwallermuseum@mts.net
www.samwallermuseum.ca
Permanent collection comprises some 70,000 items of natural history specimens, historical artifacts, books & other library materials, photographs & negatives, fine art objects, & archival resources of the Town of The Pas; temporary exhibits; special events & programming
David Raitt, Director
Sharain Jones, Curator

Pilot Mound: **Marringhurst Pioneer Park Museum**
RR#2, Pilot Mound, MB R0G 1P0
Tel: 204-825-2334
Schoolhouse with original furnishings; open year round

Pilot Mound: **Pilot Mound Museum**
Pilot Mound Library, PO Box 126, 219 Broadway Ave. West, Lower Level, Pilot Mound, MB R0G 1P0
Tel: 204-825-2035
pmlibrary@mymts.net
Pioneer household & agricultural items; natural history artifacts; open year round
Shirley Foidart, Chair, Pilot Mound Library
Allison MacAulay, Head Librarian

Plum Coulee: **Plum Coulee & District Museum**
PO Box 36, 277 Main Ave., Plum Coulee, MB R0G 1R0
Tel: 204-829-3419; Fax: 204-829-3436
pcoulee@mts.net
Artifacts & photographs portray the Ukrainian, Mennonite, Jewish, & Ukrainian pioneer history of Plum Coulee & the surrounding area. The Plum Coulee & District Museum is open during the summer, or by appointment.

Portage la Prairie: **The Fort-La-Reine Museum & Pioneer Village**
PO Box 744, 2652 Saskatchewan Ave. East, Portage la Prairie, MB R1N 3C2
Tel: 204-857-3259; Fax: 204-239-4917
enquiries@fortlareinemuseum.ca
www.fortlareinemuseum.ca; fort-la-reine.tumblr.com
twitter.com/fortlareine
www.facebook.com/1295 53080390522
Depicts native & pioneer life in the 1800s & includes a fort, trading post, village store, country church, schoolhouse, print shop, fire hall, stable, trapper's cabin & several heritage homes; also includes a railway display of a caboose, 1882 official private railcar of Sir William Van Horne, several maintenance railroad vehicles & railway crossing; Muskateer Aircraft & Allis Chalmers Museum hous
John L. Bjore, Sec.-Manager/Curator

Rapid City: **Rapid City Museum**
PO Box 271, 4th Ave., Rapid City, MB R0K 1W0
Tel: 204-826-2043
racimus@live.ca
www.rapidcitymb.ca/museum
Cundy watch display; Frederick Philip Grove display; old school building; old Rapid City Reporter building with press & back copies; open July & Aug., other times by appt.
Sue Armstrong, Contact, 204-826-2969

Reston: **Reston & District Museum**
PO Box 280, 102 - 9th St., Reston, MB R0M 1X0
Tel: 204-877-3641
Local artifacts & archival material

Riverton: **Hecla Island Heritage Home Museum**
c/o Manitoba Conservation, Riverton, MB R0C 2R0
Tel: 204-279-2056
gov.mb.ca/conservation/parks/act_interp/centres/hecla-heritage.html
Depiction of the life of an Icelandic family, 1920-1940s; located in Hecla Village, off PTH 8.

La Riviere: **Archibald Historical Museum**
Also known as: **Archibald Museum**
PO Box 97, La Riviere, MB R0G 1A0
Tel: 204-242-2825
www.rmofpembina.com/museum.htm
Other contact information: Alternate Phones: 204-242-2554; 204-242-2235
1878 log house furnished as it was during Nellie McClung's residency plus large frame home (furnished) where she lived, had the first of her family & wrote her first books; also La Rivière C.P.R. Station & more; open mid-May - Labour Day, closed Wed. & Thu. unless by appt.
R.K. Wallcraft, President

Roblin: **Keystone Pioneers Museum Inc.**
PO Box 10, Roblin, MB R0L 1P0
Tel: 204-937-2979
keystonemuseum@gmail.com
kpmroblinmb.webs.com
www.facebook.com/189524247747064
Agricultural equipment & artifacts; Elaschuk House; Makaroff Church; Sawmill
Richard Wileman, President, 204-773-6634
Sue Bellamy, Secretary, 204-937-4806
Patricia Wanner, Treasurer, 204-937-8772

Roland: **Roland 4-H Museum**
72 - 3rd St., Roland, MB R0G 1T0
Tel: 204-343-2061
info@roland4hmuseum.ca
www.roland4hmuseum.ca
History of the 4-H club in Roland, MB. Open July & Aug., Su 1:00-6:00, M-Th 1:00-4:00.

Rossburn: **Rossburn Museum**
c/o Town of Rossburn, PO Box 70, 43 Main St. North, Rossburn, MB R0J 1V0
Tel: 204-859-2762; Fax: 204-859-2959
town.rsb@mts.net
www.town.rossburn.mb.ca
The Rossburn Museum features rooms representing a pioneer kitchen, a classroom, a hospital room, a print shop, & a hairdressing salon. The museum also displays a miniature Ukrainian village, plus Ukrainian artifacts.

St Andrews: **Lower Fort Garry National Historic Site of Canada**
5925 Hwy. 9, St Andrews, MB R1A 4A8
Tel: 204-785-6050; Fax: 204-482-5887
Toll-Free: 888-773-8888
lfg.info@pc.gc.ca
pc.gc.ca/garry
twitter.com/lowerft garrynhs
www.facebook.com/lowerfortgarrynhs
1830s stone Hudson's Bay Co. fort; costumed interpreters, visitor centre, gift store, restaurant; open May 15 - Labour Day, daily from 9-5
Dawn Bronson, Superintendent

Saint-Boniface: **La Maison Gabrielle-Roy**
CP 133, 375, rue Deschambault, Saint-Boniface, MB R2H 3B4
Tél: 204-231-3853; Téléc: 204-231-3910
info@maisongabrielleroy.mb.ca
www.maisongabrielleroy.mb.ca
www.faceboo k.com/LaMaisonGabrielleRoy
François Lentz, Président
Lucienne Châteauneuf, Directrice générale

Saint-Boniface: **Le Musée de Saint-Boniface Museum**
494, av Taché, Saint-Boniface, MB R2H 2B2
Tél: 204-237-4500; Téléc: 204-986-7964
info@msbm.mb.ca
msbm.mb.ca
Médias sociaux: www.youtube.com/user/StBonifaceMuseum
twitter.com/msbm_mb_ca
www.faceb ook.com/msbm.mb.ca
Logé dans l'ancien couvent des Soeurs Grises, le musée a pour mission d'effectuer des recherches sur des objets reliés au patrimoine canadien-français et métis de l'Ouest canadien; préservation et interprétation; expositions thématiques; plus de 30 000 objets historiques et ethnologiques dans la collection; programmation; boutique.
Dr. Philippe R. Mailhot, Directeur, pmailhot@msbm.mb.ca
Pierrette Boily, Conservatrice, pboily@msbm.mb.ca

St Claude: **Manitoba Dairy Museum**
Parent: **St. Claude Historical Society**
PO Box 131, St Claude, MB R0G 1Z0
Tel: 204-379-2156; Fax: 204-379-2156
Artifacts from settlers, many of whom came from France; variety of dairy artifacts
Raymond Philippot, Curator

Sainte-Geneviève: **Site Historique Monseigneur Taché / Monseigneur Taché Historic Site**
98, rue Saltel, Sainte-Geneviève, MB R5H 1R2
Tél: 204-853-7509
Fondée en: 1989

St Joseph: **Musée St-Joseph Museum Inc.**
PO Box 34, Étienne St., St Joseph, MB R0G 2C0
Tel: 204-737-2390; Fax: 204-737-2049
www.rmofmontcalm.com/museestjoseph.html
Other contact information: Alternate Phone: 204-737-3000
Domestic & agricultural artifacts; the oldest timber house in southern Manitoba; antique tractors. Open May 15 - Sept. 15
George Perron, Contact, gdperron@mts.net

Sandy Lake: **Ukrainian Cultural Heritage Museum**
Railway Ave., Sandy Lake, MB R0J 1X0
Tel: 204-585-2168
ebaba@escape.ca
Other contact information: Alternate Phones: 204-585-5314; 204-585-2636
1899 Ukrainian settlement; traditional Ukrainian arts & crafts; open June - Sept. & by appt.

Selkirk: **Marine Museum of Manitoba (Selkirk) Inc.**
PO Box 7, 490 Eveline St., Selkirk, MB R1A 2B1
Tel: 204-482-7761
marinemuseum@mts.net
www.marinemuseum.ca
Year Founded: 1973 The museum gathers and restores marine vessels related to Manitoba's Lake Winnipeg and the Red River from about 1850 to the present. Storehouses of artifacts and records are located aboard historic vessels, including the S.S. Keenora and the C.G.S. Bradbury. Open May - Sept.; school/group tours available.
Ms Shaylene Nordal, Museum Manager
Don Gordon, Chair

Selkirk: **St. Andrews' Rectory National Historic Site**
374 River Rd., Selkirk, MB R1A 2Y1
Tel: 204-785-6050; Fax: 204-482-5887
Toll-Free: 888-773-8888
lfg.info@pc.gc.ca
www.pc.gc.ca/lhn-nhs/mb/standrews/in dex.aspx
Other contact information: TTY: 1-866-787-6221
Collection of panels & antiques; open May - Sept.

Seven Sisters: **Whiteshell Natural History Museum**
c/o Manitoba Conservation, Seven Sisters, MB R0E 1Y0
www.gov.mb.ca/conservation/parks/popular_parks/whiteshell
Year Founded: 1960 Located in the Whiteshell Provincial Park, the natural history museum contains informative displays about the wildlife in the park, the boreal forest, sturgeon & the Winnipeg River, petroforms, & the Aborignal people. The Whiteshell Natural History Museum, located in a log building at Nutimik Lake, is open from the long weekend in May to the long weekend in September.

Shilo: **Royal Canadian Artillery Museum / Le Musée national de l'Artillerie du Canada; Le Musée de l'**
Also known as: **The National Artillery Museum of Canada; The RCA Museum**
CFB Shilo, Shilo, MB R0K 2A0
Tel: 204-765-3000; Fax: 204-765-5289
stag@mts.net
www.rcamuseum.com
Three permanent galleries, one temporary exhibits gallery; archives; library; kit shop; 109 major pieces of equipment; largest collection of Canadian military-pattern vehicles; open year round
K. Christensen, Curator
R. Sanderson, Director

Shoal Lake: **The Clack Family Heritage Museum**
c/o Don Yanick, PO Box 568, Shoal Lake, MB R0J 1Z0
Tel: 204-759-2368; Fax: 204-759-2484
dsyanick@inethome.ca
www.shoallake.ca/prairiemountain
Antique cars, tractors, trucks & farm implements; Victorian china & clothing; railway, RCMP military & native artifacts; open June-Sept.

Shoal Lake: **Clegg Carriage Museum**
c/o Prairie Mountain Regional Museums Collection Inc., PO Box 568, Shoal Lake, MB R0J 1Z0
Tel: 204-759-2368; Fax: 204-759-2484
dsyanick@inethome.ca
www.shoallake.ca/prairiemountain; www.museumsmanitoba.com
Located 3 miles south of Hwy #24 in Arrow River; collection of 90 completely restored horse-drawn vehicles, including a WW1 ambulance, a covered wagon, peddlar's wagon and hearse
Don Yanick, President, Prairie Mountain Regional Museums Collection Inc.

Shoal Lake: **Prairie Mountain Regional Museums Collection Inc.**
Also known as: **Prairie Mountain Regional Museum**
PO Box 568, Shoal Lake, MB R0J 1Z0
dsyanick@inethome.ca
www.shoallake.ca/prairiemountain
Local history.
Don Yanick, President, dsyanick@inethome.ca

Shoal Lake: **Shoal Lake Police & Pioneer Museum**
PO Box 233, Shoal Lake, MB R0J 1Z0
Tel: 204-759-2429; Fax: 204-759-2704
www.shoallake.ca/MountedPoliceMuseum
Other contact information: Summer phone: 204-759-3326
A replica of an 1875 NWMP building; it houses a collection of North West Mounted Police & Royal Canadian Mounted Police displays; official Museum for the Mounted Police in Manitoba; open June-Sept. by summer staff, other times by appt.; school talks & presentations available

Snowflake: **Star Mound School Museum**
General Delivery, Snowflake, MB R0G 2K0
Tel: 204-876-4749
One-room country school c. 1886
Joan Wheeler, Contact, 204-873-2600

Souris: **Hillcrest Museum**
PO Box 1287, 26 Crescent Ave. East, Souris, MB R0K 2C0
Tel: 204-483-2008
www.sourismanitoba.com/hillcrest-museum.html
Year Founded: 1967 Includes agricultural museum & CPR caboose; open May - Sept.; collection of over 5000 butterflies on display

Souris: **The Plum - 1883 Souris Heritage Church Museum & Tea Room**
Also known as: **The Plum Museum**
PO Box 548, 142 - 1st St. South, Souris, MB R0K 2C0
Tel: 204-483-3643
www.sourismanitoba.com/plum-museum.html
Other contact information: Off-Season Phone: 204-483-2643
Housed in St. Luke's Anglican Church, circa 1883, the museum's collection focuses on local art & history. Open July-Sept., 11:00-7:00.

***Sprague:* Sprague & District Historical Museum**
PO Box 60, Sprague, MB R0A 1Z0
Tel: 204-437-2342; Fax: 204-437-2032

Local & military history; open June-Sept., Sa & Su 1:00-5:00.

***Ste Anne des Chênes:* Musée Pointe des Chênes**
208 av Centrale, Ste Anne des Chênes, MB R5H 1C9
Tel: 204-422-5639; Fax: 204-422-5514
ritchot@ccco.net
Situated in a park next to the Villa Youville; museum features old pioneer artifacts of the region
Paul-Guy Lavack, President

***Steinbach:* Mennonite Heritage Village (Canada) Inc.**
231 PTH 12 N, Steinbach, MB R5G 1T8
Fax: 204-326-5046
Toll-Free: 866-280-8741
info@mhv.ca
www.mennoniteheritagevillage.com
Includes J.J. Reimer Historical Library & Archives; historical village with traditional housebarns, semlin, blacksmith shop, printery, general store, operating windmill, farm fields, exihibition gallery; livery barn restaurant serving ethnic Mennonite food; library; gift shop; special events throughout the summer; educational programming; online bookstore on the website. Open May through September.
Barry Dyck, Executive Director, barryd@mhv.ca
Dr. Roland Sawatzky, Senior Curator, rolands@mhv.ca
Anne Toews, Program Director, annet@mhv.ca

***St-Georges:* Musée St-Georges**
19 Baie Caron, St-Georges, MB R0E 1V0
Tél: 204-367-8801; Téléc: 204-367-9970
odiled@xplornet.com
Ouvert de mai à sept.

***St-Malo:* Le Musée Pionnier St Malo**
PO Box 328, Hwy. 59 South, St-Malo, MB R0A 1T0
Tel: 204-347-5767
Depiction of early settlers' lives

***Stonewall:* Stonewall Quarry Park**
PO Box 250, Stonewall, MB R0C 2Z0
Tel: 204-467-7980; Fax: 204-467-7985
stoneqp@stonewall.ca
www.stonewall.ca
Exhibits pertain to the limestone quarries & their role in the development of the community of Stonewall

***St-Pierre-Jolys:* Musée de St-Pierre-Jolys**
CP 321, 432, rue Joubert nord, St-Pierre-Jolys, MB R0A 1V0
Tél: 204-433-7635
froy@hsd.ca
www.museestpierrejolys.ca
Le musée est un ancien couvent et sert à se rappeler le patrimoine et les contributions des religieuses au développement du village de Saint-Pierre-Jolys; on retrouve aussi la Maison Goulet, et un cabane à sucre.

***Strathclair:* Strathclair Museum**
PO Box 383, Main St., Strathclair, MB R0J 2C0
Tel: 204-365-5201
www.museumsmanitoba.com/dir/western/68.html
In a restored CPR station and residence, the museum contains material relating to the district, which includes geneaology and information on Lord Elphinstone; replica blacksmith shop and machine shed; Open July & August or by appt.
Helga Gerrard, Sec.-Treas.

***Swan River:* Swan Valley Historical Museum & Archives**
PO Box 2078, Hwy. 10, Swan River, MB R0L 1Z0
Tel: 204-734-3585
Year Founded: 1972 History of Swan River Valley, Ice Age to settlement; open mid-May - mid-Sept.; archives open by appt. Tues. 9-2, summer
Niel Brown, President, 204-734-2713
Gwen Palmer, Secretary, 204-734-2475

***Teulon:* Teulon & District Museum**
Teulon-Rockwood Green Acres Park, PO Box 44, Teulon, MB R0C 3B0
Tel: 204-886-2216
www.teulon.ca/TeulonandDistrictMuseum.htm
Site includes a log house, a caboose, two schoolhouses, a small church, a large machine shed, old shoe shop, outside bake oven & the Dr. Hunter Home, 1918 Ford car, doll house with over 300 dolls; open June - Sept., Tues. to Sun., or by appt.

***Thompson:* Heritage North Museum**
162 Princeton Dr., Thompson, MB R8N 2A4
Tel: 204-677-2216; Fax: 204-677-8953
hnmuseum@mts.net
www.heritagenorthmuseum.ca
Year Founded: 1990 The museum preserves the heritage & history of Thompson & area, where in 1956 nickel was discovered. One of the log buildings displays a taxidermy array of animals native to the region, hides, furs and fossils, while the other building focuses on the mining industry. There is a gift shop.
Tanna Teneycke, Executive Director
Sharon McLeod, President
Valerie Little, Vice-President

***Treherne:* Treherne Museum**
c/o Town Office, PO Box 30, 215 Broadway St., Treherne, MB R0G 1H0
Tel: 204-723-2621; Fax: 204-723-2719
www.treherne.ca
Year Founded: 1978

***Virden:* Currahee Military Museum**
PO Box 729, Virden, MB R0M 2C0
Tel: 204-748-1461; Fax: 204-748-1805
john@wolverinesupplies.com
Open by appt. only
John Hipwell

***Virden:* River Valley School Museum**
PO Box 2048, Virden, MB R0M 2C0
Tel: 204-748-3920
Country school furnishings & library 1896-1955

***Virden:* Virden Pioneer Home Museum Inc.**
PO Box 29, 390 King St. West, Virden, MB R0M 2C0
Tel: 204-748-1659; Fax: 204-748-2501
virden.cimnet.ca/cim/187C1_4T421T3T168.dhtm
Open summer daily
Helen Boulton-Elliott, President
Mary Jo O'Rourke, Secretary

***Wabowden:* Wabowden Historical Museum**
c/o Wabowden Community Council, PO Box 130, Wabowden, MB R0B 1S0
Tel: 204-689-2362; Fax: 204-689-2355
wabcouncil@digistar.mb.ca
The Wabowden Historical Museum preserves & displays artifacts from Wabowden & the surrounding region, such as mining, logging, fishing, & trapping items. The museum is open from Canada Day until the Labour Day weekend.
Caroline Sanofsky, President

***Wasagaming:* Riding Mountain Historical Society & Pinewood Museum**
PO Box 254, 154 Wasagaming Dr., Wasagaming, MB R0J 2H0
Tel: 204-848-2810
Records & preserves the history of humans in the Riding Mountain National Park; open daily 2-5pm in July & Aug.
Cathy Chalmers, President

***Wasagaming:* Riding Mountain National Park of Canada (RMNPC) / Parc national du Canada du Mont-Riding**
General Delivery, Wasagaming, MB R0J 2H0
Tel: 204-848-7275; Fax: 204-848-2596
rmnp.info@pc.gc.ca
www.pc.gc.ca/ridingmountain
Other contact information: TTY: 1-866-787-6221; E-mail, Friends of RMNP: friends.rmnp@pc.gc.ca
The Riding Mountain National Park of Canada covers 3,000 km2 of the Manitoba prairie & escarpment. The park provides a variety of school & interpretation programs. The Visitor Centre is open from mid May to mid October.
Scot Shellborn, Officer, Visitor Experiences, 204-848-7284

***Waskada:* Waskada Museum**
c/o Village of Waskada, PO Box 40, 103 - 2nd St., Waskada, MB R0M 2E0
Tel: 204-673-2503
www.waskada.ca/pages/Museum.htm
Other contact information: Phone, Appointments: 204-673-2557
The Waskada Museum features the following buildings: the 1914 Anglican Church, the 1906 Union (Royal) Bank, a 1927 blacksmith shop, the 1896 Menota country school, a vehicle display building, & a display building. The museum is open during July & August.

***Wawanesa:* Sipiweske Museum**
PO Box 116, 102 - 4th St., Wawanesa, MB R0K 2G0
Tel: 204-824-2289; Fax: 204-824-2244
wacomcon@mts.net
Memorabilia from pioneers, Nellie McClung, Native people & 1903 insurance company; open July-Aug.; by appointment other times

***Whitemouth:* Whitemouth Municipal Museum**
PO Box 294, Hwy. 44, Whitemouth, MB R0E 2G0
Tel: 204-348-2216
www.granite.mb.ca
Museum depicting the different ways of life in the area - farming, railway, forestry, trapping, peat moss plants, hydro, AECL, fishing, brickyard, flour mill; artifacts housed in six buildings & two pole sheds; cairn honouring Dr. Charlotte Ross (The Iron Rose), first female to practice medicine in Manitoba; turn of the century house; 1905 Anglican Church; CPR Caboose; seasonal hours.
Harvey Pischke, Contact

***Winkler:* Pembina Threshermen's Museum Inc.**
PO Box 1103, Winkler, MB R6W 4B2
Tel: 204-325-7497
info@threshermensmuseum.com
www.threshermensmuseum.com
The Pembina Threshermen's Museum preserves the area's agricultural & Mennonite heritage. The grounds of the museum feature several heritage buildings, such as the 1909 Pomeroy School, the 1905-1906 Morden CPR Sation, an 1885 log house, plus a sawmill, windmill, blacksmith shop, barbershop, & post office. The museum is open from the beginning of May to the end of September.

***Winnipeg:* 402 Squadron Association**
PO Box 42202 St. James, Winnipeg, MB R3J 0X7
Tel: 204-786-5503
Archives, photographs of #402 City of Winnipeg Squadron

***Winnipeg:* Air Force Heritage Museum & Air Park / Le Musée du patrimoine de la force aérienne et du parc aéri**
1 Canadian Air Division Headquarters, PO Box 17000 Forces, Air Force Way, Winnipeg, MB R3J 3Y5
Tel: 204-833-2500; Fax: 204-833-2512

The museum, located in the Billy Bishop building, is part of a complex that consists of an outdoor air park showcasing 14 aircraft. The air park is open year round. Museum is open daily Mon-Fri throughout the summer from 8:00-4:00 by appointment. Guided tours, with services in English and French; wheelchair accessible; food service and restrooms. Located on Air Force Way, north off Ness Ave. on Sharp Blvd.
Don Pearsons, Executive Director

***Winnipeg:* Costume Museum of Canada**
PO Box 49098 Garden City, Winnipeg, MB R2V 4G8
Tel: 204-989-0072

www.facebook.com/pages/Costume-Museum-of-Canada/948974 56640
Over 35,000 artifacts spanning over 400 years; collection of costumes, textiles & related accessories. The museum is currently closed, but seeking support to continue their efforts.
Trudy Hansford, Contact, trudyhansford@mymts.net

***Winnipeg:* Dalnavert Museum**
***Parent:* Manitoba Historical Society**
61 Carlton St., Winnipeg, MB R3C 1N7
Tel: 204-943-2835
info@mhs.mb.ca
www.mhs.mb.ca/info/museums/dalnavert/index.shtml
1895 restored Victorian home of Hugh John Macdonald, son of Sir John A. Macdonald
Dr. Annabelle Mays, President, president@mhs.mb.ca
Jacqueline Friesen, CAO
Jennifer Bisch, Chief Program Officer/Curator, dalnavert@mhs.mb.ca

***Winnipeg:* The Ed Leith Cretaceous Menagerie**
Dept. of Geological Sciences, University of Manitoba, Wallace Bldg., 125 Dysart Rd., Winnipeg, MB R3T 2N2
Tel: 204-474-9371
umanitoba.ca/geoscience/cretaceousmenagerie
The Menagerie displays four complete skeletal replicas of creatures from the Cretaceous Period. Open M-F 8:30-4:30.
Brenda Miller, Administrative Assistant, Dept. of Geological Sciences, brenda_miller@umanitoba.ca

***Winnipeg:* The Fire Fighters Museum of Winnipeg**
56 Maple St., Winnipeg, MB R3B 0Y8
Tel: 204-942-4817; Fax: 204-885-1306
firemuseum@gatewest.net
www.winnipegfiremuseum.ca
The museum's collections cover every aspect of Winnipeg's fire service. Call the museum for their hours of operation.

***Winnipeg:* Fort Garry Horse Regimental Museum & Archives Inc.**
c/o McGregor Armoury, 551 Machray Ave., Winnipeg, MB R2W 1A8
Tel: 204-586-6298
www.fortgarryhorse.ca
Depicts the history of the Fort Garry Horse from 1912 to present; open Mon. evenings 7:30-10:30; other times by appt.
Larry Lajeunesse, Chair
Gord Crossley, Director

***Winnipeg:* FortWhyte Alive**
1961 McCreary Rd., Winnipeg, MB R3P 2K9
Tel: 204-989-8355; Fax: 204-895-4700
info@fortwhyte.org
www.fortwhyte.org
twitter.com/fortwhytealive
www. facebook.com/FortWhyteAlive

74 hectares of lakes, marshes aspen parkland for environmental education; exhibit building

***Winnipeg:* Historical Museum of St. James-Assiniboia**
***Parent:* Historical Museum Association of St. James-Assiniboia**
3180 Portage Ave., Winnipeg, MB R3K 0Y5
Tel: 204-888-8706
Open year round

***Winnipeg:* Ivan Franko Museum**
200 Mc Gregor St., 595 Pritchard Ave., Winnipeg, MB R2W 5L6
Tel: 204-589-4397; Fax: 204-589-3404
History of Ivan Franko, Ukrainian poet, novelist, & social activist & Ukrainian pintings; ceramics, woodcarving, glassware, embroidery, & weaving; open year-round.

***Winnipeg:* J.B. Wallis Museum of Entomology**
Dept. of Entomology, University of Manitoba, Winnipeg, MB R3T 2N2
Tel: 204-474-9257; Fax: 204-474-7628
head_entomo@umanitoba.ca
www.umanitoba.ca/afs/entomology/jbwallis.html
250,000 species of insects
Dr. Rob Currie, Department Head Ph.D., rob_currie@umanitoba.ca

***Winnipeg:* Jewish Heritage Centre of Western Canada Inc.**
Asper Jewish Community Campus, #C140, 123 Doncaster St., Winnipeg, MB R3N 2B2
Tel: 204-477-7460; Fax: 204-477-7465
jewishheritage@jhcwc.org
www.jhcwc.org
The centre includes a library, archive collections, a Holocaust resource & education centre, artifact exhibitions, & seasonal visiting exhibits. Open M-Th 9:00-4:00.

***Winnipeg:* Manitoba Children's Museum**
The Forks, 45 Forks Market Rd., Kinsmen Building, Winnipeg, MB R3C 4T6
Tel: 204-924-4000; Fax: 204-956-2122
general@childrensmuseum.com
www.childrensmuseum.com
Year Founded: 1983 Catering to children, the site includes such hands-on exhibits as a 1950s train station with CNR diesel locomotive. Open daily, year round.
Diane Doth, Executive Director

***Winnipeg:* Manitoba Crafts Museum & Library (MCML)**
#1B, 183 Kennedy St., Winnipeg, MB R3C 1S6
Tel: 204-487-6117
info@mcml.ca
www.mcml.ca
www.facebook.com/258347936251
Year Founded: 1986 The museum's collection focuses on the development of Canadian, and particularly Manitoban, crafts since the 1920s. The library houses about 2,500 titles pertaining to crafts, including scrapbooks and design patterns. Open year round
Stephanie Cooper, Co-President, president@mcml.ca
Judy Girard, Co-President, president@mcml.ca
Andrea Reichert, Curator, curator@mcml.ca

***Winnipeg:* Manitoba Electrical Museum & Education Centre**
PO Box 815, 680 Harrow St., Winnipeg, MB R3C 2P4
Tel: 204-477-7905
www.hydro.mb.ca/about_us/electrical_museum.shtml
Year Founded: 1971 The museum explores the history of electricity in Manitoba from the 1800s. Exhibits include archival photographs, documents and electrical artifacts, including vintage household appliances and an electric streetcar. In the lower level is an interactive section with Hazard Hamlet where, children can learn about potentially hazardous situations if electricity is not used properly.

***Winnipeg:* Manitoba Military Aviation Museum**
Bldg. 66, Canadian Forces Base 17 Wing Winnipeg, 715 Wuhiri Rd., Winnipeg, MB R3J 3Y5
Tel: 204-833-2500
donnariguidel@manitobamilitaryaviationmuseum.com
www.manitobamilitaryavi ationmuseum.com
Other contact information: Historian, E-mail: normmalaney@manitobamilitaryaviationmuseum.com
The museum is dedicated to preserving Manitoba aviation heritage through its collection & exhibits. Open Tu-F, 1:00-5:00.
Lt. Donna Riguidel, Heritage Officer
Rob Iwacha, 17 Wing Heritage Assistant
Norman Malayney, Resident Miltary Aviation Historian

***Winnipeg:* Manitoba Sports Hall of Fame & Museum Inc. (MSHOF)**
***Parent:* Sport Manitoba**
Sport for Life Centre, 145 Pacific Ave., Winnipeg, MB R3B 2Z6
Tel: 204-925-5736; Fax: 204-925-5916
halloffame@sportmanitoba.ca
www.halloffame.mb.ca
twitter.com/SportMani toba
Year Founded: 1993 The museum aims to honour those people who have contributed significantly to Manitoba's rich sports history. The exhibits use various memorabilia and photos to cover such sports as athletics, basketball, baseball/softball, curling, football, golf, hockey, and the Winter Olympics.
Rick D. Brownlee, Sport Heritage Manager
Andrea Reichert, Collections Manager, andrea.reichert@sportmanitoba.ca

***Winnipeg:* Naval Museum of Manitoba**
HMCS Chippawa Bldg., 1 Navy Way, Winnipeg, MB R3C 4J7
Tel: 204-943-7745; Fax: 204-947-9533
curator@naval-museum.mb.ca
naval-museum.mb.ca
The museum honours Manitoba's contributions to the Canadian Navy. Open to visitors on Wednesdays from 9:00 to 3:00; also open Sundays 1:00 to 4:00 in the summer.

***Winnipeg:* Ogniwo Polish Museum Society Inc.**
1417 Main St., Winnipeg, MB R2W 3V3
Tel: 204-586-5070
info@polishmuseum.com
www.polishmuseum.com
Artifacts related to Polish immigrants in Canada; open year round

***Winnipeg:* Queen's Own Cameron Highlanders of Canada Regimental Museum Inc.**
Minto Armoury, #230, 969 St. Matthew's Ave., Winnipeg, MB R3G 0J7
Tel: 204-786-4330
thequeensowncameronhighlandersofcanada.net
Regimental dress, equipment & archives from 1910 to present

***Winnipeg:* Riel House National Historic Site of Canada / Parc historique national du Canada de la Maison-Riel**
c/o Parks Canada, #401, 25 Forks Market Rd., Winnipeg, MB R3C 4S8
Tel: 204-257-1783; Fax: 204-983-2221
riel.info@pc.gc.ca
www.pc.gc.ca/lhn-nhs/mb/riel/contact.aspx
Other contact information: TTY: 1-866-787-6221; Off-Season Phone: 204-983-6757
Riel family home, depicts life of Métis family in St. Vital during the 1880s; open daily mid-May - Labour Day

***Winnipeg:* Robert B. Ferguson Museum of Mineralogy**
Dept. of Geological Sciences, University of Manitoba, Wallace Bldg., 125 Dysart Rd., Winnipeg, MB R3T 2N2
Tel: 204-474-9371; Fax: 204-474-7623
umanitoba.ca/geoscience/MuseumWeb/MuseumWeb
Year Founded: 1971 The museum's collection includes mineral specimins & research papers.

***Winnipeg:* Ross House Museum**
Joe Zuken Heritage Park, 140 Meade St. North, Winnipeg, MB R2W 3K5
Tel: 204-943-3958
rosshouse@mhs.mb.ca
www.mhs.mb.ca
www.facebook.com/g roups/107918235910933
Ross House was the first post office in western Canada. It is now a museum, owned by the City of Winnipeg & operated by the Manitoba Historical Society. The museum depicts the operation of early postal service & the life of the Ross family around 1850. Ross House is open from the beginning of June to the end of August. Schools & large groups may arrange appointments at other times of the year.
Dr. Simon Lucy, Chair, Ross House Community Committee
Victor Sawelo, Museum Manager

***Winnipeg:* Royal Canadian Mint - Winnipeg Facility**
520 Lagimodiere Blvd., Winnipeg, MB R2J 3E7
Tel: 204-983-6400; Fax: 204-255-5203
www.mint.ca
Tours of the mint available year round; call for reservations
Christian Robin, Supervisor, Tour Operations, robin@mint.ca

***Winnipeg:* Royal Winnipeg Rifles Regimental Museum**
Minto Armoury, #208, 969 St. Matthews Ave., Winnipeg, MB R3G 0J7
Tel: 204-786-4300; Fax: 204-786-4384
riflesmuseum@shaw.ca
www.mintoarmoury.com
Year Founded: 1970 Collects & preserves the history of the Regiment, & also houses displays relevant to the Winnipeg Light Infantry & the Winnipeg Grenadiers; military artifacts & memorabilia, pictures, books & other documents; open Tues. & by appt.; closed Sat. June - Aug
Gerry Woodman, President & Director, cwowoodman@shaw.ca

***Winnipeg:* St. Norbert Provincial Heritage Park**
PO Box 30, 200 Saulteaux Cres., Winnipeg, MB R3J 3W3
Tel: 204-945-4375; Fax: 204-945-0012
www.gov.mb.ca/conservation/parks/popular_parks/central/norber t_info.html
Illustrates how a natural landscape used for hunting, fishing & camping by Aboriginal peoples evolved into a French-speaking Métis settlement, then a French-Canadian agricultural community of the pre-World War I period; guided tours of restored Turenne & Bohémier houses; open daily May long weekend to Labour Day weekend.

***Winnipeg:* St. Vital Museum**
***Parent:* St. Vital Historical Society Inc.**
600 St. Mary's Rd., Winnipeg, MB R2M 3L5
Tel: 204-255-2864
info@svhs.ca
www.svhs.ca
Educational centre, bringing "the history of St. Vital" to the community by way of shows & displays; museum holds artifacts
Bob Holliday, President
John Dempster, Resident Historian

***Winnipeg:* St. Volodymyr Ukrainian Catholic Museum**
***Parent:* Ukrainian Catholic Archeparchy of Winnipeg**
233 Scotia St., Winnipeg, MB R2V 1V7
Tel: 204-338-7801; Fax: 204-339-4006
Religious & cultural collection pertaining to the life of the church in Canada.

***Winnipeg:* Sandilands Forest Centre**
***Parent:* Manitoba Forestry Association**
c/o Manitoba Forestry Association, 900 Corydon Ave., Winnipeg, MB R3M 0Y4
Tel: 204-453-3182; Fax: 204-477-5765
www.thinktrees.org/Sandilands_Forest_Discovery_Centre.aspx
The Centre is sited on 122 hectares of land granted to the Manitoba Forestry Association, & is located near Hadashville, just south of the Trans Canada Highway, east of Winnipeg; information on biodiversity, forest ecology, sustainable management of forest resources, fire prevention & management; nature trails, museum, fire tower & picnic area; educational programming; commemorative tree planting
Dr. Christina McDonald, President
Patricia Pohrebniuk, Executive Director
Glenn Peterson, Director, Education

***Winnipeg:* Seven Oaks House Museum**
PO Box 25176, 1650 Main St., Winnipeg, MB R2V 4C8
Tel: 204-339-7429; Fax: 204-334-8516
Seven Oaks House is a log residence, which was built between 1851 & 1853. It has been restored to reflect life during the Red River settlement in the 19th century. The museum is open from mid May to Labour Day.

***Winnipeg:* Stewart Hay Memorial Museum**
Duff Roblin Bldg., Dept. of Zoology, University of Manitoba, Winnipeg, MB R3T 2N2
Tel: 204-474-9245; Fax: 204-474-7588
hann@ms.umanitoba.ca
Mounted & study specimens of mammals, birds, fish, reptiles, amphibians, crustaceans, mollusks & other invertebrates; casts of fossils; open year round

***Winnipeg:* Transcona Historical Museum**
141 Regent Ave. West, Winnipeg, MB R2C 1R1
Tel: 204-222-0423; Fax: 204-222-0208
info@transconamuseum.mb.ca
www.transconamuseum.mb.ca
Archives, photographs, rare books, reference files, natural history (including an 8,000 specimen lepidoptera collection), First Nations cultural artifacts (3,500 items), Euro-Canadian cultural artifacts & a clothing & textile collection
Alanna Horejda, Curator

***Winnipeg:* Ukrainian Cultural & Educational Centre**
184 Alexander Ave. East, Winnipeg, MB R3B 0L6
Tel: 204-942-0218; Fax: 204-943-2857
ucec@mts.net
www.oseredok.org
Library & historical & archival collections dealing with the history of Ukrainians in Canada & the history of Ukraine; open Tues. - Sat. year round

***Winnipeg:* University of Winnipeg Geography Museum**
515 Portage Ave., Winnipeg, MB R3B 2E9
Tel: 204-786-9485; Fax: 204-774-4134
geography@uwinnipeg.ca
geograph.uwinnipeg.ca/facilities.htm
Teaching & reference collection of rocks, minerals & fossils, with a Manitoba focus; open year round

Kim Monson, Contact, k.monson@uwinnipeg.ca

***Winnipeg:* UVAN Historical Museum & Archives**
#203, 456 Main St., Winnipeg, MB R3B 1B6
Tel: 204-942-5861
Historical, ethnological & archival material

***Winnipeg:* Western Canada Aviation Museum (WCAM) / Musée de l'aviation de l'ouest du Canada**
Hangar T-2, 958 Ferry Rd., Winnipeg, MB R3H 0Y8
Tel: 204-786-5503; Fax: 204-775-4761
info@wcam.mb.ca; events@wcam.mb.ca
www.wcam.mb.ca
Other contact information: E-mail, School Tours: programs@wcam.mb.ca; Gifts: giftshop@wcam.mb.ca
The Western Canada Aviation Museum's recovery & restoration department works to prepare aircraft for display. The museum features sights such as Canada's first helicopter, bushplanes, historic military jets, & commercial aircraft. The museum also contains an aviation reference library, with collections of books, magazines, manuals, photographs, drawings, & audio-visual materials. The library is open to the public by appointment. The museum is open year-round.

***Winnipeg:* Winnipeg Police Museum**
***Parent:* Winnipeg Police Museum & Historical Society Inc.**
PO Box 1680, 130 Allard Ave., Winnipeg, MB R3C 2Z7
Tel: 204-986-3976
wps-museum@winnipeg.ca
www.winnipeg.ca
Year Founded: 1974 The Winnipeg Police Museum exhibits items related to the Winnipeg Police Force, which formed in 1874. Objects on display include early handcuffs,& identification cameras, & a jail cell which was built in 1911. There are also exhibits surrounding the 1919 Winnipeg General Strike & Earle "The Strangler" Nelson. Located at the Winnipeg Police Academy, the Winnipeg Police Museum is open daily. Conducted group tours can be arranged.

***Winnipeg:* Winnipeg Railway Museum**
PO Box 48, 123 Main St., Winnipeg, MB R3C 1A3
Tel: 204-942-4632
wpgrail@mts.net
www.wpgrailwaymuseum.com
The museum contains artifacts, trains, & train-related vehicles & equipment. Open year-round, M, Th & Sa 9:00-12:00.

***Winnipegosis:* Medd House Museum**
***Parent:* Winnipegosis Historical Society Inc.**
c/o Winnipegosis Historical Society Inc., PO Box 336, Winnipegosis, MB R0L 2G0
Tel: 204-656-4318
winnipegosismuseum@yahoo.ca
www.winnipegosis.org
Other contact information: Alternate Phone: 204-656-4273
Historic house once owned by a local Winnipegosis doctor, Dr. Medd.

***Winnipegosis:* Winnipegosis Museum**
***Parent:* Winnipegosis Historical Society Inc.**
c/o Winnipegosis Historical Society Inc., PO Box 336, Winnipegosis, MB R0L 2G0
Tel: 204-656-4791; Fax: 204-656-4751
winnipegosismuseum@yahoo.ca
www.winnipegosis.org
Housed in former CNR Railway Station (c.1897); 65-foot freighter, the "Myrtle M"; artifacts; CNR historical material; War Memorial items; native handiwork
Pauline Riley, Contact, 204-656-4273, pauliner@mts.net

***Woodlands:* Woodlands Pioneer Museum**
PO Box 206, Hwy. 6, Woodlands, MB R0C 3H0
Tel: 204-383-5691
Other contact information: Alternate Phones: 204-383-5919; 204-383-5589
Post office; municipal office; doctor's office; church; school; log house; open July-Aug.

New Brunswick

Provincial Museums

Kings Landing Historical Settlement / Village historique de Kings Landing
5904 Rte. 102, Prince William, NB E6K 0A5
Tel: 506-363-4999; Fax: 506-363-4989
info@kingslanding.nb.ca
kingslanding.nb.ca
twitter.com/KLTeamster
ww w.facebook.com/KingsLandingHistory
Historical settlement on the St. John River with more than 100 costumed interpreters depicting rural life from 1790-1910; 65,000 artifacts; open June - Oct.

Musée Acadien (MAUM)
c/o Campus de Moncton, Université de Moncton, 18, av Antonine-Maillet, Moncton, NB E1A 3E9
Tél: 506-858-4088; Téléc: 506-858-4043
maum@umoncton.ca
www.umoncton.ca/umcm-maum
Fondée en: 1886 Le plus ancien musée acadien au monde est fondé par le père Camille Lefebvre. La collection dépasse 35,000 objets et photographies et représente tous les aspects de la vie acadienne. Exposition permanente; expositions temporaires; expositions virtuelles.
Jeanne-Mance Cormier, Conservatrice
Bernard LeBlanc, Conservateur
Nicole LeBlanc, Secrétaire administrative

New Brunswick Museum (NBM/MNB) / Musée du Nouveau-Brunswick
277 Douglas Ave., Saint John, NB E2K 1E5
Tel: 506-643-2300; Fax: 506-643-2360
Toll-Free: 888-268-9595
nbmuseum@nbm-mnb.ca
www.nbm-mnb.ca
Year Founded: 1934 Collections at the provincial museum of New Brunswick include human history, marine & technology, prints, fine & decorative arts, botany, zoology, & geology; A full range of exhibitions & programs are offered daily; Closed Christmas Day & Good Friday
Jane Fullerton, Director & Chief Executive Officer, 506-643-2346

Local Museums in New Brunswick

***Aulac:* Fort Beauséjour National Historic Site**
111 Fort Beauséjour Rd., Aulac, NB E4L 2W5
Tel: 506-364-5080; Fax: 506-536-4399
fort.beausejour@pc.gc.ca
www.pc.gc.ca/lhn-nhs/nb/beausejour/index_E.asp
Built in 1751 by the French; star-shaped fort overlooking the Bay of Fundy
Pierrette Robichaud, Manager

***Bathurst:* Musee de la Guerre / Memorial War Museum Légion Royale Canadienne, Herman J.Good V.C. Branche**
18, 575, av St-Peter, Bathurst, NB E2A 2Y5
Tél: 506-546-3135

***Bathurst:* Nepisiquit Centennial Museum & Cultural Centre**
***Also known as:* Bathurst Heritage Museum**
***Parent:* Bathurst Heritage Trust Commission Inc.**
360 Douglas St., Bathurst, NB E2A 4S6
Tel: 506-546-9449; Fax: 506-545-7050
bhtc@nb.aibn.com
www.bathurstheritage.ca
The Centre houses the Bathurst Heritage Museum, Nepisiguit Genealogy/Archives, & Multicultural Association of the Chaleur Region. Open June-Sept., M-F 10:00-4:00.

***Boiestown:* Central New Brunswick Woodmen's Museum Inc.**
6342 Rte. 8, Boiestown, NB E6A 1Z5
Tel: 506-369-7214; Fax: 506-369-9081
woodmen@nb.aibn.com
www.woodmenmuseum.com
Year Founded: 1979 16 exhibit buildings, depicts life of Central New Brunswick lumberjack & culture of Miramichi people
Megan Scammell, Executive Director

***Caraquet:* Éco-Musée de l'huître / Oyster Museum**
675, boul Saint-Pierre ouest, Caraquet, NB E1W 1A2
Tel: 506-727-3226
rmne.ca/eco-musee-huitre

***Caraquet:* Musée Acadien de Caraquet / Acadian Museum of Caraquet**
15, boul St-Pierre est, Caraquet, NB E1W 1B6
Tél: 506-726-2682; Téléc: 506-726-2660
museecaraquet.ca
Promotes the history & culture of the Acadian people from the Acadian Peninsula using its own collection as well as other collections & regional archives

***Caraquet:* Village Historique Acadien**
PO Box 5626, Caraquet, NB E1W 1B7
Tel: 506-726-2600Toll-Free: 877-721-2200
vha@gnb.ca
www.vhanb.ca
Gabriel LeBreton, Directeur général par intérim, gabriel.lebreton@gnb.ca
Philippe Basque, Historien et conservateur en chef, philippe.basque@gnb.ca

***Clair:* Société historique de Clair Inc.**
724, rue Principale, Clair, NB E7A 2H4
Tel: 506-992-3637; Fax: 506-992-6247
sochclair@nb.aibn.com
Museum & historic site guided tours; Beaux-arts, Historie humaine; visites guidées; open June to Labour Day

***Connors:* Pioneer Historical Connors Museum**
3614 Rte. 205, Connors, NB E7A 1S3
Tel: 506-992-2500; Fax: 506-992-2500
Items used in general store; blacksmith shop; Victorian mansion

***Dalhousie:* Musée Restigouche Regional Museum**
115 George St., Dalhousie, NB E8C 1R6
Tel: 506-684-7490; Fax: 506-684-7490
gurrm@nbnet.nb.ca
Local history museum, archives, gallery

***Doaktown:* Atlantic Salmon Museum**
***Also known as:* Miramichi Salmon Museum**
263 Main St., Doaktown, NB E9C 1A9
Tel: 506-365-7787; Fax: 506-365-7359
museum@nbnet.nb.ca
www.atlanticsalmonmuseum.com
Year Founded: 1982 Through interpretive displays, the Atlantic Salmon Museum shows the history of the life of the Atlantic salmon, as well as the cultural & economic value of the Atlantic salmon to the Miramichi River & New Brunswick. Conservation is also emphasized. The museum is open from June to October. Appointments for rentals can be made during other times.
Linda Gaston, Executive Director

***Doaktown:* Doak House Historic Site**
386 Main St., Doaktown, NB E9C 1E4
Tel: 506-453-2324; Fax: 506-453-2416
guy.tremblay@gnb.ca
Open end June - Early Sept.
Glen Harding, Site Manager

***Dorchester:* Westmorland Historical Society Inc.**
#5, 3497 Cape Rd., Dorchester, NB E4K 2X2
Tel: 506-379-6633; Fax: 506-379-3033
keillorhouse@nb.aibn.com
www.keillorhousemuseum.com
Operating: The Keillor House (Westmorland Centennial Museum, c. 1813), 506-379-6633; open June - Sept. or by appt.; Bell Inn (c.1811), 506-379-2580; open Apr. - Oct.; St. James Presbyterian Church Museum, 506-379-6633; Beachkirk Collection (c. 1884); open June - Sept. or by appt.; The Maritime Penetentiary Museum, 506-379-6633; open June - Sept.
Alice Folkins, Manager, joansal@nbnet.nb.ca

***Edmundston:* Antique Automobile Museum**
35 Principale St., Edmundston, NB E7B 1V6
Tel: 506-737-2637
www.tourismnewbrunswick.ca/Products/A/AntiqueAutomobileMuseum.aspx
Open June-Sept.
Jocelyne St-Onge, Contact, Jocelyne.st-onge@gnb.ca

***Edmundston:* Musée historique du Madawaska**
c/o Campus d'Edmundston, Université de Moncton, 165, boul Hébert, Edmundston, NB E3V 2S8
Tel: 506-737-5282; Fax: 506-737-5373
musee@umce.ca
www.umoncton.ca/umce/node/89
twitter.com/UMCE_UMoncton
www.facebook.com/UdeMEdmundston
Christian Michaud, Contact, 506-737-5050

***Fredericton:* 'School Days' Museum**
PO Box 752, Fredericton, NB E3B 5R6
Tel: 506-459-3738
sdmuseum@nb.sympatico.ca
museum.nbta.ca
NB's educational heritage from 19th century; located in Justice Bldg. ANNEX, off Queen St.; artifacts pertaining to NB schools & teacher training
Harry Palmer, President, hspalmer@nb.sympatico.ca

***Fredericton:* Brydone Jack Observatory Museum**
University of New Brunswick, PO Box 4400, Fredericton, NB E3B 5A3
Tel: 506-453-4723
The first astronomical observatory in Canada was built in 1851. The building is now a Nnational Historic Site & a museum on the campus of the University of New Brunswick. It houses tools & equipment used by Dr. William Brydone Jack, who was a professor of mathematics, natural philosophy, & astronomy.

***Fredericton:* Electrical Engineering Museum**
University of New Brunswick, Dept. of Electrical Engineering, Fredericton, NB E3B 5A3
Tel: 506-453-4561; Fax: 506-453-3589

***Fredericton:* Fredericton Region Museum / Musée de la région de Fredericton**
PO Box 1312 A, 571 Queen St., Fredericton, NB E3B 5C8
Tel: 506-455-6041; Fax: 506-458-8741
info@yorksunburymuseum.com
www.yorksunburymuseum.com
Social Media: www.youtube.com/user/ysmuseum
www.facebook.com/FrederictonRegionMuseum
Ruth Murgatroyd, Executive Director

***Fredericton:* Guard House & Soldiers' Barracks**
c/o Fredericton Tourism, PO Box 130, 11 Carleton St., Fredericton, NB E3B 4Y7
Tel: 506-460-2041; Fax: 506-460-2474
Toll-Free: 888-888-4768
www.tourismfredericton.ca
Historic military buildings 1828-1866

***Fredericton:* New Brunswick Sports Hall of Fame / Temple de la renommée sportive du Nouveau-Brunswick**
PO Box 6000, 503 Queen St., Fredericton, NB E3B 5H1
Tel: 506-453-3747; Fax: 506-459-0481
deborah.williams@gnb.ca
www.nbsportshalloffame.nb.ca
Open year round, hours vary; recognizes, collects, preserves, exhibits & promotes New Brunswick's sports heroes & sports heritage. Street address is 503 rue Queen St., Frederiction, NB, E3B 1B8.
Jamie Wolverton, Executive Director, jamie.wolverton@gnb.ca
Deborah Williams, Executive Assistant, deborah.williams@gnb.ca
Kelly Ross, Curator/Exhibits Director, curator@gnb.ca

***Fredericton:* Old Government House**
PO Box 6000, 51 Woodstock Rd., Fredericton, NB E3B 5H1
Tel: 506-453-2505; Fax: 506-453-2416
ogh@gnb.ca
www.gnb.ca/lg/ogh/index-e.asp
Constructed from 1826 to 1828, Government House was the residence of New Brunswick's Governors & Lieutenant-Governors. Government House also served as a school for hearing impaired students, a military barracks during World War I, a hospital for returning soldiers, & an RCMP headquarters. Since 1999, the House has been open to the public, featuring restored rooms, exhibits, & bilingual tours during the summer. Government House still contains the Lieutenant-Governor's office & residence.

***Fredericton:* Wulastook Museums Inc.**
PO Box 700, 108 Queen St., Fredericton, NB E3B 5B4
Tel: 506-451-7777; Fax: 506-451-1029

***Fredericton Junction:* Currie House**
110 Currie Lane, Fredericton Junction, NB E5L 1X7
Tel: 506-368-2818; Fax: 506-368-1900
ddupl@nbnet.nb.ca
www.tourismnewbrunswick.ca/en-CA/Product/Museum.htm?pid=401
Museum with displays of antiques and artifacts, history of area and local families. Large picnic area, nature trails through woods and by river.
Don Duplisea, Contact, 506-368-2818, Fax: 506-422-1223, ddupl@nbnet.nb.ca

***Gagetown:* Queens County Museum**
69 Front St., Gagetown, NB E5M 1A4
Tel: 506-488-2966
Gagetown's Queens County Museum is located in the Tilley Home, which was the home of Sir Leonard Tilley, a Father of Confederation, & the 1836 Queens County Courthouse. The museum contains furnishings of the Loyalist & Victorian periods, plus historical exhibits. It is open from mid June to mid September.

***Grand Falls:* Grand Falls Museum / Musée de Grand-Sault**
#103, 142 Court St., Grand Falls, NB E3Z 2R2
Tel: 506-473-5265; Fax: 506-473-7160
Local artifacts; Extensive collection of church records, genealogies, etc.; Open mid-June to end of Aug. or by appt.
Patrick McCooey, President

***Grand Manan:* Grand Manan Museum**
1141 Rte. 776, Grand Manan, NB E0G 1X0
Tel: 506-662-3524
gmadmin@grandmananmuseum.ca
www.grandmananmuseum.ca
Open June - Sept.; in winter by appt.

***Grand-Anse:* Musée des Papes**
184, rue Acadie, Grand-Anse, NB E8N 1A6
Tel: 506-732-3003; Fax: 506-732-5491
museedespapes@gmail.com
museedespapes.snappages.com
www.facebook.com/1 90968550939951
Relates the evolution of Christianity to the present religious congregations; open mid-June to end of Aug.
Edmond Landry, Directeur

***Hampton:* Kings County Museum**
***Parent:* Kings County Historical & Archival Society Inc.**
c/o Kings County Historical & Archival Society Inc., PO Box 1813, 27 Centennial Rd., Hampton, NB E5N 6N3
Tel: 506-832-6009
kingscm@nbnet.nb.ca
www.kingscountymuseum.com
Year Founded: 1968 Artifacts include textiles, clothing, china, guns, glassware, military, royalty, art & archival material

***Harvey, Albert County:* Old Bank Museum**
***Parent:* Albert County Heritage Trust**
c/o Albert County Heritage Trust, PO Box 435, Mary's Point Rd., Harvey, Albert County, NB E4H 2M9
Tel: 506-882-2015
Other contact information: Off-Season Phone: 506-882-2100
Historic bank building now a museum & information centre
Mary Majka, President, maryspt@nbnet.nb.ca

***Hillsborough:* Hon. William Henry Steeves House**
40 Mill St., Hillsborough, NB E4H 2Z8
Tel: 506-734-3102; Fax: 506-734-3452
steevesmuseum@nb.aibn.com
www.steeveshousemuseum.ca
Year Founded: 1971 Operated by Heritage Hillsborough Inc.; birthplace of William Henry Steeves, a Father of Confederation; open every day July 1 to Labour Day
Lois Snider, President

***Hillsborough:* New Brunswick Railway Museum**
2847 Main St., Hillsborough, NB E4H 2X7
Tel: 506-734-3195; Fax: 506-734-3711
info@nbrm.ca
www.nbrm.ca/en/index.shtml
Year Founded: 1993 Dedicated to preserving the history of train travel in New Brunswick, the museum has on site an extensive collection of full-sized railway cars. This is the province's only operating railway museum, with excursion trains 4 days a week along the Petitcodiac River & southeastern New Brunswick. Displays of equipment & artifacts highlight the local & area railway history. There is a gift shop. Open daily, June - Sept.
Patrick McKinley, President
J.A. Clowes, Secretary & Director

***Hopewell Cape:* Albert County Museum**
3940 Rte 114, Hopewell Cape, NB E4H 3J8
Tel: 506-734-2003; Fax: 506-734-3291
albertcountymuseum@nb.aibn.com
www.albertcountymuseum.ca
The museum is located in the UNESCO Fundy Biosphere Reserve. Experience early life in Albert County & the Shepody Bay region by visiting the original Shire Town buildings, circa 1845. Explore the former County Jail complete with cells, displays & collections relating to the early history of the area. Visit the magnificent County Courthouse & ask about the project to commemorate R.B. Bennett, Canada's 11th Prime Minister. Displays on shipbuilding, farming; gift shop; meeting rooms; research resources room.
Donald Alward, Manager/Curator

***Kingston:* John Fisher Memorial Museum**
***Parent:* Kingston Peninsula Heritage Inc.**
c/o Kingston Peninsula Heritage Inc., 874 Rte. 845, Kingston, NB E5N 1V3
Tel: 506-763-2101
jfmmuseum@nb.aibn.com
www.kingstonnb.ca/JFMM
Located in the basement of Macdonald Consolidated School. Open June-Aug.

***Kouchibouguac:* Saint Croix Island International Historic Site / Lieu historique international de l'Ile-Sainte-Croix**
c/o Kouchibouguac National Park of Canada, 186, Rte. 117, Kouchibouguac, NB E4X 2P1
Tel: 506-876-2443; Fax: 506-876-4802
kouch.info@pc.gc.ca
www.pc.gc.ca
Year Founded: 1984 Located on Rte. 127 Bayside, with a view of Saint Croix Island; site of Pierre Dugua's first attempt to found a settlement in N. America; viewing deck & self-guided interpretive trail; picnic area. The site is also a U.S. National Monument
Carole Loiselle, Unit Superintendent

***Lower Newcastle:* MacDonald Farm Historic Site**
600 Rte. 11, Lower Newcastle, NB E1V 7G1
Tel: 506-453-2324; Fax: 506-453-2416
www.gnb.ca/0007/heritage/Macdonald.asp
Year Founded: 1970 Constructed by Scottish settler, Lt. Col. Alexander MacDonald of Bartibog, between 1815 and 1820 in Georgian style, the site includes a barn, 4 outbuildings, as well as a wharf and boat house. Costumed guides demonstrate cooking, crafts and care of animals.
Mr. Guy Tremblay, Manager, Museum Services, Government of New Brunswick, 506-444-5892, guy.tremblay@gnb.ca

***Memramcook:* Monument Lefebvre National Historic Site / Lieu historique national du Monument-Lefebvre**
480, rue Centrale, Memramcook, NB E4K 3S6
Tél: 506-758-9783; Téléc: 506-758-9813
Ligne sans frais: 877-765-1896
monument@nbnet.nb.ca
www.pc.gc.ca/lhn-nhs/nb/lefebvre/index_e.asp
Fondée en: 1982 Located in the Monument LeFebvre building, in cooperation with Parks Canada, the centre focuses on the survival of the Acadian people from 1755 to present. Shows are performed in the theatre. There is a gift shop with a variety of Acadian products. Guided tours are offered.
Conrad LeBlanc, President, Monument LeFebvre Society
Hermance LeBlanc, Directrice générale

***Minto:* Minto Museum & Information Centre**
187 Main St., Minto, NB E4B 3N4
Tel: 506-327-3383; Fax: 506-327-3041
www.village.minto.nb.ca/MMIC.html
Open July 1 - Sept. 1

***Minto:* New Brunswick Internment Camp Heritage Museum**
#1, 420 Pleasant Dr., Minto, NB E4B 2T3
Tel: 506-327-3573
nbinternmentcampmuseum.ca
Artifacts & model of the Ripples Internment Camp
Ed Caissie, Project Coordinator, 506-450-9666, eccaissi@hotmail.com

***Miramichi:* Miramichi Natural History Museum**
PO Box 162, 149 Wellington St., Miramichi, NB E1N 2B5
Tel: 506-773-7305
Natural history museum built in 1909, the oldest museum of its kind in New Brunswick and the third oldest in Canada; houses the Dr. Henri Marc Ami Collection; leased to the Miramichi Natural History Association

***Miramichi:* Rankin House Museum**
2224 Wellington St., Miramichi, NB E1V 6N3
Tel: 506-773-3448
1837; example of mansions built by the early lumber & shipping barons; unique collection of historic items; tourist information centre; open July & Aug.

***Miramichi:* St. Michael's Museum Association Inc.**
PO Box 368, 10 Howard St., Miramichi, NB E1N 3A7
Tel: 506-778-5152
mmuseum@nbnet.nb.ca
Miramichi history & extensive civil & church records for most denominations; geneology; tours in June-Aug.

***Miramichi:* W.S. Loggie Cultural Centre**
222 Wellington St., Miramichi, NB E1N 1M9
Tel: 506-773-7645

***Moncton:* Free Meeting House**
c/o Moncton Museum, 20 Mountain Rd., Moncton, NB E1C 2J8
Tel: 506-856-4383; Fax: 506-856-4355
info.museum@moncton.ca
www.moncton.ca

***Moncton:* Lutz Mountain Meeting House**
Lutz Mountain Heritage Foundation, 3143 Mountain Rd., Moncton, NB E1G 2X1
Tel: 506-384-7719; Fax: 506-854-8051
lutzmtnheritage@rogers.com
www.lutzmtnheritage.ca
Year Founded: 1975 The Lutz Mountain Meeting House is open during the summer only, or by appointment.
Gerry Gillcash, President

***Moncton:* Moncton Museum / Musée de Moncton**
20 Mountain Rd., Moncton, NB E1C 2J8
Tel: 506-856-4383; Fax: 506-856-4355
info.museum@moncton.org
www.moncton.ca/Residents/Recreation_Parks_and_Culture/Museums_and_Heritage
Year Founded: 1974 The permanent exhibits showcase Moncton's history from the time of the Micmacs to the period preceding the Deportation of Acadians, when agriculture was Moncton's primary economic engine, to the golden shipbuilding years and the railway era. There are also temporary and travelling exhibits. A research library and educational programs are offered. Open year round.
Brenda Orr, Sr. Heritage Officer, Recreation, Parks & Culture Dept., City of Moncton, 506-856-4383, brenda.orr@moncton.ca

***New Denmark:* New Denmark Memorial Museum**
***Parent:* New Denmark Historical Society**
6 Main Rd., New Denmark, NB E0J 1T0
Tel: 506-553-6464
hilltown@nbnet.nb.ca
www.facebook.com/groups/82612803207
Other contact information: Alternate Phone: 506-553-6897

New Denmark Memorial Museum honours the Danish immigrants who settled in the New Denmark area of New Brunswick in 1872. It is the oldest Danish settlement in Canada. Exhibits include books, china, & farm machinery. The museum is open from mid June to the beginning of September.

***Oromocto:* Canadian Military Engineering Museum**
***Also known as:* CME Museum**
Canadian Forces School of Military Engineering, CFB / ASG Gagetown, #J-10, D215, Mitchell Bldg., Oromocto, NB E2V 4J5
Tel: 506-422-2000; Fax: 506-422-1220
cmemuseum@forces.gc.ca (Museum Staff)
www.cmemuseum.ca
Other contact information: E-mail, Research Inquiries: cme.research@sympatico.ca
Year Founded: 1957 Displays at the Canadian Military Engineering Museum date back before the 1800s, with drawings, plans, & photographs of forts built by engineers, such as the Citadel in Nova Scotia. Displays also depict trench life during World War I. Weapons & uniforms from World War II, artifacts from the Korean War, & a United Nations display are also part of the museum. A research library houses photographs, reference books, training manuals, & personal diaries. The museum is open year round.
Col. John Tattersall, Chair
Maj. Joe Gale, Museum Executive Officer
CWO Blaine Thurston, Vice-President, History & Heritage
Sgt John Wilt, Curator & Treasurer

***Oromocto:* Fort Hughes Military Blockhouse**
62 Miramichi Rd., Oromocto, NB E2V 1S2
Tel: 506-357-4400; Fax: 506-357-2266
recreation@oromocto.ca
www.oromocto.ca
Located in Sir Douglas Hazen Park, 1 Wharf Rd., Oromocto, NB.

***Oromocto:* New Brunswick Military History Museum (NBMHM) / Museum Musée d'histoire militaire du nouveau brunswick**
Bldg. A-5, PO Box 17000 Forces, Oromocto, NB E2V 4J5
Tel: 506-422-1304
info@nbmilitaryhistorymuseum.ca
www.nbmilitaryhistorymuseum.ca
Year Founded: 1973 The museum presents exhibits about the Canadian Army, the Royal Canadian Navy, & the Royal Canadian Air Force, from 1800-1968, & the Canadian Armed Forces from 1968 to the present. Since 2010 the museum has expanded its mandate to include pre-1800 New Brunswick military history.
Capt. Kevin Anderson, Director, kevin.anderson@forces.gc.ca

***Paquetville:* Salon de la renommée de Paquetville et village natal d'Edith Butler**
1094, rue du Parc, Paquetville, NB E8R 1J4
Tel: 506-764-2500
rmne.ca/salon-de-la-renommee-de-paquetville-et-village-natal-d-edith-butle r

***Petit-Rocher:* New Brunswick Mining & Mineral Interpretation Centre (CIMMNB) / Centre d'interprétation des mines & minerais du Nouveau-Bru**
397, rue Principale, Petit-Rocher, NB E8J 1L9
Tel: 506-542-2672; Fax: 506-542-2708
The Mining & Mineral Interpretation Centre features exhibitions about the mining heritage of New Brunswick, plus a simulation of an underground descent.
Marc-André Godin, Contact

***Plaster Rock:* Plaster Rock Museum & Information Centre**
81 Ridgewell St., Plaster Rock, NB E7G 2N6
Tel: 506-356-6077
Plaster Rock Museum & Information Centre features exhibits about the community's past, including the lumbering & farming activities in Plaster Rock & the surrounding region.

***Sackville:* Mary's Point Shorebird Reserve & Interpretive Centre**
***Also known as:* Shepody National Wildlife Area, Mary's Point Section**
PO Box 6227, Sackville, NB E4L 1G6
Tel: 506-882-2544
maryspt@nbnet.nb.ca
www.naturenb.ca/Eng/maryspoint.aspx
Year Founded: 1992 Located in the Shepody National Wildlife Area and administered by both Nature NB and Environment Canada's Canadian Wildlife Service, these wetlands protect large numbers of shorebird species. The Interpretation Centre educates the public on the shorebirds' habitats and their hemispheric migrations over the Bay of Fundy region.

***Sackville:* Struts Gallery & Faucet Media Arts Centre**
7 Lorne St., Sackville, NB E4L 3Z6
Tel: 506-536-1211
info@strutsgallery.ca
www.strutsgallery.ca
An artist-run centre dedicated to presenting regional & national contemporary artist-initiated activities
Dan Vogel, President
Amanda Fauteux, Program Manager
Elli Hearte, Manager, Faucet Media Arts Centre, production@strutsgallery.ca
John Murchie, Coordinator, admin@strutsgallery.ca

***Saint John:* Barbour's General Store**
St. Andrew's Sq., PO Box 1971, King St., Saint John, NB E2L 4L1
Tel: 506-658-2939
www.tourismsaintjohn.com
Other contact information: Phone, Off season: 506-658-2855
Artifacts housed at Barbour's General Store include authentic grocery items, pharmaceutical items, cooking utensils, china, farm implements, & yard goods. The restored nineteenth-century country general stored is open from mid-June to mid-September.

***Saint John:* Loyalist House Museum**
***Also known as:* Merritt House**
120 Union St., Saint John, NB E2L 1A3
Tel: 506-652-3590
info@loyalisthouse.com
www.loyalisthouse.com
Year Founded: 1960 Operated by the New Brunswick Historical Society as a national historic site, Loyalist House was built in 1817 by David Daniel Merritt, a United Empire Loyalist from Rye, NY. The house remains very much as it was built & still displays its original furniture: piano-organ, swooning divans, 'yoke-back' chairs, four-poster bed, etc. This buiding is one of the few surviving buildings of the Great Saint John Fire in 1877.

***Saint John:* Saint John Firefighters Museum**
24 Sydney St., Saint John, NB E2L 3X1
Tel: 506-633-1840; Fax: 506-633-1840
www.tourismsaintjohn.com
The museum is the site of the No. 2 Engine house, built in 1840; a collection of firefighting artifacts & photographs; includes an entire room dedicated to the Great Saint John Fire of 1877, an authentic hand pump, a 1956 LaFrance Fire Engine, a Junior Firefighters play room & much more!

***Saint John:* Saint John Jewish Historical Museum**
91 Leinster St., Saint John, NB E2L 1J2
Tel: 506-633-1833; Fax: 506-642-9926
sjjhm@nbnet.nb.ca
personal.nbnet.nb.ca/sjjhm
Year Founded: 1986 Housed in the same building with the Shaarei Zedek Synagogue, the museum collects, displays & preserves articles related specifically to the Saint John Jewish community; provides a research facility for genealogists, historians & religious scholars; 7 display areas; Jewish education outreach kits, membership program
Katherine Biggs-Craft, Curator

***Saint John:* Saint John Sports Hall of Fame**
PO Box 1971, Saint John, NB E2L 4L1
Tel: 506-658-2909; Fax: 506-658-2902
recandparks@saintjohn.ca
www.cityofsaintjohn.com/services_recreation_hal l-of-fame.cfm
Located in Harbour Station
Ian Polley, Chair

***Saint John:* St. Andrews Blockhouse National Historic Site**
454 Whipple St., Saint John, NB E2M 2R3
Tel: 506-529-4270; Fax: 506-636-4574
fundy.info@pc.gc.ca
www.pc.gc.ca
Other contact information: Off-season Tel: 506/636-4011
Blockhouse built for border defence during the War of 1812; contains elements of the oldest blockhouse in New Brunswick; located at 23 Joe's Point Rd., St. Andrews NB E5B 2J7
Anne Bardou

***St Andrews:* Ross Memorial Museum / Musée mémorial Ross**
188 Montague St., St Andrews, NB E5B 1J2
Tel: 506-529-5124; Fax: 506-529-5183
rossmuse@nb.aibn.com
www.townsearch.com/rossmuseum
Decorative arts museum in one of St. Andrews' finest early houses; open June - Oct.
Margot Magee Sackett, Director

***St Martins:* Quaco Museum & Library**
***Parent:* Quaco Historical & Library Society**
236 Main St., St Martins, NB E5R 1B8
Tel: 506-833-4740
www.quaco.ca
Year Founded: 1978 Displays the history & heritage of the Quaco-St. Martins area with a specific focus on the shipbuilding heritage of the region; archives available for historical/genealogical research; the Carson Memorial Library, located behind the museum, is a volunteer-run public reading/lending library; gift shop. Museum & archives open June-Sept., other times by apppointment. Library is open Wednesdays & Saturdays throughout the year.
Richard Parsons, President, president@quaco.ca
Barbara McIntyre, Curator, 506-833-4768, curator@quaco.ca
Elizabeth Thibodeau, Librarian, 506-833-2553, librarian@quaco.ca

***St Stephen:* Charlotte County Museum Inc.**
443 Milltown Blvd., St Stephen, NB E3L 1J9
Tel: 506-466-3295
www.town.ststephen.nb.ca
Year Founded: 1977 Exhibits on 3 floors of the 1864 James Murchie Home; collection includes china, including early Chinese porcelain dating to the 17th century; hand-crafted articles, quilts, samplers; costumes; early tools & furniture; theme rooms portray area from the late 18th - early 20th century. The museum has a satellite location at 127 Milltown Blvd., St Stephen, NB, which includes displays of lumbering & shipbuilding, past industries, 19th & 20th century gowns, kitchen artifacts, school room, & tool shed.
Irene Ritch, Executive Director

***Shippagan:* Societé historique Nicolas-Denys**
218, boul J.D. Gauthier, Shippagan, NB E8S 1P6
Tel: 506-336-3461; Fax: 506-336-3434
shnd@umcs.ca
www.acadie.net/guide/organismes3.cfm?id=40
Heures d'ouvertures et les différentes coordonnées comment nous joindre pour le centre de documentation: mardi, mercredi et jeudi de 9 h 00 à 12 h et de 13 h à 16 h, mercredi soir de 19 à 21 h.
Ivan Robichaud, Président, 506-336-0400
Nathalie M. Lanteigne, Secrétaire, 506-336-3461

***St-Isidore:* St-Isidore Museum Inc.**
3942, boul des Fondateurs, St-Isidore, NB E8M 1C2
Tel: 506-358-6003
villasti@nb.aibn.com
Exhibits depict agricultural & forestry background of the region; open in July & Aug., Thu.-Sun.

***Sussex:* Agricultural Museum of New Brunswick**
28 Perry St., Sussex, NB E4E 2N7
Tel: 506-433-6799
info@agriculturalmuseumofnb.com
www.agriculturalmuseumofnb.com
www.facebook.com/469958723016450
The museum houses agricultural equipment, military memorabilia, and furniture & housewares. Open mid-June - mid-Sept.

***Tabusintac:* Tabusintac Centennial Memorial Library & Museum**
4490 Rte. 11, Tabusintac, NB E9H 1J3
Tel: 506-779-1918
www.tabusintac.ca/library_museum.html
Other contact information: Alternate Phone: 506-779-8045
Houses historical artifacts & memorabilia from the Tabusintac area; also features a craft shop

***Tracadie-Sheila:* Musée Historique de Tracadie Inc.**
#399, 222, rue du Couvent, Tracadie-Sheila, NB E1X 1E1
Tél: 506-393-6366; Téléc: 506-395-6355
museehis@nb.sympatico.ca
www.musee-tracadie.com
Fondée en: 1968 Leprosy in the 19th century; also history of Tracadie, artifacts dating several centuries before the arrival of the white colonists, articles relating to the life of the Acadians.
L-V 9h-17h; Sa, D 12h-17h
Zélica Daigle, President, 506-393-6366, museums@nb.sympatico.ca

***Welshpool:* Roosevelt Campobello International Park / Parc international Roosevelt de Campobello**
459 Rte. 774, Welshpool, NB E5E 1A4
Tel: 506-752-2922; Fax: 506-752-6000
info@fdr.net
www.fdr.net
www.facebook.com/Roosevelt.Campobello
The Roosevelt Campobello International Park, located on Campobello Island in New Brunswick's Bay of Fundy, features the 34-room summer residence of Franklin D. Roosevelt & his wife Eleanor. Guided tours are given of the home. The park also contains the Edmund S. Muskie Visitor Center, where visitors learn the story of the former president of the United States, through displays & a film. The Roosevelt Cottage & Visitor Centre are open from mid May to mid October. The park is open year-round.

***Woodstock:* Old Carleton County Court House**
***Parent:* Carleton County Historical Society**
c/o Carleton County Historical Society, 128 Connell St., Woodstock, NB E7M 1L5
Tel: 506-328-9706
cchs@nb.aibn.com
www.cchs-nb.ca
Year Founded: 1986 The Carleton County Historical Society restored the Old County Court House which was built in 1833. The court house originally served as the County seat of justice & was also the meeting place for the first County Council in New Brunswick. Guided tours are available during the summer & by appointment at other times.
John Thompson, President

Newfoundland & Labrador

Provincial Museums

The Rooms
PO Box 1800 C, 9 Bonaventure Ave., St. John's, NL A1C 5P9
Tel: 709-757-8000; Fax: 709-757-8017
information@therooms.ca
www.therooms.ca
Other contact information: Archives: 709-757-8030; Museum: 709-757-8020; Gallery: 709-757-8040
The Rooms consists of the Newfoundland & Labrador Provincial Archives, Art Gallery, & Museum. The Archives collects records of the Government of Newfoundland & Labrador, as well as records from private sources which have value to the history of the province. Permanent exhibits at the museum depict Newfoundland & Labrador's early people, as well as Fort Townsend, the home of British soldiers &, since 1870, the Royal Newfoundland Constabulary. One level of the museum is dedicated to the birds of Newfoundland & Labrador. The Rooms Provincial Art Gallery presents more than 7,000 historical & contemporary works.
Dean Brinton, Chief Executive Officer, 709-757-8012, Fax: 709-757-8017
Anne Chafe, Director, The Rooms Provinical Museum, 709-757-8077, Fax: 709-757-8021, annechafe@therooms.ca
Deanne Fisher, Director, Marketing & Development, 709-757-8070, Fax: 709-757-8017, deannefisher@therooms.ca
Penny Houlden, Director, The Rooms Regional Museums, 709-757-8022, Fax: 709-757-8021, phoulden@therooms.ca
Vicky Lewis, Director, Finance & General Operations, 709-757-8015, Fax: 709-757-8017, vlewis@therooms.ca
Sheila Perry, Director, The Rooms Provincial Art Gallery, 709-757-8042, Fax: 709-757-8041, sheilaperry@therooms.ca
Greg Walsh, Director, Provincial Archives, 709-757-8032, Fax: 709-757-8031
Gillian Davidge, Manager, Education & Public Programming, 709-757-8109, gilliandavidge@therooms.ca

Local Museums in Newfoundland & Labrador

***Baie Verte:* Baie Verte Peninsula Miners' Museum**
#319, Rte. 410, Baie Verte, NL A0K 1B0
Tel: 709-532-8090; Fax: 709-532-4166
baievertepeda@nf.aibn.com
Year Founded: 1975 The Miners' Museum presents a replica of life & work during the mining years (1860 - 1864 & 1901-1915) on the Baie Verte Peninsula.

***Bonavista:* Bonavista Historical Society Museum**
Bldg. 2, Ryan Premises National Historic Site, PO Box 295, 10 Ryan's Hill, Bonavista, NL A0C 1B0
Tel: 709-468-2920; Fax: 709-468-2495
Year Founded: 1969 The Bonavista Historical Society Museum is situated in the restored turn-of-the-century Ryan Retail Store at the Ryan Premises National Historic Site. The collection reflects local life in the late 19th century in one of Newfoundland's inshore fishing communities. The musuem also holds a collection of medical artifacts from the early twentieth century. Bonavista Museum is open from mid-June to mid-October.

***Botwood:* Botwood Heritage Centre**
12 Airbase Pl., Botwood, NL A0H 1E0
Tel: 709-257-4612; Fax: 709-257-3022
bhsa@nf.aibn.com
town.botwood.nl.ca
The Botwood Heritage Centre depicts the time of the Beothuk, the European exploration era in the Exploits Valley, & the early railway & shipping period of Abitibi.

***Burin:* Burin Heritage House**
***Also known as:* Reddy House**
PO Box 500, Seaview Dr., Burin, NL A0E 1E0
Tel: 709-891-2355
burinheritagemuseums@nf.aibn.com
www.townofburin.com
The Burin Heritage House features artifacts related to the history of Burin, including the fishery & the tidal wave. The museum is open from mid May to the beginning of October.

***Carbonear:* Baccalieu Trail Heritage Corporation**
#2, 4 Pike's Lane, Carbonear, NL A1Y 1A7
Tel: 709-596-1906
www.baccalieudigs.ca
Year Founded: 1993 The corporation preserves, protects, & promotes the heritage of the Baccalieu Trail Region, which consists of approximately seventy communities along 240 km of coastline on Newfoundland & Labrador's Avalon Peninsula.

***Carbonear:* Carbonear C.N. Railway Station**
PO Box 64, Water St. West, Carbonear, NL A1Y 1B5
Tel: 709-596-2532; Fax: 709-596-2582
www.heritage.nf.ca/society/rhs
Other contact information: Phone, Off Season: 709-596-2849
The Carbonear Railway Station is one of Newfoundland & Labrador's Resgistered Heritage Structures. Built around 1917, the building exemplifies a station during the one hundred year era of the Newfoundland railroad. Operated by the Carbonear Heritage Society, the station contains railway artifacts, exhibits about the history of Carbonear, genealogical information, & a tourist information centre. The Carbonear C.N. Railway Station is open from June to September. Appointments may be arranged during the off season.

***Cow Head:* Dr. Henry N. Payne Community Museum**
Conservation & Heritage Inc., PO Box 238, Cow Head, NL A0K 2A0
Tel: 709-243-2466
cowhead.ca/heritage/index.htm
Restored theme home; artifacts tell story of Dr. Henry N. Payne & cultural heritage of area; gift shop. Located at the northern tip of Gros Morne National Park.
Ms Glenda Reid Bavis, Staff contact, 709-243-2466, g.bavis@nf.sympatico.ca

***Cupids:* Cupids Museum**
PO Box 200, Cupids, NL A0A 2B0
Tel: 709-528-3500
cupidshistorical@nf.sympatico.ca
www3.nf.sympatico.ca/cupidshistorical
Located on Seaforest Dr.; open June 15-Sept. 30
Linda Kane, Curator

***Deer Lake:* Heritage Museum**
PO Box 989, Rte. 1, Deer Lake, NL AOK 2E0
Tel: 709-635-4440; Fax: 709-635-5103
www.town.deerlake.nf.ca
Year Founded: 1988 The museum preserves the local history with displays related to logging, agriculture and the settlers' lives in the Humber Valley. Open May-Dec.

***Durrell:* Durrell Museum & Crafts**
17 Museum Rd., Durrell, NL A0G 1Y0
Tel: 709-884-2780
lebulgin@hotmail.com
Other contact information: Alternate Phone: 709-884-5537
Open end of May - end of Sept.; mounted polar bear exhibit & crafts
Lloyd Bulgin, President

***Ferryland:* Historic Ferryland Museum**
PO Box 7, Ferryland, NL A0A 2H0
Tel: 709-432-2711; Fax: 709-432-2209
Other contact information: Off Season: 709-432-2155
Located in the old Courthouse; exhibits depicting community life & Ferryland's role in colonization of North America; open mid-June - Labour Day
Maxine Dunne, Curator, maxinedunne@hotmail.com

***Flatrock:* Flat Rock Museum**
663 Windgap Rd., Flatrock, NL A1K 1C7
Tel: 709-437-6312; Fax: 709-437-6311
www.townofflatrock.com/museum
Open July - Sept. or by appt.

***Fogo:* Bleak House Museum**
PO Box 57, Fogo, NL A0G 2B0
Tel: 709-266-2237
Other contact information: Alternative Phone: 709-266-2487
Year Founded: 1988 Bleak House was built around 1816 for the Slade family, who were involved in the Fogo Island fish trade. The home was restored & made into a museum. The home features items that belonged to owners of the home, plus artifacts that depict the history of Fogo. Bleak House Museum is open from July to September.

***Forteau:* Point Amour Lighthouse Provincial Historic Site**
c/o Labrador Straits Historical Development Corporation, PO Box 112, Forteau, NL A0K 2P0
Tel: 709-927-5825; Fax: 709-656-3150
Toll-Free: 800-563-6353
lshdc@labradorstraits.net; info@seethesites.ca
www.pointamourlighthouse.ca; www.seethesites.ca
www.facebook.com/ProvincialHistoricSites.NL
Other contact information: Alternative Phone: 709-931-2013
Consisting of several buildings, the Point Amour Light station dates back to the 1850s. The Provincial Historic Site in Newfoundland & Labrador has been restored, & now features displays that depict the maritime history of the Labrador Straits. An interpretive trail at the site takes visitors to the site of the HMS Raleigh & HMS Lily shipwrecks. The site is open from mid May to the beginning of October.
Bonnie Goudie, Executive Director
Kim Shipp, Contact, kimshipp@gov.nl.ca

***Gander:* North Atlantic Aviation Museum**
***Parent:* North Atlantic Aviation Museum Association**
PO Box 234, 135 Trans Canada Hwy., Gander, NL A1V 1W6
Tel: 709-256-2923; Fax: 709-256-8561
info@northatlanticaviationmuseum.com
www.northatlanticaviationmuseum.com
twitter.com/NAAMGANDER
facebook.com/pages/North-Atlantic-Aviation-Museum/202379909800908
Year Founded: 1996 The North Atlantic Aviation Museum depicts important aviation moments over the North Atlantic, from the war years to commercial flying. The focus is upon Gander's involvement in aviation history. The Museum features six aircraft. Hours: Summer: M-F 9:00-7:00; Off-Season: 9:00-5:00 or by appointment (please call)
Bob Briggs, President
Brian Williams, Vice-President
Jonathan Waterman, Secretary
Harold Penney, Treasurer

***Grand Bank:* Provincial Seamen's Museum (PSM)**
***Parent:* The Rooms**
PO Box 1109, 54 Marine Dr., Grand Bank, NL A0E 1W0
Tel: 709-832-1484; Fax: 709-757-8023
psminfo@therooms.ca
Artifacts pertaining to the banks fishery

***Grand Falls-Windsor:* Logger's Life Provincial Museum**
c/o Provincial Bldg., Cromer Ave., Grand Falls-Windsor, NL A2A 1W9
Tel: 709-486-0492
mmpminfo@therooms.ca
www.therooms.ca/museum/loggers_life_museum.asp
Other contact information: Off-Season Phone: 709-757-8023
Logging exhibit is a replica of 1920s logging camp; displays tools & clothing representative of that era; located west of Grand Falls-Windsor on Trans Canada Hwy.

***Grand Falls-Windsor:* Mary March Provincial Museum**
Provincial Building, Cromer Ave., Grand Falls-Windsor, NL A2A 1W9
Tel: 709-292-4522
information@therooms.ca
www.therooms.ca/mmpm
Year Founded: 1988 From the European name of one of the last Beothuks, the aboriginal people of the island of Newfoundland, the Mary March Museum traces the Aboriginal, European, natural & geological history of the Central Newfoundland Region. Open daily 9am-4:45pm, May-Oct. It is part of The Rooms Regional Museums network.

***Happy Valley-Goose Bay:* Northern Lights Military Museum**
Northern Lights Bldg., PO Box 2168 B, 170 Hamilton River Rd., Happy Valley-Goose Bay, NL A0P 1E0
Tel: 709-896-5939
Bruce Haynes, Contact

***Harbour Grace:* Conception Bay Museum**
PO Box 298, Water St., Harbour Grace, NL A0A 2M0
Tel: 709-596-5465
cbm@nf.aibn.com
www.hrgrace.ca/museum.html
Open June - Aug; off season by appt.

***Hopedale:* Moravian Mission Museum**
***Also known as:* Agvituk Historical Society Museum**
***Parent:* Agvituk Historical Society**
PO Box 12, Hopedale, NL A0P 1G0
Tel: 709-933-3777; Fax: 709-933-3746
Moravian Mission House; archaeology artifacts from 1500-2000 years ago; items related to Labrador Inuit; European medical supplies & furniture
Patricia Pottle, Executive Director

Lewisporte: **By The Bay Museum & Craft Shop**
PO Box 569, 235 Main Rd., Lewisporte, NL A0G 3A0
Tel: 709-535-8555
lada@nf.aibn.com; btbmuseum@nf.aibn.com
Other contact information: Alternative Phone: 709-535-3900
Year Founded: 1872 Exhibits at the Bye The Bay Museum show the history of Lewisporte & its surrounding region, including Beothuk artifacts, the shipbuilding & logging industries & World War I & World War II. Owned & operated by the Lewisporte Area Development Association, the museum is open from the end of May to the end of August.
Pat Martin, Contact
Barry Porter, Contact

Little Catalina: **Mockbeggar Plantation Provincial Historic Site**
Also known as: **Bradley House**
PO Box 128, Little Catalina, NL A0C 1W0
Tel: 709-468-7300; Fax: 709-468-5044
Toll-Free: 800-563-6353
mockbeggar@nf.aibn.com
www.tcr.gov.nl.ca/tcr/heritage/ historicsites/mockbeggar.html
Other contact information: In Season Tel: 709-468-7300; Fax: 709-468-5044
Year Founded: 1990 Built in the 1870s, the museum was the home of Newfoundland statesman, Senator F. Gordon Bradley and is restored to that 1939 period. Other buildings include a carpenter shop, fish store and cod-liver oil factory from the 18 century. Museum is located on Roper St., Bonavista, NL, A0C 1B0.
Ms Linda Badcock, Historic Sites Officer, 709-729-0592, Fax: 709-729-7989
Don Johnson, Site Supervisor

Marystown: **Marystown Heritage Museum Corporation**
PO Box 688, Ville Marie Dr., Marystown, NL A0E 2M0
Tel: 709-279-1462
The museum exhibits include everyday articles from the town's historic past, from squid jiggers to priests. Open daily mid-June - Aug.; Jan.-May, Sept.-Dec. Mon.-Fri 9-5
Albert Dober, Chair

Moreton's Harbour: **Moreton's Harbour Community Museum**
PO Box 28, Main Rd., Moreton's Harbour, NL A0G 3H0
Tel: 709-684-2355
Operated by the Moreton's Harbour Women's Institute, the Moreton's Harbour Community Museum is situated in a house which was built in 1916. The museum features various artifacts, including agricultural implements & equipment used during the inshore fishery. Archives include census records, diaries, & school minute books. The community museum is open from mid June to the beginning of September. Tours may be arranged during the off season.

Mount Arlington Heights: **St. Bartholomew's Church**
c/o Mt. Arlington Hts., PO Box 25, Mount Arlington Heights, NL A0B 2L0
Tel: 709-228-2583
Church built in 1930 by parishoners

Musgrave Harbour: **Fishermen's Museum**
PO Box 159, 4 Marine Dr., Musgrave Harbour, NL A0G 3J0
Tel: 709-655-2162
Ship models, engines, photographs, accounts of local shipwrecks

Nain: **Piulimatsivik - Nain Museum**
c/o Moravian Mission, General Delivery, Nain, NL A0P 1L0
Tel: 709-922-2821
Moravian & Inuit artifacts are on display at Piulimatsivik, the Nain Museum.

Newtown: **Barbour Living Heritage Village**
PO Box 135, Newtown, NL A0G 3L0
Tel: 709-536-3220; Fax: 709-536-3150
barboursite@nf.aibn.com
www.barbour-site.com
www.facebook.com/34990249 8362983
An historic fishing village, featuring a schoolhouse, sealing interpretation centre, fisherman's stage, theatre, & art gallery. The historic Greenspond Court House is located nearby; the court house is owned by Cape Freels Heritage Trust Inc. and can be contacted at 709-536-3220.

North West River: **Labrador Heritage Museum**
Parent: **Labrador Heritage Society**
c/o Labrador Heritage Society, PO Box 99, North West River, NL A0P 1M0
Tel: 709-497-8858; Fax: 709-497-8228
info@labradorheritagemuseum.ca
www.labradorheritagemuseum.ca
Other contact information: Craft Shop Phone: 709-497-8282
Exhibit includes arifacts & infomation about the Hudson Bay Company store, trapping, exploration of Labrador & the International Grenfell Association in North West River

Old Perlican: **Howard House of Artifacts**
PO Box 100, Old Perlican, NL A0A 3G0
Tel: 709-587-2022
Located 3 miles from Old Perlican on Shore Line country road at Daniel's Cove; artifacts represent the 1890s & 1900 to 1945; collection of Newfoundland homemade furniture of the 1930s; open daily

Placentia: **O'Reilly House Museum**
Parent: **Placentia Area Historical Society**
c/o Placentia Area Historical Society, PO Box 233, 48 Orcan Dr., Placentia, NL A0B 2Y0
Tel: 709-227-5568
www.placentiahistory.ca
Year Founded: 1989 Built in 1902 as a residence for magistrate, William O'Reilly, O'Reilly House is now a museum operated by the Placentia Area Historical Society. The Victorian home displays many items from Placemtia' past. The museum is open from the beginning of June to mid October.
Tom O'Keefe, President, 709-227-0322, tokeefe@personainternet.com

Placentia Bay: **Castle Hill National Historic Site of Canada**
PO Box 10 Jerseyside, Placentia Bay, NL A0B 2G0
Tel: 709-227-2401; Fax: 709-227-2452
castle.hill@pc.gc.ca
www.pc.gc.ca/eng/lhn-nhs/nl/castlehill/index.aspx
17th & 18th century remains of French & English fortifications; picnic areas & hiking trails; special events & programming; Visitor Centre with gift shop. Off-season contact information: PO Box 1268, St John's, NL A1C 5M9; Phone: 709-468-1601; Fax: 709-468-1604.
Bill Brake, Superintendent

Port au Choix: **Port au Choix National Historic Park Site**
PO Box 140, Port au Choix, NL A0K 4C0
Tel: 709-861-3522; Fax: 709-861-3827
pac-historic-site@pc.gc.ca
www.pc.gc.ca/lhn-nhs/nl/portauchoix/index.asp x
Commemorates area's rich aboriginal history dating back 5400 years; visitors can view artifacts & exhibits on the four prehistoric cultures that occupied area; walking trails, archaeological sites, lighthouse & fossils
Peter Deering, Acting Field Unit Superintendent, Western Newfoundland & Labrador

Port au Port: **Our Lady of Mercy Museum**
PO Box 330, 103 Main St., Port au Port, NL A0N 1T0
Tel: 709-648-2745
Former rectory now holds artifacts from the Bay St. George area; open May - Sept.

Port aux Basques: **Gulf Museum**
c/o South West Coast Historical Society, PO Box 1299, Port aux Basques, NL A0M 1C0
Tel: 709-695-7560
Nautical items & the astrolabe (dated 1628): an instrument used by early navigators to determine latitude. The Society operates a refurbished train site facility consisting of a railway station & nine rail cars.

Port aux Basques: **Port aux Basques Railway Heritage Centre**
PO Box 1299, Port aux Basques, NL A0M 1C0
Tel: 709-695-7560
The Port aux Basques Railway Heritage Centre depicts the significance of the railway to Newfoundland's history. In the late 1890s, Port aux Basques became the western terminus of the Newfoundland Railway, where the railway schedule connected with steamers. Open from June to October, the heritage centre features the train station & various rail cars.

Port de Grave: **Fishermen's Museum, Porter House & School**
Port de Grave, NL A0A 3J0
Tel: 709-786-3912
hermanporter@personainternet.com
Year Founded: 1979 Museum contains artifacts depicting life & times of Newfoundland fishermen; Porter House is a traditional fisherman's house restored to early 1900s; Hibbs' Hole Schoolhouse, a restored one-room school
Herman Porter, Curator

Port Union: **Port Union Museum**
PO Box 98, Main St., Rte. 230, Port Union, NL A0C 2J0
Tel: 709-469-2728; Fax: 709-469-2728
thebungalow@eastlink.ca
Other contact information: Alternate Phone: 709-469-2159
Includes estate of the late Sir Wm. F. Coaker, founder of Port Union & Sir Wm. F. Coaker Memorial Cemetery; open mid June - Sept.; small admission fees apply

Pouch Cove: **Pouch Cove Museum**
Town Hall, PO Box 59, 660 Main Rd., Pouch Cove, NL A0A 3L0
Tel: 709-335-2848; Fax: 709-335-2840
pouchcove@nf.aibn.com
pouchcove.ca
Open year round
Barbara Tilley, Town Manager

Red Bay: **Red Bay National Historic Site of Canada**
PO Box 103, Red Bay, NL A0K 4K0
Tel: 709-920-2142; Fax: 709-920-2144
redbay.info@pc.gc.ca
www.pc.gc.ca/lhn-nhs/nl/redbay/natcul/basque.aspx
Other contact information: Phone, Summer: 709-920-2051
During the 16th century, Basque merchants & ship owners from France & Spain planned seasonal expeditions to the south coast of Labrador & the north shore of Quebec to hunt whales. The port they used most often was called Butus, which is now Red Bay. Red Bay is now a National Historic Site with a Visitor Centre. The Visitor Centre features discoveries from a marine archaeology project in the Red Bay area. Visitors learn about Labrador's 16th century history, through displays of original artifacts recovered from archaeological excavations, plus reproductions. The site is open from June to October.

Rocky Harbour: **L'Anse aux Meadows National Historic Site**
c/o Parks Canada, PO Box 70, Rocky Harbour, NL A0K 4N0
Tel: 709-458-2417; Fax: 709-623-2028
viking_lam@pch.gc.ca
www.pc.gc.ca/eng/lhn-nhs/nl/meadows/index.aspx
UNESCO World Heritage Site depicting first authenticated European presence in North America; the focal point are the reconstructions of three Norse buildings of this archaeological site. There are also exhibits the Viking lifestyle, artifacts, & the archaeological discovery of the site. Visitor centre open mid-June - early Oct.

Rocky Harbour: **Gros Morne National Park Visitor Reception Centre**
PO Box 130, Rocky Harbour, NL A0K 4N0
Tel: 709-458-2417; Fax: 709-458-2059
grosmorner.info@pc.gc.ca
www.pc.gc.ca/eng/pn-np/nl/grosmorne/index.aspx
Other contact information: TTY: 709-772-4564
Gros Morne was declared a UNSESCO World Heritage site in 1987. GM discovery centre looks at the forces of nature. The centre looks at geology, plant & animal life, marine story & human history. It is located on the south side of Bonne Bay, one hour from Deer Airport & the Trans Canada Highway.

St Anthony: **Grenfell Historic Properties**
PO Box 93, 1 Maraval Rd., St Anthony, NL A0K 4S0
Tel: 709-454-4010; Fax: 709-454-4047
info@grenfell-properties.com
www.grenfell-properties.com
Year Founded: 1998 Dr. Wilfred Grenfell's former home restored circa 1920. Seasonal Hours: M-F 9:00-6:00pm; Off-Season Hours: M-F 9:00-5:00
Cynthia Randell, Manager

St. John's: **Anglican Cathedral of St. John the Baptist**
PO Box 23112, St. John's, NL A1B 4J9
Tel: 709-726-5677; Fax: 709-726-2053
angcathedral@nf.aibn.com
www.stjohnsanglicancathedral.org
Pictures, artifacts, records, documents & books related to the history of the Cathedral & Parish; established in 1699, the parish is the oldest non-Roman Catholic religious foundation in Canada; Cathedral building is one of the finest examples of English neo-Gothic architecture in North America. The Church is located at 16 Church Hill, St. John's, NL.
Donna Hiscock, Cathedral Archivist
Very Rev. Josiah Noel, Dean

St. John's: **Beothuk Interpretation Centre Provincial Historic Site**
PO Box 8700, St. John's, NL A1B 4J6
Tel: 709-729-0592; Fax: 709-729-7989
Toll-Free: 800-563-6353
info@seethesites.ca
www.seethesites.ca/the-sites/beoth uk-interpretation-centre.aspx
www.facebook.com/ProvincialHistoricSites.N L
Year Founded: 1981 The Beothuk site at Boyd's Cove dates back to the late 17th & early 18th centuries. The site features the archaeological remains of Beothuk life, including their house pits. Visitors can learn about these extinct people at the interpretive centre, where several artifacts from the site are displayed & on the interpretive trail. The centre is open from mid June to mid October.
Kim Shipp, Contact, kimshipp@gov.nl.ca

St. John's: **Cape Bonavista Lighthouse Provincial Historic Site**
Department of Tourism, Culture & Recreation, Heritage Division, PO Box 8700, Hwy. 230, St. John's, NL A1B 4J6
Toll-Free: 800-563-6353
tourisminfo@gov.nl.ca
www.tcr.gov.nl.ca/tcr/heritage/historicsites/capebonavista.html
The Cape Bonavista Lighthouse was built in 1843. The site features guided tours & a walking trail. The lighthouse is open from mid May to the beginning of October.
Linda Badcock, Historic Sites Officer (Year Round Contact), 709-729-0592, Fax: 709-729-7989, lbadcock@gov.nl.ca
Don Johnson, Site Supervisor (Seasonal Contact), 709-468-7444, Fax: 709-468-5426, capebonavista@nf.aibn.com

St. John's: **Cape Spear National Historic Site of Canada / Lieu historique national du Canada du Cap-Spear**
PO Box 1268, St. John's, NL A1C 5M9
Tel: 709-772-5367; Fax: 709-772-6302
cape.spear@pc.gc.ca
www.pc.gc.ca/eng/lhn-nhs/nl/spear/index.aspx
Located at most easterly point in North America, the Cape Spear lighthouse is the oldest in Newfoundland & Labrador. The lighthouse has been restored to reflect 1839. Visitors can view displays about the history of lighthouses & lightkeeping. The grounds are open year round, & the lighthouse, Visitor Interpretation Centre & the Heritage Gift Shop are open from mid May to mid October.

St. John's: **Commissariat House Provincial Historic Site, St. John's, NF**
Dept. of Tourism, Culture & Recreation, Culture & Heritage Division, PO Box 8700, King's Bridge Rd., St. John's, NL A1B 4J6
Tel: 709-729-6730; Fax: 709-729-6745
Toll-Free: 800-563-6353
commissariat@nf.aibn.com
www.explorenewfoundlandandlab rador.com
Other contact information: Year-round Email: tourisminfo@gov.nl.ca
This building, one of the oldest buildings in NFLD, was built especially for the Commissariat to supply the city's garrison and has been restored back to the 1830's era complete with tradtionally dressed maids and clerks to help answer questions.
Linda Badcock, Historic Sites Officer

St. John's: **Heart's Content Cable Station Provincial Historic Site, Heart's Content NF**
Provincial Historic Sites, Arts & Culture Centre, PO Box 8700, St. John's, NL A1B 4J6
Tel: 709-583-2160; Fax: 709-583-2373
Toll-Free: 800-563-6353
heartscontent@nf.aibn.com
www.tcr.gov.nl.ca/tcr/herita ge/historicsites/heartscontentcablestation.html
Other contact information: Year-round Email: tourisminfo@gov.nf.ca
Year Founded: 1974 Located on Hwy. 80, this cable station marks the first successful transatlantic telegraph cable landing in 1866. Displays focus on the history of cable, with equipment and instrumentation on exhibit. Open May-Oct., 10:00-5:30 daily.
Scott Andrews, Historic Sites Officer, Tourism, Culture & Recreation, 709-729-0592, Fax: 709-729-7989, tourisminfo@gov.nl.ca
Bob Balsom, Site Supervisor

St. John's: **Hiscock House Provincial Historic Site, Trinity NL**
Also known as: **Mountain Ash Villa**
Dept. of Tourism, Culture & Recreation, PO Box 8700, St. John's, NL A1B 4J6
Tel: 709-464-2042; Fax: 709-464-2349
Toll-Free: 800-563-6353
trinity@nf.aibn.com
www.tcr.gov.nl.ca/tcr/heritage/his toricsites/thehiscockhouse.html
Other contact information: In Season Tel: 709/464-2042; Fax: 709/464-2349
Year Founded: 1982 Owned solely by the Hiscock family until it was reborn as a museum, the house has been restored to its 1910 style. Located on Church St., it is open late spring to early autumn, 10:00-5:30 daily.
Ms Linda Badcock, Historic Sites Officer, Tourism, Culture & Recreation, 709-729-0592, Fax: 709-729-7989, tourisminfo@gov.nl.ca
Joan Kane, Site Supervisor

St. John's: **James J. O'Mara Pharmacy Museum**
Apothecary Hall, 488 Water St., St. John's, NL A1E 1B3
Tel: 709-753-5877; Fax: 709-753-8615
inforx@nlpb.ca
www.nlpb.ca/museum.html
twitter.com/nlpharmacyboard
w ww.facebook.com/139887479372029
Drug store c. 1895; open end-June - end-Aug. or by appt.
Donald F. Rowe, Secretary-Registrar, drowe@nlpb.ca
Joan O'Mara, Museum Contact, jomara@nlpb.ca

St. John's: **Quidi Vidi Battery Provincial Historic Site**
PO Box 8700, St. John's, NL A1B 4J6
Tel: 709-729-0592; Fax: 709-729-6745
commissariat@nf.aibn.com
The Quidi Vidi Battery was built by the French in the 1700s. It was later taken over by the British, who rebuilt the guardhouse. The site is now restored to the era of 1812, when it was used to ward off a possible American attack. The Quidi Vidi Battery is located on Cuckhold's Cove Road in Quidi Vidi Village, Newfoundland & Labrador. Tours are available from guides dressed in period costumes, from late June until September.
Andrea van Nostrand, Seasonal Contact, 709-729-6745, quidividi@nf.aibn.com

St. John's: **Royal Newfoundland Constabulary Historical Society Archives & Museum**

Royal Newfoundland Constabulary Bldg., 1 Fort Townshend, St. John's, NL A1C 2G2
Tel: 709-729-8000; Fax: 709-729-8214
jlynch@commissionaires.nl.ca
www.rnchs.ca
Collects & preserves early police records; 48+ audio tapes of oral history interviews, as well as 10,000+ photographs; researchers may contact the office of the Chief of Police, indicating their area of interest, to arrange for access to the archives; photocopying available upon request, subjet to copyright protocols; open year round
Edward Roberts, Chair

St. John's: **The Royal St. John's Regatta Museum**
PO Box 214, Clancy Dr., St. John's, NL A1C 5J2
Tel: 709-576-8921; Fax: 709-576-3315
stjohnsregatta@nf.aibn.com
www.stjohnsregatta.org
The long history of rowing competition in St. John's, dating back to the early 1800s, is depicted at the Regatta Museum, through photographs, trophies, & other memorabilia. Please contact the Regatta Museum to arrange an appointment to visit.
Wayne Young, President, Regatta Committte
Paul Rogers, Secretary, Regatta Committte

St. John's: **St. Thomas' Old Garrison Church Museum**
8 Military Rd., St. John's, NL A1C 2C4
Tel: 709-576-6632; Fax: 709-576-2541
office@st-thomaschurch.com
www.st-thomaschurch.com
c. 1836
Jean E.C. Lewis, Archival Committee Member
David Edwards, Archival Committee Member
Rev. Robert Chafe, Archival Committee Member

St. John's: **Signal Hill National Historic Site of Canada / Lieu historique national du Canada de Signal Hill**
PO Box 1268, St. John's, NL A1C 5M9
Tel: 709-772-5367; Fax: 709-772-6302
Toll-Free: 888-773-8888
signal.hill@pc.gc.ca
www.pc.gc.ca/lhn-nhs/nl/signalhil l/index.aspx
In 1901, Signal Hill was the reception point of the first transatlantic wireless signal. From the 18th century to World War II, Signal Hill was also the site of harbour defence for St. John's, Newfoundland. Today, visitors can tour the Visitor Interpretation Centre & visit Cabot Tower to view the Marconi exhibit. The site is open year-round.

St. John's: **Trinity Interpretation Centre, Trinity NL**
Dept. of Tourism, Culture & Recreation, Culture & Heritage Division, PO Box 8700, St. John's, NL A1B 4J6
Tel: 709-464-2042; Fax: 709-729-7989
Toll-Free: 800-563-6353
trinity@nf.aibn.com
www.tcr.gov.nl.ca/tcr/heritage/his toricsites/index.html
Exhibits on the commercial & social history of Trinity; open June - Sept.
Linda Badcock, Historic Sites Officer
Joan Kane, Site Supervisor

St Lawrence: **St. Lawrence Miner's Memorial Museum**
PO Box 128, St Lawrence, NL A0E 2V0
Tel: 709-873-2222
wrowsell@hotmail.com
Open daily in summer
Gregory Quirke, Clerk/Manager, heritagesl@live.ca

Salvage: **Salvage Fishermens' Museum**
General Delivery, Salvage, NL A0G 3X0
Tel: 709-677-2414
www.explorenewfoundlandandlabrador.com
The museum building, a home once owned by the Lane family, dates from 1860 & is the oldest dwelling in the area; collection of fishing & domestic artifacts relates to the history & cultural life of Salvage, from the late 19th c. to the present; open daily, mid-June to Labour Day; wheelchair accessible; archive; gift shop

Springdale: **Harvey Grant Heritage Centre**
Also known as: **H.C. Grant Heritage Museum**
PO Box 57, 50 Main St., Springdale, NL A0J 1T0
Tel: 709-673-4313; Fax: 709-673-4969
Other contact information: Alternate Phone: 709-637-3439
Artifacts from 1940s, 50s & 60s, related to life of Harvey Grant; open July & Aug.

Torbay: **Torbay Museum**
Torbay Municipal Centre, PO Box 1160, 1288 Torbay Rd., Torbay, NL A1K 1K4
Tel: 709-437-6532
csmall@torbay.ca
torbay.museum.tripod.com; torbay.ca
www.facebook.com/TorbayMuseum
Year Founded: 1988 Over 500 artifacts dating from early 1800s; the collection is dedicated to produce a display of historical artifacts for public viewing, and the preservation and promotion of the heritage of Torbay. Open Mon. - Fri. 9-4, Tues. & Thu. 6:30-8:30 in summer; Tue. & Thu. 6:30-8:30 off season; otherwise by appt.
Contessa Small, Curator, csmall@torbay.ca

Trepassey: **Trepassey Area Museum**
PO Box 63, Trepassey, NL A0A 4B0
Tel: 709-436-2044
Open July & Aug.

Trinity: **Lester-Garland Premises Provincial Historic Site, Trinity NL**
Also known as: **The Ryan Shop**
Parent: **Trinity Historical Society**
c/o Trinity Historical Society, PO Box 8, Trinity, NL A0C 2S0
Tel: 709-464-3599; Fax: 709-464-3599
info@trinityhistoricalsociety.com
www.trinityhistoricalsociety.com
Mercantile bldg. including counting house restored to 1820 & retail shop restored to 1910; located on West St., Trinity following Rtes. 230 or 239; open daily June - Sept.
Linda Badcock, Historic Sites Officer

Trinity: **Trinity Museum**
Parent: **Trinity Historical Society**
PO Box 8, Trinity, NL A0C 2S0
Tel: 709-464-3599; Fax: 709-464-3599
info@trinityhistoricalsociety.com
www.trinityhistoricalsociety.com
www .facebook.com/193216850915
Year Founded: 1967 The artifacts of Trinity Museum are displayed in a salt box style house, which was built in the 1880s. The collection reflects the history of Trinity, & includes fishing, boat building, commercial, & domestic items. The site also features a fire engine shed, which displays an 1811 fire pump. Trinity Museum is owned & operated by the Trinity Historical Society. The museum is open from mid June to mid October, & by appointment at other times during the year.

Twillingate: **Twillingate Museum & Craft Shop**
PO Box 369, Twillingate, NL A0G 4M0
Tel: 709-884-2825
info@tmacs.ca
www.tmacs.ca
Other contact information: Phone, After Hours: 709-884-2044
Year Founded: 1973 Twillingate Museum is located in the former Anglican Church Rectory, which was built around 1900. Furnishings in the museum reflect the Victorian era. Examples of exhibits include Inuit, Dorset, & Beothuk First Nations artifacts. Archives include photographs, family histories, & cemetery data. The museum is open from May to October.
Linda Blondin, Contact

West St. Modeste: **Labrador Straits Museum**
PO Box 18, West St. Modeste, NL A0K 5S0
Tel: 709-931-2330; Fax: 709-931-2504
zpike@mylabrador.ca
www.labradorstraitsmuseum.ca
Hunting & fishing collections, household communication & religious items

Wesleyville: **Bonavista North Museum & Gallery**
PO Box 257, 12 Memorial Dr, Wesleyville, NL A0G 4R0
Tel: 709-536-2110
museum@nf.aibn.com
www.bonavistanorth.blogspot.com
The Bonavista North Museum & Gallery contains photographs, artifacts, & artwork from the local area. The museum is open daily from the beginning of July to the end of August. Appointments can be arranged during the off season.

Whitbourne: **Whitbourne Heritage Society, Inc.**
PO Box 166, Station Rd., Whitbourne, NL A0B 3K0
Tel: 709-759-2345; Fax: 709-759-2242

Year Founded: 1991 Open July 1 - Labour Day.
Judy Gosse, President
Curtis Sheppard, Vice-President
Susan George, Secretary
Mary Gosse, Treasurer

Northwest Territories

Territorial Museums

Prince of Wales Northern Heritage Centre (PWNHC)
c/o Government of the NWT, PO Box 1320, 4750 48th St., Yellowknife, NT X1A 2L9
Tel: 867-873-7551; Fax: 867-873-0205
www.pwnhc.ca
Other contact information: NWT Archives Phone: 867-873-7698; Fax: 867-873-0660
Located on the shores of Frame Lake, the Prince of Wales Northern Heritage Centre is open year-round. Visitors to the centre will discover various exhibits about the people, places, & natural history of the Northwest Territories.
Barb Cameron, Director, 867-873-7551, barb_cameron@gov.nt.ca
Joanne Bird, Curator of Collections, 867-873-7668, joanne_bird@gov.nt.ca
Rosalie Scott, Conservator, 867-873-7664, rosalie_scott@gov.nt.ca
Ian Moir, Territorial Archivist, 867-873-7177, ian_moir@gov.nt.ca

Local Museums in Northwest Territories

Colville Lake: **Colville Lake Museum & Gallery**
General Delivery, Colville Lake, NT X0E 1L0
Tel: 867-709-2500
Museum housing ethnographic artifacts, art gallery & archives; discovery centre; guided tours; gift shop; part of Colville Lake Lodge, a log cabin facility in a Dene community
Bern Will Brown, Curator

Fort Good Hope: **Dene Museum & Archives**
General Delivery, Fort Good Hope, NT X0E 0H0
Tel: 403-598-2331
The museum's collection includes photographs of area elders & residents, oral history tapes, written materials (including transcripts of tapes), & printed material.

Fort Smith: **Northern Life Museum & Cultural Centre**
PO Box 420, 110 King St., Fort Smith, NT X0E 0P0
Tel: 867-872-2859
nlmmanager@northwestel.net; manager@nlmcc.ca
www.nwtresearch.com/canoe/museum.htm
Year Founded: 1974 Collection, preservation & presentation of NWT culture & history; open year round

Hay River: **Hay River Heritage Centre**
39 Lakeshore Dr., Hay River, NT X0E 0R9
Tel: 867-874-3872
The museum has collections in human history, natural sciences, the arts, & an archive of photos, maps, prints & drawings, & manuscripts.

Holman: **Holman Museum**
PO Box 162, Holman, NT X0E 0S0
Tel: 867-396-3804; Fax: 867-396-3054
The museum's collection features Inuit artifacts from the Holman area.

Norman Wells: **Norman Wells Historical Centre**
PO Box 56, Norman Wells, NT X0E 0V0
Tel: 867-587-2415; Fax: 867-587-2469
www.normanwellsmuseum.com/visitor-centre
Year Founded: 1989 Dene cultural artifacts; geological history; WWI & Canol Project interpretation; Great Bear Lake & MacKenzie River explorers; local archives
Sarah Colbeck, Manager/Curator, canol.trail@theedgenw.ca

Nova Scotia

Provincial Museums

Fisheries Museum of the Atlantic
Lunenburg Waterfront, PO Box 1363, 68 Bluenose Dr., Lunenburg, NS B0J 2C0
Tel: 902-634-4794; Fax: 902-634-8990
Toll-Free: 866-579-4909
fma@gov.ns.ca
museum.gov.ns.ca/fma/
Historic buildings featuring 3 floors of exhibits & activities: Millenium Aquarium; Bluenose Memorabilia; Fishermen's Memorial Room; August Gales 1926-1927; Bank Fishery Gallery; Rum Running; life in fishing communities; Hall of Inshore Fisheries; fisherman's store; Marine Engine Room, whales, boat shop; schooner Theresa E. Connor; side trawler Cape Sable; part of the Nova Scotia Museum
Jim Tupper, General Manager
Felicia Knock, Secretary-Bookkeeper
Ralph Getson, Curator, Education

Maritime Museum of the Atlantic (MMA) / Musée Maritime d'Atlantique
1675 Lower Water St., Halifax, NS B3J 1S3
Tel: 902-429-7490
museum.gov.ns.ca/mma
Marine history branch of the Nova Scotia Museum; on waterfront; marine artifacts, memorabilia from the Titanic, Halifax explosion exhibit, restored ship chandlery, extensive small craft collection; library & gift shop; Vessel CSS Acadia at museum wharf; open year-round
Kim Reinhardt, General Manager, reinhaka@gov.ns.ca
Calum Ewing, Director, Museum Operations, ewingcn@gov.ns.ca

Nova Scotia Museum (NSM)
Heritage Division, NS Dept. of Tourism, Culture & Heritage, 1747 Summer St., Halifax, NS B3H 3A6
Tel: 902-424-7344; Fax: 902-424-0560
Toll-Free: 800-632-1114
nsmwebmaster@gov.ns.ca
museum.gov.ns.ca
twitter.com/ ns_museum
www.facebook.com/novascotiamuseum
The Nova Scotia Museum family includes 27 museums across the province, including Museum of Natural History, Halifax; Maritime Museum of the Atlantic, Halifax; Haliburton House, Windsor; Uniacke Estate Museum Park, Mount Uniacke; Prescott House, Starr's Point; Lawrence House, Maitland; Balmoral Grist Mill, Balmoral; Sutherland Steam Mill, Denmark; Fisherman's Life Museum, Jeddore; & Shand House, Windsor.
Bill Greenlaw, Executive Director

Local Museums in Nova Scotia

Amherst: **Cumberland County Museum & Archives**
150 Church St., Amherst, NS B4H 3C4
Tel: 902-667-2561; Fax: 902-667-0996
ccmuseum@ns.aliantzinc.ca
www.cumberlandcountymuseum.com
Year Founded: 1973 Exhibits & archives on the natural, social & industrial heritage of Cumberland County; located in the 1838 heritage home of Robert Barry Dickey, a Father of Confederation; the archives houses genealogical & other material; fine art collection by County artists; well maintained gardens surround the museum. Open year round.
Shirley Nickerson, Manager/Curator

Amherst: **Nova Scotia Highlanders Museum**
Col. James Layton Ralson Armoury, 36 Acadia St., Amherst, NS B4H 3L6
Tel: 902-661-6797; Fax: 902-667-4437
nshmuseum@eastlink.ca
free.hostultra.com/~ambushpaintball/nshighregmuseu m
C.W.O. (Ret'd) Ray Coulson, Curator C.D.

Annapolis Royal: **Fort Anne National Historic Site / Lieu historique national du Fort-Anne**
PO Box 9, Annapolis Royal, NS B0S 1A0
Tel: 902-532-2397; Fax: 902-532-2232
information@pc.gc.ca
www.pc.gc.ca
Other contact information: Off-Season Phone: 902/532-2321
French & English period fortifications, 1629-1854; exhibits; open May 15 - Oct. 15
Theresa Bunbury, Supt., Operations

Annapolis Royal: **Fort Edward National Historic Site / Lieu historique national du Fort Édouard**
PO Box 9, Annapolis Royal, NS B0S 1A0
Tel: 902-532-2321; Fax: 902-532-2232
www.parkscanada.gc.ca
Built in 1750 by Major Charles Lawrence, this Fort protected the route from Halifax to the Annapolis Valley and remains one of Nova Scotia's oldest buildings.
Theresa Bunbury, Director

Annapolis Royal: **North Hills Museum**
PO Box 503, 5065 Granville Rd., Annapolis Royal, NS B0S 1A1
Tel: 902-532-2168
museum.gov.ns.ca/nhm
Late 18th-century farmhouse which serves as the setting for the collection of Georgian furniture, ceramics, glass, silver & paintings of former owner Robert Patterson

Annapolis Royal: **O'Dell House Museum**
136 Saint George St., Annapolis Royal, NS B0S 1A0
Tel: 902-532-7754
historic@ns.aliantzinc.ca
www.annapolisheritagesociety.com/odell.htm
The museum is housed in a stagecoach inn & tavern from around 1869. O'Dell House is the former home of Nova Scotia Pony Express rider, Corey O'Dell & his family. Among the displays are items from Annapolis Royal's ship-building & sea-faring history. The Annapolis Heritage Society's Genealogy Centre's Archives & Collections Centre is also located at O'Dell House Museum. The Centre contains local histories, vital statistics for Annapolis & Digby counties, deeds, & church, cemetery, & probate records.
Barry Moody, Chair, Annapolis Heritage Society
Frances Rafuse, Secretary, Annapolis Heritage Society
Jane Dewolfe, Treasurer, Annapolis Heritage Society

Annapolis Royal: **Port-Royal National Historic Site of Canada / Lieu historique national de Port-Royal**
PO Box 9, Annapolis Royal, NS B0S 1A0
Tel: 902-532-2898; Fax: 902-532-2232
information@pc.gc.ca
www.pc.gc.ca/lhn-nhs/ns/portroyal/index.aspx
Other contact information: Phone, Off-Season: 902-532-2321 (mid October to mid May)
The national historic site on the coast of Nova Scotia is a reconstruction of early 17th-century buildings. The buildings represent a French colony from the era. The site features costumed interpreters & demonstrations to reflect life in one of the earliest settlements in North America.

Antigonish: **Antigonish Heritage Museum**
20 East Main St., Antigonish, NS B2G 2E9
Tel: 902-863-6160
antheritage@parl.ns.ca
www.parl.ns.ca/aheritage
Open year round
Jocelyn Gillis, Contact

Arichat: **Lenoir Forge Museum**
PO Box 223, 708 Veterans Memorial Dr., Arichat, NS B0E 1A0
Tel: 902-226-9364; Fax: 902-226-1919
Community museum; local artifacts; local artisan blacksmith

Baddeck: **Alexander Graham Bell National Historic Site of Canada / Lieu historique national Alexander-Graham-Bell du Canada**
PO Box 159, Baddeck, NS B0E 1B0
Tel: 902-295-2069; Fax: 902-295-3496
information@pc.gc.ca
www.parkscanada.gc.ca; capebretonisland.com/AGBell.html
Presents Dr. Bell's life & work, with emphasis on his accomplishments in Baddeck; open year round; Nov. 1 - Apr. 30 site visits by arrangement. The site is located on Chebucto St. (Rte 205), on the eastern edge of Baddeck.
Aynsley MacFarlane, Site Manager
Carol Whitfield, Field Unit Supt.

Baddeck: **Canso Islands & Grassy Island Fort National Historic Sites of Canada / Iles-Canso et Fort-de-l'Ile-Grassy Lieux historiques du Can**
PO Box 159, Baddeck, NS B0E 1B0
Tel: 902-295-2069; Fax: 902-295-3496
information@pc.gc.ca; atlantic.parksinfo@pc.gc.ca
www.pc.gc.ca/eng/lhn-nhs/ns/canso/index.aspx
Other contact information: Alternative Phone, Summer: 902-366-3136
The Canso Islands were a fishing base for the French during the 16th & 17th centuries. The British used the fishing port during the first half of the 18th century. The Islands were the scene of several battles between the French & English & the Mi'kmaq. In 1744, the Canso settlement was destroyed by the French. The visitor centre & interpretive trail are open from June 1st to September 15th.

Baddeck: **Marconi National Historic Site of Canada / Lieu historique national Marconi du Canada**
c/o Alexander Graham Bell National Historic Site, PO Box 159, Baddeck, NS B0E 1B0
Tel: 902-295-2069; Fax: 902-295-3496
information@pc.gc.ca
parkscanada.gc.ca/marconi
The site marks where Guglielmo Marconi initiated the age of global communications in 1902 by transmitting the first wireless message across the Atlantic Ocean. Visitors can see the Wireless Hall of Fame and walk to the original transmission station. Open June 1 - Sept.
Aynsley MacFarlane, Site Manager
Carol Whitfield, Field Unit Supt.

***Barrington:* Barrington Woolen Mill Museum**
***Parent:* Cape Sable Historical Society**
2368 Hwy. 3, Barrington, NS B0W 1E0
Tel: 902-637-2185
Year Founded: 1968 A preserved wool mill from the 1800s; open June-Sept.

***Barrington:* Cape Sable Historical Society Centre**
Old Court House, 2401 Hwy. 3, RR#1, Barrington, NS B0W 1E0
Tel: 902-637-2185; Fax: 902-637-2185
barmuseumcomplex@eastlink.ca
www.capesablehistoricalsociety.com
Year Founded: 1937 The Cape Sable Historical Society illustrates the history of Shelburne & Yarmouth Counties by collecting historical documents, genealogical records, & other items, & preserving historical sites. The Cape Sable Historical Society Centre is open year round.
Marjory Weeks, President
Brenda Maxwell, Manager

***Barrington:* Old Meeting House Museum**
***Parent:* Cape Sable Historical Society**
2408 Hwy. 3, Barrington, NS B0W 1E0
Tel: 902-637-2185
museum.gov.ns.ca/omh
A preserved New England-style meeting house c.1765; open June-Sept.

***Barss Corner, Maplewood:* Parkdale-Maplewood Community Museum**
3005 Barss Corner Rd., RR#1, Barss Corner, Maplewood, NS B0R 1A0
Tel: 902-644-2893
p-mcm@hotmail.com.ca
parkdale.ednet.ns.ca
www.facebook.com/94020106181
Founded by Thomas I. Spidell, a missionary-salesman for the New & Latter House of Israel
Carolea Kaulback, Chair
Barbara Gail, Curator

***Bedford:* Atlantic Canada Aviation Museum (ACAM) / Musée D'aviation des provinces Atlantique**
PO Box 44006, 1658 Bedford Hwy., Bedford, NS B4A 3X5
Tel: 902-873-3773
info@atlanticcanadaaviation.com
www.atlanticcanadaaviation.com
Year Founded: 1977 Located at the Halifax International Airport (20 Sky Blvd.), the Atlantic Canada Aviation Museum preserves the aviation heritage of Atlantic Canada. The aircraft collection includes the Bell 47-J-2 Ranger Helicopter, the CF-5A Freedom Fighter, a Harvard Mk II, & a CF-104 Starfighter. The museum is open from mid-May to mid-October. At other times, tours can be arranged.
Michael White, Public Affairs Officer, 902-446-7606, mga1937@hotmail.com

***Bridgetown:* James House**
c/o The Bridgetown & Area Historical Society, PO Box 645, 12 Queen St., Bridgetown, NS B0S 1C0
Tel: 902-665-4530
james.house.museum@gmail.com
Year Founded: 1979 James House was built in 1835 by Richard James, a member of the British Army who served in England & India. The house was donated to the Bridgetown & Area Historical Society. It became a Provincial Heritage Building, & now operates as the museum for the town of Bridgetown. James House features the Memorial Military Museum, which is sponsored by the Royal Canadian Legion, Branch 33. The museum is open from June to October.

***Bridgewater:* DesBrisay Museum & Exhibition Centre**
c/o 60 Pleasant St., Bridgewater, NS B4V 3X9
Tel: 902-543-4033; Fax: 902-543-4713
museum@bridgewater.ca
www.bridgewater.ca/desbrisay-museum/welcome-to-our-museum.html
Year Founded: 1902 Home of famed porcupine quill-decorated cradle; parkland & trails; open year round; located 130 Jubilee Rd., Bridgewater; admission fee
Barbara Thompson, Director, bthompson@bridgewater.ca
Linda Bedford, Curator, lbedford@bridgewater.ca

***Bridgewater:* Wile Carding Mill**
c/o DesBrisay Museum, 60 Pleasant St., Bridgewater, NS B4V 3X9
Tel: 902-543-8233; Fax: 902-543-4713
museum.gov.ns.ca/wcm
Last surviving plant of a 19th-century water-powered industrial park; part of Nova Scotia Museum; open June 1 - Sept. 30; located at 242 Victoria Rd., Bridgewater; admission fee

***Canso:* Whitman House Museum & Tourist Bureau**
Canso Historical Society, PO Box 128, 1297 Union St., Canso, NS B0H 1H0
Tel: 902-366-2170; Fax: 902-366-3093
cansotouristbureau@ns.sympatico.ca
Year Founded: 1975 Whitman House was built in 1885. The first resident was C.H. Whitman, a Baptist minister. The operation of the Whitman House Museum is now overseen by the Canso Historical Society. Exhibits at the Whitman House Museum depict the history of the town of Canso & eastern Guysborough County, & Canso Harbour. The museum is open from June 1st to September 30th. At other times of the year, appointments may be arranged.

***Cape Sable Island:* Archelaus Smith Museum & Historical Society**
915 Hwy. 330, Centreville, Cape Sable Island, NS B0W 1P0
Tel: 902-745-3361
archsmith@hotmail.ca
Portrays the history of Cape Sable Island including fishing techniques & gear, the Cape Island boat, shipwrecks, lives of sea captains, items from old kitchens, paintings by local artists, geneological & other historical records. The collection illustrates the background & growth of a pre-Loyalist fishing community
Bryant Newell, Secretary

***Cheticamp:* Musée Acadien / Acadian Museum**
CP 98, Cheticamp, NS B0E 1H0
Tél: 902-224-2170; Téléc: 902-224-2170
info@cheticamphookedrugs.com
www.cheticamphookedrugs.com/museum
Fondée en: 1963 Part of the Coopérative Artisanale, which also includes a shop & restaurant. Open May - Oct.
Diane Poirier, Manager, 902-224-3463

***Church Point:* Musée Église Sainte-Marie Museum**
PO Box 28, 1713 Hwy. 1, Church Point, NS B0W 1M0
Tel: 902-769-2832; Fax: 902-769-0048
www.museeeglisesaintemariemuseum.ca
Largest wooden church in North America; open June - Oct.
André Valotaire, Président

***Clementsport:* Old St. Edward's Anglican Loyalist Church Museum**
PO Box 171, 34 Old Post Rd., Clementsport, NS B0S 1E0
Tel: 902-638-8554
Original Loyalist, Old St. Edward's Anglican Church & Cemetery consecrated 1797; managed by volunteers; situated at 34 Old Post Rd., Clementsport, Annapolis County, NS

***Cole Harbour:* Cole Harbour Heritage Farm Museum**
471 Poplar Dr., Cole Harbour, NS B2W 4L2
Tel: 902-434-0222
farm.museum@ns.aliantzinc.ca
www.coleharbourfarmmuseum.ca
Open daily from May 15 - Oct.15; or by appt.
Elizabeth Corser

***Dartmouth:* Black Cultural Centre for Nova Scotia**
1149 Main St., Dartmouth, NS B2Z 1A8
Tel: 902-434-6223; Fax: 902-434-2306
Toll-Free: 800-465-0767
contact@bccns.com
www.bccns.com
Year Founded: 1983 Programs at the cultural education centre have include guided tours, music, plays, workshops, & lectures.
Dr. Henry V. Bishop, Chief Curator
Russell Grosse, Manager, Operations

***Digby:* Admiral Digby Museum**
PO Box 1644, 95 Montague Row, Digby, NS B0V 1A0
Tel: 902-245-6322; Fax: 902-245-5196
admuseum@ns.sympatico.ca
www.admuseum.ns.ca
Museum is housed in a Georgian-style home and is named for Rear Admiral Robert Digby. On display are period rooms, furnishings and artifacts relating to the history of Digby; costumes; Marine Room with charts, ship models, and navigational equipment; photographs; online gift shop; online archives which include family registers and other items of interest to genealogical and historical researchers. Open mid-June - mid-Oct.; two days a week in winter
Sheryl Stanton, Curator

***Dingwall:* North Highlands Community Museum & Culture Centre**
PO Box 3, Dingwall, NS B0C 1G0
Tel: 902-383-2579
community@northhighlandsmuseum.ca
www.northhighlandsmuseum.ca
Social Media: www.youtube.com/user/nhcmuseum
twitter.com/NHCmuseum
The history & culture of northern Cape Breton Island is celebrated at the North Highlands Community Museum & Culture Centre, through artifacts & documents. The collection includes maritime artifacts, such as shipwreck booty, schoolroom materials, doctor's instruments, & farming tools.
Rob Macdonald, Co-Chair
David Rasmussen, Co-Chair
Deidre Fraser, Coordinator
Esther Danielson, Secretary
Maureen Grover, Treasurer

***Englishtown:* Great Hall of The Clans, Highland Pioneers Museum**
PO Box 80, Englishtown, NS B0C 1H0
Tel: 902-295-3411; Fax: 902-295-2912
info@gaeliccollege.edu
www.gaeliccollege.edu
Open daily June - Sept.
Beth Anne MacEachen, Manager

***Glace Bay:* Cape Breton Miners' Museum**
PO Box 310, 42 Birkley St., Glace Bay, NS B1A 5T8
Tel: 902-849-4522; Fax: 902-849-8022
info@minersmuseum.com
www.minersmuseum.com
The Cape Breton Miners' Museum tells the story of the area's history of coal mining. Visitors may tour the Ocean Deeps Colliery, which is a coal mine situated beneath the museum building. Exhibits include coal mining equipment. Research inquiries will be responded to by museum staff. The museum also features the Men of the Deeps Theatre.

***Grand Pre:* Grand-Pré National Historic Site of Canada**
PO Box 150, Grand Pre, NS B0P 1M0
Tel: 902-542-3631; Fax: 902-542-1691
Toll-Free: 866-542-3631
contact@grand-pre.com
www.grand-pre.com
Bilingual guides interpret history of the Acadians; open daily May 1 - Oct. 30; entrance fee
Victor Tétrault, Executive Director

***Greenwood:* Greenwood Military Aviation Museum**
PO Box 786, Greenwood, NS B0P 1N0
Tel: 902-765-1494; Fax: 902-765-1261
gmam001@hotmail.com
gmam.ca
Year Founded: 1995 Recording the history of RAF/RCAF/CF station 1942 to present
Maj. R. Leblanc, General Manager
Bryan Nelson, Curator

***Guysborough:* Old Court House Museum & Information Centre**
***Parent:* Guysborough County Heritage Association**
c/o Guysborough County Heritage Association, PO Box 49, Guysborough, NS B0J 1N0
Tel: 902-533-4008; Fax: 902-533-2258
guysborough.historical@ns.sympatico.ca
www.guysboroughcountyheritage.ca
Open June - Oct.

***Halifax:* Africville National Historic Site**
***Parent:* Africville Genealogy Society**
Seaview Memorial Park, Halifax, NS
Tel: 902-492-0253
www.africville.ca
www.facebook.com/africville
Accessible year round
Irvine Carvery, President, Africville Genealogy Society, irvine@africville.ca

***Halifax:* Army Museum**
Cavalier Bldg., Halifax Citadel National Historic Site, PO Box 9080 A, Halifax, NS B3K 5M7
Tel: 902-422-5979; Fax: 902-426-4228
armymuseum@ns.aliantzinc.ca
Year Founded: 1953 The Army Museum preserves & promotes the military heritage of Atlantic Canada. Displays, including uniforms, decorations, weapons, & firearms, are related to the British, Canadian Regular Force, & Militia. The museum is open from May to October.

***Halifax:* Fisherman's Life Museum (FLM)**
Jeddore, Oyster Pond, 58 Navy Pool Loop, Halifax, NS B0J 1W0
Tel: 902-772-2344; Fax: 902-772-2344
monkma@gov.ns.ca
museum.gov.ns.ca/flm/
Other contact information: Summer Tel: 902/889-2053, Fax: 902/889-2053
Open daily June 1 - Oct. 15
Martha Monk, Site Manager
Judith Shiers Milne, Public Information Officer, 902/424-7398, shiersjl@gov.ns.ca

***Halifax:* Halifax Citadel National Historic Site of Canada**
PO Box 9080 A, Halifax, NS B3K 5M7
Tel: 902-426-5080; Fax: 902-426-4228
halifax.citadel@pc.gc.ca
www.pc.gc.ca/eng/lhn-nhs/ns/halifax/index.aspx
twitter.com/ParksCanada_NS
The Citadel was completed in 1856 & was the fourth in a series of British forts on the site. Now the Citadel serves as a national landmark commemorating Halifax's role as a key naval station in the British Empire. The historic site features a living history program with the 78th Highlanders & the precision of the Royal Artillery.
Linda Frank, Field Unit Superintendent

***Halifax:* HMCS Sackville**
***Also known as:* Canadian Naval Memorial Trust (CNMT)**
PO Box 99000 Forces, Halifax, NS B3K 5X5
Tel: 902-429-2132
www.hmcssackville-cnmt.ns.ca
Social Media: vimeo.com/user7544880
twitter.com/HMCSSACKVILLE1
www.facebook.com/2543 72034574664
Other contact information: Winter Phone: 902-427-2837
Canada's Naval Memorial; WWII corvette museum; open summer, downtown Halifax, open winter, HMCS Dockyard
Vice-Admiral (Ret'd) Hugh MacNeil, Chair, chair@canadasnavalmemorial.ca
LCdr. (Ret'd) Jim Reddy, Director/Commanding Officer, co@canadasnavalmemorial.ca
Doug Thomas, Executive Director, execdir@canadasnavalmemorial.ca

***Halifax:* Maritime Command Museum / Musée du Commandement Maritime**
***Also known as:* Marcom Museum**
Admiralty House, PO Box 99000 Forces, 2725 Gottingen St., Halifax, NS B3K 5X5
Tel: 902-721-8250
marcommuseum@forces.gc.ca
psphalifax.ca/marcommuseum
Year Founded: 1974 Of the Dept. of National Defence's 55 museums, this is the largest. Housed within 30 rooms of Admiralty House, a Georgian mansion, are displays representing facets of the Canadian Military. The collection consists of a research library, uniforms, model ships, medals, badges, ships' bells and other memorabilia associated with naval life. Open year round
Marilyn Gurney, Director

***Halifax:* Nova Scotia Sport Hall of Fame**
#446, 1800 Argyle St., Halifax, NS B3J 3N8
Tel: 902-421-1266; Fax: 902-425-1148
sporthalloffame@eastlink.ca
www.novascotiasporthalloffame.com
The Hall of Fame honours Nova Scotians who have made an impact on sports during the past 100 years. Inductees are addeed to the Hall of Fame each year, during The Hall of Fame Induction Night.
Bill Robinson, Executive Director, billr@eastlink.ca
Shane Mailman, Manager, Facility & Communications
Karolyn Sevcik, Coordinator, Administration & Special Events, halloffameevents@eastlink.ca
Rob Randall, Treasurer

***Halifax:* Prince of Wales Tower National Historic Site of Canada**
c/o Halifax Citadel National Historic Site, PO Box 9080 A, Halifax, NS B3K 5M7
Tel: 902-426-5080; Fax: 902-426-4228
halifax.citadel @pc.gc.ca
www.pc.gc.ca/lhn-nhs/ns/prince/index.aspx
The Prince of Wales Tower was built in 1796 & 1797. Its purpose was to protect the British from Fench attack. Over 200 years later, visitors will discover exhibits which show the tower's history. The Tower is open from the beginning of July to the end of August.
Linda Frank, Field Unit Superintendent, Mainland Nova Scotia Field Unit, Parks Canada
Dave Danskin, Manager, Heritage Presentation & Visitor Services, Mainland Nova Scotia Field Unit, Parks Canada
Tanya Taylor White, Manager, External Relations, Mainland Nova Scotia Field Unit, Parks Canada

***Halifax:* Thomas McCulloch Museum**
Biology Dept., Dalhousie University, 1355 Oxford St., Halifax, NS B3H 4J1
Tel: 902-494-3515
biology@dal.ca
biotype.biology.dal.ca/museum
Year Founded: 1883 Collection of mounted birds, artifacts, Lorenzen ceramic mushrooms, shells & insects; marine & freshwater aquaria; occasional temporary exhibits; open weekdays; free admission
Stephen Fry, Chief Curator, 902-494-3530, steve.fry@dal.ca
Karen Smith, Curator, 902-494-2785, karen.smith@dal.ca
Julie Walker, Director

***Halifax:* York Redoubt National Historic Site of Canada**
c/o Halifax Citadel National Historic Site, PO Box 9080 A, Halifax, NS B3K 5M7
Tel: 902-426-5080; Fax: 902-426-4228
halifax.citadel@pc.gc.ca
www.pc.gc.ca/lhn-nhs/ns/york/index.aspx
York Redoubt was established in 1793 to defend the Halifax Harbour. Today, it is a National Historic Site of Canada, which is part of the Halifax Defence Complex. The site is open year-round.
Linda Frank, Field Unit Superintendent, Mainland Nova Scotia Field Unit

***Hantsport:* Churchill House & Marine Memorial Room**
c/o Town of Hantsport, PO Box 399, Hantsport, NS B0P 1P0
Tel: 902-684-3461; Fax: 902-684-3227
susan@hantsportnovascotia.com
www.hantsportnovascotia.com;
nsgna.ednet.ns.ca/hantsport/churchl.htm
Other contact information: (off season) 902/684-9068
Located at 6 Main St., Hantsport; open daily July - Sept., or by appt.; classic Victorian architecture; documents local shipbuilding history
Susan Carey, Tourism Manager, Hantsport

***La Have:* Fort Point Museum**
c/o Lunenburg County Historical Society, PO Box 99, La Have, NS B0R 1C0
Tel: 902-688-2696
lchs-fortpoint@ns.sympatico.ca
www3.ns.sympatico.ca/lchs-fortpoint/
On National Historic Site of Fort Ste. Marie de Grâce, 1632

***La Have:* LaHave Island Marine Museum**
PO Box 69, 100 LaHave Islands Rd., La Have, NS B0R 1C0
Tel: 902-688-2973
limms@auracom.com
www.lahaveislandsmarinemuseum.ca
Historical treasures from a community that derived its life & livelihood from the sea
Douglas Berrigan, President
Kathy Sullivan, Curator

***Inverness:* Inverness Miners Museum**
***Parent:* Inverness Historical Society**
PO Box 598, 62 Lower Railway St., Inverness, NS B0E 1N0
Tel: 902-258-3822
www.inverness-ns.ca/inverness-miners-museum.html
Terry MacDonald, Curator, 902-258-2877

***Iona:* Highland Village Museum / An Clachan Gàidhealach**
4119 Hwy. 223, Iona, NS B2C 1A3
Tel: 902-725-2272; Fax: 902-725-2227
Toll-Free: 866-442-3542
highlandvillage@gov.ns.ca
www.museum.gov.ns.ca/hv
Year Founded: 1959 The museum's mission is to collect & preserve the Gaelic heritage of Nova Scotia, with a focus on advancing the language. Included on site are: interpretation centre & museum, carding mill, 1880-1900 frame house, schoolhouse, forge, country store, barn, frame house (1830-1875), log cabin, stone (black) house, outdoor performance centre. There is also an extensive database of genealogical information. The museum is open June - Oct., 9:30-5:30 daily.
Mr. Rodney Chaisson, Director, chaissrs@gov.ns.ca

***Kentville:* Blair House Museum**
c/o N.S. Fruit Growers' Association, Kentville Agricultural Centre, 32 Main St., Kentville, NS B4N 1J5
Tel: 902-678-1093; Fax: 902-678-1567
www.nsapples.com/museumb.htm
Year Founded: 1981 The Blair House Museum was opened by the Nova Scotia Fruit Growers' Association. The purpose of the museum is the preservation & presentation of the history of the apple growing industry. The Agriculture Canada wing of the museum displays past & present research conducted at the station. The museum is located in a 1911 building, which was the residence of the research station's first superintendent, Dr. William Saxby Blair.
Dela Erith, Executive Director, Nova Scotia Fruit Growers' Association, derith@nsapples.com
Helen Arenburg, Inspector, & Contact, Public Relations, harenburg@nsapples.com

***Kentville:* Kings County Museum**
***Parent:* Kings Historical Society**
37 Cornwallis St., Kentville, NS B4N 2E2
Tel: 902-678-6237; Fax: 902-678-2764
museum@okcm.ca
www.okcm.ca
twitter.com/Kings_Co_Museum
www.facebook. com/kingscountymuseum
Cultural & natural history of Kings County; Parks Canada commemorative exhibit to the New England Planters; genealogy & community history archives
Bria Stokesbury, Curator, curator@okcm.ca
Cathy Margeson, Office Manager

***Liverpool:* Hank Snow Country Music Centre**
PO Box 1419, 148 Bristol Ave., Liverpool, NS B0T 1K0
Tel: 902-354-4675; Fax: 902-354-5199
Toll-Free: 888-450-5525
info@hanksnow.com
www.hanksnow.com
Year Founded: 1996 A tribute to Hank Snow, legendary country/folk singer from "down east," the displays include a plethora of photos and memorabilia, from his guitar strings to his iconic toupées to his yellow 1947 Cadillac. The centre also houses the Nova Scotia Country Music Hall of Fame.

***Liverpool:* Perkins House Museum**
PO Box 1078, 105 Main St., Liverpool, NS B0T 1K0
Tel: 902-354-4058
museum.gov.ns.ca/peh
Connecticut style cottage built by merchant & diarist Simeon Perkins in 1766; open June - Oct. 15
Linda Rafuse, Director

***Liverpool:* Queens County Museum**
PO Box 1078, 109 Main St., Liverpool, NS B0T 1K0
Tel: 902-354-4058; Fax: 902-354-2050
www.queenscountymuseum.com
Year Founded: 1980 The Queens County Museum depicts the cultural history of Nova Scotia's Queens County. The south shore of the province has a strong history related to the Mi'kmaq culture, fishing, & the forest. Programs are available for schools & the public.
Linda Rafuse, Director, rafusela@gov.ns.ca

***Lockeport:* Little School Museum**
PO Box 69, Lockeport, NS B0T 1L0
Tel: 902-656-2238
townoflockeport@aura.com
www.lockeport.ns.ca
Replica of a former school room & a marine room; historical artifacts of local area

***Louisbourg:* Fortress of Louisbourg National Historic Site / Forteresse-de-Louisbourg, Lieu historique national**
259 Park Service Rd., Louisbourg, NS B1C 2L2
Tel: 902-733-2280; Fax: 902-733-2362
information@pc.gc.ca
www.pc.gc.ca/eng/lhn-nhs/ns/louisbourg/index.aspx
twitter.com/ParksCanada_NS
www.facebook.com/FortressOfLouisbourgNHS
Chip Bird, Field Unit Superintendent, Parks Canada, Cape Breton Field Unit

***Louisbourg:* S&L (Sydney & Louisburg) Railway Museum**
7330 Main St., Louisbourg, NS B1C 1P5
Tel: 902-733-2720
fortress.uccb.ns.ca/historic/s_l.html
Exhibits include railroad artifacts, models, photographs & other documentation; paintings; rolling stock, model railroad, souvenirs; open June 1 - Oct. 15; tourist information centre
Eugene Magee, Curator

***Lower Sackville:* Fultz House Museum**
***Parent:* Fultz Corner Restoration Society**
PO Box 124, 33 Sackville Dr., Lower Sackville, NS B4C 2S8
Tel: 902-865-3794
fultz.house@ns.sympatico.ca
www.fultzhouse.ca
www.facebook.com/77826276228
1860s home which belonged to the Fultz family of Sackville, NS; contains many artifacts & photographs from the Sackville area; blacksmith shop & cooperage shop from 1800s

***Lower West Pubnico:* Le Village historique acadien de la Nouvelle-Écosse / Historic Acadian Village of Nova Scotia**
PO Box 70, Lower West Pubnico, NS B0W 2C0
Tel: 902-762-2530; Fax: 902-762-2543
Toll-Free: 888-381-8999
villagehistorique@ns.aliantzinc.ca
museum.gov.ns.ca/av
A living historical village dedicated to preserving & showcasing the Acadian way of life from bygone days; open June-Oct.
Roger W. d'Entremont, Executive Director, roger@ns.aliantzinc.ca

***Mabou:* An Drochaid**
***Parent:* Mabou Gaelic & Historical Society**
Rte. 19, Mabou, NS B0E 1X0
Tel: 902-945-2311
Housed in an old general store; a centre for arts & crafts, genealogical & historical records, & research.
Theresa Beaton, Contact, 902-945-2930
Rodney MacDonald, Contact

Mahone Bay: **Mahone Bay Settlers Museum**
PO Box 583, 578 Main St., Mahone Bay, NS B0J 2E0
Tel: 902-624-6263
info@settlersmuseum.ns.ca
www.settlersmuseum.ns.ca
www.facebook.com/60254904029
Community Museum which provides vistors with a local history of the area; Open June to Sept.
Michael J. O'Connor, Acting Chair
Hannah Cody, Museum Manager
Wilma Stewart-White, Volunteer Curator

Maitland: **East Hants Historical Museum**
PO Box 51, Maitland, NS B0N 1C0
Tel: 902-261-2796
ehhs.weebly.com
Small museum containing historical Nova Scotian artifacts with local connections, historical documents, military records & cemetary records
Nancy Doane, President, East Hants Historical Society
Glenys Leck, Secretary
Olive Terris, Treasurer

Maitland: **Lawrence House Museum**
Parent: **Nova Scotia Museum**
8660 Hwy. 215, RR #1, Maitland, NS B0N 1T0
Tel: 902-261-2628
museum.gov.ns.ca/lh
c.1865 home of William D. Lawrence, shipwright; open June 1 - Oct. 15

Middleton: **Annapolis Valley Macdonald Museum**
PO Box 925, 21 School St., Middleton, NS B0S 1P0
Tel: 902-825-6116; Fax: 902-825-0531
macdonald.museum@ns.sympatico.ca
www.macdonaldmuseum.ca
Features antique clocks and pocket watches; Art Gallery featuring local artists; historical artifacts, household items, tools; recreated classroom and general store; sports heritage wall of fame; gift shop.

Milton: **Milton Blacksmith Shop Museum**
PO Box 572, 351 West St., Milton, NS B0T 1P0
Tel: 902-350-0268
www.qcis.ns.ca/blacksmith
Managed by the Milton Heritage Society, the museum is a 1903 smithy, complete with forge, ox sling & original workbenches, as well as a wide array of tools of the trade; also large display of photographs of historical Milton, NS
Ms Christine Tupper, Curator, 902-354-2550

Mount Uniacke: **Uniacke Estate Museum Park**
Parent: **Nova Scotia Museum**
PO Box 12, 758 Hwy. #1, Mount Uniacke, NS B0N 1Z0
Tel: 902-866-0032; Fax: 902-866-2560
museum.gov.ns.ca/uemp
c.1813; open June - Oct. 15
Martina Murphy, Chief Heritage Interpreter, murphyms@gov.ns.ca

Musquodoboit Harbour: **Musquodoboit Railway Museum**
Parent: **Nova Scotia Railway Heritage Society (NSRHS)**
PO Box 303, Musquodoboit Harbour, NS B0J 2L0
Tel: 902-889-2689
www.novascotiarailwayheritage.com/musquodoboit.htm
Open May 16 - Oct.

New Glasgow: **Carmichael Stewart House**
86 Temperance St., New Glasgow, NS B2H 3A7
Tel: 902-752-5583
pictoucounty@ns.sympatico.ca
www.parl.ns.ca/csmuseum
Year Founded: 1965 Operated by the Pictou County Historical Society, the Carmichael Stewart House Museum is a late Victorian home which contains collections such as photographs, clothing, & Trenton Glassware. The museum is open during the summer.
Fergie MacKay, President
Jessica MacNeil, Treasurer
George McKay, Secretary

New Glasgow: **Carmichael Stewart House Museum**
Parent: **Pictou County Historical Society**
86 Temperance St., New Glasgow, NS B2H 3A7
Tel: 902-752-5583
carmich@eastlink.ca
www.parl.ns.ca/csmuseum
Fergie MacKay, President

New Ross: **Ross Farm Museum**
4568 Rte. 12, RR#2, New Ross, NS B0J 2M0
Tel: 902-689-2210Toll-Free: 877-689-2210
rossfarm@gov.ns.ca
rossfarm.museum.gov.ns.ca
twitter.com/RossFarmMuseu m
www.facebook.com/RossFarmMuseum
Ross family farm 1817

Lisa Wolfe, Director, wolfelm@gov.ns.ca

North East Margaree: **Margaree Salmon Museum**
PO Box 21, 60 East Big Intervale Rd., North East Margaree, NS B0E 2H0
Tel: 902-248-2848
margareesalmonmuseum@yahoo.ca
www.margareens.com/margaree_salmon.html
Year Founded: 1965 Exhibits relate to salmon angling on the Margaree River. Located in a former schoolhouse; includes collections of fishing tackle, photos & memorabilia of famous anglers. Open June-Oct.
Frances Hart, Contact

Orangedale: **Orangedale Railway Museum**
Parent: **Orangedale Station Association**
PO Box 16, Orangedale, NS B0E 2K0
Tel: 902-756-3384
orangedale.station@gmail.com
www.novascotiarailwayheritage.com/orangedale.htm
Open June - mid-Oct.; railway station built in 1911
Martin Boston, President

Parrsboro: **Fundy Geological Museum**
162 Two Island Rd., Parrsboro, NS B0M 1S0
Tel: 902-254-3814; Fax: 902-254-3666
Toll-Free: 866-856-9466
fundygeo@gov.ns.ca
fundygeo.museum.gov.ns.ca
Open daily in summer; Tues.-Sat. in winter
Karen Dickinson, Chair
Kenneth Adams, Director/Curator, adamskd@gov.ns.ca

Pictou: **McCulloch House Museum (MCH)**
PO Box 1210, 100 Haliburton Rd., Pictou, NS B0K 1H0
Tel: 902-485-4563; Fax: 902-485-5213
museum.gov.ns.ca/mch
Year Founded: 1972 Administered by the Pictou County Genealogy and Heritage Society, the museum was built in 1805 as home to Rev. Dr. McCulloch, the founder of Pictou Academy & first president of Dalhousie University. The exhibits reflect the life & times of the Scottish immigrants and their influence on today's Nova Scotia.
Judith Shiers Milne, Public Information Officer, 902-424-7398, Fax: 902-424-0560, shiersjl@gov.ns.ca

Pictou: **Northumberland Fisheries Museum & Heritage Association (NFM)**
PO Box 1489, 71 Front St., Pictou, NS B0K 1H0
Tel: 902-485-4972; Fax: 902-485-6586
www.northumberlandfisheriesmuseum.com
Year Founded: 1978 Located in the historic C.N. Station; fishing artifacts from the late 1800s to present day; original fisherman's Bunkhouse; The "Silver Bullet"; photographs; boat models; fishing tools; artifacts on lobster processing; shell fish/live fish displays; sea heritage education for schools & seniors; education is based on fact & scientific data from Northumberland Strait area; local research conducted on fishing & sea heritage; recent additions to the museum include a lobster hatchery & lighthouse museum & research centre.
David MacKeil, Chair
Michelle Davey, Business Manager

Port Hastings: **Port Hastings Museum & Archives**
24 Rte. 19, Port Hastings, NS B9A 1M1
Tel: 902-625-1295
office@porthastingsmuseum.ca
www.porthastingsmuseum.ca
Located in 100-year-old Cape Breton house; displays include pioneer artifacts, photographic displays & exhibits on construction of causeway; genealogical records available
Bob MacEachern, President
Vacant , Curator

Port Hood: **Chestico Museum & Historical Society**
PO Box 144, Port Hood, NS B0E 2W0
Tel: 902-787-2244
chesticoplace.com
Year Founded: 1986 Located in Harbourview, on Rte 19 on the outskirts of Port Hood, the museum houses artifacts from the local community; house histories, historical events, people of the Port Hood area; gift shop; tea room; special programming. The museum will be housed in a new facility, Chestico Place, located in the centre of Port Hood, in the near future.
Susan Mallette, Director

Pubnico-Ouest: **Musée des Acadiens des Pubnicos et Centre de recherche**
CP 92, Pubnico-Ouest, NS B0W 3S0
Tél: 902-762-3380; Téléc: 902-762-0726
musee.acadien@ns.sympatico.ca
www.museeacadien.ca
Le Musée: #898, autoroute 335; consacré au patrimoine des Acadiens/Acadiennes de Pubnico-Ouest; articles de maison; documents; photographies; archives; potager traditionnel; boutique de souvenirs.

Paul d'Entremont, Président

Riverport: **Ovens Natural Park & Museum**
PO Box 38, 326 Ovens Rd., Riverport, NS B0J 2W0
Tel: 902-766-4621
info@ovenspark.com
www.ovenspark.com; ovenspark.tumblr.com
www.facebook.com/ovensnaturalpark
Located on the Atlantic coast of Nova Scotia, Ovens Natural Park is a reserve of coastal forest, featuring the sea caves or "Ovens". The area became known internationally during th 1861 gold rush. The Gold Rush Museum contains artifacts from that era.
Angel Chapin, Director

St Peters: **Nicolas Denys Museum**
PO Box 204, 46 Denys St., St Peters, NS B0E 3B0
Tel: 902-535-2379
Micmac, Acadien, Scottish & Irish artifacts
Judy Madden, Curator, judy_madden80@hotmail.ca

Shag Harbour: **Chapel Hill Museum**
PO Box 46, 5492 Hwy #3, Shag Harbour, NS B0W 3B0
Tel: 902-723-1313
chapelhillhistory@aliantzinc.ns.ca
chapelhill.webs.com
Located in former Baptist Church; features various displays related to local area including tools for ship building, genealogical research materials, various fishing exhibits; able to view 4 local lighthouses from observation tower; open June 1 - Sept. 15 daily; rest of the year by appt.
Douglas Shand, President, Chapel Hill Historical Society, 902-723-2949, shawimm@ns.sympatico.ca
Veronica Hopkins, Vice President/Treasurer, Chapel Hill Historical Society, vhopkins@ns.sympatico.ca

Shag Harbour: **Shag Harbour Incident Society Museum**
Also known as: **UFO Museum**
PO Box 53, Shag Harbour, NS B0W 3B0
Tel: 902-723-0174
shagharbour@gmail.com
cuun.i2ce.com/misc/shagHarbourMuseum
Year Founded: 2007 The museum displays memorabilia, TV programs, & other material related to the documented 1967 crash of a UFO in the Gulf of Maine, near Shag Harbour. The museum also details local history unrelated to the crash. Open M-F 1:00-5:00, Sa 12:00-5:00, Su 1:00-5:00; also open by appointment.
Cindy Nickerson, Chair
Dale Nickerson, Associate, 902-723-2385

Shearwater: **Shearwater Aviation Museum**
PO Box 5000 Main, 12 Wing, Shearwater, NS B0J 3A0
Tel: 902-720-1083; Fax: 902-720-2037
info@shearwateraviationmuseum.ns.ca
www.shearwateraviationmuseum.ns.ca
twitter.com/YAWmuseum
www.facebook.com/shearwateraviationmuseum

Shelburne: **The Dory Shop Museum**
Parent: **Shelburne Historical Society**
PO Box 39, 11 Dock St., Shelburne, NS B0T 1W0
Tel: 902-875-3219; Fax: 902-875-4141
museum.gov.ns.ca/dory
Restored dory factory, est. 1880; open June 1 - Sept. 30; dories still built to order
Kim Truchan, Complex Manager, truchakc@gov.ns.ca

Shelburne: **Ross-Thomson House & Store Museum**
PO Box 39, Shelburne, NS B0T 1W0
Tel: 902-875-3141; Fax: 902-875-4141
shelburne.museum@ns.sympatico.ca
www.historicshelburne.com
Located on Charlotte St. in Shelburne; 1785 Loyalist house & garden; 18th-century store & chandlery; 19th-century military artifacts; open June 1 - Oct. 15
Kim Truchan, Complex Manager, shs.kimtruchan@ns.aliantzinc.ca

Shelburne: **Shelburne County Museum**
PO Box 39, 20 Dock St., Shelburne, NS B0T 1W0
Tel: 902-875-3219; Fax: 902-875-4141
shelburne.museum@ns.sympatico.ca
www.historicshelburne.com
Cultural & economic history of Shelburne from 1783; genealogy information; open year round
Finn Bower, Curator

Sherbrooke: **Sherbrooke Village**
Parent: **Historic Sherbrooke Village Development Society**
PO Box 295, 42 Main St., Sherbrooke, NS B0J 3C0
Tel: 902-522-2400; Fax: 902-522-2974
Toll-Free: 888-743-7845
svillage@gov.ns.ca
museum.gov.ns.ca/sv
Social Media: www.youtube.com/user/sherbrookevillage
twitter.com/Sherbrooke_NS
www.facebook.com/pages/Sherbrooke-Village/1148 18421893386
Open June - mid-Oct.
Kurt Oko, Chair
Mark Sajatovich, Executive Director

Smith's Cove: **Old Temperance Hall Museum**
590 Hwy. 1, Smith's Cove, NS B0S 1S0
smithscovemuseum@gmail.com
Exhibits of the 19th and 20th century pertaining to the local community including the earliest inhabitants, the Mi'kmaq; history of the Sons of Temperance.

Springhill: **The Anne Murray Centre**
36 Main St., Springhill, NS B0M 1X0
Tel: 902-597-8614; Fax: 902-597-2001
info@annemurraycentre.com
www.annemurraycentre.com
Year Founded: 1989 Pays tribute to the achievements of Springhill's internationally acclaimed singing superstar; open May - Oct., otherwise by appt. or by chance.

Springhill: **Springhill Miner's Museum**
PO Box 610, 145 Black River Rd., Springhill, NS B0M 1X0
Tel: 902-597-3449
springhillminersmuseum@hotmail.com
www.town.springhill.ns.ca/Attractions.html
Tours of the Springhill coal mine, famous in song & legend; gift shop & picnic area; open May - Oct.
Roberta McMasters, Contact

Starr's Point: **Prescott House**
1633 Starr's Point Rd., Starr's Point, NS B0P 1T0
Tel: 902-542-3984; Fax: 902-542-3984
museum.gov.ns.ca/prh
c.1814 Georgian house, open June 1 - Oct. 15; museum shop; bus tours welcome
Diana Baldwin, Contact, baldwidj@gov.ns.ca

Stellarton: **Museum of Industry**
PO Box 2590, 147 North Foord St., Stellarton, NS B0K 1S0
Tel: 902-755-5425; Fax: 902-755-7045
industry@gov.ns.ca
museum.gov.ns.ca/moi
Atlantic Canada's largest museum; chronicles the impact of industrialization on the people, economy & landscape of Nova Scotia; features Canada's oldest steam locomotives, an historic model railway layout, a belt-driven working machine shop & a collection of Nova Scotia's Trenton glass
Debra McNabb, Director
Mary Guildford, Curator, Collections
Andrew Phillips, Curator, Education & Public Programming

Sydney: **Cape Breton Centre for Heritage & Science**
Also known as: **The Lyceum Museum**
225 George St., Sydney, NS B1P 1J5
Tel: 902-539-1572
oldsydneysociety@ns.aliantzinc.ca
www.oldsydney.com/museums/centre.html
twitter.com/OldSydney
www.facebo ok.com/OldSydneySociety
The Lyceum was built in 1904 by the Roman Catholic diocese. The Opera House contained a 900 seat theatre, as well as a library, gymnasium, billiards room, & clubrooms. Today, the Lyceum houses the Cape Breton Centre for Heritage & Science. The Old Sydney Society provides tours of the Colonial Town of Old Sydney, which was first the home to Mi'Kmaq people, then Basque fishermen, Loyalists, & later immigrating Scots. In the Cape Breton Centre for Heritage & Science, visitors will discover the natural & social histories of Cape Breton County. The museum is open year round.
Dr. Robert Morgan, President, 902-539-3951
J. Peyton Chisholm, Curator
Elaine Hummer, Bookkeeper

Sydney: **Cossit House Museum**
Parent: **Old Sydney Society**
c/o Cape Breton Centre for Heritage & Science, 225 George St., Sydney, NS B1P 4P4
Tel: 902-539-7973
museum.gov.ns.ca/ch
One of the oldest buildings on Cape Breton Island, c.1787.

Tatamagouche: **Balmoral Grist Mill**
RR#4, Tatamagouche, NS B0K 1V0
Tel: 902-657-3016; Fax: 902-657-2606
www.museum.gov.ns.ca/bgm
Located at 660 Matheson Brook Road in Balmoral Mills, the 1874 three-storey grist mill is still operational. The grist mill is open from June 1st to October 15th.
Darrell Burke, Site Manager, burked@gov.ns.ca

Tatamagouche: **Sunrise Trail Museum**
39 Creamery Rd., Tatamagouche, NS B0K 1V0
Tel: 902-657-3500; Fax: 902-657-0240
creamerysquare@ns.aliantzinc.ca
Open daily mid-June - Labour Day

Tatamagouche: **Sutherland Steam Mill Museum**
Parent: **Nova Scotia Museum**
c/o Balmoral Grist Mill, RR#4, Tatamagouche, NS B0K 1V0
Tel: 902-657-3365; Fax: 902-657-2606
museum.gov.ns.ca/ssm
Open June 1 - Oct. 15
Darrell Burke, Site Manager, 902-657-3017, burked@gov.ns.ca

Truro: **Colchester Historeum**
Parent: **Colchester Historical Society**
PO Box 412, 29 Young St., Truro, NS B2N 5C5
Tel: 902-895-6284
colchesterhistoreum.ca
twitter.com/Col_Historeum
www.facebook.com/colchesterhistoreum
Other contact information: Archives Phone: 902-895-9530
Year Founded: 1976 Museum & archive devoted to preserving the history of Colchester County; open year round.
Aidan Norton, Curator
Nan Harvey, Archivist

Truro: **The Little White Schoolhouse**
PO Box 1252, 20 Arthur St., Truro, NS B2N 5N2
Tel: 902-895-5170
littlewhiteschool.ca
Original Riverton School; commemorates schoolhouses in Nova Scotia from Confederation to the 1950s; contains books & artifacts from the era of one-room schoolhouse; requests for research on the graduates of the Provincial Normal School & College & in old copies of the NS Journal of Education, accepted; open early June - Aug. & by appt.

Tupperville: **Tupperville School Museum**
2663 Hwy. 201, Tupperville, NS B0S 1C0
Tel: 902-665-2579; Fax: 902-665-4875
tuppervillemuseum@auracom.com
www.nslocal.ca/tuppervillemuseum
Open daily mid-May - mid-Sept.
Marion L. Inglis, Chair

Wallace: **Wallace & Area Museum**
Parent: **Wallace & Area Museum Society**
PO Box 179, 13440 Rte. 6, Wallace, NS B0K 1Y0
Tel: 902-257-2191
wallacemuseum@ns.aliantzinc.ca
www.wallaceandareamuseum.com
www.facebook.com/pages/Wallace-and-Area-Mus eum/120610681314312
Year Founded: 1983 The museum collect, preserves, & displays the history of Wallace & the surrounding region. Artifacts include nineteenth century marine charts & maps, the United Empire Loyalist grant, pre-Confederation letters, & items about shipbuilding in Wallace & the Wallace sandstone quarries. Hours: June-Sep.: M-Sa 9:00-5:00; Su 1:00-4:00; Oct.-May M, Th 10:00-2:00
Doris Purdy, President
Glenda Waugh, Vice-President
David Dewar, Curator
Doug Perry, Secretary

West Bay: **Marble Mountain Library & Museum**
RR#1, West Bay, NS B0E 3K0
Tel: 902-756-3289
Wendy MacDonald, Curator

Windsor: **Haliburton House Museum**
PO Box 2683, 414 Clifton Ave., Windsor, NS B0N 2T0
Tel: 902-798-2915; Fax: 902-798-2915
museum.gov.ns.ca/hh
Open June 1-Oct. 15
Alan Dauphinee, Superintendent, dauphiar@gov.ns.ca

Windsor: **Shand House Museum**
PO Box 2683, 389 Avon St., Windsor, NS B0N 2T0
Tel: 902-798-8213; Fax: 902-798-5619
museum.gov.ns.ca/sh
Open June 1 - Oct. 15

Windsor: **West Hants Historical Society Museum**
PO Box 2335, 281 King St., Windsor, NS B0N 2T0
Tel: 902-798-4706
whhs@ns.aliantzinc.ca
www.westhantshistoricalsociety.ca
Artifacts related to the history of Hants County in Nova Scotia are collected & preserved by the West Hants Historical Society & displayed at its museum. Visitors will find information about the Mi'kmaq, the Acadians, the Loyalists, the Great Windsor Fire of 1897, & the local shipbuilding industry. The society also operates a genealogy department. The museum is open five days a week from mid June to the end of August, & one day a week from September to June. Summer tours are available of the Fort Edward Blockhouse. Appointments may be arranged for times when the museum is closed.

Wolfville: **Randall House Museum**
c/o Wolfville Historical Society, 259 Main St., Wolfville, NS B4P 1C6
Tel: 902-542-9775
randallhouse@live.ca
www.wolfvillehs.ednet.ns.ca
The Randall House is an historic farmhouse, from around 1800, which is owned & operated by the Wolfville Historical Society. The Randall House Museum reflects life in Wolfville & the surrounding area during the 18th & 19th centuries. On display are furniture, clothing, china, & a collection of Victorian greeting cards. A library is located in The Randall House for persons researching local history & genealogy.
John Whidden, President
Heather Watts, Archivist, 902-542-0307
William Bishop, Historian

Yarmouth: **Firefighters' Museum of Nova Scotia**
Nova Scotia Museum Complex, 451 Main St., Yarmouth, NS B5A 1G9
Tel: 902-742-5525
darbydl@gov.ns.ca
museum.gov.ns.ca/fm/
Artifacts date to the early 1800s; open year round
David Darby, Curator

Yarmouth: **Yarmouth County Museum & Archives**
Parent: **Yarmouth County Historical Society**
22 Collins St., Yarmouth, NS B5A 3C8
Tel: 902-742-5539; Fax: 902-749-1120
ycmuseum@eastlink.ca
yarmouthcountymuseum.ednet.ns.ca
www.facebook.com /92402018979
Also operates the Pelton-Fuller House in Yarmouth, the historic summer home of A.C. Fuller, the Fuller Brush Man & the Killam Brothers' shipping office, the oldest in Canada, during the summer months
Nadine Gates, Director/Curator
Adrienne Beaudette, Assistant Director, ycm.asst.dir@eastlink.ca
Jamie Serran, Archivist, ycarchives@eastlink.ca

Nunavut

Local Museums in Nunavut

Iqaluit: **Nuantta Sunaqutangit Museum**
Bldg. Number 212, PO Box 1900, Iqaluit, NU X0A 0H0
Tel: 867-979-5537
museum@nunanet.com
Founded in 1969; housed in a historic Hudson Bay Company warehouse building; collections focus on Inuit culture & history from the Baffin region, including historical & archeological artifacts, tools, clothing, & equipment as well as arts & crafts; also maintains a collection of archival photographs, publications & documents for exhibition & research purposes; open year-round

Pangnirtung: **Sipalaseequtt Museum Society**
Angmarlik Visitor Centre, PO Box 227, Pangnirtung, NU X0A 0R0
Tel: 867-473-8737
Inuit artifacts; whaling history in Cumberland Sound Baffin Island; Elders' meetings; craft production; tours
Ooleepika Arnaqaq, Manager, Angmarlik Centre, oarnaqaq1@gov.nu.ca

Ontario

Provincial Museums

Hockey Hall of Fame (HHOF) / Le Temple de la Renommée du Hockey
Brookfield Place, 30 Yonge St., Toronto, ON M5E 1X8
Tel: 416-360-7765; Fax: 416-360-1501
info@hhof.com
www.hhof.com
www.facebook.com/pages/Hockey-Hall-of-Fame/ 10405440140

Year Founded: 1961 The museum holds a veritable treasure of artifacts, memorabilia, films and photos, displayed in multi-media exhibits, all on a hockey theme. Also on site is the D.K. (Doc) Seaman Hockey Resource Centre which stores a vast archive. The museum offers a variety of educational programs. Visitors can also enjoy interactive games. This is the home of hockey's ultimate trophy, Lord Stanley's Cup.
Mr. William C. Hay, Chair/CEO, Board of Directors, bhay@hhof.com
Mr. Philip Pritchard, Vice-President/Curator, ppritchard@hhof.com

Royal Ontario Museum (ROM)
100 Queen's Park, Toronto, ON M5S 2C6
Tel: 416-586-8000
info@rom.on.ca
www.rom.on.ca
Year Founded: 1912 The Royal Ontario Museum (ROM) is Canada's largest museum, an internationally renowned facility & popular public attraction. Created in 1912, the ROM has an unusually broad dual mandate of collecting & preserving in the areas of natural history & human cultures, & communicating its research to the world. Today, the ROM holds in excess of 6 million objects in its collections, which include galleries of art, archaeology & science.
William Thorsell, Director & CEO
Glenn Dobbin, Deputy Director, Operations
Dr. Mark Engstrom, Deputy Director, Collections & Research
James Temerty, Chair, Board of Governors

Local Museums in Ontario

***Alliston:* Museum on the Boyne**
PO Box 910, 250 Fletcher Cres., Alliston, ON L9R 1A1
Tel: 705-435-0167; Fax: 705-434-3006
boynemuseum@town.newtecumseth.on.ca
www.motb.ca
Community museum displaying household, agricultural & industrial artifacts from 1840's to present; site features 1850's log cabin, 1860 English barn & 1915 fair building
Katie Naieb, Curator

***Almonte:* Mill of Kintail Conservation Area**
4175 Hwy 511, RR#2, Almonte, ON K0G 1K0
Tel: 613-259-2421; Fax: 613-259-3468
info@mvc.on.ca
www.mvc.on.ca/index.php/conservation-areas/mill-of-kintai l
Kintail Museum, housed in a heritage grist mill, is a collection and a conservation site on the Indian River in Lanark County. The museum showcases the life and works of Robert Tait McKenzie as the mill was his summer home and sculpture studio; the museum showcases the largest collection of McKenzie's sculptures and memorabilia in Canada.
Stephanie Kolsters, Museum Manager, 613-256-3610, ext. 2, skolsters@mvc.on.ca

***Almonte:* Mississippi Valley Textile Museum**
PO Box 784, 3 Rosamond St. East, Almonte, ON K0A 1A0
Tel: 613-256-3754; Fax: 613-256-3754
mvtm@magma.ca
www.textilemuseum.mississippimills.com
Year Founded: 1985 Museum is located in the annex of the former Rosamond Woolen Company constructed in 1867; houses information on the early mills & their owners, displays of period offices, artifacts & machinery related to the beginnings of the textile industry, and a gift shop.
Mr. Martin Ruben, President

***Ameliasburg:* Ameliasburgh Historical Museum**
PO Box 67, Ameliasburg, ON K0K 1A0
Tel: 613-968-9678; Fax: 613-966-1599
amelmuseum@pecounty.on.ca
www.pec.on.ca/ameliasburghmuseum/index.html
Year Founded: 1968 Household items, quilts, crafts, agricultural machinery & tools & a 1910 Goldie Corlis engine with an 18-foot flywheel in a village setting; lots of events during season; tea room. Located at 517 County Rd. 19, Ameliasburgh.
Janice Hubbs, Curator

***Ameliasburg:* Quinte Educational Museum & Archives**
PO Box 14, 14 Coleman St., Ameliasburg, ON K0K 1A0
Tel: 613-966-5501
info@qema1978.com
www.qema1978.com
The history of education in Prince Edward County & Ontario is preserved at the Quinte Educational Museum & Archives, through educational artifacts & archival material.
Dan Rainey, President, danrainey@qema1978.com

***Amherstburg:* Fort Malden National Historic Site of Canada (FMNHS) / Lieu historique national du Canada du Fort-Malden**
PO Box 38, 100 Laird Ave., Amherstburg, ON N9V 2Z2
Tel: 519-736-5416; Fax: 519-736-6603
ont.fort-malden@pc.gc.ca
www.parkscanada.gc.ca/malden
twitter.com/Park sCan_SWOnt
www.facebook.com/FortMaldenNHS
Riverfront site includes original earthworks, a restored soldier's barrack & a museum
John MacLeod, Resource Centre Specialist
Jennifer Duquette, Site Manager

***Amherstburg:* North American Black Historical Museum**
277 King St., Amherstburg, ON N9V 2C7
Tel: 519-736-5433; Fax: 866-622-4672
Toll-Free: 800-713-6336
nabhm@mnsi.net
www.blackhistoricalmuseum.org
The Museum allows visitors to experience Black history through the Taylor Log Cabin, a home of escaped slaves from the United States, the Nazrey African Methodist Episcopal Church, & a Cultural Centre.
Kenn Stanton, Curator & Administrator
Lyle Browning, President
Paul Hertel, Secretary
Wava Jackson, Treasurer

***Amherstburg:* Park House Museum**
Kings Navy Yard, 214 Dalhousie St., Amherstburg, ON N9V 1W4
Tel: 519-736-2511; Fax: 519-736-2511
info@ParkHouseMuseum.com
www.parkhousemuseum.com
Other contact information: E-mail, Tours: order@ParkHouseMuseum.com
Built during the 1790s by a family of Loyalists, Park House is an example of Pièce sur Pièce log construction. The Park House Museum is open year-round to display items of historical significance to the town of Amherstburg & the surrounding area. During the summer, tinsmithing is demonstrated in the pensioner's cottage.

***Ancaster:* Fieldcote Memorial Park & Museum**
64 Sulphur Springs Rd., Ancaster, ON L9G 1L8
Tel: 905-648-8144; Fax: 905-648-4857
fieldcote@hamilton.ca
www.hamilton.ca
Collection, preservation & exhibition of local history; landscaped gardens & walking trails

***Ancaster:* Griffin House National Historic Site**
733 Mineral Springs Rd., Ancaster, ON L9H 1A1
Tel: 905-546-2424; Fax: 905-546-2338
griffinhouse@hamilton.ca
www.hamilton.ca
The house commemorates the determination of black men & women who journeyed to Canada via the Underground Railroad. Open July-Sept., Su 1:00-4:00.

***Ancaster:* Ingledale**
c/o Hamilton Region Conservation Authority, PO Box 7099, Ancaster, ON L9G 3L3
Tel: 905-643-2103
c. 1812 home of Inglehart family; located at Fifty Point Conservation Area, Stoney Creek

***Ancaster:* Sulpher Springs Station/Dundas Valley Trail Centre**
c/o Hamilton Conservation Authority, PO Box 7099, Ancaster, ON L9G 3L3
Tel: 905-627-1233; Fax: 905-627-9722
Toll-Free: 888-319-4722
dvalley@conservationhamilton.ca
www.conservationhamilt on.ca
Centre is a replica of an 1800-era train station; displays/exhibits on the Niagara Escarpment, local cultural heritage & trail etiquette governing the valley's extensive, multi-use trail network; bird watching, cycling or historical tours
Paul Piett, Supt.

***Ancaster:* Valens Log Cabin Museum**
PO Box 7099, Ancaster, ON L9G 3L3
Tel: 905-659-7715
C. 1836 restored homestead located at Valens Conservation Area, 1691 Regional Rd. 97, RR#6, Cambridge ON N1R 5S7

***Appin:* Ekfrid Community Museum**
48 Wellington St., Appin, ON N0L 1A0
Tel: 519-289-2015; Fax: 519-287-2359
Located in the former Appin Post Office & Orange Hall; artifacts from late 1800s; open May-Aug., weekends & by request

***Appleton:* North Lanark Regional Museum**
647 River Rd., Appleton, ON K0A 1A0
Tel: 613-257-8503
appletonmuseum@hotmail.com
Operates a small regional museum; open May 22nd to Thanksgiving, Wed.-Sun., 10-4; admission $2

***Arnprior:* Arnprior & District Museum / Musée d'Arnprior et Région**
35 Madawaska St., Arnprior, ON K7S 1R6
Tel: 613-623-4902; Fax: 613-623-4902
www.arnpriormuseum.org/Museum.htm
Located in the former post office, which was built in 1896, the Arnprior & District Museum features local artifacts & photograpsh, a 1928 fire engine, a lumbering exhibit, & an early 19th century canon. The museum is open Monday to Saturday.
Janet Carlile, Curator, jcarlile@arnprior.ca

***Astra:* National Air Force Museum of Canada**
PO Box 1000 Forces, Astra, ON K0K 3W0
Tel: 613-965-7223; Fax: 613-965-7352
Toll-Free: 866-701-7223
publicrelations@airforcemuseum.ca
airforcemuseum.ca
www.facebook.com/120719991296340
Social history museum dedicated to the airmen & airwomen who served in Canada's Air Force; features daily viewing of the on-going restoration of the world's only fully restored Halifax bomber aircraft; an Air Park displays 14 aircraft, 21 commemorative cairns & 5,600 "Ad Astra" granite stones; a large collection of artifacts; & a specialty gift shop; open daily May 1 - Sept. 30 Wed. - Sun.
Chris Colton, Executive Director, director@airforcemuseum.ca
Kevin Windsor, Curator, curator@airforcemuseum.ca

***Atikokan:* Atikokan Centennial Museum & Historical Park**
204 East Main St., Atikokan, ON P0T 1C0
Tel: 807-597-6585; Fax: 807-597-6585
atikokancentennialmuseum@bellnet.ca
Restored logging engine & train; mining & logging exhibits; Steep Rock & Caland Iron Ore Mines; local archival & art collections
Catherine Reilly, Museum Curator
Janis McIntyre, Museum Assistant

***Aurora:* Aurora Historical Society & Hillary House, National Historic Site**
15372 Yonge St., Aurora, ON L4G 1N8
Tel: 905-727-8991
ahs@aurorahs.com
www.hhahs.space4art.biz
Year Founded: 1963 Heritage artifacts held by the Aurora Historical Society date back over 200 years. The collections are related to the history of Aurora & to Hillary House. Hillary House, the Koffler Museum of Medicine, contains a significant collection of medical instruments.
Jennifer Steen, Manager & Curator, jennifer@aurorahs.com

***Aurora:* Hillary House, Koffler Museum of Medicine**
15372 Yonge St., Aurora, ON L4G 1N8
Tel: 905-727-8991
ahs@aurorahs.com
www.hillaryhouse.ca
Built in 1862, the house was home to 3 generations of medical doctors and their families, covering the evolution of medicine from the era of leeches and bleeding to the discovery of penicillin. Exhibits include: medicial instruments, books, papers, household furnishings, and equipment dating from the early 19th century. Open May - Aug., 9:30-4:30 daily; Sept. - Apr. by appointment only.

***Aylmer:* Aylmer & District Museum Association**
14 East St., Aylmer, ON N5H 1W2
Tel: 519-773-9723; Fax: 519-773-3445
aylmermuseum@amtelecom.net
The Aylmer & District Museum Association preserves & promotes the history of Aylmer & Malahide. The museum is open from the beginning of March to the end of November.
Pat Zimmer, Curator
Jacquie Jeffery, Chair

***Aylmer:* Ontario Police College Museum**
PO Box 1190, 10716 Hacienda Rd., Aylmer, ON N5H 2T2
Tel: 519-773-5361; Fax: 519-773-5762
Year Founded: 1962 Small display of police related items including speed measuring devices, breath collection & testing equipment, handcuffs & batons, police uniforms & hats, First Nations Police display, Forensics Investigative display
Rudy Gheysen, Director, 519-773-4200, rudy.gheysen@ontario.ca
Bill Stephens, Deputy Director, 519-773-4516, bill.stephens@ontario.ca

Azilda: **Rayside-Balfour Museum**
Azilda Public Library, 120 Ste-Agnes St., Azilda, ON P0M 1B0
Tel: 705-688-3955; Fax: 705-983-4119
www.sudburymuseums.ca
The museum houses artifacts related to the agricultural history of the area. Open June-Sept., M 10:00-2:00, Tu-Th 3:00-8:00.

Baden: **Castle Kilbride National Historic Site**
60 Snyder's Rd. West, Baden, ON N3A 1A1
Tel: 519-634-8444; Fax: 519-634-5035
Toll-Free: 800-469-5576
castle.kilbride@wilmot.ca
www.castlekilbride.ca
A restored 1877 mansion originally built by industrialist James Livingston, now a National Historic Site. Open Tu-Su 1:00-4:00.

Bala: **Bala's Museum, with Memories of Lucy Maud Montgomery**
PO Box 14, 1024 Maple Ave., Bala, ON P0C 1A0
Tel: 705-762-5876Toll-Free: 888-579-7739
bala.net/museum
The museum's collection features items related to Lucy Maud Montgomery. Spring hours: May-June, Sa & Su 1:00-4:00; Summer hours: June-Sept., Tu-Th 12:00-4:00, F-Su 1:00-4:00; Fall hours: Sept.-Oct., Sa & Su 1:00-4:00.

Bancroft: **Bancroft Mineral Museum**
c/o Bancroft and District Chamber of Commerce, PO Box 539, Bancroft, ON K0L 1C0
Tel: 613-332-1513; Fax: 613-332-2119

Located at 30 Station Street in Bancroft, the Bancroft Mineral Museum is a natural science museum which features mineral specimens collected from the local area. The museum is open year-round.

Bancroft: **North Hastings Heritage Museum**
PO Box 239, 26B Station St., Bancroft, ON K0L 1C0
Tel: 613-332-1884
nhastingshertiage@bellnet.ca

www.town.bancroft.on.ca/index.php/visiting/north-hastings-heritage-museum
Log house built in 1859; documents of North Hastings area
Robert Walker, Curator

Barrie: **Grey & Simcoe Foresters Regimental Museum**
c/o Barrie Armoury, 37 Parkside Dr., Barrie, ON L4N 1W8
Tel: 705-728-3761; Fax: 705-728-1220
gsfmus@csolve.net
thegreyandsimcoeforesters.org
Grey & Simcoe Foresters Regiment artifacts on display include: period uniforms, medals, field gear, & official recognitions & documentation.
Lorne Williams, Curator

Barriefield: **Frontenac County Schools Museum**
Also known as: **Schools Museum**
414 Regent St., Barriefield, ON K7K 5R1
Tel: 613-544-9113
www.fcsmuseum.com/MuseumInfo.html
This community museum and archives has a geographical focus on Frontenac County and the City of Kingston, with a heritage schoolroom (1900-1920), a late 19th- and 20th-century archival collection and public elementary school records. Public programming includes costumed interpretive tours, educational programs and research assistance.

Bath: **Bath Museum of Loyalist County**
The Old Town Hall, 434 Main St., Bath, ON K0H 1G0
Tel: 613-352-7716
www.bathmuseum.ca
Year Founded: 1936 Local history, including aboriginal artifacts; open May-Sept., W-Sa 10:00-4:00.

Bath: **United Empire Loyalist Heritage Centre & Park**
Parent: **Bay of Quinte Br., United Empire Loyalist Association of Canada**
54 Adolphustown Park Rd., Bath, ON K0K 2S0
Tel: 613-373-2196
1784@uel.ca
www.uel.ca
The United Empire Loyalist Heritage Centre houses the H.C. Burleigh Archives. The Heritage Centre is owned & operated by the Bay of Quinte Branch of the United Empire Loyalist Association of Canada. It is open from April to October, & by appointment at other times of the year.
Brian Tackaberry, Bay of Quinte Branch President, United Empire Loyalist Association
June Dafoe, Bay of Quinte Branch Board Governor, United Empire Loyalist Association, adafoe1@cogeco.ca
Tom Riddolls, Curator, tom@uel.ca

Beachville: **Beachville District Museum**
PO Box 220, 584371 Beachville Rd., Beachville, ON N0J 1A0
Tel: 519-423-6497; Fax: 519-423-6935
bmchin@execulink.com
www.beachvilledistrictmuseum.ca
The Beachville District Museum features artifacts, such as Mastadon bones found on the O.J. Bond farm. The history of limestone quarries is also depicted at the museum, since the area is home to the largest open face quarries in Canada. A baseball display is featured because Beachville is the place where the first recorded baseball game in North America took place. The museum is open year round.

Beaverton: **Beaver River Museum**
PO Box 314, 284 Simcoe St., Beaverton, ON L0K 1A0
Tel: 705-426-9641
bte.hist.soc@bellnet.ca
www.btehs.com
Year Founded: 1976 The Beaver River Museum consists of the Old Stone Jail, a settlers' log cabin (c.1850), & a brick house (c.1900). The museum is open during weekends in May, June, & September, & daily, except on Tuesdays, in July & August.
Julie Everett, Curator
Ken Alsop, Archivist

Belleville: **Belleville Public Library & John M. Parrott Art Gallery**
254 Pinnacle St., Belleville, ON K8N 3B1
Tel: 613-968-6731; Fax: 613-968-6841
gallery@bellevillelibrary.com
bellevillelibrary.com/johnmparrottartgalle rys9.php
twitter.com/BellevillePL
www.facebook.com/219197338115817
The gallery is located on the third floor of the public library. The gallery is open Tu, W, F & Sa 9:30-5:00, & Th 9:30-8:00.
Susan Holland, Curator, sholland@bellevillelibrary.com

Belleville: **Glanmore National Historic Site**
257 Bridge St. East, Belleville, ON K8N 1P4
Tel: 613-962-2329; Fax: 613-962-6340
mwakeling@city.belleville.on.ca
www.quinte.net/glanmore/
The restored Victoria home of the Phillips-Burrows-Faulkner families; original & period furnishings displayed in principal rooms; paintings & decorative art from the Couldery Collection on permanent exhibit; lamps from the Paul Lamp Collection, as well as other exhibits; special exhibits/events held throughout the year
Rona Rustige, Curator

Belleville: **Hastings & Prince Edward Regiment Military Museum**
The Armoury, 187 Pinnacle St., Belleville, ON K8N 3A5
Tel: 613-966-2125; Fax: 613-966-2110
www.theregiment.ca/hpmuseum.html
Open year round, Tues.-Thurs. 1:00-4:00.
J. Sherry, Director
N. Smith, Curator

Blind River: **Timber Village Museum**
PO Box 628, 180 Leacock St., Blind River, ON P0R 1B0
Tel: 705-356-7544
www.blindriver.com
Other contact information: Year round: 705-356-2251
Year Founded: 1967 Provides guest with a sense of what a lumberjack's life was like at the turn of the last century; displays include axes, saws, logging tools & a portable forge; art gallery which exhibits works of contemporary local artists & artisans; workshops, children's educational programmes; lumberjack dinner, 1st Sat. in Oct.; open year round.
Christine Clark, Curator/Manager
Ken Corbiere, Clerk Administrator/Treasurer

Bobcaygeon: **The Boyd Museum**
PO Box 1221, 21 Canal St. East, Bobcaygeon, ON K0M 1A0
Tel: 705-738-9482; Fax: 705-738-0918
info@theboydmuseum.com
www.theboydmuseum.com
The museum shows, through artifacts & archival material, how the Boyd family helped develop the Bobcaygeon & Kawartha Lakes region. Open May, June, & Sept., Sa 10:00-4:00, Su 1:00-3:00; July & Aug., daily 10:00-4:00.

Bobcaygeon: **Kawartha Settlers' Village**
PO Box 755, 85 Dunn St., Bobcaygeon, ON K0M 1A0
Tel: 705-738-6163
info@settlersvillage.org
settlersvillage.org
Twelve historic homes & buildings collected on former Kawartha farm; regional arts & heritage centre offering courses in the Arts
Al Ingram, President
Gail Thomassen, General Manager, gail@settlersvillage.org
Marion Bell, Office Assistant, marion@settlersvillage.org

Borden: **Base Borden Military Museum**
Canadian Forces Base Borden, PO Box 1000 Main, 27 Ram St., Borden, ON L0M 1C0
Tel: 705-423-3531; Fax: 705-423-3623
beaton.sl@forces.gc.ca
www.borden.forces.gc.ca/998/89/46/91-eng.asp
The Base Borden Military Museum consists of several buildings & a memorial park. It features the history of CFB Borden, with a collection of armoured vehicles, artillery pieces, trucks, & aircraft from World War I, World War II, & the present. As the birthplace of the Canadian Air Force, Base Borden also displays the Avro 504 K aircraft, a Tiger Moth, a Silver Star, & a Tutor aircraft.

Bothwell: **Fairfield Museum**
14878 Longwoods Rd., RR#3, Bothwell, ON K0P 1C0
Tel: 519-692-4397
fairfield.museum@sympatico.ca
Site of Moravian Delaware mission, est. 1792, destroyed 1813 by US soldiers; artifacts from burnt village

Bowmanville: **Clarington Museums & Archives**
Municipality of Clarington, 62 Temperance St., Bowmanville, ON L1C 3A8
Tel: 905-623-2734; Fax: 905-623-5684
info@claringtonmuseums.com
www.claringtonmuseums.com
Comprised of Bowmanville Museum, Clarke Museum, Sarah Jane Williams Heritage Centre; depicts the early urban & rural roots of the Municipality of Clarington; special collections including Dominion Pianos & Organs; one of the largest doll collections in Canada
Martha Rutherford Conrad, Administrator, claringtonmuseums@rogers.com

Bracebridge: **Woodchester Villa**
PO Box 376, 15 King St., Bracebridge, ON P1L 1T7
Tel: 705-645-5501; Fax: 705-645-0385
info@octagonalhouse.com
www.octagonalhouse.com
Woodchester Villa is an octagonal house museum, which dates back to 1882. The house is designated as a historic site, under the Ontario Heritage Act. Woodchester Villa is open from Canada Day to Labour Day.

Brampton: **Lorne Scots Regimental Museum**
The Armoury, 2 Chapel St., Brampton, ON L6W 2H1
Tel: 905-451-5724
www.lornesmuseum.ca; www.lornescots.ca/museum.php
Located at 48 John St.
Maj. (Ret'd) Richard E. Ruggle, Chair, shepherd@kw.igs.net
Maj. (Ret'd) Tom Graham, Curator, tom069@sympatico.ca

Brantford: **Bell Homestead National Historic Site**
94 Tutela Heights Rd., Brantford, ON N3T 1A1
Tel: 519-756-6220; Fax: 519-759-5975
bellhomestead@brantford.ca
www.bellhomestead.ca
Displays at the Bell Homestead National Historic Site depict the 1870 to 1881 household of Alexander Graham Bell, the invention of the telephone, & the origins of Canadian telephone operations.
Brian Wood, Curator
Lorie Steiner, Chair

Brantford: **Brant Museum & Archives**
c/o Brant Historical Society, 57 Charlotte St., Brantford, ON N3T 2W6
Tel: 519-752-2483; Fax: 519-752-1931
information@brantmuseums.ca
www.brantmuseum.ca
Operated by the Brant Historical Society, the Brant Museum & Archives collects, preserves, researches, & exhibits items related to the founding, settlement, & diversity of Brant County & the surrounding area. Researchers will discover items such as photographs, diaries, letters, & maps in the archive collection. Open year round.
Stacey McKellar, Curator

Brantford: **Canadian Military Heritage Museum**
PO Box 27033, 794 Colborne St., Brantford, ON N3S 7V1
Tel: 519-759-1313
cmhm@execulink.com
www.cmhmhq.ca
A privately owned & operated museum displaying artifacts from Canada's military history. Hours of Operation: March & Apr., F-Su 10:00-4:00; May-Sept., Tu-Su 10:00-4:00; Oct. & Nov., F-Su 10:00-4:00.

Brantford: **Myrtleville House Museum**
Parent: **Brant Historical Society**
34 Myrtleville Dr., Brantford, ON N3V 1C2
Tel: 519-752-3216; Fax: 519-752-1931
information@brantmuseums.ca
www.brantmuseums.ca
http://www.facebook.co m/MyrtlevilleHouseMuseum

One of the oldest homes in Brant County (1837); the museum also promotes interactive learning & provide hands-on activities to aid students in explore the heritage of the county. Open year-round Monday-Friday 9-4 and Sat/Sun 1-4 in July and August.

Brighton: **Presqu'ile Provincial Park**
328 Presqu'ile Pkwy., Brighton, ON K0K 1H0
Tel: 613-475-4324
www.ontarioparks.com/english/pres.html
One of Ontario's oldest provincial parks (1922); displays & programs of early history of the area; working lighthouse

Brighton: **Proctor House Museum**
Parent: **Save Our Heritage Organization**
PO Box 578, 96 Young St., Brighton, ON K0K 1H0
Tel: 613-475-2144
info@proctorhousemuseum.ca
proctorhousemuseum.ca
Living museum: 1860s gentleman's home, completely furnished; open daily July & August for tours; or by appt. The Brighton Barn Theatre is housed in the Proctor-Simpson Barn adjacent to the property.
Anna Rittwage, President

Brockville: **Brockville Museum**
5 Henry St., Brockville, ON K6V 6M4
Tel: 613-342-4397; Fax: 613-342-7345
info@brockvillemuseum.com
www.brockvillemuseum.com
Year Founded: 1981 The Brockville Museum is committed to preserving and promoting the history of Brockville through quality exhibits and education programs.
Bonnie Burke, Director, 613-342-4397, bburke@brockville.com

Bruce Mines: **Bruce Mines Museum**
PO Box 220, 75 Taylor St, Bruce Mines, ON P0R 1C0
Tel: 705-785-3426; Fax: 705-785-3170
www.brucemines.ca
Year Founded: 1961 Situated in a church built in 1894, the Bruce Mines Museum features pioneer items such as an 1876 slot machine, a Victorian doll house, & a Yakaboo canoe.

Burgessville: **Thames Valley Museum School**
PO Box 37, 656 Main St. North, Burgessville, ON N0J 1C0
Tel: 519-424-9964; Fax: 519-242-9964
info@museumschool.ca
www.museumschool.ca
1905 Baronial-style two-room schoolhouse; one classroom is restored to reflect the first quarter of the 20th century; the other is a gallery for changing exhibits on educational history; tours, educational programs, archives
Sharon Meek, Curator
Ken Riehl, Chair

Burlington: **Ireland House at Oakridge Farm**
2168 Guelph Line, Burlington, ON L7P 5A8
Tel: 905-332-9888; Fax: 905-332-1714
Toll-Free: 800-374-2099
www.museumsofburlington.com
Home of Joseph Ireland, built between 1835 & 1837; open year round
Barbara Teatero

Burlington: **Joseph Brant Museum**
1240 North Shore Blvd. East, Burlington, ON L7S 1C5
Tel: 905-634-3556; Fax: 905-634-4498
Toll-Free: 888-748-5386
www.museumsofburlington.com
Year Founded: 1942 The museum is a replica of the original 1800 home of Mohawk, Captain Joseph Brant, "Thayendanegea"; exhibits relating to indigeneous culture, with emphasis on the Iroquois; history of Burlington; historical costume exhibit, one of Ontario's finest collection of Victorian clothing & accessories; open year round,
Barbara Teatero, Director of Museums, teaterob@burlington.ca

Caledonia: **Edinburgh Square Heritage & Cultural Centre**
Also known as: **Edinburgh Square**
PO Box 2056, 80 Caithness St. East, Caledonia, ON N3W 2G6
Tel: 905-765-3134
esquare.centre@haldimandcounty.on.ca
www.haldimandcoun ty.on.ca
Artifacts relating to Town of Haldimand, from pioneer times to 1970s; open year round
Anne Unyi, Curator

Cambridge: **Cambridge Sports Hall of Fame**
#444, 425 Hespeler Rd., Cambridge, ON N1R 6J2
Tel: 519-653-7071
cambridgesportshalloffame.ca
The Hall of Fame seeks to celebrate the sporting history of Cambridge through text, images, & memorabilia, as well as annually inducting athletes, teams, & builders.
Gary Hedges, Chair, gr.hedges@sympatico.ca
Jim Cox, Contact, Displays & Memorabilia, mjcox11@rogers.com
Bob Howison, Contact, jbhowison@aol.com

Cambridge: **The Fashion History Museum**
PO Box 848, Cambridge, ON N1R 5X9
Tel: 647-328-0017
www.fashionhistorymuseum.com
Year Founded: 2004 The museum's collection features over 8,000 garments & accessories, from the 1660s to the present. The museum currently lacks a permanent home, but creates travelling exhibitions & engages in research.
Kenn Norman, Chair, chair@fashionhistorymuseum.com
Jonathan Walford, Curator, curator@fashionhistorymuseum.com

Campbellford: **Campbellford-Seymour Heritage Centre**
Campbellford-Seymour Heritage Society, PO Box 1294, 113 Front St. North, Campbellford, ON K0L 1L0
Tel: 705-653-2634
csheritage@persona.ca
www.csheritage.org
Year Founded: 1989 The Campbellford-Seymour Heritage Centre is the home of the Campbellford-Seymour Heritage Society. The Society preserves & communicates the history of Campbellford / Seymour, maintains local archives, & assists with genealogical research.
Anne Linton, Contact

Cannington: **Cannington Historical Museum**
c/o Cannington Historical Society, Cannington Town Hall, PO Box 196, 38 Laidlaw St. South, Cannington, ON L0E 1E0
Tel: 705-432-3136
canningtonsecretary@brockhistoricalsocieties.ca
www.brockhistoricalsocie ties.ca
Other contact information: E-mail, President: canningtonpresident@brockhistoricalsocieties.ca
Located in Cannington's MacLeod Park on Peace Street, the Cannington Historical Museum features the following buildings: log homes (circa 1827 & 1857), an 1871 Canadian Northern Railway station, a 1929 Canadian National Railway caboose, the 1934 Derryville (LOL) Hall, & a driving shed. The museum is open from Victoria Day to Labour Day, or by appointment.
Ted Foster, President
Ray Lush, Vice-President
Margaret Crammond, Secretary
Cheryl Dillon, Publicist

Carleton Place: **Carleton Place & Beckwith Heritage Museum & Gardens**
Parent: **C.P. & Beckwith Historical Society**
267 Edmund St., Carleton Place, ON K7C 3E8
Tel: 613-253-7013
cpbheritagemuseum@bellnet.ca
cpbheritagemuseum.com
Local history of Carleton Place & Beckwith Township
Shane W.M. Edwards, President, shanewmedwards@aol.com
Jennifer Irwin, Collections Manager

Carp: **Diefenbunker, Canada's Cold War Museum**
PO Box 466, 3911 Carp Rd., Carp, ON K0A 1L0
Tel: 613-839-0007Toll-Free: 800-409-1965
www.diefenbunker.ca; diefenbunker.wordpress.com
Social Media: pinterest.com/diefenbunker;
www.youtube.com/TheDiefenbunker
twitter.com/Diefenbunker
www.facebook.com/diefenbunker
The museum is housed in a once-secret Cold War-era bunker meant to shelter members of the government in the event of a nuclear attack. The bunker is now a National Historic Site of Canada. The museum seeks to preserve the history of Canada's involvement in the Cold War, & to create interest in the Cold War in general. Open daily 11:00-4:00.
Doug Beaton, President
Henriette Riegel, Executive Director, h.riegel@diefenbunker.ca

Cayuga: **Haldimand County Museum & Archives**
PO Box 38, 8 Echo St., Cayuga, ON N0A 1E0
Tel: 905-772-5880
museum.archives@haldimandcounty.on.ca
tourism.haldiman dcounty.on.ca/museums/hcmuseum.html
twitter.com/visithaldimand
www.fac ebook.com/128909910457566
Temporary & permanent exhibits; 1835 log cabin on site; regional & genealogical archives
Karen E. Richardson, Curator

Chapleau: **Chapleau Centennial Museum**
Also known as: **Chapleau Museum & Tourist Information Centre**
PO Box 129, 94 Monk St., Chapleau, ON P0M 1K0
Tel: 705-864-1122
www.chapleau.ca/en/visit/museumsteamengine.asp
Year Founded: 1967 Located in Centennial Park, on Monk St. in Chapleau; tourist information centre; mineral collection, mounted animals, material related to Chapleau & area; archives; educational programming; bilingual services; special needs facilities; picnic area; open May 15 - Oct. 15

Chatham: **Chatham Railroad Museum**
PO Box 434, 2 McLean St., Chatham, ON N7M 5K5
Tel: 519-352-3097
CKtourism@chatham-kent.ca
www.chatham-kent.ca
Located in a CN baggage car built in 1955; contains early railroad equipment, several model trains & other memorabilia; open May through Labour Day, with group tours available all year round
Gary Shurgold

Chatham: **Chatham-Kent Black Historical Society**
177 King St. East, Chatham, ON N7M 3N1
Tel: 519-352-3565; Fax: 519-354-2642
info@ckblackhistoricalsociety.org
www.ckblackhistoricalsociety.org
Year Founded: 1992 The society offers guided tours of heritage sites around the Essex & Kent areas of Southern Ontario, as well as a Heritage Room featuring displays & archival material.

Chatham: **Chatham-Kent Museum**
Chatham Cultural Centre, 75 William St. North, Chatham, ON N7M 4L4
Tel: 519-360-1998; Fax: 519-354-4170
CKccc@chatham-kent.ca
www.chatham-kent.ca
Local history museum & archives; features a retrospective of Chatham-Kent during first half of 20th century; special exhibitions gallery with changing displays throughout year; open daily
David Benson, Heritage Co-ordinator

Chatham: **Milner Heritage House**
c/o Chatham-Kent Museum, 75 William St. North, Chatham, ON N7M 4L4
Tel: 519-360-1998; Fax: 519-354-4170
ckccc@chatham-kent.ca
www.chatham-kent.ca
Year Founded: 1943 Museum depicts the turn-of-the-century lifestyle of Robert Milner,a successful, local industrialist and carriage maker; also features award-winning artwork by Robert's wife Emma; second floor features the Rev. Sandys bird collection & the MacPhail exotic animal collection
Ms Stephanie Suitor, Curator

Cheltenham: **The Great War Flying Museum**
Brampton Airport, PO Box 27, 13691 McLaughlin Rd., RR#1, Cheltenham, ON L7C 3L7
Tel: 905-838-4936
info@GreatWarFlyingMuseum.com
www.greatwarflyingmuseum.com
Volunteer group builds, maintains & flies WWI replica fighter aircraft; artifacts from WWI

Chesterville: **Chesterville & District Historical Society Heritage Centre**
PO Box 693, 14 Victoria St., Chesterville, ON K0C 1H0
Tel: 613-938-2455
www.northdundas.com/tourism/HeritageCentre.htm
Year Founded: 1984 The centre is housed in an 1867 building, & features a collection of artifacts on local history.
Carol Goddard, President
Alec J. Ball, Vice-President, 613-821-3934
Margot Dixon, Secretary, 613-984-2880

Cloyne: **Cloyne Pioneer Museum**
Parent: **The Cloyne & District Historical Society**
PO Box 228, Hwy. 41, Cloyne, ON K0H 1K0
Tel: 613-336-2203
pioneer@mazina.on.ca
pioneer.mazinaw.on.ca
Artifacts from the pioneer days of the area including tools, clothing, kitchen and other households effects, glass bottles, flat irons, a rolling pin made from a block of solid maple, photos and old catalogues; genealogical archive. Located across from the Post Office in Cloyne. Summer Hours: M-Su 10:00-4:00
Carolyn McCulloch, President
Ian Brumell, Treasurer
Eileen Flielder, Secretary

Cobalt: **The Bunker Military Museum**
c/o Cobalt Historical Society, PO Box 309, 21 Silver St., Cobalt, ON P0J 1C0
Tel: 705-679-5220
chs@cobalthistoricalsociety.ca
www.cobalt.ca/index.php/historic-cobalt/bunker-military-museum
The museum consists of the private military memorabilia collection of Cobalt resident Jim Jones, & is housed in the Bilsky Block, in Cobalt.

***Cobalt:* Cobalt Mining Museum**
***Also known as:* Northern Ontario Mining Museum**
PO Box 215, 24 Silver St., Cobalt, ON P0J 1C0
Tel: 705-679-8301
cnomchin@ntl.sympatico.ca
Year Founded: 1953 The museum preserves the world's largest collection of native silver ore, mining & prospecting equipment & artifacts, & fluorescent rock; other displays highlight the early cultural & social life of Cobalt; unique, handcrafted silver jewelry available in the gift shop; underground tours of the Colonial Adit can be arranged. Open all year.
R.M. Holdsworth, Chairman

***Cobourg:* Sifton-Cook Heritage Centre (SCHC)**
***Parent:* Cobourg Museum Foundation (CMF)**
c/o Cobourg Museum Foundation, Victoria Hall, 55 King St. West, Cobourg, ON K9A 2M2
Tel: 905-373-7222
info@cobourgmuseum.ca
northumberlandheritage.ca
Social Media: pinterest.com/CobourgMuseum
twitter.com/CobourgMuseum
www.facebook.com /153555487994142
The centre is housed in an old barracks building; the site also includes an 1860s workman's cottage.
Joan Chalovich, Chair

***Cochrane:* Cochrane Railway & Pioneer Museum**
PO Box 490, 210 Railway St., Cochrane, ON P0L 1C0
Tel: 705-272-4361; Fax: 705-272-6068
www.town.cochrane.on.ca
Located across from the train station in Cochrane; railway artifacts & memorabilia, photographs, displays

***Coldwater:* Coldwater Canadiana Heritage Museum**
***Also known as:* Woodrow Homestead**
PO Box 125, 1474 Woodrow Rd., Coldwater, ON L0K 1E0
Tel: 705-835-5032
dougbi@sympatico.ca
www.coldwaterheritagemuseum.com
1840s log house & other buildings; open May - Oct.
Richard Jolliffe, President

***Collingwood:* Bygone Days Heritage Village**
879 - 6th St., RR#1, Collingwood, ON L9Y 3Y9
Tel: 705-429-2159
www.georgianbayselect.com/bygonedays
Year Founded: 1969 The village features 30 buildings that date from the mid-1800s, as well as costumed interpreters who walk about the village. Open June-Oct., weekends 10:00-5:00; weekdays by appointment.
Don Hounsome, Contact

***Collingwood:* The Collingwood Museum**
PO Box 556, 45 St. Paul St., Collingwood, ON L9Y 4B2
Tel: 705-445-4811; Fax: 705-445-9004
museum@collingwood.ca
www.collingwood.ca/museum
Located in the "Station"; large collection relating to history of Collingwood & area; exhibits showcasing shipping & shipbuilding & early history; archival materials & special events & activities throughout the year
Anita Miles, Manager

***Comber:* Comber & District Historical Society**
PO Box 158, RR#2, 8840 Hwy. 77, Comber, ON N0P 1J0
Tel: 519-687-3332
Pioneer articles & agricultural items; admission by donation; open Thu.-Mon.
Lila McFadden, Sec.-Treas.
Ralph Mellow, President
Kenneth Cranston, Vice-President

***Combermere:* Madonna House Pioneer Museum**
Madonna House Apostolate, 2888 Dafoe Rd., RR#2, Combermere, ON K0J 1L0
Tel: 613-756-3713; Fax: 613-756-0211
combermere@madonnahouse.org
www.madonnahouse.org
Social Media: www.youtube.com/MadonnaHouseCanada
twitter.com/madonnahouse
www.facebo ok.com/MadonnaHouse
Year Founded: 1967 History of early settlers in the area; located in century-old barn
Fr. David May, Director General
Mark Schlingerman, Director General
Susanne Stubbs, Director General

***Commanda:* Commanda Heritage Centre**
4077 Hwy. 522, Commanda, ON P0H 1J0
Tel: 705-729-2113
info@commanda.ca
www.commanda.ca
Complete with original shelves, counter & floor from the 1870s; features artifacts from 1870s - 1930s as well as a gift shops which features work from the region; tea room; open daily mid-June - mid-Oct.

***Copper Cliff:* Copper Cliff Museum**
26 Balsam St., Copper Cliff, ON P0M 1N0
Tel: 705-692-4448
www.sudburymuseums.ca
Year Founded: 1901 Located in 1890 log house; contains artifacts pertaining to the lifestyle of residents of a mining community; photographs & documents leading back to establishment of Copper Cliff

***Cornwall:* Cornwall Community Museum**
PO Box 773, 160 Water St. West, Cornwall, ON K6H 5T5
Tel: 613-936-0842
ian10@bellnet.ca
Loyalist & local history archives, local domestic manufacturing; open year round, Wed.-Sun.
Ian Bowering, Curator

***Cornwall:* Stormont, Dundas & Glengarry Highlanders Regimental Museum**
505 - 4th St. East, Cornwall, ON K6H 2J7
Tel: 613-936-9124; Fax: 613-993-8147
Open year round.

***Cornwall Island:* Ronathahon:ni Cultural Centre**
RR#3, Cornwall Island, ON K6H 5R7
Tel: 613-932-9452; Fax: 613-932-0092
Iroquois, Cree & Ojibwa artifacts

***Cumberland:* Cumberland Heritage Village Museum**
PO Box 159, 2940 Queen St., Cumberland, ON K4C 1E6
Tel: 613-833-3059; Fax: 613-830-3061
cumberlandmuseum@ottawa.ca
Representation of a rural village in the Lower Ottawa Valley, with artifacts related to period of 1880-1935; open year round

***Delhi:* Delhi Ontario Tobacco Museum & Heritage Centre**
200 Talbot Rd., Delhi, ON N4B 2A2
Tel: 519-582-0278; Fax: 519-582-0122
delhi.museum@norfolkcounty.ca
www.delhimuseum.ca
Year Founded: 1979 Tobacco-related machinery; a ginseng exhibit; multicultural exhibits & street scene depicting five historic buildings at turn of the 20th century; a large pavilion complete with barbecues is available in Quance Park nearby
Judy A. Livingstone, Curator/Director
Claire Bauslaugh, Programme Coordinator

***Delta:* The Old Stone Mill, National Historic Site (DMS)**
***Also known as:* The Delta Mill Society**
PO Box 172, Delta, ON K0E 1G0
Tel: 613-928-2584
info@deltamill.org
www.deltamill.org
www.facebook.co m/DeltaMill
Stone mill c. 1810. Part of the Family of National Historic Sites;the oldest surviving automatic stone grist mill in Ontario; showcases milling technology and 1800s industrial heritage; artifacts include buhr millstones, 48 inch Swain turbines, roller mills.
Dr. Paul Fritz, President

***Dorset:* Dorset Heritage Museum**
PO Box 111, 1040 Main St., Dorset, ON P0A 1E0
Tel: 705-766-0323
dhm@muskoka.com
www.dorsetheritagemuseum.ca
Local history; open May-July, Sa & Su 10:00-4:00; July-Oct. W-Sa 10:00-4:00.

***Dresden:* Uncle Tom's Cabin Historic Site (UTCHS)**
***Also known as:* Uncle Tom's Cabin**
29251 Uncle Tom's Rd., Dresden, ON N0P 1M0
Tel: 519-683-2978; Fax: 519-683-1256
utchs@heritagetrust.on.ca
www.uncletomscabin.org
Uncle Tom's Cabin educates visitors about fugitive slaves in the Dresden area. The site focuses on the life of the Reverend Josiah Henson, a slave who escaped with his family to Upper Canada via the Underground Railroad. The grounds feature the following attractions: the Josiah Henson Interpretive Centre, the North Star Theatre, the Underground Railroad Freedom Gallery, the Harris House, a smokehouse, a sawmill, the Josiah Henson House, a pioneer church, & the Henson Family Cemetery. Open from mid May to the end of October. At other times of the year, groups of twenty or more may make an appointment.
Steven Cook, Curator

***Dryden:* Dryden & District Museum**
15 Van Horne Ave., Dryden, ON P8N 2A5
Tel: 807-223-4671; Fax: 807-223-7354
lgardner@dryden.ca
First Nations & pioneer artifacts; minerals; archival material

***Dundas:* Dundas Historical Society Museum**
139 Park St. West, Dundas, ON L9H 1X8
Tel: 905-627-7412; Fax: 905-627-4872
mail@dundasmuseum.ca
www.dundasmuseum.ca
Celebrates & preserves the story of the Dundas community; museum features true to life displays, & a diversified collection of exhibits reflecting the varied occupations & activities of those who have contributed to the development of the community
Carolyn Westoby, Curator

***Dunvegan:* The Glengarry Pioneer Museum**
***Also known as:* Dunvegan Museum**
#30, 1645 County Rd., RR#1, Dunvegan, ON K0C 1J0
Tel: 613-527-5230
info@glengarrypioneermuseum.ca
www.glengarrypioneermuseum.ca
1840 log inn; miniature cheese factory; 1869 municipal hall; carriage shed & log barn; blacksmith shop
Jennifer Black, Curator

***Ear Falls:* Ear Falls District Museum**
PO Box 309, Ear Falls, ON P0V 1T0
Tel: 807-222-3624; Fax: 807-222-2384
eftownship@ear-falls.com
www.ear-falls.com
Dedicated to the history of exploration, transportation, & the settlement of the area

***Egmondville:* The Van Egmond House**
***Also known as:* The Van Egmond Foundation**
PO Box 1033, 80 Kippen Rd., Egmondville, ON N0K 1W0
Tel: 519-522-0413
Restored & furnished Georgian county-manor house dating to the mid-19th century with antiques indicitive of the time; founded by Constant Van Egmond.

***Elgin:* Jones Falls Defensible Lockmaster's House & Blacksmith Shop**
PO Box 10, Elgin, ON K0G 1E0
Tel: 613-359-5377; Fax: 613-359-6042
Lockmaster's house c. 1841; blacksmith shop produces hardware c. 1843
Sandy Haining, Sector Supervisor

***Elgin:* Kingston Mills Blockhouse**
PO Box 10, Elgin, ON K0G 1E0
Tel: 613-359-5377; Fax: 613-359-6042
Toll-Free: 800-230-0016
1840s animated militia barracks

***Elk Lake:* Elk Lake Heritage Museum**
c/o Corporation of Township of James, PO Box 70, Elk Lake, ON P0J 1G0
Tel: 705-678-2237; Fax: 705-678-2495
History of area, in particular, mining, lumbering, agriculture
Lionel Venne, Chair

***Elliot Lake:* Elliot Lake Nuclear & Mining Museum**
Lester B. Pearson Centre, Hwy. 108, Elliot Lake, ON P5A 2T1
Tel: 705-848-2084; Fax: 705-848-0545
darla.hennessey@city.elliotlake.on.ca
Mining heritage; northern home of the Canadian Mining Hall of Fame; Dr. Franc Joubin Mineral Collection; open Sept. - June, Mon.-Fri.; July - Aug., daily

***Emo:* Rainy River District Women's Institute Museum**
***Also known as:* Emo Women's Institute Museum**
PO Box 511, 21 Tyrell St., Emo, ON P0W 1E0
Tel: 807-482-2754
Small pioneer museum; open mid May - Oct.; other times by appointment
Sherri Stamarski, Contact, stamarsk@nwonet.net

***Englehart:* Englehart & Area Historical Museum**
67 - 6th Ave., Englehart, ON P0J 1H0
Tel: 705-544-2400
englehartandareamuseum@ntl.sympatico.ca
www.englehart.ca
Exhibits show how settlement along the Temiskaming & Northern Ontario railway created town of Englehart & brought homesteaders to the claybelt's rural communites, 1900-1950; open May 1 - Dec. 1 & exhibition room

***Essex:* Essex Railway Station**
***Parent:* Heritage Essex Inc.**
87 Station St., Essex, ON N8M 2C5
Tel: 519-776-9800; Fax: 519-776-7241
heritageessex@bellnet.ca
www.essexrailwaystation.ca
A restored stone railway station from 1887. Also on site are a heritage gardens area, & two antique railcars.

***Essex:* Maidstone Bicentennial Museum**
***Parent:* Maidstone & District Historical Society**
1093 Puce Rd., Essex, ON N8M 2X7
Tel: 519-727-8811
Year Founded: 1984 Contains artifacts from the former Maidstone Township; the New Heritage Gardens feature native plants, trees, & shrubs.
Victoria Beaulieu, President, 519-728-1587
Marg Campbell, Director, Education, 519-979-0179

***Etobicoke:* Applewood: The James Shaver Woodsworth Homestead**
***Also known as:* Shaver House**
450 The West Mall, Etobicoke, ON M9C 1E9
Tel: 416-622-4124
jswoods@bellnet.ca
www.applewoodshaverhouse.org
www.facebook.com/ApplewoodShaverHouse
The homestead is an historic building that now offers space for meetings, weddings, & other parties. Open M-F 10:00-5:00, Sa & Su by appointment.

***Exeter:* Arkona Lions Museum & Information Centre**
c/o Ausable Bayfield Conservation Authority, 71108 Morrison Line, RR#3, Exeter, ON N0M 1S5
Tel: 519-828-3071; Fax: 519-235-1963
info@abca.on.ca
www.abca.on.ca
Arkona Lions Museum & Information Centre features local First Nations artifacts, Devonian era fossils, minerals, & semi-precious stone.
Tom Prout, General Manager, tprout@abca.on.ca

***Fenelon Falls:* Fenelon Falls Museum**
PO Box 179, 50 Oak St., Fenelon Falls, ON K0M 1N0
Tel: 705-887-1044; Fax: 705-887-1532
maryboro2003@yahoo.ca
www.maryboro.ca
Open daily June 15 - Labour Day; weekends only May 20-June 15 & Labour Day to Thanksgiving
Ali Scott, Curator

***Fenelon Falls:* Horseless Carriage Museum**
1427 County Rd. 8, Fenelon Falls, ON K0M 1N0
Tel: 705-738-9576
info@horselesscarriage.net
www.horselesscarriage.net
Social Media: www.youtube.com/user/lauracbennett
The museum is privately owned & operated, & specializes in early transportation & mechanical antiquities. Please call for an appointment.

***Fergus:* Wellington County Museum & Archives**
RR#1, 0536 County Rd. 18, Fergus, ON N1M 2W3
Tel: 519-846-0916; Fax: 519-846-9630
Toll-Free: 800-663-0750
info@wcm.on.ca
www.wcm.on.ca
Other contact information: Museum: 519-846-0916, ext. 5221; Archives: 519-846-0916, ext. 5225
The Wellington County Museum reflects the history of Wellington County people. The museum is housed in the former House of Industry & Refuge, which was built in 1877. Permanent exhibits include a World War I military exhibit, a pioneer log cabin, a 1920s kitchen, & textiles. The archives feature historical & genealogical records which date back to the first settlement in Wellington County. The Couling Collection consists of architectural information.
Bonnie Callen, Administrator, bonniec@wcm.on.ca
Susan Dunlop, Curator MA, susan@wcm.on.ca
Karen Wagner, Archivist BA, MLS, karen@wcm.on.ca
Patty Whan, Conservator, patty@wcm.on.ca
Libby Walker, Coordinator, Activities, libbyw@wcm.on.ca

***Flesherton:* South Grey Museum & Historical Library**
PO Box 299, Flesherton, ON N0C 1E0
Tel: 519-924-2843; Fax: 519-986-3643
museum@greyhighlands.ca
www.greyhighlandsmuseum.com
Open Tues. - Sat. end of June - Labour Day, or by appt; Open Thurs. - Sat. Labour Day - June.
Sarah Redmond, Curator

***Forest:* Forest-Lambton Museum**
PO Box 707, 59 Broadway St., Forest, ON N0N 1J0
Tel: 519-786-3239
www.lambtononline.com/forest_lambton
Local artifacts including doll collection; flax industry; early telephone equipment; Grand Truck Railroad; First Nation's Artifacts; pictures & documents from the 1800s
Sylvia Freeman, Secretary
Ken Kingdon, President

***Fort Frances:* Fort Frances Museum & Cultural Centre**
259 Scott St., Fort Frances, ON P9A 1G8
Tel: 807-274-7891; Fax: 807-274-4103
phawley@fort-frances.com
www.fort-frances.com/museum
The community museum is housed in an 1898 schoolhouse. The exhibits of the Fort Frances Museum & Cultural Centre reflect the development of Fort Frances & the Rainy River District from pre-contact to present day.
Pam Hawley, Curator

***Frankville:* Maple Sugar House & Museum**
41 Leacock Rd., RR#1, Frankville, ON K0E 1H0
Tel: 613-275-2893Toll-Free: 877-440-7887
mail@gibbonsmaple.com
www.rideau-info.com/gibbons
The House produces & sells maple syrup, maple sugar, maple butter & other maple products. As well, there displays from the past and present of maple syrup making equipment. Tours are offered.

***Gananoque:* Arthur Child Heritage Museum of the Thousand Islands**
***Parent:* Historic Thousand Islands Village Foundation**
125 Water St., Gananoque, ON K7G 3E3
Tel: 613-382-2535; Fax: 613-382-2912
Toll-Free: 877-217-7391
ivillage@cogeco.net
www.1000islandsheritagemuseum.com
The museum building was once the main station for the Thousand Islands Railway; now it is the centrepiece of the Historic Thousand Islands Village complex. Open daily 10:00-4:00; Nov.-Dec., Sa & Su 10:00-4:00 only.
Linda Mainse, Executive Director
Timothy Compeau, Consulting Curator

***Gananoque:* Gananoque Museum**
PO Box 100, 30 King St. East, Gananoque, ON K7G 2T6
Tel: 613-382-4024; Fax: 613-382-8587
Open mid-June - mid-Sept., Mon. - Sun.

***Gloucester:* Gloucester Museum**
4550B Bank St., Gloucester, ON K1G 3W6
Tel: 613-822-2076
Domestic ware; agricultural implements; Gloucester History Society archives; City of Gloucester archives

***Goderich:* Huron County Museum & Historic Gaol**
110 North St., Goderich, ON N7A 2T8
Tel: 519-524-2686; Fax: 519-524-1922
Toll-Free: 888-524-8394
www.huroncounty.ca/museum
Local history including transportation, military, agriculture & furniture
Claus Breede, Director

***Golden Lake:* Golden Lake Algonquin Museum**
PO Box 1657A Mishomis Inamo, Golden Lake, ON K0J 1X0
Tel: 613-625-2823; Fax: 613-625-2332
mgr.economicdevelopment@pikwakanagan.ca
Algonquin artifacts; domestic & ornamental artifacts of the early settlers

***Gore Bay:* Western Manitoulin Island Historical Society Museum**
PO Box 298, 150 Water St., Gore Bay, ON P0P 1H0
Tel: 705-282-2420
Canadian 19th century artifacts, including historical & documentary art; open Mar.-Nov.

***Gormley:* Whitchurch-Stouffville Museum & Community Centre**
14732 Woodbine Ave., Gormley, ON L0H 1G0
Tel: 905-727-8954; Fax: 905-727-1282
Toll-Free: 888-290-0337
www.townofws.com/museum.asp
Year Founded: 1971 The museum is located in the hamlet of Vandorf & includes the Bogarttown Schoolhouse, a restored 1850 log cabin, the Brown House, barn, & the Vandorf Public School; special events & programming, tours, craft workshops, & research material. Open year round.
Stephanie Foley, Curator

***Gowganda:* Gowganda & Area Museum**
Lot 12, Third St., Gowganda, ON P0J 1J0
Tel: 705-624-3171
Silver mining displays; log cabin; research library & resource centre; open mid-May - mid-Sept.

***Grafton:* Barnum House Museum**
PO Box 161, 10568 Country Rd. 2, Grafton, ON K0K 2G0
Tel: 905-349-2656; Fax: 905-349-3357
barnum@heritagetrust.on.ca
www.heritagefdn.on.ca
Owned by the Ontario Heritage Trust, Barnum House was built in 1819. The home is an example of Neo-Classical architecture. The decor of Barnum House reflects an Upper Canada home between 1820 & 1840. Barnum House Museum is open from June to Labour Day.
Wayne Kelly, Manager, Public Education & Community Development, 416-314-4913

***Grand Bend:* Lambton Heritage Museum**
10035 Museum Rd., RR#2, Grand Bend, ON N0M 1T0
Tel: 519-243-2600; Fax: 519-243-2646
heritage.museum@county-lambton.on.ca
www.lclmg.org
www.facebook.com/pa ges/Lambton-Libraries/271179146270568
Year Founded: 1978 Eight buildings on a 30 acre site; extensive collection of pressed glass & Currier & Ives prints; features history of Sarnia-Lambton area including large collection of agricultural implements
Laurie Webb, Curator-Supervisor

***Gravenhurst:* Bethune Memorial House National Historic Site**
235 John St. North, Gravenhurst, ON P1P 1G4
Tel: 705-687-4261; Fax: 705-687-4935
ont-bethune@pch.gc.ca
www.pc.gc.ca/bethune
At the Bethune Memorial House National Historic Site, the life & achievements of Dr. Henry Norman Bethune are commemorated. The house is his birthplace. Dr. Bethune is recognized for his time in China, where he served as a surgeon & a teacher. The site is open from June 1st to October 31st. At other times, group tours may be arranged by phone.
Scott Davidson, Site Manager

***Gravenhurst:* Muskoka Boat & Heritage Centre**
275 Steamship Bay Rd., Gravenhurst, ON P1P 1Z9
Tel: 705-687-2115; Fax: 705-687-9408
Toll-Free: 866-687-6667
www.segwun.com
www.facebook.com/pages/Muskoka-Steamships/119101791445311
The Muskoka Boat & Heritage Centre presents the history of boat-building, Muskoka's steamship era, & life on the water in Muskoka. At the site is a large in water collection of antique boats. The RMS Segwun is the oldest operating steamship in North America. The Muskoka Boat & Heritage Centre is open year-round.

***Grimsby:* Grimsby Museum**
PO Box 244, 6 Murray St., Grimsby, ON L3M 4G5
Tel: 905-945-5292; Fax: 905-945-0715
museum-public@town.grimsby.on.ca
www.town.grimsby.on.ca
Year Founded: 1984 Owned & operated by the Town of Grimsby, the museum interprets the history of Grimsby from prehistoric times. The Gallery of the Forty explores the settlement of the United Empire Loyalists in 1787. The Grimsby museum provides educational programs, as well as local history & genealogical information. It is open year-round.
Janet Cannon, Curator

***Guelph:* C.A.V. Barker Museum of Canadian Veterinary History**
Ontario Veterinary College, University of Guelph, 50 Stone Rd., Guelph, ON N1G 2W1
Tel: 519-824-4120
www.ovc.uoguelph.ca/history
The museum details the history of the Ontario Veterinary College, as well as Canadian veterinary medicine in general, & holds more than 10,000 items in its collection. The museum is open by appointment only.

***Guelph:* Guelph Civic Museum**
25 Norfolk St., Guelph, ON N1H 4H8
Tel: 519-836-1221; Fax: 519-836-5280
museum@guelph.ca
www.guelph.ca/museum
twitter.com/guelphmuseums
Year Founded: 1967 The museum is housed in a c. 1850 limestone building and features over 30,000 artifacts and 4,000 photos relating to the istory of Guelph and area; special events and programming for children.
Katherine McCracken, Director, katherine.mccracken@guelph.ca
Bev Dietrich, Curator, bev.dietrich@guelph.ca

***Guelph:* Hammond Museum of Radio**
595 Southgate Rd., Guelph, ON N1G 3W6
Tel: 519-822-2441
www.hammondmuseumofradio.org
Year Founded: 1982 The museum's collection includes hundreds of radios; open M-F 9:00-5:00, & weekends by request.
Nori Irwin-Hahn, Curator, curator@hammondmuseumofradio.org

Guelph: **McCrae House**
108 Water St., Guelph, ON N1G 1A6
Tel: 519-836-1482; Fax: 519-836-5280
museum@guelph.ca
www.guelph.ca/museum
Year Founded: 1968 The house, built in 1858, is the 1872 birthplace of John McCrae, author of "In Flanders Fields", & a National Historic Site. Exhibitions interpret McCrae's life & times, & an award-winning historic garden is maintained by volunteers. Activities include garden teas, the Poppy Push, Teddy Bear Picnic & Canada Day celebration.
Katherine McCracken, Director

Haileybury: **Haileybury Heritage Museum**
PO Box 911, 575 Main St., Haileybury, ON P0J 1K0
Tel: 705-672-1922
hhmuseum@onlink.net
www.alexand.ca
Haileybury Heritiage Museum is focused on one of Canada's ten worst natural disasters, the Great Fire of 1922 which destroyed 90 percent of the Town of Haileybury & communities in 18 surrounding townships in South Temiskaming; features a restored 1904 Toronto Railway Company streetcar (used as housing after the '22 fire); a 1922 Ruggles Fire Pumper; & the tugboat M.V. Beauchene.

Haliburton: **Haliburton Highlands Museum**
PO Box 389, Haliburton, ON K0M 1S0
Tel: 705-457-2760
info@haliburtonhighlandsmuseum.com
haliburtonhighlandsmuseum.com
Local domestic, lumbering & agricultural history. Open year round. Hours: Summer: Tu-Su 10:00-5:00; Spring/Fall: Tu-Sa 10:00-5:00; Winter: Currently being reviewed.
Thomas Ballantine, Director
Stephen Hill, Curator

Hamilton: **Canadian Football Hall of Fame & Museum**
58 Jackson St. West, Hamilton, ON L8P 1L4
Tel: 905-528-7566; Fax: 905-528-9781
info@cfhof.ca; store@cfhof.ca
www.cfhof.ca
Year Founded: 1962 The Canadian Football Hall of Fame & Museum features exhibits which depict the history of the game at all levels. A special section is dedicated to the Hall of Famers.
Steve Howse, Chair
George Black, Chair, Selection Committee
Mark DeNobile, Executive Director, mark@cfhof.ca
Meghan Sturgeon, Curator, meg@cfhof.ca
Bob Morreale, Treasurer & Office Manager, rob@cfhof.ca

Hamilton: **Dundurn Castle**
610 York Blvd., Hamilton, ON L8R 3H1
Tel: 905-546-2872; Fax: 905-546-2875
dundurn@hamilton.ca
www.dundurncastle.com
Restored home of Sir Allan MacNab, one of Canada's first premiers; depiction of mid-19th century life in over 40 rooms; open year round

Hamilton: **Hamilton & Scourge National Historic Site**
c/o Hamilton Military Museum, 610 York Blvd., Hamilton, ON L9H 5Z9
Tel: 905-546-2872; Fax: 905-546-2875
military@hamilton.ca
www.hamilton-scourge.hamilton.ca
Research files on the Hamilton & Scourge, armed merchant schooners from the War of 1812, which capsized & lie in water off Port Dalhousie.

Hamilton: **Hamilton Children's Museum**
1072 Main St. East, Hamilton, ON L8M 1N6
Tel: 905-546-4848; Fax: 905-546-4851
childrensmuseum@hamilton.ca
www.hamilton.ca/CultureandRecreation/Arts_Culture_And_Museums
Year Founded: 1978 This is an interactive, hands-on learning centre that offers children the opportunity to explore a wide variety of themes from the natural sciences and arts. Closed on Mondays.
Karen McCartney, Curator/Site Supervisor, Education, 905-546-2424, karen.mccartney@hamilton.ca

Hamilton: **Hamilton Military Museum / Le musée militaire de Hamilton**
610 York Blvd., Hamilton, ON L8R 3H1
Tel: 905-546-2872; Fax: 905-546-2875
military@hamilton.ca
www.hamilton.ca
Uniforms, weapons & lifestyle from War of 1812, Rebellion of 1837-38, the Victorian era, Boer War, & WWI; open year round

Hamilton: **Hamilton Museum of Steam & Technology**
900 Woodward Ave., Hamilton, ON L8H 7N2
Tel: 905-546-4797; Fax: 905-546-4798
steammuseum@hamilton.ca
www.hamilton.ca
Housed in a 19th century public works building. The facility is a Civil & Power Engineering Landmark & a National Historic Site. It contains two steam engines that pumped water to Hamilton more than 140 years ago. Open year-round.

Hamilton: **Hamilton Psychiatric Hospital Museum**
c/o St. Joseph's Mountain Health Services, PO Box 585, Hamilton, ON L8N 3K7
Tel: 905-388-2511; Fax: 905-381-5601
lmuirhea@stjosham.on.ca
www.stjosham.on.ca
With a variety of artifacts and photographs, the museum preserves the history of psychiatric care & treatment in Ontario with an emphasis on events at the Hamilton Psychiatric Hospital & in the regions it serves.
Ms Betty Laird, Coordinator, Volunteer Services, 905-522-1155, x35561

Hamilton: **HMCS Haida National Historic Site of Canada**
658 Catharine St. North (Pier 9), Hamilton, ON L8L 4V7
Tel: 905-526-0911; Fax: 905-526-9734
haida.info@pc.gc.ca
www.pc.gc.ca/haida
Commissioned in 1943, and dubbed "the fightingest ship in the Royal Canadian Navy", HMCS Haida saw service in WWII and the Korean War. Canada's most famous warship and the last of the Tribal Class destroyers left in the world is berthed at Hamilton.

Hamilton: **Royal Hamilton Light Infantry Heritage Museum**
John Weir Foote VC Armoury, 200 James St. North, Hamilton, ON L8R 2L1
Tel: 905-528-2945
www.rhli.ca/museum/
Military artifacts from 1830 to present, with specific reference to the Royal Hamilton Light Infantry; library
Ed Newman, Museum Administrator

Hamilton: **Whitehern Historic House & Garden**
The McQuesten Residence, 41 Jackson St. West, Hamilton, ON L8P 1L3
Tel: 905-546-2018; Fax: 905-546-4933
whitehern@hamilton.ca
www.whitehern.ca/whitehern.php
Former home of the McQuesten family from 1852 - 1968; period rooms feature original furnishings

Hamilton: **Workers Arts & Heritage Centre (WA&HC)**
51 Stuart St., Hamilton, ON L8L 1B5
Tel: 905-522-3003; Fax: 905-522-5424
wahc@wahc-museum.ca
www.wahc-museum.ca
twitter.com/WAHC
www.facebook .com/groups/13727960716
Located at Hamilton's former Custom House, which was built in 1860, the Workers Arts & Heritage Centre celebrates the history & culture of all working people in Canada. Exhibits include the labour movement in the Hamilton area, a history of office work, & the history of life on the shop floor, which explores Canada's early industrial days to the rise of automation in the workplace. The museum is open year-round.
Elizabeth McLuhan, Executive Director, executivedirector@wahc-museum.ca
Fabiola De Vierna, Coordinator, Administration & Finance, fabiola@wahc-museum.ca
Brian Kelly, Coordinator, Building & Exhibitions, brian@wahc-museum.ca
Andrew Lochhead, Coordinator, Labour Arts, andrew@wahc-museum.ca

Harrow: **John R. Park Homestead**
915 County Rd. 50 East, RR#1, Harrow, ON N0R 1G0
Tel: 519-738-2029; Fax: 519-776-8688
Toll-Free: 888-487-4760
jrph@erca.org
www.erca.org/conservation/area.john_r_park_homestead.cfm
twitter.com/essexregionca
www.facebook.com/4608375367 0
Living history museum; open year round
Janet Cobban, Curator

Holland Centre: **Comber Pioneer Village**
Rte. 3, Holland Centre, ON N0H 1R0
Tel: 519-794-3467
First log school of Holland Township; settler's cabin; log barn; replica of Martins Inn; log smoke house

Ignace: **Ignace Heritage Centre**
PO Box 480, 36 Main St., Ignace, ON P0T 1T0
Tel: 807-934-2280; Fax: 807-934-6452
www.olsn.ca/ignace
www.facebook.com/218910864872499
Local artifacts; located in the Ignace Public Library
Pam Greenwood, Chief Librarian/CEO, ceoignacelibrary@gmail.com

Ingersoll: **Ingersoll Cheese & Agricultural Museum**
130 Oxford St., 2nd Fl., Ingersoll, ON N5C 2V5
Tel: 519-485-0120
curator@ingersoll.ca
www.ingersoll.ca
Other contact information: April-Sept. Phone: 519-485-5510
Located in Centennial Park; 6 buildings including cheese factory museum, blacksmith shop; barn; community museum featuring spectacular woodcarved scene "pathway of the giants" & Ingersoll Sports Hall of Fame houses Harold Wilson's Miss Canada IV Speedboat; open daily July - Aug.; open weekends through May & June to Thanksgiving

Iron Bridge: **Iron Bridge Historical Museum**
PO Box 460, Iron Bridge, ON P0R 1H0
Tel: 705-843-2033; Fax: 705-843-2035
Pioneer artifacts

Iroquois: **Carman House Museum**
PO Box 249, Carman Rd., Iroquois, ON K0E 1K0
Tel: 613-652-4422; Fax: 613-652-4636
Other contact information: Phone, Summertime: 613-652-4808
Carman House is a United Empire Loyalist home, which was built in 1815. It is a living history museum, which reflects life in 1835. The museum is open from late June to Labour Day.

Iroquois Falls: **Iroquois Falls Pioneer Museum**
PO Box 448, 245 Devonshire Ave., Iroquois Falls, ON P0K 1E0
Tel: 705-258-3730; Fax: 705-258-3730
www.iroquoisfalls.com
Other contact information: Phone, Tours by appointment during the off season: 705-258-3409
Year Founded: 1970 The Garden Town of the North is home of the Shay Train Engine, the workhorse of the logging industry. The Iroquois Falls Pioneer Museum offers many displays, including the history of a company which became the world's largest producer of pulp & paper, the general store, a telephone exhibit, a hands-on display for children, the 1916 fire, a replica of a tug boat, & the Iroquois Hotel, which was built by the company.
Alexa Wollan, President, Iroquois Falls Historical Society Bd., & Director, alexa.60@live.com

Jordan: **Ball's Falls Centre for Conservation**
c/o Niagara Peninsula Conservation Authority, 3292 - 6th Ave., Jordan, ON L0R 1S0
Tel: 905-562-5235; Fax: 905-788-1121
info@npca.ca
www.ballsfalls.ca; ballsfalls.wordpress.com
Social Media: www.youtube.com/user/ballsfallsca
twitter.com/BallsFallsCA
www.facebook.com/209357529103582
The Ball's Falls Centre for Conservation offers information about the Niagara Peninsula's history, the natural history of the Twenty Valley & its watershed, & the Niagara Escarpment Biosphere Reserve. Historical homes, a mill, & a church are available for touring.
Rob Winninger, Site Administrator, rwinninger@npca.ca
Rob Kuret, Site Superintendent, rkuret@npca.ca
Nicci Hingley, Administrative Assistant, nhingley@npca.ca

Kakabeka Falls: **Hymers Museum**
RR#1, Kakabeka Falls, ON P0T 1W0
Tel: 807-577-4787
Local history
Linda Turk, Contact, lindat@tbaytel.net

Kapuskasing: **Ron Morel Memorial Museum**
88 Riverside Dr., Kapuskasing, ON P5N 1B3
Tel: 705-337-4274; Fax: 705-337-1741
Museum is housed in two railway cars & a caboose headed by steam locomotive 5107; changing seasonal exhibits & permanent displays; one railway car is devoted to trains & railway history, with a large working HO-gauge model; the Heritage Caravan with its clay sculptures depict Northern Ontario history; open daily from early June to Labour Day

Kars: **Swords & Ploughshares Museum**
7500 Reeve Craig Rd. North, RR#1, Kars, ON K0A 2E0
Tel: 613-489-3447
swords@calnan.com
www.calnan.com/swords
Military artifacts, 1914-present; agricultural machinery & implements, 1840-1940; open May - Oct. & by appt.

Kenora: **Lake of the Woods Museum**
PO Box 497, 300 Main St. South, Kenora, ON P9N 3X5
Tel: 807-467-2105; Fax: 807-467-2109
museum@kmts.ca
www.lakeofthewoodsmuseum.ca
www.facebook.com/LakeOfTheW oodsMuseum
Collection of more than 20,000 articles; displays feature native & pioneer artifacts, natural history, minerals, textiles, pictorial & archival material illustrating the history of the Lake of the Woods & surrounding area
Jan Lindstrom, Chair
Lori Nelson, Director

Keswick: **Georgina Military Museum (GMM)**
26061, RR#2, Keswick, ON L4P 3E9
Tel: 905-989-9900
frontdesk@georginamilitarymuseum.ca
www.georginamilita rymuseum.ca
www.facebook.com/georginamilitarymuseum
The museum is dedicated to teaching the public about the involvement of Canadians in wartime conflicts throughout history. Open Sa & Su 10:00-4:00.
John Cannon, President/Secretary
Phil Craig, Curator/Co-Founder

Keswick: **Georgina Pioneer Village & Archives**
26557 Civic Centre Rd., RR#2, Keswick, ON L4P 3G1
Tel: 905-476-4305; Fax: 905-476-7492
www.georginapioneervillage.ca
Social Media: www.flickr.com/photos/georginapioneervillage
www.facebook.com/3536782079 78112
Late 19th century historic village; interpreters & demonstrators; special exhibitions, events, tours, workshops & genealogical archives; open June-Sept., Thur.-Sun., 10-5 or by appt.
Phillip Rose-Donahoe, Curator, curator@georgina.ca
Melissa D. Matt, Archives Coordinator

Killarney: **Killarney Centennial Museum**
32 Commissioners St., Killarney, ON P0M 2A0
Tel: 705-287-2424; Fax: 705-287-2660
Toll-Free: 888-597-2721
townkill@vianet.on.ca
www.municipality.killarney.on.ca
Year Founded: 1967 The museum preserves historical artifacts from the time of the fur trade to the present; collection includes household items, objects from local commercial fishing, logging, mining & tourism industries, & photographs. Located at 29 Commissioners St. in Killarney. Open 6 days per week from late June to early September.
Laurier Low
Rosemarie Roque

King City: **King Township Museum**
Parent: **King Township Historical Society**
2920 King Rd., King City, ON L7B 1L6
Tel: 905-833-2331; Fax: 905-833-0462
kingmuseum@king.ca
www.king.ca
Year Founded: 1982 Housed in the Old Kinghorn School SS #23

Kingston: **Bellevue House National Historic Site (BHNHS)**
35 Centre St., Kingston, ON K7L 4E5
Tel: 613-545-8666; Fax: 613-545-8721
bellevue.house@pc.gc.ca
www.pc.gc.ca/lhn-nhs/on/bellevue/index_e.asp
Other contact information: TTY: 613-545-8668
Built in the early 1840s, Bellevue House was the home of Sir John A. Macdonald. The site is closed from November to March, but groups may make reservations.

Kingston: **Canada's Penitentiary Museum (CPM) / Musée du service correctionnel du Canada**
Also known as: **Canada's Penitentiary Museum/Musée pénitentiaire du Canada**
PO Box 260, 555 King St. West, Kingston, ON K7L 4V8
Tel: 613-530-3122; Fax: 613-536-4815
fpm@cogeco.net
www.penitentiarymuseum.ca
To preserve & interpret the past & contemporary experiences of the people & places associated with the history of corrections in Canada; located at 555 King St. West
Dave St. Onge, Curator

Kingston: **Cataraqui Archaeological Research Foundation/Kingston Archaeological Centre**
611 Princess St., Kingston, ON K7L 1E1
Tel: 613-542-3483
carf@carf.info
www.carf.info
Year Founded: 1986 The Foundation was established to oversee the excavation of Fort Frontenac, and to collect and preserve artifacts from the site. It is now involved in numerous archaeological projects at sites in Eastern Ontario, and operates the Kingston Archaeological Centre; educational programming and research collection. Open Mon to Fri, 9:30-4:00.
Sue Bazely, Executive Director

Kingston: **City of Kingston Fire Department Museum**
271 Brock St., Kingston, ON K7L 1S5

Antique firefighting equipment, photographs & models

Kingston: **Fort Henry**
Also known as: **The Citadel of Upper Canada**
PO Box 213, Kingston, ON K7L 4V8
Tel: 613-542-7388; Fax: 613-542-3054
Toll-Free: 800-437-2233
john.robertson@forthenry.com, getaway@parks.on.ca
www.forthenry.com
The Citadel of Upper Canada, brought to life by the Fort Henry Guard; restaurant; gift stores; children's muster parades; festivals, events, historic dining
John Robertson, Manager

Kingston: **International Hockey Hall of Fame & Museum**
PO Box 82, 277 York St., Kingston, ON K7L 4V6
Tel: 613-544-2355
info@ihhof.com
www.ihhof.com
twitter.com/HockeyHallFame
www.facebook.com/pages/Hockey-Hall-of-Fame/10 405440140
Year Founded: 1943 Home to 10,000 sq. feet of hockey memories; open mid-June - Labour Day, daily 10-3; off-season group tours by appt.
Mark Potter, President, mark.potter@ihhof.com
Larry Paquette, Vice-President, larry.paquette@ihhof.com

Kingston: **MacLachlan Woodworking Museum**
2993 Hwy. 2 East, Kingston, ON K7L 4V1
Tel: 613-542-0543; Fax: 613-547-5968
mwmuseum@cityofkingston.ca
www.cityofkingston.ca/museum
Year Founded: 1967 Exhibits include tools & lifestyles of 19th century tradespeople; hands-on workshops, educational programs & demonstrations are offered. The gift shop stocks handmade wooden kitchenware, linen, toys and wooden ornaments.
Annabelle Girard, Program Coordinator
Caroline Petznick, Curator

Kingston: **Marine Museum of the Great Lakes at Kingston**
55 Ontario St., Kingston, ON K7L 2Y2
Tel: 613-542-2261; Fax: 613-542-0043
marmus@marmuseum.ca
www.marmuseum.ca
Year Founded: 1976 The museum showcases an original pumping station and steam engines built in 1891. Exhibits include the history of boat building, as well as Kingston's maritime history on the Great Lakes. An Eco Gallery focuses on environmental issues related to the Great Lakes. At dock is the Alexander Henry, a icebreaking ship built in 1959.

Kingston: **Military Communications & Electronics Museum**
PO Box 17000 Forces, 95 Craftsman Blvd., Hwy. #2, Kingston, ON K7K 7B4
Tel: 613-541-4675; Fax: 613-540-8111
www.c-and-e-museum.org
Preserves & inteprets the Communications & Electronics Branch military history; provides group & individual tours; responds to research requests & is available to provide expert artifact appraisals; supports community activities with mobile displays & temporary loans of artifacts
Maj. (Ret'd) Mike DeNoble, Director, Museum Operations, 613-541-4211, denoble.mp@forces.gc.ca
Annette Gillis, Curator, Artifacts & Research Inquiries, 613-541-5130, gillis.ae@forces.gc.ca

Kingston: **Miller Museum of Mineralogy & Geology**
Miller Hall, Queen's University, 36 Union St., Kingston, ON K7L 3N6
Tel: 613-533-6767; Fax: 613-533-6592
geol.queensu.ca/museum
Collection of rocks, minerals & fossils from around the world; education tour programs available by request
Dr. J. Hutchinson, Department Head
Mark Badham, Curator

Kingston: **Murney Tower Museum**
Parent: **Kingston Historical Society**
c/o Kingston Historical Society, PO Box 54, Kingston, ON K7L 4V6
Tel: 613-544-9925
kingstonhs@gmail.com
www.kingstonhistoricalsociety.ca/Murney_Tower.html
Tower, built in 1846, now houses military, agricultural, Aboriginal & early settlers' artifacts; open summer
Gordon Sinclair, Chair, Kingston Historical Society
Warren Everett, Chair, Murney Tower Committee

Kingston: **Museum of Health Care at Kingston**
Ann Baillie Bldg. National Historic Site, 32 George St., Kingston, ON K7L 2V7
Tel: 613-548-2419
museum@kgh.kari.net
www.museumofhealthcare.ca
Social Media: www.youtube.com/user/MuseumOfHealthCare
twitter.com/MuseumofHealth
www .facebook.com/9025182465
The museum, located in an early 1900s residence for student nurses, tells the story of the evolution of health care in Canada. Open Fall/Winter/Spring Tu-F 10:00-4:00.
Alan Grant, Chair
Dr. James Low, Executive Director Emeritus, lowj@kgh.kari.net
Dr. Pamela Peacock, Curator, peacockp@kgh.kari.net
Jenny Brown, Museum Manager & Program Director, brownj@kgh.kari.net

Kingston: **Princess of Wales' Own Regiment Military Museum**
The Armouries, 100 Montreal St., Kingston, ON K7K 3E8
Tel: 613-541-5010; Fax: 613-542-3894
pwormuseum.ca
Open year round.
Stuart MacDonald, Curator, curator@pwormuseum.ca

Kingston: **Pump House Steam Museum**
c/o Cultural Services Dept., City of Kingston, 216 Ontario St., Kingston, ON K7L 2Z3
Tel: 613-546-4291
phsmuseum@cityofkingston.ca
www.steammuseum.ca
twitter.com/kingstonmuseums
www.facebook.com/kingst onmuseums
Former pumping station with artifacts relating to steam power; operating steam & pump engines
Gordon Robinson, Curator

Kingston: **The Royal Military College Museum / Le musée du Collège militaire royal du Canada**
Also known as: **RMC Museum**
PO Box 17000 Forces, Kingston, ON K7K 7B4
Tel: 613-541-6000; Fax: 613-542-3565
mckenzie-r@rmc.ca
Housed in the Fort Frederick Martello Tower on the College grounds; holdings relate to the history of the College, the achievements of its ex-cadets & to the history of the Royal Navy Dockyard which once occupied the site; amongst the Museum's most treasured possessions is the superb Douglas Arms Collection; open daily last Sat. in June - Labour Day
Ross McKenzie, Curator
Dr. J.G. Pike, Committee Chair

Kingsville: **Canadian Transportation Museum & Heritage Village (CTMHV)**
6155 Arner Townline, County Rd. 23, Kingsville, ON N9Y 2E5
Tel: 519-776-6909; Fax: 519-776-8321
info@ctmhv.com
www.ctmhv.com
www.facebook.com/groups/182746380618/#!/groups/182746380618
Year Founded: 1954 Located on County Road #23 in Kingsville, Ontario, the Canadian Transportation Museum collects, restores, & exhibits modes of transportation from the mid 1800s to 1992. Examples of displays include horse drawn carts, fire trucks, & Ford Model Ts. The Heritage Village contains buildings, such as a one room schoolhouse, a train station, a log home, & a general store.
Kim Brimner, Manager, manager@ctmhv.com

Kingsville: **Jack Miner Bird Sanctuary & Museum**
PO Box 39, Kingsville, ON N9Y 2E8
Tel: 519-733-4034Toll-Free: 877-289-8328
info@jackminer.com
www.jackminer.com
Year Founded: 1904 Known as "Wild Goose Jack", Jack Miner founded the bird sanctuary in 1904 and stipulated that admission would remain free. In addition to the sanctuary and grounds, the museum holdings include memorabilia, wildlife prints, medals, manuscripts & newspaper clippings, books, a bust of Jack Miner and letter from friend Henry Ford, and baseball bats from Ty Cobb. Located at 322 Road 3 West, off Division Road in Kingsville.

Kirkland Lake: **Museum of Northern History at the Sir Harry Oakes Chateau**
PO Box 1148, 2 Chateau Dr., Kirkland Lake, ON P2N 3M7
Tel: 705-568-8800
museum@tkl.ca
www.discoverkl.ca
The Chateau, built by Sir Henry Oakes and has been preserved as a museum exhibit and is also a space to preserve northern history.
Kelly Gallagher, Town Curator

***Kitchener:* Doon Heritage Crossroads**
***Also known as:* Doon Pioneer Village**
10 Huron Rd., Kitchener, ON N2P 2R7
Tel: 519-748-1914; Fax: 519-748-0009
rtom@region.waterloo.on.ca
www.region.waterloo.on.ca
Other contact information: TTY: 519/748-0537
Turn of the century living history village; open daily May - Dec.
Thomas A. Reitz, Curator/Manager

***Kitchener:* Joseph Schneider Haus Museum**
466 Queen St. South, Kitchener, ON N2G 1W7
Tel: 519-742-7752; Fax: 519-742-0089
www.regionofwaterloo.ca/en/discoveringtheregion/josephschneiderhaus.asp
www.facebook.com/163934690313150
Other contact information: TTY: 519-575-4608
Traces back to the Schneider family, one of the first group of Pennsylvania German Mennonites in the area

***Kitchener:* Woodside National Historic Site of Canada / Lieu historique national de Woodside**
528 Wellington St. North, Kitchener, ON N2H 5L5
Tel: 519-571-5684; Fax: 519-571-5686
Toll-Free: 888-773-8888
ont-woodside@pc.gc.ca
www.pc.gc.ca/lhn-nhs/on/woodside /index.aspx
Woodside National Historic Site was the childhood home of Canada's longest-serving Prime Minister, William Lyon Mackenzie King. Today, the house is restored to the Victorian era of the 1890s. The site is open from mid May to late December. Groups may reserve tours during the off season.
Kim Seward-Hannam, Supt.

***Komoka:* Komoka Railway Museum Inc.**
PO Box 22, 133 Queen St., Komoka, ON N0L 1R0
Tel: 519-657-1912
station-master@komokarailmuseum.ca
www.komokarailmuseum.ca
Restored railroad station; site includes 1913 Shay logging locomotive, 1939 CN baggage car, 1972 caboose & a collection of CN maintenance jiggers

***Lakefield:* Christ Church Community Museum**
c/o St. John the Baptist Anglican Church, PO Box 217, 81 Queen St., Lakefield, ON K0L 2H0
Tel: 705-652-8302
stjohnslakefield.ca
History of Lakefield, & the Strickland family; The Bill Twist Collection; display of old toys, dolls & doll furniture, cards; open 1:00-4:00 daily

***Lanark:* Lanark & District Museum**
80 George St., Lanark, ON K0G 1K0
Tel: 613-259-2575
lanarkanddistrictmuseum@gmail.com
www.lanarkcountymuseums.ca
Open weekends, mid-May to mid-Oct.

***Lanark:* Middleville & District Museum**
PO Box 6, 2130 Concession Rd. 6D, Lanark, ON K0G 1K0
Tel: 613-259-5462
middlevillemuseum@gmail.com
www.middlevillemuseum.blogspot.ca
Local pioneer artifacts including items for the maple syrup, cheese & lumbering industries; open May 24-Thanksgiving
Alice Borrowman, Chair & Curator, maborrowman@gmail.com

***Latchford:* House of Memories**
PO Box 82, Latchford, ON P0J 1N0
Tel: 705-676-2417
Local artifacts from 1900-1940; WWI & WWII items; natural history exhibits

***Leamington:* Point Pelee National Park of Canada, Visitor Centre, DeLaurier Historical House, & Trail / Parc national du Canada de la Pointe-Pelée**
407 Monarch Lane, RR#1, Leamington, ON N8H 3V4
Tel: 519-322-2365; Fax: 519-322-1277
Toll-Free: 888-773-8888
pelee.info@pc.gc.ca
www.pc.gc.ca./pelee
Other contact information: TTY: 1-866-787-6221
Located at the southern tip of Canada, Point Pelee National Park features the DeLaurier Historical House. The homestead & barn depict the park's human & cultural heritage. The Visitor Centre houses exhibits, a children's discovery room, & theatre programs about the area's natural & cultural heritage.

***Limehouse:* Canadian Military Studies Museum**
Lot 23, Conc. 6, RR#1, Limehouse, ON L0P 1H0
Tel: 905-877-6522
durangedhemi@sympatico.ca
The Canadian Military Studies Museum features artifacts from the mid-17th century, the Boer War, World War I, & World War II, to the Korean & Vietnam Wars.

***Lindsay:* Old Lindsay Jail**
***Parent:* Victoria County Historical Society**
PO Box 187, 50 Victoria Ave. North, Lindsay, ON K9V 4S1
Tel: 705-324-3404; Fax: 705-324-1805
info@oldejailmusem.ca
www.oldejailmuseum.com
www.facebook.com/groups/3 5377022941
The Lindsay Jail, built in 1863, was historically known as the County Gaol. The Victoria County Historical Society collects, preserves, & exhibits the history of the County of Victoria.
John Macklem, President

***Little Current:* Centennial Museum of Sheguiandah**
Postal Bag 2000, Little Current, ON P0P 1K0
Tel: 705-368-2367; Fax: 705-368-0761
shegmus@vianet.ca
Year Founded: 1967 pioneer culture & history on Manitoulin Island
Heidi Ferguson, Curator

***London:* Banting House National Historic Site**
***Parent:* Canadian Diabetes Association**
442 Adelaide St. North, London, ON N6B 3H8
Tel: 519-673-1752; Fax: 519-660-8992
banting@diabetes.ca
www.diabetes.ca/about-us/who/banting-house
The hosue where Dr. F.G. Banting, the co-discoverer of insulin, once lived. Open Tu-Sa 12:00-4:00.

***London:* Canadian Medical Hall of Fame**
PO Box 202, 267 Dundas St., London, ON N6A 1H2
Tel: 519-488-2003; Fax: 519-488-2999
cmhf@cdnmedhall.org
www.cdnmedhall.org
Social Media: www.youtube.com/user/cdnmedhall
twitter.com/CdnMedHallFame
www.faceboo k.com/cdnmedhall
Year Founded: 2003 The Hall features a portrait gallery, featured exhibits, a wall fo quotations, a stamp display refelcting the history of Canadian health care, & a media theatre. Open Tu-F 8:30-4:30, Sa 10:00-5:00, Su 10:00-5:00 (Apr.-Oct. only).
Cecil Rorabeck, Chair M.D., F.R.C.S.C
Janet Tufts, Executive Director, jtufts@cdnmedhall.org

***London:* Eldon House**
481 Ridout St. North, London, ON N6A 5H4
Tel: 519-661-0333; Fax: 519-661-2559
ramurray@museumlondon.ca
www.eldonhouse.ca
Other contact information: Direct Line: 519-661-5169
House of the Harris family from 1834-1959
Paul Way, President
Brian Meehan, Executive Director
Tara Whittmann, Coordinator, Heritage Site, twittman@museumlondon.ca

***London:* Fanshawe Pioneer Village (FPV)**
2609 Fanshawe Park Rd. East, London, ON N5X 4A1
Tel: 519-457-1296; Fax: 519-457-3364
info@fanshawepioneervillage.ca
www.fanshawepioneervillage.ca
Costumed interpreters demonstrate life in mid-1800s to early 1900s rural Ontario crossroads community
Sheila A. Johnson, Executive Director
Shanna Dunlop, Curator & Head of Operations

***London:* First Hussars: Citizen Soldiers Museum**
399 Ridout St. North, London, ON N6A 2P1
Tel: 519-471-1538
www.firsthussars.ca/museum.html
Follows the history of the 1st Hussars from 1856 until today; includes material on the Boer War, the Great War & WWII
Alastair Neely, Curator

***London:* Forest City Gallery (FCG)**
258 Richmond St., London, ON N6B 2H7
Tel: 519-434-5875
www.forestcitygallery.com; www.fcgintern.blogspot.ca
Social Media: www.youtube.com/user/forestcitygallery
twitter.com/ForestCityGlry
www. facebook.com/forestcitygallery
An artist-run centre dedicated to showcasing national & international artists working in visual/media arts, performance, literature, & music. Open W-Sa 12:00-5:00.
Rene Vandenbrink, President
Jenna Faye Powell, Director, director@forestcitygallery.com

***London:* Grosvenor Lodge**
1017 Western Rd., London, ON N6G 1G5
Tel: 519-645-2845; Fax: 519-645-0981
info@grosvenorlodge.com
www.grosvenorlodge.com
1853 estate; operates as London Regional Resource Centre for Heritage & the Environment, administered by the Heritage London Foundation; resources available on heritage & environmental issues; venue for meetings, seminars & social events; library & display areas open to public; open Mon.-Fri. 9-4

***London:* Guy Lombardo Music Centre**
205 Wonderland Rd. South, London, ON N6K 3T3
Tel: 519-473-9003
www.guylombardomusic.com/museum.html
Memorabilia relating to bandleader & his band, the Royal Canadians, including original recordings & videotapes; open June-Aug., Wed.-Sun., 11-7; Sept. 12:30-4:30 or by appt.
Doug Flood, Director, 519-652-3417, seventyeights@aol.com

***London:* London Regional Children's Museum**
21 Wharncliffe Rd. South, London, ON N6J 4G5
Tel: 519-434-5726; Fax: 519-434-1443
info@londonchildrensmuseum.ca
www.londonchildrensmuseum.ca
Social Media: www.youtube.com/user/LdnChildrensMuseum
twitter.com/children_museum
www.facebook.com/LondonChildrensMuseum
Hands-on, interactive museum; features ten themed galleries, school programs, outreach programs, day camps, workshops, birthday parties & membership programs
Sean Galloway, Co-Chair
Kerry L. Robbins, Co-Chair
Joy Birch, Executive Director, joy@londonchildrensmuseum.ca

***London:* Museum London**
421 Ridout St. North, London, ON N6A 5H4
Tel: 519-661-0333; Fax: 519-661-2559
info@museumlondon.ca
www.londonmuseum.on.ca
Operates Eldon House; exhibits include family life, historical & contemporary art & historical artifacts from the London area from 1834 to 1960
Brian Meehan, Executive Director & Chief Curator
Cydna Mercer, Head of Administration
Melanie Townsend, Head of Exhibitions & Collections

***London:* Museum of Ontario Archaeology & Iroquoian Village Site (MOA)**
Lawson-Jury Bldg., University of Western Ontario, 1600 Attawandaron Rd., London, ON N6G 3M6
Tel: 519-473-1360; Fax: 519-473-1363
museum.of.archaeology@uwo.ca
www.uwo.ca/museum
twitter.com/MuseOntArch
www.facebook.com/99483006781
Archaeological & ethnographical collection; prehistoric archaeological Iroquois village site; museum open year round with reduced hours in fall & winter
Dr. Neal Ferris, Lawson Chair, Canadian Archaeology, nferris@uwo.ca
Joan Kanigan, Executive Director, jkanigan@uwo.ca

***London:* The Royal Canadian Regiment Museum**
Wolseley Barracks, 701 Oxford St. East, London, ON N5Y 4T7
Tel: 519-660-5102; Fax: 519-660-5344
Breede.C@forces.gc.ca
www.theroyalcanadianregiment.ca/thercrmuseum/thercrmuseum.htm
To serve as a training medium to teach regimental history; to preserve regimental history through the collection of documents, pictures, books & artifacts with emphasis on the RCR; to serve as a place of military interest for the public & Canadian Forces personnel; to provide research facilities for the study of Canadian military history.
Claus Breede, Curator
Maj. R.A. Smyth, Director

***Lucan:* Donnelly Homestead**
34937 Roman Line, RR#3, Lucan, ON N0M 2J0
Tel: 519-227-1244
rsalts@quadro.net
www.quadro.net/~donnelly
Historical on-site tours given on the original Donnelly property by current owner; artifacts & photographs; tours preferably by appt., year round; private residence
Robert Salts, Contact

***Madoc:* O'Hara Mill Pioneer Homestead**
PO Box 56, 638 Mill Rd., Madoc, ON K0K 2K0
Tel: 613-473-2084
www.ohara-mill.org
Other contact information: Phone, Membership Services: 413-473-1015
Attractions include O'Hara House, a log house, a saw mill, & a one room log schoolhouse. O'Hara House is restored to represent the Victorian era around 1840. The saw mill is a rare working English Gate or Reciprocating Frame saw mill.
Dave Little, Chair, 613-967-2466
Clara Hopkins, Vice-Chair, 613-473-2084

Karen Maguire, Secretary, 613-473-2177
Gayle Ketcheson, Treasurer, 613-473-4680

Magnetawan: **Magnetawan Historical Museum**
Also known as: **Magnetawan Heritage Centre**
PO Box 70, Hwy. 520, Magnetawan, ON P0A 1P0
Tel: 705-387-3308
www.magnetawan.com
Other contact information: Alternate Phone: 705-387-3357
Restored plant & turbine that supplied first electricity for village; log cabin; located at Biddy St. at the Magnetawan Locks.

Manitowaning: **Assiginack Museum & Heritage Park**
PO Box 238, Arthur St., Manitowaning, ON P0P 1N0
Tel: 705-859-3905
assigmuse@amtelecom.net
www.manitoulin-island.com/museums/assiginack_complex.htm
The Assiginack Museum & Heritage Park is a community & marine museum. Artifacts are from the mid-1800s to the mid-1900s. Visitors can see a pioneer home & school, a 19th century grist mill, plus the Great Lakes steamship, S.S. Norisle, which was built in 1946. The museum is open from June to October.
Jeanette Allen, Curator

Manotick: **Watson's Mill**
Also known as: **Manotick Mill**
PO Box 145, 5525 Dickinson St., Manotick, ON K4M 1A3
Tel: 613-692-6455; Fax: 613-692-5486
Toll-Free: 800-267-3504
watsonsmillmanotick@rogers.com
www.watsonsmill.com
Year Founded: 1860 19th century working gristmill, built 1860; gift shop; tours; picnic area; live interpretation, gossip tours
Bonnie Gray, President, Board of Directors
Isabelle Geoffrion, Manager, 613-692-6455
Cam Trueman, Interpretation & Education Officer, 613-692-6455

Markham: **Markham Museum & Historic Village**
9350 Hwy. 48, Markham, ON L3P 3J3
Tel: 905-294-4576; Fax: 905-294-4590
museuminfo@markham.ca
www.markham.ca/wps/portal/Markham/RecreationCultur e/MarkhamMuseum
Buildings, vehicles, furnishing & agricultural & industrial equipment that relate to Markham Township's history, from native presence to the 20th century; open year round

Marten River: **Marten River Provincial Park Logging Museum**
c/o Marten River Provincial Park, Marten River, ON P0H 1T0
Tel: 705-892-2200; Fax: 705-892-2147
ontarioparks.com/english/mart.html
Artifacts for early logging era in Northern Ontario

Massey: **Massey Area Museum**
160 Sauble St., Massey, ON P0P 1P0
Tel: 705-865-2266; Fax: 705-865-2266
info@masseyareamuseum.com
www.masseyareamuseum.com
Year Founded: 1967 The Massey Area Museum is housed in the original Bretzlaff General Store, which was built in 1909. The museum details logging history, as well as Aboriginal, Fort LaCloche, mining, farming, & early settler history. Model rooms, a chapel, a general store, & Massey's first horse-drawn fire engine are featured at the museum. There is also an historical & genealogical research centre, which includes records of the Township of Sables-Spanish River's ten cemeteries.
Carolyn Hein, Curator

Matheson: **Thelma Miles Historical Museum**
PO Box 601, 374 Hough Rd., Matheson, ON P0K 1N0
Tel: 705-273-2325; Fax: 705-273-1731
History of the communities of Val Gagné, Shillington, Wavel, Ramore, Holtyre & Matheson from 1900-1945

Mattawa: **Mattawa & District Museum**
PO Box 9, 285 First St., Mattawa, ON P0H 1V0
Tel: 705-744-5495; Fax: 705-744-5495
mattawamuseum.com
Year Founded: 1976 Open daily July - Aug.; weekends in May, June, Sept., Oct.

Mattawa: **Voyageur Heritage Centre**
Samuel de Champlain Provincial Park, PO Box 147, Hwy. 17 East, Mattawa, ON P0H 1V0
Tel: 705-744-2276
www.ontarioparks.com/english/samu.html
The Voyageur Heritage Centre tells the story of the Mattawa River & the lives of the voyageurs. The centre features one of the largest reproduced birch bark canoes.

Maxville: **Glengarry Sports Hall of Fame**
PO Box 282, Maxville, ON K0C 1T0
Tel: 613-527-1044
www.glengarrysports.com
Year Founded: 1978

Meaford: **Meaford Museum**
111 Bayfield St., Meaford, ON N4L 1N4
Tel: 519-538-5974; Fax: 519-538-5974
meafordmuseum@meaford.ca
www.meafordmuseum.ca
Year Founded: 1961 The Meaford Museum aims to collect, educate, display, conserve and feature the history of the former Town of Meaford and the surrounding area, from early settlements to the present. Hours: Open hours vary. Check website or call for details.
Pam Woolner, Curator

Meldrum Bay: **The Net Shed Museum**
Water St., Meldrum Bay, ON P0P 1R0
Tel: 705-283-3267
Open June & Aug.; artifacts of pioneer fishing, lumbering & farming; display of nursing in WWII

Merrickville: **The Blockhouse Museum**
PO Box 294, Merrickville, ON K0G 1N0
Tel: 613-269-4034
info@merrickvillehistory.org
www.merrickvillehistory.org
Built as a defence for the Rideau Canal built in 1830. Contains local pioneer artifacts.
Gillian Hammonds, Manager, The Blockhouse Museum

Midland: **Huronia Museum**
PO Box 638, 549 Little Lake Park, Midland, ON L4R 4P4
Tel: 705-526-2844; Fax: 705-527-6622
info@huroniamuseum.com
www.huroniamuseum.com
Social Media: www.flickr.com/photos/huroniamuseum
twitter.com/HuroniaMuseum
www.face book.com/huroniamuseum
Recreated Huron Village represents one of hundreds that existed in the Georgian Bay area, representing a unique & sophisticated society which lasted nearly 1,000 years; Canada's first recreated Native village; extensive exhibits on regional history, art gallery, archives & Mundys Bay Store; a large selection of native & historical books
Gary French, Chair
Jamie Hunter, Director/Curator

Midland: **Martyrs' Shrine**
PO Box 7, 16163 Hwy. 12 West, Midland, ON L4R 4K6
Tel: 705-526-3788; Fax: 705-526-1546
shrine@jesuits.ca
www.martyrs-shrine.com
Year Founded: 1926 Built in 1926 in tribute to the Jesuit missionaries who laboured among the Huron, 1625-50, and to the eight who were martyred, the interior of this church with its wooden walls and canoe-like ceiling celebrates the melding of historical cultures. Open daily, Victoria Day weekend through Thanksgiving weekend; tours &/or talks given on request.
Rev. Alex F. Kirsten, Director S.J.

Midland: **Sainte-Marie among the Hurons / Sainte-Marie-au-Pays-des-Hurons**
PO Box 160, 16164, Hwy. 12 East, Midland, ON L4R 4K8
Tel: 705-526-7838; Fax: 705-526-9193
www.saintemarieamongthehurons.on.ca
Other contact information: TTY: 705-528-7697
During the 17th century, Sainte-Marie served as the fortress & headquarters for the French Jesuit mission to the Huron nation. Based upon archaeological & historical research, Sainte-Marie was recreated on its original site. Special programs & courses are offered about the first European community in Ontario. The site is open from the end of April to the end of October.

Milford: **Mariners Park Museum**
PO Box 12, 2065 County Rd. 13, Milford, ON K0K 2P0
Tel: 613-476-8392
marinersmuseum@pecounty.on.ca
pecounty.on.ca/government/rec_parks_culture/rec_culture/muse ums/index.php
Year Founded: 1967 Indoor and outdoor exhibits distinguish the site, with displays of various artifacts from marine activity in the area, including treasures from diving expeditions, as well as pieces related to local fishing, ship building, ice harvesting and rum running days. The False Duck Lighthouse has become a memorial to the County's sailors.
Jennifer Lyons, Head Curator, Recreation, Parks & Culture, Prince Edward County, 613-476-2148, Fax: 613-476-9835, museums@pecounty.on.ca

Milton: **Country Heritage Park**
PO Box 38, Milton, ON L9T 2Y3
Tel: 905-878-8151; Fax: 905-876-4530
Toll-Free: 888-307-3276
information@countryheritagepark.com
www.countryheritag epark.com
Display of machinery & tools related to all aspects of agricultural industry in Ontario

Milton: **Halton Region Museum**
5181 Kelso Rd., RR#3 (Kelso Conservation Area), Milton, ON L9T 2X7
Tel: 905-875-2200; Fax: 905-876-4322
Toll-Free: 866-442-5866
museum@halton.ca
www.halton.ca/museum
Year Founded: 1962 Focusing on Halton's natural & cultural heritage, the main exhibits are located in Alexander Barn and in the Visitor Centre on the main floor. Both Heritage and Environmental Programmes are offered. The Reference Library stores various regional, historical records available for research purposes. Open year round.
Nancy Field, Manager, Heritage Services, Halton Region, 905-875-2200, nancy.field@halton.ca

Milton: **Streetcar & Electric Railway Museum**
c/o Ontario Electric Railway Historical Association Inc., PO Box 578, Milton, ON L9T 5A2
Tel: 519-856-9802; Fax: 519-856-1399
streetcar@hcry.org
www.hcry.org
Operating streetcar & electric railway museum
Gord McOuat, Vice-President
J. Borland, President

Mindemoya: **Central Manitoulin Historical Society Pioneer Museum**
PO Box 320, Mindemoya, ON P0P 1S0
Tel: 705-377-4994
www.centralmanitoulin.ca
The museum features a log cabin, workshop & blacksmith shop, frame barn, farm equipment, & reinactments of pioneer life. Open July & Aug., M-F 1:00-4:00, or by appointment.
Jan McQuay, Secretary, 705-377-4045

Minesing: **Simcoe County Museum**
1151 Hwy. 26, Minesing, ON L0L 1Y0
Tel: 705-728-3721; Fax: 705-728-9130
museum@simcoe.ca
www.county.simcoe.on.ca
Open daily; 9:00-4:30 Monday to Saturday and 1:00-4:30 Sunday. Admission $6.00 adults, $4.00 seniors/students

Mississauga: **Benares Historic House & Visitor Centre**
1507 Clarkson Rd. North, Mississauga, ON L5J 2W8
Tel: 905-822-2347
www.mississauga.ca/portal/discover/benareshistorichouse
Year Founded: 1995 Owned & operated by the City of Mississauga, Community Services Department, the Benares Historic House is a Georgian style home, which was built in 1857. The home has been restored to reflect the early 20th century & displays original artifacts from the Harris family & home. The Benares House is believed to be the inspiration for Mazo de la Roche's Jalna novels.

Mississauga: **Bradley House Museum**
1620 Orr Rd., Mississauga, ON L5J 4T2
Tel: 905-615-4860
www.mississauga.ca/portal/discover/bradleymuseum
The Bradley Museum is owned & operated by the City of Mississauga, Community Services Department. The museum grounds feature an early 19th century home known as The Anchorage, a farmhouse which was built in 1830, & a log cabin. The farmhouse was owned by the Bradleys, who were a United Empire Loyalist couple. The museum is open year round.

Mississauga: **Lithuanian Museum/Archives of Canada (LMAC)**
Parent: **Lithuanian Canadian Community**
2185 Stavebank Rd., Mississauga, ON L5C 1T3
Tel: 416-533-3292
info@klb.org
www.klb.org/muziejusEN.html
To collect, display, organize & preserve documents, photographs, fine art, textiles, memorabilia, souvenirs of community events, uniforms, medals, coins, maps, flags, videos, audio tapes & rare books or periodicals which pertain to Lithuania & Lithuanian Canadians; small lending library
Dr. Rasa Mazeika, Director

Mooretown: **Moore Museum**
94 Moore Line, Mooretown, ON N0N 1M0
Tel: 519-867-2020; Fax: 519-867-2020
www.mooremuseum.ca
Year Founded: 1975 Open year round; Jan. - Feb. by appt.
Laurie Mason, Curator, lmason@twp.stclair.on.ca

Morpeth: **Rondeau Provincial Park Visitor Centre**
RR#1 (Hwy. 15), Morpeth, ON N0P 1X0
Tel: 519-674-1750
rondeau@ontario.ca
www.rondeauprovincialpark.ca; ontarioparks.com/english/rond.html
www.facebook.com/pantsgloydi
Other contact information: Visitor Centre Phone: 519-674-1768
Herbarium, egg, mammal, insect, archaeological, photographic & bird collection
Anne Ondrovcik, President, Friends of Rondeau

Morrisburg: **Upper Canada Village**
13740 County Rd. 2, Morrisburg, ON K0C 1X0
Tel: 613-543-4328Toll-Free: 800-437-2233
www.uppercanadavillage.com
Other contact information: Phone, Village Library Appointments: 613-543-3704
Upper Canada Village features more than forty heritage buildings. The village depicts daily life in the 1860s, through demonstrations, talks, & hands-on activities. The site also has a library & research facility. Upper Canada Village is open from mid May to mid October.

Mount Brydges: **Ska-Nah-Doht Iroquoian Village & Museum**
8449 Irish Dr., RR#1, Mount Brydges, ON N0L 1W0
Tel: 519-264-2420; Fax: 519-264-1562
lowerthames@odyssey.on.ca
www.lowerthames-conservation.on.ca/SkaNahDoht. htm
This recreated Iroquoian village of 1,000 years ago has 18 outdoor exhibits including a palisade with maze & longhouses; museum in resource centre; displays on nature & conservation; trails, wetland boardwalks & picnic areas.There are hands on exhibits and an archaeological collection.
Karen Mattila, Curator

Mount Hope: **Canadian Warplane Heritage Museum (CWH)**
Hamilton Airport, 9280 Airport Rd., Mount Hope, ON L0R 1W0
Tel: 905-679-4183; Fax: 905-679-4186
Toll-Free: 877-347-3359
museum@warplane.com
www.warplane.com
Year Founded: 1971 The museum is dedicated to the acquisition & preservation of aircraft flown by Canadians from WWII to the present, & the collection of related aviation artifacts & memorabilia; library & archival resources; meeting room & hangar rental; special events & programming; group tours available. Open daily 9-5, year round.
David G. Rohrer, CEO/Director

Napanee: **Allan Macpherson House**
180 Elizabeth St., Napanee, ON K7R 1B5
Tel: 613-354-5982; Fax: 613-354-5285
machouse@kingston.net
www.macphersonhouse.ca
Year Founded: 1967 1826 mansion of Allan Macpherson, one of Napanee's leading citizens; reflects the taste, public & private activities of an entrepreneurial Scottish immigrant. Open May-Dec. School programs; bridal party rentals; children's summer activity days; annual whiskey tasting.
Sandra Penney, Managing Director

Napanee: **Lennox & Addington County Museum & Archives**
97 Thomas St. East, PO Bag 1000, Napanee, ON K7R 3S9
Tel: 613-354-3027; Fax: 613-354-1005
nmuseum@lennox-addington.on.ca
www.lennox-addington.on.ca
Located in former County jail (1864); genealogy & historical research centre, county's origins, Loyalist settlement & development from 1784 to present, displays & extensive archives; open year round
Jane Foster, Manager
Shelley Respondek, Archivist, archives@lennox-addington.on.ca

Napanee: **Old Hay Bay Church**
c/o Katherine Staples, 304 Staples Lane, Napanee, ON K7R 3K7
Tel: 613-373-2877; Fax: 613-373-8816
www.oldhaybaychurch.org
Other contact information: Alternate Phone: 613-373-2261
A National Historic Site, Old Hay Bay Church was erected in 1792. Located at 2365 South Shore Road in Adolphustown, Ontario, the church is the oldest Methodist building in Canada.
Katherine Staples, Contact

Nepean: **Algonquin College Museum**
Applied Museum Studies Program, Algonquin College, 1385 Woodroffe Ave., Nepean, ON K2G 1V8
Tel: 613-727-4723; Fax: 613-727-7759
www.algonquincollege.com/museum
Teaching collection
Michael Wheatley, Coordinator, wheatlm1@algonquincollege.com

Nepean: **Nepean Museum Inc.**
Parent: **Nepean Museum Inc.**
16 Rowley Ave., Nepean, ON K2G 1L9
Tel: 613-723-7936; Fax: 613-723-7936
reception@nepeanmuseum.ca
www.nepeanmuseum.ca
www.facebook.com/pages/N epean-Museum/119420948766
Year Founded: 1983 Housed in the first Nepean Library, the museum displays historical objects related to Nepean's past & present. Nepean Museum contains two meeting rooms.
Lindsay MacDonald, Director & Curator, curator@nepeanmuseum.ca
Kalle Boucher, Manager, Education & Volunteers, educationservices@nepeanmuseum.ca
Emily Bracewell, Manager, Collections, collections@nepeanmuseum.ca

New Liskeard: **Little Claybelt Homesteaders Museum**
PO Box 1718, 883356 Hwy. 65, New Liskeard, ON P0J 1P0
Tel: 705-647-9575
claybeltmuseum.ca
Displays of geological origin of Little Claybelt, pioneer activities, historical documents, artifacts & agricultural implements, pioneer family histories
Clair Shepherdson, President

Newmarket: **Elman W. Campbell Museum**
Also known as: **Newmarket Museum**
134 Main St. South, Newmarket, ON L3Y 3Y7
Tel: 905-953-5314; Fax: 905-898-2083
Toll-Free: 877-550-5575
elmanmuseum@rogers.com
www.newmarket.ca
Exhibits trace the development of Newmarket from the time of the first settlers
Elizabeth Sinyard, Curator

Niagara Falls: **Battle Gound Hotel Museum**
6137 Lundy's Lane, Niagara Falls, ON L2G 1T4
Tel: 905-358-5082
niagarafallshistorymuseum.ca/index.php/museums/battle-ground-hotel-museum
The museum is located on the site of the Lundy's Lane Battlefield, is housed in a restored 1850s tavern, & showcases artifacts related to the War of 1812. Open May-Aug., F-Su 11:00-5:00.

Niagara Falls: **Daredevil Gallery**
6170 Fallsview Blvd., Niagara Falls, ON L2G 7T8
Tel: 905-358-3611; Fax: 905-358-3613
Toll-Free: 866-405-4629
info@imaxniagara.com
www.imaxniagara.com/daredevil-gal lery
Only collection of original daredevil barrels found in Niagara Falls

Niagara Falls: **Guinness World Records Museum**
4943 Clifton Hill, Niagara Falls, ON L2G 3N5
Toll-Free: 866-656-0310
www.guinnessniagarafalls.com
Displays of human achievements; models of the extraordinary; computer databanks & videos; open year round

Niagara Falls: **Laura Secord Homestead**
c/o Oak Hall Administrative Office, Niagara Parks Commission, PO Box 150, 7400 Portage Road South, Niagara Falls, ON L2E 6T2
Tel: 905-262-4851Toll-Free: 877-642-7275
friendsoflaurasecord@hotmail.com
www.niagaraparks.com/heritage-trail/laura-secord-homestead.html
www.facebook.com/FriendsofLauraSecord
Other contact information: Niagara Parks Phone: 905-356-2241
Open May-Sept. in Queenston ON
Caroline McCormick, President, Friends of Laura Secord
David Hemmings, Contact, Research & Genealogy, hemmingsdd@gmail.com

Niagara Falls: **Louis Tussaud's Waxworks**
5907 Victoria Ave., Niagara Falls, ON L2G 3L5
Tel: 905-374-6601; Fax: 905-374-7345
www.cliftonhill.com/attractions
Year Founded: 1953 Museum displays wax models of famous and infamous people, such as artists, musicians, celebrities, politicians and religious & historical figures. Open year round.
Mr. Tim Parker, Gneral manager Manager, parker@ripleys.com
André Ross

Niagara Falls: **McFarland House**
c/o Niagara Parks Commission, PO Box 150, Niagara Falls, ON L2E 6T2
Tel: 905-295-4377; Fax: 905-295-4142
Toll-Free: 877-642-7275
www.niagaraparks.com/heritage-trail/mcfarland-house.html
www.facebook.com/niagaraparkspr
Year Founded: 1959 Built in 1800 and home to John McFarland and his family for 150 years, the house served as a hospital for both the British & American wounded during the War of 1812. Restored by the Niagara Parks Commission in period style, there are also traditional grounds and the McFarland Tea Garden to enjoy refreshments. Nature trails can be accessed from the park. The house is located at 15927 Niagara Parkway, Niagara-on-the-Lake.
Ms April Petrie, Manager, Heritage & Educational Services

Niagara Falls: **Movieland Wax Museum of the Stars**
4848 Clifton Hill, Niagara Falls, ON L2G 3N4
Tel: 905-358-3061
info@cliftonhill.com
www.cliftonhill.com/attractions/movieland-wax-museum-stars
Open year round

Niagara Falls: **Niagara Falls History Museum**
5810 Ferry St., Niagara Falls, ON L2G 1S9
Tel: 905-358-5082; Fax: 905-358-0920
llmuseum@niagarafalls.ca
www.niagarafallsmuseum.ca/lundyslanehistoricalm useum.html
Year Founded: 1961 The 1874 museum was originally located on Drummond Rd., the site of the Battle of Lundy's Lane, July 25, 1814, but was moved to its present site in 1970. Exhibits include a significant collection of War of 1812 artifacts, as well as historic prints of Niagara Falls. The Museum also houses a variety of artifacts relating to all aspects of the founding and development of the City of Niagara Falls.
Mr. Gordon West, Board Chair
Kathleen Powell, Manager

Niagara Falls: **Old Fort Erie**
c/o Hall Administrative Office, Niagara Parks Commission, PO Box 150, 7400 Portage Rd. South, Niagara Falls, ON L2E 6T2
Tel: 905-871-0540
www.niagaraparks.com/old-fort-erie
Other contact information: Niagara Parks Commission Phone: 905-356-2241
Collection of military equipment housed in a reconstructed fort. Open May-Oct.

Niagara Falls: **Ripley's Believe It or Not! Museum**
4960 Clifton Hill, Niagara Falls, ON L2G 3N4
Tel: 905-356-2238; Fax: 905-374-7345
www.ripleysniagara.com
Year Founded: 1963 Ripley's Believe It or Not! in Niagara Falls presents strange & bizarre exhibits. The museum is open year-round.
Tim Parker, General Manager

Niagara Falls: **Willoughby Historical Museum**
9935 Niagara Pkwy., Niagara Falls, ON L2E 6S6
Tel: 905-295-4036; Fax: 905-295-4036
whmuseum@niagarafalls.ca
www.niagarafallsmuseum.ca/willoughby.html
The Willoughby Historical Museum collects, preserves, interprets, & displays items related to Ontario's former Township of Willoughby, the Village of Chippawa, & the surrounding region. Examples of artifacts include household objects, school materials, toys, telephones, & a functioning magneto switchboard. The museum is open year-round. Tours & research can be arranged by phoning the museum.

Niagara-on-the-Lake: **Niagara Apothecary**
5 Queen St., Niagara-on-the-Lake, ON L0S 1J0
Tel: 905-468-3845
www.niagaraapothecary.ca
The Niagara Apothecary depicts an 1869 pharmacy. Artifacts include the Harvey bottles & jars, which were imported from Britain around 1830, mortars & pestles, a 19th century leech jar, & an early cash register.

Niagara-on-the-Lake: **Niagara Fire Museum**
PO Box 498, Niagara-on-the-Lake, ON L0S 1J0
Tel: 905-468-7279
Fire-fighting equipment dating back 140 years

Niagara-on-the-Lake: **Niagara Historical Society & Museum**
Also known as: **Niagara Historical Museum**
PO Box 208, 43 Castlereagh St., Niagara-on-the-Lake, ON L0S 1J0
Tel: 905-468-3912; Fax: 905-468-1728
contact@niagarahistorical.museum
www.niagarahistorical.museum
Year Founded: 1895 Ontario's first purpose-built museum; artifacts from Niagara's social & military history
Clark Bernat, Managing Director
Amy Klassen, Administrator, Niagara Historical Society

Nipigon: **Nipigon Museum**
PO Box 208, 40 Front St., Nipigon, ON P0T 2J0
Tel: 807-887-0356
nipigonmuseumtheblog.blogspot.ca
www.facebook.com/128774150545422

Artifacts relating to local lumbering & fur trading; rocks & minerals; bottles
Betty Brill, Curator

Nipissing: Nipissing Township Museum
General Delivery, Nipissing, ON P0H 1W0
Tel: 705-724-2938; Fax: 705-724-5385
admin@nipissingtownship.com
www.nipissingtownship.com
Housed in a former Anglican church built in late 1800s of logs; displays mostly of tools, clothing & photos pertaining to the families who first settled in the area
Joe Steele, Curator

North Bay: @DiscoveryNorthBayMuseum
Parent: Heritage North Bay
100 Ferguson St., North Bay, ON P1B 1W8
Tel: 705-476-2323
a
discoverynorthbay.weebly.com
twitter.com/discoverynbay
10,000 domestic & business objects related to settling & development of local region; open year round
Nicole Mattenley, Coordinator,
nicole.mattenley@heritagenorthbay.com

North Bay: Callander Bay Heritage Museum
PO Box 100, 107 Lansdowne St. East, North Bay, ON P0H 1H0
Tel: 705-752-2282; Fax: 705-752-3116
museum@callander.ca
www.mycallander.ca/museum
The Callander Bay Heritage Museum was the home & office of Dr. Allan R. Dafoe from 1914 to 1943. Dr. Dafoe was the doctor for the Dionne Quintuplets. The museum contains exhibits about the doctor & the quintuplets. The Alex Dufresne Gallery features the work of local artists. The museum also houses local genealogical sources & historical records for research.
Tom Fletcher, Chair

North Bay: Canadian Forces Museum of Aerospace Defence
Canadian Forces Base North Bay, 22 Wing, Hornell Heights, North Bay, ON P0H 1P0
Tel: 705-494-2011; Fax: 705-494-6222
aerospace.defence@live.ca
www.aerospacedefence.ca

North Bay: Dionne Quints Museum
c/o North Bay & District Chamber of Commerce, 1375 Seymour St., North Bay, ON P1B 9V6
Tel: 705-472-8480; Fax: 705-472-8027
Toll-Free: 888-249-8998
nbcc@northbaychamber.com
www.northbaychamber.com
The Quints Museum is a not for profit institution dedicated to the Dionne Quintuplets; artifacts from the Quints's early days and their growing up years; baby buggies, baby dresses, books, newspaper and magazine articles, artisitic reproductions, postcards. Located at Hwys 11 and 17 at Seymour Street in North Bay.
Amy Bennett, Director

North Buxton: Buxton National Historic Site & Museum
21975 A.D. Shadd Rd., North Buxton, ON N0P 1Y0
Tel: 519-352-4799; Fax: 519-352-8561
buxton@ciaccess.com
www.buxtonmuseum.com
Year Founded: 1967 The site is a memorial to the Elgin Settlement, which was the last stop on the Underground Railroad for many fugitives of the American system of slavery in the pre-Civil War years. The Raleigh (Buxton) Schoolhouse of 1861 & a settlement cabin from 1854 are now part of the museum. The museum preserves the artifacts of the original settlers of the Elgin Settlement & their descendants.
Shannon Prince, Curator

Norwich: The Norwich & District Museum & Archives
89 Stover St. North, RR#3, Norwich, ON N0J 1P0
Tel: 519-863-3101; Fax: 519-863-2343
norwichdhs@execulink.com
www.ocl.net/projects/norwich_historical/museum/
1889 Quaker Meeting House; archives & genealogical library
Janet Hilliker, Archivist
Kerrie Gill, Curator

Oakville: Canadian Golf Hall of Fame & Museum (CGHF)
Glen Abbey Golf Club, 1333 Dorval Dr., Oakville, ON L6J 4Z3
Tel: 905-849-9700
cghf@rcga.org
www.rcga.org
Year Founded: 1971 Located at Glen Abbey, the Canadian Golf Hall of Fame & Museum tells the history of golf in Canada. The Hall of Fame honours amateur & professional golfers & builders of the sport, who have made extraordinary contributions to the game of golf in Canada. The archives & library collects photographs & documents, as well as golf publications about the game, golf courses & golfers. Staff are available to assist with research. The museum also arranges travelling exhibitions. The Canadian Golf Hall of Fame & Museum is open year round.
Karen Hewson, Director, CGHF, & Executive Director, Royal Canadian Golf Association Foundation, 1-800-263-0009, khewson@rcga.org
Meggan Gardner, Curator, mgardner@rcga.org
Jordan Diacur, Museum Assistant, jdiacur@rcga.org

Oakville: Oakville Museum at Erchless Estate
8 Navy St., Oakville, ON L6J 2Y5
Tel: 905-338-4400; Fax: 905-815-5973
www.oakvillemuseum.com
The Oakville Museum at Erchless Estate features the following historical buildings: Erchless Estate (c. 1858), The Custom House & Toronto Bank (c. 1856), & The Old Post Office (c. 1835). The Thomas Museum is operated by the Oakville Historical Society.
Claire Loughheed, Senior Manager, Culture Services, cloughheed@oakville.ca
Bill Nesbitt, Museum Supervisor, bnesbitt@oakville.ca
Carolyn Cross, Curator, Collections, ccross@oakville.ca
Susan Crane, Officer, Learning & Community Development, scrane@oakville.ca
Julie Hawryszko, Mueum Programmer, Public Programs, jhawryszko@oakville.ca
Preeya Nayee, Mueum Programmer, Education Programs, pnayee@oakville.ca

Odessa: Historic Babcock Mill
100 Bridge St., Odessa, ON K0H 2H0
Tel: 613-386-7351; Fax: 613-386-3833
clawson@loyalist.ca
Restored, fully operational water-powered 1856 mill
Patrick Beyer, Contact

Ohsweken: Chiefswood National Historic Site
Also known as: Pauline Johnson House
PO Box 640, Ohsweken, ON N0A 1M0
Tel: 519-752-5005; Fax: 519-752-9578
chiefswood@execulink.com
www.chiefswood.com
The site is the location of the Chiefswood Museum, birthplace and childhood home of poet Emily Pauline Johnson (Tekahionwake); educational programming; tours; gift shop; "The Homing Bee" newsletter. Open Tues. through Sunday, 10:00-3:00, May-Oct. Open by appointment Oct.-May.
Paul Whitlow, Curator, Chiefswood Museum

Oil Springs: Oil Museum of Canada
PO Box 16, 2423 Kelly Rd., Oil Springs, ON N0N 1P0
Tel: 519-834-2840; Fax: 519-834-2840
oil.museum@county-lambton.on.ca
www.lambtononline.com/oil_museum
Situated in Oil Springs, Ontario, The Oil Museum of Canada preserves the site of the first commercial oil well in North America. Visitors learn the story of Canadian oil pioneers, through petroleum industry artifacts, working exhibits, & photographs. Visitors can also see original oil wells, which continue to produce oil.
Connie Bell, Supervisor

Orillia: Stephen Leacock Museum
PO Box 625, 50 Museum Dr., Orillia, ON L3V 6K5
Tel: 705-329-1908; Fax: 705-326-5578
www.leacockmuseum.com
www.facebook.com/104044192964809
Jenny Martynyshyn, Administrative Coordinator, 705-329-1908

Oshawa: Canadian Automotive Museum
99 Simcoe St. South, Oshawa, ON L1G 4G7
Tel: 905-576-1222
camuseum@bellnet.ca
www.oshawa.ca/tourism/can_mus.asp
Year Founded: 1961 The Canadian Automotive Museum depicts the history & future plans of the Canadian automotive industry. More than sixty vehicles, dating from 1898 to 1981 are on display. Items related to the era of the vehicles are also displayed.

Oshawa: Ontario Regiment (RCAC) Museum
Col. R.S. McLaughlin Armoury, 53 Simcoe St. North, Oshawa, ON L1G 4R9
Tel: 905-721-4000; Fax: 905-434-1328
info@ontrmuseum.ca
www.ontrmuseum.ca
L.Col. (Ret'd) Leo Morin, President C.D., president@ontrmuseum.ca
Earl Wotten, Curator, president@ontrmuseum.ca

Oshawa: Oshawa Sydenham Museum
1450 Simcoe St. South, Oshawa, ON L1H 8S8
Tel: 905-436-7624
Henry House c1849; Robinson House c1846; Guy House c1835

Oshawa: Parkwood National Historic Site, The R.S. McLaughlin Estate
270 Simcoe St. North, Oshawa, ON L1G 4T5
Tel: 905-433-4311
info@parkwoodestate.com
www.parkwoodestate.com
Built between 1915 & 1917, Parkwood was the grand estate of R. Samuel McLaughlin, who was the founder of General Motors of Canada. The McLaughlin family lived at the home from 1917 to 1972. Today, it is furnished to reflect the 1920s & 1930s. The National Historic Site is open year-round.

Ottawa: The Billings Estate National Historical Site / Lieu historique national du domaine Billings
2100 Cabot St., Ottawa, ON K1H 6K1
Tel: 613-247-4830; Fax: 613-247-4832
museums@ottawa.ca
www.ottawa.ca/museums;
www.friendsofbillingsestatemuseum.org
Home & property of Braddish & Lamira Billings, two of Ottawa's earliest settlers, c. 1828; exhibits highlight 5 generations of family & community history
Anik Després, Education Officer
Brahm Lewandowski, Education Officer

Ottawa: Bytown Museum / Musée Bytown
PO Box 523 B, Ottawa, ON K1P 5P6
Tel: 613-234-4570; Fax: 613-234-4846
program@storm.ca (Appointments)
www.bytownmuseum.com
Bytown Museum is situated in the oldest stone building in Ottawa, which was a treasury & storehouse during the construction of the Rideau Canal. Within the museum, the history of Bytown & the nation's capital is traced. The museum is open from the beginning of April to the end of November, & during March Break. From December to March, the museum is open by appointment only.
Mike Steinhauer, Director, mikesteinhauer@bytownmuseum.ca

Ottawa: Cameron Highlanders of Ottawa Regimental Museum
Cartier Sq. Drill Hall, 2 Queen Elizabeth Dr., Ottawa, ON K1A 0K2
www.camerons.ca/Org_Museum.html
The Regimental Museum contains memorabilia of the Cameron Highlanders of Ottawa. It is open one evening each week.

Ottawa: Canada Agriculture Museum / Musée de l'agriculture du Canada
Prince of Wales Dr., PO Box 9724 T, Ottawa, ON K1G 5A3
Tel: 613-991-3044; Fax: 613-993-7923
Toll-Free: 866-442-4416
www.agriculture.technomuses.ca
Other contact information: TTY: 613-991-9207; Phone, Media: 613-996-7812
The Canada Agriculture Museum is a demonstration farm & research station, which features animal barns, the Dominion Arboretum, ornamental gardens, & special exhibitions.
David Sutin, Manager, Communications & Marketing, 613-996-7812, dsutin@technomuses.ca

Ottawa: The Canadian Museum of Scouting
1345 Baseline Rd., Ottawa, ON K2C 0A7
Tel: 613-224-5131; Fax: 613-224-3571
mailbox@scouts.caca
www.scouts.ca
Year Founded: 1907 Scouting artifacts and historical memorobilia (Canada/UK/World); Open by appointment only
Robert Stewart, Exec. Commissioner & CEO, Scouts Canada
Stephen Kant, Chief Commissioner & Chair of the Board
Gary Boutilier, Director, Financial Services
John Singleton, Vice-President, Finance, Board of Governors
Lisa Nowlan, Director, Communication Services

Ottawa: Canadian Ski Museum & Canadian Ski Hall of Fame (CSMus) / Musée canadien du ski et Temple de la renommée du ski canad
#9, 2420 Bank St., Ottawa, ON K1Z 8S1
Tel: 613-422-1288
halloffame@magma.ca
www.skimuseum.ca
The Canadian Ski Museum & Canadian Ski Hall of Fame preserves Canadian skiing history & celebrates Canadian skiing & snowboarding traditions & achievements. The Hall of Fame honours Canada's accomplished skiers, snowboarders, coaches, officials, & builders of the sport.
Ivo Krupka, Chair
Walter Boyce, Director, Fundraising
Trevor Klotz, Director, Legal
Don Runge, Director, Publications
Wendy Statham, Treasurer

Ottawa: **The Canadian Wildlife & Wilderness Art Museum (CWWAM) / Musée canadien d'art naturaliste**
PO Box 98 B, Ottawa, ON K1P 6C3
Tel: 613-237-1581
Established by the Canadian Academy of Wilderness Artists (CAWA) "Hall of Fame" Art Foundation; 9,500 artifacts, drawings, prints, lithographs, carvings, sculpture & paintings. Coupled with major Canadian artists from the present and the past: Robert Bateman, Glen Loates, Ely Kish, Neil Blackwell, Norval Morriseau, A.J. Casson, Bernard Loates & many more; are several important American & European artists including Frederic Remington, Charles Marion Russell, Georgia O'Keefe, Eanger Irving Couse, Albert Bierstadt, Manfred Schatz & many more; some pieces are privately held & are on loan
Maria Amati, Executive Director
Gary Slimon, Director

Ottawa: **Governor General's Foot Guards Museum**
Drill Hall, Cartier Sq., Ottawa, ON K1A 0K2
Tel: 613-990-0620
elane22@rogers.com
www.ggfg.ottawa.on.ca
Regimental museum; brief history of regiment from 1872 to present by way of artifacts
Martin J. Lane, Curator CD

Ottawa: **J.H. Naismith Museum & Hall of Fame**
c/o Dr. James Naismith Foundation, 2729 Draper Ave., Ottawa, ON K2H 7A1
Tel: 613-256-3610
www.naismithmuseum.com
Artifacts related to life of Dr. James Naismith, originator of game of basketball; Canadian Basketball Hall of Fame exhibits & archives

Ottawa: **Laurier House National Historic Site**
335 Laurier Ave. East, Ottawa, ON K1N 6R4
Tel: 613-992-8142
laurier-house@pc.gc.ca
www.pc.gc.ca/lhn-nhs/on/laurier/index.aspx
Residence of Sir Wilfrid Laurier & the Right Honourtable William Lyon MacKenzie King, built in 1878

Ottawa: **Mackenzie King Estate / Domaine Mackenzie-King**
National Capital Commission, #202, 40 Elgin St., Ottawa, ON K1P 1C7
Tel: 819-827-2020Toll-Free: 800-465-1867
info@ncc-ccn.ca
www.canadascapital.gc.ca/places-to-visit/mackenzie-king- estate
Other contact information: TTY: 1-866-661-3530
Located in Gatineau Park; open daily from mid-May to the end of Oct.

Owen Sound: **Billy Bishop Home & Museum**
948 - 3rd Ave. West, Owen Sound, ON N4K 4P6
Tel: 519-371-0031
info@billybishop.org
www.billybishop.org
twitter.com/osmuseums
www.facebook.com/BillyBishop HomeMuseum
Year Founded: 1987 The museum, housed in the former home of Air Marshal William Avery Bishop, serves to preserve Canada's aviation history. Hours of Operation: Regular, Tu-F 11:00-5:00, Sa & Su 12:00-5:00; May-Oct., M-Sa 10:00-5:00, Su 12:00-5:00; Holidays 12:00-4:00.

Owen Sound: **Grey Roots Museum & Archives**
102599 Grey Rd. 18, RR#4, Owen Sound, ON N4K 5N6
Tel: 519-376-3690; Fax: 519-376-4654
Toll-Free: 877-473-9766
info@greyroots.com
www.greyroots.com
Collects, preserves, restores, documents, interprets & displays the material culture of Grey County & the city of Owen Sound, c. 1815 - present; research, interpretive programs, tours; gift shop
Brian Manser, Manager, brian.manser@greyroots.com

Parry Sound: **West Parry Sound District Museum (WPSDM)**
Also known as: **Museum on Tower Hill**
PO Box 337, 17 George St., Parry Sound, ON P2A 2X4
Tel: 705-746-5365; Fax: 705-746-8775
info@wpsdm.com
www.wpsdm.com
Year Founded: 1983 Situated in Tower Hill Park, the West Parry Sound District Museum displays items related to the First Nations, settlement, logging, shipping, agriculture, recreation, & natural history. The museum is open year-round.
Darcy Yanni, Museum Director, darcy@wpsdm.com
Tanya Bolwerk, Bookkeeper, accounting@wpsdm.com

Pelee Island: **Pelee Island Heritage Centre**
1073 West Shore Rd., Pelee Island, ON N0R 1M0
Tel: 519-724-2291
curator@peleeislandmuseum.ca
www.peleeislandmuseum.ca
Rare Flora & fauna exhibits; early navigation displays; local shipwreck information

Pembroke: **1st Air Defence Regiment (Lanark & Renfrew Scottish Regiment) Royal Canadian Artillery Museum**
177 Victoria St., Pembroke, ON K8A 4K2
Tel: 613-588-6166Toll-Free: 613-635-4667
rwclauson@cogeco.ca
Free admission; open year round, by appointment only.

Pembroke: **Champlain Trail Museum & Pioneer Village**
PO Box 985, 1032 Pembroke St. East, Pembroke, ON K8A 7M5
Tel: 613-735-0517; Fax: 613-629-5067
pembrokemuseum@nrtco.net
www.champlaintrailmuseum.com
Economic, political & social history of upper Ottawa Valley & Renfrew County; archival & genealogical material
Tony Cowan, Manager

Penetanguishene: **Discovery Harbour / Havre de la Découverte**
Ministry of Tourism, 93 Jury Dr., Penetanguishene, ON L9M 1G1
Tel: 705-549-8064; Fax: 705-549-4858
Toll-Free: 705-526-7697
hhp@hhp.on.ca
www.discoveryharbour.on.ca
Ontario's leading Marine Heritage Site; orginally built as a military base with its roots tracing back to the War of 1812. Tours, interactive daily activies in the summer. Open weekdays late-May to July 1; open daily July 1 to Labour Day weekend
Jan Gray, General Manager

Penetanguishene: **Penetanguishene Centennial Museum & Archives**
13 Burke St., Penetanguishene, ON L9M 1C1
Tel: 705-549-2150; Fax: 705-549-7542
info@pencenmuseum.com
www.pencenmuseum.com
www.facebook.com/1787791345 28
Other contact information: E-mail, Genealogy & History Research Ctr.: genealogy@pencenmuseum.com
Penetanguishene's museum is housed in the former C. Beck Lumber Office & General Store which was built in 1875. The location also features a Genealogy & History Research Center & Archives, which houses the the Georgian Bay Heritage League Collection with more than 500 genealogical files & local history books. Penetanguishene Centennial Museum & Archives is open year-round.
Nicole Jackson, Curator, njackson@pencenmuseum.com
Pam Tessier, Coordinator, Research, ptessier@pencenmuseum.com
Janice Gadsdon, Curatorial Assistant, jgadsdon@pencenmuseum.com

Perth: **The Perth Museum**
Also known as: **Matheson House**
11 Gore St. East, Perth, ON K7H 1H9
Tel: 613-267-1947; Fax: 613-267-5635
perthmuseum@town.perth.on.ca
www.perthcanada.com
1840 stone home of Senator Matheson; open year round; National Historic Site; 2 galleries; historic gardens
Karen Rennie, Curator

Petawawa: **Canadian Airborne Forces Museum / Musée des Forces aéroportées canadiennes**
Canadian Forces Base Petawawa, PO Box 9999 Main, 63 Colborne Rd., Petawawa, ON K8H 2X3
Tel: 613-588-6238
info@petawawamuseums.com
www.petawawamuseums.com
Other contact information: E-mail, Volunteer Coordinator: volunteers@petawawamuseums.com
The Canadian Airborne Forces Museum preserves & honours the memory of airborne forces that served Canada since World War II. Their history is presented through historical artifacts, dioramas, videos, & a large screen mini-theatre. The museum is a member of the following organizations: the Organization of Military Museums of Canada, the Canadian Museums Association, the Ontario Museums Association, the Ottawa Valley Tourist Association, & the Renfrew County Museums Network. The Canadian Airborne Forces Museum is open year-round.
Anne Lindsay, Museologist, Lindsay.A@forces.gc.ca
Ainsley Greenfield, Manager, Collections

Petawawa: **Canadian Forces Base Petawawa Military Museum**
Canadian Forces Base Petawawa, PO Box 9999 Main, 63 Colborne Rd., Petawawa, ON K8H 2X3
Tel: 613-588-6238
info@petawawamuseums.com
www.petawawamuseums.com
Other contact information: E-mail, Volunteer Coordinator: volunteers@petawawamuseums.com
The Canadian Forces Base Petawawa Military Museum collects, preserves, & interprets items related to the history of individuals & units of CFB Petawawa since 1905. Museum staff also assist with research requests.
Anne Lindsay, Museologist, Lindsay.A@forces.gc.ca
Ainsley Greenfield, Manager, Collections

Peterborough: **The Canadian Canoe Museum**
910 Monaghan Rd., Peterborough, ON K9J 5K4
Tel: 705-748-9153Toll-Free: 866-342-2663
www.canoemuseum.ca
Social Media: canoemuseum.wordpress.com
twitter.com/CndnCanoeMuseum
www.facebook.com/CndnCanoeMuseum
Collection of over 600 canoes & kayaks, plus related artifacts; open year round

Peterborough: **Hope Water-Powered Saw Mill**
Also known as: **Hope Mill**
c/o Otonabee Region Conservation Authority, 250 Milroy Dr., Peterborough, ON K9H 7M9
Tel: 705-745-5791; Fax: 705-745-7488
otonabeeca@otonabee.com
www.otonabee.com/orcf/news/events/hope_mill.htm
www.facebook.com/pages/Otonabee-Conservation/1048193862 17442
Built in 1835 by Scottish immigrant Squire William Lang, the Otonabee Conservation Authority purchased the mill from his great grandson in 1966. The saw-powered Hope Mill has been restored to its original charm and is fully functional. Demonstrations and tours are offered. A collection of 19th-century carpentry tools, as well as larger pieces of equipment (lathe, planer, drill-press), are on exhibit. The mill is located at 3414 Hope Mill Rd. on the banks of the Indian River in Lang, ON.
Richard Hunter, CAO
John Williams, Coordinator, Conservation Lands

Peterborough: **Hutchison House Museum**
Parent: **Peterborough Historical Society**
270 Brock St., Peterborough, ON K9H 2P9
Tel: 705-743-9710
info@hutchisonhouse.ca
www.hutchisonhouse.ca
www.facebook.com/120961071272046
Living history museum owned & operated by the Peterborough Historical Society open to all interested in the history of Upper Canada in the 1800s
Gale Fewings, Curator

Peterborough: **Lang Pioneer Village**
c/o County of Peterborough, Attn: Lang Pioneer Village Museum, 470 Water St., Peterborough, ON K9H 3M3
Tel: 705-295-6694; Fax: 705-295-6644
Toll-Free: 866-289-5264
info@langpioneervillage.ca
langpioneervillage.ca
Year Founded: 1967 Living history museum from 1800-1900; over 20 restored buildings with costumed interpreters; open Mon.-Fri. May 15-June 30, Sat.-Fri. July 1 to Labour Day; call or see website for hours of operation, admission prices & list of special events
Joe Corrigan, Manager, jcorrigan@county.peterborough.on.ca

Peterborough: **Lang Water Powered Grist Mill**
Also known as: **Lang Mill**
c/o Otonabee Region Conservation Authority, 250 Milroy Dr., Peterborough, ON K9H 7M9
Tel: 705-745-5791; Fax: 705-745-7488
otonabeeca@otonabee.com
www.otonabee.com
www.facebook.com/104819386217 442
Fully operational water-powered grist mill located on the west bank of the Indian River at Lang Pioneer Village (Otonabee-South Monaghan Township-County of Peterborough).

Allan K. Seabrooke, CAO/Secretary-Treasurer M.Sc., AMCT, Otonabee Conservation, aseabrooke@otonabee.com
John Williams, Manager, Conservation Lands & Resources, jwilliams@otonabee.com

Peterborough: **Peterborough Museum & Archives**
Ashburnham Memorial Park, PO Box 143, Peterborough, ON K9J 6Y5
Tel: 705-743-5180; Fax: 705-743-2614
administration@peterboroughmuseumandarchives.ca
www.peterboroughmuseuman darchives.ca
www.facebook.com/pages/Peterborough-Museum-Archives/1126 083 10308
Other contact information: E-mail, Artifacts: collections@peterboroughmuseumandarchives.ca
The heritage & culture of Peterborough & the surrounding area is preserved & presented at Peterborough Museum & Archives. The Museum houses a variety of artifacts, such as archaeological collections, technological artifacts, & military collections. The Archives holds over 2,000 fonds, including personal letters, maps, photographs, association records, early Peterborough Examiner newspapers, & the early records of Peterborough County Court. The Museum & Archives is open year-round. Appointments are required to visit the Archives (archives@peterboroughmuseumandarchives.ca).
Jon Oldham, Media Contact, joldham@peterborough.ca

Peterborough: **Trent-Severn Waterway National Historic Site of Canada, Lock 21 - Peterborough Lift Lock**
PO Box 567, Peterborough, ON K9J 6Z6
Tel: 705-750-4900; Fax: 705-742-9644
Toll-Free: 888-773-8888
Ont.Trentsevern@pc.gc.ca
www.pc.gc.ca/eng/lhn-nhs/on/t rentsevern/visit/visit6/lock21.aspx
Other contact information: Phone, Group Tours: 705-750-4950; Teletypewriter (TTY): 705-750-4949
Opened in 1904, the Peterborough Lift Lock is the highest hydraulic lift lock in the world. Located next to Lock 21 is the Peterborough Lift Lock Visitor Centre, which contains exhibits & films. The Peterborough Lift Lock Visitor Centre is open during the navigation season.
Peter Frood, Field Unit Superintendent, Parks Canada Central Ontario Field Unit
Sara Atkins, Manager, External Relations & Communications, Parks Canada Central Ontario Field Unit

Petrolia: **Petrolia Discovery**
PO Box 1480, Petrolia, ON N0N 1R0
Tel: 519-882-0897; Fax: 519-882-4209
petdisc@xcelco.on.ca
www.petroliadiscovery.com
Petrolia Discovery depicts the history of the pioneer oil men of Lambton County, Ontario. The museum is located at an oilfield which was established in the 1870s. This 19th century oilfield has been restored & is still operational. Petrolia Discovery is open from Victoria Day until Labour Day. School & educational tours may be arranged after the summer season.

Pickering: **Pickering Museum Village**
c/o City of Pickering, One The Esplanade, Pickering, ON L1V 6K7
Tel: 905-683-8401; Fax: 905-686-4079
museum@city.pickering.on.ca
www.pickering.ca/en/museum.asp
Social Media: www.youtube.com/user/PickeringMuse
twitter.com/pickeringmuse
www.faceb ook.com/pickeringmuse
Located at 2365 Concession Road #6 in Pickering, Ontario, the Pickering Museum Village features fifteen restored heritage buildings, including a schoolhouse, churches, a blacksmith shop, houses, & barns.

Picton: **Macaulay Heritage Park**
Also known as: **Prince Edward County Museum**
PO Box 2150, 35 Church St., Picton, ON K0K 2T0
Tel: 613-476-3833; Fax: 613-476-9835
macmuseum@pecounty.on.ca
www.pec.on.ca/macaulay
Year Founded: 1973 The site encompasses the 1830 Macaulay House, home of the Rev. William Macaulay, carriage house, heritage gardens & former St. Mary Magdalene Church and cemetary; open Tues.-Sun. 1-4:30 from long weekend in May to Thanksgiving; 10-4:30 (July & Aug.)
Ms Jennifer Lyons, Head Curator, 613-476-2148 ext 426, museums@pecounty.on.ca
Elizabeth Hunter, Museum Manager

Picton: **Rose House Museum**
c/o Recreation, Parks & Culture, Prince Edward County, 332 Main St., Picton, ON K0K 2T0
Tel: 613-476-2148; Fax: 613-476-9835
museums@pecounty.on.ca
www.pecounty.on.ca
www.facebook.com/museumspec
1804 original homestead; home to five generations of the Rose family; living history depicting life in 1800s; guided tours
Jennifer Lyons, Head Curator

Port Carling: **Muskoka Lakes Museum**
PO Box 432, 100 Joseph St., Port Carling, ON P0B 1J0
Tel: 705-765-5367
info@mlmuseum.com
www.mlmuseum.com
Log home from 1875; artifacts of early settlers & lumber industry; displays related to boat building & water transportation; archives of Muskoka region; open May 19 - Thanksgiving
Doug Smith, Director/Curator

Port Colborne: **Port Colborne Historical & Marine Museum**
PO Box 572, 280 King St., Port Colborne, ON L3K 5X8
Tel: 905-834-7604; Fax: 905-834-6198
museum@portcolborne.ca
www.portcolborne.ca/page/museum
The Port Colborne Historical & Marine Museum depicts the history of Port Colborne & the Welland Canala. The museum features heritage buildings, such as an 1869 home & carriage house, a log schoolhouse, & an 1850 marine blacksmith shop. A reproduction of the parapet of Port Colborne's Lighthouse contains ship models & marine artifacts. The museum, heritage village, & gift shop are open from May to December.
Stephanie Powell Baswick, Director & Curator
Lynn van Dillen, Assistant Curator, lynnvandillen@portcolborne.ca
Glenn Walker, Technician, Heritage Research, archives@portcolborne.ca

Port Dover: **Port Dover Harbour Museum**
PO Box 1298, 44 Harbour St., Port Dover, ON N0A 1N0
Tel: 519-583-2660
portdover.museum@norfolkcounty.ca
www.norfolkcounty.ca
The Port Dover Harbour Museum tells the story of Port Dover's fishing industry, ship building, Lake Erie shipwrecks, rum running, & other parts of lakeside life. The museum is open year round.

Port Hope: **Canadian Fire Fighters Museum**
PO Box 325, 95 Mill St. South, Port Hope, ON L1A 3W3
Tel: 905-885-8985; Fax: 905-885-8985
burgin@firemuseumcanada.com
www.firemuseumcanada.com
www.facebook.com/ FireMuseumCanada
Year Founded: 1985 The museum's collection represents the history of firefighting in Canada, including vehicles, gear, fire alarms, & photos. Open daily May-Oct., 10:00-4:00.

Port Hope: **Dorothy's House Museum (EDHS)**
Also known as: **East Durham Historical Society**
PO Box 116, 3632 Ganaraska Rd., Port Hope, ON L1A 3V9
Tel: 905-797-2247
info@porthopehistorical.ca
www.porthopehistorical.ca
Artifacts from the Port Hope & Hope Township area; house built around 1869; barn; driveshed; open May - Aug.
Ron Getz, President

Port Perry: **Scugog Shores Historical Museum**
Also known as: **Scugog Shores Museum Village & Archives**
16210 Island Rd., Port Perry, ON L9L 1B4
Tel: 905-985-3589; Fax: 905-985-3492
cbelfry@scugogshoresmuseum.com
www.scugogshoresmuseum.com
Historic village, comprising a log cabin, Lee House, blacksmith & woodright shops, print shop, school, church, barns, heritage flower, herb & dye plant gardens, & Ojibway Heritage Interpretive Lands; museum archives houses genealogical resources; special events & programming, themed artifact kits for rent, tours, building rentals
Craig Belfry, Manager, Culture & Heritage, Township of Scucog

Port Rowan: **Backus Heritage Conservation Area & Village (BHCA)**
c/o Long Point Region Conservation Authority, RR#1, Port Rowan, ON N0E 1M0
Tel: 519-586-2201
www.lprca.on.ca
Other contact information: Phone, Administration Office: 519-428-4623
Owned & operated by the Long Point Region Conservation Authority, the Backus Heritage Conservation Area features a conservation education centre & a heritage village. The village consists of restored & reconstructed buildings, including the John C. Backhouse Mill, the Teeterville Baptist Church, the Vittoria Carriage Shop, & the Forbes Barn. The history of the Long Point Region Watershed is depicted through exhibits & artifacts.

Prescott: **Fort Wellington National Historic Site of Canada**
PO Box 479, Prescott, ON K0E 1T0
Tel: 613-925-2896; Fax: 613-925-1536
ont-wellington@pc.gc.ca
www.pc.gc.ca/eng/lhn-nhs/on/wellington/ne/ne3.as px
Built during the War of 1812, Fort Wellington defended the St. Lawrence River shipping route between Kingston & Montréal. It was rebuilt in 1838 to once again defend against possible attack by the United States. Today, the Visitor Centre at the site displays exhibits related to the War of 1812 & the Upper Canada Rebellion. The site is open from Victoria Day weekend to the end of September. During the off-season, groups of ten or more may make an appointment.

Prescott: **The Forwarders' Museum**
PO Box 2179, 201 Water St., Prescott, ON K0E 1T0
Tel: 613-925-1861; Fax: 613-925-4381
Toll-Free: 800-218-1131
tourism@prescott.ca
www.prescott.ca
Forwarding trade; St Lawrence River & local history; open June-Labour Day

Queenston: **Brock's Monument National Historic Site**
14184 Niagara Pkwy., Queenston, ON L0S 1P0
Tel: 905-262-4759; Fax: 905-468-7681
www.friendsoffortgeorge.ca
twitter.com/fofg
www.facebook.com/102031676 507960
A 185-foot-high monument to Major-General Sir Isaac Brock, situated on the Queenston Heights battlefield.

Red Lake: **Red Lake Regional Heritage Centre**
PO Box 64, 51A Hwy. 105, Red Lake, ON P0V 2M0
Tel: 807-727-3006
heritage@redlake.ca
www.redlakemuseum.com
www.facebook.com/154411087917525
At the Red Lake Regional Heritage Centre, visitors will discover Aboriginal, fur trade, gold mining, & immigration history. The centre also provides information about Woodland Caribou Park. The Red Lake Regional Heritage Centre is open year-round.
Tannis Innes, Chair
Michele Alderton, Director/Curator
Sara Cuthbertson, Assistant Curator

Renfrew: **McDougall Mill Museum**
Also known as: **Renfrew Museum**
PO Box 554, Arthur Ave., Renfrew, ON K7V 4B1
Tel: 613-432-2129
museum@renfrewmuseum.ca
www.renfrewmuseum.ca
Other contact information: Tel. (Off-season) 613/432-7015
Year Founded: 1969 Housed in a stone, 1855 grist mill built on the Bonnechere River by Hudson's Bay Company agent, John Lorne McDougall, the museum displays 3 floors of artifacts, including early appliances from Renfrew's industrial days. There are also exhibits of military articles, Victorian clothing and a wedding dress gallery. The museum is run by the Renfrew And District Historical And Museum Society.

Renfrew: **The NHA/NHL Birthplace Museum**
Also known as: **Birthplace of the NHA/NHL**
c/o Renfrew & Area Chamber of Commerce, 161 Raglan St. South, Renfrew, ON K7V 1R2
Tel: 613-432-7015
nhlmuseum@nhlbirthplace.ca
www.nhlbirthplace.ca/Museum.html
The museum details the history of the National Hockey Association & the National Hockey League, starting with the influence of hockey enthusiast & founder of the Town of Renfrew, M.J. O'Brien.
Jim Miller, Executive Director

Richards Landing: **Fort St. Joseph National Historic Site of Canada**
PO Box 220, Richards Landing, ON P0R 1J0
Tel: 705-246-2664; Fax: 705-246-1796
fortstjoseph-info@pc.gc.ca
www.pc.gc.ca/lhn-nhs/on/stjoseph/index_e.asp
Ruins of a fort erected after 1796 to serve as a fur trade centre; artifacts from excavation of site

Richards Landing: **St. Joseph Island Museum Complex**
Also known as: **St. Joseph Island Museum Village**
RR#2, Richards Landing, ON P0R 1J0
Tel: 705-246-2672
Six artifact buildings represent the pioneer era (1820-1880) & the settlement era after the Homestead Act of 1868; over 6,000 artifacts; farming, lumbering, maple syruping & early navigation displays; 2 schools, a church, a store, a barn, an 1880 log cabin & a general store
Pat Fleming, Curator
Micheline Yandeau, Chair

Richmond Hill: **Canadian Museum of Hindu Civilization (CMOHC)**
8640 Yonge St., Richmond Hill, ON L4C 6Z4
www.cmohc.com
The museum is the first of its kind in North America, celebrating Hinduism's contributions to philosophy, the arts, & science.
Shylee Someshwar, Chair

Dr. Budhendra Doobay, President
Avinash Persaud, Director

Ridgetown: **Ridge House Museum**
PO Box 550, 53 Erie St. South, Ridgetown, ON N0P 2C0
Tel: 519-674-2223; Fax: 519-674-3747
ckridgehouse@chatham-kent.on.ca
www.chatham-kent.ca/ridgehouse
Year Founded: 1975 The Ridge Hose Museum depicts the life of a middle class family in Ridgetown around 1875. Interactive tours & interpretive programs are provided.
Nicole Gignac, Curator

Ridgeway: **Fort Erie Historical Museum**
c/o Fort Erie Museum Board, PO Box 339, 402 Ridge Rd., Ridgeway, ON L0S 1N0
Tel: 905-894-5322; Fax: 905-894-6851
museum@forterie.on.ca
www.museum.forterie.ca/historical.html
Exhibits on archaelogy, genealogy, Fenian Raids, local history & archives; open year-round Sun.-Fri.; daily in July & Aug.
Jane Davies, Curator

Ridgeway: **Fort Erie Railroad Museum**
Fort Erie Museum Board, PO Box 339, 400 Central Ave., Ridgeway, ON L0S 1N0
Tel: 905-871-1412; Fax: 905-894-6851
museum@forterie.on.ca
Located on Central Ave.; includes Steam engine #6218, caboose & 2 train stations; open daily Victoria Day - Labour Day; open weekends until Thanksgiving
Jane Davies, Curator

Ridgeway: **Ridgeway Battlefield National Historic Site**
c/o Fort Erie Historical Museum, PO Box 339, 402 Ridge Rd., Ridgeway, ON L0S 1N0
Tel: 905-894-5322; Fax: 905-894-6851
museum@forterie.on.ca
www.museum.forterie.ca/battlefield.html
The Ridgeway Battlefield national historic site site marks the location where in 1866 Irish-American soldiers, known as Fenians, fought Canadian forces in an attempt to gain Ireland's independence of England. The Fort Erie Museum maintains the original cabin at the battle site, where visitors can see a visual account of the Battle of Ridgeway.

Rockton: **Westfield Heritage Village (WHV)**
1049 Kirkwall Rd., Rockton, ON L0R 1X0
Tel: 519-621-8851; Fax: 519-621-6897
Toll-Free: 800-883-0104
westfield@speedway.ca
www.westfieldheritage.ca
The Heritage Village presents more than thirty-five historical & reproduction buildings. The site also features Ontario's oldest log cabin & a T.H. & B. steam locomotive.

Rosemont: **Dufferin County Museum & Archives**
PO Box 120, 936029 Airport Rd., Rosemont, ON L0N 1R0
Tel: 705-435-1881; Fax: 705-435-9876
Toll-Free: 877-941-7787
info@dufferinmuseum.com
www.dufferinmuseum.com
Two log structures; CPR flagging station; historic church; changing exhibits; archives
Wayne Townsend, Director/Curator
Darrell Keenie, General Manager

St Catharines: **Morningstar Mill (Mountain Mills Museum)**
22 Cliff Rd., St Catharines, ON L2R 3W1
Tel: 905-688-6050
info@morningstarmill.ca
www.morningstarmill.ca
Year Founded: 1962 Museum site is made up of a number of buildings: the water-powered gristmill (built in 1872 & known as Morningstar Mill), the turbine shed, the millers house, the icehouse, sawmill and the barn which houses the blacksmith shop and carpentry shop. School tours are welcome. Admission by donation.
Tom Wilson, St. Catharines, Recreation & Community Services, 905-688-5601, Fax: 905-646-9262

St Catharines: **St. Catharines Museum**
PO Box 3012, 1932 Welland Canals Pkwy., St Catharines, ON L2R 7C2
Tel: 905-984-8880; Fax: 905-984-6910
Toll-Free: 800-355-134
museuminfo@stcatharines.ca
www.stcatharineslock3museum. ca
Year Founded: 1965 Major collection of artifact, archival & art material related to the history of St. Catharines & the Welland Canal; collections include Girl Guides, Fred Pattison Aviation Collection (BCATP), St. Lawrence Seaway, family papers, marine photographs, Ferranti-Packard & the DeCew Falls Waterworks Collection; guided tours; summer camps, edu-fun camps; guest speakers; tours & special events
Anne Crawford, Administrative Co-ordinator, acrawford@stcatharines.ca

St. George: **Adelaide Hunter Hoodless Homestead**
359 Blue Lake Rd., RR#1, St. George, ON N0E 1N0
Tel: 519-448-1130
adelaidehoodless@gmail.com
www.adelaidehoodless.ca
www.facebook.com/130185503729776
Birthplace of Adelaide Hunter Hoodless, an educational reformer, one of Canada's early feminists and a co-founder of a number of organizations promoting the cause of women's well-being, including: the Women's Institute, the Victorian Order of Nurses, the YWCA, & the National Council of Women. Hunter Hoodless was instrumental in establishing domestic science on the curriculum of Ontario schools, & wrote the first textbook to be used. Before her untimely death at the age of 53, she was engaged in the cause of promoting technical trades education for women. Her childhood home, built in 1830, is an example of mid-nineteenth century Ontario Neo Gothic style. The homestead property includes picnic facilities & grounds that can be rented for gatherings & other special occasions. Guided tours, & school programs available. Open year round.

St Jacobs: **The Maple Syrup Museum**
Also known as: **Maple Syrup Museum of Ontario**
Country Mill, PO Box 701, 1441 King St. North, St Jacobs, ON N0B 2N0
Tel: 519-664-1232; Fax: 519-669-4259
www.stjacobs.com
History of maple syrup production; artifacts; photographs
Albert Martin, Contact, 519-669-2423

St Marys: **Canadian Baseball Hall of Fame & Museum**
PO Box 1838, 140 Queen St., St Marys, ON N4X 1C2
Tel: 519-284-1838; Fax: 519-284-1234
Toll-Free: 877-250-2255
baseball@baseballhalloffame.ca
baseballhalloffame.ca
Social Media: www.youtube.com/user/CanadianHallofFame
twitter.com/CDNBaseballHOF
www.facebook.com/135326447763
Open May - Thanksgiving; displays include exclusive collection of Ferguson Jenkins memorabilia & artifacts of the Montreal Expos & Toronto Blue Jays
Scott Crawford, Director, Operations, scott@baseballhalloffame.ca

St Marys: **St Marys Museum**
PO Box 98, 177 Church St. South, St Marys, ON N4X 1A9
Tel: 519-284-3556; Fax: 519-284-2881
museum@town.stmarys.on.ca
www.stmarysmuseum.ca
Changing exhibits; seasonal activities; research facilities for genealogy & area history in 1850s limestone house
Mary Smith, Manager
Trisha McKibbin, Curator

St Thomas: **Elgin County Museum**
450 Sunset Dr., St Thomas, ON N5R 5V1
Tel: 519-631-1460; Fax: 519-631-9209
museum@elgin-county.on.ca
www.elgin.ca/ElginCounty/CulturalServices/Muse um
Year Founded: 1957 History of Elgin County; changing exhibits in gallery, workshops & special events
Mike Baker, Curator, mbaker@elgin-county.on.ca

St Thomas: **Elgin County Railway Museum**
225 Wellington St., St Thomas, ON N5R 2S6
Tel: 519-637-6284
thedispatcher@ecrm5700.org; tours@ecrm5700.org
ecrm5700.org
The museum seeks to preserve the heritage of the St. Thomas & Elgin County railroad, & to educate the public on the railroad's contributions to the community. Open May-Sept., Tu-Su 10:00-4:00; Sept.-May, Tu-Sa 12:00-4:00.
Ron Bareham, President
Dawn Miskelly, Manager

St Thomas: **The Elgin Military Museum**
30 Talbot St., St Thomas, ON N5P 1A3
Tel: 519-633-7641
curator@elginmilitarymuseum.ca
www.elginmilitarymuseum.ca
Information on veterans from Elgin County; archive collection with military documents & publications

Sault Ste Marie: **Canadian Bushplane Heritage Centre**
50 Pim St., Sault Ste Marie, ON P6A 3G4
Tel: 705-945-6242; Fax: 705-942-8947
Toll-Free: 877-287-4752
retail@bushplane.com
www.bushplane.com
Social Media:
www.youtube.com/watch?v=aDznJUco4oo&feature=related
twitter.com/BushplaneCentre
www.facebook.com/canadian.centre
The centre celebrates the heritage of bushplanes & forest fire protection in Canada through hands-on displays, including flight simulators. Open May-Oct., daily 9:00-6:00; daily 10:00-4:00 during the rest of the year.
Hugh MacDonald, President
Mike Delfre, Executive Director, mdelfre@bushplane.com
Todd Fleet, Curator

Sault Ste Marie: **Ermatinger-Clergue National Historic Site**
c/o Historic Sites Board, PO Box 580, 99 Foster Dr., Sault Ste Marie, ON P6A 5N1
Tel: 705-759-5443; Fax: 705-541-7023
old.stone.house@cityssm.on.ca
www.ermatingerclerguenationalhistoricsite. ca
1814 stone house: features historic crop gardens, recreated rooms, costumed interpreters, hands-on activities; Blockhouse: exhibits & period furnishings; open Mid-Apr. - Nov.
Kathryn Fisher, Curator

Sault Ste Marie: **St. Mary's River Marine Heritage Centre**
Also known as: **Museum Ship Norgoma**
Roberta Bondar Dock, PO Box 23099, Sault Ste Marie, ON P6A 6W6
Tel: 705-256-7447
norgoma@shaw.ca
www.norgoma.org
Other contact information: Seasonal Phone: 705-256-7447
An 188-foot passenger/cargo vessel built in 1950; open June - Oct.
Louis Muio, President

Sault Ste Marie: **Sault Ste Marie Canal National Historic Site**
1 Canal Dr., Sault Ste Marie, ON P6A 6W4
Tel: 705-941-6205; Fax: 705-941-6206
info-saultcanal@pc.gc.ca
www.parkscanada.gc.ca/sault
Operates a recreational lock between May & Oct. & offers school programming, guided tours & a large open space for the enjoyment of visitors (boat watching, nature trail, birdwatching, cycling, fishing)
Louise Robillard, Chief, Visitor Activities, louise.robillard@pc.gc.ca

Sault Ste Marie: **Sault Ste Marie Museum**
690 Queen St. East, Sault Ste Marie, ON P6A 2A4
Tel: 705-759-7278; Fax: 705-759-3058
heritage@saultmuseum.com
www.saultmuseum.com
Maintained by the Sault St. Marie & 49th Field Regiment R.C.A. Historical Society; the museum collects & preserves artifacts & archival material illustrating the history of Sault Ste Marie & area
Kim Forbes, Curator & Administrator

Selkirk: **Cottonwood Mansion Museum**
Parent: **Cottonwood Mansion Preservation Foundation**
PO Box 56, 740 Haldimand Rd. #3, Selkirk, ON N0A 1P0
Tel: 905-776-2538
cottonwoodmansion@gmail.com
www.cottonwoodmansion.ca
www.facebook.com/cottonwood.mansion
A restored Italianate-style mansion, circa 1870. Open May-Sept., W-Sa 11:00-4:00, Su 1:00-4:00, or by appointment.
Ken Schaus, President
Jill Walters-Klamer, Curator

Selkirk: **Wilson MacDonald Memorial School Museum**
3513 Rainham Rd., Selkirk, ON N0A 1P0
Tel: 905-776-3319; Fax: 905-776-0683
wmacdonald.museum@haldimandcounty.on.ca
www.haldimandcounty.on.ca
Wilson MacDonald Memorial School Museum presents the story of poet Wilson Pugsley MacDonald, rural education, & Selkirk, Ontario & its surrounding area. Archival research is available for a fee. The museum is open from mid March to mid December.
Dana B. Stavinga, Curator

Sharon: **Sharon Temple National Historic Site & Museum**
18974 Leslie St., Sharon, ON L0G 1V0
Tel: 905-478-2389
info@sharontemple.ca
www.sharontemple.ca
The Sharon Temple National Historic Site features nine historic buildings. The centerpiece of the site is the Temple of the Children of Peace, which was completed in 1832. Sharon Temple is open from mid May to mid October. Group & scholars may make appointments at other times of the year.

***Simcoe:* Eva Brook Donly Museum & Archives**
***Parent:* Norfolk Historical Society**
109 Norfolk St. South, Simcoe, ON N3Y 2W3
Tel: 519-426-1583; Fax: 519-426-1584
office@norfolklore.com; genealogy@norfolklore.com
www.norfolklore.com
The Museum & Archives feature information about the people, heritage, & history of Norfolk County. Museum artifacts are housed in a two storey brick home which was erected in the 1840s. Archives include family histories, documents, records, & phototgraphs.
Keitha Davis, President, Norfolk Historical Society
Helen Bartens, Curator & Marager, curator@norfolklore.com

***Sioux Lookout:* Sioux Lookout Museum**
c/o Community Development Office, PO Box 158, Sioux Lookout, ON P8T 1A4
Tel: 807-737-2700; Fax: 807-737-3436
bmackinnon@siouxlookout.ca
www.siouxlookout.ca
Year Founded: 1981 First Nations artifacts; pioneer artifacts related to logging, mining, aviation & the Canadian National Railway

***Smiths Falls:* Heritage House Museum / Musée de la maison du patrimoine**
PO Box 695, 11 Old Slys Rd., Smiths Falls, ON K7A 4T6
Tel: 613-283-8560; Fax: 613-283-4764
heritagehouse@smithsfalls.ca
www.smithsfalls.ca/heritagehouse
Year Founded: 1981 Built in 1860-1861 by Joshua Bates, the house is located near the Rideau River and displays 7 rooms, including kitchen, parlor and bedroom, all restored to Victorian style. Workshops and programs for children are offered. There is a gift shop. Tours available; open year round.
Carol Miller, Curator

***Smiths Falls:* Industrial Heritage Complex Merrickville Lockstation**
34A Beckwith St. South, Smiths Falls, ON K7A 2A8
Tel: 613-283-5170
19th century construction on Rideau Canal, with emphasis on Merrickville; collection includes power generation machinery; located on County Rd. #2 in Merrickville, ON.

***Smiths Falls:* Rideau Canal National Historic Site of Canada**
34 Beckwith St. South, Smiths Falls, ON K7A 2B3
Tel: 613-283-5170; Fax: 613-283-0677
Toll-Free: 888-773-8888
RideauCanal-info@pc.gc.ca
www.pc.gc.ca/lhn-nhs/on/ride au/index.aspx
twitter.com/RideauCanalNHS
www.facebook.com/RideauCanalN HS
Other contact information: TTY: 1-866-787-6221
The historic Rideau Canal is operated by Parks Canada in an effort to preserve the canal's historic features as well as to provide a navigable waterway for boaters.

***Smiths Falls:* Smiths Falls Railway Museum of Eastern Ontario**
PO Box 962, 90 William St. West, Smiths Falls, ON K7A 5A5
Tel: 613-283-5696
info@rmeo.org
rmeo.org
www.facebook.com/rmeo.smithsfalls
Railway Museum at the historic CNR station

***Sombra:* Sombra Museum**
3470 St. Clair Parkway, Sombra, ON N0P 2H0
Tel: 519-892-3982
www.twp.stclair.on.ca/sombra_museum.htm
Local historical artifacts housed in 1881 Victorian frame home; stories of the St. Clair River illustrated through photos & artifacts in 3 rooms; log cabin circa 1830; reference collection & family archives; marine room featuring nautical equipment & photos relating to the St. Clair River & the Great Lakes; special events & programming.
Shelley Lucier, Curator, shelley.lucier@county-lambton.on.ca

***South Baymouth:* Little Schoolhouse & Museum South Baymouth**
General Delivery, South Baymouth, ON P0P 1Z0
Tel: 705-859-2344
sbmuseum@volnetmmp.net
www.manitoulin-island.com/museums/little_schoolhouse.htm
Displays the history of this fishing village through artifacts & pictures.
Bryan Gleason, Contact

***Southampton:* Bruce County Museum & Cultural Centre**
PO Box 180, 33 Victoria St. North, Southampton, ON N0H 2L0
Tel: 519-797-2080; Fax: 519-797-2191
Toll-Free: 866-318-8889
collections@brucecounty.on.ca
www.brucemuseum.ca
www .facebook.com/124282581140
Other contact information: E-mail, Archival Information: archives@brucecounty.on.ca
Permanent galleries at the Bruce County Museum & Cultural Centre include the following: Creation Stories; Our Tropical Past; Geology & The Ice Ages; First People's Gallery; A Time To Remember, featuring military exhibits; Telephone Beginnings, depicting the history of telephone service in Bruce County; Living On The Land, showcasing the area's agricultural history; The Land; Living On The Water, with information about lighthouses, shipbuilding, fishing, & shipwrecks; & Living in Balance, with information about resources & industries.
Barbara Ribey, Director & Curator, bribey@brucecounty.on.ca
Ann-Marie Collins, Archivist, acollins@brucecounty.on.ca

***Stittsville:* Goulbourn Museum**
PO Box 621, 2064 Huntley Rd., RR#3, Stittsville, ON K2S 1A7
Tel: 613-831-2393
info@goulbournmuseum.ca
www.goulbournmuseum.ca
twitter.com/GoulbournMuseum
www.facebook.com/Go ulbournMuseum
Year Founded: 1990 Collection housed in 1873 Township Hall & 1961 Clerk's Building; displays about a family farms & rural schools; exhibit of military service from 1812 to present; genealogical data & library. Hours: Tu-F, Su 1:00-4:00

***Stoney Creek:* Battlefield House Museum & Park**
PO Box 66561, 77 King St. West, Stoney Creek, ON L8G 5E5
Tel: 905-662-8458; Fax: 905-546-4141
battlefield@hamilton.ca
www.battlefieldhouse.ca
The Gage Homestead was built in 1796. During the War of 1812 & the Battle of Stoney Creek, the Gage family fled to the cellar of the home. The Battlefield Monument commemorates the soldiers who died during the battle. Each June, the Battlefield House Museum & Park is the site of a military re-enactment of the Battle of Stoney Creek. The site is open from July 1st to Labour Day.
Susan Ramsay, Curator

***Stratford:* Brocksden Country School Museum**
2719 Perth Line 37, RR#1, Stratford, ON N5A 4C7
Tel: 519-271-0499; Fax: 519-271-1978
The school which opened in 1853 presents a living history program for classes.
Wilma McCaig, Secretary

***Stratford:* Fryfogel Tavern**
Perth County Historical Foundation, 1931 Line 34, Stratford, ON N0B 2P0
Stagecoach stop & resting place 1844-45; history of Perth County's settlers; open by appt.

***Strathroy:* A.W. Campbell House Museum**
c/o St. Clair Region Conservation Authority, 205 Mill Pond Cres., Strathroy, ON N7G 3P9
Tel: 519-245-3710; Fax: 519-245-3348
stclair@scrca.on.ca
www.scrca.on.ca
The museum is located in the A.W. Campbell Conservation Area, R.R.#2 Alvinston, ON, off Nauvoo Rd. A typical 1890s southwestern Ontario rural home comprises the museum, and the conservation area also includes a campground and walking trails.
Rick Battson, Director of Communications, rbattson@scrca.on.ca

***Strathroy:* Strathroy Middlesex Museum**
34 Frank St., Strathroy, ON N7G 2R4
Tel: 519-245-0492; Fax: 519-245-1073
info@strathroymuseum.ca
www.strathroymuseum.ca
Open year round; medical theme room; military display; 1930s electric kitchen; printing shop; archival material

***Stratton:* Kay-Nah-Chi-Wah-Nung Historical Centre**
***Also known as:* The Manitou Mounds**
PO Box 100, Stratton, ON
Tel: 807-486-1163; Fax: 807-483-1263
Toll-Free: 888-992-9949
info@manitoumounds.com
www.manitoumounds.com
The Manitou Mounds are the centre's focal point. The Mounds are sacred First Nations ground, & were integral to the continent-wide aboriginal trading network. Visitors can explore the site on nature trails, & also learn about the area's history in the visitors centre.

***Sturgeon Falls:* Musée Sturgeon River House Museum**
250, ch Fort Rd., Sturgeon Falls, ON P2B 2N7
Tél: 705-753-4716; Téléc: 705-753-5476
info@sturgeonriverhouse.com
www.sturgeonriverhouse.com
Le musée se trouve sur un site de la Compagnie de la Baie d'Hudson; l'exposition traite de fourrure et les animaux de la région.
Serge Ducharme, Directeur

***Sudbury:* Anderson Farm Museum**
***Parent:* Anderson Farm Museum Heritage Society**
PO Box 6400, Sudbury, ON P3A 3B7
Tel: 705-692-4448; Fax: 705-692-4448
Open year round
Jim Fortin, Curator, Greater Sudbury Heritage Museums, 705-671-2489

***Sudbury:* Centre franco-ontarien de folklore (CFOF)**
Université de Sudbury, 935, rue du Lac Ramsay, Sudbury, ON P3E 2C6
Tél: 705-675-8986; Téléc: 705-675-5809
cfof@cfof.on.ca
www.cfof.on.ca
Fondée en: 1972 A pour mission de mettre en valeur le folklore et le patrimoine franco-ontarien; musée; activités éducatives; bibliothèque; archives; publications; magasin virtuel
Roger Gervais, Directeur général

***Sudbury:* Flour Mill Museum**
245 St. Charles St., Sudbury, ON P3C 2Z3
Tel: 705-692-4448
www.sudburymuseums.ca
Year Founded: 1974 The museum is made out of two buildings: a heritage house built in 1902 & a log cabin built in 1983 to celebrate Sudbury's centennial. Open July & Aug., W-Su 10:00-4:00.

***Sudbury:* Greater Sudbury Heritage Museums**
***Also known as:* Greater Sudbury Virtual Museum**
c/o Greater Sudbury Public Library, 74 MacKenzie St., Sudbury, ON P3C 4X8
Tel: 705-671-2489
www.sudburymuseums.ca
Greater Sudbury Heritage Museums is the collective name for the following four heritage sites located in & around Sudbury: Anderson Farm Museum, Copper Cliff Museum, Flour Mill Museum, & Rayside-Balfour Museum. The Greater Sudbury Virtual Museum is the online collection of photos, videos, archives, & more hosted on www.sudburymuseums.ca.
Jim Fortin, Curator

***Sudbury:* Irish Regiment of Canada Regimental Museum**
Sudbury Armoury, 333 Riverside Dr., Sudbury, ON P3E 1H5
Tel: 705-669-2300; Fax: 705-675-5069

***Sutton West:* Eildon Hall Sibbald Memorial Museum**
Sibbald Point Provincial Park, RR#2, Sutton West, ON L0E 1R0
Tel: 905-722-8061; Fax: 905-722-5416
Situated by the shore of Lake Simcoe, Eildon Hall was the Sibbald family home

***Teeterville:* Teeterville Pioneer Museum**
194 Teeter St., Teeterville, ON N0E 1S0
Tel: 519-426-5870; Fax: 519-428-3069
teeterville.museum@norfolkcounty.ca
teetervillemuseum.ca
www.facebook. com/teetervillemuseum
Other contact information: Victoria Day - Labour Day: 519-443-4400
Features historical buildings & picnic grounds.
Tanya Zajac, Curator
Tanya Richardson, Museum Coordinator

***Thunder Bay:* Centennial Park 1910 Logging Camp & Museum**
Parks Division, Victoria Ville Civic Centre, 111 Syndicate Ave. South, Thunder Bay, ON P7E 6S4
Tel: 807-625-2351; Fax: 807-625-3528
www.thunderbay.ca/parks
Full scale replica of a 1910 logging camp re-creates the early history of Northern Ontario's forest industry; park open year round; logging camp and museum open mid-June to Labour Day, 8:00 am.m to 8:00 p.m.; Muskeg Express logging train; Winter sleigh rides; craft shop; picnic area; trails
Bruce Phillips

***Thunder Bay:* Definitely Superior Artist-Run Centre & Gallery**
PO Box 24012, 250 Park Ave., Thunder Bay, ON P7A 8A9
Tel: 807-344-3814
defsup@tbaytel.net
www.definitelysuperior.com
Year Founded: 1988 An artist-run centre for contemporary arts, hosting exhibitions as well as workshops, lectures, film & video screenings, performance, music & literary events. Open Tu-Sa 12:00-6:00.
Tiffany Miller, President
David Karasiewicz, Director

***Thunder Bay:* Fort William Historical Park (FWHP)**
1350 King Rd., Thunder Bay, ON P7K 1L7
Tel: 807-473-2344; Fax: 807-473-2327
info@fwhp.ca
www.fwhp.ca
Social Media: www.youtube.com/user/FortWilliamHistPark
twitter.com/FWHPtweets
www.fa cebook.com/fortwilliamhistoricalpark
Year Founded: 1973 A living history site that depicts the fur trade activities of the North West Company in the early 1800s; 42 reconstructed buildings on a 225-acre site. Touts that it is the largest Fur Trade Post. Hours: 10:00-5:00
Sergio Buonocore, General Manager,
sergio.buonocore@mtr.gov.on.ca

***Thunder Bay:* Northwestern Ontario Sports Hall of Fame**
219 May St. South, Thunder Bay, ON P7E 1B5
Tel: 807-622-2852; Fax: 807-622-2736
nwosport@tbaytel.net
www.nwosportshalloffame.com
Year Founded: 1978 The Hall's mission is to preserve and honour Northwestern Ontario's sports heritage, with displays, photos, archival material, artifacts and other documentation on over 200 athletes; reference library; educational programming. Open all year.
Diane Imrie, Executive Director

***Thunder Bay:* Paipoonge Historical Museum**
RR#6, Thunder Bay, ON P7C 5N5
Tel: 807-939-1262; Fax: 807-577-3888
lgarrity@tbaytel.net
Year Founded: 1952 Reflecting the history of the Municipality of Oliver/Paipoonge & area during the late 1800s & early 1900s. Collection of pioneer material and farm machinery, old school room, kitchen and bedroom displays.
Lois Garrity, Curator & Director

***Thunder Bay:* Thunder Bay Military Museum**
The Armoury, 317 Park Ave., Thunder Bay, ON P7B 1C7
Tel: 807-343-5175; Fax: 807-346-4022
army.ca/inf/lssrmus.php
Georg Hoegel Art Collection - paintings & drawings done by Mr. Hoegel when he was a prisoner of war in Canada from 1941-1946; other military art; tri-service collection, representing all three services, rotated regularly; open 4 afternoons, 2 evenings & by request
Lt.Col./Dr. T.M.S. Kaipio, President C.D., Ph.D.
Myles G. Penny, Curator C.D., B.A., B.Ed., pennym@air.on.ca

***Thunder Bay:* Thunder Bay Museum**
***Also known as:* Thunder Bay Historical Museum Society**
425 East Donald St., Thunder Bay, ON P7E 5V1
Tel: 807-623-0801; Fax: 807-622-6880
info@thunderbaymuseum.com
www.thunderbaymuseum.com
A museum, historical society & archives for Thunder Bay & Northwestern Ontario
Dr. Tory Tronrud, Curator

***Tillsonburg:* Annandale National Historic Museum**
***Also known as:* Annandale House**
30 Tillson Ave., Tillsonburg, ON N4G 2Z8
Tel: 519-842-2294; Fax: 519-842-5355
www.tillsonburg.ca/Visitors/AnnandaleHouse.aspx
Nationally designated for its interior, representing the Victorian "Aesthetic Art Movement," Annandale House is restored to the 1880's period; location of tourist information for Tillsonburg; open year round
Patricia Phelps, Curator, pphelps@tillsonburg.ca

***Timmins:* Timmins Museum: National Exhibition Centre / Musée de Timmins: Centre national d'exposition**
***Also known as:* Timmins Museum: NEC**
325 Second Ave., Timmins, ON P4N 0B3
Tel: 705-360-2617; Fax: 705-360-2693
museum@timmins.ca
www.timmins.ca
Preserves, presents & studies the history of the Porcupine Gold Camp, Timmins Ontario. The South Porcupine location closed in 2006 due to structural damage; the new site at 325 Second Ave. will be opening soon.
Karen Bachmann, Director/Curator,
karen.bachmann@timmins.ca

***Tobermory:* The Peninsula & St. Edmunds Township Museum**
RR#1, Tobermory, ON N0H 2R0
Tel: 519-596-2479
Year Founded: 1967 Housed in the former St. Edmunds Settlement School (ca. 1898), the museum's holdings include land deeds and registers, photographs, and exhibits on lumbering, fishing, and hunting activities; the upper floor of the museum is dedicated to area marine history and includes maps, tools, and relics from shipwrecks. An 1875 furnished log house is located on the grounds and is open by appointment only. Located south of Tobermory Harbour, on the east side of Hwy 6. Open weekends from Victoria Day to Thanksgiving, and weekdays from July 1 to Labour Day.

***Toronto:* 48th Highlanders Museum**
73 Simcoe St., Toronto, ON M5J 1W9
Tel: 416-596-1382
geordie48@sympatico.ca
www.48highlanders.com/04_03.html
Year Founded: 1959 The museum seeks to collect, preserve, & present the legacy of the 48th Highlanders of Canada. Open year-round, W & Th 10:00-3:00.

***Toronto:* The Bata Shoe Museum (BSM)**
327 Bloor St. West, Toronto, ON M5S 1W7
Tel: 416-979-7799; Fax: 416-979-0078
www.batashoemuseum.ca;
astepintothebatashoemuseum.blogspot.ca
Social Media: pinterest.com/batashoemuseum;
batashoemuseum.tumblr.com
twitter.com/batashoemuseum
www.facebook.com/batashoemuseum
Explores footwear in the social & cultural life of humankind from ancient times to present. Exhibits vary but there is a permanant exhibit which includes a pair of Elton John platform shoes and shoes which date back hundreds of years.
Sonja Bata, Chair

***Toronto:* Baycrest Heritage Museum**
***Also known as:* The Morris and Sally Justein Heritage Museum**
Baycrest Hospital, 3560 Bathurst St., Main Fl., Toronto, ON M6A 2E1
Tel: 416-785-2500; Fax: 416-785-2378
www.baycrest.org
The Morris and Sally Justein Heritage Museum displays Judaica exhibits. The historical & cultural Judaica exhibits & permanent collections are designed for Baycrest Hospital & Home's elderly clients.
Lois Buckstein, Chair

***Toronto:* Beth Tzedec Reuben & Helene Dennis Museum**
c/o Beth Tzedec Synagogue, 1700 Bathurst St., Toronto, ON M5P 3K3
Tel: 416-781-3514; Fax: 416-781-0150
museum@beth-tzedec.org
www.beth-tzedec.org/museum
Year Founded: 1965 The museum features a major Judaica collection, including Jewish art & history from ancient times to the present. Appointments may be made for tours.
Dorion Liebgott, Curator

***Toronto:* Black Creek Pioneer Village**
1000 Murray Ross Pkwy., Toronto, ON M3J 2P3
Tel: 416-736-1733
bcpvinfo@trca.on.ca
www.blackcreek.ca
Operated by the Toronto & Region Conservation Authority (TRCA), Black Creek Pioneer Village is a living history experience, which spans over 30 acres. It exemplifies a small south central Ontario community between the 1790s & the 1860s. Demonstrations & special activities depict rural life. Black Creek Village also features the historic Black Creek Historic Brewery. The village is open from the beginning of May to the end of December.
Rick Sikorski, Manager, Marketing & Communications, TRCA

***Toronto:* Cabbagetown Regent Park Community Museum**
Residence House, Riverdale Farm, 201 Winchester St., Toronto, ON M4X 1B8
Tel: 416-392-6794
farm@toronto.ca
www.crpmuseum.com
The museum collects, preserves, & displays the history of the Cabbagetown & Regent Park neighbourhoods in Toronto. Open year-round, Sa & Su 11:00-4:00.

***Toronto:* Campbell House**
160 Queen St. West, Toronto, ON M5H 3H3
Tel: 416-597-0227; Fax: 416-597-0750
info@campbellhousemuseum.ca
www.campbellhousemuseum.ca
twitter.com/Cam pbellHouseTO
www.facebook.com/365449410187802
Built in 1822, the Campbell House is the oldest remaining building from the original town of York. The Sir William Campbell Foundation operates the museum. Special programs are available for groups. The Home is open from the beginning of May until Thanksgiving.
Liz Driver, campbellhouse@bellnet.ca

***Toronto:* Canadian Advertising Museum (CAM)**
c/o Bev Atkinson, Humber ITAL - Lakeshore Campus, #F102, 3199 lakeshore Boul. West, Toronto, ON M8V 1K8
Tel: 416-675-6622; Fax: 416-251-3797
info@canadianadvertisingmuseum.com
www.canadianadvertisingmuseum.com
Social Media:
www.linkedin.com/groups/Canadian-Advertising-Museum-CAM-4260094
twitter. com/cam_tweets
www.facebook.com/canadianadvertisingmuseum
The museum seeks to preserve Canadian business & culture through advertising, both online & in their physical collection.
Kate Taylor, Acting Chair,
ktaylor@canadianadvertisingmuseum.com
Bev Atkinson, Secretary-Treasurer,
batkinson@canadianadvertisingmuseum.com

***Toronto:* Canadian Air & Space Museum (TAM)**
PO Box 1, 65 Carl Hall Rd., Toronto, ON M3K 2E1
Tel: 416-638-6078; Fax: 416-638-5509
casm@casmuseum.org
www.casmuseum.org
Aviation industry & history in the Toronto region

***Toronto:* Canadian Broadcasting Corporation Museum & & Graham Spry Theatre**
***Also known as:* CBC Museum**
PO Box 500 A, 250 Front St. West, Toronto, ON M5W 1E6
Tel: 416-205-5574
www.cbc.ca/museum
The CBC Museum presents the story of CBC's broadcasting history, since 1936.

***Toronto:* The Canadian Business Hall of Fame / Le Temple de la renommée de l'entreprise canadienne**
Allan Lambert Galleria, Brookfield Place, 181 Bay St., Toronto, ON M5J 2S1
Tel: 416-622-4602; Fax: 416-622-6861
Toll-Free: 800-265-0699
rmaund@jacan.org
cbhof.org
Year Founded: 1979
Jos Wintermans, Chair
Kris Fixter, National Director, Marketing & Communications, 416-622-4602
Richard Friedman, Director, Sponsorship, rfriedman@cbhof.ca

***Toronto:* Canadian Motorsport Hall of Fame & Museum**
***Parent:* Canadian Motorsport Heritage Foundation**
Toronto, ON
archives@cmhf.ca
www.cmhf.ca
Year Founded: 1993 The CMHF seeks to honour & recognize the Canadians who have made a contribution to the area of motorsports. The CMHF is currently looking for a new location.
Dr. Hugh Scully, President/Chair
Sid Priddle, Contact, sgwpriddle@gmail.com

***Toronto:* Canadian Sculpture Centre**
***Parent:* Sculptors Society of Canada**
c/o Sculptors Society of Canada, #204, 60 Atlantic Ave., Toronto, ON M6K 1X9
Tel: 647-435-5858
gallery@cansculpt.org
cansculpt.org
Other contact information: Society Phone: 416-533-0126
The Sculptors Society of Canada hosts a sculpture gallery on Church St. in Toronto that displays temporary exhibits. Please see the website for details.

***Toronto:* Casa Loma**
1 Austin Terrace, Toronto, ON M5R 1X8
Tel: 416-923-1171; Fax: 416-923-5734
info@casaloma.org; kiwanis@casaloma.org
www.casaloma.org
Year Founded: 1937 Owned by the City of Toronto & operated by The Kiwanis Club of Casa Loma, Casa Loma is the former home of Sir Henry Pellatt, a Canadian financier, industrialist, & military man. The decorated castle contains an 800 foot tunnel, secret passages, towers, & stables. A self-guided audio tour is available in eight languages.
Richard R. Wozenilek, Chair, Board of Trustees of Casa Loma
Lou Seiler, Director, Marketing, lseiler@casaloma.org

***Toronto:* Colborne Lodge**
c/o Museum Services, Metro Hall, 55 John St., 8th Fl., Toronto, ON M5V 3C6
Tel: 416-392-6916; Fax: 416-392-0375
clodge@toronto.ca
www.toronto.ca/museums; www.highpark.org/colborne.htm
Site of the 19th century home of High Park founders, John & Jemmina Howard; contains many of their original furnishings, watercolours of early Toronto, & other artifacts; coach house, tomb & restored gardens on the property; special events & programming; party room rentals; located at the south end of High Park, Colborne Lodge Dr., just north of the Queensway. Open year round.
Cheryl Hart, Museum Coordinator

***Toronto:* Design Exchange (DX)**
234 Bay St., Toronto, ON M5K 1B2
Tel: 416-363-6121; Fax: 416-368-0684
info@dx.org
www.dx.org
Social Media: youtube.com/designexchange;
flickr.com/photos/thedesignexchange
twitter.com/designexchange
www.fac ebook.com/DesignExchange
Year Founded: 1994 The DX is the only museum in Canada dedicated to preserving design heritage. The museum is housed in the old Toronto Stock Exchange building in downtown Toronto. Hours of Operation: M, W-F 10:00-5:00, Tu 10:00-8:00, Sa & Su 12:00-5:00.
Shauna Levy, President, shauna@dx.org
Anne Marie Minardi, Acting Curator/Director, Collections, annemarie@dx.org

***Toronto:* The Enoch Turner Schoolhouse (1848)**
106 Trinity St., Toronto, ON M5A 3C6
Tel: 416-863-0010
www.enochturnerschoolhouse.ca
One of Toronto's oldest institutions & the city's first free school
P. Lynne Kurylo, Chair
Anne Mcarty, Administrator, amcarty@enochturnerschoolhouse.ca

***Toronto:* Fort York National Historic Site**
100 Garrison Rd., Toronto, ON M5V 3K9
Tel: 416-392-6907; Fax: 416-392-6917
fortyork@toronto.ca
www.toronto.ca/culture/museums/fort-york.htm
Year Founded: 1934 Built by Lieutenant-Governor John Graves Simcoe as a garrison in 1793, Fort York was purchased by the City of Toronto in 1909 and restored as a museum in 1934. Its fortified walls contain the largest collection of original War of 1812 buildings in Canada. Some of the restored interiors reflect the life of the garrison community, while others serve as exhibit space for artifacts on a military theme. The site offers seasonal guided tours as well as musket, drill, and music demonstrations.
Mr. David O'Hara, Site Administrator, 416-392-6907 ext 222, dohara@toronto.ca

***Toronto:* Gardiner Museum of Ceramic Art**
***Also known as:* Gardiner Museum**
111 Queen's Park, Toronto, ON M5S 2C7
Tel: 416-586-8080; Fax: 416-586-8085
mail@gardinermuseum.on.ca
www.gardinermuseum.on.ca
Containing 3,000+ historical and contemporary pieces, the Gardiner Museum is North America's premier specialized ceramic museum; gift shop; Gail Brooker Ceramic Research Library; Jamie Kennedy's Gardiner Restaurant; permanent and special exhibits; studio spaces and ceramic courses; talks, book launches, films and other programs.
Alexandra Montgomery, Executive Director

***Toronto:* Gibson House Museum**
5176 Yonge St., Toronto, ON M2N 5P6
Tel: 416-395-7432
gibsonhouse@toronto.ca
www.toronto.ca/culture/museums/gibson-house.htm
Gibson House, built in 1851, was the home of Scottish immigrant David Gibson and his family. Gibson, a land surveyor, played a role in the mapping of early Toronto and spent some years in exile in the U.S. for his participation in the Rebellion of 1837 in Upper Canada.
Elizabeth Nelson-Raffaele, Curator

***Toronto:* Historic Zion Schoolhouse**
1091 Finch Ave. East, Toronto, ON M2J 2X3
Tel: 416-395-7435
zionschool@toronto.ca
www.toronto.ca/culture/museums/zion-schoolhouse.htm
A City of Toronto Museum, the Zion Schoolhouse offers modern students a roleplaying experience into the lives of children circa 1910.

***Toronto:* Mackenzie House**
82 Bond St., Toronto, ON M5B 1X2
Tel: 416-392-6915; Fax: 416-392-0114
machouse@toronto.ca
www.toronto.ca/museums
Year Founded: 1950 The final home of Toronto's first mayor, William Lyon Mackenzie who gained notoriety during the 1837 Upper Canada Rebellion, this 1858 Georgian rowhouse has been refurnished in period style and also showcases a print shop.
Ms Janet Schwartz, Site Coordinator

***Toronto:* Montgomery's Inn**
4709 Dundas St. West, Toronto, ON M9A 1A8
Tel: 416-394-8113; Fax: 416-394-6027
montinn@toronto.ca
www.montgomerysinn.com
Year Founded: 1975 Built in 1830, the restored inn reflects life in 1847. Its library holds photographs, artifacts, and archival materials documenting the history of Etobicoke; tearoom; gift shop; seasonal programs; community theatre and music; workshops
Mike Lipowski, Curator, 416/394-8112

***Toronto:* Museum of Childhood (MOC)**
121 Brunswick Ave., Toronto, ON M5S 2M3
Tel: 416-368-2866; Fax: 416-504-0316
Extensive collection of childhood toys, clothes, furniture, books; opening date before year 2005; educational presentations & traveling exhibits available
Loet Vos, President

***Toronto:* MZTV Museum of Television**
64 Jefferson Ave., Toronto, ON M6K 1Y4
Tel: 416-599-7339; Fax: 416-599-3572
mztv@mztv.com
www.mztv.com
www.facebook.com/239799029379279
The museum seeks to protect & preserve television sets & related technologies, as well as books, magazines, original papers, discs, toys & ephemera of television; interactive 3D gallery; museum; e-gallery online at website; guided tours Mon.-Fri. The museum is closed until 2013 while they relocate.
Moses Znaimer, Chair
Carolyn Stewart, Curator/Archivist, carolyns@mztv.com
Kristen Maciejowski, Curatorial Assistant, kristenm@mztv.com

***Toronto:* The Queen's Own Rifles of Canada Regimental Museum**
Casa Loma, 1 Austin Terrace, Toronto, ON M5R 1X8
Tel: 416-407-3675
www.qor.com/social/museum.html
Display artifacts pertinent to the history of the regiment from 1860-present; open year round

***Toronto:* Queen's York Rangers Regimental Museum**
Fort York Armoury, 660 Fleet St., Toronto, ON M5V 1A9
Tel: 416-973-3265; Fax: 416-203-3675
qyrang.ca/about/history
Traces the history of the Queen's York Rangers, an active reconnaissance unit of the Army Reserve; displays begin wth the Seven Year's War, through the American Revolution & settlement of Upper Canada & through the campaigns of 19th century & two world wars
L.Col. Diane Kruger, Curator, qyrangcentralregistry@intern.mil.ca

***Toronto:* Redpath Sugar Museum**
95 Queen's Quay East, Toronto, ON M5E 1A3
Tel: 416-933-8341; Fax: 416-366-7550
Toll-Free: 800-267-1517
Consumer-Canada@redpathsugar.com
www.redpathsugars.com
www.facebook.com/redpathsugar
Year Founded: 1979 The Redpath Sugar Museum displays the history of sugar production & refining, models of transportation that bring sugar to the refinery, as well as the story of the Redpath family. The museum offers a program for schools.

Scott Brownrigg, Contact, Media Inquiries, 416-644-4927

***Toronto:* Royal Canadian Military Institute Museum**
426 University Ave., Toronto, ON M5G 1S9
Tel: 416-597-0286; Fax: 416-597-6919
info@rcmi.org
www.rcmi.org
Artifacts related to Canadians' participation in the military; library open to researchers & members; open year round
Gregory Loughton, Curator, gregory.loughton@rcmi.org

***Toronto:* The Royal Regiment of Canada Museum**
***Also known as:* The Royals' Museum**
Fort York Armoury, 660 Fleet St., Toronto, ON M5V 1A9
Tel: 416-755-1727
rregtc.gmail.com
www.army.dnd.ca/rregtc/coy/museum.html
Year Founded: 1996 Military artifacts, dating from 1862, of the The Royal Regiment of Canada, & predecessors: the 10th Royal Grenadiers (Toronto Regiment), & the 3rd, 123rd, 124th, 204th & 58th Battalions; archives; school tours by appointment. Located next to the Royals' WO's & Sergeants' Mess on the 2nd floor, at the east end of Fort York Armoury.
Capt. Bruce Barbeau, Curator

***Toronto:* The Salvation Army Museum**
2 Overlea Blvd., Toronto, ON M4H 1P4
Tel: 416-285-4344
heritage_centre@can.salvationarmy.org
salvationist.ca/ about-us/history/museum-archives
Open to public & gives a pictorial outline of Salvation Army history, particularly as it pertains to Canada & Bermuda, through the use of artifacts, photographs & special techniques; no fee; wheelchair accessible; open Mon.-Fri., closed all statutory holidays
Col. John E. Carew, Director

***Toronto:* Sarah & Chaim Neuberger Holocaust Education Centre**
UJA Federation of Greater Toronto, Lipa Green Centre, Sherman Campus, 4600 Bathurst St., 4th Fl., Toronto, ON M2R 3V2
Tel: 416-631-5689
neuberger@ujafed.org
www.holocaustcentre.com;
learningabouttheholocaust.blogspot.ca
Social Media: neubergerhec.tumblr.com
twitter.com/holocaust_ed
www.facebook.com/HoloCentre
The centre is dedicated to educating the public about the Holocaust & creating dialogue about civil society through programs, exhibitions, an on-site museum, & library. Open M-Th 9:00-4:30, F 9:00-1:00, or by appointment.
Honey Sherman, Chair
Mira Goldfarb, Executive Director
Rachel Libman, Head, Programs & Exhibitions
Carol Fox, Administrative Assistant, cfox@ujafed.org

***Toronto:* Scadding Cabin**
***Parent:* York Pioneeer & Historical Society**
c/o York Pioneers & Historical Society, PO Box 45026, 2482 Yonge St., Toronto, ON M4P 3E3
Tel: 416-494-0503
yorkpioneers@gmail.com; information@explace.on.ca
www.yorkpioneers.org; www.explace.on.ca
Built for John Scadding, clerk to Lieutenant-Governor John Graves Simcoe, the cabin is Toronto's oldest dwelling. Located at Exhibition Place, southeast of 25 British Columbia Rd.; wooden house, built in late 1700s, contains furniture which belonged to John Graves Simcoe; open late Aug.-Labour Day (during CNE)

***Toronto:* Scarborough Historical Museum**
1007 Brimley Rd., Toronto, ON M1P 3E8
Tel: 416-338-8807
shm@toronto.ca
www.toronto.ca/scarboroughmuseum
Includes Cornell House, McCowan Log Cabin & Hough Carriage Works; picnic area; parking
Madeleine Callaghan, Manager/Curator, 416-397-7630

***Toronto:* Sesquicentennial Museum & Archives**
Toronto District School Board, 155 College St., Toronto, ON M5T 1P6
Tel: 416-397-3680; Fax: 416-397-3685
toes.tdsb.on.ca/day/tusc/location/sesqui.asp
Preserves the history of the TDSB & its schools; collects, documents, researches, exhibits, & historical artifacts, fine art, & archival, & published material for its educational community - students, parents, staff & trustees & its citizens

***Toronto:* Spadina Museum: Historic House & Gardens**
285 Spadina Rd., Toronto, ON M5R 2V5
Tel: 416-392-6910; Fax: 416-392-0382
spadina@toronto.ca
www.toronto.ca/culture/museums/spadina.htm
1866 mansion contains four generations of décor, reflecting art movements such as Art Nouveau
Nancy Reynolds, Site Coordinator
Karen Edwards, Curator

***Toronto:* Taras H. Shevchenko Museum**
1614 Bloor St. West, Toronto, ON M6P 1A7
Tel: 416-534-8662; Fax: 416-535-1063
shevchenkomuseum@bellnet.ca
www.infoukes.com/shevchenkomuseum

The museum is dedicated to the art, life and literary legacy of Ukraine's renowned poet, Taras Schevchenko; the Toronto site is the only Shevchenko museum in the Americas; library; art exhibits; Ukrainian folk art and handicrafts. Open year round.
Wm. Harasym, President

***Toronto:* Textile Museum of Canada**
55 Centre Ave., Toronto, ON M5G 2H5
Tel: 416-599-5321; Fax: 416-599-2911
info@textilemuseum.ca
www.textilemuseum.ca
Unique exhibitions & programming; focus on the traditions & aesthetics of historic & contemporary textiles
Patricia Bentley, Sr. Curator

***Toronto:* Todmorden Mills Heritage Museum & Art Centre**
67 Pottery Rd., Toronto, ON M4K 2B8
Tel: 416-396-2819
todmorden@toronto.ca
www.toronto.ca/culture/museums/todmorden.htm
Depicts early industry in Toronto; new papermill galleries & theatre feature frequent exhibitions & is available for rental
Ulana Baluk, Administrator

***Toronto:* Toronto Police Museum & Discovery Centre**
40 College St., Toronto, ON M5G 2J3
Tel: 416-808-7020; Fax: 416-808-7023
museum@torontopolice.on.ca
www.torontopolice.on.ca
Interactive displays; collection includes uniforms, badges, communication & transportation equipment; high profile crimes; open year round
Norina D'Agostini
Gabi Voigt

***Toronto:* Toronto's First Post Office (TFPO)**
***Parent:* Town of York Historical Society**
260 Adelaide St. East, Toronto, ON M5A 1N1
Tel: 416-865-1833; Fax: 416-865-9414
tfpo@total.net
www.townofyork.com
twitter.com/tos1stpo
www.facebook. com/TOs1stPO
Year Founded: 1983 Canada's only surviving pre-1851 Post Office; restored as a museum & full postal service operation; gift shop
Jennifer McIlroy, President
Janet Walters, Curator

***Toronto:* York Museum**
Centennial Recreation Centre, 2694 Eglinton Ave. West, Toronto, ON M6M 1T9
Tel: 416-394-2759
yorkmuseum@toronto.ca
www.toronto.ca/culture/york_museum.htm
York Museum tells the story of the former City of York. Artifacts range from a 3,000 year old stone axe as a reminder of the First Nations history in the area, to a telephone switchboard. Phone 416-338-0492 to arrange a visit.

***Tweed:* Tweed & Area Heritage Centre**
***Also known as:* Houston House 1897**
PO Box 665, 40 Victoria St. North, Tweed, ON K0K 3J0
Tel: 613-478-3989; Fax: 613-478-6457
tweedheritageinfo@on.aibn.com
Year Founded: 1988 An information centre, art gallery, museum, archives & genealogical research centre; local arts & crafts promotional centre; Hours: M-Sa 9:00am-12:00pm, 1:00-5:00
Evan Morton, Curator

***Uxbridge:* Thomas Foster Memorial Temple**
PO Box 190, 51 Toronto St. South, Uxbridge, ON L9P 1T1
Tel: 905-852-9181; Fax: 905-852-9164
Toll-Free: 888-559-9022
www.town.uxbridge.on.ca
Built by former mayor of Toronto, Thomas Foster, in 1935/36 as a memorial to his wife, unique in the design of Byzantine architecture; holds tours on the 1st & 2nd Sun., June-Sept.; special concerts throughout the year, with special program in Oct.
Bev Northeast, Contact, bnortheast@powergate.ca

***Uxbridge:* Uxbridge Historical Centre**
***Also known as:* Uxbridge-Scott Museum & Archives**
PO Box 1301, 7230 Concession Rd. 6, Uxbridge, ON L9P 1R2
Tel: 905-852-5854
museum@town.uxbridge.on.ca
www.uxbridgehistoricalcentre.com
twitter.com/UxbridgeMuseum
www.facebo ok.com/uxbridgehistoricalcentre
Year Founded: 1972 Displays of artifacts & photos to help tell the story of the Uxbridge area; special display on The Oak Ridges Moraine; 10 heritage buildings on site; picnic grounds; Hours for Tours: May-Oct.: W-Su 10:00-4:00
Allan McGillivray, Curator

***Vernon:* Osgoode Township Historical Society & Museum**
PO Box 74, 7814 Lawrence St., Vernon, ON K0A 3J0
Tel: 613-821-4062
oths@magma.ca
www.magma.ca/~oths
The Osgoode Township Historical Society & Museum preserves the development of the Township of Osgoode, situated south of Ottawa, Ontario. Artifacts include indigenous Native & pioneer articles & documents, such as historic furniture & clothing, & agricultural tools & equipment. The Museum is open Tuesdays to Saturdays.
Jenn Hume, Contact

***Wallacetown:* Backus-Page House Museum**
PO Box 26, 29424 Lakeview Line, Wallacetown, ON N0L 2M0
Tel: 519-762-3072
info@backuspagehouse.ca
www.backuspagehouse.ca;
tyrconnellheritagesociety.blogspot.ca
twitter.com/BackusPageHouse
www.facebook.com/backuspagehouse
A living history museum featuring costumed interpreters & period artifacts. May-Oct., Tu-F 10:00-4:30, Sa & Su 12:00-4:30; open year-round by appointment.

***Wasaga Beach:* Nancy Island Historic Site**
c/o Wasaga Beach Provincial Park, 11 - 22nd St. North, Wasaga Beach, ON L9Z 2V9
Tel: 705-429-2516; Fax: 705-429-7983
nancyisland@wasagabeachpark.com
www.wasagabeachpark.com
Remains of the British schooner "Nancy"; replica of Upper Lakes lighthouse; artifacts related to marine aspects of War of 1812
John Fisher, Superintendent, Wasaga Beach Provincial Park

***Waterford:* Waterford Heritage & Agricultural Museum**
159 Nichol St., Waterford, ON N0E 1Y0
Tel: 519-443-4211
waterford.museum@norfolkcounty.ca
www.norfolkcounty.on.ca; www.sprucerowmuseum.ca
www.facebook.com/147540755302855
History of the Waterford & Townsend area; includes unique collection of agricultural equipment representative of southern Ontario
Melissa Collver, Curator & Director, melissa.collver@norfolkcounty.ca
James Christison, Museum Assistant, james.christison@norfolkcounty.ca

***Waterloo:* Brubacher House Museum**
c/o University of Waterloo, North Campus, Waterloo, ON N2L 3G6
Tel: 519-886-3855
bhouse@watserv1.uwaterloo.ca
www.grebel.uwaterloo.ca/bhouse
Built in 1850, the Brubacher House was later purchased by the University of Waterloo. The home's interior was rebuilt to reflect a Pennsylvania German Mennonite home from the 1850 to 1890 era. Many of the furnishings in the Brubacher House, collected from local Mennonite families, also reflect the time period. Operated by Conrad Grebel University College & the Mennonite Historical Society of Ontario, the House is open from the beginning of May to the end of October.

***Waterloo:* Earth Sciences Museum**
Centre for Environmental & Information Technology, University of Waterloo, 200 University Ave. West, Waterloo, ON N2L 3G1
Tel: 519-888-4567; Fax: 519-746-7484
esmuseum@uwaterloo.ca
uwaterloo.ca/earth-sciences-museum
Year Founded: 1967 Dinosaurs, gems, minerals & a 60-tonne rock garden
Peter Russell, Curator
Corina McDonald, Coordinator, Outreach, 519-888-4567, cmmcdonald@uwaterloo.ca

***Waterloo:* Elliott Avedon Virtual Museum & Archive of Games**
University of Waterloo, 200 University Avenue West, Waterloo, ON N2L 3G1
Tel: 519-888-4567; Fax: 519-746-6776
www.gamesmuseum.uwaterloo.ca
Specializes in the collection, presentation & display of games, both Canadian & international collections; researchers act as a resource for archiving related materials related to games & also provide research facilities & expertise to persons interested in pursuing the study of Games. The physical collection was relocated to the Canadian Museum of Civilization in 2009; the University of Waterloo currently maintains information about the collection on its website as a virtual museum.

***Waterloo:* Museum of Visual Science & Optometry**
Optometry Bldg., University of Waterloo, Waterloo, ON N2L 3G1
Tel: 519-888-4567
plofthou@uwaterloo.ca
optometry.uwaterloo.ca/museum-of-vision-science
Antique spectacles; eye examining equipment; historical documents & books; open; year round

***Wawa:* Lake Superior Provincial Park Visitor Centre**
PO Box 267, Wawa, ON P0S 1K0
Tel: 705-856-2284; Fax: 705-856-1333
www.lakesuperiorpark.ca
Open in July & Aug., this interpretive centre includes information on the Lake Superior Provincial Park's natural & cultural features & the area's recreational opportunities

***Wbbwood:* Mississagi Strait Lighthouse Museum**
c/o Kitrina Tremblay, PO Box 77, Wbbwood, ON P0P 2G0
Tel: 705-282-7258
info@themississagilighthouse.com
www.themississagilighthouse.com
Lighthouse built in 1873, includes artifacts related to seafaring & fishing; keeper's house features 19th-century furnishings; open mid-May - Sept. Lighthouse staff request to be contacted by email during the summer. Located at the western tip of Manitoulin Island, near the village of Meldrum Bay.
Mary Eadie, Manager

***Welland:* Welland Historical Museum**
140 King St., Welland, ON L3B 3J3
Tel: 905-732-2215; Fax: 905-732-9169
wellandhistoricalmuseum@cogeco.net
www.wellandmuseum.ca
twitter.com/We llandMuseum
www.facebook.com/212024838829918
History of Welland including the Welland Canal & its industries; open Tue.-Sat.; kids summer camps in July & Aug.; children's museum
Nora Reid, Executive Director, nr.wm@cogeco.net
Penny Morningstar, Curator, pm.wm@cogeco.net

***Wellington:* Wellington Heritage Museum**
290 Main St., Wellington, ON K0K 3L0
Tel: 613-399-5015; Fax: 613-476-9835
wellmuseum@pecounty.on.ca (May - September)
Other contact information: E-mail, October - April:
museums@pecounty.on.ca
The local history collection of the Wellington Heritage Museum is housed within a Quaker Meeting House, which was built in 1885. The museum features a tribute to the Society of Friends, who helped develop the county. A special collection is the Douglas A. Crawford Canning Industry Collection. Wellington Heritage Museum is open from May to mid October.
Jennifer Lyons, Head Curator, 613-476-2148
Janice Hubbs, Site Curator, 613-399-5015

***Westport:* Rideau District Museum**
PO Box 305, Westport, ON K0G 1X0
Tel: 613-273-2502; Fax: 613-273-3222
bwlaird@rideau.net
Year Founded: 1961 Housed in 1850s blacksmith & carriage shop with forges & bellows intact & showing many artifacts from the local district, including a 9-foot tall 19th-century statue of Sally Grant, the Blind Lady of Justice
Wendy Briggs-Jude, Chair, 613-273-5449

***White Lake:* Waba Cottage Museum & Gardens**
375 Peneshula Rd., White Lake, ON K0A 3L0
Tel: 613-623-8853
info@mcnabbraeside.com
www.mcnabbraeside.com
Situated in an 8-acre park amongst heritage buildings, boat launch & flower gardens; located on Burnstown Rd., White Lake, ON.
Brenda Storie, Contact, 613-623-4341

***Whitney:* Algonquin Visitor Centre & Algonquin Logging Museum**
PO Box 219, Whitney, ON K0J 2M0
Tel: 613-637-2828; Fax: 613-637-2138
info@algonquinpark.on.ca
www.algonquinpark.on.ca
Other contact information: Park Information: 705/633-5572
Visitor Centre contains exhibits on the Park's natural & human history, restaurant, & bookstore; wheelchair accessible; Logging Museum presents the history of logging from 1830's to current times; exhibits include a recreated Camboose camp & a steam powered amphibious tug. Visitor Centre open year round. Logging Museum open daily 9:00-5:00 from late June until Thanksgiving.
Rick Stronks, Chief Park Naturalist

Wiarton: **The Gallery of Early Canadian Flight**
c/o Brian Reis, RR#3, Wiarton, ON N0H 2T0
Tel: 519-534-4090; Fax: 519-534-3184
earlycanflight@sympatico.ca
www.canflightmuseum.org
Located in the Wiarton-Keppel Airport, the museum's collection includes photos, posters, & artists' prints of significant moments in Canadian aviation history, as well as models of pioneering aircraft, & historically important videos. Open year-round, daily 8:30-6:30, or by appointment.

Williamstown: **Bethune-Thompson House**
19730 John St., Williamstown, ON K0C 2J0
Tel: 613-347-7192
Year Founded: 1977 The house was first built in 1784 by an early settler to the Williamstown area, & is now a National Historic Site. Open M-F, & Sa 1:00-5:00.

Williamstown: **The Nor'Westers & Loyalist Museum**
19651 County Rd. 17, Williamstown, ON K0C 2J0
Tel: 613-347-3547
museum@bellnet.ca
norwestersandloyalistmuseum.ca
Housed in a Georgian-style building; stories of loyalist pioneers & partners of the Northwest Fur Trade Company
Gay Hamilton, Chair, gayhamilton@sympatico.ca

Windsor: **Ojibway Nature Centre**
5200 Matchette Rd., Windsor, ON N9C 4E8
Tel: 519-966-5852
www.ojibway.ca
twitter.com/OjibwayPark
The Ojibway Nature Centre presents displays about the natural history & ecology of the Ojibway Prairie Complex. Visitors will also discover a live exhibit area, featuring the Eastern Fox Snake & the Eastern Massasauga Rattlesnake. The Centre is staffed by naturalists, who provide lessons & conducted tours. Events & programs are available for all ages.

Windsor: **Serbian Heritage Museum of Windsor (SHM)**
6770 Tecumseh Rd. East, Windsor, ON N8T 1E6
Tel: 519-944-4884; Fax: 519-974-3963
members.tripod.com/swo_heritage/serbian.htm
Year Founded: 1987 Artifacts & archival material of Serbian people in Windsor dating back to 1920s; tours, educational programming & lectures; gift shop; open year round

Windsor: **Willistead Manor**
1899 Niagara St., Windsor, ON N8Y 1K3
Tel: 519-253-2365
36-room mansion, built 1904-1906; viewing by appt. Available for special events.

Windsor: **The Windsor Wood Carving Museum**
850 Ouellette Ave., Windsor, ON N9A 4M9
Tel: 519-977-0823; Fax: 519-977-1391
woodcarv@windsorpubliclibrary.com
www.windsorwoodcarvingmuseum.ca
Year Founded: 1996 Located in Windsor's Central Library, the museum holds a collection of wood carvings from around the world. Open Tu-F 10:00-5:00, Sa 10:00-4:00.

Windsor: **Windsor's Community Museum**
Also known as: **François Baby House**
254 Pitt St. West, Windsor, ON N9A 5L5
Tel: 519-253-1812; Fax: 519-253-0919
wmuseum@city.windsor.on.ca
www.citywindsor.ca
Year Founded: 1958 The Museum includes the François Baby House on Pitt St. W., and the Duff-Baby Interpretation Centre, located at 221 Mill St.; changing exhibits on the history of the Windsor region; houses over 15,000 artifacts, paintings, drawings, prints and photos, maps, newspapers and books, and a large archival collection. Open year round.
Madelyn Della Valle, Curator

Wingham: **North Huron District Museum**
PO Box 1522, 273 Josephine St., Wingham, ON N0G 2W0
Tel: 519-357-1096; Fax: 519-357-1110
nhmuseum@northhuron.ca
Special events & bi-monthly exhibits featuring the history of North Huron's writers, painters, businesses, farmers & people; Special exhibit & garden dedicated to Alice Munro

Woodstock: **Woodstock Museum National Historic Site**
Museum Square, 466 Dundas St., Woodstock, ON N4S 1C4
Tel: 519-537-8411; Fax: 519-537-7235
museum@city.woodstock.on.ca
www.woodstockmuseum.ca
Other contact information: E-mail, Registrar: apollard@city.woodstock.on.ca
The Woodstock Museum National Historic Site exhibits the local history of Woodstock from 10,000 B.C. to 2001. At the former Town Hall & Market House, which was built in 1853, visitors can see the 1879 Council Chambers & the 1889 Grand Hall. The museum contains a research room, with books & vertical files. It is open to the public by appointment only. School education programs are available, by phoning 519-539-2382, extension 2903, or e-mailing the Education Officer at the following address: kgill@city.woodstock.on.ca. The museum is open year-round.
Karen Houston, Curator, khouston@city.woodstock.on.ca

Prince Edward Island

Provincial Museums

Prince Edward Island Museum & Heritage Foundation / Le Musée et la Fondation du patrimoine de l'Ile-du-Prince-É
2 Kent St., Charlottetown, PE C1A 1M6
Tel: 902-368-6600; Fax: 902-368-6608
mhpei@gov.pe.ca
www.peimuseum.com
The organization is the operator of seven provincial museums & heritage sites across Prince Edward Island. Sites include the Elmira Railway Museum, Basin Head Fisheries Museum, Orwell Corner Historic Village & Agricultural Museum, Beaconsfield Historic House, Eptek Art & Culture Centre, The Acadian Museum of Prince Edward Island, & Green Park Shipbuilding Museum & Yeo House. Open year-round are the Beaconsfield Historic House, the Eptek Art & Culture Centre, & the The Acadian Museum of Prince Edward Island. The others are open during the summer months. The Prince Edward Island Museum & Heritage Foundation also has the responsibility for the provincial collection of over 85,000 artifacts.

Basin Head Fisheries Museum
RR#2, Souris, PE C0A 2B0
Tel: 902-357-7233
1930 cannery & inshore fishery heritage; open May - Sept.

Beaconsfield Historic House
2 Kent St., Charlottetown, PE C1A 1M6
Tel: 902-368-6603
1877 mansion restored; open year round

Elmira Railway Museum
Elmira, PE C0A 1K0
Tel: 902-357-7234
Railway station

Eptek Art & Culture Centre
Waterfront Properties, 130 Harbour Dr., Summerside, PE C1N 1A9
Tel: 902-888-8373; Fax: 902-888-8375

Green Park Shipbuilding Museum & Yeo House
Tyne Valley, RR#1, Port Hill, PE C0B 2C0
Tel: 902-831-7947
19th century furniture; shipbuilding material

Musée acadien/Acadian Museum
PO Box 159, Miscouche, PE C0B 1T0
Tel: 902-432-2880

Orwell Corner Historic Village
RR#2, Vernon Bridge, PE C0A 2E0
Tel: 902-651-8510
Open May - Oct.
Dr. David L. Keenlyside, Executive Director, 902-368-6601, Fax: 902-368-6608, dlkeenlyside@gov.pe.ca
Nora Young, Executive Assistant, njyoung@edu.pe.ca

Local Museums in Prince Edward Island

Alberton: **Alberton Museum**
PO Box 515, 457 Church St., Alberton, PE C0B 1B0
Tel: 902-853-4048
ahf@isn.net
www.townofalberton.ca/history/museum.htm
Year Founded: 1964 Genealogy resources on area families; old photo collection; history of the fox industry; Micmac Indian displays; displays of antique furniture, glassware, textiles & toys. Open June - Sept. Located at 457 Church St. in Alberton.

Charlottetown: **Car Life Museum Inc.**
45 Oak Dr., Charlottetown, PE C1A 6T6
Tel: 902-892-1754
Located on Highway 1 in Bonshaw, Prince Edward Island, the Car Life Museum features restored cars which date back to 1898. The museum also houses farm machinery from the early 1800s & the early 1900s. The Car Life Museum is open from June to September.
Doris MacKay, Contact, 902-675-3555

Charlottetown: **Green Gables House**
2 Palmers Lane, Charlottetown, PE C1A 5V6
Tel: 902-963-7874
peinp-pnipe@pc.gc.ca
www.pc.gc.ca/lhn-nhs/pe/greengables/visit/index_E.asp
Dedicated to Anne of Green Gables, a fictional but nonetheless, famous character created by Lucy Maud Montgomery for her book series "Anne of Green Gables". Open May 1 - Oct. 31

Charlottetown: **Port-la-Joye-Fort Amherst National Historic Site of Canada**
c/o Parks Canada, 2 Palmer's Lane, Charlottetown, PE C1A 5V8
Tel: 902-566-7626; Fax: 902-566-8295
pljfa.info@pc.gc.ca; information@pc.gc.ca
www.pc.gc.ca/lhn-nhs/pe/amherst/activ.aspx
Other contact information: Summer Phone: 902-675-2220
Visitors to the Port-la-Joye-Fort Amherst National Historic Site of Canada learn the history of the Mi'kmaq of Prince Edward Island. Interpretive services are available in July & August. Guided tours are offered in both English & French. The grounds are open from June to October.
Jessica Pinkham, Contact, jessica.pinkham@pc.gc.ca

Charlottetown: **Prince Edward Island Regiment (RCAC) Museum**
Queen Charlotte Armouries, PO Box 1480, Charlottetown, PE C1A 7N1
Tel: 902-368-0108; Fax: 902-368-3034
www.facebook.com/107780305912036

Charlottetown: **Province House National Historic Site of Canada**
c/o Parks Canada, 2 Palmer's Lane, Charlottetown, PE C1A 5V6
Tel: 902-566-7626; Fax: 902-566-8295
information@pc.gc.ca
www.pc.gc.ca/eng/lhn-nhs/pe/provincehouse/index.asp x
Includes Confederation Chamber, site of historic discussions regarding union of the BNA colonies; remains of the Legislative Bldg. for PEI; open year round
Jessica Pinkham, Contact, jessica.pinkham@pc.gc.ca

Charlottetown: **Spoke Wheel Car Museum**
RR#3, Charlottetown, PE C1A 7J7
Antique automobiles

Ellerslie: **Ellerslie Shellfish Museum**
Ellerslie, PE C0B 1J0
Tel: 902-853-2181
Aquariums of live fish & shellfish; history of oyster cultivation
Joanne Wallace, Director

Kensington: **Anne of Green Gables Museum at Silver Bush**
5 Gerald McCarville Dr., Kensington, PE C0B 1M0
Tel: 902-886-2884Toll-Free: 800-665-2663
george@annesociety.org
www.annemuseum.com
Open May - Thanksgiving

Kensington: **The Keir Memorial Museum**
2214 Rte. 20, Kensington, PE C0B 1M0
Tel: 902-836-3054
kmmuseum@bellaliant.com
www.malpequebay.ca/keirmuseum.htm
Open July - Sept.

Kensington: **Veterans' Memorial Military Museum**
88 Victoria St., Kensington, PE C0B 1M0
Tel: 902-836-3600
Military memorabilia mostly from WWI & WWII; Boer War items
Brian Campbell, Contact, brian.campbell@islandtelecom.com

Montague: **Garden of the Gulf Museum**
PO Box 1237, 564 Main St., Montague, PE C0A 1R0
Tel: 902-838-2467
ggmuseum@eastlink.ca
www.montaguemuseum.com
Other contact information: Off-season Phone: 902/838-2820
Year Founded: 1958 Early island history; open June - Sept. PEI's oldest Museum.

Murray Harbour: **Log Cabin Museum**
Route 18 A, Murray Harbour, PE C0A 1V0
Tel: 902-962-2201
Local history
Preston Robertson, Contact

O'Leary: **Prince Edward Island Potato Museum**
PO Box 602, O'Leary, PE C0B 1V0
Tel: 902-859-2039Toll-Free: 800-565-3457
info@peipotatomuseum.com
www.peipotatomuseum.com
www.facebook.com/grou ps/138711350502
The history of the potato industry is depicted at the Prince Edward Island Potato Museum. Visitors will see a collection of machinery & farm implements related to growing & harvesting potatoes. The museum also includes the Potato Hall of Fame. It is open from mid May to mid October.
Donna Rowley, Manager, 902-853-2312

Richmond: **The Bottle Houses / Les Maisons de Bouteilles**
PO Box 72, Richmond, PE C0B 2E0
Tel: 902-854-2987
www.teleco.org/SitesWebs/bouteilles/index.html
Other contact information: Off season: 902/854-2254
Three fantasy-like buildings made of over 25,000 vari-coloured bottles, creating a symphony of light & colour within; located in Cape Egmont; flower gardens; giftshop; bilingual service
Réjeanne Arsenault, Owner/Operator

Rustico: **Farmers' Bank of Rustico**
Hunter River, RR#3, Rustico, PE C0A 1N0
Tel: 902-963-3168
info@farmersbank.ca
www.farmersbank.ca
Other contact information: (off season): 902/963-2304
Banking artifacts; precursor to the Credit Union movement in North America
J.D. MacDonald, President

Summerside: **International Fox Museum & Hall of Fame Inc.**
286 Fitzroy St., Summerside, PE C1N 1J2
Tel: 902-436-0177
toxpei@isn.net
Located at historic Holman Homestead & Gardens; museum tells the story of the PEI silver fox industry heyday between 1894 & WWII

Tignish: **Tignish Cultural Centre**
103 School St., Tignish, PE C0B 2B0
Tel: 902-882-1999; Fax: 902-882-3144
www.tignish.com
Local history

West Point: **West Point Lighthouse**
Lot 8, 364 Cedar Dunes Park Rd., West Point, PE C0B 1V0
Tel: 902-859-3605; Fax: 902-859-1510
Toll-Free: 800-764-6854
westpointlighthouse@gmail.com
www.westpointlighthouse. com
Year Founded: 1983 The West Point Development Corporation restored the historic West Point Lighthouse, which was built in 1875 & had a keeper until 1963. The lighthouse is one of the tallest on Prince Edward Island. Today, the lighthouse continues to operate as a navigational aid.

Wood Islands: **Ripley's Believe It or Not! Museum**
c/o Mac 5 International Inc., 313 Trans Canada Hwy., Wood Islands, PE C0A 1B0
Tel: 902-969-9386
ripleys@pei.aibn.com
www.ripleyspei.com
Ripley's presents displays of unual events & things: open June - Sept.
Thom McMillan, Contact, thom.mac@pei.sympatico.ca

Quebec

Provincial Museums

Canadian Centre for Architecture (CCA) / Centre Canadien d'Architecture
1920, rue Baile, Montréal, QC H3H 2S6
Tel: 514-939-7026; Fax: 514-939-7020
info@cca.qc.ca; press@cca.qc.ca (Press Relations)
www.cca.qc.ca
Other contact information: Phone, Administration: 514-939-7000; E-mail, Tours: schools@cca.qc.ca
Year Founded: 1979 The Canadian Centre for Architecture is a museum & an international research centre. The Centre raises awareness of the role of architecture, stimulates design innovation, & promotes scholarly research.
Phyllis Lambert, Founding Director & Chair
Mirko Zardini, Director & Chief Curator
Louise Désy, Curator, Photography
Isabelle Huiban, Head, Media Relations, ihuiban@cca.qc.ca

McCord Museum of Canadian History / Musée McCord d'histoire canadienne
690, rue Sherbrooke ouest, Montréal, QC H3A 1E9
Tel: 514-398-7100; Fax: 514-398-5045
webmaster@mccord.mcgill.ca
www.mccord-museum.qc.ca
Social Media: www.youtube.com/user/MuseeMcCordMuseum
twitter.com/MuseeMcCord
www.fac ebook.com/museemccord
Year Founded: 1921 The museum started with the collections of David Ross McCord & a building from McGill University. It conserves a variety of objects reflecting the social history & material culture of Montreal, Quebec & Canada. Exhibits include over 1,440,000 pieces & range from paintings, costumes & decorative arts, to archives of texts & photographs. Open year round with summer/winter hrs.
Suzanne Sauvage, President/CEO, suzanne.sauvage@mccord.mcgill.ca
Sylvie Durand, Director, Programs, sylvie.durand@mccord.mcgill.ca
Philip Leduc, Director, Operations, philip.leduc@mccord.mcgill.ca

Musée de l'Amerique française (MAF)
2, côte de la Fabrique, Québec, QC G1R 3V6
Tél: 418-692-2843; Téléc: 418-646-9705
Ligne sans frais: 866-710-8031
mcqweb@mcq.org
www.mcq.org/en/maf/index.html
Le plus ancien musée au Canada; la collection regroupe des instruments d'enseignement des sciences, monnaies anciennes, médailles, collections de minéralogie, de géologie, de numismatique, de zoologie, de botanique, de fossiles, livres anciens, et de peinture; expositions et activités; centre de référence; boutique; café.
Danielle Poiré, Directrice-générale (intérim)

Musée de la civilisation
CP 155 B, 85, rue Dalhousie, Québec, QC G1K 7A6
Tél: 418-643-2158; Téléc: 418-646-9705
Ligne sans frais: 866-710-8031
mcq@mcq.org
www.mcq.org
Médias sociaux: www.youtube.com/mcqpromo
twitter.com/mcqorg
www.facebook.com/museedelacivilisation
Fondée en: 1988 Le musée est doté de la plus importante collection ethnographique et historique du Québec et se distingue par sa muséologie innovatrice; programmation thématique; activités éducatives et culturelles; ateliers, visites commentées; boutique; café.
Danielle Poiré, Directrice générale (intérim)

Pointe-à-Callière, Montréal Museum of Archaeology & History
Angle de la Commune, 350, place Royale, Montréal, QC H2Y 3Y5
Tel: 514-872-9150
info@pacmusee.qc.ca; rhumaines@pacmusee.qc.ca (HR)
www.pacmusee.qc.ca
Other contact information: E-mail, Public Services Department: glemay@pacmusee.qc.ca
Year Founded: 1992 The Montréal Museum of Archaeology & History is situated on the site where, in 1642, a mass celebrated the founding of Montréal. Pointe-à-Callière was also the location of a home built in 1688 by the third governor of Montréal, Chevalier Louis Hector de Callière. The site features architectural remains, & the museum houses hundreds of artifacts.
Sophie Brochu, President & CEO
Francine Lelièvre, Executive Director
John LeBoutillier, Secretary-Treasurer
Raymond Montpetit, Coordinator, Historical Research

Local Museums in Quebec

Alma: **L'Odyssée des Bâtisseurs**
1671, av du Pont Nord, Alma, QC G8B 5G2
Tél: 418-668-2606; Téléc: 418-668-5851
Ligne sans frais: 866-668-2606
info@odysseedesbatisseurs.com
www.odysseedesbatisseurs.com
Axé sur l'importance de l'eau au coeur du développement, le parc thématique L'Odyssée des Bâtisseurs vous invite à visiter des expositions vivantes, admirer un panorama naturel et industriel extraordinaire et vivre une expérience multimédia 360 saisissante à l'intérieur d'un ancien château d'eau.
Danielle Larouche, Directrice générale

Alouette: **Bagotville Air Defence Museum / Musée de la Défense aérienne de Bagotville**
PO Box 567 Main, Alouette, QC G0V 1A0
Tel: 418-677-7159; Fax: 418-677-4104
museebagotville@forces.qc.ca
www.bagotville.net
Year Founded: 1997 Canadian Military Aviation Museum
Claude Chamberland, Director
Captain Mauril Dufort, 3 Wing Heritage Officer

Angliers: **Site historique T.E Draper/Chantier de Gédéon**
Parent: **Les Promoteurs d'Angliers inc.**
CP 82, 11, rue du T.E. Draper, Angliers, QC J0Z 1A0
Tél: 819-949-4431; Téléc: 819-949-4431
tedraper@tlb.sympatico.ca
www3.telebecinternet.com/tedraper
Montez à bord du remorqueur de bois T.E. Draper; visitez le chantier de Gédéon, la reconstitution d'un camp de bûcherons des années 1930-1940.
Cathy Fraser, Contact

Anse-au-Griffon: **Manoir Le Boutillier, lieu historique national du Canada**
578, boul Griffon, Anse-au-Griffon, QC G4X 6A4
Tél: 418-892-5150; Téléc: 418-892-5189
manoir.leboutillier@lanseaugriffon.ca
www.lanseaugriffon.ca/manoir
Built in 1850s by John Le Boutillier; open June - mid-Oct.

Asbestos: **Musée minéralogique d'Asbestos / Asbestos Mineralogical Museum**
341, boul St-Luc, Asbestos, QC J1T 2W4
Tél: 819-879-6444
Minerals from the Jeffrey Mine; local mining history; exploration & survey instruments; workshops for schools; seasonal opening

Authier: **École du Rang II d'Authier**
CP 74, 269 Rang II, Authier, QC J0Z 1C0
Tél: 819-782-3289; Téléc: 819-782-2421
Ligne sans frais: 866-336-3289
ecolrgll@tlb.sympatico.ca
pwp.lino.com/ecolrgll
Représente les écoles de rang qui ont meublé le paysage rural du Québec dans les années quarantes

Batiscan: **Vieux presbytère de Batiscan**
340, rue Principale, Batiscan, QC G0X 1A0
Tél: 418-362-2051; Téléc: 418-362-1373
direction@presbytere-batiscan.com
www.presbytere-batiscan.com
Datant de 1816, propose une reconstitution fidèle de l'intérieur de la maison au milieu du 19e siècle; aperçu du quotidien du curé Fréchette et de sa ménagère Adéline, les deux habitants du presbytère à cette époque; exposition temporaire à chaque année; sentier ornithologique; aire de repos et de pique-nique; boutique souvenir.

Beauharnois: **Pointe-du-Buisson/Musée québécois d'archéologie**
333, rue Émond, Beauharnois, QC J0S 1J0
Tel: 450-429-7857; Fax: 450-429-5921
administration@pointedubuisson.com
www.pointedubuisson.com
Archaeology site; prehistoric objects which form a collection that is recognized in the scientific world as one of the most important in the NE of the continent; research, outreach education; over two million objects & fragments of artifacts & ecofacts that mark SW Quebec.
Alessandro Cassa, Directeur général, direction@pointedubuisson.com

Beaumont: **Moulin de Beaumont**
2, rte du Fleuve, Beaumont, QC G0R 1C0
Tél: 418-833-1867
pages.videotron.com/moulinb
1821 flour mill; open May 15 - June 24, Sept. & Oct., Sat & Sun., Tues. - Fri by appt.; June 24 - Aug., Tues. - Sat.

Bergeronnes: **Centre Archéo Topo**
498, rue de la Mer, Bergeronnes, QC G0T 1G0
Tél: 418-232-6286; Téléc: 418-232-6695
Ligne sans frais: 866-832-6286
archeo95@bellnet.ca
www.archeotopo.qc.ca
L'histoire de la région de La Haute-Côte-Nord; exposition interactive retrace la vie des tribus amérindiennes dans la région; jeux didactiques; ateliers pour les enfants et les jeunes; excursions; spectacle multimédia; boutique.

Les Bergeronnes: **Centre d'interprétation et d'observation de Cap-de-Bon-Désir**
13, ch du Cap-de-Bon-Désir, Les Bergeronnes, QC G0T 1G0
Tél: 418-232-6751; Téléc: 418-235-6468
Ligne sans frais: 888-773-8888
parcscanada-que.pc.qc.ca
www.quebecmaritime.ca
Promontoire naturel pour l'observation des mammifères marins; guides-interprètes; salle d'exposition, phare. Ouvert mi-juin-mi-octobre.

Berthierville: **Chapelle des Cuthbert de Berthier**
461, rue de Bienville, Berthierville, QC J0K 1A0
Tél: 450-836-7336; Téléc: 450-836-8158
www.patrimoineberthier.org
La plus ancien temple protestant au Québec; expositions, visites commentées; pique-nique sur place; ouverte tous les jours, du juin au fête du Travil, 10h-18h

Berthierville: **Musée Gilles-Villeneuve**
960, av Gilles-Villeneuve, Berthierville, QC J0K 1A0
Tél: 450-836-2714; Téléc: 450-836-3067
Ligne sans frais: 800-639-0103
museegillesvilleneuve@bellnet.ca
www.museegillesvilleneuve.com
Fondée en: 1995 Le musée a pour mandat perpétuer le souvenir de Gilles Villeneuve, le grand coureur automobile du F1; voitures, photographies, Galerie M. Trudel.
Alain Bellehumeur, Superviseur

Bonaventure: **Musée acadien du Québec à Bonaventure**
95, av Port Royal, Bonaventure, QC G0C 1E0
Tél: 418-534-4000; Téléc: 418-534-4105
reception@museeacadien.com
www.museeacadien.com
twitter.com/museeacadi en
www.facebook.com/205929912758086
Louise Cyr, Directeur, direction@museeacadien.com

Boucherville: **Maison Louis-Hippolyte Lafontaine**
314, boul Marie-Victorin, Boucherville, QC J4B 1X1
Tél: 514-449-8347
maison.lh.lafontaine@boucherville.ca

Cascapédia-Saint-Jules: **Musée de la rivière Cascapédia / The Cascapedia River Museum**
275, rte 299, Cascapédia-Saint-Jules, QC G0C 1T0
Tél: 418-392-5079; Téléc: 418-392-5070
info@cascapedia.org
www.cascapedia.org
Le musée raconte l'histoire de la région autour de la rivière Cascapédia, la pêche au saumon, et le patrimoine gaspésien; boutique.

Causapscal: **Maison Dr. Joseph-Frenette**
3, rue Frenette, Causapscal, QC G0J 1J0
Tél: 418-756-5999; Téléc: 418-756-3344
www.maisondrjosephfrenette.com
Joseph Frenette exerçait la profession, aujourd'hui disparue, de médecin de campagne. Il consacra sa vie à soigner des malades et des blessés, à faire naître des enfants, à sauver des vies. Tel un livre ouvert, cette exposition fait découvrir son univers familial et professionnel et à comprendre le rôle primordial du médecin de campagne dans l'histoire du Québec.

Causapscal: **Site historique Matamajaw**
53C, rue Saint-Jacques sud, Causapscal, QC G0J 1J0
Tél: 418-756-5999; Téléc: 418-756-3344
faucuscar@globetrotter.net
www.causapscal.net
Ancien lieu de villégiature de Sir John A. McDonald et de Lord Mount Stephen, le Matamajaw Salmon Club a attiré les membres de la haute société anglaise, américaine et canadienne durant la fin du 19e et au début du 20e siècle. Le Site Matamajaw est le seul ancien établissement privé accessible au public en Amérique du Nord.

Chambly: **Lieu historique du Fort-Chambly**
2, rue Richelieu, Chambly, QC J3L 2B9
Tél: 514-658-1585; Téléc: 514-658-7216
Ligne sans frais: 888-773-8888
parcscanada-que@pc.gc.ca
www.pc.gc.ca/lhn-nhs/qc/fortchambly
Présente l'histoire et les coutumes de la Nouvelle-France de 1665-1760; expositions; activités.

Chambord: **Village Historique de Val-Jalbert**
95, rue St-Georges, Chambord, QC G0W 1G0
Tel: 418-275-3132; Fax: 418-275-5875
Toll-Free: 888-675-3132
valjalbert@valjalbert.com
www.valjalbert.com
Social Media: www.youtube.com/user/valjalbert1901
www.facebook.com/426543094744
Partially restored ghost town; created by the 1901 opening of a pulp & paper mill; as the years went by the town flourished & several services & buildings were added including a train station, convent, hotel & general store; on Aug. 13, 1927 the plant shut down forcing workers to leave Val-Jalbert; today it's a rich historical, industrial & religious patrimony; fall height of 72 m.
Danny Bouchard, Directeur général

Château-Richer: **Centre d'interpretation de la Côte-de-Beaupré**
CP 40, 7976, av Royale, Château-Richer, QC G0A 1N0
Tél: 418-824-3677; Téléc: 418-824-5907
info@histoire-cotedebeaupre.org
www.histoire-cotedebeaupre.org
Présente les aspects culturels, géographiques, historiques et patrimoniaux qui témoignent de la beauté de la région; activités pédagogiques complémentaires au programme d'enseignement; ouvert tous les jours, 9h30-16h30
Luc Trépanier, Directeur général

Château-Richer: **Musée de l'Abeille**
Also known as: **Economusée du miel**
8862, boul Sainte-Anne, Château-Richer, QC G0A 1N0
Tél: 418-824-4411; Téléc: 418-824-4422
info@musee-abeille.com
www.musee-abeille.com
Centre d'interprétation; l'exposition Des Abeilles et Des Hommes; visites guidées; informations sur le miel; boutique.
Redmond Hayes, President

Chicoutimi: **Centre historique des Soeurs de Notre-Dame du Bon-Conseil de Chicoutimi**
700, rue Racine est (porte 688), Chicoutimi, QC G7H 1V2
Tél: 418-543-4861; Téléc: 418-543-7194
centrehistorique@sndbc.qc.ca
www.sndbc.qc.ca; www.reseaumuseal.com; www.museevirtuel.ca

Chicoutimi: **La Pulperie de Chicoutimi**
300, rue Dubuc, Chicoutimi, QC G7J 4M1
Tél: 418-698-3100; Téléc: 418-698-3158
Ligne sans frais: 877-998-3100
info@pulperie.com
www.pulperie.com
Médias sociaux: www.youtube.com/user/PulperieChicoutimi
www.facebook.com/PulperiedeChicoutimi
Collection de plus de 26 000 ojets et oeuvres; maison Arthur-Villeneuve; expositions d'art et d'ethnologie; vestiges restaurés des anciennes installations de la Compagnie de pulpe de Chicoutimi; parc.
Jacques Fortin, Directeur général

Claybank: **Claybank Brick Plant Historical Museum & National Historic Site**
Parent: **Claybank Brick Plant Historical Society**
PO Box 2-5, Claybank, S0H 0W0
Tel: 306-868-4774; Fax: 306-868-4854
claybank@sasktel.net
claybank.sasktelwebsite.net
Social Media: www.youtube.com/watch?v=eFpA_3XU7G8
The museum is a well-preserved brick plant dating from 1914, & has been designated a National Historic Site. Visitors can also explore the surrounding Massold Clay Canyons area, & hike on a variety of nature trails. Open May-Aug., daily 10:00-12:00 & 1:00-5:00, or by appointment.

Coaticook: **Beaulne Museum / Musée Beaulne**
96, rue Union, Coaticook, QC J1A 1Y9
Tel: 819-849-6560; Fax: 819-849-9519
info@museebeaulne.qc.ca
www.museebeaulne.qc.ca
Other contact information: Alternative E-mail: bonjour@museebeaulne.qc.ca
Year Founded: 1964 Beaulne Museum depicts the history & achievements of the local Norton family, who were known for manufacturing railway jacks & their philanthropy. The museum is located in Château Arthur Osmore Norton, a Victorian-style mansion which was built in 1912. Beaulne Museum is open year round from Tuesday to Sunday.

Cookshire: **Compton County Historical Museum Society / Societé d'histoire du musée du comté Compton**
PO Box 967, 374 Route 253, Cookshire, QC J0B 1M0
Tel: 819-875-5256; Fax: 819-875-3182
mus.eatoncorner@gmail.com
mus.eatoncorner.com
Housed in a former Congregationalist Church built in 1842. Address is 374 Route 253, Eaton Corner, Quebec.
Pat Boychuck, President

Coteau-du-Lac: **Lieu historique national du Canada de Coteau-du-Lac / Coteau-du-Lac National Historic Site of Canada**
308A, ch du Fleuve, Coteau-du-Lac, QC J0P 1B0
Tél: 450-763-5631; Téléc: 450-763-1654
parcscanada-que@pc.gc.ca
www.pc.gc.ca/fra/lhn-nhs/qc/coteaudulac/index.a spx
Autre numéros: TTY: 1-866-787-6221
Exposition et activités: le site stratégique de Coteau-du-Lac, le Blockhaus, coin de famille, circuit nature, jardin archéologique, reconstitution militaire, marché champêtre.

Desbiens: **Centre d'histoire et d'archéologie de la Métabetchouane**
243, rue Hébert, Desbiens, QC G0W 1N0
Tél: 418-346-5341; Téléc: 418-346-5341
cham@digicom.ca
www.chamans.com
Fondée en: 1995 Site historique et archéologique; histoire d'il y a 5,000 ans; poste de traite; salle de découverte; animation; exposition thématique; 20 juin - sept. ou par réservation

La Doré: **Le Moulin des Pionniers de La Doré**
4205, rue des Peupliers, La Doré, QC G8J 1E4
Tél: 418-256-8242Ligne sans frais: 866-272-2842
moulindespionniers@live.ca
moulindespionniers.com
Moulin à scie à pouvoir hydraulique, toujours à l'oeuvre depuis 1889; Maison de Marie, une des plus anciennes maisons de La Doré, avec un potager et une grange-étable; petite ferme avec des animaux; camp qui abrite un restaurant et un bar; auberge "La Nuit Boréale"; sentiers pédestres; tour d'observation; expositions; programmation.
Rodrigue Tremblay, Président
Guylaine Lapointe, Directrice générale, guylainemoulin@hotmail.com

Drummondville: **Le Village Québecois d'Antan inc.**
1425, rue Montplaisir, Drummondville, QC J2B 7T5
Tél: 819-478-1441; Téléc: 819-478-8155
Ligne sans frais: 877-710-0267
renseignements@villagequebecois.com
www.villagequebecois.com
Fondée en: 1977 Reconstitution d'un village canadien-français du siècle dernier (1810-1910)
Pierre Derouin, Directeur général, pierre@villagequebecois.com
France Lemoine, Trésorière, france@villagequebecois.com
Simon Bourgault, Directeur, Communications, simon@villagequebecois.com

Duhamel-Ouest: **Lieu historique national du Canada du Fort-Témiscamingue / Fort Témiscamingue National Historic Site of Canada**
834, ch Vieux-Fort, Duhamel-Ouest, QC J9V 1N7
Tél: 819-629-3222; Téléc: 819-629-2977
Ligne sans frais: 888-773-8888
fort.temiscamingue@pc.gc.ca
www.pc.gc.ca/fra/lhn-nhs/qc/temiscamingue
Rappelle la présence millénaire des algonquins et l'histoire de ce poste de traite situé au détroit du Lac Témiscamingue.

Forestville: **Petite Anglicane**
CP 147, #2, 2e rue, Forestville, QC G0T 1E0
Tél: 418-587-2109; Téléc: 418-587-6212
Archéologie locale, les gardes-feu, les remèdes d'autrefois, la vie domestique, nos pionniers, l'histoire de Forestville en photos; expositions temporaires; visites guidées

Gaspé: **Magasin générale Hyman & Sons et l'entrepôt Parc national du Canada Forillon, 122, boul Gaspé, Gaspé, QC G4X 1A9**
Tél: 418-368-5505; Téléc: 418-368-6837
parcscanada-que@pc.gc.ca
www.pc.gc.ca/Forillon
Magasin au centre du village, de l'époque 1920, autrefois la propriété de la compagnie de pêche "William Hyman and Sons", au Parc national du Canada Forillon; animation en costumes; programmation; visites guidées.

Gaspé: **Musée de la Gaspésie**
80, boul Gaspé, Gaspé, QC G4X 1A9
Tél: 418-368-1534; Téléc: 418-368-1535
info@museedelagaspesie.ca
www.museedelagaspesie.ca
Médias sociaux: www.youtube.com/user/musee1534
twitter.com/MG1534
www.facebook.com/pages/Musée-de-la-Gaspésie/11072457562 4365
Le musée favoriser la connaissance et l'appréciation de l'histoire et du patrimoine gaspésiens; activités de conservation et de recherche; collections y compris les disciplines de l'ethnologie, l'histoire, les beaux-arts, les sciences naturelles, l'archéologie; archives; boutique; programmation.
Sébastien Lévesque, Directeur général, direction@museedelagaspesie.ca

Gaspé: **Parc national du Canada Forillon / Forillon National Park of Canada**
122, boul Gaspé, Gaspé, QC G4X 1A9
Tél: 418-368-5505; Téléc: 418-368-6837
Ligne sans frais: 888-787-6221
information@pc.gc.ca
www.pc.gc.ca/pn-np/qc/forillon.aspx
twitter.com/ForillonNP
www.faceboo k.com/ForillonNP
Autre numéros: TTY: 1-866-787-6221

Gatineau: **Canadian Postal Museum (CPM)**
c/o Canadian Museum of Civilization, 100 Laurier St., Gatineau, QC K1A 0M8
Toll-Free: 800-555-5621
www.civilization.ca/exhibitions/canadian-postal-museum
Year Founded: 1971 The museum is one of a kind in Canada, collecting, researching, & interpreting the heritage of Canada's postal service. Open M-W & F 9:00-6:00, Th 9:00-8:00, Sa & Su 9:30-6:00.
Chantal Amyot, Director, Exhibitions & Canadian Postal Museum, chantal.amyot@civilization.ca

Gatineau: **Fort George National Historic Site of Canada**
Also known as: **Fort George**
c/o Parks Canada National Office, 25-7-N, rue Eddy, Gatineau, QC K1A 0M5
Tel: 905-468-6614; Fax: 905-468-4638
ont-niagara@pc.gc.ca
www.pc.gc.ca/eng/lhn-nhs/on/fortgeorge/index.aspx
twitter.com/fofg
www.facebook.com/102031676507960
Other contact information: Friends of Fort George URL: www.friendsoffortgeorge.ca
Recontructed fort built in 1799

Gatineau: **Musée de l'Auberge Symmes / Symmes Inn Museum**
Also known as: **Musée d'Aylmer Museum Inc.**
PO Box 311, 1, rue Front, Gatineau, QC J9H 5E6
Tel: 819-682-0291
symmes@ca.inter.net
www.symmes.ca
twitter.com/Charle sSymmes
www.facebook.com/130585520302457
Richard M. Bégin, President

Godbout: **Musée amérindien et inuit de Godbout**
134, ch Pascal-Comeau, Godbout, QC G0H 1G0
Tél: 418-568-7306
www.vitrine.net/godbout
Cécile Grenier, Directrice, cecilegrenier6@sympatico.ca
Claude Grenier, Directeur

Granby: **Centre d'interpretation de la Nature du Lac Boivin**
700, rue Drummond, Granby, QC J2G 8C7
Tél: 450-375-3861; Téléc: 450-375-3736
marco.lemay@cscantons.qc.ca
www.darwin.cyberscol.qc.ca/centre/cinlb/
Fondée en: 1980 A pour mission de conserver le territoire, les habitats, la faune et la flore de la région
Mario Fortin, Directeur général

Guérin: **Musée de Guérin**
913, rue Principale, Guérin, QC J0Z 2E0
Tél: 819-784-7014
musee-guerin@tlb.sympatico.ca
www.culture-at.org/musee-guerin
Le Musée de Guérin offre deux expositions permanentes: "Autour du clocher" et "Le Réveil rural" qui retracent la vie religieuse et agricole des années 1940-50. Situé sur la "Terre de la Fabrique", concédée au début de la paroisse, le site du musée comprend encore un lieu du culte et la ferme de Monsieur le Curé

Havre-Aubert: **Aquarium des Iles-de-la-Madeleine / Island Aquarium**
982 route 199, La Grave, Havre-Aubert, QC G4T 9C7
Tél: 418-937-2277
info@aquariumdesiles.ca
www.facebook.com/aquariumdesiles

Hâvre-Aubert: **Musée de la Mer Inc.**
1023, Rte. 199, Hâvre-Aubert, QC G4T 9C8
Tél: 418-937-5711; Téléc: 418-937-2449
info@museedelamer-im.com
www.ilesdelamadeleine-guidetouristique.com/Ile-du-Havre/Musee-de-la-Mer
L'histoire des Iles-de-la-Madeleine, l'évolution de la navigation, l'histoire de la pêche; collections de roches, de minéraux, de coquillages; photos et objets marins. Ouvert à l'année.
Michelle Joannette, Directrice générale

Inukjuak: **Musée commémoratif et Centre de transmission de la culture Daniel Weetaluktuk / Daniel Weetaluktuk Commemorative Museum & Cultural Transmis**
General Delivery, Inukjuak, QC J0M 1M0
Tél: 819-254-8919; Téléc: 819-254-8148
Ligne sans frais: 866-897-2287
avataq-inukjuak@avataq.qc.ca
www.avataq.qc.ca
Le centre contribue à la protection et à la diffusion de la culture des Inuits d'Inukjuak et du Nunavik; collection de plus de 400 objets anciens et contemporains présentés dans leur contexte culturel d'origine; oeuvres d'art, vêtements traditionnels, artefacts; exposition permanente; expositions temporaires.
Louis Gagnon, Conservateur, louisgagnon@avataq.qc.ca

Inverness: **Musée du Bronze d'Inverness**
1760, ch Dublin, Inverness, QC G0S 1K0
Tél: 418-453-2101; Téléc: 418-453-7711
info@museedubronze.com
www.museedubronze.com
Voué à la recherche, la mise en valeur, la diffusion, la fabrication, l'interprétation et l'éducation relative à l'art du bronze; fonderie; ateliers; visites guidées; jardin; programmation.

Michelle Joannette, Directrice générale

L'Islet-sur-Mer: **Musée maritime du Québec**
Also known as: **Musée maritime Bernier**
55, ch des Pionniers est, L'Islet-sur-Mer, QC G0R 2B0
Tél: 418-247-5001
info@mmq.qc.ca
www.mmq.qc.ca
Fondée en: 1968 Le musée a pour mission la sauvegarde, l'étude, et la mise en valeur du patrimoine maritime se rattrachant au fleuve Saint-Laurent, et de la porte des Grands Lacs; la conservation des navires historiques; expositions permanentes: "Gens du pays, gens du fleuve", "Capt. Joseph-Elzéar Bernier", "Ilititaa...Bernier, ses hommes et les Inuits", et "Pirates ou corsaires?"; boutique; visites guidées; accessible aux personnes à mobilité réduite.

Kahnawake: **Musée Kateri Tekakwitha Mission Saint-François-Xavier, PO Box 70, Kahnawake, QC J0L 1B0**
Tel: 450-632-6030; Fax: 450-632-6031
kateritekakwithasanctuary@yahoo.ca
Religious & ethnic artifacts dating back to the 17th century; historical mission buildings (rectory 1717, church 1845) contain Blessed Kateri's tomb (1656-1680) & precious works of art including the Deerfield Bell (17th - 19th cent.); open all year 10-5; Kahnawake is a native Mohawk reservation

Kamouraska: **Musée régional de Kamouraska**
69, av Morel, Kamouraska, QC G0L 1M0
Tél: 418-492-9783; Téléc: 418-492-3144
museekam@videotron.ca
www.museekamouraska.com
Fondée en: 1977 Il assume fidèlement sa mission de protection, conservation et diffusion du riche patrimoine historique et culturel de tout Kamouraska
Yvette Raymond, Directrice générale

Knowlton: **Brome County Historical Museum (BCHS)**
PO Box 690, 130 Lakeside, Knowlton, QC J0E 1V0
Tel: 450-243-6782
bchs@endirect.qc.ca
Managed by the Brome County Historical Society, the Brome County Museum presents the history of Brome County & the surrounding region. The museum's grounds feature an old fire hall from 1904, an academy building from 1854, & the Brome County Court House from 1858-1859. The court house contains the archives of the Brome County Historical Society. The museum is open from mid May to mid September. The archives are open year round.

Lac-Drolet: **Maison du Granit**
301, rte du Morne, Lac-Drolet, QC G0Y 1C0
Tél: 819-549-2566
info@maisondugranit.ca
www.maisondugranit.ca
Fondée en: 1989 A pour mission de collecter et de diffuser l'histoire de l'industrie du granit et de ses artisans les tailleurs de pierre; exposition permanente; expositions thématiques; visites guidées; jardin panoramique.

Lachine: **Centre historique des Soeurs de Sainte-Anne**
1280, boul Saint-Joseph, Lachine, QC H8S 2M8
Tél: 514-637-4616
musee@ssacong.org; chssa@bellnet.ca
www.ssacong.org/musee
Musée communautaire de la Congrégation des Soeurs de Sainte-Anne. Le musée a pour mission de faire découvrir la vie des Soeurs de Sainte-Anne marquée par les lieux et les époques où elles ont évolué; open year-round, winter by appt. only
Murielle Gagnon, Responsable du musée, murielle.gagnon@bellnet.ca

Lachine: **Lieu historique national du Canada du Commerce-de-la-fourrure-à-Lachine / The Fur Trade at Lachine National Historic Site of Canada**
1255, boul St-Joseph, Lachine, QC H8S 2M2
Tél: 514-637-7433; Téléc: 514-637-5325
parcscanada-que@pc.gc.ca
www.pc.gc.ca/lhn-nhs/qc/lachine.aspx
A bord d'un canot, découvrez le point de départ des grands explorateurs du continent nord-américain; programmes et activités; exposition sur l'apogée du commerce des fourrures; visites thématiques.

Lachine: **Musée de Lachine**
1, ch du Musée, Lachine, QC H8S 4L9
Tél: 514-634-3478; Téléc: 514-637-6784
museedelachine@lachine.ca
lachine.ville.montreal.qc.ca/musee
Includes Maison leBer-LeMoyne & the Dépendance, the oldest complete buildings on the Island of Montreal as well as the Benoît-Verdickt Pavillion, a contemporary art exhibition centre; the Pavillion de l'Entrepôt presents multidisciplinary & multicultural exhibitions; educational program available for school-aged visitors as well as others; open Wed. - Sun.; guided tours Thurs. & Fri. by appt.
Marc Pitre, Directeur

Lac-Mégantic: **Musée Namesokanjic**
#200, 5527, rue Frontenac, Lac-Mégantic, QC G6B 1H6
Tél: 819-583-2441; Téléc: 819-583-5920
greffier@ville.lac-megantic.qc.ca
www.lac-megantic.qc.ca
Outils forestiers, objets domestiques, photographies, costumes; programmation et activités.
Jean-François Grandmont, Personne ressource

Lasalle: **Moulin Fleming, centre d'interprétation historique**
9675, boul LaSalle, Lasalle, QC H8R 4A8
Tél: 514-367-6439; Téléc: 514-367-6606
ville.montreal.qc.ca/lasalle
Ouvert mai - sept.

Laval: **Musée Armand-Frappier, Centre d'interprétation des biosciences / Armand-Frappier Museum**
531, boul des Prairies, Laval, QC H7V 1B7
Tél: 450-686-5641; Téléc: 450-686-5391
musee-afrappier@iaf.inrs.ca
www.musee-afrappier.qc.ca
Fondée en: 1992 Le musée offre des activités pour favoriser la compréhension d'enjeux scientifiques reliés à la santé humaine, animale & environnementale; il fait connaître l'oeuvre du Dr Armand Frappier, microbiologiste.
Guylaine Archambault, Directrice générale, guylaine.archambault@iaf.inrs.ca
Caroline Labelle, Agente de réservation, caroline.labelle@iaf.inrs.ca

Laval: **Musée écologique - (C.J.N.) Vanier**
3995, boul Lévesque Saint-Vincent-de-Paul, Laval, QC H7E 2R3

Lévis: **Musée du College de Lévis**
9, rue Mgr Gosselin, Lévis, QC G6V 5K1
Tél: 418-837-8600
Fermé au public, ouvert sur demande

Lévis: **Musée Le Régiment de la Chaudière**
Manège militaire de Lévis, 10, rue de l'Arsenal, Lévis, QC G6V 4P7
Tél: 418-835-0340; Téléc: 418-835-0450

Lévis: **Société historique Alphonse-Desjardins (SHAD)**
Also known as: **Maison Alphonse-Desjardins**
6, rue du Mont-Marie, Lévis, QC G6V 1V9
Tél: 418-835-2090; Téléc: 418-835-9173
Ligne sans frais: 866-835-8444
info@maisonalphonsedesjardins.com
www.desjardins.com
La maison de style néo-gothique fut construite en 1883 pour Alphonse Desjardins, fondateur des caisses populaires. C'est là que Desjardins a conçu son grand projet coopératif et qu'ont débuté, en 1901, les activités de la Caisse populaire de Lévis
Esther Normand, Conservation & Administration Agent

Longueuil: **Musée Marie-Rose Durocher**
80, rue St-Charles est, Longueuil, QC J4H 1A9
Tél: 450-651-8104
centremarierose@yahoo.ca
www.snjm.org
Le Centre Marie-Rose est ouvert au public; le musée présente des expositions à caractère religieux et historique de la vie de Marie-Rose Durocher, fondatrice de la Congrégation des Soeurs des Saints Noms de Jésus et de Marie; collection de tableaux et d'artefacts.

Malartic: **Musée Régional des Mines et des arts de Malartic**
CP 4227, 650, rue de la Paix, Malartic, QC J0Y 1Z0
Tél: 819-757-4677; Téléc: 819-757-4140
museem@lino.com

La Malbaie: **Musée de Charlevoix**
10, ch du Hâvre, La Malbaie, QC G5A 2Y8
Tél: 418-665-4411; Téléc: 418-665-4560
info@museedecharlevoix.qc.ca
museedecharlevoix.qc.ca
twitter.com/Musee Charlevoix
www.facebook.com/MuseeDeCharlevoix
Main fields of interest: ethno-history & folk art; textual art; decroative arts; fine arts; history
Paul-Henri Jean, Président
Annie Breton, Directrice générale, directiongenerale@bellnet.ca

Maniwaki: **Le centre d'interprétation de l'historique de la protection de la forêt contre le feu**
8, rue Comeau, Maniwaki, QC J9E 2R8
Tél: 819-449-7999; Téléc: 819-449-5102
info@ci-chateaulogue.qc.ca
www.ci-chateaulogue.qc.ca

Le Château Logue; centre d'interprétation; expositions y compris l'histoire des grands feux de forêts au Québec, la forêt exploitée, et la forêt protégée; visites et randonnées gratuites; tour d'observation.
François Ledoux, Directeur

La Martre: **Corporation du Centre d'interprétation archéologique de la Gaspésie**
6, rue des Fermières, La Martre, QC G0E 2H0
Tél: 418-288-1318; Téléc: 418-288-1318

Interprète sur la préhistoire gaspésienne dont l'accent est mis sur la période paléoindienne récente; exposition et sentier d'interprétation
Carlos Suich, Administrateur

***Mashteuiatsh:* Musée amérindien de Mashteuiatsh / The Native Museum of Mashteuiatsh**
1787, rue Amishk, Mashteuiatsh, QC G0W 2H0
Tél: 418-275-4842; Téléc: 418-275-7494
Ligne sans frais: 888-875-4042
museeilnu@cgocable.ca
www.museeilnu.ca
Sauvegarde l'héritage ilnu et permet aux autochtones, la population et les touristes d'en prendre connaissance; expositions permanentes et temporaires; programmes éducatifs.

Jean-Denis Gill, Directeur, direction.museeilnu@cgocable.ca
Louise Siméon, Responsable, secteur muséal, archive.museeilnu@cgocable.ca

***Matane:* Musée du Vieux-Phare**
#300, 235, av Saint-Jerome, Matane, QC G4W 3A7
Tél: 418-562-1065; Téléc: 418-562-1917
cldtourisme@globetrotter.net

***Melbourne:* Richmond County Historical Society Museum (RCHS)**
1296 Rte. 243, Melbourne, QC J0B 2B0
Tél: 819-826-1332
e-dhealy@sympatico.ca
www.richmondcountyhistoricalsociety.com
To research & preserve historical facts in the Richmond County area; museum refurbished as a typical home of the late 1800s; archives centre
Esther Healy, Archivist

***Métabetchouan-Lac-à-la-Croix:* Centre d'interprétation de l'agriculture et de la ruralité**
281, rue St-Louis, Métabetchouan-Lac-à-la-Croix, QC G8G 2C8
Tél: 418-349-3633; Téléc: 418-349-5013
Ligne sans frais: 877-611-3633
ciar@cgocable.ca
www.ciar-lacalacroix.com
Fondée en: 1976 Situé au coeur d'une plaine agricole, le CIAR est un site désigné pour découvrir la richesse du patrimoine agricole du Saguenay-Lac-Saint-Jean. A travers l'exposition Gens de la terre, découvrez 150 ans d'histoire, us et coutumes des ancêtres, qui ont bâti le paysage actuel. Labyrinthe dans un Champ de Maïs; ferme pédagogique; camp d'étabissement (1868); programmes éducatifs.
France Lemoine, Directrice générale

***Mont Saint-Hilaire:* Centre de la nature Mont Saint-Hilaire**
422, ch des Moulins, Mont Saint-Hilaire, QC J3G 4S6
Tél: 450-467-1755; Téléc: 450-467-8015
info@centrenature.qc.ca
www.centrenature.qc.ca
A pour mission d'assurer l'intégrité du patrimoine naturel de la montagne, offrir un contact avec la nature et une gamme d'activités éducatives et culturelles, et promouvoir la conservation des milieux naturels de la région; ouvert 365 jours par année; offre un réseau de 24 km de sentiers, et un trottoir de bois accessible aux personnes à mobilité restreinte
Kees Vanderheyden, Directeur

***Montebello:* Lieu historique national du Canada du Manoir-Papineau / Manoir-Papineau National Historic Site of Canada**
500, rue Notre-Dame, Montebello, QC J0V 1L0
Tél: 819-423-6965; Téléc: 819-423-6455
Ligne sans frais: 888-773-8888
parcscanada-que@pc.gc.ca
www.pc.gc.ca/fra/lhn-nhs/qc/papineau
La maison de la famille Papineau, 1848-1850; plus de 800 objets, meubles, vêtements, oeuvres d'art, livres et documents; fresques de Napoléon Bourassa; Concerts d'Amédée; jardin.

***Montmagny:* Musée de l'accordéon**
***Also known as:* Manoir Couillard-Dupuis**
301, boul Taché est, Montmagny, QC G5V 1C5
Tél: 418-248-7927; Téléc: 418-248-1596
accordeonmontmagny.com
Fondée en: 1992 Research centre & collection of accordians

***Montréal:* Basilique Notre-Dame de Montréal**
110, rue Notre-Dame ouest, Montréal, QC H2Y 1T2
Tél: 514-842-2925; Téléc: 514-842-3370
info@basiliquenddm.org
www.basiliquenddm.org
Construite entre 1824 & 1829, la basilique acceuille des centaines de milliers de visiteurs chaque année; réputée pour la richesse de sa décoration intérieure: les vitraux, les éléments d'architecture, et les oeuvres d'art; visites guidées (individuels/groupes); visites scolaires; services religieux; événements; concerts; location de salles; boutique.
Yoland Tremblay, Directeur général

***Montréal:* Biodôme de Montréal**
4777, av Pierre-De Coubertin, Montréal, QC H1V 1B3
Tél: 514-868-3000; Téléc: 514-868-3065
biodome@ville.montreal.qc.ca
www2.ville.montreal.qc.ca/biodome/; www.biodome.qc.ca
Le Biodôme recrée des Écosystèmes des Amériques: forêt tropicale, forêt laurentienne, Saint-Laurent marin, monde polaire. Notez que le Biodôme est fermé pour une durée indéterminée en raison d'un conflit de travail à la Ville de Montréal.
Rachel Léger, Directrice

***Montréal:* The Black Watch of Canada (RHR) Regimental Memorial Museum**
2067, rue Bleury, Montréal, QC H3A 2K2
Tel: 514-496-1686; Fax: 514-496-2758
info@blackwatchcanada.com
www.blackwatchcanada.com
Uniforms, photographs & artifacts from early 1860s to present; open Tue. evenings, 7-9 pm & by appt.
Bruce D. Bolton, Director
Anne B. Stewart, Curator

***Montréal:* Canadian Grenadier Guards Regimental Museum**
4171, av Esplanade, Montréal, QC H2W 1S9
Tel: 514-496-1984; Fax: 514-496-2709

***Montréal:* Centre d'exposition de l'Université de Montréal Pavillon de la Faculté d'aménagement, CP 6128 Centre-ville, Montréal, QC H3C 3J7**
Tél: 514-343-6111; Téléc: 514-343-2183
www.expo.umontreal.ca
Comment s'y rendre: Pavillon de la faculté de l'Aménagement, 2940, ch d la Côte-Sainte-Catherine, local 0056, Montréal. Centre d'exposition multidisciplinaire. Comprend: collection herbier Marie-Victorin; collection du département d'anthropologie; collection du Laboratoire de recherche sur les musiques du monde; oeuvres d'art; design industriel
Louise Grenier, Directrice, l.grenier@umontreal.ca

***Montréal:* Chapelle Notre-Dame-de-Bon-Secours/Musée Marguerite Bourgeoys**
400, rue Saint-Paul est, Montréal, QC H2Y 1H4
Tél: 514-282-8670; Téléc: 514-282-8672
info@marguerite-bourgeoys.com
www.marguerite-bourgeoys.com
twitter.com /margbourg
www.facebook.com/margueritebourgeoys
Chapelle, musée d'histoire, et site archéologique; programmation diversifiée, visites guidées, boutique, location des salles.
Danielle Dubois, Director General

***Montréal:* Écomusée du fier monde**
2050, rue Amherst, Montréal, QC H2L 3L8
Tél: 514-528-8444; Téléc: 514-528-8686
ecomusee@globetrotter.net
www.ecomusee.qc.ca
Fondée en: 1980 Highlights the history of the Centre-Sud heritage, which is a mircososm of the industrial revoltuion which took place in Canada during the latter half of the 19th century.

***Montréal:* Insectarium de Montréal / Montreal Insectarium**
4581, rue Sherbrooke est, Montréal, QC H1X 2B2
Tél: 514-872-1400; Téléc: 514-872-0662
insectarium@ville.montreal.qc.ca
www.ville.montreal.qc.ca/insectarium
twitter.com/espacepourlavie
www.facebook.com/Espacepourlavie
Autre numéros: Administration, tél: 514-872-0663
Largest insectarium in North America; 140,000 scientific specimens collection; 20,000 exhibition collection (including 4,000 on public display); about 100 species of arthropods live collection

***Montréal:* Lieu historique national de Sir George-Etienne Cartier / Sir George-Étienne Cartier National Historic Site**
***Also known as:* Maison Cartier**
458, Notre-Dame est, Montréal, QC H2Y 1C8
Tel: 514-283-2282; Fax: 514-283-5560
Toll-Free: 888-773-8888
cartier.maison@pc.gc.ca
www.pc.gc.ca/lhn-nhs/qc/etienn ecartier.aspx
Other contact information: TTY: 1-866-558-2950
Commemorates the life and accomplishments of Sir George-Étienne Cartier; Cartier family homes; performances and re-enactments that vary depending on season; Open March - December

***Montréal:* Maison de Mère d'Youville**
138, rue Saint-Pierre, Montréal, QC H2Y 2L7
Tél: 514-842-9411
asscong@sgm.ca
www.sgm.qc.ca
Fondée en: 1981 Ancien couvent des Soeurs Grises; l'hospice et le couvent restauré en 1981; la chapelle mise en valeur en 1991; les anciens magasins-entrepôts rénovés; par rendez-vous.

***Montréal:* Maison Saint-Gabriel**
2146, Place Dublin, Montréal, QC H3K 2A2
Tél: 514-935-8136; Téléc: 514-935-5692
msgrcip@globetrotter.qc.ca
www.maisonsaint-gabriel.qc.ca
www.facebook. com/255220478149
Fondée en: 1966 La Maison est la maison d'accueil des Filles du Roy et pendant 300 ans, la maison de ferme de la Congrégation de Notre-Dame; un exemple de l'architecture du Régime français; expositions qui expliquent le rôle de Marguerite Bourgeoys et la vie à la colonie de l'Ile de Montréal pendant le 17e siècle; jardin; visites guidées.
Madeleine Juneau, Directrice générale

***Montréal:* Montréal History Centre / Centre d'histoire de Montréal**
***Also known as:* Fire Station**
335, Place d'Youville, Montréal, QC H2Y 3T1
Tel: 514-872-3207; Fax: 514-872-9645
chm@ville.montreal.qc.ca
www2.ville.montreal.qc.ca/chm/engl/centre-doca. shtm
Year Founded: 1983 This city museum is located in an old firehall. Here Montreal's story is told through exhibits, models, sets, videos and 8,000 photographs from 1642 until today.

***Montréal:* The Montréal Holocaust Memorial Centre / Le Centre commémoratif de l'Holocauste à Montréal**
Maison Cummings, 5151, ch. de la Côte-Sainte-Catherine, Montréal, QC H3W 1M6
Tel: 514-345-2605; Fax: 514-344-2651
info@mhmc.ca
www.mhmc.ca
To collect, research & preserve historical, cultural & ethnographic material related to Jewish communities in Europe & North Africa which fell under Nazi rule
Alice Herscovitch, Executive Director

***Montréal:* Musée de BMO Banque de Montréal / BMO Bank of Montreal Museum**
129, rue St-Jacques, Montréal, QC H2Y 1L6
Tél: 514-877-6810; Téléc: 514-877-7341

The office of the Cashier of Canada's oldest banking institution is recreated; open year round (closed on non-banking days); free, self-guided tour
Yolaine Toussaint, Archivist, yolaine.toussaint@bmo.com

***Montréal:* Musée de L'Oratoire Saint-Joseph du Mont-Royal / Museum of Saint Joseph Oratory of Mount-Royal**

3800, ch Queen Mary, Montréal, QC H3V 1H6
Tél: 514-733-8211; Téléc: 514-733-9735
Ligne sans frais: 877-672-8647
pelerinage@osj.qc.ca
www.saint-joseph.org
Fondée en: 1955 Le musée se consacre à l'art chrétien et à l'histoire et le patrimoine québécoise; expositions thématiques. L'Oratoire mise en valeur la vie et l'oeuvre de frère André; visites commentées; boutique; bibliothèque/archives/centre de recherche.
André Bergeron, Directeur

***Montréal:* Musée des Hospitalières de l'Hôtel-Dieu de Montréal**
201, av des Pins ouest, Montréal, QC H2W 1R5
Tél: 514-849-2919; Téléc: 514-849-4199
museehospitalieres@bellnet.ca
www.museedeshospitalieres.qc.ca
Fondée en: 1992 Le musée introduit l'histoire des Hospitalières de Saint-Joseph et des Hospitalières de l'Hôtel-Dieu; exposition permanent; programmation et activités; boutique; salles de conférence à louer; 20 000 objets; archives.
Louise Verdant, Directrice générale

***Montréal:* Musée des ondes Émile Berliner**
1050, rue Lacasse, local C-220, Montréal, QC H4C 2Z3
Tél: 514-932-9663
info@berliner.montreal.museum
www.berliner.montreal.museum
Fondée en: 1996 Émile Berliner a inventé le gramophone, le disque horizontal, et la matrice pour imprimer les disques. Le musée possède plus de 30 000 objets et se consacre à l'histoire de l'industrie des ondes; archives; activités.

***Montréal:* Musée du Château Ramezay / Château Ramezay Museum**
280, rue Notre-Dame est, Montréal, QC H2Y 1C5
Tél: 514-861-3708; Téléc: 514-861-8317
info@chateauramezay.qc.ca
www.chateauramezay.qc.ca
Fondée en: 1895 Le musée est consacré à la conservation, et la mise en valeur d'une collection axée sur l'histoire de Montréal et du Québec; plus de 25 000 objets, oeuvres d'art, artefacts ethnologiques et archéologiques, objets numismatiques; photographies; meubles; costumes; bibliothèque; jardin; boutique; café.
André J. Delisle, Directeur général/Conservateur

***Montréal:* Musée du Château-Dufresne**
2929, av Jeanne-d'Arc, Montréal, QC H1W 3W2
Tél: 514-259-9201; Téléc: 514-259-6466
spoirier@chateaudufresne.com
www.chateaudufresne.com
Le Château, construit entre 1915 et 1918 pour servir de résidence aux frères Oscar et Marius Dufresne, met en pratique les principes du style Beaux-Arts. Programmation culturelle; visites guidées; expositions; salles à louer pour réceptions.
Mr. Paul Labonne, Directeur général, plabonne@chateaudufresne.com

***Montréal:* Musée du Cinéma/Cinémathèque québécoise**
335, boul de la Maisonneuve est, Montréal, QC H2X 1K1
Tél: 514-842-9763; Téléc: 514-842-1816
info@cinematheque.qc.ca
www.cinematheque.qc.ca
www.facebook.com/groups /5583261239
Fondée en: 1963 La Cinémathèque a le mandat de conserver, documenter et mettre en valeur le patrimoine cinématographique et télévisuel national et international.
Yolande Racine, Directrice générale

***Montréal:* Musée Édouard-Dubeau**
Université de Montréal, #D-129, 2900, rue Édouard-Montpetit, Montréal, QC H3C 3J7
Tél: 514-343-6111; Téléc: 514-343-2233
www.expo.umontreal.ca/collections/dentaire.htm
Denis Ruel, Responsible, denis.ruel@umontreal.ca

***Montréal:* Musée régimentaire les Fusiliers Mont-Royal**
3721, av Henri-Julien, Montréal, QC H2X 3H4
Tél: 514-283-7444; Téléc: 514-496-5086
info@lesfusiliersmont-royal.com
lesfusiliersmont-royal.com

***Montréal:* Le Musée Stewart au Fort de l'Ile Sainte-Hélène / The Stewart Museum at the Fort Ile Sainte-Hélène**
CP 1200 A, Montréal, QC H3C 2Y9
Tél: 514-861-6701; Téléc: 514-284-0123
info@stewart-museum.org
stewart-museum.org
Fermeture temporaire; l'exposition permanente renouvelée du musée sera accessible au public dès l'automne 2010; activités scolaires et culturelles.
Bruce D. Bolton, Directeur
Guy Vadeboncoeur, Conservateur

***Montréal:* Phonothèque québécoise, Musée du son**
335, boul de Maisonneuve est, Montréal, QC H2X 1K1
Tél: 514-282-0703
www.phonotheque.org
Histoire des archives sonores, de l'industrie du disque, etc. History of sound archives, sound recording & radio industry.

***Montréal:* Redpath Museum**
McGill University, 859, rue Sherbrooke ouest, Montréal, QC H3A 2K6
Tel: 514-398-4086; Fax: 514-398-3185
redpath.museum@mcgill.ca
www.mcgill.ca/redpath
Social Media: pinterest.com/redpathmuseum
twitter.com/RedpathMuseum
www.facebook.com /308943939115940
Extensive collections in paleontonlogy, mineralogy, zoology & ethnology; family workshop series "Discovery Workshop"
Dr. David M. Green, Director/Curator B.Sc., M.Sc., Ph.D., Vertebrates, david.m.green@mcgill.ca
Dr. Virginie Millien, Asst. Prof./Chief Curator Ph.D., D.E.A., Paleontology & Zoology, virginie.millien@mcgill.ca

***Montréal:* Royal Canadian Ordnance Corps Museum**
***Also known as:* RCOC Museum**
Longue-Pointe Garrison, CP 4000 K, 6560, rue Hochlega, Montréal, QC H1N 3R9
Tél: 514-252-2777
www.rcocmuseum.com/RCOCMuseum.html
Fondée en: 1962 An accredited military museum of the Department of National Defence, the Royal Canadian Ordnance Corps Museum depicts the historical mission of the Royal Canadian Ordnance Corps, & other pre-unification support elements of the Canadian Army, the RCAF, & the RCN. These service elements united in 1968 to create the Logistics Branch of the Canadian Forces. The collection of the RCOC Museum is housed in a 1943 building, which originally served as Longue-Pointe Garrison's St-Barbara Catholic & Protestant chapels.
LCol (ret'd) Al Truelove, Director & President, Royal Canadian Ordnance Corps Museum Committee
Andrew Gregory, Curator PhD, agregory17@cogeco.ca
Jacques Monast, Technical Advisor

***Mont-Saint-Grégoire:* Centre d'interprétation du milieu écologique du Haut-Richelieu**
16, ch du Sous-Bois, Mont-Saint-Grégoire, QC J3B 6Z5
Tél: 450-346-0406
services@cimehautrichelieu.qc.ca
www.cimehautrichelieu.qc.ca
A pour mission la conservation du Mont-Saint-Grégoire, et d'autres sites naturels dans la région du Haut-Richelieu
Renée Gagnon, Directice générale

***Mont-Saint-Hilaire:* Maison amérindienne**
510, Montée des Trente, Mont-Saint-Hilaire, QC J3H 2R8
Tél: 450-464-2500; Téléc: 450-464-0071
info@maisonamerindienne.com
www.maisonamerindienne.com
Fondée en: 2000 Un lieu d'échanges, de partage et de rapprochement des peuples à travers des activités culturelles (expositions, contes et légendes, conférences), environnementales et gastronomiques; seul site multinations, situé dans une érablière.
André Michel, Fondateur

***New Richmond:* Gaspesian British Heritage Village**
351, boul Perron ouest, New Richmond, QC G0C 2B0
Tel: 418-392-4487; Fax: 418-392-5907
heritagevillage@globetrotter.net
www.gaspesianvillage.com
British heritage in Gaspé from 1760 to 1900s; June 24th - Aug. 22nd
Mike Geraghty, President

***Nicolet:* Musée des religions du monde**
900, boul Louis-Fréchette, Nicolet, QC J3T 1V5
Tél: 819-293-6148; Téléc: 819-293-4161
musee@museedesreligions.qc.ca
www.museedesreligions.qc.ca
www.facebook .com/museedesreligionsdumonde
Le musée se consacre à l'histoire des rites religieux du bouddhisme, de l'hindouisme, de l'islam, du judaïsme, et du christianisme; location de salle; boutique; programmation et activités; les installations du musée sont adaptées pour les personnes à mobilité réduite.
Jean-François Royal, Directeur

***Nicolet:* Musée historique des Soeurs de l'Assomption de la Sainte Vierge**
Pavillon Leduc, 251, rue St-Jean-Baptiste, Nicolet, QC J3T 1X9
Tél: 819-293-2011; Téléc: 819-293-8315
musee@sasv.ca
www.musee-soeurs-assomption.net
Fondée en: 1979 Collection permanente du patrimoine des fondatrices et des fondateurs de la Congrégation; costume religieux; tableaux; meubles; instruments de musique; sculptures; objets liturgiques.
Sr. Gisèle Saint-Louis, Directrice

***Notre-Dame-de-l'Ile-Perrot:* Parc historique Pointe-du-Moulin**
2500, boul Don-Quichotte, Notre-Dame-de-l'Ile-Perrot, QC J7V 7P2
Tél: 514-453-5936; Téléc: 514-453-8744
info@pointedumoulin.com
www.pointedumoulin.com
Ani Kataroyan, Directrice générale

***Notre-Dame-du-Nord:* Centre thématique fossilifère du lac Témiscamingue / Lake Timiskaming Fossil Centre**
CP 296, 5, rue Principale, Notre-Dame-du-Nord, QC J0Z 3B0
Tél: 819-723-2500
musee@fossiles.qc.ca
www.fossiles.qc.ca
A pour mission de mettre en valeur la période Orodovicien-Silurien dans la région; recherche; expositions; boutique.

***Nouvelle:* Musée d'histoire naturelle du parc de Miguasha**
231, rte Miguasha ouest, Nouvelle, QC G0C 2E0
Tél: 418-794-2475; Téléc: 418-794-2033
parc.miguasha@sepaq.com
maritime.musees.qc.ca/en/museums/miguasha/index. php
www.facebook.com/parcnationaldemiguasha

***Odanak:* Musée des Abénakis**
Société historique d'Odanak, 108, Waban-Aki, Odanak, QC J0G 1H0
Tél: 450-568-2600; Téléc: 450-568-5959
info@museedesabenakis.ca
www.museedesabenakis.ca
Ouvert en 1962 et complètement rénové en 2005, le premier musée amérindien au Québec vous souhaite la bienvenue. Au coeur d'un site historique, un ensemble d'activité est offert pour plaire à toute la famille. Spectacle multimédia, expositions, belvédère, église catholique, chapelle et aire de pique-nique rendront la visite inoubliable.
Michelle Bélanger, Directrice générale

***Otterburn Park:* Muséobus - Le Musée des enfants**
760, ch des Patriotes, Otterburn Park, QC J3H 1Z5
Tél: 450-464-0201; Téléc: 450-446-4644
info@museobus.qc.ca
www.museobus.qc.ca
Musée mobile aménagé dans des autobus scolaires; propose des expositions scientifiques interactives et des sentiers d'interprétation; piste d'hébertisme et aire de pique-nique; programmation; Camp Éco Nature.

***Pabos Mills:* Centre d'interprétation du Parc du Bourg de Pabos**
75, rue de la Plage, Pabos Mills, QC G0C 2J0
Tél: 418-689-6043
bourg@globetrotter.net
www.lebourgdepabos.com
Promouvoir l'histoire de la seule seigneurie de la Nouvelle-France à exploiter commercialement la pêche; ouvert tous le jours, juin-septembre.

***Paspébiac:* Site historique du Banc-de-Pêche-de-Paspébiac**
CP 430, 3e rue, rte du Banc, Paspébiac, QC G0C 2K0
Tél: 418-752-6229; Téléc: 418-752-6408
shbp@globetrotter.net
www.shbp.ca
Sea heritage & traditional trades; tours; gift shop; restaurant; open June - Oct.

***Percé:* Centre d'interprétation du Parc national de l'Ile-Bonaventure et du Rocher-Percé**
4, rue du Quai, Percé, QC G0C 2L0
Tél: 418-782-2240; Téléc: 418-782-2241
parc.ibrperce@sepaq.com
www.sepaq.com
A pour mission de protéger un refuge d'oiseaux migrateurs, et le patrimoine historique de la région
Rémi Plourde, Directeur

***Percé:* Musée Le Chafaud**
145, rte 132, Percé, QC G0C 2L0
Tél: 418-782-5100; Téléc: 418-782-5565
lebjl@globetrotter.net
www.musee-chafaud.com

***Péribonka:* Musée Louis-Hémon**
700, rte Maria-Chapdelaine, Péribonka, QC G0W 2G0
Tél: 418-374-2177; Téléc: 418-374-2516
museelh@destination.ca
www.museelh.ca
Chantale Simard, Directrice

***La Pocatière:* Musée François-Pilote**
100, 4e av, La Pocatière, QC G0R 1Z0
Tél: 418-856-3145; Téléc: 418-856-5611
museefpilote@leadercsa.com
www.leadercsa.com/museefrancoispilote
Fondée en: 1973 Voir la paroisse rurale d'autrefois sous tous ses aspects, des salles reconstituées d'habitations, de bureaux de professionnels et d'artisans, une collection de sciences naturelles, agriculture et sciences pures, enseignement agricole; expositions; programmes scolaires; rampe d'acces et ascenseur disponible.
Paul-André Leclerc, Directeur général

***Pointe-à-la-Croix:* Battle of the Restigouche National Historic Site of Canada**
PO Box 359, rte 132, Pointe-à-la-Croix, QC G0C 1L0
Tel: 418-788-5676; Fax: 418-788-5895
information@pc.gc.ca
www.pc.gc.ca/eng/lhn-nhs/qc/ristigouche/index.aspx
Other contact information: TTY: 1-866-787-6221
Located at the mouth of the Restigouche River, the Battle of the Restigouche National Historic Site is the scene of the last naval battle between France & England for possession of North America in 1760. Visitors to the site can see the vestiges of the vessel, The Machault, as well as several artifacts from the wreck. The national historic site is open daily from June to mid-October.

***La Prairie:* Société d'histoire de la Prairie de la Magdeleine (SHLM)**
249, rue Sainte-Marie, La Prairie, QC J5R 1G1
Tél: 450-659-1393
histoire@laprairie-shlm.com
shlm.info
Historical society active in the areas of genealogy, historical research & guided tours
Gaétan Bourdages, Président
Marie-Hélène Bourdeau, Coordinatrice

***Québec:* Centre d'interprétation de Place-Royale**
***Parent:* Musée de la civilisation**
27, rue Notre-Dame, Québec, QC G1K 4E9
Tél: 418-646-3167Ligne sans frais: 866-710-8031
mcqweb@mcq.org
www.mcq.org/fr/cipr
Fondée en: 1999 Site historique; le Centre est situé au premier établissement français permanent en Amérique; expositions, visites commentées, animations historiques, espace découverte, activités éducatives, ateliers.

***Québec:* La Citadelle de Québec & Le Musée du Royal 22e Régiment**
La Citadelle, 1, côte de la Citadelle, Québec, QC G1R 4V7
Tél: 418-694-2815; Téléc: 418-694-2853
information@lacitadelle.qc.ca
www.lacitadelle.qc.ca
Fondée en: 1980 Située sur le Cap Diamant, La Citadelle est un site du patrimoine mondial de l'UNESCO, et la résidence officielle du Royal 22e Régiment. Le musée offre des visites guidées, activités, et collections d'artefacts militaires (médailles, insignes, uniformes et textiles, armes).
Jocelyne Milot, Directrice

***Québec:* Commission des Champs-de-Bataille nationaux / National Battlefields Commission**
390, av de Bernières, Québec, QC G1R 2L7
Tél: 418-648-3506; Téléc: 418-648-3638
information@ccbn-nbc.gc.ca
www.ccbn-nbc.gc.ca
Les Plaines d'Abraham; Parc des Braves; Maison de la découverte des plaines d'Abraham; Exposition multimédia Odyssée Canada; Tours Martello; Souper mystère de 1814 à la tour Martello 2; Bus d'Abraham: tour guidé des plaines d'Abraham, Maison patrimoniale Louis S.-St-Laurent, Kiosque Edwin-Bélanger, Jardin Jeanne d'Arc

***Québec:* Lieu historique national du Canada Cartier-Brébeuf / Cartier-Brébeuf National Historic Site of Canada**
CP 10 B, 175, rue de l'Espinay, Québec, QC G1K 7A1
Tél: 418-648-4038; Téléc: 418-948-9181
Ligne sans frais: 888-773-8888
parcscanada-que@pc.gc.ca
www.pc.gc.ca/fra/lhn-nhs/qc/cartierbrebeuf
Commémore l'hivernage de Jacques Cartier et de ses compagnons en 1535-1536, à proximité du village iroquoïen de Stadaconé; activités.
Linda Bernier, Contact

***Québec:* Lieu historique national du Canada de la Grosse-Ile-et-le-Mémorial-des-Irlandais / Grosse-Ile & the Irish Memorial National Historic Site of C**
CP 10 B, 2, rue d'Auteuil, Québec, QC G1K 7R3
Tél: 418-248-8841; Téléc: 866-790-8991
Ligne sans frais: 888-773-8888
parcscanada-que@pc.gc.ca
www.pc.gc.ca/fra/lhn-nhs/qc/grosseile
Commémore l'importance de l'immigration au Canada, plus particulièrement via la porte d'entrée de Québec, et les événements tragiques vécus par les immigrants irlandais en ce lieu, notamment l'épidémie de typhus de 1847.

***Québec:* Lieu historique national du Canada des Fortifications-de-Québec / Fortifications of Québec National Historic Site of Canada**
CP 10 B, 2, rue d'Auteuil, Québec, QC G1K 7A1
Tél: 418-648-7016; Téléc: 418-648-2506
Ligne sans frais: 888-773-8888
www.pc.gc.ca/fra/lhn-nhs/qc/fortifications
Trésor de l'UNESCO; la Citadelle et ses environs, terrasse Dufferin, Château Frontnac; visites guidées.
Nicole Ouellet, Régisseure

***Québec:* Lieu historique national du Canada des Forts-de-Lévis**
***Also known as:* Fort Numéro-Un/Fort No.1**
CP 10 B, 41, ch du Gouvernement, Québec, QC G1K 7R3
Tél: 418-835-5182; Téléc: 418-948-9119
Ligne sans frais: 888-773-8888
parcscanada-que@pc.gc.ca
www.pc.gc.ca/fra/lhn-nhs/qc/levis/index.aspx
Autre numéros: TTY: 1-866-787-6221

***Québec:* Maison Henry-Stuart**
82, Grande Allée ouest, Québec, QC G1R 2G6
Tél: 418-647-4347; Téléc: 418-647-6483
Ligne sans frais: 800-494-4347
cmsq@cmsq.qc.ca
www.cmsq.qc.ca/mhs
Construite en 1849, la maison représente un exemple d'un type d'habitation courant aux 19e siècle à Québec; collection d'objets, meubles; visites thématiques; jardin.

***Québec:* Musée Bon-Pasteur**
14, rue Couillard, Québec, QC G1R 3S9
Tél: 418-694-0243; Téléc: 418-694-6233
info@museebonpasteur.com
www.museebonpasteur.com
Fondée en: 1992 L'histoire de la Congrégation des Servantes du Coeur Immaculé de Marie (Soeurs du Bon-Pasteur de Québec); condition féminine au XIXe siècle; meubles et peintures d'époque; visites personnalisées en français et en anglais (portugais sur demande)
Claudette Ledet, Directrice

***Québec:* Musée de géologie René-Bureau**
Pavillon Adrien Pouliot, Université Laval, Québec, QC G1K 7P4
Tél: 418-656-2131; Téléc: 418-656-7339
www2.ggl.ulaval.ca/musee/index.html
André Lévesque, Conservateur du musée, alevesqu@ggl.ulaval.ca

***Québec:* Musée des Augustines de l'Hôtel-Dieu de Québec**
32, rue Charlevoix, Québec, QC G1R 5C4
Tél: 418-692-2492; Téléc: 418-692-2668
musee@augustines.ca
www.augustines.ca
Fondée en: 1958 Tableaux canadiens et européens, meubles, vaisselle, broderies, instruments médicaux. Le musée est en réaménagement et est fermée jusqu'en 2011.
S. Nicole Perron, Directrice du Musée AMJ

***Québec:* Musée des Ursulines de Québec**
12, rue Donnacona, Québec, QC G1R 3Y7
Tél: 418-694-0694; Téléc: 418-694-2136
murq@vmuq.com
www.ursulines-uc.com
Le musée met en valeur la collection pédagogique des Ursulines de Québec; documents; instruments de musique; objets scientifiques; spécimens d'histoire naturelle; photographies; broderies; tableaux.
Christine Turgeon, Directrice

***Québec:* Musée les Voltigeurs de Québec**
Manège militaire Grande Allée, 805, av Wilfrid-Laurier est, Québec, QC G1R 2L3
Tel: 418-648-4422; Fax: 418-648-4422
info@voltigeursdequebec.net
voltigeursdequebec.net/musee.html
Social Media: www.youtube.com/voltigeursdequebec
twitter.com/voltigeurs
www.facebook.com/groups/5200064637
Raymond Falardeau, Conservateur du musee
L'adjudant-chef (r) Éric Godbout, Directeur des projets

***Québec:* Musée Naval de Québec / Naval Museum of Québec**
***Also known as:* Musée naval Stanislas-Déry**
170, rue Dalhousie, Québec, QC G1K 8M7
Tél: 418-694-5387; Téléc: 418-694-5550
info@museenavaldequebec.com
www.museenavaldequebec.com
Le musée a pour mission de conserver et communiquer l'histoire navale du Saint-Laurent, et de la Réserve navale du Canada.

***Québec:* Site patrimonial du Parc-de-L'Artillerie**
***Also known as:* Parc-de-L'Artillerie**
CP 10 B, 2, rue d'Auteuil, Québec, QC G1K 7A1
Tél: 418-648-7016; Téléc: 418-648-2506
Ligne sans frais: 888-773-8888
parcscanada-que@pc.gc.ca
www.pc.gc.ca/fra/lhn-nhs/qc/artiller/index.aspx

***Québec:* Villa Bagatelle**
1563 ch St-Louis, Québec, QC G1S 1G1
Tel: 418-654-0259; Fax: 418-654-0991
www.quebecregion.com
Exhibition Centre & garden

***Richmond:* Centre d'interprétation de l'ardoise**
5, rue Belmont, Richmond, QC J0B 2H0
Tél: 819-826-3313; Téléc: 819-826-5757
ardoise@globetrotter.net
www.centreardoise.ca; www.townshipsheritage.com
Fondée en: 1992 A pour mission de promouvoir le patrimoine de l'ardoise dans la vallée du Saint-François; le centre est logé dans une église presbytérienne construite en 1889, ayant une toiture en ardoise; métiers, techniques et divers usages de cette pierre; histoires de l'industrie sont racontées
Denise Lupien

***Rimouski:* Musée régional de Rimouski**
35, rue Saint-Germain ouest, Rimouski, QC G5L 4B4
Tél: 418-724-2272; Téléc: 418-725-4433
mrdr@globetrotter.net
www.museerimouski.qc.ca
Le musée, qui loge dans la plus ancienne église de pierre de la région, présente des collections thématiques sur l'art contemporain, histoire et sciences; oeuvres et artefacts; guides interprétifs; activités.
Franck Michel, Directeur général

***Rimouski:* Site historique maritime de la Pointe-au-Père**
1000, rue du Phare, Rimouski, QC G5M 1L8
Tél: 418-724-6214; Téléc: 418-721-0815
www.shmp.qc.ca
Fondée en: 1980 Le musée regroupe les artefacts du navire l'Empress of Ireland, et met en valeur le Phare-de-Pointe-au-Père et le sous-marin ONONDAGA, désarmé par la Défense nationale en 2000.

***Rimouski-Est:* Site historique de la Maison Lamontagne**
707, boul du Rivage, Rimouski-Est, QC G5L 1E9
Tél: 418-722-4038; Téléc: 418-722-4038
maisonlamontagne@globetrotter.net
www.maisonlamontagne.com
Open - 24 juin - 5 sept.
Fanny Côté, Directrice

***Rivière-du-Loup:* Musée des bateaux miniatures et de légendes du Bas-Saint-Laurent**
80, boul Cartier, Rivière-du-Loup, QC G5R 2M9
Tél: 418-868-0800; Téléc: 418-856-1815
Ligne sans frais: 866-868-0800
info@museedebateauxminiatures.com
www.museedebateauxminiatures.com
Exposition de 160 bateaux miniatures faits par 20 artistes de la région; boutique souvenir; petite galerie d'art; visites guidées.

***Rivière-du-Loup:* Musée du Bas-St-Laurent**
300, rue St-Pierre, Rivière-du-Loup, QC G5R 3V3
Tél: 418-862-7547; Téléc: 418-862-3019
musee@mbsl.qc.ca
www.mbsl.qc.ca
Fondée en: 1975 Consacré à la photographie ethnologique, art moderne, et à l'éducation; conservation, recherche, et diffusion; plus de 2 000 objets ethnologiques, et plus de 300 objets d'art; plus de 125 000 photographies anciennes; expositions itinérantes; publication; boutique; location de salles.
Pierre Landry, Directeur général

***Rivière-Éternite:* Centre de découverte et de services Le Béluga (secteur Baie Sainte-Marguerite)**
Parc National du Saguenay, 91, rue Notre-Dame, Rivière-Éternite, QC G0V 1P0
Tél: 418-272-1556; Téléc: 418-272-1516
Ligne sans frais: 800-665-6527
parc.saguenay@sepaq.com
www.sepaq.com/pq/sag/fr/interpretation.html
Exposition permanente "Baie comme bélugas"; l'histoire et l'importance de protéger le béluga dans son milieu naturel; activités de découverte.

***Rivière-Éternite:* Centre de découverte et de services le Fjord du Saguenay (secteur de la Baie-Éternité)**
Parc National du Saguenay, 91, rue Notre-Dame, Rivière-Éternite, QC G0P 1P0
Tél: 418-272-1556; Téléc: 418-272-3438
parc.saguenay@sepaq.com
www.sepaq.com/pq/sag/fr/interpretation.html
Découvrez les secrets du fjord; exposition permanente

***Rouyn-Noranda:* La Maison Dumulon**
CP 242, 191, av du Lac, Rouyn-Noranda, QC J9X 5C3
Tél: 819-797-7125; Téléc: 819-797-7109
maison.dumulon@rouyn-noranda.ca
www.maison-dumulon.ca
Fondée en: 1980 La maison de la famille Dumulon est une reconstitution fidèle du bâtiment d'origine; visites guidées; animation; activités spéciales; location de salles; boutique. L'église orthodoxe russe Saint-Georges est administrée par la Corporation de La maison Dumulon.
Geneviève C. Gauthier, Directrice

***Saguenay:* Musée du Fjord**
3346, boul de la Grande-Baie sud, Saguenay, QC G7G 1G2
Tél: 418-697-5077; Téléc: 418-697-5079
Ligne sans frais: 866-697-5077
info@museedufjord.com
www.museedufjord.com
www.faceb ook.com/pages/Le-Musée-du-Fjord/118098813663
Fondée en: 1960 Consacré à la préservation et la mise en valeur du patrimoine historique, naturel et artistique du territoire du fjord du Saguenay; exposition permanente; expositions temporaires thématiques; programmation; artefacts historiques; photographies; documents.

Guylaine Simard, Directrice

***Saint-André-Avellin:* Musée des Pionniers de Saint-André-Avellin**
20, rue Bourgeois, Saint-André-Avellin, QC J0V 1W0
Tél: 819-983-2624; Téléc: 819-983-3702
www.petite-nation.qc.ca/patrimoine/musee.html
Relate la vie rurale des 19e et 20e siècles; meubles, objets, outils et machines en expositions; livres du XIXe siècle; photographies.
Raymond Whissell, Sec.-Très.

***Saint-André-d'Argenteuil:* Musée régional d'Argenteuil / Caserne-de-Carillon - Lieu historique national du Canada (MRA)**
44, rte du Long-Sault, Saint-André-d'Argenteuil, QC J0V 1X0
Tel: 450-537-3861; Fax: 450-537-1983
info@museeregionaldargenteuil.ca
www.museeregionaldargenteuil.ca
twitt er.com/mrargenteuil
www.facebook.com/184512031562388
Historical exhibitions: 8 exhibition rooms; the Museum is housed in the former Caserne-de-Carillon (Carillon Barracks).
Luc Grondin, Président
Lyne St-Jacques, Directrice

***Saint-Constant:* Exporail: Musée ferroviaire canadien / Exporail: Canadian Railway Museum**
110, rue St-Pierre, Saint-Constant, QC J5A 1G7
Tel: 450-632-2410; Fax: 450-638-1563
info@exporail.org
www.exporail.org
Canada's largest collection of railway equipment (150 vehicles, a turntable, 2 train stations, a new exhibit pavilion)
Marie-Claude Reid, Directrice générale, direction.generale@exporail.org

***Saint-Denis-de-la-Bouteillerie:* Maison Chapais**
CP 70, 2, rte 132 est, Saint-Denis-de-la-Bouteillerie, QC G0L 2R0
Tél: 418-498-2353
www.maisonchapais.com
www.facebook.com/213524838684198
Fondée en: 1990 Monument historique daté de 1834; trois étages et diverses dépendances; réservations préférables pour les groupes; visites guidées de la maison et ses jardins oubliés; galerie-boutique offre cadeaux et souvenirs, livres.

***Sainte-Anne-de-Beaupré:* Musée de Sainte-Anne-de-Beaupré**
9803, boul Sainte-Anne, Sainte-Anne-de-Beaupré, QC G0A 3C0
Tél: 418-827-6873; Téléc: 418-827-6870
musee@ssadb.qc.ca
www.sanctuairesainteanne.org
Le musée retrace l'histoire d'un pèlerinage et rend hommage à la Vierge Marie; expositions permanentes et temporaires; visites guidées; jardins; magasin du Sanctuaire.

***Sainte-Foy:* Maison Hamel-Bruneau**
CP 218, 2608, ch Saint-Louis, Sainte-Foy, QC G1V 1N2
Tél: 418-641-6280; Téléc: 418-654-4151
patrimoinestefoysillery@ville.quebec.qc.ca
www.ville.quebec.qc.ca; www.paricilavisite.qc.ca
Construit vers 1857; maison historique abrite un centre de diffusion culturelle; programmation thématique variée; concerts; activités; jardins, aire de pique-nique.

***Sainte-Foy:* Musée de géologie**
Université Laval, Département de géologie, Pavillon Adrien-Pouliot, Cité Universitaire, Sainte-Foy, QC G1K 7P4
Tel: 418-656-2131; Fax: 418-656-7339
alevesqu@ggl.ulaval.ca
www2.ggl.ulaval.ca/musee/index.html
André Lévesque, Conservateur, alevesqu@ggl.ulaval.ca

***Sainte-Marie:* Maison J.A. Vachon**
383, rue de la Coopérative, Sainte-Marie, QC G6E 3X5
Tél: 418-387-4052; Téléc: 418-387-2652
Ligne sans frais: 866-387-4052
maisonjavachon@globetrotter.net
www.vachon.com/en/history/maison

***Saint-Eustache:* Moulin Légaré / Légaré Mill**
232, rue St-Eustache, Saint-Eustache, QC J7R 2L7
Tél: 450-974-5400; Téléc: 450-974-2632
www.corporationdumoulinlegare.com
Fondée en: 1975 This 1762 flour mill has never once stopped working since its completion. The miller produces wheat & buckwheat flour with the original millstones & flour is sold on site. Activities are available for students.
Mélanie Séguin, Directrice, 450-974-5001, mseguin@corporationdumoulinlegare.com

***Saint-Eustache:* Musée de Saint-Eustache et de ses Patriotes**
235, rue Saint-Eustache, Saint-Eustache, QC J7R 2L8
Tél: 450-974-5170; Téléc: 450-974-2632
mseguin@ville.saint-eustache.qc.ca

***Saint-Hyacinthe:* Musée du Centre Élisabeth-Bergeron**
805, av Raymond, Saint-Hyacinthe, QC J2S 5T9
Tél: 450-773-6067; Téléc: 450-773-8044
ceb@sjsh.org
www.sjsh.org
Présente la vie et l'oeuvre de la fondatrice des Soeurs de Saint-Joseph-de Saint-Hyacinthe; l'histoire d'une communauté de religieuses enseignantes, fondée en terre Maskoutaine; quatre salles d'exposition, visite commentée comprenant une présentation audiovisuelle, un arrêt au tombeau de la vénérable Élisabeth Bergeron ainsi qu'à la chapelle; ouvert tous les jours.

***Saint-Hyacinthe:* Musée du séminaire de Saint-Hyacinthe**
650, rue Girouard est, Saint-Hyacinthe, QC J2S 7B7
Tél: 450-774-0203; Téléc: 450-774-7101
bssh@cgocable.ca
Museum of natural sciences, archeology, ethnology, religious heritage & works of art

***Saint-Jean-Port-Joli:* Musée de sculpture sur bois des Anciens Canadiens**
CP 66, 332, av de Gaspé ouest, Saint-Jean-Port-Joli, QC G0R 3G0
Tél: 418-598-3392; Téléc: 418-598-3329
info@museedesancienscanadiens.com
www.museedesancienscanadiens.com
Collection de plus de 250 sculptures originales, et un vidéo sur la sculpture sur bois et sur neige. Le musée est ouvert du mai jusqu'au novembre.

***Saint-Jean-sur-Richelieu:* Musée Du Fort St-Jean**
15, rue Jacques-Cartier nord, Saint-Jean-sur-Richelieu, QC J3B 8R8
Tél: 450-358-6500; Téléc: 450-358-6909
info@museedufortsaintjean.ca
www.museedufortsaintjean.ca
Col. (ret.) Pierre Cadotte, Président O.M.M., M.S.M., C.D.
Eric Ruel, Conservateur

***Saint-Jean-sur-Richelieu:* Musée du Haut-Richelieu**
***Also known as:* Musée d'histoire et de la céramique québécoise**
182, Jacques-Cartier nord, Saint-Jean-sur-Richelieu, QC J3B 7W3
Tél: 450-347-0649; Téléc: 450-347-9994
info@museeduhaut-richelieu.com
www.museeduhaut-richelieu.com
L'histoire du Haut-Richelieu.

***Saint-Joseph-de-Beauce:* Musée Marius Barbeau**
139, rue Sainte-Christine, Saint-Joseph-de-Beauce, QC G0S 2V0
Tél: 418-397-4039; Téléc: 418-397-6151
info@museemariusbarbeau.com
www.museemariusbarbeau.com
Le musée a pour mission la conservation, la recherche et la mise en valeur le patrimoine de la Beauce, tant du point de vue historique, ethnologique et artistique.
Lucie Duval, Personne ressource

***Saint-Joseph-de-la-Rive:* Musée maritime de Charlevoix**
CP 1, 305, rue de l'Église, Saint-Joseph-de-la-Rive, QC G0A 3Y0
Tél: 418-635-1131; Téléc: 418-635-2600
expom@charlevoix.net
www.musee-maritime-charlevoix.com
Conserve et communique le patrimoine maritime à travers l'histoire des goélettes qui ont navigué sur le Saint-Laurent; bâtiment central thématique, scierie, atelier et magasin de l'époque; exposition sur l'astroblème; archives; boutique.

***Saint-Joseph-de-la-Rive:* Papeterie Saint-Gilles**
***Also known as:* Economusee(R) du papier**
CP 40, 304, rue Félix Antoine-Savard, Saint-Joseph-de-la-Rive, QC G0A 3Y0
Tél: 418-635-2430; Téléc: 418-635-2613
Ligne sans frais: 866-635-2430
papier@papeteriesaintgilles.com
www.papeteriesaintgilles.com
Papier fait à la main, 100% coton, sans acide et chiné de pétales de fleurs de la région, selon des techniques traditionnelles datant du XVIIe siècle

***Saint-Lambert:* Musée du costume et du textile du Québec**
349, rue Riverside, Saint-Lambert, QC J4P 1A8
Tél: 450-923-6601
info@mctq.org
www.mctq.org
Fondée en: 1979 Le musée se consacre à la recherche, la conservation, l'éducation, et la diffusion; expositions de costume, textiles, et de la fibre; boutique.
Pierre G. Bélanger, Président
Suzanne Chabot, Directrice générale, suzanne.chabot@mctq.org
Joanne Watkins, Directrice administrative, joanne.watkins@mctq.org

***Saint-Prime:* Musée du fromage cheddar**
148, av Albert-Perron, Saint-Prime, QC G8J 1L4
Tél: 418-251-4922; Téléc: 418-251-1172
Ligne sans frais: 888-251-4922
cheddar@bellnet.ca
www.museecheddar.org
La vieille Fromagerie Perron est la seule survivante de sa catégorie au Québec. Aujourd'hui transformée en lieu d'interprétation elle vous raconte la fabrication traditionnelle du cheddar; visites guidées; boutique souvenir, vente de fromage; casiers verrouillés pour vélos; ouverte au public juin - sept. et sur réservation pour le reste de l'année.
Mme Diane Hudon, Directrice générale

***Salaberry-de-Valleyfield:* Écomusée des Deux-Rives**
75, rue St-Jean-Baptiste, Salaberry-de-Valleyfield, QC J6T 1Z6
Tel: 450-370-4855; Fax: 450-370-4861
info@museedesdeuxrives.com

***Sept-Iles:* Musée Shaputuan / Shaputuan Museum**
290, boul des Montagnais, Sept-Iles, QC G4R 5R2
Tél: 418-962-4000; Téléc: 418-962-3131
www.ville.sept-iles.qc.ca
A pour mission de perpétuer la culture des Innus; le musée s'engage a acquérir, étudier et interpréter la culture; expositions; activités.

***Shawinigan:* Cité de l'Énergie**
CP 156, 1000, av Melville, Shawinigan, QC G9N 6T9
Tél: 819-536-8516; Téléc: 819-536-2982
Ligne sans frais: 866-900-2483
infocite@citedelenergie.com
www.citedelenergie.com
Médias sociaux: www.youtube.com/user/CiteEnergie
www.facebook.com/CiteEnergie
Centre de sciences, expositions, spectacle multimédia, tour d'observation Hydro-Québec

***Shawinigan-Sud:* Église Notre-Dame-de-la-Présentation**
825, av 2e, Shawinigan-Sud, QC G9P 1E1
Tél: 819-536-3652; Téléc: 819-536-4170
eglisendp@cgocable.ca
www.eglisendp.qc.ca
Lieu historique national du Canada; protection et mise en valeur des oeuvres de Leduc dans l'église
Lise Racine, Présidente
Mance Vallée, Coordonnatrice

***Sherbrooke:* Musée de la nature et des sciences de Sherbrooke**
225, rue Frontenac, Sherbrooke, QC J1H 1K1
Tél: 819-564-3200; Téléc: 819-564-7388
Ligne sans frais: 877-434-3200
info@naturesciences.qc.ca
www.naturesciences.qc.ca
Situé dans une ancienne usine de textile, le Musée renferme une collection de près de 100 000 objets dont 65 000 en sciences naturelles; expositions; théâtre d'objets intéractifs sur la fonction du cerveau; services d'animation et d'éducation et une salle multifonctionnelle disponible en location.
Mme Marie-Claude Bibeau, Directrice générale

***Sherbrooke:* Musée Régimentaire les Fusiliers de Sherbrooke**
64, rue Belvédère sud, Sherbrooke, QC J1H 4B4
Tél: 819-564-5940; Téléc: 819-564-5641

***Sherbrooke:* La Société d'histoire de Sherbrooke**
275, rue Dufferin, Sherbrooke, QC J1H 4M5
Tél: 819-821-5406
info@histoiresherbrooke.com
www.histoiresherbrooke.com
Fondée en: 1992 A pour mission de préserver le patrimoine local, et promouvoir l'histoire de Sherbrooke et les Cantons-de-l'Est
John Therriault, Président, info@histoiresherbrooke.com
Michael Harnois, Directeur général, michel.harnois@histoiresherbrooke.com
Karine Savary, Archiviste, karine.savary@histoiresherbrooke.com

***Sorel-Tracy:* Biophare**
6, rue St-Pierre, Sorel-Tracy, QC J3P 3S2
Tél: 450-780-5740; Téléc: 450-780-5734
Ligne sans frais: 877-780-5740
info@biophare.com
www.biophare.com
Fondée en: 1994 Dédiée à la réserve de la biosphère du lac Saint-Pierre; présente une exposition permanente "l'observatoire

du lac Saint-Pierre"; musée, groupes scolaires, boutique, location de salles.
Marc Mineau, Directeur général

Stanbridge East: **Missisquoi Museum / Musée Missisquoi**
2 River St., Stanbridge East, QC J0J 2H0
Tel: 450-248-3153; Fax: 450-248-0420
info@missisquoimuseum.ca
www.museemissisquoi.ca
Year Founded: 1964 Museum is house in the 1830 three-story, red brick, Cornell Mill. Exhibitions include Missisquoi County Archives, and explore the historic development of the county. Other buildings on site are the Walbridge Barn and Hodge's General Store.
Pamela Realffe, Executive Secretary
Heather Darch, Curator
Judy Antle, Archivist

Stanstead: **Stanstead Historical Society / Société Historique de Stanstead**
Also known as: **Colby-Curtis Museum**
535, rue Dufferin, Stanstead, QC J0B 3E0
Tel: 819-876-7322; Fax: 819-876-7936
info@colbycurtis.ca
www.colbycurtis.ca
Year Founded: 1929 Operates the Colby Curtis Museum & Carrollcroft Property
Pierre Rastoul, Director/Curator

St-Lin-Laurentides: **Lieu historique national du Canada de Sir-Wilfrid-Laurier / Sir Wilfrid Laurier National Historic Site of Canada**
945, 12e av, St-Lin-Laurentides, QC J5M 2W4
Tél: 450-439-3702Ligne sans frais: 888-787-8888
parcscanada-que@pc.gc.ca
www.pc.gc.ca/fra/lhn-nhs/qc/wilfridlaurier/inde x.aspx
Autre numéros: TTY: 1-866-787-6221
Centre d'interprétation; exposition présente la vie et l'oeuvre de Sir Wilfrid Laurier.

St-Paul-de-l'Ile-aux-Noix: **Lieu historique national du Canada du Fort-Lennox / Fort Lennox National Historic Site of Canada**
1 - 61st Ave., St-Paul-de-l'Ile-aux-Noix, QC J0J 1G0
Tél: 450-291-5700; Téléc: 450-291-4389
Ligne sans frais: 888-773-8888
parcscanada-que@pc.gc.ca
www.pc.gc.ca/fra/lhn-nhs/qc/lennox/index.aspx
Autre numéros: TTY: 1-866-787-6221
Visites guidées; activités; caserne, poudrière, corps de garde, et prison; expositions: "Ces messieurs les officiers", et "Le fort Lennox, Oeuvre des ingénieurs royaux".

Sutton: **Eberdt Museum of Communications**
30A, rue Principale, Sutton, QC J0E 2K0
Tél: 514-538-2649
mchs@aide-internet.org
Special collection for TV & radio

Sutton: **Musée des communications et d'histoire de Sutton**
CP 430, 32, rue Principale sud, Sutton, QC J0E 2K0
Tél: 450-538-2883
richard@publiciterre.org
www.museedesutton.com

Tadoussac: **Centre d'interprétation des mammifères marins**
Also known as: **CIMM**
108, de la Cale-Sèche, Tadoussac, QC G0T 2A0
Tél: 418-235-4701; Téléc: 418-235-4325
info@gremm.org
www.gremm.org
Fondée en: 2005 A pour mission la conservation du milieu marin & la recherche scientifique sur les mammifères marins du Saint-Laurent

Tadoussac: **La maison des Dunes**
750, ch du Moulin Baude, Tadoussac, QC G0T 2A0
Tél: 418-235-4238Ligne sans frais: 800-665-6527
Maison faisant partie du patrimoine local, transformée en centre d'interprétation; exposition permanente; présentations, par des naturalistes, sur le phénomène des dunes de sable

Tadoussac: **La Petite chapelle de Tadoussac**
Also known as: **La Chapelle des Indiens**
CP 69, rue Bord de l'Eau, Tadoussac, QC G0T 2A0
Tél: 418-235-4657; Téléc: 418-235-4433
www.tadoussac.com

Tadoussac: **Poste de Traite Chauvin Trading Post**
157, rue du Bord-de-l'Eau, Tadoussac, QC G0T 2A0
Tél: 418-235-4657; Téléc: 418-235-4433
culture@tadoussac.com
Réplique du premier poste de traite des fourrures du 17e siècle; présente des objets se rapportant à la vie des autochtones et les produits d'échange; dégustation de phoque tous les dimanches
Gaby Villeneuve

Thetford Mines: **Musée minéralogique et minier de Thetford Mines**
711, boul Frontenac ouest, Thetford Mines, QC G6E 7Y8
Tél: 418-335-2123; Téléc: 418-335-5605
service.client@museemineralogique.com
www.museemineralogique.com
Fondée en: 1976 Présente l'histoire géologique, minière & social de la région de L'Amiante; expositions; activités educatives; excursions
François Cinq-Mars, Directeur,
f.cinq-mars@museemineralogique.com

Trois-Pistoles: **Parc de l'aventure basque en Amérique (PABA)**
66, rue du Parc, Trois-Pistoles, QC G0L 4K0
Tél: 418-851-1556; Téléc: 418-851-2188
Ligne sans frais: 877-851-1556
info@aventurebasque.ca
www.aventurebasque.ca
Frédéric Jean, Président par intérim
Mélanie Paquet, Directrice-coordonnatrice

Trois-Rivières: **Centre d'exposition sur l'industrie des pâtes et papiers**
CP 368, 800, Parc portuaire, Trois-Rivières, QC G9A 5H3
Tél: 819-372-4633; Téléc: 819-374-1900
ceipp@v3r.net
www.ceipp.net
Le Centre d'exposition s'engage à vous faire découvrir l'histoire de la région papetière du Québec; activités; groupes scolaires et adultes; ouvert tous les jours 10h-18h, du 30 mai au 27 septembre (2009) et sur réservation pour les groupes

Trois-Rivières: **Lieu historique national du Canada des Forges-du-Saint-Maurice / Forges du Saint-Maurice National Historic Site of Canada**
10 000, boul des Forges, Trois-Rivières, QC G9C 1B1
Tél: 819-378-5116; Téléc: 819-378-0887
Ligne sans frais: 888-773-8888
parcscanada-que@pc.gc.ca
www.pc.gc.ca/fra/lhn-nhs/qc/saintmaurice
A 20 minutes de Trois-Rivières, commémore l'établissement de la première communauté industrielle au Canada; ouvert de mi-mai à mi-oct.; groupes sur réservation.

Trois-Rivières: **Musée des Ursulines de Trois-Rivières**
734, rue des Ursulines, Trois-Rivières, QC G9A 5B5
Tél: 819-375-7922; Téléc: 819-375-0238
info@musee-ursulines.qc.ca
www.musee-ursulines.qc.ca; www.ursulines-uc.com
Médias sociaux: www.facebook.com/pages/Trois-Rivieres-QC/Musee-des-Ursulines
twitter.com /museeursulines
www.facebook.com/musee.desursulines
Conserve et met en valeur l'histoire des Ursulines dès 1697; expositions thématiques, visites guidées, galerie d'art.

Trois-Rivières: **Musée militaire de Trois-Rivières**
Also known as: **Musée du 12e Régiment blindé du Canada**
574, rue St-François-Xavier, Trois-Rivières, QC G9A 1R6
Tél: 819-371-5290; Téléc: 819-371-5292
museemilitaire@cgocable.ca
www.mediat-muse.qc.ca/web_12e.html; www.12rbc.ca
Musée et manège militaire; exposition retraçant l'histoire du régiment; salles d'armes; collections d'uniformes, pièces d'équipements, armes blanches et armes à feu en usage dans les Forces canadiennes.

Trois-Rivières: **Musée Pierre Boucher**
Séminaire Saint-Joseph, 858, rue Laviolette, Trois-Rivières, QC G9A 5S3
Tél: 819-376-4459; Téléc: 819-378-0607
museepierre-boucher@ssj.qc.ca
Musée fondé en 1920 par Mgr Albert Tessier pour protéger et sauvegarder le patrimoine local et régional; art contemporain (québecois et canadien); un programme d'animation adapté pour les groupes scolaires et les groupes d'adultes est centré sur les expositions temporaires, consacrées aux artistes contemporains et aux collections du musée; le musée est ouvert gratuitement du mardi au dimanche

Trois-Rivières: **Musée québécois de culture populaire / Museum of Quebec Folk Culture**
200, rue Laviolette, Trois-Rivières, QC G9A 6L5
Tél: 819-372-0406; Téléc: 819-372-9907
info@culturepop.qc.ca
www.culturepop.qc.ca
www.facebook.com/culturepop
Fondée en: 2001 Le Musée propose six expositions audacieuses, non conventionnelles et empreintes de plaisir à la manière des Québécois; reliée au Musée, la Vieille prison de Trois-Rivières, offre une visite-expérience, guidée par des ex-détenus. Heures: June 24-Sep.3: 10h-18h; Automne, hiver, printemps: 10h-17h
Benoît Gauthier, Directeur

Ulverton: **Moulin à laine d'Ulverton / Ulverton Woolen Mills**
210, ch Porter, Ulverton, QC J0B 2B0
Tél: 819-826-3157; Téléc: 819-826-6266
info@moulin.ca
www.moulin.ca
Fondée en: 1982 Initie aux méthodes artisanales et industrielles de production et de traitement de la laine

Valcourt: **Musée J. Armand Bombardier**
1001, av J.A. Bombardier, Valcourt, QC J0E 2L0
Tél: 450-532-5300; Téléc: 450-532-2260
info@museebombardier.com
www.museebombardier.com
Médias sociaux: www.youtube.com/MuseeJAB
www.facebook.com/MuseeBombardier
Le musée présente la vie et l'oeuvre de Joseph-Armand Bombardier, mécanicien, inventeur et entrepreneur; retrace l'évolution de l'industrie de la motoneige; expositions; activités.

Val-d'Or: **La Cité de l'Or**
Parent: **La Corporation du Village minier de Bourlamaque**
CP 212, 90, av Perreault, Val-d'Or, QC J9P 4P3
Tél: 819-825-7616; Téléc: 819-825-9853
Ligne sans frais: 877-582-5367
courrier@citedelor.qc.ca
www.citedelor.com
Site historique du patrimoine minier en Abitibi-Témiscamingue; visites guidées à la seule mine d'or du Québec accessible à 91 mètre sous terre; expositions; boutique; par réservation.
Ghislaine Brousseau, Responsable des réservations

Vaudreuil-Dorion: **Musée régional de Vaudreuil-Soulanges (MRVS)**
431, av St-Charles, Vaudreuil-Dorion, QC J7V 2N3
Tel: 450-455-2092; Fax: 450-455-6782
Toll-Free: 877-455-2092
info@mrvs.qc.ca
www.mrvs.qc.ca
Exposition permanente et expositions temporaires; collections spécialisées; ethnologie et histoire; collection beaux-arts; circuits patrimoniaux; centre de documentation en généaologie et histoire régionale; visities guidées, activités, ateliers, programmation; location de salles; boutique; café.
Daniel Bissonnette, Directeur générale

Victoriaville: **Musée Laurier**
16, rue Laurier ouest, Victoriaville, QC G6P 6P3
Tél: 819-357-8655; Téléc: 819-357-8655
info@museelaurier.com
museelaurier.com
Fondée en: 1929 Résidence de Sir Wilfrid Laurier, ancien premier ministre du Canada, et sa femme Lady Laurier, maintenant la propriété de la Société du Musée Laurier; collection d'objets d'art et de meubles, sculpture, et oeuvres en art contemporain.
Richard Pedneault, Directeur/Conservateur

Westmount: **Royal Montreal Regiment Museum**
4625, rue Ste-Catherine ouest, Westmount, QC H3Z 1S4
Tel: 514-496-2003; Fax: 514-496-5085
royalmontrealregiment.com
twitter.com/rmtlr
www.facebook.com/royalmont realregiment

Windsor: **Parc histoique de la Poudrière de Windsor / Windsor Powder Mill Historical Park**
342, rue St-Georges, Windsor, QC J1S 2Z5
Tél: 819-845-5284
poudriere@villedewindsor.qc.ca
www.poudriere-windsor.com
www.facebook.com/195123797205009
Fondée en 1864, dans la foulée de la guerre de session, la Poudrière de Windsor s'est investie dans la fabrication de poudre noire, un composé essentiel des explosifs. Jusqu'en 1922, la ville de Windsor a vécu au rythme de cette industrie dangereuse. On peut maintenant découvir les secrets, le comment et le pourquoi de cette industrie via une toute nouvelle exposition permanente et la visite guidé

Saskatchewan

Provincial Museums

Royal Saskatchewan Museum
2445 Albert St., Regina, SK S4P 4W7
Tel: 306-787-2815; Fax: 306-787-2820
rsminfo@royalsaskmuseum.ca
www.royalsaskmuseum.ca
Saskatchewan's natural & human history; archaeology; entomology; botany; natural history; paleontology; geology. Life Sciences Gallery; Earth Sciences Gallery; First Nations Gallery; Paleo Pit interactive gallery for children ; Megamunch, a half-size robotic Tyrannosaurus rex. Publication of informational booklets & nature notes, giftshop, research library.
Harold Bryant, Curator, Earth Sciences

David Baron, Director
Keith Roney, Curator, Life Sciences
Margaret Hanna, Curator, Aboriginal History
Ron Tillie, Supervisor, Exhibits
Paula Hill, Public Programs, Education
Ferne Johnston, Administrator

Western Development Museum (WDM)
2935 Melville St., Saskatoon, SK S7J 5A6
Tel: 306-934-1400; Fax: 306-934-4467
Toll-Free: 800-363-6345
info@wdm.ca
www.wdm.ca
Social Media: www.youtube.com/user/SKWDM
twitter.com/skWDM
www.facebook.com/skwdm
The Western Development Museum preserves Saskatchewan's collective heritage, in order to raise awareness of & interest in the cultural & economic development of western Canada. The Curatorial Centre in Saskatoon coordinates services for the museum's branches in Moose Jaw, North Battleford, Saskatoon, & Yorkton. Tours of the Curatorial Centre may be arranged through the education & extension staff.

History of Transportation
50 Diefenbaker Dr., Moose Jaw, SK S6H 4N8
Tel: 306-693-5989; Fax: 306-691-0511

Heritage Farm & Village
PO Box 183, North Battleford, SK S9A 2Y1
Tel: 306-445-8033; Fax: 306-445-7211

Story of People
PO Box 98, Hwy. 16 West, Yorkton, SK S3N 2V6
Tel: 306-783-8361; Fax: 306-782-1027

1910 Boomtown
2610 Lorne Ave. South, Saskatoon, SK S7J 0S6
Tel: 306-931-1910; Fax: 306-934-0525

David Klatt, Executive Director
Cal Glasman, Director, Administration, cglasman@wdm.ca
Ruth Bitner, Curator, Collections, rbitner@wdm.ca
Warren Clubb, Curator, Exhibits, wclubb@wdm.ca
Dianne Craig, Manager, Corporate Development, dcraig@wdm.ca
Terry Thompson, Manager, Facilities, tthompson@wdm.ca
Brian Newman, Coordinator, Exhibits, bnewman@wdm.ca
Leslee Newman, Coordinator, Education & Extension, lnewman@wdm.ca
Jan Olsen, Coordinator, Marketing, jolsen@wdm.ca
Juanelle Finlay, Library Technician, jfinlay@wdm.ca

Local Museums in Saskatchewan

***Abernethy:* Abernethy Nature-Heritage Museum**
PO Box 158, Abernethy, SK S0A 0A0
Tel: 306-333-2202
anhm@sasktel.net
Heritage & antique artifacts with a core exhibit of more than 300 wildlife specimens mounted by the late Ralph Stueck (1897-1979); video presentation of Stueck's "talking goose" & other folklore; activities/hands-on displays for children; small art gallery; 1930's classroom. Open daily May - Sept. Wheelchair accessible.
Eileen Gaye, President

***Abernethy:* Motherwell Homestead Natural Historic Site**
PO Box 247, Abernethy, SK S0A 0A0
Tel: 306-333-2116; Fax: 306-333-2210
motherwell-homestead@pc.gc.ca
www.pc.gc.ca/motherwell
Year Founded: 1983 The site includes Lanark Place, the farmstead estate of pioneer farmer and politician, W.R. Motherwell, who had a significant influence on the development of scientific agriculture in Western Canada. The homestead depicts the lifestyles, costumes, and architecture of the early 20th century, with costumed guides. Open Victoria Day - Labour Day.
Flo Miller, Site Coordinator, flo.miller@pc.gc.ca

***Alameda:* Alameda & District Heritage Museum**
PO Box 195, Alameda, SK S0C 0A0
Tel: 306-483-5099
Open Wed. July-Aug., or by appointment.
Evelyn Lochart, Contact

***Alida:* Gervais Wheels Museum**
PO Box 40, Alida, SK S0C 0B0
Tel: 306-443-2303
Pioneer artifacts, music boxes, gramophones, North American automobiles

***Allan:* Allan Community Heritage Society & Museum**
326 Main St., Allan, SK S0K 0C0
Tel: 306-257-3511; Fax: 306-257-4249
kbrfitz@sasktel.net
Other contact information: Alternate Phone: 306-257-4341

***Arborfield:* Dickson Hardie Interpretive Centre at Pasquia Regional Park**
PO Box 339, Arborfield, SK S0E 0A0
Tel: 306-768-3239; Fax: 306-769-8307
rob.sus@yourlink.ca
www.pasquia.com
The museum features fossil castings of archaeological finds from around the Carrot River, & pieces from throughout the region collected by locals. Open May-Sept.

***Arcola:* Arcola Museum**
PO Box 354, Railway Ave., Arcola, SK S0C 0G0
Tel: 306-455-2462
Open May-Sept.

***Assiniboia:* Assiniboia & District Museum**
PO Box 1211, 506 - 3rd Ave. West, Assiniboia, SK S0H 0B0
Tel: 306-642-5353; Fax: 306-642-4216
assini.museum@sasktel.net
southcentralmuseums.ca/assiniboia.html
Other contact information: Phone, appointments: 306-642-4790
The Assiniboia & District Museum features vintage cars from 1916 to 1964, a grain elevator, a Pole Shed with agricultural machinery, a school room & a military display. The museum is open seven days a week during July & August, & Monday to Friday from September to June.

***Avonlea:* Avonlea Heritage Museum**
PO Box 401, 219 Main St., Avonlea, SK S0H 0C0
Tel: 306-868-2101
www.avonleamuseum.ca
Year Founded: 1980 The Avonlea Heritage Museum displays artifacts which depict the geological age, plus the history of native people, pioneers, & ranchers in the area. The Truax Anglican Church is situated on the grounds. The museum is open from June to September. At other times of the year, appointments can be arranged. Hours: June, July, Aug. 10:00-5:00 or by Appointment
Richard Geisler, President
Joyce Holland, Secretary
Debra Penner, Treasurer

***Battleford:* Fort Battleford National Historic Site of Canada**
PO Box 70, Battleford, SK S0M 0E0
Tel: 306-937-2621; Fax: 306-937-3370
battleford.info@pc.gc.ca
www.parkscanada.gc.ca/battleford
Other contact information: TTY: 306-937-3199
NWMP post, c. 1886; open May long weekend - Sept. long weekend
Glenn Ebert, Site Coordinator

***Battleford:* Fred Light Museum**
PO Box 40, Battleford, SK S0M 0E0
Tel: 306-937-7111
Pioneer artifacts, gun collection, military artifacts; open May - Sept.
Bernadette Leslie, Supervisor

***Battleford:* Saskatchewan Baseball Hall of Fame & Museum**
PO Box 1388, 292 - 22nd St., Battleford, SK S0M 0E0
Tel: 306-446-1983; Fax: 306-446-0509
saskbaseballmuseum@sasktel.net
Year Founded: 1983 Has over 3,000 artifacts dealing with baseball plus 6,000 items of archival nature such as pictures, books & magazines
Jane Shury, Executive Director

***Beauval:* Frazer's Museum**
PO Box 64, Beauval, SK S0M 0G0
Aboriginal & pioneer artifacts, including articles from Hudson's Bay Company, missionaries & Métis people

***Bengough:* Bengough & District Museum**
PO Box 122, 140 - 1st Ave. West, Bengough, SK S0C 0K0
Tel: 306-268-2909
dashby@sasktel.net
www.southcentralmuseums.ca/bengough.html
Other contact information: Alternate Phone: 306-268-2927
Local history; open daily from June-Aug., & by appointment Sept.-May.

***Big River:* Big River Memorial Museum**
PO Box 220, 205 Third Ave. North, Big River, SK S0J 0E0
Tel: 306-469-2112
The Big River Memorial Museum contains items from fishing & logging in the area.

***Biggar:* Biggar Museum & Gallery**
PO Box 1598, 105 - 3rd Ave. West, Biggar, SK S0K 0M0
Tel: 306-948-3451; Fax: 306-948-3478
biggarmuseum@sasktel.net
www.biggarmuseum.com
Year Founded: 1972 The museum collects historical artifacts from the settlement of the town of Biggar & the surrounding district. Among it collections are a general store display & a reconstruction of the Biggar train station. Biggar Museum & Gallery is open year round.
Anne Livingston, Executive Director

***Biggar:* Homestead Museum**
PO Box 542, Biggar, SK S0K 0M0
Tel: 306-948-3427
Prairie pioneer village including sod house, school, church, barn, general store, 1913 house, 1920 house & bunk house & cook car; collection of Historical Character dolls; open daily Victoria Day - Oct.
Cecile Martin, Contact

***Birch Hills:* Birch Hills & District Historical Society**
PO Box 693, 7 Wilson St., Birch Hills, SK S0J 0G0
Tel: 306-749-2262
bhmuseum@yahoo.ca
www.birchhills.ca/recreation.html
The museum's collection contains restored agricultural machines, a memorial wall, & a lending library of over 200 Saskatchewan history books. Buildings on-site include a log barn, a milk house, & a CPR station. Open Jan.-Dec., W 2:00-4:00, also by appointment.

***Blaine Lake:* Blaine Lake Museum**
PO Box 10, Blaine Lake, SK S0J 0J0
Tel: 306-497-2531
The Blaine Lake Museum is situated in the CNR station, which was built in 1912. The museum depicts the local history of the area.

***Bonnyville:* Bonnyville & District Museum**
***Parent:* Bonnyville & District Historical Society**
4401 - 54 Ave., Bonnyville, SK T9N 2H4
Tel: 780-826-4925; Fax: 780-812-3475
bvmuseum@telus.net
town.bonnyville.ab.ca
Year Founded: 1991 The museum features 250,000 artifacts pertaining to local history. Open May-Sept., daily 10:00-4:00.

***Borden:* Borden & District Historical Museum**
PO Box 5, 200 Main St., Borden, SK S0K 0N0
Tel: 306-997-4517
www.bordensask.ca/index-3.4.html
Year Founded: 1990 Artifacts housed in a one-room schoolhouse & former Masonic Lodge; site also includes a replica of the Diefenbaker homestead, as well as a butcher shop & barber shop. Open June-Sept., or by appointment.
Heather Silcox, Chair

***Briercrest:* Briercrest & District Museum**
PO Box 216, 400 Main St., Briercrest, SK S0H 0K0
Tel: 306-799-4951
villageofbriercrest.ca/museum_.html
Other contact information: Alternate Phones: 306-799-4988; 306-799-4424
Year Founded: 1987 The Briercrest & District Museum houses collections from the Briercrest area's earliest settlers & their descendants. Examples of the museum's artifacts include household items & small farm equipment. Open by appointment.

***Broadview:* Broadview Historical Museum**
PO Box 556, Broadview, SK S0G 0K0
Tel: 306-696-3244
www.broadview.ca/museum
Year Founded: 1972 Articles related to Broadview's history are collected & displayed. Visitors can see the Highland School, a blacksmith shop, a post office, a sod house, a log home, & a Canadian Pacific Railway station & caboose. Broadview Historical Museum is open from the beginning of June to the end of August.

***Cabri:* Cabri & District Museum**
PO Box 230, 202 - 1st St. South, Cabri, SK S0N 0J0
Tel: 306-587-2339
Displays include artifacts from World War I & World War II, First Nations, & household & farm items. The museum is open from May to September.

***Cadillac:* Cadillac Museum**
PO Box 118, Centre St., Cadillac, SK S0N 0K0
Tel: 306-785-2128; Fax: 306-785-2042

Household articles & early 20th century tools; clothing; fire-fighting equipment; quilt exhibit; demonstrations. Open upon request
Luanne Hancock, Contact

***Canora:* CN Station House Museum**
PO Box 180, Canora, SK S0A 0L0
Tel: 306-563-4591
stn.house.museum@sasktel.net
The museum contains CN & pioneer artifacts, & is housed in the oldest Class 2 station left in Saskatchewan. Part of the museum is being integrated into the town's new Visitor Centre. Open July-Sept., daily 10:00-4:00.

***Canwood:* Canwood Museum**
PO Box 269, 635 - 3rd Ave. East, Canwood, SK S0J 0K0
Year Founded: 1971 Canwood Museum is a community museum located in an old schoolhouse. Displays include farm artifacts, clothing, & pictures.

***Carlyle:* Rusty Relics Museum Inc.**
PO Box 840, 115 Railway Ave. W., Carlyle, SK S0C 0R0
Tel: 306-453-2266
rustyrelicsmuseum@gmail.com
Other contact information: Alternate Phone: 306-453-2363
A museum of pioneer life in Saskatchewan; artifacts relating to Carlyle area displayed in room settings in a 1910 CN railway station; includes a 1943 CPR caboose, a CN Motor car, CN tool shed with railway tools, furnished 1905 one-room country school, agricultural machinery & old church
Wilbert Hume, President

***Choiceland:* Choiceland Historical Society**
PO Box 234, Choiceland, SK S0J 0M0
Tel: 306-428-2850
emoll@sasktel.net
choiceland.ca/museum.html
Local & military history. Open May-Sept., F 1:00-4:00

***Climax:* Climax Community Museum Inc.**
PO Box 246, Climax, SK S0N 0N0
Tel: 306-293-2124; Fax: 306-293-2051
Pioneer collection - domestic, tools, farm machinery, military, hospital & sports, community archives
Victor Van Allen, President/Curator

***Consul:* Consul Museum**
PO Box 144, Consul, SK S0N 0P0
Tel: 306-299-4493
consulmuseum@gmail.com
www.consulmuseum.ca
Year Founded: 2005 The Consul Museum is the first Saskatchewan museum to exist solely as a website. The site contains pictures, videos, & stories of local history.

***Coronach:* Coronach District Museum**
PO Box 449, Coronach, SK S0H 0Z0
Tel: 306-267-4923
Features historical displays, records, photos & artifacts representing the lives of pioneers of the area
Judy Greenwood, Chair

***Craik:* Craik Oral History Museum**
PO Box 144, Craik, SK S0G 0V0
Tel: 306-734-2881
bubball@sasktel.net
Local history; collection contains photographs, slides, videos, documents & record books, & 600 hours of audio cassette recordings. Open Jan.-Dec., or by appointment.

***Craik:* Prairie Pioneer Museum**
PO Box 157, 541 Parks Rd., Craik, SK S0G 0V0
Tel: 306-734-2480
www.craik.ca/pioneer.html
Year Founded: 1966 The pioneer way of life in Craik & rural Saskatchewan is portrayed at the Prairie Pioneer Museum. Buildings include two rural schools & a heritage house, which was built in 1906. Artifacts, such as household furnishings & medical & veterinary instruments, are on display. The museum is open during the summer, & is accessible year-round by request.
Mary Eva, Contact

***Creighton:* Royal Northwest Mounted Police Post Museum**
***Also known as:* RNWMP Post Museum**
PO Box 100, 216 Creighton Ave., Creighton, SK S0P 0A0
Tel: 306-688-3538; Fax: 306-688-4110
creightontourism@sasktel.net
www.townofcreighton.ca/museum.html
A reconstruction of the original Royal Northwest Mounted Police Post in Beaver City, circa 1915. Located at the Creighton Recreation Culture & Tourism Centre. Open May-Sept.

***Cudworth:* Cudworth Museum**
PO Box 69, Cudworth, SK S0K 1B0
Tel: 306-256-3492; Fax: 306-256-3515
town.cudworth@sasktel.net
Year Founded: 2004 Local history; former CN station.

***Cupar:* Cupar & District Heritage Museum**
PO Box 164, Cupar, SK S0G 0Y0
Tel: 306-723-4324
Year Founded: 1955 Open May - Sept. or by appt.
Wes Bailey, Chair

***Cut Knife:* Clayton McLain Memorial Museum**
PO Box 8, 111A Hill Ave., Cut Knife, SK S0M 0N0
Tel: 306-398-2920; Fax: 306-398-2951
cmmmcutknife@gmail.com
www.cmmmcutknife.ca; cmmmcutknife.blogspot.com
Located in Tomahawk Park; local history, including First Nations artifacts from early life & Battle of Cutknife Hill, and McLain family collection; archives include personal papers, photgraphs, and a complete collection of the local newspaper; educational programming; research services; open June-Sept.

***Denare Beach:* Northern Gateway Museum**
PO Box 70, Beaver Dr., Denare Beach, SK S0P 0B0
Tel: 306-362-2141; Fax: 306-362-2257
Year Founded: 1957 The Northern Gateway Museum houses artifacts from fur trade excavations, First Nations life, gold rush activities, & mining operations. Archives include architectural records, photographs, & films.

***Dinsmore:* Yester-Years Community Museum**
PO Box 216, Main St., Dinsmore, SK S0L 0T0
Features the main museum, blacksmith shop, butter & post office buildings; open July & Aug. upon request

***Dodsland:* Dodsland & District Museum**
PO Box 171, Dodsland, SK S0L 0V0
Tel: 306-356-2228
Old grocery store on lower floor represents a village of the past; top floor represents living quarters of the past; located at Main St. & 1st Ave; open May-Nov., Tu & Th 1:30-4:30, or by appointment.
Weldon Bacon, President

***Duck Lake:* Duck Lake Regional Interpretive Centre**
PO Box 328, Duck Lake, SK S0K 1J0
Tel: 306-467-2057; Fax: 306-467-2257
Toll-Free: 866-467-2057
duckmuf@sasktel.net
www.dlric.org
Year Founded: 1959 Frontier of First Nation, Métis & Pioneer Society, 1870-1905; artifact & art galleries, theatre, gift shop, 24m viewing tower, conference facilities
Celine Perillat, Executive Director

***Duff:* Duff Community Heritage Museum**
PO Box 57, Duff, SK S0A 0S0
Tel: 306-728-3275
www.spreda.sk.ca/community_Duff.htm
Open by appointment only, this tourist attraction has been built out of an old church and features a recreational pioneer-era kitchen and old rural schoolhouse, along with various other historical items and photos from the village's history.

***Dysart:* Dysart & District Museum**
PO Box 327, Dysart, SK S0G 1H0
Tel: 306-432-2255
Other contact information: Alternate Phone: 306-432-2100
Local history; replicas of area country schools; Wall of Honour war memorial; open June-Sept., Th & Sa 1:30-4:00.

***Eastend:* Eastend Museum & Cultural Centre**
PO Box 214, Eastend, SK S0N 0T0
Tel: 306-295-3564
Tie Rail Ranch House, blacksmith shop, operating 1903 Cae Steam Engine, 1927 Federal Truck, & a stage coach; LaRose Building contains 1500 items; Open daily May - Labour Day
Shelly Parker, President
Glen Duke, Treasurer
Doreen Stewart, Secretary

***Eatonia:* Eatonia Heritage Park**
PO Box 189, 100 Railway Ave., Eatonia, SK S0L 0Y0
Tel: 306-967-2251
eatonia@yourlink.ca
Municipal Heritage Property featuring a train caboose & wood-frame railway station & house from the early 1900s.

***Edam:* Harry S. Washbrook Museum**
PO Box 182, 2nd Ave., Edam, SK S0M 0V0
Tel: 306-397-2260
Local pioneer & First Nations artifacts

***Elbow:* Elbow Museum & Historical Society**
PO Box 207, Elbow, SK S0H 1J0
Tel: 306-854-2277; Fax: 306-854-2229
elbow@sasktel.net
www.elbowsask.com
Housed in an old schoolhouse; sodhouse built in 1965 & July 1999; artifacts represent era of late 1800s & early 1900s
Joan Soggie, Chair

***Elrose:* Elrose Museum**
***Parent:* Elrose Heritage Society**
PO Box 556, 102 - 4th Ave., Elrose, SK S0L 0Z0
Tel: 306-378-2383
elrosemuseum@hotmail.com
Directors collect, restore & catalogue artifacts & antiques; open May-Sept.
Florence Rowley, Secretary
Betty Rudd, President

***Esterhazy:* Esterhazy Community Museum**
PO Box 371, Esterhazy, SK S0A 0X0
Tel: 306-745-2988
Pioneer artifacts, taxidermy & music rooms, old store, model of potash mine; fashion show; antique doll and toy show

***Esterhazy:* Kaposvar Historic Site**
PO Box 371, 183 Fertile Belt, Esterhazy, SK S0A 0X0
Tel: 306-745-3474
1907 church & rectory; Annual Pilgrimage on the fourth Sun. in Aug.

***Estevan:* Estevan Art Gallery & Museum**
118 - 4th St., Estevan, SK S4A 0T4
Tel: 306-634-7644; Fax: 306-634-2490
eagm@sasktel.net
www.eagm.ca
NWMP Museum, local artifacts; open summer season; plus art with 2 contemporary exhibiting galleries, with travelling exhibitions, giftshop; open year round
Griffith Aaron Baker, Director/Curator

***Eston:* Prairie West Historical Centre & Society**
PO Box 910, 946 - 2nd St. East, Eston, SK S0L 1A0
Tel: 306-962-3772
emljacobson@sasktel.net
Other contact information: Alternate Phones: 206-962-2559; 306-962-4578; 306-962-2552
Local history museum & art gallery; wildflower garden

***Foam Lake:* Foam Lake Museum**
PO Box 1041, 113 Bray Ave., Foam Lake, SK S0A 1A0
Tel: 306-272-4292
Local pioneer museum documenting the settlement of the area. Open June 1st - Aug. 31st and by appointment.
Ruth Gushulak, President
Fina Anderson, Secretary

***Fort Qu'appelle:* Fort Qu'Appelle Museum**
PO Box 1093, Fort Qu'appelle, SK S0G 1S0
Tel: 306-332-6033
valleycalls@sasktel.net
www.fortquappelle.com/history.html
1864 Hudson Bay Co. post; open June-Sept.
J. Norman, Vice-President
L. Anderson, President

***Frenchman Butte:* Frenchman Butte Museum**
PO Box 10, Frenchman Butte, SK S0M 0W0
Tel: 306-344-4478; Fax: 306-344-4566
info@frenchmanbuttemuseum.ca
www.frenchmanbuttemuseum.ca
Pioneer & CNR artifacts; arrowhead & gun collections, mounted birds

***Frobisher:* Frobisher Threshermen's Museum**
PO Box 194, Frobisher, SK S0C 0Y0
Tel: 306-486-4513
Steam engines, wooden threshing separators, gas & diesel tractors, ploughshares

***Glaslyn:* Glaslyn & District Museum**
PO Box 363, Railway Ave., Glaslyn, SK S0M 0Y0
Tel: 306-342-4657
Other contact information: Alternate Phone: 306-342-2121
Museum contains artifacts from the 1800's, housed in a restored CNR station house circa 1926; CNR water tank & caboose also on-site; taxidermy articles, including a rare two-headed calf.

***Glen Ewen:* Glen Ewen Community Antique Centre**
Glen Ewen, SK S0C 1C0
Tel: 306-925-2221
Features a collection of antique cars that includes a 1910 Ford & a 1937 Packard; also showcases guns, dishes & household articles from the early 1900s; open seasonally or by request
Arne Hansen, Director

***Glenavon:* Glenavon Museum**
General Delivery, Glenavon, SK S0G 1Y0
Tel: 306-429-2011; Fax: 306-429-2260
www.glenavonsk.ca
Open July & Aug., Tue & Th 1:00-4:00.

Glentworth: **Glentworth Museum**
PO Box 174, Glentworth, SK S0H 1V0
Tel: 306-266-4320
Local history artifacts

Goodsoil: **Goodsoil Historical Museum**
PO Box 370, Goodsoil, SK S0M 1A0
Tel: 306-238-4565; Fax: 306-238-4991
schamber@sasktel.net
Year Founded: 1977 Natural stone school building built in 1945; first teacherage built in 1934 of logs; miniature church with original steeple from church destroyed by tornado; over 2,500 artifacts, many dating from 1800s; old machinery; doll house with hundreds of dolls from around the world. Open June 30 - Aug. 31
Alex Schamber, President, schamber@sasktel.net
Rudy Leiter, Secretary

Gravelbourg: **Gravelbourg & District Museum**
PO Box 862, 300 Main St., Gravelbourg, SK S0H 1X0
Tel: 306-648-2332
Open July & Aug.
Louis Stringer, Manager

Grenfell: **Grenfell Museum Assoc.**
PO Box 1156, 711 Wolseley Ave., Grenfell, SK S0G 2B0
Tel: 306-697-2930; Fax: 306-697-2500
Restored 1904 Queen Anne turreted house; added attraction is the annex with furniture & tools of bygone days as well as an outstanding military display
Lloyd Arthur, President
Mary Christie, Secretary

Gull Lake: **Gull Lake Museum**
PO Box 305, 3570 Rutland Ave., Gull Lake, SK S0N 1A0
Tel: 306-672-4377
sbdavies@sasktel.net
gulllakesk.ca/museum.htm
The museum site features artifacts housed in three buildings: a vintage house, an old country schoolhouse, & a pole structure with farm-related items.

Hague: **Saskatchewan River Valley Museum**
PO Box 630, Hague, SK S0K 1X0
Tel: 306-225-2112; Fax: 306-225-4642
Approx. 6,000 artifacts, including First Nations & Mennonite; original European house/barn; country school; Mennonite church; horse-drawn farming machinery, blacksmith tools, pre-1950 furniture & appliances; open May long weekend - Thanksgiving

Harris: **Harris Museum**
PO Box 131, 204 Railway Ave., Harris, SK S0L 1K0
Tel: 306-656-2002; Fax: 306-656-2172
Year Founded: 1989 The volunteer operated Harris Museum features local history & archives, plus a C.N. Water Tower & a gas engine water pump. The museum is open from May to September, or by appointment.
Harvey Neil, President
RoseAnn Mireau, Past President, 306-656-4449
Betty McFarlane, Contact, 306-656-4725
Dolores Neil, Contact, 306-656-2172

Hazenmore: **Heritage Hazenmore Museum**
PO Box 103, Hazenmore, SK S0N 1C0
Tel: 306-264-5149
Local history; open on request

Hepburn: **Hepburn Museum of Wheat**
PO Box 69, Hepburn, SK S0K 1Z0
Tel: 306-947-2128
Other contact information: Alternate Phone: 306-947-2170
Museum collection housed in an original grain elevator. Open Sat. in the summer.

Herbert: **Herbert CPR Train Station Museum**
Parent: **Herbert Heritage Association**
PO Box 202, 625 Railway Ave., Herbert, SK S0H 2A0
Tel: 306-784-3411
t.o.herbert@sasktel.net
www.townofherbert.com/herbert_train_station.html
The museum's collection is housed in a restored CPR station circa 1910, with a caboose on-site. Open June-Sept.
Bill Redekop, President
Shirley Heffley, Supervisor

Herschel: **Ancient Echoes Interpretive Centre**
PO Box 130, Herschel, SK S0L 1L0
Tel: 306-377-2045
ancientechoes@sasktel.net
www.ancientechoes.ca
The Centre contains local artifacts, including petroglyph rock carvings & the remains of a Pleisosaur.

Hodgeville: **Country Craft Shoppe & Homestead Museum**
PO Box 264, 102 - 1st St. West, Hodgeville, SK S0H 2B0
Tel: 306-677-2693
Eight rooms depicting an early homestead; crafts, gifts & tearoom

Hudson Bay: **Al Mazur Memorial Heritage Park**
PO Box 37, Hudson Bay, SK S0E 0Y0
Tel: 306-865-2180
1910heritage@sasktel.net
www.townofhudsonbay.com/default.aspx?page=80
Local history; artifacts housed in original buildings; 16-acre museum park; located at the junction of Hwy. 3 & 9; open May-Sept., daily 9:00-5:00

Hudson Bay: **Hudson Bay Museum**
Parent: **Hudson Bay & District Cultural Society**
c/o Hudson Bay & District Cultural Society, PO Box 931, 512 Churchill St., Hudson Bay, SK S0E 0Y0
Tel: 306-865-2170
hbmuseum@hotmail.com
www.townofhudsonbay.com
Preserving artifacts of the area; open May 15 - Sept. 10

Humboldt: **Humboldt & District Museum & Gallery**
PO Box 2349, Humboldt, SK S0K 2A0
Tel: 306-682-5226; Fax: 306-682-1430
humboldt.museum@sasktel.net
www.humboldtmuseum.ca
Focus on the Humboldt Telegraph Station of 1878, as well as the settlement of Humboldt & district, & the spiritual influence of St. Peter's Abbey; housed in a 1912 post office building
Carol Oleksyn, Chair
Jennifer Hoesgen, Curator

Imperial: **Imperial & District Museum**
PO Box 269, Royal St., Imperial, SK S0G 2J0
Tel: 306-963-2280
Local history; open by appt.

Imperial: **Nels Berggren Museum**
PO Box 125, Royal St., Imperial, SK S0G 2J0
Tel: 306-963-2033
Lamps, clocks, sewing machines, musical instruments, & art.

Indian Head: **Bell Barn Society of Indian Head**
PO Box 1882, Indian Head, SK S0G 2K0
Tel: 306-695-2355
bellbarn.ca
The society helps preserve the Bell Barn, a 125-year-old structure that once belonged to the Qu'Appelle Valley Farming Company. Open May-Sept., daily 10:00-4:00, or by appointment.

Kay Dixon, Chair
Jerry Willerth, Barn Boss, 306-695-2086, gdwillerth@sasktel.net
Connie Billett, Secretary, 306-695-3456, cbillett@sasktel.net

Indian Head: **Indian Head Museum**
PO Box 566, 610 Otterloo St., Indian Head, SK S0G 2K0
Tel: 306-695-2234
www.townofindianhead.com/our-history/history-resources.html
1907 two-storey fire hall displaying artifacts of local pioneer days; also 1926 one-room school, 1883 Bell Farm Cottage; replica of 1930s one-bay village garage; farm implements
Terry Fuller, Contact, tlfuller@sasktel.net

Ituna: **Ituna & District Museum**
Ituna Branch, Parkland Regional Library, 518 - 5th Ave. NE, Ituna, SK S0A 1N0
Tel: 306-785-2835
www.ituna.ca/libraryandmuseum.html
Other contact information: Alternate Phones: 306-795-3458; 306-795-2484
Year Founded: 1971 Local history including Ukrainian & aboriginal artifacts; open July-Aug.

Kamsack: **Kamsack & District Museum**
Also known as: **Power House Museum**
PO Box 991, Queen Elizabeth Boul., Kamsack, SK S0A 1S0
Tel: 306-542-4415
kphmuseum@gmail.com; kphm@gmail.com
Exhibits focus on both First Nations & European history; housed in a former power plant; features one of the original diesel engines which generated the town's electricity until 1958; rooms furnished in the style of a typical 1920s pioneer dwelling. Open May - Sept.; car show & shine mid-June

Kelliher: **Kelliher & District Heritage Museum Inc.**
PO Box 111, Kelliher, SK S0A 1V0
Tel: 306-675-2183
Walter Oleksyn

Kenosee Lake: **Cannington Manor Provincial Park**
PO Box 220, Kenosee Lake, SK S0C 2S0
Tel: 306-739-5251; Fax: 306-577-2622
manor.cannington@gov.sk.ca
www.tpcs.gov.sk.ca/CanningtonManor
Other contact information: Phone, Off Season: 306-577-2600
In the late 1800s, partners in the Moose Mountain Trading Company established the village of Cannington Manor. Buildings from this village have been reconstructed or restored for visitors. Buildings at the site include a Land Titles Office, a bachelor's cabin, a Moose Mountain Trading Company store, a carpenter's shop, a blacksmith shop, a flour mill, & the Mitre Hotel. Cannington Manor is open from Victoria Day to Labour Day.

Kerrobert: **Kerrobert & District Museum**
PO Box 452, 433 Manitoba Ave., Kerrobert, SK S0L 1R0
Tel: 306-834-5277
Other contact information: Alternate Phone: 306-834-2991
Replica of the first tent store & pioneer furniture; Open May-Sept.
Darren Obritsch, President, 306-834-2934
Bobbi Hebron, Secretary, 306-834-2409

Kincaid: **Kincaid Museum**
PO Box 177, Dominion Ave., Kincaid, SK S0H 2J0
Tel: 306-264-3910
Local historical material

Kindersley: **Kindersley & District Plains Museum**
PO Box 599, 903 - 11th Ave. East, Kindersley, SK S0L 1S0
Tel: 306-463-6620
kindersleymuseum@sasktel.net
Other contact information: Alternate Phone: 306-463-3062
Wide collection of early farm machinery & tools, household items, education items & items from school & churches; fire hall & fire truck; military display, a general store, post office & print shop; an archaeological display; open May to mid-Sept.

Kinistino: **Kinistino & District Pioneer Museum Inc.**
PO Box 10, Main St., Kinistino, SK S0J 1H0
Tel: 306-864-2461
Displays of artifacts from fur trade & pioneer times; oldest purely agricultural settlement in Saskatchewan; open July-Aug. or by appt.

Kipling: **Kipling & District Historical Society**
PO Box 414, Kipling, SK S0G 2S0
Tel: 306-736-8254
e.hamelin@sasktel.net
Elaine Hamelin, Secretary

Kisbey: **Kisbey Museum**
PO Box 117, 291 Ross St., Kisbey, SK S0C 1L0
Tel: 306-462-2162
Detailed history & pictures of Kisbey's namesake, R. Claude Kisbey; 1,000+ objects; open Thu. through July & Aug. & by request

Kronau: **Kronau Bethlehem Heritage Society**
PO Box 1, Kronau, SK S0G 2T0
Tel: 306-781-3082; Fax: 306-781-2267
4efarms@sasktel.net
www.facebook.com/pages/Kronau-Heritage-Society/248288010817
The museum collection is housed in the restored Kronau Lutheran Church building, circa 1912. Open May-Sept., Wed.-Su 10:00-4:00.

Kyle: **Kyle & District Museum**
PO Box 543, Kyle, SK S0L 1T0
Tel: 304-375-2525; Fax: 206-375-2534
www.kylesaskatchewan.ca/tok_attractions.html
Local history; collection housed in former Tuberose Red Cross outpost hospital; artifacts include World War I & II items, machinery & vehicles, fossils, & items relating to Wooly Mammoth remains found in 1964.
Bill Stepple, Contact, 306-375-2336

Lancer: **Lancer Centennial Museum**
PO Box 21, Lancer, SK S0N 1G0
Tel: 306-689-2925
Open June-Sept.

Langenburg: **Langenburg Homestead Museum**
PO Box 864, 305 Carl Ave. East, Langenburg, SK S0A 2A0
Tel: 306-743-2432; Fax: 306-743-2625
langenburgt@sasktel.net
www.town.langenburg.sk.ca
Local history; open June-Aug.
Kay Klopstock, Contact, 306-743-2625

Langham: **Langham & District Heritage Village & Museum**
PO Box 516, 302 Railway St., Langham, SK S0K 2L0
Tel: 306-283-4342; Fax: 306-283-4772
www.langham.ca
Preserves & exhibits artifacts illustrating the history & culture of Langham & area; special events & programming. Open May long weekend to Sept. 30, Wed. 9-12 & Sat. 9-3, or by appointment.
Doreen Nickel, President

Lanigan: **Lanigan & District Heritage Centre**
Parent: **Lanigan & District Heritage Association**
PO Box 424, Lanigan, SK S0K 2M0
Tel: 306-365-2569; Fax: 306-365-2960
lanigan.dist.heritage@sasktel.net
www.sasktelwebsite.nat/ldha/
Year Founded: 1994 The Lanigan & District Heritage Association's mission is to preserve the Lanigan CPR Station, where the Centre is currently housed; includes a museum, tourism information, agricultural interpretive display, potash exposition, caboose, recreation & coffee area & storage. Located at 75 Railway Ave., Lanigan.
Ruth Wildeman, Secretary
Andrew Cebryk, Chair

Lashburn: **Lashburn Centennial Museum**
PO Box 275, Corner of Main St. and 1st Ave., Lashburn, SK S0M 1H0
Tel: 306-285-4145
lashburncentennialmuseum@gmail.com
Other contact information: Town Office: 306-285-3533
Vetern's Gallery with artifacts from the Boer War to Korean War; 1908 Gully School; artifacts of the Barr Colony settlers; log cabin & blacksmith shop; open July & Aug.

Leross: **Kellross Heritage Museum**
PO Box 215, 2nd Ave., Leross, SK S0A 1V0
Tel: 306-675-6144
Open by appt. from June 15
Louise Tereposky

Leroy: **Leroy & District Heritage Museum**
PO Box 47, Leroy, SK S0K 2P0
Tel: 306-286-3464
Open July & Aug.

Loon Lake: **Steele Narrows Provincial Historic Park**
PO Box 39, Loon Lake, SK S0M 1L0
Tel: 306-837-7410; Fax: 306-837-2415
makwalake@gov.sk.ca
www.saskparks.net/SteeleNarrows
The park rests on the site of the last battle of the 1885 North West Rebellion. The battle is depicted on interpretive panels located at the top of a hill overlooking the park. The burial ground containing the remains of the Cree killed in the battle is located across the road.

Lucky Lake: **Lucky Lake Museum**
PO Box 268, Lucky Lake, SK S0L 1Z0
Tel: 306-858-2641
ddayers@yourlink.ca

Lumsden: **Lumsden Heritage Museum**
c/o Lumsden Historical Society, PO Box 91, 50 Qu'Appelle Dr. West, Lumsden, SK S0G 3C0
Tel: 306-731-2905
The museum consists of five pioneer buildings, a machine shed, a livery stable, & a blacksmith shop. Four of the pioneer buildings contain artifacts depicting the district's early history.

Luseland: **Luseland & Districts Museum**
PO Box 8, 600 Grand Ave., Luseland, SK S0L 2A0
Tel: 306-372-4258
Other contact information: Alternate Phone: 306-372-4331
Year Founded: 1990 Hours: May 1-Dec.15 Sa 1:00-4:00 or open upon request
Alvin Bekemeier, Chairperson, 306-372-4621
Rev. David Mellicke, Secretary, 306-372-4980
Bev Obrigewitch, Treasurer, 306-372-4416
Valerie Finley, Past Chair, 306-372-4258
Niel Scholer, Building Committee Member, 306-372-4612
Brent Honeker, Building Committee Member, 306-372-4314
Ed Walz, Building Committee Member, 306-372-4824

Macklin: **Macklin & District Museum**
Also known as: **Eid House**
PO Box 423, 5002 Herald St., Macklin, SK S0L 2C0
Tel: 306-753-2610
town.macklin@sasktel.net
www.macklin.ca/museum.htm
Year Founded: 1990 Built in 1919 by Frank Shaw, the town's first bank manager, the house later became a hospital during the 1920s. Open Tu, Th, F, summer.

Macrorie: **Macrorie Museum**
PO Box 177, Macrorie, SK S0L 2E0
Tel: 306-243-4327
www.macrorie.com/04-history.html
Other contact information: Alternate Phones: 306-243-4507; 306-243-2037; 306-243-2149
Consists of 3 sites: an old post office, insurance office, & living quarters which depict the local farming area; an old brick school, heritage site; a caboose & jigger; open Mon. in July & Aug. 2-4, or by appt.
Gerry Torvik, Contact, 306-243-4207

Maidstone: **Maidstone & District Historical & Cultural Society Inc.**
PO Box 250, Maidstone, SK S0M 1M0
Tel: 306-893-2890
May - Sept.

Main Centre: **Main Centre Heritage Museum**
c/o Dora Wall, PO Box 42, Main Centre, SK S0H 2V0
Tel: 306-784-2903
Local history & early pioneering artifacts; school & church history; Herbert Ferry Crossing display; open by appt. Jan.-Dec.
Dora Wall, Chair

Maple Creek: **Fort Walsh National Historic Site**
PO Box 278, Maple Creek, SK S0N 1N0
Tel: 306-662-2645; Fax: 306-662-2711
fort.walsh@pc.gc.ca
www.pc.gc.ca/eng/lhn-nhs/sk/walsh/index.aspx
Other contact information: TTY: 306-662-3124
NWMP fort & Cypress Hills Massacre site; open mid May - last weekend in Sept.
Katherine Patterson, Field Unit Superintendent, Saskatchewan South, Parks Canada

Maple Creek: **Jasper Cultural & Historical Centre**
PO Box 1504, Maple Creek, SK S0N 1N0
Tel: 306-662-2434; Fax: 306-662-4359
jasper.centre@sasktel.net
www.jaspercentre.ca
Year Founded: 1988 Open Mon.-Fri. in winter; daily in summer
Heather Wickstrom, Manager/Curator

Maple Creek: **St. Victor Petroglyph Provincial Historic Park**
c/o Cypress Hills Interprovincial Park, PO Box 850, Maple Creek, SK S0N 1N0
Tel: 306-662-5411
cypresshills@gov.sk.ca; st.victor@sasktel.net
www.saskparks.net; stvictor.sasktelwebsite.net
The St. Victor Petroglyphs are an enduring mystery; their origin & purpose is unknown, yet they provide a clue as to who populated the plains in the era pre-dating written records. The petroglyphs are best viewed in the early morning on a clear day; an interpretive panel & reproduction of a few of the petroglyphs are provided for visitors at the site, which is located south of St. Victor. Admission is free.

Maple Creek: **Southwest Saskatchewan Oldtimers Museum**
PO Box 1540, 218 Jasper St., Maple Creek, SK S0N 1N0
Tel: 306-662-2474; Fax: 206-662-2711
oldtimers@sk.sympatico.ca; oldtimers@sasktel.net
Ranching, First Nations, NWMP, firearms; open May 20 to Sept. 30

Maple Creek: **Wood Mountain Post Provincial Park**
c/o Cypress Hills Interprovincial Park, PO Box 850, Maple Creek, SK S0N 1N0
Tel: 306-662-5411; Fax: 306-662-5482
cypresshills@gov.sk.ca
www.saskparks.net
The post was an important site for the North-West Mounted Police around the turn of the century, where the local detachment patrolled the Canada-USA border. Visitors to the park will find two reconstructed buildings with displays inside, & staff hosting guided tours. Open June-Aug., daily 10:00-5:00.

Maryfield: **Maryfield Museum**
PO Box 262, Stephen St., Maryfield, SK S0G 3K0
Tel: 306-646-2201
Clocks, tools, record players, telephones

McCord: **McCord & District Museum**
PO Box 82, McCord, SK S0H 2T0
Tel: 306-478-2522
ba.wilson@xplornet.com
www.southcentralmuseums.ca/mccord.html
Year Founded: 1973 Museum is housed in a 1928 CPR railway station and exibits includehistorical items from households and businesses in the area. Of note is an actual caboose on tracks beside the museum. A companion museum is the 1913 church at the opposite end of the street which displays religious articles from various churches in the region.

Meadow Lake: **Meadow Lake Museum**
PO Box 610, 120 - 1st St. East, Meadow Lake, SK S9X 1Y5
Tel: 306-236-3622; Fax: 306-236-4299
meadowlake_townml@sasktel.net
www.meadowlake.ca
Exhibits are related to pioneers, farming, lumbering, & birds. The museum is open from Victoria Day to Labour Day.
Cecil Midgett, Contact

Melfort: **Melfort & District Museum**
PO Box 3222, 401 Melfort St. West, Melfort, SK S0E 1A0
Tel: 306-752-5870; Fax: 306-752-5556
melfort.museum@sasktel.net
www.cityofmelfort.ca
www.facebook.com/32948 3827062438
Year Founded: 1971 Community museum, archives, pioneer village; agricultural machinery displays; located adjacent to the Melfort fairgrounds.
Gailmarie Anderson, Curator

Melville: **Melville Heritage Museum Inc.**
PO Box 2528, 100 Heritage Dr., Melville, SK S0A 2P0
Tel: 306-728-2070; Fax: 306-728-2038
melmus@sasktel.net
Regional museum, located in the former Luther Academy (1913-1926); artifacts & histories of local, provincial & national interest; includes chapel, library, Grand Trunk Pacific/CNR & Military; over 100 original B & W framed photographs depict Melville's first quarter century; gift shop; murals; limited wheelchair access

Melville: **Melville Railway Museum**
PO Box 2863, Melville Regional Park, Melville, SK S0A 2P0
Tel: 306-728-4205
www.city.melville.sk.ca/siteengine/activepage.asp?PageID=188
Former CNR steam locomotive #5114; a J-4-5 class 4-6-2 built in 1919; also former Grand Trunk Pacific station from Duff, Saskatchewan containing artifacts including exhibits of communications equipment, from telegraphs, and telephones. There are also records from the Grand Trunk Railway and CNR, including employee records
Jennifer Mann, Tourism Manager, 306-728-3722, Fax: 306-728-2443, jmann@melville.ca

Midale: **Souris Valley Antique Association**
PO Box 161, Main St., Midale, SK S0C 1S0
Tel: 306-458-2374
phil.st@sasktel.net
Other contact information: Alternate Phones: 306-458-2409; 306-458-2476
The association runs a 33-acre Heritage Village consisting of two pioneer houses, a barn, blacksmith shop, church, service station, & rural school. Open June-Sept.

Middle Lake: **Middle Lake Museum**
PO Box 157, Middle Lake, SK S0K 2X0
Pioneer artifacts

Milden: **Milden Community Museum**
PO Box 218, Milden, SK S0L 2L0
Tel: 306-935-4511
A community museum holding local artifacts including those of an old-time school, hospital & bedroom; open July-Aug.

Moose Jaw: **15 Wing Military Aviation Museum**
PO Box 5000, 15 Wing Moose Jaw, Moose Jaw, SK S6H 7Z8
Tel: 306-694-2222; Fax: 306-694-2813

Moose Jaw: **Moose Jaw Museum & Art Gallery**
Crescent Park, Moose Jaw, SK S6H 0X6
Tel: 306-692-4471; Fax: 306-694-8016
mjamchin@sasktel.net
www.mjmag.ca
Year Founded: 1966 The building houses art, history & science exhibits, with a wide range of human history artifacts with strong representation of First Nations beadwork, women's clothing, and clothing-related artifacts from 1880 onward. There is a gift shop. The Learning Centre offers programs for school children and art classes for all ages. Open year round; admission by donation.
Heather Smith, Curator

Moose Jaw: **Sukanen Ship Pioneer Village & Museum of Saskatchewan**
PO Box 2071, Moose Jaw, SK S6H 7T2
Tel: 306-693-7315
pmjohnson@Sasktel.net
www.sukanenmuseum.ca
38 acres of land; pioneer village of 20 buildings; antique farm with machinery; 100 collector tractors; 40 cars & trucks
Abe Giesbretch, Secretary
R. Jones, President

Moose Jaw: **Western Development Museum**
Also known as: **Moose Jaw Western Development Museum**
50 Diefenbaker Dr., Moose Jaw, SK S6J 1L9
Tel: 306-693-5989; Fax: 306-691-0511
moosejaw@wdm.ca
www.wdm.ca
Moose Jaw is one of four exhibit branches of Saskatchewan's Western Development Museum. The other branches are located in North Battleford, Saskatoon, & Yorkton. The Moose Jaw Western Development Museum displays the history of transportation, from the canoe to the railway. The museum also features the Snowbirds Gallery, which presents Canadian military aerobatic flight history.
Katherine Fitton, Manager, Moose Jaw, kfitton@wdm.ca
David Samson, Museum Technician, dsamson@wdm.ca
Jackie Hall, Officer, Programs & Education, jhall@wdm.ca
Shirley Stenko, Officer, Visitor Services, sstenko@wdm.ca

Moosomin: **Jamieson Museum**
PO Box 236, 306 Gertie St., Moosomin, SK S0G 3N0
Tel: 306-435-3156
Pre-1900 house, church, military collection; open May - Oct.

Moosomin: **Moosomin Regional Museum**
PO Box 1654, Moosomin, SK S0G 3N0
Tel: 306-435-3301; Fax: 306-435-3082
d.barry@sasktel.net
Open July & Aug.

Morse: **Morse Museum & Cultural Centre**
PO Box 308, Morse, SK S0H 3C0
Tel: 306-629-3230; Fax: 306-629-3230
morsemuseum@sasktel.net
sites.google.com/site/morsemuseum1
facebook.co m/pages/Morse-Museum-and-Cultural-Centre/8511642284
Year Founded: 1980 former school, built in 1912; May-Sep. M-F 9:00-5:00

Mortlach: **Mortlach Museum & Drop In Centre**
PO Box 163, Mortlach, SK S0H 3E0
Tel: 306-355-2268
Other contact information: Chair, Phone: 306-355-2214
Located in the town's old fire hall; pioneer & aboriginal artifacts; replica courthouse & jail cell; open year-round, M-F, or by appointment.

Mossbank: **Mossbank & District Museum Inc.**
PO Box 172, 517 Main St., Mossbank, SK S0H 3G0
Tel: 306-354-2889
django@sasktel.net
A community history museum dedicated to the history of No. 2 Bombing & Gunnery School which was located three miles east of Mossbank during WWII; blacksmith shop & blacksmith's house are now classified as provincial heritage property
Roy Tollefson, President

Naicam: **Naicam Museum**
PO Box 238, Naicam, SK S0K 2Z0
Tel: 306-874-2280; Fax: 306-874-5444
naicam@sasktel.net
www.townofnaicam.ca/museum.htm
History & archives of Naicam & District in Heritage building (pioneer school)
Ruby J. Lindsay, Contact, rjlindsay@sasktel.net

Neilburg: **Manitou Pioneers Museum**
PO Box 336, 301 - 4th Ave. East, Neilburg, SK S0M 2C0
Tel: 306-823-4264; Fax: 306-826-5407
The museum features the largest collection of arrowheads & stone hammers in Saskatchewan, as well as salt & pepper shakers, & lamps. Open July & Aug., or by appointment.

Nipawin: **Nipawin & District Living Forestry Museum**
PO Box 1917, Hwy. 35 West, Nipawin, SK S0E 1E0
Tel: 306-862-9866
Other contact information: Alternate Phone: 306-862-3317
Situated on 14 acres; open May - Aug.

Nokomis: **Nokomis District Museum & Heritage Co-op**
PO Box 417, Hwy. 20 & 3rd Ave., Nokomis, SK S0G 3R0
Tel: 306-528-2979
Displays & artifacts of early days & local history; open June 1 - Labour Day daily 10-5
Karen Lee, President

North Battleford: **Western Development Museum**
Also known as: **North Battleford Western Development Museum**
PO Box 183, North Battleford, SK S9A 2Y1
Tel: 306-445-8033; Fax: 306-445-7211
nbattleford@wdm.ca
www.wdm.ca
North Battleford is one of four exhibit branches of Saskatchewan's Western Development Museum. The other branches are located in Moose Jaw, Saskatoon, & Yorkton. The North Battleford Western Development Museum provides visitors with the opportunity to explore a Heritage Farm & Village. Sights include a Wheat Pool grain elevator, a 1910 Case 110 tractor, A Co-op store, homes, & churches.
Wayne Fennig, Manager, North Battleford, wfennig@wdm.ca
Joyce Smith, Manager, Operations, jsmith@wdm.ca
Cheryl Stewart, Coordinator, Education & Volunteers, cstewart@wdm.ca
Daniel Stewart, Museum Technician, dstewart@wdm.ca

Ogema: **Deep South Pioneer Museum**
PO Box 185, Ogema, SK S0C 1Y0
Tel: 306-459-2544
carol@ogema-agencies.ca
www.ogema.ca/ogema-attractions-museum.html
28 buildings dipicting early pioneer life in Saskatchewan. Open May-Oct., Su 1:00-5:00, or by appointment.
Harold Wiles, Contact

Outlook: **Outlook & District Heritage Museum & Gallery**
PO Box 1095, 100 Railway Ave., Outlook, SK S0L 2N0
Tel: 306-867-8285
outlookmuseum@hotmail.com
town.outlook.sk.ca/museum_home.htm
Located in a former railway station, the Outlook & District Heritage Museum & Gallery is open from June to August. Exhibits include a caboose & an old jail cell. The Museum also keeps copies of the local newspaper, entitled "The Outlook", dating back to 1910.

Oxbow: **Ralph Allen Memorial Museum**
PO Box 86, 802 Railway Ave., Oxbow, SK S0C 2B0
Tel: 306-483-5082
Open May-Sept.
Otto Neuman, President
Michael Bartolf, Contact, mbartolf@sk.sympatico.ca

Paynton: **Bresaylor Heritage Museum**
PO Box 33, Main St., Paynton, SK S0M 2J0
Tel: 306-895-4813
The Bresaylor Heritage Museum collects artifacts from the Bresaylor & Paynton area. Items date back to 1882, when the earliest residents settled in Bresaylor. The museum is open in July & August, & at other times of the year by appointment.

Pelly: **Fort Pelly Livingston Museum**
PO Box 24, 306- 1st Ave. S, Pelly, SK S0A 2Z0
Tel: 306-595-2030
www.pelly.ca/museum.html
Brian Clough

Perdue: **Perdue Museum**
PO Box 243, Perdue, SK S0K 3C0
Tel: 306-237-9161

Plenty: **Plenty & District Museum**
PO Box 99, Main St., Plenty, SK S0L 2R0
Tel: 306-932-4727
Situated in a 1911 building, which once served as Plenty's post office & hardware store, the Plenty & District Museum depicts pioneer life in the community & surrounding area. Farming equipment is featured in a separate building.

Ponteix: **Notukeu Heritage Museum**
PO Box 603, 110 Railway Ave. East, Ponteix, SK S0N 1Z0
Tel: 306-625-3530; Fax: 306-625-3536
auvergnois@sasktel.net
The museum's collection includes fossils, Paleo-Indian artifacts, & the collection of amateur archaeologist Henri Liboiron.

Porcupine Plain: **Porcupine Plain & District Museum**
PO Box 171, 137 Windsor Ave., Porcupine Plain, SK S0E 1H0
Tel: 306-278-2317
www.porcupineplain.com
Other contact information: Alternate Phone: 306-278-2073
Year Founded: 1968 The Porcupine Plain & District Museum features local pioneer artifacts, such as antique machinery & clothing. The museum also houses a bird displat, with birds from the Porcupine Plain & Somme area. The soldier settlement consists of a log home, a schoolhouse, & a church. The Porcupine Plain & District Museum is open from the beginning of July to the Labour Day weekend in September. At other times, tours may be arranged.

Prairie River: **Prairie River Museum**
Also known as: **Prairie River Heritage Society**
PO Box 86, Railway Ave., Prairie River, SK S0E 1J0
Tel: 306-889-4248
prairierivermuseum@yourlink.ca
Railway, agriculture, lumbering, trapping, First Nations artifacts. Located in an old CN railway station. Open Jan.-Dec., or by appointment.

Preeceville: **Preeceville & District Heritage Museum**
PO Box 192, 239 Highway Ave. East, Preeceville, SK S0A 3B0
Tel: 306-547-2774
l.plaxin@sasktel.net
www.townofpreeceville.ca/default.aspx?page=52
Year Founded: 1985 Local history

Prelate: **Blumenfeld & District Heritage Site**
PO Box 34, Prelate, SK S0N 2B0
Tel: 306-673-2289
Other contact information: Alternate Phone: 306-628-3614
The museum's collection includes the history of St. Peter & St. Paul Blumenfeld Church, as well as other churches in the area, & artifacts of early pioneers.

Prelate: **St. Angela's Museum & Archives**
PO Box 220, 201 - 3rd Ave., Prelate, SK S0N 2B0
Tel: 306-673-2200
To preserve valuable history of pioneer Saskatchewan & of the pioneer Ursulines of St. Angela's Convent Academy at Prelate Saskatchewan; collection tells story of Ursuline life & apostolate that were used in chapel, classroom & other departments

Prince Albert: **Cumberland House Provincial Historic Park**
Prince Albert Park Area, PO Box 3003, Prince Albert, SK S6V 6G1
Tel: 306-953-3571
cumberlandhousehistpark@gov.sk.ca

Prince Albert: **Diefenbaker House**
246 - 19th St. West, Prince Albert, SK S6V 8A9
Tel: 306-764-2992
historypa@citypa.com
historypa.com
Residence of John G. Diefenbaker immediately prior to his becoming Prime Minister of Canada; museum furnished as it was in Mr. Diefenbaker's day & also includes phtographic displays of his life & associations in Prince Albert
James Benson, Manager

Prince Albert: **Evolution of Education Museum**
10 River St. East, Prince Albert, SK S6V 8A9
Tel: 306-764-2992
historypa@citypa.com
historypa.com
Year Founded: 1963 Housed in the original Claytonville one-room rural school & features a class-room setting, plus displays of many early educational materials & artifacts
James Benson, Manager

Prince Albert: **Prince Albert Historical Museum**
Parent: **Prince Albert Historical Society**
10 River St. East, Prince Albert, SK S6V 8A9
Tel: 306-764-2992
historypa@citypa.com
historypa.com
twitter.com/histo rypa
www.facebook.com/PrinceAlbertHistoricalSociety
History, life-styles & people of Prince Albert & area; souvenir shop & tea room
James Benson, Manager

Prince Albert: **Rotary Museum of Police & Corrections**
c/o Prince Albert Historical Society, 10 River St. East, Prince Albert, SK S6V 8A9
Tel: 306-764-2992
historypa@citypa.com
historypa.com
Housed in the guardhouse of the Prince Albert division of the NorthWest Mounted Police & Royal Northwest Mounted police; features artifacts, equipment & uniforms from the RCMP, Prince Albert City Police, the Provincial Correctional Service & the Correctional Service of Canada, as well as from the Saskatchewan Provincial Police
James Benson, Manager

Prud'homme: **Prud'homme Museum**
PO Box 38, Prud'homme, SK S0K 3K0
Tel: 306-654-2001; Fax: 306-654-2007
voprud@sasktel.net
www.prudhommevillage.com
Open year-round.
Hervé Poilièvre, Contact, 306-654-2038

Punnichy: **Punnichy & District Museum**
PO Box 396, 223 Main St., Punnichy, SK S0A 3C0
Tel: 306-835-2887
Local history; open July & Aug., Tu & Th 2:00-4:00, or by appointment.

Radville: **Radville CN Station/Firefighters Museum**
PO Box 85, 227 Main St., Radville, SK S0C 2G0
Tel: 306-815-7999; Fax: 306-869-3100
jverhelst@sasktel.net
Open by appointment only.

Raymore: **Raymore Pioneer Museum Inc.**
PO Box 453, Raymore, SK S0A 3J0
Tel: 306-476-2180; Fax: 306-746-4314
raymoretown@aski.ca
Collection of local pioneer artifacts
Wayne Focht, Sec.-Treas.

Regina: **Alex Youck School Museum**
1600 - 4th Ave., Regina, SK S4R 8C8
Tel: 306-791-8200
Other contact information: Alternate Phone: 306-523-3000
Open by appt. only
Alex Youck, Director

Regina: **Government House Museum & Heritage Property (GH)**
4607 Dewdney Ave., Regina, SK S4T 1B7
Tel: 306-787-5773; Fax: 306-787-5714
governmenthouse@gov.sk.ca
www.governmenthouse.gov.sk.ca
twitter.com/Go vt_House
Former residence of the Lieutenant Governor of the Northwest Territories & the Province of Saskatchewan

***Regina:* RCMP Heritage Centre**
RCMP Academy, 'Depot' Division, 5907 Dewdney Ave., Regina, SK S4T 0P4
Tel: 306-522-7333
info@rcmphc.com; bookings@rcmphc.com
www.rcmpheritagecentre.com
twitter.com/RCMP_HC
w ww.facebook.com/RCMPHC
Year Founded: 2007 The complete history of the RCMP is told through exhibits, multimedia, & programs.
Janet Wightman, Chair

***Regina:* Regina Plains Museum**
1835 Scarth St., 2nd Fl., Regina, SK S4P 2G9
Tel: 306-780-9435; Fax: 306-565-2979
rp.museum@sasktel.net
www.reginaplainsmuseum.com
www.facebook.com/regi na.plains
Year Founded: 1960 Regina Plains Museum is the civic history museum of the city. It is open year-round.
Christa Donaldson, Executive Director
Jan Morier, Coordinator, Communications

***Regina:* Saskatchewan African Canadian Heritage Museum Inc.**
PO Box 1171 Main, Regina, SK S4P 3B4
Tel: 306-545-8824; Fax: 306-543-6181
info@sachm.org
www.sachm.org
SACHM is a virtual museum dedicated to preserving the history of people of African ancestry who lived & currently live in Saskatchewan.
Reggie Newkirk, Co-Chair, Chair1@sachm.org
Dr. Jane Ekong, Co-Chair, Chair2@sachm.org

***Regina:* Saskatchewan Military Museum**
The Armouries, 1600 Elphinstone St., Regina, SK S4T 3N1
Tel: 306-585-3771
SaskatchewanMilitaryMuseum@hotmail.ca
www.facebook.com /SaskMilitaryMuseum
Collects & preserves Saskatchewan's military history from 1885 to the present; artifacts, uniforms, badges & medals, vehicles, ammunition; photos, archival material & paintings
Maj. (Ret'd) C. Keith Inches, Curator, keithinches@sasktel.net

***Regina:* Saskatchewan Pharmacy Museum**
***Parent:* Saskatchewan Pharmacy Museum Society**
#700, 4010 Pasqua St., Regina, SK S4S 6S4
Tel: 306-584-2292; Fax: 306-584-9695
saskpharm@sk.sympatico.ca
www.skpharmacists.ca
Collection & preservation of pharmacy artifacts, documentation of pharmacy history
Bill Paterson, President

***Regina:* Saskatchewan Sports Hall of Fame & Museum**
2205 Victoria Ave., Regina, SK S4P 0S4
Tel: 306-780-9232
sasksportshalloffame.com
twitter.com/SaskSportsHF
www.facebook.com/SaskSportsHF
Year Founded: 1966 3,000 sq. ft. of exhibit space celebrating the sport heritage of Saskatchewan; open year round with extended summer hours
Sheila Kelly, Executive Director, skelly@sshfm.com

***Regina Beach:* Lakeside Heritage Museum**
PO Box 102, Regina Beach, SK S0G 4C0
Tel: 306-729-4676
john.currie@gov.sk.ca
Other contact information: Park Phone: 306-725-5203
Located beside the Cultural Centre, near South Shore School; open May-Sept., Su.

***Regina Beach:* Last Mountain House Provincial Historic Park**
PO Box 215, Regina Beach, SK S0G 4C0
Tel: 306-725-5203
www.saskparks.net/LastMountainHouse
Other contact information: July & Aug., Phone: 306-731-4409
The Last Mountain House dates from 1869, & was used by the Hudson's Bay Company as a winter outpost for its Fort Qu'Appelle fur trade operation. The museum is a reconstruction, featuring three buildings, a privy, & an ice house. Open July-Sept., Th-Su.
John Currie, Contact, john.currie@gov.sk.ca

***Riverhurst:* F.T. Hill Museum**
PO Box 201, 324 Teck St., Riverhurst, SK S0H 3P0
Tel: 306-353-2220
villageofriverhurst@sasktel.net
www.mainstayinn.ca/museum.htm
Gun collection, aboriginal artifacts, pioneer items; open June 15 - Aug. 31 & by appt.
Donna Miner, Contact, 306-353-4802

***Rocanville:* Rocanville & District Museum**
PO Box 490, Rocanville, SK S0A 3L0
Tel: 306-645-2113; Fax: 306-645-2087
roc.cap@sasktel.net
Other contact information: Phone, Appointments: 306-645-2164
Located at the corner of Qu'appelle Avenue & St. Albert Street, the Rocanville & District Museum showcases a CPR station, a church, a schoolhouse, a blacksmith shop, & a Masonic Lodge. The museum is open during July & August, & by appointment at other times of the year.

***La Ronge:* Mistasinihk Place Interpretive Centre**
c/o Saskatchewan Family Foundation, PO Box 5000, La Ronge Ave., La Ronge, SK S0J 1L0
Tel: 306-425-4350
Aboriginal artifacts, artwork by northern artists, displays about northern industries & activites

***Rose Valley:* Rose Valley & District Heritage Museum**
PO Box 123, 115 Centre St., Rose Valley, SK S0E 1M0
Tel: 306-322-4545; Fax: 306-322-5822
Museum with artifacts from area 1900 to present; open July & Aug., Mon.-Fri.; off season viewing available by request
Judi Rustad, President
Irene Martinson, Sec.-Treas.

***Rosetown:* Rosetown & District Museum**
PO Box 37, 605 Colwell Rd., Rosetown, SK S0L 2V0
Tel: 306-882-2199
rdmuseum@sasktel.net
Natural history specimens, photographs, handicrafts

***Rosthern:* Mennonite Heritage Museum**
PO Box 116, 6th Ave., Rosthern, SK S0K 3R0
Tel: 306-232-4415
Museum housed in school, artifacts from 1800 to present, collection of World Wheat champion; open May to Sept.

***Rouleau:* Rouleau & District Museum**
PO Box 132, Rouleau, SK S0G 4H0
Tel: 306-776-2363
A rural town street setting with houses, barn, blacksmith shop, school & other buildings; archives; special events, such as the annual threshing bee in Aug., & other programming. Open by appt., May - Sept.
Gareth Argue, President

***St Brieux:* Musée St. Brieux Museum**
CP 224, 300, ch Barbier, St Brieux, SK S0K 3V0
Tél: 306-275-2123
Documentation au sujet de la vie des pionniers, de leurs origines, des missions environnantes et de l'église catholique pré-Vatican II; des tournées en français ou en anglais sont offertes

***St Victor:* Le Beau Village Museum**
PO Box 58, St Victor, SK S0H 3T0
Tel: 306-642-3215
dducharme@sasktel.net
Religious & pioneer artifacts; open by appointment only.

***St Victor:* McGillis House**
St Victor, SK S0H 3T0
Tel: 306-642-3171
www.willowbunch.ca
Located in St. Victor's regional park, McGillis House was built in 1890. Artifacts in the home include Métis items, kerosene lanterns, early saddles & bridles, & a feathered buffalo skull.

***St Walburg:* St. Walburg & District Historical Museum**
PO Box 87, St Walburg, SK S0M 2T0
Tel: 306-248-3267
Local exhibits from pioneer days to 1945
David Swift, Chair
Judy Seguin, Secretary

***Saltcoats:* Saltcoats Museum**
PO Box 309, Saltcoats, SK S0A 3R0
Tel: 306-744-2977
Local history; open July & Aug., or by appointment.

***Saskatoon:* Children's Discovery Museum on the Saskatchewan**
Market Mall, #116, 2325 Preston Ave., Saskatoon, SK S7J 2G2
Tel: 306-683-2555
discovery@museumforkids.sk.ca
www.museumforkids.sk.ca
www.facebook.com/museumforkids.sk.ca
Year Founded: 2009 The museum provides hands-on exhibits & programs to children ten & under, in an effort to promote creativity, curiosity, & a love of learning.
Erica Bird, President

***Saskatoon:* Diefenbaker Canada Centre**
University of Saskatchewan, 101 Diefenbaker Pl., Saskatoon, SK S7N 5B8
Tel: 306-966-8384; Fax: 306-966-6207
dief.centre@usask.ca
artsandscience.usask.ca/diefenbaker
The Diefenbaker Canada Centre includes a museum, archives, & research centre. The centre houses artifacts, such as a personal library, papers, & memorabilia, that were bequeathed to the University of Saskatchewan by former prime minister of Canada, John G. Diefenbaker. The archives features collections of press clippings, photographs, & documents related to Diefenbaker's life & Canadian history.
Teresa Carlson, Acting Director, 306-966-8383, teresa.carlson@usask.ca
Trent Evanisky, Coordinator, Special Exhibits, 306-966-8386
Rob Paul, Coordinator, Archives, 306-966-8387, rob.paul@usask.ca

***Saskatoon:* Fort Carlton Provincial Historic Park**
#102, 112 Research Dr., Saskatoon, SK S7K 2H6
Tel: 306-467-5205; Fax: 306-933-5215
fortcarlton@gov.sk.ca
www.saskparks.net
Located 26 km. west of Duck Lake on Hwy. 212; a reconstructed Hudson's Bay Company fur trade post; open May - Sept.
Janice Crawford, Contact

***Saskatoon:* Gabriel Dumont Institute of Native Studies & Applied Research (GDI)**
c/o Saskatoon Publishing Office, #2, 604 - 22nd St. West, Saskatoon, SK S7M 5W1
Tel: 306-934-4941; Fax: 306-244-0252
Toll-Free: 877-488-6888
metismuseum@gdi.gdins.org; general@gdi.gdins.org
www.metismuseum.com; www.gdins.org
www.facebook.com/gabrieldumontinstitute
A joint project between GDI & Saskatchewan Department of Learning, the Department of Canadian Heritage's Canadian Culture Online Program, the Canada Council for the Arts, SaskCulture, the Government of Canada, & the University of Saskatchewan Division of Media & Technology; the virtual museum provides users with a comprehensive study of Métis history & culture, including many primary documents such as oral history interviews, photos, & other archival materials.
Darren R. Préfontaine, Project Leader

***Saskatoon:* Marr Residence**
326 - 11th St. East, Saskatoon, SK S7N 0E7
Tel: 306-652-1201
Year Founded: 1982 The oldest building in Saskatchewan (built in 1884) that's still on its original site, now designated a heritage site by the City of Saskatoon.

***Saskatoon:* Meewasin Valley Authority (MVA)**
402 - 3rd Ave. South, Saskatoon, SK S7K 3G5
Tel: 306-665-6888; Fax: 306-665-6117
meewasin@meewasin.com
www.meewasin.com
Year Founded: 1979 Conservation agency for the South Saskatchewan River
Susan Lamb, CEO, 306-665-6887

***Saskatoon:* Musée Ukraina Museum Inc. (MUM)**
PO Box 26072, Saskatoon, SK S7K 8C1
Tel: 306-244-4212
ukrainamuseum@sasktel.net
www.mumsaskatoon.com
Year Founded: 1955 The museum's goal is to collect & preserve Ukranian cultural heritage, & make it available to the public.
Patricia Mialkowsky, President

***Saskatoon:* Museum of Antiquities**
#116, College Bldg., University of Saskatchewan, 107 Administration Pl., Saskatoon, SK S7N 5A2
Tel: 306-966-7818; Fax: 306-966-1954
museum_antiquities.usask.ca
www.usask.ca/antiquities/
Year Founded: 1974 A collection of Near Eastern, Egyptian, Greek, Roman & Medieval sculpture in full scale replica as well as original works & coinage
Tracene Harvey, Acting Director

***Saskatoon:* Natural Sciences Museum**
Dept. of Biology & Geological Sciences, University of Saskatchewan, 112 Science Pl., Saskatoon, SK S7N 5E2
Tel: 306-966-4399; Fax: 306-966-4461
peta.bonhams@usask.ca
www.usask.ca
Designed to show evolution through time beginning with marine invertebrates & ending with evolution of animals; displays of living plants & animals correspond to fossils & create an integrated learning experience; free self-guided tours year-round; brochures downloaded from website
Dr. P. Bonham-Smith, Head, Biology, peta.bonhams@usask.ca
Dr. B. Pratt, Geology, brian.pratt@usask.ca

Saskatoon: **Royal Canadian Legion Artifacts Room**
The Royal Canadian Legion, Nutana Branch, 3021 Louise St., Saskatoon, SK S7J 3L1
Tel: 306-374-6303; Fax: 306-374-3233
nutana.legion@sasktel.net
www.nutanalegion.ca/museum.shtml
The collection is located in the basement of the Legion building, & features a variety of military memorabilia. Open Tu, W & F.

Saskatoon: **Saskatchewan Railway Museum**
PO Box 21117, Saskatoon, SK S7H 5N9
Tel: 306-382-9855
srha@saskrailmuseum.org
www.saskrailmuseum.org
Year Founded: 1990 The museum site features locomotives, cabooses, a sleeping car, & streetcars that visitors can board. Visitors can also ride the museum's "speeder." Open May-Sept., F-Su 10:00-5:00.

Saskatoon: **Ukrainian Museum of Canada (UMC)**
Parent: **Ukrainian Women's Association of Canada**
910 Spadina Cres. East, Saskatoon, SK S7K 3H5
Tel: 306-244-3800; Fax: 306-652-7620
ukrmuse@sasktel.net
www.umc.sk.ca
The Ukrainian Museum preserves & encourages Ukrainian folk arts in Canada. The permanent gallery tells the story of Ukrainian immigration to Canada with displays of folk arts, including costumes, embroideries, weaving, ceramics, & Easter eggs. The museum's collection of textiles is one of the largest of its kind in North America.

Edmonton: **Ukrainian Museum of Canada (UMC)**
St. John's Cultural Centre, 10611 - 110 Ave. NW, Edmonton, AB T5H 1H7
Tel: 780-441-1062
info@umcalberta.org
www.umcalberta.org
Open May-Aug., Mon.-Fri., or by appointment.

Vancouver: **Ukrainian Museum of Canada (UMC)**
Parent: **Ukrainian Women's Association of Canada**
154 - 10th Ave. East, Vancouver, BC V5T 1Z4
Tel: 604-876-4747

Calgary: **Ukrainian Museum of Canada (UMC)**
St. Vladimir's Ukrainian Orthodox Cultural Centre, 404 Meredith Rd. NE, Calgary, AB T2E 5A6
Tel: 403-264-3437
info@stvlads.com
www.stvlads.com/museum.html
Open Tues. 10:00-2:30, or by appointment.

Winnipeg: **Ukrainian Museum of Canada (UMC)**
1175 Main St., Winnipeg, MB R2W 3S4
Tel: 204-582-1018

Toronto: **Ukrainian Museum of Canada (UMC)**
Parent: **Ukrainian Women's Association of Canada**
620 Spadina Ave., Toronto, ON M5S 2H4
Tel: 416-923-3318; Fax: 416-923-8266
museum@stvladimir.ca
www.umcontario.com
www.facebook.com/2652318002015 46
Open Mon.-Fri., Sat.-Sun. by appointment only.
Sonia Korpus, President
Janet C.P. Danyliuk, Director & CEO

Saskatoon: **W.P. Fraser Herbarium Saskatchewan (SASK)**
Dept. of Plant Sciences, University of Saskatchewan, #3C77 Agriculture Bldg., 51 Campus Dr., Saskatoon, SK S7N 5A8
Tel: 306-966-4968; Fax: 306-966-5015
sask.herbarium@usask.ca
www.herbarium.usask.ca
The herbarium houses 180,000 specimens, the largest collection in Saskatchewan. Open by permission only.
Dr. J. Hugo Cota-Sánchez, Curator/Associate Professor

Saskatoon: **Wanuskewin Heritage Park**
Penner Rd., RR#4, Saskatoon, SK S7K 3J7
Tel: 306-931-6767; Fax: 306-931-4522
Toll-Free: 877-547-6546
wanuskewin@wanuskewin.com
www.wanuskewin.com
Year Founded: 1992 The Wanuskewin Heritage Park represents the life of the Northern Plains First Nations people. Visitors will find tipi rings, bison kill sites, a medicine wheel, & pottery fragments. The 116 hectare park operates under the leadership & guidance of First Nations people. It is open year-round.

Saskatoon: **Waskesiu Heritage Museum**
c/o Ione Langlois, 401 Surgeon Terrace, Saskatoon, SK S7K 4C6
Tel: 306-242-0883
www.waskesiu.org/heritage_museum.html
Year Founded: 2005 Located in Prince Albert National Park, in the Friends of the Park Bookstore; open July & Aug., Su-Sa 10:00-5:00.
Don Ravis, President, 306-244-6204, dmravis@shaw.ca
Ione Langlois, Curator, ionelanglois@gmail.com
Marj Matheson, Archives, 306-955-5264, almarjmath@sasktel.net

Saskatoon: **Western Development Museum**
Also known as: **Saskatoon Western Development Museum**
2610 Lorne Ave. South, Saskatoon, SK S7J 0S6
Tel: 306-931-1910; Fax: 306-934-0525
saskatoon@wdm.ca
www.wdm.ca
Saskatoon is one of four exhibit branches of Saskatchewan's Western Development Museum. The other branches are located in Moose Jaw, North Battleford, & Yorkton. The Saskatoon Western Development Museum presents a 1910 Boomtown. Visitors can explore more than thirty buildings, including a blacksmith shop & a general store. The museum is also home to the Saskatchewan Agricultural Hall of Fame.
Tom Waiser, Manager, Saskatoon, twaiser@wdm.ca
Corinne Daelick, Coordinator, Education & Volunteers, cdaelick@wdm.ca
Julie Jackson, Museum Technician, jjackson@wdm.ca

Sceptre: **Great Sandhills Museum**
PO Box 29, Sceptre, SK S0N 2H0
Tel: 306-623-4345; Fax: 306-623-4612
gshs@sasktel.net
www.greatsandhillsmuseum.com
Dedicated to collect, portray & preserve the heritage of the "Great Sandhills" District in SW Saskatchewan through natural history specimens
Gertrude Hale, President

Scout Lake: **St. Mary's Historical Society of Maxstone, Inc.**
PO Box 33, Scout Lake, SK S0H 3V0
Tel: 306-642-4079
lornesfarm@sasktel.net; lornesfarm@xplornet.ca
www.southcentralmuseums.ca/maxstone.html
Other contact information: Alternate Phone: 306-642-3150
Heritage site includes old church (1917) & graveyard, oldschool; open year round, by appt. only
Lorne Kwasnicki, Director

Semans: **Semans & District Museum**
PO Box 205, Semans, SK S0A 3S0
Tel: 306-524-2020
Year Founded: 1983 The museum is housed in an old school-turned-Oddfellows Hall. The collection contains artifacts & archives on local history. The museum is located on the corner of Main Street & 4th Ave.; open June-Sept.

Shaunavon: **Grand Coteau Heritage & Cultural Centre**
PO Box 966, Centre St., Shaunavon, SK S0N 2M0
Tel: 306-297-3882; Fax: 306-297-3668
gchcc@sasktel.net
www.shaunavonmuseum.ca
Natural history museum, heritage museum, art gallery, public library; open year round
Ingrid Cazakoff, Director

Shell Lake: **Shell Lake Museum**
c/o Shell Lake Village Office, PO Box 280, Shell Lake, SK S0J 2G0
Tel: 306-427-2272
The Shell Lake Museum is located in the historic station house. The site also features a log house. It is open on weekends during the summer.

Shellbrook: **Shellbrook & Districts Museum**
PO Box 40, Shellbrook, SK S0J 2E0
Tel: 306-747-4949; Fax: 306-747-3111
Open year-round.

Spalding: **Reynold Rapp Museum**
PO Box 308, Spalding, SK S0K 4C0
Tel: 306-287-4030
Housed in Reynold Rapp M.P.'s family home

Spiritwood: **Spiritwood & District Museum**
PO Box 34, Spiritwood, SK S0J 2M0
Tel: 306-883-2828; Fax: 306-427-4787
awasden@sasktel.net
www.townofspiritwood.ca/default.aspx?page=16
Local history, with an emphasis on agriculture & vintage machinery & vehicles. Open year-round, M-F 9:00-5:00, or by appointment.
Auralia Wasden, Contact, awasden@sasktel.net
Geraldine Lavoie, Contact, 306-883-8891, geraldinemarie65@hotmail.com

Spy Hill: **Spy Hill Museum**
PO Box 268, Spy Hill, SK S0A 3W0
Tel: 306-534-4462; Fax: 306-534-2227
Year Founded: 1954 The museum has three buildings depicting the history of Spy Hill, from prehistoric days to the present. Open July & Aug., M, Tu, Th-Su 2:00-4:00.

Spy Hill: **Wolverine Hobby & Historical Society Inc.**
PO Box 191, Spy Hill, SK S0A 3W0
Tel: 306-534-2200
Three buildings, former country school, former retail outlet & Lutheran church; touring/visiting on request
Glenn Walz, President

Star City: **Star City Heritage Museum**
PO Box 38, 217 - 5th St., Star City, SK S0E 1P0
Tel: 306-863-2309
Star City's Heritage Museum presents World War I & World War II memorabilia, personal & household items, & farm equipment. The museum is open from June to August & by appointment during the off season.

Stoughton: **Stoughton & District Museum**
PO Box 492, 327 Main St., Stoughton, SK S0G 4T0
Tel: 306-457-2413
stoughtontown@sasktel.net
Pioneer items; open June to Sept.

Strasbourg: **Strasbourg & District Museum**
PO Box 369, Main St., Strasbourg, SK S0G 4V0
Tel: 306-725-3707
www.townofstrasbourg.ca/museum.htm
Year Founded: 1971 Pioneer & First Nations artifacts, mounted animals & birds
Ingrid Youck, Curator

Sturgis: **Sturgis Station House Museum**
PO Box 255, 306 Railway Ave. SE, Sturgis, SK S0A 4A0
Tel: 306-548-5565
sturgismuseumfile@yahoo.ca
www.townofsturgis.com/tourism
Year Founded: 1986 Aboriginal & early settlers artifacts; open June-Aug.

Swift Current: **Doc's Town Heritage Village**
Parent: **Swift Current Agricultural & Exhibition Association**
Kinetic Exhibition Park, PO Box 146, 17th Ave. SE & South Railway St., Swift Current, SK S9H 3V5
Tel: 306-773-2944; Fax: 306-773-7015
kineticpark@swiftcurrent.ca
www.swiftcurrentex.com
twitter.com/SCAGEX
A reconstructed town depicting Saskatchewan life in the early 1900s.

Swift Current: **Swift Current Museum**
44 Robert St. West, Swift Current, SK S9H 4M9
Tel: 306-778-2775; Fax: 306-778-4818
www.swiftcurrent.ca
The museum hosts a featured exhibit on how human activities impact the environment, as well as temporary exhibits throughout the year. The museum also houses the Swift Current & district archives. Open year-round, M-F, 8:00-5:00.
Lloyd Begley, Contact, l.begley@swiftcurrent.ca

Tisdale: **Tisdale & District Museum**
PO Box 1528, Tisdale, SK S0E 1T0
Tel: 306-873-4999
tmuseum@hotmail.com
The museum features vintage cars, the history of Tisdale bee farming, & artifacts from a historic shoot-out between the Provincial Police & four Russian Bolsheviks. Open May-Sept., 9:00-6:00.

Turtleford: **Turtleford & District Museum**
PO Box 43, Turtleford, SK S0M 2Y0
Tel: 306-845-2433
dmbleakney@littleloon.ca
townofturtleford.ca
Local history, science & technology; located in Lions Park, south of Turtleford; open May-Sept daily.

Unity: **Unity & District Heritage Museum**
Unity Regional Park, General Delivery, Unity, SK S0K 4L0
Tel: 306-228-4464; Fax: 306-228-2149
www.townofunity.com/recreation/museum.php
The Unity & District Heritage Museum includes the following attractions: a 1909 CP Rail Station, the 1908 St. Thomas Anglican Church, the 1926 St.zwarthmore United Church, restored schools, an original home of Unity, a blacksmith shop, & a harness shop. The museum is open from mid May to October.

Vanguard: **Vanguard Centennial Museum**
General Delivery, Vanguard, SK S0N 2V0
Tel: 306-582-2244
vanguard@chinook.lib.sk.ca
Pioneer articles

Iris Minifie, Curator, 306/582-6010, harry.minifie@sasktel.net

***Veregin:* National Doukhobor Heritage Village (NDHV)**
PO Box 99, Veregin, SK S0A 4H0
Tel: 306-542-4441
ndhv@yourlink.ca
www.ndhv.ca
Year Founded: 1980 The Village is a National & Provincial Historical Site, depicting the life of the Russian Doukhobor people who immigrated to Canada in the late 1800s. The Village features 12 buildings, a gift shop, & an on-site picnic area. Open May-Sept., daily 10:00-6:00.

***Verigin:* National Doukhobour Heritage Village**
PO Box 99, Verigin, SK S0A 4H0
Tel: 306-542-4441
ndhv@yourlink.ca
www.ndhv.ca
Doukhobour artifacts, photos, handicrafts, clothing, hand tools; barns, a blacksmith shop & agricultural equipment; model of early Doukhobour village

***Verwood:* Verwood Community Museum**
PO Box 213, Main St., Verwood, SK S0H 4G0
Tel: 306-642-5767
Pioneer articles housed in former church built in 1916

***Wadena:* Wadena & District Museum & Gallery**
PO Box 1208, Wadena, SK S0A 4J0
Tel: 306-338-3454; Fax: 306-338-3804
wadena.museum@sasktel.net
townofwadena.com
Early settlers; 1904 CNR station house; 1907 Sunderland School No.1; blacksmith shop; furnishings; artifacts; open June - Aug., Tue.-Sun.

***Wakaw:* Batoche National Historic Site of Canada (BNHS)**
PO Box 1040, RR#1, Wakaw, SK S0K 4P0
Tel: 306-423-6227; Fax: 306-423-5400
batoche@pc.gc.ca
www.pc.gc.ca/eng/lhn-nhs/sk/batoche/index.aspx
Other contact information: TTD: 306-423-5540
The Batoche National Historic Site of Canada, on the banks of the South Saskatchewan River, is the scene of the last battlefield in the Northwest Rebellion of 1885. The site displays the remains & several restored buildings of the village of Batoche. The life of the Métis at Batoche between 1860 & 1900 is depicted. The site is open from May to September.

***Wakaw:* Diefenbaker Law Office**
PO Box 760, Wakaw, SK S0K 4P0
Tel: 306-233-5157
Replica of the former prime minister's law office, located in Wakaw from 1918-1925

***Wakaw:* Wakaw Heritage Society Museum**
PO Box 475, Wakaw, SK S0K 4P0
Tel: 306-233-4257
Year Founded: 1983 Collections associated with pioneer life
Mary Kostiuk, Secretary

***Waskesiu Lake:* Prince Albert National Park of Canada**
Northern Prairies Field Unit, PO Box 100, Waskesiu Lake, SK S0J 2Y0
Tel: 306-663-4522
panp.info@pc.gc.ca
www.pc.gc.ca/eng/pn-np/sk/princealbert/index.aspx
Protecting part of the boreal forest, Prince Albert National Park features the cabin of conservationist Grey Owl, a white pelican nesting colony, & a free-ranging herd of plains bison. Visitors to the park can participate in interpretive programs & special events. The park is open year-round, & the Interpretive Centre is open from the end of June to September.
Alan Fehr, Field Unit Superintendent, Northern Prairies

***Watson:* Watson & District Heritage Museum**
PO Box 736, Watson, SK S0K 4V0
Tel: 306-287-3783
The museum is housed in a National Heritage Site building, originally belonging to the Canadian Bank of Commerce, circa 1907. 2,000 artifacts are on display, including farm machinery, tools, ladies' fashion, & sports memorabilia. Open June-Aug., Tu-Sa 10:00-5:00.

***Wawota:* Wawota & District Museum**
PO Box 179, 101 Main St., Wawota, SK S0G 5A0
Tel: 306-739-2110
www.wawota.com/museum.htm
Year Founded: 1980 The Wawota & District Museum consists of the following buildings: the main building which was built in the early 1900s & used as a municipal office, a 1909 fire hall, the Bethany Schoolhouse, & a farm equipment shed. The museum is open during July & August, & by appointment at other times.

***Weekes:* Dunwell & Community Museum**
PO Box 120, Weekes, SK S0E 1V0
Tel: 306-278-2906
Restored CNR station, pioneer artifacts & Ukrainian clothes

***Weyburn:* Soo Line Historical Museum**
PO Box 1016, 411 Industrial Lane, Weyburn, SK S4H 2L2
Tel: 306-842-2922; Fax: 306-842-2922
slhm@sasktel.net
www.ascasonline.org/articoloOTTO66.html
www.facebook. com/118758801502753
Year Founded: 1960 Largest private collection of silver in the world; collection of artifacts that were used by Weyburn & District pioneers
Jacquie Mallory, Curator

***Weyburn:* Turner Curling Museum**
PO Box 370, 327 Mergens St., Weyburn, SK S4H 2K6
Tel: 306-848-3218; Fax: 306-842-2001
wneiszner@weyburn.ca
www.weyburn.ca
The museum was established by the late Don Turner & his wife Elva Turner; collection includes curling stones, brooms, clothing, pins, crests & books from around the world; tours available; open by appointment.
Elva Turner, Contact

***Weyburn:* Weyburn & Area Heritage Village**
PO Box 370, Weyburn, SK S4H 2K6
Tel: 306-842-6377
wneiszner@weyburn.ca
www.weyburn.net/attractions.html
Reproduction of a village community from the early 1900s; open May-Aug., daily 1:00-8:00.

***White Fox:* White Fox Museum**
PO Box 399, White Fox, SK S0J 3B0
Tel: 306-276-2106
villageofwhitefox@sasktel.net
Trapper's cabin, tool & harness shop, pioneer items; open June-Sept.

***Whitewood:* Whitewood Historical Museum**
PO Box 752, 603 North Railway, Whitewood, SK S0G 5C0
Tel: 306-735-2380
www.townofwhitewood.ca/tourism-and-heritage/whitewood-historical-museum
Other contact information: Alternate Phone: 306-735-2210
The museum consists of 5 buildings, including a pioneer school room & home, military display, Hungarian, French, Finnish & Swedish collections; open July - Aug.

***Wilcox:* Athol Murray College of Notre Dame Archives & Museum**
Archives / Museum Bldg., Athol Murray College of Notre Dame Campus, PO Box 100, Wilcox, SK S0G 5E0
Tel: 306-732-2080; Fax: 306-732-2008
nd.archives@notredame.sk.ca
www.notredame.sk.ca
The Athol Murray College of Notre Dame Archives & Museum collects & preserves items that tell the story of Père Athol Murray & the history of the Athol Murray College of Notre Dame. The archives & museum features Père Athol Murray's collection of Rare Books, the Rex Beach Repository, the Parthenon Frieze, the Nicholas de Grandmaison Art Portrait collection, sculptures, & stained glass windows. The archives & museum is open seven days a week in July & August, & Monday to Friday from September to June.
Terry McGarry, Curator

***Wilkie:* Wilkie & District Museum**
PO Box 868, 1st St. East, Wilkie, SK S0K 4W0
Tel: 306-843-2717
wilkiemuseum@gmail.com
Open summer; by appt. the rest of the year

***Willow Bunch:* Willow Bunch Museum**
***Parent:* Willow Bunch Museum & Heritage Society**
PO Box 157, 16 Édouard Beaupré St., Willow Bunch, SK S0H 4K0
Tel: 306-473-2806; Fax: 306-473-2789
www.willowbunch.ca
Other contact information: Phone, Mid Sept. - Mid May: 306-473-2762 or 306-473-2279
Year Founded: 1972 The Willow Bunch Museum is located in a Convent school which was built in 1914 by the Sisters of the Cross. One attraction is the display about Edouard Beaupré, an eight foot, three inch tall circus performer who was born in Willow Bunch in 1881. The museum is open from mid May to mid September. Tours may be arranged during the off-season.
Doris O'Reilly, Director

***Wolseley:* Wolseley & District Museum**
PO Box 218, Blanchard St., Wolseley, SK S0G 5H0
Tel: 306-698-2360
Local history of the Wolseley including decorative arts, furnishings, household objects, & maps.

***Wood Mountain:* Wood Mountain Rodeo Ranch Museum**
PO Box 53, Wood Mountain, SK S0H 4L0
Tel: 306-266-4953
www.woodmountain.ca/RodRanc.html
Other contact information: Phone, Tour Bookings: 306-266-2000
Located in the Wood Mountain Regional Park, Wood Mountain Rodeo Ranch Museum offers a glimpse into the life of ranchers & cowboys who arrived in the area in the 1880s. Exhibits include the history of the Wood Mountain Stampede, which is the oldest continuous rodeo in Canada. An extensive archival collection is also housed at the museum. The museum is open from May to September.
Lois Todd, Museum Contact

***Wynyard:* Frank Cameron Museum**
PO Box 734, 1st St. West, Wynyard, SK S0A 4T0
Tel: 306-554-3661
recreation.wynyard@sasktel.net
Local history; houses in a country schoolhouse; open May-Aug.

***Wynyard:* Wynyard & District Museum**
***Parent:* Wynyard & District Museum Society**
c/o Town of Wynyard, PO Box 220, Wynyard, SK S0A 4T0
Fax: 306-554-3224
CPR hand car, household accesories, farm implements, WWI materials
Fern Swimburnson, President
Val Sather, Secretary

***Yorkton:* Western Development Museum**
***Also known as:* Yorkton Western Development Museum**
PO Box 98, Hwy. 16 West, Yorkton, SK S3N 2V6
Tel: 306-783-8361; Fax: 306-782-1027
yorkton@wdm.ca
www.wdm.ca
Yorkton is one of four exhibit branches of Saskatchewan's Western Development Museum. The other branches are located in Moose Jaw, North Battleford, & Saskatoon. The Yorkton Western Development Museum presents the times when immigrants settled in western Canada, including the English, Ukrainians, Doukhobors, Germans, Swedes, & Icelanders.
Susan Mandziuk, Manager, Yorkton, smandziuk@wdm.ca
Carla Madsen, Programmer, Education & Special Events, cmadsen@wdm.ca
Phil Lane, Supervisor, Building, plane@wdm.ca

Yukon Territory

Territorial Museums

MacBride Museum
1124 First Ave., Whitehorse, YT Y1A 1A4
Tel: 867-667-2709; Fax: 867-633-6607
info@macbridemuseum.com
www.macbridemuseum.com
Year Founded: 1951 The Yukon Historical Society acquired the unoccupied Government Telegraph Office built in 1900, & in the 1960s opened it to the public as a museum to house the growing collection of cultural & natural history: Yukon heritage from pre-history to present. Exhibits include archeological & paleontological specimens; ethnographic artifacts, historic artifacts, photographs & archival materials; large industrial & transportation artifacts. Also there are outdoor displays, two heritage buildings.
Hank Moorlag, Chair, MacBride Museum Society
Patricia Cunning, Executive Director, pcunning@macbridemuseum.com
Leighann Chalykoff, Communications Coordinator & Project Manager, lchalykoff@macbridemuseum.com

Local Museums in Yukon Territory

***Burwash Landing:* Kluane Museum of Natural History**
PO Box 45, Historic Mile 1093, Alaska Hwy., Burwash Landing, YT Y0B 1V0
Tel: 867-841-5561
klvanemus@yknet.yk.ca
www.yukonmuseums.ca/museum/kluane/kluane.html
Workclass wildlife display, native handicrafts; open Victoria Day - Labour Day

***Carmacks:* Tagé Cho Hudän Interpretive Centre**
PO Box 135, Carmacks, YT Y0B 1C0
Tel: 867-863-5831; Fax: 867-863-5710
tagechohudan@northwestel.net
Other contact information: Alternate Fax: 867-863-5831
The centre's collection includes traditional boats, stone & bone tools, & traditional clothing. Visitors can also explore the outside area, which features a walking trail & a mammoth snare diorama. Open May-Sept., daily 9:00-6:00; off-season by appointment.

***Dawson City:* Dänojà Zho Cultural Centre**
PO Box 599, 1131 Front St., Dawson City, YT Y0B 1G0
Tel: 867-993-6768; Fax: 867-993-6553
cultural.centre@trondek.ca
trondekheritage.com
The centre presents Tr'ondëk Hwëch'in heritage through galleries, exhibits, & walking tours. Open June-Sept., M-Sa 10:00-6:00; by appointment in the off-season.

***Dawson City:* Dawson City Museum**
PO Box 303, Dawson City, YT Y0B 1G0
Tel: 867-993-5291; Fax: 867-993-5839
info@dawsonmuseum.ca
www.dawsonmuseum.ca
twitter.com/dcmuseum
www.facebook.com/pages/Dawson-City-Museum/118073228250444
Three main galleries include objects and photographs which tells of the story of the Klondike era through the Gold Rush; native history; open mid-May to mid- Sept.; other times by appt.
Laura Mann, Executive Director, lmann@dawsonmuseum.ca
Kathleen Sproule, Collections Coordinator, ksproule@dawsonmuseum.ca
Molly MacDonald, Archives Coordinator, mmacdonald@dawsonmuseum.ca

***Dawson City:* Klondike National Historic Sites**
PO Box 390, Dawson City, YT Y0B 1G0
Tel: 867-993-7200
dawson.info@pc.gc.ca
www.pc.gc.ca/lhn-nhs/yt/klondike/index.aspx
twitter.com/ParksCanYukon
Historic buildings; artifacts; documents; related to Klondike history, Yukon Consolidated Gold Corp. & the Dawson Daily News
G. MacMillan, Supt.

***Faro:* Campbell Region Interpretive Centre**
PO Box 580, Faro, YT Y0B 1K0
Tel: 867-994-2288
cric@faroyukon.ca
www.faroyukon.ca
Other contact information: Year-Round Phone: 867-994-2728; E-mail: erica@faroyukon.ca
The centre is housed in a log building, & offers visitors information on the area's tourist destinations, hiking trails, & heritage sites. The centre also features displays on the area's history, geology, & wildlife. Hours of Operation: May, dailt 9:00-5:00; June-Aug., daily 8:00-6:00; Sept., daily 9:00-5:00.

***Haines Junction:* Kluane National Park**
PO Box 5495, Haines Junction, YT Y0B 1L0
Tel: 867-634-7207; Fax: 867-634-7208
kluane.info@pc.gc.ca
www.pc.gc.ca/kluane
twitter.com/parkscanyukon
Other contact information: Administration Phone: 867-634-7250; Conservation Phone: 867-634-7279
Natural & cultural history of Kluane National Park & Reserve of Canada; information on park services, hiking & other activities
Luke Johnson, Chair, Kluane National Park Management Board
Anne Morin, Field Unit Superintendent, Yukon Field Unit
Sean Sheardown, Superintendent, Kluane National Park & Reserve

***Keno City:* Keno City Mining Museum**
PO Box 17, Site 1, Keno City, YT Y0B 1M0
Tel: 867-995-3103
www.yukonmuseums.ca/museum/keno/keno.html
History of mining of gold & silver in the early 1900s (tools, equipment artifacts); open June-Sept.

***Mayo:* Binet House**
PO Box 160, Mayo, YT Y0B 1M0
Tel: 867-996-2926; Fax: 867-996-2907
mayo@northwestel.net
www.yukonmuseums.ca/interp/binet/binet.html
Other contact information: Off-Season Phone: 867-996-2317
A restored heritage building with displays on area history, early medical equipment, wildlife, & geology; open May-Sept.

***Old Crow:* John Tizya Centre**
PO Box 94, Old Crow, YT Y0B 1N0
Tel: 867-966-3261; Fax: 867-966-3800
info@vgfn.net
www.vgfn.ca
Situated in the only Yukon community north of the Arctic Circle, the centre presents Vuntut Gwitchin's culture, oral history, & surrounding landscape. Open year-round, weekdays 9:00-12:00, 1:00-4:30.

***Teslin:* George Johnston Tlingit Indian Museum**
***Also known as:* Teslin Historical & Museum Society**
PO Box 146, Km 1294 Mile 804, Alaska Hwy., Teslin, YT Y0A 1B0
Tel: 867-390-2550Toll-Free: 867-390-2042
schatterton@northwestel.net
www.gjmuseum.yk.net
Inland Tlingit ethnographic & 20th centrury artifacts; open May 22-Sept. 4

***Teslin:* Teslin Tlingit Heritage Centre**
PO Box 133, Teslin, YT Y0A 1B0
Tel: 867-390-2532
Visitors to the centre can explore the Tlingit people's day-to-day life; the centre's collection includes traditional masks & artifacts. Open June-Sept., daily 9:00-5:00; off-season by appointment.

***Whitehorse:* Copperbelt Railway & Mining Museum**
***Parent:* Miles Canyon Historic Railway Society**
c/o Miles Canyon Historic Railway Society, 1127 First Ave., Whitehorse, YT Y1A 0G5
Tel: 867-667-6355; Fax: 867-667-6198
mchrs@northwestel.net
www.yukonrails.com/museum
twitter.com/MCHRSYukon
www.facebook.com/MCHRSYukon
The museum site features a working railway, station museum, & picnic area; open May-Sept.

***Whitehorse:* Fort Selkirk**
c/o Tourism & Culture, Cultural Services Branch, PO Box 2703, Whitehorse, YT Y1A 2C6
Tel: 867-667-5386
museevirtuel-virtualmuseum.ca/sgc-cms/expositions-exhibitions/fort_selkirk
Accessible only by boat or plane; co-owned & managed by the Yukon Government and the Selkirk First Nation; open mid-May - mid-Sept. URL is a portal to the virtual museum.

***Whitehorse:* Kwanlin Dün Cultural Centre**
1171 - 1st Ave., Whitehorse, YT Y1A 0G9
Tel: 867-456-5322
www.kwanlindunculturalcentre.com
twitter.com/KDCulture
www.facebook.com/KwanlinDunCulturalCentre
The centre seeks to benefit the Kwanlin Dün people by reviving & preserving their culture, heritage, & way of life. Visitors can experience Kwanlin Dün culture through programs, exhibits, & events. Open June-Sept., M-Sa 10:00-6:00, or by appointment.
Rae Mombourquette, Executive Director, rae.m@kdcc.ca

***Whitehorse:* LePage Park**
c/o Yukon Historical & Museums Association, 3126 Third Ave., Whitehorse, YT Y1A 1E7
Tel: 867-667-4704; Fax: 867-667-4506
info@heritageyukon.ca
heritageyukon.ca
www.facebook.com/155225187844868
Walking tours by interpreters in period costume, June - Aug.; free noon concerts in the summer; surrounded by heritage buildings & an art gallery; open year round
Brent Slobodin, President

***Whitehorse:* Old Log Church Museum**
PO Box 31461, 3rd Ave. & Elliot St., Whitehorse, YT Y1A 6K8
Tel: 867-668-2555; Fax: 867-667-6258
logchurch@klondiker.com
www.oldlogchurchmuseum.ca
www.facebook.com/old logchurchmuseum
Open May - Labour Day

***Whitehorse:* Yukon Beringia Interpretive Centre**
PO Box 2703, Kilometre 1423 (Mile 886), Alaska Hwy., Whitehorse, YT Y1A 2C6
Tel: 867-667-8855; Fax: 867-667-8854
beringia@gov.yk.ca
www.beringia.com
www.facebook.com/126598970843
Beringia was an ancient place, situated between two continents on the edge of the Arctic. The land connection between Siberia & Alaska was part of the larger area known as Beringia. The land of ice was home to huge mammals, such as woolly mammoths & scimitar cats, & the first people of North America. The Yukon Beringia Interpretive Centre is open from May to September. During the winter, it is open on Sundays, or by appointment.

***Whitehorse:* Yukon Historical & Museums Association**
Donnenworth House, 3126 - 3rd Ave., Whitehorse, YT Y1A 1E7
Tel: 867-667-4704; Fax: 867-667-4506
yhma@northwestel.net; info@heritageyukon.ca
www.heritageyukon.ca
www.facebook.com/155225187844868
Year Founded: 1977 The Association offers visitors a 45-minute walking tour of Whitehorse's heritage sites. Donnenworth House features a photographic display depicting various heritage sites around the Yukon. The website offers downloadable audio walking tours. Open M-F 9:00-4:00.
Marc Johnson, President
Tracey Anderson, Executive Director

***Whitehorse:* Yukon Transportation Museum**
30 Electra Cres., Whitehorse, YT Y1A 6E6
Tel: 867-668-4792; Fax: 867-633-5547
info@goytm.ca
goytm.ca
www.facebook.com/120797977963812
Transportation displays depicting the first commercial aircraft in the Yukon; construction of the Alaska Highway, the White Pass & Yukon Route Railway. Open daily 10-6, mid-May - end of August.
Casey Mclaughlin, Executive Director/Curator, casey@goytm.ca
Cathy Ritchie, Assistant Director/Curator, cathy@goytm.ca

National Parks & Outdoor Education Centres

Alberta

Local National Parks & Outdoor Education Centres in Alberta

***Banff:* Banff National Park**
PO Box 900, Banff, AB T1L 1K2
Tel: 403-762-1550; Fax: 403-762-1551
Toll-Free: 888-927-3367
banff.vrc@pc.gc.ca
www.pc.gc.ca/eng/pn-np/ab/banff/ind ex.aspx
Social Media: www.youtube.com/view_play_list?p=7ABD4B2249F753EB
twitter.com/banffnp
www.facebook.com/BanffNP
Other contact information: Backcountry Trail Reservations, Phone: 403-762-1556
Banff National Park was Canada's first national park. It spans 6,641 square kilometres (2,564 square miles) of valleys, mountains, glaciers, forests, meadows, & rivers. Hours of Operation: Winter, 9:00-5:00; Spring, 9:00-7:00; Summer, 8:00-8:00; Fall, 9:00-7:00

***Fort Saskatchewan:* Elk Island National Park**
Site 4, R.R.#1, Fort Saskatchewan, AB T8L 2N7 Canada
Tel: 780-922-5790; Fax: 780-992-2951
elk.island@pc.gc.ca
www.pc.gc.ca/pn-np/ab/elkisland/index_E.asp
Other contact information: Administration, Phone: 780-992-2950
Elk Island National Park of Canada protects the aspen parkland, which is one of the most endangered habitats in Canada. The park is home to herds of plains bison, wood bison, moose, deer, & elk. The park is also home to over 250 species of birds. Hours: Campground Reservations, Administration Building & Wardern Operations Building open year round, 8:00-3:00; Sandy Beach Campground open May-Sept. weather permitting; Golf Course open May-Sept. weather permitting; winter campground open Oct-April weather permitting.

***Jasper:* Jasper National Park of Canada**
PO Box 10, Jasper, AB T0E 1E0
Tel: 780-852-6176; Fax: 780-852-6152
pnj.jnp@pc.gc.ca
www.pc.gc.ca/pn-np/ab/jasper/index_E.asp
Social Media: www.youtube.com/ParksCanadaAgency
twitter.com/JasperNP
www.facebook.com/JasperNP
Other contact information: Backcountry Trail Reservations, Phone: 780-852-6177
Jasper is the largest & most northerly Canadian rocky mountain national park, part of a World Heritage Site. The park is comprised of carefully protected ecosystems, & includes destinations such as Sunwapta Falls, Mount Edith Cavell, Athabasca Glacier, Miette Hotsprings, & 1,000-plus kilometres of trails. Hours of Operation: Winter 9:00-5:00; Spring 9:00-7:00; Summer 8:30-8:00; Fall 9:00-6:00

***Waterton Park:* Waterton Lakes National Park of Canada**
PO Box 200, Waterton Park, AB T0K 2M0
Tel: 403-859-5133; Fax: 403-859-5152
waterton.info@pc.gc.ca
www.pc.gc.ca/eng/pn-np/ab/waterton/index.aspx
Social Media: www.youtube.com/user/ParksCanadaAgency
twitter.com/watertonlakesnp
www.facebook.com/WatertonLakesNP
Waterton Lakes National Park helps protect the unique physical, biological & cultural resources found in one of the narrowest places in the Rocky Mountains. Upper Waterton Lake is the

deepest lake in the Canadian Rockies. In 1932, the park was joined with Montana's Glacier National Park to form the Waterton-Glacier International Peace Park. Hours of Operation: Park Receptionist year round, M-F 8:00-4:00; Campsites & Parkways May-Sept.

British Columbia

Local National Parks & Outdoor Education Centres in British Columbia

***Field:* Yoho National Park of Canada**
PO Box 99, Field, BC V0A 1G0
Tel: 250-343-6783
yoho.info@pc.gc.ca
www.pc.gc.ca/eng/pn-np/bc/yoho/index.aspx
Other contact information: TTY: 1-866-787-6221
Year Founded: 1886 Yoho National Park is situated on the western slopes of the Canadian Rocky Mountains. 'Yoho' is a Cree experession of awe & wonder, given to the park because of its immense rock walls, waterfalls, & mountain peaks. Hours of Operation: Parklands are open year round; Visitor Centre open only Spring-Fall.

***Queen Charlotte:* Gwaii Haanas National Park Reserve & Haida Heritage Site**
PO Box 37, Queen Charlotte, BC V0T 1S0
Tel: 250-559-8818; Fax: 250-559-8366
Toll-Free: 877-559-8818
gwaii.haanas@pc.gc.ca
www.pc.gc.ca/eng/pn-np/bc/gwaiih aanas/index.aspx
Gwaii Haanas National Park is jointly managed by the Government of Canada & the Council of the Haida Nation, through an agreement signed in 1993, although the question of ownership is unresolved. Hours of Operation: M-F 8:00-12:00, 1:00-4:30.

***Radium Hot Springs:* Kootenay National Park of Canada**
PO Box 220, Radium Hot Springs, BC V0A 1M0
Tel: 250-347-9505; Fax: 250-347-9980
Toll-Free: 888-927-3367
kootenay.info@pc.gc.ca
www.pc.gc.ca/eng/pn-np/bc/koote nay/index.aspx
Other contact information: TTY: 1-866-787-6221
Year Founded: 1920 Kootenay National Park represents the south-western region of the Canadian Rocky Mountains. The park contains such diverse landscapes as glaciers-topped mountains & semi-arid grasslands that harbour plants such as cactus. Hours of Operation: Parklands are open year round. Hours of operation: the park is open year-round; the Kootenay National Park Visitor Centre is open May-June 9:00-5:00, June-Sept. 9:00-7:00, Sept-.Oct. 9:00-5:00, & closed Oct.-Spring.

***Revelstoke:* Glacier National Park of Canada**
PO Box 350, Revelstoke, BC V0E 2S0
Tel: 250-837-7500; Fax: 250-837-7536
www.pc.gc.ca/pn-np/bc/glacier/index_E.asp
Other contact information: TTY: 1-866-787-6221
Glacier National Park of Canada protects part of the Columbia Mountains Natural Region in British Columbia's interior, which includes stands of old-growth cedar & hemlock, & habitat for endangered species such as mountain caribou, mountain goat, & grizzly bear. Also located in the park is The Rogers Pass National Historic Site, which commemorates the construction of the country's first major national transportation route. Hours of Operation: Winter 7:00-5:00; Spring 8:30-4:30; Summer 8:00-6:00; Fall 9:00-5:00; Nov. Th-M 7:00-3:00

***Revelstoke:* Mount Revelstoke National Park of Canada**
PO Box 350, Revelstoke, BC V0E 2S0
Tel: 250-837-7500; Fax: 250-837-7536
www.pc.gc.ca/eng/pn-np/bc/revelstoke/index.aspx
Other contact information: TTY: 1-866-787-6221
Mount Revelstoke National Park contains old-growth rainforest of giant cedar & pine, subalpine forest, & alpine meadows & tundra. The Monashee & Selkirk Mountains are also in the park. Hiking trails take visitors through various landscapes, including Western Red Cedars & jungle-like wetland. Hours of Operation: The Revelstoke Office is open year-round, M-F 8:00-4:30.

***Sidney:* Gulf Islands National Park Reserve of Canada**
2220 Harbour Rd., Sidney, BC V8L 2P6
Tel: 250-654-4000; Fax: 250-654-4014
Toll-Free: 866-944-1744
gulf.islands@pc.gc.ca
www.pc.gc.ca/pn-np/bc/gulf/index _E.asp
Year Founded: 2003 Gulf Islands National Park Reserve protects part of British Columbia's southern Gulf Islands archipelago. These islands represent the Strait of Georgia Lowlands, which is one of the most ecologically sensitive regions in southern Canada. The park includes fifteen islands, many islets & reefs, & around twenty-six square kilometres of marine areas. Hours of Operation: Some parks are closed during the off-season & camping is prohibited; please see the website for detailed information.

***Ucluelet:* Pacific Rim National Park Reserve of Canada**
PO Box 280, 2040 Pacific Rim Hwy., Ucluelet, BC V0R 3A0
Tel: 250-726-3500; Fax: 250-726-3520
pacrim.info@pc.gc.ca
www.pc.gc.ca/eng/pn-np/bc/pacificrim/index.aspx
Pacific Rim National Park Reserve of Canada is backed by the Insular Mountains Range of Vancouver Island, & faces the Pacific Ocean. Pacific Rim presents the rich natural and cultural heritage of Canada's west coast. Its cool, wet maritime climate produces an abundance of life in the water & on land. Coastal temperate rainforest gives way to diverse intertidal & subtidal areas. Also presented is the history of the Nuu-chah-nulth First Nations, as well as that of European explorers & settlers. Hours of Operation: year round.
Dave McVetty, Superintendent

Manitoba

Local National Parks & Outdoor Education Centres in Manitoba

***Churchill:* Wapusk National Park of Canada**
PO Box 127, 1 Mantayo Seepee Meskanow, Churchill, MB R0B 0E0
Tel: 204-675-8863; Fax: 204-675-2026
Toll-Free: 888-773-8888
wapusk.np@pc.gc.ca
www.pc.gc.ca/eng/pn-np/mb/wapusk/in dex.aspx
Other contact information: TTY: 866-787-6221
Wapusk National Park of Canada, & is home to one of the world's largest polar bear maternity denning areas ("Wapusk" is a Cree word meaning "White Bear"). The park encompasses the Hudson James Lowlands region, bordering on Hudson Bay, & lies on the transition area between boreal forest & Arctic tundra. Note: Access to the park is via authorized commercial tour operators in Churchill. The park currently has limited visitor capacity. Parks Canada does not recommend unescorted visits to the park. For the most current list of operators, please contact the park office or visit the website.
Sheldon Kowalchuk, Contact, sheldon.kowalchuk@pc.gc.ca

***Wasagaming:* Riding Mountain National Park of Canada**
Wasagaming, MB R0J 2H0
Tel: 204-848-7275; Fax: 204-848-2596
rmnp.info@pc.gc.ca
www.pc.gc.ca/eng/pn-np/mb/riding/index.aspx
twitter .com/@RidingNP
www.facebook.com/RidingNP
Riding Mountain forms part of the Manitoba Escarpmet, & protects a variety of wildlife & vegetation. The park features many hiking trails & Agassiz Tower, which offers visitors a panoramic view of the prairies to the north. Visitor services can be found in Wasagaming, the park's town site, including accommodation, restaurants, & shopping. Hours of Operation: Administration Office M-F 8:00-12:00, 12:30-4:00; Visitor Centre, Spring & Fall M-Su 9:30-5:30, Summer 9:30-8:00.

New Brunswick

Local National Parks & Outdoor Education Centres in New Brunswick

***Alma:* Fundy National Park of Canada**
PO Box 1001, Alma, NB E4H 1B4
Tel: 506-887-6000; Fax: 506-887-6008
fundy.info@pc.gc.ca
www.pc.gc.ca/eng/pn-np/nb/fundy/index.aspx
Other contact information: TTY: 506-887-6015
Fundy National Park of Canada protects some of the only remaining wilderness in southern New Brunswick, including the Caledonia Highlands & Bay of Fundy. Inland, visitors can explore forests & stream valleys. Hours of Operation: Vistor Reception Centre, Spring & Fall 8:30-4:15; Summer 8:00 am-9:45 pm.

***Kouchibouguac National Park:* Kouchibouguac National Park of Canada**
186 Rte. 117, Kouchibouguac National Park, NB E4X 2P1
Tel: 506-876-2443; Fax: 506-876-4802
kouch.info@pc.gc.ca
www.pc.gc.ca/eng/pn-np/nb/kouchibouguac/index.aspx
twitter.com/KouchibouguacNP
www.facebook.com/KouchibouguacNP
Other contact information: TTY: 506-876-4205
Year Founded: 1969 Kouchibouguac National Park of Canada is a Canadian Heritage protected area, & is one of only two wilderness national parks in New Brunswick. The landscape of the 238 km2 park is characteristic of the Maritime Plain Natural Region in which it is located, including such features as bogs, salt marshes, tidal rivers, freshwater systems, lagoons, abandoned fields, & forests. The name Kouchibouguac is of Mi'kmaq origin & means "river of the long tides." Visitors can explore 60 km of paths for hikers & cyclists, as well as partaking in canoeing, kayaking, swimming, camping, bird watching, & cross country skiing, snowshoeing, & tobogganing in winter. Hours of operation: Park Administration, M-F 8:15-4:30year-round; Visitor Reception Centre & Park Entrance Kiosk, May-June 9:00-5:00, June-Sept. 8:00-8:00, Sept.-Oct. 9:00-5:00.

Newfoundland & Labrador

Local National Parks & Outdoor Education Centres in Newfoundland & Labrador

***Glovertown:* Terra Nova National Park of Canada**
General Delivery, Glovertown, NL A0G 2L0
Tel: 709-533-2801; Fax: 709-533-2706
info.tnnp@pc.gc.ca
www.pc.gc.ca/eng/pn-np/nl/terranova/index.aspx
Terra Nova National Park of Canada encompasses the North Atlantic Ocean & the boreal forest of Eastern Newfoundland. The park's landscape varies from cliffs & inlets to forested hills, bogs, & ponds. Visitors can also explore the remnants of sawmills & past human cultures found within the park. Hours of Operation: Administration Building, M-F 8:30-4:30; Visitor Centre, May-June 10:00-4:00, June-Sept. 10:00-6:00, Sept.-Oct. 10:00-4:00.

***Nain:* Torngat Mountains National Park of Canada**
PO Box 471, Nain, NL A0P 1L0
Tel: 709-922-1290; Fax: 709-922-1294
Toll-Free: 888-922-1290
torngats.info@pc.qc.ca
www.pc.gc.ca/eng/pn-np/nl/torng ats/index.aspx
Other contact information: French Phone: 709-458-2417
The Torngat Mountains National Park of Canada, in northern Labrador, encompasses nearly 10,000 km2. It extends from Saglek Fjord in the south, to the northern tip of Labrador; & from the province's boundary with Quebec in the west, to the Labrador Sea in the east. The national park protects an area of Arctic wilderness, featuring mountains (the highest peaks in eastern North America), small glaciers, fjords, river valleys, & rugged coastal landscapes. This land has been home to the Inuit & their ancestors for thousands of years. Hours of operation: Park office hours are M-F 8:00-4:30, except holidays. The park itself is a remote wilderness, with no on-site facilities or road access. As a result, visitors are encouraged to come only in late winter/early spring & summer.

***Rocky Harbour:* Gros Morne National Park of Canada**
PO Box 130, Rocky Harbour, NL A0K 4N0
Tel: 709-458-2417; Fax: 709-458-2059
grosmorne.info@pc.gc.ca
www.pc.gc.ca/pn-np/nl/grosmorne/index_E.asp
Other contact information: TTY: 709-772-4564
Gros Morne National Park of Canada was designated a UNESCO World Heritage Site in 1987. Visitors can hike through mountains or camp by the sea. Boat tours are offered, & waterfalls, marine inlets, sea stacks, beaches, & nearby fishing villages can all be explored. Hours of Operation: Park Headquaters, M-F 8:00-12:00, 1:00-4:30; Visitor Centre, May-June 9:00-5:00, June-Sept. 8:00-8:00, Sept-Oct. 9:00-5:00.

Northwest Territories

Local National Parks & Outdoor Education Centres in Northwest Territories

***Fort Simpson:* Nahanni National Park Reserve of Canada**
PO Box 348, 10002 - 100 St., Fort Simpson, NT X0E 0N0
Tel: 867-695-7750; Fax: 867-695-2446
nahanni.info@pc.gc.ca
www.pc.gc.ca/pn-np/nt/nahanni/index_E.asp
Nahanni National Park Reserve of Canada protects a portion of the Mackenzie Mountains Natural Region. A key feature of the park is the Naha Dehé (South Nahanni River), and the park's diverse landscape offers a home to many species of birds, fish & mammals. The Ford Simpson visitor centre features displays on the history, culture & geography of the area. The park was inscribed on UNESCO's World Heritage List in 1978. Hours of Operation: Winter, M-F 8:30-12:00, 1:00-5:00; Summer, daily 8:00-12:00, 1:00-5:00.

***Fort Smith:* Wood Buffalo National Park of Canada**
PO Box 750, 149 McDougal Rd., Fort Smith, NT X0E 0P0
Tel: 867-872-7960; Fax: 867-872-3910
wbnp.info@pc.gc.ca
www.pc.gc.ca/pn-np/nt/woodbuffalo.aspx
Other contact information: TTY: 867-872-7961; 24-Hour Hotline: 867-872-7962
Year Founded: 1922 Wood Buffalo National Park is Canada's largest national park & one of the largest in the world. It was established to protect the last herds of bison in northern Canada, & today it protects an example of Canada's Northern Boreal

Plains. Hours of Operation: Park is open year round; Fort Smith Visitor Reception Centre open seven days a week in the summer, and Mon.-Fri. in the winter; Fort Chipewyan Visitor Reception Centre open Mon.-Fri. year-round, with most weekends open in summer as well.

***Fort Smith:* Wood Buffalo National Park of Canada**
750, Fort Smith, NT X0E 0P0
Tel: 867-872-7900; Fax: 867-872-3910
wbnp.info@pc.gc.ca
www.pc.gc.ca/eng/pn-np/nt/woodbuffalo/index.aspx
Year Founded: 1922 Wood Buffalo National Park of Canada is the country's largest national park & one of the largest in the world. It was established to protect the last herds of bison in northern Canada, & today it protects Canada's Northern Boreal Plains. Hours of Operation: The park is open year-round; Fort Smith Visitor Reception Centre is open seven days a week in the summer, & M-F 9:00-5:00 the rest of the year.

***Inuvik:* Ivvavik National Park of Canada**
c/o Western Arctic Field Unit, PO Box 1840, Inuvik, NT X0E 0T0
Tel: 867-777-8800; Fax: 867-777-8820
inuvik.info@pc.gc.ca
www.pc.gc.ca/eng/pn-np/yt/ivvavik/index.aspx
Ivvavik National Park of Canada is the first national park in Canada to be created as a result of an aboriginal land claim agreement. The park protects a portion of the calving grounds of the Porcupine caribou herd and represents the Northern Yukon and Mackenzie Delta natural regions. Hours of Operation: Park is open year round, with no available services.

***Paulatuk:* Tuktut Nogait National Park of Canada**
PO Box 91, Paulatuk, NT X0E 1N0
Tel: 867-580-3233; Fax: 867-580-3234
inuvik.info@pc.gc.ca
www.pc.gc.ca/eng/pn-np/nt/tuktutnogait/index.aspx
The park is located 170 kilometres north of the arctic circle & is home to the Bluenose West caribou herd, as well as wolves, grizzly bears, muskoxen, arctic char, & a large number of raptors. Hours of Operation: open year round.

***Sachs Harbour:* Aulavik National Park of Canada**
PO Box 29, Sachs Harbour, NT X0E 0Z0
Tel: 867-690-3904; Fax: 867-690-4808
inuvik.info@pc.gc.ca
www.pc.gc.ca/eng/pn-np/nt/aulavik/index.aspx
Aulavik National Park protects more than 12,000 square kilometres of arctic lowlands on the north end of Banks Island. At the heart of the park lies the Thomsen River, one of Canada's most northerly navigable waterways, which visitors can paddle. The park is home to the endangered Peary caribou and the highest density of muskoxen in the world. Hours of operation: open year round.

Nova Scotia

Local National Parks & Outdoor Education Centres in Nova Scotia

***Ingonish Beach:* Cape Breton Highlands National Park of Canada**
Ingonish Beach, NS B0C 1L0
Tel: 902-224-2306; Fax: 902-285-2866
cbhnp.info@pc.gc.ca
www.pc.gc.ca/pn-np/ns/cbreton/index_E.asp
twitter. com/ParksCanada_NS
www.facebook.com/CBHNP
Cape Breton Highlands National Park of Canada is home to the Cabot Trail, & offers visitors scenery, wildlife, & human history stretching back to the last Ice Age. Hours of Operation: park is open year round; Visitor Centre Spring 9:00-5:00, Summer 8:00-7:00, Fall 9:00-5:00.

***Maitland Bridge, Annapolis County:* Kejimkujik National Park & National Historic Site of Canada**
PO Box 236, Maitland Bridge, Annapolis County, NS B0T 1B0
Tel: 902-682-2772; Fax: 902-682-3367
kejimkujik.info@pc.gc.ca
www.pc.gc.ca/eng/pn-np/ns/kejimkujik/index.aspx
twitter.com/ParksCanada_NS
Kejimkujik is the sole inland national park in the Maritimes, featuring lakes & rivers, woodlands, & a variety of wildlife. Visitors can explore historic canoe routes, portages, & hiking trails in the park. Hours of Operation: Visitor Reception Centre, mid-June - Labour Day 8:30-8:00, Labour Day - mid-Oct. 8:30-5:30, mid-Oct. - April 9:00-4:00, May - mid-June 8:30-5:30, closed weekends in Nov. & Dec.; Campground Kiosk mid-June - Labour day 9:00-9:00, closed in winter.

Nunavut

Local National Parks & Outdoor Education Centres in Nunavut

***Iqaluit:* Quttinirpaaq National Park of Canada**
PO Box 278, Iqaluit, NU X0A 0H0
Tel: 867-975-4673; Fax: 867-975-4674
nunavut.info@pc.gc.ca
www.pc.gc.ca/eng/pn-np/nu/quttinirpaaq/index.aspx
Hours of Operation: Warden station only staffed furing the summer field season. Parks Canada Office in Iqaluit is open M-F 8:30-12:00, 1:00-5:00 year round.
Joadamee Amagoalik, Chair, Quttinirpaaq Joint Inuit/Gov't Park Committee
Nancy Anilniliak, Field Unit Superintendent, Nunavut, Parks Canada

***Pangnirtung:* Auyuittuq National Park of Canada**
PO Box 353, Pangnirtung, NU X0A 0R0
Tel: 867-473-2500; Fax: 867-473-8612
nunavut.info@pc.gc.ca
www.pc.gc.ca/eng/pn-np/nu/auyuittuq/index.aspx
Year Founded: 1976 Auyuittuq National Park of Canada protects 19,089 km2 of terrain. Auyuittuq is an Inuktitut word meaning "land that never melts." The park is located in the eastern Arctic, on southern Baffin Island, & includes the highest peaks of the Canadian Shield, the Penny Ice Cap, coastal fiords, & Akshayuk Pass, which was a traditional corridor used by the Inuit for thousands of years. Hours of Operation: Visitor Centre open year-round, M-F 8:30-5:00; summer hours are posted in June.
Maryse Mahy, Communication Manager, 867-975-4673, Fax: 867-975-4674, maryse.mahy@pc.gc.ca

***Pond Inlet:* Sirmilik National Park of Canada**
PO Box 300, Pond Inlet, NU X0A 0S0
Tel: 867-899-8092; Fax: 867-899-8104
sirmilik.info@pc.gc.ca
www.pc.gc.ca/eng/pn-np/nu/sirmilik/contact.aspx
Year Founded: 2001 Sirmilik National Park represents the Northern Eastern Arctic Lowlands Natural Region & portions of the Lancaster Sound Marine Region. The park features wilderness hiking & camping, & a prominent seabird colony near of Baillarge Bay. Hours of Operation: Administration & Visitor Centre, M-F 8:30-12:00, 1:00-5:00.

Ontario

Local National Parks & Outdoor Education Centres in Ontario

***Heron Bay:* Pukaskwa National Park of Canada**
PO Box 212, Heron Bay, ON P0T 1R0
Tel: 807-229-0801; Fax: 807-229-2097
ont-pukaskwa@pc.gc.ca
www.pc.gc.ca/pn-np/on/pukaskwa/index_E.asp
twitt er.com/PukaskwaNP
Pukaskwa National Park is the only wilderness national park in Ontario, & protects 1878 square km of boreal forest & Lake Superior shoreline. Hours of Operation: Administration Office M-F 8:30-4:30 year-round.

***Leamington:* Point Pelee National Park of Canada**
407 Monarch Lane, RR#1, Leamington, ON N8H 3V4
Tel: 519-322-2365; Fax: 519-322-1277
Toll-Free: 888-773-8888
pelee.info@pc.gc.ca
www.pc.gc.ca/eng/pn-np/on/pelee/in dex.aspx
Other contact information: TTY: 1-866-787-6221
Point Pelee National Park is located at the southern tip of Canada, 50 km (30 miles) south-east of Windsor, Ontario. It is one of Canada's smallest national parks, but features picnic areas & a Visitor Centre, as well as the famous Tip, & Marsh Boardwalk. Hours of Operation: April-May 6:00-10:00, May 5:00-10:00, May-Oct. 6:00-10:00, Oct-March 7:00-7:00.

***Mallorytown:* St. Lawrence Islands National Park of Canada**
2 County Road 5, RR#3, Mallorytown, ON K0E 1R0
Tel: 613-923-5261; Fax: 613-923-1021
ont-sli@pc.gc.ca
www.pc.gc.ca/eng/pn-np/on/lawren/index.aspx
twitter.c om/slinationalpark
www.facebook.com/160237280773786
St. Lawrence Islands National Park was conceived in the 1870s, & is located in the heart of the Thousand Islands tourist area. Hours of Operation: Administration Office, M-F 8:00-4:30 year round; Islands, May-Oct; Mallourytown Landing Visitor Centre open weekends & holidays May-June 10:00-4:00, & Th-M June-Sept.

***Midland:* Georgian Bay Islands National Park of Canada**
PO Box 9, 901 Wye Valley Rd., Midland, ON L4R 4K6
Tel: 705-526-9804; Fax: 705-526-5939
Toll-Free: 877-737-3783
info.gbi@pc.gc.ca
www.pc.gc.ca/eng/pn-np/on/georg/inde x.aspx
twitter.com/GBINP
Other contact information: Summer Weekend & Holiday Phone: 705-427-2532
Georgian Bay Islands National Park of Canada protects the Canadian Shield, including the Honey Harbour area to Twelve Mile Bay in southern Georgian Bay. The islands are accessible by boat only. Beausoleil, the largest island, offers tent camping, overnight & day docking, heritage education programs, & hiking trails. Wheelchair accessible & reserved campsites are also available at the Cedar Spring campground on Beausoleil. Hours of Operation: Midland administration office open year-round, 8:00-4:00; Beausoleil Island Kiosk open Su-Th 9:00-5:00, F & Sa 9:00-7:00.

***Tobermory:* Bruce Peninsula National Park of Canada**
PO Box 189, Tobermory, ON N0H 2R0
Tel: 519-596-2233; Fax: 519-596-2298
bruce-fathomfive@pc.gc.ca
www.pc.gc.ca/eng/pn-np/on/bruce/index.aspx
Other contact information: Camping Office, Phone: 519-596-2263
Bruce Peninsula National Park of Canada is located inside a World Biosphere Reserve. The cliffs of the park are inhabited by thousand-year-old cedar trees, & the park is comprised of habitats ranging from alvars to forests & lakes. All together the ecosystem is the largest remaining chunk of natural habitat in southern Ontario. Hours of Operation: Administration Office, M-F 8:00-4:30; Cyprus Lake Campground Office, Fall M, Th, Su 9:00-5:00, F & Sa 9:00-8:00, Summer 8:00-12:00.

Prince Edward Island

Local National Parks & Outdoor Education Centres in Prince Edward Island

***Charlottetown:* Prince Edward Island National Park of Canada**
2 Palmers Lane, Charlottetown, PE C1A 5V8
Tel: 902-672-6350; Fax: 902-672-6370
pnipe.peinp@pc.gc.ca
www.pc.gc.ca/pn-np/pe/pei-ipe/index_E.asp
www.fac ebook.com/PEInationalpark
Other contact information: TTY: 902-566-7061
The landscape of Prince Edward Island National Park of Canada includes sand dunes, barrier islands & sand pits, beaches, sandstone cliffs, wetlands, & forests. Various plants & animals call these habitats home, including the endangered Piping Plover. The Park also features Green Gables & Dalvay-by-the-Sea National Historic Site. In 1998, six kilometres of the Greenwich Peninsula were added to the Park in order to protect unique dune formations, rare plants & animals, & archaeological discoveries dating back 10,000 years. Hours of Operation: Entrance Kiosks, June 11:00-5:00, July-Sept. 10:00-6:00; Cavendish Destination Centre Jan.-May M-F 11:00-2:30, May M-F 9:00-5:00, May-June daily 9:00-5:00, June-Sept. daily 8:00-9:00, Sept.-Oct. daily 9:00-5:00, Oct.-Dec. M-F 11:00-2:30; Greenwich Interpretation Centre, June 9:00-3:00, July-Sept. 9:00-5:00.

Quebec

Local National Parks & Outdoor Education Centres in Quebec

***Gaspé:* Forillon National Park of Canada**
122, boul Gaspé, Gaspé, QC G4X 1A9
Tel: 418-368-5505; Fax: 418-368-6837
Toll-Free: 888-773-8888
information@pc.gc.ca
www.pc.gc.ca/pn-np/qc/forillon/in dex_E.asp
twitter.com/ForillonNP
www.facebook.com/ForillonNP
Other contact information: TTY: 1-866-787-6221
Year Founded: 1970 Forillon National Park of Canada is located at the farthest point of the Gaspé Peninsula, & covers a 244 km2 area. It protects a portion of the Notre-Dame & Mégantic mountain regions, & elements of the Gulf of St. Lawrence marine region. Present in the park are ten different rock formations, colonies of seabirds, & arctic-alpine plants. The Grande-Grave National Heritage Site is located within the park & reveals the way of life of fishing families in the region. Hours of Operation: Park is open all year round, with services mostly offered between June & October; please see the website for detailed information.

Havre-Saint-Pierre: **Mingan Archipelago National Park Reserve of Canada**
1340, rue de la Digue, Havre-Saint-Pierre, QC G0G 1P0
Tel: 418-538-3331; Fax: 418-538-3595
Toll-Free: 888-773-8888
information@pc.gc.ca
www.pc.gc.ca/eng/pn-np/qc/mingan/ index.aspx
Other contact information: TTY: 1-866-787-6221
Year Founded: 1984 The Mingan Archipelago National Park Reserve of Canada is situated along the North Shore of the Gulf of St. Lawrence, & is comprised of about forty limestone islands, & and over 1,000 islets & reefs. This territory is home to an abundance of vegetation & wildlife, including seabird colonies, seals, dolphins, & whales. Hours of Operation: Havre-Saint-Pierre Reception & Interpretation Center & Longue-Pointe-de-Mingan Reception & Interpretation Centre open June-Sept.

Shawinigan: **La Mauricie National Park of Canada**
PO Box 160 Bureau-chef, 702 - 5e Rue, Shawinigan, QC G9N 6T9
Tel: 819-538-3232; Fax: 819-536-3661
Toll-Free: 888-773-8888
parkscanada-que@pc.gc.ca
www.pc.gc.ca/pn-np/qc/maurici e/index_E.asp
Year Founded: 1970 La Mauricie National Park of Canada covers an area of 536 km2, protecting a sample of the southernmost part of the Canadian Shield. Hours of Operation: Reception Centre, May & Sept-Oct. Sa-Th 9:00-4:30, F 9:00-9:30, May-Sept. every day 7:00-9:30.

Saskatchewan

Local National Parks & Outdoor Education Centres in Saskatchewan

Val Marie: **Grasslands National Park of Canada**
PO Box 150, Val Marie, SK S0N 2T0
Tel: 306-298-2257; Fax: 306-298-2042
grasslands.info@pc.gc.ca
www.pc.gc.ca/eng/pn-np/sk/grasslands/index.aspx
Other contact information: TTY: 1-866-787-6221
Grasslands is the first national park of Canada to preserve a section of the mixed prairie grasslands. Visitor activities include guided hikes, interpretive trails, bird watching, & nature photography. Hours of Operation: Parklands are open year round; Visitor Reception Centre is open daily from mid-May - Labour Day, 8:00-5:00, & from Sept-May, the Centre is open M-F, 8:00-4:30.

Waskesiu Lake: **Prince Albert National Park of Canada**
c/o Northern Prairies Field Unit, PO Box 100, Waskesiu Lake, SK S0J 2Y0
Tel: 306-663-4522
panp.info@pc.gc.ca
www.pc.gc.ca/eng/pn-np/sk/princealbert/index.aspx
Prince Albert National Park protects a portion of the boreal forest, & serves as a transition zone between the parkland & the northern forest. The park features the only protected white pelican nesting colony in Canada, the lakeside cabin of conservationist Grey Owl, & a free-ranging herd of plains bison. Special events & interpretive programs are also offered. Visitor services are provided in the townsite of Waskesiu, located in the park. Hours of Operation: Parklands are open year-round; Information Centre open daily 8:00-8:00 from mid-May - early Sept., & on weekends during peak cross country ski season.

Yukon Territory

Local National Parks & Outdoor Education Centres in Yukon Territory

Haines Junction: **Kluane National Park & Reserve of Canada**
PO Box 5495, Haines Junction, YT Y0B 1L0
Tel: 867-634-7250; Fax: 867-634-7208
kluane.info@pc.gc.ca
www.pc.gc.ca/pn-np/yt/kluane/index_E.asp
twitter. com/ParksCanYukon
Other contact information: Visitor Information Phone: 867-634-7207
Kluane National Park & Reserve of Canada covers an area of 21,980 km2, & features mountains (including Mount Logan, Canada's highest peak at 5,959 m/19,545 ft.), icefields, & valleys that are home to a variety of plant & wildlife species. Hours of Operation: Visitor Centre, mid-May-mid Sept, daily 9:00-5:00.

Old Crow: **Vuntut National Park of Canada**
PO Box 19, Old Crow, YT Y0B 1N0
Tel: 867-667-3910; Fax: 867-393-6701
vuntut.info@pc.gc.ca
www.pc.gc.ca/eng/pn-np/yt/vuntut/index.aspx
twitt er.com/ParksCanYukon
Year Founded: 1995 Vuntut National Park was established after negotiations through the Vuntut Gwitchin First Nation's Final Land Claims Agreement, between the Vuntut Gwitchin of Old Crow & the Government of Canada & the Yukon. The park encompasses 4,345. sq. km of land in the northwestern corner of the Yukon Territory. Hours of Operation: Park is open year round, with no services available.
Anne Morin, Field Unit Superintendent, Yukon Field Unit, Parks Canada
Robert Lewis, Superintendent, Vuntut National Park of Canada

Observatories

Alberta

Local Observatories in Alberta

Calgary: **Rothney Astrophysical Observatory (RAO)**
Physics & Astronomy Dept., University of Calgary, Calgary, AB T2N 1N4
Tel: 403-931-2366
rao@phas.ucalgary.ca
www.ucalgary.ca/rao
Other contact information: Open House Info: 403-220-7977; 403220-5385
The RAO is the University of Calgary's astronomical facility which is home to the following telescopes: the 0.4-m Clarke-Milone Telescope (which is controlable via the internet), the 0.5-m Baker Nunn Telescope (used to search for asteroids), & the 1.8-m A.R. Cross Telescope (one of the 3 largest in Canada). The RAO also has an Interpretive Centre which is open for drop-in visits M, Tu, & W 12:00-4:00.
Dr. Phil Langill, Director, pplangil@ucalgary.ca

Edmonton: **University of Alberta Observatory**
Dept. of Physics, University of Alberta, Edmonton, AB T6G 2J1
Tel: 780-492-5410; Fax: 780-492-0714
stars@ualberta.ca
www.ualberta.ca/~stars
twitter.com/UofAObservatory
www.facebook.com/UofAObservatory
Consists of a 0.5m-diameter telescope equipped with a prime focus CCD camera; research programs are directed toward stellar photometry & the detection of faint, extended sources such as HII regions & supernova remnants; Campus Observatory has permanently mounted 12 & 14 inch telescopes & an exhibit area; facility used for undergraduate instruction & public observing during academic year; admission is free.
Dr. Sharon Morsink, Associate Professor, Astrophysics, morsink@ualberta.ca

British Columbia

Local Observatories in British Columbia

Kamuela: **Canada-France-Hawaii Telescope**
c/o CFHT Corporation, 65-1238 Mamalahoa Hwy., Kamuela, HI 96743 USA
Tel: 808-885-7944; Fax: 808-885-7288
info@cfht.hawaii.edu
www.cfht.hawaii.edu
Other contact information: FTP: ftp.cfht.hawaii.edu
The CFH observatory hosts a world-class, 3.6 meter optical/infrared telescope. The observatory is located atop the summit of Mauna Kea, a 4,200 meter, dormant volcano located on the island of Hawaii. By appointment only.
Dr. Gregory G. Fahlman, Chair, greg.fahlmannrc@cnrc.gc.ca
Doug Simons, Executive Director, simons@cfht.hawaii.edu

Vancouver: **Gordon MacMillan Southam Observatory (GSO)**
Parent: **H.R. MacMillan Space Centre**
1100 Chestnut St., Vancouver, BC V6J 3J9
Tel: 604-738-2855; Fax: 604-736-5665
info@spacecentre.ca
www.spacecentre.ca/gms
Part of the H.R. MacMillan Space Centre.
Rob Appleton, Executive Director

Victoria: **Centre of the Universe Astronomy Interpretive Centre / Centre de l'Univers - Centre d'interprétation en astronomie**
5071 West Saanich Rd., Victoria, BC V9E 2E7
Tel: 250-363-8262; Fax: 250-363-8290
cu@nrc-cnrc.gc.ca
www.nrc-cnrc.gc.ca/eng/outreach/cu/index.html
The Centre offers telescope tours, planetarium presentations, & a multimedia theatre. Public observations are held in the summer. Open year-round.
Dr. Ken Tapping, Group Leader/Research Council Officer Ph.D., 250-497-2345, Fax: 250-497-2355

Victoria: **Climenhaga Observatory**
Dept. of Physics & Astronomy, University of Victoria, PO Box 3055, 3800 Finnerty Rd., Victoria, BC V8W 3P6
Tel: 250-721-7750; Fax: 250-721-7715
office@phys.uvic.ca
www.astro.uvic.ca
Russell Robb, Contact, robb@uvic.ca

Manitoba

Local Observatories in Manitoba

Winnipeg: **The Lockhart Planetarium**
Dept. of Physics & Astronomy, University of Manitoba, 394 University College, #380, 500 Dysart Rd., Winnipeg, MB R3T 2M8
Tel: 204-474-9785
physics@umanitoba.ca
www.umanitoba.ca/faculties/science/astronomy/lockhart/lockhart.html
Year Founded: 1964 Planetarium theatre; display area; astronomy reference library

Winnipeg: **Manitoba Planetarium**
Parent: **The Manitoba Museum**
190 Rupert Ave., Winnipeg, MB R3B 0N2
Tel: 204-956-2830; Fax: 204-942-3679
info@manitobamuseum.ca
www.manitobamuseum.ca/main/planetarium-intro
A 287 seat space theatre equipped with Zeiss MkV star projector, which is capable of reproducing the night sky as seen from any location on Earth; complimented with advanced video project & multmedia projectors; shows & programs change throughout the year
Mike Jensen, Supervisor, Science Gallery & Planetarium Programs, 204-988-0613

Nova Scotia

Local Observatories in Nova Scotia

Halifax: **Burke-Gaffney Observatory (BGO)**
Loyola Bldg., Saint Mary's University, 923 Robie St., Halifax, NS B3H 3C3
Tel: 902-420-5633; Fax: 902-420-5141
www.smu.ca/academic/science/ap/bgo.html
Other contact information: Info Line: 902-496-8257
40 cm reflecting telescope; public tours held on the 1st & 3rd Sat. of each month at 7 pm (Nov.-Mar.) or 9 pm (Apr.-Oct.), weather permitting; Mon. evenings or daytime groups by arrangement
David J. Lane, Director, dlane@ap.smu.ca

Ontario

Local Observatories in Ontario

Hamilton: **W.J. McCallion Planetarium**
Dept. of Physics & Astronomy, McMaster University, 1280 Main St. West, Hamilton, ON L8S 4M1
Tel: 905-525-9140; Fax: 905-546-1252
planetarium@physics.mcmaster.ca
www.physics.mcmaster.ca/planetarium/

London: **Hume Cronyn Memorial Observatory**
Also known as: **Cronyn Observatory**
c/o Physics & Astronomy Bldg., University of Western Ontario, 1151 Richmond St., London, ON N6A 3K7
Tel: 519-661-3283; Fax: 519-661-2033
astrooutreach@uwo.ca; physoutreach@uwo.ca
www.physics.uwo.ca/outreach/cronyn_observatory.html
Built in 1939, observatory houses a 25 cm refactor currently used for teaching & visitor programs
David F. Gray, Observatory Director, dfgray@uwo.ca

London: **University of Western Ontario Astronomical Observatory**
Also known as: **Elginfield Observatory**
Dept. of Physics & Astronomy, University of Western Ontario, 1151 Richmond St., London, ON N6A 3K7
Tel: 519-661-3283; Fax: 519-661-2033
p-a.info@uwo.ca
www.astro.uwo.ca
Dr. Jan Cami, Observatory Coordinator, jcami@uwo.ca

Richmond Hill: **David Dunlap Observatory (DDO)**
Parent: **Metrus Development Inc.**
Observatory Hill, 123 Hillsview Dr., Richmond Hill, ON L4C 1T3
Tel: 905-884-9562
info@astro.utoronto.ca
www.theddo.ca; www.observatoryhill.ca
Year Founded: 1935 The observatory was sold to Metrus Development in 2008, & is now part of the Observatory Hill site.

Public programs are scheduled throughout the summer, & Viewing Nights are held most Saturday nights for the public to drop in & use the facilities.
Paul Mortfield, Chair, paul@theddo.ca

***Sudbury:* Doran Planetarium**
Fraser Bldg., Laurentian University, 935 Ramsey Lake Rd., Sudbury, ON P3E 2C6
Tel: 705-675-1151; *Fax:* 705-675-4868
plegault@laurentian.ca
www.laurentian.ca/Laurentian/Home/Departments/Physics/Planetarium
Astronomical presentation, show & lecture in both French & English
Paul-Émile Legault, Director, plegault@laurentian.ca

Quebec

Local Observatories in Quebec

***Notre-Dame-des-Bois:* Astrolab du Parc National du Mont Mégantic**
189, rte du Parc, Notre-Dame-des-Bois, QC J0B 2E0
Tél: 819-888-2941; *Téléc:* 819-888-2943
Ligne sans frais: 800-665-6527
astrolab-parc-national-mont-megantic.org

Saskatchewan

Local Observatories in Saskatchewan

***Saskatoon:* University of Saskatchewan Observatory**
Dept. of Physics & Engineering Physics, University of Saskatchewan, 116 Science Pl., Saskatoon, SK S7N 5E2
Tel: 306-966-6429; *Fax:* 306-966-6400
artsandscience.usask.ca/physics/observatory
Open every Saturday evening after dark for public viewing through the telescope; admission is free

Performing Arts - Dance

International

The Royal Scottish Country Dance Society (RSCDS)
12 Coates Cres., Edinburgh EH3 7AF United Kingdom
info@rscds.org
www.rscds.org
To preserve & further the practice of traditional Scottish Country Dancing; to provide or assist in providing special education or instruction in the practice of Scottish Country Dances
Elspeth Gray, Secretary

Alberta

Alberta Ballet
Nat Christie Centre, 141 - 18 Ave. SW, Calgary AB T2S 0B8
Tel: 403-245-4222
schoolinfo@albertaballet.com
www.albertaballet.com
To enrich & bring beauty to people's lives through creating, performing & teaching ballet
Peter Dala, Music Director
Jean Grand-Maître, Artistic Director
Martin Bragg, Executive Director

Alberta Dance Alliance (ADA)
Percy Page Centre, 11759 Groat Rd., 2nd Fl., Edmonton AB T5M 3K6
Tel: 780-422-8107; *Fax:* 780-422-2663
Toll-Free: 888-422-8107
info@abdancealliance.ab.ca
www.abdancealliance.ab.ca
To foster & promote the appreciation & practice of dance in Alberta, through administrative, technical, & informative services, programs, advocacy, & special events
Bobbi Westman, Executive Director

Brian Webb Dance Co.
PO Box 53092, Edmonton AB T5N 48A
Tel: 780-452-3282; *Fax:* 780-497-4330
webbcdf@shaw.ca
www.bwdc.ca
The Brian Webb Dance Company is a producer and presenter of contemporary dance. The BWDC is a community-minded, dynamic, artistic builder: a team builder; we build our work through collaboration - the democratic exchange of ideas to create something new.
Brian Webb, Artistic Director

Catalyst Theatre Society of Alberta
8529 Gateway Blvd., Edmonton AB T6E 6P3
Tel: 780-431-1750; *Fax:* 780-433-3060
info@catalysttheatre.ca
www.catalysttheatre.ca
To create & present original Canadian work that explores new possibilities for theatre
Jonathan Christenson, Artistic Director

Decidedly Jazz Danceworks
1514 - 4th St. SW, Calgary AB T2R 0Y4
Tel: 403-245-3533; *Fax:* 403-245-3584
djd@decidedlyjazz.com
www.decidedlyjazz.com
Creates concert jazz dance that sustains the spirit and traditions of jazz. Mixes groove, African roots, rhythm, improvisation, interplay with musicians, and deeply human soul, has distinguished DJD on the international jazz dance stage. Offers a season of performances, touring, and jazz classes.
Vicki Adams Willis, Artistic Director
Kathi Sundstrom, General Manager

Springboard Dance
205 - 8th Ave. SE, 2nd Fl., Calgary AB T2G 0K9
Tel: 403-265-3230; *Fax:* 403-294-7457
www.springboardperformance.com
To produce, create & perform intellectually & sensually stimulating modern dance
Trina Rasmuson
Shelly Tegnazzini
Nicole Mion

Sun Ergos, A Company of Theatre & Dance
130 Sunset Way, Priddis AB T0L 1W0
Tel: 403-931-1527; *Fax:* 403-931-1534
Toll-Free: 800-743-3351
waltermoke@sunergos.com
www.sunergos.com
Social Media: www.youtube.com/user/sunergostheatre; www.flickr.com/photos/sunergos
To witness, maintain & develop the ethnocultural roots of theatre & dance, without prejudice of race, creed, sex, or cultural background, to celebrate the differences & recognize the similarities among all peoples; to provide the best possible theatre & dance within the urban & rural communities, nationally & internationally
Robert Greenwood, Artistic & Managing Director
Dana Luebke, Artistic & Production Director

Vinok Worldance
PO Box 4867, Edmonton AB T6E 5G7
Tel: 780-454-3739; *Fax:* 780-454-3436
vinok@vinok.ca
www.vinok.ca
To present music & dances of the world to audiences all across Canada; to reflect world dance as a way of celebrating life, involving dance, music, song, improvisation & the expression of a people
Doyle Marko, Artistic Director
Leanne Koziak, Executive Director

British Columbia

Ballet British Columbia
677 Davie St., 6th Fl., Vancouver BC V6G 2B6
Tel: 604-732-5003; *Fax:* 604-732-4417
info@balletbc.com
www.balletbc.com
To commission & perform a balanced repertoire rooted in classical technique, which encompasses the best new ballets & late 20th century classics
Emily Molnar, Interim Artistic Director

Dance Centre
Scotiabank Dance Centre, 677 Davie St., Level 6, Vancouver BC V6B 2G6
Tel: 604-606-6400; *Fax:* 604-606-6401
info@thedancecentre.ca
www.thedancecentre.ca
To raise the profile of dance in BC; to serve as a focal point & advocate for issues & concerns affecting the entire dance community; to coordinate the resources & activities of this wide ranging community
Heather Bray, Marketing Manager
Mirna Zagar, Executive Director

DanceArts Vancouver
Scotiabank Dance Centre, 677 Davie St., 7th Fl., Vancouver BC V6B 2G6
Tel: 604-606-6425; *Fax:* 604-606-6432
info@dancearts.bc.ca
To increase the exposure of performing arts through the presentation of interdisciplinary performances & workshops; to present contemporary dance work & interdisciplinary dance/theatre/music performances of the highest quality; to act as a catalyst & animator for dance & associated arts in the community & to offer infrastructure & presentation support of that activity
Judith Marcuse, Artistic Director

EDAM Performing Arts Society (EDAM)
303 - 8th Ave. East, Vancouver BC V5T 1S1
Tel: 604-876-9559; *Fax:* 604-876-9525
info@edamdance.org
www.edamdance.org
To explore new directions in dance & the performing arts
Peter Bingham, Artistic Director
Mona Hamill, Administrative Director

Goh Ballet Society
2345 Main St., Vancouver BC V5T 3C9
Tel: 604-872-4014; *Fax:* 604-872-4011
admin@gohballet.com
www.gohballet.com
The Goh Ballet Academy was established in 1978 with the mission to prepare aspiring dancers for professional careers by providing rigorous training in the vocabulary and artistry of classical ballet.
Fei Wong, President
Chan Hon Goh, Artistic Director

Kinesis Dance Society
Scotia Bank Dance Centre, Level 7, 677 Davie St., Vancouver BC V6B 2G6
Tel: 604-684-7844; *Fax:* 604-684-7834
info@kinesisdance.org
www.kinesisdance.org
To contribute new & provocative works of contemporary dance to the local, national & international dance scene; to educate through workshops & cultural exchanges & to collaborate with other media, such as film, video & theatre
Paras Terezakis, Artistic Director

Lola Dance
#104, 336 - 1st Ave. East, Vancouver BC V5T 4R6
Tel: 604-683-6552; *Fax:* 604-681-1431
info@loladance.org
www.loladance.org
To create an inspired creative dance environment for choreography & performance; Participating in educational initiatives, by offering instruction in dance, youth outreach programming, residencies, teaching while on tour, choreographic workshops, & special youth presentations; To enhance the growth of the arts community & the cultural heritage of Vancouver, British Columbia & Canada
Lola MacLaughlin, Artistic Director & Founder

Mascall Dance
1130 Jervis St., Vancouver BC V6E 2C7
Tel: 604-689-9339; *Fax:* 604-689-9399
admin@mascalldance.ca
www.mascalldance.ca
To provide a forum for research, creation, performance, education, documentation & dissemination of contemporary dance & related disciplines
Jennifer Mascall, Artistic Director

Vancouver Moving Theatre (VMT)
PO Box 88270, Stn. Chinatown, Vancouver BC V6A 4A4
Tel: 604-628-5672
savannahandterry@axion.net
www.vancouvermovingtheatre.com
To develop a new form of interdisciplinary art influenced by the Pacific Rim culture of Vancouver; to present services & products to affirm the importance of art in questions of healing, humanity & the soul
Savannah Walling, Artistic Director
Terry Hunter, Executive Director

Manitoba

Canadian Square & Round Dance Society (CSRDS)
115 Holly Dr., Oakbank MB R0E 1J2
Tel: 204-444-3115; *Fax:* 204-444-5768
Toll-Free: 866-206-6696
info@squaredance.ca
www.csrds.ca
To link information about Canadian square & round dancing associations together in order to promote awareness, inspire activity, & to offer information
Lorraine Kozera, Secretary
John Kozera, Secretary
Bob Ruohoniemi, President

Dance Manitoba Inc.
Pantages Playhouse Theatre, #204, 180 Market Ave. East, Winnipeg MB R3B 0P7
Tel: 204-989-5260; *Fax:* 204-989-5268
info@dancemanitoba.org
www.dancemanitoba.org
To promote the development of dance through festivals, workshops, & showcases
Nicole Langevin-Owens, Executive Director

Royal Winnipeg Ballet (RWB)
380 Graham Ave., Winnipeg MB R3C 4K2
Tel: 204-956-0183; *Fax:* 204-943-1994
Toll-Free: 800-667-4792
ballet@rwb.org
www.rwb.org
To enrich the human experience by teaching, creating & performing outstanding dance
Arlene Minkhorst, School Director
Charlene Rocke, Chair
André Lewis, Artistic Director

Ruth Cansfield Dance
806 Osborne St., Winnipeg MB R3L 2C7
Tel: 204-284-5810; *Fax:* 204-284-1131
Toll-Free: 866-405-5810
info@ruthcansfield.com
To create & perform the choreography of Ruth Cansfield; to use our collective talent & energy to create an educational experience that will benefit the community as a whole, dancers & non-dancers alike; to pursue tours that will enable the company to carry our dance message to provincial, national, & international dance audiences
Ken Manson, Vice-President
Jon McPhail, Administration Director
Ruth Cansfield, Artistic Director
Ellie Cansfield, President

Winnipeg's Contemporary Dancers
#204, 211 Bannatyne Ave., Winnipeg MB R3B 3P2
Tel: 204-452-0229; *Fax:* 204-287-8618
info@winnipegscontemporarydancers.ca
www.winnipegscontemporarydancers.ca
Winnipeg 's Contemporary Dancers' goal is to create a place on the local, national and international arts landscape that enables vital intersections, linkages and exchange among dance creators, dance interpreters, spectators and communities. Our values, programs, and activities are based on respect for our history, the ongoing development of our artists, and to our place in the community.
Brian Lott, Artistic Director

New Brunswick

Les Productions DansEncorps Inc.
#12A, 140, rue Botsford, Moncton NB E1C 4X5
Tél: 506-855-0998; *Téléc:* 506-852-3401
dencorps@nb.aibn.com
www.dansencorps.ca
Création, production, formation et diffusion de spectacles de danse; contribution au développement des arts au Nouveau-Brunswick
Chantal Cadieux, Directrice artistique

Nova Scotia

Dance Nova Scotia
1113 Marginal Rd., Halifax NS B3H 4P7
Tel: 902-422-1749; *Fax:* 902-422-0881
office@dancens.ca
www.dancens.ca
To promote, stimulate & encourage the development of dance as a cultural, educational & social activity
Dianne Milligan, Executive Director

Two Planks & a Passion Theatre Association (TP&aP)
PO Box 190, 555 Ross Creek Rd., Canning NS B0P 1H0
Tel: 902-582-3073; *Fax:* 902-582-7943
mail@twoplanks.ca
www.twoplanks.ca; www.twoplanksandpassion.blogspot.com
To develop & present high quality, professional theatre both regionally & nationally which reflects Canadian life, with strong roles for women; to develop & build an artistic centre in Canning, NS, accessible to both the local community & to artists of all disciplines & residencies
Ken Schwartz, Artistic Director

Ontario

Ballet Creole
375 Dovercourt Rd., Toronto ON M6J 3E5
Tel: 416-960-0350; *Fax:* 416-960-2067
info@balletcreole.org
www.balletcreole.org
Preserves and perpetuates traditional and contemporary African culture and increases awareness of the rich African culture that exists in Canada. Establishes a dynamic new Canadian artistic tradition based on a fusion of diverse dance and music traditions. Promotes multicultural understanding through education and quality entertainment to national and international audiences.
Patrick Parson, Artistic Director

Ballet Jörgen
c/o George Brown College, Casa Loma Campus, Room 126, Building C, 160 Kendal Ave., Toronto ON M5R 1M3
Tel: 416-961-4725; *Fax:* 416-415-2865
info@balletjorgen.ca
www.balletjorgen.ca
To operate exclusively as a charitable organization to administer & employ its property, assets & rights for the purpose of raising the public's awareness of ballet as an art form by establishing, maintaining & operating a ballet company; to advance knowledge & increase public recognition of ballet by developing a repertoire of original dance productions for performance, film & video for the benefit of the community at large; to advance artistic appreciation & education of the general public of choreography as a distinctive art form by commissioning & making available to the public presentations by a variety of choreographers
Bengt Jörgen, Artistic Director & CEO

Canada Dance Festival Society
PO Box 1376, Stn. B, 53 Elgin St., Ottawa ON K1P 5R4
Tel: 613-947-7000; *Fax:* 613-943-1399
cdffdc@nac-cna.ca
www.canadadance.ca
To hold a festival of dance every two years
Brian H. Webb, Artistic Director
Pamela Fralick, Chair

Canadian Children's Dance Theatre (CCDT)
509 Parliament St., Toronto ON M4X 1P3
Tel: 416-924-5657; *Fax:* 416-924-4141
info@ccdt.org
www.ccdt.org
The Canadian Children's Dance Theatre is a modern dance repertory company of 13 to 19-year old dancers based in Toronto, Canada. Founded in 1980 by Deborah Lundmark and Michael deConinck Smith to present gifted young artists in professional productions, the Company has staged more than one thousand performances from Barrie to Beijing.
Elizabeth Varty, Marketing, Development & Arts Education
Deborah Lundmark, Artistic Director & Resident Choreographer
Michael de Coninck Smith, Co-Artistic Director & Production Manager

Canadian Dance Teachers Association (CDTA) / Association canadienne des professeurs de danse
c/o President, 178 Barrick Rd., Port Colbourne ON L3K 4B4
Tel: 905-834-0077
donna.moreau@sympatico.ca
www.cdtanational.ca
To advance education in the field of dance & maintain throughout Canada an organization of qualified dance teachers; to promote friendship & the exchange of ideas & information among the dance teachers of Canada, to provide an organization to represent Canadian dance teachers internationally
Donna Moreau, President

Dance Ontario Association / Association Ontario Danse
Case Goods Bldg. 74, The Distillery District, #304, 55 Mill St., Toronto ON M5A 3C4
Tel: 416-204-1083; *Fax:* 416-204-1085
contact@danceontario.ca
www.danceontario.ca
To support the advancement of all forms of dance; To offer a unified voice on dance issues
Catherine Carpenko, Chair
Samara Thompson, Vice-Chair
Rosslyn Jacob Edwards, Executive Director
Jennifer Watkins, Secretary
Allison Cummings, Treasurer

Dance Oremus Danse (DOD)
240 Dovercourt Rd., Toronto ON M6J 3E1
Tel: 416-536-9002; *Fax:* 416-536-9002
pauljamesdwyer@yahoo.ca
www.danceoremusdanse.org
To increase the public's appreciation of the aesthetic arts by promoting & encouraging the philosophy, movement practices & dance forms of Isadora Duncan (1877-1927) & European neo-classical dance, via seminars, workshops, courses on dance, performance, publishing & other media
Paul James Dwyer, Founder/Artistic Director

Dance Umbrella of Ontario (DUO)
#201, 490 Adelaide St. West, Toronto ON M5V 1T2
Tel: 416-504-6429; *Fax:* 416-504-8702
Toll-Free: 800-919-5019
duo@danceumbrella.net
www.danceumbrella.net
To assist & support professional dance creators in Ontario dance centres
Christine Moynihan, Executive Director

Dancemakers
The Case Goods Warehouse, Bldg. #74, #306, 55 Mill St., Toronto ON M5A 3C4
Tel: 416-367-1800; *Fax:* 416-367-1870
info@dancemakers.org
www.dancemakers.org
To bring dance of challenging physicality & emotional impact to audiences by drawing on the diverse talents & individual strengths of its artists; to develop & support works which both provoke & entertain
Michael Trent, Artistic Director
Bradley Kulay, Administrative Manager

Dancer Transition Resource Centre (DTRC) / Centre de ressources et transition pour danseurs (CRTD)
The Lynda Hamilton Centre, #500, 250 The Esplanade, Toronto ON M5A 1J2
Tel: 416-595-5655; *Fax:* 416-595-0009
Toll-Free: 800-667-0851
nationaloffice@dtrc.ca
www.dtrc.ca
The Centre helps dancers make necessary transitions into, within & from professional performing, as well as operating a resource centre for the dance community & the public, offering seminars, education materials & information. It is a registered charity, BN: 101258077RR0001.
Amanda Hancox, Executive Director
Garry Neil, Chair

Danny Grossman Dance Company
#202, 157 Carlton St., Toronto ON M5A 2K3
Tel: 416-408-4543; *Fax:* 416-408-2518
info@dannygrossman.com
www.dannygrossman.com
To strive to build a dance legacy in Canada by preserving important dance works & undertaking residencies & workshops to educate & inspire the next generation of dancers & dance audiences
Helen Chapman, Managing Director
Danny Grossman, Artistic Director

Fringe Festival of Independent Dance Artists (FFIDA)
Toronto ON
Tel: 416-214-5854
info@ffida.org
Michael Menegon, Artistic Director

Fujiwara Dance Inventions
#201, 490 Adelaide St. West, Toronto ON M5V 1T2
Tel: 416-593-4710; *Fax:* 416-504-8702
info@fujiwaradance.com
www.fujiwaradance.com
To dance into insight, through the creation, performance, & teaching of dance; To encounter & express the mysteries of human nature as they are manifest in the body, before words
Denise Fujiwara, Artistic Director

Gina Lori Riley Dance Enterprises
401 Sunset Ave., Windsor ON N9B 3P4
Tel: 519-253-3000
riley2@uwindsor.ca
www.ginaloririleydanceenterprises.com
To advance the art of dance through the development of new work, performance & through community education in an exemplary manner as a contemporary modern professional Canadian dance company
Gina Lori Riley, Artistic Director

Le Groupe Dance Lab / Le Groupe lab de danse
#2, 2 Daly St., Ottawa ON K1N 6E2
Tel: 613-235-1492; *Fax:* 613-235-1651
info@legroupe.org
www.legroupe.org
To nurture artists & audiences, while proving a haven where choreographers can make challenging choices & venture down new roads in their working methods; to devote full-time resources to choreographers who immerse themselves in the creative process
Tony Chong, Associate Artistic Director
Peter Boneham, Artistic Director
Anthony Pan, General Manager

National Ballet of Canada
Walter Carsen Centre, 470 Queens Quay West, Toronto ON M5V 3K4
Tel: 416-345-9686; *Fax:* 416-345-8323
info@national.ballet.ca
www.national.ballet.ca
The National Ballet of Canada, a company with more than 60 dancers & its own full symphony orchestra, & ranking as one of the world's top international dance organizations, is Canada's premiere dance company. The Four Seasons Centre for the Performing Arts is the performance venue while the company is in Toronto.
Karen Kain, Artistic Director
Kevin Garland, Executive Director
David Briskin, Music Director/Principal Conductor

Ontario Ballet Theatre
1133 St. Clair Ave. West, Toronto ON M6E 1B1
Tel: 416-656-9568; *Fax:* 416-651-4803
tara@ontarioballettheatre.com
www.ontarioballettheatre.com
To nurture & develop an appreciation of contemporary & classical ballet by reaching new audiences through artistic excellence

Ontario Folk Dance Association (OFDA)
35 Touraine Ave., Toronto ON M3H 1R3
ontariofolkdancers@gmail.com
www.ofda.ca
To promote the practice of international folk arts & dance; to prepare, collect & disseminate information & material relating to folk arts & dance
Kevin Budd, Vice-President
Beverly Sidney, President

Opéra Atelier (OA)
St. Lawrence Hall, 157 King St. East, 4th Fl., Toronto ON M5C 1G9
Tel: 416-703-3767; *Fax:* 416-703-4895
opera.atelier@operaatelier.com
www.operaatelier.com
To produce opera, ballet, & drama from the 17th & 18th centuries
Jane Hargraft, General Manager

Royal Academy of Dance / Canada
#500, 1200 Sheppard Ave. East, Toronto ON M2K 2S5
Tel: 416-489-2813; *Fax:* 416-489-3222
Toll-Free: 888-709-0895
info@radcanada.org
www.radcanada.org
To provide dance education & training
Jan Garvey, National Administrator

Toronto & District Square & Round Dance Association
8 Seven Oaks Circle, St Catharines ON L2P 3N6
Tel: 905-641-1872
www3.sympatico.ca/jerry.callen/td/
To promote, encourage & foster wider knowledge of square & round dancing; to provide for mutual exchange of philosophy & material pertaining to square & round dancing between callers, teachers, & leaders; to improve quality of square & round dancing; to encourage use of standards of uniformity relating to square & round dancing
Sharron Hall, Secretary

Toronto Dance Theatre (TDT)
80 Winchester St., Toronto ON M4X 1B2
Tel: 416-967-1365; *Fax:* 416-963-4379
info@tdt.org
www.tdt.org
To develop Canadian dance works of art; to perform nationally & internationally; to explore new ideas in choreographic expression while embracing the fresh & vital aspects of inherited traditions
Jay Rankin, Managing Director
Christopher House, Artistic Director

Québec

Ballet Ouest / Ballet West
#218, 269 boul. St. Jean, Pointe-Claire QC H9R 3J1
Tel: 514-783-1245; *Fax:* 514-939-1469
centredanse@balletouest.com
www.balletouest.com
To provide a milieu that encourages young dancers to express themselves through dance & to move from amateur to professional status; educate & develop audiences; present an alternative view to counteract the mass culture that is being fed to our youth
Susan Altschul, Company Manager
Marie St-Amour, President
Margaret Mehuys, Artistic Director

BJM DANSE (BJM)
1210, rue Sherbrooke est, Montréal QC H2L 1L9
Tél: 514-982-6771; *Téléc:* 514-982-9145
info@bjmdanse.ca
www.bjmdanse.ca
Crée, produit et diffuse à l'échelle nationale et internationale des spectacles de danse contemporaine; offre à ses danseurs un entraînement professionnel; permet aux chorégraphes invités et aux danseurs de développer leur propre recherche; génère un répertoire exclusif et conserve l'esprit novateur qui anime la compagnie de puis sa création
Louis Robitaille, Directeur artistique
Bernard Lagacé, Directeur général

Le Carré des Lombes
#401, 2022, rue Sherbrooke Est, Montréal QC H2K 1B9
Tél: 514-287-9339; *Téléc:* 514-287-9415
info@lecarredeslombes.com
www.lecarredeslombes.com
Diffuser des spectacles de danse; promouvoir la danse comme discipline artistique
Suzanne Beaucaire, Coordonatrice Générale

Cercle d'expression artistique Nyata Nyata
4374, boul St-Laurent, 3e étage, Montréal QC H2W 1Z5
Tél: 514-849-9781; *Téléc:* 514-849-7199
info@nyata-nyata.org
www.nyata-nyata.org
Compagnie Danse Nyata Nyata is an enterprise of contemporary artistic expression, which defines its activities in the field of African dance, with the specific objective to explore and develop the particular aesthetics of this art form as it relates to music, poetry, mythology, ritual and the related arts, bringing forth essential aspects which link the ancestral with the contemporary. This process includes choreographic creation, dance performance, musical composition, writings, conferences, the teaching and promotion thereof in a local, national and international context.
Zab Maboungou, Directrice artistique

Compagnie de danse Migrations
880, av Pére-Marquette, Québec QC G1S 2A4
Tél: 418-684-3132; *Téléc:* 418-684-3134
migrations@qc.aira.com
www.migrationsdanse.com
Création, formation, production et diffusion de la danse et musique traditionnelle québécoise et des cultures du monde
Richard Turcotte, Directeur artistique
Blandin Garnier, Adjointe administrative

Compagnie Marie Chouinard
#715, 3981, boul St-Laurent, Montréal QC H2W 1Y5
Tél: 514-843-9036; *Téléc:* 514-843-7616
info@mariechouinard.com
www.mariechouinard.com
To be dedicated to modern & unique interpretations of dance, new artistic choreography, & expression through the movements of the human body
Marie Chouinard, Directrice artistique
Pierre Des Marais, Directeur général

Danse-Cite inc
#426, 3680, rue Jeanne-Mance, Montréal QC H2X 2K5
Tél: 514-525-3595; *Téléc:* 514-525-3536
info@danse-cite.org
www.danse-cite.org
Création et production de spectacles de danse contemporain
Daniel Soulières, Directeur artistique

Fédération des loisirs-danse du Québec
CP 1000, Succ. M, 4545, av Pierre-de Coubertin, Montréal QC H1V 3R2
Tél: 514-252-3029; *Téléc:* 514-251-8038

Fortier Danse-Création
Succ. C, #301, 2022, rue Sherbrooke Est, Montréal QC H2K 1B9
Tél: 514-529-8158; *Téléc:* 514-529-1222
admin@fortier-danse.com
www.fortier-danse.com
Création et diffusion des oeuvres du chorégraphe Paul-André Fortier
Paul-André Fortier, Directeur artistique
Gilles Savary, Directeur général

Les Grands Ballets Canadiens de Montréal (GBCM)
Maison de la Danse, 4816, rue Rivard, Montréal QC H2J 2N6
Tél: 514-849-8681; *Téléc:* 514-849-0098
info@grandsballets.com
www.grandsballets.com
Maintenir la tradition du ballet classique et élargir le champ d'expression de cette forme artistique par la création; faire connaître et apprécier la danse à tous les publics grâce à la qualité de nos presentations et de nos productions
Alain Dancyger, Directeur général
Gradimir Pankov, Directeur artistique

La La La Human Steps
#206, 5655, av du Parc, Montréal QC H2V 4H2
Tél: 514-277-9090; *Téléc:* 514-277-0862
info@lalalahumansteps.com
www.lalalahumansteps.com
Présenter les spectacles crées par Édouard Lock sur les plus grandes scènes du monde; compagnie de danse contemporaine
Édouard Lock, Directeur artistique

Louise Bédard Danse
#300, 2022, rue Sherbrooke Est, Montréal QC H2K 1B9
Tél: 514-982-4580; *Téléc:* 514-982-0613
infos@lbdanse.org
www.lbdanse.org
Louise bédard danse is a non-profit organization founded in 1990 with the aim of pursuing modern dance creation, awareness and education activities, and offering original choreographic creations to the general public.
Louise Bédard, Directrice artistique

Lucie Grégoire Danse
#405,1030, rue Cherrier, Montréal QC H2L 1H9
Tél: 514-524-7665; *Téléc:* 514-524-7584
luciegregoire3@sympatico.ca
www.luciegregoire.ca
Lucie Grégoire, Directrice artistique

Margie Gillis Dance Foundation / Fondation de danse Margie Gillis
3519, rue St-Urbain, Montréal QC H2X 2N6
Tel: 514-845-3115; *Fax:* 514-845-4526
info@margiegillis.org
www.margiegillis.org
The objective of the Margie Gillis Dance Foundation is to reach as large a public as possible with a dance program of physical and emotional integrity, directed at making the audience aware of the potential and magic of their own lives.
Margie Gillis, Artistic Director
Manon Laflamme, Administrative Director

Montréal Danse
#109, 372, rue Sainte-Catherine ouest, Montréal QC H3B 1A2
Tél: 514-871-4005; *Téléc:* 514-871-4007
info@montrealdanse.com
www.montrealdanse.com
Se voue à la création de vibrantes oeuvres chorégraphiques avec le concours de plusieurs chorégraphes nationaux et internationaux
Kathy Casey, Directrice artistique

O Vertigo Danse
175, rue Sainte-Catherine ouest, Montréal QC H2X 1Z8
Tél: 514-251-9177; *Téléc:* 514-251-7358
info@overtigo.com
www.overtigo.com
Se consacre à la création en nouvelle danse et la diffusion des oeuvres de la fondatrice et directrice artistique de la compagnie
Diane Boucher, Directrice générale
Ginette Laurin, Directrice générale

Regroupement québécois de la danse (RQD)
#440, 3680 rue Jeanne-Mance, Montréal QC H2X 2K5
Tél: 514-849-4003; *Téléc:* 514-849-3288
info@quebecdanse.org
www.quebecdanse.org
Promouvoir, encourager et soutenir le développement artistique, social et économique des danseurs, chorégraphes et de tout intervenant professionnel de la communauté de la danse au Québec

Anik Bissonette, Présidente

Saskatchewan

Dance Saskatchewan Inc.
PO Box 8789, 205A Pacific Ave., Saskatoon SK S7K 1N9
Tel: 306-931-8480; *Fax:* 306-244-1520
Toll-Free: 800-667-8480
dancesask@sasktel.net
www.dancesask.com
To support & enhance the development of all dance forms; to preserve & promote dance in Saskatchewan; to represent & educate about dance; to encourage a passion for dance; to create a viable, unified organization which represents & advocates dance interests; to foster a respect & acceptance of dance which encourages free expression of cultural identity; to establish an active, vibrant environment which focuses on job creation, performance & cultural diversity within a central dance facility
Linda Coe-Kirkham, Executive Director

Performing Arts - Music

Alberta

Alberta Band Association (ABA)
#204, 4818 - 50 Ave., Red Deer AB T4N 4A3
Tel: 403-347-2237; *Fax:* 403-237-2241
Toll-Free: 877-687-4239
www.albertabandassociation.com
To promote & develop the musical, educational & cultural values of bands & band music in Alberta
Ken Rogers, President

Alberta Choral Federation (ACF)
#103, 10612 - 124 St., Edmonton AB T5N 1S4
Tel: 780-488-7464; *Fax:* 780-488-6403
info@albertachoralfederation.ca
www.albertachoralfederation.ca
To promote choral music within the communities of Alberta; to gain support for choral music through public policy
Laurier Fagnan, President
Kathleen Skinner, Vice President

Alberta Recording Industry Association (ARIA)
1205 Energy Square, 10109-106 St NW, Edmonton AB T5J 3L7
Tel: 780-428-3372; *Fax:* 780-426-0188
Toll-Free: 800-465-3117
To assist & advance the development of the Canadian recorded music industry; to foster the excellence, diversity & vitality of Alberta artists & the Alberta sound recording industry

Calgary Opera Association
Arrata Opera Centre, 1315 - 7 St. SW, Calgary AB T2R 1A5
Tel: 403-262-7286; *Fax:* 403-263-5428
info@calgaryopera.com
www.calgaryopera.com
To enrich the cultural life of the community by celebrating musical art through the performance of professional opera
W.R. (Bob) McPhee, General Director

Calgary Philharmonic Society (CPO)
#205, 8 Ave. SE, Calgary AB T2G 0K9
Tel: 403-571-0270; *Fax:* 403-294-7424
info@cpo-live.com
www.cpo-live.com
To provide our audience with a rich, diverse & unequalled symphonic musical experience which earns broad community support
Ann Lewis-Luppino, President & CEO

Calgary Youth Orchestra
c/o Mount Royal College Conservatory, 4825 Mount Royal Gate SW, Calgary AB T3E 6K6
Tel: 403-240-5978; *Fax:* 403-240-6594
cyo@mtroyal.ca
www.cyo.ab.ca
To provide the best possible musical experience for the talented young musicians of the Calgary region, in an art form that is considered one of the highest forms of expression
George Fenwick, Orchestra Manager

Canadian Federation of Music Teachers' Associations (CFMTA) / Fédération canadienne des associations des professeurs de musique
13407 - 14A Ave., Surrey AB V4A 7P9
Tel: 604-531-8840; *Fax:* 604-531-8747
dbrigs@telus.net
www.cfmta.org
To promote high musical & academic qualifications among members
Darlene Brigidear, President

Canadian Society for Traditional Music (CSTM) / Société canadienne pour les traditions musicales (SCTM)
c/o 3-47 Arts Building, University of Alberta, Edmonton AB T6G 2E6
cstmsctm@ualberta.ca
www.yorku.ca/cstm
Study & promotion of musical traditions of all cultures & communities in all their aspects
Sherry Johnson, Secretary
Anna Hoefnagels, President
Chris McDonald, Treasurer

Country Music Foundation of Canada Inc.
8607 - 128 Ave., Edmonton AB T5E 0G3
Tel: 780-476-8230; *Fax:* 780-472-2584
To preserve & present Canadian country music; to maintain country music museum & Canadian Country Music Association's Hall of Honour
William Maxim, Chair

Edmonton Jazz Society (EJS)
11 Tommy Banks Way, Edmonton AB T6E 2M2
Tel: 780-432-0428; *Fax:* 780-433-3773
jasiek@yardbirdsuite.com
www.yardbirdsuite.com
To present, promote & develop the performance of live Jazz music in the City of Edmonton
Paul Wilde, President

Edmonton Opera Association
Winspear Centre, 9720 - 102 Ave., Edmonton AB T5J 4B2
Tel: 780-424-4040; *Fax:* 780-429-0600
edmopera@edmontonopera.com
www.edmontonopera.com
To develop & promote opera as a dynamic & progressive art form; to attract & challenge audiences & artists through a creative program of opera production & education
Brian Deedrick, Artistic Director
Mary Phillips-Rickey, General Manager

Edmonton Symphony Orchestra (ESO)
9720 - 102 Ave., Edmonton AB T5J 4B2
Tel: 780-428-1108; *Fax:* 780-425-0167
Toll-Free: 800-563-5081
info@winspearcentre.com
www.edmontonsymphony.com
To foster appreciation & enjoyment of live, professional orchestral music through presenting concert performances, educational & community programs
Rob McAlear, Artistic Administrator
Annemarie Petrov, Executive Director

Edmonton Youth Orchestra Association (EYO)
PO Box 66041, Stn. Heritage Post Office, Edmonton AB T6J 6T4
Tel: 780-436-7932; *Fax:* 780-436-7932
eyo@shaw.ca
www.eyso.com
To provide young musicians with the opportunity to develop their orchestral skills & increase their knowledge & appreciation of music, while enriching the cultural life of the community through concerts & benefit performances
Michael Massey, Music Director

Festival Chorus of Calgary
EPCOR Centre for Performing Arts, 205 - 8 Ave. SE, Calgary AB T2G 0K9
Tel: 403-294-7400
lgneufeld@shaw.ca
www.festivalchorus.ca
To present two concerts per year for the Marblehead community
Mel Kirby, Artistic Director

Lethbridge Symphony Orchestra
PO Box 1101, Lethbridge AB T1J 4A2
Tel: 403-328-6808; *Fax:* 403-380-4418
info@lethbridgesymphony.org
www.lethbridgesymphony.org
Glenn Klassen, Music Director, Artistic, Special P
Dawn Leite, General Manager

Red Deer Symphony Orchestra
Cultural Services Building, PO Box 1116, 3827, 39th St., Red Deer AB T4N 6S5
Tel: 403-340-2948; *Fax:* 403-309-4612
reddeersymphony@telus.net
www.rdso.ca
Melody McKnight, Executive Director
Claude Lapalme, Music Director

British Columbia

Canadian New Music Network (CNMN) / Réseau canadien pour les musiques nouvelles (RCMN)
416, rue McGill, Montréal BC H2Y 2G1
admin@reseaumusiquesnouvelles.ca
www.newmusicnetwork.ca
To improve communication, understanding & knowledge within the new music community; To represent the community in Canadian society, by working with the media, Canadian government & arts organizations
Emily Hall, Administrator
Tim Brady, President

Delta Youth Orchestra
PO Box 131, Delta BC V4K 3N6
Tel: 604-878-4655; *Fax:* 604-943-9603
info@dyo.bc.ca
www.dyo.bc.ca
To provide an educationally oriented experience for young musicians from the lower mainland of British Columbia
Stephen Robb, Music Director

Early Music Vancouver (EMV)
1254 - 7 Ave. West, Vancouver BC V6H 1B6
Tel: 604-732-1610; *Fax:* 604-732-1602
staff@earlymusic.bc.ca
www.earlymusic.bc.ca
To foster increased understanding & appreciation of early music by providing educational programs, high quality concerts at reasonable prices featuring both local & internationally acclaimed musicians & by providing informative publications
José Verstappen, Executive Director

Fraser Valley Symphony Society
PO Box 122, Abbotsford BC V2S 4N8
Tel: 604-859-3877
fvssorchestra@hotmail.com
www.fraservalleysymphony.ca
Lindsay Mellor, Conductor

Friends of Chamber Music
PO Box 38046, Stn. King Edward Mall, Vancouver BC V5Z 4L9
Tel: 604-437-5747; *Fax:* 604-437-4769
fcmtickets@yahoo.com
www.friendsofchambermusic.ca
To present the best in chamber music
Eric Wilson, Program Chair

Greater Victoria Youth Orchestra (GVYO)
1611 Quadra St., Victoria BC V8W 2L5
Tel: 250-360-1121; *Fax:* 250-381-3573
gvyo@telus.net
www.gvyo.org
To affirm & nourish the love of music in young people; to foster musical development of orchestra members; to serve as musical resource to the community at large
John Sterk, President
Sheila Redhead, Manager

Kamloops Intermediate Orchestra
PO Box 1387, Kamloops BC V2C 6L7
Tel: 250-554-3693
To provide training & playing opportunities for regional youth
Mark Betuzzi, Music Director

Kamloops Symphony (KSO)
PO Box 57, Kamloops BC V2C 5K3
Tel: 250-372-5000; *Fax:* 250-372-5089
info@kamloopssymphony.com
www.kamloopssymphony.com
To operate & promote a symphony orchestra for the Kamloops region
Bruce Dunn, Music Director

Okanagan Symphony Society
PO Box 20238, #239, 1899 Springfield Rd., Kelowna BC V1Y 9H2
Tel: 250-763-7544; *Fax:* 250-763-3553
admin@okanagansymphony.com
www.okanagansymphony.com
To provide the communities of the Okanagan Valley with an orchestra that is committed to excellence in the performance of classical music
Rosemary Thomson, Music Director

Pacific Opera Victoria (POV)
#500, 1815 Blanshard St., Victoria BC V8T 5A1
Tel: 250-382-1641; *Fax:* 250-382-4944
dshefsiek@pov.bc.ca
www.pov.bc.ca
To provide professional quality opera to the residents of Greater Victoria & Vancouver Island; to provide career-oriented Canadian artists with the opportunity to expand their repertoire & gain professional experience; to train community artists & technicians in the discipline of opera production; to enhance the understanding & enjoyment of opera as an art form
Timothy Vernon, Artistic Director
David Shefsiek, Executive Director

Prince George Symphony Orchestra Society (PGSO)
2880 - 15 Ave., Prince George BC V2M 1T1
Tel: 250-562-0800; *Fax:* 250-562-0844
admin@pgso.com
www.pgso.com
To provide symphonic music for Prince George & region consistent with Prince George Symphony Orchestra artistic policy that facilitates artistic development of its players; to foster & facilitate positive community image & financial responsiblity so that a wide spectrum of musical experiences is offered to players & audiences alike
Ruth Langner, General Manager

Richmond Community Orchestra & Chorus
#130, 10691 Shellbridge Way, Richmond BC V6X 2W8
Tel: 604-276-2747; *Fax:* 604-270-3644
roca.office@gmail.com
www.roca.ca
Sue Tench, Administrator

Surrey Symphony Society (SSS)
#181, 6832 King George Hwy., Surrey BC V3W 4Z9
Tel: 604-572-9225
inquiries@surreyyouthorchestra.org
www.surreyyouthorchestra.org
To expand an appreciation of orchestral music among young musicians & to share this with the community through public performance
Lucille Lewis, Music Director
Carla Birston, Intermediate Strings Conductor
Margaret LaBelle, Business Manager
Rick Dorfer, Junior Strings Conductor

Vancouver Island Symphony
PO Box 661, 150 Commercial St., Nanaimo BC V9R 5L9
Tel: 250-754-0177; *Fax:* 250-754-0165
info@vancouverislandsymphony.com
www.vancouverislandsymphony.com
To promote & present orchestra music in the Central Vancouver Island Region
Margot Holmes, Executive Director
David W. Covey, President
J. Valentine, Contact

Vancouver New Music (VNM)
837 Davie St., Vancouver BC V6Z 1B7
Tel: 604-633-0861; *Fax:* 604-633-0871
info@newmusic.org
www.newmusic.org
Regarded as Western Canada's major producer of contemporary music & sonic art, dedicated to the outstanding performance of the music of our time; fostering connections within the community to bring new music to a wider audience; commissions & premieres new works by Canadian composers; produces music-theatre, leading electroacoustic music, international composers & performers; produces an annual Vancouver New Music Festival; explores the interaction of contemporary music with other disciplines
Giorgio Magnanensi, Artistic Director
David Murphy, President
Heather McDermid, Manager, Marketing & Communications
Jim Smith, Managing Producer
Jason Dubois, Production Manager

Vancouver Opera (VOA) / Association de l'opéra de vancouver
1945 McLean Dr., Vancouver BC V5N 3J7
Tel: 604-682-2871; *Fax:* 604-682-3981
tickets@vancouveropera.ca
www.vancouveropera.ca
To share the power of opera with all who are open to receiving it, through superior performances & meaningful education programs for all ages
James W. Wright, Geneeral Director

Vancouver Philharmonic Orchestra (VPO)
PO Box 27503, Stn. Oakridge, Vancouver BC V5Z 4M4
Tel: 604-878-9989
vpo@vcn.bc.ca
www.vanphil.ca
Cathy McCashin, President
Maura Gauditis, Vice-President
Katherine Bailey, Treasurer

Vancouver Symphony Society
601 Smithe St., Vancouver BC V6B 5G1
Tel: 604-684-9100; *Fax:* 604-684-9264
customerservice@vancouversymphony.ca
www.vancouversymphony.ca
Provides stewardship for the Vancouver Symphony Orchestra to achieve recognition as one of Canada's highest quality symphony orchestras; to perform at all times with artistic distinction & thereby enrich BC's quality of life; to expand the enjoyment & appreciation of the finest orchestral music of the past & present
Jeff Alexander, President & CEO
Mary-Ann Moir, Vice-President, Finance & Administration

Vancouver Youth Symphony Orchestra Society (VYSO)
3214 - 10 Ave. West, Vancouver BC V6K 2L2
Tel: 604-737-0714; *Fax:* 604-737-0739
vyso@telus.net
www.vyso.com
To provide orchestral training & experience to music students in Greater Vancouver & the Lower Mainland from beginner to advanced level career student
Roger Cole, Artistic Director
Holly Littleford, Orchestra Manager

Victoria Symphony
#610, 620 View St., Victoria BC V8W 1J6
Tel: 250-385-9771; *Fax:* 250-385-7767
administration@victoriasymphony.ca
www.victoriasymphony.ca
To advance musical culture; to advance musical education among younger members of community; to encourage, foster, & promote performance of Canadian & other contemporary musicians
Stephen Smith, Interim Executive Director
Deedrie Ballard, President
Tania Miller, Music Director

Manitoba

Alliance Chorale Manitoba
#212, 340 Provencher Blvd., Winnipeg MB R2H 0G7
Tél: 204-233-7423; *Téléc:* 204-233-3324
Fédération provinciale sans but lucratif qui a pour mandat de promouvoir le chant choral en français et de favoriser ainsi l'épanouissement de la culture francophone du Manitoba.
Gilles Landry, Contact

Brandon University School of Music
Queen Elizabeth II Building, School of Music, Brandon University, 270 - 18th St., Brandon MB R7A 6A9
Tel: 204-728-9631; *Fax:* 204-728-6839
music@brandonu.ca
www.brandonu.ca/music/
Mark Rudoff, Director

Canadian Band Association (CBA) / Association canadienne des harmonies
15 Pinecrest Bay, Winnipeg MB R2G 1W2
Tel: 204-663-1226; *Fax:* 204-663-1226
cbaband@shaw.ca
cba.usask.ca
To promote & develop the musical educational & cultural values of band & band music in Canada
Ken Epp, Executive Director

Carl Orff Canada Music for Children (COC)
c/o Joan Linklater, 88 Tunis Bay, Winnipeg MB R3T 2X1
Tel: 204-261-1893
www.orffcanada.ca
To encourage the development of a wholistic music education evolved from the pedagogical philosophy & approach of Carl Orff
Joan Linklater, President

Manitoba Band Association
15 Pinecrest Bay, Winnipeg MB R2G 1W2
Tel: 204-663-1226; *Fax:* 204-663-1226
mbband@shaw.ca
www.mbband.org
To promote growth & development of bands in Manitoba
Wendy McCallum, President

Manitoba Chamber Orchestra (MCO)
Portage Place, 393 Portage Ave., #Y300, Winnipeg MB R3B 3H6
Tel: 204-783-7377; *Fax:* 204-783-7383
mco@mts.net
www.manitobachamberorchestra.org
To perform chamber orchestra repertoire with emphasis on premiering new Canadian works & Canadian soloists
Anne Manson, Music Director
Vicki Young, General Manager

Manitoba Opera Association Inc.
Lower Level, Centennial Concert Hall, #105, 555 Main St., Winnipeg MB R3B 1C3
Tel: 204-942-7479; *Fax:* 204-949-0377
mbopera@manitobaopera.mb.ca
www.manitobaopera.mb.ca
To present & develop appreciation for art of opera in Manitoba; to assist in development of Canadian talent, with emphasis on Manitobans
Peter George, President

Western Canadian Music Alliance (WCMA)
#340, 955 Portage Ave., Winnipeg MB R3G OP9
Tel: 204-943-8485; *Fax:* 204-453-1594
breakoutwest.ca
The music industry associations of Manitoba, Alberta, and Saskatchewan work in tandem towards the shared vision of developing the infrastructure of the independent music industry in Western Canada.
Rick Fenton, Executive Director

Winnipeg Symphony Orchestra Inc. (WSO)
#101, 555 Main St., Winnipeg MB R3B 1C3
Tel: 204-949-3999
lmarks@wso.mb.ca
www.wso.mb.ca
To perform a wide variety of orchestral music including classical, contemporary, pop & children's music in Manitoba & Northwestern Ontario
Dorothy Dobbie, Chair & President
Alexander Mickelthwate, Music Director

New Brunswick

Symphony New Brunswick / Symphonie Nouveau-Brunswick
Brunswick Square, 39 King St., Level III, Saint John NB E2L 4W3
Tel: 506-634-8379; *Fax:* 506-634-0843
symphony@nbnet.nb.ca
www.symphonynb.com
To present high-quality, live orchestral & chamber music from all periods & to promote the appreciation of music through educational activities in New Brunswick
Thomas J. Condon, President

Newfoundland and Labrador

Newfoundland Symphony Orchestra Association (NSO)
Arts & Culture Centre, PO Box 1854, St. John's NL A1C 5P9
Tel: 709-722-4441; *Fax:* 709-753-0561
nso.orchestra@nso.nfld.net
www.nso-music.com
To foster & promote in all age groups of the general public of the province an interest in & an appreciation of music; to provide the province with a symphony orchestra of the highest possible standard; to provide professional musicians, highly skilled amateur players & talented students with the opportunity of performing
Peter Gardner, General & Artistic Director
Alasdair Black, Operations Manager
G.C. (Gerry) Germain, Chair

Newfoundland Symphony Youth Orchestra (NSYO)
PO Box 1854, St. John's NL A1C 5P9
Tel: 709-722-4441; *Fax:* 709-753-0561
Youth Orchestra in Newfoundland
Peter Gardner, Director

Nova Scotia

African Nova Scotian Music Association (ANSMA)
PO Box 931, 1149 Main St., Dartmouth NS B2Z 1A8
Tel: 902-404-3036; *Fax:* 902-434-0462
ansma@eastlink.ca
www.ansma.com
The African Nova Scotian Music Association (ANSMA) is a not for profit organization dedicated to the development, promotion

and enhancement of African Nova Scotia Music locally, nationally and internationally.
Louis (Lou) Gannon Jr., President

Association of Canadian Choral Conductors (ACCC) / Association des chefs de choeur canadiens
6303 Duncan St., Halifax NS B3L 1K4
Tel: 902-442-7054; *Fax:* 902-442-7050
accc@ca.inter.net
www.choralcanada.org
To promote choral music, particularly Canadian works, in schools, post-secondary institutions, churches & communities throughout Canada
Christina Murray, Executive Director
Bridgid Coult, President

Deep Roots Music Cooperative
PO Box 2360, Wolfville NS B4P 2G9
Tel: 902-542-7668
info@deeprootsmusic.ca
www.deeprootsmusic.ca/cooperative
To develop year-round musical programs culminating in an annual festival, and to encourage meaningful connections between cultures, community groups, artists and audiences.
Peter Mowat, Chair

Music Nova Scotia
#302, 5516 Spring Garden Rd., Halifax NS B3J 1G6
Tel: 902-423-6271; *Fax:* 902-423-8841
Toll-Free: 888-343-6426
info@musicnovascotia.ca
www.musicnovascotia.ca
Social Media: www.myspace.com/musicnovascotia; www.youtube.com/user/MusicNS
To encourage the creation, development, growth and promotion of Nova Scotia's music industry.
Scott Long, Executive Director

Music NWT
Roman Empire Bldg., 5103 51st St., 2nd Fl., Yellowknife NT X1A 1S8
Tel: 867-873-5577; *Fax:* 867-873-5575
info@musicnwt.ca
www.musicnwt.ca
The association brings together musicians, offers workshops & other resources, & provides networking opportunities

Nova Scotia Band Association
355 Branch St, New Glasgow NS B2H 3A5
Tel: 902-751-5996; *Fax:* 902-755-8490
admin@novascotiabandassociation.com
www.novascotiabandassociation.com
To support and promote the development of bands throughout the province of Nova Scotia through communication, coordination, program development, advocacy and lobbying at the provincial level.
Barbara Stetter, President

Nova Scotia Youth Orchestra
6199 Chebucto Rd., Halifax NS B3L 1K7
Tel: 902-423-5984
nsyo@ns.sympatico.ca
www.novascotiayouthorchestra.com
To provide young musicians with the finest orchestral training; to provide live orchestral music to audiences in Nova Scotia
Dinuk Wijeratne, Music Director

Scotia Chamber Players
6181 Lady Hammond Rd., Halifax NS B3K 2R9
Tel: 902-429-9467; *Fax:* 902-425-6785
admin@scotiafestival.ns.ca
www.scotiafestival.ns.ca
To enhance the quality of music by producing an annual festival of world-class chamber music in study & performance for the benefit of musicians, students & audiences
Christopher Wilcox, Managing Director

Symphony Nova Scotia (SNS)
Park Lane Mall, PO Box 218, #301, 5657 Spring Garden Rd., Halifax NS B3J 3R4
Tel: 902-421-1300; *Fax:* 902-422-1209
info@symns.cohn.dal.ca
www.symphonynovascotia.ca
To enhance the quality of life of the citizens of Nova Scotia through high quality, professionally performed orchestral music
Erika Beatty, Chief Executive Officer

Ontario

Alliance for Canadian New Music Projects (ACNMP) / Alliance pour des projets de musique canadienne nouvelle
Canadian Music Centre, 20 St. Joseph St., Toronto ON M4Y 1J9
Tel: 416-963-5937; *Fax:* 416-961-7198
fbredeson@gprc.ab.ca
www.acnmp.ca
To provide young musicians with an opportunity to celebrate & enjoy the music of their own time & country through the organization's syllabus & its festival, Contemporary Showcase
Ann La Plante, General Manager
Jill Kelman, President

Bach Elgar Choral Society
86 Homewood St., Hamilton ON L8P 2M4
Tel: 905-527-5995; *Fax:* 905-527-0555
www.bachelgar.com
To provide choral music of excellent quality & broad-based appeal to the community; To act as a cultural & educational resource

Bluegrass Music Association of Central Canada (BMACC)
c/o Secretary, 339 Wellington St. N, Woodstock ON N4S 6S6
Tel: 519-539-8967
weslowe@bmacc.ca
www.bmacc.ca
The Bluegrass Music Association of Central Canada is dedicated to the preservation and promotion of Bluegrass and Old-time music throughout Central Canada. The BMACC works to support individuals, groups and organizations involved in bluegrass and old-time music and provide leadership and promote education among fans, clubs, bands and artists.
Denis Chadbourn, President

Brampton Symphony Orchestra
PO Box 93091, Stn. Brampton South, 499 Main St. South, Brampton ON L6Y 4V8
Tel: 905-459-0853
info@bramptonsymphony.com
www.bramptonsymphony.com
Michael Todd, President

Brantford Symphony Orchestra Association Inc.
PO Box 24012, 185 King George Rd., Brantford ON N3R 7X3
Tel: 519-759-8781; *Fax:* 519-759-0842
administrator@brantfordsymphony.ca
www.brantfordsymphony.ca
To provide enduring access to the best symphonic entertainment, giving people of all ages opportunities for musical growth & education
Gary Cork, Vice President
Philip Sarabura, Conductor/Music Director

Canadian Academy of Recording Arts & Sciences (CARAS) / Académie canadienne des arts et des sciences de l'enregistrement (ACASE)
345 Adelaide St. West, 2nd fl., Toronto ON M5V 1J6
Tel: 416-485-3135; *Fax:* 416-485-4978
Toll-Free: 888-440-5866
membership@carasonline.ca
www.carasonline.ca
To promote Canadian artists and music; To identify & reward the achievements of Canadian artists
Ed Robinson, Chair, CARAS & MusiCounts
Melanie Berry, President & Chief Executive Officer, CARAS & MusiCounts
Chris Topping, Vice-President, Events & Special Programming
Alex Heming, Senior Coordinator, Marketing & Fulfillment
Meghan McCabe, Senior Coordinator, Communications

Canadian Association for Music Therapy (CAMT) / Association de musicothérapie du Canada (AMC)
#230, 110 Cumberland St., Toronto ON M5R 3V5
Tel: 416-944-0421; *Fax:* 416-944-0431
Toll-Free: 800-996-2268
camt@musictherapy.ca
www.musictherapy.ca
To promote excellence in music therapy practice & education in Canadian clinical, educational, & community settings
Guylaine Vaillancourt, President

Canadian Bureau for the Advancement of Music (CBAM)
Exhibition Place, Toronto ON M6K 3C3
Tel: 416-260-6451
moreinfo@thecbam.ca
www.thecbam.ca
To promote music (piano) education program for elementary school students
Nancy Manning, CAO

Canadian Children's Opera Chorus (CCOC)
Opera Centre, #215, 227 Front St. East, Toronto ON M5A 1E8
Tel: 416-366-0467; *Fax:* 416-366-9204
info@canadianchildrensopera.com
www.canadianchildrensopera.com
To be the foremost children's operatic chorus in Canada & to achieve international recognition
Ken Hall, General Manager
Ann Cooper Gay, Artistic Director

Canadian Country Music Association (CCMA) / Association de la musique country canadienne
30B Commercial Rd., Toronto ON M4G 1Z4
Tel: 416-947-1331; *Fax:* 416-947-5924
country@ccma.org
www.ccma.org
The federally chartered non-profit professional organization protects the heritage, & advocates the development of Canadian country music both in Canada & worldwide.
Sheila Hamilton, Executive Director
Heather Ostertag, Chair
Lynne Foster, Sec.-Treas.

Canadian Disc Jockey Association (CDJA)
PO Box 92, Arva ON N0M 1C0
Fax: 519-472-0242
Toll-Free: 877-472-0653
pres@cdja.ca
www.cdja.org
To provide a forum for professional disc jockeys to meet & discuss mutual trade concerns, benefits, etc.; to improve the DJ service industry by establishing & promoting standards, procedures & benefits for disc jockey operations & operators across Canada; to promote the disc jockey to the consumer as an alternative & economical form of entertainment for a wide variety of applications; to assist & train the member in any way possible to professionally develop skills, knowledge, experience & business acumen in the disc jockey service sector; to represent the disc jockey service industry as a lobby & special interest group; to provide special service, advice & common benefit to disc jockeys across Canada
Doug Scott, President

Canadian Independent Music Association (CIMA)
30 St. Patrick St., 2nd Fl., Toronto ON M5T 3A3
Tel: 416-485-3152; *Fax:* 416-485-4373
cima@cimamusic.ca
www.cimamusic.ca
CIMA concentrates on lobbying governments for support & copyright reform. It maintains watch on Cancon regulations & other broadcast regulatory matters, and to raise the profile of Canadian music abroad, the association also promotes the industry at international events, particularly MIDEM, held annually in Cannes, France.
Duncan McKie, President & CEO
Donna Murphy, Vice-President, Operations
Sharon Hookway, Membership/Communications
Mary Vrantsidis, International Trade Shows

Canadian League of Composers / La Ligue canadienne de compositeurs
c/o Canadian Music Centre, 20 St. Joseph St., Toronto ON M4Y 1J9
Tel: 416-964-1364; *Toll-Free:* 877-964-1364
info@composition.org
www.composition.org
The oldest organization that speaks for professional composers in a professional capacity. It endeavours to represent the best interests of composers and to monitor and influence the conditions that affect their livlihood and public image.
James Rolfe, President, Ontario

Canadian Music Centre (CMC) / Centre de musique canadienne
Chalmers House, 20 St. Joseph St., Toronto ON M4Y 1J9
Tel: 416-961-6601; *Fax:* 416-961-7198
info@musiccentre.ca
www.musiccentre.ca; www.centremusique.ca
To stimulate the awareness, appreciation & performance of Canadian music
Allan G. Bell, President
Elisabeth Bihl, Executive Director

Canadian Music Educators' Association (CMEA) / Association canadienne des éducateurs de musique
#A-430A, Wilfrid Laurier University, Waterloo ON N2L 3C5
Tel: 519-884-0710
edwin.wasiak@uleth.ca
www.musiceducationonline.org
To provide leadership in establishing & maintaining high standards of school music in Canada
Betty Hanley, Membership
Ed Wasiak, President

Canadian Music Festival Adjudicators' Association (CMFAA)
c/o School of Music, Queen's University, Kingston ON K7L 3N6
Tel: 613-533-6000; *Fax:* 613-533-6808
zuki@queensu.ca
www.cmfaa.ca
John Hansen, Vice-President
Ireneus Zuk, President

Canadian Musical Heritage Society (CMHS) / Société pour le patrimoine musical canadien (SPMC)
#15, 120 Walnut Ct., Ottawa ON K1R 7W2
Tel: 613-237-0550
enquiries@cliffordfordpublications.ca
To provide research & publication of early Canadian music in a multi-volume anthology
Clifford Ford, Executive Secretary

Canadian Opera Company (COC) / Compagnie d'opéra canadienne
145 Queen St. West, Toronto ON M5A 1E8
Tel: 416-363-8231; *Fax:* 416-363-5584
Toll-Free: 800-250-4653
tickets@coc.ca
www.coc.ca
To produce opera of the highest international standard while attracting growing public support & participation in opera through increased accessibility & education; To attract, develop & promote young Canadian singers, musicians, stage directors, conductors, designers, technical personnel & administrators; To encourage Canadian librettists & composers to compose new works
Alexander Neef, General Director
Robert Lamb, Managing Director

Canadian University Music Society (CUMS) / Société de musique des universités canadiennes (SMUC)
c/o Secretariat, #202, 10 Morrow Ave., Toronto ON M6R 2J1
Tel: 416-538-1650; *Fax:* 416-489-1713
journals@interlog.com
www.cums-smuc.ca/
To stimulate research, musical performance & composition; to improve instructional methods in university teaching; to provide a forum to exchange views on common problems, scholarly research in music & other matters of professional concern; to advise on new university programs & monitor existing programs
Deanna Oye, President

Cathedral Bluffs Symphony Orchestra (CBSO)
PO Box 51074, 18 Eglinton Sq., Toronto ON M1L 2K2
Tel: 416-879-5566
info@cathedralbluffs.com
www.cathedralbluffs.com
To provide residents of Scarborough with an opportunity to hear classical symphonic music performed by a live orchestra; to provide skilled amateur musicians & young soloists with an opportunity to perform
Norman Reintamm, Artistic Director
Murray Finkelstein, President

Choirs Ontario
1442A Bayview Ave., Toronto ON M4G 3A7
Tel: 416-923-1144; *Fax:* 416-929-0415
Toll-Free: 866-935-1144
info@choirsontario.org
www.choirsontario.org
To promote choral singing in communities, schools & universities, places of worship, etc. throughout Ontario.
Dean Jobin-Bevans, President

Conservatory Canada
#M-2, 130 King St., London ON N6A 1C5
Tel: 519-433-3147; *Fax:* 519-433-7404
Toll-Free: 800-461-5367
mail@conservatorycanada.ca
www.conservatorycanada.ca
To promote achievement in music through a comprehensive program of study, evaluation & recognition for teachers & students; to foster the development of musical talent & potential
Warwick Victoria, Executive Director

Counterpoint Community Orchestra
PO Box 41, 552 Church St., Toronto ON M4Y 2E3
Tel: 416-654-9806
info@ccorchestra.org
www.ccorchestra.org
Terry Kowalczuk, Music Director

Deep River Symphony Orchestra (DRSO)
PO Box 1496, Deep River ON K0J 1P0
Tel: 613-586-9385
symphony@drso.ca
www.drso.ca
To promote the development & enjoyment of music in the Upper Ottawa Valley
Peter Morris, Music Director
Heather Butterworth, Secretary

Edward Johnson Music Foundation (EJMF)
PO Box 1718, 50 Cork St. East, 2nd Fl., Guelph ON N1H 6Z9
Tel: 519-821-7570; *Fax:* 519-821-4403
info@edwardjohnsonmusicfoundation.org
www.edwardjohnsonmusicfoundation.org
To recognize the vital role of music in the fabric of our lives & communities; To create opportunities for children & adults to learn about, create, & enjoy music in schools & throughout the community
Rosemary Smith, Executive Director

Etobicoke Philharmonic Orchestra (EPO)
PO Box 66, Stn. D, Toronto ON M9A 4X1
Tel: 416-239-5665; *Fax:* 416-239-5665
info@eporchestra.ca
www.eporchestra.ca
To provide an opportunity for trained amateur musicians to perform together & become acquainted with an orchestral repertoire; to provide the community with symphonic music, competently performed in a local setting; to assist serious music students in their studies through performance experience & a scholarship program
Tom Fleming, General Manager
Carolyn McGee, Co-President
Pat Butler, Co-President

Foundation Assisting Canadian Talent on Recordings (FACTOR)
30 Commercial Rd., Toronto ON M5V 1Z4
Tel: 416-696-2215; *Fax:* 416-351-7311
general.info@factor.ca
www.factor.ca
To provide financial assistance for production of sound recordings, videos, syndicated radio programs & international tour support; English-language counterpart of Musicaction
Duncan McKie, President
Phil Gumbley, Director of Operations

Georgian Bay Symphony (GBS)
PO Box 133, 994 - 3rd Ave. East, Owen Sound ON N4K 5P1
Tel: 519-372-0212; *Fax:* 519-372-9023
gbs@bmts.com
www.georgianbaysymphony.ca
To enhance appreciation of music which includes growth & development of regional orchestra
Richard Nancarrow, President
John Barnum, Music Director

Guild of Canadian Film Composers (GCFC) / Guilde des compositeurs canadiens de musique de film
PO Box 22059, 45 Overlea Blvd., Toronto ON M4H 1N9
Tel: 416-410-5076; *Fax:* 416-410-4516
Toll-Free: 866-657-1117
gcfc@gcfc.ca
www.gcfc.ca
To improve the status & quality of music as it applies to film/tv/new media through education & the professional development of its members & the producing community; to represent & communicate the interests of its members to the music & film/tv/new media industries as well as other institutions; to collaborate with trade & industry associations with common interests; to represent all Canadian composers within the certified territories & producer entities detailed in our certification under the Canadian Status of the Artist Act, as the exclusive organization for collective negotiations
Maria Topalovich, Executive Director

Halton Youth Symphony (HYS)
PO Box 494, Oakville ON L6J 5A8
Tel: 905-616-2760
manager@haltonyouthsymphony.com
www.haltonyouthsymphony.com
To inspire, encourage & challenge young musicians to build their musical skills through the experience of various forms of orchestral music; to create an enjoyable environment that promotes teamwork, leadership & community involvement

Hamilton Philharmonic Orchestra
#1002, 105 Main St. East, Hamilton ON L8N 1G6
Tel: 905-526-1677; *Fax:* 905-526-0616
communications@hpo.org
www.hpo.org
To provide artistically excellent music to patrons
James Sommerville, Music Director
Annelisa Pedersen, Executive Director

Hamilton Philharmonic Youth Orchestra (HPYO)
299 Fennell Ave. West, Hamilton ON L9C 1G3
Tel: 905-573-9094
info@hpyo.com
www.hpyo.com
Paul McCulloch, Music Director & Conductor

Hart House Orchestra
University of Toronto, 7 Hart House Circle, Toronto ON M5S 3H3
Tel: 416-978-5362
webmaestro@harthouseorchestra.ca
www.harthouseorchestra.ca
Zoe Dille, Programme Advisor

Huronia Symphony Orchestra (HSO)
PO Box 904, Barrie ON L4M 4Y6
Tel: 705-721-4752; *Fax:* 705-737-0679
office@huroniasymphony.ca
www.huroniasymphony.ca
To operate & support a symphony orchestra in Simcoe County; to provide symphonic music for people of the area as well as an opportunity for children & youth to receive instruction in orchestral music
David Chambers, President

International Symphony Orchestra of Sarnia, Ontario & Port Huron, Michigan
225 Davis St., Sarnia ON N7T 1B2
Tel: 519-337-7775; *Fax:* 519-337-1822
iso@rivernet.net
www.theiso.org
To provide cultural enrichment within the community by providing high calibre choral & symphonic performances
Jerome David Summers, Music Director

International Youth Symphony Orchestra
118 North Victoria St., Sarnia ON N7T 5W9
Tel: 519-337-7775; *Fax:* 519-337-1822

Kingston Symphony Association (KSA)
PO Box 1616, #206, 11 Princess St., Kingston ON K7L 5C8
Tel: 613-546-9729; *Fax:* 613-546-8580
info@kingstonsymphony.on.ca
www.kingstonsymphony.on.ca
To maintain & produce professional orchestral & symphonic music in the Kingston area
Andrea Haughton, General Manager

Kingston Youth Orchestra
PO Box 1616, #206, 11 Princess St., Kingston ON K7L 5C8
Tel: 613-546-9729; *Fax:* 613-546-8580

Kitchener-Waterloo Chamber Orchestra (KWCO)
197 Weber St. East, Kitchener ON N2H 1E5
Tel: 519-744-3828; *Fax:* 519-749-0832
kwchamberorchestra@gmail.com
www.kwchamberorchestra.ca
Joanna Armbruster, President
Graham Coles, Music Director

Kitchener-Waterloo Symphony Orchestra Association Inc. (KWSOA)
36 King St. West, Kitchener ON N2G 1A3
Tel: 519-745-4711; *Fax:* 519-745-4474
Toll-Free: 888-745-4717
info@kwsymphony.on.ca
www.kwsymphony.on.ca
To cultivate the tradition of live performance through the presentation of classical orchestral & popular music for the edification, enrichment, education & excitement of our community & beyond
Genevieve Twomey, Executive Director

Kitchener-Waterloo Symphony Youth Orchestra (KWSYO)
36 King St. West, Kitchener ON N2G 1A3
Tel: 519-745-4711; *Toll-Free:* 888-745-4717
info@kwsymphony.on.ca
www.kwsymphony.on.ca

Barbara Kaplanek, Youth Strings Conductor
Julie Baumgartel, Youth Sinfonia Conductor/Director, KWSYO Chamber Music
Paul Pulford, Youth Orchestra Conductor
Peter Maness, Valhalla Brass Conductor

Kiwanis Music Festival Association of Greater Toronto
1422A Bayview Ave., Toronto ON M4G 3A7
Tel: 416-487-5885; *Fax:* 416-487-5784
kiwanismusic@bellnet.ca
kiwanismusictoronto.org/index.html
To bring together various choirs in music competitions
Pam Allen, General Manager

Korean-Canadian Symphony Orchestra (KGSO)
#203, 703 Bloor St. West, Toronto ON M6G 1L5
Tel: 416-534-3760
info@kcso.ca
www.kcso.ca
Myung Sook Kim, President
Richard Lee, Music Director

London Community Orchestra (LCO)
c/o 838 Wellington St. North, London ON N6A 3S7
Tel: 519-433-2074
sally.vernon@odyssey.on.ca
www.ontera.net/~lco/
To give concerts & to sponsor local young artists as soloists
Leonard Ingrao, Music Director
Margaret Whitby, Manager
Ray Thomson, President

London Youth Symphony (LYS)
PO Box 553, Stn. B, London ON N6A 4W8
Tel: 519-686-8070
info@londonyouthsymphony.org
www.londonyouthsymphony.org
To provide the region's most talented young musicians with the opportunity to build self-discipline, confidence & team spirit within an outstanding symphonic environment that offers professional directorship & coaching
Len Ingrao, Musical Director
Daina Janitis, Manager

Mariposa Folk Foundation
PO Box 383, Orillia ON L3V 6J8
Tel: 705-326-3655; *Fax:* 705-329-4099
info@mariposafolk.com
www.mariposafolk.com
The promotion & preservation of folk arts in Canada through song, story, dance, & craft. Office is located at 37 Mississaga St. West in Orillia.
Christopher Lusty, President

Mississauga Youth Orchestra
159 Cavendish Ct., Mississauga ON L6J 5S3
Tel: 905-815-8125; *Fax:* 905-815-8516
email@myomusic.ca
www.myomusic.ca
Kathy Grell, Manager

Music Canada
85 Mowat Ave., Toronto ON M6K 3E3
Tel: 416-967-7272; *Fax:* 416-967-9415
info@musiccanada.com
www.musiccanada.com
CRIA develops and promotes high ethical standards in the creation, manufacture and marketing of sound recordings.
Graham Henderson, President

Music for Young Children (MYC) / Musique pour jeunes enfants
39 Leacock Way, Kanata ON K2K 1T1
Tel: 613-592-7565; *Fax:* 613-592-9353
Toll-Free: 800-561-1692
myc@myc.com
www.myc.com
To develop, deliver & support comprehensive entry level music education programs of the finest quality
Janice Reade, Manager, Public Relations

Music Industries Association of Canada (MIAC) / Association canadienne des industries de la musique
#807, 505 Consumers Rd., Toronto ON M2J 4V8
Tel: 416-490-1871; *Fax:* 416-490-0369
Toll-Free: 877-480-6422
info@miac.net
www.miac.net
To represent Canadian manufacturers, distributors, retailers & wholesalers of musical instruments & accessories, sound reinforcement/lighting products, published music & computer music software
Barbara Cole, General Manager

National Arts Centre Orchestra of Canada (NACO) / Orchestre du Centre national des Arts (OCNA)
PO Box 1534, Stn. B, 53 Elgin St., Ottawa ON K1P 5W1
Tel: 613-947-7000; *Toll-Free:* 866-850-2787
info@nac-cna.ca
www.nac-cna.ca
Pinchas Zukerman, Music Director
Alex Gazalé, Production Director
Christopher Deacon, Managing Director

National Shevchenko Musical Ensemble Guild of Canada
626 Bathurst St., Toronto ON M5S 2R1
Tel: 416-533-2725; *Fax:* 416-533-6348
info_sme@bellnet.ca
www.shevchenkomusic.com
To provide instruction in vocal, instrumental & dance for youth & adults by maintaining the Shevchenko Musical Ensemble & Shevchenko School of Dance & Music; to perpetuate Ukrainian cultural traditions
Ginger Kautto, General Manager

National Youth Orchestra Canada (NYOC) / Orchestre national des jeunes Canada (ONJC)
#500, 59 Adelaide St. East, Toronto ON M5C 1K6
Tel: 416-532-4470; *Fax:* 416-532-6879
Toll-Free: 888-532-4470
info@nyoc.org
www.nyoc.org
Social Media: www.youtube.com/nyoconjc
Barbara Smith, Executive Director
Jonathan Welmers, Manager, Production
Karen Osmond, Manager, Operations
Joan Fischer, Interim Director, Development
Mercedes Dziver, Coordinator, Development
Lauren Scobie, Coordinator, Communications
Tara Litrack, Administrative Assistant

Niagara Youth Orchestra Association
#148, 12 - 111 Fourth Ave., St Catharines ON L2S 3P5
Tel: 905-704-0559; *Fax:* 905-704-0558
nyo@vaxxine.com
www.niagarayouthorchestra.ca
To foster among youth of Niagara Region an interest in & understanding of orchestral music of high quality
Michael Newnham, Music Director

Northumberland Orchestra Society (NOC)
PO Box 1012, Cobourg ON K9A 4W4
Tel: 905-377-1477
norchestra@norchestra.org
www.norchestra.org
Michael Newnham, Music Director & Conductor

Oakville Chamber Orchestra
PO Box 76036, 1500 Upper Middle Rd. West, Oakville ON L6M 3H5
Tel: 905-483-6787
mail@oakvillechamber.org
www.oakvillechamber.org
Charlotte Meissner, President
Charles Demuynck, Music Director

Oakville Symphony Orchestra (OSO)
#114, 99 Bronte Rd., Oakville ON L6L 3B7
Tel: 905-338-1462; *Fax:* 905-338-7954
oakville.symphony@cogeco.ca
www.oakvillesymphony.com
To bring audiences a variety of music for all ages & to contribute to the cultural growth of the community
Peggy Steele, General Manager

Ontario Band Association
c/o Membership Co-ordinator, 459 Concord Ave., Toronto ON M6H 2P9
membership@onband.ca
www.onband.ca
To promote & develop musical, educational & cultural values of bands in Ontario by sponsoring annual band & solo instrument competition, composition competition, original works
Sarah Arcand, President
Sommer Buttu, Secretary

Opera Lyra Ottawa
#110, 2 Daly Ave., Ottawa ON K1N 6E2
Tel: 613-233-9200; *Fax:* 613-233-5431
Toll-Free: 877-233-5972
marketing@operalyra.com
www.operalyra.ca
To provide employment & training opportunities for musicians, singers, stage hands, directors, & young artists of the highest calibre from across Canada & abroad; To present fully staged operas & various small-scale operas & concerts each season
Elizabeth Howarth, General Director

Opera Ontario
Opera Hamilton, #905, 105 Main St. East, Hamilton ON L8N 1G6
Tel: 905-527-7627; *Fax:* 905-527-0014
Toll-Free: 800-575-1381
info@operaontario.com
www.operaontario.com
To provide a consistently improving quality of operatic experience that compares favorably with opera produced anywhere in the world, which will enrich the audience & encourage the widest possible participation; to produce quality professional opera that will contribute to the cultural, economic & educational quality of our unique multi-city community
Alice Willems, President
David Speers, General Director

Opera.ca
#410, 174 Spadina Ave., Toronto ON M5T 2C2
Tel: 416-591-7222
info@opera.ca
www.opera.ca
Opera.ca works with members across the country to advance the interests of Canada's opera community and create greater opportunity for opera audiences and professionals alike.
Christina Loewen, Executive Director
Sandra Cina, Coordinator, Membership & Communications

Orchestra London Canada Inc.
609 Wellington St., London ON N6A 3R6
Tel: 519-679-8558; *Fax:* 519-679-8914
rgloor@orchestralondon.ca
www.orchestralondon.ca
To enrich the quality of life in the London area by maintaining a professional orchestra, serving the community through a wide variety of musical activities
Robert Gloor, Executive Director
Brent Kelman, President

Orchestra Toronto (OT)
#402, 131 Beecroft Rd., Toronto ON M2N 6G9
Tel: 416-467-7142
otoronto@on.aibn.com
www.orchestratoronto.ca
To provide affordable family entertainment, music education, & full repertoire in all its programs
Judy Mann, Contact
Erroll Gay, Music Director

Orchestras Canada (OC) / Orchestres Canada
230-460 College St., Toronto ON M6G 1A1
Tel: 416-366-8834; *Fax:* 416-366-1780
info@oc.ca
www.orchestrascanada.org
To strengthen Canada's orchestral community through leadership in advocacy, education, & professional development
Katherine Carleton, Executive Director

Orchestras Mississauga
4141 Living Arts Dr., Mississauga ON L5B 4B8
Tel: 905-615-4405; *Fax:* 905-615-4402
symphony.info@livingarts.on.ca
www.mississaugasymphony.ca
To provide & promote orchestral music; to ensure its accessibility to all segments of the community
John Barnum, Music Director
Eileen Keown, General Manager

Orillia Youth Symphony Orchestra (OYSO)
168 Parkview Ave., Orillia ON L3V 4M3
Tel: 705-326-7548
www.oyso.ca
To offer opportunity to participate in symphonic orchestra for young people 8-18 years of age
Mayumi Kumagai, Music Director

Oshawa-Durham Symphony Orchestra (ODSO)
PO Box 444, Oshawa ON L1H 7L5
Tel: 905-579-6711; *Fax:* 905-987-3083
contact@odso.ca
www.odso.ca

To bring fine orchestral music to residents of the area by operating a high-quality orchestra
John G. Patte, Business Manager
Ronald H. Stead, Chair

Ottawa Symphony Orchestra Inc. (OSO) / Orchestre symphonique d'Ottawa
#250, 2 Daly Ave., Ottawa ON K1N 6E2
Tel: 613-231-7802; *Fax:* 613-231-3610
oso@on.aibn.com
www.ottawasymphony.com
To develop the highest possible artistic level of performance of symphonic repertoire among local musicians, local & Canadian soloists, Canadian music, partnership opportunities for performance with other local performing arts organizations, educational outreach opportunities for young audiences & young performers
David Currie, Music Director

Ottawa Youth Orchestra Academy (OYO) / L'Orchestre des jeunes d'Ottawa
#1, 54 Beech St., Ottawa ON K1S 3J6
Tel: 613-233-9318; *Fax:* 613-233-5038
info@oyoa-aojo.ca
www.oyoa-aojo.ca
John Gomez, Music Director

Pembroke Symphony Orchestra
PO Box 374, Pembroke ON K8A 6X6
Tel: 613-687-2660
info@pembrokesymphony.org
pembrokesymphony.org
Angus Armstrong, Concertmaster
Gail Marion, President

Peterborough Symphony Orchestra (PSO)
PO Box 1135, Peterborough ON K9J 7H4
Tel: 705-742-1992; *Fax:* 705-742-2077
Toll-Free: 877-742-1992
info@thepso.org
www.thepso.org
To perform & develop excellence in symphonic music that will enrich, stimulate & attract the widest possible audience by presenting & perpetuating quality orchestral music to the people of Peterborough & beyond
Michael Newnham, Music Director

The Queen of Puddings Music Theatre Company
The Case Good Warehouse, Bldg. 74, Studio 206, 55 Mill St., Toronto ON M5A 3C4
Tel: 416-203-4149; *Fax:* 416-203-8027
queenofpuddings@bellnet.ca
www.queenofpuddingsmusictheatre.com
Queen of Puddings has consistently produced provocative, dramatic presentations that have challenged the parameters of the opera genre. The company works solely with Canadian artists.
Dairine Ni Mheadhra, Artistic Director
John Hess, Artistic Director

Quinte Symphony
PO Box 23087, Belleville ON K8P 5J3
Tel: 613-395-3756
info@quintesymphony.com
www.quintesymphony.com
Committed to enriching the Quinte community by actively promoting an appreciation of Classical & Canadian orchestral music
Gordon Craig, Music Director
Judith Chalmers, President

Royal Canadian College of Organists (RCCO) / Collège royal canadien des organistes (CRCO)
#202, 204 St. George St., Toronto ON M5R 2N5
Tel: 416-929-6400; *Fax:* 416-929-2265
manager@rcco.ca
www.rcco.ca
To promote a high standard of organ playing, choral directing, church music & composition; to hold examinations in organ playing, choir directing, theory & general knowledge of music; to encourage recitals; to increase the understanding among church musicisans, authorities & the public of matters relating to church music
Valerie Hall, President

Royal Conservatory Orchestra
273 Bloor St. West, Toronto ON M5S 1W2
Tel: 416-408-2824; *Fax:* 416-408-3096
glenngouldschool@rcmusic.ca
www.rcmusic.ca
Mervon Mehta, Executive Director

Sault Symphony Association / Orchestre symphonique de Sault Ste-Marie
#2, 121 Brock St., Sault Ste Marie ON P6A 3B6
Tel: 705-945-5337; *Fax:* 705-945-8865
symphony@soonet.ca
www.saultsymphony.com
To promote symphonic music in Sault Ste Marie, the Algoma region, & the upper peninsula of Michigan
Patti Gardi, General Manager

Scarborough Philharmonic Orchestra
#209, 3007 Kingston Rd., Toronto ON M1M 1P1
Tel: 416-429-0007
spo@spo.ca
www.spo.ca
To enrich the cultural life of Scarborough, through the promotion & presentation of high calibre musical performances; To develop a strong & financially viable organization

Songwriters Association of Canada (SAC) / Association des auteurs-compositeurs canadiens
129 John St., Toronto ON M5V 2E2
Tel: 416-961-1588; *Fax:* 416-961-2040
Toll-Free: 866-456-7664
sacadmin@songwriters.ca
www.songwriters.ca
To protect & develop the creative & business environments for songwriters in Canada & around the world
Don Quarles, Executive Director
Eddie Schwartz, President

Soundstreams Canada
#200, 57 Spadina Ave., Toronto ON M5V 2J2
Tel: 416-504-1282; *Fax:* 416-504-1285
info@soundstreams.ca
www.soundstreams.ca
To foster & promote the development of 20th century music & music by Canadian composers, through the sponsorship of concerts, musical theatre works for young audiences, festivals & special events, recording projects, the commissioning of new works by Canadian composers & touring of Canadian artists
Jennifer Winchester, General Manager

Sudbury Symphony Orchestra Association Inc. (SSO) / Orchestre symphonique de Sudbury inc
#266, 303 York St., Sudbury ON P3E 2A5
Tel: 705-673-1280; *Fax:* 705-673-1434
symphon1@bellnet.ca
www.sudburysymphony.com
To provide the opportunity for a broad spectrum of the public in the Sudbury Region & surrounding area to attend a stimulating program of concerts; to maintain an environment & organization which encourages artistic responsibility & commitment; to attract & maintain private & public funding in order to achieve accessibility & continuity through financial stability; to increase the awareness & appreciation of music in the community; to provide a vehicle for the participation in & ongoing development of the performance of orchestral music; to increase the awareness, appreciation & performance of Canadian music in the community
Victor Sawa, Artistic Director
Marg Barry, Executive Director

Sudbury Youth Orchestra Inc.
PO Box 2241, Stn. A, Sudbury ON P3A 4S1
Tel: 705-566-8101
info@sudburyyouthorchestra.ca
www.sudburyyouthorchestra.ca
To foster an appreciation of orchestral music; to create opportunities for orchestral performance; to provide access to education & training in an orchestral setting for the youth of Sudbury & area
Jamie Arrowsmith, Music Director
Mary Salem Charette, Director

Symphony Hamilton
PO Box 89007, 991 King St. West, Hamilton ON L8S 4R5
Tel: 905-526-6690
info@symphonyhamilton.ca
www.symphonyhamilton.ca
To enrich the cultural life of the Hamilton & surrounding area by maintaining a full-size community symphony orchestra; to perform a wide repertoire of symphonic music, including works by Canadian composers; to make great symphonic music accessible to a larger public by offering attractive concert programs at affordable prices
James R. McKay, Music Director & Conductor
Brenda Sandberg, General Manager
Sydney Hassel, President

Tafelmusik Baroque Orchestra & Chamber Choir
PO Box 14, 427 Bloor St. West, Toronto ON M5S 1X7
Tel: 416-964-9562; *Fax:* 416-964-2782
info@tafelmusik.org
www.tafelmusik.org
Social Media: www.youtube.com/user/tafelmusik1979
Bringing baroque music to Toronto & the world, through concerts, recordings, & a music education programme
Andy Kenins, Chair

Tapestry New Opera Works
The Cannery, Studio 316, #58, 55 Mill St., Toronto ON M5A 3C4
Tel: 416-537-6066; *Fax:* 416-537-7841
information@tapestrynewopera.com
www.tapestrynewopera.com
To develop & produce original works of Canadian opera & music theatre
Wayne Strongman, Artistic Director

Thunder Bay Symphony Orchestra Association (TBSO)
PO Box 29192, Thunder Bay ON P7B 6P9
Tel: 807-345-4331; *Fax:* 807-622-1927
info@tbso.ca
www.tbso.ca
To maintain & nurture a professional, regional orchestra of artistic integrity & excellence; to offer a variety of programs to enrich & encourage the widest possible audience; to support the development of local young musicians
Elizabeth Poulin, President
Leanne Atkinson, General Manager
Geoffrey Moull, Music Director

Timmins Symphony Orchestra
PO Box 1365, Timmins ON P4N 7N2
Tel: 705-267-1006; *Fax:* 705-267-1006
tsoffice@ntl.sympatico.ca
www.timsym.com

Toronto Chinese Youth Orchestra
21 Holmesdale Dr., Markham ON L6C 1S9
Tel: 905-887-7828
tcyo@rogers.com
www.tcyo.ca
Tak-Ng Lai, Music Director

Toronto Downtown Jazz Society
82 Bleecker St., Toronto ON M4X 1L8
Tel: 416-928-2033; *Fax:* 416-928-0533
tdjs@tojazz.com
www.torontojazz.com
To produce the Toronto Downtown Jazz Festival, as well as many other events & programs to further develop jazz talent & audience appreciation; To operate as a registered charity (No. 12969 0269 RR0001); To promote community involvement, artistic excellence, & outstanding production standards
Patrick Taylor, CEO/Executive Producer
Josh Grossman, Artistic Director

The Toronto Mendelssohn Choir
60 Simcoe St., Toronto ON M5J 2H5
Tel: 416-598-0422; *Fax:* 416-598-2992
manager@tmchoir.org
www.tmchoir.org
Canada's world-renowned large vocal ensemble. It has maintained a tradition of performing the finest choral repertoire, and includes the Youth Choir.
Cynthia Hawkins, Executive Director

Toronto Philharmonia
#109, 1210 Sheppard Ave. East, Toronto ON M2K 1E3
Tel: 416-499-2204; *Fax:* 416-490-9739
office@torontophil.on.ca
www.torontophil.on.ca
To provide quality, affordable classical music to City of Toronto & to Ontario communities on tour
Kerry Stratton, Music Director

Toronto Philharmonia Youth Orchestra
PO Box 134, Port Hope ON L1W 3W3
Tel: 416-797-2138; *Toll-Free:* 866-460-5596
info@ljyo.ca
www.ljyo.ca
Michael Lyons, Music Director

Toronto Sinfonietta
400 St. Clair Avenue E, Toronto ON M4T 1P5
Tel: 416-410-4379; *Fax:* 416-233-1054
info@torontosinfonietta.com
www.torontosinfonietta.com
Krzysztof Liebert, President

Matthew Jaskiewicz, Music Director

Toronto Symphony Orchestra (TSO)
212 King St. West, 6th Fl., Toronto ON M5H 1K5
Tel: 416-593-7769; *Fax:* 416-977-2912
www.tso.ca
To present concerts of both established & new music at the highest artistic standard possible, while recognizing audiences' needs; to play a role in the development of future musicians & audiences
George Lewis, Chair
Andrew R. Shaw, President/CEO

Toronto Symphony Youth Orchestra (TSYO)
212 King St. West, 6th Fl., Toronto ON M5H 1K5
Tel: 416-593-7769; *Fax:* 416-977-2912
cmatt@tso.ca
www.tso.on.ca
Christy DiFelice, Manager

University of Toronto Symphony Orchestra
Faculty of Music, University of Toronto, 80 Queen's Park Cres., Toronto ON M5S 2C5
Tel: 416-978-3733; *Fax:* 416-946-3353
performance.music@utoronto.ca
www.music.utoronto.ca
David Briskin, Conductor

University of Western Ontario Symphony Orchestra (UWOSO)
Faculty of Music, University of Western Ontario, 1151 Richmond St. North, London ON N6A 3K7
Tel: 519-661-2043; *Fax:* 519-661-3531
music@uwo.ca
www.music.uwo.ca

Wilfrid Laurier University Symphony Orchestra
Faculty of Music, 75 University Ave. West, Waterloo ON N2L 3C5
Tel: 519-884-0710; *Fax:* 519-747-9129
jdupuis@wlu.ca
To train music students to be musicians who have solid knowledge of music theory & history, & are competent performers
Paul Pulford, General Manager/Music Director

Windsor Symphony Orchestra (WSO)
487 Ouellette Ave., Windsor ON N9A 4J2
Tel: 519-973-1238; *Toll-Free:* 888-327-8327
www.windsorsymphony.com
To enrich community life & serve as an educational resource through high quality live performance of orchestral music
Barb Kuker, President
Stephen Savage, First Vice President
Sandra Aversa, Second Vice President

York Symphony Orchestra Inc.
PO Box 355, Richmond Hill ON L4C 4Y6
Tel: 416-410-0860
yorksymphonyorchestra@hotmail.com
www.yorksymphony.ca
To provide musical enjoyment for audiences & musicians, with the goal of being recognized & supported throughout the region
Gregory Burton, Music Director

Prince Edward Island

East Coast Music Association (ECMA) / Association de la musique de la côte est
#70, 90 University Ave., Charlottetown PE C1A 4K9
Tel: 902-892-9040; *Fax:* 902-892-9041
ecma@ecma.ca
www.ecma.ca
To develop, foster, promote & celebrate East Coast music locally & globally

Music PEI
PO Box 2371, Charlottetown PE C1A 8C4
Tel: 902-894-6734; *Fax:* 902-894-4404
music@musicpei.com
www.musicpei.com
To promote, foster and develop artists and the music industry on PEI.
Jim Hornby, President
Rob Oakie, Executive Director

Prince Edward Island Symphony Society (PEISO)
PO Box 185, 146 Richmond St., Charlottetown PE C1A 7K4
Tel: 902-892-4333
peiso@peisymphony.com
www.peisymphony.com
To establish & promote symphonic music; to further & foster appreciation of musical education; to promote the welfare of musicians; to give & arrange performances, entertainments & concerts; to employ teachers & instructors to inform the public & awaken interest
Annette Campbell, Contact

Québec

Académie de musique du Québec (AMQ)
CP 818, Succ. C, 1231, rue Panet, Montréal QC H2L 4L6
Tél: 514-528-1961; *Téléc:* 514-528-7572
prixdeurope@videotron.ca
Promouvoir le goût et l'avancement de la musique au Québec, aux professeurs oeuvrant dans le secteur privé et soucieux à la fois d'autonomie et d'encadrement, aux élèves qui désirent une reconnaissance officielle de leur travail
Jean Marchand, Président

Alliance des chorales du Québec (ACQ)
CP 1000, Succ. M, 4545, av Pierre-de Coubertin, Montréal QC H1V 3R2
Tél: 514-252-3020; *Téléc:* 514-252-3222
Ligne sans frais: 888-924-6387
information@chorale.qc.ca
www.chorale.qc.ca
Regrouper des chorales de tous styles et de tous niveaux; donner des moyens de mieux chanter; promouvoir et développer le chant choral au Québec
Catherine Girard, Directrice générale

Association québécoise de l'industrie du disque, du spectacle et de la vidéo (ADISQ)
6420, rue Saint-Denis, Montréal QC H2S 2R7
Tél: 514-842-5147; *Téléc:* 514-842-7762
info@adisq.com
www.adisq.com
Promouvoir les intérêts des producteurs de disques, spectacles et vidéos

Canadian Amateur Musicians (CAMMAC) / Musiciens amateurs du Canada
85 Cammac Rd., Harrington QC J8G 2T2
Tel: 819-687-3938; *Fax:* 819-687-3323
Toll-Free: 888-622-8755
national@cammac.ca
www.cammac.ca
To create opportunities for musicians of all levels & ages to play music in a non-competitive environment
Harry Qualman, President
Raymond Vles, Vice-President
Rachel Gagnon, Secretary
Roland Wilk, Treasurer
Radu Kaufman, Executive Director
Patricia Abbott, Artistic Director
Johanne Guérin, Group Coordinator
Solange Marquis, Comptroller

Canadian Music Competitions Inc. / Concours de musique du Canada inc.
#220, 1450, rue City Councillors, Montréal QC H3A 2E6
Tel: 514-284-5398; *Fax:* 514-284-6828
Toll-Free: 877-879-1959
info@cmcnational.com
www.cmcnational.com
Faire participer a une véritable expérience nationale de musique, en étroite collaboration avec les institutions et les professeurs de musique du pays, les plus doués de nos jeunes musiciennes et musiciens canadiens.
Raymonde Boutet, Présidente

Chants Libres, compagnie lyrique de création
#303, 1908, rue Panet, Montréal QC H2L 3A2
Tél: 514-841-2642; *Téléc:* 514-841-2640
creation@chantslibres.org
www.chantslibres.org
Réunir des créateurs de toutes les disciplines (musique, théâtre, arts plastiques, arts électroniques, vidéo etc.) autour d'un point commun: la voix
Pauline Vaillancourt, Directrice générale

Concerts symphoniques de Sherbrooke inc. (CSS) / Sherbrooke Symphony Orchestra
Domain Howard, Pavillon 1, CP 610, 1300, boul de Portland, Sherbrooke QC J1H 5H9
Tél: 819-821-0227; *Téléc:* 819-821-1959
oss@abacom.com
www.css-oss.com
Faire connaître la musique symphonique dans la région et permettre aux musiciens de la région de jouer dans un orchestre professionnel
Michel Bédard, Président
Stéphane Laforest, Directeur artistique

Ensemble contemporain de Montréal (ECM+)
3890 rue Clark, Montréal QC H2W 1W6
Tél: 514-524-0173; *Téléc:* 514-524-0179
info@ecm.qc.ca
www.ecm.qc.ca
Natalie Watanabe, Directrice générale

Ensemble vocal Ganymède
CP 476, Succ. C, Montréal QC H2L 4K4
Tél: 514-528-6302
contacter@evganymede.com
www.evganymede.com
Choeur d'hommes
Yvan Sabourin, Directeur

Fédération des harmonies et des orchestres symphonies du Québec (FHOSQ)
CP 1000, Succ. M, 4545, av Pierre-de-Coubertin, Montréal QC H1V 3R2
Tél: 514-252-3026; *Téléc:* 514-252-3115
info@fhosq.org
www.fhosq.org
Contribuer au développement et à l'amélioration des harmonies en tant que loisir éducatif et culturel
Chantal Isabelle, Coordinatrice

Jeunesses Musicales du Canada (JMC) / Jeunesses Musicales of Canada
305, av du Mont-Royal est, Montréal QC H2T 1P8
Tel: 514-845-4108; *Fax:* 514-845-8241
Toll-Free: 877-377-7951
info@jeunessesmusicales.com
www.jeunessesmusicales.ca
To promote Canadian musical artists & develop audiences
Jacques Marquis, Directeur général et artistique
Claudia Morissette, Directrice, Concerts
Nathalie Allen, Directrice, Services financiers
Isabelle Ligot, Directrice, Communications JMC/CMIM/FJMC

Musicaction
#2, 4385, rue Saint-Hubert, Montréal QC H2J 2X1
Tél: 514-861-8444; *Téléc:* 514-861-4423
Ligne sans frais: 800-861-5561
info@musicaction.ca
www.musicaction.ca
Développement de la musique vocale francophone au Canada
Andrée Ménard, Directrice générale

L'Opéra de Montréal (ODM) / Montréal Opera
260, boul de Maisonneuve ouest, Montréal QC H2X 1Y9
Tel: 514-985-2222; *Fax:* 514-985-2219
info@operademontreal.com
www.operademontreal.com
To present opera productions of comparable quality & originality to those seen in the world's great opera houses; seeks the contribution of creative personnel from local & national levels, as well as inviting the best artists from abroad; supports the emergence of new Canadian opera talent
Pierre Dufour, General & Production Director
Christine Krebs, Administrative Director
Michel Beulac, Artistic Director
Monique Denis, Donations & Sponsorship Manager
Pierre Vachon, Communications & Marketing Director
Alexandre Taillefer, Chair
Chantal Lambert, Atelier Lyrique Program Director

Opéra de Québec
1220, av Taché, Québec QC G1R 3B4
Tél: 418-529-4142; *Téléc:* 418-529-3735
operaqc@mediom.qc.ca
www.operadequebec.qc.ca
Produire des spectacles d'opéra professionnels à Québec
Gaston Déry, Président

Orchestre de chambre de Montréal (OCM) / Montréal Chamber Orchestra (MCO)
5476 Côte St-Antoine, Montréal QC H4A 1R2
Tél: 514-871-1224; *Téléc:* 514-871-8967
info@mco-ocm.qc.ca
www.mco-ocm.qc.ca
Se consacre au répertoire pour ensemble de chambre & oeuvres canadiennes
Wanda Kaluzny, Music Director

Orchestre symphonique de Montréal
260, boul de Maisonneuve ouest, 2e étage, Montréal QC H2X 1Y9
Tél: 514-842-3402; *Téléc:* 514-842-0728
www.osm.ca

L'Orchestre doit diffuser, au plus large public possible, le répertoire mondial de la musique symphonique, & les artistes de niveau international; doit assumer son rôle social & institutionnel
Madeleine Careau, Chef de la direction
René Mandel, Directeur musical

Orchestre symphonique de Québec
401, av Grande Allée est, Québec QC G1R 2J5
Tél: 418-643-8486; *Téléc:* 418-646-9665
billetterie@osq.qc.ca
www.osq.qc.ca
Interpréter le répertoire symphonique; être le principal moteur de l'activité musicale de la région. L'OSM est reconnu comme un organisme de grande qualité, dynamique, accessible, et financièrement sain
Jean Letarte, Directeur artistique

Orchestre symphonique de Trois-Rivières (OSTR)
CP 1281, Trois-Rivières QC G9A 5K8
Tél: 819-373-5340; *Téléc:* 819-373-6693
administration@ostr.ca
www.ostr.ca
Poursuivre l'atteinte des objectifs inhérents à ses axes de développement: éducation, implication dans son milieu, diffusion de musique symphonique, création musicale et diffusion de nouveaux produits
Thérèse Boutin, Directrice générale
Jacques Lacombe, Directeur artistique
Jean-Marc Vanasse, Président

Orchestre symphonique des jeunes de la Montérégie
31, rue Lorne, Saint-Lambert QC J4P 2G7
Tél: 450-923-3733
courrier@aojm.org
www.aojm.org
Jean-Claude Paré, Président

Orchestre symphonique des jeunes de Montréal (OSJM)
CP 83566, Succ. Succursale Garnier, Montréal QC H2J 4E9
Tél: 514-645-0311; *Téléc:* 514-524-9894
osjmontreal@gmail.ca
www.osjm.org
Présenter le jeune musicien de talent à un auditoire et lui fournir une expérience formative sous la supervision d'artistes reconnus; encourager et soutenir le choix d'une carrière musicale qui peut mener à un grand orchestre; promouvoir un intérêt dans les concerts et développer un soutien plus diversifié dans les activités de l'orchestre; fournir à l'entreprise privée l'occasion de participer plus activement dans une activité culturelle d'envergure et l'aider à faire apprécier son rôle dans la communauté
Jean-Paul Lejeune, Président

Orchestre symphonique des jeunes du West Island (OSJWI) / West Island Youth Symphony Orchestra (WIYSO)
CP 1028, Succ. Pointe-Claire, Pointe-Claire QC H9S 4H9
Tél: 514-633-1128; *Téléc:* 514-633-1129
info@osjwi.qc.ca
www.osjwi.qc.ca
Permettre aux jeunes de 8-25 ans de jouer dans un orchestre regroupant tous les instruments sous la direction d'un chef professionel
Isabelle Delage, Présidente

Orchestre symphonique des jeunes Philippe-Filion
2100, boul des Hêtres, Shawinigan QC G9N 8R8
Tél: 819-539-6000; *Téléc:* 819-539-2400
morind03@cgocable.ca
Monique Gagnon Carbonneau, Directrice Musicale

Orchestre symphonique du Saguenay-Lac-St-Jean (OSSLSJ)
202, rue Jacques-Cartier est, Chicoutimi QC G7H 6R8
Tél: 418-545-3409; *Téléc:* 418-545-8287
info@lorchestre.org
www.lorchestre.org
Produire et diffuser des concerts professionnels à travers tout le Saguenay-Lac-Saint-Jean en regard des enjeux financiers et des structures d'accueil existantes. Ses qualités artistiques et administratives en constante évolution lui permettent d'exercer un leadership au sein des organismes musicaux régionaux, basé sur un partenariat serré avec le milieu, au service du développement de sa discipline et de sa communauté
Jacques Clément, Directeur artisique

Orchestre symphonique régional Abitibi-Témiscamingue
CP 2305, Rouyn-Noranda QC J9X 5A9
Tél: 819-762-0043; *Téléc:* 819-762-0274
osr@tlb.sympatico.ca
culture-at.org/osr
Diffusion de la musique classique et integration de la relève
Réginald Grenier, Président

Organization of Canadian Symphony Musicians (OCSM) / Organisation des musiciens d'orchestres symphoniques du Canada (OMOSC)
#6, 445, rue Gerard-Morrisset, Québec QC G1S 4V5
Tel: 418-688-0801
www.ocsm-omosc.org
To address issues confronting professional symphony musicians
Francine Schutzman, President
Eline Brock Sanheim, First Vice-President
David Brown, 2nd Vice-President
Robert Fraser, Secretary
Greg Sheldon, Treasurer

Société chorale de Saint-Lambert / St. Lambert Choral Society
CP 36546, Succ. CSP Victoria, Saint-Lambert QC J4P 3S8
www.chorale-stlambert.qc.ca
To offer several concerts of choral music each year
Nancy Kirkwood, President
David Christiani, Music Director
Kimberley Bartczak, Accompanist

Société Pro Musica Inc. / Pro Musica Society Inc.
#201, 3505, rue rue Ste-Famille, Montréal QC H2X 2L3
Tél: 514-845-0532; *Téléc:* 514-845-1500
Ligne sans frais: 877-445-0532
info@promusica.qc.ca
www.promusica.qc.ca
Promouvoir et présenter à Montréal la plus belle musique de chambre par les meilleurs interprètes d'ici et d'ailleurs; dans la série TOPAZE, promouvoir et offrir aux jeunes familles de meilleures conditions pour assister aux concerts avec un atelier d'animation musicale pour les enfants
Pierre Rolland, Directeur artistique
Monique Dubé, Directrice générale

Saskatchewan

Regina Symphony Orchestra (RSO)
2424 College Ave., Regina SK S4P 1C8
Tel: 306-586-9555; *Fax:* 306-586-2133
Toll-Free: 800-667-8497
info@reginasymphony.com
www.reginasymphony.com
To promote & enhance the performance & enjoyment of live orchestral music in Regina & southern Saskatchewan & contribute to the cultural life of the city, province & nation
Victor Sawa, Musical Director
Natasha Bood, Executive Director

Saskatchewan Band Association (SBA)
34 Sunset Dr. North, Yorkton SK S3N 3K9
Tel: 306-783-2263; *Fax:* 306-783-2060
Toll-Free: 877-475-2263
sask.band@sasktel.net
www.saskband.org
To promote & support instrumental music in Saskatchewan; To act as a voice on issues that affect bands in Saskatchewan
Adrian Bourgeois, President
Christa MacBride, Vice-President
Chistin Dorgan-Lee, Secretary
Aaron Sikora, Treasurer

Saskatchewan Orchestral Association, Inc. (SOA)
PO Box 87, Hanley SK S0G 2E0
Tel: 306-544-2230; *Fax:* 306-544-2718
saskorchestras@yourlink.ca
www.saskorchestras.com
To serve as resource base & coordinating body for orchestral & string programs in Saskatchewan; To procure funds to make achievement of goals & objectives of SOA possible
Kathryn Peters, Administrator

Saskatoon Symphony Society (SSO)
Standard Life Bldg., #120, 128 Fourth Ave. South, Saskatoon SK S7K 1M8
Tel: 306-665-6414; *Fax:* 306-652-3364
saskatoon.symphony@sasktel.net
www.saskatoonsymphony.org
To promote, encourage & support symphonic & classical music in Saskatoon & elsewhere in Saskatchewan
Catherine McKeehan, General Manager

Saskatoon Youth Orchestra
1610 Morgan Ave., Saskatoon SK S7H 2S1
Tel: 306-373-6408; *Fax:* 306-955-6336
syo@sasktel.net
toeww.sasktelwebsite.net/SYO.html
Wayne Toews, Music Director

South Saskatchewan Youth Orchestra (SSYO)
101 Leopold Cres., Regina SK S4T 6N5
Tel: 306-586-3007; *Fax:* 306-586-2133
ssyo.ca@gmail.com
www.ssyo.ca
To provide orchestral training to young musicians in Southern Saskatchewan
Alan Denike, Music Director

Yukon Territory

Jazz Yukon
PO Box 31307, Whitehorse YT Y1A 5P7
Tel: 867-633-3300
info@jazzyukon.ca
www.jazzyukon.ca
To promote & present jazz in the Yukon through an annual integrated program of live jazz presentations & jazz education outreach

Performing Arts - Theatre

Alberta

Alberta Playwrights' Network (APN)
2633 Hochwald Ave. SW, Calgary AB T3E 7K2
Tel: 403-269-8564; *Fax:* 403-265-6773
Toll-Free: 800-268-8564
admin@albertaplaywrights.com
www.albertaplaywrights.com
APN is a non-profit, provincial arts service organization and registered charity dedicated to fostering playwriting in Alberta.
Johanne Deleeuw, Executive Director
Brian Dooley, Edmonton Liaison

Evergreen Theatre Society
2633 Hochwald Ave. SW, Calgary AB T3E 7K2
Tel: 403-228-1384; *Fax:* 403-229-1385
Toll-Free: 877-840-9746
info@evergreentheatre.com
www.evergreentheatre.com
To create innovative, entertaining, accessible education-tangible choices for a healthy & sustainable future
Lisa Ryan, Director, Residency
Sean Fraser, Executive Director

New West Theatre Society
#111, 210A - 12A St. North, Lethbridge AB T1J 0P5
Tel: 403-381-9378
info@newwesttheatre.com
www.newwesttheatre.com
To provide Lethbridge & surrounding region with a broad-based & diverse program of professional quality theatrical, musical & dramatic performances
Nicholas Hanson, Artistic Director
Jeremy Mason, General Manager

Theatre Alberta Society
11759 Groat Rd., 3rd Fl., Edmonton AB T5M 3K6
Tel: 780-422-8162; *Fax:* 780-422-2663
Toll-Free: 888-422-8160
theatreab@theatrealberta.com
www.theatrealberta.com
To encourage the growth of theatre in Alberta through high quality support & training opportunities to theatre professionals, educators & community theatre practitioners
Marie Gynane-Willis, Executive Director

Theatre Calgary
220 - 9 Ave. SE, Calgary AB T2G 5C4
Tel: 403-294-7440; *Fax:* 403-294-7493
info@theatrecalgary.com
www.theatrecalgary.com
Produces classical and modern theatre.
Tom McCabe, President
Dennis Garnhum, Artistic Director

Theatre Network (1975) Society
10708 - 124 St., Edmonton AB T5M 0H1
Tel: 780-453-2440; *Fax:* 780-453-2596
info@theartnetwork.ca
www.attheroxy.com
To promote original regional drama
Jill Roszell, General Manager

Bradley Moss, Artistic Director

British Columbia

Bard on the Beach Theatre Society
#301, 601 Cambie St., Vancouver BC V6B 2P1
Tel: 604-737-0625; *Fax:* 604-737-0425
Toll-Free: 877-739-0559
info@bardonthebeach.org
www.bardonthebeach.org
To provide Vancouver residents & visitors with affordable, accessible Shakespearean productions of the finest quality
Christopher Gaze, Artistic Director
Robert Barr, Managing Director

British Columbia Drama Association
PO Box 2031, #7, 10 Commercial St., Nanaimo BC V9R 6X6
Tel: 250-591-0018; *Fax:* 250-591-0027
info@theatrebc.org
www.theatrebc.org
To promote the development of theatre in BC & Canada through a wide range of programs, services, activities, competitions, festivals & events
Robb Mowbray, Executive Director
Ray Mordan, President
Ray Mordan, Sec.-Treas.

First Pacific Theatre Society
1440 - 12 Ave. West, Vancouver BC V6H 1M8
Tel: 604-731-5483; *Fax:* 604-733-3880
info@pacifictheatre.org
www.pacifictheatre.org
To produce high quality theatre; to operate with artistic, spiritual, relational & financial integrity
Ron Reed, Artistic Director
Alison Chisholm, Theatre Administrator
Frank Nickel, Production Manager
Andrea Loewen, Director, Public Relations
Cindy McPherson, Business Manager

First Vancouver Theatre Space Society (FVTS)
c/o Vancouver Fringe Festival, 1398 Cartwright St., Vancouver BC V6H 3R8
Tel: 604-257-0350; *Fax:* 604-253-1924
info@vancouverfringe.com
www.vancouverfringe.com
To promoting interest in the arts in Vancouver; to nurture & support artists
Eduardo Ottoni, Production Manager
David Jordan, Executive Director

Greater Vancouver Professional Theatre Alliance (GVPTA)
1405 Anderson St., 3rd Fl., Vancouver BC V6H 3R5
Tel: 604-608-6799; *Fax:* 604-608-6923
info@gvpta.ca
www.gvpta.ca
To promote live theatre & foster a thriving environment for the continued growth & development of theatre in Greater Vancouver
Sue Porter, Executive Director

Intrepid Theatre Co. Society
#2, 1609 Blanshard St., Victoria BC V8S 4P6
Tel: 250-383-2663; *Fax:* 250-380-1999
info@intrepidtheatre.com
www.intrepidtheatre.com
To educate & enhance the public's awareness & aesthetic appreciation of contemporary & progressive styles of modern theatre by encouraging, developing & producing new or experimental works for public performance; by coordinating & producing the annual Fringe Theatre Festival in Victoria
Janet Munsil, Producer
Ian Case, General Manager

Playwrights Theatre Centre
#201, 1398 Cartwright St., Vancouver BC V6H 3R8
Tel: 604-685-6228; *Fax:* 604-685-7451
plays@playwrightstheatre.com
www.playwrightstheatre.com
Playwrights Theatre Centre is committed to developing new Canadian plays. Through dramaturgy, workshops, writers' groups and other programs, we provide support to experienced, emerging, and aspiring playwrights from across the country.
Ray Wallis, President
Martin Kinch, Executive Director/Literary Manager
Linda Gorrie, Administrator

Théâtre la Seizième
#266, 1555 - 7e av ouest, Vancouver BC V6J 1S1
Tel: 604-736-2616; *Fax:* 604-736-9151
info@seizieme.ca
www.seizieme.ca/
Promouvoir le théâtre professionnel francophone en Colombie-Britannique
Craig Holzschuh, Directeur général et artistique

Theatre Terrific Society
4397 - 2nd Ave. West, Vancouver BC V6R 1K4
Tel: 604-222-4020; *Fax:* 604-222-4020
info@theatreterrific.ca
www.theatreterrific.ca
To provide theatrical opportunities to people with disabilities
Susanna Uchatius, Artistic Director
Nina Hirlaender Hinton, General Manager

The Vancouver Summer Festival Society
#400, 873 Beatty St., Vancouver BC V6B 2M6
Tel: 604-688-1152; *Fax:* 604-688-8441
music@festivalvancouver.bc.ca
www.festivalvancouver.bc.ca
Presents a summer music celebration that explores the connections between cultures, centuries & people; internationally acclaimed artists from around the globe join forces with some of Canada's best performers in over 40 concerts featuring classical music, world music & jazz
George Laverock, Program Director
Morna Edmundson, Administrative Director

Vancouver TheatreSports League (VTSL)
#104, 1177 West Broadway, Vancouver BC V6H 1G3
Tel: 604-738-7013; *Fax:* 604-738-8013
info@vtsl.com
www.vtsl.com
To challenge & inspire the community by growing & exploring exceptional improv-based work
Jay Ono, Executive Director

Western Canada Theatre Company Society (WCT)
PO Box 329, Kamloops BC V2C 5K9
Tel: 250-372-3216; *Fax:* 250-374-7099
info@westerncanadatheatre.bc.ca
www.westerncanadatheatre.bc.ca
To provide the regional community with challenging professional theatre; to entertain, educate, enrich & interact with the cultural mosaic of its community; to promote & assist the performing arts through the provision of educational, theatrical & artistic opportunities & services & through the management & operation of facilities
Lorid Marchand, General Manager

Manitoba

Le Cercle Molière
340, boul Provencher, Saint-Boniface MB R2H 0G7
Tél: 204-233-8053; *Téléc:* 204-233-2373
reception@cerclemoliere.com
www.cerclemoliere.com
Présenter des spectacles de théâtre en français au Manitoba
Roland Mahé, Directeur artistique

Manitoba Association of Playwrights (MAP)
#503, 100 Arthur St., Winnipeg MB R3B 1H3
Tel: 204-942-8941; *Fax:* 204-942-1555
mbplay@mts.net
www.mbplays.ca
To provide support for playwrights in Manitoba through the operation of programs for emerging & established playwrights
Rory Runnells, Coordinator

Manitoba Theatre Centre (MTC)
174 Market Ave., Winnipeg MB R3B 0P8
Tel: 204-942-6537; *Fax:* 204-947-3741
Toll-Free: 877-446-4500
patronservices@mtc.mb.ca
www.mtc.mb.ca
Canada's first English-language regional theatre, with a mandate to study, practise & promote all aspects of the dramatic arts, with particular emphasis on professional production
Steven Schipper, Artistic Director
Zaz Bajon, General Manager

Prairie Theatre Exchange (PTE)
Portage Place, #Y300, 393 Portage Ave., 3rd Fl., Winnipeg MB R3B 3H6
Tel: 204-942-7291; *Fax:* 204-942-1774
pte@pte.mb.ca
www.pte.mb.ca
To operate a professional theatre of high calibre for the entertainment & edification of a broad spectrum of people; to operate a school to encourage appreciation of theatre & to provide accessible, high quality, innovative drama education; to support the development of new plays; to foster theatre arts-related endeavours of others through use of our facilities & expertise; to manage one or more community theatre arts centres
Cherry Karpyshin, General Manager
Wendy Miller, President

New Brunswick

Théâtre l'Escaouette
170, rue Botsford, Moncton NB E1C 4X6
Tél: 506-855-0001; *Téléc:* 506-855-0010
gilleslosier@nb.aibn.com
www.escaouette.com
Le théâtre l'Escaouette est un lieu privilégié de création. Avec ses 25 ans d'existence, les artistes ont porté à la scène 38 textes originaux, plus de la moitié de l'ensemble de la production dramaturgique acadienne créée au Nouveau-Brunswick.
Marcia Babineau, Direction artistique & codirection générale

Theatre New Brunswick (TNB)
#31, 55 Whitting Rd., Fredericton NB E3B 5Y5
Tel: 506-460-1381; *Fax:* 506-453-9315
Toll-Free: 800-442-9779
general@tnb.nb.ca
www.tnb.nb.ca
To provide live professional theatre to the people of New Brunswick by touring & performing in nine centres throughout the province; to entertain by providing quality theatre & acting as a theatrical resource for playwrights, actors & young people interested in the field
Heather Vanlderstine, Administrative Assistant

Théâtre populaire d'Acadie (TPA)
#302, 220, boul. St-Pierre ouest, Caraquet NB E1W 1A5
Tél: 506-727-0920; *Téléc:* 506-727-0923
Ligne sans frais: 800-872-0920
tpa@pacadie.ca
www.tpacadie.ca
Créer, produire, diffuser et faire rayonner le théâtre d'ici et d'ailleurs
Maurice Arsenault, Directeur artistique et général

Newfoundland and Labrador

Theatre Newfoundland Labrador
PO Box 655, Corner Brook NL A2H 6G1
Tel: 709-639-7238; *Fax:* 709-639-1006
www.theatrenewfoundland.com
Theatre Newfoundland and Labrador (TNL) is a not-for-profit organization dedicated to creating and producing professional theatre which reflects the lives and dirversity of our audiences on the provinces's west coast, extending to labrador and across the island of Newfoundland.
Jeff Pitcher, Artistic Director

Nova Scotia

Neptune Theatre Foundation
1593 Argyle St., Halifax NS B3J 2B2
Tel: 902-429-7300; *Fax:* 902-429-1211
Toll-Free: 800-565-7345
info@neptunetheatre.com
www.neptunetheatre.com
To pursue theatrical excellence with artistic vision; to develop local & Canadian artistic talent; to encourage the youth of our community to develop a life-long interest in live theatre
Doreen E. Malone, General Manager
George Pothitos, Artistic Director

Theatre Nova Scotia (TNS)
1113 Marginal Rd., Halifax NS B3H 4P7
Tel: 902-425-3876; *Fax:* 902-422-0881
theatrens@theatrens.ca
www.theatrens.ca
To provide services, training & resources to professional & amateur theatre community throughout Nova Scotia
Sue Leblanc-Crawford, Chair
Christopher Shore, Executive Director

Ontario

The Actors' Fund of Canada / La Caisse des acteurs du Canada inc.
#301, 1000 Yonge St., Toronto ON M4W 2K2
Tel: 416-975-0304; *Fax:* 416-975-0306
Toll-Free: 877-399-8392
contact@actorsfund.ca
www.actorsfund.ca

The Actors' Fund of Canada promotes artistic excellence for performers, creators, technicians and other members of creative and production teams in all entertainment industry sectors. The Fund carries out this mission by providing encouragement and short-term financial aid to help entertainment industry workers maintain their health, housing and ability to work after an illness, injury or sudden unemployment.
Barry Flatman, President

Association of Summer Theatres 'Round Ontario (ASTRO)
c/o Theatre Ontario, #210, 215 Spadina Ave., Toronto ON M5T 2C7
Tel: 416-408-4556; *Fax:* 416-408-3402
tim@theatreontario.org
www.summertheatre.org
To act as an information & resource network for its members; to support the professional development of its members; to act as a liaison for its membership with arts & business organizations, the media & the community; to advocate for its membership with government, government agencies & other organizations; to undertake projects to increase awareness of the activities of its membership among the general public
Steven Thomas, President

Buddies in Bad Times Theatre
12 Alexander St., Toronto ON M4Y 1B4
Tel: 416-975-9130; *Fax:* 416-975-9293
chy@artsexy.ca
www.artsexy.ca
To promote gay, lesbian, & queer theatrical expression
Brendan Healy, Artistic Director

Canadian Association for Theatre Research (CATR) / Association canadienne de la recherche théâtrale (ACRT)
#2, 40 River St., Toronto ON M5A 3N9
nicholsg@umoncton.ca
www.catr-acrt.ca
To focus on theatre, drama, & performance in a Canadian context, including acting, directing, practical matters of theatre, historiography, & the teaching, reception, theory, & literary criticism of drama
Kym Bird, Secretary
Shelley Scott, President
James Dugan, Treasurer

The Canadian Stage Company
26 Berkeley St., Toronto ON M5A 2W3
Tel: 416-367-8243; *Fax:* 416-367-1768
general@canstage.com
www.canstage.com
To develop, produce & export the best in Canadian & international contemporary theatre
Louise Plunkett, Customer Service Manager
Matthew Jocelyn, Artistic & General Director

Canadian Theatre Critics Association (CTCA) / Association des critiques de théâtre du Canada
#724, 2121 Bathurst St., Toronto ON M5N 2P3
Tel: 416-782-0966; *Fax:* 416-782-0366
scenechanges@rogers.com
www.canadiantheatrecritics.ca
To promote excellence in theatre criticism; to encourage the dissemination of information on theatre on a national level; to encourage the awareness & development of Canadian theatre nationally & internationally through theatre criticism in all the media; to promote & encourage excellence in Canadian theatre through national awards; to improve the status & working conditions of theatre critics
Jeniva Berger, Founding President
Alvina Ruprecht, Co-President
Don Rubin, Co-President

Compagnie vox théâtre
333 King Edward Ave., Ottawa ON K1N 7M5
Tél: 613-241-1090; *Téléc:* 613-241-0250
info@voxtheatre.ca
www.voxtheatre.ca
Avec son travail de création, ses productions de théâtre chanté, ses accueils de spectacle pluridisciplinaires et ses tournées, la compagnie Vox Théâtre présente une programation complète pour les enfants et leur propose aussi des activités de formation

Gryphon Theatre Foundation
PO Box 454, Barrie ON L4M 4T7
Tel: 705-728-4613; *Fax:* 705-728-4623
boxoffice@gryphontheatre.com
www.gryphontheatre.com
To promote interest, & provide opportunities for education in the performing arts in the Georgian Bay area; to encourage & support the development of a regional theatre in the Georgian Bay area; to provide opportunities for Canadian artistic talent; to operate a theatre company
Donna Kenwell, Chair

Harbourfront Centre
235 Queens Quay West, Toronto ON M5J 2G8
Tel: 416-973-4600; *Fax:* 416-973-6055
info@harbourfrontcentre.com
www.harbourfrontcentre.com
To nurture the growth of new cultural expression; to stimulte Canadian & international interchange; to provide a dynamic, accessible environment for the public to experience the marvels of the creative imagination
Bruce Hutchinson, Director, Marketing & Media Relations
William J.S. Boyle, CEO
Gregory Burke, Director, The Power Plant
Melanie Fernandez, Director, Community & Education
Tina Rasmussen, Director, Performing Arts
Geoffrey Taylor, Director, Harbourfront Reading Series

Native Earth Performing Arts Inc. (NEPA)
Bldg. 74, #300/305, 55 Mill St., Toronto ON M5A 3C4
Tel: 416-531-1402; *Fax:* 416-531-6377
Toll-Free: 877-854-9708
office@nativeearth.ca
www.nativeearth.ca
To enable Native actors, writers, designers, directors & technicians to work together to produce quality theatre that is vital to their development as artists & their identity as Native people; to encourage the use of theatre as form of communication within the Native community, including the use of the Native languages
Yvette Nolan, Artistic Director
Donna-Michelle St. Bernard, General Manager

Ontario Puppetry Association
714 Hedgerow Pl., London ON K7M 4G9
Tel: 613-389-2996; *Toll-Free:* 800-379-0446
dsmith@kos.net
www.onpuppet.org
To promote recognition of puppetry as art; to distribute information on all aspects; to assist in eventual formation of national puppet theatre
Philip Arnold, President
Mike Harding, Vice-President

Playwrights Guild of Canada (PGC)
#210, 215 Spadina Ave., Toronto ON M5T 2C7
Tel: 416-703-0201; *Fax:* 416-703-0059
Toll-Free: 800-561-3318
info@playwrightsguild.ca
www.playwrightsguild.ca
To encourage Canadian playwriting; to publish, promote & distribute Canadian plays; to provide current information of Canadian plays & their authors; to offer copyright protection; to promote the study & appreciation of Canadian plays; to safeguard freedom of expression on the stage
Robin Sokoloski, Executive Director

Professional Association of Canadian Theatres (PACT)
#555, 215 Spadina Ave., Toronto ON M5T 2C7
Tel: 416-595-6455; *Fax:* 416-595-6450
Toll-Free: 800-263-7228
marlaf@pact.ca
www.pact.ca
To gain recognition & support for professional theatre in Canada; To support the development of Canadian theatre companies by sharing resources & knowledge; to develop working standards & relationships with theatre professionals through their associations; To inform & connect theatres across Canada through a communications network; To act as a major force in influencing cultural policy at all levels of government
Lucy White, Executive Director
Eric Coates, President
Linda Gorrie, Treasurer

Resurgence Theatre Company (RTC)
211 Main St. South, Newmarket ON L3Y 5Y9
Tel: 905-953-2838; *Fax:* 905-895-0070
info@resurgence.on.ca
www.resurgence.on.ca
To present the classics & ignite contemporary & new works of theatre, utilizing the energy of young & established professionals
Anthony Leo, General Manager

Shaw Festival
PO Box 774, 10 Queen's Parade, Niagara-on-the-Lake ON L0S 1J0
Tel: 905-468-2153; *Fax:* 905-468-5438
Toll-Free: 800-657-1106
dlg@shawfest.com
www.shawfest.com
To create intellectually challenging & entertaining theatre at an affordable price
Jackie Maxwell, Artistic Director
Colleen Blake, Executive Director

Tarragon Theatre
30 Bridgman Ave, Toronto ON M5R 1X3
Tel: 416-536-5018; *Fax:* 416-533-6372
info@tarragontheatre.com
www.tarragontheatre.com
To develop & produce new Canadian plays
Richard Rose, Artistic Director
Ernest McNee, President
Giles Meikle, Treasurer

Théâtre de la Vieille 17
119, rue York, Ottawa ON K1N 5T4
Tél: 613-241-8562; *Téléc:* 613-241-9507
communications@vieille17.ca
www.vieille17.ca
Créer et diffuser des spectacles pour la jeunesse et pour les adultes à l'échelle régionale, nationale et internationale
Esther Beauchemin, Directrice artistique et générale

Théâtre du Nouvel-Ontario (TNO)
21 Lasalle Blvd., Sudbury ON P3A 6B1
Tél: 705-525-5606; *Téléc:* 705-525-1129
tno@letno.ca
www.letno.ca
Dédié à la création, à la dramaturgie franco-ontarienne et à l'accueil d'oeuvres principalement canadiennes
Geneviève Pineault, Directrice artistique et générale

Théâtre du Trillium
333 av King Edward, Ottawa ON K1N 7M5
Tél: 613-789-7643; *Téléc:* 613-789-7641
comm@theatre-trillium.com
www.theatre-trillium.com
Anne-Marie White, Directrice artistique et générale

Théâtre français de Toronto
#610, 21, rue College, Toronto ON M5G 2B3
Tél: 416-534-7303; *Téléc:* 416-534-9087
Ligne sans frais: 800-819-4981
info@theatrefrancais.com
www.theatrefrancais.com
Le Théâtre français de Toronto est un théâtre professionnel de langue française, de répertoire et de création. Il s'adresse à tous les amateurs de théâtre en français, tant les francophones que les francophiles : ce faisant, il contribue au développement culturel et pédagogique de la communauté de Toronto. Théâtre français de Toronto is a professional French-language theatre presenting repertoire as well as new work. While appealing to all lovers of French-language theatre, it contributes to the cultural and educational development of Toronto's francophone community.
Guy Mignault, Directeur artistique
Ghislain Caron, Directeur administratif

Théâtre la Catapulte
333, av King-Edward, Ottawa ON K1N 7M5
Tél: 613-562-0851; *Téléc:* 613-562-0631
communications@catapulte.ca
catapulte.ca
Créer et diffuser sur une échelle provinciale et nationale des productions pour adultes et adolescents; développer des nouvelles oeuvres; offir une formation continue des artistes de la relève; accueillir des productions
Jean Stéphane Roy, Directeur artistique
Maurice Demers, Président

Theatre Ontario
#210, 215 Spadina Ave., Toronto ON M5T 2C7
Tel: 416-408-4556; *Fax:* 416-408-3402
info@theatreontario.org
www.theatreontario.org
To promote the continued development of theatre arts & artists in Ontario; to support the continued development of vital & broadly accessible theatre training of the highest quality to all sectors of Ontario's theatre community; to encourage the continued development of high quality theatre & drama programs within the educational system of Ontario; to ensure that Ontario's community theatres & educators obtain access to the resources of professional theatre; to facilitate interaction & communication between community, educational & professional theatre

John Goddard, Executive Director

Toronto Alliance for the Performing Arts (TAPA)
#210, 215 Spadina Ave., Toronto ON M5T 2C7
Tel: 416-536-6468; *Fax:* 416-536-3463
Toll-Free: 800-541-0499
jacobak@tapa.ca
www.tapa.ca
To foster greater respect & support for the arts by advocating on behalf of Canadian theatre & dance, representing all cultural backgrounds, to government, supporters, & the general public; to provide services which enhance the artistic, technical, & administrative development of members
Jacoba Knaapen, Executive Director

Young People's Theatre (YPT)
165 Front St. East, Toronto ON M5A 3Z4
Tel: 416-862-2222
boxoffice@youngpeoplestheatre.ca;
online@youngpeoplestheatre.ca
www.youngpeoplestheatre.ca
To make a positive impact on the intellectual, social, & emotional development of young people; To produce plays for young audiences; To operate a year-round drama school for youth
Hughy Neilson, Managing Director
Alexis Buset, Technical Director
Nancy Webster, Managing Director
Allen MacInnis, Artistic Director
Craig Morash, Director, Finance & Operations
Jeff Cummings, Manager, Production
Jill Ward, Manager, Education & Participation
Megan Brady, Administrator, Ticketing Operations
Jan Borkowski, Coordinator, Marketing, & Graphic Designer
Isaac Thomas, Coordinator, Drama School
Aaron Carveth, Development Officer, Donor Acquisition & Retention

Prince Edward Island

Theatre PEI
PO Box 1573, Charlottetown PE C1A 7N3
Tel: 902-894-3558; *Fax:* 902-894-3558
To make challenging, stimulating & entertaining theatre accessible to Island audiences, including schools
Daphne Harker, Administrator
Ron Irving, Artistic Director
Rob MacLean, Associate Artistic Director

Québec

Association québécoise des marionnettistes (AQM)
Centre UNIMA-CANADA (section Québec), CP 7, Succ. de Lorimier, #300, 7755, boul Saint-Laurent, Montréal QC H2H 2N6
Tél: 514-522-1919; *Téléc:* 514-521-3737
aqm@aei.ca
www.aqm.ca
Représenter ses membres et créer un terrain propice aux échanges, aux actions communes et à la réflexion sur la pratique de l'art de la marionnette
Hélène Ducharme, Président

Black Theatre Workshop (BTW)
#432, 3680, Jeanne-Mance, Montréal QC H2X 2K5
Tel: 514-932-1104; *Fax:* 514-932-6311
www.blacktheatreworkshop.ca
To encourage & promote the development of a Black & Canadian theatre, rooted in a literature that reflects the creative will of Black Canadian writers & artists, & the creative collaborations between Black & other artists; To strive to create a greater cross-cultural understanding by its presence & the intrinsic value of its work
Quincy Armorer, Artistic Director
Jacklin Webb, President

Canadian Institute for Theatre Technology (CITT) / L'Institut Canadien des Technologies Scénographiques (ICTS)
PO Box 85041, 345 Laurier Blvd., Mont-Saint-Hilaire QC J3H 5W1
Tel: 613-482-1165; *Fax:* 613-482-1212
Toll-Free: 888-271-3383
info@citt.org
www.citt.org
To work for the betterment of the Canadian live performance community; To promote safe & ethical work practices
Adam Mitchell, President
Gerry van Hezewyk, Vice-President
Mike Dickinson, Secretary
Eric Mongerson, Treasurer
Monique Corbeil, National Coordinator

Centre des auteurs dramatiques (CEAD)
#200, 261, rue du Saint-Sacrement, Montréal QC H2Y 3V2
Tél: 514-288-3384; *Téléc:* 514-288-7043
cead@cead.qc.ca
www.cead.qc.ca
Promotion et diffusion ici et à l'étranger des textes d'auteurs québécois et d'auteurs franco-canadiens; développement dramaturgique
Marc Drouin, Directeur général
Lise Vaillancourt, Président

Conseil québécois du théâtre (CQT)
#808, 460, rue Ste-Catherine ouest, Montréal QC H3B 1A7
Tél: 514-954-0270; *Téléc:* 514-954-0165
Ligne sans frais: 866-954-0270
cqt@cqt.qc.ca
www.cqt.ca
Promouvoir et défendre les intérêts du milieu théâtral et le représenter auprès des diverses instances; concerter, animer et informer la communauté théâtrale sur toutes les questions qui touchent la pratique théâtrale; promouvoir et développer le théâtre
Martine Lévesque, Directrice générale
Marika Crête-Reizes, Adjointe

Fédération québécoise du théâtre amateur (FQTA)
CP 211, Succ. Saint-Élie-d'Orford, Sherbrooke QC J1R 1A1
Tél: 819-752-2501; *Téléc:* 819-758-4466
Ligne sans frais: 877-752-2501
info@fqta.ca
www.fqta.ca
Promouvoir le théâtre amateur en réunissant tous les individus et les groupes de théâtre pour contribuer à l'éducation artistique, esthétique et sociale de la population; établir un contact permanent entre les individus; fournir des occasions d'échange, de travaux, de recherches, de méthodes, de matériel et d'information ayant trait au théâtre
Yoland Roy, Directeur général

Théâtre des épinettes
255, rue Laframboise, Chibougamau QC G8P 2S5
Tél: 418-748-4682
Guy Lalancette

Théâtres associés inc. (TAI)
#405, 1908, rue Panet, Montréal QC H2L 3A2
Tél: 514-842-6361; *Téléc:* 514-842-9730
info@theatresassocies.ca
www.theatresassocies.ca
Théâtres associés (T.A.I.) inc. est une association qui se fait la voix d'institutions théâtrales francophones québécoises.
Jacques Vézina, Président
Jacques Cousineau, Secrétaire général

Théâtres unis enfance jeunesse (TUEJ)
#217, 911, rue Jean-Talon Est, Montréal QC H2R 1V5
Tél: 514-380-2337
tuej.org
Défendre les intérêts des producteurs dans le domaine du théâtre pour la jeunesse
Isabelle Boisclair, Présidente

Saskatchewan

Globe Theatre Society
Globe Theatre, Prince Edward Bldg., 1801 Scarth St., Regina SK S4P 2G9
Tel: 306-525-9553; *Fax:* 306-352-4194
Toll-Free: 866-954-5623
onstage@globetheatrelive.com
www.globetheatrelive.com
To create & produce professional theatre & make it accessible with a view to entertain, educate & challenge
Ruth Smillie, Artistic Director

Saskatchewan Playwrights Centre (SPC)
PO Box 3092, Saskatoon SK S7K 3S9
Tel: 306-665-7707; *Fax:* 306-244-0255
sk.playwrights@sasktel.net
www.saskplaywrights.ca
Independently incorporated and governed centre devoted to developing playwrights.
Mansel Robinson, President

Theatre Saskatchewan
1077 Angus St., Regina SK S4T 1Y4
Tel: 306-352-0797; *Fax:* 306-569-7888
info@theatresaskatchewan.com
www.theatresaskatchewan.com
Strives to build a strong foundation for theatre which allows all people in Saskatchewan accessibility to live drama

La Troupe du Jour
CP 339, 914 - 20th St. West, Saskatoon SK S7K 3L3
Tél: 306-244-1040; *Téléc:* 306-652-1725
communication@latroupedujour.ca
www.latroupedujour.ca
La Troupe du Jour Inc. develops professional and community French-language theatre through the creation of new works, training, performance, and outreach. La Troupe du Jour is dedicated to the development of French-language theatre in Saskatchewan.
Denis Rouleau, General Manager/Artistic Director

Science Centres

Alberta

Local Science Centres in Alberta

Calgary: **TELUS Spark**
Also known as: **Calgary Science Centre**
PO Box 2100 M, 220 St. George's Dr. NE, Calgary, AB T2E 5T2
Tel: 403-817-6800
info@sparkscience.ca
www.sparkscience.ca
Social Media: www.youtube.com/telusworldofscience
twitter.com/telus_spark
www.facebo ok.com/telusspark
The new TELUS Spark science centre features the following exhibits & installations: Prototype Lab; Being Human; Earth & Sky; Energy & Innovation; Open Studio; Creative Kids Museum; Presentation Theatre; Temperature Adventure; & HD Digital Dome Theatre. Open year round.
Martin Kratz, Chair
Jennifer Martin, President & CEO, ceo@sparkscience.ca

Cold Lake: **Cold Lake Air Force Museum**
PO Box 6550 Forces, Cold Lake, AB T9M 2C6
Tel: 780-594-3546; Fax: 780-840-4811
coldlakeairforcemuseum.com

Edmonton: **TELUS World of Science - Edmonton**
11211 - 142 St. NW, Edmonton, AB T5M 4A1
Tel: 780-452-9100
info@edmontonscience.com
www.edmontonscience.com
twitter.com/twosedm
www.facebook.com/EdmontonS cience
IMAX theatre; planetarium; exhibit galleries; observatory; giftshop; café; Ham Radio Station; science & computer lab
Kerry Day, Chair
George Smith, President & CEO
Mike Steger, Director, Marketing & Communication

British Columbia

Local Science Centres in British Columbia

Vancouver: **H.R. MacMillan Space Centre (HRMSC)**
Also known as: **The Planetarium**
1100 Chestnut St., Vancouver, BC V6J 3J9
Tel: 604-738-7827; Fax: 604-736-5665
info@spacecentre.ca
www.spacecentre.ca
Social Media: www.youtube.com/user/MacMillanSpaceCentre
twitter.com/AskAnAstronomer
www.facebook.com/178662617057
Western Canada's premier earth, space science & astronomy attraction & educational resource
Eric K. Pringle, President
Rob Appleton, Executive Director

Vancouver: **Science World at TELUS World of Science**
1455 Quebec St., Vancouver, BC V6A 3Z7
Tel: 604-443-7440; Fax: 604-443-7430
info@scienceworld.ca
www.scienceworld.ca
Social Media: www.youtube.com/scienceworldtv
twitter.com/scienceworldca
www.facebook .com/scienceworldca
Hands-on exhibits; demonstrations; Omnimax theatre
Andrew Harries, Chair
Bryan Tisdall, President/CEO

Vernon: **Okanagan Science Centre**
Polson Park, 2704 Hwy. 6, Vernon, BC V1T 5G5
Tel: 250-545-3644; Fax: 250-545-3644
info@okscience.ca
www.okscience.ca
twitter.com/OkanaganScience
www.f acebook.com/141544795902551
Year Founded: 1990 All of the centre's exhibits are based on scientific principals, in an effort to inspire visitors to appreciate

the universal nature of science. Hours of Operation: M-F 10:00-5:00, Sa 11:00-5:00.

Ontario

Provincial Science Centres

Ontario Science Centre / Centre des sciences de l'Ontario
770 Don Mills Rd., Toronto, ON M3C 1T3
Tel: 416-696-1000; Fax: 416-696-3166
Toll-Free: 888-696-1110
www.ontariosciencecentre.ca
Social Media: www.youtube.com/user/OntarioScienceCentre
twitter.com/ontsciencectr
ww w.facebook.com/ontariosciencecentre
Other contact information: TTY: 416-696-3202
Over 800 interactive exhibits on the environment, technology, food, chemistry, communications, sport & space; exhibits, programs, demonstrations, workshops & films for the public; special programs for school groups, children, adults & senior citizens; gift shops & restaurant; Ontario's only OMNIMAX Theatre featuring a 24-metre dome screen with wrap-around sound; open year round
Mark Cohon, Chair
Lesley Lewis, CEO

Local Science Centres in Ontario

***Sudbury:* Science North**
100 Ramsey Lake Rd., Sudbury, ON P3E 5S9
Tel: 705-522-3701Toll-Free: 800-461-4898
www.sciencenorth.ca
Social Media: www.youtube.com/user/sciencenorth
twitter.com/ScienceNorth
www.faceboo k.com/ScienceNorth
Year Founded: 1984 Science centre, IMAX Theatre, planetarium, living butterfly gallery & special exhibits hall; exhibit design & consulting services.
Guy Labine, CEO, labine@sciencenorth.ca

Quebec

Provincial Science Centres

The Montréal Science Centre
King-Edward Pier, Old Port of Montréal, 333 Commune St. West, Montréal, QC H2Y 2E2
Tel: 514-496-4724Toll-Free: 877-496-4724
information@oldportofmontreal.com
www.montrealsciencecentre.com
www.fa cebook.com/centredessciences
Visitors acquire an understanding of science & technology & how it affects daily living; three interactive science exhibition halls; IMAX TELUS Cinema

Local Science Centres in Quebec

***Laval:* Cosmodôme - Centre des sciences de l'espace et Camp spatial Canada / Cosmodôme - Space Science Centre & Space Camp**
2150, rte des Laurentides, Laval, QC H7T 2T8
Tél: 450-978-3600; Téléc: 450-978-3624
Ligne sans frais: 800-565-2267
info@cosmodome.org
www.cosmodome.org
Host to the Space Science Centre & to the Space Camp, the Cosmodôme leads its visitors on a journey through the conquest of space.
Nicole Dalpé, Director
Anne-Josée Dionne, Coordinator, Sales & Marketing, marketing@cosmodome.org

***Montréal:* Biosphère**
160, ch Tour-de-L'Isle, Montréal, QC H3C 4G8
Tel: 514-283-5000; Fax: 514-283-5021
Toll-Free: 855-773-8200
info.biosphere@ec.gc.ca
www.ec.gc.ca/biosphere
twitt er.com/biospheremtl
www.facebook.com/biospheremtl
Museum of environment; the domed structure housing the museum was built for Expo 67.

***Montréal:* Planétarium de Montréal / Montréal Planétarium**
1000, rue Saint-Jacques ouest, Montréal, QC H3C 1G7
Tél: 514-872-4530; Téléc: 514-872-8102
www.planetarium.montreal.qc.ca
www.facebook.com/Espacepourlavie
Multimedia productions about astronomy on a giant hemispheric dome 20 metres across. As of 2011 the Montréal Planetarium is closed; the new Rio Tinto Alcan Planetarium will open in Spring 2013.

***Saint-Louis-du-Ha-Ha:* Aster, La Station scientifique du BSL**
59, ch Bellevue, Saint-Louis-du-Ha-Ha, QC G0L 3S0
Tél: 418-854-2172; Téléc: 418-854-1898
Ligne sans frais: 877-775-2172
adminaster@bellnet.ca
www.asterbsl.ca
www.facebook.com/263103340448096
Scientific & technical culture; activities include: "Hélios", "Léonard, Ingénieur Créateur" & "Starlab"; educational workshops for schools
Andrée Levasseur, Présidente
Maurice Fallu-Landry, Directeur
Chantale Tardif, Directrice-adjointe

Saskatchewan

Local Science Centres in Saskatchewan

***Regina:* Saskatchewan Science Centre**
2903 Powerhouse Dr., Regina, SK S4N 0A1
Tel: 306-522-4629; Fax: 306-525-0194
Toll-Free: 800-667-6300
www.sasksciencecentre.com
Social Media: www.youtube.com/user/sasksciencecentre
twitter.com/SkScienceCentre
www .facebook.com/SaskScienceCentre
Other contact information: Administration Phone: 306-791-7900
Interactive science museum featuring hands-on exhibits, Kramer Imax theatre; open year-round
Sandy Baumgartner, Executive Director

Zoos

Alberta

Local Zoos in Alberta

***Calgary:* Bow Habitat Station**
1440 - 17A St. SE, Calgary, AB T2G 4T9
Tel: 403-297-6561; Fax: 403-592-8552
bow.habitat@gov.ab.ca
www.bowhabitat.gov.ab.ca
Social Media: www.flickr.com/photos/srdalberta/sets
www.facebook.com/BowHabitatStation
Includes: a Visitor Centre, which is an interpretive centre about fresh water, fish, and aquatic habitats; the Sam Livingston Fish Hatchery, a large trout hatchery; and the Pearce Estate Park Interpretive Wetland, a unique collection of constructed wetlands, self-guided trails and interpretive signs.

***Calgary:* Calgary Zoo, Botanical Garden & Prehistoric Park**
1300 Zoo Rd. NE, Calgary, AB T2E 7V6
Tel: 403-232-9300; Fax: 403-237-7582
Toll-Free: 800-588-9993
guestrelations@calgaryzoo.ab.ca
www.calgaryzoo.org
Social Media: www.youtube.com/calgaryzoo1
www.facebook.com/thecalgaryzoo
136 acres + 320 acre off-site breeding & conservation facility; educational programs; gift shop; open year round
Greg Turnbull, Chair
Dr. Clément Lanthier, President/CEO

***Calgary:* Inglewood Bird Sanctuary**
PO Box 2100 M, Location 59, 2425 - 9 Ave. SE, Calgary, AB T2P 2M5
Tel: 403-268-2489; Fax: 403-221-3775
www.calgary.ca
Offers more than two km. of level trails; more than 270 species of birds & 300 species of plants plus several kinds of mammals have been observed in area; visitor centre; two classrooms where nature-related programs are presented by the Sanctuary's professional naturalists

***Edmonton:* Edmonton Valley Zoo**
PO Box 2359, 13315 Buena Vista Rd., Edmonton, AB T5J 2R7
Tel: 780-442-5311
attractions@edmonton.ca
www.edmonton.ca/valleyzoo
Social Media: www.youtube.com/user/CityEdmonton
twitter.com/CityofEdmonton
www.faceb ook.com/cityofedmonton
Features more than 350 endangered & exotic animals; main zoo & children's zoo; minature train, merry-go-round & camel rides available; open daily except Christmas Day
Denise Prefontaine, Director

***Lacombe:* Ellis Bird Farm**
PO Box 5090, Lacombe, AB T4L 1W7
Tel: 403-346-2211; Fax: 403-346-2211
www.ellisbirdfarm.ca
www.facebook.com/EllisBirdFarm
Other contact information: Summer phone 403-885-4477
Nestboxes; wildlife gardens; tea house; open May - Aug.
Cliff Soper, Chair
Myrna Pearman, Biologist/Manager, Site Services
Cynthia Pohl, Head Gardener

British Columbia

Local Zoos in British Columbia

***Aldergrove:* Greater Vancouver Zoo**
5048 - 264th St., Aldergrove, BC V4W 1N7
Tel: 604-856-6825; Fax: 604-857-9008
info@gvzoo.com
www.gvzoo.com
twitter.com/GVZooChat
www.facebook.com/ 350349281684818
Over 960 animals representing 176 species; world's only albino black bear; one of North America's largest grizzly bear habitats.
Jody Henderson, General Manager, jhenderson@gvzoo.com

***Coombs:* Butterfly World & Gardens**
PO Box 36, 1080 Winchester Rd., Coombs, BC V0R 1M0
Tel: 250-248-7026; Fax: 250-752-1091
www.nature-world.com
The Butterfly World & Gardens is a nature park with tropical gardens, orchids, ponds, birds, & butterflies. The park is open from March to October.

***Creston:* Creston Valley Wildlife Management Area (CVWMA)**
PO Box 640, 1874 Wildlife Rd., Creston, BC V0B 1G0
Tel: 250-402-6900
askus@crestonwildlife.ca
www.crestonwildlife.ca
Social Media: www.flickr.com/search/?q=creston%20wildlife
twitter.com/crestonwildlife
www.facebook.com/149782131736839
17,000-acre wetland habitat. This diverse wildlife resource provides many recreational and educational opportunities. Hiking, cycling, canoeing, picnicking, wildlife viewing, hunting, fishing, and many other outdoor activities can be experienced here. Open May-September.
Marc-André Beaucher, Area Manager
Jim Collins, General Manager

***Kamloops:* British Columbia Wildlife Park**
9077 Dallas Dr., Kamloops, BC V2C 6V1
Tel: 250-573-3242; Fax: 250-573-2406
info@bczoo.org
www.bczoo.org
twitter.com/bcwildlifepark
www.facebook .com/BCzoo
A non-profit organization dedicated to the conservation of BC wildlife through display, interpretation, education, wildlife rehabilitation, endangered species & direct action.
Glenn Grant, General Manager, 250-573-3242, glenn@bczoo.org

***Kelowna:* Speedwell Bird Sanctuary**
PO Box 144, Kelowna, BC V1Y 7N3
Tel: 250-766-2081; Fax: 250-766-0617
Social Media:
www.youtube.com/playlist?list=PL24A1A0A91EC2638B
Year Founded: 1985 Breeding facility for amazon parrots, pheasants; botanical garden featuring trees, shrubs & roses; by appt.
Dan Bruce, Contact

***Richmond:* Richmond Nature Park**
11851 Westminster Hwy., Richmond, BC V6X 1B4
Tel: 604-718-6188; Fax: 604-718-6189
nature@richmond.ca
www.richmond.ca/parksrec/ptc/naturepark/about.htm
Features 5 km. of well-groomed trails through bog & forest; more than 100 species of birds, mammals, reptiles & amphibians may be sighted; seasonal programs & events
Brenda Bartley-Smith, President, Nature Park Society
Kristine Bauder, Nature Park Coordinator
Richard Kenny, Nature Park Assistant

***Vancouver:* Stanley Park Ecology Society**
PO Box 5167, Vancouver, BC V6B 4B2
Tel: 604-257-6908
info@stanleyparkecology.ca
stanleyparkecology.ca
twitter.com/StanleyPkEcoSoc
www.facebook.com/Sta nleyPkEcoSoc
Encourages stewardship of the natural world through education & action & by fostering awareness; provides public programs for adults & families, school programs, wildlife information & resources promoting coexistence between people & its wild neighbours
Patricia Thomson, Executive Director, 604-718-6523, exec@stanleyparkecology.ca

***Victoria:* Swan Lake Christmas Hill Nature Sanctuary**
3873 Swan Lake Rd., Victoria, BC V8X 3W1
Tel: 250-479-0211; Fax: 250-479-0132
info@swanlake.bc.ca
www.swanlake.bc.ca
www.facebook.com/SwanLakeChrist masHillNatureSanctuary
Nature education centre; 125 acres including marshy lowlands surrounding Swan Lake & rocky, oak-forested highlands of Christmas Hill.
Jody Watson, Chair
Terry Morrison, Executive Director

***Victoria:* Victoria Butterfly Gardens**
PO Box 190, 1461 Benvenuto Ave., Victoria, BC V8M 1R3
Tel: 250-652-3822; Fax: 250-652-4683
Toll-Free: 877-722-0272
info@butterflygardens.com
www.butterflygardens.com
w ww.facebook.com/butterfly.gardens
Indoor tropical gardens, fish, birds, & butterflies. Open Mar. 1 Oct. 31

Manitoba

Local Zoos in Manitoba

***Rennie:* Alfred Hole Goose Sanctuary & Visitor Centre (AHGS)**
c/o Manitoba Conservation, PO Box 130, Rennie, MB R0E 1R0
Tel: 204-369-5470
mschneider@gov.mb.ca

www.gov.mb.ca/conservation/parks/act_interp/centres/alf_hole.html
Other contact information: Whiteshell Park Interpreter: 204-369-3157
Year Founded: 1939 Located in Whiteshell Provincial Park; wheelchair accessible Visitor Centre interprets the history of the site as well as the biology of geese; spring, summer & fall program features hands-on activities, guided hikes, school programming & special events

***Thompson:* Thompson Zoo**
***Parent:* Thompson Zoological Society**
205 Mystery Lake Rd., Thompson, MB R8N 1S6
Tel: 204-677-7982; Fax: 204-778-4186
thompzoo@mymts.net
Other contact information: Alternate Phone: 204-677-7996
Year Founded: 1978 Over 100 animals and birds. The Thompson Zoo is the only northern Wildlife Rehab Cetnre in Manitoba. Open year round.
Erin Wilcox, Director

***Winnipeg:* Assiniboine Park Zoo**
55 Pavilion Cres., Winnipeg, MB R3P 2N7
Tel: 204-927-6000; Fax: 204-927-7603
info@assiniboinepark.ca
www.assiniboineparkzoo.ca
Social Media: www.youtube.com/user/AssiniboinePark
twitter.com/assiniboinezoo
www.fa cebook.com/assiniboineparkzoo
Year Founded: 1904 Open daily & currently has over 2,000 animals of 200 different species; main entrance located at 2595 Roblin Blvd., Winnipeg, MB.
Margaret Redmond, President & CEO, Assiniboine Park Conservancy

New Brunswick

Local Zoos in New Brunswick

***Moncton:* Magnetic Hill Zoo**
100 Worthington Ave., Moncton, NB E1C 9Z3
Tel: 506-877-7718
info.zoo@moncton.ca
www.moncton.org/zoo/
Social Media: www.youtube.com/user/ResurgoMoncton
twitter.com/CityofMoncton
www.face book.com/cityofmoncton.villedemoncton
The Magnetic Hill Zoo is committed to safeguarding animal species & raising public awareness of endangered species. The zoo is designed with the well-being of the animals, as well as the safety of the public, in mind.
Bruce Dougan, Manager

***Saint John:* Cherry Brook Zoo Inc.**
901 Foster Thurston Dr., Saint John, NB E2K 5H9
Tel: 506-634-1440; Fax: 506-634-0717
noahsark@bellaliant.net
www.cherrybrookzoo.com
www.facebook.com/127305 657323681
A non-for profit zoo situated in a 35-acre woodland that is located in the northern section of the city's 2200-acre Rockwood Park. Utilizing the unusual natural terrain of Rockwood Park, the animals are surrounded by a natural setting.
Leonard Collrin, Chief Administrative Director
Lynda Collrin, Director, Zoo Development
Hugh P. O'Hara, Senior Zoo Keeper

Newfoundland & Labrador

Local Zoos in Newfoundland & Labrador

***Glovertown:* Terra Nova National Park of Canada (TNNP) / Parc national du Canada Terra-Nova**
General Delivery, Glovertown, NL A0G 2L0
Tel: 709-533-2801; Fax: 709-533-2706
info.tnnp@pc.gc.ca
www.pc.gc.ca/pn-np/nl/terranova/index_E.asp
Represents the unique character of the eastern Newfoundland Atlantic Terrestrial Natural Region; characterized by low relief & a series of rounded hills from sea level to 200 metres; home to 12 of 14 native terrestrial mammals, 8 fish species & more than 200 bird species recorded in the park; artifacts of native & European settlement

***Holyrood:* Salmonier Nature Park**
PO Box 190, Holyrood, NL A0A 2R0
Tel: 709-229-7888; Fax: 709-229-7078
brenda.pike@gov.nl.ca
www.env.gov.nl.ca/env/snp
Other contact information: Alternate Phone: 709-229-3915
Open June to Thanksgiving

Nova Scotia

Local Zoos in Nova Scotia

***Shubenacadie:* Shubenacadie Provincial Wildlife Park**
PO Box 299, Shubenacadie, NS B0N 2H0
Tel: 902-758-2040; Fax: 902-758-7011
wildlifepark@gov.ns.ca
wildlifepark.gov.ns.ca
45 exhibits featuring native & exotic species in natural enclosures along a 2.3 km walking trail; picnic area & playground; open daily May 15-Oct. 15 & weekends only during winter season; fee

Ontario

Local Zoos in Ontario

***Bowmanville:* Bowmanville Zoo**
340 King St. East, Bowmanville, ON L1C 3K5
Tel: 905-623-5655; Fax: 905-623-0957
www.bowmanvillezoo.com
www.facebook.com/BowmanvilleZoo
Year Founded: 1919 Canada's oldest private zoo, featuring Animal Kingdom shows, elephant rides, restaurant & gift shop; CAZA accredited; open May - Sept.
Michael Hackenberger, Director, mike@bowmanvillezoo.com

***Cambridge:* African Lion Safari & Game Farm**
RR#1, Cambridge, ON N1R 5S2
Tel: 519-623-2620; Fax: 519-623-9542
Toll-Free: 800-461-9453
admin@lionsafari.com
www.lionsafari.com
African Lion Safari is a Canadian-owned family business that seeks to both entertain its guests & act as a conservation park for its animals. Open May-Oct.
Mike Takacs, General Manager

***Cambridge:* Cambridge Butterfly Conservatory**
2500 Kossuth Rd., Cambridge, ON N3H 4R7
Tel: 519-653-1234; Fax: 519-650-2582
info@cambridgebutterfly.com
www.cambridgebutterfly.com
*twitter.com/con servatory_*
www.facebook.com/CambridgeButterflyConservatory
Live butterfly conservatory & tropical garden, also featuring birds & bugs; open daily 10:00-5:00.

***Kingsville:* Jack Miner Bird Sanctuary**
360 Rd. 3 West, Kingsville, ON N9Y 2E5
Tel: 519-733-4034Toll-Free: 877-289-8328
www.jackminer.com
www.facebook.com/JackMinerMigratoryBirdSanctuary
Year Founded: 1931 Centre for the conservation of migrating Canada geese & wild ducks, originating from the waterfowl refuge management system. Open year-round, free admission; closed Sundays.
Mary E. Baruth, Executive Director, mbaruth@jackminer.com

***Midland:* Wye Marsh Wildlife Centre**
PO Box 100, 16160 Hwy. 12 E, Midland, ON L4R 4K6
Tel: 705-526-7809; Fax: 705-526-3294
info@wyemarsh.com
www.wyemarsh.com
Year Founded: 1984 Indoor & outdoor natural history exhibits; environmental education & recreation programs; fully accessible nature centre & trails; assistive equipment available
Laurie Schutt, Executive Director

***Morrisburg:* Upper Canada Migratory Bird Sanctuary (UCMBS) / Sanctuaire des oiseaux migrateurs Upper Canada**
c/o Parks of the St. Lawrence, 13740 County Rd. 2, Morrisburg, ON K0C 1X0
Tel: 613-543-4328Toll-Free: 800-437-2233
www.uppercanadabirdsanctuary.com
www.facebook.com/146312528725287
A natural area with over 8 km. of nature trails, visitor centre & gift shop, campground & group camping area; offers a duck banding program, fall goose feeding program, outdoor education topics & special events such as the Annual Waterfowl Day

***Orono:* Jungle Cat World Inc. (JCW)**
***Also known as:* Orono Exotic Cat World**
3667 Conc. Rd. 6, Orono, ON L0B 1M0
Tel: 905-983-5016; Fax: 905-983-9858
info@junglecatworld.com
www.junglecatworld.com
Social Media: www.youtube.com/user/SafariZooCamp1
twitter.com/JungleCatWorld
www.fac ebook.com/123056467776168
Year Founded: 1983 Jungle Cat World is a wildlife park located on 15 acres of land. Though Jungle Cat World is home to a variety of threatened & endangered species such as lemurs, gibbons, cotton-top tamarins & spider monkeys, the park specializes in wild felines. They include the world's largest, the Siberian tiger, to the rarest, the Amur leopard, to some of the smallest like the sand cats from the African deserts.

***St Catharines:* Happy Rolph Bird Sanctuary & Children's Petting Farm**
c/o St Catharines Recreation & Community Services, 320 Geneva St., St Catharines, ON L2R 7C2
Tel: 905-937-7210; Fax: 905-646-9262
jmclaghlin@stcatharines.ca
A 15-acre municipal park on the shores of Lake Ontario boasts gardens & pathways, petting farm (open Victoria Day to Thanksgiving weekend), picnic area & playground facilities.

***Thunder Bay:* Chippewa Wildlife Park**
Victoriaville Civic Centre, 111 Syndicate Ave. South, Thunder Bay, ON P7E 6S4
Tel: 807-625-2351; Fax: 807-625-3258
www.thunderbay.ca
The municipally operated zoological park contains bird & mammal species, which are indigenous to northwestern Ontario. The Chippewa Wildlife Park features an elevated walkway (pedestrian boardwalk) for viewing the animals.
Paul Fayrick, Manager, Parks, 807-625-2806, pfayrick@thunderbay.ca

***Toronto:* High Park Zoo**
c/o Parks, Forestry & Recreation, City Hall, 100 Queen St. West, Toronto, ON M5H 2N2
Tel: 416-392-6599
parks@toronto.ca
www.toronto.ca/parks/zoo/high_park.htm
Located on Deer Pen Road, the animal paddocks have always been one of the most popular attractions, dating back to 1890 when deer were kept in High Park. Today, visitors will find domestic & exotic species including bison, llamas, peacocks, deer, highland cattle & sheep.
Helen Sousa, Supervisor, High Park, hsousa@toronto.ca

***Toronto:* Riverdale Farm**
201 Winchester St., Toronto, ON M4X 1B8
Tel: 416-392-6794
www.toronto.ca/parks/featured-parks/riverdale-farm
Riverdale Farm is a Toronto Parks, Forestry & Recreation Division facility featuring animals & gardens in the surrounding park. Located in the heart of downtown Toronto, in the area known as Cabbagetown. Admission is free. Parking on neighbouring city streets only.

***Toronto:* Toronto Zoo**
361A Old Finch Ave., Toronto, ON M1B 5K7
Tel: 416-392-5929; Fax: 416-392-5934
tzwebmaster@torontozoo.ca
www.torontozoo.com
www.facebook.com/TheToron toZoo
The Toronto Zoo is one of Canada's premier Zoos, offering interactive education & partaking in conservation activities. The

Zoo has over 5,000 animals representing over 500 species. Open year round.
John Tracogna, CEO

***Woodbridge:* Kortright Centre for Conservation**
9550 Pine Valley Dr., Woodbridge, ON L4L 1A6
Tel: 905-832-2289
info@trca.on.ca
www.kortright.org
www.facebook.com/K ortrightCentre
Year Founded: 1982 An environmental education & demonstration centre, situated on 325 hectares of woodland.

Quebec

Local Zoos in Quebec

***Bonaventure:* Bioparc de la Gaspésie**
123, des Vieux Ponts, Bonaventure, QC G0C 1E0
Tél: 418-534-1997; Téléc: 418-534-1998
Ligne sans frais: 866-534-1997
info@bioparc.ca
www.bioparc.ca; bioparcgaspesie.blogspot.ca
Médias sociaux: www.youtube.com/user/BioparcGaspesie
twitter.com/BioparcGaspesie
www.f acebook.com/BioparcGaspesie
Gaspesian wildlife observation centre; through a one mile walk path, visitors discover a collection of fauna & flora indigenous to the region presented in their five respective ecosystems: the Bay, the Lagoon, the River, the Forest & the Tundra
Aurélien Bisson, Président
Marie-Josée Bernard, Directrice générale, mjbernard@bioparc.ca

***Granby:* Zoo de Granby / Granby Zoo**
525, rue St-Hubert, Granby, QC J2G 5P3
Tél: 450-372-9113; Téléc: 450-372-5531
Ligne sans frais: 877-472-6299
info@zoodegranby.com
www.zoodegranby.com
Médias sociaux: www.youtube.com/user/ZOOdeGRANBYOfficiel
twitter.com/zoodegranby
www.facebook.com/zoogranby
The Granby Zoo seeks to provide visitors with an exciting education experience, bringing visitors close to endangered & exotic animals, while promoting conservation & scientific development. Open June - Oct. (Thanksgiving Day).
Mario Gariépy, Président
Joanne Lalumière, Directrice-générale et secrétaire exécutive

***Hemmingford:* Parc Safari Africain (Québec) Inc.**
850, route 202, Hemmingford, QC J0L 1H0
Tél: 450-247-2727; Téléc: 450-247-3563
www.parcsafari.com
www.facebook.com/ParcSafari
Fondée en: 1972 The park strives to protect & preserve endangered species while providing visitors with a safari adventure. The park houses 500 animals from 75 different species, including elephants, rhinos, giraffes, zebras, lions, macaques, chimpanzees, white tigers, & more. Also includes a water park.

***Sainte-Anne-de-Bellevue:* Ecomuseum / Écomuséum**
21125, ch Sainte-Marie, Sainte-Anne-de-Bellevue, QC H9X 3Y7
Tél: 514-457-9449; Téléc: 514-457-0769
info@ecomuseum.ca
www.ecomuseum.ca
Open year round; wildlife interpretation centre; animals of the St. Lawrence Valley
David Rodrigue, Directeur général

***Saint-Eustache:* Ferme de Reptiles Exotarium inc.**
846, ch Fresniere, Saint-Eustache, QC J7R 4K3
Tel: 450-472-1827; Fax: 450-472-8122
info@exotarium.net
www.exotarium.net
Rare & endangered reptiles, amphibians & invertebrates
Hervé Maranda, Directeur/propriètaire

***Saint-Félicien:* Zoo Sauvage de Saint-Félicien**
2230, boul du Jardin, Saint-Félicien, QC G8K 2P8
Tél: 418-679-0543; Téléc: 418-679-3647
Ligne sans frais: 800-667-5687
info@zoosauvage.org
www.zoosauvage.org
twitter.com/zoostfelicien
www.facebook.com/zoosauvage
Displays North American wildlife in an innovative context; no cages or bars; open daily May 15 - Oct. 14., 9-5
Lauraine Gagnon, Directrice générale

***Saint-Félicien:* Zoo sauvage de Saint-Felicien**
2230, boul du Jardin, Saint-Félicien, QC G8K 2P8
Tél: 418-697-0543; Téléc: 418-679-3647
Ligne sans frais: 800-667-5687
info@zoosauvage.org
www.zoosauvage.org
twitter.com/zoostfelicien
www.facebook.com/zoosauvage
The zoo seeks to provide visitors with a memorable experience while engaging in educational, scientific, & recreational activities.

Lauraine Gagnon, Directrice Générale

***Saint-Joachim:* Centre d'interprétation faunique du Cap-Tourmente**
570, ch du Cap-Tourmente, Saint-Joachim, QC G0A 3X0
Tél: 418-827-4591; Téléc: 418-827-6225
cap.tourmente@ec.gc.ca
www.captourmente.com

Saskatchewan

Local Zoos in Saskatchewan

***Regina:* Wascana Waterfowl Park**
Wascana Centre, PO Box 7111, 2900 Wascana Dr., Regina, SK S4P 3S7
Tel: 306-522-3661; Fax: 306-565-2742
wca@wascana.sk.ca
www.wascana.sk.ca
The Wascana Waterfowl Park is a 223 hectare thriving marshland within Regina's city limits.
Bernadette McIntyre, CEO

SECTION 3
ASSOCIATIONS

Associations in this section are listed alphabetically by subject. Directly following this page is an Entry Index arranged alphabetically by entry name, regardless of subject. Many subjects are also represented in other sections throughout the book. For example, Section 2: Arts & Culture includes Art Galleries, while this section includes Art Gallery Associations.

Association Name Index

A

B

C

D

E

F

G

N

O

P

Aboriginal Peoples

Lutheran Association of Missionaries & Pilots (LAMP)
4966 - 92 Ave. NW, Edmonton AB T6B 2V4
Tel: 780-466-8507; *Fax:* 780-466-6733
Toll-Free: 800-307-4036
office@lampministry.org
www.lampministry.org
Social Media: www.facebook.com/group.php?gid=233505351133; www.youtube.com/user/LAMPMinistry/videos
To share Jesus Christ with the people of remote areas of Canada
Ron Ludke, Executive Director

Accounting

Canadian Academic Accounting Association (CAAA) / Association canadienne des professeurs de comptabilité (ACPC)
3997 Chesswood Dr., Toronto ON M3J 2R8
Tel: 416-486-5361; *Fax:* 416-486-6158
admin@caaa.ca
www.caaa.ca
To promote excellence in accounting education & research in Canada with particular reference to Canadian post-secondary accounting programs & Canadian issues
Vaughan Radcliffe, Présidente
Susan Kelsall, Vice-President
Ayesha Lahar, Vice-President
Kathy Létourneau, Treasurer
Bharat Aggrawal, Secretary

Canadian Bookkeepers Association
#482, 283 Danforth Ave., Toronto ON M4K 1N2
Fax: 866-804-4617
info@canadianbookkeepersassociation.com
www.c-b-a.ca
To promote, support, provide for & encourage Canadian bookkeepers; to promote & increase the awareness of Bookkeeping in Canada as a professional discipline; to support national, regional & local networking among Canadian Bookkeepers; to provide information on leading-edge procedures, education & technologies that enhance the industry, as well as, the Canadian bookkeeping professional; to support & encourage responsible & accurate bookkeeping practices throughout Canada
Norm Eady, President

Canadian Institute of Chartered Accountants (CICA) / Institut canadien des comptables agréés
277 Wellington St. West, Toronto ON M5V 3H2
Tel: 416-977-3222; *Fax:* 416-977-8585
www.cica.ca
Social Media: www.linkedin.com/company/canadian-institute-of-chartered-accountants
To foster public confidence in the chartered accountant profession; To assist members to excel
Kevin Dancey, President & Chief Executive Officer
Nigel Byars, Executive Vice-Presidnet
Tim Forristal, Vice-President, Education
Ron Salole, Vice-President, Standards
Heather Whyte, Vice-President, Communications & External Relations
Cairine Wilson, Vice-President, Member Services
Stephen Anisman, Controller
Tim Beauchamp, Director, Public Sector Accounting
Alan Burger, Director, Human Resources
Frank Colantonio, Director, Continuing Education
George Greer, Director, Information Technology Services
Jylan Khalil, Director, Qualification
Brian Loney, Director, Member Services
Peter Martin, Director, Accounting Standards
Elly Meister, Director, Government Relations
Suzanne Mondoux, Director, Language Services
Greg Shields, Director, Auditing & Assurance Standards
Gord Beal, Director, Guidance & Support

Canadian Insurance Accountants Association (CIAA) / Association canadienne des comptables en assurance
c/o Taylor Enterprises Ltd., #310, 2175 Sheppard Ave. East, Toronto ON M2J 1W8
Tel: 416-971-7800; *Fax:* 416-491-1670
ciaa@ciaa.org
www.ciaa.org
To promote study, research, & development of management & insurance accounting
Catherine Fleming, Executive Assistant

Certified General Accountants Association of Alberta
#100, 325 Manning Rd. NE, Calgary AB T2E 2P5
Tel: 403-299-1300; *Fax:* 403-299-1339
Toll-Free: 800-661-1078
questions@cga-alberta.org; studentservices@cga-alberta.org
www.cga-alberta.org
To represent the provincial interests of Certified General Accountants & students; To establish & enforce professional competency & ethical standards
John Carpenter, Chief Executive Officer
Paul V. Ennis, Senior Vice-President, Student Services
Larry Presiloski, Senior Vice-President, Corporate Strategy
Theresa Eliuk, Vice-President, Operations
Michelle Everett, Vice-President, Recruitment
Janice Harrington, Vice-President, Communications & Government Relations
Tom Skomorowski, Vice-President, Education
Breton Thoen, Vice-President, Business Systems
Sandy Umpherville, Vice-President, Member Services & Regulatory Standards

Certified General Accountants Association of British Columbia
#300, 1867 West Broadway, Vancouver BC V6J 5L4
Tel: 604-732-1211; *Fax:* 604-732-1252
Toll-Free: 800-565-1211
info@cga-bc.org
www.cga-bc.org
Social Media: twitter.com/cgabc
To act as the governing & regulatory body responsible for Certified General Accountants in British Columbia; To train & certify British Columbia's Certified General Accountants
John Pankratz, President
Bruce Hurst, 1st Vice-President
Bill Caulfield, Executive Director & Secretary
Stephen Spector, Treasurer

Certified General Accountants Association of Canada
#100, 4200 North Fraser Way, Burnaby BC V5J 5K7
Tel: 604-669-3555; *Fax:* 604-689-5845
Toll-Free: 800-663-1529
www.cga-canada.org
Social Media: www.facebook.com/cgacanada; twitter.com/cgacanada; www.linkedin.com/groups?gid=2111514; www.youtube.com/user/cgacdn
To represent Certified General Accountants & students in Canada, Bermuda, the nations of the Caribbean, the People's Republic of China, & Hong Kong; To establish educational standards; To advocate for accounting professional excellence & responsible policy & practices
Terry LeBlanc, Chair
Patrick Keller, Vice-Chair
Anthony Ariganello, President & Chief Executive Officer
Rock Lefebvre, Vice-President, Research & Standards
Taylore Ashlie, Director, Communications

Certified General Accountants Association of Manitoba
4 Donald St. South, Winnipeg MB R3L 2T7
Tel: 204-477-1256; *Fax:* 204-453-7176
Toll-Free: 800-282-8001
info@cga-manitoba.org; memberservices@cga-manitoba.org
www.cga-manitoba.org
To provide professional support services for the accounting profession in Manitoba; To ensure commitment to the Code of Ethical Principles & Rules of Conduct; To empower members to excel
Grant B. Christensen, Chief Executive Officer
Jamie Thomas, President
D. Scott Anderson, Director, Member Services & Practice Development
Lynn Bailey, Director, Student Services
Nadine Morrill, Director, Finance & Administration
Kathryn M. Payne, Director, Professional Regulation
Grant Christensen, Secretary
Andrea Kinsman, Treasurer

Certified General Accountants Association of New Brunswick / Association des comptables généraux accrédités du Nouveau-Brunswick
PO Box 1395, #10, 236 St. George St., Moncton NB E1C 8T6
Tel: 506-857-0939; *Fax:* 506-855-0887
Toll-Free: 877-462-4262
cganb@cga-nb.org
www.cga-nb.org
To advance the interests of Certified General Accountants & to inform the public in New Brunswick; To provide education & professional services to members; To uphold the Code of Ethical Principles & Rules of Conduct to protect the public
Trisha Fournier-Hoyt, President
Trudy Dryden, Executive Director
Jean-Yves Thériault, Secretary-Treasurer

Certified General Accountants Association of Newfoundland & Labrador (CGA-NL)
#201, 294 Freshwater Rd., St. John's NL A1B 1C1
Tel: 709-579-1863; *Fax:* 709-579-0838
Toll-Free: 800-563-2426
office@cganl.org; education@cganl.org
www.cganl.org
To protect the public through commitment to The CGA Newfoundland & Labrador Code of Ethical Principles & Rules of Conduct & The CGA Newfoundland & Labrador Independence Standard; To advocate on issues to advance the interests of Certified General Accountants in Newfoundland & Labrador
Trevor McCormick, Chair
Tracey Osmond, Vice-Chair
Michael Duah, Secretary & Registrar
Kevin Antle, Treasurer

Certified General Accountants Association of Nova Scotia
#230, 1801 Hollis St., Halifax NS B3J 3N4
Tel: 902-425-4923; *Fax:* 902-425-4983
office@cga-ns.org
www.cga-ns.org
To control the professional standards, conduct, & discipline of Certified General Accountants from Nova Scotia; To grant the exclusive right to the CGA designation
Louis Bourque, Director, Education
Stana Colovic, Director, Administration & Member Services
Kristin McLellan, Manager, Student Services
Brenda Allison, Registrar

Certified General Accountants Association of Ontario
240 Eglinton Ave. East, Toronto ON M4P 1K8
Tel: 416-322-6520; *Fax:* 416-322-6481
Toll-Free: 800-668-1454
info@cga-ontario.org
www.cga-ontario.org
Social Media: www.facebook.com/cga
To regulate qualification, performance, & discipline standards for Certified General Accountants throughout Ontario; To grant exclusive rights to the CGA designation
Blake Mercer, Chair
Janice Charko, Vice-Chair
Doug Brooks, Chief Executive Officer
Steve D'Alessandro, Vice-President, Finance
Bessie Jones, Vice-President, Information Services
J.D. Clarke, Senior Vice-President, Operations
Jennifer Spragge, Vice-President, Human resources & Strategic Planning
Delmarie Scherloski, Vice-President, Marketing & Communications
Ted Wigdor, Vice-President, Government & Corporate Affairs
Blake Mercer, Secretary-Treasurer
Amy Mulhern, Manager, Public Relations

Certified General Accountants Association of Prince Edward Island
PO Box 3, #105, 18 Queen St., Charlottetown PE C1A 4A1
Tel: 902-368-7237; *Fax:* 902-368-3627
contact@cga-pei.org
www.cga-pei.org
To provide professional support services to the accounting profession in Prince Edward Island
Jason Macdonald, President
Phillip A. Rafuse, Vice-President
Paula Gallant, Secretary
Patricia Robertson, Treasurer

Certified General Accountants Association of Saskatchewan
#209, 3502 Taylor St. East, Saskatoon SK S7H 5H9
Tel: 306-955-4622; *Fax:* 306-373-9219
Toll-Free: 800-667-4754
general@cga-saskatchewan.org
www.cga-saskatchewan.org
Social Media: www.facebook.com/cga?v=wall; twitter.com/cgaSaskatchewan; www.linkedin.com/groups?gid=3790591
To ensure members' commitment to the Certified General Accountants Association of Saskatchewan Code of Ethics; To promote excellence in accounting standards & practices; To advance the interests of Saskatchewan's Certified General Accountants
Prabha Vaidyanathan, Executive Director
Adam Burke, Manager, Education & Technology

Kayleigh Kazakoff, Coordinator, Administration & Member Support

Certified General Accountants Association of the Northwest Territories & Nunavut
Graham Bromley Bldg., PO Box 128, 5016 - 50th Ave., 3rd Fl., Yellowknife NT X1A 2N1
Tel: 867-873-5620; *Fax:* 867-873-4469
Toll-Free: 888-633-3221
admin@cga-nwt-nu.org
www.cga-nwt-nu.org
To provide training & professional support services to accountants in the Northwest Territories & Nunavut; To grant the exclusive rights to the CGA designation; To advance the interests of members; To protect the public; To advocate for the public interest
Marlene Sutton, Executive Director
Pawan Chugh, Chair & President
Andy Wong, Vice-President & Chair, Nominations Committee
Nancy Magrum, Secretary & Chair, Professional Development Committee
Biswanath Chakrabarty, Treasurer & Chair, Finance Committee

Certified General Accountants Association of Yukon
PO Box 31536, RPO Main St., Whitehorse YT Y1A 6K8
Tel: 867-668-4461; *Fax:* 867-668-8635
www.cga.org/canada/yukon

CGA Student Services - New Brunswick
Commerce House, PO Box 5100, #403, 236 St. George St., Moncton NB E1C 8R2
Tel: 506-857-0939; *Fax:* 506-855-0887
Toll-Free: 877-855-0887
cganb@cga-nb.org
www.cga-nb.org
The Certified General Accountants' Association of Canada gives the Association its unity and strength and ensures the portability of the CGA desgingation.

Chartered Accountants Institute of Bermuda (ICAB)
PO Box 1625, Hamilton HM GX Bermuda
Tel: 441-292-7479; *Fax:* 441-295-3121
icab@northrock.bm
www.icab.bm
Annarita G. Marion, President & CEO

CMA Canada / La Société des comptables en management accrédités
#1400, One Robert Speck Pkwy., Mississauga ON L4Z 3M3
Tel: 905-949-4200; *Fax:* 905-949-0888
Toll-Free: 800-263-7622
info@cma-canada.org; governance@cma-canada.org
www.cma-canada.org
Social Media: www.facebook.com/pages/CMA-Canada/108842141630; twitter.com/cmabc; www.linkedin.com/company/cma-canada
To drive value creation by developing professionals & resources to lead the advancement & integration of strategy, accounting & management
Thomas Joy, President & CEO
Cindy Ruocco, Manager, Communications & Public Affairs

CMA Canada - Alberta
#300, 1210 - 8th St. SW, Calgary AB T2R 1L3
Tel: 403-269-5341; *Fax:* 403-262-5477
Toll-Free: 877-262-2000
info@cma-alberta.com
www.cma-alberta.com
Social Media: twitter.com/CMAAlberta
To develop & advance the competencies & market relevance of CMAs through accreditation, education, & high standards
David Shaw, President

CMA Canada - British Columbia (CMABC)
Two Bentall Centre, PO Box 269, #1055, 555 Burrard St., Vancouver BC V7X 1M8
Tel: 604-687-5891; *Fax:* 604-687-6688
Toll-Free: 800-663-9646
cmabc@cmabc.com
www.cmabc.com
To be pre-eminent in management accounting by ensuring that the body of knowledge is available, by setting & enforcing the standards of competence, ensuring availability of CMAs in the defined territory, & supporting research; to optimize the performance of enterprises by driving the continuous development of financial & strategic management professionals & shaping the strategic leadership competencies of CMAs
Colin Bennett, President & CEO

CMA Canada - Manitoba
#815, 240 Graham Ave., Winnipeg MB R3C 0J7
Tel: 204-943-1538; *Fax:* 204-947-3308
Toll-Free: 800-841-7148
cmamb@cma-canada.org
www.cma-manitoba.com
Social Media: www.facebook.com/cmamb
To support members in leading organizations in the application of advanced management practices
Ron Stoesz, Chief Executive Officer

CMA Canada - Newfoundland & Labrador
PO Box 28090, Stn. Avalon Mall, #104, 31 Peet St., St. John's NL A1B 4J8
Tel: 709-726-3652; *Fax:* 709-726-5513
mbradbury@cma-nl.com
www.cma-nl.com
Mark A. Bradbury, Executive Director

CMA Canada - Northwest Territories & Nunavut
PO Box 512, Yellowknife NT X1A 2N4
Tel: 867-873-2875; *Fax:* 867-920-2503
mdemeule@cma-canada.org
www.cma-nwt.com
Michelle Demeule, Executive Director

CMA Canada - Nova Scotia, Bermuda & PEI
Sentry Place, #300, 1559 Brunswick St., Halifax NS B3J 2G1
Tel: 902-422-5836; *Fax:* 902-423-1605
Toll-Free: 800-565-7198
nforan@cmans.com
www.cmans.com
To promote standards of excellence in management accounting
Nancy Foran, Chief Executive Officer

CMA Canada - Ontario
#1100, 25 York St., Toronto ON M5J 2V5
Tel: 416-977-7741; *Fax:* 416-977-6079
Toll-Free: 800-387-2991
info@cmaontario.org
www.cmaontario.org
Social Media: www.cmaontario.org/facebook; twitter.com/becomeacma; www.cmaontario.org/linkedin
To optimize the performance of enterprises by driving the continuous development of management accounting & shaping the strategic competences of CMA's
Merv Hillier, President & CEO

CMA Canada - Québec
715, square Victoria, 3e étage, Montréal QC H2Y 2H7
Tél: 514-849-1155; *Téléc:* 514-849-9674
Ligne sans frais: 800-263-5390
administration@cma-quebec.org
www.cma-quebec.org
Protéger le public en contrôlant la compétence et l'intégrité de ceux et celles qui exercent la profession; favoriser la prééminence de ses membres dans le monde des affaires; assurer une formation de tout premier ordre; l'Ordre joue un rôle primordial dans l'acquisition et l'application du savoir de ses membres; il est responsable de l'émission des permis d'exercice aux candidats qui remplissent les conditions nécessaires, de la garde du tableau des membres, de la surveillance de l'exercice de la profession et du dépistage de la pratique illégale
François Renauld, Président/Directeur général

CMA Canada - Saskatchewan
#202, 1900 Albert St., Regina SK S4P 4K8
Tel: 306-757-9428; *Fax:* 306-347-8580
Toll-Free: 800-667-3535
sask@cma-canada.org
www.cma-saskatchewan.com
Bob Cochran, Director of Accreditation
Betty Hoffart, CEO

CMA Canada - Yukon
PO Box 31426, Whitehorse YT Y1A 6K8
Tel: 867-668-3388; *Fax:* 867-668-2402
cmayukon@internorth.com
www.cma-canada.org/yukon.asp
To promote standards of excellence in management accounting
Karen Johnson, Territorial Representative

CMA New Brunswick (CMANB) / La Société des comptables en management du Nouveau-Brunswick
#101, 570 Queen St., Fredericton NB E3B 6Z6
Tel: 506-455-2262; *Fax:* 506-455-2266
Toll-Free: 877-676-2262
www.cmanb.com
Represents over 400 CMAs in New Brunswick. A self-regulating association which maintains the highest standards of professional practice, in its mission to develop both professionals and resources in service to the public
Suzanne Tucker, CEO

Guild of Industrial, Commercial & Institutional Accountants / Guilde des comptables industriels, commerciaux et institutionnels
36 Tandian Ct., Woodbridge ON L4L 8Z9
Tel: 905-264-2713; *Fax:* 905-264-1043
iciaguild@aol.com
www.guildoficia.ca
To support & promote interest in vocational accountancy; To encourage acceptance of modern accounting methods & procedures

Institute of Chartered Accountants of Alberta (ICAA)
Manulife Place, #580, 10180 - 101 St., Edmonton AB T5J 4R2
Tel: 780-424-7391; *Fax:* 780-425-8766
Toll-Free: 800-232-9406
info@icaa.ab.ca
www.icaa.ab.ca
To protect the public interest by setting & enforcing high professional & ethical standards
Jane Halford, CEO & Executive Director
Peter R. Stephen, President
Daryl Ritchie, Vice-President
Brenda McKenzie, Director, Registrations

Institute of Chartered Accountants of British Columbia (ICABC)
One Bentall Centre, #500, 505 Burrard St., Box 22, Vancouver BC V7X 1M4
Tel: 604-681-3264; *Fax:* 604-681-1523
Toll-Free: 800-663-2677
www.ica.bc.ca
Social Media: www.facebook.com/pages/Chartered-Accountants-of-BC/231591610237242; twitter.com/icabc; www.linkedin.com/company/2129203; www.youtube.com/user/CAsofBCvideo; www.flickr.com/photos/icabc
To protect & serve the public, members, & students by providing exceptional education, regulation & member services programs so that chartered accountants may provide the highest quality of professional services
Sandy Parcher, Manager, Executive Office
Richard Rees, CEO

Institute of Chartered Accountants of Manitoba (ICAM)
#500, 161 Portage Ave. East, Winnipeg MB R3B 0Y4
Tel: 204-942-8248; *Fax:* 204-943-7119
Toll-Free: 888-942-8248
icam@icam.mb.ca
www.icam.mb.ca
To protect the public by acting as the governing body of the profession of chartered accountancy in Manitoba; To ensure the profession observes established professional practice standards, rules of professional conduct, bylaws, & regulations
Gary Hannaford, CEO
Ian R. Seymour, President & Chair
Rick M. MacKay, Sec.-Treas.
Shirley Sommer, Registrar & Director, Standards Enforcement

Institute of Chartered Accountants of Newfoundland (ICAN)
PO Box 21130, #501, 95 Bonaventure Ave., St. John's NL A1B 2X5
Tel: 709-753-7566; *Fax:* 709-753-3609
tbatstone@icanl.ca
www.icanl.ca
To serve the interests of society & the membership by providing leadership; To uphold the professional standards, integrity & preeminence of chartered accountants in Newfoundland & Labrador
Tashia Batstone, CEO
Jason Silver, Chair
Scott Shears, Vice-Chair
Dorothy Keating, Sec.-Treas.

Institute of Chartered Accountants of Nova Scotia (ICANS)
#1410, 1791 Barrington St., Halifax NS B3J 3L1
Tel: 902-425-3291; *Fax:* 902-423-4505
icans@icans.ns.ca
www.icans.ns.ca
To protect & serve the public & our members by providing exceptional services & resources within a well-regulated profession
Michele A. Wood-Tweel, CEO/Executive Director
Kathie Slaunwhite, Office Administrator

Institute of Chartered Accountants of Ontario (ICAO) / Institut des comptables agrées de l'Ontario
69 Bloor St. East, Toronto ON M4W 1B3
Tel: 416-962-1841; *Fax:* 416-962-8900
Toll-Free: 800-387-0735
customerservice@icao.on.ca
www.icao.on.ca
Mission is to foster public confidence in the Chartered Accountant profession, by acting in the public interest and helping members excel. The Institute sets and enforces the highest standards of practice, qualification and education; promotes professional excellence and ethical conduct; encourages continuous improvement of capabilities among members; promotes the profession while serving as it's primary voice in Ontario
Rod N. Barr, President/CEO
Nora Murrant, Executive Vice President/COO
Tom Warner, Vice President/Registrar

Institute of Chartered Accountants of Prince Edward Island
PO Box 301, 129 Kent St., Charlottetown PE C1A 7K7
Tel: 902-894-4290; *Fax:* 902-894-4791
www.icapei.com
To foster public confidence in the profession of chartered accountancy in Prince Edward Island; To act in the public interest; To assist members to excel in their role as leaders in senior management, advisory, finance, tax & assurance
Albert M. Ferris, Executive Director
George Mason, President
Chris Leary, Vice-President
Karen Stanley, Sec.-Treas.

Institute of Chartered Accountants of Saskatchewan
3621 Pasqua St., Regina SK S4S 6W8
Tel: 306-359-1010; *Fax:* 306-569-8288
Toll-Free: 800-268-3793
inst.ca@icas.sk.ca
www.icas.sk.ca
Represents CA's and CA students in Saskatchewan; protects the public by ensuring members adhere to high professional and ethical standards of practice
Keri McFadden, CEO

Institute of Chartered Accountants of the Northwest Territories & Nunavut (ICANWT)
c/o Indian & Northern Affairs Canada, PO Box 2433, Yellowknife NT X1A 2P8
Tel: 867-873-3680; *Fax:* 867-920-4135
www.icanwt.nt.ca
John Laratta, President

Institute of Chartered Accountants of the Yukon Territory
c/o Institute of Chartered Accountants of British Columbia, Stn. 22, #500, 505 Burrard St., One Bentall Centre, Vancouver BC V7X 1M4
Tel: 604-681-3264; *Fax:* 604-681-1523
Toll-Free: 800-663-2677
www.icayk.ca
Colleen S. Clark, President

The Institute of Internal Auditors (IIA) / L'Institut des vérificateurs internes
247 Maitland Ave., Altamonte Springs FL 32701-4201 USA
Tel: 407-937-1111; *Fax:* 407-937-1101
customerrelations@theiia.org
www.theiia.org
Social Media: www.facebook.com/TheInstituteofInternalAuditors; twitter.com/theiia
To provide leadership for the global profession of internal auditing; To advocate for the profession's value
Richard F. Chambers, President & CEO

New Brunswick Institute of Chartered Accountants (NBICA) / Institut des comptables agréés du Nouveau-Brunswick
Mercantile Centre, #250, 55 Union St., Saint John NB E2L 2B2
Tel: 506-634-1588; *Fax:* 506-634-1015
nbica@nb.aibn.com
www.nbica.org
To serve members, students & the interests of the public with integrity, objectivity & a commitment to excellence; to promote & increase the knowledge, skills & proficiency of members & students; to regulate the discipline & professional conduct of members & students; to require public practitioners to carry minimum levels of professional liability insurance; to have lay representatives sit on Council; to conduct practice inspection of its public practitioners
Jack Blackier, Executive Director

Ordre des CGA du Québec
#1800, 500, Place d'Armes, Montréal QC H2Y 2W2
Tél: 514-861-1823; *Téléc:* 514-861-7661
Ligne sans frais: 800-463-0163
ordre@cga-quebec.org
www.cga-quebec.org
Mèdia social: www.facebook.com/cgaquebec
Assurer la protection du public; contrôler l'exercice de la profession par ses membres
Stephan Robitaille, Présidente
Denise Rainville, Directrice, Finances et administration

L'Ordre des comptables agréés du Québec (OCAQ)
680, rue Sherbrooke ouest, 18e étage, Montréal QC H3A 2S3
Tél: 514-288-3256; *Téléc:* 514-843-8375
Ligne sans frais: 800-363-4688
info@ocaq.qc.ca
www.ocaq.qc.ca
Protection du public; dépister l'exercice illégal de la comptabilité publique; s'assurer de la formation adéquate des membres
Jean-Pierre Allaire, Président
Alain Côté, Vice-présidente

Petroleum Accountants Society of Canada (PASC)
PO Box 4520, Stn. C, Calgary AB T2T 5N3
Tel: 403-262-4744; *Fax:* 403-244-2340
info@petroleumaccountants.com
www.petroleumaccountants.com
To contribute to the long term success of the Canadian petroleum industry by staying abreast of the constantly changing needs of the industry & striving to satisfy those needs
Norm Wolf, President
Josh Molcak, Vice-President

The Society of Professional Accountants of Canada / La Société des comptables professionnels du Canada
#1007, 250 Consumers Rd., Toronto ON M2J 4V6
Tel: 416-350-8145; *Fax:* 416-350-8146
Toll-Free: 877-515-4447
registrar@professionalaccountant.org
www.professionalaccountant.org
To provide ongoing education & to set qualifying standards, to ensure the professional competence of its members in the practice of accountancy
William O. Nichols, President

Addiction

Addictions Foundation of Manitoba (AFM) / Fondation manitobaine de lutte contre les dépendances
1031 Portage Ave., Winnipeg MB R3G 0R8
Tel: 204-944-6236; *Fax:* 204-786-7768
Toll-Free: 866-638-2561
wpgreg@afm.mb.ca
afm.mb.ca
To be a sensitive, caring, learning organization dedicated to continuously improving our services related to addiction & to collaborate with community members in providing a holistic approach, resulting in an improved quality of life for Manitobans; provides prevention, education & treatment programs related to addictions to individuals & communities; conducts research into the negative effects of addictions
Heather Mitchell, Chair

Adult Children of Alcoholics (ACA)
PO Box 75061, 20 Bloor St. East, Toronto ON M5W 3T3
Tel: 416-631-3614
acatoronto@hotmail.com
acatoronto.org/Adult_Children_of_Alcoholics_Toronto
ACA is a 12-step program of adults who meet and share common experiences of living in an alcoholic or dysfunctional home. Past experiences are examined and their influence in the present is explored. By practising the 12 Steps and accepting a Higher Power, the aim is to improve lives today.
Sandra Frattura, Contact

Airspace Action on Smoking & Health
PO Box 18004, 1215c 56th St., Delta BC V4L 2M4
Tel: 778-899-4832; *Toll-Free:* 888-245-7722
airspace@airspace.bc.ca
airspace.bc.ca
Social Media: www.facebook.com/234024210003649; twitter.com/airspace_bc
To educate non-smokers on the effects that smoking has on them & of their legal right to smoke-free air; to help establish laws to protect the comfort, safety & health of non-smokers; to help reduce the number of future smokers

Al-Anon Family Groups (Canada), Inc. / Groupe familiaux Al-Anon
PO Box 57012, 163 Bell St. North, Ottawa ON K1R 1A1
Tel: 613-860-3431; *Fax:* 613-723-0151
Toll-Free: 888-425-2666
wso@al-anon.org
al-anon.alateen.on.ca
Social Media: www.facebook.com/172402452825446; twitter.com/AlAnon_WSO
Richard L. Buchanan, CEO

Al-Anon Groupe La Vallée de l'Espoir
CP 21, Chibougamau QC G8P 2K5
Tél: 418-748-3779
www.al-anon-quebec-est.org

Alcoholics Anonymous (GTA Intergroup) (AA)
#202, 234 Eglinton Ave. East, Toronto ON M4P 1K5
Tel: 416-487-5591; *Fax:* 416-487-5855
Toll-Free: 877-404-5591
TTY: 866-831-4657
office@aatoronto.org
www.aatoronto.org
Fellowship of men & women who share their experience, strength & hope with each other so that they may solve their common problem & help others recover from alcoholism; the primary purpose is to stay sober & help other alcoholics to achieve sobriety
Barbara H., Chair

Alcooliques Anonymes du Québec
3920, rue Rachel est, Montréal QC H1X 1Z3
Tél: 514-376-9230; *Téléc:* 514-374-2250
region87@aa-quebec.org
aa-quebec.org/AA_Quebec/index.htm
Demeurer abstinent et aider d'autres alcooliques à le devenir
Claudette Pichette

Alcooliques Anonymes Groupe La Vallée du Cuivre
CP 21, Chibougamau QC G8P 2K5
Ligne sans frais: 866-376-6279

Canadian Assembly of Narcotics Anonymous (CANA)
PO Box 25073 RPO West Kildonan, Winnipeg MB R2V 4C7
www.canaacna.org
To help the addict who suffers from the disease of addiction

Canadian Centre on Substance Abuse (CCSA) / Centre canadien de lutte contre l'alcoolisme et les toxicomanies (CCLAT)
#300, 75 Albert St., Ottawa ON K1P 5E7
Tel: 613-235-4048; *Fax:* 613-235-8101
Toll-Free: 800-559-4514
info@ccsa.ca; publications@ccsa.ca
www.ccsa.ca
Social Media: twitter.com/CCSAcanada; www.youtube.com/user/CCSACCLAT
To minimize the harm associated with addictions, including substance abuse & problem gambling
Michel Perron, CEO
Tina Barton, Advisor, Communications
Doug Beirness, Senior Analyst, Research & Policy

Centre for Addiction & Mental Health (CAMH) / Centre de toxicomanie et de santé mentale
250 College St., Toronto ON M5T 1R8
Tel: 416-535-8501; *Toll-Free:* 800-463-6273
info@camh.net
www.camh.net
Social Media: www.facebook.com/CentreforAddictionandMentalHealth; twitter.com/CAMHnews
To provide treatment for & research into substance abuse & mental health issues. Clinical & research sites in Toronto & across Ontario
Catherine Zahn, President/CEO

Council on Drug Abuse (CODA)
#505, 111 Peter St., Toronto ON M5V 2H1
Tel: 416-763-1491; *Fax:* 416-763-5343
info@drugabuse.ca
drugabuse.ca
The council is a non-profit organization that strives to prevent & reduce substance abuse, primarily among youth, by sponsoring education programs in schools. It is a registered charity, BN: 106988140RR0001.
Anne Marie Wright, Chair
Ildiko Csermely, Executive Director

MADD Canada / Les mères contre l'alcool auvolant
#500, 2010 Winston Park Dr., Oakville ON L6H 5R7
Tel: 905-829-8805; *Fax:* 905-829-8860
Toll-Free: 800-665-6233
info@madd.ca
www.madd.ca
Social Media: www.facebook.com/maddcanada.ca; twitter.com/maddcanada
To stop death & injury caused by impaired driving; To support victims of this crime
Andrew Murie, CEO
Wayne Kauffeldt, Chairperson
Denise Dubyk, President

Narcotiques Anonymes
1701, rue St-Luc, Chibougamau QC G8P 2N4
Tél: 418-770-5166

Parent Action on Drugs (PAD)
7 Hawksdale Rd., Rm. 121, Toronto ON M3K 1W3
Tel: 416-395-4970; *Fax:* 866-591-7685
pad@parentactionondrugs.org
www.parentactionondrugs.org
Social Media: www.facebook.com/pages/Parent-Action-on-Drugs-PAD/390301531674
To address issues of substance use among youth through outreach, prevention, education & parent support; enhances the capacity of parents, youth & communities to promote an environment that encourages youth to make informed choices
Diane Buhler, Executive Director

Physicians for a Smoke-Free Canada / Médecins pour un Canada sans fumée
1226A Wellington St., Ottawa ON K1Y 3A1
Tel: 613-233-4878; *Fax:* 613-233-7797
psc@smoke-free.ca
www.smoke-free.ca
Atul Kapur, President
James Walker, Sec.-Treas.

Responsible Gambling Council (Ontario) (RGC(O)) / Le Conseil ontarien pour le jeu responsable
#205, 411 Richmond St. East, Toronto ON M5A 3S5
Tel: 416-499-9800; *Fax:* 416-499-8260
Toll-Free: 888-391-1111
mail@rgco.org
www.responsiblegambling.org
RGCO is an independent, non-profit organization committed to the prevention of problem gambling. It works to increase awareness of compulsive gambling among families, community & service club leaders, & supports research into the causes & treatment. It has developed several programs to raise awareness, including high school drama tours & interactive programs for university students. And, it has created campaigns aimed at friends & spouses of those at risk. It is a registered charity, BN: 106846462RR0001.
Terry Finn, Chair
Jon E. Kelly, Executive Director

Advertising & Marketing

The Advertising & Design Club of Canada (ADCC)
#205, 344 Bloor St. West, Toronto ON M5S 3A7
Tel: 416-423-4113; *Fax:* 416-423-3362
info@theadcc.ca
www.theadcc.ca
To recognize, support & promote creative excellence in the Canadian advertising, publishing & design community
Brian Howlett, President
Dawn Wickstrom, Executive Director

Advertising Standards Canada (ASC) / Les normes canadiennes de la publicité
South Tower, #1801, 175 Bloor St. East, Toronto ON M4W 3R8
Tel: 416-961-6311; *Fax:* 416-961-7904
Toll-Free: 888-256-8646
info@adstandards.com
www.adstandards.com
To ensure the integrity & viability of advertising through industry self-regulation.
Linda J. Nagel, President/CEO

Association canadienne des annonceurs inc.
#925, 2015, rue Peel, Montréal QC H3A 1t8
Tél: 514-842-6422; *Téléc:* 514-842-6223
Ligne sans frais: 800-883-0422
info@aca-online.com
www.aca-online.com
L'ACA est la ressource de première ligne des annonceurs à la recherche d'un leadership fiable et crédible de même que pour des conseils et un soutien en matière de communications marketing. Pour ses membres, l'ACA constitute un investissement essential au succès de leur mis en marché
Ron Lund, Président/Chef de la direction

Association des agences de publicité du Québec (AAPQ) / Association of Québec Advertising Agencies
#925, 2015, rue Peel, Montréal QC H3A 1T8
Tél: 514-848-1732; *Téléc:* 514-848-1950
aapq@aapq.ca
www.aapq.ca
Promouvoir et défendre les intérêts des agences membres
Yanik Deschênes, Président-directeur général

Association of Canadian Advertisers Inc. (ACA) / Association canadienne des annonceurs
#1103, 95 St. Clair Ave. West, Toronto ON M4V 1N6
Tel: 416-964-3805; *Fax:* 416-964-0771
Toll-Free: 800-565-0109
info@aca-online.com
www.aca-online.com
Promotes the common interests of advertisers & is a valuable resource to members, providing expertise, education & information
Ronald S. Lund, President & CEO
Susan Charles, Vice President, Member Services

Audit Bureau of Circulation (ABC)
Canadian Member Service Office, #850, 151 Bloor St. West, Toronto ON M5S 1S4
Tel: 416-962-5840; *Fax:* 416-962-5844
service@accessabc.com
www.accessabc.com
To be the pre-eminent self-regulatory auditing organization, responsible to advertisers, advertising agencies, & the media they use, for the verification & dissemination of members' circulation data & other information for the benefit of the advertising marketplace in the United States & Canada
Michael J. Lavery, President & Managing Director

Canadian Advertising Research Foundation (CARF) / Fondation canadienne de recherche en publicité (FCRP)
#1005, 160 Bloor St. East, Toronto ON M4W 1B9
Tel: 416-413-3864; *Fax:* 416-413-3879
tkormann@tvb.ca
www.carf.ca
To promote greater effectiveness in advertising & marketing through completely impartial & objective research; to further, through the fostering of research, scientific practices in advertising & marketing
Tiffany James, Administrator
Lisa Eaton, Co-Chair

Canadian Automatic Merchandising Association (CAMA) / L'Association canadienne d'auto-distribution
Member Services, #100, 2233 Argentia Rd., Mississauga ON L5N 2X7
Fax: 905-826-4873
Toll-Free: 888-849-2262
info@vending-cama.com
www.vending-cama.com
CAMA repsents the intersts of Vending Operators, Machine Manufacturers, and Product and Service Suppliers in Canada. It is designed to represent, support, and enhance the vending industry.
Kim Lockie, National President
Amanda Curtis, Executive Director

Canadian Institute of Marketing / Institut canadien du marketing
205 Miller Dr., Georgetown ON L7G 6G4
Tel: 905-877-5369; *Fax:* 905-877-5369
info@cinstmarketing.ca
www.cinstmarketing.ca
Social Media: www.facebook.com/group.php?gid=8099252591
To improve the practice of marketing in Canada by encouraging the adoption of professional standards & qualifications by practitioners & employers, & by sponsoring activities related to marketing education & training; to be a means by which those engaged in all aspects of marketing as a professional activity can represent their views & interests to governments & agencies
A. Grant Lee, General Manager
Shiv Seechurn, Vice-President & Registrar
Oswald Emmanuel, Sec.-Treas.

Canadian Marketing Association (CMA) / Association canadienne du marketing (ACM)
#607, 1 Concorde Gate, Toronto ON M3C 3N6
Tel: 416-391-2362; *Fax:* 416-441-4062
info@the-cma.org
www.the-cma.org
Social Media: www.facebook.com/cdnmarketing; twitter.com/Cdnmarketing; www.linkedin.com/groups?mostPopular=&gid=47336
To be the pre-eminent marketing association in Canada representing the integration & convergence of all marketing disciplines, channels & technologies
John Gustavson, President & CEO
Wally Hill, Vice President, Public Affairs & Communications

Canadian Media Directors' Council (CMDC)
#1097, 1930 Yonge St., Toronto ON M4S 1Z4
Tel: 416-967-7282
bruce.claassen@genesismedia.com
www.cmdc.ca
To advance media advertising in Canada; To create more efficient processes to execute and administer media transactions by adopting industry-wide standards
Bruce Claassen, President
Cynthia Fleming, Secretary-Treasurer

Canadian Out-of-Home Measurement Bureau (COMB)
#500, 111 Peter St., Toronto ON M5V 2B8
Tel: 416-968-3823; *Fax:* 416-968-9396
Toll-Free: 800-866-1189
www.comb.org
Karen Best, President

Chartered Institute of Marketing Management of Ontario (CIMMO)
19 Bartley Dr., RR#3, Caledon East ON L0N 1E0
Tel: 905-880-2964
goodall@allstream.net
To provide a standard for the marketing industry & be the voice of marketing professionals in Ontario.
Nigel Goodall, Chair

Conseil des directeurs médias du Québec (CDMQ)
#925, 2015, rue Peel, Montréal QC H3A 1T8
Tél: 514-990-1899
info@cdmq.ca
www.cdmq.ca
Etre un point de convergence d'opinions et d'information, un instrument de défense des intérêts des clients/agences et un outil de promotion et de stimulation de la fonction média
Alain Tardy, Président

Institute of Communication Agencies (ICA) / Institut des communications et de la publicité (ICP)
#3002, 2300 Yonge St., Toronto ON M4P 1E4
Tel: 416-482-1396; *Fax:* 416-482-1856
Toll-Free: 800-567-7422
ica@icacanada.ca
www.ica-ad.com
To anticipate, serve & promote the collective interests of ICA members, with regard to defining, developing & helping to maintain the highest possible standards of professional practice
Jani Yates, President
Gillian Graham, CEO

Marketing Research & Intelligence Association (MRIA) / L'Association de la recherche et de l'intelligence marketing (ARIM)
Bldg. 4, #104, 2600 Skymark Ave., Mississauga ON L4W 5B2
Tel: 905-602-6854; *Fax:* 905-602-6855
Toll-Free: 888-602-6742
info@mria-arim.ca
www.mria-arim.ca
To benefit the public & its members by developing & delivering ethical, professional practice standards, promoting the industry, & advocating for public policy that balances the need for research with privacy & consumer rights.
Kimberlee Niziol Jonas, President
Brendan Wycks, Executive Director
Rick Hobbs, CMRP, Secretary-Treasurer

National Advertising Benevolent Society (NABS) / Société nationale de bienfaisance en publicité
4th Floor, 1910 Yonge Street, Toronto ON M4S 1Z5
Tel: 416-962-0446; *Fax:* 416-962-9149
Toll-Free: 800-661-6227
nabs@nabs.org
www.nabs.org
Social Media: www.facebook.com/pages/NABS-Canada/113033972042210; twitter.com/NABS_Canada; www.linkedin.com/company/nabs-canada

To relieve the suffering of individuals & their families who have derived the majority of their income from advertising
Brent Lowe-Bernie, Chair
Jim Warrington, Executive Director

National Association of Major Mail Users, Inc. (NAMMU) / Association nationale des grands usagers postaux inc. (ANGUP)
#302, 517 Wellington St. West, Toronto ON M5V 1G1
Tel: 416-977-3703; *Fax:* 416-977-4513
Toll-Free: 800-453-1308
executive@nammu.org; nammu@rogers.com
www.nammu.org
Dedicated to working in cooperation with Canada Post to improve cost & service
Kathleen Rowe, President

Out-of-Home Marketing Association of Canada (OMAC) / Association marketing canadienne de l'affichage (AMCA)
#500, 111 Peter St., Toronto ON M5V 2H1
Tel: 416-968-3435; *Fax:* 416-968-6538
rcaron@omaccanada.ca
www.omaccanada.ca
To increase out-of-home's share of ad dollars by promoting the benefits & effectiveness of out-of-home media to agencies & advertisers; to develop & implement new initiatives that serve as a resource to the industry & increase understanding of out-of-home media; to foster development of standards & guidelines that make out-of-home easier to plan & buy; to serve as the united voice of the industry through involvement in issues that represent the interests of its members
Rosanne Caron, President

Print Measurement Bureau (PMB)
#1101, 77 Bloor St. West, Toronto ON M5S 1M2
Tel: 416-961-3205; *Fax:* 416-961-5052
Toll-Free: 800-762-0899
lina@pmb.ca
www.pmb.ca
Steve Ferley, President
Hastings Withers, Executive Vice President/Research Director
Lina Di Santo, Client Services Manager

Print Production Association of Ontario (PPA)
PO Box 48027, 1881 Yonge St., Toronto ON M4S 3C0
Tel: 416-410-7841
pgonsalves@interbrand.ca
To keep print buyers abreast of latest technology
Patricia Gonslaves, Executive Member
Sonya Popovich
Patricia Gonsalves
Mark Greene
Jennifer Whitfield

Promotional Product Professionals of Canada Inc. / Professionnels en produits promotionnels du Canada
#100, 6700, Côte-de-Liesse, Saint-Laurent QC H4T 2B5
Tel: 514-489-5359; *Fax:* 514-489-7760
Toll-Free: 866-450-7722
info@pppc.ca
www.pppc.ca
Social Media: twitter.com/PPPCInc
To advance the promotional products industry; To act as the voice of the predominant advertising medium in Canada
Edward Ahad, President & Chief Executive Officer
Chantal Fontaine, Director, Professional Development & Certification
Carol Phillips, Director, Publications
Marc C. Phillips, Director, Information Technology
Debbie Pinkerton, Director, Member Services
Linda Sloan, Manager, Events

Radio Marketing Bureau (RMB)
#316, 175 Bloor St. East, Toronto ON M4W 3R8
Tel: 416-922-5757; *Fax:* 416-922-6542
Toll-Free: 800-667-2346
info@rmb.ca
www.rmb.ca
To educate advertisers on the effective use of the radio medium to achieve & surpass their advertising objectives
Gary Belgrave, President

Sign Association of Canada (SAC) / Association canadienne de l'enseigne (ACE)
#1519, 44 Victoria St., Toronto ON M5C 1Y2
Tel: 416-628-6608; *Fax:* 416-628-6607
Toll-Free: 877-470-9787
info@sac-ace.ca
www.sac-ace.ca
To represent & support association members
Bob Bronk, Executive Director

Fred Elkins, President

Trans-Canada Advertising Agency Network (T-CAAN)
#504, 4001 Bayview Ave., Toronto ON M2M 3Z7
Tel: 416-221-6984
marketingmonkey@sympatico.ca
www.tcaan.ca
To promote exchange of ideas, services & market intelligence among members; services areas include strategy, advertising, public relations & branding
Alice Zaharchuk, Executive Director
Bill Whitehead, Managing Director

Agriculture & Farming

Agricultural Alliance of New Brunswick (AANB) / Alliance agricole du Nouveau-Brunswick
#303, 259 Brunswick St., Fredericton NB E3B 1G8
Tel: 506-452-8101; *Fax:* 506-452-1085
alliance@fermenbfarm.ca
www.fermenbfarm.ca
To promote & advance the social & economic conditions of those engaged in agricultural pursuits; to formulate & promote agricultural policies to meet changing economic conditions
Nicole Arseneau, Office Manager
Mélanie Godin, Coordinator, Environmental Farm Plan

Agricultural Groups Concerned About Resources & the Environment
Ontario AgriCentre, #106, 100 Stone Rd. West, Guelph ON N1G 5L3
Tel: 519-837-1326
agcare@agcare.org
www.agcare.org
Social Media: www.facebook.com/FarmFoodCare; twitter.com/farmfoodcare; www.youtube.com/user/FarmandFoodCare
Lilian Schaer, Executive Director
Kelly Daynard, Program Manager

Agricultural Institute of Canada (AIC) / Institut agricole du Canada
#900, 9 Corvus Crt., Ottawa ON K2E 7Z4
Tel: 613-232-9459; *Fax:* 613-594-5190
Toll-Free: 888-277-7980
office@aic.ca
www.aic.ca
To provide the voice for national knowledge & expertise; To promote the creation, production, & delivery of safe foods & sustainable use of related national resources in Canada & beyond
Digvir Jayas, President
Lianne Dwyer, Vice-President
Frances Rodenburg, Manager, Administration & Communications

Agricultural Institute of Canada Foundation (AICF)
#900, 9 Corvus Crt., Ottawa ON K2E 7Z4
Tel: 613-232-9459; *Fax:* 613-594-5190
Toll-Free: 888-277-7980
office@aic.ca
www.aic.ca/about/foundation.cfm
To enhance agriculture & the role it plays in providing Canadians with a safe, affordable, nutritious food supply
Eveline Wolterson, President
Frances Rodenburg, Secretary-Treasurer & Manager (Interim)

Agricultural Producers Association of Saskatchewan (APAS)
#100, 2400 College Ave., Regina SK S4P 1C8
Tel: 306-789-7774; *Fax:* 306-789-7779
info@apas.ca
www.apas.ca
To provide farmers & ranchers with a democratically elected, grassroots, non-partisan producer organization based on rural municipal boundaries
Nial Kuyek, General Manager

Alberta Association of Agricultural Societies (AAAS)
J.G. O'Donoghue Building, #200, 7000 - 113 St., Edmonton AB T6H 5T6
Tel: 780-427-2174; *Fax:* 780-422-7755
aaas@gov.ab.ca
www.albertaagsocieties.ca
To preserve & enhance the viability of agricultural societies in Alberta
Tim Carson, Chief Executive Officer
Lisa Hardy, Executive Director
Monica Bradley, Treasurer

Alberta Canola Producers Commission (ACPC)
#170, 14315 - 118 Ave., Edmonton AB T5L 4S6
Tel: 780-454-0844; *Fax:* 780-465-5473
Toll-Free: 800-551-6652
web@canola.ab.ca
www.canola.ab.ca
Social Media: www.facebook.com/albertacanola; twitter.com/albertacanola; www.youtube.com/albertacanola
To provide leadership in a vibrant canola industry for the benefit of Alberta canola producers; to strive to improve the long-term profitability of Alberta canola producers
Ward Toma, General Manager

Alberta Institute of Agrologists
#249, 2055 Premier Way, Sherwood Park AB T8H 0G2
Tel: 780-464-9797; *Fax:* 780-464-1171
info@aia.ab.ca
www.albertaagrologists.ca
To serves as a regulatory body within the province for matters related to agrology
Twlya Jones, Chair
David Lloyds, CEO & Registrar

Alberta Milk
1303 - 91 St. SW, Edmonton AB T6X 1H1
Tel: 780-453-5942; *Fax:* 780-455-2196
Toll-Free: 877-361-1231
cblatz@albertamilk.com
www.albertamilk.com
To promote the sustainability of the dairy industry in Alberta
Bill Feenstra, Chair
Gerald Weiss, Executive Director
Mike Southwood, General Manager
Denise Brattinga, Manager, Finance
Ray Grapentine, Manager, Industry & Member Services
Katherine Loughlin, Manager, Market Development
Gerd Andres, Manager, Policy & Transportation

Animal Nutrition Association of Canada (ANAC) / Association de nutrition animale du Canada
#1301, 150 Metcalfe St., Ottawa ON K2P 1P1
Tel: 613-241-6421; *Fax:* 613-241-7970
info@anacan.org
www.anacan.org
ANAC advocates on behalf of the livestock & poultry feed industry with government regulators & policy-makers, & works to maintain high standards of feed & food safety.
Peter Bennett, Chair
Graham Cooper, Executive Director

Association des jeunes ruraux du Québec (AJRQ)
65, rang 3 est, Princeville QC G6L 4B9
Tél: 819-364-5606; *Téléc:* 819-364-5006
info@ajrq.qc.ca
www.ajrq.qc.ca
Promouvoir la formation auprès de nos membres; soutenir leur sentiment d'appartenance au milieu rural
Josiane Chabot, Présidente
Annie Chabot, Directrice générale

Association québécoise des industries de nutrition animale et céréalière (AQINAC)
#200, 4790, rue Martineau, Saint-Hyacinthe QC J2R 1V1
Tél: 450-799-2440; *Téléc:* 450-799-2445
info@aqinac.com
www.aqinac.com
Développer des relations de partenariat avec tous les paliers du Gouvernement, pour mettre en marché des aliments pour animaux de grande qualité; établir et maintenir les meilleures relations possibles entre ses membres et les divers intervenants gouvernementaux; favoriser la mise en marché d'aliments pour animaux performants et de grande qualité; diffuser toute information pertinente en agro-alimentaire et favoriser la formation continue de ses membres; collaborer avec les autres associations organismes et établissements dans la poursuite des objectifs de l'Association; négocier des avantages tangibles pour ses membres en règle; représenter ses membres en toutes matières reliées à l'approvisionnement de biens et services dans le secteur agro-alimentaire
Yvan Lacroix, Président-directeur général

Atlantic Dairy Council (ADC)
PO Box 9410, Stn. A, #700, 6009 Quinpool Rd., Halifax NS B3K 5S3
Tel: 902-425-2445; *Fax:* 902-425-2441
info@adcrecycles.com
www.adrecycles.com
To maintain good relations among those engaged in dairy processing & distribution industries; to provide opportunities for industry training courses; & to enable united action on any matter concerning the welfare of the dairy trade
John K. Sutherland, Executive Secretary

Beef Information Centre (BIC)
Plaza 4, #101, 2000 Argentia Rd., Mississauga ON L5N 1W1
Tel: 905-821-4900; *Fax:* 905-821-4915
Toll-Free: 888-248-2333
info@beefinfo.org
www.beefinfo.org
Social Media: www.facebook.com/ILoveCanadianBeef
To build consumer demand for beef
Glenn Brand, CEO

British Columbia Agriculture Council
#230, 32160 South Fraser Way, Abbotsford BC V2T 1W5
Tel: 604-854-4454; *Fax:* 604-854-4485
Toll-Free: 866-522-3477
bcac@bcagcouncil.com
www.bcac.bc.ca
To provide leadership in representing, promoting, & advocating the collective interests of all agriculture producers in the province of British Colombia; To foster cooperation & a collective response to matters affecting the future of agriculture in the province; To facilitate programs & service delivery for a number of programs that benefit the industry
Andy Dolberg, Executive Director

British Columbia Dairy Foundation
3236 Beta Ave., Burnaby BC V5G 4K4
Tel: 604-294-3775; *Fax:* 604-294-8199
Toll-Free: 800-242-6455
contactus@bcdf.ca
www.bcdairyfoundation.ca
To coordinate, plan, produce & administer dairy products promotion, education & public relations programs best suited to meet the needs of the dairy industry in British Columbia.
Robin Smith, Executive Director

British Columbia Fruit Growers' Association
1473 Water St., Kelowna BC V1Y 1J6
Tel: 250-762-5226; *Fax:* 250-861-9089
info@bcfga.com
www.bcfga.com
To represent fruit growers' interests in British Columbia
Joe Sardinha, President

British Columbia Grape Growers Association (BCGA)
451 Atwood Road, Grand Forks BC V0H 1H9
Tel: 877-762-4652; *Fax:* 250-442-4076
Toll-Free: 877-762-4652
bcga@nethop.net
www.grapegrowers.bc.ca
The Association represents all commercial Columbia on agricultural issues and concerns. It works with other industry organizations, with procincial and federal agricultural organizations and all levels of government to represent, promote and advance the interests of all grapegrowers in British Columbia.
Connie Bielert, Secretary

British Columbia Institute of Agrologists (BCIA)
2777 Claude Rd., Victoria BC V9B 3T7
Tel: 250-380-9292; *Fax:* 250-380-9233
Toll-Free: 877-855-9291
p.ag@bcia.com
www.bcia.com
Kelly McLaughlin, Financial Officer
Robert Moody, Executive Director

British Columbia Milk Producers Association (BCMPA)
3236 Beta Ave., Burnaby BC V5G 4K4
Tel: 604-294-3737; *Fax:* 604-294-8199
Toll-Free: 877-462-2672
www.bcmilkproducers.ca
The British Columbia Milk Producers Association (BCMPA) is the "voice of all dairy farmers in BC" and are advocates with governments, the media, special interest groups and environmentalists, and other industry associations. Their purpose is to advance the legitimate business interest of this province's dairy farmers and promote a vibrant, sustainable industry which supplies high quality dairy products to the consumer.
Robin Smith, Executive Director

Canada Grains Council (CGC)
#1215, 220 Portage Ave., Winnipeg MB R3C 0A5
Tel: 204-925-2130; *Fax:* 204-925-2132
office@canadagrainscouncil.ca
www.canadagrainscouncil.ca
To be the primary networking group for those involved in the grain industry
Jean-Marc Ruest, Chair

Canadian 4-H Council / Conseil des 4-H du Canada
Central Experimental Farm, #26, 930 Carling Ave., Ottawa ON K1A 0C6
Tel: 613-234-4448; *Fax:* 613-234-1112
www.4-h-canada.ca
Social Media: www.facebook.com/4HCanada;
twitter.com/4HCanada; www.youtube.com/4hcanada
To inspire youth across Canada to become contributing leaders in their communities; To support the development of Canada's rural youth
Mike Nowosad, Chief Executive Officer
Erin Brophy, Manager, Communications & Marketing
Mike Carroll, Manager, Finance
Sue Walker, Manager, Fund Development

Canadian Consulting Agrologists Association (CCAA) / Association canadienne des agronomes-conseils
502 - 45 St. West, 2nd Fl., Saskatoon SK S7L 6H2
Tel: 306-933-2974; *Fax:* 306-244-4497
info@ccaa.bz
www.ccaa.bz
To provide excellence in agricultural consulting; To promote standards of competency; To maintain Standards of Ethical Conduct
Adele Buettner, Executive Director
Terry Betker, President

Canadian Co-operative Association (CCA) / Association des coopératives du Canada (ACC)
Co-operative House, #400, 275 Bank St., Ottawa ON K2P 2L6
Tel: 613-238-6711; *Fax:* 613-567-0658
info@CoopsCanada.coop
www.coopscanada.coop
Social Media:
www.facebook.com/pages/Co-operatives-in-Canada/361648435712?ref=nf; twitter.com/CoopsCanada
To develop co-operatives throughout Canada & in other countries; To promote the co-operative model; To unite co-operatives from various industry sectors & regions of Canada
Claude Gauthier, President
Denyse Guy, Executive Director
Jo-Anne Ferguson, Senior Director, International Development
John Anderson, Director, Government Affairs & Public Policy
Julie Breuer, Director, Fundraising & Operations
Quintin Fox, Director, Consultancy & Training, & Manager, Member Services
Norma Jones, Director, Finance & Administration
Donna Balkan, Manager, Communications

Canadian Federation of Agriculture (CFA) / Fédération canadienne de l'agriculture
21 Florence St., Ottawa ON K2P 0W6
Tel: 613-236-3633; *Fax:* 613-236-5749
info@cfafca.ca
www.cfa-fca.ca
Social Media: www.facebook.com/cfafca; twitter.com/CFAFCA
To coordinate the efforts of agricultural producer organizations throughout Canada for the purpose of promoting their common interests through collective action; to promote & advance the social & economic conditions of those engaged in agricultural pursuits; to assist in formulating & promoting national agricultural policies to meet changing national & international conditions
Errol Halkai, Executive Director
Jessica Goodfellow, Director, Communications
Ron Bonnett, President

Canadian Feed Information Centre (CFIC)
PO Box 1251, Swift Current SK S9H 3X4
Tel: 306-773-5401; *Fax:* 306-773-3955
To collect, classify, & provide information on the composition & nutritive value of Canadian feeds; to act as Canadian representative to INFIC & as a coordinating agency of Canadian activities.
J.E. Knipfel, Contact

Canadian Honey Council / Conseil canadien du miel
36 High Vale Cres., Calgary AB T3A 5K8
Tel: 403-475-3882; *Toll-Free:* 877-356-8935
chc-ccm@honeycouncil.ca
www.honeycouncil.ca
To promote, develop & maintain cooperation among all persons, organizations & government personnel involved with Canadian beekeeping industry
Rod Scarlett, executive Director

Canadian Organic Growers Inc. (COG) / Cultivons Biologique Canada
323 Chapel St., Ottawa ON K1N 7Z2
Tel: 613-216-0741; *Fax:* 613-236-0743
Toll-Free: 888-375-7383
office@cog.ca
www.cog.ca
Social Media:
www.facebook.com/pages/Canadian-Organic-Growers/277231516329
To conduct research into alternatives to traditional chemical & energy-intensive food growing practices; To provide a resource base & a forum open to all farmers & food growers interested in alternative agriculture; To foster the goals of a decentralized, bio-regionally-based food system; To endorse practices which promote & maintain long-term soil fertility, reduce fossil fuel uses, reduce pollution, recycle wastes & conserve non-renewable resources; To assist the farmer, grower, food processor & consumer, through education & demonstration, in understanding the value of organic foods
Laura Telford, Executive Director

Canadian Pest Management Association (CPMA) / Association canadienne de la gestion parasitaire (ACGP)
PO Box 1748, Moncton NB E1C 9X5
Fax: 866-957-7378
Toll-Free: 866-630-2762
cpma@pestworld.org
www.pestworldcanada.org
To provide pest management information; To act as the voice of the pest management industry throughout Canada; Upholding the association's Code of Ethics
Bill Melville, President
Karen Furgiuele-Percy, Director, Business Development
Randy Hobbs, Director, Government Affairs
Sean Rollo, Treasurer

Canadian Plowing Organization
43 Ewen Dr., Uxbridge ON L9P 1L5
Tel: 905-852-6221
info@canadianplowing.ca
www.canadianplowing.ca
To preserve the art of match plowing in Canada; to promote the efficient operation & use of farm machinery; to promote improved farm productivity & yield efficiency through proper seed bed preparation & soil management
Robert Timbers, Contact

Canadian Seed Growers' Association (CSGA) / Association canadienne des producteurs de semences
PO Box 8455, #202, 240 Catherine St., Ottawa ON K1G 3T1
Tel: 613-236-0497; *Fax:* 613-563-7855
seeds@seedgrowers.ca
www.seedgrowers.ca
Dale Apolphe, Executive Director

Canadian Seed Trade Association (CSTA) / Association canadienne du commerce des semences (ACCS)
#505, 39 Robertson Rd., Ottawa ON K2H 8R2
Tel: 613-829-9527; *Fax:* 613-829-3530
csta@cdnseed.org
www.cdnseed.org
The Canadian Seed Trade Association (CSTA) is committed to fostering an environment conducive to research, developing, distributing, and trading seed and associated technologies; with the goal of bettering the choices and successes of our members and their customers. Their five key goals are as follows; fostering innovation; support for a science based regulatory system; increase the use of pedigreed seed; support the understanding and use of indentity preserved systems; improve market access and understanding for the trade of seed
W.C. Leask, Executive Vice-President
David Sippell, President

Canadian Society for Bioengineering (CSBE) / Société canadienne de génie agroalimentaire et de bioingénierie (SCGAB)
2028 Calico Crescent, Orleans ON K4A 4L7
Tel: 613-590-0975
bioeng@shaw.ca
www.bioeng.ca
To provide expertise in the areas of farm power & machinery, structures & environment, soil & water & electrical power & processing
James S. Townsend, Secretary
Ron MacDonald, President

Canadian Society of Agronomy
S.C. Sheppard, PO Box 637, Pinawa MB R0E 1L0
Tel: 204-753-2747; *Fax:* 204-753-8478
sheppards@ecomatters.com
www.agronomycanada.com
The mission of The Canadian Society of Agronomy is dedicated to enhancing cooperation and coorindation among agronomists, to recognizing significant achievements in agronomy and to providing the oppourtunity to report and evaluate information pertinent to agronomy in Canada. The goals and objects include networking; external relations and awareness; and internal communications and coordination.
Steve Sheppard, Executive Director

Canadian Sphagnum Peat Moss Association (CSPMA) / Association canadienne Tourbe de Sphaigne
#2208, 13 Mission Ave., St Albert AB T8N 1H6
Tel: 780-460-8280; *Fax:* 780-459-0939
cspma@peatmoss.com
www.peatmoss.com
To promote the benefits of peat moss to horticulturists and home gardeners throughout North America.
Paul Short, President

Canadian Sugar Beet Producers' Association Inc. (CSBPA)
4900 - 50 St., Taber AB T1G 1T3
Tel: 403-223-1110; *Fax:* 403-223-1022
sugarmb@telusplanet.net
To represent interests of Canadian sugar beet growers on provincial & federal government levels & on an international level through the World Association of Beet & Cane Growers; to raise public profile of the beet sugar industry.
Bruce Webster, General Manager

Canola Council of Canada
#400, 167 Lombard Ave., Winnipeg MB R3B 0T6
Tel: 204-982-2100; *Fax:* 204-942-1841
admin@canolacouncil.org
www.canolacouncil.org
To enhance the Canadian canola industry's ability to profitably produce & supply seed, oil, & meal products that offer superior value to customers throughout the world.
JoAnne Bluth, President

Certified Organic Associations of British Columbia (COABC)
#202, 3002 - 32nd Ave., Vernon BC V1T 2L7
Tel: 250-260-4429; *Fax:* 250-260-4436
office@certifiedorganic.bc.ca
www.certifiedorganic.bc.ca
To maintain a credible set of organic production & processing standards
Sarah Clark, Administrator
Kristy Wipperman, Office Manager

Christian Farmers Federation of Ontario (CFFO)
7660 Mill Rd., RR#4, Guelph ON N1H 6J1
Tel: 519-837-1620; *Fax:* 519-824-1835
cffomail@christianfarmers.org
www.christianfarmers.org
Social Media: twitter.com/CFFOnt;
www.youtube.com/user/ChristianFarmers
A professional organization for Christian family farm entrepreneurs; a general farm organization with an interest in a broad range of agricultural, rural & social issues that impact upon the quality of the family life & family businesses of members; as a professional organization, committed to enabling members as producers, as marketers & as citizens, developing both the entrepreneurial & community leadership of members; through involvement in public policy, promotes a family farm & stewardship perspective; as a confessional organization, committed to being upfront about the Christian value system that motivates members, in order to make the wisdom of the Christian faith available to farm practice & farm policy
John Clement, General Manager

Coalition of Rail Shippers (CRS)
#405, 580 Terry Fox Dr., Ottawa ON K2L 4C2
Tel: 613-599-3283; *Fax:* 613-599-1295
CRS provides input to government on matters affecting Canadian, rail freight transportation.
Robert H. Ballantyne, Chair

Conseil des industriels laitiers du Québec inc. (CILQ) / Québec Dairy Council Inc.
#200, 8585, boul St-Laurent, Montréal QC H2P 2M9
Tél: 514-381-5331; *Téléc:* 514-381-6677
info@cilq.ca
cilq.ca
Regrouper les entreprises laitières industrielles du Québec qui s'occupent des différentes phases de la transformation, distribution et commercialisation du lait et des produits laitiers; promotion, protection et développement de leurs intérêts économiques, sociaux et professionnels
Pierre M. Nadeau, Président-directeur général
Charles Langlois, Vice-président, Affaires économiques & Approvisionnement
Yolaine Villeneuve, Directrice, Affaires publiques & corporatives

La Coop Fédérée
#200, 9001, boul de l'Acadie, Montréal QC H4N 3H7
Tél: 514-384-6450; *Téléc:* 514-384-7176
information@lacoop.coop
www.lacoop.coop
La CFQ fournit aux agriculteurs, directement ou par l'entremise de ses coopératives sociétaires, une vaste gamme de biens et de services nécessaires à l'exploitation de leur entreprise, y compris des produits pétroliers; de plus, elle transforme et commercialise sur les marchés locaux et internationaux divers produits agricoles: viande porcine, volaille, etc.
Denis Richard, Président

CropLife Canada
#627, 21 Four Seasons Pl., Toronto ON M9B 6J8
Tel: 416-622-9771
www.croplife.ca
To represent Canada's plant science industry; To foster the developmment of the industry; To build Canadians' trust & appreciation for plant science innovations
Lorne Hepworth, President
Pierre Petelle, Executive Director, Regulatory Affairs & Non-Ag Uses
Nadine Sisk, Executive Director, Communications & Member Services
Russel Hurst, Managing Director, Stewardship & Sustainability
Cam Davreux, Vice-President, Stewardship
Annie Hsu, Vice-President, Finance & Administration
Peter MacLeod, Vice-President, Chemistry
Dennis Prouse, Vice-President, Government Affairs
Janice Tranberg, Vice-President, Western Canada

Dairy Farmers of Canada (DFC) / Les Producteurs laitiers du Canada (PLC)
21 Florence St., Ottawa ON K2P 0W6
Tel: 613-236-9997; *Fax:* 613-236-0905
info.policy@dfc-plc.ca
www.dairyfarmers.ca
To coordinate action of dairy producer organizations on all issues of national scope; to collaborate with relevant agencies in elaboration of national policies of interest to Canadian dairy industry.
Jacques Laforge, President
Bruce Saunders, 1st Vice-President
Wally Smith, 2nd Vice-President

Dairy Farmers of Nova Scotia (DFNS)
#100, 4060 Hwy. 236, Lower Truro NS B6L 1J9
Tel: 902-893-6455; *Fax:* 902-897-9768
hboyd@dfns.ca
www.dfns.ca
To provide a regulatory and administrative service to Nova Scotia's dairy producers.
Grian Cameron, General Manager
Barron Blois, Chair

Fédération d'agriculture biologique du Québec (FABQ)
#100, 555, boul Roland-Therrien, Longueuil QC J4H 3Y9
Tél: 450-679-0530; *Téléc:* 450-670-4867
fabq@upa.qc.ca
www.fabqbio.ca
Promouvoir l'étude, la défense et le développement des intérêts économiques, sociaux et moraux de ses membres; administrer tout le programme de la mise en marché; étudier des problèmes relatifs à la production; coopérer à la vulgarisation des techniques de production biologique; renseigner le producteur sur la production et la vente de produits biologiques certifiés
Gérard Bouchard, Président

Fédération des agricultrices du Québec (FAQ)
555, boul Roland-Therrien, Longueuil QC J4H 4E7
Tél: 450-679-0540; *Téléc:* 450-463-5228
fed.agricultrices@upa.qc.ca
www.agricultrices.com
Valoriser la profession; créer un réseau entre les femmes; avoir une force politique capable de défendre les intérêts des agricultrices; prodiguer de la formation
Marcel Groleau, Présidente

Fédération des producteurs de bovins du Québec (FPBQ) / Federation of Québec Beef Producers
#305, 555, boul Roland-Therrien, Longueuil QC J4H 4G2
Tél: 450-679-0530; *Téléc:* 450-442-9348
www.bovin.qc.ca
Regrouper et défendre les intérêts professionnels et économiques des producteurs de bovins du Québec; administrer et appliquer le plan conjoint des producteurs de bovins du Québec
Jean-Philippe Deschênes-Gilbert, Directeur général

Fédération des producteurs de lait du Québec (FPLQ)
555, boul Roland-Therrien, Longueuil QC J4H 3Y9
Tél: 450-679-0530; *Téléc:* 450-679-5899
fplq@upa.qc.ca
www.lait.org
Défense et promotion des intérêts professionnels et sociaux des producteurs de lait et mise en marché du lait de la ferme.
Alain Bourbeau, Directeur général

Fédération des producteurs de porcs du Québec (FPPQ)
CP 120, 555, boul Roland-Therrien, Longueuil QC J4H 4E9
Tél: 450-679-0540; *Téléc:* 450-679-0102
Ligne sans frais: 800-363-7672
fppq@upa.qc.ca
www.leporcduquebec.qc.ca
A l'ordre du jour du Plan agroenvironnemental de la production porcine on trouve; l'application de plans de fertilisation sur toutes les fermes; la diminution des rejets de phosphore et d'azote pour éviter la surfertilisation; la réduction des odeurs; l'utilisation du lisier comme matière fertilisante; mise en place d'actions collectives.
Bernard Verret, Directeur général

Flax Council of Canada
#465, 167 Lombard Ave., Winnipeg MB R3B 0T6
Tel: 204-982-2115; *Fax:* 204-942-1841
flax@flaxcouncil.ca
www.flaxcouncil.ca
To provide a central focus for industry, producers, government, research institutions & marketing organizations; to promote flax worldwide through crop, market & product development.
M. Barry Hall, President

Horticulture Nova Scotia (HORT NS)
Kentville Agricultural Centre, 32 Main St., Kentville NS B4N 1J5
Tel: 902-678-9335; *Fax:* 902-678-1280
hortns@ns.sympatico.ca
www.hortns.com
To enhance collaborative efforts among members which will strengthen & provide leadership to the horticultural industry
Donna Crawford, Administrative Coordinator
Lloyd Evans, President

Keystone Agricultural Producers (KAP)
#203, 1700 Ellice Ave., Winnipeg MB R3H 0B1
Tel: 204-697-1140; *Fax:* 204-697-1109
kap@kap.mb.ca
www.kap.mb.ca
To be a democratic & effective policy organization, promoting the social, economic & physical well-being of all Manitoban agricultural producers
Yvonne Rideout, General Manager
Ian Wishart, President

Manitoba Institute of Agrologists (MIA)
#201, 38 Dafoe Ave., Winnipeg MB R3T 2N2
Tel: 204-275-3721; *Fax:* 888-315-6661
mia@mts.net
www.mia.mb.ca
To act in accordance with the Agrologists Act of Manitoba; To regulate the practice of agrology in Manitoba; To ensure the knowledge, competence, & integrity of institute members, in order to protect the public interest; To act as the voice of the agrology profession
Richard Kieper, P.Ag., President
Jim Weir, Executive Director & Registrar
Estel Facundo, Officer, Administration

Mushrooms Canada (CMGA)
7660 Mill Rd., RR#4, Guelph ON N1H 6J1
Tel: 519-829-4125; *Fax:* 519-837-0729
info@canadianmushroom.com
www.mushrooms.ca
To encourage cooperation & communication within the Canadian industry, with various levels of government, & with related organizations internationally; To promote mushroom consumption
William Stevens, Executive Vice-President
Glenn Martin, President

National Farmers Union (NFU) / Syndicat national des cultivateurs
2717 Wentz Ave., Saskatoon SK S7K 4B6
Tel: 306-652-9465; *Fax:* 306-664-6226
nfu@nfu.ca
www.nfu.ca
Social Media: twitter.com/NFUcanada
To improve economic & social well-being of rural people & rural communities
Terry Boehm, President
Joan Brady, Women's President
Cammie Harbottle, Youth President

New Brunswick Institute of Agrologists (NBIA) / L'Institut des agronomes du Nouveau-Brunswick (IANB)
PO Box 3479, Stn. B, Fredericton NB E3B 5H2
Tel: 506-459-5536; *Fax:* 506-454-7837
nbia@nbagrologists.nb.ca
www.nbagrologists.nb.ca
To maintain high competency & professional standards for those practicing agrology in New Brunswick; To uphold the NBIA Code of Ethics; to offer advice to the public about agriculture & related areas; To formulate policies & improve the agriculture & food industry
Charles Briggs, President
Duncan Fraser, Secretary
Margaret Mann, Registrar
Rita Rattray, Office Administrator

Newfoundland & Labrador Federation of Agriculture
PO Box 1045, 308 Brookfield Rd., Bldg. 4, Mount Pearl NL A1N 3C9
Tel: 709-747-4874; *Fax:* 709-747-8827
info@nlfa.ca
www.nlfa.ca
To act as the united voice of farmers in Newfoundland & Labrador; To improve the agricultural industry in Newfoundland & Labrador; To advance the economic & social conditions of those in the agricultural industry
Paul Connors, Executive Director
Matthew Carlson, Officer, Communications
Kim O'Rourke, Administrative Assistant
Jamie Warren, Officer, Industry Development
Gerry Sullivan, Coordinator, Agriculture Awareness & Agri-Tourism
Christa Wright, Coordinator, Agriculture in the Classroom

Newfoundland & Labrador Institute of Agrologists (NLIA)
PO Box 978, Mount Pearl NL A1N 3C9
Tel: 709-772-4170
www.aic.ca/agrology/nlia.cfm
Dedicated to the professional aspects of Canadian agriculture.
Gary Bishop, President/Treasurer
Samir Debnath, Registrar

Not Far From The Tree
90 Croatia St., Toronto ON M6H 1K9
Tel: 416-363-6441
info@notfarfromthetree.org
www.notfarfromthetree.org
The group operates a residential, fruit-picking program where teams of volunteers are dispatched to harvest fruit from trees that the owners would otherwise let go to waste. The fruit is divided equally among the ownners, volunteers & a local, community food distribution organization who can make good use of it.

Nova Scotia Federation of Agriculture (NSFA)
Covington Place, 332 Willow St., 2nd Fl., Truro NS B2N 5A5
Tel: 902-893-2293; *Fax:* 902-893-7063
info@nsfa-fane.ca
www.nsfa-fane.ca
To act as the voice for the agricultural community in Nova Scotia; To ensure a competitive & sustainable future for agriculture in Nova Scotia; To build financially viable, ecologically sound, & socially responsible farm businesses in the province
Beth Densmore, President
Donna Langille, Manager, Operations

Nova Scotia Fruit Growers' Association (NSFGA)
Kentville Agricultural Centre, 32 Main St., Kentville NS B4N 1J5
Tel: 902-678-1093; *Fax:* 902-679-1567
www.nsapples.com
To serve the interests of tree fruit growers in Nova Scotia
Brian Boates, President

Nova Scotia Institute of Agrologists (NSIA)
PO Box 550, 35 Tower Rd., Truro NS B2N 5E3
Tel: 902-897-6742
nsagrologists@eastlink.ca
www.nsagrologists.ca

Ontario Agri Business Association (OABA)
#104, 160 Research Lane, Guelph ON N1G 5B2
Tel: 519-822-3004; *Fax:* 519-822-8862
info@oaba.on.ca
www.oaba.on.ca
To serve & represent firms engaged in the crop inputs, country grain elevator, & feed & farm supply industy, plus related agricultural businesses operating within Ontario
D.O. Buttenham, CEO
Gwen Paddock, President
Cory McDonald, Vice-President
Dale Cowan, Treasurer

Ontario Beekeepers' Association (OBA)
#476, 8560 Tremaine Rd., Milton ON L9T 4Z1
Tel: 905-636-0661; *Fax:* 905-636-0662
info@ontariobee.com
www.ontariobee.com
To coordinate & advance the beekeeping industry in Ontario
Virginia Steckle, Business Administrator
Brent Halsall, President

Ontario Creamerymen's Association
26 Dominion St., Alliston ON L9R 1L5
Tel: 705-435-6751; *Fax:* 705-435-6797
allistoncreamery1@bellnet.ca
Lloyd Kennedy, President

Ontario Dairy Council (ODC)
6533D Mississauga Rd., Mississauga ON L5N 1A6
Tel: 905-542-3620; *Fax:* 905-542-3624
Toll-Free: 866-542-3620
info@ontariodairies.ca
www.ontariodairies.ca
To represent interests of dairy product processors, marketers & distributors in Ontario
Tom Kane, President
Christina Lewis, Vice-President

Ontario Federation of Agriculture (OFA)
Ontario AgriCentre, #206, 100 Stone Rd. West, London ON N1G 5L3
Tel: 519-821-8883; *Fax:* 519-821-8810
Toll-Free: 800-668-3276
info@ofa.on.ca
www.ofa.on.ca
Social Media: www.facebook.com/ontariofarms; twitter.com/ontariofarms; www.youtube.com/user/ontariofarms
To represent farm families throughout Ontario; To champion the interests of Ontario farmers; To work towards a sustainable future for farmers
Mark Wales, President
Don McCabe, Vice-President
Debra Pretty-Straathof, Vice-President

Ontario Fruit & Vegetable Growers' Association (OFVGA) / L'Association des fruiticulteurs et des maraîchers de l'Ontario
#105, 355 Elmira Rd. North, Guelph ON N1K 1S5
Tel: 519-763-6160; *Fax:* 519-763-6604
info@ofvga.org
www.ofvga.org
Dedicated to the advancement of horticulture, working proactively through effective lobbying for the betterment of the industry & producers as a whole through advocacy, research, education, communication & marketing
Art Smith, CEO

Ontario Institute of Agrologists (OIA)
Ontario AgriCentre, #108, 100 Stone Rd. West, Guelph ON N1G 5L3
Tel: 519-826-4226; *Fax:* 519-826-4228
Toll-Free: 866-339-7619
info@oia.on.ca
www.oia.on.ca
OIA regulates Ontario's Professional Agrologists & ensures that competencies meet a Standard of Practice within a specific scope of agrology; ensures that business is conducted within a Code of Ethics; protects the public interest; grows the agri-life science industry; contributes to the excellence of colleagues; pursues professional development to enhance knowledge, skills & experience so they can practise science of agrology with skill, integrity & transparency.
Bruce Hobin, President
Phillis Chang, Director, Finance & Admin.
Pat Joannie, Project Manager
Terry Kingsmill, Registrar

Ontario Maple Syrup Producers' Association (OMSPA)
469 Melville Rd., Consecon ON K0K 1T0
Tel: 613-399-3300; *Fax:* 613-399-3301
Toll-Free: 866-399-3301
admin@ontariomaple.com
www.ontariomaple.com
To promote Ontario maple products through research & education
Bridget Stevenson, Business Administrator

Ontario Plowmen's Association (OPA)
188 Nicklin Rd., Guelph ON N1H 7L5
Tel: 519-767-2928; *Fax:* 519-767-2101
Toll-Free: 800-661-7569
eventadmin@plowingmatch.org
www.plowingmatch.org
Provides ledership to local plowing associations; oversees the International Plowing Match; mission is to advance interest & involvement in agriculture by promoting new technologies, environmental & safety issues; preserving the history of soil cultivation
Ray Dedman, 1st Vice-President
Robert MacLean, 2nd Vice-President
Cathy Lasby, Executive Director
Bob Hammell, President

Ordre des agronomes du Québec (OAQ)
#810, 1001, rue Sherbrooke est, Montréal QC H2L 1L3
Tél: 514-596-3833; *Téléc:* 514-596-2974
Ligne sans frais: 800-361-3833
agronome@oaq.qc.ca
www.oaq.qc.ca
Assure les utilisateurs de services agronomiques et les consommateurs de la compétence, du professionnalisme et de l'engagement des agronomes et ainsi favoriser le mieux-être de la société
René Mongeau, Président

Prince Edward Island Federation of Agriculture (PEIFA)
420 University Ave., Charlottetown PE C1A 7Z5
Tel: 902-368-7289; *Fax:* 902-368-7204
ianm@peifa.ca
www.peifa.ca
To provide a united voice for Island farmers
John Jaimeson, Executive Director

Prince Edward Island Institute of Agrologists (PEIIA)
PO Box 2712, Charlottetown PE C1A 8C3
Tel: 902-892-1943; *Fax:* 902-892-0443
peiia@pei.sympatico.ca
www.peiia.ca
To safeguard the public by ensuring its members are qualified & competent to provide knowledge & advice on agriculture & related areas
Brian Beaton, President
Bert Christie, Sec.-Treas.
Claude Gallant, Registrar

Prince Edward Island Vegetable Growers Co-op Association
PO Box 1494, 280 Sherwood Rd., Charlottetown PE C1A 7N1
Tel: 902-892-5361; *Fax:* 902-566-2383
peiveg@eastlink.ca
Don Read, Manager

Québec 4-H
6500, boulevard Arthur-Sauvé, bur. 202, Laval QC H7R 3X7
Tel: 450-314-1942; *Fax:* 450-314-1952
info@clubs4h.qc.ca
www.clubs4h.qc.ca
To develop life skills, such as leadership, cooperation, responsibility, & independence, for the English speaking rural youth of Québec, through achievement & skill-development
Tammy Oswick-Kearney, Provincial Coordinator

Québec Farmers' Association (QFA)
#255, 555, boul Roland-Therrien, Longueuil QC J4H 4E7
Tel: 450-679-0540; *Fax:* 450-463-5291
qfa@upa.qc.ca
www.quebecfarmers.org
Ivan Hale, Executive Director
Wendy Jones, Director, Operations

Ruth's Daughters of Canada
71 Elm Grove Ave., Toronto ON M6K 2J2
Tel: 416-599-7937
www.ruthsdaughters.com
The Association offers support to women who are victims of domestic violence. Its chapters center around prayer, friendship & outreach, & also develops action plans to prevent violence against women.

Cheri DiNovo, Contact

Saskatchewan Association of Agricultural Societies & Exhibitions (SAASE)
PO Box 31025, Regina SK S4R 8R6
Tel: 306-565-2121; *Fax:* 306-565-2079
gduck.saase@sasktel.net
www.saase.ca
To provide the forum for exchange of ideas among Association members; to provide educational opportunities for members; to address relevant issues affecting members; to provide for district, board & provincial meetings of members; to promote fair & agricultural industry; to help promote & form new societies; to provide a liaison with the extension program of University of Saskatchewan; to assist governments & universities to reach their agricultural & educational objectives
Glen Duck, Executive Director

Saskatchewan Beekeepers Association (SBA)
PO Box 55, RR#3, Yorkton SK S3N 2X5
Tel: 306-743-5469; *Fax:* 306-743-5528
whowland@accesscomm.ca
www.saskatchewanbeekeepers.ca
To support Saskatchewan's beekeeping industry; To represent the province's beekeeping industry at both the provincial & national levels
Calvin Parsons, President
Corey Bacon, Vice-President
Wink Howland, Secetary-Treasurer
Dennis Glennie, Coordinator, SBA Bear Fence Program

Saskatchewan Canola Growers Association (SCGA)
#210, 111 Research Dr., Saskatoon SK S7N 3R2
Tel: 306-668-2380; *Toll-Free:* 800-690-5788
www.canolagrowers.ca
To communicate the concerns of canola growers in Saskatchewan; To advance the production of canola in Saskatchewan; To increase profitability for farms; To further the marketing of canola
Wayne Thompson, Executive Director
Stan Jeeves, President
Tyler Markusson, Vice-President
Ed Schafer, Vice-President
Jeff Pylatuik, Secretary

SeCan Association / Association SeCan
#501, 300 March Rd., Kanata ON K2K 2E2
Tel: 613-592-8600; *Fax:* 613-592-9497
Toll-Free: 800-764-5487
seed@secan.com
www.secan.com
As Canada's Seed Partner, SeCan actively seeks partnerships which promote profitability in Canadian agriculture. SeCan is the largest supplier of certified seed to Canadian farmers with more than 1,000 members from coast to coast engaged in seed production, processing and marketing. They are a private, not-for-profit, member corporation with the primary goal of accessing and promoting leading genetics.
Jeff Reid, General Manager

Society of Ontario Nut Growers (SONG)
RR#3, Niagara-on-the-Lake ON L0S 1J0
Tel: 905-935-9773; *Fax:* 905-935-6887
nuttrees@grimonut.com
www.songonline.ca
To promote the interests of nut growers; to encourage scientific research in the breeding & culture of nut-bearing plants suited to Ontario conditions; to disseminate information on propagation techniques & cultural practices
Ernie Grimo, Treasurer

Union des producteurs agricoles (UPA)
#100, 555, boul. Roland-Therrien, Longueuil QC J4H 3Y9
Tél: 450-679-0530
upa@upa.qc.ca
www.upa.qc.ca
Mèdia social: www.facebook.com/pageUPA; twitter.com/upaqc; www.youtube.com/user/upa1972
Promouvoir, défendre et développer les intérêts professionnels, économiques, sociaux et moraux des producteurs agricoles et forestiers, sans distinction de race, de nationalité, de sexe, de langue et de croyance
Marcel Groleau, Président général

Vegetable Growers' Association of Manitoba (VGAM)
PO Box 984, Portage la Prairie MB R1N 3C3
Tel: 204-428-3188; *Fax:* 204-428-3245
vgam@escape.ca
To support Manitoba's vegetable growers
Doug Connery, Chair, Labour

Western Barley Growers Association (WBGA)
Agriculture Centre, 97 East Lake Ramp NE, Airdrie AB T4A 0C3
Tel: 403-912-3998; *Fax:* 403-948-2069
wbga@wbga.org
www.wbga.org
To provide farmers with an informed & effective voice in the agriculture industry of Western Canada
Brian Otto, President
Rick Strankman, Treasurer
Jeff Nielsen, Past President
Doug Robertson, Alberta Vice-President
Art Walde, Saskatchewan Vice-President

Western Canadian Shippers' Coalition (WCSC)
31 Centennial Pkwy., Delta BC V4L 2C3
Tel: 604-943-8984; *Fax:* 604-943-8936
Ian May, Chair

Wild Rose Agricultural Producers
#102, 115 Portage Close, Sherwood Park AB T8H 2R5
Tel: 780-416-6530; *Fax:* 780-416-6531
Toll-Free: 888-616-6530
info@wrap.ab.ca
www.wrap.ab.ca
To represent its members at the regional, provincial & national level for the benefit of agriculture; to create an atmosphere of cooperation & communication to ensure that areas of common concern among all producers are dealt with to the benefit of agriculture as a whole
Rod Scarlett, Executive Director

Yukon Agricultural Association
#203, 302 Steele St., Whitehorse YT Y1A 2E5
Tel: 867-668-6864; *Fax:* 867-393-9566
info@yukonag.ca
www.yukonag.ca
To provide resources and opportunities to agricultural producers in the Yukon.
Al Falle, President
Rick Tone, Executive Director

AIDS

Action Séro Zéro
CP 246, Succ. C, Montréal QC H2L 4K1
Tél: 514-521-7778; *Téléc:* 514-521-7665
www.sero-zero.qc.ca
Services gratuits de promotion de la santé et de prévention du VIH/SIDA et des infections transmissibles sexuellement et par le sang. Bureaux: 2075, rue Plessis, local 207, Montréal.
Robert Rousseau, Directeur général

The AIDS Foundation of Canada Inc.
#302, 1224 Hamilton St., Vancouver BC V6B 2S8
Tel: 604-688-7294; *Fax:* 604-689-4888
contact@aidsfoundationofcanada.com
www.aidsfoundationofcanada.com
To address the growing problem of HIV disease in Canada; to fund new & innovative ways of assisting infected/affected people with HIV; to support new ways to heighten awareness of HIV disease among the general population

AIDS Vancouver (AV)
1107 Seymour St., Vancouver BC V6B 5S8
Tel: 604-893-2201; *Fax:* 604-893-2211
TTY: 604-893-2215
Crisis Hot-Line: 604-687-2437
contact@aidsvancouver.org
www.aidsvancouver.org
Social Media: www.facebook.com/group.php?gid=48799305725
To alleviate individual & collective vulnerability to HIV & AIDS, through care, support, education, advocacy, & research
David Swan, Executive Director

AIDS Vancouver Island (AVI)
1601 Blanshard St., Victoria BC V8W 2J5
Tel: 250-384-2366; *Fax:* 250-380-9411
Toll-Free: 800-665-2437
Crisis Hot-Line: 250-384-4554
info@avi.org
www.avi.org
Social Media: www.facebook.com/group.php?gid=221277862889
To reduce the spread of, primarily, HIV/AIDS & also Hepatitis C &/or other co-infections; To improve the health & well-being of people infected & affected primarily by HIV/AIDS & also by Hepatitis C &/or other co-infections
Katrina Jensen, Executive Director

Black Coalition for AIDS Prevention
20 Victoria St., 4th Fl., Toronto ON M5C 2N8
Tel: 416-977-9955; *Fax:* 416-977-7664
info@black-cap.com
www.black-cap.com
Social Media: www.facebook.com/group.php?gid=10127593377
To reduce the spread of HIV infection in the Black communities & to enhance the quality of life for Black people living with or affected by HIV/AIDS
Shannon Thomas Ryan, Executive Director

Blood Ties Four Directions Centre
307 Strickland St., Whitehorse YT Y1A 2J9
Tel: 867-633-2437; *Fax:* 867-633-2447
Toll-Free: 877-333-2437
bloodties@klondiker.com
www.bloodties.ca
The organization acts as an information & support centre to: promote public awareness of AIDS/AIDS & hepatitis C and aid in their prevention; assist people living with HIV/AIDS & hep C.
Patricia Bacon, Executive Director

Canadian AIDS Society (CAS) / Société canadienne du sida (SCS)
#800, 190 O'Connor St., Ottawa ON K2P 2R3
Tel: 613-230-3580; *Fax:* 613-563-4998
Toll-Free: 800-499-1986
casinfo@cdnaids.ca
www.cdnaids.ca
Social Media: www.facebook.com/group.php?gid=172950011095
To strengthen the response to HIV/AIDS across Canada; To enrich the lives of people living with HIV/AIDS
Gerry McConnery, Chair
Jeffrey Keller, Vice-Chair
Monique Doolittle-Romas, Executive Director
Christal Capostinsky, Secretary
Marc Lapierre, Treasurer
Jordan Tarini, Director, Youth
Kim Thomas, Director, Programs

Canadian Foundation for AIDS Research (CANFAR) / Fondation canadienne de recherche sur le SIDA
#710, 165 University Ave., Toronto ON M5H 3B8
Tel: 416-361-6281; *Fax:* 416-361-5736
Toll-Free: 800-563-2873
www.canfar.com
Social Media: www.facebook.com/canfar; twitter.com/canfar; www.youtube.com/user/CANFAR; www.flickr.com/photos/canfar
National, privately funded, charitable foundation created to raise awareness in order to fund research into all aspects of HIV infection & AIDS
Christopher Bunting, President

Canadian HIV/AIDS Legal Network / Réseau juridique canadien VIH/sida
#600, 1240 Bay St., Toronto ON M5R 2A7
Tel: 416-595-1666; *Fax:* 416-595-0094
info@aidslaw.ca
www.aidslaw.ca
Social Media: twitter.com/aidslaw
To promote the human rights of people living with & vulnerable to HIV/AIDS, in Canada & internationally; through research, legal & policy analysis, education, advocacy & community mobilization
Janet Butler-McPhee, Director of Communications

Coalition des organismes communautaires québécois de lutte contre le sida (COCQ-SIDA)
1, rue Sherbrooke est, Montréal QC H2X 3V8
Tél: 514-844-2477; *Téléc:* 514-844-2498
Ligne sans frais: 866-535-0481
info@cocqsida.com
www.cocqsida.com
Mèdia social: www.facebook.com/COCQSIDA; twitter.com/COCQSIDA
Représenter les membres afin de favoriser l'émergence et le soutien d'une action concertée dans les dossiers d'intérêt commun; faire reconnaître l'expertise et l'apport des organismes communautaires et non-gouvernementaux dans la lutte contre le sida.
Hélène Légaré, Présidente
Ken Monteith, Directeur général

Healing Our Spirit
395 Railway St., Vancouver BC V6A 1A6
Tel: 604-605-8901; *Fax:* 604-605-8902
Toll-Free: 866-605-8901
info@fnes.ca
www.healingourspirit.org
To prevent & reduce the spread of HIV infection in First Nation communities & to support those affected by HIV/AIDS.
Norma Guerin, Executive Director
Leonard George, President

Maison Plein Coeur
1611, rue Dorion, Montréal QC H2K 4A5
Tél: 514-597-0554; *Téléc:* 514-597-2788
info@maisonpleincoeur.org
www.maisonpleincoeur.org
Contribuer à prévenir le VIH-SIDA, et à promouvoir la santé chez les personnes vivant avec la maladie; offrir des services sans aucune discrimination

Toronto PWA Foundation (TPWAF)
399 Church St., 2nd Fl., Toronto ON M5B 2J6
Tel: 416-506-1400; *Fax:* 416-506-1404
info@pwatoronto.org
www.pwatoronto.org
To promote the health & well-being of all people living with HIV/AIDS by providing accessible, direct & practical services
Murray Jose, Executive Director

Animal Breeding

Appaloosa Horse Club of Canada (ApHCC)
PO Box 940, Claresholm AB T0L 0T0
Tel: 403-625-3326; *Fax:* 403-625-2274
aphcc@appaloosa.ca
www.appaloosa.ca
Social Media:
www.facebook.com/group.php?gid=255499284509
To collect records & historical data relating to origin of the Appaloosa; To file records & issue certificates of registration; to preserve, improve & standardize the breed
Lynn Shinkewski, President
Donna Wyatt, Director
Mervin Veinot, Treasurer
Joceyln Kish, Secretary

Ayrshire Breeders Association of Canada (ABAC) / L'Associaton des éleveurs Ayrshire du Canada
4865, boul Laurier ouest, Saint-Hyacinthe QC J2S 3V4
Tel: 450-778-3535; *Fax:* 450-778-3531
info@ayrshire-canada.com
www.ayrshire-canada.com
Social Media:
www.facebook.com/profile.php?id=100000928371239
To bring Ayrshire breeders together for the purpose of cooperating in their efforts to further the interests of the breed; promote the breeding of purebred Ayrshire cattle in Canada; establish breeding standards; cooperate with industry partners to enhance programs; program services in English & French
Linda Ness, Executive Director
Chad McKell, Registrar

Canadian Angus Association (CAA) / L'Association canadienne Angus
#142, 6715 - 8 St. NE, Calgary AB T2E 7H7
Tel: 403-571-3580; *Fax:* 403-571-3599
Toll-Free: 888-571-3580
tina1@cdnangus.ca; registry@cdnangus.ca; cacp@cdnangus.ca
www.cdnangus.ca
To offer services to enhance the growth & position of the Angus breed; To maintain breed purity
Doug Fee, Chief Executive Officer
Bob Switzer, President
Sharmayne Byrgesen, Registrar

Canadian Arabian Horse Registry
#113, 37 Athabascan Ave., Sherwood Park AB T8A 4H3
Tel: 780-416-4990; *Fax:* 780-416-4860
cahr@cahr.ca
www.cahr.ca
To register purebred Arabian horses in Canada; to establish standards of breeding practices; To serve the needs of Arabian horse owners
Christine Tribe, Registrar
Marcia Friesen, President
Robert Sproule, Secretary-Treasurer

Canadian Belgian Horse Association
17150, Conc. 10, Schomberg ON L0G 1T0
Tel: 905-939-1186; *Fax:* 905-939-7547
cbha@csolve.net
www.canadianbelgianhorse.com
Promotion & betterment of the Belgian breed of horse
Gerald Hendry, President

Canadian Bison Association (CBA) / Association canadienne du bison
PO Box 3116, #200, 1660 Pasqua St., Regina SK S4P 3G7
Tel: 306-522-4766; *Fax:* 306-522-4768
cba1@sasktel.net
www.canadianbison.ca
To develop the bison industry; to maintain the production of bison in a natural state (no growth hormones, chemicals, feed lots, free-range management); to be the voice for commercial breeders; to assist in the formation of regulations & guidelines in commercial production & management of Canadian Plains Bison & to promote the product & awareness of the bison industry
Gavin Conacher, Executive Director

Canadian Blonde d'Aquitaine Association
c/o Canadian Livestock Records Corp., 2417 Holly Lane, Ottawa ON K1V 0M7
Tel: 613-731-7110; *Fax:* 613-731-0704
cbda@clrc.ca
www.canadianblondeassociation.ca
Myrna Flesch, President

Canadian Brown Swiss & Braunvieh Association / L'association canadienne de la Suisse Brune et de la Braunvieh
RR#5, Hwy. 6 North, Guelph ON N1H 6J2
Tel: 519-821-2811; *Fax:* 519-763-6582
brownswiss@gencor.ca
www.browncow.ca
To encourage, develop & regulate breeding of Brown Swiss & Braunvieh dairy cattle.
Ernst Gubelmann, President

Canadian Cattle Breeders' Association (CCBA) / Société des éleveurs de bovins canadiens (SEBC)
4865, boul Laurier ouest, Saint-Hyacinthe QC J2S 3V4
Tel: 450-774-2775; *Fax:* 450-774-9775
info@cqrl.org
www.clrc.ca/canadiancattle.shtml
Angèle Hébert, Sec.-trés.

Canadian Cattlemen's Association (CCA)
#310, 6715 - 8 St. NE, Calgary AB T2E 7H7
Tel: 403-275-8558; *Fax:* 403-274-5686
feedback@cattle.ca
www.cattle.ca
To act as the national voice of beef producers across Canada; To produce high-quality beef products; To maintain a profitable Canadian beef industry; To use management practices that protect the health of the animal & protect the environment
Travis Toews, President
John Masswohl, Director, Government & International Relations
Andrea Brocklebank, Manager, Research
Rob McNabb, General Manager, Operations
Peggy Strankman, Manager, Environmental Affairs
Gina Teel, Manager, Communications
Louis Desautels, Consultant, Animal Health

Canadian Charolais Association (CCA)
2320 - 41 Ave. NE, Calgary AB T2E 6W8
Tel: 403-250-9242; *Fax:* 403-291-9324
cca@charolais.com
www.charolais.com
Social Media: www.facebook.com/cdncharolais; twitter.com/canCharolais
To be leaders in predictable beef genetics; to register, record, transfer & promote Canadian Charolais; to provide services for membership
Wade Beck, President

Canadian Co-operative Wool Growers Ltd. (CCWG)
PO Box 130, 142 Franktown Rd., Carleton Place ON K7C 3P3
Tel: 613-257-2714; *Fax:* 613-257-8896
Toll-Free: 800-488-2714
ccwghq@wool.ca
www.wool.ca
To operate as a producer-owned wool marketing cooperative; To collect, grade, & market, the majority of the Canadian wool clip to the global market; To retail farm supplies & animal health & identification products
Eric Bjergso, General Manager

Canadian Cutting Horse Association (CCHA)
RR#3, Innisfail AB T4G 1T8
Tel: 403-227-4444; *Fax:* 403-227-3030
connie@ccha.ca
www.ccha.ca
To promote the cutting horse, a specially trained horse to isolate or cut an individual animal from large cattle herds
Les Timmons, President
Jamie Couilliard, Vice-President
Connie Couilliard, National Administrator
Geoff Thomas, Secretary-Treasurer

Canadian Dexter Cattle Association (CDCA) / Société canadienne des bovins Dexter
2417 Holly Lane, Ottawa ON K1V 0M7
Tel: 613-731-7110; *Fax:* 613-731-0704
ron.black@clrc.ca
www.dextercattle.ca
To preserve & promote the breeding of good quality Dexter cattle in Canada
Ron Black, Secretary
Glorianne Bjerland, President

Canadian Donkey & Mule Association (CDMA)
25766 - 48 Ave., Langley BC V4W 1J2
Tel: 604-857-4990
vallen@shaw.ca
www.donkeyandmule.com
To operate registry for donkeys & recordation for mules; to promote use, well-being & protection of donkeys & mules; to assist in training & placing donkeys for disabled riding.
Virginia Allen, Secretary

Canadian Fjord Horse Association
PO Box 70, Didsbury AB T0M 0W0
www.cfha.org
To operate under the Animal Pedigree Act; To assure the success of the purebred registered Norwegian Fjord Horse in Canada
Burt Shewfelt, President
Dianne Manegre, Secretary-Treasurer
LauraLee Mills, Registrar

Canadian Galloway Association (CGA) / Société canadienne Galloway
c/o CLRC, 2417 Holly Lane, Ottawa ON K1V 0M7
Tel: 613-731-7110; *Fax:* 613-731-0704
galloway@clrc.ca
www.galloway.ca
To promote & regulate the breeding of Galloways, Belted Galloways & White Galloways in Canada
John Toon, President
Ron Black, Sec.-Treas.

Canadian Gelbvieh Association (CGA)
#110, 2116 - 27 Ave. NE, Calgary AB T2E 7A6
Tel: 403-250-8640; *Fax:* 403-291-5624
gelbvieh@gelbvieh.ca
www.gelbvieh.ca
To promote Gelbvieh cattle in Canada & their registration.
Vern Pancoast, President
Wendy Belcher, Secretary Manager

Canadian Goat Society (CGS) / La Société canadienne des éléveurs de chèvres
2417 Holly Lane, Ottawa ON K1V 0M7
Tel: 613-731-9894; *Fax:* 613-731-0704
cangoatsoc@travel-net.com
www.goats.ca
The Canadian Goat Society is dedicated to maintaining the integrity of our herdbooks, providing accurate evaluation programs for performance and type and promoting the responsible and humane treatment of goats.
Sharon Hunt, Secretary Manager

Canadian Guernsey Association
5653 Hwy. 6, RR#5, Guelph ON N1H 6J2
Tel: 519-836-2141; *Fax:* 519-763-6582
info@guernseycanada.ca
www.guernseycanada.ca
To provide services to breeders of Guernsey dairy cattle including records, awards, promotion, sales & shows.
Vivianne Macdonald, Manager

Canadian Hereford Association (CHA) / Association canadienne Hereford
5160 Skyline Way NE, Calgary AB T2E 6V1
Tel: 403-275-2662; *Fax:* 403-295-1333
Toll-Free: 888-836-7242
herefords@hereford.ca
www.hereford.ca
To promote the consistent & economical production of beef; To strive to meet & exceed consumer expectations for tender, juicy, & flavourful beef products, through performance measurement, genetic selection, appropriate handling, feeding, & processing
Gordon Stephenson, General Manager

Canadian Highland Cattle Society (CHCS) / Société canadienne des éleveurs de bovins Highland
70209 Evergreen Line, RR#3, Exeter ON N0M 1S5
Tel: 519-229-6220; *Fax:* 519-229-6220
highland@chcs.ca
www.chcs.ca
To regulate & promote breeding of Highland cattle in Canada.
Terri Barr, Secretary-Manager

Canadian Icelandic Horse Federation (CIHF)
401 Ashton Cooke Rd., Enderby BC V0E 1V5
Tel: 250-838-0234
erhard@toltaway.com
www.cihf.ca

To promote & maintain the purity of the Icelandic horse; to keep record of breeding and registration of Icelandic horse under the Canadian National Livestock Record System; to promote the awareness and secure the integrity of purebred Icelandic horses.
Erhard Marenbach, President
Otmar Fueth, Vice-President

Canadian Limousin Association (CLA)
#13, 4101 - 19th St. NE, Calgary AB T2E 7C4
Tel: 403-253-7309; *Fax:* 403-253-1704
limousin@limousin.com
www.limousin.com
To provide collective service for Limousin breeders in Canada, record registration & produce Records of Performance on all registered animals; to promote & inform producers about Limousin cattle; to develop & implement educational agricultural programs
Jason Brock, President

Canadian Livestock Records Corporation (CLRC) / Société canadienne d'enregistrement des animaux
2417 Holly Lane, Ottawa ON K1V 0M7
Tel: 613-731-7110; *Fax:* 613-731-0704
Toll-Free: 877-833-7110
clrc@clrc.ca
www.clrc.ca
To serve the Canadian seed stock industry; to be responsible to the member breed associations & Agriculture Canada for the maintenance of records, issuance of certificates, endorsement of changes of ownership, enrolment of members, registration of individuals, identification letters, collection of fees & the deposit of same into the appropriate breed association account
Ron Black, General Manager

Canadian Maine-Anjou Association (CMAA)
5160 Skyline Way NE, Calgary AB T2E 6V1
Tel: 403-291-7077; *Fax:* 403-291-0274
cmaa@maine-anjou.ca
www.maine-anjou.ca
To encourage, develop, & regulate the breeding of Main-Anjou cattle in Canada
Stuart Byman, President
Murray Preece, Secretary
Brian Brown, Treasurer

Canadian Milking Shorthorn Society (CMSS)
302-400 Waterloo Ave., Guelph ON N1H 7H9
Tel: 519-824-2119; *Fax:* 519-824-2566
milking.shorthorn@gmail.com
www.cmss.on.ca
To promote & encourage the development of milking shorthorn cattle.
Ryan Barrett, Secretary-Manager
John Knox, President

Canadian Morgan Horse Association (CMHA) / Association des chevaux Morgan canadien inc.
PO Box 286, Port Perry ON L9L 1A3
Tel: 905-982-0060; *Fax:* 905-982-0097
info@morganhorse.ca
www.morganhorse.ca
Bob Watson, President
Melissa MacKenzie, Eastern Vice-President
Laurie Ann Lyons, Western Vice-President
Mark Grootelaar, Treasurer

Canadian Murray Grey Association (CMGA)
PO Box 2093, Stettler AB T0C 2L0
Tel: 403-742-3843; *Fax:* 403-742-3857
cmga@electrotel.ca
To promote the genetics of Murray Grey Beef Cattle
Barbara Groves, Secretary
Bill Tran, President
Udo Adam, Treasurer

Canadian Palomino Horse Association (CPHA)
c/o Lorraine Holdaway, 631 Hendershott Rd., RR#1, Hannon ON L0R 1P0
Tel: 905-692-4328
canadianpalomino@gmail.com
www.clrc.ca/palomino.shtml
To develop & promote the breeding of Palomino horses in Canada; To establish standards of breeding
Lorraine Holdaway, Secretary
Laura Lee Mills, Registrar

Canadian Percheron Association / Association canadienne du cheval Percheron
Tel: 250-379-2855; *Fax:* 250-379-2213
canadapercheron@uniserve.com
www.canadianpercherons.com
To develop & encourage the breeding of purebred Percheron horses in Canada; To establish standards of breeding; To regulate the breeding of purebred Percheron horses
David Logies, President
Donna Swanston, Vice-President

Canadian Pork Council (CPC) / Conseil canadien du porc (CCP)
#900, 200 Laurier Ave. West, Ottawa ON K1P 5Z9
Tel: 613-236-9239; *Fax:* 613-236-6658
info@cpc-ccp.com
www.cpc-ccp.com
To provide a leadership role in a concerted effort involving all levels of industry & government toward a common understanding & action plan for achieving a dynamic & prosperous pork industry in Canada.
Jurgen Preugschas, Chair
Martin Rice, Executive Director

Canadian Red Poll Cattle Association / Société Canadienne des Bovins Red Poll
2417 Holly Lane, Ottawa ON K1V 0M7
Tel: 613-731-7110; *Fax:* 613-731-0704
Toll-Free: 877-731-7110
redpoll@clrc.ca
www.clrc.ca/redpoll.shtml
To encourage development & regulation of breeding of purebred Red Poll cattle in Canada for improvement of Canadian beef cattle industry
Ron Black, Sec.-Treas.

Canadian Sheep Breeders' Association (CSBA) / La société canadienne des éleveurs de moutons
333 Ontario St., Toronto ON M5A 2V8
Fax: 416-972-1023
Toll-Free: 866-956-1116
www.sheepbreeders.ca
Trenholm Nelson, President
Kim MacDougall, Vice President

Canadian Sheep Federation / Fédération canadienne du mouton
130 Malcolm Rd., Guelph ON N1K 1B1
Tel: 519-824-6018; *Fax:* 866-909-5360
Toll-Free: 888-684-7739
info@cansheep.ca
www.cansheep.ca
To set national policy for the sheep industry; to endeavour to further the viability, expansion & prosperity of the Canadian sheep & wool industry.
Dwane Morvik, Chair
Jennifer MacTavish, Executive Director

Canadian Shorthorn Association
Canada Centre Bldg., Exhibition Park, PO Box 3771, Regina SK S4P 3N8
Tel: 306-757-2212; *Fax:* 306-525-5852
info@canadianshorthorn.com
www.canadianshorthorn.com
Belinda Wagner, Sec.-Treas.

Canadian Simmental Association
#13, 4101 - 19 St. NE, Calgary AB T2E 7C4
Tel: 403-250-7979; *Fax:* 403-250-5121
Toll-Free: 866-860-6051
cansim@simmental.com
www.simmental.com
To encourage, develop, & regulate the breeding of Simmental cattle in Canada
Murray Jacobson
Everett Hall, First Vice-President
Rick McIntyre, Second Vice-President
Dale Kelly, General Manager

Canadian Swine Breeders' Association (CSBA) / L'Association canadienne des éleveurs de porcs
Bldg 54, Central Experiemental Farm, 930 Carling Ave., Ottawa ON K1A 0C6
Tel: 613-731-5531; *Fax:* 613-233-8903
canswine@canswine.ca
www.canswine.ca
To improve & promote Canadian purebred swine; to lobby on behalf of purebred swine breeders in Canada; to direct & regulate purebred swine industry; to be involved in registration & transfer of following breeds: Berkshire, British Saddleback, Chester White, Duroc, Hampshire, Large Black, Pietrain, Poland China, Spotted, Tamworth, Welsh, Yorkshire, Landrace, Lacombe, Red Wattle (registration forms can be obtained from Canadian Livestock Records Corporation).
Brian Sullivan, General Manager

Canadian Tarentaise Association (CTA)
PO Box 1156, Shellbrook SK S0J 2E0
Tel: 306-773-7065; *Fax:* 306-773-7577
Toll-Free: 800-450-4181
canadiantarentaise@sasktel.net
www.canadiantarentaise.com
To develop, register & promote Tarentaise cattle in Canada.
Wayne Collette, President
Rosalyn Harris, Secretary

Canadian Thoroughbred Horse Society (CTHS) / Société canadienne du cheval Thoroughbred
PO Box 172, Toronto ON M9W 5L1
Tel: 416-675-1370; *Fax:* 416-675-9525
cths@idirect.com
www.cthsnational.com
To assist & afford a means for promotion of interests of those engaged in breeding of thoroughbreds; to protect members against unbusinesslike methods; to diffuse information among members & others; to secure uniformity in usage & business conditions; to determine requirements of horses as thoroughbreds by the Society; to promote, encourage & assist in livestock & agricultural exhibitions, fairs & racing; to sponsor, assist & conduct sales of thoroughbred stock; to compile statistics of the industry; to maintain efficient supervision of breeders of thoroughbred horses; to prevent, detect & punish fraud (ie. in registration of throughbreds).
Gordon Wilson, President
Fran Okihiro, National Executive Secretary

Canadian Trakehner Horse Society (CTHS)
PO Box 6009, New Hamburg ON N3A 2K6
Tel: 519-662-3209; *Fax:* 519-662-3209
cantrakhsivh@golden.net
www.cantrak.on.ca
To maintain a public registry of Trakehner horses, under the Canadian Livestock Records Corporation; to promote & preserve Trakehner horses in Canada
Judy Kirkby, President
Ingrid von Hausen, Registrar & Secretary
Laurel Glanfield, Treasurer

Canadian Welsh Black Cattle Society (CWBCS) / Société Canadienne des bovins Welsh Black
c/o Canadian Livestock Records Corporation, 2417 Holly Lane, Ottawa ON K1V 0M7
Tel: 613-731-7110
kaiser.randy@gmail.com
www.canadianwelshblack.com
Randy Scott, President
Randy Kaiser, Vice-President
Dale Clark, Secretary-Treasurer

GENCOR
RR#5, Guelph ON N1H 6J2
Tel: 519-821-2150; *Fax:* 519-763-6582
Toll-Free: 888-821-2150
boconnor@gencor.ca
www.gencor.ca
Gencor is farmer directed AI cooperative located in South-western Ontario
Brian O'Connor, General Manager

Holstein Canada
PO Box 610, 20 Corporate Pl., Brantford ON N3T 5R4
Tel: 519-756-8300; *Fax:* 519-756-3502
general@holstein.ca
www.holstein.ca
To improve the Holstein breed by ascertaining the most desirable characteristics of the breed for current & prospective conditions in Canada; To prepare, maintain & make available a genealogical record of the breed; To promote the best interests of breeders & owners of Holstein cattle
Brian Van Doormaal, Chief Executive Officer
Germain Lehoux, President

Jersey Canada (JC)
#9, 350 Speedvale Ave. West, Guelph ON N1H 7M7
Tel: 519-821-1020; *Fax:* 519-821-2723
info@jerseycanada.com
www.jerseycanada.com
To represent & promote the Jersey breed & encourage market development domestically & internationally; To provide & maintain a registration system, catalogues, & pedigree information; To update classification & milk production records
Adrian Haeni, President
Robert Jarrell, First Vice-President
VACANT, Second Vice-President
Kathryn Kyle, Executive Secretary
Jill Dann, Registrar

National Chinchilla Breeders of Canada (NCBC)
RR#2, Norval ON L0P 1K0
ncbc@idirect.com
www.chinnet.com/misc/ncbc.html
N.C.B.C. appoints live animal Graders in every region of Canada. These Graders will visit ranches in order to appraise and grade animals, advise ranchers and thereby ensure the high quality of breeding stock required to maintain the high standards of this Canadian Association.
Tom Riedstra, President
Marie Riedstra, Sec.-Treas.

Nova Scotia Mink Breeders' Association
RR#4, Weymouth NS B0W 3T0
Tel: 902-387-5100
To foster better mink breeding among the members; to help secure market advantage.
Karen Sabine, Secretary

The Ontario Farm Animal Council (OFAC)
#106, 100 Stone Rd. West, Guelph ON N1G 5L3
Tel: 519-837-1326; *Fax:* 519-837-3209
www.farmfoodcare.org
Social Media: www.facebook.com/FarmFoodCare; twitter.com/farmfoodcare
To support & promote the responsible production & marketing of livestock & poultry by Ontario farmers & through a variety of initiatives, to better inform the public of the excellence of animal agriculture
John Maaskant, Chairman
Crystal Mackay, Executive Director

Salers Association of Canada (SAC) / Association salers du Canada
Stn. 879, #1, 517 - 10th Ave. South, Carstairs AB T0M 0N0
Tel: 403-337-5851; *Fax:* 403-337-3143
info@salerscanada.com; salers@telusplanet.net
www.salerscanada.com
To develop & register Salers cattle
Gerald McGee, President
Brian Jones, Treasurer
Adams Kathleen (Kathy), Secretary-Manager & Registrar

Sask Pork
Bay 2, 502 - 45th St. West, Saskatoon SK S7L 6H2
Tel: 306-244-7752; *Fax:* 306-244-1712
info@saskpork.com
www.saskpork.com
To position the Saskatchewan pork industry as a preferred supplier of high quality, competitively priced pork products for the global market.
Neil Ketilson, General Manager

Saskatchewan Stock Growers Association (SSGA)
Main Floor, Canada Centre Building, Evraz Place, PO Box 4752, Regina SK S4P 3Y4
Tel: 306-757-8523; *Fax:* 306-569-8799
ssga@sasktel.net; ssga.admin@sasktel.net
www.skstockgrowers.com
To serve, protect, & advance the interests of the beef industry in Saskatchewan; To represent the cattle industry in Saskatchewan on the legislative front
Chad MacPherson, General Manager
Calvin Knoss, President

Standardbred Canada (SC)
2150 Meadowvale Blvd., Mississauga ON L5N 6R6
Tel: 905-858-3060; *Fax:* 905-858-3111
resource@standardbredcanada.ca
www.standardbredcanada.ca
To encourage & develop the breeding of Standardbred Horses
Ted Smith, President/CEO

The Western Stock Growers' Association (WSGA)
Stockmen's Centre, #232, 2116 - 27 Ave. NE, Calgary AB T2E 7A6
Tel: 403-250-9121
office@wsga.ca
www.wsga.ca
To support & protect livestock growers by lobbying the government on legislation & proposed new legislation; to promote environmentally sound range management practices
Phil Rowland, President

Animals & Animal Science

Alberta Society for the Prevention of Cruelty to Animals
10806 - 124 St., Edmonton AB T5M 0H3
Tel: 780-447-3600; *Fax:* 780-447-4748
info@albertaspca.org
www.albertaspca.org
Social Media: 1
To promote education of public about welfare of domestic animals & livestock; To deal with wildlife issues; To work on improving legislation; To concentrate on enforcement & education; To have every animal in Alberta humanely treated
Terra Johnston, Executive Director

Alberta Veterinary Medical Association (AVMA)
Weber Centre, #950, 5555 Calgary Trail NW, Edmonton AB T6H 5P9
Tel: 780-489-5007; *Fax:* 780-484-8311
Toll-Free: 800-404-2862
brenda.betnar@abvma.ca
www.avma.ab.ca
To represent Alberta veterinarians in small animal, large animal & mixed practice as well as those employed in government, industry or other institutions
Duane Landals, Registrar

Animal Alliance of Canada (AAC) / Alliance animale du Canada
#101, 221 Broadview Ave., Toronto ON M4M 2G3
Tel: 416-462-9541; *Fax:* 416-462-9647
contact@animalalliance.ca
www.animalalliance.ca
Social Media: www.facebook.com/132125293547127
To preserve & protect all animals; to promote harmonious relationship between people, animals & the environment; to address issues including pound seizure, cosmetic & product testing, puppy mills, pet overpopulation, exotic pet trade, the fur trade, sport hunting, factory farming, animals as "entertainment"
Shelly Hawley-Yan, Editor
George Dupras, Director
Jacqui Barnes, Director
Marie Crawford, Director
Barry Kent MacKay, Director
Liz White, Director

Animal Welfare Foundation of Canada (AWF) / Fondation du bien-être animal du Canada
#343, 300 Earl Grey Dr., Ottawa ON K2T 1C1
info@awfc.ca
www.awfc.ca
The Animal Welfare Foundation of Canada is a registered charity, supported by donors and administered by a volunteer Board of Directors. The Foundation seeks to improve the quality of life for animals in this country. Since the 1960s the Foundation, an independent watchdog organization, has been at the forefront of issues of humane care of animals in Canada.
Ian Duncan, President & Chair
Frances Rodenberg, Honorary Secretary

Association des propriétaires canins de Prévost (APCP)
CP 604, Prévost QC J0R 1T0
Tél: 450-224-888
apcp_wouf@yahoo.ca
www.wouflaurentides.org
Média social: www.facebook.com/145223315575911

Association des résidents du Lac Echo (ARLEQ)
CP 343, St-Hippolyte QC J8A 3P6
Tél: 450-224-4338
Michel Lamontagne, Contact

Association des résidents du Lac Renaud
Prévost QC J0R 1T0
www.lacrenaud.org
Marcelle Théoret, Présidente
Gilles Tourigny, Administrateur

Atlantic Canadian Anti-Sealing Coalition
contact@antisealingcoalition.ca
www.antisealingcoalition.ca
The Atlantic Canadian Anti-Sealing Coalition is a collection of individuals and groups from across the Atlantic Region working to end the commercial seal hunt by peaceful and legal means.

Brandon Humane Society
2200 - 17 St. East, Brandon MB R7A 7M6
Tel: 204-728-1333
info@brandonhumanesociety.ca
www.brandonhumanesociety.ca
To provide care for & homes for abused companion animals; to educate the public about the value of humane treatment of animals.
Darren Creighton, President
Tracy Munn, Shelter Manager

British Columbia Society for the Prevention of Cruelty to Animals
1245 East 7th Ave., Vancouver BC V5T 1R1
Tel: 604-681-7271; *Fax:* 604-681-7022
Toll-Free: 800-665-1868
info@spca.bc.ca
www.spca.bc.ca
Social Media: www.facebook.com/home.php#!/bcspca
To protect & enhance the quality of life for domestic, farm, & wild animals in British Columbia
Craig Daniell, CEO & General Manager

Calgary Humane Society
4455 - 110 Ave. SE, Calgary AB T2C 2T7
Tel: 403-205-4455; *Fax:* 403-723-6050
admin@calgaryhumane.ca
www.calgaryhumane.ca
To foster humane treatment of animals & to promote values which demonstrate respect for animals.
Patricia Cameron, Executive Director

Canadian Animal Health Institute (CAHI) / Institut canadien de la santé animale (ICSA)
#102, 160 Research Lane, Guelph ON N1G 5B2
Tel: 519-763-7777; *Fax:* 519-763-7407
cahi@cahi-icsa.ca
www.cahi-icsa.ca
To work closely with allied industry groups for the betterment of Canadian agriculture; To foster & maintain a regulatory & legislative climate which will encourage member companies to develop & market useful animal health products & services; To promote the proper use of animal health & nutrition products by livestock & poultry farmers through user education information programs; To develop a public information program which enhances appreciation of the contributions the animal health & nutrition industry makes to the economy & society
Jean Szkotnicki, President
Tracey Firth, Director, Programs

Canadian Association for Laboratory Animal Science (CALAS)
#640, 144 Front St., Toronto ON M5J 2L7
Tel: 416-593-0268; *Fax:* 416-979-1819
office@calas-acsal.org; membership@calas-acsal.org
www.calas-acsal.org
To elevate standards of laboratory animal science; To promote excellence in research; To eliminate inhumane & unnecessary use of animals in research; To enhance animal welfare
Teresa McKernan, President
Michelle Gillespie, Vice-President
Wendy Ansell, Administrator
Claire Smits, Treasurer, claire.smits@hli.ubc.ca
Khadijah Hewitt, Coordinator, Membership & Registry

Canadian Association of Animal Health Technologists & Technicians (CAAHTT) / Association canadienne des techniciens et technologistes en santé animale (ACTTSA)
339 Booth St., Ottawa ON K1R 7K1
Tel: 800-567-2862
info@caahtt-acttsa.ca
www.caahtt-acttsa.ca
To provide coordination & resources to support members in the delivery of animal health care services
Phyllis Mierau, Executive Director
Michele Moroz, President
Chantal Cormier, Vice-President

Canadian Association of Professional Pet Dog Trainers (CAPPDT)
PO Box 85, 156097 Highway 10, Shelburne ON L0N 1S0
Toll-Free: 877-748-7829
info@cappdt.ca
www.cappdt.ca
To further the concept of dog-friendly & humane training techniques; to provide forum whereby professional pet dog trainers can be educated, exchange & generate ideas & network with other professionals
Pat Renshaw, Chair

Canadian Association of Zoos & Aquariums (CAZA) / Association des zoos et aquariums du Canada (AZAC)
#400, 280 Metcalfe St., Ottawa ON K2P 1R7
Tel: 613-567-0099; *Fax:* 613-233-5438
Toll-Free: 888-822-2907
info@caza.ca
www.caza.ca
To promote the welfare of animals; To provide input into legislative matters & government policy affecting the zoo & aquarium industry
Robin Hale, President
Bill Peters, National Director
Greg Tarry, Manager, Special Projects
Serge Lussier, Secretary-Treasurer

Canadian Council on Animal Care (CCAC) / Conseil canadien de protection des animaux (CCPA)
#1510, 130 Albert St., Ottawa ON K1P 5G4
Tel: 613-238-4031; *Fax:* 613-238-2837
ccac@ccac.ca
www.ccac.ca
To act on behalf of the people of Canada to ensure, through programs of education, assessment & persuasion, that the use of animals in Canada, where necessary for research, teaching & testing, employs physical & psychological care according to acceptable scientific standards; To promote an increased level of knowledge, awareness, & sensitivity to the relevant ethical principles
Clément Gauthier, Executive Director
Michael Baar, Director, Assessment & Certification Program
Gilly Griffin, Director, Guidelines & Three Rs Programs
Pascale Belleau, Coordinator, Education, Training, & Communications
Emily Verlinden, Coordinator, Publications

Canadian Federation of Humane Societies (CFHS) / Fédération des sociétés canadiennes d'assistance aux animaux
#102, 30 Concourse Gate, Ottawa ON K2E 7V7
Tel: 613-224-8072; *Fax:* 613-723-0252
Toll-Free: 888-678-2347
info@cfhs.ca
www.cfhs.ca
As the national voice of societies and SPCAs, the CFHS supports its member animal welfare organizations across Canada in promoting respect & humane treatment toward all animals
Barbara Cartwright, CEO
Kim Elmslie, Communications Coordinator
Shelagh MacDonald, Program Director

Canadian Kennel Club (CKC) / Club canin canadien
#400, 200 Ronson Dr., Toronto ON M9W 5Z9
Tel: 416-675-5511; *Fax:* 416-675-6506
Toll-Free: 800-250-8040
information@ckc.ca; orderdesk@ckc.ca
www.ckc.ca
To provide registry services for all officially recognized breeds of purebred dogs; To provide governance for all CKC approved events; To encourage, guide, & advance the interests of purebred dogs & their responsible owners & breeders in Canada
Sonny Allinson, Staff Liaison, Breeder Relations Responsible Dog Ownership Committees
Leila Bahorie, Staff Liaison, Registration Committee
Diane Draper, Staff Liaison, Legislation, Appeal, & Discipline Committees
Cherie Fontbin, Staff Liaison, Audit Committee
Elio Furlan, Staff Liaison, Club Relations, Breed Standards, & Event Officiating Committees
Tara Merrimen, Staff Liaison, Strategic Planning Committee
Rachel Munthali, Staff Liaison, Genetics & Medical Committee

Canadian Society of Animal Science (CSAS) / Société canadienne de science animale
c/o Agriculture & Agri-Food Canada Research Station, CP 90, #2000, rte 108 est, Sherbrooke QC J1M 1Z3
Tél: 819-565-9171; *Téléc:* 819-564-5507
info@aic.ca
www.csas.net
To provide opportunities to discuss the problems of the Canadian animal & poultry industries, with the objective of furthering advancements in these industries; To assist in the coordination of research, teaching & technology transfer related to the animal & poultry industries; To encourage publication of scientific information; To provide an annual forum for professionals in the agricultural industry to meet & discuss the most recent technological advancements in the field of animal & poultry science
Karen Schwartzkopf-Genswein, President
Marie-France Palin, Secretary-Treasurer

Canadian Society of Zoologists (CSZ) / Société canadienne de zoologie (SCZ)
c/o Biology Department, University of Western Ontario, London ON N6A 5B7
Tel: 519-661-3869
www.csz-scz.ca
To promote advancement & public awareness of zoology; To facilitate sharing of knowledge & ideas among all persons interested in science & practice of zoology; To organize discussions & debates of general interest
Helga Guderley, Secretary
Louise Milligan, President

Canadian Veterinary Medical Association (CVMA) / Association canadienne des médecins vétérinaires (ACMV)
339 Booth St., Ottawa ON K1R 7K1
Tel: 613-236-1162; *Fax:* 613-236-9681
admin@cvma-acmv.org
www.canadianveterinarians.net
To represent the interests of the veterinary profession in Canada; commits to excellence within the profession & to the well-being of animals; promotes public awareness of the contribution of animals & veterinarians to society
Jost Am Rhyn, Executive Director

Canadians for Ethical Treatment of Food Animals (CETFA)
PO Box 18024, 2225 - 41 Ave. West, Vancouver BC V6M 4L3
care@cetfa.com
www.cetfa.com
Social Media: www.facebook.com/cetfa.news
CETFA is an investigation-based, farm animal advocacy organization that promotes the humane treatment of animals raised for food. It works to educate the public about Canada's food industry by providing information on factory farming practices.
Patricia Oswald, President
Twyla Francois, Head, Investigation

College of Veterinarians of British Columbia (CVBC)
#107, 828 Harbourside Dr., North Vancouver BC V7P 3R9
Tel: 604-929-7090; *Fax:* 604-929-7095
Toll-Free: 800-463-5399
reception@cvbc.ca
www.cvbc.ca
To serve members by promoting their professional image, providing a forum for addressing issues of importance to the profession, offering continuing education & protecting their interests & rights; to protect & serve animals & animal custodians through evaluation of veterinary competence & facility quality & by enforcing the Veterinarians Act & Bylaws
Valerie Osborne, Registrar
John Brocklebank, Deputy Registrar

College of Veterinarians of Ontario (CVO)
2106 Gordon St., Guelph ON N1L 1G6
Tel: 519-824-5600; *Fax:* 519-824-6497
Toll-Free: 800-424-2856
inquiries@cvo.org
www.cvo.org
To protect the public by regulating & enhancing the veterinary profession in Ontario
Ken Bridge, President
Christine Simpson, Acting Registrar

East Coast Aquarium Society (ECAS)
c/o 91 Deerbrooke Dr., Dartmouth NS B2V 1X2
www.eastcoastaquariumsociety.ca
To further the aquarium hobby and promote the practice of keeping tropical fish.
Kathryn Purdy, President
Kelly Lively Jones, Director, Membership

Fort McMurray Society for the Prevention of Cruelty to Animals
155 MacAlpine Cres., Fort McMurray AB T9H 4A5
Tel: 780-743-8997; *Fax:* 780-791-3772
spca@altech.ab.ca
www.fortmcmurrayspca.ca
Social Media: www.facebook.com/home.php?#!/group.php?gid=43835681529
To ensure the humane treatment of all animals in the regional municipality of Wood Buffalo.
Terri Czmuchalek, President

Horse Council British Columbia (HCBC)
27336 Fraser Hwy., Aldergrove BC V4W 3N5
Tel: 604-856-4304; *Fax:* 604-856-4302
Toll-Free: 800-345-8055
reception@hcbc.ca; membership@hcbc.ca; education@hcbc.ca
www.hcbc.ca
To represent members & work on behalf of their equine interests in British Columbia; To preserve equestrian use of public lands; To foster & promote participation in equine activities; To ensure the well-being of horses
Lisa Laycock, Executive Director
Orville Smith, President
Carol Cody, Secretary
Carolyn Farris, Treasurer

Human-Animal Bond Association of Canada (HABAC) / Association canadienne sur les relations privilégiées liant les humains et les animaux
c/o 5481 Richmond Rd., Ottawa ON K2R 1G4
Tel: 613-591-6228
colbourn@rogers.com
www.habac.ca
To promote the study of human-animal interactions & their effects; to support & advance knowledge on all aspects of animal welfare & interrelationships of skills involved in the well-being of humans & animals; To clarify the value of the human-animal bond for therapeutic purposes; To encourage & promote responsible & ethical use of animals specifically related to the human-animal bond; To sponsor the Canadian Canine Good Citizen Test; To create awareness of the value of animals in our society
Joan S. Colbourn, President

Humane Society Yukon
126 Tlingit Rd., Whitehorse YT Y1A 6J2
Tel: 867-633-6019; *Fax:* 867-633-2210
shelter@northwestel.net
www.humanesocietyyukon.ca
To foster a caring, compassionate atmosphere; to promote a humane ethic & responsible pet ownership; to prevent & suppress cruelty to animals.
Corey Roussell, Administrator

Jardin zoologique du Québec (JZQ)
9300, rue de la Faune, Charlesbourg QC G1G 5H9
Tél: 418-622-0312; *Téléc:* 418-646-9239
spsnq@spsnq.qc.ca
Contribuer à l'étude, à la mise en valeur et à la conservation de la faune et de son environnement.
Jean-Paul Bédard, Directeur

London Humane Society (LHS)
624 Clarke Rd., London ON N5V 3K5
Tel: 519-451-0630; *Fax:* 519-451-8995
administration@londonhumane.ca
www.londonhumanesociety.ca
To monitor animal welfare & treatment in London & Middlesex County; to afford our community's animals who have been abandoned, abused, neglected or injured with a facility dedicated to their well-being; to act as their advocate relating to animal welfare; to educate our community
Judy Foster, Executive Director

Manitoba Veterinary Medical Association (MVMA)
6014 Roblin Blvd., Winnipeg MB R3R 0H4
Tel: 204-832-1276; *Fax:* 204-832-1382
Toll-Free: 866-338-6862
adowd@mvma.ca
www.mvma.ca
Veterinarians working together to enhance professional excellence for the health & welfare of animals & Manitobans.
Andrea Lear, General Manager, Communications & Advocacy

Montréal SPCA
5215, rue Jean-Talon ouest, Montréal QC H4P 1X4
Tél: 514-735-2711; *Téléc:* 514-735-7448
admin@spcamontreal.com
www.spcamontreal.com
La Société recueille, héberge et soigne les animaux errants ou abandonnés; rend les animaux perdus à leurs propriétaires; met en adoption les animaux en santé; détruit de façon humanitaire ceux qui sont indésirés ou malades; inspecte et enquête sur les plaintes de cruauté.
Pierre Barnoti, Directeur général

National Retriever Club of Canada
780 East Chestermere Dr., Chestermere AB T1X 1A6
Tel: 403-248-3347
secretary@nrcc-canada.com
www.nrcc-canada.com
Gordon Benn, President
Marg Murray, Sec.-Treas.

New Brunswick Society for the Prevention of Cruelty to Animals / Société protectrice des animaux du Nouveau-Brunswick
PO Box 1412, Stn. A, Fredericton NB E3B 5E3
Tel: 506-458-8208; *Fax:* 506-458-8209
www.spca-nb.ca
Social Media:
www.facebook.com/group.php?gid=18023383071#!/group.php?gid=4629259647
To prevent cruelty to & encourage consideration for all animals; to pursue program of humane education.
Brad Horncastle, President

New Brunswick Veterinary Medical Association (NBVMA) / Association des médecins vétérinaires du Nouveau-Brunswick (AMVNB)
1700 Manawagonish Rd., Saint John NB E2M 3Y5
Tel: 506-635-8100
www.nbvma-amvnb.ca
To act as the regulatory body for the practice of veterinary medicine in New Brunswick; To establish standards of practice in the profession; To promote animal health & welfare; To prevent public health problems related to animal disease
George Whittle, Executive Director

Newfoundland & Labrador Society for the Prevention of Cruelty to Animals
PO Box 29053, St. John's NL A1A 5B5
Tel: 709-726-0301; *Fax:* 709-579-8089
spcastjohns@gmail.com
www.spcastjohns.org; www.cfhs.ca
To act as the voice for animal welfare in Newfoundland & Labrador; To promote humane treatment toward all animals
Lynn Cadigan, President & Contact, Media
Simone Browne, Vice-President
Carolyn Hickey, Secretary
Bob Noseworthy, Treasurer

Newfoundland & Labrador Veterinary Medical Association (NALVMA)
PO Box 818, Mount Pearl NL A1N 3C8
Tel: 709-576-2131
nalvma@nalvma.ca
www.nalvma.ca
To promote better animal health care; to educate the general public & strive towards continued excellence in veterinary medicine.
Martha Sweeting, President
Ellen Melvin, Sec.-Treas.

Nova Scotia Society for the Prevention of Cruelty to Animals (NS SPCA)
PO Box 38073, #200A - 11 Akerley Blvd., Dartmouth NS B3B 1X2
Tel: 902-835-4798; *Fax:* 902-835-7885
Toll-Free: 888-703-7722
animals@spcans.ca; info@spcans.ca
www.spcans.ca
Social Media:
www.facebook.com/group.php?gid=18023383071#!/nsspca
NS SPCA strives to prevent abuse & neglect of all animals in Nova Scotia. It provides leadership in humane education through outreach activities & adoption services. It also enforces laws on animal cruelty by issuing orders, warrants & laying charges. It is a registered charity, BN: 134704741RR0001.
Sean Kelly, President
Kristan Williams, Executive Director

Nova Scotia Veterinary Medical Association
15 Cobequid Rd., Lower Sackville NS B4C 2M9
Tel: 902-865-1876; *Fax:* 902-865-2001
info@nsvma.ca
www.nsvma.ca
To license Nova Scotia veterinarians in small animal, large animal & mixed practice as well as those employed in government, industry or other institutions
Frank Richardson, Secretary Registrar
Christopher MacDonald, President

Ontario Society for the Prevention of Cruelty to Animals (OSPCA)
16586 Woodbine Ave., RR#3, Newmarket ON L3Y 4W1
Tel: 905-898-7122
info@ospca.on.ca; donate@ospca.on.ca
www.ontariospca.ca
Social Media:
www.facebook.com/OntarioSPCA?v=wall&viewas=0; twitter.com/ontariospca; www.youtube.com/user/OntarioSPCA
To provide care & shelter for animals, especially pets; To enforce animal cruelty laws in the province; To investigate cruelty complaints; To carry out rescues & bring perpetrators to court; To advocates for humane laws; To promote humane education & public awareness of the humane treatment of animals; To operates a Wildlife Rehabilitation Centre in Midland, ON
Kate MacDonald, Chief Executive Officer
Tanya Firmage, Director, Operations, Animal Welfare
Connie Mallory, Chief Inspector
Alison Cross, Senior Manager, Marketing & Communications

Ontario Veterinary Medical Association (OVMA)
#205, 420 Bronte St. South, Milton ON L9T 0H9
Tel: 905-875-0756; *Fax:* 905-875-0958
Toll-Free: 800-670-1702
info@ovma.org
www.ovma.org
To represent Ontario veterinarians in small animal, large animal & mixed practice as well as those employed in government, industry or other institutions; programs include government & public relations, humane veterinary practice, continuing education in veterinary science & practice management & direct services to members.
Doug Raven, CEO
Melissa Carlaw, Manager, Communications & Public Relations

Ordre des médecins vétérinaires du Québec (OMVQ)
#200, 800, av Ste-Anne, Saint-Hyacinthe QC J2S 5G7
Tél: 450-774-1427; *Téléc:* 450-774-7635
Ligne sans frais: 800-267-1427
omvq@omvq.qc.ca
www.omvq.qc.ca
Protection du public; contribuer à l'amélioration de la santé et du bien-être des animaux; formation des membres; maintien de la qualité des services vétérinaires
Joël Bergeron, Président
Suzie Prince, Directrice générale/Secrétaire

PIJAC Canada / Conseil consultatif mixte de l'industrie des animaux de compagnie
#202, 2495 Lancaster Rd., Ottawa ON K1B 4L5
Fax: 613-730-9111
Toll-Free: 800-667-7452
information@pijaccanada.com
www.pijaccanada.com
To ensure the highest level of pet care attainable & a guarantee of a fair & equitable representation for all facets of the Canadian pet industry.
Louis McCann, Executive Director
Rénald Sabourin, Assistant Executive Director

Prince Edward Island Humane Society (PEIHS)
PO Box 20022, 309 Sherwood Rd., Charlottetown PE C1A 9E3
Tel: 902-892-1190; *Fax:* 902-892-3617
info@peihumanesociety.com
www.peihumanesociety.com
Social Media:
www.facebook.com/group.php?gid=161960057162347
To promote & provide the humane treatment of animals recognizing that each is deserving of moral concern
Kelly Mullaly, Executive Director

Prince Edward Island Veterinary Medical Association (PEIVMA)
PO Box 21097, Stn. 465 University Ave., Charlottetown PE C1A 9h6
Tel: 902-367-3757; *Fax:* 902-367-3176
admin.peivma@gmail.com
www.peivma.com
To represent PEI veterinarians in small animal, large animal & mixed practice as well as those employed in government, industry or other institutions; to licence & regulate veterinarians in PEI
Wade Sweet, President
Marti Hopson, Vice-President

Red Deer & District SPCA
#4505, 77 St., Red Deer AB T4P 2J1
Tel: 403-342-7722; *Fax:* 403-341-3147
office@reddeerspca.com
www.reddeerspca.com
Dedicated to the care & protection of companion animals & the promotion of human treatment of animals & responsible pet ownership
Julie Crawford, Executive Director

Regina Humane Society Inc.
PO Box 3143, Regina SK S4P 3G7
Tel: 306-543-6363; *Fax:* 306-545-7661
Crisis Hot-Line: 306-543-6363
info@reginahumane.ca; volunteer@reginahumane.ca
www.reginahumanesociety.ca
To be responsible for the welfare of animals
Lisa Koch, Executive Director

Responsible Dog Owners of Canada (RDOC)
160 Oakridge Blvd., Nepean ON K2G 2V2
Tel: 613-228-7764
info@responsibledogowners.ca
www.responsibledogowners.ca
To promote responsible dog ownership and public safety through education and support, cultivate respect for the rights and privileges of all members of society, both dog-owning and non-dog owning, encourage and foster recognition of the contribution that canines make in society through companionship, service/assistance and therapy and assemble a strong network of responsible dog owners to ensure the restoration and preservation of a dog-friendly society.
Candice O'Connell, Chair

Saskatchewan Society for the Prevention of Cruelty to Animals
PO Box 37, 519 - 45th St. W., Saskatoon SK S7L 5Z9
Tel: 306-382-7722; *Fax:* 306-384-3425
Toll-Free: 877-382-7722
saskspca@sasktel.netsktel.net
www.sspca.ca
Social Media:
www.facebook.com/group.php?gid=18023383071#!/group.php?gid=6741122026
Frances Wach, Executive Director

Société québécoise pour la défense des animaux (SQDA) / Québec Society for the Defense of Animals (QSDA)
#102, 847, rue Cherrier, Montréal QC H2L 1H6
Tél: 514-524-1970
info@sqda.org
www.sqda.org
Faire connaître et respecter le monde animal par tous les moyens possibles; obtenir une législation modifiée pour la protection de toute espèce; Combattre la destruction de notre faune; exposer l'aberration de l'élevage intensif; Contrôler l'expérimentation animale
Ghislain A. Arsenault, Président

Toronto Humane Society (THS)
11 River St., Toronto ON M5A 4C2
Tel: 416-392-2273; *Fax:* 416-392-9978
communications@torontohumanesociety.com
www.facebook.com/pages/Toronto-Humane-Society/8666187799
Social Media: www.facebook.com/group.php?gid=8666187799; twitter.com/THS_tweet
To promote the humane care & protection of all animals & to prevent cruelty & suffering
Linda MacKinnon, BA, BEd, MEd, Chair
Marcie Laking, President
Wendy Strickland, Vice-President
Lisa Gibbens, BA, MISt, Secretary

Toronto Zoo
361A Old Finch Ave., Toronto ON M1B 5K7
Tel: 416-392-5900; *Fax:* 416-392-5863
torontozoo@torontozoo.ca
www.torontozoo.com
To support the Toronto Zoo in its efforts to conserve species diversity through conservation, education, & research
Raymond Cho, Chair
Calvin White, CEO

Western Federation of Individuals & Dog Organizations
8160 Railway Ave., Richmond BC V7C 3K2
Tel: 604-681-1929; *Fax:* 604-277-4285
To promote & provide education & services in matters affecting the welfare of dogs & other animals; to work in conjunction with legislative bodies on matters relating to the sale, care, custody & control of dogs & other animals; to provide information & services relating to the benefits of the human-animal bond.
Frances Clark, Contact

World Society for the Protection of Animals (WSPA) / Société mondiale pour la protection des animaux
#960, 90 Eglinton Ave. East, Toronto ON M4P 2Y3
Tel: 416-369-0044; *Fax:* 416-369-0147
Toll-Free: 800-363-9772
wspa@wspa.ca
www.wspa.ca
Social Media:
www.facebook.com/group.php?gid=143249880633
To promote effective means for the prevention of cruelty to, & relief of suffering of animals in any part of the world; 15 offices worldwide
Elizabeth Sharpe, Communications Manager

Yukon Schutzhund Association
32 Maple St., Whitehorse YT Y1A 4A8
Tel: 867-668-6118
mattson@northwestel.net
www.kaltersberg.com/YSAInformationPage.htm
To promote dog training for the sport of Schutzhund in the Yukon Territory.
Randy Mattson, President

ZOOCHECK Canada Inc.
788 1/2 O'Connor Dr., Toronto ON M4B 2S6
Tel: 416-285-1744; *Fax:* 416-285-4670
zoocheck@zoocheck.com
www.zoocheck.com
Zoocheck works to improve wildlife protection in Canada and to end the abuse, neglect and exploitation of individual wild animals through: investigation & research; public education & awareness campaigns; capacity building initiatives; legal programs; legislative actions.
Lesli Bisgould, Chair
Rob Laidlaw, Executive Director

Zoological Society of Manitoba
54 Zoo Dr., Winnipeg MB R3P 2N8
Tel: 204-982-0660; *Fax:* 204-982-0673
zooquestions@zoosociety.com
www.zoosociety.com
The Zoological Society of Manitoba functions in three roles: 1. To promote the welfare and continuation of the Society; 2. To focus on the development of Assiniboine Park Zoo, making it a collection of merit and distinction; 3. To match concern with action for the preservation of earth's wildlife and their habitat
Julie Eccles, General Manager

Zoological Society of Montréal / Société zoologique de Montréal
#525, 117, rue Ste-Catherine ouest, Montréal QC H3B 1H9
Tel: 514-845-8317
contact@zoologicalsocietymtl.org
www.zoologicalsocietymtl.org
To promote & develop interest in & knowledge of wildlife; To encourage the study of biology & nature sciences; To encourage the protection of wildlife

Antiques

Antiquarian Booksellers' Association of Canada (ABAC) / Association de la librairie ancienne du Canada (ALAC)
c/o 783 Bank St., Ottawa ON K1S 3V5
info@abac.org
www.abac.org
To maintain high standards in the antiquarian book trade; To promote interest in rare books & manuscripts
Roger Auger, President
Alexandre Arjomand, Secretary

Antique Automobile Club of America (AACA)
501 West Governor Rd., Hershey PA 17033 USA
Tel: 717-534-1910; *Fax:* 717-534-9101
general@aaca.org
www.aaca.org
Steven L. Moskowitz, Executive Director
Jack Armstrong, Secretary-Treasurer

Historic Vehicle Society of Ontario (HVSO)
c/o Canadian Transportation Museum & Heritage Village, 6155 Arner Town Line, RR#2, Kingsville ON N9Y 2E4
Tel: 519-776-6909; *Fax:* 519-776-8321
Toll-Free: 886-776-6909
info@ctmhv.com
www.ctmhv.com/The_Museum/members_gallery.htm
To collect, restore & display vehicles, buildings & artifacts that serve to demonstrate the founding settlement of Essex County; to preserve the past to enhance the future.
Michelle Staley, Curator/Admin. Director

Manitoba Antique Association
PO Box 2881, Winnipeg MB R3C 4B4
manitobaantique@gmail.com
www.manitobaantiqueassociation.com
To preserve & restore antiques; To promote the admiration of all antiques
Frank Coelho, President

Vintage Locomotive Society Inc.
PO Box 33021, RPO Polo Park, Winnipeg MB R3G 3N4
Tel: 204-832-5259; *Fax:* 866-751-2348
info@pdcrailway.com
www.pdcrailway.com
To collect, restore for operation & maintain steam locomotives & rolling stock of early part of twentieth-century; to provide source of historical information relating to origin & past operation of acquired equipment & buildings
Paul Newsome, General Manager

Archaeology

Archaeological Society of Alberta (ASA)
97 Eton Rd. West, Lethbridge AB T1K 4T9
Tel: 403-381-2655
jnermc@telus.net
www.arkyalberta.com
To promote the regulations of the Alberta Historical Act & to disseminate archaeological information by means of publications & seminars
Jim McMurchy, Executive Sec.-Treas.

Archaeological Society of British Columbia (ASBC)
PO Box 520, Stn. Bentall, Vancouver BC V6C 2N3
Tel: 604-822-2567; *Fax:* 604-822-6161
asbc.president@gmail.com
www.asbc.bc.ca
To protect the archaeological heritage of British Columbia; to promote public understanding of the scientific approach to archaeology; to encourage government to preserve archaeological & pre-historic sites
Patricia Ormerod, President

Association des archéologues du Québec (AAQ)
CP 322, Succ. Haute-Ville, Québec QC G1R 4P8
info@archeologie.qc.ca
www.archeologie.qc.ca
Définir les standards de la profession; veiller à la saine gestion et la mise en valeur du patrimoine archéologique à cause d'une éthique exemplaire et de la qualité de ses membres; agir comme interlocuteur privilégié pour tout ce qui regarde la question archéologique auprès des gouvernements et des organismes, privés ou publics, qui ont à coeur la préservation de notre patrimoine collectif
Richard Fiset, Président

Canadian Archaeological Association (CAA) / Association d'archéologie canadienne
c/o Jack Brink, Royal Alberta Museum, 12845 - 102 Ave., Edmonton AB T5N 0M6
Tel: 780-453-9151
president@canadianarchaeology.com
www.canadianarchaeology.com
To publish & disseminate archaeological knowledge in Canada; To encourage archaeological research & conservation efforts; To promote cooperation among archaeological societies & agencies
Jack Brink, President
Eric Damkjar, Vice-President
Jeff Hunston, Secretary-Treasurer

Nova Scotia Archaeology Society (NSAS)
PO Box 36090, Halifax NS B3J 3S9
Tel: 902-453-4972
dkelman@crmgroup.ca
www.novascotiaarchaeologysociety.com
To promote the preservation of Nova Scotia's archaeological sites & resources
Darryl Kelman, President
Terry J. Deveau, Vice-President
Robyn Crook, Secretary
Matt Munro, Treasurer

The Ontario Archaeological Society Inc.
#102, 1444 Queen St. East, Toronto ON M4L 1E1
Tel: 416-406-5959; *Fax:* 416-406-5959
Toll-Free: 888-733-0042
oasociety@ontarioarchaeology.on.ca
www.ontarioarchaeology.on.ca
To preserve, promote, investigate, record & publish an archaeological record of the province of Ontario
Lorie Harris, Executive Director
Jean-Luc Pilon, President
Jim Keron, Sec.-Treas. & Director, Finance

Saskatchewan Archaeological Society (SAS)
#1, 1730 Quebec Ave., Saskatoon SK S7K 1V9
Tel: 306-664-4124; *Fax:* 306-665-1928
saskarchsoc@sasktel.net
www.saskarchsoc.ca
Social Media: www.facebook.com/group.php?gid=137032406371156
To promote the study, preservation & appropriate utilization of the historic & pre-historic archaeological sites & artifacts of the province; To promote & carry out educational programs
Talina Cyr-Steenkamp, Executive Director
Belinda Riehl-Fitzsimmons, Business Administrator

Save Ontario Shipwrecks (SOS)
PO Box 2389, Blenheim ON N0P 1A0
Tel: 519-676-4110; *Fax:* 519-676-7058
rjequip@on.aibn.com
www.saveontarioshipwrecks.on.ca
Social Media: www.facebook.com/group.php?gid=68638569592
To promote & preserve Ontario's marine heritage
Michael Hill, President
Jonathan Ferguson, Secretary

Underwater Archaeological Society of British Columbia (UASBC)
c/o Vancouver Maritime Museum, 1905 Ogden Ave., Vancouver BC V6J 1A3
Tel: 604-942-9908; *Fax:* 604-980-0358
uasbc@uasbc.com
www.uasbc.com
To promote the science of underwater archaeology; to conserve, preserve & protect the maritime heritage lying beneath our coastal & inland waters
Jacques Marc, President
David Stone, Executive Director

Architecture

Alberta Association of Architects (AAA)
Duggan House, 10515 Saskatchewan Dr., Edmonton AB T6E 4S1
Tel: 780-432-0224; *Fax:* 780-439-1431
info@aaa.ab.ca
www.aaa.ab.ca
To regulate the practice of architecture & interior design in Alberta for the protection of the public & the administration of the profession; to bring architects together in order to channel the energies of unique, creative individuals spiritually committed to a superior architecture
Dianne Johnstone, Executive Director

Architects Association of Prince Edward Island (AAPEI)
PO Box 1766, Charlottetown PE C1A 7N4
Tel: 902-566-3699; *Fax:* 902-566-1235
info@aapei.com
www.aapei.com
Heather Mader, President

Architects' Association of New Brunswick (AANB) / Association des architectes du Nouveau-Brunswick
PO Box 5093, Sussex NB E4E 5L2
Tel: 506-433-5811; *Fax:* 506-432-1122
inquiries@aanb.org
www.aanb.org
To govern & regulate persons in New Brunswick who offer architectural services; To advance & maintain the standards of architecture in New Brunswick
Malcolm R. Boyd, President
Donald C. Sterritt, Treasurer
Reno Soucy, Registrar

The Architectural Conservancy of Ontario (ACO)
#403, 10 Adelaide St. East, Toronto ON M5C 1J3
Tel: 416-367-8075; *Fax:* 416-367-8630
Toll-Free: 877-264-8937
manager@arconserv.ca
www.arconserv.ca
To preserve buildings & structures of architectural merit & places of natural beauty or interest
Lloyd Alter, President

Architectural Institute of British Columbia (AIBC)
#100, 440 Cambie St., Vancouver BC V6B 2N5
Tel: 604-683-8588; *Fax:* 604-683-8568
Toll-Free: 800-667-0753
info@aibc.ca
www.aibc.ca
To regulate the profession of architecture in accordance with the Architects Act; to promote & increase the knowledge, skill & proficiency of its members in all things relating to the practice of architecture; to advance & maintain high standards of qualification & professional ethics; to promote public appreciation of architecture, allied arts, sciences & the professions
Michael Ernest, Interim Executive Director
Catherine Bolter, Coordinator, Professional Development

Association des Architectes en pratique privée du Québec (AAPPQ) / Association of Architects in Private Practice of Québec
#425, 1980, rue Sherbrooke ouest, Montréal QC H3H 1E8
Tél: 514-937-4140; *Téléc:* 514-937-2329
aappq@aappq.qc.ca
www.aappq.qc.ca

Organiser en association et représenter les architectes en pratique privée du Québec; étudier, défendre et développer des intérêts économiques, sociaux et moraux de ses membres; promouvoir et développer l'utilisation des services de l'architecte en pratique privée au Québec ou ailleurs
Alain Fournier, Président
Sylvie Beaucage, Secrétaire administrative

Association of Architectural Technologists of Ontario (AATO)
#207, 1515 Matheson Blvd. East, Mississauga ON L4W 2P5
Tel: 905-238-7594; *Fax:* 905-238-6344
Toll-Free: 866-805-2286
aato@bellnet.ca
aato.on.ca
The Association is a government-legislated, licensing & regulatory body for Architectural Technologists & Technicians in the province. It strives to maintain the standard of professional conduct of its members, as well as advocates to all levels of government on behalf of them & the industry.
Brian Abbey, President
Sam Pasquale, Registrar

Canadian Architectural Certification Board (CACB) / Conseil canadien de certification en architecture (CCCA)
#710, 1 Nicholas St., Ottawa ON K1N 7B7
Tel: 613-241-8399; *Fax:* 613-241-7991
info@cacb.ca
www.cacb.ca
The Canadian Architectural Certification Board fulfills two seperate but related mandates: 1- Administer a program of accreditation of the Canadian schools of architecture in accordance with "Conditions and Procedures for Accreditation" approved by the CCAC and the CCUSA and 2- Administer a program of certification of the educational qualifications of indivdual applicants in accordance withe criteria contained within the "Education Standard" approved by the CCAC.
Gordon Richards, President
Myriam Blais, Vice-President

Design Exchange (DX)
Toronto Dominion Centre, PO Box 18, 234 Bay St., Toronto ON M5K 1B2
Tel: 416-363-6121; *Fax:* 416-368-0684
info@dx.org; membership@dx.org; education@dx.org; media@dx.org
www.dx.org
To provide a design museum & centre for design research & education; To raise awareness & understanding of design
Tim Gilbert, Interim President

Manitoba Association of Architects (MAA)
137 Bannatyne Ave. East, 2nd Fl., Winnipeg MB R3B 0R3
Tel: 204-925-4620; *Fax:* 204-925-4624
info@mbarchitects.org
www.mbarchitects.org
In fulfilling its mandate, the MAA serves to protect the public interest and advance the profession of architecture. The MAA works with its membership and other stakeholders to establish high entry standards to the profession and maintain high standards of practice.
Judy Pestrak, Executive Director

Newfoundland Association of Architects
PO Box 5204, Stn. A, 7 Downing St., St. John's NL A1C 5V5
Tel: 709-726-8550; *Fax:* 709-726-1549
nlaa@newfoundlandarchitects.com
www.newfoundlandarchitects.com
Supporting architecture and architects in Newfoundland and Labrador.
Lynda Hayward, Administrative Director
Greg Snow, President
Lynda Hayward, Administrator

Northwest Territories Association of Architects (NWTAA)
Administrative Office, Northern Frontier Visitors Centre, PO Box 1394, 4807 - 49th St., Yellowknife NT X1A 2P1
Tel: 867-766-4216; *Fax:* 867-920-2652
www.nwtaa.ca
To maintain the Register of Architects, in accordance with the NWT Architects Act
Deleigh Rausch, Executive Director
Darrell Vikse, Registrar
Harriet Burdett-Moulton, Chair, Registration & Licence Review
Stephen Cumming, Chair, Practice Review
Wayne Guy, Chair, Complaint Review
Kris Schlagintweit, Chair, Continuing Education

Nova Scotia Association of Architects (NSAA)
1359 Barrington St., Halifax NS B3J 1Y9
Tel: 902-423-7607; *Fax:* 902-425-7024
info@nsaa.ns.ca
www.nsaa.ns.ca
To administer the practice of architecture in Nova Scotia
Mark Atwood, Registrar
Therese LeBlanc, President

Ontario Association of Architects (OAA)
111 Moatfield Dr., Toronto ON M3B 3L6
Tel: 416-449-6898; *Fax:* 416-449-5756
Toll-Free: 800-565-2724
oaamail@oaa.on.ca; practiceadvisor@oaa.on.ca (Practice Advisor)
www.oaa.on.ca
To operate in accordance with the Government of Ontario's Architects Act; To serve & protect the public interest by promoting & increasing the knowledge, skill, & proficiency of members
I. Hillel Roebuck, Registrar
Gordon Masters, Director, Operations
Kristi Doyle, Director, Policy
Andrew Fuller, Administrator, Accounting & Information Technology
Gail Hanselman, Administrator, Certificate of Practice
Tamara La Pierre King, Administrator, Web site & Communications
Jessica O'Rafferty, Administrator, Admission
Ellen Savitsky, Administrator, Continuing Education
Kim Sumi, Administrator, Licence

Ordre des architectes du Québec (OAQ)
#100, 1825, boul René-Lévesque ouest, Montréal QC H3H 1R4
Tél: 514-937-6168; *Téléc:* 514-933-0242
Ligne sans frais: 800-599-6168
info@oaq.com
www.oaq.com
Sa principale fonction est d'assurer la protection du public en régissant l'exercice de la profession d'architecte au Québec.
André Bourassa, Président

Royal Architectural Institute of Canada (RAIC) / Institut royal d'architecture du Canada
#330, 55 Murray St., Ottawa ON K1N 5M3
Tel: 613-241-3600; *Fax:* 613-241-5750
info@raic.org
www.raic.org
To represent Canadian architects nationally & internationally; to foster public awareness & appreciation of architecture; to engage in architectural research & education; to lobby government on architectural issues
Jim McKee, Executive Director
Paule Boutin, President

Saskatchewan Association of Architects (SAA)
#200, 642 Broadway Ave., Saskatoon SK S7N 1A9
Tel: 306-242-0733; *Fax:* 306-664-2598
www.saskarchitects.com
To regulate the profession of architecture in Saskatchewan, in order to ensure the protection of the public interest; To advance the profession of architecture in the province; To ensure that high standards for practice & conduct are followed
Jeff Jurzyniec, President
Grant McKercher, 1st Vice-President
Jeff Jurziniec, 2nd Vice-President
John Parry, Executive Director
Reg Squires, Secretary-Treasurer

Society for the Study of Architecture in Canada (SSAC) / Société pour l'étude de l'architecture au Canada (SEAC)
PO Box 2302, Stn. D, Ottawa ON K1P 5W5
info@canada-architecture.org
canada-architecture.org
To promote the study of Canadian architecture including an examination of both historical & cultural issues relating to buildings, districts, cities & the cultural landscapes; to encourage the collection & preservation of Canada's architectural records; to encourage preservation of the built environment
Pierre du Prey, President
Andrew Waldron, Vice-President
Lucie Morisset, Vice-President

Arts

Alberta Foundation for the Arts (AFA)
10708 - 105 Ave., Edmonton AB T5H 0A1
Tel: 780-427-9968; *Fax:* 780-422-1162
www.affta.ab.ca
Social Media: www.facebook.com/AlbertaFoundationfortheArts
To create the best possible climate for the arts in Alberta; provides grant funding to artists, art organizations & cultural industries; manages an extensive art collection featuring Alberta artists
Jeffrey Anderson, Executive Director

Alliance for Arts & Culture
#100, 938 Howe St., Vancouver BC V6Z 1N9
Tel: 604-681-3535; *Fax:* 604-681-7848
info@allianceforarts.com
www.allianceforarts.com
Social Media: www.facebook.com/AllianceforArtsandCulture; twitter.com/AllianceArts; www.youtube.com/user/AllianceArtsCulture
To project a strong voice for the local arts community; To promote the activities of the arts through a variety of programs, services, & marketing strategies; To increase public awareness of & accessibility to the arts & culture
Rob Gloor, Executive Director
Kevin Dale McKeown, Director, Communications & Special Events
Kevin Teichroeb, Director, Interactive Media
Melissa Flagg, Administrator, Members Services

Assembly of BC Arts Councils
PO Box 92, Stn. A, Nanaimo BC V9R 5G6
Tel: 250-754-3388; *Fax:* 250-754-3390
Toll-Free: 888-315-2288
info@assemblybcartscouncils.ca
www.assemblybcartscouncils.ca
To promote & advance the role of arts & culture in building community; to work with community based organizations in furthering the impact & contribution of the arts locally, regionally & province-wide
Junko Sakamoto, Executive Director

Canadian Artists' Representation (CARFAC) / Le Front des artistes canadiens
#250, 2 Daly Ave., Ottawa ON K1N 6E2
Tel: 613-233-6161; *Fax:* 613-233-6162
Toll-Free: 866-344-6161
carfac@carfac.ca
www.carfac.ca
To act as a national voice for Canada's professional visual artists; To promote a socio-economic climate that is conducive to the production of visual arts
Grant McConnell, National President & Spokesperson
Deirdre Logue, Vice-President
April Britski, Executive Director
Margaret Ryall, Secretary
Julie McIntyre, Treasurer
Taylor Norris, Coordinator, Membership
Melissa Gruber, Director, Advocacy & Communications

Canadian Arts Presenting Association (CAPACOA) / Association canadienne des organismes artistiques
#200, 17 York St., Ottawa ON K1N 9J6
Tel: 613-562-3515; *Fax:* 613-562-4005
mail@capacoa.ca
www.capacoa.ca
Social Media: www.facebook.com/CAPACOA; twitter.com/capacoa
To promote the development of the presentation of the arts in Canada; to promote & encourage greater knowledge & appreciation of the presentation of the performing arts; To encourage touring of artists & attractions throughout all regions of Canada; To provide information on artists & attractions touring regionally & nationally; To assist presenters of the arts in Canada with coordination of bookings; To provide opportunities for professional development of presenters in Canada; To promote communication & understanding between presenters of the arts in Canada; To provide forum for exchange of views concerning presentation of the performing arts generally; To provide information on regional & federal policies which relate to presentation of the arts; To provide the opportunity to make contacts nationwide
Erin Benjamin, Executive Director
Mélanie Bureau, Operations Manager

Canadian Celtic Arts Association
c/o Jean Talman, 91 Stafford St., Toronto ON M6J 3R1
jean.talman@utoronto.ca
To promote Celtic culture; To serve as a link between the diverse Celtic communities in Canada
Jean Talman, President & Membership Secretary

Donald Gillies, Treasurer

Canadian Conference of the Arts (CCA) / Conférence canadienne des arts
#406, 130 Slater St., Ottawa ON K1P 6E2
Tel: 613-238-3561; *Fax:* 613-238-4849
info@ccarts.ca
www.ccarts.ca
To ensure the lively existence & continued growth of the arts & the cultural industries in Canada; to increase the Canadian materials (works created, produced, & performed by Canadians) available to Canadians; to improve the quality of life for all artists & arts groups; to unite members to work for interests of all artists & whole cultural community; to work closely with other arts service organizations to formulate policies & advocate their adoption by governments.
Alain Pineau, National Director
Alessia Bongiovanni, Executive Assistant

Chorale Les Voix de la Vallée du Cuivre de Chibougamau inc.
CP 128, Chibougamau QC G8P 2K6
Tél: 418-748-7811
Linda Marceau

Conseil des arts et des lettres du Québec
79, boul René Lévesque est, 3e étage, Québec QC G1R 5N5
Tél: 418-643-1707; *Téléc:* 418-643-4558
Ligne sans frais: 800-897-1707
info@calq.gouv.qc.ca
www.calq.gouv.qc.ca
Média social: www.facebook.com/group.php?gid=12468994038; twitter.com/LeCALQ
Soutenir, dans toutes les régions du Québec, la création, l'expérimentation et la production dans les domaines des arts visuels, des métiers d'art, de la littérature, du théâtre, de la musique, de la danse, des arts du cirque, des arts multidisciplinaires, des arts médiatiques et de la recherche architecturale et d'en favoriser le rayonnement au Québec, au Canada et à l'étranger
Marie DuPont, Président du conseil d'administration
Yvan Gauthier, Président & Directeur général

Council for Business & the Arts in Canada (CBAC) / Conseil pour le monde des affaires et des arts du Canada
#903, 165 University Ave., Toronto ON M5H 3B8
Tel: 416-869-3016; *Fax:* 416-869-0435
info@businessforarts.org
www.businessforarts.org
To make the partnership between business & the arts more effective in supporting the nation's creative minds.
James D. Fleck, Chair
Nichole Anderson, President & CEO

Federation of Canadian Artists (FCA)
1241 Cartwright St., Vancouver BC V6H 4B7
Tel: 604-681-2744; *Fax:* 604-681-2740
fcaoffice@artists.ca (Education) fcaadmin@artists.ca (Membership)
www.artists.ca
To share & promote the visual arts
Tatjana Mirkov-Popovicki, President
Andrew McDermott, 1st Vice-President
Harold Allanson, 2nd Vice-President
Bev Rushworth, Executive Director
Mila Kostic, Director, Gallery
Elaine Chatwin, Secretary
Sandy Kay, Treasurer

Governor General's Performing Arts Awards Foundation (GGPAAF) / Les Prix du Gouverneur Général pour les arts de la scène
#804, 130 Albert St., Ottawa ON K1P 5G4
Tel: 613-241-5297; *Fax:* 613-238-4849
nominations@ggpaaf.com
www.bell.ca/ggawards
To celebrate outstanding lifetime achievement in various performing arts disciplines in Canada; To raise awareness of the contributions of Canadian performing artists; To foster awareness of Francophone artists in English Canada & Anglophone artists in French Canada; To inspire future performing artists
Whitney Taylor, Director
Peter Herrndorf, President/CEO
Harold Redekopp, Co-Chair
Albert Millaire, Co-Chair

Manitoba Arts Council (MAC) / Conseil des arts du Manitoba (CAM)
#525, 93 Lombard Ave., Winnipeg MB R3B 3B1
Tel: 204-945-2237; *Fax:* 204-945-5925
Toll-Free: 866-994-2787
info@artscouncil.mb.ca
www.artscouncil.mb.ca
An arms-length agency of the provincial government dedicated to artistic excellence; offers a broad based grant program for professional artists & arts organizations; promotes, preserves, supports & advocates for the arts as essential to the quality of life of all people of Manitoba.
Douglas Riske, Executive Director

Newfoundland and Labrador Arts Council (NLAC)
PO Box 98, 1 Springdale St., St. John's NL A1C 5H5
Tel: 709-726-2212; *Fax:* 709-726-0619
Toll-Free: 866-726-2212
nlacmail@nlac.ca
www.nlac.ca
To foster & promote the arts of the province; to carry on financial assistance programs for individual artists & arts groups; to work with the government & the community for development in the arts
Reg Winsor, Executive Director
Tom Gordon, Chair

Northwest Territories Arts Council
c/o NWT Education, Culture & Employment, PO Box 1320, Stn. Main, Yellowknife NT X1A 2L9
Tel: 867-920-6370; *Fax:* 867-873-0205
boris_atamanenko@gov.nt.ca
pwnhc.learnnet.nt.ca/artscouncil
To promote and encourage the arts in the Northwest Territories.
Boris Atamanenko, Manager, Community Programs

Ontario Arts Council (OAC) / Conseil des arts de l'Ontario
151 Bloor St. West, 5th Fl., Toronto ON M5S 1T6
Tel: 416-961-1660; *Fax:* 416-961-7796
Toll-Free: 800-387-0058
info@arts.on.ca
www.arts.on.ca
Social Media: twitter.com/oac_cao
Ontario's primary funding body for professional arts activity; promotes & assists the development of the arts & artists; offers 50+ funding programs
John Brotman, Executive Director

Organization of Saskatchewan Arts Councils (OSAC)
1102 - 8th Ave., Regina SK S4R 1C9
Tel: 306-586-1250; *Fax:* 306-586-1550
info@osac.sk.ca
www.osac.sk.ca
To assist the membership in their endeavors to develop, promote & present the visual arts &/or performing arts
Kevin Korchinski, Executive Director

Performing Arts NB, Inc. (PANB)
Brunswick Sq., 3rd Level, 39 King St., Saint John NB E2L 4W3
Tel: 506-635-8019; *Fax:* 506-657-7832
performingartsnb@nb.aibn.com
www.nbinfo.ca
Social Media: WWW.FACEBOOK.COM/PAGES/pERFORMING-aRTS-nb-pan b/127945243882172
To achieve the vision of New Brunswick as a place where all residents attend a diversity of quality, live performances in their own community; all students attend performances in their own school by performing artists; artists residing in New Brunswick find a supportive arts community & the resources necessary to establish a career in the performing arts in New Brunswick & beyond; maintain a resource centre; assume an advocacy for the performing arts in the community
Nancy Schell, Executive Director
Nicole L. Gallant, President

Prince Edward Island Council of the Arts (PEICA)
115 Richmond St., Charlottetown PE C1A 1A7
Tel: 902-368-4410; *Fax:* 902-368-4418
Toll-Free: 888-734-2784
info@peica.ca
www.peiartscouncil.com
Social Media: www.facebook.com/group.php?gid=6930656373
To make the Arts integral to the lives of all Prince Edward Islanders; Through advocacy, education, distribution of funds, management of the Arts Guild & program of prizes & awards.
Greg Doran, Chair

SaskCulture Inc.
#600, 2220 - 12th Ave., Regina SK S4P 0M8
Tel: 306-780-9284; *Fax:* 306-780-9252
saskculture.info@saskculture.sk.ca
www.saskculture.sk.ca
To bring together organizations which work to further the course of culture
Rose Gilks, General Manager
Diane Ell, Communications Manager

Scarborough Arts Council (SAC)
1859 Kingston Rd., Toronto ON M1N 1T3
Tel: 416-698-7322; *Fax:* 416-698-7972
office@scarborougharts.com
www.scarborougharts.com
To develop all arts disciplines in Scarborough, Ontario; To link artists & the community
Colin Hughes, Chair
Christine Harris, Vice-Chair
Ravinder Shawe, Vice-Chair
Tim Whalley, Executive Director
Carolyn Kim, Secretary
Daniel Broome, Treasurer
Susan Dimitrakopoulos, Coordinator, Office & Membership
Benedict Lopes, Coordinator, Programs

Automotive

Alberta Motor Association (AMA)
PO Box 8180, Stn. South, Edmonton AB T6H 5X9
Tel: 780-430-5555
www.ama.ab.ca
Tania Willumsen, Chair
Don Smitten, President

Association des propriétaires d'autobus du Québec (APAQ)
#107, 225, boul Charest est, Québec QC G1K 3G9
Tél: 418-522-7131; *Téléc:* 418-522-6455
apaq@apaq.qc.ca
www.apaq.qc.ca
Défendre les intérêts des enterprises offrant des services de transport collectif de personnes par autobus et autocars
Mario St-Laurent, Directeur général
Sophie Guay, Coordonnatrice à la comptabilité
Karine Parent, Coordonnatrice, Développement et à la promotion
Diane Villeneuve, Coordonnatrice, Événements
Martin Bureau, Responsable, Communications et au marketing

Association des spécialistes du pneus et Mécanique du Québec (ASPQ)
CP 1033, Drummondville QC J2A 0B1
Tél: 514-461-1035; *Téléc:* 514-461-1035
Ligne sans frais: 866-454-0477
info@aspmq.ca
www.aspq.ca/aspq
Daniel Dubuc, Président
Danny Houle, Vice-président
Wendy Allain, Directrice éxécutive

Atlantic Recreation Vehicle Dealers Association (ARVDA)
PO Box 9410, Stn. A, Halifax NS B3K 5S3
Tel: 902-425-2445; *Fax:* 902-425-2441
matthew@hamblys.ca
www.arvda.ca
Wayne Hambly, President

Automobile Journalists Association of Canada (AJAC) / Association des journalistes automobile du Canada
PO Box 398, Stn. Main, Cobourg ON K9A 4L1
Toll-Free: 800-361-1516
beth@ajac.ca
www.ajac.ca
Association of professional automotive experts who report on new vehicles and new industry trends in various print and broadcast media.
Beth Rhind, Manager

Automobile Protection Association (APA) / Association pour la protection automobile
292, boul St. Joseph ouest, Montréal QC H2V 2N7
Tel: 514-272-5555; *Fax:* 514-273-0797
apamontreal@apa.ca
www.apa.ca
To inform & represent the public on major automobile-related issues
Antoinette Greco, Directrice générale
George Iny, Président

Automotive Industries Association of Canada (AIAC) / Association des industries de l'automobile du Canada
1272 Wellington St. West, Ottawa ON K1Y 3A7
Fax: 613-728-6021
Toll-Free: 800-808-2920
info.aia@aiacanada.com
www.aiacanada.com
Social Media: www.facebook.com/AIAofCanada
To represent the automotive aftermarket industry in Canada; To promote, educate, & represent members
Marc Brazeau, President
Deborah Moynes-Keshen, Executive Vice-President
Therese Santostefano, Director, Operations & Finance
Andrew Shepherd, Director, Collision Training
Patty Kettles, Manager, Marketing & Communications

Automotive Parts Manufacturers' Association (APMA)
#801, 10 Four Seasons Pl., Toronto ON M9B 6H7
Tel: 416-620-4220; *Fax:* 416-620-9730
info@apma.ca
www.apma.ca
To promote the manufacture in Canada of automotive parts, systems, components, materials, tools, equipment & supplies, & also the provision of services used in the automotive industry & in particular for the original equipment market; To engage in activities in support of the welfare of the members of the Association
Steve Rodgers, President
Vincent Guglielmo, Vice-President
Peter Corbyn, Director, Environment & Energy
Shaun Cott, Manager, Marketing

Automotive Retailers Association of British Columbia
#1, 8980 Fraserwood Ct., Burnaby BC V5J 5H7
Tel: 604-432-7987; *Fax:* 604-432-1756
info@ara.bc.ca
www.ara.bc.ca
To enhance the image & competitive status of association members throughout BC & ensure high quality service to protect the road safety of the motoring public
Gord Valente, President
H. Dale Finch, Executive Director

BCADA - The New Car Dealers of BC
#70, 10551 Shellbridge Way, Richmond BC V6X 2W9
Tel: 604-214-9964; *Fax:* 604-214-9965
info@newcardealers.ca
www.newcardealers.ca
To promote benefits & heighten awareness of issues of interest to members
Blair Qualey, President & CEO

British Columbia Automobile Association (BCAA)
4567 Canada Way, Burnaby BC V5G 4T1
Tel: 604-268-5000; *Fax:* 604-268-5585
Toll-Free: 800-663-1956
www.bcaa.com
To provide motoring, travel, & insurance services to members in British Columbia & the Yukon
Timothy J. Condon, President & Chief Executive Officer
Collin MacKinnon, Senior Vice-President & CFO
Ken Ontko, Senior Vice-President & CIO
Greg Oyhenart, Sr. VP & Chief Member Experience Officer
Heidi Worthington, Sr. Vice-President & Chief Marketing Officer
John Allen, Vice-President & Chief HR Officer

CAA Manitoba
870 Empress St., Winnipeg MB R3C 2Z3
Tel: 204-262-6100
contact@caamanitoba.com
www.caamanitoba.com
Social Media: www.facebook.com/caamanitoba; twitter.com/caamanitoba
Bohdan (Bud) V. Halkewycz, Chair
Michael R. Mager, President & Chief Executive Officer

CAA-Québec
444, rue Bouvier, Québec QC G2J 1E3
Tél: 418-624-2424; *Ligne sans frais:* 800-686-9243
info@caa-quebec.qc.ca
www.caaquebec.com
Veut assurer la sécurité et paix d'esprit à chacun de ses membres ainsi qu'à ses clients en leur offrant des services et des produits de très haute qualité dans les domaines de l'automobile, du voyage, de l'habitation et des services financiers
Sophie Gagnon, Vice-présidente adjointe, Relations publiques et gouvernementales de CAA-Québec
Philippe St-Pierre, Conseiller en communication

Canadian Automobile Association (CAA) / Association canadienne des automobilistes
National Office, #200, 1145 Hunt Club Rd., Ottawa ON K1V 0Y3
Toll-Free: 800-564-6222
www.caa.ca
Social Media: twitter.com/CAA; www.youtube.com/TheCAAChannel
To promote, develop & implement programs & information related to the rights, responsibilities, & needs of the motorist as a consumer
Tim Shearman, President
Jeff Walker, Vice-President, Public Affairs
Lionel Aucoin, Managing Director, E-Business
Alayne Crawford, Manager, Public Affairs
Jamie Patterson, Manager, Partnership Programs of CAA

Canadian Automobile Association Maritimes
Corporate Office & Saint John Member Service Centre, 378 Westmorland Rd., Saint John NB E2J 2G4
Tel: 506-634-1400; *Fax:* 506-653-9500
Toll-Free: 800-471-1611
www.caa.ca/atlantic
To serve New Brunswick, Newfoundland & Labrador, Nova Scotia, & Prince Edward Island

Canadian Automobile Association Niagara
3271 Schmon Pkwy., Thorold ON L2V 4Y6
Tel: 905-984-8585; *Fax:* 905-688-0289
www.caa.niagara.net

Canadian Automobile Association North & East Ontario
Administration Centre, PO Box 8350, Stn. T CSC, Ottawa ON K1G 3T2
Tel: 613-820-1890; *Fax:* 613-820-4646
Toll-Free: 800-267-8713
contactcaa@caaneo.on.ca; membership@caaneo.on.ca
www.caaneo.on.ca
To deliver automotive, travel, insurance & related services to members & advocate on their behalf
Frances Mannarino, Chair
Tim Georgeoff, President & Chief Executive Officer

Canadian Automobile Association North & East Ontario
Administration Centre, PO Box 8350, Stn. T, Ottawa ON K1G 3T2
Tel: 613-820-1890; *Fax:* 613-820-4646
Toll-Free: 800-267-8713
contactcaa@caaneo.on.ca; membership@caaneo.on.ca
www.caaneo.on.ca
Frances Mannarino, Chair
Tim Georgeoff, President & Chief Executive Officer

Canadian Automobile Association Saskatchewan
200 Albert St. North, Regina SK S4R 5E2
Tel: 306-791-4314; *Fax:* 306-949-4461
caa.admin@caasask.sk.ca
www.caasask.sk.ca
To guarantee excellent emergency road assistance, travel, & insurance services; To provide services, products, programs, & representations to government in order to meet the needs of members, clients, & employees
Fred Titanich, President

Canadian Automobile Association South Central Ontario
60 Commerce Valley Dr. East, Thornhill ON L3T 7P9
Tel: 905-771-3000; *Fax:* 905-771-3101
Toll-Free: 866-988-8878
info@caasco.ca
www.caasco.com
Social Media: www.facebook.com/pages/CAA-South-Central-Ontario/106112779480473; twitter.com/caasco; www.youtube.com/caasouthcentralON
To enrich the driving experience of members by providing travel, insurance & automotive services & information
Nick Parks, President & Chief Executive Officer
Gina Banwait, Specialist, Community Relations
Silvana Aceto, Specialist, Media & Public Relations

Canadian Automobile Association South Central Ontario
60 Commerce Valley Dr. East, Thornhill ON L3T 7P6
Tel: 905-771-3000; *Fax:* 905-771-3101
Toll-Free: 866-988-8878
info@caasco.ca
www.caasco.ca

Canadian Automobile Association Windsor
1215 Ouellette Ave., Windsor ON N8X 1J3
Tel: 519-255-1212; *Fax:* 519-255-7379
windsor@caasco.ca
www.caa.ca/csg-gce/cgs-offices-locations-e.cfm

Canadian Automobile Dealers' Association (CADA) / Corporation des associations de détaillants d'automobiles (CADA)
85 Renfrew Dr., Markham ON L3R 0N9
Tel: 905-940-4959; *Fax:* 905-940-6870
Toll-Free: 800-463-5289
www.cada.ca
To deal with issues of a national nature which affect the well-being of franchised automobile & truck dealers in Canada
Al MacPhee, Chair
Richard C. Gauthier, President & Chief Executive Officer
Stephen Chipman, Secretary-Treasurer

Canadian Automobile Sport Clubs - Ontario Region Inc. (CASC-OR)
703 Petrolia Rd., Toronto ON M3J 2N6
Tel: 416-667-9500; *Fax:* 416-667-9555
Toll-Free: 877-667-9505
office@casc.on.ca
www.casc.on.ca
To provide leadership, management, advocacy & the administrative services, facilities & equipment necessary to enable members to maximize their enjoyment & participation in motorsport; to maintain controls & standards necessary for safe competition
John Adamkowski, Secretary
Scott Ellsworth, President

Canadian Automotive Repair & Service Council
c/o Cars Knowledge Network, #6, 9120 Leslie St., Richmond Hill ON L4B 3J9
Tel: 905-709-1010; *Fax:* 905-709-1013
askus@cars-council.ca
www.cars-council.ca
CARS serves as a virtual gathering place to access training & education programs, to research industry issues, & to learn of new skills, technologies & trends.
Dan Bell, President
Jennifer Steeves, Executive Director

Canadian Vehicle Manufacturers' Association (CVMA) / Association canadienne des constructeurs de véhicules
#400, 170 Attwell Dr., Toronto ON M9W 5Z5
Tel: 416-364-9333; *Fax:* 416-367-3221
Toll-Free: 800-758-7122
info@cvma.ca
www.cvma.ca
The CVMA creates a framework within which member companies (such as Fordand General Motors) work together to achieve shared industry objectives on a range of important issues such as consumer protection, the environment, and vehicle safety. They provide research, information, industry-government advocacy, and other services aimed at building a better understanding of the importance of a healthy automotive industry to Canada's economic well-being and prosperity.
B.A. Gaunt, Chairman
Mark A. Nantais, President

Corporation des concessionnaires d'automobiles du Québec inc. (CCAQ)
#750, 140, Grande-Allée est, Québec QC G1R 5M8
Tél: 418-523-2991; *Téléc:* 418-523-3725
Ligne sans frais: 800-463-5189
info@ccaq.com
www.ccaq.com
Offre une multitude de services aux membres; représenter ses membres

Japan Automobile Manufacturers Association of Canada
#460, 151 Bloor St. West, Toronto ON M5S 1S4
Tel: 416-968-0150; *Fax:* 416-968-7095
jama@jama.ca
www.jama.ca
To promote increased understanding of economic & trade matters pertaining to the motor vehicle industry; To encourage closer cooperation between Canada & Japan; To represent the interests of members
Takashi Sekiguchi, Chairman

Manitoba Motor Dealers Association (MMDA)
#230, 530 Century St., Winnipeg MB R3H 0Y4
Tel: 204-985-4200; *Fax:* 204-775-9125
Toll-Free: 800-949-6632
info@mmda.mb.ca
www.mmda.mb.ca
To represent franchised automobile & truck dealers in Manitoba by dealing with provincial issues that affect this membership; To advance the automotive industry in Manitoba; To uphold the code of ethics
Neil Metcalfe, President
Geoff Sine, Executive Director

Motor Dealers' Association of Alberta (MDA)
9249, 48 St., Edmonton AB T6B 2R9
Tel: 780-468-9552; *Fax:* 780-465-6201
info@mdaalberta.com
www.mdaalberta.com
The Motor Dealer's Association of Alberta (MDA) strives to serve the collective interest of all its members and promote positive relationships with government, industry, suppliers, consumers and media, by offering needed and effective programs and services.
Denis Ducharme, President

Nova Scotia Automobile Dealers' Association (NSADA)
#700, 6009 Quinpool Rd., Halifax NS B3K 5S3
Tel: 902-425-2445; *Fax:* 902-425-2441
info@nsada.ca
www.nsada.ca
To assist & protect association members; To act as the voice of new vehicle franchised dealers in Nova Scotia
John K. Sutherland, Executive Vice-President

Ontario Tire Dealers Association
PO Box 516, 34 Edward St., Drayton ON N0G 1P0
Tel: 888-207-9059; *Fax:* 866-375-6832
www.otda.com
To represent & promote members
Robert Bignell, Executive Director
Glenn Warnica, President
Ron Spiewak, Secretary-Treasurer
Eric Gilbert, Chair, Ontario Tire Dealers Associaton Committee

Prince Edward Island Automobile Dealers Association
PO Box 22004, 6 Jenkins Ave., Charlottetown PE C1A 9J2
Tel: 902-566-3639; *Fax:* 902-368-7116
peiada@eastlink.ca
Lisa Doyle-MacBain, Manager

Recreation Vehicle Dealers Association of Alberta
10561 - 172 St. NW, Edmonton AB T5S 1P1
Tel: 780-455-8562; *Fax:* 780-453-3927
Toll-Free: 888-858-8787
rvda@rvda-alberta.org
www.rvda-alberta.org
To develop professionalism & customer confidence in the RV industry

Recreation Vehicle Dealers Association of British Columbia (RVDABC)
#201, 17700 - 56th Ave., Surrey BC V3S 1C7
Tel: 604-575-3868; *Fax:* 604-575-3869
info@rvda.bc.ca
www.rvda.bc.ca
To promote, protect, educate, & enhances benefits for its members
Joan Jackson, Executive Director

Recreation Vehicle Dealers Association of Canada (RVDA) / Association des commerçants de véhicules recréatifs du Canada
#204, 6411 Buswell St., Richmond BC V6Y 2G5
Tel: 604-718-6325; *Fax:* 604-204-0154
info@rvda.ca
www.rvda.ca
Social Media: www.facebook.com/#!/RVDAofCanada
To promote professionalism in the RV industry through educational programs & events; to present the views of the industry to government & the general public
Alden Kowarsky, Chair
Eleonore Hamm, President

Recreation Vehicle Dealers Association of Manitoba
69 Morin Rd., St Francois Xavier MB R4L 1A8
Tel: 204-864-2112; *Fax:* 204-864-2232
rvdamb@mts.net
www.manitobarvda.ca
To build & improve the RV industry
Kim Wozniak, Manager

Recreation Vehicle Dealers Association of Saskatchewan
342 Armstrong Way, Saskatoon SK S7N 3N1
Tel: 306-955-7832; *Fax:* 306-955-7952
info@saskatchewanrvda.ca
www.saskatchewanrvda.ca
Sheila Lardner, Manager

Saskatchewan Automobile Dealers Association (SADA)
610 Broad St., Regina SK S4R8H1
Tel: 306-721-2208; *Fax:* 306-721-1009
Susan Buckle, Executive Director

Toronto Automobile Dealers' Association (TADA)
85 Renfrew Dr., Markham ON L3R 0N9
Tel: 905-940-6232; *Fax:* 905-940-6235
info@tada.ca
www.tada.ca
Social Media:
www.facebook.com/group.php?gid=149581915142339;
twitter.com/TADA_GR
Sandy Liguori, President

Used Car Dealers Association of Ontario (UCDA)
230 Norseman St., Toronto ON M8X 6A2
Tel: 416-231-2600; *Fax:* 416-232-0775
Toll-Free: 800-268-2598
web@ucda.org
www.ucda.org
To enhance the image of the industry through member education, consumer awareness of the benefits members provide, & mediation of consumer/dealer disputes
Robert G. Beattie, Executive Director
Steve Peck, President

Aviation & Aerospace

Aéro-Club des Outardes
1455, de Biencourt, Montréal QC H4E 1T1
Tél: 514-465-7806
francisco45@gmail.com
aeroclubdesoutardes.iquebec.com
Favorise la formation au pilotage, la pratique et le développement du vol à voile au Québec.
Jacques Fairpault, Président

Aerospace Industries Association of Canada (AIAC) / Association des industries aérospatiales du Canada
#7030, 255 Albert St., Ottawa ON K1P 6A9
Tel: 613-232-4297; *Fax:* 613-232-1142
info@aiac.ca
www.aiac.ca
To promote & facilitate the continued success & growth of this strategic industry; To establish & maintain a public policy environment that enables sustained aerospace industry growth; To strengthen the international competitiveness of all aerospace firms in Canada; To strengthen Canadian aerospace SME capabilities & position them as "suppliers of choice"; To represent & involve the full range of aerospace companies that operate in Canada
Jim Quick, President & CEO
David Schellenberg, Chair

Air Transport Association of Canada (ATAC) / Association du transport aérien du Canada
#700, 255 Albert St., Ottawa ON K1P 6A9
Tel: 613-233-7727; *Fax:* 613-230-8648
atac@atac.ca
www.atac.ca
To advance the issues that affect members from the commercial aviation & flight training industries as well as avaiation industry suppliers
Fred Gaspar, Vice-President, Policy & Strategic Planning
John McKenna, President & Chief Executive Officer
Bill Boucher, Vice-President, Flight Operations
Wayne Gouveia, Vice-President, Commercial General Aviation
Cedric Paillard, Vice-President, Communications & Marketing
Mike Skrobica, Vice-President, Industry Monetary Affairs
Brian Whitehead, Vice-President, Technical Operations

Airport Management Council of Ontario
10 Geddes Cres., Barrie ON L4N 7B3
Tel: 705-726-2626; *Fax:* 705-739-8520
Toll-Free: 877-636-2626
amco@amco.on.ca
www.amco.on.ca
AMCO is committed to the sustainability of airports nationally. It monitors the airport industry, lobbies, provides networking opportunities and training to airports & businesses that work to enhance airport operations.

Mike Karsseboom, President
Bryan Avery, Executive Director

Association québécoise du transport aérien (AQTA)
Aéroport international Jean-Lesage, 600, 6e av de l'Aéroport, Québec QC G2G 2T5
Tél: 418-871-4635; *Téléc:* 418-871-8189
aqta@aqta.ca
www.aqta.ca
Média social:
www.facebook.com/group.php?gid=119190028092054;
www.linkedin.com/groups?home=&gid=2588987
Voué à la défense et la promotion des intérêts de tous les secteurs du transport aérien
Éric Lippé, Président-directeur général

British Columbia Aviation Council (BCAC)
PO Box 32366, Stn. YVR Domestic Terminal, Richmond BC V7B 1W2
Tel: 604-278-9330; *Fax:* 604-278-8210
info@bcaviationcouncil.org
www.bcaviationcouncil.org
A self-sustaining organization with the mission to "promote the safe and orderly development of aviation and aviation services to the province of British Columiba."
Mike Matthews, Chair
Donna Farquar, Executive Administrator

Canadian Aeronautics & Space Institute (CASI) / Institut aéronautique et spatial du Canada
#104, 350 Terry Fox Dr., Ottawa ON K2K 2W5
Tel: 613-591-8787; *Fax:* 613-591-7291
casi@casi.ca; membership@casi.ca
www.casi.ca
To advance the art, science, engineering, & applications of aeronautics & associated technologies in Canada; To promote Canadian competence & international competitiveness
Geoff Languedoc, Executive Director
April Duffy, Coordinator, Publications, Information & Membership Services

Canadian Airports Council (CAC) / Conseil des aéroports du Canada
#600, 116 Lisgar St., Ottawa ON K2P 0C2
Tel: 613-560-9302; *Fax:* 613-560-6599
www.cacairports.ca
To act as the voice for Canadian airports on a great range of important issues
Daniel-Robert Gooch, President
Nicole Larocque, Administrative Assistant

Canadian Aviation Historical Society (CAHS)
PO Box 2700, Stn. D, 156 St. Pierre Rd., Ottawa ON K1P 5W7
www.cahs.com
The Society collects & disseminates information about Canada's aviation heritage. It aims to foster public interest in the field. It is a registered charity, BN: 118829589RR0001.
Danielle Metcalfe-Chenail, National President
Rachel Heide, Treasurer
Jim Bell, Secretary

Canadian Aviation Maintenance Council (CAMC) / Conseil canadien de l'entretien des aéronefs (CCEA)
#155, 955 Green Valley Cres., Ottawa ON K2C 3V4
Tel: 613-727-8272; *Fax:* 613-727-7018
Toll-Free: 800-448-9715
secretariat@camc.ca
www.camc.ca
To develop occupational training standards & facilitate the implementation of a human resources strategy for the Canadian Aviation Maintenance Industry.
Raewen Borris, Leader, Communications
Robert Donald, Executive Director

Canadian Federation of AME Associations (CFAMEA)
837 Charlotte St., Fredericton NB E3B 1M7
Tel: 506-452-1809; *Fax:* 506-452-8251
www.cfamea.com
Ben L. McCarty, Chair

Canadian Flight Instructors Association
579 Kingston Rd., Ajax ON L1S 6M1
Tel: 905-683-8986; *Fax:* 905-683-6977
bill@jsdavidson.ca
Bill Davidson

Canadian Owners & Pilots Association (COPA)
71 Bank St., 7th Fl., Ottawa ON K1P 5N2
Tel: 613-236-4901; *Fax:* 613-236-8646
copa@copanational.org
www.copanational.org
The recognized voice of general aviation in Canada

Kevin Psutka, President

Canadian Seaplane Pilots Association (CSPA)
#1001, 75 Albert St., Ottawa ON K1P 5E7
Tel: 613-236-4901; *Fax:* 613-236-8646
To maintain communications among seaplane pilots; to represent them at all levels of government; to help develop regulations conducive to safe & pleasurable flying; to prepare & disseminate educational material; to advance among its members information & knowledge of seaplane flying.
Chris Bullerdick, Director

Helicopter Association of Canada (HAC)
#500, 130 Albert St., Ottawa ON K1P 5G4
Tel: 613-231-1110; *Fax:* 613-369-5097
www.h-a-c.ca
To ensure the financial viability of the Canadian civil helicopter industry; To promote flight safety; To expand utilization of helicopter transport
Teri Northcott, Chair
Fred L. Jones, BA LLB, President & Chief Executive Officer
Sylvain Seguin, Vice-President & Director, Marketing
Gary McDermid, Secretary
Maureen Crockett, Treasurer

International Air Transport Association / Association du transport aérien international
PO Box 113, 800, Place Victoria, Montréal QC H4Z 1M1
Tel: 514-874-0202; *Fax:* 514-874-9632
www.iata.org
To promote safe, regular & economical air transport for the benefit of the peoples of the world; to foster air commerce; to study the problems connected with air transport; to provide a means for collaboration among the air transport enterprises engaged directly or indirectly in international air transport service; to cooperate with the International Civil Aviation Organization & other international organizations; to furnish for governments a forum for developing industry working standards &, as appropriate, coordinating international fares & rates; to simplify the travelling process for the general public
Giovanni Bisignani, Director General & CEO
Kevin G. Dobby, Corporate Secretary
Mark Hubble, IATA Representative in Canada/Vice-, Marketing & Commercial Services

International Civil Aviation Organization: Legal Affairs & External Relations Bureau
999, rue Université, Montréal QC H3C 5H7
Tel: 514-954-8219; *Fax:* 514-954-6077
icaohq@icao.int
www.icao.int
To promote the safe & orderly development of civil aviation in the world; to set international standards & regulations necessary for the safety, security, efficiency & regularity of air transport & to serve as the medium for cooperation in all fields of civil aviation.
Denys Wibaux, Director
Raymond Benjamin, Secretary General

International Industry Working Group (IIWG)
International Air Transport Association, PO Box 113, 800, Place Victoria, Montréal QC H4Z 1M1
Tel: 514-874-0202; *Fax:* 514-874-9632
obrienm@iata.org
www.iata.org
To promote & develop an open exchange of information to minimize interface problems through well-informed design, development & operation of both aircraft & airports; to study jointly solutions to major problems which impede the development of the air transport system
Tony Tyler, Chair
Giovanni Bisignani, Director General & CEO

The Ninety-Nines Inc./International Organization of Women Pilots
4300 Amelia Earhart Rd., Oklahoma City OK 73159 USA
Tel: 405-685-7969; *Fax:* 405-685-7985
Toll-Free: 800-994-1929
99s@ninety-nines.org
www.ninety-nines.org
To promote world fellowship through flight; to provide networking & scholarship opportunities for women & aviation education in the community; to preserve the unique history of women in aviation
Margo McCutcheon, Governor, East Canada Section
Wendy Boyes, Governor, West Canada Section
Susan Larson, President

Northern Air Transport Association (NATA)
PO Box 2457, Yellowknife NT X1A 2P8
Tel: 867-920-2985; *Fax:* 867-920-2983
nata-yzf@theedge.ca
www.nata-yzf.ca
To promote safe & effective Northern air transportation

Don Douglas, Executive Director
Stephen Nourse, President
Teri Arychuk, Secretary-Treasurer

Recreational Aircraft Association (RAA) / Réseau aéronefs amateur
22 - 4881 Fountain St. North, Breslau ON N0B 1M0
Tel: 519-648-3030; *Toll-Free:* 800-387-1028
raa@raa.ca
www.raa.ca
To be a national leader in the development & advancement of recreational aviation; to promote recreational flying & building of amateur built aircraft, restorations of classic & antique aircraft
Gary Wolf, President
Dave Hadath, Treasurer

Ultralight Pilots Association of Canada (UPAC) / Association canadienne des pilotes d'avions ultra-légers
907289 Township Rd. 12, RR#4, Bright ON N0J 1B0
Tel: 519-684-7628
www.upac.ca
To promote ultralight aviation in Canada
K. Lubitz, President

University of Toronto Institute for Aerospace Studies
Faculty of Applied Science & Engineering, 4925 Dufferin St., Toronto ON M3H 5T6
Tel: 416-667-7700; *Fax:* 416-667-7799
www.utias.utoronto.ca
UTIAS is a graduate studies and research institute, forming part of the faculty of Applied Science and Engineering at the University of Toronto.
D.W. Zingg, Director
H.T. Liu, Associate Director
O.L. Gülder, Associate Director

Banking

Canadian Community Reinvestment Coalition (CCRC)
PO Box 821, Stn. B, Ottawa ON K1P 241
Tel: 613-789-5753; *Fax:* 613-241-4758
cancrc@web.net
www.canrc.org
To increase the accountability of Canada's financial institutions, increase their reinvestment in the Canadian ecomony, strengthen Canada's economy, strengthen community economic development efforts across Canada, and develop leadership in the Canadian financial services consumer movement.

Broadcasting

Audio Engineering Society (AES)
AES Toronto Section, PO Box 292, #32E, 223 Pioneer Dr., Kitchner ON N2P 1L9
Tel: 519-894-5308
torontoaes@uex.net
www.torontoaes.org
Social Media:
www.linkedin.com/groups?home=&gid=2023730&trk=anet_ug_hm
Dedicated to audio technology.
Sy Potma, Chair
Jeffery S. Bamford, Secretary
Syberen Potma, Vice Chair

BBM Canada / Sondages BBM
1500 Don Mills Rd., 3rd Fl., Toronto ON M3B 3L7
Tel: 416-445-9800; *Fax:* 416-445-8644
info@bbm.ca
www.bbm.ca
To provide broadcast measurement & consumer behaviour data to broadcasters, advertisers, & agencies
Glen Shipp, Executive Vice-President & CFO
Lisa Eaton, Senior Vice-President, Member Engagement
Anna Giagkou, Vice-President, Finance
Ricardo Gomez-Insausti, Vice-President, Research
Jane Hill, Vice-President, Operations
Randy Missen, Vice-President, Technical Implementation
Dorena Quinn, Vice-President, Human Resources & Corporate Services

Broadcast Executives Society (BES)
#100-170, 2 Bloor St. West, Toronto ON M4W 3E2
Tel: 416-413-3870; *Fax:* 416-413-3878
admin@bes.ca
www.bes.ca
To serve as forum for the broadcast industry.

John Tucker, Administrator

Broadcast Research Council of Canada (BRC)
#1005, 160 Bloor St. East, Toronto ON M4W 1B9
Tel: 416-413-3864; *Fax:* 416-413-3879
brc@tvb.ca
www.brc.ca
To provide a forum for presentations relating to the broadcast advertising business; to provide awards to the most promising students at colleges that train people to enter the advertising business.
Eva Tolkunow, President

Canadian Association of Broadcasters (CAB) / Association canadienne des radiodiffuseurs (ACR)
PO Box 627, Stn. B, #700, 45 O'Connor St., Ottawa ON K1P 1A4
Tel: 613-233-4035; *Fax:* 613-233-6961
cab@cab-acr.ca
www.cab-acr.ca
To act as the national voice of Canada's private broadcasters
Sylvie Courtemanche, Chair
Sylvie Bissonnette, Chief Financial Officer & Vice-President, Finance & Administration

Canadian Association of Ethnic (Radio) Broadcasters (CAEB) / Association canadienne des radiodiffuseurs ethniques
c/o CHIN Radio, #400, 622 College St., Toronto ON M6G 1B6
Tel: 416-531-9991; *Fax:* 416-531-5274
info@chinradio.com
www.chinradio.com
To foster & promote the development of multilingual / multicultural radio broadcasting in Canada
Lenny Lombardi, President

Canadian Broadcast Distribution Association (CBDA) / Association canadienne de distribution de radiodiffusion
#100, 2233 Argentia Rd., Mississauga ON L5N 2X7
Tel: 905-826-3451; *Fax:* 905-826-4873
info@cbda.ca
www.cbda.ca
The Association fosters interoperability of broadcasting services across multiple distribution platforms, facilitate the exchange of information on critical technical operational matters of interest to its members and provide education on topical issues.

Friends of Canadian Broadcasting (FCB)
#200-238, 131 Bloor St. West, Toronto ON M5S 1R8
Tel: 416-968-7496; *Fax:* 416-968-7406
friends@friends.ca
www.friends.ca
Social Media: twitter.com/friendscb
To defend & enhance the quality & quantity of Canadian programming in the Canadian audio-visual system
Ian Morrison, Spokesperson

National Campus & Community Radio Association (NCRA) / Association nationale des radio étudiantes et communautaires (ANREC)
#230, 325 Dalhousie, Ottawa ON K1N 7G2
Tel: 613-321-1440; *Fax:* 613-321-1442
Toll-Free: 866-859-8086
office@ncra.ca
www.ncra.ca
To encourage development of community & student radio in Canada by providing core services to community-oriented radios & representing them to government, industry & the public
Catherine Fisher, President
Shelley Robinson, Executive Director

Ontario Association of Broadcasters (OAB)
PO Box 54040, 5762 Hwy. 7 East, Markham ON L3P 7Y4
Tel: 905-554-2730; *Fax:* 905-554-2731
memberservices@oab.ca
www.oab.ca
Doug Kirk, President
Valerie Skivington, Administrator

Radio Advisory Board of Canada (RABC) / Conseil consultatif canadien de la radio
#811, 116 Albert St., Ottawa ON K1P 5G3
Tel: 613-230-3261; *Toll-Free:* 888-902-5768
rabc.gm@on.aibn.com
www.rabc-cccr.ca
An association of organizations which are concerned with the use of the radio spectrum; these in turn represent the users of radio communications & related service providers, manufacturers, & professional societies; its purpose is to consult & advise Industry Canada on behalf of industry on the development, management, & regulation of radio services in Canada

Roger Poirier, General Manager
Ron Coles, President

Radio Amateurs of Canada Inc. (RAC) / Radio Amateurs du Canada inc.
#217, 720 Belfast Rd., Ottawa ON K1G 0Z5
Tel: 613-244-4367; *Fax:* 613-244-4369
Toll-Free: 877-273-8304
rachq@rac.ca
www.rac.ca
To act as coordinating body of amateur radio organizations in Canada, liaison agency between members & other amateur organizations in Canada & other countries, coordinating & advisory agency between members & industry Canada; to promote interests of amateur radio operators through program of technical & general education in amateur matters
Geoff Bawden, President
Paul Burggraaf, Secretary

Radio Television News Directors' Association (Canada) (RTNDA Canada) / Association canadienne des directeurs de l'information en radio-télévision
#310, 2175 Sheppard Ave. East, Toronto ON M2J 1W8
Tel: 416-756-2213; *Fax:* 416-491-1670
Toll-Free: 877-257-8632
info@rtndacanada.com
www.rtndacanada.com
Social Media: www.facebook.com/group.php?gid=2366031327
RTNDA Canada is the voice of electronic journalists. It sets the standards for the field of broadcast journalism, fosters high standards of electronic news presentation, & promotes the free flow of information.
Andy LeBlanc, President
Sherry Denesha, Operations Manager

Television Bureau of Canada, Inc. (TVB) / Bureau de la télévision du Canada
#1005, 160 Bloor St. East, Toronto ON M4W 1B9
Tel: 416-923-8813; *Fax:* 416-413-3879
Toll-Free: 800-231-0051
tvb@tvb.ca
www.tvb.ca
To promote sales, marketing & research of commercial television industry in Canada
Duncan Robertson, Manager, Resource Centre
Theresa Treutler, President & CEO
Rhonda-Lynn Bagnall, Manager, Telecaster Services

Western Association of Broadcast Engineers
#300, 8120 Beddington Blvd. NW, Calgary AB T3K 2A8
Tel: 403-630-4907; *Fax:* 403-295-3135
info@wabe.ca
www.wabe.ca
Laverne Siemens, President

Women in Film & Television - Toronto
#601, 110 Eglinton Ave. East, Toronto ON M4P 2Y1
Tel: 416-322-3430; *Fax:* 416-322-3703
wift@wift.com
www.wift.com
To provide year-round training programs, industry events, & professional awards for women & men in Canadian screen based media
Susan Ross, Chair
Sadia Zaman, Executive Director

Youth Media Alliance (AMJ) / Alliance Médias Jeunesse (AET)
#107, 1400, boul René-Lévesque est, Montréal QC H2L 2M2
Tel: 514-597-5417; *Fax:* 514-597-5205
www.ymamj.org
Social Media: www.facebook.com/pages/Youth-Media-Alliance/150380741707933?sk=wall
To promote the production & carriage of quality Canadian television programming for children; to ensure the development of critical viewing skills so that families are able to use media more effectively in the home; to promote awareness of the need to help young people make the most of their experience of television & other screen-based media
Caroline Fortier, Executive Director

Building & Construction

Aggregate Producers' Association of Ontario (APAO)
#2, 365 Brunel Rd., Mississauga ON L4Z 1Z5
Tel: 905-507-0711; *Fax:* 905-507-0717
Moreen Miller, President

Alberta Construction Association (ACA)
18012 - 107 Ave., Edmonton AB T5S 2J5
Tel: 780-455-1122; *Fax:* 780-451-2152
info@abconst.org
www.albertaconstruction.net
Ken Gibson, Executive Director
Shelley Andrea, Director, Administration

Alberta Ready Mixed Concrete Association (ARMCA)
9653 - 45 Ave., Edmonton AB T6E 5Z8
Tel: 780-436-5645; *Fax:* 780-436-6503
armca@telus.net
www.armca.net
To provide industry representation for the advancement of quality concrete in Alberta; To market & promote the use of concrete; To provide a consolidated industry approach to regulatory bodies; To provide networking opportunities; to provide education & training
Laura Andre, Executive Director

Alberta Roadbuilders & Heavy Construction Association (ARHCA)
#201, 9333 - 45 Ave., Edmonton AB T6E 5Z7
Tel: 780-436-9860; *Fax:* 780-436-4910
Toll-Free: 866-436-9860
administration@arhca.ab.ca
www.arhca.ab.ca
Gene Syvenky, Chief Executive Officer
Kimberley Barrett, Director, Finance & Administration
Heidi Harris-Jensen, Director, External Affairs
Dawn Fenske, Coordinator, Communications

Alberta Roofing Contractors Association (ARCA)
2380 Pegasus Rd. NE, Calgary AB T2E 8G8
Tel: 403-250-7055; *Fax:* 403-250-1702
Toll-Free: 800-382-8515
info@arcaonline.ca
www.arcaonline.ca
To provide continuing education for roofing contractors, their personnel & interested others; to represent the roofing contracting industry in its relationships with legislative & regulating bodies; to work closely with affiliate organizations & liaison groups in advancing professionalism of roofing contracting; to provide a forum for interaction of members; to encourage high standards of professional conduct among roofing contractors; to develop a comprehensive body of knowledge about roofing management & technology, & disseminate ideas & knowledge to members & others; to monitor new products & systems; to work for cooperation & greater understanding between contracting, inspection, manufacturing & supply segments of the roofing industry

Architectural Woodwork Manufacturers Association of British Columbia (AWMA-BC)
#101, 4238 Lozells Ave., Burnaby BC V5A 0C4
Tel: 604-298-3555; *Fax:* 604-298-3558
bc.awmac.org
To advance the highest standards of education, quality workmanship, warranties & business practices in architectural woodwork manufacturing in British Columbia
Mike Harskamp, President

Architectural Woodwork Manufacturers Association of Canada (AWMAC)
516 - 4 St. West, High River AB T1V 1B6
Tel: 403-652-7685; *Fax:* 403-652-7384
info@awmac.com
www.awmac.com
To foster & advance the interests of those who are engaged in or who are directly or indirectly connected with or affected by the production & installation of architectural woodwork; to endeavour to achieve a closer relationship & a better understanding among the various branches of the industry
Rick Koehn, Vice-President
Frank VanDonzel, Secretary/Manager
Myron Jonzon, President

Architectural Woodwork Manufacturers Association of Canada - Manitoba
1447 Waverly St., Winnipeg MB R3T 0P7
manitoba@awmac.com
www.awmac.com
To foster and advance the intersts of those who are engaged in or who are directly or indirectly connected with or affected by the production and installation of architectural woodwork; to endeavor to achieve a closer relationship and a better understanding among the various branches of the industry.
Curtis Popel, President
Richard Wroblewski, Vice-President
Nancy Carpenter, Secretary
Greg Pallone, Treasurer

Architectural Woodwork Manufacturers Association of Canada - Northern Alberta
c/o Beyersbergen Interiors, 15327 - 116 Ave., Edmonton AB T5M 3Z5
Tel: 780-906-9399; *Fax:* 780-456-1050
northernalberta@awmac.com
To foster and advance the interests of those who are engaged in or who are directly or indirectly connected with or affected by the production and installation of architrcutural woodwork; to endeavor to achieve a closer relationship and a better understanding among the various branches of the industry.
Joseph George, President

Architectural Woodwork Manufacturers Association of Canada - Ontario Chapter (AWMAC-ON)
70 Leek Cres., Richmond Hill ON L4B 1H1
Tel: 416-499-4000; *Fax:* 416-499-8752
info@awmacontario.com
www.awmacontario.com
To foster & advance the interests of those engaged in the production & installation of architectural woodwork in Ontario
Micah Gingrich, Secretary-Treasurer

Architectural Woodwork Manufacturers Association of Canada - Saskatchewan
PO Box 26032, Stn. Lawson Heights, Saskatoon SK S7K 8C1
Tel: 306-652-2704; *Fax:* 306-664-2552
awmac.sask@sasktel.net
www.awmac.com
To foster and advance the interests of those who are engaged in or who are directly or indirectly connected with or affected by the production and installation of architectural woodwork; to endeavor to achieve a closer relationship and a better understanding among the various branches of the Ibirary.
Kerry DePape, President

Architectural Woodwork Manufacturers Association of Canada - Southern Alberta
PO Box 40124, #02A, 4803 Centre St. NW, Calgary AB T2G 5G5
Tel: 403-264-5979; *Fax:* 403-652-7384
southernalberta@awmac.com
www.awmac.com/chapters-home.php?region=sa
The Association works to advance the interests of those related to the production & installation of architectural woodwork. It endeavors to foster a closer relationship among the various branches of the industry.
Rod Roll, President
Rob Hodgins, Secretary
Larry White, AWNAC Director

Association de la construction du Québec (ACQ) / Construction Association of Québec
9200, boul Métropolitain est, Anjou QC H1K 4L2
Tél: 514-354-0609; *Téléc:* 514-354-8292
Ligne sans frais: 888-868-3424
info@prov.acq.org
www.acq.org
Média social: www.facebook.com/ACQprovinciale
Promotion et défense des intérêts des entreprises de construction, de gestionnaire de plans de garantie des bâtiments résidentiels neufs (Qualité Habitation) et d'agent patronal négociateur pour tous les employeurs des secteurs institutionnel/commercial et industriel (IC/I)
Jean Pouliot, Président
Manon Bertrand, Vice-présidente, IC/I
Marc Dugré, Vice-président, Finances
René Hamel, Vice-président, Habitation
Laberge Yvan, Vice-président, Régions

Association des constructeurs de routes et grands travaux du Québec (ACRGTQ) / Québec Road Builders & Heavy Construction Association
435, av Grande-Allée est, Québec QC G1R 2J5
Tél: 418-529-2949; *Téléc:* 418-529-5139
Ligne sans frais: 800-463-4672
acrgtq@acrgtq.qc.ca
www.acrgtq.qc.ca
Défendre les intérêts des entrepreneurs en génie civil et voirie du Québec
Stéphane Gauthier, Président
Maître Gisèle Bourque, Directrice générale
François Lefebvre, Trésorier

Association des entrepreneurs en construction du Québec (AECQ) / Association of Building Contractors of Québec (ABCQ)
#101, 7905, boul Louis-H. Lafontaine, Anjou QC H1K 4E4
Tél: 514-353-5151; *Téléc:* 514-353-6689
Ligne sans frais: 800-361-4304
info@aecq.org
www.aecq.org
Étudier, promouvoir, protéger et défendre les intérêts des employeurs en matière de relations de travail; négocier les clauses du tronc commun à chacune des quatre conventions collectives sectorielles
Pierre Dion, Directeur général

Association des maîtres couvreurs du Québec (AMCQ) / Québec Master Roofers Association
3001, boul Tessier, Laval QC H7S 2M1
Tél: 450-973-2322; *Téléc:* 450-973-2321
Ligne sans frais: 888-973-2322
info@amcq.qc.ca
www.amcq.qc.ca
Promouvoir les intérêts généraux des entreprises de couvertures et ceux de diverses entreprises des secteurs connexes dans la province de Québec; promouvoir la hausse de la qualité des travaux de couvertures
François Morissette, Vice-président exécutif

Association québécoise de la quincaillerie et des matériaux de construction (AQMAT) / The Building Materials Retailers Association of Québec
#200, 476, rue Jean-Neveu, Longueuil QC J4G 1N8
Tél: 450-646-5842; *Téléc:* 450-646-6171
www.aqmat.org
Promouvoir l'intérêt général de ses membres-clients engagés dans la vente au détail de matériaux de construction et de quincaillerie, en leur offrant une panoplie de produits et services visant à faciliter la gestion de leurs commerces, des Québécois et la rénovation
Richard Darveau, Président-directeur général

Atlantic Building Supply Dealers Association (ABSDA)
70 Englehart St., Dieppe NB E1A 8H3
Tel: 506-858-0700; *Fax:* 506-859-0064
Toll-Free: 800-561-7114
absda@nbnet.nb.ca
www.absda.ca
To keep membership informed of new trends & developments in the industry; to provide a forum to discuss mutual problems & ideas; to provide continuing education programs for members
Don Sherwood, President
Pamela Brennan, Chair

Atlantic Provinces Ready-Mixed Concrete Association (APRMCA) / Association des fabricants de béton préparé des provinces atlantiques
30 Damascus Rd., Bedford NS B4A 0C1
Tel: 902-443-4456; *Fax:* 902-429-6696
info@atlanticconcrete.ca
www.aprmca.com
To promote the use of ready-mixed concrete while providing leadership to the industry through the exchange of ideas & information.
Mary Macaulay, Executive Director

British Columbia Construction Association (BCCA)
#401, 655 Tyee Rd., Victoria BC V9A 6X5
Tel: 250-475-1077; *Fax:* 250-475-1078
www.bccassn.com
To provide excellence in the representation of & service to British Columbia's construction industry
Manley McLachlan, President & Chief Executive Officer
Abigail Fulton, Vice-President, Government Relations
Warren Perks, Vice-President & Director, Industry Practices
Colleen McConnell, Director, Marketing & Communications
Paul Mitchell, Manager, Special Projects

British Columbia Construction Association - North (BCCA-N)
3851 - 18 Ave., Prince George BC V2N 1B1
Tel: 250-563-1744; *Fax:* 250-563-1107
kkrenzler@nbcca.bc.ca
www.nbcca.bc.ca
To act as a united voice on behalf of all sectors of the construction industry on concerns of the industry; To promote education, training, safety, standard practices, high standards, & investment in the construction industry of northern British Columbia
Rosalind Thorn, President
Sue Zacharias, Chair
Bonnie Griffith, Secretary
Ken Morland, Treasurer

British Columbia Ready Mixed Concrete Association
26162 - 30A Ave., Aldergrove BC V4W 2W5
Tel: 604-626-4141; *Fax:* 604-626-4143
ccampbell@bcrmca.bc.ca
www.bcrmca.bc.ca
To work cooperatively with all levels of government to ensure the ready-mix concrete industry operates with a focus on the communities & the environment
Carolyn Campbell, Executive Director

British Columbia Road Builders & Heavy Construction Association (BCRB&HCA)
#307, 8678 Greenall Ave., Burnaby BC V5J 3M6
Tel: 604-436-0220; *Fax:* 604-436-2627
info@roadbuilders.bc.ca
www.roadbuilders.bc.ca
To represent the interests of member companies to government, media, other organizations, & the public
Jack W. Davidson, President
Jackson Yu, Administrator
Kate Cockerill, Manager, Communications & Membership

Building Supply Industry Association of British Columbia (BSIA of BC)
#2, 19299 - 94th Ave., Surrey BC V4N 4E6
Tel: 604-513-2205; *Fax:* 604-513-2206
Toll-Free: 888-711-5656
www.bsiabc.ca
To act as the official voice of the building supply industry in British Columbia; To provide services to members
Thomas Foreman, President
Marijoel Chamberlain, Coordinator, Member Services, & Manager, Trade Show
Jackie Trafton, Administrator

Canadian Concrete Masonry Producers Association (CCMPA)
PO Box 1345, 1500 Avenue Rd., Toronto ON M5M 3X0
Tel: 416-495-7497; *Fax:* 416-495-8939
Toll-Free: 888-495-7497
information@ccmpa.ca
www.ccmpa.ca
Works on behalf of concrete masonry producers to build an industry as strong and as enduring as the products it manufactures
Marina de Souza, Managing Director

Canadian Concrete Pipe Association (CCPA) / Association canadienne des fabricants de tuyaux de béton (ACTB)
205 Miller Dr., Halton Hills ON L7G 6G4
Tel: 905-877-5369; *Fax:* 905-877-5369
info@ccpa.com
www.ccpa.com
Social Media:
www.facebook.com/group.php?gid=106265401921
To coordinate research & development, promotion, education & federal government relations programs pertaining to the marketing of high quality precast concrete waste water & storm drainage products in Canada.
John Greer, Chair

Canadian Construction Association (CCA) / Association canadienne de la construction (ACC)
275 Slater St., 19th Fl., Ottawa ON K1P 5H9
Tel: 613-236-9455; *Fax:* 613-236-9526
cca@cca-acc.com
www.cca-acc.com
To act as the national voice of the construction industry; To serve, promote, & enhance the construction industry by acting on behalf of its members in matters of national concern
Michael Atkinson, President
Pierre Boucher, Chief Operating Officer
Eric Lee, Senior Director, Industry Practices
Mark Belton, Director, Finance
Bill Ferreira, Director, Government Relations & Public Affairs
Chantal Montpetit, Director, Meetings & Conferences
Kirsi O'Connor, Director, Marketing & Communications
Aneel Rangi, Director, Legal & Research Services

Canadian Masonry Contractors' Association (CMCA)
Canada Masonry Centre, 360 Superior Blvd., Mississauga ON L5T 2N7
Tel: 905-564-6622; *Fax:* 905-564-5744
www.canadamasonrycentre.com/cmca
CMCA works to advance masonry technology, skills development & the use of masonry products in construction across Canada. It provides managerial, technical, accounting & financial, promotional, marketing, & other services to organizations serving the masonry industry.

Canadian Paint & Coatings Association (CPCA) / Association canadienne de l'industrie de la peinture et du revêtement
#608, 170 Laurier Ave. West, Ottawa ON K1P 5V5
Tel: 613-231-3604; *Fax:* 613-231-4908
cpca@cdnpaint.org
www.cdnpaint.org
To represent the paint industry among the provincial, federal & municipal governments
Dale Constantinoff, Chair

Canadian Precast / Prestressed Concrete Institute (CPCI) / Institut canadien du béton préfabriqué et précontraint
#100, 196 Bronson Ave., Ottawa ON K1R 6H4
Tel: 613-232-2619; *Fax:* 613-232-5139
Toll-Free: 877-937-2724
info@cpci.ca
www.cpci.ca
To stimulate & advance the common interests & general welfare of the structural precast/prestressed concrete industry, the architectural precast concrete industry & the post-tensioned concrete industry in Canada
Rob Burak, President

Canadian Ready Mixed Concrete Association (CRMCA) / Association canadienne du béton préparé
#3, 365 Brunel Rd., Mississauga ON L4Z 1Z5
Tel: 905-507-1122; *Fax:* 905-890-8122
www.crmca.ca

Canadian Roofing Contractors' Association (CRCA) / Association canadienne des entrepreneurs en couverture (ACEC)
#100, 2430 Don Reid Dr., Ottawa ON K1H 1E1
Tel: 613-232-6724; *Fax:* 613-232-2893
Toll-Free: 800-461-2722
crca@on.aibn.com
www.roofingcanada.com
CRCA consists of companies actively engaged in Canada in the roofing and related sheet metal contracting business, along with companies engaged in manufactoring or supplying materials and services used in any branch of the rooofing and sheet metal industry.
John E. Hill, Executive Director

Canadian Welding Bureau (CWB)
8260 Parkhill Dr., Milton ON L9T 5V7
Tel: 905-542-1312; *Fax:* 905-542-1318
Toll-Free: 800-844-6790
info@cwbgroup.org
www.cwbgroup.org
CWB is a not-for-profit organization serving the welding & joining industry. It administers certification programs for CSA Standards W47.1, W47.2, W186, W178.1 & W48 series. It also provides support for welding-based programs in schools, education institutions, welding professionals & companies employing welding technology.
J. Doria, Chair
Douglas Luciano, President

Cement Association of Canada (CAC) / Association canadienne du ciment
#502, 350 Sparks St., Ottawa ON K1R 7S8
Tel: 613-236-9471; *Fax:* 613-563-4498
www.cement.ca
Represents all of Canada's cement producers; aims to improve & extend the uses of cement & concrete through market development, engineering, research, education, & public affairs work
Michael McSweeney, President & CEO

Construction Association of New Brunswick Inc. (CANB)
59 Avonlea Ct., Fredericton NB E3C 1N8
Tel: 506-459-5770; *Fax:* 506-457-1913
canb1@nbnet.nb.ca
www.constructnb.ca
CANB is designed to perform a co-ordinating function for reaching consensus to effectively present the Industry's collective views to various client groups, partic-ularly to relevant departments and agencies of the provincial government.
Hilary Howes, Executive Director

Construction Association of Nova Scotia
Parkway Pl., City of Lakes Business Park, #3, 260 Brownlow Ave., Dartmouth NS B3B 1V9
Tel: 902-468-2267; *Fax:* 902-468-2470
cans@cans.ns.ca
www.cans.ns.ca

The Construction Association of Nova Scotia (CANS) is an industry trade association representing contractors, suppliers and service providers comprising the non-residential construction industry. CANS was founded in 1862 as the Halifax Builders' Society. Since that time, CANS membership has grown to include firms from all over Atlantic Canada as well as other regions of the country. The primary role of CANS is to represent the interests of our 600 member companies.
Carol MacCulloch, President
Donna Cruickshank, Office Manager

Construction Association of Prince Edward Island (CAPEI)
PO Box 728, #223, 40 Enman Cres., Charlottetown PE C1E 1E6
Tel: 902-368-3303; *Fax:* 902-894-9757
admin@capei.ca
www.capei.ca
To foster, promote & advance the interests & efficiency of Prince Edward Island's construction industry
Ross D. Barnes, General Manager
Craig Ling, President

Construction Specifications Canada (CSC) / Devis de construction Canada
#312, 120 Carlton St., Toronto ON M5A 4K2
Tel: 416-777-2198; *Fax:* 416-777-2197
info@csc-dcc.ca
www.csc-dcc.ca
To improve communication, contract documentation, & technical information in the construction industry
Bruce Gillham, President

Council of Ontario Construction Associations (COCA)
#2001, 180 Dundas St. West, Toronto ON M5G 1Z8
Tel: 416-968-7200; *Fax:* 416-968-0362
info@coca.on.ca
www.coca.on.ca
To contribute to the long-term growth & profitability of the construction industry in Ontario; To speak with a unified voice to government, the industry & the public.
Ian Cunningham, President

Glass & Architectural Metals Association (GAMA)
c/o Calgary Construction Association, 2725 - 12 St. NE, Calgary AB T2E 7J2
To advance the glass & architectural metals industry
Al Ryland, President
Becky McLaughlin, Treasurer & Contact, Membership

Infrastructure Health & Safety Association (IHSA)
#400, 5110 Creekbank Rd., Mississauga ON L4W 0A1
Tel: 905-625-0100; *Fax:* 905-625-8998
Toll-Free: 800-263-5024
info@ihsa.ca
www.ihsa.ca
IHSA is part of Health & Safety Ontario. It has advisory councils that cover transportation, residential, general ICI, heavy civil & aggregates, mechanical, electrical & priority rates. IHSA cooperates with employers & workers to eliminate occupational injury & illness by offering training programs, auditing & consulting services, in addition to health & safety resources.
Al Beatie, Interim President
Donald E. Dickie, Executive Vice-President/General Manager

Lumber & Building Materials Association of Ontario (LBMAO)
#27, 5155 Spectrum Way, Mississauga ON L4W 5A1
Tel: 905-625-1084; *Fax:* 905-625-3006
Toll-Free: 888-365-2626
www.lbmao.on.ca
To promote the welfare of members so that they are able to build a competitive advantage & remain at the leading edge of the lumber & building materials industry
David W. Campbell, President
Bob Lockwood, Chair
Dwayne Sprague, Vice-Chair

Manitoba Heavy Construction Association (MHCA)
#3, 1680 Ellice Ave., Winnipeg MB R3G 0Z2
Tel: 204-947-1379; *Fax:* 204-943-2279
info@mhca.mb.ca
www.mhca.mb.ca
Social Media: twitter.com/ManitobaHeavy
To promote a safe workplace for employees in Manitoba's heavy construction industry; To represent the heavy construction industry in Manitoba
Christopher Lorenc, President
Wendy Greund Summerfield, Manager, Finance
Greg Huff, Manager, MHC Training Academy
Christine Miller, Manager, Events & Membership
Jason Rosin, Manager, Communications

Manitoba Ready Mixed Concrete Association Inc. (MRMCA)
169 Kingston Row, Winnipeg MB R2M 0T1
Tel: 204-667-8539; *Fax:* 204-237-5075
info@mrmca.com
www.mrmca.com
To represent the concrete industry in Manitoba; To advance the quality of concrete in Manitoba

Master Insulators' Association of Ontario Inc.
Building 1, #101, 2600 Skymark Ave., Mississauga ON L4W 5B2
Tel: 905-279-6426; *Fax:* 905-279-6422
manager@miaontario.org
www.miaontario.org
Malcolm D. Haylock, Office Manager

Master Painters & Decorators Association (MPDA)
2800 Ingleton Ave., Burnaby BC V5C 6G7
Tel: 604-298-7578; *Fax:* 604-298-5183
Toll-Free: 888-674-8708
info@paintinfo.com
www.paintinfo.com/assoc/mpda/
To set & raise standards of industrial organizations
Greg Boshard, President
Alan Kelly, Vice President

Mechanical Contractors Association of Alberta
#204, 2725 - 12 St. NE, Calgary AB T2E 7J2
Tel: 403-250-7237; *Fax:* 403-291-0551
Toll-Free: 800-251-0620
www.mcaalberta.com
To promote plumbing & mechanical contractors; to provide educational programs to foster improved management & productivity in mechanical contracting; to represent mechanical contractors with their various publics - governments, design authorities, labour; to foster professional advancement & profitability of the plumbing, heating & mechanical contracting industry through its member services
Hans Tiedemann, Executive Director

Mechanical Contractors Association of British Columbia (MCABC)
#223, 3989 Henning Dr., Burnaby BC V5C 6N5
Tel: 604-205-5058; *Fax:* 604-205-5075
Toll-Free: 800-663-8473
www.mcabc.org
To encourage, support & promote the advancement of the mechanical contracting industry; to provide leadership, assistance & training to members.
Dana Taylor, Executive Vice President

Mechanical Contractors Association of Canada (MCAC) / Association des entrepreneurs en mécanique du Canada
#601, 280 Albert St., Ottawa ON K1P 5G8
Tel: 613-232-0492; *Fax:* 613-235-2793
mcac@mcac.ca
www.mcac.ca
To promote plumbing & mechanical contractors; to provide educational programs to foster improved management & productivity in mechanical contracting; to represent mechanical contractors to their various publics - governments, design authorities, labour.
Richard McKeagan, President

Mechanical Contractors Association of Manitoba (MCAM)
#1, 860 Bradford St., Winnipeg MB R3H 0N5
Tel: 204-774-2404; *Fax:* 204-772-0233
mcam@mts.net
www.mca-mb.com
To continually improve mechanical industry standards while providing a high level of value performance & customer service for our members
Betty McInerney, Executive Director

Mechanical Contractors Association of New Brunswick / Association des entrepreneurs en mécanique du N.-B.
c/o Moncton Northeast Construction Association, 297 Collishaw St., Moncton NB E1C 9R2
Tel: 506-857-4128; *Fax:* 506-857-8861
info@mneca.ca
www.mneca.ca
To provide leadership & service to members; to act on behalf of members in labour relations matters, including collective bargaining; to advance & develop the industry, primarily in New Brunswick; to endeavour to improve legislation affecting the industry; to promote sound labour relations
Bill Dixon, Executive Director

Mechanical Contractors Association of Newfoundland & Labrador
PO Box 745, Mount Pearl NL A1N 2Y2
Tel: 709-747-5577; *Fax:* 709-368-5342
ddawe@nfld.net
David Dawe, Executive Director

Mechanical Contractors Association of Nova Scotia
c/o Construction Association of Nova Scotia, #3, 260 Brownlow Ave., Dartmouth NS B3B 1V9
Tel: 902-468-2267; *Fax:* 902-468-2470
cans@cans.ns.ca
www.cans.ns.ca
Donna Cruickshank, Manager

Mechanical Contractors Association of Ontario (MCAO)
#103, 10 Director Ct., Woodbridge ON L4L 7E8
Tel: 905-856-0342; *Fax:* 905-856-0385
mcao@mcao.org
www.mcao.org
Steve Coleman, Executive Vice-President

Mechanical Contractors Association of Prince Edward Island
c/o Association of Commercial & Industrial Contractors of PEI, PO Box 1685, Charlottetown PE C1A 7N4
Tel: 902-566-3456; *Fax:* 902-368-2754
wmm@wmm93.pe.ca
Mary MacDonald, Contact

Mechanical Contractors Association of Saskatchewan Inc. (MCAS)
Heritage Business Park, #105, 2750 Faithfull Ave., Saskatoon SK S7K 6M6
Tel: 306-664-2154; *Fax:* 306-653-7233
mca-sask@mca-sask.com
www.mca-sask.com
MCAS is a provincial non-profit, trade association that represents plumbing & heating contractors in relation to the construction industry, legislative departments of municipal & provincial government & other industry-related bodies.
Allan Awrey, President
Judy Nagus, Executive Director

National Building Envelope Council
c/o 5041 Regent St., Burnaby BC V5C 4H4
Tel: 604-473-9587
To pursue excellence in the design, construction & performance of the building envelope
Dominique Derome, President Elect

National Elevator & Escalator Association (NEEA)
#708, 6299 Airport Rd., Mississauga ON L4V 1N3
Tel: 905-678-9940; *Fax:* 905-677-7634
Andrew Reistetter, Executive Director

New Brunswick Roofing Contractors Association, Inc. (NBRCA) / Association des entrepreneurs en couverture du Nouveau-Brunswick
PO Box 7242, 57 King St., 3rd Fl., Saint John NB E2L 4S6
Tel: 506-652-7003; *Fax:* 506-696-0380
info@nbrca.ca
www.nbrca.ca
To protect the public's interest in relation to roofing; To act as the voice of New Brunswick's roofing industry; To facilitate a competent & profitable roofing & sealed membrane system industry in the province; To foster excellence in roofing related activities; to ensure that members uphold the code of ethics
Ron Hutton, Executive Director
Rob Paterson, President
Robert McGinn, Vice-President
Geoff Munn, Secretary
Serge Robichaud, Treasurer

Newfoundland & Labrador Construction Association (NLCA)
#201, 333 Pippy Pl., St. John's NL A1B 3X2
Tel: 709-753-8920; *Fax:* 709-754-3968
info@nfld.com
www.nlca.ca
To act as the voice of the construction industry in Newfoundland & Labrador; To enhance the professionalism & productivity of members through the development of policies
Keith McCarthy, Chair
Rhonda Neary, President & Chief Operating Officer
Frank Collins, Secretary-Treasurer
Susan Casey, Coordinator, Events
Adelle Connors, Coordinator, Member Services

Newfoundland & Labrador Road Builders / Heavy Civil Association (NLRB / HCA)
PO Box 23038, St. John's NL A1B 4J9
Tel: 709-364-8811; *Fax:* 709-364-8812
nlrbhca@nf.aibn.com; bulletin@nfld.com (Road Builders Bulletin)
www.nfld.net/roadbuilders
To act as the voice of the road construction, water & sewer, & heavy construction industries in Newfoundland & Labrador; To develop standard tendering & contractual practices & procedures
Austin Sheppard, Manager, Business
Steve Grainger, President
Brian Johnson, Vice-President
Perry Barrett, Secretary-Treasurer
Perry Barrett, Chair, Sater & Sewer

Northwest Territories Construction Association (NWTCA)
PO Box 2277, 4921 - 49th St., 3rd Fl., Yellowknife NT X1A 2P7
Tel: 867-873-3949; *Fax:* 867-873-8366
director@nwtca.ca
www.nwtca.ca
To act as a voice for construction-related business in the Northwest Territories & Nunavut
Bob Doherty, President
Niels Konge, Vice-President, Northwest Territories
Brent Crooks, Vice-President, Nunavut
Trina Rentmeister, Secretary-Treasurer

Nova Scotia Road Builders Association
#217, 11 Thornhill Dr., Dartmouth NS B3B 1R9
www.nsrba.ca
To speak for the heavy construction industry in Nova Scotia; to liaise with provincial Department of Transportation.
Grant Feltmate, Executive Director
Ken Thomas, President

Ontario Concrete Pipe Association (OCPA)
447 Frederick St., 2nd Fl, Kitchener ON N2H 2P4
Tel: 519-489-4488; *Fax:* 519-578-6060
admin@ocpa.com
www.ocpa.com
To represent the concrete pipe & maintenance hole industry throughout Ontario; to promote engineered concrete products of permanence
Brian Wood, President
Mike Leathers, Vice President
John Munro, Sec.-tres.

Ontario General Contractors Association (OGCA)
#703, 6299 Airport Rd., Mississauga ON L4V 1N3
Tel: 905-671-3969; *Fax:* 905-671-8212
info@ogca.ca
www.ogca.ca
Offers experience and expertise dealing with contracts, architects, engineers and owners
Clive Thurston, President
Mary Wademan, Office Manager

Ontario Industrial Roofing Contractors' Association (OIRCA)
#301, 940 The East Mall, Toronto ON M9B 6J7
Tel: 416-695-4114; *Fax:* 416-695-9920
Toll-Free: 888-336-4722
oirca@ontarioroofing.com
www.ontarioroofing.com
To act as the voice of the industrial-commercial roofing industry in Ontario; To promote excellence in roofing construction
Jim Norman, President
Brian Benham, 1st Vice-President
DaCosta Manuel, Treasurer

Ontario Painting Contractors Association (OPCA)
#305, 211 Consumers Rd., Toronto ON M2J 4G8
Tel: 416-498-1897; *Fax:* 416-498-6757
Toll-Free: 800-461-3630
info@opca.org
www.ontpca.org
To foster, develop & maintain unity & stability among members by acting as a bargaining agent; providing services & educational opportunities; acting as a liaison between industry groups; upholding & improving the standards of the industry; promoting the use of modern specifications; advancing an attitude of ethical responsibility & pride
Thomas Corbett, President
Andrew Sefton, Executive Director

Ontario Pipe Trades Council
Confederation Square, #203, 45 Goderich Rd., Hamilton ON L8E 4W8
Tel: 905-573-3703; *Fax:* 905-573-0804
info@optc.org
www.optc.org
To promote the many technical, commercial & environmental benefits of the Pipe Trades & maximize their use in the construction industry; to promote the interest of the plumbing, pipe fitting, sprinkler fitting & HVAC industry in the province of Ontario
Neil McCormack, Business Manager

Pipe Line Contractors Association of Canada (PLCAC)
#201, 1075 North Service Rd. West, Oakville ON L6M 2G2
Tel: 905-847-9383; *Fax:* 905-847-7824
plcac@pipeline.ca
www.pipeline.ca
To represent contractors in labour relations
O.J. Kavanaugh, President
Neil G. Lane, Executive Director
Michael J. Gallardo, Assistant Executive Director

Prince Edward Island Roadbuilders & Heavy Construction Association
PO Box 1901, Charlottetown PE C1A 7N5
Tel: 902-894-9514; *Fax:* 902-894-9512
pei.roadbuilders@pei.sympatico.ca
www3.pei.sympatico.ca/pei.roadbuilders/
"Prince Edward Island Road Builders and Heavy Construction Association is comprised of companies sharing a common goal — a strong, effective voice in the Heavy Construction Industry. The Association's business is guided by a Board of Directors made up of seven representatives from the Regular Member category and two representatives from the Associate Member category who meet monthly and a Manager who maintains the day-to-day operations on behalf of the membership. We strive to encourage business with our members and promote functions where members can gather and become acquainted as well as profiling businesses in our Newsletter, The Roadrunner."
Joe Murphy, Manager

Ready Mixed Concrete Association of Ontario (RMCAO)
#3, 365 Brunel Rd., Mississauga ON L4Z 1Z5
Tel: 905-507-1122; *Fax:* 905-890-8122
dbiffis@rmcao.org
www.rmcao.org
To promote & further the business, technology & use of quality concrete through partnership between producers & the construction & specifying industries
John D. Hull, President
Bart Kanters, P.Eng., MBA, Director, Technical Services
Ron Monsour, Director, Marketing, Eastern & Northern Ontario
Nancy Chapman, Manager, Administration & Member Services
Mick Prieur, Senior Pavement Engineer

Road Builders Association of New Brunswick (RBANB)
#5, 59 Avonlea Ct., Fredericton NB E3C 1N8
Tel: 506-454-5079; *Fax:* 506-452-7646
rbanb@nb.aibn.com
www.rbanb.com
To foster & enhance relations between the members, & between the members of other associations in construction; to acquire & disseminate information of value to the industry & to its membership; to improve & extend standards, conditions, methods & practices within the industry
Andrew Graham, President
Maurice Albert, Vice-President

Roofing Contractors Association of British Columbia (RCABC)
9734 - 201st St., Langley BC V1M 3E8
Tel: 604-882-9734; *Fax:* 604-882-1744
bporth@rcabc.org
www.rcabc.org
To provide continuing education for roofing contractors, their workers & interested others; to represent the roofing contracting industry in its relationships with legislative & regulating bodies; to work closely with affiliate organizations & liaison groups in advancing the professionalism of roofing contracting; to provide a forum for the interaction of members; to encourage high standards of professional conduct among roofing contractors; to develop a comprehensive body of knowledge about roofing management & technology; to disseminate ideas & knowledge to members & others; to monitor new products & systems; to work for cooperation & greater understanding between contracting, inspection, manufacturing & supply segments of the roofing industry
Ivan van Spronsen, Executive Vice-President

Roofing Contractors Association of Manitoba Inc. (RCAM)
290 Burnell St., Winnipeg MB R3G 2A7
Tel: 204-783-6365; *Fax:* 204-783-6446
info@rcam.ca
www.rcam.ca
R.M. Stefanick, Secretary Manager

Roofing Contractors Association of Nova Scotia (RCANS)
PO Box 141, 7 Frederick Ave., Mount Uniacke NS B0N 1Z0
Tel: 902-866-0505; *Fax:* 902-866-0506
Toll-Free: 888-278-0133
contact@rcans.ca
www.rcans.ca
RCANS is is a trade association promoting quality workmanship in the commerical, industrial & institutional roofing industry. It encourages training for roofers & was instrumental in the initiation of an apprenticeship program.
curtis Turner, President
Marg Woodworth, Office Manager

Saskatchewan Construction Safety Association Inc. (SCSA)
498 Henderson Dr., Regina SK S4N 6E3
Tel: 306-525-0175; *Fax:* 306-525-1542
Toll-Free: 800-817-2079
www.scsaonline.ca
To provide safety programs & servies to construction employers & employees in order to reduce human & financial loss associated with injuries in the construction industry
Bill Johnson, Executive Director
Dan Sherven, Manager, Operations
Kellie Lefebvre, Coordinator, Human Resources & Finance
Linda Rea-Rosseker, Coordinator, Publications & Communications

Saskatchewan Heavy Construction Association
1939 Elphinstone St., Regina SK S4T 3N3
Tel: 306-586-1805; *Fax:* 306-585-3750
slipp@saskheavy.ca
www.saskheavy.com
The Saskatchewan Heavy Construction Association is committed to the heavy construction industry by actively promoting quality, cost-effective, socially responsible services for the public and its members.
Shantel Lipp, President
Monica Faber, Membership Coordinator

Saskatchewan Ready Mixed Concrete Association Inc. (SRMCA)
#203, 1801 McKay St., Regina SK S4N 6E7
Tel: 306-757-2788; *Fax:* 306-569-9144
www.concreteworksharder.com
SRMCA works to maintain the highest quality of concrete produced by its members. It strives to improve the industry in all aspects & represents its members in relation to governments, environmental agencies & other industry-related associations.
Ken Nichols, President
Garth Sanders, Executive Director

Sealant & Waterproofing Association (SWA)
70 Leek Cres., Richmond Hill ON L4B 1H1
Tel: 416-499-4000; *Fax:* 416-499-8752
info@swao.com
www.swao.com
To promote the exchange of ideas for the development of the highest standards & operating efficiency within the sealant & waterproofing industry
Robert J. Montpetit, President
Andrew Porciello, Vice President

Southern Interior Construction Association (SICA)
#104, 151 Commercial Dr., Kelowna BC V1X 7W2
Tel: 250-491-7330; *Fax:* 250-491-3929
kelowna@sica.bc.ca
www.sica.bc.ca
To offer members' plans & specifications for viewing; to promote standard tendering practices
Debra Hicks, President

Terrazzo Tile & Marble Association of Canada (TTMAC) / Association canadienne de terrazzo, tuile et marbre
#8, 163 Buttermill Ave., Concord ON L4K 3X8
Tel: 905-660-9640; *Fax:* 905-660-0513
Toll-Free: 800-201-8599
association@ttmac.com
www.ttmac.com
To standardize terrazzo, tile, marble, & stone installation techniques, so that the industry will grow & proper; To support the hardsurface industry & its members
Elaine Cook, Eastern Editor, The Analyst

Toronto Construction Association
70 Leek Cres., Richmond Hill ON L4B 1H1
Tel: 416-499-4000; *Fax:* 416-499-8752
bmirsky@tcaconnect.com
www.tcaconnect.com
To develop & promote excellence within the construction industry of the Greater Toronto Area
Glenn Ackerkey, Chair
John G. Mollenhauer, President & CEO
Kim F. McKinney, Executive Vice-President

Western Canada Roadbuilders Association
1236 Ellice Ave., Winnipeg MB R3G 0E7
Tel: 204-947-1379; *Fax:* 204-943-2279
clorenc@mhca.mb.ca
www.wcrhca.org
Represents four western provincial roadbuilders & heavy construction associations at the provincial & federal level
Chris Lorenc, President

Western Retail Lumber Association (WRLA)
Western Retail Lumber Association Inc., #1004, 213 Notre Dame Ave., Winnipeg MB R3B 1N3
Tel: 204-957-1077; *Fax:* 204-947-5195
Toll-Free: 800-661-0253
wrla@wrla.org
www.wrla.org
To serve & promote needs & common interests of lumber, building materials & hard goods industry on the Prairies
Gary Hamilton, Executive Director
Dwight Dixon, President

Winnipeg Construction Association
290 Burnell St., Winnipeg MB R3G 2A7
Tel: 204-775-8664; *Fax:* 204-783-6446
wca@winnipegconstruction.ca
www.winnipegconstruction.ca
John Schubert, President
Ronald Hambley, Executive Vice-President

Business

Association for Corporate Growth, Toronto Chapter (ACG)
720 Spadina Ave, Toronto ON M5S 2T9
Tel: 416-868-1881; *Fax:* 416-860-0580
acgtoronto@acg.org
www.acg.org/toronto
To foster sound corporate growth by providing its members with an opportunity to gain new ideas from speakers, seminars & discussions with people working in the field of corporate growth; to develop additional skills & techniques which will contribute to the growth of their respective organizations; to meet other corporate growth professionals who can provide counsel & valuable contacts
Thomas Kaddour, Administrator
Gary A. LaBranche, President

Better Business Bureau of Central & Northern Alberta
Capitol Place, #888, 9707 - 110 St., Edmonton AB T5K 2L9
Tel: 780-482-2341; *Fax:* 780-482-1150
Toll-Free: 800-232-7298
info@edmontonbbb.org
www.edmonton.bbb.org
To handle inquiries & complaints; To provide an ad review program; To educate the public
Chris Lawrence, President & CEO

Better Business Bureau of Eastern & Northern Ontario & the Outaouais / Bureau d'éthique commerciale de l'Est et Nord de l'Ontario et l'Outaouais
#505, 700 Industrial Ave., Ottawa ON K1G 0Y9
Tel: 613-237-4856; *Fax:* 613-237-4878
info@ottawa.bbb.org; accreditation@ottawa.bbb.org
www.ottawa.bbb.org
To promote & foster the highest ethical relationship between business & the public through voluntary self regulation, consumer & business education, & service excellence
Spencer Nimmons, Vice-President, Business Relations

Better Business Bureau of Manitoba & Northwest Ontario
1030B Empress St., Winnipeg MB R3G 3H4
Tel: 204-989-9010; *Fax:* 204-989-9016
Toll-Free: 800-385-3074
bbbinquiries@mts.net
www.manitoba.bbb.org
To encourage ethical business practices through self-regulation in Manitoba.
Amaro Silva, Manager

Better Business Bureau of Mid-Western Ontario
354 Charles St., Kitchener ON N2G 4L5
Tel: 519-579-3080; *Fax:* 519-570-0072
Toll-Free: 800-459-8875
www.kitchener.bbb.org
To encourage ethical business practices through self-regulation in Mid-Western Ontario.
Ric Borski, President

Better Business Bureau of Newfoundland
#301, 360 Topsail Rd., St. John's NL A1E 2B6
Tel: 709-364-2222; *Fax:* 709-364-2255
Toll-Free: 877-663-2363
info@bbbnl.org
www.nl.bbb.org
To promote and foster the highest ethical relationships between business and the public through voluntary self-regulation, consumer and business education and service excellence.
Glenn Sullivan, President

Better Business Bureau of Saskatchewan
980 Albert St., Regina SK S4R 7601
Tel: 306-352-7601; *Fax:* 306-565-6236
Toll-Free: 888-352-7601
info@bbbsask.com
www.sask.bbb.org
To be devoted to the vitality of the free enterprise system & the concerns of the consumer public; To develop, encourage, & promote an ethical marketplace
Danny Berehula, Executive Director

Better Business Bureau of Southern Alberta
#350, 7330 Fisher St. SE, Calgary AB T2H 2H8
Tel: 403-531-8784; *Fax:* 403-640-2514
Toll-Free: 800-661-4464
info@calgary.bbb.org
www.calgary.bbb.org
To promote & encourage ethical practices in retail market for goods & services through provision of a wide range of consultative, informative & conciliatory arbitration services for businesses & consumers.
Ellen Wright, President

Better Business Bureau of the Maritime Provinces
#805, 1888 Brunswick St., Halifax NS B3J 3J8
Tel: 902-422-6581; *Fax:* 902-429-6457
bbbmp@bbbmp.ca
www.maritimeprovinces.bbb.org
To provide mutually beneficial relationships between buyer & seller based on responsible business practices
Don MacKinnon, President

Better Business Bureau of Vancouver Island
#220, 1175 Cook St., Victoria BC V8V 4A1
Tel: 250-386-6348; *Fax:* 250-386-2367
Toll-Free: 877-826-4222
info@vi.bbb.org
vi.bbb.org
Committed to the principle that fair dealing is good business for both buyer & seller & the majority of buyers & sellers are honest & responsible
Vern Fischer, President
Rosalind Scott, Executive Director

Better Business Bureau of Western Ontario
PO Box 2153, #308, 200 Queens Ave., London ON N6A 4E3
Tel: 519-673-3222; *Toll-Free:* 877-283-9222
info@westernontario.bbb.org;
complaints@westernontario.bbb.org
www.westernontario.bbb.org
To promote the vitality of the free enterprise system & ethical business practices; To serve the concerns of business & the consuming public
Jan Delaney, President
Chris Lavoie, Manager, Operations
Marlene Aquilina-Bock, Coordinator, Business Development

Better Business Bureau of Windsor & Southwestern Ontario
#302, 880 Ouellette Ave., Windsor ON N9A 1C7
Tel: 519-258-7222; *Fax:* 519-258-1198
bbb@bbbwindsor.com
www.windsorbbb.com
Thier mission is to promote and foster the highest ethical relationship between businesses and the public through voluntary self-regulation, consumer and business education, and service education.

Better Business Bureau Serving South Central Ontario
100 James St. South, Hamilton ON L8P 2Z2
Tel: 905-526-1111; *Fax:* 905-526-1225
info@thebbb.ca, membership@thebbb.ca
www.thebbb.ca
Their mission is to develop, encourage, and promote an ethical marketplace. Their mission is to promote and foster the highest ethical relationship between businessess and the public through voluntary self-regulation, consumer and business education and service excellence.

Business Council of British Columbia
#810, 1050 Pender St. West, Vancouver BC V6E 3S7
Tel: 604-684-3384; *Fax:* 604-684-7957
info@bcbc.com
www.bcbc.com
To build a competitive & growing economy that provides opportunities for all who invest, work, & live in British Columbia
Greg D'Avignon, President & Chief Executive Officer
Jock Finlayson, Executive VP & Chief Policy Officer
Herb Eibensteiner, Chief Operating Officer & Vice-President, Membership
Ken Peacock, Chief Economist & Vice-President

Canadian Association of Family Enterprise (CAFE) / Association canadienne des enterprises familiales
#112, 465 Morden Rd., Oakville ON L6K 3W6
Tel: 416-538-9992; *Fax:* 905-337-8260
Toll-Free: 866-849-0099
office@cafenational.org
www.cafenational.org
To improve succession statistics for family businesses across Canada where Canadian family businesses connect with peers & resources for success.
Lawrence Barns, National CEO

The Canadian Council for Public-Private Partnerships (CCPPP) / Le Conseil canadien pour les partenariats public-privé
1 First Canadian Place, #1600, 100 King St. West, Toronto ON M5X 1G5
Tel: 416-861-0500; *Fax:* 416-862-7661
partners@pppcouncil.ca
www.pppcouncil.ca
To act as a proponent for improvements in the quality & cost of public services provided to Canadians through innovative partnerships between the public & private sectors
Mark Romoff, President

Canadian Council for Small Business & Entrepreneurship (CCSBE) / Conseil canadien des PME et de l'entrepreneuriat (CCPME)
c/o Centre for Small Business & Entrepreneurship, Acadia University, 38 Crowell Dr., Willet House, Wolfville NS B4P 2R6
Tel: 902-585-1776; *Fax:* 902-585-1057
ccsbe.secretariat@acadiau.ca
www.ccsbe.org
The Canadian Council for Small Business and Entrepreneurship (CCSBE-CCPME) is a national membership-based organization promoting and advancing the developmet of small business and entrepreneurship through research, education and training, networking, and dissemination of scholarly and policy-oriented information.
Jean-Marie Nkongolo-Bakenda, President
Chris Pelham, Secretary

Canadian Council of Better Business Bureaus (CCBBB) / Conseil canadien des bureaux d'éthique commerciale
2 St. Clair Ave. East, Toronto ON M4T 2T5
Tel: 416-644-4936
ccbbb@ccbbb.ca
www.ccbbb.ca
To protect consumers & the vitality of the free enterprise system; To foster the highest standards of responsibility & probity in business practice by advocating truth in advertising, by assuring integrity in performance of business services, & by voluntary regulation & monitoring activities designed to enhance public trust & confidence in business
Douglas Simpson, President & Chief Executive Officer

Canadian Council of Chief Executives (CCCE) / Conseil canadien des chefs d'entreprise
#1001, 99 Bank St., Ottawa ON K1P 6B9
Tel: 613-238-3727; *Fax:* 613-238-3247
info@ceocouncil.ca
www.ceocouncil.ca
To engage in policy work in Canada, North America, & the world
John Manley, P.C., O.C., President & Chief Executive
Susan Scotti, Senior Vice-President, Planning & Operations

John R. Dillon, Corporate Counsel & Vice-President, Policy
Sam T. Boutziouvis, Vice-President, Policy, International, & Fiscal Issues
Ross H. Laver, Vice-President, Policy & Communications
Nancy Wallace, Vice-President, Corporate Services
Sarah Reid, Communications Officer

Canadian Federation of Independent Business (CFIB) / Fédération canadienne de l'entreprise indépendante
#401, 4141 Yonge St., Toronto ON M2P 2A6
Tel: 416-222-8022; *Fax:* 416-222-6103
Toll-Free: 888-234-2232
cfib@cfib.ca
www.cfib-fcei.ca
To act as the voice for small businesses in Canada
Catherine Swift, Chair, President, & CEO
Brien Gray, Executive Vice-President
Richard Fahey, Senior Vice-President, Strategic Development
Dan Kelly, Senior Vice-President, Legislative Affairs
Ted Mallett, Vice-President & Chief Economist
Doug Bruce, Vice-President, Research
Corinne Pohlmann, Vice-President, National Affairs

Canadian Franchise Association (CFA) / Association canadienne de la franchise
#116, 5399 Eglinton Ave. West, Toronto ON M9C 5K6
Tel: 416-695-2896; *Fax:* 416-695-1950
Toll-Free: 800-665-4232
info@cfa.ca
www.cfa.ca
To promote & represent franchise excellence through a national association of businesses united by a common interest in ethical franchising.
Lorraine McLachlan, President

Canadian Institute of Chartered Business Valuators (CICBV) / L'Institut canadien des experts en évaluation d'entreprises
#710, 277 Wellington St. West, Toronto ON M5V 3H2
Tel: 416-977-1117; *Fax:* 416-977-7066
admin@cicbv.ca
www.cicbv.ca
To develop high professional standards for Canadian Chartered Business Valuators; To manage the Chartered Business Valuator (CBV) designation; To govern members of the Institute with a strict Code of Ethics & Practice Standards
Jeannine Brooks, President & Chief Executive Officer
Bob Boulton, Director, Professional Affairs
Le Anh Huynh, Coordinator, Programmes
Lauren Kirshner, Coordinator, External Relations
Jennifer Warlow, Coordinator, Communications
Deborah Pelle, Manager, Events
Judith Roth, Manager, Information Technology & Member Services

Canadian International Institute of Applied Negotiation (CIIAN) / L'Institut international canadien de la négociation pratique
138 Flora St., Ottawa ON K1R 5R5
Tel: 613-237-9050; *Fax:* 613-237-6951
ciian@ciian.org
www.ciian.org
Social Media:
www.facebook.com/group.php?gid=145938635447384;
twitter.com/CIIAN
To build sustainable peace at local, national, & international levels
Benjamin Hoffman, President

Canadian Organization of Small Business Inc. (COSBI)
5405, 129 Ave. NW, Edmonton AB T5A 0A3
Tel: 780-423-2672
To support & promote the interests of small business & independent professionals throughout Canada; to protect the free enterprise system & the interests of independent business; to function as a lobby & service organization dealing with all levels of government or large bureaucracy; to provide members with access to information vital to business success & to present the owner/manager's point of view to decision makers in both political & private sectors
Donald Richard Eastcott, Managing Director
Roy E. Shannon, Chair

Canadian Professional Sales Association (CPSA) / Association canadienne des professionnels de la vente
#400, 655 Bay St., Toronto ON M5G 2K4
Tel: 416-408-2685; *Fax:* 416-408-2684
Toll-Free: 888-267-2772
customerservice@cpsa.com; salessuccess@cpsa.com
www.cpsa.com
Social Media:
www.facebook.com/CanadianProfessionalSalesAssociation
To develop & serve sales professionals
Craig Lindsay, Chair
Harvey Copeman, President/CEO
Debora Bloom, Chair, Sales Institute & Secretary
Alfred Whiffen, Vice-Chair
Bob Medland, Treasurer

Canadian Society of Customs Brokers (CSCB) / Société canadienne des courtiers en douane
#320, 55 Murray St., Ottawa ON K1N 5M3
Tel: 613-562-3543; *Fax:* 613-562-3548
cscb@cscb.ca; courseinfo@cscb.ca; students@cscb.ca
www.cscb.ca
To act as voice of the industry to all levels of government; To provide information to members on all matters affecting customs brokerage
Bedard Melanie, Chair

Canadian Youth Business Foundation (CYBF) / La Fondation canadienne des jeunes entrepreneurs
#1410, 100 Adelaide St. West, Toronto ON M5H 1S3
Tel: 416-408-2923; *Fax:* 416-408-3234
Toll-Free: 866-646-2922
info@cybf.ca
www.cybf.ca
Social Media: twitter.com/cybfcanada
CYBF helps young people who would not otherwise have the opportunity to develop their self-confidence, achieve economic independence, fulfill their ambitions, & contribute to the community through the medium of self-employment & job creation. It is a registered charity, BN: 895001261RR0001.
John Risley, Chair
Vivian Prokop, CEO

Chambre de commerce St-Félix de Valois
15, ch Joliette, Saint-Félix-de-Valois QC J0K 2M0
Tél: 450-889-8161; *Téléc:* 450-889-1590
ccst-flx@megacom.net
www.stfelixdevalois.qc.ca
La mission de la Chambre de Commerce de Saint-Félix-de-Valois est de travailler au bien-être économique, civique et social de Saint-Félix-de-Valois et au développement de ses ressources en regroupant les leaders de tout son territoire intéressés à oeuvrer en ce sens
Josée Durand, Directrice générale

Conseil du patronat du Québec (CPQ)
#510, 1010, rue Sherbrooke ouest, Montréal QC H3A 2R7
Tél: 514-288-5161; *Téléc:* 514-288-5165
Ligne sans frais: 877-288-5161
plemieux@cpa.gc.ca
www.cpq.qc.ca
Mèdia social: www.facebook.com/conseilpatronat?ref=ts;
twitter.com/conseilpatronat;
www.linkedin.com/groups/Conseil-patronat-Qu%C3%A9bec-290 8454?gid=29084
Le Conseil du patronat du Québec a pour mission de s'assurer que les entreprises puissent disposer au Québec des meilleures conditions possibles- notamment en metiére de capital humain- afin de prospereer de fason durable dans un contexte de concurrence mondiale.
Yves-Thomas Dorval, Président

Entrepreneurship Institute of Canada
PO Box 40043, 75 King St. South, Waterloo ON N2J 4V1
Tel: 519-885-1559; *Fax:* 519-885-0990
Toll-Free: 800-665-4497
entinst@sympatico.ca
www.entinst.ca
To distribute support & educational resources of interest to entrepreneurs to corporations, institutions, human resources departments, post-secondary educational institutions, training departments, business resource centres, libraries, & business owners across Canada & the United States

Hong Kong-Canada Business Association (HKCBA) / L'Association commerciale Hong Kong-Canada
#220, 1050 West Pender St., Vancouver BC V6E 3S7
Tel: 604-684-2410; *Fax:* 604-684-6208
nationaled@hkcba.com
www.hkcba.com
To encourage & promote trade & commercial activities across a broad range of industries between Canada & Hong Kong, & through Hong Kong to China & the Asia Pacific Region.
Robert A. Brown, CEO, Special Events
David Pohl, National Chair
Joyce Chung, Executive Director

Italian Chamber of Commerce of Ontario (ICCO)
1502, 80 Richmond St. West, Toronto ON M5H 2A4
Tel: 416-789-7169; *Fax:* 416-789-7160
info.toronto@italchambers.ca
www.italchambers.ca
ICCO is a private, independent, not-for-profit organization whose aim is to enhance & promote business, trade & cultural relations between Canada & Italy. It acts as a liaison between the Canadian & Italian governments & their business communities.
Ronald J. Farano, Chair
George Visintin, President
Corrado Paina, Executive Director

Kelowna Chamber of Commerce
544 Harvey Ave., Kelowna BC V1Y 6C9
Tel: 250-861-3627; *Fax:* 250-861-3624
info@kelownachamber.org
www.kelownachamber.org
To improve trade & commerce & the economic, civic & social welfare of the city of Kelowna
Norm LeCavalier, President

Lloydminster Chamber of Commerce
4419 - 52 Ave., Lloydminster AB T9V 0Y8
Tel: 780-875-9013; *Fax:* 780-875-0755
www.lloydminsterchamber.com
To enhance private enterprise in Lloydminster & surrounding area
Pat L. Tenney, Executive Director
Peggy Bosch, President

Markham Board of Trade (MBT)
#206, 80F Centurian Dr., Markham ON L3R 8C1
Tel: 905-474-0730; *Fax:* 905-474-0685
info@markhamboard.com
www.markhamboard.com
To enhance the success of members & the Markham business community.
Richard Cunningham, President/CEO

Meeting Professionals International (MPI)
#1700, 3030 Lyndon B. Johnson Freeway, Dallas TX 75234-2759 USA
Tel: 972-702-3000; *Fax:* 972-702-3070
feedback@mpiweb.org
www.mpiweb.org
Social Media: www.facebook.com/MPIfans; twitter.com/mpi
To position meetings as a primary communications vehicle & a critical component of an organization's success; To lead the industry by serving the diverse needs of all people with a direct interest in the outcome of meetings; To educate & prepare members for their changing roles in the greater business world; To validate relevant knowledge & skills while simultaneously demonstrating a commitment to meeting excellence. Canadian office: 6519-B Mississauga Rd., Mississauga, ON L5N 1A6; phone: 905-286-4807, fax: 905-567-7191
Kevin Hinton, Chair

Mission Regional Chamber of Commerce
34033 Lougheed Hwy., Mission BC V2V 5X8
Tel: 604-826-6914; *Fax:* 604-826-5916
manager@missionchamber.bc.ca
www.missionchamber.bc.ca
The Chamber fosters a network for entrepreneurial leaders to partner in education, communication & representation.
Michelle Favero, Manager
Sean Melia, President

Mouvement québécois de la qualité (MQQ)
#1710, 360, rue Saint-Jacques ouest, Montréal QC H2Y 1P5
Tél: 514-874-9933; *Téléc:* 514-866-4600
Ligne sans frais: 888-874-9933
mqq@qualite.qc.ca
www.qualite.qc.ca
Mèdia social: www.facebook.com/MouvementQuebecoisQualite
Promouvoir et rendre accessibles aux organisations les meilleures pratiques d'affaire pour accroître leur performance et leur compétitivité
Roch Dubé, Président

Muskoka Lakes Chamber of Commerce
PO Box 536, 3181 Muskoka Rd. 169, Bala ON P0C 1A0
Tel: 705-762-5663; *Fax:* 705-762-5664
info@muskokalakeschamber.com
www.muskokalakeschamber.com
Social Media:
www.facebook.com/group.php?gid=152472788107902;
twitter.com/muskokalkscc;
www.linkedin.com/company/muskoka-lakes-chamber-of-commerce
Jane Templeton, Manager
Kailey Luker, Consultant, Event & Tourism
Tracy Owen, President
Walter Moon, Vice-President
Susan McEachern, Treasurer

The National Citizens Coalition / Coalition nationale des citoyens inc.
#501, 27 Queen St. East, Toronto ON M5C 2M6
Tel: 416-869-3838; *Fax:* 416-869-1891
Toll-Free: 888-703-5553
ncc@nationalcitizens.ca
www.nationalcitizens.ca
To promote free markets, individual freedom & responsibility under limited government & a strong defence
Peter Coleman, President & CEO
Colin T. Brown, Chair

National Quality Institute (NQI) / Institut national de la qualité (INQ)
#307, 2275 Lakeshore West Blvd., Toronto ON M8V 3Y3
Tel: 416-251-7600; *Fax:* 416-251-9131
Toll-Free: 800-263-9648
info@excellence.ca
www.nqi.ca
Social Media: www.facebook.com/82765064279;
twitter.com/excellencecan
To inspire & foster excellence in Canadian organizations; to enhance Canada's national well-being & global leadership through the incorporation of quality principles in business, government, education & health care; to promote, encourage & support the understanding & adoption of total quality principles & practices in all sectors of the economy across Canada; & to recognize outstanding achievement through the Canada Awards for Excellence
Allan Ebedes, President & CEO

Ontario Public Buyers Association, Inc. (OPBA)
Ridley Square, #361, 111 Fourth Ave., St Catharines ON L2S 3P5
Tel: 905-682-2644
info@opba.ca
www.opba.ca
To promote the ethical & effective expenditure of public funds through the principles of professional procurement
Lisa Buitenhuis, President
James Macintyre, Vice President
Bart Menage, Secretary
Barbara Cosby, Treasurer

Winnipeg Chamber of Commerce (WCC) / Chambre de commerce de Winnipeg
#100, 259 Portage Ave., Winnipeg MB R3B 2A9
Tel: 204-944-8484; *Fax:* 204-944-8492
info@winnipeg-chamber.com
www.winnipeg-chamber.com
Social Media: www.facebook.com/WpgChamber;
twitter.com/wpgchamber;
www.linkedin.com/company/the-winnipeg-chamber-of-commerce?trk=fc_badge; www.youtube.com/wpgchamber
To act as the voice of business in Winnipeg; To foster an environment in which Winnipeg businesses can proper
David Angus, President & Chief Executive Officer
Chuck Davidson, Vice-President, Policy
Karen Weiss, Vice-President, Finance & Operations
Christine Ens, Director, Membership & Marketing
Wendy Stephenson, Director, Strategic Initiatives
Stacia Franz, Coordinator, Communications
Marion Wong, Coordinator, Information

Worldwide Association of Business Coaches
c/o WABC Coaches Inc., PO Box 215, Saanichton BC V8M 2C3
Fax: 250-656-8752
info@wabccoaches.com
www.wabccoaches.com
To develop, advance & promote the emerging profession of business coaching, worldwide
Wendy Johnson, President/CEO

Centraide

Centraide Abitibi Témiscamingue et Nord-du-Québec
1009, 6e rue, Val-d'Or QC J9P 3W4
Tél: 819-825-7139; *Téléc:* 819-825-7155
courrier@centraide-atnq.qc.ca
www.centraide-atnq.qc.ca
Huguette Boucher, Directrice générale

Chemical Industry

Canadian Association of Agri-Retailers (CAAR)
#628, 70 Arthur St., Winnipeg MB R3B 1G7
Tel: 204-989-9300; *Fax:* 204-989-9306
Toll-Free: 800-463-9323
info@caar.org
www.caar.org
Social Media:
www.facebook.com/group.php?gid=142300712530309
To represent & protect the interests of Canadian agricultural retailers
Delaney Ross, Manager, Communications & Marketing
Irene O'Dell, Office Coordinator
Lynda Nicol, Coordinator, Communications & Research

Canadian Association of Chemical Distributors (CACD) / Association canadienne des distributeurs de produits chimiques (ACDPC)
349 Davis Rd., #A, Oakville ON L6J 2X2
Tel: 905-844-9140; *Fax:* 905-844-5706
www.cacd.ca
Social Media:
www.facebook.com/group.php?gid=339092806129805;
www.linkedin.com/company/canadian-association-of-chemical-distributors; www.youtube.com/user/CatherineCACD
To speak for the distribution sector of the Canadian chemical industry; To reflect the collective views of members in dealing with governments, allied associations, & the public; To provide members of the association with services that assist them in conducting their business; To ensure adherence by members to a Code of Practice for Responsible Distribution
Cathy Campbell, President
Dave Saucier, Manager, Regulatory & Government Affairs
Catherine Wieckowska, Manager, Communications & Member Services
Fatima Alexander, Administrator, You Be the Chemist Program

Canadian Consumer Specialty Products Association (CCSPA)
#800, 130 Albert St., Ottawa ON K1P 5G4
Tel: 613-232-6616; *Fax:* 613-233-6350
assoc@ccspa.org
www.ccspa.org
Social Media: twitter.com/CCSPA_ACPCS
Represents the specialty chemical & formulated products industry; promotes the interests of member companies by providing a national voice, encouraging ethical practices, negotiating with government, & fostering industry cooperation
Shannon Coombs, Executive Director
Nancy Hitchins, Director, Administration & Member Services

Canadian Fertilizer Institute (CFI) / Institut canadien des engrais
#907, 350 Sparks St., Ottawa ON K1R 7S8
Tel: 613-230-2600; *Fax:* 613-230-5142
info@cfi.ca
www.cfi.ca
Roger L. Larson, President
Dave Finlayson, Vice-President, Science & Risk Management
Clyde Graham, Vice-President, Strategy & Alliances
Kristian Stephens, Senior Manager, Technical Affairs
Robert Godfrey, Manager, Policy
Catherine King, Manager, Communications
Monique MacDonald, Manager, Finance & Corporate Services

Chemical Institute of Canada (CIC) / Institut de chimie du Canada
#550, 130 Slater St., Ottawa ON K1P 6E2
Tel: 613-232-6252; *Fax:* 613-232-5862
Toll-Free: 888-542-2242
info@cheminst.ca
www.cheminst.ca
To maintain all branches of the professions of chemical sciences & chemical engineering in their proper status among other learned & scientific professions; To encourage original research & develop & maintain high standards in profession; To enhance usefulness of profession to the public
Roland Andersson, Executive Director
Joan Kingston, Director, Finance & Administration
Gale Thirlwall, Manager, Awards & Local Sections
Luke Andersson, Coordinator, Marketing
Angie Moulton, Coordinator, Membership Services
Anne Campbell, Officer, Conference Programs

International Plant Nutrition Institute (IPNI)
#550, 3500 Parkway Lane, Norcross GA 30092 USA
Tel: 770-447-0335; *Fax:* 770-448-0439
info@ipni.net
www.ipni.net
To assist in the design & implementation of agronomic research; to obtain scientific facts & education programs to tell those facts about balanced fertilization, particularly in relation to agricultural production systems; to conduct & provide on-site support of field experiments worldwide
Terry L. Roberts, President
Tom Jensen, Northern Great Plains Director, (Saskatchewan)
Tom Bruulsema, N. American-Northeastern Director, (Ontario)

Ordre des chimistes du Québec (OCQ)
Place du Parc, #2199, 300 rue Léo-Pariseau, Montréal QC H2X 4B3
Tél: 514-844-3644; *Téléc:* 514-844-9601
information@ocq.qc.ca
www.ocq.qc.ca
L'Ordre est une corporation professionnelle dont la raison d'être est la protection du public
Guy Collin, Président du Conseil d'administration

Society of Chemical Industry - Canadian Section (SCI)
#550, 130 Slater St., Ottawa ON K1P 6E2
scicanada@soci.org
www.soci.org
To encourage acquaintance & understanding among responsible individuals in the various fields of the industrial chemical process industries; to promote acquaintance & understanding between the chemical industry & the universities & governments; to encourage scientific education in universities by recognizing student achievements; to reward outstanding achievement in the Canadian chemical & allied industries & universities through awards & honorary lectureships; to promote communication between the members of the Canadian chemical & allied industries & those of other countries
Roger Hayward, Hon. Chair
Rosie Baston, Coorindator

Child & Family Services

Black Family Support Network
719, rue Des Seigneurs, Montréal QC H3J 1Y2
Tel: 514-933-1867; *Fax:* 514-933-1808
lbbfs@bell.net
Rosemary Segee, Contact

Elizabeth House / Maison Elizabeth
2131 Marlowe, Montréal QC H4A 3L4
Tel: 514-482-2488; *Fax:* 514-482-9467
info@maisonelizabethhouse.com
www.maisonelizabethhouse.com
To provide a continuum of specialized services to pregnant adolescents & women, mothers & babies, fathers, & families experiencing significant difficulty in adjusting to pregnancy & to their new roles as parents & caregivers; To support clients as they make choices & are directed to appropriate resources either in-house or in the community; To serve the anglophone community throughout the province of Quebec
Linda Schachtler, Contact

Yukon Child Care Association (YCCA)
YT
YCCA@live.com
web.mac.com/life9/YCCA
To develop a high quality, universally accessible, & affordable child care system in the Yukon; To represent caregivers & families
Cyndi Desharnais, Contact

Childbirth

Alberta Association of Midwives (AAM)
PO Box 11957, #166, 4307-130 Ave. SE, Edmonton AB T2Z 3V8
Tel: 403-214-1882
info@alberta-midwives.com
www.alberta-midwives.com
The AAM promotes awareness of the profession of midwifery, supports midwifery-centered research, participates in a provincial education program. It also represents its members in areas of remuneration, benefits and insurance.
Jane Baker, President

Association of Ontario Midwives (AOM) / Association des sages-femmes de l'Ontario
#301, 365 Bloor St. E., Toronto ON M3W 3L4
Tel: 416-425-9974; *Fax:* 416-425-6905
Toll-Free: 866-418-3773
admin@aom.on.ca
www.aom.on.ca
To represent midwives & the practice of midwifery in Ontario
Kelly Stadelbauer, Executive Director

College of Midwives of British Columbia (CMBC)
#210, 1682 West 7th Ave., Vancouver BC V6J 4S6
Tel: 604-742-2230; *Fax:* 604-730-8908
information@cmbc.bc.ca
www.cmbc.bc.ca
To serve & protect the public interest by registering competent midwives who will practise safely & ethically in British Columbia
Jane Kilthei, Registrar & Executive Director

Infant Feeding Action Coalition
6 Trinity Sq., Toronto ON M5G 1B1
Tel: 416-595-9819; *Fax:* 416-591-9355
info@infactcanada.ca
www.infactcanada.ca
To protect, promote & support breastfeeding in Canada & globally; to promote better infant & maternal health; to foster appropriate mother & infant nutrition
Elisabeth Sterken, National Director

La Leche League Canada (LLLC) / Ligue La Leche Canada
PO Box 700, Winchester ON K0C 2K0
Tel: 613-774-4900; *Fax:* 613-774-2798
ofm@LLLC.ca
www.lllc.ca
To act as a support network for breastfeeding mothers; To promote the importance of breastfeeding in Canada; To disseminate information on how to help mothers succeed in breastfeeding
Fiona Audy, Chair
Lisa Loeppky, Secretary
Wendy Dale, Treasurer

Multiple Births Canada (MBC) / Naissances multiples Canada
PO Box 432, Wasaga Beach ON L0L 2P0
Tel: 705-429-0901; *Fax:* 705-429-9809
Toll-Free: 866-228-8824
office@multiplebirthscanada.org
www.multiplebirthscanada.org
To improve the quality of life for multiple birth individuals & their families through research, education, service & advocacy
Gail Moore, Chair
Melanie Dugard, Treasurer

Serena Canada
151 Holland Ave., Ottawa ON K1Y 0Y2
Tel: 613-728-6536; *Toll-Free:* 888-373-7362
sc@serena.ca
www.serena.ca
Serena promotes a natural family planning method based on information from a woman's body. The couple can identify the fertile, infertile & relatively infertile phases, so they themselves can choose whether or not to conceive a child. Respect for human life from conception is central to its philosophy. It is a registered charity, BN: 119145621RR0001.

Children & Youth

Alberta Associations for Bright Children (AABC)
c/o Action for Bright Children Calgary Society, PO Box 36093, Stn. Lakeview, Calgary AB T3E 7C6
Tel: 403-463-9612
www.edmontonabc.org/aabc
To inform & support professionals & parents who are facing the challenge of dealing with bright, gifted, talented children; to advocate at the school board & government levels to ensure that resources & expertise are allocated in a manner that serves the children best

Alberta Child Care Association (ACCA)
#110, 10025 - 106 St., Edmonton AB T5J 1G4
Tel: 780-421-7544; *Fax:* 780-428-0080
Toll-Free: 877-421-9937
www.albertachildcare.org
ACCA is non-profit, member-based society with a mission to strengthen and advance the early learning & child care profession in Alberta.
Marg Golberg, Chair
Karen Baretta, Office Manager

Association for Bright Children (Ontario) (ABC Ontario) / Société pour enfants doués et surdoués (Ontario)
c/o 135 Brant St., Oakville ON L6K 2Z8
Tel: 416-925-6136
abcinfo@abcontario.ca
www.abcontario.ca
ABC Ontario is volunteer-based, self-support, non-profit network dedicated to providing information & support to parents of bright & gifted children. It works to increase the understanding & acceptance of bright & gifted children/youth at home, at school & in the community, & encourages society to nurture them that they may reach their full potential. It is a registered charity, BN: 118777275RR0001.
Rosanno DelGrosso, President
Claire Collins, Executive Director
Jim Hall, Sec.-Treas.

Association québécoise des centres de la petite enfance (AQCPE)
#200, 6611, rue Jarry est, Montréal QC H1P 1W5
Tél: 514-326-8008; *Téléc:* 514-326-3322
Ligne sans frais: 888-326-8008
info@aqcpe.com
www.aqcpe.com
A pour mandat la concertation des acteurs du réseau, la représentation politique de ses membres et la promotion des centres de la petite enfance, et services de soutien; représente les employeurs du secteur des CPE à l'occasion de négociations, en matière de relations du travail et de main-d'oeuvre; l'AQCPE est reconnue par le Min. de la Famille et des Aînés pour les négociations provinciales.
Louis Senécal, Directeur général
Viriya Thach, Responsable des communications

B'nai Brith Youth Organization Canada (BBYO)
4700 Bathurst St., 2nd Fl., Toronto ON M2R 1W8
Tel: 416-398-2004; *Fax:* 416-398-5780
info@bbyo.on.ca
www.bbyo.on.ca
To educate young people about the richness of Jewish culture & heritage
Kevin Goodman, Program Director

Boys & Girls Clubs of Alberta
J. Percy Page Centre, 11759 Groat Rd., Edmonton AB T5M 3K6
Tel: 780-415-1734; *Fax:* 780-415-1737
www.bgccan.com/clubresults.asp?l=e&location=ab
Social Media: www.facebook.com/group.php?gid=24403790656
The Clubs offer educational, recreational & skills development programs & services to children from pre-school to young adulthood. Activities are scheduled after school, evenings & weekends, providinge a safe, supportive place where children & youth can build positive relationships, & develop confidence & skills.
Karen McCullagh, Western Region Director
Pearl Kapitzke, Regional Services Coordinator

Boys & Girls Clubs of Canada (BGCC) / Clubs garçons & filles du Canada
#204, 7100 Woodbine Ave., markham ON L3R 5J2
Tel: 905-477-7272; *Fax:* 905-477-2056
info@bgccan.com; bgcc_communications@bgccan.com (media)
www.bgccan.com
Social Media: www.facebook.com/group.php?gid=2233316912
To provide safe, supportive place where children & youth can experience new opportunities, overcome barriers, build positive relationships, & develop confidence & skills for life
Pam Jolliffe, President & Chief Executive Officer
Marlene Deboisbriand, Vice-President, Member Services
Susan Bower, Vice-President, Business Operations
Sue Sheridan, Director, Resource Development
Denise Silverstone, Director, National Programs
Mary O'Connell, Specialist, Media Relations

Boys & Girls Clubs of Manitoba
Central Region, #204, 7100 Woodbine Ave., Markham ON L3R 5J2
Tel: 416-535-9675; *Fax:* 905-477-2056
www.bgccan.com/clubresults.asp?l=e&location=mb
The Clubs offer educational, recreational & skills development programs & services to children from pre-school to young adulthood. Activities are scheduled after school, evenings & weekends, providinge a safe, supportive place where children & youth can build positive relationships, & develop confidence & skills.
Sandra Morris, Central Region Director
Brittany Tough, Central Region Coordinator

Boys & Girls Clubs of New Brunswick
Maritime Region, c/o #204, 7100 Woodbine Ave., Markham ON L3R 5J2
Tel: 902-469-1550
www.bgccan.com/clubresults.asp?l=e&location=nb
The Clubs offer educational, recreational & skills development programs & services to children from pre-school to young adulthood. Activities are scheduled after school, evenings & weekends, providinge a safe, supportive place where children & youth can build positive relationships, & develop confidence & skills.
Wendy Johnston, Maritime Region Director

Boys & Girls Clubs of P.E.I.
PO Box 86, 1253 Port Hill Stn. Rd, Tyne Valley PE C0B 2C0
Tel: 902-831-3297; *Fax:* 902-831-3466
www.boysandgirlsclubsofpei.org
Their mission is to provide a safe, supportive place where children and youth can experience new oppourtunities, overcome barriers, build positive relationships and develop confidence and skills for life.
Wendy Johnston, Maritime Region Director
Lorraine Robinson, Provincial Coordinator

Boys & Girls Clubs of Québec / Clubs garçons et filles du Québec
Region de Québec, c/o #204, 7100 Woodbine Ave., Markham ON L3R 5J2
Tél: 905-477-7272; *Téléc:* 905-477-2056
www.bgccan.com/clubresults.asp?l=e&location=qc
Marlene Deboisbriand, Vice-President, Member Services

Boys & Girls Clubs of Saskatchewan
J. Percy Page Centre, 11759 Groat Rd., Edmonton AB T5M 3K6
Tel: 780-415-1734; *Fax:* 780-415-1737
Toll-Free: 877-615-1734
www.bgccan.com/clubresults.asp?l=e&location=sk
The Clubs offer educational, recreational & skills development programs & services to children from pre-school to young adulthood. Activities are scheduled after school, evenings & weekends, providinge a safe, supportive place where children & youth can build positive relationships, & develop confidence & skills.
Karen McCullagh, Western Region Director
Pearl Kapitzke, Regional Services Coordinator

Boys & Girls Clubs of Yukon
Pacific Region, PO Box 20222, 1434 Graham St., Kelowna BC V1Y 9H2
Tel: 250-762-3914; *Fax:* 250-762-6562
www.bgccan.com/clubresults.asp?l=e&location=yt
The Clubs offer educational, recreational & skills development programs & services to children from pre-school to young adulthood. Activities are scheduled after school, evenings & weekends, providinge a safe, supportive place where children & youth can build positive relationships, & develop confidence & skills.
Carrie Wagner-Miller, Pacific Region Director

Canadian Association for Young Children (CAYC) / Association canadienne pour les jeunes enfants (ACJE)
c/o Vicki Brown, 356B Prospect Bay Rd., Prospect Bay NS B3T 1Z7
www.cayc.ca
To influence policies & programs affecting critical issues related to the education & welfare of Canadian young children from birth through age nine
Margaret Fair, President
Iris Berger, Chair, Publications
Vicki Brown, Contact, Membership Dervice

Canadian Centre for Child Protection
615 Academy Rd., Winnipeg MB R3N 0E7
Tel: 204-945-5735; *Fax:* 204-948-2461
Toll-Free: 800-532-9135
www.protectchildren.ca; www.childfind.mb.ca
Social Media: www.facebook.com/184856436064; twitter.com/CdnChildProtect
To assist in the location & prevention of missing children; to increase the provincial awareness of issues relating to missing children & to advocate for the protection & rights of children
Lianna McDonald, Executive Director

Canadian Child Care Federation (CCCF) / Fédération canadienne des services de garde à l'enfance (FCSGE)
#201, 383 Parkdale Ave., Ottawa ON K1Y 4R4
Tel: 613-729-5289; *Fax:* 613-729-3159
Toll-Free: 800-858-1412
www.cccf-fcsge.ca
To promote excellence in child care & early learning

Don Giesbrecht, President
Lynda Kerr, Senior Director, Business Operations
Claire McLaughlin, Manager, Publications and Marketing
Linda Skinner, Treasurer

Canadian Young Judaea
788 Marlee Ave., Toronto ON M6B 3K1
Tel: 416-781-5156; *Fax:* 416-787-3100
Toll-Free: 800-804-6661
youngjudaea@bellnet.ca
www.youngjudaea.ca
Canada Young Judaea is Canada's largest Zionist youth movement and are affiliated with six resdential summer camps across Canada; they are pluralistic and apolitical.
Risa Epstein, National Executive Director

Child Find Alberta (CFA)
3751 - 21 St. NW, Calgary AB T2E 6T5
Tel: 403-270-3463; *Fax:* 403-270-8355
Toll-Free: 800-561-1733
info@childfind.ab.ca
www.childfind.ab.ca
Social Media: twitter.com/ChildFindAB
To aid in location of missing &/or abducted children & to reunite these children with their legal custodians; to offer relevant information & support to families who have been reunited; to prevent, through education, abduction of children & runaway children situations.
Brad Bostock, Executive Director
Kelly Shaw, Operations Coordinator

Child Find British Columbia
#208, 2722 Fifth St., Victoria BC V8T 4B2
Tel: 250-382-7311; *Fax:* 250-382-0227
Toll-Free: 888-689-3463
childvicbc@shaw.ca
childfindbc.com
To assist in the search & location of missing children, providing support to law enforcement & families; To educate & prevent the abduction & exploitation of children & provide awareness
Debie Byl, Executive Director

Child Find Canada Inc. (CFC)
PO Box 237, Oakville MB R0H 0Y0
Tel: 204-870-1298
childcan@aol.com
www.childfind.ca
Supports provincial Child Find organizations in the location of & education in the prevention of missing children; increases national awareness of issues relating to missing children; advocates for the protection & rights of children.
Kathryn Anderson, National Co-Ordinator

Child Find Newfoundland/Labrador
#217, 31 Peet St., St. John's NL A1B 3W8
Tel: 709-738-4400; *Fax:* 709-738-0550
childnfld@aol.com
www.childfind.ca
To prevent missing children; To support the search for missing children
Jeff Sears, President

Child Find Ontario
440A Britannia Rd. East, Mississauga ON L4Z 1X9
Tel: 905-712-3463; *Fax:* 905-712-3462
Toll-Free: 800-543-8477
mail@childfindontario.ca
www.ontario.childfind.ca
Child Find Ont. assists in the search & recovery process of missing children; educates on the dangers of abduction to minimize the risk; is a registered charity, BN : 130263502RR0001.
John, Executive Director

Child Find PEI Inc.
PO Box 21008, 106C Kensington Rd., Charlottetown PE C1A 5J5
Tel: 902-368-1678; *Fax:* 902-368-1389
Toll-Free: 800-387-7962
childfind@pei.aibn.com
www.childfindpei.com
Child Find PEI is a registered, non-profit, charitable organization that assists in the location of missing children; increases awareness of the problem of missing children; teaches ways to prevent abduction; provides assistance & support to families of a missing child.
Rob Coughlin, President

Child Find Saskatchewan Inc.
#202, 3502 Taylor St. East, Saskatoon SK S7H 5H9
Tel: 306-955-0070; *Fax:* 306-373-1311
Toll-Free: 800-513-3463
childsask@aol.com
www.childfind.sk.ca
To locate missing & abducted children & reunite them with their lawful parent or guardian; To increase public awareness of the need to protect children; To educate both parents & child on street proofing technology & to support families of missing children
Phyllis Hallatt, President

Children's Creative Response to Conflict (CCRC)
211 Bronson Ave., Ottawa ON K1R 6H5
Tel: 613-234-9019
ccrccanada@gmail.com
www.ccrc-crc.ca
To help educators, parents and those who work with young people learn creative skills of non-violent conflict resolution through cooperation, communication, affirmation, problem solving, mediation and bias awareness.

Children's Wish Foundation of Canada / Fondation canadienne rêves d'enfants
#350, 1101 Kingston Rd., Pickering ON L1V 1B5
Tel: 905-839-8882; *Fax:* 905-839-3745
Toll-Free: 800-267-9474
nat@childrenswish.ca
www.childrenswish.ca
Social Media: www.facebook.com/ChildrensWish; twitter.com/Childrens_wish; www.linkedin.com/company/children's-wish-foundation-of-canada
The Foundation grants wishes to children suffering from a high risk, life-threatening illnesses. It is a registered charity, BN: 124038878RR0001.
Chris Kotsopoulos, CEO
Linda Marco, Vice-President, Development
Paul St-Germain, Director, Communications

Desta Black Youth Network
Padua Centre, 1950, rue St-Antoine ouest, Montréal QC H3J 1A5
Tel: 514-932-7597; *Fax:* 514-932-9468
info@destanetwork.ca
www.destanetwork.ca
To provide an outreach initiative to young adults, from ages 18 to 25, within the Black community; To mentor marginalized youth in the areas of education, employment, & personal growth; To empower vision, strengthen authentic identity, & promote excellence

Enfant-Retour Québec / Missing Children Quebec
#100, 7101 av Park, Montréal QC H3N 1X9
Tél: 514-843-4333; *Téléc:* 514-843-8211
Ligne sans frais: 888-692-4673
info@enfant-retourquebec.ca
www.enfant-retourquebec.ca
Média social: www.facebook.com/182144014082
Assister les parents à la recherche de leurs enfants portés disparus; aider également les professionnels, avocats, policiers, travailleurs sociaux impliqués dans une situation de disparition d'enfant ou de prévention contre une disparition; réseau international de communication et d'aide qui oeuvre également à sensibiliser la population au problème des enfants disparus et exploités par des affiches, émissions, documents
Pina Arcamone, Directrice générale

Fondation Rêves d'Enfants, div. Nord-du-Québec
423, rue Normand, Chibougamau QC G8P 1A1
Tél: 418-748-3702
Kathy Fortin

Gifted Children's Association of British Columbia (GCABC)
c/o West Coast Child Care Resource Centre, 2772 East Broadway, Vancouver BC V5M 1Y8
info@gcabc.ca
www.gcabc.ca
To support parents & others meet the needs of gifted children across British Columbia
John Kirkness, President
Tasha Carrothers, Secretary

Girl Guides of Canada (GGC) / Guides du Canada
50 Merton St., Toronto ON M4S 1A3
Tel: 416-487-5281; *Fax:* 416-487-5570
www.girlguides.ca
Social Media: www.facebook.com/GirlGuidesofCanada.GuidesduCanada; twitter.com/girlguidesofcan; www.youtube.com/user/ggcanada; flickr.com/photos/girlguidesofcan/sets
GGC strives to prepare girls to meet the challenges of life, & in a safe environment, teaches them such skills as bandaging wounds & coping with bullies. It encourages girls to foster friendships & develop a sense of leadership, empowering them to become responsible members of the community. It is part of a global organization of 145 countries, the largest for girls in the world. It is a registered charity, BN: 118938554RR0027.
Chris Burton, Chief Commissioner

Junior Achievement Canada (JACAN) / Jeunes Entreprises du Canada
#218, 1 Eva Rd., Toronto ON M9C 4Z5
Tel: 416-622-4602; *Fax:* 416-622-6861
Toll-Free: 800-265-0699
www.jacan.org
Social Media: www.facebook.com/JAchievement; www.linkedin.com/groups?mostPopular=&gid=3027142
To provide practical business & economic education programs & experience for young people, through partnerships with business & education communities
Sandra Patterson, President & CEO
Stephen Ashworth, Senior Vice President, Operations & Education
Rob Peacock, Senior Vice President, Development
Tim Turnbull, Vice President, Fund Development
Claudia Bishop, CFO

Junior Chamber International Canada / Jeune chambre internationale du Canada
14 Bruce Farm Dr., Toronto ON M2H 1G3
Tel: 416-886-9756; *Fax:* 416-221-9926
Toll-Free: 800-265-0484
administration@jcicanada.com
www.jcicanada.com
To contribute to the advancement of the global community by providing the opportunity for young people to develop the leadership skills, social responsibility & fellowship necessary to create positive change. Chapters across Canada.
Jean-Simon Deschênes, Chairman of the Board
Leslie Shore, National President

Justice for Children & Youth (JFCY)
#1203, 415 Yonge St., Toronto ON M5B 2E7
Tel: 416-920-1633; *Fax:* 416-920-5855
Toll-Free: 866-999-5329
info@jfcy.org
www.jfcy.org
To assist & empower children & youth in obtaining fair & equal access to legal, educational, medical & social resources; to provide direct legal assistance in all areas of children's law to eligible children & youth of Metro Toronto & vicinity; to provide summary legal advice, information & assistance to young people, parents, professionals & community groups on a province-wide basis; to advocate for law & policy reform; to monitor & respond to developments & changes to the laws which affect children
Martha Mackinnon, Executive Director
Jeffery Rosekat, President & Chair

Manitoba Child Care Association (MCCA)
2350 McPhillips St., 2nd Fl., Winnipeg MB R2V 4J6
Tel: 204-586-8587; *Fax:* 204-589-5613
Toll-Free: 888-323-4676
info@mccahouse.org
www.mccahouse.org
To act as the voice of child care in Manitoba; To advocate for a quality system of child care; To advance early childhood education as a profession
Julie Skaftfeld, President
Pat Wege, Executive Director
Karen Gander, Manager, Professional Development
Monique Sutherland, Manager, Finance & Accounting
Tami Karsin, Director, Branch Services
Laurinda Neyron, Director, Public Policy & Professionalism

North America Missing Children Association Inc. (NAMCA)
Toll-Free: 800-260-0753
To become a liaison between parent/guardians & police to help find missing & abducted people; to help educate the public with prevention tips on runaways, abductions & kidnapping; recognized by the RCMP Missing Children Registry
Patricia Hughes, Executive Director

Ranch Ehrlo Society
PO Box 570, Pilot Butte SK S0G 3Z0
Tel: 306-781-1800; *Fax:* 306-757-0599
inquiries@ranchehrlo.ca
www.ehrlo.com
To provide a range of quality assessment, treatment, education & support services that improves the social & emotional functioning of children & youth referred to our program
Geoff Pawson, President & CEO

Safe Kids Canada / Sécurijeunes Canada
#2105, 180 Dundas St. West, Toronto ON M5G 1Z8
Tel: 416-813-7288; *Fax:* 416-813-4986
Toll-Free: 888-723-3847
safekids.web@sickkids.ca
www.safekidscanada.ca
Social Media: twitter.com/safekidscanada
National Injury Prevention Program of the Hospital for Sick Children; promotes effective strategies to prevent unintentional injuries; builds partnerships & uses a comprehensive approach to advance safety & reduce the burden of injuries to Canada's children & youth
Pamela Fuselli, Executive Director

Scouts Canada / Scouts du Canada
National Office, 1345 Baseline Rd., Ottawa ON K2C 0A7
Toll-Free: 888-726-8876
helpcentre@scouts.ca
www.scouts.ca
Social Media:
www.facebook.com/pages/Scouts-Canada/27747198656;
twitter.com/scoutscanada;
www.linkedin.com/company/scouts-canada;
www.youtube.com/scoutscanada
To contribute to the education of young people through a value system based on the Scout Promise & Law; To emphasize learning by doing, particularly in small groups, with outdoor activities as a learning resource
Steve Kent, Chair & Chief Commissioner
Rob Stewart, Executive Commissioner & CEO
Dylan Reinhart, National Youth Commissioner
Valarie Dillon, Executive Director, Human Resources & Volunteer Services
Fiona Livingstone, Executive Director, Financial Services
John Petitti, Executive Director, Marketing & Communications
Bethany Tory, Executive Director, Member Services

A World of Dreams Foundation Canada / La Fondation canadienne un monde de rêves
#3575, 6900, boul déCarie, Montréal QC H3A 3L4
Tel: 514-985-3003; *Fax:* 514-985-9280
Toll-Free: 800-567-7254
info@awdreams.com
www.awdreams.com
To fulfill dreams for chronically, critically & terminally ill children
Lora Cianci, Director

Citizenship & Immigration

Canadian Association of Professional Immigration Consultants (CAPIC) / Association Canadienne des Conseillers Professionnels en Immigration (ACCPI)
#602, 245 Fairview Mall Dr., Toronto ON M2J 4T1
Tel: 416-483-7044; *Fax:* 416-309-1985
info@capic.ca
www.capic.ca
Social Media:
www.facebook.com/group.php?gid=104799452895463
To represent Certified Canadian Immigration Consultants (CCIC), or full members of the Canadian Society of Immigration Consultants (CSIC)
Katarina Onuschak, Executive Director
Monica Poon, National Coordinator
Christopher Daw, Director, Lobbying
Lynn Gaudet, Director, Communications
Deepak Kohli, Director, Membership
Tanveer Sharief, Director, Education & Training

Canadian Ukrainian Immigrant Aid Society (CUIAS)
2383 Bloor St. W., 2nd Fl., Toronto ON M6S 1P9
Tel: 416-767-4595; *Fax:* 416-767-2658
cuias@cuias.org
www.cuias.org
To sponsor & aid in settlement of Ukrainian refugees.
Ludmila Kolesnichenko, Executive Director

Centre for Information & Community Services of Ontario (CICS)
c/o Immigrant Resource Centre, 2330 Midland Ave., Toronto ON M1S 5G5
Tel: 416-292-7510; *Fax:* 416-292-7579
Crisis Hot-Line: 416-292-2832
info@cicscanada.com
www.cicscanada.com
To provide a wide range of cost-effective, culturally-sensitive & professional services; to empower newcomers to settle & integrate into Canadian society; to promote active citizenship in the community; committed to excellence & to be a leading agency in settlement, education & social services
Moy Wong-Tam, Executive Director
Fina Ching, President
Samuel Luk, Vice-President

Eritrean Canadian Community Centre of Metropolitan Toronto (ECCC)
579 St. Clair Ave. W, Toronto ON M6C 1A3
Tel: 416-658-8580; *Fax:* 416-658-7442
info@eccctoronto.ca
www.eccctoronto.ca
The Eritrean Canadian Community Centre of Metropolitan Toronto (ECCC) is a non-profit charitable organization established in 1985. It provides immigrant and refugees settlement services and creates the environment for building capacity in the Eritrean community of Toronto.

Immigrant Centre Manitoba
100 Adelaide St., Winnipeg MB R3A 0W2
Tel: 204-943-9158; *Fax:* 204-949-0734
info@icmanitoba.com
www.international-centre.ca
To encourage pride in Canada & appreciation of Canadian citizenship; to encourage intercultural understanding in multicultural Canada; to support immigration & provide caring services to newcomers.
Linda Lalande, Executive Director

Jewish Immigrant Aid Services of Canada (JIAS) / Services canadiens d'assistance aux immigrants juifs
#306, 4580 Dufferin St., Toronto ON M3H 5Y2
Tel: 416-630-9051; *Fax:* 416-630-9029
national@jias.org
www.jias.org
To serve the needs of Jewish immigrants & refugees; to facilitate the legal entry of Jewish immigrants to Canada; to provide services about immigration, naturalization, resettlement & integration.
Janis Roth, Executive Director

National Organization of Immigrant & Visible Minority Women of Canada (NOIVMWC) / Organisation nationale des femmes immigrantes et des femmes appartenant à une minorité visible du Canada (ONFIFAMVC)
#412, 219 Argyle St., Ottawa ON K2P 2H4
Tel: 613-232-0689; *Fax:* 613-232-0988
noivmwc@noivmwc.org
www.noivmwc.org
To ensure equality for immigrant & visible minority women within bilingual Canada by putting into place strategies that will combat sexism, racism, poverty, isolation & violence & by acting as an advocate on issues dealing with immigrant & visible minority women.
Eva Pakyam, President

Ontario Council of Agencies Serving Immigrants (OCASI)
#200, 110 Eglinton Ave. West, Toronto ON M4R 1A3
Tel: 416-322-4950; *Fax:* 416-322-8084
generalmail@ocasi.org
www.ocasi.org; www.settlement.org
To act as a collective voice for immigrant services; to provide access for immigrants & refugees to settlement services; to provide social organizational development with community groups, policy analysis & government relations, professional development of member agency staff & research into issues facing immigrant service agencies
Josie Di Zio, President
Debbie Douglas, Executive Director

Ottawa Community Immigrant Services Organization (OCISO) / Organisme communautaire des services aux immigrants d'Ottawa
959 Wellington St. West, Ottawa ON K1Y 2X5
Tel: 613-725-0202; *Fax:* 613-725-9054
info@ociso.org
www.ociso.org
To enable newcomers & their families to fully participate in an open & welcoming Ottawa, through innovative services, community building & public engagement
Hamdi Mohamed, Executive Director

Place Benoît Bon Courage Community Centre / Centre Communautaire Bon Courage De Place Benoît
#2, 155 Place Benoît, Ville Saint-Laurent QC H4N 2H4
Tél: 514-744-0897; *Téléc:* 514-744-6205
Provides local services for immigrants
Dayonn Vann, Contact

Conservation

Nova Scotia Federation of Anglers and Hunters (NSFAH)
PO Box 654, Halifax NS B3J 2T3
Tel: 902-477-8898; *Fax:* 902-444-3883
tonyrodgers@eastlink.ca
www.nsfah.ca
The Nova Scotia Federation of Anglers and Hunters is dedicated to the conservation and propagation of the wildlife in the province for those who hunt, fish, trap or otherwise wish to enjoy the wildlife resources of Nova Scotia. This will be accomplished by education, cooperation and exchange of information will all people and by uniting provincial organizations having similar objectives.
Tony Rodgers, Executive Director

Construction

Ontario Road Builders' Association
#1, 365 Brunel Rd., Mississauga ON L4Z 1Z5
Tel: 905-507-1107; *Fax:* 905-890-8122
www.orba.org
Social Media:
www.facebook.com/OntarioRoadBuildersAssociation;
twitter.com/onroadbuilders
To act as the voice of the Ontario road building industry; To maintain high standards in the road building industry; To promote worker health & safety
Geoff Wilkinson, Executive Director
Karen Renkema, Director, Government Relations
Kathryn Thomas, Director, Member Services
Kim Le Fort, Office Manager & Coordinator, Events
Patrick McManus, Policy Analyst

Consumers

Consumers Council of Canada (CCC)
#100, 35 Madison Ave., Toronto ON M5R 2S2
Tel: 416-483-2696; *Fax:* 416-483-4128
billhuzar@consumerscouncil.com
www.consumerscouncil.com
Christina Bisanz, Executive Director
Bill Huzar, President

Consumers' Association of Canada (CAC) / Association des consommateurs du Canada
436 Gilmour St., 3rd Fl., Ottawa ON K2P 0R8
Tel: 613-238-2533; *Fax:* 613-238-2538
info@consumer.ca
www.consumer.ca
To represent & articulate the best interests of Canadian consumers to all levels of government & to all sectors of society by continually earning recognition as the trusted voice of the consumer on a national basis; to inform & educate consumers on marketplace issues; To work with government & industry to solve marketplace problems; To focus its work in the areas of food, health, trade, standards, financial services, communications industries & other marketplace issues as they emerge
Bruce Cran, President
Mel Fruitman, Vice-President

Copyright

Canadian Artists Representation Copyright Collective Inc.
109A Fourth Ave., Ottawa ON K1S 2L3
Tel: 613-232-3818; *Fax:* 613-232-8384
Toll-Free: 866-502-2722
carcc@carcc.ca
www.carcc.ca
To license and administer copyright for its affiliates, visual and media artists, in Canada.
Janice Seline, Executive Director

Culture

Albanian-Canadian Community Association
26 Six Point Rd., Toronto ON M8Z 2W9
Tel: 416-503-4704; *Fax:* 416-503-4704
info@albcan.org
www.albcan.org
Petraq Peci, Chairman

Assemblée communautaire fransaskoise (ACF)
#101, 2445 - 13 Ave., Regina SK S4P 0W1
Tél: 306-569-1912; *Téléc:* 306-781-7916
Ligne sans frais: 800-991-1912
acf@sasktel.net
www.fransaskois.sk.ca
Travaille au développement, à l'épanouissement et au rayonnement de tous ses membres; est l'entité gouvernante de la communauté fransaskoise
Michel Dubé, Présidente
Patrice N'Gouandi, Agente aux communications

Assemblée parlementaire de la Francophonie (APF)
Région Amérique, Assemblée nationale, 1020, rue des Parlementaires, 6e étage, Québec QC G1A 1A3
Tél: 418-643-7391; *Téléc:* 418-643-1865
mvermette@assnat.qc.ca
www.regionamerique-apf.org
Promouvoir la langue et la culture francaise; promouvoir les droits de l'homme et la démocratie
André Lavoie, Secrétaire administrative régionale

Association canadienne-française de l'Alberta (ACFA)
#303, Pav. II, 8627, rue Marie-Anne-Gaboury, Edmonton AB T6C 3N1
Tél: 780-466-1680; *Téléc:* 780-465-6773
acfa@acfa.ab.ca
www.acfa.ab.ca
Mèdia social: www.facebook.com/acfaab
Représenter la population francophone de l'Alberta; promouvoir le bien-être intellectuel, culturel et social des francophones de l'Alberta; encourager, faciliter et développer l'enseignement en français; entretenir des relations amicales avec les groupes de différentes origines ethniques et anglophones dans la province
Denis Perreaux, Directeur général
Mireille Péloquin, Directrice, Services communautaires

Association canadienne-française de l'Ontario, Mille-îles (ACFOMI)
Kingston ON
Tél: 613-546-7863; *Téléc:* 613-507-7794
www.acfomi.org/acfo
Appuyer le développement communautaire; rassembler les forces vives de la communauté franco-ontarienne; faire des représentations politiques
Lucie Mercier, Directrice générale

Association franco-yukonnaise (AFY)
302 rue Strickland, Whitehorse YT Y1A 2K1
Tél: 867-668-2663; *Téléc:* 867-663-3511
Ligne sans frais: 866-673-7632
afy@afy.yk.ca
www.afy.yk.ca
Le secteur culturel de l'Association franco-yukonnaise offre plusieurs activités sociales, culturelles et artistiques. La culture francophone du Yukon passe par les arts visuels, la chanson, la musique, les rires, la danse, les spectacles amateurs, la tire d'érable, les rencontres sociales et bien plus encore.
Isabelle Salesse, Codirectrice générale
Régis St-Pierre, Codirecteur général

Association of Canadian Clubs / Association des cercles canadiens
#211, 2415 Holly Lane, Ottawa ON K1V 2P2
Tel: 613-236-8288; *Fax:* 613-236-8299
support@istcl.com
www.canadianclub.ca
To promote Canadian identity; to encourage Canadian unity; to foster throughout Canada an interest in public affairs; to cultivate attachment to Canadian institutions
Lyn Goldman, National President
Christine Merrikin, Executive Secretary
Jim Waters, Regional Director, British Columbia
Marjorie Nickerson, Regional Director, Alberta
Maura Gillis-Cipywnyk, Regional Director, Saskatchewan
Jacqui Blanchard, Regional Director, Manitoba
Allan Mutart, Regional Director, Southern Ontario
Clara Edwardson, Regional Director, Eastern & Northern Ontario
Cynthia Dinsmore, Regional Director, Québec

Canada-Israel Cultural Foundation (CICF) / Fondation culturelle Canada-Israël
4700 Bathurst St., 2nd Fl., Toronto ON M2R 1W8
Tel: 416-932-2260; *Fax:* 416-398-5780
cicf@bellnet.ca
www.cicfweb.ca
The mission of the Canada-Israel Cultural Foundation is to act as a cultural bridge between Canada and Israel, promoting and supporting intercultural exchange with a special focus on young artists, and developing artistic life by awarding scholarships and grants.
Cheryl Wetstein, Executive Director

Canadian-Scandinavian Foundation (CSF) / Fondation Canada-Scandinavie
PO Box 135, Stn. B, Montréal QC H3B 3J5
Tel: 514-398-4740; *Fax:* 514-398-7356
csf-fcs@hotmail.com
www.canada-scandinavia.ca
The Foundation raises funds to distribute to Canadian students who wish to travel to Denmark, Finland, Iceland, Norway or Sweden, to undertake studies at a Scandinavian institution. It promotes study/research projects by offering travel busaries.
Derek Yaple-Schobert, Chair
Hans Moller, President

Centre culturel franco-manitobain (CCFM)
340, boul Provencher, Saint Boniface MB R2H 0G7
Tél: 204-233-8972; *Téléc:* 204-233-3324
administration@ccfm.mb.ca
www.ccfm.mb.ca
Mèdia social: www.facebook.com/people/Centre-Culturel-Franco-Manitobain/1549747456
A pour objectif de maintenir, d'encourager, de favoriser et de patronner, par tous les moyens possibles, toutes les formes d'activités culturelles de langue française, et de rendre la culture canadienne-française accesible à tous les résidents de la province.
Sylviane Lanthier, Directrice générale

Centre francophone de Toronto (CFT)
20 Lower Spadina Ave., Toronto ON M5V 2Z1
Tél: 416-203-1220; *Téléc:* 416-203-1165
www.centrefranco.org
Permettre à la population francophone du grand Toronto d'avoir accès à des services d'information, d'orientation et d'encadrement susceptibles de promouvoir la dimension humaine, culturelle et communautaire des multiples visages de la francophonie
Lise Marie Baudry, Directrice générale

Chateauguay Valley English-Speaking Peoples' Association (CVESPA)
1493, rte 138, CP 1357, Huntingdon QC J0S 1H0
Tel: 450-264-5386; *Fax:* 450-264-5387
To assure preservation, maintenance & on-going development of English-speaking population in Southwest Québec; to encourage continuous development of their institutions & cultural heritage; to assure full participation & representation of English-speaking community in all aspects of Québec society; to promote positive attitudes in English-speaking community to participate fully & harmoniously with French-speaking population; to foster activities which would bring the two communities together to improve their mutual understanding

Chinese Canadian Association of Prince Edward Island (CCAPEI)
president.ccapei@gmail.com
www.ccapei.org
Zhongyu Zhang, President

Conseil de la vie française en Amérique (CVFA)
#201, 5350, boul Henri-Bourassa, Québec QC G1H 6Y8
Tél: 418-626-5665; *Téléc:* 418-626-5663
Favoriser le développement et l'épanouissement des communautés d'origine de langue et de culture françaises en Amerique
Guy Lefebvre, Directeur général
Jean-Louis Desrochers, Président

The Council of Canadians (COC) / Le Conseil des Canadiens
#700, 170 Laurier Ave. West, Ottawa ON K1P 5V5
Tel: 613-233-2773; *Fax:* 613-233-6776
Toll-Free: 800-387-7177
inquiries@canadians.org
www.canadians.org
Social Media: www.facebook.com/groups/2228697837; twitter.com/councilofcdns; www.youtube.com/councilofcanadians
With chapters across the country, The Council of Canadians is Canada's largest citizens' organization, working to protect Canadian independence in areas such as energy & environment, health care & fair trade. The Council provides a critical voice on key national issues: safeguarding our social programs, promoting economic justice, renewing Canada's democracy, asserting Canadian sovereignty, promoting alternatives to corporate-style free trade & preserving the environment
Maude Barlow, National Chairperson

Fédération acadienne de la Nouvelle-Écosse (FANE)
La Maison acadienne, 54 Queen St., Dartmouth NS B2Y 1G3
Tél: 902-433-0065; *Téléc:* 902-433-0066
fane@federationacadienne.ca
www.federationacadienne.ca
Un regroupement d'organismes régionaux, provinciaux et institutionnels d'expression française qui s'engage à promouvoir l'épanouissement et le développement global de la communauté acadienne et francophone de la Nouvelle-Écosse.
Jean Léger, Directeur général

Fédération culturelle canadienne-française (FCCF)
Place de la Francophonie, #405, 450 Rideau St., Ottawa ON K1N 5Z4
Tél: 613-241-8770; *Téléc:* 613-241-6064
Ligne sans frais: 800-267-2005
info@fccf.ca
www.fccf.ca
Défendre et promouvoir les arts et la culture de la francophonie canadienne hors-Québec.
Éric Dubeau, Directeur général

Fédération de la jeunesse canadienne-française inc. (FJCF)
#403, 450 Rideau St., Ottawa ON K1N 5Z4
Tél: 613-562-4624; *Téléc:* 613-562-3995
Ligne sans frais: 800-267-5173
fjcf@fjcf.ca
www.fjcf.ca
Etre le porte-parole national de la jeunesse canadienne-française et acadienne; assurer l'épanouissement de la jeunesse dans les secteurs de l'éducation, des arts et communications, des loisirs et de l'économie; augmenter la visibilité de la FJCF et de ses membres auprès de leurs différentes clientèles; augmenter les occasions pour les jeunes d'utiliser la langue française; renforcer le sentiment d'appartenance des jeunes, pour qu'ils soient des agents de changement dans leur communauté.
Jean-Michel Beaudry, Président

Fédération des communautés francophones et acadienne du Canada (FCFAC)
#300, 450 rue Rideau, Ottawa ON K1N 5Z4
Tél: 613-241-7600; *Téléc:* 613-241-6046
info@fcfa.ca
www.fcfa.ca
Mèdia social: www.facebook.com/FCFACanada; twitter.com/fcfacanada
Défendre et promouvoir les droits et les intérêts des communautés francophones et acadiennes qu'elle représente.
Suzanne Bossé, Directrice générale
Marie-France Kenny, Présidente

Fondation franco-ontarienne (FFO)
#102, 559, av King Edward, Ottawa ON K1N 7N5
Tél: 613-565-4720; *Téléc:* 613-565-8539
info@fondationfranco-ontarienne.ca
www.fondationfranco-ontarienne.ca
La Fondation franco-ontarienne appuie financièrement la réalisation d'initiatives qui assurent la vitalité de la communauté franco-ontarienne
Solange Fortin, Coordonnatrice générale

Guyana Cultural Association of Montréal (GCAM)
PO Box 29640, Stn. CSP Prom du Parc, St. Hubert QC J3Y 9A9
Tel: 514-676-5771; *Fax:* 514-445-0747
gcaminfo@yahoo.com
www.gcaom.org
U. Leebert Sancho, Contact

L'Institut canadien de Québec (ICQ)
350, rue Saint-Joseph est, 4e étage, Québec QC G1K 3B2
Tél: 418-641-6788; *Téléc:* 418-641-6787
courrier@institutcanadien.qc.ca
www.icqbdq.qc.ca
Mèdia social: www.facebook.com/group.php?gid=176468254731; twitter.com/ICQ_Quebec
Démocratiser l'accès au savoir et aux oeuvres d'imagination par un service de bibliothèque universellement accessible; sensibiliser le public aux arts et à la culture; gestion de bibliothèques publiques de la Ville de Québec.
Jean Payeur, Directeur général
Gilbert Lacasse, Président
Sylvie Fortin, Secrétaire

The Japan Foundation, Toronto / Kokosai Koryu Kikin Toronto Nihon Bunka Centre
#213, 131 Bloor St. West, Toronto ON M5S 1R1
Tel: 416-966-1600; *Fax:* 416-966-9773
info@jftor.org
www.japanfoundationcanada.org
Tokyo-based foundation established by the Government of Japan to promote Japanese culture abroad; offers a broad range of programs designed to further cultural exchange with Japan, with an emphasis on Japanese studies at the post-secondary level & Japanese language study

Masayuki Suzuki, Director
Lori Lytle, Program Officer

The Royal Commonwealth Society of Canada (RCS) / La Société royale du Commonwealth du Canada
c/o RCS Ottawa, PO Box 8023, Stn. T, Ottawa ON K1G 3H6
www.rcs.ca
A charitable, non-partisan organization which promotes knowledge of the Commonwealth & its member countries; fosters unity in diversity in matters of common concern; promotes international understanding, cooperation & peace; upholds the best traditions of the Commonwealth
Ronald Goodall, Chair
Brian Marley-Clarke, Past Chair & Treasurer

St. Vincent and the Grenadines Association of Montreal Inc. (SVGA) / L'Association St.Vincent et Grenadines de Montrèal Inc.
PO Box 396, Stn. Snowdon Station, Montréal QC H3X 3T3
Tel: 514-364-3299
www.svgamontreal.com
Thomas (Tom) Austin, President

Société de développement des entreprises culturelles (SODEC)
#800, 215, rue Saint-Jacques, Montréal QC H2Y 1M6
Tél: 514-841-2200; *Téléc:* 514-841-8606
Ligne sans frais: 800-363-0401
info@sodec.gouv.qc.ca
www.sodec.gouv.qc.ca
La SODEC est une société du gouvernement du Québec qui relève du ministre de la Culture, des Communications et de la Condition féminine. Elle soutient la production et la diffusion de la culture québécoise dans le champ des industries culturelles.
François Macerola, Président et chef de la direction

Société des Acadiens et Acadiennes du Nouveau-Brunswick (SAANB)
#204, 702, rue Principale, Petit-Rocher NB E8J 1V1
Tél: 506-783-4205; *Téléc:* 506-783-0629
Ligne sans frais: 888-722-2343
saanb@nb.aibn.com
www.saanb.org
La Société vise à unir tous les Acadiens et Acadiennes du Nouveau-Brunswick et les sensibiliser aux problèmes sociaux, économiques, culturels et politiques qu'ils doivent affronter; s'occuper de tout sujet ayant trait à la protection et à la promotion des droits et à l'avancement des intérêts des Acadiens et Acadiennes du Nouveau-Brunswick; entretenir des liens aussi étroits que possible avec les groupements analogues des autres provinces canadiennes et de l'étranger.
Marie-Pierre Simard, Présidente
Bruno Godin, Directeur général

Société franco-manitobaine (SFM)
#106, 147, blvd. Provencher, Saint-boniface MB R2H 0G2
Tél: 204-233-4915; *Téléc:* 204-977-8551
Ligne sans frais: 800-665-4443
sfm@sfm-mb.ca
www.sfm-mb.ca
Porte-parole officiel de la communauté franco-manitobaine, veille à l'épanouissement de cette communauté et revendique le plein respect des droits de celle-ci; de concert avec ses partenaires, elle planifie et facilite le développement global de la collectivité et en fait la promotion
Daniel Boucher, Président/Directeur général

Société nationale de l'Acadie (SNA)
307, rue Amirault Dieppe, Dieppe NB E1A 1G1
Tél: 506-853-0404; *Téléc:* 506-853-0400
www.snacadie.org
Mène différentes activités sur les scènes interprovinciales et internationales afin de promouvoir et de défendre les droits et intérêts du peuple acadien
Martin Arseneau, Directeur, Comunications

Société Saint-Jean-Baptiste de Montréal (SSJBM)
82, rue Sherbrooke ouest, Montréal QC H2X 1X3
Tél: 514-843-8851; *Téléc:* 514-844-6369
www.ssjb.com
Média social: www.facebook.com/groups/84605646085; twitter.com/ssjbm
Une société nationale qui participe de façon non partisane à l'évolution politique, sociale, économique et culturelle du Québec par ses actions, ses études, ses interventions et ses campagnes d'opinion
Mario Beaulieu, Président général

Townshippers' Association (TA) / Association des Townshippers
#100, 257, rue Queen, Sherbrooke QC J1M 1K7
Tel: 819-566-5717; *Fax:* 819-566-0271
Toll-Free: 866-566-5717
ta@townshippers.qc.ca
www.townshippers.qc.ca
Social Media: twitter.com/townshippersTA
To promote the interests of the English-speaking community in the historical Eastern Townships; to strengthen the cultural identity of this community; to encourage the full participation of the English-speaking population in the community at large
Ingrid Marini, Executive Director
Gerald Cutting, President

L'Union culturelle des Franco-Ontariennes (UCFO)
#1, 5330, ch Canotek, Ottawa ON K1J 9C1
Tél: 613-741-1334; *Téléc:* 613-741-8577
Ligne sans frais: 877-520-8226
ucfo@on.aibn.com
www.unionculturelle.ca
Améliorer les conditions et les réalités sociales des femmes francophones de l'Ontario; faciliter l'épanouissement de la femme tout en favorisant son autonomie
Diane Brissette, Présidente provinciale

Dental

Alberta Dental Assistants Association (ADAA)
#166, 14315 - 118 Ave. NW, Edmonton AB T5L 4S6
Tel: 780-486-2526; *Fax:* 780-486-2728
Toll-Free: 800-355-8940
contact@abrda.ca
www.abrda.ca
To ensure that members are valued as essential partners in the provision of high quality oral health care
Howards Riddel, Executive Director

Alberta Dental Association & College (ADAC)
#101, 8230 - 105 St., Edmonton AB T6E 5H9
Tel: 780-432-1012; *Fax:* 780-433-4864
Toll-Free: 800-843-3848
adaadmin@telusplanet.net
www.abda.ab.ca

Association des assistant(e)s-dentaires du Québec (CDAA/AADQ)
#203, 6705, Jean-Talon est, Saint-Léonard QC H1S 1N2
Tél: 514-722-9900; *Téléc:* 514-256-8539
info@cdaa.ca
www.cdaa.ca
Aider ses membres à parfaire leurs connaissances par des cours pratiques et théoriques; moderniser le domaine dentaire; règlementer les assistants-dentaires
Johanne Longpré, Présidente

Association des chirurgiens dentistes du Québec (ACDQ)
#1425, 425, boul de Maisonneuve ouest, Montréal QC H3A 3G5
Tél: 514-282-1425; *Téléc:* 514-282-0255
Ligne sans frais: 800-361-3794
info@acdq.qc.ca
www.acdq.qc.ca
L'Association a pour objet l'étude, la défense et le développement des intérêts économiques, sociaux et moraux de ses membres.
Serge Langlois, Président

Association des denturologistes du Québec (ADQ)
Complexe Raycom, #230, 8150, boul Métropolitain est, Anjour QC H1K 1A1
Tél: 514-252-0270; *Téléc:* 514-252-0392
Ligne sans frais: 800-563-6273
denturo@adq-qc.com
www.adq-qc.com
Protéger et développer les intérêts professionnels, moraux, sociaux et économiques de ses membres

British Columbia Dental Association
#400, 1765 - 8th Ave. West, Vancouver BC V6J 5C6
Tel: 604-736-7202; *Fax:* 604-736-7588
Toll-Free: 888-396-9888
post@bcdental.org
www.bcdental.org
To act as the voice of dentistry in British Columbia; To prevent oral disease

Canadian Academy of Endodontics / L'Académie canadienne d'endodontie
c/o #301, 400 St. Mary Ave., Winnipeg MB R3C 4K5
webmaster@caendo.ca
www.caendo.ca
The goal of CAE is to advance the art & science of endodontics by providing learning experiences through lectures, providing teachers of endodontics a forum for interaction, providing information & acting as a resource to dental governing bodies, & ultimately to improving the health of the public.
Michael Gossack, President
Wayne Acheson, Executive Secretary

Canadian Association for Dental Research (CADR) / Association canadienne de recherches dentaires (ACRD)
c/o Dr. C. Birek, Faculty of Dentistry, University of Manitoba, 780 Bannatyne Ave., Winnipeg MB R3E 0W2
Tel: 204-789-3256; *Fax:* 204-789-3913
birek@ms.umanitoba.ca
www.cadr-acrd.ca
To advance research & increase knowledge in order to improve oral health in Canada; To support & represent Canadian oral health researchers
Edward Putnins, President
Michael Greene, President, CADR Student Research Group
Debora Matthews, Vice-President
Catalena Birek, Secretary-Treasurer

Canadian Association of Orthodontists (CAO) / Association canadienne des orthodontists (aco)
#310, 2175 Sheppard Ave. East, Toronto ON M2J 1W8
Tel: 416-491-3186; *Fax:* 416-491-1670
Toll-Free: 877-226-8800
cao@taylorenterprises.com
www.cao-aco.org
To advance the science & art of orthodontics; To promote the highest quality of orthodontic care in Canada; To act as the official voice of Canadian orthodontic specialists
Howard Steiman, President
Paul Major, First Vice-President
Garry A. Solomon, Second Vice-President
Michael W. Patrician, Secretary-Treasurer
Dan Pollit, Chair, Communications

Canadian Dental Assistants Association (CDAA) / Association canadienne des assistants(es) dentaires (ACAD)
#203, 2255 St. Laurent Blvd., Ottawa ON K1G 4K3
Tel: 613-521-5495; *Fax:* 613-521-5572
Toll-Free: 800-345-5137
info@cdaa.ca
www.cdaa.ca
Social Media: twitter.com/CDAA_ACAD
Strives to foster opportunities for growth, to be the voice for Canadian dental assistants, & to represent the interests of provincial & military dental associations
Mark Buzan, Executive Director
Miriam Moodley, Director, Projects
Janet Hazen, President
Sherry Hirsche, Vice-President

Canadian Dental Association (CDA) / L'Association dentaire canadienne (ADC)
1815 Alta Vista Dr., Ottawa ON K1G 3Y6
Tel: 613-523-1770; *Fax:* 613-523-7736
reception@cda-adc.ca
www.cda-adc.ca
Social Media: www.facebook.com/pages/Canadian-Dental-Health/203452689666842; twitter.com/mydentalhealth
The authoritative national voice of dentistry, dedicated to the representation & advancement of the profession, nationally & internationally, & to the achievement of optimum oral health
Robert MacGregor, President
Peter Doig, Vice President

Canadian Dental Hygienists Association (CDHA) / Association canadienne des hygiènistes dentaires
96 Centrepointe Dr., Ottawa ON K2G 6B1
Tel: 613-224-5515; *Fax:* 613-224-7283
Toll-Free: 800-267-5235
info@cdha.ca
www.cdha.ca
To act as the collective voice of dental hygiene in Canada; to advance the profession in support of our members; to contribute to the health & well-being of the public.
Susan A. Ziebarth, Executive Director

Certified Dental Assistants of BC (CDABC)
#103, 3540 West 41st Ave., Vancouver BC V6N 3E6
Tel: 604-714-1766; *Fax:* 604-714-1767
Toll-Free: 800-579-4440
info@cdabc.org
www.cdabc.org
Marlene Robinson, Executive Director
Angela Wiebe, President

College of Dental Surgeons of British Columbia (CDSBC)
#500, 1765 West 8th Ave., Vancouver BC V6J 5C6
Tel: 604-736-3621; *Fax:* 604-734-9448
Toll-Free: 800-663-9169
info@cdsbc.org
www.cdsbc.org
Registers, licenses & regulates dentists & certified dental assistants. Assures British Columbians of professional standards of health care, ethics, & competence by regulating dentistry in a fair & reasonable manner; administers the Dentists Act
Bob Coles, President

College of Dental Surgeons of Saskatchewan
#202, 728 Spadina Cres. East, Saskatoon SK S7K 4H7
Tel: 306-244-5072; *Fax:* 306-244-2476
cdss@saskdentists.com
www.saskdentists.com
To operate as a provincial licensing body
Jerod Orb, Executive Director
Bernie White, Registrar
Frank Hohn, President
Brent Dergousoff, Vice-President

College of Dental Technologists of Ontario
#300, 2100 Ellesmere Rd., Toronto ON M1H 3B7
Tel: 416-438-5003; *Fax:* 416-438-5004
info@cdto.ca
www.cdto.ca
To serve & protect the public interest by regulating & guiding the dental technology profession
E. Cheung, Registrar

Dental Association of Prince Edward Island (DAPEI)
184 Belvedere Ave., Charlottetown PE C1A 2Z1
Tel: 902-892-4022; *Fax:* 902-892-4470
dapei@pei.sympatico.ca
www.dapei.ca
DAPEI sees itself as a partner, a policy advisor, and decision maker with the public, government and its members, regarding the availability, accessibility, and affordibility of appropriate and high quality dental services for islanders.
Dana M. Coles, President
Brian Barrett, Executive Director

Dental Council of Prince Edward Island
184 Belvedere Ave., Charlottetown PE C1A 2Z1
Tel: 902-892-4470; *Fax:* 902-892-4470
Council for dentists specifically in PEI.

Denturist Association of British Columbia
#312C, 9801 King George Hwy., Surrey BC V3T 5H5
Tel: 604-582-6823; *Fax:* 604-582-0317
info@denturist.bc.ca
www.denturist.bc.ca
Maria Green, President

Denturist Association of Canada (DAC) / Association des denturologistes du Canada (ADC)
PO Box 45521, 2397 King George Hwy., Surrey BC V4A 9N3
Tel: 604-538-3123; *Fax:* 604-582-0317
Toll-Free: 877-538-3123
dacdenturist@telus.net
www.denturist.org
To promote oral health in Canada through the profession of denturism.
Michael Vout, President
Gerry Hansen, Chief Administrative Officer

Denturist Association of Manitoba
PO Box 70006, #1, 1660 Kenaston Blvd., Winnipeg MB R3P 0X6
Tel: 204-897-1087; *Fax:* 204-488-2872
Toll-Free: 866-897-1087
administrator@denturistmb.org
www.denturistmb.org
To represent Manitoba denturists & ensure high quality, low cost delivery of dentures direct to the public
Paul Hrynchuk, President
Kelli Wagner, Administrator

Denturist Association of Newfoundland & Labrador
6 Commonwealth Ave., Mount Pearl NL A1N 1W2
Tel: 709-364-3355; *Fax:* 709-364-3355
John Brown, President

Denturist Association of Northwest Territories
PO Box 1506, Yellowknife NT X1A 2P2
Tel: 867-766-3666; *Fax:* 867-669-0103

Denturist Association of Ontario (DAO)
#106, 5780 Timberlea Blvd., Mississauga ON L4W 4W8
Tel: 905-238-6090; *Fax:* 905-238-7090
Toll-Free: 800-284-7311
info@denturistassociation.ca
www.dao.on.ca
The Association is a member-oriented, diversified & innovative centre of information for denturists & the public. They develop services that address current needs & future concerns & are the primary providers of dental prosthetics & related services.
David Kostynyk, President
Kim Stilwell, Chief Administrative Officer

Denturist Society of Nova Scotia
c/o Chedabucto Denture Clinic, 3951 South River Rd., Antigonish NS B2G 2H6
Tel: 902-863-3131; *Fax:* 902-863-3131
Diane Carrigan-Weir, President

Denturist Society of Prince Edward Island
Rhyno Denture Clinic, 222 University Ave., Charlottetown PE C1A 4S7
Tel: 902-892-3253
rhynopat@hotmail.com

Manitoba Dental Assistants Association
#17, 595 Clifton St., Winnipeg MB R3G 2X5
Tel: 204-586-7378; *Fax:* 204-783-9631
mdaa@mdaa.ca
www.mdaa.ca

Manitoba Dental Association (MDA)
#103, 698 Corydon Ave., Winnipeg MB R3M 0X9
Tel: 204-988-5300; *Fax:* 204-988-5310
office@manitobadentist.ca
www.manitobadentist.ca
To act as the governing body for dentists & dental assistants in Manitoba; To ensure that that the oral health of Manitobans is met
Joel Antel, President
Allan Cogan, Vice-President
Rafi Mohammed, Sec.-Treas.

National Dental Examining Board of Canada / Le bureau national d'examen dentaire du Canada
#203, 100 Bronson Ave., Ottawa ON K1R 6G8
Tel: 613-236-5912; *Fax:* 613-236-8386
director@ndeb.ca
www.ndeb.ca
According to the Act of Parliament, the NDEB is responsible for the establishment of qualifying conditions for a national standard of dental competence for general practitioners, for establishing and maintaining an examination facility to test for this national standard of dental competence and for issuing certificates to dentists who successfully meet this national standard.

New Brunswick Dental Assistants Association (NBDAA) / Association des Assistantes Dentaires du Nouveau-Brunswick
PO Box 8997, Shediac NB E4P 8W5
Tel: 506-532-9189; *Fax:* 506-532-3635
Toll-Free: 866-530-9189
bernioff@nb.sympatico.ca
www.cdaa.ca/nbdaa
Supporting Dental Assistants in New Brunswick.
Amber Caissie, President
Bernice Léger, Office Coordinator

New Brunswick Dental Society / Société dentaire du Nouveau-Brunswick
Carleton Place, PO Box 488, Stn. A, #820, 520 King St., Fredericton NB E3B 4Z9
Tel: 506-452-8575; *Fax:* 506-452-1872
nbds@nb.aibn.com
www.nbdental.com
To regulate & promote the dentistry profession in New Brunswick. To promote professional growth, high ethical standards and quality care giving through communication, education, and regulation of denistry in New Brunswick.
Lia A. Daborn, Executive Director

New Brunswick Denturists Society / Société des denturologistes du Nouveau-Brunswick
PO Box 5566, 288 West St. Pierre Blvd., Caraquet NB E1W 1B7
Tel: 506-727-7411; *Fax:* 506-727-6728
claudetteboudreau@aibn.com
www.nbdenturistsociety.ca
Daniel J. Robichaud, President
Claudette Boudreau, Secretary

Newfoundland & Labrador Dental Association
The Fortis Bldg., #401, 139 Water St., St. John's NL A1C 1B2
Tel: 709-579-2362; *Fax:* 709-579-1250
nfdental@nfld.net
www.nlda.net
To promote & advance dentistry or dental surgery & related arts & sciences in all their branches; to increase the knowledge, skill, standard & proficiency of its members in the practice of dentistry or dental surgery; to maintain the honour & integrity of the dental profession; to aid in the furtherance of measures designed to improve dental health & prevent disease & disability; to cooperate with & to assist public & private dental associations, agencies & commissions in the task of providing or financing dental care; to promote measures designed to improve standards of dental care & the practice of dentistry or dental surgery; to improve the welfare & social standards of its members & encourage the cooperation of its members in the protection of their rights.
Anthony Patey, Executive Director

Newfoundland & Labrador Dental Board
139 Water St., 6th Fl., St. John's NL A1C 1B2
Tel: 709-579-2391; *Fax:* 709-579-1250
nfdental@nfld.net
According to the Act of Parliament, the NDEB is responsible for the establishment of qualifying conditions for a national standard of dental competence for general practitioners, for establishing and maintaining an examination facility to test for this national standard of dental competence and for issuing certificates to dentists who successfully meet this national standard.
Paul O'Brien, Sec-Reg.

Newfoundland Dental Assistants Association
#274, 38 Pearson St., St. John's NL A1A 3R1
To advance the career of dental assisting in Newfoundland
Vera Walsh, President

Northwest Territories & Nunavut Dental Association
PO Box 24, 4916 - 49 St., Yellowknife NT X1A 2N1
Tel: 867-873-6416; *Fax:* 867-920-7798
nwtnudentalassoc@theedge.ca

Nova Scotia Dental Assistants' Association (NSDAA)
PO Box 9142, Stn. A, Halifax NS B3K 5M8
Tel: 902-826-1922; *Fax:* 902-820-3015
nsdaa@ns.sympatico.ca
www.nsdaa.ca
To affiliate at local, provincial & national levels for the betterment of the dental assistant profession & patient care
Michelle Fowler, President
Lynda Foran, Executive Director

Nova Scotia Dental Association (NSDA)
#101, 1559 Brunswick St., Halifax NS B3J 2G1
Tel: 902-420-0088; *Fax:* 902-423-6537
nsda@eastlink.ca
www.nsdental.org
D.V. Pamenter, Executive Director

Ontario Dental Assistants Association (ODAA)
869 Dundas St., London ON N5W 2Z8
Tel: 519-679-2566; *Fax:* 519-679-8494
odaainfo@ody.ca
www.odnaa.org
To act as the certifying body for dental assistants in Ontario
Darlene Leiska, President
Suzanne McLachlen, Vice-President
Judy Melville, Executive Director

Ontario Dental Association (ODA)
4 New St., Toronto ON M5R 1P6
Tel: 416-922-3900; *Fax:* 416-922-9005
Toll-Free: 800-387-1393
info@oda.ca
www.oda.ca
Social Media:
www.facebook.com/pages/Canadian-Dental-Health/2034526896 66842
To represent the dentists of Ontario; to provide exemplary oral health care & promote the attainment of optimal health for the people of Ontario
Harry Höediono, President
Rick Caldwell, Vice-President

Ordre des dentistes du Québec (ODQ)
625, boul René-Lévesque ouest, 15e étage, Montréal QC H3B 1R2
Tél: 514-875-8511; *Téléc:* 514-393-9248
Ligne sans frais: 800-361-4887
dirgen@odq.qc.ca; com@odq.qc.ca
www.ordredesdentistesduquebec.qc.ca
Assurer la qualité des services en médecine dentaire par le respect de normes élevées de pratique et d'éthique et de promouvoir la santé bucco-dentaire auprès de la population du Québec
Caroline Daoust, Directrice générale et secrétaire

Ordre des denturologistes du Québec (ODQ)
395, rue du Parc-Industriel, Longueuil QC J4H 3V7
Tél: 450-646-7922; *Téléc:* 450-646-2509
Ligne sans frais: 800-567-2251
info@odq.com
www.odq.com
Monique Bouchard, Directrice générale et secrétaire

Prince Edward Island Dental Assistants Association
PO Box 404, Cornwall PE C1A 1H0
Tel: 902-566-9553; *Fax:* 902-367-2207
info@peidaa.com
Julie Ready, President

Provincial Dental Board of Nova Scotia
#102, 1559 Brunswick St., Halifax NS B3J 2G1
Tel: 902-420-0083; *Fax:* 902-492-0301
admin@pdbns.ca
www.pdbns.ca
To protect the public in the delivery of dental care by licensure & regulation
W.A. MacInnis, Registrar

Royal College of Dental Surgeons of Ontario
6 Crescent Rd., 5th Fl., Toronto ON M4W 1T1
Tel: 416-961-6555; *Fax:* 416-961-5814
Toll-Free: 800-565-4591
info@rcdso.org
www.rcdso.org
To operate as the governing body for dentists in Ontario; To protect the public's right to quality dental services by providing leadership to the dental profession in self-regulation
Ted Schipper, Chair
Peter Trainor, Vice-President

Royal College of Dentists of Canada (RCDC) / Collège Royal des Chirurgiens Dentistes du Canada
#2003, 180 Dundas St. West, Toronto ON M3G 1Z8
Tel: 416-512-6571
office@rcdc.ca
www.rcdc.ca
To provide examinations for dental sciences & for nationally recognized dental specialties in Canada
J. Richard Emery, President
Garnet Packota, Vice-President
Ernest W.N. Lam, Secretary-Treasurer
Patricia A. Main, Registrar
Paul Jackson, Examiner-in-Chief

Saskatchewan Dental Assistants' Association (SDAA)
PO Box 294, 603 - 3rd St., Kenaston SK S0G 2N0
Tel: 306-252-2769; *Fax:* 306-252-2089
sdaa@sasktel.net
www.sdaa.sk.ca
To promote excellence in dental health care; To advance public protection through enforcement of regulations, education, ethical practice, & standardization
Susan Anholt, Executive Director
Calla Effa, President
Robin McKay Ganshorn, Coordinator, Professional Development

Yukon Denturist Association
#1, 106 Main St., Whitehorse YT Y1A 2A7
Tel: 867-668-6818; *Fax:* 867-668-6811
pjallen@northwestel.net
Elsie Bagan, Registrar

Developing Countries

Canadian Consortium for International Social Development (CCISD)
Carleton University, 1719 Dunton Tower, Ottawa ON K1S 5B6
Tel: 613-520-2600; *Fax:* 613-520-2344
ccsid@ccs.carleton.ca
www.ccisd.ca
CCISD is a consortium of scholars, activists and organizations doing and promoting applied research and advocacy on international issues of social policy and social development.
Angela Laird, Contact

Mennonite Central Committee Canada (MCCC)
134 Plaza Dr., Winnipeg MB
Tel: 204-261-6381; *Fax:* 204-269-9875
Toll-Free: 888-622-6337
canada@mennonitecc.ca
canada.mcc.org
Social Media:
www.facebook.com/pages/Mennonite-Central-Committee-Canada/289561555567; twitter.com/MCCCan
To operate as a relief & development service agency; To promote relief, development, & peace
Don Peters, Executive Director

Teamwork Children's Services International
5983 Ladyburn Cres., Mississauga ON L5M 4V9
Tel: 905-542-1047
jchacha@teamworkchildrenservices.com
www.teamworkchildrenservices.com
To provide orphaned & disadvantaged children in rural areas of Africa a safe & secure faith-based home environment; To provide the children with good health, education, & vocational training, enabling them to become self-supporting & productive citizens
Joel Chacha, Program Director

Disabled Persons

AboutFace
#1003, 123 Edward St., Toronto ON M5G 1E2
Tel: 416-597-2229; *Fax:* 416-597-8494
Toll-Free: 800-665-3223
info@aboutfaceinternational.org
www.aboutfaceinternational.org
To provide emotional support & information to, & on behalf of, individuals who have a facial difference & their families
Anna Pileggi, Executive Director
Sharon Fitzpatrick, Chair

Active Living Alliance for Canadians with a Disability (ALACD) / Alliance de vie active pour les canadiens/canadiennes ayant un handicap
#104, 720 Belfast Rd., Ottawa ON K1G 0Z5
Tel: 613-244-0052; *Fax:* 613-244-4857
Toll-Free: 800-771-0663
TTY: 888-771-0663
ala@ala.ca
www.ala.ca
To promote inclusion & active living lifestyles of Canadians with disabilities by facilitating communication & collaboration among organizations, agencies & individuals
Jane Arkell, Director

Alberta Association for Community Living (AACL)
11724 Kingsway Ave., Edmonton AB T5G 0X5
Tel: 780-451-3055; *Fax:* 780-453-5779
Toll-Free: 800-252-7556
mail@aacl.org
www.aacl.org
Social Media:
www.facebook.com/group.php?gid=165187756132&ref=ts
To advocate for fully inclusive community lives for children & adults with developmental disabilities
Bruce Uditsky, Chief Executive Officer
Lori Adamchick, Executive Director
Barbara MacIntyre, President
Kim Guay, Vice-President
Dean Fowler, Treasurer
Trish Bowman, Director, Community Devlopment
Deb McLean, Manager, Operations
Colleen Storms, Manager, Business
Lisa Snyder, Librarian

Alberta Association of Rehabilitation Centres (AARC)
#19, 3220 - 5 Ave. NE, Calgary AB T2A 5N1
Tel: 403-250-9495; *Fax:* 403-291-9864
acds@acds.ca
www.acds.ca
To support organizations that provide services & supports to people with disabilities; To act as a voice for the field of community rehabilitation to the political & administrative arms of government; To focus on human resource initiatives for the services sector; To provide in-service training opportunities for people employed in the field; To accredit & certify service in Alberta
Ann Nicol, CEO
Helen Ficocelli, President
Judy Galbraith, Vice-President

Alberta Committee of Citizens with Disabilities (ACCD)
#106, 10423 - 178 St. NW, Edmonton AB T5S 1R5
Tel: 780-488-9088; *Fax:* 780-488-3757
Toll-Free: 800-387-2514
TTY: 780-488-9090
accd@accd.net
www.accd.net
To promote full participation in society for Albertans with disabilities
Beverley D. Matthiessen, Executive Director

Alberta Easter Seals Society
Baker Centre, #1408, 10025 - 106 St., Edmonton AB T5J 1G4
Tel: 780-429-0137; *Fax:* 780-429-1937
Toll-Free: 877-732-7837
edmonton@easterseals.ab.ca
www.easterseals.ab.ca
To represent interests of all people with disabilities in Alberta; to promote change at all policy-making levels through public awareness campaigns, projects, seminars; to provide mobility equipment; to conduct public awareness programs; to provide recreational activities through summer camp - Camp Horizon; to provide a residential home program - Easter Seals McQueen Residence
Jodi Zabludowski, Director, Operations
Trish Gooz, Director, Finance & Administration
Susan Law, CEO

ARCH Disability Law Centre
#110, 425 Bloor St. East, Toronto ON M4W 3R5
Tel: 416-482-8255; *Fax:* 416-482-2981
Toll-Free: 866-482-2724
TTY: 416-482-1254
archlib@lao.on.ca
www.archdisabilitylaw.ca
To defend & advance the equality rights of persons with disabilities; assisting individuals with disabilities to understand their rights & how to enforce them; working with groups representing people with disabilities throughout Ontario; representing in precedent setting cases where client cannot be represented appropriately by other legal services; summary advice & referral - lawyers who specialize in areas of law as they relate to disability provide free, confidential, basic legal advice & referral to other sources of assistance
Ivana Petricone, Executive Director

Association du Québec pour enfants avec problèmes auditifs (AQEPA)
#A446, 3700, rue Berri, Montréal QC H2L 4G9
Tél: 514-842-8706; *Téléc:* 514-842-4006
Ligne sans frais: 877-842-4006
aqepa@aqepa.org
www.aqepa.surdite.org
Regrouper les parents d'enfants sourds et malentendants; informer et sensibiliser les parents et le public
Daniel Péloquin, Directeur général

Association du Québec pour l'intégration sociale (AQIS) / Québec Association for Community Living
3958, rue Dandurand, Montréal QC H1X 1P7
Tél: 514-725-7245; *Téléc:* 514-725-2796
direction_generale@aqis-iqdi.qc.ca
Défendre les droits et promouvoir les intérêts des personnes ayant une déficience intellectuelle
Lucie Villeneuve, Présidente
Diane Milliard, Directrice générale

Association for Community Living - Manitoba
#6, 120 Maryland St., Winnipeg MB R3G 1L1
Tel: 204-786-1607; *Fax:* 204-789-9850
aclmb@aclmb.ca
www.aclmb.ca
To promote the welfare of people with handicaps & their families; To speak on behalf of people with developmental disabilities in Manitoba; To ensure that every person in Manitoba has access to supports necessary to live with dignity & to participate fully in the community of his/her choice
Val Surbey, President
Betty Hopkins, Secretary
Malanchuk Reg, Treasurer

Association for the Neurologically Disabled of Canada (AND) / Association canadienne pour les handicapés neurologiques
56 Centre St., Thornhill ON L4J 1E9
Tel: 416-244-1992; *Fax:* 416-244-4099
Toll-Free: 800-561-1497
info@and.ca
www.and.ca
To help the neurologically disabled achieve their full potential

Basil Ziv, Executive Director

Association for Vaccine Damaged Children
c/o Mary James, 67 Shier Dr., Winnipeg MB R3R 2H2
To inform parents of the risks of immunization; To support parents in any challenging situation with public health authorities
Mary James, Contact

Association québécoise pour le loisir des personnes handicapées (AQLPH)
CP 1000, Succ. M, 4545, av Pierre-de-Coubertin, Montréal QC H1V 3R2
Tél: 514-252-3144; *Téléc:* 514-252-8360
info@aqlph.qc.ca
www.aqlph.qc.ca
Promouvoir le droit à un loisir de qualité (éducatif, sécuritaire, valorisant et de détente); promouvoir la participation et la libre expression de la personne face à son loisir; promouvoir l'accès à tous les champs d'application du loisir (tourisme, plein air, sport et activité physique, loisir scientifique, socio-éducatif et socioculturel) pour toutes les personnes handicapées du Québec sans restriction d'âge, de sexe, ni de type d'handicap
Guylaine Laforest, Directrice générale

BALANCE for Blind Adults
#302, 4920 Dundas St. West, Toronto ON M9A 1B7
Tel: 416-236-1796; *Fax:* 416-236-4280
info@balancefba.org
www.balancefba.org
To provide instruction & support to individuals with visual impairment to enable them to live independently & confidently in their community; To promote independence, decision making, & self-fulfillment
Susan Archibald, Executive Director
Laura Antal, Coordinator, Office
David Kopman, Coordinator, Volunteers
Doug Poirier, Coordinator, Programs

The Bob Rumball Centre for the Deaf (BRCD)
2395 Bayview Ave., Toronto ON M2L 1A2
Tel: 416-449-9651; *Fax:* 416-449-8881
TTY: 416-449-2728
info@bobrumball.org
www.bobrumball.org
To provide opportunities for a higher quality of life for deaf people while preserving & promoting their language & culture; to foster & develop good relations with the community at large & actively promote the Centre; to work closely with the various ministries of the provincial government & related agencies.
Alistair M. Fraser, Chairman
Robert L. Rumball, Interim Executive Director
Karen Chambers, Manager of Finance
Shirley Cassel, Supervisor of Centre Programs

British Columbia Association for Community Living (BCACL)
227 - 6th St., New Westminster BC V3L 3A5
Tel: 604-777-9100; *Toll-Free:* 800-618-1119
info@bcacl.org
www.bcacl.org
Social Media:
www.facebook.com/group.php?gid=112557852110381
To enhance the lives of persons with developmental disabilities & their families; To promote the participation of people with developmental disabilities in all aspects of community life; To support activities dedicated to building inclusive communities that value the diverse abilities of all people
Annette Delaplace, President
Faith Bodnar, Executive Director
Karen De Long, Director, Community Development
Danielle Kelliher, Director, Communications
Salima Mawji, Director, Resource Development
Frank Peng, Director, Finance
Alain LeFebvre, Treasurer

Canadian Abilities Foundation
#270, 340 College St., Toronto ON M5T 3A9
Tel: 416-923-1885; *Fax:* 416-923-9829
Toll-Free: 888-700-4476
able@abilities.ca
www.abilities.ca
Social Media: www.facebook.com/group.php?gid=2384460966
To provide information, inspiration & opportunity to Canadians with disabilities
Raymond D. Cohen, President & Publisher
Jennifer Rivkin, Managing Editor
Christine Staddon, Coordinator, Special Projects

Canadian Association for Community Living (CACL) / Association canadienne pour l'intégration communautaire
Kinsmen Building, York University, 4700 Keele St., Toronto ON M3J 1P3
Tel: 416-661-9611; *Fax:* 416-661-5701
inform@cacl.ca
www.cacl.ca
Social Media: www.facebook.com/canadianacl;
twitter.com/cacl_acic; www.youtube.com/canadianacl
To ensure the following for people with intellectual disabilities: the same rights, & access to choice, services, & supports as others; the same opportunities to live in freedom & dignity with the necessary supports to do so; & the ability to articulate & realize their rights & aspirations
Michael Bach, Executive Vice-President
John Cairns, Director, Finance & Administration
Cam Crawford, Director, Research & Knowledge
Doris Rajan, Director, Social Development & Public Education
Neil Wiernik, Manager, Online Community & Communications

Canadian Association of the Deaf (CAD) / Association des sourds du Canada
#203, 251 Bank St., Ottawa ON K2P 1X3
Tel: 613-565-2882; *Fax:* 613-565-1207
TTY: 613-565-8882
info@cad.ca
www.cad.ca
Social Media: www.facebook.com/group.php?gid=57872523519
To protect & promote the rights, needs, & concerns of deaf Canadians
Doug Momotiuk, President
James D. Roots, Executive Director

The Canadian Council of the Blind (CCB) / Le Conseil canadien des aveugles
#100, 20 James St., Ottawa ON K2P 0T6
Tel: 613-567-0311; *Fax:* 613-567-2728
Toll-Free: 877-304-0968
ccb@ccbnational.net
www.ccbnational.net
Social Media:
www.facebook.com/group.php?gid=143280866736;
twitter.com/ccbnational
To promote the well-being of individuals who are blind or vision-impaired through higher education, profitable employment, & social association; To create a closer relationship between blind & sighted friends; To organize a nation-wide organization of people who are blind & vision-impaired & groups of blind persons throughout Canada; To promote measures for the conservation of sight & the prevention of blindness
Louise Gillis, National President
Jim Tokos, First Vice-President
Linda Sobey, Second Vice-President

Canadian Council on Rehabilitation & Work (CCRW) / Le Conseil canadien de la réadaptation et du travail (CCRT)
#1202, 1 Yonge St., Toronto ON M5E 1E5
Tel: 416-260-3060; *Fax:* 416-260-3093
Toll-Free: 800-664-0925
TTY: 416-260-9223
info@ccrw.org
www.ccrw.org
To improve employment opportunities for persons with disabilities in Canada; To promote the equitable & meaningful employment of persons with disabilities
Carole J. Barron, President & Chief Executive Officer
Venatius Babu, Chief Financial Officer
Georgia Whalen, Director, Information Technology & Standards
Elizabeth Smith, Manager, Employer Consultations & Partnerships
Monica Winkler, Senior Administrator

Canadian Cultural Society of The Deaf (CCSD)
Building 5, The Distillery Historic District, #101, 55 Mill St., Toronto ON M5A 3C4
Tel: 416-203-0343; *Fax:* 416-203-1086
TTY: 416-203-2294
info@deafculturecentre.ca; giftshop@deafculturecentre.ca
www.deafculturecentre.ca
To ensure that the cultural needs of deaf & hard-of-hearing people are being met; To concentrate efforts in the areas of the performing arts, sign language, deaf literature, the visual arts, & heritage resources
Joanne Cripps, CYW, Co-Director
Anita Small, M.Sc., Ed.D, Co-Director

Canadian Foundation for Physically Disabled Persons (CFPDP)
731 Runnymede Rd., Toronto ON M6N 3V7
Tel: 416-760-7351; *Fax:* 416-760-9405
whynot@sympatico.ca
www.cfpdp.com
To provide financial assistance to organizations sharing concern for physically disabled adults; to help create awareness in the public & business communities, & in government of the needs of physically disabled adults in the areas of housing, employment, education, accessibility, sports & recreation, & research.
Vim Kochhar, Chair
Dorothy Price, Executive Director

Canadian Guide Dogs for the Blind (CGDB)
PO Box 280, 4120 Rideau Valley Dr. North, Manotick ON K4M 1A3
Tel: 613-692-7777; *Fax:* 613-692-0650
cgdb@sympatico.ca
www.guidedogs.ca
To assist visually-impaired Canadians with their mobility by providing & training them in the use of professionally trained guide dogs.
Jane Thornton, COO

Canadian Hard of Hearing Association (CHHA) / Association des malentendants canadiens (AMEC)
#205, 2415 Holly Lane, Ottawa ON K1V 7P2
Tel: 613-526-1584; *Fax:* 613-526-4718
Toll-Free: 800-263-8068
TTY: 613-526-2692
chhanational@chha.ca
www.chha.ca
To act as the voice of all hard of hearing Canadians; To promote the integration of hard of hearing people into society
Robert Corbeil, Executive Director
Louise Normand, President
Michael Currie, Vice-President
Don Halpert, Treasurer

Canadian Hearing Society (CHS) / Société canadienne de l'ouïe
271 Spadina Rd., Toronto ON M5R 2V3
Tel: 416-928-2535; *Fax:* 416-928-2506
Toll-Free: 877-347-3427
TTY: 877-216-7310
info@chs.ca
www.chs.ca
Social Media:
www.facebook.com/pages/The-Canadian-Hearing-Society/1646
04840229034; twitter.com/wwwCHSca
To provide services that enhance the independence of deaf, deafened, & hard of hearing people, & that encourage prevention of hearing loss
Chris Kenopic, President/CEO & Secretary
Stephanus Greeff, CFO & Vice-President, Finance
Katherine Hum-Antonopoulos, COO & Vice-President, Programs & Services
Susan Main, Vice-President, Fundraising & Strategic Communications
Gary Prong, Director, Human Resources

Canadian National Institute for the Blind (CNIB) / INCA (INCA)
1929 Bayview Ave., Toronto ON M4G 3E8
Fax: 416-480-7700
Toll-Free: 800-563-2642
info@cnib.ca
www.cnib.ca
Social Media: www.facebook.com/myCNIB
To ameliorate the condition of persons with vision loss in Canada; To prevent blindness; To promote sight enhancement services; To direct services to more than 100,000 Canadians with vision loss, provided through a network of more than 57 service centres, within 13 provincial & territorial operating divisions; To provide library services, research, advocacy, public education, & accessible design consulting; To produce materials in alternative formats, including Braille & DAISY talking books; To supply assistive technologies for persons with vision loss
John M. Rafferty, President
Craig Lillico, CFO, Treasurer, & Vice-President
Sandra Levy, Chief People Officer Vice-President, Human Resource
Margaret McGrory, Executive Director & Vice-President, CNIB Library
Tim Alcock, Vice-President, Marketing & Communications
Keith Gordon, Vice-President, Research & Service Quality
Bill McKeown, Vice-President, Government Relations & Divisional Advancement

Centre de réadaptation Constance-Lethbridge (CRCL) / Constance Lethbridge Rehabilitation Centre
7005, boul de Maisonneuve ouest, Montréal QC H4B 1T3
Tél: 514-487-1770; *Téléc:* 514-487-0284
lharvey@ssss.gouv.qc.ca
www.constance-lethbridge.qc.ca
Offre des services spécialisés et ultraspécialisés à des adultes ayant une déficience motrice, en externe ou à domicile, de réadaptation, d'adaptation, de préparation et de support à l'intégration sociale ou professionnelle aux clientèles ayant des problèmes orthopédiques, neurologiques et rhumatologiques; offre aussi une expertise d'évaluation de la conduite automobile, d'évaluation et d'orientation des capacités de travail de la personne handicapée; un atelier de travail est accessible pour les personnes handicapées qui ne peuvent intégrer les centres de travail adapté de la communauté
Ghislaine Prata, Directrice générale

Christian Record Services Inc.
PO Box 31119, #119, 1300 King St. East, Oshawa ON L1H 8N9
Tel: 905-436-6938; *Fax:* 905-436-7102
Toll-Free: 888-899-0006
crs-ncb@hotmail.com
www.crsblindservices.ca
To enrich the lives of blind, deaf, visually, physically & hearing impaired persons regardless of race, creed, economic status or sex.
Patricia L. Page, Executive Director

Community Living Ontario (CLO) / Intégration communautaire Ontario
#403, 240 Duncan Mill Rd., Toronto ON M3B 3S6
Tel: 416-447-4348; *Fax:* 416-447-8974
Toll-Free: 800-278-8025
info@communitylivingontario.ca
www.communitylivingontario.ca
Social Media: www.facebook.com/communitylivingontario; twitter.com/CLOntario; www.youtube.com/user/comlivon
To lobby on behalf of people with intellectual disablilities in Ontario; To ensure that every person in Ontario has access to supports to live with dignity & to participate in the community of his/her choice
Alan McWhorter, Interim Executive Director
Keith Dee, Director, Membership Services
Kimberley Gavan, Director, Community Development
Gordon Kyle, Director, Social Policy & Government Relations

Council of Canadians with Disabilities (CCD) / Conseil des Canadiens avec déficiences
#926, 294 Portage Ave., Winnipeg MB R3C 0B9
Tel: 204-947-0303
TTY: 204-947-4757
ccd@ccdonline.ca
www.ccdonline.ca
To improve the status of disabled citizens in Canadian society; to promote self-help for persons with disabilities; to provide a democratic structure for disabled citizens to voice concerns; to monitor federal legislation; to share information & cooperate with disabled persons' organizations in Canada & in other countries; to establish a positive image of disabled Canadians
Laurie Beachell, National Coordinator

DisAbled Women's Network of Canada / Réseau d'Action des Femmes Handicapées du Canada
#505, 110, rue Ste. Thérèse, Montréal QC H2Y 1E6
Tel: 514-396-0009; *Fax:* 514-396-6585
Toll-Free: 866-396-0074
admin@dawncanada.net
www.dawncanada.net
DAWN Canada's mission is to end the poverty, isolation, discrimination & violence experienced by women with disabilities; to ensure that they get the services & support needed, as well as the access to opportunities granted non-disabled people.
Carmela Sebastiana Hutchison, President
Bonnie L. Brayton, National Executive Director

The Easter Seal Society (Ontario) (TESS) / Société du timbre de Pâques de l'Ontario
#700, One Concorde Gate, Toronto ON M3C 3C6
Tel: 416-421-8377; *Fax:* 416-696-1035
Toll-Free: 800-668-6252
info@easterseals.org; donations@easterseals.org
www.easterseals.org
Social Media: www.facebook.com/MoneyMart24HourRelay; twitter.com/eastersealsont
To help children with physical disabilities achieve their full individual potential & future independence
Nelson Millman, Chair
Carol Lloyd, President & CEO

Easter Seals Canada / Timbres de Pâques Canada
#401, 40 Holly St., Toronto ON M4S 3C3
Tel: 416-932-8382; *Fax:* 416-932-9844
Toll-Free: 877-376-6362
info@easterseals.ca
www.easterseals.ca
Social Media: www.facebook.com/pages/Easter-Seals-Canada/16770287059?ref=ts; twitter.com/easterseals
To enhance the quality of life, self-esteem, & self-determination of Canadians with physical disabilities; To support the social & economic integration of people with disabilities
Max Beck, Chief Executive Officer
Greg Sarney, National Director, Development
Jason Eano, Manager, Business Development
Brian Chan, Outreach Coordinator, National Programs
Lydia Chan, Coordinator, National Programs

Easter Seals Newfoundland & Labrador
Southcott Hall, #712, 100 Forest Rd., St. John's NL A1A 1E5
Tel: 709-754-1399; *Fax:* 709-754-1398
Toll-Free: 888-601-6767
info@easterseals.nf.ca
www.easterseals.nf.ca
A charitable organization dedicated to maximizing the abilities & enhancing the lives of children & youth with physical disabilities through recreational, social & other therapeutic programs, direct assistance, education & advocacy.
Deirdre Greene, Executive Director/CEO

Easter Seals Nova Scotia (AFNS)
3670 Kempt Rd., Halifax NS B3K 4X8
Tel: 902-453-6000; *Fax:* 902-454-6121
easterseals@easterseals.ns.ca
www.easterseals.ns.ca
Social Media: www.facebook.com/ESnovascotia; twitter.com/Eastersealsns
To enable Nova Scotians with physical disabilities to enhance their quality of life by realizing their individual potential
Thomas G. Merriam, President & CEO
Faye Joudrey, Co-ordinator, Client & Equipment Services

Independent Living Canada / Vie autonome Canada
#402, 214 Montréal Rd., Ottawa ON K1L 8L8
Tel: 613-563-2581; *Fax:* 613-563-3861
TTY: 613-563-4215
info@cailc.ca
www.cailc.ca
To represent & coordinate the network of independent living centres; To guide & support independent living centres in the delivery of programs & services
Kelly J. Nadeau, National Chair
Traci Walters, National Director
Cecilia Carroll, Secretary
Diane Kreuger, Treasurer
Susan Forster, Manager, Services & Accreditation

Kinsmen Foundation of British Columbia & Yukon (KRF)
PO Box 34005, Stn. D, Vancouver BC V6J 4M1
Tel: 604-233-1993; *Fax:* 604-233-1992
Toll-Free: 866-335-1234
on-track@shaw.ca
www.kinclubofvancouver.com
Committed to providing funding for services & technologies empowering British Columbians with physical disabilities to live more independently
Jim Watson, President & CEO

Nanaimo Association for Community Living (NACL)
#201, 96 Cavan St., Nanaimo BC V9L 2V1
Tel: 250-741-0224; *Fax:* 250-741-0227
nacl.office@nanaimoacl.com
www.nanaimoacl.com
To support all people with disabilities to achieve the highest quality of life through participation, independence, inclusion & education
Graham Morry, Executive Director

National Institute of Disability Management & Research (NIDMAR) / Institut national de recherche et de gestion de l'incapacité au travail
c/o Pacific Coast University for Workplace Health Sciences, 4755 Cherry Creek Rd., Port Alberni BC V9Y 0A7
Tel: 778-421-0821; *Fax:* 778-421-0823
nidmar@nidmar.ca
www.nidmar.ca
Committed to reducing the human, social, & economic cost of disability to workers, employers, & society by providing education, research, policy development, & implementation resources to promote workplace-based integration programs
Wolfgang Zimmermann, Executive Director

New Brunswick Association for Community Living / Association du Nouveau-Brunswick pour l'intégration communautaire
#201, 420 Wilsey Rd., Fredericton NB E3B 6E9
Tel: 506-453-4400; *Fax:* 506-453-4422
Toll-Free: 866-622-2548
nbacl@nbnet.nb.ca
www.nbacl.nb.ca
To promote the welfare of people with handicaps & their families; To lobby for developmentally disabled people in New Brunswick; To ensure that every person in New Brunswick has access to supports to live with dignity & participate in the community of his/her choice
Krista Carr, Executive Director
Jason Carr, Director, Strategic Initiatives
Tammy Gallant, Director, Finance, Human Resources, & Administration
Alex LeBlanc, Manager, Independent Facilitation & Social Inclusion
Christy McLean, Manager, Communications
Amy Murray, Manager, Employment Training Initiatives
Shana Soucy, Manager, Inclusive Education

Newfoundland & Labrador Association for Community Living (NLACL)
PO Box 8414, 31 Peet St., St. John's NL A1B 3N7
Tel: 709-722-0790; *Fax:* 709-722-1325
Toll-Free: 800-701-8511
nlacl@nf.aibn.com
www.nlacl.ca
To develop communities in Newfoundland & Labrador that welcome individuals with developmental disabilities
Brianna Hookey, Executive Director
Ray McIsaac, President
Vivienne Kuester, Vice-President
Joey Mackey, Secretary
Richard Chow, Treasurer

Nova Scotia Association for Community Living (NSACL)
#2, 22-24 Dundas St., Dartmouth NS B2Y 4L2
Tel: 902-469-1174; *Fax:* 902-461-0196
nsacl@accesswave.ca
www.nsacl.ca
To work for the benefit of persons of all ages who have an intellectual disability in Nova Scotia; To ensure those with an intellectual disability have the same rights & access as all other persons
Jean Coleman, Executive Director
Roger Isnor, President

Nova Scotia Hearing & Speech Foundation
#5, 1350 Bedford Hwy., Bedford NS B4A 1E1
Tel: 902-423-1947; *Fax:* 902-423-3765
Toll-Free: 866-278-5678
info@hearingandspeech.ca
www.hearingandspeech.ca
To provide hearing services to all Nova Scotians & speech-language services to preschool children & adults; To work with community volunteer leaders, the families & friends of those who are hearing or speech impaired, our partners in government, & the medical & academic communities; To raise funds to support critical Centres' needs
Cheryl MacLeod, Office Manager
Gordon Moore, Chair

Ontario Federation for Cerebral Palsy (OFCP)
#104, 1630 Lawrence Ave. West, Toronto ON M6A 1C8
Tel: 416-244-9686; *Fax:* 416-244-6543
Toll-Free: 877-244-9686
TTY: 866-246-9122
info@ofcp.on.ca
www.ofcp.on.ca
OFCP strives improve the quality of life of persons with cerebral palsy through a broad range of programs, education, support of research & the delivery of needed services to people with cerebral palsy, & other physical disabilities, & their families.
Clarence Meyers, Executive Director

Ontario March of Dimes (OMOD) / Marche des dix sous de l'Ontario
10 Overlea Blvd., Toronto ON M4H 1A4
Tel: 416-425-3463; *Fax:* 416-425-1920
Toll-Free: 800-263-3463
info@marchofdimes.ca
www.marchofdimes.ca
To maximize the independence, personal empowerment & community participation of people with physical disabilities
Andria Spindel, President & CEO
Jerry Lucas, Vice-President, Programs
Mary Lynne Stewart, Director, Communications & Fund Development

Pamiqsaiji Association for Community Living
PO Box 708, Rankin Inlet NU X0C 0G0
Tel: 867-645-2542; *Fax:* 867-645-2543
pamiqacl@qiniq.com
Yvonne Cooper, Manager

Prince Edward Island Association for Community Living (PEIACL)
161 St. Peters Rd., Charlottetown PE C1A 5P7
Tel: 902-566-4844; *Fax:* 902-368-8057
Toll-Free: 888-360-8681
info@peiacl.ca
www.peiacl.ca
To work on behalf of individuals with an intellectual disability & their families; To empower families to increase options available to Islanders with an intellectual disability
Bridget Cairns, Executive Director
Trudi Barry, Provincial Coordinator

Prince Edward Island Council of People with Disabilities (PEICOD)
Landmark Plaza, #2, 5 Lower Malpeque Rd., Charlottetown PE C1E 1R4
Tel: 902-892-9149; *Fax:* 902-566-1919
Toll-Free: 888-473-4263
peicod@peicod.pe.ca
www.peicod.pe.ca
To improve the quality of life of people with disabilities on PEI
Marcia Carroll, Executive Director

Québec Easter Seal Society / Société des timbres de Pâques du Québec
#810, 1155 University St., Montréal QC H3B 3A7
Tel: 514-866-1969; *Fax:* 514-866-6124
Toll-Free: 800-263-1969
info@easterseal.qc.ca
Funding agency which provides financial assistance to handicapped children with purchase of specialized equipment; contributes towards programs for children's camps
Robert C. Bédard, Executive Director

R.C.L. (Québec) for the Disabled / R.C.L. (Québec) pour les Handicapés
#410, 1000, rue Saint-Antoine ouest, Montréal QC H3C 3R7
Tel: 514-866-3689; *Fax:* 514-866-6303
rclqc_handicapes@lycos.com
To provide assistance to adults with physical disabilities; to assist such adults to be more independent in their lives; to provide specialized equipment for severely disabled persons; to offer loans of wheelchairs, hospital beds, walking aids; to provide transportation from rural regions to treatment centres
John S. Jamieson, President

The Roeher Institute / L'Institut Roeher
Kinsmen Bldg., York University, 4700 Keele St., Toronto ON M3J 1P3
Tel: 416-661-9611; *Fax:* 416-661-5701
Toll-Free: 800-856-2207
info@roeher.ca
www.roeher.ca
To promote the equality, participation & self-determination of people with intellectual & other disabilities, by examining the causes of marginalization & by providing research, information & social development opportunities
Cameron Crawford, President

Saskatchewan Abilities Council
2310 Louise Ave., Saskatoon SK S7J 2C7
Tel: 306-374-4448; *Fax:* 306-373-2665
provincialservices@abilitiescouncil.sk.ca
www.abilitiescouncil.sk.ca
Social Media: www.facebook.com/saskatchewanabilitiescouncil
To enhance the independence & community participation of people of varying abilities in Saskatchewan
Ian Wilkinson, Executive Director
Keith Appleton, Director, Provincial Services

Saskatchewan Association for Community Living (SACL)
3031 Louise St., Saskatoon SK S7J 3L1
Tel: 306-955-3344
sacl@sacl.org
www.sacl.org
To enhance the lives of individuals with intellectual disabilities throughout Saskatchewan; To develop programs & services to meet the needs of people with intellectual disabilities
Kevin McTavish, Executive Director
Wilda Wallace, President
Gloria Mahussier, Vice-President
Judy Anderson, Treasurer
Becky Machnee, Coordinator, Communications & Fundraising
James Sanheim, Coordinator, Employment Opportunities
Megan Wells, Coordinator, Youth Programs

Silent Voice Canada Inc.
#300, 50 St. Clair Ave. East, Toronto ON M4T 1M9
Tel: 416-463-1104; *Fax:* 416-778-1876
TTY: 416-463-3928
silent.voice@silentvoice.ca
www.silentvoice.ca
To serve deaf children, deaf youth & adults & their families in the GTA; to improve communication & relationships between the deaf & hearing in families & in our community; to provide services in a sign language environment
Maureen Haan, Executive Director
Norm Forma, President

Société pour les enfants handicapés du Québec (SEHQ) / Québec Society for Disabled Children
2300, boul René-Lévesque ouest, Montréal QC H3H 2R5
Tél: 514-937-6171; *Téléc:* 514-937-0082
Ligne sans frais: 877-937-6171
sehq@enfantshandicapes.com
www.enfantshandicapes.com
Média social: www.facebook.com/enfantshandicapes; twitter.com/SEHQ
Voué au bien-être des enfants handicapés et de leur famille; grâce aux contributions publiques qui lui sont versées et aux efforts conjugués de bénévoles et des permanents, la société offre des services directs et professionnels qui favorisent le développement personnel des enfants et leur intégration dans la communauté.
Ronald Davidson, Directeur général
Carolle Desjardins, Directrice, Financement
Nicole Amzallag, Assistant to the Director
Véronique Charlebois, Directrice des soins infirmiers

Society for Manitobans with Disabilities Inc. (SMD)
825 Sherbrook St., Winnipeg MB R3A 1M5
Tel: 204-975-3010; *Fax:* 204-975-3073
Toll-Free: 866-282-8041
TTY: 204-784-3012
info@smd.mb.ca
smd.mb.ca
To promote the full participation & equality of people with disabilities: To provide a full range of rehabilitation services; To facilitate the development of a receptive & supportive environment
David L. Steen, Executive Director/President/CEO

Special Needs Planning Group
70 Ivy Cres., Stouffville ON L4A 5A9
Tel: 905-640-8285; *Fax:* 905-640-8285
graemetreeby@sympatico.ca
www.specialneedsplanning.ca
The "Special Needs" Planning Group is an organization that is made up entirely of parents of people with disabilities. They use a team approach to planning using Planners, Lawyers and Accountants, all of whom are specialists in planning for people with disabilities.
Graeme S. Treeby, Contact

The Speech and Stuttering Institute
#2, 150 Duncan Mill Rd., Toronto ON M3B 3M4
Tel: 416-491-7771; *Fax:* 416-491-7215
info@speechandstuttering.com
www.speechandstuttering.com
To provide treatment of & foster the development of innovative speech/language therapy programs; to support education & research in communication disorders
Paul L'Heureux, Chair
Margit Pukonen, Program Director

Vecova Centre for Disability Services and Research
3304 - 33 St. NW, Calgary AB T2L 2A6
Tel: 403-284-1121; *Fax:* 403-284-1146
info@vecova.ca
www.vecova.ca
To be leaders in innovative services & research that support persons with disabilities to live as contributing & valued members of the community
Leslie Tamagi, Executive Director
Neil MacKenzie, Chair

Vision Institute of Canada (VIC)
York Mills Centre, #110, 16 York Mills Rd., Toronto ON M2P 2E5
Tel: 416-224-2273; *Fax:* 416-224-9234
visioninstitute@globalserve.net
visioninstitute.optometry.net
To improve the quality of vision care in the community; to provide eye & vision care to persons with special needs
Paul Chris, Executive Director
Catherine Chiarelli, Chief of Clinical Services

Yellowknife Association for Community Living
PO Box 981, 4912 - 53 St., Yellowknife NT X1A 2N7
Tel: 867-920-2644; *Fax:* 867-920-2348
info@ykacl.ca
www.ykacl.ca
To promote the welfare of people with handicaps & their families; to lobby on behalf of people with developmental disabilities in the Northwest Territories; to ensure that every person in Northwest Territories has access to supports to live with dignity & to participate in the community of his/her choice
Jane Whyte, Executive Director
Donna Williston, President
Pam Weeks-Beaton, Vice-President

Yukon Association for Community Living (YACL)
PO Box 31478, Whitehorse YT Y1A 6K8
Tel: 867-667-4606; *Fax:* 867-668-8169
yaclwhse@northwestel.net
To promote the welfare of people with intellectual disabilities & their families; To ensure that every person in the Yukon has access to supports necessary to live with dignity & to participate fully in the community of his/her choice
Chris Hale, President
Vicki Wilson, Coordinator

Disarmament

Coalition to Oppose the Arms Trade (COAT)
541 McLeod St., Ottawa ON K1R 5R2
Tel: 613-231-3076
overcoat@rogers.com
coat.ncf.ca
Social Media: www.facebook.com/group.php?gid=2337208773
To actively oppose the arms trade and support the anti-war movement.
Richard Sanders, Coordinator

Drilling

Alberta Water Well Drilling Association (AWWDA)
PO Box 130, Lougheed AB T0B 2V0
Tel: 780-386-2335; *Fax:* 780-386-2344
awwda@telusplanet.net
www.awwda.com
The AWWDA is a non-profit, non-sectarian organization with certain objectives including: assisting, promoting, encouraging, and supporting the interest and welfare of the water well industry in all of its phases; fostering aid and promote scientific education, standard research, and technique in order to improve methods of well construction and development and advance the science of groundwater in the province of Alberta.
Brad Meyers, Secretary Manager

Association des enterprises spécialiseés en eau du Québec
5930, boul Louis-H. Lafontaine, MontréAl QC H1M 1S7
Tél: 514-353-9960; *Téléc:* 514-353-3393
Ligne sans frais: 800-468-8160
contact@aeseq.com
www.aeseq.com
L'AESEQ est la seule association qui regroupe les entrepreneurs de construction oeuvrant dans tous les secteurs du cycle de l'eau décentralisé au Québec
Daniel Schanck, Directeur général

British Columbia Ground Water Association (BCGWA)
c/o Office Of The Secretary, 1708 - 197A St., Langley BC V2Z 1K2
Tel: 604-530-8934; *Fax:* 604-530-8934
secretary@bcgwa.org
www.bcgwa.org
To advance the ground water industry, through professional & technical leadership; To promote the responsible development & use of ground water resources in British Columbia; To protect the underground water supply
Remi Allard, President
Tim Oster, Vice-President
Dave Mellis, Treasurer
Joan Perry, Secretary

Canadian Association of Drilling Engineers (CADE)
#560, 400 - 5 Ave. SW, Calgary AB T2P 0L2
Tel: 403-532-0220; *Fax:* 403-263-2722
info@cade.ca
www.cade.ca
Social Media: twitter.com/cade_can
To provide a forum for the exchange of technical drilling knowledge & expertise
Eric Schmelzl, President

Jeff Arvidson, Chair, Technical
Mike Buker, Chair, Education
John Burnell, Chair, Membership
Graham Evans, Chair, Information Technology

Canadian Association of Oilwell Drilling Contractors (CAODC)
#800, 540 - 5 Ave. SW, Calgary AB T2P 0M2
Tel: 403-264-4311; *Fax:* 403-263-3796
info@caodc.ca; membership@caodc.ca; publications@caodc.ca
www.caodc.ca
To represent drilling rig contractors; to provide ongoing means of communication between drilling & well servicing contractors, governments, other industry sector participants, & the general public; To improve standards for safety & training, equipment & technical procedures; To coordinate programs between government bodies & contractors; To oversee the Rig Technician Trade & Apprenticeship Program in Alberta, British Columbia, & Saskatchewan
Joe Bruce, Chair
W. Ross Pickering, Vice-Chair

Canadian Diamond Drilling Association (CDDA)
City Centre Building, 101 Worthington St. East, North Bay ON P1B 1G5
Tel: 705-476-6992; *Fax:* 705-476-9494
office@cdda.ca
www.canadiandrilling.com
To foster the commercial interests of members; to promote the simplifications, standardization & interchangeability of diamond drilling equipment; to recognize the safety & health of employees; to foster the protection of the natural environment; to secure the elimination of unfair or uneconomic practices within the industry & freedom from unjust or unlawful exactions; to establish & maintain uniformity & equity in the customs & commercial usages of the diamond drilling business; to acquire & disseminate valuable business information; to promote communication among those engaged in the industry.
Louise Lowe, Secretary Manager

Canadian Ground Water Association (CGWA) / Association canadienne des eaux souterraines
#100-409, 1600 Bedford Hwy., Bedford NS B4A 1E8
Tel: 902-845-1885; *Fax:* 902-845-1886
info@cgwa.org
www.cgwa.org
To act as the national voice of the ground water industry in Canada; To encourage the management & protection of ground water
Wayne C. MacRae, Executive Officer
John Freisen, President

Manitoba Water Well Association (MWWA)
PO Box 1648, Winnipeg MB R3C 2Z6
Tel: 204-479-3777
info@mwwa.ca
www.mwwa.ca
To promote & support the water well industry in Manitoba
Jeff Bell, President
Ray Ford, Vice-President
Lynn Giersch, Business Manager
Marilyn Schneider, Secretary-Treasurer

New Brunswick Ground Water Association
31 Gray Rd., Penobsquis NB E4E 5S7
Tel: 506-433-6767; *Fax:* 506-432-6888
nbgwa@nb.sympatico.ca
www.nbgwa.ca
To preserve & protect New Brunswick's water; To promote education of members & the public; To encourage the development of ground water guidelines & strategies
Roger Roy, President
Terry Burpee, Sec.-Treas.

Newfoundland/Labrador Ground Water Association
PO Box 160, Doyles NL A0N 1J0
Tel: 709-955-2561; *Fax:* 709-955-3402
gwater@nf.sympatico.ca
To promote the protection & management of ground water in Newfoundland & Labrador
Francis Gale, Contact

Nova Scotia Ground Water Association (NSGWA)
#417, 3 - 644 Portland St., Dartmouth NS B2W 2M3
Fax: 902-435-0089
Toll-Free: 888-242-4440
nsgwa@ns.aliantzinc.ca
www.nsgwa.ca
To act as the voice of the industry to all levels of government; To encourage the management & protection of ground water
Arthur Jefferson, President
Noreene McGuire, Secretary-Treasurer

Ontario Ground Water Association (OGWA)
48 Front St. East, Strathroy ON N7G 1Y6
Tel: 519-245-7194; *Fax:* 519-245-7196
www.ogwa.ca
To protect & promote Ontario's ground water; To provide guidance to members, government representatives, & the public
Greg Bullock, President
Rob MacKinnon, Secretary-Treasurer
Anne Gammage, Office Manager

Prince Edward Island Ground Water Association
PO Box 857, RR#2, Cornwall PE C0A 1H0
Tel: 902-675-2360; *Fax:* 902-675-2360
To promote the protection of ground water in Prince Edward Island
Watson MacDonald, Contact

Saskatchewan Ground Water Association (SGWA)
PO Box 9434, Saskatoon SK S7K 7E9
Tel: 306-244-7551; *Fax:* 306-343-0001
To act as the voice of the ground water industy throughout Saskatchewan; To promote the management of ground water throughout the province
Kathleen Watson, Contact

Economics

Association des économistes québécois (ASDÉQ)
CP 6128, Succ. Centre-ville, Montréal QC H3C 3J7
Tél: 514-342-7537; *Téléc:* 514-342-3967
Ligne sans frais: 866-342-7537
national@asdeq.org
www.asdeq.org
Assurer la promotion professionnelle des économistes
Charles A. Carrier, Directeur général

Association des professionnels en développement économique du Québec (APDEQ) / Economic Development Professionals Association of Québec
CP 297, #203-B, 189, rue Tupper, Magog QC J1X 3W8
Tél: 819-868-9778; *Téléc:* 819-868-9907
Ligne sans frais: 800-361-8470
info@apdeq.qc.ca
www.apdeq.qc.ca
L'APDEQ a son siège social à Magog, en Estrie. Elle compte sur deux employés permanents qui assurent le développement de l'organisme, la gestion des dossiers, le suivi des décisions du conseil d'administration, la gestion générale et les services aux membres. Son personnel soutient également le travail des administrateurs et des autres personnes qui siègent sur les divers comités.
Patrice Gagnon, Directeur général

Atlantic Association of Applied Economists (AAAE)
PO Box 828, Stn. B, Ottawa ON K1P 5P9
Tel: 613-238-7698; *Fax:* 613-238-7698
info@cabe.ca
www.cabe.ca
To provide forums for current economic & public policy issues
David Chaundy, President
Tara Ainsworth, Sec.-Treas.

Atlantic Provinces Economic Council (APEC) / Conseil économique des provinces de l'Atlantique
#500, 5121 Sackville St., Halifax NS B3J 1K1
Tel: 902-422-6516; *Fax:* 902-429-6803
info@apec-econ.ca
www.apec-econ.ca
To be the leading advocate for the economic development of the Atlantic region and accomplishes this by: monitoring and analysing current and emerging economic trends and policies; communicating the results of this analysis to its mbmers on a regular basis; consulting with a wide audience; dissminating its research and policy analysis to business, gov't, and the community at large; advocating the appropriate public and private sector policy responses.
Elizabeth Beale, President & CEO

Canada West Foundation (CWF)
#900, 1202 Centre St. SE, Calgary AB T2G 5A5
Tel: 403-264-9535; *Fax:* 403-269-4776
cwf@cwf.ca
www.cwf.ca
To operate as a public policy research institute; To introduce western perspectives into current Canadian policy debates; To produce & disseminate objective research to serve as a catalyst for informed public debate & initiatives for active citizen education & engagement in the Canadian public policy process
Roger Gibbins, President & Chief Executive Officer
Grace Kucey, Vice-President, Operations
Robert Roach, Vice-President, Research
Peggy Porteous, Director, Finance

Rachael Strathern, Coordinator, Communication & Media

Canadian Agricultural Economics Society (CAES) / Société canadienne d'agroéconomie (SCAE)
University Of Victoria, PO Box 1700, Stn. CSC, Rm. 360, Business & Economics Bldg., Victoria BC V8W 2Y2
Fax: 866-543-7613
valcaes@telus.net
caes.usask.ca/
To address problems related to the economics of food production & marketing & the quality of rural life through extension, research, teaching, & policy making in government & private industry
Valerie Johnson, Executive Director

Canadian Association for Business Economics, Inc. (CABE) / Association canadienne de science économique des affaires, inc.
PO Box 828, Stn. B, Ottawa ON K1P 5P9
Tel: 613-238-4831; *Fax:* 613-238-7698
info@cabe.ca
www.cabe.ca
To represent the interests of business economists in Canada; To enhance the professionalism of business economists

Canadian Economics Association (CEA) / Association canadienne d'économique
Département des Sciences Économiques, Université du Québec à Montréal, PO Box 8888, Stn. Centre-Ville, Montréal QC H3C 3P8
Tel: 514-987-3000
www.economics.ca
To represent academic economists; To advance economic knowledge
Anne Motte, Executive Director
Victoria Zinde-Walsh, President
Georges Dionne, Vice-President
Steven Ambler, Secretary-Treasurer

Canadian Law & Economics Association
Faculty of Law, University of Toronto, 78 Queen's Park Cres., Toronto ON M5S 2C5
Tel: 416-978-6767; *Fax:* 416-978-7899
kristin.demuth@utoronto.ca
www.canlecon.org
Nadia Gulezko, Contact
Margaret F. Brinig, President

C.D. Howe Institute / Institut C.D. Howe
#300, 67 Yonge St., Toronto ON M5E 1J8
Tel: 416-865-1904; *Fax:* 416-865-1866
cdhowe@cdhowe.org
www.cdhowe.org
Research & educational institute identifying current & emerging economic & social policy issues facing Canadians; to recommend particular policy options; to communicate conclusions of research to domestic & international audiences.
Finn Poschmann, Vice-President, Research
Kevin Fleming, Editor
William B.P. Robson, President & CEO

Centre interuniversitaire de recherche en économie quantitative (CIREQ)
Pavillon Lionel-Groulx, Université de Montréal, CP 6128, Succ. Centre-Ville, 3150, rue Jean-Brillant, local C-6088, Montréal QC H3C 3J7
Tél: 514-343-6557; *Téléc:* 514-343-5831
cireq@umontreal.ca
www.cireq.umontreal.ca
Recherches dans les domaines de l'économétrie théorique et appliquée, de l'économie financière et de la théorie économique
Dominique Bérubé, Dirctrice générale

The Conference Board of Canada / Le Conference Board du Canada
255 Smyth Rd., Ottawa ON K1H 8M7
Tel: 613-526-3280; *Fax:* 613-526-4857
Toll-Free: 866-711-2262
www.conferenceboard.ca
To be dedicated to applied research, notably in public policy, economic trends, & organizational performance
Anne Golden, President & CEO
Glen Hodgson, Sr. VP & Chief Economist
Perry Eisenschmid, Vice-President, Marketing, Sales & IT

Economic Developers Association of Canada (EDAC) / Association canadienne de développement économique (ACDE)
#200, 7 Innovation Dr., Flamborough ON L9H 7H9
Tel: 905-689-8771; *Fax:* 905-689-5925
info@edac.ca
www.edac.ca
Social Media: wwws.twitter.com/E_D_A_C

To contribute to Canada's economic, social, & environmental well-being by advancing economic development; To enhance professional competence & ethical service
Penny A. Gardiner, Chief Executive Officer
Jay Amer, President
Cheri Kemp-Long, Vice-President
Serge Côté, Second Vice-President
John Watson, Treasurer

Economic Developers Council of Ontario Inc. (EDCO)
PO Box 8030, Cornwall ON K6H 7H9
Tel: 613-931-9827; *Fax:* 613-931-9828
Toll-Free: 877-818-7666
edco@sympatico.ca
www.edco.on.ca
To provide a forum for economic development related educational activities; to increase the profile of EDCO & the profession; to encourage & create an awareness of economic development issues with relevant government agencies; to promote & develop Ontario as a premier location for economic activity by increasing employment & prosperity, & enhancing the quality of life within the Ontario municipalities.
Aileen Murray, President
Heather Lalonde, Executive Director

The Fraser Institute
1770 Burrard St., 4th Fl., Vancouver BC V6J 3G7
Tel: 604-688-0221; *Fax:* 604-688-8539
Toll-Free: 800-665-3558
info@fraserinstitute.ca
www.fraserinstitute.ca
Social Media: twitter.com/FraserInstitute
To redirect public attention to the role competitive markets play in the economic well-being of all Canadians
Sherry Stein, Director, Development
Brett J. Skinner, President
J. Kristin McCahon, Director, Publication Production
Dean Pekley, Director, Communications
Annabel Addington, Director, Administration & Human Resources

The North-South Institute (NSI) / L'Institut Nord-Sud
#200, 55 Murray St., Ottawa ON K1N 5M3
Tel: 613-241-3535; *Fax:* 613-241-7435
nsi@nsi-ins.ca
www.nsi-ins.ca
To analyze, for Canadians & others, the economic, social, & political implications of global change & to propose policy alternatives to promote global development & justice
Roy Culpeper, President

Public Policy Forum / Forum des politiques publiques
#1405, 130 Albert St., Ottawa ON K1P 5G4
Tel: 613-238-7160; *Fax:* 613-238-7990
mail@ppforum.ca
www.ppforum.com
To promote better public policy & better public management through dialogue among leaders from the public, private, labour & voluntary sectors
David J. Mitchell, President
Yves Poisson, Vice-President
Ted Williamson, Director, Finance & Administration

Rotman Institute for International Business
University of Toronto, 105 St. George St., Toronto ON M5S 3E6
Tel: 416-978-5781
riib@utoronto.ca
www.rotman.utoronto.ca
RIIB merges the former Institute for Policy Analysis and the Institute for International Business, and focusses on research on the global business environment, enterprise decision making in the global economy, and the urban service economy.
Wendy Dobson, Co-Director
Roger L. Martin, Dean, Prof. of Strategic Management

Education

Agence universitaire de la Francophonie (AUF)
CP 49714, Succ. Musée, 3034, boul Edouard-Montpetit, Montréal QC H3T 1J7
Tél: 514-343-6630; *Téléc:* 514-343-5783
recorat@auf.org
www.auf.org
Média social: www.facebook.com/profile.php?id=1691871982; twitter.com/planeteauf; www.youtube.com/planeteauf; www.dailymotion.com/planeteauf
Le but principal est le développement, au sein de l'espace francophone, d'une coopération internationale pour assurer à la fois le dialogue permanent des cultures et la circulation des personnes, des idées, des expériences entre institutions universitaires, dans l'intérêt de l'éducation et du progrès de la science.
Bernard Cerquiglini, Recteur

Alberta Catholic School Trustees Association
#205, 9940 - 106 St., Edmonton AB T5K 2N2
Tel: 780-484-6209; *Fax:* 780-484-6248
admin@acsta.ab.ca
www.acsta.ab.ca
Social Media: twitter.com/acstanews
Stefan Michniewski, Executive Director

Alberta Home & School Councils' Association (AHSCA)
#1200, 9925 - 109 St., Edmonton AB T5K 2J8
Tel: 780-454-9867; *Fax:* 780-455-0167
Toll-Free: 800-661-3470
www.albertaschoolcouncils.ca
Social Media: www.facebook.com/180244032050548; twitter.com/ABschoolcouncil
To be the voice of parents/families committed to the best possible education for Alberta children, so that they may reach their potential to participate in society in a meaningful & responsible way
Michele Mulder, Executive Director
Marilyn Sheptycki, President
Brad Vonkeman, Vice-President

Alberta School Boards Association (ASBA)
#1200, 9925-109 St., Edmonton AB T5K 2J8
Tel: 780-482-7311; *Fax:* 780-482-5659
reception@asba.ab.ca
www.asba.ab.ca
To promote the availability of high quality schooling for all; To assist member boards in fulfilling their mission of achieving excellence in education
Jacquie Hansen, President
Jacquie Hansen, President
Cheryl Smith, Vice-President
David Anderson, Executive Director
Donna Engel, Director, Finance & Corporate Services
Suzanne Lundrigan, Director, Communications
Heather Rogers, Director, Finance & Corporate Services

Alberta Teachers' Association (ATA)
Barnett House, 11010 - 142 St., Edmonton AB T5N 2R1
Tel: 780-447-9400; *Fax:* 780-455-6481
Toll-Free: 800-232-7208
government@teachers.ab.ca
www.teachers.ab.ca
To advance the cause of education in Alberta; To improve the teaching profession; To increase public interest in & support for education; To cooperate with other bodies having similar objectives
Carol Henderson, President

Alliance canadienne des responsables et enseignants en français (langue maternelle) (ACREF) / Canadian Association for the Teachers of French as a First Language
Place de la Francophonie, Succ. A, #401, 450, rue Reideau, Ottawa ON K1N 5Z4
Tél: 613-744-3192; *Téléc:* 613-744-0154
acref@franco.ca
Développer un réseau d'identification nationale des professeurs de français langue maternelle; favoriser le développement et l'épanouissement des associations provinciales vouées à l'enseignement du français langue maternelle; promouvoir la diffusion de l'information en matière de théories pédagogiques, de formation à l'approche communicative, et de pratiques scolaires et d'idéologie visant l'identité des francophones, l'égalité en tant que groupe national et le contrôle des structures éducatives; appuyer les organismes provinciaux lors de leur rencontre annuelle; développer des instruments de diffusion de l'information à l'intention de ses membres; favoriser le développement d'une politique nationale en ce qui a trait à la gestion des institutions d'enseignement et voir à ce qu'elle respecte l'autonomie des francophones
Denise Moulun-Pasek, Présidente

Association canadienne d'éducation de langue française (ACELF)
268, rue Marie-de-l'Incarnation, Québec QC G1N 3G4
Tél: 418-681-4661; *Téléc:* 418-681-3389
info@acelf.ca
www.acelf.ca
Média social: www.facebook.com/acelf.ca
L'ACELF inspire et soutient le développement et l'action des institutions éducatives francophones du Canada
Yves St-Maurice, Président
Lucie Grégoire, Adjointe administrative

Association canadienne des professeurs d'immersion (ACPI) / Canadian Association of Immersion Teachers (CAIT)
#310, 176, rue Gloucester, Ottawa ON K2P 0A6
Tél: 613-230-9111; *Téléc:* 613-230-5940
bureau@acpi.ca
www.acpi.ca
Chantal Bourbonnais, Directrice générale

Association des cadres scolaires du Québec
#170, 1195, av Lavigerie, Québec QC G1V 4N3
Tél: 418-654-0014; *Téléc:* 418-654-1719
acsq@acsq.qc.ca
www.acsq.qc.ca
Valoriser le statut professionnel de ses membres et promouvoir leurs intérêts professionnels et éconimiques; Collaborer avec les autorités gouvernementales et les organismes intéressés, au développement ordonné du système scolaire, par une participation constante et adéquate à l'élaboration et à la mise en oeuvre des politiques relatives à l'éducation
Lucie Godbout, Directrice général
Lucie Demers, Présidente
Mario Vachon, Vice-Président
Jean-François Lussier, Secrétaire-trésorier

Association des collèges privés du Québec (ACPQ)
1940, boul Henri-Bourassa est, Montréal QC H2B 1S2
Tél: 514-381-8891; *Téléc:* 514-381-4086
Ligne sans frais: 888-381-8891
acpq@cadre.qc.ca
www.acpq.net
Défendre les intérêts de ses collèges membres et contribuer au développement de l'enseignement collégial privé au Québec
Guy Forgues, Directeur général
Lucie Leduc, Adjointe administrative

Association des directeurs généraux des commissions scolaires du Québec (ADIGECS)
a/s Directeur exécutif, #200, 195 ch de Chambly, Longueuil QC J4H 3L3
Tél: 450-674-6700; *Téléc:* 450-674-7337
www.adigecs.qc.ca
Contribuer à l'avancement de l'éducation au Québec; protéger les intérêts de ses membres notamment au chapitre des conditions de travail
Serge Pelletier, Président
Normand Lapointe, Directeur exécutif

Association des enseignantes et des enseignants franco-ontariens (AEFO) / Franco-Ontarian Teachers' Association
681 ch. Belfast, Ottawa ON K1G 0Z4
Tél: 613-244-2336; *Téléc:* 613-563-7718
Ligne sans frais: 888-609-7718
aefo@aefo.on.ca
www.aefo.on.ca
L'Association des enseignantes et des enseignants franco-ontariens (AEFO) est un syndicat francophone regroupant les travailleuses et les travailleurs au service des établissements publics et privés francophones en Ontario. Elle défend les intérêts individuels et collectifs de ses membres et fait la promotion de leur profession et du fait français.
Réjean Laroche, Directeur général
Marie-Élisabeth Brunet, Responsable des communications

Association des enseignantes et des enseignants francophones du Nouveau-Brunswick (AEFNB)
CP 712, 650, rue Montgomery, Fredericton NB E3B 5B4
Tél: 506-452-8921; *Téléc:* 506-453-9795
aefnb@nbnet.nb.ca
www.aefnb.nb.ca
Représenter les intérêts des enseignantes et des enseignants francophones de la province; favoriser et maintenir au Nouveau-Brunswick des services éducatifs de langue française de première qualité
Monique Caissie, Présidente

Association for Baha'i Studies (ABS) / Association d'études Baha'is
34 Copernicus St., Ottawa ON K1N 7K4
Tel: 613-233-1903; *Fax:* 613-233-3644
www.bahai-studies.ca
Social Media: www.facebook.com/331784303733
To foster Baha'i scholarship & to demonstrate the value of this scholarly approach; to promote courses of study on the Baha'i faith; to foster relationships with various leaders of thought & persons of capacity; to publish scholarly materials examining the Baha'i faith, especially on its application to the concerns & needs of humanity; to organize annual meetings & develop chapters of the Association around the world

Association for Canadian Studies (ACS) / Association d'études canadiennes (AEC)
1822A, rue Sherbooke ouest, Montréal QC H3H 1E4
Tel: 514-925-3099; *Fax:* 514-925-3095
general@acs-aec.ca
www.acs-aec.ca
Social Media: twitter.com/Canadianstudies
To initiate & supports activities in the areas of research, teaching, communications, & the training of students in the field of Canadian studies, especially in interdisciplinary & multidisciplinary perspectives; To strive to raise public awareness of Canadian issues; To provide the Canadian Studies community, principally within Canada, with a wide range of activities & programs
Siddharth Bannerjee, Executive Director
James Ondrick, Director, Programs & Administration

Association francophone internationale des directeurs d'établissements scolaires (AFIDES)
500, boul Crémazie est, Montréal QC H2P 1E7
Tél: 514-383-7335; *Téléc:* 514-384-2139
Ligne sans frais: 877-783-7335
afides@afides.org
www.afides.org
Promouvoir les échanges entre les responsables francophones d'établissements scolaires pour répondre à des besoins de perfectionnement international par la coopération et les échanges
Carol Bédard, Présidente

Association francophone pour le savoir (ACFAS)
425, rue de la Gauchetière est, Montréal QC H2L 2M7
Tél: 514-849-0045; *Téléc:* 514-849-5558
www.acfas.ca
Mèdia social: www.facebook.com/33532707807; twitter.com/_Acfas; linkedin.com/company/acfas—association-francophone-pour-le-savoir
Promouvoir et soutenir la science et la technologie pour encourager le développement culturel et économique de la société
Esther Gaudreault, Directrice générale

Association of Atlantic Universities (AAU) / Association des universités de l'Atlantique
#403, 5657 Spring Garden Rd., Halifax NS B3J 3R4
Tel: 902-425-4230; *Fax:* 902-425-4233
info@atlanticuniversities.ca
www.atlanticuniversities.ca
To assist in assuring the quality & coordination of higher education in Atlantic Provinces; to provide a forum for university administrators to discuss & coordinate their views, interests & concerns in support of higher education in the Atlantic provinces
Peter Halpin, Executive Director

Association of British Columbia Teachers of English as an Additional Language (B.C. TEAL)
#206, 640 West Broadway, Vancouver BC V5Z 1G4
Tel: 604-736-6330; *Fax:* 604-736-6306
admin@bcteal.org
www.bcteal.org
To foster & promote effective instruction in English as a second language in BC; to raise the professional status of BC ESL teachers; to promote communication among BC ESL professionals
Alison McBride, Director of Administration

Association of Canadian Community Colleges (ACCC) / Association des collèges communautaires du Canada
701-1 Rideau St., Ottawa ON K1N 8S7
Tel: 613-746-2222; *Fax:* 613-746-6721
info@accc.ca
www.accc.ca
To provide leadership in supporting member institutions in their provision of learning opportunities which promote both individual development & that of the society & economy
James Knight, President & CEO

Association of Canadian Faculties of Dentistry (ACFD) / Association des facultés dentaires du Canada (AFDC)
#204, 100 Bronson Ave., Ottawa ON K1R 6G8
Tel: 613-237-6505; *Fax:* 613-236-8386
director@acfd.ca
www.acfd.ca
To assure the quality of dental education & research in Canada. It also strives to keep its members informed of issues regarding University-based dental education and promote communication between its members.
John Perry, President

Association of Canadian Universities for Northern Studies (ACUNS) / Association universitaire canadienne d'études nordiques
#405, 17 York St., Ottawa ON K1N 9J6
Tel: 613-562-0515; *Fax:* 613-562-0533
office@acuns.ca
www.acuns.ca
Social Media: twitter.com/acunsaucen
The Association encourages the government & private sector to support polar scholarship, fostering programs to increase public awareness of polar sciences & research. It represents its member universities & colleges, encouraging the establishment of funds & resources to ensure a network of trained researchers, regional managers & educators.
Robert C. Baily, President
Peter Geller, Vice-President
Michael Goodyear, Sec.-Treas.
Heather Cayouette, Program Manager

Association of Colleges of Applied Arts & Technology of Ontario (ACAATO) / Association des collèges d'arts appliqués et de technologie de l'Ontario
#1010, 655 Bay St., Toronto ON M5G 2K4
Tel: 416-596-0744; *Fax:* 416-596-2364
www.collegesontario.org
To advance a strong college system for Ontario
Linda Franklin, President & CEO

Association of Deans of Pharmacy of Canada (ADPC) / Association des doyens de pharmacie du Canada (ADPC)
c/o College of Pharmacy & Nutrition, University of Saskatchewan, 110 Science Pl., Saskatoon SK S7N 5C9
Tel: 306-966-6328; *Fax:* 306-966-6377
www.afpc.info/deans
Harold Lopatka, Executive Director
David Hill, Treasurer

Association of Early Childhood Educators Ontario (AECEO)
#211, 40 Orchard View Blvd., Toronto ON M4R 1B9
Tel: 416-487-3157; *Fax:* 416-487-3758
Toll-Free: 866-932-3236
info@aeceo.ca
www.aeceo.ca
Social Media: www.facebook.com/189978994376068; twitter.com/AECEO
To support early childhood educators throughout Ontario
Rachel Langford, President
Eduarda Sousa, Executive Director
Lena DaCosta, Coordinator, Professional Development, Marketing & Advertising
Sue Parker, Coordinator, Membership Services & Office Manager
Goranka Vukelich, Secretary
Gaby Chauvet, Treasurer

Association of Educational Researchers of Ontario (AERO) / Association ontarienne des chercheurs et chercheuse en éducation
c/o Dufferin-Peel Catholic District School Board, 40 Matheson Blvd. West, Mississauga ON L5R 1C5
Tel: 905-890-0708
susan.palijan@dpcdsb.org
www.aero-ontario.org
To promote & improve research, education, planning & development pertaining to education in the Ontario school system
Lynn Kostuch, President

Association of Faculties of Medicine of Canada (AFMC) / L'Association des facultés de médecine du Canada (AFMC)
#800, 265 Carling Ave., Ottawa ON K1S 2E1
Tel: 613-730-0687; *Fax:* 613-730-1196
www.afmc.ca
Social Media: twitter.com/afmc_e
To represent the interests of members in medical research policy formulation; to promote & advance academic medicine through the review & development of standards for medical education, through the development of national policies appropriate to the aims & purposes of Canadian faculties of medicine, through the fostering of research, & through representation of Canadian faculties of medicine to professional associations & governments
Nick Busing, President & CEO

Association of Independent Schools & Colleges in Alberta (AISCA)
#201, 11830 - 111 Ave., Edmonton AB T5G 0E1
Tel: 780-469-9868; *Fax:* 780-469-9880
office@aisca.ab.ca
www.aisca.ab.ca
To defend & promote the right of parents to determine the context for their children's education; to create a positive social, fiscal & political environment in which independent schools are free to maintain their identity as they serve the public interest; to support & encourage independent schools in providing significant educational choices for parents & their children; to foster public understanding & appreciation of independent schools & their services
Duane Plantinga, Executive Director

Association of Registrars of the Universities & Colleges of Canada (ARUCC) / Association des registraires des universités et collèges du Canada
c/o University of Calgary, 2500 University Dr. NW, Calgary AB T2N 1N4
Tel: 403-220-3832; *Fax:* 403-289-1253
sekulic@ucalgary.ca
www.arucc.ca
ARUCC was developed in response to the professional needs of student administrative services personnel in universities.
Mike Sekulic, President

Association of Universities & Colleges of Canada (AUCC) / Association des universités et collèges du Canada
#600, 350 Albert St., Ottawa ON K1R 1B1
Tel: 613-563-1236; *Fax:* 613-563-9745
info@aucc.ca
www.aucc.ca
To foster & promote the interests of higher education
Paul Davidson, President/CEO
Tom Traves, Chair

Association of University Forestry Schools of Canada (AUFSC) / Association des écoles forestières universitaires du Canada
c/o School of Forestry, Lakehead University, 955 Oliver Rd., Thunder Bay ON P7B 5E1
Tel: 807-343-8511
David MacLean, President

Association provinciale des enseignantes et enseignants du Québec (APEQ) / Québec Provincial Association of Teachers (QPAT)
#1, 17035, boul Brunswick, Kirkland QC H9H 5G6
Tél: 514-694-9777; *Téléc:* 514-694-0189
Ligne sans frais: 800-361-9870
reception@qpat-apeq.qc.ca
www.qpat-apeq.qc.ca
Alan Lombard, Executive Director

Association québécoise des professeurs de français (AQPF)
#222, 2095, Frank-Carrel, Sainte-Foy QC G1N 4L8
Tél: 418-683-0947; *Téléc:* 450-332-5888
Ligne sans frais: 800-267-0947
apqf@bellnet.ca
www.aqpf.qc.ca
Les principaux champs d'intervention sont - la didactique et l'enseignement du français langue maternelle du préscolaire à l'université; l'enseignement du français aux adultes; l'alphabétisation; l'enseignement du français langue seconde; promotion de la langue française, de la culture québécoise et de la francophonie
Érick Falardeau, Présidente, Section de Québec
Réjean Leclair, Président, Section Centre du Québec
Julie Roberge, Président, Section de Montréal
Suzanne Richard, Présidente

Association québécoise des troubles d'apprentissage (AQETA) / Learning Disabilities Association of Québec (LDAQ)
#502, 740, rue Saint-Maurice, Montréal QC H3C 1L5
Tél: 514-847-1324; *Téléc:* 514-281-5187
info@aqeta.qc.ca
www.aqeta.qc.ca
Mèdia social: www.facebook.com/aqeta.provinciale; www.fr.twitter.com/#!/AQDRnationale
Faire connaître les troubles d'apprentissage; faire la promotion des besoins et des droits collectifs des enfants et des adultes qui vivent avec des troubles d'apprentissage
Lise Bibaud, Directrice générale

Association québécoise du personnel de direction des écoles (AQPDE)
#235, 3291, ch Ste-Foy, Québec QC G1X 3V2
Tél: 418-781-0700; *Téléc:* 418-781-0276
info@aqpde.ca
www.aqpde.ca
Défendre et promouvoir les intérêts professionnels, sociaux et économiques des membres, favoriser leur participation et établir une concertation avec les autres organismes du réseau de l'éducation pour assurer les meilleures conditions de ses membres
Danielle Boucher, Présidente

Black Educators Association of Nova Scotia (BEA)
2136 Gottingen St., Halifax NS B3K 3B3
Tel: 902-424-7036; *Fax:* 902-424-0636
Toll-Free: 800-565-3398
beaadulted@eastlink.ca
www.thebea.ns.ca
To monitor and ensure the development of an equitable education system, so that African Nova Scotians are able to achieve their maximum potential.

British Columbia Confederation of Parent Advisory Councils (BCCPAC)
#350, 5172 Kingsway, Burnaby BC V5H 2E8
Tel: 604-687-4433; *Fax:* 604-687-4488
Toll-Free: 866-529-4397
info@bccpac.bc.ca
www.bccpac.bc.ca
To advance the public school education & well-being of children in British Columbia
Ann Whiteacre, President
Carla Giles, COO

British Columbia School Trustees Association (BCSTA) / Association des commissaires d'écoles de Colombie-Britannique
1580 West Broadway, 4th Fl., Vancouver BC V6J 5K9
Tel: 604-734-2721; *Fax:* 604-732-4559
bcsta@bcsta.org
www.bcsta.org
To promote effective boards of public school trustees working together for BC students. It is a non-profit, voluntary organization dedicated to assisting school boards in their key work; improving student achievement through community engagement.
Stephen Hansen, Executive Director
Connie Denesiuk, President

British Columbia Teachers' Federation (BCTF) / Fédération des enseignants de la Colombie-Britannique
#100, 550 - 6th Ave. West, Vancouver BC V5Z 4P2
Tel: 604-871-2283; *Fax:* 604-871-2293
Toll-Free: 800-663-9163
benefits@bctf.ca; rovergaard@bctf.ca (Media Relations)
www.bctf.ca
Social Media: www.facebook.com/BCTeachersFederation; twitter.com/bctf
To represent 41,000 public school teachers in the province of British Columbia; To support 33 provincial specialist associations, such as the British Columbia Teacher-Librarians' Association & the British Columbia Music Educators' Association; To advocate for the professional, economic, & social goals of teachers
Susan Lambert, President
Susan Lambert, First Vice-President
Jim Iker, Second Vice-President

Canadian Alliance of Student Associations (CASA) / Alliance canadienne des associations étudiantes (ACAE)
130 Slater St., Ottawa ON K1P 6E2
Tel: 613-236-3457; *Fax:* 613-236-2386
www.casa-acae.com
Social Media: www.facebook.com/casa.acae; twitter.com/casadaily; www.youtube.com/user/CASAACAE; www.flickr.com/photos/casa-acae
Chris Saulnier, Chair
Zach Dayler, National Director
Michael McDonald, Manager, Stakeholder Relations
Matthew McMillan, Secretary
Ghislain LeBlanc, Treasurer

Canadian Asian Studies Association (CASA) / Association canadienne des études asiatiques (ACEA)
c/o Concordia University, #SB115, 1455, rue de Maisonneuve ouest, Montréal QC H3G 1M8
Tel: 514-848-2280; *Fax:* 514-848-4514
casa_acea@bellnet.ca
canadianasianstudies.concordia.ca
To expand & disseminate knowledge about Asia in Canada
Scott Simon, President
Jacques Bertrand, Vice-President
Annamaria Piccioni, Secretariat
Reeta C. Tremblay, Secretariat

Canadian Association for American Studies (CAAS) / Association d'études américaines au Canada
c/o Dana Medoro, Associate Professor, University of Manitoba, 636 Fletcher Argue, Winnipeg MB R3T 5V5
webmaster@american-studies.ca
www.american-studies.ca
Social Media: www.facebook.com/group.php?gid=75085833950
To encourage study & research concerning the United States; To examine the implications of American studies for Canada & the world
Dana Medoro, President
Jason Haslam, Vice-President
Jennifer Harris, Secretary
Percy Walton, Treasurer

Canadian Association for Co-operative Education (CAFCE) / Association canadienne de l'enseignement coopératif
#205, 834 Yonge St., Toronto ON M4W 2H1
Tel: 416-483-3311; *Fax:* 416-483-3365
cafce@cafce.ca
www.cafce.ca
To act as the voice for post-secondary co-operative education in Canada; To advance post-secondary co-operative education throughout the country; To establish national standards
Kevin Rolston, President
Stacey Cool, Secretary
Shane Phillippe, Treasurer

Canadian Association for Graduate Studies (CAGS) / Association canadienne pour les études supérieures (ACES)
#301, 260 St. Patrick St., Ottawa ON K1N 5K5
Tel: 613-562-0949; *Fax:* 613-562-9009
info@cags.ca
www.cags.ca
To promote excellence in graduate education; To foster research, scholarship, & creative activity; To provide a nationwide link for the exchange of information between graduate schools & granting councils, research, business, & industrial sectors, & all levels of government; To hold meetings & conferences; To publish materials to advance graduate education; To develop & maintain national standards for graduate degree programs; To support the regular external evaluation of these standards; To deal with other matters of concern to Deans & Associate Deans of graduate studies
Sally Rutherford, Executive Director
John Doering, President
Gary Slater, Vice-President
Sue Horton, Sec.-Treas.

Canadian Association for Pastoral Practice & Education (CAPPE) / Association canadienne pour la pratique et l'éducation pastorales (ACPEP)
660 Francklyn St., Halifax NS B3H 3B5
Tel: 902-820-3085; *Fax:* 902-820-3087
Toll-Free: 866-442-2773
office@cappe.org
www.cappe.org
To support persons involved in pastoral care & pastoral counselling in Canada; To set standards & monitor professional practice; To accredit educational centres in a range of settings
Walton Brian, President
Tony Sedfawi, Executive Director
Dawn Dyer, Secretary
King Harold, Treasurer
Kathy Greig, Office Manager

Canadian Association for Scottish Studies (CASS)
Dept. of History, Centre for Scottish Studies, University of Guelph, 1008 MacKinnon Ext., Guelph ON N1G 2W1
Tel: 519-824-4120; *Fax:* 519-766-9516
scottish@uoguelph.ca
www.uoguelph.ca/scottish
To promote interest in Scottish history, literature, & culture
Graeme Morton, General Editor, IRSS

Canadian Association for Teacher Education (CATE) / Association canadienne pour la formation des enseignants (ACFE)
c/o The Canadian Society for the Study of Education, #204, 260 Dalhousie St., Ottawa ON K1N 7E4
Tel: 613-241-0018; *Fax:* 613-241-0019
www.csse-scee.ca/cate
To encourage scholarly study & research in education, with special emphasis on teacher education; to provide for the membership a national forum for the presentation & discussion of significant studies in education, with special emphasis on teacher education
Lynn Thomas, President

Canadian Association for the Advancement of Netherlandic Studies (CAANS) / Association canadienne pour l'avancement des études néerlandaises (ACAEN)
c/o Secretary-Treasurer, 613 Huyck's Point Rd., Wellington ON K0K 3L0
www.caans-acaen.ca
With chapters across Canada, CAANS aims to stimulate awareness & interest in, & to promote the study of Netherlandic languages (Dutch, Flemish, Afrikaans), as well as Netherlandic literature, history & culture. The association provides a forum for discussion in these areas, holds an annual conference, publishes research, & sponsors relevant cultural & scholarly activities such as meetings, presentations, lectures & discussions
Linda Feldman, President
Paul de Laat, Sec.-Treas.

Canadian Association for the Study of Discourse & Writing (CASDW) / Association canadienne de rédactologie (ACR)
c/o W. Brock MacDonald, Woodsworth College, University of Toronto, 119 St. George St., Toronto ON M5S 1A9
wb.macdonald@utoronto.ca
cattw-acprts.mcgill.ca
To advance the study & teaching of discourse, writing, & communication in both academic & nonacademic settings
Doreen Starke-Meyerring, President
Anne Parker, Secretary

Canadian Association for University Continuing Education (CAUCE) / Association pour l'éducation permanente dans les universités du Canada (AEPUC)
c/o Centre for Continuing & Distance Education, U. of Saskatchewan, #464, 221 Cumberland Ave. North, Saskatoon SK S7N 1M3
Tel: 306-966-5604; *Fax:* 306-966-5590
cauce.secratariat@usask.ca
www.cauce-aepuc.ca
To enlarge the quality & scope of educational opportunities for adults at the university level
Tracey Taylor-O'Reilly, President

Canadian Association of College & University Student Services (CACUSS) / Association des services aux étudiants des universités et collèges du Canada (ASEUCC)
c/o Events Management Plus Inc., #310, 4 Cataraqui St., Kingston ON K7L 1Z7
Tel: 613-531-9210; *Fax:* 613-531-0626
contact@cacuss.ca
www.cacuss.ca
Social Media: www.facebook.com/cacuss; twitter.com/cacusstweets
To represent & serve persons who work in Canadian post-secondary institutions in student affairs & services; To offer advocacy & assistance on issues that affect the quality of student life on Canadian university & college campuses
Donna Dennison, Administrative Director
Chris McGrath, President
Janet Mee, President-Elect
Jennifer Hamilton, Executive Director

Canadian Association of Foundations of Education (CAFE) / Association canadienne des fondements de l'éducation (ACFE)
c/o The Canadian Society for the Study of Education, #204, 260 Dalhousie St., Ottawa ON K1N 7E4
Tel: 613-241-0018; *Fax:* 613-241-0019
csse-scee@csse.ca
www.csse-scee.ca/cafe
To provide a forum for discussing the contribution of the social sciences & humanities (eg. history of education, philosophy of education, sociology of education) to educational theory, research & practice
Michael O'Sullivan, President

Canadian Association of Geographers (CAG) / Association canadienne des géographes
Department of Geography, McGill University, #425, 805, rue Sherbrooke ouest, Montréal QC H3A 2K6
Tel: 514-398-4946; *Fax:* 514-398-7437
valerie.shoffey@cag-acg.ca (Executive Secretary)
www.cag-acg.ca
To promote the discipline of geography in Canada & internationally

Anne Godlewska, President
Mary-Louise Byrne, Secretary-Treasurer
Ian MacLachlan, Editor, The Canadian Geographer
Valerie Shoffey, Editor, The CAG Newsletter

Canadian Association of Independent Schools (CAIS)
12 Bannockburn Ave., Toronto ON M5M 2M8
Tel: 416-780-1779
director@cais.ca
www.cais.ca
James Christopher, Executive Director

Canadian Association of Principals (CAP) / Association canadienne des directeurs d'école
#220, 300 Earl Grey Dr., Kanata ON K2T 1C1
Tel: 613-622-0346; *Fax:* 613-622-0258
cap@bellnet.ca
www.cdnprincipals.org
To represent the professional perspectives of principals & vice-principals at the national level & to provide the leadership necessary to ensure quality educational opportunities for Canadian students.
Marie Schutt, Executive Assistant

Canadian Association of School Social Workers & Attendance Counsellors (CASSWAC)
c/o Rolling River School Div., PO Box 1170, Minnedosa MB R0J 0P0
Tel: 204-867-2754
www.casswac.ca
Rebecca Gray, President

Canadian Association of Schools of Nursing (CASN) / Association canadienne des écoles de sciences infirmières (ACESI)
#15, 99 Fifth Ave., Ottawa ON K1S 5K4
Tel: 613-235-3150; *Fax:* 613-235-4476
inquire@casn.ca
www.casn.ca
CASN/ACESI represents Canadian nursing programs. The association is the national voice for nursing education & nursing research.
Cynthia Baker, Executive Director

Canadian Association of Second Language Teachers (CASLT) / Association canadienne des professeurs de langues secondes (ACPLS)
#300, 950 Gladstone Ave., Ottawa ON K1Y 3E6
Tel: 613-727-0994; *Fax:* 613-727-3831
Toll-Free: 877-727-0994
admin@caslt.org
www.caslt.org
To promote & advance nationally learning of second languages; to encourage activities & research in field of second language
Guy Leclair, Executive Director
Louise St-Amand, Office & Membership Administrator

Canadian Association of Slavists (CAS) / Association canadienne des slavistes
Alumni Hall, Dept. of History & Classics, University of Alberta, #2, 28 Tory Bldg., Edmonton AB T6G 2H4
Tel: 780-492-2566; *Fax:* 780-492-9125
csp@ualberta.ca
www.ualberta.ca/~csp/cas/contact.html
To operate a learned society comprising scholars & professionals with interests in the social, economic, & political life of Slavic people, in addition to their languages, cultures, & histories; To promote understanding of Slavic societies & dialogue; To disseminate information about the past & present of the Slavic world
Megan Swift, President
R. Carter Elwood, Honorary President
Bohdan Nebesio, Sec.-Treas.
Elena Baraban, Vice-President
Reid Allan, Vice-President
Bohdan Nebesio, Sec.-Treas.

Canadian Association of University Business Officers (CAUBO) / Association canadienne du personnel administratif universitaire (ACPAU)
#320, 350 Albert St., Ottawa ON K1R 1B1
Tel: 613-230-6760; *Fax:* 613-563-7739
nlaporte@caubo.ca
www.caubo.ca
To promote the professional & effective management of the administrative, financial & business affairs of higher education; to have the professional standards of its members & to strengthen the contribution of higher education to the well being of Canada
Nathalie Laporte, Executive Director

Canadian Association of University Research Administrators (CAURA) / Association canadienne d'administrateurs de recherche universitaire (ACARU)
#600, 350 Albert St., Ottawa ON K1R 1B1
admin@caura-acaru.ca
www.caura-acaru.ca
CAURA is a national voice for research administrators, & is committed to improving the profession at educational institutions, hospitals & research facilties. It provides a forum for discussion & exchange of information on current issues & policies.
Barbara Crutchley, President
L'naya Hindman, Executive Director

Canadian Association of University Teachers (CAUT) / Association canadienne des professeures et professeurs d'université (ACPPU)
2705 Queensview Dr., Ottawa ON K2B 8K2
Tel: 613-820-2270; *Fax:* 613-820-7244
acppu@caut.ca
www.caut.ca
To act as the national voice for academic staff; To promote academic freedom; To improve the quality & accessibility of post-secondary education in Canada
James Turk, Executive Director
Gordon Piché, Associate Executive Director, Administration & Finance
David Robinson, Associate Executive Director, Research & Advocacy
Michael Piva, Assistant Executive Director, Collective Bargaining & Services

Canadian Bureau for International Education (CBIE) / Bureau canadien de l'éducation internationale (BCEI)
#1550, 220 Laurier Ave. West, Ottawa ON K1P 5Z9
Tel: 613-237-4820; *Fax:* 613-237-1073
info@cbie.ca
www.cbie.ca
Social Media: twitter.com/cbie_bcei
To promote international understanding & development through the free movement of people & active exchange of ideas, information & technologies across national borders
Karen McBride, President
Bashir Hassanali, Executive Vice-President
Jennifer Humphries, Vice-President, Membership, Public Policy
Margaux Béland, Vice-President, Canadian Partnerships
Monique Paquette, Executive Assistant

Canadian Catholic School Trustees' Association (CCSTA) / Association canadienne des commissaires d'écoles catholique
Catholic Education Centre, 570 West Hunt Club Rd., Nepean ON K2G 3R4
Tel: 613-224-4455; *Fax:* 613-224-3187
ccsta@ottawacatholicschools.ca
www.ccsta.ca
To protect the right to Catholic education in Canada; To promote excellence in Catholic education across Canada
John Stunt, Executive Director
Paula Peroni, President
Ted Paszek, Vice-President

Canadian Council for the Advancement of Education (CCAE) / Le Conseil canadien pour l'avancement de l'éducation
#310, 4 Cataraqui St., Kingston ON K7K 1Z7
Tel: 613-531-9213; *Fax:* 613-531-0626
admin@ccaecanada.org
www.ccaecanada.org
Social Media: www.facebook.com/group.php?gid=325169814892&ref=ts; twitter.com/CCAECanada
To promote excellence in educational advancement through networking opportunities, professional development, & mutual support
Mark Hazlett, Executive Director
Melana Soroka, President
Kathy Arney, Vice-President
Kathy Butler, Vice-President
Ivan Muzychka, Vice-President

Canadian Council of Teachers of English Language Arts (CCTELA)
#10, 730 River Rd., Winnipeg MB R2M 5A4
Tel: 204-255-1676; *Fax:* 204-253-2562
cctela@mts.net
www.cctela.ca
To provide a national voice in education relating to English Language Arts; to serve as a forum for communication among provincial councils concerning English Language Arts; to provide a system of communication & cooperation for teachers of English Language Arts at all levels in Canada; to encourage research, experimentation & investigation in English Language Arts teaching; to sponsor, promote & lobby for programs of benefit to Canadian students.
Linda Ferguson, Executive Director

Canadian Council of University Physical Education & Kinesiology Administrators (CCUPEKA) / Conseil canadien des administrateurs universitaires en éducation physique et kinésiologie (CCAUEPK)
c/o Dr. J. Starkes, Department of Kinesiology, McMaster University, Hamilton ON L8S 4K1
www.ccupeka.ca
To serve as an accrediting body for physical education & kinesiology programs at universities in Canada; To offer a voice for academics, through lobbying initiatives
Janet Starkes, Coordinator, Accreditation Council

Canadian Education & Training Accreditation Commission (CETAC)
#310, 590 Queen St., Fredericton NB E3B 7H9
Tel: 506-459-4546
info@cetac.ca
www.cetac.ca
To assure students & the general public of the quality of Canada's post-secondary institutions & the programs they offer; To assist the institutions in continuously improving themselves & the education provided to students

Canadian Education Association (CEA) / Association canadienne d'éducation (ACE)
#705, 119 Spadina Ave., Toronto ON M5V 2L1
Tel: 416-591-6300; *Fax:* 416-591-5345
Toll-Free: 866-803-9549
info@cea-ace.ca
www.cea-ace.ca
Social Media: www.facebook.com/cea.ace; twitter.com/cea_ace
CEA is a cross-Canada network of educators & education influencers who are passionate about education: those who work in classrooms & schools, district offices, research & policy circles, & not-for-profit & business sectors. CEA strives to generate & advance ideas that lead to greater student & teacher engagement; to teaching that inspires all students to learn; & to schools that ensure both equity & excellence to meet the developmental needs of all learners in our global & changing society.
Ron Canuel, Chief Executive Officer
Gilles Latour, Chief Operating Officer
Max Cooke, Director, Communications

Canadian Ethnic Studies Association (CESA) / Société canadienne d'études ethniques (SCEE)
c/o Dept. of Sociology, University of Calgary, 2500 University Dr. NW, Calgary AB T2N 1N4
Tel: 403-220-6502; *Fax:* 403-282-9298
cesa@uwinnipeg.ca
cesa.uwinnipeg.ca
To encourage scholarly debate about theoretical & practical issues in Canadian ethnic studies
Lloyd Wong, President
Lori Wilkinson, Vice-President
Amal Madibbo, Secretary-Treasurer

Canadian Faculties of Agriculture & Veterinary Medicine (CFAVM) / Facultés d'agriculture et de médecine vétérinaire du Canada
77 Townsend Dr., Nepean ON K2J 2V3
Tel: 613-825-6873
info@cfavm.ca
www.cfavm.ca

Canadian Federation for Humanities & Social Sciences (CFHSS) / Fédération canadienne des sciences humaines (FCSH)
#300, 275 Bank St., Ottawa ON K2P 2I6
Tel: 613-238-6112; *Fax:* 613-238-6114
fedcan@fedcan.ca
www.fedcan.ca
Social Media: www.facebook.com/fedcan?ref=nf; twitter.com/fedcan
The Federation represents the Canadian research community by working to support & advance research in the humanities & social sciences in Canada.
Graham Carr, President
Jean-Marc Mangin, Executive Director

Canadian Federation of Business School Deans (CFBSD) / Fédération canadienne des doyens des écoles d'administration
3000, ch de la Côte-Sainte-Catherine, Montréal QC H3T 2A7
Tel: 514-340-7116; *Fax:* 514-340-7275
info@cfbsd.ca; conferences@cfbsd.ca; surveys@cfbsd.ca
www.cfbsd.ca
To encourage the professional development of business school administrators; To promote excellence in management education; To represent management education to the government, the business community, & the media
Michel Patry, Chair
Bahram Dadgostar, Vice-Chair
Timothy Daniel Daus, Executive Director
Robert Mantha, Secretary-Treasurer

Canadian Federation of Students (CFS) / Fédération canadienne des étudiantes et étudiants (FCEE)
338C Somerset St. West, Ottawa ON K2P 0J9
Tel: 613-232-7394; *Fax:* 613-232-0276
web@cfs-fcee.ca
www.cfs-fcee.ca
To represent the collective interests of college & university students across Canada; To act as a unified voice for Canadian university & college students
Katherine Giroux-Bougard, National Chair
Noah Stewart, National Deputy Chair
Dave Molenhuis, National Treasurer
Andrea Balon, Representative, Graduate Students
Roxanne Dubois, Representative, Francophone Students
Sandy Hudson, Representative, Women
Thomas Roussin, Representative, Aboriginal Students
Krishna Saravanamuttu, Representative, Students of Colour

Canadian Federation of University Women (CFUW) / Fédération canadienne des femmes diplômées des universités (FCFDU)
Head Office, #305, 251 Bank St., Ottawa ON K2P 1X3
Tel: 613-234-8252; *Fax:* 613-234-8221
cfuwgen@rogers.com
www.cfuw.org
To pursue knowledge; to promote education; to improve the status of women & human rights; To participate actively in public affairs in a spirit of cooperation & friendship
Brenda Wallace, President
Samantha Spady, Coordinator, Advocacy & Communications

Canadian Foundation for Economic Education (CFEE) / Fondation d'éducation économique
#201, 110 Eglinton Ave. West, Toronto ON M4R 1A3
Tel: 416-968-2236; *Fax:* 416-968-0488
Toll-Free: 888-570-7610
mail@cfee.org
www.cfee.org
To enhance the economic capabilities of Canadians
Jean Olier Caron, Chair
Lori Cranson, Chair
Steve Petherbridge, Advisor

Canadian Home & School Federation (CHSF) / Fédération canadienne des associations foyer-école (FCAFE)
6067 Quinpool Rd, Halifax NS B3L 1A2
Tel: 902-864-0235
chsf@bellnet.ca
www.canadianhomeandschool.com
To improve the quality of Canadian public education available to children & youth; To act as the national voice of parents with children in public schools
Janet Walsh, President
Judith Cameron, Western Vice-President
Brian Peat, Central Vice-President
Cynthia Richards, Eastern Vice-President
Eva Cameron, Secretary-Treasurer

Canadian Interuniversity Sport (CIS) / Sport interuniversitaire canadien (SIC)
#N205, 801 King Edward, Ottawa ON K1N 6N5
Tel: 613-562-5670; *Fax:* 613-562-5669
cisoffice@universitysport.ca
www.cis-sic.ca
Social Media: twitter.com/CIS_SIC
To act as the national governing body for men's & women's university sport in Canada
Marg McGregor, CEO

Canadian Network for Innovation in Education (CNIE)
#204, 260 Dalhousie St., Ottawa ON K1N 7E4
Tel: 613-241-0018; *Fax:* 613-241-0019
cnie-rcie@cnie-rcie.ca
www.cade-aced.ca
To develop & promote the use of technologies, practices, & policies that foster access to learning for students
Maureen Baron, President
Anna Sawicki, Sec.-Treas.

Canadian School Boards Association (CSBA) / Association canadienne des commissions/conseils scolaires
1410 rue Stanley, bureau 515, Montréal QB H3A 1P8
Tel: 514-289-2988; *Fax:* 514-849-8228
info@cdnsba.org
www.cdnsba.org
To provide leadership for school boards throughout Canada by supporting the efforts of the provincial/territorial school board/trustee associations; To promote educational excellence at the elementary/secondary levels as a national imperative; To foster & promote the maintenance of the principles of local autonomy in education in Canada through elected representation; To provide for & maintain liaison with the Cabinet & all branches of the federal government & members of Parliament & to make representation on behalf of school boards in Canada; To maintain a national profile for school boards & to make representation on their behalf to other national organizations; To provide for interprovincial communication on issues & developments in public education that take place on a provincial/territorial, national or international level
Ruth Ann Furgala, President

Canadian Society for Education through Art (CSEA) / Société canadienne d'éducation par l'art (SCEA)
Faculty of Education, Department of Curriculum and Instruction, PO Box 3010, Stn. CSC, University of Victoria, Victoria BC V8W 3N4
Tel: 250-721-7896; *Fax:* 250-721-7598
info@csea-scea.ca
www.csea-scea.ca
The Canadian Society for Education through Art, is a voluntary association and is the only Canadian national organization that brings together art educators, gallery educators, and others wtih similr intersts and concerns.
Fiona Blaikie, President, Lakehead University, Orillia Campus

Canadian Society for the Study of Education (CSSE) / Société canadienne pour l'étude de l'éducation (SCEE)
#204, 260 Dalhousie St., Ottawa ON K1N 7E4
Tel: 613-241-0018; *Fax:* 613-241-0019
csse-scee@csse.ca
www.csse-scee.ca
To advance knowledge & inform practice in educational settings; to promote the advancement of Canadian research & scholarship in education; to provide for the discussion of studies, issues & trends in education, & for the dissemination of research findings; to promote exchange among members & other educational researchers in Canada & internationally; to foster partnerships &, through educational research, influence public policy & help determine the nature, structure & funding of the research agenda
Fernand Gervais, President

Canadian Society for the Study of Higher Education (CSSHE) / La Société canadienne pour l'étude de l'enseignement supérieur (SCEES)
PO Box 34091, Stn. Fort Richmond, Winnipeg MB R3T 5T5
Tel: 204-474-6404
www.ss.ucalgary.ca/csshe/
To advance the knowledge of post-secondary education through the promotion of research & its dissemination through publications & learned meetings
Stephen Kerr, Treasurer
Ester Enns, President

Canadian Society of Biblical Studies (CSBS) / Société canadienne des études bibliques (SCEB)
c/o Prof. Robert A. Derrenbacker, Jr., Regent College, 5800 University Blvd., Vancouver BC V6T 2E4
rderrenbacker@regent-college.edu
www.ccsr.ca/csbs
To stimulate the critical investigation of the classical biblical literature & related literature
Terry Donaldson, President
Francis Landy, Vice-President
Robert A. Derrenbacker, Jr., Treasurer & Membership Secretary
Richard S. Ascough, Officer, Communications

Canadian Teachers' Federation (CTF) / Fédération canadienne des enseignantes et des enseignants (FCE)
2490 Don Reid Dr., Ottawa ON K1H 1E1
Tel: 613-232-1505; *Fax:* 613-232-1886
Toll-Free: 866-283-1505
info@ctf-fce.ca
www.ctf-fce.ca
Social Media:
www.facebook.com/group.php?gid=147721021992584;
twitter.com/CanTeachersFed
To promotes a strong publicly funded education system for Canada, one that enhances the country's competitiveness in a knowledge based global economy & gives children the opportunity to become active, engaged citizens
Calvin Fraser, Secretary General
Emily Noble, President

Canadian Test Centre Inc. (CTC) / Services d'évaluation pédagogique
#7-8, 85 Citizen Ct., Markham ON L6G 1A8
Tel: 905-513-6636; *Fax:* 905-513-6639
Toll-Free: 800-668-1006
info@canadiantestcentre.com
www.canadiantestcentre.com
To publish & distribute test products; to support teachers to make their testing programs work; to invest in research & development projects which aim to improve the measurement & evaluation of student ability & achievement.
Ernest W. Cheng, Managing Director

Canadian University & College Conference Organizers Association (CUCCOA) / Association des coordonnateurs de congrès des universités et des collèges du Canada (ACCUCC)
312 Oakwood Ct., Newmarket ON L3Y 3C8
Tel: 905-954-0102; *Fax:* 905-895-1630
inquiries@cuccoa.org
www.cuccoa.org
Exists for the purpose of information sharing, professional development & group marketing
Carol Ford, Manager

Canadian University & College Counselling Association (CUCCA) / Association canadienne de counseling universitaire et collégial
c/o Canadian Association of College & University Student Services, #310, 4 Cataraqui St., Kingston ON K7K 1Z7
Tel: 613-531-9210; *Fax:* 613-531-0626
www.cacuss.ca/en/divisions/CUCCA/overview.htm
David V. Ness, President

Centre d'animation de développement et de recherche en éducation (CADRÉ)
1940, boul Henri-Bourassa est, Montréal QC H2B 1S2
Tél: 514-381-8891; *Téléc:* 514-381-4086
www.cadre.qc.ca
Paul Boisvenu, Directeur général

Centre franco-ontarien de ressources pédagogiques (CFORP)
435, rue Donald, Ottawa ON K1K 4X5
Tél: 613-747-8000; *Téléc:* 613-747-2808
Ligne sans frais: 877-742-3677
cforp@cforp.ca
www.cforp.ca
Média social: twitter.com/#!/CFORP
Le Centre franco-ontarien de ressources pédagogiques (CFORP) est un centre multiservices en éducation qui produit et diffuse des ressources pédagogiques et qui offre des services destinés à soutenir l'éducation en langue française.
Cet organisme à but non lucratif appuie le développement et l'épanouissement de l'éducation en langue française à l'aide de services, comme la formation professionnelle du personnel scolaire et l'impression de documents, et de projets novateurs, tels des ressources numériques et des cours multimédias en ligne. La Librairie du Centre, propriété du CFORP, offre depuis 1992 des services non seulement au milieu scolaire, mais aussi à toute la communauté francophone et francophile. Tous les profits des ventes à la librairie sont réinvestis dans la production de nouvelles ressources pédagogiques.
Gilles Leroux, Directeur général
Michel Goulet, Directeur, Développement et Édition
Guy Dubois, Directeur, Formation professionnelle
Hubert Lalande, Directeur, Production multimédia
Michel Levesque, Directeur, Librairie du Centre
Daniel Forget, Directeur, Imprimerie
Lise Gélinas, Directrice, Communications/Marketing
Penny Bell, Directrice, Finances et Ressources humaines

The Commonwealth of Learning (COL)
#1200, 1055 Hastings St. West, Vancouver BC V6E 2E9
Tel: 604-775-8200; *Fax:* 604-775-8210
info@col.org
www.col.org
To create & widen access to education & to improve its quality, utilising distance education techniques & associated communications technologies to meet the particular requirements of member countries
John Daniel, President & CEO
Dave Wilson, Communications Manager

Comparative & International Education Society of Canada (CIESC) / Société canadienne d'éducation comparée et internationale (SCECI)
University of Western Ontario, #2, 1151 Richmond St., London ON N6A 5B8
www.edu.uwo.ca/ciesc/
To promote international knowledge & understanding in education; To examine educational systems in international & comparative framework

Confederation of Alberta Faculty Associations (CAFA)
Univ. of Alberta, 11043 - 90 Ave., Edmonton AB T6G 2E1
Tel: 780-492-5630; *Fax:* 780-436-0516
lori.morinville@ualberta.ca
www.ualberta.ca/~cafa/
CAFA is a professional organization of faculty and faculty association in Alberta Universities and is comprised of three associations; The Association of Academic Staff; University of Alberta, Athabasca University Faculty Association; and The University of Lethbridge Faculty Association. The objects of the Conferdation are to promote the quality of education in the province and to promote the well-being of Alberta Universities and their academic staff.
John Nicholls, Executive Director
Lori Morinville, Administrative Officer

Confederation of University Faculty Associations of British Columbia (CUFA BC)
#315, 207 West Hastings St., Vancouver BC V6B 1H7
Tel: 604-646-4677; *Fax:* 604-646-4676
www.cufa.bc.ca
Robert Clift, Executive Director
David Mirhady, President

Conférence des recteurs et des principaux des universités du Québec (CREPUQ) / Conference of Rectors & Principals of Quebec Universities
c/o Conférence des recteurs et des principaux, #200, 500, rue Sherbrooke ouest, Montréal QC H3A 3C6
Tél: 514-288-8524; *Téléc:* 514-288-0554
info@crepuq.qc.ca
www.crepuq.qc.ca
Est un organisme privé qui regroupe, sur une base volontaire, tous les établissements universitaires québécois; sert de forum permanent d'échanges et de concertation qui permet aux gestionnaires de partager leurs expériences en vue d'améliorer l'efficacité générale du système universitaire québécois.
Daniel Zizian, Directeur général

Conference of Independent Schools (Ontario) (CIS)
PO Box 27, Whitby ON L1N 5R7
Tel: 905-665-8622; *Fax:* 905-665-8635
admin@cisontario.ca
www.cisontario.ca
To provide a collegial forum to promote excellence in education among its member schools
George L. Briggs, Executive Director

Council of Atlantic Ministers of Education & Training (CAMET) / Conseil atlantique des ministres de l'Éducation et de la Formation (CAMEF)
PO Box 2044, Halifax NS B3J 2Z1
Tel: 902-424-5352; *Fax:* 902-424-8976
camet-camef@cap-cpma.ca
www.camet-camef.ca
To allow the ministers responsible for education & training in New Brunswick, Nova Scotia, Newfoundland & Labrador, & Prince Edward Island to collaborate & respond to needs identified in public & post-secondary education; To enhance cooperation in public & post-secondary education to improve learning for Atlantic Canadians
Rhéal Poirier, Secretary
Sylvie Martin, Regional Coordinator

Council of Canadian Law Deans (CCLD) / Conseil des doyens et des doyennes des facultés de droit du Canada (CDFDC)
57 Louis Pasteur, Ottawa ON K1N 6N5
Tel: 613-824-9233; *Fax:* 613-824-9233
brigitteccld@rogers.com
www.ccld-cdfdc.ca
Brigitte Pilon, Executive Director

Council of Catholic School Superintendents of Alberta
AB
superintendents@ccssa.ab.ca
www.ccssa.ab.ca
Provides a forum for discussion regarding the direction & development of Catholic Education in Alberta
George Zeigner, Executive Director

Council of Ontario Universities (COU) / Conseil des universités de l'Ontario
#1100, 180 Dundas St. West, Toronto ON M5G 1Z8
Tel: 416-979-2165; *Fax:* 416-979-8635
cou@cou.on.ca
www.cou.on.ca
Social Media: www.facebook.com/CouncilofOntarioUniversities; twitter.com/OntUniv
To work with & on behalf of members to meet public policy expectations related to accountability, diversity of educational opportunity, financial self-reliance, & responsiveness to educational & marketplace needs
Alastair Summerlee, Chair
Bonnie M. Patterson, President & CEO
Nancy Sullivan, Interim Executive Director, Corporate Services
Barbara Hauser, Secretary to Council & Sr. Advisor

Dufferin Peel Educational Resource Workers' Association (DPERWA)
#106, 5805 Whittle Rd., Mississauga ON L4Z 2J1
Tel: 905-501-1622; *Fax:* 905-501-1623
www.dperwa.com
DPERWA is the official, certified bargaining body for all Educational Assistants, Designated Early Childhood Educators & Supply ERWs employed with the Dufferin Peel Catholic District School Board.
Diane Kossel, President

Elementary Teachers' Federation of Ontario (ETFO) / Fédération des enseignantes et des enseignants de l'élémentaire de l'Ontario (FEEO)
#1000, 480 University Ave., Toronto ON M5G 1V2
Tel: 416-962-3836; *Fax:* 416-642-2424
Toll-Free: 888-838-3836
glewis@etfo.org
www.etfo.ca
Social Media: www.facebook.com/ETFOprovincialoffice; twitter.com/etfonews; www.youtube.com/user/ETFOprovincial
To regulate relations between employees & employer, including but not limited to securing & maintaining, through collective bargaining, the best possible terms & conditions of employment; To advance the cause of education & the status of teachers & educational workers; To promote a high standard of professional ethics & a high standard of professional competence; To foster a climate of social justice in Ontario & continue a leadership role in such areas as anti-poverty, non-violence & equity; To promote & protect the interests of all members of the Federation & the students in their care; To cooperate with other organizations in Ontario, Canada & elsewhere, having the same or like objects
Gene Lewis, General Secretary
Ruth Alam, Manager, Human Resources Services

Fédération des cégeps
500, boul Crémazie est, Montréal QC H2P 1E7
Tél: 514-381-8631; *Téléc:* 514-381-2263
comm@fedecegeps.qc.ca
www.fedecegeps.qc.ca
Média social: www.facebook.com/monretouraucegep
De promouvoir le développement de l'enseignement collégial; au nom de ses membres, la Fédération établit des contacts et étudie des dossiers communs avec différents partenaires gouvernementaux et privés, notamment en ce qui concerne les affaires pédagogiques, étudiantes, matérielles et financières, et les ressources humaines du réseau
François Dornier, Président
Jean Beauchesne, Président-directeur général

Fédération des comités de parents du Québec inc. (FCPQ)
2263, boul Louis-XIV, Québec QC G1C 1A4
Tél: 418-667-2432; *Téléc:* 418-667-6713
Ligne sans frais: 800-463-7268
courrier@fcpq.qc.ca
www.fcpq.qc.ca
La Fédération des comités de parents du Québec (FCPQ) tire sa raison d'être de l'existence, dans chacune des commissions scolaires, d'un comité de parents représentant les parents des élèves des écoles publiques primaires et secondaires. La mission ultime de la FCPQ est de défendre et de promouvoir les droits et les intérêts des parents des élèves des écoles publiques primaires et secondaires de façon à assurer la qualité de l'éducation offerte aux enfants.
Lyne Deschamps, Présidente

La Fédération des commissions scolaires du Québec (FCSQ)
CP 10490, Succ. Sainte-Foy, 1001, av Bégon, Québec QC G1V 4C7
Tél: 418-651-3220; *Téléc:* 418-651-2574
info@fcsq.qc.ca
www.fcsq.qc.ca
Tout en conservant ses tâches premières de coordination et d'unification, la mission de la Fédération s'est élargie, au fil des ans, pour rencontrer deux objectifs principaux : contribuer à promouvoir l'éducation ainsi que représenter et défendre avec détermination les intérêts des commissions scolaires.
Josée Bouchard, Présidente
Pâquerette Gagnon, Directrice générale

Fédération des établissements d'enseignement privés (FEEP)
1940, boul Henri-Bourassa est, Montréal QC H2B 1S2
Tél: 514-381-8891; *Téléc:* 514-381-4086
Ligne sans frais: 888-381-8891
info@feep.qc.ca
www.cadre.qc.ca
Soutien des établissements membres sur les plans administratifs, pédagogiques et de la vie scolaire; représentation auprès du gouvernement
Paul Boisvenu, Directeur général

Fédération étudiante universitaire du Québec (FEUQ) / Québec University Students' Federation
15, Marie-Anne Ouest, 2e étage, Montréal QC H2W 1B6
Tél: 514-396-3380; *Téléc:* 514-396-7140
Ligne sans frais: 877-396-3380
feuq@feuq.qc.ca
www.feuq.qc.ca
Défendre et promouvoir les droits des étudiantes et étudiants universitaires du Québec
Martine Desjardins, Président
Yanick Grégoire, Vice-président exécutive

Fédération nationale des enseignants et des enseignantes du Québec (FNEEQ) / National Federation of Québec Teachers
1601, av de Lorimier, Montréal QC H2K 4M5
Tél: 514-598-2241; *Téléc:* 514-598-2190
fneeq.reception@csn.qc.ca
www.fneeq.qc.ca
Média social: www.facebook.com/FneeqCSN; twitter.com/FneeqCSN
La Fédération nationale des enseignantes et des enseignants du Québec (FNEEQ) est une fédération de la CSN qui regroupe les syndicats de l'enseignement. La mission première de la FNEEQ est l'amélioration des conditions de travail par l'entremise de la négociation et de l'application d'une convention collective entre un employeur et le personnel enseignant et salarié
Jean Trudelle, Président

Federation of Independent School Associations of BC (FISA)
150 Robson St., Vancouver BC V6B 2A7
Tel: 604-684-6023; *Fax:* 604-684-3163
fisabc@telus.net
www.fisabc.ca
To assist independent schools in maintaining their independence while seeking fair treatment for them in legislative & financial terms.
Fred Herfst, Executive Director
D. Lauson, President

Federation of New Brunswick Faculty Associations (FNBFA) / Fédération des associations de professeures et professeurs d'université du Nouveau-Brunswick (FAPPUNB)
#204, 361 Victoria St., Fredericton NB E3B 1W5
Tel: 506-458-8977; *Fax:* 506-458-5620
fnbfa@nb.aibn.com
www.fnbfa.ca
To promote interests of teachers, librarians & researchers in universities & colleges of New Brunswick; to advance standards of professions & to seek to improve quality of higher education in the Province.
Gilles Allain, Executive Director
Jean Sauvageau, Sec.-Treas.

Fédération provinciale des comités de parents du Manitoba (FPCP)
81, chemin Quail Ridge, Winnipeg MB R2Y 2A9
Tél: 204-237-9666; *Téléc:* 204-231-1436
Ligne sans frais: 866-666-8108
fpcp@fpcp.mb.ca
www.entreparents.mb.ca
Appuyer les membres dans le développement des milieux, familial, éducatif (préscolaire et scolaire) et communautaire, propices à l'épanouissement des familles francophones
Geneviève Boudreau, Directrice générale

Fédération québécoise des directeurs et directrices d'établissements d'enseignement (FQDE)
#100, 7855, boul Louis-H-Lafontaine, Anjou QC H1K 4E4
Tél: 514-353-7511; *Téléc:* 514-353-2064
Ligne sans frais: 800-361-4258
info@fqde.qc.ca
www.fqde.qc.ca
Défendre les droits des directeurs, directrices, directeurs adjoints, directrices adjointes d'établissements d'enseignement, sans oublier de promouvoir l'excellence dans la direction des établissements d'enseignement au Québec: en supportant des associations de directions d'établissement d'enseignement; en faisant en sorte que les directions d'établissement d'enseignement aient un environnement de travail favorisant la réalisation du projet éducatif; en s'assurant que les directions d'établissement d'enseignement maintiennent une compétence de gestionnaire de haute qualité.
Marc Brunelle, Secrétaire
Chantal Longpré, Présidente

Fédération québécoise des professeures et professeurs d'université (FQPPU) / Québec Federation of University Professors
#405, 4446, boul St-Laurent, Montréal QC H2W 1Z5
Tél: 514-843-5953; *Téléc:* 514-843-6928
Ligne sans frais: 888-843-5953
federation@fqppu.or
www.fqppu.org
La Fédération québécoise des professeures et professeurs d'université (FQPPU) est un organisme à vocation politique dont la mission globale est d'ouvrer au maintien, à la défense, à la promotion et au développement de l'université comme service public et de défendre une université accessible et de qualité.
Max Roy, Président

First Nations SchoolNet (FNS)
Indian & Northern Affairs Canada, Education Program Directorate, 255 Albert St., Ottawa QC K1A 0H4
Tel: 613-995-9146; *Fax:* 819-997-0632
Toll-Free: 800-567-9604
pnr-fns@ainc-inac.gc.ca
www.ainc-inac.gc.ca/edu/ep/index1-eng.asp
Established by the federal government, FNS provides internet access, computer equipment & technical support to First Nations schools on reserves across the country. Students can connect with each other, develop new skills, & participate in national & international events. Six non-profit, regional management organizations deliver the program in their respective region, working with Indian & Northern Affairs Canada.
Elinor Bradley, Director

Foundation for Educational Exchange Between Canada & the United States of America
#2015, 350 Albert St., Ottawa ON K1R 1A4
Tel: 613-688-5540; *Fax:* 613-237-2029
info@fulbright.ca
www.fulbright.ca
Social Media: www.facebook.com/pages/Fulbright-Canada/193768967190; twitter.com/FulbrightPrgrm; www.youtube.com/user/FulbrightCanada
To support outstanding graduate students, faculty, professionals, & independent researchers in order to enhance understanding between the people of Canada & the United States
Michael K. Hawes, Executive Director
Ava Kovats, Sr. Finance Officer

Halifax Education Foundation
19 Medway Court, Dartmouth NS B2W 4G4
Tel: 902-434-2322; *Fax:* 902-434-2053
To support and enhance quality public education in all areas of the Halifax Regional Municipality.

Independent Schools Canada (ISC) / Fédération canadienne des écoles privées (FCEP)
4114 Belanger Dr., Abbotsford BC V3G 1K3
Toll-Free: 888-227-8421
fisc@shaw.ca
www.independentschools.ca
To represent interests & concerns of independent schools; to support & encourage members in the promotion & enhancement of the rightful place & responsibility of independent schools.
Fred Herfst, President

Institut de coopération pour l'éducation des adultes (ICEA)
#300, 5225, rue Berri, Montréal QC H2J 2S4
Tél: 514-948-2044; *Téléc:* 514-948-2046
Ligne sans frais: 877-948-2044
icea@icea.qc.ca
www.icea.qc.ca
Promouvoir l'exercice du droit des adultes à l'éducation tout au long de la vie
Diane Dupuis, Directrice générale

Learning Disabilities Association of Alberta (LDAA) / Troubles d'apprentissage - Association de l'Alberta
PO Box 29011, Stn. Lendrum, Edmonton AB T6H 5Z6
Tel: 780-448-0360; *Fax:* 780-438-0665
info@ldaa.ca
www.ldaa.ca
Supporting people with learning disabilities so that they develop to their full potential. Chapters in Calgary, Red Deer & Edmonton.
Kathryn Burke, Executive Director

Learning Disabilities Association of Canada (LDAC) / Troubles d'apprentissage - Association canadienne (TAAC)
#616, 250 City Centre Ave., Ottawa ON K1R 6K7
Tel: 613-238-5721; *Fax:* 613-235-5391
Toll-Free: 877-238-5322
info@ldac-taac.ca
www.ldac-taac.ca
Social Media: www.facebook.com/groups/52488157512; twitter.com/ldacacta; www.youtube.com/ldacacta
To advance the education, employment, social development, legal rights & general well-being of people with learning disabilities; to create a greater public awareness & understanding of learning disabilities; to promote & develop early recognition, diagnosis, treatment & appropriate educational, social, recreational & career-oriented programs for people with learning disabilities; to promote legislation, research & training of personnel in the field of learning disabilities
Judy Kerr, CEO
Lynn Green, Chair

Learning Disabilities Association of Manitoba (LDAM) / Troubles d'apprentissage - Association de Manitoba
617 Erin St., Winnipeg MB R3G 2W1
Tel: 204-774-1821; *Fax:* 204-788-4090
ldamb@mts.net
www.ldamanitoba.org
To provide support to all those who are concerned with learning disabilities; To represent individuals & families with learning disabilities
Marilyn MacKinnon, Executive Director

Learning Disabilities Association of New Brunswick (LDANB) / Troubles d'apprentissage - Association du Nouveau-Brunswick (TA-ANB)
#203, 403 Regent St., Fredericton NB E3B 3X6
Tel: 506-459-7852; *Fax:* 506-455-9300
Toll-Free: 877-544-7852
ldanb_taanb@nb.aibn.com
www.nald.ca/ldanb
Promotes the understanding & acceptance of the ability of persons with learning disabilities to lead meaningful & successful lives. Satellite office in Saint John.
Patricia Kirby, President
Fabienne McKay, Vice President, Administration

Learning Disabilities Association of Newfoundland & Labrador Inc. (LDANL)
The Board of Trade Bldg., #301, 66 Kenmount Rd., St. John's NL A1B 3V7
Tel: 709-753-1445; *Fax:* 709-753-4747
info@ldanl.org
www.ldanl.org
Social Media: www.facebook.com/103104129749204; twitter.com/ldanl
To work towards to the advancement of legal rights, social development, education, employment, & the general well-being of people with learning disabilities
David Banfield, Executive Director
Donna Skanes, Administrative Assistant

Learning Disabilities Association of Nova Scotia (LDANS) / Troubles d'apprentissage - Association de la Nouvelle-Écosse
#601, 46 Portland St., Dartmouth NS B2Y 1H4
Tel: 902-423-2850; *Fax:* 902-423-2834
Toll-Free: 877-238-5322
info@ldans.ca
www.ldans.ca
To advance the education, employment, social development, legal rights & general well-being of people with learning disabilities.
Rachel Perrier, Executive Director
Krista McNamara, Administrative Coordinator

Learning Disabilities Association of Ontario (LDAO) / Troubles d'apprentissage - Association de l'Ontario
Box 39, #1004, 365 Bloor St. East, Toronto ON M4W 3L4
Tel: 416-929-4311; *Fax:* 416-929-3905
resource@ldao.ca
www.ldao.ca
Social Media: www.facebook.com/LDAOntario; twitter.com/ldaofontario
To provide leadership in learning disabilities advocacy, research, education & services; to advance the full participation of children, youth & adults with learning disabilites in today's society.
Lawrence Barns, President & CEO
Karen Quinn, Director, Operations

Learning Disabilities Association of Prince Edward Island (LADPEI)
#149, 40 Enman Cres., Charlottetown PE C1E 1E6
Tel: 902-894-5032
info@ldapei.ca
www.ldapei.ca
Social Media: www.facebook.com/ldapei; twitter.com/LDAPEI
To advance the interests of people with learning disabilities; To act as a voice for learning disabled people of Prince Edward Island
Nils Ling, Executive Director

Learning Disabilities Association of Saskatchewan (LDAS) / Troubles d'apprentissage - Association de la Saskatchewan
3 - 701 2nd Ave. N, Saskatoon SK S7K 2C9
Tel: 306-652-4114; *Fax:* 306-652-3220
reception@ldas.org
www.ldas.org
To advance the education, employment, social development, legal rights & general well-being of people with learning disabilities. Branches in Regina & Prince Albert.
Dale Rempel, Provincial Executive Director

Learning Disabilities Association of The Northwest Territories (LDA-NWT)
PO Box 242, Yellowknife NT X1A 2N2
Tel: 867-873-6378; *Fax:* 867-873-6378
lda-nwt@arcticdata.ca
www.nald.ca/contacts?f=76
To help people with learning disabilities achieve their potential in school, the workplace, & in society
Nancy Galway, Contact

Learning Disabilities Association of Yukon Territory (LDAY)
107 Main St., Whitehorse YT Y1A 2A7
Tel: 867-668-5167; *Fax:* 867-668-6504
ldayoffice@northwestel.net
www.ldayukon.com
To provide services & programs for Yukoners with learning disabilities so that they reach their potential & become productive members of society
Stephanie Hammond, Executive Director
Esther Chasse, President

Learning Enrichment Foundation (LEF)
116 Industry St., Toronto ON M6M 4L8
Tel: 416-769-0830; *Fax:* 416-769-9912
info@lefca.org
www.lefca.org
To provide programs & services to help individuals become contributors to their community's social & economic development
Ed Lamoureux, President
James McLeod, Vice-President
Kathleen Macdonald, Secretary

Manitoba Association of Parent Councils (MAPC)
#1005, 401 York Ave., Winnipeg MB R3C 0P8
Tel: 204-956-1770; *Fax:* 204-948-2855
Toll-Free: 877-290-4702
mapc1@mts.net
www.mapc.mb.ca
Naomi Kruse, Administrative Officer

Manitoba Association of School Business Officials (MASBO)
375 Jefferson Ave., Winnipeg MB R2V 0N3
Tel: 204-254-7570; *Fax:* 204-254-3606
masbo@mts.net
www.masbo.ca
To provide leadership in the areas of finance, maintenance & transportation
Ede Fast, Executive Director

Manitoba Association of School Superintendents (MASS)
375 Jefferson Ave., Winnipeg MB R2V 0N3
Tel: 204-487-7972; *Fax:* 204-487-7974
coralie.bryant@7oaks.org
www.mass.mb.ca
Provides leadership for public education by advocating in the best interest of learners, & supports its members through professional services.
Coralie Bryant, Executive Director

Manitoba Association of School Trustees (MAST)
191 Provencher Blvd., Winnipeg MB R2H 0G4
Tel: 204-233-1595; *Fax:* 204-231-1356
Toll-Free: 800-262-8836
www.mbschoolboards.ca
To provide services to school boards in Manitoba; To advocate for public education
Carolyn Duhamel, Executive Director
Heather Demetrioff, Associate Director, Member Services

Manitoba Federation of Independent Schools Inc. (MFIS)
630 Westminster Ave., Winnipeg MB R3C 3S1
Tel: 204-783-4481
www.mfis.ca
To support & encourage high educational standards & values unique to our various school communities; to represent interests & concerns of member independent schools in Manitoba
Susan Eberhard, Executive Director
Robert Praznik, President

Manitoba Teachers' Society (MTS)
McMaster House, 191 Harcourt St., Winnipeg MB R3J 3H2
Tel: 204-888-7961; *Fax:* 204-831-0877
Toll-Free: 800-262-8803
www.mbteach.org
Social Media: twitter.com/mbteachers
Envisions a public education system that provides equal accessibility & equal opportunity for all children, that optimizes the potential of all students as individuals & citizens, that fosters lifelong learning & that ensures a safe learning environment respectful of diversity & human dignity
Paul Olson, President

Mensa Canada Society / La Société Mensa Canada
PO Box 1570, Kingston ON K7L 5C8
Tel: 613-547-0824; *Fax:* 613-531-0626
mensa@eventsmgt.com
www.canada.mensa.org
To identify & foster human intelligence for the benefit of humanity; To encourage research; To provide an intellectual & social environment for members
Millie Norry, President

National Christian School Association
PO Box 26005, Saskatoon SK S7K 8C1
Tel: 306-280-9991
lbrunelle@aceministries.com
www.aisca.ab.ca/associations.htm
To continue to assure Canadians of the freedom to choose alternative Christian education
Lou Brunelle, President

National Educational Association of Disabled Students (NEADS) / Association nationale des étudiant(e)s handicapé(e)s au niveau postsecondaire
Carleton University, Rm. 426, Unicentre, 1125 Colonel By Dr., Ottawa ON K1S 5B6
Tel: 613-380-8065; *Fax:* 613-369-4391
Toll-Free: 877-670-1256
info@neads.ca
www.neads.ca
To encourage the self-empowerment of post-secondary students with disabilities; to advocate for increased accessibility at all levels so that disabled students may gain equal access to a college or university education; to provide an information resource base on services for disabled students nationwide according to a file of material from post-secondary institutions
Frank Smith, National Coordinator

New Brunswick Federation of Home & School Associations, Inc. (NBFHSA)
#4, 618 Queen St., Fredericton NB E3B 1C2
Tel: 506-451-6247
homeandschool.nb.aibn.com
www.nbhomeandschool.org
To ensure a quality education, enhanced by parental involvement, & a safe environment for all children.
Cynthia Richards, President
Vern Garnett, 1st Vice President

New Brunswick Teachers' Federation (Ind.) (NBTF) / Fédération des enseignants du Nouveau-Brunswick (FENB)
PO Box 752, 650 Montgomery St., Fredericton NB E3B 5G2
Tel: 506-452-8921; *Fax:* 506-453-9795
www.nbta.ca
Social Media: www.facebook.com/219814221400600
To represent the interests of the Association
Larry Jamieson, Executive Director

Newfoundland & Labrador School Boards' Association (NLSBA)
40 Strawberry Marsh Rd., St. John's NL A1B 2V5
Tel: 709-722-7171; *Fax:* 709-722-8214
www.schoolboardsnl.ca
To promote the interests of education in Newfoundland & Labrador
Brian Shortall, Executive Director
Brenda Pinto, Executive Assistant
Wayne Noseworthy, Director, Labour Relations

Newfoundland & Labrador Teachers' Association (NLTA) / Association des enseignants de Terre-Neuve
3 Kenmount Rd., St. John's NL A1B 1W1
Tel: 709-726-3223; *Fax:* 709-726-4302
Toll-Free: 800-563-3599
mail@nlta.nl.ca
www.nlta.nl.ca
Social Media: twitter.com/NLTeachersAssoc
To strive towards the professional excellence & personal well-being of teachers
Hancock Hancock, Executive Director
Lily Cole, President
James Dinn, Vice-President
Jim Fox, Treasurer

Northwest Territories Teachers' Association (NWTTA)
PO Box 2340, 5018 - 48 St., Yellowknife NT X1A 2P7
Tel: 867-873-8501; *Fax:* 867-873-2366
nwtta@nwtta.nt.ca
www.nwtta.nt.ca
The Northwest Territories Teachers' Association is the professional voice of educators as they provide quality education to Northwest Territories students. With commitment to growth, respect & security for its membership, the Association represents all regions equally, advocates for public education & promotes the teaching profession
David Reid, President

Nova Scotia Federation of Home & School Associations (NSFHSA)
6067 Quinpool Rd., Halifax NS B3L 1A2
Tel: 902-421-2663; *Fax:* 902-660-3771
Toll-Free: 800-214-8373
vanda@staff.ednet.ns.ca
www.nsfhsa.org
Social Media: www.facebook.com/group.php?gid=3295519755
To provide a forum for discussion between the home & school beyond the parent-teacher interview; to promote & secure legislation for the care & protection of & equality of educational opportunities for children; to give parents an understanding of the school & its work, assisting in interpreting the school to the public; to confer & cooperate with organizations other than the schools which concern themselves with the training & development of children & youth
Vanda Dow, President

Nova Scotia School Boards Association (NSSBA) / Association des conseils scolaires de la Nouvelle-Écosse
#395, 3 Spectacle Lake Dr., Dartmouth NS B3B 1W8
Tel: 902-491-2888; *Fax:* 902-429-7405
cnass@nssba.ednet.ns.ca
www.nssba.ca
Social Media: twitter.com/NSSchoolBoards
To act as the voice for school boards in Nova Scotia; To strive towards excellence in public education for students in the province
Ken Meech, Executive Director
Vic Fleury, President
Gin Yee, Treasurer

Nova Scotia Teachers Union (NSTU) / Syndicat des enseignants de la Nouvelle-Écosse
Dr. Tom Parker Bldg., 3106 Joseph Howe Dr., Halifax NS B3L 4L7
Tel: 902-477-5621; *Fax:* 902-477-3517
Toll-Free: 800-565-6788
nstu@nstu.ca; library@nstu.ca
www.nstu.ca
Social Media: www.facebook.com/nsteachersunion; twitter.com/NSTeachersUnion; www.youtube.com/nstuwebcast
To unify the teaching profession in Nova Scotia; To improve the quality of education
Alexis Allen, President

Nunavut Teachers Association (NTA)
PO Box 2458, Iqaluit NU X0A 0H0
Tel: 867-979-0750; *Fax:* 867-979-0780
piadmin@ntanu.ca
www.ntanu.ca
The Nunavut Teachers Association, or NTA, is the negotiating and representative organization for teachers, vice-principals, principals, and RSO and TLC coordinators in Nunavut.
Robin Langill, President
Emile Hatch, Executive Director

Ontario Alliance of Christian Schools (OACS)
790 Shaver Rd., Ancaster ON L9G 3K9
Tel: 905-648-2100; *Fax:* 905-648-2110
oacs@oacs.org
www.oacs.org
To promote independent schools in Ontario; to promote Christian education in Canada; to provide educational services for member schools; to lobby government for educational choice. Canada's largest & oldest independent school organization, representing 79 schools with approximately 14,000 students.
Adrian Guldemond, Executive Director

Ontario Association of Career Colleges (OACC)
PO Box 340, #2, 155 Lynden Rd., Brantford ON N3T 5N3
Tel: 519-752-2124; *Fax:* 519-752-3649
www.oacc.on.ca
Social Media: www.facebook.com/group.php?gid=148743424929
To act as the voice for the private career college sector in Ontario
Paul Kitchin, Executive Director
Lorna Mills, Manager, Office & Financial Aid
Laura Bailey, Coordinator, Media Communications

Ontario Association of Deans of Education (OADE)
#1100, 180 Dundas St. West, Toronto ON M5G 1Z8
Tel: 416-979-2165; *Fax:* 416-979-8635
oade.cou.on.ca
Josée Martel, Contact

Ontario Association of School Business Officials (OASBO)
#207, 144 Main St. North, Markham ON L3P 5T3
Tel: 905-209-9704; *Fax:* 905-209-9705
office@oasbo.org
www.oasbo.org
Dedicated to the pursuit & support of quality education for all students. OASBO is the professional organization for school business officials in Ontario. Our purpose is to improve the quality of school business management and the status, competency, leadership qualities and ethical standards of school business officials at all levels; focus is on information sharing, the promotion of learning at all opportunities, the optimization of operational processes, & the development of partnerships to promote & recognize business practices excellence.
Bill Blackie, Executive Director

Ontario Catholic School Trustees' Association (OCSTA)
PO Box 2064, #1804, 20 Eglinton Ave. West, Toronto ON M4R 1K8
Tel: 416-932-9460; *Fax:* 416-932-9459
ocsta@ocsta.on.ca
www.ocsta.on.ca
Social Media: www.facebook.com/CatholicEducationInOntario; twitter.com/catholicedu; www.youtube.com/user/OCSTAVideo1; www.flickr.com/photos/ocsta
Kevin Kobus, Executive Director

Ontario Confederation of University Faculty Associations (OCUFA) / Union des associations des professeurs des universités de l'Ontario
#300, 83 Yonge St., Toronto ON M5C 1S8
Tel: 416-979-2117; *Fax:* 416-593-5607
ocufa@ocufa.on.ca
www.ocufa.on.ca
To act as the voice of Ontario's approximately 15,000 university faculty & academic librarians; To advance the professional & economic interests of university faculty & academic librarians; To enhance the quality of Ontario's higher education system
Mark Langer, President
Constance Adamson, Vice-President
Henry Mandelbaum, Executive Director
Mark Rosenfeld, Associate Executive Director, Research & Communications
Glen Copplestone, Treasurer

Ontario Council for University Lifelong Learning
c/o Lakehead University, Thunder Bay ON P7B 5E1
Tel: 807-343-8210; *Fax:* 807-343-8008
www.ocull.ca
OCULL is a professional association for administrators and practitioners who develop and deliver degree and on-degree continuing education programs in Ontario universities. OCULL is an advocate for adult learners at Ontario universities, a collegial network, and a vehicle for professional development for its members.
Leslie Malcolm, President

Ontario Council on Graduate Studies (OCGS) / Conseil ontarien des études supérieures
#1100, 180 Dundas St. West, Toronto ON M5G 1Z8
Tel: 416-979-2165; *Fax:* 416-979-8635
ocgs@cou.on.ca
ocgs.cou.on.ca/
Strives to ensure quality graduate education & research across Ontario
Donna Woolcott, Executive Director

Ontario English Catholic Teachers' Association (CLC) (OECTA)
#400, 65 St. Clair Ave. East, Toronto ON M4T 2Y8
Tel: 416-925-2493; *Fax:* 416-925-7764
Toll-Free: 800-268-7230
membership@oecta.on.ca
www.oecta.on.ca
To advance Catholic education; To provide professional services, support, protection, & leadership
Kevin O'Dwyer, President
Marshall Jarvis, General Secretary

Ontario Federation of Home & School Associations Inc. (OFHSA)
51 Stuart St., Hamilton ON L8L 1B5
Tel: 905-308-9563; *Fax:* 905-308-7935
info@ofhsa.on.ca
www.ofhsa.on.ca
To provide facilities for the bringing together of members of Home & School Associations for discussion of matters of general interest & to stimulate cooperative effort; to assist in forming public opinion favorable to reform & advancement of the education of the child; to develop between educators & the general public such united effort as shall secure for every child the highest advantage in physical, mental, moral & spiritual education; to raise the standard of home & national life; to maintain a non-partisan, non-commercial, non-racial & non-sectarian organization
Lee Gowers, President
Teresa Blum, Executive Vice-President

Ontario Federation of Independent Schools (OFIS)
2199 Regency Terrace, Ottawa ON K2C 1H2
info@ofis.ca
www.ofis.ca
To secure guarantees from Ontario government for independent schools' right to exist, curricular freedom, self-governance & acceptance by government of its responsibility to let education grants follow a child to any bona fide school that meets acceptable social & educational criteria
Barbara Bierman, Executive Director
Barbara Brown, President

Ontario Principals' Council (OPC)
180 Dundas St. West, 25th Fl., Toronto ON M5G 1Z8
Tel: 416-322-6600; *Fax:* 416-322-6618
Toll-Free: 800-701-2362
admin@principals.on.ca
www.principals.on.ca
To support the work of Ontario's principals & vice-principals to provide excellent leadership in the public education system
Mike Benson, Executive Director
Vicki Shannon, President

Ontario Public School Boards Association (OPSBA)
439 University Ave., Toronto ON M5G 1Y8
Tel: 416-340-2540; *Fax:* 416-340-7571
webmaster@opsba.org
www.opsba.org
To represent Ontario's public school authorities & public district school boards; To advocate on behalf of the public school system in Ontario; To promote & enhance public education
Colleen Schenk, President
Gail Anderson, Executive Director
Florenda Tingle, Executive Coordinator

Ontario Secondary School Teachers' Federation (OSSTF) / Fédération des enseignants des écoles secondaires de l'Ontario (FEESO)
60 Mobile Dr., Toronto ON M4A 2P3
Tel: 416-751-8300; *Fax:* 416-751-3394
Toll-Free: 800-267-7867
www.osstf.on.ca
To protect & enhance Ontario's public education system; To establish working conditions for members
Ken Coran, President
Paul Elliott, Vice-President
Harvey Bischof, Vice-President
Pierre Côté, General Secretary
Earl Burt, Treasurer

Ontario Society for Education Through Art (OSEA)
c/o Membership Secretary, 37 Hopewell Ave., Toronto ON M4K 3M8
www.osea.on.ca
To promote & advocate learning through the visual arts
Jane Dewar, Vice President
Maira Herenberg, President

Ontario Teachers' Federation (OTF) / Fédération des enseignantes et des enseignants de l'Ontario (FEO)
#200, 1300 Yonge St., Toronto ON M4T 1X3
Tel: 416-966-3424; *Fax:* 416-966-5450
Toll-Free: 800-268-7061
www.otffeo.on.ca
To represent the interests of all registered teachers in Ontario's publicly funded schools
Francine LeBlanc-Lebel, President
Rhonda Kimberley-Young, Sec.-Treas.

ORT Canada
#200, 530 Wilson Ave., Toronto ON M3H 5Y9
Tel: 416-787-0339; *Fax:* 416-787-9420
Toll-Free: 866-991-3045
info@ort-toronto.org
www.ort-toronto.com
To fundraise in support of the worldwide vocational-training-school network of ORT.
Sandra Chapnik, President
Lindy Meshwork, Executive Director

Parent Co-operative Preschools International (PCPI)
8725 Westport Dr., Niagara Falls ON L2H 0A2
Tel: 905-374-6605; *Fax:* 905-374-0473
www.preschools.coop
To promote the family & community; to strengthen & expand the parent cooperative movement & community appreciation of parent education for adults & preschool education for children; to promote desirable standards for program, practices & conditions in parent cooperative preschools & encourage continuing education for parents, teachers & directors; to promote interchange of information among parent cooperative nursery schools, kindergartens & other parent-sponsored preschool programs; to cooperate with family living, adult education & early childhood educational organizations in the interest of more effective service relationships with parents of young children; to study & promote legislation designed to further the health & well-being of children & families

Parents partenaires en éducation (PPE)
#B-150, 2445, boul St-Laurent, Ottawa ON K1G 6C3
Tél: 613-741-8846; *Téléc:* 613-741-7322
Ligne sans frais: 800-342-0663
info@reseauppe.ca
www.reseauppe.ca
Média social: twitter.com/@info_ppe
Travailler en étroite collaboration avec ses partenaires en éducation, outiller les parents dans leur rôle de partenaires en éducation et agir comme porte-parole provincial des parents; promouvoir l'excellence de l'éducation de langue française et l'épanouissement global des enfants francophones
Geneviève Folliet, Présidente

Prince Edward Island Home & School Federation Inc. (PEIHSF)
PO Box 1012, 40 Enman Cres., Charlottetown PE C1A 7M4
Tel: 902-620-3186; *Fax:* 902-620-3187
Toll-Free: 800-916-0664
peihsf@edu.pe.ca
www.edu.pe.ca/peihsf/
Wendy MacDonald, President
Shirley Jay, Executive Director

Prince Edward Island School Trustees Association (PEISTA)
trusteespei@yahoo.ca
trusteespei.blogspot.com
To act as umbrella organization in coordinating & supporting efforts of school trustees in furthering education & education needs for all children in PEI
Ron Lee, President

Prince Edward Island Teachers' Federation (PEITF) / Fédération des enseignants de l'Île-du-Prince-Édouard
PO Box 6000, 24 Glen Stewart Dr., Charlottetown PE C1A 8B4
Tel: 902-569-4157; *Fax:* 902-569-3682
Toll-Free: 800-903-4157
rmacrae@peitf.com
www.peitf.com
To promote & support education as well as the professional & economic well-being of PEI teachers
Carrie St. Jean, President
Shaun MacCormac, General Secretary

Québec Association for Adult Learning Inc. (QAAL) / Association Québécoise pour l'éducation des adultes
#LB568-3, 1455 boul Maisonneuve ouest, Montréal QC H3G 1M8
Tel: 514-848-2424; *Fax:* 514-848-4520
qaal@alcor.concordia.ca
doe.concordia.ca/qaal
QAAL is a not-for-profit, English-language association that supports those who support adult learners. It promotes equality of access to information & services, & it raises public awareness of adult learning issues, notably from an English-speaker's perspective in Québec.
Michael Canuel, President
Mario Pasteris, Executive Director

Québec Association of Independent Schools (QAIS) / Association des écoles privées du Québec
PO Box 398, Stn. Snowdon, Montréal QC H3X 3T6
Tel: 514-483-6111; *Fax:* 514-483-0865
Toll-Free: 866-909-6111
qais@qc.aibn.com
www.qais.qc.ca
The Quebec Association of Independent Schools (QAIS) is an organization consisting of English elementary and secondary independent schools licensed in the public interest and located in Quebec. QAIS promotes collaboration, provides services that further educational leadership and advocates independent English language education in Quebec on behalf of its member schools.
Michel Lafrance, Executive Director

Québec English School Boards Association (QESBA) / Association des commissions scolaires anglophones du Québec (ACSAQ)
#515, 1410, rue Stanley, Montréal QC H3A 1P8
Tel: 514-849-5900; *Fax:* 514-849-9228
Toll-Free: 877-512-7522
qesba@qesba.qc.ca
www.qesba.qc.ca
Social Media: www.facebook.com/122225577919
To represent English school boards in Québec
David Birnbaum, Executive Director

Québec Federation of Home & School Associations Inc. (QFHSA) / Fédération des associations foyer-école du Québec Inc.
#560, 3285, boul Cavendish, Montréal QC H4B 2L9
Tel: 514-481-5619; *Fax:* 514-481-5610
Toll-Free: 888-808-5619
info@qfhsa.org
www.qfhsa.org
To provide facilities for the bringing together of members of Home & School Associations for discussion of matters of general interest & to stimulate cooperative effort; To assist in forming public opinion favorable to reform & advancement of the education of the child; to develop between educators & the general public such a united effort as shall secure for every child the highest advantage in physical, mental, moral & spiritual education; To raise the standard of home & national life; To maintain non-partisan, non-commercial, non-racial & non-sectarian organization
Liette Chamberland, President
Rosalind Hoenig, Secretary

Le Réseau d'enseignement francophone à distance du Canada (REFAD)
CP 47542, Succ. Plateau Mont-Royal, Montréal QC H2H 2S8
Tél: 514-284-9109; *Téléc:* 514-284-9363
refad@sympatico.ca
www.refad.ca
Favoriser la collaboration entre les personnes et les organisations intéressées par l'enseignement à distance en français; rassembler en réseau les établissements qui ont recours à la formation à distance en français; appuyer et compléter d'autres réseaux d'enseignement à distance existant déjà à travers le Canada; promouvoir et accroître la qualité et la quantité des programmes et des cours offerts dans la francophonie canadienne.
Caroll-Ann Keating, Présidente
Alain Langlois, Directeur général

The Retired Teachers of Ontario (RTO) / Les Enseignants et enseignantes retraités de l'Ontario (ERO)
#300, 18 Spadina Rd., Toronto ON M5R 2S7
Tel: 416-962-9463; *Fax:* 416-962-1061
Toll-Free: 800-361-9888
info@rto-ero.org
www.rto-ero.org
To promote the interests of persons in receipt of a pension under the Ontario Teachers' Pension Act
Howard Braithwaite, Executive Director

Saskatchewan Association for Multicultural Education (SAME)
144 Marsh Cres., Regina SK S4S 5J7
Tel: 306-780-9428
same@sasktel.net
www.same.ca
To promote multicultual & anti-racist education throughout Saskatchewan; To raise awareness & acceptance of cultural diversity in the province; To respond to changes in multicultural policies & demographics; To address social justice issues
Rhonda Rosenberg, Executive Director

Saskatchewan Association of Historical High Schools (SAHHS)
c/o Luther College High School, 1500 Royal St., Regina SK S4T 6G3
Tel: 306-791-9150; *Fax:* 306-359-6962
lutherhs@luthercollege.edu
www.luthercollege.edu
Mark Anderson, Principal

Saskatchewan Association of School Councils (SASC)
#301, 221 Cumberland Ave. North, Saskatoon SK S7N 1M3
Tel: 306-955-5723; *Fax:* 306-445-7707
www.schoolcouncils.com
To enhance the education & general well-being of children & youth; to promote the involvement of parents, students, educators & the community at large in the advancement of learning & to act as a voice for parents; to promote effective communication between the home & the school; to encourage parents to participate in educational activities & decision making
Darlene Krell, President
Deborah Agema, Executive Director

Saskatchewan School Boards Association (SSBA)
#400, 2222 - 13th Ave., Regina SK S4P 3M7
Tel: 306-569-0750; *Fax:* 306-352-9633
admin@saskschoolboards.ca
www.saskschoolboards.ca
Represents boards of education, including school division boards, conseils scolaires, & local or district boards; ensures advocacy, leadership & support for member boards of education by speaking as the voice for quality public education for all children; offers opportunities for trustee development; provides information & services
Darren McKee, Executive Director
Patti Blackburn, Administrative Officer
Andrea Ashton, Communications Officer

Saskatchewan Teachers' Federation (STF) / Fédération des enseignants et des enseignantes de la Saskatchewan
2317 Arlington Ave., Saskatoon SK S7J 2H8
Tel: 306-373-1660; *Fax:* 306-374-1122
Toll-Free: 800-667-7762
stf@stf.sk.ca
www.stf.sk.ca
Steven Allen, President
Gwen Dueck, General Secretary

Skills/Compétences Canada
#205, 260, boul Saint Raymond, Gatineau QC J9A 3G7
Tel: 819-771-7545; *Fax:* 819-771-5575
Toll-Free: 877-754-5226
skillscanada@skillscanada.com
www.skillscanada.com
Social Media: www.facebook.com/pages/Skills-Canada-Competences-Canada/11736117829828
To create dynamic synergies between industry, government, youth, educators & labour; to raise awareness of the value of a technical or skilled trade career; to champion & stimulate the development of technological & employability skills in Canadian youth to strengthen our competitive edge in the global marketplace
Donavon Elliott, President
Shaun Thorson, Executive Director
Natalee Lewis, Communications/Marketing Coordinator

Society for Educational Visits & Exchanges in Canada (SEVEC) / Société éducative de visites et d'échanges au Canada
300-950 Gladstone Ave., Ottawa ON K1Y 3E6
Tel: 613-727-3832; *Fax:* 613-727-3831
Toll-Free: 800-387-3832
info@sevec.ca
www.sevec.ca
To create, facilitate & promote enriching educational opportunities within Canada for the development of mutual respect & understanding through programs of exploration in language & culture
Mary Reeves, Chair
Sandy Dobson, Director, Finance & Administration
Michele Ténière, Director, Marketing & Communications

Society for Quality Education (SQE)
57 Twyford Rd., Toronto ON M9A 1W5
Tel: 416-231-7247; *Fax:* 416-237-0108
Toll-Free: 888-856-5535
info@societyforqualityeducation.org
www.societyforqualityeducation.org
To advance public & private education in Canada by disseminating authoritative information on educational governance & methodology.
Doretta Wilson, Executive Director
Malkin Dare, President

Society for the Promotion of the Teaching of English as a Second Language in Quebec (SPEAQ) / Société pour la promotion de l'enseignement de l'anglais, langue seconde, au Québec
#2, 6818, Rue Saint-Denis, Montréal QC H2S 2S2
Tel: 514-271-3700; *Fax:* 514-271-4587
speaq@speaq.qc.ca
www.speaq.qc.ca
To bring together persons engaged or interested in the teaching of English as a second language in Quebec; To promote & develop the professional & economic interests of its members; To create a favourable climate for the development of teaching English as a second language in Quebec//Promouvoir l'enseignement de l'anglais, langue seconde au Québec
Micheline Schinck, President
Monique Mainella, Vice President

TESL Canada Federation (TESL Canada)
#408, 4370 Dominion St., Burnaby BC V5G 4L7
Tel: 604-298-0312; *Fax:* 604-298-0372
Toll-Free: 800-393-9199
admin@tesl.ca
www.tesl.ca
To support the sharing of knowledge & experiences across Canada; To represents diverse interests in TESL nationally & internationally
Louise Aerts, Executive Director
Jennifer Pearson Terell, President
Sandie Kouritzin, Secretary

TESL Ontario
#405, 27 Carlton St., Toronto ON M5B 1L2
Tel: 416-593-4243; *Fax:* 416-593-0164
Toll-Free: 800-327-4827
administration@teslontario.org
www.teslontario.org
Social Media: www.facebook.com/101601733235647; twitter.com/TESLOntario; www.linkedin.com/groups/TESL-Ontario-1813872
Sheila Nicholas, Chair
Marilyn Johnston, Vice-Chair

United World Colleges
Lester B. Pearson College of the Pacific, 650 Pearson College Dr., Victoria BC V9C 4H7
Tel: 250-391-2411; *Fax:* 250-391-2412
admin@pearsoncollege.ca
www.pearsoncollege.ca
Through international education, shared experience & community service, the United World Colleges encourage young people to become responsible citizens, politically & environmentally aware, committed to the ideals of peace, justice, understanding & cooperation, & to the implementation of these ideals through action & personal example
David B. Hawley, Director

Yukon Teachers' Association (YTA) / Association des enseignantes et des enseignants du Yukon
2064 - 2 Ave., Whitehorse YT Y1A 1A9
Tel: 867-668-6777; *Fax:* 867-667-4324
Toll-Free: 866-668-2097
admin@yta.yk.ca
www.yta.yk.ca
To promote & support public education; To represent the professional & economic needs of Yukon educators
Katherine Mackwood, President
Dave Hobbins
Patricia Bort, Professional Development
Denise Schneider, Administrator, YTA Office
Dorothy LeBel, Finance Clerk, Finance

Electronics & Electricity

Canadian Electrical Contractors Association (CECA) / Association canadienne des entrepreneurs électriciens (ACEE)
#460, 170 Attwell Dr., Toronto ON M9W 5Z5
Tel: 416-675-3226; *Fax:* 416-675-7736
Toll-Free: 800-387-3226
ceca@ceca.org
www.ceca.org
To represent electrical contractors at the national level
Colin Campbell, President
David Mason, Vice-President
Eryl Roberts, Executive Secretary

Canadian Electrical Manufacturers Representatives Association (CEMRA)
#300, 180 Attwell Dr., Toronto ON M9W 6A9
Tel: 905-602-8877; *Fax:* 416-679-9234
info@electrofed.com
www.electrofed.com
To represent over 300 member companies that manufacture, distribute, & service electrical, electronics, & telecommunications products
Milos Janick, President & CEO

Conseil Canadien des Électrotechnologies (CCE) / Canadian Council on Electrotechnologies (CCE)
600, av de la Montagne, Shawinigan QC G9N 7N5
Tél: 819-539-1560; *Téléc:* 819-539-1558
Transfert technologique en vue de l'utilisation rationnelle et optimale de l'électricité
Richard Clayton, President-CCE
Michael P. Dudar, Vice Président-CCE

Consumer Electronics Marketers of Canada: A Division of Electro-Federation Canada (CEMC)
#300, 180 Attwell Dr., Mississauga ON M9W 6A9
Tel: 905-602-8877; *Fax:* 416-679-9234
info@electrofed.com
www.cemc-efc.ca
To represent the consumer electronic marketing industry; To provide information for CEMC members to help them make good business decisions; To report on the status of the consumer electronics market
Robert Gumiela, Chair
Susan Winter, Vice-President

Corporation des maîtres électriciens du Québec (CMEQ) / Corporation of Master Electricians of Québec
5925, boul Décarie, Montréal QC H3W 3C9
Tél: 514-738-2184; *Téléc:* 514-738-2192
Ligne sans frais: 800-361-9061
webmestre@cmeq.org
www.cmeq.org
Augmenter la compétence des membres; règlementer la conduite des membres et de la profession; faciliter et encourager les membres à se familiariser avec des nouvelles techniques; chercher des solutions pratiques aux problèmes communs de l'industrie électrique
Johanne Pulford, Directrice générale

Electrical Contractors Association of Alberta (ECAA)
11235 - 120 St., Edmonton AB T5G 2X9
Tel: 780-451-2412; *Fax:* 780-455-9815
Toll-Free: 800-252-9375
ecaa@ecaa.ab.ca
www.ecaa.ab.ca
To work towards increased contractors knowledge & efficiency; improved communication between industry sections; government liaison for training qualifications & regulations; overall improvement of the electrical industry
Sheri McLean, Executive Director

Electrical Contractors Association of BC (ECA-BC)
#201, 3989 Henning Dr., Burnaby BC V5C 6N5
Tel: 604-294-4123; *Fax:* 604-294-4120
eca@eca.bc.ca
www.eca.bc.ca
To promote use of electricity; to strengthen, encourage & promote electrical contracting industry; to promote functions assisting businessmen to become more efficient & profitable.
Deborah Cahill, Executive Director

Electrical Contractors Association of New Brunswick Inc. (ECANB)
PO Box 322, Fredericton NB E3B 4Y9
Tel: 506-452-7627; *Fax:* 506-452-1786
dwe@eca.nb.ca
www.eca.nb.ca
David Ellis, Executive Director

Electrical Contractors Association of Ontario (ECAO)
#460, 170 Attwell Dr., Toronto ON M9W 5Z5
Tel: 416-675-3226; *Fax:* 416-675-7736
Toll-Free: 800-387-3226
ecao@ecao.org
www.ecao.org
To serve & represent the interests of the electrical contracting industry
Eryl Roberts, Executive Vice President
Bill McKee, Treasurer
Lucy Roberts, Contact, Public Relations & Member Services

Electrical Contractors Association of Saskatchewan
c/o Michael Fougere, 320 Gardiner Park Ct., Regina SK S4V 1R9
Tel: 306-525-0171
To voice the concerns of electrical contractors in Saskatchewan; To improvethe electrical industry
Michael Fougere, Executive Director

Electro-Federation Canada Inc. (EFC)
#300, 180 Attwell Dr., Toronto ON M9W 6A9
Tel: 905-602-8877; *Fax:* 905-602-5686
Toll-Free: 866-602-8877
info@electrofed.com
www.electrofed.com
Social Media: twitter.com/EFC_Tweets
To represent members provincially, federally, & internationally on issues affecting the electro-technical business
Milos Jancik, President/CEO
Ken Frankum, Chair
Harald Henze, Treasurer
Larry Moore, Vice-President, Consumer Councils
Joseph Neu, Vice-President, Engineering, Codes & Standards

Institute of Electrical & Electronics Engineers Inc. - Canada
PO Box 63005, Stn. University PO, Shoppers Drug Mart #742, 102 Plaza Dr., Dundas ON L9H 4H0
Tel: 905-628-9554; *Fax:* 905-628-9554
admin@ieee.ca
www.ieee.ca
Social Media:
www.facebook.com/group.php?gid=182255135157013
To advance the theory & practice of electrical, electronics, & computer engineering & computer science
Cathie Lowell, IEEE Canada Administrator

Om Malik, President
Keith Brown, President Elect
Gerard Dunphy, Treasurer

Manitoba Electrical League Inc.
#104, 1780 Wellington Ave., Winnipeg MB R3H 1B3
Tel: 204-783-4125; *Fax:* 204-783-4216
office@meleague.net
www.meleague.net
To advise & inform all people of Manitoba on effective use of electricity toward maintenance & betterment of standards of living; to encourage cooperation of various branches of electrical industry in developing programs in support of common marketing objectives.
Dave Foreman, General Manager

Ontario Electrical League (OEL)
#300, 180 Attwell Dr., Toronto ON M9W 6A9
Tel: 905-238-1382; *Fax:* 905-238-1420
communications@oel.org
www.oel.org
To represent & strengthen the electrical industry in Ontario
Mary Ingram-Haigh, President
Sheila Sage, Manager, Operations
Cynthia Kenth, Contact, Communications

Emergency Response

Canadian Avalanche Association (CAA)
PO Box 2759, 110 MacKenzie Ave., Revelstoke BC V0E 2S0
Tel: 250-837-2435; *Fax:* 250-837-4624
Toll-Free: 800-667-1105
info@avalanche.ca
www.avalanche.ca
To foster & support a professional environment for avalanche safety operations in Canada; To represent the avalanche community to stakeholders
Ian Tomm, Executive Director
Mary Clayton, Director, Communications
Kristin Anthony-Malone, Manager, Operations
Emily Grady, Manager, Industry Training Program

Canadian Fallen Firefighters Foundation / Fondation canadienne des pompiers morts en service
#200, 440 Laurier Ave. W., Ottawa ON K1R 7X6
Tel: 613-786-3024; *Fax:* 613-782-2228
info@cfff.ca
www.cfff.ca
To serve all firefighters & their families in time of need. This registered, non-profit, charitable organization is made up of members of the Canadian Fire Service and other interested citizens dedicated to honouring Canada's fallen firefighters.
Robert Kirkpatrick, President
Douglas Wylie, 1st Vice-President
Mike McKenna, 2nd Vice-President
Doug Lock, Treasurer

Canadian Red Cross Society (CRCS) / La Société canadienne de la Croix-Rouge
#300, 170 Metcalfe St., Ottawa ON K2P 2P2
Tel: 613-740-1900; *Fax:* 613-740-1911
Toll-Free: 800-418-1111
WeCare@redcross.ca; shop@redcross.ca (online stor inquiries)
www.redcross.ca
To help people deal with situations that threaten: their survival & safety, their security & well-being, their human dignity, in Canada & around the world; To improve the lives of vulnerable people by mobilizing the power of humanity
Conrad Sauvé, Secretary General & Chief Executive Officer
Ted Tanaka, President
Alan Dean, Vice-President
Amit Mehra, Vice-President

Civil Air Search & Rescue Association (CASARA)
c/o John Kelly, National Administrator, 3025 Ness Ave., #C, Winnipeg MB R2Y 2J2
Tel: 204-953-2290
jkelly@casaranational.ca
www.casara.ca
To promote aviation safety; To support Canada's Search & Rescue (SAR) program
John Davidson, President
John Kelly, National Administrator
Brian Bishop, Vice-President, Training & Operations
Mike Daniels, Vice-President, Finance & Administration
Doug MacDonald, Vice-President, Plans & Equipment

Corporation des services d'ambulance du Québec
#205, 455, rue Marais, Vanier QC G1M 3A2
Tél: 418-681-4448; *Téléc:* 418-681-4667
A l'origine, la mission de la Corporation des services d'ambulance du Québec visait exclusivement à offrir une gamme de services et d'avantages à ses membres et à défendre les intérêts de ces derniers auprès des différentes instances gouvernementales, auprès de ses membres au Québec.

Lifesaving Society / Société de sauvetage
287 McArthur Ave., Ottawa ON K1L 6P3
Tel: 613-746-5694; *Fax:* 613-746-9929
experts@lifesaving.ca
www.lifesaving.ca
The Society is a volunteer organization that works to prevent drowning & water-related incidents by providing lifesaving, lifeguarding & leadership education. It is a registered charity, BN: 119129088RR0001.
Paul Dawe, President
Yvan Chalifour, Executive Director

Occupational First Aid Attendants Association of British Columbia (OFAAA)
#108, 2323 Boundary Rd., Vancouver BC V5M 4V8
Tel: 604-294-0244; *Fax:* 604-294-0289
Toll-Free: 800-667-4566
ofaaa@ofaaa.bc.ca
www.ofaaa.bc.ca
To enhance the professional status of first aid attendants & to promote accessibility to high standards of first aid for the workers of the province of British Columbia
Russ Brown, Vice-President
Adrian Metcalf, Treasurer
Irvin Schonbrun, Secretary
Laural Martin, Administrator
Allan Zdunic, President

REACT Canada Inc.
32 The Queensway North, Keswick ON L4P 1E3
Tel: 905-476-5231
react@react-canada.org
www.react-canada.org
To provide skilled volunteer two-way radio communications for safety; To provide volunteer emergency radio communications for travellers; To provide safety communications for walkathons & parades.; To offer speakers to community groups on correct use of radio in emergencies
Ronald W. McCracken, Director

St. John Ambulance / Ambulance Saint-Jean
#400, 1900 City Park Dr., Ottawa ON K1J 1A3
Tel: 613-236-7461; *Fax:* 613-236-2425
Toll-Free: 888-840-5646
info@nhq.sja.ca
www.sja.ca
To enable Canadians to improve their health, safety & quality of life by providing training & community service. Courses in CPR, emergency first aid, & safety training are offered, as well as community service programs (medical first response, therapy dog services, emergency preparedness, youth programs), & first aid kits
F. Richard Bruce, Chancellor
Steven Gaetz, Interim CEO

Employment & Human Resources

Association of Canadian Search, Employment & Staffing Services (ACSESS) / Association nationale des entreprises en recrutement et placement de personnel
#100, 2233 Argentia Rd., Mississauga ON L5N 2X7
Tel: 905-826-6869; *Fax:* 905-826-4873
Toll-Free: 888-232-4962
acsess@acsess.org
www.acsess.org
To promote the advancement & growth of the employment & staffing services industry in Canada
Steve Jones, National President
Amanda Curtis, Executive Director

Association of Professional Recruiters of Canada
#2210, 1081 Ambleside Dr., Ottawa ON K2B 8C8
Tel: 613-721-5957; *Fax:* 613-721-5850
Toll-Free: 888-421-0000
www.workplace.ca/resources/aprc_assoc.html
Social Media:
www.facebook.com/InstituteofProfessionalManagement
To establish standards & practices for the recruitment & selection of human resources in Canada & to provide members with the tools to practice at the highest professional levels
Nathaly Pinchuk, Executive Director
Brian Pascal, President

Canadian Association of Career Educators & Employers (CACEE) / Association canadienne des spécialistes en emploi et des employeurs (ACSEE)
#202, 720 Spadina Ave., Toronto ON M5S 2T9
Tel: 416-929-5156; *Fax:* 416-929-5256
Toll-Free: 866-922-3303
www.cacee.com
To facilitate the process of matching graduates with employment; a partnership of employer recruiters & career educators providing information, advice & services to students, employers & career centre personnel in the areas of career planning & student recruitment.
Anne Markey, Executive Director
Janine Clarke, Operations Manager

Canadian Career Information Association (CCIA) / Association canadienne de documentation professionnelle (ACADOP)
205 Humber College Blvd., Toronto ON M9W 5L7
Tel: 416-675-5030
karen.fast@humber.ca
www.ccia-acadop.ca
To promote the development & effective delivery of Canadian career information
Anna De Grauwe, Chair
Angella Nunes, Treasurer

Canadian Council of Human Resources Associations (CCHRA) / Conseil canadien des associations en ressources humaines (CCARH)
#603, 150 Metcalfe St., Ottawa ON K2P 1P1
Tel: 613-567-2477; *Fax:* 613-567-2478
Toll-Free: 866-560-1288
info@cchra-ccarh.ca
www.cchra-ccarh.ca
To establish national core standards for the human resources profession; to foster communications among participating associations; to be the recognized resource on equivalency for human resources qualifications across Canada; & to provide a national & international collective voice on human resources issues
Patrick Hartling, Chair

Human Resources Professionals Association (HRPA)
#1902, 2 Bloor St. West, Toronto ON M4W 3E2
Tel: 416-923-2324; *Fax:* 416-923-7264
Toll-Free: 800-387-1311
info@hrpa.org
www.hrpa.ca
HRPA empowers human resources professionals by providing management & leadership support, through information resources, events, professional development, & networking opportunities.
Antoinette Blunt, Chair
William (Bill) Greenhalgh, CEO
Louise Tagliacozzo, Manager, Board Relations & Administration

International Association for Human Resource Information Management (IHRIM)
PO Box 1086, Burlington MA 01803 USA
press@ihrim.org (media information)
www.ihrim.org
To operate as a clearinghouse for the HRIM industry; To enable members to achieve strategic objectives through the integration of information technology & human resource management
Lynne Mealy, President & Chief Executive Officer
Jean Andrews, Manager, Membership Marketing & Vendor Relations
Laurie Carantit, Manager, Marketing & Communications
Michelle Czosek, Manager, Education & Special Programs
Karen Murray, Manager, Membership Programs

Ordre des conseillers en ressources humaines et en relations industrielles agréés du Québec (ORHRI)
#1400, 1200, av McGill Collège, Montréal QC H3B 4G7
Tél: 514-879-1636; *Téléc:* 514-879-1722
Ligne sans frais: 800-214-1609
info@portailrh.org
www.portailrh.org
La promotion de l'importance stratégique de la gestion des ressources humaines dans la gestion des organisations ainsi que la promotion des nouveaux concepts et champs de développement qui caractérisent son évolution; la promotion des principes de gestion des ressources humaines dans les organisations en tenant compte des tendances sociales et économiques et en accord avec les valeurs de l'association; le développement des membres par le biais de programmes stratégiques de formation et de perfectionnement, des activités d'échanges et d'information et la mise en commun d'expertise professionnelle; la prise de position publique sur des sujets d'intérêt en ressources humaines; le maillage de ses membres à l'intérieur de diverses activités professionnelles et sociales
Florent Francoeur, Président-directeur général

Energy

Association of Major Power Consumers in Ontario (AMPCO)
Sterling Tower, #1702, 372 Bay St., Toronto ON M5H 2W9
Tel: 416-260-0280; *Fax:* 416-260-0442
info@ampco.org
www.ampco.org
To represent Ontario's electricity-intensive companies; To ensure reliability of power supply to support the economy of Ontario; To advocate a fair & equitable pricing system for electricity; To present views on energy matters to such groups as the Ontario Energy Board, the Ontario Government, Ontario Hydro, the news media, & the general public; To provide decision makers with recommendations on resolving issues
Adam White, President
Adam White, President
Fareeda Heeralal, Contact

Canadian Coalition for Nuclear Responsibility (CCNR) / Regroupement pour la surveillance du nucléaire (RSN)
PO Box 236, Stn. Snowdon, Montréal QC H3X 3T4
Fax: 514-489-5118
ccnr@web.ca
www.ccnr.org
Dedicated to education and research on all issues related to nuclear energy, whether civilian or military — including non-nuclear alternatives — especially those pertaining to Canada.
Gordon Edwards, President
Marc Chénier, Sec.-Treas.

Canadian Energy Research Institute (CERI)
#150, 3512 - 33 St. NW, Calgary AB T2L 2A6
Tel: 403-282-1231; *Fax:* 403-284-4181
info@ceri.ca
www.ceri.ca
To provide the public, industry, & the government with information concerning all aspects of energy
Peter Howard, President & Chief Executive Officer
David McWhinney, Director, Accounting & Operations
Dinara Millington, Director, Research
Jon Rozhon, Senior Researcher
Thorn Walden, Senior Economist

Canadian Fluid Power Association (CFPA) / Association canadienne d'énergie fluide
#310, 2175 Sheppard Ave. East, Toronto ON M2J 1W8
Tel: 416-499-1416; *Fax:* 416-491-1670
info@cfpa.ca
www.cfpa.ca
To build public awareness of fluid power technology; To provide a forum for the exchange of information & opinion; To represent the Canadian fluid power industry to government, educational institutions & other organizations; To ensure that members' concerns are known to those in government; To ensure that students are able to be properly prepared for careers in the fluid power industry; To ensure that members are kept abreast of the latest developments in the fluid power industry
Carolyne Vigon, Administrator
Mary Lou Murray, Registrar, Events

Canadian Institute of Energy (CIE)
#26, 181 Ravine Dr., Port Moody BC V3H 4T3
Tel: 604-949-1346; *Fax:* 604-469-3717
cienergybc@gmail.com
www.cienergy.org
To provide a Canadian perspective on energy technology, business & policy, nationally & internationally, for those affected professionally or personally by energy issues; To encourage energy research, education & dissemination of topical information; To provide an unbiased forum for discussion & debate
Penny Cochrane, Chair
Melissa McArthur, Administrator
John Oliver, Treasurer

Canadian Nuclear Association (CNA) / Association nucléaire canadienne
#1610, 130 Albert St., Ottawa ON K1P 5G4
Tel: 613-237-4262; *Fax:* 613-237-0989
www.cna.ca
To promote the orderly & sound development of nuclear energy for peaceful purposes in Canada & abroad; To promote & foster an environment favourable to the healthy growth of the uses of nuclear energy & radioisotopes; To encourage cooperation between various industries, utilities, educational institutions, government departments & agencies, which may have a common interest in the development of economic nuclear power & the uses of radioisotopes; To provide a forum for the discussion & resolution of problems which are of concern to the members, the industry, or the Canadian public; To stimulate cooperation with other associations with similar objectives & purposes
Denise Carpenter, President & Chief Executive Officer
Steve Coupland, Director, Environmental Affairs
George Christidis, Director, Government Affairs
Heather Kleb, Director, Regulatory Affairs
Kathleen Olson, Director, Communications
John Stewart, Director, Policy & Research
Marie-danielle Davis, Corporate Secretary

Canadian Nuclear Society (CNS) / Société nucléaire canadienne (SNC)
655 Bay St., 17th Fl., Toronto ON M5G 2K4
Tel: 416-977-7620; *Fax:* 416-977-8131
cns-snc@on.aibn.com
www.cns-snc.ca
To promote the exchange of information about nuclear science & technology & its applications; To foster the beneficial utilization of nuclear science
Adriaan Buijs, President
K.L. (Ken) Smith, Financial Administrator
Denise Rouben, Office Manager

Canadian Renewable Fuels Association (CRFA) / Association canadienne des carburants renouvelables
#605, 350 Sparks St., Ottawa ON K1R 7S8
Tel: 613-594-5528; *Fax:* 613-594-3076
l.ehman@greenfuels.org
www.greenfuels.org
To promote renewable fuel development & usage
Gordon Quaiattini, President
Deborah Elson, Director, Member Relations & Industry Promotions
Debby Marandola, Director, Operations
Alison Ouellet, Director, Government Affairs

Canadian Solar Industries Association
#605, 150 Isabella St., Ottawa ON K1S 1V7
Tel: 613-736-9077; *Fax:* 613-736-8938
Toll-Free: 866-522-6742
info@cansia.ca
www.cansia.ca
Social Media: www.facebook.com/cansia; twitter.com/CanadianSIA; www.linkedin.com/groups/Canadian-Solar-Industries-Association-4208965
To develop a strong Canadian solar energy industry; To act as the voice for the solar energy industry in Canada
Michelle Chislett, Chair
John A. Gorman, President
Wesley Johnston, Director, Policy & Research
David Samuel, Director, Member Services & Operations
Tiffany Shields, Administrator, Services & Communications

Canadian Wind Energy Association Inc. (CanWEA) / Association canadienne d'énergie éolienne
#810, 170 Laurier Ave. West, Ottawa ON K1P 5V5
Tel: 613-234-8716; *Fax:* 613-234-5642
Toll-Free: 800-922-6932
info@canwea.ca
www.canwea.ca
Social Media: twitter.com/canwindenergy
To promote the social, economic, & environmental benefits of wind energy in Canada; To encourage the appropriate development & application of wind energy; To create suitable environmental policy
Robert Hornung, President
Chris Forrest, Vice-President, Communications & Marketing
Sean Whittaker, Vice-President, Policy
Penelope Feather, Director, Finance
Janice Taylor, Director, Conference & Events

Energy Council of Canada / Conseil canadien de l'énergie
#608, 350 Sparks St., Ottawa ON K1R 7S8
Tel: 613-232-8239; *Fax:* 613-232-1079
krystal.piamonte@energy.ca
www.energy.ca
To foster a greater understanding of energy issues; To enhance the effectiveness of the Canadian energy strategy
Murray J. Stewart, President
Brigitte Svarich, Director, Operations

Energy Probe Research Foundation (EPRF)
225 Brunswick Ave., Toronto ON M5S 2M6
Tel: 416-964-9223; *Fax:* 416-964-8239
webadmin@eprf.ca
www.eprf.ca
To educate Canadians about the benefits of conservation & renewable energy; to help Canada secure long-term energy self-sufficiency in the shortest possible time with the fewest disruptive effects & with the greatest societal, environmental & economic benefits; to provide business, government & the public with information on energy & energy-related issues; to help Canada contribute to global harmony & prosperity; recipient of the 1990 Lieutenant Governor's Conservation Award, the first time that an environmental organization has been so honoured; divisions include Energy Probe, Probe International, Environment Probe, Margaret Laurence Fund, Consumer Policy Institute, Environmental Bureau of Investigations, Urban Renaissance Institute
Patricia Adams, President
Lawrence Solomon, Managing Director

Planetary Association for Clean Energy, Inc. (PACE) / Société planétaire pour l'assainissement de l'énergie
#1001, 100 Bronson Ave., Ottawa ON K1R 6G8
Tel: 613-236-6265; *Fax:* 613-235-5876
paceincnet@gmail.com
pacenet.homestead.com
To steward & facilitate the implementation of clean energy systems worldwide
Andrew Michrowski, President

Solar & Sustainable Energy Society of Canada Inc. (SESCI) / Société des énergie solaire et durable du Canada Inc.
c/o Frederic Pouyot, #173, 207 Bank St., Ottawa ON k2P 2N2
Tel: 613-686-4474; *Fax:* 613-533-6550
bruce@techonfoot.com
www.sesci.ca
To act as a voice for renewable energy in Canada; To increase the use of solar & sustainable energy in Canada; To support energy conservation
Frederic Pouyot, President

Wood Energy Technology Transfer Inc. (WETT)
#7, 296 Jarvis St., Toronto ON M5B 2C5
Tel: 416-968-7718; *Fax:* 416-968-6818
Toll-Free: 888-358-9388
WETT@funnel.ca
www.wettinc.ca
To promote the safe & effective use of wood burning systems, WETT maintains a training program designed to confirm & recognize the knowledge & skills of practising wood energy professionals; to provide training to new people entering the industry; to provide training to non-industry professionals such as inspectors; to provide training to specialty audiences such as volunteer firefighters & carpenters in remote communities
Anthony Laycock, Executive Director

Engineering & Technology

American Society of Mechanical Engineers (ASME)
3 Park Ave., New York NY 10016-5990 USA
Tel: 800-843-2763
infocentral@asme.org
www.asme.org
Social Media: www.facebook.com/ASME.org; twitter.com/ASMEmembership
To promote the art, science, & practice of multidisciplinary engineering; To focus on the technical, educational, & research issues of the engineering & technology community; To help the engineering community develop solutions to improve the quality of life
Thomas G. Loughlin, Executive Director
Victoria Rockwell, President
Wilbur J. Marner, Secretary-Treasurer
David Soukup, Managing Director, Governance

Applied Science Technologists & Technicians of British Columbia (ASTTBC)
10767 - 148 St., Surrey BC V3R 0S4
Tel: 604-585-2788; *Fax:* 604-585-2790
techinfo@asttbc.org
www.asttbc.org
To advance the profession of applied science technology & the professional recognition of applied science technologists, certified technician, & other members in a manner that serves & protects the public interest
John E. Leech, AScT, CAE, Executive Director
Cindy Aitken, Manager, Governance & Events
Garry Gaudet, Manager, Media Relations
Jason Jung, Manager, Member & Program Development
Nicky Malli, Manager, Finance
Geoff Sale, AScT, Manager, Internationally Trained Professionals
Anne Sharp, BA, Manager, Marketing
Robert Stitt, AScT, Manager, Special Projects
Karen Taylor, DipBM, Manager, Operations

Association des ingénieurs municipaux du Québec (AIMQ) / Association of Québec Municipal Engineers
CP 792, Succ. B, Montréal QC H3B 3K5
Tél: 514-845-5303
aimg.rlamarche@videotron.ca
www.aimq.net
Améliorer les connaissances et le statut de l'ingénieur municipal par l'échange d'information, la coopération entre ingénieurs municipaux et avec d'autres associations professionnelles et la promotion des intérêts communs des membres de l'Association
Dany Lachance, Président

Association des ingénieurs-conseils du Québec (AICQ) / Consulting Engineers of Québec
#930, 1440, rue Ste-Catherine ouest, Montréal QC H3G 1R8
Tél: 514-871-2229; *Téléc:* 514-871-9903
info@aicq.qc.ca
www.aicq.qc.ca
Promouvoir et développer l'industrie du génie-conseil en regroupant des membres qui offrent des services de qualité
Johanne Desrochers, Présidente-directrice générale
Pierre Nadeau, Directeur, Communications

Association of Certified Engineering Technicians & Technologists of Prince Edward Island (ACETTPEI)
PO Box 1436, 92 Queen St., Charlottetown PE C1A 7N1
Tel: 902-892-8324
info@acettpei.ca
www.acettpei.ca
To benefit society by advancing the professions of applied science & engineering technology in Prince Edward Island
Trent Collicutt, President
Alan Robison, Vice-President
Delbert Reeves, Treasurer
Tom MacDonald, Registrar

Association of Consulting Engineering Companies - Canada (ACEC) / L'Association des firmes d'ingénieurs-conseils - Canada (AFIC)
#420, 130 Albert St., Ottawa ON K1P 5G4
Tel: 613-236-0569; *Fax:* 613-236-6193
Toll-Free: 800-565-0569
info@acec.ca
www.acec.ca
To assist in promoting satisfactory business relations between its Member Firms & their clients; To promote cordial relations among the various consulting engineering firms in Canada & to foster the interchange of professional, management & business experience & information among them; To safeguard the interest of the consulting engineer; To further the maintenance of high professional standards in the consulting engineering profession
John D. Gamble, CET, P.Eng., President
Jean-Marc Carrière, Vice-President, Finance & Administration
Susie Grynol, Vice-President, Policy & Public Affairs
Nadine Boudreau, Coordinator, Communications

Association of Consulting Engineering Companies - New Brunswick (ACEC-NB)
183 Hanwell Rd., Fredericton NB E3B 2R2
Tel: 506-470-9211; *Fax:* 506-451-9629
info@acec-nb.ca
www.cenb.nb.ca
To develop & support member firms; To improve the business environment for member firms & their clients; To further the professional standards of the consulting engineering profession
John Fudge, Executive Director
David McAllister, President
Christy Cunningham, Secretary
Karen Robichaud, Treasurer

Association of Engineering Technicians & Technologists of Newfoundland & Labrador (AETTNL)
Donovan's Industrial Park, PO Box 790, 22 Sagona Ave., Mount Pearl NL A1N 2Y2
Tel: 709-747-2868; *Fax:* 709-747-2869
Toll-Free: 888-238-8600
aettnl@aettnl.com
www.aettnl.com
AETTNL's mission is to advance the profession of Applied Science/Engineering Technology & the professional recognition of Certified Technicians & Technologists. It regulates the standards of training & practice, & protects the interests of its members & the public.
Tony Scott, President
Linda Hayward, Office Manager

Association of Professional Engineers & Geoscientists of British Columbia (APEGBC)
#200, 4010 Regent St., Burnaby BC V5C 6N2
Tel: 604-430-8035; *Fax:* 604-430-8085
Toll-Free: 888-430-8035
apeginfo@apeg.bc.ca; communication@apeg.bc.ca
www.apeg.bc.ca
Social Media: twitter.com/APEGBC
To protect the public interest in matters related to geoscience & engineering; To regulate & govern the professions of professional engineers & geoscientists in British Columbia, according to the Engineers & Geoscientists Act; To strive for professional excellence, by establishing academic, experience, & professional practice standards
Derek Doyle, P.Eng., Chief Executive Officer
Jeff Holm, P.Eng., FEC, President
Janet Sinclair, Chief Operating Officer
Jennifer Cho, CGA, Director, Finance & Administration
Peter Mitchell, P.Eng., Director, Professional Practice, Standards, & Development
Gillian Pichler, P.Eng., Director, Registration
Geoff Thiele, LLB, Director, Legislation, Ethics & Compliance
Megan Archibald, Associate Director, Communications & Stakeholder Engagement
Don Gamble, Associate Director, Information Systems
Deesh Olychick, Associate Director, Member Services
Kim Bush, Generalist, Human Resources
Melinda Lau, Publications Specialist & Managing Editor

Association of Professional Engineers & Geoscientists of Manitoba (APEGM)
870 Pembina Hwy., Winnipeg MB R3M 2M7
Tel: 204-474-2736; *Fax:* 204-474-5960
Toll-Free: 866-227-9600
apegm@apegm.mb.ca; volunteer@apegm.mb.ca; events@apegm.mb.ca
www.apegm.mb.ca
To serve & protect the public interest by governing & advancing the practice of engineering in accordance with the Engineering Profession Act of Manitoba
Grant Koropatnick, P.Eng., Executive Director & Registrar
Sharon E. Sankar, Director, Admissions
Michael Gregoire, P.Eng., Officer, Professional Standards
William C. Boyce, Manager, Operations & Finance
Lorraine Dupas, Coordinator, Admissions
Angela Moore, Coordinator, Events & Communications
Diana Vander Aa, Coordinator, Volunteers

Association of Professional Engineers & Geoscientists of New Brunswick (APEGNB) / Association des ingénieurs et géoscientifiques du Nouveau-Brunswick (AINB)
183 Hanwell Rd., Fredericton NB E3B 2R2
Tel: 506-458-8083; *Fax:* 506-451-9629
Toll-Free: 888-458-8083
info@apegnb.com
www.apegnb.com
To establish, maintain & develop standards of knowledge & skill, qualification & practice, & professional ethics; To promote public awareness of the role of the association
Andrew McLeod, FEC (Hon.), Chief Executive Officer
Darryl Ford, P.Eng., President
Jean Bourdreau, P.Eng., Vice-President

Association of Professional Engineers & Geoscientists of Saskatchewan (APEGS)
#104, 2255 - 13 Ave., Regina SK S4P 0V6
Tel: 306-525-9547; *Fax:* 306-525-0851
Toll-Free: 800-500-9547
apegs@apegs.sk.ca
www.apegs.sk.ca
To achieve a safe & prosperous future through engineering & geoscience
Dennis Paddock, P.Eng., FEC, Executive Director & Registrar
Patti Kindred, P.Eng., FEC, Director, Education & Compliance
Barb Lakeman, Director, Finance & Operations
Kate MacLachlan, Ph.D., P.Geo., Director, Academic Review
Tina Maki, P.Eng., Director, Registration
Bob McDonald, P.Eng., FEC, LL, Director, Membership & Legal Services
Chris Wimmer, P.Eng., Director, Professional Standards

Association of Professional Engineers of Prince Edward Island (APEPEI)
549 North River Rd., Charlottetown PE C1E 1J6
Tel: 902-566-1268; *Fax:* 902-566-5551
info@engineerspei.com
www.engineerspei.com

Engineers PEI regulates the practice of professional engineering in the province, with authority over members, licensees, engineers-in-training, & holders of certificates of authorization.
Mark E. Victor, President
Jim Landrigan, Executive Director/Registrar

Association of Professional Engineers of the Yukon Territory (APEY)
312B Hanson St., Whitehorse YT Y1A 1Y6
Tel: 867-667-6727; *Fax:* 867-668-2142
staff@apey.yk.ca
www.apey.yk.ca
To establish, maintain & develop standards of knowledge & skill, standards of qualification & practice & standards of professional ethics; to promote public awareness of the role of the association
Gord Hamilton, President
Richard Trimble, Registrar
Sandy Birrell, Sec.-Treas.

Association of Professional Engineers, Geologists & Geophysicists of Alberta (APEGGA)
Scotia One, #1500, 10060 Jasper Ave. NW, Edmonton AB T5J 4A2
Tel: 780-426-3990; *Fax:* 780-426-1877
Toll-Free: 800-661-7020
email@apegga.org
www.apegga.org
To register & set practice standards & codes of professional conduct & ethics for professional engineers, geologists, & geophysicists in Alberta, according to The Engineering, Geological & Geophysical Professions Act
A.J. Schuld, Chief Executive Officer & Registrar
Len Shrimpton, P.Eng., FEC, Chief Operating Officer
Ray Chopiuk, P.Eng., FEC, Director, Professional Practice
Philip Mulder, APR, FEC (Hon.), Director, Communications
Neth Michael, P.Eng., Director, Compliance
Gerry O'Donnell, B. Comm., CGA, Director, Administration & Finance
Ross Plecash, P.Eng., FEC, Director, Corporate Affairs & Investigations
Mark Tokarik, LL.B., P.Eng., Director, Registration

Association of Science & Engineering Technology Professionals of Alberta (ASET)
Phipps-McKinnon Building, #1630, 10020 - 101A Ave. NW, Edmonton AB T5J 3G2
Tel: 780-425-0626; *Fax:* 780-424-5053
Toll-Free: 800-272-5619
www.aset.ab.ca
To benefit the public & the profession by regulating & promoting safe, high quality, professional technology practice; To focus on the engineering technology, applied science, & information technology fields; To issue credentials to qualified individuals; To accredit training programs
Elizabeth Mcdonald, C.E.T., President
Barry Cavanaugh, Chief Executive Officer
Jennifer McNeil Betrand, BA, Director, Education & Special Projects
Russifer Medvedev, MA, Director, Communications & Member Benefits
Heather Shewchuk, B.Comm., Director, Corporate & Government Relations
Norman Viegas, CMA, CAE, Director, Finance & Administration

Canadian Acoustical Association / Association canadienne d'acoustique
c/o C. Laroche, Faculty of Health Sciences, University of Ottawa, #3062, 451 Smyth Rd., Ottawa ON K1H 8M5
Tel: 613-562-5800; *Fax:* 613-562-5248
secretary@caa-aca.ca
www.caa-aca.ca
To foster communication among people working in all areas of acoustics in Canada; To promote the growth & practical application of knowledge in acoustics; To encourage education, research, & employment in acoustics
Christian Giguère, President
Dalila Giusti, Treasurer
Chantal Laroche, Executive Secretary

Canadian Advanced Technology Alliance (CATA Alliance) / Association canadienne de technologie de pointe
National Headquarters, #416, 207 Bank St., Ottawa ON K2P 2N2
Tel: 613-236-6550
info@cata.ca
www.cata.ca
Social Media: www.facebook.com/group.php?gid=5391503953; twitter.com/CATAAlliance
To provide members with a network to establish partnerships, to match up with global business opportunities; To offer communication & advocacy services, notably in dealing with the government; To work to ensure that policies are favourable to Canadian technology companies; To maintain a research repository where members can access information to advance their agendas
John Reid, President & Chief Executive Officer
Barry Gander, Executive Vice-President
Charles Duffet, Senior Vice-Presient & CIO Advisor
Russ Roberts, Senior Vice-President, Tax & Finance
Kevin Wennekes, Vice-President, Research

Canadian Air Cushion Technology Society (CACTS)
c/o Canadian Aeronautics & Space Institute, #104, 350 Terry Fox Dr., Kanata ON K2K 2W5
www.casi.ca/canadianaircushiontechnologysociety.aspx
To serve the air cushion technology (hovercraft) community throughout Canada; To advance the science, technologies, & applications of air cushion technology
Jacques Laframboise, Society Chair

Canadian Association for Composite Structures & Materials (CACSMA) / Association canadienne pour les structures et matériaux composites (ACSMAC)
c/o J. Denault, Industrial Materials Institute, Ntl. Research Council, Montréal QC H3G 1M6
Tel: 450-641-5105; *Fax:* 450-848-4596
Johanne.Denault@imi.cnrc-nrc.gc.ca
www.cacsma.ca
To support composites companies in Canada; To promote Canadian composites capabilities; To encourage the application of composites in all sectors
Suong V. Hoa, President
Mehdi Hojjati, Secretary
Johanne Denault, Treasurer

Canadian Council of Technicians & Technologists (CCTT) / Conseil canadien des techniciens et technologues
#295, 1101 Prince Of Wales Dr., Ottawa ON K2C 3W7
Tel: 613-238-8123; *Fax:* 613-238-8822
Toll-Free: 800-891-1140
ccttadm@cctt.ca
www.cctt.ca
Social Media: twitter.com/CCTTCanada
To advocate on behalf of Canada's certified technicians & technologists; To establish & maintain national competency standards
Isidore J. LeBlond, Chief Executive Officer
Rick Tachuk, Director, Communications & Marketing
Darlene Pilon, Manager, Finance & Events Management
Valery Vidershpan, Manager, Database Development
Jianwu Liu, Researcher, International Educational Programs

Canadian Hydrogen & Fuel Cell Association (CHFCA)
4250 Wesbrook Mall, Vancouver BC V6T 1W5
Tel: 604-822-9178; *Fax:* 604-822-8106
info@chfca.ca
www.chfca.ca
To act as the collective voice of the hydrogen & fuel cell technologies & products sector; To support Canadian corporations, educational institutions, & governments which develop & deploy hydrogen & fuel cell products & services in Canada
John W. Tak, President & Chief Executive Officer
Terry Kimmel, Vice-President
Michael Dujardin, Controller
Javis Lui, Manager, Communications & Member Relations
Sarah Richards, Manager, Conferences & Workshops

Canadian Remote Sensing Society (CRSS) / Société canadienne de télédétection
c/o Canadian Aeronautics & Space Institute, #104, 350 Terry Fox Dr., Kanata ON K2K 2W5
Tel: 613-591-8787; *Fax:* 613-591-7291
casi@casi.ca
www.casi.ca/cdn-remote-sensing-society
To advance the art, science, engineering, & application of remote sensing in Canada; To uphold the Society's Code of Ethics
Derek R. Peddle, Chair
Monique Bernier, Vice-Chair
Anne Smith, Secretary-Treasurer

Canadian Society for Civil Engineering (CSCE) / Société canadienne de génie civil
4877, rue Sherbrooke ouest, Montréal QC H3Z 1G9
Tel: 514-933-2634; *Fax:* 514-933-3504
info@csce.ca; membership@csce.ca
www.csce.ca
To develop & maintain high standard of civil engineering practice in Canada; To enhance the public image of the civil engineering profession
Doug Salloum, Executive Director
Mahmoud Lardjane, Manager, Programs
Louise Newman, Manager, Communications
Andrea Grimaud, Officer, Membership Liaison

Canadian Society for Engineering Management (CSEM) / Société canadienne de gestion en ingénierie
1295 Hwy. 2 East, Kingston ON K7L 4V1
louisem@cogeco.ca
www.csem-scgi.org
To represent the interests & enhance the capabilities of engineers in management in order to promote & advance efficient management of commerce, industry & public affairs.
John Wood, President
Dominique Janssens, Sec.-Treas.

Canadian Society for Mechanical Engineering (CSME) / Société canadienne de génie mécanique (SCGM)
1295 Hwy. 2 East, Kingston ON K7L 4V1
Tel: 613-547-5989; *Fax:* 613-547-0195
csme@cogeco.ca
www.csme-scgm.ca
To benefit Canada & the world by fostering excellence in the practice of mechanical engineering; To support members
Rama B. Bhat, President

Canadian Technical Asphalt Association (CTAA) / Association technique canadienne du bitume
#300, 895 Fort St., Victoria BC V8W 1H7
Tel: 250-361-9187; *Fax:* 250-361-9187
admin@ctaa.ca
www.ctaa.ca
To organize efforts of membership on a non-profit, public service basis; to assemble, correlate & disseminate technical information on characteristics & uses of bituminous materials; to conduct conferences at which characteristics & uses of asphaltic materials are discussed; to stimulate & encourage research on uses of asphaltic materials; to encourage colleges to teach students to study asphalt technology
Michel Paradis, President
Robert Noble, Secretary-Treasurer

Certified Technicians & Technologists Association of Manitoba (CTTAM)
#602, 1661 Portage Ave., Winnipeg MB R3J 3T7
Tel: 204-784-1088; *Fax:* 204-784-1084
admin@cttam.com
www.cttam.com
To advance the professional recognition & development of certified applied science technicians & technologists in a manner that serves the public interest
Tracey Kucheravy, CET, President
Terry Gifford, CAE, Executive Director
Robert B. Chochinov, CET, Registrar

Community Energy Association
#308, 402 West Pender St., Vancouver BC V6B 1T6
Tel: 604-628-7076; *Fax:* 778-786-1613
www.communityenergy.bc.ca
To support local governments throughout British Columbia in accelerating the application of energy efficiency and renewable energy in all aspects of community design, infrastructure and community engagement for sustainability.
Norm Connolly, Executive Director

Consulting Engineers of Alberta (CEA)
Phipps-McKinnon Building, #870, 10020 - 101A Ave., Edmonton AB T5J 3G2
Tel: 780-421-1852; *Fax:* 780-424-5225
info@cea.ca
www.cea.ca
To provide leadership to foster a positive business environment for the consulting engineering firms in Alberta; To promote the engineering industry; To enhance interests & opportunities of CEA members; To provide society with high standards of engineering design & safety
Wendy Cooper, Executive Director
Gord Johnston, President
Ken Pilip, Registrar
Sharon Moroskat, Manager, Finance & Administration
Hiju Song, Manager, Events & Communications

Consulting Engineers of British Columbia (CEBC)
#1258, 409 Granville St., Vancouver BC V6C 1T2
Tel: 604-687-2811; *Fax:* 604-688-7110
info@cebc.org
www.cebc.org
To improve the commercial environment for consulting engineering firms
Glenn Martin, Executive Director
Jack Lee, President

Glen Martin, Executive Director
Alla Samusevich, Coordinator, Accounting & Events

Consulting Engineers of Manitoba Inc. (CEM)
PO Box 1547, Stn. Main, Winnipeg MB R3C 2Z4
Tel: 204-774-5258; *Fax:* 204-779-0788
cemca@shaw.ca
www.cemanitoba.com
To promote & enhance the business interests of the consulting engineers of Manitoba; to lead in the application of technology for the benefit of society.
Shirley E. Tillett, Executive Director
H. Pankratz, President

Consulting Engineers of Nova Scotia (CENS)
PO Box 613, Stn. M, Halifax NS B3J 2R7
Tel: 902-461-1325; *Fax:* 902-461-1321
cens@eastlink.ca
www.cens.org
To enable the consulting engineering industry in Nova Scotia to capitalize on opportunities to grow; To promote employment of member firms

Consulting Engineers of Ontario (CEO)
#405, 10 Four Seasons Pl., Toronto ON M9B 6H7
Tel: 416-620-1400; *Fax:* 416-620-5803
staff@ceo.on.ca
www.ceo.on.ca
To further the maintenance of high professional standards in consulting engineering profession; to promote cordial relations among various consulting firms in Ontario; to foster interchange of professional management & business experience & information among consulting engineers; to develop regional representation & participation in affairs of the association.
Saskia Martini-Wong, Manager, Operations & Finance
David Amm, Chair

Consulting Engineers of Saskatchewan (CES)
#12, 2010 - 7 Ave., Regina SK S4R 1C2
Tel: 306-359-3338; *Fax:* 306-522-5325
ces@sasktel.net
www.ces.sk.ca
To further the maintenance of high professional standards in consulting engineering profession; To promote cordial relations among various consulting firms in Saskatchewan; To foster interchange of professional management & business experience & information among consulting engineers; To develop regional representation & participation in affairs of the association
Val Jakubowski, Executive Director

Consulting Engineers of Yukon (CEY)
c/o EBA Engineering Consultants Ltd., #6, 151 Industrial Rd., Whitehorse YT Y1A 2V3
Tel: 867-668-3068; *Fax:* 867-668-4349
cey@eba.ca
www.cey.ca
To maintain high professional standards in the consulting engineering profession; To promote cordial relations among various consulting firms in the Yukon; to foster interchange of professional management & business experience & information among consulting engineers; To develop regional representation & participation in affairs of the association
Richard Trimble, Executive Director

Continental Automated Buildings Association (CABA) / Association continentale pour l'automatisation des bâtiments
#210, 1173 Cyrville Rd., Ottawa ON K1J 7S6
Tel: 613-686-1814; *Fax:* 613-744-7833
Toll-Free: 888-798-2222
caba@caba.org
www.caba.org
Social Media:
www.facebook.com/group.php?gid=108759039149175;
twitter.com/caba_news; www.youtube.com/cabaconf
To promote advanced technologies for the automation of homes & buildings in North America; To create opportunities for members
Ronald J. Zimmer, President & Chief Executive Officer
Ken Gallinger, Director, Marketing
George Grimes, Director, Business Development
John L. Hall, Director, Research
Rawlson O'Neil King, Director, Communications

The Engineering Institute of Canada (EIC) / L'Institut canadien des ingénieurs (ICI)
1295 Hwy. 2 East, Kingston ON K7L 4V1
Tel: 613-547-5989; *Fax:* 613-547-0195
jplant1@cogeco.ca
www.eic-ici.ca
To further the development of engineering in Canada; to stimulate the advancement of the quality & scope of Canadian engineering; to meet regularly with other engineering organizations & industries to promote understanding & improvement of the profession, the diffusion of engineering information & to provide Canadian representation in specialized engineering fields; to interact with government agencies & departments for the purpose of influencing decision making on matters relating to engineering & technology; to cooperate with the provincial engineering licensing bodies, The Canadian Council of Professional Engineering, The Association of Consulting Engineers of Canada, The Canadian Academy of Engineering & other engineering organizations in matters of common interest; to promote interaction with specific interest groups; to collaborate with universities & educational institutions
B. John Plant, Executive Director
Kerry Rowe, President

Engineers Canada / Ingénieurs Canada
#1100, 180 Elgin St., Ottawa ON K2P 2K3
Tel: 613-232-2474; *Fax:* 613-230-5759
Toll-Free: 877-408-9273
info@engineerscanada.ca;
executive.office@engineerscanada.ca
www.ccpe.ca
To establish & maintain a common bond between constituent associations; To assist constituent associations to meet their common needs & those of their members by coordinating standards, procedures, & programs across Canada; To represent the engineering profession with respect to national & international affairs; To increase the profile & prestige of the engineering profession
Chantal Guay, ing., P.Eng., M, Chief Executive Officer
Marie Carter, FEC, P.Eng., Chief Operating Officer
Marc Bourgeois, FIC (Hon.), Director, Communications & Public Affairs
Gordon Griffith, FEC, P.Eng, ing, Director, Education
Ken McMartin, FEC, P.Eng., Director, Professional & International Affairs

Engineers Nova Scotia
1355 Barrington St., Halifax NS B3J 1Y9
Tel: 902-429-2250; *Fax:* 902-423-9769
Toll-Free: 888-802-7367
info@engineersnovascotia.ca
www.engineersnovascotia.ca
To establish, maintain & develop standards of knowledge & skill, standards of qualification & practice, & standards of professional ethics; To promote public awareness of the role of the association
Len White, P.Eng., Chief Executive Officer & Registrar
Perry Mitchelmore, P.Eng., President

INO / Institut national d'optique
2740, rue Einstein, Québec QC G1P 4S4
Tel: 418-657-7006; *Fax:* 418-657-7009
info@ino.ca
www.ino.ca
To be an international leader in optics & photonics R&D, promoting economic expansion in the country by providing assistance to companies seeking to be more competitive
Jean-Yves Roy, President & CEO

Institute of Power Engineers (IPE)
PO Box 878, Burlington ON L7R 3Y7
Tel: 905-333-3348; *Fax:* 905-333-9328
ipenat@nipe.ca
www.nipe.ca
To promote business relations, social activities & mutual understanding among power engineers.
Jude Rankin, National President
Bruce King, 1st National Vice President
Don Purser, National Secretary

ISIS Canada Research Network (ISIS)
Agricultural & Civil Engineering Building, University of Manitoba, #A250, 96 Dafoe Rd., Winnipeg MB R3T 2N2
muftia@cc.umanitoba.ca
www.isiscanada.com
To advance civil engineering in Canada to a world leadership position through the development & application of fibre-reinforced polymers & integrated intelligent fibre optic sensing technologies, for the benefit of all Canadians
Donald Whitmore, Chair
Aftab Mufti, President & Scientific Director
Edward Pentland, Chair, Technology Transfer & Commercialization Committee

Municipal Engineers Association (MEA)
#2, 6355 Kennedy Rd., Mississauga ON L5T 2L5
Tel: 905-795-2555; *Fax:* 905-795-2660
info@municipalengineers.on.ca
www.municipalengineers.on.ca
To provide focus & unity for licensed engineers employed by municipalities in Ontario; To address issues of common concern to members; To facilitate the dissemination of information
Rick A. Kester, President
J. David Shantz, Executive Director
Gary Carroll, Vice-President
Trevor D. Lewis, Treasurer

NACE International (NACE)
1440 South Creek Dr., Houston TX 77084-4906 USA
Tel: 281-228-6200; *Fax:* 281-228-6300
Toll-Free: 800-797-6223
firstservice@nace.org
www.nace.org
Social Media: www.facebook.com/NACEinternational;
twitter.com/NACEtweet
To protect people, assets & the environment from the effects of corrosion. Northern Area sections include: Atlantic Canada, B.C., Calgary, Canadian National Capital Section, Edmonton, Montreal, Saskatchewan & Toronto
Bob Chalker, Executive Director
Jenny Been, Section Secretary/Treasurer, Northern Area
Scott MacIntyre, Area Membership Chairman, Northern Area

New Brunswick Society of Certified Engineering Technicians & Technologists (NBSCETT) / Société des techniciens et des technologues agréés du génie du Nouveau-Brunswick (STTAGN-B)
#2, 385 Wilsey Rd., Fredericton NB E3B 5N6
Tel: 506-454-6124; *Fax:* 506-452-7076
Toll-Free: 800-665-8324
nbscett@nbscett.nb.ca
www.nbscett.nb.ca
To grant certification to applied science & engineering technology technicians & technologists; to protect titles & powers of discipline for its members
David Sheaves, President
Jennifer Lawson, Executive Assistant
Edward F. Leslie, Executive Director

Northwest Territories & Nunavut Association of Professional Engineers & Geoscientists (NAPEG)
#201, 4817 - 49 St., Yellowknife NT X1A 3S7
Tel: 867-920-4055; *Fax:* 867-873-4058
www.napeg.nt.ca
To license professional engineers & professional geoscientists in the Northwest Territories & Nunavut; To regulate the practices of professional engineering & professional geoscience; To establish & maintain standards of knowledge, skill, care, & professional ethics among registrants
Hendrik Falck, President
Linda Golding, Executive Director
Victoria James, Coordinator, Registration

Ontario Association of Certified Engineering Technicians & Technologists (OACETT)
#404, 10 Four Seasons Pl., Toronto ON M9B 6H7
Tel: 416-621-9621; *Fax:* 416-621-8694
info@oacett.org
www.oacett.org
To advance the profession of applied science & engineering technology through standards for society's benefit.
David J. Thomson, CEO
David Saunders, President

Ordre des ingénieurs du Québec (OIQ)
Gare Windsor, #350, 1100, av des Canadiens-de-Montréal, Montréal QC H3B 2S2
Tél: 514-845-6141; *Téléc:* 514-845-1833
Ligne sans frais: 800-461-6141
info@oiq.qc.ca
www.oiq.qc.ca
Faire de la promotion et s'assurer de la qualité des services rendus à la société par les ingénieurs, individuellement et collectivement, en tant que membres d'un corps professionnel; Favoriser leur épanouissement professionnel et personnel; Contribuer au développement socio-économique de la société
Maud Cohen, ing., Présidente
Stéphane Bilodeau, ing., Vice-président, Finances
Daniel Lebel, ing., PMP, Vice-président, Affaires publiques
Éric Potvin, ing., Vice-président, Affaires professionnelles

Ordre des technologues professionnels du Québec (OTPQ)
#720, 1265, rue Berri, Montréal QC H2L 4X4
Tél: 514-845-3247; *Téléc:* 514-845-3643
Ligne sans frais: 800-561-3459
info@otpq.qc.ca
www.otpq.qc.ca
Média social: www.facebook.com/TechnologuesProfessionnels;
twitter.com/otpq;
www.linkedin.com/groups?home=&gid=4134994
Promouvoir et assurer la compétence des technologues professionnels dans l'intérêt public
Denis Beauchamp, Directeur général et secrétaire

Plant Engineering & Maintenance Association of Canada (PEMAC)
#402, 6 - 2400 Dundas St. West, Mississauga ON L5K 2R8
Tel: 905-823-7255; *Fax:* 905-823-8001
mail@pemac.org
www.pemac.org
To be recognized as a nationwide centre of excellence in plant engineering & maintenance; To form positive & constructive links with industry & service sectors, in support of local & nationwide developments & productivity; To deliver strongly identifiable services & commitments across the range of disciplines embraced by the association; to educate & introduce new concepts; To provide representation at all government levels; To provide career enhancement & networking opportunities; To promote research in the field of plant engineering & maintenance
Norm Clegg, Executive Director
Brian Malloch, President

Positive Power Co-op (PPC)
#422, 2000 Appleby Line, Burlington ON L7L 7H7
Tel: 519-846-8130
www.positivepowerco-op.com
Positive Power Co-op is a not-for-profit co-operative dedicated to promoting and building community-based renewable energy projects in the Hamilton, Halton and Haldimand regions.
Stacey Hare, General Manager
Curt Hammond, Chair

Professional Engineers & Geoscientists Newfoundland & Labrador (PEG-NL)
PO Box 21207, #203, 10 Fort William Pl., St. John's NL A1A 5B2
Tel: 709-753-7714; *Fax:* 709-753-6131
main@pegnl.ca
www.pegnl.ca
To provide competent & ethical practice of engineering & geoscience in Newfoundland & Labrador; To ensure public confidence, sustainability, & stewardship of the professions; To provide leadership to enhance quality of life through the application & management of engineering & geoscience
Geoff Emberley, P. Eng., FEC, Chief Executive Officer & Registrar
Mark Fewer, B. Comm., Chief Operating Officer & Deputy Registrar
Leo White, P. Eng., Director, Professional Standards
Carl King, Councilor, Western District
Steve McLean, Executive Director

Professional Engineers Ontario (PEO)
#101, 40 Sheppard Ave. West, Toronto ON M2N 6K9
Tel: 416-224-1100; *Fax:* 416-224-9527
Toll-Free: 800-339-3716
financialservices@peo.on.ca
www.peo.on.ca
To meet the needs of Ontario society by licensing & regulating the entire practice of professional engineering in an open, transparent, inclusive manner
J. David Adams, P.Eng., MBA, President
Kim Allen, P.Eng., MBA, Chief Executive Officer & Registrar
Scott Clark, Chief Administrative Officer
Eric Brown, P.Eng., ISP, PM, Director, IT & Facilities Management
Moody Samuel Farag, M.Eng., P.Eng., Manager, Admissions
Brian MacEwen, P.Eng., Manager, Registration
Connie Mucklestone, Director, Communications

Saskatchewan Applied Science Technologists & Technicians (SASTT)
363 Park St., Regina SK S4N 5B2
Tel: 306-721-6633; *Fax:* 306-721-0112
info@sastt.ca
www.sastt.ca
To regulate the professional conduct of applied science technologists & certified technicians in Saskatchewan, in order to protect the public
Jaime Briltz, Executive Director & Registrar
Steve Oszust, President
Edward Worrall, 1st Vice-President
Kelly Ljunggren, 2nd Vice-President

SHAD Valley International
8 Young St. East, Waterloo ON N2J 2L3
Tel: 519-884-8844; *Fax:* 519-884-8191
info@shad.ca
www.shad.ca
To advance the scientific & technological capabilities of youth, integrated with the development of their entrepreneurial spirit; To collaborate with education, business & other communities, both domestic & international, to provide exceptional development opportunities
Barry Bisson, President

Society of Motion Picture & Television Engineers (SMPTE)
3 Barker Ave, 5th Fl., White Plains NY 10601 USA
Tel: 914-761-1100; *Fax:* 914-761-3115
membership@smpte.org
www.smpte.org
Peter Lude, Exec. Vice-President
Pierre Marion, Governor, Canadian Region
Kenneth C. Fuller, President

Society of Tribologists & Lubrication Engineers / Société des tribologistes et ingénieurs en lubrification
840 Busse Hwy., Park Ridge IL 60068-2302 USA
Tel: 847-825-5536; *Fax:* 847-825-1456
information@stle.org
www.stle.org
To promote study of tribology, friction, wear & lubrication; To function as resource for distribution of new information & techniques
Edward Salek, Executive Director

TechNova
#A308, Cambridge 1, 202 Brownlow Ave., Dartmouth NS B3B 1T5
Tel: 902-463-3236; *Fax:* 902-465-7567
Toll-Free: 866-723-8867
info@technova.ca
www.technova.ca
Certifying engineering & applied science technicians & technologists for the betterment of the public & the welfare of the environment
Louis LeBel, President

Environmental

Action Nord Terre
535, 4e Rue, Chibougamau QC G8P 1S4
Tél: 418-748-7056
André Naud, Président

Air & Waste Management Association (A&WMA) / Association pour la prévention de la contamination de l'air et du sol
One Gateway Center, 420 Fort Duquesne Blvd., 3rd Fl., Pittsburgh PA 15222-1435 USA
Tel: 412-232-3444; *Fax:* 412-232-3450
Toll-Free: 800-270-3444
info@awma.org
www.awma.org
Social Media: www.facebook.com/group.php?gid=33499462923; twitter.com/AirandWaste; www.linkedin.com/company/445959
To improve environmental knowledge & decisions; To assist members in critical environmental decision making & professional development; To provide a neutral forum for exchanging information & developing networking opportunities; To increase public education & outreach
Merlyn L. Hough, President
Mike Kelly, Executive Director & Secretary
Amy Gilligan, Treasurer

Alberta Environmental Network (AEN)
PO Box 4541, Edmonton AB T6E 5G4
Tel: 780-757-4872; *Fax:* 866-868-5563
admin@aenweb.ca; events@aenweb.ca
www.aenweb.ca
Social Media: twitter.com/ABEnvNet
To facilitate communication & cooperation among environmental groups in Alberta in order to contribute to the enhancement & protection of the environment
Nashina Shariff, Chair

Alberta Fish & Game Association (AFGA)
6924 - 104 St., Edmonton AB T6H 2L7
Tel: 780-437-2342; *Fax:* 780-438-6872
office@afga.org
www.afga.org
To ensure fish & wildlife habitat & resources in Alberta
Conrad Fennema, President
Martin Sharren, Executive Vice-President
Sandie Buwalda, Coordinator, Programs
Brad Fenson, Coordinator, Habitats
Kerry Grisley, Co-Manager, Operation Grassland Community
Susan Skinner, Co-Manager, Operation Grassland Community

Alberta Water Council
Petroleum Plaza, South Tower, #1400, 9915 - 108 St., Edmonton AB T5K 2G8
Tel: 780-644-7380
www.albertawatercouncil.ca
The Alberta Water Council is a stakeholder partnership that provides leadership, expertise and advocacy, to engage and empower individuals, organizations, business and governments to achieve the outcomes of the Water for Life strategy.
Gord Edwards, Executive Director

Alberta Wilderness Association (AWA)
455 - 12 St. NW, Calgary AB T2N 1Y9
Tel: 403-283-2025; *Fax:* 403-270-2743
Toll-Free: 866-313-0713
awa@shaw.ca
www.albertawilderness.ca
Social Media: www.facebook.com/AlbertaWilderness; twitter.com/ABWilderness; www.youtube.com/user/AlbertaWilderness
To promote the protection of Alberta's rivers & wildlands areas; To restore the natural ecosystems of Alberta; To educate Albertans on wilderness conservation & sustainable use of natural lands & waters
Richard Secord, President
Christyann Olson, Executive Director

Association for Literature, Environment, and Culture in Canada (ALECC) / Association pour la littérature, l'environnement et la culture au Canada
c/o Department of English, University of Calgary, 2500 University Dr. NW, 11th Fl., Calgary AB T2N 1N4
contactus@alecc.ca
www.alecc.ca
To promote and support artistic, critical and cultural studies work on a wide range of environmental issues.
Pamela Banting, President

Bedeque Bay Environmental Management Association (BBEMA)
PO Box 8310, Emerald PE C0B 1M0
Tel: 902-886-3211
www.bbema.ca
To provide a framework for citizen-based education and action that reduced soil erosion, maintained water quality and improved the ecosystem.

Big Rideau Lake Association (BRLA)
PO Box 93, Hwy. 15, Portland ON K0G 1V0
Tel: 613-272-3629
brla@brla.on.ca
www.brla.on.ca
The Big Rideau Lake Association (BRLA) is a non-profit organization committed to long-term environmental protection and service to all who use Big Rideau Lake and share its resources.
Peter Copestake, President

BIOQuébec / Québec Bio-Industries Business Network
#120, 500, Boul Cartier ouest, Laval QC H7V 5B7
Tél: 450-781-3965; *Téléc:* 450-781-3966
info@bioquebec.com
www.bioquebec.com
Òtre le porte-parole des entreprises biotechnologiques du Québec; favoriser le développement et la mise en valeur des biotechnologies et des bioindustries québécoises, et ce au bénéfice de ses membres; To promote the development & the upgrading of biotechnologies; to supply strategic information of technical & economical content as well as carry out projects, events & activities; to stimulate collaboration between private industry, governments & universities; to stimulate the growth of structuring economical activities in this field; to act as a spokesman for the bio-industry in Québec
Gilles R. Gagnon, Président
Mario Lebrun, Directeur général

British Columbia Environment Industry Association (BCEIA)
#400, 602 West Hastings St., Vancouver BC V6B 1P2
Tel: 604-683-2751; *Fax:* 604-677-5960
info@bceia.com
www.bceia.com
Social Media: twitter.com/BCEIA_
To develop the environmental industry in British Columbia; To promote technological development
Frank Came, President
Charles Bois, Secretary-Treasurer

British Columbia Environmental Network (BCEN)
#461, 1755 Robson St., Vancouver BC V6G 3B7
Tel: 604-515-1969
editor@ecobc.ca
www.ecobc.org
To facilitate communication among environmental groups & individuals so that ecological sustainability & economic stability prevail, & biological diversity & human health remain viable
David Boehm, Treasurer

British Columbia Water & Waste Association (BCWWA)
#221, 8678 Greenall Ave., Burnaby BC V5J 3M6
Tel: 604-433-4389; *Fax:* 604-433-9859
Toll-Free: 877-433-4389
contact@bcwwa.org
www.bcwwa.org
Social Media: www.facebook.com/group.php?gid=21435804125
To safeguard public health & the environment through the sharing of skills, knowledge, experience & education; To provide a voice for the water & waste community in British Columbia & the Yukon
Daisy Foster, Chief Executive Officer
David Icharia, Director, Operations
Judy Zhang, Manager, Finance
Sarah Vaughan, Manager, Communications
Kimberly Perreault, Coordinator, Member Services
TBA, Coordinator, Education & Technology

BurlingtonGreen Environmental Association
3281 Myers Lane, Burlington ON L7N 1K6
Tel: 905-466-2171
www.burlingtongreen.org
Social Media: www.facebook.com/burlington.green.environment
To advocate for local environmental issues
Amy Schnurr, Executive Director

Campaign for Nuclear Phaseout (CNP)
#412, 1 Nicholas St., Ottawa ON K1N 7B7
www.cnp.ca
The Campaign for Nuclear Phaseout (CNP) represents a coalition of Canadian public interest organizations concerned with the environmental consequences of nuclear power generation.

Canadian Arctic Resources Committee
488 Gladstone Ave., Ottawa ON K1N 8V4
Tel: 613-759-4284; *Fax:* 613-237-3845
Toll-Free: 866-949-9006
davidg@carc.org
www.carc.org
The Canadian Arctic Resources Committee (CARC) is a citizens' organization dedicated to the long-term environmental and social well being of northern Canada and its peoples.
Chuck Birchall, Chair

Canadian Association for Laboratory Accreditation Inc. (CALA)
#310, 1565 Carling Ave., Ottawa ON K1Z 8R1
Tel: 613-233-5300; *Fax:* 613-233-5501
ecummins@cala.ca
www.cala.ca
Social Media:
www.facebook.com/group.php?gid=161209647296775
To provide internationally-recognized accreditation services; To assist laboratories in the achievement of high levels of scientific & management excellence; To improve environmental quality & public health & safety
Charlie Brimley, President & CEO
Brenda Dashney, Chief Financial Officer
Ned Gravel, Manager, Quality & Training
Ken Middlebrook, Manager, Proficiency Testing
Andrew Morris, Manager, Data & Information

Canadian Association of Recycling Industries (CARI) / Association canadienne des industries du recyclage (ACIR)
#1, 682 Monarch Ave., Ajax ON L1S 4S2
Tel: 905-426-9313; *Fax:* 905-426-9314
www.cari-acir.org
To address issues facing the recycling industry in Canada & internationally; To promote commercial recycling activities
Bertrand Van Dorpe, President
Len Shaw, Executive Director
Donna Turner, Association Manager
Tracy Shaw, Manager, Communications & Membership
Chris Cassell, Secretary-Treasurer

Canadian Association on Water Quality (CAWQ) / Association canadienne sur la qualité de l'eau (ACQE)
PO Box 5050, 867 Lakeshore Rd., Burlington ON L7R 4A6
Tel: 905-336-4513; *Fax:* 905-336-6444
www.cawq.ca
To promote research on scientific, technological, legal & administrative aspects of water pollution research & control; To further the exchange of information & the practical application of such research for public benefit
Clayton Tiedemann, President
Yves Comeau, Secretary
Peter Jones, Treasurer

Canadian Centre for Pollution Prevention (C2P2) / Centre canadien pour la prévention de la pollution
#134, 215 Spadina Ave., Toronto ON M5T 2C7
Tel: 905-822-4133; *Fax:* 416-979-3936
Toll-Free: 800-667-9790
info@c2p2online.com
www.c2p2online.com
To shape the future of production & consumption; To catalyze behavioural change in order to increase sustainable practices, a healthier environment, & competitiveness
Fred Granek, Chief Operating Officer
Leah Nielsen, Coordinator, Projects
Shari Russell, Coordinator, Projects

Canadian Environment Industry Association (CEIA)
119, Concession 6 Rd., Fisherville ON N0A 1G0
Tel: 416-410-0432; *Fax:* 416-362-5231
To promote the interests and development of Canadian companies supplying environmental technologies, products and services.
Christopher Henderson, Chair

Canadian Environmental Certification Approvals Board (CECAB) / Bureau canadien de reconnaissance professionnelle des spécialistes de l'environnement
#200, 308 - 11th Ave. SE, Calgary AB T2G 0Y2
Tel: 403-233-7484; *Fax:* 403-264-6240
certification@eco.ca
www.cecab.org
CECAB is a professional autonomous body providing national certification for Canadian environmental practitioners.
Lou Locatelli, Vice Chair

Canadian Environmental Law Association (CELA) / Association canadienne du droit de l'environnement
#301, 130 Spadina Ave., Toronto ON M5V 2L4
Tel: 416-960-2284; *Fax:* 416-960-9392
articling@cela.ca (legal inquiries)
www.cela.ca
To advocate for environmental law reform; To act in court or during hearings on behalf of citizens' groups & individuals who would otherwise be unable to afford legal assistance
Theresa McClenaghan, Executive Director & Counsel
Mary Anderson, Manager, Finance
Tracy Tucker, Manager, Office
Kathleen Cooper, Senior Researcher
Burgandy Dunn, Counsel, Public Legal Education

Canadian Environmental Network (RCEN) / Réseau canadien de l'environnement
39 McArthur Ave., Level 1-1, Ottawa ON K1L 8L7
Tel: 613-728-9810; *Fax:* 613-728-2963
info@cen-rce.org
www.cen-rce.org
Social Media:
www.facebook.com/CanadianEnvironmentalNetwork;
twitter.com/#!/RCEN
To promote ecologically sound ways of life; To enhance members' work to restore, protect, & promote a clean & sustainable environment
Daniel Casselman, Coordinator, National Caucus
Jessie Sadler, Coordinator, National Caucus
Joséphine Hénault, Administrator, Office & Events

Canadian Environmental Technology Advancement Corporation - West (CETAC)
Research Park, Univ. of Calgary, 3608 - 33rd St. NW, Calgary AB T2L 2A6
Tel: 403-777-9595; *Fax:* 403-777-9599
cetac@cetacwest.com
www.cetacwest.com
Established by Environment Canada, CETAC-West is a private sector, not-for-profit corporation committed to helping small & medium-sized enterprises that are engaged in the development & commercialization of new environmental technologies. To this end, it has created a network of technology producers, industry experts, & investment sources.
Joe Lukacs, President/CEO
Margaret Kelly, Vice-President, Alberta

Canadian Institute of Resources Law (CIRL) / Institut canadien du droit des ressources
Murray Fraser Hall, University of Calgary, #3353, 2500 University Dr. NW, Calgary AB T2N 1N4
Tel: 403-220-3200; *Fax:* 403-282-6182
cirl@ucalgary.ca
www.cirl.ca
To undertake and promote research, education and publication on the law relating to Canada's renewable and non-renewable natural resources.
J. Owen Saunders, Executive Director

Clifford D. Johnson, Chair

Canadian Land Reclamation Association (CLRA) / Association canadienne de réhabilitation des sites dégradés (ACRSD)
PO Box 61047, RPO Kensington, Calgary AB T2N 4S6
Tel: 403-289-9435; *Fax:* 403-289-9435
clra@telusplanet.net
www.clra.ca
To rehabilitate disturbed lands & waterways
David Polster, President
Tracy Patterson, Vice-President
Linda Jones, Secretary-Treasurer

Canadian Network for Environmental Education & Communication (EECOM) / Réseau canadien d'éducation et de communication relatives à l'environnement
c/o 336 Rosedale Ave., Winnipeg MB R3L 1L8
nswayze@eecom.org
www.eecom.org
To advance environmental learning in Canada; To promote environmental literacy & environmental stewardship; To contribute to a sustainable future
Natalie Swayzer, Executive Director
Grant Gardner, Chair
Rick Wishart, Treasurer

Canadian Parks Partnership (CPP) / Partenaires des parcs canadiens
#360, 1414 - 8th St. SW, Calgary AB T2R 1J6
Tel: 613-567-0099
nature@canadianparkspartnership.com
To support the overall enhancement of Canada's parks, historic sites & canals system & to foster public awareness, appreciation, understanding of & involvement in the system

Canadian Peregrine Foundation (CPF)
#214, 1450 O'Connor Dr., Toronto ON M4B 2T8
Tel: 416-481-1233; *Toll-Free:* 888-709-3944
info@peregrine-foundation.ca
www.peregrine-foundation.ca
The Canadian Peregrine Foundation is a registered charity dedicated to assisting the recovery of the peregrine falcon and other raptors at risk.

Canadian Polystyrene Recycling Alliance (CPRA)
260 Peter St., Port Hope ON L1A 3V6
www.cpracanada.ca
To operate a vertically integrated polystyrene recycling facility to recycle polystyrene into picture frames & mouldings
Sam Alavy, President & Chief Executive Officer

Canadian Society of Environmental Biologists (CSEB) / Société canadienne des biologistes de l'environnement
PO Box 962, Stn. F, Toronto ON M4Y 2N9
www.cseb-scbe.org
To further the conservation of natural resources of Canada & to promote the prudent management of these resources so as to minimize adverse environmental effects; to ensure high professional standards in education, research & management related to resources & environment; to advance the education of the public & to protect public interest on matters pertaining to the use of natural resources & the protection & management of the environment; to undertake environmental research & education programs; to assess & evaluate administrative & legislative policies having ecological significance in terms of conservation of resources & quality of the environment; to develop & promote policies that seek to achieve balance among resource management & utilization, protection of the environment & quality of life; to foster liaison among environmental biologists working within governmental, industrial & educational frameworks across Canada
Robert Stedwill, President

Canadian Water & Wastewater Association (CWWA) / Association canadienne des eaux potables et usées (ACEPU)
#11, 1010 Polytek St., Ottawa ON K1J 9H9
Tel: 613-747-0524; *Fax:* 613-747-0523
tdellison@cwwa.ca
www.cwwa.ca
To represent the common interests of Canadian municipal water & wastewater systems to federal & interprovincial bodies
Schmidt Thomas, President

Canadian Water Resources Association (CWRA) / Association canadienne des ressources hydriques (ACRH)
c/o Membership Office, 9 Covus Crt., Ottawa ON K2E 7Z4
Tel: 613-237-9363; *Fax:* 613-594-5190
services@aic.ca
www.cwra.org
To encourage recognition of the high priority & value of water
F.A. (Rick) Ross, Executive Director & Editor, Water News
André Saint-Hilaire, President
Paul H. Whitfield, Co-Editor, Canadian Water Resources Journal
Brenda Toth, Secretary
Ed Dean, Treasurer

Canadian Wildlife Federation (CWF) / Fédération canadienne de la faune
350 Michael Cowpland Dr., Kanata ON K2M 2W1
Tel: 613-599-9594; *Fax:* 613-599-4428
Toll-Free: 800-563-9453
info@cwf-fcf.org
www.cwf-fcf.org
To promote the conservation of fish & wildlife, wildlife habitat & quality aquatic environments; To foster an understanding of natural processes; To ensure adequate stocks of wildlife for the use & enjoyment of all Canadians; To sponsor research; To cooperate with legislators, government & non-government agencies in achieving conservation objectives
Dave Powell, President
Lloyd Lintott, First Vice-President
Bob Morris, Second Vice-President
Guy Vezina, Secretary
John Ford, Treasurer

Carleton Sustainable Campus Network (CSCN)
Carleton University, #326 UC, 1125 Colonel By Dr., Ottawa ON K1S 5B6
Tel: 613-520-2757; *Fax:* 613-520-3989
cscn@carleton.ca
www.carleton.ca/cscn
To engage the Carleton University campus as a living laboratory and learning tool in creating a sustainable society.

Carolinian Canada Coalition
Grosvenor Lodge, 1017 Western Rd., London ON N6G 1G5
Tel: 519-433-7077; *Fax:* 519-913-2449
info@carolinian.org
www.carolinian.org
To promote the protection and conservation of the Carolinian Life Zone of Southwestern Ontario.
Gordon Nelson, Chair

Citizens for a Safe Environment (CSE)
Tel: 416-461-1092
info@csetoronto.org
www.csetoronto.org
To promomote waste management practices that protect the health of Toronto citizens, their communities and the environment.

Citizens' Clearinghouse on Waste Management (CCWM)
17 Major St., Kitchener ON N2H 4R1
www.citizenswasteinfo.org
To help citizens gain access to information that will help them solve waste management problems in their communities and across Ontario.
John Jackson, Coordinator

Citizens' Environment Watch (CEW)
#204, 147 Spadina Ave., Toronto ON M5V 2L7
Tel: 647-258-3280; *Fax:* 416-637-2717
info@citizensenvironmentwatch.org
www.citizensenvironmentwatch.org
To provide communities the tools for education, monitoring and influencing positive change and to encourage people to take an active role in restoring and sustaining nature.
Meredith Cochrane, Executive Director

Citizens' Opposed to Paving the Escarpment (COPE)
PO Box 20014, 2211 Brant St., Burlington ON L7P 0A4
mail@cope-nomph.org
www.cope-nomph.org
To preserve the Niagara Escarpment, by ensuring that no new highway corridors are paved across the Niagara Escarpment & that all viable alternatives to the proposed Mid-Peninsula Highway are fully considered

Clean Nova Scotia (CNS)
126 Portland St., Dartmouth NS B2Y 1H8
Tel: 902-420-3474; *Fax:* 902-424-5334
Toll-Free: 888-380-5008
cns@clean.ns.ca
www.clean.ns.ca
Social Media: www.facebook.com/pages/Clean-Nova-Scotia/117505381665669; twitter.com/CleanNovaScotia; www.youtube.com/user/CleanNovaScotia1
To inspire positive environmental change in Nova Scotia
Judy McMullen, Executive Director
Jill Murphy, Director, Finance
Marlene Parsons, Director, Human Resources
Gina Patterson, Director, Programs
Katie Abriel, Manager, Climate Change Education Programs
Joe Moar, Manager, Home Energy Evaluations
David Ashley, Coordinator, Ship to Shore Program
Neil Bailey, Coordinator, Waste Programs
Steve Fairbairn, Coordinator, Green Schools Nova Scotia
Spencer Fowlie, Coordinator, Farms-to-School
Valerie Francella, Coordinator, Adopt-a-Watershed
Derek Gillis, Coordinator, Drive Wiser / Fleet Wiser Program
Leann Grosvold, Coordinator, Communications
Lisa Privett, Coordinator, Environmental Home Assessment Program
Kari Riddell, Coordinator, Litterless Road Tour

Coalition on the Niagara Escarpment (CONE)
193 James St. South, Hamilton ON L8P 3A8
Tel: 905-529-4955; *Fax:* 905-529-9503
cone@niagaraescarpment.org
www.niagaraescarpment.org
CONE is a non-profit alliance of environmental groups, conservation organizations, and concerned citizens and businesses dedicated to the protection of Ontario's Niagara Escarpment.
Robert Patrick, President

Compost Council of Canada / Conseil canadien du compost
16 Northumberland St., Toronto ON M6H 1P7
Tel: 416-535-0240; *Fax:* 416-536-9892
Toll-Free: 877-571-4769
info@compost.org
www.compost.org
Social Media: www.facebook.com/people/Compost-Council/100001137258465
To advance organics residuals recycling & compost use; To contribute to environmental sustainability
Susan Antler, Executive Director

Conservation Council of New Brunswick (CCNB) / Conseil de la conservation du Nouveau-Brunswick
180 St. John St., Fredericton NB E3B 4A9
Tel: 506-458-8747; *Fax:* 506-458-1047
info@ccnbaction.ca
www.conservationcouncil.ca
To generate awareness of the ecological foundations of our quality of life; To promote public policies with respect to the integrity of natural systems & to contribute to a sustainable society; To advocate appropriate remedies to pressing environmental problems such as ground water contamination & hazardous wastes
Jamie Watson, Executive Director
Stephanie Coburn, President

Conservation Council of Ontario (CCO) / Conseil de conservation de l'Ontario
#132, 215 Spadina Ave., Toronto ON M5T 2C7
Tel: 416-533-1635; *Fax:* 416-979-3936
cco@web.ca
www.weconserve.ca/cco
To build a strong conservation movement across Ontario
Ben Marans, President
Chris Winter, Executive Director
Karen Sun, Secretary

Conservation Ontario
Box 11, 120 Bayview Pkwy., Newmarket ON L3R 4W3
Tel: 905-895-0716; *Fax:* 905-895-0751
info@conservationontario.ca
www.conservation-ontario.on.ca
Social Media: www.facebook.com/home.php?sk=group_33621230329
To represent & support a network of community-based environmental organizations; To ensure conservation, restoration, & responsible management of Ontario's wetlands, woodlands, & natural habitat
Dick Hibma, Chair
Don Pearson, General Manager
Bonnie Fox, Manager, Policy & Planning
Charley Worte, Manager, Source Water Protection Planning
Jo-Anne Rzadki, Coordinator, Watershed Stewardship
Chris Wilkinson, Coordinator, Water Resources Information Project (WRIP)
Jane Lewington, Specialist, Marketing & Communications

Cumulative Environmental Management Association (CEMA)
Morrison Center, #214, 9914 Morrison St., Fort McMurray AB T9H 4A4
Tel: 780-799-3947; *Fax:* 780-714-3081
info@cemaonline.ca
www.cemaonline.ca
To study the cumulative environmental effects of industrial development in the region and produce guidelines and management frameworks.
Glen Semenchuk, Executive Director

Ducks Unlimited Canada (DUC) / Canards Illimités Canada
PO Box 1160, Stonewall MB R0C 2Z0
Fax: 204-467-9028
Toll-Free: 800-665-3825
webfoot@ducks.ca; volunteer@ducks.ca; member@ducks.ca
www.ducks.ca
Social Media: www.facebook.com/ducksunlimitedcanada; twitter.com/ducanada
To conserve, restore, & manage wetlands & associated habitats, for the benefit of waterfowl, which in turn provide healthy environments for wildlife & people
Jeff Nelson, Chief Executive Officer
Jack H. Hole, President
David Carefoot, Chief Financial Officer
Sandy Gousseau, National Director, Communications & Marketing
Grant Monck, National Director, Development
Henry Murkin, National Director, Conservation
Loraine Nyokong, National Director, Fundraising & Membership
Gary Goodwin, Executive Corporate Secretary & Counsel

Earth Day Canada (EDC) / Jour de la terre Canada
#503, 111 Peter St., Toronto ON M5V 2H1
Tel: 416-599-1991; *Fax:* 416-599-3100
Toll-Free: 888-283-2784
info@earthday.ca; donate@earthday.ca
www.earthday.ca
Social Media: www.facebook.com/EarthDayCanada; twitter.com/earthdaycanada; www.youtube.com/user/EarthDayCanada
To improve the state of the environment by motivating & helping Canadians to achieve local solutions
Jed Goldberg, President
Keith Treffry, Director, Communications
Paul Bubelis, Chair

Ecojustice Canada
#214, 131 Water St., Vancouver BC V6B 4M3
Tel: 604-685-5618; *Fax:* 604-685-7813
Toll-Free: 800-926-7744
www.ecojustice.ca
To provide legal representation to environmental groups that cannot afford to go to court against large institutions when important wilderness values are at stake; to bring selected cases with the ultimate goal of establishing an aggregate of strong legal precedents that recognize environmental values; to provide professional advice on the development of environmental legislation
Paul Richardson, President & Chair
Cathy Wilkinson, Vice Chair
Mike Cormack, Treasurer
Ronald H. Pearson, Secretary

Ecology Action Centre (EAC)
2705 Fern Lane, Halifax NS B3K 4L3
Tel: 902-429-2202; *Fax:* 902-405-3716
info@ecologyaction.ca
www.ecologyaction.ca
Social Media: www.facebook.com/EcologyActionCentre; twitter.com/ecologyaction
To act as a voice for Nova Scotia's environment; To build a healthier, more sustainable Nova Scotia
Maggy Burns, Internal Director
Tim Roberts, Co-Chair
Karen Hollett, Co-Chair

EcoPerth
2196 Old Brooke Rd., RR#2, Maberry ON K0H 2B0
Tel: 613-267-6463; *Fax:* 613-268-2907
info@ecoperth.on.ca
www.ecoperth.on.ca
To promote local projects that are environmentally sustainable and economically efficient in the Perth, Ontario area.
Bob Argue, Executive Director

Elsa Wild Animal Appeal of Canada
PO Box 45051, 2482 Yonge St., Toronto ON M4P 3E3
Tel: 416-489-8862; *Fax:* 416-489-4769
info@elsacanada.com
www.elsacanada.com
To help save endangered wildlife species in Canada
Betty Henderson, President

Enviro-Accès Inc.
Place Andrew-Paton, #150, 85, rue Belvédère nord, Sherbrooke QC J1H 4A7
Tél: 819-823-2230; *Téléc:* 819-823-6632
enviro@enviroaccess.ca
www.enviroaccess.ca
Supporter les petites et moyennes entreprises qui oeuvrent dans le domaine de l'environnement en leur offrant les services professionnels nécessaires au développement de leurs projets et de leurs affaires.
Manon Laporte, Présidente-directrice générale

EnviroLink
PO Box 8102, Pittsburgh PA 15217 USA
www.envirolink.org
To promote a sustainable society by connecting individuals and organizations through communication technologies.

Environmental Careers Organization of Canada / L'Organisation pour les carrières en environnement du Canada
#200, 308 - 11th Ave. SE, Calgary AB T2G 0Y2
Tel: 403-233-0748; *Fax:* 403-269-9544
info@eco.ca
www.eco.ca
Social Media: www.facebook.com/ecocanada; twitter.com/ecocanada
To provide services to all participants in the environmental sector, including educators, students, practitioners, & employers
Hubert Bourque, Chair
Jon Ogryzlo, Sec.-Treas.
Grant S. Trump, President/CEO
Michael Kerford, Vice-President
Janelle Thomlinson, Director, Marketing & Communications

The Environmental Coalition of PEI
126 Richmond St., Charlottetown PE C1A 1H9
Tel: 902-566-4696; *Fax:* 902-566-4037
energy@ecopei.ca
www.ecopei.ca
To preserve & enhance the environment for all living things
Kate McDonald, Energy Coordinator

Environmental Education Association of the Yukon (EEAY)
Whitehorse YT
eeyukon@gmail.com
taiga.net/YukonEE
To promote environmental education in the Yukon and foster communication between individuals and groups with and interest in environmental education.

Environmental Health Association of British Columbia (EHABC)
PO Box 30033, Stn. Saanich Centre, Victoria BC V8X 5E1
Tel: 250-658-2027
www.ehabc.org
To raise awareness within the medical community, educational institutions, and the general public to prevent further cases of environmental sensitivity from occurring.

The Environmental Law Centre (Alberta) Society (ELC)
#800, 10025 - 106 Street, Edmonton AB T5J 1G4
Tel: 780-424-5099; *Fax:* 780-424-5133
Toll-Free: 800-661-4238
elc@elc.ab.ca
www.elc.ab.ca
To conduct research in environmental & natural resources law, policy & procedure; to educate the public on environmental law; to operate an environmental law information & referral service for the benefit of the public; to monitor relevant municipal, provincial & federal environmental laws, policies & procedures, & make recommendations for reform
Cindy Chiasson, Executive Director

Environmental Managers Association of British Columbia (EMABC)
PO Box 3741, Vancouver BC V6B 3Z8
Tel: 604-998-2226; *Fax:* 604-998-2226
info@emaofbc.com
www.emaofbc.com
To encourage education, share knowledge among members and create a forum for environmental management issues in the industrial, commercial and institutional sectors, serve as a key resource of environmental information for members and explore existing and emerging environmental issues.
Patrick Novak, President
Krista Hennebury, Executive Director

Environmental Services Association of Alberta (ESAA)
#102, 2528 Ellwood Dr. SW, Edmonton AB T6X 0A9
Tel: 780-429-6363; *Fax:* 780-429-4249
Toll-Free: 800-661-9278
info@esaa.org
www.esaa.org
To act as the voice of Alberta's environment industry
Craig Robertson, President
Randy Neumann, Secretary
Skip Kerr, Treasurer
Joe Barraclough, Director, Industry & Government Relations
Joe Chowaniec, Director, Program & Event Development

Environmental Services Association of Nova Scotia (ESANS)
Woodside Industrial Park, #211-2, 1 Research Dr., Dartmouth NS B2Y 4M9
Tel: 902-463-3538; *Fax:* 902-466-6889
contact@esans.ca
www.esans.ca
ESANS is a province-wide business organization dedicated to the promotion of environmental products, services & organizations within the environmental industry.
Adam Cooney, President

Environmental Youth Alliance (EYA)
PO Box 3601, Stn. Terminal, #517, 119 Pender St. West, Vancouver BC V6B 1S5
Tel: 604-689-4446; *Fax:* 604-689-4242
info@eya.ca
www.eya.ca
To save the earth through non-violent means; To promote change by educating people on our interconnectedness with Nature & involving youth in action projects; To create a youth movement that is activist-oriented & works towards environmental respect & protection.

Environnement jeunesse
454, rue Laurier est, Montréal QC H2J 1E7
Tél: 514-252-3016; *Téléc:* 514-254-5873
Ligne sans frais: 866-377-3016
infoenjeu@enjeu.qc.ca
www.enjeu.qc.ca
Promouvoir la conservation et l'amélioration de la qualité de l'environnement; développer chez les jeunes les qualités favorisant leur implication sociale.
Jérôme Normand, Directeur général

Evergreen
#300, 550 Bayview Ave, Toronto ON M4W 3X8
Tel: 416-596-1495; *Fax:* 416-596-1443
Toll-Free: 888-426-3138
info@evergreen.ca; donate@evergreen.ca
www.evergreen.ca
To bring communities & nature together for the benefit of both; To create sustaining, healthy, dynamic outdoor spaces by engaging people & encouraging local stewardship
Geoff Cape, Executive Director
Seana Irvine, Chief Operating officer

FaunENord
313, 3e Rue, 2e étage, Chibougamau QC G8P 1N4
Tél: 418-748-4441; *Téléc:* 418-748-1110
www.faunenord.icr.qc.ca
Une entreprise vouée à la promotion & à l'aménagement durable des ressources fauniques & des écosystèmes
Justine Desmeules

Fédération québécoise des chasseurs et pêcheurs
162, rue du Brome, Saint-Augustin-de-Desmaures QC G3A 2P5
Tél: 418-878-8901; *Téléc:* 418-878-8980
Ligne sans frais: 888-523-2863
info@fedecp.qc.ca
www.fedecp.qc.ca
Mèdia social: www.facebook.com/116805682100; twitter.com/FederationCP
Contribuer, dans le respect de la faune et de ses habitats, à la gestion du développement et à la perpétuation de la chasse et de la pêche comme activités traditionnelles et sportives
Pierre Latraverse, Président
Marjorie Alain, Responsable des relations publiques

First Nations Environmental Network
PO Box 394, Tofino BC V0R 2Z0
Tel: 250-726-5265; *Fax:* 250-725-2357
councilfire@hotmail.com
www.fnen.org
The First Nations Environmental Network is a circle of First Nations people committed to protecting, defending, and restoring the balance of all life by honouring traditional Indigenous values and the path of our ancestors. We encourage the work of protecting, defending and healing Mother Earth. We desire and need to link grassroots Indigenous people nationally and internationally to support each other on environmental struggles and concerns. We are obligated to leave footprints for our children to follow by striving to live our life with traditional values.
Steve Lawson, Coordinator

Fondation de la faune du Québec (FFQ)
#420, 1175, av Lavigerie, Sainte-Foy QC G1V 4P1
Tél: 418-644-7926; *Téléc:* 418-643-7655
Ligne sans frais: 877-639-0742
ffq@fondationdelafaune.qc.ca
www.fondationdelafaune.qc.ca
Mèdia social: www.facebook.com/fondationdelafauneduquebec
Promouvoir la conservation et la mise en valeur de la faune et de son habitat
André Martin, Président-directeur général

FortWhyte Alive
1961 McCreary Rd., Winnipeg MB R3P 2K9
Tel: 204-989-8355; *Fax:* 204-895-4700
info@fortwhyte.org
www.fortwhyte.org
Social Media: www.facebook.com/pages/FortWhyte-Alive/471614835647?ref=ts
FortWhyte Alive is dedicated to providing programming, natural settings and facilities for environmental education and outdoor recreation. In so doing, FortWhyte promotes awareness and understanding of the natural world and actions leading to sustainable living.
Bill Elliott, President/CEO

Friends of Red Hill Valley
PO Box 61536, Hamilton ON L8T 5A1
Tel: 905-381-0240; *Fax:* 905-548-6317
redhill@hwcn.org
www.hwcn.org/forhv
To protect & enhance the Red Hill Valley in Hamilton, Ontario

Friends of the Earth Canada (FoE) / Les Ami(e)s de la Terre Canada
#300, 260 St. Patrick St., Ottawa ON K1N 5K5
Tel: 613-241-0085; *Fax:* 613-241-7998
Toll-Free: 888-385-4444
foe@foecanada.org
www.foecanada.org
To serve as a national voice for the environment, working with others to inspire the renewal of our communities & the earth, through research, education, advocacy & cooperation
Beatrice Olivastri, CEO

Friends of the Greenbelt Foundation
#201, 69 Scollard St., Toronto ON M5R 1G2
Tel: 416-960-0001; *Fax:* 416-960-0030
info@greenbelt.ca
www.greenbelt.ca
The Foundation was created to help foster the Greenbelt's living countryside by nurturing and supporting activities that preserve its environmental and agricultural integrity.
Burkhard Mausberg, CEO
Jan Whitelaw, Chair

Green Action Centre (RCM)
303 Portage Ave., 3rd Fl., Winnipeg MB R3B 2B4
Tel: 204-925-3777; *Fax:* 204-942-4207
Toll-Free: 866-394-8880
info@resourceconservation.mb.ca
www.resourceconservation.mb.ca
Social Media: www.facebook.com/group.php?gid=134760813229244
To promote ecological sustainability by developing alternatives to currently unsustainable practices; our principal activity is environmental education; our partners & clients include businesses, schools, non-profit groups, governments, recyclers, home gardeners & general public
Randall McQuaker, Executive Director

Greenpeace Canada
33 Cecil St., Toronto ON M5T 1N1
Tel: 416-597-8408; *Fax:* 416-597-8422
Toll-Free: 800-320-7183
supporter.ca@greenpeace.org
www.greenpeace.org/canada
Social Media: www.facebook.com/greenpeace.canada; twitter.com/greenpeaceCA; youtube.com/user/GreenpeaceCanada; flickr.com/photos/greenpeace_canada
Greenpeace is an independent, non-profit organization best known for non-violent direct actions to raise awareness on issues such as biodiversity, pollution of the Earth, nuclear threats & disarmament; it brings public opinion to bear on decisions makers. Public protest is only one of many Greenpeace strategies; it conducts scientific, economic & political research, publicizes environmental problems, recommends environmentally sound solutions & lobbies for change.
Bruce Cox, Executive Director
Ann Rowan, Chair

Greenspace Alliance of Canada's Capital
PO Box 55085, 240 Sparks St., Ottawa ON K1P 1A1
greenspace@greenspace-alliance.ca
www.greenspace-alliance.ca
To preserve green spaces in the National Capital area.
Cheryl Doran, Chair

Hamilton Industrial Environmental Association (HIEA)
PO Box 35545, Hamilton ON L8H 7S6
Tel: 905-561-4432
info@hiea.org
www.hiea.org
To improve the local environment - air, land and water - through joint and individual activities, and by partnering with the community to enhance future understanding of environmental issues and help establish priorities for action.
Jim Stirling, Chair

Harmony Foundation of Canada / Fondation Harmonie du Canada
PO Box 50022, #15, 1594 Fairfield Rd., Victoria BC V8S 1G1
Tel: 250-380-3001; *Fax:* 250-380-0887
harmony@islandnet.com
www.harmonyfdn.ca
Social Media: www.facebook.com/117724434937243; www.youtube.com/user/harmonyfdn
To encourage development which is socially & environmentally sustainable; To strive towards ecological stability, long-term prosperity, & social harmony
Michael Bloomfield, Founder & Executive Director
Robert Bateman, Honorary Chair
Jean-Pierre Soublière, President
Nick Mosky, Secretary
Robert Van Tongerloo, Treasurer

Hope for Wildlife Society
PO Box 1, 5909 Hwy. 207, #14 R.R.#2, Head of Chezzetcook NS B0J 1N0
Tel: 902-452-3339
info@hopeforwildlife.net
www.hopeforwildlife.net
Specializing in the care, treatment and rehabilitation of injured or orphaned native fur bearing mammals, sea birds and songbirds both indigenous to the Nova Scotia area as well as non-indigenous species and pets.
Hope Swinimer, Founder & Director

Institut de recherche en biologie végétale (IRBV) / Plant Biology Research Institute (PBRI)
4101, rue Sherbrooke est, Montréal QC H1X 2B2
Tél: 514-343-2121
irbv@irbv.umontreal.ca
www.irbv.umontreal.ca
To develop a centre of excellence in plant biology; both in fundamental research and its applicaitons; train students in plant biology at the master, doctoral, and post-doctoral levels; further training and knowledge of its researchers and technical personnel; promote the technological transfer of its scientific research results to users; provide complementary services to the community in fields relevant to plant biology, where expertise in the field is lacking.
Anne Bruneau, Directrice

Institute for Sustainable Energy, Economy and Environment Student's Association (ISEEESA)
Scrubfield Hall, #199B, 2500 University Dr., Calgary AB T2N 1N4
info@iseeesa.ca
www.iseeesa.ca
Social Media: www.facebook.com/groups/iseeesa; twitter.com/iseeesa
To promote and create initiatives that reflect the growing movement to obtain a cleaner energy supply, healthy environment, and efficient economy.
Lauren Rooney, President

International Council for the Exploration of the Sea (ICES)
H.C. Andersens Blvd. 44-46, Copenhagen VDK-1553 Denmark
info@ices.dk
www.ices.dk
To coordinate research & monitor activities to understand the marine environment & resources & man's impact upon them, including the identification of priority marine contaminants, their distribution, transport & effects; to provide advice regarding marine resources & pollution to member governments & international regulatory commissions; to publish & disseminate the results of research
Gerd Hubold, General Secretary
David Gillis, ICES Delegate, Canada
Ariane Plourde, ICES Delegate, Canada

International Institute for Sustainable Development (IISD) / Institut international du développement durable (IIDD)
161 Portage Ave. East, 6th Fl., Winnipeg MB R3B 0Y4
Tel: 204-958-7700; *Fax:* 204-958-7710
info@iisd.ca
www.iisd.org
To promote sustainable development in decision-making in Canada & abroad by undertaking sustainable development research, advising government, business & organizations, analyzing & reporting on issues & events, & publishing & disseminating sustainable development information. Offices in Winnipeg, Ottawa, New York, & Geneva.
Franz Tattenbach, President/CEO
William H. Glanville, Vice-President & COO

Jasper Environmental Association (JEA)
PO Box 2198, Jasper AB T0E 1E0
Tel: 780-852-4152; *Fax:* 780-852-4152
jea2@telus.net
www.jasperenvironmental.org
To support Parks Canada in administering Jasper National Park in accordance with Canadian legislation, Parks Canada principles and policies and the wishes of the Canadian public.

Manitoba Eco-Network Inc. (MEN) / Réseau écologique du Manitoba inc.
#3, 303 Portage Ave., Winnipeg MB R3B 2B4
Tel: 204-947-6511; *Fax:* 204-989-8476
info@mbeconetwork.org
www.mbeconetwork.org
To educate the public on environmental issues; to conduct research on environmental issues; to facilitate communications between environmental groups & the general public
Anne Lindsey, Executive Director

Manitoba Environment Officers Association Inc. (MEOA)
147 Norcross Cres., Winnipeg MB R3X 1J2
meoa@mts.net
www.meoa.ca
To enhance the public health and safety of Manitobans and to protect, maintain and rehabilitate Manitoba's environment ecosystems through the diligent duties of educated Environment Officers and to obtain for Environment Officers continued education and recognition of their efforts.
Bill Barr, President

Manitoba Environmental Industries Association Inc. (MEIA)
#100, 62 Albert St., Winnipeg MB R3B 1E9
Tel: 204-783-7090; *Fax:* 204-783-6501
admin@meia.mb.ca
www.meia.mb.ca
To assist members in the business of the environment; To connect business, government, & stakeholders with environmental issues
John Fjeldsted, Executive Director
Vaughn Bullough, President
Rosemary Deans, Coordinator, Education & Training
Deb Tardiff, Coordinator, Education & Training
Sheldon McLeod, Secretary
John Pikel, Treasurer

Manitoba Wildlife Federation (MWF)
70 Stevenson Rd., Winnipeg MB R3H 0W7
Tel: 204-633-5967; *Fax:* 204-632-5200
info@mwf.mb.ca; vpHunting@mwf.mb.ca; vpPrograms@mwf.mb.ca
www.mwf.mb.ca
To devote members to the causes of conservation & the participation in the wise use of natural resources; To encourage the propagation of game & fish; To promote the enforcement of game laws; To cooperate with government departments
Reid Woods, President
Lori Thomas, Director, Administration
Rachelle Aime, Vice-President, Education
Ken MacMaster, Vice-President, Membership
Larry Millan, Vice-President, Environment & Habitat
Reg Wiebe, Coordinator, Hunter Education

Municipal Waste Association (MWA)
#100, 127 Wyndham St. North, Guelph ON N1H 4E9
Tel: 519-823-1990; *Fax:* 519-823-0084
carrie@municipalwaste.ca
www.municipalwaste.ca
To expedite the flow of information regarding 3R programs to municipalities & other community & government groups; To act as an information forum for municipal recycling coordinators; To allow member municipalities to act as a unified voice in promoting progressive waste reduction & recycling alternatives
Vivian De Giovanni, Executive Director
Ben Bennett, Manager, Projects & Communications

National Energy Conservation Association Inc. (NECA) / Association nationale pour la conservation de l'énergie
250 McDermot Ave., Winnipeg MB R3B 0S5
Tel: 204-956-5888; *Fax:* 204-956-5819
Toll-Free: 800-263-5974
neca@neca.ca
www.neca.ca
To promote energy efficiency in the building sector; To work towards a sustainable future
Ryan Dalgleish, Contact, Business Development

The Nature Conservancy of Canada (NCC) / Société canadienne pour la conservation de la nature
#400, 36 Eglinton Ave. West, Toronto ON M4R 1A1
Tel: 416-932-3202; *Fax:* 416-932-3208
Toll-Free: 800-465-0029
nature@natureconservancy.ca
www.natureconservancy.ca
Social Media: www.facebook.com/natureconservancy.ca; twitter.com/NatureConsCDA
To protect Canada's biodiversity through long-term stewardship & property securement
Laurie J. Thomson, Chair
John Lounds, President & Chief Executive Officer
Jane Gilbert, Chief Communications Officer
Lynn Gran, Chief Development Officer & Vice-President, Strategic Philanthropy
Kamal Rajani, Chief Financial Officer
John Riley, Chief Science Officer & National Director, Strategies
Ian Barnett, Vice-President, Regional Operations
Michael Bradstreet, Vice-President, Conservation
Julie Wood, Vice-President, Corporate

New Brunswick Environment Industry Association (NBEIA) / L'Association des industries de l'environnement du Nouveau-Brunswick (AIENB)
PO Box 637, Stn. A, Fredericton NB E3B 5B3
Tel: 506-455-0212; *Fax:* 506-452-0213
nbeia@nbnet.nb.ca
www.nbeia.nb.ca
To promote the growth of environmental business in New Brunswick
Pierre Landry, President
Eric Cook, Secretary-Treasurer

New Brunswick Environmental Network (NBEN) / Réseau environnemental du Nouveau-Brunswick (RENB)
167 Creek Rd., Waterford NB E4E 4L7
Tel: 506-433-6101; *Fax:* 506-433-6111
nben@nben.ca
www.nben.ca
Social Media: www.facebook.com/pages/NBEN-RENB/134259049952351
To strengthen the environmental movement throughout New Brunswick; To promote ecologically sound ways of life
Mary Ann Coleman, Executive Director
Joanna Brown, Coordinator, Youth Outreach & Events
Raissa Marks, Coordinator, Education & Outreach Programs

New Brunswick Wildlife Federation (NBWF) / Fédération de la faune du Nouveau-Brunswick
576, rue Principale, St. Leonard NB E7E 2H5
www.nbwildlifefederation.org
To foster sound management & wise use of the renewable & non-renewable natural resources of New Brunswick; to assist & encourage the enforcement of those game laws which are in keeping with the objectives of the Federation & to strive for better management & game laws where & when necessary; to educate membership & the public, with particular emphasis upon conservation & safety; to represent the interests & concerns of New Brunswick sportsmen; to cooperate with government departments & all related groups, where interests are mutual.
Roland Michaud, President
Rod Currie, Secretary

Newfoundland & Labrador Environmental Industry Association (NEIA)
Parsons Bldg., #101, 90 O'Leary Ave., St. John's NL A1B 2C7
Tel: 709-772-3333; *Fax:* 709-772-3213
info@neia.org
www.neia.org
To promote the growth & development of the environmental industry of Newfoundland & Labrador; to promote ethical behavior & high standards for environmental products & services; to provide a strong, unified voice toward all private sector, government & non-profit entities involved in the Newfoundland environmental industry.
Linda Bartlett, Executive Director
Bill Scott, President

Newfoundland & Labrador Wildlife Federation (NWLF)
15 Conran St., St. John's NL A1E 5L8
Tel: 709-368-6180
ward.sampson@nf.sympatico.ca
www.nlwf.ca
To foster awareness & enjoyment of the natural world; To promote the sustainable use of natural resources; To protect wildlife & its habitat through conservation & effective wildlife management
Bernie Rumboldt, Contact

North American Recycled Rubber Association (NARRA)
#24, 1621 McEwen Dr., Whitby ON L1N 9A5
Tel: 905-433-7769; *Fax:* 905-433-0905
narra@oix.com
www.recycle.net/recycle/assn/narra
The Association provides a unified voice, as well as a communication network & research facility, for issues of concern to those involved in rubber recycling across North America.
Diane Sarracini, Office Manager

Nova Scotia Environmental Network (NSEN)
3115 Veith St., Halifax NS B3K 3G9
Tel: 902-454-6846; *Fax:* 902-453-3633
nsen@cen-rce.org; board_nsen@cen-rce.org
www.nsen.ca
To conserve & enhance the natural environment; To achieve a sustainable future for Nova Scotia; To connect environmental & health organizations
Tamara Lorincz, Executive Director
Emma Boardman, Secretary & Agent

Nova Scotia Nature Trust (NSNT)
PO Box 2202, 2085 Maitland St., Halifax NS B3J 3C4
Tel: 902-425-5263; *Fax:* 902-429-5263
Toll-Free: 877-434-5263
nature@nsnt.ca
www.nsnt.ca
To protect Nova Scotia's outstanding natural legacy through land conservation.
Nil d'Entremont, President
Bonnie Sutherland, Executive Director

Oak Ridges Moraine Foundation (ORMF)
The Gate House, 13990 Dufferin St. North, King City ON L7B 1B3
Tel: 905-833-5733; *Fax:* 905-833-8379
support@ormf.com
www.ormf.com
To provide support and encouragement for activities that preserve, protect, and restore the environmental integrity of the Oak Ridges Moraine and support a trail along it.
Kim Gavine, Executive Director

Offshore Energy Environmental Research Association (OEER)
Bank of Montreal Building, PO Box 2664, #400, 5151 George St., Halifax NS B3J 3P7
Tel: 902-424-8479; *Fax:* 902-424-0528
Toll-Free: 888-257-8688
oeer@offshoreenergyresearch.ca
www.offshoreenergyresearch.ca
To build research capacity in Nova Scotia and to assess the potential impacts of: petroleum exploration, development and production and renewable energy technologies (ocean currents, wind, tides and waves) on the marine environment.
Wayne St-Amour, Executive Director

ONEIA - Ontario Environment Industry Association
215 Spadina Avenue, Suite 401, Toronto ON M5T 2C7
Tel: 416-531-7884; *Fax:* 416-644-0116
info@oneia.ca
www.oneia.ca
To promote the growth of environment business in Ontario
Marjan Lahuis, Operations Manager, Membership Recruitment and Sponsor Relations
Alex Gill, Executive Director

Ontario Environment Industry Association (ONEIA)
#410, 215 Spadina Ave., Toronto ON M5T 2C7
Tel: 416-531-7884
info@oneia.ca
www.oneia.ca
To represent the interests of the environmental industry in Ontario; To promote environmental business to industry & government in Ontario
Alex Gill, Executive Director

Ontario Environmental Network (OEN)
PO Box 1412, Stn. Main, North Bay ON P1B 8K6
Tel: 705-840-2888
oen@oen.ca
www.oen.ca
To encourage discussions of ways to protect the environment; To increase environmental awareness throughout Ontario; To serve the environmental non-profit, non-governmental community in Ontario
Phillip Penna, Coordinator

Ontario Federation of Anglers & Hunters (OFAH)
PO Box 2800, 4601 Guthrie Dr., Peterborough ON K9J 8L5
Tel: 705-748-6324; *Fax:* 705-748-9577
ofah@ofah.org
www.ofah.org
Social Media: www.facebook.com/127166042780; twitter.com/ofah; www.youtube.com/ofahcommunications
To save & defend from waste the natural resources of Ontario, its soils, minerals, air, water, forests & wildlife
Rob Hare, President
Mike Reader, Executive Director

Ontario Pollution Control Equipment Association (OPCEA)
PO Box 137, Midhurst ON L0L 1X0
Tel: 705-725-0917; *Fax:* 705-725-1068
opcea@opcea.com
www.opcea.com
To assist members in the promotion of their services & equipment in Ontario
Kelly Manden, Executive Administrator
Brian Allen, President
Wayne Harrison, Vice-President
Heinz Held, Treasurer

Ontario Steelheaders
PO Box 604, Brantford ON N3T 5T3
president@ontariosteelheaders.ca
www.ontariosteelheaders.ca
To improve access and habitat for migratory rainbow trout, provide young rainbow trout with suitable nursery habitat, provide relevent and appropriate input to government, agencies and other organizations, and to educate members and the public on relevent issues, conservation practices and proper angling techniques.

Ontario Streams
50 Bloomington Rd. West, Aurora ON L4G 3G8
Tel: 905-713-7399; *Fax:* 905-713-7361
www.ontariostreams.on.ca
To promote the conservation & rehabilitation of streams & wetlands, through education & community involvement
Doug Forder, Field Supervisor

Ontario Waste Management Association (OWMA) / Société ontarienne de gestion des déchets
#3, 2005 Clark Blvd., Brampton ON L6T 5P8
Tel: 905-791-9500; *Fax:* 905-791-9514
contact@owma.org
www.owma.org
To act as the voice of the private sector waste industry in Ontario; To protect the enviroment by properly managing waste & recyclable materials
Rob Cook, President
Michele Goulding, Manager, Finance & Administration

Ottawa Duck Club (ODC)
841 Kinsgmere Ave., Ottawa ON K2A 3J8
www.ottawaduckclub.com
To actively improve the nesting habitat for waterfowl and other birds along the Ottawa River.
Bill Bower, President

Ottawa Riverkeeper / Sentinelle Outaouais
#301, 1960 Scott St., Ottawa ON K1Z 8L8
Tel: 613-321-1120; *Fax:* 613-822-5258
Toll-Free: 888-953-3737
info@ottawariverkeeper.ca
www.ottawariverkeeper.ca
To protect and promote the ecological health and diversity of the Ottawa River and its tributaries; To ensure swimmable, fishable, drinkable waterways
Meredith Brown, Executive Director

Peace Valley Environment Association (PVEA)
PO Box 6062, Fort St John BC V1J 4H6
pvea@shaw.ca
www.peacevalley.ca
To protect and defend the natural environment of the Peace Valley area of British Columbia

The Pembina Institute
219 - 19 St. NW, Calgary AB T2N 2H9
Tel: 403-269-3344; *Fax:* 403-269-3377
www.pembina.org
To develop & promote public policy & educational programs which protect the environment & encourage environmentally sound resource management strategies; to implement a conserver society
Ed Whittingham, Executive Director

Pitch-In Canada (PIC) / Passons à l'action Canada
PO Box 45011, Stn. Ocean Park RPO, White Rock BC V4A 9L1
Fax: 604-535-4653
Toll-Free: 877-474-8244
www.pitch-in.ca
To improve communities & the envionment by providing programs to reduce, re-use, recycle, & properly manage & dispose waste
Misha Cook, Executive Director
Lisa Davis, Project Coordinator
Misha van Veen, Program Manager
Valerie S. Thom, Executive Director

The Pollution Probe Foundation (PPF)
#402, 625 Church St., Toronto ON M4Y 2G1
Tel: 416-926-1907; *Fax:* 416-926-1601
pprobe@pollutionprobe.org
www.pollutionprobe.org
A registered Canadian charity which seeks to define environmental problems through research; to promote understanding through education & to press for practical solutions through advocacy. The organization is non-partison & works collaboratively with government agencies, other non-profit organizations, & private business to engage key issues & find solutions. Offices in Toronto & Ottawa
Bob Oliver, CEO
Husam Mansour, COO

Prince Edward Island Eco-Net (PEIEN)
126 Richmond St., Charlottetown PE C1A 1H9
Tel: 902-566-4170; *Fax:* 902-566-4037
peien@isn.net
www.peieconet.org
Social Media: www.facebook.com/peieconet?ref=ts
To promote communication & cooperation among ENGO's (Environmental NGO's) & between ENGO's & governments; to provide referral services; to coordinate workshops & conferences; to provide consultations; to publish & distribute information
Susan Hawkins, Executive Director

Prince Edward Island Wildlife Federation
#103B, 420 University Ave., Charlottetown PE C1A 7Z5
Tel: 902-892-3332; *Fax:* 902-892-3334
peiwfft@pei.aibn.com

To foster sound management & wise use of the renewable resources of PEI; to assist & encourage the enforcement of those game laws which are in keeping with the objectives of the Federation & to strive for better management & game laws where & when necessary; to cooperate with government departments & related groups where interests are mutual; to educate membership & the public, with particular emphasis upon conservation & safety; to represent the interests & concerns of PEI sportsmen
Karl McCormack, President

Recycling Council of Alberta (RCA)
PO Box 23, Bluffton AB T0C 0M0
Tel: 403-843-6563; *Fax:* 403-843-4156
info@recycle.ab.ca
www.recycle.ab.ca
Social Media: www.facebook.com/RecyclingCouncilOfAlberta; twitter.com/3RsAB
To promote & facilitate waste reduction, recycling, & resource conservation in Alberta
Jason London, President
Sharon Howland, Vice-President
Maegan Lukian, Secretary
Anne Auriat, Treasurer

Recycling Council of British Columbia (RCBC)
#10, 119 West Pender St., Vancouver BC V6B 1S5
Tel: 604-683-6009; *Fax:* 604-683-7255
Toll-Free: 800-667-4321
rcbc@rcbc.bc.ca; hotline@rcbc.bc.ca
www.rcbc.bc.ca
Social Media:
www.facebook.com/home.php?sk=group_10340005498; twitter.com/RecyclingBC; www.youtube.com/user/RCBCTrailerTrashed
To promote the principles of zero waste; To decrease British Columbia's environmental footprint
Brock Macdonald, Executive Director
Anna Rochelle, Director, Finance
Harvinder Gill, Manager, Information Services
Ben Ramos, Manager, Member Services

Recycling Council of Ontario (RCO) / Conseil du recyclage de l'Ontario
#225, 215 Spadina Ave., Toronto ON M5T 2C7
Tel: 416-657-2797; *Toll-Free:* 888-501-9637
rco@rco.on.ca
www.rco.on.ca
Social Media: twitter.com/#!/RCOntario
To minimize impact on the environment by eliminating waste
Jo-Anne St. Godard, Executive Director
Diane Blackburn, Manager, Events
David Hanson, Program Manager, Waste Diversion Certification Program
Sarah Mills, Manager, Special Projects & Take Back the Light
Lucy Robinson, Manager, Member Relations
Catherine Leighton, Coordinator, Special Projects
Andrew Reeves, Coordinator, Outreach & Communications

Réseau environnement
#220, 911, rue Jean Talon est, Montréal QC H2R 1V5
Tél: 514-270-7110; *Téléc:* 514-270-7154
info@reseau-environnement.com
www.reseau-environnement.com
Regrouper des entreprises spécialisées dans la gestion des déchets commerciaux, industriels et des services municipaux reliés à l'environnement; Assurer l'avancement des technologies et de la science, la promotion des expertises et le soutien des activités en environnement
Stéphanie Myre, Présidente-directrice générale
Mario Laplante, Directeur général adjointé
Josianne Lafantaisie, Coordonnatrice principale, Communications et relations publiques
Romy Regis, Coordonnatrice, Événements
Lyne Dubois, Merlicom
Mihaela Sandor, Comptable

Réseau québécois des groupes écologistes (RQGE)
1557-A, avenue Papineau, Montréal QC H2K 4H7
Tél: 514-392-0096
info@rqge.qc.ca
www.rqge.qc.ca
Réseau de services et d'information pour les groupes écologiques du Québec; aider les groupes à communiquer entre eux
Yvan Croteau, Président

Resource Efficient Agricultural Production (REAP Canada)
Glenaladale House, PO Box 125, 21111, ch Lakeshore, Sainte-Anne-de-Bellevue QC H9X 3V9
Tel: 514-398-7743; *Fax:* 514-398-7972
info@reap-canada.com
www.reap-canada.com
To improve farm profits & productivity while minimizing adverse health & environmental effects
Roger Samson, Executive Director

Rideau Environmental Action League (REAL)
PO Box 1061, Smiths Falls ON K7A 5A5
Tel: 613-283-9500; *Fax:* 613-283-9500
info@realaction.ca
www.realaction.ca
To conduct community-wide environmental projects and promote environmental improvements within the Town of Smiths Falls and Lanark, Leeds and Grenville Counties.
Barb Hicks, President

Rideau Valley Conservation Authority (RVCA)
PO Box 599, 3889 Rideau Valley Dr., Manotick ON K4M 1A5
Tel: 613-692-3571; *Fax:* 613-692-0831
Toll-Free: 800-267-3504
postmaster@rvca.ca
www.rvca.ca
Social Media:
www.facebook.com/group.php?gid=108941882522595; twitter.com/RideauValleyCA
To advocate for clean water, natural shorelines and sustainable land use throughout the Rideau Valley watershed.
Alan Arbuckle, Chair
Charles Billington, Director, Community Relations

Sackville Rivers Association (SRA)
PO Box 45071, Sackville NS B4E 2Z6
Tel: 902-865-9238
sackvillerivers@ns.sympatico.ca
www.sackvillerivers.ns.ca
To promote the preservation, restoration and enhancement of the Sackville River Watershed.
Walter N. Regan, President

Sarnia-Lambton Environmental Association (SLEA)
1489 London Rd., Sarnia ON N7S 1P6
Tel: 519-332-2010; *Fax:* 519-332-2015
www.sarniaenvironment.com
To monitor ambient environmental conditions to assess the impact of its members on the local environment's air, water and soil.
Dean Edwardson, General Manager

Saskatchewan Eco-Network (SEN)
#203, 115 - 2 Ave. North, Saskatoon SK S7K 2B1
Tel: 306-652-1275; *Fax:* 306-665-2128
sen@link.ca
www.econet.sk.ca
To provide educational activities to develop an awareness of conservation & enhancement of the environment
Mike Finley, Chair
Lynn Hainsworth, Executive Director
Paddy Tutty, Administrator

Saskatchewan Environmental Industry & Managers' Association (SEIMA)
2341 McIntyre St., Regina SK S4P 2s3
Tel: 306-543-1567; *Fax:* 306-543-1568
info@seima.sk.ca
www.seima.sk.ca
Social Media:
www.facebook.com/group.php?gid=111586162187848
To act as the voice of practitioners in Saskatchewan's environmental industry on environmental matters; To promote responsible environmental management in the province; To develop the environmental industry in Saskatchewan
Kathleen Livingston, Executive Director & COO
Jim Finnigan, President
Lawrence Pinter, Vice-President
Glen J. Weisbrod, Treasurer
Cheryl Hender, Secretary

Saskatchewan Environmental Society (SES)
PO Box 1372, #203, 115 - 2nd Ave. North, Saskatoon SK S7K 3N9
Tel: 306-665-1915; *Fax:* 306-665-2128
info@environmentalsociety.ca
www.environmentalsociety.ca
The Society works to maintain the integrity of Saskatchewan's forests, farmlands and natural prairie landscapes; protect the atmosphere, and promote energy conservation and the development of renewable energy resources; and build sustainable communities, responsible waste management, and enhanced water quality in the province's lakes and rivers.
Allyson Brady, Executive Director
Peter Prebble, Director, Energy & Water Policy
Jen Antony, Coordinator, Retire Your Ride
Angie Bugg, Coordinator, Energy Conservation
Greg Rooke, Coordinator, Pesticide Reduction
Alina Siegfried, Coordinator, Water Issues

Saskatchewan Soil Conservation Association (SSCA)
PO Box 1360, Indian Head SK S0G 2K0
Tel: 306-695-4233; *Fax:* 306-695-4236
Toll-Free: 800-213-4287
info@ssca.ca
www.ssca.ca
To improve the land & environment; To increase public awareness of soil conservation; To promote conservation production systems to Saskatchewan producers
Tim Nerbas, President
Marilyn Martens, Office Manager

Saskatchewan Waste Reduction Council (SWRC)
The Two-Twenty, #208, 220 - 20th St. West, Saskatoon SK S7M 0W9
Tel: 306-931-3242; *Fax:* 306-955-5852
info@saskwastereduction.ca
www.saskwastereduction.ca
To help the people of Saskatchean reduce waste; To provide input on policies about solid & hazardous waste
Joanne Fedyk, Executive Director
Naomi Mihilewicz, Coordinator, Outreach
Martha Hollinger, Contact, Member Services & Administration

Saskatchewan Wildlife Federation (SWF)
9 Lancaster Rd., Moose Jaw SK S6J 1M8
Tel: 306-692-8812; *Fax:* 306-692-4370
Toll-Free: 877-793-9453
sask.wildlife@sasktel.net
www.swf.sk.ca
Social Media:
www.facebook.com/pages/Saskatchewan-Wildlife-Federation/178255362147
To promote the wise use & management of natural resources in Saskatchewan
Darrell Crabbe, Executive Director
Ray Wild, President
Marilee Herone, Manager, Office
Maureen Horrocks, Coordinator, Communications
Jim Kroshus, Coordinator, Habitat Trust Land
Adam Matichuk, Coordinator, Fisheries Project
JeanAnne Prysliak, Coordinator, Education Program

Sea Shepherd Conservation Society (SSCS)
PO Box 48446, Vancouver BC V7X 1A2
Tel: 604-688-7325
canada@seashepherd.org
www.seashepherd.org
Social Media:
www.facebook.com/seashepherdconservationsociety
Investigates & documents violations of international laws, regulations & treaties protecting marine wildlife species; involved with the enforcement of these laws when there is no enforcement by national governments or international regulatory organizations
Paul Watson, Founder & President

SEEDS Foundation
#400, 144 - 4th Ave. SW., Calgary AB T2P 3N4
Tel: 403-221-0835; *Fax:* 403-221-0876
Toll-Free: 800-661-8751
seeds@telusplanet.net
www.seedsfoundation.ca
Social Media:
www.facebook.com/pages/SEEDS-Foundation/117021191648133
To provide educational support materials & professional assistance to teachers in the area of energy, environment & sustainable development; To work toward the development of a society which understands & is committed to actions leading to wise stewardship of resources, resource use & the environment
Diane Field, Executive Director

Seventh Generation Community Projects
c/o Trucker House Renewal Centre, #155, 99 Fifth Ave., Ottawa ON K1S 5P5
Tel: 613-446-2117
seventhgeneration@tuckerhouse.ca
www.seventhgeneration.ca
Seventh Generation Community Projects promotes integrated sustainable living practices in the greater Ottawa area by hosting events, creating resources, networking, and supporting green businesses.

Scott McKenzie, Contact

Severn Sound Environmental Association (SSEA)
67 Fourth St., Midland ON L4R 3S9
Tel: 705-527-5166; *Fax:* 705-527-5167
www.severnsound.ca
To forge cooperative initiatives to address environmental issues by planning, designing, arranging funding and implementing environmental projects and promoting a sustainable Severn Sound community.
Keith Sherman, Executive Director

Sierra Club of Canada (SCC) / Sierre club du Canada
#412, 1 Nicholas St., Ottawa ON K1N 7B7
Tel: 613-241-4611; *Fax:* 613-241-2292
Toll-Free: 888-810-4204
info@sierraclub.ca
www.sierraclub.ca
Social Media: www.facebook.com/sierraclubcanada; twitter.com/SierraClubCan; www.youtube.com/sierraclubcanada
To develop a diverse, well-trained grassroots network, working to protect the integrity of our global ecosystems; To focus on five overriding threats: loss of animal & plant species, deterioration of the planet's oceans & atmosphere, the ever-growing presence of toxic chemicals in all living things, destruction of our remaining wilderness, spiralling population growth & overconsumption
John Bennett, Executive Director
Anowara Baqi, CFO
Tania Beriau, Development Director
Daniel Spence, Director, Communications

Small Water Users Association of BC
4167 Highway 3A, Nelson BC V1L 6N1
Tel: 250-825-4308
smallwaterusers@shaw.ca
www.smallwaterusers.com
The Small Water Users Association of BC is a new non-profit society dedicated to serving the interests of small water systems (1 to 300 connections) throughout British Columbia.
Denny Ross-Smith, Executive Director

Society Promoting Environmental Conservation (SPEC)
2150 Maple St., Vancouver BC V6J 3T3
Tel: 604-736-7732; *Fax:* 604-736-7115
admin@spec.bc.ca
www.spec.bc.ca
To address environmental issues in British Columbia, with a focus on urban communities in the Lower Mainland & the Georgia Basin; To encourage policies that lead to urban sustainability
Joanna Robinson, President
Isle Sarady, Manager, Operations
Catriona Gordon, Coordinator, School Gardens Community
Alicia Embree, Secretary
Jason Fast, Treasurer

Solid Waste Association of North America (SWANA)
#700, 1100 Wayne Ave., Silver Spring MD 20910 USA
Fax: 301-589-7068
Toll-Free: 800-467-9262
info@swana.org
www.swana.org
Social Media: www.facebook.com/MySWANA; twitter.com/SWANA; www.linkedin.com/groups?home=&gid=45037
To serve individuals & communities responsible for the operation & management of solid waste management systems; To advance professional standards in the field through training programs, technical assistance, & education
John Skinner, Executive Director & CEO

Southeast Environmental Association (SEA)
PO Box 1500, 41 Woods Islands Hill, Montague PE C0A 1R0
Tel: 902-838-3351; *Fax:* 902-838-0610
sea@pei.aibn.com
www.seapei.ca
To protect, maintain, and enhance the ecology of south eastern Prince Edward Island for the environmental, social, and economic well being of area residents.
Sarah Jane Bell, Coordinator
Edgar Dewar, Chair

Sustainable Urban Development Association (SUDA)
2637 Council Ring Rd., Mississauga ON L5L 1S6
Tel: 416-400-0553
mail@suda.ca
www.suda.ca
To foster a healthy natural environment by providing information about ways in which cities can become more efficient in the land, material, water and energy resources, and highly supportive of sustainable transportation.

TD Friends of the Environment Foundation / Fondation des amis de l'environnement TD
TD Tower, 66 Wellington St., 17th Fl., Ottawa ON M5K 1A2
Toll-Free: 800-361-5333
tdfef@td.com
www.fef.td.com
To protect & preserve the Canadian environment
Natasha Alleyne-Martin, Manager, National Programs
Ellen Dungen, Regional Manager, Saskatchewan & Manitoba
Cathy Jowsey, Regional Manager, Northern & Eastern Ontario
Mandip Kharod, Regional Manager, British Columbia, Alberta, Yukon, & Northwest Territories
Amelie Picher, Regional Manager, Québec
Yvetter Scrivener, Regional Manager, Central & Southwestern Ontario
Farzana Syed, Regional Manager, Greater Toronto Area, Surrounding Region, & Atlantic Provinces

Thousand Islands Watershed Land Trust (TIWLT)
19 Reynolds Rd., Landsdowne ON K0E 1L0
www.tiwlt.ca
To permanently protect land in the Thousand Islands watershed region through acquisition or conservation agreements, and to achieve good land management through stewardship agreements and education.
Dann Michols, President

Water Environment Association of Ontario (WEAO)
PO Box 176, Milton ON L9T 4N9
Tel: 416-410-6933; *Fax:* 416-410-1626
julie.vincent@weao.org
www.weao.org
To advance the water environment industry; To promote sound public policy
Catherine Jefferson, Executive Director
Julie A. Vincent, Executive Administrator
Anne Baliva, Admin. Assistant
John Presta, Treasurer

Western Canada Water (WCWWA)
PO Box 1708, 126 - 3rd Ave. West, Cochrane AB T4C 1B6
Tel: 403-709-0064; *Fax:* 403-709-0068
Toll-Free: 877-283-2003
member@wcwwa.ca
www.wcwwa.ca
To advance support for water professionals throughout western Canada
Audrey Arisman, Executive Director

Western Canada Wilderness Committee (WCWC)
PO Box Z205, Station Terminal, Vancouver BC V6B 3W2
Tel: 604-683-8220; *Fax:* 604-683-8229
Toll-Free: 800-661-9453
info@wildernesscommittee.org
www.wildernesscommittee.org
To work for the protection of Canadian & the Earth's wilderness through research & education; to promote the principles which achieve ecologically sustainable communities
Andrea Reimer, Executive Director
Joe Foy, Director, National Campaign
Gwen Barlee, Director, Policy

Wild Bird Care Centre (WBCC)
PO Box 11159, Nepean ON K2H 7T9
Tel: 613-828-2849
mojo@wildbirdcarecentre.org
www.wildbirdcarecentre.org
To assess, treat, and rehabilitate sick, orphaned, or injured wild birds before releasing them back to the wild.
Kathy Nihei, Founder

Wildlife Habitat Canada (WHC) / Habitat faunique Canada (HFC)
#310, 1740 Courtwood Cres., Ottawa ON K2C 2B5
Tel: 613-722-2090; *Fax:* 613-722-3318
Toll-Free: 800-669-7919
reception@whc.org
www.whc.org
Social Media: www.facebook.com/pages/Wildlife-Habitat-Canada/124492716000
To promote the conservation, restoration & enhancement of wildlife habitat to retain diversity, distribution & abundance of wildlife; To provide a funding mechanism for the conservation, restoration & enhancement of wildlife habitat in Canada; To foster coordination & leadership in the conservation, restoration & enhancement of wildlife habitat in Canada
Len Ugarenko, President

Wildlife Preservation Canada (WPC) / Conservation de la faune au Canada
RR#5, 5420 Hwy. 6 North, Guelph ON N1H 6J2
Tel: 519-836-9314; *Fax:* 519-836-8840
Toll-Free: 800-956-6608
admin@wildlifepreservation.ca
www.wildlifepreservation.ca
Social Media: www.facebook.com/group.php?gid=141989432535249
To save endangered animal species from extinction in Canada & internationally
Elaine Williams, Executive Director
H. Alec B. Monro, President
Jessica Steiner, Recovery Biologist
Ellen Reinhart, Contact, Member & Donor Relations

Wood Buffalo Environmental Association (WBEA)
#100, 330 Thickwood Blvd., Fort McMurray AB T9K 1Y1
Tel: 780-799-4420
info@wbea.org
www.wbea.org
To provide state of the art air monitoring system that meets the needs of residents and stakeholders in the Wood Buffalo Region.
Carna MacEachern, Executive Director
Ann Dort-MacLean, President

World Wildlife Fund - Canada (WWF-Canada) / Fonds mondial pour la nature
#410, 245 Eglinton Ave. East, Toronto ON M4P 3J1
Tel: 416-489-8800; *Fax:* 416-489-3611
Toll-Free: 800-267-2632
ca-panda@wwfcanada.org
www.wwf.ca
Social Media: www.facebook.com/WWFCanada
To conserve wild animals, plants & habitats for their own sake & the long-term benefit of people; to protect the diversity of life on earth; to stop, & eventually reverse, the accelerating degradation of our planet's natural environment, & to help build a future in which humans live in harmony with nature
Patricia Koval, Chair
Monte Hummel, President Emeritus
Darcy Dobell, Vice-President, Pacific Conservation
Arlin Hackman, Vice-President, Conservation & Chief Conservation Officer
Grahame Cliff, Vice-President, Finance & Administration
Christina Topp, Vice-President, Marketing & Communications
Robert Rangeley, Vice-President, Atlantic Region

Yukon Conservation Society (YCS)
302 Hawkins St., Whitehorse YT Y1A 1X6
Tel: 867-668-5678; *Fax:* 867-668-6637
ycs@ycs.yk.ca
www.yukonconservation.org
To pursue ecosystem well-being throughout the Yukon & beyond
Karen Baltgailis, Executive Director
Georgia Greetham, Coordinator, Office
Sue Kemmett, Coordinator, Forestry
Anne Middler, Coordinator, Energy
Lewis Rifkind, Coordinator, Mining

Yukon Environmental Network
PO Box 30097, Whitehorse YT Y1A 5M2
Tel: 867-668-5678; *Fax:* 867-668-6637
yukonenvironet@gmail.com
Susan Davis, Coordinator

Yukon Fish & Game Association (YFGA)
509 Strickland St., Whitehorse YT Y1A 2K5
Tel: 867-667-4263; *Fax:* 867-667-4237
www.yukonfga.ca
To ensure the long-term management of fish, wildlife, & outdoor recreational resources in the Yukon; To improve wildlife habitat
Paul Jacobs, President
Gord Zealand, Executive Director
Jillian Mclellan, Office Administrator

Equipment & Machinery

AMC - Agricultural Manufacturers of Canada
PO Box 636, Stn. Main, Regina SK S4P 3A3
Tel: 306-522-2710; *Fax:* 306-781-7293
Toll-Free: 800-959-7462
amc@a-m-c.ca
www.a-m-c.ca
To foster & promote the growth & development of the agricultural equipment manufacturing industry; to identify industry problems & take remedial action; to encourage governments to enact legislation & offer programs that enhance the growth potential of industry; to provide a forum for members to exchange ideas &

discuss their industry as it relates to the national & international economy
Jerry Engel, President

Association des marchands de machines aratoires de la province de Québec (AMMAQ)
7, rue Bernier, Bedford QC J0J 1A0
Tél: 450-248-7946; *Téléc:* 450-248-3264
info@ammaq.ca
www.ammaq.ca
Aider et regrouper tous les concessionnaires de machineries agricoles de toute la province; compiler des statistiques et des renseignements sur la vente de machines aratoires dans la province du Québec; obtenir une plus grande coopération entre les marchands de machines aratoires des diverses régions de la province; promouvoir la vente et l'utilisation des machines aratoires
Peter Maurice, Directeur général

Association des propriétaires de machinerie lourde du Québec inc. (APMLQ)
#259, 2750, ch Ste-Foy, Sainte-Foy QC G1V 1V6
Tél: 418-650-1877; *Téléc:* 418-650-3361
Ligne sans frais: 800-268-7318
apmlq@videotron.ca
www.apmlq.com/
Informer et instruire ses membres au moyen de publications; maintenir un secrétariat permanent dans un but de liaison entre les membres et de contact avec différentes autorités; négocier avec les autorités publiques toutes ententes susceptibles de promouvoir les buts de l'Association et ceux de ses membres
Richard Robitaille, Président

Association of Equipment Manufacturers - Canada (AEM-Canada)
World Exchange Plaza, PO Box 81067, #880, 111 Albert St., Ottawa ON K1P 1B1
Tel: 613-566-4568; *Fax:* 613-566-2026
www.aem.org
The Association acts as a voice for its members to the public & on a governmental level. It is also a regulatory body setting standars for safety, offering a variety of educational programs & seminars. AEM also serves as a disseminating body providing it members with current information & news on the industry.
Dennis Slater, President
Howard Mains, Canada Consultant, Public Policy

Canada East Equipment Dealers' Association (CEEDA)
64 Temperance St., Aurora ON L4G 2P8
Tel: 905-841-6888; *Fax:* 905-841-1214
info@orfeda.com
www.orfeda.com
To promote the welfare of equipment trade retailers in the Maritimes & Ontario; To represent dealer interests in government legislation & regulation; To foster cooperation among manufacturers & distributors; To promote high standards for the retail equipment industry
Craig Smith, Chair
Keith Stoltz, 1st Vice-Chair
Beverly J. Leavitt, President & CEO
Carol Schoen, Secretary-Treasurer

Canadian Association of Defence & Security Industries (CADSI) / Association des industries canadiennes de défense et de sécurité (AICDS)
#1250, 130 Slater St., Ottawa ON K1P 6E2
Tel: 613-235-5337; *Fax:* 613-235-0784
cadsi@defenceandsecurity.ca
www.defenceandsecurity.ca
To represent Canadian defence & security industries domestically & internationally
Tim Page, President
Janet Thorsteinson, Vice-President, Government Relations
Andrea Walton, Manager, Operations & Administration
Steven Hillier, Manager, Marketing & Membership
Martine Proulx, Director, Events
Stefanie van Duynhoven, Assistant, Communications

Canadian Association of Equipment Distributors (CAED)
4531 Southclark Pl., Ottawa ON K1T 3V2
Tel: 613-822-8861; *Fax:* 613-822-8862
mswan@caed.org
www.caed.org
To represent the equipment industry in Canada; To promote cooperation between distributors & manufacturers; To encourage environmentally sound business practices
Mike Christodoulou, Chair
Nancy Ellen Leu, President

Canadian Process Control Association (CPCA)
2100 Banbury Cres., Oakville ON L6H 5P6
Tel: 905-844-6822; *Fax:* 905-901-9913
cpca@cpca-assoc.com
www.cpca-assoc.com
To promote the industry & its members to customers, academia, & public bodies; To provide a forum to exchange technical, industry, & regulatory information; To develop industry statistics; To encourage professional & ethical behaviour & quality standards among members

Municipal Equipment & Operations Association (Ontario) Inc.
38 Summit Ave., Kitchener ON N2M 4W5
Tel: 519-741-2780; *Fax:* 519-741-2750
admin@meoa.org
www.meoa.org
A network of individuals working directly with equipment & operations, to exchange information, promote high standards in the field & cost effective public service in Ontario.
Don Miller, Treasurer
Bill Barr, President

Ethnic Groups

Jamaica Association of Montréal Inc.
4065, Jean-Talon ouest, Montréal QC H4P 1W6
Tel: 514-737-8229; *Fax:* 514-737-4861
jamaica_inc@yahoo.ca
www.jam-montreal.com
Educational, cultural & social activities for the Jamaican community; after-school & evening classes & programs for youth & adults; Saturday morning program for children; restaurant on site
Noel Alexander, Contact

New Brunswick African Association Inc.
www.nbafricans.com
The New Brunswick African Association Inc. is a community based organization focused on supporting the African community in New Brunswick to sustain, grow and thrive.
Donath Mrawira, President

Events

Alberta Music Festival Association
Alberta College, Edmonton AB
Tel: 780-633-3725
info@albertamusicfestival.org
www.albertamusicfestival.org
To coordinate, regulate & assist activities of local Alberta festivals of music & speech arts; to encourage formation of additional local festivals
Norma Jean Atkinson, President
Wendy Durieux, Provincial Administrator

Associated Manitoba Arts Festivals, Inc. (AMAF)
#202, 1151 Pembina Hwy., Winnipeg MB R3T 2A3
Tel: 204-945-4578; *Fax:* 204-948-2073
amaf@mts.net
www.amaf.mb.ca
To promote & encourage participation in growth & development of & appreciation for creative & performing arts in partnership with local festivals
Cynthia Warkentin, President
Arlene Baschak, Vice-President

Association des professionnels en exposition du Québec (APEQ)
868, rue Brisette, Sainte-Julie QC J3E 2B1
Tél: 514-990-0224; *Téléc:* 450-922-7238
info@apeq.org
www.apeq.org
Faire reconnaître le rôle vital de l'industrie des expositions dans la vie économique, industrielle, culturelle et sociale au Québec; promouvoir, auprès du monde des affaires, l'efficacité des expositions comme moyen de promotion, de commercialisation et de communication; favoriser l'éducation de ses membres
Jacques Perreault, Directeur général

Canadian Association of Exposition Management (CAEM) / Association canadienne des directeurs d'expositions
PO Box 218, #2219, 160 Tycos Dr., Toronto ON M6B 1W8
Tel: 416-787-9377; *Fax:* 416-596-1808
Toll-Free: 866-441-9377
info@caem.ca
www.caem.ca
To represent & improve the exposition & trade show industry in Canada
Serge Micheli, Executive Director
Stephen Dempsey, President
Isabella Wai, 1st Vice-President
Lisa McDonald, 2nd Vice-President
Robert Halasz, Secretary
Gilles Bouchard, Treasurer
Michael Dargavel, Office Manager

Canadian Association of Fairs & Exhibitions (CAFE) / Association canadienne des foires et expositions
PO Box 13161, Ottawa ON k2k 1x4
Tel: 613-233-0012; *Fax:* 613-233-1154
Toll-Free: 800-663-1714
info@canadian-fairs.ca
www.canadian-fairs.ca
To provide leadership in the development of the Canadian Fair Industry; To represent the Canadian fairs & exhibitions sector at the national level
Mavis Hanna, Executive Director

Carnaval de Québec / Québec Winter Carnival
205, boul des Cèdres, Québec QC G1L 1N8
Tél: 418-626-3716; *Téléc:* 418-626-7252
Ligne sans frais: 866-422-7628
comm@carnaval.qc.ca
www.carnaval.qc.ca
Depuis 50 ans, le Carnaval de Québec s'est donné la mission d'organiser annuellement une fête populaire hivernale dans le but de faire bénéficier à Québec une activité économique, touristique et sociale de première qualité dont les gens de la région seront fiers.
Alain Winter, Président
Jean Pelletier, Directeur général

Exhibitions Association of Nova Scotia (EANS)
40 Gateway Rd., Halifax NS B3M 1M9
Tel: 902-443-2039; *Fax:* 902-443-6721
www.eans.ca
EANS is a non-profit organization promoting such events as fairs & exhibitions across the province.
Glen E. Jefferson, Executive Director

Federation of Canadian Music Festivals (FCMF) / La Fédération canadienne des festivals de musique
C/O Executive Director, 14004 - 75th Ave. NW, Edmonton AB T5R 2Y5
Toll-Free: 877-323-3263
fcmf@shaw.ca
www.fcmf.org
Umbrella organization for 230+ local & provincial festivals; to develop & encourage Canadian talent in the performance & knowledge of classical music; to encourage the study & practice of the art of music alone or in conjunction with related arts; to organize the National Music Festival in which winners from each province participate
Pam Allen, President
Rhéal Fournier, Vice President

Federation of Music Festivals of Nova Scotia
82 High St., New Glasgow NS B2H 2W9
Tel: 902-752-9590
jessie@novaanalytics.ca
Jessie MacNeil, Provincial Secretary

Festivals & Events Ontario (FEO)
#301, 5 Graham St., Woodstock ON N4S 6J5
Tel: 519-537-2226; *Fax:* 519-537-2226
info@festivalsandeventsontario.ca
www.festivalsandeventsontario.ca
Festivals & Events Ontario (FEO) was established in 1987 as an association devoted to the growth and stability of the festival and event industry in Ontario. FEO provides festival and event organizers across the province with a networking forum offering professional development opportunities and resources aimed to encourage professionalism and excellence in the delivery of festivals and special events. The association also serves industry members whose goods and services are of use and benefit to Ontario's festivals and special events.
Gary Masters, Executive Director
Debbie Mann, Sales and Technical Coordinator

Festivals et Événements Québec (FEQ)
CP 1000, Succ. M, 4545, av Pierre-de-Coubertin, Montréal QC H1V 3R2
Tél: 514-252-3037; *Téléc:* 514-254-1617
Ligne sans frais: 800-361-7688
info@satqfeq.com
www.evenementsquebec.qc.ca
Regrouper les fêtes, festivals et événements, de les promouvoir et de leur offrir des services qui favorisent leur développement
Pierre-Paul Leduc, Directeur general
Luc Martineau, Directeur marketing
Sylvain Martineau, Dir. Ventes

Lyne Voyer, Dir. Communications
Sylvie Theberge, Dir. Services Membres
Robert Aucoin, Dir. recherche
Claude Latour, Dir. web

Greater Vancouver International Film Festival Society (VIFF)
1181 Seymour St., Vancouver BC V6B 3M7
Tel: 604-685-0260; *Fax:* 604-688-8221
viff@viff.org
viff.org
To operate the Annual Vancouver International Film Festival, bringing to British Columbia the best in current art cinema from around the world as well as buried treasures from past international cinema
Alan Franey, Festival Director

International Special Events Society - Toronto Chapter (ISES)
312 Oakwood Court, Newmarket ON L3Y 3C8
Tel: 905-898-7434; *Fax:* 905-895-1630
Toll-Free: 866-729-4737
info@isestoronto.com
www.isestoronto.com
Social Media: www.facebook.com/group.php?gid=7607457535
To educate, advance & promote the special events industry & its network of professionals along with related industries; to uphold the integrity of the special events profession to the public through "Principles of Professional Conduct & Ethics"; to acquire & disseminate useful business information; to foster a spirit of cooperation among members & other special events professionals
Carol Ford, Executive Director

New Brunswick Competitive Festival of Music Inc.
PO Box 2022, Saint John NB E2L 3T5
Tel: 506-847-7228
info@nbcfm.ca
www.nbcfm.ca
To hold a competitive & non-competitive music festival where students of all ages & music disciplines, including piano, vocal, strings, & band may meet, compete on a friendly basis & learn from expert adjudication
Elizabeth Collings, Executive Secretary
Chris Titus, President

New Brunswick Federation of Music Festivals Inc. (NBFMF) / La Fédération des festivals de musique du Nouveau-Brunswick inc. (FFMNB)
NB
info@nbfmf.org
nbfmf.org
Barbara Long, Executive Director/President

Newfoundland Federation of Music Festivals
c/o 1 Marigold Place, St. John's NL A1E 5N7
Tel: 709-722-9376
www.fcmf.org/province.htm
To coordinate activities of local music festivals & conduct a provincial music festival annually; to participate in the CIBC National Music Festival.
Joan Woodrow, Provincial Administrator

Ontario Music Festivals Association (OMFA)
c/o Pam Allen, 1422 Bayview Ave., #A, Toronto ON M4G 3A7
Toll-Free: 888-307-6632
mail@omfa.info
www.omfa.info
To promote the performance of classical music by Ontario's youth; To encourage knowledge of classical music
Martha Gregory, President
James Brough, Vice-President
Steven Fielder, Treasurer
Pam Allen, Festival Administrator

Performing Arts BC
PO Box 22042, Penticton BC V2A 8L1
Tel: 250-493-7279; *Fax:* 250-493-7279
festival@bcprovincials.com
www.bcprovincials.com
Antonia Mahon, Executive Director

Prince Edward Island Kiwanis Music Festival Association
c/o 227 Keppoch Rd., Stratford PE C1B 2J5
Tel: 902-569-2885; *Fax:* 902-569-2885
peikmfa@gmail.com
www.peikiwanismusicfestival.ca
To make possible performances of young & older musicians in a semi-professional atmosphere; to adjudicate using professionals; & to encourage performance & study in music
Diane Campbell, Provincial Administrator

Provincial Exhibition of Manitoba
115 - 10th St., Brandon MB R7A 4E7
Tel: 204-726-3590; *Fax:* 204-725-0202
Toll-Free: 877-729-0001
info@brandonfairs.com
www.brandonfairs.com
To showcase agriculture; to link urban & rural regions through education & awareness while providing entertainment, community pride & economic enhancement to the region
Karen Oliver, General Manager
Neil Thomson, President

Québec Competitive Festival of Music / Festival de concours du Québec
136 Duke of Kent St., Pointe-Claire QC H9R 1X9
Tél: 514-398-4535; *Téléc:* 514-398-8061
davidson@music.mcgill.ca
Tom Davidson, Contact

Royal Agricultural Winter Fair Association (RAWF) / Foire agricole royale d'hiver
The Ricoh Coliseum, 100 Princes' Blvd., Toronto ON M6K 3C3
Tel: 416-263-3400; *Fax:* 416-263-3488
info@royalfair.org
www.royalfair.org
To promote excellence in agricultural & equestrian activities through world class competition, exhibitions & education
Bill Duron, CEO

Saskatchewan Music Festival Association Inc.
#14, 62 Westfield Dr., Regina SK S4S 2S4
Tel: 306-757-1722; *Fax:* 306-347-7789
Toll-Free: 888-892-9929
sask.music.festival@sasktel.net
www.smfa.ca
Oldest organized cultural organization in Saskatchewan; to provide a classical competitive music festival system of the highest standard at the local, provincial & national levels
Carol Donhauser, Executive Director

Tangofest
c/o #1801, 2350 Dundas St. West, Toronto ON M6P 4B1
Tel: 416-536-8446
info@tangofest.ca
www.tangofest.ca
Musharraf Farooqi, Executive Director

Toronto International Film Festival Inc.
#1600, 2 Carlton St., Toronto ON M5B 1J3
Tel: 416-967-7371; *Toll-Free:* 877-968-3456
customerrelations@tiff.net; humanresources@tiff.net
www.tiffg.ca
To lead in creative & cultural discovery through the moving image
Paul Atkinson, Chair

Vancouver International Children's Festival
402 - 873 Beatty St., Vancouver BC V6B 2M6
Tel: 604-708-5655; *Fax:* 604-708-5661
info@childrensfestival.ca
www.childrensfestival.ca
To provide performing arts programs to young people in a festival environment; To encourage critical thinking & a lifelong interest in learning, the arts & cultural development
Ken Daskewech, Chair

Western Association of Exhibition Management (WAEM)
1475 East Georgia St., Vancouver BC V5L 2A9
Tel: 604-205-3955; *Fax:* 604-205-5490
info@waem.org
www.waem.org
Nick Szrejter, Secretary

Farming

Friends of the Central Experimental Farm (FCEF)
Building 72, Central Experimental Farm, Ottawa ON K1A 0C6
Tel: 613-230-3276; *Fax:* 613-230-1238
info@friendsofthefarm.ca
www.friendsofthefarm.ca
To preserve, maintain, protect and enhance the Arboretum, the Ornamental Gardens and other public areas of the Central Experimental Farm in Ottawa, Ontario, Canada.
Polly McColl, President

Prince Edward Island Certified Organic Producers Co-op
PO Box 1776, Charlottetown PE C1A 7N4
Tel: 902-894-9999
www.organicpei.com
To increase organic production, research and market development; invite growers into the organic industry and promote and educate Islanders about organic food.
Mark Bernard, President

Fashion & Textiles

Alberta Men's Wear Agents Association
PO Box 66037, Stn. Heritage, Edmonton AB T6J 6T4
Tel: 780-455-1881; *Fax:* 780-455-3969
amwa@shaw.ca
www.trendsapparel.com
Ken Melnychuk, President
Sue Brochu, Secretary-Treasurer

Allied Beauty Association (ABA)
#26-27, 145 Traders Blvd. East, Mississauga ON L4Z 3L3
Tel: 905-568-0158; *Fax:* 905-568-1581
Toll-Free: 800-268-6644
abacan@idirect.com
www.abacanada.com
To encourage & create a greater understanding & knowledge of the professional beauty industry to the salons, the public, the federal & provincial governments, & to members
Marc Speir, Executive Director

Apparel Manufacturers Association of Ontario
#504, 124 O'Connor St., Ottawa ON K1P 5M9
Tel: 613-231-3220; *Fax:* 613-231-2305
Bob Kirke, Executive Director

BeautyCouncil (BC)
899 West 8th Ave., Vancouver BC V5Z 1E3
Tel: 604-871-0222; *Fax:* 604-871-0299
Toll-Free: 800-663-9283
info@ciabc.net
www.ciabc.net
To strive for the highest standards of excellence in professional cosmetology services through its member enhancement programs & to service the public through education & knowledge.
Herman Schut, Chair
Tara Gilbert, CEO

Canadian Apparel Federation (CAF) / Fédération canadienne du vêtement
#708, 151 Slater St., Ottawa ON K1P 5H3
Tel: 613-231-3220; *Fax:* 613-231-2305
info@apparel.ca
www.apparel.ca
Social Media: www.facebook.com/pages/Canadian-Apparel-Federation/102242196491712; twitter.com/caf_apparel; www.linkedin.com/company/canadian-apparel-federation
To provide a forum for provincial apparel associations representing the vast majority of the country's manufacturers; To exercise leadership in relations with government, suppliers & the general public
Bob Kirke, Executive Director

Canadian Association of Wholesale Sales Representatives (CAWS) / Association canadienne des représentants de ventes en gros
PO Box 54546, 1771 Avenue Rd., Toronto ON M5M 4N5
Tel: 416-782-8961; *Fax:* 416-782-5876
caws@bellnet.ca
www.caws.ca
To represent comission sales agents on a national level. Serves as an umbrella organization for affiliate markets across Canada which are responsible for the coordination of trade shows directed towards the retail buyer.
Paul Reynard, Executive Director

Canadian Textile Association (CTA) / La Fédération canadienne du textile
4505 Paddock Trail, Niagara Falls ON L2H 3E6
Tel: 905-371-8985; *Fax:* 905-371-9238
Toll-Free: 877-897-1474
info@cdntexassoc.com
www.cdntexassoc.com
To advance & disseminate knowledge of textiles; to promote sound procedures of textile processing; to encourage & sponsor textile research & investigation; to assist in the establishment of standards in the textile industry; to promote & encourage schools, classes & libraries for the study of textile technology; to collaborate with international groups in advancing the foregoing objectives

John Secondi, President

Canadian Textiles Institute (CTI) / Institut canadien des textiles
#500, 222 Somerset St. West, Ottawa ON K2P 2G3
Tel: 613-232-7195; *Fax:* 613-232-8722
cti@textiles.ca
www.textiles.ca
Harvey L. Penner, Chair

Cosmetology Association of Nova Scotia
126 Chain Link Dr., Halifax NS B3S 1A2
Tel: 902-468-6477; *Fax:* 902-468-7147
Toll-Free: 800-765-8757
www.nscosmetology.ca
The Cosmetology Act and By-Laws ensures that all persons practicing cosmetology (i.e. hairdressing facial/make-up and manicure-pedicure services) possess the requisite skill and knowledge to properly perform all duties pertaining to these occupations.
Dana Sharkey, Office Manager & Administrator
Malcolm Norton, President

Groupe CTT Group (CTT) / CTT Group Centre for Textile & Geosynthetic Technologies
3000, rue Boullé, Saint-Hyacinthe QC J2S 1H9
Tél: 450-778-1870; *Téléc:* 450-778-3901
Ligne sans frais: 877-288-8378
www.groupecttgroup.com; www.gcttg.com
Favoriser le développement des matériaux textiles et de stimuler l'avancement technologique de l'industrie textile et géosynthétique par des activités telles que la recherche et le développement, l'assistance technique, la formation sur mesure, l'information spécialisé et l'animation du milieu
Jacek Mlynarek, President/CEO

Institut des manufacturiers du vêtement du Québec (IMVQ) / Apparel Manufacturers Institute of Québec (AMIQ)
#1514 555, rue Chabanel ouest, Montréal QC H2N 2J2
Tél: 514-382-3846; *Téléc:* 514-383-1689
sc@vetementquebec.com
www.vetementquebec.com
Vêtement Québec (IMVQ) joue des rôles multiples - elle est une source, notamment, d'information, de formation, d'inspiration et de motivation. Toutefois, d'abord et avant tout, c'est une association. Vêtement Québec est le regroupement professionnel des hommes et des femmes qui dirigent un grand nombre des entreprises de vêtements les plus progressives du pays, ainsi que d'entreprises qui offrent des produits et des services essentiels au secteur.
Patrick Thomas, Directrice générale

Luggage, Leathergoods, Handbags & Accessories Association of Canada (LLHA)
PO Box 144, Stn. A, Toronto ON M9C 4V2
Fax: 519-624-6408
Toll-Free: 866-872-2420
info@llha.ca
www.llha.ca
To promote the growth of the industry in Canada; To foster the interchange of ideas
Catherine Genge, Executive Administrator

Manitoba Fashion Institute (MFI)
c/o Sterling Glove, 165 Selkirk Ave. East, Winnipeg MB R2W 2L3
Tel: 204-586-8189; *Fax:* 204-582-2992
To increase awareness & to promote a positive image of the apparel industry in Manitoba; To ensure that the industry continues to remain an integral component of the Manitoba economy

Ontario Fashion Exhibitors (OFE)
PO Box 218, #2219, 160 Tycos Dr., Toronto ON M6B 1W8
Tel: 416-596-2401; *Fax:* 416-596-1808
Toll-Free: 800-765-7508
www.ofeshows.ca
To produce fashion marketplace events
Les Cappe, President
Jamie Finiffter, Vice-President
Serge Micheli, Executive Director
Gretchen Palmer, Secretary
Stephen Messer, Treasurer
Michael Dargavel, Show Manager

Prairie/Saskatoon Apparel Market
601 - 331 Smith St., Winnipeg MB R3C 2G9
Tel: 204-942-2060; *Fax:* 204-947-0561
pammarkt@mts.net
Eric Levi, President
Pat Herzog, Market Director

Shoe Manufacturers' Association of Canada (SMAC) / Association des manufacturiers de chaussures du Canada
#203, 90, rue Morgan, Baie d'Urfe QC H9X 3A8
Tel: 514-457-3436; *Fax:* 514-457-8004
hanna@shoecanada.com
To represent & serve Canadian footwear manufacturers; To protect the Canadian domestic shoe industry
George P. Hanna, President

Western Apparel Market
910 Mainland St., Vancouver BC V6B 1A9
Tel: 604-682-5719; *Fax:* 604-682-3892
wambc@telus.net

Western Canada Children's Wear Markets (WCCWM)
#264, 1951 Glen Dr., Vancouver BC V6A 4J6
Tel: 604-681-1719; *Fax:* 604-681-1730
jeffswartz@telus.net
Jeff Swartz, President

Film & Video

Academy of Canadian Cinema & Television (ACCT) / Académie canadienne du cinéma et de la télévision
49 Ontario St., Toronto ON M5A 2V1
Tel: 416-366-2227; *Fax:* 416-366-8454
Toll-Free: 800-644-5194
info@academy.ca
www.academy.ca
The Academy promotes & celebrates exceptional creative achievement in the Canadian film & television industries. Its mandate is to heighten public awareness & increase audience appreciation of Canadian film & television productions through its national Award programs: Genie Awards, Gemini Awards, & Prix Gémeaux. It is a registered charity, BN :106681471RR0001.
Ronald I. Cohen, Chair
Sara Morton, Executive Director

Alberta Motion Picture Industries Association (AMPIA)
#318, 8944 - 182 St. NW, Edmonton AB T5T 2E3
Tel: 780-944-0707; *Fax:* 780-426-3057
Toll-Free: 800-814-7779
info@ampia.org
www.ampia.org
Social Media: twitter.com/yourampia
To develop & sustain the motion picture industry indigenous to Alberta
Josh Miller, President
Camille Beaudoin, Director

Association des producteurs de films et de télévision du Québec (APFTQ)
Edifice City Centre, #1030, 1450, rue City Councillors, Montréal QC H3A 2E6
Tél: 514-397-8600; *Téléc:* 514-392-0232
info@apftq.qc.ca
www.apftq.qc.ca
Représente ses membres auprès des gouvernements et organismes et encourage la coopération étroite entre tous les intervenants de l'industrie cinématographique et télévisuelle
Claire Samson, President and CEO

Association des réalisateurs et réalisatrices du Québec (ARRQ)
Maison de la Réalisation, 5154, rue St-Hubert, Montréal QC H2J 2Y3
Tél: 514-842-7373; *Téléc:* 514-842-6789
secretariat@arrq.qc.ca
www.arrq.qc.ca
Défendre les intérêts et les droits professionnels, économiques, culturels, sociaux et moraux des réalisateurs pigistes membres, travaillant principalement dans les domaines du cinéma et de la télévision
Julie Forest, Directrice générale

Atlantic Filmmakers Cooperative (AFCOOP)
PO Box 2043, Halifax NS B3J 2Z1
Tel: 902-420-4572; *Fax:* 902-420-4573
membership@afcoop.ca
www.afcoop.ca
Social Media:
www.facebook.com/group.php?gid=2270148397&ref=ts
An accessible member-run centre for the production & presentation of creative films in a collaborative, learning environment
Greg Morris-Poultney, Executive Director

Canadian Association of Film Distributors & Exporters (CAFDE) / Association canadienne des distributeurs et exportateurs de films (ACDEF)
North Tower, #1400, 175 Bloor St. East, Toronto ON M4W 3R8
Tel: 416-415-7217; *Fax:* 416-944-2212
teast@cafde.ca
To foster & promote the health of the Canadian motion picture industry by strengthening the Canadian owned & controlled distribution/export sector
Ted East, President

Canadian Film Centre (CFC) / Centre canadien du film
2489 Bayview Ave., Toronto ON M2L 1A8
Tel: 416-445-1446; *Fax:* 416-445-9481
info@cdnfilmcentre.com
www.cfccreates.com
To operate as Canada's foremost film, televion, & new media institution; To advance Canadian creative talent, content, & values worldwide, through training, production, promotion & investment

Canadian Film Institute (CFI) / Institut canadien du film (ICF)
#120, 2 Daly Ave., Ottawa ON K1N 6E2
Tel: 613-232-6727; *Fax:* 613-232-6315
info@cfi-ifc.ca
www.cfi-icf.ca
To promote Canadian cinema; To assist in locating sources for rental or purchase of individual films & videos; To give subject & content information on theatrical & non-theatrical films & videos from both private & public sources; To give general information on Canadian & international film, video, & television production, distribution, exhibition, & related subjects
Jack Horwitz, Chair
Tom McSorley, Executive Director & Secretary
Jerrett Zaret, Coordinator, Sponsorship
Michael Leong, Treasurer

Canadian Filmmakers Distribution Centre (CFMDC)
#119, 401 Richmond St. West, Toronto ON M5V 3A8
Tel: 416-588-0725; *Fax:* 416-588-7956
cfmdc@cfmdc.org
www.cfmdc.org
To promote & distribute the work of independent Canadian filmmakers.
Lauren Howes, Executive Director

Canadian Media Production Association
601 Bank St., 2nd Fl., Ottawa ON K1S 3T4
Tel: 613-233-1444; *Fax:* 613-233-0073
Toll-Free: 800-656-7440
ottawa@cmpa.ca
www.cmpa.ca
Social Media: www.facebook.com/theCMPA;
twitter.com/CMPA_Updates;
www.linkedin.com/company/canadian-media-production-association-cmpa-; www.youtube.com/CMPAOnline
To represent the interests of media companies engaged in the production & distribution of English language television programs, feature films, & new media content throughout Canada
Norm Bolen, President & Chief Executive Officer
Jane Cheesman, Chief Financial Officer
Marc Séguin, Senior Vice-President, Policy
Jay Thomson, Vice-President, Broadcasting Policy & Regulatory Affairs
Susanne Vaas, Vice-President, Business Affairs
Anne Trueman, Director, Communications & Media
Sarolta Csete, Manager, National Mentorship Program & e-Services
Lisa Moreau, Manager, Member Services & Special Events

Canadian Motion Picture Distributors Association (CMPDA) / Association canadienne des distributeurs de film
#1603, 22 St. Clair Ave. East, Toronto ON M4T 2S4
Tel: 416-961-1888; *Fax:* 416-968-1016
info@cmpda.ca
www.cmpda.org
To act as the voice of U.S.A. studios who market feature films, prime time entertainment programming for television & pay TV, & pre-recorded videos & DVDs in Canada; To coordinate recommendations on matters affecting national distributors of feature films, pre-recorded videocassettes, & television programs; To protect the rights of copyright owners

Canadian Picture Pioneers (CPP)
#1762, 250 The East Mall, Toronto ON M9B 6L3
Tel: 416-368-1139
cdnpicturepioneers@rogers.com
www.canadianpicturepioneers.ca

To provide assistance for the welfare of those in the motion picture industry in Canada
John Freeborn, Executive Director
Phil May, President
Paul Wroe, Secretary-Treasurer

Canadian Society of Cinematographers (CSC)
#131, 3007 Kingston Rd., Toronto ON M1M 1P1
Tel: 416-266-0591; *Fax:* 416-266-3996
admin@csc.ca; editor@csc.ca (Communications & Publications)
www.csc.ca
To promote the art & craft of cinematography
Susan Saranchuk, Executive Director

La Cinémathèque québécoise
335, boul de Maisonneuve est, Montréal QC H2X 1K1
Tél: 514-842-9763; *Téléc:* 514-842-1816
info@cinematheque.qc.ca
www.cinematheque.qc.ca
Conservation et mise en valeur du patrimoine cinématographique et télévisuel; promouvoir la culture cinématographique; créer des archives de cinéma; acquérir et conserver des films ainsi que toute la documentation qui s'y rattache; projeter ces films et exposer ces documents de facon non commerciale à des fins historique, pédagogique et artistique.
Pierre Jutras, Directeur, Conservation et programmation
Suzanne Hénaut, Présidente
Yolande Racine, Directrice générale

Directors Guild of Canada (DGC) / La Guilde canadienne des réalisateurs
#402, 111 Peter St., Toronto ON M5V 2H1
Tel: 416-482-6640; *Fax:* 416-482-6639
Toll-Free: 888-972-0098
mail@dgc.ca
www.dgc.ca
DGC is a national labour organization representing key creative & logistical personnel in the film & television industry. The Guild began as an association of creative film directors & expanded into all areas of the production, design & editing of film & television in Canada. A primary mandate is to promote & advance the quality & vitality of Canadian feature film & television production.
Sturla Gunnarsson, President
Brian Anthony, National Executive Director

The Harold Greenberg Fund
Astral Media, BCE Place, #100, 181 Bay St., Toronto ON M5J 2T3
Tel: 416-956-5431; *Fax:* 416-363-9005
hgfund@tv.astral.com
www.astralmedia.com
To foster the development & production of feature-length movies written by Canadians & the production of family television series
John Galway, President

Independent Media Arts Alliance (IMAA) / Alliance des arts médiatiques indépendants (AAMI)
3995, rue Berri, Montréal QC H2L 4H2
Tel: 514-522-8240; *Fax:* 514-987-1862
info@imaa.ca
www.imaa.ca
To promote discussion among media art centres; To coordinate independent film & video centres
François-Xavier Tremblay, Interim National Director

The Motion Picture Theatre Associations of Canada (MPTAC) / Les associations des propriétaires des cinémas du Canada
#304, 1240 Bay St., Toronto ON M5R 2A5
Tel: 416-969-7057; *Fax:* 416-922-5667
mptac.ca@ca.inter.net
www.mptac.ca
To maintain a national trade association of motion picture theatre exhibitors, consisting of owners, operators, executives & managers; to forward & promote the general welfare & prosperity of motion picture exhibitors; to gather, receive & disseminate such information as may seem helpful to members & associatedorganizations; to interchange ideas in rendering mutual assistance & to provide helpful vocational advice & guidance, & to act as a group representing national interests.
Nuria Bronfman, Executive Director

The Moving Pictures Travelling Canadian Film Festival Society
#300, 856 Homer Street, Vancouver BC V6B 2W5
Tel: 604-681-4549; *Fax:* 604-687-4937
Toll-Free: 877-858-3456
info@movingpictures.ca
To make Canadian films available in regions of the country that have limited access to them; to develop an audience for & awareness of Canadian films in Canada by exhibiting Canada's best films
Sauching Ng, Festival Director

National Screen Institute - Canada (NSI)
#400, 141 Bannatyne Ave., Winnipeg MB R3B 0R3
Tel: 204-956-7800; *Fax:* 204-956-5811
Toll-Free: 800-952-9307
info@nsi-canada.ca
www.nsi-canada.ca
To supply innovative, focused, applied professional training, leading participants to successful careers as writers, directors & producers in Canada's film & television industry
John Gill, Chief Executive Officer

North of Superior Film Association (NOSFA)
#352, 1100 Memorial Ave., Thunder Bay ON P7B 4A3
Tel: 807-625-5450
info@nosfa.ca
www.nosfa.ca
To promote film and appreciation of film in the Thunder Bay area.
Marty Mascarin, President
Catherine Powell, Festival Coordinator

Northern Film & Video Industry Association (NFVIA)
PO Box 31340, Whitehorse YT Y1A 5P7
Tel: 867-456-2978
info@nfvia.com
www.nfvia.com
Supports the film & video sector in the Yukon by focussing on areas such as human resource development in the industry, development of infrastructure & production support, marketing, strategic alliances & partnerships, & membership services
Andy Crowther, President

On Screen Manitoba
#003, 100 Albert St., Winnipeg MB R3B 1H3
Tel: 204-927-5898; *Fax:* 204-272-8792
info@onscreenmanitoba.com
www.onscreenmanitoba.com
To build & represent the motion picture industry in Manitoba; To foster excellence & innovation in the industry
Nicole Matiation, Executive Director
Trevor Suffield, Coordinator, Communications

Saskatchewan Motion Picture Industry Association (SMPIA)
1831 College Ave., 3rd Fl., Regina SK S4P 4V5
Tel: 306-525-9899; *Fax:* 306-569-1818
Toll-Free: 877-247-6742
info@smpia.sk.ca
www.smpia.sk.ca
Social Media: www.facebook.com/group.php?gid=43556252872
Committed to the intrinsic cultural & economic value of motion pictures;to work toward the creation & advancement of opportunities for the production, promotion & appreciation of motion pictures in Saskatchewan
Vanessa Bonk, Executive Director

Yukon Film Society (YFS)
4137C, 4th Ave., Whitehorse YT Y1A 1H8
Tel: 867-393-3456
yukonfilmsociety@yknet.ca
www.yukonfilmsociety.com
To present independent and alternative media art works to Yukon audiences and to support the production and distribution of works by Yukon media artists.
Mitch Miyagawa, President
Ross Burnet, General Manager

Finance

L'Alliance des Caisses populaires de l'Ontario limitée (ACPOL)
CP 3500, 1870 Bond St., North Bay ON P1B 4V6
Tél: 705-474-5634; *Téléc:* 705-474-5326
support@acpol.com
www.caissealliance.com
Lucie Moncion, Directrice générale

Association de planification fiscale et financière (APFF) / Fiscal & Financial Planning Association
#660, 1100, boul. René-Lévesque ouest, Montréal QC H3B 4N4
Tél: 514-866-2733; *Téléc:* 514-866-0113
Ligne sans frais: 877-866-0113
apff@apff.org
www.apff.org
Regrouper les personnes intéressées à la planification fiscale successorale et financière; publier et diffuser l'information dans ces domaines; favoriser la recherche
Maurice Mongrain, Chief Executive

Association des cadres municipaux de Montréal (ACMM)
2e étage, 281, rue St-Paul, Montréal QC H2Y 1H1
Tél: 514-499-1130; *Téléc:* 514-499-1737
admin@acmm.qc.ca
www.acmm.qc.ca
A pour objet l'établissement de relations ordonnées entre l'employeur et les membres ainsi que l'étude, la défense et le développement des intérêts économiques sociaux, moraux et professionnels de ces derniers
René Boucher, Président
Normand Moussette, Directeur général

Association of Canadian Financial Corporations (ACFC) / Association des compagnies financières canadiennes
Sussex Centre, #401, 50 Burnhamthorpe Rd. West, Mississauga ON L5B 3C2
Tel: 905-949-4920; *Fax:* 905-896-9380
admin.acfc@sympatico.ca
To represent financial industry
Rita Minucci, Corporate Secretary

Association of Canadian Pension Management (ACPM) / Association canadienne des administrateurs de régimes de retraite
#304, 1255 Bay St., Toronto ON M5R 2A9
Tel: 416-964-1260; *Fax:* 416-964-0567
info@acpm.com
www.acpm.com
To act as the voice of Canada's pension industry; To foster the growth of the the national retirement income system
Christopher Brown, President
Bryan Hocking, Chief Executive Officer
Diane Bélanger, Director, Member & Stakeholder Relations
Ric Marrero, Director, Marketing & Communications
Becky J. West, Secretary, Communications

Canada's Venture Capital & Private Equity Association (CVCA) / Association canadienne du capital de risque et d'investissement (ACCR)
Heritage Bldg., MaRS Centre, #120J, 101 College St., Toronto ON M5G 1L7
Tel: 416-487-0519; *Fax:* 416-487-5899
cvca@cvca.ca
www.cvca.ca
The CVCA provides advocacy, networking, information, & professional development for venture capital & private equity professionals.
Richard M. Rémillard, Executive Director
Rick Nathan, Chair
Gregory Smith, President

Canadian Association of Insolvency & Restructuring Professionals (CAIRP) / Association canadienne des professionnels de l'insolvabilité et de la réorganisation (ACPIR)
277 Wellington St. West, Toronto ON M5V 3H2
Tel: 416-204-3242; *Fax:* 416-204-3410
info@cairp.ca
www.cairp.ca
To develop, educate, support & give value to members; To foster the provision of insolvency, business recovery service with integrity, objectivity & competence, in a manner that instils the highest degree of public trust; To advocate for a fair, transparent, & effective system of insolvency/business recovery administration throughout Canada
Mark Yakabuski, President
Bea Casey, Director, CAIRP Education Programs
Ali R. Hemani, Director, Finance & Administration
Joshua Katchen, Manager, Events

Canadian Association of Pension Supervisory Authorities (CAPSA) / Association canadienne des organismes de contrôle des régimes de retraite (ACOR)
c/o CAPSA Secretariat, PO Box 85, 5160 Yonge St., 17th Fl., Toronto ON M2N 6L9
Tel: 416-590-7081; *Fax:* 416-590-7070
capsa-acor@fsco.gov.on.ca
www.capsa-acor.org
To facilitate an efficient & effective pension regulatory system in Canada
Mario Marchand, Chair
Philip Howell, Vice-Chair
Mark Prefontaine, Vice-Chair
Christian Nordin, Manager, Policy

Canadian Association of Student Financial Aid Administrators
c/o Student Resource Centre, Grant McEwan University, PO Box 1796, Edmonton AB T5J 2P2
Tel: 780-497-4271; *Fax:* 780-497-4656
www.casfaa.ca
Represents financial aid administrators & awards officers in universities & colleges across Canada
Mark Jacober, Treasurer

Canadian Bankers Association (CBA) / Association des banquiers canadiens
PO Box 348, Stn. Commerce Court West, 199 Bay St., 30th Fl., Toronto ON M5L 1G2
Tel: 416-362-6093; *Fax:* 416-362-7705
inform@cba.ca
www.cba.ca
Social Media: twitter.com/CdnBankers
To advocate for policies that contribute to a beneficial banking system
Réjean Lévesque, Chair, Executive Council
Terry Campbell, President
Rachel Swiednicki, Manager, Media Relations

Canadian Finance & Leasing Association (CFLA) / Association canadienne de financement et de location (ACFL)
#301, 15 Toronto St., Toronto ON M5C 2E3
Tel: 416-860-1133; *Fax:* 416-860-1140
Toll-Free: 877-213-7373
info@cfla-acfl.ca
www.cfla-acfl.ca
To ensure an environment in Canada where asset-based financing, equipment & vehicle-leasing industry can be profitable
David Powell, President/CEO
Sherry Xinhua Jia-Hatheway, Director, Finance & Administration
Vanessa Foran, Director, Policy

Canadian Institute of Financial Planning (CIFPs)
#600, 3660 Hurontario St., Mississauga ON L5B 3C4
Tel: 647-723-6450; *Fax:* 647-723-6457
Toll-Free: 866-933-0233
cifps@cifps.ca
www.cifps.ca
To train & qualify advisors to become Certified Financial Planners; To represent members on matters of common interest
Keith Costello, President & Chief Executive Officer
Shirley Myers, Vice-President, Member Services & Business Development
Anthony Williams, Director, Academic Affairs
Andrew Cunningham, Manager, Information Services
Odele Burton, Corporate Secretary

Canadian Investor Relations Institute (CIRI) / Institut canadien de relations avec les investisseurs
#201, 1470 Hurontario St., Mississauga ON L5G 3H4
Tel: 905-274-1639
enquiries@ciri.org
www.ciri.org
To advance the practice of investor relations; To raise the stature of the profession in Canada; To act as the voice of investor relations professionals throughout Canada
Tom Enright, President & Chief Executive Officer
Yvette Lokker, Director, Communications & Professional Development
Karen Clutsam, Coordinator, Membership
Jennifer McInnis, Coordinator, Programming
Lisa Williams, Coordinator, Publications
Brenda McCutcheon, Bookkeeper

Canadian Payments Association (CPA) / Association canadienne des paiements (ACP)
180 Elgin St., 12th Fl., Ottawa ON K2P 2K3
Tel: 613-238-4173; *Fax:* 613-233-3385
info@cdnpay.ca
www.cdnpay.ca
To establish & operate safe & efficient national clearing & settlements systems; To facilitate the interaction of its systems with others involved in the exchange, clearing & settlement of payments; To facilitate the development of new payment methods & technologies
Janet Cosier, Chair
Ron Morrow, Deputy Chair
Guy Legault, President & Chief Executive Officer

Canadian Payroll Association (CPA) / L'Association canadienne de la paie (ACP)
#1600, 250 Bloor St. East, Toronto ON M4W 1E6
Tel: 416-487-3380; *Fax:* 416-487-3384
Toll-Free: 800-387-4693
infoline@payroll.ca; dialogue@payroll.ca (media inquiries)
www.payroll.ca
To provide payroll leadership, through advocacy & education
Patrick Culhane, President & Chief Executive Officer

Canadian Pension & Benefits Institute (CPBI) / Institut canadien de la retraite et des avantages sociaux (ICRA)
CPBI National Office, #305, 465, rue St-Jean, Montréal QC H2Y 2R6
Tel: 514-288-1222; *Fax:* 514-288-1225
info@cpbi-icra.ca; members@cpbi-icra.ca
www.cpbi-icra.ca
To provide continuing education & networking forums related to pensions, employee benefits, & investments
Peter Casquinha, CEO
Peter Buntain, Vice-Chair & Secretary
Peter Casquinha, Chief Executive Officer
Lena A. Jaoude, Manager, Marketing
Marc Tessier, Manager, Finance
Dominic Tremblay, Manager, Membership Services
Peter Buntain, Chair

Canadian Securities Institute (CSI) / L'Institut canadien des valeurs mobilières
200 Wellington St. West, 15th Fl., Toronto ON M5V 3C7
Tel: 416-364-9130; *Fax:* 416-359-0486
Toll-Free: 866-866-2601
customer_support@csi.ca; exam_scheduling@csi.ca
www.csi.ca
To enhance the knowledge of securities & financial industry professionals & promote knowledge & understanding of investing among the public
Roberta Wilton, President & Chief Executive Officer, CSI Global Education Inc.
Sandy Jespersen, Director, Marketing & Communications

Chambre de commerce Canada-Pologne
5570 Waverly Rue, Montréal QC H2T 2Y1

Credit Counselling Canada (CCC) / Conseil de Credit du Canada
Columbia Sky Train Station Bldg., #330, 435 Columbia St., New Westminster BC V3L 5N8
Tel: 604-527-8999; *Fax:* 604-527-8008
Toll-Free: 888-527-8999
contact@CreditCounsellingCanada.ca
www.creditcounsellingcanada.ca
To ensure all Canadians have access to not-for-profit credit counselling; to ensure a quality of service is provided to Canadians by member agencies; to advocate on issues relevant to money management & the wise use of credit along with public policy & legislative issues around these; to promote awareness of the existence & availability of non-profit credit counselling; to cultivate positive working relationships with stakeholders
Pat White, Executive Director

Credit Institute of Canada (CIC) / L'Institut canadien du crédit
#216C, 219 Dufferin St., Toronto ON M6K 3J1
Tel: 416-572-2615; *Fax:* 416-572-2619
Toll-Free: 888-447-3324
geninfo@creditedu.org
www.creditedu.org
Social Media: www.ncfef.com
To provide credit education for credit & financial professionals in Canada
Peter Finlay, Chair, President, & Dean
Reggie Delovtich, General Manager & Secretary
Nawshad Khadaroo, Manager, Operations, Education, & Certification
Mike MacPhee, Treasurer
Fern Bellissimo, Coordinator, Membership

Credit Union Central of Canada (CUCC) / La Centrale des caisses de crédit du Canada
Corporate Office, #500, 300 The East Mall, Toronto ON M9B 6B7
Tel: 416-232-1262; *Fax:* 416-232-9196
Toll-Free: 800-649-0222
inquiries@cucentral.com; help@cucentral.com
www.cucentral.ca
To act as the national voice for the Canadian credit union system; To facilitate the national cooperative movement; To provide services to ensure best practices are met at all credit unions; To develop opportunities for cooperative growth
David MacLean, Chair
David Phillips, President & Chief Executive Officer
Cheryl Byrne, Vice-President, Knowledge Services
Stephen Fitzpatrick, Vice-President, Finance & Operations
Brigitte Goulard, Vice-President, Policy
Gary Rogers, Vice-President, Financial Policy
Brenda O'Connor, Vice-President, General Counsel & Corporate Secretary

Fédération des caisses populaires acadiennes
Édifice Martin-J.-Légère, CP 5554, 295, boul St-Pierre ouest, Caraquet NB E1W 1B7
Tél: 506-726-4000; *Téléc:* 506-726-4001
www.acadie.com
Média social: www.facebook.com/caissespopulairesacadiennes
Améliorer la qualité de vie de ceux et celles qui y adhèrent tout en contribuant à l'autosuffisance socio-économique de la collectivité acadienne du Nouveau-Brunswick, dans le respect de son identité linguistique et ses valeurs coopératives
Camille H. Thériault, Président/Directeur général

Fédération des caisses populaires du Manitoba
#200, 605 rue Des Meurons, Winnipeg MB R2H 2R1
Tél: 204-237-8988; *Téléc:* 204-233-6405
federation@ciasse.biz
www.caisse.biz
Contribuer à l'essor économique et socio-culturel des manitobains en poursuivant le développement des services et du réseau financiers dont les avoirs sont gérés, administrés et contrôlés par des francophones
Normand Collet, President

Financial Executives International Canada (FEIC)
#1201, 170 University Ave., Toronto ON M5H 3B3
Tel: 416-366-3007; *Fax:* 416-366-3008
Toll-Free: 866-677-3007
www.feicanada.org
To promote ethical conduct in the practice of financial management; To contribute to the legal & policy making process in Canada
Karyn Brooks, Chair
Louis Marcotte, Vice-Chair
Michael Conway, National President/Chief Executive
Line Trudeau, Chief Financial Officer & Secretary
Don Comish, Director, Programs
Sydney Freeston, Coordinator, Membership

Financial Planning Standards Council (FPSC)
#902, 375 University Ave., Toronto ON M5G 2J5
Tel: 416-593-8587; *Fax:* 416-593-6903
Toll-Free: 800-305-9886
inform@fpsc.ca; communications@fpsc.ca
www.fpsc.ca
Social Media: twitter.com/FPSC_Canada
To develop, enforce, & promote competency & ethical standards in financial planning by those who have earned the designation of Certified Financial Planner (CFP)
Debbie Ammeter, Chair
James W. Kraft, Vice-Chair
Cary List, President & Chief Executive Officer
John Wickett, Senior Vice-President, Standards & Certification
Stephen Rotstein, General Counsel & Vice-President, Policy & Enforcement
Tamara Smith, Vice-President, Marketing & Consumer Affairs

Institute of Canadian Bankers (ICB) / Institut des banquiers canadiens
#400, 625, boul René-Lévesque ouest, Montréal QC H3B 1R2
Tel: 514-282-9480; *Fax:* 514-878-4260
Toll-Free: 800-361-7339
icb.info@csi.ca
www.csi.ca/icb
To provide financial services training & education, in areas such as banking, wealth management, insurance, investment, trust & management studies; To award professional designations, such as a Bachelor of Commerce degree (in partnership with Nipissing University) & a Master of Business Administration in Financial Services degree (in partnership with the University of Québec & Dalhousie University)
Marie Muldowney, Executive Director

Investment Counsel Association of Canada (ICAC) / Association des conseillers en gestion de portefeuille du Canada
#1602, 110 Yonge St., Toronto ON M5C 1T4
Tel: 416-504-1118; *Fax:* 416-504-1117
icacinfo@investmentcounsel.org
www.investmentcounsel.org
To represent the Investment Counsel and portfolio managers in Canada; To advocate high standards of unbiased portfolio management in the interest of investors
Katie Walmsley, President
Bob Hill, Chair

Investment Funds Institute of Canada (IFIC) / L'Institut des fonds d'investissement du Canada
11 King St. West, 4th Fl., Toronto ON M5H 4C7
Tel: 416-363-2150; *Fax:* 416-861-9937
Toll-Free: 866-347-1961
WebAdmin@ific.ca
www.ific.ca

To act as the voice of the investment funds industry in Canada; To enhance the integrity & growth of the Canadian mutual fund industry
Oliver Murray, Chair
Charles Sims, 1st Vice-Chair
Stéphane Langlois, President

Investment Industry Regulatory Organization of Canada (IIROC) / Organisme canadien de réglementation du commerce des valeurs mobilières (OCRCVM)
#2000, 121 King St. West, Toronto ON M5H 3T9
Tel: 416-364-6133; *Fax:* 416-364-0753
publicaffairs@iiroc.ca
www.iiroc.ca
To oversee investment dealers & trading activity on debt & equity marketplaces in Canada; To focus on regulatory & investment industry standards, protecting investors & strengthening market integrity
Susan Wolburgh Jenah, President/CEO

Investors Association of Canada (IAC)
PO Box 84, #2500, 1 Dundas St. West, Toronto ON M5G 1Z3
contact@iac.ca
www.iac.ca
To be a source of investor education
Chuck Chakrapani, Chair

Municipal Finance Officers' Association of Ontario (MFOA)
2169 Queen St. East. 2nd Fl., Toronto ON M4L 1J1
Tel: 416-362-9001; *Fax:* 416-362-9226
dan@mfoa.on.ca
www.mfoa.on.ca
To represent the interests of municipal finance officers throughout Ontario; To promote the interests of members
Dan Cowin, Executive Director
Nigel White, President
Calvin Barrett, Vice-President
Donna Herridge, Secretary
Ron Kaufman, Treasurer

Mutual Fund Dealers Association of Canada (MFDA) / Association canadienne des courtiers de fonds mutuels
#1000, 121 King St. West, Toronto ON M5H 3T9
Tel: 416-361-6332; *Toll-Free:* 888-466-6332
mfda@mfda.ca
www.mfda.ca
The Mutual Fund Dealers Association of Canada (MFDA) is the national self-regulatory organization (SRO) for the distribution side of the Canadian mutual fund industry. The MFDA is structured as a not-for-profit corporation and its Members are mutual fund dealers that are licensed with provincial securities commissions
Larry M. Waite, President & CEO
Mark T. Gordon, Executive Vice-President

Ontario Association of Credit Counselling Services (OACCS)
PO Box 189, Grimsby ON L3M 4G3
Tel: 905-945-5644; *Toll-Free:* 888-746-3328
www.indebt.org
To represent member agencies & provide them with a forum for the pursuit of common interests in order to support, strengthen & enhance not-for-profit credit counselling services; to enhance the quality & availability of not-for-profit credit counselling
Henrietta Ross, Executive Director

Pension Investment Association of Canada (PIAC) / Association canadienne des gestionnaires de fonds de retraite
39 River St., Toronto ON M5A 3P1
Tel: 416-640-0264; *Fax:* 416-646-9460
info@piacweb.org
www.piacweb.org
To promote the financial security of pension fund beneficiaries through sound investment policy & practices
Peter Waite, Executive Director

Registered Deposit Brokers Association (RDBA)
#308A, 49 High St., Barrie ON L4N 5J4
Tel: 705-730-7599; *Fax:* 705-730-0477
Toll-Free: 866-261-6263
www.rdba.ca
To represent interests of deposit clients & independent deposit brokers
Brenda Molnar, Executive Director
Brian L. Smith, President

Social Investment Organization (SIO)
184 Pearl St., 2nd Fl., Toronto ON M5H 1L5
Tel: 416-461-6042; *Fax:* 416-461-2481
info@socialinvestment.ca
www.socialinvestment.ca
To take a leadership role in coordinating the SRI agenda in Canada; to raise public awareness of SRI in Canada; to reach out to other groups interested in SRI; to provide information on SRI to our members & the public
Eugene Ellmen, Executive Director
Andrika Boshyk, Assistant Director

Women in Capital Markets (WCM) / Les femmes sur les marchés financiers
#301, 250 Consumers Rd., Toronto ON M2J 4V6
Tel: 416-502-3614; *Fax:* 416-495-8723
info@wcm.ca
www.wcm.ca
To enable capital markets professionals to reach their greatest potential for success; to advance woment within Canadian financial services
Caroline Dabau, Chair
Martha Fell, Chief Executive Officer
Cindy Gareau, Executive Director

World Lottery Association (WLA)
Montréal Office, #2000, 500, rue Sherbrooke ouest, Montréal QC H3A 3G6
Tel: 514-282-0273; *Fax:* 514-873-8999
lr@world-lotteries.org
www.world-lotteries.org
To control runaway gambling; to protect territorial integrity & promote the role of state-licensed lotteries as generators of funds for good causes
Lynne Roiter, Head

Fisheries & Fishing Industry

Association québécoise de l'industrie de la pêche (AQIP) / Québec Fish Processors Association
#860, 2600, boul Laurier, Sainte-Foy QC G1V 4W2
Tél: 418-654-1831; *Téléc:* 418-654-1376
aqip@globetrotter.net
www.quebecweb.com/aqip
Défendre les intérêts professionnels des industries québécoises de la transformation des produits marins; travailler au développement des services; aider à l'amélioration de la productivité en usines

Atlantic Canada Fish Farmers Association (ACFFA)
226 Limekiln Rd., Letang NB E5C 2A8
Tel: 506-755-3526; *Fax:* 506-755-6237
info@atlanticfishfarmers.com
atlanticfishfarmers.com
Social Media:
www.facebook.com/group.php?gid=150506105026651;
twitter.com/AtlFishFarmers
To act as the voice of Atlantic Canada's salmon farming industry; To implement fish health initiatives to produce high-quality finfish
Pamela Parker, Executive Director
Sybil Smith, Director, Operations
Betty House, Coordinator, Research & Development
Jim Hanley, Manager, Wharf

Atlantic Fishing Industry Alliance
38B John St., Yarmouth NS B5A 3H5
Tel: 902-446-4477
To represent organizations in the harvesting, processing and marketing sectors of the commercial fishing industry in the Maritime Provinces.

Atlantic Salmon Federation (ASF) / Fédération du saumon atlantique
PO Box 5200, St Andrews NB E5B 3S8
Tel: 506-529-4581; *Fax:* 506-529-4438
savesalmon@asf.ca
www.asf.ca
To protect, conserve, & restore wild Atlantic salmon & their ecosystems
Bill Taylor, President & Chief Executive Officer
Todd Dupuis, Executive Director, Regional Programs
Jonathan Carr, Director, Research & Environment
Bill Mallory, Executive Vice-President & CFO
Rob Beatty, Vice-President, Development
Sue Ann Scott, Vice-President, Communications
Muriel Ferguson, Manager, Public Information
Martin Silverstone, Editor, Atlantic Salmon Journal

British Columbia Salmon Farmers Association (BCSFA)
#302, 871 Island Hwy., Campbell River BC V9W 2C2
Tel: 250-286-1636; *Fax:* 250-286-1574
Toll-Free: 800-661-7256
info@salmonfarmers.org
www.salmonfarmers.org
To promote the interests of persons, firms & corporations growing & selling farmed salmon in BC
Mary Ellen Walling, Executive Director

British Columbia Seafood Alliance (BCSA)
#1100, 1200 West 73rd Ave., Vancouver BC V6P 6G5
Tel: 604-377-9213; *Fax:* 604-683-4510
cburridge@telus.net
www.bcseafoodalliance.com
To represent the interests & values of a majority of BC's seafood industries to the federal & provincial governments & to the general public; to promote the conservation & environmentally sustainable use & production of seafood resources in BC; to foster an economically viable & internationally competitive seafood industry
Christina Burridge, Executive Director
Gina Johansen, Safety and Assistance

British Columbia Shellfish Growers Association (BCSGA)
2002 Comox Ave., Unit F, Comox BC V9M 3M6
Tel: 250-890-7561; *Fax:* 250-890-7563
roberta@bcsga.ca
www.bcsga.ca
Advancing the sustainable growth & prosperity of the BC shellfish industry in a global economy by providing leadership & advocacy to members & stakeholders while maintaining the integrity of the marine environment
Roberta Stevenson, Executive Director

Canadian Aquaculture Industry Alliance (CAIA) / Alliance de l'industrie canadienne de l'aquiculture
PO Box 81100, Stn. World Exchange Plaza, #705, 116 Albert St., Ottawa ON K1P 1B1
Tel: 613-239-0612; *Fax:* 613-239-0619
info@aquaculture.ca
www.aquaculture.ca
To represent the interests of aquaculture operators, feed companies, suppliers, & provincial finfish & shellfish aquaculture associations on both the national & international scenes; To ensure the international competitiveness of the Canadian aquaculture industry
Ruth Salmon, Executive Director
Sherry Sadler, Coordinator, Projects

Canadian Centre for Fisheries Innovation (CCFI) / Centre canadien d'innovations des pêches
PO Box 4920, Stn. C, Ridge Rd., St. John's NL A1C 5R3
Tel: 709-778-0517; *Fax:* 709-778-0516
ccfi@mi.mun.ca
www.ccfi.ca
To work with the fishing industry to improve productivity & profitability of fishery through science & technology
Robert Verge, Managing Director
Gabe Gregory, Chair

Canadian Council of Professional Fish Harvesters (CCPFH) / Conseil canadien des pêcheurs professionnels (CCPP)
#712, 1 Nicholas St., Ottawa ON K1N 7B7
Tel: 613-235-3474; *Fax:* 613-231-4313
www.ccpfh-ccpp.org
To represent the interests of professional fish harvesters across Canada in their dealings with the federal, provincial & territorial governments on national issues of common concern; To provide organizational structure & leadership for the development of a program of professionalization for fish harvesters in collaboration with the organizations representing professional fishers across Canada; To act as a national industry sector council to plan & implement training & adjustment programs for the fish harvesting industry in Canada
John Sutcliffe, Executive Director
Earle McCurdy, President
Dan Edwards, Vice-President
Ronnie Heighton, Vice-President
Daniel Landry, Secretary
O'Neil Cloutier, Treasurer

Environment Resources Managament Association
PO Box 857, Grand Falls-Windsor NL A2A 2P7
Tel: 709-489-7350
www.exploitsriver.ca/association.php
To promote the development of the Exploits River as a major Atlantic Salmon producing river.

Fisheries Council of Canada (FCC)
#900, 170 Laurier Ave. West, Ottawa ON K1P 5V5
Tel: 613-727-7450; *Fax:* 613-727-7453
info@fisheriescouncil.org
www.fisheriescouncil.ca
To represent Canada's fish & seafood industry
Patrick McGuinness, President
Patrick McGuinness, President

Fisheries Council of Canada - British Columbia Representative
4214 - 199A St., Langley BC V3A 4V6
Tel: 604-530-7258; *Fax:* 604-530-2015
gjconsult@telus.net
Patrick McGuinness, President

Fishermen and Scientists Research Society (FSRS)
PO Box 25125, Halifax NS B3M 4H4
Tel: 902-876-1160; *Fax:* 902-876-1320
www.fsrs.ns.ca
To establish and maintain a network of fishermen and scientific personnel that are concerned with the long-term sustainability of the marine fishing industry in the Atlantic Region.
Patricia King, General Manager

Guysborough County Inshore Fishermen's Association (GCIFA)
PO Box 98, 990 Union St., Canso NS B0H 1H0
Tel: 902-366-2266; *Fax:* 902-366-2679
gcifa@gcifa.ns.ca
www.gcifa.ns.ca
To provide community based management of the fishing resource and to ensure a sustainable resource fishery and habitat, healthy fish stocks and act as an information liaison between inshore fishermen and the Dept. of Fisheries, as well as provide effective representation within the industry and other associations.
Eugene O'Leary, President

International Pacific Halibut Commission (IPHC)
#300, 2320 West Commodore Way, Seattle WA 98199 USA
Tel: 206-634-1838; *Fax:* 206-632-2983
www.iphc.int
Mandated to research and manage Pacific halibut stocks, within the Convention waters of the U.S. and Canada.
Bruce M. Leaman, Executive Director
Larry Johnson, Canadian Commissioner
Laura Richards, Canadian Commissioner
Gary Robinson, Canadian Commissioner
James Balsiger, US Commissioner
Ralph Hoard, US Commissioner
Phillip Lestenkof, US Commissioner

North Atlantic Salmon Conservation Organization (NASCO)
11 Rutland Sq., Edinburgh EH1 2AS United Kingdom
hq@nasco.int
www.nasco.int
To promote the conservation, restoration, enhancement & rational management of salmon stocks in North Atlantic
A. Isaksson, President, (NASCO Council, Iceland)
Malcolm Windsor, Secretary
Peter Hutchinson, Assistant Secretary

North Pacific Anadromous Fish Commission (NPAFC)
#502, 889 West Pender St., Vancouver BC V6C 3B2
Tel: 604-775-5550; *Fax:* 604-775-5577
secretariat@npafc.org
www.npafc.org
To promote the conservation of anadromous stocks in the North Pacific Ocean
Vladimir Fedorenko, Executive Director
Suam Kim, President, (Korea)
Guy Beaupré, Canadian Representative

Nova Scotia Salmon Association (NSSA)
PO Box 396, Chester NS B0J 1J0
nssalmo@yahoo.ca
www.novascotiasalmon.ns.ca
To further the conservation & wise management of wild Atlantic salmon & trout
Carl Purcell, President

Prince Edward Island Fishermen's Association (PEIFA)
#102, 420 University Ave., Charlottetown PE C1A 7Z5
Tel: 902-566-4050; *Fax:* 902-368-3748
adminpeifa@pei.eastlink.ca; researchpeifa@pei.eastlink.ca
www.peifa.org
To represent fishermen across Prince Edward Island; To act as a single, united voice on behalf of Island fishers on industry issues
Michael McGeoghegan, President
Ed Frenette, Manager

Seafood Producers Association of Nova Scotia
Queen Square, PO Box 991, #1801, 45 Alderney Dr., Dartmouth NS B2Y 3Z6
Tel: 902-463-7790; *Fax:* 902-469-8294
spans@ns.sympatico.ca
Roger C. Stirling, President

Food & Beverage Industry

Association des brasseurs du Québec (ABQ) / Québec Brewers Association
#888, 2000, rue Peel, Montréal QC H3A 2W5
Tél: 514-284-9199; *Téléc:* 514-284-0817
Ligne sans frais: 800-854-9199
asbq@brasseurs.qc.ca
brasseurs.qc.ca
Philippe Batani, Directeur général

Association of Canadian Biscuit Manufacturers (ACBM) / Association canadienne des manufacturiers de biscuits
#301, 885 Don Mills Rd., Toronto ON M3C 1V9
Tel: 416-510-8036; *Fax:* 416-510-8043
To effectively represent common interests & concerns of member companies who manufacture biscuits in Canada by providing a forum to exchange information & resolve issues; to establish & maintain systems sufficient to ensure early consultation & effective representation in areas of government policy & regulation which affect members' interests; to promote a balanced view of the industry's role, performance & motives; to act as a credible source of information & assistance to the biscuit industry, as a forum for developing consensus positions on issues where an industry position may usefully & legally be established; to develop an effective organization plan including structure, staff membership & finances
Ileana Lima, Executive Director

Association of Canadian Distillers (ACD) / Association des distillateurs canadiens
#704, 255 Albert St., Ottawa ON K1P 6A9
Tel: 613-238-8444
info@acd.ca
www.acd.ca
To protect & advance the interests of its members; To promote & protect, both nationally & internationally, the well-being & viability of the Canadian distilling industry; To foster responsible attitudes toward the consumption of distilled spirits (gin, vodka, rum, Canadian Whisky) in Canada; To aggressively pursue & enhance the recognition of the name & positive reputation of Canadian Whisky as Canada's unique appellation distilled spirits product; To preserve & protect the integrity & standards of all distilled products

Atlantic Food & Beverage Processors Association
500 St. George St., Moncton NB E1C 1Y3
Tel: 506-389-7892; *Fax:* 506-854-5850
info@atlanticfood.ca
www.atlanticfood.ca
To actively support the food processors in the region in their efforts to operate efficiently and profitably.
Don Newman, Executive Director

Breakfast Cereal Manufacturers of Canada (BCMC)
#301, 885 Don Mills Rd., Toronto ON M3C 1V9
Tel: 416-510-8036; *Fax:* 416-510-8044
ileanal@fcpmc.com
To provide a forum for members to review issues of significance to the breakfast industry; to represent industry with government
Kathleen Kennedy, Manager

Brewers Association of Canada / L'Association des brasseurs du Canada
#650, 100 Queen St., Ottawa ON K1P 1J9
Tel: 613-232-9601; *Fax:* 613-232-2283
info@brewers.ca
www.brewers.ca
To represent brewing companies operating in Canada; To collect information & statistics about the brewing industry; To provide information about the industry to the public
Ian Faris, President & Chief Executive Officer
André Forin, Director, Public Affairs
Edwin P. Gregory, Director, Policy & Research
Linda Andrusek, Manager, Administrative Services
Peter A.B. MacPhail, Accountant

Brewing & Malting Barley Research Institute (BMBRI) / Institut de recherche - brassage et orge de maltage
#1510, One Lombard Pl., Winnipeg MB R3B 0X3
Tel: 204-927-1407; *Fax:* 204-947-5960
info@bmbri.ca
www.bmbri.ca
Supporting the development & evaluation of new malting barley varieties in Canada
Michael Brophy, President & CEO
R. Chappell, Chair

Canadian Agencies Practicing Marketing Activation (CAPMA)
#107, 1 Eva Rd., Toronto ON M9C 4Z5
info@capma.org
www.capma.org
To raise the profile of the industry
Christine Ross, Executive Director
Mike Armstrong, President
Matthew Diamond, Vice-President
Chad Grenier, Secretary
Rick Takamatsu, Treasurer

Canadian Association of Foodservice Professionals (CAFP)
#130, 10691 Shellbridge Way, Richmond BC V6X 2W8
Tel: 604-248-0215; *Fax:* 604-270-3644
Toll-Free: 877-599-2237
national@cafp.com
www.cafp.com
Social Media: twitter.com/wearecafp
To enhance the prestige of the food service profession through improving standards of service; To promote education in the industry & to provide increased opportunity for youth to train for the food service profession; to promote research in food service & nutrition; To work for food service regulation & legislation in the public interest; To promote through good fellowship & personal association new opportunities for increased management efficiency & exchange of professional information
Carol Schell, National President
David Savage, Secretary-Treasurer
Allison Miner, Contact

Canadian Bottled Water Association (CBWA) / Association canadienne des embouteilleurs d'eau
#203-1, 70 East Beaver Creek Rd., Richmond Hill ON L4B 3B2
Tel: 905-886-6928; *Fax:* 905-886-9531
info@cbwa.ca
www.cbwa.ca
To represent the Canadian bottled water industry; To ensure a high standard of quality for bottled water
Elizabeth Griswold, Executive Director

Canadian College & University Food Service Association (CCUFSA)
c/o Drew Hall, University of Guelph, Gordon St., Guelph ON N1G 2W1
Tel: 519-824-4120; *Fax:* 519-837-9302
mcollins@hrs.uoguelph.ca
www.ccufsa.on.ca
To enhance the quality of campus life through the growth & development of food service operations in colleges & universities
Lee Elkas, President
David Boeckner, Executive Director
Gerard Hayes, Secretary-Treasurer

Canadian Council of Grocery Distributors (CCGD) / Conseil canadien de la distribution alimentaire (CCDA)
#402, 6455, rue Jean-Talon est, Montréal QC H1S 3E8
Tel: 514-982-0267
www.ccgd.ca
To advance & promote the Canadian grocery & foodservice distribution industry at regional & national levels; To act as the voice for the grocery industry in Canada, on policies such as labour laws, & environment initiatives
Andrew Walker, Chair
Nick Jennery, President & Chief Executive Officer
Win MacIntyre, Secretary-Treasurer
Cathy Gell, Contact, Communications

Canadian Federation of Independent Grocers (CFIG) / Fédération canadienne des épiciers indépendants
#902, 2235 Sheppard Ave. East, Toronto ON M2J 5B5
Tel: 416-492-2311; *Fax:* 416-492-2347
Toll-Free: 800-661-2344
info@cfig.ca; membership@cfig.ca; events@cfig.ca
www.cfig.ca
Social Media: www.facebook.com/CFIGFCEI; twitter.com/cfigfcei

To equip & enable independent, franchised, & specialty grocers for sustainable success; To act as a united voice for independent grocers across Canada
Francois Bouchard, Chair
John F.T. Scott, President & Chief Executive Officer
Ward Hanlon, Vice-President, Industry Relations
Fran Nielsen, Vice-President, Finance & Administration
Gary Sands, Vice-President, Government Relations
Sacha Lalla, Director, Member Services
Eden Minty, Director, Events
Irina Costachescu, Tradeshow Operations Manager, Expositions
Dan Leggieri, Manager, Communications
Rolster Taylor, Tradeshow Manager, Sales

Canadian Health Food Association (CHFA) / Association canadienne des aliments de santé
#302, 235 Yorkland Blvd., Toronto ON M2J 4Y8
Tel: 416-497-6939; *Fax:* 905-479-3214
Toll-Free: 800-661-4510
info@chfa.ca
www.chfa.ca
Social Media: www.facebook.com/group.php?gid=12940324924
To act as the voice of the natural products industry; To promote natural & organic products as an integral part of health & well-being; To ensure the growth of the natural & organic industry
Deborah Callbreath, Chair
Natalie Cajic, Specialist, Communications

Canadian Meat Council (CMC) / Conseil des viandes du Canada
#407, 1545 Carling Ave., Ottawa ON K1Z 8P9
Tel: 613-729-3911; *Fax:* 613-729-4997
info@cmc-cvc.com
www.cmc-cvc.com
To express the views of the membership with government, all elements of the food industry, consumer organizations, the research & academic community, & the media; To foster high standards of industry integrity, & a vast range of wholesome, nutritional meat products
James M. Laws, Executive Director
Ray Price, First Vice President-Treasurer

Canadian Meat Science Association (CMSA) / Association scientifique canadienne de la viande (ASCB)
Dept. of Agricultural, Food & Nutritional Science, Univ. of Alberta, #4-10, Agriculture / Forestry Centre, Edmonton AB T6G 2P5
Tel: 780-492-3651; *Fax:* 780-492-5771
ruth.ball@ales.ualberta.ca
www.cmsa-ascv.ca
To promote the application of science & technology to the production, processing, packaging, distribution, preparation, evaluation, & utilization of all meat & meat products; To develop & promote useful, coordinated research, educational techniques, & service activities
Peter Purslow, President
Sandra Gruber, President-Elect
Manuel Juárez, Sec.-Treas.
Sylvain Fournaise, Director at Large

Canadian National Millers Association (CNMA)
#200, 265 Carling Ave., Ottawa ON K1S 2E1
Tel: 613-238-2293; *Fax:* 613-235-5866
dwiggins@canadianmillers.ca
www.canadianmillers.ca
To serve as a vehicle for consultation between the milling industry, government departments & agencies; to promote regulatory & public policy environment that enhances international competitiveness; to provide international trade development to the industry; to disseminate information about the industry & Canadian wheat flour quality; to work directly & in cooperation with the trade offices abroad
Gordon Harrison, President
Donna Wiggins, Director, Administration

Canadian Produce Marketing Association (CPMA) / Association canadienne de la distribution de fruits et légumes
162 Cleopatra Dr., Ottawa ON K2G 5X2
Tel: 613-226-4187; *Fax:* 613-226-2984
question@cpma.ca
www.cpma.ca
To increase the market for fresh fruits & vegetables in Canada, by encouraging cooperation & information exchange in all segments, at the domestic & international level
Dan Dempster, President

Canadian Snack Food Association (CSFA) / Association canadienne des fabricants des grignotines
c/o Ileana Lima, PO Box 42252, 128 Queen St. South, Mississauga ON L5M 4Z0
Tel: 289-997-1379
ileanal@4reflections.com
canadiansnack.com
To provide the leadership required for sustained growth & competitiveness of the industry; to influence policy formulation, legislation & regulations at all levels of government in the best interests of the industry
Calum MacLeod, President
Ileana Lima, Contact

Canadian Sugar Institute (CSI) / Institut canadien du sucre
Water Park Pl., #620, 10 Bay St., Toronto ON M5J 2R8
Tel: 416-368-8091; *Fax:* 416-368-6426
info@sugar.ca
www.sugar.ca
Sandra Marsden, President
Tristin Brisbois, Manager, Nutrition & Scientific Affairs

Canadian Vintners Association (CVA) / L'Association des vignerons du Canada
#200, 440 Laurier Ave. West, Ottawa ON K1R 7X6
Tel: 613-782-2283; *Fax:* 613-782-2239
info@canadianvintners.com
www.canadianvintners.com
To formulate & promote policies that will advance the interests & goals of the Canadian wine sector.
Paul-André Bosc, President

Coffee Association of Canada (CAC) / Association du café du Canada
#301, 885 Don Mills Rd., Toronto ON M3C 1V9
Tel: 416-510-8032; *Fax:* 416-510-8044
info@coffeeassoc.com
www.coffeeassoc.com
Dedicated to addressing industry-wide issues on behalf of our members, keeping them fully informed, & allowing them to focus on the proprietary concerns of building their businesses
Sandy McAlpine, President

Confectionery Manufacturers Association of Canada (CMAC) / Association canadienne des fabricants de confiseries
#301, 885 Don Mills Rd., Toronto ON M3C 1V9
Tel: 416-510-8034; *Fax:* 416-510-8043
info@cmaconline.ca
www.confectioncanada.com
To increase confectionery consumption & production; to achieve global competitiveness; to grow confectionery consumption in a responsible manner as an enjoyable food that is part of a healthy, active lifestyle.
John Rowsome, President
Pat Gagne, Executive Assistant

Conseil de la transformation agroalimentaire et des produits de consommation (CTAC) / Council of Food Processing & Consumer Products
#102, 200, rue MacDonald, Saint-Jean-sur-Richelieu QC J3B 8J6
Tél: 450-349-1521; *Téléc:* 450-349-6923
info@conseiltac.com
www.conseiltac.com
Média social: www.linkedin.com/company/1237456
Le porte-parole officiel des manufacturiers de produits alimentaires du Québec qui s'y regroupent à titre de membres fabricants; canalise les représentations des manufacturiers, en particulier auprès des gouvernements; coordonne l'action des membres en vue de promouvoir leurs intérêts économiques, sociaux et professionnels; suscite l'éducation des consommateurs sur les valeurs d'une bonne alimentation; favorise la promotion des produits fabriqués par les membres; établit des liaisons entre les manufacturiers, les producteurs, les fournisseurs, les distributeurs, les consommateurs et les autres maillons de la chaîne alimentaire; encourage la recherche dans les domaines de l'agriculture, de l'alimentation et du marketing
Sylvie Cloutier, Présidente-directrice générale

Flavour Manufacturers Association of Canada (FMAC) / Association canadienne de fabricants des arômes
#301, 885 Don Mills Rd., Toronto ON M3C 1V9
Tel: 416-510-8036; *Fax:* 416-510-8044
ileanal@fcpmc.com
To serve the needs of the Canadian flavour industry by providing a forum for the examination of industry problems, assisting in the implementation of solutions, & fostering a global perspective for creativity, innovation & competition.
Ileana Lima, Administrator

Food & Consumer Products of Canada (FCPC) / Produits alimentaires et de consommation du Canada (PACC)
100 Sheppard Ave E., Toronto ON m2n 6Z1
Tel: 416-510-8024; *Fax:* 416-510-8043
info@fcpc.ca
www.fcpc.ca
To represent the food & consumer products industry, from small privately-owned companies to big glboal multinationals
Nancy Croitoru, President & Chief Executive Officer
Kathleen Kennedy, Vice-President, Finance & Administration
Lesley McKeever, Senior Vice-President, Industry Affairs & Membership
Errol Cerit, Senior Director, Industry Affairs
Rachel Kagan, Senior Director, Environment & Sustainability Policy
Janice Emery-Carter, Manager, Education Centre
Linda Saunby, Coordinator, Public Affairs
Heather Spencer, Coordinator, Member Services
Jami Nirenberg, Coordinator, Events

Food Processors of Canada (FPC) / Fabricants de produits alimentaires du Canada
#900, 350 Sparks St., Ottawa ON K1R 7S8
Tel: 613-722-1000; *Fax:* 613-722-1404
fpc@foodprocessors.ca; conferences@foodprocessors.ca
www.foodnet.fic.ca
To provide professional services & advice to members on matters such as manufacturing, trade, & commerce
Christopher J. Kyte, President
Mel Fruitman, Vice-President

New Brunswick Maple Syrup Association (NBMSA)
#223, 1350 Regent St., Fredericton NB E3C 2G6
Tel: 506-458-8889; *Fax:* 506-454-0652
yrp@nb.aibn.com
www.maple.infor.ca
The New Brunswick Maple Syrup Association (NBMSA) is a non-profit organization, dedicated to representing the interests of its members, and facilitating the industry through advertisement and the constant improvement of quality and standards by collaborating with various organizations towards the enrichment of the ever-growing maple industry.
Yvon Poitras, General Manager

Ontario Coffee & Vending Service Association (OCVSA)
#301, 885 Don Mills Rd., Toronto ON M3C 1V9
Tel: 416-510-8032; *Fax:* 416-510-8044
info@coffeeassoc.com
www.coffeeassoc.com/ocvsa.htm

Ontario Independent Meat Processors (OIMP)
7660 Mill Rd., RR 4, Guelph ON N1H 6J1
Tel: 519-763-4558; *Fax:* 519-763-4164
www.oimp.ca
To support & foster a safe & wholesome meat & poultry industry, maintaining viability & high quality through ongoing education, research & representation at all levels of government
Joe Abate, President
Laurie Nicol, Executive Director

Pet Food Association of Canada (PFAC) / Association des fabricants d'aliments pour animaux familiers du Canada
PO Box 35570, 2528 Bayview Ave., Toronto ON M2L 2Y4
Tel: 416-447-9970; *Fax:* 416-443-9137
info@pfac.com
www.pfac.com
To provide association members with a unified voice on issues that affect the pet food industry in Canada

Refreshments Canada / Association canadienne de l'industrie des boissons gazeuses
20 Bay St., 12th Fl., Toronto ON M5J 2N8
Tel: 416-362-2424; *Fax:* 416-362-3229
info@refreshments.ca
www.refreshments.ca
To represent soft drink bottlers, distributors, franchise houses & industry suppliers on a variety of issues
Justin Sherwood, President
Anthony Van Heyningen, Senior Director, Research & Policy
Stephanie Baxter, Senior Director, Communications

Tea Association of Canada (TAC) / Association du thé du Canada
#602, 133 Richmond St. West, Toronto ON M5H 2L3
Tel: 416-510-8647; *Fax:* 416-510-8044
info@tea.ca
www.tea.ca

To represent & advance the interests of Canada's tea industry to all levels of government in an effort to improve the conditions under which the industry operates & to promote better business relations between the industry's players
Louise Roberge, President

Wine Council of Ontario
PO Box 4000, 4890 Victoria Ave. North, Vineland ON L0R 2E0
Tel: 905-684-8070; *Fax:* 905-562-1993
info@winesofontario.org
winecountryontario.ca
Social Media: www.facebook.com/WineCountryOntario; twitter.com/winecountryont
A non-profit trade association which plays a leadership role in the marketing, promotion, and future directions of the Ontario wine industry
Magdalena Kaiser-Smit, Director, Public Relations, Marketing & Tourism

Yukon Food Processors Association (YFPA)
PO Box 20437, Whitehorse YT Y1A 7A2
Tel: 867-393-3189
processors.yukonfood.com
To represent the food processing industry in the Yukon Territory.
Michell Spittal, President

Forestry & Forest Products

Alberta Forest Products Association (AFPA)
#500, 10709 Jasper Ave., Edmonton AB T5J 3N3
Tel: 780-452-2841; *Fax:* 780-455-0505
info@albertforestproducts.ca
www.albertaforestproducts.ca
To represent companies that manufacture forest products throughout Alberta
Neil Shelly, Executive Director
Brady Whittaker, President & Chief Executive Officer
Norm Dupuis, Director, Grade Bureau
Brock Mulligan, Director, Communications
Keith Murray, Director, Policy & Regulation
Carola von Sass, Director, Health & Safety

Association of British Columbia Forest Professionals (ABCFP)
#330 - 321 Water St., Vancouver BC V6B 1B8
Tel: 604-687-8027; *Fax:* 604-687-3264
info@abcfp.ca
www.abcfp.ca
Social Media: www.facebook.com/79659811198; twitter.com/abcfp
To protect the public interest in the practice of professional forestry by ensuring the competence, independence & integrity of its members; to ensure that every person practising professional forestry is accountable to the association & to the public
Sharon Glover, Chief Executive Officer

Association of Registered Professional Foresters of New Brunswick (ARPFNB) / Association des forestiers agréés du Nouveau-Brunswick (AFANB)
#221, 1350 Regent St., Fredericton NB E3C 2G6
Tel: 506-452-6933; *Fax:* 506-450-3128
info@arpfnb.ca
www.arpfnb.ca
To manage the forest resources of New Brunswick for the sustained development of these resources; To assure the proficiency & competency of Registered Professional Foresters in New Brunswick
Jennifer Hacking, Executive Director
Doug Prosser, President
John Kershaw, Vice-President
Edwin Swift, Secretary-Treasurer

Canadian Forestry Association (CFA) / Association forestière canadienne
1027 Pembroke St. East, Pembroke ON K8A 3M4
Tel: 613-732-2917; *Fax:* 613-732-3386
Toll-Free: 866-441-4006
teachingkits@canadianforestry.com
www.canadianforestry.com
To advocate for the wise use & protection of Canada's forest, water, & wildlife resources; To nurture economic & environmental health, through the management & conservation of forest resources; To provide a national voice for provincial forestry agencies
Barry Waito, Chair
Kathy Abusow, President & Chief Executive Officer

Canadian Forestry Association of New Brunswick (CFANB) / Association forestière canadienne du Nouveau-Brunswick (AFCNB)
#248, 1350 Regent St., Fredericton NB E3C 2G6
Tel: 506-452-1339; *Fax:* 506-452-7950
Toll-Free: 866-405-7000
info@cfanb.ca
www.cfanb.ca
To champions trees & forests of New Brunswick; To promote environmental, commercial, recreational, & inspirational benefits; To encourages conservation & wise use of natural resources
Christopher Dickie, President
Valerie Archibald, Associate Director
Jennifer Geneau, Secretary
Jamie Morrison, Treasurer

Canadian Hardwood Plywood & Veneer Association (CHPVA) / Association canadienne du Contreplaqué et de Placages de bois dur (ACCPBD)
47, rue de Richelieu, Chambly QC J3L 2C3
Tel: 514-733-2777; *Fax:* 514-733-2777
michel.tremblay2@bellnet.ca
www.chpva.ca
To protect the interests & conserve the rights of those involved in the manufacture & distribution of hardwood veneer & plywood & their suppliers in Canada.
Michel G. Tremblay, Executive vice-president
Céline Brisebois, Coordinator

Canadian Institute of Forestry / Institut forestier du Canada
c/o The Canadian Ecology Centre, PO Box 430, 6905 Hwy. 17 West, Mattawa ON P0H 1V0
Tel: 705-744-1715; *Fax:* 705-744-1716
admin@cif-ifc.org; questions@cif-ifc.org
www.cif-ifc.org
Social Media: www.facebook.com/groups/53806339292; www.youtube.com/user/CIFtube
To act as the national voice of forest practitioners
John Pineau, Executive Director
Mark Kube, President
Michel Vallée, Vice-President
Brian Haddon, Research Editor, The Forestry Chronicle

Canadian Lumber Standards Accreditation Board (CLSAB)
#102, 28 Deakin St., Ottawa ON K2E 8B7
Tel: 613-482-2480; *Fax:* 613-482-6044
info@clsab.ca
www.clsab.ca
Alphonse Caouette, Chair
Chuck Dentelbeck, Secretary-Treasurer

Canadian Pallet Council (CPC) / Conseil des palettes du Canada
239 Division St., Cobourg ON K9A 3P9
Tel: 905-372-1871; *Fax:* 905-373-0230
info@cpcpallet.com
www.cpcpallet.com
Belinda Junkin, President/CEO

Canadian Plywood Association
735 - 15 St. West, North Vancouver BC V7M 1T2
Tel: 604-981-4190; *Fax:* 604-985-0342
info@canply.org
www.canply.org
Canadian plywood organization.
Judy White, Office Manager
James F. Shaw, President

Canadian Pulp & Paper Network for Innovation in Education & Research (PAPIER) / Réseau canadien de pâtes et papiers pour l'innovation en éducation et en recherche
2385 East Mall, Vancouver BC V6T 1Z4
Tel: 604-822-8561; *Fax:* 604-822-8563
www.papiernet.ca
To act as the voice of Canadian university faculty involved in teaching & research for the pulp & paper industry
Patrice Mangin, Chair
Richard Kerekes, Director

Canadian Well Logging Society (CWLS)
Scotia Centre, #2200, 700 - 2nd St. SW, Calgary AB T2P 2W1
Tel: 403-269-9366; *Fax:* 403-269-2787
www.cwls.org
Mike Seifert, Membership Chair
Harold S. Hovdebo, President

Canadian Wood Council (CWC) / Conseil canadien du bois (CCB)
#400, 99 Bank St., Ottawa ON K1P 6B9
Tel: 613-747-5544; *Fax:* 613-747-6264
www.cwc.ca
To represent Canadian manufacturers of wood products; To insure market access for wood products; To communicate technical information; To organize educational programs for students & construction professionals
Michael Giroux, President
Helen Griffin, Vice-President, Codes & Engineering
Étienne Lalonde, Vice-President, Market Development
Ioana Lazea, Manager, Events
Natalie Tarini, Manager, Communications

Canadian Wood Pallet & Container Association (CWPCA) / Association canadienne des manufacturiers de palettes et contenants (ACMPC)
#11, 1884 Merivale Rd., Ottawa ON K2G 1E6
Tel: 613-521-6468; *Fax:* 613-521-1835
Toll-Free: 877-224-3555
info@canadianpallets.com
www.canadianpallets.com
Social Media: twitter.com/canadianpallets
To promote the general welfare of the wooden pallet & container manufacturing industry; to improve services directly or otherwise; to cooperate with officers of government & business in any program considered essential to the national welfare or economy; to engage in any other lawful activities & enjoy powers, rights & privileges granted or conferred upon associations of a similar nature.
Bill Eggertson, Executive Director
Lori Devlin, Director, Member Services
Stephanie Poirier, CWPCP
Blair McEwen, President

Canadian Wood Preservers Bureau (WPC) / Préservation du bois Canada
#202, 2141 Thurston Dr., Ottawa ON K1G 6C9
Tel: 613-737-4337; *Fax:* 613-247-0540
info@woodpreservation.ca
www.woodpreservation.ca
To provide a quality assurance program for the treated wood industry
Henry Walthert, Executive Director

Christmas Tree Farmers of Ontario (CFTO)
#1, 9251 County Rd., Palgrave ON L0N 1P0
Fax: 905-729-0548
Toll-Free: 800-661-3530
ctfo@christmastrees.on.ca
www.christmastrees.on.ca
CFTO is an association devoted to farmers who specialize in Christmas tree growing.
Shirley Brennan, Executive Director

College of Alberta Professional Foresters
#209, 10544 - 106 St., Edmonton AB T5H 2X6
Tel: 780-432-1177; *Fax:* 780-432-7046
office@capf.ca
www.capf.ca
To maintain an accurate register of registered professional foresters in Alberta; To set standards of professional conduct & competence for members; To administer the title, Registered Professional Forester (RPF)
Ted Gooding, President

Conseil de l'industrie forestière du Québec (CIFQ) / Québec Forestry Industry Council (QFIC)
#200, 1175, av Lavigerie, Sainte-Foy QC G1V 4P1
Tél: 418-657-7916; *Téléc:* 418-657-7971
info@cifq.qc.ca
www.cifq.qc.ca
Représente la très grande majorité des entreprises de sciage résineux, de pâtes, papiers, cartons et panneaux oeuvrant au Québec; se consacre à la défense des intérêts de ces entreprsies, à la promotion de leur contribution au développement socio-économique, à la gestion intégrée et à l'aménagement durable des forêts, de même qu'à l'utilisation optimale des ressources naturelles; oeuvre auprès des instances gouvernementales, des organismes publics et parapublics, des organisations et de la population; encourage un comportement responsable de ses membres en regard des dimensions environnementales, économiques et sociales de leurs activités.
Claude Perron, Président-directeur général

Consulting Foresters of British Columbia
PO Box 98, Pender Island BC V0N 2M0
Tel: 250-656-8818
info@cfbc.bc.ca
www.cfbc.bc.ca

To maintain high professional standards in forestry consulting; To advance contact between its members, client groups, & the public at large
Robert Schuetz, President
Stan Price, Vice-President

Council of Forest Industries (COFI)
Pender Place I Business Building, #1501, 700 Pender St. West, Vancouver BC V6C 1G8
Tel: 604-684-0211; *Fax:* 604-687-4930
info@cofi.org
www.cofi.org
To be the voice of the British Columbia interior forest industry; To offer member companies services in areas such as international market & trade development, community relations, public affairs, quality control, & forest policy
Ken Higginbotham, Chair
John Allan, President & Chief Executive Officer
Paul J. Newman, Executive Director, Market Access & Trade
Doug Routledge, Vice-President, Forestry & Northern Operations
Anne Mauch, Director, Regulatory Issues

La Fédération des producteurs de bois du Québec (FPBQ)
#565, 555, boul Roland-Therrien, Longueuil QC J4H 4E7
Tél: 450-679-0530; *Téléc:* 450-679-4300
bois@upa.qc.ca
www.fpbq.qc.ca
Défendre les intérêts de l'ensemble des propriétaires de boisés du Québec ainsi que l'élaboration et la promotion des politiques souhaitables et nécessaires pour atteindre cet objectif; représenter les propriétaires de boisés privés auprès des pouvoirs publics et des autres groupes de la société au niveau provincial et national; coordonner l'ensemble des activités des Syndicats et Offices de producteurs de bois ainsi que l'établissement, le maintien et le développement entre eux d'une étroite collaboration
Marc-André Côté, Directeur

For Ed BC
#213, 4438 - 10th Ave. West, Vancouver BC V6R 4R8
Tel: 604-737-8555; *Fax:* 604-737-8598
info@foredbc.org
www.landscapesmag.com
To provide education to lifelong learners in all segments of society about the environment & its resources to achieve better environmental decisions & health outcomes; To engage citizens, communities, & volunteers to rehabilitate, protect, & enhance the environment
Cheryl Ziola, President
Sandra Ulmer, Contact, Education
Helen Sutherland, Contact, Administration

Forest Products Association of Canada (FPAC) / Association des produits forestiers du Canada
#410, 99 Bank St., Ottawa ON K1P 6B9
Tel: 613-563-1441; *Fax:* 613-563-4720
ottawa@fpac.ca; customercentre@fpac.ca
www.fpac.ca
To be the voice of Canada's wood, pulp & paper producers nationally & internationally in the areas of government, trade, & environmental affairs; To advance the Canadian forest products industry's global competitiveness & sustainable stewardship; To operate in a mannner which is economically viable, environmentally responsible, & socially desirable
Avrim Lazar, President & Chief Executive Officer
Andrew Casey, Vice-President, Public Affairs & International Trade
Jean-Pierre Martel, Sr. Vice-President, Sustainability
Catherine Cobden, Vice-President, Economics & Regulatory Affairs
Lori Harop, Executive Director, Environmental Reputation Project
Isabelle Des Chênes, Vice-President, Market Relations & Communications
Mark Hubert, Vice-President, Climate Change Leadership
Susan Murray, Executive Director, Public Relations
David Church, Director, Transportation & Recycling
Roger Cook, Director, Environment
Andrew DeVries, Director, Conservation Biology & Aboriginal Affairs
Jon Flemming, Director, Ecomonics & Trade Policy
Paul Lansbergen, Director, Energy, Economics, & Climate Change
Joel Neuheimer, Director, Market Affairs
Étienne Bélanger, Manager, Forestry Issues
George Wamala, Manager, Government Relations & Policy

Forest Products Association of Nova Scotia (FPANS)
PO Box 696, Truro NS B2N 5E5
Tel: 902-895-1179; *Fax:* 902-893-1197
www.fpans.ca
To act as the voice of the forest industry in Nova Scotia; To cooperate with industry, federal, provincial, & municipal governments, & other stakeholders to ensure adherence to forest management & stewardship policies; To promote sustainable management & viability of the forest industry
Steve Talbot, Executive Director
Jeff Bishop, Coordinator, Communications

Manitoba Forestry Association Inc.
900 Corydon Ave., Winnipeg MB R3M 0Y4
Tel: 204-453-3182; *Fax:* 204-477-5765
mfainc@mts.net
www.mbforestryassoc.ca
To promote the wise use & management of all natural renewable resources, with emphasis on forests; to promote the planting of trees; to promote private land forestry (woodlots); to act as liaison among government, industry & the general public.
Patricia Pohrebnuk, Executive Director
Jennifer Lidgett, President

Maritime Lumber Bureau (MLB) / Bureau de bois de sciage des Maritimes
PO Box 459, Amherst NS B4H 4A1
Tel: 902-667-3889; *Fax:* 902-667-0401
Toll-Free: 800-667-9192
mlb@ns.sympatico.ca
www.mlb.ca
An accredited quality control agency for the lumber industry in the region.
Diana L. Blenkhorn, President & CEO

National Aboriginal Forestry Association (NAFA)
#1426, 220 Laurier Ave. W, Ottawa ON K1P 5Z9
Tel: 613-233-5563; *Fax:* 613-233-4329
hbombay@nafaforestry.org
www.nafaforestry.org
To promote & support increased Aboriginal involvement in forest management & related commercial opportunities; to assist Aboriginal communities in their quest to achieve a standard of land care which is balanced, sustainable & reflective of the traditional knowledge & forest values of Aboriginal peoples; to facilitate capacity-building in forest management through the development of human resource strategies & models for increased participation in natural resource decision making; to address the need for Aboriginal forest land rehabilitation & increased Aboriginal control over forest resources through the development of appropriate policy & programming
Harry M. Bombay, Executive Director
Peggy Smith, Senior Advisor
Janet Pronovost, Office Manager

New Brunswick Forest Products Association Inc. (NBFPA) / L'Association des produits forestiers du Nouveau-Brunswick (APFNB)
Hugh John Flemming Forestry Centre, 1350 Regent St., Fredericton NB E3C 2G6
Tel: 506-452-6930; *Fax:* 506-450-3128
info@nbforestry.com
www.nbforestry.com
The New Brunswick Forest Products Association is a non-government, non-profit organization that represents its forest industry members by serving as a common voice in relations with the government and the public, promoting a healthy New Brunswick forest, raising public awareness of sustainable forest management practices, and providing a forum for the exchange of information, ideas, and concerns.
Mark Arsenault, President/CEO

Newfoundland & Labrador Forest Protection Association
PO Box 728, Mount Pearl NL A1N 2C2
Tel: 709-729-1012; *Fax:* 709-368-2740
nlfpa@nfld.com
www.nlfpa.nfol.ca
To maintain Newfoundland's forests as a productive & renewable resource;to increase public awareness, school education & natural appreciation of forests; to bring about better understanding of forests to people of all ages & backgrounds.
Doug Rex, Executive Director
William Furey, President

Nova Scotia Forestry Association (NSFA)
PO Box 6901, Port Hawkesbury NS B9A 2W2
contact@nsfa.ca
www.nsfa.ca
To conserve Nova Scotia's forests; To promote the wise use & management of forest resources
Debbie Waycott, Contact

Ontario Forest Industries Association (OFIA) / l'Industrie forestière de l'Ontario
#950, 20 Toronto St., Toronto ON M5C 2B8
Tel: 416-368-6188; *Fax:* 416-368-5445
info@ofia.com
www.ofia.com
To act as a unified voice on behalf of member companies to ensure industry positions are considered; To respond to industry issues, such as economic, environmental, & technological developments
Jamie Lim, President/CEO
Mark Holmes, Manager, Public Affairs
Scott Jackson, Manager, Forest Policy

Ontario Forestry Association (OFA) / Association forestière de l'Ontario
#700, 144 Front St. W., Toronto ON MSJ 2L7
Tel: 416-493-4565; *Fax:* 416-493-4608
Toll-Free: 800-387-0790
info@oforest.ca
www.oforest.ca
Social Media: www.facebook.com/ontarioforestryassoc; twitter.com/ontforest; www.youtube.com/user/ontforest
To promote sound land use & full development protection & utilization of Ontario's forest resources for maximum public advantage; to increase public awareness, school education & natural appreciation of forests; to bring about better understanding of forests to people of all ages & backgrounds
Tracy Smith, Acting Executive Director

Ontario Lumber Manufacturers' Association (OLMA) / Association des manufacturiers de bois de sciage de l'Ontario
PO Box 97530, #1202, 55 York St., Toronto ON M1C 4Z1
Tel: 416-367-9717; *Fax:* 416-367-3415
info@olma.ca
www.olma.ca
To ensure a sound & renewable forest economy; To oversee lumber grading licenses & quality control at member sawmills in Ontario; To ensure market access within Northern America, Europe, & Japan
Dale Kaemingh, Chair
Hartley Multamaki, Vice-Chair
David G. Milton, President & Secretary
Hal Brindley, Treasurer
Andre G. Boucher, Chief Grading Inspector

Ontario Professional Foresters Association (OPFA)
PO Box 91523, #201, 5 Wesleyan St., Georgetown ON L7G 2E2
Tel: 905-877-3679; *Fax:* 905-877-6766
opfa@opfa.ca
www.opfa.ca
NOMA Regulatory Body, authorized by the Professional Forestry Act to serve the public interest by actively contributing to the sustainability of Ontario's crown,rural and urban forests through the establishment of professional standards, encouraging the adoption & use of best practices, & ensuring the competency of those who practice professional forestry
David Milton, President
Carl Corbett, Vice-President

Ontario Urban Forest Council (OUFC)
Mount Pleasant Group of Cemeteries, #23/25, 1523 Warden Ave., Toronto ON M1R 4Z8
Tel: 416-936-6735; *Fax:* 416-291-5709
info@oufc.org
www.oufc.org
To promote & assist in the protection & preservation of shade trees; to cooperate with all associations, government agencies, industry & individuals with a mutual interest in preserving & developing Ontario's shade tree heritage & landscape; to promote management of urban forest in Ontario
Jack Radecki, Executive Director

Ordre des ingénieurs forestiers du Québec (OIFQ)
#110, 2750, rue Einstein, Québec QC G1P 4R1
Tél: 418-650-2411; *Téléc:* 418-650-2168
oifq@oifq.com
www.oifq.com
Assurer la protection du public; assurer la qualité des services rendus au public québécois; favoriser l'amélioration continue de l'expertise et de la compétence des ingénieurs forestiers; mettre en place des actions favorisant la durabilité de l'aménagement forestier pour le bénéfice de l'ensemble de la société
Denis Villeneuve, Président

Prince Edward Island Forest Improvement Association (PEIFIA)
RR#1, York PE C9A 1P0
Tel: 902-672-2114; *Fax:* 902-672-2620
Wanson Hemphill, Contact

Registered Professional Foresters Association of Nova Scotia (RPFANS)
PO Box 1031, Truro NS B2N 5G9
Tel: 902-893-0099
contact@rpfans.ca
www.rpfans.ca
To improve the holistic management of forest resources in Nova Scotia
Roger Aggas, Registrar
John Ross, President
Mike Brown, Treasurer

Regroupement des associations forestières régionales du Québec
#100, 138, rue Wellington nord, Sherbrooke QC J1H 5C5
Tél: 819-562-3388
info@afce.qc.ca
www.afce.qc.ca
Daniel Archambault

Saskatchewan Forestry Association (SFA)
#139, 1061 Central Ave., Prince Albert SK S6V 4V4
Tel: 306-763-2189; *Fax:* 306-763-6456
info@whitebirch.ca
www.whitebirch.ca
To promote the wise use, protection, & management of forests, water, & wildlife in Saskatchewan
Sindy Nicholson, President

Sustainable Forestry Initiative
#700, 900 - 17th St. NW, Washington DC 20006 USA
info@sfiprogram.org
www.sfiprogram.org
Social Media: twitter.com/sfiprogram; www.youtube.com/user/SFIProgram
To promote sustainable forest management; To maintain & improve the sustainable forestry certification program
Kathy Abusow, President & Chief Executive Officer
Dale Bischoff, Network Manager
Rick Cantrell, Vice-President & Chief Operating Officer
Danny Karch, Director, Green Building
Allison Welde, Director, Conservation Partnerships & Communications

Wood Preservation Canada (WPC) / Préservation du bois Canada
#202, 2141 Thurston Dr., Ottawa ON K1G 6C9
Tel: 613-737-4337; *Fax:* 613-247-0540
info@woodpreservation.ca
www.woodpreservation.ca
To represent, support & promote the treated wood industry in Canada
Henry Walthert, Executive Director

Fraternal

Benevolent & Protective Order of Elks of Canada
#100, 2629 - 29 Ave., Regina SK S4S 2N9
Tel: 306-359-9010; *Fax:* 306-565-2860
Toll-Free: 888-843-3557
ger@elks-canada.org
www.elks-canada.org
To promote & support community needs, through volunteer efforts of local lodges
Duane Romuld, Grand Exalted Ruler

Les Chevaliers de Colomb du Québec / Knights of Columbus of Québec
670, av Chambly, Saint-Hyacinthe QC J2S 6V4
Tél: 450-768-0616; *Téléc:* 450-768-1660
Ligne sans frais: 866-893-3681
conact@chevaliersdecolomb.com
www.chevaliersdecolomb.com
Un groupe d'entraide et une société fraternelle, qui unit des hommes de foi; l'ordre n'est pas rattaché à la structure juridique de l'Église catholique mais c'est un ordre de laïcs catholiques et exclusivement masculin

Les Chevaliers de Colomb du Québec, District No 37, Conseil 5198
CP 141, 124, rue des Forces Armées, Chibougamau QC G8P 2L5
Tél: 418-748-2411
www.chevaliersdecolomb.com
Jacques Fortin, Député de district
Reynald Bouchard, Grand Chevalier

Empire Club of Canada
Fairmont Royal York Hotel, 100 Front St. West, Level H, Toronto ON M5J 1E3
Tel: 416-364-2878; *Fax:* 416-364-7271
empireclub@bellnet.ca
www.empireclubfoundation.com
Jo-Ann McArthur, President

Foresters
Forester House, 789 Don Mills Rd., Toronto ON M3C 1T9
Tel: 416-429-3000; *Fax:* 416-467-2518
Toll-Free: 800-828-1540
service@foresters.com
www.foresters.com
A fraternal benefit society which provides life insurance & other financial products to its members
George Mohacsi, CEO

Grand Orange Lodge of Canada
94 Sheppard Ave. West, Toronto ON M2N 1M5
Tel: 416-223-1690; *Fax:* 416-223-1324
Toll-Free: 800-565-6248
secretary@grandorangelodge.ca
www.grandorangelodge.ca
To encourage its members to actively participate in the Protestant church of their choice; to actively support the Canadian system of government; to anticipate legislation & its impact on the civil & religious liberties of all Canadians; to provide social activities which will enrich the lives of its members; to participate in benevolent activities which will enrich our communities & our country
Roy Dawe, Grand Secretary

International Association of Rebekah Assemblies
c/o The Sovereign Grand Lodge IOOF, 422 Trade St., Winston-Salem NC 27101 USA
Tel: 336-725-6037; *Fax:* 336-773-1066
Toll-Free: 800-766-1838
iarasec@aol.com
www.ioof.org/rebekahs.html
The Rebekah lodges are the female auxiliary of the Independent Order of Odd Fellows, but are open to both women and men.

IODE Canada (IODE)
#219, 40 Orchard View Blvd., Toronto ON M4R 1B9
Tel: 416-487-4416; *Fax:* 416-487-4417
Toll-Free: 866-827-7428
iodecanada@bellnet.ca
www.iode.ca
To improve the quality of life for children, youth & those in need through education, social service & citizenship programs
Catherine Moore, President

Knights Hospitallers, Sovereign Order of St. John of Jerusalem, Knights of Malta, Grand Priory of Canada (OSJ)
Grand Chancery Canada, 52 Kingswood Dr., Bowmanville ON L1E 1Z3
Tel: 905-579-0326; *Fax:* 905-579-3773
To propagate the principles of chivalry; care for the sick, aged, invalid, poor & children in need; protect & defend Christianity throughout the world; combat errors; champion the truth; promote & encourage the spirit of Brotherhood & charity within the order; members are expected to be united in brotherhood & charity
Joseph Frendo Cumbo, Grand Master
M. Sillato, Secretary General
Violet Sillato, Treasurer General

Knights of Pythias - Domain of British Columbia
#B7, 7155 ETC Hwy., Kamloops BC V2C 4T1
Tel: 250-573-3056
www.members.shaw.ca/veng/
Edward J. Eagles, Grand Secretary

Ladies' Orange Benevolent Association of Canada
c/o Grand Orange Lodge of Canada, 94 Sheppard Ave. West, Toronto ON M2N 1M5
Fax: 416-223-1324
Toll-Free: 800-565-6248
www.grandorangelodge.ca/loba; www.orangenet.org/loba.htm
Chalmers John, Grand Secretary, Grand Lodge of Canada

Order of Sons of Italy in Canada
34 Lincoln St., Welland ON L3C 5J1
Tel: 905-892-3352
www.ordersonsofitalycanada.com
A fraternal organization of Canadians of Italian heritage, they work together to achieve the following purposes; SERVICE & CHARITY: To assist the needy, the ill, and disabled through financial support, the provision of housing, and other support programs; COMMUNITY INVOLVEMENT: To encourage the active participation of our members in the political, social and economic life of our community; to participate in programs combating discrimination, racism, and social injustice; HERITAGE: To promote and preserve the Italian language, culture, and traditions in our country.
Josie Cumbo, National President
Patsy Giammarco, National Administative Secretary

The Order of United Commercial Travelers of America (UCT)
#300, 901 Centre St. North, Calgary AB T2E 2P6
Tel: 403-277-0745; *Fax:* 403-277-6662
Toll-Free: 800-267-2371
www.uct.org
To provide members with affordable insurance & support through fraternal benefit & discount programs
Randy Young, President

Réseau Hommes Québec (RHQ)
#134, 911, rue Jean-Talon est, Montréal QC H2R 1V5
Tél: 514-276-4545; *Ligne sans frais:* 877-908-4545
info@rhquebec.org; communications@rhquebec.org
www.rhquebec.org
Média social: www.facebook.com/pages/Réseau-Hommes-Québec-RHQ/114381705296554
Organisme sans but lucratif; a pour mission d'entretenir un réseau de groupes autogérés d'écoute, de parole & d'entraide aux hommes
Guy Corneau, Fondateur

Royal Arch Masons of Canada
361 King St. West, Hamilton ON L8P 1B4
Tel: 905-522-5775; *Fax:* 905-522-5099
Melvyn J. Duke, Grand Scribe E.

Society of Kabalarians of Canada
1160 West 10th Ave., Vancouver BC V6H 1J1
Tel: 604-263-9551; *Fax:* 604-263-5514
Toll-Free: 866-489-1188
info1@kabalarians.com
www.kabalarians.com
The Society promotes Kabalarian philosophy, which teaches a constructive way of life through the understanding of the Mathematical Principle, encouraging people to live a more progressive, constructive life.
Lorenda Bardell, President

Sons of Scotland Benevolent Association
#801, 505 Consummers Road, Toronto ON M2J 4V8
Tel: 416-482-1250; *Fax:* 416-482-9576
Toll-Free: 800-387-3382
info@sonsofscotland.com
www.sonsofscotland.com
Undertake & support activities which promote the elements of Scottish culture in Canada; honour the history & heritage of Scots in Canada; support & raise funds for charitable organizations; provide fraternal & insurance benefits for members
Robert Stewart, Executive Director

Yukon Order of Pioneers (YOOP)
Tel: 867-667-2564
h_rwilcox@hotmail.com
www.yukon-seniors-and-elders.org/yukonorder.home.htm
The Yukon Order of Pioneers is decicated to the advancement of the Yukon Territory, the mutual protection of its members, and to uniting those members in the strong tie of Brotherhood and to preserving the names of all Yukon Pioneers on its rolls and the collecting and preservation of the literature and incidents of the Orders history.
Rob Wilcox, President

Funeral Services

Alberta Funeral Service Association (AFSA)
3030 - 55 St., Red Deer AB T4P 3S6
Tel: 403-342-2460; *Fax:* 403-342-2495
Toll-Free: 800-803-8809
inquiry@afsa.ca
www.afsa.ca
To promote & improve funeral service in Alberta
Deanna Schroeder, Executive Administrator

Cemetery & Crematorium Association of British Columbia (CCABC)
#211, 2187 Oak Bay Ave., Victoria BC V8R 1G1
Tel: 866-587-3213
info@ccabc.org
www.ccabc.org
To promote high standards of ethics & service in the cemetery & crematorium profession in British Columbia; To act as a collective voice to regulators

John Chasca, President
Blair Wallin, Vice-President

Corporation des thanatologues du Québec (CTQ)
#115, 4600, boul Henri-Bourassa, Québec QC G1H 3A5
Tél: 418-622-1717; *Téléc:* 418-622-5557
Ligne sans frais: 800-463-4935
info@corpothanato.com
www.domainefuneraire.com
Média social: www.facebook.com/corporation.thanatologues.quebec; twitter.com/corpothanato
Représenter le domaine funéraire, supporter son évolution promouvoir l'excellence et contribuer au développement d'affaire de ses membres pour le mieux être de la population
René Goyer, Président

Funeral & Cremation Services Council of Saskatchewan
3847C Albert St., Regina SK S4S 3R4
Tel: 306-584-1575; *Fax:* 306-584-1576
Toll-Free: 800-892-0116
sask.funeral@sasktel.net
www.fcscs.ca
Terry Zip, Chair
R.G. (Bob) Carter, Registrar

Funeral Advisory & Memorial Society (FAMS)
55 St. Phillips Rd., Toronto ON M9P 2N8
Tel: 416-241-6274
info@fams.ca
www.fams.ca
To provide unbiased consumer advice on funeral planning
Margaret Adamson, Chair
Paul Siemens, Vice-Chair & Secretary
Johanna Ntiforo, Office Administrator

Funeral Service Association of British Columbia (FSABC)
#211, 2187 Oak Bay Ave., Victoria BC V8R 1G1
Tel: 250-592-3213; *Fax:* 250-592-4362
Toll-Free: 800-665-3899
info@bcfunerals.com
www.bcfunerals.com
To promote, through education, communication, & leadership, the highest standards of ethics & service in the funeral profession
Ryan McLane, President

Funeral Service Association of Canada (FSAC) / L'Association des services funéraires du Canada
#6, 14845 Yonge St., Suite 192, Aurora ON L4G 6H8
Tel: 905-841-7779; *Fax:* 905-841-0997
Toll-Free: 866-941-7779
info@fsac.ca
www.fsac.ca
Social Media: www.facebook.com/FuneralAssociation
To provide a collective voice for the Canadian funeral professional; To provide high quality professional services with dignity & competence; To ensure compliance with all provisions of the law; To provide information about services
Scott MacLeod, President
Sue Lasher, Vice-President

Manitoba Funeral Service Association (MFSA)
PO Box 48067, Stn. RPO Lakewood, Winnipeg MB R2J 4A3
Tel: 204-947-0927; *Fax:* 204-269-7148
info@mfsa.mb.ca
www.mfsa.mb.ca
To serve funeral directors & funeral homes throughout Manitoba; To advance funeral service; To uphold a code of ethics
Jody Nicholson, President
Thorunn Petursdottir, Executive Director
Janice Dryden, Secretary-Treasurer

Newfoundland & Labrador Funeral Services Association (NLFSA)
PO Box 138, Winterton NL A0G 3M0
Tel: 709-586-2721; *Fax:* 709-586-2888
contact@nlfuneralboard.ca
www.nlfuneralboard.ca/nlfuneralservices.html
The Association offers funeral service support for the province of NFLD & Labrador.
Milton Peach, President
Wayne Bennett, Vice-President

Ontario Association of Cemetery & Funeral Professionals (OACFP)
PO Box 10173, 27 Legend Ct., Ancaster ON L9K 1P3
Tel: 905-383-6528; *Fax:* 905-383-2771
Toll-Free: 888-558-3335
info@oacfp.com
www.oacfp.com
To promote high standards of service & the professional operation of cemeteries, funeral homes, crematoria, & related bereavement services
Anita Mazzara, President
Terry Eccles, First Vice-President
Tim Vreman, Sec.-Treas.
Jo-Anne Rogerson, Executive Director

Ontario Funeral Service Association (OFSA)
#203, 3425 Harvester Rd., Burlington ON L7N 3N1
Tel: 905-637-3371; *Fax:* 905-637-3583
Toll-Free: 800-268-2727
info@ofsa.org
www.ofsa.org
To maintain high standards of services & ethical business practices among Ontario's funeral homes for the welfare of the public; To represent & support Ontario's independently owned funeral establishments
Myles O'Riordan, President
Cathie Turner, Vice-President
Kerri Douglas, Executive Coordinator
Lesley Bingley, Secretary-Treasurer

Prince Edward Island Funeral Directors & Embalmers Association
PO Box 540, Kensington PE C0B 1M0
Tel: 902-836-3313; *Fax:* 902-836-4461
To ensure professional services of the highest standards
Faye Doucette, President

Fur Trade

Canadian Association for Humane Trapping (CAHT)
PO Box 7115, Stn. Maplehurst, Burlington ON L7T 4J8
caht1@cogeco.ca
www.caht.ca
To reduce & eliminate suffering of animals trapped for whatever reason; To work with governments, trappers, the commercial fur industry, animal welfare organizations & the public-at-large to bring about actual trapping improvements
James H. Bandow, Executive Director
Donald Mitton, Project Director
Donna Bandow, Coordinator, Grants & Fundraising

The Fur Council of Canada (FCC) / Conseil canadien de la fourrure
#1270, 1435, rue Saint-Alexandre, Montréal QC H3A 2G4
Tel: 514-844-1945; *Fax:* 514-844-8593
info@furcouncil.com
www.furcouncil.com
To promote all aspects of the fur trade
Alan Herscovici, Executive Director
Angela Gurley, Secretary
Paula Lishman, President

Fur Institute of Canada (FIC) / Institut de la fourrure du Canada (IFC)
#701, 331 Cooper St., Ottawa ON K2P 0G5
Tel: 613-231-7099; *Fax:* 613-231-7940
info@fur.ca
www.fur.ca
To promote the sustainable & wise use of Canadian fur resources
Robert B. Cahill, Executive Director
Bruce Williams, Chair
Mary Baskin, Manager, Corporate & Communications

Fur-Bearer Defenders (FBD)
#215, 3989 Henning Dr., Burnaby BC V5C 6P8
Tel: 604-435-1850; *Fax:* 604-435-1840
fbd@banlegholdtraps.com
furbearerdefenders.com
Social Media: www.facebook.com/FURfree?ref=ts; twitter.com/FurBearers; www.youtube.com/furbearerdefenders
To stop trapping cruelty & protect fur-bearing animals
Lesley Fox, Executive Director

Furriers Guild of Canada
#211, 4174 Dundas St. West, Toronto ON M8X 1X3
Tel: 416-234-9494; *Fax:* 416-234-2244
furriersguildca@ica.net
To promote Canadian fur retailers

Galleries & Museums

Alberta Museums Association
#404, 10408, 124 St., Edmonton AB T5N 1R5
Tel: 780-424-2626; *Fax:* 780-425-1679
info@museums.ab.ca
www.museums.ab.ca
To promote understanding, access & excellence within Alberta's museums for the benefit of society
Bill Peters, President

Association Museums New Brunswick (AMNB) / Association des musées du Nouveau-Brunswick
668 Brunswick St., Fredericton NB E3B 1H6
Tel: 506-452-2908; *Fax:* 506-459-0481
amnb@nb.aibn.com
www.amnb.ca
To preserve New Brunswick's heritage by uniting, promoting & advancing our heritage workers, supporters & organizations
Barbara McIntyre, President

Association of Manitoba Museums (AMM)
#1040, 555 Main St., Winnipeg MB R3B 1C3
Tel: 204-947-1782; *Fax:* 204-942-3749
Toll-Free: 866-747-9323
info@museumsmanitoba.com
www.museumsmanitoba.com
To strengthen the museum community by promoting excellence in preserving & presenting Manitoba's heritage; To improve the AMM's ability to communicate with its members; To continue a training program
Monique Brandt, Executive Director

Atlantic Provinces Art Gallery Association (APAGA)
c/o MSVU Art Gallery, 166 Bedford Hwy., Halifax NS B3M 2J6
Tel: 902-457-6160; *Fax:* 902-457-2447
info@apaga.com
www.apaga.ca
To pursue & promote high standards of excellence in care & presentation of works of art in public art galleries in the Atlantic region; To encourage the closest possible cooperation between art galleries, museums & artists; To serve as an advisory body in matters of professional interest
Ingrid Jenkner, Director

British Columbia Museums Association (BCMA)
#204, 26 Bastion Sq., Victoria BC V8W 1H9
Tel: 250-356-5700; *Fax:* 250-387-1251
Toll-Free: 800-663-7867
bcma@museumsassn.bc.ca
www.museumsassn.bc.ca
To promote the protection & preservation of the objects, specimens, records & sites significant to the natural, creative & human history of British Columbia; to aid in the improvement of museums & galleries as educational institutions; to assist in the development of the museum profession.
Jim Harding, Executive Director
Shelley Gauthier, Member Services Coordinator

Canadian Federation of Friends of Museums (CFFM) / Fédération canadienne des amis de musées (FCAM)
#400, 280 Metcalfe St., Ottawa ON K2P 1R7
Tel: 613-567-0099; *Fax:* 613-233-5438
info@cffm-fcam.ca
www.cffm-fcam.ca
Social Media: www.facebook.com/group.php?gid=146503988697066
To serve as source of information & expertise for friends of museums; To serve as communications network & national voice for those who are dedicated to the support & promotion of museums for the benefit of all Canadians
Tony Bowland, Co-President
Marie Senécal-Tremblay, Co-President
Yves Dagenais, Treasurer

Canadian Museums Association (CMA) / Association des musées canadiens
#400, 280 Metcalfe St., Ottawa ON K2P 1R7
Tel: 613-567-0099; *Fax:* 613-233-5438
Toll-Free: 888-822-2907
info@museums.ca
www.museums.ca
Social Media: www.facebook.com/pages/Canadian-Museums-Association/107410072621904; twitter.com/musecdnCached
To advance a strong, vital, & valued Canadian museum sector
Bill Greenlaw, President
Nancy Noble, Vice-President
John G. McAvity, Executive Director & CEO

Community Museums Association of Prince Edward Island
PO Box 22002, 161 St. Peter's Rd., Charlottetown PE C1A 9J2
Tel: 902-892-8837; *Fax:* 902-892-1459
info@museumspei.ca
www.museumspei.ca
To foster & support museums, historical societies & other non-profit organizations concerned with heritage of PEI.

Barbara Boys MacCormac, President
Barry King, Executive Director

ICOM Museums Canada / ICOM Musées Canada
#400, 280 Metcalfe St., Ottawa ON K2P 1R7
Tel: 613-567-0099; *Fax:* 613-233-5438
icom@museums.ca
To advance the cause of museums throughout the world & in Canada; to provide liaison with International Council of Museums in Paris; to hold annual meeting in conjunction with Canadian Museums Association.
Francine Caron, Contact

Museum Association of Newfoundland & Labrador (MANL)
PO Box 5785, St. John's NL A1C 5X3
Tel: 709-722-9034; *Fax:* 709-722-9035
manl@nf.aibn.com
www.manl.nf.ca
To protect & preserve the cultural & natural heritage of Newfoundland & Labrador; To unite, support & promote members; To improve & promote museums
Teresita McCarthy, President
John Griffin, Vice-President
Angela Noseworthy, Treasurer
Diane Curtis, Secretary

Museums Association of Saskatchewan (MAS)
424 McDonald St., Regina SK S4N 6E1
Tel: 306-780-9279; *Fax:* 306-780-9463
mas@saskmuseums.org
www.saskmuseums.org
To work for the advancement of strong & vibrant museums in Saskatchewan; To encourage the preservation & understanding of the province's cultural & natural heritage; To serve Saskatchewan museums
Brenda Sherring, Executive Director
Royce Pettyjohn, President
Patricia Fiori, Director, Learning
Wendy Fitch, Director, Museum Operation Services

Ontario Association of Art Galleries (OAAG)
#617, 111 Peter St., Toronto ON M5V 2H1
Tel: 416-598-0714; *Fax:* 416-598-4128
oaag@oaag.com
www.oaag.org
To encourage the highest standards for the exhibition, interpretation, & conservation of the visual arts; to develop tools to assist gallery professionals in achieving institutional goals; to advance positive, responsive relations with government, its agencies, & the citizens of Ontario.
Demetra Christakos, Executive Director

Ontario Museum Association (OMA) / Association des musées de l'Ontario
George Brown House, 50 Baldwin St., Toronto ON M5T 1L4
Tel: 416-348-8672; *Fax:* 416-348-0438
Toll-Free: 866-662-8672
www.museumsontario.com
To enhance the mission of museums as significant cultural resources in the service of Ontario society & its development
Marie Lalonde, Executive Director

Organization of Military Museums of Canada, Inc. (OMMC) / L'Organisation des musées militaires du Canada inc.
PO Box 60042, Stn. Unicity, Winnipeg MB R3K 2E7
ommcinc@gmail.com
www.ommcinc.ca
To preserve the military heritage of Canada by encouraging the establishment & operation of military museums; to educate museum staffs through lectures, discussions, workshops, visits, publications & exhibits; to cooperate with others having the same or similar purposes.
Marilyn Gurney, President
Stuart Beaton, Vice President

La Société des musées québécois (SMQ)
CP 8888, Succ. Centre-Ville - UQAM, Montréal QC H3C 3P8
Tél: 514-987-3264; *Téléc:* 514-987-3379
museesadecouvrir@smq.qc.ca
www.musees.qc.ca
Au service du développement de la muséologie au Québec

Yukon Historical & Museums Association (YHMA)
3126 - 3 Ave., Whitehorse YT Y1A 1E7
Tel: 867-667-4704; *Fax:* 867-667-4506
yhma@northwestel.net
www.heritageyukon.ca
To preserve & foster an appreciation of the Yukon's history & culture; to act as forum for other museum & heritage organizations in the region
Tracey Anderson, Executive Director

Gas & Oil

Canadian Association of Petroleum Producers (CAPP) / Association canadienne des producteurs pétroliers
#2100, 350 - 7 Ave. SW, Calgary AB T2P 3N9
Tel: 403-267-1100; *Fax:* 403-261-4622
communication@capp.ca; membership@capp.ca; publications@capp.ca
www.capp.ca
Social Media: www.facebook.com/OilGasCanada; twitter.com/oilgascanada; www.youtube.com/cappvideos
To represent companies that produce Canada's natural gas & crude oil; To enhance the economic sustainability of the Canadian upstream petroleum industry; To ensure work is conducted in a safe & environmentally & socially responsible manner; To work with government to develop regulatory requirements
David Collyer, President
Janet Annesley, Vice-President, Communications
Bob Bleaney, Vice-President, External Relations
Tom Huffaker, Vice-President, Policy & Environment
David Pryce, Vice-President, Operations
Nick Schultz, Vice-President, Pipeline Regulation
Greg Stringham, Vice-President, Oil Sands & Markets

Canadian Energy Pipeline Association (CEPA)
#1860, 205 - 5th Ave. SW, Calgary AB T2P 2V7
Tel: 403-221-8777; *Fax:* 403-221-8760
info@cepa.com
www.cepa.com
The Canadian Energy Pipeline Association (CEPA) represents Canada's trasmissions pipeline companie. Their members transport 97% of Canada's daily crude oil and natural gas production from producing regions to markets throughout Canada and the United States.
Brenda Kenny, President
Myra Paul, Administrative Assistant

Canadian Gas Association (CGA) / Association canadienne du gaz
#809, 350 Sparks St., Ottawa ON K1R 7S8
Tel: 613-748-0057; *Fax:* 613-748-9078
info@cga.ca
www.cga.ca
Social Media: twitter.com/GoSmartEnergy
To act as the voice of the natural gas distribution industry in Canada
Timothy M. Egan, President & Chief Executive Officer
Paula Dunlop, Director, Public Affairs & Strategy
Bryan Gormely, Director, Policy, Economics, & Information
Jim Tweedie, Director, Operations, Safety, & Integrity Management
Valerie Prokop, Manager, Finance & Corporate Services

Canadian Propane Association (CPA) / Association canadienne du propane (ACP)
#616, 130 Albert St., Ottawa ON K1P 5G4
Tel: 613-683-2270; *Fax:* 613-683-2279
info@propane.ca
www.propane.ca
Social Media: twitter.com/Propanedotca
To act as the national voice of the Canadian propane industry; To supports its members in the development of a safe, environmentally responsible Canadian propane industry
Jim Facette, President & CEO
Steven Sparling, Chair
Allison Mallette, Manager, Research & Communications
Peter Maddox, Regional Manager, Ontario

Canadian Society of Petroleum Geologists (CSPG)
#110, 333 - 5th Ave. SW, Calgary AB T2P 1G7
Tel: 403-264-5610; *Fax:* 403-264-5898
cspg@cspg.org
www.cspg.org
Social Media: www.facebook.com/CSPGOnline; www.linkedin.com/groups/Canadian-Society-Petroleum-Geologists-4153517
To advance the science of geology, especially as it relates to petroleum, natural gas & other fossil fuels; to promote the technology of exploration for finding & producing these resources; to foster the spirit of scientific research; to develop a sense of pride & community among Canadian Petroleum Geologists; to provide the means to ensure that the Canadian Petroleum Geologist is the best trained, best supported & most skillful practitioner in the world
Lis Bjeld, Executive Director

Gas Processing Association Canada (GPAC)
#400, 1040 - 7th Ave. SW, Calgary AB T2P 3G9
Tel: 403-244-4487; *Fax:* 403-244-2340
info@gpacanada.com
www.gpacanada.com
To promote interaction & exchange of ideas & technology that will add value to those who are involved with or affected by the hydrocarbon processing industry
Josh Carter, President
Jeff McPhail, Director, Safety
Rob Nadalutti, Director, Academic
Erika Rauser, Coordinator, Events

Industrial Gas Users Association Inc. (IGUA) / Association des consommateurs industriels de gaz (ACIG)
#502, 350 Sparks St., Ottawa ON K1R 7S8
Tel: 613-236-8021; *Fax:* 613-230-9531
www.igua.ca
To provide a coordinated & effective voice for industrial firms depending on natural gas as fuel or feedstock; to represent industrial users of natural gas before regulatory boards & governments
Murray Newton, President
Ghislaine Carrière, Manager, Accounting & Office Services

NOIA
Atlantic Place, #602, 215 Water St., St. John's NL A1C 6C9
Tel: 709-758-6610; *Fax:* 709-758-6611
www.noianet.com
To assist, promote & facilitate the participation of members in ocean industries, with particular emphasis on oil & gas, to enhance their growth & development; to promote the growth of ocean industry; to act as a focal point for representations to government bodies & agencies; to act as a source of information & education for members
Robert Cadigan, President & CEO

Offshore/Onshore Technologies Association of Nova Scotia (OTANS)
#400, 1718 Argyle St., Halifax NS B3J 3N6
Tel: 902-425-4774; *Fax:* 902-422-2332
otans@otans.com
www.otans.com
To identify, promote & support the development of opportunities both offshore & onshore in the oil & gas industry
Paul McEachern, Managing Director

Ontario Petroleum Institute Inc. (OPI)
#104, 555 Southdale Rd. East, London ON N6E 1A2
Tel: 519-680-1620; *Fax:* 519-680-1621
www.ontpet.com
To promote responsible exploration & development by Ontario's oil, gas, hydrocarbon storage, & solution-mining industries
Marko Pasic, President
Joe Van Overberghe, Executive Director
Kerry O'Shea, Treasurer
Morley Salmon, Secretary

Petroleum Research Atlantic Canada (PRAC)
1321 Edward St., Halifax NS B3H 3H5
Tel: 902-494-2960; *Fax:* 902-494-2489
info@pr-ac.ca
www.pr-ac.ca
To build petroleum-related research & development capability & capacity throughout Atlantic Canada; To establish research priorities, coordinate research proposals, provide seed funding for research & development, identify opportunities & provide support in the administration of research programs
David Finn, President

Petroleum Services Association of Canada (PSAC)
#1150, 800 - 6 Ave. SW, Calgary AB T2P 3G3
Tel: 403-264-4195; *Fax:* 403-263-7174
www.psac.ca
To represent the supply, manufacturing, & service sectors of the upstream petroleum industry
Mark Salkeld, President & Chief Executive Officer
Elizabeth Aquin, Senior Vice-President
Patrick J. Delaney, Vice-President, Health & Safety
Kelly Morrison, Director, Communications & Stakeholder Relations
Heather Doyle, Manager, Meetings & Events

Gems & Jewellery

Alberta Federation of Rock Clubs (AFRC)
2073 Blackmud Creek Drive SW, Edmonton AB T6W 1G8
Tel: 780-430-6694
paulinez8@shaw.ca
www.afrc.ca

To assist member clubs by providing information & expertise; to promote the study of the Earth Sciences
Alice Watts, President
Pauline Zeschuk, Secretary

Canadian Gemmological Association (CGA)
1767 Avenue Rd., Toronto ON M5M 3Y8
Tel: 416-785-0962; *Fax:* 416-785-9043
Toll-Free: 877-244-3090
info@canadiangemmological.com
www.canadiangemmological.com
To set a standard for excellence in the practice of gemmology
Duncan Parker, President
Brad Wilson, Vice-President
Glen King, Treasurer

Canadian Institute of Gemmology (CIG) / Institut canadien de gemmologie
c/o School of Jewellery Arts, PO Box 57010, Vancouver BC V5K 5G6
Tel: 604-530-8569
wolf@cigem.ca
www.cigem.ca
To serve the jewellery industry & the general public
Wolf Kuehn, Executive Director

Canadian Jewellers Association (CJA)
#600, 27 Queen St. East, Toronto ON M5C 2M6
Tel: 416-368-7616; *Fax:* 416-368-1986
Toll-Free: 800-580-0942
cja@canadianjewellers.com
www.canadianjewellers.com
The members of CJA are entrusted with the responsibility of sale and service of jewellery, watches and related products and agree to the following: maintaining the highest level of personal integrity, honesty, and business ethics; comply with all government laws and regulations relating to the jewellery and watch industry; supoort and abide by the regulations, constitution, and objectives of the CJA and Code of Ethics; provide high standards; provide knowledge and expertise; to clearly establish the guarnatee and/or service policy regarding all merch; to adhere to sound business practices; to refrain from all forms of copyright and trademark infringement.
Ken Mulhall, President & CEO

Corporation des bijoutiers du Québec (CBQ) / Québec Jewellers' Corporation
868, rue Brissette, Sainte-Julie QC J3E 2B1
Tél: 514-485-3333; *Téléc:* 450-649-8984
info@cbq.qc.ca
www.cbq.qc.ca
La promotion des membres, la défence de leurs intérêts économiques et sociaux et le développement du professionnalisme chez les membres; garantir au public un meilleur service et l'intégrité des bijoutiers membres; accroître la compétence des gens du métier; favoriser l'exercise du métier selon l'art et la science
André Marchand, Président
Lise Petitpas, Directrice générale

Gem & Mineral Federation of Canada (GMFC) / Fédération canadienne des gemmes et des minéraux
PO Box 42015, Stn. North, Winfield BC V4V 1Z8
Tel: 250-376-4878
president@gmfc.ca
www.gmfc.ca
To promote earth sciences; to protect collecting sites; to educate collectors; to foster good will, friendship & rapport among all
Winifred Robertson, President

Jewellers Vigilance Canada Inc. (JVC)
#600, 27 Queen St. East, Toronto ON M5C 2M6
Tel: 416-368-4840; *Fax:* 416-368-5552
Toll-Free: 800-636-9536
info@jewellersvigilance.ca
www.jewellersvigilance.ca
Jewellers Vigilance Canada (JVC) was established in 1987 as an independent non-profit association with a mandate to advance ethical practices, establish a level playing field for the Canadian jewellery industry and provide crime prevention education for the trade.
Phyllis Richard, Executive Director

Government & Public Administration

Alberta Association of Municipal Districts & Counties (AAMD&C)
2510 Sparrow Dr., Nisku AB T9E 8N5
Tel: 780-955-3639; *Fax:* 780-955-3615
Toll-Free: 855-548-7233
aamdc@aamdc.com
www.aamdc.com
Social Media: twitter.com/aamdc
Gerald Rhodes, Executive Director

Alberta Municipal Clerks Association (AMCA)
c/o City of Spruce Grove, 315 Jespersen Dr., Spruce Grove AB T7X 3E8
Tel: 780-962-7634
communications@albertamunicipalclerks.com
www.albertamunicipalclerks.com
To provide a forum for exchange of ideas among the municipal clerks of the municipalities of Alberta; to provide a means for presentation of suggested amendments in legislation to senior government; to work in conjunction with any other organization, having as its objective the betterment of administration of local government
Doug Tymchyshyn, President

Alberta Rural Municipal Administrators Association
6027 - 4th St. NE, Calgary AB T2K 4Z5
Tel: 403-275-0622; *Fax:* 403-275-8179
d_vschmaltz@shaw.ca
www.armaa.ca
Valerie Schmaltz, Sec.-Treas.
Ross Rawlusyk, President

Alberta Urban Municipalities Association (AUMA)
#300, 8616 15 Ave., Edmonton AB T6E 6E6
Tel: 780-433-4431; *Fax:* 780-433-4454
Toll-Free: 800-310-2862
main@auma.ca
www.auma.ca
Social Media: twitter.com/theauma
To provide leadership in advocating local government interests to the provincial government & other organizations, & to provide services that address the needs of its membership
John McGowan, CEO

Association des directeurs généraux des municipalités du Québec
#129, 10, rue Hugues-Pommier, Beauport QC G1E 4T9
Tél: 418-660-7591; *Téléc:* 418-660-0848
adgmq@adgmq.qc.ca
www.adgmq.qc.ca/
Permettre l'amélioration des connaissances et du statut de ses membres et la promotion de la formule de gestion conseil/directeur général
Jacques Poulin, Président
Jacques Alain, Directeur Exécutif

Association des directeurs municipaux du Québec (ADMQ)
#500, 580, av Grande-Allée est, Québec QC G1R 2K2
Tél: 418-647-4518; *Téléc:* 418-647-4115
admq@admq.qc.ca
admq.qc.ca/
De voir à la promotion et à la défense des membres en plus d'offrir un soutien professionnel constant au niveau des outils de formation et de communication
Sylvie Dubois, Présidente

Association francophone des municipalités du Nouveau-Brunswick inc. (AFMNB)
#322, 702, rue Principale, Petit-Rocher NB E8J 1V1
Tél: 506-542-2622; *Téléc:* 506-542-2618
Ligne sans frais: 888-236-2622
afmnb@afmnb.org
www.afmnb.org
Promouvoir le développement des municipalités francophones du Nouveau-Brunswick
Lise Ouellette, Directrice générale
Jean Lanteigne, Président

Association internationale des maires francophones - Bureau à Québec (AIMF)
CP 700, Succ. Haute-Ville, #312, 2, rue des Jardins, Québec QC G1R 4S9
Tél: 418-641-6188; *Téléc:* 418-641-6437
Favoriser les échanges et la coopérations entre les villes membres

Association of Manitoba Municipalities (AMM)
1910 Saskatchewan Ave. West, Portage la Prairie MB R1N 0P1
Tel: 204-857-8666; *Fax:* 204-856-2370
amm@amm.mb.ca
www.amm.mb.ca
Social Media: www.facebook.com/124665930946719; twitter.com/AMMManitoba
To provide communications link between municipalities; to lobby for municipal governments with senior levels of government
Joe Masi, Executive Director
Doug Dobrowolski, President

Association of Municipal Administrators of New Brunswick (AMANB) / Association des administrateurs municipaux du Nouveau-Brunswick (AAMNB)
PO Box 30044, Stn. Prospect Plaza RPO, Fredericton NB E3B 0H8
Tel: 506-453-4229; *Fax:* 506-444-5452
amanb@nb.aibn.com
www.amanb-aamnb.ca
To promote & advance status of persons employed in field of municipal administration; to advance quality of administration of municipal services; to encourage closer official & personal relationship among members to facilitate interchange of ideas & experience; to establish & maintain standards of performance for members; to assist in provision of formal training & educational facilities
Cynthia Geldart, President
Eva Turnbull, Executive Director

Association of Municipal Administrators, Nova Scotia (AMANS)
CIBC Building, #1106, 1809 Barrington St., Halifax NS B3J 3K8
Tel: 902-423-2215; *Fax:* 902-425-5592
amans@eastlink.ca
www.amans.ca
To improve the quality of local government in Nova Scotia through the development of educational programs; To provide a forum for the exchange of ideas; to provide a resource to municipal officials; To provide service to members to improve their professional capabilities
Janice Wentzell, Executive Director
Kristy Hardie, Administrative Assistant

Association of Municipal Managers, Clerks & Treasurers of Ontario (AMCTO) / Association des directeurs généraux, secrétaires et trésoriers municipaux de l'Ontario (ASTMO)
#910, 2680 Skymark Ave., Mississauga ON L4W 5L6
Tel: 905-602-4294; *Fax:* 905-602-4295
amcto@amcto.com
www.amcto.com
To foster administrative excellence in local government; to identify & meet training & education needs in local government; to be an influential voice for local government; to provide an effective communication forum for local government; to promote public awareness of & confidence in local government; to facilitate change within AMCTO
Andy Koopmans, Executive Director

Association of Municipalities of Ontario (AMO)
#801, 200 University Ave., Toronto ON M5H 3C6
Tel: 416-971-9856; *Fax:* 416-971-6191
Toll-Free: 877-426-6527
amo@amo.on.ca; municom@amo.on.ca; policy@amo.on.ca
www.amo.on.ca
To support & enhance strong & effective municipal government in Ontario; To represent almost all of Ontario's 444 municipal governments
Pat Vanini, Executive Director
Nancy Plumridge, Director, Administration & Business Development
Monika Turner, Director, Policy
Judy Dezell, Project Manager, Gas Tax Implementation
Snezana Vukelic, Manager, Information Services

Association of Yukon Communities (AYC)
#15, 1114 - 1st Ave., Whitehorse YT Y1A 1A3
Tel: 867-668-4388; *Fax:* 867-668-7574
www.ayc-yk.ca
To further the establishment of responsible government at the community level; To provide a united approach to issues affecting local governments; To advance ambitions & goals of member communities by developing a shared common vision of the future; To represent members in matters affecting them & the welfare of their communities; To provide programs & services of common interest & benefit to members
John Pattimore, Executive Director

Association québécoise du loisir municipal (AQLM)
CP 1000, Succ. M, 4545, av Pierre-de-Coubertin, Montréal QC H1V 3R2
Tél: 514-252-5244; *Téléc:* 514-252-5220
infoaqlm@loisirmunicipal.qc.ca
www.loisirmunicipal.qc.ca
Intégrer le domaine de vie communautaire au mandat de loisir; Affirmer la maîtrise d'oeuvre de la municipalité en loisir; faire valoir le service municipal de loisir comme partenaire du réseau des organisations locales (institutionnelles et associatives); Promouvoir l'expertise des professionnels du loisir; démontrer l'utilité et les bénéfices du loisir; Développer des pratiques professionnelles en loisir
Luc Toupin, Directeur général
Pierre Waters, Directeur, Services aux membres associés
Joëlle Derulle, Conseillère, Formations et développement

Canadian Association of Municipal Administrators (CAMA)
PO Box 128, Stn. A, Fredericton NB E3B 4Y2
Tel: 866-771-2262
admin@camacam.ca
www.camacam.ca
To advance excellence in municipal management throughout Canada
Jacques Des Ormeaux, President
Ron Shaw, Treasurer

Canadian Council on Social Development (CCSD) / Conseil canadien de développement social (CCDS)
PO Box 13713, Kanata ON K2K 1X6
Tel: 613-236-8977; *Fax:* 613-482-7970
council@ccsd.ca
www.ccsd.ca
To develop & promote progressive social policies, on issues such as child well-being, poverty, housing, employment, cultural diversity, & social inclusion
Peggy Taillon, President & Chief Executive Officer
Katherine Scott, Vice-President, Research & Policy
Terrance Hunsley, Manager, Projects
Tammy Williams, Manager, Operations & Special Projects

Cities of New Brunswick Association
PO Box 1421, Stn. A, 95 Duffie Dr., Fredericton NB E3B 5E3
Tel: 506-693-0008; *Fax:* 506-693-0009
Sandra Mark, Executive Director

Corporation des officiers municipaux agréés du Québec (COMAQ) / Corporation of Chartered Municipal Officers of Québec
Édifice Lomer-Gouin, #R02, 575, rue Saint-Amable, Québec QC G1R 2G4
Tél: 418-527-1231; *Téléc:* 418-527-4462
Ligne sans frais: 800-305-1031
info@comaq.qc.ca
www.comaq.qc.ca
Regrouper les cadres municipaux des cités et villes du Québec; promouvoir la formation professionnelle par l'organisation de cours; protéger les intérêts sociaux-économiques des membres.
Erick Parent, Secrétaire général

Council of Maritime Premiers/Council of Atlantic Premiers (CMP/CAP) / Conseil des premiers ministres des Maritimes/Conseil des premiers ministres de l'Alantique
PO Box 2044, #1006, 5161 George St., Halifax NS B3J 2Z1
Tel: 902-424-7590; *Fax:* 902-424-8976
info@cap-cpma.ca
www.cap-cpma.ca
Don Osmond, Secretary

Democracy Watch
PO Box 821, Stn. B, #1210, 1 Nicholas St., Ottawa ON K1P 5P9
Tel: 613-241-5179; *Fax:* 613-241-4758
dwatch@web.net
www.dwatch.ca
To advocate for democratic reform, government accountability, and corporate responsibility.
Duff Conacher, Coordinator

Federation of Canadian Municipalities (FCM) / Fédération canadienne des municipalités
24 Clarence St., Ottawa ON K1N 5P3
Tel: 613-241-5221; *Fax:* 613-241-7440
federation@fcm.ca
www.fcm.ca
Social Media: www.facebook.com/pages/FCM/201746766534992; twitter.com/FCM_online; www.linkedin.com/company/federation-of-canadian-municipalities
FCM is the national voice of municipal government that represents the interests of municipalities on policy & program matters that fall within federal jurisdiction. Its goal in serving elected municipal officials is the improvement of the quality of life in all communities.
Berry Vrbanovic, President
Basil L. Stewart, President

Federation of Northern Ontario Municipalities (FONOM)
PO Box 2175, Stn. A, Sudbury ON P3A 4S1
Tel: 705-586-9120; *Fax:* 705-586-9195
fonom@eastlink.ca
www.fonom.org
To act as the voice for the people of northeastern Ontario communities; To work for the betterment of municipal government by striving for improved legislation respecting local government in northern Ontario
Lynne Reynolds, Executive Director
Al Spacek, President

Federation of Prince Edward Island Municipalities Inc. (FPEIM)
1 Kirkdale Rd., Charlottetown PE C1E 1R3
Tel: 902-566-1493; *Fax:* 902-566-2880
info@fpeim.ca
www.fpeim.ca
To represent the interests of the cities, towns & communities within PEI; To secure united action for the protection of individual municipalities & municipal interests as a whole; To act as a clearing house for the collection, exchange & dissemination of information of concern & interest to member municipalities; To provide training, education & development opportunities for elected & appointed municipal officials
John Dewey, Executive Director
Bruce MacDougall, President

Fédération Québécoise des Municipalités (FQM)
#560, 2954, boul Laurier, Sainte-Foy QC G1V 4T2
Tél: 418-651-3343; *Téléc:* 418-651-1127
fqm@fqm.ca
www.fqm.ca
Etre la porte-parole des régions; défendre les intérêts de ses membres
Bernard Généreux, Président

Foreign Service Community Association (FSCA) / Association de la communauté du service extérieur (ACSE)
L.B. Pearson Building, 125 Sussex Dr., Ottawa ON K1A 0G2
Tel: 613-944-5729; *Fax:* 613-995-9335
fsca.acse@international.gc.ca
www.fsca-acse.org
To support the employees, spouses, & dependants of Canadian foreign service departments; To act as a liaison between families of the Canadian Foreign Service & Foreign Affairs Canada (FAC), the Canadian International Development Agency (CIDA), International Trade Canada (ITCan), Citizenship & Immigration Canada (CIC), & the Department National Defence (DND)
Helen Boutilier-Inglis, President

Government Finance Officers Association (GFOA)
#2700, 203 North LaSalle St., Chicago IL 60601-1210 USA
Tel: 312-977-9700; *Fax:* 312-977-4806
inquiry@gfoa.org
www.gfoa.org
To serve the public finance profession in the the United States & Canada
Jeffrey Esser, Executive Director & CEO
Kenneth L. Rust, President
John Jurkash, Chief Financial Officer, Financial Administration

Institute of Public Administration of Canada (IPAC) / Institut d'administration publique du Canada (IAPC)
#401, 1075 Bay St., Toronto ON M5S 2B1
Tel: 416-924-8787; *Fax:* 416-924-4992
www.ipac.ca
To advance public service excellence, by sharing effective practices & policy in public administration; To lead public administration research in Canada; To further professional, non-artisan public service
Michael Fenn, Executive Director
Gabriella Ciampini, Director, Special Events
Wendy Feldman, Director, Research
Carole Humphries, Director, Membership & Marketing
Ann Masson, Director, International Programs
Jehan Contractor, Coordinator, Finance & Administration, Special Projects
Jennifer Dany Aubé, Coordinator, Member Services
Elisabeth Laviolette, Managing Editor & Manager, Public Sector Management Magazine
Megan Sproule-Jones, Managing Editor, Canadian Public Administration Journal

Institute On Governance (IOG) / Institut sur la gouvernance
60 George St., Ottawa ON K1N 1J4
Tel: 613-562-0090; *Fax:* 613-562-0087
info@iog.ca
www.iog.ca
Social Media: www.facebook.com/IOGca; twitter.com/IOGca; www.linkedin.com/groups/Institute-On-Governance-4179557
To explore, share & promote responsible & responsive governance in Canada & abroad
Maryantonett Flumian, President
Philip Bolger, Vice-President, Operations
Todd Cain, Vice-President, Crown & Organization Governance
Laura Edgar, Vice-President, Partnerships & International Programming
Toby Fyfe, Vice-President, Learning Lab
Marion Lefebvre, Vice-President, Aboriginal Governance

Local Government Management Association of British Columbia (LGMA)
Central Building, 620 View St., 7th Fl., Victoria BC V8W 1J6
Tel: 250-383-7032; *Fax:* 250-384-4879
office@lgma.ca; editor@lgma.ca (magazine); ads@lgma.ca
www.lgma.ca
To promote professional management & leadership excellence in local government; To create awareness of local government officers' roles in the community
Tom MacDonald, Executive Director
Elizabeth Brennan, Coordinator, Internship Program
Ana Fuller, Coordinator, Program
Renee Johansson, Accountant

Manitoba Municipal Administrators' Association Inc.
533 Buckingham Rd., Winnipeg MB R3R 1B9
Tel: 204-255-4883; *Fax:* 204-255-2623
mmaa@mts.net
www.mmaa.mb.ca
The Manitoba Municipal Administrators' Association (MMAA) is a dynamic, action-orientated organization for Municipal Employees. The MMAA focusses on the needs of our membership and are committed to their professional development.
Mel Nott, Executive Director

Municipalities Newfoundland & Labrador
460 Torbay Rd., St. John's NL A1A 5J3
Tel: 709-753-6820; *Fax:* 709-738-0071
Toll-Free: 800-440-6536
mnl@municipalitiesnl.com
www.municipalitiesnl.com
To assist communities in their endeavour to achieve & sustain strong & effective local government thereby improving the quality of life for all the people of this province.
Craig Pollett, Executive Director
Christine Cave, Administrative Officer

National Association of Federal Retirees (FSNA) / L'Association nationale des retraités fédéraux (ANRF)
1052 St. Laurent Blvd., Ottawa ON K1K 3B4
Tel: 613-745-2559; *Fax:* 613-745-5457
info@fsna.com
www.fsna.com
To protect & enhance the rights & benefits of retired federal employees, & seniors in general, & to cooperate with other seniors'/pensionsers' organizations on objectives of mutual interest
Hélian Lizotte, National President
Stan Hrabchuk, National President

Northwest Territories Association of Communities (NWTAC)
Finn Hansen Bldg., #200, 5105 - 50th St., Yellowknife NT X1A 1S1
Tel: 867-873-8359; *Fax:* 867-873-3042
Toll-Free: 866-973-8359
www.nwtac.com
To promote the exchange of information amongst the community governments of the Northwest Territories and to provide a united front for the realization of goals.
Yvette Gonzalez, CEO

Northwestern Ontario Municipal Association (NOMA)
PO Box 10308, Thunder Bay ON P7B 6T8
Tel: 807-683-6662
admin@noma.on.ca
www.noma.on.ca
To consider matters of interest to municipalities in northwestern Ontario; To procure enactment of legislation which may be advantageous to northwestern Ontario's municipalities
Charla Robinson, Executive Director
Dennis Brown, President

Iain Angus, Vice-President

Ontario Municipal Human Resources Association (OMHRA)
#307, 1235 Fairview St., Burlington ON L7S 2K9
Tel: 905-525-4000; *Fax:* 905-525-9833
admin@omhra.ca
www.omhra.ca
To provide direction on issues of human resources management; To represent the interests of the association, related to legislation & policies
Peggy Mellor, President
Kandy Webb, Vice-President
Christine A. Ball, Executive Officer

Ontario Municipal Management Institute (OMMI)
618 Balmoral Dr., Oshawa ON L1J 3A7
Tel: 905-434-8885; *Fax:* 905-434-7381
www.ommi.on.ca
To enhance management skills, in order to strengthen local government administration
Bill McKim, Executive Director
Jackie Russell, Administrator, Training & Accreditation

Ontario Small Urban Municipalities (OSUM)
c/o Association of Municipalities of Ontario, #801, 200 University Ave., Toronto ON M5H 3C6
Tel: 416-971-9856; *Fax:* 416-971-6191
Toll-Free: 877-426-6527
amo@amo.on.ca
www.amo.on.ca//AM/Template.cfm?Section=What_s_New7
To take matters which affect Ontario's small urban communities to the attention of the provincial & federal governments
Paul Grenier, Chair
Jim Collard, Vice-Chair & Conference Chair
Larry McCabe, Administrative Member, OSUM Executive Committee

The Public Affairs Association of Canada (PAAC) / Association des affaires publiques du Canada
#301, 250 Consumers Rd., Toronto ON M2J 4V6
Tel: 416-367-2223; *Fax:* 416-495-8723
info@publicaffairs.ca
www.publicaffairs.ca
To improve the professionalism of members to enhance the relations of members' organizations with their publics
John Capobianco, President
Erika Mozes, Events Chair
Chris May, Sec.-Treas.

Rural Municipal Administrators' Association of Saskatchewan (RMAA)
PO Box 130, Wilcox SK S0G 5E0
Tel: 306-732-2030; *Fax:* 306-732-4495
rmaa@sasktel.net
www.rmaa.ca
To address the needs of rural administrators in Saskatchewan
Kevin Ritchie, Executive Director
Don McCallum, President
Tim Leurer, Vice-President

Saskatchewan Association of Rural Municipalities (SARM)
2075 Hamilton St., Regina SK S4P 2E1
Tel: 306-757-3577; *Fax:* 306-565-2141
Toll-Free: 800-667-3604
sarm@sarm.ca
www.sarm.ca
To represent & advocate for rural municipal government in Saskatchewan
Dale Harvey, Executive Director
David Marit, President

Saskatchewan Urban Municipalities Association (SUMA)
#200, 2222 - 13th Ave., Regina SK S4P 3M7
Tel: 306-525-3727; *Fax:* 306-525-4373
suma@suma.org
www.suma.org
To work to enhance urban life in Saskatchewan, by providing administrative & consultative services to members, a forum for the discussion & resolution of current issues, & a negotiating vehicle for improvements in legislation, financing & programs. SUMA provides information & training for aldermen & mayors, and group benefits for its members
Laurent Mougeot, CEO
Mark Cooper, Director, Policy & Communication
Gail Meyer, Manager, Member & Administrative Services

Society of Local Government Managers of Alberta
PO Box 308, 4629 - 54 Ave., Bruderheim AB T0B 0S0
Tel: 780-796-3836; *Fax:* 780-796-2081
linda.davies@shaw.ca
www.clgm.net
Linda M. Davies, Executive Director/Registrar

Union des municipalités du Québec (UMQ)
#680, 680, rue Sherbrooke ouest, Montréal QC H3A 2M7
Tél: 514-282-7700; *Téléc:* 514-282-8893
info@umq.qc.ca
www.umq.qc.ca
Au bénéfice des citoyens, représenter les municipalités auprès du gouvernement et contribuer à l'efficience de gestion des municipalités.
Pierre Prévost, Directeur général par intérim
Robert Coulombe, Président

Union of British Columbia Municipalities
#60, 10551 Shellbridge Way, Richmond BC V6X 2W9
Tel: 604-270-8226; *Fax:* 604-270-9116
ubcm@civicnet.bc.ca
www.civicnet.bc.ca
To provide a common voice for local government
Richard Taylor, Executive Director
Brenda Binnie, President

Union of Municipalities of New Brunswick (UMNB) / Union des municipalités du Nouveau-Brunswick
#4, 79 Main St., Rexton NB E4W 1Z9
Tel: 506-523-7991; *Fax:* 506-523-7992
umnb@nb.aibn.com
www.umnb.ca
To unite the municipalities of New Brunswick through their respective councils into a body whose common efforts shall be devoted solely to the achievement of that which is the common good of all
Tom Gillett, Director

Union of Nova Scotia Municipalities (UNSM)
#1106, 1809 Barrington St., Halifax NS B3J 3K8
Tel: 902-423-8331; *Fax:* 902-425-5592
info@unsm.ca
www.unsm.ca
To research, promote & represent provincial interests of local government
Betty MacDonald, Executive Director
Judy Webber, Event Planner/Financal Officer

Urban Municipal Administrators' Association of Saskatchewan (UMAAS)
PO Box 603, Hudson Bay SK S0E 0Y0
Tel: 306-865-2825; *Fax:* 306-865-2800
umaas@sasktel.net
www.umaas.ca
Richard Dolezsar, Executive Director

Health & Medical

Acoustic Neuroma Association of Canada (ANAC) / Association pour les neurinomes acoustiques du Canada
PO Box 68028, 162 Bonnie Doon Shopping Centre, Edmonton AB T6C 4N6
Toll-Free: 800-561-2622
info@anac.ca
www.anac.ca
To provide support & information for those who have experienced acoustic neuromas or other tumors affecting the cranial nerves; To furnish information on patient rehabilitation to physicians & health care personnel; To promote & support research; To educate the public regarding symptoms suggestive of acoustic neuromas, thus promoting early diagnosis & consequent successful treatment
Cheryl Bauer, National Coordinator

Acupuncture Foundation of Canada Institute (AFCI) / Institut de la fondation d'acupuncture du Canada
#204, 2131 Lawrence Ave. East, Toronto ON M1R 5G4
Tel: 416-752-3988; *Fax:* 416-752-4398
afciweb@afcinstitute.com
www.afcinstitute.com
To define & maintain the highest professional standards for the use of acupuncture; to gain recognition of acupuncture's legitimate place in western medicine as a safe, efficient complement to conventional medical treatment; to design educational training programs for physicians, physiotherapists, RNs, dentists, chiropractors & naturopaths in the methodology & practice of acupuncture
Catherine Fuller, President/Chair
Cathy Donald, Treasurer

African Medical & Research Foundation Canada (AMREF Canada)
#407, 489 College St., Toronto ON M6G 1A5
Tel: 416-961-6981; *Fax:* 416-961-6984
info@amrefcanada.org
www.amrefcanada.org
Social Media: www.facebook.com/amrefcanada?ref=profile; twitter.com/amrefcanada
Development agency working to enhance community health in East & Southern Africa; headquartered in Nairobi, Kenya; eleven national offices in both Europe & America; acts as support office in raising private & public funds for overseas health programs & also plays active role in maintaining working relations with Canadian International Development Agency (CIDA)
Anne-Marie Kamanye, Executive Director

Alberta & Northwest Territories Lung Association
PO Box 4500, Stn. South, #208, 17420 Stony Plain Rd., Edmonton AB T5E 6K2
Tel: 780-488-6819; *Fax:* 780-488-7195
Toll-Free: 888-566-5864
info@ab.lung.ca
www.ab.lung.ca
Social Media: www.facebook.com/group.php?gid=192015860715
To educate the public & medical professionals about lung health
Anne Marie Downey, Chair
Kate Hurlburt, Vice-Chair
Tom Watts, Secretary
Paul Borrett, Treasurer

Alberta Association of Naturopathic Practitioners (AANP)
PO Box 21142, 665 - 8th St. SW, Calgary AB T2P 4H5
Tel: 403-266-2446
aanb_ab@telusplanet.net
www.naturopathic-alberta.com
Alissa Gaul, President

Alberta Association of Optometrists (AAO)
#100, 8407 Argyll Rd., Edmonton AB T6C 4B2
Tel: 780-451-6824; *Fax:* 780-452-9918
Toll-Free: 800-272-8843
www.optometrists.ab.ca
To promote excellence in the practice of Optometry, to enhance public recognition of Optometry as the primary vision care provider in Alberta, and to advance the interests of the profession.
Brian Wik, Executive Director

Alberta Heritage Foundation for Medical Research (AHFMR)
#1500, 10104 - 103 Ave., Edmonton AB T5J 4A7
Tel: 780-423-5727; *Fax:* 780-429-3509
Toll-Free: 877-423-5727
info@ahfmr.ab.ca
www.ahfmr.ab.ca
To support basic biomedical, clinical & health research in Alberta; contributes funds to scientific community to carry out research
Jacques Magnan, Interim President & CEO
Kathleen Thurber, Director, Communications & Education

Alberta Medical Association
12230 - 106 Ave. NW, Edmonton AB T5N 3Z1
Tel: 780-482-2626; *Fax:* 780-482-5445
Toll-Free: 800-272-9680
media@albertadoctors.org, amamail@albertadoctors.org
www.albertadoctors.org/home
To advocate on behalf of its physician members; to provide leadership & support for their role in the provision of quality health care
R. Michael Giuffre, President Elect
Linda M. Slocombe, President

Alberta Public Health Association (APHA)
c/o ACICR, 4075 RTF, 8308 - 114th St., Edmonton AB T6G 2E1
Tel: 780-492-6014; *Fax:* 780-492-7154
info@apha.ab.ca
www.apha.ab.ca
To promote & protect the health of the public through advocacy, partnerships, & education
Kim Raine, President
Elinor Wilson, Executive Director

Allergy Asthma Information Association (AAIA) / Allergie Asthme association d'information
#118, 295 The West Mall, Toronto ON M9C 4Z4
Tel: 416-621-4571; *Fax:* 416-621-5034
Toll-Free: 800-611-7011
admin@aaia.ca
www.aaia.ca
Social Media: www.facebook.com/AllergyAsthmaInformationAssociation
To create a safer environment for Canadians with allergies, asthma, & anaphylaxis; To assist persons coping with allergies; To act as a national voice for individuals affected by allergy, asthma, & anaphylaxis
Mary Allen, Chief Executive Officer
Louis Isabella, Treasurer

ALS Society of Canada (ALS) / La Société canadienne de la SLA (SLA)
#200, 3000 Steeles Ave. East, Markham ON L3R 4T9
Tel: 905-248-2052; *Fax:* 905-248-2019
Toll-Free: 800-267-4257
www.als.ca
Social Media: www.facebook.com/ALSCanada1; twitter.com/alsassociation
To support research towards a cure for ALS; to support ALS partners in their provision of quality care for persons affected by ALS
Lindee David, CEO
Enzo Raponi, Director, Development
Bobbi Greenberg, Director, Communications

Alzheimer Manitoba
#10, 120 Donald St., Winnipeg MB R3C 4G2
Tel: 204-943-6622; *Fax:* 204-942-5408
Toll-Free: 800-378-6699
alzmb@alzheimer.mb.ca
www.alzheimer.mb.ca/
To alleviate the individual, family & social consequences of Alzheimer type dementia while supporting the search for a cure
Sylvia Rothney, Executive Director

Alzheimer Society Canada (ASC) / Société Alzheimer Canada
#1600, 20 Eglinton Ave. West, Toronto ON M4R 1K8
Tel: 416-488-8772; *Fax:* 416-322-6656
Toll-Free: 800-616-8816
info@alzheimer.ca
www.alzheimer.ca
Social Media: www.facebook.com/AlzheimerSociety; twitter.com/AlzSociety
Identifies, develops & facilitates national priorities that enable members to alleviate personal & social consequences of Alzheimer's disease & related disorders; promotes research & leads the search for a cure
Leslie A. Beck, President

Alzheimer Society of Alberta & Northwest Territories
10531 Kingsway Ave., Edmonton AB T5H 4K1
Tel: 780-488-2266; *Fax:* 780-488-3055
Toll-Free: 866-950-5465
info@alzheimer.ab.ca
www.alzheimer.ab.ca
The Society strives to alleviate the personal & social consequences of Alzheimer disease through the development, support & coordination of local societies & chapters. It also promotes the search for a cure through education & research. It is a registered charity, BN: 129690343RR0001.
Bill Gaudette, CEO
Christene Gordon, Director, Education & Support Services

Alzheimer Society of British Columbia
#300, 828 West 8th Ave., Vancouver BC V5Z 1E1
Tel: 604-681-6530; *Fax:* 604-669-6907
Toll-Free: 800-667-3742
info@alzheimerbc.org
www.alzheimerbc.org
Social Media: www.facebook.com/AlzheimerBC; twitter.com/AlzheimerBC; www.youtube.com/AlzheimerBC
To alleviate the personal & social consequences of Alzheimer disease & related dementias; to promote public awareness & to search for the causes & the cures
Jean Blake, CEO

Alzheimer Society of New Brunswick / Société alzheimer du nouveau brunswick
#100, 320 Maple St., Fredericton NB E3B 5G2
Tel: 506-459-4280; *Fax:* 506-452-0313
Toll-Free: 800-664-8411
info@alzheimernb.ca
www.alzheimernb.ca
Social Media: www.facebook.com/127071537361985; twitter.com/AlzheimerNB
To alleviate the personal & social consequences of Alzheimer disease; to promote the search for a cause & cure
Gloria McIlveen, Executive Director

Alzheimer Society of Newfoundland & Labrador
PO Box 37013, 687 Water St., St. John's NL A1E 1C2
Tel: 709-576-0608; *Fax:* 709-576-0798
Toll-Free: 877-776-0608
alzheimersociety@nf.aibn.com
www.alzheimernl.org
To support the search for the cause & cure of Alzheimer Disease; To raise public awareness of the personal & social impact of the disease; To promote the provision of support to families & caregivers in Newfoundland
Christine Caravan, Director

Alzheimer Society of Nova Scotia
#300, 6009 Quinpool Rd., Halifax NS B3K 5J7
Tel: 902-422-7961; *Fax:* 902-422-7971
Toll-Free: 800-611-6345
alzheimer@asns.ca
www.alzheimer.ca/ns
Social Media: www.facebook.com/profile.php?id=100003124237350; twitter.com/alzheimerns
To enhance the quality of life of people with Alzheimer disease through providing & promoting public education & family support; to engage in advocacy on behalf of people with Alzheimer disease & their families; to promote research at the provincial & national levels
Lloyd O. Brown, Executive Director
Justin McDonough, President

Alzheimer Society of PEI
166 Fitzroy St., Charlottetown PE C1A 1S1
Tel: 902-628-2257; *Fax:* 902-368-2715
Toll-Free: 866-628-2257
society@alzpei.ca
www.alzpei.ca
To support & assist Islanders affected by Alzheimer Disease; To raise the level of awareness & educate the public at large about the disease
Colleen Laybolt, Executive Administrator

Alzheimer Society Of Saskatchewan Inc. (ASOS)
#301, 2550 - 12 Ave., Regina SK S4P 3X1
Tel: 306-949-4141; *Fax:* 306-949-3069
Toll-Free: 800-263-3367
office@alzheimer.sk.ca
www.alzheimer.sk.ca
Social Media: www.facebook.com/217901721605861; twitter.com/AlzheimerSK
To alleviate the personal & social consequences of Alzheimer's disease & related disorders & to promote the search for a cause & a cure
Joanne Bracken, Executive Director
Kathleen Defoe, Coordinator, Finance & Administration

Alzheimer Society Ontario / Société Alzheimer Ontario
#1600, 20 Eglinton Ave. West, Toronto ON M4R 1K8
Tel: 416-967-5900; *Fax:* 416-967-3826
Toll-Free: 800-879-4226
staff@alzheimeront.org
www.alzheimer.ca/en/on
Social Media: www.facebook.com/AlzheimerSocietyofOntario; twitter.com/alzheimeront
To improve the quality of life for persons with Alzheimer disease & their families; to inform & educate the public & health care professionals about Alzheimer disease; to coordinate a chapter network & liaison in order to present a united voice to the Government of Ontario & other provincial groups on matters relating to legal concerns, health care, research, & community needs; to raise funds for research
Bryon Gero, President

Aplastic Anemia & Myelodysplasia Association of Canada (AAMAC)
#321, 11181 Yonge St., Richmond Hill ON L4S 1L2
Tel: 905-780-0698; *Fax:* 905-780-1648
Toll-Free: 888-840-0039
info@aamac.ca
www.aamac.ca
To disseminate information concerning the disease; To form a nation-wide support network for patients, families & medical professionals; To support Canadian Blood Services & their programs; To raise funds for research
Gord Sanford, President
Joyce Burnett, Secretary
Sylvia Scow, Coordinator, British Columbia
Chris Meyer, Coordinator, Ontario

Arthritis Society / Société de l'arthrite
#1700, 393 University Ave., Toronto ON M5G 1E6
Tel: 416-979-7228; *Fax:* 416-979-8366
Toll-Free: 800-321-1433
info@arthritis.ca
www.arthritis.ca
Social Media: www.facebook.com/arthritissociety
The Society is a not-for-profit organization devoted solely to funding & promoting arthritis research, programs & patient care. There are division offices in each province & nearly 1,000 community branches throughout Canada. It is a registered charity, BN: 108071671RR0003.
Steven McNair, President/CEO
Derek Rodrigues, CFO

Association canadienne des ataxies familiales (ACAF) / Canadian Association of Friedreich's Ataxia
#110, 3800, rue Radisson, Montréal QC H1M 1X6
Tél: 514-321-8684; *Téléc:* 514-899-9158
ataxie@lacaf.org
www.lacaf.org
Recueillir des dons du public pour financer les recherches médicales qui se font sur l'Ataxie de Friedreich ainsi que d'améliorer la condition de vie des personnes ataxiques; (personne qui est affligée par la maladie de l'Ataxie de Friedreich)
Diane Limoges, Présidente

Association d'orthopédie du Québec
CP 216, #3000, 2, Complexe Desjardins, Montréal QC H5B 1G8
Tél: 514-844-0803; *Téléc:* 514-844-6786
aoq@fmsq.org
www.orthoquebec.ca/
Valoriser le statut professionnel de ses membres; promouvoir leurs intérêts économiques; contribuer au développement de la chirurgie orthopédique et de la traumatologie par le biais d'activités de formation médicale continue
Jacques Desnoyers, Président

Association d'oto-rhino-laryngologie et de chirurgie cervico-faciale du Québec
#3000, 2, Complexe Desjardins, Montréal QC H5B 1G8
Tél: 514-350-5125; *Téléc:* 514-350-5165
assorl@fmsq.org
www.orlquebec.org
Valoriser le statut professionnel de ses membres, promouvoir leurs intérêts scientifiques, économiques et professionnels, et contribuer au développement de l'oto-rhino-laryngologie
Pascal Desrochers, Secrétaire
Raynald Ferland, Président

Association de neurochirurgie du Québec (ANCQ)
#3000, 2, Complexe Desjardins, Montréal QC H5B 1G8
Tél: 514-350-5120; *Téléc:* 514-350-5100
ancq@fmsq.org
www.ancq.net
La neurochirurgie est la spécialité qui s'occupe du traitement médico-chirurgical des pathologies du système nerveux central et de ses enveloppes (cerveau, moelle épinière, crâne et rachis) ainsi que du système nerveux périphérique (nerfs). L'ANCQ a pour mission le développement des intérêts économiques, sociaux, moraux et scientifiques de ses membres
Alain Bouthillier, Président
David Mathieu, Secrétaire-trésorier
Painchaud Gisèle, Directrice

L'Association de spina-bifida et d'hydrocéphalie du Québec (ASBHQ)
#542, 3333, ch. Queen-Mary, Montréal QC H3V 1A2
Tél: 514-340-9019; *Téléc:* 514-340-9109
Ligne sans frais: 800-567-1788
info@spina.qc.ca
www.spina.qc.ca
Média social: twitter.com/ASBHQ
Promouvoir et défendre les droits, les intérêts et le bien-être des personnes ayant le spina-bifida et l'hydrocéphalie; sensibiliser le public à la nature du spina-bifida et de l'hydrocéphalie ainsi qu'aux besoins des personnes ayant ces malformations; favoriser et soutenir la recherche sur les causes, les nouveaux traitements et les techniques de prévention du spina-bifida et de l'hydrocéphalie
Marc Picard, Président

Association des Allergologues et Immunologues du Québec
CP 216, Succ. Desjardins, #3000, 2, Complexe Desjardins, Montréal QC H5B 1G8
Tél: 514-350-5101; *Téléc:* 514-350-5146
jdelisle@fmsq.org
www.allerg.qc.ca
Normand Dubé, Président

Association des cardiologues du Québec
#3000, 2, Complexe Desjardins, Montréal QC H5B 1G8
Tél: 514-350-5106; *Téléc:* 514-350-5156
acq@fmsq.org
Gaëtan Houde, Président
Louise Girard, Directrice

Association des chiropraticiens du Québec
7960, boul Métropolitain est, Montréal QC H1K 1A1
Tél: 514-355-0557; *Téléc:* 514-355-0070
Ligne sans frais: 866-292-4476
acq@chiropratique.com
www.chiropratique.com
Défendre les intérêts professionnels, sociaux et économiques de ses membres
Richard Giguère, Président
Marie-Hélène Boivin, Secrétaire
Claude Pilon, Trésorier

Association des conseils des médecins, dentistes et pharmaciens du Québec (ACMDP) / Association of Councils of Physicians, Dentists & Pharmacist of Québec
#212, 560, boul Henri-Bourassa ouest, Montréal QC H3L 1P4
Tél: 514-858-5885; *Téléc:* 514-858-6767
acmdp@acmdp.qc.ca
www.acmdp.qc.ca
Offrir l'information, la motivation, et la formation médico-administrative nécessaire aux Conseils des médecins, dentistes, et pharmaciens membres afin qu'ils accomplissent adéquatement leurs tâches
Dominique Derome, Directrice générale
Nicole Durand, Adjointe administrative

Association des dermatologistes du Québec (ADQ) / Association of Dermatologists of Québec
CP 216, Succ. Succ. Desjardins, #3000, 2, Complexe Desjardins, Montréal QC H5B 1G8
Tél: 514-350-5111; *Téléc:* 514-350-5161
www.adq.org
Syndicat professionnel: assure la défense des intérêts économiques, professionnels et scientifiques de ses membres
Chantal Bolduc, Présidente

Association des gastro-entérologues du Québec (AGEQ)
CP 216, Succ. Desjardins, 2, Complexe Desjardins, Montréal QC H5B 1G8
Tél: 514-350-5112; *Téléc:* 514-350-5146
sbergeron@FMSQ.ORG
www.ageq.qc.ca
Notre site a une mission d'information et de formation aux membres, une mission d'information et de formations aux médecins de première ligne, aux patients souffrant de pathologies gastro-intestinales et aux autres médecins intéressés par la gastro-entérologie. Enfin, notre site a la mission de créer des liens avec la communauté médicale internationale.
Victor Plourde, Président

Association des médecins biochimistes du Québec
#3000, 2, Complexe Desjardins, Montréal QC H5B 1G8
Tél: 514-350-5105; *Téléc:* 514-350-5151
ambq@fmsq.org
www.ambq.med.usherbrooke.ca
Promouvoir l'utilisation optimale des tests de laboratoire au Québec en offrant, au professionnel de la santé et au patient, les meilleurs services de diagnostic et de dépistage de maladies grâce à des techniques biochimiques et immunologiques
Elaine Letendre, Présidente

Association des médecins endocrinologues du Québec
CP 216, Succ. Desjardins, #3000, 2, Complexe Desjardins, Montréal QC H5B 1G8
Tél: 514-350-5135; *Téléc:* 514-350-5049
Ligne sans frais: 800-561-0703
ameq@fmsq.org
www.ameq.qc.ca
L'Association est un porte-parole des endocrinologues; elle favorise les intérêts scientifiques de ses membres et organise plusieurs réunions afin de permettre une formation médicale continue des endocrinologues
Jean-Hugues Brossard, Président

Association des médecins généticiens du Québec
#300, 2, Complexe Desjardins, Montréal QC H5B 1G8
Tél: 514-350-5141; *Téléc:* 514-350-5151
mfcaron@fmsq.org
Emmanuelle Lemyre, Présidente
Sandrine Guillot, Directrice

Association des médecins gériatres du Québec
CP 216, Succ. Desjardins, #3000, 2, Complexe Desjardins, Montréal QC H5B 1G8
Tél: 514-350-5145; *Téléc:* 514-350-5151
amgq@fmsq.org; clavoie@fmsq.org
www.fmsq.org/amgq
Maurice St-Laurent, Président

Association des médecins hématologistes-oncologistes du Québec (AMHOQ)
#3000, 2, Complexe Desjardins, Montréal QC H5B 1G8
Tél: 514-350-5121; *Téléc:* 514-350-5126
Ligne sans frais: 800-561-0703
amhoq@fmsq.org
Daniel Bélanger, Président

Association des médecins microbiologistes-infectiologues du Québec (AMMIQ)
#3000, 2, Complexe Desjardins, Montréal QC H5B 1G8
Tél: 514-350-5104; *Téléc:* 514-350-5144
info@ammiq.org
www.ammiq.org
L'Association regroupe des médecins (de laboratoire et dans le diagnostic clinique) spécialisés dans l'épidémiologie, le traitement et la prévention des maladies infectieuses
Charlotte Lavoie, Directrice

Association des médecins ophtalmologistes du Québec (AMOQ)
CP 216, Succ. Desjardins, 2, Complexe Desjardins, Montréal QC H5B 1G8
Tél: 514-350-5124; *Téléc:* 514-350-5174
amoq@fmsq.org
www.amoq.org
Promouvoit les intérêts professionnels et économiques de ses membres; se préoccupe du maintien de la compétence; suscite et appuie des activités scientifiques susceptibles de favoriser l'avancement de l'ophtalmologie; se préoccupe de l'accessibilité aux soins ophtalmologiques
Jean-Daniel Arbour, Président

Association des médecins rhumatologues du Québec (AMRQ)
#3000, 2, Complexe Desjardins, Montréal QC H5B 1G8
Tél: 514-350-5136; *Téléc:* 514-350-5029
amrq@fmsq.org
www.fmsq.org
La rhumatologie se consacre au diagnostic et au traitement des pathologies qui touchent les articulations, les os, les muscles et tendons et parfois tout organe dans le cadre de maladies systémiques. Ceci regroupe au-delà de 100 conditions pouvant aller de l'arthrite rhumatoïde au lupus érythémateux disséminé en passant par l'arthrose, les vasculites et l'ostéoporose.
Denis Choquette, Président

Association des médecins spécialistes en médecine nucléaire du Québec (AMSMNQ)
#3000, 2, Complexe Desjardins, Montréal QC H5B 1G8
Tél: 514-350-5133; *Téléc:* 514-350-5151
Ligne sans frais: 800-561-0703
amsmnq@fmsq.org
www.medecinenucleaire.com/
François Lamoureux, Président
Jean Guimond, Vice-président

Association des médecins spécialistes en santé communautaire du Québec (AMSSCQ)
#3000, 2, Complexe Desjardins, Montréal QC H5B 1G8
Tél: 514-350-5138; *Téléc:* 514-350-5151
amsscq@fmsq.org
www.amsscq.org
L'association a pour rôle de promouvoir les intérêts professionnels et économiques de ses membres
Jacques Ringuet, Président
Marc Rhainds, Vice-président

Association des néphrologues du Québec
#3000, 2, Complexe Desjardins, Montréal QC H5B 1G8
Tél: 514-350-5134; *Téléc:* 514-350-5151
mfcaron@fmsq.org
Robert Charbonneau, Président
Marie-France Caron, Directrice

Association des neurologues du Québec (ANQ)
CP 216, Succ. Desjardins, #3000, 2, Complexe Desjardins, Montréal QC H5B 1G8
Tél: 514-350-5122; *Téléc:* 514-350-5172
anq@fmsq.org
www.anq.qc.ca
Représente des médecins spécialistes qui diagnostique et traite les maladies affectant le système nerveux central ainsi que le système nerveux périphérique
Ginette Guilbeault, Directrice

J. Marc Girard, Président
Francine Veilleux, Secrétaire

Association des obstétriciens et gynécologues du Québec (AOGQ)
#3000, 2, Complexe Desjardins, Montréal QC H5B 1G8
Tél: 514-849-4969; *Téléc:* 514-849-5011
info@gynecoquebec.com
www.gynecoquebec.com
Promouvoir l'intérêt professionnel scientifique et économique de ses membres
Francine Charlebois, Directrice administrative

Association des optométristes du Québec (AOQ) / Québec Optometric Association
#740, 1265, rue Berri, Montréal QC H2L 4X4
Tél: 514-288-6272; *Téléc:* 514-288-7071
aoq@aoqnet.qc.ca
www.aoqnet.qc.ca
Syndicat professionnel voué au développement des meilleures conditions de pratique économiques et professionnelles pour les optométristes du Québec
Francois Charbonneau, Directeur général
Steven Carrier, Président

Association des pathologistes du Québec (APQ)
CP 216, #3000, 2, Complexe Desjardins, Montréal QC H5B 1G8
Tél: 514-350-5102; *Téléc:* 514-350-5152
Ligne sans frais: 800-561-0703
patho@fmsq.org
www.apq.qc.ca
Danielle Joncas, Directrice

Association des pédiatres du Québec
#3000, 2, Complexe Desjardins, Montréal QC H5B 1G8
Tél: 514-350-5127; *Téléc:* 514-350-5177
pediatrie@fmsq.org
www.fmsq.org
Thérèse Côté-Boileau, Présidente

Association des pharmaciens des établissements de santé du Québec (APES)
#320, 4050, rue Molson, Montréal QC H1Y 3N1
Tél: 514-286-0776; *Téléc:* 514-286-1081
info@apesquebec.org
www.apesquebec.org
Linda Vaillant, Directrice générale
France Boucher, Directrice générale adjointe

Association des physiatres du Québec (APQ)
#3000, 2, Complexe Desjardins, Montréal QC H5B 1G8
Tél: 514-350-5119; *Téléc:* 514-350-5147
apq@fmsq.org
www.fmsq.org
La physiatrie est la spécialité médicale vouée à la prévention, au diagnostic et au traitement médical des douleurs et des troubles de l'appareil locomoteur (la colonne vertébrale, les os, les muscles, les tendons, les articulations, les vaisseaux et le cerveau)
Claude Bouthillier, Président

Association des pneumologues de la province de Québec (APPQ)
#3000, 2, Complexe Desjardins, Montréal QC H5B 1G8
Tél: 514-350-5117; *Téléc:* 514-350-5153
appq@fmsq.org
www.fmsq.org; www.pneumologue.ca
Promouvoir les intérêts professionnels et économiques de ses membres; se préoccuper du maintien de leur compétence; se prononcer sur les problématiques de la pneumologie dans les meilleurs intérêts de la population
Dionne Raymonde, Directrice
Alain Beaupré, Président

Association des radiologistes du Québec
CP 216, Complexe Desjardins, Montréal QC H5B 1G8
Tél: 514-350-5129; *Téléc:* 514-350-5179
bureau@arq.qc.ca
www.arq.qc.ca
Regrouper les médecins spécialisés en radiologie; défendre leurs intérêts et promouvoir leur spécialité
Gaetan Barrette, Président

Association des radio-oncologues du Québec (AROQ)
#3000, 2, Complexe Desjardins, Montréal QC H5B 1G8
Tél: 514-350-5130; *Téléc:* 514-350-5126
aroq@fmsq.org
www.aroq.ca; www.fmsq.org
Khalil Sultanem, Président

Association des sexologues du Québec (ASQ)
#404, 7400, boul Saint-Laurent, Montréal QC H2R 2V1
Tél: 514-270-9289; *Téléc:* 514-270-6351
www.associationdessexologues.com
Susciter auprès du public une meilleure connaissance de la sexologie et du rôle du sexologue, en favorisant et en maintenant les normes scientifiques et professionnelles les plus élevées dans l'exercice de la sexologie et dans la formation des sexologues
Alain Gariépy, Président
Dominique Themens, Vice-présidente

Association des spécialistes en chirurgie plastique et esthétique du Québec (ASCPEQ)
CP 216, Succ. Desjardins, 2, Complexe Desjardins, Montréal QC H5B 1G8
Tél: 514-350-5109; *Téléc:* 514-350-5246
www.ascpeq.org
L'Association entend se consacrer essentiellement au développement continu de l'art et de la science de la chirurgie plastique et esthétique, entre autres par la diffusion de renseignements pertinents auprès du public, par la promotion d'une relation médecin-patient fondée sur la communication, la compréhension et le respect mutuel, ainsi que par une contribution active aux programmes d'éducation et de formation continue et par une participation critique aux débats relatifs au rôle et à la place des professionnels de la santé au sein de la société québécoise
André Chollet, Président

Association des spécialistes en médecine d'urgence du Québec
Tour de l'Est, #3000, 2, Complexe Desjardins, Montréal QC H5B 1G8
Tél: 514-350-5115; *Téléc:* 514-350-5116
www.asmuq.org/
François Dufresne, Président

Association des spécialistes en médecine interne du Québec
CP 216, Succ. Desjardins, #3000, 2, Complexe Desjardins, Montréal QC H5B 1G8
Tél: 514-350-5118; *Téléc:* 514-350-5168
med.interne@fmsq.org
Patrick Chagnon, Président

Association des urologues du Québec (AUQ) / Quebec Urological Association (QUA)
#3000, 2, Complexe Desjardins, Montréal QC H5B 1G8
Tél: 514-350-5131; *Téléc:* 514-350-5181
auq@fmsq.org
www.auq.org
Lorne Aaron, Président
Liliane Verret, Secrétariat

Association diabète Québec (ADQ) / Québec Diabetes Association
#300, 8550, boul Pie-IX, Montréal QC H1Z 4G2
Tél: 514-259-3422; *Téléc:* 514-259-9286
Ligne sans frais: 800-361-3504
info@diabete.qc.ca
www.diabete.qc.ca
Mèdia social: www.facebook.com/179747505687; twitter.com/DiabeteQuebec
Regrouper les diabétiques et favoriser l'entraide; les renseigner sur les façons de faire face à la maladie; informer le grand public et le sensibiliser à la condition de personnes souffrant du diabète; ouvrir de nouvelles voies dans le domaine de la recherche pour en venir à triompher du diabète
Serge Langlois, Président-directeur général

Association médicale du Québec (AMQ) / Québec Medical Association (QMA)
#3200, 380, rue Saint-Antoine ouest, Montréal QC H2Y 3X7
Tél: 514-866-0660; *Téléc:* 514-866-0670
Ligne sans frais: 800-363-3932
admin@amq.ca
www.amq.ca
Rassembler et soutenir les médecins du Québec afin de garantir à la population québécoise des conditions et des soins de santé de qualité
Claudette Duclos, Directrice générale

Association of Local Public Health Agencies (ALPHA)
#1306, 2 Carlton St., Toronto ON M5G 1T6
Tel: 416-595-0006; *Fax:* 416-595-0030
info@alphaweb.org
www.alphaweb.org
To provide leadership in public health management to health units in Ontario; To assist local public health units in the provision of efficient & effective services
Linda Stewart, Executive Director
Gordon Fleming, Manager, Public Health Issues
Tannisha Lambert, Manager, Administrative & Association Services

Association of Medical Microbiology & Infectious Disease Canada (AMMI Canada) / Association pour la microbiologie médicale et l'infectiologie Canada
#101, 298 Elgin St., Ottawa ON K2P 1M3
Tel: 613-260-3233; *Fax:* 613-260-3235
info@ammi.ca; communications@ammi.ca; manager@ammi.ca
www.ammi.ca
To represent the broad interests of researchers & physicians who specialize in the fields of infectious diseases & medical microbiology in Canada; To contribute to the health of people at risk of, or affected by, infectious diseases; To promote & facilitate research; To develop policies for the prevention, diagnosis, & management of infectious diseases
Lynn Johnston, President
Brett Filson, Executive Director
Riccarda Galioto, Office Manager & Coordinator, Special Events
Sarah Forgie, Secretary
Mel Krajden, Treasurer
Kimberley Wannamaker, Administrative Assistant, Membership
Gwen Lovagi, Contact, Communications

Association pour la santé publique du Québec (ASPQ) / Québec Public Health Association
#200, 4126, rue St-Denis, Montréal QC H2W 2M5
Tél: 514-528-5811; *Téléc:* 514-528-5590
info@aspq.org
www.aspq.org
Favoriser un regard critique sur les enjeux de santé publique au Québec en constituant un regroupement volontaire, autonome, multidisciplinaire et multisectoriel de personnes et d'organisations provenant des milieux tant institutionnels et professionnels que communautaires. L'Association constitue un forum qui offre un espace à ses membres pour développer des prises de position communes ou concertées, appuyer des politiques favorables à la santé et au bien-être et développer des coalitions et des projets en collaboration avec d'autres partenaires de santé publique ou du milieu.
Lucie Granger, Directrice Générale
Martine Deschênes, Adjointe administrative

Association Québécoise de chirurgie
#3000, 2, Complexe Desjardins, Montréal QC H5B 1G8
Tél: 514-350-5107; *Téléc:* 514-350-5157
aqc-dpc@fmsq.org
www.chirurgiequebec.ca
Objectifs sont la protection et défense des intérêts professionnels collectifs des chirurgiens et l'enseignement chirurgical continu
Richard Ratelle, Président

Association québécoise de l'épilepsie
#111, 1015, côte du Beaver Hall, Montréal QC H2Z 1S1
Tél: 514-875-5595; *Téléc:* 514-875-0077
aqe@cam.org
www.cam.org/~aqe/
Veiller au mieux-être des personnes épileptiques et à leurs familles; promouvoir les droits des personnes épileptiques; sensibiliser le public à l'épilepsie; promouvoir l'intégration scolaire et au travail
France Picard, Directrice générale

Asthma Society of Canada (ASC) / Société canadienne de l'asthme
#2306, 4680 Yonge St., Toronto ON M2N 6K1
Tel: 416-787-4050; *Fax:* 416-787-5807
Toll-Free: 866-787-4050
info@asthma.ca
www.asthma.ca
To optimize the health of people with asthma through education and asthma awareness.
Christine Hampson, President & Chief Executive Officer
Jim Martin, Director, Fund Raising
Oxana Latycheva, Vice President, Asthma Control Pro.

Autism Northwest Territories
4904 Matonabee St., Yellowknife NT X1A 1X8
Tel: 867-920-4206; *Fax:* 867-873-0235
autism@hotmail.com
Lynn Elkin, President

Autism Ontario
#004, 1179A King St. West, Toronto ON M6K 3C5
Tel: 416-246-9592; *Fax:* 416-246-9417
www.autismontario.com
To ensure that each individual with autism spectrum disorders is provided the means to achieve quality of life as a respected member of society
Marg Spuelstra, Executive Director

Autism Society Alberta (ASA)
#101, 11720 Kingsway Ave., Edmonton AB T5G 0X5
Tel: 780-453-3971; *Fax:* 780-447-4948
autism@autismedmonton.org
www.autismedmonton.org
To improve the understanding of autism throughout Alberta by the dissemination of information to parents, health care workers, educators, government, private agencies & the public
Karen Phillips, Director
Jean Ashmore, Secretary

Autism Society Canada (ASC) / Société canadienne d'autisme
PO Box 22017, 1670 Heron Rd., Ottawa ON K1V 0C2
Tel: 613-789-8943; *Fax:* 613-789-6985
info@autismsocietycanada.ca
www.autismsocietycanada.ca
To provide support on a national basis to people affected by autism & related conditions through the collective efforts of Canadian provincial & territorial autism societies; to provide information & general referrals to the public regarding autism & related conditions; to promote public awareness of autism & related conditions; to encourage research in fields related or relevant to autism & related conditions; to communicate with government, agencies, & other organizations on behalf of persons affected by autism & related conditions; to promote actions to ensure people with autism & related conditions live in an environment that supports their well-being & enables them to reach their full potential; to promote & encourage the convening of conferences focused on autism & related conditions
Kathleen Provost, Executive Director
Lynn Andrews, Information Services Coordinator

Autism Society Manitoba
825 Sherbrook St., 2nd Fl., Winnipeg MB R3A 1M5
Tel: 204-783-9563; *Fax:* 204-975-3027
Toll-Free: 800-225-9108
info@autismmanitoba.com
www.autismmanitoba.com
To promote the quality of life for people with Pervasive Developmental Disorder/Autism & their families; to promote full inclusion, dignity & development of personal skills & abilities for our members
Sandra McKay, President

Autism Society New Brunswick
PO Box 1493, Stn. A, Fredericton NB E3B 5G2
Toll-Free: 888-773-1916
autism_nb@yahoo.com
www.autismnb.org
Social Media: www.facebook.com/group.php?gid=120942775566
To promote public awareness, understanding & acceptance of persons with autism while providing support to families for the realization of services & programs within their community
Tamara Downey, President

Autism Society Newfoundland & Labrador (ASNL)
PO Box 14078, 70 Clinch Cres., St. John's NL A1B 4G8
Tel: 709-722-2803; *Fax:* 709-722-4926
Toll-Free: 866-722-2803
info@autism.nf.net
www.autism.nf.net
Social Media: twitter.com/AutismSocietyNL
To promote the diagnosis, treatment, education & integration into the community of all autistic persons; to provide information about autism; to promote research; to promote integrated care for autistic persons; to encourage the formation of parent support groups around the province
Trish Williams, Executive Director
Christopher Dedde, Aspire Program Coordinator

Autism Society of British Columbia
#301, 3701 East Hastings St., Burnaby BC V5C 2H6
Tel: 604-434-0880; *Fax:* 604-434-0801
Toll-Free: 888-437-0880
info@autismbc.ca
www.autismbc.ca
To promote awareness of autism & the needs of families with a child or adult with autism; to provide advocacy, resources, & referrals to families of people with autism in BC
Michael Lewis, Executive Director

Autism Society of Nova Scotia (ASNS)
PO Box 195, Dartmouth NS B2Y 3Y3
Tel: 902-429-5529
autismns@ns.aliantzinc.ca
www.autismsocietynovascotia.ca
To advocate for, educate the public about, & provide support to, persons with autism/pervasive developmental disorders & their families
Dana Shaw, Executive Director
Tracey Avery, Chair

Autism Society of PEI
PO Box 3243, 135 Kent St., Charlottetown PE C1A 8W5
Tel: 902-566-4844; *Toll-Free:* 888-360-8681
Nathalie@autismsociety.pe.ca
www.autismsociety.pe.ca
Austim resources available in PEI
Jeff Himelman, President
Nathalie Walsh, Executive Director

Autism Treatment Services of Canada (ATSC) / Association canadienne pour l'obtention des services aux personnes autistiques
404 - 94 Ave. SE, Calgary AB T2J 0E8
Tel: 403-253-2291; *Fax:* 403-253-6974
Toll-Free: 888-301-2872
atsc@autism.ca
www.autism.ca
The Society is an Alberta-based organization working to ensure that a comprehensive range of services exists across Canada to meet the needs of individuals with autism & their families, & that autistic people are given the opportunity to achieve maximum independence & productivity within the community. It is a registered charity, BN: 132329541RR0001.
Peter Johnson, Chair
Dave Mikkelsen, Executive Director

Autism Yukon
508F Main St., Whitehorse YT Y1A 2B9
Tel: 867-667-6406; *Fax:* 867-667-6408
info@autismyukon.org
www.autismyukon.org
Leah Davy Ryckman, Executive Director

Breast Cancer Action (BCA) / Sensibilisation au cancer du sein
Riverside Mall, 739A Ridgewood Ave., Ottawa ON K1V 6M8
Tel: 613-736-5921; *Fax:* 613-736-8422
info@bcaott.ca
www.bcaott.ca
To advocate establishment of a national resource office, directed by women affected by breast cancer, to serve as clearinghouse for information about treatment, legislative action, access to treatments & support services; to advocate for a designated centre for excellence to accelerate research; to advocate greater emphasis on developing earlier detection; to promote increased survivor participation in cancer care planning & policy making; to promote better education of family physicians & women in early detection & follow-up
Diane Ryan, President

Breast Cancer Society of Canada / Société du cancer du sein du Canada
420 East St. North, Sarnia ON N7T 6Y5
Tel: 519-336-0746; *Fax:* 519-336-5725
Toll-Free: 800-567-8767
bcsc@bcsc.ca
www.bcsc.ca
Social Media: www.facebook.com/breastcancersocietyofcanada
To support research into the prevention, detection, & treatment of breast cancer
Marsha Davidson, Executive Director
Dawn Hamilton, Coordinator, Fund Development
Bunny Caughlin, Officer, Operations
Johanne Deschamps, Officer, Communications

The British Columbia Association of Optometrists (BCAO)
#610, 2525 WILLOW Street, Vancouver BC V5Z 3N8
Tel: 604-737-9907; *Fax:* 604-737-9967
Toll-Free: 888-393-2226
info@optometrists.bc.ca
www.optometrists.bc.ca
To maintain standards; to represent membership to government & other health care professions; to raise public levels of awareness about optometry, good vision & eye care.
Cheryl Williams, CEO
Antoinette Dumalo, President

British Columbia Cancer Foundation (BCCF)
#150, 686 West Broadway, Vancouver BC V5Z 1G1
Tel: 604-877-6040; *Fax:* 604-877-6161
Toll-Free: 888-906-2873
bccfinfo@bccancer.bc.ca
www.bccancerfoundation.com
Social Media: www.facebook.com/BCCancerFoundation; twitter.com/bccancer
To reduce the incidence of cancer, reduce the mortality rate from cancer, & improve the quality of life for those living with cancer, through the acquisition, development, & stewardship of resources
Douglas Nelson, President & Chief Executive Officer
Luigi (Lou) Del Gobbo, Chief Financial Officer & Vice-President
Patsy Worrall, Vice-President, Marketing & Communications
Cindy Dopson, MBA, CHRP, Director, Human Resources

British Columbia Centre for Ability Association (BCCFA)
2805 Kingsway, Vancouver BC V5R 5H9
Tel: 604-451-5511; *Fax:* 604-451-5651
info@bc-cfa.org
www.centreforability.bc.ca; bc-cfa.org
To provide community-based services that enhance the quality of life for children, youth & adults with disabilities & their families in ways that facilitate & build competencies & foster inclusion in all aspects of life
Audrey Kwan, Manager, Communications

British Columbia Chiropractic Association (BCCA)
#125, 3751 Shell Rd., Richmond BC V6X 2W2
Tel: 604-270-1332; *Fax:* 604-278-0093
Toll-Free: 866-256-1474
info@bcchiro.com
www.bcchiro.com
D. Nixdorf, Executive Director

British Columbia Lung Association (BCLA)
2675 Oak St., Vancouver BC V6H 2K2
Tel: 604-731-5864; *Fax:* 604-731-5810
Toll-Free: 800-665-5864
info@bc.lung.ca
www.bc.lung.ca
Social Media: www.facebook.com/home.php?#!/BCLungAssociation
To support lung health research, education, prevention, & advocacy; To help people manage respiratory diseases, including asthma, COPD (chronic bronchitis and emphysema), lung cancer, sleep apnea, & tuberculosis
Scott McDonald, Executive Director
Kelly Ablog-Morrant, Director, Health Education & Program Services
Chris Lam, Manager, Development
Katrina van Bylandt, Manager, Communications
Debora Wong, Manager, Finance & Administration
Marissa McFadyen, Coordinator, Specia Events

British Columbia Lupus Society (BCLS)
#200, 1645 - 7 Ave. West, Vancouver BC V6J 1S4
Tel: 604-714-5564; *Toll-Free:* 866-585-8787
info@bclupus.org
www.bclupus.org
To provide education & support to Lupus patients & their friends & families; to increase public awareness of lupus
Michael Hinman, President

British Columbia Medical Association (BCMA)
#115, 1665 West Broadway, Vancouver BC V6J 5A4
Tel: 604-736-5551; *Fax:* 604-736-4566
Toll-Free: 800-665-2262
communications@bcma.bc.ca
www.bcma.org
To promote a social, economic & political climate in which members can provide the citizens of British Columbia with the highest standard of health care while achieving maximum professional satisfaction & fair economic reward.
Brian Brodie, President

British Columbia Naturopathic Association (BCNA)
2238 Pine St., Vancouver BC V6J 5G4
Tel: 604-736-6646; *Fax:* 604-736-6048
Toll-Free: 800-277-1128
bcna@bcna.ca
www.bcna.ca
To act on behalf of the naturopathic profession in British Columbia; To advance the welfare of members of the profession
Christoph Kind, President
Deborah Phair, Vice-President
Tonia Mitchell, Treasurer

British Columbia Transplant Society (BCTS)
555 West 12th Ave., 3rd Fl., Vancouver BC V5Z 3X7
Tel: 604-877-2240; *Fax:* 604-877-2111
Toll-Free: 800-663-6189
BCTS_Webmaster@bcts.hnet.bc.ca
www.transplant.bc.ca
To lead & coordinate all activities related to organ transplantation & donation, ensuring high standards of quality & efficient management.
Jonathan Guss, CEO
Darrel Weinkauf, Chief Operations Officier

Canada Health Infoway / Inforoute Santé du Canada
#1200, 1000, rue Sherbrooke ouest, Montréal QC H3A 3G4
Tel: 514-868-0550; *Fax:* 514-868-1120
Toll-Free: 866-868-0550
info@infoway-inforoute.ca
www.infoway-inforoute.ca
To accelerate the development of compatible electronic health information systems, which provide healthcare professionals with rapid access to complete & accurate patient information, enabling better decisions about diagnosis & treatment.
Richard C. Alvarez, President & CEO

Canadian Agency for Drugs & Technologies in Health (CADTH) / Agence canadienne des médicaments et des technologies de la santé (ACMTS)
#600, 865 Carling Ave., Ottawa ON K1S 5S8
Tel: 613-226-2553; *Fax:* 613-226-5392
info@cadth.ca; publications@cadth.ca
www.cadth.ca
To offer evidence-based information & impartial advice to health care decision makers about the effectiveness of drugs & other health technologies
Brian O'Rourke, President & CEO

Canadian Alliance of Physiotherapy Regulators / Alliance canadienne des organismes de réglementation de la physiothérapie
#501, 1243 Islington Ave., Toronto ON M8X 1Y9
Tel: 416-234-8800; *Fax:* 416-234-8820
email@alliancept.org
www.alliancept.org
To facilitate the sharing of information & build consensus on national regulatory issues in order to assist member regulators in fulfilling their mandate of protecting the public interest
Katya Duvalko, CEO

Canadian Anesthesiologists' Society (CAS) / Société canadienne des anesthésiologistes (SCA)
#208, One Eglinton Ave. East, Toronto ON M4P 3A1
Tel: 416-480-0602; *Fax:* 416-480-0320
anesthesia@cas.ca; adminservices@cas.ca
www.cas.ca
Social Media: twitter.com/CASUpdate
To advance the medical practice of anesthesia throughout Canada
Richard Chisholm, President
Richard Chisholm, Vice-President
S. Stanley Mandarich, Executive Director
Patricia Houston, Secretary
Susan O'Leary, Treasurer

Canadian Association for Clinical Microbiology & Infectious Diseases (CACMID) / Association canadienne de microbiologie clinique et des maladies contagieuses
c/o Dr. A. Petrich, St. Luke's Wing, St. Joseph's Healthcare, #424L, 50 Charlton Ave. East, Hamilton ON L8N 4A6
Tel: 905-522-1155; *Fax:* 905-521-6083
www.cacmid.ca
To enhance the cooperation of professionals specializing in clinical microbiology & infectious disease; To act as the voice for clinical microbiology & infectious disease professionals; To develop standards in the field of clinical microbiology
Karam Ramotar, President
Greg Tyrrell, Vice-President
Astrid Petrich, Secretary-Treasurer

Canadian Association for Health Services & Policy Research (CAHSPR) / Association canadienne pour la recherche sur les services et les politiques de la santé (ACRSPS)
292 Somerset St. West, Ottawa ON K2P 0J6
Tel: 613-288-9239; *Fax:* 613-599-7805
cahspr@cahspr.ca; memberships@cahspr.ca
www.cahspr.ca
To improve the quality, relevance, & application of health services & policy research
Steve Morgan, President
Adalsteinn (Steini) Brown, President-elect

Canadian Association of Cardio-Pulmonary Technologists (CACPT)
PO Box 848, Stn. A, Toronto ON M5W 1G3
contactus@cacpt.ca
www.cacpt.ca
To establish maintain high standards for Registered Cardio-Pulmonary Technologists
David Hu, Head, Pulmonary
Mike Stevenson, Head, Cardiac

Canadian Association of Centres for the Management of Hereditary Metabolic Diseases
c/o Dept. of Genetics, Childrens' Hospital of E. Ontario, 401 Smyth Rd., Ottawa ON K1H 8L1
www.garrod.ca
The GARROD Association is a national body for the coordination of the management of inherited metabolic disorders. It provides

a forum for the exchange of information & develops guidelines for the investigation & treatment of the diseases.
Murray Potter, President
Pranesh Chakraborty, Sec.-Treas.

Canadian Association of Child Neurology (CACN) / L'Association canadienne de neurologie pédiatrique (ACNP)
#709, 7015 Macleod Trail SW, Calgary AB T2H 2K6
Tel: 403-229-9544; *Fax:* 403-229-1661
www.ccns.org/society_CACN.html
To advance knowledge about the development of the nervous system from conception, as well as the diseases of the nervous system in children; To improve treatment of young people with neurological handicaps
Joseph Dooley, President
Jerome Yager, Sec.-Treas.
Sally Gregg, Managing Director

Canadian Association of Emergency Physicians (CAEP) / Association canadienne des médecins d'urgence (ACMU)
#104, 1785 Alta Vista Dr., Ottawa ON K1G 3Y6
Tel: 613-523-3343; *Fax:* 613-523-0190
Toll-Free: 800-463-1158
admin@caep.ca; board@caep.ca; committees@caep.ca
www.caep.ca
To act as the national voice of emergency medicine; To empower physicians to provide excellent emergency care, through leadership, continuing education, & advocacy
Valoree McKay, Chief Executive Officer
Chris Evans, President
Mark Reardon, Treasurer
Vera Klein, Manager, CME
Nadine Lunt, Manager, Communications & Marketing

Canadian Association of Gastroenterology / Association canadienne de gastroentérologie
#224, 1540 Cornwall Rd., Oakville ON L6J 7W5
Tel: 905-829-2504; *Fax:* 905-829-0242
Toll-Free: 888-780-0007
www.cag-acg.org
The CAG supports and engages in the study of gastroenterology; promotes patient care, research, teaching and professional development in the field; and promotes and maintains the highest ethical standards of practice.
Paul Sinclair, Executive Director

Canadian Association of General Surgeons (CAGS) / Association canadienne des chirurgiens généraux (ACCG)
PO Box 1428, Stn. B, Ottawa ON K1P 5R4
Tel: 613-882-6510
cags@cags-accg.ca
www.cags-accg.ca
To assist all general surgeons with continuing education; facilitate & promote surgical research; develop policies & new ideas in the areas of clinical care, education & research
Susan Reid, President

Canadian Association of Medical Biochemists (CAMB) / Association des médecins biochimistes du Canada (AMBC)
774 Echo Dr., Ottawa ON K1S 5N8
Tel: 613-730-8177; *Fax:* 613-730-1116
Toll-Free: 800-668-3740
camb@rcpsc.edu
www.camb-ambc.ca
Danièle Saintonge, Association Manager

Canadian Association of Medical Oncologists (CAMO) / Association canadienne des oncologues médicaux (ACOM)
c/o CAMO Secretariat Office, 774 Echo Dr., Ottawa ON K1S 5N8
Tel: 613-730-6284; *Fax:* 613-730-1116
camo@rcpsc.edu
www.cos.ca/camo/default.asp
Charles Butts, President
Kara Laing, Secretary-Treasurer

Canadian Association of Medical Radiation Technologists (CAMRT) / Association canadienne des technologues en radiation médicale (ACTRM)
#1000, 85 Albert St., Ottawa ON K1P 6A4
Tel: 613-234-0012; *Fax:* 613-234-1097
Toll-Free: 800-463-9729
editorialoffice@camrt.ca
www.camrt.ca
To act as the certifying body for medical radiation technologists & therapists throughout Canada
Charles Shields, Chief Executive Officer

Michelle Charest, Director, Finance & Administration
Elaine Dever, Director, Education
Mark Given, Director, Professional Practice
Leacy O'Callaghan O'Brien, Director, Advocacy, Communications, & Events

The Canadian Association of Naturopathic Doctors (CAND) / Association canadienne des docteurs en naturopathie
#200, 20 Holly St., Toronto ON M2S 3B1
Tel: 416-496-8633; *Fax:* 416-496-8634
Toll-Free: 800-551-4381
www.cand.ca
Social Media: www.facebook.com/NaturopathicDrs; twitter.com/naturopathicdrs
CAND is a not-for-profit professional organization that promotes naturopathic medicine to the public, insurance companies & corporations. CAND encourages professional, educational & networking activities among its members, & standardization of educational requirements for practitioners
Shawn O'Reilly, Executive Director
Alex McKenna, Marketing Director

Canadian Association of Neuropathologists (CANP) / Association canadienne de neuropathologistes
QE2 Health Sciences Centre, Rm 738, Mackenzie Bldg., 5788 University Ave., Halifax NS B3H 1V8
Tel: 902-473-3156; *Fax:* 902-473-1049
robert.macaulay@cdha.nshealth.ca
canp.medical.org
To organize the annual scientific meeting; to promote the professional & educational objectives of neuropathologists.
David Munoz, President
Rob Macaulay, Sec.-Treas.

Canadian Association of Occupational Therapists (CAOT) / Association canadienne des ergothérapeutes (ACE)
CTTC Building, #3400, 1125 Colonel By Dr., Ottawa ON K1S 5R1
Tel: 613-523-2268; *Fax:* 613-523-2552
Toll-Free: 800-434-2268
insurance@caot.ca
www.caot.ca
To develop & promote the profession of occupational therapy in Canada & abroad; To assist occupational therapists achieve excellence in their professional practice by offering services, products, events, & networking opportunities
Sue Baptiste, Preisdent
Janet Craik, Director, Professional Practice
Christiane Des Lauriers, Director, Standards
Christina Hatchard, Director, Finance
Lis Ostiguy, Director, Professional Affairs
Jeanne Salo, Coordinator, Membership

Canadian Association of Optometrists (CAO) / Association canadienne des optométristes
234 Argyle Ave., Ottawa ON K2P 1B9
Tel: 613-235-7924; *Fax:* 613-235-2025
Toll-Free: 888-263-4676
info@opto.ca
www.opto.ca
To represent & assist the profession of optometry in Canada; To improve the quality, availability, & accessibility of vision & eye care
Glenn Campbell, Executive Director
Lise Loyer, National Director, Optometric Assistants Course
Catherine Heinmiller, National Coordinator, Children's Vision Initiative & Member Programs
Doug Dean, Director, Third Party Plans
Leslie Laskarin, Director, Communications

Canadian Association of Oral & Maxillofacial Surgeons (CAOMS) / Association canadienne de spécialistes en chirurgie buccale et maxillo-faciale (ACSCBMF)
#100, 32 Colonnade Rd., Ottawa ON K2E 7J6
Tel: 613-721-1816; *Fax:* 613-721-3581
Toll-Free: 888-369-5641
caoms@caoms.com; (Secretariat); executivedirector@caoms.com
www.caoms.com
Kevin McCann, Chair, Membership

Canadian Association of Paediatric Surgeons (CAPS) / Association de la chirurgie infantile canadienne
c/o Children's Hospital Of Eastern Ontario, 401 Smyth Rd., Ottawa ON K1H 8L1
Tel: 613-737-7600; *Fax:* 613-738-4849
bass.caps@gmail.com
www.caps.ca
The aim of CAPS is to improve the surgical care of infants and children in Canada.
Juan Bass, Secretary Treasurer

Canadian Association of Pathologists (CAP) / Association canadienne des pathologistes
774 Echo Dr., Ottawa ON K1S 5N8
Tel: 613-730-6230; *Fax:* 613-730-1116
Toll-Free: 800-668-3740
cap@royalcollege.ca
cap-acp.org
Lakovina Alexopoulou, President

Canadian Association of Physical Medicine & Rehabilitation (CAPM&R) / Association canadienne de médecine physique et de réadaptation
774 Echo Dr., Ottawa ON K1S 5N8
Tel: 613-730-6245; *Fax:* 613-730-1116
capmr@rcpsc.edu
www.capmr.ca
The CAPM&R represents and promotes the interests of the speciality of physiatry in Canada by providing and maintaing a national forum and network. It advances and increases awareness of the specialty through strategic alliances and partnerships, public policy, and professional and practice development.
Patrick Potter, Chair

Canadian Association of Prosthetics & Orthotics (CAPO) / Association canadienne en prothèses et orthèses
#605, 294 Portage Ave., Winnipeg MB R3C 0B9
Tel: 204-949-4970; *Fax:* 204-947-3627
capo@mts.net
www.pando.ca
To promote the prosthetic/orthotic profession in Canada & abroad
Kathy Kostycz, Manager

Canadian Association of Radiologists (CAR) / L'Association canadienne des radiologistes
#310, 377 Dalhousie St., Ottawa ON K1N 9N8
Tel: 613-860-3111; *Fax:* 613-860-3112
membership@car.ca
www.car.ca
Voluntary organization representing the goals & the interests of imaging specialists; to promote the clinical, educational, research & political goals of Canadian radiology to members, organized radiology, medical associations, government & the public
Adele Fifield, CEO

Canadian Association of Speech-Language Pathologists & Audiologists (CASLPA) / Association canadienne des orthophonistes et audiologistes
#1000, 1 Nicholas St., Ottawa ON K1N 7B7
Tel: 613-567-9968; *Fax:* 613-567-2859
Toll-Free: 800-259-8519
caslpa@caslpa.ca
www.caslpa.ca
The Association supports & represents the professional needs & development of speech-language pathologists & audiologists. Through this support, the needs of people with communication disorders are championed.
Ondina Love, Executive Director
Linda Walsh, President
Sharon Fotheringham, Manager, Speech-Language Pathology & Standards
Chantal Kealey, Manager, Audiology & Supportive Personnel

Canadian Association of Thoracic Surgeons (CATS) / Association canadienne des chirurgiens thoraciques
c/o J. Clifton, Department of Surgery, University of British Columbia, 910 West 10th Ave., Vancouver BC V5Z 4E3
Tel: 604-875-5355
www.canats.org
To represent thoracic surgeons across Canada
Joanne Clifton, Secretariat
Donna Maziak, President
Drew Bethune, Secretary-Treasurer & Chair, Programs
Andrew Seely, Chair, Research
Rosaire Vaillancourt, Chair, Continuing Professional Development

Canadian Association of Transplantation
774 Echo Dr., Ottawa ON K1S 5N8
Toll-Free: 800-263-2833
cst@rcpsc.edu
www.transplant.ca
Health professionals committed to facilitating & enhancing the transplant process
Jan Emerton, President

Canadian Athletic Therapists Association (CATA) / Association canadienne des thérapeutes du sport
#402, 1040 - 7th Ave. SW, Calgary AB T2P 3G9
Tel: 403-509-2282; *Fax:* 403-509-2280
info@athletictherapy.org
www.athletictherapy.org
CATA is dedicated to delivery of quality care through injury prevention, emergency services & rehabilitative techniques.
Grant Slessor, Executive Director

Canadian Blood Services (CBS) / Societé canadienne du sang
1800 Alta Vista Dr., Ottawa ON K1G 4J5
Tel: 613-739-2300; *Fax:* 613-731-1411
Toll-Free: 888-236-6283
feedback@blood.ca; fundraising@blood.ca
www.bloodservices.ca
Social Media:
www.facebook.com/home.php?#!/CanadianBloodServices
To manage the blood supply for Canadians; to ensure blood safety in every branch of its structure & in every decision
Leah Hollins, Chair
Graham D. Sher, Chief Executive Officer

Canadian Brain Tumour Tissue Bank
#301, 620 Colborne St., London ON N6B 3R9
Tel: 519-642-7755; *Fax:* 519-642-7192
Toll-Free: 800-265-5106
braintumor@braintumor.ca
www.braintumor.ca
To supply optimally collected brain tumour tissue to researchers all over the country, internationally & locally in the hopes that some day the cause of & the cure for brain tumours will be found.
Susan Marshall, Executive Director

Canadian Cancer Society (CCS) / Société canadienne du cancer
National Office, #300, 55 St. Clair Ave. West, Toronto ON M4V 2Y7
Tel: 416-961-7223; *Fax:* 416-961-4189
Toll-Free: 888-939-3333
ccs@cancer.ca
www.cancer.ca
Social Media: www.facebook.com/canadiancancersociety
The Society collects donations to fund cancer research in Canada. It disseminates information on cancer prevention & treatments, advocating for healthy environment & lifestyle to reduce the incidence of cancer, and also offers individual & group support programs for caregivers, family & friends of cancer patients. It is a registered charity, BN: 118829803RR0001.
Elizabeth Newson, Chair
Peter Goodhand, President & CEO
Monique Porlier, CFO & VP, Operations

Canadian Cancer Society Research Institute
#200, 10 Alcorn Ave., Toronto ON M4V 3B1
Tel: 416-961-7223; *Fax:* 416-961-4189
ccsri@cancer.ca; research@cancer.ca; agiorgi@cancer.ca (Media)
www.cancer.ca/research
To act as a strong voice in the cancer research community; To support a broad range of projects that involve Canadian investigators across the spectrum of cancer research
Michael Wosnick, Scientific Director
Christine Williams, Director, Research
Cecilia Pangilinan, Senior Program Administrator, Programs & Awards
Joanne Reynolds, Administrator, Research
Lori Moser, Project Manager, Prevention Initiative

Canadian Cardiovascular Society (CCS) / Société canadienne de cardiologie
#1403, 222 Queen St., Ottawa ON K1P 5V9
Tel: 613-569-3407; *Fax:* 613-569-6574
Toll-Free: 877-569-3407
info@ccs.ca
www.ccs.ca
To promote cardiovascular health & care through knowledge translation, dissemination of research & encouragement of best practices, professional development & leadership in health policy
Blair O'Neill, President

Canadian Celiac Association (CCA) / L'Association canadienne de la maladie coeliaque
#400, 5025 Orbitor Dr., Bldg. 1, Mississauga ON L4W 4Y5
Tel: 905-507-6208; *Fax:* 905-507-4673
Toll-Free: 800-363-7296
info@celiac.ca
www.celiac.ca
Social Media:
www.facebook.com/groups/canadianceliacassociation; twitter.com/gfbri
CCA works to increase awareness of celiac & dermatitis herpetiformis among government institutions, health care professionals & the public. It provides information about the disease & a gluten-free diet, & encourages research through the establishment of the J.A. Campbell Research Fund. It is a registered charity, BN: 106844244RR0001.
Brian Benwell, President
Robert Beddie, Treasurer
Jim McCarthy, Executive Director

Canadian Chiropractic Association (CCA) / Association chiropratique canadienne (ACC)
#600, 30 St. Patrick St., Toronto ON M5T 3A3
Tel: 416-585-7902; *Fax:* 416-585-2970
Toll-Free: 877-222-9303
www.chiropracticcanada.ca
To see every Canadian have full & equitable access to chiropractic care; To promote the integration of chiropractic into the Canadian health care system
Eleanor White, Chair
John Corrigan, President
H. James Duncan, CAE, Executive Director
Jeffrey M. Warren, Vice-President
Allan Gotlib, Director, Research
Maureen McCandless, Director, Communications
John Tucker, Director, Government & Inter-professional Relations
Nekeisha Mohammed, Manager, Communications
Robert David, Secretary-Treasurer

Canadian Coalition for Immunization Awareness & Promotion (CCIAP) / La Coalition canadienne pour la sensibilisation et la promotion de la vaccination (CCSPV)
c/o Canadian Public Health Association, #400, 1565 Carling Ave., Ottawa ON K1Z 8R1
Tel: 613-725-3769; *Fax:* 613-725-9826
immunize@cpha.ca
www.immunize.cpha.ca
To contribute to the control/elimination/eradication of vaccine preventable diseases in Canada by increasing awareness of the benefits & risks of immunization for all ages.
Bonnie Henry, Chair
Susan Bowles, Vice-Chair

Canadian College of Health Leaders (CCHL) / Collège canadien des leaders en santé
292 Somerset St. West, Ottawa ON K2P 0J6
Tel: 613-235-7218; *Fax:* 613-235-5451
Toll-Free: 800-363-9056
info@cchl-ccls.ca; communications@cchse.org
www.cchl-ccls.ca
Social Media:
www.facebook.com/group.php?gid=154324094612698; twitter.com/CCHL_CCLS
To advance excellence in health leadership; To act as a collective voice for the profession
Ray J. Racette, President & Chief Executive Office
Jaime M. Cleroux, Vice-President, Membership & Corporate Services
Linda O'Rourke, Vice-President, Professional Standards & Leadership Development
Sylvie M. Deliencourt, Manager, Professional Designation Programs & Leadership Development
Carolyn Farrington, Manager, Finance
Kathy Ivey, Manager, Marketing & Communications

Canadian College of Medical Geneticists (CCMG) / Collège canadien de généticiens médicaux
774 Echo Dr., Ottawa ON K1S 5N8
Tel: 613-730-6250; *Fax:* 613-730-1116
ccmg@rcpsc.edu
www.ccmg.medical.org
To establish & maintain professional & ethical standards for medical genetics services in Canada; To certify individuals who provide medical genetics services; to encourage research activities
Albert Chudley, President
Gail Graham, Treasurer

Canadian Council of Food & Nutrition (CCFN) / Conseil canadien des aliments et de la nutrition
2810 Matheson Blvd. East, 1st Fl., Mississauga ON L4W 4X7
Tel: 905-625-5746; *Fax:* 905-265-9372
info@ccfn.ca
www.ccfn.ca
The multi-sectoral trusted voice for science-based food & nutrition policy & information in Canada.
Francey Pillo-Blocka, President & CEO

Canadian Critical Care Society (CCCS) / Société canadienne de soins intensifs
c/o Toronto General Hospital, 10 Eaton North, Room 220, 200 Elizabeth St., Toronto ON M5G 2C4
Tel: 416-340-4800; *Fax:* 416-340-4211
info@canadiancriticalcare.org
www.canadiancriticalcare.org
To develop training & educational guidelines
Deborah Wilson, Secretary

Canadian Dermatology Association (CDA) / Association canadienne de dermatologie (ACD)
#425, 1385 Bank St., Ottawa ON K1H 8N4
Tel: 613-738-1748; *Fax:* 613-738-4695
Toll-Free: 800-267-3376
info@dermatology.ca; member.services@dermatology.ca
www.dermatology.ca
Social Media: CDN Dermatology; @ Cdn Dermatology
To advance the science of medicine & surgery related to the health of the skin; To support & advance patient care; To represent dermatologists in Canada
Ian Landells, President
Michelle Albagli, Executive Director
Ben Barankin, Secretary
David Zloty, Treasurer
Jennifer Scott, Officer, Communications & Programs
Jason Rivers, Editor-in-Chief, Journal of Cutaneous Medicine & Surgery

Canadian Diabetes Association (CDA) / Association canadienne du diabète
#1400, 522 University Ave., Toronto ON M5G 2R5
Tel: 416-363-3373; *Toll-Free:* 800-226-8464
info@diabetes.ca; Membership@diabetes.ca; Donation@diabetes.ca
www.diabetes.ca
Social Media:
www.facebook.com/CanadianDiabetesAssociation; twitter.com/DiabetesAssoc; www.youtube.com/user/CDA1927
To advance the welfare of Canadians with diabetes; to support research into the causes, complications, treatment, & cure of diabetes; To promote & strengthen services for people affected by diabetes & their families; To work with health professionals to improve standards in care the & treatment of diabetes; To develop guidelines for diabetes education in Canada; To promote the rights of Canadians affected by diabetes in an effort to bring about positive change in the areas of public awareness, government policy, health policy issues, & employment
Doug Macnamara, Chair
Michael Cloutier, President & Chief Executive Officer
Walter Kurz, CFO & Vice-President, Organizational Excellence & Shared Services
Angelique Berg, Vice-President, Community Engagement
Glen Doucet, Vice-President, Government Relations & Public Affairs
Janelle Robertson, Vice-President, Business Operations
Jovita Sundaramoorthy, Vice-President, Research & Education
Randi Garcha, Manager, National Media Relations & External Communications

Canadian Down Syndrome Society (CDSS) / Société canadienne du syndrome de Down
#103, 2003 - 14 St. NW, Calgary AB T2M 3N4
info@cdss.ca
www.cdss.ca
Social Media:
www.facebook.com/cdndownsyndrome?ref=ts%2F; twitter.com/CdnDownSyndrome
To ensure equitable opportunities for all Canadians with Down syndrome7
Kevin Whyte, Board Chair
Kirk Crowther, Executive Director
Jonathan A. Bateman, Coordinator, Event & Fund Development
Kaitlyn Pecson, Coordinator, Design & Communication
Ashlee Stone, Coordinator, Advocacy Research

Canadian Dyslexia Association (CDA) / Association canadienne de la dyslexie
57, rue du Couvent, Gatineau QB J9H 3C8
Tel: 613-853-6539; *Fax:* 819-684-0672
info@dyslexiaassociation.ca
www.dyslexiaassociation.ca

Canadian Epilepsy Alliance (CAE) / L'Alliance canadienne de l'épilepsie (ACE)
26 O'Leary Ave., St. John's NL A1B 2C7
Tel: 709-722-0502; *Fax:* 709-722-0999
www.epilepsymatters.com
To promote independence & quality of life for people with epilepsy & their families, through support services, information, advocacy, & public awareness
Gail Dempsey, President

Canadian Foundation for the Study of Infant Deaths (CFSID) / Fondation canadienne pour l'étude de la mortalité infantile
#403, 60 James St., St Catharines ON L2R 7E7
Tel: 905-688-8884; *Fax:* 905-688-3300
Toll-Free: 800-363-7437
sidsinfo@sidscanada.org
www.sidscanada.org
To provide information & emotional support to families of infants who have died due to Sudden Infant Death Syndrome (SIDS); to carry out programs of public education & awareness; to promote & support research activities into the cause(s) of SIDS & its effects on families
Andrea Clement-Christie, Chair

Canadian Health Coalition (CHC) / Coalition canadienne de la santé
2841 Riverside Dr., Ottawa ON K1V 8X7
Tel: 613-521-3400; *Fax:* 613-521-9638
info@medicare.ca
www.healthcoalition.ca
Social Media: www.facebook.com/groups/76610717247; twitter.com/healthcoalition; www.youtube.com/user/HealthCoalition
To create good health; To preserve & strengthen the Canada Health Act, the foundation of Medicare; To make the health care system democratic, accountable & representative; To provide a continuum of care from large institutions to the home; To protect our investment in the skills & abilities of our health care workers; To ensure fair wages for all health care providers; To eliminate profit-making from illness; To reduce over-prescribing & make drugs affordable; to stop fee-for-service payments; To expand methods of health care & the role of non-physician health providers
Michael McBane, National Coordinator

Canadian Hematology Society (CHS) / Société canadienne d'hématologie
#199, 435 St. Laurent Blvd., Ottawa ON K1K 2Z8
Tel: 613-748-9613; *Fax:* 613-748-6392
cag@ca.inter.net
www.canadianhematologysociety.org
To represent members of the Society & provide information about hematology

Canadian Hemochromatosis Society (CHS) / Société canadienne de l'hémochromatose
#285, 7000 Minoru Blvd., Richmond BC V6Y 3Z5
Tel: 604-279-7135; *Fax:* 604-279-7138
Toll-Free: 877-223-4766
office@toomuchiron.ca
www.toomuchiron.ca
To increase awareness among the public & medical community with regards to the importance of family screening, early diagnosis & treatment of Hemochromatosis
Frank Erschen, President & Chair

Canadian Hemophilia Society (CHS) / Société canadienne de l'hémophilie
#400, 1255 rue University, Montréal QC H3B 3B6
Tel: 514-848-0503; *Fax:* 514-848-9661
Toll-Free: 800-668-2686
chs@hemophilia.ca
www.hemophilia.ca
To find a cure & to provide services to people with hemophilia or other inherited bleeding disorders; to serve persons infected with HIV or hepatitis through blood & blood products
David Page, National Executive Director
Hélène Bourgaize, National Director, Volunteer Development & Human Resources
Deborah Franz Currie, National Director, Resource Development

Canadian Hospice Palliative Care Association (CHPCA) / Association canadienne de soins palliatifs (ACSP)
Annex D, Saint-Vincent Hospital, 60 Cambridge St. North, Ottawa ON K1R 7A5
Tel: 613-241-3663; *Fax:* 613-241-3986
Toll-Free: 800-668-2785
info@chpca.net
www.chpca.net
CHPCA provides leadership in the pursuit of excellence in the care of people approaching death in Canada, in order to lessen suffering, loneliness, & grief. The national association works to develop national standards of practice for hospice palliative care.
Sarah Walker, President
Ed McLaren, Secretary-Treasurer
Sharon Baxter, Executive Director

Canadian Institute of Child Health (CICH) / Institut canadien de la santé infantile
#300, 384 Bank St., Ottawa ON K2P 1Y4
Tel: 613-230-8838; *Fax:* 613-230-6654
cich@cich.ca
www.cich.ca
To promote the health & well-being of Canadian children through consultation, collaboration, research & advocacy by building alliances & coalitions & by creating resources on health promotion, disease & injury prevention relevant to child & family health in Canada; To identify issues of concern by monitoring the health & well-being of children in Canada; To promote & improve the health & well-being of mothers & infants in all settings; To promote the healthy physical development of children in a safe environment & reduce childhood injuries; To promote the healthy psycho-social development of children in supportive & nurturing environments; To facilitate empowerment of individuals & communities to achieve the above goals for Canadian children & their families; To facilitate collaborative work between consumers, professional, non-professional & government agencies that results in appropriate actions for identified needs
Robin Moore-Orr, D.Sc., R.D., Chair
Lynne Westlake, Secretary
Eleonore Benesch, Treasurer

Canadian Institute of Public Health Inspectors (CIPHI) / Institut Canadien des inspecteurs en santé publique (ICISP)
#720, 999 West Broadway Ave., Vancouver BC V5Z 1K5
Tel: 604-739-8180; *Fax:* 604-738-4080
Toll-Free: 888-245-8180
questions@ciphi.ca; office@ciphi.ca
www.ciphi.ca
To protect the health of all Canadians; To advance the environmental & health sciences; To enhance the field of public health inspection through certification, information, & advocacy
Adam Grant, National President

Canadian Liver Foundation (CLF) / Fondation canadienne du foie (FCF)
#801, 3100 Steeles Ave. East, Toronto ON L3R 8T3
Tel: 416-491-3353; *Fax:* 416-491-4952
Toll-Free: 800-563-5483
clf@liver.ca
www.liver.ca
Social Media: www.facebook.com/group.php?gid=6584473365; twitter.com/CdnLiverFdtn
To reduce the incidence & impact of all liver disease by funding liver research & education; promote liver health through programs & publications
Morris Sherman, Chairman
Paul Derksen, Sec.-Treas.

Canadian Lung Association (CLA) / Association pulmonaire du Canada
National Office, #300, 1750 Courtwood Cres., Ottawa ON K2C 2B5
Tel: 613-569-6411; *Fax:* 613-569-8860
Toll-Free: 800-566-5864
info@lung.ca
www.lung.ca
To improve & promote lung health across Canada
Heather Borquez, President & Chief Executive Officer
Mary-Pat Shaw, Vice-President, National Programs & Operations
Connie Côté, Senior Director, National Lung Health Framework
Claudia Gongora, Director, Finance
Janis Hass, Director, Marketing & Communications
Janet Sutherland, Director, Canadian Thoracic Society/Canadian Respiratory Health Professiona
Anne Van Dam, Director, Research & Knowledge Translation
Christopher Wilson, Director, Public Affairs & Advocacy

Canadian Marfan Association / Association du syndrome de Marfan
PO Box 42257, Stn. Centre Plaza, 128 Queen St. S, Mississauga ON L5M 4Z0
Tel: 905-826-3223; *Fax:* 905-826-2125
Toll-Free: 866-722-1722
info@marfan.ca
www.marfan.ca
Social Media: www.facebook.com/CanadianMarfanAssociation; twitter.com/CanadianMarfan
To increase public awareness of Marfan Syndrome in Canada; to provide accurate, timely information about this condition to affected patients, their families & health care personnel; to encourage the establishment of Marfan self-help groups in communities across Canada; to support & foster research
Shirley Otway, Contact, Southern Alberta
Roy Braunberger, Contact, Lacombe, Alberta
Lisa McDonald, Contact, British Columbia
Jan Landsiedel, Contact, Manitoba & N.W. Ontario
Robert French, Contact, Newfoundland
Michelle Reid, Contact, Nova Scotia
Michael Stern, Contact, Montréal
Arleta Taylor, Contact, Saskatchewan
Eva Theofilopoulos, Executive Manager, GTA Chapter

Canadian Medical Association (CMA) / Association médicale canadienne (AMC)
1867 Alta Vista Dr., Ottawa ON K1G 5W8
Tel: 613-731-8610; *Fax:* 613-236-8864
Toll-Free: 888-855-2555
cmamsc@cma.ca; cmatechsupport@cma.ca (technical support)
www.cma.ca
Social Media: twitter.com/CMA_Docs; www.youtube.com/user/CanadianMedicalAssoc
To act as the national voice of physicians in Canada; To serve the Canadian medical community; To promote the highest standards of health & health care
John Haggie, President
Michael Golbey, Chair
Jeffrey Turnbull, President

The Canadian Medical Protective Association / Association canadienne de protection médicale
PO Box 8225, Stn. T, 875 Carling Ave., Ottawa ON K1G 3H7
Tel: 613-725-2000; *Fax:* 613-725-1300
Toll-Free: 800-267-6522
feedback@cmpa.org; mediainquiries@cmpa.org
www.cmpa-acpm.ca
Founded by a group of Canadian doctors for their mutual protection against legal actions based on allegations of malpractice or negligence
John E. Gray, Executive Director & CEO
Michael Lawrence, President
Lawrence Groves, 1st Vice-President
Edward Crosby, 2nd Vice-President

Canadian MedicAlert Foundation / Fondation canadienne MedicAlert
#800, 2005 Sheppard Ave. East, Toronto ON M2J 5B4
Tel: 416-696-0267; *Fax:* 800-392-8422
Toll-Free: 800-668-1507
www.medicalert.ca
Social Media: www.facebook.com/medicalertcanada; twitter.com/medicalertCA
To provide lifelong access to personal & medical information in order to protect & save the lives of its members; MedicAlert is a non-profit organization that provides all Canadians with medical protection in an emergency situation.
Robert Ridge, President

Canadian Memorial Chiropractic College (CMCC)
6100 Leslie St., Toronto ON M2H 3J1
Tel: 416-482-2340; *Fax:* 416-482- 362
communications@cmcc.ca
www.cmcc.ca
To advance the art, science & philosophy of chiropractic; To educate chiropractors; To further the development of the chiropractic profession; To improve the health of society
Mark Symchych, Chair
Jean A. Moss, DC, MBA, President
David Gryfe, Secretary-Treasurer

Canadian Natural Health Association (CNHA)
#105, 5 Wakunda Pl., Toronto ON M4A 1A2
Tel: 416-686-7056; *Toll-Free:* 866-686-7056
To establish leadership in healthy, natural lifestyle education & support services; to assist by providing resources to help make people healthier
Mark Ansara, Executive Director

Canadian Network of Toxicology Centres (CNTC) / Réseau canadien des centres de toxicologie
Bovey Bldg., 2nd Fl., Gordon St., Guelph ON N1G 2W1
Tel: 519-824-4120; *Fax:* 519-837-3861
uoguelph.ca/ses/content/canadian-network-toxicology-centres
To be recognized & respected for excellence in research, training, analysis & communication of information focused on critical toxicology issues for ecosystem & human health; to achieve this through innovative, multi-disciplinary teamwork & partnerships between the public & private sector
Len Ritter, Executive Director
Donna Warner, Program Coordinator

Canadian Neurological Sciences Federation (CCNS) / Fédération des sciences neurologiques du Canada
#709, 7015 Macleod Trail SW, Calgary AB T2H 2K6
Tel: 403-229-9544; *Fax:* 403-229-1661
info@cnsfederation.org
www.cnsfederation.org
To enhance the care of patients with diseases of the nervous system; To act as the umbrella organization for the following societies: Canadian Neurological Society, Canadian Neurosurgical Society, Canadian Society of Clinical Neurophysiologists, & Canadian Association of Child Neurologists
Dan Morin, Chief Executive Officer
Marika Fitzgerald, Manager, Finance & Administration
Donna Irvin, Administrator, Membership Services
Lisa Bicek, Coordinator, Professional Development
Cindy Leschyshyn, Editorial Coordinator, Journal

Canadian Neurological Society (CNS) / Société canadienne de neurologie
#709, 7015 Macleod Trail SW, Calgary AB T2H 2K1
Tel: 403-229-9544; *Fax:* 403-229-1661
www.cnsfederation.org/
To promote & encourage all aspects of neurology, including research, education, assessment & accreditation; provide for annual scientific sessions to promote the knowledge & practice of neurology
Dan Morin, CNSF CEO
Lisa Bicek, Manager
Marika Fitzgerald, Manager, Finance & Administration

Canadian Occupational Therapy Foundation (COTF) / La Fondation canadienne d'ergothérapie (FCE)
CTTC Bldg., #3401, 1125 Colonel By Dr., Ottawa ON K1S 5R1
Tel: 613-523-2268; *Fax:* 613-523-2552
Toll-Free: 800-434-2268
www.cotfcanada.org
Social Media: www.facebook.com/239464269434993
To fund & promote research & scholarship in occupational therapy in Canada
Sangita Kamblé, Executive Director
Anne McDonald, Executive Assistant

Canadian Oncology Societies
c/o 82-84 Barrie St., Kingston ON K7L 3N6
Tel: 613-533-6000; *Fax:* 613-533-2941
bvancersluis@ctg.queensu.ca
www.cos.ca
COS strives to increase and exchange knowledge in the field of oncology; to promote the application of such knowledge in the prevention and diagnosis of cancer and the care of cancer patients and their families; to promote interdisciplinary approaches to patient care and research in cancer; to provide a forum for the presentation and discussion of scientific knowledge and advances in oncology; to further continuing education for groups and indivduals involved in the care of patients who require special attention; support public cancer education programs; to support and assist the Canadian Cancer Society and the National Cancer Insitute; to advise government and other agencies on the provision of health services relevent to oncology.
Jean Maroun, Chair of COS Committee

Canadian Ophthalmological Society (COS) / Société canadienne d'opthalmologie (SCO)
#610, 1525 Carling Ave., Ottawa ON K1Z 8R9
Tel: 613-729-6779; *Fax:* 613-729-7209
cos@eyesite.ca
www.eyesite.ca
To assure the provision of optimal eye care to all Canadians by promoting excellence in ophthalmology & providing services to support its members in practice
Jennifer Brunet-Colvey, Chief Executive Officer

Canadian Organization for Rare Disorders (CORD)
#600, 151 Bloor St. West, Toronto ON M5S 1S4
Tel: 416-969-7464; *Toll-Free:* 877-302-7273
office@cord.ca
www.cord.ca
To advocate for health policy that works for people with rare disorders; to promote research & services for all rare disorders in Canada; To increase access to genetic screening & genetic counselling for rare disorders
Durhane Wong-Rieger, President
Ed Koning, Vice-President
John Adams, Treasurer

Canadian Orthopaedic Association (COA) / Association canadienne d'orthopédie
#360, 4150, rue Ste-Catherine ouest, Montréal QC H3Z 2Y5
Tel: 514-874-9003; *Fax:* 514-874-0464
cynthia@canorth.org
www.coa-aco.org
Social Media: twitter.com/CdnOrthoAssoc
To provide continuing medical education for orthopaedic surgeons
Douglas C. Thomson, CEO

Canadian Orthopaedic Foundation (COF) / Fondation orthopédique du Canada (FOC)
PO Box 7029, Innisfil ON L9S 1A8
Tel: 416-410-2341; *Toll-Free:* 800-461-3639
mailbox@canorth.org
www.canorth.org
To foster excellence in the provision of health care to patients with musculoskeletal disease or injury, in a cost effective manner, based on significant outcome studies, by supporting research, educating its members & securing funding from government & other health care funding agencies
James Waddell, Chair
Sandra Vlaar Ingram, Vice Chair

Canadian Orthoptic Council / Conseil canadien d'orthoptique
CHUL, 2705 Boul, Laurier, Ste. Foy QC G1V 4G2
Fax: 418-654-2188
info@orthopticscanada.org
www.orthopticscanada.org
To establish standards in the training of orthoptic students; to establish standards for orthoptic training centres; to provide examinations of orthoptic students in order to determine their proficiency in orthopotics & to award a certificate of competency to qualified students who pass the examinations; to require evidence of continuing education of certified orthoptists; to establish standards for the professional ethical conduct of certified orthoptists.
Louis-Etienne Marcoux, Sec.-Treas.

Canadian Paediatric Society (CPS) / Société canadienne de pédiatrie
2305 St. Laurent Blvd., Ottawa ON K1G 4J8
Tel: 613-526-9397; *Fax:* 613-526-3332
info@cps.ca
www.cps.ca
To advocate for the health needs of children & youth; to provide continuing education to paediatricians; to establish national guidelines for paediatric care & practice
Kenneth J. Henderson, President
Marie Adèle Davis, Executive Director
Elizabeth Moreau, Director, Communications & Public Education

Canadian Pain Society / Société canadienne pour le traitement de la douleur
#202, 1143 Wentworth St. West, Oshawa ON L1J 8P7
Tel: 905-404-9545; *Fax:* 905-404-3727
office@canadianpainsociety.ca
www.canadianpainsociety.ca
Social Media: www.facebook.com/CanadianPain;
twitter.com/canadianpain
To foster research on pain; To improve the management of patients with acute & chronic pain
M. Catherine Bushnell, President
Diane LaChapelle, Secretary
Michael McGillion, Treasurer
Ellen Maracle-Benton, Office Manager
Judy Watt-Watson, President Elect

Canadian Paraplegic Association (CPA) / Association canadienne des paraplégiques
#230, 1101 Prince of Wales Dr., Ottawa ON K2C 3W7
Tel: 613-723-1913; *Fax:* 613-723-1060
info@canparaplegic.org
www.canparaplegic.org
Social Media: www.facebook.com/119959731859;
twitter.com/CPA_National
To assist persons with spinal cord injuries & other physical disabilitieto to cope with the changes caused by their injury, to become independent & self-reliant, & to lead productive lives
Myrtle Jenkins-Smith, President
Ron Swan, Treasurer

Canadian Pediatric Foundation (CPF) / La fondation canadienne de pédiatrie
2305 St. Laurent Blvd., Ottawa ON K1G 4J8
Tel: 613-526-9397; *Fax:* 613-526-3332
cpf@cps.ca
www.cps.ca
To promote improved health care & social well-being for the children of Canada, particularly for disadvantaged groups; to promote better standards of health care for children throughout the world, particularly where Canadian aid is active.
Marie Adèle Davis, Executive Director

Canadian Physiotherapy Association (CPA) / L'Association canadienne de physiothérapie
955 Green Valley Cres., Ottawa ON K2C 3V4
Tel: 613-564-5454; *Fax:* 613-564-1577
Toll-Free: 800-387-8679
information@physiotherapy.ca
www.physiotherapy.ca/public; www.thesehands.ca
Social Media: www.facebook.com/CPA.ACP;
twitter.com/physiocan
To provide leadership & direction to the profession; To foster excellence in practice, education & research; To promote high standards of health in Canada
Robert Werstine, President

Canadian Podiatric Medical Association (CPMA) / Association médicale podiatrique canadienne
#2063, 61 Broadway Blvd., Sherwood Park AB T8H 2C1
Toll-Free: 888-220-3338
askus@podiatrycanada.org
www.podiatrycanada.org
To effectively serve & provide guidance to its members & the podiatry profession in Canada; to serve the public; to provide the authoritative national voice for podiatrists in Canada; to recognize a particular responsibility to contribute to the development of national positions & standards related to the podiatric medical profession through education, research, materials & personnel
Mario Turanovic, President

Canadian Porphyria Foundation Inc. (CPF) / La Fondation canadienne de la porphyrie
PO Box 1206, Neepawa MB R0J 1H0
Tel: 204-476-2800; *Fax:* 204-476-2800
Toll-Free: 866-476-2801
www.cpf-inc.ca
Dedicated to improving the quality of life for Canadians affected by the porphyrias through programs of awareness, education, service, advocacy & research; committed to promoting public & medical professional awareness; assembling, printing & distributing up-to-date educational information to physicians, health care personnel, diagnosed patients & others affected by porphyria; offering support programs to affected individuals & their families; promoting the family social welfare of affected individuals; educating & informing physicians & others in health care about the porphyrias so that early diagnosis & proper treatment will be realized; promoting & providing financial assistance for research; committed to encouraging, supporting & serving physicians & researchers in their efforts to find more effective treatments & to increasing physician, patient & community awareness & thereby cultivating support for research
Lois J. Aitken, President/Executive Director

Canadian Post-MD Education Registry (CAPER) / Système informatisé sur les stagiaires post-MD en formation clinique
#800, 265 Carling Ave., Ottawa ON K1S 2E1
Tel: 613-730-1204; *Fax:* 613-730-1196
caper@afmc.ca
www.caper.ca
To provide accurate & timely data pertaining to Post-MD training & physician resources in Canada to assist medical schools, governments & other work longitudinal research pertaining to physicians training & supply
Steve Slade, Vice-President, Research & Analysis
Hélène LeBlanc, Executive Assistant

Canadian Public Health Association (CPHA) / Association canadienne de santé publique (ACSP)
#300, 1565 Carling Ave., Ottawa ON K1Z 8R1
Tel: 613-725-3769; *Fax:* 613-725-9826
info@cpha.ca
www.cpha.ca
Social Media:
www.facebook.com/group.php?gid=159289860285?ref
To represent public health in Canada; To support universal & equitable access to the necessary conditions to achieve health for all Canadians; To provide links to the international public health community
Debra Lynkowski, Chief Executive Officer
Janet MacLachlan, Associate Chief Executive Officer
James Chauvin, Director, Policy Development
Ian Culbert, Director, Communications & Development
Greg Penney, Director, National Programs
Sarah Pettenuzzo, Manager, Conferences

Canadian Public Health Association - NB/PEI Branch
#34, 2865 Rothesay Rd., Rothesay NB E3B 4P2
Tel: 506-847-0311; *Fax:* 506-847-0311
Cristin Muecke, President

Ann Harling, Secretary-Treasurer

Canadian Public Health Association - NWT/Nunavut Branch
PO Box 1000, Stn. 1000, Iqaluit NU X0A 0H0
Tel: 867-975-5774; *Fax:* 867-975-5755
isobol@gov.nu.ca
Isaac Sobol, President

Canadian Rheumatology Association (CRA) / Société canadienne de rhumatologie
912 Tegal Pl., Newmarket ON L3X 1L3
Tel: 905-952-0698; *Fax:* 905-952-0708
cra@rogers.com
www.rheum.ca; www.rhumato.ca
To represent Canadian rheumatologists & promote their pursuit of excellence in arthritis care & research in Canada through leadership, education & communication
Jamie Henderson, President
Cory Ballie, Sec.-Treas.

Canadian Sickle Cell Society / La société de l'anémie falciforme du Canada
#33, 6999, Côte des Neiges, Montréal QC H3S 2B8
Tel: 514-735-5100; *Fax:* 514-735-5109
cslaf@total.net
To educate the public at large & at risk; to recruit & train volunteers; to provide effective lobbying for the improvement of services to the families & individuals affected by sickle cell anemia; to identify sickle disease or traits; to provide individual & family counselling.
Rosetta Cadogan, Regional Director

Canadian Society for Clinical Investigation (CSCI) / Société canadienne de recherches cliniques (SCRC)
114 Cheyenne Way, Ottawa ON K2J 0E9
Fax: 613-491-0073
Toll-Free: 877-968-9449
info@csci-scrc.ca
www.csci-scrc.ca
To promote research in the field of human health throughout Canada; to lobby for research funding; to support Canadian researchers in their endeavours & at all stages of their careers by supporting knowledge translation & fostering communities of health science researchers
Brent W. Winston, President

Canadian Society for International Health (CSIH) / Société canadienne de la santé internationale
#1105, 1 Nicholas St., Ottawa ON K1N 7B7
Tel: 613-241-5785
csih@csih.org
www.csih.org
Social Media: www.facebook.com/CSIH.org
To promote international health & development through mobilization of Canadian resources; To advocate & facilitate research, education, & service activities in international health; To further Canadian strengths of progressive health policy & programming in all fields where global & domestic health concerns meet; To contribute to the evolving global understanding of health & development
Janet Hatcher-Roberts, Executive Director

Canadian Society for Medical Laboratory Science (CSMLS) / Société canadienne de science de laboratoire médical
PO Box 2830, Stn. LCD 1, 33 Wellington Ave. North, Hamilton ON L8N 3N8
Tel: 905-528-8642; *Fax:* 905-528-4968
Toll-Free: 800-263-8277
www.csmls.org
To promote & maintain a nationally accepted standard of medical laboratory technology; To promote, maintain, & protect professional identity & interests of medical laboratory technologists
Goldie Fagan, President
Christine Nielsen, Executive Director

Canadian Society for Surgical Oncology (CSSO) / Société canadienne d'oncologie chirurgicale
c/o J. Hanes, Surgical Oncology, Princess Margaret Hospital, #3-130, 610 University Ave., Toronto ON M5G 2M9
Tel: 416-946-6583; *Fax:* 416-946-6590
jane.hanes@uhn.on.ca
www.cos.ca/csso
To encourage optimum patient care through a multi-disciplinary treatment approach; To promote surgical oncology training programs in Canadian universities
Jane Hanes, CSSO Coordinator
Richard Nason, President
Carmen Giacomantonio, Secretary-Treasurer

Canadian Society for the History of Medicine (CSHM) / Société canadienne d'histoire de la médecine (SCHM)
c/o McMaster Univ., History of Medicine, #3NIO Health Sciences Ctr, Hamilton ON L8N 3Z5
Tel: 905-525-9140; *Fax:* 905-522-9509
www.cshm-schm.ca
To promote the study & communication of the history of health & medicine
Patricia Prestwich, President
C. Peter Warren, Vice-President
Peter Twohig, Secretary-Treasurer

Canadian Society for Transfusion Medicine (CSTM) / Société canadienne de médecine transfusionnelle
774 Echo Dr., Ottawa ON K1S 5N8
Tel: 613-260-6198; *Fax:* 613-730-1116
cstm@royalcollege.ca
www.transfusion.ca
To promulgate throughout Canada a high level of ethics & professional standards; to create national & regional opportunities for the presentation & discussion of research & developments in this & allied fields; to initiate & maintain a program of continuing education; to promote good laboratory & good manufacturing practices; to establish mutually beneficial working relationships with relevant national & international societies & organizations & to be the primary voice for transfusion medicine in Canada
Kieran Biggins, President

Canadian Society for Vascular Surgery (CSVS) / Société canadienne de chirurgie vasculaire
c/o Christiane Dowsing, Society Manager, 774 Echo Dr., Ottawa ON K1S 5N8
Tel: 613-730-6263; *Fax:* 613-730-1116
csvs@royalcollege.ca
www.canadianvascular.ca
To promote vascular health for Canadians
Jerry Chen, President
Gerrit Winkelaar, Secretary
Jacques Tittley, Treasurer
Thomas Forbes, Chair, Research Committee
Ravi Sidhu, Chair, Education Committee

Canadian Society of Allergy & Clinical Immunology (CSACI) / Société canadienne d'allergie et d'immunologie clinique
774 Echo Dr., Ottawa ON K1S 5N8
Tel: 613-730-6272; *Fax:* 613-730-1116
csaci@rcpsc.edu
www.csaci.ca
To ensure optimal patient care by advancing the knowledge & practice of allergy, clinical immunology, & asthma
Charles Frankish, President
Richard Warrington, Vice-President
Stuart Carr, Secretary-Treasurer

Canadian Society of Cardiac Surgeons / Société des chirurgiens cardiaques
#1403, 222 Queen St., ottawa ON K1P 5V9
Toll-Free: 877-569-3407
cscs@ccs.ca
www.ccs.ca/cscs
Christopher Feindel, President
Roy Masters, Secretary-Treasurer

Canadian Society of Clinical Neurophysiologists (CSCN) / Société canadienne de neurophysiologistes cliniques
PO Box 5456, Stn. A, #709, 7015 Macleod Trail SW, Calgary AB T2H 2K6
Tel: 403-229-9544; *Fax:* 403-229-1661
brains@ccns.org
www.ccns.org
To promote & encourage all aspects of neurophysiology, including research & education, in addition to assessment & accreditation in the field
Donna Irvin, Secretary-Treasurer

Canadian Society of Cytology (CSC) / Société canadienne de cytologie
c/o Dr. Dirk van Niekirk, BC Cancer Agency, 600 West 10th Ave., Vancouver BC V5Z 4E6
dvanniek@bccancer.bc.ca
www.cap.medical.org/cytology.htm
To promote & support education in cytology; To maintain a high standard of practice within the discipline of cytopathology; To foster the development of cytopathology in Canada
Linda Kapusta, Chair
Michele Weir, Vice-Chair
Dirk van Niekerk, Treasurer

Canadian Society of Diagnostic Medical Sonographers (CSDMS)
PO Box 1220, Kemptville ON K0G 1J0
Tel: 613-258-0855; *Toll-Free:* 888-273-6746
info@csdms.com
www.csdms.com
To enhance patient care by promoting the science of diagnostic medical ultrasound
Tom Ball, President

Canadian Society of Endocrinology & Metabolism (CSEM) / Société canadienne d'endocrinologie et métabolisme (SCEM)
774 Echo Dr., Ottawa ON K1S 5N8
Tel: 613-730-6224; *Fax:* 613-730-1116
CSEM@rcpsc.edu
www.endo-metab.ca
To advance the discipline of endocrinology & metabolism in Canada
Cheri L. Deal, President
Ivy Fettes, Secretary-Treasurer

Canadian Society of Gastroenterology Nurses & Associates (CSGNA)
#224 - 1540 Cornwall Rd., Oakville ON L6J 7W5
Tel: 905-829-8794; *Fax:* 905-829-0242
Toll-Free: 866-544-8794
csgnaexecutiveassistant@csgna.com
www.csgna.com
To enhance the educational & professional growth of the membership within the resources available.
Joanne Glen, President
Cindy James, Treasurer

Canadian Society of Internal Medicine (CSIM) / Société canadienne de médecine interne
774 Echo Dr., Ottawa ON K1S 5N8
Tel: 613-730-6244; *Fax:* 613-730-1116
csim@royalcollege.ca
www.csimonline.com
Bert Govig, President

Canadian Society of Nephrology (CSN) / Société canadienne de néphrologie (SCN)
c/o Dr. A. Garg, Kidney Clinical Research, London Health Sciences Ctr., #ELL-101, 800 Commissioners Rd. East, London ON N6A 4G5
Tel: 519-685-8502; *Fax:* 519-685-8269
smkelly@mun.ca (CSN Secretariat)
www.csnscn.ca
To advance the practice of Nephrology; To promote the highest quality of care for patients with renal diseases, by setting high standards for medical training & education; To encourage research in biomedical sciences related to the kidney, kidney disorders & renal replacement therapies
Barbara Ballermann, President
Marcello Tonelli, Vice-President
Amit Garg, Secretary-Treasurer
James Barton, Chair, Education Committee
Braden Manns, Chair, Scientific Committee
Marcello Tonelli, Chair, Guidelines Committee
Verna Yiu, Chair, RCPSC Specialty

Canadian Society of Nuclear Medicine (CSNM) / La Société canadienne de médecine nucléaire (SCMN)
774 Echo Dr., Ottawa ON K1S 5N8
Tel: 613-730-6254; *Fax:* 613-730-1116
csnm@rcpsc.edu
www.csnm-scmn.ca
The Society is concerned with public policy & aspects of nuclear medicine practice pertaining to standards of clinical practice & training for specialists. Safety & research are also concerns of the Society.

Canadian Society of Nutrition Management / Société canadienne de gestion de la nutrition
#300, 1370 Don Mills Rd., Toronto ON M3B 3N7
Fax: 416-441-0591
Toll-Free: 866-355-2766
csnm@csnm.ca
www.csnm.ca
CSNM fosters an environment in which members can achieve success in their chosen field.
Pat Sylvain, President Elect
Heather Truber, President

Canadian Society of Orthopaedic Technologists (CSOT) / Société canadienne des technologistes en orthopedie
#715A, 18 Wynford Dr., Toronto ON M3C 3S2
Tel: 416-445-4516; *Fax:* 416-489-7356
csot@look.ca
www.pappin.com/csot
To promote & develop training programmes, professional standards; encourage uniform training programs & examinatios; promote & facilitate cooperation between Orthopaedic Technologists & the medical profession.
Pamela Smith, Registrar/Office Manager

Canadian Society of Otolaryngology - Head & Neck Surgery (CSO-HNS) / Société canadienne d'otolaryngologie et de chirurgie cervico-faciale
Administrative Office, 221 Millford Cres., Elora ON N0B 1S0
Tel: 519-846-0630; *Fax:* 519-846-9529
Toll-Free: 800-655-9533
cso.hns@sympatico.ca
www.entcanada.org
To improve patient care in otolaryngology - head & neck surgery; To maintain high professional & ethical standards
Dale Brown, President
Sam Spafford, Secretary
Martin Corsten, Treasurer
Donna Humphrey, General Manager

Canadian Society of Plastic Surgeons (CSPS) / Société canadienne des chirurgiens plasticiens
#4, 1469, boul St-Joseph est, Montréal QC H2J 1M6
Tel: 514-843-5415; *Fax:* 514-843-7005
Toll-Free: 800-665-5415
csps_sccp@bellnet.ca
www.plasticsurgery.ca
To advance the art & science of plastic surgery
Karyn Wagner, Executive Director
Patricia Bortoluzzi, President
Douglas Ross, Vice-President
Bryan Callaghan, Sec.-Treas.

Canadian Society of Respiratory Therapists (CSRT) / La Société canadienne des thérapeutes respiratoires (SCTR)
#400, 301 Cooper St., Ottawa ON K1G 3Y6
Tel: 613-731-3164; *Fax:* 613-521-4314
Toll-Free: 800-267-3422
info@csrt.com
www.csrt.com
Social Media: www.facebook.com/group.php?gid=37337032416
To provide leadership toward the advancement of cardiorespiratory care; To achieve excellence through the definition of roles, standards, & scope of clinical practice
Christiane Ménard, Executive Director
James McCormick, President
Angela Coxe, President-Elect
Jeff Dmytrowich, Treasurer

Canadian Spinal Research Organization (CSRO)
#2, 120 Newkirk Rd., Richmond Hill ON L4C 9S7
Tel: 905-508-4000; *Fax:* 905-508-4002
Toll-Free: 800-361-4004
csro@globalserve.net
www.csro.com
Social Media: www.facebook.com/196341387063476; www.youtube.com/user/CSROVideos
To improve the physical quality of life for people with spinal injuries; to reduce the incidence of spinal cord injuries through awareness programs for the public & prevention programs with targeted groups
Michael Dorman, Executive Director
Barry Munro, President

Canadian Sport Massage Therapists Association (CSMTA) / Association canadienne des massothérapeutes du sport
1030 Burnside Rd. West, Victoria BC V8Z 1N3
Tel: 250-590-9861; *Fax:* 250-388-7835
natoffice@csmta.ca
www.csmta.ca
To provide leadership in the field of sport massage therapy & education in Canada through the establishment of professional standards & qualifications of its members, as a certifying body
Kim Mark-Goldsworthy, President
Roberta Graham, National Office Coordinator
Trish Schiedel, Vice President
Monty Churchman, Secretary

Canadian Thoracic Society (CTS) / Société canadienne de thoracologie (SCT)
c/o National Office, The Lung Association, #300, 1750 Courtwood Cres., Ottawa ON K2C 2B5
Tel: 613-569-6411; *Fax:* 613-569-8860
Toll-Free: 888-566-5864
ctsinfo@lung.ca
www.lung.ca/cts
To enhance the prevention & treatment of respiratory diseases
George Fox, President
Janet Sutherland, Director
Jean Bourbeau, Secretary
Mark FitzGerald, Treasurer
Suzanne Desmarais, Manager, Communications & Membership
Suzanne McCoy, Manager, Continuing Professional Development

Canadian Transplant Association (CTA) / Association canadienne des greffes
c/o Neil Folkins, 11649 St. Albert Trail NW, Edmonton AB T5M 3L6
Toll-Free: 877-779-5991
www.organ-donation-works.org
To promote a healthy lifestyle for transplant recipients
Dave Smith, President
Neil Folkins, Director, Membership
Kathy Tachynski, Secretary
Debbie Lanktree, Treasurer

Canadian Urological Association (CUA) / Association des urologues du Canada
#1303, 1155, University St., Montréal QC H3B 3A7
Tel: 514-395-0376; *Fax:* 514-395-1664
cua@cua.org
www.cua.org
Tiffany Pizioli, Executive Director
Josephine Sciortino, Editorial Director CUAJ

Canadians for Health Research (CHR) / Les Canadiens pour la recherche médicale
PO Box 126, Westmount QC H3Z 2T1
Tel: 514-398-7478; *Fax:* 514-398-8361
info@chrcrm.org
www.chrcrm.org
To further understanding & communication among the public, the scientific community & government; To promote stability & quality in Canadian health research; to meet goals through the direct provision of information on request, & development & circulation of literature & special programming; To sponsor periodic conferences, workshops, a journalism award, & a student essay competition

CancerCare Manitoba (CCMB)
675 McDermot Ave., Winnipeg MB R3E 0V9
Tel: 204-787-2197; *Toll-Free:* 866-561-1026
donate@cancercare.mb.ca
www.cancercare.mb.ca
To provide exceptional care for patients & their families
Annitta L. Stenning, Executive Director
Sandra Tym, Director, Finance & Administration
Roberta Koscielny, Director, Communications & Public Affairs

Catholic Health Alliance of Canada / Alliance catholique canadienne de la santé
Annex C, Saint-Vincent Hospital, 60 Cambridge St. North, Ottawa ON K1R 7A5
Tel: 613-562-6262; *Fax:* 613-782-2857
challiance@bruyere.org
www.chac.ca
To strengthen & support the ministry of Catholic health care organizations & providers, through advocacy & governance
Mike Shea, Chair
James Roche, Executive Director
Nuala Kenny, Ethics & Health Policy Advisor

Catholic Health Association of British Columbia (CHABC)
9387 Holmes St., Burnaby BC V3N 4C3
Tel: 604-524-3427; *Fax:* 604-524-3428
smhouse@shawlink.ca
chabc.bc.ca
To witness to the healing ministry and abiding presence of Jesus. Inspired by the Gospel, this Association strives to have a universal concern for health as a condition for full human development.
Dianne Doyle, President

Catholic Health Association of Manitoba (CHAM) / Association catholique manitobaine de la santé (ACMS)
SBGH Education Bldg., #N5067, 409 Taché Ave., Winnipeg MB R2H 2A6
Tel: 204-235-3136; *Fax:* 204-235-3811
www.cham.mb.ca
To carry out the healing ministry of the Catholic Church in the delivery of both health & social services in Manitoba; To treat the people of Manitoba with compassion & respect for all; to recognize the spiritual dimension integral to health & healing
Wilmar Chopyk, Executive Director
Daniel Lussier, Chair

Catholic Health Association of Saskatchewan (CHAS)
1702 - 20 St. West, Saskatoon SK S7M 0Z9
Tel: 306-655-5330; *Fax:* 306-655-5333
cath.health@sasktel.net
www.chassk.ca
To provide leadership in mission, ethics, spiritual care, & social justice in Saskatchewan; To promote the sanctity of life & the dignity of all
Sandra Kary, Executive Director
Brian Martin, President
Christopher Boychuk, Vice-President
Peter Martens, Secretary-Treasurer

Catholic Health Corporation of Ontario (CHCO)
PO Box 1879, 712 College Ave. West, Guelph ON N1H 7A1
Tel: 519-767-5600; *Fax:* 519-767-5602
chco@chco.ca
www.chco.ca
Sponsors member institutions and thereby continues and strengthens Catholic health care in Ontario
Don McDermott, President
Sarah Quackenbush, Consultant, Mission & Education

Childhood Cancer Foundation Candlelighters Canada (CCCFC) / Fondation pour le Cancer chez l'enfant
#801, 21 St. Clair Ave. East, Toronto ON M4T 1L9
Tel: 416-489-6440; *Fax:* 416-489-9812
Toll-Free: 800-363-1062
info@childhoodcancer.ca
www.childhoodcancer.ca
Candlelighters Canada is a national volunteer charitable organization dedicated to improving the quality of life for families experiencing the effects of childhood cancer, through the provision of resources, parent support & the promotion of research. It is a registered charity, BN# 131897654RR0001.
Glenn Fraser, Chair
Megan Davidson, President & CEO

Chiropractic Awareness Council (CAC)
595 Woolwich St., Guelph ON N1H 3Y5
Tel: 519-822-1879; *Fax:* 519-822-1239
Toll-Free: 877-997-9927
totalhealth@chiropracticawarenesscouncil.org
www.chiropracticawarenesscouncil.org
To promote public awareness of chiropractic life principles by promoting an awareness of the devastating effects of vertebral subluxation complex on the expression of human health potential; To educate the public with the conviction that chiropractic care is a integral aspect of health for people of all ages & to society in general
Steven Silk, Chair

Christian Health Association of Alberta (CHAA)
132 Warwick Rd., Edmonton AB T5X 4P8
Tel: 780-488-8074; *Fax:* 780-475-7968
chaaa@compusmart.ab.ca
www.chaaa.ab.ca
Represents the shared vision & values of those seeking to make visible Jesus the Healer; provides support & leadership to members & the community through education, advocacy & collaboration
Glyn J. Smith, Administrator

Chronic Pain Association of Canada (CPAC)
PO Box 66017, Stn. Heritage, #130, 2323 - 111 St., Edmonton AB T6J 6T4
Tel: 780-482-6727; *Fax:* 780-433-3128
cpac@chronicpaincanada.com
www.chronicpaincanada.com
To advance the treatment & management of chronic intractable pain; to develop research projects to promote the discovery of a cure for this disease; to educate both the health care community & the public
Terry Bremner, President
Barry Ulmer, Executive Director

Collège des médecins du Québec (CMQ)
2170, boul René-Lévesque ouest, Montréal QC H3H 2T8
Tél: 514-933-4441; *Téléc:* 514-933-3112
Ligne sans frais: 888-633-3246
info@cmq.org
www.cmq.org
Mèdia social: www.facebook.com/group.php?gid=257741694238490; twitter.com/CMQ_org
Promouvoir une médecine de qualité pour protéger le public et contribuer à l'amélioration de la santé des Québécois
Charles Bernard, Président-directeur général
Yves Robert, Secrétaire

College of Chiropractors of Alberta (CCOA)
Manulife Place, 11203 - 70 St. NW, Edmonton AB T5B 1T1
Tel: 780-420-0932; *Fax:* 780-425-6583
To ensure quality chiropractic care that enhances the well-being & protects the rights of the people of Alberta; To promote the art, science, & philosophy of chiropractic & its value in the health care community
Deb Manz, Chief Executive Officer
Clark Mills, President

College of Dietitians of Alberta
#740, 10707 - 100 Ave., Edmonton AB T5J 3M1
Tel: 780-448-0059; *Fax:* 780-489-7759
Toll-Free: 866-493-4348
office@collegeofdietitians.ab.ca
www.collegeofdietitians.ab.ca
The College is the regulatory body of registered dieticians/nutritionists in Alberta, setting entry requirements, standards of practice. It is accountable to both the government & the public.
Doug Cook, Executive Director & Registrar

College of Dietitians of British Columbia (CDBC)
#409, 1367 West Broadway, Vancouver BC V6H 4A7
Tel: 604-736-2016; *Fax:* 604-736-2018
Toll-Free: 877-736-2016
info@collegeofdietitiansbc.org
www.collegeofdietitiansbc.org
To serve & protect the nutritional health of the public through quality dietetic practice
Fern Hubbard, Registrar

College of Dietitians of Manitoba
#36, 1313 Border St., Winnipeg MB R3H 0X4
Tel: 204-694-0532; *Fax:* 204-889-1755
Toll-Free: 866-283-2823
office.cdm@mts.net
www.manitobadietitians.ca
The College is the regulating body within the province for dietitians & the profession of dietetics, setting education standards, ensuring competency of members.
Michelle Hagglund, Registrar

College of Dietitians of Ontario (CDO) / L'Ordre des diététistes de l'Ontario
PO Box 30, #1810, 5775 Yonge St., Toronto ON M2M 4J1
Tel: 416-598-1725; *Fax:* 416-598-0274
Toll-Free: 800-668-4990
information@cdo.on.ca
www.cdo.on.ca
To promote awareness of & access to competent, high quality nutritional care for Ontarians.
Mary Lou Gignac, Registrar

College of Family Physicians of Canada (CFPC) / Collège des médecins de famille du Canada
2630 Skymark Ave., Mississauga ON L4W 5A4
Tel: 905-629-0900; *Fax:* 905-629-0893
Toll-Free: 800-387-6197
info@cfpc.ca
www.cfpc.ca
To improve the health of Canadians by promoting high standards of medical education & care in family practice, by contributing to public understanding of healthful living, by supporting ready access to family physician services, & by encouraging research & disseminating knowledge about family medicine
Calvin Gutkin, Executive Director/CEO
Sandy Buchman, President

College of Physicians & Surgeons of Alberta (CPSA)
Telus Plaza South, #2700, 10020 - 100 St. NW, Edmonton AB T5J 0N3
Tel: 780-423-4764; *Fax:* 780-420-0651
Toll-Free: 800-561-3899
info@cpsa.ab.ca
www.cpsa.ab.ca
To serve the public & guide the medical profession; to identify factors affecting competent medical practice; to promote quality improvement in medical practice; to ensure practitioners meet our registration standards; to resolve complaints involving practitioners fairly & effectively.
Trevor Theman, Registrar

College of Physicians & Surgeons of British Columbia (CPSBC)
#300, 699 Howe St., Vancouver BC V6C 0B4
Tel: 604-733-7758; *Fax:* 604-733-3503
Toll-Free: 800-461-3008
www.cpsbc.ca
M.A. Docherty, President

College of Physicians & Surgeons of Manitoba (CPSM)
#1000, 1661 Portage Ave., Winnipeg MB R3J 3T7
Tel: 204-774-4344; *Fax:* 204-774-0750
Toll-Free: 877-774-4344
cpsm@cpsm.mb.ca
www.cpsm.mb.ca
William Pope, Registrar

College of Physicians & Surgeons of New Brunswick / Collège des médecins et chirurgiens du Nouveau-Brunswick
#300, One Hampton Rd., Rothesay NB E2E 5K8
Tel: 506-849-5050; *Fax:* 506-849-5069
Toll-Free: 800-667-4641
info@cpsnb.org
www.cpsnb.org
Ed Schollenberg, Registrar

College of Physicians & Surgeons of Newfoundland & Labrador
#603, 139 Water St., St. John's NL A1C 1B2
Tel: 709-726-8546; *Fax:* 709-726-4725
cpsnl@cpsnl.ca
www.cpsnl.ca
To protect the public; to regulate the practice of medicine & medical practitioners
Robert W. Young, Registrar
William Moulton, Chair

College of Physicians & Surgeons of Nova Scotia (CPSNS)
#5005, 7071 Bayers Rd., Halifax NS B3L 2C2
Tel: 902-422-5823; *Fax:* 902-422-5035
Toll-Free: 877-282-7767
mmchugh@cpsns.ns.ca
www.cpsns.ns.ca
To govern the practice of medicine in the public interest
Cameron D. Little, CEO & Registrar
Pat Pettit, Director, Administration

College of Physicians & Surgeons of Ontario (CPSO)
80 College St., Toronto ON M5G 2E2
Tel: 416-967-2603; *Fax:* 416-961-3330
Toll-Free: 800-268-7096
feedback@cpso.on.ca
www.cpso.on.ca
To ensure the best quality care for the people of Ontario by the doctors of Ontario
Robert Byrick, President
Rayudu Koka, President

College of Physicians & Surgeons of Prince Edward Island
199 Grafton St., Charlottetown PE C1A 1L2
Tel: 902-566-3861; *Fax:* 902-566-3861
mmacdonald@collegeofphysicians.pe.ca
www.cpspei.ca
The College is the regulatory body for physicians in the province, responsible for licensing all medical doctors, maintaining medical standards, handling complaints from the public, & delivering disciplinary action.
Don Ling, Council President
Cyril Moyse, Registrar
Melissa MacDonald, Office Secretary

College of Physicians & Surgeons of Saskatchewan (CPSS)
#500, 321A - 21st St. East, Saskatoon SK S7K 0C1
Tel: 306-244-7355; *Fax:* 306-244-0090
cpss@quadrant.net
www.quadrant.net/cpss/
The College of Physicians and Surgeons is a statutory, self-regulating body established by legislation of the Government of Saskatchewan and charged with the responsibility of: Licencing properly qualified medical practitioners; developing and ensuring the standards of practice in all fields of medicine; investigating and disciplining of all doctors whose standards of medical care, ethical or professional conduct are questioned.
J. Wolan, Director, Communications & Education
B. Salte, Associate Registrar
K. Shaw, Deputy Registrar
D.A. Kendel, Registrar

Community & Hospital Infection Control Association Canada / Association pour la prévention des infections à l'hôpital et dans la communauté - Canada
PO Box 46125, Winnipeg MB R3R 3S3
Tel: 204-897-5990; *Fax:* 204-895-9595
Toll-Free: 866-999-7111
chicacda@mts.net
www.chica.org
To promote excellence in the practice of infection prevention & control; to employ evidence based practice & application of epidemiological principles to improve the health of Canadians
Jim Gauthier, President

Consumer Health Organization of Canada (CHOC)
#1901, 355 St. Clair Ave. West, Toronto ON M5P 1N5
Tel: 416-924-9800; *Fax:* 416-924-6404
info@consumerhealth.org
www.consumerhealth.org
To encourage the prevention of all kinds of illness through knowledge; to help the individual, the family & the community to enjoy the benefits of a more wholesome lifestyle; to promote harmony & cooperation between like-minded groups.

Crohn's & Colitis Foundation of Canada (CCFC) / Fondation canadienne des maladies inflammatoires de l'intestin
#600, 60 St. Clair Ave. East, Toronto ON M4T 1N5
Tel: 416-920-5035; *Fax:* 416-929-0364
Toll-Free: 800-387-1479
ccfc@ccfc.ca
www.ccfc.ca
Social Media: www.facebook.com/group.php?gid=181701075182303; twitter.com/isupportibd; www.youtube.com/watch?v=6xJY_Fu7o8E&lr=1
To find a cure for Crohn's disease & ulcerative colitis; To raise funds for medical research; To educate individuals with inflammatory bowel disease, their families, health professionals, & the public
Marty Cutler, President
Paul McCarten, Secretary
Byron Sonberg, Treasurer

Cystic Fibrosis Canada
National Office, #601, 2221 Yonge St., Toronto ON M4S 2B4
Tel: 416-485-9149; *Fax:* 416-485-0960
Toll-Free: 800-378-2233
info@cysticfibrosis.ca
www.cysticfibrosis.ca
Social Media: www.facebook.com/CysticFibrosisCanada; twitter.com/CFCanada; www.youtube.com/CysticFibrosisCanada
To help people with Cystic Fibrosis through funding research towards a cure or control; To support high quality care; To promote public awareness; To raise & allocate funds
Maureen Adamson, Chief Executive Officer
Ken Chan, Vice-President, Advocacy & Partnerships
Trevor Roberts, Chief Marketing & Development Officer
Aida Fernandes, Director, Medical / Scientific & Community Programs
Barb Gull, Director, Finance & Accounting
Cheryl Woods, Director, Community Development
Alice Awweh, National Events & Partner Relations Officer
Christine Beyaert, Social Media & Communications Officer

Dietitians of Canada (DC) / Les diététistes du Canada
#604, 480 University Ave., Toronto ON M5G 1V2
Tel: 416-596-0857; *Fax:* 416-596-0603
centralinfo@dietitians.ca
www.dietitians.ca
To advance health, through food & nutrition; To act as the voice of the profession in Canada
Marsha Sharp, Chief Executive Officer
Corinne Eisenbraun, Director, Professional Practice Development
Janice Macdonald, Director, Communications
Marlene Wyatt, Director, Professional Affairs
Patricia Sierra, Manager, Finance & Administration

Doctors Manitoba
20 Desjardins Dr., Winnipeg MB R3X 0E8
Tel: 204-985-5888; *Fax:* 204-985-5844
Toll-Free: 888-322-4242
www.docsmb.org
To advocate for Manitoba physicians, representing their professional & economic interests.
Debbie Bride, Communications Officer
John A. Laplume, CEO

Doctors Nova Scotia
25 Spectacle Lake Dr., Dartmouth NS B3B 1X7
Tel: 902-468-1866; *Fax:* 902-468-6578
info@doctorsns.com
www.doctorsns.com
To maintain the integrity of the medical profession; To represent members; To promote high quality health care & disease prevention in Nova Scotia
Nancy MacCready-Williams, CEO
John Chiasson, President

Dystonia Medical Research Foundation Canada / Fondation de recherches médicales sur la dystonie
#909, 100 Adelaide St. West, Toronto ON M5H 1S3
Tel: 416-488-6974; *Fax:* 416-488-5878
Toll-Free: 800-361-8061
info@dystoniacanada.org
www.dystoniacanada.org
DMRF Canada aims to advance & support research relating to dystonia; to build awareness about the illness in order to educate both medical & lay communities; and to sponsor patient & family support groups & programs. It is a registered charity, BN: 126616598RR0001.
Sarah Smith, National Director

Epilepsy & Seizure Association of Manitoba
#4, 1805 Main St., Winnipeg MB R2V 2A2
Tel: 204-783-0466; *Fax:* 204-784-9689
Toll-Free: 866-374-5377
epilepsy.seizures.mb@mts.net
www.manitobaepilepsy.org
The Association aims to improve the quality of life of persons with epilepsy through a broad range of programs, education, support of research & services. It is a registered charity, BN: 108087826RR0001.
Jim Cook, President
Phyllis Thomson, Executive Director
Tom Hansen, Vice-President
Diane Wall, Treasurer
Frances Held, Secretary

Epilepsy Canada (EC) / Épilepsie Canada
#336, 2255B Queen St. East, Toronto ON M4E 1G3
Fax: 905-764-1231
Toll-Free: 877-734-0873
epilepsy@epilepsy.ca
www.epilepsy.ca
To enhance the quality of life for persons affected by epilepsy; To promote & support research into all aspects of epilepsy; To facilitate educational initiatives; To increase public & professional awareness of epilepsy; To fund research; To encourage governments to address the needs of people with epilepsy
W. McIntyre Burnham, National President

Epilepsy Ontario / Épilepsie Ontario
#308, 1 Promenade Circle, Thornhill ON L4J 4P8
Tel: 905-764-5099; *Fax:* 905-764-1231
Toll-Free: 800-463-1119
info@epilepsyontario.org
epilepsyontario.org
EO is a non-profit, non-governmental health organization promoting optimal quality of life for people living with seizure disorders. It advocates for awareness, support services, and research into these disorders and maintains a network of local agencies, contacts & associates to provide services, counselling & referrals. It is a registered charity, BN: 118900844RR0001.
Dianna Findlay, Executive Director

Ethiopiaid
#600, 325 Dalhousie St., Ottawa ON K1N 7G2
Tel: 613-697-4843
info@ethiopiaid.ca
www.ethiopiaid.ca
Ethiopiaid aims to create lasting and positive change in Ethiopia by tackling the problems of poverty, ill health and poor education.
As a fundraising organisation, we donate directly to local community projects in Ethiopia. These partners already hold the answers, they simply need a helping hand from people like you to carry out their work.

Eye Bank of BC (EBBC)
Eye Care Centre, 2550 Willow St., Vancouver BC V5Z 3N9
Tel: 604-875-4567; *Fax:* 604-875-5316
Toll-Free: 800-667-2060
eyebankofbc@vch.ca
www.eyebankofbc.ca
To acquire human donor eye tissue for the purposes of corneal transplant, scelra grafts & medical research.
Linda Dempster, Manager
M. McCarthy, Medical Director

Eye Bank of Canada - Ontario Division
One Spadina Cres., Toronto ON M5S 2J5
Tel: 416-497-8735; *Fax:* 416-978-1522
eye.bank@utoronto.ca
eyebank.med.utoronto.ca
To provide donated eye tissue for surgical use in those whose vision can be restored or improved through corneal transplantation or other eye surgery
Fides Coloma, Manager

Fédération des médecins omnipraticiens du Québec (FMOQ) / Québec Federation of General Practitioners
#1000, 1440, rue Sainte-Catherine ouest, Montréal QC H3G 1R8
Tél: 514-878-1911; *Téléc:* 514-878-4455
Ligne sans frais: 800-361-8499
info@fmoq.org
www.fmoq.org
Étude et défense des intérêts économiques, sociaux, moraux et scientifiques des associations et de leurs membres; promouvoir et développer le rôle de l'omnipraticien dans les sphères de la vie économique, sociale, scientifique et culturelle en définissant d'une façon objective le statut propre à l'omnipraticien
Louis Godin, Président-directeur général

Fédération des médecins spécialistes du Québec (FMSQ) / Federation of Medical Specialists of Québec
CP 216, Succ. Desjardins, #3000, 2, Complexe Desjardins, Montréal QC H5B 1G8
Tél: 514-350-5000; *Téléc:* 514-350-5100
Ligne sans frais: 800-561-0703
president@fmsq.org
www.fmsq.org
Défendre et promouvoir les intérêts économiques, professionnels et scientifiques des médecins spécialistes
Gaétan Barrette, Président

Federation of Canadian Naturists (FCN)
PO Box 186, Stn. D, Toronto ON M9A 4X2
Tel: 416-410-6833; *Fax:* 416-410-6833
Toll-Free: 888-512-6833
information@fcn.ca
www.fcn.ca
To promote naturism (social nudism) as a healthy, wholesome & completely natural lifestyle
Stéphane Deschênes, President

Federation of Regulatory Authorities of Canada (FMRAC) / Fédération des ordres des médecins du Canada
#103, 2283 St. Laurent Blvd., Ottawa ON K1G 5A2
Tel: 613-738-0372; *Fax:* 613-738-9169
info@fmrac.ca
www.fmrac.ca
To provide a national structure for the provincial & territorial medical regulatory authorities; To present & pursue issues of common concern & interest; To share, consider, & develop positions on such matters
B. Ward, President

Fédération québécoise de l'autisme et des autres troubles envahissants du développement (FQATED) / Québec Federation for Autism & Other Pervasive Developmental Disorders
#104, 65, rue de Castelnau ouest, Montréal QC H2R 2W3
Tél: 514-270-7386; *Téléc:* 514-270-9261
Ligne sans frais: 888-830-2833
secretariatfqa@contact.net
www.autisme.qc.ca
Promouvoir et défendre les droits et les intérêts de la personne autiste ou ayant un trouble envahissant du développement afin qu'elle accède à une vie digne et à une meilleure autonomie sociale possible.
Jo-Ann Lauzon, Directrice générale

Fédération québécoise des massothérapeutes (FQM)
#400, 4428, boul St-Laurent, Montréal QC H2W 1Z5
Tél: 514-597-0505; *Téléc:* 514-597-0141
Ligne sans frais: 800-363-9609
administration@fqm.qc.ca
www.fqm.qc.ca
Média social: www.facebook.com/massotherapie.FQM
Regrouper les massothérapeutes afin de promouvoir la massothérapie sous l'intérêt public et de valoriser la profession de la massothérapie
Sylvie Bédard, Directrice générale

Fédération québécoise des sociétés Alzheimer (FQSA) / Federation of Québec Alzheimer Societies
#211, 5165, rue Sherbrooke ouest, Montréal QC H4A 1T6
Tél: 514-369-7891; *Téléc:* 514-369-7900
Ligne sans frais: 888-636-6473
info@alzheimerquebec.ca
www.alzheimerquebec.ca
Média social: www.facebook.com/group.php?gid=21548021978
Alléger les conséquences personnelles et sociales de la maladie d'Alzheimer; diffuser l'information auprès du public sur la maladie d'Alzheimer et sur les services offerts par notre réseau; soutenir les sociétés qui offrent aide et formation; promouvoir et encourager la recherche sur la maladie d'Alzheimer entre autres par la gestion d'un fonds provincial de la recherche; établir des relations et faire des représentations auprès des autorités concernées
Réal Leahey, Président

Fibrose kystique Québec (FKQ) / Cystic Fibrosis Québec (CFQ)
625 av du Président-Kennedy, Montréal QC H3A 1K2
Tél: 514-877-6161; *Téléc:* 514-877-6116
Ligne sans frais: 800-363-7711
www.fibrosekystiquequebec.com
Média social:
www.facebook.com/group.php?gid=162576157129896;
twitter.com/FKQuebec;
plus.google.com/106908476349956061911
Sensibiliser la population sur la fibrose kystique; amasser des fonds pour la recherche médicale; améliorer la qualité de vie des personnes atteintes de FK; découvrir un remède ou un moyen de contrôler la fibrose kystique.
Bettina Ehlers, Secrétaire de direction

A fleur de sein & Objectif Santé Mammaire
CP 518, 492, 2e Rue, Chibougamau QC G8P 2X9
Tél: 418-748-7914; *Téléc:* 418-748-4422
afleurdesein@tlb.sympatico.ca
www.cbcn.ca/afleurdesein/
Offrir solidarité, présence, écoute & entraide à ceux & celles qui sont atteints d'un cancer, quel qu'il soit
Marie Lefrançois, Présidente, A fleur de sein
Nicole Pagé, Coordonnatrice, Objectif Santé Mammaire

La Fondation canadienne du rein, section Chibougamau
CP 462, Chibougamau QC G8P 2Y8
Tél: 418-748-4730
Hélène Ross-Arseneault

Fondation de la banque d'yeux du Québec inc. / Québec Eye Bank Foundation
5415, boul de l'Assomption, Montréal QC H1T 2M4
Tél: 514-252-3886; *Téléc:* 514-252-3821
fondby@ssss.gouv.qc.ca
Financement de la recherche sur les maladies de l'oeil et plus particuliement de la cornée (greffe)
Daniel Michaluk, Coordonnatrice administrative

Fondation des maladies du coeur du Québec (FMCQ) / Heart & Stroke Foundation of Québec
#500, 1434, rue Sainte-Catherine ouest, Montréal QC H3G 1R4
Tél: 514-871-1551; *Téléc:* 514-871-9385
Ligne sans frais: 800-567-8563
www.fmcoeur.qc.ca
Forte de l'engagement de ses donateurs, de ses bénévoles et de ses employés, a pour mission de contribuer à l'avancement de la recherche et de promouvoir la santé du coeur, afin de réduire les invalidités et les décès dus aux maladies cardiovasculaires et aux accidents vasculaires cérébraux
Bobbe Wood, CEO
Richard Légaré, Président du conseil

Fondation québécoise du cancer
2075, rue de Champlain, Montréal QC H2L 2T1
Tél: 514-527-2194; *Téléc:* 514-527-1943
Ligne sans frais: 877-336-4443
cancerquebec.mtl@fqc.qc.ca
www.fqc.qc.ca
Vouée à l'amélioration de la condition de la personne atteinte de cancer et de ses proches; offrir des services d'hôtellerie, d'écoute et d'information pour gens atteints du cancer; améliorer la qualité de vie des patients et celle de leurs proches.
Michel Gélinas, Président-fondateur

The Foundation Fighting Blindness (FFB)
890 Yonge St., 12th Fl., Toronto ON M4W 3P4
Tel: 416-360-4200; *Fax:* 416-360-0060
Toll-Free: 800-461-3331
info@ffb.ca
www.ffb.ca
Social Media: www.facebook.com/187447074652378; twitter.com/FFBCanada
To support & promote research directed to finding the causes, treatments & ultimately the cures for retinitis pigmentosa, macular degeneration & related retinal diseases
Sharon M. Colle, President & CEO
Rahn Dodick, Treasurer
Andrew Burke, Secretary

GI (Gastrointestinal) Society
855 - 12th Ave., Vancouver BC V5Z 1M9
Tel: 604-875-4875; *Fax:* 604-875-4429
Toll-Free: 866-600-4875
info@badgut.org
www.badgut.org
Social Media: www.facebook.com/CISociety; twitter.com/GISociety
To improve the lives of people with GI and liver conditions, support research, advocate for appropriate patient access to healthcare & promote gastrointestinal & liver health
Gilles Larose, Chairperson
Gail Attara, Co-Founder & President/CEO

Health Action Network Society (HANS)
#202, 5262 Rumble St., Burnaby BC V5J 2B6
Tel: 604-435-0512; *Fax:* 604-435-1561
hans@hans.org; membership@hans.org; events@hans.org
www.hans.org
Social Media: twitter.com/JoinHANS
To support complementary & alternative health care; To provide resources about preventive medicine & natural therapeutics; To facilitate delivery of integrated health care; To act as a voice for natural health consumers in Canada
Lorna Hancock, Director

Health Association of African Canadians (HAAC)
1149 Main St., Dartmouth NS B2Z 1A8
Tel: 902-405-4222
haac@chebucto.ns.ca
www.haac.ca
To promote and improve the health of African Canadians in Nova Scotia through community engagement, education, policy recommendations, partnerships, and research participation.
Phyllis Marsh-Jarvis, President

Health Care Public Relations Association of Canada (HCPRA) / Association des relations publiques des organismes de la santé, Canada (ARPOS)
PO Box 36029, 1106 Wellington St., Ottawa ON K1Y 4V3
Tel: 613-729-2102; *Fax:* 613-729-7708
info@hcpra.org
www.hcpra.org
Social Media: www.facebook.com/165490196835523; twitter.com/HCPRA
To address the concerns of the public relations professionals in Canadian health care settings
Jane Petricic, National Coordinator
Judy Brown, HCPRA President

Health Sciences Centre Foundation (HSCF)
Thorlakson Building, 820 Sherbrook St., #MS1, Winnipeg MB R3A 1R9
Tel: 204-787-2022; *Fax:* 204-787-2804
Toll-Free: 800-679-8493
hsc_foundation@hsc.mb.ca
www.hscfoundation.mb.ca
To promote health care excellence by funding medical research & clinical projects to the benefit of diverse communities served by the Health Sciences Centre
F.L. (Lynn) Bishop, Chair
Dawne Smithson, Vice-President/COO

Heart & Stroke Foundation of Alberta, NWT & Nunavut (HSFA)
#100, 119 - 14 St. NW, Calgary AB T2N 1Z6
Tel: 403-264-5549; *Fax:* 403-237-0803
Toll-Free: 888-473-4636
www.hsf.ab.ca
The Association disseminates information about heart disease & stroke, & also promotes research into new drugs, therapies, treatments in disorders leading to heart disease & stroke. It conducts several events to campaign for funds. It is a registered charity, BN: 118780840RR0001.
Roderick J. McKay, Chair
Diana Krecsy, CEO

Heart & Stroke Foundation of British Columbia & Yukon (HSFBCY)
1212 West Broadway, Vancouver BC V6H 3V2
Tel: 604-736-4404; *Fax:* 604-736-8732
Toll-Free: 888-473-4636
info@hsf.bc.ca
www.heartandstroke.bc.ca
To further the study, prevention & relief of cardiovascular disease
Bobbe Wood, CEO

Heart & Stroke Foundation of Canada (HSFC) / Fondation des maladies du coeur du Canada
#1402, 222 Queen St., Ottawa ON K1P 5V9
Tel: 613-569-4361; *Fax:* 613-569-3278
www.heartandstroke.ca
To further the study, prevention & reduction of disability & death from heart disease & stroke through research, education & the promotion of healthy lifestyles
Sally Brown, CEO
Robert Brools, Chair

Heart & Stroke Foundation of Manitoba (HSFM)
The Heart & Stroke Bldg., #200, 6 Donald St., Winnipeg MB R3L 0K6
Tel: 204-949-2000; *Fax:* 204-957-1365
www.heartandstroke.mb.ca
To eliminate heart disease & stroke through education, advocacy, & research
Debbie Brown, CEO

Heart & Stroke Foundation of New Brunswick / Fondation des maladies du coeur du Nouveau-Brunswick
#606, 133 Prince William St., Saint John NB E2L 2B5
Tel: 506-634-1620; *Fax:* 506-648-0098
Toll-Free: 800-663-3600
www.heartandstroke.nb.ca
To improve the health of residents of New Brunswick by preventing & reducing disability & death from heart disease & stroke, through research, health promotion & advocacy
Daniel Connolly, CEO

Heart & Stroke Foundation of Newfoundland & Labrador
PO Box 670, 1037 Topsail Rd., Mount Pearl NL A1C 5X3
Tel: 709-753-8521; *Fax:* 709-753-3117
info@heartandstroke.nf.net
www.heartandstroke.nf.ca
To work in Newfoundland & Labrador to advance research, advocate, & promote healthy lifestyles so that heart disease & stroke will be eliminated & their impact reduced
George Tilley, CEO

Heart & Stroke Foundation of Nova Scotia (HSFNS)
Park Lane - Mall Level 3, PO Box 245, 5657 Spring Garden Rd., Halifax NS B3J 3R4
Tel: 902-423-7530; *Fax:* 902-492-1464
Toll-Free: 800-423-4432
contactus@heartandstroke.ns.ca
www.heartandstroke.ns.ca
To eliminate heart disease & stroke; To advance research; To promote healthy living; To engage in advocacy activities
Jane Farquharson, CEO

Heart & Stroke Foundation of Prince Edward Island Inc.
PO Box 279, 180 Kent St., Charlottetown PE C1A 7K4
Tel: 902-892-7441; *Fax:* 902-368-7068
Toll-Free: 888-473-4636
www.heartandstroke.pe.ca
To improve the health of Islanders through the funding of heart disease & stroke research & the provision of heart & stroke education & programs
Charlotte Comrie, CEO & Executive Director
Jason Roberts, Chair
Joan Sinclair, Director, Development
Susan Taylor-McConnell, Coordinator, Health Promotion
Sue Platts, Coordinator, School Programs & Events
Cathy Sinclair, Coordinator, Stroke Strategy

Heart & Stroke Foundation of Saskatchewan (HSFS) / Fondation des maladies du coeur de la Saskatchewan
279 - 3 Ave. North, Saskatoon SK S7K 2H8
Tel: 306-244-2124; *Fax:* 306-664-4016
Toll-Free: 888-473-4636
heart.stroke@hsf.sk.ca
www.heartandstroke.sk.ca
Social Media: www.facebook.com/heartandstroke
The Foundation is a volunteer-driven, non-profit organization with the ultimate goal to eliminate & reduce the impact of heart disease & stroke. It aims to advance research, promote healthy living, & advocates a healthy public policy. It is a registered charity, BN: 107955817RR0001.
Nikki Gerrard, President
Lucy Buller, CEO

Hepatitis Outreach Society
Halifax Shopping Centre, PO Box 29120, 2973 Oxford St., Halifax NS B3J 4T8
Tel: 902-420-1767; *Fax:* 902-463-6725
Toll-Free: 800-521-0572
info@hepatitisoutreach.com
www.hepatitisoutreach.com
To educate Nova Scotians about Hepatitis and its prevention, reduce social stigmatization and isolation; and prevent the spread of Hepatitis.
Angus Campbell, Contact

Huntington Society of Canada / Société Huntington du Canada
#400, 151 Frederick St., Kitchener ON N2H 2M2
Tel: 519-749-7063; *Fax:* 519-749-8965
Toll-Free: 800-998-7398
info@huntingtonsociety.ca
www.huntingtonsociety.ca
To aspire for a world free of Huntington disease; To maximize the quality of life of people living with HD
Bev Heim-Myers, Executive Director & CEO
Anne Brace, Chair
Sean Dewart, Secretary
Glenda Rowein, Treasurer

Hypertension Canada
c/o Judi Farrell, #211, 3780 - 14th Ave., Markham ON L3R 9Y5
Tel: 905-943-9400; *Fax:* 905-943-9401
admin@hypertension.ca
www.hypertension.ca
To advance health by preventing & controlling high blood presseure
Ross Feldman, President
Judi Farrell, Executive Director
Pierre Larochelle, Vice-President
John Blair, Secretary
Robert Brooks, Treasurer

International Association for Medical Assistance to Travellers (IAMAT)
#036, 67 Mowat Ave., Toronto ON M6K 3E3
Tel: 416-652-0137; *Fax:* 416-652-1983
www.iamat.org
Social Media: www.facebook.com/302185377896; twitter.com/IAMAT_Travel
To make competent care available to the traveller around the world; to make direct grants to medical institutions
Assunta Uffer-Marcolongo, President

Juvenile Diabetes Research Foundation Canada (JDRF)
#800, 2550 Victoria Park Ave., Toronto ON M2J 5A9
Tel: 647-789-2000; *Fax:* 416-491-2111
Toll-Free: 877-287-3533
general@jdrf.ca
www.jdrf.ca
To support research to find a cure for diabetes & its complications; To increase awareness of diabetes, particularly Juvenile (Type 1) diabetes
Aubrey Baillie, Chair
Andrew McKee, President/CEO
David Kozloff, Secretary
Alex Davidson, Treasurer

Kidney Foundation of Canada (KFOC) / Fondation canadienne du rein
#300, 5165, rue Sherbrooke ouest, Montréal QC H4A 1T6
Tel: 514-369-4806; *Fax:* 514-369-2472
Toll-Free: 800-361-7494
info@kidney.ca; webmaster@kidney.ca
www.kidney.ca
Social Media: www.facebook.com/kidneyfoundation; twitter.com/kidneycanada; www.youtube.com/kidneycanada; www.flickr.com/kidneyfoundation
To improve the health & quality of life of people living with kidney disease; To fund research & related clinical education; To provide services for the special needs of individuals living with kidney disease; To advocate for access to high quality health care; To actively promote awareness of & commitment to organ donation
Richardson Kathryn, National President
Julian Midgley, National Vice President

L.E. Society of Saskatchewan (LESS)
c/o Royal University Hospital, PO Box 88, 103 Hospital Dr., Saskatoon SK S7N 0W0
Tel: 306-781-6123; *Toll-Free:* 877-566-6123
less@sasklupus.com
www.sasklupus.com
To provide support for those affected by lupus through understanding, education, public awareness & research
Lloyd Driedger, President

Leprosy Mission Canada / La Mission évangélique contre la lèpre (Canada)
#100, 100 Mural St., Richmond Hill ON L4B 1J3
Tel: 905-886-2885
info@leprosy.ca
www.leprosy.ca
TLM Canada provides care and support to leprosy patients in many parts of the world including India, Bangladesh, and Nigeria.
Peter Derrick, Executive Director

The Leukemia & Lymphoma Society of Canada (LLSC) / Société de leucémie et lymphome du Canada
#804, 2 Lansing Square, Toronto ON M2J 4P8
Fax: 416-661-7799
Toll-Free: 877-668-8326
donatecanada@lls.org
www.llscanada.org
Social Media: www.facebook.com/LLSCanada; twitter.com/llscanada; www.youtube.com/llscanada; www.flickr.com/photos/llscanada
To cure leukemia, lymphoma, Hodgkin's disease & myeloma, & to improve the quality of life of patients & their families
Adrian Hartog, Chair

Lupus Canada
#3, 3555 14th Avenue, Markham ON L3R 0H5
Tel: 905-513-0004; *Fax:* 905-513-9516
Toll-Free: 800-661-1468
info@lupuscanada.org
www.lupuscanada.org
Social Media: www.facebook.com/group.php?gid=69263929055&ref=ts
To improve the lives of people living with lupus; To encourage cooperation among the lupus organizations in Canada
Catherine Madden, Executive Director
Kendra MacDonald, President
Tina Sarta, Treasurer

Lupus Foundation of Ontario (LFO)
PO Box 687, 294 Ridge Rd. North, Ridgeway ON L0S 1N0
Tel: 905-894-4611; *Fax:* 905-894-4616
Toll-Free: 800-368-8377
lupusont@vaxxine.com
www.vaxxine.com/lupus
To serve the lupus patient community as a charitable organization
Patricia Leece, President

Lupus New Brunswick
#17, 55 Grant St., Moncton NB E1A 3R3
Tel: 506-384-6227; *Toll-Free:* 877-303-8080
lupins@rogers.com
www.lupusnb.ca
Social Media: www.facebook.com/group.php?gid=113746565332566
The group promotes eduction & public awarness of lupus. It brings together lupus patients, friends, family, & other interested persons for a network of support.
Nancy Votour, President

Lupus Newfoundland & Labrador
PO Box 8121, Stn. A, Kenmount Rd., St. John's NL A1B 3M9
Tel: 709-368-8130
lupusnfld@nl.rogers.com
www.envision.ca/webs/lupusnfldlab
Dale Williams, President

Lupus Nova Scotia
PO Box 38038, Dartmouth NS B3B 1X2
Tel: 902-425-0358; *Fax:* 902-798-0772
Toll-Free: 800-394-0125
lubpussocietyns@ns.sympatico.ca
www.lupuscanada.org/novascotia
The Society informs, educates & supports all those afflicted with lupus. It promotes public & professional awareness of the disease as a prevalent & controllable one, as well as funding research for its cure. It is a registered charity, BN: 133533158RR0001.

Lupus Ontario (OLA)
#230, 2900 John St., Markham ON L3R 5G3
Tel: 905-415-1099; *Fax:* 905-415-9874
Toll-Free: 877-240-1099
info@lupusontario.org
www.lupusontario.org
To serve the needs of Lupus sufferers in Ontario
Julia Kane, President
Tina Sarta, Vice-President
Sharon Coslett, Secretary
Emily Leung, Treasurer

Lupus PEI
PO Box 23002, Charlottetown PE C1E 1Z6
Tel: 902-892-3875; *Fax:* 902-626-3585
Toll-Free: 800-661-1468
bargri@pei.sympatico.ca
www.lupuscanada.org/pei
The organization promotes public awareness of lupus on PEI, while offering support & educational materials to lupus patients, their families & friends.

Lupus Society of Alberta (LESA)
#200, 1301 - 8 St. SW, Calgary AB T2R 1B7
Tel: 403-228-7956; *Fax:* 403-228-7853
Toll-Free: 888-242-9182
lupuslsa@shaw.ca
www.lupus.ab.ca
To provide education & support on lupus issues & enable research to find a cure.
Rosemary E. Church, Executive Director
Marleery E. Winston, President

Lupus Society of Manitoba Inc.
#105, 386 Broadway Ave., Winnipeg MB R3C 3R6
Tel: 204-942-6825; *Fax:* 204-942-4894
Toll-Free: 888-942-6825
lupus@mts.net
To provide support, encouragement & education to lupus patients & their families
Darlene Garner, President

Manitoba Association of Optometrists (MAO)
#200B, 392 Academy Rd., Winnipeg MB R3N 0B8
Tel: 204-943-9811; *Fax:* 204-943-1208
mao@optometrists.mb.ca
www.optometrists.mb.ca
To regulate the practice of optometry in Manitoba, in accordance with The Optometry Act & Regulation; To represent optometrists in Manitoba; To protect & promote the vision care needs & eye health of Manitobans
Michelle Georgi, President
Laureen Goodridge, Executive Director
Lorne Ryall, Registrar

Manitoba Chiropractors' Association (MCA)
#610, 1445 Portage Ave., Winnipeg MB R3G 3P4
Tel: 204-942-3000; *Fax:* 204-942-3010
www.mbchiro.org
To act as both a regulatory body & a professional association to serve the public & the chiropractors of Manitoba; To foster high standards of chiropractic health care for Manitobans; To ensure that safe, ethical, & competent servicew are provided by Manitoba chiropractors
Taras Luchak, Executive Director
Ernie Miron, Registrar

Manitoba Lung Association
629 McDermot Ave., Winnipeg MB R3A 1P6
Tel: 204-774-5501; *Fax:* 204-772-5083
Toll-Free: 888-566-5864
info@mb.lung.ca
www.mb.lung.ca
To improve lung health
Margaret Bernhardt-Lowdon, Executive Director & Director, Health Initiatives
Jo-anne Douglas, Director, Tobacco Reduction Initiatives
Ron East, Director, Programming, Fund Development, & Marketing
Kris Kamenz, Director, Finance

Manitoba Medical Service Foundation Inc. (MMSF)
599 Empress St., Winnipeg MB R3G 3P3
Tel: 204-788-6801; *Fax:* 204-774-1761
info@mmsf.ca
www.mmsf.ca
To consider the provision of funds for the advancement of scientific, educational, & other activities to maintain & improve the health & welfare of the citizens of Manitoba
Greg Hammond, Executive Director
Allen Rouse, Chair

Manitoba Naturopathic Association (MNA)
PO Box 2339, Stn. Main, #2, 161 Stafford St., Winnipeg MB R3C 4A6
Tel: 204-947-0381; *Fax:* 204-452-7044
To act as a regulatory body for the profession of naturopathy, in accordance with The Naturopathic Act of Manitoba
Christopher Turner, Contact

Manitoba Paraplegia Foundation Inc.
825 Sherbrook St., Winnipeg MB R3A 1M5
Tel: 204-786-4753; *Fax:* 204-786-1140
winnipeg@canparaplegic.org
www.cpamanitoba.ca/mpf
To provide support for research & prevention activities; to provide direct aid to paraplegics & quadriplegics for home modifications, vocational aid & other items to assist spinal cord injured Manitobans to lead independent lives within the community; to provide support for special projects undertaken on behalf of spinal cord injured persons in Manitoba
Doug Finkbeiner, President

Manitoba Public Health Association (MPHA)
c/o Klinic Community Health Centre, 870 Portage Ave., Winnipeg MB R3G 0P1
manitobapha@mts.net
www.manitobapha.ca
To influence health, social, environmental, & economic policy decisions, in order to improve the well-being of people in Manitoba; To ensure that health promotion, health protection, & disease protection are part of services
Barb Wasilewski, President

Massage Therapy Alliance of Canada (MTAC) / Alliance canadienne de massothérapeutes
c/o Massage.ca, 581 Huron St., Toronto ON M5R 2R6
Tel: 416-929-9759
www.massage.ca
To foster & advance the art, science & philosophy of massage therapy through nationwide cooperation in a professional, ethical & practical manner for the betterment of health care in Canada

Médecins francophones du Canada
8355, boul Saint-Laurent, Montréal QC H2P 2Z6
Tél: 514-388-2228; *Téléc:* 514-388-5335
Ligne sans frais: 800-387-2228
www.medecinsfrancophones.ca
Conrad L. Pelletier, Président

Medical Council of Canada (MCC) / Le Conseil médical du Canada
PO Box 8234, Stn. T, #100, 2283 St. Laurent Blvd., Ottawa ON K1G 3H7
Tel: 613-521-6012; *Fax:* 613-521-9509
MCC_Admin@mcc.ca
www.mcc.ca
To establish & promote a qualification in medicine, known as the Licentiate of the Medical Council of Canada, such that the holders thereof are acceptable to medical licensing authorities for the issuance of a licence to practise medicine
Ian Bowmer, Executive Director

Medical Devices Canada
#900, 405 The West Mall, Toronto ON M9C 5J1
Tel: 416-620-1915; *Fax:* 416-620-1595
Toll-Free: 866-586-3332
info@medec.org
www.medec.org
To achieve a business & regulatory environment favourable to the growth of the industry & ensuring the availability of new cost-effective medical technologies that benefit Canadians
James Wilson, Chair
Stephen Dibert, President & CEO

Medical Society of Prince Edward Island (MSPEI)
2 Myrtle St., Stratford PE C1B 2W2
Tel: 902-368-7303; *Fax:* 902-566-3934
Toll-Free: 888-368-7303
www.mspei.org
To promote health & improvement of medical services; to prevent disease; to represent members at national bodies & government; to consider all matters concerning the professional welfare of members.
Kathy Maher, Communications Director
Sandy Irwin, Executive Director

The Michener Institute for Applied Health Sciences
222 St. Patrick St., Toronto ON M5T 1V4
Tel: 416-596-3101; *Fax:* 416-596-3168
Toll-Free: 800-387-9066
info@michener.ca
www.michener.ca
To design, develop & deliver the best educational programs, products & services in applied health sciences

Paul Bertin, Chair
Paul Gamble, Secretary/President & CEO

Multiple Sclerosis Society of Canada (MS) / Société canadienne de la sclérose en plaques
#700, 175 Bloor St. East, Toronto ON M4W 3R8
Tel: 416-922-6065; *Fax:* 416-922-7538
Toll-Free: 800-268-7582
info@mssociety.ca
www.mssociety.ca
Social Media: www.facebook.com/MSSocietyCanada; twitter.com/mssocietycanada; www.linkedin.com/company/ms-society-of-canada; www.youtube.com/MSSocietyCanada; www.flickr.com/people/28406606@N06
To be a leader in finding a cure for multiple sclerosis & enabling people affected by MS to enhance their quality of life
James Casey, Chair
Yves Savoie, President & CEO

Muscular Dystrophy Association of Canada (MDAC) / Association canadienne de la dystrophie musculaire (ACDM)
#900, 2345 Yonge St., Toronto ON M4P 2E5
Tel: 416-488-0030; *Fax:* 416-488-7523
Toll-Free: 866-687-2538
info@muscle.ca
www.muscle.ca
Social Media: www.facebook.com/muscle.ca; twitter.com/md_canada
To improve the quality of life of persons who have muscular dystrophy through a broad range of programs, education, support of research & the delivery of needed services to people with muscular dystrophy & their families
Michel Chalifoux, Chair
Catherine Sherrard, CEO

Myasthenia Gravis Association of British Columbia (MGABC)
2805 Kingsway Ave., Vancouver BC V5R 5H9
Tel: 604-451-5511; *Fax:* 604-451-5651
mgabc@centreforability.bc.ca
www.myastheniagravis.ca
To provide information & support to British Columbians who suffer from Myasthenia Gravis (Grave Muscular Disease) & to their caregivers; to increase public awareness of the disease; to gather & disseminate specific information on Myasthenia Gravis to healthcare providers in British Columbia; to foster & support research into the causes & treatment of Myasthenia Gravis
Brenda Kelsey, President

National Eating Disorder Information Centre (NEDIC)
ES 7-421, 200 Elizabeth St., Toronto ON M5G 2C4
Tel: 416-340-4156; *Fax:* 416-340-4736
Toll-Free: 866-633-4220
nedic@uhn.on.ca
www.nedic.ca
The National Eating Disorder Information Centre (NEDIC) is a non-profit organization founded in 1985 to provide information and resources on eating disorders and food and weight preoccupation. One of their main goals is to inform the public about eating disorders and related issues.
Merryl Bear, Director

National ME/FM Action Network / Réseau national d'action EM/FM encéphalomyélite myalgique/fibromyalgie
#512, 33 Banner Rd., Nepean ON K2H 8V7
Tel: 613-829-6667; *Fax:* 613-829-8518
ag922@ncf.ca
www.mefmaction.net
To offer support, advocacy, education & research into the many, varied, anomalies connected with Myalgic Encephalomyelitis/Chronic Fatigue Syndrome & Fibromyalgia (ME/FM)
Lydia E. Neilson, CEO

New Brunswick Association of Dietitians (NBAD) / Association des diététistes du Nouveau-Brunswick (ADNB)
#101, 333 Champlain St., Dieppe NB E1A 1P2
Tel: 506-856-6881; *Fax:* 506-856-6855
registrar@adnb-nbad.com; info@adnb-nbad.com
www.adnb-nbad.com
To regulate the practice of dietetics within New Brunswick.
Maryse Vautour, Registrar

New Brunswick Association of Naturopathic Doctors
2278 King George Hwy., Miramichi NB E1V 6N6
Tel: 506-773-3700; *Fax:* 506-773-3704
www.nband.ca
To educate the public on the philosophies and values of Naturopathic Medicine and to promote the profession within the province.
Crystal Charest, Contact

New Brunswick Association of Optometrists (NBAO) / Association des optométristes du Nouveau-Brunswick
#1, 490 Gibson St., Fredericton NB E3A 4E9
Tel: 506-458-8759; *Fax:* 506-450-1271
nbao@nbnet.nb.ca
www.nbao.ca
Joan Hicks, President

New Brunswick Catholic Health Association (NBCHA)
1773 Water St., Miramichi NB E1N 1B2
Tel: 506-778-5302; *Fax:* 506-778-5303
nbcha@nb.aibn.com
www.chanb.com/chanb/
The New Brunswick Catholic Health Association is a provincial Christian organization promoting health care in the tradition of the Catholic Church. The Association fosters healing in all its aspects: Physical, psychological, social and spiritual
Robert Stewart, Executive Director

New Brunswick Chiropractors' Association (NBCA) / Association des chiropraticiens du Nouveau-Brunswick
#206, 944 Prospect Street, Fredericton NB E3B 9M6
Tel: 506-445-6800; *Fax:* 506-455-4430
comments@nbchiropractic.ca
www.nbchiropractic.ca
To regulate the practice of chiropractic & govern its members in accordance with the Act & the by-laws, in order to serve & protect the public interests; to establish, maintain, develop & enforce standards of qualification for the practice of chiropractic, including the required knowledge, skill & efficiency; to establish, maintain, develop & enforce standards of professional ethics; to promote public awareness of the role of the Association & the work of chiropractic, & to communicate & cooperate with other professional organizations for the advancement of the best interests of the Association, including the publication of books, papers & journals; & to encourage studies in chiropractic & provide assistance & facilities for special studies & research
Mohamed El-Bayoumi, President

New Brunswick Lung Association / Association pulmonaire du Nouveau-Brunswick
65 Brunswick St., Fredericton NB E3B 1G5
Tel: 506-455-8961; *Fax:* 506-462-0939
Toll-Free: 800-565-5864
nblung@nbnet.nb.ca
www.nb.lung.ca
To promote wellness throughout New Brunswick & prevent lung disease
Barbara MacKinnon, President & Chief Executive Officer
Betty Barrett, Officer, Finance & Administration
Louise Steeves, Officer, Communications
Arthur Thomson, Director, Environmental Initiatives
Barbara Walls, Director, Health Initiatives

New Brunswick Medical Society (NBMS) / Société médicale du Nouveau-Brunswick
176 York St., Fredericton NB E3B 3N7
Tel: 506-458-8860; *Fax:* 506-458-9853
nbms@nb.aibn.com
www.nbms.nb.ca
To advance medical science in all its branches; to promote improvement of medical services; to prevent disease in cooperation with health officers & all others engaged in such work; to maintain high scientific & professional status for its members; to promote medical science & related arts & sciences
Robert Rae, President

Newfoundland & Labrador Association of Optometrists (NLAO)
PO Box 8042, Stn. C, St. John's NL A1B 3M7
Tel: 709-739-8284; *Fax:* 709-739-8378
nlao@nl.rogers.com
www.nao.opto.ca
The Association provides an online resource for Doctors of Optometry & other healthcare providers in Newfoundland & Labrador. It owns & operates Newfoundland Vision Services Inc., a not for profit corporation providing safety eyewear to industrial employers in the province
Grace Hwang, President

Newfoundland & Labrador Chiropractic Association
#285W, 120 Torbay Rd., St. John's NL A1A 2G8
Tel: 709-739-7762; *Fax:* 709-739-7703
nlca@nl.rogers.com
www.nlchiropractic.ca
Carl Eustace, President
Michelle Batterson, Executive Director
Linda Slaney, Secretary
Mike Witherall, Treasurer

Newfoundland & Labrador College of Dietitians (NLCD)
PO Box 1756, Stn. C, St. John's NL A1C 5P5
Tel: 709-753-4040; *Toll-Free:* 877-753-4040
www.nlcd.ca; www.dietitians.ca
To regulate Registered Dietitians & to ensure competency in the dietetic profession, in the interest of the people in Newfoundland.

Newfoundland & Labrador Lung Association (NLLA)
Carnell Building, PO Box 13457, Stn. A, 15 Pippy Pl., 2nd Fl., St. John's NL A1B 4B8
Tel: 709-726-4664; *Fax:* 709-726-2550
Toll-Free: 888-566-5864
info@nf.lung.ca; health@nf.lung.ca
www.nf.lung.ca
To achieve healthy breathing for the people of Newfoundland & Labrador
Greg Noel, Acting Executive Director

Newfoundland & Labrador Medical Association (NLMA)
164 MacDonald Dr., St. John's NL A1A 4B3
Tel: 709-726-7424; *Fax:* 709-726-7525
Toll-Free: 800-563-2003
nlma@nlma.nl.ca
www.nlma.nl.ca
To represent & support physicians in Newfoundland & Labrador; provide leadership in the promotion of good health & the provision of quality health care to the people of the province
Sandra Luscombe, President
Robert Ritter, Executive Director

Newfoundland & Labrador Public Health Association (NLPHA)
PO Box 8172, St. John's NL A1B 3M9
To advocate for the physical, emotional, social, & environmental well-being of Newfoundland & Labrador's people & communities
Fay Matthews, President
Elizabeth Wright, Secretary
Pat Murray, Treasurer

Northwest Territories Medical Association (NWTMA)
PO Box 1732, Yellowknife NT X1A 2P3
Tel: 867-920-4575; *Fax:* 867-920-4575
nwtmedassoc@ssimicro.com
www.nwtma.ca
The voice of physicians in the Territory, the Northwest Territories Medical Association (NWTMA) advocates on behalf of its members and the citizens of the North for access to high quality health care, and provides leadership and guidance to its members.
Anna Reid, President
Marlena Guzowski, Executive Director

Nova Scotia Association of Naturopathic Doctors
#16, 3514 Joseph Howe Dr., Halifax NS B3L 4H7
Tel: 902-431-8001; *Fax:* 902-542-4554
www.nsand.ca
The NSAND is the professional association representing licensed NDs in Nova Scotia.
Sarah Baille, Co-President
Jyl Bishop Veale, Co-President

Nova Scotia Association of Optometrists (NSAO)
PO Box 9410, Stn. A, #700, 6009 Quinpool Rd., Halifax NS B3K 5S3
Tel: 902-435-2845; *Fax:* 902-425-2441
nsao@accesswave.ca
www.nsoptometrists.ca
To foster excellence in the delivery of vision & eye health services in Nova Scotia; To act as the voice of optometry in Nova Scotia
Sheldon Pothier, O.D., Registrar

Nova Scotia College of Chiropractors (NSCC)
PO Box 9410, Stn. A, 6009 Quinpool Road, Halifax NS B3K 5S3
Tel: 902-425-2445; *Fax:* 902-425-2441
inquiries@chiropractors.ns.ca
www.chiropractors.ns.ca
To promote & improve the proficiency of chiropractors in all matters relating to the practice of chiropractic; to protect the public from untrained & unqualified persons acting as chiropractors; to advance the chiropractic profession
Lisa Richard, Registrar

Nova Scotia Dietetic Association (NSDA)
#212, 1496 Bedford Hwy., Bedford NS B4A 1E5
Tel: 902-835-0253; *Fax:* 902-835-0523
info@nsdassoc.ca
www.nsdassoc.ca

The Association is the regulatory body for dietitions & nutritionists in the province, & has a mandate to register & discipline (when necessary) practitioners to ensure safe, ethical & competent dietetic practice.
Jennifer Hutchinson, President

Nova Scotia Lung Association (LANS)
6331 Lady Hammond Rd., Halifax NS B3K 2S2
Tel: 902-443-8141; *Fax:* 902-445-2573
Toll-Free: 888-566-5864
info@ns.lung.ca
www.ns.lung.ca

To control & prevent lung disease in Nova Scotia; To help people who live with lung disease
Louis Brill, President & Chief Executive Officer
Johnathan Clarke, Manager, Health Initiatives
Lesley Dunn, Manager, Resource Development
Nick McBride, Manager, Finance & Special Events
Natalie Owens, Manager, Communications
Colleen MacDonald, Coordinator, Donor Relations

Occupational & Environmental Medical Association of Canada (OEMAC) / Association canadienne de la médecine du travail et de l'environnement (ACMTE)
#1430, 1101 Upper Middle Rd. East, Oakville ON L6H 5Z9
Tel: 905-849-9925; *Fax:* 905-338-8523
oemac@oemac.org
www.oemac.org

To act as the voice of the Canadian occupational & environmental medicine sector
Howard Hamer, President

Ontario Association of Naturopathic Doctors (OAND)
#603, 789 Don Mills Rd., Toronto ON M3C 1T5
Tel: 416-233-2001; *Fax:* 416-233-2924
Toll-Free: 877-628-7284
info@oand.org
www.oand.org

To act as a voice for naturopathic doctors in Ontario
Alison Dantas, CEO
Elias Markou, Chair
Alfred Hauk, Secretary
Meghan Walker, Treasurer

Ontario Association of Optometrists (OAO)
Plaza 3, #300, 2000 Argentia Rd., Mississauga ON L5N 1V9
Tel: 905-826-3522; *Fax:* 905-826-0625
Toll-Free: 800-540-3837
wbishop@optom.on.ca
www.optom.on.ca
Social Media:
www.facebook.com/pages/Ontario-Association-of-Optometrists/28166312427; www.youtube.com/user/OntarioOptometrists

To advance the profession of optometry at the government, regulatory, & public levels
Cam Jackson, Chief Executive Officer
Bethany Carey, Controller & Director, Member Services
Melissa Secord, Director, Continuing Education
Sandra Ng, Manager, Policy & Government Relations

Ontario Chiropractic Association (OCA) / Association chiropratique de l'Ontario
#200, 20 Victoria St., Toronto ON M5C 2N8
Tel: 416-860-0070; *Fax:* 416-860-0857
Toll-Free: 877-327-2273
oca@chiropractic.on.ca
www.chiropractic.on.ca

To serve its members by promoting the philosophy, art, & science of chiropractic & thereby enhance the health & well-being of the citizens of Ontario
Robert Haig, Chief Executive Officer
Valerie Carter, Director, External Relations
Kimbalin Kelly, Director, Operations
Joyce Chow Ng, Manager, Finance
Nathalie Plourde, Manager, Member Services

Ontario Lung Association (OLA)
573 King St. East, Toronto ON M5A 4L3
Tel: 416-864-9911; *Fax:* 416-864-9916
Toll-Free: 888-344-5864
olalung@on.lung.ca; donors@on.lung.ca; airquality@on.lung.ca
www.on.lung.ca

To provide lung health information & support to people affected by lung disease; To prevent & control chronic lung disease
Kelly Mu¤oz, Chair
George Habib, President & Chief Executive Officer
Eric Bentzen, Treasurer

Ontario Medical Association (OMA)
#900, 150 Bloor St. West, Toronto ON M5S 3C1
Tel: 416-599-2580; *Fax:* 416-340-2944
Toll-Free: 800-268-7215
info@oma.org; membership@oma.org
www.oma.org

To represent the clinical, political, & economic interests of Ontario physicians; To promote an accessible, quality health-care system
Mark MacLeod, President
Catherine Flaman, Contact, mentor@oma.org

Ontario Occupational Health Nurses Association (OOHNA)
#605, 302 The East Mall, Toronto ON M9B 6C7
Tel: 416-239-6462; *Fax:* 416-239-5462
Toll-Free: 866-664-6276
administration@oohna.on.ca
www.oohna.on.ca

To foster a climate of excellence, innovation & partnership enabling Ontario Occupational Health Nurses to achieve positive workplace health & safety objectives
Karen Watson, President
Brian Verrall, Executive Director

Ontario Public Health Association (OPHA) / Association pour la santé publique de l'Ontario
#1850, 439 University Ave., Toronto ON M5G 1Y8
Tel: 416-367-3313; *Fax:* 416-367-2844
Toll-Free: 800-267-6817
info@opha.on.ca
www.opha.on.ca

To provide leadership on issues affecting public health in Ontario; To strengthen the influence of persons involved in public & community health across Ontario
Siu Mee Cheng, Executive Director
Magdalena Wasilewska, Research Assistant

Opticians Association of Canada (OAC)
#2706, 83 Garry St., Winnipeg MB R3C 4J9
Tel: 204-982-6060; *Fax:* 204-947-2519
Toll-Free: 800-842-3155
canada@opticians.ca
www.opticians.ca
Social Media: www.facebook.com/215512795151373
Robert Dalton, Executive Director

Ordre des ergothérapeutes du Québec (OEQ)
#920, 2021, av Union, Montréal QC H3A 2S9
Tél: 514-844-5778; *Téléc:* 514-844-0478
Ligne sans frais: 800-265-5778
ergo@oeq.org
www.oeq.org

Protéger le public; assurer la qualité d'ergothérapie; promouvoir l'accessibilité aux services d'ergothérapie; soutenir la pratique professionnelle et son évolution; favoriser le rayonnement de la profession
Alain Bibeau, Président-directeur général
Louise Tremblay, Secrétaire générale

Ordre des orthophonistes et audiologistes du Québec (OOAQ)
#601, 235, boul René-Levesque est, Montréal QC H2X 1N8
Tél: 514-282-9123; *Téléc:* 514-282-9541
Ligne sans frais: 888-232-9123
info@ooaq.qc.ca
www.ooaq.qc.ca

L'Ordre des orthophonistes et audiologistes du Québec, un organisme régi par le code des professions, a pour mission d'assurer la protection du public en regard du domaine d'exercice de ses membres, soit les troubles de la communication humaine; surveille l'exercice professionnel des orthophonistes et des audiologistes et voit à favoriser l'accessibilité du public à des services de qualité; contribue à l'intégration sociale des individus et à l'amélioration de la qualité de vie de la population québécoise
Marie-Pierre Caouette, Présidente

Ordre professionnel des diététistes du Québec (OPDQ)
#1220, 2155, rue Guy, Montréal QC H3H 2R9
Tél: 514-393-3733; *Téléc:* 514-393-3582
Ligne sans frais: 888-393-8528
opdq@opdq.org
www.opdq.org

Assurer la protection du public en contrôlant notamment l'exercice de la profession par ses membres.
Annie Chapados, Directrice générale et secrétaire

Ordre professionnel des physiothérapeutes du Québec (OPPQ)
#1000, 7151, Jean Talon est, Anjou QC H1M 3N8
Tél: 514-351-2770; *Téléc:* 514-351-2658
Ligne sans frais: 800-361-2001
physio@oppq.qc.ca
oppq.qc.ca

Assurer la protection du public en surveillant l'exercice de la physiothérapie par ses membres et en contribuant à leur développement professionnel
Lucie Forget, Présidente
Claude Laurent, Directeur général et Secrétaire

Organ Donors Canada / Donneurs d'organes du Canada
5326 Ada Blvd. NW, Edmonton AB T5W 4N7
Tel: 780-474-9363

Information service dedicated to assisting the process of anatomical gift giving in Canada & increasing public awareness of the need for, & the human & economic advantages of all types of human organ & tissue donations for transplant, teaching & research.
Mae Cox, Executive Director

Osteoporosis Canada / Ostéoporose Canada
#301, 1090 Don Mills Rd., Toronto ON M3C 3R6
Tel: 416-696-2663; *Fax:* 416-696-2673
Toll-Free: 800-463-6842
info@osteoporosis.ca
www.osteoporosis.ca

To encourage research into the prevention, diagnosis, & treatment of osteoporosis; To improve access to osteoporosis care & support
Famida Jiwa, President & CEO
Diane Thériault, Chair
Fred Goddard, Treasurer

Ovarian Cancer Canada (OCC) / Cancer de l'ovaire Canada (COC)
#205, 145 Front St. East, Toronto ON M5A 1E3
Tel: 416-962-2700; *Fax:* 416-962-2701
Toll-Free: 877-413-7970
info@ovariancanada.org
www.ovariancanada.org
Social Media:
www.facebook.com/pages/Ovarian-Cancer-Canada/102394063730; www.youtube.com/ovariancancercanada

To support women & their families living with the disease; to raise awareness in the general public & with health care professionals; to fund research to develop reliable early detection techniques, improved treatments & ultimately, a cure.
David Livingston, Chair
Elisabeth Ross, CEO
Karen Cinq Mars, Vice-President, Marketing & Business Innovation
Hoda Brooke, Finance Director
Allyson MacQueen, National Walk Director

Parkinson Society - Maritime Region (PSMR) / Société Parkinson - Region Maritime (SPRM)
#150, 7071 Bayers Rd., Halifax NS B3L 2C2
Tel: 902-422-3656; *Fax:* 902-422-3797
Toll-Free: 800-663-2468
psmr@parkinsonmaritimes.ca
www.parkinsonmaritimes.ca
Social Media: www.facebook.com/parkinsonmaritimes; twitter.com/psmr

To give information to people with Parkinson & their family, children & caregivers
John McCarthy, Chair

Parkinson Society British Columbia (PSBC)
#600, 890 West Pender St., Vancouver BC V6C 1J9
Tel: 604-662-3240; *Fax:* 604-687-1327
Toll-Free: 800-668-3330
info@parkinson.bc.ca
www.parkinson.bc.ca

Diane Robinson, Executive Director

Parkinson Society Canada / Société Parkinson Canada
#316, 4211 Yonge St., Toronto ON M2P 2A9
Tel: 416-227-9700; *Fax:* 416-227-9600
Toll-Free: 800-565-3000
general.info@parkinson.ca
www.parkinson.ca

To raise funds for research into the causes & treatment of Parkinsons; to provide services which support Parkinsonians & their families; to disseminate information about the condition to individuals & organizations across Canada
Joyce Gordon, President & CEO

Parkinson Society Canada - Central & Northern Ontario Region
#321, 4211 Yonge St., Toronto ON M2P 2A9
Tel: 416-227-1200; *Fax:* 416-227-1520
Toll-Free: 800-565-3000
info.cno@parkinson.ca
www.cno.parkinson.ca
Debbie Davis, CEO

Parkinson Society Canada - Manitoba Region
7 - 414 Westmount Dr., Winnipeg MB R2J 1P2
Tel: 204-786-2637; *Fax:* 204-786-2327
Toll-Free: 866-999-5558
laura.asher@parkinson.ca
www.parkinson.ca
Howard Koks, Executive Director

Parkinson Society Canada - Southwestern Ontario Region
Meadowbrook Business Park, #117, 4500 Blakie Rd., London ON N6L 1G5
Tel: 519-652-9437; *Fax:* 519-652-9267
Toll-Free: 888-851-7376
info@parkinsonsociety.ca
www.parkinsonsociety.ca
Joanne Bernard, Manager of Administration

Parkinson Society Newfoundland & Labrador
#305, 136 Crosbie Rd., St. John's NL A1B 3K3
Tel: 709-574-4428; *Fax:* 709-754-5868
Toll-Free: 800-567-7020
parkinson@nf.aibn.com
Patricia Morrissey, Executive Director

Parkinson Society of Canada - Toronto Chapter
#321, 4211 Yonge St., Toronto ON M2P 2A9
Tel: 416-227-1200; *Fax:* 416-227-1520
Toll-Free: 800-565-3000
communications@parkinson.ca
www.parkinson.ca
Parkinson Society Canada is the national voice of Canadians living with Parkinson's whose purpose is to ease the burden and find a cure through research, education, advocacy, and support services. Their vision revolves around wanting people with Parkinson's to have access to more uniform services across the country; to work to ensure greater consistency and equitable access; to address gaps in the isolated and disadvantages regions; to maximize the funds available to support people living w/ Parkinson's by adopting best practices; and by spending donor money in the most effective way.
Debbie Davis, CEO (Central & Northern Ontario)
Sarah Rooje, CNO Admin./Client Services

Parkinson Society of Ottawa
1053 Carling Ave., Ottawa ON K1Y 4E9
Tel: 613-722-9238; *Fax:* 613-722-3241
psoc@lri.ca
www.parkinsons.ca
Dennise Taylor-Gilhen, Executive Director

The Parkinson's Society of Southern Alberta (PSSA)
#102, 5636 Burbank Cres. SE, Calgary AB T2H 1Z6
Tel: 403-243-9901; *Fax:* 403-243-8283
Toll-Free: 800-561-1911
pssa@parkinsons-society.org
www.parkinsons-society.org
PSSA is dedicated to helping people and families of Southern Alberta who live with Parkinson's and related disorders
John Petryshen, CEO

Post-Polio Awareness & Support Society of BC (PPASS/BC)
102 - 9775 - 4th St., Sidney BC V8L 2Z8
Tel: 250-655-8849; *Fax:* 250-655-8859
ppass@ppassbc.com
www.ppassbc.com
To develop awareness, communication & education between society & community; to disseminate information concerning research & treatment about Post-Polio Syndrome; to support polio survivors other than through direct financial aid
Joan Toone, President

Post-Polio Network Manitoba Inc. (PPN-MB)
#204, 825 Sherbrook St., Winnipeg MB R3A 1M5
Tel: 204-975-3037; *Fax:* 204-975-3027
www.smd.mb.ca/post_polio_network_manitoba_inc.aspx
To serve as a support group & information centre for polio survivors throughout Manitoba, especially those suffering from post-polio syndrome; To acquaint the medical community & those responsible for government services as to the nature & extent of the problems associated with the late effects of polio
Charlene Craig, President
Dolores Horobetz, Treasurer

Clare Simpson, Secretary

Prince Edward Island Association of Optometrists (PEIAO)
PO Box 1812, Charlottetown PE C1A 7N5
Tel: 902-626-3937; *Fax:* 902-626-3973
info@peioptometrists.ca
www.peioptometrists.ca
To promote the professional interests of optometrists in Prince Edward Island Association; To improve optometrists' proficiency
Susan Judson, President
Catherine Arsenault, Vice-President
Murray Rusk, Secretary
J.E. Hickey, Treasurer

Prince Edward Island Chiropractic Association (PEICA)
228 Grafton St., Charlottetown PE C1A 1L5
Tel: 902-894-4400; *Fax:* 902-894-3762
chiro.whitty@pei.aibn.com
To represent the chiropractic profession in Prince Edward Island; To advance the chiropractic profession in the province; To encourage high standards of service; To protect the residents of Prince Edward Island from unqualified individuals acting as chiropractors
David Whitty, President
Darren MacLean, Registrar

Prince Edward Island Dietetic Association
153 Spring St., Summerside PE C1N 3G2
Tel: 902-436-2438
peidrb@pei.sympatico.ca
To promote, encourage & improve the status of dietitians & nutritionists in the province of PEI; to promote & increase the knowledge & proficiency of its members in all matters relating to nutrition & dietetics; to promote public awareness
Rita Arsenault, President

Prince Edward Island Lung Association
#2, 1 Rochford St., Charlottetown PE C1A 9L2
Tel: 902-892-5957; *Fax:* 902-566-9901
Toll-Free: 888-566-5864
info@pei.lung.ca
www.pei.lung.ca
To improve the respiratory health of Islanders through education, advocacy & research; To raise funds to support medical research
Margaret Munro, President
Judy Hansen, Vice-President
Joanne Ings, Executive Director
Bev McCormick, Treasurer

Psoriasis Society of Canada / Société psoriasis du Canada
National Office, PO Box 25015, Halifax NS B3M 4H4
Tel: 902-443-8680; *Fax:* 902-443-2073
Toll-Free: 800-656-4494
www.psoriasissociety.org
To provide programs & services to people who suffer from psoriasis in Canada; to encourage formation of support groups where individual sufferers may share experiences & exchange information; to provide facts about psoriasis to medical community, general public & teaching profession; to promote & encourage research directed towards treatment & cure for psoriasis
Judy Misner, President

Public Health Association of British Columbia (PHABC)
#210, 1027 Pandora Ave., Victoria BC V8V 3P6
Tel: 250-595-8422; *Fax:* 250-595-8622
staff@phabc.org
www.phabc.org
To constitute a special resource in BC for the betterment & maintenance of the population's health at the community & personal level
Ted Bruce, President

Public Health Association of Nova Scotia (PHANS)
PO Box 33074, Halifax NS B3L 4T6
Tel: 902-477-2960; *Fax:* 902-477-4584
phans@cpha.ca
www.phans.ca
Marie McCully Collier, President

Québec Black Medical Association
#101, 1832 Sherbrooke St. W, Montréal QC H3H 1C4
Tel: 514-937-8822
www.qbma.org
The Québec Black Medical Association aims to enable young people from the Black community to pursue careers as health professionals and to advance medical practice and research in Quebec.

E.C. Tucker, Contact

Québec Lung Association (QLA) / Association pulmonaire du Québec (APQ)
5790, av Pierre-de-Coubertin, Montréal QC H1N 1R4
Tel: 514-287-7400; *Fax:* 514-287-1978
Toll-Free: 888-768-6669
info@pq.lung.ca; info@pq.poumon.ca
www.pq.poumon.ca
To provide resources in Québec about lung cancer, chronic obstructive pulmonary disease, sarcoidosis, tuberculosis, asthma, chronic bronchitis, sleep apnea, pneumonia, & emphysema
Dominique Massie, Executive Director
Raymond Jabbour, Chief Financial Officer & Director, Direct Marketing & Information Technology
Mireille Chéry, Director, Development & Communications
Lynda Monière, Coordinator, Media Relations & Major Events
Lise Vaillancourt, Respiratory Therapist & Coordinator, Programs

The Royal College of Physicians & Surgeons of Canada (RCPSC) / Le Collège royal des médecins et chirurgiens du Canada (CRMCC)
774 Echo Dr., Ottawa ON K1S 5N8
Tel: 613-730-8177; *Fax:* 613-730-8830
Toll-Free: 800-668-3740
info@royalcollege.ca
rcpsc.medical.org
Social Media: www.facebook.com/TheRoyalCollege; twitter.com/Royal_College
To oversee the medical education of specialists in Canada; To set the highest standards in postgraduate medical education, through national certification examinations & lifelong learning programs; To promote sound health policy
Andrew Padmos, CEO
Danielle Fréchette, Director, Health Policy & Governance Support
Karen McCarthy, Director, Communications & External Relations
Tim Julien, CFO

Saint Elizabeth Health Care (SEHC) / Les soins de santé Sainte-Elizabeth
#300, 90 Allstate Pkwy., Markham ON L3R 6H3
Tel: 905-940-9655; *Fax:* 905-940-9934
communications@saintelizabeth.com
www.saintelizabeth.com
To serve the physical, emotional, & spiritual needs of people in their homes & communities
Shirlee M. Sharkey, President & CEO
Noreen Taylor, Chair
Theodore Freedman, Vice-Chair
Heather Gomes, Treasurer
Ron Yamada, Secretary

Saskatchewan Association of Naturopathic Practitioners (SANP)
1814 Lorne Ave., Saskatoon SK S7H 1Y4
Tel: 306-955-2633; *Fax:* 306-955-2638
naturdoctor@sasktel.net
www.sanp.ca
To act as the governing body for naturopathic doctors in Saskatchewan; To license & regulate naturopathic physicians in the province; To ensure members are educated & trained according to strict standards
Leshia Ferguson, President
Kent Bailey, Vice-President
Tanya Gokavi, Secretary
Jacqui Fleury, Treasurer
Vanessa DiCicco, Registrar
Julie Zepp Rutledge, Liaison, Government, Media, & Public

Saskatchewan Association of Optometrists (SAO)
#108, 2366 Ave. C North, Saskatoon SK S7L 5X5
Tel: 306-652-2069; *Fax:* 306-652-2642
Toll-Free: 877-660-3937
sao@sasktel.net
www.optometrists.sk.ca
To license the delivery of optometric care in Saskatchewan; To regulate doctors of optometry throughout the province; To ensure excellence in the delivery of vision & eye health services across Saskatchewan; To enforce high standards of optometric eye care, in order to protect the public; To act as the voice of optometry in Saskatchewan
Sheila Spence, Executive Director
Janann Blackburn, Coordinator, Vision Care Program

Saskatchewan Dietitians Association (SDA)
PO Box 3894, #17, 2010 - 7th Ave., Regina SK S4R 1C2
Tel: 306-359-3040; *Fax:* 306-359-3046
registrar@saskdietitians.org
www.saskdietitians.org

To protect the public by registering competent dietitians; To set standards of practice; To uphold codes of conduct; To provide a framework for continuing competence, consisting of a self-assessment tool, a learning plan, & a quality assurance audit
Victoria Jurgens, President
Lana Moore, Registrar

Saskatchewan Families for Effective Autism Treatment (SASKFEAT)
PO Box 2150, Tisdale SK S0E 1T0
Tel: 306-862-4768
saskfeat@hotmail.com
www.saskfeat.com
To act as a voice for the concerns & needs of parents & families of autistic children & individuals in Saskatchewan; To find the most effective treatment for autistic children & individuals
Tim Verklan, President
Carolyn Forsey, Vice-President
Ron Luciw, Secretary
Brad Hayes, Treasurer

Saskatchewan Lung Association
1231 - 8 St. East, Saskatoon SK S7H 0S5
Tel: 306-343-9511; *Fax:* 306-343-7007
Toll-Free: 888-566-5864
info@sk.lung.ca
www.sk.lung.ca
To improve respiratory health & overall quality of life; To advocate for support of education & research
Frank Scott, Chair
Helen Cotton, Vice-Chair
Brian Graham, President & Chief Executive Officer
Jan Haffner, Vice-President, Health Initiatives
Sharon Kremeniuk, Vice-President, Development
Jennifer Miller, Vice-President, Health Education
Leah Sullivan, Vice-President, Finance & Operations
Pat Smith, Treasurer

Saskatchewan Medical Association (SMA)
#402, 321A - 21st St. East, Saskatoon SK S7K 0C1
Tel: 306-244-2196; *Fax:* 306-653-1631
Toll-Free: 800-667-3781
sma@sma.sk.ca
www.sma.sk.ca
To represent physicians in Saskatchewan; To advance the professional, educational, & economic welfare of physicians in the province
George Miller
Martin Vogel, Executive Director
Ed Hobday, Administrative Director
Phillip Fourie, Treasurer

Saskatchewan Parkinson's Disease Foundation (SPDF)
PO Box 21010, Stn. Gardiner Park, Regina SK S4V 1J4
Tel: 306-545-4400; *Fax:* 306-790-9605
Toll-Free: 888-685-0059
pss@sasktel.net
To provide education & support services in Saskatchewan to ease the burdens of people living with Parkinson's disease & their families; To support research to find a cure for Parkinson's disease

Saskatchewan Public Health Association Inc.
PO Box 845, Regina SK S4P 3B1
terry.gibson@saskatoonhealthregion.ca
To constitute a resource in Saskatchewan for the improvement & maintenance of health
Saqib Shahab, President

Société canadienne de la sclérose en plaques (Division du Québec) (SCSP) / Multiple Sclerosis Society of Canada (Québec Division)
Tour Est, #1010, 550, rue Sherbrooke ouest, Montréal QC H3A 1B9
Tél: 514-849-7591; *Téléc:* 514-849-8914
Ligne sans frais: 800-268-7582
info.qc@mssociety.ca
www.mssociety.ca/qc
Soutenir la recherche sur la SP; offrir des services aux personnes atteintes de la maladie et à leurs familles; sensibiliser le public à la sclérose en plaques et maintenir les relations avec les gouvernements.
Louis Adam, Executive Director

Société Huntington du Québec (SHQ) / Huntington Society of Québec (HSQ)
2300, boul René-Lévesque ouest, Montréal QC H3H 2R5
Tél: 514-282-4272; *Téléc:* 514-937-0082
Ligne sans frais: 877-282-4272
shq@huntingtonqc.org
www.hsc-ca.org
Francine Lacroix, Directrice générale

Société Parkinson du Québec / Parkinson Society Québec
#1470, 550 rue Sherbrooke ouest, Montréal QC H3A 1B9
Tél: 514-861-4422; *Téléc:* 514-861-4510
Ligne sans frais: 800-720-1307
infos@parkinsonquebec.ca
www.parkinsonquebec.ca
Nathalie Ross, Directrice générale

Society of Obstetricians & Gynaecologists of Canada (SOGC) / Société des obstétriciens et gynécologues du Canada
780 Echo Dr., Ottawa ON K1S 5R7
Tel: 613-730-4192; *Fax:* 613-730-4314
Toll-Free: 800-561-2416
helpdesk@sogc.com
www.sogc.org
To promote excellence in the practice of obstetrics & gynaecology; To produce national clinical guidelines for medical education on women's health issues; To promote optimal, comprehensive women's health care
Michel Fortier, President
André Lalonde, Executive Vice-President
Vyta Senikas, Associate Executive Vice President
Linda Desjardins, Director, Finance & Information Technology
Natalie Wright, Director, Communications Division
Mark Heywood, Treasurer

Society of Rural Physicians of Canada (SRPC) / Société de la médecine rurale du Canada
PO Box 893, 269 Main St., Shawville QC J0X 2Y0
Tel: 819-647-7054; *Fax:* 819-647-2485
Toll-Free: 877-276-1949
admin@srpc.ca
www.srpc.ca
To provide equitable medical care for rural communities; to provide sustainable working conditions for rural physicians
Karl Stobbe, President
Lee Teperman, Administrative Officer

Spina Bifida & Hydrocephalus Association of Canada (SBHAC) / Association de spina-bifida et d'hydrocephalie du Canada
#428, 167 Lombard Ave., Winnipeg MB R3B 0V3
Tel: 204-925-3650; *Fax:* 204-925-3654
Toll-Free: 800-565-9488
info@sbhac.ca
www.sbhac.ca
To improve the quality of life of all individuals with spina bifida &/or hydrocephalus & their families through awareness, education, advocacy & research; to reduce the incidence of neural tube defects
Colleen Talbot, President

The Terry Fox Foundation / La Fondation Terry Fox
#303, 46165 Yale Rd., Chilliwack BC V2P 2P2
Tel: 604-701-0246; *Fax:* 604-701-0247
Toll-Free: 888-836-9786
national@terryfoxrun.org
www.terryfoxrun.org
Social Media: www.facebook.com/TheTerryFoxFoundation
To maintain the vision & principles of Terry Fox while raising money for cancer research through the annual Terry Fox Run, memoriam donations & planned gifts. All money raised by the Foundation is distributed through the National Cancer Institute of Canada
Darrell Fox, National Director
Judith Fox-Alder, International Director

Thalidomide Victims Association of Canada (TVAC) / Association canadienne des victimes de la thalidomide (ACVT)
Centre commercial Joseph Renaud, #211, 6830, boul Joseph Renaud, Montréal QC H1K 3V4
Tel: 514-355-0811; *Fax:* 514-355-0860
mercedes.acvt@sympatico.ca
www.thalidomide.ca
To monitor the drug thalidomide & to meet the needs of thalidomide survivors; to empower & enhance the quality of life of Canadian thalidomidors
Mercedes Benegbi, Executive Director

Thyroid Foundation of Canada / La Fondation canadienne de la Thyroïde
c/o National Treasurer, PO Box 9, Manotick ON K4M 1A2
Fax: 514-630-9815
Toll-Free: 800-267-8822
www.thyroid.ca
To provide leadership to the fight against thyroid disease
Mabel Miller, President
Donna Miniely, Treasurer

Toronto Children's Care Inc. (TCC)
26 Gerrard St. East, Toronto ON M5B 1G3
Tel: 416-977-0458; *Fax:* 416-977-8807
info@rmhtoronto.org
www.rmhtoronto.org
To provide a home away from home for out-of-town families whose children are receiving treatment in Toronto hospitals for serious illness; we strongly believe that when a child is seriously ill, the love & support of family can be as important as any course of treatment
Jane Marco, Executive Director
John Davis, President

Tourette Syndrome Foundation of Canada (TSFC) / La Fondation canadienne du syndrome de Tourette
#195, 5945 Airport Rd., Mississauga ON L4V 1R9
Tel: 905-673-2255; *Fax:* 905-673-2638
Toll-Free: 800-387-0120
tsfc@tourette.ca
www.tourette.ca
Through education, advocacy, self-help, & the promotion of research, the TSFC assists individuals affected by Tourette Syndrome & its associated disorders.
Lynn McLarnon, Executive Director

Trillium Gift of Life Network
#900, 522 University Ave., Toronto ON M5G 1W7
Tel: 416-363-4001; *Fax:* 416-363-4002
Toll-Free: 800-263-2833
info@giftoflife.on.ca
www.giftoflife.on.ca
To enable every Ontario resident to make an informed decision to donate organs & tissue; to support healthcare professionals in implementing their wishes; maximize organ & tissue donation in Ontario in a respectful & equitable manner through education, research, services & support
Frank Markel, President & CEO

Turner's Syndrome Society (TSS) / Société du syndrome de Turner
323 Chapel St., Ottawa ON K1N 7Z2
Tel: 613-321-2267; *Fax:* 613-321-2268
Toll-Free: 800-465-6744
www.turnersyndrome.ca
To improve the quality of life for individuals & families affected by Turner's Syndrome; to strive to accomplish this through providing public & professional awareness about the needs & concerns of individuals with Turner's Syndrome & their families through the development of communication networks to provide mutual support

United Ostomy Association of Canada Inc. (UOAC)
#501, 344 Bloor St. West, Toronto ON M5S 3A7
Tel: 416-595-5452; *Fax:* 416-595-9924
Toll-Free: 888-969-9698
info1@ostomycanada.ca
www.ostomycanada.ca
Social Media: www.facebook.com/groups/39109880405/
To assist all persons with gastrointestinal or urinary diversions, & their families & caregivers, by providing emotional & practical support & help, information & instruction
Les Kehoe, President
Janet Paquet, Vice-President

Vocational Rehabilitation Association of Canada (VRA Canada)
#310, 4 Cataraqui St., Kingston ON K7K 1Z7
Tel: 613-507-5530; *Fax:* 888-441-8002
Toll-Free: 888-876-9992
info@vracanada.com
www.vracanada.com
To support members in promoting & providing the professional delivery of rehabilitation services
Garry Derenoski, National President

Yukon Medical Association
5 Hospital Rd., Whitehorse YT Y1A 3H7
Tel: 867-393-8749
yma@yukondoctors.ca; office@yukondoctors.ca
www.yukondoctors.ca
A voluntary association of Yukon doctors; advocates on behalf of members; promotes professionalism in medical practice & accessibility to quality health care for Yukoners
Rao Tadepalli, President

Yukon Public Health Association (YPHA)
Tel: 867-393-8784
Established to strengthen the impact of people who are active in public and community health throughout the Yukon through education, awareness, public participation and building of partnerships and networks
Ron Pearson, Contact
Val Pike, President

Heating, Air Conditioning, Plumbing

Canadian Institute of Plumbing & Heating (CIPH) / Institut canadien de plomberie et de chauffage
#330, 295 The West Mall, Toronto ON M9C 4Z4
Tel: 416-695-0447; *Fax:* 416-695-0450
Toll-Free: 800-639-2474
info@ciph.com
www.ciph.com
To act as a unified voice for plumbing, heating, hydronic, PVF, & waterworks across Canada
Ralph Suppa, President & General Manager
Elizabeth McCullough, General Manager, Trade Shows
Kevin Wong, Coordinator, Member Services
Stephen Apps, Contact, Education & Training
Ken Tomihiro, Contact, Hydronics, Codes, & Standards

Heating, Refrigeration & Air Conditioning Institute of Canada (HRAI) / Institut canadien du chauffage, de la climatisation et de la réfrigération (ICCCR)
Bldg. 1, #201, 2800 Skymark Ave., Mississauga ON L4W 5A6
Tel: 905-602-4700; *Fax:* 905-602-1197
Toll-Free: 800-267-2231
hraimail@hrai.ca
www.hrai.ca
To serve the HRAI membership & HVACR industry in Canada by facilitating industry solutions, coordinating a strong national membership, representing the industry to their publics, conducting accountable association activities, providing quality member/customer services, & educating & training industry members
Warren J. Heeley, President
Martin Luymes, Vice-President
Andrew Hall, Director, Energy Conservation/Demand Management Programs
Joanne Spurrell, Director, Education & Market Development
Heather Grimoldby-Campbell, Manager, Administration & Wholesalers Division
Daisy Del Prado, Communications Coordinator

Ontario Plumbing Inspectors Association (OPIA)
129 Dumble Ave., Peterborough ON K9H 5A9
Tel: 705-748-0120
opia@opia.info, secretary@opia.info
www.opia.info/members
To promote uniform enforcement of plumbing regulations; close liaison & interchange of ideas & knowledge between members of the OPIA & members of other associations; provide education & training to members & the industry
Doug Flucker, President
Rainier Blundel, Vice President

Ontario Refrigeration & Air Conditioning Contractors Association (ORAC)
#43, 6770 Davand Dr., Mississauga ON L5T 2G3
Tel: 905-670-0010; *Fax:* 905-670-0474
info@orac.ca
www.orac.ca
To represent Ontario's contractor practitioners in the refrigeration & air conditioning trade; To enhance quality & efficiency in the industry to benefit customers
David Irwin, President
Grant Sheahan, Vice-President
Dave Honsberger, Managing Director
Ted Martin, Treasurer

Refrigeration Service Engineers Society (Canada) (RSES Canada)
PO Box 3, Stn. B, Toronto ON M9W 5K9
Tel: 905-842-9199; *Toll-Free:* 877-955-6255
www.rsescanada.com
To lead all segments of the HVAC industry by providing superior educational & training programs; to create an environment that encourages maximum member participation in the development & decision process of the Society
David Chafe, President
Nick Reggi, Secretary

Thermal Environmental Comfort Association (TECA)
PO Box 73105, Stn. Evergreen RO, Surrey BC V3R 0J2
Tel: 604-594-5956; *Fax:* 604-594-5091
Toll-Free: 888-577-3818
training@teca.ca
www.teca.ca
To offer the residential heating, cooling and ventilation industry up-to-date training courses and a collective voice in local and provincial issues.
Kim Savage, Executive Director
Gary Fabbro, President
Kathryn Kubossek, Administrator

History, Heritage, Genealogy

Alberta Family History Society (AFHS)
712 - 16 Ave. NW, Calgary AB T2M 0J8
Tel: 403-214-1447
www.afhs.ab.ca
To encourage accuracy & thoroughness in family histories & genealogical research; to establish relations with related societies to promote common interests
Irene Oickle, Membership Chair
Lorna Loughton, President

Alberta Historical Resources Foundation (AHRF)
Old St. Stephen's College, 8820 - 112 St., Edmonton AB T6G 2P8
Tel: 780-431-2300; *Fax:* 780-427-5598
culture.alberta.ca/ahrf/default.aspx
To assist in the preservation of Alberta's historic sites, buildings & objects; to encourage & promote public awareness of the province's past; grants are awarded in the spring & fall at each year to a wide variety of community-based heritage initiatives
David Link, Director

Alberta Pioneer Railway Association
PO Box 70014, Stn. Londonderry, Edmonton AB T5C 3R6
Tel: 780-472-6229; *Fax:* 780-968-0167
www.railwaymuseum.ab.ca
To collect, preserve, restore, exhibit & interpret artifacts which represent the history & social impact of the railways in Western Canada, with emphasis on Canadian National Railways & Northern Alberta Railways & their predecessors in northern & central Alberta
Herb Dixon, Contact

Antique Motorcycle Club of Manitoba Inc. (AMCM)
1377 Niakwa Rd. East, Winnipeg MB R2J 3T3
Tel: 204-831-8165
www.amcm.ca
Ross Metcalfe, President
Mike Baraschuk, Librarian

Architectural Heritage Society of Saskatchewan (AHSS)
202 - 1275 Broad St., Regina SK S4R 1Y2
Tel: 306-359-0933; *Fax:* 306-359-3899
sahs@sasktel.net
www.ahsk.ca
To promote, support & facilitate the preservation, conservation, restoration & reuse of distinct architectural & historical heritage properties (designated or potential) throughout the province, ensuring that our built heritage is maintained for present & future citizens to appreciate the contributions & craftsmanship of past generations; to enhance the current social, economic & environmental quality of life

Association québécoise d'interprétation du patrimoine (AQIP)
CP 11003, Succ. Le Plateau, Gatineau QC J9A 0B6
Tél: 819-595-2190
aqip@aqip.ca
www.aqip.ca
Stimuler la communication entre les individus et les organismes intéressés à l'interprétation du patrimoine naturel, culturel, historique et industriel; promouvoir l'interprétation du patrimoine québécois auprès des gouvernements, des organismes, des médias et du public en général; stimuler l'acquisition de connaissances et la recherche liée à l'interprétation du patrimoine
Denis Lavoie, Président

British Columbia Genealogical Society (BCGS)
PO Box 88054, Stn. Lansdowne Mall, Richmond BC V6X 3T6
Tel: 604-502-9119; *Fax:* 604-502-9119
bcgs@bcgs.ca
www.bcgs.ca
To perpetuate the heritage of BC; to collect, preserve & publish material relevant to promotion of ethical principles, scientific methods & effective techniques in genealogical & historical research.
Jean List, President
Kenneth Livingstone, Corresponding Secretary

British Columbia Historical Federation (BCHF)
PO Box 5254, Stn. B, Victoria BC V8R 6N4
Tel: 604-277-2627; *Fax:* 604-277-2657
info@bchistory.ca
www.bchistory.ca
To offer assistance to writers of BC history; to disburse loans for publishing to members only; to offer a scholarship for undergraduate history major; to sponsor an annual competition for writers of BC history; to stimulate public interest & to encourage historical research in BC history
Barb Hynek, President
Jean Wilson, Secretary
Ken Welwood, Treasurer

British Columbia Railway Historical Association (BCRHA)
1148 Balmoral Rd., Victoria BC V8T 1B1
Tel: 250-383-7063
bcrha@shaw.ca
www.trainweb.org/bcrha
To preserve railway exhibits, manuscripts & film of BC railways
Paul J. Smith, President

Bus History Association, Inc. (BHA)
965 McEwan Ave., Windsor ON N9B 2G1
Tel: 519-977-0664
bdrouillard3@cogeco.ca
www.bus-history.org
To preserve & record data, information & other related materials of the bus industry, both within North America & worldwide

Canada's National History Society (CNHS) / Société d'histoire nationale du Canada
Bryce Hall, 515 Portage Ave., Main Fl., Winnipeg MB R3B 2E9
Tel: 204-988-9300; *Fax:* 204-988-9309
Toll-Free: 866-952-3444
memberservices@canadashistory.ca
www.historysociety.ca
To promote greater popular interest in Canadian history
Deborah Morrison, Publisher, President & CEO

Canadian Association for Conservation (CAC) / Association canadienne pour la conservation et la restauration (ACCR)
c/o Danielle Allard, #419, 207 Bank St., Ottawa ON K2P 2N2
Tel: 613-231-3977; *Fax:* 613-231-4406
coordinator@cac-accr.com
www.cac-accr.ca
To promote conservation of Canadian cultural property
Sylvia Kindl, President
Jessica Lafrance, Vice-President
Jennifer Mills, Secretary
Kyla Ubbink, Treasurer

Canadian Association of Heritage Professionals (CAPHC) / Association canadienne d'experts-conseils en patrimoine (ACECP)
George Brown House, #211, 50 Baldwin St., Toronto ON M5T 1L4
Tel: 416-515-7450; *Fax:* 416-515-0961
admin@cahp-acecp.ca
www.caphc.ca
To represent & further the professional interests of heritage consultants active in both the private & public sectors; To establish & maintain principles & standards of practice for heritage consultants; To enhance awareness & appreciation of heritage resources, & the contribution of heritage consultants; To foster communication among private practitioners, public agencies, & the public at large in matters related to heritage conservation
Fernando Pellicer, President & Chair, Communications Committee
Eileen Costello, Treasurer & Secretary

Canadian Catholic Historical Association - English Section (CCHA) / Société canadienne d'histoire de l'église catholique - Section anglaise
c/o St. Michael's College, 81 St. Mary St., Toronto ON M5S 1J4
Tel: 905-893-9754; *Fax:* 416-934-3444
www.umanitoba.ca/colleges/st_pauls/ccha/ccha.html
The Association promotes interest & research in the history of the Canadian Catholic Church, its dioceses, religious communities, institutions, parishes, buildings, sites, & personalities. It is divided into English & French sections.
Peter Meehan, President-General
Edward Jackman, Secretary-General

Canadian Heritage Information Network (CHIN) / Réseau canadien d'information sur le patrimoine (RCIP)
#2F1, 15 rue Eddy, Gatineau QC K1A 0M5
Tel: 819-994-1200; *Fax:* 819-994-9555
Toll-Free: 800-520-2446
service@chin.gc.ca
www.chin.gc.ca; www.virtualmuseum.ca
To engage national & international audiences in Canadian heritage, through leadership & innovation in digital content, partnerships, & lifelong learning opportunities
Gabrielle Blais, Director General
Paul Lima, Senior Policy Advisor
Louise Filiatrault, Director

Nancy Larivière, Assistant to the Director

Canadian Historical Association (CHA) / Société historique du Canada (SHC)
#501, 130 Albert St., Ottawa ON K1P 5G4
Tel: 613-233-7885; *Fax:* 613-565-5445
cha-shc@cha-shc.ca
www.cha-shc.ca
To encourage historical research; To stimulate public interest in history; To promote the preservation of Canadian heritage
Lyle Dick, President
Michel Duquet, Executive Director
Martin Laberge, Secretary, French Language
Amber Loydlangston, Secretary, English Language

Canadian Oral History Association (COHA) / Société canadienne d'histoire orale (SCHO)
c/o University of Winnipeg, 515 Portage Ave., Winnipeg MB R3B 2E9
janisthiessen@shaw.ca
www.canoha.ca
To encourage & support the creation & preservation of sound recordings which document the history & culture of Canada; to develop standards of excellence & increase competence in the field of oral history through study, education & research.
Nolan Reilly, President
Janis Thiessen, Sec.-Tres.

Canadian Railroad Historical Association (CRHA) / Association canadienne d'histoire ferroviaire
110, rue St-Pierre, Saint-Constant QC J5A 1G7
Tel: 450-632-2410; *Fax:* 450-638-1563
info@exporail.org
www.exporail.org
To collect, preserve & disseminate information/items relating to the history of railways in Canada

Canadian Society for the Study of Names (CSSN) / Société canadienne d'onomastique (SCO)
c/o GNBC Secretariat, Centre for Topographic Information, #634, 615 Booth St., Ottawa ON K1A 0E9
Tel: 613-992-3892; *Fax:* 613-943-8282
TTY: 613-996-4397
geonames@NRCan.gc.ca
geonames.rncan.gc.ca/info/cssn_e.php
CSSN promotes the study of all aspects of names & naming in Canada & elsewhere.
Wolfgang Ahrens, President
Léo LaBrie, Sec.-Treas.

Canadian Society of Church History (CSCH) / Société canadienne d'histoire de l'Église
c/o Robynne R. Healey, Dept. of History, Trinity Western University, 7600 Glover Rd., Langley BC V2Y 1Y1
robynne.healey@twu.ca
www.augustana.ab.ca/csch/
To encourage research in the history of Christianity, especially the history of Christianity in Canada
Todd Webb, President
Marguerite Van Die, Vice-President & Program Chair
Robynne Rogers Healey, Administrative Secretary
John H. Young, Treasurer

Canadian Society of Mayflower Descendants
deb121clarke@rogers.com
www.rootsweb.com/~canms/canada.html
Joyce Cutler, Governor

Canadian Vintage Motorcycle Group (CVMG)
33 Station Rd., Toronto ON M8V 2R1
secretary@cvmg.ca
www.amcm.ca
Bill Hoar, President
Betty Anne Clark, Correspondence Secretary
Anthony Petti, Membership Secretary

Canadian Warplane Heritage (CWH)
9280 Airport Rd., Mount Hope ON L0R 1W0
Tel: 905-679-4183; *Fax:* 905-679-4186
Toll-Free: 877-347-3359
museum@warplane.com
www.warplane.com
To acquire documents; perserve & maintain a complete collection of aircraft that were flown by Canadians & the Canadian military services from the beginning of World War II to the present, including other related aviation artifacts & memorabilia of significant historic importance to this period; to instruct, educate & entertain the general public through the maintenance & rotation of displays, flight demonstrations, special events & activities, & to encourage Canadians of all ages to become actively involved in the preservation of these aircraft & artifacts; to provide facilities for the restoration & protection, interpretation & exhibits of the collection; to maintain supportive exhibits in tribute to the thousands of men & women who built, serviced & flew these aircraft & in memory of those who did not return
Pamela Rickards, Vice President of Operations
Al Mickeloff, Manager, Marketing

Canadiana
#200, 440 Laurier Ave. West, Ottawa ON K1R 7X6
Tel: 613-235-2628; *Fax:* 613-235-9752
info@canadiana.org
www.canadiana.ca
Social Media: www.facebook.com/pages/Canadiana/115437585187018; twitter.com/CanadianaCA
To specialize in the digitization of, preservation of, & access to documentary heritage
Lynn Copeland, President
Leslie Weir, Vice-President
Sylvie Belzile, Treasurer

Conseil des monuments et sites du Québec (CMSQ)
82, Grande-Allée ouest, Québec QC G1R 2G6
Tél: 418-647-4347; *Téléc:* 418-647-6483
Ligne sans frais: 800-494-4347
cmsq@cmsq.qc.ca
www.cmsq.qc.ca
Oeuvrer à valoriser et faire connaître les monuments et les sites aux autorités et à la population du Québec; rassembler les individus, organismes et groupes partageant sa mission; entreprendre les actions appropriées à la mise en valeur et à la sauvegarde des éléments patrimoniaux
Louise Mercier, Présidente

The CRB Foundation (CRBF) / La Fondation CRB
1170, rue Peel, 8e étage, Montréal QC H3B 4P2
Tel: 514-878-5250; *Fax:* 514-878-5299
To encourage young people to strengthen their knowledge & appreciation of their history, heritage & cultural identity
Charles R. Bronfman, Chair
Johanne McDonald, Director of Operations

Family History Society of Newfoundland & Labrador
#101A, 66 Kenmount Rd., St. John's NL A1B 3V7
Tel: 709-754-9525; *Fax:* 709-754-6430
fhs@fhsnl.ca
www.fhsnl.ca
Social Media: www.facebook.com/144749998869923; twitter.com/fhsnl
To encourage & promote the study of family history in Newfoundland & Labrador; To collect & preserve local genealogical & historical records & materials; to foster education in genealogical research
Don Tarrant, President
John Fitzgerald, Secretary

Fédération des sociétés d'histoire du Québec
CP 1000, Succ. M, 4545, av Pierre-De Coubertin, Montréal QC H1V 3R2
Tél: 514-252-3031; *Téléc:* 514-251-8038
Ligne sans frais: 866-691-7207
fshq@histoirequebec.qc.ca
www.histoirequebec.qc.ca
Regrouper les organisations historiques de Québec.
Richard M. Bégin, Président

Federation of Nova Scotian Heritage (FNSH)
1113 Marginal Rd., Halifax NS B3H 4P7
Tel: 902-423-4677; *Fax:* 902-422-0881
Toll-Free: 800-355-6873
fnsh@hfx.andara.com
To support, promote & link NS heritage groups; to be a leader in heritage issues; to promote heritage awareness in Nova Scotia; to coordinate professional & volunteer development.
Anita Price, Executive Director

Fédération québécoise des sociétés de généalogie (FQSG)
CP 9454, Succ. Sainte-Foy, 1055, av du Séminaire, Québec QC G1V 4B8
Tél: 418-653-3940; *Téléc:* 418-653-3940
federationgenealogie@bellnet.ca
www.federationgenealogie.qc.ca
Représenter les sociétés de généalogie locales et régionales; la promotion et l'épanouissement de la généalogie au Québec et son rayonnement à l'étranger sont les buts visés
Albert J. Cyr, Président

Genealogical Association of Nova Scotia (GANS) / Association généalogique de la Nouvelle-Écosse
#222, 3045 Robie St., Halifax NS B3K 4P6
Tel: 902-454-0322
gans@chebucto.ns.ca
www.chebucto.ns.ca/Recreation/GANS
To encourage interest in & to raise standards of research in genealogy through workshops & publications; to acquaint members with research materials & methods to serve as medium of exchange for genealogical information; to support the collection & preservation of documents & other genealogical materials; to foster recognition of the value of genealogy to a proper study of the social sciences.
Allan Marble, President

Genealogical Institute of The Maritimes (GIM) / Institut généalogique des Provinces Maritimes
PO Box 36022, 5675 Spring Garden Rd., Halifax NS B3J 1G0
don.clark@ns.sympatico.ca
nsgna.ednet.ns.ca/gim/
The Genealogical Institute of the Maritimes, a non-profit organization, was established in 1983 under the auspices of the Council of Maritime Premiers. As well as pursuing geneaology, the play an educational role in upgrading the quality of professional family history research in the Maritimes and strive for excellence in research and encourage others to do the same.
Allen Marble, President
Robert Pierce, Registrar

Halifax Citadel Regimental Association (HCRA)
PO Box 9080, Stn. A, Halifax NS B3M 5K7
Tel: 902-426-1990
info@regimental.com
www.regimental.com
To assist Parks Canada in the administration and delivery of the historical interpretive program and associated activities at the Halifax Citadel National Historic Site of Canada and raise funds in support of that program.
Brian Andrecyk, President
Roderick MacLean, Administrative Officer

Heritage Canada Foundation (HCF) / Fondation Héritage Canada
190 Bronson Ave., Ottawa ON K1R 6H4
Tel: 613-237-1066; *Fax:* 613-237-5987
Toll-Free: 866-964-1066
heritagecanada@heritagecanada.org
www.heritagecanada.org
Social Media: www.facebook.com/heritagecanadafoundation; twitter.com/HeritageCanada
To foster & ensure the understanding, protection & sustainable evolution of Canada's heritage buildings & historic places
Natalie Bull, Executive Director
Carolyn Quinn, Director, Communications & Editor

L'Héritage canadien du Québec (HCQ) / The Canadian Heritage of Québec (CHQ)
1181, rue de la Montagne, Montréal QC H3G 1Z2
Tél: 514-393-1417; *Téléc:* 514-393-9444
chq@total.net
www.hcq-chq.org/french/
Organisme qui se consacre à la préservation des terrains & des constructions revêtant une valeur historique/architecturale dans la province du Québec
John Molson, Président

Heritage Foundation of Newfoundland & Labrador
PO Box 5171, 1 Springdale St., St. John's NL A1C 5V5
Tel: 709-739-1892; *Fax:* 709-739-5413
Toll-Free: 888-739-1892
info@heritagefoundation.ca
www.heritagefoundation.ca
To stimulate an understanding of & appreciation for the architectural heritage of Newfoundland & Labrador; To support & contribute to the preservation, maintenance & restoration of buildings of architectural or historical significance; To designate buildings & structures as Registered Heritage Structures; may make grants for purpose of preservation, maintenance, or restoration (Deadline for submitting grant application is Mar. 1 & Sept. 1 of each year)
George Chalker, Executive Director
Robert Parsons, Chairperson

Heritage Society of British Columbia
914 Garthland Pl. West, Victoria BC V9A 4J5
Tel: 250-384-4840
hsbc@islandnet.com
www.heritagebc.ca
Social Media: www.facebook.com/pages/Heritage-BC/191841050874008
To represent groups involved with heritage projects & issues
Rick Goodacre, Executive Director
Eric Pattison, President
Jan Thomas, Office Manager, Surrey

Historic Sites Association of Newfoundland & Labrador (HSANL)
PO Box 5542, St. John's NL A1C 5W4
Tel: 709-753-9262; *Fax:* 709-753-0879
Toll-Free: 877-753-9262
info@historicsites.ca
www.historicsites.ca
To preserve, promote, & interpret the history & heritage of Newfoundland & Labrador, in partnership with Parks Canada
Catherine Dempsey, Executive Director

Historic Theatres' Trust (HTT) / Société des salles historiques
PO Box 387, Stn. Victoria Station, Montréal QC H3Z 2V8
Tel: 514-933-8077; *Fax:* 514-933-8012
theatres@total.net
To develop an increased appreciation within the Canadian public concerning the preservation of historic Canadian theatres; To provide technical documentation & expertise to encourage improved methods of preserving, restoring, maintaining, operating & researching historic theatres
Janet MacKinnon, President

Historical Society of Alberta (HSA)
Lancaster Building, PO Box 4035, Stn. C, #622, 304 - 8th Ave. SW, Calgary AB T2P 1C5
Tel: 403-261-3662; *Fax:* 403-269-6029
albertahistory@telus.net
www.albertahistory.org
To preserve & promote the history of Alberta; to encourage the study & preservation of Canadian & Albertan history; to rescue from oblivion the memories, experiences & knowledge of early inhabitants.
William Baergen, President

Huguenot Society of Canada / Société Huguenote du Canada
#105 - 4936 Yonge St., Toronto ON M2N 6S3
To perpetuate the memory of the Huguenots; to keep in touch with Huguenot descendants & Huguenots worldwide
Peter Dupuy, President

ICOMOS Canada
PO Box 737, Stn. B, Ottawa ON K1P 5P8
Tel: 613-749-0971; *Fax:* 613-749-0971
canada@icomos.org
canada.icomos.org
To further the conservation, protection, rehabilitation, & enhancement of monuments, groups of buildings & sites; To encourage primary research in many important fields
Dinu Bumbaru, President
Alain Dejeans, Vice-président, Comité francophone
John Ward, Vice President, English Speaking Committee

J. Douglas Ferguson Historical Research Foundation
PO Box 5079, Shediac NB E4P 8T8
Tel: 506-532-6025; *Fax:* 506-532-6025
www.nunet.ca/jdfhrf/main.php
The Foundation is a non-profit, educational organization that gives financial support to a broad range of activities aimed at preserving the heritage of early historical currency, banks & other issuers of money, coins, tokens & paper money issued throughout Canada since the 18th century. It is a registered charity, BN: 118973437RR0001.
Geoffrey G. Bell, Chair
Cliff Beattie, President
Len Buth, Treasurer

Jewish Genealogical Society of Canada (JGSC)
PO Box 91006, 2901 Bayview Ave., Toronto ON M2K 2Y6
Tel: 647-247-6414
info@jgstoronto.ca
www.jgstoronto.ca
To foster interest in Jewish genealogical research; To facilitate the pursuit of Jewish genealogical research domestically & internationally; To provide a forum for the exchange of knowledge & information among people interested in Jewish genealogy
Harvey Glasner, President
Faye Blum, Secretary
Sid Disenhouse, Treasurer

Literary & Historical Society of Québec (LHSQ) / Société littéraire et historique de Québec
44, chaussée des Écossais, Québec QC G1R 4H3
Tel: 418-694-9147; *Fax:* 418-694-0754
info@morrin.org
www.morrin.org
To preserve, develop & share the diverse cultural life of the Québec City region's English-speaking community through innovative, responsive & effective services
Simon Auclair, Library Manager

Manitoba Genealogical Society Inc. (MGS)
1045 St. James St., #E, Winnipeg MB R3H 1B1
Tel: 204-783-9139; *Fax:* 204-783-0190
contact@mbgenealogy.com
www.mbgenealogy.com
Social Media: www.facebook.com/group.php?gid=8750026759; twitter.com/MbGenealogy
To collect & preserve local genealogical & historical records & materials; To foster education in genealogical research through society workshops & seminars; To encourage production of genealogical publications relating especially to Manitoba
Kathy Stokes, President
Mary Bole, Library Chair

Manitoba Historical Society (MHS)
61 Carlton St., Winnipeg MB R3C 1N7
Tel: 204-947-0559; *Fax:* 204-943-2565
info@mhs.mb.ca
www.mhs.mb.ca
To promote public interest in, and preservation of Manitoba's historical resources; To encourage research relating to the history of Manitoba
Annabelle Mays, President
James Kostuchuk, First Vice-President
Victor Sawelo, Manager, Ross House

Monarchist League of Canada (MLC) / Ligue Monarchiste du Canada
PO Box 1057, Oakville ON L6J 5E9
Tel: 905-912-0916
domsec@monarchist.ca
www.monarchist.ca
Social Media: www.facebook.com/canadamonarchist; twitter.com/monarchist
To promote loyalty to the Sovereign & a broader understanding of constitutional monarchy as part of Canada's parliament, history, social fabric, culture & traditions
Robert Finch, Dominion Chairman
Gavin Guthrie, Vice-Chairman
Robert Finch, Chairman

New Brunswick Genealogical Society Inc. (NBGS, Inc.) / Société Généalogique du Nouveau-Brunswick Inc.
PO Box 3235, Stn. B, Fredericton NB E3A 5G9
sbalch@nbnet.nb.ca
www.nbgs.ca
To promote & facilitate family historical research in New Brunswick
Stanley Balch, President
David Fraser, Treasurer
Dianne N. Mullin, Secretary, Membership

New Brunswick Historical Society
Loyalist House, 120 Union St., Saint John NB E2L 1A3
Tel: 506-652-3590
www.loyalisthouse.com
To promote the study, research & discussion of New Brunswick history; to collect & preserve New Brunswick history; to publish & educate. The Society owns & operates Loyalist House.
Erma Hadzic, Secretary
George F. Teed, Treasurer
David Goss, Vice-President
Kathy Wilson, President

New Westminster Hyack Festival Association
204, 6th St., New Westminster BC V3L 3A1
Tel: 604-522-6894; *Fax:* 604-522-6094
info@hyack.bc.ca
www.hyack.bc.ca
The New Westminster Hyack Festival Association organizes and facilitates events in the City of New Westminster while preserving history and tradition, in order to promote the City, stimulate the local economy, and entertain and involve people in a fun-filled atmosphere. Its events are recognized both locally and internationally, fostering a positive image for the City of New Westminster and its surrounding areas.
Melanie Vogel, Executive Director

Newfoundland Historical Society (NHS)
Office: #15, 90 Military Rd., PO Box 23154 Churchill Sq., St. John's NL A1B 4J9
Tel: 709-722-3191; *Fax:* 709-729-7989
nhs@nf.aibn.com
www.infonet.st-johns.nf.ca/providers/nfldhist
To promote study, research & public discussion of Newfoundland & Labrador's history; to record the history of the province; to promote preservation of historic sites
Melanie Martin, President

Ontario Black History Society (OBHS) / Société historique des Noirs de l'Ontario
Ontario Heritage Centre, #402, 10 Adelaide St. East, Toronto ON M5C 1J3
Tel: 416-867-9420; *Fax:* 416-867-8691
admin@blackhistorysociety.ca
www.blackhistorysociety.ca
To study Black history in Canada; to recognize, preserve & promote the contribution of Black peoples & their collective histories through education, research & cooperation; to promote the inclusion of material on Black history in school curricula; to sponsor & support educational conferences & exhibits in this field.
Rosemary J. Sadlier, President

Ontario Electric Railway Historical Association
PO Box 578, 13629 Guelph Line Rd., Milton ON L9T 5A2
Tel: 519-856-9802; *Fax:* 519-856-1399
streetcar@hcry.org
www.hcry.org
To collect & return to operating capacity, electric railway equipment representing North American city & interurban systems
J. Borland, President
Ian Campbell, Vice-President

Ontario Genealogical Society (OGS) / Société de généalogie de l'Ontario
#102, 40 Orchard View Blvd., Toronto ON M4R 1B9
Tel: 416-489-0734; *Fax:* 416-489-9803
provoffice@ogs.on.ca
www.ogs.on.ca
To encourage, bring together & assist all those interested in the pursuit of family history; to promote genealogical research; to set standards for genealogical excellence; to make available the knowledge, availability, diversity & comprehensiveness of the genealogical resources of Ontario; to share expertise in other geographic areas
Nancy Trimble, President
Shirley Sturdevant, Vice-President

Ontario Historical Society (OHS) / La Société historique de l'Ontario
34 Parkview Ave., Willowdale ON M2N 3Y2
Tel: 416-226-9011; *Fax:* 416-226-2740
ohs@ontariohistoricalsociety.ca
www.ontariohistoricalsociety.ca
To bring people together who are interested in preserving some aspect of Ontario's history; to encourage & assist museums, historical societies & other heritage groups to research, preserve & interpret artifacts, architecture, archaeological sites & archival resources of local communities; to provide a forum to exchange ideas, research & experiences related to the history of Ontario; to sponsor programs & projects with a wide general appeal that help discover Ontario history
Robert Leverty, Executive Director

Pier 21 Society
1055 Marginal Rd., Halifax NS B3H 4P6
Tel: 902-425-7770; *Fax:* 902-423-4045
info@pier21.ca
www.pier21.ca
To preserve & share information about the Canadian immigration experience through history
John E. Oliver, Chair
Robert Moody, Chief Executive Officer
Kristine Kovacevic, Manager, Museum Visitor Services
Carrie-Ann Smith, Manager, Research
Peter Malloy, Treasurer

Postal History Society of Canada (PHSC)
PO Box 562, Stn. B, Ottawa ON K1P 5P7
secretary@postalhistorycanada.net
www.postalhistorycanada.net
To promote the study of postal history of Canada
Chris Green, Contact

Prince Edward Island Genealogical Society Inc. (PEIGS)
PO Box 2744, Charlottetown PE C1A 8C4
peigs_queries@yahoo.ca
www.peigs.ca
To encourage & promote the study of family history in PEI; to collect & preserve local genealogical & historical records & materials; to foster education in genealogical research

Prince Edward Island Museum & Heritage Foundation (PEIMHF) / Le Musée et la fondation du patrimoine de l'Ile-du-Prince-Édouard
2 Kent St., Charlottetown PE C1A 1M6
Tel: 902-368-6600
mhpei@gov.pe.ca
www.gov.pe.ca/peimhf
Social Media: www.facebook.com/124989037532122; twitter.com/#!/PEIMUSEUM
To study, preserve, interpret & protect the human & natural heritage of PEI
Nora J. Young, Contact

Québec Family History Society (QFHS) / Société de l'histoire des familles du Québec
PO Box 1026, Pointe-Claire QC H9S 4H9
Tel: 514-695-1502; *Fax:* 514-695-3508
qfhs@bellnet.ca
www.qfhs.ca
To promote genealogy & genealogical research in Québec (particularly English & Protestant records) to collect & preserve books, manuscripts & other related material; To conduct workshops & seminars & discuss topics of interest to members
Gary Schroder, President
Joan Benoit, Executive Secretary

Réseau du patrimoine franco-ontarien (RPFO)
#B151, 2445 boul St-Laurent, Ottawa ON K1G 6C3
Tél: 613-729-5769; *Téléc:* 613-729-2209
Ligne sans frais: 866-307-9995
www.rpfo.ca
Permettre à ses membres de découvrir le patrimoine franco-ontarien par l'entremise de l'histoire et de la généalogie
Alexandre Ranger, Coordonnateur administratif
Richard St-Georges, Président
Andréanne Joly, Vice-présidente

Réseau du patrimone franco-ontarien (RPFO)
2445, boul. Saint-Laurent, Ottawa ON K1G 6C3
Tél: 613-729-5769; *Ligne sans frais:* 866-307-9995
www.rpfo.ca
Promouvoir la conservation du patrimoine franco-ontarien
Alexandre Ranger, Coordonnateur administratif

Richard III Society of Canada
c/o 156 Drayton Ave., Toronto ON M4C 3M2
richardiii@cogeco.ca
home.cogeco.ca/~richardiii/
In the belief that traditional accounts of the character & career of Richard III are neither supported by sufficient evidence nor reasonably tenable, the Society aims to promote research into his life & times to secure a re-assessment of the material relating to this period & this monarch's role in English history.
Tracy Bryce, Secretary

Royal Heraldry Society of Canada / Société royale héraldique du Canada
PO Box 8128, Stn. T, Ottawa ON K1G 3H9
Tel: 613-998-1976
secretary@heraldry.ca
www.heraldry.ca
Social Media: www.facebook.com/group.php?gid=35284796074
To maintain, foster & develop the heraldic traditions of Canadians by: increasing public awareness of heraldry & the society; advocating with governments for the protection & proper use of heraldry in Canada; advising the Canadian Heraldic Authority on matters of mutual concern
David M. Cvet, President
David E. Rumball, 1st Vice-President
Carl A. Larsen, 2nd Vice-President

The Royal Nova Scotia Historical Society (RNSHS)
PO Box 2622, Halifax NS B3J 3P7
david.sutherland@dal.ca
nsgna.ednet.ns.ca/rnshs
To promote an understanding & appreciation of Nova Scotia's history & cultural development; to encourage the preservation of published & archival materials & artifacts; to read papers pertaining to Nova Scotia's history at meetings of the society; to publish selected papers in the society's periodical
David Sutherland, President

Saskatchewan Cultural Exchange Society (SCES)
2431 - 8 Ave., Regina SK S4R 5J7
Tel: 306-780-9494; *Fax:* 306-780-9487
sces@sasktel.net
www.sces.ca
Social Media: www.facebook.com/groups/5599472389; twitter.com/TheExchangeClub; www.youtube.com/user/theexchangeclub; www.myspace.com/the_exchange
To support & facilitate cultural exchange & communication by providing a base for sharing community cultural experiences; to attract & involve practising artists in a cultural exchange in Saskatchewan; to enhance the opportunities for residents of smaller communities in Saskatchewan to experience & learn about contemporary cultural production; to provide an alternative for artists to interact with the public
Margaret Fry, CEO
Carol Morin, Chair

Saskatchewan Genealogical Society (SGS)
PO Box 1894, #110, 1514 - 11th Ave., Regina SK S4P 3E1
Tel: 306-780-9207
saskgenealogy@sasktel.net
www.saskgenealogy.com
To provide assistance in researching family history throughout the world; to preserve heritage documents; to collect materials for study
Linda Dunsmore-Porter, Executive Director
Celeste Rider, Provincial Librarian

Société canadienne d'histoire de l'Église Catholique - Section française (SCHEC) / Canadian Catholic Historical Association - French Section
SCHEC, Université du Québec à Trois-Rivières, 3351, boul des Forges, Trois-Rivières QC G9A 5H7
Tél: 819-376-5011; *Téléc:* 819-376-5179
schec.cieq.ca
Grouper les personnes intéressées à l'histoire de l'Église catholique au Canada; stimuler l'intérêt pour cette histoire dans le grand public; tenir des congrès annuels dans diverses régions du Canada afin de susciter un dialogue entre chercheurs participants et de promouvoir les travaux d'histoire régionale
René Hardy, Président

Société d'histoire régionale de Chibougamau
646, 3e Rue, Chibougamau QC G8P 1P1
Tél: 418-748-3124
Christian Claveau, Président

Société généalogique canadienne-française (SGCF)
3440, rue Davidson, Montréal QC H1W 2Z5
Tél: 514-527-1010; *Téléc:* 514-527-0265
info@sgcf.com
www.sgcf.com
Regrouper toutes les personnes désireuses de partager des connaissances généalogiques et leur histoire de famille par les conférences et la publication de travaux de recherche
Gisèle Monarque, Présidente

La Société historique de Québec
1070, De La Chevrotière, Québec QC G1R 3J4
Tél: 418-692-0556; *Téléc:* 418-692-0614
shq1@bellnet.ca
www.societehistoriquedequebec.qc.ca
Étudier et diffuser l'histoire de la ville de Québec et de sa région; relever et mettre en valeur le patrimoine de la même région
Jean Dorval, Président
Jean-François Caron, Trésorier
Doris Drolet, Secrétaire

United Empire Loyalists' Association of Canada (UELAC)
Dominion Office, The George Brown House, #202, 50 Baldwin St., Toronto ON M5T 1L4
Tel: 416-591-1783; *Fax:* 416-591-7506
uela@becon.org
www.uelac.org
To unite together descendants of those families who, as a result of the American revolutionary war, sacrificed their homes in retaining their loyalty to the British Crown; to keep alive the knowledge of the early contributions of hundreds of thousands of Loyalists of many cultures, creeds & colours
Fredrick H. Hayward, President
Carl Stymiest, Sr. Vice-President

West Coast Railway Association (WCRA)
PO Box 2790, Vancouver BC V6B 3X2
Tel: 604-524-1011; *Fax:* 604-876-4104
Toll-Free: 800-722-1233
info@wcra.org
www.wcra.org
Collects, preserves, restores, operates & exhibits artifacts relating to the history of railways, especially those of BC; the West Coast Railway Heritage Park in Squamish BC develops educational exhibits on railway heritage for all age groups; the tour program encourages the public to travel today's railways to see Canada
Don Evans, Executive Director

Homosexuality

Alliance des gais et lesbiennes Laval-Laurentides (AGLLL Inc.)
CP 98030, 95, boul Labelle, Sainte-Thérèse QC J7E 5R4
aglll@hotmail.com
www.algi.qc.ca/asso/aglll/
Groupe de discussion; activités

AlterHéros
CP 476, Succ. C, Montréal QC H2L 4K4
Tél: 514-846-1398
info@alterheros.com
www.alterheros.com
Organisme communautaire bénévole à but non lucratif qui favorise l'insertion sociale des personnes d'orientation homosexuelle, bisexuelle et d'identité transsexuelle
Marc-Olivier Ouellet, Fondateur

Amazones des grands espaces
Montréal QC
Tél: 514-525-3663
info@plein-air-amazones.org
www.plein-air-amazones.org
Club de plein air pour lesbiennes

ARC: Aînés et retraités de la communauté
Montréal QC
Tél: 514-529-7471
arcmontreal@hotmail.com
www.algi.qc.ca/asso/retraitesgais
Groupement de personnes gaies aînées ou retraitées; activités sociales, culturelles ou sportives. Contactez Raymond B. au 514-529-7471 ou Nicholas au 514-343-1117

Archives gais du Québec
#202, 4067, boul St-Laurent, Montréal QC H2W 1Y7
Tél: 514-287-9987
www.agq.qc.ca
Organisme communautaire à but non lucratif qui a le mandat de recevoir, conserver et préserver tout document de l'histoire des gais et lesbiennes du Québec - revues, journaux, coupures de presse, livres et vidéos, photos
Ian Blair, Président

Association des Gais et Lesbiennes du Bas-St-Laurent
info_aglbsl@yahoo.ca
www.algi.qc.ca/asso/aglbsl/
Activités sociales et sportives; contact: Jean-François, administrateur.

Association des lesbiennes et des gais sur Internet (ALGI)
CP 476, Succ. C, Montréal QC H2L 4K4
Tél: 514-528-8424; *Téléc:* 514-528-9708
info@algi.qc.ca
www.algi.qc.ca
Favoriser l'expression des lesbiennes et des gais au moyen de l'Internet; favoriser l'échange entre les individus et les organismes de la communauté gaie et lesbienne dans un esprit d'entraide

Association des pères gais de Montréal inc. (APGM) / Gay Fathers of Montréal Inc.
4245, rue Laval, Montréal QC H2W 2J6
Tél: 514-528-8424; *Téléc:* 514-528-9708
peresgais@yahoo.ca
www.algi.qc.ca/asso/apgm/
Regrouper les hommes qui sont à la fois pères et gais; offrir support et aide aux hommes gais soucieux d'éduquer leurs enfants; permettre au père gai de se situer face à la condition de vie au moyen d'échanges, de discussion et d'information; promouvoir la condition des pères gais et la défense de leurs intérêts communs

Bi Unité Montréal (BUM)
CP 476, Succ. C, Montréal QC H2L 4K4
webmaster@biunitemontreal.org
www.algi.qc.ca/asso/bum/
Association à but non lucratif; a pour mission de faire connaître la bisexualité et de rassembler les bisexuel(le)s dans un lieu commun pour qu'ils/qu'elles puissent s'informer, se divertir, et se supporter.

Les Bolides
Montréal QC
info@lesbolides.org
www.lesbolides.org
Ligue de quilles
Fernand

Canadian Lesbian & Gay Archives (CLGA)
PO Box 699, Stn. F, 34 Isabella St., Toronto ON M4Y 1N1
Tel: 416-777-2755
queeries@clga.ca
www.clga.ca
To acquire, preserve & make available to the public information in any medium about lesbians & gays, with an emphasis on Canada.
Martin Lanigan, President

Centre communautaire des gais et lesbiennes de Montréal
CP 476, Succ. C, Montréal QC H2L 4K4
Tél: 514-528-8424; *Téléc:* 514-528-9708
info@ccglm.org
www.ccglm.org
Organisme sans but lucratif qui agit pour améliorer la condition des membres de nos communautés - lesbiennes, gais, bisexuel(les), transexuel(les), transgenres, et allosexuel(les); bibliothèque

Centre d'orientation sexuelle de l'université McGill (COSUM) / McGill University Sexual Identity Centre (MUSIC)
Dép. de psychiatrie, Hôpital général de Montréal, #A2-160, 1650, av Cedar, Montréal QC H3G 1A4
Tél: 514-934-1934; *Téléc:* 514-934-8471
music-cosum@mcgill.ca
www.mcgill.ca/cosum; www.algi.qc.ca/asso/cosum
Offre des psychothérapies individuelles à court terme, psychothérapies de groupe & de couple ou familiales
Karine J. Igartua, Psychiatre

Centre de solidarité lesbienne
#301, 4126, rue St-Denis, Montréal QC H2W 2M5
Tél: 514-526-2452; *Téléc:* 514-526-3570
info@solidaritelesbienne.qc.ca
www.solidaritelesbienne.qc.ca
Le Centre est accessible aux personnes à mobilité réduite; organisme sans but lucratif qui a pour mission d'améliorer les conditions de vie des lesbiennes en leur offrant des services et des interventions adaptés à leur réalité et ce, dans les domaines de la violence conjugales, du bien-être et de la santé.

Coalition des familles homoparentales
Montréal QC
Tél: 514-846-1543
info@familleshomoparentales.org
www.familleshomoparentales.org
Milite pour la reconnaissance légale et sociale des familles homoparentales; groupe bilingue de parents lesbiens, gais, bisexuels et transgenres. Québec: 418-523-5572
Mona Greenbaum, Directrice

Coalition for Lesbian & Gay Rights in Ontario (CLGRO) / Coalition pour les droits des lesbiennes et personnes gaies en Ontario
PO Box 822, Stn. A, Toronto ON M5W 1G3
Tel: 416-392-6878
www.clgro.org
To work towards feminism, lesbian, gay & bisexual liberation by engaging in public struggle for full human rights, by promoting access & diversity within our communities, & by strengthening cooperative networks for lesbian, gay & bisexual activism

Comité des gais et lesbiennes du conseil central du Montréal métropolitain (CSN) (CGLCCMM-CSN)
Montréal QC
Tél: 514-598-2012
www.algi.qc.ca/asso/cglccmm
Jacques Tricot

Community One Foundation
PO Box 760, Stn. F, Toronto ON M4Y 2N6
Tel: 416-920-5422
info@communityone.ca
www.communityone.ca
To raise & disburse funds for the advancement of lesbian, gay, bisexual & transgender projects, artists & organizations; to fund projects in the areas of health & social services, arts & culture, research & education, political & legal
Philip Wong, Executive Director
Lenore MacAdam, Board Co-Chair
Larry Hughsam, Board Co-Chair/Treasurer

Conseil québécois des gais et lesbiennes du Québec (CQGL)
CP 182, Succ. C, Montréal QC H2L 4K1
Tél: 514-759-6844
info@cqgl.ca
www.cqgl.ca
A pour mission concrétiser notre leitmotive 'S'engager pour l'égalité sociale'. Adresse civique: #105, 4360, rue d'Iberville, Montréal, QC.
Steve Foster, Président

Council on Homosexuality & Religion (CHR) / Conseil de l'homosexualité et la religion
PO Box 1912, Winnipeg MB R3C 3R2
Tel: 204-772-8215; *Fax:* 204-478-1160
Toll-Free: 888-399-0005
cvogel@mts.net
To foster the welfare of homosexually-oriented persons & promote the understanding & acceptance of homosexuality within religious institutions; To provide counselling & referral services; To conduct workshops, seminars & lectures; To provide a library & a range of publications on homosexuality & religion; To assist others in the same activities
Chris Vogel, Sec.-Treas.
A.E. Millward, President

Dignity Canada Dignité
PO Box 2102, Stn. D, Ottawa ON K1P 5W3
Tel: 613-746-7279; *Fax:* 613-746-0353
info@dignitycanada.org
www.dignitycanada.org
To voice the concerns of Roman Catholic sexual minorities; To promote the development of sexual theology, justice, & acceptance of the lesbian & gay community; To reinforce a sense of dignity & to encourage gay men & lesbian women to become more active members in the Church & society
Frank Testin, President
Norman Prince, Secretary

Egale Canada
185 Carlton St., Toronto ON M5A 2K7
Tel: 416-964-7887; *Fax:* 416-963-5665
Toll-Free: 888-204-7777
egale.canada@egale.ca
www.egale.ca
Social Media: www.facebook.com/EgaleCanada; twitter.com/egalecanada
To advance equality & justice for lesbian, gay, bisexual & transgendered persons, & their families in Canada
Hilary Cook, Director

Fondation Mario-Racine / Mario Racine Foundation
2075, rue Plessis, Local 110, Montréal QC H2L 2Y4
Tél: 514-528-5940
info@fondation-mario-racine.qc.ca
www.fondation-mario-racine.qc.ca
A pour mission de favoriser le développement communautaire et culturel des gais et lesbiennes à Montréal; est engagée dans la réalisation du Centre communautaire des gais et lesbiennes de Montréal.
Michel Durocher, Président

Gai-Côte-Sud
#100, 708, 4e Av, La Pocatière QC G0R 1Z0
gaicotesud@hotmail.com
www.algi.qc.ca/asso/gcs/
Favoriser le bien-être des gais, lesbiennes, bisexuel(les) et transgenres de la région.
Magella Dionne, Président

GRIS-Centre-du-Québec
Tél: 819-477-3953
risennev@cgocable.ca
Richard Senneville, Président

Groupe de discussion au masculin (GDM)
CP 476, Succ. C, Montréal QC H2L 4K4
Tél: 514-528-8424
gdminfo@gmail.com
www.gai-gdm.org

Groupe de recherche et d'intervention sociale (GRIS-Montréal)
CP 476, Succ. C, Montréal QC H2L 4K4
Tél: 514-590-0016; *Téléc:* 514-590-0764
info@gris.ca
www.gris.ca
Favoriser un meilleure connaissance des réalités homosexuelles et de faciliter l'intégration des gais, lesbiennes et bisexuel(les) dans la société
Robert Pilon, Président

Groupe gai de l'Outaouais
Gatineau QC
Tél: 819-776-2727
marlan@videotron.ca
www.algi.qc.ca/asso/gdhgfo/
Discussions, rencontres, activités sociales; les rencontres ont lieu les mercredis soir à 19h30, au Bureau régional d'action sida, 109, rue Wright, local 003 (Gatineau, secteur Hull).

Groupe gai de l'Université Laval
Pavillon Mauice-Pollack, 2305, rue de l'Université, Québec QC G1V 0A6
Tél: 418-656-2131
ggul@public.ulaval.ca
www.algi.qc.ca/asso/ggul/

Groupe régional d'intervention social - Québec (GRIS-Québec)
363, rue de la Couronne, local 202, Québec QC G1K 6E9
Tél: 418-523-5572; *Téléc:* 418-523-9758
gris@grisquebec.org
www.grisquebec.org
Guy Lefebvre, Coordonnateur

Hors sentiers
5828, rue de Normanville, Montréal QC H2S 2B4
Tél: 450-963-9710
hors_sentiers@yahoo.ca
www.algi.qc.ca/asso/horssentiers/
Groupe de plein air

Jeunesse Lambda
a/s Centre communautaire des gais et lesbiennes de Montréal, 2075, rue Plessis, 3e étage, Montréal QC H2L 2Y4
Tél: 514-528-7535
info@jeunesselambda.org
www.algi.qc.ca/asso/jlambda/
Groupe d'accueil francophone de discussion et d'activités par et pour les jeunes gais, lesbiennes, bisexuel(les). Adresse postale: CP 32125, CSP Saint-André, Montréal QC H2L 4Y5
Gabriel Boisvert, Président

Projet 10 / Project 10
#218, 2000, Northcliffe, Montréal QC H4A 3K5
Tél: 514-989-4585; *Téléc:* 514-989-0001
questions@p10.qc.ca
www.p10.qc.ca; www.myspace.com/p10montreal
Ligne d'entraide anonyme et confidentielle; services pour les jeunes lesbiennes, gais, bisexuel(le)s, intersexuel(le)s, allosexuel(le)s, trans, et bispirituel(le)s
Carly Boyce, Co-coordinatrice
Shauna Thomas, Co-coordinatrice

Réseau des lesbiennes du Québec (RLQ) / Québec Lesbian Network
#110, 2075, rue Plessis, Montréal QC H2L 2Y4
Tél: 514-528-8424
rlqln.info@gmail.com
rlq-qln.algi.qc.ca
Diane Heffernan, Coordonnatrice

TimeOut / TempsLibre
PO Box 1087, Stn. B, Ottawa ON K1P 5R1
timeout@gayottawa.com
www.gayottawa.com
Sporting, social and recreational events for the gay community in Ottawa and area.

La Trame
CP 845, Succ. Desjardins, Montréal QC H5B 1B9
Tél: 514-374-0227
la.trame@hotmail.com
www.latrame.blogspot.com
Regroupement pour lesbiennes dans le domaine des arts, de la culture et du loisir
Mireille Robillard, Contact

Horticulture & Gardening

Les Amis du Jardin botanique de Montréal / Friends of the Montréal Botanical Garden
#A-206, 4101, rue Sherbrooke est, Montréal QC H1X 2B2
Tél: 514-872-1493; *Téléc:* 514-872-3765
www.amisjardin.qc.ca
Média social: www.facebook.com/LesAmisduJardinbotaniquedeMontreal
Promouvoir une culture scientifique et une culture générale concernant la nature, l'environnement et la botanique; supporter, par des actions concrètes, le Jardin botanique dans sa mission afin d'assurer son développement; informer les membres, de façon privilégiée, des plus récents progrès scientifiques; présenter au public les différentes composantes du Jardin botanique et en vulgariser le rôle, les actions et le contenu; valoriser la flore mondiale, particulièrement celle du Québec et promouvoir la conservation de la nature; représenter le grand public auprès des instances du Jardin
Michèle-E. Hogue, Directrice générale
Paule Lamontagne, Présidente

British Columbia Landscape & Nursery Association (BCLNA)
#102, 5783 - 176A St., Surrey BC V3S 6S6
Tel: 604-574-7772; *Fax:* 604-574-7773
Toll-Free: 800-421-7963
www.bclna.com
To work together to improve quality & standards of the industry
Lesley Tannen, Executive Director

Canadian Horticultural Council (CHC) / Conseil canadien de l'horticulture
9 Corvus Ct., Ottawa ON K2E 7Z4
Tel: 613-226-4880; *Fax:* 613-226-4497
webmaster@hortcouncil.ca
www.hortcouncil.ca
To improve horticultural & allied industries including production, grading, packing, transportation, storage & marketing
Anne Fowlie, Executive Vice-President

Canadian Iris Society (CIS)
c/o Ed Jowett, 1960 Sideroad 15, RR#2, Tottenham ON L0G 1W0
Tel: 905-936-9941
cdn-iris@rogers.com
www.cdn-iris.ca
To encourage, improve & extend the cultivation of the Iris & to collaborate with other societies for this purpose, as well as to regulate the nomenclature & colour classification of this flower.
Ed Jowett, President
Ann Granatier, Secretary

Canadian Nursery Landscape Association (CNLA)
Stn. Main, 7856 Fifth Line South, R.R.#4, Milton ON L9T 2X8
Tel: 905-875-1399; *Fax:* 905-875-1840
Toll-Free: 888-446-3499
info@canadanursery.com
www.canadanursery.com
Social Media: twitter.com/cnlavictor
To coordinate provincial member groups in the Canadian horticultural industry; to set national standards; to work with government; to develop national priorities
Victor Santacruz, Executive Director

Canadian Ornamental Plant Foundation (COPF) / Fondation canadienne des plantes ornementales
5A - #218, 975 McKeown Ave., North Bay ON P1B 9P2
Tel: 705-495-2563; *Fax:* 705-495-1449
Toll-Free: 800-265-1629
info@copf.org
www.copf.org
To encourage new plant development by strengthening relations between growers & breeders for the benefit of the horticulture industry
Peggy Walsh Craig, Managing Director

Canadian Rose Society (CRS)
#100, Chancellor Ave., Victoria BC V8Z 1R4
Tel: 416-266-6303
info@canadianrosesociety.org
www.canadianrosesociety.org
To provide information about rose growing, speakers, judges, nurseries & suppliers, & rose shows; To correspond with people with similar interests throughout Canada & around the world
Barb Munton, Membership Sec.-Treas.

Canadian Society for Horticultural Science (CSHS) / Société canadienne de science horticole
#1112, 141 Laurier Ave. West, Ottawa ON K1P 5J3
Tel: 613-232-9459; *Fax:* 613-594-5190
services@aic.ca
www.cshs.ca
To advance research, teaching, information, & technology related to all horticultural crops
David Percival, President
Denis Charlebois, Vice-President
Samir Debnath, Secretary-Treasurer

City Farmer - Canada's Office of Urban Agriculture
PO Box 74567, Stn. Kitsilano, Vancouver BC V6K 4P4
Tel: 604-685-5832
cityfarm@interchange.ubc.ca
www.cityfarmer.org
Social Media: cityfarmer.info
City Farmer encourages gardening in an urban environment. The website carries information for communities & schools about organic farming, composting, pest control.
Michael Levenston, Executive Director

Fédération des sociétés d'horticulture et d'écologie du Québec (FSHÉQ)
CP 1000, Succ. M, 4545, av Pierre-de-Coubertin, Montréal QC H1V 3R2
Tél: 514-252-3010; *Téléc:* 514-251-8038
fsheq@fsheq.com
www.fsheq.com
Regrouper tous les organismes voués à l'horticulture; faire la promotion de l'horticulture.
Thérèse Tourigny, Directrice générale

Fédération interdisciplinaire de l'horticulture ornementale du Québec (FIHOQ)
#300E, 3230, rue Sicotte ouest, Saint-Hyacinthe QC J2S 7B3
Tél: 450-774-2228; *Téléc:* 450-774-3556
fihoq@fihoq.qc.ca
www.fihoq.qc.ca
Grouper en fédération les associations professionnelles qui s'occupent d'horticulture ornementale au Québec; étudier, promouvoir, protéger et développer de toutes manières les intérêts économiques, sociaux et professionnels de ses membres; imprimer, éditer des revues, journaux, périodiques et plus généralement, toutes publications du domaine de l'horticulture ornementale aux fins d'information, de culture professionnelle et de propagande; organiser et tenir des cours, conférences, congrès, assemblées, expositions et autres réunions pour la promotion, le développement et la vulgarisation de l'horticulture ornementale; promouvoir la protection du consommateur dans le domaine de l'horticulture ornementale; assurer une répresentation tant sur le plan local et national, que sur le plan international des personnes oeuvrant dans le domaine de l'horticulture ornementale au Québec.
Luce Daigneault, Directrice générale
Jean Grégoire, Président

Flowers Canada (FC) / Fleurs Canada
Retail & Distribution Sector, #305, 99 Fifth Ave., Ottawa ON K1S 5P5
Fax: 866-671-8091
Toll-Free: 800-447-5147
flowers@flowerscanada.org
www.flowerscanada.org
To act as the voice of the Canadian floriculture industry; To improve the Canadian floriculture industry
James Fuller, Chairman

Landscape Alberta Nursery Trades Association (LANTA)
#200, 10331 - 178 St., Edmonton AB T5S 1R5
Tel: 780-489-1991; *Fax:* 780-444-2152
Toll-Free: 800-378-3198
info@landscape-alberta.com
www.landscape-alberta.com
To advance the Alberta ornamental horticulture industry through unity, education & professionalism
Nigel Bowles, Executive Director

Landscape New Brunswick Horticultural Trades Association (LNBHTA)
PO Box 742, Saint John NB E2L 4B3
Fax: 506-633-1621
Toll-Free: 866-752-6862
nbhta@nbnet.nb.ca
www.nbhta.ca
The mission of LNB is to further the development of the ornamental horticulture industry by focusing on the environment, education, promotion and professionalism. LNB is here to represent our members and to help them achieve their goals what so ever those goals may be.
John Evans, President

Landscape Newfoundland & Labrador (LNL)
PO Box 8062, St. John's NL A1B 3M9
Tel: 709-726-5651; *Fax:* 709-726-8441
davek@nl.rogers.com
www.landscapenf.org
Our vision is one that promotes professionalism at all levels of the Industry, and achieves the highest standards of excellence in delivery of services and products across all sectors of our industry.
David Kiell, Executive Director

Landscape Nova Scotia
Executive Plus Business Centre, #44, 201 Brownlow Ave., Dartmouth NS B3B 1W2
Tel: 902-463-0519; *Fax:* 902-463-6308
Toll-Free: 877-567-4769
info@landscapenovascotia.ca
www.landscapenovascotia.ca
Landscape Nova Scotia's mission is to promote high standards in product quality, professional service and conduct in the landscape and horticulture industry. We have been a voice for the landscape and horticultural industry for more than 20 years in Nova Scotia, and are committed to providing consumers with options to make informed decisions.
Scott Mosher, President

Landscape Ontario Horticultural Trades Association (LOHTA)
7856 Fifth Line South, RR#4, Milton ON L9T 2X8
Tel: 905-875-1805; *Fax:* 905-875-3942
Toll-Free: 800-265-5656
www.horttrades.com
To be a leader in representing, promoting & fostering a favourable environment for the advancement of the horticultural industry in Ontario
Tony DiGiovanni, Executive Director

North American Native Plant Society (NANPS)
PO Box 84, Stn. D, Toronto ON M9A 4X1
Tel: 416-631-4438
nanps@nanps.org
www.nanps.org
Dedicated to the study, conservation & cultivation of North America's wild flora.
Ruth Zaugg, Secretary

Ontario Horticultural Association (OHA)
448 Paterson Ave., London ON N5W 5C7
secretary@gardenontario.org
www.gardenontario.org
Social Media:
www.facebook.com/home.php?sk=group_167342733299811; twitter.com/gardenontario
To promote civic beautification, preservation of the environment, youth work & education of many aspects of horticulture
Carol Dunk, President

Prince Edward Island Horticultural Association
404 Mount Edward Rd, Charlottetown PE C1E 2A1
Tel: 902-566-2733; *Fax:* 902-566-5637
peihort@pei.aibn.com

Rhododendron Society of Canada (RSC)
RR#2, St George Brant ON N0E 1N0
Tel: 519-448-1537
To share information on rhododendrons
H.G. Hedges, Contact

Royal Botanical Gardens (RBG) / Les jardins botaniques royaux
680 Plains Rd. West, Hamilton ON L7T 4H4
Tel: 905-527-1158; *Fax:* 905-577-0375
Toll-Free: 800-694-4769
info@rbg.ca
www.rbg.ca
Social Media:
www.facebook.com/pages/Royal-Botanical-Gardens/140038459379746; twitter.com/RBGCanada; www.youtube.com/user/royalbotanicalgarden
To be recognized in Canada & throughout the world for its unique contribution to the collection, research, exhibition, & interpretation of the plant world & for the development of public understanding & appreciation of the relationship between the plant world, humanity, & the rest of nature
Mark C. Runciman, CEO

Saskatchewan Nursery Landscape Association (SNLA)
c/o Landscape Alberta Nursery Trades Association, #200, 10331 - 178 St., Edmonton AB T5S 1R5
Tel: 780-489-1991; *Fax:* 780-444-2152
Toll-Free: 866-383-4711
rebecca@canadanursery.com
www.snla.ca

Seeds of Diversity Canada (SoDC) / Semences du patrimoine Canada
PO Box 36, Stn. Q, Toronto ON M4T 2L7
Toll-Free: 866-509-7333
mail@seeds.ca
www.seeds.ca
To search out & preserve rare & endangered varieties of vegetables, fruits, flowers, herbs & grains
Bob Wildfong, Executive Director

Société d'Horticulture et d'Écologie de Prévost
CP 611, Prévost QC J0R 1T0
Tél: 450-224-9252
Florence Frigon, Présidente

Hospitals

Accreditation Canada / Agrément Canada
1150 Cyrville Rd., Ottawa ON K1J 7S9
Tel: 613-738-3800; *Fax:* 613-738-7755
Toll-Free: 800-814-7769
learning@accreditation.ca
www.accreditation.ca
To improve quality in health services through accreditation; To provide health care organizations with a voluntary, external peer review to assess the quality of their services
Wendy Nicklin, President & Chief Exectuive Officer
Gilles Lanteigne, Executive Vice-President & COO
Donna Anderson, Vice-President, Strategic Communications & External Relations
Danielle Dorschner, Director, National Services

Alberta Continuing Care Association (ACCA)
#120, 9405 - 50 St. NW, Edmonton AB t6b 2t4
Tel: 780-435-0699; *Fax:* 780-436-9785
info@ab-cca.ca
www.ab-cca.ca
To represent owners & operators of long term care & designated assisted living facilities & home care
Bruce West, Executive Director
Denise MacDonald, Director, Communications & Special Projects
Kailey O'Neill, Analyst, Planning & Research

Association des établissements privés conventionnés - santé services sociaux (AEPC)
#200, 204, rue Notre-Dame ouest, Montréal QC H2Y 1T3
Tél: 514-499-3630; *Téléc:* 514-873-7063
info@aepc.qc.ca
www.aepc.qc.ca
Promouvoir l'amélioration continue de la qualité des soins et des services donnés au sein des entreprises membres; protéger et promouvoir l'entreprise privée dans le domaine de la santé et du bien-être
Jean Hébert, Directeur Général

Association of Canadian Academic Healthcare Organizations (ACAHO)
780 Echo Dr., Ottawa ON K1S 5R7
Tel: 613-730-5818; *Fax:* 613-730-4314
brimacombe@acaho.org
www.acaho.org
To lobby for health care research & teaching hospitals
Glenn Brimacombe, CEO

Association of Ontario Health Centres (AOHC) / Association des centres de santé de l'Ontario (ACSO)
#500, 907 Lawrence Ave. West, Toronto ON M6A 3B6
Tel: 416-236-2539; *Fax:* 416-236-0431
mail@aohc.org
www.aohc.org
To promote community based primary care, health promotion, & illness prevention services, focusing on the broader determinants of health such as education, employment, poverty, isolation, & housing
Adrianna Tetley, Executive Director
Sophie Bart, Manager, Membership & Organizational Health
Mary MacNutt, Manager, Strategic Communications & Campaigns
Anjali Misra, Manager, Performance Management
Carolyn Poplak, Manager, Education & Capacity Building

Association québécoise d'établissements de santé et de services sociaux (AQESSS) (AQESS) / Québec Hospital Association
#400, 505, boul de Maisonneuve ouest, Montréal QC H3A 3C2
Tél: 514-842-4861; *Téléc:* 514-282-4271
Ligne sans frais: 800-361-4661
www.aqesss.qc.ca
Représenter et promouvoir les intérêts de ses membres et leur fournir des services qui répondent à leurs besoins
Lise Denis, Directrice générale

Auxiliaires bénévoles de l'Hôpital de Chibougamau
51, 3e Rue, Chibougamau QC G8P 1N1
Tél: 418-748-2676
Marie-Ange Fréchette, Présidente

Canadian Association of Healthcare Auxiliaries (CAHA) / L'association des auxiliaires bénévoles des soins de santé du Canada
c/o Canadian Healthcare Assn., #100, 17 York St., Ottawa ON K1N 9J6
Tel: 613-236-9364; *Fax:* 613-236-9350
caha.office@rogers.com
www.caha.freeservers.com
To assist provincial members in providing support to local auxiliaries through leadership, education, advocacy, communication & representation
Joyce Nash, President

Canadian Association of Paediatric Health Centres (CAPHC) / Association canadienne des centres de santé pédiatriques
c/o Canadian Association of Paediatric Health Centres, #104, 2141 Thurston Dr., Ottawa ON K1G 6C9
Tel: 613-738-4164; *Fax:* 613-738-3247
eorbine@caphc.org
www.caphc.org
To improve the health of children within Canada through research activities & through advocacy with governments & health care organizations; to provide information exchange amongst members.
Elaine Orrbine, CEO

Canadian Healthcare Association (CHA) / Association canadienne des soins de santé
#100, 17 York St., Ottawa ON K1N 9J6
Tel: 613-241-8005; *Fax:* 613-241-5055
tneuman@cha.ca
www.cha.ca
Social Media: twitter.com/CHA_ACS
To improve the delivery of health services in Canada through policy development, advocacy & leadership
Pamela C. Fralick, President/CEO
Teresa Neuman, Communications Specialist

Canadian Home Care Association (CHCA) / Association canadienne de soins et services à domicile
#707, 10 Kingsbridge Garden Circle, Mississauga ON L5R 3K6
Tel: 905-361-3277; *Fax:* 905-361-3274
chca@cdnhomecare.ca
www.cdnhomecare.ca
Social Media: twitter.com/CdnHomeCare
To promote the development, integration, delivery, public awareness & evaluation of quality home care services in Canada; to provide national leadership to strengthen & unify the home care sector; to collect & disseminate information about home care; to encourage or commission research; to influence policy & legislation; to establish a code of ethics
John Schram, President

Continuing Care Association of Nova Scotia (CCANS)
c/o Sunshine Personal Home Care, 38A Withrod Dr., Halifax NS B3N 1B1
Tel: 902-956-0090
ccans@eastlink.ca
www.nsnet.org/ccans
To represent continuing care facilities throughout Nova Scotia
Debra Leigh, COO

Health Association of PEI (HAPEI)
10 Pownal St., Charlottetown PE C1A 3V6
Tel: 902-368-3901; *Fax:* 902-368-3231
emholmes@ihis.org
To influence the change & development of the health delivery system; to provide services which assist members in managing their human, financial & physical resources.

Health Employers Association of British Columbia (HEABC)
#200, 1333 West Broadway, Vancouver BC V6H 4C6
Tel: 604-736-5909; *Fax:* 604-736-2715
contact@heabc.bc.ca
www.heabc.bc.ca
To serve a diverse group of over 300 publicly funded healthcare employers; To represent the entire spectrum of healthcare employers
Lee Doney, CEO

Hospital Auxiliaries Association of Ontario (HAAO)
#2800, 200 Front St. West, Toronto ON M5V 3L1
Tel: 416-205-1407; *Fax:* 416-205-1337
Toll-Free: 800-598-8002
jroth@haao.com
www.haao.com
Social Media: www.facebook.com/193203857388754
To advocate for community partnerships to support health care in Ontario; To promote volunteer services
Elayne Meharg, President
Joan Farlinger, Vice-President
Janet Simms-Baldwin, Secretary
Margaret Anne Robertson, Treasurer

New Brunswick Association of Healthcare Auxiliaries
220 Driftwood Loop, Fredericton NB E3B 7P2
Tel: 506-452-5432
r3jbooker@health.nb.ca
R. John Booker, President

New Brunswick Association of Nursing Homes, Inc. (NBANH) / Association des foyers de soins du Nouveau-Brunswick, inc. (AFSNB)
#206, 1113 Regent St., Fredericton NB E3B 3Z2
Tel: 506-460-6262; *Fax:* 506-460-6253
www.nbanh.com
Social Media: www.facebook.com/group.php?gid=157312207644040; twitter.com/NBANH_AFSNB
To assist members in the provision of quality & efficient care to their residents
Brian Harris, President
Michael Keating, Executive Director
Ken McGeorge, Treasurer

New Brunswick Healthcare Association (NBHA) / L'Association des soins de santé du Nouveau-Brunswick (ASSNB)
861 Woodstock Rd., Fredericton NB E3B 7R7
Tel: 506-451-0750; *Fax:* 506-451-0760
nbha@nbhealthcare.com
www.nbhealthcare.com
To improve health services delivery in New Brunswick by influencing health policy; to strive to be a well respected and influential leader in healthcare in New Brunswick, and a major driver for change.
Robert Simpson, CEO
Norah Wilson, Executive Secretary

Newfoundland & Labrador Health Boards Association (NLHBA)
2nd Fl. Beothuck Bldg., 20 Crosbie Pl., St. John's NL A1B 3Y8
Tel: 709-364-7701; *Fax:* 709-364-6460
nlhba@nlhba.nf.ca
www.nlhba.nl.ca
To work collaboratively with the province's publicly-funded health system through dynamic leadership in advocacy, the creation & exchange of ideas, & development of consistent policies, standards, & guidelines. The Association also provides collective bargaining & labour relations services to provincial Residential Boards, & facilitates physician recruitment & group purchasing
John F. Peddle, Executive Director
Cindy Parsons, Secretary

Northwest Territories Health Care Association (NWTHCA)
c/o Hay River Community Health Board, 3 Gaetz Dr., Hay River NT X0E 0R0
Tel: 867-874-7110; *Fax:* 867-874-7109
Working together for wellness
Wes Drodge, NWT Representative

Nova Scotia Association of Health Organizations (NSAHO)
Bedford Professional Centre, 2 Dartmouth Rd., Halifax NS B4A 2K7
Tel: 902-832-8500; *Fax:* 902-832-8505
sandi@nsaho.ns.ca
www.nsaho.ns.ca
To promote an effective, efficient & integrated quality health system for all Nova Scotians through leadership in influencing the development of public policy, representing & advocating members' interests & providing services to assist its members meet the health care needs of their communities
Mary Lee, President/CEO

Ontario Association of Medical Laboratories (OAML)
#1802, 5000 Yonge St., Toronto ON M2N 7E9
Tel: 416-250-8555; *Fax:* 416-250-8464
oaml@oaml.com
www.oaml.com
To act as the voice of Ontario's community laboratory sector; To promote professionalism, technical excellence, & accountability in the delivery of laboratory services throughout Ontario

Ontario Association of Non-Profit Homes & Services for Seniors (OANHSS)
#700, 7050 Weston Rd., Woodbridge ON L4L 8G7
Tel: 905-851-8821; *Fax:* 905-851-0744
www.oanhss.org
To support members in the provision of quality non-profit long term care, seniors' community services, & housing
Kevin Queen, Board Chair
Donna A. Rubin, Chief Executive Officer

Ontario Hospital Association (OHA)
#2800, 200 Front St. West, Toronto ON M5V 3L1
Tel: 416-205-1300; *Fax:* 416-205-1301
Toll-Free: 800-598-8002
info@oha.com
www.oha.com
To build a strong, innovative, & sustainable health care system that meets patient care needs throughout Ontario; To promote an efficent & effective health care system
Kevin P.D. Smith, Chair
Tom Closson, President & Chief Executive Officer
Warren DiClemente, Chief Operating Officer & VP, Educational Services
Julie Giraldi, Chief Human Resources & Officer, Information Technology
Doug Miller, Chief Financial Officer
Paul Davies, Treasurer

Ontario Long Term Care Association (OLTCA)
345 Renfrew Dr., 3rd Fl., Markham ON L3R 9S9
Tel: 905-470-8995; *Fax:* 905-470-9595
info@oltca.com
www.oltca.com
Provides professional leadership to the long-term care sector; to empower long-term care facilities to provide high quality & cost-effective health care & accommodation services
Gail Paech, Chief Executive Officer (Interim)
Brian Baillie, Director, Corporate Affairs & Member Services

The Regional Health Authorities of Manitoba (RHAM)
#2, 203 Duffield St., Winnipeg MB R3J 0H6
Tel: 204-833-1721; *Fax:* 204-940-2042
mebbitt@rham.mb.ca
www.rham.mb.ca
Tom Kapac, Program Manager

Saskatchewan Association of Health Organizations (SAHO)
#800, 2002 Victoria Ave., Regina SK S4P 0R7
Tel: 306-347-5500; *Fax:* 306-525-1960
info@saho.org
www.saho.org
To serve members through services, support, & programs
Susan Antosh, President/CEO
Alex Taylor, Chair

Housing

Association of Condominium Managers of Ontario (ACMO)
#100, 2233 Argentia Rd., Mississauga ON L5N 2X7
Tel: 905-826-6890; *Fax:* 905-826-4873
Toll-Free: 800-265-3263
rcm@acmo.org
www.acmo.org
To enhance the quality performance of condominium property managers & management companies in Ontario
Chris Antipas, President
Amanda Curtis, Executive Director

Association provinciale des constructeurs d'habitations du Québec inc. (APCHQ) / Provincial Association of Home Builders of Québec
5930, boul Louis-H.-Lafontaine, Anjou QC H1M 1S7
Tél: 514-353-9960; *Téléc:* 514-353-4825
Ligne sans frais: 800-468-8160
www.apchq.com
Depuis 1997, l'APCHQ est la plus importante gestionnaire de mutuelles de prévention du domaine de la construction. Étant le seul agent négociateur patronal des relations de travail dans le secteur résidentiel, elle défend les intérêts de quelque 12 000 employeurs et 25 000 travailleurs
Marc Savard, Directeur général
Frédéric Birtz, Directeur des opérations

Canadian Association of Home & Property Inspectors (CAHPI) / Association canadienne des inspecteurs de biens immobiliers
PO Box 13715, Ottawa ON K2K 1X6
Tel: 613-839-5344; *Fax:* 613-839-2554
Toll-Free: 888-748-2244
info@cahpi.ca
www.cahpi.ca
To promote & enhance the professionalism & competency of professional home & property inspectors
Bill Sutherland, President
Sharry Featherston, Administrator/Registrar
Blaine Swan, Treasurer

Canadian Condominium Institute (CCI)
#310, 2175 Sheppard Ave. East, Toronto ON M2J 1W8
Tel: 416-491-6216; *Fax:* 416-491-1670
Toll-Free: 866-491-6216
cci.national@taylorenterprises.com; mediaenquiries@cci.ca
www.cci.ca
To serve as a central clearinghouse & research centre on condominium issues & activities across the country; To provide objective research for practitioners & government agencies regarding all aspects of condominium operations; To offer professional assistance; To improve legislation & represent condominiums; to develop standards
Janice Pynn, RCM, ARP, ACCI, Chair
Jim MacKenzie, MBA, DAA, FCIP, National President
F. Diane Gaunt, Executive Director
Alison Nash, Manager, Operations
Peter K. Harris, C.A., ACCI, FCC, Secretary-Treasurer

Canadian Federation of Apartment Associations (CFAA) / Fédération canadienne des Associations de propriétaires immobiliers
#640, 1600 Carling Ave., Ottawa ON K1Z 1G3
Tel: 613-235-0101; *Fax:* 613-238-0101
admin@cfaa-fcapi.org
www.cfaa-fcapi.org
To represent members on political & economic issues at the national level & to facilitate the exchange of information & materials amongst members while maintaining the highest professional & ethical standards in all activities
John Dickie, President
David Benes, Administrator

Canadian Home Builders' Association (CHBA) / Association canadienne des constructeurs d'habitations
#500, 150 Laurier Ave. West, Ottawa ON K1P 5J4
Tel: 613-230-3060; *Fax:* 613-232-8214
chba@chba.ca
www.chba.ca
To assist its members in serving the needs & meeting the aspirations of Canadians for housing; To be the voice of the residential construction industry in Canada; To achieve an environment in which members can operate profitably; To promote affordability & choice in housing for all Canadians; To support the professionalism of members
Nichael Gough, National Coordinator, Association Services
Jack Mantyla, National Coordinator, Education & Training
John Kenward, Chief Operating Officer
Don Johnston, Senior Director, Technology & Policy
Lynda Barrett, Director, Conferences & Special Events
John Bos, Director, Finance
David Crenna, Director, Urban Issues
David Foster, Director, Environmental Affairs

Canadian Housing & Renewal Association (CHRA) / Association canadienne d'habitation et de rénovation urbaine (ACHRU)
#310, 130 Slater St., Ottawa ON K1P 6E2
Tel: 613-594-3007; *Fax:* 613-594-9596
info@chra-achru.ca
www.chra-achru.ca
To provide access to adequate & affordable housing.
Sharon Chisholm, Executive Director

Canadian Manufactured Housing Institute (CMHI)
#500, 150 Laurier Ave. West, Ottawa ON K1P 5J4
Tel: 613-563-3520; *Fax:* 613-232-8600
cmhi@cmhi.ca
www.cmhi.ca
To be the voice of the manufactured housing industry in Canada; to seek, identify & solidify the development of new, profitable market opportunities for manufactured housing, both domestically & internationally; to promote housing affordability for all Canadians.

Confederation of Resident & Ratepayer Associations (CORRA)
231 Dunvegan Rd., Toronto ON M5P 2P3
Fax: 416-483-0122
The association coordinates the activities of & lobbies for member associations to promote better urban life & beneficial legislation. It acts as watchdog to protect city neighbourhoods, parks & waterfront.
Brian Maguire, Chair

Cooperative Housing Association of Newfoundland & Labrador
PO Box 453, #206, 75 Barbour Dr., Mount Pearl NL A1N 2C4
Tel: 709-747-5615; *Fax:* 709-747-5606
chanal@nl.rogers.com
chanal.no-ip.org
Bill Vardy, President

Cooperative Housing Federation of British Columbia (CHF BC)
#200, 5550 Fraser St., Vancouver BC V5W 2Z4
Tel: 604-879-5111; *Fax:* 604-879-4611
Toll-Free: 866-879-5111
info@chf.bc.ca
www.chf.bc.ca
Social Media:
www.facebook.com/pages/CHF-BC/123651397671685;
twitter.com/chfbc; www.youtube.com/user/coopsbc;
www.flickr.com/photos/bchousingcoops
To expand non-profit co-operative housing; to promote better housing conditions in BC; to share skills & information with the co-operative housing community; represent housing co-ops to governments & the general public
Thom Armstrong, Executive Director

Cooperative Housing Federation of Canada (CHF Canada) / Fédération de l'habitation coopérative du Canada (FHCC)
#311, 225 Metcalfe St., Ottawa ON K2P 1P9
Tel: 613-230-2201; *Fax:* 613-230-2231
Toll-Free: 800-465-2752
info@chfcanada.coop
www.chfc.ca
Social Media: www.facebook.com/105594649486310;
twitter.com/CHFCanada; www.youtube.com/user/coophousing;
flickr.com/groups/coophousingcanada
To unite, represent, & serve the co-op housing community across Canada
Nicholas Gazzard, Executive Director
David Granovsky, Coordinator, Government Relations

Federation of Metro Toronto Tenants' Associations (FMTA)
#500, 27 Carlton St., Toronto ON M5B 1L2
Tel: 416-646-1772
Crisis Hot-Line: 416-921-9494
hotline@torontotenants.org
www.torontotenants.org
To inform & educate tenants; To encourage the organization of tenants; To lobby for tenant protection laws; To promote affordable housing

Ontario Association of Property Standards Officers Inc.
#1000, 1 Municipal Dr., Aurora ON L4G 6J1
www.oapso.org
Garry Anderson, President

Ontario Non-Profit Housing Association (ONPHA)
#400, 489 College St., Toronto ON M6G 1A5
Tel: 416-927-9144; *Fax:* 416-927-8401
Toll-Free: 800-297-6660
mail@onpha.org; communications@onpha.org;
municipal@onpha.org
www.onpha.on.ca
To build a strong non-profit housing sector in Ontario; To strive for excellence in non-profit housing management; To represent non-profit housing
Keith Ward, President
Sharad Kerur, Executive Director
Jo Ferris-Davies, Director, Member Development & Education
Alice Radley, Treasurer
Diana Summers, Manager, Policy, Research, & Government Relations
Rhona Duncan, Coordinator, Communications & Marketing

ShareOwner Education Inc.
#806, 4 King St. West, Toronto ON M5H 1B6
Tel: 416-595-9600; *Fax:* 416-595-0400
Toll-Free: 800-268-6881
customercare@shareowner.com
www.shareowner.com

To offer practical education & portfolio training to individual investors & investment clubs, so that they may invest successfully in quality growth stocks; To increase stock market literacy
John Bart, Chief Mentor

Human Rights & Civil Liberties

Alberta Civil Liberties Research Centre (ACLRC)
c/o Faculty of Law, University of Calgary, 2500 University Dr. NW, Calgary AB T2N 1N4
Tel: 403-220-2505; *Fax:* 403-284-0945
aclrc@ucalgary.ca
www.aclrc.com
To promote awareness among Albertans about civil liberties & human rights through research & education
Linda McKay-Panos, Executive Director

Amnesty International - Canadian Section (English Speaking)
312 Laurier Ave. East, Ottawa ON K1N 1H9
Tel: 613-744-7667; *Fax:* 613-746-2411
Toll-Free: 800-266-3789
info@amnesty.ca
www.amnesty.ca
AI Canada is part of a worldwide movement which is independent of any government, political grouping, ideology, economic interest or religious creed. It's primary aim is to bring public attention to abuses of human rights standards, particularly cases where people are imprisoned for their beliefs, or "prisoners of conscience." It holds that mass public pressure, expressed through effective forms of action, is critical to preventing & ending human rights violations. It also works to abolish the death penalty, torture, & other cruel treatment of prisoners, to end political killings & "disappearances." It is a registered charity, BN: 118785914RR0001.
Michael Boissin, Chair
Sarah Beamish, President
Robert Goodfellow, Executive Director

Amnistie internationale, Section canadienne (Francophone) / Amnesty International, Canadian Section (Francophone)
50 rue Ste-Catherine Ouest bureau 500, Montréal QC H2X 3V4
Tél: 514-766-9766; *Téléc:* 514-766-2088
Ligne sans frais: 800-565-9766
info@amnistie.ca
www.amnistie.ca
Mouvement d'intervention directe formé de bénévoles qui visent à la libération des prisonniers d'opinion, la tenue de procès équitables pour les prisonniers politiques, l'abolition de la torture et la cessation des "disparitions" et assassinats politiques
Beatrice Vaugrante, Direction

Black Coalition of Québec / La Ligue des Noirs du Québec
5201, boul Decarie, Montréal QC H3W 3C2
Tel: 514-489-3830; *Fax:* 514-489-2843
info.ligue@videotron.ca
www.liguedesnoirs.org
The Coalition speaks for the Black community in the defence of individual human rights and against all forms of discrimination
Dan Philip, Président

British Columbia Civil Liberties Association (BCCLA)
#550, 1188 West Georgia St., Vancouver BC V6E 4A2
Tel: 604-687-2919; *Fax:* 604-687-3045
info@bccla.org
www.bccla.org
Social Media:
www.facebook.com/pages/BC-Civil-Liberties-Association/884126 3601; twitter.com/bccla; www.youtube.com/user/BCCivilLiberties
To protect & enhance civil liberties & human rights in British Columbia
David Eby, Executive Director
Michael Vonn, Policy Director

Canada Tibet Committee (CTC)
#2250, 300 Léo-Pariseau, Montréal QC H2X 4B3
Tel: 514-487-0665; *Fax:* 514-487-7825
ctcoffice@tibet.ca
www.tibet.ca
Social Media: www.facebook.com/groups/31692752904; twitter.com/canadatibetcomm; www.youtube.com/tibetchannel
To create a structure where concerned Canadians can work together with their Tibetan friends to develop increased awareness in Canada.

The Canadian Centre/International P.E.N. (PEN)
#301, 24 Ryerson Ave., Toronto ON M5T 2P3
Tel: 416-703-8448; *Fax:* 416-703-3870
info@pencanada.ca
www.pencanada.ca
To foster understanding among writers of all nations; to fight for freedom of expression wherever it is endangered; to work for preservation of world's literature
Ellen Seligman, President
Isobel Harry, Executive Director
Kendra Ward, Office Manager

Canadian Civil Liberties Association (CCLA) / Association canadienne des libertés civiles
#506, 360 Bloor St. West, Toronto ON M5S 1X1
Tel: 416-363-0321; *Fax:* 416-861-1291
mail@ccla.org
www.ccla.org
Nathalie Des Rosiers, General Counsel
Marsha Hanen, President

Canadian Tribute to Human Rights (CTHR) / Monument canadien pour les droits de la personne (MCDP)
#170, 99 - 5th Ave., Ottawa ON K1P 5P5
Tel: 613-828-5492; *Fax:* 613-828-3647
info@cthr-mcdp.com
www.cthr-mcdp.com
To ensure public awareness of the presence in Ottawa of the Tribute monument as a symbol of Canadians' committment to preserving & fostering human rights; To promote use of the site as a focal point for all groups working for human rights in Canada & internationally; To spread the concept of public places dedicated to human rights in other capital cities of countries that have affirmed the UN Universal Declaration of Human Rights.
Andrew Fenus, Vice-President
George Wilkes, Sec.-Treas.
Teena Hendelman, President

Citizens for Public Justice (CPJ)
#501, 309 Cooper St., Ottawa ON K2P 0G5
Fax: 613-232-1275
Toll-Free: 800-667-8046
cpj@cpj.ca
www.cpj.ca
To promote public justice in Canada by shaping key public policy debates through research and analysis, publishing and public dialogue. CPJ encourages citizens, leaders in society and governments to support policies and practices which reflect God's call for love, justice and stewardship.
Joe Gunn, Executive Director

CPJ Corp. (CPJ)
#501, 309 Cooper St., Ottawa ON K2P 0G5
Fax: 613-232-1275
Toll-Free: 800-867-8046
cpj@cpj.ca
www.cpj.ca
To promote public justice in Canada byshaping key public policy debates through research & analysis, publishing & public dialogue; CPJ encourages citizens, leaders in society & governments to support policies & practices which reflect God's call for love, justice & stewardship
Joe Gunn, Executive Director

Equitas - International Centre for Human Rights Education / Equitas - Centre international d'éducation aux droits humains
#1100, 666, rue Sherbrooke ouest, Montréal QC H3A 1E7
Tel: 514-954-0382; *Fax:* 514-954-0659
info@equitas.org
www.equitas.org
To provide human rights education in Canada & abroad, based on the principles elaborated in the Universal Declaration of Human Rights
Rob Yalden, President
Ian Hamilton, Executive Director

Human Rights Institute of Canada (HRIC) / Institut canadien des droits humains
#905, 280 Albert St., Ottawa ON K1P 5G8
Tel: 613-232-2920; *Fax:* 613-232-3735
hric@humanrightsinstitute.com
www.humanrightsinstitute.com
To advance the Canadian quest for freedom, justice & equality in a democratic society; to do so by cooperation with other groups & individuals, public meetings & conferences, submissions to parliamentary & other bodies, publicity, complaint to United Nations; to use independent, non-partisan professional research as a basis for all positions that may be taken; based on universal declaration of human rights, applies in-depth legal techniques to determine & recommend solutions.
Marguerite E. Ritchie, President

International Centre for Human Rights & Democratic Development (ICHRDD) / Centre international des droits de la personne et du développement démocratique
#1100, 1001, boul de Maisonneuve est, Montréal QC H2L 4P9
Tel: 514-283-6073; *Fax:* 514-283-3792
dd-rd@dd-rd.ca
www.dd-rd.ca
To work with civil society organizations & governments, in Canada & abroad, for the benefit of developing countries; to act as a mediator, to facilitate dialogue & to work on projects where consensus between civil society & governments has not yet been built; to promote human rights & strengthen democratic institutions around the world through partnerships with human rights, indigenous peoples' & women's rights groups, as well as democratic movements & governments.
Gérard Latulippe, President

League for Human Rights of B'nai Brith Canada / Ligue des droits de la personne de B'nai Brith Canada
15 Hove St., Toronto ON M3H 4Y8
Tel: 416-633-6224; *Fax:* 416-630-2159
Toll-Free: 800-892-2624
league@bnaibrith.ca
www.bnaibrith.ca/league/league.htm
To strive for human rights for all Canadians; to improve inter-community relations; to combat racism & racial discrimination; to prevent bigotry & anti-Semitism.
Frank Dimant, CEO

Macedonian Human Rights Movement of Canada (MHRMC) / Mouvement canadien de défense des droits de la personne dans la communauté macédonienne
#434, 157 Adelaide St., Toronto ON M5H 4E7
Tel: 416-850-7125; *Fax:* 416-850-7127
info@mhrmi.org
www.mhrmi.org
To secure & maintain the human rights of all Macedonians wherever they live through advocacy & education
Andy Plukov, Treasurer
Luby Vidinovski, Vice-President
Bill Nicholov, President
Mark Opashinov, Secretary

Minority Rights Association of Greater Châteauguay
#310, 155 boul. St.-Jean Baptiste, Châteauguay QC J6K 3B1
Tel: 450-699-5910
Margaret Wilheim, Contact

Industry

Canadian Mechanical Contracting Education Foundation (CMCEF)
#601, 280 Albert St., Ottawa ON K1P 5G8
Tel: 613-232-5169; *Fax:* 613-235-2793
cmef@cmcef.org
www.cmcef.org
To ensure a stronger Mechanical Contracting Industry by initiating and conducting essential educational and research programs which enhance this industry's ability to operate efficiently and economically for the benefit of those served by the industry.
Tania Johnston, Executive Director

Information Technology

Association for Image & Information Management International - 1st Canadian Chapter (AIIM Canada)
c/o Teranet Inc., #600, 1 Adelaide St. East, Toronto ON M5C 2V9
winnie.tsang@teranet.ca
www.aiim.org/chapters/firstcanadian
To connect users & suppliers of e-business technologies & services
Winnie Tsang, President
Darin Davis, Secretary

Association of Professional Computer Consultants - Canada (APCC)
#400, 2323 Yonge St., Toronto ON M4P 2C9
Tel: 416-545-5275; *Toll-Free:* 800-487-2722
info@apcconline.com
www.apcconline.com
To promote the interests of independent computer consultants; to provide cost-saving services to members; to provide members with a forum for interaction & exchange

Canadian Association of Internet Providers (CAIP) / Association canadienne des fournisseurs internet (ACFI)
#416, 207 Bank St., Ottawa ON K2P 2N2
Tel: 613-236-6550; *Fax:* 613-236-8189
info@cata.ca
www.caip.ca
To foster the growth of a healthy & competitive Internet service industry in Canada through collective & cooperative action on issues of mutual interest.
Tom Copeland, Chair

Canadian Association of SAS Users (CASU) / Association canadienne des utilisateurs SAS (ACUS)
#500, 280 King St. East, Toronto ON M5A 1K7
Tel: 416-363-4424; *Fax:* 416-363-5399
To provide support to all Canadian SAS user groups; to assist them in the most efficient & effective use of the SAS system for information delivery; to provide updates on research & development of institute software & services.
Carl Farrell, President

Canadian Community of Computer Educators (CCCE)
15 Lone Oak Ave., Brampton ON L6S 5V4
info@ccce.on.ca
www.ccce.on.ca
To ensure excellence in education & training to support information technology

Canadian Image Processing & Pattern Recognition Society (CIPPRS) / Association canadienne de traitement d'images et de reconnaissance des formes (ACTIRF)
Dept. of Computer Sciences, Univ. of Western Ontario, Middlesex College 383, London ON N6A 5B7
Tel: 519-661-2111; *Fax:* 519-661-3515
barron@csd.uwo.ca
www.cipprs.org
To promote research & development activities in image & signal processing for solving pattern recognition problems.
John Barron

Canadian Information Processing Society (CIPS) / L'Association canadienne de l'informatique (ACI)
National Officer, #801, 5090 Explorer Dr., Mississauga ON L4W 4T9
Tel: 905-602-1370; *Fax:* 905-602-7884
Toll-Free: 877-275-2477
info@cips.ca
www.cips.ca
Social Media: www.facebook.com/group.php?gid=2459351719; twitter.com/cips; www.linkedin.com/groups?about=&gid=71785&trk=anet_ug_grp pro
To define & foster the IT profession; To encourage & support the IT practitioner; To advance the theory & practice of IT, while safeguarding the public interest
Jon Nightingale, Chair, Governance Committee

CANARIE
#500, 45 O'Connor St., Ottawa ON K1P 1A4
Tel: 613-943-5454; *Fax:* 613-943-5443
info@canarie.ca
www.canarie.ca
Canada's advanced internet development organization; to facilitate & promote the development of Canada's communications infrastructure; to stimulate next-generation products, applications & services; to communicate the benefits of an information-based society. CANARIE also intends to act as a catalyst and partner with governments, industry and the research community to increase overall IT awareness, ensure continuing promotion of Canadian technological excellence and ultimately, foster long-term productivity and improvement of living standards.
Guy Bujold, President & CEO

Centre international pour le développement de l'inforoute en français (CIDIF)
165, Blvd. Hébert, Edmundston NB E3V 2S8
Tél: 506-737-5280; *Téléc:* 506-737-5281
info@cidif.org
www.cidif.org
Fournir des outils et des services spécialisés afin de contribuer à rendre l'utilisation de logiciels et l'internet transparente aux usagers de différentes cultures et de différentes langues
Roger Gervais, Directeur général

Chinese Canadian Information Processing Professionals (CIPro)
PO Box 316, 7305 Woodbine Ave., Markham ON L3R 3V7
info@cipro.ca
www.cipro.ca
Scaven Liow, President

COACH - Canada's Health Informatics Association (COACH)
#301, 250 Consumers Rd., Toronto ON M2J 4V6
Tel: 416-494-9324; *Fax:* 416-495-8723
Toll-Free: 888-253-8554
info@coachorg.com
www.coachorg.com
Social Media: www.facebook.com/group.php?gid=196625113752686; twitter.com/COACH_HI; www.linkedin.com/company/coach-canada's-health-informatics-a ssociation
To improve the health of Canadians & enhance the management of Canada's health system by advancing the practice of health information management & effective utilization of associated technologies
Don Newsham, Chief Executive Officer
Shannon Bott, Executive Director, Operations
Linda Miller, Executive Director, CHIEF: Canada's Health Informatics Executive Forum
John Schinbein, Executive Director, CTF Telehealth Forum
Lydia Lee, President
Neil Gardner, President-Elect
Mike Barron, Sec.-Tres.

Communications & Information Technology Ontario (CITO)
#200, 2625 Queensview Dr., Ottawa ON K2B 8K2
Tel: 613-726-3420; *Fax:* 613-726-3424
Toll-Free: 566-759-6014
To be a catalyst for innovation & entrepreneurship in Ontario's communications & information technology industry; To promote the interchange of people, ideas & technologies between industry & universities by advancing university-based research & supporting universities in graduating students in communications & information technology
Don Wilford, Managing Director, Centre of Excellence for Photonics

Digital Nova Scotia (ITANS)
Technology Innovation Centre, 1 Research Dr., Dartmouth NS B2Y 4M9
Tel: 902-423-5332; *Fax:* 877-282-9506
info@digitalnovascotia.com
www.digitalnovascotia.com
Social Media: www.facebook.com/groups/2384141607; twitter.com/digitalns; www.youtube.com/user/digitalnovascotia
To be dedicated to the development & growth of the digital technologies industry in Nova Scotia
Michael McConnell, Chief Executive Officer
Jason K. Powell, President
John Leahy, Vice-President
Ken Lee, Director, Events
David T. Fraser, Secretary
Steven Carr, Treasurer

Electronic Frontier Canada Inc. (EFC) / Frontière électronique du Canada
20 Richmond Ave., Kitchener ON N2G 1Y9
Tel: 905-525-9140; *Fax:* 905-546-9995
damien@efc.ca
www.efc.ca
EFC works to ensure that the principals embodied in the Canadian Charter of Rights & Freedoms are protected as new computing, communications & information technologies emerge.
David Jones, President
Jeffrey Shallit, Vice-President/Treasurer
Richard Rosenberg, Vice-President

GS1 Canada
#800, 1500 Don Mills Rd., Toronto ON M3B 3L1
Tel: 416-510-8039; *Fax:* 416-510-1916
Toll-Free: 800-567-7084
info@gs1ca.org
www.gs1ca.org
To act as a facilitator for the use of electronic information transactions in support of Canadian users.
N. Arthur Smith, President/CEO

Information & Communications Technology Council of Canada (ICTC) / Conseil des technologies de l'information et des communications du Canada (CTIC)
#300, 116 Lisgar St., Ottawa ON K2P 0C2
Tel: 613-237-8551; *Fax:* 613-230-3490
info@ictc-ctic.ca
www.ictc-ctic.ca
To serve the software development profession by developing joint ventures in courseware design & delivery, by integrating training & education processes, by helping to ensure sufficient supply & quality of new entrants to the profession & by promoting an attractive image & definition of software workers
Faye West, Chair

Information Resource Management Association of Canada (IRMAC)
PO Box 5639, Stn. A, Toronto ON M5W 1N8
Tel: 416-712-9932
www.irmac.ca
To provide a forum for members to exchange information about data administration & information resource management
Ron Klein, President
Ruxandra Petolescu, Vice-President
Jonathan Pinchefsky, Secretary
Rezelline Tan, Treasurer

Information Technology Association of Canada (ITAC) / Association canadienne de la technologie de l'information
#801, 5090 Explorer Dr., Mississauga ON L4W 4T9
Tel: 905-602-8345; *Fax:* 905-602-8346
info@itac.ca
www.itac.ca
Represents 1,300 companies in the computing & telecommunications hardware, software, services & electronic content sectors; identifies & leads on issues that affect the industry; advocates initiatives to enable continued growth & development.
Karna Gupta, President
Bill Munson, Vice President
Carlo Viola, Director, Finance
Alberta Fraccaro, Accounting Coordinator

The Instrumentation, Systems & Automation Society of America (ISA)
PO Box 12277, 67 T.W. Alexander Dr., Research Triangle Park NC 27709 USA
Tel: 919-549-8411; *Fax:* 919-549-8288
info@isa.org
www.isa.org
Social Media: www.facebook.com/InternationalSocietyOfAutomation; twitter.com/ISA_Interchange
To be the foremost worldwide society involved with the science & application of measurement & control technologies; To advance members' competence, professionalism & recognition
Patrick Gouhin, Executive Director
Ken Hilgers, Director, Finance & Administration, Customer Service, & Facility Operations

National Capital FreeNet (NCF) / Libertel de la Capitale Nationale
Trailhead Building, #302, 1960 Scott St., Ottawa ON K1Z 8L8
Tel: 613-520-9001; *Fax:* 613-520-3524
ncf@ncf.ca
www.ncf.ca
Free, computer-based information sharing network; links the people & organization of the National Capital region; provides useful information & enables an open exchange of ideas with the world; prepares people for full participation in a rapidly changing communications environment

Newfoundland & Labrador Association of Technology Companies (NLATC)
#5, 391 Empire Ave., St. John's NL A1E 1W6
Tel: 709-772-8324; *Fax:* 709-757-6284
info@nati.net
www.nati.net
Social Media: twitter.com/NATI_NL
To act collectively for technical organizations in Newfoundland industry in cooperation with educational & public sectors to promote the growth of innovative technical industries in Newfoundland & Labrador & the rest of Canada
Ron Taylor, Chief Executive Officer

reBOOT Canada
#110, 136 Geary Ave., Toronto ON M6H 4H1
Tel: 416-534-6017; *Fax:* 416-534-6083
rose@rebootcanada.ca
www.rebootcanada.ca

Refurbishes old computers received from individual & corporate donors & distributes them, free of charge, to other charitable organizations
Nicholas Brinckman, Executive Director

Insurance Industry

Advocis
#209, 390 Queens Quay West, Toronto ON M5V 3A2
Tel: 416-444-5251; *Fax:* 416-444-8031
Toll-Free: 800-563-5822
info@advocis.ca
www.advocis.ca
To represent what our members do best - Advice & Advocacy; to carry on the tradition of effectively representing our members' interests with all levels of government, regulators, & industry, always with the intention of putting the interests of consumers first
Dean Owen, Chair
Greg Pollock, President & CEO

Canadian Association of Blue Cross Plans (CABCP) / Association Canadienne des Croix Bleue (ACCB)
Stn. 2000, Toronto ON M9C 5P1
Toll-Free: 888-261-4033
www.bluecross.ca
To maintain & monitor standards of performance by association members; to ensure members manage effectively supplementary health, dental, life insurance, & disability income products on an individual and group basis

Canadian Association of Mutual Insurance Companies (CAMIC) / Association canadienne des compagnies d'assurance mutuelles (ACCAM)
#205, 311 McArthur Ave., Ottawa ON K1L 6P1
Tel: 613-789-6851; *Fax:* 613-789-7665
nlafreniere@camic.ca
www.camic.ca
To provide information, research, advocacy to its members in areas of general concerns & to negotiate supply agreements for goods & services of common needs. Objectives: to promote a strong, health and competitive insurance market; to support regulatory efficiency and legislative change; to inform member companies on matters affecting the industry and to build consensus on action plans; to promote self-regulation for the property and casualty insurance industry
Normand Lafrenière, President

Canadian Board of Marine Underwriters (CBMU)
#100, 2233 Argentia Rd., Mississauga ON L5N 2X7
Tel: 905-826-4768; *Fax:* 905-826-4873
info@cbmu.com
www.cbmu.com
To procure & disseminate information of interest to marine underwriters & others; To facilitate the exchange of views & ideas which work to improve the marine underwriting industry & marine insurance; To promote & protect the interest of the underwriting community
Brent Chorney, President
Halyna Troian, Administrator
Amanda Curtis, Secretary-Treasurer

Canadian Independent Adjusters' Association (CIAA) / Association canadienne des experts indépendants (ACEI)
Centennial Centre, #100, 5401 Eglinton Ave. West, Toronto ON M9C 5K6
Tel: 416-621-6222; *Fax:* 416-621-7776
Toll-Free: 877-255-5589
info@ciaa-adjusters.ca
www.ciaa-adjusters.ca
To provide leadership for independent adjusters in Canada; To develop & maintain high standards of professionalism; To represent the interests of independent adjusters at the regional, provincial, & national levels
Patricia M. Battle, Executive Director
Patti M. Kernaghan, President
Mary Charman, 1st Vice-President
Greg G. Merrithew, 2nd Vice-President
Marie C. Gallagher, Secretary
Randy P. LaBrash, Treasurer, Randy.Labrash@crawco.ca

Canadian Institute of Actuaries (CIA) / Institut canadien des actuaires (ICA)
Secretariat, #1740, 360 Albert St., Ottawa ON K1R 7X7
Tel: 613-236-8196; *Fax:* 613-233-4552
secretariat@actuaries.ca
www.actuaries.ca
To set & ensure educational & professional standards for members; To operate a review & disciplinary system; To maintain liaison with government authorities & other professions & organizations; To promote research
Michel C. Simard, Executive Director
Lynn Blackburn, Director, Member Services & Standards Development
Les Dandridge, Director, Communications & Public Affairs
Jacques Leduc, Director, Operations, Finance, & Administration
Alicia Rollo, Director, Education & Professional Development

Canadian Life & Health Insurance Association Inc. (CLHIA) / Association canadienne des compagnies d'assurances de personnes inc.
#1700, 1 Queen St. East, Toronto ON M5C 2X9
Tel: 416-777-2221; *Fax:* 416-777-1895
info@clhia.ca
www.clhia.ca
To represent the interests of member life & health insurance companies
George Mohacsi, Chair
Frank Swedlove, President
Wendy Hope, Vice-President, External Relations

Centre for Study of Insurance Operations (CSIO) / Centre d'étude de la pratique d'assurance (CEPA)
#500, 110 Yonge St., Toronto ON M5C 1T4
Tel: 416-360-1773; *Fax:* 416-364-1482
Toll-Free: 800-463-2746
helpdesk@csio.com
www.csio.com
To act as the national standards association for property & casualty insurance by representing property & casualty industry initiatives; To provide a competitive advantage for the independent broker distribution channel
Robert Fitzgerald, Chair
Steven Kaukinen, President
Francine Davis, Manager, EDI & Forms Standards
Sebastian Penalosa, Manager, Network & Membership Services
Connie Strange, Manager, XML Standards

Chambre de l'assurance de dommages (CHAD)
#1200, 999, boul de Maisonneuve ouest, Montréal QC H3A 3L4
Tél: 514-842-2591; *Téléc:* 514-842-3138
Ligne sans frais: 800-361-7288
info@chad.qc.ca
www.chad.ca
Assurer la protection du public en matière d'assurance de dommages et d'expertise en règlement de sinistres; encadrer de façon préventive et disciplinaire la pratique professionnelle des individus et des organisations oeuvrant dans ces domaines
Jacques Yelle, Chairman
Serge Lyras, Président

Chambre de la sécurité financière (CSF)
300, rue Léo-Pariseau, 26e étage, Montréal QC H2X 4B8
Tél: 514-282-5777; *Téléc:* 514-282-2225
Ligne sans frais: 800-361-9989
renseignements@chambresf.com
www.chambresf.com
Mèdia social: www.facebook.com/130907696934893
Assurer la protection du public en maintenant la discipline et en veillant à la formation et à la déontologie de ses membres
Luc Labelle, Président et chef de la direction

Facility Association
PO Box 121, #2400, 777 Bay St., Toronto ON M5G 2C8
Tel: 416-863-1750; *Fax:* 416-868-0894
Toll-Free: 800-268-9572
mail@facilityassociation.com
www.facilityassociation.com
To ensure the availability of automobile insurance for owners & licensed drivers of motor vehicles who may otherwise have difficulty obtaining such insurance.
David J. Simpson, President & CEO

Financial Services Commission of Ontario (FSCO) / Commission des services financiers de l'Ontario (CSFO)
PO Box 85, 5160 Yonge St., 17th Fl., Toronto ON M2N 6L9
Tel: 416-250-7250; *Fax:* 416-590-7070
Toll-Free: 800-668-0128
contactcentre@fsco.gov.on.ca
www.fsco.gov.on.ca
To provide regulatory services that protect the public interest; to make recommendations to the Min. of Finance about the regulared sectors; to provide resources for the proper functioning of the Tribunal
John Solursh, Chair

GAMA International Canada / GAMA International du Canada
#209, 390 Queens Quay West, Toronto ON M4V 3A2
Tel: 416-444-5251; *Fax:* 416-444-8031
Toll-Free: 800-563-5822
info@gamacanada.com
www.gamacanada.com
To focus on professional development for leaders involved in the distribution of financial services
Greg D. Powell, President

Groupement des assureurs automobiles (GAA)
Tour de la Bourse, CP 336, #2410, 800 Place-Victoria, Montréal QC H3A 3C6
Tél: 514-288-4321; *Ligne sans frais:* 877-288-4321
cinfo@gaa.qc.ca
www.gaa.qc.ca
Administrer, de façon efficace et selon les décisions du conseil d'administration, tous les mandats certifiés au Groupement des assureurs automobiles par la Loi sur l'assurance automobile du Québec
Brigitte Corbeil, Directeur général

L'Institut d'assurance de dommages du Québec (IADQ)
#2230, 1200, av McGill College, Montréal QC H3B 4G7
Tél: 514-393-8156; *Téléc:* 514-393-9222
montrealcourriel@institutdassurance.ca
www.iadq.qc.ca/informa/
Organiser des cours, des séminaires et des conférences; promouvoir le rayonnement des titres professionnels PAA et FPAA d'assurance du Canada (AIAC & FIAC). Organisme sans but lucratif, qui a été mis sur pied par l'industrie de l'assurance de dommages pour donner la formation professionnelle à tous ceux qui oeuvrent dans ce secteur au Québec
Nancy LaMontagne, Présidente

Insurance Brokers Association of Alberta (IBAA)
3010 Calgary Trail, Edmonton AB T6J 6V4
Tel: 780-424-3320; *Fax:* 780-424-7418
Toll-Free: 800-318-0197
ibaa@ibaa.ca; education@ibaa.ca; convention@ibaa.ca
www.ibaa.ca
To preserve & strengthen insurance brokers
Ginny Bannerman, Chief Executive Officer
Karen Dyberg, President
Dean Bailey, Vice-President

Insurance Brokers Association of British Columbia (IBABC)
#1300, 1095 West Pender St., Vancouver BC V6E 2M6
Tel: 604-606-8000; *Fax:* 604-683-7831
www.ibabc.org
To promote the member insurance broker as the premiere distributor of general insurance products & services in British Columbia
Charles (Chuck) Byrne, Executive Director
Trudy Lancelyn, Deputy Executive Director

Insurance Brokers Association of Manitoba (IBAM)
#205, 530 Kenaston Blvd., Winnipeg MB R3N 1Z4
Tel: 204-488-1857; *Fax:* 204-489-0316
Toll-Free: 800-204-5649
info@ibam.mb.ca
www.ibam.mb.ca
To promote insurance brokers as the primary providers of insurance products & services in Manitoba
David Schioler, Chief Executive Officer

Insurance Brokers Association of New Brunswick (IBANB) / Association des courtiers d'assurances du Nouveau-Brunswick
PO Box 1523, #201, 590 Brunswick St., Fredericton NB E3B 5G2
Tel: 506-450-2898; *Fax:* 506-450-1494
ibanb@nbinsurancebrokers.ca
www.ibanb.org
To champion the professional, independent insurance broker system in New Brunswick
Georges Leger, President
Linda M. Dawe, CEO

Insurance Brokers Association of Newfoundland (IBAN)
Chimo Bldg., 151 Crosbie Rd., 3rd Floor, St. John's NL A1B 4B4
Tel: 709-726-4450; *Fax:* 709-754-4399
iban@nfld.net
www.iban.ca
Association of insurance brokers in Newfoundland. Insurance brokers work on behalf of clients to secure the best coverage in the market from federally regulated insurance companies
Mary Geralyn Rahal, Office Administrator

Insurance Brokers Association of Nova Scotia (IBANS)
380 Bedford Hwy, Halifax NS B3M 2L4
Tel: 902-876-0526; *Fax:* 902-876-0527
info@ibans.com
www.ibans.com
To promote the independent insurance broker as the premier distributor of property & casualty insurance products & other related insurance services in Nova Scotia
Stephen Greene, Executive Director

Insurance Brokers Association of Ontario (IBAO)
#700, 1 Eglinton Ave. East, Toronto ON M4P 3A1
Tel: 416-488-7422; *Fax:* 416-488-7526
Toll-Free: 800-268-8845
contact@ibao.com
www.ibao.org
To act as the authoritative voice of independent brokers in Ontario; To serve the interests of member brokers; To preserve & enhance the value & integrity of the independent broker insurance distribution system
Randy Carroll, CEO
Bryan Yetman, President
Peter Blodgett, Chair

Insurance Brokers Association of Prince Edward Island
c/o Hyndman & Co. Limited, PO Box 790, 57 Queen St., Charlottetown PE C1A 4A5
Tel: 902-566-4244; *Fax:* 902-566-5990
hyndmaninsurance@anchorgroup.com
Helen Hyndman, Contact

Insurance Brokers' Association of Saskatchewan (IBAS)
#305, 2631 - 28 Ave., Regina SK S4S 6X3
Tel: 306-525-5900; *Fax:* 306-569-3018
IBASinfo@ibas.sk.ca
www.ibas.sk.ca
Social Media: www.facebook.com/270988899613418
To promote & preserve the independent insurance brokerage system as a secure, knowledgeable, cost-effective, customer-oriented, professional method of insurance delivery
Barry Seaborn, President

Insurance Institute of British Columbia (IIBC)
#1110, 800 West Pender St., Vancouver BC V6C 2V6
Tel: 604-681-5491; *Fax:* 604-681-5479
Toll-Free: 888-681-5491
IIBCmail@insuranceinstitute.ca
www.iibc.org
Danielle Bolduc, General Manager
Shaun Sinclair, President
Pierre Chavigny, Sec.-Treas.

Insurance Institute of Canada (IIC) / Institut d'assurance du Canada (IAC)
18 King St. East, 16th Fl., Toronto ON M5C 1C4
Tel: 416-362-8586; *Fax:* 416-362-4239
Toll-Free: 866-362-8585
GTAmail@insuranceinstitute.ca
www.insuranceinstitute.ca
To design, develop, & delivers insurance educational programs & texts; To prepare examinations & awards diplomas; To provide a graduate society; To develop career information on behalf of the property/casualty insurance industry
Peter G. Hohman, President & CEO

Insurance Institute of Manitoba (IIM)
#533, 167 Lombard Ave., Winnipeg MB R3B 0V3
Tel: 204-956-1702; *Fax:* 204-956-0758
iimmail@insuranceinstitute.ca
www.insuranceinstitute.ca
To provide educational services in the general insurance industry in both English and French, such as the Chartered Insurance Professional (CIP), & Fellow Chartered Insurance Professional (FCIP) programs
Ted Teterenko, President
Jennifer Tougas, Manager

Insurance Institute of New Brunswick (IINB)
#101, 1010 St-George Blvd., Moncton NB E1E 4R5
Tel: 506-386-5896; *Fax:* 506-386-1130
IINBmail@insuranceinstitute.ca
www.insuranceinstitute.ca
Monique LeBlanc, Manager
Darrel Coates, President

Insurance Institute of Newfoundland & Labrador Inc. (IINL)
Chimo Bldg., 151 Crosbie Rd., St. John's NL A1B 4B4
Tel: 709-754-4398; *Fax:* 709-754-4399
www.insuranceinstitute.ca
Cathy Mercer, Manager

Insurance Institute of Northern Alberta (IINA)
202 Solar Court, 10350 - 124 St., Edmonton AB T5N 3V9
Tel: 780-424-1268; *Fax:* 780-420-1940
IINAmail@insuranceinstitute.ca
www.insuranceinstitute.ca
The Insurance Institute of Northern Alberta provides products and sevices to the general insurance industry, and ensures the maintenance of a uniform standard of education for the general Insurance Business throughout Canada
Dawn Horne, Manager

Insurance Institute of Nova Scotia (IINS)
#503, 73 Tacoma Dr., Dartmouth NS B2W 3Y6
Tel: 902-433-0070; *Fax:* 902-433-0072
IINSmail@insuranceinstitute.ca
www.insuranceinstitute.ca
To provide educational products & services to the general insurance industry, such as the Chartered Insurance Professional (CIP) & the Fellow Chartered Insurance Professional (FCIP) designation programs
Sandra Reinders, President
Susanne Paulsen, Treasurer
Jenny Renyo, Manager

Insurance Institute of Ontario (IIO)
18 King St. East, 16th Fl., Toronto ON M5C 1C4
Tel: 416-362-8586; *Fax:* 416-362-8081
agervasio@insuranceinstitute.ca
www.insuranceinstitute.ca
To deliver general insurance educational services in English & French, which are consistent with the standardized curriculum offered throughout Canada, such as the Fellow Chartered Insurance Professional (FCIP) & the Fellow Chartered Insurance Professional (FCIP) designation programs
André Fredette, President
Paul Martin, Sr. Vice-President
Linda Wahrer, Secretary
Randy Bushey, Treasurer
Peter Hohman, Manager

Insurance Institute of Prince Edward Island (IIPEI)
PO Box 811, 51 University Ave., Charlottetown PE C1A 4K8
Tel: 902-892-1692; *Fax:* 902-368-7305
IIPEImail@insuranceinstitute.ca
www.insuranceinstitute.ca
Monique LeBlanc, Manager

Insurance Institute of Saskatchewan (IIS)
#310, 2631 - 28 Ave., Regina SK S4S 6X3
Tel: 306-525-9799; *Fax:* 306-569-3018
IISmail@insuranceinstitute.ca
www.insuranceinstitute.ca
To offer educational products & services to the general insurance industry in both English & French, such as the Fellow Chartered Insurance Professional (FCIP) & the Chartered Insurance Professional (CIP) designation programs
Jennifer Meshka, President
Lisa Todd, Secretary
Joanne Duke, Manager

Insurance Institute of Southern Alberta (IISA)
#1110, 833 - 4 Ave. SW, Calgary AB T2P 3T5
Tel: 403-266-3427; *Fax:* 403-269-3199
IISAmail@insuranceinstitute.ca
www.insuranceinstitute.ca
To advance the efficiency, expertise & ability of people employed in the insurance & financial services industry
Caroline Logan, Manager

LOMA Canada
675 Cochrane Dr., East Tower, 6th Floor, Markham ON L3R 0B8
Tel: 905-530-2302; *Fax:* 905-530-2001
lomacanada@loma.org
www.lomacanada.org
To serve its member companies by encouraging & assisting individuals to acquire knowledge & understanding of business of life & health insurance & related financial services.
Brent Lemanski, Resident Director, Canada

Marine Insurance Association of British Columbia (MIABC)
c/o Coast Underwriters Ltd., #1610, 200 Granville St., Vancouver BC V6C 1S4
Tel: 604-629-3820; *Fax:* 604-629-8561
www.m-i-a-b-c.org
To represent the goals & interests of the marine insurance industry in British Columbia

Nuclear Insurance Association of Canada (NIAC) / Association canadienne d'assurance nucléaire
c/o CGI, 150 Commerce Valley Dr. West, Lock Box 200, Markham ON L3T 7Z3
Tel: 905-695-6657; *Fax:* 905-771-5312
NIAC is a voluntary, non-profit association of insurers. Members may provide insurance protection by participation in property and liability pools; the association underwrites and accepts nuclear risks located within Canadian territorial limits for Nuclear Liability and Physical Damage (liability &/or property insurance)
Colleen P. DeMerchant, Assistant Manager

Ontario Insurance Adjusters Association (OIAA)
29 De Jong Dr., Mississauga ON L5M 1B9
Tel: 905-542-0576; *Fax:* 905-542-1301
Toll-Free: 888-259-1555
manager@oiaa.com
www.oiaa.com
To promote & maintain a high standard of ethics in the business of insurance claims adjusting
Norman McGlashan, President

Ontario Mutual Insurance Association (OMIA)
PO Box 3187, 350 Pinebush Rd., Cambridge ON N3H 4S6
Tel: 519-622-9220; *Fax:* 519-622-9227
information@omia.com
www.omia.com
To assist mutual insurance companies to achieve excellence in service provision

Regroupement des cabinets de courtage d'assurance du Québec (RCCAQ) / Insurance Brokers Association of Québec - Assembly
Complexe Saint-Charles, #550, 1111 rue Saint-Charles Ouest, Tour Est, Longueuil QC J4K 8G4
Tél: 450-674-6258; *Téléc:* 450-674-3609
Ligne sans frais: 800-516-6258
info@rccaq.com
www.rccaq.com
Promouvoir les intérêts socio-économiques des membres
Mario Lanouette, Président
Johanne Lamanque, Directrice générale

Reinsurance Research Council (RRC) / Conseil de recherche en réassurance (CRR)
#7, 296 Jarvis St., Toronto ON M5B 2C5
Tel: 416-968-0183; *Fax:* 416-968-6818
mail@rrccanada.org
www.rrccanada.org
Represents the majority of professional reinsurers registered in Canada; conducts research into all lines of property/casualty reinsurance, presents the views of its members where appropriate, and provides liaison with governments, the primary insurance market, & other interested parties; promotes high standards of service and ethical business practices; develops and maintains cordial relations among members and with kindred associations and the public
Anthony Laycock, General Manager

Risk & Insurance Management Society Inc. (RIMS)
c/o Thomas Oystrick, RIMS Canada Council, Mount Royal University, 4825 Mount Royal Gate SW, Calgary AB T3E 6K6
canada@rims.org; membership@rims.org
www.rimscanada.ca
Social Media:
www.facebook.com/group.php?gid=258125305110;
twitter.com/rimsorg
To advance the practice of risk management in Canada
Bonnie Wasser, Canadian Consultant
Tino Brambilla, Chair, RIMS Canada Council
Thomas Oystrick, Treasurer, RIMS Canada Council
Bruce Tainsh, Membership Coordinator, RIMS Canada Council
Phil Corbeil, Chair, Communications & External Affairs Committee
Marley Drainville, Chair, National Conference Committee
Dave Jackson, Chair, National Education Committee

Saskatchewan Municipal Hail Insurance Association (SMHI)
2100 Cornwall St., Regina SK S4P 2K7
Tel: 306-569-1852; *Fax:* 306-522-3717
Toll-Free: 877-414-7644
smhi@smhi.ca
www.smhi.ca
To provide spot-loss hail insurance coverage to Saskatchewan grain farmers at cost
Rodney Schoettler, CEO
Mark Holfeld, COO

Society of Public Insurance Administrators of Ontario (SPIAO)
c/o The Municipality Of Clarington, 40 Temperance St., Bowmanville ON L1C 3A6
info@spiao.ca
www.spiao.ca
To exchange knowledge & pursue matters dealing with risk & insurance management; to promote cooperation among all local government bodies which have interests in the field of risk & insurance management; to encourage development of educational training programs; to collect & disperse information
Nancy Taylor, Treasurer

Underwriters' Laboratories of Canada (ULC) / Laboratoires des assureurs du Canada
7 Underwriters Rd., Toronto ON M1R 3A9
Tel: 416-757-3611; *Fax:* 416-757-8727
Toll-Free: 866-937-3852
ulcinfo@ulc.ca
www.ulc.ca
ULC is an independent product safety testing, certification & inspection organization. It supports domestic governmental product safety regulations, & works with international safety systems to help further trade with adherence to local safety requirements. It develops & publishes standards, classifications & specifications for products as they relate to fire, accident or property hazards, electrical safety.
Martin Oughton, President & Gen. Mgr.

Interior Design

Associated Designers of Canada (ADC)
#201, 192 Spadina Ave., Toronto ON M5T 2C2
Tel: 416-410-4209; *Fax:* 416-703-6601
Toll-Free: 800-361-2721
www.designers.ca
To promote, pursue & protect the interests & needs of set, costume, lighting & sound designers working in Canada
Jackie McAlpine, Contact

Association des designers industriels du Québec (ADIQ)
CP 182, Succ. Rosemont, Montréal QC H1X 3B7
Tél: 514-287-6531; *Téléc:* 514-278-3049
info@adiq.ca (Noémi Marquis)
www.adiq.ca
Mission est du soutenir, représenter et promourvoir les membres professionels et mettre en valeur la profession.
Mario Gagnon, Président
Assam Michel Daoud, Vice-président

Association of Canadian Industrial Designers (ACID) / Association des designers industriels du Canada
157 Adelaide St. West, Toronto ON M5H 4E7
info@designcanada.org
www.designcanada.org
To represent Canadian industrial designers throughout world. The ACID represents the collective interests of designers and is dedicated to increasing the knowledge, skill and proficiency of its members through networking, discussion forums, seminars and trade events.

Association of Interior Designers of Nova Scotia (IDNS)
PO Box 2042, Halifax NS B3J 3B4
Tel: 902-425-4367
info@idns.ca
www.idns.ca
Interior Designers of Nova Scotia (IDNS) is a professional association of registered Interior Designers. IDNA promotes the profession and its mandate acts to serve both the interests of public and the interior design industry. IDNS: protects the health, safety, and well-being of the general public, develops and maintains standards of practice of interior design; encourages the continuing education of practicing interior designers; upholds the Code of Ethics for the professional practice of interior design; promotes and extends the profession of interior design by providing a liaison between the profession and the public.
Keri Koch, President

Association of Registered Interior Designers of New Brunswick (ARIDNB) / Association des designers d'intérieur immatriculés du Nouveau-Brunswick (ADIINB)
PO Box 1541, Fredericton NB E3B 5G2
Tel: 506-459-3014
info@aridnb.ca
www.aridnb.ca
To establish & maintain standards of knowledge, skill, & professional ethics among association members; To serve the public interest by governing the practice of interior design in New Brunswick
Daphne Rae, President
Louise Duguay, Vice-President
Sara Dunton, Treasurer & Registrar
Lyn Van Tassel, Secretary

Association of Registered Interior Designers of Ontario (ARIDO)
#220, 6 Adelaide St. East, Toronto ON M5C 1H6
Tel: 416-921-2127; *Fax:* 416-921-3660
Toll-Free: 800-334-1180
adminoffice@arido.ca
www.arido.ca
To govern the conduct & professional standards of members; To increase awareness of the profession & ensure rights of interior designers & the public they serve
Susan Wiggins, Executive Director

Association professionnelle des designers d'intérieur du Québec (APDIQ)
#101, 465, rue Saint-Jean, Montréal QC H2Y 2R6
Tél: 514-284-6263
www.apdiq.com
Promouvoir la reconnaissance des designers d'intérieur comme ordre professionnel; assurer la qualité de leurs services; les regrouper pour faire évoluer leur profession; veiller aux intérêts du public; édicter et assurer le respect des règles d'éthique professionnelle
André Lapointe, Président

British Columbia Industrial Designer Association (BCID)
PO Box 33943, Vancouver BC V6J 4L7
Tel: 604-608-3204; *Fax:* 604-608-3204
email@bcid.com
www.bcid.com
The Association is the public voice for its members, representing their interests nationally. It maintains a set of standards to preserve the integrity of the profession, and keeps a register of professional industrial designers in the province.

Interior Designers Association of Saskatchewan (IDAS)
PO Box 32005, Stn. Erindale, Saskatoon SK S7S 1N8
Tel: 306-343-3311; *Fax:* 306-249-3011
char.vaughn@sasktel.net
www.idas.ca
To promote an understanding of the profession to the public & to support members in their profession through continuing education & networking
Charlene Vaughn, President

Interior Designers Institute of British Columbia (IDIBC)
#400, 601 West Broadway, Vancouver BC V5Z 4C2
Tel: 604-298-5211; *Fax:* 604-421-5211
info@idibc.org
www.idibc.org
To act as the single representative voice of the Interior Design profession in British Columbia; to advance the profession through public recognition & provide leadership & services to members through programs, communication & education; to benefit public health, safety & welfare, contribute to the enhancement of the environment & increase the perception, appreciation & value of design in the community.
Alyssa Myshok, President

Interior Designers of Alberta (IDA)
PO Box 21171, Edmonton AB T6R 2V4
Tel: 780-413-0013; *Fax:* 780-413-0076
info@interiordesignalberta.com
www.interiordesignalberta.com
Michele Gunn, President
Jill Lane, Association Manager

Interior Designers of Canada (IDC) / Designers d'intérieur du Canada
#220, 6 Adelaide St. East, Toronto ON M5C 1H6
Tel: 416-649-4425; *Fax:* 416-921-3660
Toll-Free: 877-443-4425
www.idcanada.org
Social Media: www.facebook.com/147037918674277?v=info; twitter.com/IDCanadaTweets
To advance the interior design industry in Canada through high standards of education for the profession, professional responsibility, professional development, & communication
Susan Wiggins, Executive Director

Professional Interior Designers Institute of Manitoba
137 Bannatyne Ave. East, 2nd Fl., Winnipeg MB R3B 0R3
Tel: 204-925-4625; *Fax:* 204-925-4624
pidim@shaw.ca
www.pidim.ca

International Cooperation/International Relations

AFS Interculture Canada (AFSIC)
1425, boul René-Lévesque ouest, Montréal QC H3G 1T7
Tel: 514-288-3282; *Fax:* 514-843-9119
Toll-Free: 800-361-7248
info-canada@afs.org
www.afscanada.org
Social Media: www.facebook.com/afsinterculturecanada
To promote global education & international development through intercultural exchange programs for both young people & adults; To offer international internships; To work as part of the largest network of international exchange programs in the world
M. Miklos Fulop, National Director
Bernard Roy, Executive Director

Aga Khan Foundation Canada
The Delegation of the Ismaili Imamat, 199 Sussex Dr., Ottawa ON K1N 1K6
Tel: 613-237-2532; *Fax:* 613-567-2532
Toll-Free: 800-267-2532
info@akfc.ca
www.akfc.ca
To support cost-effective development projects in Asia & Africa in the fields of primary health care, education & rural development, with special attention paid to the needs of women. Major initiatives include: The Pakistan-Canada Social Institutions Development Program; the Tajikistan Institutional Support Program and the Non-Formal Education Program of the Bangladesh Rural Advancement Committee.
Khalil Z. Shariff, CEO

Atlantic Council of Canada (ACC) / Conseil atlantique du Canada (CAC)
Stn. 701, 165 University Ave., Toronto ON M5H 3B8
Tel: 416-979-1875; *Fax:* 416-979-0825
info@atlantic-council.ca
www.atlantic-council.ca
To inform Canadians of the purpose & benefits of Canada's membership in the Atlantic Alliance & NATO.
Julie Lindhout, President
Goran S. Pesic, Executive Director

Canada World Youth (CWY) / Jeunesse Canada Monde (JCM)
2330, rue Notre-Dame ouest, 3e étage, Montréal QC H3J 1N4
Tel: 514-931-3526; *Fax:* 514-939-2621
Toll-Free: 800-605-3526
recruitment@cwy-jcm.org
www.canadaworldyouth.org
Social Media: www.facebook.com/group.php?gid=6244934985
To increase people's ability to participate actively in the development of just, harmonious & sustainable societies; To create exceptional learning opportunities for communities, groups & individuals wishing to acquire skills & explore new ideas.
Iris Almeida-Côté, President & CEO
Iris Almeida-Côté, President/CEO

Canadian Association for Latin American & Caribbean Studies (CALACS) / Association canadienne des études latino-américaines et caraïbes (ACELAC)
c/o Juan Pablo Crespo Vasquez, York Research Tower, York University, #8-17, 4700 Keele St., Toronto ON M3J 1P3
Tel: 416-736-2100; *Fax:* 519-971-3610
calacs@yorku.ca
www.can-latam.org
To facilitate networking & the exchange of information among those engaged in teaching & research on Latin America & the Caribbean in Canada & abroad; To foster throughout Canada, especially within the universities, colleges, & other centres of higher education, the expansion of information on & interest in Latin America & the Caribbean; To represent the academic & professional interest of Canadian Latin Americanists
Pablo Crespo Vasquez Juan, Contact, Administration
Steven Palmer, Secretary-Treasurer

Canadian Association for the Study of International Development (CASID) / L'Association canadienne d'études du développement international (ACEDI)
c/o The North-South Institute, #500, 55 Murray St., Ottawa ON K1N 5M3
Tel: 613-241-3535; *Fax:* 613-241-7435
charmain.levy@uqo.ca
www.casid-acedi.ca
National, bilingual, interdisciplinary & pluralistic association devoted to the study of international development in all parts of the world
Charmain Lévy, President, charmain.levy@uqo.ca

Canadian Commission for UNESCO / Commission canadienne pour l'UNESCO
PO Box 1047, 350 Albert St., Ottawa ON K1P 5V8
Tel: 613-566-4414; *Fax:* 613-566-4405
Toll-Free: 800-263-5588
info@unesco.ca
www.unesco.ca
An arm's length agency of the Government of Canada; to promote Canadian participation in the programmes & activities of UNESCO; to advise the government of Canada on its policies toward UNESCO; to act as a forum for Canadian civil society & government to discuss matters relating to UNESCO
David A. Walden, Secretary-General

Canadian Council for International Co-operation (CCIC) / Conseil canadien pour la coopération internationale
#200, 45 Rideau St., Ottawa ON K1N 5Z4
Tel: 613-241-7007; *Fax:* 613-241-5302
info@ccic.ca
www.ccic.ca
To work globally to achieve sustainable human development; To seek to end global poverty; To promote social justice & human dignity for all
Jim Cornelius, Chair
Julia Sánchez, President & Chief Executive Officer
Anna Campos, Officer, Finance & Administration
Chantal Havard, Officer, Government Relations & Communications
Fraser Reilly-King, Policy Analyst, Aid & International Co-operation
Shams Alibhai, Treasurer

Canadian Foundation for the Americas (FOCAL) / Fondation canadienne pour les Amériques
#720, 1 Nicholas St., Ottawa ON K1N 7B7
Tel: 613-562-0005; *Fax:* 613-562-2525
focal@focal.ca
www.focal.ca
To foster informed & timely debate & dialogue on issues of importance to decision-makers throughout Canada & the Americas; to develop a greater understanding of important hemispheric issues & to help build a stronger community of the Americas
Carlo Dade, Executive Director
Madeleine Bélanger, Director, Communications

Canadian Friends of Burma (CFOB) / Les Amis canadiens de la Birmanie
#206, 145 Spruce St., Ottawa ON K1R 6P1
Tel: 613-237-8056; *Fax:* 613-563-0017
cfob@cfob.org
www.cfob.org
To promote democracy & human rights in Burma by working within the global movement, & educating & activating Canadian involvement in the struggle for peace in Burma
Tin Maung Htoo, Executive Director
Toe Kyi, Director, Information Technology
Ashley Stewart, Director, Media & Community Relations
Kevin McLoed, Researcher

Canadian Friends of Ukraine (CFU)
South Bldg., 620 Spadina Ave., 2nd Fl., Toronto ON M5S 2H4
Tel: 416-964-6644; *Fax:* 416-964-6085
canfun@interlog.com
www.canadianfriendsofukraine.com
To strengthen Canadian-Ukrainian relations; To promote democracy & reform in Ukraine
Margareta Shpir, President
John Pidkowich, Vice-President
Lisa Shymko, Executive Director
Walentina Rodak, Treasurer
John Kuzyk, Chair, Canada-Ukraine Library Centres

Canadian Hunger Foundation (CHF)
323 Chapel St., Ottawa ON K1N 7Z2
Tel: 613-237-0180; *Fax:* 613-237-5969
Toll-Free: 866-242-4243
www.chf-partners.ca
To assist local NGOs in developing countries, with particular emphasis on food production, water supply security, & energy
Tony Breuer, Executive Director
Cynthia Farrell, Director, Technical Services
Mary Forbes, Director, Finance
Sandra Kiviaho, Director, Public Engagement
Neil Leslie, Director, Fundraising
Sue MacPherson, Director, Human Resources
Michael Jones, Officer, Communications

Canadian Institute for Conflict Resolution (CICR) / Institut canadien pour la résolution des conflits
c/o St. Paul University, 223 Main St., Ottawa ON K1S 1C4
Tel: 613-235-5800; *Fax:* 613-235-5801
Toll-Free: 866-684-2427
info@cicr-icrc.ca
www.cicr-icrc.ca
To foster, develop & communicate resolution processes for individuals, organizations & communities in Canada & internationally; to embody, within the conflict resolution process, the positive attributes of common sense, sensitivity, compassion & spirituality.
Brian Strom, Executive Director

Canadian Institute of Cultural Affairs / Institut canadien des affaires culturelles
655 Queen St. East, Toronto ON M4M 1G4
Tel: 416-691-2316; *Fax:* 416-691-2491
Toll-Free: 877-691-1422
ica@icacan.ca
www.icacan.ca
To empower people to develop leadership capacity; To contribute to positive social change
Nan Hudson, Executive Director
Staci Kentish, Director, Youth as Facilitative Leaders

Canadian International Council (CIC) / Conseil international du Canada
#210, 45 Willcocks St., Toronto ON M5S 1C7
Tel: 416-946-7209; *Fax:* 416-946-7319
info@opencanada.org; technical@opencanada.org (technical issues)
www.opencanada.org
Social Media: www.facebook.com/CanadianInternationalCouncil; twitter.com/TheCIC; www.youtube.com/user/onlinecicvideos
To strengthen Canada's role in international affairs; To advance research & dialogue on international affairs
Jennifer Jeffs, President
Laura Sunderland, Vice-President, Programs
Deborah Shields, Director, Operations
Kathryn McBride, Administrator, Office

Canadian Peace Alliance (CPA) / Alliance canadienne pour la paix
#13, 427 Bloor St. West, Toronto ON M5S 1X7
Tel: 416-588-5555; *Fax:* 416-588-5556
cpa@web.ca
www.acp-cpa.ca
To involve Canadians in the worldwide movement to stop the arms race, ensure the non-violent settlement of disputes & guarantee the security & well-being of all peoples.
Sid Lacombe, Coordinator

Canadian Physicians for Aid & Relief (CPAR)
1425 Bloor St. West, Toronto ON M6P 3L6
Tel: 416-369-0865; *Fax:* 416-369-0294
Toll-Free: 800-263-2727
info@cpar.ca
www.cpar.ca
Social Media: twitter.com/cpar
To help impoverished communities in developing nations become prosperous, while maintaining harmony with the environment; To tackle all aspects of poverty; To emphasize healthy community empowerment & integrated community based development
Kevin O'Brien, Executive Director
Todd Carmichael, Director, Programs
Dwight Peters, Director, Development
Zemede Russom, Director, Finance
Kathy Johnston, Manager, Human Resources
Roxane Tracey, Manager, Communications & Fundraising

CARE Canada
#200, 9 Gurdwara Rd., Ottawa ON K2E 7X6
Tel: 613-228-5600; *Fax:* 613-226-5777
Toll-Free: 800-267-5232
info@care.ca
www.care.ca
Social Media: www.facebook.com/carecanada; twitter.com/CARE_CAN
To defend dignity and fight poverty by empowering the world's most vulnerable and greatest agent for change: women and girls
Kevin McCort, President/CEO
Gillian Barth, Executive Vice-President

Carrefour de solidarité internationale inc.
165, rue Moore, Sherbrooke QC J1H 1B8
Tél: 819-566-8595; *Téléc:* 819-566-8076
info@csisher.com
www.csisher.com
Susciter la solidarité de la population de l'Estrie pour la justice sociale au plan international.
Marco Labrie, Directeur général

Centre canadien d'étude et de coopération internationale (CECI) / Canadian Centre for International Studies & Cooperation
3000, rue Omer-Lavallée, Montréal QC H1Y 3R8
Tél: 514-875-9911; *Téléc:* 514-875-6469
Ligne sans frais: 877-875-2324
info@ceci.ca
www.ceci.ca
Mèdia social: www.facebook.com/cecicooperation; twitter.com/CECI_Canada; www.youtube.com/commceci
Le CECI combat la pauvreté et l'exclusion; renforce les capacités de développment des communautés défavorisées; appuie des initiatives de paix, de droits humains et d'équité; mobilise des ressources et favorise l'échange de savoir-faire.
Mario Renaud, Executive Director
Suzanne Laporte, Chair

Child Haven International / Accueil international pour l'enfance
19014 - 7th Conc., RR#1, Maxville ON K0C 1T0
Tel: 613-527-2829; *Fax:* 613-527-1118
fred@childhaven.ca
www.childhaven.ca
To assist any child of any nationality who needs in-country care or a private family home; To provide institutions & cottage or village industries for giving training in handcrafts, music, agricultural methods; To promote the integrity of the family by providing help for adolescents or adults who have special needs & by community development & medical aid projects
Fred Cappuccino, Director
Bonnie Cappuccino, Director

Children's International Summer Villages (Canada) Inc. (CISV) / Villages internationaux d'enfants
PO Box 1384, Stn. B, Ottawa ON K1P 5R4
Tel: 613-230-2949
canada@cisv.org
www.cisv.ca
To promote cross-cultural friendship, through educational programs for youth & adults in 60 countries; To prepare indivduals to become active & contributing members of a peaceful society; To stimulate the life-long development of amicable relationships & effective & appropriate leadership towards a fair & just world
Coreen Blackburn, National Secretary

Christian Blind Mission International (CBMI)
PO Box 800, 3844 Stoufville Rd., Stouffville ON L4A 7Z9
Tel: 905-640-6464; *Fax:* 905-640-4332
Toll-Free: 800-567-2264
cbm@cbmcanada.org
www.cbmcanada.org
With core values based on Christian faith, CBMI serves the blind & disabled in the developing world, irrespective of nationality, race, sex, or religion; prevents & treats blindness & other disabilities through medical care, rehabilitation training & integration programs; helps people to help themselves.
Ted Dueck, Chair
Ed Epp, Executive Director

CNEC - Partners International
#56, 8500 Torbram Rd., Brampton ON L6T 5C6
Tel: 905-458-1202; *Fax:* 905-458-4339
Toll-Free: 800-883-7697
info@partnersinternational.ca
www.partnersinternational.ca
Harry Doxsee, Chair

CODE
321 Chapel St., Ottawa ON K1N 7Z2
Tel: 613-232-3569; *Fax:* 613-232-7435
Toll-Free: 800-661-2633
codehq@codecan.org; donor.donateur@codecan.org
www.codecan.org
To enable people to learn by developing partnerships that provide resources for learning, to promote awareness & understanding & to encourage self-reliance; To support training for teachers & librarians; To coordinate book donations from North American publishers to schools & libraries in the developing world
Scott Walter, Executive Director
Brian Coburn, Director, Finance & Administration
Ann Collins, Director, Marketing & Public Engagment
Sean Maddox, Director, Development
Dominique Naud, Manager, Communications

CoDevelopment Canada (CODEV)
#260, 2747 East Hastings St., Vancouver BC V5K 1Z8
Tel: 604-708-1495; *Fax:* 604-708-1497
codev@codev.org
www.codev.org
CoDev is a BC-based, non-profit agency that works for social change in Latin American, facilitating relationships between Northern & Southern organizations that share a commitment to workers' rights, community development & women's rights. It helps organizations involve disenfranchised groups in local decision-making processes, develop policy, & lobby both the public & private sectors. It is a registered charity, BN: 130153463RR0001.
Joey Hartman, President
Barbara Wood, Executive Director

Compassion Canada
PO Box 5591, London ON N6A 5G8
Tel: 519-668-0224; *Fax:* 519-685-1107
Toll-Free: 800-563-5437
info@compassion.ca
www.compassion.ca
To provide sponsors for children in Third World countries; to aid community development projects in cooperation with Canadian International Development Agency; to be an advocate for children, to release them from their spiritual, economic, social & physical poverty & to enable them to become responsible & fulfilled Christian adults
Barry Slauenwhite, President

Conseil canadien de la coopération et de la mutualité (CCCM)
275, rue Bank, 4e étage, Ottawa ON K2P 2L6
Tél: 613-789-5492; *Téléc:* 613-789-0743
info@cccm.coop
www.cccm.coop
Le Conseil vise à promouvoir la coopération en vue du développement socio-économique des communautés francophones du Canada.
Brigitte Gagné, Directrice générale

Conseil de coopération de l'Ontario (CCO)
#201, 435, boul St-Laurent, Ottawa ON K1K 2Z8
Tél: 613-745-8619; *Téléc:* 613-745-4649
Ligne sans frais: 866-290-1168
info@cco.coop
www.cco.coop
Favoriser la prise en charge socio-économique de la communauté francophone de l'Ontario par le biais de la coopération
Luc Morin, Directeur général

Conseil québécois de la coopération et de la mutualité (CCQ)
#204, 5955, rue Saint-Laurent, Lévis QC G6V 3P5
Tél: 418-835-3710; *Téléc:* 418-835-6322
info@coopquebec.coop
www.coopquebec.qc.ca
Organisme de regroupement, sur une base volontaire, des organisations coopératives du Québec pour favoriser l'action concertée de ses membres, promouvoir l'authenticité coopérative, défendre les intérêts de ses membres
Hélène Simard, Présidente

CUSO-VSO
200-44 Eccles St., Ottawa ON K1R 6S4
Tel: 613-829-7445; *Fax:* 613-829-7996
Toll-Free: 888-434-2876
questions@cusointernational.org
www.cusointernational.org
Social Media: www.facebook.com/cusovso; twitter.com/CusoIntl
CUSO-VSO is a non-profit development agency that works through skilled volunteers to aid global social justice; to address poverty, human rights violations, HIV/AIDS, inequity & environmental degradation; to give Canadians information, the experiences & the tools they need to become active global citizens.
Derek Evans, Executive Director
Derek Evans, Executive Director

Forum for International Trade Training (FITT) / Forum pour la formation en commerce international
#300, 116 Lisgar St., Ottawa ON K2P 0C2
Tel: 613-230-3553; *Fax:* 613-230-6808
Toll-Free: 800-561-3488
info@fitt.ca
www.fitt.ca
Committed to providing quality programs' training & certification in international trade designed to prepare businesses & individuals to compete successfully in world markets.
Caroline Tompkins, President

Group of 78 / Groupe des 78
#206, 145 Spruce St., Ottawa ON K1R 6P1
Tel: 613-230-0860; *Fax:* 613-563-0017
group78@web.net
www.web.net/~group78
The association advocates peace, disarmament, sustainable development & strengthening of the United Nations. It is a registered charity, BN : 130562085RR0001.
Richard Harmston, Chair

HOPE International Development Agency
214 Sixth St., New Westminster BC V3L 3A2
Tel: 604-525-5481; *Fax:* 604-525-3471
Toll-Free: 866-525-4673
hope@hope-international.com
www.hope-international.com
Social Media: twitter.com/HOPEInt
To help the poverty-stricken section of Third World people to attain the basic necessities of life; To inform Canadians regarding issues related to the developing world & HOPE's activities; To provide alternative technological & educational support to people in developing countries where enviornmental, economic, &/or social circumstances have interfered with the ability of local communities to sustain themselves by using traditional methods. Other offices in Afghanistan, Australia, Cambodia, Ethiopia, Japan, Myanmar, New Zealand, the U.K., & the U.S.
David S. McKenzie, Executive Director
Aklilu Mulat, COO
John King, Director of Development

Horizons of Friendship (HOF)
PO Box 402, Stn. Main, 50 Covert St., Cobourg ON K9A 4L1
Tel: 905-372-5483; *Fax:* 905-372-7095
Toll-Free: 888-729-9928
info@horizons.ca
www.horizons.ca
To address the root causes of poverty & injustice through the cooperation of people from the south & north; To support Central American & Mexican partner organizations which undertake local initiatives; To raise awareness in Canada of global issues; To work with Canadian organizations at the local & national levels
Patricia Rebolledo, Executive Director

Inter Pares / Among Equals
221 Laurier Ave. East, Ottawa ON K1N 6P1
Tel: 613-563-4801; *Fax:* 613-594-4704
Toll-Free: 866-563-4801
info@interpares.ca
www.interpares.ca
To build equality of people, North & South, by collaborating with & supporting justice for people around the world; Inter Pares applies 4 principles: Leadership by Women, Participation, Sustainability & Respect for Cultural Values
Rita Morbia, Executive Director

International Relief Agency Inc. (IRA)
#84, 95 Wood St., Toronto ON M4Y 2Z3
Tel: 416-928-0901
ira@ica.net
To promote free enterprise, national freedoms & democracy
Adam A. Budzanowski, Director General
Olivia Aquino, Chair
Eileen Brown, Office Manager

Mahatma Gandhi Canadian Foundation for World Peace
PO Box 60002, RPO University of Alberta, Edmonton AB T6G 2S4
Tel: 780-492-5504; *Fax:* 780-492-0113
yhong@ualberta.ca
www.gandhi.ca
To conduct programs & activities that promote the teachings & philosophy of Mahatma Gandhi in order to advance peace & understanding amongst peoples of the world
Prem Kalia, Chair

Manitoba Council for International Cooperation (MCIC) / Conseil du Manitoba pour la coopération internationale
#302, 280 Smith St., Winnipeg MB R3C 1K2
Tel: 204-987-6420; *Fax:* 204-956-0031
info@mcic.ca; mcic@web.ca
www.mcic.ca
Social Media: www.facebook.com/mcic.ca; twitter.com/MCIC_CA
To promote international development that protects the environment; To coordinate the development work of member agencies
Janice Hamilton, Executive Director

The Marquis Project, Inc.
912 Rosser Ave., Brandon MB R7A 0L4
Tel: 204-727-5675; *Fax:* 204-727-5683
marquisp@mts.net
www.marquisproject.com
To inform rural Manitobans of global issues; to link concerns to those of Third World peoples; to encourage concrete positive action in response to global concerns
Lynn Slobogian, Executive Director

Ontario Council for International Cooperation (OCIC) / Conseil de l'Ontario pour la coopération internationale
#209, 344 Bloor St. West, Toronto ON M5S 3A7
Tel: 416-972-6303; *Fax:* 416-972-6996
info@ocic.on.ca
www.ocic.on.ca
Community of Ontario-based international development and global education organizations and individual associate members working globally for social justice
Kimberly Gibbons, Executive Director

Operation Eyesight Universal
4 Parkdale Cres. NW, Calgary AB T2N 3T8
Tel: 403-283-6323; *Fax:* 403-270-1899
Toll-Free: 800-585-8265
info@operationeyesight.ca
www.operationeyesight.ca
Social Media: www.facebook.com/OperationEyesightUniversal; twitter.com/OpEyesight; www.linkedin.com/company/operation-eyesight
To eliminate avoidable blindness through the development & support of permanent, self-sustaining, quality blindness prevention & sight restoration programs for those people in greatest need
Pat Ferguson, President & CEO

Oxfam Canada
39 McArthur Ave., Ottawa ON K1L 8L7
Tel: 613-237-5236; *Fax:* 613-237-0524
Toll-Free: 800-466-9326
info@oxfam.ca; donor_relations@oxfam.ca
www.oxfam.ca
To build solutions for the creation of a fair world, without poverty & injustice
Margaret Hancock, Chair
Don MacMillan, Treasurer

Peace Brigades International (Canada) (PBI)
145 Spruce St., Ottawa ON K1R 6P1
Tel: 613-237-6968
info@pbicanada.org
www.pbicanada.org/home
To explore & implement non-violent approaches to peacekeeping & support for basic human rights; to provide protective accompaniment & peace education training in Colombia, Indonesia, & Mexico
Christine Jones, National Coordinator

Physicians for Global Survival (Canada) (PGS) / Médecins pour la survie mondiale (Canada)
#208, 145 Spruce St., Ottawa ON K1R 6P1
Tel: 613-233-1982; *Fax:* 613-233-9028
pgsadmin@web.ca
www.pgs.ca
Committed to the abolition of nuclear weapons, the prevention of war, the promotion of non-violent means of conflict resolution & social justice in a sustainable world
Nancy Covington, President

Project Peacemakers
745 Westminster Ave., Winnipeg MB R3G 1A5
Tel: 204-775-8178; *Fax:* 204-784-1339
info@projectpeacemakers.org
www.projectpeacemakers.org
Social Media: www.facebook.com/pages/project-peacemakers/108617822532 248

Project Peacemakers is a group of people working for peace from a faith perspective. Its activities are varied, from peace delegations in war zones to educational forums on such issues as child soldiers & violent video games.
Dianne Cooper, Chair

Project Ploughshares
57 Erb St. West, Waterloo ON N2L 6C2
Tel: 519-888-6541; *Fax:* 519-888-0018
plough@ploughshares.ca
www.ploughshares.ca
Ecumenical peace agency of the Canadian Council of Churches that identifies, develops & advances approaches that build peace & prevent war
John Siebert, Executive Director

Saskatchewan Council for International Co-operation (SCIC) / Conseil de la Saskatchewan pour la co-opération internationale
2138 McIntyre St., Regina SK S4P 2R7
Tel: 306-757-4669; *Fax:* 306-757-3226
scic@earthbeat.sk.ca
www.earthbeat.sk.ca
To act as the umbrella organization for international development agencies in Saskatchewan; To distribute international development funds provided by the Government of Saskatchewan; To facilitate communications among member agencies in Saskatchewan and across Canada; To support cooperative government relations, public education, & fundraising

Save a Family Plan (SAFP)
PO Box 3622, London ON N6A 4L4
Tel: 519-672-1115; *Fax:* 519-672-6379
safpinfo@safp.org
www.safp.org
Social Media: twitter.com/SaveaFamilyPlan
Implements sustainable family & community development programs in 5 states in India, with 41 social service societies, 26 homes of health, approximately 10,550 grass roots community organiziations & 15,000 poor families; programs are developed through needs assessments; within all aspects of programming, environmental & gender impact assessments are undertaken. Offices in Canada, the U.S. & India
Lesley Porter, Executive Director
Lois Côté, President

Save the Children - Canada (SCC) / Aide à l'enfance - Canada
#300, 4141 Yonge St., Toronto ON M2P 2A8
Tel: 416-221-5501; *Fax:* 416-221-8214
Toll-Free: 800-668-5036
sccan@savethechildren.ca
www.savethechildren.ca
Social Media: www.facebook.com/savethechildren.ca; twitter.com/SaveChildrenCan
To fight for children's rights; To deliver immediate & lasting improvements to children's lives worldwide in Canada & 10 countries overseas
Patricia Erb, President/CEO

Science for Peace (SfP) / Science et paix
c/o University College, #306A, 15 King's College Circle, Toronto ON M5S 3H7
Tel: 416-978-3606; *Fax:* 416-978-3606
sfp@physics.utoronto.ca
www.scienceforpeace.ca
To understand & act against forces of militarism, social injustice, & environmental destruction
Judith Deutsch, President
Margrit Eichler, Secretary
Chandler Davis, Treasurer

United Nations Association in Canada (UNAC) / Association canadienne pour les Nations-Unies (ACNU)
#300, 309 Cooper St., Ottawa ON K2P 0G5
Tel: 613-232-5751; *Fax:* 613-563-2455
info@unac.org
www.unac.org
To study international problems & Canada's relationship to them as a member of the UN & its related agencies; To foster mutual understanding, goodwill & cooperation between the people of Canada & those of other countries, with the object of promoting peace & justice; To study possible courses of action in the field of international affairs; To work for support by the government & the people of Canada for desirable policies; To furnish information about & stimulate public interest in the UN & its various agencies which have been established for direct or indirect promotion of international order, justice & security; To foster national commitment to principles of multilateralism & international cooperation
Kathryn White, Executive Director

World Federalist Movement - Canada (WFMC)
#207, 145 Spruce St., Ottawa ON K1R 6P1
Tel: 613-232-0647; *Fax:* 613-563-0017
wfcnat@web.ca
www.worldfederalistscanada.org
Education, research, political support for strengthening the United Nations & rule of law in world affairs
Warren Allmand, President
Fergus Watt, Executive Director
Simon Rosenblum, Chair

World University Service of Canada (WUSC) / Entraide universitaire mondiale du Canada (EUMC)
1404 Scott St., Ottawa ON K1Y 2N2
Tel: 613-798-7477; *Fax:* 613-798-0990
Toll-Free: 800-267-8699
wusc@wusc.ca
www.wusc.ca
We believe that all peoples are entitled to the knowledge & skills necessary to contribute to a more equitable world; to foster human development & global understanding through education & training
Chris Eaton, Executive Director
Ravi Gupta, Associate Executive Director

World Vision Canada (WVC) / Vision Mondiale
1 World Dr., Mississauga ON L5T 2Y4
Tel: 905-565-6100; *Fax:* 866-219-8620
Toll-Free: 866-595-5550
info@worldvision.ca
www.worldvision.ca
An international partnership of Christians committed to the poor; a Christian relief organization dedicated to children, families and communities, with a mission to overcome poverty and injustice, and serve all people regardless of religion, race, ethnicity or gender; active in 90+ countries around the world.
Dave Toycen, President & CEO

Labour Relations

ADR Institute of Canada (ADRIC) / Institut d'arbitrage et de médiation du Canada
#405, 234 Eglinton Ave. East, Toronto ON M4P 1K5
Tel: 416-487-4733; *Fax:* 416-487-4429
Toll-Free: 877-475-4353
admin@adrcanada.ca
www.adrcanada.ca
To promote the use of arbitration & mediation (ADR - alternative dispute resolution) to settle disputes; to provide information & education on ADR to practitioners, parties, the public, & the business, professional & government communities; to assist those wishing to use ADR through the provision of Arbitration & Mediation Rules, administrative services, & information about the process & member arbitrators & mediators
Mary Anne Harnick, Executive Director

Association canadienne des relations industrielles (ACRI) / Canadian Industrial Relations Association
Département des relations industrielles, Université Laval, Pavillon J.-A.-deSève, Sainte-Foy QC G1K 7P4
Tél: 418-656-2468; *Téléc:* 418-656-3175
acri-cira@rlt.ulaval.ca
www.cira-acri.ca
Promouvoir la discussion, la recherche, et la formation dans le domaine des relations industrielles
Guy Bellemare, Président
Jean-Noël Grenier, Sec.-trés.

Association of Workers' Compensation Boards of Canada (AWCBC) / Association des commissions des accidents du travail du Canada
6551B Mississauga Rd., Mississauga ON L5N 1A6
Tel: 905-542-3633; *Fax:* 905-542-0039
contact@awcbc.org
www.awcbc.org
To facilitate cooperation among Canadian Boards & Commissions; to foster greater public understanding or dialogue about workplace health & safety & workers' compensation
Brenda Croucher, Executive Director

Canadian Association of Administrators of Labour Legislation (CAALL) / Association canadienne des administrateurs de la législation ouvrière (ACALO)
CAALL Secretariat, Phase II, Place du Portage, 165, rue Hôtel-de-Ville, 8e étage, Gatineau QC K1A 0J2
Tel: 819-953-0969; *Fax:* 819-953-9779
CAALL-secretariat@hrsdc-rhdsc.gc.ca
www.caall-acalo.org/home_e.shtml
To provide a forum for federal, provincial, & territorial senior officials; to develop agenda, background papers, & logistics for meetings of Ministers responsible for Labour; To follow-up on issues as directed by Ministers
Margaret MacDonald, President
Debra Young, Secretary
Sandy Jones, Acting Manager, Intergovernmental Relations & Social Dialogue
Nina Chretien, Officer, Research & Project, Intergovernmental Relations & Social Dialogue

Canadian Association of Labour Media (CALM) / Association canadienne de la presse syndicale (ACPS)
76 Westmount Ave., Toronto ON M6H 3K1
Tel: 416-656-2256; *Fax:* 416-656-7649
Toll-Free: 888-290-2256
editor@calm.ca
www.calm.ca
To provide training, labour-friendly news, & graphics for labour communicators
Pat Van Horne, President
Mikael Swayze, Secretary-Treasurer
Rosemarie Bahr, CALM Editor

Canadian Committee on Labour History (CCLH) / Comité canadien sur l'histoire du travail
c/o Canadian Committee on Labour History, Athabasca University, #1200, 10011 - 109 St., Edmonton AB T5J 3S8
cclh@athabascau.ca
www.cclh.ca
To promote & publish scholarly research in the area of Canadian labour history & related topics
Alvin Finkel, President
G.S. Kealey, Treasurer

Canadian Injured Workers Alliance (CIWA) / L'Alliance canadienne des victimes d'accidents et de maladies du travail (ACVAMT)
PO Box 10098, 1201 Jasper Dr., Thunder Bay ON P7B 6T6
Tel: 807-345-3429; *Fax:* 807-344-8683
Toll-Free: 877-787-7010
www.ciwa.ca
To support & strengthen the work of local & provincial groups by providing a forum for exchanging information & experiences; To provide training & educational resources in partnership with these groups to ensure that injured workers maintain control over their destinies & that the groups themselves be democratically controlled by the workers
Bill Cheodore, National Coordinator

Cape Breton Injured Workers' Association (CBIWA)
714 Alexandra St., Sydney NS B1S 2H4
Tel: 902-539-4650; *Fax:* 902-539-4171
cbiwa@hotmail.ca
The Cape Breton Injured Workers Association is a volunteer group, located in Sydney, Nova Scotia working on behalf of injured workers by providing information, assisting with claims and appeals, and continuing a dialogue with the Workers' Compensation Board of Nova Scotia.

Centre canadien d'arbitrage commercial (CCAC) / Canadian Commercial Arbitration Centre (CCAC)
Place du Canada, #905, 1010, rue de la Gauchetière ouest, Montréal QC G1K 5V6
Tél: 514-448-5980; *Téléc:* 514-448-5948
Ligne sans frais: 877-909-3794
www.ccac-adr.org
Fournir des services de conciliation, de médiation et d'arbitrage pour les activités commerciales et de consommation; offrir des activités de formation aux arbitres et médiateurs; analyse de dossiers litigieux et études pour des organismes privés et publics
Michel A. Jeanniot, Président
Julie Houle, Coordonnatrice

Construction Labour Relations - An Alberta Association (CLRA)
#207, 2725 - 12 St. NE, Calgary AB T2E 7J2
Tel: 403-250-7390; *Fax:* 403-250-5516
Toll-Free: 800-308-9466
www.clra.org
To represent construction employers in collective bargaining, collective agreement administration, administrative labour law, lobbying.
R. Neil Tidsbury, President

Construction Labour Relations Association of British Columbia
PO Box 820, 97 - 6 St., New Westminster BC V3L 4Z8
Tel: 604-524-4911; *Fax:* 604-524-3925
wendym@clra-bc.com
www.clra-bc.com
Clyde Scollan, President
Wendy Mazur, Office Manager

Construction Labour Relations Association of Newfoundland & Labrador Inc. (CLRA)
Ultramar Bldg., Main Floor, PO Box 8144, Stn. A, 39 Pippy Pl., St. John's NL A1B 3M9
Tel: 709-753-5770; *Fax:* 709-753-5771
nchaplin@clra.nf.net
Neil Chaplin, President

Institut de médiation et d'arbitrage du Québec (IMAQ)
CP 874, Succ. B, Montréal QC H3B 3k5
Tél: 514-282-3327; *Téléc:* 514-282-2214
info@imaq.org
www.imaq.org
Promouvoir les méthodes alternatives de résolution de conflits (médiation, arbitrage); donner accès par internet à la population et aux entreprises à une banque de médiateurs et d'arbitres accrédités selon leur: spécialité (médiateur ou arbitre), région, langue de communication, catégorie de membre, profession, domaine d'expertise
Serge Pisapia, Président
Thierry Bériault, Vice-président

Inter-American Commercial Arbitration Commission (IACAC)
OAS Administrative Bldg., Rm. 211, 19th & Constitution Ave. NW, Washington DC 20006 USA
Tel: 202-458-3249; *Fax:* 202-458-3293
sice@sice.oas.org
To promote conciliation, amicable composition & arbitration in the international commercial settling of disputes in the Western hemisphere
Julio Gonzales Soria, President
Guillermo Fernandez de Soto, Director General

Provincial Building & Construction Trades Council of Ontario
35 International Blvd., Toronto ON M9W 6H3
Tel: 416-679-8887; *Fax:* 416-679-8882
info@ontariobuildingtrades.com
www.ontariobuildingtrades.com
Patrick J. Dillon, Business Manager

Pulp & Paper Employee Relations Forum
c/o Westcott Consulting, 6627 Westcott Rd., Duncan BC V9L 6A4
Tel: 250-748-9445; *Fax:* 250-709-8715
Toll-Free: 888-273-7148
westcot@telus.net
paperforum.com
To act primarily as a research & information service for the industry; to service the pulp & paper industry in job evaluation, benefit & pension plan administration & trusteeship, contract interpretation & any other matters relating to labour relations
Fred Oud, Executive Director

Union of Injured Workers of Ontario, Inc.
2888 Dufferin St., Toronto ON M6B 3S6
Tel: 416-785-8787; *Fax:* 416-785-6390
Serving injured workers & their families; advocacy, counselling, information & referral
Philip Biggin, Executive Director

Western Employers Labour Relations Association
#203, 27126 Fraser Hwy., Langley BC V4W 3P6
Tel: 604-857-5540; *Fax:* 604-857-5547
westernemployers@welra.ca
www.welra.com
Employee relations services for both union & non-union employers
Jim Halliday, Director, Labour Relations

World at Work
PO Box 4520, Stn. A, Toronto ON M5W 4M4
Tel: 480-951-9191; *Fax:* 480-483-8352
Toll-Free: 877-951-9191
customerrelations@worldatwork.com
www.worldatwork.org
Social Media: www.facebook.com/WorldatWorkAssociation; twitter.com/worldatwork; www.linkedin.com/groups?about=&gid=84761; www.youtube.com/worldatworktv
To promote the education of compensation & benefits professionals
Anne Ruddy, President
Marcia Rhodes, Contact, Media Relations

Labour Unions

Agriculture Union
#1000, 233 Gilmour St., Ottawa ON K2P 0P2
Tel: 613-560-4306; *Fax:* 613-235-0517
www.agrunion.com
To advance the workplace interests of its membership; To fight for a society that recognizes the value of the important public services provided by Agriculture Union members
Bob Kingston, National President

Air Canada Pilots Association (ACPA) / L'Association des pilotes d'Air Canada
#205, 6299 Airport Rd., Mississauga ON L4V 1N3
Tel: 905-678-9008; *Fax:* 905-678-9016
Toll-Free: 800-634-0944
info@acpa.ca
www.acpa.ca
Paul Strachan, President
Jon Webster, Secretary-Treasurer
Paul Strachan, Chair, Master Executive Council

Air Line Pilots Association, International - Canada (ALPA)
#1715, 360 Albert St., Ottawa ON K1R 7X7
Tel: 613-569-5668; *Fax:* 613-569-5681
www.alpa.org
Social Media: www.facebook.com/pages/We-Are-ALPA/200676905671
To promote & represent the interests of the airline pilot profession; To safeguard the rights of individual members; To promote & maintain the highest standards of flight safety; To function as a trade union & professional association
Lee Moak, President
W. Randolph Helling, Sec.-Treas.

Alberta Federation of Labour (AFL) / Fédération du travail de l'Alberta
10654 - 101 St., Edmonton AB T5H 2S1
Tel: 780-483-3021; *Fax:* 780-484-5928
Toll-Free: 800-661-3995
afl@afl.org
www.afl.org
Social Media: www.facebook.com/group.php?gid=149042028439970
To act as a central labour body, representing Alberta's organized workers & their families; To improve conditions for Alberta's workers, their families, & communities
Gil McGowan, President
Nancy Furlong, Secretary-Treasurer
Linda Robinson, Financial Administrator
Terry Inigo-Jones, Senior Staff Contact, Communications

Alberta Union of Provincial Employees / Syndicat de la fonction publique de l'Alberta
10451 - 170 St., Edmonton AB T5P 4S7
Tel: 780-930-3300; *Fax:* 780-930-3392
Toll-Free: 800-232-7284
www.aupe.org
Social Media: www.facebook.com/yourAUPE
Ron Hodgins, Executive Director
Jamie Oyarzun, Director, Labour Relations

Alliance des professeures et professeurs de Montréal (APPM)
8225, boul Saint-Laurent, Montréal QC H2P 2M1
Tél: 514-384-5756; *Téléc:* 514-383-4880
presidence@alliancedesprofs.qc.ca
www.alliancedesprofs.qc.ca
Alain Marois, Président

Alliance du personnel professionnel et technique de la santé et des services sociaux (APTS)
#1050, 1111 rue Saint-Charles Ouest, Longueuil QC J4K 5G4
Tél: 450-670-2411; *Téléc:* 450-679-0107
Ligne sans frais: 866-521-2411
info@aptsq.com
www.aptsq.com
Regrouper les organisations syndicales représentant toutes les catégories des personnes salariées professionnelles ou paramédicales travaillant dans le domaine de la santé; défendre, promouvoir et sauvegarder les intérêts collectifs des membres
Dominique Verreault, Présidente
Dominique Aubertin, Directrice générale

Alliance of Canadian Cinema, Television & Radio Artists (ACTRA) / Alliance des artistes canadiens du cinéma, de la télévision et de la radio
#300, 625 Church St., Toronto ON M4Y 2G1
Tel: 416-489-1311; *Fax:* 416-489-8076
Toll-Free: 800-387-3516
national@actra.ca
www.actra.ca
Social Media: twitter.com/ACTRAnat
To represent performers in recorded media; To negotiate & administer collective agreements which set minimum rates & basic conditions governing work; To advocate public policies designed to create strong Canadian broadcasting & film industries in order to provide work opportunities for members in their own country
Daintry Dalton, Regional Executive Director
Stephen Waddell, National Executive Director
Ferne Downey, National President
Theresa Tova, National Treasurer

Amalgamated Transit Union (AFL-CIO/CLC) / Syndicat uni du transport (FAT-COI/CTC)
5025 Wisconsin Ave. NW, Washington DC 20016 USA
Tel: 202-537-1645; *Fax:* 202-244-7824
Toll-Free: 888-240-1196
www.atu.org
Social Media: www.facebook.com/ATUInternational; twitter.com/#!/ATUComm
Oscar Owens, Sec.-Treas.
Lawrence J Hanley, President

American Federation of Musicians of the United States & Canada (AFL-CIO/CLC) (AFM) / Fédération des musiciens des États-Unis et du Canada (FAT-COI/CTC)
#600, 1501 Broadway, New York NY 10036 United States
Tel: 212-869-1330; *Fax:* 212-764-6134
www.afm.org
Social Media: www.facebook.com/afm.org; twitter.com/MusiciansUnion
The largest organization in the world which represens of professional musicians in both Canada and the US. Helps in negotiating fair agreements, protectingownership of recorded music, securing benefits such as health care and pension or lobbying our legislators. AFM is committed to raising industry standards and placing the professional musician in the foreground of the cultural landscape.
Ray Hair, President

Association canadienne des métiers de la truelle, section locale 100 (CTC) / Trowel Trades Canadian Association, Local 100 (CLC)
a/s FTQ-Construction, #2900, 565, rue Crémazie est, Montréal QC H2M 2V6
Tél: 514-381-7300; *Téléc:* 514-381-5173
Ligne sans frais: 877-666-4060
www.ftqconstruction.org
La FTQ-Construction a, bien entendu, de manière très précise le mandat de négocier les conventions collectives applicables dans les sous secteurs d'activités (industriel, commercial et institutionnel, génie civil et voirie, résidentiel) et de voir à leur application. Mais bien au-delà de ce mandat traditionnel, la FTQ-Construction veut s'assurer d'être présent dans l'ensemble des débats représentant un intérêt pour les travailleurs et les travailleuses qu'il représente.
Yves Mercure, Président

Association nationale des peintres et métiers connexes, section locale 99 (CTC) (ANPMC) / National Association of Painters & Allied Trades, Local 99 (CLC)
#200, 5275, rue Jean-Talon est, Saint-Léonard QC H1S 1L2
Tél: 514-593-5413; *Téléc:* 514-727-8331
Aider nos membres dans leur métier; faire respecter les conventions collectives sur les chantiers

Association of Allied Health Professionals: Newfoundland & Labrador (Ind.) (AAHP) / Association des professionnels unis de la santé: Terre-Neuve et Labrador (ind.)
6 Mount Carson Ave., Mount Pearl NL A1N 3K4
Tel: 709-722-3353; *Fax:* 709-722-0987
Toll-Free: 800-728-2247
info@aahp.nf.ca
www.aahp.nf.ca
Sharon King, Executive Director
Bruce Callahan, President

Association of Canadian Film Craftspeople
Local 2020 Communications, Energy & Paperworkers Union of Canada, #108, 3993 Henning Dr., Burnaby BC V5C 6P7
Tel: 604-299-2232; *Fax:* 604-299-2243
info@acfcwest.com
www.acfcwest.com
Benoit Lamarche, President
Richard Chilton, Ssecretary/Treasurer
Greg Chambers, Business Manager

Association of Canadian Financial Officers (ACFO) / Association canadienne des agents financiers
#400, 2725 Queensview Dr., Ottawa ON K2B 0A1
Tel: 613-728-0695; *Fax:* 613-761-9568
Toll-Free: 877-728-0695
information@acfo-acaf.com
www.acfo-acaf.com
To unite in a democratic organization all public service financial administrators for which the association becomes or applies to become a bargaining agent; to serve the welfare of its members through effective collective bargaining with their employers; to obtain for members the best levels of compensation for services rendered to their employers & the best terms & conditions of employment; to protect the rights & interests of all members in all matters upon their employment or upon their relationship with their employers; to seek to maintain high professional standards & promote their professional development; to affiliate as appropriate with other associations, unions or labour organizations for the purpose of enhancing the interests of members in the attainment of their professional & bargaining goals
Milt Isaacs, President & Chair
Karen Hall, Executive Vice-President
Raoul Andersen, Vice-President
Tony Bourque, Vice-President
Rob Hawkins, Vice-President
Nicole Bishop-Tempke, Vice-President
Dany Richard, Vice-President
Daniel J. Larose, Executive Director

Association of New Brunswick Professional Educators (ANBPE) / Association des éducateurs professionnels du Nouveau-Brunswick
c/o Wayne Milner, Counselling Services, NBCC Moncton, #1101A, 1234 Mountain Rd., Moncton NB E1C 8H9
To operate as a bargaining unit of the New Brunswick Union of Public & Private Employees (NBUPPE / NUPGE)
Wayne Milner, President & Director

Association professionnelle des ingénieurs du gouvernement du Québec (ind.) (APIGQ) / Association of Professional Engineers of the Government of Québec (Ind.)
Complexe Iberville, #600, 2954, boul Laurier, Sainte-Foy QC G1V 4T2
Tél: 418-683-3633; *Téléc:* 418-683-6878
lepont@apigq.qc.ca
www.apigq.qc.ca
Association professionnelle des ingénieurs du Gouvemement de Québec.
Michel Gagnon, Président

Association professionnelle des inhalothérapeutes du Québec (ind.) / Professional Association of Inhalation Therapists of Québec (Ind.)
#201, 4101, rue Molson, Montréal QC H1Y 3L1
Tél: 514-251-8050; *Téléc:* 514-259-8084
négocier une convention collective adaptée aux besions des membres; voir à l'application de la convention collective; défendre et promouvoir les intérêts sociaux économiques des membres; améliorer les conditions de travail des membres; faciliter des relations de travail harmonieuses au niveau local grâce à la tenue de comités de relations professionnelles (CRP); adapter les conditions de travail des membres au vécu et aux impératifs du milieu; promourvoir une vie syndicale active.

Association professionnelle des technologistes médicaux du Québec (ind.) / Québec Professional Association of Medical Technologists (Ind.)
1595, rue St-Hubert, 3e étage, Montréal QC H2L 3Z2
Tél: 514-524-3734; *Téléc:* 514-524-7863
L'étude, la sauvegarde et le développement des intérêts économiques, sociaux, moraux, éducatifs et professionnels de ses membres et particulièrement la négotiation et l'application de la convention collective

Atlantic Communication & Technical Workers' Union (Ind.) (AC&TWU) / Syndicat des travailleurs en communication et des techniciens de l'Atlantique (ind.)
#7, 50 Akerley Blvd., Dartmouth NS B3B 1R8
Tel: 902-453-2058; *Fax:* 902-422-4647
Toll-Free: 800-565-2289
Bruce W. Lambert, Business Manager & Financial Secret

Atlantic Federation of Musicians (AFM)
32-B St. Margaret's Bay Road, Halifax NS B3N 1J7
Tel: 902-479-3200; *Fax:* 902-479-1312
Toll-Free: 866-240-4809
571@bellaliant.com
www.afm571.ca
Kenneth R. MacKay, President

Bricklayers, Masons Independent Union of Canada (CLC) / Syndicat indépendant des briqueteurs et des maçons du Canada (CTC)
#200, 1263 Wilson Ave., Toronto ON M3M 3G3
Tel: 416-241-1183; *Fax:* 416-241-9845
Giuseppe Bellotto, President
John Meiorin, Secretary

British Columbia Carpenters Union (BCPCC)
#305, 2806 Kingsway, Vancouver BC V5R 5T5
Tel: 604-437-0471; *Fax:* 604-437-1110
info@bccarpentersunion.com
www.bccarpentersunion.com
The objects of the Council are to organize workers; encourage an apprenticeship system & higher standard of skill; to develop, improve & enforce the program & standards of occupational safety & health; to cultivate friendship; to develop good public relations with the community; to assist each other to secure employment & to reduce the hours of daily labour
Jan Noster, President
Pat Haggarty, Sec.-Treas.

British Columbia Federation of Labour (BCFL) / Fédération du travail de la Colombie-Britannique
#200, 5118 Joyce St., Vancouver BC V5R 4H1
Tel: 604-430-1421; *Fax:* 604-430-5917
bcfed@bcfed.ca; admin@bcfed.ca; media@bcfed.ca;
educate@bcfed.ca
www.bcfed.com
To promote the interests of affiliated unions & their members; To advance the economic & social welfare of the workers of British Columbia; To act as the single voice for workers' rights in British Columbia
Jim Sinclair, President
Jim Chorostecki, Executive Director
Gord Lechner, Director, Occupational Health & Safety Education Centre
Summer McFadyen, Director, Political Action
Nina Hansen, Director, Occupational Health & Safety
Jane Staschuk, Director, Women's Rights, Education, & Training
Michael Gardiner, Director, Communications, Transportation, & First Nations
Jason Mann, Director, Young Workers & Human Rights
Jessie Uppal, Director, Campaigns, Community, & Social Action

British Columbia Ferry & Marine Workers' Union (CLC) (BCFMWU) / Syndicat des travailleurs marins et de bacs de la Colombie-Britannique (CTC)
1511 Stewart Ave., Nanaimo BC V9S 4E3
Tel: 250-716-3454; *Fax:* 250-716-3455
Toll-Free: 800-663-7009
mailroom@bcfmwu.com
www.bcfmwu.com
To unite in the Union all workers eligible for membership; to seek the best possible wage standards & improvements in the conditions of employment for these workers & to represent members in protecting & maintaining their rights; to act as the representative of the membership; to establish free child day care for all individuals; to engage in educational, legislative, political, civic, social, welfare, community & other activities to safeguard & promote economic & social benefits & justice for all workers, unionized & non-unionized.
Kelly Carson, Sec.-Treas.
Richard Goode, President

British Columbia Government & Service Employees' Union (BCGEU) / Syndicat des fonctionnaires provinciaux et de service de la Colombie-Britannique
4911 Canada Way, Burnaby BC V5G 3W3
Tel: 604-291-9611; *Fax:* 604-291-6030
Toll-Free: 800-663-1674
www.bcgeu.ca
Judi Filion, Treasurer
Darryl Walker, President

Canada Employment & Immigration Union (CEIU) / Syndicat de l'emploi et de l'immigration du Canada (SEIC)
#1004, 233 Gilmour St., Ottawa ON K2P 0P2
Tel: 613-236-9634; *Fax:* 613-236-7871
courchs@ceiu-seic.ca
www.ceiu-seic.ca
To unite all the union members in the Canada Employment & Immigration Commission, the Department of Employment & Immigration & the Immigration Appeal Board, & anyone who wishes to join in a single union acting on their behalf by processing appeals & grievances; To unite all members by fostering an understanding of the fundamental differences between the interests of the members & those of the employer; To assure a union presence at the workplace through collective strength of membership
Don Rogers, National President
Steve McCuaig, National Executive Vice-President

Canadian Actors' Equity Association (CLC) (CAEA)
44 Victoria St., 12th Fl., Toronto ON M5C 3C4
Tel: 416-867-9165; *Fax:* 416-867-9246
info@caea.com; membership@caea.com; reception@caea.com
www.caea.com
CAEA negotiates & administers collective agreements, provides benefit plans, information & support, & acts as an advocate for its membership.
Allan Teichman, President
Arden R. Ryshpan, Executive Director
Lynn McQueen, Director, Communications

Canadian Association of Professional Employees (CAPE)
World Exchange Plaza, 100 Queen St., 4th Fl., Ottawa ON K1P 1J9
Tel: 613-236-9181; *Fax:* 613-236-6017
Toll-Free: 800-265-9181
general@acep-cape.ca
www.acep-cape.ca
To negotiate & monitor collective agreement for all federal government economists, sociologists & statisticians.
Claude Poirier, President

Canadian Auto Workers (CAW-Canada)
205 Placer Ct., Toronto ON M2H 3H9
Tel: 416-497-4110; *Fax:* 416-495-6552
Toll-Free: 800-268-5763
caw@caw.ca
www.caw.ca
Social Media:
www.facebook.com/pages/Canadian-Auto-Workers/1040059063 01666; twitter.com/CAWCommunicate
To improve the working conditions & general economic & social conditions of Canadian workers in the industries of: aerospace, mining, fishing, auto & specialty vehicle assembly, auto parts, hotels, airlines, rail, education, hospitality, retail, road transportation, health care, manufacturing, shipbuilding, & others
Ken Lewenza, National President
Peter Kennedy, National Secretary-Treasurer
Jean-Pierre Fortin, Québec Director

Canadian Federal Pilots Association (CFPA) / Association des pilotes fédéraux du Canada (APFC)
#509, 350 Sparks St., Ottawa ON K1R 7S8
Tel: 613-230-5476; *Fax:* 613-230-2668
cfpa@cfpa-apfc.ca
www.cfpa-apfc.ca
Daniel Slunder, Chair
Denis Brunelle, Vice-Chair
Michel Brulotte, Secretary-Treasurer

Canadian Federation of Nurses Unions (CFNU) / La Fédération canadienne des syndicats d'infirmières/infirmiers
2841 Riverside Dr., Ottawa ON K1V 8X7
Tel: 613-526-4661; *Fax:* 613-526-1023
Toll-Free: 800-321-9821
cfnu@nursesunions.ca
www.nursesunions.ca
Social Media: www.facebook.com/NursesUnions;
twitter.com/CFNU
To advance the social, economic & general welfare of its members; To act on national matters of significant concern to the Federation; To promote unity among nurses' unions & other allied health care workers who share the objectives of the CFNU; To provide a national forum to promote desirable legislation on matters of national significance; To preserve free democratic unionism & collective bargaining in Canada; To support other organizations sharing the Union's objectives
Linda Silas, President

Canadian Football League Players' Association (CFLPA) / Association des joueurs de la ligue de football canadienne
#207, 603 Argus Rd., Oakville ON L6J 6G6
Tel: 905-844-7852; *Fax:* 905-844-5127
Toll-Free: 800-616-6865
admin@cflpa.com
www.cflpa.com
The Canadian Football League Players' Association ("C.F.L.P.A.") was established in 1965 and has since that time represented the professional football players in the Canadian Football League ("C.F.L.") with the objective of establishing fair and reasonable working conditions for the players.
Stu Laird, President
Mike O'Shea, 1st Vice-President
Jay McNeil, 2nd Vice-President
Sean Fleming, Member-at-Large
Edward Molstad, Legal Counsel
Fred James, Benefits Chairman
Deanne Mitchell, Executive Assistant

Canadian Iron, Steel & Industrial Workers' Union (Ind.)
17 East Broadway, Vancouver BC V5T 1V4
Tel: 604-681-6002; *Fax:* 604-873-9112

Canadian Labour Congress (CLC) / Congrès du travail du Canada (CTC)
National Headquarters, 2841 Riverside Dr., Ottawa ON K1V 8X7
Tel: 613-521-3400; *Fax:* 613-521-4655
www.canadianlabour.ca
Social Media: www.facebook.com/clc.ctc
To represent the interests of affiliated workers across Canada; To act as an umbrella organization for affiliated regional labour councils, provincial federations, Canadian unions, & international unions
Ken Georgetti, President
Barbara Byers, Executive Vice-President
Marie Clarke Walker, Executive Vice-President
Hassan Yussuff, Secretary-Treasurer
Karl Flecker, Director, Anti-Racism & Human Rights
Andrew Jackson, Director, Social & Economic Policy
Daniel Mallett, Director, Political Action
Lucien Royer, Director, International
Colleen Kilty, Manager, Human Resources
Dennis Gruending, Contact, Communications, Media Calls

Canadian Marine Officers' Union (AFL-CIO/CLC) / Syndicat canadien des officiers de la marine marchande (FAT-COI/CTC)
9670, Notre-Dame East, Montreal QC H1L 3P8
Tel: 514-354-8321; *Fax:* 514-354-8368
info@cmou.ca
www.cmou.ca
Richard Vezina, President

Canadian Marine Pilots' Association (CMPA) / Association des pilotes de la marine canadienne
#1302, 155 Queen St., Ottawa ON K1P 6L1
Tel: 613-232-7777; *Fax:* 613-232-7667
cmpa@tnpa.ca
www.marinepilots.ca
To represent Canadian marine pilots; To raise awareness of marine pilots' role to protect public safety; To ensure a healthy Canadian marine sector
Simon Pelletier, President
Bernard Boissonneault, Vice-President
Mike Burgess, Vice-President
Fred Denning, Vice-President
Andrew Rae, Vice-President

Canadian Media Guild (CMG) / La Guilde canadienne des médias
#810, 310 Front St. West, Toronto ON M5V 3B5
Tel: 416-591-5333; *Fax:* 416-591-7278
Toll-Free: 800-465-4149
info@cmg.ca
www.cmg.ca
Social Media: www.facebook.com/pages/Canadian-Media-Guild/108304249197614
To advance the interests of Guild members through collective bargaining
Carmel Smyth, National President
Karen Wirsig, Coordinator, Communications

Canadian Merchant Service Guild (CMSG) / Guilde de la marine marchande du Canada (GMMC)
#150, 1150 Morrison Dr., Ottawa ON K2H 8S9
Tel: 613-829-9531; *Fax:* 613-596-6079
cmsgott@on.aibn.com
www.cmsg-gmmc.ca
To promote the social, economic, cultural, educational & material interests of ships' masters, chief engineers, officers, pilots & of other persons whose employment is directly related to maritime operations
Mark Boucher, National President
Joy Thomson, National Sec.-Treas.

Canadian National Federation of Independent Unions (CNFIU) / Fédération canadienne nationale des syndicats indépendants (FCNSI)
PO Box 416, 36 Main Street N., Campbellville ON L0P 1B0
Tel: 905-854-6868; *Fax:* 905-854-6869
Toll-Free: 800-638-9438
info@cnfiu.com
www.cnfiu.com
To encourage & promote the formation of independent unions
Ann Waller, President
Paul Dickson, Treasurer

Canadian Postmasters & Assistants Association (CPAA) / Association canadienne des maîtres de poste et adjoints (ACMPA)
281 Queen Mary St., Ottawa ON K1K 1X1
Tel: 613-745-2095; *Fax:* 613-745-5559
mail@cpaa-acmpa.ca
www.cpaa-acmpa.ca
Leslie A. Schous, National President
Pierre Charbonneau, National Vice-President
Shirley L. Dressler, National Vice President
Daniel L. Maheux, National Secretary-Treasurer

Canadian Telephone Employees' Association (Ind.) / Association canadienne des employés de téléphone (ind.)
PO Box 103, #1903, 777 Bay St., Toronto ON M5G 2C8
Tel: 416-977-2251; *Fax:* 416-977-9738
Toll-Free: 800-595-2696
CTEA Mission is to be the best union for our members. Their strategy is to depend on responsible elected Representatives and District Committees to develop and reflect membership opinion; to provide membership control of their union through the General Council; to remain independent in the labour movement.
Brenda Knight, President

Canadian Union of Postal Workers (CUPW) / Syndicat des travailleurs et travailleuses des postes (STTP)
377 Bank St., Ottawa ON K2P 1Y3
Tel: 613-236-7238; *Fax:* 613-563-7861
feedback@cupw-sttp.org
www.cupw-sttp.org
CUPW is a democratic union. They are involved with various campaigns and activities which help support their members.
Denis Lemelin, National President
George Kuehnbaum, National Sec.-Treas.

Canadian Union of Public Employees (CUPE) / Syndicat canadien de la fonction publique (SCFP)
1375 St. Laurent Blvd., Ottawa ON K1G 0Z7
Tel: 613-237-1590; *Fax:* 613-237-5508
cupemail@cupe.ca
www.cupe.ca
To advance the social, economic, & general welfare of both active & retired employees; To promote required legislation
Paul Moist, National President
Charles Fluery, National Secretary-Treasurer
Daniel Légère, General Vice-President
Lucie Levasseur, General Vice-President
Barry O'Neill, General Vice-President
Tom Graham, General Vice-President, Saskatchewan
Fred Hahn, General Vice-President, Ontario

Centrale des syndicats démocratiques (CSD)
#300, 801, 4e rue, Québec QC G1J 2T7
Tél: 418-529-2956; *Téléc:* 418-529-6323
info@csd.qc.ca
www.csd.qc.ca
CSD est composée des associations de salariés constituées ou non en vertu de la Loi des syndicats professionnels qui y adhèrent et souscrivent aux objectifs de la CSD; CSD a comme première croyance la liberté de la personne humaine, tant dans son intelligence que dans la recherche de la satisfaction de ses besoins matériels; elle est donc libre de toute attache politique et se reconnaît comme un mouvement de fraternité et de solidarité dédié entièrement à la formation, à l'information, à la défense et à la promotion collective des travailleuses et des travailleurs.
François Vaudreuil, Président

Centrale des syndicats du Québec (CSQ)
9405, rue Sherbrooke est, Montréal QC H1L 6P3
Tél: 514-356-8888; *Téléc:* 514-356-9999
Ligne sans frais: 800-465-0897
communications.montreal@csq.qc.net
www.csq.qc.net
Média social: www.facebook.com/lacsq; twitter.com/CSQ_centrale
De regrouper dans un même mouvement des personnels salariés ayant des aspirations et des intérêts communs et de promouvoir leurs intérêts professionnels, sociaux, et économiques; dans cette perspective, elle travaille à établir un environnement syndical et professionnel exempt de harcèlement sexuel et favorise la vie syndicale par le partage des ressources; elle intervient au soutien direct de ses affiliés et assure différents services liés aux relations de travail et à la vie professionnelle (recherche dans le domaine de l'éducation, etc.)
Gabriel Marchand, Directeur général
Réjean Parent, Président

CEP Local 2003
#105, 2065 Dundas St. East, Mississauga ON L4X 2W1
Tel: 905-238-0877; *Fax:* 905-238-9567
Toll-Free: 800-263-0855
cuoe@cuoe.org
www.ceplocal2003.org
Paul Sauve, National President
George Reid, National Vice-President
Kenneth B. Spiece, National Treasurer
Larry Lynch, National Recording Secretary

Christian Labour Association of Canada (CLAC) / Association chrétienne du travail du Canada
2335 Argentia Rd., Mississauga ON L5N 5N3
Tel: 905-812-2855; *Fax:* 905-812-5556
Toll-Free: 800-268-5281
headoffice@clac.ca
www.clac.ca
Social Media: www.facebook.com/clacunion; twitter.com/clacnewlabour; www.youtube.com/user/CLACunion
To promote labour relations based on the social principles of justice, respect & dignity; To stand up for fair wages, reasonable work hours, good benefits, a dependable retirement savings plan, job security, professional development & opportunities for advancement
Dick Heinen, Executive Director
Hank Beekhuis, Ontario Provincial Director
Wayne Prins, Prairies Director
David Prentice, BC Provincial Director

Communications, Energy & Paperworkers Union of Canada (CEP) / Syndicat canadien des communications, de l'énergie et du papier (SCEP)
301 Laurier Ave. West, Ottawa ON K1P 6M6
Tel: 613-230-5200; *Fax:* 613-230-5801
Toll-Free: 877-230-5201
info@cep.ca
www.cep.ca
Social Media: www.facebook.com/group.php?gid=14453572223
To improve pay & working conditions through collective bargaining & to represent members at grievance hearings; To present a common front with other unions & community groups to governments on issues that affect all workers, from minimum wage to medicare
Gaétan Ménard, Sec.-Treas.
Dave Coles, President

Compensation Employees' Union (Ind.) (CEU) / Syndicat des employés d'indemnisation (ind.)
#200, 8120 Granville Ave., Richmond BC V6Y 1P3
Tel: 604-278-4050; *Fax:* 604-278-5002
www.ceu.bc.ca
The Compensation Employees' Union was certified in 1974. The CEU is an all inclusive bargaining unit representing all workers at the Workers' Compensation Board that are not excluded by law. The membership ranges from cleaners, support positions, technicial positions, officer level positions, physiologists, and lawyers.
Sandra Wright, President
Carol Velon, Secretary

Confédération des syndicats nationaux (CSN) / Confederation of National Trade Unions
1601, av De Lorimier, Montréal QC H2K 4M5
Tél: 514-598-2155; *Téléc:* 514-598-2089
csncommunications@csn.qc.ca
www.csn.qc.ca
Média social: www.facebook.com/LaCSN; twitter.com/laCSN
La Confédération limite ses activités principalement au Québec, quoique certains locaux soient établis hors de la province; comprend 9 fédérations, 13 conseils centraux et 2 800 syndicats

Pierre Patry, Trésorier
Louis Roy, Présidente
Jean Lortie, Secrétaire générale

Congress of Union Retirees Canada (CURC) / Association des syndicalistes retraités du Canada (ASRC)
2841 Riverside Dr., Ottawa ON K1V 8X7
Tel: 613-526-7422; *Fax:* 613-521-4655
curc.clc-ctc.ca
To ensure that the concerns of senior citizens & union retirees are heard across Canada
Pat Kerwin, President
Len Hope, First Vice-President
Doug MacPherson, Second Vice-President
Bob McGarry, Secretary
Betty Ann Bushell, Treasurer

Customs Excise Union Douanes Accise (CEUDA)
1741 Woodward Dr., Ottawa ON K2C 0P9
Tel: 613-723-8008; *Fax:* 613-723-7895
web@ciu-sdi.ca
www.ceuda.psac.com
Social Media: twitter.com/ciusdi_en
To address CEUDA members' concerns on a timely basis
Ron Moran, National President
Michelle Tranchemontagne, Legal Counsel & Director, Office
Jonathan Choquette, Officer, Communications & Political Coordination

Employees' Association, St. Mary's of the Lake Hospital (CNFIU) / Association des employés, l'Hôpital Saint Mary's of the Lake (FCNSI)
PO Box 207, Kingston ON K7L 4V8
Tel: 613-544-5220

Fédération autonome du collégial (ind.) (FAC) / Autonomous Federation of Collegial Staff (Ind.)
#400, 1259, rue Berri, Montréal QC H2L 4C7
Tél: 514-848-9977; *Téléc:* 514-848-0166
Ligne sans frais: 800-701-1369
fac@lafac.qc.ca
Défendre et développer les intérêts économiques, sociaux, pédagogiques et professionnels du personnel enseignant des cégeps; défendre le droit d'association, la libre négociation et la liberté d'action syndicale; négocier et s'assurer de l'application des conventions collectives; de représenter ses syndicats affiliés partout où leurs intérêts sont débattus.
Alain Dion, Président

Fédération CSN - Construction (CSN) / CNTU Federation - Construction (CNTU)
2100B, boul de Maisonneuve est, 4e étage, Montréal QC H2K 4S1
Tél: 514-598-2421; *Téléc:* 514-598-2425
sec-montreal@csnconstruction.qc.ca
www.csnconstruction.qc.ca
Alain Mailhot, Président
François Trépanier, Secrétaire général
Yves Coté, Coordonateur

Fédération de la métallurgie (CSN) / Federation of Metal Trades (CNTU)
#204, 2100, boul de Maisonneuve est, Montréal QC H2K 4S1
Tél: 514-529-4937; *Téléc:* 514-529-4935
fm@csn.qc.ca
www.metallurgie.csn.qc.ca
Alain Lampron, Président
Yvan Gamelin, Secrétaire-Trésorier

Fédération de la santé et des services sociaux (FSSS)
1601, av de Lorimier, Montréal QC H2K 4M5
Tél: 514-598-2210; *Téléc:* 514-598-2223
fsss@fsss.qc.ca
www.fsss.qc.ca
De promouvoir et sauvegarder la santé, la sécurité et les intérêts des personnes employées des établissements affiliés ou en voie d'affiliation; de représenter ses membres auprès de la Confédération des syndicats nationaux en lui soumettant toutes questions d'intérêt général; de représenter ses membres, de concert avec le CSN, partout où les intérêts généraux des travailleuses et travailleurs le justifient; d'aider à conclure, en faveur des syndicats affiliés, des conventions collectives de travail et en favoriser l'application; de collaborer à l'éducation des travailleuses et travailleurs et à la formation de responsables et militantes et militants syndicaux; d'assurer les services à ses syndicats affiliés; de favoriser et d'établir des liens inter-syndicaux avec les autres travailleuses et travailleurs dans le secteur public et para-public et dans le secteur privé du Québec et du Canada
Francine Lévesque, Présidente
Denyse Paradis, Secrétaire-trésorière

Fédération des employées et employés de services publics inc. (CSN) (FEESP) / Federation of Public Service Employees Inc. (CNTU)
1601, av de Lorimier, Montréal QC H2K 4M5
Tél: 514-598-2231
feesp.courrier@csn.qc.ca
www.feesp.csn.qc.ca
Il est composé de quatre personnes élues, du coordonnateur ou coordonnatrice des services et de la personne déléguée syndicale.
Danielle Beaulieu, Présidente

Fédération des enseignants de cégeps
9405, rue Sherbrooke est, Montréal QC H1L 6P3
Tél: 514-356-8888; *Téléc:* 514-354-8535
fec@csq.qc.net
www.fec.csq.qc.net
Elle reste donc, encore aujourd'hui, une organisation qui jouit, à l'intérieur de la CSQ, d'une autonomie totale pour tout ce qui touche la négociation et l'application de la convention collective, les orientations concernant les dossiers professionnels et les politiques collégiales de même que pour ce qui touche la gestion de son personnel et de son budget. Plus encore aujourd'hui qu'hier, la FEC et ses syndicats participent aux décisions de la Centrale puisque celle-ci a multiplié, au cours des années, ses instances décisionnelles et consultatives auxquelles participent directement la FEC et ses syndicats.

Fédération des intervenantes en petite enfance du Québec (FIPEQ)
9405, rue Sherbrooke est, Montréal QC H1L 6P3
Tél: 514-356-8888; *Téléc:* 514-356-9999
Ligne sans frais: 800-465-0897
fipeq@csq.qc.net
www.petitmonde.com
La Fédération des intervenantes en petite enfance du Québec (FIPEQ) est vouée à la promotion de la profession, à la défense des droits et des intérêts ainsi qu'à l'amélioration des conditions de vie de toutes les intervenantes, tant travailleuses autonomes que salariées, oeuvrant au service des centres de la petite enfance.
Sylvie Tonnelier, Présidente

Fédération des médecins résidents du Québec inc. (ind.) (FMRQ) / Québec Federation of Residents (Ind.)
#510, 630, rue Sherbrooke ouest, Montréal QC H3A 1E4
Tél: 514-282-0256; *Téléc:* 514-282-0471
Ligne sans frais: 800-465-0215
fmrq@fmrq.qc.ca
www.fmrq.qc.ca
L'étude, la défense et le développement des intérêts économiques, sociaux, moraux et scientifiques des syndicats et des leurs membres.
Jean Gouin, Executive Director
Patrick Labelle, Administrative Director

Fédération des policiers et policières municipaux du Québec (ind.) (FPMQ) / Québec Federation of Policemen (Ind.)
7955, boul Louis-Hippolyte-La Fontaine, Anjou QC H1K 4E4
Tél: 514-356-3321; *Téléc:* 514-356-1158
Ligne sans frais: 800-361-0321
info@fpmq.org
www.fpmq.org
L'étude et la défense des intérêts économiques, professionnels, sociaux et moraux de ses associations-membres et de tous les policiers que celles-ci regroupent.
Denis Côté, Président
Christine Beaulieu, Directrice, Communications

Fédération des professionnèles (FPCSN) / Quebec Federation of Managers & Professional Salaried Workers (CNTU)
1601, av de Lorimier, Montréal QC H2K 4M5
Tél: 514-598-2143; *Téléc:* 514-598-2491
Ligne sans frais: 888-633-2143
www.fpcsn.qc.ca
Regroupe plus de 7000 professionnèles oeuvrant dans différents secteurs d'activités: santé et services sociaux, organismes gouvernementaux, éducation, secteur municipal, médecines alternatives, secteur juridique, intégration à l'emploi, professionnèles autonomes, organismes communautaires, etc
Michel Tremblay, Président
Lucie Dufour, Secrétaire générale

Fédération des professionnelles et professionnels de l'éducation du Québec (FPPE) / Québec Federation of Professional Employees in Education
9405, rue Sherbrooke est, Montréal QC H1L 6P3
Tél: 514-356-8888; *Téléc:* 514-356-9999
Ligne sans frais: 800-465-0897
infos@fppe.qc.ca
www.fppe.qc.ca
De promouvoir et de développer les intérêts professionnels, sociaux et économiques des professionnelles et professionnels de l'éducation du Québec ainsi que de défendre les droits fondamentaux compris à l'intérieur des chartes, le droit d'association, le droit à la libre négociation et le droit à la liberté d'action syndicale; de représenter ses syndicats affiliés à un niveau national; d'orienter et de coordonner la représentation de ses syndicats affiliés auprès des instances de la Centrale; de diriger et de coordonner la négociation des conventions collectives; de concilier les conflits qui peuvent naître entre les syndicats affiliés; de mettre à la disposition des syndicats affiliés et de leurs membres des services de qualité en matière de négociation et d'application des conditions de travail et des droits sociaux, d'information et de formation syndicale.
Réjean Parent, Président
Louise Chabot, Vice-présidente
Sylvie Simoneau, 2e Vice-président
Pierre Jobin, 3e Vice-président

Fédération des Syndicats de l'Enseignement (FSE)
CP 100, 320, rue Saint-Joseph est, Québec QC G1K 9E7
Tél: 418-649-8888; *Téléc:* 418-649-1914
fse@csq.qc.net
www.fse.qc.net
Média social: www.facebook.com/FSECSQ; twitter.com/FSECSQ
Promouvoir les intérêts professionnels, sociaux et économiques du personnel enseignant des commissions scolaires; orienter et coordonner la représentation des syndicats affiliés auprès des instances de la Centrale et de représenter les syndicats affiliés là où leurs intérêts et leurs droits sont débattus; assumer prioritairement la responsabilité des négociations, les aspects sectoriels des relations du travail et de l'action juridique ainsi que les questions professionnelles à caractère sectoriel; favoriser la concertation entre les syndicats affiliés et concilier les divergences qui pourraient naître entre eux.
Laurier Caron, Directeur général

Fédération des syndicats de la santé et des services sociaux (F4S-CSQ)
9405, rue Sherbrooke est, Montréal QC H1L 6P3
Tél: 514-356-8888; *Téléc:* 514-356-2845
f4s@csq.qc.net
www.sante.csq.qc.net/index.cfm/2,0,1672,9553,2883,0,html
Réunis en congrès les 7 et 8 juin 2007, les déléguées et délégués de la Fédération du personnel de la santé et des services sociaux (FPSSS-CSQ) et de la Fédération des syndicats de professionnelles et professionnels de la santé et des services sociaux (FSPPSSS-CSQ) ont décidé à l'unanimité d'unir leurs forces et de fonder une nouvelle fédération : la Fédération des syndicats de la santé et des services sociaux (F4S-CSQ), affiliée à la Centrale des syndicats du Québec (CSQ).
René Beauséjour, Président

Fédération des travailleurs et travailleuses du Québec - Construction
#2900, 565, boul Crémazie est, Montréal QC H2M 2V6
Tél: 514-381-7300; *Téléc:* 514-381-5173
Ligne sans frais: 877-666-4060
www.ftqconstruction.org
Média social: www.facebook.com/pages/FTQ-Construction/166936194129; twitter.com/FTQConstruction; www.youtube.com/user/FTQconstruction
On peut facilement affirmer que la mission d'une association syndicale est quasi sans limite. La FTQ-Construction a, bien entendu, de manière très précise le mandat de négocier les conventions collectives applicables dans les sous secteurs d'activités (industriel, commercial et institutionnel, génie civil et voirie, résidentiel) et de voir à leur application. Mais bien au-delà de ce mandat traditionnel, la FTQ-Construction veut s'assurer d'être présent dans l'ensemble des débats représentant un intérêt pour les travailleurs et les travailleuses qu'il représente.
Yves Ouellette, Directeur général

Fédération des travailleurs et travailleurs du papier et de la forêt (CSN) (FTPF) / Federation of Paper & Forest Workers (CNTU)
#350, 155, boul Charest est, Québec QC G1K 3G6
Tél: 418-647-5775; *Téléc:* 418-647-5884
direction.ftpf@videotron.net
www.ftpf.csn.qc.ca

Groupe CNW exploite sept bureaux au Canada, dont deux bureaux CNW Telbec au Québec. De ses bureaux de Vancouver, de Calgary, de Toronto, d'Ottawa, de Montréal, de Québec et de Halifax, CNW répond avec efficacité aux besoins du marché canadien, et ce, 24 heures par jour, 365 jours par année, tout en assurant un service en anglais et en français.
Suzanne Lareau, Présidente-directrice générale
Claire Chouinard, Directrice, Communications & marketing

Fédération du personnel de l'enseignement privé (FPEP)
9405, rue Sherbrooke est, Montréal QC H1L 6P3
Tél: 514-356-8888; *Téléc:* 514-356-1866
fpep@csq.qc.net
www.fpep.csq.qc.net
Promouvoir les intérêts professionnels, sociaux et économiques de ses membres; défendre le droit d'association, de libre négociation et la liberté d'action syndicale; représenter ses syndicats membres
Francine Lamoureux, Présidente
Martine Dion, Vice-Présidente
Denis Benoit, Vice-Président
Denis Benoit, Vice-Président
Josée Noël, Tresorière

Fédération du personnel de soutien scolaire (CSQ) (FPSS) / Federation of Support Staff
9405, rue Sherbrooke est, 4e étage, Montréal QC H1L 6P3
Tél: 514-356-8888; *Téléc:* 514-493-3697
webfpss@csq.qc.net
www.fpss.csq.qc.net
Mèdia social: www.facebook.com/fpss.csq; twitter.com/FPSSCSQ
Le seul regroupement au Québec représentant exclusivement du personnel de soutien scolaire des écoles et des centres. Elle est affiliée à la Centrale des syndicats du Québec (CSQ)
Diane Cinq-Mars, Présidente

Fédération du personnel du loisir, de la culture et du communautaire (CEQ) (FPLCC)
9405, rue Sherbrooke est, Montréal QC H1L 6P3
Tél: 514-356-8888; *Téléc:* 418-649-8888
Ligne sans frais: 877-850-0897
fplcc@csq.qc.net
www.csq.qc.net
Regroupe les syndicats qui représentent le personnel oeuvrant dans les secteurs du loisir, du sport, de la culture du tourisme et du communautaire
Réjean Parent, Président

Fédération du personnel professionnel des collèges (FPPC)
9405, rue Sherbrooke est, Montréal QC H1L 6P3
Tél: 514-356-8888; *Téléc:* 514-356-3377
fppc@csq.qc.net
www.fppc.csq.qc.net
Mèdia social: www.facebook.com/166365983458347; twitter.com/fppc_csq
Défendre et promouvoir la fonction professionnelle dans les collèges
Bernard Bérubé, Président

Fédération du personnel professionnel des universités et de la recherche (FPPU)
867, du Haut-Boc., Trois-Rivières QC G9A 4W7
Tél: 819-840-4544; *Téléc:* 819-840-4294
fppu@uqtr.ca
www.fppu.ca
La FPPU est la seule organisation syndicale regroupant exclusivement le personnel professionnel des universités et de la recherche
Bernard Gaucher, Président

Fédération indépendante des syndicats autonomes (FISA) / Independent Federation of Autonomous Unions
#201, 1778, boul Wilfrid-Hamel, Québec QC G1N 3Y8
Tél: 418-529-4571; *Téléc:* 418-529-4695
Ligne sans frais: 800-407-3472
info@fisa.ca
www.fisa.ca
Fournir des services d'organisation, de conseils, de représentation et d'aide financière aux associations membres.
Jean Gagnon, Président

Fédération nationale des communications (CSN) (FNC) / National Federation of Communication Workers (CNTU)
1601, av de Lorimier, Montréal QC H2K 4M5
Tél: 514-598-2132; *Téléc:* 514-598-2431
fnc@fncom.org
www.fncom.org
La défense des intérêts économiques, sociaux, politiques et professionnels des membres.
Chantale Larouche, Présidente

Fraternité interprovinciale des ouvriers en électricité (CTC) (FIPOE) / Interprovincial Brotherhood of Electrical Workers (CLC)
#11100, 565, boul Crémazie est, Montréal QC H2M 2W2
Tél: 514-385-3476; *Téléc:* 514-385-9298
info@fipoe.org
www.fipoe.org
Regrouper des électriciens de construction, des installateurs de systèmes d'alarmes et des monteurs de ligne.
Benjamin Otis, Président
Gérald Castilloux, Directeur général

Fraternité nationale des forestiers et travailleurs d'usine (CTC) / National Brotherhood of Foresters & Industrial Workers (CLC)
Locale 299, #101, 2, boul Desaulniers, Saint-Lambert QC J4P 1L2
Tél: 450-465-2218; *Téléc:* 450-465-1301
Ligne sans frais: 800-317-1818
fnftu@qc.aira.com
L'étude, la sauvegarde et le développement des intérêts économiques, et l'application de conventions collectives
Sylvie Labelle, Adjointe au président
Yves Guérette, Président

Government Services Union (GSU) / Syndicat des services gouvernementaux
#100, 1770 Woodward Dr., Ottawa ON K2C 0P8
Tel: 613-226-5983; *Fax:* 613-226-8241
gsu-ssg@psac.com
www.gsu-ssg.ca
Their members provide compensation, audit, procurement, disposal telecommunications and informatics, translation, real property and reciever general services to some 100 federal government departments and agencies. They also provide information about government programmes and research the opinions of Canadians.
Mark Brunell, President

Grain Services Union (CLC) (GSU) / Syndicat des services du grain (CTC)
2334 McIntyre St., Regina SK S4P 2S2
Tel: 306-522-6686; *Fax:* 306-565-3430
Toll-Free: 866-522-6686
gsu.regina@sasktel.net
www.gsu.ca
They represent Saskatchewan Wheat Pool Workers and represent members working for a variety of companies within Canada.
Carolyn Illerbrun, President
Hugh J. Wagner, Secretary/Manager

Health Sciences Association of Alberta (HSAA) / Association des sciences de la santé de l'Alberta (ind.)
10212 - 112 St., Edmonton AB T5K 1M4
Tel: 780-488-0168; *Fax:* 780-488-0534
Toll-Free: 800-252-7904
www.hsaa.ca
To conduct activities as a labour union to enhance the quality of life for HSAA members & society
Elisabeth Ballermann, President
Patricia Heffel, Director, Administrative Services
Lynette McAvoy, Director, Labour Relations
Roni Hermanutz, Manager, Human Resources
Joanne Monro, Officer, Occupational Health & Safety
Scott Pattison, Officer, Communications

Health Sciences Association of Saskatchewan (HSAS) / Association des sciences de la santé de la Saskatchewan (ind.)
#42, 1736 Quebec Ave., Saskatoon SK S7K 1V9
Tel: 306-955-3399; *Fax:* 306-955-3396
Toll-Free: 888-565-3399
hsasstoon@sasktel.net; hsasregina@sasktel.net
www.hsa-sk.com
Social Media: www.facebook.com/124779960928913
To conduct activities as an independent union representing its members who are health sciences professionals in Saskatchewan
Bill Craik, Executive Director
Karen Wasylenko, President
Anne Robins, Vice-President
Cara McDavid, Secretary
Karen Kinar, Treasurer

Hospital Employees' Union (HEU) / Syndicat des employés d'hôpitaux
5000 North Fraser Way, Burnaby BC V5J 5M3
Tel: 604-438-5000; *Fax:* 604-739-1510
Toll-Free: 800-663-5813
info@heu.org
www.heu.org
Social Media: twitter.com/HospEmpUnion
To unite & associate together all employees employed in hospital, medical or related work for the purpose of securing concerted action in whatever may be regarded as conducive to their best interests; to embrace the concept of equality of treatment for all in hospital, medical or related employment, with respect to wages & job opportunities, recognizing their obligation to provide high-quality care; to defend & preserve the right of all persons to high standards of medical & hospital treatment
Ken Robinson, President
Bonnie Pearson, Secretary & Business Manager

International Alliance of Theatrical Stage Employees, Moving Picture Technicians, Artists & Allied Crafts of the U.S., Its Territories & Canada (IATSE)
1430 Broadway, 20th Fl., New York NY 10018 USA
Tel: 212-730-1770; *Fax:* 212-921-7699
webmaster@iatse-intl.org
www.iatse-intl.org
Matthew D. Loeb, International President
John M. Lewis, Director, Canadian Affairs

International Association of Bridge, Structural, Ornamental & Reinforcing Iron Workers (AFL-CIO) / Association internationale des travailleurs de ponts, de fer structural et ornemental (FAT-COI)
#400, 1750 New York Ave. NW, Washington DC 20006 USA
Tel: 202-383-4800; *Fax:* 202-638-4856
iwmagazine@iwintl.org
www.ironworkers.org
Social Media: www.facebook.com/unionironworkers; twitter.com/TheIronworkers; www.youtube.com/user/IronworkersIMPACT
This union represents ironworkers and works for employment oppourtunties, fair pay, health and welfare benefits, continuing education, and other workers' rights since 1896.
Walter Wise, General President

International Association of Fire Fighters (AFL-CIO/CLC) (IAFF) / Association internationale des pompiers (FAT-COI/CTC)
#300, 1750 New York Ave. NW, Washington DC 20006-5395 USA
Tel: 202-737-8484; *Fax:* 202-737-8418
www.iaff.org
IAFF has established professional standards for the North American fire service with active political & legislative programs, & with experts in the fields of occupational health & safety, fire-based emergency medical services & hazardous materials training. It provides a voice in the development & implementation of new training & equipment, & has worked to ensure the staffing of fire & EMS departments.
Harold A. Schaitberger, General President

International Association of Machinists & Aerospace Workers (IAMAW) / Association internationale des machinistes et des travailleurs de l'aérospatiale
Machinists Bldg., 9000 Machinists Pl., Upper Marlboro MD 20772-2687 USA
Tel: 301-967-4500
www.goiam.org; www.iamaw.ca
Social Media: www.facebook.com/machinistsunion; twitter.com/machinistsunion
To work as the negotiating body for its members
R. Thomas Buffenbarger, President

International Brotherhood of Boilermakers, Iron Ship Builders, Blacksmiths, Forgers & Helpers (AFL-CIO) (IBB) / Fraternité internationale des chaudronniers, constructeurs de navires en fer, forgerons, forgeurs et aides (FAT-COI)
New Brotherhood Bldg., #570, 753 State Ave., Kansas City KS 66101 USA
Tel: 913-371-2640; *Fax:* 913-281-8101
www.boilermakers.org
The Brotherhood is a diverse union representing boilermakers and other workers in the U.S. and Canada in construction, repair, maintenance, manufacturing, professional emergency medical services, and related industries. The Western Canadian Section serves the territory from Thunder Bay west, including Manitoba, Saskatchewan, Alberta, British Columbia, Yukon & NWT. The Eastern Canadian Section serves territory east of Thunder Bay, including Ontario, Quebec, New Brunswick, Nova Scotia, PEI, & Newfoundland & Labrador

Newton B. Jones, International President
Joseph Maloney, International Vice President, Western Canada
Edward Power, International Vice President, Eastern Canada

International Brotherhood of Electrical Workers (AFL-CIO/CFL) (IBEW) / Fraternité internationale des ouvriers en électricité (FAT-COI/FCT)
900 Seventh St. NW, Washington DC 20001 USA
Tel: 202-833-7000; *Fax:* 202-728-7676
www.ibew.org
Social Media: www.facebook.com/IBEWFB; twitter.com/IBEW_IP
The International Brotherhood of Electrical Workers (IBEW) represents approximately 725,000 members who work in a wide variety of fields, including utilities, construction, telecommunications, broadcasting, manufacturing, railroads and government.
Salvatore J. Chilia, International Secretary-Treasurer
Edwin d. Hill, International President

International Federation of Professional & Technical Engineers (AFL-CIO/CLC) (IFPTE) / Fédération internationale des ingénieurs et techniciens (FAT-COI/CTC)
#701, 501 3rd St. NW, Washington DC 20001 USA
Tel: 202-239-4880; *Fax:* 202-239-4881
generalinfo@ifpte.org
www.ifpte.org
To represent employees in a wide variety of occupations in the technical, administrative & professional fields
Gregory J. Junemann, President

International Longshore & Warehouse Union (CLC) / Syndicat international des débardeurs et magasiniers (CTC)
1188 Franklin St., 4th Fl., San Francisco CA 94109 USA
Tel: 415-775-0533; *Fax:* 415-775-1302
info@ilwu.org
www.ilwu.org
ILWU is an international warehouse union representing the rights of their members.
Robert McEllrath, President

International Longshoremen's Association (AFL-CIO/CLC) (ILA) / Association internationale des débardeurs (FAT-COI/CTC)
#930, 17 Battery Pl., New York NY 10004 USA
Tel: 212-425-1200; *Fax:* 212-425-2928
jmcnamara@ilaunion.org
ilaunion.org
Richard P. Hughes, President
Robert E. Gleason, Sec.-Treas.

International Union of Bricklayers & Allied Craftworkers (AFL-CIO/CFL) (BAC) / Union internationale des briqueteurs et métiers connexes (FAT-COI/FCT)
620 F St. NW, Washington DC 20004 USA
Tel: 202-783-3788; *Toll-Free:* 888-880-8222
askbac@bacweb.org
www.bacweb.org
John J. Flynn, President

International Union of Elevator Constructors (AFL-CIO/CFL) (IUEC) / Union internationale des constructeurs d'ascenseurs (FAT-COI/FCT)
7154 Columbia Gateway Dr., Columbia MD 21046 USA
Tel: 410-953-6150; *Fax:* 410-953-6169
contact@iuec.org
www.iuec.org
Kevin P. Stringer, General Sec.-Treas.
Dana A. Brigham, General President

International Union of Operating Engineers (AFL-CIO/CFL) / Union internationale des opérateurs de machines lourdes (FAT-COI/FCT)
1125 - 17 St. NW, Washington DC 20036 USA
Tel: 202-429-9100; *Fax:* 202-778-2613
www.iuoe.org
Vincent J. Giblin, President

International Union of Painters & Allied Trades (AFL-CIO/CFL) / Syndicat international des peintres et métiers connexes (FAT-COI/FCT)
1750 New York Ave. NW, Washington DC 20006 USA
Tel: 202-637-0700
mail@iupat.org
www.iupat.org
James A. Williams, President

International Union, United Automobile, Aerospace & Agricultural Implement Workers of America, Local 251 (CLC) (UAW) / Syndicat international des travailleurs unis de l'automobile, de l'aérospatiale et de l'outillage agricole d'Amérique (C
8000 East Jefferson Ave., Detroit MI 48214 USA
Tel: 313-926-5000; *Toll-Free:* 800-243-8829
www.uaw.org
UAW is one of the largest & most diverse unions in North America, with members in virtually every sector of the economy. It is the collective bargaining body for its members, negotiating for wages & benefits.
Bob King, President
Dennis Williams, Sec.-Treas.

Laborers' International Union of North America (AFL-CIO/CLC) (LiUNA) / Union internationale des journaliers d'Amérique (FAT-COI/CTC)
905 - 16 St. NW, Washington DC 20006 USA
Tel: 202-737-8320; *Fax:* 202-737-2754
communications@liuna.org
www.liuna.org
Social Media: www.facebook.com/LaborersInternationalUnionofNorthAmerica; twitter.com/LIUNA; www.youtube.com/user/liunavideo
Union fighting for better wages and benefits, safer jobsites, more successful employers, and a strong voice for the people.
Richard Metcalf, Director, Corporate Affairs
Richard Greer, Director, Strategic Communications

Major League Baseball Players' Association (Ind.) / Association des joueurs de la Ligue majeure de baseball (ind.)
12 East 49th St., 24th Fl., New York NY 10017 USA
Tel: 212-826-0808; *Fax:* 212-752-4378
feedback@mlbpa.org
www.mlb.com/pa
To represent and protect the interests of professional baseball players in the United States.
Michael Weiner, Executive Director
Martha Child, CAO

Management & Professional Employees Society of BC Hydro (Ind.) (MAPES) / Société des employés professionnels et administratifs (ind.)
12388 - 88 Ave., Surrey BC V3W 7R7
Tel: 604-590-7454; *Fax:* 604-597-6656
john.vandermaar@powertech.bc.ca
To bargain collectively with Powertech Labs Inc. & its subsidiaries or successors on behalf of the members of the society with respect to all matters concerning terms & conditions of employment; to encourage & promote innovative concepts & procedures in the field of industrial relations; to adopt such procedures to the resolution of disputes between the society & the companies
Livio Gambone, President

Manitoba Association of Health Care Professionals (MAHCP) / Association des professionnels de la santé du Manitoba
#101, 1500 Notre Dame Ave., Winnipeg MB R3E 0P9
Tel: 204-772-0425; *Fax:* 204-775-6829
Toll-Free: 800-315-3331
info@mahcp.ca
www.mahcp.com
MAHCP is a union of health care professionals dedicated to protecting, advocating for, and advancing the rights of its members through labour relations activities.
Wendy Despins, President

Manitoba Federation of Labour / Fédération du travail du Manitoba
#303, 275 Broadway, Winnipeg MB R3C 4M6
Tel: 204-947-1400; *Fax:* 204-943-4276
www.mfl.mb.ca
To advance economic & social welfare of working people in Manitoba; To encourage workers to vote & exercise full rights & responsibilities
Darlene Dziewit, President

Maritime Fishermen's Union (CLC) (MFU) / Union des pêcheurs des Maritimes (CTC) (UPM)
408 Main St., Shediac NB E4P 2G1
Tel: 506-532-2485; *Fax:* 506-532-2487
shediac@mfu-upm.com
www.mfu-upm.com
The Maritime Fishermen's Union (MFU) represents over 1,800 fishermen/owner-operators, in New Brunswick and Nova Scotia. The MFU works to maintain a sustainable inshore fishery and defends the principal of the fishermen/owner-operator. Most MFU fishers practice a multi-species fishery with vessels under 15 meters.

Christian Brun, Executive Secretary

Mechanical Service Contractors of Canada (MSCC)
#601, 280 Albert St., Ottawa ON K1P 5G8
Tel: 613-232-0492; *Fax:* 613-235-2793
Toll-Free: 877-622-2668
daryl@mcac.ca
www.servicecontractor.ca
The Mechanical Service Contractors of Canada (MSCC), a division of the Mechanical Contractors Association of Canada, is dedicated to mechanical service, repair and retrofit contractors.
Daryl Sharkey, Chief Operating Officer

Native Brotherhood of British Columbia (NBBC) / Fraternité des Indiens de la Colombie-Britannique
#710, 100 Park Royal South, Vancouver BC V7T 1A2
Tel: 604-913-3372; *Fax:* 604-913-3374
nbbc@nativevoice.bc.ca
www.nativevoice.bc.ca
To advance the social, spiritual, economic & physical conditions of its members, including higher standards of education, health & living conditions; to cooperate with other organizations which concern themselves with the advancement of Indian welfare; focus is on capacity building, including fisheries, marine resources, tourism & eco-tourism, forestry & other resources with economic potential & opportunities

Natural Resources Union (NRU)
#600, 233 Gilmour St., Ottawa ON K2P 0P2
Tel: 613-560-4378; *Fax:* 613-233-7012
www.nru-srn.com
Mike Sargent, National President

New Brunswick Federation of Labour (NBFL) / Fédération des travailleurs et travailleuses du Nouveau-Brunswick
#314, 96 Norwood Ave., Moncton NB E1C 6L9
Tel: 506-857-2125; *Fax:* 506-383-1597
nbfl@nbnet.nb.ca; fttnb@nbnet.nb.ca
www.nbfl-fttnb.ca
To act as the central voice of labour in New Brunswick; To build solidarity & support between unions; To advance the economic & social welfare of New Brunswick's workers
Michel Boudreau, President
Ron Oldfield, First Vice-President
Thérèse Tremblay, Second Vice-President
Alex Bailey, Vice-President, Youth
Sandy Harding, Vice-President, Women's Issues
Danny King, Secretary-Treasurer

Newfoundland & Labrador Association of Public & Private Employees (NAPE)
PO Box 8100, 330 Portugal Cove Pl., St. John's NL A1B 3M9
Tel: 709-754-0700; *Fax:* 709-754-0726
Toll-Free: 800-563-4442
inquiries@nape.nf.ca
www.nape.nf.ca
The largest union in Newfoundland & Labrador
Bert Blundon, Secretary-Treasurer
Carol Furlong, President
Arlene Sedlickas, Vice President
David Curtis, Vice-President

Newfoundland & Labrador Federation of Labour (NLFL) / Fédération du travail de Terre-Neuve et du Labrador
NAPE Bldg., PO Box 8597, Stn. A, 330 Portugal Cove Pl., 2nd Fl., St. John's NL A1B 3P2
Tel: 709-754-1660; *Fax:* 709-754-1220
fed@nlfl.nf.ca
www.nlfl.nf.ca
The voice of labour in the province, with 30 affiliated unions, & over 500 locals in 6 district labour councils
Lana Payne, President
Linda Rideout, Executive Secretary

Northern Territories Federation of Labour / Fédération du travail des Territoires du Nord
PO Box 2787, Yellowknife NT X1A 2R1
Tel: 867-873-3695; *Fax:* 867-873-6979
ntfl@yk.com
www.ntfl.yk.com
An umbrella labour organization serving workers in the NWT & Nunavut, & the voice of all unions & workers in Canada's northern region; office located at 9 Stanton Plaza, 100 Borden Dr. in Yellowknife.
Mary Lou Cherwaty, President

Nova Scotia Federation of Labour / Fédération du travail de la Nouvelle-Écosse
#225, 3700 Kempt Rd., Halifax NS B3K 4X8
Tel: 902-454-6735; *Fax:* 902-454-7671
info@nsfl.ns.ca
www.nsfl.ns.ca
The Federation speaks on behalf of and represents the interests of organized and unorganized workers. It promotes decent wages and working conditions, improved health and safety laws and lobbies for fair taxes and strong social programs. It works for social equality, and to end racism and discrimination.
Rick Clarke, President
Ivy Shaw, Sec.-Treas.

Nova Scotia Government & General Employees Union (NSGEU) / Syndicat de la fonction publique de la Nouvelle-Écosse
100 Eileen Stubbs Ave., Dartmouth NS B3B 1Y6
Tel: 902-424-4063; *Fax:* 902-424-2111
Toll-Free: 877-556-7438
inquiry@nsgeu.ns.ca
www.nsgeu.ns.ca
The Nova Scotia Government & General Employees Union (NSGEU) is the largest union in the province of Nova Scotia and is the recognized bargaining agent for 26,000 public and private sector employees. Our members work in the civil service, school boards, universities, hospitals, liquor stores, correctional facilities, Regional Health Boards, municipalities, and other establishments across the Province.
Joan Jessome, President

Nova Scotia Union of Public & Private Employees (CCU) (NSUPE) / Syndicat des employés du secteur public de la Nouvelle-Écosse (CCU)
6309 Chebucto Rd., Halifax NS B3L 1K9
Tel: 902-422-9495; *Fax:* 902-429-7655
nsupe@ns.sympatico.ca
www.nsupe.ca
NSUPE is a trade union dedicated to bettering and protecting the livelihood and the social and economic well-being of its members, their families and fellow citizens.
John Hanrahan, President
Nancy Travis, Vice-President

Nunavut Employees Union (NEU)
PO Box 869, Iqaluit NU X0A 0H0
Tel: 867-979-4209; *Fax:* 867-979-4522
Toll-Free: 877-243-4424
info@neu.ca
www.neu.ca
The Nunavut Employees Union represents the interests of the employees of the Government of Nunavut, the Northwest Territories Power Corporation who live in Nunavut, Workers Compensation Board in Nunavut, Nunavut Housing Corporation, and the unionized employees of Nunavut municipalities and Housing Associations. Most of our members work for the Government of Nunavut and live all across the territory. Others belong to Canada Labour Code bargaining units representing Housing Associations and Authorities, Hamlet and town employees, and support staff in schools. NEU members are social workers and nurses, health care professionals, power plant workers, security guards, hamlet bylaw officers, renewable resource officers, engineers, and many more.
Doug Workman, President
Brian Boutilier, Executive Director

Office & Professional Employees International Union (AFL-CIO/CLC) / Union internationale des employés professionnels et de bureau (FAT-COI/CTC)
1660 L St. NW, Washington DC 20036 USA
Tel: 202-393-4464
opeiu@opeiu.org
www.opeiu.org
Michael Goodwin, President

Ontario Federation of Labour (OFL) / Fédération du travail de l'Ontario
#202, 15 Gervais Dr., Toronto ON M3C 1Y8
Tel: 416-441-2731; *Fax:* 416-441-0722
Toll-Free: 800-668-9138
TTY: 416-443-6305
info@ofl.ca
www.ofl.ca
To represent the interests of organized workers in Ontario; To provide support services to its affiliated local unions & labour councils
Sid Ryan, President
Nancy Hutchinson, Sec.-Treas.

Ontario Professional Fire Fighters Association (OPFFA) / Association des pompiers professionnels de l'Ontario (ind.)
292 Plains Rd. East, Burlington ON L7T 2C6
Tel: 905-681-7111; *Fax:* 905-681-1489
www.opffa.org
Fred LeBlanc, President
Mark McKinnon, Executive Vice-President
Barry Quinn, Secretary-Treasurer
Jeff Braun-Jackson, Office Manager & Researcher

Ontario Public Service Employees Union (OPSEU) / Syndicat des employées et employés de la fonction publique de l'Ontario
100 Lesmill Rd., Toronto ON M3B 3P8
Tel: 416-443-8888; *Fax:* 416-443-9670
Toll-Free: 800-268-7376
opseu@opseu.org
www.opseu.org
To negotiate collective agreements; to conduct membership education; to lobby governments to maintain & improve public services; to defend the principle of social unionism by speaking out on public policy issues such as taxes, free trade, privatization, health care, social services, occupational health & safety, & employment equity.
Smokey Thomas, President

Operative Plasterers' & Cement Masons' International Association of the US & Canada (AFL-CIO/CFL) - Canadian Office
Varette Bldg., #1902, 130 Albert St., Ottawa ON K1P 5G4
Tel: 613-236-0653; *Fax:* 613-230-5138
cdnoffice@buildingtrades.ca
www.buildingtrades.ca
We represent over 400,000 construction workers who belong to the 15 affiliated international Building Trades unions in Canada.
Robert Blakely, Director, Canadian Affairs

Prince Edward Island Federation of Labour / Fédération du travail de l'Île-du-Prince-Édouard
22 Enman Cres., Charlottetown PE C1A 1E6
Tel: 902-368-3068; *Fax:* 902-368-3192
peifed@pei.aibn.com
www.peifl.ca
Carl Pursey, President

Prince Edward Island Union of Public Sector Employees / Syndicat de la fonction publique de l'Île-du-Prince-Édouard
PO Box 1116, 4 Enman Cres. South, Charlottetown PE C1A 7M8
Tel: 902-892-5335; *Fax:* 902-569-8186
Toll-Free: 800-897-8773
peiupse@peiupse.ca
www.peiupse.ca
Shelly Ward, President

Professional Association of Foreign Service Officers (Ind.) (PAFSO) / L'Association professionnelle des agents du service extérieur (ind.) (APASE)
#412, 47 Clarence St., Ottawa ON K1N 9K1
Tel: 613-241-1391; *Fax:* 613-241-5911
info@pafso.com
www.pafso.com
Ron Cochrane, Executive Director

Professional Association of Internes & Residents of Newfoundland (PAIRN) / Association professionnelle des internes et résidents de Terre-Neuve
c/o Student Affairs, Health Sciences Complex, Memorial University, #2867, 300 Prince Philip Dr., St. John's NL A1B 3V6
Tel: 709-777-7118; *Fax:* 709-777-6968
pairn@mun.ca
www.pairn.nl.ca
To collaborate with local & national health care organizations to advocate on behalf of internes, resident physicians, & fellows of Newfoundland & Labrador; To advocate for the acknowledgement of the resident's role in medical education
Chris Smith, President
Pamela Hebbard, Vice-President
Deanna Murphy, Secretary
Sohaib Al-Asaaed, Treasurer

Professional Association of Interns & Residents of Saskatchewan (PAIRS) / Association professionnelle des internes et résidents de la Saskatchewan (ind.)
C Wing, Royal University Hospital, PO Box 23, #5687, 103 Hospital Dr., 5th Fl., Saskatoon SK S7N 0W8
Tel: 306-655-2134; *Fax:* 306-655-2134
pairs.sk@usask.ca
www.usask.ca/pairs
To represent resident physicians of Saskatchewan at the university & hospital levels, as well as provincially & nationally; To improve education, salaries, & other benefits for resident physicians
Gavin Beck, President
Sue Sidhu, Vice-President
Nove Kalia, Secretary-Treasurer
Joan Cheyne, Executive Director

Professional Association of Residents & Interns of Manitoba (PARIM) / Association professionnelle des résidents et internes du Manitoba
#AD107, 720 McDermot Ave., Winnipeg MB R3E 0T3
Tel: 204-787-3673; *Fax:* 204-787-2692
parim@mts.net
www.parim.org
To represent the concerns of all residents & interns in Manitoba; To advocate for the well-being of residents & interns; To promote quality medical education & excellent patient care
Marc Fournier, Co-President
Paul Wawryko, Co-President
Jay Hingwala, Vice-President, Internal Affairs & Finance
Fatemeh Kojori, Vice-President, Social & Well-being
Kanwal Kumar, Vice-President, Communications

Professional Association of Residents in the Maritime Provinces (PARI-MP) / Association professionnelle des résidents des provinces maritimes
Halifax Professional Centre, #460, 5991 Spring Garden Rd., Halifax NS B3H 1Y6
Tel: 902-404-3595; *Fax:* 902-404-3599
Toll-Free: 877-972-7467
sandi@parimp.ca
www.parimp.ca
To represent the interests of resident physicians who train at Dalhousie University; To improve the well-being & working conditions of residents in the Maritimes; To advocate on the behalf of residents
Laine Green, President
Matt Smith, Vice-President
Bryan Chung, Secretary
Kerri Purdy, Treasurer
Sandi Carew Flemming, Executive Director
Leanne Bryan, Coordinator, Benefits & Events

Professional Association of Residents of Alberta (PARA) / Association professionnelle des résidents de l'Alberta
Garneau Professional Center, #340, 11044 - 82 Ave., Edmonton AB T6G OJ2
Tel: 780-432-1749; *Fax:* 780-432-1778
para-ab@shawbiz.ca
www.para-ab.ca
To represent physicians completing further training in residency programs; To promote excellence in education & patient care; To advocate for health care issues & for improvement in working conditions, salary, & benefits for resident physicians of Alberta
Michelle Carle, President
Henry Conter, Vice-President, Internal Affairs
Kenman Gan, Vice-President, Operations & Finance
Jillian Schwartz, Vice-President, External Affairs
Sarah Thomas, Executive Director
Tana Findlay, Executive Director, Operations

Professional Association of Residents of British Columbia (PAR-BC) / Association professionnelle des résidents de la Colombie-Britannique
#2010, 401 West Georgia St., Vancouver BC V6B 5A1
Tel: 604-876-7636; *Fax:* 604-876-7690
Toll-Free: 888-877-2722
par@par-bc.org
www.par-bc.org
To bargain collectively on behalf of residents in British Columbia; To foster the personal well-being of members
Mark Masterson, President
Sam Gharbi, Vice-President
Sana Ahmed, Director, Communications
May Tee, Director, Finance

Professional Employees Association (Ind.) (PEA) / Association des employés professionnels (ind.)
#505, 1207 Douglas St., Victoria BC V8W 2E7
Tel: 250-385-8791; *Fax:* 250-385-6629
Toll-Free: 800-779-7736
jjensen@pea.org
www.pea.org
Social Media: www.facebook.com/peaonline; twitter.com/pea_online; www.youtube.com/user/PEAblogger
To provide collective bargaining representation to professionals employed in the provincial public service & elsewhere in the BC public sector
Frank Kohlberger, President

Professional Engineers Government of Ontario
#206, 3199 Bathurst St., Toronto ON M6A 2B2
Tel: 416-784-1284; *Fax:* 416-784-1366
pego@pego.on.ca
www.pego.on.ca
The Professional Engineers Government of Ontario (PEGO) is a certified bargaining association representing Professional Engineers and Ontario Land Surveyors working directly for the Government of the Province of Ontario.
John Gasbarri, President

The Professional Institute of the Public Service of Canada (PIPSC) / Institut professionnel de la fonction publique du Canada
250 Tremblay Rd., Ottawa ON K1G 3J8
Tel: 613-228-6310; *Fax:* 613-228-9048
Toll-Free: 800-267-0446
www.pipsc.ca
To serve members by serving as their collective bargaining agent & by providing representational services
Gary Corbett, President
Edward Gillis, COO/Executive Secretary

Public Service Alliance of Canada (CLC) (PSAC) / Alliance de la Fonction publique du Canada (CTC) (AFPC)
233 Gilmour St., Ottawa ON K2P 0P1
Tel: 613-560-4200; *Fax:* 613-567-0385
Toll-Free: 888-604-7722
www.psac.com
To unite all workers in a single democratic organization; To obtain for all public service employees the best standards of compensation & other conditions of employment & to protect the rights & interests of all public service employees; To maintain & defend the right to strike
John Gordon, National President
Jeannie Baldwin, Regional Executive Vice-President, Atlantic
Bob Jackson, Regional Executive Vice-President, B.C.
Robyn Benson, Regional Executive Vice-President, Prairies
Patty Ducharme, National Vice-President
Sharon DeSpousa, Regional Executive Vice-President, Ontario
Jérôme Turcq, Vice-président exécutif régional, Québec
Julie Docherty, Regional Executive Vice-President, North
Larry Rousseau, Regional Executive Vice-President, National Capital Region

Pulp, Paper & Woodworkers of Canada (CCU) (PPWC)
#201, 1184 - 6 Ave. West, Vancouver BC V6H 1A4
Tel: 604-731-1909; *Fax:* 604-731-6448
Toll-Free: 888-992-7792
louise@web.net
www.ppwc.ca
Chris Elias, President

Research Council Employees' Association (Ind.) (RCEA) / Association des employés du conseil de recherches (ind.) (AECR)
PO Box 8256, Ottawa ON K1G 3H7
Tel: 613-746-9341; *Fax:* 613-745-7868
office@rcea.ca
www.rcea.ca
The RCEA is the certified bargaining agent for six groups and categories and represents the majority of NRC employees. These groups and categories are: AD (Administrative Support) Group, AS (Administrative Services) Group, CS (Computer Systems Administration) Group, OP (Operational) Category, PG (Purchasing and Supply) Group, and TO(Technical) Category.
Serge Croteau, President
Laurette T. Ernst, Office Manager

Royal Newfoundland Constabulary Association (RNCA) / Fraternité des policiers de la gendarmerie royale de Terre-Neuve
125 East White Hills Rd., St. John's NL A1A 5R7
Tel: 709-739-5946; *Fax:* 709-739-6276
office@rnca.ca
www.rnca.ca
The goals and objectives of the RNCA are to improve benefits and working conditions for police officers, improve public safety and strive to create a positive relationship between the police and the community they protect.
Todd Barron, President

Saskatchewan Government & General Employees' Union (SGEU) / Syndicat de la fonction publique de la Saskatchewan
1440 Broadway Ave., Regina SK S4P 1E2
Tel: 306-522-8571; *Fax:* 306-352-1969
Toll-Free: 800-667-5221
general@sgeu.org
www.sgeu.org
Bob Bymoen, President

Saskatchewan Joint Board, Retail, Wholesale & Department Store Union (CLC) / Conseil mixte du syndicat des employés de gros, de détail et de magasins à rayons de la Saskatchewan (CTC)
1233 Winnipeg St., Regina SK S4R 1K1
Tel: 306-569-9311; *Fax:* 306-569-9521
Toll-Free: 877-747-9378
rwdsu.regina@sasktel.net
www.rwdsu.sk.ca
Chris Banting, Secretary-Treasurer

Schneider Employees' Association (Ind.) / Association des employés de Schneider (ind.)
321 Courtland Ave. East, Kitchener ON N2G 3X8
Tel: 519-741-5000; *Fax:* 519-744-5099
schneider@cwa-scacanada.ca
Sandy Russell, National President

Seafarers' International Union of Canada (AFL-CIO/CLC) / Syndicat international des marins canadiens (FAT-COI/CTC)
1333, rue Saint-Jacques, Montréal QC H3C 4K2
Tel: 514-931-7859; *Fax:* 514-931-3667
siuofcanada@seafarers.ca
www.seafarers.ca
Michel Desjardins, President

Service Employees International Union (AFL-CIO/CLC) / Union internationale des employés des services (FAT-COI/CTC)
1800 Massachusetts Ave. NW, Washington DC 20036 USA
Tel: 202-730-7000; *Fax:* 202-898-3402
Toll-Free: 800-424-8592
TTY: 202-730-7481
www.seiu.org
Social Media: www.facebook.com/SEIU; twitter.com/SEIU; www.youtube.com/user/SEIU; www.flickr.com/photos/seiu
SEIU is focused on uniting workers in 3 sectors: healthcare, property services, & public services. The union aims to improve the lives of its members, their families, & the services they provide.
Mary Kay Henry, President

Sheet Metal Workers' International Association (AFL-CIO/CFL) (SMWIA) / Association internationale des travailleurs du métal en feuilles (FAT-COI/FCT)
1750 New York Ave. NW, 6th Fl., Washington DC 20006 USA
Tel: 202-783-5880
info@smwia.org
www.smwia.org
SMWIA aims to establish & maintain desirable working conditions for its members, & is their collective bargaining agent.
Mike Sullivan, General President

Shipyard General Workers' Federation of British Columbia (CLC) / Fédération des ouvriers des chantiers navals de la Colombie-Britannique (CTC)
#130, 111 Victoria Dr., Vancouver BC V5L 4C4
Tel: 604-254-8204; *Fax:* 604-254-7447
office@bcshipyardworkers.com
www.bcshipyardworkers.com
George MacPherson, President
Quentin Del Vecchio, General Secretary

Société des Auteurs de Radio, Télévision et Cinéma (SARTEC) / Society of Writers in Radio, Television & Cinema
1229, rue Panet, Montréal QC H2L 2Y6
Tél: 514-526-9196; *Téléc:* 514-526-4124
information@sartec.qc.ca
www.sartec.qc.ca
Regroupe les auteurs de langue française oeuvrant au Canada dans les domaines de la radio, de la télévision, du cinéma ou de l'audiovisuel; a pour objet l'étude, la défense et le développement des intérêts économiques, sociaux et moraux de ses membres
Yves Légaré, Directeur général
Sylvie Lussier, Présidente

Société des technologues en nutrition (STN)
895, boul Charest ouest, Québec QC G1N 2C9
Tél: 418-990-0309
stn@stnq.ca
www.stnq.ca
Signer des contrats collectifs de travail; surveiller la mise en application des conditions de travail des membres; promouvoir la défense et les intérêts économiques et professionnels des membres

The Society of Energy Professionals
#300, 425 Bloor St. East., Toronto ON M4W 3R4
Tel: 416-979-2709; *Fax:* 416-979-5794
Toll-Free: 866-288-1788
society@society.on.ca
www.thesociety.ca
To represent the interests of the professional, administrative, & associated employees in all aspects of their employment with Ontario Hydro
Rodney Sheppard, President

Society of Professional Engineers & Associates (SPEA) / Société des ingénieurs professionnels et associés
#2, 2275 Speakman Dr., Mississauga ON L5K 1B1
Tel: 905-823-3606; *Fax:* 905-823-9602
www.spea.ca
To represent scientists, engineers, technologists, & tradespeople who work for Atomic Energy of Canada Limited (AECL) in Mississauga, Ontario & abroad
Ritu Luther, Office Administrator
Peter White, President
Val Aleyaseen, Chair, Membership
Vincent Tume, Secretary
Brian Girard, Treasurer

Space Systems Engineers & Scientists Association (SSESA) / Association des ingénieurs et des scientifiques des systèmes spatiaux (AISSS)
1073, rue Saint-Denis, Montréal QC H2X 3J3
Tel: 514-844-1347; *Fax:* 514-844-8037
lauzon.d@ems-t.ca
www.aisss-ssesa.org
Dominick Lauzon, President

Syndicat de la fonction publique du Québec inc. (ind.) (SFPQ) / Québec Government Employees' Union (Ind.)
5100, boul des Gradins, Québec QC G2J 1N4
Tél: 418-623-2424; *Téléc:* 418-623-6109
communication@sfpq.qc.ca
www.sfpq.qc.ca
Assurer la défense des intérêts économiques, politiques et sociaux des membres et le développement de leurs conditions de vie; faire la promotion des services publics comme moyen démocratique de répondre aux besoins de la population
Lucie Martineau, Présidente général

Syndicat de professionnelles et professionnels du gouvernement du Québec (SPGQ) / Union of Professional Employees of the Québec Government
7, rue Vallière, Québec QC G1K 6S9
Tél: 418-692-0022; *Téléc:* 418-692-1338
Ligne sans frais: 800-463-5079
courrier@spgq.qc.ca
www.spgq.qc.ca
Média social: www.facebook.com/lespgq; twitter.com/spgq
Gilles Dussault, Président
Michael Isaacs, Secrétaire

Syndicat des agents de la paix en services correctionnels du Québec (ind.) (SAPSCQ) / Union of Prison Guards of Québec (Ind.)
4906, boul Gouin est, Montréal QC H1G 1A4
Tél: 514-328-7774; *Téléc:* 514-328-0889
Ligne sans frais: 800-361-3559
www.sapscq.com
Service syndical pour les agents de la paix en services correctionnels du Québec
Stéphane Lemaire, Président national
Tony Vallières, Vice-président
Sylvain Maltais, Secrétaire général

Syndicat des agents de maîtrise de TELUS (ind.) (SAMT) / TELUS Professional Employees Union (Ind.) (TPEU)
#605, 2, St-Germain est, Rimouski QC G5L 8T7
Tél: 418-722-6144; *Téléc:* 418-724-0765
samt2@globetrotter.net

La sauvegarde et la promotion des intérêts professionnels, scientifiques, économiques, sociaux, culturels et politiques de ses membres; faire bénéficier les membres et les travailleurs en général des avantages de l'entraide et des négociations collectives; obtenir pour ses membres un meilleur niveau de vie et de meilleures conditions de travail; représenter les membres auprès de l'employeur
Harold Morrissey, Président
Lynda Fortin, Secrétaire

Syndicat des employé(e)s de magasins et de bureau de la Société des alcools du Québec (ind.) / Québec Liquor Board Store & Office Employees Union (Ind.)
1065, rue St-Denis, Montréal QC H2X 3J3
Tél: 514-849-7754; *Téléc:* 514-849-7914
Ligne sans frais: 800-361-8427
info@semb-saq.com
www.semb-saq.com/index.html
Katia Lelièvre, Présidente

Syndicat des employés en radio-télédiffusion de Télé-Québec (CSQ) / Télé-Québec Television Broadcast Employees' Union
1000, rue Fullum, Montréal QC H2K 3L7
Tél: 514-529-2805; *Téléc:* 514-873-0826
sert@colba.net
sert.csq.qc.net/
Philippe Ouimet, Président

Syndicat des pompiers et pompières du Québec (CTC) (SPQ) / Québec Union of Firefighters (CLC)
#3900, 565, boul Crémazie est, Montréal QC H2M 2V6
Tél: 514-383-4698; *Téléc:* 514-383-6782
Ligne sans frais: 800-461-4698
spq@spq-ftq.com
www.spq-ftq.com
Gilles Raymond, Président

Syndicat des professeures et professeurs de l'Université de Sherbrooke (SPPUS)
2500, boul Université, Sherbrooke QC J1K 2R1
Tél: 819-821-7656; *Téléc:* 819-821-7995
sppus@usherbrooke.ca
www.usherbrooke.ca/sppus
Voir à l'application de la convention collective; défendre les intérêts des membres
Bernard Héraud, Secrétaire général

Syndicat des professeurs de l'État du Québec (ind.) (SPEQ) / Union of Professors for the Government of Québec (Ind.)
#1003, 2120, rue Sherbrooke est, Montréal QC H2K 1C3
Tél: 514-525-7979; *Téléc:* 514-525-4655
Ligne sans frais: 877-525-7979
info@speq.org
www.speq.org
Le Syndicat des professeurs de l'État du Québec (SPEQ) a été accrédité le 8 septembre 1965 pour représenter les fonctionnaires enseignants salariés.
Claude Tanguay, Président

Syndicat des professionnels et des techniciens de la santé du Québec (SPTSQ) / Québec Union of Health Professionals & Technicians
#850, 1001, rue Sherbrooke est, Montréal QC H2L 1L3
Tél: 514-521-4469; *Téléc:* 514-521-0086
Défense des intérêts socio-économiques de ses membres
Carolle Dubé, Présidente

Syndicat des technicien(ne)s et artisan(e)s du réseau français de Radio-Canada (ind.) (STARF) / CBC French Network Technicians' Union (Ind.)
1250, rue de la Visitation, 1er étage, Montréal QC H2L 3B4
Tél: 514-524-1100; *Téléc:* 514-524-6023
Ligne sans frais: 888-838-1100
secretariat@starf.qc.ca
www.starf.qc.ca
Benoît Celestino, Président
Marie-France Clément, Secrétaire-trésorier

Syndicat des technologues en radiologie du Québec (ind.) (STRQ) / Union of Radiology Technicians of Québec
#850, 1001, rue Sherbrooke est, Montréal QC H2L 1L3
Tél: 514-521-4469; *Téléc:* 514-521-0086
Étude, développement et la défense des intérêts professionnels, économiques, sociaux et éducatifs de ses membres et particulièrement la négociation et l'application de conventions collectives.

Syndicat des travailleurs de la construction du Québec (CSD)
#300, 801, 4e rue, Québec QC G1J 2T7
Tél: 418-522-3918; *Téléc:* 418-529-6323
www.csdconstruction.qc.ca
Défendre et promouvoir les intérêts sociaux et économiques de ses membres
Patrick Daigneault, Président
Guy Terrault, Vice-président
Gilles C. Coulombe, Secrétaire

Syndicat du personnel technique et professionnel de la Société des alcools du Québec (ind.) (SPTPSAQ) / Québec Liquor Board's Union of Technical & Professional Employees (Ind.)
905, rue de Lorimier, Montréal QC H2K 3V9
Tél: 514-873-5878; *Téléc:* 514-873-5896
sptp@bellnet.ca
Yves St-Georges, Président

Syndicat général du cinéma et de la télévision - Section Office national du film (ind.) (SGCT)
#25A, 2340, ch Lucerne, Mont-Royal QC H3R 2J8
Tél: 514-344-9399; *Téléc:* 514-344-9509
Représenter les cinéastes et techniciens employés par l'Office National du Film du Canada

Syndicat interprovincial des ferblantiers et couvreurs, la section locale 2016 à la FTQ-Construction
#400, 8550, boul Pie IX, Montréal QC H1Z 4G2
Tél: 514-374-1515; *Téléc:* 514-374-2282
Ligne sans frais: 866-374-1515
administration@ftq2016.org
www.ftq2016.org
Voir à la promotion et à la défense des intérêts économiques et sociaux des membres; assurer l'intégrité du métier de ferblantier et couvreur en défendant sa juridiction professionnelle et en assurant sa sécurité d'emploi; représenter les travailleurs, que leur travail soit effectué à l'intérieur du chantier de construction ou non; cultiver des sentiments de solidarité parmis les travailleurs; obtenir des améliorations dans les conditions de travail de ses membres
Dorima Aubut, Directeur provincial

Syndicat professionnel des diététistes et nutritionnistes du Québec (SPDNQ) / Québec Professional Union of Dieticians (Ind.)
2665, rue Beaubien est, Montréal QC H1Y 1G8
Tél: 514-725-5535; *Téléc:* 514-725-4433
Claudette Péloquin-Antoun, Présidente

Syndicat professionnel des ingénieurs d'Hydro-Québec (ind.) (SPIHQ) / Hydro-Québec Professional Engineers Union (Ind.)
bureau #1400, 1255 rue University, Montréal QC H3B 3X1
Tél: 514-845-4239; *Téléc:* 514-845-0082
Ligne sans frais: 800-567-1260
spihq@spihq.qc.ca
www.spihq.qc.ca
Le Syndicat travaille pour la défense & le développement des intérêts économiques, sociaux, & professionnels des membres
Carole Leroux, Président
Yvon Filion, Secrétaire

Syndicat professionnel des médecins du gouvernement du Québec (ind.) (SPMGQ) / Professional Union of Government of Québec Physicians (Ind.)
1390, rue du Père-Jamet, Sainte-Foy QC G1W 3G5
Tél: 418-266-4670; *Téléc:* 418-266-4672
christine.gagne@csst.qc.ca
Représenter les médecins à l'emploi du gouvernement du Québec
Christine Gagné, Présidente

Syndicat québécois de la construction (SQC) / North Shore Construction Inc. (Ind.)
2121, av Sainte-Anne, Saint-Hyacinthe QC J2S 5H5
Tél: 450-773-8833; *Téléc:* 450-773-2232
Ligne sans frais: 888-773-8834
info@sqc.ca
www.sqc.ca
Sylvain Gendron, Président

Teaching Support Staff Union (TSSU)
Simon Fraser University, AQ 5129/5130, 8888 University Dr., Burnaby BC V5A 1S6
Tel: 604-291-4735; *Fax:* 604-291-5369
tssu@tssu.ca
www.tssu.ca
Social Media: twitter.com/TSSU
Scott Drake, Organizer

Teamsters Canada (CLC)
#804, 2540, boul Daniel Johnson, Laval QC H7T 2S3
Tél: 450-682-5521; *Téléc:* 450-681-2244
Ligne sans frais: 866-888-6466
info@teamsters-canada.org
www.teamsters.ca
Média social: www.facebook.com/group.php?gid=5512214518
Robert Bouvier, Président
Tom Fraser, Vice-président
Stan Hennessey, Vice-président

Teamsters Canada Rail Conference (TCRC) / Conference ferroviaire de Teamsters Canada (CFTC)
#1710, 130 Albert St., Ottawa ON K1P 5G4
Tel: 613-235-1828; *Fax:* 613-235-1069
info@teamstersrail.ca
www.teamstersrail.ca
Dan Shewchuk, President

Telecommunications Employees Association of Manitoba (Ind.) (TEAM) / Association des employés en télécommunications du Manitoba (ind.)
#200, 1 Wesley Ave., Winnipeg MB R2H 1K1
Tel: 204-984-9470; *Fax:* 204-231-2809
Toll-Free: 877-984-9470
team@teamunion.mb.ca
www.teamunion.mb.ca
Misty Hughes-Newman, President

Telecommunications Workers' Union (CLC) (TWU) / Syndicat des travailleurs en télécommunications (CTC) (STT)
5261 Lane St., Burnaby BC V5H 4A6
Tel: 604-437-8601; *Fax:* 604-435-7760
Toll-Free: 888-986-3971
twu@twu-stt.ca
www.twu-stt.ca
John Carpenter, Vice-President
Betty Carrasco, Vice-President
George Doubt, President
Sherryl Anderson, Sec.-Treas.

Union canadienne des travailleurs en communication (ind.) / Canadian Union of Communication Workers (Ind.)
502, 90e av, Lasalle QC H8R 2Z7
Tél: 514-595-9095; *Téléc:* 514-595-8911

Union des artistes (UDA) / Artists' Union
#400, 1441, boul. René-Lévesque ouest, Montréal QC H3G 1T7
Tél: 514-288-6682; *Téléc:* 514-285-6789
info@uda.ca
www.uniondesartistes.com
Identification, étude, défense et développement des intérêts économiques, sociaux et moraux de ses membres
Raymond Legault, Président
François Ferland, Directeur général

Union of Canadian Transportation Employees (UCTE) / Union canadienne des employés des transports (UCET)
#702, 233 Gilmour St., Ottawa ON K2P 0P2
Tel: 613-238-4003; *Fax:* 613-236-0379
buschml@psac-afpc.comm
www.ucte.com
The Union represents members working in the public & private sectors of the Canadian transportation industry (ports, airports, NAV Canada, pilotage authorities, transportation companies, canals, the Dept. of Transport, lighthouses, ships and Canadian Coast Guard bases)
Gardenia Li, Finance & Administration Officer

Union of National Defence Employees (UNDE) / Union des employés de la Défense nationale (UEDN)
#700, 116 Albert St., Ottawa ON K1P 5G3
Tel: 613-594-4505; *Fax:* 613-594-8233
Toll-Free: 866-594-4505
www.unde-uedn.com
John MacLennan, National President

Union of Northern Workers / Syndicat des travailleurs du Nord
#200, 5112 - 52 St., Yellowknife NT X1A 3Z5
Tel: 867-873-5668; *Fax:* 867-920-4448
Toll-Free: 877-906-4447
www.unw.ca
Todd Parsons, President

Union of Postal Communications Employees (UPCE) / Syndicat des employés des postes et des communications (SEPC)
#701, 233 Gilmour St., Ottawa ON K2P 0P2
Tel: 613-560-4342; *Fax:* 613-594-3849
sepc-upce@psac.com
www.upce.ca
Represents Canada Post members employed in administrative, clerical, technical & professional capacities
Patty Ducharme, National Executive Vice President

Union of Solicitor General Employees (USGE) / Syndicat des employés du Solliciteur général (SESG)
#603, 233 Gilmour St., Ottawa ON K2P 0P2
Tel: 613-232-4821; *Fax:* 613-232-3311
info@usge-sesg.com
www.usge-sesg.com
Mireille Laniel, Operations Manager

Union of Taxation Employees (UTE) / Syndicat des employé(e)s de l'impôt (SEI)
#602, 233 Gilmour St., Ottawa ON K2P 0P2
Tel: 613-235-6704; *Fax:* 613-234-7290
www.ute-sei.org
Betty Bannon, National President

Union of Veterans' Affairs Employees (UVAE) / Syndicat des employé(e)s des affaires des anciens combattants (SEAC)
#703, 233 Gilmour St., Ottawa ON K2P 0P2
Tel: 613-560-5460; *Fax:* 613-237-8282
thauvey@psac.com
uvae-seac.ca
Yvan Thauvette, National President

UNITE HERE Canada
460 Richmond St. West, 2nd Fl., Toronto ON M5V 1Y1
Tel: 416-510-0887; *Fax:* 416-510-0891
Toll-Free: 800-268-4046
info@unitehere.ca
www.unitehere.ca

United Association of Journeymen & Apprentices of the Plumbing & Pipe Fitting Industry of the United States & Canada (UA)
3 Park Place, Annapolis MD 21401 USA
Tel: 410-269-2000; *Fax:* 410-267-0262
ua.org
Social Media:
www.facebook.com/pages/United-Association/103644036958; twitter.com/UAPoliticalEd; www.youtube.com/uaweb901
The union for plumbers, fitters, welders and HVAC Service Techs
William P. Hite, General President
Patrick R. Perno, General Sec.-Treas.
Stephen F. Kelly, Assistant General President

United Brotherhood of Carpenters & Joiners of America (AFL-CIO/CLC) / Fraternité unie des charpentiers et menuisiers d'Amérique (FAT-COI/CTC)
101 Constitution Ave. NW, Washington DC 20001 USA
Tel: 202-546-6206; *Fax:* 202-543-5724
webmaster@carpenters.org
www.carpenters.org
Douglas J. McCarron, General President

United Food & Commercial Workers Canada (UFCW CANADA)
#300, 61 International Blvd., Toronto ON M9W 6K4
Tel: 416-675-1104; *Fax:* 416-675-6919
ufcw@ufcw.ca
www.ufcw.ca
Social Media: www.facebook.com/ufcwcanada; twitter.com/ufcwcanada
One of Canada's largest private sector unions
Wayne Hanley, National President

United Food & Commercial Workers' International Union (UFCW) / Union internationale des travailleurs et travailleuses unis de l'alimentation et du commerce
1775 K St. NW, Washington DC 20006 USA
Tel: 202-223-3111; *Fax:* 202-466-1562
ufcw@ufcw.ca
www.ufcw.org
Social Media: www.facebook.com/group.php?gid=19812849944
Joseph T. Hansen, International President
Anthony M. Perrone, International Sec.-Treas.

United Mine Workers of America (CLC) / Mineurs unis d'Amérique (CTC)
8315 Lee Hwy., Fairfax VA 22031 USA
Tel: 703-208-7200
www.umwa.org
Cecil Roberts, President

United Steelworkers of America (AFL-CIO/CLC) / Métallurgistes unis d'Amérique (FAT-COI/CTC)
5 Gateway Center, Pittsburgh PA 15222 USA
Tel: 412-562-2400
webmaster@uswa.org
www.uswa.org
Social Media: www.facebook.com/steelworkers?ref=ts; twitter.com/steelworkers
Leo W. Gerard, International President

United Transportation Union (AFL-CIO/CLC) - Canada
71 Bank St., 7th Fl., Ottawa ON K1P 5N2
Tel: 613-747-7979; *Fax:* 613-747-2815

Yukon Employees Union (YEU) / Syndicat des employés du Yukon
#201, 2285 Second Ave., Whitehorse YT Y1A 1C9
Tel: 867-667-2331; *Fax:* 867-667-6521
admint@yeu.ca
www.yeu.ca
To unite all members of the Alliance over which this Union has jurisdiction into a single union capable of acting on their behalf; to obtain through democratic means for all members the best possible standards of wages, salaries & other conditions of employment, & to protect the interests, rights & privileges of all such employees
Laurie Butterworth, President
Denise L. Norman, Executive Director

Yukon Federation of Labour (YFL) / Fédération du travail du Yukon
#102, 106 Strickland St., Whitehorse YT Y1A 2J5
Tel: 867-667-6676; *Fax:* 867-633-5558
yfl@yukonfed.com
www.yukonfed.com
Doug Rody, Director, Policy & Legislative Affairs

Landscape Architecture

Alberta Association of Landscape Architects (AALA)
PO Box 21052, Edmonton AB T6R 2V4
Tel: 780-435-9902; *Fax:* 780-413-0076
aala@aala.ab.ca
www.aala.ab.ca
To advance the quality of the professional practice of landscape architecture in Alberta
Jill Lane, Manager
Mark Nolan, Registrar
Brian Charanduk, Treasurer
Michelle Lefebre, Secretary

Association des architectes paysagistes du Québec (AAPQ)
4655, De Lorimier, Montréal QC H2H 2B4
Tél: 514-990-7731; *Téléc:* 877-990-7731
info@aapq.org
www.aapq.org
Promouvoir la création et la valorisation du paysage en milieu naturel et construit dans le but de constituer un cadre de vie sain, fonctionnel, esthétique, axé sur les besoins de la population et répondant aux exigences écologiques
Marie-Claude Robert, Directrice générale

Atlantic Provinces Association of Landscape Architects (APALA)
PO Box 653, Stn. Halifax CRO, Halifax NS B3J 2Z1
info@apala.ca
www.apala.ca
To promote, improve & advance the profession; to maintain standards of professional practice & conduct consistent with the need to serve & to protect the public interest; to support improvement &/or conservation of the natural, cultural, social & built environment
Edward Versteeg, Sec.-Treas.
Gordon Smith, President

British Columbia Society of Landscape Architects (BCSLA)
#110, 355 Burrard St., Vancouver BC V6C 2G8
Tel: 604-682-5610; *Fax:* 604-681-3394
admin@bcsla.org
www.bcsla.org
To promote, improve & advance the profession; to maintain standards of professional practice & conduct consistent with the need to serve & protect the public interest; to support the improvement &/or conservation of the natural, cultural, social & built environment.
Pawel Gradowski, President

Canadian Society of Landscape Architects (CSLA) / Association des architectes paysagistes du Canada (AAPC)
PO Box 13594, Ottawa ON K2K 1X6
Tel: 866-781-9799; *Fax:* 866-871-1419
info@csla.ca
www.csla.ca
To support the improvement &/or conservation of the natural, cultural, social & built environment; to promote visibility, recognition, acceptance & understanding of the profession by communicating its value in relation to that of the public good
Elizabeth A. Sharpe, Executive Director

Manitoba Association of Landscape Architects (MALA)
131 Callum Cres., Winnipeg MB R2G 2C7
Tel: 204-663-4863; *Fax:* 204-668-5662
www.mala.net
To promote, improve & advance the profession; to maintain standards of professional practice & conduct consistent with the need to serve & protect public interest; to support improvement &/or conservation of the natural, cultural, social & built environment
Emeka Nnadi, President

Newfoundland & Labrador Association of Landscape Architects (NLALA)
77 Gower St., St. John's NL A1C 1N6
Tel: 709-579-7744
www.nlala.com
Jim Floyd, President

Northwest Territories Association of Landscape Architects (NWTALA)
PO Box 1394, Yellowknife NT X1A 2P1
Tel: 867-920-2986; *Fax:* 867-920-2986
atborow@internorth.com
To represent landscape architects in the Northwest Territories

Ontario Association of Landscape Architects (OALA)
#407, 3 Church St., Toronto ON M5E 1M2
Tel: 416-231-4181; *Fax:* 416-231-2679
oala@oala.ca
www.oala.ca
To promote, improve & advance the profession; to maintain standards of professional practice & conduct consistent with the need to serve & to protect the public interest; to support improvement &/or conservation of the natural, cultural, social & built environment
Linda MacLeod, Registrar
Glenn O'Connor, President

Saskatchewan Association of Landscape Architects (SALA)
#200, 642 Broadway Ave., Saskatoon SK S7N 1A9
www.sala.sk.ca
To promote, improve, & advance the profession of landscape architecture; To maintain standards of professional practice & conduct
Arnold Thiessen, President
Ray Foret, Treasurer

Language, Linguistics, Literature

ABC Life Literacy Canada
#604, 110 Eglinton Ave. East, Toronto ON M4P 2Y1
Tel: 416-218-0010; *Fax:* 416-218-0457
Toll-Free: 800-303-1004
info@abclifeliteracy.ca
www.abc-canada.org
Social Media: www.facebook.com/abclifeliteracycanada; twitter.com/Life_Literacy; www.linkedin.com/groups?home=&gid=2805444; www.youtube.com/user/abccanadavideo
A joint initiative of business & labour, supporting the development of an educated & adaptable workforce through the fostering of a lifelong learning culture; ABC CANADA supports the development of a fully literate Canadian population
Margaret Eaton, President
Anthony Alfred, Director, Communications & Marketing

Association canadienne de traductologie (ACT) / Canadian Association for Translation Studies (CATS)
a/s École de traduction et d'interprétation, Université d'Ottawa, 70, av Laurier est, Ottawa ON K1N 6N5
www.uottawa.ca/associations/act-cats/
Société savante qui regroupe des chercheurs, des professeurs et des praticiens qui se consacrent ou s'intéressent à l'étude ou à l'enseignement de la traduction et des disciplines apparentées
Georges Bastin, Président
Denise Nevo, Vice-présidente

Association of Canadian Corporations in Translation & Interpretation (ACCTI) / Association canadienne de compagnies de traductions et d'interpretation
#306, 421 Bloor St. East, Toronto ON M4W 3T1
Tel: 416-975-5000; *Fax:* 416-975-0505
english_info@accti.org; info_francais@accti.org
www.accti.org
To unite the Canadian translation industry, providing a quality standard to protect the public & service providers alike; to arrange for arbitration in the event of a dispute; to operate in the best interest of members
Paul Penzo, President
Maryse M. Benhoff, Vice-President

Association of Translators & Interpreters of Alberta (ATIA) / Association des traducteurs et interprètes de l'Alberta
PO Box 546, Stn. Main, Edmonton AB T5J 2K8
Tel: 780-434-8384; *Toll-Free:* 888-434-2842
bernadette.david@shaw.ca
www.atia.ab.ca
Allettie Bastiaansen, President

Association of Translators & Interpreters of Nova Scotia (ATINS) / Association des traducteurs et interprètes de la nouvelle-écosse
PO Box 372, Halifax NS B3J 2P8
Tel: 902-443-0350
info@atins.org
www.atins.org
To ensure that clients have access to a body of qualified professionals; to promote the profession & the development of its members
Bruce Knowlden, President

Association of Translators & Interpreters of Ontario (ATIO) / Association des traducteurs et interprètes de l'Ontario
#1202, 1 Nicholas St., Ottawa ON K1N 7B7
Tel: 613-241-2846; *Fax:* 613-241-4098
Toll-Free: 800-234-5030
info@atio.on.ca
www.atio.on.ca
To promote a high degree of professionalism & to protect the interest of those who use the language services provided by its members; to organize professional development activities & to encourage exchanges among its members
Catherine Bertholet, Executive Director
Nancy McInnis, President

Association of Translators & Interpreters of Saskatchewan (ATIS) / Association des traducteurs et interprètes de la Saskatchewan
2341 Broad St., Regina SK S4P 1Y9
Tel: 306-522-2847
www.atis-sk.ca
To provide a collective voice for members; to ensure that members exercise the profession in accordance with their code of ethics; to administer admission procedures of national certification examination; to provide a list of current certified members
Elisabet Ráfouls-Sagués, President
Brigitte Haguès, Vice-President

Association of Translators, Terminologists & Interpreters of Manitoba (ATIM) / Association des traducteurs, terminologues et des interprètes du Manitoba
PO Box 83, 200, av de la Cathédrale, Winnipeg MB R2H 0H7
Tel: 204-797-3247
info@atim.mb.ca
www.atim.mb.ca
ATIM is a non-profit association whose objectives are to provide a collective voice for its members, ensure that members exercise their profession in accordance with its Code of Ethics, & protect the public interest by ensuring the quality of the services rendered by its members.
Carmen Roberge, President

Association of Visual Language Interpreters of Canada (AVLIC) / Association des interprètes en langage visuel du Canada
#110, 39012 Discovery Way, Squamish BC V8B 0E5
Tel: 604-617-8502; *Fax:* 604-567-8502
avlic@avlic.ca
www.avlic.ca
Social Media: www.facebook.com/AVLIC; www.youtube.com/user/TheAVLIC
To represent interpreters whose working languages are English & American Sign Language (ASL); To promote high standards & uniformity within the profession of interpreting
Christie Reaume, President
Caroline Tetreault, Secretary
Cindy Haner, Treasurer
Jane Pannell, Administrative Manager

The Brontë Society - Canada
142 Glenforest Rd., Toronto ON M4N 1Z9
Tel: 416-488-0888
judith_watkins@rogers.com
To bring closer together all who honour the Brontë sisters; to act as the guardian of such letters, writings & personal belongings as could be acquired for the Museum; to dispel legend & false sentiments regarding the Brontë story
Judith Watkins, Canadian Representative

Canadian Association for Commonwealth Literature & Language Studies (CACLALS) / Association canadienne pour l'étude des langues et de la littérature du Commonwealth
c/o Kristina Fagan, Department of English, University of Saskatchewan, 9 Campus Dr., Saskatoon SK S7N 5A5
ww.caclals.ca
To promote the study of Commonwealth literature in Canada; To encourage the reading of Canadian literature abroad
Susan Gingell, President
Kristina Fagan, Secretary-Treasurer
Neil ten Kortenaar, Editor, Chimo

Canadian Comparative Literature Association (CCLA) / Association canadienne de littérature comparée (ACLC)
c/o Markus Reisenleitner, Department of Humanities, York University, 217 Vanier College, Toronto ON M3H 1P3
www.complit.ca
Karin Beeler, President
Susan Ingram, Vice-President
Pascal Gin, Secretary
Markus Reisenleitner, Treasurer

Canadian Linguistic Association (CLA) / Association canadienne de linguistique (ACL)
c/o University of Toronto Press, Journals Division, 5201 Dufferin Ave., Toronto ON M3H 5T8
www.chass.utoronto.ca/~cla-acl
To advance scientific study of linguistics & language in Canada
France Martineau, President
Ileana Paul, Secretary
Carrie Dyck, Treasurer

Canadian Literary & Artistic Association / Association littéraire et artistique canadienne inc.
PO Box 61534, Stn. Tétreault-Ville, Montréal QC H1L 6R1
Tel: 514-993-1556
alaican@aei.ca
www.alai.ca
Promoting and protecting copyright as well as to study questions regarding the protection and the applicability of these rights.
Ysolde Gendreau, President

Canadian Parents for French (CPF)
#310, 176 Gloucester St., Ottawa ON K2P 0A6
Tel: 613-235-1481; *Fax:* 613-230-5940
cpf@cpf.ca
www.cpf.ca
To provide educational opportunities for young Canadians to learn & use the French language; To recognize & support English & French as Canada's two official languages; To create & promote opportunities for young Canadians to learn & use French as a second language

Canadian Translators, Terminologists & Interpreters Council (CTTIC) / Conseil des traducteurs, terminologues et interprètes du Canada (CTTIC)
#1202, One Nicholas St., Ottawa ON K1N 7B7
Tel: 613-562-0379; *Fax:* 613-241-4098
info@cttic.org
www.cttic.org
To ensure uniform standards for the practice of the profession; to make available to the public a body of reliable professionals in translation, terminology & interpretation

Kristel Blais, Administrative Director
Faith Cormier, President

Centre interdisciplinaire de recherches sur les activités langagières (CIRAL)
Pavillon Charles-de-Koninck, Université Laval, #2260-A, Faculté des lettres, Québec QC G1V 0A6
Tél: 418-656-3040; *Téléc:* 418-656-7144
ciral@ciral.ulaval.ca
www.ciral.ulaval.ca
Le Centre interdisciplinaire de recherches sur la activités langagières (CIRAL) regroupe cinq équipes régulières, une vingtaine de chercheurs et quelque soixante-dix étudiants de deuxième et troisième cycles. Tous partagent la même conception des questions linguistiques : la langue est indissociable de l'histoire et de la culture des groupes qui la parlent, et elle évolue en fonction des contacts interethniques et des pressions socioculturelles qui s'exercent sur elle.
Johanna-Pascale Roy, Directrice

Corporation des traducteurs, traductrices, terminologues et interprètes du Nouveau-Brunswick (CTINB) / Corporation of Translators, Terminologists & Interpreters of New Brunswick
CP 427, Fredericton NB E3B 4Z9
Tél: 506-458-1519
ctinb@nbnet.nb.ca
www.ctinb.nb.ca
Donner à ses membres une voix collective; promouvoir le perfectionnement professionnel de ses membres; veiller à ce que ses membres respectent son Code de déontologie; faire connaître le rôle professionnel de ses membres dans la société; protéger l'intérêt public en faisant subir des examens d'admission à la CTINB et d'agrément des membres ainsi qu'en examinant les plaintes reçues à l'égard des membres; entretenir des liens avec les organismes semblables et avec les établissements de formation universitaire dans les domaines de la traduction, de la terminologie et de l'interprétation

Esperanto Association of Canada (KEA) / Association canadienne d'esperanto
6358-A, rue de Bordeaux, Montréal QC H2G 2R8
www.esperanto.ca/en/kea
To promote & teach the neutral international language of Esperanto
Normand Fleury, President

Fédération canadienne pour l'alphabétisation en français (FCAF)
#205, 235 ch Montréal, 2e étage, Ottawa ON K1L 6C7
Tél: 613-749-5333; *Téléc:* 613-749-2252
Ligne sans frais: 888-906-5666
info@fcaf.net
www.fcaf.net
Promouvoir l'alphabétisation en français au Canada; assurer une concertation des intervenantes en alphabétisation en français au Canada.
Normand Lévesque, Directeur général
Colette Arseneault, Présidente
Isabelle Salesse, Vice-présidente

Internatial Unio For Kanadio (sic) (IUK)
92 Glenholm Av., Toronto ON M6H 3B1
Tu tranzform el deifektik inggligh langweij intu el rasional kanadio [sic]
Jonathan Keitz, Prezzident

Jane Austen Society of North America (JASNA)
#105, 195 Wynford Dr., Toronto ON M3C 3P3
Tel: 416-425-2195; *Toll-Free:* 800-836-3911
info@jasna.org
www.jasna.org
Dedicated to the appreciation of Jane Austen & her writings
Nancy Stokes, Canadian Membership Secretary

L. M. Montgomery Institute (LMMI)
University of Prince Edward Island, 550 University Ave., Charlottetown PE C1A 4P3
Tel: 902-628-4346; *Fax:* 902-628-4345
lmmi@upei.ca
www.lmmontgomery.ca
With a focus on scholarship & teaching, the Institute provides resources & educational opportunities to students & scholars researching the life, works & influence of L.M. Montgomery
Mark Leggott, Chair

Literary Translators' Association of Canada (LTAC) / Association des traducteurs et traductrices littéraires du Canada (ATTLC)
Concordia University LB 601, 1455, boul de Maisonneuve ouest, Montréal QC H3G 1M8
Tel: 514-848-2424; *Fax:* 514-848-4514
info@attlc-ltac.org
www.attlc-ltac.org
To promote literary translation & interests of literary translators.
Jo-Anne Elder, President

Movement for Canadian Literacy (MCL) / Rassemblement canadien pour l'alphabétisation (RCA)
342A Elgin St., Ottawa ON K2P 1M6
Tel: 613-563-2464; *Fax:* 613-563-2504
clln@literacy.ca
www.literacy.ca
Social Media: twitter.com/Cdn_Literacy
To act as a national voice for literacy for Canadians
Lindsay Kennedy, President & CEO

National Adult Literacy Database (NALD) / Base de données en alphabétisation des adultes (BDAA)
Sterling House, 767 Brunswick St., Fredericton NB E3B 1H8
Tel: 506-457-6900; *Fax:* 506-457-6910
Toll-Free: 800-720-6253
contactnald@nald.ca
www.nald.ca
Social Media: twitter.com/NALD_BDAA
To provide an information network, in both official languages; to support the Canadian literacy community: adult learners, practitioners, organizations & governments
Bill Stirling, CEO

Ordre des traducteurs, terminologues et interprètes agréés du Québec (OTTIAQ)
#1108, 2021, rue Union, Montréal QC H3A 2S9
Tél: 514-845-4411; *Téléc:* 514-845-9903
Ligne sans frais: 800-265-4815
info@ottiaq.org
www.ottiaq.org
Promouvoir la qualité et l'efficacité de la communication en s'assurant de la compétence de ses membres dans les domaines de la traduction, de la terminologie et de l'interprétation. L'Ordre remplit ainsi son mandat de protection du public
Claude Laurent, Directeur général

Quebec English Literacy Alliance (QELA)
PO Box 3542, Knowlton QC J0E 1V0
Tel: 450-242-2360; *Fax:* 450-242-2543
Toll-Free: 866-242-7352
qelamail@gmail.com
www.qela.qc.ca
To be the unified voice of Quebec English literacy providers nationally & provincially
Louise Quinn, Executive Director

Saskatchewan Elocution & Debate Association (SEDA) / Association d'élocution et des débats de la Saskatchewan
1860 Lorne St., Regina SK S4P 2L7
Tel: 306-780-9243; *Fax:* 306-781-6021
info@saskdebate.com
www.saskdebate.com
To foster debate & public speaking
Lorelie DeRoose, Executive Director

Saskatchewan Organization for Heritage Languages Inc. (SOHL)
2144 Cornwall St., Regina SK S4P 2K7
Tel: 306-780-9275; *Fax:* 306-780-9407
sohl@sasktel.net
www.heritagelanguages.sk.ca
To promote & develop teaching of heritage languages in Saskatchewan; to act in advocacy capacity to make representation to government, institutions & boards regarding matters pertaining to heritage languages; to promote cooperation with & mutual support of provincial organizations with similar aims & objectives; to encourage inter-provincial & national liaison
Tamara Ruzic, Executive Director

Société québécoise d'espéranto (SQE) / Québec Esperanto Society (QES)
6358A, rue de Bordeaux, Montréal QC H2G 2R8
informo@esperanto.qc.ca
www.esperanto.qc.ca
Faire connaître et aider à l'apprentissage de l'espéranto; organiser des rencontres et favoriser l'utilisation de la langue; présenter les avantages de la langue et le mouvement mondial
Boris-Antoine Legault, Président
Sylvain Auclair, Trésurer
Jérôme-Frédéric Bouchard, Secretaire

Society of Translators & Interpreters of British Columbia (STIBC)
PO Box 33, #511, 850 West Hastings St., Vancouver BC V6C 1E1
Tel: 604-684-2940; *Fax:* 604-684-2947
www.stibc.org
To promote the interests of translators & interpreters in BC; to serve the public by applying a Code of Ethics members must comply with; by setting & maintaining high professional standards through education & certification
Golnaz Aliyarzadeh, President

Sweetgrass First Nations Language Council
PO Box 1506, 184 Mohawk St., Brantford ON N3T 5V6
Tel: 519-759-2650; *Fax:* 519-759-8912
amos@woodland-centre.on.ca
www.woodland-centre.on.ca
To provide overall leadership in the retention & revitalization of First Nations languages; to identify resources, both human & material, for the maintenance of Anishinaabeg (Algonkian) & Ogwehowe (Iroquoian) cultural values, traits & institutions of these First Nations: Delaware, Cree, Odawa, Potawotomi, Ojibwe/Chippewa, Cayuga, Mohawk, Onondaga, Seneca & Tuscarora
Amos Key, Director

Universala Esperanto Asocio
Stn. BJ, Nieuwe Binnenweg 176, Rotterdam 3015 Netherlands
info@uea.org
www.uea.org
To promote the use of the international language Esperanto; to work toward the solution to the language problem within international relations; to help improve human relations by making every effort to diminish national, racial, religious, & political tensions; to promote solidarity among all Esperantists & respect for all people

World Literacy of Canada (WLC) / Alphabétisation mondiale Canada
#236, 401 Richmond St. West, Toronto ON M5V 3A8
Tel: 416-977-0008; *Fax:* 416-977-1112
info@worldlit.ca
www.worldlit.ca
To promote international development & social justice through support of community-based programs that emphasize adult literacy & non-formal education
Sandra Onufryk, President
Marguerite Pigott, Vice-President
Jamie Zeppa, Secretary
Mamta Mishra, Executive Director

Law

The Advocates' Society
#1700, 480 University Ave., Toronto ON M5G 1V2
Tel: 416-597-0243; *Fax:* 416-597-1588
mail@advocates.ca
www.advocates.ca
Social Media: www.facebook.com/TheAdvocatesSociety; twitter.com/Advocates_Soc; www.linkedin.com/company/the-advocates%27-society?trk=fc_badge
To teach the skills & ethics of advocacy through information sharing, educational programs, seminars, conferences, & workshops; To speak out on behalf of advocates; To protect the right to representation by an independent bar; To initiate appropriate reforms to the legal system
Peter H. Griffin, President
Alexandra Chyczij, Executive Director

Alberta Civil Trial Lawyers' Association (ACTLA)
#550, 10055 - 106 St., Edmonton AB T5J 2Y2
Tel: 780-429-1133; *Fax:* 780-429-1199
Toll-Free: 800-665-7248
admin@actla.com
www.actla.com
To advocate for a strong civil justice system that protects the rights of all Albertans
Lyn Bromilow, Executive Director
James D. Cuming, President

Alberta Federation of Police Associations (AFPA)
Energy Square, #100, 7024 - 101 Ave., Edmonton AB T6A 0H7
Fax: 403-795-7173
information@albertapolice.ca
www.albertapolice.ca
To address local, provincial, & national police association issues
Bob Walsh, President

Alberta Government Civil Lawyers Association (AGCLA)
Bowker Building, Civil Law Division, Alberta Justice, 9833 - 109 St., 5th Fl., Edmonton AB T5K 2E8
Tel: 780-422-0500; *Fax:* 780-425-0307
To promote & provide continuing education to members in all spheres of civil law

Alberta Law Foundation (ALF)
#300, 407 - 8 Ave. SW, Calgary AB T2P 1E5
Tel: 403-264-4701; *Fax:* 403-294-9238
info@albertalawfoundation.org
www.albertalawfoundation.org
To conduct research into & recommend reform of law & administration of justice; to establish, maintain & operate law libraries; to contribute to legal education & knowledge of people of Alberta; to provide assistance to Native people's legal & student programs
David Aucoin, Executive Director
Diana M. Porter, Administrative Assistant

Association des juristes d'expression française de l'Ontario (AJEFO)
#201, 214 ch Montréal, Ottawa ON K1L 8L8
Tél: 613-842-7462; *Téléc:* 613-842-8389
bureau@ajefo.ca
www.ajefo.ca
Représenter les intérêts des avocates, des avocats, des juges, des fonctionnaires de la justice, des professeures, des professeurs, des étudiantes et des étudiants en droit, et des autres participants et participantes du monde juridique, qui travaillent à la promotion des services juridiques en français sur le territoire de l'Ontario; viser à assurer un accès égal à la justice, sans pénalité, délai, obstacle ou hésitation à l'utilisation du français par l'appareil judiciaire, les membres du Barreau ou la population francophone de notre province
Sean McGee, Président
Sonia Ouellet, Directrice générale

Association des juristes d'expression française de la Saskatchewan (AJEFS) / French Jurists Association of Saskatchewan
#6, 4625, rue Albert, Regina SK S4S 6B6
Tél: 306-924-8543; *Téléc:* 306-569-2609
Ligne sans frais: 800-991-1912
ajefs@sasktel.net
www.ajefs.ca
Développer et promouvoir les droits et services en français auprès des instances juridiques et gouvernementales; informer et sensibiliser la population fransaskoise sur la vulgarisation des lois et l'utilisation des services juridiques en français
Roger Lepage, Président

Association des policières et policiers provinciaux du Québec (ind.) (APPQ) / Québec Provincial Police Association (Ind.)
1981, rue Léonard-De Vinci, Sainte-Julie QC J3E 1Y9
Tél: 450-922-5414; *Téléc:* 450-922-5417
www.appq-sq.qc.ca
Média social: www.youtube.com/watch?v=2AWQQrHbx20
Promouvoir le bien-être de ses membres et voir à leurs intérêts sociaux, moraux et culturels
Pierre Veilleux, Président
Jocelyn Boucher, Vice-président, Ressources humaines
Luc Fournier, Vice-président, Finances
Jacques Painchaud, Vice-président, Discipline et déontologie
Pierre Lemay, Vice-président, Griefs et formation
Daniel Rolland, Vice-président, Ress. matérielles et santé et sécurité du travail

Association of Black Lawyers & Notaries
#10, 10, rue Notre-Dame est, Montréal QC H2Y 1B7
Tel: 514-878-9112
Provides referrals to Black lawyers & notaries in the Montréal area
Sharon Sandiford, Contact

Association of Canadian Court Administrators (ACCA) / Association des administrateurs judiciaires du Canada
#518B, 45 Main St. East, Hamilton ON L8P 1H4
Tel: 905-645-5333; *Fax:* 905-645-5375
www.acca-aajc.ca
To improve the administration of justice through the application of modern management techniques; to promote coordination of research activities relating to court administration & furnish a forum for the interchange of practical information relating to court administration; to aid in the improvement of court administration in general, with particular emphasis on the study, development,

& use of scientific & technological methods; to increase the proficiency of court managers
Debbie Baker, President
Christine Mosher, Secretary
Anne Roland, Treasurer
Linda Bogard, Vice-President

Association of Legal Court Interpreters & Translators (ALCIT) / Association des traducteurs et interprètes judiciares (ATIJ)
483, rue Saint-Antoine est, Montréal QC H2Y 1A5
Tel: 514-845-3113; *Fax:* 514-845-3006
admin@atij.ca
www.atij.ca; www.alcit.ca
The members of the Association work for numerous organizations and Law Courts, although most commonly for the Municipal Court of Montréal and the City of Montréal Police Department. The members currently translate and interpret in 102 languages.
Henri Keleny, President

Barreau de Montréal / Bar of Montréal
Palais de Justice, #980, 1, rue Notre Dame est, Montréal QC H2Y 1B6
Tél: 514-866-9392; *Téléc:* 514-866-1488
info@barreaudemontreal.qc.ca
www.barreaudemontreal.qc.ca
Administrer une corporation professionnelle
Doris Larrivée, Directrice générale
Gislaine Dufault, Directrice des communications

British Columbia Federation of Police Officers (Ind.)
PO Box 42601, #105, 1005 Columbia St., New Westminster BC V3M 6H5
Tel: 604-650-1510; *Fax:* 604-850-1303
www.bcfedpolice.com
Daryl Tottenhan, Director

British Columbia Law Institute (BCLI)
University of British Columbia, 1822 East Mall, vancouver BC V6T 1Z1
Tel: 604-822-0142; *Fax:* 604-822-0144
Toll-Free: 800-565-5297
bcli@bcli.org
www.bcli.org
A not-for-profit law reform agency that performs research & studies to change & modernize British Columbian law.
D. Peter Ramsay, Q.C., Chair
R.C. (Tino) DiBella, Vice-Chair
W. James Emmerton, Executive Director
Krista James, National Director

Canadian Association of Black Lawyers (CABL) / L'Association des Avocats Noirs du Canada
#300, 20 Toronto St., Toronto ON M5C 2B8
www.cabl.ca
Andrew Alleyne, President

Canadian Association of Chiefs of Police (CACP) / Association canadienne des chefs de police (ACCP)
#100, 300 Terry Fox Dr., Kanata ON K2K 0E3
Tel: 613-595-1101; *Fax:* 613-383-0372
cacp@cacp.ca
www.cacp.ca
To encourage & develop cooperation among all Canadian police organizations & members in pursuit & attainment of common objects to create & develop the highest standards of efficiency in law enforcement through the fostering & encouragement of police training, education & research; To promote & maintain a high standard of ethics, integrity, honour & conduct in profession of law enforcement; To encourage & advance the study of modern & progressive practices in prevention & detection of crime; To foster uniformity of police practices & cooperation for the protection & security of the people of Canada
Dale McFee, O.O.M., President

Canadian Association of Legal Translators / Association canadienne des juristes-traducteurs
PO Box 919, Stn. B, Ottawa ON K1P 5P9
To promote double qualification as lawyer (or jurist) & as translator for the translation of legal documents.
Mario Pelletier, President

Canadian Association of Police Boards (CAPB) / Association canadienne des commissions de police
PO Box 4670, Stn. E, Ottawa ON K1S 5H8
Tel: 819-682-1440; *Fax:* 819-682-4569
jlanzon.capb.ca
www.capb.ca
To express views & positions of municipal governing authorities; To provide means for collection & sharing of information & discussion of matters relating to policing services; To consider matters of national interest; To comment on social, economic, cultural, & legislative questions which may affect the quality, efficiency, & costs of policing services; To promote the quality & uniformity of policing services; To educate the public on matters relating to the governance of policing services; To act as a lobbying group to liaise between federal, provincial & municipal governmental authorities, & the federal & provincial solicitors general; To provide a forum for participation by civilian governors of municipal policing services & other agencies; To promote & encourage greater cooperation to serve the interest of the public; To advance criminal justice
Jennifer Lanzon, Executive Director

Canadian Association of Provincial Court Judges (CAPCJ) / L'Association canadienne des juges de cours provinciales
c/o Judge Alan T. Tufts, Nova Scotia Provincial Court, 87 Cornwallis St., Kentville NS B4N 2E5
Tel: 902-679-6070; *Fax:* 902-679-6190
atufts@judicom.ca (Judge Alan T. Tufts)
www.judges-juges.ca
To ensure the soundness of provincial & territorial courts across Canada
Robert Prince, President
Russell J. Otter, Executive Director
Robin Finlayson, Co-Chair, National Education Committee
Ronald LeBlanc, Co-Chair, National Education Committee
David Orr, Chair, Committee on the Law
Odette Perron, Co-Chair, Provincial Judges' Journal / Journal des juges provinciaux
Robert Prince, Chair, Communications Committee
Karen Ruddy, Chair, CAPCJ Newsletter Editorial Committee
David C. Walker, Co-Chair, Provincial Judges' Journal / Journal des juges provinciaux

Canadian Bar Association (CBA) / Association du barreau canadien
#500, 865 Carling Ave., Ottawa ON K1S 5S8
Tel: 613-237-2925; *Fax:* 613-237-0185
Toll-Free: 800-267-8860
info@cba.org
www.cba.org
To promote improvements in the law; to promote improvements in the administration of justice; to promote individual lawyer training; to advocate in the public interest; to represent the profession on a national & international level; to promote the interests of the CBA; to promote equality in the profession
John Hoyles, Chief Executive Officer
Bernard Amyot, President

The Canadian Corporate Counsel Association (CCCA) / L'Association canadienne des conseillers juridiques d'entreprises
#410, 20 Toronto St., Toronto ON M5C 2B8
Tel: 416-869-0522; *Fax:* 416-869-0946
ccca@ccca-cba.org
www.cancorpcounsel.org
To provide quality education, information & other services & resources of specific interest to corporate counsel in Canada, & to facilitate communication & networking among such counsel
Derek Edward Patterson, President
Kari F. Horn, Treasurer

Canadian Council on International Law (CCIL) / Conseil canadien de droit international (CCDI)
275 Bay St., Ottawa ON K1R 5Z5
Tel: 613-235-0442; *Fax:* 613-232-8228
manager@ccil-ccdi.ca
www.ccil-ccdi.ca
To bring together scholars of international law & organizations engaged in teaching & research at Canadian universities; To encourage & conduct studies in international law with a view to its progressive development & codification; To foster the study of legal aspects of Canada's international problems & to advocate their solution in accordance with existing or developing principles of international law.
Craig Forcese, President
Elizabeth Macaulay, Manager

Canadian Criminal Justice Association (CCJA) / Association canadienne de justice pénale (ACJP)
#101, 320 Parkdale Avenue, Ottawa ON K1Y 4X9
Tel: 613-725-3715; *Fax:* 613-725-3720
ccja-acjp@rogers.com
www.ccja-acjp.ca
Social Media: www.facebook.com/186547581359601
To promote a humane, equitable and effective criminal justice system in Canada
Irving Kulik, Executive Director

Canadian Institute for the Administration of Justice (CIAJ) / Institut canadien d'administration de la justice (ICAJ)
Faculté de droit, Univ. de Montréal, PO Box 6128, Stn. Centre-Ville, #3421, 3101, chemin de la Tour, Montréal QC H3C 3J7
Tel: 514-343-6157; *Fax:* 514-343-6296
ciaj@ciaj-icaj.ca
www.ciaj-icaj.ca
Social Media: www.facebook.com/ciaj.icaj; twitter.com/ciaj_icaj; www.linkedin.com/groups?about=&gid=4113891
To improve the quality of justice for all Canadians
Christine Huglo Robertson, Executive Director

Canadian Law & Society Association (CLSA) / Association canadienne de droit et société (ACDS)
c/o Journals Division, University of Toronto Press, 5201 Dufferin St., Toronto ON M3H 5T8
Tel: 416-667-7810; *Fax:* 416-667-7881
Toll-Free: 800-221-9985
www.acds-clsa.org
To encourage socio-legal inquiry both domestically & internationally

Canadian Maritime Law Association / Association canadienne de droit maritime
#900, 1000, rue de la Gauchetiére ouest, Montréal QC H3B 5H4
Tel: 514-849-4161; *Fax:* 514-849-4167
cmla@cmla.org
www.cmla.org
To represent all Canadian commercial maritime interests for the uniform development of Canadian & international maritime law affecting marine transportation & related aspects
Robert C. Wilkins, Secretary-Treasurer
Christopher J. Giaschi, President
John G. O'Connor, National Vice-President

Canadian Petroleum Law Foundation
PO Box 4143, Stn. C, Calgary AB T2T 5M9
Tel: 403-237-2423
lara.h.pella@esso.ca
www.cplf.org
To study oil & gas laws
Ben Rogers, President
Miles Pittman, Treasurer

Canadian Police Association (CPA) / L'Association canadienne des policiers (ACP)
#100, 141 Catherine St., Ottawa ON K2P 1C3
Tel: 613-231-4168; *Fax:* 613-231-3254
cpa-acp@cpa-acp.ca
www.cpa-acp.ca
Charles Momy, President
Tom Stamatakis, Vice-President

Chambre des notaires du Québec
#600, 1801, av McGill College, Montréal QC H3B 3L2
Tél: 514-879-1793; *Téléc:* 514-879-1923
Ligne sans frais: 800-668-2473
information@cdnq.org
www.cdnq.org
La Chambre des notaires doit, conformément à la loi et sous la surveillance de l'Office des professions du Québec, assurer principalement la protection du public utilisateur des services professionnels de notaire.
Pierre Cléroux, Directeur général

Church Council on Justice & Corrections (CCJC) / Conseil des églises pour la justice et la criminologie
#303, 200 Isabella St., Ottawa ON K1S 1V7
Tel: 613-563-1688; *Fax:* 613-237-6129
info@ccjc.ca
www.ccjc.ca
To strengthen churches' ministry in fields of crime prevention, justice & corrections; to initiate, encourage & support programs which sensitize congregations & educate volunteer groups to participate in development of community responses to crime, justice & corrections; to promote a healing justice; to examine & respond to policy concerns with assistance of churches; to call on churches to address issues; to provide resources to churches & other related organizations.
Laurent Champagne, President
Lorraine Berzins, Communication Chair of Justice

Community Legal Education Association (Manitoba) Inc. (CLEA) / Association d'éducation juridique communautaire (Manitoba) inc.
#205, 414 Graham Ave., Winnipeg MB R3C 0L8
Tel: 204-943-2382; *Fax:* 204-943-3600
mctroszko@communitylegal.mb.ca
To provide legal education & information programs to Manitobans

Mary Troszko, Executive Director
Heather Dixon, President

Community Legal Education Ontario (CLEO)
#600, 119 Spadina Ave., Toronto ON M5V 2L1
Tel: 416-408-4420; *Fax:* 416-408-4424
cleo@cleo.on.ca
www.cleo.on.ca
To provide public legal education services & programs that benefit the low income community, disadvantaged persons, such as immigrants & refugees, seniors, women, & injured workers in Ontario

Community Legal Information Association of Prince Edward Island (CLIA)
Sullivan Bldg., 1st Fl., PO Box 1207, Charlottetown PE C1A 7M8
Tel: 902-892-0853; *Fax:* 902-368-4096
Toll-Free: 800-240-9798
clia@cliapei.ca
www.cliapei.ca
To provide Islanders with understandable, useful information about the Canadian laws & the justice system

Congress of Black Lawyers and Jurists of Québec
#500, 445, boul St-Laurent, Côte-Des-Neiges N QC H3S 2B8
Tel: 514-954-3471; *Fax:* 514-954-3451
Please call prior to visit

Continuing Legal Education Society of BC
#500, 1155 West Pender Street, Vancouver BC V6E 2P4
Tel: 604-669-3544; *Fax:* 604-669-9260
Toll-Free: 800-663-0437
custserv@cle.bc.ca
www.cle.bc.ca
To meet the present & future educational needs of the legal profession in British Columbia
Ronald G. Lamperson, Chair

Criminal Lawyers' Association (CLA)
#1, 189 Queen St. East, Toronto ON M5A 1S2
Tel: 416-214-9875; *Fax:* 416-968-6818
www.criminallawyers.ca
To be the voice for criminal justice & civil liberties in Canada
Anthony Laycock, Executive Director
Norm Boxall, President

Federation of Law Reform Agencies of Canada
c/o Manitoba Law Reform Commission, 405 Broadway, 12th Fl., Winnipeg MB R3C 3L6
Tel: 604-822-0142; *Fax:* 604-822-0144
Collection of 8 law reform agencies, from various provinces, who meet yearly to exchange information.
Jeffrey A. Schnoor, President

Federation of Law Societies of Canada (FLSC) / Fédération des ordres professionnels de juristes du Canada
World Exchange Plaza, #1810, 45 O'Connor St., Ottawa ON K1P 1A4
Tel: 613-236-7272; *Fax:* 613-236-7233
info@flsc.ca
www.flsc.ca
To coordinate the law societies of Canada; To act as a voice for Canadian law societies
John Campion, President
Ian Donaldson, Vice-President
Ronald J. MacDonald, Vice-President
Bob Linney, Director, Communications

Fondation du barreau du Québec
Maison du Barreau, #404, 445, boul Saint-Laurent, Montréal QC H2Y 3T8
Tél: 514-954-3400; *Téléc:* 514-954-3449
Ligne sans frais: 800-361-8495
fondation@barreau.qc.ca
www.barreau.qc.ca
Média social: www.facebook.com/barreauduquebec
Subventionner, primer et supporter des travaux axés vers l'intérêt public et utiles à la pratique du droit.
Gilles Ouimet, Président

Foundation for Legal Research / La foundation pour la recherche juridique
c/o Law Foundation of British Columbia, #1340, 605 Robsen St., Vancouver BC V6B 5J3
Toll-Free: 800-267-8860
www.cba.org
To support & maintain scholarships, bursaries & prizes in the field of legal research
John R.R. Jennings, Chair
Francois Letourneaux, Secretary
Stephen Bresolin, Treasurer

Institute of Law Clerks of Ontario (ILCO)
#502, 20 Adelaide St. East, Toronto ON M5C 2T6
Tel: 416-214-6252; *Fax:* 416-214-6255
reception@ilco.on.ca
www.ilco.on.ca
To provide an organized network for promoting unity, cooperation & mutual assistance among Law Clerks in Ontario; to advance & protect their status & interests; to promote their education for the purpose of increasing their knowledge, efficiency & professional ability.
Lisa Matchim, President
Jacqueline Cummins, Vice-President

International Centre for Criminal Law Reform & Criminal Justice Policy (ICCLR)
1822 East Mall, Vancouver BC V6T 1Z1
Tel: 604-822-9875; *Fax:* 604-822-9317
icclr@law.ubc.ca
www.icclr.law.ubc.ca
To improve the quality of justice through reform of criminal law, policy & practice; to provide advice, information, research & proposals for policy development & legislation
Kathleen Macdonald, Executive Director

International Commission of Jurists (Canadian Section) (ICJ) / La Commission internationale de juristes (section canadienne) (CIJ)
#500, 865 Carling Ave., Ottawa ON K1S 5S8
Tel: 613-237-2925; *Fax:* 613-237-0185
patw@cba.org
www.icjcanada.org
To works internationally with the parent organization to monitor & promote the rule of law & the impartiality & independence of the judiciary in countries where these are threatened or non-existent; to act nationally & locally to promote awareness of these issues & human rights generally
Paul D.K. Fraser, President
Pat Whiting, Executive Director

Law Foundation of British Columbia
#1340, 605 Robson St., Vancouver BC V6B 5J3
Tel: 604-688-2337; *Fax:* 604-688-4586
info@lawfoundationbc.org
www.lawfoundationbc.org
To allocate funds to programs that will benefit the general public of British Columbia; To act in accordance with The Legal Profession Act & distribute income in areas that promote & advance a just society & the rule of law, such as legal aid, law libraries, legal education, legal research, & law reform; To conduct operations with recognition of the diverse population of British Columbia
Wayne Robertson, Executive Director
Margaret Sasges, Chair
Jo-Anne Kaulius, Director, Finance

Law Foundation of Newfoundland & Labrador
Murray Premises, 2nd Fl., PO Box 5907, #49, 55 Elizabeth Ave., St. John's NL A1C 5X4
Tel: 709-754-4424; *Fax:* 709-754-4320
www.atyp.com/lawfoundationnl
To provide grants for the following services in Newfoundland & Labrador that advance public understanding of the law & access to legal services: the Legal Aid Commission as established under the Legal Aid Act; law libraries; legal research; legal education; scholarships for studies relevant to law; law reform; & legal referral services

Law Foundation of Nova Scotia
PO Box 325, Halifax NS B3J 2N7
Tel: 902-422-8335; *Fax:* 902-492-0424
nslawfd@nslawfd.ca
www.nslawfd.ca
To establish & maintain a fund to be used for the examination, research, revision & reform of & public access to the law, legal education, the administration of justice in the province & any other purposes incidental or conducive to or consequential upon the attainment of any such objects
Kerry L. Oliver, Executive Director

Law Foundation of Ontario / La fondation du droit de l'Ontario
PO Box 19, #3002, 20 Queen St. West, Toronto ON M5H 3R3
Tel: 416-598-1550; *Fax:* 416-598-1526
general@lawfoundation.on.org
www.lawfoundation-on.org
Mark J. Sandler, Chair
Elizabeth Goldberg, Chief Executive Officer

Law Foundation of Prince Edward Island
49 Water St., Charlottetown PE C1A 7K2
Tel: 902-566-1666
To establish & maintain a fund & use the proceeds thereof for the purposes of: legal education & research on law reform; the editing & printing of decisions of the Supreme Court & the Provincial Court of PEI; the promotion of legal aid; aid in the establishment, operation & maintenance of law libraries in PEI
M. Jane Ralling, Chair

Law Foundation of Saskatchewan
#200, 2208 Scarth St., Regina SK S4P 2J6
Tel: 306-352-1121; *Fax:* 306-522-6222
lfsk@virtusgroup.ca
www.lawfoundation.sk.ca
To maintain a fund to support legal aid, law reform, law libraries, legal education, & legal research
Robert Arscott, Secretary
Patricia Quaroni, Chair
Bob Watt, Treasurer

Law Society of Alberta (LSA)
#500, 919 - 11th Ave. SW, Calgary AB T2R 1P3
Tel: 403-229-4700; *Fax:* 403-228-1728
Toll-Free: 800-661-9003
www.lawsocietyalberta.com
To serve the public by promoting a high standard of legal services & professional conduct through the governance & regulation of an independent legal profession; to govern all lawyers who practise law in Alberta; responsible for admitting lawyers to the Bar, professional conduct & discipline of lawyers
Don Thompson, Executive Director
Sheila Serup, Manager
Douglas R. Mah, Q.C., President

Law Society of British Columbia
845 Cambie St., 8th Fl., Vancouver BC V6B 4Z9
Tel: 604-669-2533; *Fax:* 604-669-5232
Toll-Free: 800-902-5300
TTY: 604-443-5700
communications@lsbc.org
www.lawsociety.bc.ca
Social Media: twitter.com/LawSocietyofBC
To ensure that the public is well served by a competent, honourable & independent legal profession
Timothy E. McGee, CEO & Executive Director
Bruce A. LeRose, President

Law Society of Manitoba (LSM) / La Société du Barreau du Manitoba
219 Kennedy St., Winnipeg MB R3C 1S8
Tel: 204-942-5571; *Fax:* 204-956-0624
admin@lawsociety.mb.ca
www.lawsociety.mb.ca
To ensure the public in Manitoba is well served by the legal profession
Allan Fineblit, CEO
Marilyn Billinkoff, Deputy CEO

Law Society of New Brunswick / Barreau du Nouveau-Brunswick
68 Avonlea Court, Fredericton NB E3C 1N8
Tel: 506-458-8540; *Fax:* 506-451-1421
general@lawsociety-barreau.nb.ca
www.lawsociety-barreau.nb.ca
The Law Society was officially created in 1846. The Provincial Legislative Assembly adopted Chapter 48 of the Provincial Statutes which in effect incorporated what was then called the "Barristers' Society" for the "purpose of securing in the Province a learned and honourable legal profession, for establishing order and good conduct among its members and for promoting knowledgeable development and reform of the law".
Mark Canty, President
Marc L. Richard, Executive Director

Law Society of Newfoundland & Labrador
PO Box 1028, St. John's NL A1C 5M3
Tel: 709-722-4740; *Fax:* 709-722-8902
CLE@lawsociety.nf.ca
www.lawsociety.nf.ca
The Law Society is the regulatory body for the legal profession in the province. It ensures that law students are appropriately educated and trained through articling and Bar Admission programs and exams, and provides continuing legal education to practitioners. Office is located at 196-198 Water St., St. John's.
Peter G. Ringrose, Executive Director

Law Society of Nunavut (LSNU)
PO Box 149, Iqaluit NU X0A 0H0
Tel: 867-979-2330; *Fax:* 867-979-2333
lawsociety@qiniq.com
www.lawsociety.nu.ca
To govern our membership & protect the public. Office is located at Bldg. 812, Unit 4, Iqualuit.
Craig Goebel, CEO

Law Society of Prince Edward Island
PO Box 128, 49 Water St., Charlottetown PE C1A 7K2
Tel: 902-566-1666; *Fax:* 902-368-7557
lawsociety@lspei.pe.ca
www.lspei.pe.ca
To uphold & protect the public interest in the administration of justice; to establish standards for the education, professional responsibility & competence of members & applicants for membership; to ensure the independence, integrity & honour of the society & its members; to regulate the practice of law; to uphold & protect the interests of members.
Susan M. Robinson, Executive Director & Sec.-Treas.

Law Society of Saskatchewan
#1100, 2002 Victoria Ave., Regina SK S4P 0R7
Tel: 306-569-8242; *Fax:* 306-352-2989
reception@lawsociety.sk.ca
www.lawsociety.sk.ca
To govern the legal profession by upholding high standards of competence & integrity; ensuring the independence of the profession; advancing the administration of justice, the profession & the rule of law, all in the public interest
A. Kirsten Logan, Secretary & Co-Director, Administration
Allan T. Snell, General Counsel & Co-Director, Administration

Law Society of the Northwest Territories / Le Barreau des Territoires du Nord-Ouest
Diamond Plaza, PO Box 1298, Stn. Main, 5204 - 50th Ave., 4th Fl., Yellowknife NT X1A 2N9
Tel: 867-873-3828; *Fax:* 867-873-6344
info@lawsociety.nt.ca
www.lawsociety.nt.ca
To serve the public by an independent, responsible & responsive legal profession.
Linda Whitford, Executive Director

Law Society of Upper Canada / Barreau du Haut-Canada
Osgoode Hall, 130 Queen St. West, Toronto ON M5H 2N6
Tel: 416-947-3300; *Fax:* 416-947-3924
Toll-Free: 800-668-7380
TTY: 416-644-4886
lawsociety@lsuc.on.ca
www.lsuc.on.ca
Social Media:
www.facebook.com/pages/Law-Society-of-Upper-Canada/110214529001232; twitter.com/LawsocietyLSUC; www.linkedin.com/company/the-law-society-of-upper-canada; www.youtube.com/lawsocietylsuc
To govern the legal profession in the public interest by ensuring that the people of Ontario are served by lawyers who meet high standards of learning, competence & professional conduct.
Malcolm L. Heins, CEO
Diana Miles, Director, Professional Development & Competence

Law Society of Yukon (LSY)
#202, 302 Steele St., Whitehorse YT Y1A 2C5
Tel: 867-668-4231; *Fax:* 867-667-7556
info@lawsocietyyukon.com
www.lawsocietyyukon.com
To govern legal profession in the Yukon.
Lynn Daffe, Executive Director

Legal Education Society of Alberta (LESA)
#2610, 10104 - 103 Ave., Edmonton AB T5J 0H8
Tel: 780-420-1987; *Fax:* 780-425-0885
Toll-Free: 800-282-3900
www.lesa.org
To educate providers of legal services in Alberta; To increase awareness of issues affecting the legal profession; To maintain & increase professional responsibility & competence; To develop & provide education in law, skills, & ethics
Thomas Achymichuk, Chair
Daniel T. Gallagher, Sec-Tres.
Paul Wood, Executive Director & Director, Canadian Centre for Professional Legal Education (CPLED) Alberta

Legal Information Society of Nova Scotia (LISNS)
5523B Young St., Halifax NS B3K 1Z7
Tel: 902-454-2198; *Fax:* 902-455-3105
Toll-Free: 800-665-9779
lisns@legalinfo.org
www.legalinfo.org
To provide Nova Scotians easy access to information & resources about the law
Kevin A. MacDonald, President

The Manitoba Law Foundation / La Fondation manitobaine du droit
412 McDermot Ave., Winnipeg MB R3A 0A9
Tel: 204-947-3142; *Fax:* 204-942-3221
bpalace@gatewest.net
To provide funds for legal education, legal research, legal aid, law reform & the establishment, operation & maintenance of law libraries
Barbara Palace, Executive Director

Municipal Law Enforcement Officers' Association (Ontario) Inc.
c/o Randy Berg, 100 Ross St., Welland ON N1H 3A1
Tel: 705-739-4241; *Fax:* 705-739-4279
mleo@mleoa.ca
www.mleoa.ca
Social Media:
www.facebook.com/group.php?gid=215037141887694
To bring members into helpful association with each other to maintain professional standards; to encourage & assist in the education & training programs for Municipal Law Enforcement Officers
Randy Berg, President

New Brunswick Law Foundation / La Fondation pour l'avancement du droit au Nouveau-Brunswick
66, rue Avonlea Court, Fredericton NB E3C 1N8
Tel: 506-453-7776; *Fax:* 506-451-1421
amartin@lawsociety-barreau.nb.ca
www.lawsociety.nb.ca
To receive the interest earned on lawyers' mixed trust accounts & to use these funds to support law-related projects to benefit residents of New Brunswick
Alban Martin, Executive Director

Northwest Territories Association of Provincial Court Judges
c/o Territorial Court of Northwest Territories, PO Box 550, 4093 - 49th St., Yellowknife NT X1A 2N4
Tel: 867-873-7604; *Fax:* 867-873-0203
Robert Gorin, Northwest Territories Director, Canadian Association of Provincial Court Judges

Northwest Territories Law Foundation
PO Box 2594, 5212 - 55th St., Yellowknife NT X1A 2P9
Tel: 867-873-8275; *Fax:* 867-873-6383
www.lawsociety.nt.ca/LawFoundation
To provide funding in the Northwest Territories in the following areas: the establishment & operation of law libraries; the provision of legal education; research in law & the administration of justice; recommendations for law reform; legal aid programs & similar programs; & the Assurance Fund
Wendy Carter, Executive Manager
Emerald Murphy, Chair

Nova Scotia Barristers' Society (NSBS)
#1101, 1645 Granville St., Halifax NS B3J 1X3
Tel: 902-422-1491; *Fax:* 902-429-4869
www.nsbs.org
To set & enforce standards of professional responsibility & ethics for lawyers; To license & discipline members of the profession, in accordance with the Legal Profession Act
Darrel I. Pink, Executive Director
Jacqueline L. Mullenger, Director, Admissions & Professional Development
Victoria Rees, Director, Professional Responsibility

Ontario Association of Corrections & Criminology
PO Box 949, Stn. K, Toronto ON M4P 2V3
Tel: 416-304-1974; *Fax:* 416-304-1977
info@oacconline.org
www.oacconline.org
The Association effects co-operation among individuals, groups & governmental organizations interested & active in the field of correctional & criminal justice. It works to further the study of correctional, criminological & criminal justice issues.
Brian Smegal, President

Ontario Association of Police Services Boards (OAPSB)
Suite A, 10 Peel Centre Dr., Brampton ON L6T 4B9
Tel: 905-458-1488; *Fax:* 905-458-2260
Toll-Free: 800-831-7727
admin@oapsb.ca
www.oapsb.ca
To act as the voice of police services boards to government; To provide services to assist police services boards in Ontario
Alok Mukherjee, President
Fred Kaustinen, Executive Director

Ontario Crown Attorneys Association (OCAA)
PO Box 30, #1015, 180 Dundas St. West, Toronto ON M5G 1Z8
Tel: 416-977-4517; *Fax:* 416-977-1460
reception@ocaa.ca
www.ocaa.ca
To promote & protect the professional interests of crown counsels, assistant crown attorneys, & articling students
William K. Lightfoot, President

People's Law School
#150, 900 Howe St., Vancouver BC V6Z 2M4
Tel: 604-331-5400; *Fax:* 604-331-5401
staff@publiclegaled.bc.ca
www.publiclegaled.bc.ca
To make law & legal system understandable & accessible to people of British Columbia

Police Association of Nova Scotia (PANS) / Association des policiers de la Nouvelle-Écosse
#22, 1000 Windmill Rd., Dartmouth NS B3B 1L7
Tel: 902-468-7555; *Fax:* 902-468-2202
Toll-Free: 888-468-2798
David W. Fisher, CEO

Police Association of Ontario (PAO) / Association des policiers de l'Ontario
#1-3, 6730 Davand Dr., Mississauga ON L5T 2K8
Tel: 905-670-9770; *Fax:* 905-670-9755
pao@pao.on.ca
www.pao.on.ca
To preserve safe communities
Ronald Middel, CAO
David McFadden, President
Edward Parent, Chair

Probation Officers Association of Ontario (POAO)
#6245, 2100 Bloor St. West, Toronto ON M6S 5A5
Tel: 905-329-3219
info@poao.org
www.poao.org
POAO is a voluntary, non-profit organization representing the professional interests of the probation & parole Officers across the province. It is not a union, but it provides representation on legislative issues to policy makers. It is also a forum for exchange of experience & information.
Patricia Giroux, President
Kimberley Ridgers, Vice-President

The Public Interest Advocacy Centre (PIAC) / Centre pour la défense de l'intérêt public
#1204, One Nicholas St., Ottawa ON K1N 7B7
Tel: 613-562-4002
piac@piac.ca
www.piac.ca
To provide legal services on a non-profit basis to groups & individuals addressing public interest issues of broad concern who would not otherwise have access to such services; the centre's special interests are telecommunications, energy, transportation, broadcasting, privacy, technical services & consumer protection
Michael Janigan, Executive Director

Public Legal Education Association of Saskatchewan, Inc. (PLEA Sask.)
#500, 333 - 25th St. East, Saskatoon SK S7K 0B8
Tel: 306-653-1868; *Fax:* 306-653-1869
www.plea.org
To educate & inform the people of Saskatchewan about the law & the legal system
Joel Janow, Executive Director
Glenda Cooney, President

Public Legal Information Association of Newfoundland (PLIAN)
Tara Place, #227, 31 Peet St., St. John's NL A1B 3W8
Tel: 709-722-2643; *Fax:* 709-722-0054
Toll-Free: 888-660-7788
info@publiclegalinfo.com
www.publiclegalinfo.com
To provide plain language legal information to the general public of Newfoundland, in both official languages, through a telephone enquiry line, public speaking engagements, publications, & a lawyer referral service
Kristen O'Keefe, Executive Director

Saskatchewan Federation of Police Officers (SFPO)
SK
Tel: 306-539-0960
www.saskpolice.com
To advance police work as a profession; To support members in their police careers
Bernie Eiswirth, Executive Officer
Evan Bray, President
Jason Stonechild, Executive Vice-President

Société de criminologie du Québec (SCQ)
#201, 2000, boul Saint-Joseph est, Montréal QC H2H 1E4
Tél: 514-529-4391; *Téléc:* 514-529-6936
crimino@societecrimino.qc.ca
www.societecrimino.qc.ca
Média social: www.facebook.com/SocieteCrimino; twitter.com/societecrimino
Mission: de contribuer à l'évolution du système de justice pénale, de favoriser les échanges & les débats entre tous les intéressés à l'avancement de la justice pénale, & de favoriser & encourager la recherche
Caroline Savard, Directrice générale

The Society of Notaries Public of British Columbia
PO Box 44, #1220, 625 Howe St., Vancouver BC V6C 2T6
Tel: 604-681-4516; *Fax:* 604-681-7258
Toll-Free: 800-663-0343
society@notaries.bc.ca
www.notaries.bc.ca
Val Wilson, Editor-In-Chief
Susan Davis, President
John Eastwood, First Vice President

Toronto Lawyers Association (TLA)
Court House Library, 361 University Ave., Toronto ON M5G 1T3
Tel: 416-327-5700; *Fax:* 416-947-9148
library@tlaonline.ca
www.tlaonline.ca
Social Media: www.facebook.com/124864490954414
Provides lawyers with key services; timely & relevant information; education about issues & opportunities affecting members; advocacy on behalf of the profession
Joan Rataic-Lang, Executive Director

Yukon Law Foundation
PO Box 31789, Whitehorse YT Y1A 6L3
Tel: 867-667-7500; *Fax:* 867-393-3904
execdir@yukonlawfoundation.com
www.yukonlawfoundation.com
The objects of the Foundation are to maintain and manage a fund accumulated primarily from the interest on lawyers' trust accounts
Deana Lemke, Executive Director
Malcolm Campbell, Chair

Yukon Public Legal Education Association (YPLEA)
PO Box 2799, Yukon College, Whitehorse YT Y1A 5K4
Tel: 867-668-5297; *Toll-Free:* 866-667-4305
www.yplea.com
To provide free legal information to Yukoners & promote greater accessibility to the legal system

Libraries & Archives

Administrators of Small Public Libraries of Ontario (ASPLO)
c/o Brant County Public Library, 12 William St., Paris ON N3L 1K7
Tel: 519-442-2433; *Fax:* 519-442-7582
gay.kozakselby@county.brant.on.ca

Alberta Association of College Librarians (AACL)
c/o Red Deer College, PO Box 5005, Red Deer AB T4N 5H5
Tel: 403-342-3306
alice.mcnair@rdc.ab.ca
www.aacl.engineseven.com
Geoff Owens, Chair
Lillian Li, Sec.-Treas.
Karin Hering, Director-at-Large

Alberta Association of Library Technicians (AALT)
PO Box 700, Edmonton AB T5J 2L4
Toll-Free: 866-350-2258
marketing@aalt.org; membership@aalt.org; journal@aalt.org
www.aalt.org
Social Media: www.facebook.com/AALTLibraryTec; twitter.com/AALTLibraryTech
To foster & enhance the professional image of library technicians in Alberta; To support library technicians throughout the province
Kirsten Livingstone, President
Kristian McInnis, Director, Membership
Joanne Shum, Director, Marketing
Lynda Shurko, Secretary
Nicole Penton, Treasurer

Alberta Library Trustees Association (ALTA)
#6-24, 7 Sir Winston Churchill Sq., Edmonton AB T5J 2V5
Tel: 780-761-2582; *Fax:* 866-419-1451
admin@librarytrustees.ab.ca; president@librarytrustees.ab.ca
www.librarytrustees.ab.ca
Social Media: twitter.com/librarytrustees
To act as the collective voice for library trustees in Alberta; To develop effective trustees
Heather Mayor, Executive Director
Dwight Nagel, President
Kiann McNeill, Vice-President
Kelly Aisenstat, Treasurer

Archives Association of British Columbia (AABC)
#249, 34A-2755 Lougheed Hwy., Port Coquitlam BC V3B 5Y9
aabc@aabc.bc.ca
www.aabc.bc.ca
AABC is the voice of archivists & archival institutions in British Columbia. It undertakes projects that strengthen the archival network in the province, through preservation & promotion of access to British Columbia's documentary heritage
Lara Wilson, President
Lisa Glandt, Secretary
Sharon Walz, Treasurer

Archives Association of Ontario (AAO) / L'Association des archives de l'Ontario
#202, 10 Morrow Ave., Toronto ON M6R 2J1
Tel: 416-538-1650; *Fax:* 416-489-1713
aao-archivists.ca
To encourage, through the establishment of networks, the public knowledge & appreciation of archives & their function; to promote the advancement of general education in the preservation of the cultural heritage & identity of the various regions of the province; to represent the interests of the archival community before the government of Ontario, local government & other provincial institutions of a public or private nature; to provide professional guidance & leadership through communication & cooperation with all persons, groups & associations interested in the preservation & use of records of the human experience in Ontario
Danielle Hughes, President
Ann-Marie Collins, Secretary

Archives Council of Prince Edward Island
Public Archives, George Coles Bldg., PO Box 1000, Charlottetown PE C1A 7M4
Tel: 902-368-4290; *Fax:* 902-368-6327
acpei@gov.pe.ca
www.archives.pe.ca
To facilitate the development of the archival system in PEI; To make recommendations about the system's operation & financing; To develop & facilitate the implementation & management of programs to assist the archival community; To communicate archival needs & concerns to decision-makers, researchers & the general public
Fred Horne, President

Archives Society of Alberta (ASA)
PO Box 4067, Stn. South Edmonton, Edmonton AB T6E 4S8
Tel: 780-424-2697; *Fax:* 780-425-1679
www.archivesalberta.org
To provide professional leadership among persons engaged in practice of archival science; to promote development of archives & archivists in Alberta; to encourage cooperation of archivists & archives with all those interested in preservation & use of documents of human experience
Debby Shoctor, President

Art Libraries Society of North America (ARLIS/NA)
Technical Enterprises, Inc., 7044 S. 13th St., Oak Creek WI 53154 USA
Tel: 414-768-8000; *Fax:* 414-768-8001
Toll-Free: 800-817-0621
info@arlisna.org
www.arlisna.org
The Society's mission is to foster excellence in art & design librarianship & image management.
Elizabeth Clarke, Executive Director
Amy Lucker, President
Marilyn Russell, Vice-President
Edward (Ted) Goodman, Treasurer

Association des archivistes du Québec (AAQ)
CP 9768, Succ. Sainte-Foy, Québec QC G1V 4C3
Tél: 418-652-2357; *Téléc:* 418-646-0868
infoaaq@archivistes.qc.ca
www.archivistes.qc.ca
Regrouper les personnes qui offrent aux organisations et à leurs clientèles des services liés à la gestion de leur information organique et consignée; offrir à ses membres des services en français et propres à assurer le développement, l'enrichissement et la promotion de leur profession et de leur discipline; assurer aux membres les services susceptibles de favoriser et d'accroître les échanges et la communication internes et externes des idées et des connaissances; promouvoir le développement professionnel des membres en s'impliquant activement au plan de la formation et du perfectionnement, en favorisant la recherche et le développement et en assurant une représentation adéquate de la profession au sein de la société et auprès des corps politiques
Michel Lèvesque, Président
Andrée Gingras, Directrice générale

Association des bibliothécaires du Québec (ABQ) / Québec Library Association (QLA)
CP 1095, Pointe-Claire QC H9S 4H9
Tél: 514-697-0146; *Téléc:* 514-697-0146
abqla@abqla.qc.ca
www.abqla.qc.ca
Média social: www.facebook.com/group.php?gid=52867661827
Susan Perles, Présidente

Association des bibliothécaires francophones de l'Ontario (ABFO)
c/o #303, 100 Lombard St., Toronto ON M5C 1M3
Tél: 416-363-3388; *Téléc:* 416-941-9581
cmarcouxhamade@torontopubliclibrary.ca
204.200.206.210/site/showPage.cgi?page=about/abfo.html
L'ABFO est l'Association des Bibliothécaires Francophones de l'Ontario qui oeuvrent dans le domaine public, collégial, universitaire ou scolaire et qui ont à coeur la culture francophone.
Céline Marcoux-Hamade, Présidente

Association des bibliothécaires professionnel(le)s du Nouveau-Brunswick (ABPNB) / Association of Professional Librarians of New Brunswick (APLNB)
CP 423, Succ. A, Fredericton NB E3B 4Z9
Tél: 506-458-7058; *Téléc:* 506-453-4831
info@abpnb-aplnb.ca
www.abpnb-aplnb.ca
Promouvoir les bibliothécaires et les services de bibliothèques au Nouveau-Brunswick; to promote librarians & library services in New Brunswick.
Victoria Volkanova, Présidente
Hector Alvarez, Secrétaire
Robin Sexton-Mayes, Trésorier

Association des bibliothèques de droit de Montréal (ABDM) / Montréal Association of Law Libraries (MALL)
Tour de la Bourse, CP 482, 800, Square Victoria, Montréal QC H4Z 1J7
www.abdm-mall.org
Vise à permettre aux gens qui travaillent dans les bibliothèques de droit et qui exercent des fonctions connexes de communiquer et d'échanger des idées; d'encourager l'avancement de la profession; de maintenir et d'accroître l'utilité des bibliothèques de droit; promouvoir la coopération
Nathalie Bélanger, Présidente

Association des bibliothèques publiques de l'Estrie (ABIPE)
5086, rue Frontenac, Lac-Mégantic QC G6B 1H3
Tél: 819-845-7115; *Téléc:* 819-845-5516
mpmorin@abacom.com
www.bpq-estrie.qc.ca
Regrouper les bibliothèques publiques d'Estrie pour en favoriser le développement; informer les membres et échanger sur toute question pertinente au dossier des bibliothèques; représenter les intérêts des bibliothèques membres de la région 05 en étant leur porte-parole officiel auprès des instances gouvernementales et autres; organiser et réaliser des activités d'animation culturelle; sensibiliser le milieu au rôle et à l'importance de la bibliothèque publique dans la communauté
Marie-Pascale Morin, Présidente
Karine Corbeil, Vice-présidente

Association for Manitoba Archives (AMA)
PO Box 26005, Stn. Maryland, Winnipeg MB R3G 3R3
Tel: 204-942-3491; *Fax:* 204-942-3492
ama1@mts.net
mbarchives.ca
To promote understanding & awareness of the role & use of archives; to promote standards, procedures & practices in the management of archives; to provide assistance & education to persons seeking to improve their skills in the development, management or operation of archives
Christy Henry, Chair

Association of Canadian Archivists (ACA) / Association canadienne des archivistes
PO Box 2596, Stn. D, Ottawa ON K1P 5W6
Tel: 613-234-6977; *Fax:* 613-234-8500
aca@archivists.ca
www.archivists.ca
Social Media: www.facebook.com/AssociationofCanadianArchivists; twitter.com/archivistsdotca; www.linkedin.com/groups?home=&gid=3704759
To ensure the preservation & accessibility of Canada's documentary heritage; To provide professional leadership among persons engaged in the discipline & practice of archival science; To promote the development of archives & archivists in Canada; To encourage cooperation of archivists with all those interested in the preservation & use of documents of human experience
Duncan Grant, Executive Director
Loryl MacDonald, President

Association of Canadian Map Libraries & Archives (ACMLA) / Association des cartothèques et archives cartographiques du Canada (ACACC)
c/o Legal Deposit, Maps, Published Heritage, Library & Archives Canada, 550, boul de la Cité, Gatineau ON K1N 0N4
membership@acmla.org; president@acmla.org; secretary@acmla.org
www.acmla.org
To represent Canadian map librarians & cartographic archivists, as well as others who are interested in geographic information; To develop professional standards & international cataloguing rules for the management & access to geographic information; To promote the contributions of map libraries & cartographic archives
Andrew Nicholson, President
Dan Duda, First Vice-President
Wenonah Van Heyst, Second Vice-President
Susan McKee, Secretary
Susan Greaves, Treasurer

Association of Newfoundland & Labrador Archives (ANLA)
PO Box 23155, RPO Churchill Sq., St. John's NL A1B 4J9
Tel: 709-726-2867; *Fax:* 709-729-7989
anla@nf.aibn.com
www.anla.nf.ca
To provide professional leadership among persons engaged in practice of archival science; to promote development of archives & archivists in Newfoundland & Labrador; to encourage cooperation of archivists with all those interested in preservation & use of documents of human experience
Stephanie Harlick, President

Association of Parliamentary Libraries in Canada (APLIC) / Association des bibliothèques parlementaires au Canada (ABPAC)
c/o Melissa Bennett, Librarian, Saskatchewan Legislative Library, #234, 2405 Legislative Dr., Regina SK S4S 0B3
mbennett@legassembly.sk.ca (President)
www.aplic-abpac.ca
To improve parliamentary library service in Canada; To encourage cooperation with related officials & organizations
Melissa Bennett, President

Association pour l'avancement des sciences et des techniques de la documentation (ASTED)
#387, 2065 rue Parthenais, Montréal QC H2K 3T1
Tél: 514-281-5012; *Téléc:* 514-281-8219
info@asted.org
www.asted.org
Promouvoir l'excellence des services documentaires et de leur personnel; inspirer la législation et promouvoir les intérêts des services documentaires et d'information; exercer au sein de la francophonie nord-américaine le leadership documentaire
Robin Dumais, Président
Francine Benoit-Plamondon, Directrice générale

Atlantic Provinces Library Association (APLA)
c/o School of Information Management, Kenneth C. Rowe Management Bldg., 6100 University Ave., Halifax NS B3H 3J5
executive@yahoo.ca
www.apla.ca
Social Media: www.facebook.com/group.php?gid=10792140537
To promote library & information service & workers throughout the Atlantic region; To represent & support the interests of persons who work in libraries in the Atlantic provinces; To cooperate with other library associations & similar organizations; To develop & offer effective continuing education programs
Jocelyne Thompson, President
Lou Duggan, Vice-President
Jocelyne Thompson, Vice-President
Ann Smith, Vice-President, Membership
Debbie Costelo, Secretary
Bill Slauenwhite, Treasurer

The Banff Centre - Library & Archives
PO Box 1020, Banff AB T1L 1H5
Tel: 403-762-6100; *Fax:* 403-762-6444
communications@banffcentre.ca
www.banffcentre.ca
To offer educational activities, performances, exhibitions, & special events
Jeff Melanson, President

Bibliographical Society of Canada (BSC) / Société bibliographique du Canada (SBC)
PO Box 575, Stn. P, Toronto ON M5S 2T1
gretagolick@rogers.com
www.library.utoronto.ca/bsc
To promote the scholarly study of history, description & transmission of texts in all media & formats; To promote the study & practice of bibliography; To further the study, research & publication of book hisory & print culture; To promote preservation & conservation of manuscript, archival & published materials in various formats; To encourage utilization & analysis of relevant manuscript & archival sources as a foundation of bibliographical scholarship & book history
David McKnight, President
Greta Golick, Secretary

Les bibliothèques publiques des régions de Québec et Chaudière-Appalaches
4705, rue de la Promenade-des-Soeurs, Cap-Rouge QC G1Y 2W2
Tél: 418-641-6143; *Téléc:* 418-650-7795
info@bibliotheques.qc.ca
www.bibliotheques.qc.ca
Regrouper les responsables des bibliothèques publiques de ces régions; promouvoir et défendre les intérêts de ces bibliothèques; représenter le secteur des bibliothèques publiques des ces régions au sein des organismes à caractères culturel et social.
Suzanne Rochefort, Présidente

Les bibliothèques publiques du Québec (BPQ)
4155, rue Brodeur, Sherbrooke QC J1L 1K4
Tél: 819-565-9744; *Téléc:* 819-565-9157
crsbpe@reseaubiblioastrie.qc.ca
www.bibliothequespubliquesduquebec.ca
Agit à titre de représentant officiel des bibliothèques publiques du Québec
Suzanne Payette, Présidente
Lachapelle Lucie, Directrice générale

British Columbia Courthouse Library Society
800 Smithe St., Vancouver BC V6Z 2E1
Tel: 604-660-2841; *Fax:* 604-660-9418
Toll-Free: 800-665-2570
librarian@courthouselibrary.ca
www.bccls.bc.ca
Johanne Blenkin, Executive Director

British Columbia Library Association (BCLA)
#150, 900 Howe St., Vancouver BC V6Z 2M4
Tel: 604-683-5354; *Fax:* 604-609-0707
Toll-Free: 888-683-5354
www.bcla.bc.ca
Social Media: twitter.com/bclibassoc
To encourage library development throughout British Columbia; To coordinate library services to various parts of the province; To promote cooperation between libraries; To advance the mutual interests of libraries & library personnel
Errin Morrison, Executive Director
Marjorie Mitchell, President
Christopher Kevlahan, Vice-President
Adrienne Wass, Second Vice-President
Chris Middlemass, Treasurer
Allie Douglas, Office Manager

British Columbia Library Trustees' Association (BCLTA)
PO Box 4334, Stn. Terminal, Vancouver BC V6B 3Z7
Tel: 604-913-1424; *Fax:* 604-913-1413
admin@bclta.org
www.bclta.org
To develop & support library trustees who govern local public libraries in British Columbia; To advance public library service in the province
Andy Ackerman, President
Ivan Idzan, Vice-President
Philip Mantler, Secretary-Treasurer

Canadian Association for Information Science (CAIS) / Association canadienne des sciences de l'information (ACSI)
c/o Nadia Caidi, Faculty of Information, #335, 45 Willcocks St., Toronto ON M5S 1C7
Tel: 416-978-4664
nadia.caidi@utoronto.ca
www.cais-acsi.ca
To advance information science in Canada by encouraging & facilitating the exchange of information on the use, access, retrieval, organization, management, & dissemination of information
Nadia Caidi, President
Siobhan Stevenson, Vice-President
Heather Hill, Director, Membership
Dinesh Rathi, Director, Communications
Heather O'Brien, Secretary
Ali Shiri, Treasurer

Canadian Association for School Libraries (CASL)
c/o Canadian Library Association, 328 Frank St., Ottawa ON K2P 0X8
Tel: 613-232-9625; *Fax:* 613-563-9895
info@cla.ca; membership@cla.ca; cpd@cla.ca (Continuing Education)
www.cla.ca/AM/Template.cfm?Section=CASL2
To promote school library programs throughout Canada as an important element in the educational process; To encourage excellence in every aspect of school libraries
Linda Shantz-Keresztes, President
Diana Gauthier, Secretary-Treasurer
Derrick Grose, Editor, School Libraries in Canada: A Journal of the CASL
Victoria Pennell, Editor, Impact

Canadian Association of Children's Librarians (CACL)
c/o Canadian Library Association, 328 Frank St., Ottawa ON K2P 0X8
Tel: 613-232-9625
www.cla.ca/AM/Template.cfm?Section=CAPL2
To address issues of interest to librarians who work with & for children
Lita Barrie, President
Ann Foster, Secretary-Treasurer

Canadian Association of College & University Libraries (CACUL)
c/o Canadian Library Association, 328 Frank St., Ottawa ON K2P 0X8
Tel: 613-232-9625; *Fax:* 613-563-9895
info@cla.ca; membership@cla.ca; cpd@cla.ca (Continuing Education)
www.cla.ca/AM/Template.cfm?Section=CACUL
To develop & promote high standards of librarianship & of library & information services in post-secondary education institutions
Pam Ryan, President
Gillian Byrne, Vice-President & Director, Membership
Wendy Rodgers, Director, Awards
Carol Shepstone, Director, Grants
Christine E. Sammon, Secretary-Treasurer

Canadian Association of Family Resource Programs / Association canadienne des programmes de ressources pour la famille
#707, 331 Cooper St., Ottawa ON K2P 0G5
Tel: 613-237-7667; *Fax:* 613-237-8515
Toll-Free: 866-637-7226
info@frp.ca
www.frp.ca
Social Media: www.facebook.com/frpcanada
To promote the well-being of families, through provision of leadership, consultation, & resources to organizations which care for children & support families; To act as the national voice for family resource programs; To advance social policy, research, resource development, & training for those who support the capacity of families to raise their children
Janice MacAulay, Executive Director
Crystal Elliott, President
Natalie Chapman, Vice-President
Trish Plant, Secretary
Stéphane Rivest, Treasurer
Jill Heckman, Director, Operations

Canadian Association of Law Libraries (CALL) / Association canadienne des bibliothèques de droit (ACBD)
PO Box 1570, #310, 4 Cataraqui St., Kingston ON K7L 5C8
Tel: 613-531-9338; *Fax:* 613-531-0626
office@callacbd.ca
www.callacbd.ca

To promote law librarianship; To develop Canadian law libraries; To promote access to legal information
Elizabeth Hooper, National Officer
Rosalie Fox, President
Cyndi Murphy, Vice-President
Ann Marie Melvie, Secretary
Sandra Wilkins, Treasurer

Canadian Association of Music Libraries, Archives & Documentation Centres (CAML) / Association canadienne des bibliothèques, archives et centres de documentation musicaux inc. (ACBM)
c/o Music Section, Library & Archives Canada, 395 Wellington St., Ottawa ON K1A 0N4
kirsten.walsh@ubc.ca (President); sacassin@yorku.ca (Webmaster)
www.yorku.ca/caml
To represent librarians, researchers, & archivists in the field of music
Kirsten Walsh, President
Rob van der Bliek, Treasurer
Laura Snyder, Secretary
Kyla Jemison, Membership Secretary
Stacy Allison-Cassin, Officer, Communications

Canadian Association of Public Libraries (CAPL)
c/o Canadian Library Association, 328 Frank St., Ottawa ON K2P 0X8
Tel: 613-232-9625; *Fax:* 613-563-9895
info@cla.ca
www.cla.ca/AM/Template.cfm?Section=CAPL2
Social Media: www.facebook.com/group.php?gid=7514940812
To further & improve public library service throughout Canada
Andre Gagnon, President
Nancy Mackenzie, Vice-President
Maureen Sawa, Secretary-Treasurer

Canadian Association of Research Libraries (CARL) / Association des bibliothèques de recherche du Canada (ABRC)
Morisset Library, University of Ottawa, #239, 65 University St., Ottawa ON K1N 9A5
Tel: 613-562-5385; *Fax:* 613-562-5297
carladm@uottawa.ca
www.carl-abrc.ca
To provide leadership to the Canadian research library community; To address issues affecting research libraries, such as federal research policy, copyright, open access publication, & preservation; To encourage broad access to scholarly information; To seek public policy encouraging of research
Ernie Ingles, President
Brent Roe, Executive Director
Diego Argáez, Officer, Research
Katherine McColgan, Coordinator, Programs

Canadian Association of Special Libraries & Information Services (CASLIS)
c/o Canadian Library Association, #400, 1150 Morrison Dr., Ottawa ON K2H 8S9
Tel: 613-232-9625; *Fax:* 613-563-9895
info@cla.ca; membership@cla.ca; cpd@cla.ca (Continuing Education)
www.cla.ca/caslis
Social Media: www.facebook.com/group.php?gid=27554915813
To support information professionals across Canada who work in special libraries & information services; To strengthen the special library community
Karen Adams, President
Pilar Martinez, Vice-President
Mary-Jo Romaniuk, Treasurer

Canadian Council of Archives (CCA) / Conseil canadien des archives
#501, 130 Albert St., Ottawa ON K1P 5G4
Tel: 613-565-1222; *Fax:* 613-565-5445
Toll-Free: 866-254-1403
cca@archivescanada.ca
www.cdncouncilarchives.ca
To facilitate development of Canadian archival system & its coordination; to make recommendations to system's operation & financing; to develop & facilitate implementation & management of programs to assist archival community; to communicate archival needs & concerns to decision-makers, researchers & the general public.
Ian Forsyth, Chairperson
Leslie Latta-Guthrie, Vice-Chair

Canadian Health Information Management Association (CHIMA)
#1404, 148 Fullarton St., London ON N6A 5P3
Tel: 519-438-6700; *Fax:* 519-438-7001
Toll-Free: 877-332-4462
www.echima.ca
To contribute to the promotion of wellness & the provision of quality healthcare through excellence in health information management; to assure competency of practice through credentialling, standards & continuing education; to promote value of health record professionals within the relevant publics
Gail Crook, CEO & Registrar

Canadian Health Libraries Association (CHLA) / Association des bibliothèques de la santé du Canada (ABSC)
39 River St., Toronto ON M5A 3P1
Tel: 416-646-1600; *Fax:* 416-646-9460
info@chla-absc.ca
www.chla-absc.ca
To lead health librarians towards excellence
Miriam Ticoll, President
Jeff Mason, Vice-President
Lindsay Glynn, Director, Continuing Education
Laurie Blanchard, Director, Public Relations
Shauna-Lee Konrad, Secretary

Canadian Library Association (CLA) / Association canadienne des bibliothèques (ACB)
#400, 1150 Morrison Dr., Ottawa ON K2H 8S9
Tel: 613-232-9625; *Fax:* 613-563-9895
info@cla.ca; membership@cla.ca; publishing@cla.ca; orders@cla.ca
www.cla.ca
Social Media: www.facebook.com/group.php?gid=2229890224; twitter.com/cla_web; www.linkedin.com/groups?gid=4137241
To develop high standards of librarianship & of library & information services across Canada
Karen Adams, President
Kelly Moore, Executive Director
Judy Green, Manager, Marketing & Communications
Geraldine Hyland, Manager, Member Services
Wendy Walton, Manager, Conference & Events
Penny Warne, Manager, Web & IT Infrastructure
Mary-Jo Romaniuk, Treasurer
Beverly Bard, Coordinator, Book Reviews
Stephanie Bowa, Coordinator, Young Canada Works Program
Carla Chami, Coordinator, Conference Registration
Maria Blake, Administrator, Orders

Canadian Library Trustees Association (CLTA)
c/o Canadian Library Association, 328 Frank St., Ottawa ON K2P 0X8
Tel: 613-232-9625; *Fax:* 613-563-9895
info@cla.ca; membership@cla.ca; cpd@cla.ca (Continuing Education)
www.cla.ca/AM/Template.cfm?Section=CLTA
To represent the interests of public library trustees in Canada; To foster excellence in public library service & public library trusteeship; To support communication among library trustee associations in Canada & abroad
Jan Harder, President
Betty Thomas, Vice-President
Elaine Kivisto, Secretary-Treasurer

Canadian Urban Libraries Council (CULC)
2006 Queen St E, no 7, Toronto ON M4L 1J3
Tel: 416-699-1938; *Fax:* 416-699-1937
www.culc.ca
To identify the issues & choices available in developing urban public library services; to explore the philosophy & principles that govern public library service in urban areas; to comment on the state of public library service in Canada; to facilitate the exchange of ideas & information between member libraries; to influence legislation & financing of urban public libraries; to promote & work in conjunction with other library organizations in Canada to achieve an urban public library service which is comprehensive, economic & efficient; to provide the means for communication & information sharing between members of the public library community; to promote formal & informal cooperation with organizations & institutions in Canada & outside Canada whose goals & objectives are relevant to large urban public library service
Catherine Bliss, Chair
Maureen Sawa, Vice-Chair

Church Library Association of Ontario (CLAO)
c/o Margaret Godefroy, CLAO Membership Secretary, #603, 155 Navy St., Oakville ON L6J 2Z7
Tel: 905-845-0222
agodefroy@cogeco.ca (Membership Secretary)
www.churchlibraries.ca
Social Media: www.facebook.com/group.php?gid=117754255215
To help church libraries in Ontario make the most of their resources
Arthur McClelland, President & Archivist
Marcella Haanstra, Coordinator, Outreach
Margaret Godefroy, Membership Secretary
Jane Rocoski, Coordinator, Resources
Mary Ryan, Coordinator, Conferences
Jo-Anne Vandermey, Treasurer
Margaret Godefroy, Secretary, Membership
Michelle Rickard, Editor, Newsletter

Corporation des bibliothécaires professionnels du Québec (CBPQ) / Corporation of Professional Librarians of Québec
#103, 353, rue St. Nicolas, Montréal QC H2Y 2P1
Tél: 514-845-3327; *Téléc:* 514-845-1618
info@cbpq.qc.ca
www.cbpq.qc.ca
Développer les services de bibliothèques; établir des normes de compétence; encourager et stimuler la recherche en bibliothéconomie; promouvoir et développer les intérêts professionnels de ses membres
Régine Horinstein, Directrice générale
Louis Houle, Président
Luc Jodoin, Vice-President
Mohammed Harti, Trésorier

Council of Archives New Brunswick (CANB) / Conseil des archives du Nouveau-Brunswick
PO Box 1204, Stn. A, 23 Dineen Dr., Fredericton NB E3B 5C8
Tel: 506-453-4327; *Fax:* 506-453-3288
archives.advisor@gnb.ca
www.canbarchives.ca/canb
To address the needs of the archival institutions in New Brunswick; To provide training & information on developments in the profession; To encourage information sharing & cooperation in educational opportunities with Maritime sister provinces & national associations
Anne LeClair, Archives Advisor

Council of Nova Scotia Archives (CNSA)
6016 University Ave., Halifax NS B3H 1W4
Tel: 902-424-7093; *Fax:* 902-424-0628
advisor@councilofnsarchives.ca
www.councilofnsarchives.ca
To foster education of archival standards & practices to preserve Nova Scotia's documentary heritage; To promote archival standards, procedures, & practices
Karen White, Advisor, Archives

Council of Prairie & Pacific University Libraries (COPPUL)
2005 Sooke Rd., Victoria BC V9B 5Y4
Tel: 250-391-2554; *Fax:* 250-391-2556
www.coppul.ca
To coordinate the activities of the Prairie & Pacific university libraries in promoting enhanced information services by means of cooperative collection development, resource sharing, rapid document delivery, & other such methods of transmitting or sharing resources; to act as an information sharing body
Sandy Slade, Executive Director

Federal Libraries Coordination Secretariat
Place de la Cité, 550 de la Cité Blvd., Gatineau PQ K1A 0N4
Tel: 819-934-4358; *Fax:* 819-934-7534
FLCS-SCBGF@lac-bac.gc.ca
www.collectionscanada.gc.ca/flcs-scbgf/index-e.html
To coordinate federal libraries service reports to the Recordkeeping & Library Coordination Office of the Government Records Branch
Fabio Onesi, Director
Deane Zeeman, Manager, Federal Libraries Consortium

Golden Horseshoe Health Libraries Association
c/o BCHS Resource Library, 200 Terrace Hill St., Brantford ON N3R 1G9
Tel: 905-519-5544
www.chla-absc.ca/?q=en/node/71
The Association's mission is to improve health and health care by promoting excellence in access to information.
Barbara Gray, President

Halifax Library Association
c/o 5940 South St., Halifax NS B3H 1S6
www.smu.ca/administration/archives/hla
Social Media: www.facebook.com/group.php?gid=20160077946
To promote libraries and their services, and to encourage more extensive cooperation and interdependence among libraries in the geographic area of Halifax Regional Municipality.
Collette Saunders, President

Health Libraries Association of British Columbia (HLABC)
c/o Devon Greyson, UBC Centre for Health Services & Policy Research, #201, 2206 East Mall, Vancouver BC V6T 1Z3
Tel: 604-822-7353; *Fax:* 604-822-5690
devon-at-chspr.ubc.ca (President)
www.hlabc.bc.ca
Social Media: www.facebook.com/group.php?gid=2347253553
To support the work of health librarians throughout British Columbia
Devon Greyson, President
Brooke Ballantyne-Scott, Vice-President
Elisheba Muturi, Secretary
Anne Allgaier, Treasurer & Contact, Membership

Indexing Society of Canada / Société canadienne d'indexation
PO Box 664, Stn. P, Toronto ON M5S 2Y4
www.indexers.ca
To encourage the production & use of indexes & abstracts; to promote the recognition of indexers & abstractors; to improve indexing & abstracting techniques; to improve communication among individual indexers & abstractors.
Mary Newberry, Co-President
Gillian Watts, Co-President
Audrey McClellan, Membership Secretary
Merridy Cox Bradley, Treasurer
Tia Leschke, Representative, British Columbia
Chris Blackburn, Representative, Central Canada
Anna Olivier, Representative, Eastern Canada
Moira Calder, Representative, Prairies & Northern Canada

Library Association of Alberta (LAA)
80 Baker Cres. NW, Calgary AB T2L 1R4
Tel: 403-284-5818; *Fax:* 403-282-6646
Toll-Free: 877-522-5550
info@laa.ca; info@albertalibraryconference.com
www.laa.ca
To facilitate the improvement of library services in Alberta; To promote library service throughout Alberta; To encourage cooperation among libraries & information centres across the province; To promote intellectual freedom in Alberta
Mary Jane Bilsland, President
Pat Sandercock, First Vice-President
Linda Williams, 2nd Vice-President
Julia Reinhart, Treasurer

Library Boards Association of Nova Scotia (LBANS)
c/o Janet Ness, Secretary, Library Boards Association of Nova Scotia, 53 Sherwood Dr., Wolfville NS B4P 2K5
Tel: 902-542-7386
janet_ness@hotmail.com
www.standupforlibraries.ca
To preserve & support quality public library service throughout Nova Scotia
Gary Archibald, Executive Director
Mary MacLellan, President
Shirley McNamara, Vice-President
Janet Ness, Secretary
Marie Hogan Loker, Treasurer

London Area Health Libraries Association (LAHLA)
c/o South Huron Hospital, Shared Library Services, 24 Huron St. West, Exeter ON N0M 1S2
Tel: 519-235-5168; *Fax:* 519-235-4476
linda.wilcox@shha.on.ca
Linda Wilcox, President

Manitoba Association of Health Information Providers (MAHIP)
c/o J.W. Crane Memorial Library, University of Manitoba, 2109 Portage Ave., Winnipeg MB R3J 0L3
Tel: 204-831-2107
angela_osterreicher@umanitoba.ca
www.chla-absc.ca/?q=en/node/75
To promote the provision of quality library service to the health community in Manitoba by communication & mutual assistance.
Angela Osterreicher, President

Manitoba Association of Library Technicians (MALT)
PO Box 1872, Winnipeg MB R3C 3R1
malt.mb.ca@gmail.com
www.malt.mb.ca
Social Media: www.facebook.com/malt.mb.ca
To promote & advance the role of library technicians throughout Manitoba; To respond to issues that relate to the library & information services community
Catherine Taylor, President
Marge Dyck, Secretary
Elizabeth Stregger, Treasurer
Katie McKee, Coordinator, Communications
Candice Phillips, Coordinator, Membership
Eric Wesselius, Editor, Newsletter

Manitoba Library Association (MLA)
#606, 100 Arthur St., Winnipeg MB R3B 1H3
Tel: 204-943-4567; *Fax:* 866-202-4567
manitobalibrary@gmail.com
www.mla.mb.ca
Social Media: www.facebook.com/group.php?gid=6003904478
To develop, support, & promote library & information services in Manitoba for the benefit of the library community & Manitoba residents
Emma Hill Kepron, President
Alex Homanchuk, Vice-President
Katherine Penner, Secretary
Kathy Rusnak, Treasurer
Dawn Bassett, Director, Professional Development
Lesley Mackie, Director, Membership
Evelyn Bruneau, Director, Fund Development
Stephen Carney, Director, Communications
Ian Fraser, Director, Advocacy
Vera Keown, Director, Conferences
Alison Pattern, Director, Membership

Manitoba School Library Association (MSLA)
c/o Claudia Klausen, Emerson Elementary School, 323 Emerson Ave., Winnipeg MB R2G 1V3
www.manitobaschoollibraries.com
To advocate for school library programs in Manitoba; To provide professional development opportunities for members
Vivianne Fogarty, President
Heather Eby, Secretary
Rhonda Morrissette, Webmaster
Claudia Klausen, Treasurer
Jeff Anderson, Co-Chair, Conferences
Lorie Battershill, Chair, Publications
Jo-Anne Gibson, Chair, Awards
Kim Marr, Chair, Membership
Christine Robinson, Co-Chair, Conferences

Maritimes Health Libraries Association (MHLA) / Association des bibliothèques de la santé des Maritimes (ABSM)
Horizon Health Network, 135 MacBeath Ave, Moncton NB E1C 6Z8
Tel: 506-857-2546; *Fax:* 506-857-5785
lori.leger@horizonNB.ca
ww.chla-absc.ca
To support members in the provision of quality information services for the health care community in the maritime provinces
Shelley McKibbon, President

New Brunswick Library Trustees' Association (NBLTA) / Association des commissaires de bibliothèque du Nouveau-Brunswick, inc.
c/o Doug Goss, 209 Saunders Rd., McAdam NB E6J 1M3
gossdj@nbed.nb.ca
To promote the public libraries of New Brunswick & to develop greater understanding of library trustees' responsibilities.
Doug Goss, Chair

Newfoundland & Labrador Health Libraries Association (NLHLA)
c/o Health Sciences Library, Memorial Univ. of Newfoundland, St. John's NL A1B 3V6
Tel: 709-777-8951
www.chla-absc.ca/?q=en/node/78
To promote the provision of a high quality library service to the health community in Newfoundland & Labrador through mutual assistance & communication; to provide professional support to the membership by offering continuing education opportunities
Shannon Gordon, President

Northern Alberta Health Libraries Association
c/o J.W. Scott Health Sciences Library, University of Alberta, 2K3.28 Walter MacKenzie Ctr., Edmonton AB T6G 2R7
nahla@nahla.ca
www.chla-absc.ca/nahla
This chapter of NAHLA exists to provide a forum for networking among libararians, library technicians and other interested in health libraries and health information.
Thane Chambers, President

Northern Lights Health Library Association
c/o Sault Area Hospital, 969 Queen Street East, Sault Ste Marie ON P6A 2C4
Tel: 705-759-3434; *Fax:* 705-759-3847
aslettk@sah.on.ca
Kim Aslett, President

Northwest Territories Archives Council (NWTAC)
c/o Northwest Territories Archives, Gov't of Northwest Territories, PO Box 1320, Yellowknife NT X1A 2L9
Tel: 867-873-7698; *Fax:* 867-873-0205
peter_harding@gov.nt.ca
www.pwnhc.ca/nwtac
To facilitate development of the archival system in the Northwest Territories; To make recommendations about the system's operation & financing; to develop & facilitate implementation & management of programs to assist the archival community; To communicate archival needs & concerns to decision-makers, researchers & the general public.
Ian Moir, President

Nova Scotia Government Libraries Council (NSGLC)
c/o Dept. of Justice Library
Tel: 902-424-7699; *Fax:* 902-424-0546
lamietm@gov.ns.ca
www.nsglc.ednet.ns.ca
To provide a forum for government libraries to discuss common problems & share information
Ruth Hart, Chair
Natalie MacPherson, Secretary
Anne Van Iderstine, Treasurer

Nova Scotia Library Association (NSLA)
c/o Kelli WooShue, Halifax Public Libraries, 60 Alderney Dr., Dartmouth NS B2Y 4P8
Tel: 902-490-5710
wooshuk@halifax.ca; nslanewsletter@gmail.com (Newsletter)
www.nsla.ns.ca
To promote the value of libraries; To facilitate the exchange of ideas & information among library workers in Nova Scotia
Faye MacDougall, President
Denise Corey, Secretary
Carin Cress, Treasurer
Jeremy Henderson, Convenor, Newsletter
Rachel Crosby, Contact, Membership
Debbie Kaleva, Convenor, Continuing Education
Theresa MacDonald, Convenor, Conferences
Lori Noseworthy, Contact, Newsletter
Jeff Mercer, Convenor, Membership
Kelli Wooshue, Convenor, Public Relations & Promotions

Ontario Association of Library Technicians (OALT) / Association des bibliotechniciens de l'Ontario (ABO)
Abbey Market, PO Box 76010, 1500 Upper Middle Rd. West, Oakville ON L6M 3H5
info@oaltabo.on.ca
www.oaltabo.on.ca
To promote the interests of library & information technician graduates & students throughout Ontario; To advance library & information technician graduates & students
Michael David Reansbury, President
Daisy Collins, Treasurer
Donna Brown, Coordinator, External Communications
Lisa Eschli, Coordinator, Internal Communications
Amna Hussain, Coordinator, Internal Communications
Amy Dwyer, Coordinator, Membership
Maria Ripley, Coordinator, Chapters
Millie Yip, Coordinator, Chapters
Kathi Vandenheuvel, Archivist

Ontario College & University Library Association (OCULA)
#201, 50 Wellington St. East, Toronto ON M5E 1C8
Tel: 416-363-3388; *Fax:* 416-941-9581
Toll-Free: 800-387-1181
info@accessola.com
www.accessola.com
To support librarians & to improve Library Science in Ontario's college & university libraries
Nathalie Soini, Vice-President
Shelagh Paterson, President

Ontario Council of University Libraries (OCUL)
c/o Library, University of Toronto, 130 St. George Street, Toronto ON M5S 1A5
Tel: 416-978-4211; *Fax:* 416-978-6755
www.ocul.on.ca

Faye Abrams, Projects Officer

Ontario Library & Information Technology Association (OLITA)
#201, 50 Wellington St. E, Toronto ON M5E 1C8
Tel: 416-363-3380; *Fax:* 416-941-9581
info@accessola.com
www.accessola.com/olita/
Social Media: www.facebook.com/accessola; twitter.com/onlibraryassoc; olastaff.tumblr.com/
Planning, development, design, application & integration of technology in the library & information environment with the impact of emerging technologies on library service, & with the effect of automated technologies on people
Michael Vandenburg, President

Ontario Library Association (OLA)
#201, 50 Wellington St. East, Toronto ON M5E 1C8
Tel: 416-363-3388; *Fax:* 416-941-9581
Toll-Free: 866-873-9867
info@accessola.com; olaprograms@accessola.com
www.accessola.com
Social Media: www.facebook.com/group.php?gid=2233680329; twitter.com/ollibraryassoc; www.linkedin.com/groups/Ontario-Library-Association
To provide opportunities for people in the library & information field to share experience & expertise, & to create innovative solutions
Shelagh Paterson, Executive Director
Karen McGrath, President
Paul Takala, Treasurer
Helios He, Manager, Operations
Beckie MacDonald, Manager, Member Services
Michelle Arbuckle, Coordinator, Education
Liz Kerr, Coordinator, Conferences
Meredith Tutching, Coordinator, Programs
Carla Wintersgill, Coordinator, Marketing & Communications

Ontario Library Boards' Association (OLBA)
c/o Ontario Library Association, #201, 50 Wellington St. East, Toronto ON M5E 1C8
Tel: 416-363-3388; *Fax:* 416-941-9581
Toll-Free: 866-873-9867
info@accessola.com; membership@accessola.com
www.accessola.com/olba
To represent Ontario public library board members on issues that affect library board leadership; To advance public library board development & improve the management & services of libraries throughout Ontario; To enhance the visibility of library boards
Joyce Cunningham, President
Frances Ryan, Vice-President

Ontario Public Library Association (OPLA)
#201, 50 Wellington St. East, Toronto ON M5E 1C8
Tel: 416-363-3388; *Fax:* 416-941-9581
Toll-Free: 866-873-9867
info@accessola.com
www.accessola.com/opla/bins/index.asp
To foster the expansion & improvement of public library service in Ontario; To support public librarians throughout Ontario; To encourage standards & certification for public library workers
Tammy Robinson, President
Lila Saab, Vice-President
Joanna Aegard, Secretary
Laura Carter, Treasurer
Rudi Denham, Editor, HoOPLA

Ontario School Library Association (OSLA)
c/o Ontario Library Association, #201, 50 Wellington St. East, Toronto ON M5E 1C8
Tel: 416-363-3388; *Fax:* 416-941-9581
Toll-Free: 866-873-9867
www.accessola.com/osla
To act as the voice of elementary & secondary school teacher-librarians in Ontario; To promote teacher-librarians as curriculum leaders; To support student success
Ruth Hall, President
Beth McEwen, Secretary-Treasurer

Ottawa Valley Health Libraries Association (OVHLA) / Association des bibliothèques de santé de la Vallée d'Outaouais
c/o Children's Hospital of Eastern Ontario, 401 Smyth Rd., Ottawa ON K1H 8L1
Tel: 613-737-7600
msampson@cheo.on.ca
www.chla-absc.ca/ovhla
The Ottawa Valley Health Libraries Association / l'Association des Bibliothèques de la Santé de la Vallée de l'Outaouais is an association of over twenty health-related libraries whose purpose is to promote the provision of quality library services in the health sciences throughout the Ottawa Valley and the Outaouais. It was formed in 1994 through the amalgamation of the Ottawa-Hull Health Libraries Association and the OHA Region 9 chapter of the Ontario Health Libraries Association and is a chapter of the Ontario Health Libraries Association (OHLA) and the Canadian Health Libraries Association (CHLA).
Margaret Sampson, President
Amanda Hodgson, Secretary

Prince Edward Island Professional Librarians Association (PEIPLA)
c/o Holland College Library Services, Manager Library Services, Charlottetown PE
Tel: 902-566-9350; *Fax:* 902-566-9522
pmdoucette@hollandcollege.com
peipla.wordpress.com
Patricia Doucette, President
Liam O'Hare, Sec.-Treas.

Regroupement des bibliothèques publiques de l'Abitibi-Témiscamingue (RBPAT)
201, ave. Dallaire, Rouyn-Noranda QC J9X 4T5
Tél: 819-762-4305; *Téléc:* 819-762-5903
info@crsbpat.qc.ca
www.biblrn.qc.ca/rbpat/
Promotion du livre et de la lecture en Abitibi-Témiscamingue; promotion des bibliothèques

Regroupement des bibliothèques publiques de la Côte-Nord
Bibliothèque centrale de prêt de la Côte-Nord, 59, rue Napoléon, Sept-Iles QC G4R 5C5
Tél: 418-962-1020
info@rbpcn.com
Yvon Grondin, Président

Regroupement Les bibliothèques publiques du Saguenay-Lac-Saint-Jean (RABLES)
100, rue Price ouest, Alma QC G8B 4S1
Tél: 418-662-6425; *Téléc:* 418-662-7593
Ligne sans frais: 800-563-6425
sbolduc@reseaubiblioslsj.qc.ca
catweb.crsbpslsj.biblio.qc.ca
Promouvoir les bibliothèques publiques; concertation dans des dossiers concernant les bibliothèques publiques; faire connaître nos services
Sophie Bolduc, Directrice générale (par intérim)

Réseau des archives du Québec (RAQ)
a/s Archives nationales du Québec à Montréal, 535 av Viger est, local 5.27.1, Montréal QC H2L 2P3
Tél: 514-864-9213
raq@bellnet.ca
www.raq.qc.ca
Promouvoir le développement et la mise en valeur des archives historiques; favoriser l'échange et la mise en commun d'information, d'expérience et de ressources; devenir un instrument de consultation et un groupe de pression reconnu des divers intervenants des milieux archivistiques
Diane Baillargeon, Présidente
Bernard Savoie, Secrétaire

Saskatchewan Association of Library Technicians, Inc. (SALT)
PO Box 24019, Saskatoon SK S7K 8B4
Fax: 306-543-4487
salt@lib.sk.ca
www.lib.sk.ca/salt
To promote the value of library technicians in Saskatchewan
Dorothy Richard, President
Carole-Anne Wilson-Hough, Secretary

Saskatchewan Council for Archives & Archivists (SCAA)
#202, 2080 Broad St., Regina SK S4P 1Y3
Tel: 306-780-9414
scaa@sasktel.net
www.scaa.sk.ca
To facilitate the development of the archival system in Saskatchewan; To develop standard archival policies & practices; To promote public awareness of the use of archives
Carey Isaak, Executive Director & Advisor, Archives
Tim Hutchinson, President
May Chan, Treasurer

Saskatchewan Health Libraries Association (SHLA)
c/o Regina-Qu'Appelle Health Region, Health Sciences Library, 1440 - 14th Ave., Regina SK S4P 0W5
Tel: 306-766-3833; *Fax:* 306-766-3839
kelly.mcivor@usask.ca
www.lib.sk.ca/shla/
To promote access to health care literature for physicians & allied health care staff
Kelly McIvor, President

Saskatchewan Library Association (SLA)
#15, 2010 - 7th Ave., Regina SK S4R 1C2
Tel: 306-780-9413; *Fax:* 306-780-9447
slaexdir@sasktel.net; slaprograms@sasktel.net
www.saskla.ca
Social Media: www.facebook.com/group.php?gid=106445391816
To further the development of library services in Saskatchewan
Jeff Mason, President
Caroline Selinger, Executive Director
Kirsten Hansen, Program Administrator
Brett Waytuck, Treasurer

Saskatchewan Library Trustees Association (SLTA)
c/o Wendy Thienes, PO Box 573, Shaunavon SK S0N 2M0
Tel: 306-297-6368; *Fax:* 306-297-3668
wendy.thienes@gmail.com
www.libraries.gov.sk.ca/slta
To foster the development of libraries & library services throughout Saskatchewan
Wendy Thienes, Executive Director
Bev Dubois, President
Dennis Taylor, Vice-President
Kae Campbell, Treasurer

Southern Alberta Health Libraries Association (SAHLA)
c/o Health Sciences Library, University of Calgary, 3330 University Dr. NW, Calgary AB T2N 4N1
Tel: 403-220-6858; *Fax:* 403-282-7992
sahla@sahla.org
www.sahla.org
Taryn Lenders, President

Southwestern Ontario Health Library Information Network
c/o Hotel Dieu Grace Hospital Medical Library, 1030 Ouellette Ave., Windsor ON N9A 1E1
Tel: 519-973-4411
linda.wilcox@shha.on.ca
www.chla-absc.ca/sohlin
Linda Wilcox, President

Special Libraries Association (SLA)
331 South Patrick St., Alexandria VA 22314-3501 USA
Tel: 703-647-4900; *Fax:* 703-647-4901
cschatz@sla.org (Public Relations); membership@sla.org
www.sla.org
To promote & strengthen information professionals from around the globe
Janice R. Lachance, Chief Executive Officer
Linda Broussard, Chief Community Officer
Quan O. Logan, Chief Technology Officer
Doug Newcomb, Chief Policy Officer

Toronto Health Libraries Association (THLA)
PO Box 94056, 3409 Yonge St., Toronto ON M4N 2L0
Tel: 416-485-0377; *Fax:* 416-485-6877
president@thla.ca
www.thla.ca
To promote the provision of quality library service to the health community; to encourage communication & cooperation among members & to foster their professional development; to consult & collaborate with other professional, technical & scientific organizations in matters of mutual interest
Weina Wang, President

Yukon Council of Archives (YCA)
PO Box 31089, Whitehorse YT Y1A 5P7
Tel: 867-667-5321; *Fax:* 867-393-6253
yukoncouncilofarchives@yahoo.ca
www.yukoncouncilofarchives.ca
To facilitate the development of the archival system in the Yukon; To make recommendations about the system's operation & financing; To develop & facilitate implementation & management of programs to assist the archival community; To communicate archival needs & concerns to decision-makers, researchers & the general public
Clara Rutherford, President
Vanessa Thorson, Vice-President

Yukon Teacher-Librarians' Association (YTLA)
2064 - 2nd Ave., Whitehorse YT Y1A 1A9
Tel: 867-668-6777; *Fax:* 867-667-4324
admin@yta.yk.ca
www.yta.yk.ca
A committee of Yukon Teachers' Association
Sandra Henderson, President

Literacy

Regroupement de Bouches à Oreilles (RBO)
265, rue Lanctôt, Chibougamau QC G8P 1C1
Tél: 418-748-2239; *Téléc:* 418-748-2735
www.abc02.org/chibougamau/
Formation de base: compter, lire, écrire
Céline Laliberté, Coordonnatrice

Literary Arts

L'arc-en-ciel littéraire
CP 180, Succ. C, Montréal QC H2L 4K1
arcenciellitteraire@yahoo.ca
arcenciellitteraire.site.voila.fr
Le seul regroupement d'écrivains GLBT au Québec; promouvoit la littérature gaie et des auteurs gais
Réjean Roy, Président fondateur

Long-Term Care

New Brunswick Special Care Home Association Inc.
c/o Seely Lodge Inc., 2443 Westfield Rd., Saint John NB E2M 6L4
Tel: 506-738-8514; *Fax:* 506-738-0892
janseely@rogers.com
www.nbscha.com
To assist licensed members of the New Brunswick Special Care Home Association Inc. in providing quality, cost effective long term care for seniors and special needs adults in cooperation with the Department of Social Development.
Jan Seely, President

Management & Administration

Administrative Sciences Association of Canada (ASAC) / Association des sciences administratives du Canada
c/o Sobey School of Business, Saint Mary's University, Halifax NS B3H 3C3
Tel: 902-496-8139
jean.mills@smu.ca
www.asac.ca
To develop teaching & research in management studies at Canadian universities
Tanya Mark, Secretary, markt@uoguelph.ca
Travor Brown, President

Alberta Institute Purchasing Management Association of Canada (AIPMAC)
Centre 104, #612, 5241 Calgary Trail, Edmonton AB T6H 5G8
Tel: 780-944-0355; *Fax:* 780-944-0356
Toll-Free: 866-610-4089
info@aipmac.ab.ca
www.aipmac.ab.ca
To develop the profession by ensuring that professional status is accessible to all purchasing practitioners in the province; high standards of eligibility & professional conduct will be developed, maintained & enforced to enhance the profession & protect public interest in the province of Alberta
Darren Caines, Executive Director
Jerome Ferber, President
Sherri Peleskey, Treasurer

ARMA Canada (ARMA)
PO Box 6000, Fredericton NB E3B 5H1
Tel: 506-453-5618; *Fax:* 506-462-2046
www.armacanada.org
Social Media: www.facebook.com/group.php?gid=14876329775; twitter.com/armacanada
ARMA is a not-for-profit, professional association focussed on managing records & information - both paper & electronic. It works to advance records & information management as a discipline & a profession, & organizes programs of research, education, training & networking.
Bernita Cogswell, Canadian Regional Manager
Fred Wideman, Sec.-Treas.
Dierdre Bradshaw, Manager, Mountain/Pacific Region
Steve Neilly, Manager, Western Region
Katherine Chornoboy, Manager, Central Region
Brenda Prowse, Manager, Eastern Region

Association des MBA du Québec (AMBAQ)
#900, 500, rue Sherbrooke ouest, Montréal QC H3A 3C6
Tél: 514-282-3810; *Téléc:* 514-844-7556
mba@affaires.com
www.ambaq.com
Ôtre le porte-parole des MBA du Québec; constituer un réseau actif de diplômés et étudiants MBA; favoriser le développement personnel et professionnel des membres; valoriser et promouvoir le diplôme MBA
Jean-Guy Renaud, Directeur général

Association of Administrative Assistants (AAA) / Association des adjoints administratifs
c/o 11110 - 108 St., Edmonton AB T5G 2T2
Tel: 780-423-2929; *Fax:* 780-407-3340
info@aaa.ca
www.aaa.ca
To establish a national standard of qualifications for an administrative assistant; to help assistants to reach this standard by providing opportunities for advanced education; to make management aware of the value of the fully-qualified administrative assistant
Doris Kurtz, Director

Association of Cultural Executives (ACE) / Association des cadres d'institutions culturelles (ACIC)
PO Box 22044, Stn. Westmount, Waterloo ON N2L 6J7
Tel: 519-579-8564; *Fax:* 519-743-6773
Toll-Free: 888-363-3591
info@acecontact.org
www.acecontact.org
To develop professional cultural executives; to manage Canada's cultural resources with priorities on training, recognition & improved working conditions for cultural managers in Canada
Dan Donaldson, Co-President
Jane Needles, Co-President

Association of Fundraising Professionals (AFP)
#412, 260 King St. East, Toronto ON M5A 4L5
Tel: 416-941-9212; *Fax:* 416-941-9013
Toll-Free: 800-796-7373
info@afptoronto.org
www.afptoronto.org
Social Media: www.facebook.com/AFPFan; twitter.com/afptoronto; www.linkedin.com/company/association-of-fundraising-professionals; www.youtube.com/AFPToronto
To advance philanthropy by enabling people & organizations to practice effective & ethical fundraising
Susan Horvath, President

Association of Professional Executives of the Public Service of Canada (APEX) / L'Association professionnelle des cadres de la fonction publique du Canada
#508, 75 Albert St., Ottawa ON K1P 5E7
Tel: 613-995-6252; *Fax:* 613-943-8919
info@apex.gc.ca
www.apex.gc.ca
Denise Amyot, President
Hanny Toxopeus, Chief Executive Officer

British Columbia Institute of the Purchasing Management Association of Canada
#300, 435 Columbia St., New Westminster BC V3L 5N8
Tel: 604-540-4494; *Fax:* 604-540-4023
Toll-Free: 800-411-7622
info@bcipmac.ca
www.bcipmac.ca
BC Institute PMAC is an incorporated, not-for-profit association that maintains a code of ethics for the profession to regulate quality & integrity.
Geraldine Kennedy, Executive Director
Deana Trudeau, Acting President

Canadian Association of Management Consultants (CMC - Canada) / Association canadienne des conseillers en management
#815, 4 King St. West, Toronto ON M5H 1B6
Tel: 416-860-1515; *Fax:* 416-860-1535
Toll-Free: 800-268-1148
consulting@cmc-canada.ca
www.cmc-canada.ca
To foster excellence & integrity in the management consulting profession; To administer the Certified Management Consultant (CMC) designation in Canada; To advance the practice & profile of the profession of management consulting in Canada; To promote ethical standards
Mauro Meneghetti, Chair
Lynn Bennett, Vice Chair
Glenn Yonemitsu, CEO

Canadian Association of School Administrators (CASA) / Association canadienne des administrateurs et des administratrices scolaires (ACAS)
1123 Glenashton Dr., Oakville ON L6H 5M1
Tel: 905-845-2345; *Fax:* 905-845-2044
www.casa-acas.ca
To promote & enhance effective administration & leadership in provision of quality education in Canada; to provide a national voice on educational matters; to promote & provide opportunity for professional development to the membership; to promote communication & liaison with national & international organizations having an interest in education; to provide a variety of services to the membership; to recognize outstanding contributions to education in Canada
Frank Kelly, Executive Director

Canadian Executive Service Organization (CESO) / Service d'assistance canadienne aux organismes (SACO)
PO Box 328, #800, 700 Bay St., Toronto ON M5G 1Z6
Tel: 416-961-2376; *Fax:* 416-961-1096
Toll-Free: 800-268-9052
toronto@ceso-saco.com
www.ceso-saco.com
Social Media: www.facebook.com/cesosaco; twitter.com/cesosaco; www.youtube.com/CESOSACO
To enhance the socio-economic well-being of the peoples & the communities of Canada, developing nations & emerging market economies
Wendy Harris, President & Chief Executive Officer
Patrick Kelly, Vice-President, National Services
Gale Lee, Vice-President, International Services
Ryan Blackwell, Manager, Business Development
Jason Laing, Manager, Recruitment

Canadian Institute of Certified Administrative Managers (CICAM)
#800, 2 St. Clair Ave. East, Toronto ON M4T 2T5
Tel: 416-921-7962; *Fax:* 416-921-3959
Toll-Free: 800-233-5864
mailbox@cicam.org
www.cicam.org
To advance science of management & administration; to develop & recognize competent professional managers & to gain recognition for members.
Phil Russo
Sal Mian, President

Canadian Institute of Management (CIM) / Institut canadien de gestion
National Office, 15 Collier St., Lower Level, Barrie ON L4M 1G5
Tel: 705-725-8926; *Fax:* 705-725-8196
Toll-Free: 800-387-5774
office@cim.ca
www.cim.ca
To promote the senior management profession by offering a series of educational programs from single courses to professional certification
Paul Markle, President
Patrick B. Dunne, Sec.-Treas.
Paul J. Walsh, Academic Dean

Canadian Management Centre
150 York St., 5th Fl., Toronto ON M5H 3S5
Fax: 416-214-6047
Toll-Free: 877-262-2519
cmcinfo@cmctraining.org
www.cmctraining.org
To play a key role in strengthening the ability of Canada's business leaders, managers & organizations to compete & succeed in today's challenging & changing business environment; To provide a full range of professional development & management education services to companies, government agencies, & individuals
John Wright, President & Managing Director
Jo Bouchard, Vice-President, Business Development
Andre Proulx, Vice-President, Marketing
Bernadette Smith, Vice-President, Learning Solutions

Canadian Public Relations Society Inc. (CPRS) / La Société canadienne des relations publiques
#346, 4195 Dundas St. West, Toronto ON M8X 1Y4
Tel: 416-239-7034; *Fax:* 416-239-1076
admin@cprs.ca
www.cprs.ca
Social Media: twitter.com/CPRSNational
To oversee the practice of public relations practitioners in Canada, to ensure the protection of the public interest; To advance the professional stature of public relations practitioners;

To promote the ethical practice of public relations & communications management
Karen Dalton, Executive Director
Jorge de Mendonca, Director, Finance & Information Systems
Monica Simmie, Director, Professional Development & Sponsorship
Elizabeth Tang, Manager, Membership, Communications, & Awards

Canadian Society of Association Executives (CSAE) / Société canadienne des directeurs d'association (SCDA)
#1100, 10 King St. East, Toronto ON M5C 1C3
Tel: 416-363-3555; *Fax:* 416-363-3630
Toll-Free: 800-461-3608
csae@csae.com
www.csae.com
To provide members with the environment, knowledge, & resources to develop excellence in not-for-profit leadership, through networking, education, advocacy, information, & research
Michael Anderson, CAE, President & Chief Executive Officer
Dave Cybak, Executive Vice-President
Josette Forde, Director, Chapter Relations & Education
Michele Haché, Director, Finance & Administration
Gail McHardy, CMP, Director, Conference & Events

Canadian Society of Corporate Secretaries (CSCS)
#255, 55 St. Clair Ave. West, Toronto ON M4V 2Y7
Tel: 416-921-5449; *Fax:* 416-967-6320
Toll-Free: 800-774-2850
info@cscs.org
www.cscs.org
To provide members with the tools necessary to become expert in corporate secretarial practice & to strengthen the corporate secretary's profile in the company.
Pamela Smith, Administrative Director
Lynn Beauregard, President

Canadian Society of Physician Executives (CSPE) / Société canadienne des médecins gestionnaires
PO Box 59005, 1559 Alta Vista Dr., Ottawa ON K1G 5T7
Tel: 613-731-9331; *Fax:* 613-731-1779
carol.rochefort@cma.ca
www.cspexecs.com
To develop physician leaders to be successful in health care leadership & management roles
Carol Rochefort, Director

Confédération nationale des cadres du Québec (CNCQ)
e/s Association des cadres des collèges du Québec, 2430, ch Ste-Foy, Québec QC G1V 1TZ
Tél: 418-877-1500; *Téléc:* 418-877-4469
www.cncq.qc.ca/
Venir en aide et supporter les associations affiliées de cadres.
Jean Perron, Chef

Corporation des approvisionneurs du Québec (CAQ)
Complexe Tassé, #302, 895, boul Séminaire nord, Saint-Jean-sur-Richelieu QC J3A 1J2
Tél: 450-357-0033; *Téléc:* 450-357-0044
Ligne sans frais: 800-977-1877
info@caq.qc.ca
www.caq.qc.ca
La Corporation des approvisionneurs du Québec assure le développement professionnel de ses membres et veille à promouvoir et favoriser l'implantation des meilleures pratiques en matière de gestion de la chaîne d'approvisionnement au sein des entreprises québécoises afin que la valeur stratégique de l'approvisionnement puisse contribuer pleinement à l'essor des entreprises et à la société québécoise.
Pierre St-Jean, Président

Couchiching Institute on Public Affairs (CIPA)
#301, 250 Consumers Rd., Toronto ON M2J 4V6
Tel: 416-642-6374; *Fax:* 416-495-8723
Toll-Free: 866-647-6374
couch@couch.ca
www.couch.ca
To bring together interested Canadians to discuss important public policy issues with experts & other members of the general public
Gwen Burrows, President
Ruth Abrahamson, Executive Director

Fédération des secrétaires professionnelles du Québec (FSPQ)
#300-11, 1173, boul Charest ouest, Québec QC G1N 2C9
Tél: 418-527-5041
info@fspq.qc.ca
www.fspq.qc.ca
Travail à la valorisation de la profession.
Line Ross, Présidente

Institute of Certified Management Consultants of Alberta (CMC-Alberta)
c/o CMC-Canada National Office, #815, 4 King St. West, Toronto ON M5H 1B6
Tel: 416-860-1515; *Fax:* 416-860-1535
Toll-Free: 800-268-1148
consulting@cmc-canada.ca
www.cmc-canada.ca/provincial_institutes.cfm?Portal_ID=1; www.icmc
To act under the regulations of the Professional & Occupational Associations Registration Act; To work as the regulatory authority for provisional registrants, certified management consultants, & fellow certified management consultants in Alberta; To ensure that members abide by professional & ethical standards
Mark Brown, President
David Wartman, Vice-President
John Pascoe, Registrar

Institute of Certified Management Consultants of Atlantic Canada
c/o CMC-Canada National Office, #815, 4 King St. West, Toronto ON M5H 1B6
Tel: 416-860-1515; *Fax:* 416-860-1535
Toll-Free: 800-268-1148
consulting@cmc-canada.ca
www.cmc-canada.ca/provincial_institutes.cfm?Portal_ID=2
CMC-Atlantic Canada is a provincial institute which fosters excellence & integrity in the management consulting profession.
Kathy-Jane Elton, President

Institute of Certified Management Consultants of British Columbia (CMC-BC)
c/o CMC-Canada National Office, #815, 4 King St. West, Toronto ON M5H 1B6
Tel: 416-860-1515; *Fax:* 416-860-1535
Toll-Free: 800-268-1148
consulting@camc.com; cmc-bc@shaw.ca
www.cmc-canada.ca/provincial_institutes.cfm?Portal_ID=3
To protect the general public & clients by ensuring that the Institute's Code of Professional Conduct is followed by the certified management consultant profession; To ensure that certified members comply with all applicable legislation & laws
Simon Wong, President
Mary Colak, Vice-President
Ken Lee, Treasurer

Institute of Certified Management Consultants of Manitoba (CMC-Manitoba) / Institut manitobain des conseillers en administration agréés
c/o CMC-Canada National Office, #815, 4 King St. West, Toronto ON M5H 1B6
Tel: 416-860-1515; *Fax:* 416-860-1535
Toll-Free: 800-268-1148
consulting@cmc-canada.ca
www.cmc-canada.ca/provincial_institutes.cfm?Portal_ID=4
To foster & promote the development & acceptance of the profession of management consulting; to promote excellence in the practice of the profession for the benefit of members, clients & the community at large.
Ken Howell, President

Institute of Certified Management Consultants of Saskatchewan
c/o CMC-Canada National Office, #815, 4 King St. West, Toronto ON M5H 1B6
Tel: 416-860-1515; *Fax:* 416-860-1535
Toll-Free: 800-662-2972
consulting@cmc-canada.ca
www.cmc-canada.ca/provincial_institutes.cfm?Portal_ID=7
Frank Hart, President
Peggie Koenig, Registrar

Institute of Chartered Secretaries & Administrators - Canadian Division (ICSA Canada) / Institut des secrétaires et administrateurs agréés au Canada
#202, 300 March Rd., Ottawa ON K2K 2E2
Tel: 613-595-1151; *Fax:* 613-595-1155
Toll-Free: 800-501-3440
info@icsacanada.org
www.icsacanada.org
The organization represents and serves Chartered Secretaries & Administrators, professionals who are hired by organizations to administer key areas such as corporate governance, director/officer/shareholder matters, compliance & regulatory matters, & financial matters.
Nancy Barrett, Executive Director

Institute of Corporate Directors (ICD) / Institut des administrateurs de sociétés
#602, 40 University Ave., Toronto ON M5J 1T1
Tel: 416-593-7741; *Fax:* 416-593-0636
Toll-Free: 877-593-7741
admin@icd.ca
www.icd.ca
To enhance the quality of corporate governance in Canada
Stan Magidson, President & CEO
Vicki Jordan, Vice President, Marketing & Membership Services

Institute of Professional Management (IPM)
#2210, 1081 Ambleside Dr., Ottawa ON K2B 8C8
Tel: 613-721-5957; *Fax:* 613-721-5850
info@workplace.ca
www.workplace.ca
Social Media: www.facebook.com/InstituteofProfessionalManagement
Nathaly Pinchuk, Executive Director
Brian Pascal, President

International Personnel Management Association - Canada (IPMA-Canada)
National Office, 20 Edwards Pl., Mount Pearl NL A1N 3V5
Fax: 613-226-2298
Toll-Free: 888-226-5002
national@ipma-aigp.ca
www.ipma-aigp.ca
Social Media: www.facebook.com/IPMACanada
To promote excellence in the practice of human resource management; to promote & enhance the HR profession in Canada & globally; to provide professional development & training for the HR community; to maintain a code of ethics & standards of practice; to recognize excellence through national & local awards programs
Glenn Saunders, Executive Director
Rick Brick, President
Heather Bowser, Director, Communications

Manitoba Institute of the Purchasing Management Association of Canada (MIPMAC)
#200, 5 Donald St., Winnipeg MB R3L 2T4
Tel: 204-231-0965; *Fax:* 204-233-1250
Toll-Free: 877-231-0965
mbpmac@mts.net
www.mb.pmac.ca
MIPMAC is committed to offering a professional development program coupled with networking opportunities to advance supply chain management.
Peter Buscemi, President
Jocelyn Wilson, Office Representative

New Brunswick Purchasing Management Institute (NBPMI)
#402, 527 Dundonald St., Fredericton NB E3B 1X5
Tel: 506-458-9414
info@pmacnb.com
www.pmacnb.com
Social Media: www.facebook.com/NBPMI
NBPMI is dedicated to being the leading source of education, training, & development in the field of purchasing & supply chain management. It provides members with networking opportunities & offers them training for a Supply Chain Management Professional (SCMP) designation.
Bill D'Donnell, President
Wendy Piercy, Administrator

Newfoundland & Labradour Institute of the Purchasing Management Association of Canada (NLIPMAC)
PO Box 29011, Stn. Torbay Road, St. John's NL A1A 5B5
Tel: 709-778-4033; *Fax:* 709-724-5625
info@pmacnl.org
www.pmacnl.org
To deliver education, training, & professional development programs in the province, so members may earn a Supply Chain Management Professional (SCMP) designation
Rick Squires, President

Northwest Territories Institute of the Purchasing Management Association of Canada (NWTIPMAC)
PO Box 2736, Yellowknife NT X1A 2R1
Tel: 867-873-9324
www.nt.pmac.ca
A non profit organization registered with the Societies Act in the Northwest Territories. We provide information and Education leading to a professional designation as a C.P.P. (Certified Professional Purchaser) the only accredited and legally recognized designation in the fields of Purchasing and Supply Management in Canada.
Howard Nowell, President

Nova Scotia Institute of the Purchasing Management Association of Canada (NSIPMAC)
PO Box 21, Stn. CRO, Halifax NS B3J 2L4
Tel: 902-425-4029; *Fax:* 902-431-7220
info@nsipmac.com
www.nsipmac.com
NSIPMAC delivers education, training & professional development programs in the province, so members may earn a Supply Chain Management Professional (SCMP) designation.
Peter Chaffey, President
Nancy Christian, Program Coordinator

Ontario Institute of the Purchasing Management Association of Canada (OIPMAC)
PO Box 64, #2704, 1 Dundas St. West, Toronto ON M5G 1Z3
Tel: 416-977-7566; *Fax:* 416-977-4135
Toll-Free: 877-726-6968
info@oipmac.ca
www.ontarioinstitute.com
Social Media:
www.facebook.com/group.php?gid=147482001988201;
twitter.com/oipmac;
www.linkedin.com/groups?about=&gid=1286497&trk=anet_ug_grppro; www.youtube.com/user/OIPMAC
The preeminent supply chain managemen organisation in Ontario, supporting a growing global SCM community of over 20,00 active members and program participants in meeting their professional and lifelong learning goals. Their programs taught by leading North American academics and professional trainers, are designed to build/enhance the professional competence and strategic perspective of practitioners at all levels of career progression, from entry-, to mid-, to senior/executive levels of functional responsibility.
R. David Fletcher, President & CEO

Ordre des administrateurs agréés du Québec (OAAQ)
#100, 910, rue Sherbrooke ouest, Montréal QC H3A 1G3
Tél: 514-499-0880; *Téléc:* 514-499-0892
Ligne sans frais: 800-465-0880
info@adma.qc.ca
www.adma.qc.ca
Favorise auprès des professionnels de l'administration, l'innovation et l'atteinte d'un niveau de compétence supérieur pour qu'ils contribuent de façon proactive et dynamique au développement des entreprises et des organisations; assure la protection du public en garantissant le respect des normes et standards professionnels en administration, en conformité avec le code de déontologie et par le biais des mécanismes prévus au code des professions; contribue à l'avancement de l'administration, discipline essentielle au développement social et économique du Québec.
Denise Brosseau, Directrice générale et Secrétaire

Purchasing Management Association of Canada (PMAC) / Association canadienne de gestion des achats (ACGA)
PO Box 112, #2701, 777 Bay St., Toronto ON M5G 2C8
Tel: 416-977-7111; *Fax:* 416-977-8886
Toll-Free: 888-799-0877
info@pmac.ca
www.pmac.ca
Social Media: www.facebook.com/pmacnational;
twitter.com/pmacnational;
www.linkedin.com/groups?about=&gid=2888933
To advance strategic supply chain management by providing training, education, & professional development for supply chain management professionals in Canada
Cheryl Paradowski, President & CEO
Cori Ferguson, Director, Public Affairs & Communications
Keith Carruthers, Chair

Saskatchewan Institute of the Purchasing Management Association of Canada (SIPMAC)
#221A, 3521 - 8th Street E, Saskatoon SK S7H 0W5
Tel: 306-653-8899; *Fax:* 306-653-8870
Toll-Free: 866-665-6167
sipmac@sasktel.net
www.si.pmac.ca
To promote & improve supply management practices in the profession through education & raising the awareness of the supply management profession within Saskatchewan
Nicole Burgess, Executive Director
Candace Finch, Administrative Assistant

Strategic Leadership Forum, The Toronto Society for Strategic Management (SLF)
75 Dunkirk Rd., Toronto ON M4C 2M5
Tel: 416-574-1832; *Fax:* 647-436-3599
membership@slftoronto.com
strategicleadershipforum.camp9.org
To provide our community of members with an independent & intellectually challenging forum that delivers practical insights & interactions on strategic management & leadership
Keith Beveridge, President
Debbie Powell, Manager, Administration

Manufacturing & Industry

Association de la recherche industrielle du Québec (ADRIQ)
#901, 1155, rue University, Montréal QC H3B 3A7
Tél: 514-337-3001; *Téléc:* 514-337-2229
adriq@adriq.com
www.adriq.com
Claude Demers, Président

Association for Operations Management (APICS)
#300, 1370 Don Mills Rd., Toronto ON M3B 3N7
Tel: 416-366-5388; *Fax:* 416-381-4054
info@apics.ca
www.apics.ca
To offer programs & materials on business management techniques; To promotes education in resource management
Shari Bricks, Executive Director
Lina DeMatteo, Manager, Events
Anthony Nijmeh, Manager, Technical Support
Greg Mulroney, Coordinator, Membership Support

Association of Independent Corrugated Converters
PO Box 73063, Stn. White Shields, 2300 Lawrence Ave. East, Toronto ON M1P 4Z5
Tel: 905-727-9405; *Fax:* 905-727-1061
info@aicc11.com
www.aiccbox.org
To provide a forum for the independent corrugated converter on legitimate matters of mutual interest; To enhance the level of professionalism of the independent converter in the operation of his/her business; To implement democratically determined goals on matters civil & governmental which have a positive effect on all independent corrugated converters

British Columbia Paint Manufacturers' Association (BCPMA)
c/o Cloverdale Paint Inc., 6950 King George Hwy., Surrey BC V3W 4Z1
Tel: 604-596-6261; *Fax:* 604-597-2677
www.bcpma.bc.ca
To act as the voice of paint manufacturers in British Columbia; To promote the welfare of association members
Ed Linton, President
Ron Vanderdrift, Vice-President
Deryk Pawsey, Secretary
Yvon Poitras, Treasurer

Canadian Appliance Manufacturers Association (CAMA)
c/o Electro-Federation Canada, #200, 5800 Explorer Dr., Mississauga ON L4W 5K9
Tel: 905-602-8877; *Fax:* 905-602-5686
Toll-Free: 866-602-8877
info@electrofed.com
www.electrofed.com/councils/CAMA/
To represent member interests in the establishment of product standards & in environmental legislation; To advocate the safe removal of mercury & other ozone depleting substances from older appliances; To support the development of energy efficient products
Sharon Borda, Manager, CAMA
Larry Moore, Vice-President, Consumer Councils

Canadian Association of Mould Makers (CAMM)
c/o St. Clair College (FCEM), PO Box 16, 2000 Talbot Rd. West, Windsor ON N9A 6S4
Tel: 519-255-7863; *Fax:* 519-255-9446
info@camm.ca
www.camm.ca
To address the concerns of Canadian mould making companies & to present a united voice on legislative issues to provincial & federal governments
Dan Moynahan, President
Diane Deslippe, Executive Director, Office

Canadian Carpet Institute / Institut canadien du tapis
#200, 435 St. Laurent Blvd., Ottawa ON K1K 2z8
Tel: 613-749-3265; *Fax:* 613-745-8753
info@canadiancarpet.org
www.canadiancarpet.org
To serve as a forum in developing industry consensus for action on common problems & opportunities; To enhance the well-being of the Canadian carpet industry by any & all means consistent with the members, & the public interest
Walter Eckhardt, President
Karel Vercruyssen, Vice-President
Raymonde Lemire, Manager, Administration

Canadian Cosmetic, Toiletry & Fragrance Association (CCTFA) / Association canadienne des cosmétiques, produit de toilette et parfums
#102, 420 Britannia Rd. East, Mississauga ON L4Z 3L5
Tel: 905-890-5161; *Fax:* 905-890-2607
cctfa@cctfa.ca
www.cctfa.ca
To encourage trust & confidence in the Canadian cosmetic, toiletry & fragrance industry & in the safety, efficacy & quality of its products; To be the princiapal voice of the personal care industry, including cosmetic-like drug products & cosmetic-like natural health products (NHP), interfacing on a timely basis with governemtn & elected representatives, to ensure development & effective representationof industry positions on a ll regulatory issues; to have the personal care industyr perceived by consumers at large as being socially concerned, responsible & involved with Canadian society; this will be primarily achieved through the CCTFA Foundation &;the Look Good Feel Better program.
Myles Robinson, Chair

Canadian Council of Furniture Manufacturers (CCFM) / Conseil canadien des fabricants de meubles
c/o Accro Furniture Industries, 305 McKay Ave., Winnipeg MB R2G 0N5
Tel: 204-654-1114; *Fax:* 204-654-2792
info@accro-acmechrome.com
Terry J. Clark, President

Canadian Hardware & Housewares Manufacturers' Association (CHHMA) / Association canadienne des fabricants de produits de quincaillerie et d'articles ménagers
#101, 1335 Morningside Ave., Toronto ON M1B 5M4
Tel: 416-282-0022; *Fax:* 416-282-0027
Toll-Free: 800-488-4792
www.chhma.ca
To assist members to sell more & do it more profitably
Vaughn Crofford, President
Maureen Hizaka, Director, Operations
Michael Jorgenson, Manager, Marketing & Communications
Pam Winter, Coordinator, Events

Canadian Innovation Centre (CIC)
c/o Waterloo Research & Technology Park, #15, 295 Hagey Blvd., Waterloo ON N2L 6R5
Tel: 519-885-5870; *Fax:* 519-513-2421
Toll-Free: 800-265-4559
info@innovationcentre.ca
www.innovationcentre.ca
To advance innovation by helping our clients make better business decisions through information, education & commercialization.
Ted Cross, Chair & CEO

Canadian Kitchen Cabinet Association (CKCA) / Association canadienne de fabricants d'armoires de cuisine (ACAC)
130 Albert St., Ottawa ON K1P 5G4
Tel: 613-567-9171; *Fax:* 613-567-4664
info@ckca.ca
www.ckca.ca
To promote the interests & conserve the rights of those engaged in the manufacture of kitchen cabinets, bathroom vanities & related millwork as well as their suppliers & dealers.
Caroline Castrucci, President
Melissa Lemay, Association Affaris Officer

Canadian Laboratory Suppliers Association (CLSA) / Association canadienne de fournisseurs de laboratoire
#131, 525 Highland Rd. West, Kitchener ON N3M 5P4
Tel: 519-579-7598; *Fax:* 519-579-8134
jhowes@clsassoc.com
www.clsassoc.com
The Canadian Laboratory Suppliers Association is a group of scientific companies committed to promoting and serving the Canadian laboratory marketplace. It provides a non-competitive environment for executives of Canada's leading scientific suppliers to share ideas and concepts. The CLSA's objective is to provide market analysis on the scientific industry, and to understand and discuss issues that influence the Canadian laboratory scientific market.
Wayne England, President

Canadian Manufacturers & Exporters (CME) / Manufacturiers et Exportateurs Canada
#1500, 1 Nicholas St., Ottawa ON K1N 7B7
Tel: 613-238-8888; *Fax:* 613-563-9218
www.cme-mec.ca
Social Media: twitter.com/cme_mec
To continuously improve the competitiveness of Canadian industry & to expand export business by: aggressive, effective advocacy to government at all levels; delivering timely, relevant information, programs & support of superior quality & value; providing opportunities for education, learning & professional growth; & promoting the development & implementation of advanced technology
Jayson Myers, President & Chief Executive Officer
Jeff Sholdice, Chief Financial Officer & Vice-President, Operations
Jeff Brownlee, Vice-President, Public Affairs & Partnerships
Joanne Heighway, Vice-President, Organizational Excellence
John Knox, Vice-President, Sales & Marketing
Jean-Michel Laurin, Vice-President, Global Business Policy
Craig Williams, Vice-President, National Programs
Mathew Wilson, Vice-President, National Policy

Canadian Office Products Association
#402, 2800 Skymark Ave., Mississauga ON L4W 5A6
Tel: 905-624-9462; *Fax:* 905-624-0830
Toll-Free: 800-267-7524
info@copa.ca
www.copa.ca

Canadian Plastics Industry Association (CPIA) / Association canadienne de l'industrie des plastiques
#125, 5955 Airport Rd., Mississauga ON L4V 1R9
Tel: 905-678-7748; *Fax:* 905-678-0774
national@cpia.ca
www.cpia.ca
Social Media: www.facebook.com/IntelligentPlastics; twitter.com/intellplastics
To advance the prosperity & international competitiveness of the Canadian plastics industry in an environmentally & socially responsible manner
Carol Hochu, President & CEO
Judy Mark, Executive Vice President

Canadian Sanitation Supply Association (CSSA) / Association canadienne des fournisseurs de produits sanitaires
PO Box 10009, 910 Dundas St. West, Whitby ON L1P 1P7
Tel: 905-665-8001; *Fax:* 905-430-6418
Toll-Free: 866-684-8273
www.cssa.com
Social Media: www.facebook.com/group.php?gid=183837499478; twitter.com/CSSA_Canada
To provide a high degree of professionalism, technical knowledge & business ethics within the membership; To promote greater public awareness, appreciation & understanding of the sanitation industry
Mike Nosko, Executive Director
Catherine Fedak, Contact, Sales
Diane Mason, Contact, Accounting
Tanya Nowotny, Contact, Production

Canadian Tooling & Machining Association (CTMA)
#3, 140 McGovern Dr., Cambridge ON N3H 4R7
Tel: 519-653-7265; *Fax:* 519-653-6764
Toll-Free: 888-437-3661
info@ctma.com
www.ctma.com
To be an effective, broad-based, respected organization, representing the Canadian tooling & machining industry, nationally & internationally
Les Payne, Executive Director

Canadian Toy Association / Canadian Toy & Hobby Fair (CTA) / L'Association canadienne du Jouet
#212, 7777 Keele St., Concord ON L4K 1Y7
Tel: 905-660-5690; *Fax:* 905-660-6103
info@cdntoyassn.com
www.cdntoyassn.com
Carol McDonald, Contact, Media Relations

Canadian Urethane Manufacturers Association (CUMA)
PO Box 5281, Penetanguishene ON L9M 2G4
Tel: 705-427-5383; *Fax:* 705-549-8197
www.cumahome.org
Scott Woodworth, President
Noel Campbell, Manager

Door & Hardware Institute in Canada
#310, 2175 Sheppard Ave. East, Toronto ON M2J 1W8
Tel: 416-492-6502; *Fax:* 416-491-1670
maryloum@taylorenterprises.com
www.dhicanada.ca
A professional organization that serves the Canadian member as the professional development, information, advocate & certification resource for the total distribution process in the architectural openings industry.
Milt Allred, President
Carolyne Vigon, Administrator

Fenestration Canada
#1208, 130 Albert St., Ottawa ON K1P 5G4
Tel: 613-235-5511; *Fax:* 613-235-4664
info@fenestrationcanada.ca
www.fenestrationcanada.ca
To represents its members in all aspects of the window & door manufacturing industry, including formulating & promoting high standards of quality in manufacturing, design, marketing, distribution, sales, & application of all types of window & door products
Yvan Banman, President
Eva Ryterband, Treasurer

National Floor Covering Association (NFCA) / Association nationale des revêtements de sol
987 Clarkson Rd. South, Mississauga ON L5J 2V8
Tel: 905-822-2280; *Fax:* 905-822-2494
www.nfcaonline.ca
To unite the Canadian regional & provincial associations in a spirit of cooperation; to improve & enhance the floorcovering industry; to share information & ideas; to undertake & support programs which will improve communications at all levels of the industry

Organization of CANDU Industries (OCI) / Association des industries CANDU
#2, 1730 McPherson Ct., Pickering ON L1W 3E6
Tel: 905-839-0073; *Fax:* 905-839-7085
www.oci-aic.org
To represent companies in the Canadian private sector engaged in the supply of goods & services for CANDU power plants in export markets; to provide a focal point for industrial collaboration between the private sector of Canada's nuclear industry & foreign purchasers of a CANDU plant; functions separately from AECL, but participates with it in the design, manufacture, construction & commissioning of CANDU facilities in foreign countries
Ron Oberth, President
Marina Oeyangen, Manager, Member Services

Paint & Decorating Retailers Association Canada (PDRA)
1401 Triad Center Dr., St. Peters MO 63376 USA
Tel: 636-326-2636
info@pdra.org
www.pdra.org
Social Media: twitter.com/PaintDecoRetail
To educate, promote & represent the interests of decorating products dealers in Canada
Jeff Baggaley, President
Dan Simon, Executive Vice-President & Publisher
Larry DeWitt, Senior Director, Art & Marketing
Renée Nolte, Director, Finance & Human Resources

The Rubber Association of Canada (RAC) / Association canadienne de l'industrie du caoutchouc
Plaza 4, #250, 2000 Argentia Rd., Mississauga ON L5N 1W1
Tel: 905-814-1714; *Fax:* 905-814-1085
info@rubberassociation.ca
www.rubberassociation.ca
Social Media: twitter.com/GTRadials; www.linkedin.com/company/the-rubber-association-of-canada
To upgrade & maintain good industry/government working relations; to explore ways of improving industry competitiveness & efficiency; To promote safety in members' products, in their use & in the workplace; To promote expansion & profitability of Canadian rubber manufacturing units; To enhance standing of Canadian rubber industry worldwide; To provide members with industry marketing statistics
Glenn Maidment, President
Ralph Warner, Director, Operations
Gilles Paquette, Communications Manager

Saskatchewan Trade & Export Partnership Inc. (STEP)
PO Box 1787, #320, 1801 Hamilton St., Regina SK S4P 3C6
Tel: 306-933-6551; *Fax:* 306-933-6556
Toll-Free: 888-976-7875
inquire@sasktrade.com
www.sasktrade.com
To work in partnership with Saskatchewan exporters & emerging exporters to maximize commercial success in global ventures; To deliver custom export solutions & market intelligence to member companies; To coordinate international development projects
Lionel LaBelle, President & Chief Executive Officer
Angela Krauss, Executive Director, Export Services
Brad Michnik, Executive Director, Trade Development
Pam Bartoshewski, Controller

Marine Trades

Association of Canadian Port Authorities (ACPA)
#1502, 85 Albert St., Ottawa ON K1P 6A4
Tel: 613-232-2036; *Fax:* 613-232-9554
leroux@acpa-ports.net
www.acpa-ports.net
To encourage, mentor & stimulate the development of excellence within Canadian ports
Gary Leroux, Executive Director

British Columbia Marine Trades Association (BCMTA)
#300, 1275 West 6th Ave., Vancouver BC V6H 1A6
Tel: 604-683-5191; *Fax:* 604-893-8808
info@bcmta.com
www.bcmta.com
To act as the voice of the BC recreational marine industry
Alan Stovell, President
Kim Barbero, Executive Director
Chris Goulder, Treasurer

British Columbia Maritime Employers Association (BCMEA)
349 Railway St., Vancouver BC V6A 1A4
Tel: 604-688-1155; *Fax:* 604-684-2397
www.bcmea.com
Andy Smith, President & Chief Executive Officer
John Beckett, Vice-President, Training, Safety, & Recruitment
Terry Duggan, Vice-President, Finance & Secretary
Mike Leonard, Vice-President, Labour Relations
Eleanor Marynuik, Vice-President, Human Resources
Greg Vurdela, Vice-President, Marketing & Information Services

Canadian Centre for Marine Communications (CCMC)
PO Box 8454, 155 Ridge Rd., St. John's NL A1B 3N9
Tel: 709-579-4872; *Fax:* 709-579-0495
ccmc@ccmc.nf.ca
www.ccmc.nf.ca
CCMC's mission is to develop the Canadian marine information and communications technology (ICT) industry in cooperation with industry, government, and academia.
Ronald V. Newhook, President & CEO
Randy Gillespie, Vice-President
Clayton S. Burry, Director, Industry Development

Canadian Navigation Society (CNS)
c/o Canadian Aeronautics & Space Institute, #104, 350 Terry Fox Dr., Kanata ON K2K 2W5
www.casi.ca/canadiannavigationsociety.aspx
To advance the science, technologies, & applications of navigation
Susan Skone, Society Chair

Chamber of Marine Commerce (CMC) / Chambre du commerce maritime (CCM)
#700, 350 Sparks St., Ottawa ON K1R 7S8
Tel: 613-233-8779; *Fax:* 613-233-3743
email@cmc-ccm.com
www.cmc-ccm.com
To bring together all sectors of the economy that rely on a cost efficient & safe marine transportation system
Ray Johnston, President
Stephen J. Brooks, Vice-President
Julia Fields, Manager, Communications

The Great Lakes Marine Heritage Foundation
55 Ontario St., Kingston ON K7L 2Y2
Tel: 613-542-2261; *Fax:* 613-542-0043
marmus@marmuseum.ca
www.marmuseum.ca
Mark Siemons, Chair

National Marine Manufacturers Association (NMMA)
#5100, 200 E. Randolph Dr., Chicago IL 60601 USA
Tel: 312-946-6200
www.nmma.org
NMMA is dedicated to creating, promoting and protecting an environment where members can achieve financial success through excellence in manufacturing, in selling, and in servicing their customers.

Thomas Dammrich, President
Linda Waddell, Vice President, Northern Shows

National Marine Manufacturers Association Canada (NMMA)
#8, 14 McEwan Dr., Bolton ON L7E 1H1
Tel: 905-951-0009; *Fax:* 905-951-0018
sanghel@nmma.org
www.cmma.ca
The CMMA is committed to being a leader; in promoting boating, advocacy with government and providing value added services to foster the financial success of the marine industry.
Rick Layzell, Chair

Shipbuilding Association of Canada / Association de la construction navale du Canada
#1502, 222 Queen St., Ottawa ON K1P 5V9
Tel: 613-232-7127; *Fax:* 613-238-5519
Represents the interests of the Canadian shipbuilding, ship repair & associated marine equipment & services industries
Peter Cairns, President
David Reid, Chair

Mental Health

Association des médecins-psychiatres du Québec (AMPQ) / Québec Psychiatrists' Association
CP 216, Succ. Desjardins, 2, complexe Desjardins, Tour de l'Est, 30e étage, Montréal QC H5B 1G8
Tél: 514-350-5128; *Téléc:* 514-350-5198
sbresse@fmsq.org; ampq@fmsq.org
www.ampq.org
Promouvoir les intérêts professionnels et économiques de ses membres
Brian G. Bexton, Président, Administration
Gérard Cournoyer, Secrétaire

Canadian Art Therapy Association (CATA) / L'association canadienne d'art thérapie
26 Earl Grey Rd., Toronto ON M4J 3L2
www.catainfo.ca
To promote the development & maintenance of professional standards of art therapy training, registration, research, & practice in Canada; To heighten awareness of art therapy as an important mental health discipline
Nick Zwaagstra, President
Lori Boyko, Registrar
Marie Alexander, Chair, Ethics
Olena Darewych, Chair, Membership

Canadian Association for Suicide Prevention (CASP) / L'Association canadienne pour la prévention du suicide (ACPS)
870 Portage Ave., Winnipeg MB R3G 0P1
Tel: 204-784-4073; *Fax:* 204-772-7998
casp@casp-acps.ca; admin@casp-acps.ca
www.casp-acps.ca
To reduce the suicide rate; To minimize the harmful consequences of suicide
Marion Cooper, President
Joan Seabrook, Vice-President
Tim Wall, Executive Director
Yvonne Bergmans, Secretary
Ian Ross, Treasurer

Canadian Centre for Stress & Well-Being
#1801, 1 Yonge St., Toronto ON M5E 1W7
Tel: 416-363-6204; *Fax:* 416-658-9536
smcen@yahoo.com
To provide education about stress management; To increase health & wellness
Lucille Peszat, Executive Director

Canadian Group Psychotherapy Association (CGPA)
Tel: 416-736-5225; *Fax:* 416-736-5782
tsimonik@rogers.com
www.cgpa.ca
To promote excellence in standards of training, practice, & research; To encourage & provide for the education of mental health professionals in group psychotherapy
Terry Simonik, President
Linda McFadyen, Secretary
Alina Isaac, Treasurer

Canadian Institute of Stress (CIS)
PO Box 665, Stn. U, Toronto ON M8Z 5Y9
info@stresscanada.org
www.stresscanada.org
To provide programs & tools for individuals & workplaces to handle stress
Richard C.B. Earle, Director

Canadian Mental Health Association (CMHA) / Association canadienne pour la santé mentale (ACSM)
Phenix Professional Building, #303, 595 Montreal Rd., Ottawa ON K1K 4L2
Tel: 613-745-7750; *Fax:* 613-745-5522
www.cmha.ca
To promote mental health as well as support the resilience & recovery of people experiencing mental illness, through advocacy, education, research & service
Peter Coleridge, CEO
Judith Watson, President
David Alge, Controller

Canadian Psychiatric Association (CPA) / Association des psychiatres du Canada
#701, 141 Laurier Ave. West, Ottawa ON K1P 5J3
Tel: 613-234-2815; *Fax:* 613-234-9857
Toll-Free: 800-267-1555
cpa@cpa-apc.org
www.cpa-apc.org
To forge a strong, collective voice for Canadian psychiatrists & to promote an environment that fosters excellence in the provision of clinical care, education & research
Ted Callanan, Sec.-Treas.
Alex Saunders, CEO

Canadian Psychiatric Research Foundation (CPRF) / Fondation canadienne de recherche en psychiatrie (FCRP)
#200, 133 Richmond St., Toronto ON M5H 2L3
Tel: 416-351-7757; *Fax:* 416-351-7765
Toll-Free: 800-915-2773
admin@cprf.ca
www.cprf.ca
To discover better treatments & cures for mental illness & addiction, by funding mental health & addiction research to improve the health of Canadians
Jean Milligan, Executive Director
Andrea Swinton, Director, Fund Development & Marketing

Canadian Psychoanalytic Society (CPS) / Société canadienne de psychanalyse (SCP)
7000, ch Côte-des-Neiges, Montréal QC H3S 2C1
Tel: 514-738-6105; *Fax:* 514-738-6393
psyanal@qc.aira.com
www.psychoanalysis.ca
The Canadian Umbrella organization for Psychoanalynists.
Martin Gauthier, President

Canadian Psychological Association (CPA) / Société canadienne de psychologie (SCP)
#702, 141 Laurier Ave. West, Ottawa ON K1P 5J3
Tel: 613-237-2144; *Fax:* 613-237-1674
Toll-Free: 888-472-0657
cpa@cpa.ca
www.cpa.ca
Social Media:
www.facebook.com/group.php?gid=146082642130174;
twitter.com/CPA_SCP;
www.linkedin.com/groups?about=&gid=3766289&trk=anet_ug_grppro
To improve the health & welfare of Canadians by promoting psychological research, education, & practice
Karen R. Cohen, Acting Executive Director
David Dozois, President
Jennifer Frain, President-Elect
Philippe Ramsay, Chief Financial Officer & Director, Administration
John Service, Director, Practice Directorate
Melissa Tiessen, Registrar & Director, Education Directorate

Centre de ressources et d'intervention pour hommes abusés sexuellement dans leur enfance (CRIPHASE) / Resource and Intervention Center for Men Sexually Abused during their Childhood
#100, 8105, rue de Gaspé, Montréal QC H2P 2J9
Tél: 514-529-5567; *Téléc:* 514-529-0571
info@criphase.org
www.criphase.org
Services et ressources pour hommes abusés sexuellement dans leur enfance; groupes, activités/ateliers
Benoit St-Jean, Directeur général

Child & Parent Resource Institute (CPRI)
600 Sanatorium Rd., London ON N6H 3W7
Tel: 519-858-2774; *Fax:* 519-858-3913
Gillian.Kriter@ontario.ca
www.cpri.ca
To enhance the quality of life of children & youth with complex mental health or developmental challenges; to assist their families so these children & youth can reach their full potential
Anne Stark, Administrator

Children's Mental Health Ontario (CMHO) / Santé Mentale pour Enfants Ontario (SMEO)
#309, 40 St. Clair Ave. East, Toronto ON M4T 1M9
Tel: 416-921-2109; *Fax:* 416-921-7600
Toll-Free: 888-234-7054
info@cmho.org
www.kidsmentalhealth.ca
To promote, support & strengthen a sustainable system of mental health services for children, youth & their families
Gordon Floyd, Executive Director & CEO

Fédération des familles et amis de la personne atteinte de maladie mentale (FFAPAMM) / Federation of Families & Friends of Persons with a Mental Illness
#203, 1990, rue Jean-Talon nord, Sainte-Foy QC G1N 4K8
Tél: 418-687-0474; *Téléc:* 418-687-0123
Ligne sans frais: 800-323-0474
info@ffapamm.qc.ca
www.ffapamm.qc.ca
La FFAPAMM se veut le porte-parole provincial des associations de familles et amis de la personne atteinte de maladie mentale. Tout en ayant à coeur de défendre et promouvoir les intérêts de ses membres, elle a également le mandat de les soutenir dans leur développement, de sensibiliser l'opinion publique aux problèmes reliés à la maladie mentale et de créer des programmes de communication et d'éducation.
Hélène Fradet, Directrice générale

International Schizophrenia Foundation
16 Florence Ave., Toronto ON M2N 1E9
Tel: 416-733-2117; *Fax:* 416-733-2352
centre@orthomed.org
www.orthomed.org/isf/isf.html
To raise the levels of diagnosis, treatment & prevention of the schizophrenias & related disorders; to reduce the fear & stigma; to provide the best possible treatment & rehabilitation services.

Mood Disorders Association of Ontario (MDAO)
#602, 36 Eglinton Ave., Toronto ON M4R 1A1
Tel: 416-486-8046; *Fax:* 416-486-8127
Toll-Free: 888-486-8236
info@mooddisorders.on.ca
www.mooddisorders.on.ca
To provide information, education & support to those affected by depression & manic depression, their families & friends; to develop & maintain a network of supportive self-help groups; to improve the quality of life of people who experience mood disorders, their families & friends; to advocate for a flexible & responsive system of care
Karen Liberman, Executive Director

Mood Disorders Society of Canada (MDSC) / La Société pour les troubles de l'humeur du Canada
#736, 3-304 Stone Rd. West, Guelph ON N1G 4W4
Tel: 519-824-5565; *Fax:* 519-824-9569
info@mooddisorderscanada.ca
www.mooddisorderscanada.ca
Social Media:
www.facebook.com/MoodDisordersSocietyCanada;
twitter.com/#!/MoodDisordersCa
The MDSC works nationally to ensure that issues related to mood disorders are understood and considered in the setting of research priorities, the development of treatment strategies, and the creation of government programs and policies. The Mood Disorders Society of Canada is one of the leading national, voluntary health organizations in the fields of depression, bipolar illness, and associated mood disorders
Phil Upshall, National Executive Director
John Starzynski, President

Ontario Psychological Association (OPA)
#221, 730 Yonge St., Toronto ON M4Y 2B7
Tel: 416-961-5552; *Toll-Free:* 800-268-0069
info@psych.on.ca; opa@psych.on.ca
www.psych.on.ca
To advance the practice & science of psychology in Ontario communities; To promote the highest ethical standards in the profession
Mary Broga, President
Ruth Berman, Executive Director
Connie Kushnir, Financial Officer
Carla Mardonet, Administrative Officer
Anna DiDonato, Coordinator, Membership Services
Jenna Barclay, Secretary, Referral Service

L'Ordre des psychologues du Québec (OPQ)
#510, 1100, av Beaumont, Montréal QC H3P 3H5
Tél: 514-738-1881; *Téléc:* 514-738-8838
Ligne sans frais: 800-363-2644
www.ordrepsy.qc.ca

Assurer la protection du public; contrôler l'exercice de la profession par ses membres; veiller à la qualité des services dispensés par ses membres; favoriser le développement de la compétence professionnelle, le respect des normes déontologiques et l'accessibilité aux services psychologiques
Rose-Marie Charest, Présidente

The Organization for Bipolar Affective Disorders Society (OBAD)
1019 - 7th Ave. SW, Calgary AB T2P 1A8
Tel: 403-263-7408; *Toll-Free:* 866-263-7408
obad@obad.ca
www.obad.ca
Their mission is to help people affected directly or indirectly by Bipolar Disorder, Depression, and Anxiety live better lives
Kaj Korvela, Executive Director

Saskatchewan Psychiatric Association
c/o Dhanapal Natarajan, Regina Qu'Appelle Health Region, 2180 - 23rd Ave., Regina SK S4S 0A5
kidsdoctor@accesscomm.ca
To increase psychiatric knowledge in Saskatchewan
Dhanapal Natarajan, Provincial Director

Schizophrenia Society of Canada (SSC) / Société canadienne de schizophrénie
#100, 4 Fort St., Winnipeg MB R3C 1C4
Tel: 204-786-1616; *Fax:* 204-783-4898
Toll-Free: 800-263-5545
info@schizophrenia.ca
www.schizophrenia.ca
To improve the quality of life for those affected by schizophrenia & psychosis; To advocate on behalf of individuals & families affected by schizophrenia for improved treatment & services
Jim Adamson, President
Chris Summerville, Chief Executive Officer
Catherine Willinsky, Manager, National Programs & Projects

Survivors of Suicide Support Program
10 Trinity Sq., Toronto ON M5G 1B1
Tel: 416-595-1716
karen@torontodistresscentre.com
To ensure the best possible mental health services & resources in Peterborough & area; to ensure best possible care, support & community reintegration of mentally ill & emotionally distressed; to encourage growth of community mental health services; to increase public awareness & understanding of mental health illness; to act in an advocacy capacity on issues related to mental health
Karen Lefotsky, Contact

Mentally Challenged Persons

Autism Resolution Ontario
Tel: 416-352-8813
info@autismresolutionontario.com
www.autismresolutionontario.com
Sharon Aschaiek, Founder

Military & Veterans

Air Cadet League of Canada / Ligue des cadets de l'air du Canada
66 Lisgar St., Ottawa ON K2P 0C1
Tel: 613-991-4349; *Fax:* 613-991-4347
Toll-Free: 877-422-6359
webadmin@aircadetleague.com
www.aircadetleague.com
Social Media: www.facebook.com/groups/19248248746
To promote & encourage a practical interest in aeronautics among young people; To assist those intending to pursue a career in aviation
Sarah Matresky, Executive Director

Air Force Association of Canada (AFAC) / L'Association des forces aériennes du Canada
PO Box 2460, Stn. D, Ottawa ON K1P 5W6
Tel: 613-232-2303; *Fax:* 613-232-2156
Toll-Free: 866-351-2322
director@airforce.ca
www.airforce.ca
To promote a viable well-equipped air force & a strong Canadian aerospace industry
Terry Chester, National President
John Melbourne, National President

Army Cadet League of Canada (ACLC) / Ligue des cadets de l'armée du Canada
66 Lisgar St., Ottawa ON K2P 0C1
Tel: 613-991-4348; *Fax:* 613-990-8701
Toll-Free: 877-276-9223
national@armycadetleague.ca
www.armycadetleague.ca
The League is a civilian, non-profit organization working in partnership with local communities & Canadian Forces to support the Royal Canadian Army Cadets. Together with the Dept. of National Defense, it is a supervisory sponsor for 450 cadet corps across Canada, providing accommodation, transportation, & financial support for the 21,000 army cadets. It promotes the corps & assists in recruitment. The League is a registered charity, BN: 108071564RR0001.
Terry Whitty, Executive Director

Army, Navy & Air Force Veterans in Canada (ANAVETS) / Les Anciens combattants de l'armée, de la marine et des forces aériennes au Canada
#2, 6 Beechwood Ave., Ottawa ON K1L 8B4
Tel: 613-744-0222; *Fax:* 613-744-0208
anavets@storm.ca
www.anavets.ca
The Association unites veterans & their supporters to maintain entitlements & benefits. It provides a fraternal milieu for its members by acquiring & operating clubs & homes. It also strives to promote patriotism in Canada, & nurture cooperation & unity within the British Commonwealth.
Neil McKinnon, President
Lorne McCartney, Sec.-Treas.

Canadian Association of Veterans in United Nations Peacekeeping
PO Box 46026, 2339 Ogilvie Rd., Gloucester ON K1J 9M7
Tel: 902-538-3399
griffisgrove@xcountry.tv
www.cavunp.org
To perpetuate the memories of fallen comrades; to provide assistance to serving & retired Canadian peacekeepers & their families; to provide education about peacekeeping & peacekeepers
Ronald R. Griffis, National President
J. Robert O'Brien, Chair
Paul Greensides, National Secretary-Treasurer

Canadian Battlefields Foundation
c/o Canadian War Museum, 1 Vimy Pl., Ottawa ON K1R 1C2
Tel: 613-731-7767
gruchy@canadianbattlefieldsfoundation.ca
www.canadianbattlefieldsfoundation.ca
To act with Le Mémorial to educate the international public with respect to Canada's role in the Second World War & to educate Canadians through providing scholarships, bursaries & prizes to carry on research into military history; to raise & disburse funds to support these activities.
H.G. Needham, Treasurer
Charles Belzile, President
Antonio Lamer, Honorary Patron

Canadian Corps Association
201 Niagara St., Toronto ON M5V 1C9
Tel: 416-504-6694
E.V. Heesaker, President
Shirley Wood Heesaker, Dominion Secretary

The Canadian Corps of Commissionaires / Le Corps Canadien des Commissionnaires
#201, 100 Gloucester St., Ottawa ON K2P 0A4
Tel: 613-688-0710; *Fax:* 613-688-0719
Toll-Free: 888-688-0715
info@commissionaires.ca
www.commissionaires.ca
To create meaningful employment opportunities for former members of the Canadian Forces, the Royal Canadian Mounted Police & others who wish to contribute to the security & well-being of Canadians
Doug Briscoe, Executive Director
Greg Richardson, Business Manager

Canadian Merchant Navy Veterans Association Inc. (CMNVA) / L'Association des Anciens Combattants de la marine marchande canadienne Inc.
2108 Melrick Pl, Sooke BC V9Z 0M9
Tel: 250-642-2638
To renew old friendships & bring together ex-Canadian merchant seamen; to promote increased recognition of the role of the merchant navy during wartime; to liaise with government to obtain full benefits & pension as recognized veterans
Bruce Ferguson, President

Canadian Peacekeeping Veterans Association (CPVA)
PO Box 905, Kingston ON K7L 4X8
Tel: 506-627-6437
info@cpva.ca
www.cpva.ca
To assist Canadians who have served on peacekeeping missions
Ray Kokkonen, President

Commission canadienne d'histoire militaire (CCHM) / Canadian Commission of Military History (CCMH)
Quartier général de la Défense nationale, 101 Colonel By Dr., Ottawa ON K1A 0K2
Téléc: 613-990-8579
La CCHM est une organisation bénévole, ne comptant qu'un Conseil de direction, sans membres, collaborant à la Commission internationale d'histoire militaire (CIHM) du Comité international des Sciences historiques (CISH) de Genève, Suisse; La Commission canadienne cherche à servir de lien entre les historiens militaires canadiens et la communauté internationale des chercheurs et écrivains en histoire militaire; La Commission canadienne travaille aussi à mieux faire connaître l'histoire militaire canadienne au Canada et à l'étranger
R. Legault, Président, Direction - Histoire et patrimoine (DHP)

Commonwealth War Graves Commission - Canadian Agency (CWGC) / Commission des sépultures de guerre du Commonwealth (CSGC)
#1707, 66 Slater St., Ottawa ON K1A 0P4
Tel: 613-992-3224; *Fax:* 613-995-0431
cwgc-canada@vac-acc.gc.ca
www.cwgc.org; www.cwgc-canadianagency.ca
To ensure Commonwealth War Burials in the Americas (including the Caribbean) are marked & maintained; to ensure maintenance of memorials to the missing; to keep records & registers; the Canadian Agency is responsible to discharge Commission duties for Commonwealth war graves in the Americas (this comprises some 3,350 cemeteries & over 20,000 commemorations).
Bradley N. Hall, Secretary General

Conference of Defence Associations (CDA) / Conférence des associations de la défense
#400B, 222 Somerset St. West, Ottawa ON K2P 2G3
Tel: 613-236-1252; *Fax:* 613-236-8191
cda@cda-cdai.ca
cda-cdai.ca
To place before people of Canada problems of defence & the well-being of Canada's Armed Forces
Gord Metcalfe, Executive Secretary
Alain Pellerin, Executive Director

Federation of Military & United Services Institutes of Canada (FMUSIC) / Fédération des instituts militaires et des instituts des services unis du Canada (FIMIC)
PO Box 1700, Stn. Forces, Kingston ON K7K 7B4
To support development & maintenance of effective Canadian military & non-military defence & security policies & capabilities; to further the aims of individual member institutes in a collective manner; to promote a better understanding by the general public in Canada of the need to meet the defence commitments of Canada
A. Cooper, Executive Vice-Chair

Korea Veterans Association of Canada Inc. (KVA) / Association canadienne des vétérans de la Corée (ACVC)
#511, 835 Oxford St., Oshawa ON L1J 3W2
Tel: 905-579-0751; *Fax:* 905-579-0527
www.kvacanada.com
To promote awareness of Canada's role in the Korean War; To represent veterans & their families
John Bishop, President
Gordon J.H. Strathy, National Secretary
Ed Hadel, National Treasurer

Military Collectors Club of Canada (MCC of Canada)
c/o John Zabarylo, Secretary-treasurer, PO Box 64009, 525 London St., Winnipeg MB R2K 3Y4
Tel: 204-669-0871
militarycollectorsclubofcanada@yahoo.ca
www.mccofc.org
John Zabarylo, Sec.-Treas.
Jim Simmons, President

National Council of Veteran Associations (NCVA)
c/o The War Amps Of Canada, 2827 Riverside Dr., Ottawa ON K1V 0C4
Tel: 613-731-3821; *Fax:* 613-731-3234
Toll-Free: 800-465-2677
communications@waramps.ca
www.waramps.ca/cliff/ncva.html
The NCVA was formed following the end of the Second World War. In this way, presentations to the Government of Canada would be considerably enhanced. Submissions to Parliamentary Committees have included issues such as opposition to the CBC-TV series The Valour and The Horror; the Canadian War Museum, and compensation for Merchant Seamen and Canadian Far East PoWs. This joint action has resulted in compensation being granted to the latter two groups as well as increased benefits to members of the Canadian Armed Forces.
H. Clifford Chadderton, Chair

The Naval Officers' Association of Canada (NOAC) / L'Association des officiers de la marine du Canada
12 Zokol Cres., Kanata ON K2K 2K5
Tel: 613-270-9597
noacexdir@msn.com
www.noac-national.ca/noac
To maintain active interest in the Maritime affairs of Canada; To oversee 15 member branches in major cities from coast to coast & a member branch in Brussels, Belgium
Ray Zuliani, President
Richard Archer, Executive Director

Navy League of Canada / Ligue navale du Canada
66 Lisgar St., Ottawa ON K2P 0C1
Tel: 613-302-1744; *Fax:* 613-990-8701
Toll-Free: 800-375-6289
info@navyleague.ca
www.navyleague.ca
Social Media: twitter.com/NavyLeagueCA
To promote an interest in maritime affairs generally throughout Canada; To prepare, publish & disseminate information & encourage debate relating to the role & importance of maritime matters in the interests of Canada; To promote, organize, sponsor, support & encourage the education & training of the youth of the country through Cadet movements & other youth groups with a maritime orientation; To hold conferences, symposia & meetings for the discussion & exchange of views in matters relating to the objects of The League; To raise funds as may be deemed necessary, for the welfare & benefit of seamen, for their dependents & for Seamen's Homes, Hostels & other institutions in Canada, including the establishment, operation & maintenance thereof; To co-operate with any kindred society having either in whole or in part comparable objects to The League
Douglas J. Thomas, National Executive Director
Jerrod Riley, National Deputy Director

New Brunswick Signallers Association (NB Sigs)
c/o Fred LeBlanc, 17 Dewitt Acres, Fredericton NB E3A 6S3
Tel: 506-472-3215
fredleb@nbnet.nb.ca
www.nbsigs.ca
Claude Jodouin, President

Princess Patricia's Canadian Light Infantry Association
PO Box 210, Denwood AB T0B 1B0
Tel: 780-842-1363; *Fax:* 780-842-4106
www.army.gc.ca/ppclic
Bud Hawkins, President, Manitoba/Northwest Ontario Branch

The Royal Canadian Legion (RCL) / La Légion royale canadienne
Dominion Command, 86 Aird Place, Ottawa ON K2L 0A1
Tel: 613-591-3335; *Fax:* 613-591-9335
info@legion.ca
www.legion.ca
To serve veterans, ex-military & military members, their families, communities & Canada
Pat Varga, Dominion President
Gordon Moore, Dominion 1st Vice President
Michael Cook, Dominion Treasurer
Bradley Kenneth White, Dominion Secretary

Royal Canadian Military Institute (RCMI)
426 University Ave., Toronto ON M5G 1S9
Tel: 416-597-0286; *Fax:* 416-597-6919
Toll-Free: 800-585-1072
info@rcmi.org
www.rcmi.org
Promotion of navy, army & air force art, science, literature & interests; promotion of good fellowship & esprit de corps amongst the officers of the various branches of the services; maintenance of a clubhouse for the accommodation, recreation, enlightenment, convenience & entertainment of its members.
Chris Corrigan, Executive Director

Royal Canadian Mounted Police Veterans' Association / Association des anciens de la Gendarmerie royale du Canada
1200 Vanier Pkwy., Ottawa ON K1A 0R2
Tel: 613-993-8633; *Fax:* 613-993-4353
Toll-Free: 877-251-1771
rcmp.vets@rcmp-grc.gc.ca
www.rcmpvetsnational.ca

Royal Canadian Naval Benevolent Fund (RCNBF)
PO Box 505, Stn. B, Ottawa ON K1P 5P6
Tel: 613-996-5087; *Fax:* 613-236-8830
Toll-Free: 888-557-8777
rcnbf@sympatico.ca
www.rcnbf.ca
To relieve distress & promote the well-being of members & former members of the naval forces of Canada & Canadian merchant navy war veterans & of their dependants
L.F. Harrison, Secretary-Treasurer

Ste. Anne's Association of War Veterans Inc. / Association Ste-Anne des anciens combattants inc.
305, boul des Anciens Combattants, Sainte-Anne-de-Bellevue QC H9X 1Y9
Tel: 514-457-3440; *Fax:* 514-457-8412
Toll-Free: 800-361-9287
steanne@vac-acc.gc.ca
To provide qualified veterans, civilians & their families with benefits & services to which they are entitled; to promote their well-being & self-sufficiency as participating members of their communities; to keep the memory of their acheivements & sacrifice alive for all Canadians
Ivette Glimont, Secretary

Mines & Mineral Resources

Association de l'exploration minière de Québec (AEMQ)
#203, 132, avenue du Lac, Rouyn-Noranda QC J9X 4N5
Tél: 819-762-1599; *Téléc:* 819-762-1522
aemq@aemq.org
www.aemq.org
Développer, défendre et promouvoir l'exploration minière au Québec
Ghislain Poirier, Président
Mélissa Desrochers, Vice-présidente, Communications

Association for Mineral Exploration British Columbia (AMEBC)
#800, 889 West Pender St., Vancouver BC V6C 3B2
Tel: 604-689-5271; *Fax:* 604-681-2363
info@amebc.ca
www.amebc.ca
To promote & assist development & growth of mining of mineral exploration in BC
Gavin C. Dirom, President & CEO

Association minière du Québec (AMQ) / Québec Mining Association
Place de la Cité - Tour Belle Cour, #720, 2590, boul Laurier, Québec QC G1V 4M6
Tél: 418-657-2016; *Téléc:* 418-657-2154
mines@amq-inc.com
www.amq-inc.com
Promouvoir le développement de l'industrie des mines, de la métallurgie et des industries connexes; défendre les intérêts généraux de ses membres; soutenir les efforts de ses membres quant au bien-être, à la sécurité et à la prévention des accidents au travail
Dan Tolgyesi, Président-directeur général
Carole Côté, Directrice, Administration

Association of Applied Geochemists (AEG)
PO Box 26099, 72 Robertson Rd., Nepean ON K2H 9R0
Tel: 613-828-0199; *Fax:* 613-828-9288
office@appliedgeochemists.org
www.appliedgeochemists.org
To promote interest in the applications of geochemistry to mineral & petroleum exploration, resource evaluation & related fields
David R. Cohen, President
Betty Arseneault, Business Manager

Canadian Copper & Brass Development Association
#415, 49 The Donway West, Toronto ON M3C 3M9
Tel: 416-391-5599; *Fax:* 416-391-3823
Toll-Free: 877-640-0946
coppercanada@onramp.ca
www.coppercanada.ca
To promote, foster & stimulate use of products of Canadian copper & brass industry. To represent and support the primary producers fabricators, manufacturers, and consumers of copper and copper alloys in Canada, by increasing industry and public awareness of copper's capabilites and advantages compared to other metals and materials, and by providing technical services related to copper's use.
Stephen A.W. Knapp, Executive Director

Canadian Institute of Mining, Metallurgy & Petroleum (CIM) / Institut canadien des mines, de la métallurgie et du pétrole
CIM National Office, #1250, 3500, boul de Maisonneuve ouest, Westmount QC H3Z 3C1
Tel: 514-939-2710; *Fax:* 514-939-2714
cim@cim.org
www.cim.org
To act as a source of leadership for its members, by offering conferences & courses, liaising with government departments, commissioning special volumes & reports, & publishing technical papers
Jean Vavrek, Executive Director
Chuck Edwards, President
Jean-Marc Demers, Deputy Executive Director
Lise Bujold, Director, Conferences & Exhibitions
Marjolaine Dugas, Director, Membership
Gérard Hamel, Director, Information Technology
Angela Hamlyn, Director, Media & Communications
Serge Major, Director, Finance & Admininstration
Deborah Sauvé, Manager, Canadian Mining Metallurgical Foundation

Canadian Mineral Analysts (CMA) / Analystes des minéraux canadiens
444 Harold Ave. West, Winnipeg MB R2C 2E2
Tel: 204-224-1443
jgregorchuk@shaw.ca
www.canadianmineralanalysts.com
To promote communication among analysts in the mining industry & persons engaged in analytical procedures & the development of methods
John Gregorchuk, Managing Secretary
Sean Murry, Treasurer
Eric Arseneault, Executive Secretary

Chamber of Mineral Resources of Nova Scotia (CMRNS)
PO Box 2171, Windsor NS B0N 2T0
Tel: 902-798-0187; *Fax:* 902-798-2141
terry.daniels@ns.sympatico.ca
To ensure Nova Scotia is recognized internationally as having mineral resources worthy of investment; to develop mineral deposits; to work for government policies that provide a framework for a competitive mining industry within the global marketplace; to promote mining as a corporate industry creating wealth & long-term stable employment, with responsible environmental & social attitudes
Terry Daniels, Managing Director

Chamber of Mines of Eastern British Columbia
215 Hall St., Nelson BC V1L 5X4
Tel: 250-352-5242; *Fax:* 250-352-7227
chamberofminesebc@netidea.com
www.cmebc.com
To act as advocate for the mining industry in British Columbia; to provide a collective voice on behalf of prospectors & miners; to provide information on exploration & mining; to educate the public through accessibility to mineral museum & library.
Jack Denny, President
Dennis Llewellyn, Chamber Manager

Chrysotile Institute
#1640, 1200, av McGill College, Montréal QC H3B 4G7
Tel: 514-877-9797; *Fax:* 514-877-9717
info@chrysotile.com
www.chrysotile.com/
To promote the implementation & enforcement of effective regulations, standards, work practices & techniques for the safe use of asbestos.
Denis Hamel, Director General

Coal Association of Canada
#150, 205 - 9th Ave. SE, Calgary AB T2G 0R3
Tel: 403-262-1544; *Fax:* 403-265-7604
Toll-Free: 800-910-2625
info@coal.ca
www.coal.ca
To promote coal as a vital energy source that is abundant, safe, reliable, environmentally and economically acceptable.
Allen Wright, President & CEO
George White, Chair

East Kootenay Chamber of Mines
#201, 12 - 11th Avenue South, Cranbrook BC V1C 2P1
Tel: 250-489-2255; *Fax:* 250-426-8755
www.ekcm.org/chamber2
Ross Stanfield, President

Mineralogical Association of Canada (MAC) / Association minéralogique du Canada
490, rue de la Couronne, Québec QC G1K 9A9
Tel: 418-653-0333; *Fax:* 418-653-0777
office@mineralogicalassociation.ca
www.mineralogicalassociation.ca
To promote & advance knowledge of mineralogy & the allied disciplines of petrology, crystallography, mineral deposits, & geochemistry
Iain M. Samson, President
Lee A. Groat, Vice-President
Michelle DeWolfe, Secretary
Marc Constantin, Treasurer
Ronald C. Peterson, Chair, Finance Committee
Robert F. Martin, Principal Editor, The Canadian Mineralogist
Pierrette Tremblay, Managing Editor, Elements Magazine

Mining Association of British Columbia (MABC)
#900, 808 West Hastings St., Vancouver BC V6C 2X4
Tel: 604-681-4321; *Fax:* 604-681-5305
mabcinfo@mining.bc.ca
www.mining.bc.ca
To speak on behalf of mineral producers; To represent the interests of British Columbia's mining industry; To communicate with senior government decision-makers, communities, NGOs, First Nations, & the media; To act as the industry's voice regarding issues such as environmental regulations, taxation, infrastructure demands, labour issues, health & safety, & international trade
Pierre Gratton, President/CEO
Zoe Younger, Vice-President, Corporate Affairs
Ben Chalmers, Vice-President, Environmental & Technical Affairs

Mining Association of Canada (MAC) / Association minière du Canada
#1105, 350 Sparks St., Ottawa ON K1R 7S8
Tel: 613-233-9392; *Fax:* 613-233-8897
communications@mining.ca
www.mining.ca
Social Media:
www.facebook.com/group.php?gid=193636270672849;
twitter.com/theminingstory
To represent the interests of member companies engaged in mineral exploration, extraction & refining; To work with governments on public policy pertaining to minerals
Pierre Gratton, President & CEO
Marilyn Fortin, Office Manager & Member Services
Monique Laflèche, Executive Assistant

Mining Association of Manitoba Inc. (MAMI)
#700, 305 Broadway Ave., Winnipeg MB R3C 3J7
Tel: 204-989-1890
pmarsden@mines.ca
www.mines.ca
To represent mining & exploration companies in Manitoba.
Ed Huebert, Executive Vice President

Mining Society of Nova Scotia
88 Leeside Dr., Sydney NS B1R 1S6
Tel: 902-567-2147; *Fax:* 902-567-2147
florence@ns.sympatico.ca
Dan McLeod, President

New Brunswick Mining Association / L'Association minière du Nouveau-Brunswick
#312, 236 St. George Blvd., Moncton NB E1C 1W1
Tel: 506-857-3056; *Fax:* 506-857-3059
Blaine Lewis, Manager

NWT & Nunavut Chamber of Mines
PO Box 2818, #103, 5102-50 Ave., Yellowknife NT X1A 2R1
Tel: 867-873-5281; *Fax:* 867-920-2145
info@miningnorth.com
www.miningnorth.com
To promote & assist the development & growth of mining & mineral exploration in NWT & Nunavut
Tom Hoefer, Executive Director

Ontario Mining Association (OMA)
#520, 5775 Yonge St., Toronto ON M2M 4J1
Tel: 416-364-9301; *Fax:* 416-364-5986
pmcbride@oma.on.ca
www.oma.on.ca
To help improve the competitiveness of the Ontario mineral industry
Chris Hodgson, President

Prospectors & Developers Association of Canada (PDAC) / Association canadienne des prospecteurs & entrepreneurs
135 King St. East, Toronto ON M5C 1G6
Tel: 416-362-1969; *Fax:* 416-362-0101
info@pdac.ca
www.pdac.ca
To protect & promote the interests of the Canadian mineral exploration & development sector
Ross Gallinger, Executive Director
Lisa J. McDonald, Chief Operations Officer
Philip Bousquet, Senior Program Director, Finance & Taxation & Securities
Sheriden Barnett, Program Director, Land Use Planning & Resource Development
Scott Cavan, Program Director, Aboriginal Affairs
Nicole Sampson, Director, Convention
Steve Virtue, Director, Communications
Lesley Williams, Program Manager, Advvocacy & Issues Management
Florence MacLeod, Coordinator, Membership

Saskatchewan Mining Association (SMA)
#1500, 2002 Victoria Ave., Regina SK S4P 0R7
Tel: 306-757-9505; *Fax:* 306-569-1085
saskmining@sasktel.net
www.saskmining.ca
To ensure the safe & profitable development of mineral resources in Saskatchewan; To act as the voice of the mining industry throughout the province; To promote understanding of the development of mineral resources in Saskatchewan
Kelvin Dereski, President
Pamela Schwann, Executive Director
David Neuburger, 1st Vice-President
Stewart Brown, 2nd Vice-President
Tracey Irwin, Manager, Communications & Membership

Yukon Chamber of Mines (YCM)
3151B - 3rd Ave., Whitehorse YT Y1A 1G1
Tel: 867-667-2090; *Fax:* 867-668-7127
info@yukonminers.ca
www.yukonminers.ca
To provides services to members, with a focus on the mining industry; To promote responsible exploration & sustainable mining practices
Mark Ayranto, President
Hugh Kitchen, Vice President

Yukon Mine Training Association (YMTA)
#120, 205 Black St., Whitehorse YT Y1A 2M8
Tel: 867-633-6463; *Fax:* 867-633-2605
info@ymta.org
www.yukonminetraining.com
To maximize employment opportunities emerging from the growth of the mining and related resource sectors in the North for First Nations and other Yukoners.
Al Doherty, Chair
Tracy Thomas, Executive Director

Yukon Prospectors' Association (YPA)
3151B - 3rd Ave., Whitehorse YT Y1A 1G1
north-land.com/ypa
To promote and advocate for the mining industry and miners of the Yukon Territory
Jim McFaull, President

Multiculturalism

Affiliation of Multicultural Societies & Service Agencies of BC (AMSSA)
#205, 2929 Commercial Dr., Vancouver BC V5N 4C8
Tel: 604-718-2777; *Fax:* 604-298-0747
Toll-Free: 888-355-5560
amssa@amssa.org
www.amssa.org
To provide leadership in advocacy & education in British Columbia for anti-racism, human rights & social justice; to support members in serving immigrants, refugees & culturally diverse communities
Tim Welsh, Program Director
Lynn Moran, Executive Director

The Atlantic Jewish Council
#508, 5670 Spring Garden Rd., Halifax NS B3J 1H6
Tel: 902-422-7491; *Fax:* 902-425-3722
atlanticjewishcouncil@theajc.ns.ca
theajc.ns.ca

Australia-New Zealand Association (ANZA)
3 - 8 Ave. West, Vancouver BC V5Y 1M8
Tel: 604-876-7128
info@anzaclub.org
www.anzaclub.org
To foster friendly relations between British Columbia, Canada, Australia & New Zealand
Chari Keet, Manager

B'nai Brith Canada (BBC)
15 Hove St., Toronto ON M3H 4Y8
Tel: 416-633-6224; *Fax:* 416-630-2159
bnb@bnaibrith.ca
www.bnaibrith.ca
Social Media: www.facebook.com/bnaibrithcanada
To bring men & women of the Jewish faith together in fellowship to serve the Jewish community through combating anti-Semitism, bigotry & racism in Canada & abroad; carrying out & supporting activities which ensure the security & survival of the State of Israel & Jewish communities worldwide; community service through various volunteer activities, cultivation of leadership, charitable work, advocacy & government relations
Frank Dimant, Executive Vice President
Eric Bissell, President

B'nai Brith Canada Institute for International Affairs
15 Hove St., Toronto ON M3H 4Y8
Tel: 416-633-6224; *Fax:* 416-630-2159
institute@bnaibrith.ca
www.bnaibrith.ca/institute.html
To identify & fight human rights abuses throughout the world, with special emphasis on Jewish communities worldwide
Frank Dimant, CEO
Ruth Klein, National Director

Baltic Federation in Canada
1590 Stewart Cres., Milton ON L9T 6P9
Tel: 905-693-8780
www.balticfederation.ca
To provide political representation for its member organizations of Estonian, Latvian & Lithuanian Canadians
Peter Meiklejohn, President

Belgo-Canadian Association (BCA)
121 Chillery Ave., Toronto ON M1K 4T5
Tel: 416-261-4603
www.belgo-canadian.com

Black Cultural Society for Nova Scotia
1149 Main St., Dartmouth NS B2Z 1A8
Tel: 902-434-6223; *Fax:* 902-434-2306
Toll-Free: 800-465-0767
contact@bccns.com
www.bccns.com
To create among members of the Black community an awareness of their past, their heritage & identity; to provide programs & activities to explore, learn about, understand & appreciate Black history, achievements & experiences in Canadian life.
Henry V. Bishop, Director & Chief Curator
Leslie Oliver, President

Canadian Arab Federation (CAF) / La Fédération Canado-Arabe
1057 McNicoll Ave., Toronto ON M1W 3W6
Tel: 416-493-8635; *Fax:* 416-493-9239
Toll-Free: 866-886-4675
info@caf.ca
www.caf.ca
To represent Canadian Arabs on issues related to public policy; To protect civil liberties & the equality of human rights
Mohamed Boudjenane, Executive Director
Sara Amash, Manager, Projects
Nora Abdulkarim, Coordinator, Job Search Workshop Program

The Canadian Doukhobor Society (CDS)
#27, Comp 4, R.R.#1, South Slocan BC V0G 2G0
Tel: 250-428-9634; *Fax:* 250-428-3519
awishlow@kootenay.com
To promote brotherhood, universal peace & the spiritual growth of our members
Marion Verigin, Secretary
Anne Stormes, Treasurer
Alex Wishlow, Chair

Canadian Ethnocultural Council (CEC) / Conseil ethnoculturel du Canada
#400, 176 Gloucester St., Ottawa ON K2P 0A6
Tel: 613-230-3867; *Fax:* 613-230-8051
cec@web.net
www.ethnocultural.ca
The Canadian Ethnocultural Council (CEC) is a non-profit, non-partisan coalition of national ethnocultural umbrella

organizations which, in turn, represent a cross-section of ethnocultural groups across Canada.
Peter Ferreira, President
Emmanuel J. Dick, Director

Canadian Institute for Jewish Research (CIJR) / Institut canadien de recherche sur le Judaïsme
PO Box 175, Stn. H, Montréal QC H3G 2K7
Tel: 514-486-5544; *Fax:* 514-486-8284
cijr@isranet.org
www.isranet.org
To increase public understanding of Jewish Israel & general Jewish world issues
Irwin G. Beutel, National Chair
Clara Balinsky, International Chair
Baruch Cohen, Research Chair
Frederick Krantz, Director

Canadian Latvian Business & Professional Association (CLBPA)
123 Overland Dr., Toronto ON M3C 2C7
Tel: 416-444-5201; *Fax:* 416-444-5208
alex@budrevics.com
Alexander Budrevics, President

Canadian Polish Congress (CPC) / Congrès canadien polonais
288 Roncesvalles Ave., Toronto ON M6R 2M4
Tel: 416-532-2876; *Fax:* 416-532-5730
kongres@kpk.org
www.kpk.org
To represent Polish-Canadians & to defend their interests; To coordinate & support the work of Polish-Canadian organizations in Canada; To foster Polish culture & assist Polish immigrants; To inform Canadians about Poland's contribution to culture & to maintain liaisons with Poland
Teresa Berezowski, President
Jan Cytowski, First Vice-President, Polish Affairs
Jerzy Barycki, Vice-President, Youth Affairs
Ludwik Klimkowski, Vice-President, Canadian Affairs
Stanislaw Godziszski, Secretary-General
Elizabeth Morgan, Treasurer

Canadian Slovak League
#6, 259 Traders Blvd. East, Mississauga ON L4Z 2E5
Tel: 905-507-8004
info@ksliga.com
www.ksliga.com
Mary Ann Doucette, Acting President

Canadian Tibetan Association of Ontario (CTAO)
#201, 160 Springhurst Ave., Toronto ON M6K 1C2
Tel: 416-410-5606; *Fax:* 416-410-5606
info@ctao.org
www.ctao.org
To represent Tibetans in Ontario; To serve the needs of the Tibetan community in the province; To promote cross-cultural understanding
Norbu Tsering, President
Lhakpa Tsering, Manager, Administration
Tashi Dhondup, Coordinator, Culture & Education
Woeser Jongdong, Coordinator, Education & Public Relations
Tenzin Ngodupng, Coordinator, Youth & Sports
Jampa Nyendak, Coordinator, Spiritual
Lobsang Mentuh, Treasurer

Canadian Zionist Federation (CZF) / La fédération sioniste canadienne
#206, 1, carré Cummings, Montréal QC H3W 1M6
Tel: 514-739-7300; *Fax:* 514-739-9412
czfnational@fedcjamtl.org
www.doingzionism.org/federations/fed_home.asp?fed=czf
To promote the Zionist ideal among the Jewish population in Canada; To assist in strengthening the Jewish State of Israel; To enrich Canadian Jewish life through the provision of Jewish education & information on Israel & Zionism, through the promotion of Aliyah & activities among Jewish youth in Canada.
Florence Simon, National Executive Director
Norman Stern, President
Shya Finestone, Treasurer
Norma Rubin, Secretary

Canadian-Croatian Congress / Kanadsko-Hrvatski Kongres
3550 Commercial St., Vancouver BC V5A 4E9
Tel: 604-871-7190; *Fax:* 604-879-2256
www.canada.crocc.org
To represent the Croatian Canadian community before the people & Government of Canada
Ivan Curman, President

The Centre for Israel & Jewish Affairs (CIJA)
PO Box 19514, Stn. Postal Outlet Manulife Centre, 55 Bloor St. West, Toronto ON M4W 3T9
Tel: 416-925-7499
contact@cija.ca
www.cija.ca
To act as decision-making body of the Jewish community in Canada; to act on behalf of Canadian Jewish community on issues & concerns affecting Jews in Canada & around the world; to foster interaction between interests & needs of Jewish community in Canada & Canadian society at large on a broad range of political, charitable & social justice issues
Paul Michaels, Director, Research & Senior Media Relations

Chinese Canadian National Council (CCNC) / Conseil national des canadiens chinois
#507, 302 Spadina Ave., Toronto ON M5T 2E7
Tel: 416-977-9871; *Fax:* 416-977-1630
national@ccnc.ca
www.ccnc.ca
To promote the rights of all individuals, in particular, those of Chinese Canadians & to encourage their full & equal participation in Canadian society; to create an environment in Canada in which the rights of all individuals are fully recognized & protected; to promote understanding & cooperation between Chinese Canadians & all other ethnic, cultural, & racial groups in Canada; to encourage & develop in persons of Chinese descent, a desire to know & respect their historical & cultural heritage, & to educate them in adopting a creative & positive attitude towards the Chinese Canadian contribution to society & the Chinese Canadian heritage
Victor Wong, Executive Director

Clans & Scottish Societies of Canada (CASSOC)
c/o Secretary, #78, 24 Fundy Bay Blvd., Scarborough ON M1W 3A4
Tel: 416-492-1623
editor@cassoc.ca
www.cassoc.ca
To foster the organization of & cooperation between Scottish associations, federations, clans, societies & groups through initiation & coordination of projects & undertakings; to advance Scottish cultural heritage in Canada
Ian A. Munro, Chair
Jo Ann M. Tuskin, Secretary

Cypriot Federation of Canada / Fédération chypriote du Canada
6 Thorncliff Park Dr., Toronto ON M4H 1H1
Tel: 416-696-7400; *Fax:* 416-696-9465
cypriotfederation@rogers.com
Kyriacos Elles, President

Czech & Slovak Association of Canada
PO Box 564, 3044 Bloor St. West, Toronto ON M8X 2Y8
Tel: 416-925-2241; *Fax:* 416-925-1940
ustredi@cssk.ca
www.cssk.ca
To develop the highest standards of citizenship in Canadians of Czech or Slovak origin by encouraging, carrying on & participating in activities of national, patriotic, cultural & humanitarian nature; to act in matters affecting status rights & welfare of Canadians of Czech or Slovak origin; to cultivate in members appreciation of their mother tongue, cultural heritage & historical traditions; to promote growth of spirit in toleration, understanding & goodwill between all ethnic elements in Canada; to conduct research & encourage studies.
Milos Suchma, President
Radmila Locher, Contact

Federation for Scottish Culture in Nova Scotia (FSCNS)
PO Box 811, Lower Sackville NS B4C 3V3
info@scotsns.ca
www.scotsns.ca
To act as the voice for Nova Scotia's clans, Scottish-cultural communities, & cultural associations; To create appreciation for the Scottish culture, traditions, & heritage
Thomas (Tom) E.S. Wallace, President
Daniel G. Campbell, 1st Vice-President
Audrey Manzer, Secretary
Al Matheson, Treasurer

Federation of Canada-China Friendship Associations
#705, 175, rue Laurier, Gatineau QC J8X 4G3
Tel: 819-777-8434
lolan.merklinger@sympatico.ca
www.fccfa.ca
To work with students from the Peoples' Republic of China studying in Canada; To take groups to China; To welcome delegations coming from China; To promote cultural exchanges
Lolan Wang Merklinger, President

Federation of Canadian Turkish Associations (FCTA)
#15, 1170 Sheppard Ave. West, Toronto ON M3K 2A3
Tel: 647-955-1923; *Fax:* 647-776-3111
info@turkishfederation.ca
www.turkishfederation.ca/en/home_en.html
To support & encourage activities of member associations aimed at making Turkish culture & Turks better known; To promote closer relations with Canadians & other ethnic communities
Mehmet Bor, Chair
Celal Ucar, Secretary
Hussein Nurgel, Treasurer

Federation of Chinese Canadian Professionals (Ontario) (FCCP)
Coral Place, 55 Glenn Hawthorne Blvd., Mississauga ON L5R 3S6
Tel: 905-890-3235; *Fax:* 905-568-5293
webmaster@fccpontario.com
www.fccpontario.com
Dennis Woo, President

Federation of Chinese Canadian Professionals (Québec) (FCCP Québec) / Fédération des professionnels chinois canadiens (Québec)
PO Box 1004, Stn. B, Montréal QC H3B 3K5
Tel: 514-747-2488
htan222@yahoo.ca
www.fccp.ca
To promote the well-being of Chinese Canadian professionals in Québec; To liaise & cooperate with Chinese Canadian professionals in other parts of Canada & throughout the world; To provide a strong voice for the group
Howard Tan, President
John Chen, Vice-President
Renee Chin, Treasurer

Federation of Danish Associations in Canada / Fédération des associations danoises du Canada
679 Eastvale Ct., Gloucester ON K1J 6Z7
home.ca.inter.net/~robuch/dan-fed.htm
To promote cooperation among Danish Canadian organizations; To promote preservation & understanding of Danish tradition & heritage
Rolf Buschardt Christensen, National President
Ole D. Larsen, National Vice-President
Ella Wolder, National Secretary
Sue Anne Nielsen, National Treasurer

Federation of Korean Canadian Associations
1133 Leslie St., Toronto ON M3L 2J6
Tel: 416-383-0777; *Fax:* 416-383-1113
koreancanadian@canada.org
www.koreancanadian.org

Finnish Canadian Cultural Federation / Fédération culturelle finno-canadienne
128 Quartz Ave., Timmins ON P4N 4L6
margaretk@personainternet.com
www.finnishcanadian.com
To act as non-political coordinator between associations, congregations, clubs & other groups of Finnish ethnic background; To promote Finland & Canadians of Finnish origin; To promote Canada & its Finnish ethnic community in Finland; To support Annual Finnish Canadian Grand Festival
Margaret Kangas, Treasurer

Finnish Organization of Canada
PO Box 65070, Toronto ON M4K 3Z2
Tel: 416-651-0317; *Fax:* 416-651-0236
Elsie Jokinen, Chair

German-Canadian Congress (GCC) / Congrès germano-canadien
#58, 81 Garry St., Winnipeg MB R3C 4J9
Tel: 204-989-8300
gccmb@hotmail.com
www.gccmb.com
To serve as official voice for 2.7 million Canadians of German-speaking background

Goethe-Institut (Montréal)
418, rue Sherbrooke est, Montréal QC H2L 1J6
Tel: 514-499-0159; *Fax:* 514-499-0905
info@montreal.goethe.org
www.goethe.de/montreal
The Goethe-Institur is the cultural institue of the Federal Republic of Germany with a global reach. They promote knowledge of the German language abroad and foster international cultural cooperation. They convey a comprehensive picture of Germany by providing information on Germany's cultural, social, and political life. They perform the principle talks of cultural and educational policy, they work in partnership with

public and private cultural bodies, the German federal states and municipalities, and the corporate sector.
Manfred Stoffl, Directeur

Goethe-Institut (Toronto)
PO Box 136, #201, 100 University Ave., Toronto ON M5J 1V6
Tel: 416-593-5257; *Fax:* 416-593-5145
info@toronto.goethe.org
www.goethe.de/toronto
To provide cultural programs, international cultural cooperation, German language teaching, & library & information services
Sonja Griegoschewski, Director
Hannah Day, Program & Office Assistant

Greater Vancouver Japanese Canadian Citizens' Association
Nikkei Heritage Centre, #200, 6688 Southoaks Cres., Burnaby BC V5E 4M7
Tel: 604-777-5222; *Fax:* 604-777-5223
gvjcca@shaw.ca
Ron Nishimura, President

Hellenic Canadian Congress / Congrès hellénique du Québec
846 Pape Ave., 2nd Fl., Toronto ON M4K 3T6
Tel: 416-461-0824; *Fax:* 416-463-9514
To collect as many names of individuals & businesses as possible in order to get an accurate & up-to-date census of Canadians of Hellenic heritage & their activities
Jimmy Sidiropoulos, President

Holocaust Education Centre
Lipa Green Centre, Sherman Campus, 4600 Bathurst St., 4th Fl., Toronto ON M2R 3V2
Tel: 416-635-2883; *Fax:* 416-635-0925
neuberger@ujafed.org
www.holocaustcentre.com
The Centre provides regular educational & remembrance activities, including workshops for teachers, students, community commemorations & survivor testimony to fufill its mandate of preserving the past & educating future generations on the lessons of the Holocaust.
Lorraine Sandler, Chair
Mira Goldfarb, Executive Director

Hungarian Canadian Cultural Centre
840 St. Clair Ave. West, Toronto ON M6C 1C1
Tel: 416-654-4926; *Fax:* 416-654-4927
office@hccc.org
www.hccc-e.org
The Centre preserves & showcases Hungarian heritage in the Canadian mosaic.
Gabor Vaski, President

Icelandic National League of North America (INL/NA)
#103, 94 - 1st Ave., Gimli MB R0C 1B1
Tel: 204-642-5897
inl@mymts.net
www.inlofna.org
Social Media: www.facebook.com/115047545201629
To foster & promote good citizenship among people of Icelandic descent; to foster & strengthen a mutual understanding of kinship, language, literature & cultural bonds among people of Icelandic origin & descent in North America & the people of Iceland; to cooperate with organizations which have similar purposes & objectives; to actively support various cultural & ethnic developments including education, history, publishing & the arts
Gail Einarson-McCleery, President
Gwen Grattan, Executive Secretary

Irish Canadian Cultural Association of New Brunswick (ICCA NB)
c/o 189 Carlisle Rd., Douglas NB E3A 7M8
info@newirelandnb.ca
www.newirelandnb.ca
To recognize & honour the contributions made by our ancestors to Canada by holding an annual Irish Festival, promoting an Irish Studies program at universities & sponsoring Irish cultural & social programs & events
Pat Murphy, President

Islamic Foundation of Toronto
441 Nugget Ave., Toronto ON M1S 5E1
Tel: 416-321-0909; *Fax:* 416-321-1995
info@islamicfoundation.ca
www.islamicfoundation.ca
Shakil Akhter, Administrator
Zaib Mirza, Social Services Coordinator

Islamic Information Foundation (IIF)
8 Laurel Lane, Halifax NS B3M 2P6
Tel: 902-445-2494; *Fax:* 902-445-2494
To promote better understanding of Islam among Muslims & Christians through information provided in print, audio & video forms & through lecture, seminars & interfaith dialogues
Jamal Badawi, Chairperson

Italian Cultural Institute / Istituto Italiano di Cultura
496 Huron St., Toronto ON M5R 2R3
Tel: 416-921-3802; *Fax:* 416-962-2503
www.iictoronto.esteri.it
To promote Italian culture & language in its many expressions in a spirit of vital interaction with the host country; to provide information on Italy's cultural heritage & contemporary cultural production; classrooms & library; offices in Toronto & Woodbridge.
Martin Stiglio, Director

Jamaican Canadian Association (JCA)
995 Arrow Rd., Toronto ON M9M 2Z5
Tel: 416-746-5772; *Fax:* 416-746-7035
info@jcassoc.com
www.jcassoc.org
To provide social interaction among members & to facilitate desirable relations with Canadian society; to represent the Caribbean community on public matters; to respond to the diverse social service needs of members; to facilitate economic, social & cultural integration of Caribbean people within Canadian society
Audrey Campbell, President

Japanese Canadian Association of Yukon (JCAY)
531 Grove St., Whitehorse YT Y1A 5J9
Tel: 867-393-2588
Fumi Torigai, Contact

Jewish Federation of Ottawa
21 Nadolny Sachs Private, Ottawa ON K2A 1R9
Tel: 613-798-4696; *Fax:* 613-789-4695
jewishottawa.com
Mitchell Bellman, President & CEO

Kashmiri Canadian Council (KCC)
#44516, 2376 Eglinton Ave. East, Toronto ON M1K 5K3
Tel: 416-282-6933; *Fax:* 416-282-7488
kcc@kashmiri-cc.ca
www.kashmiri-cc.ca

Latvian National Federation in Canada / Fédération nationale lettone au Canada
4 Credit Union Dr., Toronto ON M4A 2N8
Tel: 416-755-2353; *Fax:* 416-913-1631
inak@inak.org
www.lnak.org
LNFC is the unifying central organization for all Latvians across Canada, representing their interests at the city, provincial & federal levels. It maintains contacts with other Canadian non-governmental organizations, & expedites projects both in Canada & in Latvia.
Andris Kesteris, Chair
Vilnis Pètersons, Administrator

League of Ukrainian Canadians
83-85 Christie St., Toronto ON M6G 3B1
Tel: 416-516-8223; *Fax:* 416-516-4033
Toll-Free: 866-714-4132
luc@lucorg.com
www.lucorg.com
The League is a cultural & political organization to aid Ukrainian people living in Canada & in Ukraine; dedicated to the continued growth & development of a prosperous Ukrainian community in Canada.
Volodymyr Paslavskyi, Executive Director

The Lithuanian Canadian Community / La Communauté lithuanienne du Canada
1 Resurrection Rd., Toronto ON M9A 5G1
Tel: 416-533-3292; *Fax:* 416-533-2282
info@klb.org
www.klb.org
To promote, maintain, & encourage the survival of the Lithuanian culture & language in Canada & abroad
Joana Kuraite-Lasiene, President

Lithuanian Canadian R.C. Cultural Society
Anapilis Christian Community Centre, 2185 Stavebank Rd., Mississauga ON L5C 1T3
Tel: 905-275-4672; *Fax:* 905-275-4364
tevzib@rogers.com
www.tevzib.com
The Society provides news & information for Canadians of Lithuanian origin or descent.
P. Gaida, Editor in Chief
Joana Kuras, President

Maltese-Canadian Society of Toronto, Inc. (MCST)
235 Medland St., Toronto ON M6P 2N6
Tel: 416-767-3645; *Fax:* 416-767-5707
mcst@intiss.com
The organization strives for the betterment of the Maltese community in Toronto. It also preserves & promotes the Maltese language & culture in Canada.
J. Zammit, Contact
C. Grixti, Contact
R. Cumbo, Contact

Manitoba Multicultural Resources Centre Inc. (MMRC)
#101, 1555 St. James St., Winnipeg MB R3H 1B5
Tel: 204-831-6672
Helps Canadians express their cultural identity through research & documentation of our common heritage, thereby creating a positive intercultural relationship among Canadian groups.

Mizrachi Organization of Canada
296 Wilson Ave., Toronto ON M3H 1S8
Tel: 416-630-9266; *Fax:* 416-630-2305
mizrachi@rogers.com
www.mizrachi.ca
A religious Zionist organization which coordinates Zionist-oriented programming for the Orthodox Jewish communities in Canada; fundraising for educational & social welfare institutions in Israel; offices in Toronto & Montréal
Jack Kahn, National President

Multicultural Association of Northwestern Ontario (MANWO)
511 Victoria Ave. East, Thunder Bay ON P7C 1B1
Tel: 807-622-4666; *Fax:* 807-622-7271
Toll-Free: 800-692-7692
manwoyc@tbaytel.net
my.tbaytel.net/manwoyc/manwo.html
MANWO is a regional umbrella organization for multicultural organizations, cultural groups, & ethno-cultural communities working together to promote the concept of multiculturalism. It serves as the region's resource centre for information, training & resources on citizenship, multiculturalism & race relations. It delivers settlement services to newcomers, & is also the parent organization of the Regional Multicultral Youth Centre, an inclusive group linking youths in small & isolated communities. The Youth Centre develops proactive programs to enhance the quality of life & improve social conditions of children & young adults.
Moffat S. Makuto, Executive Director

Multicultural Association of Nova Scotia (MANS) / Association multiculturelle de la Nouvelle-Écosse
1113 Marginal Rd., Halifax NS B3H 4P7
Tel: 902-423-6534; *Fax:* 902-422-0881
admin@mans.ns.ca; communications@mans.ns.ca
www.mans.ns.ca
To develop & influence multicultural policy & to promote equality; To create a sense of belonging & respect for all cultures
Sylvia Parris, Vice-President

Multicultural History Society of Ontario (MHSO)
c/o Oral History Museum, #307, 901 Lawrence Ave. West, Toronto ON M5S 1C3
Tel: 416-979-2973; *Fax:* 416-979-7947
mhso.mail@utoronto.ca
www.mhso.ca
Working with communities, schools, cultural agencies and institutions to preserve, record and make accessible archival and other material which demonstrate the role of immigration and ethnicity in shaping the culture and economic growth of Ontario and Canada. Library is located at St. Michael's College, University of Toronto.
Jennifer Harrington, Contact, Oral History Museum

Muslim Association of Canada (MAC)
#332, 1568 Merivale Rd., Ottawa ON K2G 5Y7
Tel: 613-321-5000; *Fax:* 613-321-5001
mac@macnet.ca
www.macnet.ca
Seeks to promote a balanced, constructive & integrated Islamic presence in Canada; operates in 11 Canadian cities

Muslim Education & Welfare Foundation of Canada (MEWFC)
Southbourne Centre, #101, 6125 Sussex Ave, Burnaby BC V5H 4G1
Tel: 604-715-4096
al.iman.education.metrotown@gmail.com
To provide for the educational, religious & welfare needs of the Muslim community
Abdellah Seddiki, Teacher

Muslim World League - Canada
#3, 6680 Campobello Rd., Mississauga ON L5N 2L8
Tel: 905-542-1050; *Fax:* 905-542-1054
mwl@mwlcanada.org
www.mwlcanada.org
The League is a non-profit, non-governmental organization that serves the religious needs of Muslims in Canada. It promotes Islam & Islamic teachings among Canadian Muslims & helps non-Muslims grasp an accurate understanding of the religion. It also serves as a resource centre, publishing booklets & flyers on current issues.
Mohamad Khatib, Director

National Association of Canadians of Origin in India (NACOI) / Association nationale des Canadiens d'origine indienne
PO Box 2308, Stn. D, Ottawa ON K1P 5W5
dbdavis@web.net
www.nacoi.ca
To encourage Canadians of origins in India to fully participate in Canadian society; to provide a national voice to Canadian of origins in India; to provide a forum for exchanges of ideas, issues, & common concerns; to facilitate communication within & with other organizations; to assure & protect rights of Canadians of origins in India
Dharam Pal Verma, President

National Association of Japanese Canadians (NAJC)
#1, 222 Osborne St., Winnipeg MB R3L 1Z3
Tel: 204-943-2910; *Fax:* 204-947-3145
national@najc.ca
www.najc.ca
To promote & develop a strong Japanese Canadian identity, thereby strengthening local communities & the national organization; to strive for equal rights & liberties for all persons & racial & ethnic minorities in particular.
Terumi Kuwada, President

National Congress of Italian Canadians (NCIC) / Congrès national des italo-canadiens
c/o Director Court, #201, Woodbridge ON L4L 4S5
Tel: 416-809-5564; *Fax:* 905-850-4516
www.canadese.org
Michael Tibollo, President

National Council of Trinidad & Tobago Organizations in Canada (NCTTOC)
#1, 66 Oakmeadow Blvd., Toronto ON M1E 4G5
Tel: 416-283-9672; *Fax:* 416-283-9672
manniedick@hotmail.com
To provide a national focus for representing the concerns of Trinidad & Tobago Nationals; to advocate on behalf of Trinidad & Tobago Nationals & their families in Canada; to develop & maintain a system of communication, information sharing & networking among Trinidad & Tobago organizations; to provide information, referrals, advocacy, & support to new arrivals from Trinidad & Tobago
Emmanuel J. Dick, President

National Federation of Pakistani Canadians Inc. (NFPC)
#1100, 251 Laurier Ave. W, Ottawa ON K1P 5J6
Tel: 613-232-5346; *Fax:* 613-232-6607
www.cool.mb.ca/nfpc
To preserve & promote the heritage, culture & language of Pakistani Canadians; to generate goodwill & understanding among ethnic & mainstream communities; to provide support to new immigrants; to create awareness of Canadian issues in the Pakistani community

New Brunswick Multicultural Council (NBMC) / Conseil multiculturel du Nouveau-Brunswick (CMNB)
#200, 361 Victoria Street, Fredericton NB E3B 1W5
Tel: 506-453-1091; *Fax:* 866-644-1956
nbmc@nb-mc.ca
www.nb-mc.ca
To represent multicultural & multi-racial interests of all member associations; to encourage development & formation of new associations; to encourage member associations in their multicultural, inter-cultural & inter-racial progarams & activities
Dexter Noel, President

Pacific Peoples Partnership (PPP)
#407, 620 View St., Victoria BC V8W 1J6
Tel: 250-381-4131; *Fax:* 250-388-5258
info@pacificpeoplespartnership.org
www.pacificpeoplespartnership.org
To promote increased understanding of social justice, environment, development, health & other issues of importance to the people of the Pacific Islands; To support equitable, environmentally sustainable development & social justice in the region
Glenn Raynor, Executive Director

Polish Alliance of Canada
1015 Barton St. East, Hamilton ON L8L 3C8
Tel: 905-545-0799
Stanislaw Glogowski, President

Scotiabank Caribana Festival
263 Davenport Rd., Toronto ON M5R 1J9
Tel: 416-391-5608; *Fax:* 416-391-5693
info@caribanafestival.com
www.caribanafestival.com
Social Media: www.facebook.com/scotiabankcaribana
Organized by the Festival Management Committee, the event is a weeks-long, city-wide celebration of everything Caribbean, from food to arts & crafts, culminating with a parade of costumed dancers from regional dance schools & clubs, mas bands & a kaleidoscope of music genres, including calypso, soca, reggae, hip hop, chutney, steel pan.
Joe Halstead, Chair & CEO, Festival Mgmt. Committee

Serbian National Shield Society of Canada
#303, 1900 Sheppard Ave. East, Toronto ON M2J 4T4
Tel: 416-496-7881; *Fax:* 416-493-0335
diddra@sympatico.ca
To promote & inform about interests & heritage of Canadian Serbs
Bora Dragasevich, President

UIA Federations Canada
#315, 4600 Bathurst St., Toronto ON M2R 3V3
Tel: 416-636-7655; *Fax:* 416-636-9897
info@uiafed.org
www.jewishcanada.org
To manage funds destined for Israel & to ensure that these funds are managed in Israel in accordance with terms set by Revenue Canada
Steven Ain, Executive Vice-President

UJA Federation of Greater Toronto
4600 Bathurst St., Toronto ON M2R 3V2
Tel: 416-635-2883; *Fax:* 416-635-9565
Toll-Free: 888-635-2424
info@ujafed.org
www.jewishtoronto.net
Social Media:
www.facebook.com/UJAFederationToronto?sk=app_184498014941265; twitter.com/#!/ujafederation
To preserve & strengthen Jewish life in Toronto, Canada & Israel, through philanthropic, volunteer & professional leadership. The UJA is committed to social justice on behalf of the Jewish poor & vulnerable locally & internationally, to strengthening ties with Israel & its people, to supporting Israel's struggle to meet its social welfare needs, to combatting antisemitism in all its forms around the world, to nurturing shared values with Canadians of all faiths, to promoting Jewish education, to building a vibrant Jewish communal life. The following Pillars identify main areas of focus for UJA: Jewish Education & Identity; Strategic Planning & Community Engagement; Integrated Development; Operations & Corporate Relations; Business & Finance
Ted Sokolsky, President & CEO
Elizabeth Wolfe, Chair

Ukrainian Canadian Congress (UCC) / Congrès des ukrainiens canadiens
#203, 952 Main St., Winnipeg MB R2W 3P4
Tel: 204-942-4627; *Fax:* 204-947-3882
Toll-Free: 866-942-4627
ucc@ucc.ca
www.ucc.ca
To protect, promote & enhance cultural identity of Ukrainians throughout Canada & beyond; to maintain, develop & enhance Ukrainian culture & language as integral elements of Canada's multicultural mosaic; to encourage participation of Ukrainian Canadians in cultural, social, economic, & political life in Canada; to actively advance better communication, understanding & mutual respect between Ukrainian Canadians & other ethnocultural communities; to foster sense of unity, cohesiveness & cooperation among member organizations
Paul Grod, President

Ukrainian Canadian Research & Documentation Centre (UCRDC) / Centre canadien-ukrainien de recherches et de documentation
#200, 620 Spadina Ave., Toronto ON M5S 2H4
Tel: 416-966-1819; *Fax:* 416-966-1820
info@ucrdc.org
www.ucrdc.org
To collect, store & promote information pertaining to Ukrainian historical events & Ukrainian Canadian experiences
Wsevolod Isajiw, Chair

Urban Alliance on Race Relations (UARR)
#507, 302 Spadina Ave., Toronto ON M5T 2E7
Tel: 416-703-6607; *Fax:* 416-703-4415
info@urbanalliance.ca
www.urbanalliance.ca
To promote a stable & healthy multiracial environment in the community, by creating awareness of current issues, assisting institutions to develop solid policies & practices, & promoting full participation by the community to dismantle barriers to equal opportunity
Sharon Simpson, President
Yumei Lin, Administrative Assistant

Vietnamese Canadian Federation / Fédération vietnamienne du Canada
249 Rochester St., Ottawa ON K1R 7M9
Tel: 613-230-8282; *Fax:* 613-230-8281
vietfederation@yahoo.ca
www.vietfederation.ca
To provide focal point for activities of the Vietnamese community in the National Capital Region & across Canada; to serve as resource centre on Vietnamese culture & issues related to resettlement & integration of Vietnamese refugees & immigrants in Canada; to maintain solidarity among the Vietnamese associations across Canada; to harmonize their activities for a better achievement of their common objectives; to work for the preservation & development of Vietnamese culture & for the enrichment of Canadian culture; to foster the spirit of mutual help & community responsibility
Diep Trinh, Executive Director
Ut V. Ngo, President
Duc Q. Duong, Treasurer

Museums

Museum London
421 Ridout St. North, London ON N6A 5H4
Tel: 519-661-0333; *Fax:* 519-661-2559
info@museumlondon.ca
www.museumlondon.ca
To enrich public knowledge & enjoyment of the art & history of the London region & Canada
Brian Meehan, Executive Director

Native Peoples

Aboriginal Friendship Centres of Saskatchewan
1615, 29th St., Saskatoon SK S7L 0N6
Tel: 306-955-0762; *Fax:* 306-955-0972
www.afcs.ca
The objectives of the Aboriginal Friendship Centres (AFC) of Sask. are: the promotion of the goals and objectives of its member Friendship Centres; the facilitation of communication and cooperation amongst all Centres w/in SK,.; the providing of information regarding the operation and dvlp. of AFCs to the public; negotiation with all tiers of gov't on matters of concern to the member Centres; assistance in Program Dvlp.; and assistance to all members in terms of funding information, debt recovery plans, financial negotiation, and networking.

Aboriginal Nurses Association of Canada (ANAC) / Association des infirmières et infirmiers autochtones du Canada
#600, 16 Concourse Gate, Ottawa ON K2E 7S8
Tel: 613-724-4677; *Fax:* 613-724-4718
Toll-Free: 866-724-3049
info@anac.on.ca
www.anac.on.ca
Social Media: www.facebook.com/group.php?gid=8896466083; twitter.com/aboriginalnurse
To work with & on behalf of Aboriginal nurses to promote the development & practice of Aboriginal nursing in order to improve the health of Aboriginal people
Evelyn Voyageur, President
Rhonda Goodtrack, Vice-President
Lisa Bourque-Bearskin, Secretary-Treasurer

Aboriginal Women's Association of Prince Edward Island
PO Box 145, Lennox Island PE C0B 1P0
Tel: 902-831-3059; *Fax:* 902-831-3468
awapei@pei.aibn.com
The purpose of the project is to address issues of concern to off-reserve Aboriginal women and to improve the educational, social and economic environments in which they live. The resource centre offers culturally sensitive programs and services to off-reserve Aboriginal families and children from birth to age 6.
Marilyn Sark

Alberta Aboriginal Women's Society
PO Box 5168, Stn. Main, Peace River AB T8S 1R8
Tel: 780-624-3416; *Fax:* 780-624-3409
aaws@telusplanet.net
Ruth Kidder, President

Alberta Native Friendship Centres Association (ANFCA)
10336 - 121 St., Edmonton AB T5N 1K8
Tel: 780-423-3138; *Fax:* 780-425-6277
info@anfca.com
www.anfca.com
To assist friendship centres in communication, funding & training
S. Graystone, Fund Development Officer

Alliance autochtone du Québec inc. / Native Alliance of Québec Inc.
21, rue Brodeur, Gatineau QC J8Y 2P6
Tél: 819-770-7763; *Téléc:* 819-770-6070
info@aaqnaq.com
www.aaqnaq.com
Robert Bertrand, Président Grand Chef

Assembly of First Nations (AFN) / Assemblée des Premières Nations (APN)
Trebla Building, 473 Albert St., Ottawa ON K1R 5B4
Tel: 613-241-6789; *Fax:* 613-241-5808
Toll-Free: 866-869-6789
imcleod@afn.ca
www.afn.ca
Social Media: www.facebook.com/AFN.APN;
twitter.com/AFN_Updates
The AFN Secretariat acts as an advocate for First Nations on many issues, including Aboriginal & Treaty Rights, economic development, education, languages & literacy, health, housing, social development, justice, land claims & the environment
Shawn Atleo, National Chief

Assembly of Manitoba Chiefs
#200, 260 St. Mary Ave., Winnipeg MB R3C 0M6
Tel: 204-956-0610; *Fax:* 204-956-2109
Toll-Free: 888-324-5483
assembly@manitobachiefs.com
www.manitobachiefs.com/
The AMC Chiefs work to promote and preserve our inherent Aboriginal and treaty rights while striving to improve the quality of life of the First Nation citizens in Manitoba.
Irene Linklater, Executive Director

Association for Native Development in the Performing & Visual Arts (ANDPVA)
#171, 601 Christie St., Toronto ON M6G 4C7
Tel: 416-535-4567; *Fax:* 416-535-9331
info@andpva.com
www.andpva.com
To coordinate & develop programs that will encourage Indigenous peoples & communities to become more actively involved in the arts; to act as liaison for Native groups & individuals who are seeking funds for specific arts projects
Harmony Rice, President

Association of Iroquois & Allied Indians
387 Princess Ave., London ON N6B 2A7
Tel: 519-434-2761; *Fax:* 519-679-1653
general@aiai.on.ca
www.aiai.on.ca
Randall Phillips, Grand Chief

British Columbia Association of Aboriginal Friendship Centres (BCAAFC)
#200, 506 Fort St., Victoria BC V8W 1E6
Tel: 250-388-5522; *Fax:* 250-388-5502
Toll-Free: 800-990-2432
admin@bcaafc.com
www.bcaafc.com
Social Media:
www.facebook.com/group.php?gid=160027657353593
To promote the betterment of Aboriginal Friendship Centres in British Columbia by acting as a unifying body for the Centres; To establish & maintain communications between Aboriginal Friendship Centres, other associations, & government
Annette Morgan, President
Barb Ward-Burkitt, Vice-President
Christopher Phillips, Treasurer
Richard Samuel, Second Vice-President
Paul Lacerte, Executive Director

British Columbia Native Women's Society
4213 Alexis Park Dr., Vernon BC V1T 7T8
Crisis Hot-Line: e - -
Barb Morin

Canadian Aboriginal & Minority Supplier Council (CAMSC)
95 Berkeley St., Toronto ON M5A 2W8
Tel: 416-941-0004; *Fax:* 416-941-9282
info@camsc.ca
www.camsc.ca
Dedicated to the economic empowerment of Aboriginal & visible minority communities through business development & employment; to identify & certify Aboriginal & minority-owned businesses, & to integrate them into the supply chain of major corporations in Canada.
Garth Scully, Chair
Orrin O. Benn, President

Canadian Association for the Study of Indigenous Education (CASIE) / Association canadienne pour l'etude de l'education des autochtones (ACÉFÉ)
c/o Canadian Society for the Study of Education, #204, 260 Dalhousie St., Ottawa ON K1N 7E4
Dwayne Donald, President

Canadian Council for Aboriginal Business (CCAB) / Conseil canadien pour le commerce autochtone
#204, 250 The Esplanade, Toronto ON M5A 1J2
Tel: 416-961-8663; *Fax:* 416-961-3995
info@caab.com
www.ccab.com
To promote full participation of Aboriginal communities in the Canadian economy
Clint Davis, President/CEO

Canadian Native Friendship Centre (CNFC)
11205 - 101 St. NW, Edmonton AB T5G 2A4
Tel: 780-479-1999; *Fax:* 780-479-0043
cnfc@shawbiz.ca
www.cnfc.ca
To improve the quality of life of Aboriginal Peoples in an urban environment by supporting self-determined activities encouraging equal access to & participation in Canadian society while respecting Aboriginal cultural distinctiveness
Barb Maytwayashing, Management Director

Centre indien cri de Chibougamau
95, rue Jaculet, Chibougamau QC G8P 2G1
Tél: 418-748-7667
Centre social pour les Autochtones de la région; centre d'exposition pour les artisans cri
Jo-Ann Toulouse, Directice générale

Chiefs of Ontario
#804, 111 Peter St., Toronto ON M5V 2H1
Tel: 416-597-1266; *Fax:* 416-597-8365
Toll-Free: 877-517-6527
margaret@coo.org
www.chiefs-of-ontario.org
Chiefs of Ontario is a coordinating body for 134 First Nation communities located within the boundaries of the province of Ontario. The purpose of the Chiefs of Ontario office is to enable the political leadership to discuss regional, provincial and national priorities affecting First Nation people in Ontario and to provide a unified voice on these issues.
Lori Jacobs, Executive Director

Confederacy of Mainland Mi'kmaq (CMM)
PO Box 1590, 57 Martin Cresc., Truro NS B2N 6N7
Tel: 902-895-6385; *Fax:* 902-893-1520
Toll-Free: 877-892-2424
www.cmmns.com
To proactively promote and assist Mi'kmaw communities' initiatives toward self determination and enhancement of community.
Donald M. Julien, Executive Director

Congress of Aboriginal Peoples (CAP) / Congrès des Peuples Autochtones
867 St. Laurent Blvd., Ottawa ON K1K 3B1
Tel: 613-747-6022; *Fax:* 613-747-8834
gilles@abo-peoples.org
www.abo-peoples.org
To represent approximately 3/4 million Aboriginal people living off-reserve in Canada
Betty Ann Lavellee, National Chief
Libby Williams, Director of Operations

Council of Yukon First Nations (CYFN)
11 Nisutlin Dr., Whitehorse YT Y1A 3S4
Tel: 867-393-9200
www.cyfn.ca
The Council of Yukon First Nations is the central political organization for the First Nation people of the Yukon. It's mission is to serve the needs of First Nations within the Yukon and the MacKenzie delta.
Andy Carvill, Grand Chief

Federation of Newfoundland Indians
CIBC Bldg., PO Box 956, #7, 9 Main St., 3rd Fl., Corner Brook NL A2H 6J3
Tel: 709-634-0996; *Fax:* 709-634-3477
Toll-Free: 800-563-2549
adminasst@fni.nf.ca
www.fni.nf.ca
Brendan Sheppard, President

Federation of Saskatchewan Indian Nations
Asimakaniseekan Askiy Reserve, #100, 103A Packham Ave., Saskatoon SK S7N 4K4
Tel: 306-665-1215; *Fax:* 306-244-4413
www.fsin.com
The Federation represents 74 First Nations in Saskatchewan & honours the spirit & intent of the Treaties & their rights. It is committed to fostering the economic, educational & social endeavours of the First Nation people, & adhernece to democratic procedure & civil law.
Guy Lonechild, Chief

Femmes autochtones du Québec inc. (FAQ) / Québec Native Women's Association Inc.
CP 1989, Kahnawake QC J0L 1B0
Tél: 450-632-0088; *Téléc:* 450-632-9280
Ligne sans frais: 800-363-0322
info@faq-qnw.org
www.faq-qnw.org
Appuyer les efforts des femmes autochtones pour l'amélioration de leurs conditions de vie par la promotion de la non-violence, de la justice et de l'égalité des droits et de les soutenir dans leur engagement au sein de leur communauté.
Carole Bussière, Executive Director

First Nations Confederacy of Cultural Education Centres
#302, 666 Kirkwood Ave., Ottawa ON K1Z 5X9
Tel: 613-728-5999; *Fax:* 613-728-2247
info@fnccec.ca; cecp@fnccec.ca
www.fnccec.com
Social Media: wwww.facebook.com/134419529944964;
twitter.com/fnccec; .
To advocate for the recovery, maintenance, enhancement & preservation of First Nations languages, cultures, & traditions
Claudette Commanda, Executive Director
Donna Goodleaf, National President
Tiffany Sark-Carr, Vice-President
Dorothy Myo, Secretary-Treasurer

Grand Council of the Crees / Grand Conseil des Cris
2, rue Lakeshore, Némiscau QC J0Y 3B0
Tel: 819-673-2600; *Fax:* 819-673-2606
cra@lino.ca
www.gcc.ca
Social Media: www.facebook.com/gcccra
The Council is the political body representing the Cree people. It also fosters, promotes, protects & assists in preserving the way of life, values & traditions of the Cree people of Quebec.
Mathew Coon Come, Grand Chief
Bill Namagoose, Executive Director

Indian Council of First Nations of Manitoba, Inc. (ICFNM)
PO Box 10299, Opaskwayak MB R0B 2J0
Tel: 204-623-7227; *Fax:* 204-623-4041
To organize non-status & off-reserve Indians of Manitoba; to represent to all levels of Canadian government the constitutional position of non-status Indians in Manitoba; to ensure access for non-status & off-reserve Indians in all programs & services of federal, provincial & municipal governments of Canada; to promote democratic participation in constitutional processes for members; leadership development within non-status & off-reserve Indian community; to provide historical & pertinent information on non-status & off-reserve Indians to membership; to organize community groups throughout Manitoba; to develop constitutional position paper for non-status & off-reserve Indians in Manitoba; to organize & conduct annual assemblies; to attend constitutional workshops & first Ministers' meetings.
Andrew Kirkness, Grand Chief

Indigenous Bar Association
70 Pineglen Cres., Ottawa ON K2G 0G8
Tel: 613-224-1529
www.indigenousbar.ca
To recognize & respect the spiritual basis of our Indigenous laws, customs & traditions; to promote the advancement of legal & social justice for Indigenous peoples in Canada; to promote reform of policies & laws affecting Indigenous peoples in Canada; to foster public awareness within the legal community, the Indigenous community & the general public in respect of legal & social issues of concern to Indigenous peoples in Canada; to provide a forum & network amongst Indigenous lawyers

Koren Lightning-Earle, President
Drew Lafond, Secretary
Anne Chalmers, Administrative Support

Inuit Art Foundation (IAF) / Fondation d'art Inuit
2081 Merivale Rd., Ottawa ON K2G 1G9
Tel: 613-224-8189; *Fax:* 613-224-2907
Toll-Free: 800-830-3293
iaf@inuitart.org
www.inuitart.org
To facilitate the creative expression of Inuit artists; To foster an increased understanding of this expression in a local & global context; To assist in the marketing of Inuit art; To promote Inuit art through exhibits, publications & public events
Marybelle Mitchell, Executive Director

Inuit Tapiriit Kanatami
#1101, 75 Albert St., Ottawa ON K1P 5E7
Tel: 613-238-8181; *Fax:* 613-234-1991
Toll-Free: 866-262-8181
info@itk.ca
www.itk.ca
Social Media:
www.facebook.com/group.php?gid=149359161748927; twitter.com/ITK_CanadaInuit; www.youtube.com/inuitofcanada
To ensure the survival of Inuit culture in Canada
Mary May Simon, President
Jim Moore, Executive Director
Stephen Hendrie, Communications Director

Labrador Native Women's Association
PO Box 542, Stn. B, Happy Valley-Goose Bay NL A0P 1S0
Tel: 709-896-5071; *Fax:* 709-896-5071
mnha@nf.aibn.com

Makivik Corporation / Société Makivik
PO Box 179, Kuujjuaq QC J0M 1C0
Tel: 819-964-2925; *Toll-Free:* 877-625-4825
info@makivik.org
www.makivik.org
A non-profit organization owned by the Inuit of Nunavik, the Corporation promotes the social & economic interests of the Inuit people; receives, administers & invests Inuit compensation funds received under the James Bay & Northern Québec Agreement, & promotes the political, social & economic development of the Nunavik region. Offices in Kuujjuaq, Montreal, Ottawa, Quebec City
Pita Aatami, President
Anthony Ittoshat, Treasurer
Andy Moorhouse, Corporate Secretary

Manitoba Association of Friendship Centres (MAC)
#200, 388 Donald St., Winnipeg MB R3B 2J4
Tel: 204-942-6299; *Fax:* 204-942-6308
info@mac.mb.ca
www.mac.mb.ca
To assist friendship centres in communication, funding & training.
Sheena Reed, President
Ella Mayer, Provincial Coordinator

Manitoba Indian Cultural Education Centre (MICEC)
119 Sutherland Ave., Winnipeg MB R2W 3C9
Tel: 204-942-0228; *Fax:* 204-947-6564
micec@shawcable.com
www.micec.com
To stimulate, reidentify, maintain, expand & promote the cultural interests, lives & identity of Manitoba First Nations in every manner & respect whatsoever, & to promote an awareness of the traditional history of the First Nation Peoples of Manitoba; to advance the interests of First Nation Peoples who are registered members of the reserves within Manitoba, whether residing on or outside them; to cooperate with other organizations concerned with the interests of First Nation Peoples; to establish & promote research services; to assist in the development of accurate curriculum for use in schools within Manitoba; to produce audio, visual, & written materials relevant to cultural education development
Dennis Daniels, Executive Director

Manitoba Métis Federation / Fédération des Métis du Manitoba
Head Office, #300, 150 Henry Ave., Winnipeg MB R3B 0J7
Tel: 204-586-8474; *Fax:* 204-947-1816
mmf@mmf.mb.ca
www.mmf.mb.ca
Objectives include: promoting and instilling pride in the history and culture of the Métis people; educating members with respect to their legal, political, social and other rights; promoting the participation and representation of the Métis people in key political and economic bodies and organizations; promoting the political, legal, social and economic interests and rights of its members.
David Chartrand, President

Maritime Aboriginal Peoples Council (MAPC)
172 Truro Heights Rd., Truro NS B6L 1X1
Tel: 902-895-2982; *Fax:* 902-895-3844

Métis Nation - Saskatchewan
406 Jessop Ave., Saskatoon SK S7N 2S5
Tel: 306-343-8285; *Fax:* 306-343-0171
Toll-Free: 888-343-6667
reception@mnsask.ca
www.mn-s.ca
Robert G. Doucette, President, Provincial Métis Council

Métis Nation Northwest Territories
PO Box 1375, 5125 - 50 St., Yellowknife NT X1A 2P1
Tel: 867-873-3505; *Fax:* 867-873-3395
metisnwt@internorth.com
Gary Bohnet, President

Métis Nation of Alberta
Delia Gray Bldg., #100, 41738 Kingsway Ave., Edmonton AB T5G 0X5
Tel: 780-455-2200; *Fax:* 780-452-8948
Toll-Free: 800-252-7553
www.albertametis.com
Social Media:
www.facebook.com/pages/Metis-Nation-of-Alberta/339682308115; twitter.com/AlbertaMetis
To represent the interests of the Métis people of Alberta & ensure the advancement of their culture & well-being
Audrey Poitras, President

Métis Nation of Ontario
#3, 500 Old St. Patrick St., Ottawa ON K1N 9G4
Tel: 613-798-1488; *Fax:* 613-722-4225
Toll-Free: 800-263-4889
ottawareception@metisnation.org
www.metisnation.org
The Métis Nation of Ontario (MNO) brings Métis people together to celebrate and share their rich culture and heritage and to forward the aspirations of the Métis people in Ontario as a collective.
Gary Lipinski, President

Métis National Council (MNC) / Ralliement national des Métis
#4, 340 MacLaren St., Ottawa ON K2P 0M6
Tel: 613-232-3216; *Fax:* 613-232-4262
Toll-Free: 800-928-6330
info@metisnation.ca
www.metisnation.ca
To represent the Métis both nationally & internationally; To secure a healthy space for the Métis Nation's existence within Canada
Clément Chartier, President

Métis National Council of Women (MNCW) / Conseil national des femmes métisses, inc. (CNFM)
PO Box 293, Woodlawn ON K0A 3M0
Tel: 613-567-4287; *Fax:* 613-567-9644
Toll-Free: 888-867-2635
info@metiswomen.ca
www.metiswomen.ca
To unite & organize Métis women in Canada; to maintain & promote respect for the individual rights, freedoms & gender equality of Métis women; to foster & promote the image of Métis women; to promote the preservation & enhancement of Métis culture; to facilitate & promote the development of services generally for the Métis & specifically for Métis women; to influence policy & to be actively involved in policy development in all organizations & at all levels that impact upon Métis women & their children; to establish & maintain cooperative & productive working relationships with the federal & provincial governments & all their related organizations as well as with other Aboriginal organizations; to actively seek funding for the Organization & its projects & activities; to represent the cultural, legal, political, social & economic issues of Métis women& their families & address their issues & concerns.
Sheila D. Genaille, President

Métis Provincial Council of British Columbia
#905, 1130 West Pender St., Vancouver BC V6E 4A4
Tel: 604-801-5853; *Fax:* 604-801-5097
Toll-Free: 800-940-1150
traceyt@mnbc.ca
www.mpcbc.bc.ca
Supporting the Métis population in British Columbia.
Bruce Dumont, President

Métis Settlements General Council
#200, 10335 - 172 St., Edmonton AB T5S 1K9
Tel: 780-822-4096; *Fax:* 780-489-9558
Toll-Free: 888-213-4400
reception@msgc.ca
www.msgc.ca
The Council represents 8 settlements, addresses socio-economic issues on their behalf, & promotes good governance & community involvement
Gerald Cunningham, President

Mi'Kmaq Association for Cultural Studies (MACS)
47 Maillard St., Membertou NS B1S 2P5
Tel: 902-567-1752; *Fax:* 902-567-0776
macs@mikmaq-assoc.ca
www.mikmaq-assoc.ca
To promote, maintain & protect the customs, language, history, tradition & culture of the Mi'Kmaq people; to facilitate & promote understanding & awareness of our culture among the public; to teach the culture, language & history of the Mi'Kmaq people to others

Mi'kmaq Native Friendship Centre
2158 Gottingen St., Halifax NS B3K 3B4
Tel: 902-420-0686; *Fax:* 902-423-6130
Social Media: www.facebook.com/group.php?gid=8114695398
The Centre promotes the educational & cultural advancement of native people in & about the Halifax/Dartmouth area. It assists people of native descent who have newly arrived in the area to settle in. Also, it strives to create & improve mutual understanding between people of native descent & others.
Gordon V. King, Executive Director

Mother of Red Nations Women's Council of Manitoba (MORN)
#300, 141 Bannatyne Ave., Winnipeg MB R3B 0R3
Tel: 204-942-6676; *Fax:* 204-942-7639
Toll-Free: 866-258-6726
morn@morn.ca
morn.cimnet.ca
MORN represents the voice of Aboriginal women in Manitoba. It serves as their primary political & advocacy organization. The association strives to promote, protect & support the spiritual, emotional, physical & mental well-being of all Aboriginal women & children in the province.
Susie McPherson, Provincial Speaker

National Aboriginal Achievement Foundation
#759, 2160 Fourth Line Rd., Oshweken ON N0A 1M0
Tel: 416-926-0775; *Fax:* 416-926-7554
Toll-Free: 800-329-9780
info@naaf.ca
www.naaf.ca
Roberta Jamieson, CEO
John Kim Bell, Founder

National Aboriginal Circle Against Family Violence
Kahnawake Business Complex, PO Box 2169, Kahnawake QC J0L 1B0
Tel: 450-638-2968; *Fax:* 450-638-9415
www.nacafv.ca
To reduce & eliminate family violence in our Aboriginal communities; programs are culturally appropriate, & support shelters & family violence prevention centres
Brenda Combs, Chair

National Association of Friendship Centres (NAFC) / Association nationale des centres d'amitié
275 MacLaren St., Ottawa ON K2P 0L9
Tel: 613-563-4844; *Fax:* 613-594-3428
nafcgen@nafc.ca
www.nafc-aboriginal.com
To assist friendship centres in communication, funding & training
Peter Dinsdale, Executive Director

Native Addictions Council of Manitoba (NACM)
160 Salter St., Winnipeg MB R2W 4K1
Tel: 204-586-8395; *Fax:* 204-589-3921
nacm@escape.ca
www.mts.net/~nacm/
To provide traditional holistic healing services to First Peoples through treatment of addictions; each member of First Peoples has the right to wellness.
Elizabeth Fontaine, Supervisor/Rehab
Bertha Fontaine, Executive Director

Native Council of Nova Scotia (NCNS)
129 Truro Heights Rd., Truro NS B6L 1X2
Tel: 902-895-1523; *Fax:* 902-895-0024
Toll-Free: 800-565-4372
www.ncns.ca
To aid & assist people of Aboriginal ancestry in Nova Scotia; to work with all levels of government, public & private agencies, &

industry to improve social, educational & employment opportunities for Aboriginal people; to foster & strengthen cultural identity & pride; to inform the public of the special needs of Native People; to cooperate with other Native organizations
Grace Conrad, Chief & President
Theresa Hare, Finance

Native Council of Prince Edward Island
6 F.J. McAuley Ct., Charlottetown PE C1A 9M7
Tel: 902-892-5314; *Fax:* 902-368-7464
Toll-Free: 877-591-3003
admin@ncpei.com
www.ncpei.com
Welcome to the Native Council of Prince Edward Island (NCPEI) The Native Council of Prince Edward Island is a Community of Aboriginal People residing off reserve in traditional Mi'kmaq territory. NCPEI is the self governing authority for all off reserve Aboriginal people living on Epekwitk (PEI).
Jamie Thomas, President
Rikki Schock, Vice-President

Native Counselling Services of Alberta (NCSA)
10975 - 124 St., Edmonton AB T5M 0H9
Tel: 780-451-4002; *Fax:* 780-428-0187
www.ncsa.ca
A non-profit organization with a mandate to promote wellness for Aboriginal individuals, families and communities. The services provided include restorative justice, social programming, community development and wellness initiatives.
Allen Benson, CEO

Native Friendship Centre of Montréal Inc. (NFCM) / Centre d'amitié autochtone de Montréal Inc.
2001, boul St-Laurent, Montréal QC H2X 2T3
Tel: 514-499-1854; *Fax:* 514-499-9436
info@nfcm.org
www.nfcm.org
To promote, develop & enhance the quality of life of the urban Aboriginal community of Montréal
Leandro Tolentino, Interim Executive Director

Native Investment & Trade Association (NITA)
6520 Salish Dr., Vancouver BC V6N 2C7
Tel: 604-275-6670; *Fax:* 604-275-0307
Toll-Free: 800-337-7743
nita@express.ca
www.native-invest-trade.com
To promote, establish & maintain trade/investment opportunities in Native communities; encourages free enterprise solutions to economic & social problems confronting Native communities, but remains sensitive to their special cultural heritage, needs, requirements; views non-governmental business involvement with First Nations as a vital step towards greater self-reliance; fosters business ventures with high employment potential; promotes projects with potential for sustainable economic growth; conducts research into innovative approaches to economic development of Native communities
Calvin Helin, President

Native Women's Association of Canada (NWAC) / L'Association des femmes autochtones du Canada (AFAC)
Six Nations of the Grand River, PO Box 331, 1721 Chiefswood Rd., Ohsweken ON N0A 1M0
Tel: 519-445-0990; *Fax:* 519-445-0924
www.nwac-hq.org
To enhance, promote & foster the social, economic, cultural & political well-being of First Nations & Métis women with First Nations & Canadian societies; to help empower women by being involved in developing & changing legislation which affects them, & by involving them in the development & delivery of programs promoting equal opportunity for Aboriginal women. Satellite office located at 1292 Wellington St. West, Ottawa, 613-722-3033.
Karen Green, CEO

New Brunswick Aboriginal Peoples Council (NBAPC)
320 St. Mary's St., Fredericton NB E3A 2S4
Tel: 506-458-8422; *Fax:* 506-451-6130
www.nbapc.org
The off-reserve Aboriginal voice for 28,255 Status & Non-status First Nations who reside in New Brunswick
Bruce Harquail, Interim Chief & President

New Brunswick Aboriginal Women's Council
29 Big Cove Rd., Elsipogtog NB E4W 2S5
Tel: 506-523-9518; *Fax:* 506-523-8350
nbawca@nb.aibn.com
Mary Jane Peters, President

Newfoundland Native Women's Association
PO Box 22, Benoits Cove NL A0L 1A0
Tel: 709-789-3430; *Fax:* 709-789-2207
nf.nativewomen@nf.aibn.com
The Native Womens Association of Canada (NWAC) is founded on the collective goal to enhance, promote, and foster the social, economic, cultural and political well-being of First Nations and Métis women within First Nation, Métis and Canadian societies.

Northwest Territories Council of Friendship Centres
c/o Soaring Eagle Friendship Centre, #2, 8 Gagnier St., Hay River NT X0E 1G1
Tel: 867-874-2792; *Fax:* 867-874-2894
To assist friendship centres in the Northwest Territories

Nova Scotia Native Women's Society
PO Box 805, Truro NS B2N 5E8
Tel: 902-893-7402; *Fax:* 902-897-7162
Social Media: www.facebook.com/nsnwa

Ontario Coalition of Aboriginal Peoples (OCAP)
PO Box 189, Wabigoon ON P0V 2W0
Tel: 807-938-1321
www.o-cap.ca
A not-for-profit advocacy organization representing the rights & interests of Métis, Status & Non-Status Aboriginal peoples living off-reserve in urban, rural or remote areas. Focus is on training programs & employment services
Brad Maggrah, President
Brad Maggrah, President
Ronald Swain, Chair

Ontario Federation of Indian Friendship Centres (OFIFC)
219 Front St. East, Toronto ON M5A 1E8
Tel: 416-956-7575; *Fax:* 416-956-7577
Toll-Free: 800-772-9291
ofifc@ofifc.org; oahai@ofifc.org (health advocacy initiative)
www.ofifc.org
To represent the collective interests of Ontario's friendship centres; To administer programs delivered by friendship centres, such as justice, health, employment, & family support; To improve the quality of life for Aboriginal people for equal access & participation in Canadian society
Sylvia Maracle, Executive Director
Celeste Hayward, Director, Programme
Juliette Nicolet, Director, Policy
Meri Saunders, Director, Finance

Ontario Native Women's Association (ONWA)
212 Miles St. East, Thunder Bay ON P7C 1J6
Tel: 807-623-3442; *Fax:* 807-623-1104
Toll-Free: 800-667-0816
www.nwac-hq.org
To foster & promote the economic, social, cultural, & political well-being of First Nations & Métis women in Ontario; To represent Native women on issues that affect their lives
Marianne Borg, Executive Director

Quaker Aboriginal Affairs Committee (QAAC)
60 Lowther Ave., Toronto ON M5R 1C7
Tel: 416-920-5213; *Fax:* 416-920-5214
qaac@quaker.ca
cfsc.quaker.ca/pages/contact_abor.html
Support for Aboriginal fights & justice, public education & campaigns
Jennifer Preston, Program Coordinator

Regroupement des centres d'amitié autochtone du Québec (RCAAQ)
#250, 225, rue Max-Gros-Louis, Wendake QC G0A 4V0
Tél: 418-842-6354; *Téléc:* 418-842-9795
Ligne sans frais: 877-842-6354
infos@rcaaq.info
www.rcaaq.info
Etre la voix provinciale des centres existants ou en voie de développement et de leurs communautés; appuyer ses membres dans l'atteinte de leurs objectifs; favoriser leur concertation et les représenter collectivement pour qu'ils remplissent au mieux leur mandat
Josée Goulet, Directrice générale

Saskatchewan Aboriginal Women's Circle Corporation
PO Box 1174, 89 Broadway St. East, Yorkton SK S3N 2X3
Tel: 306-783-1228; *Fax:* 306-783-1771
sawcc@hotmail.com
www.sawcc.sk.ca
To walk in balance with guidance by the creator; to unite people together as healthy nations to ensure a better life for future generations
Judy Hughes, President

Society of Yukon Artists of Native Ancestry (SYANA)
#205, 302 Steele St., Whitehorse YT Y1A 2C5
Tel: 867-668-2695
To promote greater knowledge & appreciation of Native art & artists; To develop Native arts; To encourage Native & public participation in the arts
Linda Polyck, Contact

2-Spirited People of the First Nations (TPFN)
#202, 593 Yonge St., Toronto ON M4Y 1Z4
Tel: 416-944-9300; *Fax:* 416-944-8381
info@2spirits.com
www.2spirits.com
To create a place where Aboriginal 2-Spirited people can grow & learn together as a community, fostering a positive, self-sufficient image, honouring our past & building a future; to work together toward bridging the gap between the 2-Spirited, Lesbian, Gay, Bisexual & Transgendered community & our Aboriginal identity
Art Zoccole, Executive Director

Union of British Columbia Indian Chiefs
#500, 342 Water St., Vancouver BC V6B 1B6
Tel: 604-684-0231; *Fax:* 604-684-5726
ubcic@ubcic.bc.ca
www.ubcic.bc.ca
To settle land claims & aboriginal rights in BC; to improve the social, economic, health, education of Aboriginal people in BC; to provide a political voice for Aboriginal people in BC
Stewart Phillip, President

Union of Nova Scotia Indians (UNSI)
PO Box 961, 47 Maillard St., Membertou NS B1S 2P5
Tel: 902-539-4107; *Fax:* 902-564-2137
rec@unsi.ns.ca
www.unsi.ns.ca
To promote welfare & progress of Native people in Nova Scotia; to liaise with all Native people on relevant issues; to defend & advise on Native rights; to cooperate with Native & non-Native agencies & organizations to the benefit of Nova Scotia Native people
Joe B. Marshall, Executive Director

Union of Ontario Indians (UOI)
Nipissing First Nation, 1 Miigizi Mikan, North Bay ON P1B 8J8
Tel: 705-497-9127; *Fax:* 705-497-9135
Toll-Free: 877-702-5200
info@anishinabek.ca
www.anishinabek.ca
The UOI represents 42 First Nations throughout the province of Ontario from Golden Lake in the east, Sarnia in the south, Thunder Bay and Lake Nipigon in the north. The 42 First Nations have an approximate combined population of 42,000 citizens, one third of the province of Ontario's aboriginal population.
Patrick Madahbee, Grand Council Chief

United Native Nations Society
#341, 1979 Marine Dr., North Vancouver BC V7G 3G2
Tel: 604-688-1821; *Fax:* 604-980-0324
Toll-Free: 800-555-9756
unn@unns.bc.ca
www.unns.bc.ca
George Holem, President
Lillian George, Vice-President

Woodland Cultural Centre (WCC)
PO Box 1506, 184 Mohawk St., Brantford ON N3T 5V6
Tel: 519-759-2650; *Fax:* 519-759-8912
woodlandcentre@execulink.com
www.woodland-centre.on.ca
To preserve the values & practices of First Nation cultures through the storage & exhibits of First Nation National Treasures; to bring about acceptable positive change in our communities & in the interaction with western Euro-society; to provide a place where people can receive teachings & guidance from our First Nation existence; to instill pride in self, children & our existence as Nations in the world community
Amos Key Jr., Executive Director

Yukon Aboriginal Women's Council
#102, 307 Jarvis St., Whitehorse YT Y1A 2H3
Tel: 867-667-6162; *Fax:* 867-668-7539
Toll-Free: 866-667-6162
yawc@northwestel.net
Louise Bouvier, President

Naturalists

Avicultural Advancement Council of Canada (AACC)
28 Greene Dr., Brampton on L6V 2R6
www.aacc.ca
To establish & maintain a national association of interested societies & individuals to promote the advancement of aviculture in Canada; To represent the Canadian avicultural community internationally; To disseminate information; to support recognized expert aviculturalists; To assist all levels of government in preparing informed legislation & policy relating to aviculture; To establish standards for the exhibition of birds in Canada; To provide a national identification leg band registry; To establish an avian species preservation program in Canada
Dunstan H. Browne, President
Denise Antler, Ring Registrar
Roslynne Webb, Secretary

British Columbia Nature (Federation of British Columbia Naturalists) (FBCN)
c/o Parks Heritage Centre, 1620 Mount Seymour Rd., North Vancouver BC V7G 2R9
Tel: 604-985-3057
manager@bcnature.ca
www.bcnature.ca
To protect biodiversity, species at risk, & natural areas throughout British Columbia; To present a unified voice on conservation & environmental issues
Betty Davison, Office Manager
Bev Ramey, President
Rosemary Fox, Chair, Conservation
Elisa Kreller, Treasurer
Maria Hamann, Office Manager
Joan Snyder, Chair, Education
Pat Westheuser, Chair, Awards

British Columbia Waterfowl Society
5191 Robertson Rd., RR#1, Delta BC V4K 3N2
Tel: 604-946-6980; *Fax:* 604-946-6980
www.reifelbirdsanctuary.com/bcws2.html
To encourage conservation of wetlands; to spur public awareness on importance of conservation of estuaries; to operate George C. Reifel Migratory Bird Sanctuary.
Kathleen Fry, Acting Manager
Jack Bates, President

Federation of Alberta Naturalists (FAN)
11759 Groat Rd., Edmonton AB T5M 3K6
Tel: 780-427-8124; *Fax:* 780-422-2663
info@fanweb.ca
www.fanweb.ca
To encourage Albertans to increase knowledge & understanding of natural history & ecological processes; to provide a unified voice for naturalists on conservation issues; to organize field meetings, conferences, nature camps, research symposia, & other activities.

Jack Miner Migratory Bird Foundation, Inc.
PO Box 39, Kingsville ON N9Y 2E8
Tel: 519-733-4034; *Toll-Free:* 877-289-8328
info@jackminer.com
www.jackminer.com
The sanctuary provides food, shelter & protection to migratory water fowl, tags birds & tracks migration patterns
Kirk W. Miner, Executive Director

Natural History Society of Newfoundland & Labrador
c/o The Osprey, PO Box 1013, Stn. C, St. John's NL A1C 5M3
Tel: 709-754-0455
nhs@nhs.nf.ca
www.nhs.nf.ca
The Natural History Society is a province-wide organization with a primary interest in promoting the enjoyment and protection of all wildlife and natural history resources in the Province of Newfoundland and Labrador and surrounding waters.
Allan Stein, Acting Vice-President
Don Steele, Secretary

Nature Canada / Canada Nature
#300, 75 Albert St., Ottawa ON K1P 5E7
Tel: 613-562-3447; *Fax:* 613-562-3371
Toll-Free: 800-267-4088
info@naturecanada.ca
www.naturecanada.ca
Social Media: www.facebook.com/NatureCanada; twitter.com/NatureCanada; www.youtube.com/user/NatureCanada1
To protect & conserve wildlife & habitats throughout Canada
Ian Davidson, Executive Director
Ruth Catana, Chief Operating Officer
Dave Spooner, Director, Finance & Administration
Chris Sutton, Director, Communications
Ted Cheskey, Manager, Bird Conservation Programs
Jodi Joy, Manager, Major & Planned Giving
Katherine Lim, Manager, Outreach & Engagement
Alex MacDonald, Manager, Protected Areas Campaigns
Carla Sbert, Manager, Conservation Programs
Andrew Van Iterson, Manager, Green Budget Coalition

Nature Manitoba (MNS)
Hammond Building, #401, 63 Albert St., Winnipeg MB R3B 1G4
Tel: 204-943-9029; *Fax:* 204-943-9029
info@naturemanitoba.ca; editor@naturemanitoba.ca (Newsletter)
www.naturemanitoba.ca
Social Media: www.facebook.com/pages/Nature-Manitoba/67945358869
To foster the popular & scientific study of nature; To preserve the natural environment; To act as a voice for people interested in the outdoors & natural history
Roger Turenne, President
Donald Himbeault, Executive Vice-President
Alain Louer, Secretary
Sean Worden, Treasurer
Susan McLarty, Office Administrator

Nature NB
#110, 924 Prospect St., Fredericton NB E3B 2T9
Tel: 506-459-4209; *Fax:* 506-459-4209
nbfn@nb.aibn.com
www.naturenb.ca
To preserve wildlife & protect its natural habitat; to promote a public interest in & a knowledge of natural history; to promote, encourage & cooperate with organizations & individuals who have similar interests & objectives; to consider matters of environmental concern.
Vanessa Roy-McDougall, Executive Director

Nature Nova Scotia (Federation of Nova Scotia Naturalists)
c/o Nova Scotia Museum of Natural History, 1747 Summer St., Halifax NS B3H 3A6
Tel: 902-582-7176
doug@fundymud.com
www.naturens.ca
To support the interests of naturalists clubs; To represent naturalists clubs throughout Nova Scotia
Bob Bancroft, President
Sue Abbot, Vice-President
Doug Linzey, Secretary
Jean Gibson, Treasurer

Nature Québec
#207, 870, av de Salaberry, Québec QC G1R 2T9
Tél: 418-648-2104; *Téléc:* 418-648-0991
conservons@naturequebec.org
www.naturequebec.org
Média social: www.facebook.com/167559993283868; twitter.com/NatureQuebec
Regrouper les individus et les sociétés oeuvrant en sciences naturelles et en environnement; maintenir des processus écologiques essentiels; préserver la diversité génétique; utiliser soutenablement des espèces et des écosystèmes
Christian Simard, Directeur général

Nature Saskatchewan
#206, 1860 Lorne St., Regina SK S4P 2L7
Tel: 306-780-9273; *Fax:* 306-780-9263
Toll-Free: 800-667-4668
info@naturesask.ca
www.naturesask.ca
Social Media: www.facebook.com/NatureSask; twitter.com/naturesask; www.linkedin.com/pub/nature-sask-gary-seib/38/7b6/39a
To foster appreciation & understanding for the natural environment; To document & protect the biological diversity of Saskatchewan; To preserve the natural eco-systems of the province
Gary Seib, General Manager
Deanna Trowsdale-Mutafov, Manager, Conservation & Education
Melissa Ranalli, Coordinator, Habitat Stewardship (Rare Plant Rescue)
Ellen Bouvier, Office Coordinator

Ontario Nature
#612, 214 King St West, Toronto ON M5H 3S6
Tel: 416-444-8419; *Fax:* 416-444-9866
Toll-Free: 800-440-2366
info@ontarionature.org
www.ontarionature.org
Social Media: www.facebook.com/OntarioNature?ref=ts; twitter.com/#!/ontarionature
To promote knowledge, understanding & respect for Ontario's natural heritage & commitment to its conservation & protection on the part of the FON membership, landowners, decision makers & the general public; To seek legislation, policies, practices & institutions which permanently protect Ontario's natural ecosystem & indigenous biodiversity, including the establishment of a comprehensive natural heritage system for Ontario with an enlarged system of parks & other protected areas linked by a network of existing & rehabilitated natural corridors
Brendon Larson, President
Caroline Schultz, Executive Director

Society of Canadian Ornithologists (SCO) / Société des ornithologistes du Canada (SOC)
a/s Thérèse Beaudet, SCO Membership Secretary, 1281, ch des Lièges, St-Jean de l'Ile d'Orléans QC G0A 3W0
beaudet.lamothe@sympatico.ca
www.sco-soc.ca
To support research to understand & conserve Canadian birds; To represent Canadian ornithologists
Erica Nol, President
Joe Nocera, Vice-President
Thérèse Beaudet, Membership Secretary
Pierre Lamothe, Treasurer

Nursing

Academy of Canadian Executive Nurses (ACEN)
c/o Association Strategy Group, #1, 136 Lewis St., Ottawa ON K2P 0S7
Tel: 613-235-3033; *Fax:* 613-233-6158
info@acen.ca
www.acen.ca
To advance nursing practice, education, research, & leadership; To work in partnership with other national organizations to influence health policy & set direction of healthcare in Canada to assure quality of care to Canadians
Noreen Linton, President
Marcia James, Admininistrative Coordinator

Association of Registered Nurses of Prince Edward Island (ARNPEI)
53 Grafton St., Charlottetown PE C1A 1K8
Tel: 902-368-3764; *Fax:* 902-628-1430
info@arnpei.ca
www.arnpei.ca
Professional Association for Registered Nurses in P.E.I.
Becky Gosbee, Executive Director
Paul Boudreau, Coordinator, Regulatory Services

British Columbia Nurses' Union (BCNU) / Syndicat des infirmières de la Colombie-Britannique
4060 Regent St., Burnaby BC V5C 6P5
Tel: 604-433-2268; *Fax:* 604-433-7945
Toll-Free: 800-663-9991
contactbcnu@bcnu.org
www.bcnu.org
Debra McPherson, Vice-President
Debra McPherson, President

Canadian Association for Nursing Research (CANR) / Association canadienne pour la recherche infirmière
c/o P. Petrucka, College of Nursing, University of Saskatchewan, 107 Wiggins Rd., Saskatoon SK S7N 5E5
Tel: 306-337-2228; *Fax:* 306-966-6221
pammla.petrucka@usask.ca
www.canr.ca
To foster practice-based nursing research & research-based nursing practice across Canada
Pamela Hawranik
Pammla Petrucka, Secretary
Riek van den Berg, Treasurer

Canadian Association for the History of Nursing (CAHN) / Association canadienne pour l'histoire du nursing
723 Colborne St., New Westminster BC V3L 5V6
www.cahn-achn.ca
To promote interest in the history of nursing; To develop scholarship in the field
Marion McKay, President
Beverley Hicks, Vice-President

Canadian Association of Burn Nurses (CABN) / Association canadienne des infirmières et infirmiers en soins aux brûlés
c/o Shannon Bonn, IWK Health Centre, PO Box 9700, 5850-5980 University Ave., Halifax NS B3K 6R8
shannon.bonn@iwk.nshealth.ca
www.cabn.ca
To provide education related to burn care; To research & develop national burn standards; To promote & support nurses & other care providers
Shannon Bonn, President
Amelia Potter, Vice-President
Judy Sleith, Treasurer

Canadian Association of Critical Care Nurses (CACCN) / Association canadienne des infirmières et infirmiers en soins de phase aiguë
PO Box 25322, London ON N6A 1X6
Tel: 519-649-5284; *Fax:* 519-649-1458
Toll-Free: 866-477-9077
caccn@caccn.ca
www.caccn.ca
To maintain & enhance the quality of patient & family centered care throughout Canada; To develop standards of critical care nursing practice
Cecilia St. George-Hyslop, President
Kate Mahon, Vice-President, Publications & Research
Pamela Cybulski, Secretary & Contact, Membership
Joanne Baird, Treasurer
Tricia Bray, Director, Awards & Corporate Sponsorship
Christine R. Halfkenny-Zellas, National Administrator

Canadian Association of Nephrology Nurses & Technologists (CANNT) / Association canadienne des infirmières et infirmiers et technologues de néphrologie (ACITN)
#322, 336 Yonge St., Barrie ON L4N 4C8
Tel: 705-720-2819; *Fax:* 705-720-1451
Toll-Free: 877-720-2819
cannt@cannt.ca
www.cannt.ca
To improve the care of renal patients through support of educational opportunities for association members; To evaluate the performance & competence of nephrology nurses & technologists against the CANNT Standards of Practice
Alison Thomas, President
Susan Placko, Treasurer & Coordinator, Website

Canadian Association of Neuroscience Nurses (CANN) / Association canadienne des infirmiers et infirmières en sciences neurologiques (ACIISN)
c/o Aline Mayer, Membership Chairperson, CANN, 30 Chantilly Gate, Stittsville ON K2S 2B1
canninfo@cann.ca; cjnn@cann.ca (Journal)
www.cann.ca
To prevent illness & to improve health outcomes for people with, or at risk for, neurological disorders; To establish standards of practice for neuroscience nurses
Sandra Bérubé, President
Deb Holtom, Vice-President & Secretary
Mark Bonin, Treasurer
Aline Mayer, Chair, Membership

Canadian Association of Nurses in AIDS Care (CANAC) / Association canadienne des infirmières et infirmiers en sidologie
PO Box 93, Pontypool ON L0A 1K0
info@canac.org
www.canac.org
The Canadian Association of Nurses in AIDS Care (CANAC) is a national professional nursing organization committed to fostering excellence in HIV/AIDS nursing, promoting the health, rights and dignity of persons affected by HIV/AIDS and to preventing the spread of HIV infection.
Jennifer Shaw, Executive Assistant

Canadian Association of Nurses in Oncology (CANO) / Association canadienne des infirmières en oncologie (ACIO)
#201, 375 West 5th Ave., Vancouver BC V5Y 1J6
Tel: 604-874-4322; *Fax:* 604-874-4378
cano@malachite-mgmt.com
www.cano-acio.ca
The organization advocates for improved cancer care for all Canadians.
Kim Chapman, President
Jeanne Robertson, Treasurer

Canadian Council of Cardiovascular Nurses (CCCN) / Conseil canadien des infirmières et infirmiers en nursing cardiovasculaire (CCINC)
#202, 300 March Rd., Ottawa ON K1P 5V9
Tel: 613-599-9210; *Fax:* 613-595-1155
info@cccn.ca
www.cccn.ca
Social Media: www.facebook.com/group.php?gid=136766926352459
To promote & maintain high standards of cardiovascular nursing through education, research, health promotion, strategic alliances, & advocacy
Wes Clark, Executive Director
Jocelyn Reimer-Kent, President
Sandra Lauck, Sec.-Treas.

Canadian Council of Practical Nurse Regulators (CCPNR)
c/o College Of LPN's of Alberta (CLPNA), #13163, 143 St., Edmonton AB T5L 4S8
Tel: 780-484-8886; *Fax:* 780-484-9069
chair@ccpnr.ca
www.ccpnr.ca
Responsible for the safety of the public through the regulation of Licensed/Registered Practical Nurses.
Linda Stranger, Chair

Canadian Federation of Mental Health Nurses (CFMHN) / Fédération canadienne des infirmières et infirmiers en santé mentale
#109, 1 Concorde Gate, Toronto ON M3C 3N6
Tel: 416-426-7029; *Fax:* 416-426-7280
info@cfmhn.ca
www.cfmhn.ca
The CFMHN is a national voice for psychiatric and mental health (PMH) nursing. They wish to assure leadership in the development and application of nursing standards that inform and affect psychiatric and mental health nursing practice; examine and influence government policy, and address national issues related to mental health and mental illness; communicate and collaborate with national and international groups that share our professional interests; faciliate excellence in psychiatric and mental health nursing by providing members with educational and networking resources.
Chris Davis, President

Canadian Gerontological Nursing Association (CGNA) / Association canadienne des infirmières et infirmiers en gérontologie
c/o Membership, #370, 101-1001 West Broadway, Vancouver BC V6H 4E4
cgna@cgna.net
www.cgna.net
To promote high standards of gerontological nursing practice; to promote educational programs in gerontological nursing; to participate in affairs which promote the health of elderly persons; to promote networking opportunities for nurses; to promote & disseminate gerontological nursing research; to present the views of the Association to government, education, professional & other appropriate bodies.
Beverly Laurila, President

Canadian Holistic Nurses Association (CHNA) / Association canadienne des infirmières en soins holistiques
c/o Marie Knapp, RR#7, Owen Sound ON N4K 6V5
Tel: 519-371-1255
info@chna.ca
www.chna.ca
To further the development of holistic nursing practice; To promote CHNA standards of practice
Marie Knapp, President
Michele Bourgeois, Secretary

Canadian Nurses Association (CNA) / Association des infirmières et infirmiers du Canada
50 Driveway, Ottawa ON K2P 1E2
Tel: 613-237-2133; *Fax:* 613-237-3520
Toll-Free: 800-361-8404
info@cna-aiic.ca; executiveoffice@cna-aiic.ca; media@cna-aiic.ca
www.cna-aiic.ca
Social Media: www.facebook.com/CNA.AIIC; twitter.com/canadanurses; www.youtube.com/user/CNAVideos; www.flickr.com/photos/cma-amc/sets
To advance the discipline of nursing; to advocate for public policy that incorporates the principles of primary health care & respects the principles, conditions & spirit of the Canada Health Act; To advance the regulation of Registered Nurses in the interest of the public; To advance international health policy & development in Canada
Judith Shamian, President
Barbara L. Mildon, President Elect
Rachel Bard, CEO
Anne Sutherland Boal, Chief Operating Officer

Canadian Nurses Foundation (CNF) / Fondation des infirmières et infirmiers du Canada
50 Driveway, Ottawa ON K2P 1E2
Tel: 613-237-2133; *Fax:* 613-237-3520
Toll-Free: 800-361-8404
info@cnf-fiic.ca
www.cnf-fiic.ca
CNF promotes the health of Canadians by enhancing nursing education & research.
Hélène Sabourin, Executive Director
Jonelle Istead, Director, Fundraising

Canadian Nurses Protective Society (CNPS) / Société de protection des infirmières et infirmiers du Canada (SPIIC)
50 Driveway, Ottawa ON K2P 1E2
Tel: 613-237-2092; *Fax:* 613-237-6300
Toll-Free: 800-267-3390
info@cnps.ca
www.cnps.ca
To offer legal liability protection related to nursing practice to eligible Registered Nurses

Canadian Occupational Health Nurses Association (COHNA) / Association canadienne des infirmières et infirmiers en santé du travail (ACIIST)
karen.mazerolle@imperialgroup.ca
www.cohna-aciist.ca
To promote national standards for occupational health nursing practice; to advance the profession by providing a national forum for the exchange of ideas & concerns; to enhance the profile of occupational health nurses; to improve the health & safety of workers; to contribute to the health of the community by providing quality health services to workers; to encourage continuing education
Karen Mazerolle, President
Marg Creen, Secretary/Treasurer
Ellen Coe, Vice President

Canadian Orthopaedic Nurses Association (CONA) / Association canadienne des infirmières et infirmiers en orthopédie
2035 Rosealle In, West Kelowna BC V1Z 3Z5
Tel: 250-769-3640
www.cona-nurse.org
To foster professional growth of the membership in the assessment, treatment & rehabilitation of individuals with neuromuscular & skeletal alterations; to promote nursing research related to orthopaedics
Deb McCullough, President

Canadian Vascular Access Association (CVAA) / Association canadienne d'Accès Vasculaire
PO Box 66572, 685 McCowan Rd., Toronto ON M1J 3N8
Tel: 416-696-7761; *Fax:* 416-696-8437
www.cvaa.info
To establish & promote standards of intravenous therapy to enhance patient care & safety
Diane Sharp, President
Michele Bellows, Vice-President & Secretary

The College & Association of Registered Nurses of Alberta (CARNA)
11620 - 168 St., Edmonton AB T5M 4A6
Tel: 780-451-0043; *Fax:* 780-452-3276
Toll-Free: 800-252-9392
carna@nurses.ab.ca
www.nurses.ab.ca
To set nursing practice standards & to ensure Albertans receive safe, competent, & ethical nursing services
Joan Petruk, President

College of Licensed Practical Nurses of Alberta (CLPNA)
13163 - 146 St., Edmonton AB T5L 4S8
Tel: 780-484-8886; *Fax:* 780-484-9069
Toll-Free: 800-661-5877
info@clpna.com
www.clpna.com
To regulate & lead the profession in a manner that protects & serves the public through excellence in Practical Nursing.
Linda L. Stanger, Executive Director/Registrar

College of Licensed Practical Nurses of BC (CLPNBC)
#260, 3480 Gilmore Way, Burnaby BC V5G 4Y1
Tel: 778-373-3100; *Fax:* 778-373-3102
Toll-Free: 877-373-2201
info@clpnbc.org; executivedirector@clpnbc.org
www.clpnbc.org
To regulate practical nursing in the public interest

College of Licensed Practical Nurses of Manitoba (CLPNM)
463 St. Anne's Rd., Winnipeg MB R2M 3C9
Tel: 204-663-1212; *Fax:* 204-663-1207
Toll-Free: 877-663-1212
info@clpnm.ca
www.clpnm.ca
The governing body for the Licensed Practical Nurses in Manitoba. The College's duty is to carry out its activities and govern its members in a manner that serves and protects the public interest. The College establishes requirements to enter the profession and assures the quality of the practice of LPNs through the development and enforcement of standards and practice and continuing competence programs.
Verna Holgate, Executive Director

College of Licensed Practical Nurses of Newfoundland & Labrador
9 Paton St., St. John's NL A1B 4S8
Tel: 709-579-3843; *Fax:* 709-579-8268
Toll-Free: 888-579-2576
info@clpnnl.ca
www.clpnnl.ca
The College for Licensed Practical Nurses of Newfoundland and Labrador (CLPNNL), in accordance with the Licensed Practical Nurses' Act, has the legislative responsibility for regulating the practice of Licensed Practical Nurses in NFLD. The mission of CLPNNL is to promote safety and protection of the general public through the provision of safe, competent and ethical nursing care.
Paul D. Fisher, Executive Director/Registrar

College of Licensed Practical Nurses of Nova Scotia (CLPNNS)
Cogswell Tower, #1212, 2000 Barrington St., Halifax NS B3J 3K1
Tel: 902-423-8517; *Fax:* 902-425-6811
info@clpnns.ca
www.clpnns.ca
To represent licensed practical nurses within the health care system; to protect the public by providing safe, competent nursing care.
Ann Mann, Executive Director/Registrar

College of Nurses of Ontario (CNO) / Ordre des infirmières et infirmiers de l'Ontario
101 Davenport Rd., Toronto ON M5R 3P1
Tel: 416-928-0900; *Fax:* 416-928-6507
Toll-Free: 800-387-5526
cno@cnomail.org
www.cno.org
To protect the public's right to quality nursing services by providing leadership to the nursing profession in self-regulation
Anne Coghlan, Executive Director

College of Registered Nurses of British Columbia (CRNBC)
2855 Arbutus St., Vancouver BC V6J 3Y8
Tel: 604-736-7331; *Fax:* 604-738-2272
Toll-Free: 800-565-6505
info@crnbc.ca
www.crnbc.ca
To provide safe & appropriate nursing practice regulated by nurses in the public interest; To promote good practice, prevent poor practice & intervene when practice is unacceptable
Laurel Brunke, CEO
Val Cartmel, President
Laurel Brunke, Executive Director

College of Registered Nurses of Manitoba (CRNM)
890 Pembina Hwy., Winnipeg MB R3M 2M8
Tel: 204-774-3477; *Fax:* 204-775-6052
Toll-Free: 800-665-2027
info@crnm.mb.ca
www.crnm.mb.ca
To regulate the practice of registered nurses & to advance the quality of nursing to protect the public interest
Kathy Doerksen, President
Susan D. Neilson, Executive Director
Glenn Hildebrand, Director, Communications, Member & Government Relations

College of Registered Nurses of Nova Scotia (CRNNS)
#4005, 7071 Bayers Rd., Halifax NS B3L 2C2
Tel: 902-491-9744; *Fax:* 902-491-9510
Toll-Free: 800-565-9744
info@crnns.ca
www.crnns.ca
Registered nurses regulating their profession to promote excellence in nursing practice.
Donna Denney, Executive Director

College of Registered Psychiatric Nurses of Alberta
#201, 9711 - 45 Ave., Edmonton AB T6E 5V8
Tel: 780-434-7666; *Fax:* 780-436-4165
Toll-Free: 877-234-7666
crpna@crpna.ab.ca
www.crpna.ab.ca
The mission of CRPNA is to; protect and servce the public interest by ensuring members provide safe, competent and ethical practice; address the needs of members and the public through education, regulation, advocacy.
Pamela Gulay, President

College of Registered Psychiatric Nurses of British Columbia
#307, 2502 St. Johns St., Port Moody BC V3H 2B4
Tel: 604-931-5200; *Fax:* 604-931-5277
Toll-Free: 800-565-2505
www.crpnbc.ca
To serve & protect the public; to assure a safe, accountable & ethical level of psychiatric nursing practice
Dorothy Jennings, Chair
Kyong-ae Kim, Executive Director & Registrar

College of Registered Psychiatric Nurses of Manitoba (CRPNM)
1854 Portage Ave., Winnipeg MB R3J 0G9
Tel: 204-888-4841; *Fax:* 204-888-8638
www.crpnm.mb.ca
To ensure that members of the profession provide safe & effective psychiatric nursing services to the public of Manitoba, in accordance with the Registered Psychiatric Nurses Act
Laura Panteluk, Executive Director

Community Health Nurses of Canada (CHNC) / Infirmières et infirmiers en santé communautaire au Canada
182 Clendenan Ave., Toronto ON M6P 2X2
Tel: 647-239-9554; *Fax:* 416-426-7280
info@chnc.ca
www.chnc.ca
To act as the voice of community health nurses across Canada; To respond to issues which affect community health nurses
Kate Thompson, President
Evelyn Butler, Administrative Manager
Ruth Schofield, Secretary
Anne Clarotto, Treasurer
Yvette Laforet-Fliesser, Officer, Communications

Fédération interprofessionnelle de la santé du Québec (FIQ)
1234, av Papineau, Montréal QC H2K 0A4
Tél: 514-987-1141; *Téléc:* 514-987-7273
Ligne sans frais: 800-363-6541
info@fiqsante.qc.ca
www.fiqsante.qc.ca
Média social: www.facebook.com/FIQSante; WWW.twitter.com/FIQSante
Améliorer les conditions de travail des infirmières, infirmiers & cardiorespiratoires; s'associer aux luttes des femmes et être présente dans les débats concernant les orientations du système de santé
Régine Laurent, présidente
Lina Bonamie, Présidente

Gerontological Nursing Association of Ontario (GNA)
PO Box 368, Stn. K, Toronto ON M4P 2G7
info@gnaontario.org
www.gnaontario.org
To promote a high standard of nursing care & related health services for older adults; To enhance professionalism in the practice of gerontological nursing
Lori Schindel Martin, President
Gwen Harris, Treasurer

Licensed Practical Nurses Association & Regulatory Board of PEI
PO Box 20058, 161 St. Peter's Rd., Charlottetown PE C1A 9E1
Tel: 902-566-1512; *Fax:* 902-892-6315
info@lpna.ca
www.lpna.ca
To represent practical nurses within the health care system
Genevieve Poole, Registrar

Manitoba Nurses' Union (MNU) / Syndicat des infirmières du Manitoba
#301, 275 Broadway, Winnipeg MB R3C 4M6
Tel: 204-942-1320; *Fax:* 204-942-0958
Toll-Free: 800-665-0043
www.nursesunion.mb.ca
To represent & support all categories of licensed nurses in Manitoba; To safeguard the role of nurses in the health care system of Manitoba
Sandi Mowat, President
Donna MacKenzie, Vice President
Holly Cadieux, Sec.-Treas.
Janice Grift, Director, Operations

National Emergency Nurses Affiliation (NENA) / Affiliation des infirmières et infirmiers d'urgence
112 Old River Rd., RR#2, Mallorytown ON K0E 1R0
www.nena.ca
To represent the Canadian emergency nursing specialty.
Landon James, President

New Brunswick Nurses Union (NBNU) / Syndicat des infirmières et infirmiers du Nouveau-Brunswick (SIINB)
103 Woodside Lane, Fredericton NB E3C 2R9
Tel: 506-453-0820; *Fax:* 506-453-0828
Toll-Free: 800-442-4914
www.nbnu-siinb.nb.ca
The New Brunswick Nurses Union is a labour organization for nurses employed in the province. It is an open and democratic organization which promotes the participation of the maximum number of members in decision-making. Their mission is to enhance the social, economic, and general worklife of nurses and their vision is NBNU as a professional, credible, and respected voice advocating for nurses and quality health care.
David Brown, Executive Director
Marilyn Quinn, President

Newfoundland & Labrador Nurses' Union (NLNU) / Syndicat des infirmières de Terre-Neuve et du Labrador
PO Box 416, Stn. C, 229 Major's Path, St. John's NL A1C 5J9
Tel: 709-753-9961; *Fax:* 709-753-1210
Toll-Free: 800-563-5100
info@nlnu.ca
www.nlnu.ca
John Vivian, Executive Director
Karyn Murphy, Communications Specialist

Nova Scotia Nurses' Union (NSNU)
30 Frazee Ave., Dartmouth NS B3B 1X4
Tel: 902-469-1474; *Fax:* 902-466-6935
Toll-Free: 800-469-1474
www.nsnu.ns.ca
The NSNU represents Registered Nurses and Licensed Practical Nurses working in acute and long term care, with the VON and Canadian Blood Services
Jean Candy, Executive Director
Janet Hazelton, President

Nurses Association of New Brunswick (NANB) / Association des infirmières et infirmiers du Nouveau-Brunswick (AIINB)
165 Regent St., Fredericton NB E3B 7B4
Tel: 506-458-8731; *Fax:* 506-459-2838
Toll-Free: 800-442-4417
www.nanb.nb.ca
To act as the professional voice & regulatory body of nursing in New Brunswick; To protect the public by maintaining standards for nursing education & practice
France Marquis, President

Ontario Nurses' Association (ONA) / Association des infirmières et infirmiers de l'Ontario
#400, 85 Grenville St., Toronto ON M5S 3A2
Tel: 416-964-8833; *Fax:* 416-964-8864
Toll-Free: 800-387-5580
onamail@ona.org
www.ona.org
Social Media: www.facebook.com/OntarioNurses; twitter.com/ontarionurses
To improve the socio-economic welfare of members
Linda Haslam-Stroud, President
Linda Haslam-Stroud, President

Operating Room Nurses Association of Canada (ORNAC) / Association des infirmières et infirmiers de salles d'opération du Canada

Tel: 604-466-7965
info@ornac.ca
www.ornac.ca
To promote operating nursing for the betterment of surgical patient care
Karen Frenette, President
Alaine Young, Treasurer

Ordre des infirmières et infirmiers auxiliaires du Québec (OIIAQ)
531, rue Sherbrooke est, Montréal QC H2L 1K2
Tél: 514-282-9511; *Téléc:* 514-282-0631
Ligne sans frais: 800-283-9511
oiiaq@oiiaq.org
www.oiiaq.org
Favoriser le développement professionnel des infirmières et infirmiers auxiliaires du Québec pour viser l'excellence dans l'exercice professionnel et tendre à une plus grande humanisation des soins
Jacques Gaulin, Président

Ordre des infirmières et infirmiers du Québec (OIIQ)
4200, boul Dorchester ouest, Westmount QC H3Z 1V4
Tél: 514-935-2501; *Téléc:* 514-935-1799
Ligne sans frais: 800-363-6048
inf@oiiq.org
www.oiiq.org
Média social: www.facebook.com/Ordre.infirmieres.infirmiers.Quebec; twitter.com/OIIQ
Assurer la protection du public; contrôler l'exercice de la profession par ses membres
Gyslaine Desrosiers, Présidente
Lise Racette, Vice-présidente
Claudia Gallant, Administratrice

Practical Nurses Canada
#255, 55 St. Clair Ave. West, Toronto ON M1E 4X9
Tel: 416-922-5968; *Fax:* 416-967-6320
Toll-Free: 866-454-5968
info@pncanada.ca
www.pncanada.ca
To promote competent, safe, holistic practical nursing care throughout Canada
Linda Gould, President
Barbara Boudreau, Vice-President
Sue O'Hare, Treasurer

Practical Nurses Federation of Ontario (PFNO)
Building 4, #200, 5025 Orbitor Dr., Mississauga ON L4W 4Y5
Tel: 905-602-6705; *Fax:* 905-602-4666
To conduct the business of a trade union, representing registered practical nurses in Ontario; To improve the working conditions of registered practical nurses throughout the province

Prince Edward Island Nurses' Union (PEINU) / Syndicat des infirmières de l'Île-du-Prince-Édouard
10 Paramount Dr., Charlottetown PE C1E 0C7
Tel: 902-892-7152; *Fax:* 902-892-9324
Toll-Free: 866-892-7152
office@peinu.com
www.peinu.com
To regulate employment relations between nurses & employers through collective bargaining & negotiation of written contracts with employers implementing progressively better conditions of employment
Mona O'Shea, President

Registered Nurses Association of Ontario (RNAO) / L'Association des infirmières et infirmiers autorisés de l'Ontario
158 Pearl St., Toronto ON M5H 1L3
Tel: 416-599-1925; *Fax:* 416-599-1926
Toll-Free: 800-268-7199
info@rnao.org
www.rnao.org
Social Media: www.facebook.com/group.php?gid=30442334943; twitter.com/rnao
To promote excellence in nursing practice; Ro advocate the role of nursing in empowering the people of Ontario to achieve & maintain their optimal health; To provide membership-centred services
David McNeil, President
Doris Grinspun, Executive Director

The Registered Nurses Association of the Northwest Territories & Nunavut (RNANT/NU)
PO Box 2757, Yellowknife NT X1A 2R1
Tel: 867-873-2745; *Fax:* 867-873-2336
admin@rnantnu.ca
www.rnantnu.ca
To promote & ensure competent nursing practice for the people of the NWT
Barb Round, Executive Director/Registrar/PR Cou

Registered Practical Nurses Association of Ontario (RPNAO)
Bldg. 4, #200, 5025 Orbitor Dr., Mississauga ON L4W 4Y5
Tel: 905-602-4664; *Fax:* 905-602-4666
Toll-Free: 877-602-4664
info@rpnao.org
www.rpnao.org
Social Media: www.facebook.com/group.php?gid=131233263620139; twitter.com/rpnao
Dedicated to decisions that enhance professional practical nursing
Dianne Martin, Executive Director
Beth McCracken, Director, Recruitment & Professional Practice
Linda Gould, President

Registered Psychiatric Nurses Association of Saskatchewan (RPNAS)
2055 Lorne St., Regina SK S4P 2M4
Tel: 306-586-4617; *Fax:* 306-586-6000
karen@rpnas.com
www.rpnas.com
To regulate psychiatric nursing as a distinct profession
Mary K. Renwick, President
Robert Allen, Executive Director

Saskatchewan Association of Licensed Practical Nurses (SALPN)
#700A, 4400 - 4th Ave., Regina SK S4T 0H8
Tel: 306-525-1436; *Fax:* 306-347-7784
Toll-Free: 888-257-2576
lpnadmin@salpn.com (general); praccon@salpn.com (practice)
www.salpn.com
To regulate Licensed Practical Nurses (LPNs) in Saskatchewan, in order to ensure public safety; To ensure that Saskatchewan's Licensed Practical Nurses provide professional nursing care; To maintain an efficient investigation & disciplinary process
Colin Hein, Executive Director
Kim Kehrig, President
Cara Brewster, Registrar
Bonnie Downes, Assistant Registrar
Della Bartzen, Investigator

Saskatchewan Registered Nurses' Association (SRNA)
2066 Retallack St., Regina SK S4T 7X5
Tel: 306-359-4200; *Fax:* 306-525-0849
Toll-Free: 800-667-9945
info@srna.org; SRNAnewsbulletin@srna.org; register@srna.org
www.srna.org
To ensure competent, knowledge-based, & ethical nursing in Saskatchewan, for the protection of the public; To establish registration & licensure requirements
David Kline, President
Karen Eisler, Executive Director

Saskatchewan Union of Nurses (SUN) / Syndicat des infirmières de la Saskatchewan
2330 - 2nd Ave., Regina SK S4R 1A6
Tel: 306-525-1666; *Fax:* 306-522-4612
Toll-Free: 800-667-7060
regina@sun-nurses.sk.ca
www.sun-nurses.sk.ca
To advocate to protect the rights of members; to enhance the socio-economic & general welfare of members through collective bargaining, research, & education
Rosalee Longmoore, President

Union of Psychiatric Nurses / Syndicat des infirmières psychiatriques
#200, 508 Clarke Rd., Coquitlam BC V3J 3X2
Tel: 604-931-2471; *Fax:* 604-931-1070
Toll-Free: 877-931-2471
dmclaren@telus.net
www.upnbc.org
Sherry Moller, President
Philip Oosterman, Director, Operations & Membership Services

Union québécoise des infirmières et infirmiers (UQII) / Québec Union of Nurses
9405, rue Sherbrooke est, Montréal QC H1L 6P3
Tél: 514-356-8888; *Téléc:* 514-356-9999
uqii@csq.qc.net
L'UQII assure la représentation de ses membres, donne aux syndicats une structure politique et fournit, en collaboration avec la CSQ, des services aux membres en matière de relations de travail, de professionnel, de négociation et de formation
Monique Bélanger, Présidente

United Nurses of Alberta (UNA) / Infirmières unies de l'Alberta
700-11150 Jasper Ave., Edmonton AB T5K 0L1
Tel: 780-425-1025; *Fax:* 780-426-2093
Toll-Free: 800-252-9394
provincialoffice@una.ab.ca
www.una.ab.ca
Social Media: www.facebook.com/UnitedNurses; twitter.com/unitednurses; www.youtube.com/user/UnitedNursesAlberta
To advance the social, economic & general welfare of nurses & other allied personnel
Heather Smith, President

Victorian Order of Nurses for Canada (VON Canada) / Infirmières de l'Ordre de Victoria du Canada
110 Argyle Ave., Ottawa ON K2P 1B4
Tel: 613-233-5694; *Fax:* 613-230-4376
Toll-Free: 888-866-2273
national@von.ca
www.von.ca
VON is dedicated to being a leader in the delivery of innovative comprehensive health & social services & to influencing the development of health & social policy in Canada; to meet rapidly changing social & external challenges; VON is accredited by Canadian Council on Health Services Accreditation
Judith Shamian, President & CEO
Diane McLeod, Executive Vice President

Yukon Registered Nurses Association (YRNA)
#204, 4133 - 4th Ave., Whitehorse YT Y1A 1H8
Tel: 867-667-4062; *Fax:* 867-668-5123
www.yrna.ca
YRNA is the regulatory body and professional association for registered nurses in the Yukon. YRNA is responsible for establishing and promoting standards of practice for registered nurses, for regulating nursing practice and for advancing professional excellence. YRNA speaks out on health care issues, advocating for the development of healthy public policy in the interest of the public.
Patricia McGarr, Executive Director
Peggy Heynen, President

Oil

Enform: The Safety Association for the Upstream Oil & Gas Industry
Head Office, 5055 - 11th St. NE, Calgary AB T2E 8N4
Tel: 403-516-8000; *Fax:* 403-516-8166
Toll-Free: 800-667-5557
customerservice@enform.ca
www.enform.ca
To improve the Canadian upstream oil & gas industry's safety performance; To prevent work-related injuries in the upstream oil & gas industry in Canada
Duane Mather, Chair
Wallace E. Baer, President
L. Harman, Vice President, Operations
R. Ogilvie, Vice President, Corporate Services

Packaging

Packaging Association of Canada (PAC) / Association canadienne de l'emballage
#607, 1 Concorde Gate, Toronto ON M3C 3N6
Tel: 416-490-7860; *Fax:* 416-490-7844
pacinfo@pac.ca
www.pac.ca
To represent both users & suppliers on the strength of environmental & economic policy
James D. Downham, President & CEO
Jan McCallum, Communications Director

Paper Packaging Canada
#3, 1995 Clark Blvd., Brampton ON L6T 4W1
Tel: 905-458-1247; *Fax:* 905-458-2052
info@paperpackaging.ca
www.paperpackaging.ca
The association represents containerboard mill sites, corrugator plants, sheet plants and related industries; works together with other players in the paper industry to develop an agenda of common concerns and issues.
John Mullinder, President & CEO

Patents & Copyright

Access Copyright
#800, One Yonge St., Toronto ON M5E 1E5
Tel: 416-868-1620; *Fax:* 416-868-1621
Toll-Free: 800-893-5777
info@accesscopyright.ca
www.accesscopyright.ca
To licence copyright users who wish to reproduce copyright-protected works; to collect a fee for this service & to distribute royalties to the copyright owners whose works have been copied; to provide protection for copyright owners as well as legal access to published works for copyright users
Maureen Cavan, Executive Director
Brian O'Donnell, Director, Business Development
Roanie Levy, Director, Legal & External Affairs

Canadian Copyright Institute (CCI)
#107, 192 Spadina Ave., Toronto ON M5T 2C2
Tel: 416-975-1756; *Fax:* 416-975-1839
info@thecci.ca
www.canadiancopyrightinstitute.ca
To encourage a better understanding of the law of copyright on the part of members, public & users of copyright material; To engage in & foster research in copyright law
Anne McClelland, Administrator

Canadian Musical Reproduction Rights Agency (CMRRA) / Agence canadienne des droits de production musicaux limitée
#320, 56 Wellesley St. West, Toronto ON M5S 2S3
Tel: 416-926-1966; *Fax:* 416-926-7521
inquiries@cmrra.ca
www.cmrra.ca
Represents the majority of music publishers & copyright owners doing business in Canada; on their behalf, issues licences & collects royalties for the reproduction of copyrighted musical works on CDs, cassettes & other sound carriers, & in films, TV programs & advertising; owned by the Canadian Music Publishers Association
David A. Basskin, President
Fred Merritt, Vice-President, Finance & Administration

Copyright Collective of Canada (CCC) / Société de perception de droit d'auteur du Canada (SPDAC)
#1603, 22 St. Clair Ave. East, Toronto ON M4T 2S3
Tel: 416-961-1888; *Fax:* 416-968-1016
speacock@ccofcan.org
The Copyright Collective of Canada represents owners (producers and distributors) of the U.S. independent motion picture and television production industry for all drama and comedy programming (such as companies represented by the Motion Picture Association of America), except for that carried on the PBS network stations.
Susan Peacock, Vice-President

Intellectual Property Institute of Canada (IPIC) / Institut de la Propriété Intellectuelle du Canada (IPIC)
#606, 60 Queen St., Ottawa ON K1P 5Y7
Tel: 613-234-0516; *Fax:* 613-234-0671
info@ipic.ca
www.ipic.ca
To promote the protection of intellectual property in Canada & abroad in order to enhance Canada's economic prospects as a sovereign nation & to foster cooperation between Canada & its trading partners around the world.

Society of Composers, Authors & Music Publishers of Canada (SOCAN) / Société canadienne des auteurs, compositeurs et éditeurs de musique
41 Valleybrook Dr., Toronto ON M3B 2S6
Tel: 416-445-8700; *Fax:* 416-445-7108
Toll-Free: 800-557-6226
socan@socan.ca
www.socan.ca
Social Media: www.facebook.com/SOCANmusic; twitter.com/SOCANmusic; www.youtube.com/SOCANmusic
SOCAN is the Canadian copyright collective that administers the performing rights of members & of affiliated international organizations by licensing the use of music in Canada
David Wood, CFO
Jennifer Brown, Vice-President, Licensing
C. Paul Spurgeon, Vice-President, Legal Services & General Counsel
Janice Scott, Vice-President, Information Technology
Randy Wark, CAO/Vice-President, Human Resources
France Lafleur, Vice-President, Member Operations
Eric Baptiste, CEO

Pharmaceutical

Alberta College of Pharmacists (ACP)
#1100, 8215 - 112 St. NW, Edmonton AB T6G 2C8
Tel: 780-990-0321; *Fax:* 780-990-0328
Toll-Free: 877-227-3838
acpinfo@pharmacists.ab.ca
www.pharmacists.ab.ca
Greg Eberhart, Registrar

Association of Faculties of Pharmacy of Canada (AFPC) / Association des facultés de pharmacie du Canada
14612 - 64 Ave., Edmonton AB T6H 1T8
Tel: 780-868-5530
www.afpc.info
To develop & implement policies & programs which will provide a forum for exchange of ideas, ensure a liaison with other organizations; to foster & promote excellence in pharmaceutical education & research in Canada
Harold Lopatka, Executive Director

Association professionnelle des pharmaciens salariés du Québec (APPSQ)
3560, rue la Verendrye, Sherbrooke QC J1L 1Z6
Tél: 819-563-6464; *Téléc:* 819-563-6464
appsq@hotmail.com
Syndicat professionnel voué à la défense des intérêts des pharmaciens salariés du Québec
Denis Godin, Président

Association québécoise des pharmaciens propriétaires (AQPP) / Québec Association of Pharmacy Owners
4378, av Pierre-de Coubertin, Montréal QC H1V 1A6
Tél: 514-254-0676; *Téléc:* 514-254-1288
Ligne sans frais: 800-361-7765
info@aqpp.qc.ca
www.aqpp.qc.ca
Assure l'étude, la défense et le développement des intérêts économiques, sociaux et professionnels de ses membres.
Normand Cadieux, Directeur général

British Columbia Pharmacy Association (BCPhA)
#1530, 1200 West 73rd Ave., Vancouver BC V6P 6G5
Tel: 604-261-2092; *Fax:* 604-261-2097
Toll-Free: 800-663-2840
info@bcpharmacy.ca
www.bcpharmacy.ca
To support & advance the economic & professional well-being of members, with the goal that they will provide improved health care in British Columbia
Marnie Mitchell, Chief Executive Officer
Parkash Ragsdale, Deputy Chief Executive Officer & Director, Professional Services
Kate Hunter, Director, Communications
Cyril Lopez, Director, Member & Corporate Services

Canada's Research-Based Pharmaceutical Companies (Rx&D) / Les companies de recherche pharmaceutique du Canada
#1220, 55 Metcalfe St., Ottawa ON K1P 6L5
Tel: 613-236-0455; *Toll-Free:* 800-363-0203
info@canadapharma.org
www.canadapharma.org
To discover new medicines that improve the quality of health care available for every Canadian
Philip Blake, Chair
Russell Williams, President

Canadian Association for Pharmacy Distribution Management (CAPDM) / Association canadienne de la gestion de l'approvisionnement pharmaceutique (ACGAP)
#301A, 3800 Steeles Ave. West, Woodbridge ON L4L 4G9
Tel: 905-265-1706; *Fax:* 905-265-9372
www.capdm.ca
Social Media: www.facebook.com/group.php?gid=182173808506667
To act as a resource & an advocacy voice for its members to advance the pharmacy distribution system as an effective, efficient, & safe delivery system for patient health care in Canada
Brent Teulon, Chair
David W. Johnston, President & CEO
Allan Reynolds, Vice-President, Industry & Member Relations
Allison Chan, Manager, Member Services & Events

Canadian Association of Pharmacy Students & Interns (CAPSI) / Association canadienne des étudiants et internes en pharmacie (ACEIP)
PO Box 68552, 360A Bloor St. West, Toronto ON M5S 1X0
president@capsi.ca
www.capsi.ca
To prepare members for moral, social, ethical obligations to be upheld in the profession of pharmacy; to promote high standards of pharmacy education throughout Canada; to promote means by which members may enhance their professional knowledge & skills; to promote mutual interests & liaison with international pharmacy students, interns & society at large
Brad Elliott, President

Canadian Association of Pharmacy Technicians (CAPT)
#164, 9-6975 Meadowvale Town Centre Circle, Mississauga ON L5N 2V7
Tel: 416-410-1142
info@capt.ca; members@capt.ca
www.capt.ca
To act as the voice of pharmacy assistants
Mary Bozoian, President
Robert Solek, Vice-President
Colleen Norris, Director, Membership
Cathy Schuster, Director, Promotions & Public Relations
Angela Silva, Director, Administration

The Canadian Council for Accreditation of Pharmacy Programs (CCAPP) / Le Conseil canadien de l'agrément des programmes de pharmacie
#1207 - 144 College St., Toronto BC M5S 3M2
Tel: 416-746-5055; *Fax:* 416-978-8511
ccappinfo@phm.utoronto.ca
www.ccapp-accredit.ca
To assess the quality of professional pharmacy degree programs in Canadian universities; to promote the continued improvement of such programs
David Hill, Executive Director

The Canadian Council on Continuing Education in Pharmacy (CCCEP) / Le conseil canadien de l'éducation permanente en pharmacie
#102, 4010 Pasqua St., Regina SK S4S 7B9
Tel: 306-545-7790; *Fax:* 306-545-7795
info@cccep.ca; admin.assistant@cccep.ca
www.cccep.ca
To act as the national coordinating & accrediting body for continuing education in pharmacy in Canada; To enhance the quality of continuing pharmacy education; To advance pharmacy practice
Arthur Whetstone, Executive Director
Anick Minville, President
Bev Zwicker, Vice-President

Canadian Foundation for Pharmacy (CFP) / Fondation canadienne pour la pharmacie
5809 Fieldon Rd., Mississauga ON L5M 5K1
Tel: 905-997-3238; *Fax:* 905-997-4264
www.cfpnet.ca
To provide programs for the advancement of the pharmacy profession in Canada
Ryan D. Itterman, President
Dayle Acorn, Executive Director

Canadian Generic Pharmaceutical Association (CGPA) / L'Association canadienne du médicament générique (ACMG)
#409, 4120 Yonge St., Toronto ON M2P 2B8
Tel: 416-223-2333; *Fax:* 416-223-2425
info@canadiangenerics.ca
www.canadiangenerics.ca
Social Media: www.facebook.com/CanadianGenerics; twitter.com/CdnGenerics
To promote an environment which supports & enhances the provision of affordable generic & innovative medications to Canadians & patients around the world through research, development & manufacturing of pharmaceuticals & fine chemicals in Canada
Jeff Connell, Director, Public Affairs

Canadian Pharmacists Association (CPhA) / Association des pharmaciens du Canada
1785 Alta Vista Dr., Ottawa ON K1G 3Y6
Tel: 613-523-7877; *Fax:* 613-523-0445
Toll-Free: 800-917-9489
info@pharmacists.ca; members@pharmacists.ca
www.pharmacists.ca
Social Media: twitter.com/CPhAAPhC
To advance the profession of pharmacy to contribute to the health of Canadians; To represent & support pharmacists across Canada

Jeff Poston, Executive Director
Ackerman Ruth, President

Canadian Society of Hospital Pharmacists (CSHP) / Société canadienne des pharmaciens d'hôpitaux
#3, 30 Concourse Gate, Ottawa ON K2E 7V7
Tel: 613-736-9733; *Fax:* 613-736-5660
info@cshp.ca
www.cshp.ca
To advance safe, effective medication use & patient care in hospitals & related health care settings throughout Canada; To act as an influential voice for hospital pharmacy; To encourge professional growth & practice excellence
Myrella Roy, Executive Director
Desarae Davidson, Administrator, Conferences
Colleen Drake, Administrator, Publications
Anna Dudek, Administrator, Finance
Robyn Rockwell, Administrator, Membership

College of Pharmacists of British Columbia
#200, 1765 - 8 Ave. West, Vancouver BC V6J 5C6
Tel: 604-733-2440; *Fax:* 604-733-2493
Toll-Free: 800-663-1940
info@bcpharmacist.org
www.bcpharmacists.org
Safe & effective pharmacy practice outcomes for the people of British Columbia.
Marshall Moleschi, Registrar
Ashifa Keshavji, Director, Professional Development

Council for Continuing Pharmaceutical Education (CCPE) / Conseil de formation pharmaceutique continue (CFPC)
3489, rue Ashby, Saint-Laurent QC H4R 2K3
Tel: 514-333-8362; *Fax:* 514-333-1119
Toll-Free: 888-333-8362
info@ccpe-cfpc.com
www.ccpe-cfpc.com
To provide educational programs to establish improved professional standards within the Canadian pharmaceutical industry; To better meet the needs & expectations of our internal & external stakeholders in the healthcare industry
Michelle Austin, Coordinator, Corporate Customers

Manitoba Pharmaceutical Association
200 Tache Ave., Winnipeg MB R2H 1A7
Tel: 204-233-1411; *Fax:* 204-237-3468
info@mpha.mb.ca
napra.ca/pages/manitoba
The Association administers the Manitoba Pharmaceutical Act. It gives license to & monitors pharmacists in the province, setingt standards of practice & investigating complaints.
Shawn Bugden, President
Ronald Guse, Registrar

Manitoba Society of Pharmacists Inc. (MSP)
#202, 90 Garry St., Winnipeg MB R3C 4H1
Tel: 204-956-6680; *Fax:* 204-956-6686
Toll-Free: 800-677-7170
info@msp.mb.ca
www.msp.mb.ca
To act as the voice of pharmacists in Manitoba on economic & professional issuess
Scott Ransome, Executive Director
Mel Baxter, President
Elmer Kuber, Vice-President
Michelle Glass, Secretary-Treasurer

National Association of Pharmacy Regulatory Authorities (NAPRA) / Association nationale des organismes de réglementation de la pharmacie
#750, 220 Laurier Ave. West, Ottawa ON K1P 5Z9
Tel: 613-569-9658; *Fax:* 613-569-9659
info@napra.ca
www.napra.ca
To facilitate the activities of provincial pharmacy regulatory authorities in their service of public interest
Carole Bouchard, Executive Director

NDMAC, Advancing Canadian Self-Care
#406, 1111 Prince of Wales Dr., Ottawa ON K2C 3T2
Tel: 613-723-0777; *Fax:* 613-723-0779
ndmac@ndmac.ca
www.ndmac.ca
To contribute to quality of life & cost-effective health care for Canadians by creating & maintaining an environment for the growth of responsible self-medication.
David S. Skinner, President
Mary McEwen, Director, Communications & Member Services

New Brunswick Pharmaceutical Society (NBPhS) / Ordre des pharmaciens du N.-B.
#8, 1224 Mountain Rd., Moncton NB E1C 2T6
Tel: 506-857-8957; *Fax:* 506-857-8838
Toll-Free: 800-463-4434
info@nbpharmacists.ca
www.nbpharmacists.ca
To protect the public by regulating the profession of pharmacy in New Brunswick.
Sam Lanctin, Registrar
Cynthia Cormier, Office Coordinator

New Brunswick Pharmacists' Association (NBPA) / Association des pharmaciens du Nouveau-Brunswick (APNB)
#410, 212 Queen St., Fredericton NB E3B 1A8
Tel: 506-459-6008; *Fax:* 506-453-0736
Toll-Free: 888-358-2345
nbpa@nbnet.nb.ca; newsroom@nbpharma.ca
www.nbpharma.ca
To advance the profession of pharmacy in New Brunswick; To represent the interests of members & the profession of pharmacy
Paul Blanchard, Executive Director

Nova Scotia College of Pharmacists (NSCP)
#200, 1559 Brunswick St., Halifax NS B3J 2G1
Tel: 902-422-8528; *Fax:* 902-422-0885
info@nspharmacists.ca
www.nspharmacists.ca
To govern the practice of pharmacy in Nova Scotia to benefit the health & well being of the public
Craig Connolly, President
Susan Wedlake, Registrar

Ontario College of Pharmacists (OCP)
483 Huron St., Toronto ON M5R 2R4
Tel: 416-962-4861; *Fax:* 416-847-8200
Toll-Free: 800-220-1921
ocpclientservices@ocpinfo.com
www.ocpinfo.com
To administer the Regulated Health Professions Act; To regulate the practice of pharmacy, in accordance with standards of practice; To ensure that members provide quality pharmaceutical service & care to the public
Stephen Clement, President & Chair
Bonnie Hauser, Vice-President

Ontario Pharmacists' Association (OPA)
#800, 375 University Ave., Toronto ON M5G 2J5
Tel: 416-441-0788; *Fax:* 416-441-0791
mail@opatoday.com
www.opatoday.com
To promote excellence in the practice of pharmacy & the wellness of patients; To act as the voice of pharmacists throughout Ontario
Dennis Darby, Chief Executive Officer
Amedeo Zottola, CFO & COO
Allan H. Malek, Vice-President, Professional Affairs
Lisa Mayeski, Director, Corporate Development & Partnerships
Deborah McNorgan, Director, Communications
Eija Kanniainen, Manager, Insurance Services
Eric Li, Manager, Pharmacy Policy
Wendy Furtenbacher, Coordinator, Membership

Ordre des pharmaciens du Québec (OPQ)
#301, 266, rue Notre Dame ouest, Montréal QC H2Y 1T6
Tél: 514-284-9588; *Téléc:* 514-284-3420
Ligne sans frais: 800-363-0324
ordrepharm@opq.org
www.opq.org
Protection du public en matières de services pharmaceutiques.
Diane Lamarre, Présidente

Pharmacy Association of Nova Scotia (PANS)
#225, 170 Cromarty Dr., Dartmouth NS B3B 0G1
Tel: 902-422-9583; *Fax:* 902-422-2619
pans@pans.ns.ca
www.pans.ns.ca
To advance the professional, academic, & commercial aspects of pharmacy & pharmacists throughout Nova Scotia; To represent the interests of Nova Scotia's pharmacists; To improve public health in Nova Scotia
Allison Bodnar, Executive Director

The Pharmacy Examining Board of Canada (PEBC) / Le Bureau des examinateurs en pharmacie du Canada (BEPC)
717 Chursh St., Toronto ON M4W 2M4
Tel: 416-979-2431; *Fax:* 416-599-9244
pebcinfo@pebc.ca
www.pebc.ca
To establish qualifications for pharmacists; To provide for examinations of those qualifications
Tena Taylor, President
Peter Gdyczynski, Vice-President

Prince Edward Island Pharmacy Board
PO Box 89, Trans Canada Hwy., Crapaud PE C0A 1J0
Tel: 902-658-2780; *Fax:* 902-658-2528
peipharm@pei.aibn.com
To prescribe qualifications, grant authorization & monitor adherence to established standards, so as to promote high standards & safeguard the public with regard to pharmaceutical service
Neila I. Auld, Registrar

Saskatchewan College of Pharmacists (SCP)
#700, 4010 Pasqua St., Regina SK S4S 7B9
Tel: 306-584-2292; *Fax:* 306-584-9695
info@saskpharm.ca
www.napra.ca/pages/Saskatchewan
To regulate pharmacists, pharmacies, & drugs in Saskatchewan; To register pharmacists who meet the education & training qualifications specified in "The Pharmacy Act, 1996"; To issue permits to operate pharmacies
Randy Wiser, President
Joan Bobyn, Vice-President
Ray Joubert, Registrar

Photography

Alberta Professional Photographers Association (APPA)
9404 - 129A Ave., Edmonton AB T5E 0N7
Tel: 780-483-4275; *Fax:* 780-472-7720
es@ppoc-alberta.ca
www.ppoc-alberta.ca
The organization has been formed to establish a strong national identity for all those involved in the photographic industry and includes provincial factions which abide by a specific code of ethics.
Ian Grant, President

Canadian Association for Photographic Art (CAPA) / L'Association canadienne d'art photographique
PO Box 357, Logan Lake BC V0K 1W0
Tel: 604-824-9490; *Fax:* 604-824-9496
capa@capacanada.ca
capacanada.ca
To promote the advancement of photography as an art form in Canada
Jacques S. Mailloux, President

Canadian Association of Photographers & Illustrators in Communications (CAPIC) / Association canadienne de photographes et illustrateurs de publicité
Case Goods Bldg. 74, #302, 55 Mill St., Toronto ON M5A 3C4
Tel: 416-462-3677; *Fax:* 416-462-9570
Toll-Free: 888-252-2742
info@capic.org; administrator@capic.org
www.capic.org
Social Media: www.facebook.com/group.php?gid=33315648062
To safeguard & promote the rights of photographers, illustrators, & digital artists who work in the Canadian communications industry
John Harquail, Managing Director
Ewan Nicholson, President
Brian Summers, Treasurer

Canadian Imaging Trade Association (CITA) / Association canadienne de l'industrie de l'imagerie
PO Box 71058, 570 Mulock Dr., Newmarket ON L3X 1Y8
Tel: 416-226-2750; *Fax:* 416-226-3347
cita2@sympatico.ca
www.citacanada.ca
To promote traditional & emerging imaging technologies (manufacturers/importers & distributors of photographic & electronic imaging equipment & sensitized materials)
Dori Gospodaric, General Manager

Corporation des maîtres photographes du Québec inc. (CMPQ) / Québec Corporation of Master Photographers Inc.
358, rue Brock, Drummondville QC J2B 1C8
Tél: 514-990-7313; *Téléc:* 819-663-7850
information@cmpq.qc.ca
www.cmpq.qc.ca
La Corporation des Maîtres Photographes du Québec inc. est un organisme sans but lucratif qui s'est donné comme objectif l'avancement de la photographieprofessionnelle tout en assurant aux consommateurs la protection et un haut niveau de qualité.

Daniel Osborne, Président
Lorraine Lacroix, Adjointe administrative

Paved Arts New Media Inc.
424 - 20th St. West, Saskatoon SK S7M 0X4
Tel: 306-652-5502
www.pavedarts.ca
To develop photography & photo-based art
Laura Margita, Executive Director
David LaRiviere, Artistic Director

Photo Marketing Association International - Canada (PMAI)
PO Box 81191, Ancaster ON L9G 4X2
Tel: 905-304-8800; *Fax:* 905-304-7700
Toll-Free: 800-461-4350
bmoggach@pmai.org
www.pmai.org/content.aspx?id=110
To disseminate timely information while providing market research & business improvement products & services that contribute to increased profitability & business growth for its membership
Bob Moggach, Director of Canadian Activities

Photographic Historical Society of Canada (PHSC)
PO Box 239, 6021 Yonge St., Toronto ON M2M 3W2
Tel: 416-691-1555; *Fax:* 416-693-0018
info@phsc.ca
www.phsc.ca
To facilitate the sharing of photographic knowledge; To help research & preserve Canada's photographic heritage
Clint Hyrorijiw, President

Professional Photographers Association of Canada - Atlantic / Atlantique (PPAC Atlantic)
136 Russell Lake Dr., Dartmouth NS B2W 6J5
Tel: 902-462-1502; *Fax:* 902-468-7818
beth@tenwoldephoto.com
www.mppaphoto.com
To uphold the association's code of ethics
Sib Pye, President
Peter Tenwolde, Treasurer
Beth Tenwolde, Executive Secretary

Professional Photographers of Canada - British Columbia (PPOC-BC)
PO Box 1329, 4543 - 201 St., Langley BC V3A 6M5
Tel: 604-857-1569; *Fax:* 604-857-1570
Toll-Free: 877-857-1569
contact@ppoc-bc.ca
www.ppoc-bc.ca
Social Media: twitter.com/PPOC_BC
To promote & foster the personal ethics & professional development of the working photographer &/or specialist through education, fellowship & public awareness
Jillian Chateauneuf, PPOC Director, British Columbia
Melissa Walsh, President

Professional Photographers of Canada 1970 Incorporated (PPOC) / Photographes Professionnels du Canada
209 Light St., Woodstock ON N4S 6H6
Tel: 519-537-2555; *Fax:* 519-537-5573
Toll-Free: 888-643-7762
www.ppoc.ca
To promote excellence in professional imaging; To elevate professional standards & ethics; To act as a voice for the photographic profession on legal matters & legislative issues
Tanya Thompson, Executive Director
Chris Stambaugh, President
Brian Boyle, Vice-President
John Beesley, Corporate Secretary
Cam Colclough, Corporate Treasurer

Professional Photographers of Ontario Inc. (PPO)
209 Light St., Woodstock ON N4S 6H6
Tel: 519-537-2555; *Fax:* 519-537-5573
Toll-Free: 888-643-7762
info@ppontario.com
www.ppontario.com
To provide an educational, business & creative environment for professional photographers & with the purpose of promoting the highest standard of personal & creative excellence within the craft
Luis Jeronimo, President

Saskatchewan Professional Photographers Association Inc.
2057 Athol St., Regina SK S4T 3E6
Tel: 306-757-1470; *Toll-Free:* 888-643-7762
admin@sppa.org
www.sppa.org
To advance professional photography through educational seminars, fellowship & competitions
Larry Raynard, President
Tanya Thompson, Administrative Coordinator

Planning & Development

Alberta Professional Planners Institute (APPI)
PO Box 596, Edmonton AB T5J 2K8
Tel: 780-435-8716; *Fax:* 780-452-7718
Toll-Free: 888-286-8716
admin@albertaplanners.com
www.albertaplanners.com
To expand the depth & enhance the credibility of the association; To promote professional growth of practicing planners throughout Alberta, the Northwest Territories, & Nunavut; To maximize membership potential; To provide an effective level of service to the membership
Beth Sanders, RPP, MCIP, President
MaryJane Alanko, Executive Director
Vicki Hackl, Contact, Membership Enquiries

Association of Professional Community Planners of Saskatchewan
2424 College Ave., Regina SK S4P 1C8
Tel: 306-584-3879; *Fax:* 306-352-6913
president@apcps.ca
www.apcps.ca
To promote & maintain professionalism in planning field
Marilyn Steranka, Executive Director
Bill Delainey, Secretary
Ryan Walker, Treasurer

Atlantic Planners Institute (API) / Institut des Urbanistes de l'atlantique (IVA)
57 Parkside Dr., Charlottetown PE C1E 1N1
Tel: 902-892-3684; *Toll-Free:* 800-207-2138
krlewis@pei.eastlink.ca
www.atlanticplanners.org
Represents professional planners in New Brunswick, Prince Edward Island, Nova Scotia, Newfoundland & Labrador. They provide the processing of membership applications, maintenance of the membership roster, production of a regularly-scheduled newsletter, funding guarantess for the annual conference organizing committee.
Kingsley Lewis

Canadian Association of Certified Planning Technicians (CACPT)
PO Box 3844, Stn. C, Hamilton ON L8H 7R6
Tel: 905-578-4681; *Fax:* 905-578-9581
director@cacpt.org
www.cacpt.org
To maintain high standards for Planning Technicians & other related planning professionals
Diane LeBreton, Executive Director
Julie Owens, President
Norman Pearson, Registrar

Canadian Institute of Planners (CIP) / Institut canadien des urbanistes (ICU)
#1112, 141 Laurier Ave. West, Ottawa ON K1P 5J3
Tel: 613-237-7526; *Fax:* 613-237-7045
Toll-Free: 800-207-2138
general@cip-icu.ca
www.cip-icu.ca
To advance professional planning excellence, through the delivery of membership & public services in Canada & abroad
Steven Brasier, CAE, Executive Director

Intergovernmental Committee on Urban & Regional Research (ICURR) / Comité intergouvernemental de recherches urbaines et régionales (CIRUR)
#210, 40 Wynford Dr., Toronto ON M3C 1J5
Tel: 647-345-6454; *Fax:* 647-345-6991
www.muniscope.ca
ICURR supports local and regional governments, as well as private and non-profit companies through subsidized information and networking services. Muniscope is Canada's national resource on municipal issues, with subscription-based research and library services available on economic development, finance and taxation, housing and infrastructure, transportation, planning, and sustainability.
Katherine d'Entremont, Director

Manitoba Professional Planners Institute (MPPI)
137 Bannatyne Ave., 2nd Fl., Winnipeg MB R3B 0R3
Tel: 204-943-3637; *Fax:* 204-925-4624
mjohnson@mts.net
www.mppi.mb.ca
MPPI is responsible for handling membership applications and services, and for the enforcement of the Code of Professional Conduct. MPPI, along with the Association of Community Planners of Saskatchewan, jointly publishes the membership newsletter SCENARIO and sponsors workshops and seminars for the purpose of informing the membership of relevant developments and issues in the planning field.
Valdene Buckley, President

Ontario Professional Planners Institute (OPPI) / Institut des planificateurs professionnels de l'Ontario
#201, 234 Eglinton Ave. East, Toronto ON M4P 1K5
Tel: 416-483-1873; *Fax:* 416-483-7830
Toll-Free: 800-668-1448
info@ontarioplanners.on.ca
www.ontarioplanners.on.ca
To act as the voice of Ontario's planning profession; To provide leadership on policies related to planning & development
Sue Cumming, President
Mary Ann Rangam, Executive Director
Robert Fraser, Manager, Finance & Administration
Loretta Ryan, Manager, Policy & Communications
Ron Keeble, Registrar

Ordre des urbanistes du Québec (OUQ)
#410, 85, rue St-Paul ouest, Montréal QC H2Y 3V4
Tél: 514-849-1177; *Téléc:* 514-849-7176
info@ouq.qc.ca
www.ouq.qc.ca
Assurer la protection du public dans l'exercice de la profession par ses membres et la promotion de la pratique de l'urbanisme au Québec
Claude Beaulac, Directeur général
Odette Michaud, Secrétaire de l'Ordre
Nathalie Corso, Coordonnatrice, Admission et qualité

Planning Institute of British Columbia (PIBC)
#110, 355 Burrard St., Vancouver BC V6C 2G8
Tel: 604-696-5031; *Fax:* 604-696-5032
Toll-Free: 866-696-5031
info@pibc.bc.ca
www.pibc.bc.ca
To promote orderly use of land, buildings & natural resources; to maintain high standard of professional competence; to protect rights & interests of those engaged in planning profession
Lindsay Chase, President
Dave Crossley, Executive Director

Urban Development Institute of Canada (UDI) / Institut de développement urbain du Canada
200-602 West Hastings St., Vancouver BC V6B 1P2
Tel: 604-669-9585; *Fax:* 604-689-8691
info@udi.org
www.udi.bc.ca
To promote wise, efficient & productive urban growth; To be an effective voice of the land development & property management industry at all levels of government; To serve as a forum for the exchange of knowledge, experience & research on land use planning & development
Maureen Enser, Executive Director
Jeff Fisher, Deputy Executive Director

Police

Ontario Association of Chiefs of Police (OACP)
#605, 40 College St., Toronto ON M5G 2J3
Tel: 416-926-0424; *Fax:* 416-926-0436
Toll-Free: 800-816-1767
oacpadmin@oacp.ca
www.oacp.on.ca
The Association coordinates police training & education. It advocates on behalf of its membership, expressing concerns & priorities to the government, public & to any other bodies.
Ron Bain, Executive Director
Joe Couto, Director, Government Relations & Communications

Politics

Alberta Greens
PO Box 61251, Stn. Brentwood, Calgary AB T2L 2K6
Tel: 403-282-4788; *Fax:* 403-289-6658
secretary@albertagreens.ca
albertagreens.ca
To encourage the development of an attitude that everyone is part of the land; to encourage strict control of all forms of pollution; to promote programs teaching consensus & facilitation; to facilitate the process of all interested community members becoming involved in education, both learning & teaching, guided by the long-term sustainability of the Earth community; to create the opportunity for Albertans to become involved in the strategic planning process

David Crowe, Treasurer/Chief Financial Officer
Grant Neufeld, President
George Read, Leader

Alberta Liberal Party
10247 - 124 St. NW, Edmonton AB T5N 1P8
Tel: 780-414-1124; *Toll-Free:* 800-661-9201
office@albertaliberal.com
www.albertaliberal.com
To elect Liberals to the Legislative Assembly of Alberta; to enunciate & promote liberal principles & policies; to initiate & maintain effective electoral constituencies
Raj Sherman, Leader
Todd van Vliet, President

Bloc québécois (BQ)
3750, boul Crémazie est, 4e étage, Montréal QC H2A 1B4
Tél: 514-526-3000; *Téléc:* 514-526-2868
www.blocquebecois.org
Gilles Duceppe, Chef

Canadian Political Science Association (CPSA) / Association canadienne de science politique (ACSP)
#204, 260 Dalhousie St., Ottawa ON K1N 7E4
Tel: 613-562-1202; *Fax:* 613-241-0019
cpsa@csse.ca
www.cpsa-acsp.ca
To encourage & develop political science & its relationship with other disciplines
Sally Rutherford, Executive Director
Reeta Tremblay, President
Michelle Hopkins, Administrator

Christian Heritage Party of Canada (CHP) / Parti de l'héritage du Canada
PO Box 4958, Stn. E, Ottawa ON K1S 5J1
Tel: 819-281-6686; *Fax:* 819-281-7174
Toll-Free: 888-868-3247
nationaloffice@chp.ca
www.chp.ca
To provide true Christian leadership & uphold biblical principles in federal legislation; To attain the leadership of the federal government of Canada through the existing democratic process
Jim Hnatiuk, National Leader
Tom Kroesbergen, President

Communist Party of Canada (CPC) / Parti Communiste du Canada
Central Committee, 290A Danforth Ave., Toronto ON M4K 1N6
Tel: 416-469-2446; *Fax:* 416-469-4063
info@cpc-pcc.ca
www.communist-party.ca
The Party aims to establish a socialist society in Canada, in which the principal means of producing & distributing wealth will be the common property of society as a whole.
Miguel Figueroa, Party Leader

Communist Party of Canada (Marxist-Leninist) (CPC(ML)) / Parti communiste du Canada (marxiste-léniniste)
National Headquarters, 1876, rue Amherst, Montréal QC H2L 3L7
Tel: 514-522-1373; *Fax:* 514-522-1373
Toll-Free: 800-263-4203
office@cpcml.ca
www.cpcml.ca
The Party holds that the attainment of communism will bring the complete emancipation of the working class. It holds that all people have claims on the society by virtue of being human and that this is the overriding principle of society, along with gender equality and freedom of conscience & lifestyle.
Anna Di Carlo, Party Leader
Hélène Héroux, Chief Agent

Conservative Party of Canada / Parti conservateur du Canada
#1204, 130 Albert St., Ottawa ON K1P 5G4
Tel: 613-755-2000; *Fax:* 613-755-2001
Toll-Free: 866-808-8407
www.conservative.ca
Social Media: www.facebook.com/group.php?gid=5661704203; www.facebook.com/pmharper; twitter.com/CPC_HQ; www.twitter.com/PMHarper; www.youtube.com/cpcpcc; www.flickr.com/photos/30107029@N04
The Conservative Party provided Canadians with an alternative to the Liberal government. It developed innovative and practical new policy ideas such as the Federal Accountability Act, the Public Transit Tax Credit and the Apprenticeship Incentive Grant- ideas Conservatives would later implement in government.
Stephen Harper, Leader

Green Party of British Columbia (GPBC)
PO Box 8088, Stn. Central, #312, 895 Fort St., Victoria BC V8W 3R7
Toll-Free: 888-473-3686
info@greenparty.bc.ca
www.greenparty.bc.ca
Social Media: www.facebook.com/groups/bcgreens; twitter.com/janesterk
To form healthy communities with diverse economies by involving the citizens of British Columbia in the political process; To offer voters in British Columbia fiscal responsibility, socially progressive policies, & environmental sustainability
Murray Weisenberger, Party Chair
Jane Sterk, Leader
David Pearce, Treasurer & Financial Agent

Green Party of Canada (GPC) / Parti vert du Canada
PO Box 997, Stn. B, #204, 396 Cooper St., Ottawa ON K1P 5R1
Tel: 613-562-4916; *Fax:* 613-482-4632
Toll-Free: 888-868-3447
info@greenparty.ca
www.greenparty.ca
Social Media: twitter.com/canadiangreens
To promote a platform that includes debt reduction, eco-jobs, saving Canada's forests, supporting small business, use of soft energies, sovereignty for First Nations, & a guarantee of full rights for women
Elizabeth May, Leader
Maureen Murphy, Executive Director

The Green Party of Manitoba
PO Box 26023, Stn. Maryland, Winnipeg MB R3C 3R3
Tel: 204-488-2831; *Fax:* 204-992-2712
Toll-Free: 866-742-4292
info@greenparty.mb.ca
www.greenparty.mb.ca
James Beddome, President

Green Party of New Brunswick
PO Box 3723, Stn. B, Fredericton NB E3A 5L8
Tel: 506-447-8499; *Fax:* 506-447-8489
Toll-Free: 888-662-8683
info@greenpartynb.ca
www.greenpartynb.ca
Jack MacDougall, Leader

The Green Party of Ontario (GPO) / Parti Vert d'Ontario
PO Box 1132, Stn. F, Toronto ON M4Y 2T8
Tel: 416-977-7476; *Fax:* 416-977-5476
Toll-Free: 888-647-3366
admin@gpo.ca
www.gpo.ca
Mike Schreiner, Leader
Becky Smit, Executive Director

International Political Science Association (IPSA) / Association internationale de science politique (AISP)
#331, 1590, av Docteur-Penfield, Montréal QC H3G 1C5
Tel: 514-848-8717; *Fax:* 514-848-4095
info@ipsa.ca
www.ipsa.ca
To promote the advancement of political science through the collaboration of scholars in different parts of the world; IPSA has consultative status with the Economic & Social Council of the United Nations & with UNESCO
Guy Lachapelle, Secretary General
Leonardo Morlino, President

The Liberal Party of Canada (LPC) / Le Parti Libéral du Canada (PLC)
#600, 81 Metcalfe St., Ottawa ON K1P 6M8
Tel: 613-237-0740; *Fax:* 613-235-7208
info@liberal.ca
www.liberal.ca
Social Media: www.facebook.com/LiberalCA; twitter.com/Liberal_party
To seek a common ground of understanding among the people of the provinces & territories of Canada; To advocate liberal philosophies, principles & policies; To promote the election of candidates of the Liberal Party to the Parliament of Canada
Bob Rae, Leader
Alfred Apps, National President
Rocco Rossi, National Director
Stephen Kukucha, National Vice-President, English
Brigitte Garceau, National Vice-President, French

The Liberal Party of Canada (British Columbia) (LPC(BC)) / Parti libéral du Canada (Colombie-Britannique)
#460, 580 Hornby St., Vancouver BC V6C 3B6
Tel: 604-664-3777; *Fax:* 604-874-8966
Toll-Free: 888-411-6511
info@lpcbc.com
www.lpcbc.com; www.teambc.ca
Diane Rabbani, Executive Director

The Liberal Party of Canada (Manitoba) / Parti libéral au Manitoba
635 Broadway, Winnipeg MB R3C 0X1
Tel: 204-988-9540; *Fax:* 204-988-9549
lpcmb@liberalpartyofcanada-mb.ca
www.liberalpartyofcanada-mb.ca
Sharon MacArthur, President

Liberal Party of Canada (Ontario) (LPC(O)) / Parti libéral du Canada (Ontario)
#205, 10 St. Mary St., Toronto ON M4Y 1P9
Tel: 416-921-2844; *Fax:* 416-921-3880
Toll-Free: 800-361-3881
admin@lpco.ca
www.lpco.ca
The Liberal Party of Canada (Ontario) represents the Federal Liberal Party and its 106 Electoral District Associations in Ontario. LPC(O) works with the thousands of members and volunteers in Ontario to ensure that it is a healthy and vibrant political organization.
Mike Crawley, President
Judi Longfield, Executive Director

The Liberal Party of Canada in Alberta (LPC(A))
Guardian Bldg., #50, 10240 - 124 St. NW, Edmonton AB T5N 3W6
Tel: 780-424-1984; *Fax:* 780-424-1966
Toll-Free: 800-879-8294
office@liberalalberta.ca
alberta.liberal.ca
Carole Halko, Executive Director
George Hodgson, President

Liberal Party of Newfoundland & Labrador / Parti libéral de Terre-Neuve et du Labrador
Beothuk Bldg., #205, 20 Crosbie Place, St. John's NL A1B 3Y8
Tel: 709-754-1813; *Fax:* 709-754-0820
Toll-Free: 866-726-7116
libcan@nf.aibn.com
www.nlliberals.ca.perfectdaycanada.com
Social Media: twitter.com/nlliberals
The Liberal Party in Newfoundland and Labrador has been the dominant political party since confederation in 1949 and are responsible for many of the major social transformations that has occurred in this province in the last half century. Those developments, which include Memorial University, countless new schools across the province and an greatly improved standard of living, have made the Liberal Party the voice of social development in Newfoundland and Labrador.
Yvonne Jones, Leader
Judy Morrow, President

Liberal Party of Nova Scotia
PO Box 723, #304, 1660 Hollis St., Halifax NS B3J 2T3
Tel: 902-429-1993; *Fax:* 902-423-1624
TTY: 902-429-1772
office@liberal.ns.ca
www.liberal.ns.ca
Social Media: twitter.com/StephenMcNeil
Stephen McNeil, Leader
Derek M. Wells, President

Liberal Party of Prince Edward Island / Parti libéral de l'Ile du Prince Édouard
PO Box 2559, #205, 129 Kent St., Charlottetown PE C1A 8C2
Tel: 902-368-3449; *Fax:* 902-368-3687
Toll-Free: 877-740-3449
office@liberal.pe.ca
www.liberal.pe.ca
Social Media: www.facebook.com/group.php?gid=38261891616
Representing the Liberal Party of PEI.
Barrie Harris, President

The Libertarian Party of Canada
2938E More Cres., Regina SK S4V 0T7
Tel: 416-443-5423
info@libertarian.ca
www.libertarian.ca
Dennis Young, Leader

New Brunswick Liberal Association
715 Brunswick St., Fredericton NB E3B 1H8
Tel: 506-453-3950; *Fax:* 506-453-2476
Toll-Free: 800-442-4902
www.nbliberal.ca
Léopold Mallet, Executive Director

New Democratic Party (NDP) / Nouveau Parti Démocratique
Federal Office, #300, 279 Laurier West, Ottawa ON K1P 5J9
Tel: 613-236-3613; *Fax:* 613-230-9950
Toll-Free: 866-525-2555
TTY: 866-776-7742
www.ndp.ca
Social Media: www.facebook.com/group.php?gid=190502667652613; twitter.com/NDP_HQ; www.twitter.com/nycole_turmel; www.youtube.com/user/NDPCanada; www.flickr.com/photos/ndpcanada
To offer Canadians an alternative political vision based on the principles of democratic socialism; To protect & expand programs such as Medicare & the Old Age Pension through prudent & effective government, & through a truly fair tax system
Nycole Turmel, Leader
Brigitte Sansoucy, Associate President
Hassan Yussuff, Associate President, Labour

Nunavut Liberal Party
PO Box 1059, Iqaluit NU X0A 0H0
Tel: 867-979-1488; *Fax:* 867-979-1478
Representing the Liberal Party in Nunavut
Alain Carrière, Riding President

Parti communiste du Québec
CP 482, Succ. Place d'Armes, Montréal QC H2Y 3H3
Tél: 514-528-6142
info@pcq.qc.ca
www.pcq.qc.ca
Unifier avec la classe ouvrière et les couches populaires pour que s'installe le pouvoir populaire dans le but de construire le socialisme
André Parizeau, Party Leader

Parti libéral du Québec (PLQ) / Québec Liberal Party (QLP)
7240, rue Waverly, Montréal QC H2R 2Y8
Tél: 514-288-4364; *Téléc:* 514-288-4364
Ligne sans frais: 800-361-1047
reception@lpcq.qc.ca
www.plq.org
Jean Charest, Chef du Parti
Marc Tanguay, Président

Parti québécois (PQ)
#150, 1200 ave. Papineau, Montréal QC H2K 4R5
Tél: 514-526-0020; *Téléc:* 514-526-0272
Ligne sans frais: 800-363-9531
info@pq.org
www.pq.org
Média social: www.facebook.com/lepartiquebecois; twitter.com/PartiQuebecois
Réaliser démocratiquement la souveraineté du Québec pour s'épanouir comme peuple francophone, pour ne plus être minoritaire, pour mettre fin au gaspillage, pour se doter d'une politique économique qui répond aux intérêts du Québec; donner au Québec une place dans le monde
Pauline Marois, Chef du Parti Québécois
Jonathan Valois, Président

Parti Vert du Québec (PVQ) / Green Party of Québec
#220, 10000 rue Lajeunesse, Montréal QC H3L 2E1
Tél: 514-303-7750; *Ligne sans frais:* 888-998-8378
info@partivertquebec.org
www.partivertquebec.org
Média social: www.facebook.com/partivert; twitter.com/claudesabourin_
Guy Rainville, Chef

Saskatchewan Liberal Association / Association libérale de la Saskatchewan
845A McDonald St., Regina SK S4N 2X5
Tel: 306-522-8507; *Fax:* 306-569-9271
contact@saskliberals.ca
www.saskliberal.ca
Social Media: www.facebook.com/group.php?gid=2399956913
Sharice Billett Niedermeyer, President

Socialist Party of Canada (SPC) / Parti Socialiste du Canada
PO Box 4280, Victoria BC V8X 3X8
spc@iname.com
www.worldsocialism.org/canada/
To promote the establishment of socialism - a system of society based upon the common ownership & democratic control of the means & instruments for producing & distributing wealth by & in the interest of society as a whole
John Ayers, Contact

Western Arctic Liberal Party
PO Box 965, Yellowknife NT XIA 2N7
Tel: 867-445-2377; *Fax:* 867-766-4915
lroeland@iandd.ca
Lana Roeland, President

Yukon Liberal Party
PO Box 183, #108 Elliot St., Whitehorse YT Y1A 2C6
Tel: 867-667-4748; *Fax:* 867-667-4720
info@ylp.ca
www.ylp.ca
Kirk Cameron, President

Poultry & Eggs

Alberta Egg Producers' Board (AEPB)
#101, 90 Freeport Blvd. NE, Calgary AB T3J 5J9
Tel: 403-250-1197; *Fax:* 403-291-9216
Toll-Free: 877-302-2344
info@eggs.ab.ca
eggs.ab.ca
To be the best producers & marketers of eggs
Michael Froese, Chair

Atlantic Provinces Hatchery Federation
PO Box 550, Truro NS B2N 5E3
Tel: 902-893-6532; *Fax:* 902-893-6035
aoderkirk@gov.ns.ca
Alex Oderkirk, Sec.-Treas.

British Columbia Broiler Hatching Egg Producers' Association (BCBHEC)
#180, 32160 South Fraser Way, Abbotsford BC V2T 1W5
Tel: 604-850-1854; *Fax:* 604-850-1683
info@bcbhec.com
www.bcbhec.com
The Association has the following responsibilities: to establish a better understanding & appreciation with the public & other interested parties regarding the industry; to stimulate & encourage improvements related to sales & scientific development in the field; to promote the exchange of ideas in an effort to find solutions to problems in the broiler hatching egg industry; to encourage economical plans to assists producers; & to provide better contact with hatcheries, feed suppliers, processors, & broiler growers.
Brian Ens, President
Dave Cherniwchan, General Manager

Canadian Broiler Hatching Egg Marketing Agency (CBHEMA) / Office canadien de commercialisation des oeufs d'incubation de poulet à chair (OCCOIPC)
21 Florence St., Ottawa ON K2O 0W6
Tel: 613-232-3023; *Fax:* 613-232-5241
info@chep-poic.ca
www.chep-poic.ca
To ensure that our members produce enough hatching eggs to meet the needs of the broiler industry
Jack Greydanus, Chair
Giuseppe Caminiti, General Manager

Chicken Farmers of Canada (CFC) / Les Producteurs de poulet du Canada
#1007, 350 Sparks St., Ottawa ON K1R 7S8
Tel: 613-241-2800; *Fax:* 613-241-5999
cfc@chicken.ca
www.chicken.ca
Social Media: www.facebook.com/chickenfarmers
To build an evidence-based, consumer driven Canadian chicken industry that provides opportunities for profitable growth for all stakeholders
David Fuller, Chair

Éleveurs de volailles du Québec
#250, 555, boul Roland-Therrien, Longueuil QC J4H 4G1
Tél: 450-679-0530; *Téléc:* 450-679-5375
evq@upa.qc.ca
volaillesduquebec.qc.ca
A pour mission l'étude, la défense et le développement des intérêts économiques, sociaux et moraux de ses membres; favorise et stimule la mobilisation et la participation de ses membres tout en les consultant et en les informant; développe et renforce la mise en marché collective des poulets et des dindons produits au Québec, en mettant en place des services garantissant le fonctionnement optimal du plan conjoint et des autres outils de mise en marché
Jean-Paul Bouchard, Président

Fédération des producteurs d'oeufs de consommation du Québec (FPOCQ)
#320, 555, boul Roland-Therrien, Longueuil QC J4H 4E7
Tél: 450-679-0530; *Téléc:* 450-679-0855
www.oeuf.ca
Média social: www.facebook.com/lesoeufs?v=wall
Favoriser le développement durable de l'industrie québécoise des oeufs et ce par: le respect de l'environnement et le bien-être des animaux; en procurant un revenu équitable aux intervenants du secteur; en répondant aux attentes des consommateurs avec des oeufs et produits de haute qualité
Serge Lefebvre, Président

Turkey Farmers of Canada (TFC) / Les éleveurs de dindon du Canada (ÉDC)
Bldg. One, #202, 7145 West Credit Ave., Mississauga ON L5N 6J7
Tel: 905-812-3140; *Fax:* 905-812-9326
info@tfc-edc.ca
www.turkeyfarmersofcanada.ca
Social Media: www.facebook.com/TastyTurkey; twitter.com/tastyturkey
To develop & strengthen the Canadian Turkey market through an effective supply management systems that stimulates growth & profitability for stakeholders
Philip J. Boyd, Executive Director
Mark Davies, Chair

Printing Industry & Graphic Arts

British Columbia Printing & Imaging Association (BCPIA)
PO Box 75218, Stn. WRPO, White Rock BC V4B 5L4
Tel: 604-542-0902; *Fax:* 604-538-8581
mknoch@bcpia.org
www.bcpia.org
To be the voice of the BC printing industry & its employees; to provide services & benefits which encourage fellowship, education, community involvement & high standards in business conduct.
Marilynn Knoch, Executive Director

Canadian Printing Industries Association (CPIA) / Association canadienne de l'imprimerie (ACI)
#1110, 151 Slater St., Ottawa ON K1P 5H3
Tel: 613-236-7208; *Fax:* 613-232-1334
Toll-Free: 800-267-7280
info@cpia-aci.ca
www.cpia-aci.ca
Social Media: www.linkedin.com/company/canadian-printing-industries-association
To advance the quality of management in the printing & allied trades; to offer services through a network of local & related organizations including representations to various sectors; to enhance the image & profile of the industry
Anateresa Mendes-Collins, Executive Assistant
Bob Elliott, President
Jamie Barbieri, Secretary-Treasurer

Canadian Printing Ink Manufacturers Association (CPIMA)
Tel: 905-556-1808; *Fax:* 647-439-1572
mconnolly@cpima.org
www.cpima.org
To exchange information that will be of benefit to members, the ink industry, & the printing industry
Vivy DaCosta, President

Ontario Printing & Imaging Association (OPIA)
#14, 2601 Matheson Blvd. East, Mississauga ON L4W 5A8
Tel: 905-602-4441; *Fax:* 905-602-9798
info@opia.on.ca
www.opia.on.ca
To provide leadership for a successful printing & imaging industry in Ontario
Mike McInnes, Chair
Kim Stewart, Vice-Chair
Tracey Preston, President
Ryan Anderson, Treasurer

Printing & Graphics Industries Association of Alberta (PGIA)
PO Box 61229, RPO Kensington, Calgary AB T2N 4S6
Tel: 403-281-1421; *Fax:* 403-225-1421
info@pgia.ca
www.pgia.ca
Committed to the advancement of a healthy, effective & ethical graphic arts industry by providing leadership in the development of imaged communications; by enabling members to work to strengthen the industry

Caron Evans, Association Manager
Dean McElhinney, President

Printing Equipment & Supply Dealers' Association of Canada (PESDA)
11 Alderbrook Place, Bolton ON L7E 1V3
Tel: 416-524-1954; *Fax:* 905-951-6374
bkirk@pesda.com
www.pesda.com
To promote & advance the interests of the printing equipment, consumables & related services industries in Canada
Evan Cambray, President
Bob Kirk, General Manager

Saskatchewan Graphic Arts Industries Association (SGAIA)
PO Box 7152, Saskatoon SK S7K 4J1
Tel: 306-373-3202; *Fax:* 306-373-3246
sgaia@sasktel.net
www.sgaia.org
To promote the interests of Saskatchewan's printing & allied industries; To increase the influence of graphic arts industry to the government & the general business community; To promote programs for the graphic arts industry at universities & technical institutions
Daryl Schaffer, President
Don Breher, Executive Director
Daryl Breckner, Secretary-Treasurer

Society of Graphic Designers of Canada (GDC) / Société des designers graphiques du Canada
Arts Court, 2 Daly Ave., Ottawa ON K1N 6E2
Tel: 613-567-5400; *Fax:* 613-564-4428
Toll-Free: 877-496-4453
info@gdc.net
www.gdc.net
Social Media: twitter.com/gdcntl
To maintain a defined, recognized & competent body of graphic designers; To promote high standards of graphic design for benefit of Canadian industry, commerce, public service & education
Roderick CJ Roodenburg, President
Melanie MacDonald, Administrative Director

Prisoners & Ex-Offenders

Canadian Association of Elizabeth Fry Societies (CAEFS) / Association canadienne des sociétés Elizabeth Fry (ACSEF)
#701, 151 Slater St., Ottawa ON K1P 5H3
Tel: 613-238-2422; *Fax:* 613-232-7130
caefs@web.net
www.elizabethfry.ca
A federation of autonomous societies which work with & on behalf of women & girls involved with the justice system, in particular criminalized women; dedicated to offering services & programs to women in need, advocating for reforms & offering fora within which the public may be informed about & participate in all aspects of the justice system as it affects women
Kim Pate, Executive Director
Ailsa Watkinson, President

Canadian Coalition Against the Death Penalty (CCADP) / Coalition canadien contre la peine de mort
80 Lillington Ave., Toronto ON M1N 3K7
Tel: 416-693-9112; *Fax:* 416-693-9112
info@ccadp.org
www.ccadp.org
To provide information about abuses of the death penalty internationally; To ensure Canada does not return to the death penalty
Tracy Lamourie, Director & Founder
Dave Parkinson, Director & Founder

The John Howard Society of Canada / Société John Howard du Canada
809 Blackburn Mews, Kingston ON K7P 2N6
Tel: 613-384-6272; *Fax:* 613-384-1847
national@johnhoward.ca
www.johnhoward.ca
To promote effective, just, & humane responses to the causes & consequences of crime
Craig Jones, Executive Director
Gordon Cook, President

Operation Springboard
#800, 2 Carlton St., Toronto ON M5B 1J3
Tel: 416-977-0089; *Fax:* 416-977-2840
info@operationspringboard.on.ca
www.operationspringboard.on.ca
To design & provide services & programs that effectively reintegrate offenders into the community as responsible individuals; to develop crime prevention strategies; To promote community involvement in design & provision of services along with continuous effort to encourage understanding & support; To bring forward recommendations that will improve effectiveness of the criminal justice system.
Margaret Stanowski, Executive Director
Liz Conrad, Director of Programs

Quakers Fostering Justice (QFJ)
PO Box 20057, Stn. RPO Mission Hills, Mission BC V2V 7P8
Tel: 604-832-0954
qfj@quaker.ca
To build caring community without need for prisons; to explore alternatives to prison based on economic, social justice & fulfillment of human needs; to foster awareness within & outside Quaker community of roots of crime & violence in society; to reach & support prisoners, guards, victims & families
Meredith Egan, Program Coordinator

St. Leonard's Society of Canada (SLSC) / Société St-Léonard du Canada
Bronson Centre, #208, 211 Bronson Ave., Ottawa ON K1R 6H5
Tel: 613-233-5170; *Fax:* 613-233-5122
Toll-Free: 888-560-9760
www.stleonards.ca
Social Media: www.facebook.com/SLSCanada
Committed to the prevention of crime through programs which promote responsible community living & safer communities
Elizabeth White, Executive Director

Seventh Step Society of Canada
PO Box 85040, Stn. Albert Park, Calgary AB T2A 7R7
Tel: 403-995-4029
seventh@7thstep.ca
www.7thstep.ca
Self-help organization dedicated to help adult & young offenders to become useful & productive members of society; to provide follow-up to those who wish to use organization as means to maintain freedom
Patrick Graham, Executive Director

Public Utilities

Canadian Association of Members of Public Utility Tribunals (CAMPUT) / Association canadienne des membres des tribunaux d'utilité publique
#646, 200 North Service Rd. West, Oakville ON L6M 2Y1
Tel: 905-827-5139; *Fax:* 905-827-3260
info@camput.org
www.camput.org
To improve public utility regulation in Canada
Terry Rochefort, Executive Director
Peter Gurnham, Chair
Alison Rhodes, Secretary-Treasurer

Canadian Public Works Association (CPWA) / Association Canadienne des Travaux Publics
#191, 253 College St., Toronto ON M5T 1R5
Tel: 202-408-9541; *Fax:* 202-408-9542
cpwa@cpwa.net
www.cpwa.net
Their mission statement is to be recognized as the "voice of public works" in Canada; to create a forum for public works professionals in Canada to exchange inforamation, develop ideas, and share skills, knowledge, and technologies on issues unique to Canada; to increase membership and participation.
W. Gary Losier, President

Electricity Distributors Association (EDA)
#1100, 3700 Steeles Ave. West, Vaughan ON L4L 8K8
Tel: 905-265-5300; *Fax:* 905-265-5301
Toll-Free: 800-668-9979
email@eda-on.ca
www.eda-on.ca
To be the voice of Ontario's electricity distributors, the publicly & privately owned companies that deliver electricity to Ontario homes, businesses & public institutions. Focus is on advocacy & representation to government, analysis of legislation & market regulations, communication & networking among members & industry colleagues
C.C. (Charlie) Macaluso, President & CEO, Administration
Tanya Fobear, Coordinator, Communications & Member Relations
Charlie Macaluso, President & CEO

Ontario Municipal Water Association (OMWA)
c/o Doug Parker, 43 Chelsea Cres., Belleville ON K8N 4Z5
Tel: 613-966-1100; *Fax:* 613-966-3024
Toll-Free: 888-231-1115
www.omwa.org
To act as the voice of municipal water supply in Ontario; To ensure the safety, quality, reliability, & sustainability of drinking water in Ontario
Ed Houghton, President
Douglas Parker, Executive Director

Utility Contractors' Association of Ontario Inc. (UCA)
#201, 1075 North Service Rd. West, Oakville ON L6M 2G2
Tel: 905-847-7305; *Fax:* 905-847-7824
info@pipeline.ca
www.uca.on.ca
Barry L. Brown, General Manager

Publishing

Alberta Weekly Newspapers Association (AWNA)
3228 Parsons Rd., Edmonton AB T6H 5R7
Tel: 780-434-8746; *Fax:* 780-438-8356
Toll-Free: 800-282-6903
info@awna.com; display@awna.com (ad material); releases@awna.com
www.awna.com
To assist members to publish high quality community newspapers; To serve advertisers by providing information about the markets of community newspapers in Alberta
Dennis Merrell, Executive Director
Ossie Sheddy, President
Murray Elliott, Vice-President
Chrissie Hamblin, Controller
Maurizia Hinse, Coordinator, Professional Development & Communication
Fred Gorman, Corporate Secretary

Alcuin Society
PO Box 3216, Vancouver BC V6B 3X8
info@alcuinsociety.com
www.alcuinsociety.com
To sponsor educational programs; Yo publish a journal; To offer awards & citations for excellence in book arts
Howard Greaves, Chair

Association des libraires du Québec (ALQ)
#580, 1001, boul de Maisonneuve est, Montréal QC H2L 4P9
Tél: 514-526-3349; *Téléc:* 514-526-3340
info@alq.qc.ca
www.alq.qc.ca
Regrouper, pour leur bénéfice mutuel, les libraires engagées dans la vente au détail au Québec et celles engagées dans la vente du livre en langue française au Canada; fournir des services, faire des études, fournir de l'information, tenir des réunions et des rencontres et contribuer à des programmes pour le bénéfice et l'amélioration de ses membres; encourager la vente au détail du livre au Québec; encourager la communication et la collaboration entre les éditeurs, les distributeurs et les autres participants de l'industrie du livre; aider les libraires à encourager la lecture; lutter contre toute forme de censure

Association nationale des éditeurs de livres (ANEL)
2514, boul Rosemont, Montréal QC H1Y 1K4
Tél: 514-273-8130; *Téléc:* 514-273-9657
Ligne sans frais: 866-900-2635
info@anel.qc.ca
www.anel.qc.ca
Soutenir le développement d'une industrie nationale de l'édition québécoise et canadienne de langue française; établir entre ses membres des rapports de bonne confraternité; étudier et défendre les intérêts tant généraux que politiques et économiques de ses membres; étudier toute question relative à la profession et diffuser l'information auprès de ses membres; constituer une représentation réelle et efficace de la profession à toute les instances pertinentes
Pierre Le François, Directeur général

Association of Book Publishers of British Columbia (ABPBC)
#600, 402 West Pender St., Vancouver BC V6B 1T6
Tel: 604-684-0228; *Fax:* 604-684-5788
e.admin@books.bc.ca
www.books.bc.ca
To encourage writing, publishing, distribution & promotion of books written by BC & Canadian authors; to cooperate with other associations & organizations to further the reading & studying of books; to work for the development & maintenance of strong competitive book publishing houses owned & controlled

in BC & Canada; to further professional training for individuals engaged in book publishing
Margaret Reynolds, Executive Director
Andrew Wooldridge, President

Association of Canadian Publishers (ACP) / Association des éditeurs canadiens
#306, 174 Spadina Ave., Toronto ON M5T 2C2
Tel: 416-487-6116; *Fax:* 416-487-8815
admin@canbook.org
www.publishers.ca
To encourage writing, publishing, distribution & promotion of books written by Canadian authors in particular, & reading & study of books in general; To represent the members at international book fairs; To facilitate the exchange of information & professional expertise among members
Margie Wolfe, President
Carolyn Wood, Executive Director
Kate Edwards, Manager, Programs

Association of Canadian University Presses (ACUP) / Association des presses universitaires canadiennes (APUC)
#700, 10 St. Mary St., Toronto ON M4Y 2W8
Tel: 416-978-2239; *Fax:* 416-978-4738
clarose@utpress.utoronto.ca
To support scholarly publishing by university presses in Canada.
Bill Harnum, President

Association of English Language Publishers of Québec (AELAQ) / Association des éditeurs de langue anglaise du Québec
#3, 1200, av Atwater, Montréal QC H3Z 1X4
Tel: 514-932-5633; *Fax:* 514-932-5456
info@aelaq.org
www.aelaq.org
To raise the profile of English-language books published in Québec
Aparna Sanyal, Executive Director

Association of Manitoba Book Publishers (AMBP)
#404, 100 Arthur St., Winnipeg MB R3B 1H3
Tel: 204-947-3335; *Fax:* 204-956-4689
ambp@mts.net
www.bookpublishers.mb.ca
To promote Manitoba publishing industry
Michelle Peters, Executive Director

Association québécoise des salons du livre (AQSL)
CP 353, #105, 110 rue de l'Évêche est, Rimouski QC G5L 7C3
Tél: 418-723-7456; *Téléc:* 418-725-4543
Ligne sans frais: 888-542-2075
info@aqsl.ca
www.aqsl.org
Association sans but lucratif, qui a pour mission la promotion du livre, du périodique et de la lecture; elle défend les intérêts des Salons membres et favorise la recherche, la documentation, les contacts professionnels, la création et la diffusion du livre
Robin Doucet, Directeur général

Atlantic Community Newspapers Association (ACNA)
#216, 7075 Bayers Rd., Halifax NS B3L 2C2
Tel: 902-832-4480; *Fax:* 902-832-4484
Toll-Free: 877-842-4480
info@acna.com
www.acna.com
To promote excellence, credibility, & the economic well-being of member community newspapers throughout Atlantic Canada
Shawn Woodford, President
Fred Fiander, Secretary
Leith Orr, Treasurer

Atlantic Publishers Marketing Association (APMA)
1484 Carlton St., Halifax NS B3H 3B7
Tel: 902-420-0711; *Fax:* 902-423-4302
apma.admin@atlanticpublishers.ca
www.atlanticpublishers.ca
To promote the growth & development of Canadian-owned publishing houses based in Atlantic Canada
Peggy Walt, Executive Director
Donna Francis, Executive Director
Robin MacGregor, Vice-President
Terrilee Bulger, Treasurer
Beverely Rach, Secretary

Book & Periodical Council (BPC)
#107, 192 Spadina Ave., Toronto ON M5T 2C2
Tel: 416-975-9366; *Fax:* 416-975-1839
info@thebpc.ca
www.thebpc.ca
To increase the level of awareness & the use of Canadian materials by the general public & in educational systems at all levels; To ensure the public has an adequate & representative range of Canadian books & periodicals in sales outlets, library systems & educational institutions; To strengthen book & periodical distribution systems; To support the development of new & existing Canadian-owned companies & encourage their growth & expansion; To improve market conditions & contractual arrangements as well as promotion & publicity given to Canadian writers & their work; To encourage the development of writing & publishing projects of social & cultural importance; To improve the cultural & economic climate in which the Canadian book & periodical industries exist; To discourage expansion of foreign ownership in all sectors of the book & periodical publishing industries
Anita Purcell, Chair

Book Promoters Association of Canada (BPAC)
PO Box 75115, Stn. Hudson Bay Postal Outlet, "The Wicket", 20 Bloor St. East, Toronto ON M4W 3T3
Tel: 905-430-5134
bookpromoters@gmail.com
bookpromotersassociationofcanada.blogspot.com
To enhance the professional skills of members; To foster professional attitudes & business practices within its membership; To raise the public & industry profile of book promotion as an integral part of the book publishing & selling process; To reward & encourage BPAC members & potential members, & those connected to the publishing industry, through the regular endowment of various awards
David Leonard, President
Selina Rajani, Director, West Coast
Miranda Snyder, Membership Director
Nadia de Freitas, Network News Managing Editor
Doug Blair, Treasurer

Book Publishers Association of Alberta (BPAA)
10523 - 100 Ave., Edmonton AB T5J 0A8
Tel: 780-424-5060; *Fax:* 780-424-7943
info@bookpublishers.ab.ca
www.bookpublishers.ab.ca
To work for maintenance & growth of strong book publishing houses owned & controlled in Alberta; to speak for common interests of constituent members; to liaise & cooperate with other associations for the good of the Canadian publishing industry
Kieran Leblanc, Executive Director

British Columbia & Yukon Community Newspapers Association (BCYCNA)
9 West Broadway, Vancouver BC V5Y 1P1
Tel: 604-669-9222; *Fax:* 604-684-4713
Toll-Free: 866-669-9222
info@bccommunitynews.com
www.bccommunitynews.com
Social Media:
www.linkedin.com/company/220705?goback=%2Efcs
To encourage excellence in the publishing of community newspapers
George Affleck, General Manager
Kerry Slater, Manager
Naomi Zwier
Sylvia Males, Accounting Manager

Canadian Bookbinders & Book Artists Guild (CBBAG) / Guilde canadienne des relieurs et des artisans du livre
#112, 60 Atlantic Ave., Toronto ON M6K 1X9
Tel: 416-581-1071; *Fax:* 416-581-1053
cbbag@cbbag.ca
www.cbbag.ca
Social Media: www.facebook.com/group.php?gid=77394956232
To create a spirit of community among hand workers in the book arts & those who love books; to promote greater awareness of the book arts; to increase educational opportunities, & foster excellence through exhibitions, workshops, lectures, & publications.
Scott Duncan, President

Canadian Booksellers Association (CBA)
#902, 1255 Bay St., Toronto ON M5R 2A9
Tel: 416-467-7883; *Fax:* 416-467-7886
Toll-Free: 866-788-0790
enquiries@cbabook.org
www.cbabook.org
To promote a high standard of business methods & ethics among members; to define & expand the role of booksellers within the Canadian publishing process; to provide professional advice to prospective & practising booksellers
Mark Lefebvre, President
Christopher Smith, Vice-President
Ellen Pickle, Treasurer

Canadian Children's Book Centre (CCBC)
#101, 40 Orchard View Blvd., Toronto ON M4R 1B9
Tel: 416-975-0010; *Fax:* 416-975-8970
info@bookcentre.ca
www.bookcentre.ca
Social Media:
www.facebook.com/pages/the-canadian-childrens-book-centre/169843829712
The Centre promotes the reading, writing, & illustrating of Canadian books for young readers, providing programs, publications & resources for teachers, librarians, authors, illustrators, publishers, booksellers & parents. It is a registered charity, BN: 124389164RR0001.
Jo-Anne Naslund, President
Charlotte Teeple, Executive Director
Dawn Todd, General Manager

Canadian Circulations Audit Board Inc. (CCAB) / Office canadien de vérification de la diffusion
Div. of BPA International, #800, 1 Concorde Gate, Toronto ON M3C 3N6
Tel: 416-487-2418; *Fax:* 416-487-6405
www.bpaww.com
To issue standardized statements of data reported by a member; to verify the figures shown in these statements by auditors' examination of any & all records considered by the corporation to be necessary; to disseminate these data for the benefit of any individual or company requiring such information
Richard Matte, General Manager

Canadian Community Newspapers Association (CCNA)
#200, 890 Yonge St., Toronto ON M4W 3P4
Tel: 416-482-1090; *Fax:* 416-482-1908
Toll-Free: 877-305-2262
info@ccna.ca
www.communitynews.ca
The Canadian Community Newspapers Association (CCNA) is the national voice of the community press in Canada.
John Hinds, Chief Executive Officer

Canadian Newspaper Association (CNA) / Association canadienne des journaux (ACJ)
c/o Newspapers Canada, #200, 890 Yonge St., Toronto ON M4W 3P4
Tel: 416-923-3567; *Fax:* 416-923-7206
Toll-Free: 877-305-2262
info@newspaperscanada.ca; publisher@newspaperscanada.ca
www.newspaperscanada.ca
To ensure the continuance of a free press to serve readers effectively, by combining the experience, expertise, & dedication of members; To increase the profile & effectiveness of Canada's newspaper industry
Natalie Larivière, Chair
John Hinds, President & Chief Executive Officer
Suzanne Raitt, Vice-President, Marketing & Innovation
Eileen Barak, Director, Government Affairs
Susan Down, Managing Director, Dailies
Tina Ongkeko, Managing Director, Community Media

The Canadian Press (CP) / La presse canadienne
36 King St. East, Toronto ON M5C 2L9
Tel: 416-364-0321; *Fax:* 416-364-0207
www.thecanadianpress.com
Social Media: twitter.com/CdnPress_News
To operate as a national news cooperative, owned & financed by Canada's daily newspapers
Scott White, Editor-in-Chief
Philippe Mercure, Business Director, CPimages
Graeme Roy, Director, News Photography
James McCarten, Senior National Editor
Andrea Baillie, Editor, Entertainment
Neil Davidson, Editor, Sports
Paul Loong, Editor, World
John Valorzi, Editor, Business

Canadian Publishers' Council (CPC)
#203, 250 Merton St., Toronto ON M4S 1B1
Tel: 416-322-7011; *Fax:* 416-322-6999
bpellas@pubcouncil.ca
www.pubcouncil.ca
Canada's main English-language book publishing trade association, representing the interests of 21 companies who publish books & other media for elementary & secondary schools, colleges & universities, professional & reference, retail, & library markets
Jacqueline Hushion, Executive Director
Colleen O'Neill, Executive Director, Trade (Consumer) & Higher Education Publishers' Groups

Canadian Telebook Agency
#401, 110 Eglinton Ave. West, Toronto ON M4R 1A3
Tel: 416-545-1595; *Fax:* 416-545-1590
admin@cta.geis.com
To simplify the complex task of sourcing books that are published &/or distributed in Canada; to provide an automated vehicle for ordering these books.
Elizabeth Bryant, Executive Director

Canadian University Press (CUP) / Presse universitaire canadienne
#503, 920 Yonge St., Toronto ON M4W 3C7
Tel: 416-962-2287; *Fax:* 416-966-3699
Toll-Free: 866-250-5595
president@cup.ca
www.cup.ca
To elevate the standard of post-secondary student journalism; to foster communication among post-secondary student newspapers; to provide a national press service for post-secondary student newspapers; to provide facilities for the dissemination of news of importance to post-secondary students
Emma Godmere, National Bureau Chief
James Michael McDonald, President

Circulation Management Association of Canada (CMC) / Association canadienne des chefs de tirage
PO Box 349, #6, 50 Main St. East, Beeton ON L0G 1A0
Tel: 905-729-1046; *Fax:* 905-729-4432
cmc@tamicirc.ca
www.circ.org
CMC provides professional development, promotes fellowship within the circulation profession, & raises the profile of circulation professionals by rewarding outstanding achievement.
Tuppy Carnie, President
Ron Sellwood, Director, Communications

Connexions Information Sharing Services
#305, 489 College St., Toronto ON M6G 1A5
Tel: 416-964-1511
www.connexions.org
To link people striving to create positive solutions to social, environmental, economic & international problems; To encourage development of a more just & democratic society; To disseminate information & ideas that contribute to this goal
Ulli Diemer, Coordinator

Conseil de presse du Québec (CPQ) / Québec Press Council
#A208, 1000, rue Fullum, Montréal QC H2K 3L7
Tél: 514-529-2818; *Téléc:* 514-873-4434
Ligne sans frais: 877-250-3060
info@conseildepresse.qc.ca
www.conseildepresse.qc.ca
Défendre la liberté de la presse, le droit du public à l'information; recevoir les plaintes du public concernant l'information journaux, télé, radio, internet.
Guy Amyot, Secrétaire général

Hebdos Québec
538, place Saint-Henri, Montréal QC H4C 2R9
Tél: 514-861-2088; *Téléc:* 514-861-1966
Ligne sans frais: 866-861-2088
communications@hebdos.com
www.hebdos.com
Mèdia social: www.facebook.com/hebdosqc; twitter.com/HebdosQuebec
Favoriser et stimuler le développement du secteur des hebdomadaires en offrant à ses membres divers services en matière de recherche, de marketing et de formation; projeter une image crédible de la presse hebdomadaire, de la défendre, et de la rendre plus visible et plus accessible
Paul Brisson, Directeur général
Angèle Marcoux-Prévost, Présidente

International Board on Books for Young People - Canadian Section (IBBY - Canada) / Union internationale pour les livres de jeunesse
c/o Canadian Children's Book Centre, #217, 40 Orchard View Blvd., Toronto ON M4R 1B9
Tel: 416-975-0010; *Fax:* 416-975-8970
info@ibby-canada.org
www.ibby-canada.org
To promote the belief that all children everywhere should have the ability to read a wide & rich selection of books at the level of their needs & interests; To build bridges of understanding & tolerance through children's books
Brenda Halliday, President
Randi Robin, Secretary, Membership

The Literary Press Group of Canada (LPG)
#501, 192 Spadina Ave., Toronto ON M5T 2C2
Tel: 416-483-1321; *Fax:* 416-483-2510
info@lpg.ca
www.lpg.ca
A not-for-profit association of Canadian literary book publishers, with a mandate to advocate on behalf of its members, & to foster the survival, growth & maintenance of strong Canadian-owned & controlled literary book publishing houses
Jack Illingworth, Executive Director
Petra Morin, Sales & Marketing Manager

Livres Canada Books
#504, 1 Nicholas St., Ottawa ON K1N 7B7
Tel: 613-562-2324; *Fax:* 613-562-2329
info@livrescanadabooks.com
www.livrescanadabooks.com
The association defends the interests of Canadian book publishers by providing market intelligence products and services, information and resources on digital publishing, as well as financial, promotion and logisitical support; the association administers the Foreign Rights Marketing Assistance Program, a component of the Canada Book Fund, as well as mentoring programs and other funding initiatives
François Charette, Executive Director
Francine Bélec, Manager, Finance & Operations
Philip Cercone, Chair, Board of Directors

Magazines Canada
#700, 425 Adelaide St. West, Toronto ON M5V 3C1
Tel: 416-504-0274; *Fax:* 416-504-0437
info@magazinescanada.ca
www.magazinescanada.ca
Social Media: www.facebook.com/MagazinesCanada; twitter.com/magscanada
To promote the value of Canadian magazine publishing industry; To serve Canadian magazines through advocacy & special initiatives; To foster an environment where new magazines are nurtured; To support established magazines; To protect the Canadian consumer magazine industry
Mark Jamison, CEO
Gary Garland, Executive Director, Advertising Services
Jim Everson, Executive Director, Public Affairs

Manitoba Community Newspapers Association (MCNA)
943 McPhillips St., Winnipeg MB R2X 2J9
Tel: 204-947-1691; *Fax:* 204-947-1919
Toll-Free: 800-782-0051
www.mcna.com
To serve community newspaper publishers in Manitoba; To act as the industry voice for the issues of community newspaper publishers; To encourage high standards in publishing
Tanis Hutchinson, Manager, Display Ad Sales

Manitoba Press Council Inc.
#101, 2033 Portage Ave., Winnipeg MB R3J 0K8
Tel: 204-888-5189; *Fax:* 204-831-6359
query@mbpress.org
www.mbpress.org
To promote professional & ethical standards of journalism; To consider complaints against member newspapers; to make findings of complaints public; To assist in the preservation of the freedom of the press
John Cochrane, Chair
Diane Cullen, Executive Secretary-Treasurer

National Magazine Awards Foundation (NMAF) / Fondation nationale des prix du magazine canadien
#700, 425 Adelaide St. West, Toronto ON M5V 3C1
Tel: 416-422-1358; *Fax:* 416-504-0437
staff@magazine-awards.com
www.magazine-awards.com
Social Media: twitter.com/natmagawards
To promote excellence in the communication arts industry in Canada through an awards program for Canadian magazine writers, editors, photographers, illustrators & art directors
Patrick Walsh, President

Ontario Community Newspapers Association (OCNA)
#103, 3050 Harvester Rd., Burlington ON L7N 3J1
Tel: 905-639-8720; *Fax:* 905-639-6962
www.ocna.org
Social Media: www.facebook.com/group.php?gid=171125688577
To support members with information about the Ontario community newspaper industry & market; To improve the competitive position of the industry
Don MacLeod, President
Anne Lannan, Executive Director
Todd Frees, Controller
Karen Shardlow, Coordinator, Member Services
Lucia Shepherd, Coordinator, Newsprint
David Harvey, Treasurer

Ontario Press Council / Conseil de presse de l'Ontario
#1706, 2 Carlton St., Toronto ON M5B 1J3
Tel: 416-340-1981; *Fax:* 416-340-8724
info@ontpress.com
www.ontpress.com
To receive & adjudicate complaints from the public against Ontario newspapers; to defend freedom of expression on behalf of the public & press
Don McCurdy, Executive Secretary

Periodical Marketers of Canada (PMC)
South Tower, #1007, 175 Bloor St. East, Toronto ON M4W 3R8
Tel: 416-968-7311; *Fax:* 416-968-6281
To represent Canadian wholesalers; To promote Canadian magazines
Ray Argyle, Executive Director

Québec Community Newspaper Association (QCNA) / Association des journaux régionaux du Québec (AJRQ)
#5, 400, boul Grand, L'Ile-Perrot QC J7V 4X2
Tel: 514-453-6300; *Fax:* 514-453-6330
info@qcna.qc.ca
www.qcna.org
To promote Québec community English media; To serve as clearinghouse for information; To promote good journalism among members; to enhance the role of the media as social catalysts; To represent its members to pertinent government departments; To interact with other provincial & national newspaper associations in Canada; To help members better their financial condition
Greg Duncan, Executive Director

Saskatchewan Publishers Group (SPG)
2405 - 11th Ave., Regina SK S4P 0K4
Tel: 306-780-9808; *Fax:* 306-780-9810
spg@saskpublishers.sk.ca
www.saskpublishers.sk.ca
To promote the Saskatchewan book publishing industry; to provide a forum for sharing information & ideas; to speak for the common interests of its members; to undertake specific projects, programs & studies; to work closely with other publishing & cultural organizations across Canada
Brenda Niskala, Co-Executive Director
Jillian Bell, Co-Executive Director

Saskatchewan Weekly Newspapers Association (SWNA)
#14, 401 - 45th St. West, Saskatoon SK S7L 5Z9
Tel: 306-382-9683; *Fax:* 306-382-9421
Toll-Free: 800-661-7962
www.swna.com
To assist persons to issue press releases, buy advertising, & place classifieds in member newspapers in central Saskatchewan & the Northwest Territories
Steven Nixon, Executive Director
Clark Pepper, President
Louise Simpson, Treasurer & Office Manager
Julie Schau, Officer, Communications, Market Research, & Sales

Société de développement des périodiques culturels québécois (SODEP)
#716, 460, rue Ste-Catherine ouest, Montréal QC H3B 1A7
Tél: 514-397-8669; *Téléc:* 514-397-6887
info@sodep.qc.ca
www.sodep.qc.ca
Mèdia social: www.facebook.com/sodep.qc.ca?ref=ts; twitter.com/cultureenrevues
Travailler à l'essor et au rayonnement des revues culturelles; établir et entretenir des liens avec le milieu de l'enseignement, les bibliothèques, les médias et les maisons de distribution; représenter et promouvoir les intérêts professionnels, éthiques et économiques des éditeurs; favoriser les échanges internationaux
Yves Beauregard, Président
Éric Perron, Vice-président
Francine Bergeron, Directrice générale
Daniel Sernine, Secrétaire-trésorier

Toronto Press Club (TPC)
PO Box 262, Stn. Commerce Court South, Toronto ON M4L 1E8
Tel: 416-363-0651; *Fax:* 416-363-9717
www.torontopressclub.net
Bill Somerville, President

Radio Broadcasting

Halifax Amateur Radio Club (HARC)
PO Box 663, Halifax NS B3J 2T3
Tel: 902-490-6421
www.halifax-arc.org
To promote amateur radio and Ham radio and provide a forum for the exchange of ideas and information related to radio communications and technical experimentation in Nova Scotia.
Murray MacDonald, President

Real Estate

Alberta Association of the Appraisal Institute of Canada (AA-AIC)
#245, 495 - 36 St. NE, Calgary AB T2A 6K3
Tel: 403-207-7892; *Fax:* 403-207-7857
info@appraisal.ab.ca
www.appraisal.ab.ca
To maintain professional ethics & standards in real estate valuation; to qualify real estate appraisers
Ken Morris, President
Suzanne E. Teal, Executive Director

Alberta Building Officials Association
PO Box 27058, City Centre RPO, Red Deer AB T4N 6X8
www.aboa.ab.ca
Goals of the organization are to improve standards of building inspection; to be a discussion forum for shared issues and concerns; to assit in the education of building inspector in the areas of administration, technical, and other branches of the profession; to promote the importance of the building official's role.
Bob Clarke, President
Ken Prusky, Secretary

Alberta Real Estate Association (AREA)
#300, 4954 Richard Rd. SW, Calgary AB T3E 6L1
Tel: 403-228-6845; *Fax:* 403-228-4360
Toll-Free: 800-661-0231
info@areahub.ca; communications@areahub.ca
www.areahub.ca
Dan Russel, CEO

Annapolis Valley Real Estate Board
PO Box 117, 2110 Hwy. 1, Auburn NS B0P 1A0
Tel: 902-847-9336; *Fax:* 902-847-9869
Cathy Simpson, Executive Officer

Appraisal Institute of Canada (AIC) / Institut canadien des évaluateurs
#403, 200 Catherine St., Ottawa ON K2P 2K9
Tel: 613-234-6533; *Fax:* 613-234-7197
info@aicanada.ca
www.aicanada.ca
Social Media: www.facebook.com/AppraisalInstitute.Canada; twitter.com/aic_canada
To grant professional designations in real estate appraisal; To strive to maintain high standards in real estate appraisal to protect the public interest
Keith Lancastle, CEO

Association des propriétaires du Québec inc. (APQ) / Quebec Landlords Association (QLA)
8350, boul St-Laurent, Montréal QC H2P 2M3
Tél: 514-382-9670; *Téléc:* 514-382-9676
Ligne sans frais: 888-382-9670
info@apq.org
www.apq.org
Défendre les droits et les intérêts des propriétaires de logements locatifs du Québec

L'Association du Québec de l'Institut canadien des évaluateurs (AQICE) / Québec Association of the Appraisal Institute of Canada
587, ch Rhéaume, Saint-Michel QC J0L 2J0
Tél: 450-454-0377; *Téléc:* 450-454-1166
Ligne sans frais: 877-454-0377
aqice@qc.aira.com
www.aqice.ca
La mission de l'Institut canadien des évaluateurs est de protéger l'intérêt du public en s'assurant que ses membres offrent des services d'expert-conseil selon des normes élevées de pratique professionnelle
Ginette St-Jean, Executive Director

Association of Battlefords Realtors
PO Box 611, North Battleford SK S9A 2Y7
Tel: 306-445-6300; *Fax:* 306-445-9020
To advance & promote interest of those engaged in real estate as brokers, agents, valuators, examiners, & experts; To increase public confidence in & respect for those engaged in real estate
Rick Cann, Executive Officer

Association of Regina Realtors Inc.
1854 McIntyre St., Regina SK S4P 2P9
Tel: 306-791-2700; *Fax:* 306-781-7940
arr@reginarealtors.com
www.reginarealtors.com
Ian Johnston, President

Association of Saskatchewan Realtors (ASR)
2811 Estey Dr., Saskatoon SK S7J 2V8
Tel: 306-373-3350; *Fax:* 306-373-5377
Toll-Free: 877-306-7732
info@saskatchewanrealestate.com
www.saskatchewanrealestate.com
Social Media: www.facebook.com/69418510914; twitter.com/saskREALTORS
Represents real estate boards & their realtor members on government affairs & provincial issues; develops standards of professional practice; administers training; provides information to members, governments & the public; provides support services to members; registers brokers & salespeople; develops special projects for the educational benefit of all registrants in Saskatchewan
Bill Madder, Executive Vice President
Patty Kalytuk, Director, Communication & Administration
Arvid Kuhnle, Director, Professional Development
Linda Minor, Member Services Coordinator

Bancroft District Real Estate Board
PO Box 1522, 69 Hastings St. North, Bancroft ON K0L 1C0
Tel: 613-332-3842
bdreb@bancroftrealestate.on.ca
www.bancroftrealestate.on.ca
Dana Yonemitsu, Executive Officer

Barrie & District Real Estate Board Inc.
30 Mary St., Barrie ON L4N 1S8
Tel: 705-739-4650; *Fax:* 705-721-9101
info@barrie.mls.ca
www.barrie.mls.ca
Provides continuing education, Multiple Listing Service (MLS), statistical information and many other services to its members. The geographical area served by the Association includes the City of Barrie and part or all of the surrounding townships including Springwater, Oro-Medonte, Innisil, Essa, Bradford-West Gwillimbury, and Clearview.
Catherine Garbe, President
Frances Clarke, Executive Officer

Brampton Real Estate Board (BREB)
#10, 35 Van Kirk Dr., Brampton ON L7A 1A5
Tel: 905-791-9913; *Fax:* 905-791-9430
info@breb.org
www.breb.org
Social Media: twitter.com/thebreb
The Brampton Real Estate Board is dedicated to helping members achieve their real estate related goals.
Chris Luxemburger, President
Lynn M. Martin, CEO

Brandon Real Estate Board (BREB)
907 Princess Ave., Brandon MB R7A 6E3
Tel: 204-727-4672; *Fax:* 204-727-8331
info@breb.mb.ca
www.breb.mb.ca
Real estate support for Realtors in Brandon.
Tim Melnyk, President

Brantford Regional Real Estate Association Inc. (BRREA)
106 George St., Brantford ON N3T 2Y4
Tel: 519-753-0308; *Fax:* 519-753-8638
brantfordreb@rogers.com
www.brrea.com
Real estate support for Realtors working in Brantford.
Louise Sharland, Executive Officer

British Columbia Association of the Appraisal Institute of Canada (BCAAIC)
#210, 10451 Shellbridge Way, Richmond BC V6X 2W8
Tel: 604-284-5515; *Fax:* 604-284-5514
Toll-Free: 888-707-8287
info@appraisal.bc.ca
www.appraisal.bc.ca
To represent, promote & support our members as leaders in the counselling, analysis & evaluation of real property. Chapters: Fraser Valley, Nanaimo, Okanagan, Vancouver, Kamloops, Northwest, Prince George, Victoria, and Kootenay
Craig Barnsley, President
Janice P. O'Brien, Executive Director

British Columbia Northern Real Estate Board
2609 Queensway, Prince George BC V2L 1N3
Tel: 250-563-1236; *Fax:* 250-563-3637
inquiries@bcnreb.bc.ca
boards.mls.ca/bcnreb/
Dorothy Friesen, President

British Columbia Real Estate Association (BCREA)
#1420, 701 Georgia St. West, Vancouver BC V7Y 1C6
Tel: 604-683-7702; *Fax:* 604-683-8601
bcrea@bcrea.bc.ca
www.bcrea.bc.ca
To promote the interests of & advocate for the real estate profession; To secure public support & trust in the profession; To promote property rights & real estate related issues; To ensure high standards of ethics & professionalism through ongoing education of realtors
Robert Laing, Chief Executive Officer
Melinda Entwistle, Chief Operating Officer
Cameron Muir, Chief Economist
Marla Gerein, Director, Education
Borg Jorgensen, Director, Finance & Systems
Damian Stathonikos, Director, Communications

Brooks Real Estate Board
PO Box 997, Brooks AB T1R 1B8
Tel: 403-362-4643; *Fax:* 403-362-3276
brecoop@telusplanet.net
Carol Breakell, Executive Officer
Creitia Morishita, President

Building Owners & Managers Association - Canada
#850, 36 Toronto St., Toronto ON M5C 2C5
Tel: 416-214-1912; *Fax:* 416-360-3838
info@bomacanada.ca
www.bomacanada.ca
To represent the Canadian commerical real estate industry on matters of national concern; To develop a strong communications network between local associations; To promote professionalism of members through education programs & effective public relations activity
Deb Cross, Executive Vice-President
Diana Osler-Zortega, President

Calgary Real Estate Board Cooperative Limited (CREB)
300 Manning Rd. NE, Calgary AB T2E 8K4
Tel: 403-263-0530; *Fax:* 403-218-3688
info@creb.com
www.creb.com
Alan Tennant, CEO

Canadian Institute of Professional Home Inspectors Inc.
#720, 999 West Broadway, Vancouver BC V5Z 1K5
Tel: 604-732-0617
info@edwitzke.com
www.edwitzke.com
To inspect all components of building for structural soundness, damage assessment, dry rot, pest problems, energy efficiency, compliance with grading, zoning, legal requirements & safety laws; to inspect all manner of the buildings, including new or existing residential or commercial buildings to determine the condition of a building, for contractors in recommending procedures for compliance with legal requirements, or for insurance companies in assessing damages & general public
Ed R.R. Witzke, President

The Canadian Real Estate Association (CREA) / Association canadienne de l'immeuble
200 Catherine St., 6th Fl., Ottawa ON K2P 2K9
Tel: 613-237-7111; *Fax:* 613-234-2567
Toll-Free: 800-842-2732
info@crea.ca
www.crea.ca
To enhance member professionalism, competency & profitability; To advocate government policies which improve the industry's market environment & enhance individual rights with respect to the ownership of real property
Gary Simonsen, Chief Executive Officer
Gary Morse, President
Laura Leyser, Vice-President

Cariboo Real Estate Association
2609 Queensway, Prince George BC V2L 1N3
Tel: 250-563-1236; *Fax:* 250-563-3637
Supporting Real Estate Agents and buyers in Cariboo, B.C.
John Castle, Chair

Central Alberta Realtors Association
4922 - 45 St., Red Deer AB T4N 1K6
Tel: 403-343-0881; *Fax:* 403-347-9080
office@CARAssociation.ca
www.rdreb.ca
Nancy A. MacKie, Executive Officer
Sandi Gouchie, President

Chambre immobilière Centre du Québec Inc.
139C, rue Hériot, Drummondville QC J2C 2B1
Tél: 819-477-1033; *Téléc:* 819-474-7913
Ligne sans frais: 877-546-8320
chambre@cgocable.ca
www.immobiliercentreduquebec.com
Marie-Paule Landry, Adjointe exécutive
Denis A. Jackson, Présidente

Chambre immobilière de l'Abitibi-Témiscamingue Inc. (CIAT)
#203, 33, av Horne, Rouyn-Noranda QC J9X 4S1
Tél: 819-762-1777; *Téléc:* 819-762-4030
ciat@cablevision.qc.ca
www.ciat.qc.ca
Raynald Rail, Président
Gilles Langlais, Directeur général

Chambre immobilière de l'Estrie inc.
19, rue King ouest, Sherbrooke QC J1H 1N4
Tél: 819-566-7616; *Téléc:* 819-566-7688
info@mon-toit.net
www.mon-toit.net
Promouvoir et protéger les intérêts de l'industrie immobilière du Québec afin que les Chambres et les membres accomplissent avec succès leurs objectifs d'affaires.
Johanne Beaudoin, Secrétaire exécutive

Chambre immobilière de l'Outaouais
106, boul Sacré-Coeur, Gatineau QC J8X 1E1
Tél: 819-771-5221; *Téléc:* 819-771-8715
info@avecunagent.com
www.avecunagent.com
Chantal Legault, Directrice générale

Chambre immobilière de la Haute Yamaska Inc. (CIHY) / Haute Yamaska Real Estate Board
#3, 45, rue Centre, Granby QC J2G 5B4
Tél: 450-378-6702; *Téléc:* 450-375-5268
administration.cihy@videotron.ca
Offrir des services de formation et d'information pour les agents immobiliers.

Chambre immobilière de la Mauricie Inc. / Trois-Rivières Real Estate Board
#102, 1640 - 6e rue, Trois-Rivières QC G8Y 5B8
Tél: 819-379-9081; *Téléc:* 819-379-9262
cimauricie@cgocable.ca
www.cimauricie.com
Lise Girardeau, Adjointe exécutive

Chambre immobilière de Lanaudière Inc.
765, boul Manseau, Joliette QC J6E 3E8
Tél: 450-759-8511; *Téléc:* 450-759-6557
www.immobilierlanaudiere.com
Élise Roch, Directrice générale

Chambre immobilière de Québec
990, av Holland, Québec QC G1S 3T1
Tél: 418-688-3362; *Téléc:* 418-688-3577
Ligne sans frais: 866-688-3362
info@ciq.qc.ca
www.fciq.ca
Promouvoir et protéger les intérêts de l'industrie immobilière du Québec afin que les Chambres et les membres accomplissent avec succès leurs objectifs d'affaires.
Gina Gaudreault, Directrice générale

Chambre immobilière de Saint-Hyacinthe Inc.
CP 667, Saint-Hyacinthe QC J2S 7P5
Tél: 450-799-2210; *Téléc:* 450-799-2230
chimmob@cgocable.ca
Promouvoir et protéger les intérêts de l'industrie immobilière du Québec afin que les Chambres et les membres accomplissent avec succès leurs objectifs d'affaires.

Chambre immobilière des Laurentides (CIL)
570, boul. des Laurentides, Piedmont QC J0R 1K0
Tél: 450-240-0006; *Téléc:* 450-240-0096
optionlaurentides@cgocable.ca
www.chambreimmobilieredeslaurentides.ca
Sa mission est la promotion, la représentation et le développement des intérêts professionnels, économiques et sociaux de ses membres
Francine Soucy, Présidente
Rose Girard, Directrice générale

Chambre immobilière du Grand Montréal / Greater Montréal Real Estate Board
600, ch du Golf, Ile-des-Soeurs QC H3E 1A8
Tél: 514-762-2440; *Téléc:* 514-762-1490
Ligne sans frais: 888-762-2440
cigm@cigm.qc.ca
www.cigm.qc.ca
Michel Beauséjour, Directeur général

Chambre immobilière du Saguenay-Lac St-Jean Inc. (CISL)
#140, 2655, boul du Royaume, Jonquière QC G7S 4S9
Tél: 418-548-8808; *Téléc:* 418-548-2588
chambre@immobiliersaguenay.com
www.immobiliersaguenay.com
Média social: www.facebook.com/immobilier.saguenay
Regrouper les membres afin de leur fournir des services, assurer la qualité de leur travail, défendre et promouvoir leurs intérêts; protéger et promouvoir le commerce de l'immobilier et encourager l'accès à la propriété; offrir de la formation et du perfectionnement dans le domaine immobilier afin d'assurer et de garantir le professionnalisme de l'industrie; faciliter au public en général l'accès à l'information dans le domaine immobilier
Ginette Gaudreault, Directrice générale

Chatham-Kent Real Estate Board
PO Box 384, 252 Wellington St. W., Chatham ON N7M 5K5
Tel: 519-352-4351; *Fax:* 519-351-1498
ckreb@mnsi.net
boards.mls.ca/chatham
Sylvia Rintjema, President

Chilliwack & District Real Estate Board
#1, 8433 Harvard Pl., Chilliwack BC V2P 7Z5
Tel: 604-792-0912; *Fax:* 604-792-6795
cadreb@telus.net
cadreb.com
Real estate board serving Chilliwack, Agassiz, Hope, Boston Bar and Harrison.
Sharon J. Labiuk, Executive Officer

Cornwall & District Real Estate Board
407B Pitt St., Cornwall ON K6J 3R3
Tel: 613-932-6457; *Fax:* 613-932-1687
cdreb@cogeco.net
boards.mls.ca/cornwall
Real estate board for Cornwall and area.

Durham Region Association of REALTORS (DRAR)
#14, 50 Richmond St. East, Oshawa ON L1G 7C7
Tel: 905-723-8184; *Fax:* 905-723-7531
drar@durhamrealestate.org
www.durhamrealestate.org
Social Media: www.facebook.com/DurhamRegionalAssociationofREALTORS
To pursue excellence & professionalism in real estate through commitment & service
Christine Marquis, President
Smith Ian, President-Elect

Edmonton Real Estate Board Co-operative Listing Bureau Ltd.
14220 - 112 Ave., Edmonton AB T5M 2T8
Tel: 780-451-6666; *Fax:* 780-452-1135
connection@ereb.com
www.ereb.com
Marc Perras, President
Ron Hutchinson, Executive Vice-President

Estevan Real Estate Board
PO Box 445, 403 - 9th Ave., Estevan SK S4A 2A4
Tel: 306-634-7885; *Fax:* 306-634-8610
boards.mls.ca/estevan
The Estevan Real Estate Board is a participant in the on-line Multiple Listing Service for the province of Saskatchewan, which provides marketing services for members. This includes postings on the residential properties web site mls.ca and the similar site for commercial and agribusiness listings, CLS.CA.
Jody Fornwald, Executive Officer

Fédération des Chambres immobilières du Québec (FCIQ)
600, ch du Golf, Ile-Des-soeurs QC H3E 1A8
Tél: 514-762-0212; *Téléc:* 514-762-0365
Ligne sans frais: 866-882-0212
info@fciq.ca
www.fciq.ca
Promouvoir et protéger les intérêts de l'industrie immobilière du Québec afin que les Chambres et les membres accomplissent avec succès leurs objectifs d'affaires
Claude Charron, Président du conseil d'administration
Chantal de Repentigny, Directrice adjointe, Communication et relations avec l'industrie

Fort McMurray Realtors Association
9909 Sutherland St., Fort McMurray AB T9H 1V3
Tel: 780-791-1124; *Fax:* 780-743-4724
moskalykc@shaw.ca
boards.mls.ca/fortmcmurray
Greg Walsh, President
Chris Moskalyk, Executive Officer

Fraser Valley Real Estate Board
PO Box 99, 15463 - 104 Ave., Surrey BC V3T 4W4
Tel: 604-930-7600; *Fax:* 604-588-0325
Toll-Free: 800-906-0258
mls@fvreb.bc.ca
www.fvreb.bc.ca
To provide the most efficient real estate marketing service.
Paul Penner, President

Georgian Triangle Real Estate Board
54 Third St., Collingwood ON L9Y 1K3
Tel: 705-445-7295; *Fax:* 705-445-7253
realestate@gtreb.com
www.gtreb.com
The Georgian Triangle Real Estate Board is dedicated to embracing new technologies, advancing quality education and high ethical standards in support of their membership while delivering MLS and real estate services consistant with the chaning regulations and market dynamics of our profession.
Sandy Raymer, Executive Officer

Greater Moncton Real Estate Board Inc.
541 St. George Blvd., Moncton NB E1E 2B6
Tel: 506-857-8200; *Fax:* 506-857-1760
gmreb@nb.aibn.com
www.monctonrealestateboard.com
The Greater Moncton Real Estate Board provides its members with the strcuture and services to enhance REALTOR professionalism, standards of business practice and ethics in meeting the real estate needs of the community.
Faye Andersen, Executive Officer
Chris Constantine, President

Guelph & District Real Estate Board
400 Woolwich St., Guelph ON N1H 3X1
Tel: 519-824-7270; *Fax:* 519-824-6730
info@gdar.ca
www.gdreb.ca
A real estate board representing Guelph, Elora, and Fergus.

Hamilton-Burlington & District Real Estate Board (HBDREB)
505 York Blvd., Hamilton ON L8R 3K4
Tel: 905-529-8101; *Fax:* 905-529-4349
info@rahb.ca
www.rahb.ca
To pursue excellence & professionalism in real estate through commitment & service

Highland Real Estate Board
c/o The Prudential Highland Properties, #104, 219 Main St., Antigonish NS B2G 2C1
Tel: 902-863-1878; *Fax:* 902-863-1933
Valerie Chugg, President

Huron Perth Real Estate Board
#6, 55 Lorne Ave. East, Stratford ON N5A 6S4
Tel: 519-271-6870; *Fax:* 519-271-3040
hpreb@wightman.ca
boards.mls.ca/huron
"The Board enforces a strict Code of Ethics and Standards of Business Practice to it's members to maintain the integrity of organized real estate; to promote interest in the marketing of real estate; and to promote, encourage and protect the ownership of real property to the public."
Gwen Kirkpatrick, Executive Officer

Institute of Municipal Assessors
#206, 10720 Yonge St., Richmond Hill ON L4C 3C9
Tel: 905-884-1959; *Fax:* 905-884-9263
Toll-Free: 877-877-8703
info@assessorsinstitute.ca
www.assessorsinstitute.ca
The IMA is the largest Canadian professional association representing members that practice in the field of Property Assessment and related Property Taxation functions.
Terry Tomkins, President
Colleen Vercouteren, 1st Vice President

Kamloops & District Real Estate Association (KADREA)
#101, 418 St. Paul St., Kamloops BC V2C 2J6
Tel: 250-372-9411; *Fax:* 250-828-1986
cboer@kadrea.com
www.boards.mls.ca/kamloops

Cathy Boer, Executive Director
Craig McIntyre, President

Kawartha Lakes Real Estate Association
31 Kent St. East, Lindsay ON K9V 2C3
Tel: 705-324-4515; *Fax:* 705-324-3916
sschell@kawarthalakes-mls.ca
www.kawarthalakes-mls.ca
Members are actively involved in a variety of community projects through the association's sponsorship and other local organizations as they promote the wonderful lifestyle that the Kawartha Lakes area affords them.
Susan Schell, Executive Officer
Mike Barkwell, President

Kingston & Area Real Estate Association
720 Arlington Park Pl., Kingston ON K7M 8H9
Tel: 613-384-0880; *Fax:* 613-384-0863
info@karea.ca
www.karea.ca
A not-for-profit organization that represents 494 real estate professionals who are also members of the Canadian Real Estate Association (CREA) and the Ontario Real Estate Association (OREA).
Susan Swann, Executive Officer

Kootenay Real Estate Board (KREB)
#208, 402 Baker St., Nelson BC V1L 4H8
Tel: 250-352-5477; *Fax:* 250-352-7184
kreb@netidea.com; kreb@telus.net
The Association promotes interest in real estate markets in all aspects through service to members & the public.
Jim Barber, President
Marianne Bond, Acting Executive Officer

Lethbridge & District Association of Realtors
522 - 6 St. South, Lethbridge AB T1J 2E2
Tel: 403-328-8838; *Fax:* 403-328-8906
lreb2@telus.net
www.ldar.ca
LDAR is a member service organization providing real estate information on the Lethbridge area. It serves as a forum to network & build connections within the real estate community.
Stan Mills, President
Margaret Van, Executive Officer

London & St. Thomas Real Estate Board
342 Commissioners Rd. West, London ON N6J 1Y3
Tel: 519-641-1400; *Fax:* 519-641-4613
mls@lstreb.com
www.lstreb.com
Greg Harris, President

Manitoba Association of the Appraisal Institute of Canada (MB AIC)
#193, 162 - 2025 Corydon Ave., Winnipeg MB R3P 0N5
Tel: 204-934-1177; *Fax:* 204-947-1332
mbaic@mts.net
www.aimanitoba.ca
Lynne Smith Dark, Executive Director
Brett Ferguson, President

Manitoba Building Officials Association
PO Box 2063, Winnipeg MB R3C 3R4
Tel: 204-832-1512; *Fax:* 204-897-8094
info@mboa.mb.ca
www.mboa.mb.ca
John Barnes, President

Manitoba Real Estate Association (MREA)
1873 Inkster Blvd., Winnipeg MB R2R 2A6
Tel: 204-772-0405; *Fax:* 204-775-3781
Toll-Free: 800-267-6019
cduheme@mrea.mb.ca; rfinch@mrea.mb.ca (education)
www.realestatemanitoba.com
Social Media: www.facebook.com/144040815612760
To represent the interest of Manitoba's licensed realtors
Brian M. Collie, Executive Director

Medicine Hat Real Estate Board Co-operative Ltd.
403 - 4 St. SE, Medicine Hat AB T1A 0K5
Tel: 403-526-2879; *Fax:* 403-526-0307
mhreb@telus.net
boards.mls.ca/medicinehat/
Dennis Schlenker, President
Brian Patterson, Executive Officer

Melfort Real Estate Board
c/o Royal Lepage Hodgins Realty, PO Box 3070, 101 Burrows Ave. West, Melfort SK S0E 1A0
Tel: 306-752-5751; *Fax:* 306-752-5754
Derwood Dodds, President

Midland-Penetang District Real Estate Board Inc.
PO Box 805, 578 King St., Midland ON L4R 4P4
Tel: 705-526-8706; *Fax:* 705-526-0701
info@midland-penetang-mls.ca

Mississauga Real Estate Board
#29, 3355 The Collegeway, Mississauga ON L5L 5T3
Tel: 905-608-6732; *Fax:* 905-608-9988
administration@mreb.ca
www.mreb.ca
Organization of Realtors, it is dedicated to the beneficial visibility of the industry.
Donna Metcalfe, Executive Director
Gay Napper, Membership Coordinator

Moose Jaw Real Estate Board
79 Hochelaga St. West, Moose Jaw SK S6H 2E9
Tel: 306-693-9544; *Fax:* 306-692-4463
mjreb@sasktel.net
www.moosejawrealestateboard.com
The Board promotes the real estate sector in the area & provides a forum for local realtors to exchange information.
Derek McRitchie, Chair
Jamie Thorn, President

Muskoka & Haliburton Association of Realtors (MHAR)
34 Cairns Cres., Huntsville ON P1H 1Y3
Tel: 705-788-1504; *Fax:* 705-788-2040
spond@mhar.on.ca
www.mhar.on.ca
Within the boundaries of the Muskoka & Haliburton Association of REALTORSr, there are seven major geographical areas: Gravenhurst in the south, Bracebridge, Muskoka Lakes in the western part of the area, Huntsville & Almaguin Highlands in the north and Lake of Bays and Haliburton in the eastern part of the area. Each of the areas contains a unique blend of both prestigious year-round recreational properties on large lakes, and lower and mid-range prized cottage properties on the smaller serene lakes.
Susan Pond, Executive Officer

New Brunswick Association of Real Estate Appraisers (NBAREA) / Association des évaluateurs immobiliers du Nouveau-Brunswick (AEIN-B)
#204, 403 Regent St., Fredericton NB E3B 3X6
Tel: 506-450-2016; *Fax:* 506-450-3010
nbarea@nb.aibn.com
www.nbarea.org
To enhance the profession & to protect the public
Jennifer Nemeth, Executive Director

New Brunswick Building Officials Association (NBBOA) / L'Association des officiels de la construction du Nouveau-Brunswick
PO Box 3193, Stn. B, Fredericton NB E3A 5G9
Tel: 506-658-2911; *Fax:* 506-632-6199
secretary@nbboa.ca
www.nbboa.ca
To achieve & maintain the highest levels of professionalism in membership, education & qualifications; legislative interpretation; building inspection service; building & construction safety.
Sherry Sparks, President
David Somerville, Secretary

New Brunswick Real Estate Association (NBREA) / Association des agents des immeubles du Nouveau-Brunswick
#1, 22 Durelle St., Fredericton NB E3C 1N8
Tel: 506-459-8055; *Fax:* 506-459-8057
Toll-Free: 800-762-1677
info@nbrea.ca
www.nbrea.ca
To strengthen & promote standards of professionalism in the real estate industry
Jamie Ryan, CEO

Newfoundland & Labrador Association of Realtors
28 Logy Bay Rd., St. John's NL A1A 1J4
Tel: 709-726-5110
boards.mls.ca/nl/index.htm

Newfoundland & Labrador Association of the Appraisal Institute of Canada
PO Box 1571, Stn. C, St. John's NL A1C 5P3
Tel: 709-753-7644; *Fax:* 709-753-7627
naaic@nf.aibn.com
To promote the appraisal profession throughout Newfoundland & Labrador
Sherry House, Executive Director
Neil Tedstone, President

Niagara Association of REALTORS (NAR)
116 Niagara St., St Catharines ON L2R 4L4
Tel: 905-684-9459; *Fax:* 905-684-4778
www.mls-niagarafalls.com
To provide members with the structure & services to facilitate the marketing of real estate; to ensure a high standard of business practices & ethics; to effectively serve the real estate needs of the members
Brad Johnstone, President

North Bay Real Estate Board
926 Cassells St., North Bay ON P1B 4A8
Tel: 705-472-6812; *Fax:* 705-472-0529
nbreb@nbreb.com
www.nbreb.com
Represents real estate agents and member offices in North Bay.
Brian Graham, President

Northern Lights Real Estate Board
1101 - 103 Ave., Dawson Creek BC V1G 2G8
Tel: 250-782-4876; *Fax:* 250-782-8574
nlreb@shawcable.com
Al Mattishaw, President
Marie Chilton, Executive Officer

Northern New Brunswick Real Estate Board Inc. / Chambre immobilière du nord du Nouveau-Brunswick
PO Box 185, #5, 360 Parkside Dr., Bathurst NB E2A 3Z2
Tel: 506-548-3045; *Fax:* 506-548-4002
nnbreb@nb.sympatico.ca
boards.mls.ca/n-newbrunswick/index.htm
Covers a large and diverse geographic area that includes the cities of Bathurst, Miramichi, Campbellton, and Dalhousie.
Carmelle F. Mallet, Executive Officer

Northumberland Hills Association of Realtors
#23, 1011 Elgin St. West, Cobourg ON K9A 5J4
Tel: 905-372-8630; *Fax:* 905-372-1443
districtrealestate@bellnet.ca
boards.mls.ca/northumberland
The real estate board covers the municipalities of Cobourg & Port Hope, from Lake Ontario to Rice Lake, & as far east as the Township of Cramahe & Hwy. 115.
Sharon Martin, President

Nova Scotia Association of REALTORS (NSAR)
#100, 7 Scarfe Ct., Dartmouth NS B3B 1W4
Tel: 902-468-2515; *Fax:* 902-468-2533
Toll-Free: 800-344-2001
info@nsar.ns.ca
www.nsar-mls.ca
Provides Realtors with services & representation to enable them to best serve the public in real estate transactions
Arnold G. Jones, Executive Officer

Nova Scotia Real Estate Appraisers Association (NSREAA)
#602, 5670 Spring Garden Rd., Halifax NS B3J 1H6
Tel: 902-422-4077; *Fax:* 902-422-3717
nsreaa@nsappraisal.ns.ca
www.nsappraisal.ns.ca
The Association regulates the practice of real estate appraisal in Nova Scotia, establishes and promotes the interests of appraisers, develops and maintains high standards of knowledge and best practices in the field, develops and enforces professional ethics, promotes public awareness of the profession, and encourages studies in real estate appraisal
Andre C. Pouliot, President
Davida Mackay, Executive Director & Registrar
Phillip Smith, Vice President

The Oakville, Milton & District Real Estate Board
125 Navy St., Oakville ON L6J 2Z5
Tel: 905-844-6491; *Fax:* 905-844-6699
info@omdreb.on.ca
www.omdreb.on.ca

Okanagan Mainline Real Estate Board (OMREB)
#112, 140 Commercial Dr., Kelowna BC V1X 7X6
Tel: 250-491-4560; *Fax:* 250-491-4580
admin@omreb.com
www.omreb.com
To provide a forum for the exchange of property-related information between members so that they may provide the public with outstanding service; to establish & maintain optimum standards of business practices; to provide continuing education for the betterment of the members' knowledge; to monitor proposed & legislated laws which inhibit or restrict the right of Canadians or British Columbians to own or use real property
Janice Myers, Executive Director

Ontario Association of the Appraisal Institute of Canada (OA-AIC)
#108, 16 Four Seasons Place, Toronto ON M9B 6E5
Tel: 416-695-9333; *Fax:* 416-695-9321
Toll-Free: 800-771-8087
info@oaaic.on.ca
www.oaaic.on.ca
To serve the public interest by advancing high standards in the analysis & valuation of real property matters by enhancing the professional competence of its members.
Signe Holstein, Executive Director
Peter McLean, President

Ontario Building Officials Association Inc. (OBOA) / Association de l'Ontario des officers en bâtiment inc.
#8, 200 Marycroft Ave., Woodbridge ON L4L 5X4
Tel: 905-264-1662; *Fax:* 905-264-8696
admin@oboa.on.ca
www.oboa.on.ca
To foster & cooperate in the establishment of uniform regulations relating to the fire protection & structural adequacy of buildings & the safety & health of the occupants; to promote the understanding & uniform interpretation & enforcement of these regulations & their companion documents; to provide assistance in the development & improvement of these regulations & their companion documents; to promote a close liaison & interchange of ideas on these regulations with related associations, the building industry, government & the consumer public
Ronald M. Kolbe, CAO
Leo Cusumano, President

Ontario Real Estate Association (OREA)
99 Duncan Mill Rd., Toronto ON M3B 1Z2
Tel: 416-445-9910; *Fax:* 416-445-2644
Toll-Free: 800-265-6732
info@orea.com
www.orea.com
Social Media: www.facebook.com/OREAinfo; twitter.com/oreainfo; www.youtube.com/OREAinfo
To represent the vocational interests of members; To advocate for a better working environment; To communicate with members & the public; To develop educational opportunities for the betterment of the real estate profession; To develop programs to assist members in providing quality services to the public; To develop & administer the educational courses required for registration to trade in real estate on behalf of The Real Estate Council of Ontario
Edward Barisa, Chief Executive Officer
Barbara Sukkau, President
Dinaz Garda, Manager, Executive Office Operations
Ozzie Logozzo, Executive Director, OREA Real Estate College

Orangeville & District Real Estate Board
228 Broadway Ave., Orangeville ON L9W 1K5
Tel: 519-941-4547; *Fax:* 519-941-8482
odreb@bellnet.ca
www.odreb.com

Organisme d'autoréglementation du courtage immobilier du Québec (OACIQ) / Québec Real Estate Association
#2200, 4905, boul Lapinière, Brossard QC J4Z 0G2
Tél: 450-676-4800; *Téléc:* 450-676-7801
Ligne sans frais: 800-440-5110
www.oaciq.com
Protéger le public par l'encadrement des activités professionnelles de tous les courtiers et agents immobiliers exerçant au Québec
Serge Brousseau, Chef de la direction

Orillia & District Real Estate Board
PO Box 551, #7, 3 Progress Dr. S., Orillia ON L3V 6H1
Tel: 705-325-9958; *Fax:* 705-325-0605
realtor.mls.ca/boards/orillia
To provide a governing body for professional standards & business practices; to provide multiple listing services.

Ottawa Real Estate Board (OREB) / Chambre d'immeuble d'Ottawa
1826 Woodward Dr., Ottawa ON K2C 0P7
Tel: 613-225-2240; *Fax:* 613-225-6420
orebadmin@ottawarealestate.org
www.ottawarealestate.org

Parry Sound Real Estate Board
47A James St., Parry Sound ON P2A 1T6
Tel: 705-746-4020; *Fax:* 705-746-2955
psreb@vianet.on.ca
www.parrysoundrealestateboard.ca

Peterborough & the Kawarthas Association of Realtors Inc. (PKAR)
PO Box 1330, 273 Charlotte St., Peterborough ON K9J 7H5
Tel: 705-745-5724; *Fax:* 705-745-9377
info@peterbororealestate.com
www.peterbororealestate.com
Carolyn J. Mills, Executive Officer

Portage La Prairie Real Estate Board
39 Royla Rd. North, Portage la Prairie MB R1N 1T9
Tel: 204-857-4111
preb@escape.ca

Powell River Sunshine Coast Real Estate Board
PO Box 307, 4699 Marine Avenue, Powell River BC V8A 5C2
Tel: 604-485-6944; *Fax:* 604-485-6944
prscreb@shaw.ca
Geri Powell, Board Administrator

Prince Albert & District Association of Realtors
615 Branion Dr., Prince Albert SK S6V 2R9
Tel: 306-764-8755; *Fax:* 306-763-0555
pareb@sasktel.net
www.princealbertrealtors.ca
Supporting Realtors in the Prince Albert Real Estate community.
Charlene Welch, Executive Officer

Prince Edward Island Association of the Appraisal Institute of Canada
PO Box 1796, Charlottetown PE C1A 7N4
Tel: 902-368-3355; *Fax:* 902-368-3582
peiaic@xplornet.com
Scott Wilson, President
Suzanne Pater, Executive Director

Prince Edward Island Real Estate Association
75 St. Peter's Rd., Charlottetown PE C1A 5N7
Tel: 902-368-8451; *Fax:* 902-894-9487
office@peirea.com
www.peirea.com
Danny Moase, President
Fred Ripley, First Vice-President, Education
Ron MacLean, Second Vice-President, Finance
Dorothy Smith, Executive Officer

Quinte & District Real Estate Board
PO Box 128, 51 Cannifton Rd. North, Cannifton ON K0K 1K0
Tel: 613-969-7873; *Fax:* 613-962-1851
quinte.MLS@reach.net
www.quinterealestate.ca

Real Estate Board of Cambridge
75 Ainslie St. North, Cambridge ON N1R 3J7
Tel: 519-623-3660; *Fax:* 519-623-8253
cambridge-admin@rogers.com
www.realestateboardcambridge.com

Real Estate Board of Greater Vancouver
2433 Spruce St., Vancouver BC V6H 4C8
Tel: 604-730-3000; *Fax:* 604-730-3100
www.rebgv.org
Robert K. Wallace, CEO

Real Estate Board of the Fredericton Area Inc. (FREB)
544 Brunswick St., Fredericton NB E3B 1H5
Tel: 506-458-8163; *Fax:* 506-459-8922
freb01@rogers.com
www.frederictonrealestateboard.com
To address member education, motivation & appreciation
Edie Whitman, Executive Officer

Real Estate Institute of Canada (REIC) / Institut canadien de l'immeuble (ICI)
#208, 5407 Eglinton Ave. West, Toronto ON M9C 5K6
Tel: 416-695-9000; *Fax:* 416-695-7230
Toll-Free: 800-542-7342
infocentral@reic.com
www.reic.ca
To advance opportunities for persons involved in real estate
Maura McLaren, Executive Director
Elaine Leibner, Associate Director, Education
Lee Arbon, Manager, Marketing & Communications

Real Property Association of Canada
#1410, One University Ave., Toronto ON M5J 2P1
Tel: 416-642-2700; *Fax:* 416-642-2727
Toll-Free: 855-732-5722
info@realpac.ca
www.realpac.ca
Social Media: www.facebook.com/111245762249174; twitter.com/realpac_news; www.linkedin.com/company/realpac; www.youtube.com/user/REALpacVideos
To represent the real estate industries point of view to government at all levels on legislative & regulatory matters
Paul Morse, CEO
Deborah Prestwich, Manager, Events & Office Services
Julia St. Michael, Manager, Research & Environmental Programs

REALTORS Association of Grey Bruce Owen Sound (RAGBOS)
517 - 10 St., Hanover ON N4N 1R4
Tel: 519-364-3827; *Fax:* 519-364-6800
info@ragbos.com
www.ragbos.ca
To provide a web-based multiple listing service for its members
Karen Cox, President

Realtors Association of Lloydminster & District
#203, 5009 - 48 St., Lloydminster AB T9V 0H7
Tel: 780-875-6939; *Fax:* 780-875-5560
lloydreb@telus.net
boards.mls.ca/lloydminster
Harpreet Saini, President
Eileen Rohs, Executive Officer

Renfrew County Real Estate Board
197 Pembroke St. East, Pembroke ON K8A 3J6
Tel: 613-735-5840; *Fax:* 613-735-0405
orebadmin@ottawarealestate.org
www.ottawarealestate.org/about_rcreb.shtml
Ann Anderson, Executive Officer

Rideau-St. Lawrence Real Estate Board
#12, 1275 Kensington Pkwy., Brockville ON K6V 6C3
Tel: 613-342-3103; *Fax:* 613-342-1637
rideau@bellnet.ca
boards.mls.ca/rideau

Saint John Real Estate Board Inc.
Hilyard Place, #120, 600 Main St., Saint John NB E2K 1J5
Tel: 506-634-8772; *Fax:* 506-634-8775
www.sjrealestateboard.ca
To provide services to & set standards for members; to preserve & promote the MLS marketing system to benefit buyers & sellers of real property
Jason Stephen, President

Sarnia-Lambton Real Estate Board (SLREB)
555 Exmouth St., Sarnia ON N7T 5P6
Tel: 519-336-6871; *Fax:* 519-344-1928
slreb@fonenet.ca
www.mls-sarnia.com
Donna Mathewson, President

Saskatchewan Association of the Appraisal Institute of Canada
3803 Lakeview Ave., Regina SK S4S 1H3
Tel: 306-352-4195; *Fax:* 306-352-6913
skaic@sasktel.net
www.skaic.org
Dave R. Gabruch, President
Marilyn Sterdnica, Executive Director

Saskatchewan Building Officials Association Inc. (SBOA)
PO Box 460, North Battleford SK S9A 2Y6
Tel: 306-445-1733; *Fax:* 306-445-1739
membership@sboa.sk.ca; conference@sboa.sk.ca
www.sboa.sk.ca
Dan Knutson, President
LeRoy Evenson, Secretary-Treasurer

Saskatoon Region Association of REALTORS (SRAR)
1149 - 8 St. East., Saskatoon SK S7H 0S3
Tel: 306-244-4453; *Fax:* 306-343-1420
info@srar.ca
www.srar.ca
To represent the real estate interests of its members & the public; to provide services & programs to enhance the professionalism, competency & effectiveness of its members; to advocate public policy towards improving the real estate market environment
Harry H. Janzen, Executive Officer

Sault Ste Marie Real Estate Board (SSMREB)
#206, 477 Queen St. East, Sault Ste Marie ON P6A 1Z5
Tel: 705-949-4560; *Fax:* 705-949-5935
www.saultstemarierealestate.ca
Claudia Devoe, President

Simcoe & District Real Estate Board
191 Queensway West, Simcoe ON N3Y 2M8
Tel: 519-426-4454; *Fax:* 519-426-9330
realsim@kwic.com
www.norfolk-mls.ca
Ray Ferris, President

South Okanagan Real Estate Board (SOREB)
365 Van Horne St., Penticton BC V2A 8S4
Tel: 250-492-0626; *Fax:* 250-493-0832
soreb@vip.net
www.soreb.org
To pursue excellence & professionalism in real estate, through quality education & high ethical standards; To protect the interest of the membership & the public
Louise Baier, Executive Officer

Sudbury Real Estate Board
190 Elm St., Sudbury ON P3C 1V3
Tel: 705-673-3388; *Fax:* 705-673-3197
sreb@vianet.on.ca
www.sudburyrealestateboard.on.ca
Myra Lahti, Executive Officer

Swift Current Real Estate Association
#211, 12 Cheadle St. West, Swift Current SK S9H 0A9
Tel: 306-773-4326; *Fax:* 306-773-3917
screa@sasktel.net
Nancy Hunter, President

Thompson Real Estate Board
55 Selkirk Ave., Thompson MB R8N 0M5
Tel: 204-778-6303; *Fax:* 204-778-5652
brealt@norcom.mb.ca
Wayne Grier, President

Thunder Bay Real Estate Board
1135 Barton St., Thunder Bay ON P7B 5N3
Tel: 807-623-8422; *Fax:* 807-623-0375
info@thunderbay-MLS.on.ca
www.thunderbay-mls.on.ca
Erin Nadon, Executive Officer

Tillsonburg District Real Estate Board
#202, 1 Library Lane, Tillsonburg ON N4G 4W3
Tel: 519-842-9361; *Fax:* 519-688-6850
tburgreb@bellnet.ca
www.tburgreb.ca
Linda Coldham, President

Timmins Real Estate Board
225 Algonquin Blvd. East, Timmins ON P4N 1B4
Tel: 705-268-5451; *Fax:* 705-264-6420
treb@ntl.sympatico.ca
Anne Marie Vaillancourt, Executive Officer

Toronto Real Estate Board (TREB)
1400 Don Mills Rd., Toronto ON M3B 3N1
Tel: 416-443-8100
www.torontorealestateboard.com
Social Media: www.facebook.com/TorontoRealEstateBoard; twitter.com/TREBhome; www.youtube.com/TREBChannel
Richard Silver, President

Valley Real Estate Board Inc. / Association Immobilière de la Vallée Ltée
PO Box 192, 72 Daigle St., Edmundston NB E3V 1M1
Tel: 506-737-8083; *Fax:* 506-737-8145
valleyboard@nb.aibn.com
Lyne LeBel, Executive Officer

Vancouver Island Real Estate Board (VIREB)
6374 Metral Dr., Nanaimo BC V9T 2L8
Tel: 250-390-4212; *Fax:* 250-390-5014
bbenoit@vireb.com
www.vireb.com
To provide cost-effective tools, services & information necessary to foster professionalism & maintain the realtor's position as the primary focus in the real estate industry
Subhadra Ghose, President
Ray Francis, Vice-President
Bill Benoit, Executive Officer

Victoria Real Estate Board (VREB)
3035 Nanaimo St., Victoria BC V8T 4W2
Tel: 250-385-7766; *Fax:* 250-385-8773
vreb@vreb.org
www.vreb.org
To promote & enhance the use of the real estate services that its members provide to the public
Glenn Terrell, Executive Officer
Tony Joe, President

West Central Alberta Real Estate Board
162 Athabasca Ave., Hinton AB T7V 2A5
Tel: 780-865-7511; *Fax:* 780-865-7517
wcareb@shaw.ca
Sandy Atfield, Executive Officer
Marcel Dery, President

Weyburn Real Estate Board
110 Souris Ave., Weyburn SK S4H 2Z8
Tel: 306-848-1000; *Fax:* 306-842-3989
remax.weyburn@sasktel.net
Shelly Baudria, Vice-President
Lyle Leonard, President

Windsor-Essex County Real Estate Board
3020 Deziel Dr., Windsor ON N8W 5H8
Tel: 519-966-6432; *Fax:* 519-966-4469
info@windsorrealestate.com
www.windsorrealestate.com
Krista Del Gatto, Executive Officer

Winnipeg Real Estate Board (WREB)
1240 Portage Ave., Winnipeg MB R3G 0T6
Tel: 204-786-8854; *Fax:* 204-784-2343
jwood@winnipegrealtors.ca
www.winnipegrealtors.ca
To serve members & to promote the benefits of organized real estate
Peter Squire, Contact

Woodstock-Ingersoll & District Real Estate Board
#6, 65 Springbank Ave., Woodstock ON N4S 8V8
Tel: 519-539-3616; *Fax:* 519-539-1975
widreb@bellnet.ca
boards.mls.ca/woodstock
Carol Smith-Gee, Executive Officer

Yellowknife Real Estate Board
#201, 5204 - 50 Ave., Yellowknife NT X1A 1E2
Tel: 867-920-4624; *Fax:* 867-873-6387
officecomp@ssimicro.com
boards.mls.ca/yellowknife
Nicole Chernish, Secretary/Treasurer & Executive Off

Yorkton Real Estate Association Inc. (YREA)
#040, 41 Broadway West, Yorkton SK S3N 0L6
Tel: 306-783-3067; *Fax:* 306-782-3231
yrea@sasktel.net
To promote a high level of professionalism among members by providing leadership in the real estate industry & in the community
Judy Pfeifer, Executive Officer
Ron Skinner, President

Yukon Real Estate Association
49 Waterfront Pl., Whitehorse YT Y1A 6V1
Tel: 867-633-4290; *Fax:* 867-667-2299
colleen@yrea.ca; president@yrea.ca
www.yrea.yk.ca
To promote interest in marketing of real estate in all its aspects & to advance & improve relations of members of society with public

Recreation, Hobbies & Games

Alberta Camping Association (ACA)
Percy Page Centre, 11759 Groat Rd., Edmonton AB T5M 3K6
Tel: 780-427-6605; *Fax:* 780-427-6695
info@albertacamping.com
www.albertacamping.com
Social Media: www.facebook.com/AlbertaCampingAssociation
To promote & coordinate organized camping in Alberta by providing camp information & leadership direction as well as promoting high standards of camp programs & activities for all populations; to take a leading role in the recognition & promotion of professional standards for organized camps in Alberta
Jon Olfert, President
Les Waite, Secretary-Treasurer

Alberta Recreation & Parks Association (ARPA)
11759 Groat Rd., Edmonton AB T5M 3K6
Tel: 780-415-1745; *Fax:* 780-451-7915
Toll-Free: 877-544-1747
arpa@arpaonline.ca
www.arpaonline.ca
Social Media: www.facebook.com/arpaonline; twitter.com/#!/arpaonline
To promote accessibility to recreation & parks & their benefits to Albertans; To work toward economic sustainability, natural resource protection, & conservation within provincial parks & natural environments
Rick Curtis, Executive Director
Steve Allan, Manager, Finance & Operations
Shelley Shea, President
Carol Petersen, Manager, Recreation & Community Development
Terry Welsh, Secretary
Judi Frank, Treasurer
Lisa Tink, Manager, Children & Youth Programs
Mandi Wise, Coordinator, Communications

Alberta Snowmobile Association (ASA)
11759 Groat Rd., Edmonton AB T5M 3K6
Tel: 780-427-2695; *Fax:* 780-415-1779
info@altasnowmobile.ab.ca
www.altasnowmobile.ab.ca
To promote safe recreational snowmobiling in the province of Alberta
Darryl Copithorne, President, president@altasnowmobile.ab.ca
Janet Riopel, Vice-President, mriopel@mcsnet.ca

Alberta Sport Parachuting Association (ASPA)
#63, 2505 - 42 St., Edmonton AB T6L 7G8
admin@aspa.ca
www.aspa.ca
To promote & facilitate the development of the sport of skydiving in Alberta
Henry Komant, Acting President
Tina Connolly, Program Coordinator

Alberta Sprint Racing Canoe Association
11759 Groat Rd., Edmonton AB T5M 3K6
Tel: 780-203-3987
arsca@shaw.ca
www.albertasprintcanoe.com
Rick Hill, President

Alberta Whitewater Association (AWA)
Percy Page Centre, 11759 Groat Rd., Edmonton AB T5M 3K6
Tel: 780-427-6717; *Fax:* 780-427-0524
www.albertawhitewater.ca
To encourage whitewater paddlesport activities
Sue Azofeifa, President

All Terrain Vehicle Association of Nova Scotia (ATVANS)
PO Box 46020, Stn. Novalea, Halifax NS B3K 5V8
Tel: 902-241-3200; *Toll-Free:* 877-288-4244
admin@atvans.org
www.atvans.org
To represent the interest of ATV'ers to Government, Land owners, other recreation user groups and the general public and educate, inform and organize ATV'ers to preserve and expand ATV recreational opportunities to promote safe family activities.
Mike Marriott, President
Ray Gouthro, Executive Director

Association des camps du Québec inc. (ACQ) / Québec Camping Association
CP 1000, Succ. M, 4545, av Pierre-de-Coubertin, Montréal QC H1V 3R2
Tél: 514-252-3113; *Téléc:* 514-252-1650
Ligne sans frais: 800-361-3586
info@camps.qc.ca
www.camps.qc.ca
Média social: www.facebook.com/130062375961
Assurer le développement, la promotion et la qualité des camps de vacances; s'assurer de la formation du personnel des camps

Association of Canadian Mountain Guides (ACMG) / Association des guides de montagne canadiens
PO Box 8341, Canmore AB T1W 2V1
Tel: 403-678-2885; *Fax:* 403-609-0070
acmg@acmg.ca
www.acmg.ca
The Association represents mountain guides in dealing with both public & private official bodies. It is the regulatory body, maintaining standards of guiding, & acts as a public relations body to promote the sport in a safe & educational manner.
Keith Reid, President
Peter Tucker, Executive Director

Association québécoise de canoë-kayak de vitesse (AQCKV)
CP 1000, Succ. M, 4545, av Pierre-de Coubertin, Montréal QC H1V 3R2
Tél: 514-252-3086; *Téléc:* 514-252-3094
directeur.technique@aqckv.qc.ca
www.aqckv.qc.ca
Promouvoir les activités de canoë-kayak de vitesse au Québec
Luc Therrien, Président

British Columbia Camping Association
c/o Sasamat Outdoor Centre, 3302 Senkler Rd., Belcarra BC V3H 4S3
Tel: 604-931-6449; *Fax:* 604-939-8522
info@bccamping.org
www.bccamping.org
To facilitate the development of organized camping in order to provide educational, character-building & constructive recreational experiences for all people; to develop awareness & appreciation of the natural environment
Hart Banack, President

British Columbia Fishing Resorts & Outfitters Association (BCFROA)
PO Box 3301, Kamloops BC V2C 6B9
Tel: 250-374-6836; *Fax:* 250-374-6640
Toll-Free: 800-374-6836
bcfroa@bcfroa.ca
www.bcfroa.ca
Works with the public & private sector to protect areas currently in use; to preserve the wildlife experience in BC for the enjoyment of future generations; a lobby group whose members are dedicated to providing a quality outdoor experience
Jan Lingford, Executive Director

British Columbia Hang Gliding & Paragliding Association (BCHPA)
www.bchpa.ca
The focus of BCHPA is the protection, maintenance & improvement of flying sites throughout the province.
Nance Margit, President

British Columbia Recreation & Parks Association (BCRPA)
#101, 4664 Lougheed Hwy., Burnaby BC V5C 5T5
Tel: 604-629-0965; *Fax:* 604-629-2651
Toll-Free: 866-929-0965
bcrpa@bcrpa.bc.ca; registration@bcrpa.bc.ca
www.bcrpa.bc.ca
To establish & sustain healthy lifestyles & communities in British Columbia
Dean Gibson, President
Suzanne Allard Strutt, Chief Executive Officer
Holly-Ann Burrows, Manager, Communication
Sandra Couto, Manager, Finance
Kara Misra, Manager, Parks & Recreation
Misty Thomas, Manager, Fitness Program

British Columbia Sailing Association
#223, 3820 Cessna Dr., Richmond BC V7B 0A2
Tel: 604-333-3628; *Fax:* 604-333-3626
crew@bcsailing.bc.ca
www.bcsailing.bc.ca
The provincial sport authority for sailing.
Tine Moberg-Parker, Executive Director

British Columbia Snowmobile Federation (BCSF)
Stn. 400, 2439 Poulton Ave., Houston BC V0Y 1Z0
Tel: 250-845-7705; *Fax:* 250-845-7715
Toll-Free: 877-537-8716
office@bcsf.org
www.bcsf.org
To encourage & promote the sport of operating snowmobiles in BC by enhancing cooperation & communication between & among snowmobile clubs, recreation industry & racing divisions, the provincial government, other motorized recreational organizations & groups supportive of snowmobiling
Les Auston, Executive Director

The Bruce Trail Conservancy
PO Box 857, Hamilton ON L8N 3N9
Tel: 905-529-6821; *Fax:* 905-529-6823
Toll-Free: 800-665-4453
info@brucetrail.org
www.brucetrail.org
Social Media:
www.facebook.com/group.php?gid=111645892194726
To secure, develop & manage the Bruce Trail as a public footpath along the Niagara Escarpment from Queenston to Tobermory, thereby promoting preservation of the escarpment's ecological & cultural integrity & fostering an appreciation of its natural beauty. The Bruce Trail, designated as a UNESCO World Biosphere Reserve, is Canada's oldest and longest footpath.
Beth Kümmling, Executive Director

Campground Owners Association of Nova Scotia (COANS)
c/o Arm of Gold Campground, 24 Church Rd., Little Bras d'Or, Cape Breton NS B1Y 2Y2
Tel: 902-736-6671
info@campingnovascotia.com
www.campingnovascotia.com
To provide the best camping experience possible throughout our diverse province; to improve standards at all the province's campgrounds; to provide leadership to this important segment of the provincial economy.
John Brennick, President
Chris Miller, Vice-President

Canadian Aerophilatelic Society (CAS) / La société canadienne d'aérophilatélie (SCA)
203A Woodfield Dr., Nepean ON K2G 4P2
www.aerophilately.ca
To represent Canadian aerophilatelists nationally & internationally
Chris Hargreaves, President
Neil Hunter, Vice-President
Brian Wolfenden, Secretary-Treasurer

The Canadian Association of Fitness Professionals / Association canadienne des professionnels en conditionnement physique
#110, 255 Consumers Rd., Toronto ON M2J 1R4
Tel: 416-493-3515; *Fax:* 416-493-1756
Toll-Free: 800-667-5622
info@canfitpro.com
www.canfitpro.com
Social Media: www.facebook.com/group.php?gid=2524100816
Can-Fit-Pro takes today's fitness professionals' challenges & creates tomorrow's solutions through ongoing relative knowledge & personal enrichment
Maureen Hagan, Executive Director
Kathy Ash, Contact, Administration

Canadian Association of Numismatic Dealers (CAND) / Association canadienne des marchands numismatiques
c/o Jo-Anne Simpson, Executive Secretary, PO Box 10272, Stn. Winona, Stoney Creek ON L8E 5R1
Tel: 905-643-4988; *Fax:* 905-643-6329
email@cand.org
www.cand.org
To ensure professionalism by members of the association
Michael Findlay, President
Paul Koolhaas, Vice-President
Wendy Hoare, Secretary-Treasurer

Canadian Association of Wooden Money Collectors (CAWMC)
c/o Norm Belsten, 86 Hamilton Dr., Newmarket ON L3Y 3E8
nbelsten@sympatico.ca
Norm Belsten, Contact

Canadian Baton Twirling Federation (CBTF) / Fédération baton canadienne
c/o Gail Ashcroft, PO Box 700, Trochu AB T0M 2C0
info_cbtf@canada.com
www.cbtf.ca
Social Media: www.facebook.com/CBTFCA; twitter.com/cbtfca
Jeff Johnson, President
Lisa Wilde, Secretary
Michelle Bretherick, Treasurer

Canadian Boating Federation / Fédération nautique du Canada
410, rue Victoria, Valleyfield QC J6K 4M3
Tel: 450-377-4122; *Fax:* 450-377-5282
cbfnc@bellnet.ca
www.cbfnc.ca
Lise Haineault, President
Derek Anderson, Vice-President, Racing
Pierre Foucher, Vice-President, Public Relations
Scott Toole, Vice-President, Outboard
Natalie Bourdeau, Secretary
Denise Mack, Treasurer

Canadian BodyBuilding Federation (CBBF) / Fédération canadienne de culturisme
info@cbbf.ca
www.cbbf.ca
To act as the governing body for amateur bodybuilding, fitness, & body fitness (figure) competition
Mark Smishek, President
Karen MacLean, Vice-President
John MacLellan, Secretary-Treasurer

Canadian Bridge Federation (CFB) / La Fédération canadienne incorporée de bridge
2719 East Jolly Pl., Regina SK S4V 0X8
Tel: 306-761-1677; *Fax:* 306-789-4919
jan@cbf.ca
www.cbf.ca
To conduct grassroot bridge events in Canada; to select & subsidize teams to World Championships.
Janice Anderson, Executive Director
Nader Hanna, President

Canadian Camping Association (CCA) / Association des camps du Canada (ACC)
43975 Watt Rd., Lindell Beach BC V2R 4X9
Toll-Free: 877-427-6958
hedwards@stillwood.ca
www.ccamping.org
Social Media:
www.facebook.com/CanadianCampingAssociation; twitter.com/ccampingorg
To develop & promote organized camping for all populations across Canada; To further the interests & welfare of children, youth, & adults through camping; To encourage high standards in camping
Harry Edwards, President

Canadian Casting Federation
c/o Toronto Sportsmen's Association, 17 Mill St., Toronto ON M2P 1B3
Tel: 416-487-4477; *Fax:* 416-487-4478
www.torontosportsmens.ca/Casting.html
To teach casting skills, covering fly, bait, & spinning

Canadian Correspondence Chess Association (CCCA) / L'Association canadienne des échecs par correspondance (ACEC)
#4, 1669 Country Rd., L'Orignal QC K0B 1K0
Tel: 613-632-3166
ccca@cogeco.ca
correspondencechess.com/ccca/index.htm
Manny Migicovsky, President

Canadian Council of Snowmobile Organizations (CCSO) / Conseil canadien des organismes de motoneige (CCOM)
PO Box 21059, Thunder Bay ON P7A 8A7
Tel: 807-345-5299
ccso.ccom@tbaytel.net
www.ccso-ccom.ca
Social Media:
www.facebook.com/group.php?gid=126035004176384
To provide leadership & support to organized snowmobiling in Canada
Dennis Burns, Executive Director

Canadian Fitness & Lifestyle Research Institute (CFLRI) / Institut canadien de la recherche sur la condition physique et le mode de vie
#201, 185 Somerset St. West, Ottawa ON K2P 0J2
Tel: 613-233-5528; *Fax:* 613-233-5536
www.cflri.ca
To conduct research, monitor trends, & make recommendations to increase physical activity & improve health in Canada
Nancy Dubois, Chair
Christine Cameron, Acting President
Mathilde Costa, Senior Manager, Finance, Administration, & Human Resources
Cora Lynn Craig, Senior Researcher

Canadian Flag Association (CFA) / Association canadienne de vexillologie (ACV)
50 Heathfield Dr., Toronto ON M1M 3B1
Tel: 416-267-9618; *Fax:* 416-267-9618
kevin.harrington@sympatico.ca
www.crwflags.com/fotw/flags/vex-cfa.html
To gather, organize & disseminate flag information with particular emphasis on flags having some association with Canada; to promote vexillology; to encourage & facilitate exchange of ideas between flag scholars, flag makers, flag collectors, flag designers & flag historians
Kevin Harrington, President

Canadian International DX Club (CIDX)
PO Box 67063, Stn. Lemoyne, Saint-Lambert QC J4R 2T8
cidxclub@yahoo.com
www.anarc.org/cidx
To serve radio enthusiasts throughout the world
Sheldon Harvey, President

Canadian Motorcycle Association (CMA) / Association motocycliste canadienne
PO Box 448, Hamilton ON L8L 8C4
Tel: 905-522-5705; *Fax:* 905-522-5716
registration@canmocycle.ca
www.canmocycle.ca
To encourage & develop motorcycling for the benefit & enjoyment of its members
Marilyn Bastedo, CEO
Joseph Godsall, President

Canadian Orienteering Federation (COF) / Fédération canadienne de course d'orientation
1239 Colgrove Ave. NE, Calgary AB T2C 5C3
Tel: 403-283-0807; *Fax:* 403-451-1681
info@orienteering.ca
www.orienteering.ca
Social Media: www.facebook.com/group.php?gid=64406548384; twitter.com/orienteeringcan
Charlotte MacNaughton, Executive Director
Alex Kerr, Vice-President
Dave Graupner, Secretary-Treasurer

Canadian Paper Money Society (CPMS)
Attn: Dick Dunn, PO Box 562, Pickering ON L1V 2R7
Tel: 905-509-1146
info@cpmsonline.ca
www.nunetcan.net/cpms.htm
The aims and ojectives of the Society are to encourage and support historical studies of banks and other paper money issuing authorities in Canada, to preserve their history and statistical records, and through research and publishing the results thereof, ensure that information, documents, and other evidence of Canada's financial development will be preserved.
Dick Dunn, Sec.-Treas.

Canadian Parks & Recreation Association (CPRA) / Association canadienne des parcs et loisirs
PO Box 83069, 1180 Walkley Rd., Ottawa ON K1V 2M5
Tel: 613-523-5315
info@cpra.ca
www.cpra.ca
To advocate on the benefits of parks & recreation services
Shelley Shea, President
CJ Noble, Executive Director
Sarah Wayne, Accountant

Canadian Parks & Wilderness Society (CPAWS) / Société pour la nature et les parcs du Canada (SNAP)
#506, 250 City Centre Ave., Ottawa ON K1R 6K7
Tel: 613-569-7226; *Fax:* 613-569-7098
Toll-Free: 800-333-9453
info@cpaws.org
www.cpaws.org
Social Media: www.facebook.com/cpaws; twitter.com/#!/cpaws
To act as the Canadian voice for public wilderness protection
Alison Woodley, National Director, Conservation
Ellen Adelberg, Director, Communications & Marketing
Chris Henschel, National Manager, Domestic & International Affairs
Sabine Jessen, National Manager, Oceans & Great Freshwater Lakes Program
Chris Miller, National Manager, Wilderness Conservation & Climate Change

Canadian Power & Sail Squadrons (Canadian Headquarters) (CPS) / Escadrilles canadiennes de plaisance (ECP)
26 Golden Gate Ct., Toronto ON M1P 3A5
Tel: 416-293-2438; *Fax:* 416-293-2445
Toll-Free: 888-277-2628
hqg@cps-ecp.ca
www.cps-ecp.ca
Social Media: www.facebook.com/groups/6654534451; twitter.com/cpsboat; www.youtube.com/CPSECP
To increase awareness & knowledge of safe boating by educating & training members & the general public, by fostering fellowship among members, & establishing partnerships & alliances with organizations & agencies interested in boating
Alain Brière, Executive Director
John Gullick, Manager, Government & Special Programs

Canadian Racing Pigeon Union Inc.
#C, 261 Tillson Ave., Tillsonburg ON N4G 5X2
Tel: 519-842-9771; *Fax:* 519-842-8809
Toll-Free: 866-652-5704
crpu@crpu.ca
www.crpu.ca
To promote the sport of pigeon racing in Canada
Oscar DeVries, President
Shannon Beadow, Office Manager

Canadian Sport Parachuting Association (CSPA) / Association canadienne du parachutisme sportif (ACPS)
300 Forced Rd., Russell ON K4R 1A1
Tel: 613-445-1881; *Fax:* 613-445-2698
office@cspa.ca
www.cspa.ca
David Hodge, President
Christopher Charlesworth, Vice-President
Nicole Demers, Secretary

Canadian Stamp Dealers' Association (CSDA) / Association canadienne des négociants en timbres-poste (ACNTP)
PO Box 81, Stn. Lambeth, London ON N6P 1P9
director@csdaonline.com
www.csdaonline.com
John Sheffield, Executive Director
Rick Day, President
Lyse Rousseau, Vice-President
John Beddows, Secretary
Isidore Baum, Treasurer

Canadian Table Soccer Federation
8311, rue Ouimet, Brossard QC J4Y 3B3
Tel: 514-668-2326
secretary@canadafoos.com
To oversee & monitor the growth of foosball in Canada.
Eric Dunn, President
Adam Imanpoor, Secretary

Canadian Table Tennis Association (CTTA) / Association canadienne de tennis de table
#400, 2211 Riverside Dr., Ottawa ON K1H 7X5
Tel: 613-733-6272; *Fax:* 613-733-7279
ctta@ctta.ca
www.ctta.ca
To increase the popularity of the sport of table tennis through programs & activities; to increase participation in table tennis at all levels
Manali Haridas, Office Administrator
Tony Kiesenhofer, Director General

Canadian Toy Collectors' Society Inc. (CTCS)
#245, 91 Rylander Blvd., Unit 7, Toronto ON M1B 5M5
ctcsweb@hotmail.com
www.ctcs.org
To promote interest in the collection & display of all types of toys, childhood memorabilia & literature; to acquire, maintain & house a collection of toys & to restore & preserve Canadian toys of historic significance.
Ron Blair, President

Canadian Trapshooting Association (CTA)
RR#1, Penhold AB T0M 1R0
Tel: 403-886-2600; *Fax:* 403-886-2600
To promote clay target shooting as a recreational sport among shooters of every age, both sexes, & at every level of ability, the ultimate objective being to compete in the world championships held each year in Ohio
Bob Brown, President

Canadian Yachting Association (CYA) / Association canadienne de yachting
Portsmith Olympic Harbour, 53 Yonge St., Kingston ON K7M 6G4
Tel: 613-545-3044; *Fax:* 613-545-3045
Toll-Free: 877-416-4720
sailcanada@sailing.ca
www.sailing.ca
To promote the sport of sailing in Canada
Gerry Giffin, President

Canoe Kayak New Brunswick
c/o Doug Forbes, 42 Third St., Rothesay NB E2H 1M9
Tel: 506-849-0793
communications@canoekayaknb.org
www.canoekayaknb.org
Canoe-Kayak New Brunswick is a non-profit volunteer organization dedicated to the promotion of safe recreational paddling in the province of New Brunswick.
Tim Humes, President

Canoe Kayak Nova Scotia (CKNS)
5516 Spring Garden Rd., Halifax NS B3J 1G6
Tel: 902-425-5454; *Fax:* 902-425-5606
canoens@sportnovascotia.ca
www.ckns.ca

Canoe Kayak Saskatchewan (CKS)
1870 Lorne St., Regina SK S4P 2L7
Tel: 306-729-4220; *Fax:* 306-729-4216
cks@accesscomm.ca
www.saskcanoe.ca
To operate as the provincial sport governing body for canoe & kayak in Saskatchewan
Jan Hanson, Executive Director
Fiona Vincent, President
Jeanette Hamilton, Treasurer

Canoe Newfoundland & Labrador
PO Box 23072, Stn. Churchill Sq., St. John's NL A1B 4J9
Tel: 709-364-1601; *Fax:* 709-368-8357
tumblehome.nfld@gmail.com
www.canoenfld.ca
Tumblehome Canoe Club is a local canoeing club that welcomes members from all parts of the province. It is a non-profit group of canoeing enthusiasts who get together regularly to enjoy the sport of canoeing and socialize with other canoeing lovers.
Corey Locke, President

Canoe Ontario
c/o OCSRA, 2078 Lemay Cres., Ottawa ON K1G 2X4
Tel: 613-618-1715
www.canoeontario.org

CanoeKayak BC
#102A, 11410 Kingston St., Maple Ridge BC V2X 0Y5
Tel: 604-465-5268; *Fax:* 604-460-0587
info@canoekayakbc.ca
www.canoekayakbc.ca
Social Media: www.facebook.com/canoekayakbc; twitter.com/CanoeKayakBC
Mary Jane Abbot, Executive Director

CanoeKayak Canada (CKC)
#700, 2197 Riverside Dr., Ottawa ON K1H 7X3
Tel: 613-260-1818; *Fax:* 613-260-5137
www.canoekayak.ca
Social Media: www.facebook.com/CanoeKayakCAN?ref=profile; twitter.com/CanoeKayakCAN
To increase the number of Canadians participating in canoeing & kayaking; To enable participants to realize excellence by providing sound athlete development programs & membership support systems
Lorraine Lafrenière, Director General
John Edwards, Director, Domestic Development
Peter Niedre, Director, Coaching Development & Education
Barney Wainwright, Director, High Performance

CanoeKayak Canada - Atlantic Division
c/o Sport NS, 5516 Spring Garden Rd., 4th Fl., Halifax NS B3J 3G6
Tel: 902-425-5450; *Fax:* 902-425-5606
ccaatlantic@sportnovascotia.ca
www.ccaatlantic.ca
Liz Orton, Program Coordinator

Charlottetown Duplicate Bridge Club
500 Queen St., Charlottetown PE C1A 8K9
Tel: 902-894-3067

Chess Federation of Canada / Fédération canadienne des échecs
#E1, 2212 Gladwin Cres., Ottawa ON K1B 5N1
Tel: 613-733-2844; *Fax:* 613-733-5209
Toll-Free: 800-563-4476
info@chess.ca
www.chess.ca
To coordinate chess play across Canada
Peter Palsson, President

Citizens for Safe Cycling (CfSC)
PO Box 248, Stn. B, Ottawa ON K1P 6C4
Tel: 613-722-4454; *Fax:* 613-722-4454
info@safecycling.ca
www.safecycling.ca
To promote cycling as fun, healthy, safe, economical, and environmentally-friendly transportation and recreation.
Zlatko Krstulich, President

Classical & Medieval Numismatic Society (CMNS)
PO Box 956, Stn. B, Toronto ON M2K 2T6
Tel: 416-490-8659; *Fax:* 416-490-6452
billmcdo@idirect.com
www.cmns.ca
To promote & encourage study & research in the field of numismatics & history as they relate to ancient & medieval coinage & related subjects; to publish the writings that are the result of such activity.
W.H. McDonald, Executive Sec.-Treas.

Climb Yukon Association
climbyukon@gmail.com
www.climbyukon.net
To develop to the climbing community in the Yukon as a recreational opportunity for adults and youth, to raise awareness of, and address access and safety concerns.
Ryan Agar, President

Dominion of Canada Rifle Association (DCRA) / L'Association de tir dominion du canada
45 Shirley Blvd., Ottawa ON K2K 2W6
Tel: 613-829-8281; *Fax:* 613-829-0099
office@dcra.ca
www.dcra.ca
Jim Thompson, Executive Director
Stan E. Frost, Executive Vice-President
T.F. deFaye, President

Fédération de saut de barils du Canada / Canadian Barrel Jumping Federation
1465, Place Louis-Fréchette, Saint-Bruno QC J3V 2T8
Tél: 450-653-9460
Promotion du sport du saut de barils; tenir le championnat canadien annuellement; reconnaître nos champions et les records
Gilles Leclerc, Président

Fédération des clubs de motoneigistes du Québec (FCMQ)
CP 1000, Succ. M, 4545, av Pierre-de Coubertin, Montréal QC H1V 3R2
Tél: 514-252-3076; *Téléc:* 514-254-2066
info@fcmq.qc.ca
www.fcmq.qc.ca
La Fédération des clubs de motoneigistes du Québec est un organisme à but non lucratif, voué au développement et à la promotion de la pratique de la motoneige dans tout le Québec
Dany Quirion, Président

Federation of Mountain Clubs of British Columbia
PO Box 19673, 130 West Broadway, Vancouver BC V5T 4E7
Tel: 604-873-6096; *Fax:* 604-873-6086
fmcbc@mountainclubs.bc.ca
www.mountainclubs.bc.ca
To promote hiking & mountaineering
Patrick R. Harrison, President
Ron Ford, Registrar
Brian Jones, Manager
Peter Rothermel, Vice-President

Federation of Ontario Cottagers' Associations (FOCA)
#201, 159 King St., Peterborough ON K9J 2R8
Tel: 705-749-3622; *Fax:* 705-749-6522
info@foca.on.ca
www.foca.on.ca
To ensure a healthy future for waterfront Ontario; To support the interests of Ontario's cottagers
Terry Rees, Executive Director
Lara Griffin, Contact, Membership
Tracy Logan, Contact, Programs

Fédération québécoise de camping et de caravaning inc. (FQCC)
CP 100, 1560, rue Eiffel, Boucherville QC J4B 5Y1
Tél: 450-650-3722; *Téléc:* 450-650-3721
Ligne sans frais: 877-650-3722
info@fqcc.ca
www.fqcc.ca
Unir les adepts du camping et du caravaning; entreprendre et coordonner des actions relatives au camping et au caravaning.
Louise Saindon, Présidente
Claude Cournoyer, Trésorier

Fédération québécoise de canoë-kayak d'eau vive
CP 1000, Succ. M, 4545, av Pierre-de Coubertin, Montréal QC H1V 3R2
Tél: 514-252-3099; *Téléc:* 514-252-3094
fqckev@kayak.qc.ca
www.kayak.qc.ca
Promouvoir le sport et la pratique d'activités en eau vive au Québec
Patrick Lévesque, Coordonnateur

Fédération québécoise de la marche
CP 1000, Succ. M, 4545, av Pierre-de Coubertin, Montréal QC H1V 3R2
Tél: 514-252-3157; *Téléc:* 514-252-5137
Ligne sans frais: 866-252-2065
infomarche@fqmarche.qc.ca
www.fqmarche.qc.ca
Mèdia social: www.facebook.com/138582999548977
Promotion de la marche et de la randonnée pedestre; support au développement de lieux de marche

Fédération québécoise des échecs (FQE) / Québec Chess Federation
CP 1000, Succ. M, Montréal QC H1V 3R2
Tél: 514-252-3034; *Téléc:* 514-251-8038
info@fqechecs.qc.ca
www.fqechecs.qc.ca
Mèdia social: www.facebook.com/eqechecs; twitter.com/fqechecs
Promouvoir l'étude, l'enseignement et la pratique du jeu d'échecs au Québec
Richard Bérubé, Directeur Général

Fédération québécoise des jeux récréatifs (FQJR)
CP 1000, Succ. M, 4545, av Pierre-de Coubertin, Montréal QC H1V 3R2
Tél: 514-252-3032
jeuxrecr@fqjr.qc.ca
www.fqjr.qc.ca
La Fédération oeuvre activement à l'avènement d'une école autonome et responsable où l'élève est le centre de toutes les préoccupations et de toutes les décisions. Cette école rend possible, en véritable partenariat, le travail de tous ses intervenants : directeur, enseignants, parents et administrateurs, concertés dans l'élaboration, la mise en oeuvre et la réussite d'un projet éducatif correspondant aux besoins de son milieu. Le rôle de chacun y est reconnu à la valeur de sa contribution.
André Leclerc, Directeur général

Fédération québécoise du canot et du kayak (FQCK)
CP 1000, Succ. M, 4545, av Pierre-de Coubertin, Montréal QC H1V 3R2
Tél: 514-252-3001; *Téléc:* 514-252-3091
info@canot-kayak.qc.ca
www.canot-kayak.qc.ca
Mèdia social: www.facebook.com/group.php?gid=254842564559812
Regrouper les organismes et individus intéressés à la pratique du canotage récréatif et du canot-camping et de promouvoir la pratique de ces activités en utilisant le canot ouvert de type amérindien autrement appelé Canot Canadien
Pierre Trudel, Directeur général
Bernard Hugonnier, Directeur, Technique
Magalie Bernard, Agente, L'Information et aux communications
Philippe Pelland, Agent, Développement

Guide Outfitters Association of British Columbia (GOABC)
PO Box 94675, Richmond BC V6Y 4A4
Tel: 604-278-2688; *Fax:* 604-278-3440
info@goabc.org
www.goabc.org
Dale Drown, General Manager

Halifax North West Trails Association (HNWTA)
c/o 27 Warwick Lane, Halifax NS B3M 4J3
Tel: 902-443-5051
info@halifaxnorthwesttrails.ca
www.halifaxnorthwesttrails.ca
To promote the creation, protection and maintenance of trails within the Halifax Mainland North area.
Todd Beal, Chair

Hang Gliding & Paragliding Association of Atlantic Canada (HPAAC)
General Delivery, Diligent River NS B0M 1H0
Tel: 902-254-2972
jnewman@eastlink.ca
www.hpaac.ca
To develop & promote the sports of hang glinding & paragliding in Atlantic Canada
Judith Newman, Contact

Hang Gliding & Paragliding Association of Canada (HPAC) / Association canadienne de vol libre (ACVL)
5 Millennium Dr., Stratford PE C1B 2H2
Fax: 902-367-3358
Toll-Free: 877-370-2078
admin@hpac.ca
www.hpac.ca
To promote unpowered foot-launched flight in hang gliders & paragliders.
Domagoj Juretic, President
Sam Jeyes, Business Manager

Hike Ontario
#800, 165 Dundas St. West, Mississauga ON L5B 2N6
Tel: 905-277-4453; *Toll-Free:* 800-894-7249
info@hikeontario.com
www.hikeontario.com
To act as the voice for hikers & walkers in Ontario; To encourage hiking, walking & trail development in Ontario; To promote trail maintenance. best practices, & safe hiking; To enhance environmental awareness, conservation & sustainable trails
Bill Wilson, President
Fran Rawlings, Secretary
Asvin Parsad, Treasurer

Ikaluktutiak Paddling Association
PO Box 125, Cambridge Bay NU X0B 0C0
Tel: 867-983-2068
ipanorth69@gmail.com
Rob Harmer, President

International Computer Games Association (ICGA)
c/o David N.L. Levy, 34 Courthope Rd., Hampstead, London NW3 2LD England
info@icga.org; board@icga.org; journal@icga.org
To promote computer games; To share technical knowledge; To foster developments in the man-machine area
David N.L. Levy, President
Yngvi Björnsson, Vice-President
Hiroyuki Iida, Secretary-Treasurer

Manitoba Camping Association (MCA)
#302, 960 Portage Ave., Winnipeg MB R3G 0R4
Tel: 204-784-1134; *Fax:* 204-784-4177
sunshinefund@mbcamping.ca
www.mbcamping.ca
Social Media: www.facebook.com/sunshinefundmb
To act as a coordinating body for organized camping in Manitoba; To promote organized camping as an educational and recreational experience
Bryan Ezako, Executive Director
Janis Banman, Coordinator, General Office Administration & Sunshine Fund Program

Manitoba Paddling Association Inc. (MPA)
145 Pacific Ave., Winnipeg MB R3B 2Z6
Tel: 204-925-5681; *Fax:* 204-925-5792
mpa@sportmanitoba.ca
www.mpa.mb.ca
To act as the governing body for all competitive paddling sports in Manitoba, including kayak, canoe, & dragon boat; To develop high performance athletes to compete for Manitoba nationally & to qualify for the national team; To develop coaches to coach from the grassroots to the high performance levels; To service paddlers from beginners to elite athletes; To ensure the existence of paddling clubs in Manitoba

Manitoba Provincial Handgun Association (MPHA)
PO Box 314, Stn. Corydon Ave., Winnipeg MB R3M 3S7
Tel: 204-925-5682; *Fax:* 204-925-5703
mbhndgn@shaw.ca
www.handgun.mb.ca
The Manitoba Provincial Handgun Association shall provide opportunity for, as well as actively promote and support, effective programming for handgun athletes, coaches and officials affiliated with the MPHA so that they may learn, practice and develop expertise in the sport of handgun shooting, within the parameters essential for effective handgun sport development.
Randy Myrdal, President

Manitoba Sport Parachute Association (MSPA)
#309, 200 Main St., Winnipeg MB R3C 4M2
Tel: 204-925-5682; *Fax:* 204-925-5703
president@mspa.mb.ca
www.mspa.mb.ca
To promote awareness & participation in skydiving in Manitoba
Jill Forbes, President

Model Aeronautics Association of Canada Inc. (MAAC) / Modélistes Aéronautiques Associés du Canada
#9, 5100 South Service Rd., Burlington ON L7L 6A5
Tel: 905-632-9808; *Fax:* 905-632-3304
Toll-Free: 855-359-6222
www.maac.ca
Social Media: www.facebook.com/group.php?gid=112219502126070
To foster, enhance, assist, aid & engage in scientific development; To provide central organization to record & disseminate information relating to model aeronautics; To guide & direct national model aviation activities; To direct technical organization of national & international model aircraft contests
Ronald R. Dodd, President
Linda Patrick, Secretary-Treasurer

National Association of Watch & Clock Collectors (NAWCC)
514 Poplar St., Columbia PA 17512-2130 USA
Tel: 717-684-8261; *Fax:* 717-684-0878
research@nawcc.org
www.nawcc.org

To stimulate interest in timepieces; to collect & preserve horological materials & information; to work with others in exhibiting timepieces; to encourage timepiece collection; to disseminate information on timepieces; to facilitate timepiece markets.
J. Steven Humphrey, Executive Director
Chuck Auman, Controller

National Darts Federation of Canada (NDFC) / Fédération nationale de dards du Canada
2417, rue Montante, Ascot QC J1H 6M3
Tel: 819-823-1392; *Fax:* 819-821-3539
secretary@ndfc.ca
www.ndfc.ca
To promote & organize Darts events & promote the betterment of the game
Bill Hatter, President
Mary Dezan, General Secretary

National Firearms Association (NFA)
PO Box 52183, Edmonton AB T6G 2T5
Tel: 780-439-1394; *Fax:* 780-439-4091
Toll-Free: 877-818-0393
membership@nfa.ca
www.nfa.ca
Sheldon Clare, President

New Brunswick Competitive Canoe Association
c/o Sport New Brunswick, 181 Kennebecasis River Rd., Hampton NB E5N 6L1
nbcca_m@hotmail.com
J. Timothy Flood, President

Newfoundland & Labrador Camping Association
27 Earle Dr., Pasadena NL A0L 1K0
Tel: 709-686-2363; *Fax:* 709-639-1636
To facilitate the development of organized camping in order to provide educational, character-building & constructive recreational experiences for all people; to develop awareness & appreciation of the natural environment

Newfoundland & Labrador Paddling Association (NLPA)
PO Box 181, 27 Lakeview Dr., Goulds NL A1S 1G4
Tel: 709-745-6482
www.kayakers.nf.ca/nlpa
To promote recreational canoeing & kayaking in Newfoundland & Labrador; to represent the interests of the canoeing & kayaking public
Allan Goodridge, President
Brian Hemeon, Vice-President, Canoeing
Darren MacDonald, Vice-President, Kayaking
Neil Burgess, Secretary
Alex Mcgruer, Treasurer

Northwest Territories Recreation & Parks Association (NWTRPA)
PO Box 841, Yellowknife NT X1A 2N6
Tel: 867-873-5340; *Fax:* 867-669-6791
admin@nwtrpa.org
www.nwtrpa.org
To increase public awareness of recreation & parks; to enhance the quality of life of residents of the NWT through fostering the development of recreation & parks services
Robin Langille, President
Geoff Ray, Executive Director

Nova Scotia Trails Federation (NSTF)
5516 Spring Garden Rd., 4th Fl., Halifax NS B3J 1G6
Tel: 902-425-5450; *Fax:* 902-425-5606
nstrails@sportnovascotia.ca
www.novascotiatrails.com
Social Media:
www.facebook.com/pages/Nova-Scotia-Trails-Federation/17631 8735774687; twitter.com/NSTrails
To promote the development and responsible use of recreational trails for the benefit and enjoyment of all Nova Scotians and visitors to our province.
Vanda Jackson, President

Ontario Camps Association (OCA)
#403, 250 Merton St., Toronto ON M4S 1B1
Tel: 416-485-0425; *Fax:* 416-485-0422
info@ontariocamps.ca
www.ontariocamps.ca
To promote youth camping throughout Ontario; To maintain high standards for organized camping; To advocate on issues which impact members
Rick Howard, President
Aruna Ogale, Executive Director

Ontario Federation of Snowmobile Clubs (OFSC)
#9, 501 Welham Rd., Barrie ON L4N 8Z6
Tel: 705-739-7669; *Fax:* 705-739-5005
www.ofsc.on.ca
To support member snowmobile clubs & volunteers; To establish & maintain quality snowmobile trails; To further the enjoyment of organized snowmobiling

Ontario Marine Operators Association (OMOA)
15 Laurier Rd., Penetanguishene ON L9M 1G8
Tel: 705-549-1667; *Fax:* 705-549-1670
Toll-Free: 888-547-6662
omoa@marinasontario.com
www.marinasontario.com
To promote recreational boating throughout Ontario
Dick Peever, President
Graham Lacey, Vice-President
Al Donaldson, Executive Director
Ed Leeman, Secretary
Bob Eaton, Director, Environmental Services

Ontario Numismatic Association (ONA)
c/o Bruce Raszmann, PO Box 40033, Stn. Waterloo Square, 75 King St. South, Waterloo ON N2J 4V1
www.ontario-numismatic.org
Paul Petch, President
Len Trakalo, Secretary, secretary@ontario-numismatic.org
Bruce Raszmann, Treasurer & Chair, Membership

Ontario Parks Association (OPA)
7856 - 5th Line South, RR#4, Milton ON L9T 2X8
Tel: 905-864-6182; *Fax:* 905-864-6184
Toll-Free: 866-560-7783
opa@ontarioparksassociation.ca
www.ontarioparksassociation.ca
To develop & protect parks & green spaces in Ontario
Paul Ronan, Executive Director
Eric Trogdon, Executive Director
Shelley May, Coordinator, Operations & Administration
Maureen Sinclair, President
Bill Harding, Vice-President

Ontario Recreation Facilities Association Inc. (ORFA)
#102, 1 Concorde Gate, Toronto ON M3C 3N6
Tel: 416-426-7062; *Fax:* 416-426-7385
Toll-Free: 800-661-6732
info@orfa.com; admin@orfa.com
www.orfa.com
To provide leadership for the recreation facility profession in Ontario; To promote the professional operation of recreation facilities throughout the province
Rob Lilbourne, President & Chair
John Milton, Chief Administrative Officer
Remo Petrongolo, Director, Business Development
Terry Piche, Director, Technical
Hubie Basilio, Coordinator, Public Relations & Communications
Rebecca Russell, Facilities Librarian

Ontario Recreational Canoeing & Kayaking Association (ORCKA)
#209, 3 Concorde Gate, Toronto ON M3C 3N7
Tel: 416-426-7016; *Fax:* 416-426-7363
info@orcka.on.ca
www.orcka.on.ca
Social Media:
www.facebook.com/group.php?gid=228950560506530
To promote development of safe, competent & knowledgeable recreational paddlers
Bruce Hawkins, President

Ontario Research Council on Leisure (ORCOL) / Conseil Ontarien de Recherche en Loisir
c/o Recreation & Leisure Studies, Faculty of Applied Health Sciences, University of Waterloo, Waterloo ON N2L 3G1
smale@healthy.uwaterloo.ca
www.orcol.uwaterloo.ca
To disseminate research about leisure & recreation, including culture, tourism, fitness, & sports
Bryan Smale, President
Don Reid, Treasurer

Ontario Sportfishing Guides' Association (OSGA)
c/o Fish 'n' Fun, 4504 Trent Trail, RR2, Washago ON L0K 2B0
info@ontariofishcharters.ca
www.ontariofishcharters.ca
The Association monitors & participates in any regulation reform regarding sportfishing in the province. It lobbies as a unified voice on behalf of its members, & serves as a network where members can promote & learn from each other.
George Watkins, Secretary

Ontario Trails Council
PO Box 500, Deseronto ON K0K 1X0
ontrails@gmail.com
www.ontariotrails.on.ca
Social Media: www.facebook.com/OntarioTrails?ref=mf; twitter.com/ontrails; www.youtube.com/user/ontrails
To promote the creation, development, preservation, management & use of an integrated, recreational, multi-seasonal trail network in Ontario; To show interest in all types of trails for non-motorized & motorized (where applicable) use in all seasons; To acquire & convert Ontario's abandoned railway rights-of-way to linear greenways for year-round recreational activities for the people of Ontario
Chris Laforest, President
Forbes Symon, Vice-President
Patrick Connor, CAE, Executive Director
Damian Braley, Secretary

Ontario Vintage Radio Association (OVRA)
197 Humberside Ave., Toronto ON M6P 1K7
Tel: 416-769-9627
www.ovra.ca
The Association acts to preserve Canada's radio history, literature & equipment. It serves as a forum for members to exchange information & continue the legacy of the original club.
Ted Catton, President

Orienteering Association of British Columbia (OABC)
4337 San Cristo Pl., Victoria BC V8N 5G5
www.orienteeringbc.ca
John Rance, President
Alex Kerr, Secretary

Outdoor Recreation Council of British Columbia (ORC)
47 West Broadway, Vancouver BC V5Y 1P1
Tel: 604-873-5546
outdoorrec@orcbc.ca
www.orcbc.ca
To advise industry & government in the development & implementation of outdoor recreation & conservation plans for BC; to contribute to the coordination of regional outdoor recreation by assisting in the establishment of a provincial network of outdoor recreationists to address recreational use conflicts & to advise government & industry on local & regional needs for noncompetitive outdoor recreation; to encourage active participation by the residents of BC in outdoor recreation activities; to promote the quality & diversity of outdoor recreation opportunities in BC by working cooperatively with government, industry, business & the public.
Robert Gunn, Chair
Jeremy McCall, Director/Treasurer

Outward Bound Canada
996 Chetwynd Rd., RR #2, Burks Falls ON P0A 1C0
Fax: 705-382-5959
Toll-Free: 888-688-9273
www.outwardbound.ca
To promote self-reliance, care & respect for others, responsibility to community & concern for the environment
Dave Wolfenden, Executive Director

Paddle Canada (PC) / Pagaie Canada
PO Box 126, Stn. Main, Kingston ON K7L 4V6
Tel: 613-547-3196; *Fax:* 613-547-4880
Toll-Free: 888-252-6292
info@paddlecanada.com
www.paddlingcanada.com
To promote all forms of recreational paddling to Canadians of diverse abilities, culture or age; to advocate for a healthy natural environment; To develop an appreciation for the canoe & the kayak in our Canadian heritage
Blair Doyle, President & Regional Director
Rick Wise, Vice-President & Chair, Member Services Committee
Corey Locke, Regional Director & Chair, Communications (Marketing & Promotions)

Paddle Manitoba
PO Box 2663, Winnipeg MB R3C 4B3
Tel: 204-338-6722
info@paddle.mb.ca
www.paddle.mb.ca
Paddle Manitoba is a non-profit association, the advocate & instructional organization promoting safe canoeing & kayaking in the province. It encourages new entrants into paddling by supporting activities necessary to develop skills.
Catherine Holmen, President

Parks & Recreation Ontario (PRO) / Parcs et loisirs de l'Ontario
#302, 1 Concorde Gate, Toronto ON M3C 3N6
Tel: 416-426-7142; *Fax:* 416-426-7371
pro@prontario.org
www.prontario.org
To enhance the quality of life, health & well-being of people, their communities & their environments; To advocate provincially for parks & recreation issues; To provide networking as well as multi-discipline professional development opportunities
Larry Ketcheson, CEO

Prince Edward Island Canoe Kayak Association
RR#4, Alliston, Montague PE C0A 1R0
Tel: 902-962-3883; *Fax:* 902-962-3883
justin.heidi@windsinc.com
www.windsinc.com/canoekayak/canoekayak.htm
Justin Richard Batten, President

Prince Edward Island Recreational Canoeing Association
PO Box 5604, RR#5, Charlottetown PE C1A 7J8
Tel: 902-368-6355; *Fax:* 902-368-6186

Prince Edward Island Underwater Council
c/o Sport PEI, 3 Queen St., Charlottetown PE C1A 7K7
Tel: 902-368-4110
a.cannon@pei.sympatico.ca
The PEI Underwater Council's mission is to help support and promote the sport of scuba diving in Prince Edward Island through safety, advocacy, cultural & environmental awareness, self-governance and education.

Recreation and Parks Association of the Yukon (RPAY)
4061, 4th Ave., Whitehorse YT Y1A 1H1
Tel: 867-668-3010; *Fax:* 867-668-2455
rpay@klondiker.com
www.rpay.org
To promote, encourage and foster the growth and development of all areas of recreation throughout the Yukon Territory.
Ian Spencer, President
Anne Morgan, Executive Director

Recreation Facilities Association of British Columbia (RFABC)
PO Box 320, #110, 174 Wilson St., Victoria BC V9A 7N7
Fax: 604-414-0068
Toll-Free: 877-285-3421
info@rfabc.com
www.rfabc.com
To promote safe & successful operating standards for community centres, swimming pools, arenas, stadiums, & parks in British Columbia; To encourage professionalism among recreation facility operators
Lori Blackman, President
Karin Carlson, Chair, Marketing
Garry Rushton, Chair, Membership
Shallon Touet, Chair, Education

Recreation New Brunswick
#34, 55 Whiting Rd., Fredericton NB E3B 5Y5
Tel: 506-459-1929; *Fax:* 506-450-6066
www.recreationnb.ca
Social Media: www.facebook.com/RecreationNB;
twitter.com/RecreationNB
To develop a professional organization for members; To enhance the image of recreation to government & the general public; To develop liaisons with other recreation groups; To affect legislation in the field of recreation & parks; to expand the NB Skills Program for Management Volunteers; To promote the need for education for leisure
Sarah Wagner, Executive Director

Recreation Newfoundland & Labrador
Bldg. 810, Pleasantville, PO Box 8700, Stn. A, St. John's NL A1B 4J6
Tel: 709-729-3892; *Fax:* 709-729-3814
www.recreationnl.com
To promote, foster & develop recreation; to provide a full range of services to enrich the concept of leisure throughout Newfoundland & Labrador; to enable individual citizens to improve their quality of life.
Wanda Wight, President
Gary Milley, Executive Director

Recreation Nova Scotia (RNS)
#309, 5516 Spring Garden Rd., Halifax NS B3J 1G6
Tel: 902-425-1128; *Fax:* 902-422-8201
info@recreationns.ns.ca
www.recreationns.ns.ca
To build healthier futures through programs & services that promote the benefits of recreation
Rhonda Lemire, Executive Director
Laurene Rehman, President
Bev Mahon, Coordinator, Communications & Fund Development

Recreational Canoeing Association BC (RCABC)
1755 East 7th Ave., Vancouver BC V5N 1S1
Tel: 604-253-5410; *Fax:* 604-253-5490
sec@bccanoe.com
www.bccanoe.com
Alan Thomson, President
Jean Chandler, Secretary

Roller Sports Canada / Sports à roulettes du Canada
c/o Roller Sports Manitoba, #312, 200 Main St., Winnipeg MB R3C 4M2
Tel: 204-925-5699; *Fax:* 204-925-5703
rollersportsmb@shawbiz.ca
www.rollersport.mb.ca

Royal Canadian Numismatic Association (RCNA)
#432, 5694 Hwy. 7 East, Markham ON L3P 1B4
Tel: 647-401-4014; *Fax:* 905-472-9645
info@rcna.ca
www.canadian-numismatic.org
To encourage & promote education in the science of numismatics, through the study of coins, paper money, medals, tokens, & all other numismatic items, with special emphasis on material pertaining to Canada
Kevin McCann, Chair, Membership

The Royal Philatelic Society of Canada (RPSC) / La Société royale de philatélie du Canada (SRPC)
PO Box 929, Stn. Q, Toronto ON M4T 2P1
Tel: 416-921-2077; *Fax:* 416-921-1282
Toll-Free: 888-285-4143
info@rpsc.org
www.rpsc.org
To promote the hobby of stamp collecting; to use stamps & postal history in education for youths & adults
George Pepall, President
Peter Butler, Executive Director

S.A.L.T.S. Sail & Life Training Society (SALTS)
PO Box 5014, Stn. B, Victoria BC V8R 6N3
Tel: 250-383-6811; *Fax:* 250-383-7781
Toll-Free: 888-383-6811
info@salts.ca
www.salts.ca
Social Media: www.facebook.com/saltsvictoria?ref=ts
Christian organization that believes through the medium of sail training both spiritual & physical development is encouraged in each individual
Loren Hagerty, Executive Director

Saskatchewan Association of Recreation Professionals (SARP)
2205 Victoria Ave., Regina SK S4P 0S4
Tel: 306-780-9267; *Fax:* 306-525-4009
Toll-Free: 800-667-7780
sarp.sk@sasktel.net
www.sarp-online.ca
To represent & support present & future recreation professionals; To promote the pursuit of excellence in the profession; To advocate for the profession
Nicole Goldsworthy, Chair

Saskatchewan Camping Association (SCA)
3950 Castle Rd., Regina SK S4S 6A4
Tel: 306-586-4026; *Fax:* 306-790-8634
info@saskcamping.ca
www.saskcamping.ca
To promote the development of quality organized camping in Saskatchewan; To act as the voice for leaders of organized camps throughout Saskatchewan
Donna Wilkinson, Executive Director

Saskatchewan Parks & Recreation Association (SPRA)
#100, 1445 Park St., Regina SK S4N 4C5
Tel: 306-780-9231; *Fax:* 306-780-9257
Toll-Free: 800-563-2555
office@spra.sk.ca; resourcecentre@spra.sk.ca
www.spra.sk.ca
To stimulate & advance parks, recreation & leisure activities, facilities, & programs in Saskatchewan

Saskatchewan Snowmobile Association (SSA)
PO Box 533, 221 Centre St., Regina Beach SK S0G 4C0
Tel: 306-729-3500; *Fax:* 306-729-3505
Toll-Free: 800-499-7533
sasksnow@sasktel.net
www.sasksnowmobiling.sk.ca
Social Media:
www.facebook.com/people/Sask-Snow/100001758383580;
twitter.com/sasksnow
To promote the benefits of snowmobiling & increase access & participation; To provide leadership & support to members; To establish & maintain safe, high quality trails; To provide support to club development
Chris Brewer, President & Chief Executive Officer
Chelsie Stuermer, Club Coordinator
Jeannie Brewer, Comptroller

Shooting Federation of Canada (SFC) / Fédération de tir du Canada (FTC)
45 Shirley Blvd., Nepean ON K2K 2W6
Tel: 613-727-7483; *Fax:* 613-727-7487
info@sfc-ftc.ca
www.sfc-ftc.ca
National governing body of recreational & Olympic shooting sports, representing firearms users in matters of legislation, shooting sports promotion, & program activities
Asmir Arifovic, President

Snowmobilers Association of Nova Scotia (SANS)
5516 Spring Garden Rd., 4th Fl., Halifax NS B3J 3G6
Tel: 902-425-5450; *Fax:* 902-425-5606
info@snowmobilersNS.com
www.snowmobilersns.com
To provide leadership & support to member snowmobile clubs so that they may enjoy quality recreational snowmobiling opportunities on a province-wide network of safe & well-developed snowmobile trails
John Cameron, General Manager

Snowmobilers of Manitoba Inc.
2121 Henderson Hwy., Winnipeg MB R2G 1P8
Tel: 204-940-7533; *Fax:* 204-940-7531
info@snoman.mb.ca
www.snoman.mb.ca
To provide strong leadership & support to member clubs; to develop & maintain safe & environmentally responsible snowmobile trails; to further the enjoyment of organized snowmobiling throughout Manitoba
Duncan Stokes, Executive Director

Soaring Association of Canada (SAC) / Association canadienne de vol à voile (ACVV)
c/o COPA National Office, 71 Bank St., 7th Fl., Ottawa ON K1P 5N2
Tel: 613-236-4901; *Fax:* 613-236-8646
sac@sac.ca
www.sac.ca
To promote, enhance & protect the sport of soaring in Canada; To provide information & services to the soaring community: licensing, medical requirements for glider pilots, aircraft certification, technical issues, courses & training, insurance plan, & services to clubs
Sylvain Bourque, President
John Mulder, Vice-President & Secretary

Sport Parachute Association of Saskatchewan
PO Box 37056, Regina SK S4S 7K3
Tel: 306-934-8528
www.skydive.sk.ca
Craig Skihar, President
Burk Reiman, Vice-President

Trail Riders of the Canadian Rockies
PO Box 6742, Stn. D, Calgary AB T2P 2E6
Tel: 403-652-8672; *Fax:* 403-261-2813
admin@trail-rides.ca
www.trail-rides.ca
To encourage travel on horseback through the Canadian Rockies; to foster the maintenance & improvement of old trails & the building of new trails; to promote good fellowship among those who visit & live in the Canadian Rockies; to encourage the appreciation of outdoor life & the study & conservation of mountain ecology; to assist in every way possible to ensure the preservation of the National Parks of Canada for the use & enjoyment of the public; to cooperate with other organizations with similar aims
Terry Stowell, Executive Director
Penny Egeland, Secretary

Trans Canada Trail Foundation (TCTF) / Fondation du sentier transcanadian
43, Westminster Ave. North, Montréal QC H4X 1Y8
Tel: 514-485-3959; *Fax:* 514-485-4541
Toll-Free: 800-465-3636
info@tctrail.ca
www.tctrail.ca
To promote & coordinate the planning, designing & building of a continuous, shared-use recreation trail that winds its way through every Province & Territory
Gail Urquhart, Vice President, Resource Development & Government Relations

Tunnelling Association of Canada (TAC) / Association canadienne des tunnels
8828 Pigott Rd., Richmond ON V7A 2C4
Tel: 604-241-1297; *Fax:* 604-241-1399
admin@tunnelcanada.ca
www.tunnelcanada.ca
To promote Canadian tunnelling & underground excavation technologies, & safe design, construction & maintenance; to facilitate information exchange; to represent the tunnelling community in matters of public & technical concern; to publish a Canadian registry of tunnels, underground excavations & similar works
Derek Zoldy, Secretary-Treasurer
Rick Staples, President

Velo Halifax Bicycle Club
PO Box 125, Dartmouth NS B2Y 3Y2
www.velohalifax.ca
Walton Watt, Registrar

Whitewater Kayaking Association of British Columbia (WKABC)
PO Box 91549, Stn. West Vancouver, Vancouver BC V7V 3P2
Tel: 604-515-6376
admin@whitewater.org
www.whitewater.org
To encourage & expand the safety & enjoyment of river kayaking
Don Butler, President

Whitewater Ontario
411 Carnegie Beach Rd., Port Perry ON L9L 1B6
Tel: 905-985-4585; *Fax:* 905-985-5256
Toll-Free: 888-322-2849
info@whitewaterontario.ca
www.whitewaterontario.ca
Whitewater Ontario is the sport governing body in the province, and represents provincial interests within the national body Whitewater Canada and the Canadian Canoe Association
Claudia Kerkoff, Vice-President

Wilderness Canoe Association (WCA)
PO Box 91068, 2901 Bayview Ave., Toronto ON M2K 2Y6
Tel: 416-223-4646
info@wildernesscanoe.ca
www.wildernesscanoe.ca
Organization of individuals interested in wilderness travel, mainly by canoe, kayak, and backpacking and, in winter, by skis and snowshoes
Aleks Gusev, Chair

YMCA Canada
#601, 1867 Younge Street, Toronto ON M4S 1Y5
Tel: 416-967-9622; *Fax:* 416-967-9618
www.ymca.ca
Social Media: twitter.com/YMCA_Canada
Dedicated to the growth of all persons in spirit, mind & body, & in a sense of responsibility to each other & the global community; fosters & stimulates the development of strong member associations & advocates on their behalf regionally, nationally & internationally
Scott Haldane, President/CEO
Marilyn Kapitany, Chair

Yukon Canoe & Kayak Club
PO Box 40080, 3 Sitka Cres., Whitehorse YT Y1A 6M6
Tel: 867-456-4827
current@yckc.ca
www.yckc.ca
Eyvi Smith, President

Yukon Outdoors Club
4061, 4th Ave., Whitehorse YT Y1A 1H1
yukonoutdoorsclub@gmail.com
www.yukonoutdoorsclub.ca
The Yukon Outdoors Club is a non-profit society whose activities include co-ordinating trips to promote the enjoyment of the outdoors.
Tony Gonda, President

YWCA Canada / Association des jeunes femmes chrétiennes du Canada
104 Edward St., 1st Fl., Toronto ON M5G 0A7
Tel: 416-962-8881; *Fax:* 416-962-8084
national@ywcacanada.ca
www.ywcacanada.ca
Social Media: www.facebook.com/ywcacanada; twitter.com/YWCA_Canada
A charitable, voluntary organization which coordinates the YWCA movement in Canada, and has a mission to advocate for the equity and equality rights and needs of women. The YWCA works actively to raise awareness on the prevention of violence against women, and the need for universal, accessible and quality child care.
Elizabeth Bourns, President
Paulette Senior, CEO
Lynne Kent, President
Francine Piché, Vice President
Cathy Riggall, Vice President

Recycling

Association of Alberta Coordinated Action for Recycling Enterprises
5212 - 49 St., Leduc AB T9E 7H5
Tel: 780-980-0035; *Fax:* 780-980-0232
Toll-Free: 866-818-2273
www.albertacare.org
To support waste management & recycling activities at the community level in Alberta
Linda McDonald, Executive Director

New Brunswick Solid Waste Association (NBSWA) / l'Association des déchets solides du Nouveau-Brunswick (ADSNB)
32 Wedgewood Dr., Rothesay NB E2E 3P7
Tel: 506-849-4218; *Fax:* 506-847-1369
Toll-Free: 877-777-4218
nbswa@nbnet.nb.ca
www.recyclenb.ca
The New Brunswick Solid Waste Association is a non-profit group dedicated to promoting and furthering the principles of solid waste management in New Brunswick. Made up of volunteer members of the regional Solid Waste Commissions and Corporations in the province, the NBSWA is actively involved in numerous environmental issues surrounding solid waste and waste diversion
Don Shea, Executive Director

Reproductive Issues

Birthright International / Accueil Grossesse
777 Coxwell Ave., Toronto ON M4C 3C6
Tel: 416-469-1111; *Fax:* 416-469-1772
Toll-Free: 800-550-4900
info@birthright.org
www.birthright.org
A tax-exempt, charitable, interdenominational organization, Birthright provides non-judgmental support to women facing an unplanned pregnancy, helping them carry their baby to term. It is unaffliated with any religous, political or public agency.
Louise R. Summerhill, Co-President & Founder
Mary Berney, Co-President

Canadian Federation for Sexual Health (CFSH) / Fédération canadienne pour la santé sexuelle
#403, 2198 Riverside Dr., Ottawa ON K1N 7X3
Tel: 613-241-4474; *Fax:* 613-241-7550
Toll-Free: 888-270-7444
admin@cfsh.ca
www.cfsh.ca
CFSH envisions a global society that celebrates healthy sexuality, its diversity of expression & reproductive choice as fundamental human rights for individuals throughout life. CFSH is a national network that takes leadership in advancing sexual & reproductive health & rights in Canada & abroad through: Public education & awareness; Support for the delivery of programs & services in Canada; Advocacy; International projects & liaison with the International Planned Parenthood Federation
Jolanta Scott-Parker, Executive Director

Canadian Fertility & Andrology Society (CFAS) / Société canadienne de fertilité et d'andrologie
#1107, 1255, rue University, Montréal QC H3B 3W7
Tel: 514-524-9009; *Fax:* 514-524-2163
info@cfas.ca
www.cfas.ca
To speak on behalf of interested parties in the field of assisted reproductive technologies & research in reproductive sciences
Carl A. Laskin, President
Mathias Gysler, Vice-President
Agneta Holländer, Executive Director
Jeff Roberts, Director, Continuing Professional Development
Janet Fraser, Secretary-Treasurer

Canadians for Choice (CFC) / Association Canadien(ne)s pour la liberté de choix
PO Box 539, Stn. B, Ottawa ON K1P 5P6
Tel: 613-789-9958; *Fax:* 613-789-9960
Toll-Free: 888-642-2725
info@canadiansforchoice.ca
www.canadiansforchoice.ca
Social Media: www.facebook.com/pages/Canadians-for-Choice/396972525557 ; twitter.com/Cdns4Choice
Dedicated to ensuring reproductive choice for all Canadians through education, research, training & public policy
Agathe Gramet-Kedzior, Acting Executive Director
Shelley Melanson, Project Officer
Norman Barwin, President
Sandeep Prasad, Vice-President

Fédération du Québec pour le planning des naissances (FQPN)
#405, 110, rue Ste-Thérèse, Montréal QC H2Y 1E6
Tél: 514-866-3721; *Téléc:* 514-866-1100
info@fqpn.qc.ca
www.fqpn.qc.ca
Promouvoir les droits des femmes dans le domaine de la santé, particulièrement la reproduction et la sexualité; promouvoir l'accès à une information critique et fiable, la liberté de choix et le consentement des femmes face à leur propre corps.
Natalie Parent, Coordonnatrice

Infertility Awareness Association of Canada (IAAC) / Association canadienne de sensibilisation à l'infertilité (ACSI)
2160 av Nightingale, Montréal QC H9S 1E4
Tel: 514-484-2891; *Fax:* 514-484-0454
Toll-Free: 800-263-2929
info@iaac.ca
www.iaac.ca
Social Media: www.facebook.com/57435550753
To offer assistance, support & education to individuals with infertility concerns; to increase the awareness & understanding of the causes, treatments & the emotional impact of infertility through the development of educational programs.
Jocelyn Smith, President

Life's Vision
#5, 130 Marion St., Winnipeg MB R2H 0T4
Tel: 204-233-8047; *Fax:* 204-233-0523
lifesvision@shaw.ca
lifesvision.ca
To engage in non-sectarian educational activities in order to encourage & promote among the general public an understanding & awareness of the dignity & worth of each individual human life, whatever its state & circumstances; to foster respect for all human life. Life's Vision provides information & referral services dealing with pregnancy & end of life issues, such as abortion, euthanasia & assisted suicide, & provides a voice for those opposed to abortion.
Heather White, Executive Director

Natural Family Planning Association
#205, 3050 Yonge St., Toronto ON M4N 2K4
Tel: 416-481-5465
nfptoronto@primus.ca
www.naturalfamilyplanning.ca
The Association promotes the Billings Ovulation Method of natural family planning which is based on an awareness of a woman's physical systems to gauge optimum fertility state. It is a registered charity, BN: 129904280RR0001.
Merrilyn Currie, Executive Director

Newfoundland & Labradour Right to Life Association
PO Box 5427, St. John's NL A1C 5W2
Tel: 709-579-1500; *Fax:* 709-579-1600
nffriendsforlife@nl.rogers.com
www.nlprolife.org; www.nlfriendsofrighttolife.net
The Association upholds the sacredness & inviolability of human life from conception to natural death. It disseminates information on such to authorities & the public, supporting mothers during & after pregnancy. It networks with similar organizations, & promotes medical research to support its beliefs.
Linda Holden, President

Ontario Coalition for Abortion Clinics (OCAC)
PO Box 495, Stn. P, 427 Bloor St. West, Toronto ON M5S 2Z1
Tel: 416-969-8463; *Fax:* 416-789-0762
ocac@sympatico.ca
To work for reproductive rights & access to abortions

Carolyn Egan, Coordinating Committee Member

Options for Sexual Health (OPT)
3550 East Hastings St., Vancouver BC V5K 2A7
Tel: 604-731-4252; *Fax:* 604-731-4698
info@optbc.org
www.optionsforsexualhealth.org
To promote optimal sexual health for all British Columbians by supporting reproductive choice, reducing unplanned pregnancy, & providing quality education, information & clinical services
Siobhan Aspinall, President

Planned Parenthood - Newfoundland & Labrador Sexual Health Centre (NLSHC)
203 Merrymeeting Rd., St. John's NL A1C 2W6
Tel: 709-579-1009; *Toll-Free:* 877-666-9847
info@nlsexualhealthcentre.org
www.nlsexualhealthcentre.org
To promote positive sexual health attitudes & practices throughout Newfoundland & Labrador; To support & respect individual choice
Rolanda Ryan, President
Costa Kasimos, Executive Director
Andrea Murphy, Secretary
Terri Hancock, Treasurer

Planned Parenthood Alberta (PPA)
#102, 1212 1st St. SE, Calgary AB T2G 2H8
Tel: 403-283-8591; *Fax:* 403-283-8563
ppalberta@plannedparenthoodalta.com
www.plannedparenthoodalta.com
To support reproductive choice & promote sexual health for all Albertans
Melanie Anderson, Executive Director

Planned Parenthood Saskatoon Centre (PPSC)
Macro Bldg., #301, 115 2nd Ave. North, Saskatoon SK S7K 1M1
Tel: 306-244-7989; *Fax:* 306-652-4034
info@sexualhealthcentresaskatoon.ca
www.sexualhealthcentresaskatoon.ca
To ensure that information, resources & support services of the highest quality regarding sexuality, contraception & reproduction are available & accessible to all in our community who need them; to encourage responsible decision-making & behaviour which is respectful of the needs & of the choices available to each individual
Evelyn Reisner, Executive Director

Pro-Life BC (PLBC)
#112, 32868 Ventura Ave., Abbotsford BC V2S 6J3
Tel: 604-853-3425; *Fax:* 604-853-3413
Toll-Free: 877-774-4625
life@prolifebc.ca
www.prolifebc.ca
To educate the people of British Columbia regarding the sanctity & value of all human life from conception to natural death
Yvonne Douma, Executive Director
Michelle Doherty, President
Monique Van Berkel, Assistant to Executive Director

Right to Life Association of Toronto
#302, 120 Eglinton Ave., Toronto ON M4P 1E2
Tel: 416-483-7869; *Fax:* 416-483-7052
office@righttolife.to
www.rtl-toronto.org
Social Media: www.facebook.com/righttolifeto
To uphold the right to life as the basic human right on which all others depend; to provide information & services to that end

Sexuality Education Resource Centre Manitoba (SERC)
#200, 226 Osborne St. North, Winnipeg MB R3C 1V4
Tel: 204-982-7800; *Fax:* 204-982-7819
info@serc.mb.ca
www.serc.mb.ca
To promote universal access to comprehensive, reliable information & services on sexuality & related health issues by fostering awareness, understanding, & support through education
Lori S. Johnson, Executive Director
Gina Sylvestre, President

World Organization Ovulation Method Billings Inc.
1506 Dansey Ave., Coquitlam BC V3K 3J1
Tel: 604-936-4472; *Fax:* 604-936-5690
info@woomb.ca
www.woomb.ca
To teach fertility awareness & natural family planning
Lou Specken, President

Research & Scholarship

Advanced Foods & Materials Network / Réseau des aliments et des matériaux d'avant-garde
#215, 150 Research Lane, Guelph ON N1G 4T2
Tel: 519-822-6253; *Fax:* 519-824-8453
www.afmnet.ca
Rickey Yada, Scientific Director

AllerGen NCE Inc.
Michael DeGroote Centre for Learning & Discovery, McMaster University, #3120, 1200 Main St. West, Hamilton ON L8N 2A5
Tel: 905-525-9140; *Fax:* 905-524-0611
info@allergen-nce.ca
www.allergen-nce.ca
To support research, capacity building activities, & networking regarding allergic disease in Canada; To reduce the morbidity, mortality & socio-economic impacts of allergy, asthma, & related immune diseases
Judah Denburg, CEO & Scientific Director
Diana Royce, Chief Operating Officer & Managing Director
Mark Mitchell, Manager, Research & Partnerships
Marta Rudyk, Manager, Communications & Coordinator, Knowledge Mobilization
Allison Brown, Coordinator, Research
Michelle Harkness, Coordinator, Highly Qualified Personnel & Events

AquaNet - Network in Aquaculture
Ocean Sciences Centre, Memorial University of Newfoundland, St. John's NL A1C 5S7
Tel: 709-737-3245; *Fax:* 709-737-3500
info@aquanet.ca
www.aquanet.ca
To foster a sustainable aquaculture sector in Canada through high quality research & education

ArcticNet Inc.
Pavillon Alexandre-Vachon, Université Laval, #4081, 1045, av de la Médecine, Québec QC G1V 0A6
Tel: 418-656-5830; *Fax:* 418-656-2334
arcticnet@arcticnet.ulaval.ca
www.arcticnet-ulaval.ca
To study the impacts of climate change in the coastal Canadian Arctic; To engage Inuit organizations, northern communities, universities, research institutes, industry, government, & international agencies as partners in the scientific process
Martin Fortier, Executive Director
Louis Fortier, Scientific Director
Réal Choquette, Administrative Director
Jean-Luc Bernier, Officer, Communications
Keith Levesque, Coordinator, Ship-based Research
Josée Michaud, Coordinator, Data

AUTO21 Network of Centres of Excellence
754 California Ave., Windsor ON N9B 2Z2
Tel: 519-253-3000; *Fax:* 519-971-3626
info@auto21.ca
www.auto21.ca
Social Media: www.facebook.com/AUTO21; twitter.com/auto21nce; www.linkedin.com/groups?about=&gid=2804256&trk=anet_ug_grppro; www.youtube.com/user/AUTO21NCE
To partner the public & private secotrs in applied automotive R&D
Peter Frise, CEO & Scientific Director
Michelle Watters, COO & Executive Director
Stephanie Campeau, Director, Public Affairs & Communications

Canadian Arthritis Network (CAN) / Le Réseau canadien de l'arthrite
#1002, 522 University Ave., Toronto ON M5T 1W7
Tel: 416-586-4770; *Fax:* 416-586-8395
can@arthritisnetwork.ca
www.arthritisnetwork.ca
Social Media: www.facebook.com/102841629761794; twitter.com/commcan
To improve the quality of life for people with arthritis; To support integrated, trans-disciplinary research & development, with a focus upon inflammatory joint diseases, osteoarthritis, & bioengineering for restoration of joint function
Robin Armstrong, Chair
John Riley, Managing Director
Claire Bombardier, Co-Scientific Director
Monique Gignac, Co-Scientific Director
Kate Lee, Director, Research & Development
Everdina Carter, Administrative Assistant

Canadian Association for Research in Nondestructive Evaluation (CARNDE) / Association canadienne de recherches en évaluation non-destructive (ACREND)
75, boul de Montagne, Boucherville QC J4B 6Y4
Tel: 450-641-5252; *Fax:* 450-641-5106
jean.bussiere@nrc.ca
www.nrc.ca
To foster, coordinate & disseminate results of research, development & application of new or advanced NDE techniques in Canada; to promote technology transfer by encouraging collaboration between universities, research organizations & industrial or governmental users; to raise the profile of NDE research in Canada by publicizing the need for & economic benefits arising from advances in NDE
Jean Bussière, Research Editor

Canadian Carbonization Research Association (CCRA)
PO Box 2460, Burlington ON L8N 3J5
Tel: 905-548-4796
www.cancarb.ca
To fund coke & coal research in Canada for benefit of member companies
Ted Todoschuk, Chairman
G.A. Chapman, Treasurer

Canadian Centre for Policy Alternatives (CCPA) / Centre canadien de politique alternative
#205, 75 Albert St., Ottawa ON K1P 5E7
Tel: 613-563-1341; *Fax:* 613-233-1458
ccpa@policyalternatives.ca
www.policyalternatives.ca
To promote research on economic & social issues facing Canada; to monitor current developments in economy & study important trends that affect Canadians; to demonstrate thoughtful alternatives to the limited perspectives of business, research institutes & government agencies; to put forward research that reflects concerns of women & men, labour & business, churches, cooperatives & voluntary agencies, governments, minorities, disadvantaged & fortunate individuals
Bruce Campbell, Executive Director
Diane Touchette, Director, Operations

Canadian Committee of Byzantinists
Talbot College, Univ. of Western Ontario, London ON N6A 3K7
Tel: 519-661-3045; *Fax:* 519-850-2388
splinter@uwo.ca
To network among Canadian Byzantinists; to promote communications & exchange of information; to promote Byzantine Studies in Canada
A.R. Littlewood, Contact

Canadian Federation for Robotics / Fédération canadienne de robotique
#301, 126 York St., Ottawa ON K1N 5T5
To promote interest in the use of & the application of robotics technologies by Canadian firms
Paul Johnston, Director

Canadian Genetic Diseases Network (CGDN) / Réseau canadien sur les maladies génétiques (RCMG)
#201, 2150 Western Pkwy., Vancouver BC V6T 1Z4
Tel: 604-221-7300; *Fax:* 604-221-0778
info@cgdn.ca
www.cgdn.ca
A nation-wide consortium of Canada's top investigators & core-technology facilities in human genetics, partnered with colleagues from industry to conduct leading-edge research within an "Institute without Walls"; to achieve international competitiveness in scientific research with social & economic benefits
Rob Abbott, CEO

Canadian Institute for Advanced Research (CIFAR) / Institut canadien de recherches avancées (ICRA)
#1400, 180 Dundas St. West, Toronto ON M5G 1Z8
Tel: 416-971-4251; *Fax:* 416-971-6169
info@cifar.ca
www.ciar.ca
To stimulate leading-edge research projects vital to Canada's future prosperity.
Richard W. Ivey, Chair
Chaviva Hosek, President/CEO

Canadian Institute for Mediterranean Studies (CIMS) / Institut canadien d'études méditerranéennes
c/o Carr Hall, Department of Italian Studies, University of Toronto, 100 St. Joseph St., Toronto ON M5S 1J4
www.utoronto.ca/cims

To study all aspects of Mediterranean culture & civilization, past & present
Alex Gropper, President
Mario Crespi, Executive Director
Cliff Goldfarb, Secretary
Philip Charles, Treasurer

Canadian Institute for Photonics Innovations (CIPI)
Université Laval, Pavillion d'optique-photonique, #2111, 2375 rue de la Terrasse, Québec QC G1V 0A6
Tel: 418-656-3013; *Fax:* 418-656-2995
cipi@cipi.ulaval.ca
www.cipi.ulaval.ca
Photonics - science of generating, manipulating, transmitting & detecting light
Robert Corriveau, President

Canadian Institute of Strategic Studies (CISS) / Institut canadien d'études stratégiques
#702, 165 University Ave., Toronto ON M5H 3B8
Tel: 416-322-8128; *Fax:* 416-322-8129
Toll-Free: 800-831-5695
info@ciss.ca
www.ciss.ca
To stimulate research, study, analysis & discussion of the strategic implications of major national & international issues, events & trends as they affect Canada & Canadians; to enhance the national security of Canada, that is, the preservation of a way of life acceptable to the Canadian people & compatible with needs & legitimate aspirations of others.
Alex Morrison, President

Canadian Institute of Ukrainian Studies (CIUS) / Institut canadien d'études ukrainiennes
#4-30, Pembina Hall, University of Alberta, Edmonton AB T6G 2H8
Tel: 780-492-2972; *Fax:* 780-492-4967
cius@ualberta.ca
www.cius.ca
To develop Ukrainian scholarship in Canada; To organize research in Ukrainian & Ukrainian-Canadian studies
Zenon E. Kohut, Director, CIUS, & Director, Kowalsky Program for the Study of Eastern Ukraine
John-Paul Himka, Director, Religion & Culture Program
David R. Marples, Director, Stasiuk Program for the Study of Contemporary Ukraine
Marusia Petryshyn, Director, Ukrainian Language Education Centre
Bohdan Klid, Assistant Director, CIUS & Media Relations
Alla Martchouk, Financial Officer, CIUS
Jars Balan, Administrative Coordinator, Kule Ukrainian Canadian Studies Centre

Canadian Language & Literacy Research Network
Elborn College, University of Western Ontario, 1201 Western Rd., London ON N6G 1H1
Tel: 519-661-3619; *Fax:* 519-661-4223
info@cllrnet.ca
www.cllrnet.ca
The Canadian Language and Literacy Research Network will improve language and literacy skills in Canadian children, enabling them to contribute more effectively to the social and economic lfie of their communities.
Donald G. Jamieson, CEO/Scientific Director

Canadian Mathematical Society (CMS) / Société mathématique du Canada
#105, 1785 Alta Vista Dr., Ottawa ON K1G 3Y6
Tel: 613-733-2662; *Fax:* 613-733-8994
office@cms.math.ca
www.cms.math.ca
To promote & advance the discovery, learning & application of mathematics.
Johan Rudnick, Executive Director

Canadian Mining Industry Research Organization (CAMIRO)
935 Ramsey Lake Rd., Sudbury ON P3E 2C6
Tel: 705-673-6595; *Fax:* 705-671-6606
info@camiro.org
www.camiro.org
To manage collaborative mining research in the divisions of exploration, mining, & metallurgical processing; To contribute to the safety, growth, & competitiveness of the Canadian mineral industry
Larry Urbanoski, Director, Research, Metallurgical Division
Tom Lane, Director, Research Development, Exploration Division
Charles Graham, Contact, Mining Division

Canadian Nautical Research Society (CNRS) / Société canadienne pour la recherche nautique
PO Box 34029, Ottawa ON K2J 4B0
www.cnrs-scrn.org
Social Media: www.facebook.com/150946001632212
To stimulate & promote nautical research in Canada; to enhance Canada's understanding of its maritime heritage; to foster communication in nautical affairs, to organize meetings, & to cooperate with other agencies promoting nautical research
Marice D. Smith, President

Canadian Numismatic Research Society (CNRS)
PO Box 1351, Victoria BC V8W 2W7
Fax: 250-598-5539
www.nunetcan.net/cnrs/cnrs.htm
To promote reseach & study of numismatics
Ronald Greene, Secretary

Canadian Operational Research Society (CORS) / Société canadienne de recherche opérationelle (SCRO)
PO Box 2225, Stn. D, Ottawa ON K1P 5W4
cors@uwindsor.ca
www.cors.ca
To advance the theory & practice of O.R. in Canada; to stimulate & promote contacts between people interested in the subject
Vinh Quan, President
Corinne MacDonald, Secretary

Canadian Philosophical Association (CPA) / Association canadienne de philosophie
c/o Louise Morel, Saint Paul University, 223 Main St., Ottawa ON K1S 1C4
Tel: 613-236-1393; *Fax:* 613-782-3005
acpa@ustpaul.ca
www.acpcpa.ca
To advance the discipline of philosophy in Canada
Ronald de Sousa, President
Louise Morel, Executive Director
Judy Pelham, Secretary
Patrice Philie, Treasurer
Eric Dayton, English Editor, Dialogue: Canadian Philosophical Review
Mathieu Marion, Éditeur Francophone, Dialogue: Revue canadienne de philosophie

Canadian Quaternary Association / Association canadienne pour l'étude du Quaternaire
c/o Joshua Kurek, Department of Biology, Queen's University, 116 Barrie St., Kinsgton ON K7L 3N6
www.canqua.com
To study & advance knowledge of the quaternary period
Irene Gregory-Eaves, President
Scott Lamoureux, Vice-President
Joshua Kurek, Secretary-Treasurer

Canadian Research Institute for the Advancement of Women (CRIAW) / Institut canadien de recherches sur les femmes (ICREF)
c/o Institute of Women's Studies, University of Ottawa, 143 Séraphin-Marion, Ottawa ON K1N 6N5
Tel: 613-562-5800
info@criaw-icref.ca
www.criaw-icref.ca
To advance the position of women in society through feminist & women-centred research; to encourage, coordinate & communicate research about the reality of women's lives & ensure an equal place for women & their experiences in the body of knowledge about Canada; to recognize & affirm the diversity of women's experiences; to demystify the research process & promote connections between research, social action & social change; to facilitate communication among feminist researchers & research organizations world-wide
Maria-Héléna Pacelli, Administrative Officer
Ann Denis, President

Canadian Society for Aesthetics (CSA) / Société canadienne d'esthétique (SCE)
c/o Dawson College, 4729, av de Maisonneuve, Westmount QC H3Z 1M3
info@csa-sce.ca
www.csa-sce.ca
To keep aesthetic theorists in close touch with the creative & critical practices that are the basis of their discipline; to increase awareness of aesthetic issues among Canadian citizens & develop the intellectual & conceptual resources for dealing with them.
Ira Newman, Anglophone President
François Chalifour, Francophone President
Victor Y. Haines, Secretary

Canadian Society for Eighteenth-Century Studies (CSECS) / Société canadienne d'étude du dix-huitième siècle (SCEDS)
c/o Department of English, Laurentian University, 935 Ramsey Lake Road, Sudbury ON P3E 2C6
sglover@laurentian.ca
www.csecs.ca
To sustain, in Canada, interest in eighteenth-century civilization in Europe & the New World; to encourage, from a wide interdisciplinary base, research on the eighteenth-century; to make known to eighteenth-century specialists the work done in this area in Canada.
Marc André Bernier, President
Armelle St-Martin, Secretary
Susan Paterson Glover, Treasurer

The Canadian Society for Mesopotamian Studies (CSMS) / La Société canadienne des études mésopotamiennes
c/o Dept. of Near & Middle Eastern Civilizations, 4 Bancroft Ave., 4th Fl., Toronto ON M5S 1C1
Tel: 416-978-4531; *Fax:* 416-978-3305
gframe@chass.utoronto.ca
To stimulate interest among the general public in the culture, history & archaeology of Mesopotamia, in particular the civilizations of Sumer, Babylon & Assyria, as well as neighbouring ancient civilizations
N.J. Johnson, Administrator
G. Frame, President
R. Thomas, Sec.-Treas.

Canadian Society for the Study of Religion (CSSR) / Société canadienne pour l'étude de la religion (SCER)
c/o Dr. Mark D. Chapman, #100, 30 Carrier Dr., Toronto ON M9W 5T7
mchapman@alumni.uwaterloo.ca
www.ccsr.ca/cssr
To promote research in the study of religion, with particular reference to Canada; To encourage a critical examination of the teaching of the discipline
Michel Desjardins, President
Mark Chapman, Membership Secretary
Richard Mann, Treasurer

Canadian Society of Patristic Studies (CSPS) / Association canadienne des études patristiques
c/o Dr. S. Muir, Religious Studies, Concordia University College of AB, 7128 Ada Blvd., Edmonton AB T5B 4E4
www.ccsr.ca/csps
To encourage the academic study of the Church Fathers
Tim Hegedus, President
Lorraine Buck, Vice-President
George Bevan, Secretary
Steven Muir, Treasurer

Canadian Sociological Association (CSA)
PO Box 98014, 2126 Burnhamthorpe Rd. West, Mississauga ON L5L 5V4
Tel: 438-880-2182
office@csa-scs.ca
www.csa-scs.ca
Social Media: www.facebook.com/134213209935255; www.linkedin.com/groups?mostPopular=&gid=3188569
To promote research, publication & teaching in sociology in Canada
J.S. Frideres, President

Canadian Stroke Network (CSN) / Réseau canadien contre les accidents cérébrovasculaires
#301, 600 Peter Morand Cres., Ottawa ON K1G 5Z3
Tel: 613-562-5696; *Fax:* 613-521-9215
info@canadianstrokenetwork.ca
www.canadianstrokenetwork.ca
To reduce the physical, social, & economic consequences of stroke on individuals & society through leadership in research; To develop & implement national strategies in stroke research; To maximize health & economic benefits; To build a consensus across Canada on stroke policy
Michael Cloutier, Chair
Antoine Hakim, CEO & Scientific Director
Katie Lafferty, Executive Director
Mike Sharma, Deputy Director

Canadian Technion Society
#206, 970 Lawrence Ave. West, Toronto ON M6A 3B6
Tel: 416-789-4545; *Fax:* 416-789-0255
Toll-Free: 800-935-8864
info@cdntech.org
www.cdntech.org
Social Media:
www.facebook.com/pages/Canadian-Technion-Society/1200727 21377514
To support Technion Israel Institute of Technology; to promote exchange of scientific information between Israel & Canada, scholarships, research, etc.
Harold Goldberg, National President
Cheryl Koperwas, National Executive Director
Natana Shek Dor, National Vice-President, Fundraising & Development

Canadian Theosophical Society Inc. / Association théosophique canadienne inc.
c/o National Secretary, 3519 Spruce Dr. SW, Calgary AB T3C 3A5
Tel: 403-217-6934
www.theosophical.ca
To form a nucleus of the Universal Brotherhood of Humanity, without distinction of race, creed, sex, caste, or colour; to encourage the study of comparative religion, philosophy, & science; to investigate unexplained laws of nature & the powers latent in man
Medardo Martinez Cruz, President
Elaine Pederzolli, National Secretary

Canadian Water Network (CWN) / Réseau canadien de l'eau
University of Waterloo, 200 University Ave. West, Waterloo ON N2L 3G1
Tel: 519-888-4567; *Fax:* 519-883-7574
info@cwn-rce.ca
www.cwn-rce.ca
To create a national partnership in innovation that promotes environmentally responsible stewardship & opportunities with respect to Canada's water resources resulting in sustained prosperity & improved quality of life for Canadians.
Bernadette Conant, Director of Programs
Mark Servos, Scientific Director
David Cotter, Director of Communications

Cancer Research Society (CRS) / Société de recherche sur le cancer
#402, 625, av Président-Kennedy, Montréal QC H3A 3S5
Tel: 514-861-9227; *Fax:* 514-861-9220
Toll-Free: 866-343-2262
info@src-crs.ca
src-crs.ca
CRS is a not-for-profit organization that supports basic cancer research through funding & seed money. Grants & fellowships are allocated to universities & hospitals involved in research across Canada. It is a registered charity, BN: 119153229RR0001.
Mario Chevrette, President
Andy Chabot, Executive Director

Centre for Research on Latin America & The Caribbean (CERLAC)
8th Fl., York Research Tower, 4700 Keele St., Toronto ON M3J 1P3
Tel: 416-736-5237; *Fax:* 416-736-5688
www.yorku.ca/cerlac
To offer an interdisciplinary research unit concerned with economic development, political & social organization & cultural contributions of Latin America & the Caribbean; to build academic & cultural links between these regions & Canada; informs researchers, policy advisors & public on matters concerning the regions; to assist in development of research & teaching institutions that directly benefit people of the regions
Eduardo Canel, Director

Classical Association of Canada (CAC) / Société canadienne des études classiques (SCEC)
Vari Hall, Department of History, York University, #2178, 4700 Keele St., Toronto ON M3J 1P3
Tel: 416-736-2100
www.cac-scec.ca
John Serrati, Secretary
Jonathan Edmundson, President
Annabel Robinson, Treasurer

Commission canadienne pour la théorie des machines et des mécanismes (CCToMM) / Canadian Committee for the Theory of Machines & Mechanisms
Faculté d'ingénierie, Univ. de Moncton, Moncton NB E1A 3E9
me.queensu.ca/people/notash/CCToMM/
Promouvoir le développement dans le domaine des machines et des mécanismes par la recherche théorique et expérimentale et leurs applications pratiques.
Roger Boudreau, Secrétaire général
Leila Notash, Responsable des communications

FPInnovations
580, boul Saint-Jean, Pointe-Claire QC H9R 3J9
Tel: 514-630-4100; *Fax:* 514-630-4134
info@fpinnovations.ca
www.feric.ca
To develop & assist with the implementation of innovative & safe forest operational solutions, which encompass areas such as the engineering, environmental, & human aspects of forestry & wildland fire operations; To improve sustainable forest operations in Canada; To provide members with knowledge & technology, based on research, to conduct cost-competitive, quality forest operations
Lynn M. Dyer, President

Geomatics for Informed Decisions Network
Pavillon Louis-Jacques-Casault, Cité Universitaire, #2306, 1055, av du Séminaire, Québec QC G1V 0A6
Tel: 418-656-7758; *Fax:* 418-656-2611
info@geoide.ulaval.ca
www.geoide.ulaval.ca
Chantal Arguin, President
Nicholas Chrisman, Scientific Director

Great Lakes Institute for Environmental Research (GLIER)
University of Windsor, 401 Sunset Ave., Windsor ON N9B 3P4
Tel: 519-253-3000; *Fax:* 519-971-3616
glier@uwindsor.ca
cronus.uwindsor.ca/glier
Brian Fryer, Contact

Humanist Association of Canada (HAC) / Association humaniste du Canada
401B Weber St. North, Waterloo ON N2J 3J2
Fax: 613-739-5969
Toll-Free: 877-486-2671
hac_memberships@yahoo.ca
www.humanistcanada.com
To bring together people who share a non-theistic view of the world; to educate the public about humanism & its ethics & values.
Dorothy Hays, President

Innovation Management Association of Canada (IMAC) / Association canadienne de la gestion de l'innovation (ACGI)
c/o CATAAlliance, #416, 207 Bank St., Ottawa ON K2P 2N2
Tel: 613-236-6550; *Fax:* 613-236-8189
info@cata.ca
www.cata.ca/imac/
To enhance the productivity & effectiveness of Canadian research development & technology-based innovations
Cathi Malette, Membership Coordinator

Institute for Research on Public Policy / Institut de recherche en politiques publiques
#200, 1470, rue Peel, Montréal QC H3A 1T1
Tel: 514-985-2461; *Fax:* 514-985-2559
irpp@irpp.org
www.irpp.org
To improve public policy in Canada by generating research, providing insight, & sparking debate that will contribute to the public policy decision-making process & strengthen the quality of public policy decisions made by Canadian governments, citizens, institutions, & organizations
Graham Fox, President

Institute for Robotics & Intelligent Systems (IRIS) / Institut de robotique et d'intelligence des systèmes
Precarn Incorporated, #510, 1525 Carling Ave., Ottawa ON K1Z 8R9
Tel: 613-727-9576; *Fax:* 613-727-5672
crawhall@precarn.ca
www.precarn.ca
To promote collaborative applied research in intelligent systems of importance to Canadian industry; to strengthen the research & development interaction between universities & industry.
Robert Crawhall, Vice Presidnt
Henri Rothschild, President

Institute for Stuttering Treatment & Research & the Communication Improvement Program (ISTAR, CIP)
College Plaza, #1500, 8215 - 112 St., Edmonton AB T6G 2C8
Tel: 780-492-2619; *Fax:* 780-492-8457
istar@ualberta.ca
www.istar.ualberta.ca
To provide the best possible treatment for stuttering children & adults; to conduct research into the nature & treatment of stuttering; to provide advanced professional training for speech pathologists; to increase public awareness & understanding of stuttering. The Communication Improvement Program offers assessment & treatment services on speech & language delays or disorders.
Marilyn Langevin, Acting Executive Director
Sheri Ruffo, Office Manager
Holly Lamheim, Clinical Director

Institute of Urban Studies (IUS)
University of Winnipeg, #103, 520 Portage Ave., Winnipeg MB R3C 0G2
Tel: 204-982-1140; *Fax:* 204-943-4695
ius@uwinnipeg.ca
ius.uwinnipeg.ca
To undertake policy-oriented research in the field of Urban Studies; to serve as a resource centre for the community; to provide educational services to the University community & the community-at-large.
Jino Distasio, Director

International Council for Canadian Studies (ICCS) / Conseil international d'études canadiennes (CIEC)
#303, 250 City Centre Ave., Ottawa ON K1R 6K7
Tel: 613-789-7834; *Fax:* 613-789-7830
lise.nichol@iccs-ciec.ca
www.iccs-ciec.ca
Social Media: www.facebook.com/ICCS.CIEC.page; twitter.com/ICCS_CIEC
To promote scholarly study, research, teaching & publication about Canada in all disciplines & all countries; to enhance communications among its members to facilitate & develop such scholarly activities; to disseminate research results & to publicize researchers' activities in the area of Canadian Studies; to encourage the development of an international community of Canadianists.
Patrick James, President
Susan Hodgett, Secretary

International Council for Central & East European Studies (Canada) (ICCEES) / Conseil international d'études de l'Europe centrale et orientale (Canada)
Intl. Studies Program, Glendon College, York University, 2275 Bayview Ave., Toronto ON M4N 3M6
Tel: 416-736-2100; *Fax:* 416-487-6852
stankosk@glendon.yorku.ca
www.rusin.fi/ICCEES
To foster study of East European affairs & to encourage dissemination of this knowledge among specialists; To create an international community of scholars.

International Geographical Union - Canadian Committee
Simon Fraser Univ., Dept. of Geography, 8888 University Dr., Burnaby BC V5A 1S6
Tel: 604-291-3321; *Fax:* 604-291-5841
agill@sfu.ca
www.igu-net.org/uk/what_is_igu/nationalcommittees.html
To promote international programs in geography within Canada; to promote activities within IGU programs relevant to Canada & to coordinate Canadian participation; to formulate Canadian position & advise the National Research Council on Canadian participation in IGU activities
Alison Gill

International Society for Research in Palmistry Inc. / Société internationale de recherches en chirologie inc.
576, rte 315, ChéNéVille QC J0V 1E0
Tel: 819-428-4298; *Fax:* 819-428-4495
Toll-Free: 866-428-3799
info@birlacenter.com
www.birlacenter.com/palmistry
The Society offers individual & group counselling through palmistry & astrology based on Eastern Vedic System.

Lakehead Social History Institute (LSHI)
c/o Lakehead University, 955 Oliver Rd., Thunder Bay ON P7B 5E1
Tel: 807-767-0934; *Fax:* 807-767-0934
epp@swedesincanada.ca
www.swedesincanada.ca
To encourage & promote research in the social history of Thunder Bay specifically & Northwestern Ontario generally

Ernie Epp, Chief Officer
Donald W. Sjöberg, Chief Officer

Mathematics of Information Technology & Complex Systems (MITACS)
Technology Enterprise Facility, University of British Columbia, #301, 6190 Agronomy Rd., Vancouver BC V6T 1Z3
Tel: 604-822-9189; *Fax:* 604-822-3689
mitacs@mitacs.ca
www.mitacs.math.ca
MITACS leads Canada's effort in the generation, application and commercialization of new mathematical tools and methodologies within a world-class research program. The network initiates and fosters linkages with industrial, governmental, and not-for-profit organizations that require mathematical technologies to deal with problems of strategic importance to Canada. MITACS is driving the recruiting, training, and placement of a new generation of highly mathematically skilled personnel that is vital to Canada's future social and economic wellbeing. Offices in Vancouver, Toronto, Montréal, St. John's & Fredericton.
Arvind Gupta, CEO & Scientific Director

The M.S.I. Foundation
#12230, 106 Avenue NW, Edmonton AB T5N 3Z1
Tel: 780-421-7532; *Fax:* 780-425-4467
info@msifoundation.ca
www.msifoundation.ca
To foster & support research into any aspect of the provision of medical & allied health services to the people of Alberta
M. Yates, Associate Secretary
L.H. Le Riche, Chairperson

Ontario Centres of Excellence - Centre for Earth & Environmental Technologies (OCE-ETech)
#200, 156 Front St. West, Toronto ON M5J 2L6
Tel: 416-861-1092; *Fax:* 416-971-7164
Toll-Free: 866-759-6014
anne.wettlaufer@oce-ontario.org
www.oce-ontario.org
ETech engages firms, clients & academic partners in the following areas: clean water technologies, resource management, sustainable agricultue & agri-food, sustainable infrastructure, clean air technologies, waste management & sustainable infrastrucutre; organizations & academics are encouraged to contact ETech to find out how to access the broad range of services available
Tom Corr, President & CEO
Tanya Dunn, Executive Assistant, Office of President

Ontario Public Interest Research Group (OPIRG) / Groupe de recherche d'intérêt public de l'Ontario
North Borden Building, #101, 563 Spadina Ave., Toronto ON M5S 2J7
Tel: 416-978-7770; *Fax:* 416-971-2292
opirg.toronto@utoronto.ca
www.opirg.org
To make information available to the general public that enables them to make informed decisions on issues & understand & possibly influence decisions made by others on their behalf; to provide an alternative to the information provided by the academic community, government & business; to offer an analysis of environmental & social issues aimed at motivating change & placing issues in the broader social, economic & political perspective in which they need to be understood
, Chief Returning Officer

Pearson Peacekeeping Centre (PPC) / Centre pour le maintien de la paix Pearson (CPMP)
HCI Bldg., #5110, 1125 Colonel By Dr., Ottawa ON K1S 5B6
Tel: 613-520-5617; *Fax:* 613-520-3787
info@peaceoperations.org
www.peaceoperations.org
To enhance the Canadian contribution to international peace & security through education, training & research in in all aspects of peace operations
Suzanne Monaghan, President

Pulp & Paper Technical Association of Canada (PAPTAC) / Association technique des pâtes et papiers du Canada
#1070, 740, rue Notre-Dame ouest, Montréal QC H3C 3X6
Tel: 514-392-0265; *Fax:* 514-392-0369
ccrotogino@paptac.ca
www.paptac.ca
To provide means for the interchange of knowledge & expertise among its members; to improve the skill levels & effectiveness of present & future employees through training & education; to provide technical & practical information on pulp & paper manufacture & use
Greg Hay, Executive Director
André Bernier, Chair

The Royal Canadian Geographical Society (RCGS) / La Société géographique royale du Canada
#200, 1155 Lola St., Ottawa ON K1K 4C1
Tel: 613-745-4629; *Fax:* 613-744-0947
Toll-Free: 800-267-0824
rcgs@rcgs.org
www.rcgs.org
Social Media: www.facebook.com/theRCGS
To impart a broader knowledge of Canada, including its environmental, economic, & social challenges, as well as it natural & cultural heritage
John Geiger, President
Beth Dye, Secretary
Keith Exelby, Treasurer

Royal Canadian Institute (RCI)
#H7D, 700 University Ave., Toronto ON M5G 1X6
Tel: 416-977-2983; *Fax:* 416-962-7314
royalcanadianinstitute@sympatico.ca
www.royalcanadianinstitute.org
To increase public understanding of science; to create an environment in which science can flourish & be appreciated
Roy Pearson, President
John A.G. Grant, Treasurer

The Royal Society for the Encouragement of Arts, Manufactures & Commerce (RSA)
8 John Adam St., London WC2N 6EZ United Kingdom
general@rsa.org.uk
www.rsa.org.uk
Social Media: www.facebook.com/theRSAorg; twitter.com/theRSAorg
To encourage the development of a principled, prosperous society & the release of human potential
Matthew Taylor, Chief Executive
Philip Duke of Edinburgh, President

The Royal Society of Canada (RSC) / La Société royale du Canada
170 Waller St., Ottawa ON K1N 9B9
Tel: 613-991-6990; *Fax:* 613-991-6996
theacademies@rsc.ca
www.rsc.ca
To promote learning & research in the arts, humanities & sciences in Canada; in its role as a National Academy, to draw on the breadth of knowledge & expertise of its members to recognize & honour distinguished accomplishments; to advise on the state of scholarship & culture across Canada; to inform the public on noteworthy social, scientific & ethical questions of the day; it is organized into three academies covering the arts & humanities, the social sciences, & the natural & applied sciences
Darren Gilmour, Executive Director

Society for the Study of Egyptian Antiquities (SSEA) / Société pour l'Étude de l'Égypte Ancienne
PO Box 578, Stn. P, Toronto ON M5S 2T1
Tel: 647-520-4339
info@thessea.org; toronto@thessea.org
www.thessea.org
To stimulate interest in Egyptology; To assist with research & training in the field; To sponsor & promote archaeological expeditions to Egypt
Lyn Green, National President
Zoe McQuinn, Chapter President
Mark Trumpour, Chapter Secretary

Stem Cell Network (SCN) / Réseau de cellules souches
#501 Smyth Rd., Room CCW-6189, Ottawa ON K1H 8L6
Tel: 613-739-6675
info@stemcellnetwork.ca
www.stemcellnetwork.ca
To investigate the immense therapeutic potential of stem cells for the treatment of diseases currently incurable by conventional approaches
Drew Lyall, Executive Director
Lisa Willemse, Director of Communications

Traffic Injury Research Foundation (TIRF) / Fondation de recherches sur les blessures de la route
#200, 171 Nepean St., Ottawa ON K2P 0B4
Tel: 613-238-5235; *Fax:* 613-238-5292
Toll-Free: 877-238-5235
tirf@tirf.ca
www.tirf.ca
To reduce traffic related deaths & injuries, through the design, promotion, & implementation of prevention programs & policies based on sound research
Robyn D. Robertson, President & CEO
Sara Oglestone, Manager, Marketing & Communications

Restaurants & Food Services

Association des fournisseurs d'hôtels et restaurants inc. (AFHR) / Hotel & Restaurant Suppliers Association Inc. (HRSA)
#230, 9300, boul Henri-Bourassa ouest, Saint-Laurent QC H4S 1L5
Tel: 514-334-3404; *Fax:* 514-334-1279
info@afhr.com
www.afhr.com
Informer et parfaire les connaissances des professionnels de l'industrie; offrir une vitrine aux fournisseurs par le biais du site web de l'association; centre d'information pour les hôtels, restaurants et institutions à la recherche de fournisseurs; programme d'escomptes pour les membres sur divers services; l'AFHR organise le Salon Rendez-vous HRI
Victor Francoeur, President & CEO
Isabelle Julien, Operation Manager
Hughes Moisan, Vice-President, Business Development

Association des restaurateurs du Québec (ARQ) / Québec Restaurant Association
6880, Louis-H.-La Fontaine, Montréal QC H1M 2T2
Tél: 514-527-9801; *Téléc:* 514-527-3066
Ligne sans frais: 800-463-4237
arqc@arqc.qc.ca
www.restaurateurs.ca
Fournir à l'ensemble des restaurateurs du Québec des services complets d'information, de formation, d'escomptes, d'assurances et de représentation gouvernementale
Bernard Fortin, Président directeur général

British Columbia Restaurant & Foodservices Association (BCRFA)
439 Helmcken St., Vancouver BC V6B 2E6
Tel: 604-669-2239; *Fax:* 604-669-6175
Toll-Free: 800-663-4482
info@bcrfa.com
www.bcrfa.com
To be the voice of the hospitality industry in British Columbia; the advocat of the restaurant industry.
Ian Tostenson, President & CEO

Canadian Culinary Federation (CCFCC) / Fédération Culinaire Canadienne
c/o Roy Butterworth, National Administrator, 30 Hamilton Ct., Riverview NB E1B 3C3
admin@ccfcc.ca; membership@ccfcc.ca; marketing@ccfcc.ca
www.ccfcc.ca
Social Media: www.facebook.com/CCFCC; twitter.com/@CdnChefs
To promote a Canadian food culture both nationally & internationally; To encourage professional excellence among chefs & cooks throughout Canada
Judson Simpson, Chair
Donald A. Gyurkovits, President
Roy Butterworth, National Administrator
Blake Chapman, Secretary
Robert Harrison, Treasurer
Tim Appleton, Chair, Junior Membership
Don (Busch) Dubay, Chair, Finance

Canadian Restaurant & Foodservices Association (CRFA) / Association canadienne des restaurateurs et des services alimentaires
316 Bloor St. West, Toronto ON M5S 1W5
Tel: 416-923-8416; *Fax:* 416-923-1450
Toll-Free: 800-387-5649
info@crfa.ca
www.crfa.ca
Social Media: www.facebook.com/group.php?gid=206094859412053; twitter.com/CDNRestaurants
To create a favourable business environment & deliver tangible value to members in all sectors of Canada's foodservice industry
Garth Whyte, President & Chief Executive Officer
Joyce Reynolds, Executive Vice-President, Government Affairs
Jill Holroyd, Senior Vice-President, Marketing & Communications
Stephanie Jones, Vice-President, Membership
Tamara Kapel, Vice-President, Finance
Justin Taylor, Vice-President, Labour & Supply
Natalie Angeja, Coordinator, Member Services
Prasanthi Vasanthakumar, Specialist, Communications

Manitoba Restaurant & Food Services Association (MRFA)
103-D Scurfield Blvd., Winnipeg MB R3Y 1M6
Tel: 204-783-9955; *Fax:* 204-783-9909
Toll-Free: 877-296-2909
info@mrfa.mb.ca
www.mrfa.mb.ca

The MRFA has four primary objectives; to lobby government and other regulatory bodies on issues affecting you and your business; to present educational seminars and social programs; to provide member services such as insurance programs and credit card savings; to represent the restaurant and foodservice industry effectively through a large membership.
Scott Jocelyn, Executive Director

Société des chefs, cuisiniers et pâtissiers du Québec (SCCPQ)
3577, rue Sainte-Catherine est, Montréal QC H1W 2E6
Tél: 514-528-1083; *Téléc:* 514-528-1037
www.sccpq.ca
Mise en valeur et émulation de la profession; reconnaissance professionnelle au niveau national
René Derrien, Président de chapitre
Patrick Gerome, Secrétaire

Retail Trade

Association des détaillants en alimentation du Québec (ADA) / Québec Food Retailers' Association
Place du parc, #1100, 300 rue Léo-Pariseau, Montréal QC H2X 4C1
Tél: 514-982-0104; *Téléc:* 514-849-3021
info@adaq.qc.ca
www.adaq.qc.ca
Représenter et défendre les intérêts professionnels, socio-politiques et économiques de tous les détaillants du Québec, et ce, quels que soient leur bannière et le type de surface qu'ils opèrent
Florent Gravel, Président-directeur général
Ginette Desjardins, Adjointe au Président-directeur général
Pierre-Alexandre Blouin, Vice-président, Affaires publiques
Manon Dextras, Directrice, Finances et administration

Association nationale des distributeurs aux petites surfaces alimentaires (ANDPSA) / National Convenience Stores Distributors Association (NACDA)
#410, 1695, boul Laval, Laval QC H7S 2M2
Tel: 450-967-3858; *Fax:* 450-967-8839
Toll-Free: 800-686-2823
nacda@nacda.ca
www.nacda.ca
Promouvoir le bien-être et les intérêts de nos membres distributeurs-grossistes ainsi que de l'industrie
Raymond Bouchard, Président du conseil d'administration

Canadian Association of Chain Drug Stores (CACDS) / Association canadienne des chaînes de pharmacies (ACCP)
#301, 45 Sheppard Ave. East, Toronto ON M2N 5W9
Tel: 416-226-9100; *Fax:* 416-226-9185
cacds@cacds.com
www.cacds.com
Social Media:
www.linkedin.com/company/canadian-association-of-chain-drug-stores
CACDS strives to ensure a strong chain drug store sector access to high quality products & health care services to Canadians.
Nadine Saby, President/CEO
Steve Wilton, Vice-President
Reza Farmand, Treasurer
Nancy Bagworth, Director, Communications

Canadian Gift & Tableware Association (CGTA) / Association canadienne de cadeaux et d'accessoires de table
42 Voyager Ct. South, Toronto ON M9W 5M7
Tel: 416-679-0170; *Fax:* 416-679-0175
Toll-Free: 800-611-6100
info@cgta.org
www.cgta.org
To create & manage sales opportunities for the gift industry

Canadian Sporting Goods Association (CSGA) / Association canadienne d'articles de sport (ACAS)
#420, 300, rue du Saint-Sacrement, Montréal QC H2Y 1X4
csga@csga.ca
www.csga.ca
To conduct quality trade shows; To provide forum responsive to the professional needs of its members; To initiate programs designed to stimulate sports activity participation as considered feasible
Andrew Prendergast, Chair
Michael Tadgell, Executive Director

Conseil québécois du commerce de détail (CQCD) / Retail Council of Québec
#910, 630, rue Sherbrooke ouest, Montréal QC H3A 1E4
Tél: 514-842-6681; *Téléc:* 514-842-7627
Ligne sans frais: 800-364-6766
cqcd@cqcd.org
www.cqcd.org
Promouvoir, représenter et valoriser le secteur du commerce de détail au Québec et les détaillants qui en font partie afin d'assurer le sain développement et la prospérité du secteur
Gaston Lafleur, Président-directeur général

Direct Sellers Association of Canada (DSA) / Association de ventes directes du Canada
#250, 180 Attwell Dr., Toronto ON M9W 6A9
Tel: 416-679-8555; *Fax:* 416-679-1568
info@dsa.ca
www.dsa.ca
The Association represents companies that manufacture & distribute goods & services through independent sales contractors, away from a fixed retail location; encourages strong consumer protection, through Codes of Ethics & Business Practices; engages in discussion with government & industry; acts as the voice of the direct selling industry to government in pursuit of better business opportunities for Canadian entrepreneurs.
Greg Neath, Chair
Ross Creber, President & Secretary

Gift Packaging & Greeting Card Association of Canada (GPGCA) / Association canadienne du papier cadeau et de la carte de voeux
1407 Military Trail, Toronto ON M1C 1A7
Tel: 416-281-8147; *Fax:* 416-286-4868
greetingcardoffice@rogers.com
To foster the well-being of manufacturers & distributors of gift packaging products, greeting cards & related paper products in Canada.
Jim Driscoll, Chairman
Clancy Delbarre, Executive Director
Jerry Seligman, Vice-Chairman

Pool & Hot Tub Council of Canada / Conseil canadien des piscines et spas
5 MacDougall Dr., Brampton ON L6S 3P3
Tel: 905-458-7242; *Fax:* 905-458-7037
Toll-Free: 800-879-7066
office@poolcouncil.ca
www.poolcouncil.ca
To promote the image & sales of the pool, spa & hot tub industry throughout Canada; to promote & enhance consumer awareness of the industry's products; to encourage & promote increased health & safety standards within the industry; to support efforts to improve pool, hot tub & spa equipment facilities, services & products; &, generally, to promote & advance the common interests of members
Robert Wood, National Executive Director

Retail Council of Canada (RCC) / Conseil canadien du commerce de détail
#800, 1255 Bay St., Toronto ON M5R 2A9
Tel: 416-922-6678; *Fax:* 416-922-8011
Toll-Free: 888-373-8245
mboydbonsu@retailcouncil.org
www.retailcouncil.org
Social Media: www.facebook.com/retailcouncil; twitter.com/RetailCouncil
To be the best at delivering the services our retail members value most; To serve, promote & represent the diverse needs of Canada's retailing industry to the highest standards of quality
David Russell, President/CEO
Bill Yetman, COO
Ruth Thorkelson, Senior Vice-President, Public Affairs
Terrance Oakey, Vice-President, Federal Government Relations

Shelfspace, the Association for Retail Entrepreneurs
#208 - 1730 - West 2nd Ave., Vancouver BC V6J 1H6
Tel: 604-736-0368; *Fax:* 604-736-3154
Toll-Free: 800-663-5135
inquiry@shelfspace.ca
www.shelfspace.ca
Social Media:
www.facebook.com/pages/Shelfspace/149758123522
To enhance the professionalism & profitability of our members
Mark Startup, President & CEO

Surrey Board of Trade (SBOT)
#101, 14439 - 104 Ave., Surrey BC V3R 1M1
Tel: 604-581-7130; *Fax:* 604-588-7549
Toll-Free: 866-848-7130
info@businessinsurrey.com
www.businessinsurrey.com
Social Media:
www.facebook.com/pages/Surrey-Board-of-Trade/14153105258 1905; twitter.com/SBofT
Provides advocacy, resources, experience & networking to members & fosters best business practices to ensure growth & prosperity of members
Anita Huberman, CEO
Anita Huberman, Chief Executive Officer
Nigel Watkinson, President
Mary Jane Stanberg, Vice-President

Retirees

McMaster University Retirees Association (MURA)
c/o McMaster University, Gilmour Hall, #B108, 1280 Main St. W, Hamilton ON L8S 4L8
Tel: 905-525-9140
mura@mcmaster.ca
mura.mcmaster.ca
The McMaster University Retirees Association seeks to contribute in as many ways as possible to the welfare, prestige, and excellence of the University and to encourage and promote a spirit of fraternity and unity among the members of the Association, and to provide means for continuing the associations which retirees enjoyed as employees of the University.

Safety & Accident Prevention

Alberta Safety Council
4831 - 93 Ave. NW, Edmonton AB T6B 3A2
Tel: 780-462-7300; *Fax:* 780-462-7318
Toll-Free: 800-301-6407
info@safetycouncil.ab.ca
www.safetycouncil.ab.ca
Social Media:
www.facebook.com/group.php?gid=189043441145255
To create awareness & provide educational & training programs to citizens of Alberta on how to maintain a safe environment at home, in traffic, at work & at play
Laurie Billings, Executive Director

Association de la santé et de la sécurité des pâtes et papiers et des industries de la forêt du Québec (ASSIFQ-ASSPPQ)
Place Iberville II, #210, 1175, av Lavigerie, Sainte-Foy QC G1V 4P1
Tél: 418-657-2267; *Téléc:* 418-651-4622
Ligne sans frais: 888-632-9326
info@santesecurite.org
www.santesecurite.org
A pour mission de soutenir et d'accompagner les entreprises dans l'amélioration continue de la santé et de la sécurité du travail
Jacques Laroche, Président-directeur général
Suzanne Lavoie, Adjointe administrative

Association des chefs en sécurité incendie du Québec (ACSIQ) / Québec Association of Fire Chiefs
5, rue Dupré, Beloeil QC J3G 3J7
Tél: 450-464-6413; *Téléc:* 450-467-6297
Ligne sans frais: 888-464-6413
www.acsiq.qc.ca
Regroupe les personnes détanant un poste de commande dans le domaine de la prévention et de la lutte contre les incendies
Jean-Claude Bolduc, Président

Association paritaire pour la santé et la sécurité du travail - Administration provinciale
#10, 1220, boul Lebourgneuf, Québec QC G2K 2G4
Tél: 418-624-4801; *Téléc:* 418-624-4858
apssap@apssap.qc.ca
www.apssap.qc.ca
L'Association a pour mission de supporter la prise en charge paritaire de la prévention en matière de santé, de sécurité et d'intégrité physique des personnes du secteur de l'Administration provinciale.
Colette Trudel, Directrice générale

Association paritaire pour la santé et la sécurité du travail - Affaires municipales (APSAM)
#710, 715, carré Victoria, Montréal QC H2Y 2H7
Tél: 514-849-8373; *Téléc:* 514-849-8873
Ligne sans frais: 800-465-1754
info@apsam.com
www.apsam.com
Développer et promouvoir les moyens nécessaires pour protéger la santé et la sécurité des personnes à l'emploi des municipalités et des organismes qui y sont reliés, dans l'ensemble du Québec; fournir aux employeurs et travailleurs des municipalités du Québec des services de formation, d'information, de recherche et de conseil
Alain Langlois, Directeur général

Association paritaire pour la santé et la sécurité du travail - Affaires sociales
#950, 5100, rue Sherbrooke est, Montréal QC H1V 3R9
Tél: 514-253-6871; *Téléc:* 514-253-1443
Ligne sans frais: 800-361-4528
info@asstsas.qc.ca
www.asstsas.qc.ca
Une association sectorielle paritaire vouée exclusivement à la prévention en santé et en sécurité du travail dans le secteur de la santé et des services sociaux
Diane Parent, Directrice générale

Association paritaire pour la santé et la sécurité du travail - Habillement
#301, 2271, boul Fernand-Lafontaine, Longueuil QC J4G 2R7
Tél: 450-442-7763; *Téléc:* 450-442-2332
info@aspme.org
www.asp-habillement.org/
To prevent work-related injuries in the apparel sector
Jacques Barbeau, Coprésident
Denis Dufour, Coprésident

Association paritaire pour la santé et la sécurité du travail - Imprimerie et activités connexes
#450, 7450, boul Galeries d'Anjou, Anjou QC H1M 3M3
Tél: 514-355-8282; *Téléc:* 514-355-6818
info@aspimprimerie.qc.ca
www.aspimprimerie.qc.ca
Fournir aux employeurs et aux travailleurs du secteur imprimerie et activités connexes des services d'information, de formation, de conseil et de recherche pour favoriser la prise en charge de la prévention dans les entreprises
Marie Ménard, Directrice générale

Association paritaire pour la santé et la sécurité du travail - Mines et services miniers (APSM)
#570, 979, av de Bourgogne, Sainte-Foy QC G1W 2L4
Tél: 418-653-1933; *Téléc:* 418-653-7726
info@apsam.com
www.apsam.com
Pierre Lapointe, Directeur général

Association paritaire pour la santé et la sécurité du travail - Produits en métal et électriques
#301, 2271, boul Fernand-Lafontaine, Longueuil QC J4G 2R7
Tél: 450-442-7763; *Téléc:* 450-442-2332
jarsenault@aspme.org
www.aspme.org
Jocelyne Arsenault, Conseillère en gestion
Éric Bélanger, Conseiller technique

Association paritaire pour la santé et la sécurité du travail - Services automobiles
#150, 8, rue de la Place-Du-Commerce, Brossard QC J4W 3H2
Tél: 450-672-9330; *Téléc:* 450-672-4835
Ligne sans frais: 800-363-2344
info@autoprevention.qc.ca
www.autoprevention.qc.ca
Depuis 1983, Auto Prévention aide les travailleurs et les employeurs du secteur des services automobiles à prendre en charge la santé et la sécurité au travail, afin d'éliminer les risques d'accidents et de maladies professionnelles.
Jean-Guy Trottier, Directeur général

Association québécoise des pompiers volontaires et permanents
#460, 9401, des Saints Côte, Mirabel QC J7N 2X4
Tél: 514-990-1338
Média social: www.facebook.com/group.php?gid=27982231370
Aider à promouvoir la prévention des incendies; aider, soutenir et susciter des efforts en vue de réduire les pertes de vie; favoriser le perfectionnement en vue de combattre plus efficacement les incendies; promouvoir l'éducation populaire en général sur la protection et la prévention des incendies; faire des recommandations auprès des corps politiques et gouvernementaux
Eric Lacasse, Président

Association sectorielle - Fabrication d'équipement de transport et de machines (ASFETM) / Sectorial Association - Transportation Equipment & Machinery Manufacturing (SATEMM)
#202, 3565, rue Jarry est, Montréal QC H1Z 4K6
Tél: 514-729-6961; *Téléc:* 514-729-8628
Ligne sans frais: 888-527-3386
info@asfetm.com
www.asfetm.com
Aider les employeurs et les travailleurs à prévenir les accidents du travail et les maladies professionnelles, en faisant pour eux de la recherche, en leur dispensant de l'information, de la formation et de l'assistance technique qui visent essentiellement à rendre impossibles les accidents et les maladies au travail, et en privilégiant, à cette fin, l'élimination de cette possibilité à sa source même selon un processus de participation paritaire
Arnold Dugas, Directeur général
Suzanne Ready, Chargée de l'information

Association Sectorielle Transport Entreposage (ASTE)
#301, 6455, boul Jean-Talon est, Montréal QC H1S 3E8
Tél: 514-955-0454; *Téléc:* 514-955-0449
Ligne sans frais: 800-361-8906
info@aste.qc.ca
www.aste.qc.ca
L'Association Sectorielle Transport Entreposage est une organisme en prèvention, autonome et paritaire, sans but lucratif, fondé et administré par des reprétants des employeurs et des syndicats.
Alain Lajoie, Directeur général

Board of Canadian Registered Safety Professionals (BCRSP) / Conseil canadien des professionnels en securité agréés
6519B Mississauga Rd., Mississauga ON L5N 1A6
Tel: 905-567-7198; *Fax:* 905-567-7191
Toll-Free: 888-279-2777
info@bcrsp.ca
www.bcrsp.ca
To protect & promote occupational health & safety, environmental safety, & public safety, through the registration of qualified health & safety professionals committed to a code of ethics
Ron Durdle, Chair
Peter Fletcher, Executive Director

Canada Safety Council (CSC) / Conseil canadien de la sécurité (CCS)
1020 Thomas Spratt Pl., Ottawa ON K1G 5L5
Tel: 613-739-1535; *Fax:* 613-739-1566
csc@safety-council.org
canadasafetycouncil.org
Social Media: www.facebook.com/canada.safety; twitter.com/CanadaSafetyCSC
To exercise leadership in a national effort to prevent death, injury & economic loss caused by accidents in the traffic, occupational & public environments; focus is on safety education & support of safety legislation
Jack Smith, President
Raynard Marchand, General Manager, Programs

Canadian Association of Fire Chiefs (CAFC) / Association canadienne des chefs de pompiers (ACCP)
#702, 280 Albert St., Ottawa ON K1P 5G8
Tel: 613-270-9138; *Toll-Free:* 800-775-5189
www.cafc.ca
Social Media: twitter.com/cafc2; ca.linkedin.com/pub/canadian-association-of-fire-chiefs/2a/a05/82b
To lead & represent the Canadian Fire Service on public safety issues with the vision of being nationally recognized as the fire service voice of authority
Robert Simonds, President
Pierre Voisine, Secretary
Lee Grant, Treasurer

Canadian Association of Road Safety Professionals (CARSP) / Association canadienne des professionnels de la sécurité routière (ACPSER)
c/o Joseph Chan, Transportation Centre, University of Saskatchewan, 57 Campus Dr., Saskatoon SK S7N 5A9
Tel: 306-966-7010; *Fax:* 306-966-7014
info@casp.ca
www.carsp.ca
The association preserves & shares professional experience regarding road safety. It promotes research & professional development & facilitates communication & cooperation among road safety groups & agencies.
Margaret Parkhill, Treasurer
Lyne Vezina, President
Mavis Johnson, Vice-President

Canadian Automatic Sprinkler Association (CASA)
#302, 335 Renfrew Dr., Markham ON L3R 9S9
Tel: 905-477-2270; *Fax:* 905-477-3611
info@casa-firesprinkler.org
www.casa-firesprinkler.org
To advance the fire sprinkler art as applied to the conservation of life & property from fire.
John Galt, President

Canadian Centre for Occupational Health & Safety (CCOHS) / Centre canadien d'hygiène et de sécurité au travail (CCHST)
135 Hunter St. East, Hamilton ON L8N 1M5
Tel: 905-572-2981; *Fax:* 905-572-2206
Toll-Free: 800-668-4284
clientservices@ccohs.ca
www.ccohs.ca
Social Media: www.facebook.com/CCOHS; twitter.com/ccohs
Promotes the total well-being—physical, psychological & mental health—of working Canadians by providing information, training, education, management systems & solutions that support health, safety, & wellness programs
S. Len Hong, President/CEO
Patabendi K. Abeytunga, Vice-President

Canadian Fire Safety Association (CFSA)
#310, 2175 Sheppard Ave. East, Toronto ON M2J 1W8
Tel: 416-492-9417; *Fax:* 416-491-1670
cfsa@taylorenterprises.com
www.canadianfiresafety.com
To promote fire safety through seminars, safety training courses, scholarships & regular meetings.
Leo Grellette, President

Canadian Radiation Protection Association (CRPA) / Association canadienne de radioprotection (ACRP)
PO Box 83, Carleton Place ON K7C 3P3
Tel: 613-253-3779; *Fax:* 888-551-0712
secretariat2007@crpa-acrp.ca
www.crpa-acrp.ca
To develop scientific knowledge for protection from the harmful effects of radiation; To encourage research; To assist in the development of professional standards in the discipline
Gary Wilson, President
Wayne Tiefenbach, Treasurer

Canadian Security Association (CANASA) / L'Association canadienne de la sécurité
National Office, #201, 50 Acadia Ave., Markham ON L3R 0B3
Tel: 905-513-0622; *Fax:* 905-513-0624
Toll-Free: 800-538-9919
staff@canasa.org
www.canasa.org
Social Media: twitter.com/CANASA_News
To act as the national voice of the security industry; To promote & protect the interests of members; To increase public awareness of the security industry's effectiveness in reducing risk; To develop & promote programs consistent with the needs of members; To develop & promote programs which will lead to the reduction of false dispatches & improved response; To influence regulations affecting the members
JF Champagne, Executive Director
Steve Basnett, Director, Trade Shows & Events
Mona Emond, Director, Marketing & Communications
Lynne Hewitson, Manager, Membership Services
Dave Kushner, Manager, Finance

Canadian Society of Air Safety Investigators (CSASI)
139 West 13th Ave., Vancouver BC V5Y 1V8
avsafe@rogers.com
To ensure air safety through investigation
Barbara M. Dunn, President
Barry Wiszniowski, Vice-President
Elaine Parker, Secretary-Treasurer

Canadian Society of Safety Engineering, Inc. (CSSE) / Société canadienne de la santé et de la sécurité, inc.
39 River St., Toronto ON M5A 3P1
Tel: 416-646-1600; *Fax:* 416-646-9460
www.csse.org
Social Media: www.facebook.com/39373429711; twitter.com/csse; www.linkedin.com/groups?gid=1558517
To be the voice of safety in Canada
Wayne Glover, Executive Director
Peter Sturm, President

Centre patronal de santé et sécurité du travail du Québec (CPSSTQ) / Employers Center for Occupational Health & Safety of Quebec
e, #1000, 500, rue Sherbrooke ouest, Montréal QC H3A 3C6
Tél: 514-842-8401; *Téléc:* 514-842-9375
www.centrepatronalsst.qc.ca
Fournir de l'information et de la formation en SST aux entreprises regroupées par les associations patronales membres du Centre patronal
Denise Turenne, Direction générale

Council of Canadian Fire Marshals & Fire Commissioners (CCFMFC) / Conseil canadien des directeurs provinciaux et des commissaires des incendies
c/o 491 McLeod Hill Rd., Fredericton NB E3A 6H6
Tel: 506-453-1208; *Fax:* 506-457-0793
CCFMFC@rogers.com
www.ccfmfc.ca
To contribute to a reduction in the number of fire deaths
Ben Laroche, President
Christopher Jones, Vice-President
Philippa Gourley, Secretary-Treasurer

Council of Private Investigators - Ontario (CPIO)
#200, 148 York St., London ON N6A 1A9
Tel: 416-955-9450
www.cpi-ontario.com
To represent the interests of private investigators in Ontario
Bill Joynt, President
Charlie Robb, Administration Manager

Federal Association of Security Officials (FASO) / Association fédérale des représentants de la sécurité
PO Box 2384, Stn. D, Ottawa ON K1P 5W5
Tel: 613-990-2615; *Fax:* 613-990-8297
Toll-Free: 888-330-3276
info@faso-afrs.ca
www.faso-afrs.ca
To enhance the performance & career development of federal security officers through enhancing the security function in government & improving the professionalism of security officers.
Claude J.G. Levesque, President

Fire Prevention Canada (FPC)
PO Box 47037, Ottawa ON K1B 5P9
Tel: 613-749-3844; *Fax:* 613-749-0109
Toll-Free: 877-906-6651
info@fiprecan.ca
www.fiprecan.ca
Working with the public & private sectors to achieve fire safety through education.
E. David Hodgins, President

Industrial Accident Victims Group of Ontario (IAVGO)
#203, 489 College St., Toronto ON M6G 1A5
Tel: 416-924-6477; *Toll-Free:* 877-230-6311
www.iavgo.org
Social Media: www.facebook.com/167369409975545
Our community legal clinic provides free services to injured workers in Ontario including legal advice, legal representation, public legal education, advocacy training and community development.
Mary DiNucci, Coordinator

Institut de recherche Robert-Sauvé en santé et en sécurité du travail (IRSST) / Robert Sauvé Occupational Health & Safety Research Institute
505, boul de Maisonneuve ouest, 15e étage, Montréal QC H3A 3C2
Tél: 514-288-1551; *Téléc:* 514-288-7636
communications@irsst.qc.ca
www.irsst.qc.ca
Média social: www.facebook.com//207703664186; twitter.com/IRSST
Contribuer par la recherche et le développement à l'amélioration de la santé et de la sécurité des travailleurs et plus spécifiquement, à l'élimination à la source des dangers pour leur santé, leur sécurité et leur intégrité physique ainsi qu'à la réadaptation des travailleurs victimes d'accidents ou de maladies professionnelles; fournir au Réseau public québécois de la prévention en santé et en sécurité du travail - composé de CSST, des Centres locaux de services communautaires, des Régies de la santé et des services sociaux et des associations sectorielles paritaires - les services et l'expertise nécessaires à leur action; diffuser les connaissances issues de ces recherches et de ces expertises auprès des milieux de travail et en favoriser le transfert; accorder des bourses d'études supérieures en santé et en sécurité du travail; agir comme laboratoire de référence au Québec, dans le domaine de l'hygiene industrielle.
Marie Larue, Présidente/Directrice générale

Newfoundland & Labrador Safety Council
Regatta Plaza II, #84, 86 Elizabeth Ave., 2nd Fl., St. John's NL A1A 1W7
Tel: 709-754-0210; *Fax:* 709-754-0010
info@safetycouncil.net
The Newfoundland and Labrador Safety Council is dedicated to the prevention of injuries and fatalities; represents all the major sectors of the province's industry, business, government departments, volunteer organizations and many individuals who have a personal interest in safety, both on and off the job.

Ontario Association of Fire Chiefs (OAFC)
#14, 530 Westney Rd. South, Ajax ON L1S 6M3
Tel: 905-426-9865; *Fax:* 905-426-3032
Toll-Free: 800-774-6651
www.oafc.on.ca
To ensure that Ontario has a well trained & well equipped fire service
Tim Beckett, President
Frank Lamie, Treasurer
Barry Malmsten, Executive Director

Ontario Industrial Fire Protection Association (OIFPA)
193 James St. South, Hamilton ON L8P 3A8
Tel: 905-527-0700; *Fax:* 905-527-6254
oifpa@interlynx.net
www.oifpa.org
To unite individuals with a concern for fire protection within Ontario's industrial community
Roy Graham, President
Jim Belrose, Vice-President
Todd Wilson, 2nd Vice-President
George Fawcett, Treasurer

Ontario Safety League (OSL) / Ligue de sécurité de l'Ontario
#212, 2595 Skymark Ave., Mississauga ON L4W 4L5
Tel: 905-625-0556; *Fax:* 905-625-0677
www.ontariosafetyleague.com
Safety through education with an emphasis on traffic & child safety
Brian J. Patterson, President & General Manager

Opération Nez rouge / Operation Red Nose
Maison Couillard, Université Laval, 2539, rue Marie-Fitzbach, Québec QC G1V 0A6
Tél: 418-653-1492; *Téléc:* 418-653-3315
Ligne sans frais: 800-463-7222
info@operationnezrouge.com
www.operationnezrouge.com
Mèdia social: www.facebook.com/OperationNezrouge; twitter.com/ORNose; www.youtube.com/user/OperationNezrouge
Service de chauffeur privé gratuit & bénévole offert pendant la période des Fêtes à tout automobiliste qui a consommé de l'alcool, our qui ne se sent pas en état de conduire son véhicule.
Stéphane Thériault, Directeur général

Préventex - Association paritaire du textile
1936, rue Rossignol, Brossard QC J4X 2C6
Tél: 450-671-6925; *Téléc:* 450-671-9267
info@preventex.qc.ca
www.preventex.qc.ca
Amener les employeurs et les travailleurs du secteur à prendre charge activement de la prévention des accidents du travail et des maladies professionnelles
Lise Laplante, Directrice générale

Radiation Safety Institute of Canada / Institut de radioprotection du Canada
Head Office & National Education Centre, #300, 165 Avenue Rd., Toronto ON M5R 3S4
Tel: 416-650-9090; *Fax:* 416-650-9920
Toll-Free: 800-263-5803
info@radiationsafety.ca
www.radiationsafety.ca
Social Media: www.facebook.com/group.php?gid=143472245714096
To be an independent source for knowledge about radiation safety in the environment, the community, & the workplace
Fergal Nolan, President & Chief Executive Officer
R. Moridi, Vice-President, Chief Scientist
Bruce Sylvester, Vice-President, Finance & Administration
Mike Haynes, Scientific Director
Natalia Mozayani, Program Manager
Tara Hargreaves, Scientist & Coordinator, Training

Safe Communities Foundation (SCF)
#201, 64 Charles St. East, Toronto ON M4Y 1T1
Tel: 416-964-0008; *Fax:* 416-964-0089
info@safecommunities.ca
www.safecommunities.ca
To help people come together in the community to create a sense of awareness, understanding, support & leadership to implement effective local programs to eliminate injuries & suffering; to improve the health & safety of workers & people of all ages throughout the community
Paul Kells, Founder & President
Jocelyne Achat, Vice-Chair

Safety Services Manitoba (SSM)
#3, 1680 Notre Dame Ave., Winnipeg MB R3H 1H6
Tel: 204-949-1085; *Fax:* 204-949-2897
Toll-Free: 800-661-3321
registrar@safetyservicesmanitoba.ca
www.safetyservicesmanitoba.ca
To prevent accidental injury or occupational illness in Manitoba by providing effective safety & health programs.
Mike Waite, Executive Director

Safety Services New Brunswick (SSNB) / Services de Sécurité Nouveau-Brunswick
#204, 440 Wilsey Rd., Fredericton NB E3B 7G5
Tel: 506-458-8034; *Fax:* 506-444-0177
Toll-Free: 877-762-7233
info@safetyservicesnb.ca
www.safetyservicesnb.ca
To promote traffic, occupational & public safety issues & practices through safety training courses & programs, educational material, public information, safety campaigns & conferences.
Bill Walker, President & CEO
Jim Arsenault, Director of OSH & Traffic Training

Safety Services Nova Scotia (SSNS)
Vantage Point 3, #3F, 110 Chain Lake Dr., Halifax NS B3S 1A9
Tel: 902-454-9621; *Fax:* 902-454-6027
www.safetyservicesns.com
The Safety Council develops & provides quality safety & health services, education & training programs to improve the quality of life of Nova Scotians.
Jackie Norman, Executive Director

Saskatchewan Safety Council
445 Hoffer Dr., Regina SK S4N 6E2
Tel: 306-757-3197; *Fax:* 306-569-1907
ssc@sasksafety.org
sasksafety.org
Harley P. Toupin, CEO
Dianne Wolbaum, Director, Operations

Workplace Safety & Prevention Services (WSPS)
Centre for Health & Safety Innovation, #300, 5110 Creekbank Rd., Mississauga ON L4W 0A1
Tel: 905-614-1400; *Fax:* 905-614-1414
Toll-Free: 877-494-9777
customercare@wsps.ca
www.wsps.ca
WSPS is a not-for-profit organization with a mandate to meet the health & safety needs of businesses in the agricultural, manufacturing & service industries. It provides programs, products, & services for the prevention of injury & illness.
Elizabeth Mills, CEO

Scholarly

Canadian Association for the Study of Humanities and the Environment
c/o Institute for Governance Studies, Simon Fraser University, Burnaby BC V5A 1S6
Tel: 778-782-4293; *Fax:* 778-782-4786
igs@sfu.ca
www.sfu.ca/igs/cashe.html
Rebecca Raglon, Secretary

Scientific

Alberta Society of Professional Biologists (ASPB)
PO Box 21104, Edmonton AB T6R 2V4
Tel: 780-434-5765; *Fax:* 780-413-0076
pbiol@aspb.ab.ca
www.aspb.ab.ca
To promote excellence in the practice of biology; To provide a voice for professional biologists in Alberta
P. Ross Bradford, Executive Director
Robin Leech, Executive Director

Bette Beswick, Registrar
Carol Engstrom, President
Gary Ash, Treasurer
Monika Burak, Coordinator, Finance
Shauna Prokopchuk, Coordinator, Membership & Communications
Joy Sager, Coordinator, Association & Events

Arctic Institute of North America (AINA)
University of Calgary, 2500 University Dr. NW, Calgary AB T2N 1N4
Tel: 403-220-7515; *Fax:* 403-282-4609
arctic@ucalgary.ca
www.arctic.ucalgary.ca
To encourage & support scientific research pertaining to the polar regions
Michel Scott, Board Chair
Benoît Beauchamp, Executive Director

Association des microbiologistes du Québec (AMQ)
5094A, av. Charlemagne, Montréal QC H1X 3P3
Tél: 514-728-1087; *Téléc:* 514-374-3988
amq@microbiologistes.ca
www.microbiologistes.ca
L'association regroupe les microbiologistes du Québec oeuvrant principalemtn en environnement, en alimentaire et en pharmaceutique. Elle a pour but d'étudier, de protéger et de développer les intérêts économiques, sociaux et professionnels des microbiologistes et de promouvoir l'essor de la microbiologie en général; est impliquée au niveau de l'accréditation des laboratoires d'analyses microbiologiques et elle est représentée au sein de plusieurs comités ou associations.
Stéphane Bourget, Président

Association of Canadian Ergonomists (ACE) / L'Association canadienne d'ergonomie
#1003, 105-150 Crowfoot Cres. NW, Calgary AB T3G 3T2
Tel: 403-219-4001; *Fax:* 403-451-1503
Toll-Free: 888-432-2223
info@ace-ergocanada.ca
www.ace-ergocanada.ca
To advance human factors/ergonomics through encouraging a high quality of practice, education & research; To facilitate communication among members; To represent the discipline; To increase awareness of human factors/ergonomics; To identify resources
Margo Fraser, Executive Director
Brenda Mallat, President

Association of Professional Biology (APB)
#300, 1095 McKenzie Ave., Victoria BC V8P 2L5
Tel: 250-483-4283; *Fax:* 250-483-3439
apbbc@apbbc.bc.ca
www.apbbc.bc.ca
To promote & assist professional practitioners of applied biology
Megan Hanacek, Managing Director & Registrar
Gerry Leering, President
Linda Stordeur, Registrar
Linda Michaluk, Executive Director

Atlantic Provinces Council on the Sciences (APCS) / Conseil des provinces atlantiques pour les sciences (CPAS)
1390 Le Marchant St., Halifax NS B3H 3P9
Tel: 902-494-3421; *Fax:* 902-494-6643
apics@dal.ca
www.apics.dal.ca
To advance science & technology through education & public awareness & the promotion of scientific literacy education & research throughout the region
Lois Whitehead, Executive Director

Biophysical Society of Canada (BSC) / La société de biophysique du Canada
a/s Dept. de chimie, Univ. Laval, 1045 Avenue de la médecine, Québec QC G1V 0A6
Tel: 418-656-3393; *Fax:* 418-656-7916
info@biophysicalsociety.ca
www.biophysicalsociety.ca
To promote biophysical research & education; to encourage cross-feeding of ideas between the physical & biological sciences; to foster & support scientific meetings, workshops & discussions in biophysics; to represent Canadian biophysics & biophysicists
Bruce C. Hill, President

BIOTECanada
#600, 1 Nicholas St., Ottawa ON K1n 7B7
Tel: 613-230-5585; *Fax:* 613-563-8850
info@biotech.ca
www.biotech.ca
To provide a unified voice fostering an environment that responds to the needs of the biotechnology industry & research community, both nationally & internationally
Peter Brenders, President & CEO

Canadian Association for Anatomy, Neurobiology, & Cell Biology (CAANCB) / Association canadienne d'anatomie, de neurobiologie et de biologie cellulaire (ACANBC)
Dr. W.H. Baldridge, Department of Anatomy, Faculty of Medicine, Dalhousie University, Halifax BC B3H 4H7
Tel: 613-533-2864; *Fax:* 613-533-2566
www.caancb.blogspot.com
To advance knowledge of anatomy; To represent anatomical sciences throughout Canada
William H. Baldridge, Secretary

Canadian Association of Palynologists (CAP) / Association canadienne des palynologues
c/o Dr. Mary A. Vetter, Luther College, University of Regina, Regina SK S4S 0A2
www.scirpus.ca/cap/cap.shtml
To advance all aspects of palynology in Canada
Matthew Peros, President
Mary A. Vetter, Secretary-Treasurer
Terri Lacourse, Editor, CAP Newsletter

Canadian Association of Physicists (CAP) / Association canadienne des physiciens et physiciennes (ACP)
MacDonald Bldg., #112, 150 Louis Pasteur Priv., Ottawa ON K1N 6N5
Tel: 613-562-5614; *Fax:* 613-562-5615
cap@uottawa.ca
www.cap.ca
CAP is a broadly-based national network of physicists working in Canadian educational, industrial, and research settings. They are a strong advocacy group for support of, and excellence in, physics research and education.
Francine M. Ford, Executive Director

Canadian Astronomical Society (CASCA) / Société canadienne d'astronomie
c/o R. Hanes, Dept. of Physics, Engineering, Physics & Astronomy, 64 Bader Lane, Stirling Hall, Queen's University, Kingston ON K7L 3N6
Tel: 613-533-6000; *Fax:* 613-533-6463
casca@astro.queensu.ca
www.casca.ca
Gilles Joncas, President
Nadine Manset, Secretary
Leslie Sage, Press Officer

Canadian Botanical Association (CBA) / Association botanique du Canada (ABC)
PO Box 160, Aberdeen SK S0K 0A0
Tel: 613-364-4074; *Fax:* 613-364-4027
lconsaul@mus-nature.ca
www.cba-abc.ca
Representing Canadian Botany & botanists nationally & internationally, the Association responds quickly & professionally on matters that are of concern to Canadian botanists.
Hugues Massicotte, President
Marian Munro, Vice-President
Laurie Consaul, Secretary
Jane Young, Treasurer

Canadian College of Physicists in Medicine (CCPM) / Collège canadien des physiciens en médecine
PO Box 72024, Kanata North RPO, Kanata ON K2K 2P4
Tel: 613-599-1948; *Fax:* 613-599-1949
www.ccpm.ca
To identify, through certification, individuals who have acquired & maintained a standard of knowledge & skill essential to the practice of medical physics, in order to serve the public
Nancy Barrett, Executive Director
Wayne A. Beckham, CCPM Registrar
Rasika Rajapakshe, Chair, Accreditation Committee on Physics of Mammography

Canadian Federation of Earth Sciences (CFES) / Fédération canadienne des sciences de la Terre
c/o Managing Director, 210 Main St., Wolfville NS B4P 1C4
Tel: 902-542-6125
cfes@magma.ca
www.geoscience.ca
To promote coordination & cooperation in activities in Canadian geoscientific education; to advise on science policy involving the earth sciences; to provide an informed opinion to the public of Canada on matters of public concern.
Bill Mercer, President

Canadian Hydrographic Association (CHA) / Association canadienne d'hydrographie
867 Lakeshore Rd., Burlington ON L7R 4A6
Tel: 905-336-4491
www.hydrography.ca
The scientific & technical group has the following objectives: to advance the development of hydrography & associated activities in Canada; to further the knowledge & professional development of members; to enhance & demonstrate the public need for hydrography; & to help the development of hydrographic sciences in developing countries; & to embrace the desciplines of marine cartography, hydrographic surveying, offshore exploration, marine geodesy, & tidal studies.
George McFarlane, National President
Terese Herron, National Secretary
Christine Delbridge, National Treasurer

Canadian Institute of Food Science & Technology (CIFST) / Institut canadien de science et technologie alimentaires (ICSTA)
#1311, 3-1750 The Queensway, Toronto ON M9C 5H5
Tel: 905-271-8338; *Fax:* 905-271-8344
cifst@cifst.ca
www.cifst.ca
To advance food science & technology; To act as a voice for scientific issues related to the Canadian food industry
Carol Ann Burrell, Executive Director
Charles Powell, President

Canadian Medical & Biological Engineering Society (CMBES) / Société canadienne de génie biomédical inc. (SCGB)
1485 Laperrière Ave., Ottawa ON K1Z 7S8
Tel: 613-728-1759
secretariat@cmbes.ca
www.cmbes.ca
To advance the theory & practice of medical device technology; To advance individuals who are engaged in interdisciplinary work involving medicine, engineering, & the life sciences; To represent the interests of biomedical & clinical engineering to government agencies
Murat Firat, President
Mike Capuano, Chair, Professional Affairs
Tim J. Zakutney, Chair, Awards
Martin Poulin, Treasurer
Melanie Chayra, Secretariat

Canadian Meteorological & Oceanographic Society (CMOS) / Société canadienne de météorologie et d'océanographie (SCMO)
PO Box 3211, Stn. D, Ottawa ON K1P 6H7
Tel: 613-990-0300; *Fax:* 613-990-1617
cmos@cmos.ca
www.cmos.ca
Social Media:
www.facebook.com/group.php?v=wall&gid=338431655320
To advance meteorology & oceanography in Canada
Ian D. Rutherford, Executive Director
Norman Mcfarlane, President
Bourque Sheila, Director, Education & Outreach
Qing Liao, Office Manager

Canadian Physiological Society (CPS) / Société canadienne de physiologie
c/o Dr. Melanie Woodin, Dept. of Cell & Systems Biology, U. of Toronto, 25 Harbord St., Toronto ON M5S 3G5
www.cpsscp.ca
To disseminate & discuss scientific information of interest to researchers in physiology & biological sciences
Steven Barnes, President
Melanie Woodin, Secretary

Canadian Phytopathological Society (CPS) / Société Canadienne de Phytopathologie (SCP)
c/o Crop Protection & Food Research Ctr Agriculture & Agri-Food Canada, 1391 Sandford St., London ON N5V 4T3
connk@agr.gc.ca
www.cps-scp.ca
To encourage & support research, education, & dissemination of knowledge on the nature, cause, & control of plant diseases; To promote communication among plant pathologists; To broaden educational opportunities for members
Kenneth Conn, Contact

Canadian Science & Technology Historical Association (CSTHA) / Association pour l'histoire de la science et de la technologie au Canada (AHSTC)
PO Box 8502, Stn. T, Ottawa ON K1G 3H9
cstha-ahstc.ca
To foster the study of Canada's scientific & technological heritage through research, publication, teaching & preservation of artifacts & records

Suzanne Beauvais, Secretary
Bertrum H. MacDonald, President

Canadian Society for Analytical Sciences & Spectroscopy
PO Box 46122, 2339 Ogilvie Rd., Ottawa ON K1J 9M7
Fax: 204-954-5984
www.csass.org
To organize programs of scientific & general interest for the educational benefit of members & the public; to organize annual scientific conferences & workshops on various aspects of pure & applied spectroscopy in the chemical, biological, geochemical & metallurgical sciences
Graeme Spiers, President
Ana Delgado, Treasurer

Canadian Society for Biochemistry & Molecular & Cellular Biology (CSBMCB) / Société canadienne de biochimie et de biologie moléculaire et cellulaire
c/o Rofail Conference & Management Services, 17 Dossetter Way, Ottawa ON K1G 4S3
Tel: 613-421-7229; *Fax:* 613-421-9811
contact@csbmcb.ca
www.csbmcb.ca
James Davie, President
Arthur Hilliker, Vice President

Canadian Society for the History & Philosophy of Science (CSHPS) / Société Canadienne d'Histoire et Philosophie des Sciences (SCHPS)
c/o Dr. Andrew Reynolds, Department of Philosphy & Religious Studies, Cape Breton University, Sydney NS B1P 6L2
andrew_reynolds@cbu.ca
www.cshps.ca; www.schps.ca
To explore all aspects of science, past & present
Kathleen Okruhlik, President
Andrew Reynolds, Secretary-Treasurer

The Canadian Society for the Weizmann Institute of Science (CSWIS)
4700 Bathurst St., 2nd Fl., Toronto ON M2R 1W8
Tel: 416-733-9220; *Fax:* 416-733-9430
Toll-Free: 800-387-3894
weizmann@ca.inter.net
www.weizmann.ac.il; www.weizmann.ca
To marshal Canadian support for the Weizmann Institute of Science in Rehovot, Israel; to help build & maintain scientific facilities; to acquire costly up-to-date research equipment & instrumentation; to set up endowments for research centres; to establish professional chairs & scholarships
Sheri Federman, Director, Programs & Operations
Michael E. Meyer, National Executive Vice-President

Canadian Society of Exploration Geophysicists (CSEG)
#600, 640 - 8th Ave. SW, Calgary AB T2P 1G7
Tel: 403-262-0015
cseg.office@shaw.ca
www.cseg.ca
To promote the science of geophysics
John Townsley, President
Larry Herd, Vice-President
Jim Racette, Managing Director
John Fernando, Director, Educational Services
Kelly Jamison, Director, Finance
Kristy Manchul, Director, Communications
Dave Nordin, Director, Member Service

Canadian Society of Forensic Science (CSFS)
PO Box 37040, 3332 McCarthy Rd., Ottawa ON K1V 0W0
csfs@bellnet.ca
www.csfs.ca
To promote the study of forensic science; To maintain professional standards in the discipline of forensic science
G. Anderson, President
G. Verret, Secretary
D. Camellato, Treasurer

Canadian Society of Microbiologists (CSM) / Société canadienne des microbiologistes
CSM-SCM Secretariat, 17 Dossetter Way, Ottawa ON K1G 4S3
Tel: 613-421-7229; *Fax:* 613-421-9811
info@csm-scm.org
www.csm-scm.org
To advance microbiology in all its aspects; to facilitate interchange of ideas between microbiologists
Ivan Oresnik, President
Ayush Kumar, Secretary-Treasurer

Canadian Society of Pharmacology & Therapeutics (CSPT) / Société de pharmacologie du Canada
Dept. of Physiology & Pharmacology, University of Western Ontario, M216 Medical Services Bldg., London ON N6A 5C1
Tel: 519-661-3312
www.pharmacologycanada.org
To promote research & education in the disciplines of pharmacology & experimental therapeutics
Gaebel Kathryn, Executive Administrator
Richard Kim, President
Fiona Parkinson, Vice-President
Cindy Woodland, Secretary-Treasurer

Canadian Society of Plant Physiologists (CSPP) / Société canadienne de physiologie végétale (SCPV)
c/o Dr. Harold Weger, Department of Biology, University of Regina, 3737 Wascana Pkwy., Regina SK S4S 0A2
treasurer@cspp-scpvca.ca
www.cspp-scpv.ca
To promote the teaching & public awareness of plant physiology in Canada
Priti Krishna, Senior Director
Peter Pauls, President
Line Lapointe, Secretary
Harold G. Weger, Treasurer

Canadian Society of Soil Science (CSSS) / Société canadienne de la science du sol
Business Office, PO Box 637, Pinawa MB R0E 1L0
Tel: 204-753-2747; *Fax:* 204-753-8478
sheppards@ecomatters.com
www.csss.ca
To be actively engaged in land use, soils research, & classification
Gordon Price, President
Barbara Cade-Menun, Secretary
Paul Bullock, Treasurer

Canadian Space Society (CSS) / La société canadienne de l'espace
Parc Downsview Park, 65 Carl Hall Rd., Toronto ON M3K 2E1
www.css.ca
To conduct technical & outreach projects; to promote the involvement of Canadians in space development
Kevin Shortt, President
Vivian Lee, Coordinator, Membership

Citizen Scientists
c/o Rouge Valley Conservation Centre, 1749 Meadowvale Rd., Toronto ON M1B 5W8
info@citizenscientists.ca
www.citizenscientists.ca
Social Media: www.facebook.com/group.php?gid=2259994028
To monitor local watersheds, foster local environmental stewardship, and educate volunteers and the public.

Club d'astronomie Quasar de Chibougamau
783, 6e Rue, Chibougamau QC G8P 2W4
Tél: 418-748-4642
www.faaq.org/clubs/quasar/
Pierre Bureau, Président

Genetics Society of Canada (GSC) / Société de génétique du Canada
c/o The Snider's Web, 59 Aulac Rd., Aulac NB E4L 2V6
Tel: 506-536-1768; *Fax:* 902-484-5694
gsc@thesndersweb.com
life.biology.mcmaster.ca/GSC/
To provide means of liaison between geneticists for coordination & development of genetics & science policy in Canada; to promote facilities for reporting, exchanging & disseminating knowledge related to genetics & to make known theSociety's views on genetic knowledge which is of direct concern to the Canadianpublic.
Paul Lasko, President
Elizabeth Stendel, Contact

Geological Association of Canada (GAC) / Association géologique du Canada (AGC)
Department of Earth Sciences, Memorial University of Newfoundland, #ER4063, Alexander Murray Bldg., St. John's NL A1B 3X5
Tel: 709-737-7660; *Fax:* 709-737-2532
gac@mun.ca
www.gac.ca
To advance the wise use of geoscience in academic, professional, & public circles
Stephen Rowins, President
Stephen Rowins, Vice-President
Toby Rivers, Secretary-Treasurer
Karen Johnston, Manager, Finance & Administration
Karen Dawe, Director, Publications

Innovation and Technology Association of Prince Edward Island (ITAP)
PO Box 241, Charlottetown PE C1A 7K4
Tel: 902-894-4827; *Fax:* 902-894-4867
itap@itap.ca
www.itap.ca
To provide advocacy and support to our members, through projects in the key areas of export development, communication and leadership development.
Kelly Dawson, President

Institute of Textile Science (ITS) / Institut des sciences textiles
c/o Jerry Bauerle, BodyCote Ortech Inc., 2395 Speakman Dr., Mississauga ON L5K 1B3
Tel: 905-822-4111; *Fax:* 905-823-1446
info@textilescience.ca
www.textilescience.ca
To promote the dissemination & interchange of knowledge concerning textile science; to encourage research & development related to textile science & technology, including the establishment & granting of awards
Kasper Van Veen, President

International Association of Hydrogeologists (IAH)
IAH Secretariat, PO Box 4130, Stn. Goring, Reading RG8 6BJKOA 1L0 UK
info@iah.org
www.iah.org
To advance the science of hydrogeology & exchange hydrogeologic information internationally
John Chilton, Executive Manager, IAH Secretariat

International Association of Hydrogeologists - Canadian National Chapter (IAH-CNC)
c/o WESA, 3108 Carp Rd., Carp ON K0A 1L0
Tel: 613-839-3053
www.iah.ca
To advance the science of hydrogeology & exchange hydrogeologic information internationally
Nell van Walsum, Secretary

International Association of Science & Technology for Development (IASTED)
Bldg B6, #101, 2509 Dieppe Ave. SW, Calgary AB T3E 7J9
Tel: 403-288-1195; *Fax:* 403-247-6851
calgary@iasted.com
www.iasted.org
Social Media:
www.facebook.com/pages/IASTED/130963346917239;
twitter.com/IASTED_Calgary
To further economic development by promoting science & technology

International Oceans Institute of Canada (IOIC)
c/o Dalhousie Univ., 1226 LeMarchant St., Halifax NS B3H 3P7
Tel: 902-494-6918; *Fax:* 902-494-1334
ioi@dal.ca
internationaloceaninstitute.dal.ca
To promote responsible management of the world's oceans & sustainable development of marine resources; to protect the integrity of the ocean environment; to promote sustainable resource development; to improve the quality of ocean-dependent human life, including health & safety of maritime communities; to further these objectives, all aspects of the ocean environment are pursued - resource management & development, marine environmental quality, ocean law & policy, high seas management, coastal zone management, marine transportation, ocean science & technology, tourism & recreation, ocean industries & maritime boundary delimitation

Life Science Association of Manitoba (LSAM)
1000 Waverley St., Winnipeg MB R3T 0P3
Tel: 204-272-5095; *Fax:* 204-272-2961
info@lsam.ca
www.lsam.ca
Association representing the life science industry in Manitoba; provides services for companies in the industry; promotes economic development
Dawson Reimer, President

Microscopical Society of Canada (MSC) / Société de Microscopie du Canada
Brockhouse Inst. of Mat.Res., McMaster Univ., 1280 Main St. West, Hamilton ON L8S 4M1
Tel: 905-525-9140; *Fax:* 905-521-2773
butcher@mcmaster.ca
msc.rsvs.ulaval.ca
Randy Mikula, President
Chris Butcher, Treasurer
Frances Leggett, Executive Secretary

North Pacific Marine Science Organization (PICES)
c/o Institute of Ocean Sciences, PO Box 6000, Sidney BC V8L 4B2
Tel: 250-363-6366; *Fax:* 250-363-6827
secretariat@pices.int
www.pices.int
To promote & coordinate marine research in the northern North Pacific & adjacent seas especially northward of 30 degrees North; to advance scientific knowledge about the ocean environment, global weather & climate change, living resources & their ecosystems & the impacts of human activities; to promote the collection & rapid exchange of scientific information on these issues
Alexander Bychkov, Executive Secretary

Nova Scotian Institute of Science (NSIS)
Science Services, Killam Library, Dalhousie Univ., 6225 University Ave., Halifax NS B3H 4H8
Tel: 902-494-3621; *Fax:* 902-494-2062
nsis@chebucto.ns.ca
www.chebucto.ns.ca/Science/NSIS
To provide a forum for scientists & those interested in science
John Rutherford, President
Michelle Paon, Vice-President
Linda Marks, Secretary
Elaine McCullogh, Treasurer

Ontario Kinesiology Association (OKA)
6519B Mississauga Rd., Mississauga ON L5N 1A6
Tel: 905-567-7194; *Fax:* 905-567-7191
info@oka.on.ca
www.oka.on.ca
Social Media: www.oka.on.ca/index.php?page=facebook
To promote the application of the science of human movement to other professionals & to the community; to uphold the standards of the profession of kinesiology; to assist kinesiologists in the performance of their duties & responsibilities
Janice Ray, President

Royal Astronomical Society of Canada (RASC) / Société royale d'astronomie du Canada
203 - 4920 Dundas St. West, Toronto ON M9A 1B7
Tel: 416-924-7973; *Fax:* 416-924-2911
Toll-Free: 888-924-7272
nationaloffice10000@rasc.ca
www.rasc.ca
Social Media: www.facebook.com/groups/2393127970/; twitter.com/rasc
To promote the advancement of astronomy across Canada
Mary Lou Whitehorne, President
Deborah Thompson, Executive Director

Science Alberta Foundation
#260, 3512 - 33 St. NW, Calgary AB T2L 2A6
Tel: 403-220-0077; *Fax:* 403-284-4132
info@sciencealberta.org
www.sciencealberta.org
Social Media: twitter.com/sciencealberta
To increase science literacy by creating innovative programs for all Albertans
Arlene Ponting, CEO
Jill Maryniuk, Manager, Marketing & Communications

Society of Toxicology of Canada (STC) / Société de toxicologie du Canada
PO Box 55094, Montréal QC H3G 2W5
Tel: 514-697-9219; *Fax:* 514-697-9309
stcsecretariat@mcgill.ca
www.stcweb.ca
To promote acquisition, facilitate dissemination & encourage utilization of knowledge in the science of toxicology
Genevieve Bondy, President
Elise Boivin-Ford, Executive Secretary

Southern Ontario Seismic Network (SOSN)
c/o University of Western Ontario, London ON N6A 5B7
Tel: 519-661-3605; *Fax:* 519-661-3198
www.gp.uwo.ca
To obtain information on the seismicity and seismic hazards of a region of southern Ontario in which a number of nuclear power facilities are located.
R.F. Mereu, Administrator

Statistical Society of Canada (SSC) / Société statistique du Canada
#209, 1725 St. Laurent Blvd., Ottawa ON K1G 3V4
Tel: 613-733-2662; *Fax:* 613-733-1386
info@ssc.ca; admin@ssc.ca
www.ssc.ca
To promote the development & use of statistics & probability; To ensure that decisions that affect society are based upon valid & appropriate statistics & interpretation; To encourage high standards for statistical education & practice
John Brewster, President
John J. Koval, Treasurer
Julie Trépanier, Executive Secretary

Youth Science Canada (YSF) / Fondation sciences jeunesse Canada (FSJ)
#213, 1550 Kingston Road, Pickering ON L1V 1C3
Tel: 416-341-0040; *Fax:* 866-613-2542
Toll-Free: 866-341-0040
info@ysf-fsj.ca
www.youthscience.ca
YSF assists Canadian youth to develop skills & knowledge for excellence in science & technology.
Reni Barlow, Executive Director
Lorne Heslop, Chair
Thomas C. Lee, Sec.-Treas.

Search & Rescue

New Brunswick Ground Search and Rescue Association (NBGSARA)
c/o President
Tel: 506-850-3461; *Fax:* 506-462-2105
www.nbgsara.nb.ca
The New Brunswick Ground Search and Rescue Association (NBGSARA) represents the Province of New Brunswick's 11 regional ground search and rescue teams. Comprised entirely of volunteers, these teams provide assistance to the RCMP and local police departments in locating and extracting missing persons in wilderness locations.
Joseph LaBelle, President

Senior Citizens

Active Living Coalition for Older Adults (ALCOA) / Coalition d'une vie active pour les ainé(e)s
PO Box 143, Shelburne ON L0N 1S0
Tel: 519-925-1676; *Fax:* 905-925-3955
Toll-Free: 800-549-9799
alcoa@uniserve.com
www.alcoa.ca
To encourage older Canadians to maintain & enhance their well-being & independence through a lifestyle that embraces daily physical activities
Patricia Clark, Executive Director

Advocacy Centre for the Elderly (ACE)
#701, 2 Carlton St., Toronto ON M5B 1J3
Tel: 416-598-2656; *Fax:* 416-598-7924
www.acelaw.ca
To provide legal services to low income senior citizens
Judith Wahl, Executive Director
Timothy Banks, Chair

Alberta Council on Aging
#232, 11808 St. Albert Trail, Edmonton AB T5L 4G4
Tel: 780-423-7781; *Fax:* 780-425-9246
Toll-Free: 888-423-9666
info@acaging.ca
www.acaging.ca
To define the needs of aging & the aged & to bring the current needs to the attention of government or voluntary agencies & to take action where appropriate; to identify & encourage relevant areas of research & systematic compilation of information affecting aging; to encourage & develop discussion on all problems affecting aging; to inform government at any level on the potential impact of policies & legislation on the aging; to print, publish, distribute & sell publications related to aging; to foster interagency liaison & cooperation
Gary Pool, President
Paul Lemay, Vice-President

Alberta Provincial Pensioners & Senior Citizens Organization (APSCO)
#334, 1237 - 4 Ave. South, Lethbridge AB T1J 0P9
Tel: 403-327-3264
gwaldern@uleth.ca
To improve & maintain the well being of all pensioners & senior citizens; To present & represent needs to all levels of governments
Violet Segouin, Treasurer
Betty Waldern, President

Alberta Senior Citizens Sport & Recreation Association (ASCSRA)
#400, 7015 Macleod Trail., Calgary AB T2H 2K6
Tel: 403-803-9852; *Fax:* 403-800-5599
info@alberta55plus.ca
www.alberta55plus.ca
To promote sport & recreation development for seniors (55+) across Alberta; to act as a provincial voice to ensure input by age categories for seniors in Alberta Winter & Summer Games; to promote future Alberta Seniors' Games
Pat Covington, President

Association des personnes en perte d'autonomie de Chibougamau inc. & Jardin des aînés
101, av du Parc, Chibougamau QC G8P 3A5
Tél: 418-748-4411
Chantal Lessard, Directrice générale

Canadian Association on Gerontology (CAG) / Association canadienne de gérontologie
#328, 263 McCaul St., Toronto ON M5T 1W7
Toll-Free: 855-224-2240
cagacg@igs.net
www.cagacg.ca
Social Media: www.facebook.com/group.php?gid=187077537979477; twitter.com/cagacg
To develop the theoretical & practical understanding of individual & population aging through multidisciplinary research, practice, education & policy analysis in gerontology; To seek the improvement of the conditions of life of elderly people in Canada
Neena Chappell, President
Anthony Lombardo, PhD, Executive Director
Margaret Denton, Secretary-Treasurer

Canadian Pensioners Concerned Inc. (CPC) / Retraités canadiens en action (RCA)
6 Trinity Sq., Toronto ON M5G 1B1
Tel: 416-368-5222; *Fax:* 416-368-0443
Toll-Free: 888-822-6750
canpension@gmail.com; info@cpcnational.ca
www.canpension.ca
To provide joint action on seniors issues; To collect authoritative factual material & distribute it in usable form to relevant persons & authorities
Barbara Kilbourn, President
Sylvia Hall, Corporate Secretary
Jane Miller, Treasurer

CARP
30 Jefferson Ave., Toronto ON M6K 1Y4
Tel: 416-363-8748; *Fax:* 416-363-8747
Toll-Free: 888-363-2279
support@carp.ca
www.carp.ca
Social Media: www.facebook.com/CARP; twitter.com/carpnews; www.zoomers.ca/group/CARP
The Association is a national, non-partisan organization that promotes the rights & quality of life of Canadians as they age through advocacy, education, information & CARP-recommended services & programs
Moses Znaimer, President
Eric Vengroff, General Manager & VP, Benefits
Susan Eng, Vice-President, Advocacy
Ross Mayot, Vice-President, Community

Club de l'âge d'or Les intrépides de Chibougamau
126, rue des Forces-Armées, Chibougamau QC G8P 3A1
Tél: 418-748-7541
Henriette Roy, Présidente

Council for Black Aging
3021 Delisle, Montréal QC H4C 1M8
Tel: 514-935-4951; *Fax:* 514-935-8466
The Council for Black Aging works as an advocate for the needs of Black seniors, undertaking activities designed to advance the interests of Black elders, keeping Black seniors better informed of issues relating to the availability of health and social services, and developing a unique day centre and a nursing home for Black elders.
Elisee Faure, Contact

Elder Active Recreation Association (ERA)
4061, 4th Ave., Whitehorse YT Y1A 1H1
Tel: 867-633-5010
www.yukon-seniors-and-elders.org/era.home.htm
To enhance the quality of life of Yukon seniors and elders by supporting them in living healthy lives with independence and dignity; to support seniors and elders in helping other seniors and elders to live full, active and healthy lives, and to develop active communities throughout the Yukon where seniors and elders can make positive lifestyle choices, exchange wisdom and connect with others in friendship, recreation and creativity.
Bill Simpson, President

Fédération des aînées et aînés francophones du Canada (FAAFC)
#300, 450 rue Rideau, Ottawa ON K1N 5Z4
Tél: 613-564-0212; *Téléc:* 613-564-0212
info@faafc.ca
www.faafc.ca/fr
Défendre les droits des personnes à la retraite; défendre les droits des préretraités; programmes intergénérationnels; protection de la langue et la culture française
Roger Doiron, Président
Jean-Luc Racine, Directeur général
Michel Vézina, Premier vice-président, Saskatchewan
André Faubert, Deuxième vice-présidente, Québec
Richard Martin, Trésorier, Terre-Neuve & Labrador
Mélina Gallant, Secrétaire, Ile-du-Prince-Édouard
Marie-Christine Aubrey, Administratrice, Territoire du Nord-Ouest
Louis Bernardin, Administrateur, Manitoba
Roland Gallant, Administrateur, Nouveau-Brunswick
Charles Gaudet, Administrateur, Nouvelle-Écosse
Claire Grisé, Administratrice, Colombie-Britannique
Germaine Lehodey, Administratrice, Alberta
Francine Poirier, Administratrice, Ontario
Roxanne Thibaudeau, Administratrice, Yukon

Help the Aged (Canada) (HTA) / Aide aux aînés (Canada)
#205, 1300 Carling Ave., Ottawa ON K1Z 7L2
Tel: 613-232-0727; *Fax:* 613-232-7625
Toll-Free: 800-648-1111
info@helptheaged.ca; adoptagran@helptheaged.ca
www.helptheaged.ca; www.aideauxainescanada.ca
To meet the needs of poor or destitute elderly people in Canada & the developing world
Jacques Bertrand, Executive Director
Jacqueline A. Bannister, Chair
Pierrette Leonard, Vice-Chair
Peter Hamilton, Secretary
Jacqueline Hallé, Treasurer

Manitoba Association on Gerontology (MAG)
884 William Ave., Winnipeg MB R3E 0Z6
Tel: 204-783-8389
To sustain the social values & philosophy which strengthen & advance human dignity & personal fulfillment during the course of aging; to cooperate with a variety of service providers to address common issues in the field of gerontology
Pamela Hawranik, President

Manitoba Society of Seniors (MSOS)
#202, 323 Portage Ave., Winnipeg MB R3B 2C1
Tel: 204-942-3147; *Fax:* 204-943-1290
Toll-Free: 800-561-6767
membership@msos.mb.ca
www.msos.mb.ca
To represent Manitobans age 50+ by advocating for their needs & concerns & by promoting a positive image of aging in the community.
Kimberly Weihs, Executive Director
Harry Paine, President

National Pensioners & Senior Citizens Federation (NPSCF) / Fédération nationale des retraités et citoyens âgés
c/o Fern Haight, PO Box 393, Hanley SK S0G 2E0
Tel: 306-544-2737; *Fax:* 306-544-2757
fern.h@sasktel.net
www.npscf.org
To act as an advisory body providing central contacts, facilities for research, surveys, uniform objectives & a national expansion of the pensioners movement; To stimulate public interest in the welfare of senior citizens by means of adequate pensions & social security that will provide comfortable housing & decent living; To protect the rights & interests of pensioners & prospective pensioners; To prevent discrimination & undue delay in granting pensions; To project a social friendly fellowship among the pensioners of Canada
Barry Thorsteinson, President
Fern Haight, Secretary

New Brunswick Senior Citizens Federation Inc. (NBSCF) / Fédération des citoyens aînés du Nouveau-Brunswick inc. (FCANB)
#214, 23 - 451 Paul St., Dieppe NB E1A 6W8
Tel: 506-857-8242; *Fax:* 506-857-0315
Toll-Free: 800-453-4333
horizons@nbnet.nb.ca
www.nbscf.ca
To promote the general welfare & leadership of NB's senior citizens regardless of language, race, colour, sex, or creed; to elevate the social, moral, & intellectual standing of NB's senior citizens; to provide information, coordination, communication, & advocating services to members
Isabelle Thériault-Arseneault, Director, Operations

Older Adult Centres' Association of Ontario (OACAO) / Association des centres pour aînés de l'Ontario
PO Box 65, Caledon East ON L7C 3L8
Tel: 905-584-8125; *Fax:* 905-584-8126
Toll-Free: 866-835-7693
sue@oacao.org
www.oacao.org
To ensure that seniors in Ontario have opportunities & choices that lead to healthy, active lifestyles
Sue Hesjedahl, Executive Director
Ellen Hope, President
Marilyn Latham, Treasurer
Debra Prescott, Secretary

Ontario Coalition of Senior Citizens' Organizations (OCSCO) / Coalition des organismes d'aînés et d'aînées de l'Ontario (COAAO)
#406, 333 Wilson Ave., Toronto ON M3H 1T2
Tel: 416-785-8570; *Fax:* 416-785-7361
Toll-Free: 800-265-0779
ocsco@web.net
www.ocsco.ca
To improve the quality of life for Ontario's seniors by encouraging seniors' involvement in all aspects of society, by keeping them informed of current issues, & by focusing on programs to benefit an aging population
Morris Jesion, Executive Director
Lisa Hems, Program Coordinator

Prince Edward Island Senior Citizens Federation Inc. (PEISCF)
#117, 40 Enman Cres., Charlottetown PE C1E 1E6
Tel: 902-368-9008; *Fax:* 902-368-9006
Toll-Free: 877-368-9008
peiscf@pei.aibn.com
www.peiscf.com
To advance the education opportunities for seniors on PEI; to improve the quality of life for seniors by advising government & other decision making bodies regarding seniors' concerns; to improve the quality of life for seniors; to increase societal understanding of seniors & the aging process through positive role modelling
Linda Jean Nicholson, Executive Director

Réseau FADOQ / Québec Federation of Senior Citizens
CP 1000, Succ. M, 4545, av Pierre-de Couberin, Montréal QC H1V 3R2
Tél: 514-252-3017; *Téléc:* 514-252-3154
Ligne sans frais: 800-828-3344
info@fadoq.ca
www.fadoq.ca
Promouvoir un concept positif du vieillissement; encourager le maintien et l'amélioration de la qualité de vie et de l'autonomie des aînés; initier et soutenir l'organisation d'activités physiques et de loisirs; redonner aux aînés une nouvelle fierté en les revalorisant à leurs propres yeux comme à ceux de la société; remettre entre les mains des aînés la gestion de leurs affaires
Danis Prud Homme, Directeur Générale
Lyne Remillard, Directeur adjointe

Routes to Learning Canada (RLC)
4 Cataraqui St., Kingston ON K7K 1Z7
Fax: 613-530-2096
Toll-Free: 866-745-1690
information@routestolearning.ca
www.routestolearning.ca
To develop, manage & facilitate educational experiences for older adults through cooperative partnership with educational agents; to balance education & travel in an environment of comradeship & respect; to continue to experiment with pilot projects to reach broader populations of older adults; to be a "learner-centered" organization that responds to the learning needs of older adults; to work towards a better understanding of our relationship with our current populations; to use new methods of reaching out to an ever more diverse multicultural Canada; to promote cost-effective educational opportunities to an ever widening group of older adults
Victoria Pearson, President/CEO

Seniors Association of Greater Edmonton (SAGE)
15 Sir Winston Churchill Sq., Edmonton AB T5J 2E5
Tel: 780-423-5510; *Fax:* 780-426-5175
info@mysage.ca
www.mysage.ca
To enhance the quality of life of older persons through service, innovation, advocacy & voluntarism
Brent Abbott, President

United Senior Citizens of Ontario Inc. (USCO)
3033 Lakeshore Blvd. West, Toronto ON M8V 1K5
Tel: 416-252-2021; *Fax:* 416-252-5770
Toll-Free: 888-320-2222
office@uscont.ca
www.uscont.ca
To further the interests & promote the welfare of the senior population in Ontario; To provide for an exchange of ideas for member groups; To assist in the formation of senior citizens clubs
Ken Cunningham, President

Service Clubs

Association des Grands Frères et Grandes Soeurs de Québec (GFGS) / Big Brothers & Big Sisters of Québec
#201, 2380, av du Mont-Thabor, Québec QC G1J 3W7
Tél: 418-624-3304; *Téléc:* 418-624-4013
gfgsquebec@videotron.ca
www.gfgs.qc.ca
Favoriser l'épanouissement de jeunes âgés de 6 à 16 ans privés de la presence d'un de leurs parents en les jumelant avec un adulte mature, qui s'engage à le rencontrer 3-4 heures par semaine pour échanger et faire des activités, selon leurs goûts réciproques

Big Brothers Big Sisters of Canada (BBBSC) / Les Grands Frères Grandes Soeurs du Canada
#113E, 3228 South Service Rd., Burlington ON L7N 3H8
Tel: 905-639-0461; *Fax:* 905-639-0124
Toll-Free: 800-263-9133
www.bbbsc.ca
To provide leadership to member agencies as they develop programs to meet the changing needs of young people
Bruce MacDonald, President
Anne Blandford, Regional Director, Atlantic
David Pickersgill, Regional Director & Board Chair, Alberta
Deirdre Speers, Regional Director, Ontario

British Columbia Lions Society for Children with Disabilities (BCLS)
3981 Oak St., Vancouver BC V6H 4H5
Tel: 604-873-1865; *Fax:* 604-873-0166
Toll-Free: 800-818-4483
info@lionsbc.ca
www.lionsbc.ca
To provide as many services as possible to children with disabilities; to enhance the lives of children with special needs; to continue building, not only specialized services & facilities, but challenging young hearts & minds as well; giving children with disabilities self-esteem, self-confidence & a sense of independence
Stephen J. Miller, President
Surinder Gahir, Chair
Beth McInnis, Financial Advisor

Canadian Federation of Junior Leagues / Fédération canadienne des jeunes ligues
4 Steeplehill Cres., Carlisle ON L0R 1H3
Tel: 905-659-9339
info@cfjl.org
www.cfjl.org
The Canadian Federation of Junior Leagues has served as the link amoung Junior Leagues within Canada for the purpose networking and sharing best practices amoungst Canadian Leagues. The Principle purpose of the Federation is to promote a strong national presence in Canada and to increase the international input to the Association of Junior Intertional, Inc.
Deborah Maw, National Coordinator

Canadian Progress Club / Club progrès du Canada
#143, 75 Lavinia St., New Glasgow NS B2H 1N5
Fax: 888-337-9826
Toll-Free: 877-944-4726
info@progressclub.ca
www.progressclub.ca
To assist those in need as well as creating & preserving a spirit of friendship that is sincere; to advance the best interests of the community in which that club is located.
Sharon Ward, National President
Carmel Kinder, National Club Administrator

Club Kiwanis Chibougamau
CP 61, Chibougamau QC G8P 2K5
Tél: 418-748-2231
Roy Lavoie, Président

Club Lions de Chibougamau
CP 11, Chibougamau QC G8P 2K5
lionschibougamau@hotmail.com
lionschibougamau.icr.qc.ca

Robin Pearson

Club Optimiste Chibougamau
1614, rue St-Jacques, Chibougamau QC G8P 2L7
Tél: 418-748-7272
Sylvie Cayouette, Présidente

Club Optimiste de Rivière-du-Loup inc.
CP 1344, Rivière-du-Loup QC G5R 4L9
Tél: 418-862-8454; *Téléc:* 418-862-3366
service@optimiste.org
www.optimiste.org
Les clubs Optimistes ® Inspirent le meilleur chez les jeunes depuis 1919 en rencontrant les besoins des jeunes de toutes les collectivités du monde. Ils organisent des projets de service communautaire positifs qui visent à tendre la main à la jeunesse.
Denise Desbiens, Présidente

Kin Canada
PO Box 3460, 1920 Rogers Dr., Cambridge ON N3H 5C6
Tel: 519-653-1920; *Fax:* 519-650-1091
Toll-Free: 800-742-5546
kinhq@kincanada.ca
www.kincanada.ca
Social Media: www.facebook.com/kincanada; twitter.com/kincanada
To enrich communities through service, while embracing national pride, positive values, personal development, & lasting friendships; To support Cystic Fibrosis research & care in Canada
Ric McDonald, Executive Director
David W. Ronson, National President

Last Post Fund (LPF) / Fonds du Souvenir
#401, 505, boul René-Lévesque ouest, Montréal QC H2Z 1Y7
Tel: 514-866-2727; *Fax:* 514-866-1471
Toll-Free: 800-465-7113
lpfinfo@lastpost.ca
www.lastpostfund.ca
To ensure that no war veterans, or certain other persons who meet the wartime service eligibility criteria, are denied a funeral & burial due to lack of funds
Evelyn Kelly, National President
Kenneth C. Garbutt, Vice President (West)
Daniel O'Connor, Vice President (East)
Jean-Pierre Goyer, Executive Director

Soroptimist Foundation of Canada
c/o #104, 13311 Yonge Street, Richmond Hill ON L4E 3L6
corinne@cmrlaw.ca
www.soroptimistfoundation.ca
To provide bursaries, scholarships & fellowships to Canadian students & Canadian schools, colleges & universities for the advancement of education & in particular to further the appreciation of social needs, & the study of community, national & international problems
Connie Rivers, Chair

Variety - The Children's Charity (Ontario)
3701 Danforth Ave., Toronto ON M1N 2G2
Tel: 416-367-2828; *Fax:* 416-367-0028
info@varietyontario.ca
www.varietyontario.ca
Variety will be the leading charity for children with special needs & their families; remain committed to improving their quality of life & integration into society
Maureen Burgess, Executive Director

Variety - The Children's Charity of BC
4300 Still Creek Dr., Burnaby BC V5C 6C6
Tel: 604-320-0505; *Fax:* 604-320-0535
Toll-Free: 800-381-2040
info@variety.bc.ca
www.variety.bc.ca
To raise funds throughout the province of B.C. for the benefit of B.C.'s children with special needs; to provide funds for capital costs; to create new centres or improve existing facilities & purchase specialized equipment
Barbara Hislop, Executive Director

Variety - The Children's Charity of Manitoba, Tent 58 Inc.
#2 - 1313 Border St., Winnipeg MB R3H 0X4
Tel: 204-982-1050; *Fax:* 204-475-3198
businessmanager@varietymanitoba.com
www.varietymanitoba.com
To raise funds for the immediate, tangible needs of the disabled & disadvantaged children of Manitoba, by mobilizing volunteer initiatives
Wayne Rogers, Executive Director

Variety Club of Northern Alberta, Tent 63
#1205 Energy Square, 10109 - 106th St., Edmonton AB T5J 3L7
Tel: 780-448-9544; *Fax:* 780-448-9289
Raises funds for the children of Northern Alberta who have disabilities or are disadvantaged
Sue McEachern, Executive Director

Variety Club of Southern Alberta
#201 - 1740B, 11A St. NE, Calgary AB T2E 6M6
Tel: 403-228-6168; *Fax:* 403-245-9282
info@varietyalberta.ca
www.varietyclub61.ab.ca
To provide disabled & disadvantaged children with the means to enjoy quality life experiences; to support research for below the knee amputee children; to provide assistance & bursaries to children in special situations
Audrey Garratt, Chief
Graham Kuntz, Executive Director

Social Clubs

Brunch-rencontre pour personnes seules
#102, 161, rue du Parc, Chibougamau QC G8P 2H3
Tél: 418-748-4951
Réjeanne Lalancette

Canadian Black Community Association
#30, 6999, Côte-des-Neiges, Montréal QC H3S 2B6
Tel: 514-737-8321; *Fax:* 514-737-6893
Cultural, recreational & social activities for youth & adults; after-school tutorials; summer camp; Teen Leadership Program; adult classes & sports activities
Michael Gittens, Contact

Social Response/Social Services

Agincourt Community Services Association (ACSA)
#100, 4155 Sheppart Ave. East, Toronto ON M1S 1T4
Tel: 416-321-6912; *Fax:* 416-321-6922
info@agincourtcommunityservices.com
www.agincourtcommunityservices.com
To address a variety of issues including systemic poverty, hunger, housing, homelessness, unemployment, accessibility and social isolation in the Scarborough community.
Gael Gilbert, Executive Director
Paul Rook, Chair

Alberta Association of Marriage & Family Therapy (AAMFT)
420 Norway Cres., Sherwood Park AB T8A 5Z4
Tel: 403-524-0873; *Fax:* 780-434-7511
Toll-Free: 877-435-5070
info@aamft.ab.ca
www.aamft.ab.ca
To provide individual marriage & family therapy; to provide educational seminars for therapists
Peter Doherty, President

Alberta Association of Services for Children & Families (AASCF)
Bonnie Doon Mall, #255, 8330 - 82nd Ave., Edmonton AB T6C 4E3
Tel: 780-428-3660; *Fax:* 780-428-3844
aascf@aascf.com
www.aascf.com
To provide opportunities for deliverers of services to meet with each other to exchange views & develop quality service in Alberta; to establish a structure which can provide information to membership & the public in support of social policy on behalf of Alberta children & families; to create a mechanism for action in social policy & public attitudes relating to the welfare of children & families; to support ongoing development & implementation of standards of service for human service providers & maintain accountability to these standards through an accreditation process; to advocate on behalf of the membership; to promote professional development of member agencies; to support research into child & family welfare issues relevant to member agencies; to advise government on social policy
Rhonda Barraclough, Executive Director

Alberta Block Parent Association
220 Doveview Crescent SE, Calgary AB T2B 1Y6
Tel: 403-262-2864; *Fax:* 403-262-5221
Toll-Free: 866-586-7666
alberta@hotmail.com
www.albertablockparent.ca/
To assist with the start-up of new programs; To provide ongoing support & resources for established programs; To ensure that faltering programs are properly closed down

Alberta College of Social Workers (ACSW) / Association des travailleurs sociaux de l'Alberta
#550, 10707 - 100 Ave. NW, Edmonton AB T5J 3M1
Tel: 780-421-1167; *Fax:* 780-421-1168
Toll-Free: 800-661-3089
acsw@acsw.ab.ca
www.acsw.ab.ca
To promote, regulate & govern the profession of social work in the Province of Alberta; To advocate for skilled & ethical social work practices & for policies, programs & services that promote the profession & protect the best interests of the public
Rod Adachi, Executive Director/Registrar
Alison MacDonald, Associate Registrar & Director, Complaints

Applegrove Community Complex
60 Woodfield Rd., Toronto ON M4L 2W6
Tel: 416-461-8143
applegrove@applegrovecc.ca
www.applegrovecc.ca
To provide social service programs for infants, children, teens, adults and seniors living in the Queen-Greenwood area of Toronto.
Susan Fletcher, Executive Director
Pierre Trudel, Chair

Association des services de réhabilitation sociale du Québec inc. (ASRSQ) / Association of Social Rehabilitation Agencies of Québec Inc.
2000, boul St-Joseph est, Montréal QC H2H 1E4
Tél: 514-521-3733; *Téléc:* 514-521-3753
info@asrsq.ca
www.asrsq.ca
Promouvoir la participation des citoyens dans l'administration de la justice, la prévention du crime et la réhabilitation des délinquants adultes
Josée Rioux, Présidente
Philippe Létourneau, Vice-président
Ruth Gagnon, Secrétaire
Serge Arel, Trésorier

The Association of Social Workers of Northern Canada (ASWNC) / L'Association des travailleurs sociaux du Nord canadien (ATSNC)
PO Box 2963, Yellowknife NT X1A 2R2
Tel: 867-699-7964
geried@socialworknorth.com
www.socialworknorth.com
Dana Jennejohn, President

Association québécoise des personnes de petite taille (AQPPT) / Association of Little People of Quebec
#308, 6300, av du Parc, Montréal QC H2V 4H8
Tél: 514-521-9671; *Téléc:* 514-521-3369
info@aqppt.org
www.aqppt.org
Promouvoir des intérêts et défendre les droits des personnes de petite taille et faciliter leur intégration scolaire, sociale et professionnelle.
Louiselle St-Pierre, Directrice générale

Association québécoise Plaidoyer-Victimes (AQPV)
#201, 4305, rue d'Iberville, Montréal QC H2H 2L5
Tél: 514-526-9037; *Téléc:* 514-526-9951
aqpv@aqpv.ca
www.aqpv.ca
Défense des droits et des intérêts des victimes d'actes criminels par la discussion, la sensibilisation, la formation, la concertation et la recherche
Marie-Hélène Blanc, Directrice générale

Battlefords United Way Inc.
PO Box 904, #93, 891 - 99th St., North Battleford SK S9A 2Z3
Tel: 306-445-1717; *Fax:* 306-445-1720
buw@sasktel.net
www.battlefords.unitedway.ca
To improve lives & build community by engaging individuals & mobilizing collective action
Treena Rathwell, Executive Director
Michael Brokop, Treasurer

Bereaved Families of Ontario (BFO)
PO Box 10015, Stn. Watline, Mississauga ON L4Z 4G5
Tel: 416-440-0290; *Fax:* 416-440-0304
Toll-Free: 800-236-6364
info@bereavedfamilies.net
www.bereavedfamilies.net
To create programs, services & resources to support bereaved families; committed to self-help & mutual aid; focus is on families who have experienced the death of a child
Bill Allan, Chair
Melissa Mould, President

Birchmount Bluffs Neighbourhood Centre (BBNC)
93 Birchmount Rd., Toronto ON M1N 3J7
Tel: 416-396-4310; *Fax:* 416-396-4314
info@bbnc.ca
www.bbnc.ca
The mission of the Birchmount Bluffs Neighbourhood Centre (BBNC) is to provide programs and supports and foster social inclusion within the community, with a focus on individuals that face a barrier to service.
Enrique Robert, Executive Director

Block Parent Program of Canada Inc. (BPPCI) / Programme Parents-Secours du Canada inc.
PO Box 7, 50 Dunlop St. East, Lower Level, Barrie ON L4N 6S7
Tel: 705-792-4245; *Fax:* 705-792-4245
Toll-Free: 800-663-1134
info@blockparent.ca
www.blockparent.ca
To provide immediate assistance through a safety network; To offer supporting community education programs
Donna Ducey, Newfoundland Contact
Linda Patterson, President

Block Watch Society of British Columbia (BCBPS)
#120, 12414 - 82nd Ave., Surrey BC V3W 3E9
Tel: 604-418-3827; *Fax:* 604-501-2509
Toll-Free: 877-602-3358
blockwatch@blockwatch.com
www.blockwatch.com
To build safe neighbourhoods across British Columbia; To encourage bonds among local residents & businesses to create a crime free area through community participation; To assist in the reduction of crime; To improve relations between police & communities
Colleen Staresina, President
Michelle Wulff, Vice-President
Jenniffer Sanford, Secretary
Ed Araki, Treasurer

Brant United Way (BUW)
30 Brant Ave., Brantford ON N3T 3C6
Tel: 519-752-7848; *Fax:* 519-752-7913
info@brantunitedway.org
www.brantunitedway.org
To help people in their time of need
Dianne Austin, Executive Director

British Columbia Association of Social Workers (BCASW) / Association des travailleurs sociaux de la Colombie-Britannique
#402, 1755 West Broadway, Vancouver BC V6J 4S5
Tel: 604-730-9111; *Fax:* 604-730-9112
Toll-Free: 800-665-4747
bcasw@bcasw.org
www.bcasw.org
Represents member concerns regarding the practice of social work in BC, professional education & regulation.
Dianne Heath, Executive Director
Jocelyn Chee, Manager, Member Services & Administration

British Columbia Council for Families (BCCF)
#204, 2590 Granville St., Vancouver BC V6H 3H1
Tel: 604-660-0675; *Fax:* 604-732-4813
Toll-Free: 800-663-5638
bccf@bccf.bc.ca
www.bccf.bc.ca
To strengthen, encourage & support families through information, education, research & advocacy
Sylvia Tremblay, President
Glenn Hope, Executive Director

British Columbia Federation of Foster Parent Associations (BCFFPA)
#207, 22561 Dewdney Trunk Rd., Maple Ridge BC V2X 3K1
Tel: 604-466-7487; *Fax:* 604-466-7490
Toll-Free: 800-663-9999
bcffpa@istar.ca
www.bcfosterparents.ca
To be the collective voice for all foster parents & to promote fostering; to act as a channel of communication between authorized child welfare agencies & foster parents concerning children & foster children in particular
Sheila Davis, Secretary
Melanie Filiatrault, President

Campbell River & District United Way
PO Box 135, Campbell River BC V9W 5A7
Tel: 250-702-2911
A non-profit organization that raises and distributes funds to member agencies that are providing support and services to residents in the Campbell River area. They are committed to building a strong and healthy community for all. The role of the United Way is to match the resources (and fundraising campaign) to those areas of greatest need.
Brad Bayly, Community Development Coordinator

Canada Without Poverty / Canada Sans Pauvreté
#1210, 1 Nicholas St., Ottawa ON K1N 7B7
Tel: 613-789-0096; *Fax:* 613-244-5777
Toll-Free: 800-810-1076
www.cwp-csp.ca
To eradicate poverty in Canada by promoting income and social security for all Canadians, and by promoting poverty eradication as a human rights obligation.
Rob Rainer, Executive Director
Kelly Law, Associate Director

Canadian Association for the Prevention of Discrimination & Harassment in Higher Education (CAPDHHE) / Association canadienne pour la prévention de la discrimination et ou harcèlement en milieu d'enseignement supérieur (ACPDHMES)
c/o University of British Columbia, Vancouver BC V6T 1Z2
Tel: 604-822-4859; *Fax:* 604-822-3260
amlong@ubc.ca
www.capdhhe.org
To provide professional development for individuals employed at colleges & universities in the area of discrimination & harassment, including harassment as identified under human rights law
Anne-Marie Long, President

Canadian Association of Sexual Assault Centres (CASAC) / Association canadienne des centres contre les agressions à caractère sexuel (ACCCACS)
77 East 20th Ave., Vancouver BC V5V 1L7
Tel: 604-876-2622; *Fax:* 604-876-8450
casac01@shaw.ca
www.casac.ca
To work for an end to violence against women & toward women's equality; to provide a national voice for anti-rape workers.

Canadian Association of Social Workers (CASW) / Association canadienne des travailleurs sociaux (ACTS)
#402, 383 Parkdale Ave., Ottawa ON K1Y 4R4
Tel: 613-729-6668; *Fax:* 613-729-9608
casw@casw-acts.ca
www.casw-acts.ca
To represent Canadian professional social workers; To strengthen & advances the social work profession in Canada; To preserve excellence within the profession
Eugenia Repetur Moreno, Executive Director

Canadian Career Development Foundation (CCDF) / Fondation canadienne pour le développement de carrière (FCDC)
#202, 119 Ross Ave., Ottawa ON K1Y 0N6
Tel: 613-729-6164; *Fax:* 613-729-3515
Toll-Free: 877-729-6164
information@ccdf.ca
www.ccdf.ca
To advance the understanding & practice of career development.
Lynne Bezanson, Executive Director
Sareena Hopkins, Co-Executive Director

Canadian Centre for Victims of Torture (CCVT)
194 Jarvis St., 2nd Fl., Toronto ON M5B 2B7
Tel: 416-363-1066; *Fax:* 416-363-2122
mabai@ccvt.org
www.ccvt.org
To offer support & arrange medical, legal & social care for torture victims & their families; to increase public awareness in Canada & abroad of torture & its effects upon survivors & their families
Mulugeta Abai, Executive Director

Canadian Council for Refugees (CCR) / Conseil canadien pour les réfugiés
#302, 6839, rue Drolet, Montréal QC H2S 2T1
Tel: 514-277-7223; *Fax:* 514-277-1447
info@ccrweb.ca; media@ccrweb.ca; publications@ccrweb.ca
www.ccrweb.ca
Social Media: www.facebook.com/ccrweb; twitter.com/ccrweb; www.youtube.com/ccrwebvideos
To be committed to the rights & protection of refugees in Canada & around the world & to the settlement of refugees & immigrants in Canada
Janet Dench, Executive Director
Marisa Berry-Méndez, Director, Settlement Policy
Cynthia Beaudry, Coordinator, Youth
Colleen French, Coordinator, Communications & Networking

Canadian Counselling & Psychotherapy Association (CCPA) / L'Association canadienne de counseling et de psychothérapie (ACCP)
#114, 223 Colonnade Rd. South, Ottawa ON K2E 7K3
Tel: 613-237-1099; *Fax:* 613-237-9786
Toll-Free: 877-765-5565
info@ccpa-accp.ca
www.ccpa-accp.ca
CCPA is a national, bilingual organization dedicated to the enhancement of the counselling profession in Canada. It promotes policies & practices which support the provision of accessible, competent, & accountable counselling services throughout the human lifespan, & in a manner sensitive to the pluralistic nature of society.
Lorna Martin, President
Barbara MacCallum, Executive Director

Canadian Crossroads International (CCI) / Carrefour canadien international
#201, 49 Bathurst St., Toronto ON M5V 2P2
Tel: 416-967-1611; *Fax:* 416-967-9078
Toll-Free: 877-967-1611
info@cintl.org
www.cintl.org
Social Media: www.facebook.com/CanadianCrossroads; twitter.com/Crossroads_CCI; www.youtube.com/user/CanadianCrossroads
CCI is a development organization that is reducing poverty & increasing women's rights around the world. It works with local organizations in West Africa, Southern Africa & South America. Organizations in developing countries select Canadian, partner organizations working on similar issues, so that they can help develop programs & meet their development goals. CCI supports the exchange of skilled volunteers. It is a registered charity, BN: 129814570RR0001.
Darlene Bessey, Chair
Karen Takacs, Executive Director
Aranka Somlo, Executive Assistant

Canadian Feed The Children (CFTC)
174 Bartley Dr., Toronto ON M4A 1E1
Tel: 416-757-1220; *Fax:* 416-757-3318
Toll-Free: 800-387-1221
contact@canadianfeedthechildren.ca
www.canadianfeedthechildren.ca
To alleviate the impact of poverty on children; we work with local partners overseas & in Canada to enhance the well-being of children & the self-sufficiency of their families & communities.
Jim Dahl, Executive Director

Canadian Grandparents' Rights Association (CGRA)
#207, 14980 - 104 Ave., Surrey BC V3R 1M9
Tel: 604-585-8242; *Fax:* 604-585-8241
Toll-Free: 866-585-8242
cgra222@vcn.bc.ca
www.vcn.bc.ca/cgra222/
Promotes, supports, and assists Grandparents and their families in maintaining or re-establishing family ties and family stability where the family has been disrupted; especially those ties between grandparents and grandchildren.
Nancy Wooldridge, National President
Florence Knight, National Director

Canadian Social Work Foundation (CSWF) / Fondation canadienne du service social
PO Box 64177, 1620 Scott St., Ottawa ON K1Y 4V2
Tel: 613-729-6668; *Fax:* 613-729-9608
casw@casw-acts.ca
www.casw-acts.ca
To edit & publish books, papers, journals & other forms of literature respecting social work in order to disseminate information to the public; to encourage studies; to promote, develop & sponsor activities strengthening social work
Ellen Oliver, President

Canadian Society for the Prevention of Cruelty to Children (CSPCC)
PO Box 700, 362 Midland Ave., Midland ON L4R 4P4
Tel: 705-526-5647; *Fax:* 705-526-0214
cspcc@bellnet.ca
www.empathicparenting.org
To increase public awareness of the long-term consequences of child abuse & neglect; to encourage primary prevention initiatives for improved nurturing of children in their earliest years of life
E.T. Barker, President

Canadian Urban Institute (CUI)
PO Box 612, #402, 555 Richmond St. West, Toronto ON M5V 3B1
Tel: 416-365-0816; *Fax:* 416-365-0650
cui@canurb.com
www.canurb.com
The Canadian Urban Institute (CUI) is a non-profit organization dedicated to providing solutions to important issues that have an impact on the quality of life in urban areas and communicating those solutions to a wide audience through a variety of media.
Glen Murray, President & CEO

Canadians Addressing Sexual Exploitation (CASE) / Canadiens opposés à l'exploitation sexuelle (COES)
360 County Rd. 31, Belle River ON N0R 1A0
Tel: 519-728-3432
case@4case.ca
www.4case.ca
C.A.S.E believes that pornography has a negative impact on men, children, women, and communities and therefore their mission is to exist to protect all children from sexual explotation and their vision is to education, influence, and partner.
Mary Hawkley, President

Canadians Concerned About Violence in Entertainment (C-CAVE)
167 Glen Rd., Toronto ON M4W 2W8
Tel: 416-961-0853; *Fax:* 416-929-2720
info@c-cave.com
www.c-cave.com
To provide public education on research findings related to media violence through popular culture, commodities marketed primarily to children, adolescents & adults.
Rose Anne Dyson, Chairperson

Carrefour communautaire de Chibougamau
CP 163, 512, rte 167, Chibougamau QC G8P 2K6
Tél: 418-748-7266
Brigitte Rosa, Coordonnatrice
Huguette Fradet, Présidente

Castlegar United Way
1995 - 6 Ave., Castlegar BC V1N 4B7
Tel: 250-365-7331; *Fax:* 250-365-5778
office@castlegar.unitedway.ca
www.castlegar.unitedway.ca
To build & help sustain a quality of community life that is good for families & business.
Steve Martin, President

Catholic Charities of The Archdiocese of Toronto
#400, 1155 Yonge St., Toronto ON M4T 1W2
Tel: 416-934-3401; *Fax:* 416-934-3402
info@catholiccharitiestor.org
www.catholiccharitiestor.org
Catholic Charities of the Archidiocese of Toronto is dedicated to ensuring the provision of health and social sciences and to provide leadership and advocacy on behalf of the member agencies and those in need. The people served live and work throughout the Greater Toronto Area, as well as, in Simcoe, Durham, Peel, and York.
Maryann Burton, Association Administrator

Centraide Bas St-Laurent
#303, 1555, boul. Jacques Cartier, Mont-Joli QC G5H 2W1
Tél: 418-775-5555; *Téléc:* 418-775-5525
direction@centraidebsl.org
www.centraidebsl.org
Organisme sans but lucratif de lutte à la pauvreté et de soutien aux personnes démunies.
Michel Daigle, Directeur général

Centraide Centre du Québec
#200, 154, rue Dunkin, Drummondville QC J2B 5V1
Tél: 819-477-0505; *Téléc:* 819-477-6719
bureau@centraide-cdq.ca
www.centraide-cdq.ca
Média social: www.facebook.com/pages/Centraide_cdq/152071968150658; twitter.com/centraide_cdq
Rassembler les personnes et les ressources du Centre-du-Québec afin de contribuer au développement social de la communauté et d'améliorer la qualité de vie de ses membres les plus vulnérables et ce, en lien avec les organismes communautaires.
Annie Jean, Directrice générale

Centraide du Grand Montréal / Centraide of Greater Montréal
493, rue Sherbrooke ouest, Montréal QC H3A 1B6
Tél: 514-288-1261; *Téléc:* 514-350-7282
communications@centraide-mtl.org
centraide-mtl.org
To maximize financial & volunteer resources in order to promote mutual aid, social commitment, & self-reliance as effective means of improving the quality of life of the community, & especially of its neediest members
Michèle Thibodeau-DeGuire, Présidente et Directrice générale

Centraide Duplessis
#217, 456, rue Arnaud, Sept-Iles QC G4R 3B1
Tel: 418-962-2011; *Fax:* 418-968-4694
administration@centraideduplessis.org
Denis Miousse, Directeur général

Centraide Estrie
1150, rue Belvédère sud, Sherbrooke QC J1H 4C7
Tél: 819-569-9281; *Téléc:* 819-569-5195
centraide_estrie@qc.aibn.com, bureau@estrie.centraide.ca
www.estrie.centraide.ca
Vise à soutenir les organismes bénévoles et communautaires engagés directement auprès des clientèles les plus démunies et vulnérables.
Claude Forgues, Directeur général

Centraide Gaspésie Iles-de-la-Madeleine
#E216, 230, rte du Parc, Sainte-Anne-des-Monts QC G4V 2C4
Tél: 418-763-2171; *Téléc:* 418-763-7677
centraidegim@globetrotter.net
www.gim.centraide.ca
Soulager la misère et la souffrance humaine.
Yvon Lemieux, Directeur général

Centraide Gatineau-Labelle-Hautes-Laurentides
671, rue de la Madone, Mont-Laurier QC J9L 1T2
Tél: 819-623-4090; *Téléc:* 819-623-7646
bureau@glhl.centraide.ca
www.gatineaulabellehlaurentides.centraide.ca
Annie Lajoie, Directrice générale

Centraide Haute-Côte-Nord/Manicouagan
#301, 858, rue de Puyjalon, Baie-Comeau QC G5C 1N1
Tél: 418-589-5567; *Téléc:* 418-295-2567
info@centraidehcnmanicouagan.ca
www.centraidehcnmanicouagan.ca
Christine Brisson, Directrice générale

Centraide KRTB-Côte-du-Sud
100, 4e av, La Pocatière QC G0R 1Z0
Tél: 418-856-5105; *Téléc:* 418-856-4385
centraideportage@bellnet.ca
centraidekrtbcotedusud.org
Notre mission est d'aider les gens, d'affecter les ressources en fonction des besoins, d'améliorer la qualité de vie de chacun et de renforcer le soutien communautaire. Donnez un coup de main au destin et participez aux efforts déployés par le Mouvement Centraide Portage-Taché.
Sylvain Roy, Directeur général

Centraide Lanaudière
674, rue St-Louis, Joliette QC J6E 2Z6
Tél: 450-752-1999
www.centraide-lanaudiere.com
Média social: www.facebook.com/275362692481275
Promouvoir l'entraide, le partage et l'engagement bénévole et communautaire
Sylvie Savoie, Directrice générale

Centraide Laurentides
CP 335, 281, rue Brière, Saint-Jérôme QC J7Z 5T9
Tél: 450-436-1584; *Téléc:* 450-436-3025
bureau@laurentides.centraide.ca
www.centraidelaurentides.org
Contribuer, par la promotion du partage et de l'engagement bénévole et communautaire, à la construction d'une société d'entraide vouée à l'amélioration de la qualité de vie des personnes en difficulté
Suzanne M. Piché, Directrice générale
Monique Richer, Présidente
Violette Gingras, Directrice de communications

Centraide Mauricie
880, Place Boland, Trois-Rivières QC G8Z 4H2
Tél: 819-374-6207; *Téléc:* 819-374-6857
centraide.mauricie@bellnet.ca
www.centraidemauricie.ca
Travailler à un changement social pour une société plus juste, plus humaine et plus démocratique à travers la promotion de l'entraide, la solidarité et l'engagement bénévole afin de répondre aux besoins socio-économiques de notre communauté.
Lise Beaulieu, Directrice générale

Centraide Outaouais
74, boul. Montclair, Gatineau QC J8Y 2E7
Tél: 819-771-7751; *Téléc:* 819-771-0301
information@centraide-outaouais.qc.ca
www.centraide-outaouais.qc.ca
Mobiliser le gens et rassembler les ressources pour améliorer la qualité de vie de personnes plus vulnérables et contribuer au développement de collectivités solidaires.
Guylaine Beaulieu, Directrice générale

Centraide Québec
#101, 3100, av Bourg-Royal, Québec QC G1C 5S7
Tél: 418-660-2100; *Téléc:* 418-660-2111
centraide@centraide-quebec.com
www.centraide-quebec.com
Média social: www.facebook.com/centraidequebec; www.youtube.com/user/CentraideQuebec
Levées de fonds et attribution de subventions à 166 organismes communautaires pour aider les personnes les plus démunies
Bruno Marchand, Président/Directeur général

Centraide Richelieu-Yamaska
320, ave. de la Concorde nord, Saint-Hyacinthe QC J2S 4N7
Tél: 450-773-6679; *Téléc:* 450-773-4734
bureau@centraidery.org
www.richelieuyamaska.centraide.ca
Centraide Portage-Taché, c'est une organisation charitable, qui repose sur l'engagement bénévole et qui se donne comme mission d'améliorer les conditions de vie des plus démuni(e)s de son territoire.
Manon Bouthot, Directrice générale

Centraide Saguenay-Lac St-Jean
#107, 475, boul. Talbot, Chicoutimi QC G7H 4A3
Tél: 418-543-3131; *Téléc:* 418-543-0665
centraideslsj@bellnet.ca
www.centraidesaglac.ca
Rassembler et développer des ressources financières et bénévoles afin d'aider les diverses communautés du Saguenay-Lac-St-Jean à organiser et à promouvoir l'entreaide, l'engagement social et la prise en charge afin d'améliorer la qualité de vie de sa collectivité et de ses membres les plus démunis et les plus vulnérables.
Martin St-Pierre, Directeur général

Centraide sud-ouest du Québec
#200, 100, rue Ste-Cécile, Salaberry-de-Valleyfield QC J6T 1M1
Tél: 450-371-2061; *Téléc:* 450-377-2309
centraid@rocler.qc.ca
www.centraidesudouest.org
Grâce à votre don, il y a du changement possible. En effet, la misère qu'elle soit physique, morale, psychologique ou matérielle peut toucher tout le monde, peu importe la classe sociale. Donner à Centraide Sud-Ouest, c'est susciter un changement positif dans notre communauté
Steve Hickey, Directeur général

Centre for Suicide Prevention
#320, 1202 Centre St. SE, Calgary AB T2G 5A5
Tel: 403-245-3900; *Fax:* 403-245-0299
csp@suicideinfo.ca
www.suicideinfo.ca
To acquire & distribute suicide prevention information.
Diane Yackel, Executive Director

The Child Abuse Survivor Monument Project (CASMP)
274 Rhodes Ave., Toronto ON M4L 3A3
Tel: 416-469-4764; *Fax:* 416-963-8892
mci@irvingstudios.com
www.childabusemonument.org
To build a memorial monument for & by survivors of child abuse to assist with the personal & social healing of the ravages of child abuse
Michael C. Irving, Artistic Director

Child Care Advocacy Association of Canada (CCAAC) / Association canadienne pour la promotion des services de garde à l'enfance (ACPSGE)
#704, 151 Slater St., Ottawa ON K1P 5H3
Toll-Free: 866-878-3096
info@ccaac.ca
www.ccaac.ca
To work toward expanding the child care system & improving its quality; To advocate for the development of an affordable, comprehensive, high-quality, not-for-profit child care system that is supported by public funds & accessible to every Canadian family who wishes to use it
Ann McCrorie, Chair
Sue Delanoy, Coordinator

Child Welfare League of Canada (CWLC) / Ligue pour le bien-être de l'enfance du Canada (LBEC)
226 Argyle Ave., Ottawa ON K2P 1B9
Tel: 613-235-4412; *Fax:* 613-235-7616
info@cwlc.ca
www.cwlc.ca
To provide public education on the needs of all children, youth & their families through research, information & other services directed toward enhancing & improving public awareness; to facilitate the development of standards in services to children, youth & their families; to encourage excellence in the delivery of these services
Peter M. Dudding, Chief Executive Officer

Christie-Ossington Neighbourhood Centre (CONC)
854 Bloor St. West, Toronto ON M6G 1M2
Tel: 416-534-8941; *Fax:* 416-534-8704
www.conccommunity.org
The Christie Ossington Neighbourhood Centre is dedicated to improving the quality of life in the Christie Ossington community by working in collaboration with residents, community institutions, agencies, local businesses and stakeholders to create a safe and healthy community.
Lynn Daly, Executive Director
Danny Anckle, Chair

Community Action Resource Centre (CARC)
1652 Keele St., Toronto ON M6M 3W3
Tel: 416-652-2273; *Fax:* 416-652-8992
info@communityarc.ca
www.communityarc.ca
The Community Action Resource Centre works to build the capacity of communities by mobilizing resources and providing supportive social services, for the empowerment of individuals and groups with a focus on serving the most vulnerable and disadvantaged. Services are offered in English, Portugese and Spanish.

Community Social Planning Council of Toronto (CSPC)
#1001, 2 Carlton St., Toronto ON M5B 1J3
Tel: 416-351-0095; *Fax:* 416-351-0107
info@socialplanningtoronto.org
www.socialplanningtoronto.org
Social Media: twitter.com/planningtoronto
The Council is an independent body that promotes community-based, social policy, planning & civic participation at both the local & city-wide levels through analysis & action-oriented research on social issues.
John Campey, Executive Director
Maria Serrano, Director, Operations

Comox Valley United Way
PO Box 3097, Courtenay BC V9N 5N3
Tel: 250-338-1151; *Fax:* 250-897-1099
June Munro, Executive Director

Confédération des organismes familiaux du Québec (COFAQ)
#205, 4360 rue D'Iberville, Montréal QC H2H 2L8
Tél: 514-521-4777; *Téléc:* 514-521-6272
famille@cofaq.qc.ca
www.cofaq.qc.ca
Représenter les familles et revendiquer leurs droits auprès des diverses instances publiques et privées; promouvoir des projets innovateurs et le développement d'expertises satisfaisant aux besoins des familles et leurs organisations; réaliser des activités de soutien auprès des membres
Henri Lafrance, Président
Paule Blain Clotteau, Vice-présidente
Suzette East, Secrétaire
Franciene Mucci, Trésorière

Cooper Institute / L'Institut Cooper
81 Prince St., Charlottetown PE C1A 4R3
Tel: 902-894-4573; *Fax:* 902-368-7180
www.cooperinstitute.ca
Cooper Institute is an education and community development centre in the province of Prince Edward Island, Canada. The main program areas of our organization are focussed on livable income for all, food sovereignty and cultural diversity and inclusion. Within these programs, we conduct research and popular education projects on provincial, national, and international level.
Joe Byrne, President

COSTI Immigrant Services
Education Centre, 1710 Dufferin St., Toronto ON M6E 3P2
Tel: 416-658-1600; *Fax:* 416-658-8537
info@costi.org
www.costi.org
COSTI provides educational, social & employment support to help immigrants in the greater Toronto area attain self-sufficiency in Canadian society. Services are provided in over 60 languages.
Bruno M. Suppa, President
Mario J. Calla, Executive Director

Cowichan United Way
#102, 435 Trunk Rd., Duncan BC V9L 2P5
Tel: 250-748-1312; *Fax:* 250-748-7652
office@cowichan.unitedway.ca
www.cowichan.unitedway.ca
To fundraise for charities; To provide guidance & counsel to charitable organization; To take leadership role in raising awareness of community needs
Jackie Scott, Secretary
Carol Stenberg, Executive Secretary

Deep River District United Way
PO Box 188, Deep River ON K0J 1P0
Tel: 613-584-3985
office@deepriver.unitedway.ca
www.deepriver.unitedway.ca
To unite the major fund-raising campaigns of benevolent, charitable, health & community welfare agencies in the Deep River district by means of an annual campaign & other fundraising activities
Bob French, President
Nancy Bourgoin, Treasurer
Sue Deon, Secretary

Delta Family Resource Centre
Jane & Sheppard Mall, #14, 2721 Jane St., Toronto ON M3L 1S3
Tel: 416-747-1172; *Fax:* 416-747-7415
contactus@dfrc.ca
www.dfrc.ca
To support the needs of families & children within the community; Offering services in English, Spanish, Italian, Hindi, Punjabi, Laotian, Gujarati, Somali, Cantonese, Tamil, Mandarin, Thi, Ewe, Twi, Urdu, Dari, & Ga
Rosalyn Miller, Executive Director

Distress Centres Ontario (DCO)
#1016, 30 Duke St. West, Kitchener ON N2H 3W5
Tel: 416-486-2242; *Fax:* 519-342-0970
info@dcontario.org
www.dcontario.org
To transfer best practices between member centres; To promote, support & sustain member agencies
Sheena Carpenter, Secretary-Treasurer

Doorsteps Neighbourhood Services
PO Box 95, #211, 1700 Wilson Ave., Toronto ON M3L 1B2
Tel: 416-243-5480; *Fax:* 416-243-7406
mbeckford@doorsteps.ca
www.doorsteps.ca
To focus on community education, prevention, & the enhancement of resiliency of individuals & communities
Morris Beckford, Executive Director

Dying with Dignity (DWD) / Mourir dans la dignité
#802, 55 Eglinton Ave. East, Toronto ON M4P 1G8
Tel: 416-486-3998; *Fax:* 416-486-5562
Toll-Free: 800-495-6156
info@dyingwithdignity.ca
www.dyingwithdignity.ca
To improve the quality of dying for all Canadians in accordance with their own wishes, values & beliefs
Donald Babey, President

Edmonton Social Planning Council (ESPC)
#37, 9912 - 106 St., Edmonton AB T5K 1C5
Tel: 780-423-2031; *Fax:* 780-425-6244
info@edmontonsocialplanning.ca
www.edmontonsocialplanning.ca
Social Media: www.facebook.com/pages/Edmonton-Social-Planning-Council/37296571206; twitter.com/edmontonspc
To provide leadership within the community by addressing & researching social issues, informing public discussion & influencing social policy
Susan Morrissey, Executive Director
John Pater, President

Elgin-St.Thomas United Way Services
300 South Edgeware Rd., St Thomas ON N5P 4L1
Tel: 519-631-3171; *Fax:* 519-631-9253
office@stthomasunitedway.ca
www.stthomasunitedway.ca
To be a leader in improving the quality of life for all people in Elgin County.
Sharon Lechner, CEO

Eston United Way
PO Box 23, Eston SK S0L 1A0
Tel: 306-962-3612
Raising money in order to create positive and lasting changes in communities.
Brenda Myer, President

Family & Community Support Services Association of Alberta (FCSSAA)
Belmead Professional Bldg., #106, 8944 - 182 St., Edmonton AB T5T 2E3
Tel: 780-415-4790; *Fax:* 780-415-4793
fcssaa@telus.net
www.fcssaa.ab.ca
To advocate on behalf of local communities & programs to the general public, municipal governments, regional services, provincial & national agencies, & authorities; To educate individuals, communities, boards, & staff
Sharlyn White, Executive Director
Jeff Carlson, President
Judy Macknee, Executive Assistant

Family Mediation Canada (FMC) / Médiation Familiale Canada
#180, 55 Northfield Dr. East, Waterloo ON N2K 3T6
Tel: 519-585-3118; *Fax:* 416-849-0643
Toll-Free: 877-362-2005
fmc@fmc.ca
www.fmc.ca
To improve the provision for cooperative conflict resolution in areas such as separation & divorce, child welfare, adoption, parent & teen counselling, age-related issues, & wills & estates
Mary Damianakis, President
Linda Bonnell, Secretary
Carrie Cekerevac, Manager, Operations

Family Service Canada (FSC) / Services à la famille - Canada
c/o 312 Parkdale Ave., Ottawa ON K1Y 4X45
Tel: 613-722-9006; *Fax:* 613-722-8610
Toll-Free: 800-668-7808
info@familyservicecanada.org
www.familyservicecanada.org
To promote families as the primary source of nurturing & development of individuals, their relationship in families & communities, through promoting & ensuring the best policies & services for families in Canada.
Margaret Fietz, President & CEO
Judi Varga-Toth, National Programs Manager
Sylvie M. Charron, Executive Assistant

Family Service Toronto (FST)
355 Church St., Toronto ON M5B 1Z8
Tel: 416-595-9230; *Fax:* 416-595-0242
sau@familyservicetoronto.org
www.fsatoronto.com
FST is a social service agency that helps low-income individuals & families in need. It is a registered charity, BN: 107376063RR0001.
Fran Odette, President
Margaret Hancock, Executive Director

Fédération des associations de familles monoparentales et recomposées du Québec (FAFMRQ) / Federation of Single-Parent Family Associations of Québec
584, rue Guizot est, Montréal QC H2P 1N3
Tél: 514-729-6666; *Téléc:* 514-729-6746
fafmrq.info@videotron.ca
www.fafmrq.org
Travailler à améliorer les conditions socio-économiques des familles monoparentales et recomposées du Québec.
Sylvie Lévesque, Directrice générale

Fédération des centres d'action bénévole du Québec (FCABQ)
1557, av Papineau, Montréal QC H2K 4H7
Tél: 514-843-6312; *Téléc:* 514-843-6485
Ligne sans frais: 800-715-7515
info@fcabq.org
www.fcabq.org
Promouvoir l'action bénévole au Québec; former un centre d'action bénévole; organiser la semaine de l'action bénévole.
Pierre Riley, Directeur général

Findhelp Information Services
#125, 543 Richmond St. W., Toronto ON M5V 1Y6
Tel: 416-392-4605; *Fax:* 416-392-4404
www.211toronto.ca
To provide comprehensive information & referral services in English, French & other languages; resources for information & referral professionals; call centre; newcomer services;

Possibilities online employment resource centre; training & outreach
Janice Hayes, Executive Director
Bruce Reynolds, President

Flemingdon Neighbourhood Services
#104, 10 Gateway Blvd., Toronto ON M3C 3A1
Tel: 416-424-2900; *Fax:* 416-424-3455
info@fnservices.org
www.fnservices.org
Committed to enhancing the over-all quality of life for residents of Flemingdon Park and the City of Toronto by increasing access to information and community resources for our clients through advocacy, empowerment and education.
John Carey, Executive Director

Food Banks Canada / Banques alimentaires Canada
#303, 2968 Dundas St. West, Toronto ON M6P 1Y8
Tel: 416-203-9241; *Fax:* 416-203-9244
info@cafb-acba.ca
www.foodbankscanada.ca
To act as the voice for the hungry in Canada; To find short term & long term solutions for Canadians who are assisted by food banks
Katharine Schmidt, Executive Director
Ron L'Esperance, Chair
Robin Garrett, Vice-Chair
Riki Turofsky, Secretary
Brian Meagher, Treasurer
Marzena Gersho, Director, National Partnerships & Programs
Shawn Pegg, Senior Manager, Policy & Research

Foster Parent Support Services Society (FPSS)
145 - 735 Goldstream Ave., Victoria BC V9B 2X4
Tel: 778-430-5459; *Fax:* 778-430-5463
admin@fpsss.com
www.fpsss.com
The FPSS Foster Parent Support Services Society is a Grass Roots organization committed to providing meaningful and accessible support, education and networking services which will continually enhance the skills and abilities of foster parents to deliver the best care possible to the children in their homes.
Margaret Howley, Executive Director

Fred Victor Centre
59 Adelaide St. East, Toronto ON M5C 1K6
Tel: 416-364-8228; *Fax:* 416-364-4728
www.fredvictor.org
To offer a continuum of community services, housing options and advocacy for adults who are experiencing homelessness, marginalization and poverty. Over 150 beds and spaces are available across 6 sites and programs.
Mark Aston, Executive Director

Frontiers Foundation (FF/OB) / Fondation Frontière
419 Coxwell Ave., Toronto ON M4L 3B9
Tel: 416-690-3930; *Fax:* 416-690-3934
Toll-Free: 800-668-4130
marcoguzman@frontiersfoundation.ca
www.frontiersfoundation.ca
Social Media: www.facebook.com/pages/Frontiers-Foundation/66661443145
To implement the enduring relief of human poverty throughout Canada & also abroad in tangible advancement projects.
Marco A. Guzman, Executive Director
Lawrence Gladue, President

Good Jobs for All Coalition
Toronto ON
Tel: 416-937-9378
communications@goodjobsforall.ca
goodjobsforall.ca
Social Media: www.facebook.com/groups/goodjobs; twitter.com/goodjobsforall
The Good Jobs for All Coalition is an alliance of community, labour, social justice, youth and environmental organizations in the Toronto region. It was formed in 2008 to start a focused dialogue on how to improve living and working conditions in Canada's largest urban centre.
Preethy Sivakumar, Coordinator

Goodwill Industries of Alberta
8761 - 51 Ave., Edmonton AB T6E 5H1
Tel: 780-944-1414; *Fax:* 780-463-7396
goodwill@goodwill.ab.ca
www.goodwill.ab.ca
Social Media: twitter.com/goodwillab
To help persons with disabilities & disadvantages; To build a strong future through rehabilitation & training
Wendy Doughty, Chair
Heather Rennebohm, President & CEO

Goodwill Industries of Toronto
#1400, 365 Bloor St. East, Toronto ON M4W 3L4
Tel: 416-362-4711; *Fax:* 416-362-0720
TTY: 416-815-4791
info@goodwill.on.ca
www.goodwill.on.ca
To provide effective vocational programs & services to people who face employment barriers to enable them to become as independent as possible
Myna Kota, Manager, External Relations

GRAND Society
c/o #509, 14 Spadina Rd., Toronto ON M5R 3M4
Tel: 416-513-9404
To provide emotional support to grandparents who have been denied access to their grandchildren; to make the public & professionals aware of this problem; to influence provincial family law to recognize the rights of grandparents
Joan Brooks, President/Chair
L. Watson, Vice-President

Grande Prairie & Region United Way
#213, 11330 - 106 St., Grande Prairie AB T8V 7X9
Tel: 780-532-1105; *Fax:* 780-532-3532
info@gpunitedway.org
www.gpunitedway.org
United Ways brings people together to strenghten our community- nuturing health and well being, building self-sufficiency, reducing barriers to independence, creating oppourtunities for children and youth, promoting understanding, dignity and respect. All dollars are raised locally are allotted to local and regional agencies.
Gladys Blackmore, President/Executive Director

Groupe d'entraide des personnes séparées/divorcées
#106, 161, av du Parc, Chibougamau QC G8P 2H3
Tél: 418-748-2777
Rita Tremblay

Human Concern International (HCI)
PO Box 3984, Stn. C, 877 Shefford Rd., Ottawa ON K1Y 4P2
Tel: 613-742-5948; *Fax:* 613-742-7733
Toll-Free: 800-587-6424
info@humanconcern.org
www.humanconcern.org
Social Media: www.facebook.com/HumanConcern; twitter.com/humanconcernint
To help alleviate human suffering by investing in humanity, through long-term development projects for sustainability, & emergency relief assistance during times of dire need
Kaleem Akhtar, Executive Director
Garnayl Abdi, Program Officer
Dalia Adballah, Administrative & Child Sponsorship Officer

Huron United Way
PO Box 211, #207, 35A East St., Goderich ON N7A 3Z2
Tel: 519-524-7900; *Fax:* 519-524-1121
huronunitedway@tcc.on.ca
www.huronunitedway.ca
United Way is a registered charitable organization. They are a community of people with a common goal of caring. By heling people in their community, they are changing lives. Fundraising is an essential part of the United Way's mission.
Jerry McDonnell, Chair

Imagine Canada
#600, 2 Carlton St., Toronto ON M5B 1J3
Tel: 416-597-2293; *Fax:* 416-597-2294
Toll-Free: 800-263-1178
info@imaginecanada.ca
www.imaginecanada.ca
Social Media: www.facebook.com/ImagineCanada; twitter.com/ImagineCanada; www.linkedin.com/groups?about=&gid=1866345&trk=anet_ug_grppro; www.youtube.com/ImagineCanada
To support Canada's charities, non-profit organizations, & socially conscious businesses
Marcel Lauzière, President & Chief Executive Officer
Cathy Barr, Senior Vice-President
Stephen Faul, Vice-President, Strategic Communications & Business Development
Michelle Gauthier, Vice-President, Public Policy & Community Engagement

InformOntario (IO)
3010 Forest Glade Dr., Windsor ON N8R 1L5
info@informontario.on.ca
www.informontario.on.ca
Represents 65 community information centres around the province; assists the Centres by developing subject & name authorities for database management, standards for statistical data gathering & standards for management of information centres; encourages professional development through annual conferences & workshops; supports local fundraising efforts; community information centres (CICs) provide information about human services & make referrals appropriate to the needs of the individual; the service blends resources & expertise in information technology with a committment to the individual; some CIC's also provide a social reporting service by analyzing inquiry data, trends & gaps in human services & reporting these findings to appropriate agencies & governments
Trudy Beaulne, President
Cathy Gowland, Treasurer

International Social Service Canada (ISSC) / Service Social International Canada (SSIC)
#506, 1580 Merivale Rd., Ottawa ON K2G 4B5
Tel: 613-236-6161; *Fax:* 613-233-7306
issc@issc-ssic.ca
www.issc-ssic.ca
To provide linkages to social service organizations worldwide; To help resolve individual & family problems resulting from the movement of people across national borders
Richard Chamney, President

Kids First Parent Association of Canada
3916 32nd St. NW, Edmonton AB T6T 1J9
Tel: 604-291-0088
info@kidsfirstcanada.org
www.kidsfirstcanada.org
Concerned with the care & well-being of children; parents lobbying to protect their right & choice to raise children in a family setting; to provide support to anyone wanting to further this cause in other communities
Helen Ward, President

Kids Help Phone (KHP) / Jeunesse j'écoute
#300, 439 University Ave., Toronto ON M5G 1Y8
Tel: 416-586-5437; *Fax:* 416-586-0651
Toll-Free: 800-668-6868
info@kidshelpphone.ca
kidshelpphone.ca
Social Media: www.facebook.com/KidsHelpPhone; twitter.com/kidshelpphone
To provide a national, bilingual, 24-hours a day, 365 days of the year, toll-free, professionally staffed, confidential counselling service to young people; To help young people deal with concerns large or small; To contribute to awareness of children's issues & the development of policies & practices to help Canadian children
Alisa Simion, Vice-President

Lakeland United Way
PO Box 8369, #204, 1301 - 8th Ave., Cold Lake AB T9M 1N3
Tel: 780-826-0045; *Fax:* 780-639-2699
luw2699@telus.net
www.lakelandunitedway.com
Umbrella fundraising organization for a variety of local charities & social services.
Ajaz Quraishi, President

Lawyers for Social Responsibility (LSR) / Avocats en faveur d'une conscience sociale (AFCS)
c/o 5120 Carney Rd. NW, Calgary AB T2L 1G2
Tel: 403-282-8260
bevdelong@shaw.ca
www.peacelawyers.ca
To advise the public, politicians, & government officials on the application of the law to foreign & defence policies; To call for use of law, not use of force, to resolve conflicts
Beverley Delong, President

Lloydminster & District United Way
4419 - 52nd Ave., Lloydminster AB T9V 0Y8
Tel: 780-875-3743; *Fax:* 780-875-3793
luw@telusplanet.net
www.lloydminster.unitedway.ca
Eric Rounce, President

Manitoba Association of Women's Shelters (MAWS)
c/o Genesis House, PO Box 389, Winkler MB R6W 4A6
Tel: 204-325-9957; *Fax:* 204-325-5889
Crisis Hot-Line: 877-977-0007
www.maws.mb.ca
MAWS is dedicated to the elimination of violence against women. It was created to provide support to member shelters for abused women & their children. It works to share information & resources with its member shelters, increase training of staff & increase services for clients. By acting as a unified voice for its members, the association also aims to enhance negotiations with funders. It is a registered charity, BN: 880786892RR0001.
Angela Braun, Chair
Jen Kehler, Provinicial Coordinator

Manitoba Block Parent Program
466 Gertrude Ave., Winnipeg MB R3L 0M8
Tel: 204-284-7562
bppw@mts.net
www.winnipegblockparents.mb.ca
It is the mission of the Block Parent Program to provide a network of police-screened easily recognizable, safe places for the members of the community, primarily children.
George Jarvis, President

Manitoba Institute of Registered Social Workers (MIRSW)
#101, 2033 Portage Ave., Winnipeg MB R3J 0K6
Tel: 204-888-9477; *Fax:* 204-831-6359
www.mirsw.mb.ca
To certify members; To act as the regulatory arm of the social work profession; To encourage ethical standards of practice to protect the public
Liz McLeod, President

La Mine d'Or, entreprise d'insertion sociale
449, 3e Rue, Chibougamau QC G8P 1N6
Tél: 418-748-4183; *Téléc:* 418-748-2837
informations@laminedor.org
www.laminedor.org
Organisme sans but lucratif, qui a pour mission l'insertion sociale & professionnelle des personnes en situation d'exclusion; offre une passerelle aux participants vers le marché du travail, la formation ou d'autres alternatives
Suzan Amyot, Présidente

Mouvement ATD Quart Monde Canada / ATD Fourth World Movement Canada
6747, rue Drolet, Montréal QC H2S 2T1
Tél: 514-279-0468; *Téléc:* 514-279-7759
www.atdquartmonde.ca
Développer un courant de refus de la misère en donnant la priorité aux plus pauvres, dans le respect des droits et de la dignité de la personne; contribuer à l'action du Mouvement dans le monde
Monique Morval, Présidente

Neepawa & District United Way
PO Box 1545, Neepawa MB R0J 1H0
Tel: 204-476-5803
office@neepawa.unitedway.ca
www.neepawa.unitedway.ca
Local United Way Chapter raising funds to help community organization.
Angela Pearen-Burnside, President

Nelson & District United Way
PO Box 89, Nelson BC V1L 5P7
Tel: 250-352-6012
united_way@netidea.com
www.uw.kics.bc.ca
Local chapter of the United Way raising funds for community organizations.
Carol-Joy Kaill, President

New Brunswick Association of Food Banks
c/o Grand Falls Regional Food Bank Inc., 363 Portage Rd., Grand Falls NB E3Z 1M2
Tel: 506-473-2001; *Fax:* 506-473-6883
To support member agencies in their efforts to alleviate hunger; to serve as a provincial voice for same.
Max Oates, Provincial Coordinator

New Brunswick Association of Social Workers (NBASW) / Association des travailleurs sociaux du Nouveau-Brunswick
PO Box 1533, Stn. A, Fredericton NB E3B 5G2
Tel: 506-459-5595; *Fax:* 506-457-1421
Toll-Free: 877-495-5595
nbasw@nbasw-atsnb.ca
www.nbasw-atsnb.ca
To regulate the profession of social work; to protect the public; To set standards; To promote the profession
Miguel LeBlanc, Executive Director

New Brunswick Block Parent Association (NBBPAI)
#47, 100 Howe Crt., Oromocto NB E2V 2R3
Fax: 506-446-5992
Toll-Free: 800-665-4900
info@blockparent.ca
www.blockparent.ca
To provide immediate assistance to community members, especially children & seniors, through a safety network; To serve 35 communities & 500 homes throughout New Brunswick
Linda Patterson, President

Newfoundland & Labrador Association of Social Workers (NLASW) / Association des travailleurs sociaux de Terre-Neuve et Labrador
PO Box 39039, 177 Hamlyn Rd., St. John's NL A1E 5Y7
Tel: 709-753-0200; *Fax:* 709-753-0120
info@nlasw.ca
www.nlasw.ca
To ensure excellence in social work in Newfoundland & Labrador; To speak out & take appropriate action on issues of social concern; To disseminate information & provide opportunities for continuing education; To provide consultation to agencies involved in training for or delivering human services; To promote the development & the enhancement of social service delivery system suited to the needs of Newfoundlanders
Lisa Crockwell, Executive Director

Non-Smokers' Rights Association (NSRA) / Association pour les droits des non-fumeurs
#221, 720 Spadina Ave., Toronto ON M5S 2T9
Tel: 416-928-2900; *Fax:* 416-928-1860
toronto@nsra-adnf.ca
www.nsra-adnf.ca
To promote public health by stopping illness & death due to tobacco, including second-hand smoke
Lorraine Fry, Executive Director
Peter Holt, Coordinator, Membership

Northumberland United Way
#203, 1005 Elgin St. West, Cobourg ON K9A 5J4
Tel: 905-372-6955; *Fax:* 905-372-4417
office@northumberland.unitedway.ca
www.northumberland.unitedway.ca
To raise & allocate funds in an efficient manner & to promote the effective delivery of services in response to current & emerging social needs in Northumberland County.
Lynda Kay, Executive Director
Cathy Cavanagh, Manager, Finance & Operations

Nova Scotia Association of Social Workers (NSASW) / Association des travailleurs sociaux de la Nouvelle-Écosse
Plaza 1881, #106, 1891 Brunswick St., Halifax NS B3J 2G8
Tel: 902-429-7799; *Fax:* 902-429-7650
nsasw@nsasw.org
www.nsasw.org
To promote & regulate the practice of social work so the members can provide a high standard of service that respects diversity, promotes social justice & enhances the worth, self-determination & potential of individuals, families & communities
Robert R. Shepherd, Executive Director

Nova Scotia Block Parent Advisory Board
Tel: 902-849-3525
michael.byrne@novascotiablockparent.com
www.novascotiablockparent.com
Jean Hiltz, Chairman

One Parent Families Association of Canada / Association des familles uniparentales du Canada
PO Box 111, Pickering ON L1V 2R2
Tel: 905-831-7098; *Fax:* 905-831-2580
Toll-Free: 877-773-7714
opfa222@aol.com
www.opfa.net
To develop & provide a broad comprehensive program for the enlightenment & guidance of single parents & their children on the special problems they encounter & for assistance on the various readjustments involved.
R. Bounds, President

Ontario Association for Marriage & Family Therapy (OAMFT)
PO Box 693, Tottenham ON L0G 1W0
Toll-Free: 800-267-2638
admin@oamft.on.ca
www.oamft.on.ca
To serve members of the association, the profession of marriage & family therapy, & the public; To uphold the Code of Ethics of the American Association for Marriage & Family Therapy
Marion Goertz, President
Ed Santana, Executive Director
Donna Chamberlain, Contact, Membership Information
Anita Pal, Contact, Media Relations

Ontario Association of Children's Aid Societies (OACAS) / Association ontarienne des sociétés de l'aide à l'enfance
75 Front St. East, 2nd Fl., Toronto ON M5E 1V9
Tel: 416-987-7725; *Fax:* 416-366-8317
info@oacas.org
www.oacas.org
The voice of child welfare in Ontario, dedicated to providing leadership for the achievement of excellence in the protection of children & in the promotion of their well-being within their families & communities
Jeanette Lewis, Executive Director
Dennis Nolan, President

Ontario Association of Interval & Transition Houses (OAITH)
#1404, 2 Carleton St., Toronto ON M5B 1J3
Tel: 416-977-6619
oaith2@web.ca
www.oaith.ca
To work towards social change by ensuring that the voices of abused women are heard; To remove barriers to equality for women & children
Paula Valois, Chair, Board of Directors
Lee-Ann Lee, Chair, Member Education & Training
Michelle Reis-Amores, Chair, Membership

Ontario Association of Social Workers (OASW) / Association des travailleuses et travailleurs sociaux de l'Ontario (ATTSO)
410 Jarvis St., Toronto ON M4Y 2G6
Tel: 416-923-4848; *Fax:* 416-923-5279
info@oasw.org
www.oasw.org; www.findasocialworker.ca; www.socialworkjobs.ca
To act as the voice of social workers in Ontario
Pina Simonetta, Communications Coordinator

Ontario Block Parent Program Inc. (OBPPI)
902 Maitland St., London ON N5Y 2X1
Tel: 519-438-2016; *Toll-Free:* 800-563-2771
obppi@live.com
www.blockparent.on.ca
To provide immediate assistance through a safety network & to offer supportive community education programs; to provide a network of police screened, easily recognizable safe homes for members of the community, especially children, to turn to in times of distress; to educate children about the program, safety on the streets & safety within the home; to develop promotions & materials to educate the community about the program, latch key children & streetproofing; to work together with the police, educators & other community groups toward safer communities
Marg Rooke, Acting Chair

Ontario Coalition for Better Child Care (OCBCC)
#206, 489 College St., Toronto ON M6G 1A5
Tel: 416-538-0628; *Fax:* 416-538-6737
Toll-Free: 800-594-7514
info@childcareontario.org
www.childcareontario.org
Social Media: twitter.com/ChildCareON
Advocates on behalf of Ontario's non-profit, licensed child care programs
Tracy Saarikoski, President
Carrol Anne Sceviour, Vice-President

Ontario Coalition of Rape Crisis Centres (OCRCC) / Coalition des centres anti-viol de l'Ontario
PO Box 6597, Stn. A, Toronto ON M5S 1A8
Tel: 416-597-1171
Crisis Hot-Line: 416-597-8808
www.ocrcc.ca
To work for prevention & eradication of sexual assault; to implement legal, social & attitudinal changes regarding sexual assault; to provide mechanism for communication, education & mobilization to alleviate political & geographical isolation of rape crisis centres in Ontario; to encourage, direct & generate research into sexual violence; to work with Canadian Association of Sexual Assault Centres (see listing) on developing national policies; to liaise with other provincial organizations addressing similar issues
Jacqueline Benn-John, President

Ontario Community Support Association (OCSA) / Association ontarienne de soutien communautaire
#104, 970 Lawrence Ave. West, Toronto ON M6A 3B6
Tel: 416-256-3010; *Fax:* 416-256-3021
Toll-Free: 800-267-6272
ocsainfo@ocsa.on.ca
www.ocsa.on.ca
To support & represent the common goals of community-based, not-for-profit health & social service organizations which assist individuals to live at home in their own community
Susan Thorning, CEO

Ontario Municipal Social Services Association (OMSSA) / Association des services sociaux des municipalités de l'Ontario
#2500, 1 Dundas St West, Toronto ON M5G 1Z3
Tel: 416-642-1659; *Fax:* 416-979-4627
info@omssa.com
www.omssa.com
To promote high standards of competency within the profession to ensure quality delivery of human services in communities; To improve social policies & programs in the areas of affordable housing, homelessness prevention, children's services, & social assistance; To act as the voice for Consolidated Municipal Service Managers in Ontario
Kira Heineck, Executive Director
Brenda Patterson, President
Patti Moore, Vice-President
David Rennie, Secretary-Treasurer

The Ontario Trillium Foundation / La Fondation Trillium de l'Ontario
45 Charles St. East, 5th Fl., Toronto ON M4Y 1S2
Tel: 416-963-4927; *Fax:* 416-963-8781
Toll-Free: 800-263-2887
TTY: 416-963-7905
trillium@trilliumfoundation.org
www.trilliumfoundation.org
To work with others to make strategic investments to build healthy, sustainable & caring communities in Ontario
L. Robin Cardozo, CEO

Ordre professionnel des travailleurs sociaux du Québec (OPTSQ)
#520, 255, boul. Crémazie est, Montréal QC H2M 1M2
Tél: 514-731-3925; *Téléc:* 514-731-6785
Ligne sans frais: 888-731-9420
info.general@optsq.org
www.optsq.org
Assurer la protection du public par le contrôle de l'exercice de la profession, par la formation continue, et le développement professionnel.
Claude Leblond, Président

Parcelles de tendresse
CP 582, Chibougamau QC G8P 2Y8
Tél: 418-748-3644
Pierette Boulay

Parent Finders of Canada
19 English Bluff Rd., Delta BC V4M 2M4
Tel: 604-948-1069; *Fax:* 604-948-2036
www.parentfinders.org
To assist adult adoptees/foster persons & birth relatives to obtain background information from adoption files kept in social services departments; To assist in search & reunion; To promote a feeling of openness about the adoption experience & a better understanding about the longing for a reunion between adult adoptees & birth relatives
Joan E. Vanstone, National Director

Parent Support Services Society of BC (PSSS)
#204, 5623 Imperial St., Burnaby BC V5J 1G1
Tel: 604-669-1616; *Fax:* 604-669-1636
Toll-Free: 877-345-9777
office@parentsupportbc.ca
www.parentsupportbc.ca
The Society promotes parent support circles to help parents & guardians learn positive parenting skills & receive emotional support. The circles are anonymous, confidential self-help groups that meet weekly to learn effective, non-abusive ways to discipline their children. It is a registered charity, BN: 106778780RR0001.
Cheryl MacDonald, President
Carol Ross, Executive Director

Parents-secours du Québec inc. (PSQI)
#203, 17, rue Fusey, Trois-Rivières QC G8T 2T3
Ligne sans frais: 800-588-8173
info@parentssecours.ca
www.parentssecours.ca
Parents-Secours du Québec inc. (PSQI) est un organisme à but non lucratif qui assure la sécurité et la protection des enfants et des aînés-es en offrant un réseau de foyers-refuges sécuritaires tout en contribuant à promouvoir la prévention par l'information et l'éducation.

People, Words & Change (PWC) / Monde des mots
Heartwood House, 153 Chapel St., Ottawa ON K1N 1H5
Tel: 613-234-2494; *Fax:* 613-234-4223
info@pwc-ottawa.ca
www.nald.ca/pwc
To teach adults to read & write in English
Kae McColl, Coordinator

Petites-Mains
7595 St.-Laurent Boul., Montréal QC H2R 1W9
Tél: 514-738-8989; *Téléc:* 514-738-6193
info@petitesmains.com
www.petitesmains.com
Petites-Mains a pour mission de venir en aide aux gens, surtout les femmes immigrantes, monoparentales, sans revenu et prestataires de l'Assistance-Emploi. Il aide ces femmes à sortir de leur isolement, à échanger avec d'autres, à apprendre un métier, à intégrer le marché du travail et à vivre en dignité dans la société.
Nahid Aboumansour, Contact

PFLAG Canada Inc.
PO Box 29211, 1633 Mountain Rd., Moncton NB E1G 4R3
Tel: 506-869-8191; *Fax:* 506-387-8349
Toll-Free: 888-530-6777
execdirector@pflagcanada.ca
www.pflagcanada.ca
Social Media: www.facebook.com/PFLAGcanada
To support individuals with questions & concerns about sexual orientation or gender identity; to make Canada a more accepting place for persons of all gender identities & sexual orientations
Cherie MacLeod, Executive Director
Stacy Green, Executive Director
Jayme Harper, Vice-President
Ryan Walkinshaw, Treasurer

Plan Canada
#1001, 95 St. Clair Ave. West, Toronto ON M4V 3B5
Tel: 416-920-1654; *Fax:* 416-920-9942
Toll-Free: 800-387-1418
info@plancanada.ca
plancanada.ca
Social Media: www.facebook.com/PlanCanada; twitter.com/PlanCanada
To help children, their families, & communities in developing countries; To raise funds through sponsorship program & implement programs in health, education, & community development overseas
Rosemary McCarney, President & CEO

Porcupine United Way
PO Box 984, #312, 60 Wilson Ave., Timmins ON P4N 7H6
Tel: 705-268-9696; *Fax:* 705-268-9700
puw@ntl.sympatico.ca
porcupineunitedway.com
To promote the organized capacity of people to care for one another
Jean Warren, Executive Director

Portage Plains United Way
224 Saskatchewan Ave. East, Portage la Prairie MB R1N 0K9
Tel: 204-857-4440; *Fax:* 204-239-1740
ppuw@mts.net
www.portageplainsuw.ca
To unite our community to enhance the quality of life for those in need
Darrell Lee, President
Tara Pettinger, Executive Director

Powell River & District United Way
PO Box 379, Powell River BC V8A 5C2
Tel: 604-485-2791
bennobabe@shaw.ca
www.unitedwayofpowellriver.ca
Pat Hull, President

Prince Edward Island Association of Social Workers / Association des travailleurs sociaux de l'Ile-du-Prince-Édouard
81 Prince St., Charlottetown PE C1A 4R3
Tel: 902-368-7337; *Fax:* 902-368-7080
vrc@eastlink.cat
To acknowledge & promote the work of social workers in Prince Edward Island; To advance the social work profession throughout the province, to ensure well-being for residents
Kelly MacWilliams, President

Prince Edward Island Block Parent Advisory Board
RR#3 Middleton, Summerside PE C1N 4J9
Tel: 902-887-2480; *Fax:* 902-887-2874
kjoffer@eastlink.ca
www.blockparent.ca
To create safer environment for children & others by designating & creating awareness of safe Block Parent homes in the community.

Prince George United Way
1600 - 3rd Ave., Prince George BC V2L 3G6
Tel: 250-561-1040; *Fax:* 250-562-8102
trevorw@pguw.bc.ca
www.pguw.bc.ca

To promote the organized capacity of persons to care for one another through voluntarism, leadership & education; To ensure the effective raising & allocation of charitable funds for community-based social services; To foster the effective provision of services that are in the best interest of the community
Trevor Williams, Executive Director
Scotty Raitt, President

Project Genesis
4735 Côte-Ste.-Catherine, Montréal QC H3W 1M1
Tel: 514-738-2036; *Fax:* 514-738-6385
Community group that provides community organization, advocacy, and education, as well as legal advice involving tenant rights, debt & bankruptcy, family law, and immigration
Michael Chervin, Contact

Québec Association of Marriage & Family Therapy (QAMFT) / Association québécoise pour la thérapie conjugale et familiale
#300, 360 Victoria Avenue, Westmount QC H3H 2N4
info@qamft.org
www.qamft.org
To promote understanding, research & education in the field of couple & family therapy & to ensure that public needs are met by practitioners of the highest quality
Andrew Sofin, President

Reena
927 Clark Ave. West, Thornhill ON L4J 8G6
Tel: 905-889-6484; *Fax:* 905-889-3827
Toll-Free: 877-324-4114
info@reena.org
www.reena.org
To integrate developmentally disabled people towards independent living within community, with emphasis on Judaic programming
Sandy Keshen, President & CEO
Minnie Ross, Manager, Communications

Regroupement des Auberges du Coeur
#32, 2000, boul Saint-Joseph est, Montréal QC H2H 1E4
Tél: 514-523-8559; *Téléc:* 514-523-5148
info@aubergesducoeur.com
www.aubergesducoeur.com
Défendre l'existence & l'autonomie des ressources communautaires d'hébergement pour jeunes adolescents & jeunes adultes en difficulté ou sans abri; agir comme porte-parole des jeunes sans abri; favoriser entre les maisons, les jeunes & les partenaires des communautés d'appartenance de chacune des Auberges des échanges sur les besoins des jeunes
Rémi Fraser, Directeur général

The Right to Die Society of Canada (RTDSC) / Société Canadienne pour le Droit de Mourir (SCDM)
145 Macdonell Ave., Toronto ON M6R 2A4
Tel: 416-535-0690; *Toll-Free:* 866-535-0690
contact-rtd@righttodie.ca
www.righttodie.ca
To work with legislators, policy makers & the public to expand the range of humane options for people who are suffering intolerably from incurable conditions & who want a self-directed dying; to work with sufferers to expand their awareness of the options that are legal & may be appropriate for them
Ruth von Fuchs, President & Secretary

Ronald McDonald House Charities of Canada (RMHC) / Oeuvres pour enfants Ronald McDonald du Canada
McDonald's Place, Toronto ON M3C 3L4
Tel: 416-443-1000; *Fax:* 416-446-3762
Toll-Free: 800-387-8808
www.rmhc.ca
To help children in need by improving the physical & emotional quality of life for children with serious illnesses, disabilities &/or chronic conditions, allowing them to lead happier, healthier & more productive lives
Richard Ellis, President
Rem Langan, Chair
Devon Friedman, Manager, Communications & Development

Samaritan's Purse Canada
20 Hopewell Way NE, Calgary AB T3J 5H5
Tel: 403-250-6565; *Fax:* 403-250-6567
Toll-Free: 800-663-6500
info@samaritan.org
www.samaritanspurse.ca
A nondenominational evangelical Christian international relief organization with projects around the globe, meeting both physical & spiritual needs of people who are victims of war, poverty, natural disasters, disease & famine. Focus is on emergency relief & development programs, medical projects.

International offices in Canada, Australia, Germany, Ireland, the Netherlands, the U.S. & the U.K.
Jeff Adams, Communications Director
Franklin Graham, President & CEO
Sean P. Campbell, Executive Director

Saskatchewan Association of Social Workers (SASW) / Association des travailleurs sociaux de la Saskatchewan
Edna Osborne House, 2110 Lorne St., Regina SK S4P 2M5
Tel: 306-545-1922; *Fax:* 306-545-1895
Toll-Free: 877-517-7279
sasw@accesscomm.ca
www.sasw.ca
To conduct the work of a professional regulator; To act as the voice of social workers in Saskatchewan; To develop & maintain standards of knowledge, skill, conduct, & competence among members to serve & protect the public interest
Carole Bryant, President
Richard Hazel, Executive Director
Bill Tingley, Registrar
Diane Lauritzen, Secretary
Leann Keach, Treasurer

Secours aux lépreux (Canada) inc. (SLC) / Leprosy Relief (Canada) Inc. (LR)
#305, 1805, rue Sauvé ouest, Montréal QC H4N 3H4
Tél: 514-744-3199; *Téléc:* 514-744-9095
Ligne sans frais: 866-744-3199
info@slc-lr.ca
www.slc-lr.ca
Venir en aide médicalement et socialement aux personnes affectées par la lèpre.
Paul E. Legault, Président
Jacques Chopleau, Vice-Président
Marie Gilbert, Secretaire
Christiane Beauvois, Trésorière

Sex Information & Education Council of Canada (SIECCAN) / Conseil d'information et éducation sexuelles du Canada
850 Coxwell Ave., Toronto ON M4C 5R1
Tel: 416-466-5304; *Fax:* 416-778-0785
sieccan@web.ca
www.sieccan.org
To inform & educate public & professionals about all aspects of human sexuality in order to support the positive integration of sexuality into people's lives
Michael Barrett, Executive Director
Stephen Holzapfel, Chair
Alexander McKay, Research Coordinator

ShareLife
1155 Yonge St., Toronto ON M4T 1W2
Tel: 416-934-3411; *Fax:* 416-934-3412
Toll-Free: 800-263-2595
sharelife@archtoronto.org
www.sharelife.org
ShareLife is the Catholic Community's response to helping the whole community through Catholic agencies by effectively raising & allocating funds
Arthur Peters, Executive Director
Bill Steinburg, Communications Manager

Social Planning & Research Council of BC (SPARC)
4445 Norfolk St., Burnaby BC V5G 0A7
Tel: 604-718-7733; *Fax:* 604-736-8697
info@sparc.bc.ca
www.sparc.bc.ca
Social Media: twitter.com/SPARC_BC
To promote the social, economic & environmental well-being of citizens & communities; to advocate the principles of social justice, equality & the dignity & worth of all people in our multicultural society; to conduct research & planning for public information, education & citizen participation in developing social policies & programs
Clement Woo, Executive Director
Daniel Hill, President

Social Planning Council of Ottawa-Carleton / Conseil de planification sociale d'Ottawa-Carleton
#501, 280 Metcalfe St., Ottawa ON K2P 1R7
Tel: 613-236-9300; *Fax:* 613-236-7060
office@spcottawa.on.ca
www.spcottawa.on.ca
To provide the residents of Ottawa-Carleton with the means to exercise informed leadership on issues affecting their social & economic well-being
Diane Urquhart, Executive Director

Social Planning Council of Winnipeg
412 McDermot Ave., Winnipeg MB R3A 0A9
Tel: 204-943-2561; *Fax:* 204-942-3221
info@spcw.mb.ca
www.spcw.mb.ca
Social Media: www.facebook.com/group.php?gid=54256670713
To identify & define social planning issues, needs & resources in the community; to develop & promote policy & program options to policy-makers; to support community groups & the voluntary human service sector; to raise community awareness of social issues & human service needs, social policy options & service delivery alternatives; to serve as a link between the three levels of government & community neighbourhoods
Wayne Helgason, Executive Director

Society of Transition Houses - BC & Yukon
#325, 119 West Pender St., Vancouver BC V6B 1S5
Tel: 604-669-6943; *Fax:* 604-682-6962
Toll-Free: 800-661-1040
admin@bcysth.ca
www.bcysth.ca
To educate, promote & advocate on issues of violence against women; to support an organization that provides or seeks to provide shelter &/or services to women & their children who experience violence
Shabna Ali, Executive Director

SOS Children's Villages Canada / SOS Villages d'Enfants Canada
#200, 244 Rideau St., Ottawa ON K1N 5Y3
Tel: 613-232-3309; *Fax:* 613-232-6764
Toll-Free: 800-767-5111
info@soschildrensvillages.ca
www.soschildrensvillages.ca
To assist SOS-Children's Villages in Canada & abroad through financial & operating support; to care for orphaned, abandoned & other children in need of long-term placement; to create opportunities for children to become happy, stable, responsible members of society
Boyd McBride, National Director

Springtide Resources
PO Box 7, #220, 215 Spadina Ave., Toronto ON M5T 2C7
Tel: 416-968-3422; *Fax:* 416-968-2026
TTY: 416-968-7335
info@womanabuseprevention.com
www.springtideresources.org
Social Media: www.facebook.com/springtide.resources
The non-profit organization aims to increase public awareness of the many aspects of violence against women & its effect on children. It works to change the social conditions that subject women to abuse by providing training & resources proactively. It is a registered charity, BN: 108053653RR0001.
Marsha Sfeir, Executive Director

Streetkids' Foundation (SKF)
First Global Place, #201, 7 Concorde Pl., Toronto ON M3C 3N4
Tel: 416-391-1801; *Fax:* 416-391-2616
To assist street kids to become self-sufficient; to reduce the number of teens who take to the streets both in Canada & abroad
J.H. Vowles, President
Robert Atkinson, Treasurer

Swift Current United Way
PO Box 485, #203B Professional Bldg. - 12 Cheadle St. West, Swift Current SK S9H 0A9
Tel: 306-773-4828; *Fax:* 306-773-4870
unitedway@sasktel.net
Jennifer Olfert, Executive Director

Thompson Crisis Centre
PO Box 1226, Thompson MB R8N 1P1
Tel: 204-677-9668; *Fax:* 204-677-9042
Toll-Free: 800-442-0613
To provide immediate assistance through a walk-in facility & a 24-hour emergency telephone service; to provide a safe place for the women & their children who are victims of physical/emotional abuse; to provide services to women & their children needing longer term support

Thompson, Nicola, Cariboo United Way
#203, 239 Victoria St., Kamloops BC V2C 2A1
Tel: 250-372-9933; *Fax:* 250-372-5926
office@unitedwaytnc.ca
www.unitedwaytnc.ca
To enable all citizens to join in a community wide effort to fund & provide in consort with others, effective delivery of health & social services & programs in response to the needs of the community
Brenda Aynsley, Executive Director

Toronto Community Foundation (TCF)
#1603, 33 Bloor St. East, Toronto ON M4W 3H1
Tel: 416-921-2035; *Fax:* 416-921-1026
info@tcf.ca
www.tcf.ca
To connect philanthropic individuals and families to charitable organizations in Toronto. TCF invests charitable gifts from donors into income-earning endowment funds, and makes grants from the earnings to support a range of charities
John B. MacIntyre, Chair
Rosalyn Morrison, VP, Community Initiatives
Carol Turner, VP, Finance

United Generations Ontario (UGO) / Générations Unies Ontario
1185 Eglinton Ave. East, Toronto ON M3C 3C6
Tel: 416-426-7115; *Fax:* 416-426-7421
info@unitedgenerations.ca
www.unitedgenerations.ca
Coalition of human service organizations & individuals who are dedicated to promoting programs that bring young & old together in a spirit of cooperation, mutual support, shared affection & regard; to empower people to take a constructive part in the life of their own communities & to create a vital volunteer exchange in caring & sharing
Russ De Cou, Executive Director
Richard Cox, Chief Operating Officer

United Way Central & Northern Vancouver Island
3156 Barons Rd., Nanaimo BC V9T 4B5
Tel: 250-729-7400; *Fax:* 250-729-8084
info@uwcnvi.ca
www.uwcnvi.ca
To improve lives by engaging individuals & mobilizing collective action
Lynne Brown, COO

United Way Community Services of Guelph & Wellington
85 Westmount Rd., Guelph ON N1H 5J2
Tel: 519-821-0571; *Fax:* 519-821-7847
info@unitedwayguelph.com
www.unitedwayguelph.com
Steve Allen, President
Ken Dardano, Executive Director

United Way for the City of Kawartha Lakes (UWVC)
50 Mary St. West, Lindsay ON K9V 2N6
Tel: 705-878-5081; *Fax:* 705-878-0475
office@ckl.unitedway.ca
www.ckl.unitedway.ca
To promote the organized capacity of people & groups in Victoria County to care for each other
Penny Barton Dyke, Executive Director

United Way of Ajax-Pickering-Uxbridge
#303, 230 Westney Rd. West, Ajax ON L1S 7J5
Tel: 905-686-0606; *Fax:* 905-686-0609
office@uwayapu.org
www.uwayapu.org
To increase the ability of the people of Ajax & Pickering to care for one another through leadership in community problem solving including generation & allocation of financial & other resources
Edna Klazek, Executive Director

United Way of Brandon & District Inc.
Scotia Towers, 201-1011 Rosser Ave., Brandon MB R7A 0L5
Tel: 204-571-8929; *Fax:* 204-727-8939
office@brandonuw.ca
www.brandonuw.ca
Debbie Arsenault, CEO

United Way of Burlington & Greater Hamilton
177 Rebecca St., Hamilton ON L8R 1B9
Tel: 905-527-4543; *Fax:* 905-527-5152
uway@uwaybh.ca
www.uwaybh.ca
To empower a diverse community to achieve positive social development
Len Lifchus, CEO

United Way of Calgary & Area
#600, 1202 Centre St. SE, Calgary AB T2G 5A5
Tel: 403-231-6265; *Fax:* 403-355-3135
uway@calgaryunitedway.org
www.calgaryunitedway.org
To invest in 250 programs offered by 130 agencies in Calgary, Airdrie, Cochrane, High River, Okotoks & Strathmore
Linda Hohol, Chair
Ruth Ramsden-Wood, President

United Way of Cambridge & North Dumfries
150 Main St., Cambridge ON N1R 6P9
Tel: 519-621-1030; *Fax:* 519-621-6220
ron@uwcambridge.on.ca
www.uwcambridge.on.ca
To enhance the quality of life in Cambridge & North Dumfries by caring for & contributing to community needs
Heidi Duarte, Manager, Development & Marketing
Brad Park, Director, Development
Ron Dowhaniuk, Executive Director

United Way of Canada - Centraide Canada
#404, 56 Sparks St., Ottawa ON K1P 5A9
Tel: 613-236-7041; *Fax:* 613-236-3087
Toll-Free: 800-267-8221
info@unitedway.ca
www.unitedway.ca; www.centraide.ca
To increase the organized capacity of people to care for one another
Peter Doig, Chair
Al Hatton, President/CEO

United Way of Cape Breton
Cabot House, PO Box 1929, 500 Kings Rd., 2nd Fl., Sydney NS B1P 6W4
Tel: 902-562-5226; *Fax:* 902-562-5721
unitedway@ns.aliantzinc.ca
www.sydney.unitedway.ca
Allister Taylor, Executive Director

United Way of Central Alberta
4811 - 48th St., Red Deer AB T4N 1S6
Tel: 403-343-3900; *Fax:* 403-309-3820
info@caunitedway.ca
www.caunitedway.ca
To improve lives & build community by engaging individuals & mobilizing collective action
Heather Gardiner, CEO

United Way of Chatham-Kent County
PO Box 606, 425 McNaughton Ave. West, Chatham ON N7M 5K8
Tel: 519-354-0430; *Fax:* 519-354-9511
united.way@united-kent.on.ca
unitedway.chatham-kent.on.ca
To build the organized capacity of people to care for one another
Karen S. Kirkwood-Whyte, Executive Director
Patrick Weaver, President

United Way of Cranbrook & Kimberley
PO Box 657, 930 Baker St., Cranbrook BC V1C 4J2
Tel: 250-426-8833; *Fax:* 250-426-5455
cranunitedway@shaw.ca; office@cranbrook.unitedway.ca
www.cranbrook.unitedway.ca
To ensure the effective raising & allocation of charitable funds for community based social services that are in the best interest of the community
Donna Brady, Executive Director

United Way of Cumberland County
PO Box 535, 43 Prince Arthur St., Amherst NS B4H 4A1
Tel: 902-667-2203; *Fax:* 902-667-3819
unitedway.cumberland@ns.aliantzinc.ca
Jeff Brennan, Chair
Cathy Skinner, Executive Director

United Way of Elrose & District Corp.
PO Box 123, Elrose SK S0L 0Z0
Tel: 306-378-2532
Jack Elliott, Chair

United Way of Estevan
PO Box 611, Estevan SK S4A 2A5
Tel: 306-634-7348; *Fax:* 306-634-2197
secretary@unitedwayofestevan.com
James Lainton, Chair

United Way of Fort McMurray
#207, 9912A Franklin Ave., Fort McMurray AB T9H 2K5
Tel: 780-791-0077; *Fax:* 780-791-0088
office@fortmcmurray.unitedway.ca
fmunitedway.com
To provide effective support for social health & welfare services in the community of Fort McMurray
Diane Shannon, Executive Director

United Way of Greater Moncton & Southeastern NB Region Inc. / Centraide de la région du Grand Moncton et du Sud-Est du NB Inc.
PO Box 768, 123 Halifax St., Moncton NB E1C 8M9
Tel: 506-858-8600; *Fax:* 506-858-0584
office@moncton.unitedway.ca
www.gmsenbunitedway.ca
Social Media: www.facebook.com/group.php?gid=76467525679
To raise funds to increase the organized capacity of people to care for one another
Debbie McInnis, Executive Director

United Way of Greater Saint John Inc.
61 Union St., 2nd Fl., Saint John NB E2L 1A2
Tel: 506-658-1212; *Fax:* 506-633-7724
office@saintjohn.unitedway.ca
www.saintjohn.unitedway.ca
Elizabeth Jadoo, Executive Director

United Way of Greater Simcoe County
#100, 136 Bayfield St., Barrie ON L4M 3B1
Tel: 705-726-2301; *Fax:* 705-726-4897
info@unitedwaysimcoecounty.on.ca
www.unitedwaysimcoecounty.on.ca
United Way of Greater Simcoe County has been making a difference in our community for over 47 years by assessing local needs and distributing resources to help those most in need.
Seija Suutari, CEO
Bethany Obermayer, Director, Finance & Administration

United Way of Haldimand-Norfolk
PO Box 472, #3, 39 Kent St. North, Simcoe ON N3Y 3L5
Tel: 519-426-5660; *Fax:* 519-426-0017
Toll-Free: 866-792-7394
uw@unitedwayhn.on.ca
www.unitedwayhn.on.ca
To improve people's lives & to strengthen the community
Evelyn Nobbs, Executive Director
Mark Liota, President

United Way of Halifax Region
Royal Bank Bldg., 46 Portland St., 7th Fl.., Halifax NS B2Y 1H4
Tel: 902-422-1501; *Fax:* 902-423-6837
info@unitedwayhalifax.ca
www.unitedwayhalifax.ca
To strengthen neighbourhoods & communities by providing programs & services that link people & resources, encourage participation & increase giving
Catherine J. Woodman, President/CEO

United Way of Halton Hills
PO Box 286, Georgetown ON L7G 4Y5
Tel: 905-877-3066; *Fax:* 905-877-3067
office@haltonhills.unitedway.ca
www.haltonhills.unitedway.ca
To provide leadership in the raising & responsible allocation of funds to meet human needs & to improve social conditions in a caring community
Janet Foster, Executive Director

United Way of Kingston, Frontenac, Lennox & Addington
417 Bagot St., Kingston ON K7K 3C1
Tel: 613-542-2674; *Fax:* 613-542-1379
uway@unitedwaykfla.ca
www.unitedwaykfla.ca
To strengthen & support the organized capacity of our diverse community to care for one another
Bhavana Varma, President
Clara Lambert, Director, Finance
Maura Doyle, Campaign Manager

United Way of Kitchener-Waterloo & Area
20 Erb St. West, 11th Fl., Waterloo ON N2L 1T2
Tel: 519-888-6100; *Fax:* 519-888-7737
info@united-way-kw.org
www.uwaykw.org
Through collaboration, build on our community's resources & strengthen our capacity to improve the quality of life for all
Dave Fitzpatrick, Board Chair
Jan Varner, CEO

United Way of Lanark County
15 Bates Dr., Carleton Place ON K7C 4J8
Tel: 613-253-9074; *Fax:* 613-235-9075
unitedway@trytel.com
www.lanarkunitedway.com
Sarah Bridson, Executive Director

United Way of Leeds & Grenville
PO Box 576, 42 George St., Brockville ON K6V 5V7
Tel: 613-342-8889; *Fax:* 613-342-8850
unitedway@ripnet.com
www.uwlg.org
Judi Baril, Executive Director

United Way of Lethbridge & South Western Alberta
1277 - 3 Ave. South, Lethbridge AB T1J 0K3
Tel: 403-327-1700; *Fax:* 403-317-7940
uwaysw@telusplanet.net
www.lethbridgeunitedway.ca
To build a better community by organizing the capacity of people to care for one another

United Way of London & Middlesex
409 King St., London ON N6B 1S5
Tel: 519-438-1721; *Fax:* 519-438-9938
uwl@uwlondon.on.ca
www.uwlondon.on.ca
To exercise leadership in coordinating people & organizations to assist those in need in our community
Andrew Lockie, CEO

United Way of Milton
PO Box 212, 1 Chris Hadfield Way, Milton ON L9T 4N9
Tel: 905-875-2550; *Fax:* 905-875-2402
office@milton.unitedway.ca
www.miltonunitedway.ca
To act as a voluntary fundraising organization to serve the people of the Milton area, reaching out for & with the recognized charitable agencies to ensure human services that enhance the quality of life in our community
Anne Eadie, Executive Director

United Way of Morden & District Inc.
114 Nelson St., Morden MB R6M 1S2
Tel: 204-822-6992
mordendistrictuw@gmail.com
To serve as an umbrella group representing 17 charitable agencies in Morden & perform only one community-wide canvassing campaign on their behalf
Cindy Kolwalski, Chair

United Way of Niagara Falls & Greater Fort Erie
MacBain Community Ctr., 7150 Montrose Rd., Niagara Falls ON L2H 3N3
Tel: 905-354-9342; *Fax:* 905-354-2717
unitedway@mail.caninet.com
www.unitedwayniagara.org
Carol Stewart-Kirkby, Executive Director

United Way of North Okanagan Columbia Shuswap
3304 - 30th Ave., Vernon BC V1T 2C8
Tel: 250-549-1346; *Fax:* 250-549-1357
office@vernon.unitedway.ca
www.unitedwaynocs.com
To promote a healthy, caring inclusive community; To strenghten our community's capacity to address social issues
Linda Yule, Executive Director

United Way of Oakville (UWO)
#200, 466 Speers Rd., Oakville ON L6K 3W9
Tel: 905-845-5571; *Fax:* 905-845-0166
info@uwoakville.org
www.uwoakville.org
Bringing people & resources together to strengthen our community
Barbara Burton, CEO
Tim Johnston, Chair

United Way of Oshawa-Whitby-Clarington-Brock & Scugog
345 Simcoe St. South, Oshawa ON L1H 4J2
Tel: 905-436-7377; *Fax:* 905-436-6414
mail@unitedwayowc.com
www.unitedwayowc.com
Cindy J. Murray, Executive Director
Robert Howard, Campaign Director

United Way of Oxford
#2, 65 Springbank Ave. North, Woodstock ON N4S 8V8
Tel: 519-539-3851; *Fax:* 519-539-3209
Toll-Free: 877-280-1391
info@unitedwayoxford.ca
www.unitedwayoxford.ca
To build the organized capacity of the community to care for one another
Kelly Gilson, Executive Director

United Way of Peel Region
#408, 90 Burnhamthorpe Rd. West, Mississauga ON L5B 3C3
Tel: 905-602-3650; *Fax:* 905-602-3651
TTY: 905-602-3653
jpereira@unitedwaypeel.org
www.unitedwaypeel.org
Social Media: twitter.com/Unitedwaypeel
United Way of Peel Region was established in 1967 and serves the communities of Mississauga, Brampton and Caledon, improving social conditions so that everyone can thrive. United Way provides a strong voice for social change that strengthens communities and improves lives.
Shelley White, President/ CEO
Shirley Crocker, Vice President, Finance & Administration
Doris Mohrhardt, Vice President, Communications & Marketing

Anita Stellinga, Vice President, Community Investment

United Way of Perth County
32 Erie St., Stratford ON N5A 2M4
Tel: 519-271-7730; *Fax:* 519-273-9350
Toll-Free: 877-818-8867
info@unitedwayperth.on.ca
www.unitedwayperth.on.ca
To strengthen & support the ability of the people of our community to care for one another
Ellen Balmain, Executive Director
Shelley Groenestege, President

United Way of Peterborough & District
277 Stewart St., Peterborough ON K9J 3M8
Tel: 705-742-8839; *Fax:* 705-742-9186
office@uwpeterborough.ca
www.uwpeterborough.ca
Social Media: www.facebook.com/15103169591; twitter.com/UnitedWayPtbo
To improve lives & build community by engaging individuals & mobilizing collective action; to provide resources, services & programs for community leadership
Jim Russell, CEO

United Way of Pictou County
Victoria Plaza, PO Box 75, #1, 342 Stewart St., New Glasgow NS B2H 5E1
Tel: 902-755-1754; *Fax:* 902-755-0853
info@pictoucountyunitedway.ca
www.pictoucountyunitedway.ca
Social Media: www.facebook.com/UWPictouCounty; twitter.com/UWPictouCo
To strengthen communities by facilitating programs & services that link people & resources; encourage participation; increase giving
Jessica Smith, Executive Director

United Way of Prince Edward Island / Centraide PEI
PO Box 247, 180 Kent St., Charlottetown PE C1A 7K4
Tel: 902-894-8202; *Fax:* 902-894-9643
Toll-Free: 877-902-4438
inquiries@peiunitedway.com
www.peiunitedway.com
To provide funds needed to meet community needs & build stronger communities
Clair F. Smith, Executive Director
Paul Chaulk, President

United Way of Quinte
Sears Unity Place, PO Box 815, 249 William St., Belleville ON K8N 5B5
Tel: 613-962-9531; *Fax:* 613-962-4165
office@belleville.unitedway.ca
www.unitedwayofquinte.ca
Social Media: www.facebook.com/group.php?gid=75482448853
To provide leadership in a collaborative endeavor with our member agencies & others to increase the capacity of our community to respond to human service needs
Julia Gosson, Executive Director

United Way of Regina
1440 Scarth St., Regina SK S4R 2E9
Tel: 306-757-5671; *Fax:* 306-522-7199
office@unitedwayregina.ca
www.unitedwayregina.ca
To improve lives & to build the community by engaging individuals & mobilizing collective action
Joanne Grant, CEO
Tracey Mann, Vice-President, Community Impact & Investments
Kristin Gushuliak, Campaign Manager

United Way of St Catharines & District
#3, 80 King St., Ground Fl., St Catharines ON L2R 7G1
Tel: 905-688-5050; *Fax:* 905-688-2997
office@stcatharines.unitedway.ca
www.unitedwaysc.ca
To increase the organized capacity of people to care for one another
Frances Hallworth, Executive Director

United Way of Sarnia-Lambton
PO Box 548, 420 East St. North, Sarnia ON N7T 6Y5
Tel: 519-336-5452; *Fax:* 519-383-6032
info@theunitedway.on.ca
www.theunitedway.on.ca
To generate resources enabling the community to respond to human care priorities in Sarnia-Lambton
Dave Brown, Executive Director
Paddy Roach, Manager, Resource Development
Pamela Bodkin, Director, Community Investment & Finance

United Way of Saskatoon & Area
100, 506 - 25 St. East, Saskatoon SK S7K 4A7
Tel: 306-975-7700; *Fax:* 306-244-0583
office@unitedwaysaskatoon.ca
www.unitedwaysaskatoon.ca
Sheri Benson, Executive Director

United Way of Sault Ste Marie
7A Oxford St., Sault Ste Marie ON P6B 1R7
Tel: 705-256-7476; *Fax:* 705-759-5899
uwssm@ssmunitedway.ca
www.saultstemarie.unitedway.ca
To improve lives & build community by engaging individuals & mobilizing collective action
Gary Vipond, Executive Director

United Way of Slave Lake Society
PO Box 1985, Slave Lake AB T0G 2A0
Tel: 780-849-3820

United Way of South Eastern Alberta
PO Box 783, Stn. M, #101, 928 Allowance Ave., Medicine Hat AB T1A 7G7
Tel: 403-526-5544; *Fax:* 403-526-5244
utdway@telus.net
www.utdway.ca
Cam Jacques, President of the Board
Holly Beauchamp-Stadnicki, Director, Fund Development

United Way of South Georgian Bay
PO Box 284, #9, 275 First St., Collingwood ON L9Y 3Z5
Tel: 705-444-1141; *Fax:* 705-444-0981
dkunitedwaysgb@gmail.com
www.unitedwaysgb.ca
To serve the south Georgian Bay area by promoting, supporting & facilitating the organized capacity of people to help one another
Debbie Kesheshian, Executive Director

United Way of Stormont, Dundas & Glengarry / Centraide de Stormont, Dundas & Glengarry
331 Water St. East, Cornwall ON K6H 1A5
Tel: 613-932-2051; *Fax:* 613-932-7534
info@unitedwaysdg.com
www.unitedwaysdg.com
To improve lives & build our community by working together
Claudette Blanchard, Campaign Clerk
Kevin Wilson, President
Karen Turchetto, Executive Director

United Way of the Alberta Capital Region
15132 Stony Plain Rd., Edmonton AB T5P 3Y3
Tel: 780-990-1000; *Fax:* 780-990-0203
united@myunitedway.ca
www.unitedthisistheway.ca
To bring people & resources together to build caring, vibrant communities
Lynne Duncan, Director
Robert Ascah, Vice-President, Government Relations, Research & Analysis
Anne Smith, Secretary/Treasurer

United Way of the Central Okanagan & South Okanagan/Similkameen
202-1456 St. Paul St., Kelowna BC V1Y 2E6
Tel: 250-860-2356; *Fax:* 250-868-3206
info@unitedwaycso.com
unitedwaycso.com
Social Media: www.facebook.com/unitedwaycso; twitter.com/UnitedWayCSO; www.youtube.com/user/UnitedWayCSO
To increase the organized capacity of people in our community to care for one another
Harry Grossmith, Executive Director
Judy Doucette, Office & Finance Manager

United Way of the Fraser Valley (UWFV)
#201, 31667 South Fraser Way, Abbotsford BC V2T 1T8
Fax: 604-852-2316
Toll-Free: 888-251-7777
wayne@uwfv.bc.ca
www.uwfv.bc.ca
To promote the organized capacity of people to care for one another
Wayne Green, Executive Director

United Way of the Lower Mainland
4543 Canada Way, Burnaby BC V5G 4T4
Tel: 604-294-8929
info@uwlm.ca
www.uwlm.ca
Michael McKnight, President & CEO

United Way of Thompson Inc.
PO Box 202, Thompson MB R8N 1N1
Tel: 204-778-5564; *Fax:* 204-778-5564
uway@mts.net
To promote the organized capacity of people to care for one another
Bobbie Montean, Executive Director

United Way of Trail
792 Rossland Ave., Trail BC V1R 3T3
Tel: 250-364-0999; *Fax:* 250-364-1564
unitedw@telus.net
To raise funds which are allocated to 26 affiliated non-profit organizations
Trish Milne, Executive Director

United Way of Windsor-Essex County
#A1, 300 Giles Blvd. East, Windsor ON N9A 4C4
Tel: 519-258-0000; *Fax:* 519-258-2346
united@weareunited.com
www.weareunited.com
To promote & strengthen the organized capacity of people to care for one another
Sheila Wisdom, Executive Director

United Way of Winnipeg / Winnipeg Centraide
5 Donald St., 3rd Fl., Winnipeg MB R3L 2T4
Tel: 204-477-5360; *Fax:* 204-453-6198
uway@unitedwaywinnipeg.mb.ca
www.unitedwaywinnipeg.mb.ca
To support & strengthen the organized capacity of people to care for one another
Susan Lewis, President

United Way of York Region (UWYR)
#200, 80F Centurian Dr., Markham ON L3R 8C1
Tel: 905-474-9974; *Fax:* 905-474-0051
Toll-Free: 877-241-4516
vnorman@uwyr.on.ca
www.uwyr.on.ca
To improve the quality of life in the communities of York Region; to ascertain & address critical human needs by fostering innovative, responsible & inclusive partnerships of financial & other resources
Daniele Zanotti, CEO

United Way South Niagara (UWSN) / Centraide de Niagara Sud
Seaway Mall, 800 Niagara St., Welland ON L3C 5Z4
Tel: 905-735-0490; *Fax:* 905-735-5432
office@southniagara.unitedway.ca
www.unitedwaysouthniagara.ca
Social Media: www.facebook.com/pages/United-Way-of-South-Niagara/227801910292; twitter.com/NiagaraSouthpaw; www.youtube.com/UWSouthNiagara
To promote, develop & support the organized capacity of our community members to care for one another; to mobilize volunteer & financial resources in a common cause of caring
Bill Auchterlonie, Executive Director

United Way Toronto
26 Wellington St. East, 2nd Fl., Toronto ON M5E 1W9
Tel: 416-777-2001; *Fax:* 416-777-0962
TTY: 416-359-2083
www.unitedwaytoronto.com; www.uwgt.org
Social Media: www.facebook.com/group.php?gid=108587420188
To meet urgent human needs & improve social conditions by mobilizing the community's volunteer & financial resources in a common cause of caring
Frances Lankin, President & CEO
Alnasir Samji, Chair

United Way/Centraide (Central NB) Inc.
#400, 1133 Regent St., Fredericton NB E3B 3Z2
Tel: 506-459-7773; *Fax:* 506-451-1104
unitedwy@nbnet.nb.ca
www.unitedwaycentral.com
To be a leader in helping to create & sustain a caring & healthy community
Frank Russell, Executive Director

United Way/Centraide of the Upper Ottawa Valley Inc.
PO Box 727, 214 Church St., Pembroke ON K8A 6X9
Tel: 613-735-0436; *Fax:* 613-735-8362
Toll-Free: 888-592-2213
unitedw@nrtco.net; office@pembroke.unitedway.ca
www.pembroke.unitedway.ca
To identify & address the needs of our community by organizing the resources of community members to care for one another
Etienne Lantos, Chair

Sheila Bucholtz, Executive Director

United Way/Centraide Ottawa (UW/CO)
363 Coventry Rd., Ottawa ON K1K 2C5
Tel: 613-228-6700; *Fax:* 613-228-6730
info@unitedwayottawa.ca
www.unitedwayottawa.ca
Social Media: www.facebook.com/group.php?gid=35673670196
To bring people & resources together to build a strong, healthy, safe community for all; to build & support a network of high priority, results-oriented community services; to offer leadership in bringing the community together; to excel in fundraising; to invest resources & charitable funds in partnership with the community; to inform & engage community stakeholders
Michael Allen, President/CEO

United Way/Centraide Sudbury & District
#E6, 105 Elm St., Sudbury ON P3C 1T3
Tel: 705-560-3330; *Fax:* 705-560-3337
office@unitedwaysudbury.com
www.unitedwaysudbury.com
To increase the organized capacity of people to care for one another through effective fundraising & allocation of these funds
Michael Cullen, Executive Director

Vanier Institute of The Family (VIF) / Institut Vanier de la famille
94 Centrepointe Dr., Ottawa ON K2G 6B1
Tel: 613-228-8500; *Fax:* 613-228-8007
Toll-Free: 800-331-4937
webmaster@vifamily.ca
www.vifamily.ca
To create awareness of, & to provide leadership on the importance & strengths of families in Canada, & the challenges families face in all their diverse structures; information from the institute's research, consultation & policy development is conveyed through advocacy, education & communications vehicles to elected officials, policymakers, educators, the media, the public & Canadian families themselves
Clarence Lochhead, Executive Director
Verna Bruce, President

Victims of Violence Canadian Centre for Missing Children (VOV)
211 Pretoria Ave., Ottawa ON K1S 1X1
Tel: 613-233-0052; *Fax:* 613-233-2712
Toll-Free: 888-606-0000
vofv@victimsofviolence.on.ca
www.victimsofviolence.on.ca
To help crime victims regain control of their lives by reducing fear & trauma; to prevent future victimization through crime prevention information; to strengthen local efforts to assist crime victims & witnesses
Gary Rosenfeldt, Executive Director

Volunteer Canada / Bénévoles Canada
353 Dalhousie St. 3rd floor, Ottawa ON K1N 7G1
Tel: 613-231-4371; *Fax:* 613-231-6725
Toll-Free: 800-670-0401
info@volunteer.ca
www.volunteer.ca
Social Media: www.facebook.com/VolunteerCanada; twitter.com/VolunteerCanada; www.youtube.com/VolunteerCanada
To support volunteerism & civic participation through special projects & programs

Volunteer Grandparents (VIP)
#203, 2101 Holdom Ave., Burnaby BC V5B 0A4
Tel: 604-736-8271; *Fax:* 604-294-6814
info@volunteergrandparents.ca
www.volunteergrandparents.ca
To support & encourage multigenerational relationships & the concept of extended family by matching screened volunteers (50+) with families with children between the age of 3-14
Stephen Sjoberg, President

The War Amputations of Canada / Les Amputés de guerre du Canada
1 Maybrook Dr., Scarborough ON M1V 5K9
Tel: 416-412-0600; *Fax:* 800-219-8988
Toll-Free: 800-250-3030
customerservice@waramps.ca
www.waramps.ca
Social Media: www.facebook.com/TheWarAmps; twitter.com/thewaramps; www.youtube.com/warampsofcanada
To provide a wide range of assistance to all Canadian war amputees & child amputees; promotes the advancement of prosthetics & prosthetic research through grants to facilities undertaking research in field of prosthetics
H. Clifford Chadderton, CEO
Danita Chisholm, Director, Communications

Weyburn & District United Way
PO Box 608, Weyburn SK S4H 2K7
Tel: 306-842-7880
weyburn.unitedway@accesscomm.ca
www.weyburnunitedway.com
Gary Erickson, President

Winkler & District United Way
PO Box 1528, Winkler MB R6W 4B4
Tel: 204-829-3843
ron@wiband.ca
Karen Schellenberg, President

Yonge Street Mission (YSM)
306 Gerrard St. East, Toronto ON M5A 2G7
Tel: 416-929-9614; *Fax:* 416-929-7204
Toll-Free: 800-416-5111
info@ysm.ca
www.ysm.ca
Social Media: www.facebook.com/YongeStreetMission; twitter.com/YSM_TO
To bring God's peace, love & justice to people living with economic, social & spiritual poverty in Toronto
Andrew Williams, Mission Program Officer
Ann Barnard Ball, Mission Development Officer
Paul Davidson, Mission Operations Officer
Bill Ryan, Director, Staff Care
Jon Unger Brandt, Director, Development

Yorkton & District United Way Inc.
PO Box 44, Yorkton SK S3N 2V6
Tel: 306-783-2582; *Fax:* 306-783-2502
bandgofyorkton@sasktel.net
To unite & facilitate community fundraising on behalf of our membership of local, charitable organizations
Brian Pohorelic, Chair
Lisa Washington, Secretary

Sports

Abbotsford Female Hockey Association (AFHA)
2167 Essex Dr., Abbotsford BC V2S 7R8
info@abbotsfordfemalehockey.com
www.abbotsfordfemalehockey.com
The Abbotsford Female Hockey Association seeks to provide an opportunity for females of all ages and all skill levels to play hockey in Abbotsford in an all female league.
Jerry Ward, President

ACUC International
PO Box 1179, #3, 101 Nelson St. East, Port Dover ON N0A 1N0
Tel: 519-583-9798; *Fax:* 519-583-3247
acuchq@acuc.ca
www.acuc.es
Social Media: www.facebook.com/acucinternational
To supply quality training for sport scuba divers & instructors; To teach the highest standards in safety, sport, & marine conservation
Juan Rodriguez, President & Chief Executive Officer
Nancy Cronkwright, Vice-President & Officer Manager
Patricia Molina, Vice-President & Manager, Clinet Service

Alberta 5 Pin Bowlers' Association (A5-PBA)
Bowling Headquarters, 432 - 14 St. South, Lethbridge AB T1J 2X7
Tel: 403-320-2695; *Fax:* 403-320-2676
Toll-Free: 800-762-3075
communications@edmonton5pin.ca
www.alberta5pin.com
Annette Bruneau, President
Julie Kind, Secretary
Don MacIver, Treasurer
Brian Sudbury, Director, Technical

Alberta Amateur Speed Skating Association (AASSA)
2500 University Dr. NW, Calgary AB T2N 1N4
Tel: 403-220-7911; *Fax:* 403-220-9226
aassa@ucalgary.ca
www.albertaspeedskating.ca
Wendy Walker, Office Administrator

Alberta Bicycle Association (ABA)
Percy Page Centre, 11759 Groat Rd., Edmonton AB T5M 3K6
Tel: 780-427-6352; *Fax:* 780-427-6438
Toll-Free: 877-646-2453
info@albertabicycle.ab.ca
www.albertabicycle.ab.ca
To promote all aspects of cycling in Alberta
Heather Lothian, Executive Director

Alberta Bobsleigh Association
Bob Niven Training Centre, #205, 88 Canada Olympic Rd. SW, Calgary AB T3B 5R5
Tel: 403-297-2721; *Fax:* 403-286-7213
slide@albertabobsleigh.com
www.albertabobsleigh.com
Social Media: www.facebook.com/group.php?gid=68082934483&ref=search
To develop a broad interest in bobsleigh in Alberta; to provide opportunities for all Albertans to participate in bobsleigh; to provide opportunities for Albertans to progress to national & international levels
Tim Dyrgas, President

Alberta Broomball Association
Percy Page Centre, 11759 Groat Rd., Edmonton AB T5M 3K6
Tel: 780-459-7668; *Fax:* 780-460-0527
neigel@telus.net
Greg Mastervick, President

Alberta Curling Federation (ACF)
Percy Page Centre, 11759 Groat Rd., 3rd Floor, Edmonton AB T5M 3K6
Tel: 780-643-0809; *Fax:* 780-427-8103
www.albertacurling.ab.ca
J.W. (Jim) Pringle, Executive Director
Debi Vion, Programs & Office Administrator

Alberta Deaf Sports Association (ADSA)
11404 - 142 St., Edmonton AB T5M 1V1
www.albertadeafsports.ca
Social Media: www.facebook.com/AlbertaDeafSports
To coordinate sport & recreation activities for the deaf in Alberta; To promote competition at the local, provincial, regional, & national levels; To select Alberta athletes to compete in national championships for the World Games of the Deaf
Arista Haas, President
Calvin Novak, Vice-President
Kimberley Keba, Secretary
Nyla Kurylowich, Treasurer

Alberta Diving
426 Reeves Cres., Edmonton AB T6R 2A4
Tel: 780-988-5571; *Fax:* 780-988-7753
www.albertadiving.ca
To act as the governing body in Alberta for the Olympic sport of amateur diving; to strive for personal & organizational excellence in all areas of diving
Cindy Casper, President
Susan Zwaenepoel, Vice-President
Barbara Dauphinais, Executive Director
Jim MacDonald, Secretary
Curtis Yano, Treasurer

Alberta Equestrian Federation (AEF)
#100, 251 Midpark Blvd. SE, Calgary AB T2X 1S3
Tel: 403-253-4411; *Fax:* 403-252-5260
Toll-Free: 877-463-6233
info@albertaequestrian.com
www.albertaequestrian.com
Social Media: www.facebook.com/group.php?gid=107271125975133
Dixie Crowson, President
Sonia Dantu, Executive Director

Alberta Golf Association (AGA)
#22, 11410 - 27 St. SE, Calgary AB T2Z 3R6
Tel: 403-236-4616; *Fax:* 403-236-2915
Toll-Free: 888-414-4849
info@albertagolf.org
www.albertagolf.org
Social Media: www.facebook.com/pages/Alberta-Golf/144026188016; twitter.com/AGinthenews
To fulfill the needs of members
Brent Ellenton, Executive Director
Jack Lane, Manager, Championships
Eric Rogers, Accountant

Alberta Luge Association (ALA)
Rm 201, BNTC, 88 Canada Olympic Rd. SW, Calgary AB T3B 5R5
Tel: 403-202-6570; *Fax:* 403-247-5497
admin@albertaluge.com
www.albertaluge.com
To ensure the continued successful growth of the sport of luge in Alberta through the development of its athletes, coaches & volunteers at the recreational & elite levels
Darryl Gunn, President

Alberta Northern Lights Wheelchair Basketball Society
8944 - 182 St. NW, Edmonton AB T5T 2E3
Tel: 780-433-4310; *Fax:* 780-431-1764
Toll-Free: 800-465-2992
programs@albertanorthernlights.com
www.albertanorthernlights.com
Social Media: www.facebook.com/172864392765380
To develop health, fitness, & sport for men, women, & children with physical disabilities

Alberta Rugby Football Union
Percy Page Centre, 11759 Groat Rd., Edmonton AB T5M 3K6
Tel: 780-415-1773; *Fax:* 780-422-5558
www.rugbyalberta.com
Social Media: www.facebook.com/groups/92155233636/
John Seaman, President
Simon Chi, Vice-President
Debby Ashmore, Executive Director
Sandy Nesbitt, Director, Finance & Administration

Alberta Schools' Athletic Association (ASAA)
Percy Page Centre, 11759 Groat Rd., Edmonton AB T5M 3K6
Tel: 780-427-8182; *Fax:* 780-415-1833
info@asaa.ca
www.asaa.ca
To provide leadership in the promotion of high school sport; to regulate sports competition & promote the belief that education includes development of the whole person
John F. Paton, Executive Director
Joyce Loucks, President

Alberta Soaring Council
PO Box 13, Black Diamond AB T0L 0H0
Tel: 403-813-6658
asc@stade.ca
www.soaring.ab.ca
To promote soaring sports provincially in all aspects; To plan & support local & provincial events & national competitions
Phil Stade, Executive Director

Alberta Soccer Association
#203, 9440 - 49th St., Edmonton AB T6B 2M9
Tel: 780-474-2200; *Fax:* 780-474-6300
Toll-Free: 866-250-2200
www.albertasoccer.com
To govern & promote the sport of soccer in Alberta
Richard Adams, Executive Director
Anthony Traficante, Manager, Operations
Carmen Charron, Coordinator, Program
Federico Sanmartin, Coordinator, Technical Operations

Alberta Sports & Recreation Association for the Blind (ASRAB)
#007, 15 Colonel Baker Pl. NE, Calgary AB T2E 4Z3
Tel: 403-262-5332; *Fax:* 403-265-7221
Toll-Free: 888-882-7722
info@asrab.ab.ca
www.asrab.ab.ca
To provide recreation & sports opportunities for Albertans who are blind & partially sighted
Marilyn McIntosh, Executive Director
Peter Wettlaufer, President

Alberta Tennis Association (ATA)
11759 Groat Rd., Edmonton AB T5M 3K6
Tel: 780-415-1661; *Fax:* 780-415-1693
info@tennisalberta.com
www.tennisalberta.com
To facilitate participation, development, & visibility of tennis throughout Alberta
Ken Rutherford, Executive Director
Jill Groves, Manager, Administration & Programs
Charlie McLean, Coordinator, High Performance
Jeff Spiers, Coordinator, Community Development

Alberta Volleyball Association (AVA)
Percy Page Centre, 11759 Groat Rd., Edmonton AB T5M 3K6
Tel: 780-415-1703; *Fax:* 780-415-1700
info@albertavolleyball.com
www.albertavolleyball.com
To promote volleyball in Alberta; To provide competitive opportunities for members
Terry Gagnon, Executive Director
Jim Plakas, Director, Technical
Terri Dorfman, Office Manager

Alberta Water Polo Association (AWPA)
PO Box 54, 2225 Macleod Trail SE, Calgary AB T2G 5B6
office@albertawaterpolo.ca
www.albertawaterpolo.ca
Social Media:
www.facebook.com/group.php?gid=143394719017308
To provide a safe & positive environment for the ongoing development & growth of water polo in Alberta for the recreational to the elite athlete
Martin Thumwood, President
Dayna Christmas, Executive Director
Sherry Schaefer, Secretary
Nicolas Youngblud, Treasurer

Alpine Canada ALPIN
#153, 401 - 9th Ave. SW, Calgary AB T2P 3C5
Tel: 403-777-3200; *Fax:* 403-777-3213
info@alpinecanada.org
alpinecanada.org
The ACA is the governing body for ski racing in Canada. Founded in 1920 and accounting for close to 200,000 supporting members, ACA represents coaches, officials, supporters and athletes, including elite racers of the Canadian Alpine Ski Team and the Canadian Disabled Alpine Ski Team.
Max Gartner, President
Jennifer Duggan, Manager, National Services

The Alpine Club of Canada (ACC) / Club alpin du Canada
PO Box 8040, 201, Indian Flats Rd., Canmore AB T1W 2T8
Tel: 403-678-3200; *Fax:* 403-678-3224
info@alpineclubofcanada.ca
www.alpineclubofcanada.ca
Social Media: www.facebook.com/alpineclubofcanada;
twitter.com/alpineclubcan
To encourage & promote mountaineering & mountain crafts; To educate Canadians in the appreciation of mountain heritage; To explore alpine & glacial regions primarily in Canada; To preserve the natural beauty of mountains & their fauna & flora; to promote mountain art & literature; To disseminate scientific & educational knowledge concerning mountains & mountaineering through meetings & publications; To conduct summer & ski mountaineering camps
Lawrence White, Executive Director
Peter Muir, President
Toby Harper, Director, Programs
Emma Varga, Manager, Finance

Aquatic Federation of Canada / Fédération aquatique du Canada
c/o Martin Richard, Director, Communications, Swimming Canada, #B140, 2445 St-Laurent Blvd., Ottawa ON K1G 6C3
Tel: 613-260-1348; *Fax:* 613-260-0804
www.aquaticfederation.ca
Bill Hogan, President

Arctic Winter Games International Committee (AWGIC)
#400, 5201 - 50 Ave., Yellowknife NT X1A 3S9
Tel: 867-873-7245; *Fax:* 867-920-6467
www.awg.ca
To provide common ground for developing Northern athletes; to promote cultural & social exchanges among Northern regions of the continent
Lloyd Bentz, Secretary
Gerry Thick, President
Wendell Shiffler, Vice-President
Ian D. Legaree, Technical Director

Association chasse & pêche de Chibougamau
CP 171, Chibougamau QC G8P 2K6
Tél: 418-748-2021
info@acpcchibougamau.com
www.acpcchibougamau.com
Favoriser et développer parmi les membres l'esprit sportif en préservant la conservation des richesses naturelles
Serge Picard, Président

Association de taekwondo du Québec
CP 1000, Succ. M, 4545, av Pierre-de Coubertin, Montréal QC H1V 3R2
Tél: 514-252-3198; *Téléc:* 514-254-7075
Ligne sans frais: 800-762-9565
info@taekwondo-quebec.ca
www.taekwondo-quebec.ca
Favoriser le développement du taekwondo québécois
Jean Faucher, Président
Elise Paradis, Vice-président

Association des plongeurs de Chibougamau
535, 4e Rue, Chibougamau QC G8P 1S4
Tél: 418-748-7056
André Naud

Association sportive des aveugles du Québec inc. (ASAQ)
CP 1000, Succ. M, 4545, av Pierre-de Coubertin, Montréal QC H1V 3R2
Tél: 514-252-3178; *Téléc:* 514-254-1303
infoasaq@sportsaveugles.qc.ca
www.sportsaveugles.qc.ca
Promouvoir la pratique du sport amateur auprès des personnes handicapées de la vue et de favoriser ainsi leur intégration
Nathalie Chartrand, Directrice générale

Association sportive des sourds du Québec inc. (ASSQ)
CP 1000, Succ. M, 4545, av Pierre-de Coubertin, Montréal QC H1V 3R2
Tél: 514-252-3069; *Téléc:* 514-252-3049
info@assq.org
www.assq.org
Promouvoir le sport, les loisirs et l'activité physique chez les personnes sourdes et malentendantes du Québec
Gérard Labrecque, Président

Athabasca Landing Pool Association (ALPA)
4705 - 48th Ave., Athabasca AB T9S 1R3
Tel: 780-675-5656; *Fax:* 780-675-4700
To provide the facilities & services, for all members of the community, to promote the education, enjoyment, health, safety, fitness & quality of aquatics
Jaymie Mullin, Manager
Alan Fisher, President

Athletics Canada / Athlétisme Canada
#B1-110, 2445 St-Laurent Blvd., Ottawa ON K1G 6C3
Tel: 613-260-5580; *Fax:* 613-260-0341
athcan@athletics.ca
www.athletics.ca
Social Media: www.facebook.com/Canadatrackandfield;
twitter.com/athleticscanada
To promote & encourage participation via competitions from the grass roots level through to the very highest level of proficiency; To assist coaches, officials & executives in fulfilling their goals through courses, conferences & clinics; To provide regular communication lines with members; To continually review & update technical programs; To assist in the research & investigation of potential new facilities; To engender more public awareness, interest & acceptance of the sport of track & field
Rob Guy, Chief Executive Officer
Larry Clough, Director, Finance
Mathieu Gentès, Director, Public Relations & Corporate Services
Donna Harris, Director, Coach Development
Scott MacDonald, Director, National Team Programs

Atlantic Canada Trail Riding Association
Sylvia Gillies, #344 Route 875, Belleisle Creek NB E5P 1C8
To promote safe horsemanship & friendly competition in the long distance trail competition
Roy Drinnan, Chair

Badminton Alberta
c/o Alberta Badminton Centre, 60 Patterson Blvd. SW, Calgary AB T3H 2E1
Tel: 403-297-2722; *Fax:* 403-297-2706
Toll-Free: 888-397-2722
tech@badmintonalberta.ca
www.badmintonalberta.ca
Social Media:
www.facebook.com/pages/Badminton-Alberta/170234779702176
To promote the sport of badminton
Jeff Bell, Executive Director

Badminton BC
#252, 3820 Cessna Dr., Richmond BC V7B 0A2
Tel: 604-333-3595; *Fax:* 604-333-3594
Toll-Free: 800-483-2473
info@badmintonbc.com
www.badmintonbc.com
To provide leadership to develop & promote badminton in BC by increasing the membership base, facilitating a higher standard of participation through competitive & development opportunities for players, coaches, officials & volunteers
Phil Weier, Acting Executive Director
Ken Thiesen, Acting Executive Director

Badminton Canada
#99, 2201 Riverside Dr., Ottawa ON K1H 8K9
Tel: 613-569-2424; *Fax:* 613-569-3232
badminton@badminton.ca
www.badminton.ca
To provide centralized support, &/or leadership in furthering member association objectives, act as custodian of the laws of badminton & to foster outstanding player development; to act for its members in helping to assure national & international class

competition for Canada's outstanding badminton players, & to establish Canada as a leading participant in international badminton
Sonia Blanchard, Office Administrator
Kyle Hunter, Executive Director

Badminton New Nouveau Brunswick
PO Box 355, Stn. Main, Bathurst NB E2A 3Z3
Tel: 506-783-4654
badminton@bnnb.ca
www.bnnb.ca
Badminton NB is a registered, non-profit organization which organizes junior and senior badminton tournaments.
Maurice Boudreau, President
Daryl Beers, Executive Director

Badminton Newfoundland & Labrador Inc.
PO Box 21248, #213, 810 East White Hills Rd., St. John's NL A1A 5B2
Tel: 709-576-7606; *Fax:* 709-576-7493
badminton@sportnl.ca
www.sportnl.ca/badminton/index.html
Social Media: www.facebook.com/group.php?gid=3468211930
BNL is the non-profit, volunteer, sports governing body for badminton in Newfoundland and Labrador.
Janice Reid Boland, Executive Director

Badminton Québec
4940, rue Hochelaga est, Montréal QC H1V 1E7
Tél: 514-252-3066; *Téléc:* 514-252-3175
badmintonquebec@videotron.ca
www.badmintonquebec.com
Promouvoir et développer le sport sur tout le territoire québécois en regroupant tous ses membres, les personnes et associations intéressées au rayonnement de notre discipline
Chantal Brouillard, Directrice générale
Christian Guibourt, Directeur technique
Alexandre Grosleau, Coordonnateur des services aux membres

Badminton World Federation (BWF)
Amoda Bldg., #17.05, 22 Jalan Imbi, L. 17, Kuala Lumpur 55100 Malaysia
bwf@bwfbadminton.org
www.bwfbadminton.org
Social Media: www.facebook.com/bwfbadminton; twitter.com/bwfmedia
To control the game of badminton, from an international aspect, in all countries; to uphold the Laws of Badminton as at present adopted
Kang Young Joong, President

Baseball Alberta (BA)
Percy Page Centre, 11759 Groat Rd., Edmonton AB T5M 3K6
Tel: 780-427-8943; *Fax:* 780-427-9032
registrar@baseballalberta.com
www.baseballalberta.com
Social Media: www.facebook.com/pages/Baseball-Alberta/130042917037092
To offer the opportunity for youth from 6-60 to participate in the great game of baseball, both recreational & competitive, in all areas of the province, large or small & by so doing, make baseball the premier sport in the Province of Alberta
Don Paulencu, President

Baseball BC
#310, 15225 - 104th Ave., Surrey BC V3R 6Y8
Tel: 604-586-3310; *Fax:* 604-586-3311
info1@baseball.bc.ca
www.baseball.bc.ca
Social Media: www.facebook.com/pages/Baseball-BC/233202485008
To support the development of baseball & the aspirations of its members; To offer oppourtunities & setting procedures, standards, & policies
John Berry, President

Baseball Canada / Fédération canadienne de baseball amateur
2212 Gladwin Cres., #A7, Ottawa ON K1B 5N1
Tel: 613-748-5606; *Fax:* 613-748-5767
info@baseball.ca
www.baseball.ca
To promote the development of baseball across Canada through support of provincial organizations & design of programs, including athletes, coaches, events, umpires & partner groups
Ray Carter, President
Jason Dickson, Vice President

Baseball New Brunswick (BNB) / Baseball Nouveau-Brunswick
#13, 900 Hanwell Rd., Fredericton NB E3B 6A2
Tel: 506-451-1329; *Fax:* 506-451-1325
director@baseballnb.ca
www.baseballnb.ca
Social Media: www.facebook.com/pages/Baseball-NB/87671406193
Brian Richard, Chair

Baseball Nova Scotia (BNS)
5516 Spring Garden Rd., 4th Fl., Halifax NS B3J 1J
Tel: 902-425-5450; *Fax:* 902-425-5606
www.baseballnovascotia.com
To represent baseball teams & leagues under the jurisdiction of BaseballCanada.
Brad Lawlor, Executive Director

Baseball Ontario
#3, 131 Sheldon Dr., Cambridge ON N1R 6S2
Tel: 519-740-3900; *Fax:* 519-740-6311
baseball@baseballontario.com
www.baseballontario.com
Mary-Ann Smith, Administrative Director

Basketball Alberta
Percy Page Centre, 11759 Groat Rd., 2nd Fl., Edmonton AB T5M 3K6
Tel: 780-427-9044; *Fax:* 780-427-9124
bballab@basketballalberta.ab.ca
www.basketballalberta.ca
Social Media: www.facebook.com/BasketballAlberta; twitter.com/BasketballAB
Vision: "To be premier facilitators of participation, development, and excellence in basketball". Mission: "To champion the sport of basketball as a game for life by inspiring unity facilitating development and delivering superior value".
Bob Mitchell, President
Paul Sir, Executive Director

Basketball BC
#210, 7888 - 200th St., Langley BC V2Y 3J4
Tel: 604-718-7852; *Fax:* 604-888-8323
www.basketball.bc.ca
Social Media: twitter.com/BasketballBC
To be British Columbia's leading resource for basketball; To build the game of basketball
Lawrie Johns, Executive Director, Youth Development Manager

Basketball Manitoba
145 Pacific Ave., Winnipeg MB R3B 2Z6
Tel: 204-925-5775; *Fax:* 204-925-5929
info@basketball.mb.ca
www.basketball.mb.ca
Social Media: www.facebook.com/basketballmanitoba; twitter.com/basketballmb; www.youtube.com/user/baskmanbaskman?feature=mhum
To operate as the provincial sport governing body for basketball in Manitoba; To ensure all Manitobians have access to the programs run by the association & that the game of basketball is enjoyed by as many people as possible
Adam Wedlake, Executive Director

Basketball New Brunswick (BNB) / Basketball Nouveau-Brunswick
#13, 900 Hanwell Rd., Fredericton NB E2E 6A2
Tel: 506-849-4667; *Fax:* 506-451-1325
info@basketball.nb.ca
www.basketball.nb.ca
To promote, develop & encourage sport & recreation aspects of basketball in New Brunswick; To assist in establishment of basketball clubs throughout New Brunswick; To liaise with government & private agencies interested in promoting & supporting basketball
Carolyn Peppin, Executive Director
Kim Flemming, Office Administrator

Basketball Nova Scotia
5516 Spring Garden Rd., 4th Fl., Halifax NS B3J 1G6
Tel: 902-425-5450; *Fax:* 902-425-5606
bnsadmin@basketball.ns.ca
www.basketball.ns.ca
To promote & encourage the game of basketball throughout the province
Peter Halpin, President
Liam Blanchard, Executive Director

Basketball NWT
info@bnwt.ca
www.bnwt.ca
The Association encourages maximum participation in basketball, develops athletes, & provides opportunities for cultural & social interchange among all involved in the sport.
Website is under development, please check back regularly for updates!

Basketball PEI
PO Box 302, 40 Enman Cres., Charlottetown PE C1A 7K7
Tel: 902-368-4208; *Fax:* 902-368-4208
Toll-Free: 800-247-6712
info@basketballpei.ca
www.basketballpei.ca
To develop basketball in the province of Prince Edward Island in a fun environment
Stephen Marchbank, Executive Director

Basketball Saskatchewan (BSI)
2205 Victoria Ave., Regina SK S4P 0S4
Fax: 306-525-4009
basketball@basketballsask.com
www.basketballsask.com
To support & improve basketball opportunities in Saskatchewan
Greg Lucas, Executive Director, glucas@basketballsask.com
Nathan Schellenberg, Director, Basketball Development
Stacey Silzer, Coordinator, Program
Dave Werry, Coordinator, High Performance

Basketball Yukon
4061, 4th Ave., Whitehorse YT Y1A 1H1
Tel: 867-668-3802
bballyukon@klondiker.com
www.basketballyukon.ca
To be leading a unified basketball community in the territory that is delivering quality programs and services from entry level to national competitions.
Tim Brady, President
Linda Sutherland, Administrative Assistant

Biathlon Alberta
Bob Niven Training Centre, #102, 88 Canada Olympic Rd. SW, Calgary AB T3B 5R5
Tel: 403-202-6548
info@biathlon.ca
www.biathlon.ca
To promote, develop & maintain biathlon in Alberta
Ken Davies, President
Andy Holmwood, Executive Director

Biathlon Canada
#111, 2197 Riverside Dr., Ottawa ON K1H 7X3
Tel: 613-748-5608; *Fax:* 613-748-5762
information@biathloncanada.ca
www.biathloncanada.ca
To achieve consistent international podium performance by leading, promoting, developing & governing biathlon in Canada to the highest standard of excellence
Joanne Thomson, Executive Director
Chris Lindsay, Director, High Performance
Katie Dobson, Coordinator, Technical Programs

Biathlon Yukon
PO Box 31673, Whitehorse YT Y1A 6L3
www.sportyukon.com/membership/?member=11
To enhance opportunities for all Yukon persons in their pursuit of excellence & in their enjoyment of participation in biathlon
Keith Clarke, President
Katrina Brogden, Secretary

Bicycle Newfoundland & Labrador
PO Box 2127, Stn. C, St. John's NL A1C 5R6
Tel: 709-738-2597
admin@bnl.nf.ca
www.bnl.nf.ca
Social Media: www.facebook.com/pages/Bicycle-NL/144379652267580
Leon Organ, President

Bicycle Nova Scotia (BNS)
5516 Spring Garden Rd., 4th Fl., Halifax NS B3J 1G6
Tel: 902-425-5454; *Fax:* 902-425-5606
staff@bicycle.ns.ca
www.bicycle.ns.ca
The coordinating body for sport, recreational & transportation cycling in Nova Scotia
Tamara Stephen, Office Administrator

Bicycle Trade Association of Canada (BTAC) / Association canadienne de l'industrie du vélo (ACIV)
17 Main St. North, Newmarket ON L3Y 3Z6
Tel: 905-853-5031; *Fax:* 905-853-7632
Toll-Free: 866-528-2822
info@btac.org
www.btac.org
Janet O'Connell, Executive Director

Blind Sports Nova Scotia
c/o CNIB, 6136 Almon St., Halifax NS B3K 1T8
Tel: 902-453-1480; *Fax:* 902-454-6570
info@blindsportsnovascotia.ca
www.blindsportsnovascotia.ca
Blind Sports Nova Scotia is an organization that presents sport and recreational activities for visually impaired athletes in Nova Scotia.
Yvon Clement, President

Bobsleigh Canada Skeleton
140 Canada Olympic Rd. SW, Calgary AB T3B 5R5
Tel: 403-247-5950; *Fax:* 403-247-5951
ddreher@bobsleigh.ca
www.bobsleigh.ca/
To strive to create Olympic & world champions
Don Wilson, CEO

Bowling Federation of Canada / Fédération des quilles du Canada
c/o Administrator, #206, 720 Belfast Rd., Ottawa ON K1G 0Z5
Tel: 613-744-5090; *Fax:* 613-744-2217
info@canadabowls.ca
www.canadabowls.ca
To promote & foster the sport of bowling in Canada; To promote among the recognized national organizations in Canada, sportmanship, good fellowhsip, & the continued interest in the future development of bowling throughout Canada
Bryan Sargeant, President
Sheila Carr, Administrator

Bowling Federation of Saskatchewan
#101, 1805 - 8th Ave., Regina SK S4R 1E8
Tel: 306-780-9412; *Fax:* 306-780-9455
bowling@sasktel.net
saskbowl.com
Working together through cooperation & harmonization to access & allocate funding for our members programs & services in order to enhance the sport of bowling
Rhonda Sereda, Executive Director

Bowling Proprietors' Association of BC
#209, 332 Columbia St., New Westminster BC V3L 1A6
Tel: 604-522-2990; *Fax:* 604-522-2055
bowl4fun@bowlbc.com
www.bowlbc.com
Ken Clarke, President

Bowling Proprietors' Association of Canada (BPAC)
#10A, 250 Shields Ct., Markham ON L3R 9W7
Tel: 905-479-1560; *Fax:* 905-479-8613
info@bowlcanada.ca
www.bowlcanada.ca
The aim of this association is to improve general conditions in the bowling industry, to promote to the general public the benefits of bowling, to create a better relationship between the many bowling establishments across Canada and to encourage any and all practices which are in the best interests of the game.
Mariano Meconi, President
Paul Oliveira, Executive Director

Bowling Proprietors' Association of Ontario (BPAO)
#202, 500 Alden Rd., Markham ON L3R 5H5
Tel: 905-940-8200; *Fax:* 905-940-8201
info@bowlontario.ca
www.bowlontario.ca
To improve conditions in bowling industry; To protect members from unreasonable legislation; To bring attention to the pleasures of bowling
Filippo Corradi, President
Melanie Girard, Director, Administration

Bowls British Columbia
#501, 1710 Bayshore Dr., Vancouver BC V6G 3G4
www.bowlsbc.ca
To foster & promote the game of Lawn Bowls; To make the game available to all in accordance within the Canadian Human Rights Code within the Province of British Columbia
Jim Aitken, President
Dave Muir, Vice-President
Judith Parkes, Secretary
Pat Cutt, Treasurer

Bowls Canada Boulingrin (BCB)
#207, 720 Belfast Rd., Ottawa ON K1G 0Z5
Tel: 613-244-0021; *Fax:* 613-244-0041
Toll-Free: 800-567-2695
office@bowlscanada.com
www.bowlscanada.com
To promote, foster & safeguard the sport of indoor & outdoor lawn bowling in all its forms in Canada, through events & programs
Kevin Penny, Executive Director

Bowls Manitoba
145 Pacific Ave., Winnipeg MB R3B 2Z6
Tel: 204-925-5694; *Fax:* 204-925-5703
bowls@shawbiz.ca
www.bowls.mb.ca
To promote lawnbowling in the province of Manitoba; To host various lawnbowling events
Cathy Derewianchuk, Executive Director

Bowls Saskatchewan Inc.
#102, 1860 Lorne St., Regina SK S4P 2L7
Tel: 306-780-9426; *Fax:* 306-781-6021
bowlsask@sasktel.net
www.bowls.sk.ca
To promote & expand the sport of bowls, which contains programs that accommodate/challenge all those interested, with the result that bowls becomes a high profile sport
Karen Swanson, Executive Director
Jean Roney, President

Boxing Alberta
Percy Page Centre, 11759 Groat Rd., Edmonton AB T5M 3K6
Tel: 780-427-6515; *Fax:* 780-427-1205
www.boxingalberta.com
Jim Titley, President
Dennis Belair, Executive Director

Boxing BC Association
481 - 23rd St. NE, Salmon Arm BC V1E 1Y8
Tel: 250-832-7759; *Fax:* 250-832-7769
boxingbc@telus.net
www.boxing.bc.ca
To provide all citizens of British Columbia access to & participation in the opportunities, programs & activities
Scotty Jackson, President

Boxing Ontario
#202, 3 Concorde Gate, Toronto ON M3C 3N7
Tel: 416-426-7250; *Fax:* 416-426-7367
info@boxingontario.com
www.boxingontario.com
This is the only governing body for amateur boxing in Ontario. It aims to organize, promote, develop interest and participation in the sport in the province.
Tom Hennessey, President
Matt Kennedy, Executive Director

Boxing Saskatchewan
PO Box 4711, Regina SK S4P 3Y3
Tel: 306-525-6678; *Fax:* 306-569-3454
skboxing@accesscomm.ca
www.boxingsask.com
This is a non-profit society that enforces rules and regulations governing amateur boxing in the province. It also promotes the formation of new clubs.
Frank Fiacco, President
Graham Craig, Executive Director

British Columbia Amateur Hockey Association (BCAHA) / Association de hockey amateur de la Colombie-Britannique
6671 Oldfield Rd., Saanichton BC V8M 2A1
Tel: 250-652-2978; *Fax:* 250-652-4536
info@bchockey.net
www.bchockey.net
To foster, improve & perpetuate amateur hockey in BC.
Barry Petrachenko, Executive Director
Ed Mayert, President

British Columbia Ball Hockey Association (BCBHA)
1302 Cliveden Ave., Delta BC V3M 6G4
Tel: 604-812-6720; *Fax:* 604-588-7760
www.bcbha.com
To govern the sport of ball hockey in British Columbia; To establish bylaws & regulations, in order to ensure a safe & fun activity; To uphold the rules& regulations of ball hockey
Wade Traversy, President
Kris Little, Vice-President
Rob Moxness, Secretary
Roger Sidhu, Treasurer

British Columbia Blind Sports & Recreation Association (BCBSRA)
#330, 5055 Joyce St., Vancouver BC V5R 6B2
Tel: 604-325-8638; *Fax:* 604-325-1638
info@bcblindsports.bc.ca
www.bcblindsports.bc.ca
To provide sports, physical recreation & fitness activities & programs for persons of all ages who are blind/visually impaired; to alleviate isolating & inhibiting effects of blindness/visual impairment; to improve physical capabilities & self-image of blind/visually impaired individuals by providing opportunities for them to learn; to encourage, promote & maintain interest in & cooperation with all such amateur sports & recreation organizations. Toll free number 0-604-325-8638, after the tone enter 7617.
Brian Cowie, President
Tami Grenon, Vice President

British Columbia Broomball Society
c/o 5356 Lochside Dr., Victoria BC V8Y 2G7
www.bcbroomball.ca
Rick Przybysz, President
Bruce MacRae, Sec.-Treas.

British Columbia Competitive Trail Riders Association (BCCTRA)
c/o 2980 Giovando Road, Nanaimo BC V9X 1K5
Tel: 250-245-4405
nicole.vaugeois@viu.ca
www.bcctra.ca
To promote & improve the rapidly growing sport of competitive trail riding in BC
Nicole Vagueois, Sec.-Treas.

British Columbia Deaf Sports Federation (BCDSF)
#254, 3820 Cessna Dr., Richmond BC V7B 0A2
Tel: 604-333-3606; *Fax:* 604-333-3450
TTY: 604-333-3606
info@bcdeafsports.bc.ca
www.bcdeafsports.bc.ca
Social Media: www.facebook.com/139556792849947; twitter.com/bcdeafsports
To provide & support the development of competitive sporting events in BC among deaf & hard of hearing athletes; to encourage training for deaf coaches; to provide financial assistance to deaf athletes to participate in local, provincial & national competitions
Johnson Leonor, Administrator

British Columbia Diving
#114, 15272 Croydon Dr., Surrey BC V3S 0Z5
Tel: 604-531-5576; *Fax:* 604-542-0387
bcdiving.sportbc.com
Developing and promoting diving throughout British Columbia by encouraging participation, growth and personal success for everyone.
Jayne McDonald, Executive Director
Beverley Boys, Technical Director

British Columbia Golf Association (BCGA)
#2110, 13700 Mayfield Pl., Richmond BC V6V 2E4
Tel: 604-279-2580; *Fax:* 604-207-9535
Toll-Free: 888-833-2242
info@bcga.org
www.britishcolumbiagolf.org
Social Media: www.facebook.com/BritishColumbiaGolf; twitter.com/bc_golfer
To promote interest in golf in BC; To protect the mutual interests of member clubs & their members; To establish & enforce uniformity in the rules of the game; To establish, control, & conduct amateur championships, matches & competitions; To interest & develop junior golfers; To select all teams to represent BC in national & international matches
Kris Jonasson, Executive Director
Deborah Pyne, Managing Director, Player Development
Andy Fung, Director, Finance & Administration
Susan White, Director, Rules, Competitions, & Education
Christopher McGrath, Manager, Communications & Marketing
Shirley Simmons-Doyle, Manager, Member Services

British Columbia Ringette Association (BCRA) / Association de ringuette de Colombie-Britannique
#319, 789 West Pender St., Vancouver BC V6C 1H2
Fax: 604-629-0876
www.bcringette.org
Glen Ritchie, President
Donna Mihalcheon, Vice President

British Columbia Rugby Union
#203, 210 West Broadway, Vancouver BC V5Y 3W2
Tel: 604-737-3065; *Fax:* 604-737-3916
bcrugby@telus.net
www.bcrugby.com
To promote, sustain & manage the game of rugby in BC in a manner that will ensure wide participation & the continuous development in a safe & responsible manner
Louise Wheeler, Manager, Member Services
Jeff Sauvé, CEO

British Columbia School Sports (BCSS)
PO Box 97, 20800 Lougheed Hwy., Maple Ridge BC V2X 7E9
Tel: 604-477-1488; *Fax:* 604-477-1484
info@bcschoolsports.ca
www.bcschoolsports.ca

To encourage student participation in extra-curricular athletics, assist schools in the development & delivery of their programs & provide governance for interschool competition
Sue Keenan, Executive Director
Raj Puri, President

British Columbia Soccer Association
#510, 375 Water St., Vancouver BC V6B 5C6
Tel: 604-299-6401; *Fax:* 604-299-9610
bcsoccer@gmail.com
www.bcsoccer.net
Bjorn Osieck, Executive Director

British Columbia Speed Skating Association
PO Box 2023, Stn. A, Abbotsford BC V2T 3T8
Tel: 604-746-4349; *Fax:* 604-746-4549
lorna@speed-skating.bc.ca
www.speed-skating.bc.ca
The organization wishes to foster the growth and development of Speed Skating in B.C. by providing quality services and support programs to all members in their pursuit of a healthy lifestyle while encouraging challenges and promoting excellence.
Ted Houghton, Executive Director

British Columbia Water Polo Association (BCWPA)
#227, 3820 Cessna Dr., Richmond BC V7B 0A2
Tel: 604-333-3480; *Fax:* 604-333-3450
bcwaterpolo@telus.net
www.bcwaterpolo.com; www.bcwaterpolo.ca
Social Media:
www.facebook.com/group.php?gid=257337230951081;
twitter.com/bcwaterpolo
To develop water polo in BC; to train provincal team & national team athletes
Dave Soul, Executive Director

British Columbia Wrestling Association (BCWA)
#335, 2416 Main St., Vancouver BC V5T 3E2
Tel: 604-737-3092; *Fax:* 604-737-6043
info@bcwrestling.com
www.bcwrestling.com
To promote & enhance the well-being of young people through their participation in wrestling
MaryAnn DeCorby, Executive Director

Broomball Newfoundland & Labrador
734 Birch St., Labrador City NL A2V 1C8
Tel: 709-944-5780; *Fax:* 709-944-5780
clarkep@nf.sympatico.ca
Harold Clarke, President

Calgary Boxing & Wrestling Commission (CBWC)
PO Box 2100, Stn. M #63, Calgary AB T2P 2M5
Tel: 403-268-5367
The CBWC acts as a regulation body for professional boxing & wrestling within the City of Calgary.
Candy S. Schacter, Chair

Canada Basketball
#11, 1 Westside Dr., Toronto ON M9C 1B2
Tel: 416-614-8037; *Fax:* 416-614-9570
info@basketball.ca
www.basketball.ca
Basketball Canada is the national sport governing body for amateur basketball in Canada; to develop the sport of basketball domestically & to contribute to the development of basketball internationally
Wayne Parrish, President & CEO

Canada Games Council (CGC) / Conseil des jeux du Canada
#701, 2197 Riverside Dr., Ottawa ON K1H 7X3
Tel: 613-526-2320; *Fax:* 613-526-4068
canada.games@canadagames.ca
www.canadagames.ca
Social Media: www.facebook.com/CanadaGames;
twitter.com/CanadaGames
The Canada Games Council is a well-established, national organization that fosters on-going partnerships with organizations at the municipal, provincial and national levels. It allocates resources in support of the following mission and strategic directions.
Sue Hylland, President/CEO
Kelly-Ann Paul, Director of Sport

Canada's Sports Hall of Fame / Temple de la renommée des sports du Canada
Exhibition Place, 115 Princes' Blvd., Toronto ON M6K 3C3
Tel: 416-260-6789; *Fax:* 416-260-9347
info@cshof.ca
www.cshof.ca
To inspire Canadian identity and national pride by telling the compelling stories of those outstanding achievements that make up Canada's sports history.
Sheryn Posen, COO
J. Trevor Eyton, Chair

Canadian 5 Pin Bowlers' Association (C5PBA) / Association canadienne des cinq quilles (AC5Q)
#206, 720 Belfast Rd., Ottawa ON K1G 0Z5
Tel: 613-744-5090; *Fax:* 613-744-2217
c5pba@c5pba.ca
www.c5pba.ca
The sports organization of male & female 5 pin bowlers provides programs & services to its members for their participation in organized 5-pin bowling. It also regulates bowling systems to standardize the sport.
Sheila Carr, Executive Director
Mel Osmond, President
Don MacIver, Corporate Sec.-Treas.

Canadian Academy of Sport Medicine (CASM) / Académie canadienne de médecine du sport (ACMS)
#4, 5330 Canotek Rd., Ottawa ON K1J 9C1
Tel: 613-748-5851; *Fax:* 613-748-5792
Toll-Free: 877-585-2394
bfalardeau@casm-acms.org
www.casm-acms.org
To promote excellence in the practice of medicine, as it applies to physical activity; To advance the art & science of sport medicine
Dawn Haworth, Executive Director

Canadian Adult Recreational Hockey Association (CARHA)
#610, 1420 Blair Pl., Ottawa ON K1J 9L8
Tel: 613-244-1989; *Fax:* 613-244-0451
Toll-Free: 800-267-1854
hockey@carhahockey.ca
www.carhahockey.ca
To develop & provide a wide range of innovative hockey benefits & solutions to customers; To build & retain relationships among the adult recreational hockey community across Canada
Michael S. Peski, President
Patti Kenny, Director, Finance
Lori Lopez, Director, Business Operations
Karen Salaj, Manager, Member Services
Laurie Snider, Manager, Service & Administration

Canadian Amateur Boxing Association (CABA) / Association canadienne de boxe amateur (ACBA)
888 Belfast Rd., Ottawa ON K1G 0Z6
Tel: 613-238-7700; *Fax:* 613-238-1600
caba@boxing.ca
www.boxing.ca
To develop & maintain uniform rules & regulations to govern amateur boxing competitions in Canada; To develop coaches & officials; To organize national team programs, including development, training, & competition
Robert G. Crête, Executive Director
Daniel Trépanier, Coordinator, Technical
Michelle Ethier, Registrar & Accountant

Canadian Amateur Wrestling Association (CAWA) / Association canadienne de lutte amateur
#7, 5370 Canotek Rd., Gloucester ON K1J 9E6
Tel: 613-748-5686; *Fax:* 613-748-5756
info@wrestling.ca
www.wrestling.ca
To operate as the national sport governing body for Olympic style wrestling in Canada; To implement a long term athlete development model; To develop coaches, officials, & administrators; To achieve podium finishes for Canadian wrestlers at World Championships & Olympic Games
Tamara Medwidsky, Executive Director
Doug Cox, President
Clint Kingsbury, Manager, Domestic Development
Dave Mair, Manager, High Performance
Dave McKay, National Coach, Senior Men
Leigh Vierling, National Coach, Senior Women

Canadian Amputee Sports Association (CASA) / Association canadienne des sports pour amputés
c/o Dale Murphy, 1126 Millcove Rd., RR#1, Mount Stewart PE C0A 1T0
www.canadianamputeesports.ca
To promote & organize amateur sport competitions in Canada for persons who are without a limb or part of a limb; To promote research in prosthetic devices for sport activities; To select a Canadian national team for participation in international sports events for amputees
James Reilly, President
Dale Murphy, Secretary
Wayne Epp, Treasurer

Canadian Aquafitness Leaders Alliance Inc. (CALA)
125 Lilian Dr., Toronto ON M1R 3W6
Tel: 416-751-9823; *Fax:* 416-755-1832
Toll-Free: 888-751-9823
cala_aqua@mac.com
www.calainc.org
Social Media:
www.facebook.com/profile.php?id=100001107894346
To provide high quality training, certification & communication network for aquafitness leaders & aquatic rehabilitation specialists; to promote professionalism & excellence through careful integration of the mind, body & spirit
Charlene Kopansky, President

Canadian Association for Disabled Skiing (CADS) / Association canadienne pour les skieurs handicapés (ACSH)
91 Nelson St., Barrie ON L4M 4K4
Tel: 705-725-4845; *Fax:* 705-725-4804
michelle.bavington@sympatico.ca
www.disabledskiing.ca
To assist individuals with a disability to participate in recreational & competitive snow skiing & snowboarding
David O'Brien, Executive Director
Al Matile, President
Helen Grimm, Secretary
Jeff Laidlaw, Treasurer

Canadian Association for Disabled Skiing - Alberta (CADS Alberta)
11759 Groat Rd., Edmonton AB T5M 3K6
Tel: 780-427-8104; *Fax:* 780-427-0524
info@cadsalberta.ca
www.cadsalberta.ca
CADS Alberta is a volunteer-based organization assisting individuals with a disability to lead fuller lives through active participation in recreational & competitive snow skiing & snowboarding. It is a registered charity, BN: 133967406RR0001.
Mike Low, President
Allyson Szafranski, Executive Coordinator

Canadian Association for Disabled Skiing - Newfoundland & Labrador Division
6 Albany Pl., St. John's NL A1E 1Y2
Tel: 709-753-3625; *Fax:* 709-777-4884
margaret.tibbo@easternhealth.ca
Marg Tibbo, Secretary

Canadian Association for Disabled Skiing Nova Scotia
c/o Alpine Ski Nova Scotia, 5516 Spring Garden Rd., Halifax NS B3J 1G6
Tel: 902-425-5450; *Fax:* 902-425-5606
alpinens@sportnovascotia.ca
disabledskiing.ca
Linda Scott

Canadian Association of Nordic Ski Instructors (CANSI)
c/o Secrétariat, 8 Douglas Rd., Chelsea QC J9B 1K4
Tel: 819-360-6700; *Fax:* 819-827-0017
office@cansi.ca; membership@cansi.ca
www.cansi.ca
CANSI promotes & advances cross-country & Telemark skiing in Canada, establishing standards, & offering levels of certification in technique & training. Its primary focus is certifying instructors to teach the general public.
Jeff Hampshire, President
Françoise Chatenoud, Office Coordinator

Canadian Association of Snowboard Instructors (CASI) / Association canadienne des moniteurs de surf des neiges (ACMS)
60 Canning Cres., cambridge on N1T 1X2
Tel: 877-976-2274; *Fax:* 866-471-6594
headoffice@casi-acms.com
www.casi-acms.com
Social Media: www.facebook.com/CASIACMS;
twitter.com/casiacms
To promote the sport of snowboarding, snowboard instruction & coaching & the professions of snowboard teaching & coaching in Canada by training & certifying snowboard instructors & coaches; to ensure that a standard of safe & efficient snowboard instruction is maintained.
Dan Genge, Executive Director

Canadian Ball Hockey Association / Association canadienne de hockey-balle
9107 Norum Rd., Delta BC V4C 3H9
Tel: 604-638-1480; *Fax:* 604-998-1410
info@cbha.com
www.cbha.com
To promote the sport of ball hockey; To arrange championships

George Gortsos, Executive Director
Shelley Callaghan, Vice-President, Women's
Connie Liosis, Vice-President, Men's
Steve Rumsey, Vice-President, Minor's

Canadian Blind Sports Association Inc. / Association canadienne des sports pour aveugles inc.
#325, 5055 Joyce St., Vancouver BC V5R 6B2
Tel: 604-419-0480; *Fax:* 604-419-0481
Toll-Free: 866-604-0480
jane@canadianblindsports.ca
www.canadianblindsports.ca
To facilitate opportunities for Canadians who are legally blind to participate in amateur sport at the national/international level, & to thereby enhance a healthy lifestyle & individual well-being.
Jane D. Blaine, Executive Director

Canadian Broomball Federation / Fédération canadienne de ballon sur glace
#302, 200 Main St., Winnipeg MB R3C 4M2
Tel: 204-925-5656; *Fax:* 204-925-5703
cbfbroomball@shaw.ca
www.broomball.ca

Canadian Centre for Ethics in Sport (CCES) / Centre canadien pour l'éthique dans le sport
#350, 955 Green Valley Cr., Ottawa ON K2C 3V4
Tel: 613-521-3340; *Fax:* 613-521-3134
Toll-Free: 800-672-7775
info@cces.ca
www.cces.ca
Foster ethical sport for all Canadians
Louise Walker, Chair
Paul Melia, CEO

Canadian Cerebral Palsy Sports Association (CCPSA) / Association canadienne de sport pour paralytiques cérébraux (ACPSA)
PO Box 41009, 1910 St. Laurent Blvd., Ottawa ON K1G 5K9
Tel: 613-748-1430; *Fax:* 613-748-1355
Toll-Free: 866-247-9934
info@ccpsa.ca
www.ccpsa.ca
Social Media: www.facebook.com/112866075626
To act as umbrella group for all provincial cerebral palsy sport organizations; To design programs that are designed for athletes with cerebral palsy & non-progressive head injuries
Earl Church, Executive Director

Canadian Colleges Athletic Association / Association canadienne du sport collégial
c/o St. Lawrence College, 2 Belmont St., Cornwall ON K6H 4Z1
Tel: 613-937-1508; *Fax:* 613-937-1530
sandra@ccaa.ca
www.ccaa.ca
To operate as the national governing body for men's & women's college sport in Canada
Sandra Murray-MacDonell, Executive Director

Canadian Curling Association (CCA) / Association canadienne de curling
1660 Vimont Ct., Orleans ON K4A 4J4
Tel: 613-834-2076; *Fax:* 613-834-0716
Toll-Free: 800-550-2875
boc@curling.ca (business of curling); championships@curling.ca
www.curling.ca
Social Media: www.facebook.com/ccacurling
To attract, retain & advance participants to grow the sport of curling
Greg Stremlaw, Chief Executive Officer
Pat Ray, Chief Operating Officer
Warren Hansen, Director, Event Operations & Media
Danny Lamoureux, Director, Championship Services & Curling Club Development
Gerry Peckham, Director, High Performance

Canadian Cycling Association (CCA) / Association cycliste canadienne
#203, 2197 Riverside Dr., Ottawa ON K1H 7X3
Tel: 613-248-1353; *Fax:* 613-248-9311
general@canadian-cycling.com
www.canadian-cycling.com
To organize & promote cycling in Canada, including road racing, track, & mountain biking, for sport & fitness
Greg Mathieu, Chief Executive Officer & Secretary General
Jacques Landry, Director, High Performance
Mathieu Boucher, Director, Development
Brett Stewart, Director, Finance & Administration

Canadian Deaf Ice Hockey Federation (CDIHF)
c/o C. Cooper, #137, 201 Queen Victoria Dr., Hamilton ON L8W 1W7
cdihf@rogers.com
www.cdihf.deafhockey.com
Social Media: www.facebook.com/group.php?gid=152070790142
To offer ice hockey programs for deaf & hard of hearing participants; To administer a hockey team to represent Canada internationally
Danny Daniels, President
Eugene Franciosi, Vice-President
Brenda Stanley, Secretary
Raymond Patterson, Treasurer

Canadian Deaf Sports Association (CDSA) / Association des sports des sourds du Canada (ASSC)
#202A, 10217, boul Pie IX, Montréal QC H1H 3Z5
Tel: 514-321-8686
TTY: 514-321-2937
info@assc-cdsa.com
www.assc-cdsa.com
Social Media: www.facebook.com/assc.cdsa; twitter.com/ASSC_CDSA
To promote & facilitate the practice of fitness, amateur sports & recreation among deaf people of all ages in Canada from the local recreational level to Olympics calibre.
Kimberley D. Rizzi, Executive Director
Ghysline "Gigi" Fiset, Project Coordinator
Mark Kusak, President

Canadian Fencing Federation (CFF) / Fédération canadienne d'escrime
10 Masterson Dr., St Catharines ON L2T 3P1
Tel: 647-476-2401; *Fax:* 647-476-2402
cff@fencing.ca
www.fencing.ca
To promote & develop the sport of fencing in Canada.
Stephen Symons, President
Ron Dewar, Vice-President

Canadian Football League (CFL) / Ligue canadienne de football (LCF)
50 Wellington St. East, 3rd Fl., Toronto ON M5E 1C8
Tel: 416-322-9650; *Fax:* 416-322-9651
www.cfl.ca
Social Media: www.facebook.com/CFL; twitter.com/CFL
Mark Cohon, Commissioner
Michael Copeland, Chief Operating Officer
Doug Allison, Vice-President, Finance & Business Operations
Matt Maychak, Vice-President, Communications & Broadcast
Kevin McDonald, Vice-President, Football Operations

Canadian Freestyle Ski Association / Association canadienne de ski acrobatique
808 Pacific St., Vancouver BC V6Z 1C2
Tel: 604-714-2233; *Fax:* 604-714-2232
info@freestyleski.com
www.freestyleski.ca
The national governing body of the sport of freestyle skiing with a mandate to develop the sport within Canada; to represent our country internationally; to promote the safe development of the sport; to promote excellence in national & international competitions
Peter Judge, CEO

Canadian Golf Superintendents Association (CGSA) / Association canadienne des surintendants de golf
#205, 5520 Explorer Dr., Mississauga ON L4W 5L1
Tel: 905-602-8873; *Fax:* 905-602-1958
Toll-Free: 800-387-1056
cgsa@golfsupers.com
www.golfsupers.com
Social Media: www.facebook.com/group.php?gid=151227228150; twitter.com/GolfSupers
To promote excellence in golf course management & environmental responsibility; To uphold the Canadian Golf Superintendents Association Principles Of Professional Practice & Code of Ethics & Conduct
Kenneth S. Cousineau, Executive Director
Tim Kubash, President
John Mills, Vice-President
Christian Pilon, Secretary-Treasurer

Canadian Handball Association (CHA) / Fédération de balle au mur du Canada
30 Melwood Ave., Halifax NS B3N 1E3
Tel: 902-477-2902; *Fax:* 902-431-3145
handball@cdnhandball.org
www.canadianhandballcourts.ca
To promote handball in Canada
Doug Santha, President
Heather Mueller, Treasurer

Canadian Jiu-jitsu Council
PO Box 543, Madoc ON K0K 2K0
Tel: 613-473-4366
www.jiujitsucouncil.ca
A non-profit educational Martial Arts organization under the Canadian Province of Ontario Charter. The CJC is administered by a volunteer group of senior Black Belts whose objective is to guide and assist the growth of Jiujitsu in a friendly, healthy environment and to help more people get more benefits, knowledge and pleasure from the Martial Art and Science of Jiujitsu.
Robert Walthers, President

Canadian Kendo Federation (CKF) / Fédération canadienne de kendo
8013 Hunter St., Burnaby BC V5A 2B8
Tel: 604-420-0438; *Fax:* 604-420-1971
hokusa@kendo-canada.com
www.kendo-canada.com
Hiro Okusa, President
Yoshiaki Taguchi, Vice-President
Christian d'Orangeville, 2nd Vice-President
Kim Taylor, Secretary
John Maisonneuve, Treasurer

Canadian Lacrosse Association (CLA) / Association canadienne de crosse (ACC)
Gladstone Sports & Health Centre, #101, 18 Louisa St., Ottawa ON K1R 6Y6
Tel: 613-260-2028; *Fax:* 613-260-2029
info1@lacrosse.ca
www.lacrosse.ca
Social Media: www.facebook.com/CanadianLacrosseAssociation; twitter.com/LacrosseCanada
To promote, develop & preserve the sport of Lacrosse & its heritage as Canada's national summer sport.
Melissa McKenzie, Executive Director

Canadian Luge Association / Association canadienne de luge
88 Canada Olympic Rd. SW, Calgary AB T3B 5R5
Tel: 403-202-6581; *Fax:* 403-247-8820
hpprchris@comcast.net
www.luge.ca
Social Media: www.facebook.com/138340422883168; twitter.com/LugeCanada
To provide leadership & pursue success in promotion & development of all aspects of luge.
Tim Farstad, Executive Director

Canadian Masters Athletic Association (CMAA)
Tel: 416-380-2503
canadianmasters.ca
Paul Osland, President
Sherry Watts, Membership

Canadian Masters Cross-Country Ski Association (CMCSA) / Association canadienne des maîtres en ski de fond
c/o 2 MacNeil Cres., Stephenville NL A2N 3E3
www.canadian-masters-xc-ski.ca/en_index.htm
Th Association promotes Masters cross-country skiing across Canada, establishing rules & regulations for activities, & representing members at meetings at the WMA.
Bruce Legrow, National Director

Canadian Modern Pentathlon Association (CAMPA) / Association canadienne du pentathlon moderne
70 Como Gardens, Hudson QC J0P 1H0
Tel: 450-458-7974; *Fax:* 450-458-1746
president@pentathloncanada.ca
www.pentathloncanada.ca
Social Media: www.facebook.com/pages/Pentathlon-Canada/168702639822958
To promote multi-discipline Olympic sport
Angela Ives, President
Blaine Dombowsky, Vice-President
Aline Lafrenière, Vi-ce President
Bob Noble, Vice-President & Director, High Performance
Colin Peace, Vice-President & Chair, Technical Committee

Canadian Olympic Committee (COC) / Comité olympique canadien
#900, 21 St Clair Ave. East, Toronto ON M4T 1L9
Tel: 416-962-0262; *Fax:* 416-967-4902
www.olympic.ca
Social Media: twitter.com/CDNOlympicTeam

To develop & advance sports & the Olympic Movement for all Canadians from coast-to-coast
Chris Rudge, CEO

Canadian Paralympic Committee (CPC) / Comité paralympique canadien
#310, 225 Metcalfe St., Ottawa ON K2P 1p9
Tel: 613-569-4333; *Fax:* 613-569-2777
www.paralympic.ca
Social Media: www.facebook.com/CDNParalympics?ref=ts; twitter.com/CDNParalympics
The CPC is responsible for creating an optimal environment for high-performance Canadian Paralympic Athletes to compete and win in the Paralympic and Parapan American Games, and by promoting their success, inspire all Canadians with a disability to get involved in sport.
Henry Storgaard, CEO & Secretary General
Karen Poapst, Senior Coordinator, Special Events & Project

Canadian Polo Association (CPA)
PO Box 17, Stn. 9, R.R.2, Okotos AB T1S 1A2
Tel: 430-995-1987; *Fax:* 403-938-8205
Toll-Free: 855-995-1987
info@polocanada.ca
www.polocanada.ca
To develop & maintain standards of excellence for the sport of polo in Canada; To promote polo across the nation
Justin R. Fogarty, Chair
Cam Clark, President
Don. B. Pennycook, Vice-President
Ada Pally, Secretary
Dave Offen, Treasurer

Canadian Pony Club (CPC)
PO Box 127, Baldur MB R0K 0B0
Tel: 204-535-2368; *Fax:* 204-535-2289
Toll-Free: 888-286-7669
info@canadianponyclub.org
www.canadianponyclub.org
The Club encourages & instructs young people to ride & care for their horses, while promoting loyalty, character & sportsmanship.
Cathy Miller, National Chair
Val Crowe, Administrator

Canadian Powerlifting Organization (CPO)
PO Box 51180 RPO Beddington, Calgary AB T3K EV9
Fax: 403-698-2434
powerlifting@gmail.com; info@wpc-canada.com
www.worldpowerlifting.com/cpo
Promoting powerlifting in Canada

Canadian Powerlifting Union (CPU)
c/o Mike Armstrong, 4709 Fordham Cres. SE, Calgary AB T2A 2A5
www.powerlifting.ca
Social Media: www.facebook.com/CDNpowerliftingunion
To oversee & regulate all IPF style powerlifting in Canada
Ryan Stinn, President
Louis Levesque, Chair, Coaching
Mike Armstrong, Secretary
Barry Antoniow, Treasurer

Canadian Professional Golfers' Association (CPGA) / Association canadienne des golfeurs professionnels
13450 Dublin Line, RR#1, Acton ON L7J 2W7
Tel: 519-853-5450; *Fax:* 519-853-5449
Toll-Free: 800-782-5764
cpga@cpga.com
www.cpga.com
The Canadian Professional Golfer's Association is a member based non-profit organization representing golf professionals across Canada.
Gary Bernard, Interim Executive Director

Canadian Racquetball Association (CRA) / Association canadienne de racquetball
145 Pacific Ave., Winnipeg MB R3B 2Z6
Tel: 613-692-5394
ed.rbcanada@sportmanitoba.ca
www.racquetball.ca
To promote racquetball as a sport & physical activity; To provide leadership by developing & coordinating services & programs designed to meet the needs of the racquetball community
Ron Brown, President
Darrell Davis, Vice-President, High Performance
Manny Gregorio, Vice-President, Marketing & Communications
Jack McBride, Vice-President, Technical
Bob Papineau, Vice-President, Finance

Canadian Rhythmic Sportive Gymnastic Federation (CRSGF) / Fédération canadienne de gymnastique rythmique sportive
c/o 2288 Covington Pl., Victoria BC V8N 5N6
Tel: 250-472-3322; *Fax:* 250-472-2659
dfrattaroli@shaw.ca
To promote Rhythmic Gymnastics for lifetime growth, fitness & the pursuit of excellence.
Danielle Frattaroli, GCG-RG Program Coordinator

Canadian Ski Council (CSC) / Conseil canadien du ski
21 Fourth St. East, Collingwood ON L9Y 1T2
Tel: 705-445-9140; *Fax:* 705-445-0525
info@skicanada.org
www.skicanada.org
Social Media: www.facebook.com/pages/Canadian-Ski-Council/152259956560 ; twitter.com/cdnskicouncil
To encourage participation in recreational skiing & snowboarding.

Canadian Ski Instructors' Alliance (CSIA) / Alliance des moniteurs de ski du Canada
#220, 4900, rue Jean Talon ouest, Montréal QC H4P 1W9
Tel: 514-748-2648; *Fax:* 514-748-2476
Toll-Free: 800-811-6428
national@snowpro.com
www.snowpro.com/csia/e
Social Media: www.facebook.com/CSIAAMSC; www.youtube.com/user/CSIAAMSC
To promote professionalism & high standards for the profession of ski instruction; To certify ski instructors across Canada
Dan Ralph, Managing Director
Lisa Cambise, Director, Shared Services
Martin Jean, Director, Education & Membership Services
Benoit Fournier, Coordinator, National Programs

Canadian Ski Instructors' Alliance (CSIA) / Fédération des entraîneurs de ski du Canada
#220, 4900 Jean Talon ouest, Montréal QC H4P 1W9
Tel: 514-748-2648; *Fax:* 514-748-2476
Toll-Free: 800-811-6428
national@snowpro.com
www.snowpro.com/en
To help produce the best skiers in the world for Canada
Otto Kamstra, Chair

Canadian Ski Marathon (CSM) / Marathon canadien de ski
#200, 81 Jean-Prolux, Gatineau QC J8Z 1W2
Tel: 819-770-6556; *Fax:* 819-770-7428
Toll-Free: 877-770-6556
ski@csm-mcs.com
www.csm-mcs.com
The Canadian Ski Marathon is an historic cross-county ski tour for people of all ages in celebration of Canadian winter. Their mission is to organize an annual and fully supported weekend in the wilderness, the Canadian Ski Marathon provides a uniquely Canadian cross-country skiing event with a broad appeal.
Gregory Koegl, President

Canadian Ski Patrol System (CSPS) / Patrouille canadienne de ski (OPCS)
4531 Southclark Pl., Ottawa ON K1T 3V2
Tel: 613-822-2245; *Fax:* 613-822-1088
Toll-Free: 900-565-2777
info@skipatrol.ca
www.csps.ca
To provide first aid & safety programs throughout Canada
Renée Scanlon, Office Manager
Brian Low, Chair
John Leu, National President

Canadian Snowsports Association (CSA) / L'Association canadienne des sports d'hiver (ACSH)
#202, 1451 West Broadway, Vancouver BC V6H 1H6
Tel: 604-734-6800; *Fax:* 604-669-7954
info@canadiansnowsports.com
www.canadiansnowsports.com
To develop elite amateur athletes; To pursue excellence at national & international level competition
Lillian Alderton, Administrator
David Pym, Managing Director

Canadian Soccer Association (CSA) / Association canadienne de soccer
Place Soccer Canada, 237 Metcalfe St., Ottawa ON K2P 1R2
Tel: 613-237-7678; *Fax:* 613-237-1516
info@soccercan.ca
www.canadasoccer.com
Social Media: www.facebook.com/canadasoccer; twitter.com/CanadaSoccerEN; www.youtube.com/CanadaSoccerTV
To promote the growth & development of soccer for all Canadians at all levels; To provide leadership & good governance for the sport
Peter Montopoli, General Secretary
Joe Guest, Deputy General Secretary
Sean Hefferman, Chief Financial Officer
Ray Clark, Director, Coaching & Player Development
Cathy Breda, Manager, Administration
Michèle Dion, Manager, Communications

Canadian Society for Exercise Physiology (CSEP) / Société canadienne de physiologie de l'exercice (SCPE)
#370, 18 Louisa St., Ottawa ON K1R 6Y6
Tel: 613-234-3755; *Fax:* 613-234-3565
Toll-Free: 877-651-3755
info@csep.cap
www.csep.ca
Social Media: www.facebook.com/group.php?gid=291577755198; twitter.com/CSEPdotCA
To promote the generation, synthesis, transfer & application of knowledge & research related to exercise physiology, encompassing physical activity, fitness, health, nutrition, epidemiology & human performance; To act as the voice for exercise physiology in Canada
Earl Noble, President
Brian MacIntosh, Executive Director
Mike Plyley, Vice-President, Research
Panagiota Klentrou, Treasurer

Canadian Society for Psychomotor Learning & Sport Psychology (CSPLSP) / Société canadienne d'apprentissage psychomoteur et de psychologie du sport (SCAPPS)
c/o Dr. N. Holt, Faculty of Physical Ed. & Rec., University of Alberta, Van Vliet Centre, Edmonton AB T6G 2H9
nick.holt@ualberta.ca
www.scapps.org
To promote the study of motor development, motor learning, motor control, & sport psychology
Nick Holt, President
Sean Horton, Secretary-Treasurer

Canadian Sport Horse Association (CSHA)
PO Box 970, 7904 Franktown Rd., Richmond ON K0A 2Z0
Tel: 613-686-6161; *Fax:* 613-686-6170
csha@canadian-sport-horse.org
www.c-s-h-a.org
Social Media: www.facebook.com/group.php?gid=10649610317
To ensure the production and promotion of a sound, solid horse, with a good disposition, capable of competing successfully in the Olympic Disciplines at all levels of competition.
Paul Morgan, President
David Lancaster, Treasurer

Canadian Team Handball Federation (CTHF) / Fédération canadienne de handball olympique (FCHO)
453, rue Jacob-Nicol, Sherbrooke QC J1J 4E5
Tel: 819-563-7937; *Fax:* 819-563-5352
f.lebeau@videotron.ca
www.handballcanada.ca
François LeBeau, COO
Ward Hrabi, President

Canadian Tenpin Federation, Inc. (CTF) / Fédération canadienne des dix-quilles, inc.
916 - 3 Ave. North, Lethbridge AB T1H 0H3
Tel: 403-381-2830; *Fax:* 403-381-6247
www.gotenpinbowling.ca
To promote & foster the sport of tenpin bowling in Canada by maintaining active membership in the world's appropriate affiliated tenpin organizations, providing competitive opportunities for all skill levels, culminating in the selection of a National Team; To encourage the development of skills through a national coaching certification program
Stan May, Executive Director
Gus Badali, Manager, Domestic Team

Canadian Therapeutic Riding Association / Association canadienne d'équitation thérapeutique
#11, 5420 Hwy. 6 North, RR#5, Guelph ON N1H 6J2
Tel: 519-767-0700; *Fax:* 519-767-0435
ctra@golden.net
www.cantra.ca
To foster therapeutic riding for persons with disabilities by establishing riding standards in collaboration with the medical profession; To accredit programs, certify instructors & promote research; To promote equestian sport & competition for persons with disabilities
Daphne Davey, President
Donna Naylor, Executive Director
Nanci Picken, Coordinator, Development
Anita LeMaître, Secretary
Neil Mahnke, Treasurer

Canadian Ultimate Players Association (CUPA)
4382 Shelbourne St., Vancouver BC V8N 3G3
Toll-Free: 888-691-1080
info@canadianultimate.com
www.canadianultimate.com
Social Media: www.facebook.com/UltimateCanada?ref=ts; twitter.com/Ultimate_Canada

Canadian University Football Coaches Association (CUFCA)
c/o Huskies Football, St. Mary's University, Halifax NS B3H 3C3
Tel: 902-420-5550
To improve the coaching of Canadian Interuniversity Athletic Union (CIAU) football teams; to improve the technical aspects of play in CIAU football
Blake Nill, President

Canadian Wheelchair Basketball Association (CWBA) / Association canadienne de basketball en fauteuil roulant (ACBFR)
#8, 6 Antares Dr., Phase 1, Ottawa ON K2E 8A9
Tel: 613-260-1296; *Fax:* 613-260-1456
Toll-Free: 877-843-2922
info@wheelchairbasketball.ca
www.wheelchairbasketball.ca
Social Media: www.facebook.com/wheelchairbasketball; twitter.com/WCBballCanada
To promote & develop opportunities in the game of wheelchair basketball
Wendy Gittens, Executive Director
Steven Bach, President

Canadian Wheelchair Sports Association (CWSA) / Association canadienne des sports en fauteuil roulant (ACSFR)
#108, 2255 St. Laurent Blvd., Ottawa ON K1G 4K3
Tel: 613-523-0004; *Fax:* 613-523-0149
info@cwsa.ca
www.cwsa.ca/en/site/
To promote excellence & develop opportunities for Canadians in wheelchair sport
Cathy Cadieux, Executive Director
Duncan Campbell, Director, National Development
Andy Van Neutegem, Director, High Performance
Don Lane, Manager, Program
Arley McNeney, Coordinator, Communications

Cape Breton County Minor Hockey Association (CBCMHA)
PO Box 6003, 95 Keltic Dr., Coxheath NS B1S 3V9
Tel: 902-562-1767; *Fax:* 902-562-1833
www.cbcmha.ca
The Cape Breton County Minor Hockey Association is dedicated to the advancement of minor hockey and promoting the development and personal growth of all participants through progressive leadership, by ensuring meaningful and equal opportunities, and providing enjoyable experiences in a safe and respectful environment.
Pam Reid, Executive Director

Centre de plein air du Mont Chalco
CP 55, Chibougamau QC G8P 2K5
Tél: 418-748-7162
Adresse: 264, rte 167, Chibougamau, QC.
Serge Boutin, Directeur des opérations

Cerebral Palsy Sports Association of British Columbia (CPSABC)
6235A - 136th St., Surrey BC V3X 1H3
Tel: 604-599-5240; *Fax:* 604-599-5241
sportinfo@sportabilitybc.ca
www.cpsports.com
To provide sports & recreational opportunities for people with cerebral palsy, head injury, stroke & similar disabilities at the local, regional, provincial & national level; To provide access to appropriate programming for members including segregated & integrated opportunities
Terri Moore, Executive Director

Charlottetown Minor Baseball Association
c/o 42 Trafalgar St., Charlottetown PE C1A 3Z1
Tel: 902-628-4028
daleclair@pei.eastlink.ca
David LeClair, President

Club 'Les Pongistes d'Ungava'
109, rue Obalski, Chibougamau QC G8P 2E8
Tél: 418-748-4903
Lynn Labbé

Club d'auto-neige Chibougamau inc.
CP 43, Chibougamau QC G8P 2K5
Tél: 418-748-3065
Mario Simard

Club de boxe Chibougamau
224, rue Mgr Houe, Chibougamau QC G8P 2Y5
Tél: 418-748-2592
David Pelletier, Président

Club de football Troilus de Chibougamau-Chapais
CP 622, Chibougamau QC G8P 2Y8
Tél: 418-748-3554
footballchibougamau.com
Serge Bouchard, Président

Club de golf de Chibougamau inc.
CP 81, Chibougamau QC G8P 2K5
Tél: 418-748-3249
Adresse: 130, rue des Forces Armées, Chibougamau, QC; Club: 418-748-4709
Richard Simard

Club de karaté Shotokan
417, rue Demers, Chibougamau QC G8P 1E8
Tél: 418-748-3639
France Bélanger, Présidente

Club de nage synchronisée Synchrogamau de Chibougamau
CP 181, Chibougamau QC G8P 2K6
Tél: 418-748-3198
Maureen Tanguay

Club de natation Natchib inc.
CP 213, Chibougamau QC G8P 2K7
Tél: 418-748-3214
Jean Boulanger, Président
Denise Caron

Club de patinage artistique Les lames givrées inc.
CP 453, Chibougamau QC G8P 2X9
Tél: 418-748-2339
Joline Bélanger

Club nautique de Chibougamau inc.
CP 395, Chibougamau QC G8P 2X8
Tél: 418-748-6628
Marcel Steinmetzer

Club Vélogamik
CP 594, Chibougamau QC G8P 2Y8
Tél: 418-748-6406
Fabien Laprise, Président

Coaches Association of British Columbia (CABC)
#200, 3820 Cessna Drive, Richmond BC V7B 0A2
Tel: 604-333-3600; *Fax:* 604-333-3450
info@coaches.bc.ca
www.coaches.bc.ca
Social Media: www.facebook.com/media/set/?set=o.22542167140&ref=mf#!/CoachesBC; twitter.com/CoachesBC
To ensure the development, certification & ongoing education of all BC coaches through the provision of the best possible programs & services
Gordon May, Executive Director

Coaches Association of PEI (CAPEI)
PO Box 302, Charlottetown PE C1A 7K7
Tel: 902-569-0583; *Fax:* 902-368-4548
Toll-Free: 800-247-6712
cgcrozier@sportpei.pe.ca
www.coachespei.ca
To educate, develop & promote coaching & coaches for the benefit of athletes, sport & the community in general; To encourage fair play, integrity & the pursuit of excellence
Cheryl G. Crozier, Executive Director

Coaching Association of Canada (CAC) / Association canadienne des entraîneurs
#300, 141 Laurier Ave. West, Ottawa ON K1P 5J3
Tel: 613-235-5000; *Fax:* 613-235-9500
www.coach.ca
Social Media: www.facebook.com/coach.ca
To improve implementation & delivery of National Coaching Certification Program; To establish coaching as viable career within the Canadian sports system; To increase the number of qualified full-time & part-time remunerated coaches at various levels within the sport system
John Bales, Chief Executive Officer
Cyndie Flett, Vice-President, Research & Development
Nancy Spotton, Vice-President, Sales & Marketing
Marc Schryburt, Director, Finance & Administration, International Programs
Julie Parkins-Forget, Manager, Marketing & Communications

Commission de Ski pour Personnes Handicapées du Québec (CSPHQ)
165 Place Lilas, Pincourt QC J7V 5B6
Tél: 514-425-8894; *Téléc:* 514-425-8894
hwohler@yahoo.com
Promouvoir et pratiquer le ski alpin
Henry Wohler, President

The Commonwealth Games Association of Canada Inc. (CGAC) / Association canadienne des jeux du Commonwealth inc.
#120, 2255 St. Laurent Blvd., Ottawa ON K1G 4K3
Tel: 613-244-6868; *Fax:* 613-244-6826
info@commonwealthgames.ca
www.commonwealthgames.ca
Kelly Laframboise, Administrative Coordinator
Thomas Jones, CEO

Cricket Canada
#301, 3 Concorde Gate, Toronto ON M3C 3N7
Tel: 416-426-7209
cricketcanada@gmail.com
www.gocricketgocanada.com
Social Media: www.facebook.com/GoCricketCanada; twitter.com/canadiancricket
To foster growth & development of cricket in Canada
Ranjit Saini, President

Cross Country Canada (CCC) / Ski de fond Canada (SFC)
c/o Bill Warren Training Centre, #100, 1995 Olympic Way, Canmore AB T1W 2T6
Tel: 403-678-6791; *Fax:* 403-678-3644
Toll-Free: 877-609-3215
info@cccski.com
www.cccski.com
Social Media: www.facebook.com/CrossCountryCanada; twitter.com/cccsk
To develop & deliver programs designed to achieve international excellence in cross-country skiing; to provide national programs for continuous development of cross-country skiing from introductory experience to international excellence, for participants of all ages & abilities, fostering the principles of ethical conduct & fair play
Jim McCarthy, President
Davin MacIntosh, Executive Director
Cathy Sturgeon, Director, Administration & Communication

Curl BC
#293, 3820 Cessna Dr., Richmond BC V7B 0A2
Tel: 604-737-3040; *Fax:* 604-737-1476
Toll-Free: 800-667-2875
curling@curlbc.ca
www.curlbc.ca
Social Media: www.facebook.com/318254030482; twitter.com/curlbc
To deliver all curling programs & services in British Columbia
Scott Braley, Executive Director & CEO
Terry Vandale, President

Curling Chibougamau
733, boul Campbell, Chibougamau QC G8P 1L2
Tél: 418-748-2671
Serge Boutin, Directeur

Curling Québec
CP 1000, Succ. M, 4545, av Pierre-de Coubertin, Montréal QC H1V 3R2
Tél: 514-252-3088; *Téléc:* 514-252-3342
Ligne sans frais: 888-292-2875
info@curling-quebec.qc.ca
www.curling-quebec.qc.ca
Offrir aux amateurs de curling, et à tous ceux désirant le devenir, la possibilité de jouer au curling à l'intérieur d'une structure organisée appuyée par divers services

Marco Berthelot, Directeur général

Cycling Association of the Yukon
4061, 4th Avenue, Whitehorse YT Y1A 1H1
Tel: 867-668-4990; *Fax:* 867-668-8212
sue.richards@gov.yk.ca
Sue Richards, President

Cycling British Columbia (CBC)
#201, 210 West Broadway, Vancouver BC V5Y 3W2
Tel: 604-737-3034; *Fax:* 604-737-3141
info@cyclingbc.net
www.cycling.bc.net
To enable, enhance, & encourage cycling in British Columbia
Keith Ryan, Chief Executive Officer
Colin Campbell, Director, Race & Business Development
Conan Cooper, Director, Development
Diana Hardie, Director, Finance & Administration
Kevin MacCuish, Director, Road & Technical
Adam Muys, Director, BMX
Richard Wooles, Director, High Performance

Cycling PEI (CPEI)
Sport PEI, PO Box 302, 40 Enman Cresent, Charlottetown PE C1A 7K7
Tel: 902-368-4985; *Fax:* 902-368-4548
mconnolly@sportpei.pe.ca
www.cpei.ca
To develop cycling in PEI
Mike Connolly, Executive Director

Disabled Skiers Association of BC (DSABC)
#220, 3820 Cessna Dr., Richmond BC V7B 0A2
Tel: 604-333-3630; *Fax:* 604-333-3450
disabledskiers@telus.net
www.disabledskiingbc.com
To contribute to the quality of life by promoting the sport of skiing for disabled persons
Brian Forrester, Executive Director
Kevin ter Kuile, President

Distance Riders of Manitoba Association (DRMA)
PO Box 47, Gr 36, RR#2, Dugald MB R0E 0K0
Tel: 204-444-2314
www.kucera.mb.ca/drma
DRMA promotes endurance riding in the province of Manitoba & brings together equestrians interested in the sport.
Myna Cryderman, President
Linda Cruden, Membership Director

Dive Ontario
216 Gilwood Park Dr., Penetang ON L9M 1Z6
Tel: 705-355-3483; *Fax:* 705-355-4663
contactus@diveontario.com
www.diveontario.com
Social Media: www.facebook.com/groups/7005127562
Janice Moore, President

Diving Plongeon Canada (DPC) / Association canadienne du plongeon amateur Inc.
#312, 700 Industrial Ave., Ottawa ON K1G 0Y9
Tel: 613-736-5238; *Fax:* 613-736-0409
cada@diving.ca
www.diving.ca
To promote the growth & awareness of diving in Canada; To contribute to the development of globally accepted standards of diving; To support the rules & regulations of international competition
Penny Joyce, Chief Operating Officer
Mitch Geller, Chief Technical Officer
Scott Cranham, Director, High Performance
Jeff Feeney, Manager, Events & Communications

Dr. James Naismith Basketball Foundation / La fondation de basketball Dr James Naismith
PO Box 1030, 14 Bridge St., Almonte ON K0A 1A0
Tel: 613-256-0492; *Fax:* 613-256-7883
info@naismithminorbasketball.ca
www.naismithbasketball.ca
To establish & operate the Naismith International Basketball Centre which will reflect the remarkable heritage & development of Naismith's game in Canada & around the world.
John Gosset, Executive Director
Kevin Hickey, President

Drive Canada
PO Box 2062, Vancouver BC V6B 3S3
Tel: 604-875-1905; *Fax:* 604-857-9582
drivecanada@shaw.ca
www.drivecanada.org
Simon Rosenman, President

Edmonton Bicycle & Touring Club (EBTC)
PO Box 52017, Stn. Garneau, Edmonton AB T6G 2T5
Tel: 780-424-2453
info@bikeclub.ca
www.bikeclub.ca
Social Media: www.facebook.com/group.php?gid=21002145481
Sid Bennett, President

Edmonton Combative Sports Commission (ECSC)
10250 - 101 St. NW, 13th Fl., Edmonton AB T6J 3P4
Tel: 780-495-0382; *Fax:* 780-429-6976
ecsc.ca
The ECSC regulates, governs & controls boxing, wrestling & full-contact karate bouts & contests within Edmonton; enforces the CPBF safety code.
Pat Reid, Executive Director

Endurance Riders Association of British Columbia (ERABC)
c/o 1624 Duncan Dr., Delta BC V4L 1S2
info@erabc.com
www.erabc.com
ERABC fosters interest in the equestrian sport of endurance riding & promotes training & competition opportunities for beginning & advanced riders. It also assists in the development & preservation of courses or terrain suitable for endurance competitions.
Terre O'Brennan, Ride Manager

Endurance Riders of Alberta (ERA)
c/o President, PO Box 418, Seba Beach AB T0E 2B0
Tel: 780-797-5404
www.enduranceridersofalberta.com
Carol Wadey, Treasurer
Owen Fulcher, President

Equestrian Association for the Disabled
8360 Leeming Rd., RR#3, Mount Hope ON L0R 1W0
Tel: 905-679-8323; *Fax:* 905-679-1705
www.tead.on.ca
To enhance the life of children & adults with physical, mental, & emotional handicaps, through equestrian therapy
Jim Sykes, Chair & President
Patrick Warner, Vice-President
Hilary Webb, Executive Director
Gord Hyland, Treasurer
Trish Brakewell, Coordinator
Pat Bullock, Instructor, Riding

Equine Canada (EC) / Canada Hippique
#100, 2685 Queensview Dr., Ottawa ON K2B 8K2
Tel: 613-248-3433; *Fax:* 613-248-3484
Toll-Free: 866-282-8395
inquiries@equinecanada.ca
www.equinecanada.ca
Social Media:
www.facebook.com/group.php?gid=385910086067; twitter.com/Equine_Canada
To promote & develop a unified Canadian Equine Community, an economically viable horse industry, & access to the use of horses for leisure, sport & commerce
Mike Gallagher, President
Craig Andreas, Chief Operating Officer
Michael Arbour, CMA, Chief Financial Officer

Fédération de basketball du Québec (FBBQ) / Québec Basketball Federation
CP 1000, Succ. M, 4545, av Pierre-De Coubertin, Montréal QC H1V 3R2
Tél: 514-252-3057; *Téléc:* 514-252-3357
Ligne sans frais: 866-557-3057
www.basketball.qc.ca
Développement et promotion de la discipline; Formation de joueurs, entraîneurs et arbitres; organisation de compétitions provinciales; Programme Poursuite de l'Excellence (Équipes et Espoirs du Québec)
Daniel Grimard, Directeur général
Francis Jetté, Agent, Communications & marketing

Fédération de patinage artistique du Québec (FPAQ)
CP 1000, Succ. M, 4545, av Pierre-de-Coubertin, Montréal QC H1V 3R2
Tél: 514-252-3073; *Téléc:* 514-252-3170
patinage@patinage.qc.ca
www.patinage.qc.ca
Rendre accessible à tous, les programmes de Patinage Canada, que ce soit par amour, par plaisir ou pour atteindre l'excellence; a l'unisson, nous contribuons ainsi à l'avancement de notre sport.
Josée Beauséjour, Directeur exécutif

Fédération de Patinage de Vitesse du Québec
930, av Roland Beaudin, Sainte-Foy QC G1V 4H8
Tél: 418-651-1973; *Téléc:* 418-651-1977
fpvq@fpvq.org
www.fpvq.org
Depuis un peu plus d'un mois déjà, les athlètes du Centre national courte piste sont en entraînement hors glace sous la surveillance des entraîneurs et avec la grande collaboration du groupe Actiforme.
Robert Dubreuil, Directeur général

Fédération de pétanque du Québec
CP 1000, Succ. M, 4545, av Pierre-de-Coubertin, Montréal QC H1V 3R2
Tél: 514-252-3077
petanque@loisirquebec.qc.ca
www.petanque.qc.ca
Développement du sport de pétanque
Denise Coutu, Secrétaire administrative

Fédération de rugby du Québec (FRQ) / Quebec Rugby Union
CP 1000, Succ. M, 4545, av Pierre-de-Coubertin, Montréal QC H1V 3R2
Tél: 514-252-3189; *Téléc:* 514-252-3159
info@rugbyquebec.qc.ca
www.rugbyquebec.qc.ca
Média social:
www.facebook.com/pages/Rugby-Qu%C3%A9bec/9877948776 8; twitter.com/RugbyQuebec
Promouvoir le sport et la santé physique en général, et sans limiter ce qui précède le sport du rugby; organiser des tournois de Rugby dans la province de Québec; regrouper les associations régionales et les clubs de Rugby du Québec
Nicholas Clapinson, Directeur

Fédération de soccer du Québec
#210, 955, av Bois-de-Boulogne, Laval QC H7N 4G1
Tél: 450-975-3355; *Téléc:* 450-975-1001
www.federation-soccer.qc.ca
Martial Prud'homme, Président
Brigitte Frot, Directrice générale
Edward Witkowskie, Vice-Président
Bruno Bédard, Responsable, Technique
Robert Ganache, Responsable, Finances
Pierre Marchand, Responsable, Compétition

Fédération de volleyball du Québec (FVBQ)
CP 1000, Succ. M, 4545, av Pierre-de Coubertin, Montréal QC H1V 3R2
Tél: 514-252-3065; *Téléc:* 514-252-3176
info-fvbq@volleyball.qc.ca
www.volleyball.qc.ca
Régir le volleyball à l'intérieur et à l'extérieur du Québec; promouvoir le volleyball; former les intervenants impliqués dans l'encadrement du participant; offrir des services aux membres
Alain D'Amboise, Directeur général
Charles H. Cardinal, Président

Fédération du baseball amateur du Québec
CP 1000, Succ. M, 4545, av Pierre-de Coubertin, Montréal QC H1V 3R2
Tél: 514-252-3075; *Téléc:* 514-252-3134
info@baseballquebec.qc.ca
www.baseballquebec.qc.ca
La mission de la Fédération du baseball amateur du Québec inc. est de : Donner un cadre général d'ordre et de discipline à tous les intervenants du baseball québécois; Reconnaître le droit pour tous les joueurs d'évoluer au baseball selon des normes et critères précis; Donner un cadre pour l'application d'une réglementation uniforme dans tout le Québec; Fournir les moyens à chacun de s'amuser, de participer et de se perfectionner afin de donner un idéal à ceux qui aspirent à une carrière.

Fédération du plongeon amateur du Québec (FPAQ)
CP 1000, Succ. M, 4545, av Pierre-de-Coubertin, Montréal QC H1V 0b2
Tél: 514-252-3096; *Téléc:* 514-252-3094
info@plongeon.qc.ca
www.plongeon.qc.ca
Régir le plongeon sur l'ensemble du territoire québécois; promouvoir le plongeon et sa pratique; tenir et organiser des stages de formation et des compétitions de plongeon; regrouper les associations de plongeon
Isabelle Cloutier, Directrice exécutive

Fédération équestre du Québec inc. (FEQ)
CP 1000, Succ. M, 4545, av Pierre-de Coubertin, Montréal QC H1V 3R2
Tél: 514-252-3053; *Téléc:* 514-252-3068
Ligne sans frais: 866-575-0515
infocheval@feq.qc.ca
www.feq.qc.ca
Mèdia social: www.facebook.com/386728291214
Promotion et développement de l'activité équestre au Québec
Richard Mongeau, Directeur général

Fédération internationale de bobsleigh et de tobogganing
Via Piranesi, 44/B, Milan 120137 Italy
egarde@tin.it
www.fibt.com
Ivo Ferriani, Président
Ermanno Gardella, Secrétaire général

Fédération Internationale de Luge de Course (FIL) / International Luge Federation
Rathausplatz 9, Berchtesgaden 83471 Germany
office@fil-luge.org
www.fil-luge.org
Promotion et participation aux compétitions de la luge dans le monde; organise des championnats du monde, des coupes du monde, des championnats régionaux; organise des cours et séminaires pour des arbitres et des entraîneurs
Josef Fendt, Président
Svein Romstad, Secrétaire général

Federation of Broomball Associations of Ontario
515 Gascon St., Russell ON K4R 1C6
Tel: 613-445-0904; *Fax:* 613-445-9844
www.ontariobroomball.ca
To serve broomball players, coaches, & leagues in Ontario
Gerry Wever, President

Federation of Canadian Archers Inc. (FCA) / Fédération canadienne des archers inc.
#108, 2255 St. Laurent Blvd., Ottawa ON K1G 4K3
Tel: 613-260-2113
information@archerycanada.ca
www.archerycanada.ca
Social Media: www.facebook.com/ArcheryCanada; twitter.com/ArcheryCanada
To promote & develop the sport of archery in a safe & ethical manner; To act as the official representative for archery to the federal government, & national & international sport organizations
Scott Ogilvie, Executive Director

Fédération québécoise de ballon sur glace
4545, av Pierre-de Coubertin, Montréal QC H1V 3R2
Tél: 514-252-3078; *Téléc:* 888-455-8547
www.fqbg.net
La Fédération Québecoise de Ballon sur Glace a pour but de promouvoir le sport du ballon sur glace dans la province de Québec
Richard Mimeau, Président

Fédération québécoise de boxe olympique (FQBO)
CP 1000, Succ. M, 4545, av Pierre-de Coubertin, Montréal QC H1V 3R2
Tél: 514-252-3047; *Téléc:* 514-254-2144
Ligne sans frais: 866-241-3779
info@fqbo.qc.ca
www.fqbo.qc.ca
Kenneth Piché, Directeur général
Victoria Sullivan-Smith, Adjointe administrative

Fédération québécoise des activités subaquatiques (FQAS)
CP 1000, Succ. M, 4545, av Pierre-de Coubertin, Montréal QC H1V 3R2
Tél: 514-252-3009; *Téléc:* 514-254-1363
Ligne sans frais: 866-391-8835
info@fqas.qc.ca
www.fqas.qc.ca
Regrouper les adeptes de la plongée et des activités subaquatiques; promouvoir la sécurite dans la pratique des activités subaquatiques; informer et renseigner ses membres et la population sur les bienfaits de la pratique; promouvoir ces activités comme moyen de formation et comme loisir
Jean-Sébastien Naud, Directeur général

Fédération québécoise des sports cyclistes (FQSC) / Québec Cycling Sports Federation
4545, av Pierre-de-Coubertin, Montréal QC H1V 3R2
Tél: 514-252-3071; *Téléc:* 514-252-3165
reception@fqsc.net
www.fqsc.net
Régie et promotion des sports cyclistes au Québec
Simon Thériault, Directeur technique
Louis Barbeau, Directeur général
André Michaud, Président

Fédération québécoise du sport étudiant (FQSE)
CP 1000, Succ. M, 4545, av Pierre-De Coubertin, Montréal QC H1V 3R2
Tél: 514-252-3300; *Téléc:* 514-254-3292
www.fqse.qc.ca; www.sportetudiant.com
Favoriser les actions éducatives dans le domaine de l'activité physique et sportive que se donne le milieu de l'éducation dans le but de contribuer, et cela dans les trois ordres d'enseignement, au développement intégral des élèves, des étudiantes et des étudiants du Québec.
Yves Paquette, Président

Fédération sportive de ringuette du Québec
CP 1000, Succ. M, 4545, av Pierre-de-Coubertin, Montréal QC H1V 3R2
Tél: 514-252-3085; *Téléc:* 514-254-1069
ringuette@ringuette-quebec.qc.ca
www.ringuette-quebec.qc.ca
Promouvoir le sport de la ringuette au Québec
Florent Gravel, Président

Field Hockey Canada (FHC) / Hockey sur gazon Canada
#240, 1101 Prince of Wales Dr., Ottawa ON K2C 3W7
Tel: 613-521-8774; *Fax:* 613-521-0261
fhc@fieldhockey.ca; communications@fieldhockey.ca (media)
www.fieldhockey.ca
Social Media: www.facebook.com/FHCanada; twitter.com/FieldHockeyCan; www.youtube.com/user/hockeysurgazoncanada
To promote the development & growth of field hockey in Canada; To provide coaching, training, & competitive opportunities to prepare Canada's national teams
Carole Lemire, Lead, Finance & Operations
Dawn Phillips, Manager, High Performance
Amy van Hemmen, Coordinator, Communications

Field Hockey Manitoba (FHM)
145 Pacific Ave., Winnipeg MB R3B 2Z6
Tel: 204-925-5794; *Fax:* 204-925-5792
info@fieldhockeymb.org
www.fieldhockeymb.org
Social Media: www.facebook.com/group.php?gid=7322580942
The Association fosters growth & development of field hockey & indoor hockey in Manitoba.
Kim Knowles, President

Football Canada
#100, 2255 St. Laurent Blvd., Ottawa ON K1G 4K3
Tel: 613-564-0003; *Fax:* 613-564-6309
info@footballcanada.com
footballcanada.com
Through its members, to initate, regulate, & manage the programs, services & activities that promote participation & excellence in Canadian Amateur Football.
Richard Munro, CEO
Bob Swan, Technical Consultant
Cara Lynch, Manager, Non-Contact Programs
Josh Sacobie, Technical Coordinator
Christine Piché, Administrative Coordinator

Football PEI
40 Enman Cres., Charlottetown PE C1E 1E6
Tel: 902-368-4262; *Fax:* 902-368-4548
www.footballpei.ca
Social Media: www.facebook.com/home.php?sk=group_113018508765757
To operate as the provincial sport governing body for amateur football in Prince Edward Island; To promote & further the development of the sport in its three forms - flag, tackle, & touch
Glen Flood, Executive Director
Brian Tacowny, President

Golf Association of Ontario (GAO)
PO Box 970, Uxbridge ON L9P 1N3
Tel: 905-852-1101; *Fax:* 905-852-8893
administration@gao.ca
www.gao.ca
Social Media: www.facebook.com/GAOGolf; twitter.com/GAOGolf
To develop & promote golf in the province
David Mills, Executive Director
Dave Colling, Director, Rules & Competitions
Mike Kelly, Director, Sport Development
Craig Loughryne, Director, Handicapping & Course Rating
Kyle McFarlane, Director, Marketing & Communications
Kate Sheldon, Director, Administration

Golf Manitoba Inc.
420 - 145 Pacific Ave., Winnipeg MB R3B 2Z6
Tel: 204-925-5730; *Fax:* 204-925-5731
golfmb@golfmanitoba.mb.ca
golfmanitoba.mb.ca
The Association determines policies & standards relating to the development & promotion of golf in the province.
Rob MacDonald, President
Dave Comaskey, Executive Director

Golf Newfoundland & Labrador (GNL)
PO Box 174, Gander NL A1V 1W6
Tel: 709-424-3102
golf@hnl.ca
www.golfnewfoundland.ca
Greg Hillier, President

Golf Québec
4545, av Pierre-de-Coubertin, Montréal QC H1V 3R2
Tél: 514-252-3345; *Téléc:* 514-252-3346
golfquebec@golfquebec.org
www.golfquebec.org
Assurer le leadership; Favoriser la croissance et le développement du golf amateur dans toute la province tout en préservant l'intégrité et les traditions du jeu
Jean-Pierre Beaulieu, President
François Roy, Directeur général adjoint
Patrice Clément, Directeur, Développement des joueurs
Éric Couture, Directeur, Tournois
Gladys V. Iodio, Coordonnatrice, Services aux membres

Gymnastics Canada Gymnastique (GCG)
#120, 1900 City Park Dr., Ottawa ON K1J 1A3
Tel: 613-748-5637; *Fax:* 613-748-5691
info@gymcan.org
www.gymcan.org
Social Media: www.facebook.com/gymcan; twitter.com/GymnasticsCan
To lead, promote, facilitate & guide gymnastics in Canada as a sport for the pursuit of excellence & world prominence, & as an activity for lifelong participation; To act as the national umbrella organization for provincial & territorial associations which are members; To publish & enforce a standard set of rules & regulations to serve as guidelines for all members; To represent Canadian gymnastics as a member of national & international agencies & federations; To coordinate application of regulations in Canada; To promote, develop & direct high performance gymnastics programs; To promote, facilitate & guide development of national gymnastics programs; To promote, guide & encourage general gymnastics activities; Yo promote gymnastics as a healthy & safe sport/activity
Jean-Paul Caron, President & Chief Executive Officer
Cathy Haines, Chief Technical Officer
Stephan Duchesne, Director, High Performance
Annie Gagnon, Coordinator, Events

Halifax County United Soccer Club
#7, 102 Chain Lake Dr., Halifax NS B3S 1A7
Tel: 902-876-8784; *Fax:* 902-446-3620
info@hcusoccer.ca
www.hcusoccer.ca
To foster a love of soccer and help individuals of all ages achieve their full potential.
Mike Maddalena, President
Laura Yost, Administrator

Halifax Sport and Social Club (HSSC)
PO Box 8821, Halifax NS B3K 5M5
Tel: 902-431-8326
info@halifaxsport.ca
www.halifaxsport.ca
To offer co-ed recreational sport leagues, tournaments and social events for adults.
Lael Morgan, General Manager

Hockey Alberta / Hockey l'Alberta
#1, 7875 - 48 Ave., Red Deer AB T4P 2K1
Tel: 403-342-6777; *Fax:* 403-346-4277
www.hockey-alberta.ca
Social Media: www.facebook.com/group.php?gid=43831380491; twitter.com/HockeyAlberta
To serve those who serve the athletes by providing good governance, quality services, programs & education
Rob Litwinski, General Manager
Mike Olesen, Senior Manager, Systems & Administration
Tim Leer, Senior Manager, Hockey Development

Hockey Canada
#204N, 801 King Edward Ave., Ottawa ON K1N 6N5
Tel: 613-562-5677; *Fax:* 613-562-5676
Toll-Free: 877-648-7465
customerservice@store.hockeycanada.ca
www.hockeycanada.ca
Social Media: www.facebook.com/HockeyCanada
To advance amateur hockey for all individuals through progressive leadership, ensuring meaningful opportunities & enjoyable experiences in a safe, sustainable environment
Sean Kelly, General Counsel
Glen McCurdie, Vice-President, Member Services

Hockey Manitoba
508 - 145 Pacific Ave., Winnipeg MB R3B 2Z6
Tel: 204-925-5755; *Fax:* 204-925-5761
info@hockeymanitoba.mb.ca
www.hockeymanitoba.mb.ca
Social Media: www.facebook.com/pages/Hockey-Manitoba/296995075852?
To foster, develop, & promote amateur hockey throughout Manitoba; To encourage fair play; To secure the enforcement of rules as adopted by by the assosication; To conduct games between member clubs to determine provincial champions
Brian Franklin, President
Peter Woods, Executive Director
Bernie Reichardt, Director, Hockey Development

Hockey New Brunswick (HNB) / Hockey Nouveau-Brunswick
PO Box 456, 861 Woodstock Rd., Fredericton NB E3B 4Z9
Tel: 506-453-0089; *Fax:* 506-453-0868
www.hnb.ca
Brian Whitehead, Executive Director
Tom Donovan, President
Pat MacFadzen, Director, Administration

Hockey Newfoundland & Labrador (NLHA) / Association de hockey de Terre-Neuve et Labrador
PO Box 176, 13B High St., Grand Falls-Windsor NL A2A 2J4
Tel: 709-489-5512; *Fax:* 709-489-2273
office@hockeynl.ca
www.hockeynl.ca
Support for hockey in Canada including minor, junior, senior, female and development.
Craig Tulk, Executive Director
Tamar Hobbs, Administrative Assistant

Hockey North
3506 McDonald Dr., Yellowknife NT X1A 2H1
Tel: 867-874-6903; *Fax:* 867-874-4603
ccarriere@northwestel.net
www.hockeynorth.ca
Cheryl Carriere, Executive Director

Hockey Northwestern Ontario (HNO)
#100, 216 Red River Rd., Thunder Bay ON P7B 1A6
Tel: 807-623-1542; *Fax:* 807-623-0037
info@hockeyhno.com
www.hockeyhno.com
John Pucci, General Manager
Ron MacKinnon, Development Coorindator

Hockey Nova Scotia
#200, 6300 Lady Hammond Rd., Halifax NS B3K 2R6
Tel: 902-454-9400; *Fax:* 902-454-3883
www.hockeynovascotia.ca
Social Media: www.facebook.com/group.php?gid=2222858784
Darren Cossar, Executive Director

Hockey PEI
PO Box 302, 40 Enman Cres., Charlottetown PE C1A 7K7
Tel: 902-368-4334; *Fax:* 902-368-4337
info@hockeypei.com
www.hockeypei.com
Rob Newson, Executive Director

Hockey Québec (FQHG)
#210, 7450, boul. les Galeries d'Anjou, Montréal QC H1M 3M3
Tél: 514-252-3079; *Téléc:* 514-252-3158
info@hockey.qc.ca
www.hockey.qc.ca
Mèdia social: www.facebook.com/group.php?gid=66611750398
Assurer l'encadrement du hockey sur glace; favoriser la promotion et le développement de la personne qui pratique le hockey
Gérard Bélanger, Président
Sylvain B. Lalonde, Directeur général

Horse Trials New Brunswick
c/o Donna Lee Cole, 7515 Rte.102, Browns Flat NB E5M 2N8
Tel: 506-468-2098
www.htnb.org
Donna Lee Cole, President
Louise McSheffrey, Secretary

Horse Trials Nova Scotia (HTNS)
60 Rockwell Drive, Mount Uniacke NS B0N 1Z0
Tel: 902-866-3889
www.htns.org
To foster & encourage safe & fun enjoyment of the sport of Horse Trials (eventing) through regular training & education of riders, coaches, horses & officials
Kim Elliott-Foster, President

International Curling Information Network Group (ICING)
73 Appleford Rd., Hamilton ON L9C 6B5
Tel: 905-389-7781
psmith@icing.org
www.icing.org
To provide information about the sport of curling worldwide
Peter M. Smith, Contact

International Masterathlete Federation (IMAF)
PO Box 185, Richmond Hill ON L4B 4R5
Tel: 905-473-9714; *Fax:* 905-473-9715
Toll-Free: 888-883-3315
To promote health, fitness, & longevity through participation in sport
Liz Roach, President
Iain Douglas, Vice-President

Island Horse Council (IHC)
PO Box 302, Charlottetown PE C1A 7K7
www.islandhorsecouncil.ca
Social Media: www.facebook.com/islandhorsecouncil
The objectives of Island Horse Council are: to promote, conduct and manage a Council for the benefit of Prince Edward Island equestrians; to provide a unified voice for the horse industry on Prince Edward Island; to establish a liaison with any authorities, including federal, provincial, and municipal governments, and provincial or national Horse Councils or Equestrian Federations; and to encourage the development of all aspects of horsemanship, health, education, training, competition, breeding, facilities and humane practices.
Wendell Grasse, Chair
Marg Younker, Treasurer

Japan Karate Association of Yukon
4061, 4th Ave., Whitehorse YT Y1A 1H1
Tel: 867-334-9009
www.sportyukon.com/membership/?member=80
To promote and facilitate Karate in the Yukon Territory.
Mike Tribes, President

Jeux Olympiques Spéciaux du Québec Inc. (OSQ) / Québec Special Olympics
5311, de Maisonneuve ouest, 2e étage, Montréal QC H4A 1Z5
Tél: 514-843-8778; *Téléc:* 514-843-8223
Ligne sans frais: 877-743-8778
info@olympiquesspeciaux.qc.ca
www.olympiquesspeciaux.qc.ca
Mèdia social: www.facebook.com/olympiquesspeciauxquebec?ref=mf; twitter.com/athletesOSQ
Les Olympiques spéciaux, actifs dans plus de 170 pays, ont pour mission d'enrichir, par le sport, la vie des personnes présentant une déficience intellectuelle. Plus de 3.7 millions d'athlètes spéciaux, de tous âges, sont inscrits dans le monde dont plus de 31,000 au Canada et 4,850 aux programmes récréatifs scolaine ou compétitifs offerts dans toutes les régions du Québec. Les 14 sports officiels sont pratiqués à l'intérieur d'un réseau de compétitions annuelles, comptant plus de 80 événements conçus pour tous les niveaux d'habiletés.
Daniel Granger, Chair

Jockey Club of Canada / Jockey Club du Canada
PO Box 66, Stn. B, Toronto ON M9W 5K9
Tel: 416-675-7756; *Fax:* 416-675-6378
jockeyclub@bellnet.ca
www.jockeyclubcanada.com
Social Media: twitter.com/jockeyclubofCAN
Promote good quality racing throughout Canada
James Lawson, Chief Steward
Stacie Roberts, Executive Director

Judo Canada
#212, 1725 St. Laurent, Ottawa ON K1G 3V4
Tel: 613-738-1200; *Fax:* 613-738-1299
Toll-Free: 877-738-5836
info@judocanada.org
www.judocanada.org
Social Media: www.facebook.com/judocanada; twitter.com/judocanada; www.youtube.com/judocanada2012
To promote the principles & teachings of the sport of Kodokan Judo; To work towards the advancement of Judo throughout Canada
Yves Régimbald, Director, Operations & Finance
Andrzej Sadej, Director, Sports
Gosselin Nathalie, Coordinator, Eclipse
Francine Latreille, Officer, Administration

Judo Nova Scotia
224 Victoria Rd., Bridgewater NS B4V 2P1
Tel: 902-543-2836; *Fax:* 902-527-4847
tim.lohnes@abitibibowater.com
www.judons.ca
Social Media: www.facebook.com/judons
Promotes the principles of judo and, in collaboration with members and interested parties, works towards the advancement of judo, at all levels and areas of Nova Scotia.
Gordon Brown, Administrative Manager
Bill Anderson, Chair
Peter Croxall, Co-Chair

Judo-Québec inc
CP 1000, Succ. M, 4545, av Pierre-de-Coubertin, Montréal QC H1V 3R2
Tél: 514-252-3040; *Téléc:* 514-254-5184
info@judo-quebec.qc.ca
www.judo-quebec.qc.ca
Assurer la promotion et le développement du judo au Québec; éduquer, développer et servir nos membres
Daniel De Angelis, Président
Patrick Esparbès, Directeur général
Patrick Vesin, Coordonnateur technique

Karate Manitoba
PO Box 2519, 266 Graham Ave., Winnipeg MB R3C 4A7
Tel: 204-925-5605; *Fax:* 204-925-5916
info@karatemanitoba.ca
www.karatemanitoba.ca
To promote & develop karate in the province of Manitoba at all levels (grassroots to elite athlete) & as recreation.
Daniel Piché, President
Ron Porath, Secretary

Karate Ontario
#8, 531 Atkinson Ave., Thornhill ON L4J 8L9
Tel: 647-706-4835
info@karate-ontario.com
karate-ontario.com
Social Media: www.facebook.com/309961174058?ref=mf; twitter.com/KarateOntario
To promote & perpetuate karate as a martial art & lifetime activity; to promote karate for physical fitness, mental fitness, & as a way of life; to develop provincial standards & programs; to encourage all participants in safely achieving their maximum at the recreational or competitive level; to provide safe competitive opportunities for karate-ka wishing to participate in the sport aspect of karate; to govern the amateur sport of karate & the conduct of all karate-ka under its jurisdiction
Dragan Kljenak, President

Lawn Bowls Association of Alberta
Percy Page Centre, 11759 Groat Rd., 3rd Fl., Edmonton AB T5M 3K6
Tel: 780-427-8119; *Fax:* 780-452-5932
lawnbowl@telusplanet.net
www.bowls.ab.ca
Fred Kodnar, President
Gayell Slater, Vice-President
Pete Wilson, Treasurer

Ligue de dards Ungava
712, 6e Rue ouest, Chibougamau QC G8P 2V1
Tél: 418-748-6732
Claire Patoine

Little League Canada / Petite ligue Canada
235 Dale Ave., Ottawa ON K1G 0H6
Tel: 613-731-3301; *Fax:* 613-731-2829
canada@littleleague.org
www.littleleague.ca
Social Media: www.facebook.com/pages/Little-League-Baseball-Canada/137589529592785; twitter.com/LittleLgeCanada
To provide baseball & softball programs to every boy or girl wishing to participate

Roy Bergerman, President & Chair
Marthe Dubroy, Secretary
Bruce Campbell, Treasurer

Lloydminster & District Fish & Game Association
PO Box 116, Lloydminster AB T9V 0X9
Tel: 780-875-3641
admin@lloydfishandgame.org
www.lloydfishandgame.org
To advocate for & assist in the conservation & management of fish, wildlife & habitat for the continuing benefit of association members & the general public
Gerry Russell, President

Lutte NB Wrestling (LNBW)
www.luttenbwrestling.com
Lutte New Brunswick Wrestling (LNBW) is a non-profit, equal opportunity organization, dedicated to the development, administration and promotion of amateur wrestling throughout the Province.
Mary Singh, Executive Director
Kevin Scully, President

Manitoba Amateur Boxing Association
#302, 200 Main St., Winnipeg MB R3C 4M2
Tel: 204-925-5658
Rosemary Broadbent

Manitoba Amateur Broomball Association (MABA)
145 Pacific Ave., Winnipeg MB R3B 2Z6
Tel: 204-925-5668; *Fax:* 204-925-9792
www.mbbroomball.com
To promote the sport of broomball in Manitoba; to offer opportunities to members in competing in provincial & national championships
Raymond Massinon, President
Ron Marohn, Vice President

Manitoba Amateur Wrestling Association (MAWA)
c/o Sport Manitoba, 145 Pacific Ave., Winnipeg MB R3B 2Z6
Tel: 204-925-5670; *Fax:* 204-925-5703
mawawrestling@mts.net
www.mawawrestling.ca
The Manitoba Amateur Wrestling Association (MAWA) is the recognised provincial sport organization (PSO) for the sport of wrestling in Manitoba. MAWA is dedicated to the continuing development of wrestling across the province and to maintain a safe, fun environment for all its members. MAWA is an organization that promotes teamwork, leadership and healthy lifestyles through wrestling in Manitoba for all ages.

Manitoba Badminton Association (MBA)
#323, 145 Pacific Ave., Winnipeg MB R3B 2Z6
Tel: 204-925-5679; *Fax:* 204-925-5703
badminton@shawbiz.ca
www.badminton.mb.ca
To provide the leadership that promotes the growth of badminton throughout Manitoba as a lifelong sport.
Ron Waterman, President
Ryan Giesbrecht, Executive Director

Manitoba Ball Hockey Association
306-145 Pacific Ave., Winnipeg MB R3B 2Z6
Tel: 204-925-5602
mbha1@hotmail.com
www.manitobaballhockey.com
Social Media: www.facebook.com/group.php?gid=50027852199
To promote & encourage the development of competitive & recreational ball hockey in Manitoba
Kelly Huff, Executive League Director

Manitoba Baseball Association
145 Pacific Ave., Winnipeg MB R3B 2Z6
Tel: 204-925-5763; *Fax:* 204-925-5928
baseball.morgan@sportmanitoba.ca
www.baseballmanitoba.ca
Social Media: www.facebook.com/pages/Baseball-Manitoba/171229052909245; twitter.com/BaseballMB
To foster the participation, development & competition of amateur baseball in Manitoba
Morgan de Pe¤a, Executive Director

Manitoba Blind Sport Association
#311, 200 Main St., Winnipeg MB R3C 4M2
Tel: 204-925-5694; *Fax:* 204-925-5703
blindsport@shawbiz.ca
www.blindsport.mb.ca
Since 1976, the Manitoba Blind Sports Association has been the recognized not-for-profit sport governing body for blind and visually impaired athletes in the province. Our mission is to encourage participation in sport at all levels of skill and ability by blind and visually impaired Manitobans, and to develop athletes of a national and international calibre.

Cathy Drewianchuk, Executive Director

Manitoba Boxing Commission
#420, 213 Notre Dame Ave., Winnipeg MB R3B 1N3
Tel: 204-945-1788; *Fax:* 204-948-3649
www.manitobaboxingcommission.com
The Manitoba Combative Sports Commission (MCSC) regulates professional boxing, kickboxing and mixed martial arts throughout the Province by licensing all participants, promoters, athletes, and supervising events.
Henry Janzen, Chair
Joel Fingard, Executive Director

Manitoba Cerebral Palsy Sports Association (MCPSA)
145 Pacific Ave., Winnipeg MB R3B 2Z6
Tel: 204-925-5682; *Fax:* 204-925-5703
To assist in the development of sport for the disabled in Manitoba by providing an opportunity for a wider participation for persons with cerebral palsy & other neuromuscular disorders

Manitoba Curling Association (MCA)
#309, 145 Pacific Ave., Winnipeg MB R3B 2Z6
Tel: 204-925-5723; *Fax:* 204-925-5720
mca@curlmanitoba.org
www.curlmanitoba.org
To promote the sport of curling in Manitoba.
Shane Ray, Executive Director
Cole Skinner, Event/Media Coordinator
Cindy Maddock, President

Manitoba Diving Association
145 Pacific Ave., Winnipeg MB R3B 2Z6
Tel: 204-925-5654; *Fax:* 204-925-5703
headcoach@panamdiving.com
www.manitobadiving.com
Provides strong ethical and values driven foundation for diving throughout Manitoba and Canada, and supports athletic development, personal growth and community awareness through excellence in leadership
Jim Lambie, Head Coach

Manitoba Fencing Association (MFA)
#308, 145 Pacific Ave., Winnipeg MB R3B 2Z6
Tel: 204-925-5696; *Fax:* 204-925-5703
fencingmb@shawbiz.ca
www.fencing.mb.ca
To promote & develop the sport of fencing in Manitoba
Monica Feist, President
Robert Hornford, Vice-President, Technical
Jane Solomon, Vice-President

Manitoba Five Pin Bowling Federation, Inc.
#219, 200 Main St., Winnipeg MB R3C 4M2
Tel: 204-925-5766; *Fax:* 204-925-5767
Toll-Free: 800-282-8069
www.mfpbf.org
To provide services & resources to its members which enable them to increase membership & promote bowling as a lifetime sport through effective programs at all levels of participation
Deanne Zilinsky, Executive Director

Manitoba Gymnastics Association (MGA)
145 Pacific Ave., Winnipeg MB R3B 2Z6
Tel: 204-925-5781; *Fax:* 204-925-5932
mga@sportmanitoba.ca
www.gymnastics.mb.ca
To develop, promote & guide gymnastics as a lifetime activity in Manitoba
Kathy Stoesz, Executive Director

Manitoba High Schools Athletic Association (MHSAA)
145 Pacific Ave., Winnipeg MB R3B 2Z6
Tel: 204-925-5640; *Fax:* 204-925-5624
info@mhsaa.ca
www.mhsaa.mb.ca
To promote the value of sports in Manitoba secondary schools; To provide athletic & educational opportunities so that students reach their full potential
Morris Glimcher, Executive Director
Scott Kwasnitza, President

Manitoba Horse Council Inc.
145 Pacific Ave., Winnipeg MB R3B 2Z6
Tel: 204-925-5718; *Fax:* 204-925-5703
admin@manitobahorsecouncil.ca
www.manitobahorsecouncil.ca

Geri Sweet, President
Bruce Rose, Executive Director

Manitoba Orienteering Association Inc. (MOA)
145 Pacific Ave., Winnipeg MB R3B 2Z6
Tel: 204-925-5706; *Fax:* 204-925-5792
info@orienteering.mb.ca
www.orienteering.mb.ca
Promotes and supports orienteering in Manitoba.
Jennifer Hamilton, President
Dave Graupner, Treasurer

Manitoba Riding for the Disabled Association Inc. (MRDA)
145 Pacific Ave., Winnipeg MB R3B 2Z6
Tel: 204-925-5905; *Fax:* 204-925-5792
exedir@mrda.cc
www.mrda.cc
Social Media: www.facebook.com/105010909544565
Provides a therapeutic horseback riding program for children with disabilities.
Peter Manastyrsky, Executive Director

Manitoba Ringette Association (MRA) / Association de ringuette du Manitoba
145 Pacific Ave., Winnipeg MB R3B 2Z6
Tel: 204-925-5710; *Fax:* 204-925-5925
ringette.admin@sportmanitoba.ca
www.manitobaringette.ca
Social Media: twitter.com/MBRingette
To develop, encourage and promote Ringette for the enjoyment of all Manitobans through the provision of programs, services and resources that inform, educate and teach skills.
Laralle Higginson, Executive Director
Melanie Reimer, Technical Director

Manitoba Soaring Council
145 Pacific Ave., Winnipeg MB R3B 2Z6
Tel: 204-925-5682; *Fax:* 204-925-5703
www.wgc.mb.ca/msc/Manitoba_Soaring_Council_Home_Page.htm
To foster the art of soaring as an environmentally friendly safe & competitive life sport accessible to all Manitobans

Manitoba Speed Skating Association
145 Pacific Ave., Winnipeg MB R3B 2Z6
Tel: 204-925-5657; *Fax:* 204-925-5792
Toll-Free: 888-628-9921
office@mbspeedskating.ca
www.mbspeedskating.org
The MSSA is dedicated to the development, growth and effective administration of the sport of speed skating in Manitoba through the provision of leadership, support and promotion of its members and clubs.
Paul Daeninck, President

Manitoba Sports Hall of Fame & Museum (MSHF&M)
145 Pacific Ave., Winnipeg MB R3B 2Z6
Tel: 204-925-5735; *Fax:* 204-925-5792
halloffame@sportmanitoba.ca
www.halloffame.mb.ca
The mandate of the Manitoba Sports Hall of Fame is to recognize and honour those people who have made their mark in Manitoba's rich sports history through their activities and achievements. The core business of the Hall of Fame is to honour people by telling their story through articles and exhibits, or right here on this website.
Rick Brownlee, Sport Heritage Manager

Manitoba Tae Kwon-Do Association
145 Pacific Ave., Winnipeg MB R3B 2Z6
Tel: 204-925-5682; *Fax:* 204-925-5703
tkd-exec@rainyday.mb.ca
To promote and govern the sport of Tae Kwon Do in Manitoba.
K.S. Cho, President

Manitoba Trail Riding Club Inc. (MTRC)
838 Alfred Ave., Winnipeg MB R2X 0T6
www.mbtrailridingclub.ca
To meet the needs of a growing number of horse people who wanted a type of riding other than in the show ring which could demonstrate good horsemanship and promote sound, sensible trail horses
Kelli Hayhurst, President
Mary Anne Kirk, Treasurer

Manitoba Underwater Council (MUC)
PO Box 711, Winnipeg MB R3C 2K3
Tel: 204-632-8508
info@manunderwater.com
www.manunderwater.com
To coordinate, preserve, support & promote sport diving clubs & associations; to promote safety in diving; to exchange & disseminate information concerning the sport of skin & scuba diving & to foster conservation

Manitoba Volleyball Association (MVA)
#412, 145 Pacific Ave., Winnipeg MB R3B 2Z6
Tel: 204-925-5783; *Fax:* 204-925-5786
volleyball.ed@sportmanitoba.ca
www.volleyballmanitoba.ca
Social Media: www.facebook.com/pages/Volleyball-Manitoba/150460355015535
To govern the sport of volleyball in Manitoba; To promote the development & growth of volleyball in the province
Ron Betts, Executive Director

Manitoba Wheelchair Sports Association
145 Pacific Ave., Winnipeg MB R3B 2Z6
Tel: 204-925-5790; *Fax:* 204-925-5792
mwsa@sportmanitoba.ca
www.mwsa.ca
Committed to leadership in the promotion of well being and a healthy lifestyle through the development of sport and fitness related opportunities for physically disabled Manitobans.
Tricia Klassen, Executive Director

Minor Hockey Alliance of Ontario
71 Albert St., Stratford ON N5A 3K2
Tel: 519-273-7209; *Fax:* 519-273-2114
alliance@alliancehockey.com
www.alliancehockey.com
Social Media: www.facebook.com/group.php?gid=114981545258512
To organize, coordinate & develop hockey programs for all ages
Tony Martindale, Executive Director

National Snow Industries Association (NSIA) / Association nationale des industries de la neige
#810, 245, av Victoria, Montréal QC H3Z 2M6
Tel: 514-939-7370; *Fax:* 514-939-7371
Toll-Free: 800-263-6742
central.station@nsia.ca
www.nsia.ca
To promote the sport of skiing, snowboarding & outdoor winter-related products
Anna Di Meglio, President
Nicole Garand, Administration & Customer Service

New Brunswick Ball Hockey Association (NBBHA)
16 Reflection Lane, Quispamsis NB E2E 6E7
Tel: 506-333-7772; *Fax:* 506-847-8585
sheila@committedtoyourgoals.com
Sheila Elliott, Contact

New Brunswick Broomball Association
c/o Daniel Savoie
Tel: 506-381-0919
Daniel Savoie, Contact

New Brunswick Candlepin Bowlers Association
PO Box 4315, 11 Sawyer Rd., Woodstock NB E7M 6B7
Tel: 506-328-8418
To promote candlepin bowling, a sport unique to the Maritimes & New England

New Brunswick Curling Association (NBCA) / Association de Curling du Nouveau-Brunswick (ACNB)
PO Box 812, Moncton NB E1C 8N6
Tel: 506-854-9143; *Fax:* 506-388-5708
Toll-Free: 800-592-2875
nbca@nb.sympatico.ca
www.nbcurling.com
To promote curling in New Brunswick; To establish & govern rules for curling competitions in New Brunswick
Marg Maranda, Executive Director
Jerry McCann, President
Catherine MacLean, Treasurer

New Brunswick Equestrian Association (NBEA)
#13, 900 Hanwell Rd., Fredericton NB E3B 6A3
Tel: 506-454-2353; *Fax:* 506-454-2363
www.nbea.ca
Deanna Phelan, President
Bonnie Robertson, Secretary

New Brunswick Golf Association (NBGA) / Association de golf du nouveau brunswick
PO Box 1555, Stn. A, Fredericton NB E3B 5G2
Tel: 506-451-1324; *Fax:* 506-451-1348
nbgolf@nb.aibn.com
www.nbga.nb.ca
To determine policies & standards relating to the development & promotion of amateur golf in New Brunswick
Tyson Flinn, Executive Director

New Brunswick Lawn Bowling Association
929A Cloverdale Rd., Riverview NB E1B 5E6
Tel: 506-386-5568; *Fax:* 506-386-5567
Ruth Katagi, Secretary

New Brunswick Sailing Association (NBSA)
c/o Executive Director, 105 Bird Ave., Fredericton NB E2A 2H8
Tel: 506-472-2117
www.nbsailing.nb.ca
The New Brunswick Sailing Association (NBSA) is the provincial governing body for boating and the sport of sailing in the province and is the Canadian Yachting Association's representative in New Brunswick. NBSA is a non-profit volunteer association with a mission to provide leadership, coordination and training to meet the needs of all New Brunswick boaters.
Sharon Mills, Executive Director

Newfoundland & Labrador Amateur Wrestling Association (NLAWA)
1 Wade's Ln., Flatrock NL A1K 1C3
Fax: 709-643-5103
contact@nlawa.com
www.nlawa.com
The NLAWA is a small organization comprised of coaches, officials, parents and athletes who are dedicated to advancing the sport of wrestling in Newfoundland and Labrador
Randy Ralph, President

Newfoundland & Labrador Ball Hockey Association (NLBHA)
PO Box 2579, Stn. C, St. John's NL A1C 6K1
Tel: 709-729-0689
paulbarron@gov.nl.ca
To promote the sport of ball hockey in Newfoundland & Labrador; To maintain rules & regulations of the sport
Paul Barron, President

Newfoundland & Labrador Basketball Association
The Didham Building, PO Box 21029, 1296A Kenmount Rd., Paradise NL A1L 1N3
Tel: 709-576-0247; *Fax:* 709-576-8787
nlba@sportnf.com
www.nlba.nf.ca
Social Media: www.facebook.com/nlbasketball; twitter.com/nlbasketball
To develop & promote the sport of basketball across Newfoundland; to assest in the establishment of basketball clubs throughout Newfoundland & Labrador.
Bill Murphy, Executive Director
Bas Kavanagh, President

Newfoundland & Labrador Curling Association
c/o Bob Osborne, 54 Hoyles Ave., St. John's NL A1B 1E3
Tel: 709-738-3640
www.curlingnl.ca
Bob Osborne, President
Roy Hodder, Vice-President
Baxter House, Secretary
Carl C. Loughlin, Treasurer
Jean Blackie, Coordinator, Technical
Len Kostaszek, Coordinator, Tournament

Newfoundland & Labrador Soccer Association
39 Churchill Ave., St. John's NL A1A 0H7
Tel: 709-576-0601; *Fax:* 709-576-0588
info@nlsa.ca (business); nlsatechnical@sportnl.ca (technical)
www.nlsa.ca
To provide opportunities for the general public to engage in the game of soccer while having fun & competition
Doug Redmond, President
Dragan Mirkovic, Director, Technical
Rob Comerford, Manager, Business

Newfoundland & Labrador Speed Skating Association (NLSSA)
81 Birchy Cove Dr., Corner Brook NL A2H 6W8
Tel: 709-785-1403
rzrenos@gmail.com

Newfoundland & Labrador Volleyball Association (NLVA)
PO Box 21248, St. John's NL A1A 5B2
Tel: 709-576-0817; *Fax:* 709-576-7493
nlvaruss@sportnl.ca
www.nlva.net
To promote volleyball in Newfoundland & Labrador; to provide competitive opportunities for its members
Russell Jackson, Executive Director
Eric Hiscock, President
Mike Murrran, Elite Development Chair

Newfoundland Baseball
83 Ashford Dr., Mount Pearl NL A1N 3N7
Tel: 709-368-2819; *Fax:* 709-368-6080
nlbaseball@nl.rogers.com
www.sport.ca/nlbaseball
Supports amatuer baseball in Newfoundland.
John Janes, President

Newfoundland Equestrian Association (NEA)
PO Box 372, Stn. C, St. John's NL A1C 5J9
www.horsenewfoundland.com
Katrina Butler, President
Sheila Anstey, Vice-President & Director, Competitions
Katie Murray, Secretary
Cathy Favre, Treasurer

North American Riding for the Handicapped Association (NARHA)
PO Box 33150, Denver CO 80233 USA
Tel: 303-452-1212; *Fax:* 303-252-4610
Toll-Free: 800-369-7433
narha@narha.org
www.narha.org
Promotes the benefit of the horse riding for individuals with physical, emotional & learning disabilities
Carol Nickell, CEO

Northern Alberta Curling Association (NACA)
#110, 9440 - 49 St., Edmonton AB T6B 2M9
Tel: 780-440-4270; *Fax:* 780-463-4519
naca@planet.eon.net
northernalbertacurling.com
Marylynn Morris, Executive Director

Northern Ontario Curling Association
PO Box 940, Unit #4, 214 Main St. West, Atikokan ON P0T 1C0
Tel: 807-597-8730; *Fax:* 888-622-8884
Toll-Free: 888-597-8730
info@curlnoca.ca
www.curlnoca.ca
Social Media: www.facebook.com/curlnoca?sk=wall; twitter.com/curlnoca
Leslie Kerr, Executive Director
Al Gemmell, President

Northern Ontario Hockey Association (NOHA)
108 Lakeshore Dr., North Bay ON P1A 2A8
Tel: 705-474-8851; *Fax:* 705-474-6019
noha@noha.on.ca
www.noha.on.ca
To foster the sport of amateur hockey in northern Ontario
Bryce Kulik, President
Chris May, Executive Director

Northwest Territories 5 Pin Bowlers' Association (NWT5PBA)
PO Box 2643, Yellowknife NT X1A 2P9
Tel: 867-873-8189; *Fax:* 867-873-8237
www.nwt5pba.ca
To promote 5 pin bowling
Gary Black, President

Northwest Territories Broomball Association
529 Range Lake Road, Yellowknife NT X1A 3Y1
justjan529@theedge.ca
www.nwtbroomball.com
Jan Vallillee, President

Northwest Territories Curling Association
PO Box 11089, Yellowknife NT X1A 3X7
Tel: 867-669-8339; *Fax:* 867-669-8327
Toll-Free: 800-661-0797
mnorburn@sportnorth.com
www.nwtcurling.com
Social Media: www.facebook.com/pages/NWT-Curling/316251248400802; twitter.com/nwt_curling
Maureen Miller, President

Northwest Territories Ringette / Association de ringuette des Territoires Nord-Ouest
#2, 496 Range Lake Rd., Yellowknife NT X1A 3R5
Tel: 867-920-7419; *Fax:* 867-920-2843
Miles Harris, President

Northwest Territories Soccer Association (NWTSA)
PO Box 11089, Yellowknife NT X1A 3X7
Tel: 867-669-8326; *Fax:* 867-669-8327
Toll-Free: 800-661-0797
www.nwtkicks.ca
The NWT Soccer Association is a volunteer-run organization and the governing body for all soccer activities in the NWT;

focus is on the grassroots development of our game, as well as the promotion of high performance
Melanie Kornacki, Sport Consultant
Ryan Fequet, President

Northwest Territories Volleyball Association (NWTVA)
c/o Sport North Federation, PO Box 11089, 4909 - 49 St., 3rd Fl., Yellowknife NT X1A 3X7
Tel: 867-669-8326; *Fax:* 867-669-8327
To develop athletes & coaches to compete as Team NWT in the Arctic Winter Games & the Canada Games
Doug Rentmeister, Executive Director, Sport North

Northwestern Ontario Curling Association (NWOCA)
433 Catherine St., Thunder Bay ON P7E 1K9
Tel: 807-622-8254; *Fax:* 807-626-9622
www.norontcurl.tripod.com
Colleen Syrja, Sec.-Treas.
Don R. MacLeod, President

Northwestern Québec Curling Association (NWQCA) / Association de curling du Nord-Ouest québécois
281, 3e rue est, Amos QC J9T 2A7
Tel: 819-732-2089; *Fax:* 819-732-1617
Claude Noel, Secretary

Nova Scotia Badminton Association
5516 Spring Garden Rd., Halifax NS B3J 1G6
Tel: 902-425-5450; *Fax:* 902-425-5606
nsbadminton@sportnovascotia.ca
www.nsba.ca
Jennifer Petrie, Executive Director
Linda Pride, President

Nova Scotia Ball Hockey Association
100 Auburn Drive, Dartmouth NS B2W 3S6
Tel: 902-462-5433; *Fax:* 902-477-0243
To promote ball hockey in Nova Scotia & to host provincial tournaments
Bill Davidson, Contact

Nova Scotia Boxing Authority (NSBA)
c/o Amanda Noonan, PO Box 864, 5516 Spring Garden Rd., 2nd Fl., Halifax NS B3J 2V2
Tel: 902-457-0413; *Fax:* 902-484-6937
anoonan@micco.ca
The Nova Scotia Boxing Authority (NSBA) was established in 1975 to regulate professional boxing. In 1981 the authority superseded local boxing commissions. The object and purpose of the authority are to supervise and regulate boxing, establish and enforce uniform rules for the conduct of boxing, and train officials in accordance with nationally established standards. The NSBA, which answers to the minister of health promotion and protection, is now responsible for regulating all combat sports.
Michael MacDonald, Chairman
Hubert Earle, Director, Combat Sports

Nova Scotia Broomball Association (NSBA)
c/o Rob McKellar, PO Box 3010, Stn. South, Halifax NS
Tel: 902-548-2600

Nova Scotia Curling Association (NSCA)
5516 Spring Garden Rd., 4th Fl., Halifax NS B3J 1G6
Tel: 902-421-2875; *Fax:* 902-425-5606
nsca@sportnovascotia.ca
www.nscurl.com
Jeremiah Anderson, Executive Director
Shirley Osborne, President

Nova Scotia Distance Riding Association (NSDRA)
RR#3, Site 802, Newport NS B0N 2A0

Nova Scotia Equestrian Federation
5516 Spring Garden Rd., 4th Fl., Halifax NS B3J 1G6
Tel: 902-425-5450; *Fax:* 902-425-5606
nsef@sportnovascotia.ca
www.horsenovascotia.ca
Heather Myrer, Executive Director

Nova Scotia Golf Association (NSGA)
#4, 24 Simmonds Dr., Dartmouth NS B3B 1R3
Tel: 902-468-8844; *Fax:* 902-484-5327
www.nsga.ns.ca
Social Media: www.facebook.com/pages/The-Nova-Scotia-Golf-Association/64019542477; twitter.com/novascotiagolf
To promote, foster & develop golf at all levels in Nova Scotia; to provide a liaison between member clubs & the Royal Canadian Golf Association; to consult & assist with member clubs on turf maintenance, handicap procedures, slope ratings, rule interpretations & junior development; to organize tournaments, in cooperation with member clubs, that determine provincial champions.

David Campbell, Executive Director
Jan Gaudette, Executive Assistant

Nova Scotia Powerlifting Association
Sydney NS B1P 3W7
Tel: 902-567-0893
johnfraser56@hotmail.com
To provide opportunities for lifters to learn the sport of powerlifting through seminars, gyms & clubs; to participate in meets locally, nationally & internationally
John Fraser, President

Nova Scotia Rugby Football Union
5516 Spring Garden Rd., Halifax NS B3J 1G6
Tel: 902-425-5450; *Fax:* 902-425-5606
rugby@sportnovascotia.ca
www.rugbyns.ns.ca
To promote, control, encourage & develop the game of rugby union football throughout Nova Scotia
Marty Williams, CEO

Nova Scotia School Athletic Federation
5516 Spring Garden Rd., Halifax NS B3J 3G6
Tel: 902-425-8662; *Fax:* 902-425-5606
dweston@sportnovascotia.ca
nssaf.ednet.ns.ca
Motto: "Education Through Sport" which thus emphasises the value of sport in relation to the multitude of benefits that participation gives to their students.
Darrell Dempster, Executive Director
Dianne Weston, Secretary

Nova Scotia Table Tennis Association (NSTTA)
9 Londra Ct., Dartmouth NS B2W 5A5
Tel: 902-406-6286
www.freewebs.com/nstta
Erica Ans, President

Nova Scotia Tennis Association
5516 Spring Garden Rd., Halifax NS B3J 1G6
Tel: 902-425-5454
tennisns@sportnovascotia.ca
www.tennisnovascotia.ca
Andrew Oxner, President
Roger Keating, Executive Director
Paul Richard, Chair, Communications

Nunavut Speed Skating Association
PO Box 761, Iqaluit NU X0A 0H0
Tel: 867-979-1226; *Fax:* 867-975-3384
jtmaurice@northwestel.net
www.nunavutspeedskating.ca
John Maurice, President

NWT Badminton Association
c/o Sport North Federation, PO Box 11089, 4908 - 49th St., 3rd Fl., Yellowknife NT X1A 3X7
Tel: 867-669-8326; *Fax:* 867-669-8327
Toll-Free: 800-661-0797
www.nwtbadminton.ca
Julie Jeffery, President

NWT Speed Skating Association
PO Box 2664, Yellowknife NT X1A 2P9
pamela@ssimicro.com
www.nwtspeedskating.ca
To promote the sport of speed skating in the NWT
Pam Dunbar, President

Ontario 5 Pin Bowlers' Association (O5PBA)
#302, 3 Concorde Gate, Toronto ON M3C 3N7
Tel: 416-426-7167; *Fax:* 416-426-7364
o5pba@o5pba.ca
www.o5pba.ca
Johnda Cresswell, President
Heather Dwinnell, Coordinator, Administration
Rhonda Gifford, Coordinator, Program
Jackie Henriques, Coordinator, Finances
Al Hong, Coordinator, Events

Ontario Amateur Wrestling Association (OAWA)
#213, 3 Concorde Gate, Toronto ON M3C 3N7
Tel: 416-426-7274; *Fax:* 416-426-7343
admin@oawa.ca
www.oawa.ca
To provide essential services & programs dedicated to developing amateur wrestling at all age levels within Ontario
Tim MaGarrey, Provincial Director

Ontario Badminton Association (OBA)
#209, 3 Concorde Gate, Toronto ON M3C 3N7
Tel: 416-426-7192; *Fax:* 416-426-7346
info@ontariobadminton.on.ca
www.ontariobadminton.on.ca
To provide an organized, structured environment for the activity of badminton
Val Butler, Executive Director

Ontario Ball Hockey Association (OBHA)
#5, 56 Pennsylvania Ave., Concord ON L4K 3V9
Tel: 905-738-3320; *Fax:* 905-738-3321
www.ontarioballhockey.ca
Social Media: www.facebook.com/group.php?gid=2374843443
To promote & increase participation in the sport of ball hockey in Ontario; to improve opportunities for competition at all levels of participation; to create & implement leadership opportunities for officials, coaches & administrators; to establish standards of play & for quality of equipment to ensure good sport & safety for all participants
Mauro Cugini, Executive Director

Ontario Basketball
#311, 3 Concorde Gate, Toronto ON M3C 3N7
Tel: 416-426-7200; *Fax:* 416-426-7360
info@basketball.on.ca
www.basketball.on.ca
To promote & develop basketball on an amateur basis in the province of Ontario.
Michele O'Keefe, Executive Director
Ken Urbach, President
Greg Verner, Vice President

Ontario Blind Sport Association (OBSA)
#104, 3 Concorde Gate, Toronto ON M3C 3N6
Tel: 416-426-7191; *Fax:* 416-426-7361
Toll-Free: 888-711-1112
matt@osrc.com
www.blindsports.on.ca
Shirley Shelby, President

Ontario Competitive Trail Riding Association Inc. (OCTRA)
R.R.#4, Tottenham ON L0G 1W0
Tel: 905-936-3362
webmaster@octra.on.ca
www.octra.on.ca
To encourage the growth & popularity of competitive trail, endurance riding & Ride'n'Tie; to establish a set of rules & quality for managing & judging same; to encourage & maintain a high standard of horsemanship & sportsmanship amongst competitors; to encourage the selection, care, training & conditioning of horses for long distance riding; to provide guidance & help to clubs & groups in establishing & running competitive rides; to ensure that all rides are run humanely so as to avoid cruelty & suffering to competing animals; to formulate promotional & educational programs; to foster goodwill & understanding between horse owners, land owners & conservation authorities with a view to opening up more land for riding trails
Mark Ford, President
Joe Mezenberg, Vice-President
Marg Murray, Secretary
Kelly Corbyn, Treasurer

Ontario Curling Association (OCA)
Office Mall 2, #2B, 1400 Bayly St., Pickering ON L1W 3R2
Tel: 905-831-1757; *Fax:* 905-831-1083
Toll-Free: 877-668-2875
doug@ontcurl.com
www.ontcurl.com
The Ontario Curling Association is an association of curling clubs covering the southern part of Ontario. Services and programs, including a variety of competitions are supplied to the clubs and their members
Doug Bakes, Executive Director

Ontario Cycling Association (OCA) / Association cycliste ontarienne
#307, 3 Concorde Gate, Toronto ON M3C 3N7
Tel: 416-426-7416; *Fax:* 416-426-7349
info@ontariocycling.org; ocamagazine@ontariocycling.org
www.ontariocycling.org
To act as the provincial governing body for road, track & cyclocross, mountain biking, & BMX racing in Ontario; To develop & deliver quality programs & services for the sport of cycling in Ontario
Duncan Vipond, President
Malcolm Eade, Vice-President, Administration & Finance
Glenn Meeuwisse, Vice-President, High Performance
Matthias Schmidt, Vice-President, Development
Jim Crosscombe, Executive Director
Denise Kelly, Director, Provincial Coaching
Chris Baskys, Coordinator, Membership
Nicky Pearson, Coordinator, BMX Growth & Development

Ontario Deaf Sports Association
#303, 3 Concorde Gate, Toronto ON M3C 3N7
Tel: 416-413-0299
office@ontariodeafsports.on.ca
www.ontariodeafsports.on.ca
Rohan Smith, President

Ontario Equestrian Federation (OEF)
#203, 9120 Leslie St., Richmond Hill ON L4B 3J9
Tel: 905-709-6545; *Fax:* 905-709-1867
Toll-Free: 877-441-7112
horse@horse.on.ca
www.horse.on.ca
Committed to equine welfare & to providing leadership & support to the individuals, associations & industries in Ontario's horse community
Deborah Thompson, Executive Director
Gary Yaghdjian, President
Kathy Fremes, Secretary

Ontario Federation of School Athletic Associations (OFSAA) / Fédération des associations du sport scolaire de l'Ontario
#204, 3 Concorde Gate, Toronto ON M3C 3N7
Tel: 416-426-7391; *Fax:* 416-426-7317
lindsey@ofsaa.on.ca (Newsletter)
www.ofsaa.on.ca
Social Media: www.facebook.com/group.php?gid=57198022397
To enhance school sport in Ontario; To handle issues that affect students, coaches, schools, & communities; To work with volunteer teacher-coaches to offer provincial championships & festivals for student-athletes across Ontario
Martin Ritsma, President
Lynn Kelman, Vice-President
Doug Gellatly, Executive Director
Lindsey Evanoff, Coordinator, Marketing & Communications

Ontario Hockey Federation (OHF)
#9, 400 Sheridon Dr., cambridge ON N1T 2H9
Tel: 226-533-9070; *Fax:* 519-620-7476
info@ohf.on.ca
www.ohf.on.ca
Social Media: www.facebook.com/OHFHockey; twitter.com/ohfhockey
Phillip McKee, Executive Director
Bill Bowman, President

Ontario Horse Trials Association (OHTA)
#186, 3-304 Stone Rd. West, Guelph ON N1G 4W4
ohta@hotmail.ca
www.horsetrials.on.ca
OHTA is a volunteer, not-for-profit organization whose main functions are to support, develop & promote events in Ontario.
Glenn McMechan, President
Robin Campbell, Secretary

Ontario Lawn Bowls Association
c/o Elaine Stevenson, 23018 Lakeridge Rd., RR#2, Sunderland ON L0C 1H0
Tel: 705-228-8058
olba@olba.ca
www.olba.ca
Arja Nesbitt, President
Elaine Houtby, Vice-President
Alan Dean, 2nd Vice-President
Bob O'Neil, Executive Director
Edith Pedden, Secretary
Richard Peart, Treasurer

Ontario Minor Hockey Association (OMHA)
#3, 25 Brodie Dr., Richmond Hill ON L4B 3K7
Tel: 905-780-6642; *Fax:* 905-780-0344
omha@omha.net
www.omha.net
Social Media: twitter.com/HometownHockey
To provide community-based minor hockey programming for men, women, & children; To monitor the safety of the game, from equipment to rules
Marg Ensoll, President
Richard Ropchan, Executive Director
Kevin Boston, Director, Marketing & Events
Ian Taylor, Director, Development
Bill Rowney, Treasurer
Mark Dickie, Manager, Communications & IT

Ontario Ringette Association (ORA) / Association de ringuette de l'Ontario
#207, 3 Concorde Gate, Toronto ON M3C 3N7
Tel: 416-426-7204; *Fax:* 416-426-7359
www.ontario-ringette.com
To promote fun, fitness, & friendship in a safe play environment; To be dedicated to quality performance & fair play opportunity for all ages
Keith Kaiser, President
Michael Beaton, Executive Director
Karla Romphf, Director, Technical
Stephanie Corrado, Coordinator, Administration

Ontario Soaring Association
10 Courtwood Pl., Toronto ON M2K 1Z9
Tel: 416-223-6487
Walter Chmela, Contact

Ontario Soccer Association (OSA)
7601 Martin Grove Rd., Vaughan ON L4L 9E4
Tel: 905-264-9390; *Fax:* 905-264-9445
TheOSA@soccer.on.ca
www.soccer.on.ca
Social Media: www.facebook.com/TheOntarioSoccerAssociation; twitter.com/OSA_Tweeter
To provide leadership & support for the advancement of soccer; To provide programs & services
Ron Smale, President
Lisa Beatty, Executive Director

Ontario Speed Skating Association (OSSA)
PO Box 1179, 2 Queen St., 2nd Fl., Lakefield ON K0L 2H0
Tel: 705-652-9490; *Fax:* 705-652-1227
ontariospeedskating.ca
Social Media: www.facebook.com/OntarioSpeedSkating; twitter.com/OSSA
To promote & develop the sport of speed skating in Ontario.
Jacqueline Deschenes, Executive Director
Sarah Leslie, Manager, Sport

Ontario Tennis Association (OTA)
#200, 1 Shoreham Dr., Toronto ON M3N 3A7
Tel: 416-514-1100; *Fax:* 416-514-1112
Toll-Free: 800-387-5066
ota@tennisontario.com
www.tennisontario.com
To act as the provincial governing body for tennis in Ontario; To promote participation in tennis in Ontario; To create tennis opportunities for players of every level, from grassroots to national calibre athlete; To encourage the quest for excellence for all players
Michel Lecavalier, President
Jim Boyce, Executive Director
Simon Bartram, Vice-President
Scott Fraser, Vice-President, Finance & Administration
Glenna Poick, Vice-President, Marketing & Communications
Liz Wood, Vice-President, Membership & Regional Development

Ontario Trail Riders Association (OTRA)
PO Box 3038, Elmvale ON L0L 1P0
www.otra.ca
To identify, develop, & preserve multi-use trails throughout Ontario
Janice Clegg, President

Ontario Underwater Council (OUC)
#104, 1185 Eglinton Ave. East, Toronto ON M3C 3C6
Tel: 416-426-7033; *Fax:* 416-426-7280
ouc@underwatercouncil.com
www.underwatercouncil.com
To represent all divers in Ontario; to promote the sport of scuba diving
Raimund Krob, President

Ontario Volleyball Association (OVA)
#304, 3 Concorde Gate, Toronto ON M3C 3N7
Tel: 416-426-7316; *Fax:* 416-426-7109
Toll-Free: 800-563-5938
ova@ontariovolleyball.org
www.ontariovolleyball.org
Social Media: twitter.com/ova_updates
To lead in the promotion & development of volleyball in Ontario
Kristine Drakich, President
Linda Melnick, Secretary & Vice-President, Operations
Gord Ley, Vice-President, Beach
Jos Nederveen, Vice-President, Indoors

Ontario Water Polo Association (OWPA) / L'Association de water polo d'Ontario
#206, 3 Concorde Gate, Toronto ON M3C 3N7
Tel: 416-426-7028; *Fax:* 416-426-7356
info@ontariowaterpolo.ca
www.ontariowaterpolo.ca
Ross McDonald, Technical Director

Ontario Women's Hockey Association (OWHA) / Association de hockey féminin de l'Ontario
#3, 5155 Spectrum Way, Mississauga ON L4W 5A1
Tel: 905-282-9980; *Fax:* 905-282-0499
info@owha.on.ca; stats@owha.on.ca
www.owha.on.ca
To provide & develop opportunities for girls & women to play female hockey in all aspects of female hockey; To foster & encourage leadership programs in all areas related to the development of female hockey in Ontario; To promote hockey as a game played primarily for enjoyment while also fostering sportsmanship
Suzanne Essex, Chair
Fran Rider, President
Mary Ann Blunt, Secretary
Debbie MacDonald, Treasurer

Ottawa District Minor Hockey Association (ODMHA)
#300, 1247 Kilborn Place, Ottawa ON K1H 6K9
Tel: 613-224-3589; *Fax:* 613-224-4625
www.odmha.on.ca
Social Media: www.facebook.com/group.php?gid=2228819818
The Ottawa & District Minor Hockey Association is dedicated to promoting and fosyering minor hockey through fair play and maintaining and increasing interest in the game of hockey by ensuring that all organized minor hockey is developed within the Branch in accordance to prescribed standards.
Dodie Malcolm, President

Ottawa Valley Curling Association (OVCA)
PO Box 40129, Ottawa ON K1V 0W8
Tel: 613-521-5822; *Fax:* 613-521-5344
Toll-Free: 800-385-6621
events@ovca.com
www.ovca.com
To foster curling in the Ottawa & St. Lawrence Valleys & Outaouais
Perry Anderson, President
Lily Ooi, Coordinator, Events

Paralympic Sports Association (Alberta) (PSA)
10024 - 79 Ave., Edmonton AB T6E 1R5
Tel: 780-439-8687; *Fax:* 780-432-0486
info@parasports.net
www.parasports.net
To provide sports & recreation programs for people with a physical disability
Kim McDonald, Executive Director
Suzanne Harrison, Coordinator, Programs

ParaSport and Recreation PEI
Royalty Center House Of Sport, PO Box 841, #115, 40 Enman Cres., Charlottetown PE C1A 7L9
Tel: 902-368-4540; *Fax:* 902-368-4548
info@parasportpei.ca
www.parasportpei.ca
To ensure the ample provision of sport & recreation opportunities for persons who are physically challenged
Tracy Stevenson, Executive Director

ParaSport Ontario
#104, 3 Concorde Gate, Toronto ON M3C 3N7
Tel: 416-426-7187; *Fax:* 416-426-7361
Toll-Free: 800-265-1539
info@parasportontario.ca
www.parasportontario.ca
Social Media: www.facebook.com/parasportontario; twitter.com/parasport_ont
To provide leadership, resources, & opportunities to ensure a strong community for persons with a disability in the Ontario sport & recreation community
Cathy Vincelli, Executive Director

Patrouille de ski St-Jean
651, 6e Rue ouest, Chibougamau QC G8P 2T8
Tél: 418-748-6914
Patrice Bolduc

Peace Curling Association (PCA)
PO Box 265, Grande Prairie AB T8V 3A4
Tel: 780-532-4782; *Fax:* 780-538-2485
peaccurl@telusplanet.net
www.peacecurl.org
Bob Cooper, President

Pemberton Soaring Centre
Pemberton BC V0N 2L1
Tel: 604-894-5727; *Fax:* 604-894-5776
Toll-Free: 800-831-2611
info@pembertonsoaring.com
www.pembertonsoaring.com
To coordinate soaring activities in BC; To encourage formation of new clubs & training of new instructors

Rudy Rozsypalek

Physical & Health Education Canada / Éducation physique et santé Canada
#301, 2197 Riverside Dr., Ottawa ON K1H 7X3
Tel: 613-523-1348; *Fax:* 613-523-1206
Toll-Free: 800-663-8708
info@phecanada.ca
www.phecanada.ca
To promote quality school health programs & the healthy development of Canadian children & youth
Mark Jones, President
Andrea Grantham, Executive Director
Sharon May, Director, Programs

Prince Edward Island Alpine Ski Association
PO Box 2026, Charlottetown PE CIA 7N7
Tel: 902-368-4110; *Fax:* 902-368-4548
Toll-Free: 800-247-6712
sports@sportpei.pe.ca
www.sportpei.pe.ca
Fred Horrelt, President

Prince Edward Island Amateur Baseball Association
PO Box 302, 40 Enman Cres., Charlottetown PE C1A 7K7
Tel: 902-569-0583; *Fax:* 902-368-4548
Toll-Free: 800-247-6712
www.baseballpei.ca
To promote & develop minor & amateur baseball in PEI
Cheryl Crozier, Executive Director
Don LeClair, President

Prince Edward Island Amateur Boxing Association
2595 Horne Cross Rd., Wilsloe PE C1E 1Z3
Tel: 902-394-1574; *Fax:* 902-628-3865
Holly Morrison, President

Prince Edward Island Badminton Association
c/o Sport PEI, PO Box 302, Charlottetown PE C1A 7K7
Tel: 902-368-4262; *Fax:* 902-368-4548
Dawna Woodside, President

Prince Edward Island Curling Association (PEICA)
PO Box 302, 40 Enman Cres., Charlottetown PE C1A 7K7
Tel: 902-368-4208; *Fax:* 902-368-4548
info@peicurling.com
www.peicurling.com
Social Media: www.facebook.com/peicurling; twitter.com/peicurling
To advance & promote curling as a competitive & recreational sport in Prince Edward Island
Amy Duncan, Executive Director

Prince Edward Island Five Pin Bowlers Association Inc.
c/o Sport PEI, PO Box 302, Charlottetown PE C1A 7K7
Tel: 902-368-4110; *Fax:* 902-368-4548
Toll-Free: 800-247-6712
sports@sportpei.pe.ca
www.sportpei.pe.ca
Nina Costain, President

Prince Edward Island Golf Association
PO Box 51, Charlottetown PE C1A 7K2
Tel: 902-393-3293; *Fax:* 902-628-2260
peiga@peiga.ca
www.peiga.ca
The total improvement of golf on PEI
Don Chandler, Executive Director
Jean Kelly, President

Prince Edward Island Hockey Referees Association
c/o Hockey PEI, 40 Enman Cres., Charlottetown PE C1A 7K7
Tel: 902-367-8373
troyhowatt@eastlink.ca
www.peihra.com
Troy Howatt, Chair

Prince Edward Island Lawn Bowling Association
Sport PEI, PO Box 302, Charlottetown PE C1A 7K7
Tel: 902-368-4110; *Fax:* 902-368-4548
Toll-Free: 800-247-6712
sports@sportpei.pe.ca
To provide guidance to bowlers and all people interested in the sport. They wish to assit in the growth and development of Lawn Bowling on PEI Island, they wish to promote and encourage fair play in the sport at club level and at National lvel, they wish to develop leadership and to provide oppourtunities for development in the field of coaching, umpiring, and administration. They also provide interesting tournaments and events throughout the playing season.
Sharon Renner, President

Prince Edward Island Roadrunners Club
40 Villa Ave., Charlottetown PE C1A 2B1
runners@peiroadrunners.ca
www.peiroadrunners.ca
The PEI RoadRunners Club is an organization whose objective is to promote and encourage running as a sport and healthful exercise. The Club welcomes all runners, regardless of ability and attempts to meet the needs of the competitive, as well as, the recreational runner.
Kim Bailey, President

Prince Edward Island Sailing Association (PEISA)
PO Box 6708, York Point PE C0A 1H0
www.peisailing.com
The PEI Sailing Association is a volunteer organization that promotes sailing in the province of Prince Edward Island, Canada. As the provincial chapter of the Canadian Sailing Association the PEI Sailing Association provides support and training to anybody interested in learning to sail or expanding their sailing.
Ellen McPhail, Executive Director

Prince Edward Island School Athletic Association (PEISAA)
109 Water St., Summerside PE C1N 1A8
Tel: 902-888-8037; *Fax:* 902-432-2659
grturtle@gov.pe.ca
www.edu.pe.ca/peisaa
Supporting sports including but not exclusive to, badminton, softball, wrestling, golf, cross country, curling, and volleyball, in PEI.
Garth Turtle, Executive Director
Lona Ryan, Game Reporting
Gerald MacCormack, Secretary-Treasurer

Prince Edward Island Soccer Association (PEISA)
PO Box 1863, 40 Enman Cres., Charlottetown PE C1A 7N5
Tel: 902-368-6251; *Fax:* 902-569-7693
admin@peisoccer.com
www.peisoccer.com
To promote & regulate soccer in PEI; to provide competitive opportunities for members.
Gerald MacDonald, President
Daphne Andrews, Secretary/Registrat
Colleen Arsenault, Treasurer

Prince Edward Island Tennis Association
PO Box 302, 40 Enman Cres., Charlottetown PE C1A 7K7
Tel: 902-368-4985; *Fax:* 902-368-4548
mconnolly@sportpei.pe.ca
www.tennispei.ca
To promote the sport of tennis on PEI.
Mike Connolly, Executive Director
Brian Hall, Technical Director

Prince Edward Island Track & Field Association
c/o Sport PEI, 3 Queen St., Charlottetown PE C1A 7K7
Tel: 902-368-4110

Prince Edward Island Water Ski Association
c/o Regional President, 8 Falconwood Rd., Charlottetown PE C1A 6B5
Tel: 902-894-5740
Stuart Smith, President

Provincial Water Polo Association (PWPA)
c/o Sport Nova Scotia, 5516 Spring Garden Rd., Halifax NS B3J 1G6
lavoie.ghg@forces.gc.ca
www.hfxh2o.ca
The Provincial Water Polo Association (PWPA) was created in late 2006, and its prime mission is to promote the sport of water polo in Nova Scotia.
Guy Lavoie, Contact

Québec Ball Hockey Association (QBHA)
#203, 5960 Jean-Talon E, St. Leonard QC H1S 1M2
Tel: 514-251-9346; *Fax:* 514-251-8285
Tony Iannitto

Québec Lawn Bowling Federation / Fédération de Boulingrin du Québec
#662 Oak Ave., Saint-Lambert QC J4P 2R6
www.qlbf.org
Debbie Smits, Contact

Rhythmic Gymnastics Alberta (RGA)
c/o Percy Page Centre, 11759 Groat Rd., 3rd Fl., Edmonton AB T5M 3K6
Tel: 780-427-8152; *Fax:* 780-427-8153
Toll-Free: 800-881-2504
rga@rgalberta.com
www.rgalberta.com
Social Media: www.facebook.com/pages/Rhythmic-Gymnastics-Alberta/298160665303?ref=ts
To foster & encourage participation & the development of excellence in rhythmic gymnastics
Joan Jack, President
Odette Lindstrom, Treasurer
Helen Marchak, Vice-President

Rhythmic Gymnastics Manitoba Inc. (RGM)
145 Pacific Ave., Winnipeg MB R3B 2Z6
Tel: 201-492-5573
rhythmic@sportmanitoba.ca
www.rgmanitoba.com
To support & promote rhythmic gymnastic programs
Katherine Kwiecien, Executive Director
Raymond Chu, President
Zdravka Tchonkova, Vice-President, Marketing
Susan Yurkiw, Vice-President, Finance
John Matthews, Director, Events

Ringette Association of Saskatchewan (RAS) / Association de ringuette de Saskatchewan
1860 Lorne St., Regina SK S4P 2L7
Tel: 306-780-9432; *Fax:* 306-780-9460
www.ringettesask.com
To develop, promote, communicate, & administer programs, policies & procedures which will enhance the development & participation of coaches, players, officals, volunteers, & administrators from all levels throughout Saskatchewan
Denise Treslan, President
Crystal Gellner, Executive Director
Keith Doering, Director, Technical

Ringette Canada (RC) / Ringuette Canada
#201, 5510 Canotek Rd., Ottawa ON K1J 9J4
Tel: 613-748-5655; *Fax:* 613-748-5860
ringette@ringette.ca
www.ringette.ca
To formulate, publish & administer national policies beneficial to the sport; To enforce laws & regulations governing ringette; To encourage ringette participants to strive for excellence in teamwork, team spirit & team discipline
David Patterson, Executive Director
Frances Losier, Director, Sport Development
Nathalie Muller, Director, Technical
Monty Aldous, Coordinator, Club Development
Alayne Martel, Contact, Media & Public Relations

Ringette New Brunswick (RNB) / Ringuette Nouveau-Brunswick
c/o Marise Aufrey, Administrative Assistant, 940 Centrale St., Memramcook NB E4K 3T4
Tel: 506-758-2546
MariseA@rrsb.nb.ca
www.sport.nb.ca/ringette/
To ensure the well-being & development of ringette athletes in New Brunswick
Ron Richard, President
Hélène L. Beaulieu, Vice-President

Ringette Nova Scotia
5516 Spring Garden Rd., 4th Fl., Halifax NS B3J 1G6
Tel: 902-425-5450; *Fax:* 902-425-5606
ringette@sportnovascotia.ca
www.ringette.ns.ca
To promote, develop & administer the sport of ringette within Nova Scotia
Lindsay Bennett, Executive Director
Dennis Barnhart, President

Rowing Canada Aviron (RCA) / Association canadienne d'aviron amateur
#321, 4371 Interurban Rd., Victoria BC V9E 2C5
Fax: 250-220-2503
Toll-Free: 877-722-4769
rca@rowingcanada.org
www.rowingcanada.org
Social Media: www.facebook.com/pages/Rowing-Canada-Aviron/81982893039?ref=ts; twitter.com/rowingcanada
To encourage the formation of rowing clubs & provincial associations; To encourage the organization of national regattas; To define & to maintain the principles of amateurism in all competitions; To organize, develop, & select national rowing teams to represent Canada internationally

Donna Atkinson, Executive Director

Royal Canadian Golf Association (RCGA) / Association royale de golf du Canada
#1, 1333 Dorval Dr., Oakville ON L6M 4X7
Tel: 905-849-9700; *Fax:* 905-845-7040
Toll-Free: 800-263-0009
info@golfcanada.ca; members@golfcanada.ca
www.golfcanada.ca
Social Media: www.facebook.com/group.php?gid=61328126412
To work with the provincial golf associations & member clubs to foster the growth & development of golf
Scott Simmons, Executive Director & CEO
Dave Lafleur, Chief Financial Officer
Larry Thomas, Chief Commercial Officer
Jeff Thompson, Chief Sport Development Officer
Rick Desrochers, Senior Director
Bill Paul, Managing Dir, Professional Championships
Sean Van Kesteren, Managing Dir, Professional Championships
Brent McLaughlin, Director, Rules, Competitions & Amateur Status

Royal Canadian Golf Association Foundation
#1, 1333 Dorval Dr., Oakville ON L6M 4X7
Tel: 905-849-9700; *Fax:* 905-845-7040
Toll-Free: 800-263-0009
info@golfcanada.ca
www.golfcanada.ca
Social Media: www.facebook.com/TheGolfCanada; twitter.com/TheGolfCanada
To raise & grant funds for the betterment of golf in Canada
Karen Rackel, President

Rugby Ontario
#307, 3 Concorde Gate, Toronto ON M3C 3N7
Tel: 416-426-7050; *Fax:* 416-426-7369
www.rugbyontario.com
Social Media: www.facebook.com/RugbyOntario; twitter.com/rugbyontario
Andrew Backer, Executive Director
Andrew Hall, Director
Fran Mason, Manager, Member Services

Sask Sport Inc.
1870 Lorne St., Regina SK S4P 2L7
Tel: 306-780-9300; *Fax:* 306-781-6021
sasksport@sasksport.sk.ca
www.sasksport.sk.ca
To ensure the total development of amateur sport through the provincial sport governing bodies; to promote extensive participation towards excellence
Jim Burnett, General Manager

Saskatchewan 5 Pin Bowlers' Association
#100, 1805 - 8th Ave., Regina SK S4R 1E8
Tel: 306-780-9412; *Fax:* 306-780-9455
bowling@sasktel.net
saskbowl.com
To develop trust & harmony among member organizations; to assist in the development & promotion of the sport of bowling through the provision of stable funding
Rhonda Sereda, Executive Director

Saskatchewan Amateur Speed Skating Association (SASSA)
2205 Victoria Ave., Regina SK S4P 0S4
Tel: 306-780-9400; *Fax:* 306-525-4009
sassa@sasktel.net
www.saskspeedskating.ca
Working together to develop & promote the sport of speed skating at all levels as a fun, competitive, healthy, family activity
Shawn MacLennan, Executive Director

Saskatchewan Amateur Wrestling Association (SAWA)
510 Cynthia St., Saskatoon SK S7L 7K7
Tel: 306-975-0822; *Fax:* 306-242-8007
sk.wrestling@shaw.ca
www.saskwrestling.com
To govern and promote the sport of wrestling in Saskatchewan.
Anna-Beth Zulkoskey, Executive Director

Saskatchewan Badminton Association (SBA)
3615 Pasqua St., Regina SK S4S 6W8
Tel: 306-780-9368; *Fax:* 306-780-9369
saskbadminton@sasktel.net
www.saskbadminton.ca
Dedicated to the development of badminton in Saskatchewan.
Frank Gaudet, Executive Director

Saskatchewan Baseball Association (SBA)
1870 Lorne St., Regina SK S4P 2L7
Tel: 306-780-9237; *Fax:* 306-352-3669
mramage@sasktel.net
www.saskbaseball.ca
To provide quality baseball programs to interested participants at whatever level they may choose
Mike Ramage, Executive Director

Saskatchewan Blind Sports Association Inc.
510 Cynthia St., Saskatoon SK S7L 7K7
Tel: 306-975-0888; *Toll-Free:* 877-772-7798
sbsa.sk@shaw.ca
www.saskblindsports.ca
To assist persons who are blind or with visual impairment to achieve excellence in sport, satisfaction in recreation, independence, self-reliance & full community participation
Tony Badger, Executive Director
Jerry Johnson, President

Saskatchewan Broomball Association (SBA)
2205 Victoria Ave., Regina SK S4P 0S4
Tel: 306-780-9215; *Fax:* 306-525-4009
saskbroomball@sasktel.net
www.saskbroomball.ca
To promote multi-level programs to members & non-member groups in both competitive & recreational settings; to promote broomball within the province of Saskatchewan
Greg Perreaux, Executive Director

Saskatchewan Curling Association (SCA)
613 Park St., Regina SK S4N 5N1
Tel: 306-780-9202; *Fax:* 306-780-9404
Toll-Free: 877-722-2875
saskcurling@sasktel.net
www.saskcurl.com/sca/scahome.htm
To govern and promote the sport of curling in Saskatchewan.
Del Jones, President

Saskatchewan Cycling Association
2205 Victoria Ave., Regina SK S4P 0S4
Tel: 306-780-9299; *Fax:* 306-525-4009
cycling@accesscomm.ca
www.saskcycling.ca
To promote and enhance the Saskatchewan cycling experience while recognizing its benefits to the individual and society.
Wayne Walker, President

Saskatchewan Deaf Sports Association
1860 Lorne St., Regina SK S4P 2L7
Toll-Free: 800-855-0511
www.saskdeafsports.ca
SDSA is a provincial organization that fosters sporting opportunities to members of the deaf & hard-of-hearing communities. With the aid of local clubs, it selects & trains deaf & hard-of-hearing athletes for international competitions.
Kenneth Hoffman, President
Dale Birley, Administrator

Saskatchewan Diving
1870 Lorne St., Regina SK S4P 2L7
Tel: 306-780-9405; *Fax:* 306-781-6021
info@divesask.ca
www.saskdiving.ca
Social Media: www.facebook.com/DIVESASK; twitter.com/divesask
To develop & promote safe diving; To ensure that diving clubs operate with safety & integrity; To provide opportunities for self fulfillment & the pursuit of excellence
Jaime Valentine, President

Saskatchewan Golf Association Inc.
510 Cynthia St., Saskatoon SK S7L 7K7
Tel: 306-975-0850; *Fax:* 306-975-0840
info@saskgolf.ca
www.saskgolf.ca
To promote & maintain amateur golf in Saskatchewan by providing access to information & clinics on golf skills development, rules, handicapping, & etiquette
Brian Lee, Executive Director
Candace Dunham, Manager, Programs & Member Services
Phil Grosse, Manager, Marketing & Sport Development
Dan Ukrainetz, Manager, Tournaments & Player Services

Saskatchewan Hockey Association (SHA) / Association de hockey de la Saskatchewan
#2, 575 Park St., Regina SK S4N 5B2
Tel: 306-789-5101; *Fax:* 306-789-6112
carissal@sha.sk.ca
www.sha.sk.ca
To administer the operation of amateur hockey in the Province of Saskatchewan; To foster & promote amateur hockey within the province & to assist in the promotion of amateur hockey outside the province; To promote, supervise & administer all competitions for amateur hockey within the jurisdiction of the SAHA
Al Hubbs, President
Kelly McClintock, General Manager

Saskatchewan Horse Federation (SHF)
2205 Victoria Ave., Regina SK S4P 0S4
Tel: 306-780-9244; *Fax:* 306-525-4009
sk.horse@sasktel.net
www.saskhorse.ca
Mae Smith, Executive Director

Saskatchewan Long Riders
c/o Brian Zwaan, PO Box 41, St. Denis SK S0K 3W0
Tel: 306-978-1225
www.sasklongriders.com
To govern & promote the sport of Long Distance Riding in Saskatchewan
Trisha Dowling, President
Burt Sutherland, Contact

Saskatchewan Rugby Union (SRU)
510 Cynthia St., Saskatoon SK S7L 7K7
Tel: 306-975-0895; *Fax:* 306-242-8007
sru@sasktel.net
www.saskrugby.com
To encourage, promote, organize, administer & otherwise regulate the sport of Rugby Union Football in the province of Saskatchewan in accordance with the laws of the game in a safe & proper manner

Saskatchewan Ski Association - Skiing for Disabled (SASKI)
1860 Lorne St., Saskatoon SK S4P 2L7
Tel: 306-780-9236; *Fax:* 306-781-6021
sask.ski@sasktel.net
www.saski.ca
To promote all aspects of winter skiing in Saskatchewan, including alpine, biathlon, cross country & skiing for disabled, & to provide assistance to clubs & individual athletes, instruction & training, adaptive equipment, & a resource library

Saskatchewan Soccer Association Inc. (SSA)
1870 Lorne St., Regina SK S4P 2L7
Tel: 306-780-9225; *Fax:* 306-780-9480
k.sumner@sasksoccer.com
www.sasksoccer.com
Social Media: www.facebook.com/pages/Saskatchewan-Soccer-Association/83226704916
Bonnie Lee Copeman, Business Administrator

Saskatchewan Volleyball Association
1750 McAra St., Regina SK S4N 6L4
Tel: 306-780-9250; *Fax:* 306-780-9288
officemanager@saskvolleyball.ca
www.saskvolleyball.ca
Social Media: www.facebook.com/group.php?gid=121947301797
To develop interest, participation & excellence in volleyball through the promotion & provision of quality services for all
Dalene Phillips, President
Dan Medford, Executive Director
Tammy Schneider, Office Manager

School Sports Newfoundland & Labrador (SSNL)
c/o Dennis Lush, President, PO Box 400, Gambo NL A0G 1T0
Tel: 709-674-5336; *Fax:* 709-674-4244
www.schoolsportsnl.ca
Social Media: www.facebook.com/141101766485
To organize, promote & govern all high school sports within the province; to assist student athletes in reaching their full physical, educational & social potential through participation & sportsmanship in interscholastic sports
Karen Richard, Executive Director
Dennis Lush, President

Skate Canada / Patinage Canada
865 Shefford Rd., Ottawa ON K1J 1H9
Tel: 613-747-1007; *Fax:* 613-748-5718
Toll-Free: 888-747-2372
skatecanada@skatecanada.ca; memberservices@skatecanada.ca
www.skatecanada.ca
Social Media: www.facebook.com/group.php?gid=129815677038
To enable all Canadians to participate in skating throughout their lifetime for fun, fitness, & achievement
William Thompson, Chief Executive Officer
Cheryl McEvoy, Chief Operating Officer
Barbara Draper, Director, Member Services

Barb MacDonald, Director, Corporate Communications
Michael Slipchuk, Director, High Performance
Jackie Stell-Buckingham, Director, Events

Snowboard Yukon
72 Teslin Rd., Whitehorse YT Y1A 3M6
Tel: 867-456-2174
info@snowboardyukon.com
www.snowboardyukon.com
To organize and sanction events, train athletes and coaches, form and administer teams for out of territory competitions, and represent Yukon riders in the Canadian Snowboard Federation.
Chris McNutt, President

Soccer New Brunswick
#2, 125 Russ Howard Dr., Moncton NB E1C 0L7
Tel: 506-382-7529; *Fax:* 506-382-5621
office@soccernb.org
www.soccernb.org
Social Media:
www.facebook.com/group.php?gid=183461681180
To foster & promote the development & growth of the sport of soccer in New Brunswick & to assure equitable accessibility through quality programs
Jeff Salvis, Executive Director

Soccer Nova Scotia (SNS)
210 Thomas Raddall Dr., Halifax NS B3S 1K3
Tel: 902-445-0265; *Fax:* 902-445-0258
admin@soccerns.ns.ca; programs@soccerns.ns.ca
www.soccerns.ns.ca
To promote the sport of soccer in Nova Scotia; To provide information & resources to aid player training, coaching education, & referee programs
George Athanasiou, Chief Executive Officer
Daniel Worthington, Director, High Performance
Carman King, Officer, Referee Development

Softball Canada
#212, 223 Colonnade Rd., Ottawa ON K1H 7X3
Tel: 613-523-3386; *Fax:* 613-523-5761
info@softball.ca
www.softball.ca
Social Media:
www.facebook.com/pages/Softball-Canada/203017655217
To develop & promote softball in Canada
Hugh Mitchener, CEO
Kevin Quinn, President

Softball Manitoba
#321, 145 Pacific Ave., Winnipeg MB R3B 2Z6
Tel: 204-925-5673; *Fax:* 204-925-5703
softball@softball.mb.ca
www.softball.mb.ca
To promote & develop softball at all levels by providing leadership, programs & services
Bill Finch, President

Southern Alberta Curling Association (SACA)
#720, 3 St. NW, Calgary AB T2N 1N9
Tel: 403-246-9300; *Fax:* 403-246-9349
curling@saca.ca
www.saca.ca
To encourage active participation for residents of all ages in our communities by helping member curling clubs offer a wide variety of programs. To assist in providing opportunities to participate in curling.
Brent Syme, General Manager

Special Olympics Alberta (SOA)
Percy Page Centre, 11759 Groat Rd., Edmonton AB T5M 3K6
Tel: 780-415-0719; *Fax:* 780-422-2663
Toll-Free: 800-444-2883
info@specialolympics.ab.ca
www.specialolympics.ab.ca
To enrich the lives of Albertans with an intellectual disability, through sport
Carmen Wyton, President & CEO

Special Olympics BC (SOBC)
#210, 3701 East Hastings St., Burnaby BC V5C 2H6
Tel: 604-737-3078; *Fax:* 604-737-3080
Toll-Free: 888-854-2276
info@specialolympics.bc.ca
www.specialolympics.bc.ca
Social Media: www.facebook.com/specialolympicsbc;
twitter.com/sobcsociety
The Association provides individuals with intellectual disability the opportunity to enhance their lives & celebrate personal achievement through positive sport experiences.
Dan Howe, President & CEO
Betty J. Simpson, Office Administrator

Special Olympics Canada (SOC) / Olympiques spéciaux
#600, 21 St. Clair Ave. East, Toronto ON M4T 1L9
Tel: 416-927-9050; *Fax:* 416-927-8475
Toll-Free: 888-888-0608
www.specialolympics.ca
To provide sport training & competition for people with a mental disability, at local, regional, provincial, national & international levels, year round
Frank Selke, Executive Vice-President
Sharon Bollenbach, Vice-President, Sport
Karen Forrest, Director, Financial Administration
Jennifer Gosen, Director, Program Development
Alexius D'Cruze, Coordinator, Marketing

Special Olympics Manitoba (SOM)
#304, 145 Pacific Avenue, Winnipeg MB R3B 2Z6
Tel: 204-925-5628; *Fax:* 204-925-5635
Toll-Free: 888-333-9179
som@specialolympics.mb.ca
www.specialolympics.mb.ca
Social Media: www.facebook.com/Special Olimpics Manitoba;
twitter.com/SpecOManitoba
To enrich the lives of Manitobans with an intellectual disability, through active participation in sport
Simon Mundey, President & CEO

Special Olympics New Brunswick
#13, 900 Hanwell Rd., Fredericton NB E3B 6A2
Tel: 506-455-0404; *Fax:* 506-455-0410
infosonb@specialolympics.ca
www.specialolympicsnb.ca
Social Media: www.facebook.com/specialolympicsnb;
twitter.com/SpecialONB
Josh Astle, Executive Director

Special Olympics Newfoundland & Labrador
#426, 354 Water St., St. John's NL A1C 1C4
Tel: 709-738-1923; *Fax:* 709-738-0119
Toll-Free: 877-738-1913
sonl@sonl.ca
www.sonl.ca
To provide sport, fitness & recreation programs for individuals with a mental handicap
Ken Marshall, Chair

Special Olympics Northwest Territories (SONWT)
PO Box 1691, Yellowknife NT X1A 2N1
Tel: 867-873-6906; *Fax:* 867-669-0225
www.sonwt.ca
Special Olympics N.W.T. is the territorial sport governing body responsible for the delivery of sport for people with intellectual disabilities in the Northwest Territories.
Lynn Elkin, Executive Director

Special Olympics Nova Scotia (SONS)
PO Box 3010, #201, 5516 Spring Garden Rd., Halifax NS B3J 1G6
Tel: 902-429-2266; *Fax:* 902-425-5606
Toll-Free: 866-299-2019
www.sons.ca
Social Media:
www.facebook.com/pages/Special-Olympics-Nova-Scotia/43431
2063275851; twitter.com/SpecialONS
Special Olympics is a non-profit organization dedicated to providing year-round sports training and athletic competition in a variety of Olympic-type sports for children and adults with an intellectual disability.
Mike Greek, President/CEO

Special Olympics Ontario (SOO)
#300, 18 Wynford Dr., Toronto ON M3C 3S2
Tel: 416-447-8326; *Fax:* 416-447-6336
Toll-Free: 888-333-5515
www.specialolympicsontario.com
Social Media: www.facebook.com/specialolympicsontario;
www.youtube.com/specialolympicson
To provide sports training & competition for people with an intellectual disability through community-based programs
Glenn MacDonell, President & Chief Executive Officer
Linda Ashe, Vice-President
Linda Miller, Manager, Marketing Services
James Noronha, Manager, Program Services

Special Olympics Prince Edward Island (SOPEI)
PO Box 822, #240, 40 Enman Cres., Charlottetown PE C1A 7L9
Tel: 902-368-8919; *Fax:* 902-892-4553
Toll-Free: 800-287-1196
sopei@sopei.com
www.sopei.com
To provide sport, recreation & fitness for the mentally disabled in PEI; to provide competitive opportunities for its members
Valerie Downe, President

Special Olympics Saskatchewan
353 Broad St., Regina SK S4R 1X2
Tel: 306-780-9247; *Fax:* 306-780-9441
Toll-Free: 888-307-6226
sos@specialolympics.sk.ca
www.specialolympics.sk.ca
Howard Schweitzer, CEO

Special Olympics Yukon (SOY) / Les Jeux Olympiques Spéciaux du Yukon
#102, 221 Hanson St., Whitehorse YT Y1A 1H1
Tel: 867-668-6511; *Fax:* 867-667-4237
info@specialolympicsyukon.ca
To provide a full continuum of sport apportunities for Yukoners with a mental disability
Serge Michaud, Executive Director
James Tucker, President

Speed Skate New Brunswick
246 St. Pierre East Blvd., Caraquet NB E1E 1B1
Tel: 506-727-6334; *Fax:* 506-727-6334
speedskatenb@gmail.com
ssnb.homestead.com
The association provides members with access to coaching & chances to compete. It serves as a hub for information on the sport & for members to network.
Ray Harris, President
Peter Steele, Provincial Coach

Speed Skate Nova Scotia
10 Thistle Dr., North Sydney NS B2A 3R1
Tel: 902-794-8954
laurolea@ns.sympatico.ca
Terri Dixon, President

Speed Skate PEI
PO Box 383, Charlottetown PE C1A 7K7
Tel: 902-628-6606
info@speedskatepei.ca
www.speedskatepei.com
Supporting the sport of speedskating in PEI.
Wendy A. Francis, President
Alban Moran, Secretary

Speed Skating Canada (SSC) / Patinage de vitesse Canada
#402, 2781 Lancaster Rd., Ottawa ON K1B 1A7
Tel: 613-260-3669; *Fax:* 613-260-3660
ssc@speedskating.ca
www.speedskating.ca
To develop & promote long & short track speed skating in Canada; To prepare athletes, coaches, officials, & volunteers to make contributions to speed skating & to Canada's image abroad through development & international programs
John-Paul Cody-Cox, Chief Executive Officer
Mark Mathies, Executive Director, Sport
Patricia Brennan, Director, Finance & Administration
Douglas Duncan, Director, Leadership Eduation
Phil Legault, Director, Communications

Sport Alliance of Ontario
3 Concorde Gate, Toronto ON M3C 3N7
Tel: 416-426-7000; *Fax:* 416-426-7381
jjoseph@sportalliance.com
www.sportalliance.com
To provide facilities, services & business expertise to enable provincial sport, recreation & fitness organizations to serve the people of Ontario
Jim Bradley, CEO
Larry Rudner, Interim CFO

Sport BC
#295, 3820 Cessna Dr., Richmond BC V7B 0A2
Tel: 604-333-3400; *Fax:* 604-333-3401
info@sportbc.com
sport.bc.com
Social Media: www.facebook.com/SportBC; twitter.com/SportBC
To provide leadership, direction, & support to member organizations in their delivery of sport opportunities to all British Columbians
Pete Quevillon, Director, KidSport BC

Sport Manitoba
145 Pacific Ave., Winnipeg MB R3b 2Z6
Tel: 204-925-5600; *Fax:* 204-925-5916
Toll-Free: 866-774-2220
info@sportmanitoba.ca
www.sportmanitoba.ca
Social Media: www.facebook.com/sportmb;
twitter.com/SportManitoba;
www.youtube.com/user/sportmanitoba

To create the best sport community in Canada through provision of resources to recognized sport organizations, enabling them to encourage participation in sport at all levels of skill & ability & to develop athletes of national & international calibre
Jeff Hnatiuk, President/CEO
Tara Skibo, Communications/Public Relations

Sport New Brunswick / Sport Nouveau-Brunswick
#13, 900 Hanwell Rd., Fredericton NB E3B 6A2
Tel: 506-451-1320; *Fax:* 506-451-1325
director@sportnb.com
www.sportnb.com
To promote the development of amateur sport in New Brunswick through services, programs, advocacy
Jason Dickson, Executive Director

Sport Newfoundland & Labrador
PO Box 8700, St. John's NL A1B 4J6
Tel: 709-576-4932; *Fax:* 709-576-7493
sportnl@sportnl.ca
www.sportnl.ca
To promote & advance amateur sport throughout Newfoundland & Labrador; to represent collective interests & goals of members; to provide various programs & services; to liaise & lobby with government, communities, media & other representative organizations; to provide direction & leadership on issues which affect members
Troy Croft, Executive Director

Sport North Federation
Don Cooper Building, PO Box 11089, 4908 - 49 St., Yellowknife NT X1A 3X7
Tel: 867-669-8326; *Fax:* 867-669-8327
Toll-Free: 800-661-0797
www.sportnorth.com
Doug Rentmeister, Executive Director

Sport Nova Scotia (SNS)
PO Box 3010, Stn. South, 5516 Spring Garden Rd., Halifax NS B3J 1G6
Tel: 902-425-5450; *Fax:* 902-425-5606
sportns@sportnovascotia.ca
www.sportnovascotia.ca
To promote the development of amateur sport in Nova Scotia through services, programs, advocacy & technical consultation
Jamie Ferguson, CEO

Sport PEI Inc.
PO Box 302, Charlottetown PE C1A 7K7
Tel: 902-368-4110; *Fax:* 902-368-4548
Toll-Free: 800-247-6712
sports@sportpei.pe.ca
www.sportpei.pe.ca
To assist in the development & promotion of amateur sport in the province of Prince Edward Island; To offer services & programs to meet the needs of the membership
Lyall Huggan, Special Projects
Gemma Koughan, Executive Director
Wendy Reid, President
Nick Murray, Communications
Lisa MacKay, Finance & Administration

Sport Physiotherapy Canada (SPC)
#416, 11411A Carling Ave., Ottawa ON K1Z 1A7
Tel: 613-748-5794; *Fax:* 613-748-5792
info@sportphysio.ca
www.sportphysio.ca
To promote professional development of members; To ensure high-quality health care for Canada's athletes

Sport Yukon
4061 - 4 Ave., Whitehorse YT Y1A 1H1
Tel: 867-668-4236; *Fax:* 867-667-4237
news@sportyukon.com
www.sportyukon.com
To promote the development of amateur sport in the Yukon through services, programs, advocacy
George Arcand, President

Sports-Québec
CP 1000, Succ. M, 4545, av Pierre-De Coubertin, Montréal QC H1V 3R2
Tél: 514-252-3114; *Téléc:* 514-254-9621
sports@sportsquebec.com
www.sportsquebec.com
Assurer la synergie de ses membres et de ses partenaires du système sportif québécois et du système sportif canadien pour favoriser le développement et l'épanouissement de l'athlète et la promotion de la pratique sportive
Luc Denis, Directeur général
Jean Couvrette, Directeur, Développement des affaires et partenariats
Isabelle Ducharme, Directrice, Programmes
Pierre Bégin, Coordonnateur, Développement sportif
Michelle Gendron, Coordonnatrice, Communications stratégiques

Squash Canada
#401, 2197 Riverside Dr., Ottawa ON K1H 7X3
Tel: 613-731-7385; *Fax:* 613-731-6291
info@squash.ca
www.squash.ca
Social Media: www.facebook.com/squashcanada; twitter.com/squashcanada; www.youtube.com/user/Squashcanada2011
Danny Da Costa, Executive Director
Jamie Hickox, Director, Performance
Whitney Fuller, Coordinator, Sport Development
Judith Post, Coordinator, Finance

Summerside & Area Minor Hockey Association (SAMHA)
PO Box 1454, Summerside PE C1N 4K4
info@summersideminorhockey.com
www.summersideminorhockey.com
Bruce Cameron, President

Swim Yukon
4061, 4th Ave., Whitehorse YT Y1A 1H1
www.swimyukon.ca
Swim Yukon is the Sport Governing Body for competitive swimming in the Yukon.
Ron Sumanik, President

Swimming / Natation Canada
#B140, 2445 St-Laurent Blvd., Ottawa ON K1G 6C3
Tel: 613-260-1348; *Fax:* 613-260-0804
natoffice@swimming.ca
www.swimming.ca
Social Media: www.facebook.com/group.php?gid=56320144853
To direct & develop competitive swimming in Canada; To represent Canada in international organizations & events
Pierre Lafontaine, Chief Executive Officer & National Coach
Mark Hahto, Chief Operating Officer
Lance Cansdale, Director, Domestic Operation
Ken Radford, Director, High Performance
Martin Richard, Director, Communications
Craig McCord, National Para-swimming Coach
Ken McKinnon, National Junior Coach

Synchro Canada / Association canadienne de nage synchronisée amateur
#200, 1010 Polytek St., Unit 14, Gloucester ON K1J 9H9
Tel: 613-748-5674; *Fax:* 613-748-5724
catherine@synchro.ca
www.synchro.ca
To develop and operate the sport of synchronized swimming in Canada, through a variety of programs designed to develop athletes, coaches & officials
Kristen Brawley, High Performance Manager

Synchro Manitoba
145 Pacific Ave., Winnipeg MB R3B 2Z6
Tel: 204-925-5693; *Fax:* 204-925-5703
execdirector@synchromb.ca
www.synchromb.ca
To promote, teach, foster, encourage, & improve, synchronized swimming in Manitoba; to regulate synchro swim in Manitoba in accordance with the constitution by-laws & rules
Allison Gervais, Executive Director

Synchro Yukon Association
4061, 4th Ave., Whitehorse YT Y1A 1H1
Tel: 867-668-7441
specialk@northwestel.net
www.sportyukon.com/membership/?member=34
To promote the sport of Synchronized Swimming in the Yukon.
Sandra Duncan, President

Table Tennis Yukon
4061, 4th Ave, Whitehorse YT Y1A 1H1
Tel: 867-668-3358
stockdale@yknet.ca
www.sportyukon.com/membership/?member=72
To promote the sport of Table Tennis in the Yukon.
David Stockdale, President

Tennis BC
#204, 210 West Broadway, Vancouver BC V5Y 3W2
Tel: 604-737-3086; *Fax:* 604-737-3124
tbc@tennisbc.org
www.tennisbc.org
Social Media: www.facebook.com/pages/Tennis-BC/189016975927; twitter.com/intent/user?screen_name=TennisBC; www.youtube.com/user/TennisBC1#g/a
Ryan Clark, Chief Executive Officer
Sarah Kadi, Director, Community Development
Lois Ker, Director, Events
Chee Ng, Director, Finance
Lanei Lee, Manager, Member Services & Marketing Communications

Tennis Canada
Rexall Centre, #100, 1 Shoreham Dr., Toronto ON M3N 3A6
Tel: 416-665-9777; *Fax:* 416-665-9017
Toll-Free: 877-283-6647
www.lovemeansnothing.ca
Social Media: www.facebook.com/TennisCanada; twitter.com/Tennis_Canada; www.youtube.com/user/TCtenniscanada
To stimulate participation & excellence in the sport at the local, provincial, national, & international levels; To provide encouragement, support, & leadership to organizations & individuals who seek to enhance the enjoyment, quality & image of Canadian tennis
Roger Martin, Chair
Michael S. Downey, President & Chief Executive Officer
Derek Strang, Chief Operating Officer
Heather Waldman, Chief Financial Officer & Vice-President, Finance & Administration
Hatem McDadi, Vice-President, Tennis Development

Tennis Manitoba
#419, 145 Pacific Ave., Winnipeg MB R3B 2Z6
Tel: 204-925-5660; *Fax:* 204-925-5703
info@tennismanitoba.com
www.tennismanitoba.com
Social Media: twitter.com/tennismanitoba
To stimulate participation & advancement in tennis by all Manitobans
Alexandra Gomez, Chair, Resource Development Committee
Mohamed Ismath, Chair, High Performance Committee
David Scrapneck, Chair, Competitive Structure Committee
Selvi Varathappan, Chair, Community Development Committee

Tennis New Brunswick
PO Box 604, Fredericton NB E3B 5A6
Tel: 506-444-0885
tnb@tennisnb.net
www.tennisnb.net

Tennis Newfoundland & Labrador
PO Box 728, Stn. C, 114 Newtown Rd., St. John's NL A1C 5L4
Tel: 709-765-0426; *Fax:* 709-722-1670
tennis@sportnl.ca
www.tennisnl.ca
To grow & promote the sport of tennis throughout Newfoundland & Labrador; To increase participation at levels consistent with the personal goals & aspirations of competitors in all age groups
Derrick Rowe, President
Ryan Maarschalk, Executive Director

Tennis Northwest Territories
PO Box 671, Yellowknife NT X1A 2N5
Tel: 867-873-2018
eastarm@ssimicro.com
www.tennisnwt.ca
Fran Hurcomb, President

Tennis Québec (TQ)
285, rue Faillon ouest, Montréal QC H2R 2W1
Tél: 514-270-6060; *Téléc:* 514-270-2700
courrier@tennis.qc.ca
www.tennis.qc.ca
Promotion et développement du tennis au Québec auprès de toutes les catégories d'âge et de tous les calibres
Jean François Manibal, Directeur général
Réjean Genois, Président

Tennis Saskatchewan
2205 Victoria Ave., Regina SK S4P 0S4
Tel: 306-780-9410; *Fax:* 306-525-4009
tennissask@sasktel.net
www.tennissask.com
To advance tennis throughout Saskatchewan by stimulating participation & excellence in the sport; To provide players throughout Saskatchewan with systematic opportunities to participate in tennis & to achieve a level of competence consistent with their abilities & aspirations, with particular emphasis on youth; To stage tennis events; To produce teams & athletes capable of winning national championships
Rory Park, Executive Director

Tennis Yukon Association
4 Kluhini Cres., Whitehorse YT Y1A 3P3
Tel: 867-393-2621; *Fax:* 867-393-2621
www.courtsidecanada.ca/communities/Yukon
To promote the sport of Tennis in the Yukon.

Stacy Lewis, President

Toronto Bicycling Network
PO Box 279, #200, 131 Bloor St. West, Toronto ON M5S 1R8
Tel: 416-760-4191
info@tbn.ca
www.tbn.ca
Brian Mclean, President

Trail Riding Alberta Conference (TRAC)
738 Wheeler Road, Edmonton AB T6M 2E8
Tel: 403-486-0957
shanharms@shaw.ca
www.trailriding.ab.ca
To finish is to win
Brent Seufert, President

Triathlon Canada
#106, 3 Concorde Gate, Toronto ON M3C 3N7
Tel: 416-426-7180; *Fax:* 416-426-7294
info@triathloncanada.com
www.triathloncanada.com
To function as the National Federation for triathlon & duathlon in Canada, & to represent Canada internationally; to promote the triathlon & duathlon, both competitive & non-competitive in Canada; to encourage support of Triathlon Canada programmes by the public generally; to provide guidance, information & assistance to the provincial triathlon associations, zones & clubs in respect to these objects & in the development of programmes for competitive & non-competitive triathletes & duathletes; to affiliate all provincial associations to Triathlon Canada who are the Provincial Sports Governing Bodies, or who are in the process of becoming the Provincial Sports Governing Bodies in their province; to organize training courses for triathletes, duathletes, coaches & administrators to national & international standards; to promote other multi-disciplined endurance events & excluding the traditional decathlon, pentathlon, heptathlon, modern pentathlon & biathlon, which are part of existing National Federations
Alan Trivett, Executive Director

Vélo New Brunswick
536 McAllister Rd., Riverview NB E1B 4G1
Tel: 506-474-0214
www.velo.nb.ca
Social Media:
www.facebook.com/home.php?sk=group_171814622867730
To promote all aspects of the activity of bicycling, competitive & recreational, both on & off the road
Kelly Murray, President
Michelle Chase, Vice-President
Sheila Colbourne, Executive Director

Vélo Québec
1251, rue Rachel est, Montréal QC H2J 2J9
Tél: 514-521-8356; *Téléc:* 514-521-5711
Ligne sans frais: 800-567-8356
www.velo.qc.ca
Mèdia social: www.facebook.com/VeloQuebec; twitter.com/VeloQuebec
Jean-François Pronovost, Directeur général

Volleyball BC
Harry Jerome Sports Centre, 7564 Barnet Hwy., Burnaby BC V5A 1E7
Tel: 604-291-2007; *Fax:* 604-291-2602
communications@volleyballbc.ca
www.volleyballbc.ca
To promote volleyball in British Columbia; To provide competitive opportunities for members
Chris Densmore, Executive Director
Chris Berglund, Director, Technical & High Performance
Jenny Graham, Manager, Programs
Brian Hiebert, Manager, Communications

Volleyball Canada (VC)
#202, 5510 Canotek Rd., Gloucester ON K1J 9J5
Tel: 613-748-5681; *Fax:* 613-748-5727
info@volleyball.ca
www.volleyball.ca
Social Media: www.facebook.com/VolleyballCanada?ref=ts; twitter.com/VBallCanada
To lead the growth of & excellence in the sport of volleyball for all Canadians
Mark Eckert, Executive Director
Hugh Wong, President
Linden Leung, Manager, Finance & Operations
James Sneddon, Director, Domestic Development

Volleyball New Brunswick
#13, 900 Hanwell Rd., Fredericton NB E3B 6A3
Tel: 506-451-1346; *Fax:* 506-451-1325
vnb@nb.aibn.com
www.vnb.nb.ca
To promote volleyball in New Brunswick; To provide competitive opportunities for members
John Richard, President
Mike Gallagher, Executive Director & Technical Director
Catherine Boudreau, Coordinator, Indoor & Beach Programs

Volleyball Nova Scotia
5516 Spring Garden Rd., 4th Fl., Halifax NS B3J 1G6
Tel: 902-425-5450; *Fax:* 902-425-5606
vns@sportnovascotia.ca
www.volleyballnovascotia.ca
To promote volleyball in Nova Scotia; To provide competitive opportunities for members
Dave Swetnam, President
Al Scott, Executive Director
Brock Pehar, Director, Technical

Volleyball Prince Edward Island
PO Box 302, Charlottetown PE C1N 7K7
Tel: 902-569-0583; *Fax:* 902-368-4548
Toll-Free: 800-247-6712
cgcrozier@sportpei.pe.ca
www.volleyballpei.com
To promote volleyball in PEI; to provide competitive opportunities for members
Cheryl Crozier, Executive Director
Krista Walsh, President
Harvey Mazerolle, Vice-President

Volleyball Yukon
4061 - 4th Ave., Whitehorse YT Y1A 1H1
Tel: 867-334-4592; *Fax:* 867-667-4237
www.volleyballyukon.com
To promote volleyball in the Yukon; to provide competitive opportunities for its members
Michael Hanson, President

Water Polo Canada (WPC)
#12, 1010 Polytek St., Gloucester ON K1G 9H9
Tel: 613-748-5682; *Fax:* 613-748-5777
office@waterpolo.ca
www.waterpolo.ca
Social Media:
www.facebook.com/pages/Water-Polo-Canada/193992167322377; twitter.com/waterpolocanada; www.youtube.com/waterpolocanada
To promote growth in sport of water polo in Canada; to administer Canada's high performance programs (Olympics, Pan Am Games, etc.) in water polo
Ahmed El-Awadi, Executive Director

Water Polo Saskatchewan Inc. (WPS)
1860 Lorne St., Regina SK S4P 2L7
Tel: 306-780-9260; *Fax:* 306-780-9467
admin@wpsask.ca
www.wpsask.ca
Social Media: www.facebook.com/waterpolosask?sk=wall
Cyril Dorgigne, Executive Director
Amanda Walton, Office Administrator

Water Ski - Wakeboard Manitoba (WSWM)
#415, 145 Pacific Ave., Winnipeg MB R3B 2Z6
Tel: 204-925-5700; *Fax:* 204-925-5792
info@wswm.ca
www.wswm.ca
To meet the needs of all those interested in the sport of water skiing by providing the resources necessary to help them achieve their goals & to encourage fun, friendship, fitness & fair play for skiers at all ability levels
Alanna Boudreau, Executive Director
Kevin Polley, President

Water Ski & Wakeboard Canada / Ski nautique et planche Canada
#210, 223 Colonnade Rd. South, Ottawa ON K2E 7K3
Tel: 613-526-0685; *Fax:* 613-526-4380
wswc@waterski-wakeboard.ca
www.waterski-wakeboard.ca
To promote & organize water skiing in Canada
Glenn Bowie, President
Dan Wolfenden, Executive Director

Whitehorse Cross Country Ski Club
#200, 1 Sumanik Dr., Whitehorse YT Y1A 6J6
Tel: 867-668-4477
info@xcskiwhitehorse.ca
www.xcskiwhitehorse.ca
To maintain high quality ski trails and facilities, maintain a safe environment, ensure the long-term viability of the club and secure land tenure for the Yukon's trail system.
Mike Gladish, Manager
Tom Ullyett, President

Whitehorse Minor Hockey Association
4061, 4th Ave., Whitehorse YT Y1A 1H1
Tel: 867-393-4698
www.whitehorseminorhockey.ca
Promotes and coordinates minor hockey leagues in Whitehorse.
John Grant, President

Whitehorse Minor Soccer Association (WMS)
4061, 4th Ave., Whitehorse YT Y1A 1H1
Tel: 867-667-2445
wms@sportyukon.com
www.yukonsoccer.yk.ca/minor
Provides low-cost, easily accessible indoor and outdoor soccer opportunities to the youth of Whitehorse.
Gerald Haase, President

Wild Rose Ball Hockey Association
7604 - 182 St., Edmonton AB T5T 1Y9
Tel: 780-970-0637; *Fax:* 780-484-9957
wrbha@telus.net
www.wrballhockey.com
Connie Liosis, Executive Director

World Curling Federation (WCF)
74 Tay St., Perth PH2 8NP Scotland
info@worldcurling.org
www.worldcurling.org
To represent curling internationally & to facilitate the growth of the sport through a network of member nations
Lester Harrison, President
Kate Caithness, Vice-President
Mike Thomson, Secretary General

Wrestling Nova Scotia
General Delivery, Bear River NS B0S 1B0
Tel: 902-857-1761
wrestlingns@canada.com
www.wrestlingnovascotia.ca
Peter Coulthard, President
Scott Aldridge, Vice-President
Debbie MacDonald, Sec.-Treas.

Youth Bowling Canada (YBC)
c/o Bowl Canada, #10A, 250 Shields Ct., Markham ON L3R 9W7
Tel: 905-479-1560; *Fax:* 905-479-8613
info@bowlcanada.ca
www.youthbowling.ca; www.bowlcanada.ca
Social Media:
www.facebook.com/pages/youth-bowling-canada/103402153046873
YBC is a program operating under the auspices of the Bowling Proprietors' Association of Canada (Bowl Canada), a not-for-profit organization comprised of 500 member centres across the country. The YBC league is divided in 5-pin & 10-pin, & further broken down in 3 age groups: bantam, junior & senior.
Mariano Meconi, President, Bowl Canada
Paul Oliveira, Executive Director, Bowl Canada

Yukon Aboriginal Sport Circle (YASC)
2166 - 2nd Ave., Whitehorse YT Y1A 4p1
Tel: 867-668-2840; *Fax:* 867-668-6577
aboriginalsport@yasc.ca
www.yasc.ca
Social Media:
www.facebook.com/pages/Yukon-Aboriginal-Sports-Circle/343599029002109
The Yukon Aboriginal Sport Circle is a non-profit society dedicated to the advancement of Aboriginal recreation and sport in the Yukon through a variety of programs to increase participation and skill levels and to increase awareness.
Gael Marchand, Executive Director
Justin Ferbey, President

Yukon Amateur Hockey Association
4061, 4th Ave., Whitehorse YT Y1A 1H1
Tel: 867-393-4501
yaha@sportyukon.com
www.yukonhockey.ca
The Yukon Amateur Hockey Association is the sports governing body for amateur hockey in the Yukon.
Walter Brennan, President

Yukon Badminton Association
4061 - 4th Ave., Whitehorse YT Y1A 1H1
Tel: 867-668-4821
bluestone@northwestel.net
Michael Muller, President

Randy Carlson, Vice-President

Yukon Broomball League
4061, 4th Ave., Whitehorse YT Y1A 1H1
Tel: 867-668-3589
biz@yukonbroomball.com
www.yukonbroomball.com
To promote and facilitate Broomball in the Yukon Territory.
Allan Milford, President

Yukon Curling Association (YCA)
4061 - 4th Ave., Whitehorse YT Y1A 1H1
Tel: 867-668-7121; *Fax:* 867-667-4237
yca@sportyukon.com
yukoncurling.inthehack.com
Gord Zealand, President

Yukon Freestyle Ski Association
4061, 4th Ave., Whitehorse YT Y1A 1H1
Tel: 867-633-5615; *Fax:* 867-393-8779
www.sportyukon.com/membership/?member=71
To promote and facilitate freestyle skiing in the Yukon Territory.
Laura Wilson, Registrar

Yukon Golf Association
4061, 4th Ave., Whitehorse YT Y1A 1H1
Tel: 867-633-3364
zealandg@northwestel.net
www.sportyukon.com/membership/?member=57
The Yukon Golf Association is an organization that enhances opportunities for all Yukonners in their pursuit of excellence and in their enjoyment of participation.
Gordon Zealand, President

Yukon Horse and Rider Association (YHRA)
PO Box 31482, Whitehorse YT Y1A 6K8
Tel: 867-456-2030
info@yhra.ca
www.yhra.ca
The YHRA is dedicated to the sport of horseback riding in the Yukon Territory, Canada. The Association aims to encourage good horsemanship and help promote interest in the light horse industry.
Paul Choquette, President

Yukon Indian Hockey Association (YIHA)
PO Box 31769, Whitehorse YT Y1A 6L3
Tel: 867-456-7294; *Fax:* 867-456-7290
info@yiha.ca
www.yiha.ca
Social Media:
www.facebook.com/group.php?gid=169614299786
The Yukon Indian Hockey Association is a non-profit organization created to establish a hockey league in the Yukon to enable Native athletes to compete with other Canadian Provinces and Territories in the sport.
Karee Vallevand, President

Yukon Schools' Athletic Association (YSAA)
c/o Porter Creek Secondary School, 1405 Hickory St., Whitehorse YT V1A 4M4
paul.macdonald@yesnet.yk.ca
www.yesnet.yk.ca/ysaa/ysaainside.html
To encourage participation of students in inter school athletics, emphasize interschool athletics as an integral part of the total educational process and plan, promote, supervise and administer a program of inter-school athletics in all approved competitions.
Paul MacDonald, President

Yukon Shooting Federation
4061, 4th Ave., Whitehorse YT Y1A 1H1
Tel: 867-668-6776
www.sportyukon.com/membership/?member=64
To promote and facilitate air rifle and air pistol shooting in the Yukon Territory.
Jim Sias, President

Yukon Soccer Association
4061 - 4th Ave., Whitehorse YT Y1A 1H1
Tel: 867-633-4625; *Fax:* 867-667-4237
yukonsoccer@sportyukon.com
www.yukonsoccer.yk.ca
The Yukon Soccer Association is the sport governing body for the sport of soccer in the Yukon Territory. It is a volunteer based organization that coordinates and administers various programs devoted to the promotion and development of soccer.
Kim King, Administrator

Yukon Speed Skating Association
11 Buttercup Pl., Whitehorse YT Y1A 5V1
Tel: 867-668-4591; *Fax:* 867-393-8101
Bruce Henry, Branch President

Yukon Underwater Diving Association (YUDA)
alyon@yukon.net
www.yukonweb.com/community/yuda/
The Yukon Underwater Diving Association (YUDA) is a non-profit organization created by sport divers to promote the sport of underwater diving in the Yukon, Northern British Columbia and South East Alaska.
Allyn Lyon, President

Yukon Weightlifting Association
4061, 4th Ave., Whitehorse YT Y1A 1H1
www.sportyukon.com/membership/?member=79
To promote and facilitate competitive weightlifting in the Yukon Territory.
Moira Lassen, President

Standards & Testing

Cable Television Standards Foundation / Fondation des normes de télévision par câble
#515, 350 Albert St., Ottawa ON K1P 5G4
Tel: 613-230-5442; *Fax:* 613-230-5679
To provide basic structure & facilitate cable industry membership for purpose of self-regulation & adjudicative role of its second body (Cable Television Standards Council)
Claudette Cardinal, Chair

Canadian Educational Standards Institute (CESI) / Institut canadien des normes d'enseignement
PO Box 3013, 2 Ridley Rd., St Catharines ON L2R 7C3
Tel: 905-684-5658; *Fax:* 905-684-5057
execdir@cesi.edu
www.cesi.edu
To develop & promote educational standards & to foster compliance with those standards related to independent elementary & secondary school education.
Anne-Marie Kee, Executive Director

Canadian Evaluation Society (CES) / Société canadienne d'évaluation
1485 Laperriere Ave., Ottawa ON K1Z 7S8
Tel: 613-725-2526; *Fax:* 613-729-6206
secretariat@evaluationcanada.ca
www.evaluationcanada.ca
To advance evaluation for its members & the public; To establish & maintain CES as the recognized national organization which represents the evaluation community; To provide a forum for the advancement of theory & practice of evaluation; To develop competencies, ethics, & standards to improve the practice of evaluation; To advocate for high-quality evaluation with practitioners, local chapters, nationally & internationally; To promote the use of evaluation in society
Martha McGuire, President

Canadian General Standards Board (CGSB) / Office des normes générales du Canada (ONGC)
CGSB, #6B1, Place Du Portage III, Gatineau QC K1A 1G6
Tel: 819-956-0425; *Fax:* 819-956-1634
Toll-Free: 800-665-2472
ncr.cgsb-ongc@pwgsc.gc.ca
www.ongc-cgsb.gc.ca
To develop standards, through accreditation with the Standards Council of Canada; To offer conformity assessment services, including product certification & registration of quality & environmental management systems, conforming to ISO standards
Terrence Davies, Acting Director

Canadian Institute for NDE
135 Fennell Ave. West, Hamilton ON L8N 3T2
Tel: 905-387-1655; *Fax:* 905-574-6080
Toll-Free: 800-964-9488
info@cinde.ca
www.cinde.ca
Social Media: www.facebook.com/297023083473
To advance scientific, engineering, technical knowledge in the field of nondestructive testing; to gather & disseminate information relating to nondestructive testing useful to individuals & beneficial to the general public; to promote nondestructive testing through courses of instruction, lectures, meetings, publications, conferences, etc.
Larry Cote, President & CEO

Canadian Metric Association (CMA) / Association métrique canadienne
PO Box 35, Fonthill ON L0S 1E0
Tel: 905-892-3800
albertjmettler@gmail.com
To promote nationwide adoption of metric system & its modern expanded version; to contribute to better understanding of metric system; to provide guidance in correct use of metric units & symbols; to support introduction of international metric standards; to encourage implementation of other international standards & practices; to advocate rational choice of numerical values for sizes of food package & other consumer products
Albert J. Mettler, Secretary
John Douglas Bailes, President

Steel & Metal Industries

Canadian Die Casters Association (CDCA) / Association canadienne des mouleurs sous pression
#3, 247 Barr St., Renfrew ON K7V 1J6
Fax: 613-432-6840
Toll-Free: 866-809-7032
info@diecasters.ca
www.diecasters.ca
To assist die casters in dealing with governments & other organizations on industry issues; To provide a united voice for members
Bonnie James, Executive Director
Murray Abramovitch, President
Yahia Reguieg, Vice-President
Danny Di Liello, Treasurer

Canadian Foundry Association (CFA) / Association des fonderies canadiennes (AFC)
#1500, 1 Nicholas St., Ottawa ON K1N 7B7
Tel: 613-789-4894; *Fax:* 613-789-5957
www.foundryassociation.ca
To assist & represent the membership in dealing with government on industry specific issues; To communicate information to the industry, which will assist its members in strengthening their own competitive position & ensuring a strong Canadian foundry industry
Judith Arbour, Executive Director
William Monaghan, Secretary-Treasurer

Canadian Institute of Steel Construction (CISC) / Institut canadien de la construction en acier (ICCA)
#200, 3760 - 14th Ave., Markham ON L3R 3T7
Tel: 905-946-0864; *Fax:* 905-946-8574
info@cisc-icca.ca
www.cisc-icca.ca
To promote good design & safety, together with efficient & economical use of steel as a means of expanding the construction markets for structural steel, joists & platework
E. Whalen, President

Canadian Sheet Steel Building Institute (CSSBI) / Institut canadien de la tôle d'acier pour le bâtiment (ICTAB)
#2A, 652 Bishop St. North, Cambridge ON N3H 4V6
Tel: 519-650-1285; *Fax:* 519-650-8081
info@cssbi.ca
www.cssbi.ca
The CSSBI's vision statement is to make steel the material of choice for building construction in Canada.

Canadian Steel Construction Council (CSCC) / Conseil canadien de la construction en acier
#300, 201 Consumers Rd., Toronto ON M2J 4G8
Tel: 416-491-9898; *Fax:* 416-491-6461
To represent the manufacturers of steel products, including: open-web steel joists, steel platework, corrugated steel pipe, sheet steel, & steel fasteners; to promote the use of steel in construction through research & engineering

Canadian Steel Producers Association (CSPA) / Association canadienne des producteurs d'acier (ACPA)
#906, 350 Sparks St., Ottawa ON K1R 7S8
Tel: 613-238-6049; *Fax:* 613-238-1832
info@canadiansteel.ca
www.canadiansteel.ca
Social Media: www.facebook.com/220022834730294; twitter.com/CSPA_ACPA
To represent the steel producers that melt & pour steel in Canada
Ron Watkins, President

Canadian Steel Trade & Employment Congress
#501, 234 Eglinton Ave. East, Toronto ON M4P 1K7
Tel: 416-480-1797; *Fax:* 416-480-2986
general@cstec.ca
www.cstec.ca
To provide a forum for communication among steel companies, steelworkers, & governments to work for the betterment of the industry & its workforce
Robert Jones, Executive Director

Corrugated Steel Pipe Institute (CSPI) / Institut pour tuyaux de tôle ondulée
#2A, 652 Bishop St. North, Cambridge ON N3H 4V6
Tel: 519-650-8080; *Fax:* 519-650-8081
info@cspi.ca
www.cspi.ca
To promote & encourage general & wider use of corrugated steel pipe for drainage & other uses across Canada; to initiate & support research, marketing, promotion, public relations & advertising programs designed to broaden the markets for CSP products; to cooperate with public & private agencies engaged in the formulation of specifications & designs for drainage & other underground structures; to provide the industry & the public with documented experience & up-to-date technical information on CSP products & their proper use & application; to enhance, through responsible public relations practices, the reputation & image of the Canadian CSP industry; to cooperate with allied industry & government authorities; to encourage & participate in educational endeavours in colleges & universities.
David J. Penny, Marketing Manager

Nickel Institute
#2700, 161 Bay St., Toronto ON M5J 2S1
Tel: 416-591-7999; *Fax:* 416-591-7987
ni_toronto@nickelinstitute.org
www.nickelinstitute.org
Market development & applications oriented non-profit research organization of international nickel industry; to provide information for nickel users, designers, specifiers, educators & others interested in nickel-containing materials & their applications
Tim Aiken, Chairman
Stephen Barnett, President

Ontario Sheet Metal Contractors Association (OSM)
#26, 30 Wertheim Ct., Richmond Hill ON L4B 1B9
Tel: 905-886-9627; *Fax:* 905-886-9959
shtmetal@bellnet.ca
www.osmca.org
OSM is a not-for-profit association & the accredited, employer bargaining agency responsible for the negotiation & administration of all provincial collective agreements between OSM, the Ontario Sheet Metal Workers' & Roofers' Conference & the Sheet Metal Workers International Association. It is the lobbying voice for all national, provincial & corporate issues which directly affect its membership.
Steve Koutsonicolas, President
Wayne Peterson, Executive Director

Reinforcing Steel Institute of Ontario (RSIO)
PO Box 40620, Stn. RPO Six Points Plaza, Toronto ON M9B 6K8
Tel: 416-239-7746; *Fax:* 416-239-7745
administrator@rebar.org
www.rebar.org
Nancy Clarkson, Administrator

Surveying & Mapping

Alberta Land Surveyors' Association (ALSA)
#1000, 10020 - 101A Ave., Edmonton AB T5J 3G2
Tel: 780-429-8805; *Fax:* 780-429-3374
Toll-Free: 800-665-2572
info@alsa.ab.ca
www.alsa.ab.ca
The ALSA is a self-governing professional association which regulates the practice of land surveying.
Brian Munday, Executive Director
David McWilliam, Registrar
Brian D. Ross, President
John Haggerty, Secretary-Treasurer

Association of British Columbia Land Surveyors (ABCLS)
#301, 2400 Bevan Ave., Sidney BC V8L 1W1
Tel: 250-655-7222; *Fax:* 250-655-7223
office@abcls.ca
www.abcls.ca
To set educational requirements for land surveyors; To regulate professional land surveyors in British Columbia
Janice Henshaw, Executive Director
Chuck Salmon, Secretary & Registrar
Gord Gamble, Manager, Practice Advisory

Association of Canada Lands Surveyors / Association des arpenteurs des terres du Canada
100E, 900 Dynes Rd., Ottawa ON K2C 3L6
Tel: 613-723-9200; *Fax:* 613-723-5558
www.acls-aatc.ca
To establish & maintain standards of qualification for Canada Lands Surveyors; to regulate Canada Lands Surveyors; To establish & maintain standards of conduct, knowledge & skill among members of the Association & permit holders; to govern the activities of members of the Association & permit holders; To cooperate with other organizations for the advancement of surveying; To perform the duties & exercise the powers that are imposed or conferred on the Association by the Act
Jean-Claude Tétreault, Executive Director

Association of Manitoba Land Surveyors
#202, 83 Gary St., Winnipeg MB R3C 4J9
Tel: 204-943-6972; *Fax:* 204-957-7602
amls@mts.net
www.amls.ca
To license qualified persons becoming commissioned land surveyors; To protect public interests concerning land boundary matters
Kelly Tole, Executive Officer

Association of New Brunswick Land Surveyors (ANBLS) / Association des arpenteurs-géomètres du Nouveau-Brunswick (AA-GN-B)
#312, 212, Queen St., Fredericton NB E3B 1A8
Tel: 506-458-8266; *Fax:* 506-458-8267
anbls@nbnet.nb.ca
www.anbls.nb.ca
To regulate & govern the practice of land surveying in New Brunswick; To develop & maintain standards of knowledge, skill, & professional ethics
Louise McSheffrey, Executive Director

Association of Newfoundland Land Surveyors
#203, 62-64 Pippy Pl., St. John's NL A1B 4H7
Tel: 709-722-2031; *Fax:* 709-722-4104
anls@nf.aibn.com
www.surveyors.nf.ca
To establish & maintain standards of knowledge, skill, & professional conduct in the practice of land surveying, in order to serve & protect the public interest in Newfoundland; to regulate & govern the practice of land surveying in the province
Robin Davis, President
Paula Baggs, Executive Director

Association of Nova Scotia Land Surveyors (ANSLS)
325A Prince Albert Rd., Dartmouth NS B2Y 1N5
Tel: 902-469-7962; *Fax:* 902-469-7963
ansls@accesswave.ca
www.ansls.ca
To establish & maintain standards of professional ethics among its members, student members & holders of a certificate of authorization, in order that the public interest may be served & protected; & knowledge & skills among its members, student members & holders of a certificate of authorization; to regulate the practice of professional land surveying & govern the profession in accordance with the Act, the regulations & the by-laws; & to communicate & cooperate with other professional organizations for the advancement of the best interests of the surveying profession
Fred Hutchinson, Executive Director

Association of Ontario Land Economists
#205, 555 St. Clair Ave. West, Toronto ON M4V 2Y7
Tel: 416-283-0440; *Fax:* 416-283-1399
admin@aole.org
www.aole.org
To continue attracting membership-quality professionals engaged in land economics pursuits; To broaden & enrich the professional development of members; To promote & maintain high ethical work standards throughout our membership; To make submissions to government for improvements in law & public administration bearing on land economics
Andrea Calla, President
John Blackburn, Vice-President & Secretary
Naomi Irizawa, Treasurer

Association of Ontario Land Surveyors (AOLS)
1043 McNicoll Ave., Toronto ON M1W 3W6
Tel: 416-491-9020; *Fax:* 416-491-2576
Toll-Free: 800-268-0718
blain@aols.org
www.aols.org
AOLS is responsible for the licensing and governance of professional land surveyors, in accordance with the Surveyors Act. The self-governing association ensures that public interest is paramount.
Blain W. Martin, Executive Director
William D. Buck, Registrar

Association of Prince Edward Island Land Surveyors (APEILS)
PO Box 20100, Charlottetown PE C1A 9E3
Tel: 902-566-9966
Wayne Tremblay, Sec.-Treas.

Canadian Cartographic Association (CCA) / Association canadienne de cartographie
c/o Department of Geography, University of Victoria, PO Box 3050, Stn. CSC, Victoria BC V8W 3P5
awood@mun.ca
www.cca-acc.org
To promote interest in cartographic materials; To encourage research in the field of cartography; To advance education in cartography
Alberta Auringer Wood, Secretary
Paul Heersink, Treasurer

Canadian Geophysical Union (CGU) / Union géophysique canadienne (UGC)
c/o Dept. of Geology & Geophysics, University of Calgary, ES #278, 2500 University Dr. NW, Calgary AB T2N 1N4
Tel: 403-220-5596; *Fax:* 403-284-0074
cgu@ucalgary.ca
www.cgu-ugc.ca
To bring together & promote the geophysical sciences; To provide a focus for geophysicists at Canadian universities, government agencies, & industry in fields of study encompassing the composition & processes of the whole earth, including hydrology, space studies, & geology
Gail Atkinson, President
Jim Craven, Treasurer
Masaki Hayashi, Secretary

Canadian Institute of Quantity Surveyors (CIQS)
#19, 90 Nolan Ct., Markham ON L3R 4L9
Tel: 905-477-0008; *Fax:* 905-477-6774
Toll-Free: 866-345-1168
info@ciqs.org
www.ciqs.org
To represent the quantity surveying & construction estimating profession in Canada
Lois Metcalfe, Executive Director
Ian Duncan, President

Geomatics Industry Association of Canada (GIAC) / Association canadienne des entreprises de géomatique
Covent Glen, PO Box 62009, 6491 Jeanne D'Arc Blvd., Ottawa ON K1C 2S0
Fax: 613-851-1256
dhtessier@giac.ca
www.giac.ca
To strengthen business climate; to maintain cooperative relations with government; to promote expanded role for members in provision of geomatics products & services; to encourage adoption by governments of improved policies & practices for procurement of geomatics products & services; to promote member firms as source of high quality, professional services; to promote Canadian geomatics industry abroad.
Dave Gariepy, Chairman

Ordre des arpenteurs-géomètres du Québec (OAGQ) / Québec Land Surveyors Association
Iberville Quatre, #350, 2954, boul Laurier, Québec QC G1V 4T2
Tél: 418-656-0730; *Téléc:* 418-656-6352
oagq@oagq.qc.ca
www.oagq.qc.ca
La protection du public et le contrôle de la profession

Professional Surveyors Canada / Géomètres professionnels du Canada
#303, 1390 Prince of Wales Dr., Ottawa ON K2C 3N6
Tel: 613-695-8333
www.psc-gpc.ca/surveyors
To foster cooperation amongst surveyors in Canada; To advocate for an integrated Canadian surveying profession
Sarah Cornett, BSc, OLS, Executive Director

Saskatchewan Land Surveyors' Association (SLSA)
#230, 408 Broad St., Regina SK S4R 1X3
Tel: 306-352-8999; *Fax:* 306-352-8366
info@slsa.sk.ca
www.slsa.sk.ca
To uphold the stewardship & standards of the legal survey profession in Saskatchewan; To regulate & govern members in the practice of professional land surveying & professional surveying; To ensure the competency of members; To administer the profession to protect the public
D.L. Gurnsey, President
A. Carl Shiels, Executive Director & Registrar
Ron J. Eichel, Vice-President

Taxation

Association of Municipal Tax Collectors of Ontario
#119, 14845 - 6 Yonge St., Aurora ON L4G 6H8
Tel: 905-725-0019
amtco@sympatico.ca
www.amtco.on.ca
To bring those persons in the municipal field of tax collecting into helpful association with each other; To promote improved standards of ethics & efficiency in tax collection methods & procedures: To consider, resolve, & recommend amendments to Provincial Acts which may improve the tax billing & collection administration; To encourage submissions & disseminate information of interest to its members; To encourage & assist in the development of educational training programs for collection personnel; To cooperate with other municipal associations; To foster good public relations
Ken Hughes, President

Canadian Property Tax Association, Inc. (CPTA) / Association canadienne de taxe foncière, inc
#225, 6 Lansing Sq., Toronto ON M2J 1T5
Tel: 416-493-3276; *Fax:* 416-493-3905
cpta@on.aibn.com
www.cpta.org
To facilitate the exchange of information about industrial & commercial property tax issues throughout Canada
Gerry I.G. Divaris, President
James D. Fraser, Executive Vice-President
Grace L. Marsh, Vice-President, Administration
J. Bradford Nixon, Vice-President, Communication
Viviane Marcotte, Managing Director

Canadian Tax Foundation (CTF) / Foundation canadienne de fiscalité (FCF)
#1200, 595 Bay St., Toronto ON M5G 2N5
Tel: 416-599-0283; *Fax:* 416-599-9283
Toll-Free: 877-733-0283
www.ctf.ca; www.fcf-ctf.ca
To create a greater understanding of the Canadian tax system; To improve the Canadian tax system
Charles J.R. Taylor, Chair
Scott Wilkie, Vice-Chair
Larry Chapman, Director & Chief Executive Officer
Jane Meagher, Director, Québec Office
Debbie Selley, Treasurer
Judy Singh, Librarian

Canadian Taxpayers Federation (CTF)
#105, 438 Victoria Ave. East, Regina SK S4N 0N7
Tel: 306-352-7199; *Fax:* 306-352-7203
admin@taxpayer.com
www.taxpayer.com
Social Media: www.facebook.com/TaxpayerDOTcom; twitter.com/taxpayerdotcom; www.youtube.com/taxpayerdotcom
To advocate for the common interest of taxpayers; To effect public policy change
Michael Binnion, Chair
Troy Lanigan, President & Chief Executive Officer
Shannon Morrison, Vice-President, Operations
Melanie Harvie, Manager, Finance

Canadian Taxpayers Federation - Alberta (CTF)
#202, 10621 - 100th Ave., Edmonton AB T5J 0B3
Tel: 800-661-0187; *Fax:* 877-482-1744
ab.director@taxpayer.com
www.taxpayer.com
Social Media: twitter.com/scotthennig
To advocate on behalf of taxpayers across Alberta
Scott Hennig, Director, Alberta

Canadian Taxpayers Federation - British Columbia (CTF)
PO Box 20539, Stn. Howe St. RPO, Vancouver BC V6Z 2N8
Tel: 800-699-2282; *Fax:* 604-608-6773
bc.director@taxpayer.com
www.taxpayer.com
To advocate lower taxes, less waste & accountable government
Maureen Bader, Director, British Columbia

Canadian Taxpayers Federation - Ontario (CTF)
Varette Bldg., #512, 130 Albert St., Ottawa ON K1P 5G4
Tel: 800-265-0442; *Fax:* 613-234-7748
federal.director@taxpayer.com
www.taxpayer.com
Social Media: twitter.com/KevinGaudet
To engage in advocacy activities specific to Ontario
Kevin Gaudet, Director, Federal & Ontario

Canadian Taxpayers Federation - Saskatchewan & Manitoba (CTF)
#212, 428 Portage Ave., Winnipeg MB R3C 0E2
Tel: 204-982-2150; *Fax:* 204-982-2154
Toll-Free: 800-772-9955
ccraig@taxpayer.com
www.taxpayer.com
Social Media: twitter.com/colincraig1
To advocate on behalf of taxpayers in the prairie provinces
Colin Craig, Director, Prairies

Teaching

Québec Board of Black Educators (QBBE)
#310, Cavendish Blvd., Montréal QC H4B 2M5
Tel: 514-481-9400; *Fax:* 514-481-0611
qbbe@videotron.ca
www.qbbe.org
The Quebec Board of Black Educators mission is to promote the development of educational services for Black Youth and other youth between the ages of 5 to 25 who reside in the Greater Montreal area.
Phylicia Burke, Contact
Clarence Bayne, President

Telecommunications

Bell Aliant Pioneers
PO Box 1430, Saint John NB E2L 4K2
Toll-Free: 800-565-1436
The Bell Aliant Pioneer Volunteers is the largest corporate based volunteer organization in Atlantic Canada and is comprised of current and former Bell Aliant employees and its predecessor companies.
Sandra King, President

Canadian Association of Telecom Dealers (CATD)
39 Parisian Rd., Brampton ON L6P 2T2
Tel: 416-273-8797
The Canadian Association of Telecom Dealers is a national association of independent telecommunication service providers, dealers and manufacturers.

Canadian Call Management Association (CAM-X)
#10, 24 Olive St., Grimsby ON L3M 2B6
Tel: 905-309-0224; *Fax:* 905-309-0225
Toll-Free: 800-896-1054
info@camx.ca
www.camx.ca
To promote the welfare of the message-handling industry & related services through the encouragement & maintenance of high standards of ethics & services; the exchange of information & the rendering of mutual aid & assistance between member organizations.
Linda Osip, Executive Director

Canadian Independent Telephone Association (CITA) / Association canadienne du téléphone indépendant
1402 Queen St. West, Alton ON L7K 0C3
Tel: 519-940-0460; *Fax:* 519-940-1137
mhtaylor@allstream.net
www.cita.ca
To promote the increase & improvement of telephone service in Canada; to promote & protect the common business interest of members; to produce & distribute literature; to represent the industry before regulatory bodies, either federal or provincial.
Margi Taylor, General Manager/Administrator
Rob Figliuzzi, Director

Canadian Internet Registration Authority (CIRA)
#306, 350 Sparks St., Ottawa ON K1R 7S8
Tel: 613-237-5335; *Fax:* 800-285-0517
www.cira.ca
CIRA is a not for profit Canadian corporation responsible for operating the dot-ca internet country code.
Byron Holland, President & CEO

Canadian Telecommunications Consultants Association (CTCA)
PO Box 361, St. Davids ON L0S 1P0
Tel: 289-477-1465; *Fax:* 866-584-2822
Toll-Free: 866-584-2822
admin@ctca.ca; membership@ctca.ca
www.ctca.ca
CTCA advocates high standards of professionalism & expertise in the provision of telecommunications solutions. Towards this vision, the association encourages the dissemination & exchange of information among telecommunications consultants & organizations.
Michael Rozender, President

Canadian Wireless Telecommunications Association (CWTA) / Association canadienne des télécommunications sans fil (ACTS)
#1110, 130 Albert St., Ottawa ON K1P 5G4
Tel: 613-233-4888; *Fax:* 613-233-2032
info@cwta.ca
www.cwta.ca
The authority on wireless issures, trends & developments in Canada; represents cellular, PCS, messaging, mobile radio, fixed wireless & movile satellite service providers as well as companies that develop & produce products & services for the industry.

Frequency Co-ordination System Association (FCSA) / Association pour la coordination des fréquences
#700, 1 Nicholas St., Ottawa ON K1N 7B7
Tel: 613-241-3080; *Fax:* 613-241-9632
amoreno.fcsa@sympatico.ca
www.fcsa.ca
To operate & administer computerized Microwave Information & Coordination System (MICS); to provide cost-effective, timely & high quality centralized administrative & technical services to allow members to be able to effectively plan & coordinate frequencies for microwave communication systems on national basis.
A. Moreno, General Manager/Sec.-Treas.

Halifax Regional CAP Association (HRCAP)
c/o 1673 Barrington St., 2nd Fl., Halifax NS B3J 1Z9
Tel: 902-482-4729; *Fax:* 902-482-5014
admin@hrca.ns.ca
www.halifaxcap.ca
Social Media: twitter.com/hrcap
To deliver quality service to communities through their locally operated Community Access Program (CAP) sites.
Ryan Deschamps, Chair

Ontario Pioneers
21 Meadowland Dr., Brampton ON L6W 2R5
Tel: 905-451-5607; *Fax:* 905-453-3996
she.rob@sympatico.ca
Sheila O'Donoghue, Manager

SaskTel Pioneers
2121 Saskatchewan Dr., 12th Fl., Regina SK S4P 3Y2
Tel: 306-777-2515; *Toll-Free:* 866-944-4442
sasktel.pioneers@sasktel.sk.ca
www.sasktelpioneers.com
Darrell Liebrecht, Manager

Telecommunities Canada Inc.
c/o President, #220, 4252 Commerce Circle, Victoria BC V8Z 4M2
Tel: 250-479-2851; *Fax:* 250-727-6418
shearman@victoria.tc.ca
www.tc.ca
To ensure that all Canadians are able to participate in community-based communications & electronic information services by promoting and supporting local community network initiatives; to represent & promote Canadian community networking movement at the national & international level
Gareth Shearman, President

TelecomPioneers
1801 California St., 44th Fl., Denver CO 80202 USA
Tel: 303-571-1200; *Fax:* 303-572-0520
Toll-Free: 800-872-5995
info@pioneersvolunteer.org
www.telecompioneers.org
Social Media: www.facebook.com/pages/Pioneers-Volunteer-Network/111882325524028
TelecomPioneers is the largest industry-related volunteer organizationin the world, comprising of over 600,000 current and retired telecommunications employees who have joined together to make their communities better places to live and work.
Carey Wirtzfeld, President

TelecomPioneers of Alberta
9 Munro Cresc., Red Deer AB T4N 0H8
Tel: 403-343-1201
chap46@telus.net
Ken Davies, Manager

TelecomPioneers of Canada
PO Box 880, 1505 Barrington St., Halifax NS B3J 2W3
Fax: 902-484-5189
Toll-Free: 888-994-3232
www.telecompioneers.ca

The TelecomPioneers of Canada is a network of current and former telecom industry employees, their partners and their families and are commited to improving the quality of life in Canada's communities.

Tenants & Landlords

Action Dignité de Saint-Léonard
9089A, boul Viau, Saint-Léonard QC H1R 2V6
Tél: 514-251-2874; *Téléc:* 514-251-2874
actdigsl@cooptel.qc.ca
Groupe de défense des droits des locataires

Association des locataires de l'×le-des-Soeurs (ALIS/NITA) / Nuns' Island Tenants Association
CP 63008, 40, Place du Commerce, Verdun QC H3E 1V6
Tél: 514-667-0914; *Téléc:* 514-995-2773
alis_nita@yahoo.com
Défense des droits des locataires

Comité d'action des citoyennes et citoyens de Verdun
3972, rue de Verdun, Verdun QC H4G 1K9
Tél: 514-769-2228; *Téléc:* 514-769-0825
cacv@videotron.ca
www.cacv-verdun.org
Le CACV soutien les personnes les plus démunies afin qu'elles améliorent leurs conditions de vie dans une optique de prise en charge
Chantal Lamarre, Directrice

Comité d'action Parc Extension (CAPE)
#9, 419, St-Roch, Montréal QC H3N 1R8
Tél: 514-278-6028; *Téléc:* 514-278-0900
cape@cooptel.qc.ca
www.comitelogement.org
A pour mission d'améliorer les conditions de vie de tous les citoyens/citoyennes du quartier Parc Extension

Comité des citoyens et citoyennes du quartier Saint-Sauveur
301, rue Carillon, Québec QC G1K 5B3
Tél: 418-529-6158
cccqss@bellnet.ca
www.cccqss.org

Comité logement de Lacine-Lasalle
426, rue St-Jacques, Lachine QC H8R 1E8
Tél: 514-544-4294; *Téléc:* 514-366-0505
logement.lachine-lasalle@videotron.ca

Comité logement du Plateau Mont-Royal
4450, St-Hubert, local 328, Montréal QC H2J 2W9
Tél: 514-527-3495; *Téléc:* 514-527-6653
clplateau@yahoo.ca

Comité logement Rosemont
5350, rue Lafond, local R-145, Montréal QC H1X 2X2
Tél: 514-597-2581; *Téléc:* 514-524-9813
info@comitelogement.org
www.comitelogement.org
Défendre et promouvoir les droits des locataires du quartier Rosemont
Martine Poitras, Coordonnatrice

Conseil communautaire Notre-Dame-de-Grâce / Notre-Dame-de-Grâce Community Council
5964, av Notre-Dame-de-Grâce, Montréal QC H4A 1N1
Tél: 514-484-1471; *Téléc:* 514-484-1687
ndgcc@ndg.ca
www.ndg.ca
Gillian Keefe, Directrice

POPIR-Comité logement (St-Henri, Petite Bourgogne, Ville Émard, Côte St-Paul)
4017, rue Notre-Dame ouest, Montréal QC H4C 1R3
Tél: 514-935-4649; *Téléc:* 514-935-4067
popir@videotron.ca

Tourism & Travel

Alberta Hotel & Lodging Association
2707 Ellwood Dr. SW, Edmonton AB T6X 0P7
Tel: 780-436-6112; *Fax:* 780-436-5404
Toll-Free: 888-436-6112
www.ahla.ca
Social Media: www.facebook.com/171333316227097; www.linkedin.com/company/alberta-hotel-&-lodging-association
To enhance the image, the quality & efficiency of the hotel industry in Alberta
Dave Kaiser, President & CEO

Algoma Kinniwabi Travel Association (AKTA)
#204, 485 Queen St. East, Sault Ste Marie ON P6A 1Z9
Tel: 705-254-4293; *Fax:* 705-254-4892
Toll-Free: 800-263-2546
info@algomacountry.com
www.algomacountry.com
To promote the Algoma Country region to the travelling public
Lori Johnson, President

Almaguin-Nipissing Travel Association
1375 Seymour St., North Bay ON P1B 9V6
Tel: 705-474-6634; *Fax:* 705-474-9271
Toll-Free: 800-387-0516
info@ontariosnearnorth.on.ca
www.ontariosnearnorth.on.ca
Social Media: www.facebook.com/ontariosnearnorth; twitter.com/ONearNorth
To market Ontario's Near North as a four-seasons family-oriented outdoor vacation destination on behalf of the organized tourist industry
Pat Lagacé, Executive Administrator

Association des hôteliers du Québec (AHQ) / Québec Hoteliers' Association
#1004, 425, boul De Maisonneuve ouest, Montréal QC H3A 3G5
Tél: 514-448-6215; *Téléc:* 514-849-1157
Ligne sans frais: 877-769-9776
info@hoteliersquebec.org
www.hoteliers-quebec.org
Mèdia social: www.facebook.com/HoteliersQuebecAHQ
Regrouper les établissements hôteliers pour les représenter, défendre leurs intérêts et leurs fournir des services et ce, tout en collaborant au développement de la qualité de la profession hôtelière et de l'industrie touristique en général
Danielle Chayer, Vice-présidente/Directrice générale

Association moto-tourisme Chibougamau
CP 580, Chibougamau QC G8P 2Y8
Tél: 418-745-3765
Jean-Paul Mercier

Association of Canadian Travel Agencies (ACTA) / Association canadienne des agences de voyages
#328, 2560 Matheson Blvd. East, Mississauga ON L4W 4Y9
Tel: 905-282-9294; *Fax:* 905-282-9826
Toll-Free: 866-725-2282
actacan@acta.travel
www.acta.ca
To provide leadership for the retail travel professional
David McCaig, President & CEO
David McCaig, President/COO

Association of Canadian Travel Agencies - Atlantic (ACTA)
PO Box 21007, Quispamsis NB E2E 4Z4
Tel: 506-847-4030; *Fax:* 506-847-4048
Toll-Free: 866-725-2282
actaatlantic@acta.travel
www.acta.ca
To represent & defend the interests of the retail travel services industry; To serve as the focal point for the retail travel services industry, where ideas & resources are pooled into initiatives designed to create & maintain a healthly business & legislative environment
Lorie Cohen Hackett, Regional Manager

Association of Canadian Travel Agents - Alberta/NWT
PO Box 73034, 6290 - 199 St., Edmonton AB T5T 3X1
Tel: 780-756-6606; *Fax:* 780-756-6639
Toll-Free: 800-667-8314
cgannon@acta.ca
To represent the retail travel sector of Canada's tourism industy, with a focus on Albertan travel agents
Allan Ronneseth, Regional, Chair
Colleen Gannon, Regional Manager

Association of Canadian Travel Agents - British Columbia/Yukon
#213, 5760 Minoru Blvd., Richmond BC V6X 2A9
Tel: 604-231-0544; *Fax:* 604-231-6020
David McCaig, President & CEO

Association of Canadian Travel Agents - Manitoba
#700, 177 Lombard Ave., Winnipeg MB R3B 0W5
Tel: 204-831-0831; *Fax:* 204-925-8000
actambsk@acta.ca
Shelley Morris, Regional Manager

Association of Canadian Travel Agents - Ontario
#328, 2560 Matheson Blvd. East, Mississauga ON L4W 4Y5
Tel: 905-282-9294; *Fax:* 905-282-9826
Toll-Free: 888-257-2282
actaon@on.aibn.com
www.acta.ca
To represent the retail travel sector of Canada's tourism industry, with a focus on Ontario travel agents
Heather Craig-Peddie, Director of Operations
Mike Foster, Regional Chair

Association of Canadian Travel Agents - Québec / Association des agents de voyages du Québec
CP 50043, Succ. Dagenais, Laval QC H7M 0A1
Tél: 450-933-4802; *Téléc:* 450-933-4803
Défense des droits et intérêts de l'industrie du voyage
Jean Luc Beauchemin, Directeur régional

Association touristique des Laurentides (ATL) / Laurentian Tourist Association
14 142, rue de la Chapelle, Mirabel QC J7J 2C8
Tél: 450-436-8532; *Téléc:* 450-436-5309
Ligne sans frais: 800-561-6673
info-tourisme@laurentides.com
www.laurentides.com
Mèdia social: www.facebook.com/TourismeLaurentides; www.youtube.com/notredecor
Unir tous les agents, corporations, corps publics et municipaux, associations et organismes, entreprises, oeuvrant dans le domaine touristique dans la région nord de Montréal; orienter et favoriser le développement et l'activité touristique régionale dans le meilleur intérêt régional; obtenir au nom de toute la région des interventions gouvernementales ou autres propres à favoriser son développement touristique

Association touristique régionale de Charlevoix
495, boul de Comporté, La Malbaie QC G5A 3G3
Tél: 418-665-4454; *Téléc:* 418-665-3811
Ligne sans frais: 800-667-2276
info@tourisme-charlevoix.com
www.tourisme-charlevoix.com/fr/accueil/index.asp
Acceuil, promotion, développement de Charlevoix en tourisme

Association touristique régionale de Duplessis (ATRD)
312, av Brochu, Sept-Iles QC G4R 2W6
Tél: 418-962-0808; *Téléc:* 418-962-6518
Ligne sans frais: 888-463-0808
info@tourismeduplessis.com
www.tourismeduplessis.com
Regrouper efficacement, sur une base géographique et sectorielle, les diverses entreprises touristiques de la région; proposer un plan d'action annuel dans lequel sont déterminés les priorités, les programmes et les services offerts à ses membres
Marie-Soleil Vigneault, Directrice générale
Danys Jomphe, Président

Association touristique régionale du Saguenay-Lac-Saint-Jean
#100, 412, boul. Saguenay Est, Chicoutimi QC G7H 7Y8
Tél: 418-543-9778; *Téléc:* 418-543-1805
Ligne sans frais: 800-463-9651
info@tourismesaglac.net
www.saguenaylacsaintjean.net
Mèdia social: www.facebook.com/TourismeSaguenayLacSaintJean; twitter.com/TourismeSagLac
Au service et à l'écoute de ses membres et de l'industrie touristique régionale dans son ensemble, elle est une organisation de concertation dont les principales activités visent à promouvoir à développer la qualité de l'expérience touristique, à assurer l'accueil et l'information et la mise en marché
Carol Martel, Directeur général
Robert Bilodeau, Président

Association touristique régionale Manicouagan
#304, 337, boul LaSalle, Baie-Comeau QC G4Z 2Z1
Tél: 418-294-2876; *Téléc:* 418-294-2345
Ligne sans frais: 888-463-5319
atrmanic@globetrotter.net
www.tourismemanicouagan.com/fr/
Promouvoir la région comme destination touristique et mettre en valeur ses attraits
Denis Cardinal, Directeur général

Associations touristiques régionales associées du Québec (ATRAQ) / Québec Regional Tourist Associations Inc.
#330, 1575, boul de l'Avenir, Laval QC H7S 2N5
Tél: 450-686-8358; *Téléc:* 450-686-9630
Ligne sans frais: 877-686-8358
information@atrassociees.com
www.atrassociees.com
Regroupe l'ensemble des associations touristiques régionales oeuvrant au Québec en vue de les représenter et défendre leurs intérêts collectifs; les promouvoir et leur offrir des services; entend contribuer ainsi au développement de l'industrie touristique québécoise
Louis Rome, Directeur général

British Columbia Lodging & Campgrounds Association (BCLCA)
#209, 3003 St. John's St., Port Moody BC V3H 2C4
Tel: 778-383-1037; *Fax:* 604-945-7606
www.bclca.com
Social Media: www.facebook.com/TravellinginBritishColumbia; twitter.com/TravellinginBC
To promote the public's utilization of member lodging & campground businesses; to monitor & make representation to governments on legislation affecting the interests of British Columbia's lodging & campground businesses; to speak for the membership on matters of general or specific interest; to encourage members to strive for excellence in accommodation & service
Joss Penny, Executive Director

Cambridge Tourism
750 Hespeler Rd., Cambridge ON N3H 5L8
Tel: 519-622-2336; *Fax:* 519-622-0177
Toll-Free: 800-749-7560
visit@cambridgetourism.com
www.cambridgetourism.com
To develop tourism initiatives & build partnerships that pool ideas & resources to promote Cambridge as a viable travel destination, generating greater economic impact for the city & other tourism stakeholders.
Greg Durocher, President, Chamber of Commerce
Jeanette Mahoney, Visitor Services Coordinator, Chamber of Commerce

Camping in Ontario
#206, 305 Milner Ave., Toronto ON M1B 3V4
Tel: 416-820-2714; *Fax:* 647-352-0900
Toll-Free: 877-672-2226
opca@campinginontario.ca
www.campinginontario.ca
Social Media: www.facebook.com/pages/Camping-In-Ontario/119145788133338
To support & improve the operation of private campgrounds in Ontario by establishing standards, disseminating information & by representation in the tourist industry & at all levels of government
Alexandra Anderson, Executive Director

Camping Québec
#700, 2001, rue de la Metropole, Longueuil QC J4G 1S9
Tél: 450-651-7396; *Téléc:* 450-651-7397
Ligne sans frais: 800-363-0457
www.destinationcamping.ca
Défendre les intérêts de nos membres; offrir des services de publications et promotion, des activitées, des escomptes sur achats et programmes divers.
Maryse Catellier, Vice-président exécutif

Canadian Hotel Marketing & Sales Executives (CHMSE)
26 Avonhurst Rd., Toronto ON M9A 2G8
Tel: 416-252-9800; *Fax:* 416-252-7071
info@chmse.com
www.chmse.com
Social Media: twitter.com/CHMSE; www.linkedin.com/groups?home=&gid=3020813
To be the leading association in providing professional development opportunities to sales & marketing executives within the Canadian hospitality industry
Shelley Macdonald, Executive Director
Julie Wiggins, Vice-President
Susan Aguilo, Vice-President
Monika Nowak, Vice-President
Linda Stott, President

Canadian Institute of Travel Counsellors (CITC) / Institut canadien des conseillers en voyages
#406, 505 Consumers Rd., Toronto ON M2J 4V8
Tel: 416-484-4450; *Fax:* 416-484-4140
Toll-Free: 800-589-5776
info@citc.ca
www.citc.ca
To lead the Canadian travel industry to be the most skilled & professional work force in the industry, & to ensure that the CTC/CTM designations are recognized, accepted & valued by the travel industry & consumers as the ultimate achievement in professionalism.
Steve Gillick, President/COO

Canadian Recreational Vehicle Association (CRVA) / Association canadienne du véhicule récréatif
110 Freelton Rd., Freelton ON L0R 1K0
Fax: 905-656-9900
www.crva.ca
To promote recreational vehicle lifestyle

Canadian Resort Development Association (CRDA)
147 Liberty St., Toronto ON M6K 3G3
Tel: 416-960-4930; *Fax:* 416-533-0591
Toll-Free: 800-646-9205
crda@rogers.com
www.crda.com
To engender a better understanding of the value of the vacation ownership product; to ensure fair & ethical treatment by all industry participants, through legislation or industry self-management; to educate & inform within the membership & outwardly to the public.
Ross Perlmutter, Executive Director

Canadian Tourism Research Institute
255 Smyth Rd., Ottawa ON K1H 8M7
Tel: 613-526-3280; *Fax:* 613-526-4857
Toll-Free: 866-711-2262
ctri@conferenceboard.ca
www.conferenceboard.ca/ctri/
Gregory Hermus, Associate Director

Cariboo Chilcotin Coast Tourism Association
#204, 350 Barnard St., Williams Lake BC V2G 4T9
Tel: 250-392-2226; *Fax:* 250-392-2838
Toll-Free: 800-663-5885
info@landwithoutlimits.com
www.landwithoutlimits.com
The Association promotes tourism products of the Cariboo Chilcotin Coast region of BC. Products & services include, access to an extensive image bank, travel guide & DVD, familiarization tour assistance, itinerary planning assistance, property inspection/recommendations, regional knowledge.
Wylie Bystedt, Chair
Amy Thacker, CEO

Central Nova Tourist Association (CNTA)
65 Treaty Trail, Millbrook NS B6L 1W3
Tel: 902-893-8782; *Fax:* 902-893-2269
Toll-Free: 800-895-1177
info@centralnovascotia.com
www.centralnovascotia.com
To contribute to the Central Nova area becoming the most important tourist destination in Nova Scotia, resulting in new tourism initiatives & strengthened businesses; we will accomplish this by working as a team dedicated to effective communication & production of our community
Joyce Mingo, Executive Director

Cornwall & Seaway Valley Tourism
11 Water St. West, Cornwall ON K6J 1A1
Tel: 613-938-4748; *Fax:* 613-938-4751
Toll-Free: 800-937-4748
info@cornwalltourism.com
www.cornwalltourism.com
To promote Cornwall & Seaway Valley as a viable visitor & convention destination
Michael Lalonde, Executive Manager

Council of Tourism Associations of British Columbia (COTA)
PO Box 3636, 349 West Georgia St., Vancouver BC V6B 3Y8
Tel: 604-685-5956
www.cotabc.com
To advocate the interests of members to provincial & federal governments, businesses & media, in order to inform them of the opportunities & concerns of the tourism industry; To promote tourism in British Columbia
Stephen Regan, President & CEO
Kitka Neyedli, Coordinator, Membership & Industry Relations Coordinator
Peter Larose, Director, Policy & Planning

Economic Development Winnipeg Inc.
#300, 259 Portage Ave., Winnipeg MB R3B 2A9
Tel: 204-954-1997; *Fax:* 204-942-4043
Toll-Free: 800-665-0204
wpginfo@economicdevelopmentwinnipeg.com
www.economicdevelopmentwinnipeg.com
To act as Winnipeg's economic development & tourism services agency, by marketing the city & providing related economic development & tourism services
Marina R. James, President & Chief Executive Officer
Greg Dandewich, Senior Vice-President
Chantal Sturk-Nadeau, Senior Vice-President, Tourism
Kathryn Maycher, Vice-President, Finance & Administration

Evangeline Trail Tourism Association (ETTA)
5518 Prospect Rd., New Minas NS B4N 3K8
Tel: 902-861-1645
To represent the private sector of tourism industry; To promote tourism in the Nova Scotia area of Evangeline Trail; To publish articles, pamphlets & books about the area; To administer & operate local tourist bureaus in cooperation with various Boards of Trade & local tourism committees
Beth Caldwell, Executive Director

Fondation Tourisme Jeunesse
3514, av Lacombe, Montréal QC H3T 1M1
Tél: 514-252-3208; *Téléc:* 514-252-3024
fondationtourismejeunesse@gmail.com
www.tourismejeunesse.org
Rendre accessible le tourisme aux jeunes, en développant divers outils et services, notamment par le biais des bureaux d'information voyages et des auberges de jeunesse du Québec
Veronica Gomez, Directrice de la Fondation

Fredericton Tourism
PO Box 130, 11 Carleton St., Fredericton NB E3B 4Y7
Tel: 506-460-2041; *Fax:* 506-460-2474
Toll-Free: 888-888-4768
www.tourismfredericton.ca
The organization is a division of the Dept. of Development Services of the City of Fredericton, & it is responsible for marketing the city & surrounding area as a tourism destination. It develops & runs a variety of cultural programs largely focused in the Historic Garrison District. Also, it operates 2 municipal Visitor Information Centres, Lighthouse on the Green, & River Valley Crafts retail shop.
David Seabrook, Tourism Manager
Frank Flanagan, Director, Development Services

The Georgian Triangle Tourist Association & Tourist Information Centre
30 Mountain Rd., Collingwood ON L9Y 5H7
Tel: 705-445-7722; *Toll-Free:* 888-227-8667
info@georgiantriangle.com
www.georgiantriangle.com
Social Media: www.facebook.com/group.php?gid=99129054579
To promote tourism & convention industries in the Georgian Triangle
Nancy Kindler, Executive Director

Halifax Tourism, Culture & Heritage
PO Box 1749, Halifax NS B3J 3A5
Tel: 902-490-5948; *Fax:* 902-490-5950
ivc@region.halifax.ns.ca
www.halifaxinfo.com
The entire Halifax region delights with its impressive array of entertainment, museums, galleries, historic sites, fine restaurants, colourful gardens and lively nightlife. Through our 188 communities, explore charming seaside towns, sun-drenched beaches, sparkling coves and miles of rugged shoreline guarded by graceful lighthouses. Imagine the vivacity of city living, the charms of small town life and the pristine beauty of nature - all in one place.
Lewis M. Rogers, Director

HomeLink International Home Exchange (HLCA)
1707 Platt Cres., North Vancouver BC V7J 1X9
Tel: 604-987-3262
info@homelink.ca
www.homelink.ca
To produce directories listing homes for vacation exchange worldwide
Jack Graber, Director

Hospitality Newfoundland & Labrador (HNL)
ICON Bldg., 187 Kenmonunt Rd., 2nd Fl., St. John's NL A1B 3P9
Tel: 709-722-2000; *Fax:* 709-722-8104
Toll-Free: 800-563-0700
hnl@hnl.ca
www.hnl.ca
To develop & promote tourism & hospitality industry throughout Newfoundland & Labrador.

Carol-Ann Gilliard, Chief Executive Officer

Hotel Association of Canada Inc. (HAC) / Association des hôtels du Canada
#1206, 130 Albert St., Ottawa ON K1P 5G4
Tel: 613-237-7149; *Fax:* 613-237-8928
info@hotelassociation.ca
www.hotelassociation.ca
Social Media: twitter.com/hotelassoc
To represent members both nationally & internationally; to provide cost-effective services which stimulate & encourage a free market accommodation industry
Anthony Pollard, President
Anthony P. Pollard, President
Walter Willett, Director, Business Development

Hotel Association of Nova Scotia (HANS)
PO Box 473, Stn. M, Halifax NS B3J 2P8
Tel: 902-425-4890
www.novascotiahotels.ca
To make Nova Scotia a year-round travel destination; To act as the official voice of the collective member hotels; To provide support for appropriate advisory boards & committees; To develop & encourage a coordinated joint marketing effort
Jeff Ransome, President

Hotel Association of Prince Edward Island
c/o 129 Queen St., Charlottetown PE C1A 4B3
Tel: 902-368-3688; *Fax:* 902-368-3108
Elaine Thompson, President

Institut de tourisme et d'hôtellerie du Québec (ITHQ)
3535, rue Saint-Denis, Montréal QC H2X 3P1
Tél: 514-282-5107; *Téléc:* 514-873-4529
Ligne sans frais: 800-361-5111
webmestre@ithq.qc.ca
www.ithq.qc.ca
Formation professionnelle en hôtellerie, restauration et tourisme.
Lucille Daoust, Directrice générale
Robert Gagnon, Président

Klondike Visitors Association (KVA)
PO Box 389C, Dawson City YT Y0B 1G0
Tel: 867-993-5575; *Fax:* 867-993-6415
kva@dawson.net
www.dawsoncity.ca
Social Media: www.facebook.com/pages/dawson-city-yukon/182559814930
The Association responds to visitor information requests & liaises with municipal & territorial governments to encourage Tourism-related initiatives. It promotes Dawson City, Yukon & the Klondike Region as a year-round tourist destination.
Gary Parker, Executive Director

Kootenay Rockies Tourism
PO Box 10, 1905 Warren Ave., Kimberley BC V1A 2Y5
Tel: 250-427-4838; *Fax:* 250-427-3344
Toll-Free: 800-661-6603
info@kootenayrockies.com
www.kootenayrockies.com
To coordinate & execute tourism marketing initiatives of private sector partners.
Chris Dadson, President

Muskoka Tourism
1342 Hwy. 11 North, RR#2, Kilworthy ON P0E 1G0
Tel: 705-689-0660; *Fax:* 705-689-9118
Toll-Free: 800-267-9700
info@muskokatourism.ca
www.discovermuskoka.ca
To market the region's tourism resources to the public, media & group tour travel markets

Niagara Falls Tourism
5400 Robinson St, Niagara Falls ON L2G 2A6
Tel: 905-356-6061; *Fax:* 905-356-5567
Toll-Free: 800-563-2557
www.niagarafallstourism.com
Social Media: www.facebook.com/niagarafallstourismcanada; twitter.com/nfallstourism; www.youtube.com/user/niagarafallstourism
Niagara Falls Tourism (Visitor and Convention Bureau) is the official tourism marketing organization of the Community, responsible for developing public and private sector programs that produce incremental visitor business and resulting economic development returns for the City, its residents and the business community
Toni Williams, Director, Operations

North of Superior Tourism Association (NOSTA)
119 South May St., Thunder Bay ON P7E 1A9
Tel: 807-346-1130; *Fax:* 807-346-1135
Toll-Free: 800-265-3951
info@nosta.on.ca
www.nosta.on.ca
Social Media: www.facebook.com/group.php?gid=55057890985
To market the tourism opportunities for vacationing in Northwestern Ontario.
Done Pearl, Executive Director

Northern British Columbia Tourism Association (NBCTA)
PO Box 2373, 1274 - 5th Ave., Prince George BC V2N 2S6
Tel: 250-561-0432; *Fax:* 250-561-0450
Toll-Free: 800-663-8843
info@nbctourism.com
www.nbctourism.com
To promote & develop the tourism industry of northern British Columbia
Anthony Everett, CEO

Northern Frontier Visitors Association (NFVA)
#4, 4807 - 49 St., Yellowknife NT X1A 3T5
Tel: 867-873-4262; *Fax:* 867-873-3654
Toll-Free: 877-881-4262
info@northernfrontier.com
www.northernfrontier.com
To promote the Northern Frontier Region as an attractive area for tourism; to foster, encourage & assist in any way the growth of tourism into & within the Northern Frontier Region; to increase awareness within the Northern Frontier Region of the potential tourism holds as a viable, clean, labour intensive industry.
Denie Olmstead, Executive Director

Northern Rockies Alaska Highway Tourism Association (NRAHTA)
PO Box 6850, Stn. Main, #300, 9523 - 100 St., Fort St John BC V1J 4J3
Tel: 250-785-2544; *Fax:* 250-785-4424
Toll-Free: 888-785-2544
info@hellonorth.com
www.hellonorth.com
To coordinate opportunites for sustainable tourism growth & development by fostering memorable year round visitor experiences; promoting social & economic benefits to members & wider community.
April Moi, Executive Director

Northwest Ontario Sunset Country Travel Association
PO Box 647W, Kenora ON P9N 3X6
Tel: 807-468-5853; *Fax:* 807-468-5484
Toll-Free: 800-665-7567
info@ontariossunsetcountry.ca
www.ontariossunsetcountry.ca
To develop, promote & advertise through cooperation, coordination & communication with clients & organizations for the betterment of tourism in Sunset Country & the province.
Gerry Cariou, Executive Director

Northwest Territories Tourism (NWTT)
PO Box 610, Yellowknife NT X1A 2N5
Toll-Free: 800-661-0788
info@spectacularnwt.com
www.spectacularnwt.com
Social Media: twitter.com/spectacularnwt
To support the development of a strong tourism sector in the Northwest Territories for the benefit of tourists, residents, & communities; To promote pan-territorial tourism; To act as a voice for the tourism industry; To preserve the integrity of the cultural & natural heritage of the Northwest Territories
Brian Desjardins, Executive Director
Ron Ostrom, Director, Marketing
Julie Warnock, Coordinator, Communications
Margo Thorne, Officer, Finance

Nunavut Tourism
PO Box 1450, Iqaluit NU X0A 0H0
Tel: 867-979-6551; *Fax:* 867-979-1261
Toll-Free: 866-686-2888
info@nunavuttourism.com
www.nunavuttourism.com
To represent the tourism industry for the private sector in Nunavut; to promote & market Nunavut tourism products
Bill Lyall, Chair
Paul Lewis, CEO
Betty Ann Eaton, Vice-Chair

NWC, the Business Travellers' Association (NWC)
PO Box 336, 28 Queen Elizabeth Way, Winnipeg MB R3C 2H6
Tel: 204-284-8900; *Fax:* 204-284-8909
Toll-Free: 800-665-6928
nwcta@nwcta.com
www.nwcta.com
To protect & introduce benefits for individual business travellers
Terry D. Carruthers, CEO & General Manager
Diane McDonald, Membership Services Coordinator

Office du tourisme et des congrès de Québec (OTCQ) / Québec City & Area Tourism & Convention Board
399, rue St-Joseph est, Québec QC G1K 8E2
Tél: 418-641-6654; *Téléc:* 418-641-6578
Ligne sans frais: 877-783-1608
www.quebecregion.com
Média social: www.facebook.com/QuebecRegion
Organisme responsable de la mise en marché de la région touristique de Québec
Gabriel Savard, Directeur général
Daniel Gagnon, Directeur, Communication et publicité

Ontario Accommodation Association (OAA)
#2, 347 Pido Rd., RR#6, Peterborough ON K9J 6X7
Tel: 705-745-4982; *Fax:* 705-745-4983
Toll-Free: 800-461-1972
www.ontarioaccommodation.com
Social Media: www.facebook.com/210817732276423
To serve Ontario's independent accommodation industry

Ontario East Tourism Association (OETA)
PO Box 730, #200, 104 St. Lawrence St., Merrickville ON K0G 1N0
Tel: 613-269-4113; *Fax:* 613-659-4306
Toll-Free: 800-567-3278
info@realontario.ca
www.realontario.ca
To encourage visitation to Eastern Ontario by means of cooperative tourism marketing
Rose Bertoia, Executive Director
John Bonser, President

Ontario Restaurant, Hotel & Motel Association (ORHMA)
#8-201, 2600 Skymark Ave., Mississauga ON L4W 5B2
Tel: 905-361-0268; *Fax:* 905-361-0288
Toll-Free: 800-668-8906
info@orhma.com
www.orhma.com
To foster a positive business climate for the hospitality industry in Ontario; To represent members before municipal & provincial governments
David Blades, Chair
Tony Elenis, President & CEO
Al Richards, Secretary-Treasurer
Michelle Saunders, Manager, Government Relations
Alice Tjan, Manager, Membership Services

Ontario's Wilderness Region
PO Box 920, 76 McIntyre Rd., Schumacher ON P0N 1G0
Tel: 705-360-1989; *Fax:* 705-268-5526
Toll-Free: 800-461-3766
info@ontarioswildernessregion.com
www.ontarioswildernessregion.com
To increase awareness in target markets of tourism possibilities in our geographic region.
Jennifer Rowe, Executive Director
Sean Mackey, President

Ottawa Tourism / Tourisme Ottawa
#1800, 130 Albert St., Ottawa ON K1P 5G4
Tel: 613-237-5150; *Fax:* 613-237-7339
Toll-Free: 800-363-4465
info@ottawatourism.ca
www.ottawatourism.ca
To maximize the number of visits to Ottawa & Canada's Capital Region through effective marketing & communication programs; to help develop & promote awareness of the contribution of tourism in the community; to facilitate the development & promotion of the products, services & needs of members
Noel Buckley, President & CEO

Ottawa Valley Tourist Association (OVTA)
9 International Dr., Pembroke ON K8A 6W5
Tel: 613-732-4364; *Fax:* 613-735-2492
Toll-Free: 800-757-6580
adventureplayground@ottawavalley.org
The Ottawa Valley Tourist Association (OVTA) is a non-profit organization designed to stimulate and promote tourism in Renfrew County. Our goal is to create a presence in the tourism marketplace. In order to position the Ottawa Valley as an

interesting and popular travel destination in the minds of travelers, a joint effort among tourism suppliers and OVTA's dedicated tourism staff is required.
Mitchell Wilkie, Manager
Charlotte Gebhart, President

Peterborough & the Kawarthas Tourism
1400 Crawford Dr., RR#5, Peterborough ON K9J 6X6
Tel: 705-742-2201; *Fax:* 705-742-2494
Toll-Free: 800-461-6424
info@thekawarthas.net
www.thekawarthas.net
Barbara van Vierzen, Manager, Customer Service

Pictou County Tourist Association
980 East River Rd., New Glasgow NS B2H 3S8
Tel: 902-752-6383; *Fax:* 902-752-6503
Toll-Free: 877-816-2326
admin@tourismpictoucounty.com
www.tourismpictoucounty.com
To promote the county to residents & visitors

Rainbow Country Travel Association (RCTA)
2726 Whippoorwill Ave., Sudbury ON P3G 1E9
Tel: 705-522-0104; *Fax:* 705-522-3132
Toll-Free: 800-465-6655
info@rainbowcountry.com
www.rainbowcountry.com
Social Media: www.facebook.com/group.php?gid=100931223286939; twitter.com/RainbowCountry
Donna MacLeod, Executive Director
Al Douglas, President
Kris Puhvel, Vice-President

Regina Regional Opportunities Commission (RROC)
1925 Rose St., Regina SK S4P 3P1
Tel: 306-789-5099; *Fax:* 306-352-1630
Toll-Free: 800-661-5099
www.reginaroc.com
Social Media: www.facebook.com/ReginaRoc; twitter.com/ReginaRoc; www.youtube.com/user/ReginaRoc; www.flickr.com/photos/54562633@N05
Providing information & services to visitors & meeting planners, the RROC is a non-profit organization dedicated to promoting tourism in Regina, & business opportunities for its members
Jennifer Nelson, Director, Communications
Andrea Soby, Office Manager

Resorts Ontario
29 Albert St. North, Orillia ON L3V 5J9
Tel: 705-325-9115; *Fax:* 705-325-7999
Toll-Free: 800-363-7227
escapes@resorts-ontario.com
www.resorts-ontario.com
To serve & promote the collective interests of resorts, lodges & inns of Ontario

Saskatchewan Hotel & Hospitality Association (SHHA)
#302, 2080 Broad St., Regina SK S4P 1Y3
Tel: 306-522-1664; *Fax:* 306-525-1944
Toll-Free: 800-667-1118
lorane.has@sasktel.net
www.hotelsofsask.com
Bill Nelson, Executive Director

Stratford Tourism Alliance (STA)
47 Downie St., Stratford ON N5A 1W7
Tel: 519-271-5140; *Fax:* 519-273-1818
Toll-Free: 800-561-7926
info@visitstratford.ca
www.welcometostratford.com
A marketing organization promoting Stratford as a destination for leisure travelers & others; provides services to members, assistance, information & guidance to visitors, convention planners, & media contacts about the advantages of Stratford & surrounding area as a destination
Eugene Zakreski, Executive Director
Christina Phillips, Coordinator, On-line & Membership Programme
Cathy Rehberg, Coordinator, Marketing

Sudbury Tourism
PO Box 5000, Stn. A, 200 Brady St., Sudbury ON P3A 5P3
Tel: 705-674-4455; *Fax:* 705-671-6767
Toll-Free: 877-304-8222
www.sudburytourism.ca
Social Media: www.facebook.com/sudburytourism; twitter.com/sudburytourism
Bruno Fabris, Contact

Thompson Okanagan Tourism Association (TOTA)
2280-D Leckie Rd., Kelowna BC V1X 6G6
Tel: 250-860-5999; *Fax:* 250-860-9993
Toll-Free: 800-567-2275
info@totabc.com
www.totabc.org/corporatesite
Social Media: www.facebook.com/totabc; twitter.com/totamedia; www.youtube.com/user/thompsonokanagan
To increase members' revenue & sustainability through cooperative marketing, ongoing education & government liaison
Glenn Mandziuk, CEO

Tourism Brantford
399 Wayne Gretzky Pkwy., Brantford ON N3R 8B4
Tel: 519-751-9900; *Fax:* 519-751-2617
Toll-Free: 800-265-6299
tourism@brantford.ca
www.visitbrantford.ca
To ensure quality visitor services through awareness, education, marketing & communications; to enhance the development of the tourism industry as an economic generator & to enhance the quality of life in our community
Susan Sager, Manager, Tourism & Marketing

Tourism Burlington
414 Locust St., Burlington ON L7S 1T7
Tel: 905-634-5594; *Fax:* 905-634-7220
Toll-Free: 877-499-9989
info@tourismburlington.com
www.tourismburlington.com
Social Media: www.facebook.com/TourismBurlington; twitter.com/burlingtontour
To increase tourism, resulting in economic benefits through utilization of recreational, cultural, commercial & personal resources
Pam Belgrade, Executive Director
Gord Langford, Chair

Tourism Calgary
#200, 238 - 11 Ave. SE, Calgary AB T2G 0X8
Tel: 403-263-8510; *Fax:* 403-262-3809
Toll-Free: 800-661-1678
www.visitcalgary.com
Social Media: www.facebook.com/visitcalgary; twitter.com/calgary
A non-profit destination marketing organization, providing services to members to promote Calgary as a destination for travel industry professionals, as well as leisure & business travelers
Randy Williams, President & CEO

Tourism Cape Breton
PO Box 1448, Sydney NS B1P 6R7
Tel: 902-563-4636; *Fax:* 902-564-5422
Toll-Free: 800-565-0000
info@cbisland.com
www.cbisland.com
Sandra MacDonald, General Manager

Tourism Hamilton
34 James St. South, Hamilton ON L8P 2X8
Tel: 905-546-2666; *Fax:* 905-546-2667
Toll-Free: 800-263-8590
tourism@hamilton.ca
www.tourismhamilton.com
To promote & increase the tourism & convention industries in Greater Hamilton
David Adames, Executive Director

Tourism Industry Association of Canada (TIAC) / Association de l'industrie touristique du Canada (AITC)
#600, 116 Lisgar St., Ottawa ON K2P 0C2
Tel: 613-238-3883; *Fax:* 613-238-3878
info@tiac.travel
www.tiac-aitc.ca
To enhance Canada's tourism industry by removing regulatory & legislative barriers to growth
David F. Goldstein, President/CEO
Kevin Desjardins, Vice President, Public Affairs

Tourism Industry Association of New Brunswick Inc. (TIANB) / Association de l'industrie touristique du Nouveau-Brunswick inc. (AITNB)
#440, 500 Beaverbrook Ct., Fredericton NB E3B 5X4
Tel: 506-458-5646; *Fax:* 506-459-3634
Toll-Free: 800-668-5313
info@tianb.com
www.tianb.com
Social Media: www.facebook.com/pages/TIANB-AITNB/127475440600650?sk=wall&filter=12; twitter.com/tianb_aitnb
To act as the provincial tourism & hospitality organization of New Brunswick, existing to fulfill the needs of its membership, in cooperation with both private & public sector partners; committed to be a representative, industry driven organization which provides leadership & direction, making tourism & hospitality the leading & most viably sustainable industry in New Brunswick
Réal Robichaud, Executive Director
Joanne Bérubé-Gagné, President

Tourism Industry Association of Nova Scotia (TIANS)
2089 Maitland St., Halifax NS B3K 2Z8
Tel: 902-423-4480; *Fax:* 902-422-0184
Toll-Free: 800-948-4267
information_central@tians.org
www.tians.org
To lead, support, represent & enhance the Nova Scotia tourism industry
Darlene Grant Fiander, President
Danny Morton, Chair
Bill Walsh, Sec.-Treas.

Tourism Industry Association of PEI (TIAPEI)
PO Box 2050, 25 Queen St., 3rd Fl., Charlottetown PE C1A 7N7
Tel: 902-566-5008; *Fax:* 902-368-3605
Toll-Free: 866-566-5008
tiapei@tiapei.pe.ca
www.tiapei.pe.ca
To represent tourism related businesses, associations, institutions, & individuals; to encourage tourism to & within PEI
Thom MacMillan, President

Tourism Industry Association of the Yukon
#3, 1109 - 1st Ave., Whitehorse YT Y1A 5G4
Tel: 867-668-3331; *Fax:* 867-667-7379
info@tiayukon.com
www.tiayukon.com
Social Media: www.facebook.com/232432356772503
To represent all sectors & businesses of the tourism industry; to foster & promote travel in Yukon; to encourage increase & improvement of visitor facilities, services & attractions; to enhance & stimulate business climate in industry; to enhance awareness of importance of tourism; to design & deliver marketing programs
Krista Prochazka, Executive Director

Tourism London
696 Wellington Rd. South, London ON N6C 4R2
Tel: 519-661-5000; *Fax:* 519-661-6160
Toll-Free: 800-265-2602
tourism@londontourism.ca
www.londontourism.ca
To promote London through co-operative partnerships as the tourism, sports tourism & meeting destination of choice resulting in positive economic impact on the city of London
John Winston, General Manager

Tourism Saint John / Bureau de tourisme et de congrés de Saint John
PO Box 1971, 15 Market Sq., 11th Fl., Saint John NB E2L 4L1
Tel: 506-658-2990; *Fax:* 506-632-6118
Toll-Free: 866-463-8639
visitsj@saintjohn.ca
www.tourismsaintjohn.com; www.venuesaintjohn.com
To position Saint John as the premier all-season, visitor, meeting & event destination on New Brunswick's Bay of Fundy; to generate revenues & publicity for the city of Saint John & its tourism operators & businesses through increased visitation, service excellence & the provision of advice & partnering opportunities
Margaret Totten, Manager

Tourism Sarnia Lambton (TSL)
556 North Christina St., Sarnia ON N7T 5W6
Tel: 519-336-3232; *Fax:* 519-336-3278
Toll-Free: 800-265-0316
info@tourismsarnialambton.com
www.tourismsarnialambton.com
To promote tourism to Lambton County, creating economic value for the entire community
Leona Allen, Office Administrator
John Dickson, General Manager/Executive Director

Tourism Saskatoon
#101, 202 Fourth Ave. North, Saskatoon SK S7K 0K1
Tel: 306-242-1206; *Fax:* 306-242-1955
Toll-Free: 800-567-2444
info@tourismsaskatoon.com
www.tourismsaskatoon.com

To operate as Saskatoon's destination management organization, maximizing the economic benefit for Saskatoon through tourism
Todd Brandt, CEO

Tourism Simcoe County
Simcoe County Museum, 1151 Hwy. 26 West, Minesing ON L0L 1Y2
Tel: 705-726-8502; *Fax:* 705-728-9130
Toll-Free: 800-487-6642
tourism@simcoe.ca
discover.simcoe.ca
The association promotes & develops the tourism industry of Simcoe County & area.
Bryan MacKell, Director, Planning, Development & Tourism, Simcoe County
Tori Martin, Administrator

Tourism Thunder Bay
500 Donald St. East, Thunder Bay ON P7E 5V3
Tel: 807-625-2149; *Toll-Free:* 800-667-8386
TTY: 807-622-2225
visit@thunderbay.com
www.visitthunderbay.com
Social Media: twitter.com/visitthunderbay
To market Thunder Bay as a destination for individuals & groups
Paul Pepe, Tourism Manager
Rose Marie Mancusa, Partnership Marketing Officer

Tourism Toronto (TCVA)
Queen's Quay Terminal at Harbourfront, PO Box 126, 207 Queen's Quay West, Toronto ON M5J 1A7
Tel: 416-203-2600; *Fax:* 416-203-6753
Toll-Free: 800-499-2514
toronto@torcvb.com
www.torontotourism.com
Social Media: www.facebook.com/visittoronto
To promote Toronto as a convention & visitor destination; To position Toronto as one of the world's great cities & a year-round destination for leisure & business
David Whitaker, President/CEO
Andrew Weir, Vice-President, Communications

Tourism Vancouver/Greater Vancouver Convention & Visitors Bureau
#210, 200 Burrard St., Vancouver BC V6C 3L6
Tel: 604-682-2222; *Fax:* 604-682-1717
www.tourismvancouver.com
Social Media: www.facebook.com/insidevancouver
To lead the cooperative effort of positioning Greater Vancouver as a preferred travel destination in all targeted markets worldwide, thereby creating opportunities for member & community sharing of the resulting economic, environmental, social & cultural benefits
Rick Antonson, President/CEO
Paul Vallee, Exec. Vice-President
Ted Lee, CFO

Tourism Victoria/Greater Victoria Visitors & Convention Bureau
Administration Office, 31 Bastion Sq., 4th Fl., Victoria BC V8W 1J1
Tel: 250-414-6999; *Fax:* 250-361-9733
Toll-Free: 800-663-3883
info@tourismvictoria.com
www.tourismvictoria.com
To oversee the development & promotion of the tourism industry in Greater Victoria
Robert Gialloreto, CEO
Helen Welch, Vice-President, Marketing

Tourism Windsor Essex Pelee Island
City Centre, #103, 333 Riverside Dr. West, Windsor ON N9A 5K4
Tel: 519-255-6530; *Fax:* 519-255-6192
Toll-Free: 800-265-3633
info@tourismwindsoressex.com
www.visitwindsoressex.com
Helps make the most of your visit to Windsor, Essex County & Pelee Island.
Gordon Orr, Managing Director

Tourisme Abitibi-Témiscamingue
#100, 155 av Dallaire, Rouyn-Noranda QC J9X 4T3
Tél: 819-762-8181; *Téléc:* 819-762-5212
Ligne sans frais: 800-808-0706
info@tourisme-abitibi-temiscamingue.org
www.abitibi-temiscamingue-tourism.org
Promotion du tourisme en Abitibi-Témiscamingue
Randa Napky, Directeur général
Jocelyn Carrier, Présidente

Tourisme Baie-James (TBJ) / James Bay Tourism
CP 134, 1252, rte 167 sud, Chibougamau QC G8P 2K6
Tél: 418-748-8140; *Téléc:* 418-748-8150
Ligne sans frais: 888-748-8140
info@tourismebaiejames.com
www.tourismebaiejames.com
Assure dans le cadre de ses responsabilités corporatives, des mandats en matière de concertation régionale, d'accueil, d'information, de signalisation, de promotion et de développement touristique
Christian Claveau, Président

Tourisme Bas-Saint-Laurent
148, rue Fraser, 2e étage, Rivière-du-Loup QC G5R 1C8
Tél: 418-867-1272; *Téléc:* 418-867-3245
Ligne sans frais: 800-563-5268
info@bassaintlaurent.ca
www.tourismebas-st-laurent.com
Accueil, développement et promotion touristique
Pierre Laplante, Directeur général
Gaston Gendreau, Président

Tourisme Cantons-de-l'Est
20, rue Don-Bosco sud, Sherbrooke QC J1L 1W4
Tél: 819-820-2020; *Téléc:* 819-566-4445
Ligne sans frais: 800-355-5755
info@atrce.com
www.cantonsdelest.com
Média social: www.facebook.com/cantonsdelest; twitter.com/cantonsdelest
A pour mission de faire de la région des Cantons-de-l'Est une des meilleures destinations touristique du Québec en toutes saisons
Alain Larouche, Directeur général
Francine Patenaude, Directrice, Marketing & développement

Tourisme Centre-du-Québec
20, boul Carignan ouest, Princeville QC G6L 4M4
Tél: 819-364-7177; *Téléc:* 819-364-2120
Ligne sans frais: 888-816-4007
info@tourismecentredoquebec.com
www.tourismecentreduquebec.com
Guylaine Turcotte, Adjointe administrative

Tourisme Chaudière-Appalaches (ATCA)
800, autoroute Jean-Lesage, Saint-Nicolas QC G7A 1E3
Tél: 418-831-4411; *Téléc:* 418-831-8442
Ligne sans frais: 888-831-4411
info@chaudiereappalaches.com
www.chaudiereappalaches.com
Média social: www.facebook.com/ChaudiereAppalaches; twitter.com/ChaudApp
Favoriser le développement et la promotion de l'industrie touristique de son territoire tout en contribuant à la réussite des entreprises qui en sont members
Richard Moreau, Director général

Tourisme Gaspésie
1575, boul. de l'Avenir, bureau 330, Laval QC H7S 2N5
Tél: 450-686-8358; *Téléc:* 450-686-9630
Ligne sans frais: 877-686-8358
information@atrassociees.com
www.atrassociees.com
Orienter et favoriser la promotion, le développement et l'activité touristique dans le meilleur intérêt de la Gaspésie; promouvoir, organiser et coordonner divers programmes de promotion et de développement touristique ayant comme conséquence d'accroître la clientèle touristique et prolongation des séjours dans la Gaspésie
Louis Rome, Directeur général
Joëlle Ross, Directrice adjointe

Tourisme Iles de la Madeleine
128, ch Principal, Cap-aux-Meules QC G4T 1C5
Tél: 418-986-2245; *Téléc:* 418-986-2327
Ligne sans frais: 877-624-4437
info@tourismeilesdelamadeleine.com
www.tourismeilesdelamadeleine.com/magdalen-islands/index.cfm
Média social: www.facebook.com/tourismeilesdelamadeleine; www.youtube.com/TourismeIDM
Regrouper les entreprises de l'industrie touristique de l'archipel afin d'accroître les efforts de développement et de promotion
Michel Bonato, Directrice générale

Tourisme Lanaudière
3568, rue Church, Rawdon QC J0K 1S0
Tél: 450-834-2535; *Téléc:* 450-834-8100
Ligne sans frais: 800-363-2788
info@lanaudiere.ca
www.lanaudiere.ca/fr/
Média social: www.facebook.com/tourismelanaudiere; twitter.com/tourlanaud
Faire la promotion, développement, commercialisation de l'offre touristiques de la région auprès des clienteles des différents marchés; améliorer l'accueil & l'information touristique
Évangéline Richard, Présidente

Tourisme Laval
2900, boul Saint-Martin ouest, Laval QC H7T 2J2
Tél: 450-682-5522; *Téléc:* 450-682-7304
Ligne sans frais: 877-465-2825
info@tourismelaval.com
www.tourismelaval.com
Andrée Courteau, Directeur général
Jean-Louis Bédard, Président

Tourisme Mauricie
1882, rue Cascade, Shawinigan QC G9N 8S1
Tél: 819-536-3334; *Téléc:* 819-536-3373
Ligne sans frais: 800-567-7603
info@tourismemauricie.com
www.tourismemauricie.com
M. André Nollet, Directeur général

Tourisme Montérégie
2001, Boul. De Rome, 3e étage, Brossard QC J4W 3K5
Tél: 450-466-4666; *Téléc:* 450-466-7999
Ligne sans frais: 866-469-0069
info@tourisme-monteregie.qc.ca
www.tourisme-monteregie.qc.ca
Éric Fournier, Directeur général
Brigitte Marcotte, Coordonnatrice, Communications

Tourisme Montréal/Office des congrès et du tourisme du Grand Montréal / Greater Montréal Convention & Tourism Bureau
CP 979, #100, 1255 Peel St., Montréal QC H3C 2W3
Tél: 514-873-2015; *Téléc:* 514-864-3838
Ligne sans frais: 877-266-5687
info@tourisme-montreal.org
www.tourism-montreal.org; www.tourisme-montreal.org
François Goulet, Vice-président exécutif

Tourisme Outaouais
103, rue Laurier, Gatineau QC J8X 3V8
Tél: 819-778-2222; *Téléc:* 819-778-7758
Ligne sans frais: 800-265-7822
info@tourisme-outaouais.ca
www.tourisme-outaouais.ca
Prospérité économique de la région par le développement et la promotion du produit touristique; structurer, organiser, orchestrer tout projet susceptible de générer des activités touristiques à retombées économiques importantes; assumer un accueil de qualité et une diffusion de l'information
Louise Boudrias, Présidente
Gilles Picard, Directeur général

Travellers' Aid Society of Toronto (TAS)
#B19-23, Union Station, 65 Front St. West, Toronto ON M5J 1E6
Tel: 416-366-7788; *Fax:* 416-366-0829
exec.director@travellersaid.ca
www.travellersaid.ca
To provide a base of needed information for travellers as well as shelter & other help in crisis situations
I.A.J. Sloan, President

Vancouver Coast & Mountains Tourism Region
#600, 210 West Broadway St., Vancouver BC V5Y 3W2
Tel: 604-638-6927; *Fax:* 604-739-0153
Toll-Free: 800-667-3306
info@vcmbc.com
www.vcmbc.com
Social Media: twitter.com/vcmbc
Kevan Ridgway, Executive Director
Doleen Dean, Coordinator

Wilderness Tourism Association of the Yukon (WTAY)
#4, 1114 First Ave., Whitehorse YT Y1A 1A3
Tel: 867-668-3369; *Fax:* 867-668-3370
www.wtay.com
The Wilderness Tourism Association of the Yukon represents the wilderness and adventure tourism industry in the Yukon Territory, Canada. The organization provides marketing, advocacy, research, consultation, referral and education resources.
Neil Hartling, President

Trade

Asia Pacific Foundation of Canada (APFC) / Fondation Asie Pacifique du Canada
#220, 890 West Pender St., Vancouver BC V6C 1J9
Tel: 604-684-5986; *Fax:* 604-681-1370
info@asiapacific.ca
www.asiapacific.ca
Social Media: www.facebook.com/asiapacificfoundationofcanada; twitter.com/AsiaPacificFdn
Independent think tank on Canada's relations with Asia; to bring together people & knowledge to provide the most current & comprehensive research, analysis & information on Canada's transpacific relations; to promote dialogue on economic, security, political & social issues, helping to influence public policy & foster informed decision-making in the Canadian public, private & non-governmental sectors
Yuen Pau Woo, President & CEO
Jill Price, Executive Director

Association of International Automobile Manufacturers of Canada (AIAMC) / Association des fabricants internationaux d'automobiles du Canada
PO Box 5, #1804, 2 Bloor St. West, Toronto ON M4W 3E2
Tel: 416-595-8251; *Fax:* 416-595-2864
auto@aiamc.com
www.aiamc.com
To represent before federal, provincial, & territorial governments the interests of members engaged in the manufacturing, importation, distribution, & servicing of light-duty vehicles
David C. Adams, President
Mary Hogarth, Director, Policy Development & Corporate Affairs
Andrew Morin, Director, Technical & Regulatory Affairs

British Canadian Chamber of Trade & Commerce
Dominion Centre, Royal Trust Tower, #2401, 77 King Street, Toronto ON M5K 1G8
Tel: 416-816-9154; *Fax:* 647-435-3436
central@bcctc.ca
www.bcctc.ca
Social Media: twitter.com/bcctc
To foster reciprocal trading between Canada & the U.K.
Thomas O'Carroll, Vice-President, Central
Liam J. Hopkins, Vice President, Western
John Hoblyn, Contact, Eastern

Canada Beef Export Federation
#235, 6715 - 8th St. NE, Calgary AB T2E 7H7
Tel: 403-274-0005; *Fax:* 403-274-7275
canada@cbef.com
www.cbef.com
The Canada Beef Export Federation facilitates the expansion of strategic global markets for Canadian beef products and identifies and develops key export markets to increase the sale of Canadian beef products. Their objective revolves around securing and increasing markets outside the USA for Canadian beef products in order to decrease export dependence on the United States.
Ted Haney, President
Gib Drury, Chairman

Canada China Business Council (CCBC) / Conseil commercial Canada Chine
#1501, 330 Bay St., Toronto ON M5H 2S8
Tel: 416-954-3800; *Fax:* 416-954-3806
ccbc@ccbc.com
www.ccbc.com
CCBC is a private, not-for-profit business association dedicated to building business success in China & Canada by offering service & support, from direct operational support in China, to trade & investment advocacy on its members' behalf. Specifically, it aims to stimulate investment, trade in goods & services, & technology transfer.
Peter Kruyt, Chair
Sarah Kutulakos, Executive Director
Eumie Leung, Director, Operations

Canadian Association of Footwear Importers (CAFI)
c/o Canadian Association of Importers & Exporters, #300, 160 Eglinton Ave. East, Toronto ON M4P 3B5
Tel: 416-595-5333; *Fax:* 416-595-8226
info@iecanada.com
www.importers.ca/about_us/cafi.html
To represent the interests of the footwear importing community across Canada
Amesika Baeta, Director, Committee

Canadian Association of Importers & Exporters / Association canadienne des importateurs & exportateurs
#200, 10 St. Mary St., Toronto ON M4Y 1P9
Tel: 416-595-5333
info@iecanada.com
www.importers.ca
To act as the voice of Canadian importers & exporters; To support Canadian importers & exporters so that they remain profitable & competitive in a global market
Joy Nott, CCS, P.Log, President
Keith Mussar, VP, Regulatory Affairs & Co-Chair, Food Committee
Carol Osmond, Vice-President, Policy
Amesika Baeta, Director, Member Relations & Development
Andrea MacDonald, Contact, Media Inquiries, I.E. Now, & Special Publications

Canadian Association of Regulated Importers (CARI) / Association canadienne des importateurs règlementés
#203, 2525 St. Laurent Blvd., Ottawa ON K1H 8P5
Tel: 613-738-1729; *Fax:* 613-733-9501
devalk@magma.ca
www.cariimport.org
The CARI ensures the right and ability for importers to do business like other businesses, and to create one voice for commodities on the import control list or otherwise controlled by regulations.
Robert De Valk, Executive Secretary

Canadian Council for the Americas (CCA) / Conseil Canadien pour les Amériques
#2300, 1066 West Hastings St., Vancouver BC V6E 3X2
Tel: 778-388-5206; *Fax:* 604-806-6112
info@cca-bc.com
www.cca-bc.com
Principal private sector link between Canada & the countries of Latin America & the Caribbean.
André Nudelman, Chair
Leon Teicher, Secretary

Canadian Courier & Logistics Association (CCLA)
#119-660 Eglinton Ave. East, Box 333, Toronto ON M4G 2K2
Tel: 416-696-9995; *Fax:* 416-696-9993
Toll-Free: 877-766-6604
info@canadiancourier.org
www.canadiancourier.org
To serve the needs, promote the interests & concerns, & enhance the reputation of the courier industry in Canada regardless of size or type of operation
David Turnbull, President & CEO

Canadian Meat Importers & Exporters Committee (CMIC) / Comité canadien des importeurs de viande
#300, 160 Eglinton Ave. East, Toronto ON M4P 3B5
Tel: 416-595-5333; *Fax:* 416-595-8226
info@iecanada.com
www.caie.ca/about_us/cmiec.html
To act as the representative voice of Canadian meat importers with respect to the activities of the federal & provincial governments & agencies & other bodies affecting the commercial interests of meat importers in Canada.
Amesika Baeta, Contact

Citizens Concerned About Free Trade (CCAFT)
PO Box 1983, Saskatoon SK S7K 3S5
Tel: 306-664-8443; *Fax:* 306-244-3790
Toll-Free: 877-937-8263
davidorchard@sasktel.net
www.davidorchard.com
To provide information & mobilize those opposed to the Free Trade Agreements & the loss of Canadian sovereignty; to have Canada exercise the termination clauses of both the FTA & NAFTA so that we can protect our resources & play an independent role in world affairs.

Electronics Import Committee (EIC)
#300, 160 Eglinton Ave. East, Toronto ON M4P 3B5
Tel: 416-595-5333; *Fax:* 416-595-8226
info@iecanada.com
www.iecanada.com
The Electronic Import Committee (EIC) focuses on the needs of members who import electronic goods. The EIC represents members' interests before government and regulatory bodies.
Joy Nott, President
Amesika Baeta, Director

Groupe export agroalimentaire Québec - Canada (GEAQC) / Agri-Food Export Group Québec - Canada
668, montée Montarville, Saint-Bruno QC J3V 6B1
Tél: 450-461-6266; *Téléc:* 450-461-6255
Ligne sans frais: 800-563-9767
info@groupexport.ca
www.clubexport.ca
Développer des services adaptés aux besoins réels de nos membres afin d'augmenter leurs ventes sur les marchés internationaux; faciliter l'accès aux programmes gouvernementaux dont nous avons la gestion.
André A. Coutu, Président-directeur général

Hong Kong Trade Development Council
Office Tower, Convention Plaza, 1 Harbour Rd., 38th Fl., Wanchai Hong Kong
hktdc@tdc.org.hk
www.tdctrade.com
to promote external trade in goods & services; to create & facilitate opportunities in international trade for Hong Kong companies; to strengthen Hong Kong as the global trade platform of Asia; to assist manufacturers, traders & service providers through marketing opportunities, trade contacts, market knowledge & competitive skills; network of over 40 offices worldwide

International Cheese Council of Canada (ICCC)
c/o Canadian Association of Importers & Exporters, PO Box 189, Toronto ON M3C 2S2
To act as the representative voice of Canadian importers of cheese, with respect to the activities of the federal & provincial governments & agencies & all other bodies affecting the commercial interests of cheese importers in Canada; To monitor & analyze all developments relating to the importation of cheese into Canada; To contribute to the formulation, revision & amendment of government policy relating to the commercial regulatory framework within which Canadian cheese importers operate their businesses; To promote the commercial interests of members in a public relations capacity; To liaise with other industry & trade associations working in cheese-related sectors
Amesika Baëta, Director, Member Relations & Development

Ontario Association of Trading Houses (OATH)
PO Box 43086, 4841 Yonge St., Toronto ON M2N 6N1
Tel: 416-223-2028; *Fax:* 416-223-5707
info@oath.on.ca
www.oath.on.ca
To develop & expand international trade; To help Canadian companies to increase their international trade & investment
Karel Urban, President
David Archer, Vice-President
Saeed Omar, Vice-President
Louis Papp, Vice-President

The Parliamentary Centre / Le Centre parlementaire
#802, 255 Albert St., Ottawa ON K1P 6A9
Tel: 613-237-0143; *Fax:* 613-235-8237
parlcent@parl.gc.ca
www.parlcent.ca
To strengthen legislatures through continuous learning & innovation in parliamentary development, mutual sharing & practical parliamentary experience, & the provision of advisory services
Amelita Armit, President/CEO

Trade Facilitation Office Canada (TFOC) / Bureau de promotion du commerce Canada
#300, 56 Sparks St., Ottawa ON K1P 5A9
Tel: 613-233-3925; *Fax:* 613-233-7860
Toll-Free: 800-267-9674
info@tfocanada.ca
www.tfocanada.ca
To help improve the economic well-being of developing countries through increased integration into the global economy
Dwayne Wright, Executive Director

World Trade Centre Montréal (WTCM)
#6000, 380, rue St-Antoine ouest, Montréal QC H2Y 3X7
Tél: 514-871-4002; *Téléc:* 514-849-3813
Ligne sans frais: 877-590-4040
wtcmontreal@ccmm.qc.ca
www.ccmm.qc.ca/fr/lachambre-World_Trade_Centre_Montreal
Appuyer, former et conseiller les entreprises, associations, institutions et organismes de développement économiques dans leurs démarches sur les marchés internationaux
Michel Leblanc, Président et chef de la direction
Lise Aubin, Vice-présidente, Exploitation & Administration

Translation

Wycliffe Bible Translators of Canada, Inc. (WBTC)
4316 - 10th St. NE, Calgary AB T2E 6K3
Tel: 403-250-5411; *Fax:* 403-250-2623
Toll-Free: 800-463-1143
info@wycliffe.ca
www.wycliffe.ca
Social Media: www.facebook.com/WycliffeCanada; twitter.com/wycliffe_canada; www.linkedin.com/WycliffeBibleTranslatorsCanada; www.youtube.com/wycliffecanada; www.godtube.com/wycliffecanada
To serve minority language groups worldwide by fostering an understanding of God's Word through Bible translation, while encouraging literacy, education & stronger communities
David Ohlson, Executive Director

Transportation & Shipping

Alberta Construction Trucking Association (ACTA)
#400, 1040 - 7 Ave. SW, Calgary AB T2P 3G9
Tel: 403-244-4487; *Fax:* 403-244-2340
info@myacta.ca
www.myacta.ca
To develop & promote the business of transporting construction & construction-related material
Jennifer Singer, President

Alberta Motor Transport Association (AMTA)
#1, 285005 Wrangler Way, Rocky View AB T1X 0K3
Fax: 403-243-4610
Toll-Free: 800-267-1003
amtamsc@amta.ca
www.amta.ca
To take a leadership role in fostering a healthy, vibrant industry
Don Wilson, Executive Director
Lorri Christensen, Director, Partners in Compliance
Peter Vaudry, Director, Corporate Services
Kathleen Brown, Administrator, Registration & Certificates
William Raccah, Administrator, Program Development

Association du camionnage du Québec inc. (ACQ) / Québec Trucking Association Inc.
#200, 6450, rue Notre Dame ouest, Montréal QC H4C 1C4
Tél: 514-932-0377; *Téléc:* 514-932-1358
Ligne sans frais: 800-361-5813
info@carrefour-acq.org
www.carrefour-acq.org
Favoriser l'amélioration des normes de sécurité, d'efficacité et d'éthique dans l'industrie du camionnage; maintenir un contact avec l'autorité gouvernementale, les usagers des services de camionnage et le public en général; soutenir le perfectionnement professionnel; soutenir les entreprises dans la défense de leurs intérêts.
Éric Gignac, Président du conseil
Michel Robert, 1er vice-président du conseil
René Rouillard, Secrétaire du conseil
Bernard Boutin, Trésorier du conseil
Jean-Claude Fortin, Vice-President
Yves Marchand, Vice-President

Association du transport écolier du Québec (ATEQ)
#300, 5300, boul des Galeries, Québec QC G2K 2A2
Tél: 418-622-6544; *Téléc:* 418-622-6595
Ligne sans frais: 877-622-6544
courrier@ateq.qc.ca
www.ateq.qc.ca
Gaston Lemay, Président

Association du transport urbain du Québec (ATUQ)
#8090, 800, rue de la Gauchetière, Montréal QC H5A 1J6
Tél: 514-280-4640; *Téléc:* 514-280-7053
info@atuq.com
www.atuq.com
Organisme de concertation et de représentation politique qui a pour mandat d'assurer la promotion du transport en commun et la défense des intérêts de ses membres auprès des partenaires de l'industrie et des différentes instances gouvernementales
Jean-Jacques Beldié, Président
France Vézina, Directrice générale

Association nationale des camionneurs artisans inc. (ANCAI)
#235, 670, rue Bouvier, Québec QC G2J 1A7
Tél: 418-623-7923; *Téléc:* 418-623-0448
infos@ancai.com
www.ancai.com
Défendre les intérêts des transporteurs en vrac (gravier et forêts) auprès des gouvernements, organismes patronaux et entreprises privées
Guy Laplante, Président
Gaétan Légaré, Directeur général
Ghislain Bernier, Directeur du bureau juridique
Sylvain Lacombe, Conseiller juridique

Association québécoise du transport et des routes inc. (AQTR)
Bureau de Montréal, #200, 1255, rue University, Montréal QC H3B 3B2
Tél: 514-523-6444; *Téléc:* 514-523-2666
info@aqtr.qc.ca
www.aqtr.qc.ca
Assumer un leadership technique; définir des règles en matière de sécurité et d'environnement; Favoriser l'échange international des expertises; promouvoir la recherche et le développement des expertises et des produits en transport; promouvoir la formation dans le domaine des transports; Assumer la représentativité de l'AQTR par la participation aux principaux forums sur les transports; Contribuer à servir la société par l'éducation et l'information du grand public
Dominique Lacoste, Présidente-directrice générale
Mathieu Charbonneau, Directeur général adjoint

Atlantic Provinces Trucking Association (APTA)
#400, 725 Champlain St., Dieppe NB E1A 1P6
Tel: 506-855-2782; *Fax:* 506-853-7424
Toll-Free: 866-866-1679
apta@apta.ca
www.apta.ca
To promote an efficient, safe & environmentally sound trucking industry in Atlantic Canada. PUBLICATIONS: Atlantic Trucking Magazine (quaterly); Atlantic Report Newsletter (monthly) (only to members).
Ralph Boyd, President
Peter Nelson, Executive Director
Georgia Smallwood, Marketing/Membership Services
Chris McKee, Managing Editor- Atlantic Trucking
Shane Esson, Chairperson

British Columbia Supercargoes' Association
#206, 3711 Delbrook Ave., North Vancouver BC V7N 3Z4
Tel: 604-878-1258; *Fax:* 604-904-6545
admin@supercargoes.bc.ca; president@supercargoes.bc.ca
www.supercargoes.bc.ca
To provide expert marine cargo planning & onsite management & supervision of shiploading & discharge of all types of cargoes & vessels on the west coast of North America
Terry Stuart, President
David Hood, Director
Magnus Fjortoft, Director

British Columbia Trucking Association (BCTA)
#100, 20111 - 93A Ave., Langley BC V1M 4A9
Tel: 604-888-5319
bcta@bctrucking.com
www.bctrucking.com
To act as the recognised voice of the commercial road transportation industry in British Columbia, by consulting & communicating with the industry, government, & the public; To promote a prosperous, safe, efficient & responsible road transportation industry; To provide programs & services to members
Louise Yako, President & Chief Executive Officer
Trace Acres, Vice-President
Greg Kolesniak, Director, Policy
Michele Nicol, Director, Business Operations
Veena Nanubhai, Coordinator, Accounting
Sandra Stashuk, Coordinator, Member Services
Shelley McGuinness, Specialist, Communications

Bytown Railway Society (BRS)
PO Box 47076, Ottawa ON K1B 5P9
Tel: 613-745-1201; *Fax:* 613-745-1201
info@bytownrailwaysociety.ca
www.bytownrailwaysociety.ca
To promote an interest in railways & railway history, with particular emphasis on Canadian railways. PUBLICATIONS: Canadian Trackside Guide, The Quebec Railway Light and Power Company, Montreal Streetcars- Vol.2. People and Places, Montreal and Southern Counties Railway Co., The Ottawa Streetcar Company, Hamilton's Other Railway.
David Stremes, President
Leslie Goodwin, Treasurer
Paul Bown, Vice-President

Canadian Association of Movers (CAM) / Association canadienne des déménageurs (ACD)
PO Box 30039, Stn. New Westminster, Thornhill ON L4J 0C6
Tel: 905-848-6579; *Fax:* 905-848-8499
Toll-Free: 866-860-0065
admin@mover.net
www.mover.net
To further the interests of the owner-managed moving & storage companies by providing for its members leadership, motivation, research, education, programs of mutual benefit, consultation & technical advice
Levi John, President

Canadian Association of Railway Suppliers / Association canadienne des fournisseurs de chemins de fer
#901, 99 Bank St., Ottawa ON K1P 6B9
Tel: 613-237-3888; *Fax:* 613-237-4888
info@railwaysuppliers.ca
www.railwaysuppliers.ca
Jay Nordenstrom, Executive Director

Canadian Bus Association (CBA) / Association canadienne de l'autobus
c/o #2001, 45 O'Connor St., Ottawa ON K1P 1A4
Tel: 613-238-1800; *Fax:* 613-241-4936
mresnick@rothwellgroup.ca
To act as the national voice of the Canadian bus industry; to act as a national forum for the discussion of bus-related issues & the establishment of positions in relation to industry-wide areas of concern; to function as a technical & operational information gathering & exchange mechanism; to further the objectives of safety, convenience & quality of the motor coach industry.

Canadian Business Aviation Association (CBAA) / Association canadienne de l'aviation d'affaires (ACAA)
#430, 55 Metcalfe St., Ottawa ON K1P 6L5
Tel: 613-236-5611; *Fax:* 613-236-2361
info@cbaa.ca
www.cbaa.ca
CBAA acts as a collective voice for the business aviation community in Canada, assisting its members in all aviation related matters, & promoting the Canadian business community globally.
Rob Madden, Chair
Sam Barone, President & CEO

Canadian Council of Motor Transport Administrators (CCMTA) / Conseil canadien des administrateurs en transport motorisé (CCATM)
2323 St. Laurent Blvd., Ottawa ON K1G 4J8
Tel: 613-736-1003; *Fax:* 613-736-1395
ccmta-secretariat@ccmta.ca (general information & membership)
www.ccmta.ca
To coordinate operational matters dealing with the administration, regulation, & control of motor vehicle transportation & highway safety
Ward Keith, President
Methusalah Kunuk, Vice-President

Canadian Ferry Operators Association (CFOA) / Association canadienne des opérateurs de traversiers
c/o Anthonie A. de Hoog, CFOA Executive Director, 21 Meredith Dr., Sussex Corner NB E4E 2T8
Tel: 506-433-4810; *Fax:* 506-432-9505
adehoog@cfoa.ca
www.cfoa.ca
To establish & maintain a standard of professional & technical excellence in the operation of Canadian ferries; To promote & protect the interests of members of the association
Anthonie A. de Hoog, Executive Director
David Miller, President

Canadian Heartland Training Railway
PO Box 1174, Camrose AB T4V 1X2
Tel: 780-679-4008; *Fax:* 780-672-4032
www.chtr.ca
To support the practical training needs of the railway industry in Canada & around the world
Joe Bracken, President

Canadian Industrial Transportation Association (CITA) / Association canadienne de transport industriel (ACTI)
#405, 580 Terry Fox Dr., Ottawa ON K2L 4C2
Tel: 613-599-3283; *Fax:* 613-599-1295
info@cita-acti.ca
www.cita-acti.ca
CITA-ACTI actively promotes a competitive and cost effective North American transportation system serving Canada and its NAFTA allies. Their vision is to be recognized as the "National Voice" of industrial transportation in Canada through increased membership and member representation in all regions of the county.
Bob Ballantyne, President
Denise Fata, Manager, Marketing and Events
Cindy Hick, Vice-President

Canadian Institute of Traffic & Transportation (CITT) / Institut canadien du trafic et du transport
#400, 10 King St. East, Toronto ON M5C 1C3
Tel: 416-363-5696; *Fax:* 416-363-5698
info@citt.ca
www.citt.ca
Social Media:
www.facebook.com/group.php?gid=148552441716
Designation granting body in logistics management.
Patrick K. Bohan, Chair
Catherine Viglas, President
Chrissy Aitchison, Marketing Manager
Jennifer Barry, Membership/Events Coordinator
Maria Murjani, Customer Service Representative
Sue MacMillan, Program Manager

Canadian International Freight Forwarders Association, Inc. (CIFFA) / Association des transitaires internationaux canadiens, inc. (ATIC)
#480, 170 Attwell Dr., Toronto ON M9W 5Z5
Tel: 416-234-5100; *Fax:* 416-234-5152
Toll-Free: 866-282-4332
ciffa@ciffa.com; membership@ciffa.com
www.ciffa.com
To represent & support members of the Canadian international freight forwarding industry in providing the highest level of quality & professional services to their clients
Marc D. Bibeau, President
Donna Letterio, First Vice-President
Mark Soubry, Second Vice-President
Paul Glionna, Third Vice-President
H. Ruth Snowden, Executive Director
Gary Vince, Treasurer
Paul Lobas, Secretary

Canadian National Railways Police Association (Ind.) (CNRPA) / Association des policiers des chemins de fer nationaux du Canada (ind.)
6479 Miller's Grove, Mississauga ON L5N 3E5
Tel: 905-824-0856; *Fax:* 905-824-4584
fjmorgan@ica.net
www.cnrpa.ca
Frank Morgan, National President

Canadian Northern Society (CNoS)
PO Box 1174, Camrose AB T4V 1X2
Tel: 780-672-3099
canadiannorthern@telus.net
www.canadiannorthern.ca
To preserve prairie heritage
Leslie S. Kozma, President
Lorrie R. Tiegs, Vice-President
Shawn I. Smith, Treasurer

Canadian Parking Association (CPA)
#350, 2255 St. Laurent Blvd., Ottawa ON K1G 4K3
Tel: 613-727-0700; *Fax:* 613-727-3183
info@canadianparking.ca
www.canadianparking.ca
The Association is the national organization that represents the parking industry & provides a dynamic forum for learning & sharing to enhance member's ability to serve the public & improve the economic vitality of communities.
Carole Whitehorne, Executive Director

Canadian Ports Clearance Association
#500, 101 Syndicate Ave. North, Thunder Bay ON P7C 3V4
Tel: 807-623-8491; *Fax:* 807-623-2676
Shipping agent

Canadian Professional Logistics Institute / Institut canadien des professionnels de la logistique
#200, 160 John St., Toronto ON M5V 2E5
Tel: 416-363-3005; *Fax:* 416-363-5598
Toll-Free: 877-363-3005
loginfo@loginstitute.ca
www.loginstitute.ca
To establish professional standards, certification & a program of professional development for the Logistics community.
Victor S. Deyglio, President
Jim Davidson, P.Log Chair
Ruth Snowden, Managing Director
Karyn Ferguson, P.Log., Program Director
Jackie Denholm, Finance/Administrator
Giselle S. Carasco, P.Log., Program Administrator
Karyn Milne, Communications/Member Services
Robyn Short, Office Coordinator

Canadian Shipowners Association (CSA) / Association des armateurs canadiens (AAC)
#705, 350 Sparks St., Ottawa ON K1R 7S8
Tel: 613-232-3539; *Fax:* 613-232-6211
csa@shipowners.ca
www.shipowners.ca
To promote an economic & competitive Canadian marine transportation industry; to support a national policy conducive to the development & maintenance of the Canadian flag merchant fleet in the inland, coastal & Arctic waters of Canada & foster the growth of a Canadian flag deep sea merchant fleet.
Bruce Bowie, President
Silvie Dagenais, Sec.-Treas.
Michel Drolet, Vice-President, Operations
Shane Foreman, Policy/Research Manager

Canadian Transport Lawyers Association
c/o S.S.T. Thibault, Heenan Blaikie LLP, #600, 900, rue René-Lévesque ouest, Québec QC G1R 2B5
www.ctla.ca
Geoffrey L. Spencer, President
Louis A. Amato-Gauci, Vice-President & Secretary
Douglas I. Evanchuk, Treasurer
Stephanie S.T. Thibault, Director, Communications

Canadian Transport Workers Union (Ind.) (CTWU) / Syndicat canadien des travailleurs du transport (ind.)
c/o Local #213, 73 Misty St., Kitchener ON N2B 3V6
Tel: 519-896-2671
Don White, President

Canadian Transportation Equipment Association (CTEA) / Association d'équipement de transport du canada (AETC)
#3B, 16 Barrie Blvd., St Thomas ON N5P 4B9
Tel: 519-631-0414; *Fax:* 519-631-1333
transportation@ctea.on.ca
www.ctea.ca
To promote excellence in commercial vehicle manufacturing; to develop standard practices
Don Moore, Executive Director
John Michel, President
Stan Delaney, Administrator, Communications

Canadian Transportation Research Forum (CTRF) / Groupe de recherches sur les transports au Canada
PO Box 23033, Woodstock ON N4T 1R0
Tel: 519-421-9701; *Fax:* 519-421-9319
feedback@ctrf.ca, cawoudsma@ctrf.ca
www.ctrf.ca
To promote the development of research in transportation & related fields; to publish research papers through media & through national & regional forum meetings.
Doug Johnson, President
Carole Ann Woudsma, Secretary
Malcolm Cairns, Executive Vice-President
Mark Hemmes, Vice-President External
Gerry Kolaitis, VP Finance/Treasurer
Vijay Gill, Vice-President Program/Publications
Linda McAusland, Vice-President Meetings
Gordon E. Tufts, VP Organization/Development

Canadian Trucking Alliance (CTA) / L'Alliance canadienne du camionnage (ACC)
324 Somerset St. West, Ottawa ON K2P 0J9
Tel: 613-236-9426; *Fax:* 866-823-4076
info@cantruck.ca
www.cantruck.com
To promote business excellence in trucking; to participate in the development of public policy which supports the economic growth, safety & prosperity of the industry; to provide services, including research, development, products & information to meet the needs of the industry.
PUBLICATIONS: Dangerous Goods: A Trucker's Guide; Crossing International Borders:A Trucker's Guide; National Safety Code: A Trucker's Guide.
Dietmar Krause, Chairperson
Paul Landry, President/CEO
Louise Yako, Director Policy/Communications
Michele Nicol, Director Business Programs
Sandra Stashuk, Member Services Coordinator
Susan Van Egdom, Accounting Coordinator

Canadian Trucking Human Resources Council (CTHRC) / Conseil canadien des ressources humaines en camionnage
#203, 720 Belfast Rd., Ottawa ON K1G 0Z5
Tel: 613-244-4800; *Fax:* 613-244-4535
info@cthrc.com
www.cthrc.com
To respond to the human resource needs of the trucking industry

Canadian Urban Transit Association (CUTA) / Association canadienne du transport urbain (ACTU)
#1401, 55 York St., Toronto ON M5J 1R7
Tel: 416-365-9800; *Fax:* 416-365-1295
www.cutaactu.ca
To represent the public transit community throughout Canada; To strengthen the industry
Michael W. Roschlau, President & Chief Executive Officer
Becky Benaissa, Director, Finance & Administration
Patrick Leclerc, Director, Marketing & Public Affairs
Paré Jean, Director, Research & Technical Services
Nancy Ortenburg, Director, Training & Membership Development
Maureen Shuell, Director, Events & Publications

Canadians for Responsible & Safe Highways (CRASH)
PO Box 1042, Stn. B, Ottawa ON K1P 5R1
Tel: 613-860-0529; *Fax:* 613-567-6204
Toll-Free: 800-530-9945
CRASH strives to ensure that safety, environmental & economic concerns are fully considered by governments when the latter establish & administer regulations pertaining to trucking operations on public highways.
Harry Gow, President

Carefree Society Transportation Service
2832 Queensway St., Prince George BC V2L 4M5
Tel: 250-562-1394; *Fax:* 250-562-1393
carefree_society@telus.net
To provide transportation services for the disabled in our community
Cathy Hickman, Executive Director
Lynnelle Sutherland, President

Central British Columbia Railway & Forest Industry Museum Society
850 River Rd., Prince George BC V2L 5S8
Tel: 250-563-7351; *Fax:* 250-563-3697
trains@pgrfm.bc.ca
www.pgrfm.bc.ca
Administers Prince George Railway & Forest Industry Museum
Laura Williams, General Manager

Chartered Institute of Logistics & Transport (CILT)
Earlstrees Court, Earlstrees Rd., Corbyn NN17 4Ax United Kingdom
enquiry@ciltuk.org.uk
www.cilt-international.com
To promote, encourage & coordinate the study & advancement of the science & art of transportation in all its branches
Bernard Auton, Director General

The Chartered Institute of Logistics & Transport in North America (CILT) / Institut agréé de la logistique et des transports Amérique du Nord
#900, 275 Slater St., Ottawa ON K1P 5H9
Tel: 613-688-1438; *Fax:* 613-688-0966
requestinfo@ciltna.com
www.ciltna.com
To promote, encourage, coordinate study & advancement of science & art of transportation.
David Collenette, Vice-Chairman
Ed Coylits, Executive Director
Edgar Courtemanch, Vice-Chairman
Tom Maville, Treasurer
Gilles Legault, Chair

Chatham Railroad Museum Society
PO Box 434, 2 McLean St., Chatham ON N7M 5K5
Tel: 519-352-3097
To present history from a retired CN baggage car

Club de trafic de Québec
CP 72, Saint-Jean-Chrysostome QC G6Z 2L3
Tél: 418-654-5446; *Téléc:* 418-619-1044
jcoulombe@videotron.ca
www.clubtraficqc.org
Regrouper les représentants oeuvrant dans le domaine du transport de la grande région de Québec
Allain Gagnon, Président
Julie Coulombe, Secrétaire-trésorière

Company of Master Mariners of Canada
c/o R. Wallace, 305 Michigan St., Victoria BC V8V 1R6
www.mastermariners.ca
The Company is a central body of command-level mariners that represents senior officers of the Canadian Merchant Service. It maintains the standard of ability & professional conduct of the officers, & also develops education, training & qualifications for young cadets. It helps liaison between Canada's commercial, governmental & military fleets.
Jim Calvesbert, National Master

Ratch Wallace, Secretary
Yezdee Kooka, Membership Chair

Dewdney-Alouette Railway Society (DARS)
22520 - 116 Ave., Maple Ridge BC V2X 0S4
Tel: 604-463-5311; *Fax:* 604-463-5317
mrmuseum@telus.net
The Society preserves the railway history of Maple Ridge, promotes the craft of model railroading, & offers advice to the public who are engaged in the building & operating of model railroads.
Dick Sutcliff, Contact

Edmonton Radial Railway Society (ERRS)
PO Box 76057, Stn. Southgate, Edmonton AB T6H 5Y7
Tel: 780-437-7721; *Fax:* 780-437-3095
info@edmonton-radial-railway.ab.ca
www.edmonton-radial-railway.ab.ca
The Society collects, preserves & restores vintage streetcars, primarily those from 1908-1951.
Hans Ryffel, President

Electric Vehicle Council of Ottawa Inc. (EVCO)
PO Box 4044, Stn. E, Ottawa ON K1S 5B1
info@evco.ca
www.evco.ca
To provide information about electric road vehicles, in Canada & worldwide

Electric Vehicle Society of Canada (EVS)
21 Burritt Rd., Toronto ON M1R 3S5
Tel: 416-755-4324; *Fax:* 416-755-4324
info@evsociety.ca
www.evsociety.ca
To investigate & promote clean transportation technologies
Howard W. Hutt, President
Joel Clemens, Treasurer
Emile Stevens, Contact, Membership
Robert Weekley, Editor, EVSurge

Freight Carriers Association of Canada (FCA)
#3-4, 427 Garrison Rd., Fort Erie ON L2A 6E6
Tel: 905-994-0560; *Fax:* 905-994-0117
Toll-Free: 800-559-7421
info@fca-natc.org
www.fca-natc.org
To provide quality information, products & services to users, providers & third parties involved in motor carrier transportation.
PUBLICATIONS: Fuel Price and Surcharge Information Bulletin (weekly); Currency Exchange Bulletin (2X/month -14th and last day of the month).
David J. Sirgey, President
Ken Leising, Manager Rate Research/Development
Diane Sheppard, Accountant
Jon Ainsworth, Senior Analyst/Programmer
Mary Anne Vehrs, Sales/Marketing

Hope Air / Vols d'espoir
#207, 124 Merton St., Toronto ON M4S 2Z2
Tel: 416-222-6335; *Fax:* 416-222-6930
Toll-Free: 877-346-4673
mail@hopeair.ca
www.hopeair.ca
Social Media: www.facebook.com/pages/Hope-Air; http://twitter.com/Hope_Air
To provide free air transportation to Canadians in financial need who must travel between their own communities & recognized facilities for medical care
Doug Keller-Hobson, Executive Director
Wayne Twaits, Chair
Robert Reeves, Vice-Chair

Huntsville & Lake of Bays Railway Society
88 Brunel Rd., Huntsville ON P1H 1R1
Tel: 705-789-7576; *Fax:* 705-789-6169
nicholls@vianet.ca
www.portageflyer.org
Maintains & displays original artifacts of the old Huntsville & Lake of Bays Railway, plus vintage railway equipment of the turn of the century
Russell A.F. Nicholls, President

Industrial Truck Association (ITA)
#460, 1750 K St. NW, Washington DC 20006 USA
Tel: 202-296-9880; *Fax:* 202-296-9884
www.indtrk.org
Represents the manufacturers of lift trucks & their suppliers who do business in Canada, the United States or Mexico
William Montwieler, Executive Director

INFORM Inc.
5 Hanover Sq., 19th Fl., New York NY 10004 USA
Tel: 212-361-2400; *Fax:* 212-361-2412
ramsey@informinc.org
www.informinc.org
Social Media: www.facebook.com/199694845376; twitter.com/informinc
To examine the effects of business practices on the environment & human health
Virginia Ramsey, Executive Director

Intermodal Association of North America (IANA)
#1100, 11785 Beltsville Dr., Calverton MD 20705 USA
Tel: 301-982-3400; *Fax:* 301-982-4815
info@intermodal.org
www.intermodal.org
To represent the combined interests of intermodal freight transportation companies & their suppliers
Joanne F. Casey, President/CEO
Thomas J. Malloy, Vice-President, Policy & Communications
Constance M. Sheffield, Vice-President, Administration & Programs
James R. Morrow, Assistant Vice-President, Member Services
Debbie Sasko, Assistant Vice-President, Contract Administration Services

Locomotive & Railway Historical Society of Western Canada
#4104, 2120 Southland Dr. SW, Calgary AB T2V 4W3
Tel: 403-265-9229; *Fax:* 403-261-1057
laniganj@telus.net
To promote the preservation of railway equipment integral to the history of Western Canada; to act in a consultative capacity on heritage rail projects
James E. Lanigan, President

Manitoba Trucking Association (MTA)
25 Bunting St., Winnipeg MB R2X 2P5
Tel: 204-632-6600; *Fax:* 204-694-7134
info@trucking.mb.ca
www.trucking.mb.ca
Develops and maintains a safe and healthy business environment for its members
Earl Coleman, President
Susan Snyder, 1st Vice President
Tom Payne, Jr., 2nd Vice President
Bob Dolyniuk, General Manager
Susan Green, Coordinator, Program & Member Services

Motorcycle & Moped Industry Council (MMIC) / Le Conseil de l'industrie de la motocyclette et du cyclomoteur (CIMC)
#201, 3000 Steeles Ave. East, Markham ON L3R 4T9
Tel: 416-491-4449; *Fax:* 416-493-1985
Toll-Free: 877-470-6642
info@mmic.ca
www.mmic.ca
The Motorcycle and Moped Industry Council (MMIC) is a national, non-profit trade association that represents the manufacturers and distributors of street legal motorcycles and related products and services in Canada.
Jo-Anne Farquhar, Director, Communications & Public Affairs
Luc Fournier, Director, Policy & Government Relations

National Association of Railroad Passengers (NARP)
#308, 900 - 2 St. NE, Washington DC 20002-3557 USA
Tel: 202-408-8362; *Fax:* 202-408-8287
narp@narprail.org
www.narprail.org
To encourage & promote a more balanced US transporation system including promotion of federal & state policies beneficial to all forms of rail service, urban rail transit, rural public transporation & intermodal terminals
Ross Capon, President

National Transportation Brokers Association (NTBA)
PO Box 238, Markham ON L3P 3J7
Tel: 905-568-4400; *Fax:* 905-640-9260
info@ntba-brokers.com
www.ntba-brokers.com
Promotes & continually improves business relationships among shippers, carriers, government & freight brokers
William Tackaberry, Chair

New Brunswick Potato Shippers Association
8824 Route 2, Grand Falls NB E3Z 1P8
Tel: 506-473-5520; *Fax:* 506-473-6701
tatered@nbnet.nb.ca
The shippers association monitors industry growth
Ed Kavanaugh, President

North America Railway Hall of Fame
RPO Centre, PO Box 20040, St Thomas ON N5P 4H4
Tel: 519-633-2535; *Fax:* 519-633-3087
info@narhf.org
www.narhf.org
To establish a tribute to those who have made significant contributions relating to the railway industry in North America; To honour railway organizations, related innovations & technical accomplishments; To preserve & display a collection of library materials & railway heritage artifacts related to the Hall of Fame inductees; To educate the public about the impact of railway transportation on history & the development of communities, nations & international relations
Paul Corriveau, President

Northwestern Ontario Air Carriers Association (NOACA)
PO Box 4075, 143 Cedar Point Dr., Sioux Lookout ON P8T 1J9
Tel: 807-737-7470; *Fax:* 807-583-2812
Jennifer Chwastyk, Vice-Chair

Ontario Community Transit Association (OCTA)
#306, 4141 Yonge St., Toronto ON M2P 2A8
Tel: 416-229-6222; *Fax:* 416-229-6281
www.octa.on.ca
To strengthen & improve public transit services in Ontario; To ensure excellence & sustainability in public transit
Kelly Paleczny, Chair
Ted Galinis, Vice-Chair
Norman Cheesman, Chief Executive Officer
Pat Delmore, Secretary
Chris Prentice, Treasurer

Ontario Good Roads Association (OGRA)
#22, 1525 Cornwall Rd., Oakville ON L6J 0B2
Tel: 289-291-6472; *Fax:* 289-291-6477
info@ogra.org
www.ogra.org
Social Media: twitter.com/Ont_Good_Roads; ca.linkedin.com/pub/ontario-good-roads-association/43/b08/829
To represent the transportation & public works-related interests of Ontario's municipalities & First Nation communities; To deliver programs & services that meet the needs of members; To support municipalities in the provision of effective & efficient transportation systems throughout Ontario
Joseph W. Tiernay, Executive Director
Brian Anderson, Manager, MEmber & Technical Services
Scott Butler, Manager, Policy & Research
Heather Crewe, Manager, Education & Training
Rayna Gillis, Manager, Finance & Administration
Colette Caruso, Coordinator, Communications & Marketing
Roni Kean, Coordinator, Curriculum
Cherry-Lyn Sales, Coordinator, Training Services
Fahad Shuja, Coordinator, Member Services & OPS
James Smith, Coordinator, Member Services & Infrastructure

Ontario Milk Transport Association (OMTA)
#301, 660 Speedvale Ave. West, Guelph ON N1K 1E5
www.milk.org/Corporate/View.aspx?Content=Students/Transportation
John Johnston, General Manager

Ontario Traffic Conference (OTC)
#2, 6355 Kennedy Rd., Mississauga ON L5T 2L5
Tel: 647-346-4050; *Fax:* 647-346-4060
info@otc.org
www.otc.org
Social Media: twitter.com/ontariotraffic
To improve traffic conditions & traffic safety in municipalities of Ontario
Marco D'Angelo, Executive Director
Ron Hamilton, President
Keith Haines, Vice-President
Mike Pelzowski, Secretary/Treasurer
Heide Schlegl, Director Engineering
Robyn Zutis, Director of Education
Kimberly Rossi, Director Marketing

Ontario Trucking Association (OTA)
555 Dixon Rd., Toronto ON M9W 1H8
Tel: 416-249-7401; *Fax:* 866-713-4188
publicaffairs@ontruck.org; membership@ontruck.org
www.ontruck.org
To represent companies & industry suppliers; To provide political advocacy, education, & information services to North American freight transport companies
Brian Taylor, Chair
David H. Bradley, President
Jeff Bryan, Secretary
Scott Tilley, Treasurer
Barrie Montague, Senior Policy Advisor
Doug Switzer, Manager Government Relations

Rebecka Torn, Manager Communications
Rolf VanderZwaag, Manager Maintenance/Tech. Issues

Ontario Trucking Association Education Foundation Inc.
555 Dixon Rd., Toronto ON M9W 1H8
Tel: 416-249-7401; *Fax:* 416-245-6152
education.foundation@ontruck.org

Operation Lifesaver (OL) / Opération Gareautrain
#1401, 99 Bank St., Ottawa ON K1P 6B9
Tel: 613-564-8100; *Fax:* 613-567-6726
admin@operationlifesaver.ca
www.operationlifesaver.ca
To create an awareness by the general public of the potential hazards of rail/highway crossings; to improve drivers' & pedestrians' behaviour at these intersections; to inform the public of the dangers associated with trespassing on railway property; & to reduce the number of accidents resulting in fatalities, injuries & monetary losses
Dan Di Tota, National Director

Pharmaceutical & Personal Care Logistics Association (PPCLA) / Association de logistique des soins personnels et pharmaceutiques
PO Box 40568, Stn. Six Points Plaza, Toronto ON M9B 6K8
Tel: 416-232-6817; *Fax:* 416-232-6818
Toll-Free: 866-293-1238
ppcla@ppcla.org
www.ppcla.org
To develop & promote the interchange of ideas & information concerning traffic & transportation matters of the pharmaceutical & toilet preparations industry; To foster fair dealings & cordial relationships among members & between representatives of the various modes of transportation employed by members
Doris Hamel, President

Private Motor Truck Council of Canada (PMTC) / Association canadienne du camionnage d'entreprise (ACCE)
#115, 1660 North Service Rd. East, Oakville ON L6H 7G3
Tel: 905-827-0587; *Fax:* 905-827-8212
Toll-Free: 877-501-7682
info@pmtc.ca
www.pmtc.ca
Recognized as the leader of the private trucking community in Canada; represents the varied interests of private fleet operators with integrity & sound business practices.
Bruce J. Richards, President
Richard Lalonde, Québec Director

The Railway Association of Canada (RAC) / L'Association des chemins de fer du Canada (ACFC)
#901, 99 Bank St., Ottawa ON K1P 6B9
Tel: 613-567-8591; *Fax:* 613-567-6726
rac@railcan.ca
www.railcan.ca
To promote the commercial viability & the safe & efficient operation of the Canadian railway industry; to act on behalf of, or work jointly with, member companies to promote public policy & regulation that provides equitable treatment between shipping modes; to provide factual information on the railway industry for the public, government & industry, & to provide the views of the industry on public policy issues.
PUBLICATIONS: Interchange; Canadian Railway Medical Rules Handbook; Locomotive Emissions Monitoring Program 2009; Canada's Railway Lead North America.
Cliff Mackay, President & CEO
Bruce Burrows, Vice-President, Public & Corporate Affairs

Saskatchewan Trucking Association (STA)
1335 Wallace St., Regina SK S4N 3Z5
Tel: 306-569-9696; *Fax:* 306-569-1008
Toll-Free: 800-563-7623
ttoope@sasktrucking.com
www.sasktrucking.com
Helps the industry fight its battles in everything from deregulation to weights and measures. Represents the industry in discussions with government
Al Rosseker, Executive Director

The Shipping Federation of Canada / La Fédération maritime du Canada
#326, 300, rue St-Sacrement, Montréal QC H2Y 1X4
Tel: 514-849-2325; *Fax:* 514-849-8774
Toll-Free: 877-534-7367
info@shipfed.ca
www.shipfed.ca
Karen Kancens, Director of Communications
Michael H. Broad, President
David Cardin, Chairman
Ivan A. Lantz, Director Marine Operations
James Moram, Director Marine Administration
Anne Legars, Director Policy/Public Affairs
Caroline Gravel, Director Environmental Affairs
Mario Minotti, Director Finance/Administration

Société des traversiers du Québec (STQ)
250, rue Saint-Paul, Québec QC G1K 9K9
Tél: 418-643-2019; *Téléc:* 418-643-7308
Ligne sans frais: 877-787-7483
stq@traversiers.gouv.qc.ca
www.traversiers.gouv.qc.ca
Contribuer à la mobilité des personnes et des marchandises en assurant des services de transport maritime de qualité, sécuritaires et fiables, favorisant ainsi l'essor social, économique et touristique du Québec
Georges Farrah, Président/directeur général

Sydney & Louisburg Railway Historical Society / Le Musée de chemin de fer de Sydney à Louisburg
7330 Main St., Louisbourg NS B1C 1P5
To commemorate the history of the S&L Railway by preserving & displaying the artifacts & documents which survive; to commemorate the people who worked for the S&L Railway; to explain the local & commercial history of the area which relates to the S&L Railway; to explain & commemorate the general themes of railway & transportation history & technology
William Bussey, President

Toronto Transportation Society (TTS)
PO Box 5187, Stn. A, Toronto ON M5W 1N5
ttswebmaster@torontotransportationsociety.org
www.torontotransportationsociety.org
To afford persons interested in transportation by land, facilities for discussion & exchange of information
Kevin Nichol, President

Transport Action Canada
Bronson Centre, PO Box 858, Stn. B, #303, 211 Bronson Ave., Ottawa ON K1P 5P9
Tel: 613-594-3290; *Fax:* 613-594-3271
info@transport-action.ca
www.transport-action.ca
National federation of environmental & consumer groups concerned about the importance of transportation on our environment & quality of life; to inform Canadians of the need for a coherent national transport policy which recognizes that conservation of resources must be a priority & that access to good public transportation is a right of all Canadians; to work for the improvement & greater use of bus & rail transportation in the interests of public safety, social equity & the protection of the environment; to press for the coordination of all transport services for the benefit of users; to demand more attention to the needs of pedestrians, cyclists & public transport users; to maximize the use of the energy-efficient rail & marine modes for the shipment of freight. PUBLICATIONS: National Transport Newsletter.
David Jeanes, President
Justin Bur, VP East
Peter Lacey, VP West
Tony Turrittin, Secretary
Klaus Beltzner, Treasurer
Bert Titcomb, Manager

Transportation Association of Canada (TAC) / Association des transports du Canada (ATC)
2323 St. Laurent Blvd., Ottawa ON K1G 4J8
Tel: 613-736-1350; *Fax:* 613-736-1395
secretariat@tac-atc.ca
www.tac-atc.ca
To promote the provision of safe, efficient, effective & environmentally sustainable transportation services in support of Canada's social & economic goals; To act as a neutral forum for the discussion of transportation issues & matters; to act as a technical focus in the highway transportation area
Michel Gravel, Executive Director
Guylaine Brousseau, Manager, Finance & Administration
Sarah Wells, Director, Technical Programs
Erica Andersen, Director, Communications & Member Services
John Law, President
Joseph K. Lam, Vice-President
Alex Turnbull, Treasurer

Truck Training Schools Association of Ontario Inc. (TTSAO)
Fax: 519-858-0920
Toll-Free: 866-475-9436
training@ttsao.com
www.ttsao.com
To provide the trucking industry with the highest quality driver training programs for entry level individuals that earn & maintain public confidence, adhering to sound & ethical business practices
Gus Rahim, President

Truckers Association of Nova Scotia (TANS)
PO Box 1527, 184 Arthur St., Truro NS B2N 5V2
Tel: 902-895-7447; *Fax:* 902-897-0487
Toll-Free: 800-232-6631
contact@tans.ca
www.tans.ca
Promotes all matters aiding the development and improvement of the trucking industry and the allied trades in Nova Scotia, including social, recreational, benevolent, educational and charitable activities. In addition, the Truckers Association of Nova Scotia makes presentations to government and other regulatory bodies in relation to the economic welfare of the trucking industry and is the main proponent in gaining access to the provincial haul rates and beneficial changes to the contract specifications used by the contractors
Wayne Onda, Executive Director

Upper Canada Railway Society
PO Box 122, Stn. A, Toronto ON M5W 1A2
Tel: 416-921-4023
ucrs@btinternet.com
To work to preserve history & railways of Canada
Scott Haskill, President

The Van Horne Institute for International Transportation & Regulatory Affairs
#620 Earth Sciences Bldg., 2500 University Dr. NW, Calgary AB T2N 1N4
Tel: 403-220-8455; *Fax:* 403-282-4663
vanhorne@ucalgary.ca
www.vanhorne.info/
To contribute to public policy development & education in the areas of transportation & regulated industries.
PUBLICATIONS: On-Trac.
Peter C. Wallis, President & CEO
Sarah Ingram, Programs Manager
Carla Frede, Webmaster
Mel Belich, Chairman

Western Transportation Advisory Council (WESTAC)
#1140, 800 Pender St. West, Vancouver BC V6C 2V6
Tel: 604-687-8691; *Fax:* 604-687-8751
infoservices@westac.com
www.westac.com
To advance Western Canadian economy through the improvement of the region's transportation system.
Lisa Baratta, Director, Strategy
Ruth Sol, President
Marcella Szel, Chairman (Executive Committee)
Lois Jackson, Chairman of the Board

Universities

African Students Association of Concordia (ASAC)
Concordia Hall Building, Concordia University, #1031-7, 1455 boul de Maisonneuve ouest, Montréal QC H4A 1M8
Tel: 514-848-2424
asacextcomm@gmail.com
asac.concordia.ca
To represent the students of African descent at Concordia University; To facilitate the social networking of African students; To promote African culture & awareness at Concordia University & in the greater Montreal community
Yves F. Nimbona, President

Visual Art, Crafts, Folk Arts

AICA Canada Inc.
172 Roselawn Ave., Toronto ON M4R 1E6
www.artfocus.com/aicacanada.com/index.html
To broaden communication about the visual arts; To promote the values of art criticism as a discipline; To act on behalf of the physical & moral defense of works of art

Alberta Craft Council (ACC)
10186 - 106 St., Edmonton AB T5J 1H4
Tel: 780-488-6611; *Fax:* 780-488-8855
Toll-Free: 800-362-7238
acc@albertacraft.ab.ca
www.albertacraft.ab.ca
To stimulate, develop & support craft in Alberta through communication, education, exhibition, & participation
Tom McFall, Executive Director
James Lavoie, Chair

Art Dealers Association of Canada Inc. (ADAC) / Association des marchands d'art du Canada
#302, 511 King St. West, Toronto ON M5V 1K4
Tel: 416-934-1583; *Fax:* 416-934-1584
Toll-Free: 866-435-2322
info@ad-ac.ca
www.ad-ac.ca
To promote & encourage public awareness of visual arts in Canada & abroad
Johanna Robinson, Executive Director
Jeanette Langmann, President

Artists in Stained Glass (AISG)
www.aisg.on.ca
Artists in Stained Glass (AISG) is a not-for-profit association established to encourage the development of stained glass as a contemporary art form, in Ontario & throughout Canada. It exists only online, & has no contact address other than its url.
Julia Williamson, Treasurer
Robert Brown, President

Association des collections d'entreprises / Corporate Art Collectors Association
Secrétariat: Banque Nationale du Canada, 600, rue de la Gauchetière ouest, 8e étage, Montréal QC H3C 4L2
Tél: 514-394-8533; *Téléc:* 514-394-6258
Ligne sans frais: 800-361-6266
joann.kane@bnc.ca
Réunir les conservateurs et les propriétaires de collections corporatives; favoriser l'échange d'information, d'idées, d'expériences, d'expertise, de systèmes ou de services; représenter de façon générale les intérêts de ses membres; favoriser la diffusion de l'art au Québec
JoAnn Kane, Présidente et secrétaire
Louis Pelletier, Vice-président
François Rochon, Trèsorier
Anne-Claude Bacon, Administratrice

The Canadian Art Foundation
#320, 215 Spadina Ave., Toronto ON M5T 2C7
Tel: 416-368-8854; *Fax:* 416-368-6135
Toll-Free: 800-222-4762
info@canadianart.ca
www.canadianart.ca
The Foundation is a charitable organization established to foster & support the visual arts in Canada and to celebrate artists & their creativity with a program of events, lectures, competitions, publications & educational initiatives. Programs include: Room with a View; International Art Tours; Anne Lind International Program; RBC Canadian Painting Competition; the Canadian Art Editorial Residency; the Canadian Art School Hop; and the Youth Arts Bursary
Ann Webb, Executive Director
Elaine Gaito, Manager, Marketing & Communications
Ann Webb, Publisher, Canadian Art
Richard Rhodes, Editor, Canadian Art

Canadian Association of Professional Conservators (CAPC) / Association canadienne des restaurateurs professionnels (ACRP)
c/o Canadian Museums Association, #400, 280 Metcalfe St., Ottawa ON K2P 1R7
Fax: 613-233-5438
swarren@technomuses.ca (Applications)
www.capc-acrp.ca
To foster high standards within the conservation profession through accreditation; To facilitate public access to professional conservators
Greg Hill, President
Diana Komejan, Vice-President
Anne Maheux, Treasurer

Canadian Craft & Hobby Association (CCHA)
Mono Plaza, PO Box 101, 633419 Hwy 10 N., Orangeville ON L9W 2Z5
Tel: 519-940-5969; *Fax:* 519-941-0492
Paul.laplante@asi-tapedots.com
www.cdncraft.org
To further the success of every business engaged in Canada's craft & hobby industry by providing an arena for the discussion of goals & plans; to foster industry expansion through development & implementation of dynamic programs & activities; to provide a forum for meeting new people, learning new ideas & profiting from benefits of working together
Paul Laplante, President

Canadian Crafts Federation (CCF) / Fédération canadienne des métiers d'art (FCMA)
PO Box 1231, Fredericton NB E3B 5C8
Tel: 506-462-9560
info@canadiancraftsfederation.ca
www.canadiancraftsfederation.ca
To represent provincial & territorial crafts councils & the Canadian crafts sector; to advance & promote the vitality & excellence of Canadian crafts nationally & internationally to the benefit of Canadian craftspeople & the community at large
Deborah Dumka, President

Canadian Guild of Crafts / Guilde canadienne des métiers d'art
1460, rue Sherbrooke ouest, #B, Montréal QC H3G 1K4
Tel: 514-849-6091; *Fax:* 514-849-7351
Toll-Free: 866-477-6091
info@canadianguild.com
www.canadianguildofcrafts.com
To preserve, encourage & promote Canadian crafts; to organize & sponsor exhibitions of the work of recognized & promising artists in the fields of arts & crafts; to educate interested groups about Canadian & native crafts through tours & lectures
Diane Labelle, Managing Director

Canadian Quilters Association (CQA) / Association canadienne de la courtepointe (ACC)
c/o 6 Spruce St., Pasadena NL A0L 1K0
Tel: 709-686-5882; *Fax:* 709-686-5883
Toll-Free: 877-672-8777
administration@canadianquilter.com
www.canadianquilter.com
The promotion of a greater understanding, appreciation & knowledge of the art, techniques & heritage of patchwork, appliqué & quilting; the promotion of the highest standards of workmanship & design in both traditional & innovative work the fostering of a climate of cooperation amongst quiltmakers across the country.
Johanna Alford, President
Vivian Kapusta, Secretary/Publicist

Canadian Society of Painters in Water Colour (CSPWC) / Société canadienne de peintres en aquarelle (SCPA)
#102, 258 Wallace Ave., Toronto ON M6P 3M9
Tel: 416-533-5100
info@cspwc.com
www.cspwc.com
To promote the use of experimentation with water-based media; To encourage new artists

Conseil des arts de Montréal (CAM)
1210, rue Sherbrooke est, Montréal QC H2L 1L9
Tél: 514-280-3580; *Téléc:* 514-280-3784
info-cam@cum.qc.ca
www.artsmontreal.org
Média social: twitter.com/ConseilArtsMtl
Soutenir, encourager et harmoniser les initiatives d'ordre artistique et culturel sur le territoire de la ville de Montréal.
Danielle Sauvage, directrice générale et sec. conseil
Line Lampron, secrétaire de direction

Conseil des arts textiles du Québec (CATQ)
811A, rue Ontario est, Montréal QC H2L 2T2
Tél: 514-524-6645; *Ligne sans frais:* 800-524-6645
info@catq.qc.ca
www.catq.qc.ca
Regrouper les artistes en arts textiles et encourager la collaboration entre eux; favoriser le développement des arts textiles par la promotion, la diffusion, documentation et l'information; fournir des services aux membres en rapport avec les buts de la corporation; organiser des activités dans le but d'atteindre les objectifs de la corporation.
Isabel Moreau, Coordanatrice Administrative

Conseil des métiers d'art du Québec (ind.) (CMA) / Québec Crafts Council (Ind.)
#400, 350, rue St-Paul est, Montréal QC H2Y 1H2
Tél: 514-861-2787; *Téléc:* 514-861-9191
cmaq@metiers-d-art.qc.ca
www.metiers-d-art.qc.ca
Pour distribuer les créations métiers d'art auprès des grossistes canadiens et étrangers.
Serge Demers, Directeur général

Craft Council of Newfoundland & Labrador
Devon House, 59 Duckworth St., St. John's NL A1C 1E6
Tel: 709-753-2749; *Fax:* 709-753-2766
info@craftcouncil.nf.ca
www.craftcouncil.nf.ca
To produce high quality work; To assist & advise members in wide variety of craft-related areas
Anne Manuel, Executive Director

Crafts Association of British Columbia (CABC) / Conseil de l'artisanat de la Colombie-Britannique
Granville Island, 1386 Cartwright St., Vancouver BC V6H 3R8
Tel: 604-687-6511; *Fax:* 604-687-6711
Toll-Free: 888-687-6511
info@cabc.net
www.cabc.net
To develop excellence in crafts
Yvonne Chui, Executive Director

Embroiderers' Association of Canada, Inc. (EAC)
c/o EAC President, PO Box 341, Lakefield ON K0L 2H0
www.eac.ca
The Association is a national, non-profit organization that aims to preserve traditional techniques & promote new challenges in embroidery through education & networking. It offers course in embroidery & certifies teachers. It is a registered charity, BN: 136380672RR0001.
Sue Thomas, President
Marilyn Marshall, Treasurer

Folklore Canada International (FCI)
2040, rue Alexandre-de-Sève, Montréal QC H2L 2W4
Tel: 514-524-8552; *Fax:* 514-524-0262
patrimoine@qc.aira.com
www.folklore-canada.org
Social Media:
www.facebook.com/group.php?gid=84023872908&v=wall
The Association is a non-profit organization committed to showcasing Canadian cultural pluralism. It promotes folk arts; organizes cultural exhanges between groups at national & international levels; organizes international folk arts festivals.
Jean-Claude Ménard, President
Guy Landry, General Director

Manitoba Crafts Council (MCC)
c/o Arts & Cultural Industries Assn of Manitoba, #501, 62 Albert St., Winnipeg MB R3B 1E9
Tel: 204-927-2787
mcc@mts.net
www.manitobacrafts.ca
To promote the development & appreciation of fine craft; to facilitate a supportive environment in which fine, contemporary craft may flourish.
Judy Jennings, President
Donna L. Turner, Executive Director

The Metal Arts Guild of Canada (MAGC)
88 Elm Grove Ave., Toronto ON M6K 2J3
Tel: 416-252-6242
maguild@interlog.com
www.metalartsguild.ca
Social Media: twitter.com/MAGcanada
To be committed to the exchange of information & ideas encouraging appreciation for the metal arts; To promote & develop the metal arts; To further education in the metal arts; To encourage members to experiment with all the forms that metal takes
Sarah Dougal-Hamel, President
Kathryn Dieroff, Treasurer

New Brunswick Crafts Council / Conseil d'artisanat du Nouveau-Brunswick
PO Box 1231, Stn. A, Fredericton NB E3B 5C8
Tel: 506-450-8989; *Fax:* 506-457-6010
Toll-Free: 866-622-7238
nbcrafts@nb.aibn.com
www.nbcraftscouncil.ca
Social Media:
www.facebook.com/#!/group.php?gid=2411474486
To provide opportunities & support to members by developing, promoting & fostering an appreciation of excellence in craft.
Beth Biggs, Executive Director
Kitty Bourne, Administrator

Nova Scotia Designer Crafts Council (NSDCC)
1113 Marginal Rd., Halifax NS B3H 4P7
Tel: 902-423-3837; *Fax:* 902-422-0881
office@nsdcc.ns.ca
www.nsdcc.ns.ca
To encourage & promote the craft movement in Nova Scotia; to increase public awareness & appreciation of craft products & activities
Susan Hanrahan, Executive Director

Ontario Crafts Council (OCC)
990 Queen St. West, Toronto ON M6J 1H1
Tel: 416-925-4222; *Fax:* 416-925-4223
info@craft.on.ca
www.craft.on.ca

To have craft recognized as a valuable part of life and the excellence of Ontario craft and craftspeople acknowledged across Canada and around the world.
Emma Quin, Executive Director

Prince Edward Island Crafts Council (PEICC)
PO Box 20071, Stn. Sherwood, Charlottetown PE C1A PE3
Tel: 902-892-5152; *Fax:* 902-628-8740
info@peicraftscouncil.com
www.peicraftscouncil.com
To promote the making & acceptance of quality handcrafted items through the provision of programs & services
Darrin White, President
Barb Boss, Executive Director

Royal Canadian Academy of Arts (RCA) / Académie royale des arts du Canada
#375, 401 Richmond St. West, Toronto ON M5V 3A8
Tel: 416-408-2718; *Fax:* 416-408-2286
rcaarts@interlog.com
www.rca-arc.ca
To celebrate the achievement of excellence & innovation by visual artists across Canada; to encourage the new generation of artists; to facilitate the exchange of ideas about visual culture for the benefit of all Canadians
Ann McCall, President

Saskatchewan Craft Council (SCC)
813 Broadway Ave., Saskatoon SK S7N 1B5
Tel: 306-653-3616; *Fax:* 306-244-2711
Toll-Free: 866-653-3616
saskcraftcouncil@sasktel.net
www.saskcraftcouncil.org
To promote, support & develop excellence in craft
Larry Trask, Chair
Rodney Peterson, Vice-Chair

Sculptors Society of Canada (SSC) / Société des sculpteurs du Canada
c/o J.M. Young, #204, 60 Atlantic Ave., Toronto ON M6K 1X9
Tel: 416-533-0126
gallery@cansculpt.org
www.cansculpt.org
Social Media:
www.facebook.com/#!/pages/Sculptors-Society-of-Canada/116512211729231
To promote Canadian sculpture; to provide encouragement to sculptors through public exhibitions & discussions in Canada & other countries
Judi Michelle Young, President

Society of Canadian Artists (SCA) / Société des artistes canadiens (SAC)
Lawrence Plaza, PO Box 54029, 500 Lawrence Ave. West, Toronto ON M6A 3B7
Tel: 416-584-9823
info@societyofcanadianartists.com
www.societyofcanadianartists.com
To promote recognition of its member-artists through exhibitions, seminars, workshops, travelling shows
Dorothy Chisholm, Vice-President, Finance

Visual Arts Nova Scotia (VANS)
1113 Marginal Rd., Halifax NS B3H 4P7
Tel: 902-423-4694; *Fax:* 902-422-0881
Toll-Free: 866-225-8267
vans@visualarts.ns.ca
vans.ednet.ns.ca
To promote a better understanding of arts & artists in Nova Scotia; to provide practical assistance to artists; to act in an advisory capacity to public & private interests
Briony Carros, Executive Director

Visual Arts Ontario (VAO)
PO Box 1159, Stn. TDC, 77 King St. West, Toronto ON M5K 1P2
Tel: 416-591-8883; *Fax:* 416-591-2432
info@vao.org
www.vao.org
To assist working artists & to provide information on art to the general public; to facilitate municipal/community involvement in the visual arts; to forge links between the visual arts & the informal & formal education systems; to provide access to groups traditionally underserviced for the reasons of geography, gender, race or linguistic distinctions
Hennie L. Wolff, Executive Director

Wildlife

Club d'ornithologie de Mirabel (COMIR)
CP 3418, 9009, Rte Arthur-Sauvé, Mirabel QC J7N 2T8
Tél: 450-258-4924
info@comirabel.org
comirabel.org
Le territoire couvert part le COMIR s'étend de la rivière des Mille-Iles au Sud, Prévost au Nord, la rivière des Outaouais (Rivière Rouge) à l'Ouest et la route 117 à l'Est.
Normande Lapensée, Présidente
Denis Lauzon, Vice-président

Spruce City Wildlife Association (SCWA)
Stn. 1384 River Rd., Prince George BC V2L 5S8
Tel: 250-563-5437; *Fax:* 250-563-5438
info@scwa.bc.ca
www.scwa.bc.ca
The Spruce City Wildlife Association is a non-profit organization made up of families, individuals and corporations in Prince George concerned about public involvement in local environmental and conservation matters.
Denise Collett, President/Treasurer

Women

Alberta Women's Institutes (AWI)
5405 - 36 Ave., Wetaskiwin AB T9A 3C7
Tel: 780-312-2440; *Fax:* 780-312-2482
evelyne@athabascau.ca
awi.athabascau.ca
An organization of women of all ages who achieve change through personal growth, communication & education
Fern Killeen, Executive Director

Alliance des femmes de la francophonie canadienne (AFFC)
Place de la francophonie, #302, 450, rue Rideau, Ottawa ON K1N 5Z4
Tél: 613-241-3500; *Téléc:* 613-241-6679
Ligne sans frais: 866-535-9422
www.affc.ca
Média social: www.facebook.com/229810340365531; twitter.com/AFFCfemmes
Favorise l'autonomie des femmes canadiennes-françaises sur tous les plans; assure le respect des droits des femmes francophones vivant en milieu minoritaire; soutien le développement de l'action collective et politique des femmes au Canada français; souligne la spécificité des femmes francophones auprès des instances gouvernementales, des diverses associations et du grand public
Manon Beaulieu, Directrice générale

Association féminine d'éducation et d'action sociale (AFEAS) / Feminine Association for Education & Social Action
5999, rue de Marseille, Montréal QC H1N 1K6
Tél: 514-251-1636; *Téléc:* 514-251-9023
info@afeas.qc.ca
www.afeas.qc.ca
Média social:
www.facebook.com/pages/Afeas/181581728519026; twitter.com/afeas1966; www.youtube.com/results?search_query=afeas&aq=f
Avec ses Activités femmes d'ici organisées sur tout le territoire québécois, l'Afeas informe ses membres, suscite des échanges et des débats et les incite à participer davantage aux différentes structures de la société

Association féminine d'éducation et d'action sociale - Chibougamau
CP 293, Chibougamau QC G8P 2K7
Tél: 418-748-2031
Martine Savard

Association Marie-Reine de Chibougamau
CP 295, Chibougamau QC G8P 2K7
Tél: 418-748-4289
Aider les femmes & les enfants victimes de violence
Fernande Fiset

Association of Canadian Women Composers (ACWC) / L'Association des femmes compositeurs canadiennes (AFCC)
20 St. Joseph St., Toronto ON M4Y 1J9
Tel: 416-239-5195
info@acwc.ca
www.acwc.ca
To promote the music of Canadian women composers through concerts, commissions, publications, recordings, etc.

British Columbia Women's Institutes (BCWI)
#203B, 750 Cottonwood Ave., Kamloops BC V2B 3X2
Tel: 250-554-5406; *Fax:* 250-554-5406
info@bcwi.org
www.bcwi.org
To help discover, stimulate & develop leadership among women; to assist, encourage & support women to become knowledgeable & responsible citizens; to ensure basic human rights for women & to work towards their equality; to be a strong voice through which matters of utmost concern can reach the decision makers; to network with organizations sharing similar objectives; to promote the improvement of agricultural & other rural communities & to safeguard the environment

Canadian Association for the Advancement of Women & Sport & Physical Activity (CAAWS) / Association canadienne pour l'avancement des femmes du sport et de l'activité physique (ACAFS)
#202N, 801 King Edward Ave., Ottawa ON K1N 6N5
Tel: 613-562-5667; *Fax:* 613-562-5668
caaws@caaws.ca
www.caaws.ca
To promote an equitable sport & physical activity system, in which girls & women are participants & leaders; To foster equitable support & diverse opportunities, in sport & physical activity for females across Canada
Karin Lofstrom, Executive Director
Sydney Millar, Manager, National Program
Stéphanie Legault, Manager, Marketing & Projects
Jessica Lowe, Administrator & Office Coordinator

Canadian Association of Women Executives & Entrepreneurs (CAWEE) / Association canadienne des femmes cadres et entrepreneurs
#1600, 401 Bay St., Toronto ON M5H 2Y4
Tel: 416-756-0000; *Fax:* 416-756-0000
contact@cawee.net
www.cawee.net
To provide an environment for successful businesswomen to grow & develop, both professionally & personally, through business & community involvement
Melvine Baird, President
Lara Bazant, Director, Policy & Administration
Susan Quinn, Director, Sponsorship
Faith Seekings, Director, Membership

Canadian Federation of Business & Professional Women's Clubs (CFBPWC) / Fédération canadienne des clubs des femmes de carrières commerciales et professionnelles (FCCFCCP)
45 Brixham Rd., London ON N6K 1P5
Tel: 519-473-3505
www.bpwcanada.com
Social Media: www.facebook.com/bpw.canada; twitter.com/bpwcan; www.ca.linkedin.com/in/bpwcanada
To develop & encourage women to pursue business, the professions & industry; To work toward the improvement of economic, employment & social conditions for women; To work for high standards of service in business, the professions, industry & public life; To stimulate interest in federal, provincial & municipal affairs; To encourage women to participate in the business of government at all levels; To encourage & assist women & girls to acquire further education & training
Doris Hall, President
Valerie Clarke, First Vice-President
Sue Calhoun, Second Vice President
Sheila Crook, Secretary
Karin Gorgerat, Treasurer

Canadian Hadassah WIZO
#900, 1310, av Greene, Montréal QC H3Z 2B8
Tel: 514-937-9431; *Fax:* 514-933-6483
info@chw.ca
www.chw.ca
Social Media:
www.facebook.com/group.php?gid=190277547652411; www.chwblog.tumblr.com
Canada's leading Jewish women's philanthropic organization extends material & moral support of Jewish women of Canada to needy individuals in Hadassah-WIZO welfare institutions in Israel; encourages Jewish & Hebrew culture in Canada; cooperates with other organizations; promotes Canadian ideals of democracy. Forty locations across Canada
Marla Dan, National President
Freda Ginsberg, National Executive Vice-President

Canadian Women in Communications (CWC) / Association canadienne des femmes en communication (AFC)
#804, 67 Yonge St., Toronto ON M5E 1J8
Tel: 416-363-1880; *Fax:* 416-363-1882
Toll-Free: 800-361-2978
cwcafc@cwc-afc.com
www.cwc-afc.com
To advance the role of women in the communications sector
Nicole Lang, Chair, Calgary Chapter
Lisa Woznica, Co-Chair, GTA Chapter
Angela J. Wheldon, Co-Chair, NCR Chapter
Judith Campbell, Vice-President
Diane Johnson, Chair, BC Chapter
Sue Timanson, Chair, Edmonton Chapter
Claire A. Cockell, Co-Chair, GTA Chapter
Marye Menaard-Bos, Co-Chair, NCR Chapter
Christianne Vaillancourt, Chair, NB Chapter
Loraine Dumas, Chair, Québec
Nathalie Noël, Chair, SW Ontario Chapter
Stephanie MacKendrick, President
Robin Hildebrandt, Chair, Manitoba Chapter

Canadian Women's Foundation / Fondation canadienne des femmes
#504, 133 Richmond St. West, Toronto ON M5H 2L3
Tel: 416-365-1444; *Fax:* 416-365-1745
Toll-Free: 866-293-4483
TTY: 416-365-1732
info@canadianwomen.org
www.cdnwomen.org
Social Media:
www.facebook.com/#!/CanadianWomensFoundation
To raise money to research, fund & share the best approaches to ending violence against women, moving low-income women out of poverty & building strong, resilient girls
Beverley Wybrow, President & CEO

Caribbean Pioneer Women of Canada
PO Box 51, Stn. Snowdon, Montréal QC H3X 3T3
Tel: 514-488-3716
jntsmith@yahoo.com
Social & cultural events & activities
Janet Smith, Contact

Centre Afrique au Féminin
419, rue St-Roch, Montréal QC H3N 1K2
Tél: 514-272-3274; *Téléc:* 514-272-8617
www.familis.org
Offre un lieu de recontres pour toutes les femmes, ces familles & ce dans une ambiance conviviale; classes, activités, halte-garderie, dépannage alimentaire
Valerie Balton

Centre de Femmes Les Elles du Nord
#2, 570, 3e Rue, Chibougamau QC G8P 1N9
Tél: 418-748-7171
Ghyslaine Bergeron, Présidente
Linda Boulanger, Coordonnatrice

Cercle des Fermières - Chibougamau
CP 123, Chibougamau QC G8P 2K6
Tél: 418-748-2126
www.cfq.qc.ca
Keri Dallaire

Comité condition féminine Baie-James
#203, 552, 3e Rue, Chibougamau QC G8P 1N9
Tél: 418-748-4408; *Téléc:* 418-748-2486
ccfbj@tlb.sympatico.ca
ccfbj.com
A pour mission l'amélioration des conditions de vie des Jamésiennes
Gérald Lemoine, Présidente

Coverdale Centre for Women Inc.
10 Culloden Court, Saint John NB E2L 3B9
Tel: 506-634-1649; *Fax:* 506-634-1647
coverdalesj@yahoo.ca
Coverdale Center for Women Inc. provides programs and services for women including self-development programs in groups and individual counseling. It is a drop-in center where women can find support, referrals to community services, general counseling, addiction counselling, positive recreation, and self-improvement courses.
Lynda Hanson, Acting Executive Director

Les EssentiElles
Centre de la francophonie, 302, rue Strickland, Whitehorse YT Y1A 2K1
Tél: 867-668-2636; *Téléc:* 867-668-3511
elles@yknet.ca
www.lesessentielles.org
Organisme à but non lucratif qui représente les intérêts des femmes francophones du Yukon.
Julie Ménard, Coordonnatrice

Federated Women's Institutes of Canada (FWIC) / Fédération des instituts féminins du Canada
PO Box 209, 359 Blue Lake Rd., St George ON N0E 1N0
Tel: 519-448-3873; *Fax:* 519-448-3506
fwican@gmail.com
www.fwic.ca/
To act as a united voice for Women's Institutes of Canada; To promote Canadian agriculture & community living
Ruth Blenkhorn, President
Sheila Needham, President

Federated Women's Institutes of Ontario (FWIO)
7382 Wellington Rd. 30, RR#5, Guelph ON N1H 6J2
Tel: 519-836-3078; *Fax:* 519-836-9456
fwio@fwio.on.ca
www.fwio.on.ca
Social Media:
www.facebook.com/home.php?sk=group_7156866227
To assist & encourage women to become more knowledgeable & responsible citizens; To promote & develop good family life skills; To help discover, stimulate & develop leadership; To help identify & resolve need in the community
Lynn Ruigrok, Executive Director

Fédération des femmes du Québec (FFQ)
#309, 110, rue St-Thérèse, Montréal QC H2Y 1E6
Tél: 514-876-0166; *Téléc:* 514-876-0162
info@ffq.qc.ca
www.ffq.qc.ca
Alexa Conradi, Présidente
Nancy Burrows, Coordonnatrice

Federation of Medical Women of Canada (FMWC) / Fédération des femmes médecins du Canada
780 Echo Dr., Ottawa ON K1S 5R7
Tel: 613-569-5881; *Fax:* 613-569-4432
Toll-Free: 877-771-3777
fmwcmain@fmwc.ca
www.fmwc.ca
Committed to the professional, social, & personal advancement of women physicians & to the promotion of the well-being of women in the medical profession & in society at large
Nahid Azad, President

Halifax Women's Network
PO Box 48030, Bedford NS B4A 3Z2
info@halifaxwomensnetwork.com
www.halifaxwomensnetwork.com
To provide opportunities for professional women to enhance their careers, increase their contacts, create a positive image, and strengthen their links to the community.
Lee Ross, President

Immigrant Women Services Ottawa (IWSO) / Services pour femmes immigrantes d'Ottawa
#400, 219 Argyle St., Ottawa ON K2P 2H4
Tel: 613-729-3145; *Fax:* 613-729-9308
infomail@immigrantwomenservices.com
www.immigrantwomenservices.com
To empower & enable immigrant women in the Ottawa region to participate in the elimination of all forms of abuse against women; to raise awareness among immigrant women who are abused, in order to break down their isolation & enable them to advocate on their own behalf; to develop a crisis service for immigrant women who are abused to give them full access to mainstream resources; to develop cross-cultural training for shelters & mainstream agencies regarding the special needs of immigrant women in order to ensure that existing services are accessible & appropriate to them & their families; to educate immigrant communities to work toward ending violence against women.

Interval House
#200, 131 Bloor St., Toronto ON M5S 1R8
Tel: 416-924-1411; *Fax:* 416-928-9020
info@intervalhouse.ca
www.intervalhouse.ca
To provide a continuum of services that enable abused women & children to have access to safe shelter & responsive services that help them establish lives free from violence; To provide integrated & specialized services related to counselling, advocacy, outreach, legal & housing support, as well as programs to help build economic self-sufficiency

Jewish Women International of Canada (JWIC)
#210, 638A Sheppard Ave. West, Toronto ON M3H 2S1
Tel: 416-630-9313; *Fax:* 416-630-9319
Toll-Free: 866-333-5942
jwic@jwicanada.com
www.jwicanada.com
Works locally, nationally & internationally to strengthen the effectiveness of women in the Jewish community & society; to foster the emotional well-being of children; to perpetuate Jewish values & secure world Jewry. Programs include ending violence towards women, sexual assault awareness, emergency housing for women & children, & advocacy to end child poverty in Canada. Offices in Toronto & Montréal, & chapters in Toronto, Montréal, B.C., Windsor & Winnipeg.
Jill Lieberman, President
Penny Krowitz, Executive Director

Korean Canadian Women's Association (KCWA)
2, 27 Madison Ave., Toronto ON M5R 2S2
Tel: 416-340-1234; *Fax:* 416-340-8114
kcwa@kcwa.net
www.kcwa.net
To empower Korean Canadian families and other vulnerable members of the community-at-large to live free from violence, poverty and inequity through the provision of culturally sensitive and linguistically appropriate services for the purpose of enhancing the well-being of immigrant families and promoting their successful integration into Canadian society.

Manitoba Women's Institutes (MWI)
1129 Queens Ave., Brandon MB R7A 1L9
Tel: 204-945-8976; *Fax:* 204-328-5294
mbwi@mts.net
www.gov.mb.ca/agriculture/organizations/wi/
Focuses on personal development, the family, agriculture, rural development & community action, locally & globally
Shirley Bell, Executive Administrator

MATCH International Centre / Centre international Match
#310, 411 Roosevelt Ave., Ottawa ON K2A 3X9
Tel: 613-238-1312; *Fax:* 613-238-6867
Toll-Free: 888-414-8717
info@matchinternational.org
www.matchinternational.org
Social Media:
www.facebook.com/pages/Match-International/149004639694?v=info
Guided by a feminist vision of sustainable development which recognizes the diversity of women & respects their efforts toward self-determination; works in partnership with women's groups in Africa, Asia, the Caribbean, & South America toward the empowerment of women through political, economic, social, & cultural justice.
Kim Bulger, Executive Director

Mouvement des Femmes Chrétiennes
3013, ch des Trois-Cantons, Nicholas Denys NB E3K 3C1
Tél: 506-783-4745; *Téléc:* 506-783-4745
secretariat@mfcnational.net
www.mfcnational.net
A pour mission former des femmes efficaces & dynamiques sur le plan familial, paroissial, social & chrétien; développer une mentalité chrétienne en faisant l'union de la vie & de la foi; transformer le milieu de vie par des projets concrets

Na'amat Canada Inc.
National Office, #6, 7005 Kildare Rd., Montréal QC H4W 1C1
Tel: 514-488-0792; *Fax:* 514-487-6727
Toll-Free: 888-278-0792
naamat@total.net
www.naamat.com
To enhance the status of women, children & families in Israel & Canada; as part of a world-wide progressive Jewish women's organization in partnership with Na'amat Israel, we believe that every person is entitled to self-respect & equal opportunity within a just society. Councils across Canada, including Calgary (Susan Inhaber, President; naamatcalgary@yahoo.ca), & Hamilton (Deena Sacks & Tory Metzger, Co-Presidents; naamathamilton@gmail.com)
Orit Tobe, National President

National Action Committee on the Status of Women (NAC) / Comité canadien d'action sur le statut de la femme (CCA)
#417, 215 Spadina Ave., Toronto ON M5T 2C7
Tel: 416-932-1718; *Fax:* 416-979-3936
nac@web.ca
www.nac-cca.ca
To shape public opinion, influence decision makers & mobilize membership & the Canadian public to work for equality & justice for all women
Sandra Carnegie Douglas, Executive Coordinator

Denise Andrea Campbell, President

National Association of Women & the Law (NAWL) / Association nationale de la femme et du droit (ANFD)
PO Box 46008, 2339 Ogilvie Rd., Gloucester ON K1J 9M7
Tel: 613-241-7570
www.nawl.ca
To promote the equality rights of women through legal education, research & law reform advocacy; to improve the legal status of women in Canada through law reform; to dismantle barriers to all women's equality
Alison Dewar, Chair, National Steering Committee
Jane Bailey, Member, National Steering Committee
Samantha Henrickson, Member, National Steering Committee

National Council of Jewish Women of Canada
#118, 1588 Main St., Winnipeg MB R2V 1Y3
Tel: 204-339-9700; *Fax:* 204-334-3779
info@ncjwc.org
www.ncjwc.org
To further human welfare in the Jewish & general communities; To help fulfill unmet needs & to serve the individual & the community

The National Council of Women of Canada (NCWC) / Le Conseil national des femmes du Canada
PO Box 67099, Ottawa ON K2A 4E4
Tel: 613-232-5025; *Fax:* 613-232-8419
Toll-Free: 877-319-0993
ncwc@magma.ca
www.ncwc.ca
Social Media: www.facebook.com/thencwc
To empower all women to work together towards improving the quality of life for women, families & society through a forum of member organizations & individuals
Karen Dempsey, President
Catherine Tillsley, Executive Director

Native Women's Association of the N.W.T.
PO Box 2321, 5017 49th St., Yellowknife NT
Tel: 867-873-5509; *Fax:* 867-873-3152
www.nativewomens.com
Provides training & education programs for native women in the Western Arctic
Nancy Peel, Executive Director

New Brunswick Women's Institute (NBWI)
Victoria Health Centre, #279, 65 Brunswick St., Fredericton NB E3B 1G5
Tel: 506-454-0798; *Fax:* 506-451-8949
nbwi@nb.aibn.com
www.nbwi.ca
To help discover, stimulate & develop leadership among women; to assist, encourage & support women to become knowledgeable & responsible citizens; to ensure basic human rights for women & work towards their equality; to network with other organizations sharing similar objectives; to promote the improvement of agricultural & other rural communities & to safeguard the environment
Debbie Johnson, Administrative Officer
Glenna Geer, President

Newfoundland & Labrador Women's Institutes
PO Box 1854, St. John's NL A1C 5P9
Tel: 709-753-8780; *Fax:* 709-753-8780
nlwi@nfld.com
www.nlwi.ca
The present day Newfoundland and Labrador Women's Institutes is an informal, educational organization for women to work together to expand their skills, broaden their interests, plan meetings, workshops and conferences, and strengthen the quality of life for themselves, their families and their communities. The NLWI is a non-partisan, non-sectarian, non-racial organization
Barbara Taylor, President

NSERC/Petro-Canada Chair for Women in Science & Engineering
c/o Faculty of Engineering & Applied Sciences, Memorial University, St. John's NL A1B 3X5
Tel: 709-737-7960; *Fax:* 709-737-7658
cwse@morgan.ucs.mun.ca
www.mun.ca/cwse/
To encourage women in Canada to enter careers in science, engineering, mathematics & computer sciences; to encourage women in Canada to attain high levels of professional achievement in these fields; to serve as an information centre for & about women in these fields; to make people aware of Canadian women scientists & engineers & of career opportunities available to them; to provide a forum for discussion of subjects of interest to members
Carolyn J. Emerson, Chair, Atlantic Region

The Older Women's Network (OWN) / Réseau des femmes aînées
115 The Esplanade, Toronto ON M5E 1Y7
Tel: 416-214-1518; *Fax:* 416-214-1541
info@olderwomensnetwork.org
www.olderwomensnetwork.org
To initiate & support discussion on issues relevant to the well-being of older women; To develop & support legislation to expand opportunities for housing, economic security, & optimum health; To monitor the media in order to encourage a more realistic & positive portrayal of older women; To support the efforts of young women to achieve equal opportunity, freedom from discrimination, abuse & exploitation, & the right to reproductive choice; To support the needs of children; To liaise with movements for social justice in Canada & abroad
Janice Tait, Chair
Andrea Brigneti, Provincial Coordinator

Prince Edward Island Business Women's Association (PEIBWA)
161 St. Peter's Rd., Charlottetown PE C1A 5P7
Tel: 902-892-6040; *Fax:* 902-892-6050
Toll-Free: 866-892-6040
office@peibwa.org
www.peibwa.org
To assist women in business to succeed by providing services and programs to meet their objectives.
Michelle Ryder-MacEwen, President

Prince Edward Island Women's Institute (PEIWI)
40 Enman Cres., Charlottetown PE C1E 1E6
Tel: 902-368-4860; *Fax:* 902-368-4439
wi@gov.pe.ca
www.womensinstitute.pe.ca
To help discover, stimulate & develop leadership among women; to assist, encourage & support women to become knowledgeable & responsible citizens; to ensure basic human rights for women & to work towards their equality; to be a strong voice through which matters of utmost concern can reach the decision makers; to network with organizations sharing similar objectives; to promote the improvement of agricultural & other rural communities & to safeguard the environment
Carol MacLellan, President

Québec Women's Institutes (QWI)
c/o Linda Hoy, 77, rte 108, Cookshire-Eaton QC J0B 1M0
Tel: 819-566-2105; *Fax:* 819-822-3145
To help discover, stimulate & develop leadership among women; To assist, encourage & support women to become knowledgeable & responsible citizens; To ensure basic human rights for women & to work toward their equality; To be a strong voice through which matters of utmost concern can reach the decision makers; To promote the improvement of agricultural & other rural communities & to safeguard the environment
Linda Hoy, Executive Officer

Réseau des femmes d'affaires du Québec inc. (RFAQ)
#100, 10794, rue Lajeunesse, Montréal QC H3L 2E8
Tél: 514-521-2441; *Téléc:* 514-521-1410
Ligne sans frais: 800-332-2683
info@rfaq.ca
www.rfaq.ca
Ce réseau de plus de 2 000 membres est le seul réseau d'affaires qui s'est donné comme mission de faire reconnaître l'importance et les mérites des femmes dans le milieu des affaires ici comme sur les quatre autres continents afin de contribuer à leur succès et au développement de leur rôle et de leur influence dans toutes les sphères de l'activité économique.
Nicole Beaudoin, Présidente/Directrice générale

Réseau Femmes Québec (RFQ)
#134, 911, rue Jean-Talon est, Montréal QC H2R 1V5
Tél: 514-484-2375
reseau.femmes.quebec@gmail.com
www.reseau-femmes-quebec.qc.ca
Ruth Vachon, Présidente

Réseau national d'action-éducation des femmes (RNAEF)
#302, 450, rue Rideau, Ottawa ON K1N 5Z4
Tél: 613-241-3500; *Téléc:* 613-241-6679
affc@franco.ca
www.affc.ca/rnaef
Obtenir des changements sociaux et économiques qui apporteront une société égalitaire et équitable en privilégiant, chez les femmes francophones du Canada, l'éducation en français sous toutes ses formes pour ainsi améliorer leurs conditions de vie

Saskatchewan Women's Institutes (SWI)
c/o Shirley Wenaas, PO Box 42, Robsart SK S0N 2G0
Tel: 306-299-4520; *Fax:* 306-299-4520
To help discover, stimulate & develop leadership among women; to assist, encourage & support women to become knowledgeable & responsible citizens; to ensure basic human rights for women & to work towards their equality; to be a strong voice through which matters of the utmost concern can reach the decision makers; to promote the improvement of agricultural & other rural communities & to safeguard the environment
Shirley Wenaas, Executive Officer

Society for Canadian Women in Science & Technology (SCWIST) / Société des canadiennes dans la science et la technologie
#471, 411 Dunsmuir St., Vancouver BC V6B 1X4
Tel: 604-893-8657; *Fax:* 604-893-8692
scwist@sfu.ca
www.harbour.sfu.ca/scwist/
To promote equal opportunities for women in scientific, technical & engineering careers; to educate public about careers in science & technology particularly to improve social attitudes on the stereotyping of careers in science; to assist educators by providing current information on careers & career training in sciences & scientific policies
Elana Brief, President

South Asian Women's Centre (SAWC)
8163 Main St., Vancouver BC V5X 3L2
Tel: 604-325-6637; *Fax:* 604-322-6675
sawc@asia.com
www.sawc.8m.com
The South Asian Women's Centre is a space for South Asian women to work actively for social change. The centre strongly believes that women can change their own lives and the lives of others in our communities, in our society, and even globally. The centre supports the development of non-oppressive attitudes and behaviours by critiquing and combating sexism, racism, homophobia, caste/classism, ageism and ableism.

Transition House Association of Nova Scotia (THANS)
#215, 2099 Gottingen St., Halifax NS B3K 3B2
Tel: 902-429-7287; *Fax:* 902-429-0561
coordinator@thans.ca
www.thans.ca
The Transition House Association of Nova Scotia (THANS) member organizations provide transitional services to women (and their children) who are experiencing violence and abuse, including culturally relevant services to Mi'kmaw people. THANS eleven member organizations work with women and their children in thirteen locations across Nova Scotia.
Pamela Harrison, Provincial Coordinator

Western Businesswomen's Association (WBA)
#302, 1107 Homer St., Vancouver BC V6B 2Y1
Tel: 604-688-0951; *Fax:* 604-681-4545
Teena Keizer, Administrator

Women Business Owners of Manitoba (WBOM)
PO Box 2748, Winnipeg MB R3C 4B3
Tel: 204-775-7981; *Fax:* 204-897-8094
info@wbom.ca
www.wbom.ca
Supports & inspires excellence, learning & growth in business
Yvonne Thompson, President
Christine Dubyts, Vice-President
Charlene Hiebert, Treasurer

Women Entrepreneurs of Canada (WEC) / Les Femmes chefs d'entreprises du Canada
Toronto Chapter & Head Office, 202, 720 Spadina Ave., Toronto ON M5S 2T9
Tel: 416-921-5150; *Fax:* 416-929-5256
Toll-Free: 866-207-4439
wec@wec.ca
www.wec.ca
Social Media: www.facebook.com/group.php?gid=5398494151
To bring together all women who own or control an industry, company, retail trade or service entreprise, who have been in business a minimum of four years; to foster communication & trade among members; to represent women entrepreneurs to government & the media; to encourage professional growth & continuing education; to provide networking, social support, advocacy & business opportunities for members
Carissa Reiniger, President

Women on the Rise Telling her story (WORTH)
5775 rue Saint-Jacques, Montréal QC H4A 2E8
Tel: 514-485-7418; *Fax:* 514-485-7418
womenontherise@bellnet.cs
To promote the well-being of women and their children, especially in the Black anglophone community, by offering them self-help activities and encouraging them to develop their potential.
Grace Campbell, Director

Women's Art Association of Canada (WAAC)
23 Prince Arthur Ave., Toronto ON M5R 1B2
Tel: 416-922-2060; *Fax:* 416-922-4657
womensart@bellnet.ca
www.womensartofcanada.ca
To provide scholarships for the arts through the following schools & colleges: The Royal Conservatory of Music of Toronto; The Ontario College of Art; The Faculty of Music, University of Toronto; The National Ballet School; Sheridan College
Karin Ungar, President

Women's Art Resource Centre (WARC)
#122, 401 Richmond St. West, Toronto ON M5V 3A8
Tel: 416-977-0097; *Fax:* 416-977-7425
warc@warc.net
www.warc.net

Women's Centre of Montreal / Centre des femmes de Montréal
3585, rue Saint-Urbain, Montréal QC H2X 2N6
Tél: 514-842-1066; *Téléc:* 514-842-1067
cfmwcm@centredesfemmes.com
www.centredesfemmesdemtl.org
The mission of the Women's Centre of Montréal is to provide services to help women help themselves. To accomplish its mission, the Centre offers educational and vocational training, information, counselling and referral services. The Centre communicates women's concerns to the public and acts as a catalyst for change regarding women's issues.
Johanne Bélisle, Directrice générale

Women's Counselling & Referral & Education Centre (WCREC)
#303B, 489 College St., Toronto ON M6G 1A5
Tel: 416-534-7501
generalmail@wcrec.org; phoneline@wcrec.org; resources@wcrec.org
www.wcrec.org
To promote the mental & emotional well-being of women; To provide free community-based, alternative, non-medical mental health services in Toronto & in other areas through contact by phone & e-mail

Women's Healthy Environments Network
#400, 215 Spadina Ave., Toronto ON M5T 2C7
Tel: 416-928-0880; *Fax:* 416-644-0116
office@womenshealthyenvironments.ca
www.womenshealthyenvironments.ca
To provide a forum for communication; to conduct research on issues relating to women in their environments of planning, health, ecology, workplace design, community development & urban & rural sociology & economy

Women's Institutes of Nova Scotia (WINS)
NSAC, PO Box 550, 35 Rock Garden Rd., Truro NS B2N 5E3
Tel: 902-893-6520; *Fax:* 902-893-6393
wins@gov.ns.ca
www.gov.ns.ca/agri/wi/
To provide women with opportunities to enhance their lives through community service & involvement, education & leadership development
Lauren Seaton, President

Women's Inter-Church Council of Canada (WICC) / Conseil oecuménique des chrétiennes du Canada
47 Queen's Park Cres. East, Toronto ON M5S 2C3
Tel: 416-929-5184; *Fax:* 416-929-4064
wicc@wicc.org
www.wicc.org
To focus on national & international issues affecting women, growth in ecumenism, action for social justice, & the sharing of spirituality & prayer
Janet Anstead, President

Women's International League for Peace & Freedom (WILPF)
#901, 6659 Southoak Cres., Burnaby BC V5E 4M9
Tel: 604-517-0581
joangord@shaw.ca
www.wilpf.int.ch/world/canada.htm
To unite women throughout the world into a force working to put an end to war; to work for social, economic & political equality for all people in all nations.
Ellen Woodsworth, President
Bruna Nota, Vice-President

Women's Legal Education & Action Fund (LEAF) / Fonds d'action et d'éducation juridiques pour les femmes (FAEJ)
#703, 60 St. Clair Ave. East, Toronto ON M4T 1N5
Tel: 416-595-7170; *Fax:* 416-595-7191
Toll-Free: 888-824-5323
info@leaf.ca
www.leaf.ca
The Fund promotes equality for women, primarily by using the gender equality provisions of the Canadian Charter of Rights & Freedoms. It sponsors test cases before the Canadian courts, human rights commissions & government agencies on behalf of women, & provides public education on the issue of gender equality. It is a registered charity, BN: 108219916RR0001.
Jennifer Tomaszewski, Chair
Kate Zavitz, Toronto Contact

Women's Network PEI
PO Box 233, 40 Enman Cres., Charlottetown PE C1A 7K4
Tel: 902-368-5040; *Fax:* 902-368-5039
Toll-Free: 888-362-7373
wnpei@wnpei.org
www.wnpei.org
To strengthen & support the efforts of PEI women to improve their status in society
Michelle MacCallum, Executive Director

Writers & Editors

Association de la presse francophone (APF) / Association of Francophone Newspapers
267, rue Dalhousie, Ottawa ON K1N 7E3
Tél: 613-241-1017; *Téléc:* 613-241-6313
apf@apf.ca
www.apf.ca
Promouvoir l'existence d'une presse communautaire écrite en langue française aussi vigoureuse et aussi répandue que possible dans les communautés de langue française à l'extérieur du Québec; Contribuer à l'amélioration de sa qualité et de son rayonnement; défendre énergiquement les principes de la liberté de parole et de la presse écrite
Francis Potié, Directeur général
Geneviève Gazaille, Directrice, Communications et des relations gouvernementales
Michelle Laliberté, Gestionnaire, Opérations financières
Pascale Castonguay, Coordonnatrice, Service de nouvelles

Canadian Association of Journalists (CAJ) / L'Association canadienne des journalistes
PO Box 36030, 1106 Wellington Ave, Ottawa ON K1Y 4V3
Tel: 613-526-8061; *Fax:* 613-521-3904
caj@caj.ca
www.caj.ca
To promote excellence in journalism; to encourage & promote investigative journalism
Hugo Rodrigues, National Director

Canadian Authors Association (CAA)
74 Mississaga St. East, Orillia ON L3V 1V5
Tel: 705-653-0323; *Toll-Free:* 866-216-6222
admin@canauthors.org
www.canauthors.org
To promote & protect Canadian authors & their works; To act as a voice for writers
Anita Purcell, Interim Executive Director

Canadian Ethnic Media Association (CEMA)
24 Tarlton Rd., Toronto ON M5P 2M4
Tel: 416-260-3625; *Fax:* 416-260-3810
madeline.ziniak@rci.rogers.com
www.canadianethnicmedia.com
To promote & preserve the value of the ethnic media in Canada; To advance understanding of Canada's cultural diversity
Ace Alvarez, President
Madaine Ziniak, Chair
Doreen Vanini, Secretary
Irene Chu, Treasurer

Canadian Farm Writers' Federation (CFWF)
PO Box 250, Ormstown QC J0S 1K0
Fax: 450-829-2226
Toll-Free: 877-782-6456
office@cfwf.ca
www.cfwf.ca
To serve the interests of agricultural journalists
Myrna Stark-Leader, President
Tamara Leigh, Vice-President
Hugh Maynard, Secretary-Treasurer
Christina Franc, Administrator

Canadian Journalism Foundation (CJF) / La Fondation pour le journalisme canadien
117 Peter St., 3rd Fl., Toronto ON M5V 2G9
Tel: 416-955-0394; *Fax:* 416-955-0395
info@cijf-fjc.ca
www.cjf-fjc.ca
To honour outstanding achievements in the field of journalism in Canada through grants, awards & scholarships; to promote & support programs & seminars at or in conjunction with qualified educational institutions in journalism.
Jody Jacobson, Executive Director
Heather McCall, Program Manager

Canadian Science Writers' Association (CSWA) / Association canadienne des rédacteurs scientifiques
PO Box 75, Stn. A, Toronto ON M5W 1A2
Toll-Free: 800-796-8595
office@sciencewriters.ca
www.sciencewriters.ca
To foster excellence in science communication; To increase public awareness of Canadian science & technology
Kristina Bergen, Executive Director
Tim Lougheed, President

Canadian Society of Children's Authors, Illustrators & Performers (CANSCAIP) / La société canadienne des auteurs, illustrateurs et artistes pour enfants
#104, 40 Orchard View Blvd., Toronto ON M4R 1B9
Tel: 416-515-1559
office@canscaip.org
www.canscaip.org
Social Media: www.facebook.com/groups/18960022544; twitter.com/CANSCAIP
To promote the growth of children's literature by establishing the rapport with teachers, librarians & children; to establish communication between publishers & society; to encourage the development of new writers, illustrators & performers
Karen Krossing, President

The Crime Writers of Canada (CWC)
PO Box 113, 3007 Kingston Rd., Toronto ON M1M 1P1
Tel: 416-597-9938
info@crimewriterscanada.com
www.crimewriterscanada.com
To promote Canadian crime writing
Cheryl Freedman, Sec.-Treas.

Editors' Association of Canada (EAC) / Association canadienne des réviseurs (ACR)
#505, 27 Carlton St., Toronto ON M5B 1L2
Tel: 416-975-1379; *Fax:* 416-975-1637
Toll-Free: 866-226-3348
info@editors.ca; webmaster@editors.ca
www.editors.ca; www.reviseurs.ca
Social Media: twitter.com/eac_acr
EAC is a federally incorporated, not-for-profit association that promotes & maintains standards of professional editing & publishing. It sets guidelines to help editors secure fair pay & good working conditions, fosters networking among editors, & cooperates with other publishing associations in areas of common concern.
Michelle Boulton, President
Sheila Mahoney, Secretary & Treasurer
Carolyn L. Burke, Executive Director

Federation of British Columbia Writers (FBCW)
PO Box 3887, Stn. Terminal, Vancouver BC V6B 2Z3
Tel: 604-683-2057
info@bcwriters.ca
www.bcwriters.ca
To develop, support, inform, & promote writers in British Columbia; To foster a community for writing in British Columbia
Sylvia Taylor, Executive Director

Fédération québécoise du loisir littéraire (FQLL)
CP 1000, Succ. M, 4545, av Pierre-de Coubertin, Montréal QC H1V 3R2
Tél: 514-252-3033; *Ligne sans frais:* 866-533-3755
www.litteraire.ca
Offre au grand public l'accès à toutes les formes de l'expression littéraire et artistique dans un contexte de loisir, d'éducation et de perfectionnement
Diane Robert, Présidente

The League of Canadian Poets (LCP)
#312, 192 Spadina Ave., Toronto ON M5T 2C2
Tel: 416-504-1657; *Fax:* 416-504-0096
admin@poets.ca
www.poets.ca
To develop the art of poetry; to enhance the status of poets & nurture a professional poetic community; to facilitate the teaching of Canadian poetry at all levels of education; to enlarge

the audience for poetry by encouraging publication, performance & recognition of poetry nationally & internationally; to uphold freedom of expression
Joanna Poblocka, Executive Director

Manitoba Writers' Guild Inc. (MWG)
#218, 100 Arthur St., Winnipeg MB R3B 1H3
Tel: 204-944-8013
info@mbwriter.mb.ca
www.mbwriter.mb.ca
To provide services & support writers in Manitoba
Darcia Senft, President
Sharron Arksey, Secretary
Mickey Cuthbert, Treasurer

The Ontario Poetry Society (TOPS)
c/o I.B. Iskov, 31 Marisa Ct., Thornhill ON L4J 6H9
Tel: 905-738-0309
ibiskov_tops2000@yahoo.ca
www.theontariopoetrysociety.ca
To establish a democratic organization for members to unite in friendship for emotional support & encouragement in all aspects of poetry, including writing, editing, performing & publishing
Kate Marshall Flaherty, Secretary
Shirley A. McCormick, President
Debbie Okun Hill, Vice-President
Bunny Iskov, Treasurer

Professional Writers Association of Canada (PWAC)
#123, 215 Spadina Ave., Toronto ON M5T 2C7
Tel: 416-504-1645; *Fax:* 416-913-2327
info@pwac.ca
www.pwac.ca
To protect & promote interests of periodical writers in Canada; to develop & maintain professional standards in editor/writer relationships by instituting use of standard publication agreement in all freelance assignments; to improve quality of periodical writing in Canada; to work actively for survival of periodical writing in a highly competitive communications market; to lobby for higher standard fees for freelance magazine & newspaper writing; to mediate grievances between writers & editors; to provide professional development workshops; to lobby for freedom of press & expression; to offset isolation of freelance writers by circulating news, information on market
Tanya Gulliver, President
Sandy Crawley, Executive Director

Québec Writers' Federation (QWF) / Fédération des Écrivaines et Écrivains du Québec
1200, av Atwater, Montréal QC H3Z 1X4
Tel: 514-933-0878
admin@qwf.org
www.qwf.org
The Federation encourages & supports English-language writing in Québec to ensure a lasting place for English literature in the province's cultural scene. It sponsors events, writing programs, & it honours literary excellence through annual awards. The organization is a registered charity, BN: 140319518RR0001.
Elise Moser, President
Lori Schubert, Executive Director

Saskatchewan Writers Guild (SWG)
PO Box 3986, Regina SK S4P 3R9
Tel: 306-757-6310; *Fax:* 306-565-8554
info@skwriter.com
www.skwriter.com
Social Media: www.facebook.com/groups/5067566475; twitter.com/SKWritersGuild
To promote excellence in writing by Saskatchewan writers; to advocate for Saskatchewan writers; to promote the teaching of Saskatchewan & Canadian literature & instruction in the art of writing at all levels of education; to improve public access to writers & their work; to develop professionalism in the business of writing; to improve the economic status of Saskatchewan writers
Judith Silverthorne, Executive Director
Milena Dzordeski, Administrative Assistant

Société des écrivains canadiens (SEC)
#105, 870, av Salaberry, Québec QC G1R 2T9
Tél: 418-843-9816; *Téléc:* 418-843-9816
www.culture-quebec.qc.ca/sec/
Grouper en association les écrivains de langue française, de nationalité canadienne, domiciliés ou non au Canada, auteurs d'un ou de plusieurs livres publiés au Canada ou ailleurs par des éditeurs homologués; servir et défendre les intérêts de la littérature canadienne; prendre toutes les mesures nécessaires ou opportunes pour assurer le respect de la propriété littéraire de ses membres.
Georges Hélal, Président général
Louis Lasnier, Secrétaire général

Société professionnelle des auteurs et des compositeurs du Québec (SPACQ)
#115, 4030, rue St-Ambroise, Montréal QC H4C 2C7
Tél: 514-845-3739; *Téléc:* 514-845-1903
Ligne sans frais: 866-445-3739
info@spacq.qc.ca
www.spacq.qc.ca
Défendre les droits et les intérêts moraux, professionnels et économiques des auteurs et des compositeurs, ainsi que les droits qui se rapportent aux oeuvres, auprès des autorités gouvernementales.
Jean-Christian Céré, Directeur général
Nancy Hamelin, Adjointe comptable
Suzan Thibault, Administratrice de contrats
Mario Chenart, Président

Society of American Travel Writers - Canadian Chapter (SATW)
24 Louisa St., Toronto ON M8V 2K6
Tel: 416-521-7462; *Fax:* 416-521-7467
bea@bcpictures.com
www.satw.ca
Jane Stokes, Chair

Union des écrivaines et écrivains québécois (UNEQ)
La Maison des écrivains, 3492, av Laval, Montréal QC H2X 3C8
Tél: 514-849-8540; *Téléc:* 514-849-6239
Ligne sans frais: 888-849-8540
ecrivez@uneq.qc.ca
www.uneq.qc.ca
Élaborer des politiques et administrer des programmes en vue de favoriser le développement de la littérature québécoise et sa diffusion au Québec comme à l'étranger, en vue également de faire reconnaître la profession d'écrivain de telle sorte que les intérêts moraux, sociaux et économiques des auteurs soient respectés
Stanley Péan, Président
Pierre Lavoie, Directeur général

Writers Association for Resourceful Minds (WARM)
614, rue Martel, Longueuil QC J4J 1C5
Tel: 450-651-7044
warmwriters@yahoo.com
geocities.com/warmwriters
To provide both established authors & aspiring writers in the Montréal area with conferences, seminars & workshops on all aspects of writing both fiction & non-fiction
Jeanette Paul, President
Alex MacLeod, Vice-President
Harry Ghosh, Treasurer

Writers Guild of Alberta (WGA)
Percy Page Centre, 11759 Groat Rd., Edmonton AB T5M 3K6
Tel: 780-422-8174; *Fax:* 780-422-2663
Toll-Free: 800-665-5354
mail@writersguild.ab.ca
www.writersguild.ab.ca
Social Media: www.facebook.com/139496766118754; twitter.com/WritersGuildAB
To provide a meeting ground & collective voice for the writers of Alberta; to promote excellence in writing in Alberta
Carol Holmes, Executive Director
Patricia MacQuarrie, President
Julie Sedivy, Vice-President

Writers Guild of Canada (WGC)
#401, 366 Adelaide St. West, Toronto ON M5V 1R9
Tel: 416-979-7907; *Fax:* 416-979-9273
Toll-Free: 800-567-9974
info@wgc.ca
www.wgc.ca
Voice of professional Canadian screenwriters; to lobby on their behalf; to protect their interests; to raise the profile of screenwriters & screenwriting
Maureen Parker, Executive Director

Writers' Alliance of Newfoundland & Labrador (WANL)
PO Box 2681, Stn. C, #102, 155 Water St., St. John's NL A1C 6K1
Tel: 709-739-5215; *Fax:* 709-739-5931
wanl@nfld.com
www.writersalliance.nf.ca
Social Media: twitter.com/WANL
To enhance the quality of writing in Newfoundland & Labrador through such programmes as workshops, meetings, readings; to encourage & develop public awareness & appreciation for the work of writers in Newfoundland & Labrador
Théa Morash, Executive Director

Writers' Federation of New Brunswick (WFNB)
PO Box 37, Stn. A, Fredericton NB E3B 4Y2
Tel: 506-459-7228; *Fax:* 506-459-7228
wfnb@nb.aibn.com
www.umce.ca/wfnb
To promote New Brunswick writing; to assist writers of New Brunswick at all stages of their development by providing services; to uphold the right to free artistic expression; to provide additional educational services to schools & libraries; to contribute to the enhancement of literary arts
Grace Morris, Secretary
Marilyn Lerch, President
Laurie Glenn Norris, Treasurer
Lee Thompson, Executive Director

Writers' Federation of Nova Scotia (WFNS)
1113 Marginal Rd., Halifax NS B3H 4P7
Tel: 902-423-8116; *Fax:* 902-422-0881
talk@writers.ns.ca
www.writers.ns.ca
Social Media: www.facebook.com/groups/7093286492; twitter.com/WFNS
To foster creative & professional writing; to provide advice & assistance to writers; to encourage greater public recognition of Nova Scotia writers

The Writers' Trust of Canada
#200, 90 Richmond St. East, Toronto ON M5C 1P1
Tel: 416-504-8222; *Fax:* 416-504-9090
info@writerstrust.com
www.writerstrust.com
Is a national charitable organization providing support to writers through various programs & awards; celebrates the talents & achievements of our country's writers; is committed to exploring & introducing to future generations the traditions that will enrich our common literary heritage & strengthen Canada's cultural foundations
Peter Kahnert, Chair
Don Oravec, Executive Director
Amanda Hopkins, Program Coordinator

The Writers' Union of Canada (TWUC)
#200, 90 Richmond St. East, Toronto ON M5C 1P1
Tel: 416-703-8982; *Fax:* 416-504-9090
info@writersunion.ca
www.writersunion.ca
To unite writers for the advancement of their common interests; to foster writing in Canada; to maintain relations with publishers; to exchange information among members; to safeguard the freedom to write & to publish; to advance good relations with other writers & their organizations in Canada & all parts of the world
Erna Paris, Chair
Deborah Windsor, Executive Director

Youth

Black Community Resource Centre (BCRC)
#497, 6767, ch de la Côte-des-Neiges, Montréal QC H3S 2T6
Tel: 514-342-2247; *Fax:* 514-342-2283
bcrc@qc.aira.com
www.bcrcmontreal.com/bcrc/; www.blackyouthproject.org/bcrc/
BCRC is a resource-based organization committed to helping English-speaking visible minority youth rekindle their dreams and achieve their full potential. The Centre takes a comprehensive approach, with a strategy that is progressive, multi-interventionist and holistic; emphasis is on infrastructure support and training, prevention and empowerment, community-building, collaboration, and an inclusive perspective. BCRC has a mandate to provide support services to individuals, communities, para-public and public organizations, and develops and implements health, education, socio-cultural and economic development programs.

Centre Afrika
1644, rue St-Hubert, Montréal QC H2L 3Z3
Tél: 514-843-4019
centreafrika@centreafrika.com
www.centreafrika.com
Activités sociales & culturelles et activités spirituelles/religieuses
Jean-François Bégin

Club Richelieu Boréal de Chibougamau
CP 522, Chibougamau QC G8P 2X9
Tél: 418-748-3008
portail.richelieu.org
Josée Bélanger

Force Jeunesse

#322, 1000, rue Saint-Antoine ouest, Montréal QC H3C 3R7

Tél: 514-384-8666; *Téléc:* 514-384-6442
info@forcejeunesse.qc.ca
www.forcejeunesse.qc.ca

Force Jeunesse est un regroupement de jeunes travailleurs issus de différents milieux dont le principe fondateur est l'équité intergénérationnelle; agit concrètement en revendiquant des mesures qui améliorent la situation économique et sociale des jeunes.
Jonathan Plamondon, Président

Head and Hands / A deux mains

5833, rue Sherbrooke ouest, Montréal QC H4A 1X4

Tel: 514-481-0277; *Fax:* 514-481-2336
info@headandhands.ca
www.headandhands.ca

Medical, social & legal services for youth; Young Parents Program; information & referral
Marlo Turner-Ritchie, Contact

Jeunes canadiens pour une civilisation chrétienne

CP 6453, Succ. A, Toronto ON M5W 1X3

Tél: 418-683-5222

Travailler avec la jeunesse pour préserver les principes catholiques et éducatifs
Sébastien Bolduc

Jeunes en partage

Succ. 204, 2e Avenue, Chibougamau QC G8P 2Z5

Tél: 418-748-2935

Dany Larouche

Richelieu International (RI)

#25, 1010 rue Polytek, Ottawa ON K1J 9J1

Tél: 613-742-6911; *Téléc:* 613-742-6916
Ligne sans frais: 800-267-6525
international@richelieu.org
www.richelieu.org

A pour mission l'épanouissement de la personalité de ses membres & au développement de leurs aptitudes personnelles & collectives; la promotion de la langue française; aider la jeunesse
Laurier Thériault, Directeur général
Denis Daigle, Directeur administratif

SECTION 4
BROADCASTING

The listings in this section are arranged by province, then city within province, except the Major Broadcasting Companies, which are arranged alphabetically by company name.

Major Broadcasting Companies

Arctic Radio
316 Green Street, Flin Flon, MB R8A 0H2
Tel: 204-687-3469; cfar@arcticradio.ca
www.arcticradio.ca
Operates 3 AM Radio stations in Northern Manitoba.
Maureen Kozar, Manager, mkozar@arcticradio.ca

Astral Broadcasting Group Inc.
Also known as: Astral TVPlus
***Owned by:** Astral Media Inc.**
#2000, 2 St-Clair Ave. West, Toronto, ON
Tel: 416-924-6664; *Fax:* 416-924-9031
www.astraltvplus.com
Owns 29 radio stations, including 21 French-language FM stations in Québec

Astral Media Inc.
PO Box 2700, 1800, av McGill College, Montréal, QC H3A 3J6
Tel: 514-939-5000; *Fax:* 514-939-1515
www.astral.com
Canada's largest broadcaster of English-and French-language pay and specialty television services and is currently involved, on its own or with partners, in 20 television services. Astral Media and its television networks also play a vital role as the largest private sector investor in Canadian feature films. Astral Media owns 82 radio stations. Astral Media employs more than 8,000 people at its facilities in Montréal, Toronto, and a number of cities throughout Québec and the Atlantic provinces
André Bureau, Chairman of the Board
Ian Greenberg, President/CEO
Sidney Greenberg, Vice-President

Astral Media Radio Atlantic
***Owned by:** Astral Media Radio Inc.**
206 Rockwood Avenue, Fredericton, NB E3B 2M2
Tel: 506-455-1069; *Fax:* 506-452-2345
www.astral.com
Owns 8 radio stations located in Fredericton, Bathurst, Woodstock and Grand Falls in New Brunswick, and Truro, Nova Scotia. These stations are focused on serving the local communities in which they are based.
André Bureau, Chairman of the Board
Ian Greenberg, President/CEO

Astral Media Radio G.P.
Also known as: Standard Radio Office
***Owned by:** Astral Media Inc.**
435 Bernard Ave., Kelowna, BC V1Y 6N8
Tel: 250-860-8600; *Fax:* 250-860-8856
info@thesun.net; info@silk.fm; info@am1150.ca
www.thesun.net; www.silk.fm; www.am1150.ca
99.9 Sun FM/CHSU-FM; 101.5 Silk FM/CILK-FM; AM 1150/CKFR-AM

Astral Media Radio Inc.
***Owned by:** Astral Media Inc.**
1700, boul René-Lévesque Est, Montréal, QB H2L 4T9
Tel: 514-529-3200;
www.astral.com
Owns 29 radio stations, including 21 French-language FM stations in Québec
Ian Greenberg, President/CEO
André Bureau, Chairman of the Board
Sidney Greenberg, Vice-President

Atlantic Television Network (ATV)
2885 Robie St., Halifax, NS B3K 5Z4
Tel: 902-453-4000; *Fax:* 902-454-3302
admin@atlantistv.eu
atlantictv.net
Social Media: twitter.com/AtlantisATV
The ATV (Atlantic Television Network) launched September 13, 1972. It is an online television network providing 24/7 output

B.C. Ltd.
Corus Conventional Television
***Owned by:** Corus Premium Television Ltd.**
170 Queen St., Kingston, ON K7K 1B2
Tel: 613-544-2340; *Fax:* 613-544-5508
www.corusent.com

Bayshore Broadcasting Corporation
270 Ninth St. East, Owen Sound, ON N4K 5P5
Tel: 519-376-2030; *Fax:* 519-371-4242
bayshore@radioowensound.com
www.radioowensound.com
Bayshore Broadcasting Corporation is an independent broadcaster. It operates radio stations in Grey, Bruce, Simcoe, & Huron counties in southern Ontario. The following stations are operated by Bayshore Broadcasting: 560 CFOS, Mix 106 (CIXK-FM), Country 93 (CKYC-FM), 98 the Beach (CFPS-FM), 97.7 the Beach (CHGB-FM), 104.9 the Beach (CHWC-FM), & Sunshine 89 (89.1 FM).
Doug Caldwell, President

Bell Media Inc.
Headquarters
299 Queen St. West, Toronto, ON M5V 2Z5
Tel: 416-384-8000;
bellmediacommunications@bellmedia.ca
www.bellmedia.ca

Bell Media Radio
***Owned by:** Bell Media Inc.**
299 Queen St. West, Toronto, ON M5V 2Z5
Tel: 416-384-8000;
bellmediacommunications@bellmedia.ca
www.bellmedia.ca

Bell Media Television
***Owned by:** Bell Media Inc.**
299 Queen St. West, Toronto, ON M5V 2Z5
Tel: 416-384-8000;
bellmediacommunications@bellmedia.ca
www.bellmedia.ca
Kevin Crull, President
Gary Anderson, Senior Vice-President
Steven Bickley, Executive Vice-President, Marketing & Business Development

Blackburn Radio Inc.
#204, 700 Richmond St., London, ON N6A 5C7
Tel: 519-679-8680; *Fax:* 519-679-5321
info@630cfco.com
www.blackburnradio.com
Social Media: www.facebook.com/country929cfco, twitter.com/BLACKBURNRADIO
Blackburn Radio is an AM-FM radio broadcaster which operates stations in Chatham, Leamington, London, Sarnia, Windsor, & Wingham.
Richard Costley-White, President/CEO
Ron Dann, General Manager, Sarnia, rdann@blackburnradio.com

Camosun College
3100 Foul Bay Road, Victoria, BC V8P 5J2
Tel: 250-370-3658; *Fax:* 250-370-3679
info@villagenow.net
www.village900.ca
Social Media: www.facebook.com/VillageNow
Village 900 is a non-profit campus/instructional radio station located at Camosun College in Victoria, British Columbia.

Canadian Broadcasting Corporation - Canadian Broadcasting Centre
Société Radio-Canada
***Owned by:** Canadian Broadcasting Corporation**
PO Box 500 A, 250 Front St. West, Toronto, ON M5W 1E6
Tel: 416-205-3311;
Toll-Free: 866-306-4636
cbcinput@cbc.ca
www.cbc.ca
Other information: TDD: 416-205-6688
The CBC is a Canadian crown corporation & serves as Canada's national public radio & television broadcaster; in French, the CBC is called la Société Radio-Canada (SRC), & the corporation also operates Radio Canada International (RCI); offers programming in English, French & 8 Aboriginal languages on radio, & in 9 languages on RCI; provides regional & local television programming in both official languages; broadcasts locally produced programs in English & native languages for people living in the far north; primarily funded by federal statutory grants.
Timothy W. Casgrain, Chair, Board of Directors

Canadian Broadcasting Corporation - Head Office (CBC)
Société Radio-Canada
PO Box 3220 C, 181 Queen St., Ottawa, ON K1Y 1E4
Tel: 613-288-6000;
liaison@cbc.ca
www.cbc.radio-canada.ca
Social Media: www.facebook.com/CBCRadioCanada
CBC/Radio-Canada is Canada's national public broadcaster & one of its largest cultural institutions. Services are offered on radio, television, the Internet, satellite radio, digital audio, as well as through its record & music distribution service & wireless WAP & SMS messaging services.
Timothy W. Casgrain, Chair, Board of Directors
Hubert T. Lacroix, President/CEO, CBC/Radio-Canada

Cégep De Rimouski
60, rue de lévêché Quest, Rimouski, QC G5L 4H6
Tel: 418-723-1880; *Fax:* 418-724-4961
infoscol@cegep-rimouski.qc.ca
www.cegep-rimouski.qc.ca

CKCR-FM
***Owned by:** Astral Media Radio G.P.**
PO Box 1420, #207 - 555 Victoria Rd., Revelstoke, BC V0E 2F0
Tel: 250-837-2149; *Fax:* 250-837-5577
www.revelstoke.myezrock.com

CKIK-FM Ltd.
Corporate Head Office
***Owned by:** Corus Premium Television Ltd.**
#300, 630-3rd Ave. SW, Calgary, AB T2P 4L4
Tel: 403-444-4244; *Fax:* 406-444-4242
www.corusent.com

CKUA Radio Network
10526 Jasper Ave., 4th Fl., Edmonton, AB T5J 1Z7
Tel: 403-428-7595; *Fax:* 403-428-7624
Toll-Free: 800-494-2582
www.ckua.com
CKUA Radio Network operates on the University of Alberta campus in Edmonton. CKUA is Canada's first educational broadcaster & Canada's first public broadcaster, is carried province-wide on AM & FM, & broadcasts in western Canada on some satellite providers & globally through ckua.com.
Ken Regan, General Manager
Wanda Bornn, Sales Manager

CKPR Inc.
87 Hill Street North, Thunder Bay, ON P7A 5V6
Tel: 807-346-2600; *Fax:* 807-345-9923
radio@ckpr.com
www.ckpr.com
A community radio station serving Thunder Bay, Ontario.
Brad Hilgers, Program Director, bhilgers@dougallmedia.com

COGECO Inc.
#100, 612 rue Saint-Jacques, Montréal, QC H3C 5R1
Tél: 450-664-4646; *Téléc:* 450-664-1777
www.cogeco.ca
COGECO is a diversified telecommunication company which strives to meet the communication needs of consumers and advertisers through broadcasting, in Québec and cable distribution in Canada and Portugal. Second largest cable system operator in Ontario, Québec and Portugal, in terms of the number of basic cable service customers served. COGECO is the controlling shareholder of the TQS network serving Québec's major markets in the French language through the operation of nine television stations
Louis Audet, President/CEO
Pierre Gagné, Vice-President/CFO, Finances

Concordia University Centre for Broadcasting Studies
SB-313 1590 Dr. Penfield, Montreal, QC H3G 1C5
Tel: 514-848-2424;
ccbs@alcor.concordia.ca
ccbs.concordia.ca
Operates CJLO, a not-for-profit instructional radio station operating out of the Loyola Campus of Concordia University.

Corus Entertainment Inc.
Corporate Executive Head Office
Corus Quay, 25 Dockside Dr., Toronto, ON M5A 0B5
Tel: 416-479-7000; *Fax:* 416-479-7006
www.corusent.com
Corus Entertainment is one of Canada's most successful integrated media and entertainment companies. Television services include: YTV, Treehouse, W Network, CMT, The Documentary Channel, SCREAM, Discovery Kids, Telelatino and TELETOON (50%); Western Canada's exclusive pay-TV movie service on six thematic channels under the Movie Central brand; three local over-the-air television stations; Corus Custom Networks advertising services for television and Max Trax, a residential subscription digital music service. They also operate 52 radio stations throughout Canada
John Cassady, President, CEO
Tom Peddie, President, Chief Financial Officer

Corus Premium Television Ltd.
***Owned by:** Corus Entertainment Inc.**
Corus Quay, 25 Dockside Dr., Toronto, ON M5A 0B5
Tel: 416-479-7000;
www.corusent.com

† French language station

Corus Radio Company
Owned by: *Corus Entertainment Inc.**
Corus Quay, 25 Dockside Dr., Toronto, ON M5A 0B5
Tel: 416-479-7078; *Fax:* 416-479-7002
www.corusent.com

CTV Inc.
Old Name: **CTVglobemedia Inc.**
Owned by: *Bell Media TV**
PO Box 9 O, Toronto, ON M4A 2M9
Tel: 416-384-5000;
Toll-Free: 866-690-6179
news@ctv.ca
www.ctv.ca
Other information: TTY: 800-461-1542
CTVglobemedia, Canada's largest private broadcaster, offers a wide range of news, sports, information, and entertainment programming, via radio and television; CTVglobemedia's main broadcast media asset is CTV Television Inc.; it also owns CHUM, now called CTV Limited, and operates Toronto radio stations CP24 Radio 1050 (formerly 1050 CHUM), and CHUM-FM; the CHUM Radio Network is a subsidiary of CTVglobemedia, as is The Globe and Mail newspaper.
Ivan Fecan, President/CEO

Dauphin Broadcasting Co. Ltd.
27 - 3 Avenue NE, Dauphin, MB R7N 0Y5
Tel: 204-638-3230; *Fax:* 204-638-8257
ckdm.reception@730ckdm.com
730ckdm.ca
Social Media: www.facebook.com/730CKDM
Operates 730 CKDM, a community radio station serving Dauphin, Manitoba for over 50 years.
Cade Malone, News Director
Christian Laughland, Sports Director

Evanov Radio Group (ERG)
Also known as: Evanov Radio
5312 Dundas St. West, Toronto, ON M9B 1B3
Tel: 416-213-1035; *Fax:* 416-233-8617
info@evanov.radio.com
www.evanovradio.com
Owns 10 radio stations spread across Cetral & Atlantic Canada; promotes independent radio broadcasting

Fairchild Radio
#7-8, 135 East Beaver Creek Rd., Richmond Hill, ON L4B 1E2
Tel: 905-763-3360; *Fax:* 905-889-7553
www.fairchildradio.com
Chinese Canadian multicultural radio network with stations in Toronto, Vancouver, and Calgary. Provides program schedules and internet simulcasting
Thomas Fung, Chairman

Fairchild Television Ltd. (FTV)
Aberdeen Centre, #3300, 4151 Hazelbridge Way, Vancouver, BC V6X 4J7
Tel: 604-295-1313; *Fax:* 604-295-1300
info@fairchildtv.com
www.fairchildtv.com
Provides programming mainly in Cantonese and Mandarin, broadcast through cable and satellite across Canada and part of the U.S.
Joe Chan, President

GlassBox Television Inc.
#400, 130 Merton St., Toronto, ON M4S 1A4
Tel: 416-486-0303; *Fax:* 416-486-0404
glassbox.tv
Raja Khanna, Chief Executive Officer
Jeffrey Elliot, Founder, President & Chief Strategy Officer
Joseph Arcuri, CFO

Global National
Owned by: *Shaw Media Inc.**
7850 Enterprise St., Burnaby, BC V5A 1V7
Tel: 604-420-2288; *Fax:* 604-422-6466
viewers@globalnational.com
www.globalnational.com

Global Television Network
Also known as: GlobalTV
Owned by: *Shaw Media Inc.**
c/o Shaw Media, 121 Bloor St. East, Toronto, ON M4W 3M5
Toll-Free: 877-307-1999
www.globaltv.com
Social Media: twitter.com/Global_TV

Golden West Broadcasting Ltd.
Radio Head Office
#201, 125 Centre Ave., Altona, MB R0G 0B0
Tel: 204-324-6464; *Fax:* 888-765-7039
www.gwm.ca
Headquartered in Altona, Manitoba. Golden West has 28 radio stations scattered across Manitoba, Saskatchewan, and Alberta
Myron Dyck, 866-324-2302, Fax: 204-324-8918
David Wiebe, General Manager

Groupe Radio Antenne 6
568, boul St-Joseph, Roberval, QC G8H 2K6
Tel: 418-275-1831; *Fax:* 418-275-2475
Operates 5 stations in Lac-Saint-Jean region; also has a presence in Abitibi, Outaouais, and Montreal
Marc-André Levesque, President

Groupe TVA inc.
1600, boul de Maisonneuve est, Montréal, QC H2L 4P6
groupetva.ca
Groupe TVA fondée en 1960 sous le nom de Corporation Télé-Métropole inc., est une entreprise de communication intégrée active dans les secteurs de la diffusion, de la production de produits audiovisuels, de la publication de magazines, de l'édition ainsi que de la distribution de films.
Pierre Dion, Président/Chef de la direction
Yves Beaupré, Vice-président, Exploitation

Harvard Broadcasting Inc.
2060 Halifax St., Regina, SK S4P 1T7
Tel: 306-546-6200; *Fax:* 306-781-7338
www.harvardbroadcasting.com
Harvard Broadcasting came into being in 1977, when The Hill Companies purchased CKCK-TV, the Regina-based CTV affiliate station. In 1981, Harvard expanded into radio with the purchase of CKRM and CFMQ, also both local stations. Today, Harvard Broadcasting Inc. includes 620 CKRM, Lite 92 FM, and 104.9 The Wolf in Regina and CFEX-FM, X92.9, in Calgary and CFVR-FM in Fort McMurray
Jason Huschi, General Manager, jasonh@harvardbroadcasting.com

Hector Broadcasting Co. Ltd.
Also known as: East Coast FM
84 Provost Street, PO Box 519, New Glasgow, NS B2H 5E7
Tel: 902-752-4200; *Fax:* 902-755-2468
info@ecfm.com
ecfm.ca
Operates 1320 CKEC, a community radio station serving Pictou County, NS

Home & Garden Television Canada (HGTV)
Also known as: HGTV
Owned by: *Shaw Media Inc.**
#200, 121 Bloor St. East, Toronto, ON M4W 3M5
Tel: 416-967-3246; *Fax:* 416-967-0971
www.hgtv.ca
Social Media: www.facebook.com/hgtv.ca, twitter.com/hgtvcanada

Inuit Broadcasting Corporation (IBC)
Administrative Office
#301, 331 Cooper St., Ottawa, ON K2P 0G5
Tel: 613-235-1892; *Fax:* 613-230-8824
info@inuitbroadcasting.ca
www.inuitbroadcasting.ca
The Inuit Broadcasting Corporation provides a window to the Arctic by producing television programming by Inuit, for Inuit. IBC has 5 production centres scattered across Nunavut, with 34 Inuit staff at every level of the production chain, from director of network programming to technical producer to administrative assistant. IBC is a founding member of Television Northern Canada & the Aboriginal Peoples Television Network.
Debbie Brisebois, Executive Director

Island Radio Ltd.
Old Name: **Central Island Broadcasting Ltd.**
4550 Willingdon Rd., Nanaimo, BC V9T 2H3
Tel: 250-758-1131; *Fax:* 250-758-4644
info@islandradio.bc.ca
www.islandradio.bc.ca
Island Radio consists of six radio stations on Vancouver Island, British Columbia
Paul Larsen, President

The Jim Pattison Broadcast Group
460 Pemberton Terrace, Kamloops, BC V2C 1T5
Tel: 250-372-3322; *Fax:* 250-374-0445
info@jpbroadcast.com
www.jpbroadcast.com
The Jim Pattison Broadcast Group is Canada's largest private western-based broadcasting company
Rick Arnish, President
Joel Simmons, Technical Director
Bruce Davis, VP Sales

Klondike Broadcasting Ltd.
203-4103 4th Avenue, Whitehorse, YK Y1A 1H6
Tel: 867-668-6100; *Fax:* 867-668-4209
Toll-Free: 867-668-6100
admin@ckrw.com
www.ckrw.com
Operates CKRW-FM in Whitehorse, YK.
Jennifer Johnstone, General Manager, ckrwcopy@ckrw.com
Eva Birdman, Sales & Ad Copy, marketing@ckrw.com

Learning Skills Television of Alberta
Also known as: ACCESS - The Education Station
3720 - 76 Ave., Edmonton, AB T6B 2N9
Tel: 780-440-7777; *Fax:* 780-440-8899
Toll-Free: 800-828-2298
access@incentre.net
www.accesslearning.com
Social Media: twitter.com/AccessLearning
Television broadcasting and multimedia learning company based in Edmonton, AB. Established in 1994 to privatize Alberta's provincial educational television service. LTA is the designated educational broadcasting Authority for Alberta as defined in the Broadcasting Act
Ronald Keast, President
Peter Palframan, Vice-President, Finance & Administration

Mainstream Broadcasting Corporation
#100-1200 West 73rd Avenue, Vancouver, BC V6P 6G5
Tel: 604-263-1320; *Fax:* 604-261-0310
www.am1320.com
Social Media: www.facebook.com/AM1320, twitter.com/AM1320chmb
Mainstream Broadcasting Corporation is a British Columbia media company owned and operated by local Vancouver resident and businessman, James Ho. In 1993, OCV programming was incorporated into the multicultural AM radio station of CHMB AM 1320, serving the needs of Vancouver's multicultural community.
James Ho, President
Teresa Wat, CEO/COO
George Feng, VP Business Development

Maritime Broadcasting System
5121 Sackville St., Halifax, NS B3J 1K1
Tel: 902-425-1225; *Fax:* 902-423-2093
mail@mbsradio.com
www.mbsradio.com
Originally established in 1969 as Eastern Broadcasting Limited, MBS Radio is a 100% maritime owned, private broadcasting company, with 25 radio stations and 410 employees serving communities in the three Maritime Provinces of Nova Scotia, New Brunswick and Prince Edward Island
Merv Russell, President

NewCap Inc.
745 Windmill Rd., Dartmouth, NS B3B 1C2
Tel: 902-468-7557; *Fax:* 902-468-7558
ncc@newcapradio.com
www.ncc.ca
NewCap is one of Canada's leading radio broadcasters with 76 licences across Canada
Robert G. Steele, President & CEO
David J. Murray, COO
Scott Weatherby, CFO & Corporate Secretary

Newfoundland Broadcasting Co. Ltd.
PO Box 2020, 446 Logy Bay Rd., St. John's, NL A1C 5S2
Tel: 709-722-5015; *Fax:* 709-726-5017
greetings@ntv.ca
www.ntv.ca
Reaches 8 million households across Canada via digital cable & satellite

Okalakatiget Society
PO Box 160, Nain, NL A0P 1L0
Tel: 709-922-2955; *Fax:* 709-922-2293
www.oksociety.com
The OKalaKatiget Society was incorporated in 1982. Stationed in Nain, Labrador the Society provides a regional, native communication service for the people on the North Coast and the Lake Melville region of Labrador. People have come to rely on the Society for information and entertainment via radio and television. Their mandate is to preserve and promote the language and culture of the Inuit within the region
Sarah Leo, Exec. Director

† French language station

Quinte Broadcasting Co. Ltd.
PO Box 149, 10 Front St. South, Belleville, ON K8N 4Z9
Tel: 613-969-5555; *Fax:* 613-969-8122
www.quinteradio.com
Myles Morton, President
Stephen Morton, Community Programming Director
Virginia Porter, Manager

Radio Canada International
Owned by: *Canadian Broadcasting Corporation**
1400, boul René-Lévesque est, Montréal, QC H2L 2M2
Tel: 514-597-7500; *Fax:* 514-597-6607
www.rcinet.ca
Social Media: www.facebook.com/CBCRadioCanada, twitter.com/cbcradiocanada
Radio Canada International has been broadcasting around the World since 1945, with live radio in English, French, Spanish, Portuguese, Arabic, Mandarin, and Russian. RCI's mandate is to increase awareness of Canadian values, as well as its social, economic and cultural activities to specific geographic areas as determined in consultation with the government of Canada. RCI also has the complementary mandate of addressing these same topics to new immigrants to Canada.
Hubert T. Lacroix, President & CEO

RAWLCO Radio Ltd.
715 Saskatchewan Cres. West, Saskatoon, SK S7M 5V7
Tel: 306-934-2222; *Fax:* 306-477-0002
www.rawlco.com
Rawlco Radio Ltd. is a Saskatchewan company with radio stations in Saskatoon, Regina, Prince Albert, North Battleford, and Meadow Lake. Operates 12 radio stations
Michael Zaplitny, Vice-President

RNC MEDIA Inc.
Old Name: **Radio Nord Communications inc.**
#1523, 1, Place Ville Marie, Montréal, QC H3B 2B5
Tél: 514-866-8686; *Téléc:* 514-866-8056
www.rncmedia.ca
Radiodiffusion (Planète Radio, Radio X); télédiffusion (TVA Gatineau-Ottawa et Abitibi-Témiscamingue; TQS Gatineau-Ottawa et Abitibi-Témiscamingue; SRC Abitibi-Témiscamingue); programmation de haute qualité et services de publicité.
Raynald Brière, Président/Chef de la direction, rbriere@rncmedia.ca
Pierre R. Brosseau, Président exécutif du conseil, pbrosseau@rncmedia.ca

Rogers Broadcasting Ltd.
777 Jarvis St., Toronto, ON M4Y 3B7
Tel: 416-935-8200; *Fax:* 416-935-8202
www.rogers.com
Rogers Broadcasting has 46 AM and FM radio stations across Canada. Television properties include Toronto multicultural television broadcasters OMNI.1 (CFMT) and OMNI.2, televised and electronic shopping service, The Shopping Channel, Rogers Sportsnet and manages two digital television services
Anthony P. Viner, President/CEO
Chuck McCoy, Exec. Vice-President, Programming

Saskatoon Media Group
Old Name: **Hildebrand Communications**
366 - 3 Ave. South, Saskatoon, SK S7K 1M5
Tel: 306-244-1975;
www.saskatoonhomepage.ca
Operates 600 CJWW out of Saskatoon.
Vic Dubois, General Manager
Ken McFarlane, General Sales Manager
Myles Myrol, Retail Sales Manager

Seneca College
1750 Finch Avenue East, Toronto, ON M2J 2X5
Tel: 416-491-5050; *Fax:* 416-493-3958
www.senecac.on.ca
Home of Radio CS, a not-for-profit instructional radio station.
Dr. Rick Miner, President
Jean Anne McLeod BA, Chair of the Board of Governors

Shaw Communications Inc.
Also known as: Shaw Cablesystems
Old Name: **Rogers Cablesystems**
www.shaw.ca
Social Media: www.facebook.com/shaw, twitter.com/shawinfo
Brad Shaw, Chief Executive Officer

Shaw Media Inc.
Also known as: Shaw Cable
#900, 630 - 3rd Ave. SW, Calgary, AB T2P 4L4
Tel: 403-750-4500; *Fax:* 403-750-4501
Toll-Free: 888-750-7429
www.shaw.ca
Shaw Communications Inc. is a diversified communications company. Its core business is the provision of broadband cable television, high-speed Internet, digital phone, telecommunications services, & satellite direct-to-home services to more than 3 million customers throughout Canada.
J.R. Shaw, Executive Chair
Peter Bissonnette, President & CEO

Showcase Television Inc.
Owned by: *Shaw Media Inc.**
#200, 121 Bloor St. East, Toronto, ON M4W 3M5
www.showcase.ca

Société Radio-Canada
Radio-Canada
Détenteur: *Canadian Broadcasting Corporation**
1400, boul René-Lévesque est, Montréal, QC H2L 2M2
Tél: 514-597-6000; *Téléc:* 514-597-5545
Ligne san frais: 866-306-4636
auditoire@radio-canada.ca
www.radio-canada.ca
Médias sociaux: www.facebook.com/CBCRadioCanada
Radio-Canada est le radiodiffuseur public national du Canada et l'une des plus grandes institutions culturelles du pays. Avec ses 28 services offerts sur des plateformes comme la radio, la télévision, Internet, la radio par satellite, l'audio numérique, sans compter son service de distribution de disques et de musique et ses services de messagerie sans fil WAP et SMS, CBC/Radio-Canada est maintenant accessible aux Canadiens à leur convenance.
Hubert T. Lacroix, Président/Chef de la direction, CBC/Radio-Canada

Steele Communications
PO Box 8-590, 391 Kenmount Rd., St. Johns, NL A1B 3P5
Tel: 709-726-5590; *Fax:* 709-726-4633
www.vocm.com
Steele Communications is the broadcast leader in Newfoundland and Labrador, with a network of 26 radio licenses across the province. Providing both AM and FM networks in a variety of formats, delivering to listeners, consistent quality programming with a local focus
Greg Hinton, VP/General Manager

Télé Inter-Rives ltée
Inter-Riverbank Television
15, rue de la Chute, Rivière-du-Loup, QC G5R 5B7
Tél: 418-867-8080; *Téléc:* 418-867-4710
Tele Inter-Rives Ltd. dirige 4 stations de télévision régionales dans l'est du Québec; CKRT-TV (SRC), CIMT-TV, CHAU (TVA), et CFTF (V).

Télé-Québec
Also known as: Société de télédiffusion du Québec
1000, rue Fullum, Montréal, QC H2K 3L7
Tél: 514-521-2424; *Téléc:* 514-873-2601
info@telequebec.tv
www.telequebec.tv
La Société a pour objet d'exploiter une entreprise de télédiffusion éducative et culturelle afin d'assurer, par tout mode de diffusion, l'accessibilité de ses produits au public. Télé-Québec est une société publique de production et de diffusion, desservant plus de 92 % de la population québécoise à travers son réseau riche de 17 émetteurs, alimenté par un lien satellite portant sa programmation de Montréal.
Michèle Fortin, Présidente/Directrice générale

TELETOON Canada Inc.
Owned by: *Corus Entertainment Inc.**
Brookfield Place, PO Box 787, 181 Bay St., Toronto, ON M5J 2T3
Tel: 416-956-2060; *Fax:* 416-956-2070
www.teletoon.com
Len Cochrane, President
Darrell Atherley
Leslie Krueger
Carole Bonneau
Trent Locke

TVOntario (OECA)
Also known as: Ontario Educational Communications Authority
PO Box 200 Q, 2180 Yonge St., Toronto, ON M4T 2T1
Tel: 416-484-2600; *Fax:* 416-484-6285
Toll-Free: 800-613-0513
ww3.tvo.org
Social Media: twitter.com/tvo
In 1970, TVOntario was established as the Ontario Educational Communications Authority (OECA) by the government of Ontario, for the purpose of using technology to support the province's education priorities. TVO, TVOntario's English-language service, is Canada's oldest educational broadcaster, and is available to over 98% of Ontario homes. TVO provides educational programming and online resources that enhance and extend learning at home and in the classroom, as well as promoting Ontario's rich cultural identity
Lisa de Wilde, CEO

V
Also known as: V Télé
Old Name: **TQS inc.**
85, rue St-Paul ouest, Montréal, QC H3C 5R1
Tél: 514-390-6100; *Téléc:* 514-390-6056
vtele.ca
Médias sociaux: www.facebook.com/vtele.ca, twitter.com/vtele
René Guimond, President/CEO
Monique Lacharité, Exec. Vice-President, Finance & Administration

Vista Broadcasting Group
Also known as: Vista Radio
130 Trans Canada Hwy., Duncan, BC V9L 3P7
Tel: 250-746-0897;
www.vistaradio.ca
Margot M. Micallef, President & Chief Executive Officer
Bryan Edwards, Sr. Executive Vice President, Business Development
Paul Mann, Sr. Executive Vice President, Sales & Training

VOCM Radio Newfoundland Ltd.
Owned by: *NewCap Inc.**
PO Box 8-590, 391 Kenmount Rd., St. John's, NL A1B 3P5
Tel: 709-726-5590; *Fax:* 709-726-4633
www.vocm.com

Wawatay Native Communications Society
PO Box 1180, 16 Fifth Ave., Sioux Lookout, ON P8T 1B7
Tel: 807-737-2951; *Fax:* 807-737-3224
Toll-Free: 800-243-9059
christinec@wawatay.on.ca
www.wawataynews.ca
Social Media: www.facebook.com/wawataynews, twitter.com/wawataynews
Wawatay Native Communications Society is a self-governing, independent community-driven entrepreneurial native organization dedicated to using appropriate technologies to meet the communication needs of people of Aboriginal ancestry in Northern Ontario
David Neegan, CEO, davidn@wawatay.on.ca

Wawatay Radio Network
Owned by: *Wawatay Native Communications Society**
PO Box 1180, 16 Fifth Ave., Sioux Lookout, ON P8T 1B7
Tel: 807-737-2951; *Fax:* 807-737-3224
Toll-Free: 800-243-9059
www.wawataynews.ca
Jerry Sawanas, Radio Programming Coordinator, jerrys@wawatay.on.ca
Bill Morris, Broadcaster & Producer, billm@wawatay.on.ca

YTV Canada Inc.
Owned by: *Corus Entertainment Inc.**
#18, 64 Jefferson Ave., Toronto, ON M6K 3H3
Tel: 416-534-1191;
www.ytv.com
Paul Robertson, President

AM Radio Stations

Alberta

Athabasca: **CKBA-AM** (Freq: 850)
Owned by: *NewCap Inc.**
#1, 4907 - 49 St., Athabasca, AB T9S 1C2
Tel: 780-675-5301, *Fax:* 780-675-4938
www.941theriver.ca
Mark Maheau, Vice-President

** For details on this company see listing in Major Broadcasting Companies section; † French language station*

***Blairmore:* CJEV** (Freq: 1340)
Owned by: *NewCap Inc.**
PO Box 840, 13213 - 20 Ave., Blairmore, AB T0K 2E2
Tel: 403-562-2806, *Fax:* 403-562-8114

***Brooks:* CIBQ-AM** (Freq: 1340)
Owned by: *NewCap Inc.**
PO Box 180, #8, 403 - 2nd Ave. West, Brooks, AB T1R 0S3
Tel: 403-362-3418, *Fax:* 403-362-8168
q1057@newcap.ca
www.q1057.ca
John Petrie, Station Manager

***Calgary:* CBR** (Freq: 1010)
Owned by: *Canadian Broadcasting Corporation**
PO Box 2640 D, 1724 Westmount Blvd. NW, Calgary, AB T2P 2M7
Tel: 403-521-6000,
www.cbc.ca/calgary

***Calgary:* CFAC-AM** (Freq: 960)
Owned by: *Rogers Broadcasting Ltd.**
#240, 2723 - 37 Ave. NE, Calgary, AB T1Y 5R8
Tel: 403-246-9696,
www.sportsnet.ca/960
Social Media: www.facebook.com/sportsnet960
Kelly Kirch, Program Director

***Calgary:* CFFR-AM** (Freq: 660)
Owned by: *Rogers Broadcasting Ltd.**
2723 - 37 Ave. NE, Calgary, AB T1Y 5R8
Tel: 403-291-0000, *Fax:* 403-291-4368
tips@660news.com
www.660news.com

***Calgary:* CHQR-AM** (Freq: 770)
Owned by: *CKIK-FM Limited**
#105, 630 - 3 Ave. SW, Calgary, AB T2P 4L4
Tel: 403-716-6500, *Fax:* 403-716-2111
Toll-Free: 800-563-7770
www.am770chqr.com
John Vos, Program Director

***Calgary:* CKMX-AM** (Freq: 1060)
Owned by: *Astral Media Radio G.P.**
#300, 1110 Centre St. NE, Calgary, AB T2E 2R2
Tel: 403-240-5800, *Fax:* 403-240-5801
www.classiccountryam1060.com

***Camrose:* CFCW** (Freq: 790)
Owned by: *NewCap Inc.*
5708 - 48 Ave., Camrose, AB
Tel: 780-672-8255
Randy Lemay, General Manager, rlemay@newcap.ca

***Drumheller:* Q91 Country** (Freq: 910)
Owned by: *NewCap Inc.**
PO Box 1480, 515 Hwy. 10 East, Drumheller, AB T0J 0Y0
Tel: 403-823-3384, *Fax:* 403-823-7241
Q91@newcap.ca
www.q91country.com
Social Media:
www.facebook.com/pages/Q91-Country-AM-910/79998194149
Linda Scheffelmaier, Station Manager, 403-823-3384, lindas@newcap.ca

***Edmonton:* CBX** (Freq: 740)
Owned by: *Canadian Broadcasting Corporation**
123 Edmond City Centre, 10062-102 Ave., Edmonton, AB T5J 2Y8
Tel: 780-468-7500,
www.cbc.ca/edmonton
Judy Piercey, Managing Director, 780-468-7526

***Edmonton:* CFCW-AM** (Freq: 790)
Owned by: *NewCap Inc.**
2394 West Edmonton Mall (Entrance 55), 8882 - 170 St., Edmonton, AB T5T 4M2
Tel: 780-468-3939, *Fax:* 780-435-0844
www.cfcw.com
Randy Lemay, General Manager, rlemay@newcap.ca

***Edmonton:* CFRN-AM** (Freq: 1260)
Owned by: *Astral Media Radio G.P.**
#100, 18520 Stony Plain Rd., Edmonton, AB T5S 2E2
Tel: 780-486-2800, *Fax:* 780-489-6927
ldickau@astral.com
www.theteam1260.com
Social Media: www.facebook.com/TheTeam1260, twitter.com/TheTeam1260
Pat Cardinal, General Manager, pcardinal@astral.com

***Edmonton:* CHED-AM** (Freq: 630)
Owned by: *Corus Premium Television Ltd.**
5204 - 84 St., Edmonton, AB T6E 5N8
Tel: 780-440-6300, *Fax:* 780-469-5937
info@630ched.com
www.630ched.com
Bob Layton, News Director, blayton@630ched.com
Daryl Hooke, Director of Client Services, daryl.hooke@corusent.com

***Edmonton:* CHQT-AM** (Freq: 880)
Owned by: *Corus Radio Company**
5204 - 84 St., Edmonton, AB T6E 5N8
Tel: 780-440-6300, *Fax:* 780-469-5937
News@iNews880.com
www.inews880.com
Syd Smith, Program Director, ssmith@630ched.com

***Edson:* CJYR-AM** (Freq: 970)
Owned by: *NewCap Inc.**
PO Box 7800, 4813 - 4th Ave., Edson, AB T7E 1V8
Tel: 780-723-4461, *Fax:* 780-723-3765

***High Prairie:* CKVH-AM** (Freq: 1020)
Owned by: *NewCap Inc.**
PO Box 2219, High Prairie, AB T0G 1E0
Tel: 780-523-5111, *Fax:* 780-523-3360
ckvh@ab.ncc.ca

***High River:* CHRB-AM** (Freq: 1140)
Owned by: *Golden West Broadcasting Ltd.**
11 - 5th Ave. SE, High River, AB T1V 1G2
Tel: 403-652-2472, *Fax:* 403-652-7861
Toll-Free: 866-652-2472
am1140@am1140.com
www.am1140radio.com
Don McCracker, Sports Director

***Lethbridge:* CLCC-AM** (Freq: closed circuit)
Owned by: *Lethbridge College*
Student Service Centre, 3000 College Dr. South, Lethbridge, AB T1K 1L6
Tel: 413-320-3373

***Peace River:* CKYL-AM** (Freq: 610)
Peace River Office
PO Box 300, 9807-100th Ave., Peace River, AB T8S 1T5
Tel: 780-624-2535, *Fax:* 780-624-5424
Toll-Free: 800-610-3610
www.ylcountry.com
Chris Black, General Manager, 780-681-4230
Rod Webb, 780-618-7629

***Stettler:* CKSQ** (Freq: 1400)
Owned by: *NewCap Inc.**
PO Box 2050, 4812A - 50th St., Stettler, AB T0C 2L0
Tel: 403-742-2930, *Fax:* 403-742-0660
www.q14country.com
Vicki Leuck, General & Sales Manager

***Wainwright:* CKKY** (Freq: 830)
Owned by: *NewCap Inc.**
1037 - 2nd Ave.. 2nd Fl., Wainwright, AB T9W 1K7
Tel: 780-842-4311, *Fax:* 780-842-4636
Chad Tabish, General Manager, ctabish@newcap.ca
Hugh MacDonald, hmacdonald@newcap.ca

***Westlock:* CKWB** (Freq: 97.9)
Owned by: *NewCap Inc.**
#17, 10030 - 106 St., Westlock, AB T7P 2K4
Tel: 780-349-4421, *Fax:* 780-349-6259
www.979therange.ca
Wray Betts, Station Manager
Dave Schuk, General Manager, dave@theeagle.ca

***Wetaskiwin:* CKJR** (Freq: 1440)
Owned by: *NewCap Inc.**
5214A - 50 Ave., Wetaskiwin, AB T9A 0S8
Tel: 780-352-0144, *Fax:* 780-352-5656
Toll-Free: 866-352-3555
www.w1440.com
Larry Donohue, Program Director, 780-490-2487, ldonohue@newcap.com

British Columbia

***Burns Lake:* CFLD** (Freq: 760)
Owned by: *CFBV*
PO Box 600, Burns Lake, BC V0J 1E0
Tel: 250-692-3414

***Dawson Creek:* CJDC-AM** (Freq: 890)
Owned by: *Astral Media Radio G.P.**
901 - 102 Ave., Dawson Creek, BC V1G 2B6
Tel: 250-782-3341, *Fax:* 250-782-3154
jlaing@astral.com
www.cjdccountry.com
Tracy Gard

***Fort St. James:* CIFL-AM** (Freq: 94.7)
Owned by: *CIVH-AM*
Fort St. James, BC

***Golden:* CKGR-FM** (Freq: 1400)
Owned by: *Astral Media Radio G.P.**
PO Box 1403, 825 - 10th Ave. South, Golden, BC V0A 1H0
Tel: 250-344-7177, *Fax:* 250-344-8138
myezrock.com

***Granisle:* The Peak** (Freq: 1480)
Owned by: *CIRX-FM*
Granisle, BC
thepeak@thepeak.ca
www.thepeak.ca

***Kamloops:* CHNL-AM** (Freq: 610)
611 Lansdowne St., Kamloops, BC V2C 1Y6
Tel: 250-372-2292, *Fax:* 250-372-2293
info@radionl.com
www.radionl.com
Robbie Dunn, General Manager, rdunn@radionl.com
Jim Reynolds, Manager, Operations, programming@radionl.com
Peter Angle, Manager, Sales, advertising@radionl.com

***Kelowna:* CKFR-AM** (Freq: 1150)
Owned by: *Astral Media Radio G.P.**
#300, 435 Bernard Ave., Kelowna, BC V1Y 6N8
Tel: 250-860-8600, *Fax:* 250-880-8856
info@am1150.ca
www.am1150.ca
Paul Brain, Creative Director, pbrain@astral.com
Jeff Winskell, Brand Director, jwinskell@astral.com

***Osoyoos:* CJOR-AM** (Freq: 1240)
Owned by: *Astral Media Inc.*
Osoyoos, BC

***Penticton:* CKOR-AM** (Freq: 800)
Owned by: *Astral Media Radio G.P.*
33 Carmi Ave., Penticton, BC V2A 3G4
Tel: 250-492-2800, *Fax:* 250-493-0370
Mark Burley, Brand Director, mburley@astral.com
Janet Burley, General Manager, Sales Manager, jburley@astral.com

***Port Hardy:* The Port 1240 AM** (Freq: 1240)
Owned by: *Vista Radio**
7035 A Market St., Port Hardy, BC V0N 2P0
Tel: 250-949-6500, *Fax:* 250-949-6580
onair@theport.ca
www.theport.ca
Doug Zackodnik, Coast Group General Manager, doug@jetfm.ca
Greg Phelps, Operations Manager

***Richmond:* CISL-AM** (Freq: 650)
Owned by: *Astral Media Radio G.P.**
#20, 11151 Horseshoe Way, Richmond, BC V7A 4S5
Tel: 604-280-0650, *Fax:* 604-272-0917
rstanton@astral.com
www.am650radio.com

***Richmond:* CJVB** (Freq: 1470; Fairchild Radio Group)
Owned by: *Fairchild Radio**
#2090, 4151 Hazelbridge Way, Richmond, BC V6X 4J7
Tel: 604-295-1234, *Fax:* 604-295-1201
general@am1470.com
www.am1470.com
George Lee, Sr. Vice-President & General Manager

***Smithers:* The Peak** (Freq: 870)
Owned by: *CIRX-FM*
Smithers, BC
thepeak@thepeak.ca
www.thepeak.ca

***Summerland:* CHOR-FM** (Freq: 1450)
Owned by: *Astral Media Radio G.P.*
PO Box 1170, #200,9901 Main St., Summerland, BC V0H 1Z0
Tel: 250-494-0333, *Fax:* 250-493-0370
www.am1450.ca
Mark Burley, Brand Director, mburley@astral.com

** For details on this company see listing in Major Broadcasting Companies section; † French language station*

Janet Burley, General Manager, Sales Manager, jburley@astral.com

***Trail:* CFNI-AM** (Freq: 104.1)
Owned by: *CFPW-FM*
Trail, BC

***Vancouver:* CBU** (Freq: 690)
Owned by: *Canadian Broadcasting Corporation**
PO Box 4600, Vancouver, BC V6B 4A2
Tel: 604-662-6801, *Fax:* 604-662-6088
www.cbc.ca/bc

***Vancouver:* CFTE** (Freq: 1410)
Owned by: *Bell Media Radio**
#300, 380 West 2nd Ave., Vancouver, BC V5Y 1C8
Tel: 604-871-9000, *Fax:* 604-871-2901
www.teamradio.ca
James Stuart, Vice President/General Manager, CHUM Radio Vancouver

***Vancouver:* CHMB** (Freq: 1320)
Owned by: *Mainstream Broadcasting Corp.**
#100, 1200 West 73 Ave., Vancouver, BC V6P 6G7
Tel: 604-263-1320, *Fax:* 604-263-0320
info@am1320.com
www.am1320.com
Wayne Lee, General Manager

***Vancouver:* CHMJ** (Freq: 730)
Owned by: *Corus Radio Company**
#2000, 700 West Georgia St., Vancouver, BC V7Y 1K9
Tel: 604-681-7511, *Fax:* 604-331-2722
programming@am730traffic.com
www.am730traffic.com
Social Media: www.facebook.com/am730traffic, twitter.com/AM730Traffic
Mike Searson, Director of Sales, 604-693-3053

***Vancouver:* CKNW-AM** (Freq: 980)
Owned by: *Corus Premium Television Ltd.**
#2000, 700 West Georgia St., Vancouver, BC V7Y 1K9
Tel: 604-331-2711, *Fax:* 604-331-2722
info@cknw.com
www.cknw.com
J.J. Johnston, General Manager

***Vancouver:* CKST** (Freq: 1040)
Owned by: *Bell Media Radio**
#300, 380 West 2nd Ave., Vancouver, BC V5Y 1C8
Tel: 604-871-9000, *Fax:* 604-871-2901
www.teamradio.ca
Social Media: twitter.com/TEAM1040
James Stuart, Vice President/General Manager, CHUM Radio Vancouver

***Vancouver:* CKWX** (Freq: 1130)
Owned by: *Rogers Broadcasting Ltd.**
2440 Ash St., Vancouver, BC V5Z 4J6
Tel: 604-873-2599, *Fax:* 604-873-0877
news1130@news1130.rogers.com
www.news1130.com
Social Media: www.facebook.com/News1130, twitter.com/news1130radio

***Vanderhoof:* CIFJ-AM** (Freq: 95.9)
Owned by: *CIVH-AM*
Vanderhoof, BC

***Victoria:* C-FAX** (Freq: 1070)
Owned by: *Bell Media Radio**
1420 Broad St., Victoria, BC V8W 2B1
Tel: 250-920-4616, *Fax:* 250-920-4633
sonia.lowe@bellmedia.ca
www.cfax1070.com
Social Media: www.facebook.com/cfax1070, twitter.com/cfax1070
Kevin Bell, General Manager, 250-920-4613, kevin.bell@bellmedia.ca
Alan Brown, Senior Account Manager

***Victoria:* CKMO** (Freq: 900)
Owned by: *Camosun College**
3100 Foul Bay Rd., Victoria, BC V8P 5J2
Tel: 250-370-3658, *Fax:* 250-370-3679
info@villagenow.net
www.villagenow.net
Social Media: www.facebook.com/VillageNow, twitter.com/VillageNowNet
Doug Ozeroff, General Manager

***White Rock:* KARI** (Freq: 550)
PO Box 75150, White Rock, BC V4B 5L3
Toll-Free: 866-901-1885
info@kari55.com
www.kari55.com

Manitoba

***Altona:* CFAM-AM** (Freq: 950)
Owned by: *Golden West Broadcasting Ltd.**
#201, 125 Centre Ave., Altona, MB R0G 0B0
Tel: 204-324-6464, *Toll-Free:* 800-374-3315
cfam@goldenwestradio.com
www.cfamradio.com

***Boissevain:* CJRB-AM** (Freq: 1220)
Owned by: *Golden West Broadcasting Ltd.**
Boissevain, MB
Elmer Hildebrand, President & CEO

***Brandon:* CKLQ-AM** (Freq: 880)
Owned by: *Westman Communications Group*
624 - 14 St. East, Brandon, MB R7A 7E1
Tel: 204-725-0515, *Fax:* 204-726-1270
qcountry@cklq.mb.ca
www.cklq.mb.ca
David Baxter, President
Don Kille, General Manager

***Dauphin:* CKDM-AM** (Freq: Broadcasting classic rock, adult contemporary & new country music at 730 AM in Dauphin)
Owned by: *Dauphin Broadcasting Co. Ltd.**
27 - 3rd Ave., Dauphin, MB R7N 0Y5
Tel: 204-638-3230, *Fax:* 204-638-8257
Toll-Free: 866-997-2536
ckdm.reception@730ckdm.com
www.730ckdm.ca
Allan Truman, General Manager

***Flin Flon:* CFAR-AM** (Freq: 590)
Owned by: *Arctic Radio**
316 Green St., Flin Flon, MB R8A 0H2
Tel: 204-687-3469, *Fax:* 204-687-6786
cfar@arcticradio.ca
www.arcticradio.ca

***Portage la Prairie:* CFRY-AM** (Freq: 920)
Owned by: *Golden West Broadcasting Ltd.**
PO Box 920, 350 River Rd., Portage la Prairie, MB R1N 0N6
Tel: 204-239-5111,
wneufeld@goldenwestradio.com
www.cfryradio.ca

***The Pas:* CJAR** (Freq: 1240)
Owned by: *Arctic Radio**
PO Box 2980, 130 - 3rd St. West, The Pas, MB R9A 1R7
Tel: 204-623-5307, *Fax:* 204-623-5337
cjar@arcticradio.ca
www.thepasonline.com

***Thompson:* CHTM** (Freq: 610)
Owned by: *Arctic Radio**
103 Cree Rd., Thompson, MB R8N 0B9
Tel: 204-778-7361, *Fax:* 204-778-5252
chtm@arcticradio.ca
www.thompsononline.ca
Social Media: www.facebook.com/610CHTM, twitter.com/610CHTM

***Winkler:* CKMW-AM** (Freq: 1570)
Owned by: *Golden West Broadcasting Ltd.**
277 1st, Winkler, MB R6W 4A6
Tel: 800-355-7065,
bhildebrand@goldenwestradio.com
www.ckmwradio.com

***Winnipeg:* CBW** (Freq: 990)
Owned by: *Canadian Broadcasting Corporation**
PO Box 160, 541 Portage Ave., Winnipeg, MB R3C 2H1
Tel: 204-788-3222, *Fax:* 204-788-3227
www.cbc.ca/manitoba
Leona Johnson, Communications & Partnerships Executive, 204-788-3124

***Winnipeg:* CFRW-AM** (Freq: 1290)
Owned by: *Bell Media Radio**
1445 Pembina Hwy., Winnipeg, MB R3T 5C2
Tel: 204-477-5120, *Fax:* 204-453-0815
info@cfrw.ca
www.cfrw.ca
Chris Brooke, Program Director
Lorne Anderson, Technical Director

***Winnipeg:* CHFC** (Freq: 1230)
Owned by: *Canadian Broadcasting Corporation**
c/o CBC Winnipeg, 541 Portage Ave., Winnipeg, MB R3B 2G1
Tel: 204-788-3222,
Other information: TTY/Teletypewriter: 866-220-6045
John Bertrand, General Manager

***Winnipeg:* CJOB-AM** (Freq: 680)
Owned by: *Corus Premium Television Ltd.**
#200, 1440 Jack Blick Ave., Winnipeg, MB R3G 0L4
Tel: 204-786-2471, *Fax:* 204-783-4512
www.cjob.com
Kevin Wallace, Program Director, kwallace@cjob.com
Steve Dubois, General Sales Manager, sdubois@cjob.com

***Winnipeg:* CKJS** (Freq: 810)
Owned by: *NewCap Inc.**
520 Corydon Ave., Winnipeg, MB R3L 0P1
Tel: 204-477-1221, *Fax:* 204-453-8244
info@ckjs.com
www.ckjs.com

New Brunswick

***†Bathurst:* CKLE** (Freq: 810)*Détenteur:* **CKLE-FM**
#10, 195, rue Main, Bathurst, NB E2A 1A7
Tél: 506-546-4600, *Téléc:* 506-546-6611
superstation@ckle.fm
www.ckle.fm

***Campbellton:* CKNB-AM** (Freq: 950)
Owned by: *Maritime Broadcasting System**
74 Water St., Campbellton, NB E3N 3G7
Tel: 506-753-4415, *Fax:* 506-789-9505
95cknb.ca
Claude Arseneault, Manager
Mark Firth, Program Director

***Fredericton:* CKHJ-AM** (Freq: 1260)
Owned by: *Astral Media Radio Atlantic Inc.**
206 Rookwood Ave., Fredericton, NB E3B 2M2
Tel: 506-451-9111, *Fax:* 506-452-2345
khjnews@astral.com
www.khj.ca
Pat Brennan, General Manager, 506-452-2334
Ryan Zimmerman, Operations Manager, 506-452-2317

***Moncton:* CBA** (Freq: 1070)
Owned by: *Canadian Broadcasting Corporation**
PO Box 950, 250 University Ave., Moncton, NB E1C 8N8
Tel: 506-853-6666, *Fax:* 506-853-6400
www.cbc.ca/nb
Social Media: twitter.com/cbcnb
Dan Goodyear, Executive Producer, CBC, New Brunswick
Mary-Pat Schutta, Program Manager, CBC, New Brunswick
John Channing, Sales Manager, CBC, New Brunswick

***Saint John:* CFBC** (Freq: 930)
Owned by: *Maritime Broadcasting System**
226 Union St., Saint John, NB E2L 1B1
Tel: 506-658-5100, *Fax:* 506-658-5116
mail@mbsradio.com
www.mbsradio.com

***Sussex:* CJCW** (Freq: 590)
Owned by: *Maritime Broadcasting System**
PO Box 5900, 6 Marble St., Sussex, NB E4E 5M2
Tel: 506-432-2529, *Fax:* 506-433-4900
www.590cjcw.com
Social Media: www.facebook.com/590CJCW

Newfoundland & Labrador

***Carbonear:* CHVO-AM** (Freq: 560)
Owned by: *VOCM Radio Newfoundland Ltd.**
1 CHVO Dr., Carbonear, NL A1Y 1A2
Tel: 709-596-7144, *Fax:* 709-596-8626
Toll-Free: 800-595-1560
www.vocm.com

***Corner Brook:* CBY** (Freq: 990)
Owned by: *Canadian Broadcasting Corporation**
PO Box 610, 162 Premier Dr., Corner Brook, NL A2H 6G1
Tel: 709-637-1151, *Fax:* 709-634-8506
www.cbc.ca/nl

** For details on this company see listing in Major Broadcasting Companies section; † French language station*

***Corner Brook:* CFCB-AM** (Freq: 570)
Owned by: *NewCap Inc.**
PO Box 570, 345 O'Connell Dr., Corner Brook, NL A2H 6H5
Tel: 709-634-4570, *Fax:* 709-634-4081
onair@cfcbradio.com
www.cfcbradio.com
Daryl Stevens, Operation Manager
Darlene Myers, Sales Manager
Mike Murphy, General Manager

***Corner Brook:* CFLW** (Freq: 1340)
Owned by: *Steele Communications**
PO Box 570, 345 O'Connel Dr., Corner Brook, NL A2H 6H5
Tel: 709-282-3601, *Toll-Free:* 800-356-4570
info@bigland.fm
www.bigland.fm
Social Media: twitter.com/biglandfm

***Gander:* CBG-AM** (Freq: 1400)
Owned by: *Canadian Broadcasting Corporation (CBC)**
PO Box 369, Gander, NL A1V 1W7
Tel: 709-256-4311, *Fax:* 709-651-2021
Toll-Free: 800-563-7933
www.cbc.ca/nl; www.cbc.ca/radio
Social Media: www.facebook.com/radiocbc; www.twitter.com/cbcradio,
Other information: Phone, Transmission Information: 1-888-353-7006; TTY: 1-866-220-6045
Maureen Anonsen, Manager, Partnership & Communications
Debbie Hynes, Senior Officer, Communications, 709-576-5150
Wayne Tilley, Manager, Accounts, 709-576-5019

***Grand Falls-Windsor:* CBT-AM** (Freq: 540)
Owned by: *Canadian Broadcasting Corporation (CBC)**
PO Box 218, 2 Harris Ave., Grand Falls-Windsor, NL A2A 2Y2
Tel: 709-489-2102, *Fax:* 709-489-1055
Toll-Free: 800-563-7933
www.cbc.ca/nl; www.cbc.ca/radio
Social Media: www.facebook.com/radiocbc; www.twitter.com/cbcradio,
Other information: Phone, Transmission Information: 1-888-353-7006
Denise Wilson, Managing Director, Newfoundland & Labrador
Kathy Porter, Executive Producer, English Radio
Debbie Hynes, Senior Officer, Communications, 709-576-5150

***Grand Falls-Windsor:* CKCM-AM** (Freq: 620)
Owned by: *NewCap Inc.**
PO Box 620, 35A Grenfell Heights, Grand Falls-Windsor, NL A2A 2K2
Tel: 709-489-2192, *Fax:* 709-489-8626
ckxgnews@vocm.com
www.vocm.com

***Happy Valley-Goose Bay:* CFLN** (Freq: 1230)
Owned by: *NewCap Inc.**
PO Box 160 C, 176 Hamilton River Rd., Happy Valley-Goose Bay, NL A0P 1C0
Tel: 709-896-2968, *Fax:* 709-896-8708

***Marystown:* CHCM-AM** (Freq: 740)
Owned by: *NewCap Inc.**
PO Box 560, Ville Marie Dr., Marystown, NL A0E 2M0
Tel: 709-279-2560,
chcm.sales@vocm.com
www.vocm.com
Russell Murphy, Station Manager

***Mount Pearl:* VOAR** (Freq: 1210)
1041 Topsail Rd., Mount Pearl, NL A1N 5E9
Tel: 709-745-8627, *Fax:* 709-745-1600
Toll-Free: 800-563-1991
voar@voar.org
www.voar.org
Sherry Griffin, Station Manager

***St. John's:* CBN-AM** (Freq: 640)
Owned by: *Canadian Broadcasting Corporation (CBC)**
PO Box 12010 A, St. John's, NL A1B 3T8
Tel: 709-576-5000, *Fax:* 709-576-5234
Toll-Free: 800-563-7933
www.cbc.ca/nl; www.cbc.ca/radio
Social Media: www.facebook.com/radiocbc; www.twitter.com/cbcradio,
Other information: Phone, CBC Radio One Newsroom: 709-576-5225
Denise Wilson, Managing Director, Newfoundland & Labrador
Kathy Porter, Executive Producer, English Radio
Maureen Anonsen, Manager, Partnership & Communications, 709-576-5013
Debbie Hynes, Senior Officer, Communications, 709-576-5150

***St. John's:* CKVO** (Freq: 710)
Owned by: *NewCap Inc.**
VOCM(AM), PO Box 8590 A, 391 Kenmount Rd., St. John's, NL A1B 3P5
Tel: 709-726-5590, *Fax:* 709-726-8626
feedback@vocm.com
www.vocm.com
John Murphy, General Manager

***St. Johns:* VOWR** (Freq: 800)
PO Box 7430, Patrick St., St. Johns, NF A1E 3Y5
Tel: 709-579-9233,
vowr@vowr.org
www.vowr.org
JG Joyce, Founder of VOWR

***Stephenville:* CFGN** (Freq: 1230)
Owned by: *NewCap Inc.**
60 West St., Stephenville, NL A2N 1C6
Tel: 709-643-2191, *Fax:* 709-643-5025
cfsx@vocm.com
Katherine Hogan, Contact

***Stephenville:* CFSX** (Freq: 870)
Owned by: *NewCap Inc.**
60 West St., Stephenville, NL A2N 1C6
Tel: 709-643-2191, *Fax:* 709-643-5025
cfsx@vocm.com
www.cfsxradio.com
Katherine Hogan, Sales, 709-214-0258

Northwest Territories

***Hay River:* CKBX-AM** (Freq: 100.1)
Owned by: *CKWL-AM*
Hay River, NT
Toll-Free: 867-873-4663
www.mix100.ca

***Yellowknife:* CFYK** (Freq: 1340)
Owned by: *Canadian Broadcasting Corporation**
PO Box 160, Yellowknife, NT X1A 2N2
Tel: 867-920-5400, *Fax:* 867-920-5440
www.cbc.ca/north

***Yellowknife:* CHAK** (Freq: 860)
Owned by: *Canadian Broadcasting Corporation**
PO Box 160, Yellowknife, NT X1A 2N2
Tel: 867-920-5400, *Fax:* 867-777-7640
www.cbc.ca/north

***Yellowknife:* CKWL-AM** (Freq: 100.1)
Owned by: *Vista Radio**
5114 49th St., Yellowknife, NT X1A 1P8
Tel: 867-920-4636, *Fax:* 867-920-4033
info@cjcd.ca
www.mix100.ca

Nova Scotia

***Amherst:* CKDH-AM** (Freq: 900)
Owned by: *Maritime Broadcasting System**
PO Box 670, Amherst, NS B4H 4B8
Tel: 902-667-3875,
ckdh@ckdh.net
www.ckdh.net
Social Media: www.facebook.com/101.7CKDH

***Digby:* CKDY** (Freq: 1420)
Owned by: *Maritime Broadcasting System**
PO Box 1420, 53 Sydney St., Digby, NS B0V 1A
Tel: 902-245-2111, *Fax:* 902-245-9720
avr@avrnetwork.com
www.avrnetwork.com

***Halifax:* CJCH-AM** (Freq: 920)
Owned by: *Bell Media Radio**
PO Box 9316, RPO, CSC, Halifax, NS B3K 6A7
Tel: 902-453-2524, *Fax:* 902-453-3132
Scott Bodnarchuck, General Manager

***Middleton:* CKAD** (Freq: 1350)
Owned by: *Maritime Broadcasting System**
PO Box 550, 10 Bridge St., Middleton, NS B0S 1P0
Tel: 902-825-3429, *Fax:* 902-825-6009
www.avrnetwork.com
Social Media: www.facebook.com/pages/AVR/264050766956087
Dianne Best, General Manager

***New Glasgow:* CKEC-AM** (Freq: 1320)
Owned by: *Hector Broadcasting Co. Ltd.**
PO Box 519, 84 Provost St., New Glasgow, NS B2H 5E7
Tel: 902-752-4200, *Fax:* 902-755-2468
info@ecfm.com
ecfm.ca
Ann MacGregor, Program Director
Doulas Freeman, CEO

***Sydney:* CBI** (Freq: 1140)
Owned by: *Canadian Broadcasting Corporation**
500 George St., Sydney, NS B1P 1K6
Tel: 902-539-5050,
www.cbc.ca
Andrew Cochran, Managing Director for the Maritimes, CBC Programming

***Sydney:* CHER** (Freq: 950)
Owned by: *Maritime Broadcasting System**
318 Charlotte St., Sydney, NS B1P 1C8
Tel: 902-564-5596, *Fax:* 902-562-1873
949thecape.com

***Sydney:* CJCB** (Freq: 1270)
Owned by: *Maritime Broadcasting System**
318 Charlotte St., Sydney, NS B1P 1C8
Tel: 902-564-5596, *Fax:* 902-564-1873
www.cjcbradio.com

***Windsor:* CFAB** (Freq: 1450)
Owned by: *Maritime Broadcasting System**
PO Box 278, 169A Water St., Windsor, NS B0N 2T0
Tel: 902-798-2111, *Fax:* 902-798-8140
www.avrnetwork.com

Nunavut

***Iqaluit:* CFFB** (Freq: 1230)
Owned by: *Canadian Broadcasting Corporation**
PO Box 490, Iqaluit, NU X0A 0H0
Tel: 867-979-6100, *Fax:* 867-979-6147
cbc.ca/north

Ontario

***Belleville:* CJBQ-AM** (Freq: 800)
Owned by: *Quinte Broadcasting Co. Ltd.**
PO Box 488, 10 Front St. South, Belleville, ON K8N 5B2
Tel: 613-969-5555, *Fax:* 613-969-8122
www.cjbq.com
Bill Morton

***Brantford:* CKPC-AM** (Freq: 1380)
Owned by: *Evanov Radio Group**
571 West St., Brantford, ON N3T 5P8
Tel: 519-759-1000, *Fax:* 519-753-1470
am1380@ckpc.on.ca
www.am1380.ca
Social Media: www.facebook.com/pages/News-Country-AM-1380/1148393885 74219
Richard Buchanan, President/General Manager

***Chatham:* CFCO-AM** (Freq: 630)
Owned by: *Blackburn Radio Inc.**
PO Box 100, 117 Keil Dr. South, Chatham, ON N7M 5K1
Tel: 519-354-2200, *Fax:* 519-354-2880
info@country929.com
country929.com

***Cornwall:* CJUL** (Freq: 1220)
Owned by: *Corus Entertainment Inc.**
709 Cotton Mill St., Cornwall, ON K6H 7K7
Tel: 613-932-5180, *Fax:* 613-938-0355
Toll-Free: 888-678-8122
www.am1220.ca
Scott Armstrong, General Manager, scott@seawayvalley.com

***Guelph:* CJOY-AM** (Freq: 1460)
Owned by: *B.C. Ltd.**
75 Speedvale Ave. East, Guelph, ON N1E 6M3
Tel: 519-824-7000, *Fax:* 519-824-4118
studio@cjoy.com
www.cjoy.com
Chris Sisam, General Manager

** For details on this company see listing in Major Broadcasting Companies section; † French language station*

***Hamilton:* CHAM-AM** (Freq: 820)
Owned by: *Astral Media Radio G.P.**
#401, 883 Upper Wentworth St., Hamilton, ON L9A 4Y6
Tel: 905-574-1150, *Fax:* 905-575-6429
Toll-Free: 866-559-7677
www.820cham.com
Jeff Storey, Program Director, jstorey@900chml.com

***Hamilton:* CHML-AM** (Freq: 900)
Owned by: *Corus Premium Television Ltd.**
#900, 875 Main St. West, Hamilton, ON L8S 4R1
Tel: 905-521-9900, *Fax:* 905-521-2306
News@900chml.com
www.900chml.com
Social Media: www.facebook.com/AM900CHML, twitter.com/AM900CHML

***Hamilton:* CKOC-AM** (Freq: 1150)
Owned by: *Astral Media Radio G.P.**
#401, 883 Upper Wentworth St., Hamilton, ON L9A 4Y6
Tel: 905-574-1150, *Fax:* 905-575-6429
www.oldies1150.com
Peter Hobbs, General Sales Manager, 905-575-6428

***Kitchener:* CKGL-AM** (Freq: 570)
Owned by: *Rogers Broadcasting Ltd.**
PO Box 936, 305 King St. West, 11th Fl., Kitchener, ON N2G 4E4
Tel: 519-743-2611, *Fax:* 519-743-7510
news570@rogers.com
www.570news.com
Pete Travers, pete.travers@kitchenerradio.rogers.com

***London:* CFPL-AM** (Freq: 980)
Owned by: *Corus Radio Company**
380 Wellington St., London, ON N6A 5B5
Tel: 519-931-6000, *Fax:* 519-679-1967
www.am980.ca
Social Media: facebook.com/pages/AM980-Londons-Breaking-News-Station/7858569300, twitter.com/AM980News
Kent Guy, Promotional Director

***London:* CJBK-AM** (Freq: 1290)
Owned by: *Astral Media Radio G.P.*
743 Wellington Rd. South, London, ON N6C 4R5
Tel: 519-686-2525,
bkbxnews@cjbk.com
www.cjbk.com
Social Media: www.facebook.com/1290cjbk, twitter.com/CJBK
Tom Cooke, President & General Manager, 519-686-2525

***London:* CKSL-AM** (Freq: 1410)
Owned by: *Astral Media Radio G.P.**
743 Wellington St. South, London, ON N6C 4R5
Tel: 519-686-2525, *Fax:* 519-686-2556
www.funny1410.ca
Tom Cooke, President & General Manager, 519-686-2525

***North Bay:* CKAT** (Freq: 600)
Owned by: *Rogers Broadcasting Ltd.**
PO Box 3000, 743 Main St. East, North Bay, ON P1B 8K8
Tel: 705-474-2000, *Fax:* 705-474-7761
Northbay.RadioHelp@rci.rogers.com
www.600ckat.com
Peter McKeown, General Manager

***Oakville:* CJMR-AM** (Freq: 1320)
284 Church St., Oakville, ON L6J 7N2
Tel: 905-271-1320, *Fax:* 905-842-1250
contact@cjmr1320.ca
www.cjmr1320.ca
Social Media: twitter.com/CJMR1320
Harry H. McDonald, Vice-President & General Manager

***Oakville:* CJYE** (Freq: 1250)
Broadcast Centre, 284 Church St., Oakville, ON L6J 7N2
Tel: 905-845-2821, *Fax:* 905-842-1250
contact@joy1250.ca
www.joy1250.ca
Harry H. McDonald, General Manager
Michael H. Caine, President

***Ottawa:* CBOF-1** (Freq: 990)
Owned by: *Canadian Broadcasting Corporation**
PO Box 3220 C, 181, rue Queen, Ottawa, ON K1P 1K9
Toll-Free: 866-306-4636
www.radio-canada.ca/regions/ottawa
Richard Simoens, Directeur, 613-288-6705, Fax: 613-288-6703, richard.simoens@radio-canada.ca
Chantal Jolicoeur, Chef de la programmation et des affaires publiques, 613-288-6547, Fax: 613-288-6703, chantal.jolicoeur@radio-canada.ca

***Ottawa:* CFGO-AM** (Freq: 1200)
Owned by: *Bell Media Radio**
87 George St., Ottawa, ON K1N 9H7
Tel: 613-750-1200, *Fax:* 613-739-4040
webmaster@chumottawa.com
www.team1200.com
Social Media: www.facebook.com/TEAM1200, twitter.com/TEAM1200Ottawa

***Ottawa:* CFRA-AM** (Freq: 580)
Owned by: *Bell Media Radio**
87 George St., Ottawa, ON K1N 9H7
Tel: 613-789-2486, *Fax:* 613-523-6423
www.cfra.com

***Ottawa:* CIWW-AM** (Freq: 1310)
Owned by: *Rogers Broadcasting Ltd.**
2001 Thurston Dr., Ottawa, ON K1G 6C9
Tel: 613-736-2001, *Fax:* 613-736-2002
tips1310@rogers.com
www.1310news.com
Social Media: twitter.com/1310news
Scott Parsons, General Manager

***Owen Sound:* CFOS-AM** (Freq: 560)
Owned by: *Bayshore Broadcasting Corporation**
PO Box 280, 270 - 9th St. East, Owen Sound, ON N4K 5P5
Tel: 519-376-2030, *Fax:* 519-371-4242
bayshore@bayshorebroadcasting.ca
www.bayshorebroadcasting.ca
Ross Kentner, General Manager, rkentner@bayshorebroadcasting.ca
Kevin Brown, General Sales Manager, kbrown@bayshorebroadcasting.ca
Rob Brignell, Director, Marketing & Business Development, rbrignell@bayshorebroadcasting.ca

***Peterborough:* CKRU** (Freq: 980)
Owned by: *B.C. Ltd.**
#200, 151 King St., Peterborough, ON K9J 2R8
Tel: 705-748-6101, *Fax:* 705-742-7708
www.980kruz.ca
Social Media: twitter.com/KruzFM
Rob Seguin, Program Director, Brand Manager

***Richmond Hill:* CHKT** (Freq: 1430)
Owned by: *Fairchild Radio**
#7-8, 135 East Beaver Creek Rd., Richmond Hill, ON L4B 1E2
Tel: 905-763-3360, *Fax:* 905-889-9828
www.fairchildradio.com
Cyril Lai, General Manager

***Sarnia:* CHOK** (Freq: 1070)
Owned by: *Blackburn Radio Inc.**
1415 London Rd., Sarnia, ON N7S 1P6
Tel: 519-542-5500, *Fax:* 519-542-1520
www.chok.com
Social Media: www.facebook.com/country1039chok, twitter.com/country1039chok

***St Catharines:* CHSC** (Freq: 1220)
36 Queenston St., St Catharines, ON L2R 2Y9
www.1220chsc.ca

***St Catharines:* CKTB-AM** (Freq: 610)
Owned by: *Astral Media Radio G.P.*
12 Yates St., St Catharines, ON L2R 6Z4
Tel: 905-684-1174, *Fax:* 905-684-4800
newsroom@610cktb.com
www.610cktb.com
Tim Parent, Brand/News Director, tparent@astral.com
Laurie Graham, General Manager, lgraham@astral.com

***Stratford:* CJCS** (Freq: 1240)
376 Romeo St. South, Stratford, ON N5A 4T9
Tel: 519-271-2450, *Fax:* 519-271-3102
www.cjcsradio.com

***Thunder Bay:* CKPR-AM** (Freq: 580)
87 Hill St. North, Thunder Bay, ON P7A 5V6
Tel: 807-346-2600, *Fax:* 807-345-9923
radio@ckpr.com
www.ckpr.com
Social Media: www.facebook.com/915ckpr, twitter.com/915ckpr
Brad Hilgers, Program Director, bhilgers@dougallmedia.com

***Toronto:* AM 740** (Freq: 740)
#205, 550 Queen St. East, Toronto, ON M5A 1V2
Tel: 416-544-0740,
www.zoomerradio.ca
Social Media: www.facebook.com/zoomerradio, twitter.com/am740
George Grant, President/CEO, G.Grant@MZMedia.com
Gene Stevens, Director, Programming & Operations, gstevens@am740radio.ca
Christopher Randall, Director, Promotions, christopher@mzmedia.com
Steven J. Shiaman, Director, Retail Sales, sshiaman@am740radio.ca

***Toronto:* CFMJ-AM** (Freq: 640)
Owned by: *Corus Premium Television Ltd.**
25 Dockside Dr., Toronto, ON M5A 0B5
Tel: 416-221-6400,
www.640toronto.com
Gord Harris, Program Director

***Toronto:* CFRB** (Freq: 1010)
Owned by: *Astral Media Radio G.P.**
2 St. Clair Ave. West, 2nd Fl., Toronto, ON M4V 1L6
Tel: 416-924-5711,
informationoffice@astral.com
www.newstalk1010.com
Pat Holiday, Vice-President & General Manager

***Toronto:* CFTR** (Freq: 680)
Owned by: *Rogers Broadcasting Ltd.**
777 Jarvis St., Toronto, ON M4Y 3B7
Tel: 416-935-8468, *Fax:* 416-935-8480
680info@680news.com
www.680news.com
Social Media: www.facebook.com/pages/680News/204410527704, twitter.com/680news

***Toronto:* CHIN** (Freq: 1540)
622 College St., Toronto, ON M6G 1B6
Tel: 416-531-9991, *Fax:* 416-531-5274
info@chinradio.com
www.chinradio.com
Social Media: www.facebook.com/chinradiocanada, twitter.com/chinradiocanada

***Toronto:* CHWO-AM** (Freq: 740)
PO Box 740 A, Toronto, ON M5W 4K6
Tel: 416-544-0740, *Fax:* 905-842-1250
www.zoomerradio.ca

***Toronto:* CJCL** (Freq: 590)
Owned by: *Rogers Broadcasting Ltd.**
The Fan, 777 Jarvis St., Toronto, ON M4Y 3B7
Tel: 416-935-0590, *Fax:* 416-413-4116
www.sportsnet.ca/590
Social Media: www.facebook.com/fan590, twitter.com/FAN590

***Toronto:* CP24 Radio 1050** (Freq: 1050)
Owned by: *Bell Media Radio**
299 Queen St. West, Toronto, ON M5V 2Z5
Tel: 416-384-2700,
now@cp24.com
www.cp24.com
Robert McLaughlin, Vice President/General Manager, CP24

***Toronto:* CSCA** (Freq: closed circuit)
Owned by: *Seneca College**
#2051, 70 The Pond Rd., Toronto, ON M3J 3M6
Tel: 416-491-5050, *Fax:* 416-739-1856
sayradio@gmail.com
csca.senecac.on.ca

***Waterloo:* CKKW-AM** (Freq: 1090)
Owned by: *Bell Media Radio**
#207, 255 King St. North, Waterloo, ON N2J 4V2
Tel: 519-884-4470, *Fax:* 519-884-6482
www.oldies1090.com

†*Windsor:* CBEF (Freq: 540)*Détenteur:* **Canadian Broadcasting Corporation (CBC)***
825 Riverside Dr. West, Windsor, ON N9A 5K9
Tél: 519-255-3411, *Ligne sans frais:* 800-551-2985
auditoire@radio-canada.ca; liaison@radio-canada.ca
www.radio-canada.ca/radio

***Windsor:* CKLW-AM** (Freq: 800)
Owned by: *Bell Media Radio**
1640 Ouellette Ave., Windsor, ON N8X 1L1
Tel: 519-258-8888, *Fax:* 519-258-0182
www.am800cklw.com

** For details on this company see listing in Major Broadcasting Companies section; † French language station*

Eric Proksch, Vice President/General Manager, ericp@am800cklw.com
Keith Chinnery, Program Director, kwc@am800cklw.com

***Windsor:* CKWW-AM** (Freq: 580)
Owned by: *Bell Media Radio**
1640 Ouellette Ave., Windsor, ON N8X 1L1
Tel: 519-258-8888, *Fax:* 519-258-0182
info@am580radio.com
www.am580radio.com
Eric Proksch, Vice President/General Manager

***Wingham:* CKNX** (Freq: 920)
Owned by: *Blackburn Radio Inc.**
215 Carling Terrace, Wingham, ON N0G 2W0
Tel: 519-357-1310, *Fax:* 519-357-1897
www.am920.ca
John Weese, General Manager, 800-265-3030

Prince Edward Island

***Charlottetown:* CFCY-AM** (Freq: 630)
Owned by: *Maritime Broadcasting System**
5 Prince St., Charlottetown, PE C1A 4P4
Tel: 902-892-1066, *Fax:* 902-566-1338
cfcy.fm
Social Media: www.facebook.com/951fmcfcy, twitter.com/cfcy

Québec

***Baie-Comeau:* CFRP** (Freq: 620)
907, rue de Puyjalon, Baie-Comeau, QC G5C 1N3
Tel: 418-589-3771, *Fax:* 418-589-9086
chlcfm97@globetrotter.net
www.chlc.com
George Daviault, Directeur generale, direction971-1005@globetrotter.net

†*Chibougamau:* CJMD-AM (Freq: 1240)*Détenteur:* **Groupe Radio Antenne 6***
539, 3e rue, Chibougamau, QC G8P 1N8
Tél: 418-275-1831, *Téléc:* 418-275-2475
www.cjmdradio.com
Marc-André Levesque

†*Chicoutimi:* CKRS (Freq: 590)*Détenteur:* **Corus Québec***
CP 1090, 121, rue Racine est, Chicoutimi, QC G7H 5G4
Tél: 418-545-2577, *Téléc:* 418-545-9186
auditoire@ckrs.ca
www.lefm98.com
Médias sociaux: www.facebook.com/FM98Saguenay
Yves Hebert, Dir. gen., yhebert@lefm98com

†*Gaspé:* CHGM (Freq: 1150)*Détenteur:* **CHNC**
155 rue de la Reine, Gaspé, QC

†*Gatineau:* CJRC-AM (Freq: 1150)*Détenteur:* **Corus Entertainment Inc.***
150, rue Edmonton, Gatineau, QC J8Y 3S6
Tél: 819-561-8801, *Téléc:* 819-561-3333
www.ckoi.com

†*La Tuque:* CFLM-AM (Freq: 1240)
CP 850, 529, rue St-Louis, La Tuque, QC G9X 3P6
Tél: 819-523-4575, *Téléc:* 819-676-8000
www.cflm.ca
Philippe Boulianne, philcflm@hotmail.com

†*Laval:* Diffusion Laval inc. (Freq: 1570)
2040, Autoroute Laval, Laval, QC H7S 2M9
Tél: 450-680-1570, *Téléc:* 450-680-1598
info@laval1570am.com
www.boomer1570.ca
Michel Mathieu, Président/Directeur général

†*Montréal:* CFMB-AM (Freq: 1280)
35, rue York, Montréal, QC H3Z 2Z5
Tél: 514-790-0251, *Téléc:* 514-483-1362
info@cfmb.ca
www.cfmb.ca
Anne-Marie Stanczykowski, Vice-President
Andrew Mielewczyk

***Montréal:* CJAD-AM** (Freq: 800)
Owned by: *Astral Media Radio G.P.*
1411, rue du Fort, Montréal, QC H3H 2R1
Tel: 514-989-2523, *Fax:* 514-989-3868
infodesk@cjad.com
www.cjad.com
Social Media: www.facebook.com/cjad800

Rob Braide, Vice-President & General Manager

***Montréal:* CJLO-AM** (Freq: closed circuit)
Owned by: *Concordia University**
#CC-430, 7141, rue Sherbrooke ouest, Montréal, QC H4B 1R6
Tel: 514-848-8663, *Fax:* 514-848-7450
feedback@cjlo.com
www.cjlo.com
Social Media: www.facebook.com/cjlo1690am, twitter.com/CJLO1690AM
Stephanie Saretsky, Station Manager, manager@cjlo.com

†*Montréal:* CJWI (Freq: 1610)*Détenteur:* **CPAM Radio Union.com Inc**
3390 blvd Crémazie est, Montréal, QC H2A 1A4
Tél: 514-790-2726, *Téléc:* 514-287-3299
info@cpam1610.com
www.cpam1610.com
Jean-Ernest Pierre

†*Montréal:* CKAC-AM (Freq: 730)
#1100, 800, rue de la Gauchetière Ouest, Montréal, QC H5A 1M1
Tél: 514-787-0730, *Téléc:* 514-787-7943
www.ckac.com

***Montréal:* CKGM-AM** (Freq: 990)
Owned by: *Bell Media Radio**
#300, 1310, av Greene, Montréal, QC H3Z 2B5
Tel: 514-931-4487, *Fax:* 514-931-4079
writetous@team990.com
www.team990.com
Jim Waters, President, CHUM Limited

†*Québec:* CHRC (Freq: 800)
250W, boulevard Wilfrid-Hamel Colisée Pepsi, Entrée nord-ouest, 4e étage, Québec, QC G1V 1R8
Tél: 418-688-8080, *Téléc:* 418-780-3780
nouvelles@quebec800.com
www.chrc.com
Louis Painchaud, Program Director, louis.painchaud@remparts.com

†*Rimouski:* CAJT
Détenteur: **CEGEP de Rimouski***
Cégep de Rimouski, 60, rue de l'Évêché ouest, Rimouski, QC G5L 4H6
Tél: 418-723-1880, *Téléc:* 418-724-4961
Ligne sans frais: 800-463-0617
infoscol@cegep-rimouski.qc.ca
www.cegep-rimouski.qc.ca
Philippe Daigle, Contact

†*Rimouski:* CJBR (Freq: 900)*Détenteur:* **Canadian Broadcasting Corporation***
273, rue St-Jean Baptiste ouest, Rimouski, QC G5L 4J8
Tél: 418-723-2217,
www.radio-canada.ca

Saskatchewan

***Estevan:* CJSL-AM** (Freq: 1280)
Owned by: *Golden West Broadcasting Ltd.**
#200, 1236 - 5th St., Estevan, SK S4A 0Z6
Tel: 306-634-1280,
mhenderson@goldenwestradio.com
www.cj1280radio.com
Laverne Pappel, Station Manager

†*Gravelbourg:* CBKF-1 (Freq: 690)*Détenteur:* **CBKF-FM; Société Radio-Canada**
Gravelbourg, SK

***Kindersley:* CFYM** (Freq: 1210)
Owned by: *CJYM*
Kindersley, SK

***Melfort:* CKJH** (Freq: 750)
Radio CJVR Ltd., PO Box 750, 611 Main St. North, Melfort, SK S0E 1A0
Tel: 306-752-2587, *Fax:* 306-752-5932
Toll-Free: 800-668-2587
sales@cjvr.com
www.ck750.com
Ken Singer, Vice President

***Moose Jaw:* CHAB-AM** (Freq: 800)
Owned by: *Golden West Broadcasting Ltd.**
1704 Main St. North, Moose Jaw, SK S6J 1L4
Tel: 306-694-0800,
www.chabradio.com

***North Battleford:* CJNB-AM** (Freq: 1050)
PO Box 1460, 1711 - 100th St., North Battleford, SK S9A 2Z5
Tel: 306-445-2477,
www.cjnb.com
David Dekker

***Prince Albert:* CKBI-AM** (Freq: 900)
Owned by: *RAWLCO Radio Ltd.**
1316 Central Ave., Prince Albert, SK S6V 7R4
Tel: 306-763-7421, *Toll-Free:* 800-667-9000
900ckbi@rawlco.com
www.900ckbi.com
Neil Headrick, Program Director, nheadrick@rawlco.com

***Regina:* CBK-FM** (Freq: 96.9)
Owned by: *Canadian Broadcasting Corporation (CBC)**
PO Box 540 Main, 2440 Broad St., Regina, SK S4P 4A1
Tel: 306-347-9540,
www.cbc.ca/sask; www.cbc.ca/radio2
Social Media: www.facebook.com/cbcsask, www.twitter.com/cbcradio2; www.twitter.com/cbcsask
Other information: Phone, Regina Radio: 306-347-9692
Lenora Sturge, Coordinator, Program Marketing, 306-347-9714
Justin Anders, Regional Web Developer, 306-788-3285

***Regina:* CJME-AM** (Freq: 980)
Owned by: *RAWLCO Radio Ltd.**
#210, 2401 Saskatchewan Dr., Regina, SK S4P 4H8
Tel: 306-525-0000, *Fax:* 306-347-8557
www.cjme.com
Kristy Werner, General Manager

***Regina:* CKRM** (Freq: 620)
Owned by: *Harvard Broadcasting Inc.**
1900 Rose St., Regina, SK S4P 0A9
Tel: 306-546-6200, *Fax:* 306-781-7338
Toll-Free: 866-767-0620
news@620ckrm.com
www.620ckrm.com
Jason Huschi, General Manager, jasonh@harvardbroadcasting.com
Grant Biebrick, Program Director, gbiebrick@harvardbroadcasting.com

***Rosetown:* CJYM** (Freq: 1330)
Owned by: *Dace Broadcasting Corp.*
PO Box 490, 208 Highway 4 North, Rosetown, SK S0L 2V0
Tel: 306-882-2686, *Fax:* 306-882-3037
bbell@goldenwestradio.com
www.cjym.com

†*Saskatoon:* CBKF-2 (Freq: 860)*Détenteur:* **CBKF-FM; Société Radio Canada***
144 - 2nd Ave., Saskatoon, SK S7K 1K5
Tél: 306-956-7400, *Téléc:* 306-956-7476
David Kyle, General Manager

***Saskatoon:* CJWW** (Freq: 600)
Owned by: *Saskatoon Media Group**
366 - 3 Ave. South, Saskatoon, SK S7K 1M5
Tel: 306-244-1975, *Fax:* 306-665-5501
www.cjwwradio.com
Vic Dubois, General Manager

***Saskatoon:* CKOM-AM** (Freq: 650)
Owned by: *RAWLCO Radio Ltd.**
715 Saskatchewan Cres. West, Saskatoon, SK S7M 5V7
Tel: 306-934-2222, *Fax:* 306-477-0002
www.ckom.com
Social Media: www.facebook.com/NewsTalk650CKOM, twitter.com/CKOMNews
Kristy Werner, General Manager
John Himpe, Program Director

***Swift Current:* CJSN-AM** (Freq: 1490)
Owned by: *Golden West Broadcasting Ltd.**
134 Central Ave. North, Swift Current, SK S9H 0L1
Tel: 306-297-2671, *Fax:* 306-297-3051
Toll-Free: 800-821-8073
ccongdon@goldenwestradio.com
www.ckswradio.ca

***Swift Current:* CKSW-AM** (Freq: 570)
Owned by: *Golden West Broadcasting Ltd.**
134 Central Ave. North, Swift Current, SK S9H 0L1
Tel: 306-773-4605, *Toll-Free:* 800-821-8073
ccongdon@goldenwestradio.com
www.ckswradio.ca
Kurtis Bakanec, Music Director

***Weyburn:* CFSL-AM** (Freq: 1190)
Owned by: *Golden West Broadcasting Ltd.**

** For details on this company see listing in Major Broadcasting Companies section; † French language station*

PO Box 340, 305 Souris Ave., Weyburn, SK S4H 2K2
Tel: 306-848-1190, *Fax:* 306-842-2720
am1190radio.com
Social Media: www.facebook.com/pages/AM-1190/111247462239648
Laverne Pappel, Station Manager

***Yorkton:* CJGX** (Freq: 940)
120 Smith St. East, Yorkton, SK S3N 3V3
Tel: 306-782-2256, *Fax:* 306-783-4994
ykt-reception@harvardbroadcasting.com
www.gx94radio.com
Social Media: www.facebook.com/groups/188922356730
Angie Norton, General Manager, anorton@harvardbroadcasting.com
Lyle Walsh, General Manager

Yukon Territory

***Whitehorse:* CFWH** (Freq: 570)
Owned by: *Canadian Broadcasting Corporation**
3103 - 3rd Ave., Whitehorse, YT Y1A 2A2
Tel: 867-668-8400,
cbcnorth@cbc.ca
www.cbc.ca/north
Social Media: www.facebook.com/CBCNorth, twitter.com/cbcnorth
Doug Caldwell, Area Manager
Mike Linder, Sr. News Editor

***Whitehorse:* CKRW** (Freq: 610)
Owned by: *Klondike Broadcasting Co.Ltd.**
#203, 4103 - 4th Ave., Whitehorse, YT Y1A 1H6
Tel: 867-668-6100, *Fax:* 867-668-4209
admin@ckrw.com
www.ckrw.com
Jennifer Jonstone, General Manager

FM Radio Stations

Alberta

***Blairmore:* CJPR-FM** (Freq: 94.9)
Owned by: *NewCap Inc.**
PO Box 840, Blairmore, AB T0K 0E0
Tel: 403-562-2806, *Fax:* 403-562-8114
www.mountainradiofm.com
Barb Kelly, Station Manager

***Calgary:* CBR-FM** (Freq: 102.1)
Owned by: *Canadian Broadcasting Corporation**
PO Box 2640, 1724 Westmount Blvd. NW, Calgary, AB T2P 2M7
Tel: 403-521-6000,
www.cbc.ca/calgary
Helen Henderson, Deputy Regional Director of Radion

***Calgary:* CFGQ-FM** (Freq: 107.3)
Owned by: *CKIK-FM Limited**
#105, 630 - 3 Ave. SW, Calgary, AB T2P 4L4
Tel: 403-716-6500, *Fax:* 403-716-2111
www.q107fm.ca
Social Media: www.facebook.com/Q107Calgary, twitter.com/q107calgary
Tim Morgan, Program Director, tim.morgan@corusent.com

***Calgary:* CFXL-FM** (Freq: 103.1)
Owned by: *NewCap Inc.**
#100, 1110 Centre St. NE, Calgary, AB T2E 2R2
Tel: 403-271-6366, *Fax:* 403-278-6772
feedback@XL103Calgary.com
www.xl103calgary.com
Vinka Dubroja, General Manager, vinka@XL103Calgary.com

***Calgary:* CHFM-FM** (Freq: 95.9)
Owned by: *Rogers Broadcasting Ltd.**
#240, 2723 - 37 Ave. NE, Calgary, AB T1Y 5R8
Tel: 403-246-9696,
www.lite96.ca

***Calgary:* CIBK-FM** (Freq: 98.5)
Owned by: *Astral Media Radio G.P.**
#300, 1110 Centre St. NE, Calgary, AB T2E 2R2
Tel: 403-240-5800,
calgaryweb@virginradio.ca
calgary.virginradio.ca
Social Media: www.facebook.com/virginradiocalgary, twitter.com/VirginRadioYYC
Stewart Meyers, General Manager, smeyers@astral.com

***Calgary:* CJAY-FM** (Freq: 92.1)
Owned by: *Astral Media Radio G.P.**
300 - 1110 Centre St. North, Calgary, AB T2E 2R2
Tel: 403-240-5850, *Fax:* 403-240-5801
www.cjay92.com
Stewart Meyers, General Manager, smeyers@astral.com

***Calgary:* CJSI-FM** (Freq: 88.9)
4510 Macleod Trail South, Calgary, AB T2G 0A4
Tel: 403-276-1111, *Fax:* 403-276-1114
www.cjsi.ca
Social Media: www.facebook.com/virginradiocalgary, twitter.com/VirginRadioYYC

***Calgary:* CJSW-FM** (Freq: 90.9)
#312, MacEwan Hall, University of Calgary, Calgary, AB T2N 1N4
Tel: 403-220-3902, *Fax:* 403-289-8212
office@cjsw.com
www.cjsw.com
Social Media: www.myspace.com/cjsw, www.facebook.com/CJSWFM, twitter.com/cjsw
Myke Atkinson, Station Manager, 403-220-3904, cjswadm@ucalgary.ca
Joe Burima, Program Director, 403-220-3903, cjswpd@ucalgary.ca
Kat Dornian, Music Director, 403-220-3085, cjswfm@ucalgary.ca
Marc Affeld, News Director, 403-220-8033, news@cjsw.com
Geneviève Dale, Office Coordinator, 403-220-6563, office@cjsw.com

***Calgary:* CKIS-FM** (Freq: 96.9)
Owned by: *Rogers Broadcasting Ltd.**
#240, 2723 - 37 Ave. NE, Calgary, AB T1Y 5R8
Tel: 403-250-9797, *Fax:* 403-291-4368
www.jackfm.ca
Social Media: www.facebook.com/jackfmcalgary

***Calgary:* CKRY-FM** (Freq: 105.1)
Owned by: *Corus Radio Company**
#105, 630 - 3rd Ave. SW, Calgary, AB T2P 4L4
Tel: 403-716-6500, *Fax:* 403-716-2111
www.country105.com
Social Media: www.facebook.com/Country105
Phil Kallsen, Program Director

***Calgary:* CMRC-FM** (Freq: 107.5)
4825 Richard Rd. SW, Calgary, AB T3E 6K6
Tel: 403-440-6119, *Fax:* 403-440-6563
www.cmrcradio.ca
Jillian Hunter, Station Manager

***Camrose:* CLCR-FM** (Freq: closed circuit)
4901 - 46 Ave., Camrose, AB T4V 2R3
Tel: 780-679-1541, *Fax:* 780-672-5252
aucsa@augustana.ca
www.augustana.ab.ca/sa

***Canmore:* CHMN-FM** (Freq: 106.5)
Owned by: *Rogers Broadcasting Ltd.**
749 Railway Ave., Canmore, AB T1W 1P2
Tel: 403-678-2222, *Fax:* 403-678-6844
www.mountainfm.ca

***Cold Lake:* CJXK-FM** (Freq: 95.3)
Owned by: *NewCap Inc.**
B-5414 - 55 St., Cold Lake, AB T9M 1R5
Tel: 780-594-2459, *Fax:* 780-594-3001
news@k-rock953.com
www.953krock.com
Chad Tabish, General Manager, ctabish@newcap.ca
Jeff Murray, Program Director, jmurray@newcap.ca

***Drayton Valley:* CIBW-FM** (Freq: 92.9)
Owned by: *The Jim Pattison Broadcast Group**
PO Box 929, 5164 - 52 Ave., Drayton Valley, AB T7A 1V3
Tel: 780-542-9290, *Fax:* 780-542-9319
Toll-Free: 888-884-2448
jocks@bigwestcountry.ca
www.bigwestcountry.ca
Social Media: www.facebook.com/pages/929-Big-West-Country/167537829943069
Cindy Andersen, Marketing Executive

***Edmonton:* CBX-FM** (Freq: 90.9)
Owned by: *Canadian Broadcasting Corporation**
Edmonton, AB
Toll-Free: 866-306-4636

***Edmonton:* CFBR-FM** (Freq: 100.3)
Owned by: *Astral Media Radio G.P.**
#100, 18520 Stony Plain Rd., Edmonton, AB T5S 2E2
Tel: 780-486-2800, *Fax:* 780-489-6927
www.thebearrocks.com
Pat Cardinal, General Manager, pcardinal@astral.com

***Edmonton:* CFMG-FM** (Freq: 104.9)
Owned by: *Astral Media Radio G.P.**
#100, 18520 Stony Plain Rd., Edmonton, AB T5S 2E2
Tel: 780-435-1049,
edmonton.virginradio.ca
Pat Cardinal, General Manager, pcardinal@astral.com
Tammy Cole, Brand Director, tcole@astral.com

***Edmonton:* CFWE-FM** (Freq: 89.9)
13245 - 146th St., Edmonton, AB T5L 4S8
Tel: 780-447-2393, *Fax:* 780-454-2820
www.ammsa.com/cfwe
Social Media: www.facebook.com/windspeakernews, twitter.com/windspeakernews
Bert Crowfoot, General Manager

***Edmonton:* CHBN-FM** (Freq: 91.7)
Owned by: *Rogers Broadcasting Ltd.*
10212 Jasper Ave., Edmonton, AB T5J 5A3
Tel: 780-424-2222, *Fax:* 780-401-1600
www.thebounce.ca
Gisele Sowa, General Manager

***Edmonton:* CIRK-FM** (Freq: 97.3)
Owned by: *NewCap Inc.**
2394 West Edmonton Mall, #8882, 170 St., Edmonton, AB T5T 4M2
Tel: 780-437-4996, *Fax:* 780-435-0844
www.k-rock973.com
Social Media: www.facebook.com/K97Edmonton, twitter.com/k97
Randy Lemay, General Manager, rlemay@newcap.ca
James "Gruff" Gushnowski, Program Director

***Edmonton:* CISN-FM** (Freq: 103.9)
Owned by: *Corus Radio Company**
5204 - 84 St., Edmonton, AB T6E 5N8
Tel: 780-428-1104, *Fax:* 780-469-5937
info@cisnfm.com
www.cisnfm.com
Chris Scheetz, Program Director, cscheetz@cisnfm.com

***Edmonton:* CJRY-FM** (Freq: 105.9)
5316 Calgary Trail, Edmonton, AB T6H 4J8
Tel: 780-466-4930, *Fax:* 780-469-5335
www.shinefm.com
Malcolm Hunt, Program Director
Carlo Bruno, Business Manager

***Edmonton:* CJSR-FM** (Freq: 88.5)
#0-09 Students Union Bldg., University of Alberta, Edmonton, AB T6G 2J7
Tel: 780-492-2577, *Fax:* 780-492-3121
www.cjsr.com
Sarah Edwards, Station Manager, admin@cjsr.com

***Edmonton:* CKER World FM** (Freq: 101.7)
10212 Jasper Ave., Edmonton, AB T5J 5A3
Tel: 780-424-2222, *Fax:* 780-401-1600
www.worldfm.ca

***Edmonton:* CKNG-FM** (Freq: 92.5)
Owned by: *Corus Premium Television Ltd.**
5204 - 84 St., Edmonton, AB T6E 5N8
Tel: 780-440-6300, *Fax:* 780-469-5937
www.joefm.ca
Greg Johnson, Program Director, greg.johnson@corusent.com

***Edmonton:* CKRA-FM** (Freq: 96.3)
Owned by: *NewCap Inc.**
2394 West Edmonton Mall, 8882 - 170 St., Edmonton, AB T5T 4M2
Tel: 780-437-4996, *Fax:* 780-435-0844
www.963capitalfm.com
John Roberts, Program Director, jroberts@newcap.ca

***Edmonton:* CKUA-FM** (Freq: 94.9)
10526 Jasper Ave., 4th Fl., Edmonton, AB T5J 1Z7
Tel: 780-428-7595, *Fax:* 780-428-7624
www.ckua.com
Ken Regan, Chief Executive Officer
Katrina Regan-Ingram, Chief Operations Officer

** For details on this company see listing in Major Broadcasting Companies section; † French language station*

†*Falher:* CKRP-FM (Freq: 95.7; 102.9; 90.3)
CP 718, Falher, AB T0H 1M0
Tél: 780-837-2346, *Téléc:* 780-837-2092
Ligne sans frais: 866-837-2346
ckrp_fm@yahoo.ca
www.acfa-ckrp.ca
Éric Charron
Julie Cadieux

***Fort McMurray:* CJOK-FM** (Freq: 93.3)
9912 Franklin Ave., Fort McMurray, AB T9H 2K5
Tel: 780-743-2246, *Fax:* 780-791-7250
mymcmurray.com
Craig Picton, Program Director
Jim Schneider, Sales Manager
Kelly Boyd, General Manager

***Fort Vermilion:* CIAM-FM** (Freq: 92.7; 104.3; 95.5; 94.1; 102.9)
PO Box 609, 4709 River Rd., Fort Vermilion, AB T0H 1N0
Tel: 780-927-2426, *Fax:* 780-927-2427
Toll-Free: 866-927-2426
info@ciamradio.com
www.ciamradio.com
Michael Sandstrom, General Manager

***Fox Creek:* CFFC-FM** (Freq: 92.1)
***Owned by:** CKKX-FM*
Fox Creek, AB

***Grande Praire:* CJUI-FM** (Freq: 104.7)
***Owned by:** Vista Radio**
#1-11002 104 Ave., Grande Praire, AB T8V 7W5
Tel: 780-357-3733, *Fax:* 780-830-7815
www.1047freefm.com

***Grande Prairie:* CJXX-FM** (Freq: 93.1)
***Owned by:** The Jim Pattison Broadcast Group**
Big Country 93.1 FM, #202, 9817 - 101 Ave., Grande Prairie, AB T8V 0X6
Tel: 780-532-0840, *Fax:* 780-538-1266
info@bigcountryxx.com
www.bigcountryxx.com
Social Media: twitter.com/bigcountry931

***High Level:* CKHL-FM** (Freq: 102.1)
PO Box 3759, High Level, AB T0H 1Z0
Tel: 780-926-4530, *Fax:* 780-926-4564
www.ylcountry.com
Chris Black, General Manager, 780-618-4230

***La Crete:* CKLA-FM** (Freq: 92.1)
***Owned by:** CKYL*
La Crete, AB

***Lethbridge:* CFRV-FM** (Freq: 107.7)
***Owned by:** Rogers Broadcasting Ltd.**
PO Box 820, 1015 - 3rd Ave. South, Lethbridge, AB T1J 0J3
Tel: 403-328-1077, *Fax:* 403-380-1539
www.1077theriver.ca
Social Media: www.facebook.com/1077theriver
Terry Voth, General Manager

***Lethbridge:* CHLB-FM** (Freq: 95.5)
***Owned by:** The Jim Pattison Broadcast Group**
401 Mayor Magrath Dr. South, Lethbridge, AB T1J 3L8
Tel: 403-329-0995, *Fax:* 403-329-0195
www.country95.fm
Gary Dorosz, General Manager, gdorosz@country95.fm
Reid Morgan, Director of Programming, pd@country95.fm

***Lethbridge:* CJBZ-FM** (Freq: 93.3)
***Owned by:** The Jim Pattison Broadcast Group**
401 Mayor Magrath Dr. South, Lethbridge, AB T1J 3L8
Tel: 403-394-9300, *Fax:* 403-329-0195
info@b93.fm
www.b93.fm
Reid Morgan, Director of Programming, r@b93.fm
Gary Dorosz, General Manager, gdorosz@country95.fm

***Lethbridge:* CJRX-FM** (Freq: 106.7)
***Owned by:** Rogers Broadcasting Ltd.**
PO Box 820, 1015 - 3rd Ave. South, Lethbridge, AB T1J 3Z9
Tel: 403-320-1220, *Fax:* 403-380-1539
www.rock106.ca
Terry Voth, General Manager, Tvoth2@rci.rogers.com

***Lloydminster:* CJCD-FM** (Freq: 106.1)
***Owned by:** Vista Radio**
PO Box 21 Atrium Centre, 5012 - 49th St., Lloydminster, AB T9V 0K2
Tel: 780-875-5400, *Fax:* 780-875-4628
www.borderrock.com

***Lloydminster:* CKLM-FM** (Freq: 106.1; 99.7)
Atrium Center, PO Box 21, 5012 - 49th St., Lloydminster, AB T9V 0K2
Tel: 780-875-5400, *Fax:* 780-875-4628
request@borderrock.com; shotgun@borderrock.com
www.borderrock.com
Marvin Perry, General Manager, marvin@borderrock.com

***Lloydminster:* CKSA-FM** (Freq: 95.9)
***Owned by:** NewCap Inc.**
5026 - 50 St., Lloydminster, AB T9V 1P3
Tel: 780-875-3321, *Fax:* 780-875-4704
Lloyd@newcap.ca
www.959lloydfm.com
Social Media: www.facebook.com/959LLOYDFM, twitter.com/lloydfm
Chad Tabish, ctabish@newcap.ca
Dean Martin, Creative Director, dmartin@newcap.ca

***Nordegg:* CHBW-FM-1** (Freq: 93.9)
***Owned by:** CIBW-FM*
Nordegg, AB

***Okotoks:* CFXL-FM** (Freq: 100.9)
***Owned by:** Golden West Broadcasting Ltd.**
PO Box 1889, 42 McRae St., 2nd Fl., Okotoks, AB T1S 1B7
Tel: 403-995-9611,
pmacdonald@goldenwestradio.com
www.theeagle1009.com

***Peace River:* CKKX-FM** (Freq: 106.1)
PO Box 300, 9807 - 100 Ave., Peace River, AB T8S 1T5
Tel: 780-624-2535, *Fax:* 780-624-5424
www.kix106.net

***Red Deer:* CFDV-FM** (Freq: 106.7)
***Owned by:** The Jim Pattison Broadcast Group**
2840 Bremner Ave., Red Deer, AB T4R 1M9
Tel: 403-343-7105, *Fax:* 403-343-2573
news@big105.fm
www.1067thedrive.fm
Paul Mason, General Manager

***Red Deer:* CHUB-FM** (Freq: 105.5)
***Owned by:** The Jim Pattison Broadcast Group**
2840 Bremner Ave., Red Deer, AB T4R 1M9
Tel: 403-343-7105, *Fax:* 403-343-2573
news@big105.fm
www.big105.fm
Paul Mason, General Manager

***Red Deer:* CIZZ-FM** (Freq: 98.9)
***Owned by:** Corus Entertainment Inc.**
PO Bag 5339, Red Deer, AB T4N 6W1
Tel: 403-343-1303, *Fax:* 403-346-1230
zed99@newcap.ca
www.zed99.com
Social Media: www.facebook.com/ZED99FM, twitter.com/zed99reddeer
R.C. (Ron) Thompson, General Manager
John Hayes, President

***Red Deer:* CKGY-FM** (Freq: 95.5)
***Owned by:** Corus Entertainment Inc.**
PO Bag 5339, Red Deer, AB T4N 6W1
Tel: 403-348-0955, *Fax:* 403-346-1230
kgmornings@kgcountry.ca, middays@kgcountry.ca
www.ckgy.com
Hilary Montobourquette, General Manager, hilarym@newcap.com
John Hayes, President

***Redcliffe:* CFMY-FM** (Freq: 96.1)
***Owned by:** The Jim Pattison Broadcast Group**
PO Box 1270, 10 Boundary Rd., Redcliffe, AB T0J 2P0
Tel: 403-548-8282, *Fax:* 403-548-8270
my96fm@jpbg.com
www.my96fm.com
Social Media: www.facebook.com/my96fm, twitter.com/my96fm
Dwaine Dietrich, General Manager

***Siksika:* CHDH-FM** (Freq: 97.7)
PO Box 1490, Siksika, AB T0J 3W0
siksikamedia@siksikanation.com
www.siksikamedia.com

***Slave Lake:* CKWA-FM** (Freq: 92.7)
***Owned by:** NewCap Inc.**
PO Box 2470, #207, 201 Main St. NE, Slave Lake, AB T0G 2A0
Tel: 780-849-2569, *Fax:* 780-849-4833
news@lakefm.ca
Social Media: www.facebook.com/927LAKEFM, twitter.com/927LakeFM
Wray Betts, wbetts@newcap.ca

***Wainwright:* CKWY-FM** (Freq: 93.7)
***Owned by:** NewCap Inc.**
#2, 1037 - 2nd Ave., Wainwright, AB T9W 1K7
Tel: 780-842-4311, *Fax:* 780-842-4636
www.waynefm.com
Chad Tabish, General Manager, ctabish@newcap.ca

British Columbia

***100 Mile House:* CFFM-FM-2** (Freq: 99.7)
***Owned by:** CFFM-FM*
100 Mile House, BC

***Abbotsford:* CKQC-FM** (Freq: 107.1)
#318, 31935 South Fraser Way, Abbotsford, BC V2T 5N7
Tel: 604-853-4756, *Fax:* 604-853-1071
Toll-Free: 866-468-1071
country1071.com
Social Media: www.facebook.com/Country1071, twitter.com/country1071
Ken Geiger, General Manager

***Burnaby:* CJSF-FM** (Freq: 90.1)
TC216, Simon Fraser University, Burnaby, BC V5A 1S6
Tel: 604-291-3727, *Fax:* 604-291-3695
cjsfmgr@sfu.ca
www.cjsf.ca
Magnus Thyrold, Station Manager
Elvira Balakshin, Program Coordinator

***Campbell River:* CFCP-FM** (Freq: 99.7)
***Owned by:** Vista Radio**
470 - 13th Ave, Campbell River, BC V9W 7J4
Tel: 250-287-7106, *Fax:* 250-287-7170
onair@997theriver.ca
www.997theriver.ca
Social Media: www.facebook.com/997theriver, twitter.com/997theriver

***Campbell River:* Coast Radio**
909 Ironwood Street, Campbell River, BC V9W 3E5
Tel: 250-287-7106, *Fax:* 250-287-7170
www.coastradio.com

***Castlegar:* CFPW-FM** (Freq: 100.3)
***Owned by:** Vista Radio**
1101A 4th St., Castlegar, BC V1N 2A8
Tel: 250-365-7600, *Fax:* 250-365-8480
www.mountainfm.net

***Castlegar:* CKGF-FM-2** (Freq: 96.7)
525 - 11th Ave., Castlegar, BC V1N 1J6
Tel: 250-365-7600, *Fax:* 250-365-8480
Dennis Gerein, General Manager

***Castlegar:* CKQR-FM** (Freq: 99.3)
1101A 4th St., Castlegar, BC V1N 2A8
Tel: 250-365-7600, *Fax:* 250-365-8480
Toll-Free: 877-560-1010
requests@mountainfm.net
www.mountainfm.net
Dennis Gerein, General Manager

***Chetwynd:* CHAD-FM** (Freq: 104.1)
PO Box 214, 4612 North Access Rd., Chetwynd, BC V0C 1J0
Tel: 250-788-9452, *Fax:* 250-788-9402
info@peacefm.ca
www.chetchad.com
Leo Sabulsky, General Manager

***Chetwynd:* CHET-FM** (Freq: 94.5)
PO Box 214, #102, 4612 North Access Rd., Chetwynd, BC V0C 1J0
Tel: 250-788-9452, *Fax:* 250-788-9402
Toll-Free: 800-788-5330
info@peacefm.ca
www.peacefm.ca
Social Media: www.facebook.com/pages/Peace-FM/178391508895881, twitter.com/Peace_FM
Leo Sabulsky, General Manager

***Chilliwack:* CKSR-FM** (Freq: 98.3)
***Owned by:** Rogers Broadcasting Ltd.**

** For details on this company see listing in Major Broadcasting Companies section; † French language station*

#309, 46167 Yale Rd., Chilliwack, BC V2P 2N2
Tel: 604-795-5711, *Fax:* 604-795-2983
starnews@starfm.rogers.com
www.starfm.com
Social Media: www.facebook.com/983starfm, twitter.com/983StarFM
Mike Hellinger, News Director

***Christina Lake:* CKQR-FM** (Freq: 93.3)
Owned by: *CFPW-FM*
Christina Lake, BC

***Courtenay:* CKLR-FM** (Freq: 97.3)
Owned by: *Island Radio Ltd.**
801B - 29th St., Courtenay, BC V9N 7Z5
Tel: 250-703-2200, *Fax:* 250-703-9611
info@973theeagle.com
www.973theeagle.com
Social Media: www.facebook.com/pages/The-Eagle-973/160156290730199, twitter.com/theeagle973
Bob Johnstone, Program Director

***Courtenay:* JetFM** (Freq: 98.9)
Owned by: *Vista Radio**
1625A McPhee Ave., Courtenay, BC V9N 3A6
Tel: 250-334-2421, *Fax:* 250-334-1977
info@jetfm.ca
www.jetfm.ca

***Cranbrook:* CHBZ-FM** (Freq: 104.7)
Owned by: *The Jim Pattison Broadcast Group**
19 - 9 Ave. South, Cranbrook, BC V1C 2L9
Tel: 250-426-2224, *Fax:* 250-426-5520
info@b104.ca
www.b104.ca

***Cranbrook:* CHDR-FM** (Freq: 102.9)
Owned by: *The Jim Pattison Broadcast Group**
19 - 9 Ave. South, Cranbrook, BC V1C 2L9
Tel: 250-426-2224, *Fax:* 250-426-5520
info@thedrivefm.ca
www.thedrivefm.ca

***Cranbrook:* CJDR-FM** (Freq: 99.1)
19 - 9th Ave. South, Cranbrook, BC V1C 2L9
Tel: 250-426-2224,
info@thedrivefm.ca
www.thedrivefm.ca
Rene Ross, Program Director, rross@thedrivefm.ca

***Crawford Bay:* CBTE-FM** (Freq: 89.9)
Owned by: *Canadian Broadcasting Corporation (CBC)**
Crawford Bay, BC
Toll-Free: 866-306-4636
www.cbc.ca/bc; www.cbc.ca/radio
Social Media: www.facebook.com/radiocbc; www.twitter.com/cbcradio

***Crawford Bay:* CKGF-FM-1** (Freq: 91.9)
Owned by: *CKGF-FM*
Crawford Bay, BC
www.1035thebridge.com

***Duncan:* CJSU-FM** (Freq: 89.7)
Owned by: *Vista Radio**
130 Trans Canada Hwy., Duncan, BC V9L 2P7
Tel: 250-746-0897, *Fax:* 250-748-1517
onair@897sunfm.com
www.897sunfm.com
Tracy Hamilton, General Manager, tracy@897sunfm.com

***Egmont:* CIEG-FM** (Freq: 104.7)
Owned by: *CISQ-FM*
Egmont, BC

***Fort Nelson:* CKRX-FM** (Freq: 102.3)
Owned by: *CKNL-FM*
Fort Nelson, BC

***Fort St John:* CHRX-FM** (Freq: 98.5)
Owned by: *Astral Media Radio G.P.**
10532 Alaska Rd., Fort St John, BC V1J 1B3
Tracey Gard

***Fort St John:* CKFU-FM** (Freq: 100.1)
10423 - 101 Ave., Fort St John, BC V1J 2B7
Tel: 250-787-7100,
reception@moosefm.ca
energeticcity.ca/moosefm
Russ Beerling, General Manager

***Fort St John:* CKNL-FM** (Freq: 101.5)
Owned by: *Astral Media Radio G.P.*
10532 Alaska Rd., Fort St John, BC V1J 1B3
Tel: 250-785-6634, *Fax:* 250-785-4544
www.1015thebear.com
Terry Shepherd, General Manager, tshepherd@astral.com
Dave Lewis, Creative Director, dlewis@astral.com
Andre Da Costa, News Director, adacosta@astral.com

***Fort St. James:* CHNV-FM-1** (Freq: 1480)
Owned by: *CKGF-FM*
Fort St. James, BC
www.thevalleywolf.ca

***Fraser Lake:* CJCI-FM** (Freq: 1450)
Owned by: *CKGF-FM*
Fraser Lake, BC
www.thevalleywolf.ca

***Gold River:* CJJR-FM** (Freq: 101.1)
Owned by: *CFWB*
Gold River, BC

***Gold River:* The River FM**

Owned by: *Vista Radio**
Gold River, BC

***Grand Forks/Greenwood:* CFPA-FM** (Freq: 96.7)
Owned by: *CFPW-FM*
Grand Forks/Greenwood, BC

***Kamloops:* CFBX-FM** (Freq: 92.5)
900 McGill Rd., House 8, Kamloops, BC V2C 5N3
Tel: 250-377-3988,
radio@tru.ca
www.theX.ca
Brant Zwicker, Station Manager

***Kamloops:* CIFM-FM** (Freq: 98.3)
Owned by: *The Jim Pattison Broadcast Group**
460 Pemberton Terrace, Kamloops, BC V2C 1T5
Tel: 250-372-3322, *Fax:* 250-374-0445
info@98.3cifm.com
www.98.3cifm.com
Rick Arnish, President & General Manager

***Kamloops:* CKBZ-FM** (Freq: 100.1)
Owned by: *The Jim Pattison Broadcast Group**
460 Pemberton Terrace, Kamloops, BC V2C 1T5
Tel: 250-372-3322, *Fax:* 250-374-0445
cheryl@b100.ca
www.b100.ca
Cheryl Blackwell, Goodmorning Kamloops Host

***Kamloops:* CKRV-FM** (Freq: 97.5)
611 Lansdowne St., Kamloops, BC V2C 1Y6
Tel: 250-372-2197, *Fax:* 250-372-2293
river@ckrv.com
www.ckrv.com
Robbie Dunn

***Kelowna:* CBTK-FM** (Freq: 88.9)
Owned by: *Canadian Broadcasting Corporation (CBC)**
Kelowna, BC
Toll-Free: 866-306-4636
www.cbc.ca/bc; www.cbc.ca/radio
Social Media: www.facebook.com/radiocbc; www.twitter.com/cbcradio
Jennifer Smith, Director, Sales & Marketing, Western Canada, 604-662-6616

***Kelowna:* CILK-FM** (Freq: 101.5)
1598 Pandosy St., Kelowna, BC V1Y 1P4
Tel: 250-860-1010, *Fax:* 250-860-0505
info@silk.fm
www.silk.fm

***Kelowna:* CKCQ-FM** (Freq: Broadcasts at 920 AM in Quesnel, and at 570 AM in Williams Lake)
Owned by: *Vista Radio**
1729 Gordon Dr., Kelowna, BC V1Y 3H3
Tel: 250-980-9009, *Fax:* 250-980-1038
1039thejuice.com
Brian Edwards, President

***Kelowna:* CKLZ-FM** (Freq: 104.7)
Owned by: *The Jim Pattison Broadcast Group**
3805 Lakeshore Rd., Kelowna, BC V1W 3K6
Tel: 250-763-1047, *Fax:* 250-762-2141
info@power104.fm
www.power104.fm

***Lillooet:* CHLS-FM** (Freq: 100.5)
PO Box 2124, #415 Main St., Lillooet, BC V0K 1V0
Tel: 250-256-2113, *Fax:* 250-256-2113
station@radiolillooet.ca
radiolillooet.ca

***Mackenzie:* CHMM-FM** (Freq: 103.5)
PO Box 547, 86 Centennial Ave., Mackenzie, BC V0J 2C0
Tel: 250-997-6277, *Fax:* 250-997-6222
chmm1035@gmail.com
www.chmm.ca
J. D. MacKenzie, Station Manager

***Merritt:* Merritt Broadcasting Ltd.**
PO Box 1630, #201, 2196 Quilchena Avenue, Merritt, BC V1K 1B8
Tel: 250-378-4288, *Fax:* 250-378-6979
info@q101.ca
www.q101.ca

***Nanaimo:* CHLY-FM** (Freq: 101.7)
The Radio Malaspina Society, #2, 34 Victoria Rd., Nanaimo, BC V9R 5B8
Tel: 250-716-3410, *Fax:* 250-716-1082
www.chly.ca
Dylan Perry, Program Manager, programdirector@chly.ca

***Nanaimo:* CHPQ-FM** (Freq: 99.9)
Owned by: *Island Radio Ltd.**
4550 Wellington Rd., Nanaimo, BC V9P 2H3
Tel: 850-758-1131, *Fax:* 250-758-4644
info@islandradio.bc.ca
www.islandradio.bc.ca
Paul Larsen, President

***Nanaimo:* CHWF-FM** (Freq: 106.9)
Owned by: *Island Radio Ltd.**
4550 Wellington Rd., Nanaimo, BC V9T 2H3
Tel: 250-758-1131, *Fax:* 250-758-4644
info@1069thewolf.com
www.1069thewolf.com
Social Media: www.facebook.com/1069thewolf, twitter.com/1069thewolf
Rob Bye, General Manager

***Nanaimo:* CKWV-FM** (Freq: 102.3)
Owned by: *Island Radio Ltd.**
4550 Wellington Rd., Nanaimo, BC V9T 2H3
Tel: 250-758-1131, *Fax:* 250-758-4644
info@1023thewave.com
www.1023thewave.com
Rob Bye, General Manager

***Nelson:* CJLY-FM** (Freq: 93.5; 96.5)
308a Hall St., Nelson, BC V1L 1Y8
Tel: 250-352-9600, *Fax:* 250-352-9663
www.kootenaycoopradio.com

***Nelson:* CKGF-FM** (Freq: 103.5)
Owned by: *Vista Radio**
312 Hall St., Nelson, BC V1L 1Y8
Tel: 250-352-1902, *Fax:* 250-352-0301
www.1035thebridge.com

***Nelson:* CKKC-FM** (Freq: 106.9)
513C Front St., Nelson, BC V1L 4B4
Tel: 250-368-5510, *Fax:* 250-368-8471
kootenays.myezrock.com
Nicole Beetstra, General Manager, 250-368-5510

***Parksville:* CIBH-FM** (Freq: 88.5)
Owned by: *Island Radio Ltd.**
PO Box 1370, 166 E. Isl Highway, Parksville, BC V9P 2H3
Tel: 250-248-4211, *Fax:* 250-248-4210
info@885thebeach.com
885thebeach.com
Rob Bye, General Manager
Kent Wilson, Program Director

***Penticton:* CIGV-FM** (Freq: 100.7)
201-1301 Main St., Penticton, BC V2A 5E9
Tel: 250-493-6767, *Fax:* 250-493-0098
Toll-Free: 888-493-6767
okanagancountry.com
James Robinson, General Manager

***Penticton:* CJMG-FM** (Freq: 97.1)
Owned by: *Astral Media Radio G.P.**

** For details on this company see listing in Major Broadcasting Companies section; † French language station*

33 Carmi Ave., Penticton, BC V2A 3G4
Tel: 250-492-2800, *Fax:* 250-493-0370
www.thesun.net

***Port Alberni:* CJAV-FM** (Freq: 93.3)
Owned by: *Island Radio Ltd.**
3296 - 3rd Ave., Port Alberni, BC V9Y 4E1
Tel: 250-723-2455, *Fax:* 250-723-0797
info@933thepeak.com
www.933thepeak.com
Social Media: www.facebook.com/933thepeak
Bye Rob, General Manager

***Port Hardy:* CKGR-FM** (Freq: 100.3)
Owned by: *Vista Radio**
7035 A Market St., Port Hardy, BC V0N 2P0
Tel: 205-949-6500, *Fax:* 250-949-6580
www.theport.ca

***Port Hardy:* The Port FM** (Freq: 1240)
Owned by: *Vista Radio**
7035 A Market St., Port Hardy, BC V0N 2P0
Tel: 205-949-6500, *Fax:* 250-949-6580
www.theport.ca

***Powell River:* CIQC-FM** (Freq: 95.7)
Owned by: *Vista Radio**
103-4675 Marine Ave., Powell River, BC V8A 2L2
Tel: 604-485-4207, *Fax:* 604-485-4210
onair@957sunfm.ca
www.957sunfm.ca
Social Media: www.facebook.com/957sunfm

***Powell River:* CJMP-FM** (Freq: 90.1)
4476 Marine Ave., Powell River, BC V8A 2K2
Tel: 604-485-2688, *Fax:* 604-485-2683
onair@cjmp.ca
cjmp.ca
Social Media: www.facebook.com/CJMP90.1FM, twitter.com/cjmpfm
Angela Lafortune, Operations Director

***Prince George:* CBYG-FM** (Freq: 91.5)
Owned by: *Canadian Broadcasting Corporation**
#1, 890 Victoria St., Prince George, BC V2L 5P1
Tel: 250-562-6701, *Fax:* 250-562-4777
daybreaknorth@cbc.ca
www.cbc.ca/bc

***Prince George:* CFUR-FM** (Freq: 88.7)
3333 University Way, Prince George, BC V2N 4Z9
Tel: 250-960-7664, *Fax:* 250-960-5995
fhayes@cfur.ca
www.cfur.ca
Fraser Hayes, Station Manager

***Prince George:* CIVH-AM** (Freq: 94.3)
Owned by: *Vista Radio**
1940 - 3 Ave., Prince George, BC V2M 1G7
Tel: 250-564-2524, *Fax:* 250-562-6611
onair@94xfm.com
www.94xfm.com
Social Media: www.facebook.com/94XRockRadioRules, twitter.com/94xfm
Terry Shepherd, President & General Manager

***Prince George:* CKDV-FM** (Freq: 99.3)
Owned by: *The Jim Pattison Broadcast Group**
1810 - 3rd Ave., 2nd Fl., Prince George, BC V2M 1G4
Tel: 250-564-8861, *Fax:* 250-562-8768
www.993thedrive.com
Ken Kilcullen, General Manager, kkilcullen@ckpg.com
Kelli Moorhead, General Sales Manager, kmoorhead@ckpg.com

***Prince George:* CKGF-FM-2** (Freq: 97.3)
Owned by: *CKGF-FM*
Prince George, BC
www.1035thebridge.com

***Prince George:* CKKN-FM** (Freq: 101.3)
Owned by: *The Jim Pattison Broadcast Group**
1810 3rd Ave., 2nd Fl., Prince George, BC V2M 1G4
Tel: 250-564-8861, *Fax:* 250-562-8768
ckpgmail@ckpg.bc.ca
1013theriver.com

***Quesnel:* CFFM-FM** (Freq: 100.3)
Owned by: *Vista Radio**
502-410 Kinchant St., Quesnel, BC V2J 7J5
Tel: 250-992-7046, *Fax:* 250-992-2354
www.thewolfonline.ca

***Quesnel:* CFFM-FM-2** (Freq: 94.9)
Owned by: *CFFM-FM*
Quesnel, BC

***Richmond:* CHKG-FM** (Freq: 96.1)
Owned by: *Fairchild Radio**
#2090 Aberdeen Centre, 4151 Hazelbridge Way, Richmond, BC V6X 4J7
www.fm961.com
Seme Ho, Assistant Vice-President, 604-295-1230, Fax: 604-295-1201, semeho@am1470.com
Leela Donna, Creative and Promotions Co-ordinator, 604-295-1252, Fax: 604-295-1201, leela@fm961.com

***Rock Creek/Osoyoos/Oliver:* CKQR-FM-1** (Freq: 103.7)
Owned by: *CFPW-FM*
Rock Creek/Osoyoos/Oliver, BC

***Salmon Arm:* CKXR-FM** (Freq: 91.5)
Owned by: *Astral Media Radio G.P.**
PO Box 69, 360 Ross St. NE, Salmon Arm, BC V1E 4N2
Tel: 250-832-2161, *Fax:* 250-832-2240
www.myezrock.com

***Smithers:* CIRX-FM** (Freq: 106.5)
Owned by: *Vista Radio**
1139 Queen St., Smithers, BC V0J 2N0
Tel: 250-847-2521,
www.thepeak.ca
Social Media: www.facebook.com/peakfanpage, twitter.com/thepeakonair

***Squamish:* CISC-FM** (Freq: A component of Mountain FM, the station broadcasts at 107.5 FM in Gibsons)
Owned by: *Rogers Communications**
#202, 40147 Glenalder Place, Squamish, BC V8B 0G2
Tel: 604-892-1021, *Fax:* 604-892-6383
mountainfm@mountainfm.com
www.mountainfm.com
Joe Polito, Manager

***Squamish:* CISP-FM** (Freq: The station is a component of Mountain FM & broadcasts at 104.5 FM in Pemberton)
Owned by: *Rogers Communications**
#202, 40147 Glenalder Place, Squamish, BC V8B 0G2
Tel: 604-892-1021, *Fax:* 604-892-6383
Toll-Free: 888-429-2724
mountainfm@mountainfm.com
www.mountainfm.com
Gary Miles, President
Joe Polito, Manager

***Squamish:* CISQ-FM** (Freq: A component of Mountain FM, the station broadcasts at 107.1 FM in Squamish, and at 102.1 FM in Whistler.)
Owned by: *Rogers Communications**
#202, 40147 Glenalder Place, Squamish, BC V8B 0G2
Tel: 604-892-1021, *Fax:* 604-892-6383
Toll-Free: 888-429-2724
moutainfm@mountainfm.com
www.mountainfm.com
Joe Polito, Manager

***Squamish:* CISW-FM** (Freq: 102.1)
#202, 40147 Glenalder Place, Squamish, BC V8B 0G2
Tel: 604-892-1021, *Fax:* 604-892-6383
www.mountainfm.com

***Terrace:* CJFW-FM** (Freq: 103.1)
Owned by: *Astral Media Radio G.P.**
4625 Lazelle Ave., Terrace, BC V8G 1S4
Tel: 250-635-6316, *Fax:* 250-638-6320
www.cjfw.ca
Brian Langston, General Manager, blangston@astral.com

***Terrace:* CKTK-FM** (Freq: 1230)
Owned by: *Astral Media Radio G.P.**
4625 Lazelle Ave., Terrace, BC V8G 1S4
Tel: 250-635-6316, *Fax:* 250-638-6320
kitimat.myezrock.com
Brian Langston, General Manager, blangston@astral.com

***Trail:* CJAT-FM** (Freq: 95.7)
Owned by: *Astral Media Radio G.P.**
1560 Second Ave., Trail, BC V1R 1M4
Tel: 250-368-5510, *Fax:* 250-368-8471
www.kbsradio.ca
Nicole Beetstra, General Manager, 250-368-5510

***Trail:* CKZX-FM** (Freq: 93.5)
Owned by: *Astral Media Radio G.P.*
1560 - 2nd Ave., Trail, BC V1R 1M4
Tel: 250-368-5510, *Fax:* 250-368-8471
kootenays.myezrock.com
Lee Sterry, Operations Manager

†*Vancouver:* CBUF-FM (Freq: 97.7)*Détenteur:* **Canadian Broadcasting Corporation***
CP 4600, 700, rue Hamilton, Vancouver, BC V6B 4A2
Tél: 604-662-6135,
www.radio-canada.ca
Pierre Guerin, Directeur des services francais dans l'ouest, 204-788-3237, pierre.guerin@radio-canada.ca

***Vancouver:* CBU-FM** (Freq: 105.7)
Owned by: *Canadian Broadcasting Corporation**
Vancouver, BC
music.cbc.ca/#/radio2

***Vancouver:* CBUX-FM** (Freq: 90.9)
Owned by: *Canadian Broadcasting Corporation**
PO Box 4600, 700 rue Hamilton, Vancouver, BC V6B 4A2
Tel: 604-662-6135,
www.radio-canada.ca/regions/colombie-britannique

***Vancouver:* CFBT-FM** (Freq: 94.5)
Owned by: *Bell Media Radio**
#300, 380 West 2nd Ave., Vancouver, BC V5Y 1C8
Tel: 604-871-9000, *Fax:* 604-871-2901
www.thebeat.com

***Vancouver:* CFMI-FM** (Freq: 101.1)
Owned by: *Corus Premium Television Ltd.**
#2000, 700 West Georgia St., Vancouver, BC V7Y 1K9
Tel: 604-331-2808, *Fax:* 604-331-2722
www.rock101.com
Social Media: www.facebook.com/ClassicRock101, twitter.com/ClassicRock101
Andy Ross, Program Director

***Vancouver:* CFOX-FM** (Freq: 99.3)
Owned by: *Corus Radio Company**
#2000, 700 West Georgia St., Vancouver, BC V7Y 1K9
Tel: 604-684-7221, *Fax:* 604-331-2722
www.cfox.com

***Vancouver:* CFRO-FM** (Freq: 102.7)
#110, 360 Columbia St., Vancouver, BC V6A 4J1
Tel: 604-684-8494,
www.coopradio.org
McNabb Robin, Membership & Outreach Coordinator

***Vancouver:* CHQM-FM** (Freq: 103.5)
Owned by: *Bell Media Radio**
#300, 380 West 2nd Ave., Vancouver, BC V5Y 1C8
Tel: 604-871-9000, *Fax:* 604-871-2901
www.qmfm.com
Mel Kemmis, Program Director

***Vancouver:* CITR-FM** (Freq: 101.9)
#233, 6138 Sub Blvd., Vancouver, BC V6T 1Z1
Tel: 604-882-1242, *Fax:* 604-882-9364
stationmanager@citr.ca
www.citr.ca
Social Media: www.facebook.com/groups/5245040262/, twitter.com/CiTRradio
Brenda Grunau, Station Manager

***Vancouver:* CJJR-FM** (Freq: 93.7)
Owned by: *The Jim Pattison Broadcast Group**
#300, 1401 - 8th Ave. West, Vancouver, BC V6H 1C9
Tel: 604-731-7772, *Fax:* 604-731-0493
cjjr@jfrm.com
www.jrfm.com
Social Media: www.facebook.com/937jrfm, twitter.com/jrfm

***Vancouver:* CKLG-FM** (Freq: 96.9)
Owned by: *Rogers Broadcasting Ltd.**
2440 Ash St., Vancouver, BC V5Z 4J6
Tel: 604-872-2557,
www.jackfm.com
Wolfgang von Petrie

***Vanderhoof:* CHNV-FM** (Freq: 1340)
Owned by: *CKGF-FM*
150 West Columbia St., Vanderhoof, BC T0J 3A0
Tel: 250-567-4914, *Fax:* 250-567-4909
www.thevalleywolf.ca

** For details on this company see listing in Major Broadcasting Companies section; † French language station*

***Vanderhoof:* The Valley Wolf** (Freq: Owns and operates several radio stations serving the British Columbia Interior.)
150 West Columbia Street, PO Box 1370, Vanderhoof, BC V0J 3A0
Tel: 250-567-4914, *Fax:* 250-567-4982
www.thevalleywolf.ca

***Vernon:* CICF-FM** (Freq: 105.7)
Owned by: *Astral Media Radio G.P.**
2800 - 31 St., Vernon, BC V1T 5H4
Tel: 250-545-9222, *Fax:* 250-542-2083
reception@thesunonline.ca
www.thesunonline.ca

***Vernon:* CKIZ-FM** (Freq: 107.5)
Owned by: *Rogers Broadcasting Ltd.**
3313 - 32 Ave., Vernon, BC V1T 2E1
Tel: 250-545-2141, *Fax:* 250-545-9008
www.1075kiss.com
Social Media: www.linkedin.com/pub/107-5-kiss-fm/28/916/409, www.facebook.com/1075.KISS, twitter.com/1075KISSFM

***Victoria:* CFUV-FM** (Freq: 101.9)
University of Victoria, PO Box 3035, Victoria, BC V8W 3P3
Tel: 250-721-8702,
director@uvic.ca
cfuv.uvic.ca
Randy Gelling, Station Manager, 250-721-8607, cfuvman@uvic.ca

***Victoria:* CHBE-FM** (Freq: 107.3)
Owned by: *Bell Media Radio**
1420 Broad St., Victoria, BC V8W 2B1
Tel: 250-382-1073,
www.1073kool.fm
Robin Haggar, Program Director

***Victoria:* CHTT-FM** (Freq: 103.1)
Owned by: *Rogers Broadcasting Ltd.**
817 Fort St., Victoria, BC V8W 1H6
Tel: 250-382-0900, *Fax:* 250-382-4358
www.1031jackfm.com

***Victoria:* CIOC-FM** (Freq: 98.5)
Owned by: *Rogers Broadcasting Ltd.**
817 Fort St., Victoria, BC V8W 1H6
Tel: 250-382-0900, *Fax:* 250-382-4358
www.ocean985.com

***Victoria:* CJZN-FM** (Freq: 91.3)
2750 Quadra St., Top Floor, Victoria, BC V8T 4E8
Tel: 250-475-6611, *Fax:* 250-475-3299
www.thezone.fm
Social Media: www.TheZone.fm/facebook, www.TheZone.fm/twitter
Dan McAllister, General Manager

***Victoria:* CKKQ-FM** (Freq: 100.3)
2750 Quadra St., 3rd Fl., Victoria, BC V8T 4E8
Tel: 250-475-0100, *Fax:* 250-475-3299
www.theq.fm
Stu Morton, President/General Manager

***Williams Lake:* CFFM-FM1** (Freq: 570)
Owned by: *Vista Radio**
83 South First Ave., Williams Lake, BC V2G 1H4
Tel: 250-392-6551, *Fax:* 250-392-4142
tgard@vistaradio.ca
www.thewolfonline.ca
Social Media: www.facebook.com/pages/The-Wolf-Online/164187966948000

Manitoba

***Brandon:* CIWM-FM** (Freq: 91.5)
Owned by: *CINC-FM*
Brandon, MB

***Brandon:* CJJJ-FM** (Freq: 106.5)
1430 Victoria Ave. East, Brandon, MB R7A 2A9
Tel: 204-725-8700, *Fax:* 204-726-7014
Toll-Free: 800-862-6307
info@assiniboine.net
www.assiniboine.net
Social Media: www.facebook.com/accmanitoba, twitter.com/ACCMB
Bob Crighton, Station Manager

***Brandon:* CKLF-FM** (Freq: 94.7)
624 - 14 St. East, Brandon, MB R7A 7E1
Tel: 204-726-8888, *Fax:* 204-726-1270
starfm@starfmradio.com
www.starfmradio.com
David Baxter, President
Cam Clark, General Manager

***Brandon:* CKXA-FM** (Freq: 101.1)
Owned by: *Astral Media Radio G.P.**
2940 Victoria Ave., Brandon, MB R7B 3Y3
Tel: 204-728-1150, *Fax:* 204-725-3794
www.1011thefarm.com
Taylor Sharon, General Manager

***Brandon:* CKX-FM** (Freq: 96.1)
Owned by: *Astral Media Radio G.P.**
2940 Victoria Ave., Brandon, MB R7B 3Y3
Tel: 204-728-1150, *Fax:* 204-725-3794
kx96@kx96online.com
www.kx96online.com
Social Media: www.facebook.com/KX96FM
Alan Cruise, CEO & President
Sharon Taylor, General Manager, staylor@astral.com
Janet Trecarten, Operations Manager, jtrecarten@astral.com

***Cross Lake:* CFNC-FM** (Freq: 1490)
PO Box 129, Cross Lake, MB R0B 0J0
Tel: 204-676-2331, *Fax:* 204-676-2911
Joyce Halcrow, Station Manager

***Portage la Prairie:* CFRY-FM** (Freq: 93.1)
Owned by: *CFRY*
Portage la Prairie, MB

***Pukatawagan:* CFPX-FM** (Freq: 98.3)
General Delivery, Pukatawagan, MB R0B 1G0
Tel: 204-553-2155
John Colomb, General Manager

***†Saint-Boniface:* CKXL-FM** (Freq: 91.1)
340, boul Provencher, Saint-Boniface, MB R2H 0G7
Tél: 204-233-4243, *Téléc:* 204-233-3646
Ligne sans frais: 866-894-3691
www.envol91.mb.ca

***Steinbach:* CILT-FM** (Freq: 96.7)
Owned by: *Golden West Broadcasting Ltd.**
#105, 32 Brandt St., Steinbach, MB R5G 2J7
Tel: 204-326-3737, *Fax:* 204-326-2299
www.steinbachonline.com
Social Media: www.facebook.com/MIX96.7FM, twitter.com/mix967fm

***The Pas:* CITP-FM** (Freq: 92.7)
Owned by: *CINC-FM*
The Pas, MB

***Thompson:* CBWK-FM** (Freq: 100.9)
Owned by: *Canadian Broadcasting Corporation**
Thompson, MB
www.cbc.ca/manitoba
Social Media: www.facebook.com/cbcmanitoba, twitter.com/CBCManitoba

***Thompson:* CINC-FM** (Freq: 96.3)
Owned by: *CINC-FM*
1507 Inkster Blvd., Thompson, MB R2X 1R2
Tel: 204-772-8255,
www.ncifm.com

***Winkler:* CJEL-FM** (Freq: 93.5)
Owned by: *Golden West Broadcasting Ltd.**
PO Box 399, 277 1st, Winkler, MB R6W 4A6
Tel: 204-331-9300, *Fax:* 204-325-2206
www.eagle935fm.com
Social Media: www.facebook.com/Eagle935FM, twitter.com/Eagle935FM

***Winnipeg:* CBW-FM** (Freq: 98.3)
Owned by: *Canadian Broadcasting Corporation**
541 Portage Ave., Winnipeg, MB R3C 2G1
Tel: 204-788-3222,
www.cbc.ca/manitoba
Other information: TTY: 866-220-6045

***Winnipeg:* CFEQ-FM** (Freq: 107.1)
1 - 741 St. Mary's Rd., Winnipeg, MB R2M 3N5
Tel: 204-452-9602, *Toll-Free:* 866-951-2486
www.freq107.com
Social Media: www.facebook.com/ignite107
Tom Hiebert, General Manager

***Winnipeg:* CFQX-FM** (Freq: 104.4)
177 Lombard Ave., 3rd Fl., Winnipeg, MB R3B 0W5
Tel: 204-944-1031, *Fax:* 204-989-5291
www.qx104fm.com
Lee Sterry, General Manager

***Winnipeg:* CFWM-FM** (Freq: 99.9)
Owned by: *Bell Media Radio*
1445 Pembina Hwy., Winnipeg, MB R3T 5C2
Tel: 204-477-5120, *Fax:* 204-453-0815
www.999bobfm.com
Mark Maheu, General Manager, bobweb13@chumradio.com
David Drake, Program Director, bobweb13@chumradio.com

***Winnipeg:* CHIQ-FM** (Freq: 94.3)
Owned by: *Bell Media Radio**
1445 Pembina Hwy., Winnipeg, MB R3T 5C2
Tel: 204-477-5120, *Fax:* 204-453-0815
www.curve943.com

***Winnipeg:* CHVN-FM** (Freq: 95.1)
Owned by: *Golden West Broadcasting Ltd.**
1 - 741 St. Mary's Rd., Winnipeg, MB R2M 3N5
Tel: 204-452-9602,
www.chvnradio.com
Els Fenton, Station & General Sales Manager, efenton@goldenwestradio.com

***Winnipeg:* CHWE-FM**

Owned by: *Evanov Radio Group**
520 Corydon Ave., Winnipeg, MB R3L 0P1
Tel: 204-477-1221, *Fax:* 204-453-8244
www.energy106.ca

***Winnipeg:* CICY-FM** (Freq: 105.5)
1507 Inkster Blvd., Winnipeg, MB R2X 1R2
Tel: 204-772-8255,
www.ncifm.com
Hoa Bui, Broadcast Technical Manager

***Winnipeg:* CINC-FM** (Freq: 105.5 fm)
1507 Inkster Blvd., Winnipeg, MB R2X 1R2
Tel: 204-772-8255,
www.ncifm.com
David McLeod, General Manager
Marshall Lank, Director, Sales & Marketing

***Winnipeg:* CJKR-FM** (Freq: 97.5)
Owned by: *Corus Premium Television Ltd.**
#200, 1440 Jack Blick Ave., Winnipeg, MB R3G 0L4
Tel: 204-786-2471, *Fax:* 204-783-4512
www.power97.com
Matt Cundill, Program Director, mcundill@power97.com

***Winnipeg:* CJUM-FM** (Freq: 101.5)
University of Manitoba, #308, University Centre, Winnipeg, MB R3T 2N2
Tel: 204-474-7027, *Fax:* 204-269-1299
cjum@cjum.com
www.umfm.com
Social Media: twitter.com/UMFM
Jared McKetiak, Station Manager, jared@umfm.com
Jared McKetiak, Program Director

***Winnipeg:* CKMM-FM** (Freq: 103.1)
177 Lombard Ave., 3rd Fl., Winnipeg, MB R3B 0W5
Tel: 204-944-1031, *Fax:* 204-989-5291
www.hot103live.com
Sharon Taylor, General Manager, staylor@astral.com
Ace Burpee, Program Director, ace@hot103.astral.com

***Winnipeg:* CKUW-FM** (Freq: 95.9)
University of Winnipeg, #4CM11, 515 Portage, Winnipeg, MB R3B 2E9
Tel: 204-786-9782, *Fax:* 204-783-7080
ckuw@uwinnipeg.ca
www.ckuw.ca
Rob Schmidt, Station Manager

***Winnipeg:* CKY-FM** (Freq: 102.3)
Owned by: *Rogers Broadcasting Ltd.**
#4, 166 Osborne St., Winnipeg, MB R3L 1Y8
Tel: 204-780-3400, *Fax:* 204-788-3401
www.102clearfm.com
Social Media: www.facebook.com/1023clearfm, twitter.com/1023clearfm

** For details on this company see listing in Major Broadcasting Companies section; † French language station*

***Winnipeg:* Red River College** (Freq: Home of 92.9 KICK-FM, a non-profit instructional radio station based at Red River College in Winnipeg, Manitoba.)
2055 Notre Dame Avenue, Winnipeg, MB R3H 0J9
Tel: 204-632-3960,
www.rrc.mb.ca

New Brunswick

†*Balmoral:* CIMS-FM (Freq: 103.9)
CP 2561, 1991, av des Pionniers, Balmoral, NB E8E 2W7
Tél: 506-826-1040, *Téléc:* 506-826-2400
info@cimsfm.ca
cimsfm.com
Rico Levesque, President

***Bathurst:* CKBC-FM** (Freq: 104.9)
***Owned by:** Astral Media Radio Atlantic**
#1, 640 St. Peter Ave., Bathurst, NB E2A 2Y7
Tel: 506-547-1360, *Fax:* 506-547-1367
maxfm@radioatl.ca
www.max1049.ca
Jamie Robichaud

†*Bathurst:* CKLE-FM (Freq: 92.9)
#10, 195 rue Main, Bathurst, NB E2A 1A7
Tél: 506-546-4600, *Téléc:* 506-546-6611
superstation@ckle.fm
www.ckle.fm

†*Edmundston:* CFAI-FM (Freq: 101.1; 105.1)
165, boul Hebert, 6e étage, Edmundston, NB E3V 2S8
Tél: 506-737-5060,
radio@cfai.fm
www.cfai.fm
Serge Parent, Dir de la Station

†*Edmundston:* CJEM-FM (Freq: 92.7)
64, rue Rice, Edmundston, NB E3V 1T2
Tél: 506-735-3351, *Téléc:* 506-739-5803
cjem@cjemfm.com
cjemfm.com
Julie Berube, 506-735-3351

†*Edmundston:* CKMV-FM (Freq: 95.1)
64, rue Rice, Edmundston, NB E3V 1T2
Tél: 506-735-3351, *Téléc:* 506-739-5803
cjem@cjemfm.com
cjemfm.com
Murillo Soucy, General Manager, 506-737-3766

***Fredericton:* CBZF-FM** (Freq: 99.5)
***Owned by:** Canadian Broadcasting Corporation**
PO Box 2200, 1160 Regent St., Fredericton, NB E3B 5G4
Tel: 506-451-4000, *Fax:* 506-451-4170
www.cbc.ca/nb

***Fredericton:* CFXY-FM** (Freq: 105.3)
***Owned by:** Astral Media Radio Atlantic**
206 Rookwood Ave., Fredericton, NB E3B 2M2
Tel: 506-454-2444, *Fax:* 506-452-2345
khjnews@astral.com
www.foxrocks.ca
Social Media: www.facebook.com/105TheFox,
twitter.com/105TheFox
John Eddy, Exec. Vice-President

***Fredericton:* CHSR-FM** (Freq: 97.9)
PO Box 4400, 223-21 Pacey Dr., Fredericton, NB E3B 5A3
Tel: 506-453-4985,
stationmanager@chsrfm.ca
chsrfm.ca
Social Media:
www.facebook.com/pages/CHSR-FM-Official/238304316821,
twitter.com/CHSR979

***Fredericton:* CIBX-FM** (Freq: 106.9)
***Owned by:** Astral Media Radio Atlantic Inc.**
206 Rookwood Ave., Fredericton, NB E3B 2M2
Tel: 506-455-1069, *Fax:* 506-452-2345
khjnews@astral.com
www.capitalfm.ca
Pat Brennan, General Manager, 506-452-2334

***Fredericton:* CIXN-FM** (Freq: 96.5)
#10, 1010 Hanwell Rd., Fredericton, NB E3B 6A4
Tel: 506-454-9600, *Fax:* 506-454-0991
welcome@joyfm.ca
www.joyfm.ca
Garth McCrea, General Manager

***Fredericton:* CJPN-FM** (Freq: 90.5)
715, rue Priestman, Fredericton, NB E3B 5W7
Tel: 506-454-2576, *Fax:* 506-453-3958
cjpn@live.ca
www.cjpn.ca

***Fredericton:* CKTP-FM** (Freq: 95.7)
PO Box R13, 150 Cliffe St., Fredericton, NB E3A 0A1
Tel: 506-474-2795, *Fax:* 506-206-3301
info@957thewolf.ca
www.cktpradio.com
Social Media: www.facebook.com/957WOLF
Timothy Paul, General Manager

***Grand Falls:* CIKX-FM** (Freq: 93.5)
***Owned by:** Astral Media Radio Atlantic**
399 Broadway Blvd., Grand Falls, NB E3Z 2K5
Tel: 506-473-9393, *Fax:* 506-473-3893
K93@astral.com
www.k93.ca
Rick McGuire, Programming Director, 506-325-3035
Rick McGuire, Program Director
Jacques LaFrance, Sales Manager

***Kedgwick:* CFJU-FM** (Freq: French language community radio at 90.1 FM in Kedgwick & in St. Quentin)
PO Box 1043, Kedgwick, NB E8B 1Z9
Tel: 506-235-9000, *Fax:* 506-235-9001
cfjufm@rogers.com
Lucille Thériault, General Manager

***Miramichi:* CFAN-FM** (Freq: 99.3)
***Owned by:** Maritime Broadcasting System**
396 Pleasant St., Miramichi, NB E1V 1X5
Tel: 506-622-3311, *Fax:* 506-627-0335
www.993theriver.com

†*Moncton:* CBAF-FM (Freq: Radio-Canada Première Chaîne 88.5 MHz (FM) à Moncton; 102.3 FM à Fredericton/Saint-Jean; 105.7 FM à Bathurst; 91.5 FM à Campbellton; 100.3 FM à Edmunston; 90.3 FM à Lamèque/Caraquet; et 91.7 FM à Bon Accord.)*Détenteur:* **Canadian Broadcasting Corporation***
250, av Université, Moncton, NB E1C 5K3
Tél: 506-853-6666, *Téléc:* 506-853-8000
Ligne sans frais: 800-561-7010
www.radio-canada.ca/regions/acadie

†*Moncton:* CBAL-FM (Freq: 98.3; 95.3; 101.9; 98.9)*Détenteur:* **Canadian Broadcasting Corporation***
CP 950, 250, av Université, Moncton, NB E1C 8N8
Tél: 506-853-6666, *Téléc:* 506-853-6739
Ligne sans frais: 800-561-7010
www.radio-canada.ca/espace_musique
Susan Mitton, Regional Director-Radio

***Moncton:* CFQM-FM** (Freq: 103.9)
***Owned by:** Maritime Broadcasting System**
1000 St. George Blvd., Moncton, NB E1E 4M7
Tel: 506-858-1220, *Fax:* 506-858-1209
1039maxfm.com
Social Media: www.facebook.com/monctonsgreatesthits

†*Moncton:* CHOY-FM (Freq: 99.9)*Détenteur:* **Maritime Broadcasting System***
Choix 99, 1000, boul St-George, Moncton, NB E1E 4M7
Tél: 506-384-2469,
choix999.com

***Moncton:* CJMO-FM** (Freq: 103.1)
***Owned by:** NewCap Inc.**
27 Arsenault Ct., Moncton, NB E1E 4J8
Tel: 506-858-5525, *Fax:* 506-858-5539
c103@c103.com
www.c103.com
Social Media: www.facebook.com/c103moncton,
twitter.com/c103
Dave Ostler, Sales Manager
Andrew Stewart, Program Director
Hilary Montbourquette, General Manager

***Moncton:* CJXL-FM** (Freq: 96.9)
27 Arsenault Ct., Moncton, NB E1E 4J8
Tel: 506-858-5525, *Fax:* 506-858-5539
www.xl96.com
Social Media: www.facebook.com/xl969,
twitter.com/scottyandtony
Hilary Montbourquette, General Manager

***Moncton:* CKOE-FM** (Freq: 107.3)
3030 Mountain Rd., Moncton, NB E1G 2W8
Tel: 506-384-1009, *Fax:* 506-383-9699
info@ckoefm.com
www.ckoefm.com
Kurk Parks, Station Manager

***Pokemouche:* CKRO-FM** (Freq: 97.1)
142 Rte 113, Pokemouche, NB E8P 1K7
Tel: 506-336-9706, *Fax:* 506-336-9058
info@ckro.ca
www.ckro.ca
Donald Noel, Dir de la Station

***Sackville:* CHMA-FM** (Freq: 106.9)
62 York St., Sackville, NB E4L 1E2
Tel: 506-364-2221,
chma@mta.ca
www.mta.ca/chma
Ian Sterling, Program Director
Lianne Young, Assistant Program Director

***Saint John:* CBD-FM** (Freq: 91.3)
***Owned by:** Canadian Broadcasting Corporation (CBC)**
PO Box 2358, 560 Main St., Saint John, NB E2L 3V6
Tel: 506-632-7750, *Fax:* 506-632-7761
Toll-Free: 866-306-4636
www.cbc.ca/nb; www.cbc.ca/radio
Social Media: www.facebook.com/radiocbc;
www.twitter.com/cbcradio,
Other information: TTY: 1-866-220-6045
Andrew Cochran, Managing Director, Maritimes
Dan Goodyear, Executive Producer, News, New Brunswick
Deborah Irvine, Executive Producer, Radio Saint John
Janet Irwin, Senior Regional Manager, News & Current Affairs
Nadine Antle, Regional Manager, Partnerships, Communications, Brand, & Promot, 506-451-4054
John Channing, Manager, Sales
Mary-Pat Schutta, Manager, Programs
Lori Wheeler, Senior Officer, Communications, 506-451-4080

***Saint John:* CFMH-FM** (Freq: 92.5)
Student Services, PO Box 5050, Saint John, NB E2L 4L5
Tel: 506-648-5667, *Fax:* 506-648-5541
cfmh@unbsj.ca
www.unbsj.ca/cfmh
Linda Pelletier, Station Manager

***Saint John:* CHSJ-FM** (Freq: 94.1)
PO Box 2000, Saint John, NB E2L 3T4
Tel: 506-633-3323, *Fax:* 506-644-3485
mail@country94.ca
www.country94.ca
Social Media: www.facebook.com/country94,
twitter.com/country94chsj

***Saint John:* CHWV-FM** (Freq: 97.3)
PO Box 2000, 58 King St., Saint John, NB E2L 3T4
Tel: 506-633-3323, *Fax:* 506-644-3485
mail@thewave.ca
www.thewave.ca
Jim MacMillin, Genera; Manager

***Saint John:* CINB-FM** (Freq: 96.1)
PO Box 96, Saint John, NB E2L 3X1
Tel: 506-657-9600, *Fax:* 506-657-7664
staff@newsongfm.com
www.newsongfm.com
Don Mabee, Station Manager

***Saint John:* CIOK-FM** (Freq: Broadcasts adult contemporary music of the 70's, 80's, 90's and now at 100.5 FM in Saint John. Sister stations: CFBC AM & CJYC FM)
***Owned by:** Maritime Broadcasting System**
226 Union St., Saint John, NB E2L 1B1
Tel: 506-658-5100, *Fax:* 506-658-5116
mailbag@k100.ca
www.k100.ca

***Saint John:* CJEF-FM** (Freq: 103.5)
#3E, 28 King St., Saint John, NB E2L 1G3
Tel: 506-657-1035, *Fax:* 506-642-7408
Gary Stackhouse, General Manager
Geoffrey Rnett, CEO

***Saint John:* CJYC-FM** (Freq: Broadcasting "everything that rocks" at 98.9 FM in Saint John. Sister stations: CFBC AM & CIOK FM)
***Owned by:** Maritime Broadcasting System**

** For details on this company see listing in Major Broadcasting Companies section; † French language station*

226 Union St., Saint John, NB E2L 1B1
Tel: 506-658-5100, *Fax:* 506-658-5116
mailbag@989bigjohnfm.com
www.989bigjohnfm.com

***Shédiac:* CJSE-FM** (Freq: 89.5, 101.7, 107.5)
51, Cornwall, Shédiac, NB E4P 8T8
Tel: 506-532-0080, *Fax:* 506-532-0120
Toll-Free: 800-604-0080
cjse@cjse.ca
www.cjse.ca
Gilles Arsenault

***St Stephen:* CHDT-FM** (Freq: 98.1)
112 Milltown Blvd., St Stephen, NB E3L 1G6
Tel: 506-466-1000, *Fax:* 506-466-4500
www.thetide.ca
Jim MacMillin, General Manager

***St Stephen:* WQDY-FM** (Freq: 92.7)
PO Box 305, St Stephen, NB E3L 2X2
Tel: 207-454-7545, *Fax:* 207-454-3062
Toll-Free: 888-855-2992
wqdy@wqdy.fm
www.wqdy.fm
Bill McVicar

***Woodstock:* CJCJ-FM** (Freq: 104.1)
Owned by:** Astral Media Radio Atlantic Inc.
#1, 131 Queen St., Woodstock, NB E7M 2M8
Tel: 506-325-3030, *Fax:* 506-325-3031
cj104@astral.com
www.cj104.com
Rick McGuire, Program Director, 506-325-3035

Newfoundland & Labrador

***Corner Brook:* CKOZ-FM** (Freq: 92.3)
***Owned by:** Newfoundland Broadcasting Co. Ltd.**
Corner Brook, NL
www.ozfm.com
Biran O'Connell, Station Manager

***Corner Brook:* CKXX-FM** (Freq: 103.9)
***Owned by:** NewCap Inc.**
PO Box 570, 345 O'Connell Dr., Corner Brook, NL A2H 6H5
Tel: 709-634-4570, *Fax:* 709-634-4081
www.k-rock1039.com
Stanley Kruchka, General Manager, stan.kruchka@vocm.com

***Deer Lake:* CFDL-FM** (Freq: 97.9)
***Owned by:** CFCB*
Deer Lake, NL
Tel: 709-634-4570, *Fax:* 706-634-4081
onair@cfcbradio.com
www.cfcbradio.com

***Gander:* CKXD-FM** (Freq: 98.7)
***Owned by:** NewCap Inc.**
PO Box 650, Gander, NL A1V 1X2
Tel: 709-651-3650, *Fax:* 709-651-2542
OnAir@987krock.com
www.987krock.com
Social Media: www.facebook.com/groups/987krock, twitter.com/987krock

***Grand Falls-Windsor:* CKMY-FM** (Freq: 95.9)
***Owned by:** Newfoundland Broadcasting Co. Ltd.**
Grand Falls-Windsor, NL
www.ozfm.com
Brian O'Connell, Station Manager

***Grand Falls-Windsor:* CKXG-FM** (Freq: 102.3; 101.3)
***Owned by:** NewCap Inc.**
35A Grenfell Heights, Grand Falls-Windsor, NL A2A 2K2
Tel: 709-489-2192, *Fax:* 709-489-8626
onair@krocknl.com
www.krocknl.com
Social Media: www.facebook.com/krock.grandfallswindsor, twitter.com/krockgfw

***Happy Valley-Goose Bay:* CFGB-FM** (Freq: 89.5)
***Owned by:** Canadian Broadcasting Corporation**
PO Box 1029 C, Happy Valley-Goose Bay, NL A0P 1C0
Tel: 709-896-2911, *Fax:* 709-896-8900
www.cbc.ca/nl

***Labrador City:* CBDQ-FM** (Freq: 96.3)
***Owned by:** Canadian Broadcasting Corporation (CBC)**
PO Box 12010, Labrador City, NL A2V 2L3
Tel: 709-944-3616, *Fax:* 709-944-5472
Toll-Free: 800-563-7933
labradormorning@cbc.ca
www.cbc.ca/nl
Social Media: www.facebook.com/radiocbc, www.twitter.com/cbcradio
Other information: Phone, Transmission Information: 1-888-353-7006; TTY: 1-866-220-6045
Denise Wilson, Managing Director, Newfoundland & Labrador
Kathy Porter, Executive Producer, English Radio
Maureen Anonsen, Manager, Partnership & Communications, 709-576-5013
Wayne Tilley, Account Manager, 709-576-5019
Debbie Hynes, Senior Officer, Communications, 709-576-5150

***Marystown:* CIOZ-FM** (Freq: 96.3)
***Owned by:** Newfoundland Broadcasting Co. Ltd.**
Marystown, NL
www.ozfm.com

***Red Rocks:* CKSS-FM** (Freq: 96.9)
***Owned by:** Newfoundland Broadcasting Co. Ltd.**
Red Rocks, NL
www.ozfm.com
Brian O'Connell, Station Manager

***St Anthony:* CFNN-FM** (Freq: 97.9)
***Owned by:** CFCB*
St Anthony, NL

***St. John's:* CBN-FM** (Freq: 106.9)
***Owned by:** Canadian Broadcasting Corporation (CBC)**
PO Box 12010 A, St. John's, NL A1B 3T8
Tel: 709-576-5000, *Toll-Free:* 800-563-7933
www.cbc.ca/nl; www.cbc.ca/radio2
Social Media: www.facebook.com/CBC.Radio2.Official?ref=nf, www.twitter.com/cbcradio2
Other information: Phone, Transmission: 888-353-7006
Denise Wilson, Managing Director, Newfoundland & Labrador
Kathy Porter, Executive Producer, English Radio
Maureen Anonsen, Manager, Partnership & Communications, 709-576-5013
Wayne Tilley, Manager, Accounts, 709-576-5019
Debbie Hynes, Senior Officer, Communications, 709-576-5150

***St. John's:* CFOZ-FM** (Freq: 100.3)
***Owned by:** Newfoundland Broadcasting Co. Ltd.**
PO Box 2020, 446 Logy Bay Rd., St. John's, NL A1C 5S2
Tel: 709-726-2922, *Fax:* 709-726-3300
www.ozfm.com
Social Media: www.facebook.com/OZFM.Newfoundland, twitter.com/CHOZFM
Brian O'Connell, Station Manager

***St. John's:* CHMR-FM** (Freq: 93.5)
PO Box A-119, Memorial University, St. John's, NL A1C 5S7
Tel: 709-737-4777, *Fax:* 709-737-7688
chmr@mun.ca
www.mun.ca/chmr
Kathy Rowe, Station Manager

***St. John's:* CHOZ-FM** (Freq: 94.7)
***Owned by:** Newfoundland Broadcasting Co. Ltd.**
PO Box 2020, 446 Logy Bay Rd., St. John's, NL A1C 5S2
Tel: 709-726-2922, *Fax:* 709-726-3300
www.ozfm.com
Social Media: www.facebook.com/OZFM.Newfoundland, twitter.com/CHOZFM
Doug Neal, General Manager

***St. John's:* CHOZ-FM** (Freq: 92.3)
***Owned by:** Newfoundland Broadcasting Co. Ltd.**
PO Box 2020, 446 Logy Bay Rd., St. John's, NL A1C 5S2
www.ozfm.com
Social Media: www.facebook.com/OZFM.Newfoundland, twitter.com/CHOZFM
Brian O'Connell, Station Manager

***St. John's:* CJOZ-FM** (Freq: 92.1)
***Owned by:** Newfoundland Broadcasting Co. Ltd.**
PO Box 2020, 466 Logy Bay Rd., St. John's, NL A1C 5S2
Tel: 709-726-2922, *Fax:* 709-726-3300
www.ozfm.com
Brian O'Connell, Station Manager

***St. John's:* CKIX-FM** (Freq: 99.1)
***Owned by:** NewCap Inc.**
PO Box 8590, 391 Kenmount Rd., St. John's, NL A1B 3P5
Tel: 709-726-5590, *Fax:* 709-726-4633
hitsmail@991hitsfm.com
www.991hitsfm.com
Hilary Montbourquette, Operations Manager
Bob Templeton, President
John Murphy, General Manager

***St. John's:* CKSJ-FM** (Freq: 101.1)
#201, 95 Bonaventure Ave., St. John's, NL A1B 2X5
Tel: 709-754-6748, *Fax:* 709-754-6749
onair@coast1011.com
www.coast1011.com

***St. John's:* VOCM-FM** (Freq: 97.5)
***Owned by:** NewCap Inc.**
PO Box 8590 A, 391 Kenmount Rd., St. John's, NL A1B 3P5
Tel: 709-726-5590, *Fax:* 709-726-4633
email@krockrocks.com
www.k-rock975.com
Social Media: www.facebook.com/975krock, twitter.com/975krock

***Stephenville:* CIOS-FM** (Freq: 98.5)
***Owned by:** Newfoundland Broadcasting Co. Ltd.**
Stephenville, NL
www.ozfm.com
Brian O'Connell, Station Manager

Northwest Territories

†*Yellowknife:* CIVR-FM (Freq: 103.5)
CP 1586, 5106-48th St., Yellowknife, NT X1A 2P2
Tél: 867-766-5172,
www.radiotaiga.ca
Sylvie Boisclair, General Manager

***Yellowknife:* CJCD-FM** (Freq: 100.1)
PO Box 218, Yellowknife, NT X1A 2N2
Tel: 867-920-4636, *Fax:* 867-920-4033
info@cjcd.ca
www.cjcd.ca
Tim Jaworski, Retail Sales Manager, tim@cjcd.ca

***Yellowknife:* CKLB-FM** (Freq: 101.9)
PO Box 2193, Yellowknife, NT X1A 2P6
Tel: 867-873-2977,
www.ncsnwt.com
Les L. Carpenter, Chief Executive Officer, 867-873-2977, ncsceo@gmail.com
Karen Pandke, Executive Assistant, 867-873-2911, ncsnwt.arctic@gmail.com

Nova Scotia

***Antigonish:* CFXU-FM** (Freq: 92.5)
PO Box 948, St. Francis Xavier University, Antigonish, NS B2G 2X1
Tel: 902-867-3941,
thefox@stfx.ca
radiocfxu.ca
John Sloat, Station Manager, cfxu@stfx.ca

***Antigonish:* CJFX-FM** (Freq: 98.9)
PO Box 5800, 85 Kirk St., Antigonish, NS B2G 2R9
Tel: 902-863-4580, *Fax:* 902-863-6300
www.989xfm.ca
Social Media: www.facebook.com/pages/989-XFM/228101459666, twitter.com/989xfm
Ken Farrell, General Manager, ken@989xfm.ca

***Bridgewater:* CKBW-FM** (Freq: 98.1)
#200, 135 North St., Bridgewater, NS B4V 2V7
Tel: 902-543-2401, *Fax:* 902-543-1208
www.ckbw.com
Michael Prud'homme, General Manager

***Bridgewater:* CKBW-FM-2** (Freq: 93.1)
#200, 135 North St., Bridgewater, NS B4V 2V7
Tel: 902-543-2401, *Fax:* 902-543-1208
ckbw@ckbw.com
www.ckbw.ca
John Wiles, General Manager

†*Cheticamp:* CKJM-FM (Freq: 106.1)
CP 699, Cheticamp, NS B0E 1H0
Tél: 902-224-1242, *Téléc:* 902-224-1770
info@ckjm.ca
www.ckjm.ca
Auguste LeFort, Station Manager

** For details on this company see listing in Major Broadcasting Companies section; † French language station*

***Dartmouth:* CITA-FM** (Freq: 105.9)
101 Isley Ave., Dartmouth, NS B3B 1S8
Tel: 902-468-8854, *Fax:* 902-468-8851
Toll-Free: 866-944-2558
info@cjlufm.com
www.citafm.com

***Digby:* CKDY-FM-1** (Freq: 103.3)
Owned by:* *CKDY
Digby, NS

***Eastern Passage:* CFEP-FM** (Freq: 94.7)
PO Box 196, Eastern Passage, NS B3G 1M5
Tel: 902-469-9231, *Fax:* 902-463-1935
seasidefm@ns.sympatico.ca
www.seasidefm.com
Wayne Harrett, General Manager, wharrett@seasidefm.com

***Halifax:* C100-FM** (Freq: 100.1)
PO Box 9316 A, 2900 Agricola St., Halifax, NS B3K 6B2
Tel: 902-453-2524, *Fax:* 902-453-3132
www.c100fm.com
Social Media: www.facebook.com/C100FM, twitter.com/C100FM
Trent McGrath, General Manager, 902-493-2731
Chris Duggan, Program Manager, chris.duggan@chumradio.com

†*Halifax:* CBAX-FM (Freq: 91.5)
CP 3000, Halifax, NS B3J 3E9
Tél: 902-420-8311, *Ligne sans frais:* 866-306-4636
www.radio-canada.ca
Andrew Cochran, Managing Director, Maritimes
Nadine Antle, Regional Manager, Partnerships, Communications, Brand, & Promot, 506-451-4054
John Channing, Manager, Nova Scotia Sales & Marketing
Kathy Large, Manager, Nova Scotia Programs
Chantal Bernard, Senior Officer, Communications, 902-420-4306

***Halifax:* CBHA-FM** (Freq: 90.5)
Owned by:* *Canadian Broadcasting Corporation (CBC)*
PO Box 3000, Halifax, NS B3J 3E9
Tel: 902-420-8311, *Fax:* 902-420-4357
Toll-Free: 866-306-4636
www.cbc.ca/ns; www.cbc.ca/radio
Social Media: www.facebook.com/radiocbc; www.twitter.com/cbcradio,
Other information: Phone, CBC Radio One Newsroom, Halifax: 902-420-4350
Andrew Cochran, Managing Director, Maritimes
Janet Irwin, Senior Manager, News & Current Affairs
John Channing, Manager, Sales, Nova Scotia
Kathy Large, Manager, Programs
Chantal Bernard, Senior Officer, Communications, 902-420-4306

***Halifax:* CBH-FM** (Freq: 102.7)
Owned by:* *Canadian Broadcasting Corporation (CBC)*
PO Box 3000, Halifax, NS B3J 3E9
Tel: 902-420-8311, *Toll-Free:* 866-306-4636
www.cbc.ca/ns; www.cbc.ca/radio2
Social Media: www.facebook.com/CBC.Radio2.Official?ref=nf, www.twitter.com/cbcradio2
Andrew Cochran, Managing Director, Maritimes
Nancy Waugh, Executive Producer, Nova Scotia News
Chantal Bernard, Senior Officer, Communications, 902-420-4306

***Halifax:* CFRQ-FM** (Freq: 104.3)
Owned by:* *NewCap Inc.*
#200, 3770 Kempt Rd., Halifax, NS B3K 4X8
Tel: 902-453-4004, *Fax:* 902-453-3132
www.q104.ca
Ron Ryan, General Manager
J.C. Douglas, Program Director

***Halifax:* CHFX-FM** (Freq: Halifax's only country music station, broadcasting at 101.9 FM)
Owned by:* *Maritime Broadcasting System Limited*
5121 Sackville St., 3rd Fl., Halifax, NS B3J 1K1
Tel: 902-422-1651, *Fax:* 902-422-5330
chfx@mbsradio.com
www.fx1019.ca
Robert Pace, Chairman
Ian Kent, General Sales Manager, ian.kent@mbsradio.com

***Halifax:* CHNS-FM** (Freq: 89.9)
Owned by:* *Maritime Broadcasting System*
#300, 5121 Sackville St., Halifax, NS B3J 1K1
Tel: 902-422-1651,
www.899halfm.com
Social Media: www.facebook.com/89.9HALFM

***Halifax:* CKDU-FM** (Freq: 88.1)
Student Union Bldg., 6136 University Ave., Halifax, NS B3H 4J2
Tel: 902-494-6479,
info@ckdu.ca
www.ckdu.ca

***Halifax:* CKUL-FM** (Freq: 96.5)
Owned by:* *NewCap Inc.*
#200, 3770 Kempt Rd., Halifax, NS B3K 4X8
Tel: 902-453-4004, *Fax:* 902-453-3120
www.planetkool.ca
Social Media: www.facebook.com/965KOOLFMhalifax, twitter.com/Kool965
Ken Geddes, General Manager, kgeddes@newcap.ca

***Inverness:* CJFX-FM** (Freq: 102.5)
Owned by:* *CJFX-FM
Inverness, NS

***Kentville:* CKEN-FM** (Freq: 97.7)
Owned by:* *Maritime Broadcasting System*
PO Box 310, 29 Oakdene Ave., Kentville, NS B4N 1H5
Tel: 902-678-2111, *Fax:* 902-678-9894
www.avrnetwork.com
Social Media: www.facebook.com/pages/AVR/264050766956087

***Kentville:* CKWM-FM** (Freq: 94.9)
Owned by:* *Maritime Broadcasting System*
PO Box 310, 29 Oakdene Ave., Kentville, NS
Tel: 902-678-2111, *Fax:* 902-678-9894
avr@avrnetwork.com
www.magic949.ca
Dianne Best, General Manager

***Port Hawkesbury:* CIGO-FM** (Freq: 101.5)
#201, 609 Church St., Port Hawkesbury, NS B9A 2X4
Tel: 902-625-1220, *Fax:* 902-625-2664
bob@1015thehawk.com
www.1015thehawk.com
Social Media: www.facebook.com/pages/1015-The-Hawk, twitter.com/1015_The_Hawk
Bob MacEachern, President & General Manager
Brenda MacEachern

†*Saulnierville:* CIFA-FM (Freq: 104.1)
CP 8, Saulnierville, NS B0W 2Z0
Tél: 902-769-2432, *Téléc:* 902-769-3101
cifafm.com
Darlene Comeau, General Manager

***Shelburne:* CJLS-FM-1** (Freq: 96.3)
Owned by:* *CJLS-FM
Shelburne, NS

†*Sydney:* CBI-FM (Freq: CBC Radio 2; 105.1)*Détenteur:* **Canadian Broadcasting Corporation***
Sydney, NS

***Sydney:* CKPE-FM** (Freq: 94.9)
Owned by:* *Maritime Broadcasting System*
318 Charlotte St., Sydney, NS B1P 1C8
Tel: 902-564-5596, *Fax:* 902-564-1873
949thecape.com
Social Media: www.facebook.com/thecape949

***Truro:* CKTO-FM** (Freq: Broadcasting adult contemporary & classic rock at 100.9 FM in Truro)
Owned by:* *Astral Media Radio Atlantic Inc.*
187 Industrial Ave., Truro, NS B2N 6V3
Tel: 902-893-6060, *Fax:* 902-893-7771
Toll-Free: 877-891-6060
www.bigdog1009.ca
Chris Van Tassel, Brand Director, 902-893-6060, cvtassel@astral.com

***Truro:* CKTY-FM** (Freq: Broadcasting country music at 99.5 FM in Truro)
Owned by:* *Astral Media Radio Atlantic Inc.*
187 Industrial Ave., Truro, NS B2N 6V3
Tel: 902-893-6060, *Fax:* 902-893-7771
Toll-Free: 877-891-6060
www.catcountry995.ca
Mike Worsley, Sales Manager, mworsley@radioatl.ca

***Yarmouth:* CJLS-FM** (Freq: 95.5)
#201, 328 Main St., Yarmouth, NS B5A 1E4
Tel: 902-742-7175, *Fax:* 902-742-3143
cjls@cjls.com
www.cjls.com
Jim Grattan, Program Manager, 902-742-7175, pr3@cjls.com

Nunavut

***Iqaluit:* CBQR-FM** (Freq: 105.1)
Owned by:* *Canadian Broadcasting Corporation*
PO Box 490, Iqaluit, NU X0A 0H0
Tel: 867-979-6100,
www.cbc.ca/north

†*Iqaluit:* CFRT-FM (Freq: 107.3)
CP 880, Iqaluit, NU X0A 0H0
Tél: 867-979-4606,
cfrt@nunafranc.ca
www.franconunavut.ca
Daniel Cuerrier, General Manager

***Iqaluit:* CKIQ-FM** (Freq: 99.9)
PO Box 417, Iqaluit, NU X0A 0H0
icefmiqaluit@gmail.com
Social Media: www.facebook.com/pages/Ice-Fm/208026069253058
Glenn Craig, Station Manager

Ontario

***Aylmer:* CHPD-FM** (Freq: 107.7)
16 Talbot St., Aylmer, ON N5H 1H4
Tel: 519-773-8555, *Fax:* 519-773-8606
www.mcson.org

***Barrie:* CFJB-FM** (Freq: 95.7)
#205, 400 Bayfield St., Barrie, ON L4M 5A1
Tel: 705-725-7304, *Fax:* 705-792-7858
www.rock95.com
Social Media: www.facebook.com/Rock95Barrie, twitter.com/rock95barrie

***Barrie:* CHAY-FM** (Freq: 93.1)
Owned by:* *Corus Radio Company*
PO Box 937, 1125 Bayfield St. North, Barrie, ON L4M 4Y6
Tel: 705-737-3511, *Fax:* 705-737-0603
www.chaytoday.ca
Other information: Newsroom Phone: 705/726-1597; Fax: 705/722-5631
JJ Johnston, General Manager

***Barrie:* CJLF-FM** (Freq: 100.3)
#111, 115 Bell Farm Rd., Barrie, ON L4M 5G1
Tel: 705-735-3370, *Fax:* 705-735-3301
www.lifeonline.fm
Scott Jackson, Station Manager, scott@lifeonline.fm
Simon Slessor, Director
Janice Baird, CFO

***Barrie:* CKMB-FM** (Freq: 107.5)
#205, 400 Bayfield St., Barrie, ON L4M 5A1
Tel: 705-725-7304, *Fax:* 705-792-7858
www.1075koolfm.com
Social Media: www.facebook.com/koolfmbarrie
Tom Manton, General Manager, 705-797-8702, tmanton@bmts.com

***Belleville:* CHCQ-FM** (Freq: 100.1)
497 Dundas St. West, Belleville, ON K8P 1B6
Tel: 613-966-0955,
www.cool100.fm
John Sherratt, President & Owner

***Belleville:* CIGL-FM** (Freq: 97.1)
PO Box 488, 10 Front St. South, Belleville, ON K8N 5B2
Tel: 613-969-5555, *Fax:* 613-969-8122
www.mix97.com
Social Media: www.facebook.com/mix97fm, twitter.com/MIX97radio

***Belleville:* CJLX-FM** (Freq: 91.3)
PO Box 4200, Belleville, ON K8N 5B9
Tel: 613-969-0923, *Fax:* 613-966-1993
contact@91x.fm; sales@91x.fm; music@91x.fm
www.91x.fm
Other information: Phone, Newsroom: 613-966-6797; Fax, News: 613-969-9382
Greg Schatzmann, General Manager

***Belleville:* CJOJ-FM** (Freq: 95.5)
497 Dundas St West, Belleville, ON K8P 1B6
Tel: 613-966-0955, *Fax:* 613-967-2565
www.classichits955.fm
Social Media: www.facebook.com/955hitsfm, twitter.com/955hitsfm

** For details on this company see listing in Major Broadcasting Companies section; † French language station*

John Sherratt, President

Bracebridge: CFBG-FM (Freq: 99.5)
#50, 2 Balls Dr., Bracebridge, ON P1L 1T1
Tel: 705-645-2218, *Fax:* 705-645-6957
Toll-Free: 705-645-3079
www.moosefm.com
Dave Keeble, Creative Director, 705-645-2218

Brantford: CFWC-FM (Freq: 93.9)
271 Greenwich St., Brantford, ON N3S 2X9
Tel: 519-759-2339, *Fax:* 519-753-1157
info@power93.ca
www.power93.ca
Tony Schleifer, Station Manager, aschleifer@power93.ca

Brantford: CKPC-FM (Freq: 92.1)
571 West St., Brantford, ON N3T 5P8
Tel: 519-759-1000, *Fax:* 519-753-1470
www.jewel92.com
Richard Buchanan, President/General Manager
Mike Rose, Operations Manager, mike@ckpcradio.com

Brockville: CFJR-FM (Freq: 104.9)
Owned by: *Bell Media Inc.*
PO Box 666, 601 Stewart Blvd., Brockville, ON K6V 5V9
Tel: 613-345-1666, *Fax:* 613-342-2438
www.1049jrfm.com
Greg Hinton, Vice President/General Manager

Brockville: CJPT-FM (Freq: 103.7)
Owned by: *Bell Media Radio*
PO Box 666, 601 Stewart Blvd., Brockville, ON K6V 5V9
Tel: 613-345-1666, *Fax:* 613-342-2438
www.bob.fm
Greg Hinton, Vice President/General Manager

Campbellford: CKOL-FM (Freq: 93.7)
PO Box 551, 15 Raglan St. South, Campbellford, ON K0L 1L0
Tel: 705-653-1089,
ckol-radio@excite.com
www.ckolradio.ca
Dave Lockwood, General Manager

Chatham: CFCO-FM (Freq: 92.9)
Owned by: *CFCO*
Chatham, ON

Chatham: CKSY-FM (Freq: 94.3)
Owned by: *Blackburn Radio Inc.**
PO Box 100, 117 Keil Dr., Chatham, ON N7M 5K1
Tel: 519-354-2200, *Fax:* 519-354-2880
info@cksyfm.com
www.cksyfm.com
Social Media: www.facebook.com/943CKSY,
twitter.com/943cksy
Walter Ploegman, General Manager,
wploegman@blackburnradio.com
Jay Poole, Program Director, jpoole@blackburnradio.com

Chatham: CKUE-FM (Freq: 95.1)
Owned by: *Blackburn Radio Inc.**
PO Box 100, 117 Keil Dr., Chatham, ON N7M 5K1
Tel: 519-354-2200, *Fax:* 519-354-2880
info@canadasrock.ca
www.therock951.com
Dave Lockbau,, Assistant Program Director,
dave@canadasrock.ca

Cobourg: CHUC-FM (Freq: 107.9)
PO Box 520, Cobourg, ON K9A 4L3
Tel: 905-372-5401, *Fax:* 905-372-6280
www.1079thebreeze.com
Don Conway, President

Cobourg: CKSG-FM (Freq: 93.3)
PO Box 520, Cobourg, ON K9A 4L3
Tel: 905-372-5401, *Fax:* 905-372-6280
Toll-Free: 866-782-7933
info@star933.com
www.star933.com
Don Conway, President, don.conway@star933.com
Dave Hughes, General Sales Manager,
dave.hughes@star933.com

Cochrane: CHPB-FM (Freq: 98.1)
171-6th Ave., Cochrane, ON P0L 1C0
Tel: 705-272-6467, *Fax:* 705-272-2520
www.moosefm.com/chpb

Collingwood: CKCB-FM (Freq: 95.1)
Owned by: *B.C. Ltd.**
#200, 186 Hurontario St., Collingwood, ON L9Y 4T4
Tel: 705-446-9510, *Fax:* 705-444-6776
www.thepeakfm.com
John Eaton, General Manager

Cornwall: CFLG-FM (Freq: 104.5)
Owned by: *Corus Radio Company**
709 Cotton Mill St., Cornwall, ON K6H 7K7
Tel: 613-932-5180, *Fax:* 613-938-0355
variety104@seawayvalley.com
www.seawayvalley.com
JJ Johnston, General Manager

†Cornwall: CHOD-FM (Freq: 92.1)
#202, 1111 Montreal Rd., Cornwall, ON K6H 1E1
Tél: 613-936-2463, *Téléc:* 613-936-2568
chodfm@chodfm.ca
chodfm.ca
Marc Charbonneau, Contact, marc@chodfm.ca

Cornwall: CJSS-FM (Freq: 101.9)
Owned by: *Corus Entertainment Inc.**
709 Cotton Mill St., Cornwall, ON K6H 7K7
Tel: 613-932-5180, *Fax:* 613-938-0355
Toll-Free: 888-678-8122
www.cjssfm.com
Tim Wieczorek, General Manager

Cornwall: CKON-FM (Freq: 97.3)
PO Box 1496, Cornwall, ON K6H 5V5
Tel: 613-575-2100, *Fax:* 613-575-2566
ckonfm@yahoo.com
www.ckonfm.com

Dryden: CJIV-FM (Freq: 97.3)
PO Box 112, Dryden, ON P8N 2Y7
Tel: 807-216-6811,
cjivradio.jacob@gmail.com
www.cjiv973.net

Dryden: CKDR-FM (Freq: 92.7)
Owned by: *Fawcett Broadcasting Ltd.*
PO Box 580, 122 King St., Dryden, ON P8N 2Z3
Tel: 807-223-2355, *Fax:* 807-223-5090
mail@ckdr.net
www.ckdr.net
Roxanne McGee, roxanne@ckdr.net

Elliot Lake: CKNR-FM (Freq: Broadcasting adult contemporary music at 94.1 FM in Elliot Lake)
144 Ontario Ave., Elliot Lake, ON P5A 1Y3
Tel: 705-848-3608, *Fax:* 705-848-1378
Toll-Free: 800-565-7359
moose941@moosefm.com
www.moosefm.com/cknr
Erika MacLellan, Operations Manager/Sales Executive,
emaclellan@moosefm.com
Bob Alexander, Promotions Director/Host,
balexander@moosefm.com

Fort Frances: CFOB-FM (Freq: 93.1)
Owned by: *Fawcett Broadcasting Ltd.*
210 Scott St., Fort Frances, ON P9A 1G7
Tel: 807-274-5341, *Fax:* 807-274-2033
info@931theborder.ca
www.b93.ca
Social Media: www.facebook.com/931TheBorder
Hugh Syrja

Guelph: CFRU-FM (Freq: 93.3)
University Centre, Level 2, University of Guelph, Guelph, ON N1G 2W1
Tel: 519-824-4120,
info@cfru.ca
www.cfru.ca
Social Media: www.facebook.com/groups/2221470650,
twitter.com/cfru_radio
Lori Guest, Music Programming Coordinator
Ignace Ntirushwamaboko, Spoken Word Coordinator
John Leacock, Music Coordinator/Advertising Coordinator
Richard Watson, Promotions Coordinator
Kim Iezzi, Operations Coordinator

Guelph: CIMJ-FM (Freq: 106.1)
Owned by: *B.C. Ltd.**
75 Speedvale Ave. East, Guelph, ON N1E 6M3
Tel: 519-824-7000, *Fax:* 519-824-4118
studio@magic106.com
www.magic106.com
Kevin Kelly, Program Director

Haliburton: CKHA-FM (Freq: 100.9)
PO Box 1125, Haliburton, ON K0M 1S0
Tel: 705-457-1009, *Fax:* 705-457-9522
canoefmadmin@bellnet.ca
www.canoefm.com
Roxanne Casey, Station Manager, roxanne@canoefm.com

Hamilton: CING-FM (Freq: 107.9)
Owned by: *Corus Premium Television Ltd.**
875 Main St. West, Hamilton, ON L8S 4R1
Tel: 905-521-9900, *Fax:* 905-521-1691
www.vinyl953.com
Jim McCourtie, Program Director, jim.mccourtie@corusent.com

Hamilton: CIOI-FM (Freq: 101.5)
#F111, 135 Fennell Ave., Hamilton, ON L8N 3T2
Tel: 905-575-2175, *Fax:* 905-575-2385
music@indifm.ca
www.mohawkcollege.ca/msa/cioi
Les Palango, Station Manager
Jamie Smith, Program & Music Director
Jeff Cudahy, Chief Engineer

Hamilton: CIWV-FM (Freq: 94.7)
589 Upper Wellington, Hamilton, ON L9A 3P8
Tel: 905-388-8911, *Fax:* 905-388-7947
www.wave947.fm
Douglas E. Kirk, President

Hamilton: CJXY-FM (Freq: 107.9)
Owned by: *Corus Radio Company**
#900, 875 Main St. West, Hamilton, ON L8S 4R1
Tel: 905-645-1079,
News@900chml.com
www.y108.ca
Social Media: www.facebook.com/Y108Rocks,
twitter.com/Y108Rocks
Jim McCourtie, Program Director, jim.mccourtie@corusent.com

Hanover: CFBW-FM (Freq: 91.3 FM; Radio Station)
267 - 10th St., Hanover, ON N4N 1P1
Tel: 519-364-0200, *Fax:* 519-364-5175
bluewaterradio@on.aibn.com
www.bluewaterradio.ca
Andrew McBride, Station Manager, 519-370-9090

†Hawkesbury: CHPR-FM (Freq: 102.1)
#37, 115 Main St., Hawkesbury, ON K6A 1A1
Tél: 613-632-1000, *Téléc:* 514-632-1110
planetelov.ca
Médias sociaux:
www.facebook.com/pages/Planète-Lov-1049-et-1021/22962929
0417310

†Hearst: CINN-FM (Freq: 91.1)
CP 2648, 1004, rue Prince, Hearst, ON P0L 1N0
Tél: 705-372-1011, *Téléc:* 705-362-7411
Ligne sans frais: 866-362-5168
cinnfm@cinnfm.com
www.cinnfm.com
Gaetane Morrissette

Huntsville: CFBK-FM 105.5 (Freq: 105.5)
#2, 7 John St., Huntsville, ON P1H 2C6
Tel: 705-789-4461, *Fax:* 705-789-1269
Karen Broad, General Manager

Kapuskasing: CKAP-FM (Freq: 100.9)
Moose FM, #2A, 22 Queen St., Kapuskasing, ON P5N 1G8
Tel: 705-335-2379, *Fax:* 705-337-6391
Toll-Free: 866-505-2379
moose1009@hbgradio.com
www.moosefm.com/ckap
Social Media:
facebook.com/pages/Moose-FM-CKAP-1009-Kapuskasing-CKH
T-945-Hearst
Rob Wills, General Manager
Valerie Isaac, News Director, 705-335-2379

†Kapuskasing: CKGN-FM (Freq: 89.7 FM Kapuskasing et 94.7 FM Smooth Rock Falls)
77, ch Brunelle nord, Kapuskasing, ON P5N 2M1
Tél: 705-335-5915, *Téléc:* 705-335-3508
Ligne sans frais: 800-385-2741
ckgn-fm@nt.net
www.ckgn.ca
Claude Chabot, Directeur général, claudechabot@ckgn.ca

Kenora: CJRL 89.5 Mix FM
Owned by: *Northwoods Broadcasting Ltd.*

* *For details on this company see listing in Major Broadcasting Companies section; † French language station*

128 Main St. South, Kenora, ON P9N 1S9
Tel: 807-468-3181, *Fax:* 807-468-4188
cjrl@cjrl.ca
www.cjrl.ca/89fm

***Kenora:* CJRL-FM** (Freq: 89.5)
Owned by: *89.5 Mix FM*
301 1st Ave. South, Kenora, ON P9N 1W2
Tel: 807-468-3181, *Fax:* 807-468-4188
www.cjrl.ca
Social Media: www.facebook.com/pages/895-The-Lake/357569390926298, twitter.com/thetide981
Timry Davidson, News Director

***Killaloe:* CHCR-FM** (Freq: 102.9; 104.5)
PO Box 195, A, 14 Lake St., Killaloe, ON K0J 2A0
Tel: 613-757-0657,
radio@chcr.org
www.chcr.org
Ambrose Mullin, Station Manager

***Kingston:* CBBK-FM** (Freq: 92.9)
Owned by: *Canadian Broadcasting Corporation (CBC)**
Kingston, ON
Toll-Free: 866-306-4636
www.cbc.ca/radio2
Social Media: www.facebook.com/CBC.Radio2.Official?ref=nf,
Other information: Twitter: www.twitter.com/cbcradio2

***Kingston:* CFFX** (Freq: 104.3)
Owned by: *Corus Entertainment Inc.**
170 Queen St., Kingston, ON K7K 1B2
Tel: 613-544-2340, *Fax:* 613-544-5508
www.lite1043.ca
Mike Ferguson, General Manager
Brad Gibb, Program Director

***Kingston:* CFLY-FM** (Freq: 98.3)
Owned by: *Bell Media Radio**
#10, 993 Princess St., Kingston, ON K7L 1H3
Tel: 613-544-1380, *Fax:* 613-546-9751
heydeejay@983flyfm.com
flyfmkingston.com
Social Media: www.facebook.com/983FLYFM, twitter.com/983FLYFM
Greg Hinton, Vice President/General Manager, greg.hinton@bellmedia.ca

***Kingston:* CFMK-FM** (Freq: 96.3)
Owned by: *B.C. Ltd.**
170 Queen St., Kingston, ON K7K 1B2
Tel: 613-544-2340, *Fax:* 613-544-5508
www.fm96.ca
Mike Ferguson, General Manager
Brad Gibb, Program Director

***Kingston:* CFRC-FM** (Freq: 101.9)
Lower Carruthers Hall, 62 Fifth Field Company Lane, Kingston, ON K7L 3N6
Tel: 613-533-2121,
www.cfrc.ca
Social Media: twitter.com/CFRC
Maureen Plunkett, Station Manager

***Kingston:* CHUM Radio Kingston** (Freq: Operates 3 radio stations in the Kingston area: 103.7 BOB FM, 98.3 FLY FM, and 98.9 The Drive.)
Owned by: *Bell Media Inc.**
#10, 993 Princess St., Kingston, ON K7L 1H3
Tel: 613-544-1380, *Fax:* 613-546-9751
www.chumkingston.com
Greg Hinton, Vice President/General Manager, greg.hinton@chumkingston.com
Brian Johnston, Sales Manager, brian.johnston@chumkingston.com
Jennifer Yascheshyn, Program Director, jennifer.yascheshyn@chumkingston.com

***Kingston:* CIKR-FM** (Freq: 105.7)
#301, 863 Princess St., Kingston, ON K7L 5N4
Tel: 613-549-1057, *Fax:* 613-549-5302
www.krock1057.ca

***Kingston:* CKVI-FM** (Freq: 91.9)
#119, 235 Frontenac St., Kingston, ON K7L 3S7
ckvi@limestone.ca
www.thecave.ca
Max Lienhard, Station Manager

***Kingston:* The Drive** (Freq: 98.9)
Owned by: *Bell Media Radio**
PO Box 1380, #10, 993 Princess St., Kingston, ON K7L 1H3
Tel: 613-544-1380, *Fax:* 613-546-9751
onair@989thedrive.com
www.989thedrive.com
Gary Perrin, General Manager

***Kirkland Lake:* CJKL-FM** (Freq: 101.5)
PO Box 430, 5 Kirkland St., Kirkland Lake, ON P2N 3J4
Tel: 705-567-3366, *Fax:* 705-567-6101
cjkl@cjklfm.com
cjklfm.com
Rob Connelly, President, General Manager, Programming Director

***Kitchener:* CFCA-FM** (Freq: 105.3)
Owned by: *CFCA-FM*
Kitchener, ON
Tel: 519-884-1053

***Kitchener:* CHYM-FM** (Freq: 96.7)
Owned by: *Rogers Broadcasting Ltd.**
PO Box 936, 305 King St. West, Kitchener, ON N2G 4E4
Tel: 519-743-2611, *Fax:* 519-743-7510
www.chymfm.com

***Kitchener:* CJDV-FM** (Freq: 107.5)
Owned by: *B.C. Ltd.**
50 Sportsworld, #210, Crossing Rd., Kitchener, ON N2P 0A4
Tel: 519-772-1212, *Fax:* 519-772-1213
www.davefm.com

***Kitchener:* CJIQ-FM** (Freq: 88.3)
299 Doon Valley Dr., Kitchener, ON N2G 4M4
Tel: 519-748-5220, *Fax:* 519-748-5971
www.cjiq.fm
Mike Thurnell, Program Director, 519-748-5220, mthurnell@conestogac.on.ca
Mark Burley, Station Manager

***Kitchener:* CJTW-FM** (Freq: 94.3)
PO Box 1433 C, 207, 659 King St. East, Kitchener, ON N2G 4H6
Tel: 519-575-9090, *Fax:* 519-575-9119
Toll-Free: 877-741-9430
info@faithfm.org
www.faithfm.org
Dave MacDonald, Station Manager

***Leamington:* CHYR-FM** (Freq: 96.7)
Owned by: *Blackburn Radio Inc.**
100 Talbot St. East, Leamington, ON N8H 1L3
Tel: 519-326-6171, *Fax:* 519-322-1110
mix967.ca
Social Media: www.facebook.com/mix967, twitter.com/themix967

***Lindsay:* CKLY-FM** (Freq: 91.9)
Owned by: *Bell Media Radio**
249 Kent St. West, Lindsay, ON K9V 2Z3
Tel: 705-324-9103, *Fax:* 705-324-4149
www.919bobfm.com
Steve Fawcett, General Manager

***London:* CBBL-FM** (Freq: 100.5)
Owned by: *Canadian Broadcasting Corporation (CBC)**
#4, 208 Piccadilly St., London, ON N6A 1S1
Toll-Free: 866-306-4636
www.cbc.ca/radio2
Social Media: www.facebook.com/CBC.Radio2.Official?ref=nf,
Other information: Twitter: www.twitter.com/cbcradio2

***London:* CBCL-FM** (Freq: 93.5)
Owned by: *Canadian Broadcasting Corporation (CBC)**
#4, 208 Piccadilly St., London, ON N6A 1S1
Tel: 519-667-1990, *Toll-Free:* 866-306-4636
www.cbc.ca/radio
Social Media: www.facebook.com/radiocbc; www.twitter.com/cbcradio,
Other information: TTY: 1-866-220-6045

***London:* CFHK-FM** (Freq: 103.1)
Owned by: *Corus Radio Company**
#222, 380 Wellington Rd., London, ON N6A 5B5
Tel: 519-931-6000, *Fax:* 519-679-1967
www.1031freshfm.com
Social Media: www.facebook.com/1031freshfm

***London:* CFPL-FM** (Freq: 95.9)
Owned by: *Corus Radio Company**
#222, 380 Wellington St., London, ON N6A 5B5
Tel: 519-931-6000, *Fax:* 519-679-1967
www.fm96.com

Rick Moss

***London:* CHJX-FM** (Freq: 105.9)
254 Adelaide St. South, London, ON N5Z 3L1
Tel: 519-679-9882, *Fax:* 519-679-2459
www.inspirefm.ca
Dave Wettlaufer, General Manager

***London:* CHRW-FM** (Freq: 94.9)
#250, UCC Bldg., London, ON N6A 3K7
chrwradio.ca
Social Media: www.facebook.com/chrwradio, twitter.com/chrwradio
Grant Stein, Station Manager
Zoltan Haraszthy, Program Director
James McMillan, News & Sports Director

***London:* CHST-FM** (Freq: 102.3)
Owned by: *Rogers Broadcasting Ltd.**
1 Communications Rd., London, ON N6J 4Z1
Tel: 519-690-0102,
www.1023bob.com
Ann LaRocque, General Manager, 519-690-0102
David Jones, Operations Manager, Program Director, 519-690-0102
Janice Pearce, Business Manager, 519-690-0102
Jan White, Promotions Manager, 519-690-0102

***London:* CIQM-FM** (Freq: 97.5)
Owned by: *Astral Media Radio G.P.**
743 Wellington Rd. South, London, ON N6C 4R5
Tel: 519-686-2525, *Fax:* 519-686-2556
www.975ezrock.com
Braden Doerr, General Manager

***London:* CIXX-FM** (Freq: 106.9)
PO Box 7005, 1001 Fanshaw College Blvd., London, ON N5Y 5R6
Tel: 519-453-2810,
www.fanshawemedia.ca
Social Media: www.youtube.com/user/1069TheX, www.facebook.com/1069TheX, twitter.com/1069TheX
Bob Collins, Contact

***London:* CJBX-FM** (Freq: 92.7)
Owned by: *Astral Media Radio G.P.**
743 Wellington Rd. South, London, ON N6C 4R5
Tel: 519-685-2525, *Fax:* 519-686-2556
bx93@bx93.com
www.bx93.com
Braden Doerr, General Manager

***Marathon:* CFNO-FM** (Freq: 93.1; 100.7)
PO Box 1000, 93 Evergreen Dr., Marathon, ON P0T 2E0
Tel: 807-229-1010, *Fax:* 807-229-1686
www.cfno.fm
S. Spencer Bell, President

***Midland:* CICZ-FM** (Freq: 104.1)
PO Box 609, 355 Cranston Cres., Midland, ON L4R 4L3
Tel: 705-526-2268, *Fax:* 705-526-3060
1041thedock.com

***Mississauga:* CFRE-FM** (Freq: closed circuit)
Erindale Campus Radio, #131, 3359 Mississauga Rd., Mississauga, ON L5L 1C6
Tel: 905-369-0504,
info@cfreradio.com
www.cfreradio.com

†*Montréal:* CBOX-FM (Freq: 102.5)***Détenteur:*** **Canadian Broadcasting Corporation***
CP 6000 Centre-ville, Montréal, ON H3C 3A8
Tél: 613-288-6000, *Ligne sans frais:* 866-306-4636
CommentairesEM@radio-canada.ca
www.radio-canada.ca/espace_musique

***New Liskeard:* CJTT-FM** (Freq: 104.5)
PO Box 1058, 55 Whitewood Ave., New Liskeard, ON P0J 1P0
Tel: 705-647-7334, *Fax:* 705-647-8660
cjtt@cjttfm.com
www.cjttfm.com
Other information: Phone, News & Sports: 705-647-7171; Phone, Studio: 705-647-6565

***Niagara Falls:* CFLZ-FM** (Freq: 101.1)
PO Box 710, 4668 St. Claire Ave., Niagara Falls, ON L2E 6X7
Tel: 905-356-6710, *Fax:* 905-356-0644
z101.fm
Dave Universal, Program Director, daveuniv@niagara.com

** For details on this company see listing in Major Broadcasting Companies section; † French language station*

***Niagara Falls:* CJED-FM** (Freq: 105.1)
PO Box 710, 4668 St. Clair Ave., Niagara Falls, ON L2E 6X7
Tel: 905-356-6710, *Fax:* 905-356-0644
www.1051edfm.com

***North Bay:* CHUR-FM** (Freq: 100.5)
Owned by: *Rogers Broadcasting Ltd.**
PO Box 3000, 743 Main St. East, North Bay, ON P1B 8K8
Tel: 705-479-2000,
www.ezrocknorthbay.com

***North Bay:* CKFX-FM** (Freq: 101.9)
Owned by: *Rogers Broadcasting Ltd.**
743 Main St. East, North Bay, ON P1B 1C2
Tel: 705-474-2000, *Fax:* 705-474-7761
www.foxradio.ca
Mitch Belanger, Program Director
Mike Belanger, Program Director

***North Bay:* CRFM-FM** (Freq: 89.9)
Canadore College, PO Box 5001, 100 College Dr., North Bay, ON P1B 8K9
Tel: 705-474-7601,
www.ThePanther.ca

***Orillia:* CICX-FM** (Freq: 105.9)
Owned by: *Rogers Broadcasting Ltd.**
PO Box 550, 7 Progress Dr., Orillia, ON L3V 6K2
Tel: 705-326-3511, *Fax:* 705-326-1816
events@kicxfm.com
kicx106.com

***Orillia:* CIKZ-FM** (Freq: 106.7)
7 Progress Dr., RR #1, Orillia, ON L3V 6H1
Tel: 705-722-5429, *Fax:* 705-326-1816
www.kicx106.com
Mora Austin, General Manager, Vice President,
mora.austin@larchecom.com

***Oshawa:* CJKX-FM** (Freq: 95.9; 89.9)
#207, 1200 Airport Blvd., Oshawa, ON L1J 8P5
Tel: 905-428-9600, *Fax:* 905-571-1150
steve@kx96.fm
www.kx96.fm
Steve Kassay, Operations Manager

***Oshawa:* CKDO-FM** (Freq: 107.7; 1350; 96.0)
#207, 1200 Airport Blvd., Oshawa, ON L1J 8P5
Tel: 905-571-0949, *Fax:* 905-571-1150
cartunes@kx96.fm; jeunesse@kx96.fm
www.kx96.fm
Steve Kassay, Vice President, Programming, steve@kx96.fm

***Oshawa:* CKGE-FM** (Freq: 94.9)
#207, 1200 Airport Blvd., Oshawa, ON L1J 8P5
Tel: 905-571-0949, *Fax:* 905-579-1150
Toll-Free: 866-799-7625
steve@therock.fm
www.therock.fm
Social Media: www.facebook.com/949therock.fm,
twitter.com/949therock
Steve Kassav, Operations Manager
Stephen A. Kassay, Vice-President, Operations

***Ottawa:* CBO-FM** (Freq: 91.5)
Owned by: *Canadian Broadcasting Corporation**
PO Box 3220 C, 181 Queen St., Ottawa, ON K1Y 1E4
Tel: 613-288-6445,
cbcnewsottawa@cbc.ca
www.cbc.ca/ottawa
Laurence Wall, Producer
Tom New, Communications Officer

***Ottawa:* CBOQ-FM** (Freq: 103.3)
Owned by: *Canadian Broadcasting Corporation**
PO Box 500 A, Ottawa, ON M5W 1E6
Toll-Free: 866-306-4636

***Ottawa:* CHBM-FM** (Freq: 97.3)
Owned by: *Astral Media Radio G.P.**
1504 Merivale Rd., Ottawa, ON K2E 6Z5
Tel: 613-225-1069,
www.boom997.com
Morgan Prue, Brand Director, mprue@astral.com

***Ottawa:* CHEZ-FM** (Freq: 106.1)
Owned by: *Rogers Broadcasting Ltd.**
2001 Thurston Dr., Ottawa, ON K1G 6C9
Tel: 613-736-2001, *Fax:* 613-736-2002
www.chez106.com
Social Media: www.facebook.com/Chez106

***Ottawa:* CHRI-FM** (Freq: 99.1)
#3, 1010 Thomas Spratt Pl., Ottawa, ON K1G 5L5
Tel: 613-247-1440, *Fax:* 613-247-7128
Toll-Free: 866-247-1440
chri@chri.ca
www.chri.ca
Bill Stevens, General Manager
Robert Du Broy, Director & General Manager

***Ottawa:* CHUO-FM** (Freq: 89.1)
#0038, 65 University Pvt., Ottawa, ON K1N 9A5
Tel: 613-562-5965,
info@chuo.fm
www.chuo.fm
Chris Jack, Interim Station Manager

***Ottawa:* CIHT-FM** (Freq: 89.9)
Owned by: *NewCap Inc.**
#100 6 Antares Drive, Phase I, Ottawa, ON
Tel: 613-723-8990, *Fax:* 613-723-7016
www.hot899.com
Social Media: www.facebook.com/TheNewHot899,
twitter.com/newhot899

***Ottawa:* CISS-FM** (Freq: 105.3)
Owned by: *Rogers Broadcasting Ltd.**
2001 Thurston Dr., Ottawa, ON K1G 6C9
Tel: 613-736-2001, *Fax:* 613-736-2002
www.1053kissfm.com
Danny Kingsbury, Station Manager/Program Director

***Ottawa:* CJLL-FM** (Freq: 97.9)
#100, 30 Murray St., Ottawa, ON K1N 5M4
Tel: 613-244-0979, *Fax:* 613-244-3858
chinottawa@chinradio.com
www.chinradio.com
Ed Ylanen, General Manager

***Ottawa:* CJMJ-FM** (Freq: 100.3)
Owned by: *Bell Media Radio**
87 George St., Ottawa, ON K1N 9H7
Tel: 613-789-2486, *Fax:* 613-750-0100
www.majic100.fm
J.R. Ello, Promotion Director, jr.ello@bellmedia.ca

***Ottawa:* CKCU-FM** (Freq: 93.1)
#517, University Centre, Carleton University, 1125 Colonel By Dr., Ottawa, ON K1S 5B6
Tel: 613-520-2898,
info@ckcufm.com
www.ckcufm.com
Matthew Croiser, Station Manager, 613-520-2600,
manager@ckcufm.com

***Ottawa:* CKDJ-FM** (Freq: 107.9)
Algonquin College, 1385 Woodroffe Ave., Ottawa, ON K2G 1V8
Tel: 613-750-2535, *Fax:* 613-727-7689
mellond@algonquincollege.com
www.ckdj.net
Social Media: www.facebook.com/CKDJ1079,
twitter.com/ckdj1079
Kyra Kratzmann, Station Manager

***Ottawa:* CKKL-FM** (Freq: 93.9)
Owned by: *Bell Media Radio**
87 George St., Ottawa, ON K1N 9H7
Tel: 613-789-2486, *Fax:* 613-739-5626
www.939bobfm.com
Al Smith, Program Director

***Ottawa:* CKQB-FM** (Freq: 106.9 The Bear)
Owned by: *Astral Media Radio G.P.**
1504 Merivale Rd., Ottawa, ON K2E 6Z5
Tel: 613-225-1069, *Fax:* 613-226-3381
Toll-Free: 800-754-1069
www.thebear.fm
Social Media: www.facebook.com/106.9TheBEAR,
twitter.com/thebear1069
Denis Bouchard, General Manager,
dbouchard@radio.astral.com
Kath Thompson, Music, Director
Scott Broderick, General Sales Manager
Rebecca Crow, Promotion Director
Eric Stafford, General Manager

***Owen Sound:* CIXK-FM** (Freq: 106.5)
Owned by: *Bayshore Broadcasting Corporation**
PO Box 280, 270 - 9 St. East, Owen Sound, ON N4K 5P5
Tel: 519-376-2030, *Fax:* 519-371-4242
bayshore@radioowensound.com
www.radioowensound.com
Ross Kentner, General Manager,
rkentner@bayshorebroadcasting.ca
Kevin Brown, General Sales Manager,
kbrown@bayshorebroadcasting.ca
Rob Brignell, Director, Marketing & Business Development,
rbrignell@bayshorebroadcasting.ca

***Owen Sound:* CKYC-FM** (Freq: 93.7)
Owned by: *Bayshore Broadcasting Corporation**
PO Box 280, 270 - 9 St. East, Owen Sound, ON N4K 5P5
Tel: 519-376-2030, *Fax:* 519-371-4242
bayshore@radioowensound.com
www.radioowensound.com
Ross Kentner, General Manager,
rkentner@bayshorebroadcasting.ca
Kevin Brown, General Sales Manager,
kbrown@bayshorebroadcasting.ca
Rob Brignell, Director, Marketing & Development,
rbrignell@bayshorebroadcasting.ca

***Parry Sound:* CKLP-FM** (Freq: 103.3)
#301, 60 James St., Parry Sound, ON P2A 1T5
Tel: 705-746-2163, *Fax:* 705-746-4292
moose1033@hbgradio.com
www.hbgradio.com
Social Media:
www.facebook.com/pages/Moose-FM-CKLP-1033-Parry-Sound/17000189969
Kimberley Ward-Grossman, Vice-President
Dave Keeble, Operations Manager
Christopher Grossman, President

***Pembroke:* CHVR-FM** (Freq: 96.7)
Owned by: *Astral Media Radio G.P.**
595 Pembroke St. East, Pembroke, ON K8A 3L7
Tel: 613-735-9670, *Fax:* 613-735-7748
star96@sri.ca
www.star96.ca
Denis Bouchard, General Manager, dbouchard@astral.com
Tracy McBride, Sales Manager, tmcbride@astral.com

†*Penetanguishene:* CFRH-FM (Freq: 88.1)
CP 5099, 63, rue Main, Penetanguishene, ON L9M 2G3
Tél: 705-549-8288, *Téléc:* 705-549-6463
www.cfrh.ca
Médias sociaux:
www.facebook.com/pages/CFRH-881-VAGUE-FM/104742480799
Peter Hominuk, General Manager

***Peterborough:* CFFF-FM** (Freq: 92.7)
Trent University, 715 George St. North, Peterborough, ON K9H 3T2
Tel: 705-741-4011,
Info@TrentRadio.cadio.ca
www.trentu.ca/org/trentradio
Other information: Studio: 705-748-4761

***Peterborough:* CKPT-FM** (Freq: 99.7)
Owned by: *Bell Media Radio**
PO Box 177, 59 George St. North, Peterborough, ON K9J 6Y8
Tel: 705-742-8844, *Fax:* 705-742-1417
energy997@chumradio.com
www.energy997.ca
Steve Fawcett, General Manager

***Peterborough:* CKQM-FM** (Freq: 105.1)
Owned by: *Bell Media Radio**
Country 105, PO Box 177, 59 George St. North, Peterborough, ON K9J 6Y8
Tel: 705-742-8844, *Fax:* 705-742-1417
www.country105.fm
Steve Fawcett, General Manager, steve.fawcett@bellmedia.ca
Brian Young, Program Director

***Peterborough:* CKWF-FM** (Freq: 101.5)
Owned by: *B.C. Ltd.**
159 King St., Peterborough, ON K9J 2R8
Tel: 705-748-6101, *Fax:* 705-742-7708
www.thewolf.ca
Social Media: twitter.com/thewolfca
Kathleen McNair, General Manager

***Port Elgin:* CFPS-FM** (Freq: 97.9)
Owned by: *Bayshore Broadcasting Corporation**
382 Goderich St., Port Elgin, ON N0H 2C1
Tel: 519-832-9800, *Fax:* 519-832-9808
Toll-Free: 877-652-9800
thebeach@98thebeach.ca
www.98thebeach.ca

** For details on this company see listing in Major Broadcasting Companies section; † French language station*

***Red Lake:* CKDR-5** (Freq: 97.1)
Owned by: *CKDR-FM*
Red Lake, ON

***Sarnia:* CBEG-FM** (Freq: 90.3)
Owned by: *Canadian Broadcasting Corporation (CBC)**
Sarnia, ON
Toll-Free: 866-306-4636
www.cbc.ca/windsor; www.cbc.ca/radio
Social Media: www.facebook.com/radiocbc; www.twitter.com/cbcradio,
Other information: TTY: 1-866-220-6045
Sandra Porteous, Managing Editor, Radio & Television, 519-255-3563
David Daigneault, Executive Producer, Radio & Television, 519-255-3410

***Sarnia:* CFGX-FM** (Freq: 99.9)
Owned by: *Blackburn Radio Inc.**
1415 London Rd., Sarnia, ON N7S 1P6
Tel: 519-542-5500, *Fax:* 519-542-1520
www.foxfm.com
Social Media: www.facebook.com/foxfmsarnia, twitter.com/foxfmsarnia

***Sarnia:* CHKS-FM** (Freq: 106.3)
Owned by: *Blackburn Radio Inc.**
1415 London Rd., Sarnia, ON N7S 1P6
Tel: 519-542-5500, *Fax:* 519-542-1520
www.k106fm.com
Social Media: www.facebook.com/K1063, twitter.com/k1063sarnia

***Sault Ste Marie:* CHAS-FM** (Freq: 100.5)
Owned by: *Rogers Broadcasting Ltd.**
642 Great Northern Rd., Sault Ste Marie, ON P6B 4Z9
Tel: 705-759-9200, *Fax:* 705-946-3575
www.ezrocksoo.com
Scott Sexsmith, General Manager, scott.sexsmith@ssmradio.rogers.com

***Sault Ste Marie:* CJQM-FM** (Freq: 104.3)
Owned by: *Rogers Broadcasting Ltd.**
642 Great Northern Rd., Sault Ste Marie, ON P6B 4Z9
Tel: 705-759-9200, *Fax:* 705-946-3575
www.qcountry.ca
Scott Sexsmith, General Manager, scott.sexsmith@ssmradio.rogers.com

***Simcoe:* CHCD-FM** (Freq: 98.9)
PO Box 98, 55 Park Rd., Simcoe, ON N3Y 4K8
Tel: 519-426-7700, *Fax:* 519-426-8574
Toll-Free: 888-273-1067
www.cd989.com
Blair Daggett, General Manager, 519-426-7700

***Sioux Lookout:* CKWT-FM** (Freq: 89.1)
PO Box 1180, 16 - 5 Ave., Sioux Lookout, ON P8T 1B7
Tel: 807-737-2951, *Fax:* 807-737-3224
www.wawataynews.ca/radio

***Smith Falls:* CKBY-FM** (Freq: 101.1)
Owned by: *Rogers Broadcasting Ltd.**
6A Beckwith St. North, Smith Falls, ON K7A 4T4
Tel: 613-736-2001, *Fax:* 613-736-2002
Toll-Free: 613-750-1011
www.y101.fm
Al Campagnola, General Manager, acampagn@rci.rogers.com

***Smiths Falls:* CJET-FM** (Freq: 92.3)
Owned by: *Rogers Broadcasting Ltd.**
PO Box 430, Smiths Falls, ON K7A 4T4
Tel: 613-283-4630, *Fax:* 613-283-7243
www.923jackfm.com
Social Media: www.facebook.com/923jackfm
Mark Hunter, General Manager, 613-736-2001, markp.hunter@rci.rogers.com
Kalum Figura, Sales Manager, 613-736-2001, kalum.figura@rci.rogers.com

***St Catharines:* CFBU-FM** (Freq: 103.7)
500 Glenridge Ave., St Catharines, ON L2S 3A1
Tel: 905-688-2644,
pd@cfbu.ca
www.cfbu.ca
Social Media: www.facebook.com/groups/17630362305, twitter.com/#%21/cfbu1037
Russell Gragg, Station Manager

***St Catharines:* CHRE-FM** (Freq: 105.7)
Owned by: *Astral Media Radio G.P.**
12 Yates St., St Catharines, ON L2R 5R2
Tel: 905-688-1057, *Fax:* 905-684-4800
www.1057ezrock.com
Madelyn Hamilton, General Manager

***St Catharines:* CHTZ-FM** (Freq: 97.7)
Owned by: *Astral Media Radio G.P.**
12 Yates St., St Catharines, ON L2R 5R2
Tel: 905-684-0977, *Fax:* 905-684-4800
www.htzfm.com
Bruce Gilbert, Program Director, pd@htzfm.com

***Sturgeon Falls:* CFSF-FM** (Freq: 99.3)
#7, 12006 Hwy. 17, Sturgeon Falls, ON P2B 3K8
Tel: 705-753-6776, *Fax:* 705-753-6776
www.moosefm.com/cfsf
Mike Trahan, General Manager, 705-475-9991

***Sudbury:* CBBS-FM** (Freq: 90.1)
Owned by: *Canadian Broadcasting Corporation (CBC)**
15 MacKenzie St., Sudbury, ON P3C 4Y1
Tel: 705-688-3200, *Fax:* 705-688-3220
Toll-Free: 866-306-4636
www.cbc.ca/sudbury; www.cbc.ca/radio2
Social Media: www.facebook.com/CBC.Radio2.Official?ref=nf,
Other information: Twitter: www.twitter.com/cbcradio2
Fiona Christensen, Managing Editor, Sudbury, 705-688-3232

†*Sudbury:* CBBX-FM (Freq: 90.9)*Détenteur:* **Canadian Broadcasting Corporation (CBC)***
15 Mackenzie St., Sudbury, ON P3C 4Y1
Tél: 705-688-3200, *Ligne sans frais:* 866-306-4636
www.cbc.ca/sudbury; www.radio-canada.ca
Fiona Christensen, Managing Editor, Sudbury, 705-688-3232

***Sudbury:* CBCS-FM** (Freq: 99.9)
Owned by: *Canadian Broadcasting Corporation (CBC)**
15 MacKenzie St., Sudbury, ON P3C 4Y1
Tel: 705-688-3200, *Toll-Free:* 866-306-4636
www.cbc.ca/sudbury; www.cbc.ca/radio
Social Media: www.facebook.com/radiocbc; www.twitter.com/cbcradio,
Other information: Phone, Sudbury News: 705-688-3240; Toll-Free: 1-800-461-1138
Fiona Christensen, Managing Editor, 705-688-3232

†*Sudbury:* CBON-FM (Freq: 98.1)*Détenteur:* **Canadian Broadcasting Corporation***
15 MacKenzie St., Sudbury, ON P3C 4Y1
Tél: 705-688-3200,
www.radio-canada.ca/regions/ontario
Médias sociaux: www.facebook.com/fm1017.ca, twitter.com/Fm1017Info

***Sudbury:* CJMX-FM** (Freq: 105.3)
Owned by: *Rogers Broadcasting Ltd.**
880 Lasalle Blvd., Sudbury, ON P3A 1X5
Tel: 705-566-4480, *Fax:* 705-560-7232
www.ezrocksudbury.com
Social Media: www.facebook.com/1053EZRock
Gary Miles, CEO
Rick Doughty, General Manager

***Sudbury:* CJRQ-FM** (Freq: 92.7)
Owned by: *Rogers Broadcasting Ltd.**
880 Lasalle Blvd., Sudbury, ON P3A 1X5
Tel: 705-566-4480, *Fax:* 705-560-7232
www.q92rocks.com
Gary Miles, President
Rick Doughty, General Manager

***Sudbury:* CJTK-FM** (Freq: 95.5)
2150 Lasalle Blvd., Sudbury, ON P3A 2A7
Tel: 705-674-2585, *Fax:* 705-688-1081
mail@kfmradio.ca
www.cjtk.com
Curtis L. Belcher, General Manager

***Sudbury:* CKLU-FM** (Freq: 96.7)
935 Ramsey Rd., Sudbury, ON P3E 2C6
Tel: 705-673-6538, *Fax:* 705-675-4878
traffic@cklu.ca
www.cklu.ca
Carrie Grahamni, General Manager, gm@cklu.ca
Carl Jorgensen, Operations Director
Tara Lévesque, Music Director

***Thunder Bay:* CBQ-FM** (Freq: 101.7)
Owned by: *Canadian Broadcasting Corporation**
213 East Miles St., Thunder Bay, ON P7C 1J5
Tel: 807-625-5000, *Fax:* 807-625-5035
www.cbc.ca/thunderbay

***Thunder Bay:* CBQT-FM** (Freq: 88.3)
Owned by: *Canadian Broadcasting Corporation**
213 East Miles St., Thunder Bay, ON P7C 1J5
Tel: 807-625-5000, *Fax:* 807-625-5035
www.cbc.ca/thunderbay/
Jolene Banning, Administration Assistant, 807-625-5026

***Thunder Bay:* CBQX-FM** (Freq: 98.7)
Owned by: *Canadian Broadcasting Corporation**
213 East Miles St., Thunder Bay, ON P7C 1J5
Tel: 807-625-5000, *Fax:* 807-625-5035
www.cbc.ca/thunderbay
Social Media: twitter.com/CBCTBay
Tom Grand, General Manager

***Thunder Bay:* CFQK-FM** (Freq: 103.5; 104.5)
87 North Hill St., Thunder Bay, ON P7A 5V6
Tel: 807-346-2600,
thunder@thethunder.ca
www.thethunder.ca
Bill Malcolm, Program Director, bmalcolm@dougallmedica.com

***Thunder Bay:* CJOA-FM** (Freq: 95.1)
#42, 63 Carrie St., Thunder Bay, ON
Tel: 807-344-9525, *Fax:* 807-344-9525
info@cjoa.org
www.cjoa.org
Social Media:
www.facebook.com/Cjoa95.1FmChristianRadioThunderBayOntario
Bonnie Gauthier, Music Director

***Thunder Bay:* CJSD-FM** (Freq: 94.3)
87 Hill St. North, Thunder Bay, ON P7A 5V6
Tel: 807-346-2600, *Fax:* 807-345-9923
rock@rock94.com
www.rock94.com
Brad Hilgers, Program Director, bhilgers@rock94.com

***Thunder Bay:* CJUK-FM** (Freq: 99.9)
Owned by: *NewCap Inc.**
#200, 180 Park Ave., Thunder Bay, ON P7B 6J4
Tel: 807-344-2000, *Fax:* 807-345-9925
magic@magic999.ca
www.magic999.ca
Dennis Landriault, General Manager

***Tillsonburg:* CKOT-FM** (Freq: 101.3)
PO Box 10, Tillsonburg, ON N4G 4H3
Tel: 519-842-4281, *Fax:* 519-842-4284
info@easy101.com
www.easy101.com
John Lamars, President & General Manager

***Timmins:* CHIM-FM** (Freq: 102.3)
226 Delnite Rd., Timmins, ON P4N 7C2
Tel: 705-264-2150,
chimfm@vianet.ca
www.chimfm.com
Roger de Brabant

***Timmins:* CHMT-FM** (Freq: 93.1)
49 Cedar St. South, Timmins, ON P4N 2G5
Tel: 705-267-6070, *Fax:* 705-267-6095
Toll-Free: 866-728-9636
www.moosefm.com/chmt
Social Media:
www.facebook.com/pages/Moose-FM-CHMT-931-Timmins/117620021634651, twitter.com/moosefmchmt
Chris Nimigon, National Sales Manager, 416-925-0488

†*Timmins:* CHYK (Freq: 104.1)
#103, 32 Mountjoy St. North, Timmins, ON P4N 4V6
Tél: 705-269-8307, *Téléc:* 705-269-8305
www.leloupfm.com/Timmins

***Timmins:* CJQQ-FM** (Freq: 92.1)
Owned by: *Rogers Broadcasting Ltd.**
260 - 2nd Ave., Timmins, ON P4N 8A4
Tel: 705-264-2351, *Fax:* 705-264-2984
www.q92timmins.com

***Timmins:* CKGB-FM** (Freq: 99.3)
Owned by: *Rogers Broadcasting Ltd.**
260 - 2nd Ave., Timmins, ON P4N 8A4
Tel: 705-264-2351, *Fax:* 705-264-2984
www.ezrocktimmins.com

***Toronto:* CBLA-FM** (Freq: 99.1)
Owned by: *Canadian Broadcasting Corporation (CBC)**

** For details on this company see listing in Major Broadcasting Companies section; † French language station*

PO Box 500 A, 205 Wellington St. West, Toronto, ON M5W 1E6
Tel: 416-205-3311, *Fax:* 416-205-6336
Toll-Free: 866-306-4636
www.cbc.ca/toronto; www.cbc.ca/radio
Social Media: www.facebook.com/radiocbc, www.twitter.com/cbcradio
Other information: Phone, Radio Newsroom: 416-205-5808; TTY: 1-866-220-6045
Susan Marjetti, Managing Director, 416-205-5791
Don Ioi, Team Manager, Toronto Sales, 416-205-2732

***Toronto:* CBL-FM** (Freq: 94.1)
Owned by: *Canadian Broadcasting Corporation (CBC)**
PO Box 500 A, 205 Wellington St. West, Toronto, ON M5W 3G7
Tel: 416-205-3311, *Toll-Free:* 866-306-4636
www.cbc.ca/toronto; www.cbc.ca/radio2
Social Media: www.facebook.com/cbcsask; www.twitter.com/cbcradio2
Susan Marjetti, Managing Director, 416-205-5791
Don Ioi, Team Manager, Toronto Sales

***Toronto:* CFIE-FM** (Freq: 106.5)
PO Box 87 E, Toronto, ON M6H 4E1
Tel: 416-703-1287, *Fax:* 416-703-4328
www.aboriginalradio.com

***Toronto:* CFMX-FM** (Freq: 96.3; 103.1)
#205, 550 Queen St. East, Toronto, ON M5A 1V2
Tel: 416-367-5353, *Fax:* 416-367-1742
www.classical963fm.com
John van Driel, General Manager/CEO

***Toronto:* CFNY-FM** (Freq: 102.1)
Owned by: *Corus Radio Company**
25 Dockside Dr., Toronto, ON M5A 0B5
Tel: 416-479-7000,
info@edge.ca
www.edge.ca

***Toronto:* CFXJ-FM** (Freq: 93.5)
299 Queen St. West, Toronto, ON M5V 2Z5
Tel: 416-214-5000,
websupport@flow935.com
www.flow935.com

***Toronto:* CHFI-FM** (Freq: 98.1)
Owned by: *Rogers Broadcasting Ltd.**
1 Ted Rogers Way, Toronto, ON
Tel: 416-935-8298, *Fax:* 416-935-8260
www.chfi.com
Social Media: www.facebook.com/981CHFI, twitter.com/981chfi
Chuck McCoy, Toronto Market Manager
Paul Fisher, Vice-President & General Manager

***Toronto:* CHIN-FM** (Freq: 100.7)
622 College St., Toronto, ON M6G 1B6
Tel: 416-531-9991, *Fax:* 416-531-5274
info@chinradio.com
www.chinradio.com
Social Media: www.facebook.com/chinradiocanada, twitter.com/chinradiocanada
Leonard Lombardi, President

***Toronto:* CHKT-FM** (Freq: 88.9)
Owned by: *Fairchild Radio**
Toronto, ON
www.am1430.com

***Toronto:* CHMS-FM** (Freq: 97.7)
Corporate Office
#201, 60 St. Clair East, Toronto, ON M4T 1N5
Tel: 416-925-0488, *Fax:* 416-925-6256
Toll-Free: 866-690-9990
www.hbgradio.com

***Toronto:* CHRY-FM** (Freq: 105.5)
York University, Student Centre, #413, 4700 Keele St., Toronto, ON M3J 1P3
Tel: 416-736-5293, *Fax:* 416-650-8052
chry@yorku.ca
www.chry.fm

***Toronto:* CHUM-FM** (Freq: 104.5)
Owned by: *Bell Media Radio**
299 Queen Street West, Toronto, ON M5V 2Z5
Tel: 416-925-6666,
www.chumfm.com

***Toronto:* CIDC-FM** (Freq: 103.5)
Owned by: *Evanov Radio Group**
5312 Dundas St. West, Toronto, ON M9B 1B2
Tel: 416-213-1035, *Fax:* 416-233-8617
info@z1035.com
www.z1035.com
Social Media: www.facebook.com/Z103.5, twitter.com/Z1035Toronto

***Toronto:* CILQ-FM** (Freq: 107.1)
Owned by: *Corus Premium Television Ltd.**
25 Dockside Dr., Toronto, ON M5A 0B5
Tel: 416-479-7000,
www.q107.com
J. Hayes, President

***Toronto:* CIRV-FM** (Freq: 88.9)
1087 Dundas St. West, Toronto, ON M6J 1W9
Tel: 416-537-1088, *Fax:* 416-537-2463
info@cirvfm.com
www.cirvfm.com
Alberto Elmir, Station Manager

***Toronto:* CIUT-FM** (Freq: 89.5)
89.5 Tower Rd., Toronto, ON M5S 0A2
Tel: 416-978-0909, *Fax:* 416-946-7004
www.ciut.fm
Ken Stowar, Station Manager & Program Director, kenthepd@gmail.com
Melissa Rodway, Office Administrator, officeadmin@ciut.com

***Toronto:* CJAQ-FM** (Freq: 92.5)
Owned by: *Rogers Broadcasting Ltd.**
1 Ted Rogers Way, Toronto, ON M4Y 3B7
Tel: 416-935-8392,
www.kiss925.com
Social Media: facebook.com/kiss925, twitter.com/kiss925toronto
Steve Kennedy, General Manager

***Toronto:* CJBC-FM** (Freq: 90.3)
Owned by: *Canadian Broadcasting Corporation**
PO Box 500 A, Toronto, ON M5W 1E6
Tel: 416-205-3311,
www.radio-canada.ca/regions/ontario

***Toronto:* CJRT-FM** (Freq: 91.1)
#100, 4 Pardee Ave., Toronto, ON M6K 3H5
Tel: 416-595-0404, *Toll-Free:* 888-595-0404
info@jazz.fm
www.jazz.fm
Social Media: twitter.com/JAZZFM91
Bernard Webber, Chair
Ross Porter, President & CEO

***Toronto:* CKFM-FM** (Freq: 99.9)
Owned by: *Astral Media Radio G.P.**
2 St. Clair Ave. West, Toronto, ON M4V 1L6
Tel: 416-922-9999,
info@virginradio999.com
www.virginradio999.com

***Toronto:* CKHC-FM** (Freq: 96.9)
205 Humber College Blvd., Toronto, ON M9W 5L7
Tel: 416-675-6622,
radiohumber@humber.ca
radio.humber.ca
Social Media: twitter.com/RadioHumber

***Toronto:* CKLN-FM** (Freq: 88.1)
55 Gould St., Toronto, ON M5B 1E9
www.ckln.fm
David Barnard, Chair

***Toronto:* CSCR-FM** (Freq: 90.3)
University of Toronto Scarborough Campus, 1265 Military Trail, Toronto, ON M1C 1A4
Tel: 416-287-7051,
www.fusionradio.ca
Piro Dhimitri, Station Manager, stationmanager@fusionradio.ca

***Waterloo:* CFCA-FM** (Freq: 105.3)
Owned by: *Bell Media Radio**
#207, 255 King St. North, Waterloo, ON N2J 4V2
Tel: 519-884-4470, *Fax:* 519-884-6482
www.koolfm.com
Paul Cugliari, Vice President/General Manager

***Waterloo:* CKMS-FM** (Freq: 100.3)
142 Waterloo St., Waterloo, ON N2J 1Y2
Tel: 519-886-2567,
soundfm.ca
Den Kellar, President

***Waterloo:* CKWR-FM** (Freq: 98.5)
375 University Ave. East, Waterloo, ON N2K 3M7
www.ckwr.com

***Waterloo:* KFUN** (Freq: 99.5)
#207, 255 King St. North, Waterloo, ON N2J 4V2
Tel: 514-884-1090, *Fax:* 519-884-6482
Social Media: www.facebook.com/KFUN995, twitter.com/995kfun
Dave Schneider, Program Director, 519-884-4470

***Wawa:* CJWA-FM** (Freq: 107.1)
PO Box 1447, 55 Broadway Ave., Wawa, ON P0S 1K0
Tel: 705-856-4555, *Fax:* 705-856-1520
Rick Labbe, President, ceojjam@onlink.net

***Welland:* CHOW-FM** (Freq: 91.7)
43, 1st Ave. East, Welland, ON J9T 1H2
Tel: 819-732-6991, *Fax:* 819-732-6988
Toll-Free: 877-342-5917
coordonnatrice@radioboreale.com
radioboreale.abitemis.info
Pat St John, President

***Welland:* CRNC-FM** (Freq: 90.1)
300 Woodlawn Rd., Welland, ON L3C 7L3
Tel: 905-735-2211, *Fax:* 905-736-6002
www.broadcasting.niagarac.on.ca
Ron Tufts, rtufts@niagarac.on.ca

***Wiarton:* CHFN-FM** (Freq: 100.1)
RR#5, Wiarton, ON N0H 2T0
Tel: 519-843-4542,
info@georgeloney.com
www.georgeloney.com
Jessica Nadjiwon, Station Manager

***Windsor:* CBE-FM** (Freq: 89.9)
Owned by: *Canadian Broadcasting Corporation (CBC)**
825 Riverside Dr. West, Windsor, ON N9A 5K9
Tel: 519-255-3411, *Toll-Free:* 866-306-4636
www.cbc.ca/windsor; www.cbc.ca/radio2
Social Media: www.facebook.com/cbcsask; www.twitter.com/cbcradio2,
Other information: Phone, Newsroom: 519-255-3456
Sandra Porteous, Managing Editor, Radio & Television, 519-255-3563
David Daigneault, Executive Producer, Radio & Television, 519-255-3410
Nancy Lauzon, Manager, Windsor Accounts, 519-255-3510

***Windsor:* CIDR-FM** (Freq: 93.9)
Owned by: *Bell Media Radio**
1640 Ouellette Ave., Windsor, ON N8X 1L1
Tel: 519-258-8888, *Fax:* 519-258-0182
www.939theriverradio.com
Eric Proksch, Vice President/General Manager

***Windsor:* CIMX-FM** (Freq: 88.7)
Owned by: *Bell Media Radio**
1640 Ouellette Ave., Windsor, ON N8X 1L1
Tel: 519-258-8888, *Fax:* 519-258-0182
www.89xradio.com
Social Media: www.facebook.com/89XFANS
Eric Proksch, Vice President/General Manager

***Windsor:* CJAM-FM** (Freq: 91.5)
401 Sunset Ave., Windsor, ON N9B 3P4
Tel: 519-971-3606, *Fax:* 519-971-3605
statcjam@uwindsor.ca
www.cjam.ca
Vernon Smith, Station Manager, statcjam@uwindsor.ca

***Wingham:* CKNX-FM** (Freq: 101.7)
Owned by: *Blackburn Radio Inc.**
215 Carling Terrace, Wingham, ON N0G 2W0
Tel: 519-357-1310, *Fax:* 519-357-1897
www.1017theone.ca
Craig Picton, Program Director, 519-357-1310

***Woodstock:* CJFH-FM** (Freq: 94.3)
1038 Parkinson Rd., Woodstock, ON N4S 7V6
Tel: 519-539-2304, *Fax:* 519-539-2011
www.hopefm.ca
Chris Gordon, Music Director

***Woodstock:* CKDK-FM** (Freq: 103.9)
Owned by: *Corus Radio Company**

** For details on this company see listing in Major Broadcasting Companies section; † French language station*

290 Dundas St., Woodstock, ON N4S 1B7
Tel: 519-539-1040, *Fax:* 519-539-7479
www.thehawk.ca
Social Media: www.facebook.com/pages/More-1039-FM/202642683093622, twitter.com/More1039
Brad Gibb, Program Director

Prince Edward Island

***Charlottetown:* CBCT-FM** (Freq: 96.1)
Owned by: *Canadian Broadcasting Corporation (CBC)**
PO Box 2230, 430 University Ave., Charlottetown, PE C1A 8B9
Tel: 902-629-6400, *Fax:* 902-629-6518
Toll-Free: 866-306-4636
www.cbc.ca/pei; www.cbc.ca/radio
Social Media: www.facebook.com/radiocbc; www.twitter.com/cbcradio,
Other information: Phone, News: 902-629-6402; TTY: 1-866-220-6045
Andrew Cochran, Managing Director, Maritimes
Donna Allen, Executive Producer, Prince Edward Island News
Janet Irwin, Senior Regional Manager, News & Current Affairs
Lenny Jackson, Station Manager, Prince Edward Island
Nadine Antle, Regional Manager, Partnerships, Communications, Brand, & Promot, 506-451-4054
John Channing, Manager, Sales
Heather McGrath, Senior Officer, Communications, 902-629-6416

***Charlottetown:* CHLQ-FM** (Freq: 93.1)
Owned by: *Maritime Broadcasting System**
5 Prince St., Charlottetown, PE C1A 4P4
Tel: 902-892-1066, *Fax:* 902-566-1338
q93.fm
Social Media: www.facebook.com/Q93ROCKS, twitter.com/Q93ROCKS

***Charlottetown:* CHTN-FM** (Freq: 100.3)
Owned by: *NewCap Inc.**
#320, 90 University Ave., Charlottetown, PE C1A 4K9
Tel: 902-569-1003, *Fax:* 902-569-8693
www.ocean1003.com
Social Media: www.facebook.com/ocean100, twitter.com/ocean100

Québec

†*Alma:* CKYK-FM (Freq: 95.7)
#200, 460, Sacré-Coeur ouest, Alma, QC G8B 1L9
saguenay.radiox.com
Marc-André Levesque, Président

***Amqui:* CFVM-FM** (Freq: 99.9)
Owned by: *Astral Media Radio Inc.**
111, rue de l'Hopital, Amqui, QC G5J 2K1
Tel: 418-629-2025, *Fax:* 418-629-2599
amqui.rougefm.ca

†*Asbestos:* CJAN-FM (Freq: 99.3)
1, rue Hilaire, Asbestos, QC J1T 0A3
Tél: 819-879-5439, *Téléc:* 819-879-7922
info@fm993.ca
fm993.ca

***Baie-Comeau:* CBMI-FM** (Freq: 93.7)
Owned by: *Canadian Broadcasting Corporation (CBC)**
Baie-Comeau, QC
Toll-Free: 866-306-4636
www.cbc.ca/montreal; www.cbc.ca/radio
Social Media: www.facebook.com/radiocbc; www.twitter.com/cbcradio,
Other information: TTY: 1-866-220-6045

†*Baie-Comeau:* CBSI-FM-24 (Freq: 106.1)*Détenteur:* **Canadian Broadcasting Corporation (CBC)***
Baie-Comeau, QC
Ligne sans frais: 866-954-1341
auditoire.quebec@radio-canada.ca
www.radio-canada.ca/regions/quebec

†*Baie-Comeau:* CHLC-FM (Freq: 97.1)
907, rue de Puyjalon, Baie-Comeau, QC G5C 1N3
Tél: 418-589-3771, *Téléc:* 418-589-9086
chlcfm97@globetrotter.net
www.chlc.com
Georges Daviault, Directeur Général

***Baie-Saint-Paul:* CHOX-FM-1** (Freq: 94.1)
Owned by: *CHOX-FM*
Baie-Saint-Paul, QC

†*Cap-aux-Meules:* CFIM-FM (Freq: 92.7)
CP 8192, Cap-aux-Meules, QC G4T 1R3
Tél: 418-986-5233, *Téléc:* 418-986-5319
administration@cfim.ca
www.cfim.ca
Charles Eugene Cyr, Directeur général, direction@cfim.ca

†*Carleton:* CIEU-FM (Freq: 94.9; 106.1)
1645, boul Perron est, Carleton, QC G0C 1J0
Tél: 418-364-7094, *Téléc:* 418-364-3150
administration@cieufm.com
www.cieufm.com
Claude Roy, Directeur général, direction@cieufm.com

***Châteauguay:* CHAI-FM** (Freq: 101.9)
25, boul St-Francis, Châteauguay, QC J6J 1Y2
Tel: 450-698-3131, *Fax:* 450-698-3339
info@Chaifm.com
chaifm.com
Social Media: www.facebook.com/pages/1019-Chai-FM/171051749593931
Sylvain Poirier

†*Chicoutimi:* CBJ-FM (Freq: 93.7FM)*Détenteur:* **Canadian Broadcasting Corporation (CBC)***
500, rue des Sagueneens, Chicoutimi, QC G7H 6N4
Tél: 418-696-6600,
auditoire.slsj@radio-canada.ca
www.radio-canada.ca/regions/saguenay-lac
Michel Gagné, Chef des services français, 418-696-6600, michel.gagne-SAG@radio-canada.ca

†*Chicoutimi:* CBJX-FM (Freq: Saguenay, QC; 100.9FM)*Détenteur:* **Société Radio-Canada; Canadian Broadcasting Corporation***
500, rue des Saguenéens, Chicoutimi, QC G7H 6N4
Tél: 418-696-6600,
www.radio-canada.ca/regions/saguenay-lac

†*Chicoutimi:* CFIX-FM (Freq: 96.9)*Détenteur:* **Astral Media Inc.***
CP 8390, 267, rue Racine est, Chicoutimi, QC G7H 5C2
Tél: 418-543-9797, *Téléc:* 418-543-7968
webmestre-saguenay@astral.com
www.rockdetente.com

†*Chicoutimi:* CJAB-FM (Freq: 94.5)*Détenteur:* **Astral Media Radio Inc.***
CP 1506, 267, rue Racine est, Chicoutimi, QC G7H 5K3
Tél: 418-545-9450, *Téléc:* 418-543-7968
saguenay.radionrj.ca
Médias sociaux: www.facebook.com/nrj945, twitter.com/NRJ945

†*Dégelis:* CFVD-FM (Freq: 95.5)
654, 6e rue est, Dégelis, QC G5T 1Y1
Tél: 418-853-3370, *Téléc:* 418-853-3321
CFVD@FM95.ca
Gilles Caron

†*Dolbeau-Mistassini:* CHVD-FM (Freq: 100.3)*Détenteur:* **Groupe Radio Antenne 6***
1975, boul Wallberg, Dolbeau-Mistassini, QC G8L 1J5
Tél: 418-276-3333, *Téléc:* 418-276-6755
chvd@antenne6.com
www.dolbeau-mistassini.planeteradio.ca
Médias sociaux: www.facebook.com/pages/Planète-1003/115354181826762
Marc-André Levesque, Président

***Donnacona:* CHXX-FM** (Freq: 100.9)
274, rue Notre-Dame, Donnacona, QC G6M 1G7
Tel: 418-285-2568

†*Drummondville:* CHRD-FM (Freq: 105.3)*Détenteur:* **Astral Media Radio Inc.***
2070, St-Georges, Drummondville, QC J2C 5G6
Tél: 819-475-1480, *Téléc:* 819-747-6610
receptionchrd@boomfm.com
www.boomfm.com

†*Drummondville:* CJDM-FM (Freq: 92.1)*Détenteur:* **Astral Media Radio Inc.***
2070 rue St-Georges, Drummondville, QC J2C 5G6
Tél: 819-474-1892, *Téléc:* 819-474-6610
drummondville.radionrj.ca

***Fermont:* CBMR-FM** (Freq: 105.1)
Owned by: *Canadian Broadcasting Corporation (CBC)**
Fermont, QC
Toll-Free: 866-306-4636
www.cbc.ca/montreal; www.cbc.ca/radio
Social Media: www.facebook.com/radiocbc, www.twitter.com/cbcradio
Other information: TTY: 1-866-220-6045

†*Fermont:* CFMF-FM (Freq: 103.1)
CP 280, 20, Place Daviault, Fermont, QC G0G 1J0
Tél: 418-287-5147, *Téléc:* 418-287-5776
infocfmf@diffusionfermont.ca
www.cfmf.ca
Nadia Larrivée, Directrice générale, n.larrivee@diffusionfermont.ca

†*Fort-Coulonge:* CHIP-FM (Freq: 101.7)
CP 820, 138, rue Principale, Fort-Coulonge, QC J0X 1V0
Tél: 819-683-3155, *Téléc:* 819-683-3211
Ligne sans frais: 888-775-3155
admin@chipfm.com
www.chipfm.com
Frank Doyle

***Gaspé:* CJRE-FM** (Freq: 97.9)
162, rue Jacques Cartier, Gaspé, QC G4X 1M9
Tel: 418-368-3511, *Fax:* 418-368-1663
Toll-Free: 866-360-3511
accueil@radiogaspesie.ca
www.radiogaspesie.ca
Jacques Chartier, General Manager

†*Gaspé:* CJRG-FM (Freq: 94.5)
162, rue Jacques Cartier, Gaspé, QC G4X 1M9
Tél: 418-368-3511, *Téléc:* 418-368-1663
Ligne sans frais: 866-360-3511
accueil@radiogaspesie.ca
www.radiogaspesie.ca

†*Gatineau:* CHLX-FM (Freq: 97.1)
171A, rue Jean-Proulx, Gatineau, QC J8Z 1W5
Tél: 819-770-1040, *Téléc:* 819-770-9740
Ligne sans frais: 819-503-8965
www.gatineau.planeteradio.ca

†*Gatineau:* CIMF-FM (Freq: 94.9)*Détenteur:* **Astral Media Radio Inc.***
15, rue Taschereau, Gatineau, QC J8Y 2V6
Tél: 819-770-2463, *Téléc:* 819-770-9338
webmestre-gatineau@astral.com
gatineau.rougefm.ca

***Gatineau:* CKTF-FM** (Freq: 104.1)
Owned by: *Astral Media Radio Inc.**
15, rue Taschereau, Gatineau, QC J8Y 2V6
Tel: 819-243-5555, *Fax:* 819-243-6816
webmestre-gatineau@astral.com
gatineau.radionrj.ca

†*Havre-Saint-Pierre:* CBSI-FM-7 (Freq: 92.5)*Détenteur:* **Canadian Broadcasting Corporation (CBC)***
Havre-Saint-Pierre, QC
Ligne sans frais: 866-954-1341
auditoire.quebec@radio-canada.ca
www.radio-canada.ca/regions/quebec

†*Hâvre-Saint-Pierre:* CILE-FM (Freq: 95.1)
992, rue du Bouleau, Hâvre-Saint-Pierre, QC G0G 1P0
Tél: 418-538-2451, *Téléc:* 418-538-3870
info@cilemf.com
www.cilemf.com

†*Joliette:* CJLM-FM (Freq: 103.5)
540, rue Thomas, Joliette, QC J6E 3R4
Tél: 450-756-1035, *Téléc:* 450-756-8097
radio@m1035fm.com
www.m1035fm.com
Médias sociaux: www.facebook.com/pages/M1035FM-Radio-de-Lanaudière/1019 6265652621, twitter.com/m1035fm
Normand Masse

†*Jonquière:* CKAJ-FM (Freq: 92.5)
3877, boul. Harvey, 2e étage, Jonquière, QC G7X 0A6
Tél: 418-546-2525, *Téléc:* 418-546-2528
ckaj@ckaj.org
www.ckaj.org
Médias sociaux: www.facebook.com/ckajfm, twitter.com/ckaj925

** For details on this company see listing in Major Broadcasting Companies section; † French language station*

***Kahnawake:* CKRK-FM** (Freq: 103.7)
PO Box 1050, Kahnawake, QC J0L 1B0
Tel: 450-638-1313, *Fax:* 450-638-4009
programming@k103radio.com
info@k103radio.com

***Kuujjuaq:* CKUJ-FM** (Freq: 97.3)
PO Box 1082, Kuujjuaq, QC J0M 1C0
Tel: 819-964-2921, *Fax:* 819-964-2229

***L'Annonciation:* CFLO-FM** (Freq: 101.9)
***Owned by:** CFLO-FM*
L'Annonciation, QC

†*La Pocatière:* CHOX-FM (Freq: 97.5)
#50, 601, 1ère av, La Pocatière, QC G0R 1Z0
Tél: 418-856-1310, *Téléc:* 418-856-3747
chox@chox97.com
www.chox97.com

***Lac-Etchemin:* CFIN-FM** (Freq: 100.5)
#11, 201, rue Claude-Bilodeau, Lac-Etchemin, QC G0R 1S0
Tel: 418-625-3737, *Fax:* 418-625-3730
cfinfm@sogetel.net
www.cfin-fm.com
Jacques Thériault

†*Lac-Mégantic:* CFJO-FM (Freq: 101.7)*Détenteur:* **CFJO-FM**
Lac-Mégantic, QC
www.o973.com
Médias sociaux:
www.facebook.com/pages/O-973-Le-meilleur-de-la-musique/1824948969, twitter.com/o973

†*Lac-Mégantic:* CJIT-FM (Freq: 106.7)
4766, rue Laval, Lac-Mégantic, QC G6B 1C7
Tél: 819-583-0663, *Téléc:* 819-583-0665
www.cjitfm.com
Ritha Breton

***Lachute:* CJLA-FM** (Freq: 104.9)
11, rue Argenteuil, Lachute, QC J8H 1X8
Tel: 450-562-8862,
www.planetelov.ca

†*Laval:* CFGL-FM (Freq: 105.7)
#100, 2830, boul St-Martin est, Laval, QC H7E 5A1
Tél: 450-664-4647, *Téléc:* 450-664-4138
www.rythmefm.com
Médias sociaux:
www.facebook.com/pages/1057-rythme-FM/124140938458,
twitter.com/rythmefm1057S
Jacques Boiteau, General Manager

***Les Escoumins:* CHME-FM** (Freq: 94.9)
34, rue de la Reserve, Les Escoumins, QC G0T 1K0
Tel: 418-233-2700, *Fax:* 418-233-3326
chme@B2B2C.ca
chme949.jimdo.com
Social Media:
www.facebook.com/pages/CHME-Rock-ma-vie/174431196087
Gilles Labelle

***Listuguj:* CFIC-FM** (Freq: 105.1)
PO Box 304, 44A Riverside ouest, Listuguj, QC
Tel: 418-788-5166, *Fax:* 418-788-3524
www.105hotcountry.com
Jake Dedan, General Manager

***Listuguj:* CHRQ-FM** (Freq: 106.9)
Listuguj, QC G0C 2R0
Sandra Bulmer, Station Manager

***Longueuil:* CHAA-FM** (Freq: 103.3)
91, rue St-Jean, Longueuil, QC J4H 2W8
Tel: 450-646-6800, *Fax:* 450-646-7378
admin@fm1033.ca
www.fm1033.ca
Eric Tetreault

†*Maniwaki:* CFOR-FM (Freq: Pur rock à 99.3 FM Maniwaki)
139, rue Principal sud, Maniwaki, QC J9E 1Z8
Tél: 819-441-0993, *Téléc:* 819-441-3488
cfor993@b2b2c.ca
www.cforfm.com
Laure Voilquin, Directrice commerciale, laure@cforfm.com

†*Maniwaki:* CHGA-FM (Freq: 97.3)
158, rue Laurier, Maniwaki, QC J9E 2K7
Tél: 819-449-9730, *Ligne sans frais:* 866-767-9730
www.chga.qc.ca
Lise Morrissette, Directrice générale, lmorrissette@chga.fm

***Maniwaki:* CKWE-FM** (Freq: 103.9)
PO Box 309, Maniwaki, QC J9E 3C9
Tel: 819-449-5170, *Fax:* 819-449-5097
Anita Penasco, General Manager

†*Mashteuiatsh:* CHUK-FM (Freq: 107.3)
1491, rue Ouiatchouan, Mashteuiatsh, QC G0W 2H0
Tél: 418-275-4684, *Téléc:* 418-275-7964
chuk@chukfm.ca
www.chukfm.ca
Marc Gill, General Manager

†*Matagami:* CHEF-FM (Freq: 99.9)
CP 39, 110, boul Matagami, Matagami, QC J0Y 2A0
Tél: 819-739-9990, *Téléc:* 819-739-6003
chef99fm@lino.com
www.chef99.ca
Marie-Eve C. Gallant, General Manager

†*Matane:* CBGA-FM (Freq: 102.1)*Détenteur:* **Canadian Broadcasting Corporation (CBC)***
Matane, QC
Tél: 514-597-6000, *Téléc:* 514-597-5545
Ligne sans frais: 800-306-4636
auditoire@radio-canada.ca
www.radio-canada.ca/radio

†*Matane:* CHOE-FM (Freq: 95.3)
800, av du Phare ouest, Matane, QC G4W 1V7
Tél: 418-562-8181, *Téléc:* 418-562-0778
www.choefm.com
Kenneth Gagné Jr.

†*Matane:* CHRM-FM (Freq: 105.3)
800, av du Phare ouest, Matane, QC G4W 1V7
Tél: 418-562-4141, *Téléc:* 418-562-0778
www.chrmfm.com
Médias sociaux:
www.facebook.com/pages/CHRM-1053-Matane/115997205081095
Michel Desrosiers, Directeur commercial, micheldesrosiers@choefm.com

†*Mont-Laurier:* CFLO-FM (Freq: 104.7)
456, rue du Pont, Mont-Laurier, QC J9L 2R9
Tél: 819-623-6610, *Téléc:* 819-623-7406
www.cflo.ca
Dominic Bell, CEO, 819-623-6610, dbell@cflo.ca

†*Montréal:* CBF-FM (Freq: 95.1)*Détenteur:* **Canadian Broadcasting Corporation (CBC)***
CP 6000 Centre-ville, 1400, boul René-Lévesque est, Montréal, QC H3C 3A8
Tél: 514-597-6000, *Ligne sans frais:* 866-306-4636
auditoire@radio-canada.ca; liaison@radio-canada.ca
www.radio-canada.ca/radio
Autre information: TDD: 514-597-6013
Pia Marquard, Managing Director, Radio & Television, Québec
Sally Caudwell, Executive Producer, Montréal News, 514-597-4089, Fax: 514-597-4511
Kenny King, Senior Manager, CBC Media Sales & Marketing
Helen Evans, Program Manager, Radio Current Affairs

†*Montréal:* CBFX-FM (Freq: 100.7)*Détenteur:* **Canadian Broadcasting Corporation (CBC)***
CP 6000 Centre-ville, 1400, boul René-Lévesque est, Montréal, QC H3C 3A8
Tél: 514-597-6000, *Téléc:* 514-597-5545
Ligne sans frais: 866-306-4636
auditoire@radio-canada.ca
www.radio-canada.ca/espace_musique
Pia Marquard, Managing Director, Radio & Television, Québec Region
Hugh Brodie, Manager, Partnerships & Communications, Québec, 514-597-5813
Helen Evans, Program Manager, Radio Current Affairs

***Montréal:* CBJE-FM** (Freq: CBC Radio One, Chicoutimi, QC, 102.7FM)
***Owned by:** Canadian Broadcasting Corporation**
PO Box 6000, 1400, boul René Lévesque est, Montréal, QC H3C 3A8
info@radio.cbc.ca
www.cbc.ca/radio
Social Media: www.facebook.com/radiocbc, twitter.com/cbcradio

Patricia Pleszczynska, General Manager

***Montréal:* CBME-FM** (Freq: 88.5)
***Owned by:** Canadian Broadcasting Corporation (CBC)**
PO Box 6000, Montréal, QC H3C 3A8
Tel: 514-597-6000, *Fax:* 514-597-6510
www.cbc.ca/radio
Social Media: www.facebook.com/radiocbc;
www.twitter.com/cbcradio,
Other information: Phone, CBC Radio One Newsroom: 514-597-6300; TTY: 1-866-220-6045
Pia Marquard, Managing Director, Radio & Television, Québec Region
Sally Caudwell, Executive Producer, News, Montréal, 514-597-4089, Fax: 514-597-4511
Mary-Jo Barr, News Director, English Services
Kenny King, Senior Manager, CBC Media Sales & Marketing
Hugh Brodie, Manager, Partnership & Communications, Québec, 514-597-5813
Helen Evans, Program Manager, Radio Current Affairs
Carolyn Warren, Regional Manager, Cultural Programming, Integrated Content

***Montréal:* CBM-FM** (Freq: 93.5)
***Owned by:** Canadian Broadcasting Corporation (CBC)**
Maison Radio-Canada, PO Box 6000 Centre-ville, 1400, boul René-Lévesque est, Montréal, QC H3C 3A8
Tel: 514-597-6000, *Fax:* 514-597-5545
Toll-Free: 866-306-4636
auditoire@radio-canada.ca
www.cbc.ca/montreal; www.cbc.ca/radio2
Social Media: www.facebook.com/CBC.Radio2.Official?ref=nf,
www.twitter.com/cbcradio2
Pia Marquard, Managing Director, Radio & Television, Québec Region
Kenny King, Senior Manager, CBC Media Sales & Marketing
Hugh Brodie, Manager, Partnership & Communications, Québec
Helen Evans, Program Manager, Radio Current Affairs

***Montréal:* CFQR-FM** (Freq: 92.5)
***Owned by:** Corus Entertainment Inc.**
#100, 800, rue de la Gauchetière ouest, Montréal, QC H5A 1K6
Tel: 514-767-9250, *Fax:* 514-766-9569
www.925thebeat.ca
Social Media: www.facebook.com/TheBeatofMontreal,
twitter.com/925thebeatmtl
Mark Dickie, General Manager, 514-787-7946

***Montréal:* CHOM-FM** (Freq: 97.7)
***Owned by:** Astral Media Radio G.P.**
1411, rue Fort, 3e étage, Montréal, QC H3H 2R1
Tel: 514-937-2466, *Fax:* 514-846-4741
infodesk@chom.com
www.chom.com
Matthew Wood, Promotions, mwood@astral.com

†*Montréal:* CIBL-FM (Freq: 101.5)
#201, 2 Ste-Catherine est, Montréal, QC H2K 1K4
Tél: 514-526-2581, *Téléc:* 514-526-3583
infoscommunautaires@cibl1015.com
www.cibl1015.com
Éric Lefebvre, Directeur général

***Montréal:* CINQ-FM** (Freq: 102.3)
5212, boul St-Laurent, 2e étage, Montréal, QC H2T 1S1
Tel: 514-495-2597, *Fax:* 514-495-2429
cinqfm@radiocentreville.com
www.radiocentreville.com
Magalie Pare

***Montréal:* CIRA-FM** (Freq: 91.3)
#199, 4020,rue Saint-Ambroise, Montréal, QC H4C 2C7
Tel: 514-382-3913, *Fax:* 514-858-0965
cira@radiovm.com
www.radiovm.com
Jean-Guy Roy, Dir de la Station

†*Montréal:* CISM-FM (Freq: 89.3)
CP 6128 Downtown, #C-1509, 2332, Edouard-Montpetit, Montréal, QC H3C 3J7
Tél: 514-343-7511, *Téléc:* 514-343-2418
www.cism.umontreal.ca
Médias sociaux: www.facebook.com/cism893,
twitter.com/cism893
Dave Ouellet

***Montréal:* CJFM-FM** (Freq: 95.9)
***Owned by:** Astral Media Radio G.P.**
1411, rue du Fort, Montréal, QC H3H 2R1
Tel: 514-790-9696,
montreal.virginradio.ca

** For details on this company see listing in Major Broadcasting Companies section; † French language station*

Gary Slaight, President
Rob Braide, Vice-President

***Montréal:* CJPX-FM** (Freq: 99.5)
124, ch. du Chenal-Le-Moyne, Ile Notre-Dame, Montréal, QC H3C 1A9
Tel: 514-871-0995, *Fax:* 514-871-0990
cjpx@radioclassique.ca
www.cjpx.ca
Francois Pare

***Montréal:* CKLX-FM** (Freq: 91.9)
#250, 200, av Laurier ouest, Montréal, QC H2T 2N8
montreal.radiox.com
Guy Banville

†*Montréal:* CKMF-FM (Freq: 94.3)*Détenteur:* **Astral Media Radio Inc.***
#050, 1717, boul René-Lévesque est, Montréal, QC H2L 4T9
Tél: 514-529-3229, *Téléc:* 514-529-9308
saguenay.radionrj.ca

†*Montréal:* CKOI-FM (Freq: 96.9)*Détenteur:* **Corus Entertainment Inc.***
#1100, 800, rue de la Gauchetière ouest, Montréal, QC H5A 1K6
Tél: 514-789-2564, *Téléc:* 514-787-7982
www.ckoi.com

***Montréal:* CKUT-FM** (Freq: 90.3)
3647, rue University, Montréal, QC H3A 2B3
Tel: 514-448-4041, *Fax:* 514-398-8261
programming@ckut.ca
www.ckut.ca

***Montréal:* MIKE-FM, CKIN-FM** (Freq: 105.1)
5899, av du Parc, Montréal, QC H2V 4H4
Tel: 514-273-2481, *Fax:* 514-273-3707
info@mikefm.ca
www.ckdgfm.ca
Marie Griffiths, Station Manager

†*Natashquan:* CKNA-FM (Freq: 104.1)
CP 9, 29, ch d'en Haut, Natashquan, QC G0G 2E0
Tél: 418-726-3284, *Téléc:* 418-726-3367
ckna@globetrotter.net
pages.globetrotter.net/ckna

†*New Carlisle:* CHNC-FM (Freq: 107.1)
153, boul Gérard-D.-Levesque, New Carlisle, QC G0C 1Z0
Tél: 418-752-2215, *Téléc:* 418-752-6939
radiochnc@globetrotter.net
www.radiochnc.com
Francis Rémillard, General Manager, francis@radiochnc.com
Brigitte Paquet, Sales Director, brigitte@radiochnc.com

***Pikogan:* CKAG-FM** (Freq: 100.1)
30, rue David Kistabish, Pikogan, QC J9T 3A3
Tel: 819-727-3237, *Fax:* 819-727-4432
ckagfm@cableamos.com
www.ckagfm.com

†*Port-Cartier:* CIPC-FM (Freq: Rock contemporain, franco/anglo, à 99.1 FM, Port-Cartier/Sept-×les)
52, rue Élie-Rochefort, Port-Cartier, QC G5B 1N2
Tél: 418-766-6869, *Téléc:* 418-766-6870
info@laradioactive.com
www.laradioactive.com

†*Port-Menier:* CJBE-FM (Freq: 90.1)
CP 15, Port-Menier, QC G0G 2Y0
Tél: 418-535-0292, *Téléc:* 418-535-0497
Denis Tremblay, Dir de la Station

***Québec:* CBVE-FM** (Freq: 104.7)
***Owned by:** Canadian Broadcasting Corporation**
PO Box 18800, 888, rue Saint-Jean, Québec, QC G1K 9L4
Tel: 866-691-3620, *Fax:* 418-691-3610

†*Québec:* CBV-FM (Freq: 106.3)*Détenteur:* **Canadian Broadcasting Corporation***
CP 18800, 888, rue St-Jean, Québec, QC G1R 5H6
Tél: 418-656-8206,
nouvelles.quebec@radio-canada.ca
www.radio-canada.ca/regions
Louise Cordeau, Directrice de Radio-Canada, Québec

†*Québec:* CBV-FM (Freq: 106.3)*Détenteur:* **Canadian Broadcasting Corporation***
CP 18800, 888, rue Saint-Jean, Québec, QC G1K 9L4
Tél: 418-654-1341,
www.radio-canada.ca/regions
Susan Campbell, General Manager

***Québec:* CBVX-FM** (Freq: 95.3)
***Owned by:** Canadian Broadcasting Corporation**
PO Box 18800, 888, rue Saint-Jean, Québec, QC G1K 9L4
Tel: 418-691-3620, *Fax:* 418-691-3610
www.radio-canada.ca/espace_musique

†*Québec:* CHIK-FM (Freq: 98.9)*Détenteur:* **Astral Media Radio Inc.***
900, rue d'Youville, 1er étage, Québec, QC G1R 3P7
Tél: 418-687-9900, *Téléc:* 418-687-3106
quebec.radionrj.ca

***Québec:* CION-FM** (Freq: 90.9; 102.5; 106.7)
3196, ch Sainte-Foy, Québec, QC G1X 1R4
Tel: 418-659-9090, *Fax:* 418-650-3306
Toll-Free: 800-447-2466
cionfm@radiogalilee.qc.ca
www.radiogalilee.com
Denis Veilleux

†*Québec:* CITF-FM (Freq: 107.5)*Détenteur:* **Astral Media Radio Inc.***
900, rue d'Youville, 1er étage, Québec, QC G1R 3P7
Tél: 418-527-3232, *Téléc:* 418-687-3106
quebec.rougefm.ca

***Québec:* CJEC-FM** (Freq: 91.9)
#505, 815 boul. Lebourgneuf, Québec, QC G2J 0C1
Tel: 418-688-0919, *Fax:* 418-682-8431
Toll-Free: 877-670-9000
www.wknd.fm
Social Media: www.facebook.com/wknd.fm
Jean-Paul Lemire, General Manager

†*Québec:* CJMF-FM (Freq: 93.3)
1305, ch Ste-Foy, 4e étage, Québec, QC G1S 4Y5
Tél: 418-687-9330, *Téléc:* 418-687-0211
commentaire@le933.com
www.le933.com
Jean-Paul Lemire

†*Québec:* CKIA-FM (Freq: 88.3)
335, rue Saint-Joseph, Québec, QC G1K 3B4
Tél: 418-529-9026,
www.ckiafm.org
Andrée Pomerleau

†*Québec:* CKRL-FM (Freq: 89.1)
405, 3e av, Québec, QC G1L 2W2
Tél: 418-640-2575, *Téléc:* 418-640-1588
programmation@ckrl.qc.ca
www.ckrl.qc.ca
Médias sociaux: www.facebook.com/CKRL891,
twitter.com/CKRL891
Jean-Pierre Bédard

†*Radisson:* CIAU-FM (Freq: 103.1)
CP 285, 143, rue Jolliet, Radisson, QC J0Y 2X0
Tél: 819-638-7033, *Téléc:* 819-638-7033
ciaufm@lino.com
www.ciaufm.ca
Martin Beaucage, Station Manger

†*Rimouski:* CBRX-FM (Freq: 101.5)*Détenteur:* **Canadian Broadcasting Corporation (CBC)***
Rimouski, QC
Ligne sans frais: 866-954-1341
auditoire.quebec@radio-canada.ca
www.radio-canada.ca/espace_musique;
www.radio-canada.ca/regions/quebec

†*Rimouski:* CIKI-FM (Freq: 98.7)*Détenteur:* **Astral Media Radio Inc.***
CP 3875, 875, boul St-Germain ouest, Rimouski, QC G5L 7P3
Tél: 418-724-9870, *Téléc:* 418-722-7508
rimouski.radionrj.ca

†*Rimouski:* CJOI-FM (Freq: 102.9)*Détenteur:* **Astral Media Radio Inc.***
502, 287, rue Pierre-Saindon, Rimouski, QC G5L 9A7
Tél: 418-723-2323, *Téléc:* 418-722-7508
rimouski.rougefm.ca
Mario Fournier, Directeur générale

†*Rimouski:* CKMN-FM (Freq: 96.5)
323, Montée industrielle, Rimouski, QC G5M 1A7
Tél: 418-722-2566, *Téléc:* 418-724-7815
ckmn-fm@cgocable.ca
www.ckmn.fm
Vic Talbot

†*Rivière-du-Loup:* CIBM-FM (Freq: 107.1)
64, rue Hôtel-de-Ville, Rivière-du-Loup, QC G5R 1L5
Tél: 418-867-1071, *Téléc:* 418-867-4940
ventes@cibm107.com
www.cibm107.com

†*Rivière-du-Loup:* CIEL-FM (Freq: 103.7)
64, rue Hôtel-de-Ville, Rivière-du-Loup, QC G5R 1L5
Tél: 418-867-1071, *Téléc:* 418-867-4940
www.cibm107.com
Médias sociaux:
www.facebook.com/pages/CIEL-FM-1037/208658131206
Clermont Labrie, Controller, clabrie@cibm107.com
Daniel St-Pierre, Program Director, dstpierre@cibm107.com

†*Roberval:* CHRL-FM (Freq: 99.5)*Détenteur:* **Groupe Radio Antenne 6***
568, boul St-Joseph, Roberval, QC G8H 2K6
Tél: 418-275-1831, *Téléc:* 418-275-2475
Médias sociaux:
www.facebook.com/pages/Planète-995/176702051800

***Rouyn-Noranda:* CHIC-FM** (Freq: 88.7)
PO Box 2185, 120, 9e Rue, Rouyn-Noranda, QC J9X 5A6
Tel: 819-797-4242, *Fax:* 819-797-3803
887@chicfm.org
chicfm.org
Jocelyn Côté, General Manager, ccechic@cablevision.qc.ca

†*Rouyn-Noranda:* CHLM-FM (Freq: 90.7)
70, av Principal, Rouyn-Noranda, QC J9X 4P2
Tél: 819-762-8155, *Ligne sans frais:* 877-666-8155
abitibi@radio-canada.ca
www.radio-canada.ca/regions/abitibi

***Rouyn-Noranda:* CJMM-FM** (Freq: 99.1)
***Owned by:** Astral Media Radio Inc.**
191, ave. Murdoch, Rouyn-Noranda, QC J9X 1E3
Tel: 819-797-2566, *Fax:* 819-797-1664
webmestre-abitibi@astral.com
www.radioenergie.com
Pat Brennan, General Manager, 506-452-2334

***Saint-Gabriel-de-Brandon:* CFNJ-FM** (Freq: 99.1)
245, rue Beauvilliers, Saint-Gabriel-de-Brandon, QC J0K 2N0
Tel: 450-835-3437,
www.cfnj.net
Denis Roch

†*Saint-Hilarion:* CIHO-FM (Freq: 96.3)
315, ch Cartier nord, Saint-Hilarion, QC G0A 3V0
Tél: 418-457-3333, *Téléc:* 418-457-3518
ciho@charlevoix.net
www.cihofm.com

†*Saint-Hyacinthe:* CFEI-FM (Freq: 106.5)*Détenteur:* **Astral Media Radio Inc.***
2596, boul Casavant ouest, Saint-Hyacinthe, QC J2S 7R8
Tél: 450-774-6486, *Téléc:* 450-774-7785
www.boomfm.com

†*Saint-Jean-sur-Richelieu:* CFZZ-FM (Freq: 104.1)*Détenteur:* **Astral Media Radio Inc.***
104, rue Richelieu, Saint-Jean-sur-Richelieu, QC J3B 6X3
Tél: 450-346-0104, *Téléc:* 450-348-2274
www.boomfm.com
Médias sociaux: www.facebook.com/radioboom

†*Saint-Jérôme:* CIME-FM (Freq: 101.3; 103.9)*Détenteur:* **Corus Entertainment Inc.***
120, de la Gare, Saint-Jérôme, QC J7Z 2C2
Tél: 450-431-2463, *Téléc:* 450-664-4138
www.cime.fm
Médias sociaux: www.facebook.com/cime.fm, twitter.com/cimefm

***Saint-Régis:* CKON-FM** (Freq: 97.3)
***Owned by:** CKON-FM
Saint-Régis, QC

†*Saint-Rémi:* CHOC-FM (Freq: 104.9)
93, rue Lachapelle est, Saint-Rémi, QC J0L 2L0
Tél: 450-454-5500, *Téléc:* 450-454-9435
www.chocfm.com

†*Sainte-Anne-des-Monts:* CJMC-FM (Freq: 100.3)
170, boul Ste-Anne est, Sainte-Anne-des-Monts, QC G4V 1N1
Tél: 418-763-5522, *Téléc:* 418-763-7211
www.bleufm.ca

** For details on this company see listing in Major Broadcasting Companies section; † French language station*

Sainte-Foy: CHYZ-FM (Freq: 94.3)
2305 rue de l'Université, 0236 Pavillon Maurice Pollack, Université Laval, Sainte-Foy, QC G1K 7P4
Tel: 418-656-2131, *Fax:* 450-656-3660
chyz@public.ulaval.ca
www.chyz.qc.ca
Jean-Philippe Lessard, General Manager

Sainte-Perpétue: CHOX-FM-2 (Freq: 101.1)
Owned by: *CHOX-FM*
Sainte-Perpétue, QC

†Salaberry-de-Valleyfield: CKOD-FM (Freq: 103.1)
249, rue Victoria, Salaberry-de-Valleyfield, QC J6T 1A9
Tél: 450-373-0103, *Téléc:* 450-373-8103
fm103@ckod.qc.ca
www.ckod.qc.ca
Robert Brunet, Propriétaire

†Senneterre: CIBO-FM (Freq: 100.5)
CP 1150, 121, 1re rue Est, Senneterre, QC J0Y 2M0
Tél: 819-737-2222, *Téléc:* 819-737-8599
cibo.fm@moncourrier.com
cibofm.com
Guy Bilodeau, General Manager

†Sept-Iles: CBSI-FM (Freq: 98.1)*Détenteur:* **Canadian Broadcasting Corporation (CBC)***
Sept-Iles, QC
Ligne sans frais: 866-954-1341
auditoire.quebec@radio-canada.ca
www.radio-canada.ca/regions/quebec

Sept-Iles: CKAU-FM (Freq: 90.1; 104.5)
PO Box 338, Sept-Iles, QC G4R 4K6
Tel: 418-927-2476, *Fax:* 418-927-2800
info@ckau.com
www.ckau.com
Reginald Wheel, CEO, 418-927-2476, reginaldv@ckau.com

†Sept-Iles: CKCN-FM (Freq: 94.1)
365 boul Laure, Sept-Iles, QC G4R 1X2
Tél: 418-962-3838, *Téléc:* 418-968-6662
ckcn@globetrotter.net
www.le941.com
Médias sociaux:
www.facebook.com/pages/FM-941-Sept-Iles/156789646061, twitter.com/FM941
Carmen Vaillancourt, Comptabe
Caroline Michaud, Directeur des programmes

Sherbrooke: CFAK-FM (Freq: 88.3)
2500, boul de Université, Sherbrooke, QC J1K 2R1
Tel: 819-821-8000, *Fax:* 819-821-7930
cfak883.usherbrooke.ca
Serge Langlois, Directeur général, dg.cfak883@usherbrooke.ca

†Sherbrooke: CFLX-FM (Freq: 95.5)
67, rue Wellington Nord, Sherbrooke, QC J1H 5A9
Tél: 819-566-2787, *Téléc:* 819-566-7331
commentaire@cflx.qc.ca
www.cflx.qc.ca
Médias sociaux: www.facebook.com/groups/5055014089, twitter.com/@cflx955
Jose Deschenes

†Sherbrooke: CIMO-FM (Freq: 106.1)*Détenteur:* **Astral Media Radio Inc.***
#200, 1845, rue King ouest, Sherbrooke, QC J1J 2E4
Tél: 819-347-1414, *Téléc:* 819-347-1061
contact-sherbrooke@astral.com
sherbrooke.radionrj.ca

†Sherbrooke: CITE-FM-1 (Freq: 102.7)*Détenteur:* **Astral Media Radio Inc.***
#200, 2185, rue King ouest, Sherbrooke, QC J1L 2E4
Tél: 819-347-1414, *Téléc:* 819-566-1011
estrie.rougefm.ca
Médias sociaux: www.facebook.com/1027Rougefm

Sherbrooke: CJMQ-FM (Freq: 88.9)
184 Queen St., Sherbrooke, QC J1M 1J9
Toll-Free: 819-570-2094
cjmqnews@yahoo.ca
www.cjmq.fm
David Teasdale, Station Manager, 819-570-2094
Maureen Dillon, Program & Music Director, 819-822-1838

†Sillery: CHOI-FM (Freq: 98.1)
#300, 1134, ch St-Louis, Sillery, QC G1S 1E5
Tél: 418-687-9810, *Téléc:* 418-682-8427
reception@radiox.com
www.radiox.com

Patrice Demers

†Sorel-Tracy: CJSO-FM (Freq: 101.7)
52, rue du Roi, Sorel-Tracy, QC J3P 4M7
Tél: 450-743-2772, *Téléc:* 450-743-0293
Ligne sans frais: 888-489-1017
cjso@cjso.qc.ca
www.cjso.qc.ca
Médias sociaux: www.facebook.com/fm1017.ca, twitter.com/Fm1017Info

†Squatec: CFVD-FM-3 (Freq: 92.1)*Détenteur:* **CFVD-FM**
Squatec, QC

St. Augustine: CJAS-FM (Freq: 93.5)
PO Box 100, 558 rue Principal, St. Augustine, QC G0G 2R0
Tel: 418-947-2239, *Fax:* 418-947-2664
cjasradio@gmail.com
www.lnscommunityradio.com/CJAS
Lorette Gallibois, General Manager

†St-Georges-de-Beauce: CHJM-FM (Freq: 99.7)
CP 100, 11760, 3e av, St-Georges-de-Beauce, QC G5Y 5C4
Tél: 418-227-0997, *Téléc:* 418-228-0096
www.mix997.com
Médias sociaux: www.facebook.com/groups/8780877809/

†St-Georges-de-Beauce: CKRB-FM (Freq: 103.3)
CP 100, 11760, 3e av, St-Georges-de-Beauce, QC G5Y 5C4
Tél: 418-227-0997, *Téléc:* 418-228-0096
www.coolfm.biz

†Ste-Marie-de-Beauce: CHEQ-FM (Freq: 101.3)
#101, 1068, boul Vachon Nord, Ste-Marie-de-Beauce, QC G6E 1M6
Tél: 418-387-1013, *Téléc:* 418-387-3757
Ligne sans frais: 877-387-1013
info@cheqfm.qc.ca
www.cheqfm.qc.ca
Mario Paquin, Directeur général, mpaquin@cheqfm.qc.ca

†Témiscaming: CKVM-FM-1 (Freq: 92.1)*Détenteur:* **CKVM-FM**
Témiscaming, QC

†Thetford Mines: CFJO-FM (Freq: 97.3)
CP 69, 327, rue Labbé, Thetford Mines, QC G6G 5S3
Tél: 418-338-1009,
www.o973.com
Annie Labbé, Directrice générale

†Thetford Mines: CKLD-FM (Freq: 105.5)
327, rue Labbé, Thetford Mines, QC G6G 1Z2
Tél: 418-335-7533, *Téléc:* 418-335-9009
info@passionrock.com
www.passionrock.com
Médias sociaux:
facebook.com/pages/Passion-Rock-1055-Thetford-Mines/11321 85887169

†Trois-Rivières: CHEY-FM (Freq: 94.7)*Détenteur:* **Astral Media Radio Inc.***
#260, 1500, boul Royale, Trois-Rivières, QC G9A 6J4
Tél: 819-378-1023, *Téléc:* 819-378-1360
webmastertr@astral.com
mauricie.rougefm.ca
Marc Thibault, Directeur de la programmation, marc.thibault@astral.com

†Trois-Rivières: CIGB-FM (Freq: 102.3)*Détenteur:* **Astral Media Radio Inc.***
#260, 1500, rue Royal, Trois-Rivières, QC G9A 6J4
Tél: 819-378-1023, *Téléc:* 819-378-1360
mauricie.radionrj.ca

†Val-d'Or: CJMV-FM (Freq: 102.7)*Détenteur:* **Astral Media Radio Inc.***
1610, 3e Avenue, Val-d'Or, QC J9P 1V8
Tél: 819-825-2568, *Téléc:* 819-825-2840
webmestre-abitibi@astral.com
valdor.radionrj.ca
Marlene Trottier, General Manager

†Verdun: CHMP-FM (Freq: 98.5)*Détenteur:* **Corus Entertainment Inc.***
#1100, 800, rue de la Gauchetière Ouest, Verdun, QC H4G 2R2
Tél: 514-789-0985,
www.985fm.ca
Médias sociaux: www.facebook.com/985fm, twitter.com/le985fm
Philippe Aubry, Directeur des ventes, 514-787-7850
Yves Delisle, Directeur adjoint, émissions

†Victoriaville: CFDA-FM (Freq: 101.9)
55, rue St-Jean Baptiste, Victoriaville, QC G6P 6T3
Tél: 819-752-5545, *Téléc:* 819-752-7552
info@passionrock.com
www.passionrock.com

†Victoriaville: CFJO-FM (Freq: 97.3; 101.7)
CP 490, 55, rue St-Jean-Baptiste, Victoriaville, QC G6P 6T3
Tél: 819-752-2785,
info@o973.com
www.o973.com
Annie Labbé, Diectrice Général

†Ville-Marie: CKVM-FM (Freq: 93.1)
62, rue Ste-Anne, Ville-Marie, QC J9V 2B7
Tél: 819-629-2710, *Téléc:* 819-622-0716
ckvm@ckvm.qc.ca
www.ckvmfm.com
Médias sociaux: www.facebook.com/ckvmfm
Tanya Neveau, Directrice générale, dg@ckvmfm.com

Windsor: CIAX-FM (Freq: 98.3)
49 Sixth Ave., Windsor, QC J1S 1T2
Tel: 819-845-2692, *Fax:* 819-845-2692
unitewindsor@qc.aira.com
www.ciaxfm.net
Marc Savoy, Directeur des ventes et publicités, ventes@ciaxfm.net

Saskatchewan

Carlyle Lake: CIDD-FM (Freq: 97.7)
PO Box 121, Carlyle Lake, SK A0C 2S0
Tel: 306-577-2450
Lana Littlechief, General Manager

Hudson Bay: CFMQ-FM (Freq: 98.1)
PO Box 1272, Hudson Bay, SK S0E 0Y0
Tel: 306-865-3065, *Fax:* 306-865-2227
cfmq@sasktel.net
www.townofhudsonbay.com
Dan Brann, General Manager

La Ronge: CBKA-FM (Freq: CBC Radio 1; 105.9FM)
Owned by: *Canadian Broadcasting Corporation**
PO Box 959, La Ronge, SK S0J 1L0
Tel: 306-425-3324,
www.cbc.ca/sk

La Ronge: CJLR-FM (Freq: 89.9)
PO Box 1529, 712 Finlayson St., La Ronge, SK S0J 1L0
Tel: 306-425-4003, *Fax:* 306-425-3123
mbcradio@mbcradio.com
www.mbcradio.com

Meadow Lake: CFDM-FM (Freq: 105.7)
PO Box 8168, Flying Dust Reserve, Meadow Lake, SK S9X 1T8
Tel: 306-236-1445, *Fax:* 306-236-2821
cfdmradio@hotmail.com

Melfort: CJVR-FM (Freq: 105.1)
PO Box 750, 611 Main St. North, Melfort, SK S0E 1A0
Tel: 306-752-2587, *Fax:* 306-752-5932
Toll-Free: 800-668-2587
info@cjvr.com
www.yourtownnews.ca
Linda Rheaume, Station Manager, 306-752-2587, linda@cjur.com

Nipawin: CJNE-FM (Freq: 94.7)
PO Box 220, Nipawin, SK S0E 1E0
Tel: 306-862-9478, *Fax:* 306-862-2334
pro.cjne@sasktel.net
www.cjnefm.com
Norman Rudock, General Manager

†North Battleford: CBKF-FM-5 (Freq: Première Chaîne; 96.9FM)*Détenteur:* **CBKF-FM; Société Radio Canada***
North Battleford, SK

North Battleford: CJCQ-FM (Freq: 98.1)
Owned by: *CJNB*
1711 100th St. North, North Battleford, SK

** For details on this company see listing in Major Broadcasting Companies section; † French language station*

***Prince Albert:* CFMM-FM** (Freq: 99.1)
1316 Central Ave., Prince Albert, SK S6V 6P5
power99fm@rawlco.com
www.power99fm.com
Social Media: www.facebook.com/pages/Power-99/175060595871715
Garth Kalin, Operations Manager

***Prince Albert:* CHQX-FM** (Freq: 101.5)
PO Box 900, 1316 Central Ave., Prince Albert, SK S6V 7R4
www.mix101fm.com

†*Regina:* CBKF-FM (Freq: Première Chaîne; 97.7FM)*Détenteur:* **Société Radio Canada***
CP 540, 2440, rue Broad, Regina, SK S4P 4A1
Tél: 306-347-9540, *Téléc:* 306-347-9635
tjsask@radio-canada.ca
www.radio-canada.ca/saskatchewan
Pierre Guérin, Directeur des services français dans l'Ouest, 204 788-3237, pierre.guerin@radio-canada.ca

***Regina:* CBK-FM** (Freq: CBC Radio 2; 96.9FM)
Owned by: *Canadian Broadcasting Corporation**
2440 Broad St., Regina, SK S4P 4A1
Tel: 306-347-9540,
www.cbc.ca/sask
David Kyle, News Director

***Regina:* CFWF-FM** (Freq: 104.9)
Owned by: *Harvard Broadcasting Inc.**
1900 Rose St., Regina, SK S4P 0A9
Tel: 306-546-6200, *Fax:* 306-781-7338
jasonh@harvardbroadcasting.com
www.thewolfrocks.com
Michael Olstrom

***Regina:* CHMX-FM** (Freq: 92.1)
Owned by: *Harvard Broadcasting Inc.**
1900 Rose St., Regina, SK S4P 0A9
Tel: 306-936-0092, *Fax:* 306-546-6200
dholien@lite92fm.com
www.lite92fm.com
Social Media: www.facebook.com/pages/My-921-Feel-Good-Now/249363191756352, twitter.com/my921feelgood
Michael Olstrom

***Regina:* CIZL-FM** (Freq: 98.9)
Owned by: *RAWLCO Radio Ltd.**
#210, 2401 Saskatchewan Dr., Regina, SK S4P 4H8
Tel: 306-525-0000, *Fax:* 306-347-8557
www.z99.com
Social Media: www.facebook.com/Z99Regina, twitter.com/z99regina
Tom Newton, Program Director

***Regina:* CJTR-FM** (Freq: 91.3)
PO Box 334 Main, Regina, SK S4P 3A1
Tel: 306-525-7274, *Fax:* 306-525-9741
radius@cjtr.ca
www.cjtr.ca
Keith Colhoun

***Regina:* CKCK-FM** (Freq: 94.5)
Owned by: *RAWLCO Radio Ltd.**
#210, 2401 Saskatchewan Dr., Regina, SK S4P 4H8
Tel: 306-525-0000, *Fax:* 306-547-8557
www.jackfmregina.com
Tom Newton, General Manager, tnewton@rawlco.com
Tim Harrison, Program Director, tharrison@rawlco.com

***Saskatoon:* CFCR-FM** (Freq: 90.5)
PO Box 7544, Saskatoon, SK S7K 4L4
Tel: 306-664-6678,
cfcr@cfcr.ca
www.cfcr.ca
Social Media: www.facebook.com/pages/CFCR-905-FM-Saskatoon-Community-Radio, twitter.com/CFCRSASKATOON
Ron Spizziri

***Saskatoon:* CFMC-FM** (Freq: 95.1)
715 Saskatchewan Cres. West, Saskatoon, SK S7M 5V7
Tel: 306-934-2222, *Fax:* 306-477-0002
www.c95.com
Jamie Wall, General Manager

***Saskatoon:* CJDJ-FM** (Freq: 102.1)
715 Saskatchewan Cres. West, Saskatoon, SK S7M 5V7
Tel: 306-934-2222, *Fax:* 306-477-0002
www.rock102rocks.com
Social Media: www.facebook.com/rock102rocks, twitter.com/rock102twits
Kristy Werner, General Manager, kwerner@rawlco.com

***Saskatoon:* CJMK-FM** (Freq: 98.3)
Owned by: *Saskatoon Media Group**
366 - 3rd Ave. South, Saskatoon, SK S7K 1M5
Tel: 306-244-1975, *Fax:* 306-665-8484
magic@magic983.fm
www.magic983.fm
Social Media: twitter.com/magic983fm

***Saskatoon:* CKBL-FM** (Freq: 92.9)
Owned by: *Saskatoon Media Group**
366 - 3rd Ave. South, Saskatoon, SK S7K 1M5
Tel: 306-244-1975, *Fax:* 306-665-8484
thebull@929thebullrocks.com
www.929thebullrocks.com
Social Media: www.facebook.com/929theBULL, twitter.com/929TheBull
Vic Dubois, President & General Manager

***Swift Current:* CIMG-FM** (Freq: 94.1)
Owned by: *Golden West Broadcasting Ltd.**
134 Central Ave. North, Swift Current, SK S9H 0L1
Tel: 306-773-4605, *Toll-Free:* 800-821-8073
ccongdon@goldenwestradio.com
www.eagle94.com
Deborah Gauger, Station General Manager & Sales

***Whitehorse:* CIAY-FM** (Freq: 100.7)
91806 Alaska Hwy., Whitehorse, SK Y1A 5B7
Tel: 867-393-2429, *Fax:* 867-393-2439
info@lifewhitehorse.com
lifewhitehorse.com
Rod Carby, Station Manager

***Wynyard:* CJVR-FM** (Freq: 100.3)
Owned by: *CJVR-FM*
Wynyard, SK

***Yorkton:* CFGW-FM** (Freq: 94.1)
Owned by: *Harvard Broadcasting*
120 Smith St. East, Yorkton, SK S3N 3V3
Tel: 306-782-2256, *Fax:* 306-783-4994
ykt-reception@harvardbroadcasting.com
www.941thefox.com
Angie Norton, General Manager, anorton@harvardbroadcasting.com

†*Zenon Park:* CBKF-FM-3 (Freq: Première Chaîne; 93.5FM)*Détenteur:* **CBKF-FM; Société Radio Canada***
Zenon Park, SK

Yukon Territory

***Whitehorse:* CHON-FM** (Freq: 98.1; 90.5)
#6, 4230A - 4 Ave., Whitehorse, YT Y1A 1K1
Tel: 867-668-6629, *Fax:* 867-668-6612
nnby@nnby.net
www.nnby.net

Television Stations

Alberta

***Athabasca:* CFRN-TV-12**(Channel: 13)
Owned by: *CFRN-TV*
Athabasca, AB

***Banff:* CBRT-TV-1**(Channel: 5 VHF)
Owned by: *Canadian Broadcasting Corporation (CBC)*
Banff, AB
Toll-Free: 866-306-4636
www.cbc.ca/calgary; www.cbc.ca/television
Social Media: www.twitter.com/cbccalgary,
Other information: TTY: 1-866-220-6045

***Bellevue:* CBRT-TV-10**(Channel: 57 UHF)
Owned by: *Canadian Broadcasting Corporation (CBC)*
Bellevue, AB
Toll-Free: 866-306-4636
www.cbc.ca/calgary; www.cbc.ca/television
Social Media: www.twitter.com/cbccalgary,
Other information: TTY: 1-866-220-6045

***Bonnyville:* CKSA-TV-2**(Channel: 9)
Owned by: *CKSA-TV*
Bonnyville, AB

***Burmis:* CBRT-TV-8**(Channel: 47 UHF)
Calgary
Owned by: *Canadian Broadcasting Corporation (CBC)*
Burmis, AB
Toll-Free: 866-306-4636
www.cbc.ca/calgary; www.cbc.ca/television
Social Media: www.twitter.com/cbccalgary,
Other information: TTY: 1-866-220-6045

***Calgary:* CBRT-TV**(Channel: 9 VHF)
Owned by: *Canadian Broadcasting Corporation (CBC)**
PO Box 2640, 1724 Westmount Blvd. NW, Calgary, AB T2P 2M7
Tel: 403-521-6000, *Fax:* 403-521-6079
Toll-Free: 866-306-4636
www.cbc.ca/calgary; www.cbc.ca/television
Social Media: www.twitter.com/cbccalgary,
Other information: Phone, TV Newsroom: 403-521-6055; TTY: 1-866-220-6045
Diane Humber, Director, Calgary Centre, 403-521-6252
Dave Budge, Director, News, 403-521-6016
Helen Henderson, Director, Programs, 403-521-6221
Jim Haskins, Manager, Calgary Sales Team, 403-521-6184
Shawna Kelly, Manager, Communications, 403-521-6207
Del Simon, Senior Officer, Communications, 403-521-6008

***Calgary:* CFCN-TV**(Channel: 3)
Owned by: *Bell Media TV**
80 Patina Rise SW, Calgary, AB T3H 2W4
Tel: 403-240-5600,
cfcnweb@bellmedia.ca
www.cfcn.ca
Patricia McDougall, Vice-President & General Manager, pmcdougall@ctv.ca

***Calgary:* CICT-TV**(Channel: 7)
Owned by: *Global Television Network**
222 - 23 St. NE, Calgary, AB T2E 7N2
Tel: 403-235-7777,
Calgary@globalnews.ca
www.globaltvcalgary.com

***Calgary:* CKAL-TV**(Channel: 5)
Owned by: *Rogers Broadcasting Ltd.**
535 - 7th Ave. SW, Calgary, AB T2P 0Y4
Tel: 403-508-2222,
citytvcalgaryfeedback@rci.rogers.com
www.citytv.com/calgary

***Cardston:* CBRT-TV-12**(Channel: 6 VHF)
Owned by: *Canadian Broadcasting Corporation (CBC)*
Cardston, AB
Toll-Free: 866-306-4636
www.cbc.ca/calgary; www.cbc.ca/television
Social Media: www.twitter.com/cbccalgary,
Other information: TTY: 1-866-220-6045

***Coleman:* CBRT-TV-11**(Channel: 17 UHF)
Owned by: *Canadian Broadcasting Corporation (CBC)*
Coleman, AB
Toll-Free: 866-306-4636
www.cbc.ca/calgary; www.cbc.ca/television
Social Media: www.twitter.com/cbccalgary,
Other information: TTY: 1-866-220-6045

***Coutts:* CBRT-TV-16**(Channel: 4 VHF)
Owned by: *Canadian Broadcasting Corporation (CBC)*
Coutts, AB
Toll-Free: 866-306-4636
www.cbc.ca/calgary; www.cbc.ca/television
Social Media: www.twitter.com/cbccalgary,
Other information: TTY: 1-866-220-6045

***Cowley:* CBRT-TV-15**(Channel: 27 UHF)
Calgary
Owned by: *Canadian Broadcasting Corporation (CBC)*
Cowley, AB
Toll-Free: 866-306-4636
www.cbc.ca/calgary; www.cbc.ca/television
Social Media: www.twitter.com/cbccalgary,
Other information: TTY: 1-866-220-6045

***Drumheller:* CBRT-TV-2**(Channel: 6 VHF)
Owned by: *Canadian Broadcasting Corporation (CBC)*

** For details on this company see listing in Major Broadcasting Companies section; † French language station*

Drumheller, AB
Toll-Free: 866-306-4636
www.cbc.ca/calgary; www.cbc.ca/television
Social Media: www.twitter.com/cbccalgary,
Other information: TTY: 1-866-220-6045

***Drumheller:* CFCN-TV-1**(Channel: 12)
Calgary

Owned by: *CFCN-TV*
Drumheller, AB

†*Edmonton:* CBXFT-TV(Channel: 11)*Détenteur:* **Canadian Broadcasting Corporation***
Edmonton City Centre, CP 555, #123, 10062 - 102 Ave., Edmonton, AB T5J 2Y8
Tél: 780-468-7790, *Téléc:* 780-468-7870
Ligne sans frais: 888-680-2432
lecarnet@radio-canada.ca-canada.ca
www.radio-canada.ca/regions/alberta/

***Edmonton:* CFRN-TV**(Channel: 3)
Owned by: *Bell Media TV**
18520 Stony Plain Rd., Edmonton, AB T5S 1A8
Tel: 780-483-3311,
edmonton.ctvnews.ca
Lloyd Lewis, General Manager & Vice-President

***Edmonton:* CKEM-DT**(Channel: 57)
Owned by: *Rogers Broadcasting Ltd.**
10212 Jasper Ave., Edmonton, AB T5J 5A3
Tel: 780-424-2222,
citytvedmontonfeedback@rci.rogers.com
www.citytv.com

***Exshaw:* CBRT-TV-17**(Channel: 34 UHF)
Owned by: *Canadian Broadcasting Corporation (CBC)*
Exshaw, AB
Toll-Free: 866-306-4636
www.cbc.ca/calgary; www.cbc.ca/television
Social Media: www.twitter.com/cbccalgary,
Other information: TTY: 1-866-220-6045

***Exshaw:* CBRT-TV-3**(Channel: 6 VHF)
Owned by: *Canadian Broadcasting Corporation (CBC)*
Exshaw, AB
Toll-Free: 866-306-4636
www.cbc.ca/calgary; www.cbc.ca/television
Social Media: www.twitter.com/cbccalgary,
Other information: TTY: 1-866-220-6045

***Harvie Heights:* CBRT-TV-13**(Channel: 22 UHF)
Owned by: *Canadian Broadcasting Corporation (CBC)*
Harvie Heights, AB
Toll-Free: 866-306-4636
www.cbc.ca/calgary; www.cbc.ca/television
Social Media: www.twitter.com/cbccalgary,
Other information: TTY: 1-866-220-6045

***Jasper:* CFRN-TV-11**(Channel: 11)
Owned by: *CFRN-TV*
Jasper, AB

***Lac La Biche:* CFRN-TV-5**(Channel: 2)
Edmonton

Owned by: *CFRN-TV*
Lac La Biche, AB

***Lake Louise:* CBRT-TV-4**(Channel: 12 VHF)
Owned by: *Canadian Broadcasting Corporation (CBC)*
Lake Louise, AB
Toll-Free: 866-306-4636
www.cbc.ca/calgary; www.cbc.ca/television
Social Media: www.twitter.com/cbccalgary,
Other information: TTY: 1-866-220-6045

***Lethbridge:* CBRT-TV-6**(Channel: 10)
Owned by: *Canadian Broadcasting Corporation (CBC)*
Lethbridge, AB
Toll-Free: 866-306-4636
www.cbc.ca/calgary; www.cbc.ca/television
Social Media: www.twitter.com/cbccalgary,
Other information: TTY: 1-866-220-6045

***Lethbridge:* CFCN-TV**(Channel: 13)
Owned by: *Bell Media TV**
640-13 Street North, Lethbridge, AB T1H 2S8
Tel: 403-329-3644, *Fax:* 403-317-2420
www.cfcn.ca

***Lethbridge:* CFCN-TV-5**(Channel: 13)
Owned by: *CFCN-TV*
Lethbridge, AB
Dave Lelek, General & Sales Manager
Terry Vogt, News Director
Dale Munro, Chief Engineer & Operations Manager

***Lethbridge:* CISA-DT**(Channel: 7)
Owned by: *Global Television Network**
1401 - 28 St. North, Lethbridge, AB T1H 6H9

www.globallethbridge.com
Peter Deys, General Manager

***Lethbridge:* CJIL-TV**(Channel: 17)
PO Box 1566, 450-31 St. N., Lethbridge, AB T1H 3Z3
Tel: 403-380-3399, *Fax:* 403-380-3322
info@miraclechannel.ca
www.miraclechannel.ca
Leon Fontaine, Chief Executive Officer

***Lethbridge:* CKAL-TV**(Channel: 6)
Owned by: *CKAL-TV*
Lethbridge, AB

***Lloydminster:* CITL-TV**(Channel: 4)
Owned by: *NewCap Inc.**
5026 - 50th St., Lloydminster, AB T9V 1P3
Tel: 780-875-3321, *Fax:* 780-875-4704
www.newcaptv.com
Social Media: twitter.com/NewcapTVNews
Chad Tabish, General Manager, ctabish@newcap.ca

***Lloydminster:* CKSA-TV**(Channel: 2)
Owned by: *NewCap Inc.**
5026 - 50 St., Lloydminster, AB T9V 1P3
Tel: 780-875-3321, *Fax:* 780-875-4704
Toll-Free: 800-565-2572
cksatv.ca
Mike Keller

***Lougheed:* CFRN-TV-7**(Channel: 7)
Edmonton

Owned by: *CFRN-TV*
Lougheed, AB

***Medicine Hat:* CFCN-TV-8**(Channel: 8)
Calgary

Owned by: *CFCN-TV*
Medicine Hat, AB

***Peace River:* CFRN-TV-2**(Channel: 3)
Edmonton

Owned by: *CFRN-TV*
Peace River, AB

***Pincher Creek:* CBRT-TV-9**(Channel: 15 UHF)
Owned by: *Canadian Broadcasting Corporation (CBC)*
Pincher Creek, AB
Toll-Free: 866-306-4636
www.cbc.ca/calgary; www.cbc.ca/television
Social Media: www.twitter.com/cbccalgary,
Other information: TTY: 1-866-220-6045

***Provost:* CKSA-TV-4**(Channel: 12)
Owned by: *CKSA-TV*
Provost, AB

***Red Deer:* CFRN-TV-6**(Channel: 8)
Edmonton

Owned by: *CFRN-TV*
Red Deer, AB

***Red Deer:* CKEM-TV**(Channel: 8)
Owned by: *CKEM-TV*
Red Deer, AB

***Redcliff:* CHAT-TV**(Channel: 6)
Owned by: *The Jim Pattison Broadcast Group**
10 Boundary Rd. S.E., Redcliff, AB T0J 2P0

info@chattv6-3.com
www.chattv6-3.com
Dwaine Dietrich, General Manager

***Rocky Mountain House:* CFRN-TV-10**(Channel: 12)
Edmonton

Owned by: *CFRN-TV*
Rocky Mountain House, AB

***Rosemary:* CBRT-TV-5**(Channel: 11 VHF)
Owned by: *Canadian Broadcasting Corporation (CBC)*
Rosemary, AB
Toll-Free: 866-306-4636
www.cbc.ca/calgary; www.cbc.ca/television
Social Media: www.twitter.com/cbccalgary,
Other information: TTY: 1-866-220-6045

***Wainwright:* CKSA-TV-3**(Channel: 8)
Owned by: *CKSA-TV*
Wainwright, AB

***Waterton Park:* CBRT-TV-7**(Channel: 4 VHF)
Owned by: *Canadian Broadcasting Corporation (CBC)*
Waterton Park, AB
Toll-Free: 866-306-4636
www.cbc.ca/calgary; www.cbc.ca/television
Social Media: www.twitter.com/cbccalgary,
Other information: TTY: 1-866-220-6045

***Waterton Park:* CFCN-TV-17**(Channel: 6)
Calgary

Owned by: *CFCN-TV*
Waterton Park, AB

***Whitecourt:* CFRN-TV-3**(Channel: 12)
Edmonton

Owned by: *CFRN-TV*
Whitecourt, AB

British Columbia

***100 Mile House:* CFJC-TV-6**(Channel: 5)
Kamloops

Owned by: *CFJC-TV*
100 Mile House, BC

***100 Mile House:* CITM-TV**(Channel: 3)
Owned by: *CHAN-TV*
100 Mile House, BC

***Apex Mountain:* CHNJ-TV-1**(Channel: 11)
Vancouver

Owned by: *CHAN-TV*
Apex Mountain, BC

***Blue River:* CH2531**(Channel: 13)
Owned by: *CHAN-TV*
Blue River, BC

***Burnaby:* CHAN-DT**(Channel: 7)
Owned by: *Global Television Network**
7850 Enterprise St., Burnaby, BC V5A 1V7
Tel: 604-420-2288, *Fax:* 604-422-6466
viewercontact.bc@globaltv.com
www.globaltvcalgary.com

***Burnaby:* KVOS-TV**(Channel: 12)
#217, 4259 Canada Way, Burnaby, BC V5G 1H3
Tel: 604-681-1212, *Fax:* 604-736-4510
metvnetwork.com

***Celista:* CHBC-TV-6**(Channel: 3)
Kelowna

Owned by: *CHBC-TV*
Celista, BC

***Chase:* CFJC-TV-8**(Channel: 11)
Kamloops

Owned by: *CFJC-TV*
Chase, BC

***Chilliwack:* CHAN-TV-1**(Channel: 11)
Vancouver

Owned by: *CHAN-DT*
Chilliwack, BC

** For details on this company see listing in Major Broadcasting Companies section; † French language station*

Clinton: CFJC-TV-4(Channel: 9)
Kamloops

Owned by: *CFJC-TV*
Clinton, BC

Courtenay: CHAN-TV-4(Channel: 13)
Vancouver

Owned by: *CHAN-DT*
Courtenay, BC

Creston: CKTN-TV-4(Channel: 12)
Vancouver

Owned by: *CHAN-TV*
Creston, BC

Dawson Creek: CJDC-TV(Channel: 5)
Owned by: *Astral Media Radio G.P.**
901 - 102 Ave., Dawson Creek, BC V1G 2B6
Tel: 250-782-3341, *Fax:* 250-782-3154
www.cjdctv.com
Terry Shepherd, General Manager, tshepherd@astral.com

Enderby: CFEN-TV-2(Channel: 11)
Vancouver

Owned by: *CHAN-TV*
Enderby, BC

Enderby: CHBC-TV-5(Channel: 4)
Kelowna

Owned by: *CHBC-TV*
Enderby, BC

Fort St James: CFFS-TV(Channel: 10, 3)
Vancouver

Owned by: *CHAN-TV*
Fort St James, BC

Fountain: CFDF-TV-1(Channel: 5)
Vancouver

Owned by: *CHAN-TV*
Fountain, BC

Fraser Lake: CFFL-TV-1(Channel: 9)
Vancouver

Owned by: *CHAN-TV*
Fraser Lake, BC

Grand Forks: CISR-TV-1(Channel: 7)
Vancouver

Owned by: *CHAN-TV*
Grand Forks, BC

Granisle: CH2798(Channel: 7)
Vancouver

Owned by: *CHAN-TV*
Granisle, BC

Hixon: CKPG-TV-1(Channel: 10)
Prince George

Owned by: *CKPG-TV*
Hixon, BC

Houston: CFHO-TV(Channel: 8)
Vancouver

Owned by: *CHAN-TV*
Houston, BC

Hudson's Hope: CJDC-TV-1(Channel: 11)
Dawson Creek

Owned by: *CJDC-TV*
Hudson's Hope, BC

Kamloops: CHKM-TV(Channel: 6)
Vancouver

Owned by: *CHAN-TV*
Kamloops, BC

Kelowna: CHBC-DT(Channel: 2)
Owned by: *Global Television Network**
342 Leon Ave., Kelowna, BC V1Y 6J2
Tel: 250-762-4535, *Fax:* 250-868-0662
Toll-Free: 888-762-4535
www.chbcnews.ca

Kelowna: CHKL-TV(Channel: 5)
Vancouver

Owned by: *CHAN-TV*
Kelowna, BC

Keremeos: CHBC-DT(Channel: 4)
Kelowna

Owned by: *CHBC-TV*
Keremeos, BC

Kildala: CFTK-TV(Channel: 5)
Terrace

Owned by: *CFTK-TV*
Kildala, BC

Kitwanga: CFTK-TV(Channel: 13)
Terrace

Owned by: *CFTK-TV*
Kitwanga, BC

Lillooet: CFDF-TV-2(Channel: 13)
Vancouver

Owned by: *CHAN-TV*
Lillooet, BC

Little Fort: CKTV-TV-1(Channel: 12)
Kamloops

Owned by: *CFJC-TV*
Little Fort, BC

Logan Lake: CFJC-TV(Channel: 11)
Kamloops

Owned by: *CFJC-TV*
Logan Lake, BC

Logan Lake: CH2518(Channel: 13)
Vancouver

Owned by: *CHAN-TV*
Logan Lake, BC

Lytton: CILY-TV-2(Channel: 8)
Vancouver

Owned by: *CHAN-TV*
Lytton, BC

Mackenzie: CIMK-TV-1(Channel: 9)
Vancouver

Owned by: *CHAN-TV*
Mackenzie, BC

Mackenzie: CKPG-TV-4(Channel: 6)
Prince George

Owned by: *CKPG-TV*
Mackenzie, BC

Malakwa: CFFI-TV-2(Channel: 11)
Vancouver

Owned by: *CHAN-TV*
Malakwa, BC

McBride: CH2013(Channel: 12)
Owned by: *CHAN-TV*
McBride, BC

Merritt: CFJC-TV-3(Channel: 8)
Kamloops

Owned by: *CFJC-TV*
Merritt, BC

Nakusp: CJNP-TV-3(Channel: 7)
Vancouver

Owned by: *CHAN-TV*
Nakusp, BC

Nelson: CKTN-TV-3(Channel: 3)
Vancouver

Owned by: *CHAN-TV*
Nelson, BC

New Denver: CH5668 / CH5669(Channel: 13)
Vancouver

Owned by: *CHAN-TV*
New Denver, BC

Nicola Valley: CFJC-TV-12(Channel: 10)
Kamloops

Owned by: *CFJC-TV*
Nicola Valley, BC

Olalla: CHKC-TV-5(Channel: 11)
Vancouver

Owned by: *CHAN-TV*
Olalla, BC

Oliver: CKKM-TV(Channel: 3)
Owned by: *CHAN-TV*
Oliver, BC

Peachland: CIPL-TV(Channel: 9)
Vancouver

Owned by: *CHAN-TV*
Peachland, BC

Penticton: CHBC-TV-1(Channel: 13)
Kelowna

Owned by: *CHBC-TV*
Penticton, BC

Penticton: CHBC-TV-7(Channel: 7)
Kelowna

Owned by: *CHBC-TV*
Penticton, BC

Penticton: CHKL-TV-1(Channel: 10)
Vancouver

Owned by: *CHAN-TV*
Penticton, BC

Port Alberni: CHEK-TV-3(Channel: 11)
Victoria

Owned by: *CHEK-TV*
Port Alberni, BC

Prince George: CIFG-TV(Channel: 12)
Vancouver

Owned by: *CHAN-TV*
Prince George, BC

Prince George: CKPG-TV(Channel: 2)
Owned by: *The Jim Pattison Broadcast Group**
1810 - 3rd Ave., 2nd Fl., Prince George, BC V2M 1G4
Tel: 250-564-8861, *Fax:* 250-562-7681
www.993thedrive.com
Social Media:
facebook.com/pages/993-The-Drive-Prince-Georges-Classic-Hits/1121
Ken Kilcullen, General Manager, kkilcullen@ckpg.bc.ca

Pritchard: CFJC-TV-19(Channel: 5)
Kamloops

Owned by: *CFJC-TV*
Pritchard, BC

** For details on this company see listing in Major Broadcasting Companies section; † French language station*

Pritchard: **CHKM-TV-1**(Channel: 9)
Vancouver

Owned by: *CHAN-TV*
Pritchard, BC

Queen Charlotte: **CFTK-TV**(Channel: 4)
Owned by: *CFTK-TV*
Queen Charlotte, BC

Quesnel: **CFJC-TV-11**(Channel: 7)
Kamloops

Owned by: *CFJC-TV*
Quesnel, BC

Quesnel: **CITM-TV-2**(Channel: 8)
Vancouver

Owned by: *CHAN-TV*
Quesnel, BC

Quesnel: **CKPG-TV-5**(Channel: 13)
Prince George

Owned by: *CKPG-TV*
Quesnel, BC

Revelstoke: **CHKL-TV-3**(Channel: 7)
Vancouver

Owned by: *CHAN-TV*
Revelstoke, BC

Rimrock: **CKRR-TV-2**(Channel: 11)
Vancouver

Owned by: *CHAN-TV*
Rimrock, BC

Salmon Arm: **CFSA-TV-1**(Channel: 13)
Vancouver

Owned by: *CHAN-TV*
Salmon Arm, BC

Salmon Arm: **CHBC-TV-4**(Channel: 9)
Kelowna

Owned by: *CHBC-TV*
Salmon Arm, BC

Santa Rosa: **CISR-TV**(Channel: 83)
Vancouver

Owned by: *CHAN-TV*
Santa Rosa, BC

Savona: **CFSC-TV-1**(Channel: 13)
Vancouver

Owned by: *CHAN-TV*
Savona, BC

Shoulder Mtn.: **CFTK-TV**(Channel: 9)
Terrace

Owned by: *CFTK-TV*
Shoulder Mtn., BC

Smithers: **CFHO-TV-1**(Channel: 13)
Vancouver

Owned by: *CHAN-TV*
Smithers, BC

Spences Bridge: **CJNA-TV-2**(Channel: 7)
Vancouver

Owned by: *CHAN-TV*
Spences Bridge, BC

Squamish: **CHAN-TV-3**(Channel: 7)
Vancouver

Owned by: *CHAN-DT*
Squamish, BC

Surrey: **CHNU-TV**(Channel: 10)
Owned by: *Rogers Broadcasting Ltd.**
#204, 5668 192 St., Surrey, BC V3S 2V7
Tel: 604-576-6880, *Fax:* 604-576-6895
audience@joytv10.ca
www.joytv10.ca
Terry Mahoney, Station Manager

Taghum: **CKTN-TV-2**(Channel: 23)
Vancouver

Owned by: *CHAN-TV*
Taghum, BC

Terrace: **CFTK-TV**(Channel: 3)
Owned by: *Astral Media Radio G.P.**
4625 Lazelle Ave., Terrace, BC V8G 1S4
Tel: 250-635-6316, *Fax:* 250-638-6320
www.cftktv.com
Brian Langston, General Manager, blangston@astral.com

Trail: **CKTN-TV**(Channel: 8)
Vancouver

Owned by: *CHAN-TV*
Trail, BC

Tuktakamin Mountain: **CFAW-TV**(Channel: 12)
Vancouver

Owned by: *CHAN-TV*
Tuktakamin Mountain, BC

Vancouver: **CBUT-TV**(Channel: 2)
Owned by: *Canadian Broadcasting Corporation**
PO Box 4600, 700 Hamilton St., Vancouver, BC V6B 4A2
Tel: 604-662-6000, *Fax:* 604-662-6414
canadanow@vancouver.cbc.ca
www.vancouver.cbc.ca

Vancouver: **CIVT-TV**(Channel: 32)
Owned by: *Bell Media TV**
#300, 750 Burrard St., Vancouver, BC V6Z 1X5
Tel: 604-608-2868, *Fax:* 604-609-5799
bccomments@ctv.ca
bc.ctvnews.ca
Jim Rusnak, Vice-President & General Manager

Vancouver: **CKVU-TV**(Channel: 10)
Owned by: *Rogers Broadcasting Ltd.**
180 West 2nd St., Vancouver, BC V5Y 3T9
Tel: 604-876-1344, *Fax:* 604-874-8225
Toll-Free: 888-336-9978
citytvvancouverfeedback@rci.rogers.com
www.citytv.com/vancouver
Social Media: www.facebook.com/Citytv, twitter.com/city_tv
Brad Phillips

Vavenby: **CKVA-TV-1**(Channel: 8)
Vancouver

Owned by: *CHAN-TV*
Vavenby, BC

Vernon: **CHBC-TV-2**(Channel: 7)
Kelowna

Owned by: *CHBC-TV*
Vernon, BC

Vernon: **CHKL-TV-2**(Channel: 12)
Vancouver

Owned by: *CHAN-TV*
Vernon, BC

Victoria: **CHEK-TV**(Channel: 6)
780 Kings Rd., Victoria, BC V8T 5A2
Tel: 250-383-2435, *Fax:* 250-384-7766
info@cheknews.ca
www.cheknews.ca
John Pollard, President, 250-480-3702, jpollard@cheknews.ca

Williams Lake: **CFBV-FM-1**(Channel: 97.5)
Owned by: *Vista Radio**
83 South First Ave., Williams Lake, BC V2G 1H4
Tel: 250-392-6551, *Fax:* 250-392-4142
www.therushfm.ca

Williams Lake: **CFJC-TV-5**(Channel: 8)
Kamloops

Owned by: *CFJC-TV*
Williams Lake, BC

Williams Lake: **CITM-TV-1**(Channel: 13)
Vancouver

Owned by: *CHAN-TV*
Williams Lake, BC

Manitoba

Flin Flon: **CKYF-TV**(Channel: 13)
Owned by: *CKY-DT*
Flin Flon, MB

McCreary: **CKX-TV-3**(Channel: 11)
Owned by: *CKX-TV*
McCreary, MB

The Pas: **CKYP-TV**(Channel: 12)
Owned by: *CKY-DT*
The Pas, MB

Thompson: **CKYT-TV**(Channel: 9)
Owned by: *CKY-DT*
Thompson, MB

†Winnipeg: **CBWFT-TV**(Channel: 3)*Détenteur:*
Canadian Broadcasting Corporation*
CP 160 Main, 541 Portage Ave., Winnipeg, MB R3C 2H1
Tél: 204-788-3262, *Téléc:* 204-788-3255

Winnipeg: **CBWT-TV**(Channel: 6)
Owned by: *Canadian Broadcasting Corporation**
PO Box 160, 541 Portage Ave., Winnipeg, MB R3B 2H1
Tel: 204-788-3222
John Bertrand, Regional Director
Dave White, TV Operation Manager

Winnipeg: **CHMI-DT**(Channel: 57)
Owned by: *Rogers Broadcasting Ltd.**
8 Forks Market Rd., Winnipeg, MB R3C 4Y3
Tel: 204-947-9613,
citytvwinnipegfeedback@rci.rogers.com
www.citytv.com

Winnipeg: **CKND-DT**(Channel: 2)
Owned by: *Global Television Network**
603 St. Mary's Rd., Winnipeg, MB R2M 3L8
Tel: 204-233-3304, *Fax:* 204-233-5615
newsroom@globaltv.ca
globalwinnipeg.com
Tim Schellenberg

Winnipeg: **CKY-DT**(Channel: 5)
Owned by: *Bell Media TV**
400-345 Graham Ave., Winnipeg, MB R3C 5S6
Tel: 204-788-3300, *Fax:* 204-788-3399
winnipegnews@ctv.ca
winnipeg.ctvnews.ca
Social Media: twitter.com/ctvwinnipeg
Hanson Bill, Vice-President & General Manager,
whanson@ctv.ca
Tara Vosbourgh, Human Resources Manager,
tvosbourgh@ctv.ca

New Brunswick

Boiestown: **CKLT-TV-2**(Channel: 7)
Owned by: *CKLT-DT*
Boiestown, NB

Chatham: **CKAM-TV-2**(Channel: 10)
Moncton

Owned by: *CKCW-TV*
Chatham, NB

Doaktown: **CKAM-TV-4**(Channel: 10)
Moncton

Owned by: *CKCW-TV*
Doaktown, NB

** For details on this company see listing in Major Broadcasting Companies section; † French language station*

†*Edmundston:* CIMT-DT-1(Channel: 4)*Détenteur:* **CIMT-TV**
7 Ch. Canada, Edmundston, NB E3V 1T9
Tél: 506-737-9810

***Fredericton:* CBAT-TV**(Channel: 4 antenna; 3 cable)
Owned by: *Canadian Broadcasting Corporation (CBC)**
PO Box 2200, 1160 Regent St., Fredericton, NB E3B 5G4
Tel: 506-451-4000, *Toll-Free:* 866-306-4636
www.cbc.ca/nb; www.cbc.ca/television
Other information: Phone, CBC News: 506-451-4044; Fax: 506-451-4170
Andrew Cochran, Managing Director, Maritimes
Janet Irwin, Senior Regional Manager, News & Current Affairs
Nadine Antle, Regional Manager, Partnerships, Communications, Brand, & Promot, 506-451-4054
John Channing, Manager, New Brunswick Sales
Mary-Pat Schutta, Manager, New Brunswick Programs
Lori Wheeler, Senior Officer, Communications, 506-451-4080

***Fredericton:* CIHF-DT-1**(Channel: 11)
Owned by: *CIHF-TV*
Fredericton, NB

†*Kedgwick:* CHAU-DT-11(Channel: 3)*Détenteur:* **CHAU-TV**
Kedgwick, NB

***Miramichi:* CIHF-TV-13**(Channel: 40)
Owned by: *CIHF-TV*
Miramichi, NB

†*Moncton:* CBAFT-TV(Channel: La chaîne 11 à Moncton; programmation régionale.)*Détenteur:* **Canadian Broadcasting Corporation***
250, av Université, Moncton, NB E1C 5K3
Tél: 506-853-6666, *Téléc:* 506-867-8031
Ligne sans frais: 800-561-7010
www.radio-canada.ca/regions/acadie
Médias sociaux: www.facebook.com/CBCRadioCanada
Louise Imbeault, Director & Station Manager

†*Moncton:* CBAFT-TV-1 - Fredericton/Saint-Jean(Channel: La chaîne 5 à Frederiction et à Saint-Jean, N-B; programmation régionale.)*Détenteur:* **CBAFT-TV/Canadian Broadcasting Corporation**
a/s CBAFT-TV, 250, av Université, Moncton, NB E1C 5K3
Ligne sans frais: 800-561-7010
www.radio-canada.ca/regions/acadie
Médias sociaux: www.facebook.com/CBCRadioCanada

†*Moncton:* CBAFT-TV-10 - Fredericton(Channel: La chaîne 19 à Frederiction, N-B; programmation régionale.)*Détenteur:* **CBAFT-TV/Canadian Broadcasting Corporation**
a/s CBAFT-TV, 250, av Université, Moncton, NB E1C 5K3
Ligne sans frais: 800-561-7010
www.radio-canada.ca/regions/acadie
Médias sociaux: www.facebook.com/CBCRadioCanada

†*Moncton:* CBAFT-TV-2 - Edmundston(Channel: La chaîne 13 à Edmunston, N-B; programmation régionale.)*Détenteur:* **CBAFT-TV/Canadian Broadcasting Corporation**
a/s CBAFT-TV, 250, av Université, Moncton, NB E1C 5K3
Ligne sans frais: 800-561-7010
www.radio-canada.ca/regions/acadie
Médias sociaux: www.facebook.com/CBCRadioCanada

†*Moncton:* CBAFT-TV-4 - Grand Falls(Channel: La chaîne 12 à Grand Falls, N-B; programmation régionale.)*Détenteur:* **CBAFT-TV/Canadian Broadcasting Corporation**
a/s CBAFT-TV, 250, av Université, Moncton, NB E1C 5K3
Ligne sans frais: 800-561-7010
www.radio-canada.ca/regions/acadie
Médias sociaux: www.facebook.com/CBCRadioCanada

†*Moncton:* CBAFT-TV-5 - Charlottetown(Channel: La chaîne 31 à Charlottetown, I-P-É; programmation régionale.)*Détenteur:* **CBAFT-TV/Canadian Broadcasting Corporation**
a/s CBAFT-TV, 250, av Université, Moncton, NB E1C 5K3
Ligne sans frais: 800-561-7010
www.radio-canada.ca/regions/acadie
Médias sociaux: www.facebook.com/CBCRadioCanada

†*Moncton:* CBHFT-TV - Halifax(Channel: La chaîne 13 à Halifax; programmation régionale.)*Détenteur:* **CBAFT-TV/Canadian Broadcasting Corporation**
a/s CBAFT-TV, 250, av Université, Moncton, NB E1C 5K3
Ligne sans frais: 800-561-7010
www.radio-canada.ca/regions/acadie
Médias sociaux: www.facebook.com/CBCRadioCanada

†*Moncton:* CBHFT-TV-1 - Yarmouth(Channel: La chaîne 3 à Yarmouth, N-É; programmation régionale.)*Détenteur:* **CBAFT-TV/Canadian Broadcasting Corporation**
a/s CBAFT-TV, 250, av Université, Moncton, NB E1C 5K3
Ligne sans frais: 800-561-7010
www.radio-canada.ca/regions/acadie
Médias sociaux: www.facebook.com/CBCRadioCanada

†*Moncton:* CBHFT-TV-2 - Mulgrave(Channel: La chaîne 7 à Mulgrave, N-É; programmation régionale.)*Détenteur:* **CBAFT-TV/Canadian Broadcasting Corporation**
a/s CBAFT-TV, 250, av Université, Moncton, NB E1C 5K3
Ligne sans frais: 800-561-7010
www.radio-canada.ca/regions/acadie
Médias sociaux: www.facebook.com/CBCRadioCanada

†*Moncton:* CBHFT-TV-3 - Sydney(Channel: La chaîne 13 à Sydney, N-É; programmation régionale.)*Détenteur:* **CBAFT-TV/Canadian Broadcasting Corporation**
a/s CBAFT-TV, 250, av Université, Moncton, NB E1C 5K3
Ligne sans frais: 800-561-7010
www.radio-canada.ca/regions/acadie
Médias sociaux: www.facebook.com/CBCRadioCanada,

†*Moncton:* CBHFT-TV-4 - Chéticamp(Channel: La chaîne 10 à Chéticamp, N-É; programmation régionale.)*Détenteur:* **CBAFT-TV/Canadian Broadcasting Corporation**
a/s CBAFT-TV, 250, av Université, Moncton, NB E1C 5K3
Ligne sans frais: 800-561-7010
www.radio-canada.ca/regios/acadie
Médias sociaux: www.facebook.com/CBCRadioCanada

†*Moncton:* CBHFT-TV-5 - Middleton(Channel: La chaîne 46 à Middleton, N-É; programmation régionale.)*Détenteur:* **CBAFT-TV/Canadian Broadcasting Corporation**
a/s CBAFT-TV, 250, av Université, Moncton, NB E1C 5K3
Ligne sans frais: 800-561-7010
www.radio-canada.ca/regions/acadie
Médias sociaux: www.facebook.com/CBCRadioCanada

†*Moncton:* CBHFT-TV-6 - Digby(Channel: La chaîne 58 à Digby, N-É; programmation régionale.)*Détenteur:* **CBAFT-TV/Canadian Broadcasting Corporation**
a/s CBAFT-TV, 250, av Université, Moncton, NB E1C 5K3
Ligne sans frais: 800-561-7010
www.radio-canada.ca/regions/acadie
Médias sociaux: www.facebook.com/CBCRadioCanada

†*Moncton:* CBHFT-TV-7 - New Glasgow(Channel: La chaîne 15 à New Glasgow, N-É; programmation régionale.)*Détenteur:* **CBAFT-TV/Canadian Broadcasting Corporation**
a/s CBAFT-TV, 250, av Université, Moncton, NB E1C 5K3
Ligne sans frais: 800-561-7010
www.radio-canada.ca/regions/acadie
Médias sociaux: www.facebook.com/CBCRadioCanada

***Moncton:* CIHF-DT-3**(Channel: 27)
Dartmouth

Owned by: *CIHF-TV*
Moncton, NB

***Moncton:* CKCW-DT**(Channel: 94.5)
Owned by: *Bell Media TV**
1000 St. George Blvd., Moncton, NB E1E 4M7
Tel: 506-858-1220, *Fax:* 506-858-1209
k945.ca

***Newcastle:* CKAM-TV-1**(Channel: 10)
Moncton

Owned by: *CKCW-TV*
Newcastle, NB

***Saint John:* CIHF-DT-2**(Channel: 12)
Dartmouth

Owned by: *CIHF-TV*
Saint John, NB

†*Saint-Quentin:* CBAFT-TV-8(Channel: 21)*Détenteur:* **CBAFT-TV**
Saint-Quentin, NB

†*Saint-Quentin:* CHAU-DT-2(Channel: 31)*Détenteur:* **CHAU-TV**
Saint-Quentin, NB

***St Stephen:* CIHF-TV-12**(Channel: 21)
Owned by: *CIHF-TV*
St Stephen, NB

***St. John's:* CKLT-DT**(Channel: 9)
Owned by: *CTV Inc.**
St. John's, NB
atlantic.ctvnews.ca

***Woodstock:* CIHF-TV-11**(Channel: 38)
Owned by: *CIHF-TV*
Woodstock, NB

Newfoundland & Labrador

***Cartwright:* CBNT-TV-21**(Channel: 9)
St. John's

Owned by: *CBNT-TV*
Cartwright, NL

***Centreville-Wareham-Trinity:* CBNT-TV-16**(Channel: 2)
St. John's

Owned by: *CBNT-TV*
Centreville-Wareham-Trinity, NL

***Clarenville:* CBNT-TV-10**(Channel: 7)
St. John's

Owned by: *CBNT-TV*
Clarenville, NL

***Conche:* CBNAT-TV-8**(Channel: 13)
St. John's

Owned by: *CBNT-TV*
Conche, NL

***Corner Brook:* CJWN-TV**(Channel: 10)
St. John's

Owned by: *CJON-TV*
Corner Brook, NL

***Deer Lake:* CJLW-TV-7**(Channel: 7)
St. John's

Owned by: *CJON-TV*
Deer Lake, NL

***Elliston:* CBNT-TV-7**(Channel: 4)
St. John's

Owned by: *CBNT-TV*
Elliston, NL

***Fermeuse:* CBNT-TV-5**(Channel: 11)
St. John's

Owned by: *CBNT-TV*
Fermeuse, NL

***Ferryland:* CBNT-TV-38**(Channel: 4)
St. John's

Owned by: *CBNT-TV*
Ferryland, NL

***Fogo Island:* CBNAT-TV-6**(Channel: 2)
Owned by: *CBNT-TV*
Fogo Island, NL

***Fortune:* CBNT-TV-33**(Channel: 9)
St. John's

Owned by: *CBNT-TV*
Fortune, NL

* *For details on this company see listing in Major Broadcasting Companies section; † French language station*

Glovertown: **CBNT-TV-13**(Channel: 3)
St. John's

Owned by: *CBNT-TV*
Glovertown, NL

Harbour Breton: **CBNT-TV-22**(Channel: 13)
Owned by: *CBNT-TV*
Harbour Breton, NL

Harbour Mille: **CBNT-TV-29**(Channel: 13)
St. John's

Owned by: *CBNT-TV*
Harbour Mille, NL

Hermitage: **CBNT-TV-24**(Channel: 4)
St. John's

Owned by: *CBNT-TV*
Hermitage, NL

Hickman's Harbour: **CBNT-TV-18**(Channel: 4)
St. John's

Owned by: *CBNT-TV*
Hickman's Harbour, NL

Lamaline: **CBNT-TV-35**(Channel: 18 UHF)
St. John's

Owned by: *CBNT-TV*
Lamaline, NL

Lawn: **CBNT-TV-36**(Channel: 6)
St. John's

Owned by: *CBNT-TV*
Lawn, NL

Lord's Cove: **CBNT-TV-34**(Channel: 9)
St. John's

Owned by: *CBNT-TV*
Lord's Cove, NL

Lumsden: **CBNT-TV-20**(Channel: 12)
St. John's

Owned by: *CBNT-TV*
Lumsden, NL

Marystown: **CBNT-TV-3**(Channel: 5)
St. John's

Owned by: *CBNT-TV*
Marystown, NL

Marystown: **CJMA-TV-11**(Channel: 11)
St. John's

Owned by: *CJON-TV*
Marystown, NL

Musgravetown: **CBNT-TV-17**(Channel: 9)
St. John's

Owned by: *CBNT-TV*
Musgravetown, NL

North West Brook: **CBNT-TV-11**(Channel: 4)
St. John's

Owned by: *CBNT-TV*
North West Brook, NL

Petty Harbour: **CBNT-TV-37**(Channel: 13)
St. John's

Owned by: *CBNT-TV*
Petty Harbour, NL

Placentia: **CBNT-TV-2**(Channel: 12)
St. John's

Owned by: *CBNT-TV*
Placentia, NL

Port Blandford: **CBNT-TV-32**(Channel: 2)
St. John's

Owned by: *CBNT-TV*
Port Blandford, NL

Port Rexton: **CBNT-TV-1**(Channel: 13)
St. John's

Owned by: *CBNT-TV*
Port Rexton, NL

Ramea: **CBNT-TV-25**(Channel: 13)
St. John's

Owned by: *CBNT-TV*
Ramea, NL

Random Island: **CBNT-TV-19**(Channel: 43 UHF)
St. John's

Owned by: *CBNT-TV*
Random Island, NL

Red Rock: **CJRR-TV-11**(Channel: 11)
St. John's

Owned by: *CJON-TV*
Red Rock, NL

St Alban's: **CBNT-TV-4**(Channel: 9)
Owned by: *CBNT-TV*
St Alban's, NL

St Bernard's: **CBNT-TV-30**(Channel: 6)
Owned by: *CBNT-TV*
St Bernard's, NL

St Mary's: **CBNT-TV-6**(Channel: 10)
St. John's

Owned by: *CBNT-TV*
St Mary's, NL

St Vincent's: **CBNT-TV-26**(Channel: 7)
St. John's

Owned by: *CBNT-TV*
St Vincent's, NL

St. John's: **CBNT-TV**(Channel: 8)
Owned by: *Canadian Broadcasting Corporation**
PO Box 12010 A, 95 University Ave., St. John's, NL A1B 3T8
Tel: 709-576-5000,
www.cbc.ca/nl
Social Media: www.facebook.com/cbcnl; twitter.com/cbcnl
Maureen Anonsen, Manager, Partnership & Communications, CBC, 709-576-5013
Debbie Hynes, Senior Communications Officer, CBC, 709-576-5050

St. John's: **CJON-TV**(Channel: 6)
Owned by: *Newfoundland Broadcasting Co. Ltd.**
PO Box 2020, 499 Logy Bay Rd., St. John's, NL A1C 5S2
Tel: 709-722-5015, *Fax:* 709-726-5107
greetings@ntv.ca
www.ntv.ca
Social Media: twitter.com/ntvnewsnl
G. Scott Stirling, President
Douglas W. Neal, General Manager
Keith Soper, Sales Manager

St. Lawrence: **CBNT-TV-28**(Channel: 12)
St. John's

Owned by: *CBNT-TV*
St. Lawrence, NL

Swift Current: **CBNT-TV-31**(Channel: 5)
St. John's

Owned by: *CBNT-TV*
Swift Current, NL

Wesleyville: **CBNT-TV-9**(Channel: 5)
St. John's

Owned by: *CBNT-TV*
Wesleyville, NL

Nova Scotia

Antigonish: **CIHF-TV-15**(Channel: 21)
Owned by: *CIHF-TV*
Antigonish, NS

Bay St. Lawrence: **CBIT-TV-17**(Channel: 13)
Sydney

Owned by: *Canadian Broadcasting Corporation*
Bay St. Lawrence, NS

Bridgewater: **CIHF-TV-6**(Channel: 9)
Owned by: *CIHF-DT*
Bridgewater, NS

Cheticamp: **CBIT-TV-2**(Channel: 2)
Sydney

Owned by: *Canadian Broadcasting Corporation*
Cheticamp, NS

Dartmouth: **CIHF-DT**(Channel: 8)
Owned by: *Global Television Network**
14 Akerley Blvd., Dartmouth, NS B3B 1J3
Tel: 902-481-7400,
www.globalmaritimes.com
Barry Saunders, General Manager

Dingwall: **CBIT-TV-16**(Channel: 12)
Sydney

Owned by: *Canadian Broadcasting Corporation*
Dingwall, NS

Dingwall: **CJCB-TV-3**(Channel: 9)
Sydney

Owned by: *CJCB-TV*
Dingwall, NS

Halifax: **CBHT-TV**(Channel: 3)
Owned by: *Canadian Broadcasting Corporation**
PO Box 3000, 1840 Bell Rd., Halifax, NS B3J 3E9
Tel: 902-420-8311, *Toll-Free:* 866-306-4636
www.cbc.ca/ns
Social Media: twitter.com/cbcns
Andrew Cochran, Managing Director for the Maritimes, CBC
Kathy Large, Program Manager, CBC, Nova Scotia
Chantal Bernard, Senior Communications Officer, 902-420-4306

Halifax: **CIHF-TV**(Channel: 8)
Dartmouth

Owned by: *CIHF-TV*
Halifax, NS

Halifax: **CJCH-DT**(Channel: 9)
Owned by: *CTV Inc.**
PO Box 1653, 2885 Robie St., Halifax, NS B3K 5Z4
atlantic.ctvnews.ca
Michael Elgie, General Manager

Halifax: **CKHY-FM**

Owned by: *Evanov Radio Group**
5527 Cogswell St., Halifax, NS B3J 1R2
Tel: 902-429-1035, *Fax:* 902-425-8637
www.live105.ca

Halifax: **CKHZ-FM**

Owned by: *Evanov Radio Group**
5527 Cogswell St., Halifax, NS B3J 1R2
Tel: 902-429-1035, *Fax:* 902-425-8637
www.energy1035.ca
Social Media: www.facebook.com/energy1035, twitter.com/energy1035hfx

Ingonish: **CBIT-TV-15**(Channel: 2)
Sydney

Owned by: *Canadian Broadcasting Corporation*
Ingonish, NS

Inverness: **CJCB-TV-1**(Channel: 6)
Sydney

Owned by: *CJCB-TV*

** For details on this company see listing in Major Broadcasting Companies section; † French language station*

Inverness, NS

***Liverpool:* CBHT-TV-1**
Halifax

Owned by: *Canadian Broadcasting Corporation*
Liverpool, NS

***Mabou:* CBIT-TV-4**(Channel: 10)
Sydney

Owned by: *Canadian Broadcasting Corporation*
Mabou, NS

***Margaree:* CBIT-TV-5**(Channel: 8)
Sydney

Owned by: *Canadian Broadcasting Corporation*
Margaree, NS

***Middleton:* CBHT-TV-6**(Channel: 8)
Halifax

Owned by: *Canadian Broadcasting Corporation*
Middleton, NS

***Mulgrave:* CBHT-TV-11**(Channel: 12)
Sydney

Owned by: *Canadian Broadcasting Corporation*
Mulgrave, NS

***Mulgrave:* CIHF-TV-16**(Channel: 28)
Owned by: *CIHF-TV*
Mulgrave, NS

***New Glasgow:* CBHT-TV-5**(Channel: 4)
Halifax

Owned by: *Canadian Broadcasting Corporation*
New Glasgow, NS

***New Glasgow:* CIHF-TV**(Channel: 34)
Owned by: *CIHF-TV*
New Glasgow, NS

***North East Margaree:* CBIT-TV-6**(Channel: 13)
Sydney

Owned by: *Canadian Broadcasting Corporation*
North East Margaree, NS

***Pleasant Bay:* CBIT-TV-3**(Channel: 8)
Sydney

Owned by: *Canadian Broadcasting Corporation*
Pleasant Bay, NS

***Sheet Harbour:* CBHT-TV-4**(Channel: 11)
Halifax

Owned by: *Canadian Broadcasting Corporation*
Sheet Harbour, NS

***Sheet Harbour:* CJCH-TV-5**(Channel: 2)
Halifax

Owned by: *CJCH-TV*
Sheet Harbour, NS

***Shelburne:* CBHT-TV-2**(Channel: 7)
Halifax

Owned by: *Canadian Broadcasting Corporation*
Shelburne, NS

***Shelburne:* CIHF-TV**(Channel: 10)
Owned by: *CIHF-TV*
Shelburne, NS

***Sherbrooke:* CBHT-TV-16**(Channel: 4)
Sydney

Owned by: *Canadian Broadcasting Corporation*
Sherbrooke, NS

***Sunnybrae:* CBHT-TV-17**(Channel: 6)
Sydney

Owned by: *Canadian Broadcasting Corporation*
Sunnybrae, NS

***Sydney:* CBIT-TV**(Channel: 5)
Owned by: *Canadian Broadcasting Corporation**
285 Alexandra St., Sydney, NS B1S 2E8
Tel: 902-563-4100, *Fax:* 902-539-1562
www.cbc.ca/ns

***Sydney:* CIHF-TV-7**(Channel: 11)
Owned by: *CIHF-TV*
Sydney, NS

***Sydney:* CJCB-TV**(Channel: 4)
Owned by: *CTV Inc.**
PO Box 469, 1283 George St., Sydney, NS B1P 1N7
Tel: 902-562-5511, *Fax:* 902-562-9714
www.ctv.ca
Glenn McLanders, 902-562-5511

***Truro:* CBHT-TV-8**(Channel: 55)
Halifax

Owned by: *Canadian Broadcasting Corporation*
Truro, NS

***Truro:* CIHF-TV**(Channel: 18)
Owned by: *CIHF-TV*
Truro, NS

***Wolfville:* CIHF-TV-5**(Channel: 20)
Owned by: *CIHF-TV*
Wolfville, NS

***Yarmouth:* CIHF-TV-10**(Channel: 45)
Owned by: *CIHF-TV*
Yarmouth, NS

***Yarmouth:* CJCH-TV-7**(Channel: 40)
Halifax

Owned by: *CJCH-TV*
Yarmouth, NS

Ontario

***Barrie:* CKVR-TV**(Channel: Broadcasting on analog channel 3 (VHF) & digital channel 10 (VHF))
Owned by: *Bell Media TV**
33 Beacon Rd., Barrie, ON L4M 4T9
Tel: 705-734-3300, *Fax:* 705-733-0302
Toll-Free: 800-461-5820
barrieinbox@ctv.ca
ctvbarrie.ca
Other information: TTY: 800-721-9110
Peggy Hebden, Station Manager, peggy.hebden@atv.ca

***Belleville:* CICO-DT-53**(Channel: 26)
Owned by: *TVOntario**
Belleville, ON

ww3.tvo.org

***Brantford:* Jewel 92**

Owned by: *Evanov Radio Group**
571 West St., Brantford, ON N3R 7C5
Tel: 519-759-1000, *Fax:* 519-753-1470
www.jewel92.com

***Chapleau:* CITO-TV-4**(Channel: 9)
Owned by: *CITO-TV*
Chapleau, ON

***Cloyne:* CICO-DT-92**(Channel: 44)
Owned by: *TVOntario**
Cloyne, ON

ww3.tvo.org

***Cornwall:* CJOH-TV-8**(Channel: 8)
Owned by: *CJOH-DT*
Cornwall, ON

***Deseronto:* CJOH-TV-6**(Channel: 6)
Owned by: *CJOH-DT*
Deseronto, ON

***Elliot Lake:* CICI-TV-1**(Channel: 3)
Owned by: *CICI-TV*
Elliot Lake, ON

***Greater Sudbury:* CICI-TV**

Owned by: *Bell Media TV**
699 Frood Rd., Greater Sudbury, ON P3C 5A3
Tel: 705-674-8301,
www.ctv.ca

***Halifax:* BMTV TVU**

Owned by: *Atlantic Television Network**
2885 Robie St., Halifax, ON B3K 5Z4

www.atlantictv.net

***Halifax:* BMTV Veetle**

Owned by: *Atlantic Television Network**
2885 Robie St., Halifax, ON B3K 5Z4

www.atlantictv.net

***Hamilton:* CHCH-TV**(Channel: 11; Oldest privately owned T.V. station and has been an independent station for most of its existence.)
PO Box 2230 A, 163 Jackson St. West, Hamilton, ON L8N 3A6
Tel: 905-522-1101, *Toll-Free:* 888-632-6688
contact@chch.com
www.chch.com
Social Media: www.facebook.com/CHCHSuperstation, twitter.com/CHCHTV

***Hearst:* CITO-TV-3**(Channel: 4)
Owned by: *CITO-TV*
Hearst, ON

***Kapuskasing:* CFCL-TV-3**(Channel: 2)
Owned by: *CFCL-TV*
Kapuskasing, ON

***Kapuskasing:* CITO-TV-1**(Channel: 10)
Owned by: *CITO-TV*
Kapuskasing, ON

***Kearns:* CFCL-TV-2**(Channel: 2)
Owned by: *CFCL-TV*
Kearns, ON

***Kearns:* CITO-TV-2**(Channel: 11)
Owned by: *CTVglobemedia Inc.*
Kearns, ON

***Keewatin:* CJBN-TV**(Channel: 13)
102 - 10th St., Keewatin, ON P0X 1C0
Tel: 807-547-2853, *Fax:* 807-547-2348
www.gokenora.com
Kyle Glieheisen, Station Manager, 807-547-2887, kyle.glieheisen@sjrb.ca
Darryl Michaluk, Station Manager, darryl.michaluk@sjrb.ca

***Kingston:* CKWS-TV**(Channel: 11)
Owned by: *YTV Canada Inc.**
170 Queen St., Kingston, ON K7K 1B2
Tel: 613-544-2340, *Fax:* 613-544-5508
newswatch@corusent.com (News room)
www.ckwstv.com
Other information: Phone, News Department: 613-542-9232; Fax, Sales Dept.: 613-544-3587
Mike Ferguson, General Manager
Jay Westman, News Director

***Kitchener:* CBLN-TV-1**(Channel: 56 antenna)
Owned by: *Canadian Broadcasting Corporation (CBC)*
Kitchener, ON
Toll-Free: 866-306-4636
www.cbc.ca/television
Other information: TTY: 1-866-220-6045

***Kitchener:* CICO-DT-28**(Channel: 28)
Owned by: *TVOntario**
Kitchener, ON

ww3.tvo.org

***Kitchener:* CKCO-DT**(Channel: 13)
Owned by: *Bell Media TV**
PO Box 91026 C, 864 King St. West, Kitchener, ON N2G 4E9
Tel: 519-578-1314,
viewermail@kitchener.ctv.ca
kitchener.ctvnews.ca
Watson Dennis, VP,GM, dwatson@ctv.ca

** For details on this company see listing in Major Broadcasting Companies section; † French language station*

***London:* CBLN-TV**(Channel: 40 antenna)
Owned by: *Canadian Broadcasting Corporation (CBC)*
London, ON
Toll-Free: 866-306-4636
www.cbc.ca/television
Other information: TTY: 1-866-220-6045

***North Bay:* CKNY-TV**(Channel: 10)
Owned by: *Bell Media TV**
245 Oak St. East, North Bay, ON P1B 8P8
Tel: 705-476-3111, *Fax:* 705-495-4474
Toll-Free: 877-303-6288
northernontario.ctvnews.ca
Scott Lund, General Manager

†*Ottawa:* CBOFT-TV(Channel: 9)*Détenteur:* **Canadian Broadcasting Corporation***
CP 3220 C, Ottawa, ON K1Y 1E4
Ligne sans frais: 866-306-4636
standard@radio-canada.ca
www.radio-canada.ca/ottawa/

***Ottawa:* CBOT-TV**(Channel: 4)
Owned by: *Canadian Broadcasting Corporation**
PO Box 3220 C, Ottawa, ON K1Y 1E4
Tel: 613-724-1200, *Fax:* 613-724-5512
www.cbc.ca/ottawa

***Ottawa:* CICO-DT-24**(Channel: 24)
Owned by: *TVOntario**
Ottawa, ON
ww3.tvo.org

***Ottawa:* CJOH-DT**(Channel: 13)
Owned by: *Bell Media TV**
87 George St., Ottawa, ON K1N 9H7
Tel: 613-224-1313, *Fax:* 888-770-2192
ctvottawa@ctv.ca
ottawa.ctvnews.ca
Social Media: www.facebook.com/CTVNewsOttawa
Louis Douville, Vice-President/General Manager

***Peterborough:* CHEX-TV**(Channel: 22)
Owned by: *YTV Canada Inc.**
743 Monaghan Rd., Peterborough, ON K9J 5K2
Tel: 705-742-0451, *Fax:* 705-742-7274
viewermail@chextv.com
www.chextv.com
Social Media: www.facebook.com/CHEXTV, twitter.com/chextvdotcom
Other information: TDD: 705-749-2179
Michael Harris, Vice-President & General Manager, michael.harris@corusent.com

***Sarnia:* CBLN-TV-2**(Channel: 34 antenna)
Owned by: *Canadian Broadcasting Corporation (CBC)*
Sarnia, ON
Toll-Free: 866-306-4636
www.cbc.ca/television
Other information: TTY: 1-866-220-6045

***Sarnia:* CKCO-TV-3**(Channel: 42)
Owned by: *CKCO-DT*
Sarnia, ON

***Sault Ste. Marie:* CHBX-TV**
PO Box 370, Sault Ste. Marie, ON P6A 5M2
Tel: 705-759-8232,
www.ctv.ca

***Sioux Lookout:* Wawatay TV**

Owned by: *Wawatay Native Communications Society**
PO Box 1180, 16 Fifth Ave., Sioux Lookout, ON P8T 1B7
Tel: 807-737-2951, *Fax:* 807-737-3224
Toll-Free: 800-243-9059
www.wawataynews.ca
Michael Dube, Producer & Editor, michaeld@wawatay.on.ca
Victor Lyon, Producer & Editor, victorl@wawatay.on.ca

***Thunder Bay:* CHFD-TV**(Channel: 4)
87 North Hill St., Thunder Bay, ON P7A 5V6
Tel: 807-346-2600, *Fax:* 807-345-9923
www.ckprthunderbay.com
Social Media: twitter.com/ckprthunderbay

***Thunder Bay:* CICO-DT-9**(Channel: 9)
Owned by: *TVOntario**
Thunder Bay, ON
ww3.tvo.org

***Thunder Bay:* CKPR-TV**(Channel: 2)
Owned by: *CKPR Inc.*
87 North Hill St., Thunder Bay, ON P7A 5V6
Tel: 807-346-2600, *Fax:* 807-345-9923
www.ckprthunderbay.com
Social Media: twitter.com/ckprthunderbay
Bryan Wyatt, News & Sports Director

***Timmins:* CITO-TV**

Owned by: *Bell Media TV**
681 Pine North, Timmins, ON P4N 7L6
Tel: 705-264-4211,
www.ctv.ca

†*Toronto:* CBLFT-TV(Channel: 25 UHF; 24 UHF)*Détenteur:* **Canadian Broadcasting Corporation (CBC)***
Société Radio-Canada, CP 500, 205 Wellington St. West, Toronto, ON M5V 3G7
Tél: 416-205-2887, *Téléc:* 416-205-2500
Ligne sans frais: 800-551-2985
auditoire@radio-canada.ca
www.radio-canada.ca/regions/ontario
Médias sociaux: www.twitter.com/RC_TV,
Autre information: Phone, Television Newsroom: 416-205-2500

***Toronto:* CBLT-TV**(Channel: 5 antenna; 6 cable)
Owned by: *Canadian Broadcasting Corporation (CBC)**
PO Box 500, 205 Wellington St. West, Toronto, ON M5W 1E6
Tel: 416-205-3311, *Fax:* 416-205-2500
Toll-Free: 866-306-4636
www.cbc.ca/toronto; www.cbc.ca/television
Other information: Phone, Television Newsroom: 416-205-2500
Susan Marjetti, Managing Director, 416-205-5791
Don Ioi, Team Manager, Toronto Sales, 416-205-2732

***Toronto:* CFMT-TV**(Channel: 47)
Administration

Owned by: *Rogers Broadcasting Ltd.**
545 Lakeshore Blvd. West, Toronto, ON M5V 1A3
Tel: 416-260-0060,
info@omnitv.ca
www.omnitv.ca
Leslie A. Sole, Exec. Vice-President
Madeline Ziniak, Vice-President & Exec. Producer
Jim Nelles, Vice-President, Marketing
Kelly Colasanti, Vice-President, Operations
Anthony P. Viner, President

***Toronto:* CFTO-TV**(Channel: 9)
Owned by: *Bell Media TV**
9 Channel Nine Ct., Toronto, ON M1S 4B5
Tel: 416-384-5000, *Toll-Free:* 800-668-0060
newsonline@ctv.ca
www.ctv.ca

†*Toronto:* CHLF-TV(Channel: 13)
CP 3005 F, 21, rue College, Toronto, ON M4Y 2M5
Tél: 416-968-3536, *Ligne sans frais:* 800-387-8435
vos_questions@tfo.org
www3.tfo.org
Louise Jourdain

***Toronto:* CICA-DT**(Channel: 19)
Owned by: *TVOntario**
PO Box 200 Q, 2180 Yonge St., Toronto, ON M4T 2T1
Tel: 416-484-2600,
ww3.tvo.org

***Toronto:* CIRR-FM**

Owned by: *Evanov Radio Group**
5312 Dundas St. West, Toronto, ON M9B 1B3
Tel: 416-922-1039, *Fax:* 416-922-3692
www.proudfm.com

***Toronto:* CITY-TV**(Channel: 57)
Owned by: *Rogers Broadcasting Ltd.**
33 Dundas St. East, Toronto, ON M5B 1B8
Tel: 416-599-2489,
citytvtorontofeedback@rci.rogers.com
www.citytv.com

***Toronto:* CJMT-TV**(Channel: 44, 14)
Owned by: *Rogers Broadcasting Ltd.**
545 Lakeshore Blvd. West, Toronto, ON M5V 1A3
Tel: 416-260-0060,
info@omni2.ca
www.omnitv.ca

***Toronto:* CKDX-FM**

Owned by: *Evanov Radio Group**
c/o Evanov Radio, 5312 Dundas St. West, Toronto, ON M9B 1B3
Tel: 416-213-1035, *Fax:* 416-233-8617
info@885thejewel.com
www.jewelradio.com/885

***Toronto:* Global Reality Channel**

Owned by: *Global National**
c/o Shaw Media, 121 Bloor St. East, 15th Fl., Toronto, ON M4W 3M5
Toll-Free: 866-967-3248
feedback@globalreality.ca
www.globalreality.ca
Social Media: www.facebook.com/globalrealitychannel, twitter.com/globalrealitytv

***Toronto:* MovieTime**

Owned by: *Global National**
c/o Shaw Media, 121 Bloor St. East, 15th Fl., Toronto, ON M4W 3M5
feedback@movietimetv.ca
www.movietimetv.ca
Social Media: www.facebook.com/movietimetv, twitter.com/MovieTimeTV

***Wawa:* CHBX-TV-1**(Channel: 7)
Owned by: *CHBX-TV*
Wawa, ON

***Windsor:* CBET-TV**(Channel: 9)
Owned by: *Canadian Broadcasting Corporation (CBC)**
825 Riverside Dr. West, Windsor, ON N9A 5K9
Tel: 519-255-3411, *Toll-Free:* 866-306-4636
www.cbc.ca/windsor
Other information: Phone, Windsor Newsroom: 519-255-3456
Sandra Porteous, Managing Edior, Radio & Television, 519-255-3563
David Daigneault, Executive Producer, Radio & Television, 519-255-3410
Nancy Lauzon, Manager, Windsor Accounts, 519-255-3510

***Windsor:* CICO-DT-32**(Channel: 32)
Owned by: *TVOntario**
Windsor, ON
ww3.tvo.org

***Windsor:* CKCO-TV**(Channel: 42)
Kitchener

Owned by: *CKCO-TV*
Windsor, ON

***Wingham:* CBLN-TV-4**(Channel: 45 antenna)
Owned by: *Canadian Broadcasting Corporation (CBC)*
Wingham, ON
Toll-Free: 866-306-4636
www.cbc.ca/television
Other information: TTY: 1-866-220-6045

Prince Edward Island

***Charlottetown:* CBCT-TV**(Channel: 13 antenna)
Owned by: *Canadian Broadcasting Corporation (CBC)**
PO Box 2230, 430 University Ave., Charlottetown, PE C1A 8B9
Tel: 902-629-6400, *Toll-Free:* 866-306-4636
www.cbc.ca/pei; www.cbc.ca/television
Other information: Phone, CBC News Compass: 902-629-6403; Toll-Free: 1-800-671-2228
Andrew Cochran, Managing Director, Maritimes
Donna Allen, Executive Producer, News, Prince Edward Island
Janet Irwin, Senior Regional Manager, News & Current Affairs
Nadine Antle, Regional Manager, Partnerships, Communications, Brand, & Promot, 506-451-4054
Lenny Jackson, Station Manager, Prince Edward Island
John Channing, Manager, Sales
Heather McGrath, Senior Officer, Communications, 902-629-6416

***Charlottetown:* CIHF-DT-14**(Channel: 42)
Owned by: *CIHF-TV*
Charlottetown, PE

** For details on this company see listing in Major Broadcasting Companies section; † French language station*

Québec

***Alma:* CBJET-TV-1**(Channel: 32)
Montréal

Owned by: *CBMT-TV; Canadian Broadcasting Corporation*
Alma, QC

***Baie-Comeau:* CBMIT-TV**(Channel: 28 UHF)
Owned by: *Canadian Broadcasting Corporation (CBC)*
Baie-Comeau, QC
Toll-Free: 866-306-4636
www.cbc.ca/television
Other information: TTY: 1-866-220-6045

†*Carleton:* CHAU-TV(Channel: 5)*Détenteur:* **Télé Inter-Rives ltée***
349, boul Perron, Carleton, QC G0C 1J0
Tél: 418-364-3344, *Téléc:* 418-364-7168
nousjoindre@chautva.com
www.chautva.com
Thibault Octave, Directeur de l'information, othibault@chautva.com
Arseneault Chantale, Journaliste, carseneault@chautva.com

†*Chandler:* CHAU-TV-4(Channel: 6)*Détenteur:* **CHAU-TV**
Chandler, QC

†*Chapais:* CBFAT-TV-1(Channel: 12)*Détenteur:* **Canadian Broadcasting Corporation (CBC)**
Chapais, QC
Tél: 514-597-6000, *Téléc:* 514-597-5545
Ligne sans frais: 866-306-4636
auditoire@radio-canada.ca
www.radio-canada.ca/television
Médias sociaux: www.twitter.com/RC_TV

†*Chibougamau:* CBFAT-TV(Channel: 5)*Détenteur:* **Canadian Broadcasting Corporation (CBC)**
Chibougamau, QC
Tél: 514-597-6000, *Téléc:* 514-597-5545
Ligne sans frais: 866-306-4636
auditoire@radio-canada.ca
www.radio-canada.ca/television
Médias sociaux: www.twitter.com/RC_TV

***Chibougamau:* CBMCT-TV**(Channel: 4)
Owned by: *Canadian Broadcasting Corporation (CBC)*
Chibougamau, QC
Toll-Free: 866-306-4636
www.cbc.ca/television
Other information: TTY: 1-866-220-6045

***Chicoutimi:* CBJET-TV**(Channel: 58)
Montréal

Owned by: *CBMT-TV; Canadian Broadcasting Corporation*
Chicoutimi, QC

†*Cloridorme:* CHAU-TV-8(Channel: 11)*Détenteur:* **CHAU-TV**
Cloridorme, QC

†*Gaspé:* CHAU-TV-6(Channel: 7)*Détenteur:* **CHAU-TV**
Gaspé, QC

†*Gatineau:* CHOT-TV(Channel: 40)
171-A, rue Jean-Proulx, Gatineau, QC J8Z 1W5
Tél: 819-770-1040,
www.rncmedia.ca
Robert H. Parent

***Harrington-Harbour:* CBMUT-TV**(Channel: 13 VHF)
Owned by: *Canadian Broadcasting Corporation (CBC)**
Harrington-Harbour, QC
Toll-Free: 866-306-4636
www.cbc.ca/television
Other information: TTY: 1-866-220-6045

†*Jonquière:* CFRS-DT(Channel: 35)*Détenteur:* **V***
2303 Sir Wilfrid-Laurier, Jonquière, QC G7X 5Z2
Tél: 418- 54-2455, *Téléc:* 418- 54-2721
vtele.ca

†*Jonquière:* CIVV-TV(Channel: 8)*Détenteur:* **Télé-Québec***
CP 23041, Jonquière, QC G7X 9Z8
Tél: 418-695-8152, *Téléc:* 418-695-8155
lgagnon@telequebec.qc.ca
telequebec.tv

†*Kuujjuarapik:* CBFK-TV(Channel: 9)*Détenteur:* **Canadian Broadcasting Corporation (CBC)**
Kuujjuarapik, QC
Tél: 514-597-6000, *Téléc:* 514-597-5545
Ligne sans frais: 866-306-4636
auditoire@radio-canada.ca
www.radio-canada.ca/television
Médias sociaux: www.twitter.com/RC_TV

†*L'Anse-à-Valleau:* CHAU-TV(Channel: 12)*Détenteur:* **CHAU-TV**
L'Anse-à-Valleau, QC

***La Tabatière:* CBMLT-TV**(Channel: 10)
Owned by: *Canadian Broadcasting Corporation (CBC)*
La Tabatière, QC
Toll-Free: 866-306-4636
www.cbc.ca/television
Other information: TTY: 1-866-220-6045

***La Tuque:* CBMET-TV**(Channel: 9)
Owned by: *Canadian Broadcasting Corporation (CBC)*
La Tuque, QC
Toll-Free: 866-306-4636
www.cbc.ca/television
Other information: TTY: 1-866-220-6045

†*Montréal:* CBFT-TV(Channel: 2 VHF; 19 UHF)*Détenteur:* **Canadian Broadcasting Corporation (CBC)***
Maison de Radio-Canada, CP 6000 Centre-ville, 1400, boul René-Lévesque est, Montréal, QC H3C 3A8
Tél: 514-597-6000, *Téléc:* 514-597-5545
Ligne sans frais: 866-306-4636
auditoire@radio-canada.ca
www.radio-canada.ca/television
Médias sociaux: www.twitter.com/RC_TV,
Autre information: Phone, Montréal TV Newsroom: 514-597-6371; Fax: 514-597-6354
Pia Marquard, Managing Director, Radio & Television, Québec Region
Sally Caudwell, Executive Producer, Montréal News, 514-597-4089, Fax: 514-597-4511

***Montréal:* CBMT-TV**(Channel: 6 VHF; 20 UHF)
Owned by: *Canadian Broadcasting Corporation (CBC)**
PO Box 6000, Montréal, QC H3C 3A8
Tel: 514-597-6000, *Fax:* 514-597-6354
www.cbc.ca/montreal; www.cbc.ca/television
Other information: Phone, CBC Montréal TV Newsroom: 514-597-6371
Pia Marquard, Managing Director, Radio & Television, Québec Region
Sally Caudwell, Executive Producer, News, Montréal, 514-597-4089, Fax: 514-597-4511
Mary-Jo Barr, News Director, English Services
Laura Tarulli, Senior Manager, Production & Resources
Carolyn Warren, Regional Manager, Cultural Programming & Integrated Content
Hugh Brodie, Manager, Partnership & Communications, Québec, 514-597-5813

†*Montréal:* CFTM-DT(Channel: 10)*Détenteur:* **Groupe TVA inc.***
1600 Est, boul de Maisonneuve, Montréal, QC H2L 4P2
groupetva.ca
Médias sociaux: www.facebook.com/ReseauTVA

†*Montréal:* CIVB-TV(Channel: 8)*Détenteur:* **Télé-Québec***
#1000, rue Fullum, Montréal, QC G5L 1X7
Tél: 514-521-2424, *Téléc:* 514-873-2601
info@telequebec.tv
www.telequebec.tv
Diane Dube

†*Montréal:* CIVM-TV(Channel: 17)*Détenteur:* **Télé-Québec***
1000, rue Fullum, Montréal, QC H2K 3L7
Tél: 514-521-2424, *Téléc:* 514-873-2601
Ligne sans frais: 800-361-4362
info@telequebec.tv
www.telequebec.tv
Claude Dufault, Directeur de la commandite et des ventes, cdufault@telequebec.tv
Desroches Gérard, Représentant, gdesroche@telequebec.tv

***Montreal:* CKMI-TV**(Channel: 5)
Owned by: *Global Television Network*
1600 de Maisonneuve E., Montreal, QC H2L 4P2
Tel: 514-521-4923,
quebecprog@globaltv.ca, globalnews.que@globaltv.co
www.globalmontreal.com
Maureen Rogers, General Manager
Karen MacDonald, Station Manager

***Murdochville:* CBMMT-TV**(Channel: 21 UHF)
Owned by: *Canadian Broadcasting Corporation (CBC)*
Murdochville, QC
Toll-Free: 866-306-4636
www.cbc.ca/television
Other information: TTY: 1-866-220-6045

†*Percé:* CHAU-TV-5(Channel: 13)*Détenteur:* **CHAU-TV**
Percé, QC

†*Plessisville:* CKYQ-FM(Channel: 95.7)
1646, av St-Laurent, Plessisville, QC G6L 2Y6
Tél: 819-362-3737, *Téléc:* 819-362-3414
studio@kyqfm.com
www.kyqfm.com

†*Pointe-au-Père:* CFER-TV(Channel: 5, 11)*Détenteur:* **Groupe TVA inc.***
465, boul Ste-Anne, Pointe-au-Père, QC G5M 1G1
groupetva.ca

†*Port-Daniel:* CHAU-TV-3(Channel: 10)*Détenteur:* **CHAU-TV**
Port-Daniel, QC

†*Québec:* CBVT-TV(Channel: 11)*Détenteur:* **Canadian Broadcasting Corporation***
CP 18800, 888, rue Saint-Jean, Québec, QC G1K 9L4
Tél: 418-654-1341, *Ligne sans frais:* 866-954-1341
nouvelles.quebec@radio-canada.ca
www.radio-canada.ca
Genevieve Goulet, Relations ave l'auditoire, auditoire.quebec@radio.canada.ca

†*Quebec:* CFAP-DT(Channel: 35)*Détenteur:* **V***
#025, 330 St-Vallier Est, Quebec, QC G9K 9C5
Tél: 418-624-2222, *Téléc:* 418-624-8930
vtele.ca

†*Rimouski:* CFER-TV(Channel: 11)*Détenteur:* **CFER-TV**
Rimouski, QC

***Rivière-Saint-Paul:* CBMPT-TV**(Channel: 11)
Owned by: *Canadian Broadcasting Corporation (CBC)*
Rivière-Saint-Paul, QC
Toll-Free: 866-306-4636
www.cbc.ca/television
Other information: TTY: 1-866-220-6045

†*Rivière-au-Rénard:* CHAU-TV-7(Channel: 4)*Détenteur:* **CHAU-TV**
Rivière-au-Rénard, QC

†*Rivière-du-Loup:* CFTF-TV(Channel: 29)
103, rue des Équipements, Rivière-du-Loup, QC G5R 5W7
Tél: 418-862-2909, *Téléc:* 418-862-8147
stevensimard@qc.aira.com
www.tqs.ca
Nancy Fortin, Production Director
Marc Simard, Président
Ginette Dumont, Administrative Secretary
Stéphane Grégoire, Vice-President, Finances
Michel Bélanger, Vice-President, Operations

†*Rivière-du-Loup:* CIMT-TV(Channel: 9; Groupe TVA owns 45% stake in the company)*Détenteur:* **Télé Inter-Rives ltée***
Rivière-du-Loup, QC

†*Rivière-du-Loup:* CKRT-TV(Channel: 9; Radio-Canada owns part stake of the company)*Détenteur:* **Télé Inter-Rives ltée***
15, rue de la Chute, Rivière-du-Loup, QC G5R 5B7
Tél: 418-867-1341, *Téléc:* 418-867-4710
nousjoindre@cimt.ca
Marc Simard, President
Ginette Dumont, Administrative Secretary

** For details on this company see listing in Major Broadcasting Companies section; † French language station*

Germain Gélinas, Vice-President, Operations
Stéphane Grégoire, Vice-President, Finances

†Rivière-du-Loup: CKRT-TV(Channel: 7)*Détenteur:* **Canadian Broadcasting Corporation***
15, rue de la Chute, Rivière-du-Loup, QC G5R 5B7
Tél: 418-867-8080, *Téléc:* 418-867-4710
info@ckrt.ca
www.ckrt.ca
Marc Simard, President
Ginette Dumont, Administrative Secretary
Germain Gélinas, Vice-President, Operations
Stéphane Grégoire, Vice-President, Finances

†Rouyn-Noranda: CFEM-DT(Channel: 13)
380, av Murdoch, Rouyn-Noranda, QC J9X 1G5
Tél: 819-762-0744, *Téléc:* 819-762-2280
nouvelles@rncmedia.ca
www.cfem.ca
Ghislain Beaulieu

†Rouyn-Noranda: CIVA-TV(Channel: 8)
Montréal
Détenteur: **CIVM-TV**
Rouyn-Noranda, QC

†Rouyn-Noranda: CKRN-DT(Channel: 4)
380, av Murdoch, Rouyn-Noranda, QC J9X 1G5
Tél: 819-762-0744, *Téléc:* 819-762-2280
www.rncmedia.ca
Ghislain Beaulieu

†Saguenay: CJPM-DT(Channel: 6)*Détenteur:* **Groupe TVA inc.**
Saguenay, QC
groupetva.ca

Saint-Augustin: CBMXT-TV(Channel: 7)
Owned by: *Canadian Broadcasting Corporation (CBC)*
Saint-Augustin, QC
Toll-Free: 866-306-4636
www.cbc.ca/television
Other information: TTY: 1-866-220-6045

†Sainte-Foy: CFCM-DT(Channel: 4)*Détenteur:* **Groupe TVA inc.***
CP 2026, 1000, av Myrand, Sainte-Foy, QC G1V 2W3
Tél: 418-688-9330, *Téléc:* 418-681-4239
Ligne sans frais: 800-463-5608
groupetva.ca
Richard Renaud, Vice-President, Regional Stations & General Manager, CFCM

†Sainte-Marguerite-Marie: CHAU-TV-1(Channel: 3)*Détenteur:* **CHAU-TV**
Sainte-Marguerite-Marie, QC

Sherbrooke: CBMT-TV-3(Channel: 50 UHF)
Owned by: *Canadian Broadcasting Corporation (CBC)*
Sherbrooke, QC
Toll-Free: 866-306-4636
www.cbc.ca/television
Other information: TTY: 1-866-220-6045

Sherbrooke: CFKS-DT(Channel: 30)
Owned by: *V**
3720, boul Industriel, Sherbrooke, QC J1L 1Z9
Tel: 819-565-9232, *Fax:* 819-822-4205
vtele.ca
Social Media: www.facebook.com/vtele.ca, twitter.com/vtele

†Sherbrooke: CHLT-DT(Channel: 7)*Détenteur:* **Groupe TVA inc.***
3330, rue King ouest, Sherbrooke, QC J1L 1C9
Tél: 819-565-7777, *Téléc:* 819-565-4650
groupetva.ca

†Sherbrooke: CIVS-DT(Channel: 24)
Montréal
Détenteur: **CIVM-TV**
Sherbrooke, QC

†Sherbrooke: CKSH-DT(Channel: 9)*Détenteur:* **Société Radio-Canada***
3720, boul Industriel, Sherbrooke, QC J1L 1Z9
Tél: 819-565-9232, *Téléc:* 819-822-4205
www.radio-canada.ca

Thetford Mines: CBMT-TV-4(Channel: 32 UHF)
Owned by: *Canadian Broadcasting Corporation (CBC)*
Thetford Mines, QC
Toll-Free: 866-306-4636
www.cbc.ca/television
Other information: TTY: 1-866-220-6045

†Tracadie: CHAU-TV-10(Channel: 9)*Détenteur:* **CHAU-TV**
Tracadie, QC

Trois-Rivières: CBMT-TV-1(Channel: 28 UHF)
Owned by: *Canadian Broadcasting Corporation (CBC)*
Trois-Rivières, QC
Toll-Free: 866-306-4636
www.cbc.ca/television
Other information: TTY: 1-866-220-6045

†Trois-Rivières: CFKM-DT(Channel: 16)*Détenteur:* **V***
926, rue Notre Dame Centre, Trois-Rivières, QC G9A 4W8
Tél: 819-377-6053,
vtele.ca
Médias sociaux: www.facebook.com/vtele.ca, twitter.com/vtele
Michel Cloutier, General Manager

†Trois-Rivières: CHEM-DT(Channel: 8)*Détenteur:* **Groupe TVA inc.***
3625, boul Chanoine-Moreau, Trois-Rivières, QC G8Y 5N6
Tél: 819-376-8880, *Téléc:* 819-376-2906
groupetva.ca

†Trois-Rivières: CIVC-TV(Channel: 45)
Trois-Rivières, QC

Vieux-Fort: CBMVT-TV(Channel: 13)
Owned by: *Canadian Broadcasting Corporation (CBC)*
Vieux-Fort, QC
Toll-Free: 866-306-4636
www.cbc.ca/television
Other information: TTY: 1-866-220-6045

Saskatchewan

Beauval: CBKBT-TV(Channel: 7)
Owned by: *CBKST-TV; Canadian Broadcasting Corporation*
Beauval, SK

Buffalo Narrows: CBKDT-TV(Channel: 11)
Owned by: *CBKST-TV; Canadian Broadcasting corporation*
Buffalo Narrows, SK

Carlyle Lake: CIEW-TV(Channel: 7)
Owned by: *CFQC-DT*
Carlyle Lake, SK

Colgate: CKCK-TV-1(Channel: 12)
Owned by: *CKCK-TV*
Colgate, SK

Fort Qu'Appelle: CBKT-TV-3(Channel: 4)
Regina

Owned by: *CBKT-TV*
Fort Qu'Appelle, SK

Fort Qu'appelle: CKCK-TV-7(Channel: 7)
Owned by: *CKCK-DT*
Fort Qu'appelle, SK

Golden Prairie: CKMC-TV-1(Channel: 10)
Owned by: *CKCK-DT*
Golden Prairie, SK

Humboldt: CIWH-TV-1(Channel: 32)
Owned by: *CFQC-DT*
Humboldt, SK

Ile-a-la-Crosse: CBKCT-TV(Channel: 9)
Owned by: *CBKST-TV; Canadian Broadcasting Corporation*
Ile-a-la-Crosse, SK

La Loche: CBKDT-TV-2(Channel: 13)
Owned by: *CBKST-TV; Canadian Broadcasting Corporation*
La Loche, SK

La Ronge: CBKST-TV-2(Channel: 12)
Owned by: *CBKST-TV*
La Ronge, SK

Leoville: CBKST-TV-3(Channel: 12)
Owned by: *CBKST-TV*
Leoville, SK

Maple Creek: CHAT-TV-2(Channel: 4)
Medicine Hat

Owned by: *CHAT-TV*
Maple Creek, SK

Meadow Lake: CBCS-TV-1(Channel: 8)
Owned by: *CKSA-TV*
Meadow Lake, SK

Meadow Lake: CITL-TV3(Channel: 3)
Lloydminster

Owned by: *CITL-TV*
Meadow Lake, SK

Montreal Lake: CBKST-TV-5(Channel: 11)
Owned by: *CBKST-TV*
Montreal Lake, SK

Moose Jaw: CBKT-TV-1(Channel: 4)
Regina

Owned by: *CBKT-TV*
Moose Jaw, SK

Moose Jaw: CKMJ-TV(Channel: 7)
Owned by: *CKCK-DT*
Moose Jaw, SK

North Battleford: CFQC-TV-2(Channel: 6)
Owned by: *CFQC-DT*
North Battleford, SK

North Battleford: CKBI-TV-2(Channel: 7)
Prince Albert

Owned by: *CKBI-TV*
North Battleford, SK

Palmbere Lake: CBKDT-TV-1(Channel: 8)
Owned by: *CBKST-TV; Canadian Broadcasting Corporation*
Palmbere Lake, SK

Pinehouse Lake: CBKST-TV-6(Channel: 10)
Owned by: *CBKST-TV*
Pinehouse Lake, SK

Prince Albert: CIPA-TV(Channel: 9)
Owned by: *Bell Media TV**
22 - 10 St. West, Prince Albert, SK S6V 3A5
Tel: 306-922-6066, *Fax:* 306-763-3041
Social Media: www.facebook.com/ctvsaskatoon, twitter.com/ctvsaskatoon

Prince Albert: CKBI-TV(Channel: 5)
Owned by: *Canadian Broadcasting Corporation**
22 - 10 St. West, Prince Albert, SK S6V 3A5
Tel: 306-922-6066, *Fax:* 306-763-3041

†Regina: CBKFT-TV(Channel: 13)*Détenteur:* **Société Radio Canada***
CP 540, 2440 Broad St., Regina, SK S4P 4A1
Tél: 306-347-9540,
rene_fountaine@radio-canada.ca
www.radio-canada.ca/regions/saskatchewan
Fontaine René, 204-788-3236, rene_fountaine@radio-canada.ca

Regina: CBKT-TV(Channel: 9)
Owned by: *Canadian Broadcasting Corporation**
PO Box 540, 2440 Broad St., Regina, SK S4P 4A1
Tel: 306-347-9540, *Fax:* 306-347-9635
audienceinfo@regina.cbc.ca
www.sask.cbc.ca
Social Media: www.facebook.com/cbcsask; twitter.com/cbcsask
Lenora Sturge, Program Marketing Co-ordinator, 306-347-9714

Regina: CFRE-TV(Channel: 5)
Owned by: *Global Television Network**
370 Hoffer Dr., Regina, SK S4N 7A4
Tel: 306-775-4000, *Fax:* 306-721-4817
www.globalregina.com

Regina: CKCK-DT(Channel: 2)
Owned by: *Bell Media TV**

** For details on this company see listing in Major Broadcasting Companies section; † French language station*

PO Box 2000, Regina, SK S4P 3E5
Tel: 306-569-2000, *Fax:* 306-522-0090
ckck@ctv.ca
regina.ctvnews.ca
Dennis Dunlop, Vice-President, General Manager, General Sales Manager, CTV Saskatchewan

***Regina:* SCN Television**(Channel: SCN operates as an agency of the Government of Saskatchewan, in accordance with The Communications Network Corporation Act (1989). The Minister of Culture Youth and Recreation serves as the Minister Responsible for SCN)
Owned by: *Bluepoint Investments Inc.**
#E-313, 2440 Broad St., Regina, SK S4P 0A5
Tel: 306-779-2726, *Fax:* 306-545-8649
inquiries@scn.ca
www.scn.ca
Jim Johns, Manager, Information Systems
David Stanchuk, Manager, Technology
Ken Alecxe, President & CEO
Richard Gustin, Executive Director, Programming
Twyla MacDougall, Executive Director, Finance & Human Resources & Strategic Plannin
Maureen MacDonald, Manager, Communications

***Saskatoon:* CBKST-TV**(Channel: 11)
Owned by: *Canadian Broadcasting Corporation**
144 - 2nd Ave. South, Saskatoon, SK S7K 1K5
Tel: 306-956-7430,
www.cbc.ca/sask
Social Media: www.facebook.com/cbcsask; twitter.com/cbcsask

***Saskatoon:* CFQC-DT**(Channel: 8)
Owned by: *Bell Media TV**
216 - 1 Ave. North, Saskatoon, SK S7K 3W3
Tel: 306-665-8600, *Fax:* 306-665-0450
saskatoon.ctvnews.ca
Dennis Dunlop, General Manager

***Saskatoon:* CFSK-DT**(Channel: 4)
Owned by: *Global Television Network**
218 Robin Cres., Saskatoon, SK S7L 7C3
Tel: 306-665-6969, *Fax:* 306-665-6069
globalnews.sask@globaltv.com
www.globalsaskatoon.com
Wayne Rorke, Station Manager, wrorke@globaltv.com
Lisa Ford, News Director, lford@globaltv.com

***Southend:* CBKST-TV-8**(Channel: 13)
Owned by: *CBKST-TV*
Southend, SK

***Spiritwood:* CKBI-TV-6**(Channel: 2)
Prince Albert

Owned by: *CKBI-TV*
Spiritwood, SK

***Stanley Mission:* CBKST-TV-4**(Channel: 8)
Owned by: *CBKST-TV*
Stanley Mission, SK

***Stranraer:* CBKST-TV-1**(Channel: 9)
Owned by: *CBKST-TV*
Stranraer, SK

***Stranraer:* CFQC-TV-1**(Channel: 3)
Owned by: *CFQC-DT*
Stranraer, SK

***Swift Current:* CBKT-TV-4**(Channel: 5)
Owned by: *CBKT-TV*
Swift Current, SK

***Swift Current:* CKMC-TV**(Channel: 12)
Owned by: *CKCK-DT*
Swift Current, SK

***Willow Bunch:* CBKT-TV-2**(Channel: 10)
Regina

Owned by: *CBKT-TV*
Willow Bunch, SK

***Willow Bunch:* CKCK-TV-2**(Channel: 6)
Owned by: *CKCK-TV*
Willow Bunch, SK

***Wynyard:* CIWH-TV**(Channel: 12)
Owned by: *CFQC-DT*
Wynyard, SK

Cable Companies

Alberta

***Calgary:* Shaw Rocket Fund**

Owned by: *Shaw Media Inc.**
#210, 2421-37th Ave. N.E., Calgary, AB T2E 6Y7
Tel: 403-750-4517,
info@rocketfund.ca
www.rocketfund.ca
Annabel Slaight, Chairperson

***Calgary:* Western Association of Broadcasters**
Calgary, AB
Tel: 877-814-2719, *Fax:* 877-814-2749
info@wab.ca
www.wab.ca

***Camrose:* Cable TV of Camrose**
4910 - 46 St., Camrose, AB T4V 1H1
Tel: 780-672-8839, *Fax:* 780-672-8830
www.cable-lynx.net

***Edmonton:* Alberta Music Industry Association**
#102, 10722-103 Ave., Edmonton, AB T5J 5G7
Tel: 780-428-3372,
info@amia.ca
www.amia.ca
Carly Klassen, Acting Executive Director, Program Manager, carly@amia.ca

***Edmonton:* Shaw TV - Edmonton**
10450 - 178 St. NW, Edmonton, AB T5S 1S2
Tel: 780-490-3555, *Fax:* 780-490-3510
www.shaw.ca/ShawTV/Edmonton

***Fort McMurray:* Shaw TV - Fort McMurray**

Owned by: *Shaw Communications Ltd.**
#200, 208 Beaconhill Dr., Fort McMurray, AB T9H 2R1
Tel: 780-714-5355,
www.shaw.ca/ShawTV/FortMcMurray

***High Prairie:* KBS TV**
PO Box 29, 5319 - 48th St., High Prairie, AB T0G 1E0
Tel: 780-523-3223

***Lethbridge:* Shaw TV - Lethbridge**

Owned by: *Shaw Communications Ltd.**
1232 - 3 Ave. South, Lethbridge, AB T1J 0J9
Tel: 403-310-7429,
shawtv.lethbridge@sjrb.ca
www.shaw.ca/ShawTV/Lethbridge

***Oyen:* Oyen Cable**
PO Box 95, Oyen, AB T0J 2J0
Tel: 403-664-3811, *Fax:* 403-664-3811
aberg@telusplanet.net; es1016@telusplanet.net
Art Berg, Owner/Operator

***Rainbow Lake:* Rainbow Lake Cable TV**
PO Box 149, Rainbow Lake, AB T0H 2Y0
Tel: 780-956-3934, *Fax:* 780-956-3570
admin@rainbowlake.ca
www.rainbowlake.ca

***Red Deer:* Shaw TV - Central Alberta**

Owned by: *Shaw Media Inc.**
4761 - 62 St., Red Deer, AB T4N 2R4
Tel: 403-340-6400, *Fax:* 403-340-6414
Toll-Free: 888-270-2433
shawtvcentralalberta@shaw.ca
www.shaw.ca/ShawTV/RedDeer
Peter Bissonnette, President

***Slave Lake:* Cable TV Slave Ltd**
PO Box 1008, 800 Main St. North, Slave Lake, AB T0G 2A0
Tel: 403-849-5188, *Fax:* 403-849-6809
ctvslave@cable-lynx.net
www.cable-lynx.net

***Veteran:* Veteran Television Society**
PO Box 470, Veteran, AB T0C 2S0
Tel: 406-575-3754

British Columbia

: Western Association of Broadcast Engineers
Calgary AB
Tel: 403-630-4907,
info@wabe.ca
www.wabe.ca
Brad Hooper, President

***Ashcroft:* Copper Valley Cablevision Ltd.**
PO Box 1120, 312 - 4th St., Ashcroft, BC V0K 1A0
Tel: 250-453-2616,
yourlink@coppervalley.bc.ca
www.coppervalley.ca

***Brackendale:* Britannia Cablevision**
PO Box 461, Brackendale, BC V0N 1H0
Tel: 604-898-9767
G.C. Pickard

***Campbell River:* Sayward Valley Communications Ltd.**
#112, 1720 - 14th Ave., Campbell River, BC V9W 8B9
Tel: 250-287-4199,
cs@saywardvalley.net
saywardvalley.net

***Castlegar:* Shaw TV - Castlegar**

Owned by: *Shaw Communications Ltd.**
1951 Columbia Ave., Castlegar, BC V2N 2W8
www.shaw.ca/ShawTV/Cranbrook

***Chilliwack:* Shaw TV - Chilliwack**

Owned by: *Shaw Communications Ltd.**
9275 Nowell St., Chilliwack, BC V2P 7G7
Tel: 604-792-8182, *Fax:* 604-792-0966
TheExpress@sjrb.ca
www.shaw.ca/ShawTV/Chilliwack

***Courtenay:* Shaw TV - Courtenay**
1591 McPhee Ave., Courtenay, BC V9N 3A6
Tel: 604-334-0888

***Cranbrook:* Shaw TV - Cranbrook**

Owned by: *Shaw Communications Ltd.**
720 Kootenay St. North, Cranbrook, BC V1C 3V2
Tel: 250-342-9415,
www.shaw.ca/ShawTV/Cranbrook

***Dawson Creek:* Shaw TV - Dawson Creek**
#204, 9817 - 100 Ave., Dawson Creek, BC V1J 1Y4
Tel: 250-785-9296, *Fax:* 250-785-9777
kevin.charach@sjrb.ca; dianne.townsend@sjrb.ca
www.shaw.ca/ShawTV/PrinceGeorge

***Delta:* Delta Cable**
5381 Ladner Trunk Rd., Delta, BC V4K 1W7
Tel: 604-946-1144, *Fax:* 604-946-5627
admin@deltacable.com
www.deltacable.com

***Duncan:* Shaw TV - Duncan**

Owned by: *Shaw Media Inc.**
35 Queens Rd., Duncan, BC V9L 2W1
Tel: 250-782-9113

***Hope:* Hope Cable Television**
PO Box 489, 360 Wallace St., Hope, BC V0X 1L0
www.rainbowcountry.bc.ca/archive/hopecable

***Kaslo:* Kaslo Cable Ltd.**
PO Box 637, Kaslo, BC V0G 1M0
Tel: 250-353-2547, *Fax:* 250-353-2547
kascable@netidea.com
M. Knight, President
K. Nijjar, Program Director, General Manager

***Kelowna:* Shaw TV - Okanagan**

Owned by: *Shaw Communications Ltd.**
2350 Hunter Rd., Kelowna, BC V1X 7H6
Tel: 250-979-6565,
www.shaw.ca/ShawTV/Kelowna

** For details on this company see listing in Major Broadcasting Companies section; † French language station*

Logan Lake: **Logan Lake TV Society**
PO Box 56, Logan Lake, BC V0K 1W0
Tel: 250-523-9339, *Fax:* 250-523-9339
admin@LLTVS.com
www.lltvs.com
Dean Neighbour, Vice President

Lower Post: **Daylu Dena Council**
PO Box 10, Lower Post, BC V0C 1W0
Tel: 250-779-3161,
dayludenacouncil.com
Roma Walker, Executive Director

Masset: **Masset Haida Television Society**
PO Box 602, 1356 Main St., Masset, BC V0T 1M0
Tel: 250-626-3994, *Fax:* 250-626-3941
mhtv@mhtv.ca
www.mhtv.ca
Alfred Brockley, President
Gerald Jennings, Vice-President

Merritt: **Shaw TV - Merritt**
PO Box 908, 2 Thorpe Ave., Merritt, BC V1K 1B8
Tel: 250-378-4919, *Fax:* 250-378-5233
MerrittTV@shaw.ca
www.shaw.ca/ShawTV/Merritt

Nanaimo: **Shaw TV - Nanaimo**

Owned by: *Shaw Communications Ltd.**
4316 Boban Dr., Nanaimo, BC V8A 2N5
Tel: 250-760-1999

Penticton: **Shaw TV - Penticton**
1372 Fairview Rd., Penticton, BC V2A 5Z8
Tel: 250-492-5940

Port Alberni: **Shaw TV - Port Alberni**

Owned by: *Shaw Communications Ltd.**
4278 - 8 Ave., Port Alberni, BC V9Y 7S8
Tel: 250-723-6295

Port Hardy: **Keta Cable**
PO Box 63, 7020 Market St., Port Hardy, BC V0N 2P0
Tel: 250-949-6109, *Fax:* 250-949-6566
ketacable@cablerocket.com
www.ketacable.com

Prince George: **Shaw TV - Prince George**

Owned by: *Shaw Communications Ltd.**
2519 Queensway St., Prince George, BC V2L 1N1
Tel: 250-614-7325, *Fax:* 250-614-7347
pgshawtv@shaw.ca
www.shaw.ca/ShawTV/PrinceGeorge

Quesnel: **Shaw TV - Quesnel**
156 Front St., Quesnel, BC V2J 2K1
Tel: 250-992-8363,
john.mackenzie@sjrb.ca
www.shaw.ca/ShawTV/PrinceGeorge

Revelstoke: **Revelstoke Cable TV**
PO Box 651, 416 - 2nd St. West, Revelstoke, BC V0E 2S0
Tel: 250-837-5246, *Fax:* 250-837-2900
rctv@rctvonline.net
www.revelstokecable.net
Don Gillespie

Riondel: **Riondel Community Cable & Video Society**
PO Box 59, 232 Fowler Ave., Riondel, BC V0B 2B0
Tel: 250-225-3433, *Fax:* 250-225-3443
riondelcable@bluebell.ca
www.bluebell.ca

Salmon Arm: **Mascon Communications Corp.**
PO Box 3386, 4901 Auto Rd. SE, Salmon Arm, BC V1E 4S2
Tel: 250-832-6000, *Fax:* 250-832-5575
Toll-Free: 866-832-6020
info@masconcable.ca
www.masconcable.ca
Social Media: www.facebook.com/MasconCable,
twitter.com/masconcable

Valemount: **Valemount Entertainment Society/CHVC-TV Community Television**
PO Box 922, Valemount, BC V0E 2Z0
Tel: 250-566-8288, *Fax:* 250-566-4645
tv@vctv.ca
www.vctv.ca
Andru McCracken, Station Manager
Barb Riswok, Vice-President

Penni Osadchuk, Station Manager

Vancouver: **British Columbia Association of Broadcasters (BCAB)**
Vancouver, BC
Tel: 604-681-2153, *Fax:* 604-681-1049
bcab@icsevents.com
www.bcab.ca
Ken Kilcullen, President, kkilcullen@ckpg.com

Vancouver: **Music BC Industry Association**
530-425 Carrall St., Vancouver, BC V6B 6E3
Tel: 604-873-1914,
info@musicbc.org
www.musicbc.org
Social Media: www.facebook.com/MusicBC, twitter.com/musicbc
Bob D'Eith, Executive Director, bob@musicbc.org

Vancouver: **Okanagan Skeena Group Ltd.**
1130 West Pender St., Vancouver, BC V6E 4A4
Tel: 604-685-1160, *Fax:* 604-684-3537
H. McKinnon, President

Vancouver: **Women in Film & Television Vancouver**
207 West Hastings St., Vancouver, BC V6B 1H7
Tel: 604-685-1152,
info@womeninfilm.ca
www.womeninfilm.ca
Social Media: www.facebook.com/Womeninfilm,
twitter.com/WIFTV
Carolyn Combs, Executive Director

Washington: **National Association of Broadcasters**
1771 N Street, N.W., Washington, DC 20036
Tel: 204-429-5300,
nab@nab.org
www.nab.org
Social Media: www.facebook.com/Broadcasters?ref=ts,
twitter.com/nabtweets
Paul Karpowicz, President

Manitoba

Brandon: **Westman Communications Group**
1906 Park Ave., Brandon, MB R7B 0R9
Tel: 204-725-4300, *Fax:* 204-726-0853
info@westmancom.com
www.westmancom.com
David Baxter, CEO & President
Sharon Bickford, Assistant, Marketing & Communications, bickfords@westmancom.com

Thompson: **Shaw TV - Thompson**

Owned by: *Shaw Media Inc.**
50 Selkirk Ave., Thompson, MB R8N 0M7
Tel: 204-778-8949, *Fax:* 204-677-9953
shawcable11@yahoo.ca
www.shaw.ca
Social Media: www.facebook.com/pages/Shaw-TV-Thompson,
twitter.com/ShawTVThompson

Winnipeg: **Manitoba Music**
1-376 Donald St., Winnipeg, MB R3B 2J2
Tel: 204-942-8650,
info@manitobamusic.com
www.manitobamusic.com
Social Media: www.facebook.com/manitobamusic,
twitter.com/manitobamusic

Winnipeg: **On Screen Manitoba**
003-100 Arthur St., Winnipeg, MB R3B 1H3
Tel: 204-927-5898, *Fax:* 204-272-8792
info@onscreenmanitoba.com
www.onscreenmanitoba.com
Nicole Matiation, Executive Director, 204-927-5893, nicole@onscreenmanitoba.com

New Brunswick

Fredericton: **RogersTV Fredericton**

Owned by: *Rogers Broadcasting Ltd.**
377 York St., Fredericton, NB E3B 3P6
Tel: 506-462-3642, *Fax:* 506-452-2846
twillis@rci.rogers.com
www.rogerstv.com
Scott Jackson, Regional Station Manager, 888-462-3680, scott.jackson@rci.rogers.com

Miramichi: **RogersTV Miramichi**

Owned by: *Rogers Broadcasting Ltd.**
454 King George Hwy., Miramichi, NB E1V 1M1
Tel: 506-778-3009, *Fax:* 506-778-3035
charles.olscamp@rci.rogers.com
www.rogerstv.com
Scott Jackson, Regional Station Manager, 888-462-3680

Moncton: **Music New Brunswick**
PO Box 1638, Moncton, NB E1C 9X4
Tel: 506-383-4662,
contact@musicnb.org
www.musicnb.org
Social Media: www.facebook.com/MusicMusiqueNB?ref=ts,
twitter.com/musicmusiquenb
Richard Hornsby, President, richard@musicnb.org

Moncton: **RogersTV Moncton**

Owned by: *Rogers Broadcasting Ltd.**
70 Assomption Blvd., Moncton, NB E1C 1A1
Tel: 506-388-8405, *Fax:* 506-388-8622
scott.jackson@rci.rogers.com
www.rogerstv.com
Scott Jackson, Regional Station Manager, 888-462-3680

Quispamsis: **Canadian Cable Systems Alliance**
447 Gondola Point Rd., Quispamsis, NB E2E 1E1
Tel: 516-849-1334,
info@ccsa.cable.ca
www.ccsa.cable.ca

St. John's: **RogersTV St. John's**

Owned by: *Rogers Broadcasting Ltd.**
58 Kenmount Rd., St. John's, NB A1B 1W2
Tel: 709-753-7175, *Fax:* 709-753-7541
outofthefog@rci.rogers.com
www.rogerstv.com
Linda Lambe, Station Manager, 709-753-7349

Newfoundland & Labrador

Burgeo: **Burgeo Broadcasting System**
147 Reach Rd., Burgeo, NL A0M 1A0
Tel: 709-886-2935, *Fax:* 709-886-1243
www.bbsict.com/bbs/bbs.html
Claude Strickland, Operations Manager, claude@bbsict.ca
Marie Rose, Program Director

Glovertown: **Glovertown Cable TV Ltd.**
PO Box 131, 51 Main St. South, Glovertown, NL A0G 2L0
Tel: 709-533-2377, *Fax:* 709-533-2702
Terry Burry, President

Labrador City: **Community Recreation Rebroadcasting Service Association/CRRS TV**
208 Amherst Ave., Labrador City, NL A2V 2Y5
Tel: 709-944-7676, *Fax:* 709-944-7675
www.crrstv.net

Ramea: **Ramea Broadcasting Co.**
PO Box 23, Ramea, NL A0M 1N0
Tel: 709-625-2618, *Fax:* 709-625-2048
Samuel Fiander

St. John's: **MUSICNL**
186 Duckworth St., St. John's, NL A1C 1G5
Tel: 709-754-2574,
www.musicnl.ca
Social Media: www.facebook.com/MusicNL,
twitter.com/#!/_MusicNL_
Denis Parker, Executive Director
Jen Winsor, Communications, Programs Officer

St. John's: **St. John's International Women's Film Festival**
PO Box 984 C, St. John's, NL A1C 5M3
Tel: 705-754-3141, *Fax:* 709-754-0049
info@womensfilmfestival.com
www.womensfilmfestival.com
Social Media: www.facebook.com/womensfilmfestival,
twitter.com/sjiwff

Northwest Territories

Deline: **Great Bear Co-operative**
PO Box 159, Deline, NT X0E 0G0
Tel: 867-589-3361, *Fax:* 867-589-4517

** For details on this company see listing in Major Broadcasting Companies section; † French language station*

Fort McPherson: **Tetlit Service Co-operative**
PO Box 27, Fort McPherson, NT X0E 0J0
Tel: 867-952-2417, *Fax:* 867-952-2602
manager.tetlit@ArcticCo-op.com

Fort Simpson: **HR Thomson Consultants**
PO Box 313, 74 Cazon Cres, Fort Simpson, NT X0E 0N0
Tel: 867-695-3107, *Fax:* 867-695-2144
fortsim@cancom.net
Ivan Simons, Contact

Yellowknife: **Northwestel Cable Inc.**
PO Box 790, 5201 - 50th St., Yellowknife, NT X1A 2R3
Tel: 867-920-3500, *Fax:* 867-920-2625
customerservice@nwtel.ca
www.nwtel.ca
Mark Walker, Vice President, Government & Aboriginal Affairs

Nova Scotia

Canning: **Cross Country TV Ltd.**
PO Box 310, Canning, NS B0P 1H0
Tel: 902-678-2395, *Fax:* 902-678-2455
wireless@xcountry.tv
www.xcountry.tv

Cheticamp: **Acadian Communications Ltd.**
PO Box 648, Cheticamp, NS B0E 1H0
Tel: 902-224-3204, *Fax:* 902-224-2382
www.aclnet.ca/home/default.asp
Eric Chiasson, President, Director, 902-224-3328, Fax: 902-224-2772

Digby: **Eastlink Cable**
88 Warwick St., Digby, NS B0V 1A0
Tel: 902-245-2519, *Fax:* 902-245-6511
www.eastlink.ca

Halfix: **Music Nova Scotia**
302-5516 Spring Garden Rd., Halfix, NS B3J 1G6
Tel: 902-423-6271,
info@musicnovascotia.ca
www.MusicNovaScotia.ca
Social Media: www.facebook.com/MusicNovaScotia, twitter.com/musicnovascotia
Scott Long, Executive Director, 902-423-6271, scott@musicnovascotia.ca

Halifax: **EastLink**
PO Box 8660 A, Halifax, NS B3K 5M3
Tel: 902-453-2800, *Fax:* 902-446-4171
Toll-Free: 888-345-1111
www.eastlink.ca
Lee Bragg
Dan McKeen

Liverpool: **Eastlink Cable**
PO Box 449, 4130 Highway #3, Liverpool, NS B0T 1K0
bill.barnaby@corp.eastlink.ca
www.eastlink.ca

Lower Sackville: **Eastlink Cable**
367 Sackville Dr., Lower Sackville, NS B4C 2R7
Tel: 902-446-3588, *Fax:* 902-453-5714
www.eastlink.ca

New Minas: **Eastlink Television**
PO Box 4000, 1001 How Ave., New Minas, NS B4N 4S8
www.eastlink.ca

Reserve: **Seaside Communications**
PO Box 4558, 1318 Grand Lake Rd., Reserve, NS B1E 1L2
Tel: 902-539-6250, *Fax:* 902-539-2597
Toll-Free: 866-872-2253
psa@seaside.ns.ca
www.seaside.ns.ca
Mora MacDonald, Office Manager, moram@seaside.ns.ca

Sydney: **Eastlink**
PO Box 8660 A, Sydney, NS B3K 5M3
Tel: 902-539-9611,
www.eastlink.ca

Truro: **Eastlink**
69 Walker St., Truro, NS B2N 4A8
www.eastlink.ca

Nunavut

Arctic Bay: **Taqqut Co-operative**
General Delivery, Arctic Bay, NU X0A 0A0
Tel: 867-439-9934, *Fax:* 867-439-8765

Arviat: **Padlei Co-operative Association**
PO Box 90, Arviat, NU X0C 0E0
Tel: 867-857-2933, *Fax:* 867-857-2762

Baker Lake: **Sanavik Co-op**
PO Box 69, Baker Lake, NU X0C 0A0
Tel: 867-793-2912, *Fax:* 867-793-2594
www.arcticco-op.com

Cambridge Bay: **Ikaluktutiak Cooperative Limited**
PO Box 38, Cambridge Bay, NU X0B 0C0
Tel: 867-983-2201, *Fax:* 867-983-2085
manager.ikaluktutiak@ArcticCo-op.com
www.arcticco-op.com

Chesterfield Inlet: **Pitsiulak Co-operative**
PO Box 500, General Delivery, Chesterfield Inlet, NU X0C 0B0
Tel: 867-898-9975, *Fax:* 867-898-9056
info@arcticco-op.com
www.arcticco-op.com

Coral Harbour: **Katudgevik Cooperative Association Ltd.**
PO Box 201, Coral Harbour, NU X0C 0C0
Tel: 867-925-9969, *Fax:* 867-925-8308
info@arcticco-op.com
www.arcticco-op.com/acl-keewatin-coral-habour.htm

Gjoa Haven: **Kekertak Co-operative**
PO Box 120, General Delivery, Gjoa Haven, NU X0E 1J0
Tel: 867-360-7271, *Fax:* 867-360-6018
manager.qikiqtaq@ArcticCo-op.com

Kugluktuk: **Kugluktuk Co-operative**
PO Box 279, Kugluktuk, NU X0E 0E0
Tel: 867-982-4231, *Fax:* 867-982-3070
manager.kugluktuk@ArcticCo-op.com
www.arcticco-op.com

Qikiqtarjuaq: **Tulugaq Co-Op**
PO Box 8, Qikiqtarjuaq, NU X0A 0B0
Tel: 867-927-8061, *Fax:* 867-927-8044
www.arcticco-op.com

Rankin Inlet: **Kissarvik Co-Op**
PO Box 40, Rankin Inlet, NU X0C 0G0
Tel: 867-645-2801, *Fax:* 867-645-2280
info@arcticco-op.com

Repulse Bay: **Naujat Co-operative**
General Delivery, Repulse Bay, NU X0C 0H0
Tel: 867-462-9943, *Fax:* 867-462-4152
info@arcticco-op.com
www.arcticco-op.com/acl-keewatin-repulse-bay.htm

Whale Cove: **Issatik Eskimo Co-op Ltd.**
PO Box 60, Whale Cove, NU X0C 0J0
Tel: 867-896-9956, *Fax:* 867-896-9087
www.arcticco-op.com

White Plains: **Society of Motion Picture & Television Engineers**
3 Barker Ave., 5th Fl., White Plains, NY 10601
Tel: 914-761-1100,
www.smpte.org

Ontario

Beardmore: **Beardmore Television**
PO Box 102, Beardmore, ON P0T 1G0
Tel: 807-875-2096

Brampton: **RogersTV Brampton**

Owned by: *Rogers Broadcasting Ltd.**
8200 Dixie Rd., Brampton, ON L6T 0C1
Tel: 905-270-2124, *Fax:* 905-848-2831
rogerstv.brampton@rci.rogers.com
www.rogerstv.com
Alex Wood, Producer, 647-747-0043

Brechin: **Central Canada Broadcast Engineers**
102 Turtle Path, Brechin, ON L0K 1B0
Fax: 705-484-2112
Toll-Free: 800-481-4649
information@ccbe.ca
www.ccbe.ca
Larry Keats, President, larry@ccbe.ca

Brockville: **TVCOGECO Brockville/Prescott**
#13A, 333 California Ave., Brockville, ON K6V 5W1
Fax: 613-342-6521
Toll-Free: 866-709-5098
www.tvcogeco.com/brockville
Ron Harrison, Program Manager, ron.harrison@cogeco.com

Burlington: **COGECO Cable Canada LP**
950 Syscon Rd., Burlington, ON L7R 4S1
Tel: 905-333-5343, *Fax:* 905-332-8426
Toll-Free: 800-267-9000
www.cogeco.com
Louis Audet, President & Chief Executive Officer
Louise St-Pierre, Vice-President, Customer Services & Ontario Operations
Maureen Tilson Dyment, Senior Director, Programming & Communications
Glenda Lloyd, Manager, Communications, Glenda.Lloyd@cogeco.com

Burlington: **TVCogeco**
PO Box 5076 Main, 950 Syscon Rd., Burlington, ON L7R 4S6
Tel: 905-878-9306, *Fax:* 905-878-7927
www.cogeco.ca
Mike Hancock, Producer
Sandy French, Producer

Chatham: **TVCOGECO Chatham**
491 Richmond St., Chatham, ON N7M 1R2
Tel: 519-352-5241, *Fax:* 519-352-8274
www.tvcogeco.com/chatham
Zach Lawton, Producer, zach.lawton@cogeco.com

Clifford: **Maitland Cable TV**
PO Box 70, 100 Elora St. North, Clifford, ON N0G 1M0
Tel: 519-327-8012, *Fax:* 519-327-8010
mcatv@wightman.ca
www.wightman.ca
Social Media: www.facebook.com/wightmantelecom

Collingwood: **RogersTV Collingwood**

Owned by: *Rogers Broadcasting Ltd.**
4 Sandford Fleming Dr., Collingwood, ON L9Y 4V9
Tel: 705-445-3400, *Fax:* 705-445-9949
www.rogers.com
David R. Scott, System Manager

Cornwall: **TVCOGECO Cornwall**
517 Pitt St., Cornwall, ON K6J 3R4
Tel: 613-937-2506, *Fax:* 613-932-3176
viewer@cogeco.ca
www.tvcogeco.com/cornwall

Dryden: **Shaw TV - Dryden**

Owned by: *Shaw Communications Ltd.**
75 Queen St., Dryden, ON P8N 1A1
Tel: 807-223-5525, *Fax:* 807-223-4445
www.shaw.ca/ShawTV/Dryden

Dublin: **Mitchell-Seaforth Cable TV Ltd.**
123 Ontario St., Dublin, ON N0K 1E0
Tel: 519-345-2341, *Fax:* 519-345-2873
cabletv@ezlink.ca
www.ezlink.ca

Fenelon Falls: **Cable Cable Inc.**
16 Cable Rd., Fenelon Falls, ON K0M 1M0
Tel: 705-887-6433, *Fax:* 705-887-2580
Toll-Free: 866-887-6434
info@cablecable.net
www.cablecable.net
Tony Fiorini, President

Fergus: **COGECO Cable Canada LP**
475 St. Patrick St. West, Fergus, ON N1M 1M2
Tel: 519-843-3700, *Fax:* 519-843-2312
www.tvcogeco.com/fergus

Geraldton: **Astrocom Cablevision Inc.**
PO Box 910, 109 Greer Ave. West, Geraldton, ON P0T 1M0
Tel: 807-854-1569, *Fax:* 807-854-2169
jim@astrocom-on.com
www.astrocom-on.com

** For details on this company see listing in Major Broadcasting Companies section; † French language station*

John S. Emmans, President

***Goderich:* EastLink TV**
PO Box 305, 141 Huckins St., Goderich, ON N7A 4C6
Tel: 519-482-9233, *Fax:* 519-482-7098
Toll-Free: 888-345-1111
cable@cabletv.on.ca
www.cabletv.on.ca

***Gore Bay:* Gore Bay Community TV**
PO Box 371, Gore Bay, ON P0P 1H0
Tel: 705-282-1595, *Fax:* 705-282-1595

***Gravenhurst:* TVCOGECO Huntsville/Gravenhurst 10**
20 West St. South, Gravenhurst, ON P1H 1P2
Tel: 705-687-8818, *Fax:* 705-687-4789
www.tvcogeco.com/huntsville-gravenhurst
Social Media: www.facebook.com/TVCMuskoka
Scott Acton, Manager, Programming & Communications Relations, scott.acto@cogeco.com

***Guelph:* RogersTV Guelph**

Owned by:** Rogers Broadcasting Ltd.
130 Silvercreek Pkwy., Guelph, ON N1H 7Y5
Tel: 519-824-1900, *Fax:* 519-824-4210
Toll-Free: 888-410-2020
www.rogerstv.com
Charles Wechsler, Station Manager, 519-894-8120, Fax: 888-329-0329, charles.wechsler@rci.rogers.com
Al Haggith, Manager, Network Operations
Gregory K. Grimes, Station Manager

***Hamilton:* Source Cable Ltd.**
1090 Upper Wellington St., Hamilton, ON L9A 3S6
Tel: 905-574-6464, *Fax:* 905-574-4909
Toll-Free: 866-785-7851
techsupport@sourcecable.net
www.sourcecable.ca
Social Media: www.facebook.com/SourceCableHamilton, twitter.com/sourcecable

***Hamilton:* TV Hamilton**
150 Dundurn St. South, Hamilton, ON L8P 4K3
Tel: 905-523-1414, *Fax:* 905-523-8141
www.cable14.com
Brent Rickert, General Manager

***Hawkesbury:* TVCOGECO Hawkesbury**
1444 Aberdeen St., Hawkesbury, ON K6A 1K7
Tel: 613-632-2625, *Fax:* 613-632-8531
www.tvcogeco.com/hawkesbury-en; www.tvcogeco.com/hawkesbury-fr
Louis Audet, CEO

***Kincardine:* Kincardine Cable TV Ltd.**
223 Bruce Ave., Kincardine, ON N2Z 2P2
Tel: 519-396-8880, *Toll-Free:* 800-265-3064
kctv@tnt21.com
www.tnt21.com

***Kingston:* TVCOGECO Kingston 13**
170 Colborne St., Kingston, ON K7L 5M7
Tel: 613-544-6311, *Fax:* 613-545-0169
www.tvcogeco.com/kingston

***Kitchener:* RogersTV Kitchener**

Owned by:** Rogers Broadcasting Ltd.
85 Grand Crest Pl., Kitchener, ON N2G 4A8
Tel: 519-893-4400,
www.rogerstv.com

***London:* RogersTV London**

Owned by:** Rogers Broadcasting Ltd.
800 York St., London, ON N6A 5B1
Tel: 519-672-0030, *Fax:* 519-672-0199
www.rogerstv.com

***Markdale:* Markdale Cable TV**
PO Box 160, 20 Eliza St., Markdale, ON N0C 1H0
Tel: 519-986-2262, *Fax:* 519-986-2612
Toll-Free: 866-686-2262
marcable@cablerocket.com
www.markdalecabletv.com
Dave Armstrong, President

***Markham:* Ontario Association of Broadcasters**
PO Box 54040, 5762 Hwy. 7 East, Markham, ON L3P 7Y4
Tel: 905-554-2730,
memberservices@oab.ca
www.oab.ca
Doug Kirk, President, Membership, Government, 905-571-0949, Fax: 905-571-1150, president@oab.ca
John Hinnen, Vice President, General Manager, 416-935-8487, Fax: 416-935-8260

***Mississauga:* Canadian Music Week**
5355 Vail Court, Mississauga, ON L5M 6G9
Tel: 905-858-4747, *Fax:* 905-858-4848
info@cmw.net
www.cmw.net
Neill Dixon, President

***Mississauga:* Electro-Federation Canada**
#300, 180 Attwell Dr., Mississauga, ON M9W 6A9
Tel: 905-602-8877,
www.electrofed.com
Jim Taggart, President, CEO, 647-260-3093, jtaggart@electrofed.com

***Mississauga:* RogersTV Mississauga**

Owned by:** Rogers Broadcasting Ltd.
3573 Wolfedale Rd., Mississauga, ON L5C 3T6
Tel: 905-270-2124, *Fax:* 905-848-2831
rogerstv.mississauga@rci.rogers.com
Jane Dheer, Station Manager, 905-897-3928

***Moose Factory:* Mocreebec Development Corporation Ltd.**
PO Box 4, 62 Hospital Dr., Moose Factory, ON P0L 1W0
Tel: 705-658-4769, *Fax:* 705-658-4487
www.mocreebec.com

***Newmarket:* RogersTV Newmarket**

Owned by:** Rogers Broadcasting Ltd.
395-A Mulock Dr., Newmarket, ON L3Y 8P3
Tel: 905-780-7114,
yorkregion@rci.rogers.com
www.rogerstv.com

***Niagara Falls:* TVCOGECO Niagara 10**
7170 McLeod Rd., Niagara Falls, ON L2G 3H2
Tel: 905-374-2248, *Fax:* 800-807-8113
Toll-Free: 800-706-4221
www.tvcogeco.com/niagara

***North Bay:* TVCOGECO North Bay 12**
PO Box 3170 Main, 240 Fee St., North Bay, ON P1B 8S4
Tel: 705-472-9868, *Fax:* 705-472-7854
www.tvcogeco.com/north-bay
Melanie Miller, Production Supervisor

***Norwich:* Nor-Del Cablevision**
PO Box 296, Norwich, ON N0J 1P0
Tel: 519-879-6527, *Fax:* 519-879-6387
Toll-Free: 800-563-1954
nordel@nor-del.com
www.nor-del.com
Glenn I. Baxter, President

***Oshawa:* RogersTV Durnham Region**

Owned by:** Rogers Broadcasting Ltd.
301 Marwood Dr., Oshawa, ON L1H 1J4
Tel: 905-436-4120, *Fax:* 905-579-5559
durhamregion@rogerstv.com
www.rogerstv.com
Steve Simic, Station Manager

†*Ottawa:* ARC du Canada et RFA
325, rue Dalhousie, 2e ét., Ottawa, ON K1N 7G2
Tél: 613-562-0000,
www.radiorfa.com
François Côté, Secrétaire général, 613-562-0000

***Ottawa:* Broadcast Educators Association of Canada**
Ottawa, ON
www.beac.ca
Yvonne Colbert, President, Atlantic Director, yvonne.colbert@cbc.ca

***Ottawa:* The Canadian Association of Broadcasters**
PO Box 627 B, 770-45 rue O'Connor, Ottawa, ON K1P 5S2
Tel: 613-233-4035,
www.cab-acr.ca

***Ottawa:* Canadian Association of Internet Providers**
#416, 207 Bank St., Ottawa, ON K2P 2N2
Tel: 613-236-6550,
info@cata.ca
www.caip.ca

***Ottawa:* Canadian Broadcast Standards Council**
PO Box 3265 D, Ottawa, ON K1P 6H8
Tel: 643-233-4607, *Toll-Free:* 866-696-4718
info@cbsc.ca
www.cbsc.ca

***Ottawa:* Canadian Film Institute**
#120, 2 Daly Ave., Ottawa, ON K1N 6E2
Tel: 613-232-6727,
info@cfi-icf.ca
www.cfi-icf.ca
Tom McSorley, Executive Director

***Ottawa:* Canadian Media Production Association**
601 Bank St., 2nd Fl., Ottawa, ON K1S 3T4
Tel: 613-233-1444,
ottawa@cmpa.ca
www.cmpa.ca
David MacLeod, Executive Producer

***Ottawa:* Canadian Wireless Telecommunications Association**
#1110, 130 Albert St., Ottawa, ON K1P 5G4
Tel: 613-233-4888,
info@cwta.ca
www.cwta.ca

***Ottawa:* Media Smarts**
#120, 950 Gladstone Ave., Ottawa, ON K1Y 3E6
Tel: 613-224-7721, *Fax:* 613-761-9024
Toll-Free: 800-896-3342
info@mediasmarts.ca
mediasmarts.ca
Jane Tallim, Co-Executive Director
Cathy Wing, Co-Executive Director

***Ottawa:* National Campus and Community Radio Association**
#230, 325 Dalhousie, Ottawa, ON K1N 7G2
Tel: 613-321-1440,
office@ncra.ca
www.ncra.ca
Shelley Robinson, Executive Director, shelley@ncra.ca

***Ottawa:* Radio Advisory Board of Canada**
811-116 Albert St., Ottawa, ON K1P 5G3
Tel: 613-230-3261, *Toll-Free:* 888-902-5768
rabc.gm@on.aibn.com
www.rabc-cccr.ca
Wayne Stacey, Chair, Broadcasting
Norm Rashleigh, Chair, Electromagnetic Compatibility
Viet Nguyen, Chair, Fixed Wireless Communications
Bob Simmonds, Chair, Mobile & Personal Communications, bsimmonds@lenbrook.com

***Ottawa:* RogersTV Ottawa**

Owned by:** Rogers Broadcasting Ltd.
475 Richmond Rd., Ottawa, ON K2A 3Y8
Tel: 613-728-2222, *Fax:* 613-728-9793
ottawa22@rci.rogers.com
www.rogerstv.com
Crystal Todd, Manager, Creative Services, 613-759-8544

***Pembroke:* TVCOGECO Pembroke**
185 Lake St., Pembroke, ON K8A 5M1
Tel: 613-735-1228, *Fax:* 613-735-6177
www.tvcogeco.com/pembroke

***Port Perry:* Compton Cable TV Ltd.**
PO Box 73 Main, Port Perry, ON L9L 1A2
Tel: 905-985-8171, *Fax:* 905-985-0010
www.compton.net

***Richmond Hill:* RogersTV Richmond Hill**

Owned by:** Rogers Broadcasting Ltd.
244 Newkirk Rd., Richmond Hill, ON L4C 3S5
Tel: 905-780-7060, *Fax:* 905-780-7072
Toll-Free: 905-780-7114
www.rogerstv.com

** For details on this company see listing in Major Broadcasting Companies section; † French language station*

***Sault Ste Marie:* ShawTV - Sault Ste. Marie**
23 Manitou Dr., Sault Ste Marie, ON P6B 6GN
Tel: 705-946-2234,
shaw.ca/ShawTV/saultstemarie
Kevin Boll, Technical Manager

***Thunder Bay:* Fibre-Tel Enterprises**
1043 Gorham St., Thunder Bay, ON P7B 4A5
Tel: 807-622-0100

***Thunder Bay:* Shaw TV - Thunder Bay**

Owned by:* *Shaw Media Inc.*
1635 Paquette Rd., Thunder Bay, ON P7G 2J2
Tel: 807-766-7010,
shawtvthunderbay@shaw.ca
www.shaw.ca/ShawTV/Thunder-Bay

***Toronto:* Actors' Fund of Canada**
#301, 1000 Yonge St., Toronto, ON M4W 2K2
Tel: 416-975-0304,
contact@actorsfund.ca
www.actorsfund.ca
Social Media: www.facebook.com/ActorsFund,
twitter.com/ActorsFund
David Hope, Executive Director, execdir@actorsfund.ca

***Toronto:* ACTRA**
625 Church St., 3rd Fl., Toronto, ON M4Y 2G1
Tel: 416-489-1311, *Toll-Free:* 800-387-3516
national@actra.ca
www.actra.ca
Stephen Waddell, Executive Director

***Toronto:* Association of Canadian Advertisers**
#1103, 95 St. Clair Ave. West, Toronto, ON M4V 1N6
Tel: 416-964-3805,
www.acaweb.ca
Ron Lund, President, CEO, rlund@ACAweb.ca

***Toronto:* The Audio Engineering Society - Toronto Section**
Toronto, ON
www.torontoaes.org

***Toronto:* Broadcast Executives Society**
PO Box 75150, 20 Bloor St. East, Toronto, ON M4W 3T3
Tel: 416-899-0370,
admin@bes.ca
www.bes.ca
John Tucker, Administrator

***Toronto:* Canada Media Fund**
50 Wellington St. E., 4th Fl., Toronto, ON M5E 1C8
Tel: 416-214-4400, *Fax:* 416-214-4420
Toll-Free: 877-975-0766
info@cmf-fmc.ca
www.cmf-fmc.ca
Pierre Campeau, Communications Manager, 416-214-4402, Fax: 416-214-4420, pcampeau@cmf-fmc.ca

***Toronto:* Canadian Advertising Research Foundation**
#1005, 160 Bloor St. East, Toronto, ON M4W 1B9
Tel: 416-413-3864,
www.carf.ca
Tiffany James, Administrator, 416-413-3864, Fax: 416-413-3879, TJames@tvb.ca

***Toronto:* The Canadian Association of Professional Image Creators**
#202, 720 Spadina Ave., Toronto, ON M5S 2T9
Tel: 416-462-3677,
administrator@capic.org
www.capic.org
Dean Casavechia, President, 902-434-1119, nationalpresident@capic.org

***Toronto:* Canadian Communications Foundation**
Toronto, ON
Tel: 416-221-7965,
www.broadcasting-history.ca

***Toronto:* Canadian Country Music Association**
#200, 120 Adelaide St. East, Toronto, ON M5C 1K9
Tel: 416-947-1331,
country@ccma.org
www.ccma.org

***Toronto:* Canadian Ethnic Media Association**
24 Tarlton Rd., Toronto, ON M5P 2M4
Tel: 416-764-3081,
www.canadianethnicmedia.com
Dat Nguyen, Contact, datnguyen@webnewsprinting.com

***Toronto:* Canadian Independent Music Association**
30 St. Patrick St., 2nd Fl., Toronto, ON M5T 3E3
Tel: 416-485-3152,
cima@cimamusic.ca
www.cimamusic.ca
Stuart Johnston, President, 416-485-3152, stuart@cimamusic.ca

***Toronto:* The Canadian Journalism Foundation**
#500, 59 Adelaide St. East, Toronto, ON M5C 1K6
Tel: 416-955-0394,
www.cjf-fjc.ca
Social Media: www.facebook.com/groups/30389998615/,
twitter.com/cjffjc
Robert Lewis, Chair

***Toronto:* Canadian Retransmission Collective**
74 The Esplanade, Toronto, ON M5E 1A9
Tel: 416-304-0290,
info@crc-scrc.ca
www.crc-scrc.ca

***Toronto:* Canadian Society of Cinematographers**
#131, 3007 Kingston Rd., Toronto, ON M1M 1P1
Tel: 416-266-0591,
admin@csc.ca
www.csc.ca

***Toronto:* Canadian Women in Communications**
#804, 67 Yonge St., Toronto, ON M5E 1J8
Tel: 416-363-1880, *Toll-Free:* 800-361-2978
cwcafc@cwc-afc.com
www.cwc-afc.com
Stephanie MacKendrick, President, 416-363-1880, smackendrick@cwc-afc.com

***Toronto:* CARAS**
345 Adelaide St. West, 2nd Fl., Toronto, ON M5V 1R5
Tel: 416-485-3135,
info@carasonline.ca
www.carasonline.ca
Melanie Berry, President, CEO

***Toronto:* CIRAA**
118 Berkeley St., Toronto, ON M5A 2W9
Tel: 416-203-1011,
info@ciraa.ca
www.ciraa.ca
Andy McLean, Managing Director

***Toronto:* Concerned Children's Advertisers**
#300, 1920 Yonge St., Toronto, ON M4S 3E6
Tel: 416-484-0871,
info@cca-arpe.ca
www.cca-kids.ca

***Toronto:* Documentary Organization of Canada**
#126, 215 Spadina Ave., Toronto, ON M5T 2C7
Tel: 416-599-3844,
info@docorg.ca
www.docorg.ca
Katie McKenna, Chair, At Large

***Toronto:* FACTOR**
30 Commercial Rd., Toronto, ON M4G 1Z4
Tel: 416-696-2215, *Toll-Free:* 877-696-2215
www.factor.ca
Social Media: www.facebook.com/FACTORCanada,
twitter.com/FACTORCanada
Duncan McKie, duncan.mckie@factor.ca

***Toronto:* FilmOntario**
625 Church St., 2nd Fl., Toronto, ON M4Y 2G1
Tel: 416-642-6704,
www.filmontario.ca

***Toronto:* Friends of Canadian Broadcasting**
PO Box 200;238, 131 Bloor St. West, Toronto, ON M5S 1R8
Tel: 416-923-8201,
www.friends.ca
Ian Morrison, Spokesperson, friends@friends.ca

***Toronto:* Independent Production Fund**
#1709, 2 Carlton St., Toronto, ON M5B 1J3
Tel: 416-977-8966,
info@ipf.ca
www.ipf.ca
Charles Ohayon, Chair

***Toronto:* Institute of Communication Agencies**
#3002, 2300 Yonge St., Toronto, ON M4P 1E4
Tel: 416-482-1396,
ica@icacanada.ca
www.icacanada.ca
Gillian Graham, CEO

***Toronto:* Interactive Ontario**
#411, 99 Atlantic Ave., Toronto, ON M6K 3J8
Tel: 416-516-0077,
info@interactiveontario.com
www.interactiveontario.com
Donald Henderson, President, CEO, 416-516-0077, donald@interactiveontario.com

***Toronto:* Liason of Independent Filmakers of Toronto**
1137 Dupont St., Toronto, ON M6H 2A3
Tel: 416-588-6444,
www.lift.on.ca
Kathryn MacKay, Chair
Ben Donoghue, Executive Director, 416-588-6444

***Toronto:* Music Canada**
85 Mowat Ave., Toronto, ON M6K 3E3
Tel: 416-967-7272,
info@musiccanada.com
www.musiccanada.com
Social Media: twitter.com/Music_Canada
Amy Terrill, Contact, Media Inquiries, aterrill@musiccanada.com

***Toronto:* Music Industries Association of Canada**
#807, 505 Consumers Rd., Toronto, ON M2J 4V8
Tel: 416-490-1871, *Fax:* 416-490-0369
Toll-Free: 877-490-6422
www.miac.net
Social Media:
www.facebook.com/pages/MIAC-Show/127195590711806,
twitter.com/MIAC_Show
Barbara Cole, Executive Director, 416-490-1871, Fax: 416-490-0369, barbara@miac.net

***Toronto:* Music Managers Forum Canada**
1731 Lawrence Ave. East, Toronto, ON M1R 2X7
Tel: 416-462-9160,
www.musicmanagersforum.ca

***Toronto:* NABET 700 CEP**
#203, 100 Lombard St., Toronto, ON M5C 1M3
Tel: 416-536-4827,
info@nabet700.com
www.nabet700.com
Jayson Mosek, Business Agent, 416-536-4827

***Toronto:* National Advertising Benevolent Society**
1910 Yonge St., 4th Fl., Toronto, ON M4S 1Z5
Tel: 416-962-0446,
nabs@nabs.org
www.nabs.org
Social Media:
www.facebook.com/pages/NABS-Canada/113033972042210,
twitter.com/nabs_canada

***Toronto:* North American Broadcasters Association**
#6C300, 205 Wellington St. West, Toronto, ON M5V 3G7
Tel: 416-598-9877,
contact@nabanet.com
www.nabanet.com
Michael McEwen, Director General

***Toronto:* Radio Starmaker Fund**
#302, 372 Bay St., Toronto, ON M5H 2W9
Tel: 416-597-6622,
info@starmaker.ca
www.starmaker.ca

***Toronto:* Re:Sound**
#900, 1235 Bay St., Toronto, ON M5R 3K4
Tel: 416-968-8870,
info@resound.ca
www.resound.ca
Ian MacKay, President

***Toronto:* ReelWorld Film Festival**
#300, 438 Parliament St., Toronto, ON M5A 3A2
Tel: 416-598-7933,
www.reelworld.ca
Social Media:
www.facebook.com/pages/ReelWorld-Film-Festival/109983872346997, twitter.com/#!/ReelWorldFilm
Tonya Lee Williams, Founder, Executive Director, tonya@reelworld.ca

** For details on this company see listing in Major Broadcasting Companies section; † French language station*

Toronto: **RogersTV Toronto**

Owned by: *Rogers Broadcasting Ltd.**
855 York Mills Rd., Toronto, ON M3B 1Z1
Tel: 416-446-6500, *Fax:* 416-446-6658
rogerstv@rci.rogers.com
www.rogerstv.com
Annie Hadida, Station Manager, 416-446-7061

Toronto: **RTDNA Canada**
#310, 2175 Sheppard Ave. East, Toronto, ON M2J 1W8
Tel: 416-756-2213, *Fax:* 416-491-1670
Toll-Free: 877-257-8632
www.rtdnacanada.com
Social Media: www.facebook.com/rtdna.canada, twitter.com/#!/RTDNA_Canada
Ian Koenigsfest, President

Toronto: **SOCAN Society of Composers, Authors, & Music Publishers of Canada**
41 Valleybrook Dr., Toronto, ON M3B 2S6
Tel: 416-445-8700, *Toll-Free:* 800-557-6226
info@socan.ca
www.socan.ca
Eric Baptiste, CEO

Toronto: **Television Bureau of Canada Inc.**
#1005, 160 Bloor St. East, Toronto, ON M4W 1B9
Tel: 416-923-8813, *Toll-Free:* 800-231-0051
tvb@tvb.ca
www.tvb.ca

Toronto: **Toronto Musicians' Association**
#500, 15 Gervais Dr., Toronto, ON M3C 1Y8
Tel: 416-421-1020,
info@tma149.ca
www.torontomusicians.org
Social Media: www.facebook.com/pages/Toronto-Musicians-Association-Local-149-of
Jim Biros, Executive Director, Theatre, 416-421-1020, jbiros@tma149.ca

Toronto: **Women in Film & Television**
#601, 110 Eglinton Ave., Toronto, ON M4P 2Y1
Tel: 416-322-3430,
wift@wift.com
www.wift.com
Social Media: www.facebook.com/WIFT.Toronto, twitter.com/WIFT
Prentiss Fraser, Chair

Toronto: **Writers Guild of Canada**
#401, 366 Adelaide St. West, Toronto, ON M5V 1R9
Tel: 416-979-7907,
info@wgc.ca
www.wgc.ca
Social Media: twitter.com/WGCtweet
Jill Golick, President, j.golick@wgc.ca

Windsor: **COGECO Cable Canada LP**
2525 Dougall Ave., Windsor, ON N8X 5A7
Tel: 519-972-6677, *Fax:* 519-972-6688
www.cogeco.ca
Robert Scussolin, Programming and Community Relations Manager

Woodbridge: **Children's Miracle Network**
#C10, 4220 Steeles Ave. West, Woodbridge, ON L4L 3S8
Tel: 905-264-9750,
radio@cmn.org
www.childrensmiraclenetwork.ca

Woodstock: **RogersTV Woodstock**

Owned by: *Rogers Broadcasting Ltd.**
21 Ridgeway Circle, Woodstock, ON N4V 1C9
Tel: 519-533-5550, *Fax:* 519-533-5560
russell.archer@rci.rogers.com
www.rogerstv.com

Prince Edward Island

Charlottetown: **East Coast Music Association**
PO Box 40028, Charlottetown, PE C1E 0J2
Toll-Free: 800-513-4953
ecma@ecma.ca
www.ecma.com
Social Media: www.facebook.com/EastCoastMusicAssociation, twitter.com/eastcoastmusic
Mike Kennedy, Chair

Summerside: **Eastlink**
PO Box 4 Main, Summerside, PE C1N 4P6
Tel: 902-724-2800

Québec

†*Albanel:* Télé-câble Albanel inc.
227, rue Principale, Albanel, QC G8M 3K3
Tél: 418-279-5940,
info@tcalbanel.com
www.tcalbanel.com
Fernand Plourde, Fondateur

†*Betsiamites:* Télécâble Pessamit
18, rue Messek, Betsiamites, QC G0H 1B0
Tél: 418-567-8863,
www.pessamit.ca

†*Brossard:* Cablevision SDM-TRP inc.
8285, boul Pelletier, Brossard, QC J4X 1P6
Tél: 450-671-4251, *Téléc:* 450-923-1873
Ligne sans frais: 800-465-9215
www.totalsat.qc.ca

†*Chisasibi:* Ginwat Cable Television Inc.
CP 420, Chisasibi, QC J0M 1E0
Tél: 819-855-2191, *Téléc:* 819-855-3186

†*Drummondville:* COGECO Cable Canada LP
1970, boul Lemire, Drummondville, QC J2B 6X5
Tél: 819-477-3978, *Téléc:* 819-474-5313
www.cogeco.ca
Reno Longpré, Contact

†*Fermont:* Coopérative de la télévision communautaire de Fermont
CP 1379, 20, place Daviault, Fermont, QC G0G 1J0
Tél: 418-287-5443, *Téléc:* 418-287-5776

†*Grande-Rivière-Ouest:* Briand et Moreau Câble inc.
CP 63, 205 B, rue du Parc, Grande-Rivière-Ouest, QC G0C 1W0
Tél: 418-385-2680, *Téléc:* 418-385-3705
bmcable@bmcable.ca
www.bmcable.ca

†*Havre-Saint-Pierre:* R&T Communautaire Hâvre-St-Pierre
992, rue du Bouleau, Havre-Saint-Pierre, QC G0G 1P0
Tél: 418-538-2451, *Téléc:* 418-538-3870
info@cilemf.com
www.cilemf.com

†*La Malbaie:* Coopérative de câblodistribution de St-Fidèle
8, ch St-Paul, La Malbaie, QC G5A 2G6
Tél: 418-434-2486, *Téléc:* 418-434-1076
marcel.couturier@sympatico.ca
Marcel Couturier, Secrétaire

†*Labelle:* Télécâble Nordique inc.
CP 630, 128, boul Curé-Labelle, Labelle, QC J0T 1H0
Tél: 819-686-2662, *Ligne sans frais:* 800-293-8093

†*Lennoxville:* Groupe Transvision Réseau
#105, 175 Queen St., Lennoxville, QC J1M 1K1
Tél: 819-563-1001, *Téléc:* 819-563-3116
support@gtvr.com
www.gtvr.com

†*Lourdes-de-Blanc-Sablon:* Coopérative de câblodistribution de Brest
1147, boul Dr.-Camille-Marcoux, Lourdes-de-Blanc-Sablon, QC G0G 1W0
Tél: 418-461-2003, *Téléc:* 418-461-2703

†*Magog:* Cable Axion inc.
250, ch de l'Axion, Magog, QC J1X 6J2
Tél: 819-843-0611, *Téléc:* 819-868-4249
Ligne sans frais: 866-552-9466
info@axion.ca
www.axion.ca
Paul Girard, Président

†*Magog:* COGECO Cable Canada LP
15, rue St-Patrice ouest, Magog, QC J1X 1V8
Tél: 819-843-3370, *Téléc:* 819-843-0698
www.cogeco.ca
Médias sociaux: www.facebook.com/CogecoQC, twitter.com/CogecoQC

†*Matagami:* Cablevision Matagami
3, rue Vanier, Matagami, QC J0Y 2A0
Tél: 819-739-2148, *Téléc:* 819-739-2612

†*Matane:* Tele-Cable Multi-Vision inc.
655, ch de la Greve, Matane, QC G4W 7A1
Tél: 418-562-1950
Raymond Vachon, Contact

Montreal: **ADISQ**
6420, rue St. Denis, Montreal, QC H2S 2R7
Tel: 514-842-5147,
info@adisq.com
www.adisq.com
Social Media: www.facebook.com/galaadisq

Montréal: **Alliance québécoise des techniciens de l'image et du son**
#300, 533, rue Ontario est, Montréal, QC H2L 1N8
Tel: 514-844-2113,
info@aqtis.qc.ca
www.aqtis.qc.ca
Bernard Arseneau, Président, barseneau@aqtis.qc.ca

†*Montreal:* Bureau de la television du Canada
Montreal, QC
Tél: 514-284-0425,
tvb@bellnet.ca
www.tvb.ca
Theresa Treutler, President, CEO, ttreutler@tvb.ca

†*Montréal:* Cable VDN Inc.
#206, 2600, rue Ontario est, Montréal, QC H2K 4K4
Tél: 514-522-1590, *Téléc:* 514-522-1568
info@cablevdn.ca
web.vdn.ca

†*Montréal:* COGECO and Cogeco Cable Head office, Montréal
#915, 5 Place Ville-Marie, Montréal, QC H3B 2G2
Tél: 514-874-2600, *Téléc:* 514-874-2625
carriere@cogeco.com
www.cogeco.ca

†*Montreal:* Conseil québécois des arts médiatiques
3995, rue Berri, Montreal, QC H2L 4H2
Tél: 514-527-5116,
www.cqam.org

†*Montreal:* Média Jeunesse
#106, 1400, boul. Rene-Levesque est, Montreal, QC H2L 2M2
Tél: 514-597-5417, *Téléc:* 514-597-5205
alliance@ymamj.org
www.ymamj.org
Médias sociaux: www.facebook.com/pages/Youth-Media-Alliance/150380741707933
Chantel Bowen, Directrice générale, 514-597-5417, cbowen@ymamj.org

†*Montréal:* Vidéotron ltée
612, rue St-Jacques, Montréal, QC H3C 4M8
Tél: 514-281-1711,
www.quebecor.com
Robert Dépatie, Président/Chef de la direction

†*Percé:* Télédistribution de la Gaspésie
CP 234, 155, Place du Quai, Percé, QC G0C 2L0
Tél: 418-782-5355, *Téléc:* 418-782-5407
TDG01@bmcable.ca
www.bmcable.ca

†*Québec:* Coopérative de câblodistribution de l'arrière-pays
20860, boul Henri-Bourassa, Québec, QC G2N 1P7
Tél: 418-849-7125, *Téléc:* 418-849-7128
info@ccapcable.com
www.ccapcable.com
Jacques Perron, Directeur général
Stephane Arseneau, Directeur, Service à la clientèle

†*Rimouski:* COGECO Cable Canada LP
384, av de la Cathédrale, Rimouski, QC G5L 5L1
Tél: 418-724-6058, *Téléc:* 418-724-7167
www.cogeco.com

†*Rivière-Saint-Jean:* Télévision communautaire Rivière-St-Jean inc.
376, St-Jean/Poste Restante, Rivière-Saint-Jean, QC G0G 2N0
Tél: 418-949-2340
Jacques Lévesque, Président

** For details on this company see listing in Major Broadcasting Companies section; † French language station*

†*Saint-Gabriel-de-Valcarti:* Valcartier Cable
1743, boul Valcartier, Saint-Gabriel-de-Valcarti, QC G0A 4S0
Tél: 418-844-1218, *Téléc:* 418-844-3030
admin@munsgdv.caa
www.saint-gabriel-de-valcartier.ca

†*Saint-Just-de-Bretenières:* Coopérative de câblodistribution de Saint-Just-de-Bretenières
11, rue du Couvent, Saint-Just-de-Bretenières, QC G0R 3H0
Tél: 418-244-3560, *Téléc:* 418-244-3560
Réjean Poulin, Président

†*Sainte-Adèle:* COGECO Cable Canada LP
CP 1375, 605, Pierre-Péladeau, Sainte-Adèle, QC J8B 1Z3
Tél: 450-229-7668, *Téléc:* 450-229-7910
tvcogeco.laurentides@cgocable.ca
www.cogeco.ca
Guy Goyer, Contact

***Sanikiluaq:* Mitiq Co-operative**
General Delivery, Sanikiluaq, QC X0A 0W0
Tel: 867-266-8860, *Fax:* 867-266-8844
info@arcticco-op.com
www.arcticco-op.com/acl-baffin-region-sanikiluaq.htm

***Sept-Iles:* TVCOGECO Sept-Iles**
410, rue Evangeline, Sept-Iles, QC G4R 2N5
Tel: 418-962-3508, *Fax:* 418-962-3531
Patrick Delobel, Directeur regional

†*Shannon:* Shannon Vision inc.
438 Boul. Jacques Cartier, Local 103, Shannon, QC G0A 4N0
Tél: 418-844-3849, *Téléc:* 418-844-0347
gestion@cableshannon.com
www.cableshannon.com

***Shawinigan:* COGECO Cable Canada LP**
1222, 47e rue, Shawinigan, QC G9N 5B4
Tel: 819-539-9501, *Fax:* 819-539-6785
www.cogeco.ca

***St-Georges-de-Beauce:* COGECO Cable Canada LP**
11197 - 2e av, St-Georges-de-Beauce, QC G5Y 1V9
Tel: 418-228-9828, *Fax:* 418-228-3015
www.cogeco.ca

†*St-Zacharie:* Cablovision ACL Enr
515, 9e Avenue, St-Zacharie, QC G0M 2C0
Tél: 418-593-5262, *Téléc:* 418-593-3260

†*Ste-Catherine-de-la-Jacques-Cartier:* Coopérative de câblodistribution Ste-Catherine-Fossambault
130, rue Désiré-Juneau, Ste-Catherine-de-la-Jacques-Cartier, QC G3N 2X3
Tél: 418-875-1118, *Téléc:* 418-875-1971
gestion@coopcscf.com
www.coopcscf.com

†*Thetford Mines:* COGECO Cable Canada LP
39 - 10e Rue Sud, Thetford Mines, QC G6G 7X6
Tel: 418-338-2079, *Téléc:* 418-335-9125
www.tvcogeco.com/thetford-mines

†*Trois-Rivières:* COGECO Câble Québec inc.
1630 - 6e rue, Trois-Rivières, QC G8Y 5B8
Tél: 819-693-8353, *Téléc:* 819-379-2232
www.cogeco.ca
Martin Leuere, Responsable

†*Val-D'Or:* Cablevision du Nord de Québec inc. une Division de Bell Aliant
45, boul de Hôtel de Ville, Val-D'Or, QC J9P 2M5
Tél: 819-825-5133, *Ligne sans frais:* 800-567-6353
www.cablevision.qc.ca
Bernard Gauthier, Président

†*Warwick:* Cablovision Warwick inc.
CP 999, 14, boul Beaumier, Warwick, QC J0A 1M0
Tél: 819-358-5858, *Téléc:* 819-358-5592
service@cablovision.com
www.cablovision.com

Saskatchewan

***Craik:* Craik Cablevision**
PO Box 60, Craik, SK S0G 0V0
Tel: 306-734-2250, *Fax:* 306-734-2688
townofcraik@craik.ca
www.craik.ca
Jeff Murray, Administrator
Jason Kemp

***Ile-a-la-Crosse:* Ile a la Crosse Communications Society Inc.**
PO Box 480, Ile-a-la-Crosse, SK S0M 1C0
Tel: 306-833-2173, *Fax:* 306-833-2042

***Imperial:* Imperial Cable System**
310 Royal St., Imperial, SK
Tel: 306-963-2220,
www.imperial.ca/business.htm

***Limerick:* Village of Limerick**
PO Box 129, Limerick, SK S0H 2P0
Tel: 306-263-2020, *Fax:* 306-263-2013
rm73@sasktel.net
www.rmstonehenge.ca

***Moose Jaw:* Shaw TV - Moose Jaw**

Owned by:** Shaw Communications Ltd.
201 Manitoba St. East, Moose Jaw, SK S6H 0A4
Tel: 306-691-7395, *Fax:* 306-692-4859
www.shaw.ca/ShawTV/Moosejaw
Bob Anderson, Regional Manager
Jim Shaw Jr., Chief Officer

***North Battleford:* Access Communications Co-operative Ltd.**
1192 - 99 St., North Battleford, SK S9A 0P3
Tel: 306-445-4045, *Fax:* 306-445-0755
Toll-Free: 866-363-2225
help@accesscomm.ca
www.accesscomm.ca
Jim Deane, President/CEO
Trevor Derksen, Vice-President, Marketing & Sales
Carmela Haines, Vice-President, Finance & Administration

***Prince Albert:* Shaw TV - Prince Albert**

Owned by:** Shaw Communications Ltd.
2990 - 2nd Ave. West, Prince Albert, SK S6V 7E9
Tel: 306-922-5622, *Fax:* 306-922-7122
shawtv10@shaw.ca
www.shaw.ca/ShawTV/Saskatoon

***Regina:* Access Communications Co-operative Ltd.**
2250 Park St., Regina, SK S4N 7K7
Tel: 306-569-3510, *Fax:* 306-565-5395
Toll-Free: 866-363-2225
help@accesscomm.ca
www.accesscomm.ca
Jim Deane, President & CEO
Trevor Derksen, Vice-President, Marketing & Sales
Carmela Haines, Vice-President, Finance & Administration

***Regina:* Saskatchewan Motion Picture Association**
W211-2440 Broad St., Regina, SK S4P 4A1
info@smpia.sk.ca
www.smpia.sk.ca
Social Media: twitter.com/smpiaoffice
Vanessa Bonk, Executive Director, 306-525-4583, vanessa@smpia.sk.ca

***Regina:* SaskFilm & Video Development Corporation**
1831 College Ave., Regina, SK S4P 4V5
Tel: 306-798-9800,
www.saskfilm.com
Social Media: www.facebook.com/pages/SaskFilm/148650991834609, twitter.com/saskfilm
Susanne Bell, CEO, Film Commissioner, 306-798-3457, bell@saskfilm.com
Joel Barton, Director, Finance & Operations, 306-798-1291, joel@saskfilm.com

***Regina:* SaskMusic**
#210, 2300 Dewdney Ave., Regina, SK S4R 1H5
Tel: 306-347-0676,
info@saskmusic.org
www.saskmusic.org
John-Paul (J.P.) Ellson, CEO, General Legal Counsel, jpellson@saskmusic.org

***Rouleau:* Rouleau Cable TV**
PO Box 250, Rouleau, SK S0G 4H0
Tel: 306-776-2270, *Fax:* 306-776-2482
Shawn Duncan, President

***Saskatoon:* Askivision Systems Inc.**
826 - 57th St. East, Saskatoon, SK S7K 5Z1
Tel: 519-686-0909, *Fax:* 519-686-1916
Toll-Free: 800-819-9718
cs@aski.ca
www.aski.ca

***Saskatoon:* Image Wireless Communications - a division of YOURLINK Inc.**
204 Cardinal Cres., Saskatoon, SK S7L 6H8
Tel: 306-955-3122, *Fax:* 306-955-3148
Toll-Free: 888-671-5465
moreinfo@yourlink.ca
www.yourlink.ca

***Saskatoon:* Shaw TV - Saskatoon**

Owned by:** Shaw Media Inc.
2326 Hanselman Ave., Saskatoon, SK S7L 5Z3
Tel: 306-665-3796, *Fax:* 306-665-3738
shawtv10@shaw.ca
www.shaw.ca/ShawTV/Saskatoon

***Swift Current:* Shaw TV - Swift Current**
15 Dufferin St. West, Swift Current, SK S9H 5A1
Tel: 306-773-7218, *Fax:* 306-773-6421

***Weyburn:* Access Communications Co-operative Ltd.**
120 - 10th Ave., Weyburn, SK S4H 1G9
Tel: 306-842-0320, *Fax:* 306-842-3465
Toll-Free: 866-363-2225
help@accesscomm.ca
www.accesscomm.ca
Jim Deane, President & CEO
Carmela Haines, Vice-President, Finance & Administration

***Young:* Village of Young**
PO Box 359, Young, SK S0K 4Y0
Tel: 306-259-2242, *Fax:* 306-259-2247
www.young.ca
Robert Speiser, Mayor

Yukon Territory

***Dawson City:* Dawson City Cable**
PO Box 308, Dawson City, YT Y0B 1G0
Tel: 867-993-7400, *Fax:* 867-993-7434

***Whitehorse:* Music Yukon**
#416, 108 Elliott St., Whitehorse, YT Y1A 6C4
Tel: 867-456-8742,
www.musicyukon.com

Specialty Broadcasters

British Columbia

***Burnaby:* Knowledge Network**
4355 Mathissi Pl., Burnaby, BC V5G 4S8
Tel: 604-431-3222, *Fax:* 604-431-3387
Toll-Free: 877-456-6988
info@knowledge.ca
www.knowledgenetwork.ca
Wayne Robert, General Manager

***Richmond:* Talentvision TV**
3300-4151 Hazelbridge Way, Richmond, BC V6X 4J7
Tel: 604-295-1328, *Fax:* 604-295-1300
info@talentvisiontv.com
www.talentvisiontv.com
Joseph Chan

Manitoba

***Winnipeg:* Aboriginal Peoples Television Network**
339 Portage Ave., Winnipeg, MB R3B 2C3
Tel: 204-947-9331, *Fax:* 204-947-9307
Toll-Free: 888-330-2786
info@aptn.ca
www.aptn.ca
Social Media: www.facebook.com/pages/APTN/88781789916
Jean LaRose, CEO
Peter Strutt, Director, Programming
Vera Houle, Director, News & Current Affairs
Ken Earl, Director, Human Resources
Wayne McKenzie, Director, Operations
Sky Bridges, Director, Marketing
Jamie Veilleux, CFO

** For details on this company see listing in Major Broadcasting Companies section; † French language station*

Winnipeg: **Dejaview**

Owned by: *Global National**
#2100, One Lombard Pl., Winnipeg, MB R3B 0X3
Toll-Free: 866-967-3248
feedback@dejaviewtv.ca
www.dejaviewtv.ca

Newfoundland & Labrador

Nain: **Okalakatiget Society Radio**
PO Box 160, Nain, NL A0P 1L0
Tel: 709-922-2187, *Fax:* 709-922-2293
okradio@oksociety.com
www.oksociety.com

Nain: **Okalakatiget Society Television**
PO Box 160, Nain, NL A0P 1L0
Tel: 709-922-2187, *Fax:* 709-922-2293
oktv@oksociety.com
www.oksociety.com

Nova Scotia

Halifax: **Independent Film Channel Canada**

Owned by: *Showcase Television Inc.**
#103, 1649 Brunswick St., Halifax, NS B3J 2G3
Toll-Free: 866-977-3663
IFCCanada@shawmedia.ca
www.ifctv.ca
John Gill, Sr. Vice-President, Drama
Emily Morgan, Vice-President, Programming, Showcase Action, Showcase Diva

Nunavut

Yellowknife: **CBC North**
CBC Mackenzie, PO Box 160, 5002 Forrest Dr., Yellowknife, NWT X1A 2N2
Tel: 867-920-5400, *Toll-Free:* 866-306-4636
www.cbc.ca/north
Social Media: www.facebook.com/group.php?gid=481521000412
Sue Glowach, Senior Officer, Communications, 867-669-3531, Fax: 867-669-3573
Donna Lee, Contact, CBC North News, 867-920-5448

Ontario

Burlington: **CTS - Crossroads TV System**
1295 North Service Rd., Burlington, ON L7R 4X5
Tel: 905-331-7333, *Fax:* 905-332-6005
ontactus@ctstv.com
www.ctstv.com
Rob Sheppard, Program Manager, rsheppard@ctstv.com

Hamilton: **SHOPTV Canada**
44 Frid St., 3rd Fl., Hamilton, ON L8N 3G3
Tel: 905-526-4600, *Fax:* 905-526-3698
info@tmgtv.ca
www.shoptvcanada.com

Mississauga: **BITE Television**

Owned by: *GlassBOX Television Inc.**
2196 Dunwin Dr., Mississauga, ON L5L 1C7
info@bite.ca
www.bitetv.ca
Social Media: www.facebook.com/bitetv, twitter.com/BiteTV
Jeffrey Elliot, Co-CEO/Manager, Marketing & Sales
Raja Khanna, Co-CEO, Finance
Simon Foster, Director, Sales, 905-828-2483, simon@glassbox.tv
Sharon Stevens, Director, Programming, 905-828-2483, sharon@glassbox.tv

Mississauga: **Shaw Broadcast Services**

Owned by: *Shaw Media Inc.**
2055 Flavelle Blvd., Mississauga, ON L5K 1Z8
Tel: 905-403-2020, *Fax:* 905-403-2022
Toll-Free: 800-268-2943
www.shawbroadcast.com

Mississauga: **The Shopping Channel**
59 Ambassador Dr., Mississauga, ON L5T 2P9
Tel: 905-362-2020, *Toll-Free:* 888-202-0888
www.theshoppingchannel.com

Newmarket: **Asian Television Network**
130 Pony Dr., Newmarket, ON L3Y 7B6
Tel: 905-836-6460, *Fax:* 905-853-5212
atn@asiantelevision.com
www.asiantelevision.com
Shan Chandrasekar, President/CEO/Founder
Jaya Chandrasekar, Executive Vice-President/Vice-President, Programming
Prakash Naidoo, Vice-President, Operations/General Manager

North York: **Telelatino Network Inc.**
5125 Steeles Ave. West, North York, ON M9L 1R5
Tel: 416-744-8200, *Fax:* 416-744-0966
Toll-Free: 800-551-8401
info@tlntv.com
www.tlntv.com
Social Media: www.facebook.com/TLNTelelatino, twitter.com/TLNTV
Aldo DiFelice, President

Oakville: **The Weather Network**
2655 Bristol Circle, Oakville, ON L6H 7W1
Tel: 905-829-1159, *Fax:* 905-829-5800
www.theweathernetwork.com
Pierre L. Morrissette

Ottawa: **CPAC**
PO Box 81099, Ottawa, ON K1P 1B1
Tel: 613-567-2722, *Fax:* 613-567-2741
Toll-Free: 877-287-2722
www.cpac.ca

Toronto: **Adult Swim**

Owned by: *TELETOON Canada Inc.**
c/o TELETOON Canada Inc., PO Box 787, 181 Bay St., Toronto, ON M5J 2T3
Tel: 416-956-2060, *Fax:* 416-956-2070
www.adultswimcanada.com
Social Media: www.facebook.com/AdultSwimCAN, twitter.com/AdultSwimCAN

Toronto: **Animal Planet**

Owned by: *Bell Media Inc.**
9 Channel Nine Ct., Toronto, ON M1S 4B5
Tel: 416-332-5000, *Fax:* 416-332-4230
comments@animalplanet.ca
www.animalplanet.ca
Social Media: twitter.com/animalplanetca

Toronto: **BBC Canada**
#200, 121 Bloor St. East, Toronto, ON M4W 3M5
Tel: 416-967-3249, *Fax:* 416-967-0044
Toll-Free: 866-813-3222
www.bbccanada.com

Toronto: **BBC Kids**
#200, 121 Bloor St. East, Toronto, ON M4W 3M5
Tel: 416-967-3250, *Toll-Free:* 866-322-2543
www.bbckids.ca

Toronto: **The Biography Channel**
545 Lakeshore Blvd. West, Toronto, ON M5V 1A3
Toll-Free: 866-260-0033
www.thebiographychannel.ca
Joe Hurley, Vice-President, 416-764-6420, joe.hurley@rci.rogers.com
Kamaldi Badlu, Sales Specialist, 416-764-6836, kamaldi.badlu@rci.rogers.com

Toronto: **BookTelevision**

Owned by: *Bell Media Inc.**
299 Queen St. West, Toronto, ON M5V 2Z5
Tel: 416-591-7400, *Fax:* 416-591-5117
info@booktelevision.com
www.booktelevision.com
Catherine McCutcheon, Director, Specialty Sales, CTVglobemedia, sales@ctv.ca

Toronto: **BPM: TV**
105 Gordon Baker Rd., 8th Fl., Toronto, ON M2H 3P8
Tel: 416-756-2404, *Fax:* 416-756-5526
info@bpmtv.com
www.bpmtv.com
Social Media: www.facebook.com/bpmtv, twitter.com/bpmtv

Kate Tinnerman, Marketing/Advertising/Distributor Relations, ktinnerman@stornoway.com
David Vowell, Director, Marketing, dvowell@stornoway.com
Cindy Boyd, Operations Manager, cboyd@stornoway.com

Toronto: **Bravo! The New Style Arts Channel**

Owned by: *Bell Media Inc.**
299 Queen St. West, Toronto, ON M5V 2Z5
bravomail@bravo.ca
www.bravo.ca
Social Media: www.facebook.com/bravoCanada

Toronto: **Business News Network**
299 Queen St. West, Toronto, ON M5V 2Z5
Tel: 416-957-8100, *Fax:* 416-657-8181
info@bnn.ca
www.bnn.ca

Toronto: **Cartoon Network**

Owned by: *TELETOON Canada Inc.**
c/o TELETOON Canada Inc., PO Box 787, 181 Bay St., Toronto, ON M5J 2T3
Tel: 416-956-2060, *Fax:* 416-956-2070
www.cartoonnetwork.ca
Social Media: www.facebook.com/cartoonnetworkCAN

Toronto: **CBC News Network**

Owned by: *Canadian Broadcasting Corporation (CBC)**
PO Box 500 A, Toronto, ON M5W 1E6
Toll-Free: 866-306-4636
www.cbc.ca/news; www.cbc.ca/programguide/daily/today/cbc_news_network
Social Media: www.facebook.com/newscbc; www.twitter.com/cbcnews,
Other information: TTY: 1-866-220-6045
Roger Ramalsingh, Affiliate Relations Officer

Toronto: **The Comedy Network**

Owned by: *Bell Media Inc.**
9 Channel Nine Ct., Toronto, ON M1S 4B5
Tel: 416-332-5300, *Fax:* 416-332-5301
mail@thecomedynetwork.ca
www.thecomedynetwork.ca
Social Media: www.facebook.com/comedynetwork, twitter.com/comedynetwork
Ed Robinson, President & General Manager

Toronto: **Country Music Television**

Owned by: *Corus Entertainment Inc.**
#18, 64 Jefferson Ave., Toronto, ON M6K 3H4
www.cmt.ca
Social Media: facebook.com/CMTCanada, twitter.com/CMTCanada

Toronto: **CP24**

Owned by: *Bell Media Inc.**
299 Queen St. West, Toronto, ON M5V 2Z5
Tel: 416-591-5757, *Fax:* 416-593-6397
now@cp24.com
www.cp24.com

Toronto: **CTV News Channel**

Owned by: *Bell Media Inc.**
9 Channel Nine Ct., Toronto, ON M1S 4B5
Tel: 416-384-5000,
ctvcommunications@ctv.ca
www.ctv.ca/newschannel/

Toronto: **The Discovery Channel**
PO Box 1200, 9 Channel Nine Ct., Toronto, ON M1S 5R6
Tel: 416-332-5000,
comments@discovery.ca
discoverychannel.ca

Toronto: **Discovery Health Channel**

Owned by: *Shaw Media Inc.**
Toronto, ON
Toll-Free: 866-967-3248
health.discovery.com
Social Media: www.facebook.com/DiscoveryHealth, twitter.com/disc_health

* *For details on this company see listing in Major Broadcasting Companies section; † French language station*

***Toronto:* Discovery Science**

Owned by:* Bell Media Inc.
PO Box 1200, 9 Channel Nine Ct., Toronto, ON M1S 4R6
Tel: 416-332-5000, *Fax:* 416-332-4245
comments@discoverycivilization.ca
discoverycivilization.ca

***Toronto:* Distribution Access**
#702, 27 Queen St. East, Toronto, ON M5C 2M6
Tel: 416-363-6765, *Fax:* 416-363-7834
ontariosales@distributionaccess.com
www.distributionaccess.com/new/main.cfm
Doug Connolly, President/COO,
doug.connolly@distributionaccess.com
Peter Palframan, CEO/Secretary-Treasurer

***Toronto:* DIY Network**

Owned by:* Home & Garden TV
Toronto, ON

www.diynetwork.com

***Toronto:* DIY Network**
#200, 121 Bloor St. East, Toronto, ON M4W 3M5
Tel: 416-967-3260, *Fax:* 416-960-0971
Toll-Free: 866-967-4488
feedback@diy.ca
www.diy.ca

***Toronto:* documentary**
PO Box 500 A, Toronto, ON M6W 1E6
Toll-Free: 866-306-4636
www.cbc.ca/documentarychannel/
Michael Burns, Director of Programming

***Toronto:* ESPN Classic Canada**

Owned by:* Bell Media Inc.
9 Channel Nine Ct., Toronto, ON M1S 4B5

www.tsn.ca/classic

***Toronto:* The Family Channel Inc.**

Owned by:* Corus Entertainment Inc.
Brookfield Place, PO Box 787, 181 Bay St., Toronto, ON M5J 2T3
Tel: 416-956-2030, *Fax:* 416-956-2035
Toll-Free: 800-893-4862
info@family.ca
www.family.ca
Joe Tedesco, Vice-President & General Manager

***Toronto:* Fashion TV**

Owned by:* Bell Media Inc.
299 Queen St. West, Toronto, ON M5V 2Z5
Tel: 416-384-7400, *Fax:* 416-384-0080
fashiontelevision@ctv.ca
www.fashiontelevision.com

***Toronto:* Food Network Canada**

Owned by:* Shaw Media Inc.
121 Bloor St. East, Toronto, ON M4W 3M5

www.foodnetwork.ca

***Toronto:* G4techTV**
545 Lakeshore Blvd. West, Toronto, ON M5V 1A3
www.g4techtv.ca
Social Media: www.facebook.com/G4TVCanada,
twitter.com/G4TVCanada
Andrea Gagliardi, Director, Consumer Marketing & Public Relations
Malcolm Dunlop, Vice-President, Marketing & Programming

***Toronto:* Grace TV**
190 Railside Rd., Toronto, ON M3A 1A3
Tel: 416-497-4940, *Fax:* 416-497-3987
info@gracetelevision.net
gracetelevision.net
Mark Prasuhn, President & General Manager

***Toronto:* History Television Inc.**

Owned by:* Shaw Media Inc.
#200, 121 Bloor St. East, Toronto, ON M4W 3M5
Tel: 416-967-3252, *Fax:* 416-960-0971
www.history.ca
Phyllis Yaffe, President/CEO
Bill Dawson, Senior Vice-President

***Toronto:* HPItv Canada**
555 Rexdale Blcd., Toronto, ON M9W 5L2
Tel: 416-675-8886, *Fax:* 416-213-2130
Toll-Free: 888-675-8886
hpi@WoodbineEntertainment.com
www.horseplayerinteractive.com

***Toronto:* HPItv International**
555 Rexdale Blvd., Toronto, ON M9W 5L2
Tel: 416-675-8886, *Fax:* 416-213-2130
www.horseplayerinteractive.com

***Toronto:* HPItv Odds**
PO Box 156, 555 Rexdale Blvd., Toronto, ON M9W 5L2
Tel: 416-675-8886,
www.horseplayerinteractive.com

***Toronto:* HPItv West**
555 Rexdale Blvd., Toronto, ON M9W 5L2
Tel: 416-675-3993, *Fax:* 416-213-2138
www.horseplayerinteractive.com

***Toronto:* Ichannel**
Stornoway Communications, #800, 105 Gordon Baker Rd., Toronto, ON M2G 3R6
Tel: 416-756-2404, *Fax:* 416-756-5526
comments@ichannel.ca
www.ichannel.ca

***Toronto:* Investigation Discovery**
Toronto, ON

comments@investigationdiscovery.ca
www.investigationdiscovery.ca

***Toronto:* Leafs TV**
#500, 50 Bay St., Toronto, ON M5J 2L2
Tel: 416-815-5400, *Fax:* 416-851-6050
mapleleafs.nhl.com

***Toronto:* Movie Central**

Owned by:* Corus Entertainment Inc.
Corus Quay, 25 Dockside Dr., Toronto, ON M5A 0B5
Tel: 416-479-6784,
info@moviecentral.ca
www.moviecentral.ca
Social Media: www.facebook.com/moviecentral,
twitter.com/moviecentral

***Toronto:* The Movie Network**

***Owned by:* Astral Media Inc.**
BCE Place, PO Box 787, #100, 181 Bay St., Toronto, ON M5M 3G5
Tel: 416-956-2010, *Fax:* 416-956-2018
Toll-Free: 800-565-6684
www.themovienetwork.ca

***Toronto:* Movieola - The Short Film Channel**
2844 Dundas St. West, Toronto, ON M6P 1Y7
Tel: 416-492-1595, *Fax:* 416-492-9539
info@movieola.ca
www.movieola.ca
Romen Podzyhun, Chairman & CEO

***Toronto:* MOVIEPIX**

Owned by:* Astral Media Inc.
PO Box 787, #100, 181 Bay St., Toronto, ON M5J 2T3
Tel: 416-956-2010, *Fax:* 416-956-2018
www.mpix.ca
Karen Spierkel, Vice-President, Communications
Lisa de Wilde, President & CEO

***Toronto:* MTV Canada**

Owned by:* Bell Media Inc.
888 Yonge St., Toronto, ON M4W 2J2
Toll-Free: 866-536-5483
feedback@mtv.ca
www.mtv.ca
Social Media: www.facebook.com/MTVCanada,
twitter.com/mtvcanada

***Toronto:* MuchLOUD**

Owned by:* Bell Media Inc.
299 Queen St. West, Toronto, ON M5V 2Z5
Tel: 416-591-7400,
muchloud@muchmusic.com
www.muchloud.com

***Toronto:* MuchMore Music**

Owned by:* Bell Media Inc.
299 Queen St. West, Toronto, ON M5V 2Z5
Tel: 416-591-5757,
muchmoremail@muchmusic.com
www.muchmoremusic.com
Social Media: twitter.com/MuchMore

***Toronto:* MuchMoreRetro**

Owned by:* Bell Media Inc.
299 Queen St. West, Toronto, ON M5V 2Z5

www.muchmoreretro.com
Other information: TTY: 416-340-7207

***Toronto:* MuchMusic**

Owned by:* Bell Media Inc.
299 Queen St. West, Toronto, ON M5V 2Z5
Fax: 416-384-6824
Toll-Free: 800-265-6824
muchmail@muchmusic.com
www.muchmusic.com
Denise Donlon, Vice-President/General Manager

***Toronto:* MuchVibe**

Owned by:* Bell Media Inc.
299 Queen St. West, Toronto, ON M5V 2Z5
Tel: 416-591-5757,
muchvibe@muchmusic.com
www.muchvibe.ca

***Toronto:* National Geographic Channel**
#200, 121 Bloor St. East, Toronto, ON M4W 3M5
Tel: 416-967-3251, *Toll-Free:* 866-967-3251
www.nationalgeographic.ca
Social Media: www.facebook.com/NatGeoWildCanada

***Toronto:* NHL Network**
9 Channel Nine Ct., Toronto, ON M1S 4B5

www.nhl.com
Social Media: twitter.com/NHLNETWORK

***Toronto:* Odyssey**
#300, 437 Danforth Ave., Toronto, ON M4K 1P1
Tel: 416-462-1200, *Fax:* 416-462-1818
info@odysseytv.ca
www.odysseytv.ca
Peter Maniatakos

***Toronto:* One: the Body, Mind & Spirit Channel**
The Brand New ONE, 64 Jefferson Ave., Toronto, ON M6K 1Y4
Tel: 416-368-3194, *Fax:* 416-368-9774
www.onebodymindspirit.com
Social Media: www.facebook.com/thebrandnewone
Bill Roberts, Chair/CEO
Mark Prasuhn, General Manager/COO

***Toronto:* Ontario Legislature Broadcast & Recording Service**
Legislative Bldg., Queen's Park, Toronto, ON M7A 1A2
Tel: 416-325-7500, *Fax:* 416-325-9426
www.ontla.on.ca
Other information: TTY: 416-325-9426
Bill Somerville

***Toronto:* Outdoor Life Network Canada**

Owned by:* Rogers Broadcasting Ltd.
9 Channel Nine Ct., Toronto, ON M1S 4B5
Tel: 416-332-7660, *Fax:* 416-332-5861
olncanada@ctv.ca
www.tsn.ca/oln

***Toronto:* OUTtv**
130 Merton St., 2nd Fl., Toronto, ON M4S 1A4

www.outtv.ca

** For details on this company see listing in Major Broadcasting Companies section; † French language station*

***Toronto:* The Pet Network**
105 Gordon Baker Rd., Toronto, ON M2H 3R6
Tel: 416-756-2404, *Fax:* 416-756-5526
comments@thepetnetwork.tv
www.thepetnetwork.tv
Social Media: www.facebook.com/mypetnetwork, twitter.com/mypetnetwork

***Toronto:* Raptors NBA TV**
307 Lakeshore Blvd. East, Toronto, ON M5A 1C1
Tel: 416-366-3865,
www.nba.com/raptors
Social Media: www.facebook.com/TorontoRaptors

***Toronto:* The Score Television Network**
PO Box 10, #435, 370 King St. West, Toronto, ON M5V 1J9
Tel: 416-977-6787, *Fax:* 416-977-7851
www.thescore.ca
Social Media: www.facebook.com/thescore, twitter.com/theScore

***Toronto:* Showcase Action**

Owned by: *Showcase Television Inc.**
#200, 121 Bloor St. East, Toronto, ON M4W 3M5
Tel: 416-967-3254, *Fax:* 416-967-0044
Toll-Free: 866-977-3663
feedback@showcase.ca
www.action-tv.ca

***Toronto:* Showcase Diva**

Owned by: *Showcase Television Inc.**
121 Bloor St. East, Toronto, ON M4S 3M5
Toll-Free: 866-977-3663
feedback@showcase.ca
www.diva-tv.ca

***Toronto:* Silver Screen Classics**
2844 Dundas St. West, Toronto, ON M6P 1Y7
Tel: 416-492-1595, *Fax:* 416-492-9539
info@silverscreenclassics.ca
www.silverscreenclassics.com

***Toronto:* Slice**

Owned by: *Shaw Media Inc.**
#1500, 121 Bloor St. East, Toronto, ON M4W 3M5
Tel: 416-967-0022, *Fax:* 416-960-0971
Toll-Free: 886-457-4433
info@slice.ca
www.slice.ca

***Toronto:* Space - The Imagination Station**

Owned by: *Bell Media Inc.**
299 Queen St. West, Toronto, ON M5V 2Z5
Tel: 416-591-5757, *Fax:* 416-591-6619
innerspace@spacecast.com
www.spacecast.com
Social Media: www.facebook.com/SPACEchannel, twitter.com/spacechannel

***Toronto:* Sports Net**
One Mount Pleasant Rd., Toronto, ON M4Y 3A1
Toll-Free: 888-451-6363
www.sportsnet.ca

***Toronto:* The Sports Network**

Owned by: *Bell Media Inc.**
9 Channel Nine Ct., Toronto, ON M1S 4B5
Tel: 416-332-5000,
webmaster@tsn.ca
www.tsn.ca

***Toronto:* Sundance Channel**
Corus Quay, 25 Dockside Dr., Toronto, ON M5A 0B5
Tel: 416-479-6785,
info@sundancechannel.ca
www.sundancechannel.ca
Social Media: www.facebook.com/sundancecanada, twitter.com/sundancecanada
Other information: TTY: 416-214-0110

***Toronto:* Teletoon At Night**

Owned by: *TELETOON Canada Inc.**
c/o TELETOON Canada Inc., PO Box 787, 181 Bay St., Toronto, ON M5J 2T3
Tel: 416-956-2060, *Fax:* 416-956-2070
teletoonatnight.com
Social Media: www.facebook.com/TeletoonAtNight

***Toronto:* Teletoon Retro**

Owned by: *TELETOON Canada Inc.**
c/o TELETOON Canada Inc., PO Box 787, 181 Bay St., Toronto, ON M5J 2T3
Tel: 416-956-2060, *Fax:* 416-956-2070
teletoonretro.com

†*Toronto:* TFO
CP 3005 F, 21, rue College, Toronto, ON M4Y 2M5
Tél: 416-484-2636, *Téléc:* 416-484-2705
Ligne sans frais: 800-463-6886
vos_questions@tfo.org
www.tfo.org

***Toronto:* Travel + Escape**
299 Queen St. West, Toronto, ON M5V 2Z5
Tel: 416-384-5000, *Fax:* 416-384-4375
insidetravel@ctv.ca
www.travelandescape.ca

***Toronto:* Treehouse TV**

Owned by: *YTV Canada Inc.**
#18, 64 Jefferson Ave., Toronto, ON M6K 3H3
info@treehousetv.com
www.treehousetv.com

***Toronto:* TVtropolis**

Owned by: *Shaw Media Inc.**
#1700, 250 Yonge St., Toronto, ON M5B 2L7
Toll-Free: 866-967-3248
feedback@tvtropolis.ca
www.tvtropolis.com

***Toronto:* Viewer's Choice Canada**
PO Box 787, #100, 181 Bay St., Toronto, ON M5J 2T3
Tel: 416-565-2010, *Toll-Free:* 800-565-6684
www.viewerschoice.ca
Other information: TTY/TDD: 416-956-2083

***Toronto:* Vision TV**
64 Jefferson Ave., Toronto, ON M6K 1Y4
Tel: 416-368-3194, *Fax:* 416-368-9774
Toll-Free: 888-321-2567
visiontv@visiontv.ca
www.visiontv.ca

Bill Roberts, President & CEO

***Toronto:* W Network**

Owned by: *Corus Entertainment Inc.**
Corus Quay, 25 Dockside Dr., Toronto, ON M5A 0B5
Tel: 416-479-6786,
www.wnetwork.com

John Cassidy, President & CEO

Québec

†*Longueuil:* Canal Evasion
992, rue Joliette, Longueuil, QC J4K 4V9
Tél: 450-677-0054, *Téléc:* 450-677-9964
www.evasion.tv
Médias sociaux: www.facebook.com/Evasion.tv?ref=ts, twitter.com/Evasion_tv

Christine Hill, Directrice générale
Chantal Fortier, Directrice de la programmation
Michel Chamberland, Président et chef de la direction

†*Montréal:* ARGENT
1600, boul de Maisonneuve est, Montréal, QC H2L 4P2
relations.auditoire@tva.ca
www.argent.canoe.com; tva.canoe.ca
Médias sociaux: twitter.com/GeorgesPothier

Yves Daoust, Directeur général

†*Montréal:* ARTV
#A 53-1, 1400, boul René-Lévesque est, Montréal, QC H2L 2M2
Tél: 514-597-3636, *Téléc:* 514-597-3633
Ligne sans frais: 800-363-3307
www.artv.ca
Médias sociaux: www.facebook.com/artv.ca

Marie Côté, Directrice générale

†*Montréal:* Canal D
#1600, 1800, ave. McGill College, Montréal, QC H3A 3J6
Tél: 514-983-3330, *Ligne sans frais:* 800-361-5194
info@chaines.astral.com
www.canald.com

Sylvain Beauregard, Director, Communications
Jean-Pierre Laurendeau, Vice-President, Programming
Judith Brosseau, Sr. Vice-President, Programming & Communications

***Montréal:* Canal Indigo**
#900, 2100, rue Sainte-Catherine ouest, Montréal, QC H3H 2T3
Tel: 514-939-5090,
info@canalindigo.com
www.canalindigo.com

Johanne Saint-Laurent, Vice-président et Directeur général, Astral Télé Reseaux

†*Montréal:* Le Canal Nouvelles TVA (LCN)
1600, boul de Maisonneuve est, Montréal, QC H2L 4P2
Tél: 514-598-2869, *Téléc:* 514-598-6073
nouvelles@tva.ca
tvanouvelles.ca

Martin Cloutier, Dir.-gén., LCN et Argent

†*Montréal:* Canal Savoir
Canal Savoir, 2200, rue Sainte-Catherine Est, 1e etage, Montréal, QC H2K 2J1
Tél: 514-509-2222, *Téléc:* 514-509-2299
Ligne sans frais: 888-640-2626
info@canalsavoir.tv
www.canalsavoir.tv

Sylvie Godbout, General Director, sgodbout@canalsavoir.tv

†*Montréal:* Canal Vie
#1600, 1800, ave. McGill College, Montréal, QC H3A 3J6
Tél: 514-938-3330,
auditoire@canalvie.com
www.canalvie.com

Véronique Lussier, Director, Communications
Lyne Denault, Vice-President, Programming
Marie Collin, Sr. Vice-President, Programming & Communications

†*Montréal:* Les Chaines Télé Astral
#1600, 1800, av McGill College, Montréal, QC H3A 3J6
Tél: 514-938-3320,
www.astral.com

Nathalie Roy, Relationniste, Canal Vie/Historia, nroy@chaines.astral.com
Christine Marceau, Relationniste, Canal D/Séries+, cmarceau@chaines.astral.com
Ian Greenberg, Président/Chef de la direction, Astral Media inc.
André Bureau, Président du Conseil, Astral Media inc.

***Montréal:* Galaxie, Your Musical Universe**
730, rue Wellington, Montréal, QC H3C 1T4
Fax: 514-664-1143
Toll-Free: 877-425-2943
www.galaxie.ca
Social Media: www.facebook.com/GalaxieMusic, www.twitter.com/galaxiemusic

†*Montréal:* Historia
Détenteur: **Astral Broadcasting Group Inc.***
#1600, 1800, ave. McGill College, Montréal, QC H3A 3J6
Tél: 514-938-3330, *Ligne sans frais:* 800-361-5194
info@chaines.astral.com
www.historiatv.com

Judith Brosseau, Sr. Vice-President, Programming & Communications
Fabrice Brasier, Vice-President, Programming
Sophie Dufort, Director, Communications

†*Montréal:* MétéoMédia
#251, 1755, boul René-Lévesque est, Montréal, QC H2K 4P6
Tél: 514-597-0232, *Téléc:* 514-597-1591
www.meteomedia.com

** For details on this company see listing in Major Broadcasting Companies section; † French language station*

***Montréal:* MusiMax**
MusiquePlus / MusiMax, 355, rue Ste-Catherine ouest, Montréal, QC H3B 1A5
Tel: 514-284-7587, *Fax:* 514-284-1889
auditoire@musimax.com
www.musimax.com

†*Montréal:* MusiquePlus
Détenteur: **Astral Broadcasting Group Inc.***
355, rue Ste-Catherine ouest, Montréal, QC H3B 1A5
Tél: 514-284-7587, *Téléc:* 514-284-1889
www.musiqueplus.com; www.musimax.com; www.astral.com
Ian Greenberg, Président/Chef de la direction, Astral Media inc.

†*Montréal:* Quebecor Media inc.
612, rue St-Jacques, Montréal, QC H3C 4M8
www.quebecor.com
Pierre Karl Péladeau, Président/Chef de la direction

†*Montréal:* RDI - Le réseau de l'information
CP 6000 Centre-Ville, 1400, boul René-Lévesque est, Montréal, QC H3C 3A8
Tél: 514-597-6000,
rdi@montreal.radio-canada.ca
radio-canada.com
Médias sociaux: www.facebook.com/radiocanada.info, twitter.com/RadioCanadaInfo
Martin Cloutier, Director
Gilles Desjardins, Director, Business Development

***Montréal:* Le Réseau des Sports**
#300, 1755, boul René-Lévesque est, Montréal, QC H2K 4P6
Tel: 514-599-2244, *Fax:* 514-599-2299
Toll-Free: 888-737-6363
info@rds.ca
www.rds.ca
Gerry Frappier, President & General Manager

†*Montréal:* Séries+
Détenteur: **Astral Broadcasting Group Inc.***
#1600, 1800, av McGill College, Montréal, QC H3A 3J6
Tél: 514-939-3150, *Téléc:* 514-939-3151
info@chaines.astral.com
www.astral.com
Ian Greenberg, Président/Chef de la direction, Astral Media inc.
André Bureau, Président du Conseil, Astral Media inc.

***Montréal:* Super Écran**
#1600, 1800, ave McGill College, Montréal, QC H3A 3J6
Toll-Free: 877-873-7327
redaction@superecran.com
www.superecran.com
Pierre Roy, Président et chef de la direction

†*Montréal:* TV5 Québec Canada
#101, 1755, boul René-Lévesque est, Montréal, QC H2K 4P6
Tél: 514-522-5322, *Téléc:* 514-522-6572
Ligne sans frais: 877-522-6660
info@tv5.ca
www.tv5.ca
Suzanne Gouin, Présidente/Directrice générale

***Montréal:* Vrak.TV**
2100, rue Ste-Catherine ouest, Montréal, QC H3H 2T3
www.vrak.tv
Véronique Lussier, Director, Communications
Marie Collin, Sr. Vice-President, Programming & Communications
Denis Dubois, Vice-President, Programming

†*Montréal:* Ztélé
Détenteur: **Astral Broadcasting Group Inc.***
a/s Astral Media, #1600, 1800, av McGill College, Montréal, QC H3A 3J6
Tél: 514-939-3150, *Téléc:* 514-939-3151
info@chaines.astral.com
www.ztele.com; www.astral.com
Médias sociaux: www.facebook.com/ztele
Ian Greenberg, Président/Chef de la direction, Astral Media inc.
André Bureau, Président du conseil, Astral Media inc.
Sidney Greenberg, Vice-Président, Astral Media inc.

†*Québec:* Assemblée nationale du Québec - Canal de l'Assemblée
Édifice Pamphile-Le May, #211, Direction de la diffusion des débats, Québec, QC G1A 1A3
Tél: 418-643-4272, *Téléc:* 418-646-8498
diffusion.debats@assnat.qc.ca
www.assnat.qc.ca
Martin-Philippe Côté, Directeur

** For details on this company see listing in Major Broadcasting Companies section; † French language station*

SECTION 5
BUSINESS & FINANCE

The listings in this section are arranged alphabetically unless otherwise indicated below.

Accounting Firms

Major Accounting Firms

BDO Dunwoody LLP

#600, 36 Toronto St.
Toronto, ON M5C 2C5

Tel: 416-865-0111; Fax: 416-367-3912
national@bdo.ca
www.bdo.ca
Social Media: www.facebook.com/BDOCanada; twitter.com/BDO_Canada

Ownership: Private
Year Founded: 1921
Number of Employees: 3,000
Revenues: 393 million Year End: 20101231
Profile: Canada's sixth-largest accounting firm concentrates on the special needs of independent business & community-based organizations. The firm provides a full range of comprehensive business advisory services.
Executives:
Keith Farlinger, Chief Executive Officer
Russ Weir, Chief Operating Officer
Ronn Watts, Chief Financial Officer
Offices:

Abbotsford
#100, 2890 Garden St.
Abbotsford, BC V2T 4W7 Canada
Tel: 604-853-6677; Fax: 604-853-4876
abbotsford@bdo.ca
Donald Gillialand, Partner

Alexandria
55 Anik St.
Alexandria, ON K0C 1A0 Canada
Tel: 613-525-1585; Fax: 613-525-1436
alexandria@bdo.ca

Alfred
PO Box 539
497 St-Philippe St.
Alfred, ON K0B 1A0 Canada
Tel: 613-679-1332; Fax: 613-679-1801
alfred@bdo.ca

Alliston
#13, 169 Dufferin St. South
Alliston, ON L9R 1E6 Canada
Tel: 705-435-5585; Fax: 705-435-5587
alliston@bdo.ca

Altona
26 Centre Ave. East
Altona, MB R0G 0B0 Canada
Tel: 204-324-8653; Fax: 204-324-1629
altona@bdo.ca
Robert Martins, Partner

Barrie
#300, 300 Lakeshore Dr.
Barrie, ON L4N 0B4 Canada
Tel: 705-726-6331; Fax: 705-722-6588
barrie@bdo.ca

Boissevain
372 South Railway St.
Boissevain, MB R0K 0E0 Canada
Tel: 204-534-6935
boissevain@bdo.ca
Tony DeVligere, Partner & Trustee

Bracebridge
#1, 239 Manitoba St.
Bracebridge, ON P1L 1S2 Canada
Tel: 705-645-5215; Fax: 705-645-8125
bracebridge@bdo.ca

Brandon
117 - 10th St.
Brandon, MB R7A 4E7 Canada
Tel: 204-727-0671; Fax: 204-726-4580
brandon@bdo.ca
Tony DeVliegere, Partner & Trustee

Brantford
#110B, 325 West St.
Brantford, ON N3R 3V6 Canada
Tel: 519-759-8320; Fax: 519-759-8421
brantford@bdo.ca

Calgary
#1900, 801 - 6 Ave. SW
Calgary, AB T2P 3W2 Canada
Tel: 403-266-5608; Fax: 403-233-7833
calgary@bdo.ca
Richard Edwards, Partner & Senior Vice-President

Cambridge
764 King St. East
Cambridge, ON N3H 3N9
Tel: 519-653-7126; Fax: 519-653-8218
cambridge@bdo.ca
Don Laird, Chartered Accountant

Cardston
259 Main St.
Cardston, AB T0K OKO Canada
Tel: 403-653-4137
cardston@bdo.ca

Charlottetown
PO Box 2158
91 Water St.
Charlottetown, PE C1A 1A5 Canada
Tel: 902-892-5365; Fax: 902-892-0383

Chatham
375 St. Clair St.
Chatham, ON N7L 3K3 Canada
Tel: 519-354-1560; Fax: 519-354-9346
chatham@bdo.ca

Cobourg
PO Box 627
204 Division St.
Cobourg, ON K9A 3P7 Canada
Tel: 905-372-6863; Fax: 905-372-6650
cobourg@bdo.ca

Collingwood
#202, 186 Hurontario St.
Collingwood, ON L9Y 3Z5 Canada
Tel: 705-445-4421; Fax: 705-445-6691
collingwood@bdo.ca
Pierre Vaillancourt, Partner

Cornwall
PO Box 644
113 Second St. East
Cornwall, ON K6H 1Y5 Canada
Tel: 613-932-8691; Fax: 613-932-7591
cornwall@bdo.ca

Cranbrook
#200, 35 - 10 Ave. South
Cranbrook, BC V1C 2M9 Canada
Tel: 250-426-4285; Fax: 250-426-8886
cranbrook@bdo.ca
Harley Lee, Partner; 250-426-4285

Dryden
37 King St.
Dryden, ON P8N 1B4 Canada
Tel: 807-223-5321; Fax: 807-223-2978
dryden@bdo.ca

Edmonton
First Edmonton Pl.
#1000, 10665 Jasper Ave. NW
Edmonton, AB T5J 3S9 Canada
Tel: 780-423-4353; Fax: 780-424-2110
edmonton@bdo.ca

Embrun
PO Box 128
991 Limoges Rd.
Embrun, ON K0A 1W0 Canada
Tel: 613-443-5201; Fax: 613-443-2538
embrun@bdo.ca

Essex
180 Talbot St. South
Essex, ON N8M 1B6 Canada
Tel: 519-776-6488; Fax: 519-776-6090
essex@bdo.ca

Fort Frances
375 Scott St.
Fort Frances, ON P9A 1H1 Canada
Tel: 807-274-9848; Fax: 807-274-5142
fortfrances@bdo.ca
Marie Allan, Partner

Golden
PO Box 1709
#205, 421 - 9th Ave. North
Golden, BC V0A 1H0 Canada
Tel: 250-344-5845; Fax: 250-344-7131
golden@bdo.ca
John Wilkey, Partner

Grande Prairie
Grande Prairie Place
9909 - 102 St., 5th Fl.
Grande Prairie, AB T8V 2V4 Canada
Tel: 780-539-7075; Fax: 780-538-1890
grandeprairie@bdo.ca
Don Blonke, Partner

Guelph
#201, 660 Speedvale Ave. West
Guelph, ON N1K 1E5 Canada
Tel: 519-824-5410; Fax: 519-824-5497
Toll-Free: 877-236-4835

Hamilton
#2, 505 York Blvd.
Hamilton, ON L8R 3K4 Canada
Tel: 905-525-6800; Fax: 905-525-6566
Toll-Free: 888-236-2383
hamilton@bdo.ca

Hanover
485 - 10th St.
Hanover, ON N4N 1R2 Canada
Tel: 519-364-3790; Fax: 519-364-5334
hanover@bdo.ca

Huntsville
PO Box 5484
2 Elm St.
Huntsville, ON P1H 1L1 Canada
Tel: 705-789-4469; Fax: 705-789-1079
huntsville@bdo.ca

Kamloops
#300, 272 Victoria St.
Kamloops, BC V2C 1Z6 Canada
Tel: 250-372-9505; Fax: 250-374-6323
kamloops@bdo.ca

Kelowna
Landmark Technology Centre
#300, 1632 Dickson Ave.
Kelowna, BC V1Y 7T2 Canada
Tel: 250-763-6700; Fax: 250-763-4457
kelowna@bdo.ca

Kenora
#300, 301 First Ave. South
Kenora, ON P9N 4E9 Canada
Tel: 807-468-5531; Fax: 807-468-9774
kenora@bdo.ca

Kincardine
970 Queen St.
Kincardine, ON N2Z 2Y2 Canada
Tel: 519-396-3425; Fax: 519-396-9829
kincardine@bdo.ca

Kitchener
#501, 305 King St. West
Kitchener, ON N2G 1B9 Canada
Tel: 519-570-4000; Fax: 519-576-5227
kitchenerwaterloo@bdodebthelp.ca

Langley
#220, 19916 - 64th Ave.
Langley, BC V2Y 1A2 Canada
Tel: 604-534-8691; Fax: 604-534-8900
langley@bdo.ca

Lethbridge
Southland Terrace
#200, 220 - 3rd Ave. South
Lethbridge, AB T1J 0G9 Canada
Tel: 403-328-5292; Fax: 403-328-9534
lethbridge@bdo.ca

Lindsay
PO Box 358
165 Kent St. West
Lindsay, ON K9V 4S3 Canada
Tel: 705-324-3579; Fax: 705-324-0774
lindsay@bdo.ca

London
Station Park
#201, 252 Pall Mall St.
London, ON N6A 5P6 Canada
Tel: 519-672-8940; Fax: 519-672-5562
london@bdo.ca

MacGregor
78 Hampton St.
MacGregor, MB R0H 0R0 Canada
Tel: 204-685-2323; Fax: 204-685-2341
macgregor@bdo.ca
Bernard Lapchuk, Partner

Manitou
330 Main St.
Manitou, MB R0G 1G0 Canada
Tel: 204-242-2637
manitou@bdo.ca
Ron Westfall, Partner

Markham
#400, 60 Columbia Way
Markham, ON L3R 0C9 Canada
Tel: 905-946-1066; Fax: 905-946-9524
markham@bdo.ca

Minnedosa
39 Main St. South
Minnedosa, MB R0J 1E0 Canada
Tel: 204-867-2957
minnedosa@bdo.ca
Jeanne Mills, Partner

Mississauga
4255 Sherwoodtowne Blvd.
Mississauga, ON L4Z 1Y5 Canada
Tel: 905-270-7700; Fax: 905-671-7915
mississauga@bdo.ca

Mitchell
PO Box 792
11 Victoria St.
Mitchell, ON N0K 1N0 Canada
Tel: 519-348-8412; Fax: 519-348-4300
mitchell@bdo.ca
Montréal
Westmount Premier
#600, 4150, rue Ste-Catherine ouest
Montréal, QC H3Z 2Y5 Canada
Tel: 514-931-0841; Fax: 514-931-9491
montreal@bdo.ca
Morden
133 - 7th St.
Morden, MB R6M 1S3 Canada
Tel: 204-822-5486; Fax: 204-822-4828
morden@bdo.ca
Sam Andrew, Partner
Mount Forest
PO Box 418
191 Main St. South
Mount Forest, ON N0G 2L0 Canada
Tel: 519-323-2351; Fax: 519-323-3661
mountforest@bco.ca
Nakusp
PO Box 1078
220 Broadway St.
Nakusp, BC V0G 1R0 Canada
Tel: 250-265-4750; Fax: 250-837-7170
nakusp@bdo.ca
Ken Davidson, Partner
Newmarket
Gates of York Plaza
#2, 17310 Yonge St.
Newmarket, ON L3Y 7R8 Canada
Tel: 905-898-1221; Fax: 905-898-0028
Toll-Free: 866-275-8836
newmarket@bdo.ca
Michael Jones, Partner
North Bay
PO Box 20001
142 Main St. West
North Bay, ON P1B 2T5 Canada
Tel: 705-495-2000; Fax: 705-495-2001
Toll-Free: 800-461-6324
northbay@bdo.ca
Oakville
#212, 345 Lakeshore Rd. East
Oakville, ON L6J 1J5 Canada
Tel: 905-849-4149; Fax: 905-615-1333
oakville@bdodebthelp.ca
Orangeville
77 Broadway Ave., 2nd Fl.
Orangeville, ON L9W 1K1 Canada
Tel: 519-938-8630; Fax: 519-372-0189
orangeville@bdodebthelp.ca
Orillia
PO Box 670
19 Front St. North
Orillia, ON L3V 4R6 Canada
Tel: 705-325-1386; Fax: 705-325-6649
orillia@bdo.ca
Oshawa
Oshawa Executive Centre
#502, 419 King St. West
Oshawa, ON L1J 2K5 Canada
Tel: 905-576-3430; Fax: 905-436-9138
oshawa@bdo.ca
Ottawa
#204, 260 Centrum Blvd
Ottawa, ON K1E 3P4 Canada
Tel: 613-837-3300; Fax: 613-837-7733
Toll-Free: 800-754-1579
ottawa@bdo.ca
Owen Sound
PO Box 397
1717 - 2nd Ave. East
Owen Sound, ON N4K 6V4 Canada
Tel: 519-376-6110; Fax: 519-376-4741
owensound@bdo.ca
Penticton
#102, 100 Front St.
Penticton, BC V2A 1H1 Canada
Tel: 250-492-6020; Fax: 250-492-8110
penticton@bdo.ca
Peterborough
PO Box 1018, Main Sta. Main
#202, 201 George St. North
Peterborough, ON K9J 7A5
Tel: 705-742-4271; Fax: 705-742-3420
Toll-Free: 888-369-6600
peterborough@bdo.ca

Petrolia
PO Box 869
4495 Petrolia Line
Petrolia, ON N0N 1R0 Canada
Tel: 519-882-3333; Fax: 519-882-2703
petrolia@bdo.ca
Doug Johnston, Partner
Picture Butte
339 Highway Ave.
Picture Butte, AB T0K 1V0 Canada
Tel: 403-732-4469; Fax: 403-732-5701
picturebutte@bdo.ca
Phillip Wever, Sr. Manager
Port Elgin
PO Box 1390
625 Mill St.
Port Elgin, ON N0H 2C0 Canada
Tel: 519-832-2049; Fax: 519-832-5659
portelgin@bdo.ca
Portage La Prairie
480 Saskatchewan Ave. West
Portage La Prairie, MB R1N 0M4 Canada
Tel: 204-857-2856; Fax: 204-239-1664
portagelaprairie@bdo.ca
John Chapman, Partner; mverwey@bdo.ca
Red Deer
4719 - 48 Ave., 3rd Fl.
Red Deer, AB T4N 3T1 Canada
Tel: 403-346-1566; Fax: 403-343-3070
reddeer@bdo.ca
James Scott, Partner
Red Lake
PO Box 234
207 Discovery Centre
Red Lake, ON P0V 2M0 Canada
Tel: 807-727-3227; Fax: 807-727-1172
redlake@bdo.ca
Revelstoke
PO Box 2100
#202, 103 - 1st St. East
Revelstoke, BC V0E 2S0 Canada
Tel: 250-837-5225; Fax: 250-837-7170
revelstoke@bdo.ca
Ridgetown
211 Main St. East
Ridgetown, ON N0P 2C0 Canada
Tel: 519-674-5418; Fax: 519-674-5410
ridgetown@bdo.ca
Rockland
#5, 2784 Laurier St.
Rockland, ON K4K 1A2 Canada
Tel: 613-446-6497; Fax: 613-446-7117
rockland@bdo.ca
Judith Gratton, Partner
St Pierre Jolys
Place Lavergne
#6, 467, rue Sabourin
St Pierre Jolys, MB R0A 1V0 Canada
Tel: 204-433-7508; Fax: 204-433-7181
saintpierrejolys@bdo.ca
Mona Marcotte, Partner
Salmon Arm
#201, 571 - 6th St. NE
Salmon Arm, BC V1E 1R6 Canada
Tel: 250-832-7171; Fax: 250-832-2429
salmonarm@bdo.ca
Sarnia
PO Box 730
250 Christina St. North
Sarnia, ON N7T 7V3 Canada
Tel: 519-336-9900; Fax: 519-332-4828
sarnia@bdo.ca
Sault Ste Marie
PO Box 1109
747 Queen St. East
Sault Ste Marie, ON P6A 2A8 Canada
Tel: 705-945-0990; Fax: 705-942-7979
ssm@bdo.ca
Selkirk
378 Main St.
Selkirk, MB R1A 1T8 Canada
Tel: 204-482-5626; Fax: 204-482-4969
selkirk@bdo.ca
Bill Findlater, Partner
Sicamous
PO Box 392
314 Finlayson St.
Sicamous, BC V0E 2V0 Canada
Tel: 250-836-4493; Fax: 250-837-7170
sicamous@bdo.ca
Ken Davidson, Partner

Sioux Lookout
PO Box 1239
#1A, 76 1/2 Front St.
Sioux Lookout, ON P8T 1B8 Canada
Tel: 807-737-1500; Fax: 807-737-4443
siouxlookout@bdo.ca
Slave Lake
PO Box 297
#303, Lakeland Centre
Slave Lake, AB T0G 2A0 Canada
Tel: 780-849-3622; Fax: 780-849-3625
slavelake@bdo.ca
Ray McComb, Partner
Sorrento
PO Box 59
#2, 1266 Trans Canada Hwy.
Sorrento, BC V0E 2W0 Canada
Tel: 250-675-3288; Fax: 250-832-2429
sorrento@bdo.ca
Squamish
PO Box 168
#202, 38147 Cleveland Ave.
Squamish, BC V8B 0A2 Canada
Tel: 604-892-9424; Fax: 604-892-9356
squamish@bdo.ca
St-Claude
76 First St.
St-Claude, MB R0G 1Z0 Canada
Tel: 204-379-2332; Toll-Free: 800-268-3337
stclaude@bdo.ca
Henri Magne, Partner
Stratford
134 Waterloo St. South
Stratford, ON N5A 4B4 Canada
Tel: 519-271-2491; Fax: 519-271-4013
stratford@bdo.ca
Montagu J. Smith, Managing Partner
Strathroy
28636 Centre Rd., RR#5
Strathroy, ON N7G 3H6 Canada
Tel: 519-245-1913; Fax: 519-245-5987
strathroy@bdo.ca
Sudbury
#202, 888 Regent St.
Sudbury, ON P3E 6C6 Canada
Tel: 705-671-3336; Fax: 705-671-9552
Toll-Free: 877-820-0404
sudbury@bdo.ca
Summerland
c/o Bell Jacoe & Co.
13211 North Victoria Rd.
Summerland, BC V0H 1Z0 Canada
Tel: 250-494-9255; Fax: 250-494-9755
summerland@bdo.ca
David Braumberger, Partner
Surrey
#200, 15225 - 104 Ave.
Surrey, BC V3R 6Y8 Canada
Tel: 604-584-2121; Fax: 604-584-3823
surrey@bdo.ca
Thunder Bay
1095 Barton St.
Thunder Bay, ON P7B 5N3 Canada
Tel: 807-625-4444; Fax: 807-623-8460
thunderbay@bdo.ca
Tiverton
84 Main St.
Tiverton, ON N0G 2T0 Canada
Tel: 519-368-5331
tiverton@bdo.ca
Toronto
Royal Bank Plaza, 33rd Fl.
PO Box 32
Toronto, ON M5J 2J8 Canada
Tel: 416-865-0200; Fax: 416-865-0887
toronto@bdo.ca
Treherne
274 Railway Ave.
Treherne, MB R0G 2V0 Canada
Tel: 204-723-2454
treherne@bdo.ca
Allan Nichol, Partner
Uxbridge
#1, 1 Brock St. East
Uxbridge, ON L9P 1P6 Canada
Tel: 905-852-9714; Fax: 905-852-9898
uxbridge@bdo.ca
Vancouver
#600, 925 West Georgia St.
Vancouver, BC V6L 3L2 Canada
Tel: 604-688-5421; Fax: 604-688-5132
vancouver@bdo.ca

Vernon
3201 - 30th Ave.
Vernon, BC V1T 2C6 Canada
Tel: 250-545-2136; Fax: 250-545-3364
vernon@bdo.ca
Brian Cockburn, Partner
Virden
PO Box 1900
255 Wellington St. West
Virden, MB R0M 2C0 Canada
Tel: 204-748-1200; Fax: 204-748-1976
virden@bdo.ca
Bob Lawrence, Partner
Vulcan
122 Centre St.
Vulcan, AB T0L 2B0 Canada
Tel: 403-485-2923; Fax: 403-485-6098
vulcan@bdo.ca
Walkerton
PO Box 760
121 Jackson St.
Walkerton, ON N0G 2V0 Canada
Tel: 519-881-1211; Fax: 519-881-3530
walkerton@bdo.ca
Welland
37 Dorothy St.
Welland, ON L3B 3V6 Canada
Tel: 905-735-6433; Fax: 905-735-6514
welland@bdo.ca
Whistler
#104, 1080 Millar Creek Rd.
Whistler, BC V0N 1B1 Canada
Tel: 604-932-3799; Fax: 604-932-3764
whistler@bdo.ca
Theresa Walterhouse, Partner
Whitehorse
#201, 3059 - 3rd Ave.
Whitehorse, YT Y1A 1E2 Canada
Tel: 867-667-7907; Fax: 867-668-3087
whitehorse@bdo.ca
Ben Baartman, Partner
Wiarton
PO Box 249
663 Berford St.
Wiarton, ON N0H 2T0 Canada
Tel: 519-534-1520; Fax: 519-534-3454
wiarton@bdo.ca
Windsor
3630 Rhodes Dr.
Windsor, ON N8W 5A4 Canada
Tel: 519-944-6900; Fax: 519-944-6116
windsor@bdo.ca
Wingham
PO Box 1420
152 Josephine St.
Wingham, ON N0G 2W0 Canada
Tel: 519-357-3231; Fax: 519-357-3230
wingham@bdo.ca
Winkler
#2, 583 Main St.
Winkler, MB R6W 1A4 Canada
Tel: 204-325-4787; Fax: 204-325-8040
winkler@bdo.ca
Frank Wiebe, Partner
Winnipeg
Wawanesa Bldg.
#700, 200 Graham Ave.
Winnipeg, MB R3C 4L5 Canada
Tel: 204-956-7200; Fax: 204-926-7201
winnipeg@bdo.ca
Woodstock
PO Box 757
94 Graham St.
Woodstock, ON N4S 6J7 Canada
Tel: 519-539-2081; Fax: 519-539-2571
woodstock@bdo.ca

Deloitte & Touche LLP

PO Box 8
#1200, 2 Queen St. East
Toronto, ON M5C 3G7
Tel: 416-874-3874; Fax: 416-874-3888
www.deloitte.ca

Ownership: Private partnership; Deloitte in Canada is a member firm of Deloitte Touche Tohmatsu.
Year Founded: 1861
Number of Employees: 5,568
Revenues: $500m-1 billion
Profile: Deloitte & Touche LLP is one of Canada's leading firms, providing a range of auditing, tax, financial advisory, & consulting services. Deloitte's offices in Québec operate under the corporate name Samson Bélair/Deloitte & Touche.
Partners:
John Bowey, Chair
Alan MacGibbon, Managing Partner & CEO
Branches:
Alma
Complexe Jacques Gagnon
#110, 100, rue St-Joseph sud
Alma, QC G8B 7A6 Canada
Tel: 418-669-6969; Fax: 418-668-2966
Amos
#200, 101, av 1re est
Amos, QC J9T 1H4 Canada
Tel: 819-732-8273; Fax: 819-732-9143
Baie-Comeau
1191, boul Laflèche, 2e étage
Baie-Comeau, QC G5C 1E1 Canada
Tel: 418-589-5761; Fax: 418-589-5764
Burlington
#202, 1005 Skyview Dr.
Burlington, ON L7P 5B1 Canada
Tel: 905-315-6770; Fax: 905-315-6700
Toll-Free: 866-836-6770
Calgary
Scotia Centre
#3000, 700 - 2nd St. SW
Calgary, AB T2P 0S7 Canada
Tel: 403-267-1700; Fax: 403-264-2871
Chicoutimi
#400, 901, boul Talbot
Chicoutimi, QC G7H 0A1 Canada
Tel: 418-549-6650; Fax: 418-549-4694
Dolbeau-Mistassini
110, 8e av
Dolbeau-Mistassini, QC G8L 1Y9 Canada
Tel: 418-276-0133; Fax: 418-276-8559
Edmonton
Manulife Place
#2000, 10180 - 101st St.
Edmonton, AB T5J 4E4 Canada
Tel: 780-421-3611; Fax: 780-421-3782
Farnham
149, rue Desjardins est
Farnham, QC J2N 2W6 Canada
Tel: 450-293-5327; Fax: 450-293-2817
Granby
PO Box 356
74, rue Court
Granby, QC J2G 4Y5 Canada
Tel: 450-372-3347; Fax: 450-372-8643
Grand-Mère
PO Box 280
1671, 6e av
Grand-Mère, QC G9T 5K8 Canada
Tel: 819-538-1721; Fax: 819-538-1882
Halifax
Purdy's Wharf Tower II
#1500, 1569 Upper Water St.
Halifax, NS B3J 3R7 Canada
Tel: 902-422-8541; Fax: 902-423-5820
Hawkesbury
300, rue McGill
Hawkesbury, ON K6A 1P8 Canada
Tel: 613-632-4178; Fax: 613-632-7703
Jonquière
Complexe A E Fortin
2266, boul René-Lévesque
Jonquière, QC G7S 6C5 Canada
Tel: 418-542-9523; Fax: 418-542-8814
Kitchener
4210 King St. East
Kitchener, ON N2P 2G5 Canada
Tel: 519-650-7600; Fax: 519-650-7601
La Baie
365, rue Victoria
La Baie, QC G7B 3M5 Canada
Tel: 418-544-7313; Fax: 418-544-0275
La Sarre
226, 2e rue est
La Sarre, QC J9Z 2G9 Canada
Tel: 819-339-5764; Fax: 819-333-2517
Langley
#225, 20316 - 56th Ave.
Langley, BC V3A 3Y7 Canada
Tel: 604-534-7477; Fax: 604-534-4220
Laval
Les Tours Triomphe
#300, 2450, boul Daniel-Johnson
Laval, QC H7T 2S3 Canada
Tel: 514-978-3500; Fax: 514-382-4984
London
One London Place
#700, 255 Queen's Ave.
London, ON N6A 5R8 Canada
Tel: 519-679-1880; Fax: 519-640-4625
Longueuil
Tour Est
#550, 1111, rue St-Charles ouest
Longueuil, QC J4K 5G4 Canada
Tel: 450-670-4270; Fax: 450-670-6420
Magog
#203, 101, rue du Moulin
Magog, QC J1X 4A1 Canada
Tel: 819-843-6596; Fax: 819-843-6931
Markham
#400, 15 Allstate Pkwy.
Markham, ON L3R 5B4 Canada
Tel: 905-948-6200; Fax: 905-948-6250
Matane
750, av du Phare ouest
Matane, QC G4W 3W8 Canada
Tel: 418-566-2637; Fax: 418-566-2839
Mississauga - Britannia Rd. East
#132, 425 Britannia Rd. East
Mississauga, ON L4Z 3E7 Canada
Tel: 416-601-6150; Fax: 416-601-6151
Mississauga - City Centre Dr.
#1100, 1 City Centre Dr.
Mississauga, ON L5B 1M2 Canada
Tel: 905-601-6150; Fax: 905-803-5101
Montréal
#3000, 1, Place Ville-Marie
Montréal, QC H3B 4T9 Canada
Tel: 514-393-7115; Fax: 514-390-4100
Ottawa
#800, 100 Queen St.
Ottawa, ON K1P 5T8 Canada
Tel: 613-236-2442; Fax: 613-236-2195
Prince Albert
#5, 77 - 15 St. East
Prince Albert, SK S6V 1E9 Canada
Tel: 306-763-7411; Fax: 306-763-0191
Prince George
#500, 299 Victoria St.
Prince George, BC V2L 5B8 Canada
Tel: 250-564-1111; Fax: 250-562-4950
Québec
#400, 925, ch Saint-Louis
Québec, QC G1S 4Z4 Canada
Tel: 418-624-3333; Fax: 418-624-0414
Regina
Bank of Montreal Bldg.
#900, 2103 - 11th Ave.
Regina, SK S4P 3Z8 Canada
Tel: 306-525-1600; Fax: 306-525-2244
Rimouski
287, rue Pierre-Saindon
Rimouski, QC G5L 8V5 Canada
Tel: 418-724-4136; Fax: 418-724-3807
Roberval
713, boul St-Joseph
Roberval, QC G8H 2L3 Canada
Tel: 418-275-2111; Fax: 418-275-6398
Rouyn-Noranda
155, av Dallaire
Rouyn-Noranda, QC J9X 4T3 Canada
Tel: 819-762-5764; Fax: 819-797-1471
Saint John
Brunswick House
PO Box 6549
44 Chipman Hill, 7th Fl.
Saint John, NB E2L 4R9 Canada
Tel: 506-632-1080; Fax: 506-632-1210
St Catharines
25 Corporate Park Dr., 3rd Fl.
St Catharines, ON L2S 3W2 Canada
Tel: 905-323-6000; Fax: 905-323-6001
Saint-Hyacinthe
2200, av Léon-Pratte
Saint-Hyacinthe, QC J2S 4B6 Canada
Tel: 450-774-4000; Fax: 450-774-1709
St. John's
Fort William Bldg.
10 Factory Lane
St. John's, NL A1C 6H5 Canada
Tel: 709-576-8480; Fax: 709-576-8460
Saskatoon
PCS Tower
#300, 122 - 1st Ave.
Saskatoon, SK S7K 7E5 Canada
Tel: 306-343-4400; Fax: 306-343-4480

Sept-Iles
#200, 421, av Arnaud
Sept-Iles, QC G4R 3B3 Canada
Tel: 418-962-2513; Fax: 418-968-6422
Sherbrooke
#300, 2727, rue King ouest
Sherbrooke, QC J1L 1C2 Canada
Tel: 819-823-1616; Fax: 819-564-8078
St-Félicien
1133, rue Notre-Dame
St-Félicien, QC G8K 1Z7 Canada
Tel: 418-679-4711; Fax: 418-679-8723
Toronto - Bay St.
BCE Place, Bay Wellington Tower
#1400, 181 Bay St.
Toronto, ON M5J 2V1 Canada
Tel: 416-601-6150; Fax: 416-601-6151
Toronto - King St.
#300, 121 King St.
Toronto, ON M9N 1L6
Tel: 416-601-6150; Fax: 416-874-4401
Toronto - Wellington St. West
30 Wellington St. West
Toronto, ON M5L 1B1 Canada
Tel: 416-601-6150; Fax: 416-601-5901
Toronto - Yonge St.
North York City Centre
#1700, 5140 Yonge St.
Toronto, ON M2N 6L7 Canada
Tel: 416-601-6150; Fax: 416-229-2524
Trois-Pistoles
546a Jean Rioux
Trois-Pistoles, QC G0L 4K0 Canada
Tel: 418-851-2232; Fax: 418-851-4244
Trois-Rivières
PO Box 1600
1500, rue Royale
Trois-Rivières, QC G9A 5L9 Canada
Tel: 819-691-1212; Fax: 819-691-1127
Val-d'Or
#240, 450 - 3e av
Val-d'Or, QC J9P 1S2 Canada
Tel: 819-825-4101; Fax: 819-825-1155
Vancouver
4 Bentall Centre
#2800, 1055 Dunsmuir St.
Vancouver, BC V7X 1P4 Canada
Tel: 604-669-4466; Fax: 604-685-0395
Windsor
#200, 150 Ouellette Pl.
Windsor, ON N8X 1L9
Tel: 519-967-0388; Fax: 519-967-0324
Winnipeg
#2300, 360 Main St.
Winnipeg, MB R3C 3Z3 Canada
Tel: 204-942-0051; Fax: 204-947-9390

EPR Canada (EPR)

National Administration Office
PO Box 21148, Maple Ridge Square Stn. Maple Ridge Square
Maple Ridge, BC V2X 17P
Tel: 604-476-2009; Fax: 604-467-1219
eprnat@epr.ca
www.epr.ca

Former Name: Evancic Perrault Robertson
Profile: EPR Canada is a group of public accounting firms. Accounting, taxation, & management consulting services are provided.
CPA-USA Network & IECnet are the organizations international affiliates.
Executives:
Paul Walker, Chair; pwalker@eprcga.com
Jeannine Brooks, Executive Director; jbrooks@epr.ca
Verle Spindor, National Administrator; vspindor@eprcga.com
Branches:
Bathurst
1935 St. Peter Ave.
Bathurst, NB E2A 7J5
Tel: 506-548-1984; Fax: 506-548-0904
eprbath@eprbathurst.ca

Note: EPR Bathurst is a full-service management counsulting & accounting firm that focusses upon medium sized organizations in the professional, governmental, & non-profit sectors.
Gilles Deveaux, BBA, CA, Partner; gdeveaux@eprbathurst.ca

André Doucet, CGA, Partner; adoucet@eprbathurst.ca
Denis St-Pierre, BBA, CGA, Partner; dstpierre@eprbathurst.ca
Calgary
#110, 7330 Fisher St. SE
Calgary, AB T2H 2H8
Tel: 403-278-5800; Fax: 403-253-9479

Note: Tax, accounting, audit & business advisory services are provided.
Keith Corrigan, Partner; keith@foundationspa.com
Tina Weis, Partner; tina@foundationspa.com
Les Willms, Partner; les@foundationspa.com
Caraquet
#13, 445, boul St-Pierre ouest
Caraquet, NB E1W 1B2
Tel: 506-727-2010; Fax: 506-727-2088
eprbath@eprbathurst.ca
Chatham
Centre Square
40 Centre St.
Chatham, ON N7M 5W3
Tel: 519-436-0556; Fax: 519-436-1291
Sandy Bray, Partner; sandyb@eprchatham.com
Lance Rieger, Partner
Sandra Hohl, Partner; sandra@eprchatham.com
Coquitlam
566 Lougheed Hwy., 2nd Fl.
Coquitlam, BC V3K 3S3
Tel: 604-936-4377; Fax: 604-936-8376
eprcoq@eprcoq.com
www.eprcoq.com

Note: Accounting & business advisory services are provided to the mid-market.
Sheralynne Merritt, Partner; smerritt@eprcoq.com
Ken Richardson, Partner; ken@eprcoq.com
Trevor Sutherland, Partner; tsutherland@eprcoq.com
Bob Tanaka, Partner; btanaka@eprcoq.com
Devon
35 Athabasca Ave.
Devon, AB T9G 1G5
Tel: 780-987-2280; Fax: 780-987-2131
Trina Fritz, Partner; rstewart@faberllp.com
Rob Stewart, Partner; rstewart@faberllp.com
Edmonton
#200, 17510 - 107 Ave.
Edmonton, AB T5S 1E9
Tel: 780-432-5262; Fax: 780-436-0115
Dan Faber, Partner; dfaber@faberllp.com
Peter Johnson, Partner; pjohnson@faberllp.com
Mark Reschke, Partner; mreschke@faberllp.com
Rob Stewart, Partner; rstewart@faberllp.com
Fredericton
#205, 206 Rookwood Ave.
Fredericton, NB E3B 2M2
Tel: 506-458-8620; Fax: 506-450-8286
eprfred@nbnet.nb.ca

Note: Clients include firms from the retail, agricultural, fishing, natural resources, manufacturing, financial, & transportation sectors, as well as municipal entities & not for profit enterprises.
Don Daye, Partner; d_daye@eprdayekelly.com
Larry Johnston, Partner; l_johnson@eprdayekelly.com
Dan Nicholson, Partner; d_nicholson@eprdayekelly.com
Elaine Stairs, Partner; e_stairs@eprdayekelly.com
Gatineau
128, boul Saint-Raymond
Gatineau, QC J8Y 1T2
Tel: 819-420-3512; Toll-Free: 888-404-9853

Note: The Quebec clientele consists of municipal & public organizations, non-profit organizations, the agricultural sector, the aviation industry, construction companies, & financial services.
Pierre Brochu, Partner; pierre.brochu@eprquebec.com
Grand Falls
PO Box 7845
381, rue McCormick
Grand Falls, NB E3Z 3E8
Tel: 506-475-9440; Fax: 506-475-9449
Denis Ouellette, Partner; deniscga@nb.aibn.com
Grande Prairie
#215, 10006 - 101st Ave.
Grande Prairie, AB T8V 0Y1
Tel: 780-539-3400; Fax: 780-538-1544
Marlin Lucuk, Partner; mlucuk@faberllp.com
Duncan McNabb, Partner; dmcnabb@faberllp.com
Hamilton
PO Box 30082
176 Rymal Rd. East
Hamilton, ON L9B 2Y5
Tel: 905-388-7453; Fax: 905-388-7397
eprhamilton@iprimus.ca

Note: The Hamilton office provides accounting, income tax, & consulting services to a wide range of clients.
Andrew Barber, Partner; andy@epr-consulting.com
Langley
21542 - 48th Ave.
Langley, BC V3A 3M5
Tel: 604-534-1441; Fax: 604-534-1491
www.eprcga.com

Note: Clients in Langley include entertainment businesses, construction companies, franchisees, farming organizations, the equine industry, non-profit organizations, & associations.
Paul Walker, Partner; pwalker@eprcga.com
Christine Kisser, Partner; ckiss@eprcga.com
London
#804, 150 Dufferin Ave.
London, ON N6A 5N6
Tel: 519-434-5847; Fax: 519-645-0727
Don DiCarlo, Partner; don@eprlon.com
Maple Ridge
22377 Dewdney Trunk Rd.
Maple Ridge, BC V2X 3J4
Tel: 604-467-5561; Fax: 604-467-1219
eprmr@eprcga.com
www.eprcga.com

Note: Maple Ridge's clientele includes professional services firms, construction companies, real estate developers, insurance agencies. social & correctional services providers, & non-profit organizations.
Kathi Halpin, Partner; khalpin@eprcga.com
Betty Johansen, Partner; bjohansen@eprcga.com
Patrick Smith, Partner; psmith@eprcga.com
Moncton
84 Brandon St.
Moncton, NB E1C 7E9
Tel: 506-850-5045;
Marc Allain, Partner; marc@allainassociates.ca
Marc Nadeau, Partner; marc@allainassociates.ca
North Vancouver
#102, 1975 Lonsdale Ave.
North Vancouver, BC V7M 2K3
Tel: 604-987-8101; Fax: 604-987-1794
cga@eprnv.ca

Note: Specialties include personal & small business services, such as general accounting, tax preparation, & management consulting.
Andrea Agnoloni, Partner; andrea@eprnv.ca
Lawrence Low, Partner; lklow@eprrmd.com
Saint-Hyacinthe
#200, 450 ave St-Joseph
Saint-Hyacinthe, QC J2S 8K5
Tel: 450-774-7165; Fax: 450-774-1589
reception.sthyacinthe@eprquebec.com
Rene Benoit, Partner; rene.benoit@eprquebec.com
Luc Bergeron, Partner; luc.Bergeron@eprquebec.com
St. John's
74 O'Leary Ave.
St. John's, NL A1B 2C7
Tel: 709-726-0000; Fax: 709-726-2200

Note: Clients include nursing & personal care homes & construction companies.
Gerald Kirby, Partner
Saskatoon
259 Robin Cres.
Saskatoon, SK S7L 6M8
Tel: 306-934-3944; Fax: 306-934-3409
www.eprsk.ca

Note: ERP Saskatoon's clients are mainly owner managed businesses that operate in all sectors of the economy. Specialties of this location include financial management & strategic financial consulting services.
Colin Taylor, B. Comm., CMA, FCGA, Partner; colin.taylor@eprsk.ca
Kristen Walter, B. Comm., CGA, Manager
Justin Young, B. Comm., CGA, Manager
Slave Lake
405 - 6th Ave. SW
Slave Lake, AB T0G 2A4
Tel: 780-849-4949; Fax: 780-849-3401
Gordon Ferguson, Partner; epr@gcferguson.com
St-Jérôme
34, rue de Martigny ouest
Saint-Jérome, QC J7Y 2E9
Tel: 450-569-2641; Fax: 450-569-2647
François Marchand, Partner; francois.marchand@eprquebec.com

Stonewall
Westside Plaza
PO Box 1038
333 Main St.
Stonewall, MB R0C 2Z0
Tel: 204-467-5566; Fax: 204-467-9133
eprstonewall@shawcable.com

Note: Specialties of EPR Stonewall are as follows: financial statements, personal & corporate taxation, business financing, farm accounting, estate planing, & computer consulting.
Ryan Smith, Partner; rsmith.eprstonewall@shawcable.com

Terrebonne
3300, boul des Entreprises
Terrebonne, QC J6X 4J8
Tel: 450-477-0377; Fax: 450-477-4023
Yves Bastien, Partner; yves.bastien@eprquebec.com
Christian Pimpare, Partner; christian.pimpare@eprquebec.com

Tilbury
PO Box 130
40 Queen Sq.
Tilbury, ON N0P 2L0
Tel: 519-682-2300; Fax: 519-682-0705
reiger@ciaccess.com

Welland
250 Division St.
Welland, ON L3B 4A4
Tel: 905-735-7933; Fax: 905-735-2419
jks@bellnet.ca
Jeffrey Spicer, Partner

White Rock
#104, 1656 Martin Dr.
White Rock, BC V4A 6E7
Tel: 604-536-7778; Fax: 604-536-7745
Glenn Parks, Partner; gparks@eprcga.com

Whitecourt
PO Box 569
#101, 5011 - 51 Ave.
Whitecourt, AB T7S 1N6
Tel: 780-778-3981; Fax: 780-778-6226
Ken Ferguson, Partner; krfpc@telus.net
Rob Stewart, Partner; rstewart@faberllp.com

Winnipeg
#1010, 1661 Portage Ave.
Winnipeg, MB R3J 3T7
Tel: 204-938-9696; Fax: 204-775-5609
eprwpg@mts.net
Barry Edmond, Partner; bemond@mts.net

Dieppe:
Dieppe
#301, 1040 Champlain St.
Dieppe, NB E1A 8L8
Tel: 506-855-3098; Fax: 506-855-3099

Note: EPR Dieppe offers accounting, auditing, tax, forecasting, business financing, & advisory services. It serves government & public agencies, as well as small & medium sized businesses.
Paul Robichaud, Partner; probichaud@eprdieppe.com

Ernst & Young LLP

Ernst & Young Tower, Toronto-Dominion Centre
PO Box 251
222 Bay St.
Toronto, ON M5K 1J7
Tel: 416-864-1234; Fax: 416-864-1174
www.ey.com

Ownership: Private
Year Founded: 1864
Number of Employees: 2,907
Profile: The following services are offered: assurance & advisory business services; corporate finance; tax; & other services. It is affiliated with Ernst & Young Orenda Corporate Finance/EGAN LLP.
Executives:
Louis P. Pagnutti, Chair/CEO
Irene David, Contact
Guy Fréchette, Contact
Murray McDonald, Contact
Fiona Macfarlane, Contact
Paul Roberts, Contact
Affiliated Companies:
Ernst & Young Orenda Corporate Finance
Offices:
Calgary
Ernst & Young Tower
1000, 440 2nd Ave. SW
Calgary, AB T2P 5E9 Canada
Tel: 403-290-4100; Fax: 403-290-4265

Dieppe
11 Englehart St.
Dieppe, NB E1A 7Y7 Canada
Tel: 506-853-3097; Fax: 506-859-7190

Note: The Dieppe office of the firm LeBlanc Nadeau Bujold merged with Ernst & Young in Sept., 2009.

Edmonton - Scotia Place
TELUS House
#2200, 10020 - 100 St.
Edmonton, AB T5J 0N3 Canada
Tel: 780-423-5811; Fax: 780-428-8977

Edmonton - Stony Plain Rd.
300, 12220 Stony Plain Rd.
Edmonton, AB T5N 3Y4 Canada
Tel: 780-482-2349; Fax: 780-452-9060

Halifax
1959 Upper Water St., 13th Fl
Halifax, NS B3J 2Z1 Canada
Tel: 902-420-1080; Fax: 902-420-0503

Kitchener
515 Riverbend Dr.
Kitchener, ON N2K 3S3 Canada
Tel: 519-744-1171; Fax: 519-744-9604

London
One London Place, #1800
255 Queens Ave.
London, ON N6A 5S7 Canada
Tel: 519-672-6100; Fax: 519-438-5785

Montréal
#1900, 800, boul René-Lévesque O
Montréal, QC H3B 1X9 Canada
Tel: 514-875-6060; Fax: 514-879-2600

Ottawa
#1600, 100 Queen St.
Ottawa, ON K1P 1K1 Canada
Tel: 613-232-1511; Fax: 613-232-5324

Québec
#1200, 150, boul René-Lévesque
Québec, QC G1R 6C6 Canada
Tel: 418-524-5151; Fax: 418-524-0061

Saint John
#1209, 1 Germain St.
Saint John, NB E2L 4V1 Canada
Tel: 506-634-7000; Fax: 506-634-2129

St. John's
The Fortis Building
139 Water St., 7th Fl
St. John's, NL A1C 1B2 Canada
Tel: 709-726-2840; Fax: 709-726-0345

Thornhill
#600, 175 Commerce Valley Dr. West
Thornhill, ON L3T 7P6 Canada
Tel: 905-731-1500; Fax: 905-882-3050

Vancouver
Pacific Centre
700 West Georgia St.
Vancouver, BC V7Y 1C7 Canada
Tel: 604-891-8200; Fax: 604-643-5422

Winnipeg
Commodity Exchange Tower, #2700
360 Main St.
Winnipeg, MB R3C 4G9 Canada
Tel: 204-947-6519; Fax: 204-956-0138

Grant Thornton LLP

50 Bay St., 12th Fl.
Toronto, ON M5J 2Z8
Tel: 416-366-4420; Fax: 416-360-4944
Toll-Free: 800-366-0100
national@grantthornton.ca
www.grantthornton.ca

Ownership: Private
Year Founded: 1939
Number of Employees: 1,172
Revenues: $100-500 million
Executives:
Phil Noble, CEO & Exec. Partner
John Garritsen, Partner, Administration; jgarritsen@grantthornton.ca
John Holdstock, Partner, Client & Services; jholdstock@grantthornton.ca
Dave Peneycad, Chief Operating Officer
Bill Brushett, Partner, Client Services
Sharon Healy, Director, Human Resources; shealy@grantthornton.ca
Anita Ferrari, Regional Managing Partner; aferrari@grantthornton.ca
Kevin Ladner, Regional Managing Partner; kladner@grantthornton.ca
Rick Mudie, Regional Managing Partner; rmudie@grantthornton.ca

Branches:
Antigonish
#204, 220 Main St.
Antigonish, NS B2G 2C2 Canada
Tel: 902-863-4587; Fax: 902-863-0917

Barrie
#201, 85 Bayfield St.
Barrie, ON L4M 3A7 Canada
Tel: 705-730-6574; Fax: 705-730-6575
R.D. Woodman, Partner

Bathurst
Harbourview Pl.
PO Box 220
#500, 275 Main St.
Bathurst, NB E2A 3Z2 Canada
Tel: 506-546-6616; Fax: 506-548-5622

Bridgewater
197 Dufferin St.
Bridgewater, NS B4V 2G9 Canada
Tel: 902-543-8115; Fax: 902-543-7707
Jeff Sabean, Partner; 902-530-3425

Calgary
#900, 833 - 4th Ave. SW
Calgary, AB T2P 3T5 Canada
Tel: 403-260-2500; Fax: 403-260-2571
Dale Brown, Partner; 403-260-2817

Charlottetown
PO Box 187, Central Sta. Central
#710, 98 Fitzroy St.
Charlottetown, PE C1A 7K4
Tel: 902-892-6547; Fax: 902-566-5358

Corner Brook
#49, 51 Park St.
Corner Brook, NL A2H 2X1
Tel: 709-634-4382; Fax: 709-634-9158

Digby
Basin Place
PO Box 848
68 Water St.
Digby, NS B0V 1A0 Canada
Tel: 902-245-2553; Fax: 902-245-6161
Digby@GrantThornton.ca
M. Rutherford, Partner

Edmonton
Scotia Place 2
#1401, 10060 Jasper Ave. NW
Edmonton, AB T5J 3R8 Canada
Tel: 780-422-7114; Fax: 780-426-3208
G.G. McFarlane, Partner; 403-260-2500

Fredericton
PO Box 1054
570 Queen St., 4th Fl.
Fredericton, NB E3B 5C2 Canada
Tel: 506-458-8200; Fax: 506-453-7029
Bruce Lewis, Partner; 506-460-8430

Grand Falls - Windsor
PO Box 83
5B Harris Ave.
Grand Falls-Windsor, NL A2A 2J3 Canada
Tel: 709-489-6622; Fax: 709-489-6625
Tom Boone, Partner; 709-489-5334

Halifax
Cogswell Tower
#1100, 2000 Barrington St.
Halifax, NS B3J 3K1 Canada
Tel: 902-421-1734; Fax: 902-420-1068
Michele Williams, Partner

Hamilton
Standard Life Centre
#1040, 120 King St. West
Hamilton, ON L8P 4V2 Canada
Tel: 905-525-1930; Fax: 905-527-4413
D.A. MacLean, Partner

Kelowna
#200, 1633 Ellis St.
Kelowna, BC V1Y 2A8 Canada
Tel: 250-712-6800; Fax: 250-661-3416

J.P. Mills, Partner

Kentville
PO Box 68
15 Webster St.
Kentville, NS B4N 3V9 Canada
Tel: 902-678-7307; Fax: 902-679-1870
Gordon Caldwell, Partner; 902-690-2001

Langley
#320, 8700 - 200th St.
Langley, BC V2Y 0G4 Canada
Tel: 604-532-3761; Fax: 604-532-8130
T.G. Davies, Partner

London
#406, 140 Fullarton St.
London, ON N6A 5P2 Canada
Tel: 519-672-2930; Fax: 519-672-6455
Robbie Peters, Partner; 519-642-5158
Markham
#200, 15 Allstate Pkwy.
Markham, ON L3R 5B4 Canada
Tel: 905-475-1100; Fax: 905-475-8906
A.R. Byrne, Partner
Marystown
PO Box 518
2 Queen St.
Marystown, NL A0E 2M0 Canada
Tel: 709-279-2300; Fax: 709-279-2340
Marystown@GrantThornton.ca
Miramichi
135 Henry St.
Miramichi, NB E1V 2N5 Canada
Tel: 506-622-0637; Fax: 506-622-5174
H.K. Raper, Partner
Mississauga
#401, 350 Burnhamthorpe Rd. West
Mississauga, ON L5R 3J1 Canada
Tel: 905-804-0905; Fax: 905-804-0509
G.R. Popp, Partner
Moncton
PO Box 1005
#500, 633 Main St.
Moncton, NB E1C 8P2 Canada
Tel: 506-857-0100; Fax: 506-857-0105
Jean Marc Delaney, Partner; 506-858-2500
Montague
PO Box 70
1 Bailey Dr.
Montague, PE C0A 1R0 Canada
Tel: 902-838-4121; Fax: 902-838-4802
C. Chapman, Partner
New Glasgow
Aberdeen Business Centre
PO Box 427
#270, 610 East River Rd.
New Glasgow, NS B2H 5E5 Canada
Tel: 902-752-8393; Fax: 902-752-4009
Wade Taylor, Partner; 902-752-7056
New Liskeard
PO Box 2170
17 Wellington St.
New Liskeard, ON P0J 1P0 Canada
Tel: 705-647-8100; Fax: 705-647-7026
R.R. Hacquard, Partner
New Westminster
628 - 6th Ave., 6th Fl.
New Westminster, BC V3M 6Z1 Canada
Tel: 604-521-3761; Fax: 604-521-8170
R.W. Mudie, Partner
North Bay
#200, 222 McIntyre St. West
North Bay, ON P1B 2Y8 Canada
Tel: 705-472-6500; Fax: 705-472-7760
G.G. Weckwerth, Partner
Orillia
#300, 6 West St. North
Orillia, ON L3V 5B8 Canada
Tel: 705-326-7605; Fax: 705-326-0837
R.D. Woodman, Partner
Port Colborne
PO Box 336, Main Sta. Main
222 Catharine St, #B
Port Colborne, ON L3K 5W1
Tel: 905-834-3651; Fax: 905-834-5095
J. Brennan, Principal
Saint John
Brunswick House
44 Chipman Hill, 4th Fl.
Saint John, NB E2L 2A9 Canada
Tel: 506-634-2900; Fax: 506-634-4569
Glenn Dewar, Partner; 506-634-4560
St. John's
PO Box 8037
187 Kenmount Rd.
St. John's, NL A1B 3P9 Canada
Tel: 709-722-5960; Fax: 709-722-7892
Jeff Pardy, Partner
Sault Ste Marie
Station Tower
421 Bay St., 5th Fl.
Sault Ste Marie, ON P6A 1X3 Canada
Tel: 705-945-9700; Fax: 705-945-9705
Theresa Cassan, Partner; 705-945-6581
Summerside
Royal Bank Bldg.
PO Box 1660
220 Water St.
Summerside, PE C1N 2V5 Canada
Tel: 902-436-9155; Fax: 902-436-6913
Kevin MacLeod, Partner; 902-432-3547
Sydney
George Place
#200, 500 George St.
Sydney, NS B1P 1K6 Canada
Tel: 902-562-5581; Fax: 902-562-0073
J. MacNeil, Partner
Thunder Bay
#300, 979 Alloy Dr.
Thunder Bay, ON P7B 5Z8 Canada
Tel: 807-345-6571; Fax: 807-345-0032
D. Vanderwey, Partner
Truro
PO Box 725
#400, 35 Commercial St.
Truro, NS B2N 5E8 Canada
Tel: 902-893-1150; Fax: 902-893-9757
G.D. Hutchings, Partner
Vancouver
#1600, 333 Seymour St.
Vancouver, BC V6B 0A4 Canada
Tel: 604-687-2711; Fax: 604-685-6569
Vancouver@GrantThornton.ca
P.B. Noble, Partner
Victoria
888 Fort St., 3rd Fl.
Victoria, BC V8W 1H8 Canada
Tel: 250-383-4191; Fax: 250-381-4623
S. Mehinagic, Partner
Wetaskiwin
5108 - 51st Ave.
Wetaskiwin, AB T9A 0V2 Canada
Tel: 780-352-1679; Fax: 780-352-2451
T.R. Bolivar, Partner
Winnipeg
94 Commerce Drive
Winnipeg, MB R3P 0Z3 Canada
Tel: 204-944-0100; Fax: 204-957-5442
D.H. Anthony, Partner
Yarmouth
PO Box 297
328 Main St.
Yarmouth, NS B5A 4B2 Canada
Tel: 902-742-7842; Fax: 902-742-0224
Paul Comeau, Partner; 902-749-0033

KPMG

Bay Adelaide Centre
#4600, 333 Bay St.
Toronto, ON M5H 2S5
Tel: 416-777-8500; Fax: 416-777-8818
www.kpmg.ca

Ownership: Private
Year Founded: 1860
Number of Employees: 5,000
Assets: $500m-1 billion
Revenues: $500m-1 billion
Executives:
Bill Thomas, Chief Executive Officer; 416-777-8144; bbthomas@kpmg.ca
Mary Lou Maher, Chief Financial Officer; 416-777-3303; mmaher@kpmg.ca
Robert Brouwer, Managing Partner, Clients & Markets
John A. Gordon, Managing Partner, Audit
John Herhalt, Managing Partner, Advisory Services; 416-777-8778; jherhalt@kpmg.ca
Elio Luongo, Managing Partner, Tax
Mario Paron, Managing Partner, Region East National; 416-777-8373; mparon@kpmg.ca
Vancouver - Burnaby
#2400, 4720 Kingsway
Burnaby, BC V5H 4N2
Branches:
Abbotsford
32575 Simon Ave.
Abbotsford, BC V2T 4W6 Canada
Tel: 604-854-2200; Fax: 604-853-2756
Calgary
Bow Valley Square II
#2700, 205 - 5th Ave. SW
Calgary, AB T2P 4B9 Canada
Tel: 403-691-8000; Fax: 403-691-8008
Jason Brown, Partner, Audit
Curtis Lester, Partner, Tax
Chilliwack
#200, 9123 Mary St.
Chilliwack, BC V2P 4H7 Canada
Tel: 604-793-4700; Fax: 604-793-4747
Edmonton
Commerce Pl.
10125 - 102 St.
Edmonton, AB T5J 3V8 Canada
Tel: 780-429-7300; Fax: 780-429-7379
Robert Borrelli, Partner, Audit
Fredericton
Frederick Sq., TD Tower
#700, 77 Westmorland St.
Fredericton, NB E3B 6Z3 Canada
Tel: 506-452-8000; Fax: 506-450-0072
Todd MacIntosh, Partner, Tax
Halifax
Purdy's Wharf, Tower One
#1500, 1959 Upper Water St.
Halifax, NS B3J 3N2 Canada
Tel: 902-429-6000; Fax: 902-423-1307
Gregory Simpson, Partner, Tax
Hamilton
Commerce Place
#700, 21 King St. West
Hamilton, ON L8P 4W7 Canada
Tel: 905-523-8200; Fax: 905-523-2222
Kamloops
#200, 206 Seymour St.
Kamloops, BC V2C 6P5 Canada
Tel: 250-372-5581; Fax: 250-828-2928
Kelowna
#300, 1674 Bertram St.
Kelowna, BC V1Y 9G4 Canada
Tel: 250-763-5522; Fax: 250-763-0044
Kingston
PO Box 1600
#400, 863 Princess St.
Kingston, ON K7L 5C8 Canada
Tel: 613-549-1550; Fax: 613-549-6349
Lethbridge
Lethbridge Centre Tower
#500, 400 - 4th Ave. South
Lethbridge, AB T1J 4E1 Canada
Tel: 403-380-5700; Fax: 403-380-5760
London
#1400, 140 Fullarton St.
London, ON N6A 5P2 Canada
Tel: 519-672-4880; Fax: 519-672-5684
Moncton
Place Marvin's
One Factory Lane
Moncton, NB E1C 9M3 Canada
Tel: 506-856-4400; Fax: 506-856-4499
Montréal
#1500, 600 boul de Maisonneuve Ouest
Montréal, QC H3A 0A3 Canada
Tel: 514-840-2100; Fax: 514-840-2187
Philippe Grubert, Partner, Audit
Brian Mustard, Partner, Tax
North Bay
PO Box 990
#300, 925 Stockdale Rd.
North Bay, ON P1B 8K3 Canada
Tel: 705-472-5110; Fax: 705-472-1249
Ottawa
World Exchange Plaza
#2000, 160 Elgin Street
Ottawa, ON K2P 2P8 Canada
Tel: 613-212-5764; Fax: 613-212-2896

Andrew Newman, Partner, Audit
Prince George
#400, 177 Victoria St.
Prince George, BC V2L 5R8 Canada
Tel: 250-563-7151; Fax: 250-563-5693
Regina
McCallum Hill Centre, Tower II
1881 Scarth St., 20th Fl.
Regina, SK S4P 4K9 Canada
Tel: 306-791-1200; Fax: 306-757-4703
Saint John
Harbour Bldg.
PO Box 2388
#306, 133 Prince William St.
Saint John, NB E2L 3V6 Canada
Tel: 506-634-1000; Fax: 506-633-8828
St Catharines
#901, One Saint-Paul St.
St Catharines, ON L2R 7L2 Canada
Tel: 905-685-4811; Fax: 905-682-2008

Saskatoon
#600, 128 - 4th Ave. South
Saskatoon, SK S7K 1M8 Canada
Tel: 306-934-6200; Fax: 306-934-6233
Sault Ste Marie
#200, 111 Elgin St.
Sault Ste Marie, ON P6A 6L6 Canada
Tel: 705-949-5811; Fax: 705-949-0911
Sudbury
Claridge Executive Centre
144 Pine St.
Sudbury, ON P3C 1X3 Canada
Tel: 705-675-8500; Fax: 705-675-7586
Laurie Bissonette, Partner, Audit
Toronto
Yonge Corporate Centre
#200, 4100 Yonge St.
Toronto, ON M2P 2H3 Canada
Tel: 416-228-7000; Fax: 416-228-7123
Vancouver
Pacific Centre
PO Box 10426
777 Dunsmuir St.
Vancouver, BC V7Y 1K3 Canada
Tel: 604-691-3000; Fax: 604-691-3031
Jim Bennett, Partner, Audit
Carlo De Mello, Partner, Audit
Vernon
Credit Union Bldg.
3205 - 32 St., 3rd Fl.
Vernon, BC V1T 9A2 Canada
Tel: 250-503-5300; Fax: 250-545-6440
Waterloo
Marsland Centre
115 King St. South
Waterloo, ON N2J 5A3 Canada
Tel: 519-747-8800; Fax: 519-747-8811
Shelley Wickenheiser, Partner, Tax
Windsor
Greenwood Centre
#618, 3200 Deziel Dr.
Windsor, ON N8W 5K8 Canada
Tel: 519-251-3500; Fax: 519-251-3530
Winnipeg
#2000, One Lombard Place
Winnipeg, MB R3B 0X3 Canada
Tel: 204-957-1770; Fax: 204-957-0808

MacKay LLP
#1100, 1177 West Hastings St.
Vancouver, BC V6E 4T5
Tel: 604-687-4511; Fax: 780-425-8780
Toll-Free: 800-351-0426
HughLivingstone@Van.MacKayLLP.ca
www.mackay.ca
Other Contact Information: Fax: 604-687-5805
Ownership: Private
Year Founded: 1969
Number of Employees: 220
Profile: Services provided include bookkeeping, audit & accounting, taxation, corporate financing, executive financial planning, microcomputer support, management consulting, business investigation, valuation & litigation support, solvency & restructuring, & international affiliations.
Executives:
Deborah Graystone, Partner
Peter Busch, Partner
Sean Gilbert, Partner
Russell D. Law, Partner
Hugh G. Livingstone, Partner
Craig Elliott, Partner
Matthew So, Partner
York Wong, Partner
Hugh Livingstone, Manager
Branches:
Calgary - 7 Avenue
Iveagh House
#1700, 717 - 7 Ave. SW
Calgary, AB T2P 0Z3 Canada
Tel: 403-294-9292; Fax: 403-294-9262
Calgary@Cal.MacKay.ca
Calgary - Macleod Trail
Southcentre Executive Tower
#400, 11012 MacLeod Trail SE
Calgary, AB T2J 6A5 Canada
Tel: 403-640-2227; Fax: 403-640-2505
calgary@cal.mackay.ca
Christine Heemskerk, General Manager
Edmonton
Highfield Place
#705, 10010 - 106th St.
Edmonton, AB T5J 3L8 Canada
Tel: 780-420-0626; Fax: 780-425-8780
Toll-Free: 800-622-5293
edmonton@edm.mackay.ca
Don Smith, General Manager
Donald J. Smith
Bob McAneeley
Brent Penner
Kelowna
#500, 1620 Dickson Ave.
Kelowna, BC V1Y 9Y2 Canada
Tel: 250-763-5021; Fax: 250-763-3600
Toll-Free: 866-763-5021
kelowna@kel.mackay.ca
Don Turri, General Manager
Don Turri
Ken Laloge
Chris White
Dan Basso
Angela C. Bailey
Surrey
#112, 7565 - 132nd St.
Surrey, BC V3W 1K5 Canada
Tel: 604-591-6181; Fax: 604-591-5676
surrey@van.mackay.ca
Keith Gagnon, Manager
Jack Arnold
Bill Gill
Keith Gagnon
Whitehorse
#200, 303 Strickland St.
Whitehorse, YT Y1A 2J9 Canada
Tel: 867-667-7651; Fax: 867-668-3797
Mark Pike, Managing Director; MarkPike@whi.mackay.ca
Blaine Anderson
Erik Hoenisch
Norman McIntyre
Yellowknife
PO Box 727
#301, 5120 - 49th St
Yellowknife, NT X1A 1P8 Canada
Tel: 867-920-4404; Fax: 867-920-4135
Toll-Free: 866-920-4404
yellowknife@yel.mackay.ca
John Laratta
Gillian Lee

Meyers Norris Penny (MNP)
715 - 5th Ave. SW, 7th Fl.
Calgary, AB T2P 2X6
Tel: 403-444-0150; Fax: 403-444-0199
www.mnp.ca
Year Founded: 1945
Number of Employees: 1300
Revenues: $100-500 million
Profile: MNP is a leading Western Canadian chartered accountancy & business advisory firm. In addition to traditional accounting services like taxation & assurance, MNP offers business services including corporate financing, human resource consulting, business & strategic planning, succession planning, valuations support, information technology consulting, self-employment training, & agricultural advisory services.
Executives:
Daryl Ritchie, FCA, Chief Executive Officer; daryl.ritchie@mnp.ca
Kelly Bernakevitch, FCA, Executive Vice-President, Operations; kelly.bernakevitch@mnp.ca
Ted Poppitt, CA, Executive Vice-President, Practice Development; ted.poppitt@mnp.ca
Laurel Wood, CMC, Executive Vice-President, Advisory Services; laurel.wood@mnp.ca
Steve Kerr, CMA, Chief Financial Officer; steve.kerr@mnp.ca
Randy Mowat, Vice-President, Marketing; randy.mowat@mnp.ca

Phil O'Brien-Moran, Vice-President, Technology; phil.obrienmoran@mnp.ca
Bob Twerdun, CA, Vice-President, Human Capital; bob.twerdun@mnp.ca
Charmaine Toms, General Counsel; charmaine.toms@mnp.ca
Affiliated Companies:
Tamarack Capital Advisors Inc.
Offices:
Abbotsford
#300, 2975 Gladwin Rd.
Abbotsford, BC V2T 5T4 Canada
Tel: 604-853-9471; Fax: 604-850-3672
Darrell P. Tracey, Contact; darrell.tracey@mnp.ca
Airdrie
#110A, 400 Main St. NE
Airdrie, AB T4B 2N1 Canada
Tel: 403-912-6235; Fax: 403-912-6332
Brandon
1401 Princess Ave.
Brandon, MB R7A 7L7 Canada
Tel: 204-727-0661; Fax: 204-726-1543
Toll-Free: 800-446-0890
Jeff Cristall, Contact; jeff.cristall@mnp.ca
Burnaby
Metrotower II
#900, 4720 Kingsway
Burnaby, BC V5H 4N2 Canada
Tel: 604-435-4317; Fax: 604-435-4319
Calgary - Bantrel
#900, 700 6th Ave. SW
Calgary, AB T2P 0T8 Canada
Tel: 403-263-3385; Fax: 403-648-4115
Kelly Brook, Contact; kelly.brook@mnp.ca
Calgary - North
#210, 5010 - 4th St. NE
Calgary, AB T2K 5X8 Canada
Tel: 403-275-8457; Fax: 403-275-8416
Don Isaman, Contact; don.isaman@mnp.ca
Calgary Downtown - MNP Place
#300, 622 - 5th Ave. SW
Calgary, AB T2P 0M6 Canada
Tel: 403-263-3385; Fax: 403-269-8450
Durell Wiley, Contact; durell.wiley@mnp.ca
Cambridge
#600, 73 Water St. N.
Cambridge, ON N1R 7L6 Canada
Tel: 519-623-3820; Fax: 519-622-3144
Rhonda Lovell, CA; rhonda.lovell@mnp.ca
Campbell River
#201, 990 Cedar St.
Campbell River, BC V9W 7Z8 Canada
Tel: 250-287-2131; Fax: 250-287-2134
Toll-Free: 800-450-9977
Chilliwack
#1, 45780 Yale Rd.
Chilliwack, BC V2P 2N4 Canada
Tel: 604-792-1915; Fax: 604-795-6526
Toll-Free: 800-444-4070
Darrell P. Tracey, Contact; darrell.tracey@mnp.ca
Courtenay
467 Cumberland Rd.
Courtenay, BC V9N 2C5 Canada
Tel: 250-338-5464; Fax: 250-338-0609
Toll-Free: 800-445-9988
Ben Vanderhorst, Contact
Dauphin
PO Box 6000
32 - 2nd Ave. SW
Dauphin, MB R7N 1S3 Canada
Tel: 204-638-6767; Fax: 204-638-8634
Toll-Free: 877-500-0790
Gerry Musey, Contact; gerry.musey@mnp.ca
Deloraine
PO Box 528
130 Broadway St. North
Deloraine, MB R0M 0M0 Canada
Tel: 204-747-2842; Fax: 204-747-2956
Julee Galvin, CA; julee.galvin@mnp.ca
Drumheller
PO Box 789
365 - 2nd St. East
Drumheller, AB T0J 0Y0 Canada
Tel: 403-823-7800; Fax: 403-823-8914
Toll-Free: 877-932-3387
Jeff Hall; jeffhall@mnp.ca
Duncan
372 Coronation Ave.
Duncan, BC V9L 2T3 Canada
Tel: 250-748-3761; Fax: 250-746-1712
Gordon John, CA; gordon.john@mnp.ca
Edmonton - City Centre
#400, 10104 - 103 Ave. NW
Edmonton, AB T5J 0H8 Canada
Tel: 780-451-4406; Fax: 780-454-1908
Gordon Reid, Contact; gordon.reid@mnp.ca
Edmonton - South
#201, 9426 - 51 Ave. NW
Edmonton, AB T6E 5A6 Canada
Tel: 780-462-8626; Fax: 780-462-8643
Murray Gray, Contact; murray.gray@mnp.ca
Estevan
#100, 1219 - 5th St.
Estevan, SK S4A 0Z5 Canada
Tel: 306-634-2603; Fax: 306-634-8708
Brian Drayton; brian.drayton@mnp.ca

Fort McMurray
9707 Main St.
Fort McMurray, AB T9H 1T5 Canada
Tel: 780-791-9000; Fax: 780-791-9047
Pat Olivier; pat.olivier@mnp.ca
Fort St. John
#2, 10611 - 102nd St.
Fort St. John, BC V1J 5L3 Canada
Tel: 250-785-8166; Fax: 250-785-5660
Marvin Beaumont, Contact; marvin.beaumont@mnp.ca
Grande Prairie
214 Place
PO Box 43
9909 - 102 St.
Grande Prairie, AB T8V 2V4 Canada
Tel: 780-831-1700; Fax: 780-539-9600
Toll-Free: 888-831-2870
Bridget Henniger; bridget.henniger@mnp.ca
Hope
PO Box 1689
100-E Fort St.
Hope, BC V0X 1L0 Canada
Tel: 604-869-9599; Fax: 604-869-3044
Toll-Free: 800-969-6060
Keith Britz, Contact; keith.britz@mnp.ca
Humboldt
PO Box 2590
701 - 9th St.
Humboldt, SK S0K 2A0 Canada
Tel: 306-682-2673; Fax: 306-682-5910
Toll-Free: 877-500-0789
Larry Rode, Contact; larry.rode@mnp.ca
Kelowna
600 - 1628 Dickson Ave.
Kelowna, BC V1Y 9X1 Canada
Tel: 250-763-8919; Fax: 250-763-1121
John Orisko, Contact; john.orisko@mnp.ca
Kenora
315 Main St. South
Kenora, ON P9N 1T4 Canada
Tel: 807-468-3338; Fax: 807-468-1418
Joseph Fregeau; jfregeau@fregeauandtompkin.ca
Killarney
501 Broadway Ave.
Killarney, MB R0K 1G0 Canada
Tel: 204-523-4633; Fax: 204-523-4538
Toll-Free: 877-500-0760
Lacombe
#5, 5265 - 45th St.
Lacombe, AB T4L 2A2 Canada
Tel: 403-782-7790; Fax: 403-782-7703
Gerald Wasylyshen; gerald.wasylyshen@mnp.ca
Leduc
#200, 5019 - 49th Ave.
Leduc, AB T9E 6T5 Canada
Tel: 780-986-2626; Fax: 780-986-2621
Deborah A. Sarnecki; deborah.sarnecki@mnp.ca
Lethbridge
3425 - 2nd Ave. South
Lethbridge, AB T1J 4V1 Canada
Tel: 403-329-1552; Fax: 403-329-1540

Gordon Tait, Contact; gord.tait@mnp.ca
Lloydminster
2905 - 50 Ave.
Lloydminster, SK S9V 0N7 Canada
Tel: 306-825-9855; Fax: 306-825-9640
Ralph Cormack; ralph.cormack@mnp.ca
Maple Ridge
#201 - 11939 224th St.
Maple Ridge, BC V2X 6B2 Canada
Tel: 604-463-8831; Fax: 604-463-0401
Tere Stykalo, Contact; tere.stykalo@mnp.ca
Medicine Hat
PO Box 580
666 - 4 St. SE
Medicine Hat, AB T1A 0K9 Canada
Tel: 403-527-4441; Fax: 403-526-6218
Toll-Free: 877-500-0786
Michael Keck, Managing Partner; michael.keck@mnp.ca
Melfort
PO Box 2020
601 Main St.
Melfort, SK S0E 1A0 Canada
Tel: 306-752-5800; Fax: 306-752-5933
Toll-Free: 877-500-0787
John Harder, Contact; john.harder@mnp.ca
Moosomin
PO Box 670
715 Main St.
Moosomin, SK S0G 3N0 Canada
Tel: 306-435-3347; Fax: 306-435-2494
Toll-Free: 877-500-0784

Layne McFarlane, Contact; layne.mcfarlane@mnp.ca
Nanaimo
PO Box 514
96 Wallace St.
Nanaimo, BC V9R 5L5 Canada
Tel: 250-753-8251; Fax: 250-754-3999
Toll-Free: 877-340-3330
Garth Busch, Regional Managing Partner; garth.busch@mnp.ca
Neepawa
PO Box 760
251 Davidson St.
Neepawa, MB R0J 1H0 Canada
Tel: 204-476-2326; Fax: 204-476-3663
Toll-Free: 877-500-0795
Marvin Beaumont, Contact; marvin.beaumont@mnp.ca
Peace River
99132 - 98 Ave.
Peace River, AB T8S 1J5 Canada
Tel: 780-624-3252; Fax: 780-624-8758
Bridget Hennigar, Regional Managing Partner; bridget.hennigar@mnp.ca
Port Moody
#601 - 205 Newport Dr.
Port Moody, BC V3H 5C9 Canada
Tel: 604-949-2088; Fax: 604-949-0509
Harry Gross; harry.gross@mnp.ca
Portage La Prairie
780 Saskatchewan Ave. West
Portage La Prairie, MB R1N 0M7 Canada
Tel: 204-239-6117; Fax: 204-857-3972
Jerry Lupkowski, Contact; jerry.lupkowski@mnp.ca
Prince Albert
25 - 11th St. East
Prince Albert, SK S6V 0Z8 Canada
Tel: 306-764-6873; Fax: 306-763-0766
Garth Busch; garth.busch@mnp.ca
Red Deer
4922 - 53 St.
Red Deer, AB T4N 2E9 Canada
Tel: 403-346-8878; Fax: 403-341-5599
Toll-Free: 877-500-0779
Tim Dekker, Contact; tim.dekker@mnp.ca
Red Lake
179 Howey St.
Red Lake, ON P0V 2M0 Canada
Tel: 807-727-1114;
Gary Porter; gary.porter@mnp.ca
Regina
Royal Bank Bldg.
#900, 2010 - 11th Ave.
Regina, SK S4P 0J3 Canada
Tel: 306-790-7900; Fax: 306-790-7990
Toll-Free: 877-500-0780
Don Stewart, Contact; don.stewart@mnp.ca
Richmond Hill
#4, 10 West Pearce
Richmond Hill, ON L4B 1B6 Canada
Tel: 905-763-2436; Fax: 905-709-9952

Kris Holbeck; kris.holbeck@mnp.ca
Rimbey
PO Box 317
4714 - 50th Ave.
Rimbey, AB T0C 2J0 Canada
Tel: 403-843-4666; Fax: 403-843-4616
Chris Simpson, Contact; chris.simpson@mnp.ca
Saskatoon
800 - 119 4th Ave. South
Saskatoon, SK S7K 5X2 Canada
Tel: 306-665-6766; Fax: 306-665-9910
Toll-Free: 877-500-0778
David Kunaman, Contact; david.kunaman@mnp.ca
Steinbach
#100 - 250 Main St.
Steinbach, MB R5G 1Y8 Canada
Tel: 204-326-9816; Fax: 204-326-9586
Alyson Kennedy; alyson.kennedy@mnp.ca
Surrey
#316, 5455 - 152 St.
Surrey, BC V3S 5A5 Canada
Tel: 604-574-7211; Fax: 778-571-3549
Rick Bisson; rick.bisson@mnp.ca
Swift Current
50 - 1st Ave. NE
Swift Current, SK S9H 4W4 Canada
Tel: 306-773-8375; Fax: 306-773-7735
Toll-Free: 877-500-0762
Thunder Bay
#210, 1205 Amber Dr.
Thunder Bay, ON P7B 6M4 Canada
Tel: 807-623-2141; Fax: 807-622-1282
Ed Stromsmoe; ed.stromsmoe@mnp.ca

Toronto
#701, 85 Richmond St. West
Toronto, ON M5H 2C9 Canada
Tel: 416-596-1711; Fax: 416-596-7894
Toll-Free: 877-251-2922
Paul Dunnett, Regional Managing Partner; paul.dunnett@mnp.ca
Vancouver
PO Box 49148
#2300, 1055 Dunsmuir St.
Vancouver, BC V7X 1J1 Canada
Tel: 604-685-8408; Fax: 604-685-8594
Toll-Free: 877-688-8408
Mackenzie Kyle, Regional Managing Partner; mackenzie.kyle@mnp.ca
Vernon
#100, 2903 - 35th Ave.
Vernon, BC V1T 2S7 Canada
Tel: 778-475-5678; Fax: 778-475-5618
Tom Plishka; tom.plishka@mnp.ca
Virden
PO Box 670
233 Queen St. West
Virden, MB R0M 2C0 Canada
Tel: 204-748-1340; Fax: 204-748-3294
Tom Kirkup, Contact; tom.kirkup@mnp.ca
Waterloo
554 Weber St. N.
Waterloo, ON N2L 5C6 Canada
Tel: 519-725-7700; Fax: 519-725-7708
Heather Farfard; heather.farfard@mnp.ca
Weyburn
#301 - 117 3rd St. NE
Weyburn, SK S4H 0W3 Canada
Tel: 306-842-8915; Fax: 306-842-1966
Sean Wallace, CA, CFP; sean.wallace@mnp.ca
Winnipeg
#2500, 201 Portage Ave.
Winnipeg, MB R3B 3K6 Canada
Tel: 204-775-4531; Fax: 204-783-8329
Dena Weiss; dena.weiss@mnp.ca
Winnipeg - Polo Park
#301, 1661 Portage Ave.
Winnipeg, MB R3J 3T7 Canada
Tel: 204-336-6167; Fax: 204-772-9687
Toll-Free: 877-500-0795
Wayne McWhirter, Contact; wayne.mcwhirter@mnp.ca

Welch LLP

151 Slater St., 12th Fl.
Ottawa, ON K1P 5H3
Tel: 613-236-9191; Fax: 613-236-8258
www.welchllp.com

Former Name: Welch & Company LLP
Ownership: Private
Year Founded: 1918
Number of Employees: 200
Profile: The firm serves business, government, & not-for-profit clients. Taxation, accounting, auditing, personal financial planning, & wealth management services are provided.
Executives:
Micheal Burch, CA, CFP, Managing Partner, Ottawa; mburch@welchllp.com
Don Timmins, CA, Partner, Ottawa; dtimmins@welchllp.com
Branches:
Belleville
525 Dundas St. East
Belleville, ON K8N 1G4 Canada
Tel: 613-966-2844; Fax: 613-966-2206
Glenn Collins, CA, Partner; gcollins@welch.on.ca
Campbellford
PO Box 1209
57 Bridge St. East
Campbellford, ON K0L 1L0 Canada
Tel: 705-653-3194; Fax: 705-653-1703
Marie Northey, CA, Partner; mnorthey@welch.on.ca
Cornwall
36 Second St. East
Cornwall, ON K6H 1Y3 Canada
Tel: 613-932-4953; Fax: 613-932-1731
Ron Mulligan, CA, Partner; rmulligan@welchllp.com
Gatineau
#201, 975, boul St-Joseph
Gatineau, QC J8Z 1W8 Canada
Tel: 819-771-7381; Fax: 819-771-3089
Guy Coté, CA, Partner; gcote@levesquemarchand.ca
Napanee
36 Bridge St. East
Napanee, ON K7R 1J8 Canada
Tel: 613-354-2169; Fax: 613-354-2160
Dan Atkinson, FCA, Partner; datkinson@welch.on.ca

Pembroke
PO Box 757
270 Lake St.
Pembroke, ON K8A 6X9 Canada
Tel: 613-735-1021; Fax: 613-735-2071
Hal Ward, CA, Partner; hward@welchllp.com
Picton
290 Main St.
Picton, ON K0K 2T0 Canada
Tel: 613-476-3283; Fax: 613-476-1627
Charles Thompson, CA, Partner; cthompson@welch.on.ca
Renfrew
101 Raglan St. North
Renfrew, ON K7V 1N7 Canada
Tel: 613-432-8399; Fax: 613-432-9154
Dan Amyotte, CA, Partner; damyotte@welchllp.com
Trenton
#4, 290 Dundas St. West
Trenton, ON K8V 3S1 Canada
Tel: 613-392-1287; Fax: 613-392-5456
John Bailey, CA, Partner; jbailey@welch.on.ca
Tweed
PO Box 807
63 Victoria St. North
Tweed, ON K0K 3J0 Canada
Tel: 613-478-5051; Fax: 613-478-3069
Marie Northey, CA, Partner; mnorthey@welch.on.ca

Accounting Firms by Province

Alberta

Banff: Collins Barrow Chartered Accountants - Banff
Cascade Plaza
PO Box 1000
#370, 317 Banff Ave.
Banff, AB T1L 1H4
Tel: 403-762-8383; Fax: 403-762-8384
cbbanff@cbrockies.com
www.cbrockies.com

Banff: Kenway Mack Slusarchuk Stewart Bow Valley LLP Chartered Accountants
PO Box 930
201 Bear St.
Banff, AB T1L 1A9
Tel: 403-762-2271; Fax: 403-762-8817
info@kmss.ca
www.kmss.ca

Calgary: Alger & Associates Inc.
#900, 833 - 4th Ave. SW
Calgary, AB T2P 3T5
Tel: 403-310-8888; Fax: 403-260-2571
Toll-Free: 310-8888
www.alger.ca

Calgary: Bernard Martens Professional Corp.
38 West Springs Gate SW
Calgary, AB T3H 4P5
Tel: 403-255-1262; Fax: 403-640-4652

Calgary: Buchanan Barry LLP
#800, 840 - 6th Ave. SW
Calgary, AB T2P 3E5
Tel: 403-262-2116; Fax: 403-265-0845
mailbox@buchananbarry.ca
www.buchananbarry.ca

Calgary: Catalyst Chartered Accountants & Consultants
#250, 200 Quarry Park Blvd. SE
Calgary, AB T2C 5E3
Tel: 403-296-0082; Fax: 403-296-0088
inquire@catalystsolutions.ca
www.catalystsolutions.ca

Calgary: CompassTAX Chartered Accountants
Dorchester Square
#600, 1333 - 8th St. SW
Calgary, AB T2R 1M6
Tel: 403-531-2200; Fax: 403-263-1826
Toll-Free: 866-531-2281
www.compasstax.ca

Calgary: Daunheimer Lynch Anderson LLP
6620 Crowchild Trail SW
Calgary, AB T3E 5R8
Tel: 403-217-5925; Fax: 403-217-5934
Toll-Free: 888-452-5925
www.dlallp.com

Calgary: Dick Cook Whyte Schulli Chartered Accountants
#555, 999 - 8th St. SW
Calgary, AB T3K 2L2
Tel: 403-245-1717; Fax: 403-244-9306

Calgary: DNTW Chartered Accountants, LLP
5917 - 1A St. SW
Calgary, AB T2H 0G4
Tel: 403-209-2248; Fax: 403-539-2248
calgary.help@dntw.com
www.dntw.com

Calgary: D.W. Robart Professional Corporation
#1800, 540 - 5th Ave. SW
Calgary, AB T2P 0M2
Tel: 403-266-2611; Fax: 403-265-8626

Calgary: Flood & Associates Consulting Ltd.
#410, 840 - 6 Ave. SW
Calgary, AB T2P 3E5
Tel: 403-263-1523; Fax: 403-263-1524
flood_co@telusplanet.net

Calgary: Garrett Gray Chartered Accountants
Parkside Place
#920, 602 - 12 Ave. SW
Calgary, AB T2R 1J3
Tel: 403-806-2850; Fax: 403-806-2854
info@garrettgray.com
www.garrettgray.com

Calgary: Hamilton & Rosenthal Chartered Accountants
1034 - 8th Ave. SW
Calgary, AB T2P 1J2
Tel: 403-266-2175; Fax: 403-514-2211
www.hamrose.com

Calgary: Kenway Mack Slusarchuk Stewart LLP
#220, 333 - 11 Ave. SW
Calgary, AB T2R 1L9
Tel: 403-233-7750; Fax: 403-266-5267
info@kmss.ca
www.kmss.ca

Calgary: Kirk Wormley Chartered Accountant
#806, 7015 Macleod Trail SW
Calgary, AB T2H 2K6
Tel: 403-266-5607; Fax: 403-201-0248
kirkwormley@shaw.ca
www.kirkwormley.ca

Calgary: Lalani & Co.
#101, 4707 - 1 St. SW
Calgary, AB T2G 0A1
Tel: 403-693-3310; Fax: 403-214-7869

Calgary: Laurie Mounteer Professional Corp.
560 Parkridge Dr. SE
Calgary, AB T2J 4Z3
Tel: 403-249-9944
laurie@mounteer.ca
www.expatax.ca

Calgary: Lo Porter Hétu
#601, 2535 - 3 Ave. SE
Calgary, AB T2A 7W5
Tel: 403-283-1088; Fax: 403-283-1044
calgary@porterhetu.com
www.porterhetu.com

Calgary: The Matthews Group
#201, 1508 - 8th St. SW
Calgary, AB T2R 1R6
Tel: 403-229-0066; Fax: 403-229-2817
matthewsgrp@telus.net
www.matthewsgrp.com

Calgary: McKinnon & Co., Chartered Accountants
740, 10655 Southport Rd. SW
Calgary, AB T2W 4Y1
Tel: 403-262-9260;

Calgary: Mitchell Kelly Jones & Associates Inc.
#1070, 340 - 12 Ave. SW
Calgary, AB T2R 1L5
Tel: 403-265-8545; Fax: 403-265-8554

Calgary: PricewaterhouseCoopers LLP, Canada - Calgary
Suncor Energy Centre
#3100, 111 - 5th Ave. SW
Calgary, AB T2P 5L3
Tel: 403-509-7500; Fax: 403-781-1825
www.pwc.com/ca

Calgary: Vertefeuille Rempel Chartered Accountants
#401, 304 - 8 Ave. SW
Calgary, AB T2P 1C2
Tel: 403-294-0733; Fax: 403-294-0734
Toll-Free: 877-794-0733
www.vertrempel.com

Canmore: Collins Barrow Chartered Accountants - Canmore
#1, 714 - 10th St.
Canmore, AB T1W 2A6
Tel: 403-678-4444; Fax: 403-678-5163
cbcanmore@cbrockies.com
www.cbrockies.com

Cochrane: W. Callaway Professional Corporation
PO Box 61
Site 5, RR#1
Cochrane, AB T4C 1A1
Tel: 403-932-5433; Fax: 403-932-5577
bill@wcallaway.com
www.wcallaway.com

Edmonton: Bernhard Brinkmann Chartered Accountant
PO Box 82090, Yellowbird Stn. Yellowbird
#200, 3205 - 97 St. NW
Edmonton, AB T6N 1B7
Tel: 780-434-2756; Fax: 780-463-7605
bhbrinkmann@brinkmann.ca
www.brinkmann.ca

Edmonton: Collins Barrow Chartered Accountants - Edmonton
Commerce Place
#2380, 10155 - 102 St. NW
Edmonton, AB T5J 4G8
Tel: 780-428-1522; Fax: 780-425-8189
edmonton@collinsbarrow.com

Edmonton: DFK Canada Inc.
1923 - 151 Ave.
Edmonton, AB T5Y 1W1
Tel: 780-472-4334; Fax: 780-472-4334
exec@dfk.ca
www.dfk.ca

Edmonton: Givens LLP, Edmonton
#201, West Chambers - 12220 Stony Plain Rd.
Edmonton, AB T5N 3Y4
Tel: 780-482-7337; Fax: 780-482-7423
edmonton@porterhetu.com
www.porterhetu.com

Edmonton: Hawkings Epp Dumont Chartered Accountants
Mayfield Square I
10476 Mayfield Rd.
Edmonton, AB T5P 4P4
Tel: 780-489-9606; Fax: 780-484-9689
www.hawkings.com

Edmonton: King & Company
#1201, Energy Sq.
10109 - 106 St.
Edmonton, AB T5J 3L7
Tel: 780-423-2437; Fax: 780-426-5861

Edmonton: Koehli Wickenberg Chartered Accountants
#105, 4990 - 92nd Ave.
Edmonton, AB T6B 2V4
Tel: 780-466-6204; Fax: 780-466-6262

Edmonton: Liu Raymond C S Chartered Accountant
#410, 10665 Jasper Ave.
Edmonton, AB T5J 3S9
Tel: 780-429-1047;

Edmonton: PricewaterhouseCoopers LLP, Canada - Edmonton
Toronto-Dominion Tower, Edmonton City Centre
#1501, 10088 - 102 Ave. NW
Edmonton, AB T5J 3N5
Tel: 780-441-6700; Fax: 780-441-6776
www.pwc.com/ca

Edmonton: Romanovsky & Associates, Chartered Accountants
10260 - 112 St.
Edmonton, AB T5K 1M4
Tel: 780-447-5830; Fax: 780-451-6291
Toll-Free: 800-861-5830
www.romanovsky.com

Edmonton: SVS Group LLP
#100, 17010 - 103 Ave.
Edmonton, AB T5S 1K7
Tel: 780-486-3357; Fax: 780-486-3320
dvisser@svsgroup.ca
www.svsgroup.ca

Fort Saskatchewan: Givens LLP, Fort Saskatchewan
9928 - 99 Ave.
Fort Saskatchewan, AB T8L 4G8
Tel: 780-998-2110; Fax: 780-998-0276
fortsask@porterhetu.com
www.porterhetu.com

High River: Muth & Company
PO Box 5039
19 - 3 Ave. SE
High River, AB T1V 1M3
Tel: 403-652-4272; Fax: 403-652-2339
highriver@porterhetu.com
www.porterhetu.com

Lacombe: Cookson Kooyman Chartered Accountants
#220, 5001 - 52nd St.
Lacombe, AB T4L 2A6
Tel: 403-782-3361; Fax: 403-782-3070
lacombe@ckca.net

Leduc: Luchak Wright Wnuk Chartered Accountants
4716 - 51 Ave.
Leduc, AB T9E 6Y8
Tel: 780-986-8383; Fax: 780-986-4499
Toll-Free: 888-986-8383
lww@lwwca.com
www.lwwca.com

Lethbridge: John Van Dyk, Professional Corporation
#801B, 3 Ave. South
Lethbridge, AB T1J 2B9
Tel: 403-317-4500; Fax: 403-317-4501
justin.vandyk@telus.net

Lethbridge: Young Parkyn McNab LLP (YPM)
#100, 530 - 8 St. South
Lethbridge, AB T1J 2J8
Tel: 403-382-6800; Fax: 403-327-8990
Toll-Free: 800-665-5034
www.ypm.ca

Red Deer: Collins Barrow Chartered Accountants - Red Deer
Collins Barrow Centre
#300, 5010 - 43 St.
Red Deer, AB T4N 6H2
Tel: 403-342-5541; Fax: 403-347-3766
reddeer@collinsbarrow.com
www.collinsbarrowreddeer.ab.ca

Slave Lake: Nash & Company
PO Box 129
Slave Lake, AB T0G 2A0
Tel: 780-849-3977; Fax: 780-849-3244
slavelake@porterhetu.com
www.porterhetu.com

St Paul: Desjardins & Company
PO Box 1600
4440 - 50 Ave.
St Paul, AB T0A 3A0
Tel: 780-645-5516; Fax: 780-645-6010
office@desjardins-co.com
www.desjardins-co.com

Stettler: Gitzel Krejci Dand Peterson
PO Box 460
4912 - 51 St.
Stettler, AB T0C 2L0
Tel: 403-742-4431; Fax: 403-742-1266
Toll-Free: 877-742-4431
gkdpca@gkdpca.com
www.gkdpca.com

Sundre: Valerie L. Burrell Chartered Accountant
#201, 101 - 6 St. SW
Sundre, AB T0M 1X0
Tel: 403-638-3116; Fax: 403-638-9166
valb@telusplanet.net
www.sundre-cornerbrook.com/Accountant/

Vegreville: Wilde and Company
PO Box 70
4902 - 50th St.
Vegreville, AB T9C 1R1
Tel: 780-632-3673; Fax: 780-632-6133
Toll-Free: 800-808-0998
office@wildeandco.com
www.wildeandco.com

Wainright: Hall & Company
291 - 10th St.
Wainright, AB T9W 1N7
Tel: 780-842-6106; Fax: 780-842-5540
Toll-Free: 888-842-6106
barry@hallco.ca
www.hallco.ca

British Columbia

Abbotsford: McDonald & Co.
#301, 2955 Gladwin Rd.
Abbotsford, BC V2T 5T4
Tel: 604-853-5225;

Burnaby: Barkman & Tanaka
Lougheed Plaza
#225, 9600 Cameron St.
Burnaby, BC V3J 7N3
Tel: 604-421-2591; Fax: 604-421-1171

Burnaby: Kanester Johal Chartered Accountants
#208, 3993 Henning Dr.
Burnaby, BC V5C 6P7
Tel: 604-451-8300; Fax: 604-451-8301
info@kjca.com
www.kjca.com

Burnaby: Kemp Harvey Goodison Inc.
#210, 6400 Roberts St.
Burnaby, BC V5G 4C9
Tel: 604-291-1470; Fax: 604-291-0264
Burnaby@khgcga.com
www.khgcga.com

Burns Lake: M. McPhail & Associates Inc.
PO Box 597
Burns Lake, BC V0J 1E0
Tel: 250-692-7595; Fax: 250-692-3872
mcphail@mcphailcga.com
www.mcphailcga.com

Campbell River: Chase Sekulich Chartered Accountants
#101, 400 Tenth Ave.
Campbell River, BC V9W 4E3
Tel: 250-287-8331; Fax: 250-287-7224
Toll-Free: 866-317-8331
office@chasesekulich.com
www.chasesekulich.com

Campbell River: Eidsvik & Co.
#303, 1100 Island Hwy.
Campbell River, BC V9W 8C6
Tel: 250-286-6629; Fax: 250-286-6779

Castlegar: Craig Gutwald Inc.
880 Waterloo Rd.
Castlegar, BC V1N 4K8
Tel: 250-365-0434; Fax: 250-365-0469
www.gutwald.ca

Duncan: Atchison Palmer Leslie Chartered Accountants
#301, 394 Duncan St.
Duncan, BC V9L 3W4
Tel: 250-748-1426; Fax: 250-748-9724
www.aplaccountants.com

Grand Forks: Kemp Harvey Burch Kientz Inc.
PO Box 2020
619 Central Ave.
Grand Forks, BC V0H 1H0
Tel: 250-442-2121; Fax: 250-442-5825
GrandForks@khgcga.com
www.khgcga.com

Kelowna: Chun & Company
#202, 3320 Richter St.
Kelowna, BC V1W 4V5
Tel: 250-860-8687; Fax: 250-860-8413
www.chun.ca

Kelowna: Wahl & Associates
#103, 1441 Ellis St.
Kelowna, BC V1Y 2A3
Tel: 250-762-3362; Fax: 250-762-3409
info@wahlcga.com
www.wahlcga.com

Madeira Park: Bonnie Murray Inc.
PO Box 70
Madeira Park, BC V0N 2H0
Tel: 604-883-2857; Fax: 604-883-2861

Maple Ridge: Choquette & Company Accounting Group
10662 - 240A St.
Maple Ridge, BC V2W 2B1
Tel: 604-463-8202; Fax: 604-463-8210
Toll-Free: 800-667-9254
info@choquetteco.com
www.choquetteco.com
Other Contact Information: Skype: 604-463-8202

Nanaimo: Church Pickard & Co.
#301, 17 Church St.
Nanaimo, BC V9R 5H5
Tel: 250-754-6396; Fax: 250-754-8177
Toll-Free: 866-754-6396
mail@churchpickard.com
www.churchpickard.com

Nanaimo: Gary Ruffle Ltd.
5107 Somerset Dr., #C
Nanaimo, BC V9T 2K5
Tel: 250-758-5557; Fax: 250-758-5720
garyruffleltd@shaw.ca
www.garyruffleltd.com

Nanaimo: Robert F. Fischer & Company Inc., C.G.A.
#13, 327 Prideaux St.
Nanaimo, BC V9R 2N4
Tel: 250-753-7287; Fax: 250-753-7453

Nelson: Carmichael, Toews, Irving Inc.
247 Baker St.
Nelson, BC V1L 4H4
Tel: 250-354-4451; Fax: 250-354-4427
admin@cti-cga.com
www.cti-cga.com

New Denver: Mark Adams Ltd.
316 6th Ave.
New Denver, BC V0G 1S0
Tel: 250-358-2411;

North Vancouver: Gray & Associates
#201, 1075 West 1st St.
North Vancouver, BC V7P 3T4
Tel: 604-990-0550; Fax: 604-990-0509
Toll-Free: 800-990-0550
info@grayandassociates.ca
grayandassociates.ca

North Vancouver: J. Casperson & Associates Ltd.
221 Rondoval Cres.
North Vancouver, BC V7N 2W6
Tel: 604-983-2113; Fax: 604-983-2114
jindra@jcasperson.com
jcaspersonassociatesltd.supersites.ca

North Vancouver: MacDonald Tash & Associates
#120, 889 Harbourside Dr.
North Vancouver, BC V7P 3S1
Tel: 604-987-2300; Fax: 604-987-2888
taxmatters@taxmatters.ca
www.taxmatters.ca

North Vancouver: Misam Canada Consulting Ltd.
#107, 998 Harbourside Dr.
North Vancouver, BC V7P 3T2
Tel: 604-984-3309; Fax: 604-984-3308
info@misamcanada.com
www.misamcanada.com
Social Media: www.twitter.com/MCS_Consulting

Oliver: Kemp Harvey Casorso Inc.
PO Box 1478
34864 - 97th St.
Oliver, BC V0H 1T0
Tel: 250-498-4977; Fax: 250-498-4330
Oliver@khgcga.com
www.khgcga.com

Osoyoos: Kemp Harvey Kemp - Osoyoos
8901 Main St.
Osoyoos, BC V0H 1V0
Tel: 250-495-3223; Fax: 250-495-3559
Toll-Free: 888-9850-5595
Osoyoos@khgcga.com
www.khgcga.com

Osoyoos: White Kennedy, Chartered Accountants - Osoyoos
PO Box 260
#204, 8309 Main St.
Osoyoos, BC V0H 1V0
Tel: 250-495-2688; Fax: 250-495-3525
osoyoos@whitekennedy.com
www.whitekennedy.com

Penticton: Harvey Lister & Webb Incorporated
502 Ellis St.
Penticton, BC V2A 4M3
Tel: 250-492-8821; Fax: 250-492-8288
info@harveylisterwebb.com
www.harveylisterwebb.com

Penticton: Kemp Harvey Kemp - Penticton
445 Ellis St.
Penticton, BC V2A 4M1
Tel: 250-492-8800; Fax: 250-492-6921
Penticton@khgcga.com
www.khgcga.com

Penticton: White Kennedy, Chartered Accountants - Penticton
#201, 99 Padmore Ave. East
Penticton, BC V2A 7H7
Tel: 250-493-0600; Fax: 250-493-4709
penticton@whitekennedy.com
www.whitekennedy.com

Port Coquitlam: Kemp Harvey de Roca Chan Inc.
#2300, 2850 Shaughnessy St.
Port Coquitlam, BC V3C 6K5
Tel: 604-552-4388; Fax: 604-552-7709
poco@khgcga.com
www.khgcga.com

Port Moody: Gregory & Associates
#402, 130 Brew St.
Port Moody, BC V3H 0E3
Tel: 604-939-2929; Fax: 604-936-4002
info@gregorywhittle.ca
www.gregorywhittle.ca

Prince George: Terlesky Braithwaite Janzen, Certified General Accountants
#300, 180 Victoria St.
Prince George, BC V2L 2J2
Tel: 250-564-2014; Fax: 250-564-5613
Toll-Free: 888-564-2014
tbjpg@tbjcga.com
www.tbjcga.com

Richmond: Bruce Dunn & Company Inc., Chartered Accountants
#200, 5760 Minoru Blvd.
Richmond, BC V6X 2A9
Tel: 604-241-8824; Fax: 604-241-8800
info@brucedunn.ca
www.brucedunn.ca

Richmond: Greig Sheppard Ltd.
5090 - 8171 Ackroyd Rd.
Richmond, BC V6X 3K1
Tel: 604-270-7601; Fax: 604-270-3314
cga@greigsheppard.com
www.greigsheppard.com

Richmond: Jerry's Accounting Ltd.
#530, 130 - 8191 Westminster Hwy.
Richmond, BC V6X 1A7
Tel: 604-273-7789; Fax: 604-273-9449
jerryky@shaw.ca
www.jerryaccounting.com

Richmond: Sunny Sun & Associates Inc.
#708, 6081 No. 3 Rd.
Richmond, BC V6Y 2B2
Tel: 604-270-4610; Fax: 604-270-4618
info@sunnycga.com
www.sunnycga.com

Squamish: McMillan Thorn, Certified General Accountants - Squamish
PO Box 2120
38013 - 3rd Ave.
Squamish, BC V0N 3G0
Tel: 604-892-5281; Fax: 604-892-5276
squamish@mcmillanthorn.com
www.mcmillanthorn.com

Surrey: Heming, Wyborn & Grewal
#200, 17618 - 58 Ave.
Surrey, BC V3S 1L3
Tel: 604-576-9121; Fax: 604-576-2890
hwgca@hwgca.com
www.hwgca.com

Surrey: Luckett Wenman & Associates
#204, 10252 - 135th St.
Surrey, BC V3T 4C2
Tel: 604-584-3566; Fax: 604-584-0629
Toll-Free: 866-584-3566
contact@luckettwenman.com
www.luckettwenman.com

Surrey: PricewaterhouseCoopers LLP, Canada - Surrey
#1400, 13450 - 102nd Ave.
Surrey, BC V3T 5X3
Tel: 604-806-7000; Fax: 604-806-7806
www.pwc.com/ca

Surrey: Sharma & Associates
#205, 8388 - 128th St.
Surrey, BC V3W 4G2
Tel: 604-597-5612; Fax: 604-590-5808
satish@sharmacga.com; hari@sharmacga.com
www.sharmacga.com

Surrey: Sunny Sun & Associates Inc. - Surrey
#200, 10193 - 152A St.
Surrey, BC V3R 4H6
Tel: 604-270-4613; Fax: 604-270-4618
info@sunnycga.com
www.sunnycga.com

Surrey: Van Wensem, Eakins & George
17678 - 58A Ave.
Surrey, BC V3S 8V7
Tel: 604-576-9242; Fax: 604-576-9258
info@vweg-cga.com
www.vweg-cga.com

Terrace: Demers & Associates
#201, 4716 Lazelle Ave.
Terrace, BC V8G 1T2
Tel: 250-638-8705; Fax: 250-638-0600
info@demerscga.com
www.demerscga.com

Vancouver: Bing C. Wong & Associates Ltd.
124 East Pender St., 3rd Fl.
Vancouver, BC V6A 1T3
Tel: 604-682-7561; Fax: 604-682-7665

Vancouver: Blair Crosson Voyer Chartered Accountants
Commerce Pl.
#1650, 400, Burrard St.
Vancouver, BC V6C 3A6
Tel: 604-684-3371; Fax: 604-684-9832

Vancouver: Campbell, Saunders Ltd.
#1000, 570 Granville St.
Vancouver, BC V6C 3P1
Tel: 604-915-5550; Fax: 604-915-5560
jmccracken@csvan.com
www.csvan.com

Vancouver: Cawley & Associates
1622 - 7th Ave. West, 3rd Fl.
Vancouver, BC V6J 1S5
Tel: 604-731-1191; Fax: 604-731-3511
bcawley@cawley.ca
www.cawley.ca

Vancouver: Collins Barrow Chartered Accountants - Vancouver
Burrard Bldg.
#800, 1030 West Georgia St.
Vancouver, BC V6E 3B9
Tel: 604-685-0564; Fax: 604-685-2050
vancouver@collinsbarrow.com

Vancouver: D&H Group
1333 West Broadway St., 10th Fl.
Vancouver, BC V6H 4C1
Tel: 604-731-5881; Fax: 604-731-9923
info@dhgroup.ca
www.dhgroup.ca

Vancouver: David Lin, Certified General Accountant
5728 East Blvd.
Vancouver, BC V6M 4M4
Tel: 604-267-0381
dlin@telus.net
www3.telus.net/davidlin

Vancouver: Davidson & Co.
Stock Exchange Tower
PO Box 10372
#1200, 609 Granville St.
Vancouver, BC V7Y 1G6
Tel: 604-687-0947; Fax: 604-687-6172
davidson@davidson-co.com
www.davidson-co.com

Vancouver: Equity Business Services Inc.
#200, 1892 West Broadway
Vancouver, BC V6J 1Y9
Tel: 604-874-9080; Fax: 604-874-9080
ehoy@equityinc.ca
www.equityinc.ca

Vancouver: Galloway Botteselle & Company
Maple Place Professional Centre
#300, 2000 West 12th Ave.
Vancouver, BC V6J 2G2
Tel: 604-736-6581; Fax: 604-736-0152
vancouver@porterhetu.com
www.porterhetu.com

Vancouver: Greenberg Associates
North Office Tower, Oakridge Centre
#489, 650 West 41st Ave.
Vancouver, BC V5Z 2M9
Tel: 604-264-5170; Fax: 604-264-5101
general@cga-gb.com
www.cga-gb.com

Vancouver: Lam Lo Nishio Chartered Accountants
659-G Moberly Rd.
Vancouver, BC V5Z 4B2
Tel: 604-872-8883; Fax: 604-872-8889
info@lamlonishio.ca
www.lamlonishio.ca

Vancouver: Lancaster & David, Chartered Accountants
PO Box 10122, Pacific Centre Stn. Pacific Centre
#510, 701 West Georgia St.
Vancouver, BC V7Y 1C6
Tel: 604-717-5526; Fax: 604-717-5560
admin@lancasteranddavid.ca
www.lancasteranddavid.ca

Vancouver: Manning Elliott
1050 West Pender, 11th Fl.
Vancouver, BC V6J 3S7
Tel: 604-714-3600; Fax: 604-714-3669
info@manningelliott.com
www.manningelliott.com

Vancouver: N.I. Cameron Inc.
#303, 475 Howe St.
Vancouver, BC V6C 2B3
Tel: 604-669-9631; Fax: 604-669-1848
info@nicameroninc.com
www.nicameroninc.com

Vancouver: PricewaterhouseCoopers LLP, Canada - Vancouver
PricewaterhouseCoopers Place
250 Howe St., 7th Fl.
Vancouver, BC V6C 3S7
Tel: 604-806-7000; Fax: 604-806-7806
www.pwc.com/ca

Vancouver: Quantum Accounting Services Inc.
#205, 873 Beatty St.
Vancouver, BC V6B 2M6
Tel: 604-662-8985; Fax: 604-662-8986
www.qas.bc.ca

Vancouver: Rolfe, Benson Chartered Accountants
#1400, 900 West Hastings St.
Vancouver, BC V6C 1E3
Tel: 604-684-1101; Fax: 604-684-7937
admin@rolfebenson.com
www.rolfebenson.com

Vancouver: Smythe Ratcliffe Chartered Accountants
#700, 355 Burrard St.
Vancouver, BC V6C 2G8
Tel: 604-687-1231; Fax: 604-688-4675
reception@smytheratcliffe.com
www.smytheratcliffe.com

Vancouver: Stan W. Lee
North Tower
#628, 650 West 41st Ave.
Vancouver, BC V5Z 2M9
Tel: 604-291-6016; Fax: 604-291-2018
stan@stanwleeca.com
www.stanwleeca.com

Vancouver: Strategex Group
#210, 1075 West Georgia St.
Vancouver, BC V6E 3C9
Tel: 604-688-2355; Fax: 604-688-2315
www.strategexgroup.ca

Vancouver: Watson Dauphinee & Masuch Chartered Accountants
#420, 1501 West Broadway Ave.
Vancouver, BC V6J 4Z6
Tel: 604-734-3247; Fax: 604-734-4802
info@wdmca.com
www.wdmca.com

Vernon: Clark Robinson
3109 - 32nd Ave.
Vernon, BC V1T 2M2
Tel: 250-545-7264; Fax: 250-542-5116
info@clarkrobinson.com
www.clarkrobinson.com

Vernon: Kemp Harvey Laidman-Betts Inc.
#204, 3334 - 30th Ave.
Vernon, BC V1T 2C8
Tel: 250-545-1544; Fax: 250-260-3641
Toll-Free: 877-547-1544
Vernon@khgcga.com
www.khgcga.com

Vernon: Willis Associates
#100, 2903 - 35th Ave.
Vernon, BC V1T 2S7
Tel: 250-549-2922; Fax: 250-542-8300
Toll-Free: 888-333-2922
www.willisassociates.ca

Victoria: Burkett & Abercrombie Chartered Accountants
#200, 3561 Shelbourne St.
Victoria, BC V8P 4G8
Tel: 250-370-9718; Fax: 250-370-9179
accountants@burkett.ca
www.burkett.ca

Victoria: Feil & Co.
1580 Cook St.
Victoria, BC V8T 3N8
Tel: 250-382-6177; Fax: 250-385-0154
email@feilnco.com
www.feilnco.com

Victoria: Ian B. Lawson & Co. Inc.
Shamrock Professional Centre
#201, 830 Shamrock St.
Victoria, BC V8X 2V1
Tel: 250-475-0222; Fax: 250-475-0229
victoria@porterhetu.com
www.porterhetu.com; www.iblawson.shawbiz.ca

Westbank: White Kennedy, Chartered Accountants - Westbank
#1, 2429 Dobbin Rd.
Westbank, BC V4T 2L4
Tel: 250-768-3400; Fax: 240-768-3445
westbank@whitekennedy.com
www.whitekennedy.com

Whistler: Gershon & Company
#207A, 4368 Main St.
Whistler, BC V0N 1B0
Tel: 604-938-1892; Fax: 604-938-1870
www.gershonandco.com

Whistler: Gordon J. Wiber & Associates Inc.
#22, 1212 Alpha Lake Rd.
Whistler, BC V0N 1B2
Tel: 604-935-1114; Fax: 604-935-1154
www.whistlerca.com

Whistler: J. Casperson & Associates Ltd. - Whistler
2509 Whistler Road
Whistler, BC V7X 1B0
Tel: 604-932-2450
jindra@jcasperson.com
jcaspersonassociatesltd.supersites.ca

Whistler: McMillan Thorn, Certified General Accountants - Whistler
#204, 1085 Millar Creek Rd.
Whistler, BC V0N 1B1
Tel: 604-938-1544; Fax: 604-938-1577
mail@mcmillanthorn.com
www.mcmillanthorn.com

Manitoba

Carman: Nakonechny & Power Chartered Accountants Ltd.
PO Box 880
31 Main St. South
Carman, MB R0G 0J0
Tel: 204-745-2061; Fax: 204-745-6322
www.nakandpow.com

Souris: Karen G. Duthie, CGA
PO Box 927
Souris, MB R0K 2C0
Tel: 204-483-3903; Fax: 204-483-2489
kduthie@porterhetu.com
www.porterhetu.com

Swan River: Pacak Kowal Hardie & Company, Chartered Accountants
PO Box 1660
#100, 4th Avenue North
Swan River, MB R0L 1Z0
Tel: 204-734-9331; Fax: 204-734-4785
Toll-Free: 800-743-8447
pkhl@pkhl.ca
www.pacakkowalhardie.com

Swan River: Reimer & Company Inc.
PO Box 146
359 Kelsey Trail
Swan River, MB R0L 1Z0
Tel: 204-734-2599; Fax: 204-734-3184
info@reimerco.ca
www.reimerco.ca

Thompson: Kendall Wall Pandya, Chartered Accountants
118 Cree Rd.
Thompson, MB R8N 0C1
Tel: 204-778-7312; Fax: 204-778-7919

Winnipeg: A.L. Schellenberg, Chartered Accountant
474 Panet Rd.
Winnipeg, MB R2C 3B9
Tel: 204-669-5143; Fax: 204-669-5145
leon@mts.net

Winnipeg: BCCA LLP Chartered Accountants
#1505, 444 St. Mary Ave.
Winnipeg, MB R3C 3T1
Tel: 204-957-7000; Fax: 204-949-1191
mail@bccallp.com
www.bccallp.com

Winnipeg: Booke & Partners
#500, 5 Donald St.
Winnipeg, MB R3L 2T4
Tel: 204-284-7060; Fax: 204-284-7105
www.bookeandpartners.ca

Winnipeg: Chochinov Porter Hétu
#1250, 363 Broadway Ave.
Winnipeg, MB R3C 3N9
Tel: 204-956-1685; Fax: 204-957-7694
schochinov@porterhetu.com
www.porterhetu.com

Winnipeg: Craig & Ross Chartered Accountants
#1515, 1 Lombard Place
Winnipeg, MB R3B 0X3
Tel: 204-956-9400; Fax: 204-956-9424
info@craigross.com
www.craigross.com

Winnipeg: Craig R. Burgess, CGA
383 McMillan Ave.
Winnipeg, MB R3L 0N3
Tel: 204-334-8972; Fax: 204-334-8448
cburgess@porterhetu.com
www.porterhetu.com

Winnipeg: The Exchange Chartered Accountants LLP
#100, 123 Bannatyne Ave.
Winnipeg, MB R3B 0R3
Tel: 204-943-4584; Fax: 204-957-5195
info@exg.ca
www.exg.ca

Winnipeg: Gaudette Elvers LLP
738 Osborne St.
Winnipeg, MB R3L 2C2
Tel: 204-489-2781; Fax: 204-452-5956
gelvers@porterhetu.com; egaudette@porterhetu.com
www.porterhetu.com

Winnipeg: Knowles Warkentin & Bridges, Chartered Accountants
#800, 125 Garry St.
Winnipeg, MB R3C 3P2
Tel: 204-982-3878; Fax: 204-982-3888
connor@kwb.ca
www.kwb.ca

Winnipeg: Lazer Grant LLP Chartered Accountants & Business Advisors
#300, 309 McDermot Ave.
Winnipeg, MB R3A 1T3
Tel: 204-942-0300; Fax: 204-957-5611
Toll-Free: 800-220-0005
LazerGrant@lazergrant.ca
www.lazergrant.ca

Winnipeg: M Group Chartered Accountants
710 Corydon Ave.
Winnipeg, MB R3M 0X9
Tel: 204-992-7200; Fax: 204-992-7208
info@mgroup.ca
www.mgroup.ca

Winnipeg: Magnus & Buffie Chartered Accountants
#1810, 444 St. Mary Ave.
Winnipeg, MB R3C 3T1
Tel: 204-942-4441; Fax: 204-944-0400

Winnipeg: PKBW Group, Chartered Accountants & Business Advisors Inc.
219 Fort St.
Winnipeg, MB R3C 1E2
Tel: 204-942-0861; Fax: 204-947-6834
senez@pkbwgroup.ca
www.pkbwgroup.ca

Winnipeg: Pope & Brookes, DFK LLP, Chartered Accountants
#300, 530 Kenaston Blvd.
Winnipeg, MB R3N 1Z4
Tel: 204-487-7957; Fax: 204-487-1243
advice@pb-dfk.com
www.pb-dfk.com

Winnipeg: PPW Chartered Accountants LLP
#209, 1661 Portage Ave.
Winnipeg, MB R3J 3T7
Tel: 204-772-4936; Fax: 204-774-4462
solutions@ppw.ca
www.ppw.ca

Winnipeg: PricewaterhouseCoopers LLP, Canada - Winnipeg
Richardson Bldg.
#2300, 1 Lombard Pl.
Winnipeg, MB R3B 0X6
Tel: 204-926-2400; Fax: 204-994-1020
www.pwc.com/ca

Winnipeg: RDK Chartered Accountant Ltd.
5 Whitkirk Place
Winnipeg, MB R3R 2A2
Tel: 204-885-5280; Fax: 204-831-6670
admin@rdkcharteredaccountant.com
www.rdkcharteredaccountant.com

Winnipeg: Scarrow & Donald LLP
#100, 5 Donald St.
Winnipeg, MB R3L 2T4
Tel: 204-982-9800; Fax: 204-474-2886
sd@scarrowdonald.mb.ca
www.scarrowdonald.mb.ca

New Brunswick

Campbellton: Allen, Paquet & Arseneau LLP
PO Box 519
207 Roseberry St.
Campbellton, NB E3N 3G9
Tel: 506-789-0820; Fax: 506-759-7514
apada@apa-ca.com
www.apa-ca.com

Edmundston: LeBlanc Nadeau Bujold - Edmundston
25 Carrier St.
Edmundston, NB E3V 4A3
Tel: 506-735-1820; Fax: 506-735-1821
edmundston@lnb.ca
www.lnb.ca

Florenceville: McCain & Company Chartered Accountants
PO Box 437
393 Main St.
Florenceville, NB E7L 1Y9
Tel: 506-392-5517; Fax: 506-392-5341
fhmccain@mccainandco.com
www.mccainandco.com

Fredericton: Bringloe Feeney
#401, 212 Queen St.
Fredericton, NB E3B 1A8
Tel: 506-458-8326; Fax: 506-458-9293

Fredericton: Bringloe Feeney LLP
#401, 212 Queen St.
Fredericton, NB E3B 1A8
Tel: 506-458-8326; Fax: 506-458-9293
shawn.bringloe@bringloefeeney.ca

Fredericton: Thornton VanTassel Chartered Accountants - Fredericton
514 Queen St.
Fredericton, NB E3B 1B9
Tel: 506-451-9261; Fax: 506-459-7595
edwin.corey@thorntonvantassel.com
www.thorntonvantassel.com

Grand Falls: LeBlanc Nadeau Bujold - Grand Falls
796, boul Éverard H. Daigle
Grand Falls, NB E3Z 3C8
Tel: 506-473-4240; Fax: 506-473-9450
grand-falls@lnb.ca
www.lnb.ca

Grand Falls: Thornton VanTassel Chartered Accountants - Grand Falls
#201, 218 Broadway Blvd.
Grand Falls, NB E3Z 2J9
Tel: 506-473-5068; Fax: 506-473-7077
joe.mcphail@thorntonvantassel.com
www.thorntonvantassel.com

Moncton: Boudreau Porter Hétu
66 Donald Ave.
Moncton, NB E1A 3B1
Tel: 506-857-0262; Fax: 506-857-0232
eboudreau@porterhetu.com
www.porterhetu.com

Moncton: PricewaterhouseCoopers LLP, Canada - Moncton
#100, 1199 Main St.
Moncton, NB E1C 0L9
Tel: 506-859-8822; Fax: 506-859-8829
www.pwc.com/ca

Perth-Andover: Thornton VanTassel Chartered Accountants - Perth-Andover
#2, 15 Station St.
Perth-Andover, NB E7H 4Y2
Tel: 506-273-2276; Fax: 506-273-2033
jim.vantassel@thorntonvantassel.com
www.thorntonvantassel.com

Plaster Rock: Thornton VanTassel Chartered Accountants - Plaster Rock
240A Main St.
Plaster Rock, NB E7G 2E1
Tel: 506-356-2641; Fax: 506-356-8493
theresa.wark@thorntonvantassel.com
www.thorntonvantassel.com

Riverview: Stevenson & Partners LLP
567 Coverdale Rd.
Riverview, NB E1B 3K7
Tel: 506-387-4044; Fax: 506-387-7270
sp@parternsnb.com
www.acgca.ca

Rothesay: Steeves Porter Hétu
Professional Centre
PO Box 4591
9 Scott Ave.
Rothesay, NB E2E 5X3
Tel: 506-847-7471; Fax: 506-847-3151
dsteeves@porterhetu.com
www.porterhetu.com

Saint John: Beers Neal LLP
#301, 53 King St.
Saint John, NB E2L 1G5
Tel: 506-632-9020; Fax: 506-632-9030
www.acgca.ca

Saint John: Curry & Betts
Admiral Beatty Building
PO Box 6789, A Stn. A
72 Charlotte St., 1st Fl.
Saint John, NB E2L 4S2
Tel: 506-635-8181; Fax: 506-633-5943
Toll-Free: 888-635-8181
www.curry-betts.ca

Saint John: PricewaterhouseCoopers LLP, Canada - Saint John
Brunswick House
PO Box 789
#300, 44 Chipman Hill
Saint John, NB E2L 4B9
Tel: 506-632-1810; Fax: 506-632-8997
www.pwc.com/ca

Saint John: Ralph H. Green & Associates
#200, 53 King St.
Saint John, NB E2L 1G5
Tel: 506-632-3000; Fax: 506-632-1007
igreen@rhgreenassociates.ca
www.rhgreenassociates.ca

St. Stephen: L K Toombs Chartered Accountants
#207, 73 Milltown Blvd.
St. Stephen, NB E3L 1G5
Tel: 506-466-3291; Fax: 506-466-9825
lktpc@nb.aibn.com
www.acgca.ca

Sussex: Turnbull & Kindred
PO Box 4608
44 Moffett Ave.
Sussex, NB E4E 5L8
Tel: 506-433-4202
aturnbull@porterhetu.com; jkindred@porterhetu.com
www.porterhetu.com

Newfoundland & Labrador

Corner Brook: J. Pike & Company Ltd.
A98-98 Broadway
Corner Brook, NL A2H 4C8
Tel: 709-639-7774; Fax: 709-639-7775

Creston: Jody Murphy, Chartered Accountant
PO Box 508
437 Creston Blvd.
Creston, NL A0E 1K0
Tel: 709-279-1888; Fax: 709-279-1895
jmurphyca@nf.sympatico.ca

Gander: Walters Hoffe
PO Box 348
30 Roe Ave.
Gander, NL A1V 1W7
Tel: 709-651-4100; Fax: 709-256-2957
info@waltershoffe.com
waltershoffe.com

Mount Pearl: Feltham Attwood
#202, 39 Commonwealth Ave.
Mount Pearl, NL A1N 1W7
Tel: 709-364-7300; Fax: 709-364-7731
debra@feltham-attwood.ca
www.porterhetu.com

St. John's: Belanger Clarke Follett & McGettigan
53 Bond St.
St. John's, NL A1C 1S9
Tel: 709-579-2161; Fax: 709-738-2391

St. John's: PricewaterhouseCoopers LLP, Canada - St. John's
Atlantic Place
#802, 215 Water St.
St. John's, NL A1C 6C9
Tel: 709-722-3883; Fax: 709-722-5874
www.pwc.com/ca

Northwest Territories

Yellowknife: Avery Cooper & Co.
Laurentian Building
PO Box 1620
4918, 50th St.
Yellowknife, NT X1A 2P2
Tel: 867-873-3441; Fax: 867-873-2353
Toll-Free: 800-661-0787
avery@averyco.nt.ca
www.averyco.nt.ca

Nova Scotia

Amherst: sj mcisaac Chartered Accountants
PO Box 217
Amherst, NS B4H 3Z2
Tel: 902-661-1027; Fax: 902-667-0884
Toll-Free: 877-282-6632
www.sjmcisaac.ca

Bedford: David B. Etter
117 Brentwood Dr.
Bedford, NS B4A 3S3
Tel: 902-456-1031; Fax: 902-835-5431
detter@porterhetu.com
www.porterhetu.com

Bedford: WBLI Chartered Accountants
26 Union St.
Bedford, NS B4A 2B5
Tel: 902-835-7333; Fax: 902-835-5297
www.wbli.ca

Bridgewater: Belliveau Veinotte Inc.
PO Box 29
11 Dominion St.
Bridgewater, NS B4V 2W6
Tel: 902-543-4278; Fax: 902-543-1818
office@bvca.ca
www.acgca.ca

Cheticamp: Harold Patrick Aucoin CGA, Inc.
15262 Cabot Trail
Cheticamp, NS B0E 1H0
Tel: 902-224-3748; Fax: 902-224-2092
haroldaucoin@haroldaucoincga.ca
www.haroldaucoincga.ca; www.porterhetu.com

Dartmouth: Connor & Associates Limited
244 Colby Dr.
Dartmouth, NS B2V 1K1
Tel: 902-482-9482; Fax: 902-435-6192
Toll-Free: 888-666-5764
www.connoraccounting.com

Dartmouth: Hunter Tellier Belgrave Adamson
Cambridge 1
#200, 202 Brownlow Ave.
Dartmouth, NS B3B 1T5
Tel: 902-468-1949; Fax: 902-468-4865
service@achba.ca

Dartmouth: Jean-Marc Chassé Inc.
#44, 201 Browlow Ave.
Dartmouth, NS B3B 1W2
Tel: 902-468-0282; Fax: 902-468-6150
jmchasse@porterhetu.com
www.porterhetu.com

Dartmouth: McNeil Porter Hétu
344 Prince Albert Rd.
Dartmouth, NS B2Y 1N6
Tel: 902-464-9300; Fax: 902-464-7246
dmcneil@porterhetu.com
www.porterhetu.com

Halifax: Dockrill Horwich Rossiter
#440, 36 Solutions Dr.
Halifax, NS B3S 1N2
Tel: 902-835-0232; Fax: 902-835-0060
www.acgca.ca

Halifax: Lyle Tilley Davidson
#720, 1718 Argyle St.
Halifax, NS B3J 3N6
Tel: 902-423-7225; Fax: 902-422-3649
info@ltdca.com; ward@ltdca.com
www.ltdca.com

Halifax: PricewaterhouseCoopers LLP, Canada - Halifax
#400, 1601 Lower Water St.
Halifax, NS B3J 3P6
Tel: 903-491-7400; Fax: 903-422-1166
www.pwc.com/ca

New Glasgow: Williams MacDonald Inc.
400 East River Rd.
New Glasgow, NS B2H 3P7
Tel: 902-752-0463; Fax: 902-755-2823
www.acgca.ca

Sydney: MGM & Associates Chartered Accountants
PO Box 1
Sydney, NS B1P 6G9
Tel: 902-539-3900; Fax: 902-564-6062
www.mgm.ca

Sydney: MGM Inc.
Commerce Tower
15 Dorchester St.
Sydney, NS B1P 6G9
Tel: 902-539-3900; Fax: 902-564-6062
trustee@mgm.ca
www.mgmtrustee.ca

Sydney: PricewaterhouseCoopers LLP, Canada - Sydney
#220, 500 George St.
Sydney, NS B1P 1K6
Tel: 902-564-0802; Fax: 902-564-1470
www.pwc.com/ca

Truro: PricewaterhouseCoopers LLP, Canada - Truro
PO Box 632, Prince Stn. Prince
710 Prince St.
Truro, NS B2N 5E5
Tel: 902-895-1641; Fax: 902-893-0460
www.pwc.com/ca

Wolfville: Bishop & Company Chartered Accountants Inc.
189 Dykeland St.
Wolfville, NS B4P 1A3
Tel: 902-542-7665; Fax: 902-542-4554
rbishop@bcica.ca

Ontario

Ajax: Thomas & Chase
#211, 50 Commercial Ave.
Ajax, ON L1S 2H5
Tel: 905-686-2407; Fax: 905-686-2276
thomaschase@on.aibn.com
www.thomasandchase.com; www.porterhetu.com

Almonte: Colby McGeachy PC
PO Box 970
258 Greystone Cres.
Almonte, ON K0A 1A0
Tel: 613-259-2878; Fax: 613-256-7569
Toll-Free: 866-259-2878
ecolby@porterhetu.com
www.porterhetu.com

Ancaster: Brownlow & Associates
259 Wilson St. East
Ancaster, ON L9G 2B8
Tel: 905-648-0404; Fax: 905-648-0403
Toll-Free: 888-648-0404
info@brownlowcas.com
www.brownlowcas.com

Arnprior: Dave H. Laventure Professional Corporation
106 McGonigal St. West, #B
Arnprior, ON K7S 1M4
Tel: 613-623-3181; Fax: 613-623-4299
www.porterhetu.com

Aylmer: Den Harder McNames Button CGA
174 Sydenham St. East
Aylmer, ON N5H 1L7
Tel: 519-773-5348; Fax: 519-773-7409
cbutton@epraylmer.com

Bancroft: Dale Rose, CGA and Peter Stone, CA
PO Box 1209
294 Hastings St. North
Bancroft, ON K0L 1C0
Tel: 613-332-0834; Fax: 613-332-4154
Toll-Free: 800-333-0834
drose@porterhetu.com; pstone@porterhetu.com
www.porterhetu.com

Barrie: Alan Martin Associates - Barrie
72 Ross St.
Barrie, ON L4N 1G3
Tel: 705-727-0407; Fax: 705-727-7677

Barrie: Powell, Jones
121 Anne St. South
Barrie, ON L4N 7B6
Tel: 705-728-7461; Fax: 705-728-8317
Toll-Free: 888-828-7461
info@powelljones.ca
www.powelljones.ca

Belleville: Soden & Co.
25 Campbell St.
Belleville, ON K8N 1S6
Tel: 613-968-3495; Fax: 613-968-7359

Belleville: Wilkinson & Company LLP
PO Box 757
139 Front St.
Belleville, ON K8N 5B5
Tel: 613-966-5105; Fax: 613-962-7072
Toll-Free: 888-728-3890
bellevil@wilkinson.net
www.wilkinson.net

Brampton: Buttar & Associates Inc.
Jaipur Chrysler Centre
#1, 470 Chrysler Dr.
Brampton, ON L6S 0C1
Tel: 905-866-6543; Fax: 905-866-6566
www.buttar.ca

Brampton: Kenneth Bell CA Business Advisory Group
#34, 18 Regan Rd.
Brampton, ON L7A 1C2
Tel: 905-453-0844; Fax: 905-453-1530
www.kenbell.ca

Brampton: SMCA Professional Corporation
#201, 197 County Court Blvd.
Brampton, ON L6W 4P6
Tel: 905-451-4034; Fax: 905-451-7158
Toll-Free: 888-524-4844
carrollm@smca.ca
www.smca.ca

Brantford: Millard, Rouse & Rosebrugh LLP
PO Box 367
96 Nelson St.
Brantford, ON N3T 5N3
Tel: 519-759-3511; Fax: 519-759-7961
csmith@millards.com
www.millards.com

Brantford: Susan L. Rice
#15, 340 Henry St.
Brantford, ON N3S 7V9
Tel: 519-752-8290; Fax: 519-752-9784
srice@obwr.ca

Brockville: G.A. Porter, CA
21 Ormond St.
Brockville, ON K6V 2K2
Tel: 613-865-9664
gporter@porterhetu.com
www.porterhetu.com

Brockville: George Caners Chartered Accountant
#210, 9 Broad St.
Brockville, ON K6V 6Z4
Tel: 613-342-1555; Fax: 613-342-2845
Toll-Free: 888-829-9952
www.caners.com

Burlington: Bateman MacKay
PO Box 5015
4200 South Service Rd.
Burlington, ON L7R 3Y8
Tel: 905-632-6400; Fax: 905-639-2285
Toll-Free: 866-787-1117
info@batemanmackay.com
www.batemanmackay.com
Other Contact Information: Toronto Phone: 416-360-6400

Burlington: Durward Jones Barkwell & Company LLP
#103, 3430 South Service Rd.
Burlington, ON L7N 3T9
Tel: 905-681-6900; Fax: 905-681-6874
Toll-Free: 866-407-5318
burl@djb.com
www.djb.com

Burlington: Prapavessis Jasek
3410 South Service Rd., Lower Fl.
Burlington, ON L7N 3T2
Tel: 905-634-8999; Fax: 905-634-5057
jim@pj.on.ca
www.pj.on.ca

Burlington: Scott & Pichelli Ltd.
#109, 3600 Billings Ct.
Burlington, ON L7N 3N6
Tel: 905-632-5853; Fax: 905-632-6113
www.bankruptcy-trustees.ca/

Burlington: Steven J. Obranovich
650 Plains Rd. East
Burlington, ON L7T 2E9
Tel: 905-632-8400; Fax: 905-632-9505
sobranovich@obwr.ca

Burlington: Stevenson & Lehocki
310 Plains Rd. East
Burlington, ON L7T 4J2
Tel: 905-632-0640; Fax: 905-632-0645
joe@stevensonlehocki.com
www.stevensonlehocki.com

Burlington: Wade & Partners LLP, Chartered Accountants
#102, 5096 South Service Rd.
Burlington, ON L7L 5H4
Tel: 905-333-9888; Fax: 905-333-9583
ca@wadegroup.ca
www.wadegroup.ca

Cambridge: Graham Mathew & Partners LLP
PO Box 880
150 Pinebush Rd.
Cambridge, ON N1R 5X9
Tel: 519-623-1870; Fax: 519-623-9490
admin@gmpca.com
www.gmpca.com

Carleton Place: Collins Barrow Chartered Accountants - Carleton Place
52 Lansdowne Ave.
Carleton Place, ON K7C 2T8
Tel: 613-253-0014; Fax: 613-253-0129
carletonplace@collinsbarrow.com

Chatham: Collins Barrow Chartered Accountants - Chatham
62 Keil Dr. South
Chatham, ON N7M 3G8
Tel: 519-351-2024; Fax: 519-351-8831
chatham@collinsbarrow.com

Chatham: Gilhula & Grant
141 Grand Ave. East
Chatham, ON N7L 1W1
Tel: 519-352-3470; Fax: 519-352-7344
gilgrant@ciaccess.com

Chelmsford: Collins Barrow Chartered Accountants - Chelmsford
PO Box 673
48 Main St. East
Chelmsford, ON P0M 1L0
Tel: 705-560-5592; Fax: 705-855-3693
chelmsford@cbsn.ca

Concord: Burghout Viola, Chartered Accountants
#105, 7941 Jane St.
Concord, ON L4K 4L6
Tel: 905-738-6402; Fax: 905-738-1805
john@burghoutviola.com
www.burghoutviola.com

Concord: Miller, Saperia & Company
#418, 1600 Steeles Ave. West
Concord, ON L4K 4M2
Tel: 905-660-6840; Fax: 905-660-6729

Concord: Starkman Salsberg & Feldberg
#316, 1600 Steeles Ave. West
Concord, ON L4K 4M2
Tel: 905-669-9900; Fax: 905-669-9901

Elginburg: Randy E. Brown CGA
2908 Leeman Rd.
Elginburg, ON K0H 1M0
Tel: 613-542-0151; Fax: 613-549-1427
rbrown@porterhetu.com

Elmvale: Alan Martin Associates
42 Queen St.
Elmvale, ON L0L 1P0
Tel: 705-322-2440; Fax: 705-322-1462

Elora: Collins Barrow Chartered Accountants - Elora
PO Box 580
342, Gerrie Rd.
Elora, ON N0B 1S0
Tel: 519-846-5315; Fax: 519-846-9120
info@collinsbarrow.com

Fort Erie: Durward Jones Barkwell & Company, Fort Erie
#15, 1264 Garrison Rd.
Fort Erie, ON L2A 1P1
Tel: 905-871-3565; Fax: 905-871-9232
Toll-Free: 866-720-2194
forterie@djb.com
www.djb.com

Fredericton: Nicholson & Beaumont Chartered Accountants
328 King St.
Fredericton, ON E3B 5C2
Tel: 506-458-9815; Fax: 506-459-7575
jbeaumont@porterhetu.com
www.porterhetu.com

Gravenhurst: C.R. Barclay, CA, CMA, MBA
10 Woods Hollow
Gravenhurst, ON P1P 1Y7
Tel: 705-684-8115; Fax: 705-684-8227
Toll-Free: 877-644-4838
cbarclay1@cogeco.ca

Grimsby: Durward Jones Barkwell & Company, Grimsby
PO Box 261
8 Christie St.
Grimsby, ON L3M 4G5
Tel: 905-945-5439; Fax: 905-945-1103
Toll-Free: 866-830-7531
grimsby@djb.com
www.djb.com

Grimsby: Southcott Davoli Professional Corporation
76 Main St. West
Grimsby, ON L3M 4G1
Tel: 905-945-4942; Fax: 905-945-0306

Guelph: Bairstow, Smart & Smith LLP
100 Gordon St.
Guelph, ON N1H 4H6
Tel: 519-822-7670; Fax: 519-822-6997
bss@bssllp.ca
www.bssllp.ca

Guelph: Embree & Co. LLP
#8, 350 Speedvale Ave. West
Guelph, ON N1H 7M7
Tel: 519-821-1555; Fax: 519-821-6168
Toll-Free: 866-531-1555
www.embreelp.ca

Guelph: Robinson, Lott & Brohman LLP
15 Lewis Rd.
Guelph, ON N1H 1E9
Tel: 519-822-9933; Fax: 519-822-9212
Toll-Free: 866-822-9992
guelph_inquiries@rlb.ca
www.rlb.ca

Guelph: Weiler & Company
#3, 512 Woolwich St.
Guelph, ON N1H 3X7
Tel: 519-837-3111; Fax: 519-837-1049
Toll-Free: 888-239-3111
weiler@weiler.ca
www.weiler.ca

Hamilton: BC&C Professional Corporation
20 Jackson St. West
Hamilton, ON L8P 1L2
Tel: 905-570-1370; Fax: 905-570-1212
fred@bccpc.ca
www.bccpc.ca

Hamilton: Durward Jones Barkwell & Company, Hamilton
Standard Life Bldg.
#780, 120 King St. West
Hamilton, ON L8P 4V2
Tel: 905-525-9520; Fax: 905-522-3113
Toll-Free: 866-358-8240
hamilton@djb.com
www.djb.com

Hamilton: Galano, Enzo & Associates
#400, 20 Hughson St. South
Hamilton, ON L8N 2A1
Tel: 905-528-0144; Fax: 905-528-0144
enzo@netinc.ca

Hamilton: MacGillivray Partners, LLP
33 Main St. East
Hamilton, ON L8N 4K5
Tel: 905-523-7732; Fax: 905-572-9333
hamilton@macgillivray.com
www.macgillivray.com

Hamilton: PricewaterhouseCoopers LLP, Canada - Hamilton
21 King St. West, Main Fl.
Hamilton, ON L8P 4W7
Tel: 905-777-7000; Fax: 905-777-7060
www.pwc.com/ca

Hamilton: Taylor Leibow LLP, Accountants & Advisors
#700, 105 Main St. East
Hamilton, ON L8N 1G6
Tel: 905-523-0000; Fax: 905-523-4681
hamilton@taylorleibow.com
www.taylorleibow.com

Hearst: Collins Barrow Chartered Accountants - Hearst
PO Box 637
1021 George St.
Hearst, ON P0L 1N0
Tel: 705-362-4261; Fax: 705-362-4641
hearst@collinsbarrow.com

Jackson's Point: Duncan Goodwin, CGA
#4, 915 Lake Dr.
Jackson's Point, ON L0E 1L0
Tel: 905-722-8587; Fax: 904-722-6519
dgoodwin@porterhetu.com
www.porterhetu.com

Kapuskasing: Collins Barrow Chartered Accountants - Kapuskasing
2 Ash St.
Kapuskasing, ON P5N 3H4
Tel: 705-337-6411; Fax: 705-335-6563
kapuskasing@collinsbarrow.com

Kelowna: Kemp Harvey Hunt Ward Inc.
#101, 1593 Sutherland Ave.
Kelowna, ON V1Y 5Y7
Tel: 250-763-8029; Fax: 250-763-5155
Kelowna@khgcga.com
www.khgcga.com

Kenora: Claudette M. Edie, CGA
685 Lakeview Dr.
Kenora, ON P9N 3P6
Tel: 807-468-8899; Fax: 807-468-6800
cedie@porterhetu.com
www.porterhetu.com

Kingston: Collins Barrow Chartered Accountants - Kingston
#301, 1471 John Counter Blvd.
Kingston, ON K7M 8S8
Tel: 613-544-2903; Fax: 613-544-6151
kingston@collinsbarrow.com

Kingston: Davies & Wyngaarden Chartered Accountants
Clock Tower Plaza
819 Norwest Rd.
Kingston, ON K7P 2N4
Tel: 613-389-8177; Fax: 613-389-7789
Toll-Free: 888-715-3555
acctg@dwca.com
www.dwca.com

Kitchener: Clarke Starke & Diegel (CSD)
#202, 871 Victoria St. North
Kitchener, ON N2B 3S4
Tel: 519-579-5520; Fax: 519-570-3611
www.csdca.com

Kitchener: YNC LLP
650 Riverbend Dr., Suite A1
Kitchener, ON N2K 3S2
Tel: 519-772-0125; Fax: 519-772-0428
info@yncllp.ca
www.youngandcompany.ca

Leamington: Collins Barrow Leamington LLP
92 Talbot St. East
Leamington, ON N8H 1L3
Tel: 519-326-2666; Fax: 519-326-7008
leamington@collinsbarrow.com
www.collinsbarrow.com

Lindsay: Collins Barrow Chartered Accountants - Lindsay
237 Kent St. West
Lindsay, ON K9V 2Z3
Tel: 705-324-5031; Fax: 705-328-3121
lindsay@collinsbarrow.com
www.collinsbarrowkawarthas.com

London: Collins Barrow Chartered Accountants - London
PO Box 5005
#700, 495 Richmond St.
London, ON N6A 5G4
Tel: 519-679-8550; Fax: 519-679-1812
london@collinsbarrow.com
www.cbhealthcaregroup.com

London: Davis Martindale LLP
373 Commissioners Rd. West
London, ON N6J 1Y4
Tel: 519-673-3141; Fax: 519-645-1646
Toll-Free: 800-668-2167
info@davismartindale.com
www.davismartindale.com
Social Media:
www.facebook.com/pages/Davis-Martindale-LLP/169872989703871; twitter.com/Davismartindale

London: MacNeill Edmundson
82 Wellington St.
London, ON N6B 2K3
Tel: 519-660-6060; Fax: 519-672-6416
info@meb.on.ca
www.meb.on.ca

London: Michael A. King, Chartered Accountant
#502, 383 Richmond St.
London, ON N6A 3C4
Tel: 519-679-8391; Fax: 519-679-1446
mike@michaelkingca.ca
www.michaelkingca.ca

London: Neal, Pallett & Townsend LLP Chartered Accountants
#300, 633 Colborne St.
London, ON N6B 2V3
Tel: 519-432-5534; Fax: 519-432-6544
www.nptca.com

London: PricewaterhouseCoopers LLP, Canada - London
#300, 465 Richmond St.
London, ON N6A 5P4
Tel: 519-640-8000; Fax: 519-640-8015
www.pwc.com/ca

Manotick: Collins Barrow Chartered Accountants - Manotick
PO Box 291
1136 Clapp Lane
Manotick, ON K4M 1A3
Tel: 613-692-2553; Fax: 613-692-2995
manotick@collinsbarrow.com
www.collinsbarrowottawa.com

Manotick: Newton & Co.
PO Box 978
5494 Manotick Main St.
Manotick, ON K4M 1A8
Tel: 613-236-2939; Fax: 613-692-2874
www.newtonco.com

Markham: Kestenberg, Rabinowicz & Partners
2797 John St.
Markham, ON L3R 2Y8
Tel: 905-946-1300; Fax: 905-946-9797
rrabinowicz@krp.ca
www.krp.ca

Markham: Sheldon & Brates Tax Consultants Ltd.
#220, 60 Renfrew Dr.
Markham, ON L3R 0E1
Tel: 905-475-5400; Fax: 905-475-4246
www.sheldonmilstein.ca
Social Media: www.youtube.com/SheldonGroupTaxFirms;

Milton: Mercer & Mercer
245 Commercial St.
Milton, ON L9T 2J3
Tel: 905-876-1144; Fax: 905-876-4209
mail@mercerandmercer.com
www.mercerandmercer.com

Mississauga: Bimal Shah
#14, 5484 Tomken Rd.
Mississauga, ON L4W 2Z6
Tel: 905-629-2653; Fax: 905-629-8701
info@shah-cga.com
www.shah-cga.com

Mississauga: Bolton & Dignan, Chartered Accountants
6509 Mississauga Rd., Unit D
Mississauga, ON L5N 1A6
Tel: 905-858-5006; Fax: 905-858-3392

Mississauga: Clarkson Rouble LLP
5190 Shuttle Dr.
Mississauga, ON L4W 4J8
Tel: 905-629-4047; Fax: 905-629-3070
office@crllp.ca
clarksonrouble.on.ca/

Mississauga: Clewes & Associates Life Insurance Consultancy Inc.
#803, 251 Queen St. South
Mississauga, ON L5M 1L7
Tel: 416-493-5586; Fax: 416-493-5061
www.clewesconsult.com

Mississauga: H&A Forensic Accounting
#400, 2680 Matheson Blvd. East
Mississauga, ON L4W 0A5
Tel: 416-233-5577; Fax: 416-233-5578
www.haforensics.com

Mississauga: Kutum & Associates
#A1, 5659 McAdam Rd.
Mississauga, ON L4Z 1N9
Tel: 905-276-1154; Fax: 905-276-2003
info@kutum.com
www.kutum.com

Mississauga: Laurel L. Stultz
#211, 1425 Dundas St. East
Mississauga, ON L4X 2W4
Tel: 905-602-0001
info@certifiedgeneralaccountant.ca
www.certifiedgeneralaccountant.ca
Other Contact Information: Cell: 416-996-3919

Mississauga: Lemoine Hyland Group LLP
#100, 1599 Hurontario St.
Mississauga, ON L5G 4S1
Tel: 905-891-5339; Fax: 905-891-1513
Toll-Free: 866-547-2666
lhgroup.com

Mississauga: MDP Chartered Accountants (MDP LLP)
#200, 4230 Sherwoodtowne Blvd.
Mississauga, ON L4Z 2G6
Tel: 905-279-7500; Fax: 905-279-9300
mdp@mdp.on.ca
www.mdp.on.ca

Mississauga: PricewaterhouseCoopers LLP, Canada - Mississauga
Mississauga Executive Centre
#1100, 1 Robert Speck Pkwy.
Mississauga, ON L4Z 3M3
Tel: 905-949-7400; Fax: 905-949-7415
www.pwc.com/ca

Mississauga: S+C Partners LLP
#204, 6465 Millcreek Dr.
Mississauga, ON L5N 5R3
Tel: 905-821-9215; Fax: 905-821-8212
info@scpllp.com; hr@scpllp.com
scpllp.com
Social Media: www.facebook.com/scpllp;

Montréal: PricewaterhouseCoopers LLP, Canada - Montréal
1250, boul. René-Lévesque ouest
Montréal, ON H3B 2G4
Tel: 514-205-5000; Fax: 514-938-5709
www.pwc.com/ca

Nepean: Jack R. Bowerman, CA - Professional Corporation
#10, 28 Concourse Gate
Nepean, ON K2E 7T7
Tel: 613-723-8202; Fax: 613-723-1216
Toll-Free: 800-282-1879
info@jrbowerman.com
www.jrbowerman.com

Niagara Falls: Durward Jones Barkwell & Company, Niagara Falls
PO Box 873
#1, 6100 Thorold Stone Rd.
Niagara Falls, ON L2E 6V6
Tel: 905-357-5711; Fax: 905-357-7932
Toll-Free: 866-223-8459
nfalls@djb.com
www.djb.com

North Bay: Collins Barrow Chartered Accountants - North Bay
1850 Bond, Unit A
North Bay, ON P1B 4V6
Tel: 705-494-9336; Fax: 705-494-8783
northbay@csbn.ca

Orleans: Andrews & Company, Chartered Accountants
540 Lacolle Way
Orleans, ON K4A 0N9
Tel: 613-837-8282; Fax: 613-837-7482
website@andrews.ca
www.andrews.ca; www.porterhetu.com

Orleans: Pyndus & Associates Ltd.
1813 Woodhaven Heights
Orleans, ON K1E 2W3
Tel: 613-834-5054; Fax: 613-837-1591
pyndus.associates@sympatico.ca
www3.sympatico.ca/cpyndus/

Ottawa: Charles Ghadban Accounting
544 Bronson Ave.
Ottawa, ON K1R 6J9
Tel: 613-234-7856
info@ghadbanaccounting.com
www.ghadbanaccounting.com

Ottawa: Collins Barrow Chartered Accountants - Ottawa
#400, 301 Moodie Dr.
Ottawa, ON K2H 9C4
Tel: 613-820-8010; Fax: 613-820-0465
collinsbarrowottawa@collinsbarrow.com
www.collinsbarrowottawa.com

Ottawa: David Ingram & Associates
329 Waverly St.
Ottawa, ON K2P 0V9
Tel: 613-234-8023; Fax: 613-234-8925
www.gro-net.com

Ottawa: Gary G. Timmons, Chartered Accountant
#105, 2442 St. Joseph Blvd.
Ottawa, ON K1C 1G1
Tel: 613-830-0200; Fax: 613-830-8824
gtimmons@gtimmons.com
www.gtimmons.com

Ottawa: Ginsberg Gluzman Fage & Levitz, LLP
287 Richmond Rd.
Ottawa, ON K1Z 6X4
Tel: 613-728-5831; Fax: 613-728-8085
info@ggfl.ca
www.ggfl.ca

Ottawa: Hartel Financial Management Corporation
540 Lacolle Way
Ottawa, ON K4A 0N9
Tel: 613-837-8282; Fax: 613-837-7482
jleblanc@hartel.ca; brighten@hartel.ca
www.hartel.ca; www.porterhetu.com

Ottawa: Logan Katz LLP
#105, 6 Gurdwara Rd.
Ottawa, ON K2E 8A3
Tel: 613-228-8282; Fax: 613-228-8284
office@logankatz.com
www.logankatz.com

Ottawa: McLarty & Co.
#110, 495 Richmond Rd.
Ottawa, ON K2A 4B2
Tel: 613-726-1010; Fax: 613-726-9009
info@mclartyco.ca
www.mclartyco.ca

Ottawa: Newton & Co.
#1205, 150 Isabella St.
Ottawa, ON K1S 1V7
Tel: 613-236-2939; Fax: 613-236-1220
nco@newtonco.com
www.newtonco.com

Ottawa: Newton & Co., Ottawa
#1205, 150 Isabella St.
Ottawa, ON K1S 1V7
Tel: 613-236-2939; Fax: 613-236-1220
www.newtonco.com

Ottawa: PricewaterhouseCoopers LLP, Canada - Ottawa
#800, 99 Bank St.
Ottawa, ON K1P 1E4
Tel: 613-237-3702; Fax: 613-237-3963
www.pwc.com/ca

Ottawa: Robertson Sharpe & Associates
#2, 200 Colonnade Rd.
Ottawa, ON K2E 7M1
Tel: 613-727-3845; Fax: 613-727-7075
info@robertson-sharpe.com
www.robertson-sharpe.com

Ottawa: Rosalind Schlessinger Certified General Accountant
332 Gilmour St.
Ottawa, ON K2P 0R3
Tel: 613-235-1807; Fax: 613-235-2253

Ottawa: Scott Rankin & Gardiner Chartered Accountants
#207, 2650 Queensview Dr.
Ottawa, ON K2B 8H6
Tel: 613-596-2767; Fax: 613-596-2775

Ottawa: Surgeson Carson Associates Inc.
#8, 99 Fifth Ave.
Ottawa, ON K1S 5K4
Tel: 613-567-6434; Fax: 613-567-0752
www.surgesoncarson.com

Ottawa: Swindells & Company
#101, 1700 Woodward Dr.
Ottawa, ON K2C 3R8
Tel: 613-230-1010; Fax: 613-230-1957
www.swindellsandwheatley.com

Ottawa: Thomas R. West CGA Professional Corporation
21 Perrin Ave.
Ottawa, ON K2J 2Y1
Tel: 613-825-8871; Fax: 613-825-4089
Tom@Thomasrwestcga.com
www.thomasrwestcga.com

Owen Sound: Gaviller & Company LLP
PO Box 460
#201, 945 - 3rd Ave. East
Owen Sound, ON N4K 5P7
Tel: 519-376-5850; Fax: 519-376-5532
Toll-Free: 800-567-7234
www.gaviller.com

Penetanguishene: Alan Martin Associates - Penetanguishene
75 Main St.
Penetanguishene, ON L9M 1S8
Tel: 705-549-3146; Fax: 705-549-5736

Peterborough: Collins Barrow Chartered Accountants - Peterborough
272 Charlotte St.
Peterborough, ON K9J 2V4
Tel: 705-742-3418; Fax: 705-742-9775
peterborough@collinsbarrow.com

Peterborough: Jon S. Thornton, Chartered Accountant
PO Box 2402
294 Rink St.
Peterborough, ON K9J 7Y8
Tel: 705-742-2308; Fax: 705-748-4824
jon@thorntonca.com
www.thorntonca.com

Richmond Hill: MDS LLP
#4, 30 Wertheim Ct.
Richmond Hill, ON L4B 1B9
Tel: 905-881-2244; Fax: 905-881-8006
reception@mdsllp.com
www.mdsllp.com

Richmond Hill: Truster Zweig LLP
#200, 66 West Beaver Creek Rd.
Richmond Hill, ON L4B 1G5
Tel: 416-222-5555; Fax: 905-707-1322
tzcas@trusterzweig.com
www.trusterzweig.ca

Richmond Hill: Willington Martin Professional Corporation
#510. 100 York Blvd.
Richmond Hill, ON L4B 1J8
Tel: 905-770-3532; Fax: 905-770-4128
jwillington@porterhetu.com; tmartin@porterhetu.com
www.porterhetu.com; www.inbalance.org

Sarnia: Collins Barrow Chartered Accountants - Sarnia
1350 L'Heritage Dr.
Sarnia, ON N7S 6H8
Tel: 519-542-7725; Fax: 519-542-8321
sarnia@collinsbarrow.com

Sarnia: Hazlitt Steeves Harris LLP
301 Front St. North
Sarnia, ON N7T 5S6
Tel: 519-336-6133; Fax: 519-336-9995
www.hshca.com

Sarnia: TurnerMoore LLP, Certified General Accountants
316 George St.
Sarnia, ON N7T 7H9
Tel: 519-344-1271; Fax: 519-344-1268
www.turnermoore.com

St Catharines: Durward Jones Barkwell & Company, St. Catharines
PO Box 505
69 Ontario St.
St Catharines, ON L2R 6V9
Tel: 905-684-9221; Fax: 905-684-0566
Toll-Free: 866-219-9431
stcath@djb.com
www.djb.com

St Catharines: Finucci Watters LLP
58 St. Paul St. West
St Catharines, ON L2S 2C5
Tel: 905-682-2406; Fax: 905-682-1466
rwatters@porterhetu.com; afinucci@porterhetu.com
www.porterhetu.com

St Thomas: Kee, Perry & Lassam
15 Barrie Blvd.
St Thomas, ON N5P 4B9
Tel: 519-631-6360; Fax: 519-631-2198
info@kpl-accountants.ca
www.kpl-accountants.ca

Stoney Creek: Durward Jones Barkwell & Company, Stoney Creek
PO Box 56062
#7C, 45 Goderich Rd.
Stoney Creek, ON L8G 5C9
Tel: 905-561-2992; Fax: 905-561-7152
Toll-Free: 866-897-2965
screek@djb.com
www.djb.com

Stouffville: Joe Nemni Financial Services
33 Katherine Cres.
Stouffville, ON L4A 1K4
Tel: 905-640-0065
jnemni@sympatico.ca
www.joenemni.com

Stratford: Collins Barrow Chartered Accountants - Stratford
413 Hibernia St.
Stratford, ON N5A 5W2
Tel: 519-272-0000; Fax: 519-272-0030
stratford@collinsbarrow.com

Sturgeon Falls: Collins Barrow Chartered Accountants - Sturgeon Falls
#7, 12006 Hwy. 17 East
Sturgeon Falls, ON P2B 3K8
Tel: 705-753-1830; Fax: 705-753-2496
sturgeonfalls@cbsn.ca
www.collinsbarrowsudburynipissing.com

Sudbury: Collins Barrow Chartered Accountants - Sudbury
1174 St. Jerome St.
Sudbury, ON P3A 2V9
Tel: 705-560-5592; Fax: 705-560-8832
sudbury@cbsn.ca
cbsn.ca

Thornhill: Brockman & Partners Forensic Accountants Inc.
10 Maxwell Ct.
Thornhill, ON L4J 6Y3
Tel: 905-764-3851; Fax: 905-764-3537
jay.brockman@brockmanandpartners.ca
www.brockmanandpartners.ca

Thornhill: Harendorf, Lebane, Moss LLP
#200, 8500 Leslie St.
Thornhill, ON L3T 7M8
Tel: 905-886-8812; Fax: 905-886-6034
Toll-Free: 888-337-9222
hsm@hsmllpcas.com
www.hsmca.ca

Thornhill: Herb Kokotow, Chartered Accountant
3 German Mills Rd.
Thornhill, ON L3T 4H4
Tel: 905-764-6175
kokotow6175@rogers.com
www.charteredaccountantontario.ca

Thornhill: Ralph Lando Orvitz
#300, 8500 Leslie St.
Thornhill, ON L3T 7M8
Tel: 905-889-1549; Fax: 905-889-2054
Ralph@ralphlandoorvitz.ca
www.ralphlandoorvitz.ca

Thunder Bay: Fukushima Enstrom LLP
577 Eleventh Ave.
Thunder Bay, ON P7B 2R5
Tel: 807-345-1393; Fax: 807-345-4630
mail@fe-llp.com

Toronto: Albert L. Stal
#301, 1370 Don Mills Rd.
Toronto, ON M3B 3N7
Tel: 416-449-0130; Fax: 416-449-6694

Toronto: Bass & Murphy Chartered Accountants LLP
885 Progress Ave., #LPH1
Toronto, ON M1H 3G3
Tel: 416-431-3030; Fax: 416-431-3340
tom@bassmurphy.com
www.bassmurphy.com

Toronto: Bennett Gold LLP, Chartered Accountants
#900, 150 Ferrand Dr.
Toronto, ON M3C 3E5
Tel: 416-449-2249; Fax: 416-449-4133
rygold@bennettgold.ca
www.bennettgold.ca

Toronto: Brief Rotfarb Wynberg Cappe
#402, 3854 Bathurst St.
Toronto, ON M3H 3N2
Tel: 416-635-9080; Fax: 416-635-0462
lcappe@brwc.com
www.brwc.com

Toronto: Cadesky & Associates LLP - King St.
Toronto-Dominion Centre, Royal Trust Tower
PO Box 93
#2401, 77 King St. West
Toronto, ON M5K 1G8
Tel: 416-594-9500; Fax: 416-594-9501
taxpros@cadesky.com
www.cadesky.com

Toronto: Cadesky & Associates LLP - Sheppard Ave. East
Atria III
#1001, 2225 Sheppard Ave. East
Toronto, ON M2J 5C2
Tel: 416-498-9500; Fax: 416-498-9501
taxpros@cadesky.com
www.cadesky.com

Toronto: Canham Rogers Chartered Accountants
#500, 2 Lansing Sq.
Toronto, ON M2J 4P8
Tel: 416-494-8000; Fax: 416-494-8032
Info@CanhamRogers.com
www.canhamrogers.com

Toronto: Chaplin & Co. Chartered Accountants
#710, 1110 Finch Ave. West
Toronto, ON M3J 2T2
Tel: 416-667-7060; Fax: 416-663-3746
ca@chaplinco.com
www.chaplinco.com

Toronto: Cholkan & Stepczuk LLP
#300, 1 Eva Rd.
Toronto, ON M9C 4Z5
Tel: 416-695-9500; Fax: 416-695-3837
Toll-Free: 800-3639500
info@c-s.ca
www.cholkan.com

Toronto: The Clarke Henning Group
#801, 10 Bay St.
Toronto, ON M5J 2R8
Tel: 416-364-4421; Fax: 416-367-8032
Toll-Free: 888-422-1241
ch@clarkehenning.com
www.clarkehenning.com

Toronto: Cole & Partners
#2000, 80 Richmond St. West
Toronto, ON M5H 2A4
Tel: 416-364-9700; Fax: 416-364-9707
www.coleandpartners.com

Toronto: Collins Barrow Toronto LLP
#1900, 390 Bay St.
Toronto, ON M5H 2Y2
Tel: 416-361-1622; Fax: 416-480-2646
www.collinsbarrowtoronto.com

Toronto: Cooper & Company Ltd.
#108, 1120 Finch Ave. West
Toronto, ON M3J 3H7
Tel: 416-665-3383; Fax: 416-665-0897
info@cooperco.ca
www.cooperco.ca

Toronto: Cunningham LLP
#810, 2001 Sheppard Ave. East
Toronto, ON M2J 4Z8
Tel: 416-496-1051; Fax: 416-496-1546
Toll-Free: 800-461-4618
info@cunninghamca.com
www.cunninghamca.com

Toronto: Duffy, Allain & Rutten LLP
908 The East Mall
Toronto, ON M9B 6K2
Tel: 416-620-7740;

Toronto: Emondson Ball Davies LLP, Chartered Accountants
#501, 10 Milner Business Ct.
Toronto, ON M1B 3C6
Tel: 416-293-5560; Fax: 416-293-5377
www.ebdcas.com

Toronto: Finucci Watters LLP (Toronto)
#802, 390 Bay St.
Toronto, ON M5H 2Y2
Tel: 647-259-1766; Fax: 647-259-1776
afinucci@finucciwatters.com
www.porterhetu.com

Toronto: Galloway Consulting Group Inc.
#703, 1200 Eglinton Ave. East
Toronto, ON M3C 1H9
Tel: 416-803-5638; Fax: 416-449-7342
info@gallowayconsulting.ca
www.gallowayconsulting.ca

Toronto: Gardner Zuk Dessen, Chartered Accountants
#205, 265 Rimrock Rd.
Toronto, ON M3J 3C6
Tel: 416-631-9800; Fax: 416-631-9183
info@gzd.ca
www.gzd.ca

Toronto: Hilborn Ellis Grant LLP
PO Box 49
#3100, 401 Bay St.
Toronto, ON M5H 2Y4
Tel: 416-364-1359; Fax: 416-364-9503
www.heg.ca

Toronto: Kelly Porter Hétu
475 Queen St. East
Toronto, ON M5A 1T9
Tel: 416-955-0060; Fax: 416-955-0061
jkelly@porterhetu.com
www.porterhetu.com

Toronto: Kenneth Michalak
1576 Bloor St. West
Toronto, ON M6P 1A4
Tel: 416-588-2808; Fax: 416-588-3634
Toll-Free: 866-258-4788
info@kjmcga.coma
www.kjmcga.com

Toronto: Klingbaum Barkin LLP
The Madison Centre
#1906, 4950 Yonge St.
Toronto, ON M2N 6K1
Tel: 416-512-1221; Fax: 416-512-1284
mk@klingbaumbarkin.com
www.klingbaumbarkin.com

Toronto: Koster, Spinks & Koster LLP (KSK)
4 Glengrove Ave. West
Toronto, ON M4R 1N4
Tel: 416-489-8100; Fax: 416-489-9194
info@ksk.ca
www.ksk.ca

Toronto: Kwan Chan Law Chartered Accountants Professional Corporation
#910, 4950 Yonge St.
Toronto, ON M2N 6K1
Tel: 416-226-6862;

Toronto: M. Schwab Accounting Services Ltd.
#606, 94 Cumberland St.
Toronto, ON M5R 1A3
Tel: 416-324-9933; Fax: 416-324-8733

Toronto: McGovern, Hurley, Cunningham LLP
#300, 2005 Sheppard Ave. East
Toronto, ON M2J 5B4
Tel: 416-496-1234; Fax: 416-496-0125
info@mhc-ca.com
www.mhc-ca.com

Toronto: Mehl & Reynolds LLP
#200, 1 Yorkdale Rd.
Toronto, ON M6A 3A1
Tel: 416-787-0681; Fax: 416-787-7630
webhome.idirect.com/~gmr

Toronto: Michael Argue, Chartered Accountant, Professional Corporation
#206, 1210 Sheppard Ave. East
Toronto, ON M2K 1E3
Tel: 416-490-8544; Fax: 416-490-8096
michaelargue@bellnet.ca
www.argueca.com

Toronto: Michael I. Atlas, Chartered Accountant
#2500, 120 Adelaide St. West
Toronto, ON M5H 1T1
Tel: 416-860-9175; Fax: 416-860-9189
matlas@taxca.com
www.taxca.com

Toronto: Mintz & Partners LLP
#200, 1 Concorde Gate
Toronto, ON M3C 4G4
Tel: 416-391-2900; Fax: 416-391-2748
info@mintzca.com
www.mintzca.com

Toronto: Nevcon Accounting Services
PO Box 43541
1531 Bayview Ave.
Toronto, ON M4G 4G8
Tel: 416-487-7996; Fax: 416-946-1098
Toll-Free: 888-463-8366
info@nevcon.com
www.nevcon.com

Toronto: PKF Hill LLP
#200, 41 Valleybrook Dr.
Toronto, ON M3B 2S6
Tel: 416-449-9171; Fax: 416-449-7401
info@pkfhill.com
www.pkfhill.com

Toronto: PricewaterhouseCoopers LLP, Canada
PwC Tower
#2600, 28 York St.
Toronto, ON M5J 0B2
Tel: 416-863-1133; Fax: 416-365-8178
www.pwc.com/ca

Toronto: PricewaterhouseCoopers LLP, Canada - Toronto - Yorkdale
#412, 1 Yorkdale Rd.
Toronto, ON M6A 3A1
Tel: 416-222-6408; Fax: 416-222-3263
www.pwc.com/ca

Toronto: PricewaterhouseCoopers LLP, Canada - Toronto - Yonge St.
North American Life Bldg.
#1900, 5700 Yonge St.
Toronto, ON M2M 4K7
Tel: 416-218-1500; Fax: 416-218-1499
www.pwc.com/ca

Toronto: Renée S. Karn, CGA
86 Acton Ave.
Toronto, ON M3H 4H1
Tel: 416-499-0012; Fax: 416-499-0194
rkarn@porterhetu.com
www.porterhetu.com

Toronto: Rich Rotstein LLP
South Tower
#303, 175 Bloor St. East
Toronto, ON M4W 3R8
Tel: 416-863-1400; Fax: 416-863-4881
lsr@richrotstein.com; lwr@richrotstein.com
www.richrotstein.com

Toronto: Rosen & Associates Limited
PO Box 101
#2200, 121 King St. West
Toronto, ON M5H 3T9
Tel: 416-363-4515; Fax: 416-363-4849
l.gallant@rosen-associates.com
www.rosen-associates.com

Toronto: Rosenberg Smith & Partners LLP
#200, 2000 Steeles Ave. West
Toronto, ON L4K 3E9
Tel: 416-798-4997; Fax: 905-660-3064
rsp@rsp.ca
www.rsp.ca

Toronto: Rosenthal Consulting Group
13 Balmoral Ave.
Toronto, ON M4V 1J5
Tel: 416-617-9966; Fax: 416-964-2371
hsrosenthal@alumni.uwaterloo.ca

Toronto: Rumanek & Company Ltd.
#714, 1280 Finch Ave. West
Toronto, ON M3J 3K6
Tel: 416-665-3328; Fax: 416-665-7634
info@trustee-in-bankruptcy.com
www.rumanek.com; www.trustee-in-bankruptcy.com
Social Media: rumanek.com/blog;

Toronto: SBLR LLP Chartered Accountants
#300, 2345 Yonge St.
Toronto, ON M4P 2E5
Tel: 416-488-2345; Fax: 416-488-3765
www.sblr.ca

Toronto: Segal & Partners Inc.
#120, 2001 Sheppard Ave. East
Toronto, ON M2J 4Z8
Tel: 416-391-1460; Fax: 416-391-2285
rmerpaw@trustee.ca
www.segalbankruptcy.com

Toronto: Serbinski Partners PC
183 Sheppard Ave. West
Toronto, ON M2N 1M9
Tel: 416-733-0300; Fax: 416-352-6004
Toll-Free: 888-878-2937
mtscpa@serbinski.com
www.serbinski.com

Toronto: SF Partnership, LLP
The Madison Centre
#400, 4950 Yonge St.
Toronto, ON M2N 6K1
Tel: 416-250-1212; Fax: 416-250-1225
general@sfgroup.ca
www.sfgroup.ca

Toronto: Sloan Partners LLP
#6, 4646 Dufferin St.
Toronto, ON M3H 5S4
Tel: 416-665-7735; Fax: 416-649-7725
www.sloangroup.ca
Social Media: www.facebook.com/SloanGroup;

Toronto: Soberman LLP Chartered Accountants
#1100, 2 St. Clair Ave. East
Toronto, ON M4T 2T5
Tel: 416-964-7633; Fax: 416-964-6454
Toll-Free: 866-964-7633
info@soberman.com
www.soberman.com

Toronto: Sone & Rovet
#406, 1200 Sheppard Ave. East
Toronto, ON M2K 2S5
Tel: 416-498-7200; Fax: 416-498-6877
www.sonerovet.com

Toronto: Spergel Inc.
#200, 505 Consumers Rd.
Toronto, ON M2J 4V8
Tel: 416-497-1660; Fax: 416-494-7199
Toll-Free: 855-773-7435
jadiken@spergel.ca
www.spergel.ca

Toronto: Stern Cohen Shier Inc.
#1400, 45 St. Clair Ave. West
Toronto, ON M4V 1L3
Tel: 416-967-5100; Fax: 416-967-4372
contact@sterncohen.com
www.sterncohen.com

Toronto: Stewart & Kett Financial Advisors Inc.
Citicorp Place
#911, 123 Front St. West
Toronto, ON M5J 2M2
Tel: 416-362-6322; Fax: 416-362-6302
www.stewartkett.com

Toronto: Tomlin Associates
#445, 700 Lawrence Ave. West
Toronto, ON M6A 3B4
Tel: 416-488-6969; Fax: 416-783-9117
larry.tomlin@gmail.com
www.tomlin.ca
Other Contact Information: Cell: 416-302-8169

Toronto: V.B. Sharma Professional Corporation, Chartered Accountants
#200, 3390 Midland Ave.
Toronto, ON M1V 5K3
Tel: 416-292-4431; Fax: 416-292-7247
vbsharma@vbsharma.ca
www.vbsharma.ca

Toronto: Zeifman & Company
201 Bridgeland Ave.
Toronto, ON M6A 1Y7
Tel: 416-256-4000; Fax: 416-256-4001
info@zeifman.ca
www.zeifman.ca

Toronto: Zwaig Associates Inc.
PO Box 53
#801, 20 Adelaide St. East
Toronto, ON M5C 2T6
Tel: 416-863-0140; Fax: 416-863-0428

Trenton: Wilkinson & Company LLP
PO Box 400
71 Dundas St. West
Trenton, ON K8V 5R6
Tel: 613-392-2592; Fax: 613-392-8512
Toll-Free: 888-713-7283
www.wilkinson.net

Vaughan: Collins Barrow Chartered Accountants - Vaughan
#600, 3300 Hwy. 7 West
Vaughan, ON L4K 4M3
Tel: 416-213-2600; Fax: 905-669-8705
vaughan@collinsbarrow.com

Vaughan: Domenic Galati CGA
#510, 3100 Steeles Ave. West
Vaughan, ON L4K 3R1
Tel: 416-745-0245
dgalati@porterhetu.com
www.porterhetu.com

Waterloo: PricewaterhouseCoopers LLP, Canada - Waterloo
#201, 95 King St. South
Waterloo, ON N2J 5A2
Tel: 519-570-5700; Fax: 519-570-5730
www.pwc.com/ca

Waterloo: PricewaterhouseCoopers LLP, Canada - Waterloo
#201, 95 King St. South
Waterloo, ON N2J 5A2
Tel: 519-570-5700; Fax: 519-570-5730

Waterloo: Transport Financial Services Ltd.
105 Bauer Pl.
Waterloo, ON N2L 6B5
Tel: 519-886-8070; Fax: 519-886-5214
Toll-Free: 800-461-5970
www.tfsgroup.com/tfs

Welland: Durward Jones Barkwell & Company, Welland
PO Box 9
171 Division St.
Welland, ON L3B 5N9
Tel: 905-735-2140; Fax: 905-735-4706
Toll-Free: 866-552-0997
welland@djb.com
www.djb.com

Welland: Lifestyle Financial Planning & Management Services Ltd.
190 Division St.
Welland, ON L3B 4A2
Tel: 905-732-1640; Fax: 905-732-1397
stalosi@lifestylefinancial.com
www.lifestylefinancial.com

Windsor: Collins Barrow Windsor LLP
3260 Devon Dr.
Windsor, ON N8X 4L4
Tel: 519-258-5800; Fax: 519-256-6152
windsor@collinsbarrow.com

Windsor: Hyatt Lassaline LLP
#203, 2510 Ouellette Ave.
Windsor, ON N8X 1L4
Tel: 519-966-4626; Fax: 519-966-9206
www.hyattlassaline.com

Windsor: PricewaterhouseCoopers LLP, Canada - Windsor
245 Ouellette Ave., 3rd Fl.
Windsor, ON N9A 7J4
Tel: 519-985-8900; Fax: 519-258-5457
www.pwc.com/ca

Windsor: Roth Mosey & Partners LLP
#300, 3100 Temple Dr.
Windsor, ON N8W 5J6
Tel: 519-977-6410; Fax: 519-977-7083
info@roth-mosey.com
www.roth-mosey.com

Woodbridge: Rashid & Quinney Chartered Accountants
#401, 216 Chrislea Rd.
Woodbridge, ON L4L 8S5
Tel: 905-856-2677; Fax: 905-856-2679
rick@randg.ca

Woodstock: Thornton VanTassel Chartered Accountants - Woodstock
318 Connell St.
Woodstock, ON E7M 6B7
Tel: 506-324-8040; Fax: 506-325-2262
stephen.thornton@thorntonvantassel.com
www.thorntonvantassel.com

Prince Edward Island

Charlottetown: Beaton Fitzpatrick Murray
PO Box 2158
#200, 155 Belevedere Ave.
Charlottetown, PE C1A 8B9
Tel: 902-892-5365; Fax: 902-892-0383
bfm@bfm.pe.ca
www.bfm.pe.ca

Summerside: Peter M. Baglole, Chartered Accountant
PO Box 1373
#7, 293 Water St.
Summerside, PE C1N 4K2
Tel: 902-436-1663; Fax: 902-436-1604
peter@baglole.ca
www.baglole.ca

Summerside: Schurman Sudsbury & Associates Ltd.
189 Water St.
Summerside, PE C1N 1B2
Tel: 902-436-2171; Fax: 902-436-0960
schurman-sudsbury@isn.net

Quebec

Anjou: Brunet, Roy, Dubé, Comptables agrées
#1200, 7100 rue Jean-Talon
Anjou, QC H1M 3S3
Tél: 514-255-1001;

Blainville: Lévesque CA, Comptables agréés
#204, 10, boul. de la Seigneurie est
Blainville, QC J7C 3V5
Tél: 450-437-8969; Téléc: 450-437-8996
infos@levesqueca.com
www.levesqueca.com

Drummondville: Samson Bélair/Deloitte & Touche s.e.n.c.r.l.
212, rue Heriot
Drummondville, QC J2C 1J8
Tel: 819-477-6311; Fax: 819-477-9572
www.deloitte.com

Joliette: Martin, Boulard & Associés, sencrl
#200, 37, Place Bourget sud
Joliette, QC J6E 5G1
Tél: 450-759-2825; Téléc: 450-752-1235
jvarin@mba.qc.ca

Lachine: Martin & Cie
1100, rue Notre-Dame
Lachine, QC H8S 2C4
Tel: 514-637-7887; Fax: 514-637-3566
l.martin@martin-cie.com
www.martin-cie.com

Longueuil: Dubé & Tétreault, Comptables agréés, S.E.N.C.
#200, 3065, ch. de Chambly
Longueuil, QC J4L 1N3
Tel: 450-442-0944; Fax: 450-442-2166
richard@dube-tetreault.com
www.dube-tetreault.com

Montréal: A. Bertucci, Chartered Accountant
1445, rue Lambert Closse
Montréal, QC H3H 1Z5
Tel: 514-932-3229; Fax: 514-932-4634
abertucci@abertucci.com
www.abertucci.com

Montréal: Accountatax Inc./ Comptataxe inc.
147, rue Spring Garden
Montréal, QC H9B 2T7
Tel: 514-685-7394; Fax: 514-685-7411
Toll-Free: 877-685-7394
www.accountatax.ca

Montréal: Aubry, Hijazi, CA - s.e.n.c.r.l.
#215, 1331, av. Green
Montréal, QC H3Z 2A5
Tel: 514-935-7787; Fax: 514-935-5865

Montréal: Beauchemin Trépanier Comptables agréés inc.
#1102, 4200, boul. St-Laurent
Montréal, QC H2W 2R2
Tel: 514-847-0182; Fax: 514-849-9082
bt@btca.qc.ca
www.btca.qc.ca

Montréal: Bessner Gallay Kreisman
#600, 4150, rue Ste-Catherine Ouest
Montréal, QC H3Z 2Y5
Tel: 514-908-3600; Fax: 514-908-3630
www.bgsk.com

Montréal: Collins Barrow Montréal S.E.N.C.R.L/LLP
#1100, 625, boul. René-Lévesque ouest
Montréal, QC H3B 1R2
Tel: 514-866-8553; Fax: 514-866-8469
montreal@collinsbarrow.com
www.collinsbarrow.com/montreal

Montréal: Fine et associés/ Fine & Associates
5101, rue Buchan
Montréal, QC H4P 1S4
Tél: 514-731-0761; Téléc: 514-731-4639

Montréal: Gestion Tellier St-Germain
PO Box 324, P.A.T. Stn. P.A.T.
11536, rue de la Gauchetière
Montréal, QC H1B 5J5
Tel: 514-640-8922; Fax: 514-640-4801
ghislaine@gestionrg.qc.ca
www.gestionrg.qc.ca

Montréal: Goldsmith Hersh s.e.n.c.r.l.
#200, 1411, rue Fort
Montréal, QC H3H 2N6
Tel: 514-933-8611; Fax: 514-933-1142
info@ghmca.com
www.gmhca.com

Montréal: Le Groupe Belzile Tremblay
2675, rue Masson
Montréal, QC H1Y 1W3
Tel: 514-384-3620; Fax: 514-384-3710
bt@belziletremblay.ca
www.belziletremblay.ca

Montréal: H&A eDiscovery
#401, 360, rue Notre Dame ouest
Montréal, QC H2Y 1T9
Tel: 514-844-5577; Fax: 514-844-1088
www.haediscovery.com; www.haforensics.com

Montréal: Info Comptabilité Plus
#201, 2035, Côte de Liesse
Montréal, QC H4N 2M5
Tel: 514-337-2677; Fax: 514-337-1594
info@infocplus.com
www.infocplus.com

Montréal: J. Kromida, Chartered Accountant
750, av. Sainte-Croix
Montréal, QC H4L 3Y2
Tel: 514-747-3413; Fax: 514-747-0799
jamesk@kromida.com
www.kromida.com

Montréal: Jacques Davis Lefaivre & Associés
#1900, 1080, côte du Beaver Hall
Montréal, QC H2Z 1S8
Tél: 514-878-2600; Téléc: 514-878-2600
Ligne sans frais: 800-363-6800
jdl@jdl.ca

Montréal: JDM Consultation Inc.
#203, 759, carré Victoria
Montréal, QC H2Y 2J7
Tel: 514-844-4536; Fax: 514-849-8647
jimmy@menegakis.ca
www.menegakis.ca

Montréal: Jean J. Drouin, CGA
#201, 6455, rue Christophe-Colomb
Montréal, QC H2S 2G5
Tel: 514-274-6831; Fax: 514-274-8128
info@drouin-cga.com

Montréal: Leclerc Forensic Accountants - Montréal
#2821, 1, Place Ville-Marie
Montréal, QC H3B 4R4
Tel: 514-798-5874; Fax: 514-788-4837
www.leclerc-ifa.com

Montréal: Martel Desjardins
Édifice de la Banque Nationale de Paris
#1440, 1981, av. McGill College
Montréal, QC H3A 2Y1
Tel: 514-849-2793; Fax: 514-849-7104
md@marteldesjardins.com
www.marteldesjardins.com

Montréal: Mazars Harel Drouin
#1200, 215, rue Saint-Jacques
Montréal, QC H2Y 1M6
Tel: 514-845-9253; Fax: 514-845-3859
www.mazars.ca

Montréal: MCA Consulting Group
5240-B, rue Saint Denis
Montréal, QC H2J 2M2
Tel: 514-277-8081; Fax: 514-276-9150
info@groupemca.com
www.groupemca.com

Montréal: Padgett Business Services
88, boul. Brunswick
Montréal, QC H9B 2C5
Tel: 514-684-8086; Fax: 514-684-0884
www.padgettwestisland.com

Montréal: Perreault, Wolman, Grzywacz & Co.
#814, 5250, rue Ferrier
Montréal, QC H4P 2N7
Tél: 514-731-7987; Téléc: 514-731-8782
www.pwgca.com

Montréal: Petrie Raymond Inc.
#1000, 255, boul. Crémazie est
Montréal, QC H2M 1M2
Tél: 514-342-4740; Téléc: 514-737-4049
info@petrieraymond.qc.ca
www.petrieraymond.qc.ca/

Montréal: Porter Hétu International
5800, av. Monkland, 2ième étage
Montréal, QC H4A 1G1
Tel: 514-369-7529; Fax: 514-482-0036
www.porterhetu.com

Montréal: PSB Boisjoli Inc.
#400, 3333, boul. Graham
Montréal, QC H3R 3L5
Tél: 514-341-5511; Téléc: 514-342-0589
info@psbboisjoli.ca
www.psbboisjoli.ca

Montréal: RSM Richter
#2000, 2, Place Alexis Nihon
Montréal, QC H3Z 3C2
Tel: 514-934-3400; Fax: 514-934-3408
mtlinfo@rsmrch.com
www.richter.ca

Montréal: Ruby Stein Wagner S.E.N.C. Chartered Accountants
Place du Parc
#1900, 300, rue Léo-Pariseau
Montréal, QC H2X 4B5
Tel: 514-842-3911; Fax: 514-849-3447
Toll-Free: 866-842-3911
info@rswca.com
www.rswca.com

Montréal: Schwartz Levitsky Feldman LLP (SLF)
1980, rue Sherbrooke ouest, 10e étage
Montréal, QC H3H 1E8
Tel: 514-937-6392; Fax: 514-933-9710
www.slf.ca

Montréal: Stamos Porter Hétu
800, av. Ste. Croix
Montréal, QC H4L 3Y2
Tel: 514-744-1100; Fax: 514-744-2200
jstamos@porterhetu.com
www.porterhetu.com

Montréal: Victor & Gold Chartered Accountants
#400, 759, carré Victoria
Montréal, QC H2Y 2J7
Tel: 514-282-1836; Fax: 514-282-6640
www.victorgold.com

Montréal: WAKED
#2825, 500, Place d'Armes
Montréal, QC H2Y 2W2
Tel: 514-875-6400; Fax: 514-861-6301
info@wakedcma.com
www.wakedcma.com

Québec: Bergeron Lavigne SENC
1780, Damiron
Québec, QC G2E 5S8
Tel: 418-877-8705; Fax: 418-877-0057
michelbergeronca@videotron.ca
www.guideformationquickbooks.com

Québec: Blouin, Julien, Potvin Comptables agréés, S.E.N.C.
#300, 2795, boul. Laurier
Québec, QC G1V 4M7
Tel: 418-651-0405; Fax: 418-651-0285
groupe@boulinjulienpotvin.qc.ca

Québec: Brassard Carrier, Comptables Agréés
#200, 1651, ch. Ste-Foy
Québec, QC G1S 2P1
Tel: 418-682-2929; Fax: 418-682-0282
info@groupebca.com
www.groupebca.com

Québec: Cauchon Turcotte Thériault Latouche
Place Iberville Un
#310, 1195, av. Lavigerie
Québec, QC G1V 4N3
Tel: 418-658-8808; Fax: 418-658-3136
equipe@cttlca.com
www.cttlca.com

Québec: Choquette Corriveau, Chartered Accountants
Place Iberville I
#300, 1195, av. Lavigerie
Québec, QC G1V 4N3
Tel: 418-658-5555; Fax: 418-658-1010
courrier@choquettecorriveau.com
choquettecorriveau.com

Québec: Dallaire Forest Kirouac S.E.N.C.R.L.
#580, 1175, av. Lavigerie
Québec, QC G1V 4P1
Tel: 418-650-2266; Fax: 418-650-2529
Toll-Free: 877-650-2266
comptable@dfk.qc.ca
www.dfk.qc.ca

Québec: Gagnon, Moisan, Comptables agréés
#227, 945, av. Newton
Québec, QC G1P 4M3
Tel: 418-871-6262; Fax: 418-871-9526
www.fortune1000.ca/gagnon-moisan/

Québec: Gariépy, Gravel, Larouche comptables agréés S.E.N.C.
601, av. du Cénacle
Québec, QC G1E 6W4
Tel: 418-666-3704; Fax: 418-666-6913
www.gglca.qc.ca

Québec: Laberge Lafleur Brown S.E.N.C.R.L.
Place de la Cité
#1060, 2590, boul. Laurier
Québec, QC G1V 4M6
Tel: 418-659-7265; Fax: 418-659-5937
www.llbca.com

Québec: Leclerc Forensic Accountants - Québec
#360, 580, Grande-Allée est
Québec, QC G1R 2K2
Tel: 418-780-5874; Fax: 418-780-3191
www.leclerc-ifa.com

Québec: Legaré Porter Hétu
#201, 3181 ch. Ste-Foy
Québec, QC G1X 1R3
Tel: 418-780-1333; Fax: 418-780-1339
miclegar@porterhetu.com
www.porterhetu.com

Québec: Malenfant Dallaire Comptables Agréés
Place de la Cité
#872, 2600, boul. Laurier
Québec, QC G1V 4W2
Tel: 418-654-0636; Fax: 418-654-0639
maldal@malenfantdallaire.com
www.malenfantdallaire.com

Québec: PricewaterhouseCoopers LLP, Canada - Québec
Place de la Cité, Tour Cominar
#1700, 2640, boul. Laurier
Québec, QC G1V 5C2
Tel: 418-522-7001; Fax: 418-522-5663
www.pwc.com/ca

Québec: Roy, Labrecque, Busque, Comptables Agréés
#160, 5055, boul. Hamel ouest
Québec, QC G2E 2G6
Tel: 418-871-0013; Fax: 418-871-0162
rlb@roylabrecquebusque.com
www.roylabrecquebusque.com

Québec: Signature comptable Mc Nicoll CA inc.
#210, 1220, boul. Lebourgneuf
Québec, QC G2K 2G4
Tel: 418-622-6666; Fax: 418-622-3904
mcnicollp@signaturecomptable.ca
www.signaturecomptable.ca

Saint-Hubert: Hébert, Turgeon, CGA Inc.
7695, ch. de Chambly
Saint-Hubert, QC J3Y 5K2
Tel: 450-676-0624; Fax: 450-676-7677
info@htcga.qc.ca
www.htcga.qc.ca

Saint-Rémi: Lefaivre Labrèche Gagné, sencrl
151, rue Perras
Saint-Rémi, QC J0L 2L0
Tél: 450-454-3974; Téléc: 450-454-7320
info@lefaivre-labreche.com
www.lefaivre-labreche.com

Shawville: Smith Porter Hétu
PO Box 896
389, rue Main
Shawville, QC J0X 2Y0
Tel: 819-647-2403; Fax: 819-647-3103
pbsmith@porterhetu.com
www.porterhetu.com; www.thetaxsmith.com

St-Laurent: Porter Hétu International (Québec) inc.
790, boul. Marcel-Laurin
St-Laurent, QC H4M 2M6
Tel: 514-744-1500; Fax: 514-744-6441
mplaliberte@porterhetu.com; esauve@porterhetu.com
www.porterhetu.com

Ste-Thérèse: Marcil Girard Porter Hétu International
8, rue St-Charles
Ste-Thérèse, QC J7E 2A2
Tel: 450-430-7526; Fax: 450-430-6809
guylaine@porterhetu.com
www.porterhetu.com

Saskatchewan

Esterhazy: Skilnick Miller Moar Grodecki & Kreklewich, Chartered Accountants - Esterhazy
Bank of Montreal Bldg.
420 Main St.
Esterhazy, SK S0A 1X0
Tel: 306-745-6611; Fax: 306-745-2899
www.skilnick.ca

Melville: Skilnick Miller Moar Grodecki & Kreklewich, Chartered Accountants
PO Box 1660
#155, 3rd Ave. East
Melville, SK S0A 2P0
Tel: 306-728-4525; Fax: 306-728-2599
melvilleoffice@skilnick.ca
www.skilnick.ca

Saskatoon: Byron J. Reynolds, Chartered Accountant
PO Box 32029, Erindale Stn. Erindale
Saskatoon, SK S7S 1N8
Tel: 306-384-1130; Fax: 306-373-6431
br@byronjreynolds.ca
www.byronjreynolds.ca

Saskatoon: Hergott Duval Stack LLP
Saskatoon Square
#1200, 410 - 22nd St. East
Saskatoon, SK S7K 5T6
Tel: 306-934-8000; Fax: 306-653-5859
www.hergott.com

Saskatoon: Hounjet Tastad Harpham
1633A Quebec Ave.
Saskatoon, SK S7K 1V6
Tel: 306-653-5100; Fax: 306-653-5141
www.hth-accountants.ca

Saskatoon: Lizée Gauthier Certified General Accountants
473 - 2nd Ave. North
Saskatoon, SK S7K 2C1
Tel: 306-653-4444; Fax: 306-665-5662
lizee@sasktel.net

Saskatoon: PricewaterhouseCoopers LLP, Canada - Saskatoon
#200, 123 - 2nd Ave. South
Saskatoon, SK S7K 7E6
Tel: 306-668-5900; Fax: 306-652-1315
www.pwc.com/ca

Domestic Banks: Schedule I

See Index for Bank of Canada, and the Federal Business Development Bank, which are Crown Corporations, listed in the Government Section. *Chartered banks in Canada are incorporated by letters patent. They are governed by the Bank Act, which establishes the legislative framework for Canada's banking system. The Bank Act provides for the incorporation of banks. The Office of the Superintendent of Financial Institutions Canada regulates and supervises the Canadian financial system.*

Domestic banks are federally regulated Canadian banks. The subsidiaries of foreign banks are federally regulated foreign banks. Both domestic and foreign banks have the same powers, restrictions and obligations under the Bank Act.

Foreign bank representative offices are established by foreign banks in Canada. They act as a liaison between the foreign bank and its clients in Canada. These offices generally promote the services of the foreign bank, and do not accept deposits in Canada.

Foreign bank branches are federally regulated. They are permitted to establish specialized, commercially-focused branches in Canada, in accordance with the Bank Act. Full service branches generally are not permitted to accept deposits of less than $150,000.

ATB Financial exemplifies a savings bank in Canada. In Alberta, ATB Financial operates under the authority of the Alberta Treasury Branches Act Chapter A-37.9, 1997 and Treasury Branches Regulation 187/97.

Alterna Bank
400 Albert St., 3rd Fl.
Ottawa, ON K1R 5B2
Tel: 613-560-0120; Toll-Free: 866-560-0120
questions@alterna.ca
www.alterna.ca
Former Name: CS Alterna Bank
Ownership: Wholly owned subsidiary of Alterna Savings & Credit Union Limited.
Year Founded: 2000

The Bank of Nova Scotia (BNS)/ La Banque de Nouvelle-Écosse
Scotia Plaza
44 King St. West
Toronto, ON M5H 1H1
Tel: 416-866-6161; Fax: 416-866-3750
email@scotiabank.com
www.scotiabank.com
Other Contact Information: Telex: WUI6719400
Also Known As: Scotiabank
Ownership: Public
Year Founded: 1832
Number of Employees: 42,046

Bank West
PO Box 5328
#1010, 24th St. SE
High River, AB T1V 1A7
Tel: 403-652-2107; Fax: 403-652-2237
Toll-Free: 888-440-2265
info@bankwest.ca
www.bankwest.ca
Ownership: Owned by Western Financial Group
Year Founded: 2002
Number of Employees: 15
Assets: $50-100 million
Revenues: Under $1 million

BMO Financial Group (BMO)
119, rue St-Jacques ouest
Montréal, QC H2Y 1L6
Tel: 514-877-7373; Fax: 514-877-7399
Toll-Free: 877-225-5266
feedback@bmo.com; remarque@bmo.com (French); mutualfunds@bmo.com
www.bmo.com
Other Contact Information: 1-877-225-5266 (French); 1-800-665-8800 (Cantonese & Mandarin); 1-866 889-0889 (TTY service); mosaik@bmo.com (Credit cards)
Former Name: Bank of Montréal
Ownership: Public
Year Founded: 1817
Number of Employees: 37,000+
Assets: $412,000,000,000 Year End: 20081031

Bridgewater Bank
Also listed under: *Financing & Loan Companies*
#150, 926 - 5th Ave. SW
Calgary, AB T2P 0N7
Tel: 403-232-6556; Fax: 403-233-2609
Toll-Free: 888-837-2326
www.bridgewaterfinancial.ca
Former Name: Bridgewater Financial Services Ltd.
Ownership: Private. Wholly owned subsidiary of Alberta Motor Association.
Year Founded: 1997
Number of Employees: 170

Canadian Imperial Bank of Commerce (CIBC)/ Banque Canadienne Impériale de Commerce
Commerce Court
PO Box 1, Stn Commerce Court
Toronto, ON M5L 1A2
Tel: 416-980-2211; Fax: 416-218-9440
Toll-Free: 800-465-2422
customer.care@cibc.com; investorrelations@cibc.com
www.cibc.com
Other Contact Information: 1-800-465-2255 (Customer Care); 1-800-465-4653 (Credit Cards); 1-888-264-6843 (Mortgages); 416-980-4523 (Corporate Communications & Public Affairs)
Ownership: Public
Year Founded: 1858
Number of Employees: 40,000
Assets: 3,700,000,000 Year End: 20081031

Canadian Tire Financial Services Ltd. (CTAL)
Also listed under: *Financial Planning & Investment Management Companies*
PO Box 2000
Welland, ON L3B 5S3
Toll-Free: 800-387-8803
www.ctfs.com
Other Contact Information: Line of Credit: 1-877-609-4872; Insurance Claims: 1-800-480-1853
Ownership: Wholly owned subsidiary of Canadian Tire Corporation Limited
Year Founded: 1966
Number of Employees: 1,300

Canadian Western Bank (CWB)/ Banque Canadienne de l'Ouest
#3000, 10303 Jasper Ave.
Edmonton, AB T5J 3X6
Tel: 780-423-8888; Fax: 780-423-8897
comments@cwbank.com
www.cwbank.com
Also Known As: Canada's Western Bank
Ownership: Widely held Canadian corporation
Year Founded: 1984
Number of Employees: 1,000
Assets: $9,525,040,000 Year End: 20081031
Revenues: $561,756,000 Year End: 20081031

Citizens Bank of Canada
#401, 815 West Hastings St.
Vancouver, BC V6C 1B4
Tel: 604-682-7171; Fax: 604-708-7790
Toll-Free: 888-708-7800
service@citizensbank.ca
www.citizensbank.ca
Ownership: Subsidiary of Vancouver City Savings Credit Union
Year Founded: 1997
Number of Employees: 120

Dundee Bank of Canada (DBC)
44 King St. West
Toronto, ON M5H 1H1
Fax: 416-849-1700
Toll-Free: 866-884-3434
support@dbc.ca
www.dbc.ca
Former Name: Dundee Wealth Bank
Ownership: Member of Dundee Financial Group (DFG), a division of DundeeWealth Inc.
Year Founded: 2006

First Nations Bank of Canada
224 - 4th Ave. South
Saskatoon, SK S7K 5M5
Tel: 306-931-2409; Fax: 306-955-6811
Toll-Free: 888-454-3622
service@firstnationsbank.com
www.firstnationsbank.com
Ownership: Private
Year Founded: 1996
Number of Employees: 05
Assets: $100-500 million
Revenues: $5-10 million

General Bank of Canada(GBC)
c/o LeMarchand Mansion
#6, 11523 - 100 Ave.
Edmonton, AB T5K 0J8
Tel: 780-443-5626; Fax: 780-443-5628
Toll-Free: 877-443-5620
info@generalbank.ca
www.generalbank.ca
Ownership: Parent company is Firstcan Management Inc.
Year Founded: 2005

Laurentian Bank of Canada/ Banque Laurentienne du Canada
1981, av. McGill College
Montréal, QC H3A 3K3
Toll-Free: 877-522-3863
www.laurentianbank.ca
Other Contact Information: 1-866-262-2231 (TTY service); 514-284-4500, ext. 7511 or 8143 (Investors & analysts); 514-284-4500, ext. 7511 (Media)
Ownership: Public
Year Founded: 1846
Number of Employees: 3,393
Assets: $19,000,000,000+ Year End: 20081031
Revenues: $630,500,500 Year End: 20081031

Manulife Bank of Canada
PO Box 1602, Waterloo Stn. Waterloo
#500MA, 500 King St. North
Waterloo, ON N2J 4C6
Tel: 519-747-7000; Toll-Free: 877-765-2265
manulife_bank@manulife.com
www.manulifebank.ca
Ownership: Private. Wholly-owned subsidiary of Manulife Financial.
Year Founded: 1993
Number of Employees: 200+
Assets: $1-10 billion

National Bank of Canada (NBC)/ Banque Nationale du Canada(BNC)
National Bank Tower
600, rue de La Gauchetière ouest
Montréal, QC H3B 4L2
Tél: 514-394-6081; Téléc: 514-394-8434
www.nbc.ca
Former Name: The Provincial Bank of Canada; The Mercantile Bank of Canada
Ownership: Public
Year Founded: 1859
Number of Employees: 18,322

Pacific & Western Bank of Canada
#2002, 140 Fullarton St.
London, ON N6A 5P2
Tel: 519-645-1919; Fax: 519-645-2060
Toll-Free: 866-979-1919
www.pwbank.com
Ownership: Parent company is Pacific & Western Credit Corp., a public company.
Year Founded: 1979
Assets: $1-10 billion
Revenues: $5-10 million

President's Choice Financial
431 King St. West
Toronto, ON M5V 1K5
Tel: 416-204-2600; Toll-Free: 888-723-8881
www.banking.pcfinancial.ca
Also Known As: PC Bank
Ownership: PC Financial is a joint venture between Loblaw Companies & CIBC.

Royal Bank of Canada (RBC)
200 Bay St.
Toronto, ON M5J 2S5
Tél: 416-974-5151; Téléc: 416-955-7800
www.rbc.com
Also Known As: RBC Financial Group
Year Founded: 1869
Number of Employees: 65,045

The Toronto-Dominion Bank
TD Centre
PO Box 1
Toronto, ON M5K 1A2
Tel: 416-982-8222; Toll-Free: 866-222-3456
www.td.com
Also Known As: TD Bank; TD Canada Trust
Ownership: Public
Year Founded: 1855
Number of Employees: 51,163

Foreign Banks: Schedule II

Amex Bank of Canada
***Also listed under:** Credit Card Companies*
101 McNabb St.
Markham, ON L3R 4H8
Tel: 905-474-0870; Toll-Free: 800-668-2639
www.americanexpress.com/canada
Other Contact Information: Toll-Free TTY/TDD: 1-866-549-6426; Local TTY/TDD: 905-940-7702
Ownership: Wholly owned subsidiary of American Express Travel Related Services Company, Inc., New York, USA.
Year Founded: 1853
Number of Employees: 3,700

Bank of China (Canada)
The Exchange Tower
PO Box 356
#2730, 130 King St. West
Toronto, ON M5X 1E1
Tel: 416-362-2991; Fax: 416-362-3047
www.boc.cn/cn/html/canada/en_s1.html
Ownership: Wholly owned subsidiary of the Bank of China Limited, Beijing, China.
Year Founded: 1992
Number of Employees: 85
Assets: $100-500 million
Revenues: $10-50 million

The Bank of East Asia (Canada)
East Asia Centre
#102-103, 350 Hwy. 7 East
Richmond Hill, ON L4B 3N2
Tel: 905-882-8182; Fax: 905-882-5220
info@hkbea.com, OsEnquiry@hkbea.com
ca.hkbea.com
Other Contact Information: (852) 3608 0200 (Phone, Overseas Branch Operations & Development Department in Hong Kong)
Ownership: Private. Member of The Bank of East Asia Group, Hong Kong.
Year Founded: 1991

Bank of Tokyo-Mitsubishi UFJ (Canada)
#1700, South Tower, Royal Bank Plaza
PO Box 42
Toronto, ON M5J 2J1
Tel: 416-865-0220; Fax: 416-865-0196
www.bk.mufg.jp/english
Ownership: Foreign. Part of The Bank of Tokyo-Mitsubishi UFJ, Ltd., Tokyo,Japan.
Year Founded: 1996

BNP Paribas (Canada)
1981, av. McGill College
Montréal, QC H3A 2W8
Tél: 514-285-6000; Téléc: 514-285-6278
Ligne sans frais: 866-277-6100
bnpp.canada@americas.bnpparibas.com
www.bnpparibas.ca
Former Name: Banque Nationale de Paris (Canada)
Ownership: Foreign. Wholly owned subsidiary of BNP Paribas, Paris, France
Year Founded: 1961
Number of Employees: 240
Assets: $1-10 billion

Citibank Canada
Citigroup Place
#1700, 123 Front St. West
Toronto, ON M5J 2M3
Tel: 416-947-5500; Fax: 416-947-5387
www.citibank.com/canada
Ownership: Wholly owned indirect subsidiary of Citibank, N.A.
Year Founded: 1982
Number of Employees: 5,000+

CTC Bank of Canada (CTCB)
1518 West Broadway
Vancouver, BC V6J 1W8
Tel: 604-683-3882; Fax: 604-683-3723
service@ctcbank.com
www.ctcbank.com
Ownership: Private. Part of Chinatrust Commercial Bank.

Habib Canadian Bank
#1B, 918 Dundas St. East
Mississauga, ON L4Y 4H9
Tel: 905-276-5300; Fax: 905-276-5400
info@habibcanadian.com
www.habibcanadian.com
Ownership: Private. Foreign. Wholly owned by Habib Bank of AG Zurich, Switzerland.
Year Founded: 1967
Assets: $50-100 million
Revenues: $1-5 million

HSBC Bank Canada
#300, 885 West Georgia St.
Vancouver, BC V6C 3E9
Tel: 604-525-4722; Fax: 604-641-1849
Toll-Free: 888-310-4722
info@hsbc.ca
www.hsbc.ca
Ownership: Subsidiary of HSBC Holdings plc, London, UK.
Year Founded: 1981
Number of Employees: 7,500
Assets: $62,931,000,000 Year End: 20081231
Revenues: $3,772,000,000 Year End: 20081231

ICICI Bank Canada
PO Box 396
Toronto, ON M3C 2S7
Toll-Free: 888-424-2422
customercare.ca@icicibank.com
www.icicibank.ca
Ownership: Wholly owned subsidiary of ICICI Bank Limited, Mumbai, India.

ING Bank of Canada
111 Gordon Baker Rd.
Toronto, ON M2H 3R1
Tel: 416-758-5344; Fax: 416-756-2422
Toll-Free: 800-464-3473
clientservices@ingdirect.ca
www.ingdirect.ca
Other Contact Information: 1-866-464-3473 (Toll Free, French service)
Social Media: www.facebook.com/superstarsaver; twitter.com/superstarsaver
Also Known As: ING DIRECT
Ownership: Wholly owned subsidiary of ING Group, Netherlands
Year Founded: 1997
Number of Employees: 850+
Assets: $10-100 billion

J.P. Morgan Bank Canada
South Tower, Royal Bank Plaza
PO Box 80
#1800, 200 Bay St.
Toronto, ON M5J 2J2
Tel: 416-981-9200; Fax: 416-981-9133
www.jpmorgan.com

Korea Exchange Bank of Canada (KEBOC)
Madison Centre
#103, 4950 Yonge St.
Toronto, ON M2N 6K1
Tel: 416-222-5200; Fax: 416-222-5822
www.kebcanada.com
Year Founded: 1981
Number of Employees: 90

MBNA Canada Bank
1600 James Naismith Dr.
Ottawa, ON K1B 5N8
Tel: 613-907-4800; Fax: 613-907-3501
Toll-Free: 800-404-1319
www.mbna.com/canada
Other Contact Information: 1-877-862-7759 (Toll-Free for card applications); 1-800-872-5758 (TTY/TTD)
Ownership: Private. MBNA Corporation, Wilmington, Delaware, USA.
Year Founded: 1997

Mega International Commercial Bank (Canada)
Madison Centre
#1002, 4950 Yonge St.
Toronto, ON M2N 6K1
Tel: 416-947-2800; Fax: 416-947-9964
megato@ipoline.com
www.megabank.com.tw
Former Name: International Commercial Bank of Cathay (Canada)
Ownership: Wholly owned subsidiary of Mega International Commercial Bank Co., Ltd., Taipei City, Taiwan.

Mizuho Corporate Bank (Canada) (MHCB)
PO Box 29
#1102, 100 Yonge St.
Toronto, ON M5C 2W1
Tel: 416-874-0222; Fax: 416-367-3452
Toll-Free: 800-668-5917
www.mizuhocbk.co.jp/english
Former Name: Mizuho Bank (Canada)
Ownership: Foreign. Part of Mizuho Corporate Bank, Ltd., Tokyo, Japan.
Year Founded: 2000

Société Générale (Canada)
#1800, 1501, av. McGill College
Montréal, QC H3A 3M8
Tél: 514-841-6000
www.societegenerale.com
Ownership: Wholly owned subsidiary of Société Générale Group, Paris, France.
Year Founded: 1974

State Bank of India (Canada)
#1600, Royal Bank Plaza, North Tower
PO Box 81, Royal Bank Stn. Royal Bank
200 Bay St.
Toronto, ON M5J 2J2
Tel: 416-865-0414; Fax: 416-865-1735
Toll-Free: 800-668-8947
sbican@sbicanada.com
www.sbicanada.com
Ownership: Subsidiary of State Bank of India
Year Founded: 1982
Number of Employees: 45
Assets: $100-500 million
Revenues: $1-5 million

Sumitomo Mitsui Banking Corporation of Canada
#1400, Ernst & Young Tower
PO Box 172, TD Centre Stn. TD Centre
Toronto, ON M5K 1H6
Tel: 416-368-4766; Fax: 416-367-3565
www.smbc.co.jp/aboutus/english
Former Name: Sakura Bank (Canada); The Sumitomo Bank of Canada
Ownership: Private. Foreign. Wholly owned subsidiary of Sumitomo Mitsui Banking Corporation, Tokyo, Japan.
Year Founded: 2001
Number of Employees: 32

UBS Bank (Canada)
Also listed under: *Financial Planning & Investment Management Companies; Investment Management*
#800, 154 University Ave.
Toronto, ON M5H 3Z4
Tel: 416-343-1800; Fax: 416-343-1900
Toll-Free: 800-268-9709
www.ubs.com/canada
Also Known As: UBS Canada
Ownership: Foreign. Public.
Year Founded: 1856
Number of Employees: 70,000
Assets: $100 billion +
Revenues: $10-100 billion

Foreign Banks: Schedule III

ABN AMRO Bank N.V., Canada Branch
Toronto-Dominion Centre
PO Box 114, T-D Centre Stn. T-D Centre
#1500, 79 Wellington St. West, 15th Fl.
Toronto, ON M5K 1G8
Tel: 416-367-0850; Fax: 416-367-7937
canada.branch@abnamro.com
www.abnamro.ca
Other Contact Information: canada.jobs@abnamro.com (Employment Enquiries); 416-367-7943 (Business & Commercial Fax); 416-367-7937 (Corporate & Institutional Fax)
Ownership: Branch of ABN AMRO Bank N.V.
Year Founded: 1824

Bank of America, National Association
#2500, 200 Front St. West
Toronto, ON M5V 3L2
Tel: 416-349-4100; Fax: 416-349-4278
Toll-Free: 800-387-1729
www.bankofamerica.com

Capital One Bank (Canada Branch)
Also listed under: *Credit Card Companies*
#1300, 5650 Yonge St.
Toronto, ON M2M 4G3
Fax: 416-228-5113
Toll-Free: 800-481-3239
ombudsman@capitalone.com
www.capitalone.ca
Other Contact Information: Customer Relations Address: PO Box 503, Stn. D, Toronto, ON M1R 5L1; Payment Address: PO Box 521, Stn. D, Toronto, ON M1R 5S4
Ownership: Foreign. Part of Capital One Services, Inc., McLean, VA, USA.

Comerica Bank
South Tower, Royal Bank Plaza
PO Box 61
#2210, 200 Bay St.
Toronto, ON M5J 2J2
Tel: 416-646-4797; Fax: 416-367-6435
www.comerica.com
Ownership: Foreign. Branch of Comerica Bank, Detroit, Michigan, USA.

Credit Suisse Securities (Canada), Inc.
PO Box 301, First Canadian Pl. Stn. First Canadian Pl.
#3000, 1 First Canadian Pl.
Toronto, ON M5X 1C9
Tel: 416-352-4500; Fax: 416-352-4680
www.csfb.com
Ownership: Part of Credit Suisse Group, Zurich, Switzerland.

Deutsche Bank AG
Commerce Court West
PO Box 263
#4700, 199 Bay St.
Toronto, ON M5L 1E9
Tel: 416-682-8000; Fax: 416-682-8383
deutsche.bank@db.com
www.db.com
Ownership: Foreign. Branch of Deutsche Bank AG, Frankfurt, Germany.

Dexia Crédit Local S.A. Canada
PO Box 201
#1620, 800, carré Victoria
Montréal, QC H4A 1E3
Tel: 514-868-1200
webmaster@dexia.com
www.dexia.com
Ownership: Branch of Dexia Crédit Local, Paris, France.

Fifth Third Bank
20 Bay St., 12th Fl.
Toronto, ON M5J 2N8
Tel: 416-216-4638
www.53.com
Ownership: Foreign. Branch of Fifth Third Bank, Cincinnati, Ohio, USA

First Commercial Bank
#100, 5611 Cooney Rd.
Richmond, BC V6X 3J6
Tel: 604-207-9600; Fax: 604-207-9638
www.firstbank.com
Ownership: Foreign. Branch of First Commercial Bank, Taiwan.

HSBC Bank USA, National Association
70 York St., 4th Fl.
Toronto, ON M5J 1S9
Tel: 416-868-8000
www.us.hsbc.com, www.hsbc.ca

JPMorgan Chase Bank, National Association
South Tower, Royal Bank Plaza
PO Box 80
#1800, 200 Bay St.
Toronto, ON M5J 2J2
Tel: 416-981-9200; Fax: 416-981-9175
Toll-Free: 888-430-9844
www.jpmorganchase.com
Former Name: The Chase Manhattan Bank; Morgan Guaranty Trust Co. of New York; Sears Bank Canada
Ownership: Branch of J.P. Morgan Chase & Co. Inc., Chicago, IL, USA.

Maple Bank GmbH
c/o Maple Financial Group Inc., Maritime Life Tower, TD Centre
PO Box 328
#3500, 79 Wellington St. West
Toronto, ON M5K 1K7
Tel: 416-350-8200; Fax: 416-350-8226
info@maplefinancial.com
www.maplebank.com; www.maplefinancial.com
Former Name: First Marathon Bank GmbH
Ownership: Subsidiary of Maple Financial Group Inc.

Mellon Bank, N.A., Canada Branch
PO Box 16
#1710, 95 Wellington St. West
Toronto, ON M5J 2N7
Tel: 416-860-0777
www.mellon.com
Ownership: Foreign. Branch of Mellon Financial Corp., Pittsburgh, PA, USA.
Year Founded: 1983

National City Bank - Canada Branch
The Exchange Tower
PO Box 462
#2140, 130 King St. West
Toronto, ON M5X 1E4
Tel: 416-361-1744; Fax: 416-361-0085
www.nationalcity.com
Ownership: owned by National City Bank, Cleveland, Ohio
Year Founded: 1845
Number of Employees: 5

Ohio Savings Bank, Canadian Branch
Centre Tower, Clarica Centre
#3110, 3300 Bloor St. West
Toronto, ON M8X 2X3
Toll-Free: 800-696-2222
www.ohiosavings.com
Ownership: Foreign. Branch of Ohio Savings Bank, Cleveland, OH, USA.

Rabobank Nederland
Royal Trust Tower
#4520, 77 King St. West
Toronto, ON M5K 1E7
Tel: 416-941-9777; Fax: 416-941-9750
www.rabobank.com
Former Name: Rabobank Canada
Ownership: Cooperative. Foreign. Branch of Rabobank Nederland, Netherlands
Year Founded: 2001
Number of Employees: 14
Assets: $1-10 billion

State Street Bank & Trust Company - Canada
Also listed under: *Trust Companies*
#1100, 30 Adelaide St. East
Toronto, ON M5C 3G6
Tel: 416-362-1100; Fax: 416-956-2525
Toll-Free: 888-287-8639
www.statestreet.com
Former Name: State Street Trust Company Canada
Ownership: State Street Corporation
Year Founded: 1990
Number of Employees: 700

Union Bank of California, N.A.
#730, 440 - 2 Ave. SW
Calgary, AB T2P 5E9
Tel: 403-264-2700; Fax: 403-264-2770
www.uboc.com
Ownership: Parent Union BanCal Corporation
Year Founded: 1864

United Overseas Bank Limited (UOB)
Vancouver Centre
PO Box 11616
#1680, 650 West Georgia St.
Vancouver, BC V6B 4N9
Tel: 604-662-7055; Fax: 604-662-3356
UOB.Vancouver@uobgroup.com
www.uobgroup.com
Ownership: Foreign. Branch of United Overseas Bank Limited, Singapore.
Year Founded: 1987

U.S. Bank National Association - Canada Branch
Adelaide Centre
#2300, 120 Adelaide St. West
Toronto, ON M5H 1T1
Toll-Free: 877-332-7461
www.usbankcanada.com
Ownership: Part of U.S. Bank, Minneapolis, MN, USA.

WestLB AG
North Tower, Royal Bank Plaza
PO Box 41
#2301, 200 Bay St.
Toronto, ON M5J 2J1
Tel: 416-216-5000; Fax: 416-216-5020
info@westlb.de
www.westlb.com
Ownership: Foreign. Branch of WestLB AG, Düsseldorf, Germany.

Foreign Banks Representative Offices

Allied Irish Banks, p.l.c. (AIB)
20 Bay St., 12th Fl.
Toronto, ON M5J 2N8
www.aib.ie
Ownership: Foreign. Office of Allied Irish Banks p.l.c., Dublin, Ireland.

American Express Bank Ltd.
#1350, 1090 West Georgia St.
Vancouver, BC V6E 3V7
Ownership: Foreign. Office of American Express Bank, New York, NY, USA.

Banco Comercial dos Açores
836 Dundas St. West
Toronto, ON M6J 1V5
Tel: 416-603-0802; Fax: 416-603-8892
www.bca.pt

Banco Espirito Santo e Comercial de Lisboa, SA
860C College St.
Toronto, ON M6H 1A2
Tel: 416-530-1700
www.bes.pt
Ownership: Private

Banco Santander Totta, SA
1110 Dundas St. West
Toronto, ON M6J 1X2
Tel: 416-538-7111
www.santandertotta.pt

Bank Hapoalim B.M.
#2105, 4950 Yonge St.
Toronto, ON M2N 6K1
Tel: 416-398-4250; Fax: 416-398-4246
www.bankhapoalim.com

Bank Leumi Le-Israel, B.M.
#400, 1 carré Westmount
Montréal, QC H3Z 2P9
Tel: 514-931-4457; Fax: 514-931-5240
english.leumi.co.il
Ownership: Office of Bank Leumi Le-Israel, B.M., Tel Aviv, Israel.
Year Founded: 1902
Assets: $10-100 billion
Revenues: $100-500 million

Bank of Cyprus, Canada Representative Office
#302, 658 Danforth Ave.
Toronto, ON M4J 5B9
Tel: 416-461-5570; Fax: 416-461-6062
Toll-Free: 888-529-2265
info@bankofcyprus.ca
www.bankofcyprus.ca
Ownership: Office of the Bank of Cyprus Group, Cyprus.
Year Founded: 1997

Bank of Ireland Asset Management (U.S.) Limited
#2460, 1800, av. McGill College
Montréal, QC H3A 3J6
Tel: 514-849-6868; Fax: 514-849-8118
canada@biam.boi.ie
www.biam.ie
Year Founded: 1987

Bank of Valletta p.l.c., Canada Representative Office
West Tower
#625, 3300 Bloor St. West, 6th Fl.
Toronto, ON M8X 2X2
Tel: 416-234-2265; Fax: 416-234-2281
Toll-Free: 800-567-2265
bovcanada@bov.com
www.bov.com

Bank Vontobel AG
#1760, 999 West Hastings St.
Vancouver, BC V6C 2W2
Tel: 604-688-1122; Fax: 604-688-1123
www.vontobel.com
Ownership: Office of Bank Vontobel AG, Zürich, Switzerland.

Banque Centrale Populaire du Maroc
#1514, 1010 rue Sherbrooke ouest
Montréal, QC H3A 2R7
Tel: 514-281-1855; Fax: 514-281-1974
gbpmaroc@qc.aira.com
www.bp.co.ma

Baring Asset Management Inc.
TD Canada Trust Tower, Brookfield Place
161 Bay St., 27th Fl.
Toronto, ON M5J 2S1
Tel: 416-572-2400; Fax: 416-572-4100
william.tsotsos@barings.com
www.baring-asset-can.com
Ownership: Private
Year Founded: 1977

Bayerische Landesbank
#2060, 1501, av. McGill College
Montréal, QC H3A 3M8
Tel: 514-985-0047; Fax: 514-985-3459
info.montreal@bayernlb.com
www.bayernlb.de
Ownership: Foreign. Part of Bayerische Landesbank (BayernLB), Munich, Germany.

Caixa Economica Montepio Gual
1286 Dundas St. West
Toronto, ON M6J 1X7
Tel: 416-588-7776; Fax: 416-588-0030
mg503@montepio.pt
www.montepio.pt

Calyon
#1900, 2000, av McGill College
Montréal, QC
Ownership: Office of Credit Agricole Group, Paris, France.
Year Founded: 2004

Centurion Bank of Punjab, Ltd.
#337, 1515 Britannia Rd. East
Mississauga, ON L4W 4K1
Tel: 905-696-0943; Fax: 905-696-0976
nri.services@centurionbop.co.in
www.centurionbop.co.in
Ownership: Office of Centurion Bank of Punjab, India.

Crédit Libanais S.A.L. Representative Office (Canada)
Place du Canada
#1325, 1010, rue de la Gauchetière ouest
Montréal, QC H3B 2N2
Tel: 514-866-6688; Fax: 514-866-6220
Toll-Free: 800-864-5512
info@creditlibanais.com
www.creditlibanais.com
Ownership: Office of Credit Libanais S.A.L., Beirut, Lebanon.

Cyprus Popular Bank Ltd.
484 Danforth Ave., 2nd Fl.
Toronto, ON M4K 1P6
Tel: 416-466-8180; Fax: 416-466-9609
Toll-Free: 877-524-5422
laiki.toronto@laiki.com, laikiebank@laiki.com
www.laiki.com
Also Known As: Laiki Bank
Ownership: Office of Laiki Group, Cyprus.

Jamaica National Overseas (Canada) Ltd.
1672 Eglinton Ave. West
Toronto, ON M6E 2H2
Tel: 416-784-2075; Fax: 416-784-2076
Toll-Free: 800-462-9003
info@jnocanada.com, rosbourne@jnocanada.com, sstamp@jnocanada.com
www.jnbs.com
Ownership: Office of Jamaica National Building Society, Kingston Jamaica.

Japan Bank for International Cooperation - Toronto Liaison Office (JBIC)
Exchange Tower
PO Box 493, 2 First Canadian Pl. Stn. 2 First Canadian Pl.
#3660, 130 King St. West
Toronto, ON M5X 1E5
Tel: 416-865-1700; Fax: 416-865-0124
www.jbic.go.jp
Ownership: Office of Japan Bank for International Cooperation, Tokyo, Japan.

JS Trasta komercbanka
#800, St. Clair Ave. East
Toronto, ON M4T 2T5
Tel: 416-644-4941; Fax: 416-644-4946
canada@tkb.lv, info@tkb.lv
www.tkb.lv
Ownership: Office of JS Trasta komercbanka, Riga, Latvia.

Landsbanki Islands hf
George Mitchell House
5112 Prince St.
Halifax, NS B3J 1L3
Tel: 902-576-3100
info@landsbanki.is
www.landsbanki.is
Ownership: Office of Landsbanki Islands hf, Reykjavik, Iceland.

Lebanese Canadian Bank, s.a.l.
#1508, 1, Place Ville-Marie
Montréal, QC H3B 2B5
Tel: 514-871-3999; Fax: 514-871-2079
www.lebcanbank.com
Other Contact Information: Alternative Phone Numbers: 514-871-1905; 514-871-1913; 514-871-1926

National Bank of Pakistan
#210, 175 Commerce Valley Dr. West
Thornhill, ON L3T 7P6
Tel: 905-707-0244; Fax: 905-707-1040
chiefrep@nbpcanada.com, enquiries@nationalbank.com.pk
www.nbp.com.pk
Ownership: Office of National Bank of Pakistan, Karachi, Pakistan.

Schroder Investment Management North America Limited - Canadian Representative Office
Also listed under: *Financial Planning & Investment Management Companies*
875 Third Ave., 22nd floor
New York, NY 10022-6225
Tel: 212-641-3830
canada@schroders.com
www.schroders.com/ca
Former Name: Schroder Investment Management Canada Limited
Ownership: Office of Schroders plc, London, UK.

Stanford International Bank Ltd. (SIBL)
#3010, 1800, av. McGill College
Montréal, QC H3A 3J6
Tel: 514-985-3600
www.stanfordinternational.com
Ownership: Office of Stanford International Bank Ltd., St. Johns, Antigua, West Indies.
Year Founded: 2004

UBS AG
PO Box 3
#650, 999 West Hastings St.
Vancouver, BC V6C 2W2
Tel: 604-691-8061; Fax: 604-691-8098
www.ubs.com
Ownership: Office of UBS AG, Zürich, Switzerland.

Victoria Mutual Building Society - Canadian Representative Office (VMBS)
3117A Dufferin St.
Toronto, ON M6A 2S9
Tel: 416-652-8652; Fax: 416-652-5266
Toll-Free: 800-465-6500
manager@vmbs.com
www.vmbs.com
Ownership: Office of Victoria Mutual Building Society, Kingston, Jamaica.

Westdeutsche Landesbank Girozentrale
North Tower, Royal Bank Plaza
PO Box 41
#2301, 200 Bay St.
Toronto, ON M5J 2J1
Tel: 416-216-5000; Fax: 416-216-5020
info@westlb.de
www.westlb.de
Also Known As: WestLB
Ownership: Office of Westdeutsche Landesbank Girozentrale, Düsseldorf, Germany

Savings Banks

ATB Financial
ATB Place
9888 Jasper Ave. NW
Edmonton, AB T5J 1P1
Tel: 780-408-7000; Fax: 780-422-4178
Toll-Free: 800-332-8383
atbinfo@atb.com
www.atb.com
Former Name: Alberta Treasury Branches
Ownership: Crown. 100% owned by the Provincial Government of Alberta
Year Founded: 1938
Number of Employees: 5,000

Boards of Trade & Chambers of Commerce

International Chambers & Business Councils

Belgian Canadian Business Chamber (BCBC)
PO Box 508, 161 Bay St., 27th Fl., Toronto ON M5J 2S1
info@belgiumconnect.com
www.belgiumconnect.com

Peter Van Praet, President
André van der Heyden, Vice-President & Board Secretary
Elly De Winne, Treasurer
Klaus Koeppen, Assistant Treasurer
Christian Frayssignes, EUCOCIT Representative
Jacques Druart, Membership Secretary
Vincent van der Heijden, Assistant Membership Secretary
Jan Carpentier, New Media Coordinator
Pieter-Jan Michielsen, Events Coordinator
Michael Green, Director
Mieke Pynnaert, Honourary Director

British Canadian Chamber of Trade & Commerce
Dominion Centre, Royal Trust Tower, #2401, 77 King Street, Toronto ON M5K 1G8
Tel: 416-816-9154; Fax: 647-435-3436
central@bcctc.ca
www.bcctc.ca

Thomas O'Carroll, Vice-President, Central
Liam J. Hopkins, Vice President, Western
John Hoblyn, Contact, Eastern

Canada China Business Council (CCBC) / Conseil commercial Canada Chine
#1501, 330 Bay St., Toronto ON M5H 2S8
Tel: 416-954-3800; Fax: 416-954-3806
ccbc@ccbc.com
www.ccbc.com

Peter Kruyt, Chair
Sarah Kutulakos, Executive Director
Eumie Leung, Director, Operations

Canada China Business Council
#600, 890 West Pender St., Vancouver BC V6C 1J9
Tel: 604-281-8838; Fax: 604-281-8831
ccbcvan@ccbc.com

Canada China Business Council
1250, boul, René-Lévesque ouest, Montréal QC
Tel: 514-585-8487

Canada Czech Republic Chamber of Commerce (CNACC)
Stn. A, 115 George St, Oakville ON L6J 0A2
Tel: 905-845-9606
admin@ccrcc.net
www.ccrcc.net

Miroslav Princ, Chamber President

Canada Eurasia Russia Business Association (CERBA)
c/o Heenan Blaikie LLP, #2900, 333 Bay St., Toronto ON M5H 2T4
Tel: 416-360-2299; Fax: 416-360-8425
katherine@cerbanet.org; joanna@cerbanet.org
www.cerbanet.org

Piers Cumberlege, National Chair
Katherine Balabanova, Regional Director, Toronto

Publications: CERBA [Canada Eurasia Russia Business Association] Newsletter

Canada-Arab Business Council (CABC) / Conseil de commerce canado-arabe (CCCA)
#702, 116 Albert St., Toronto ON K1P 5G3
Tel: 613-680-3888; Fax: 613-565-3013
info@canada-arabbusiness.org
www.canada-arabbusiness.org

Affiliation(s): Canadian Chamber of Commerce
Hugh O'Donnell, Chairman & CEO

Canada-Finland Chamber of Commerce
c/o Finnish Credit Union, 191 Eglinton Ave. East, Toronto ON M4P 1K1
Tel: 416-486-1533; Fax: 416-486-1592
info@canadafinlandcc.com
www.canadafinlandcc.com

Peter Auvien

Canada-India Business Council (C-IBC) / Conseil de commerce Canada-Inde
#302, 1 St. Clair Ave. East, Toronto ON M4T 2V7
Tel: 416-214-5947; Fax: 416-214-9081
info@canada-indiabusiness.ca
www.canada-indiabusiness.ca

Roy MacLaren, Chair
Rana Sarkar, President & Executive Director

Canada-Indonesia Business Council
PO Box 11-C, #110, 260 Adelaide St. East, Toronto ON M5A 1N1
Tel: 416-366-8490; Fax: 416-947-1534

Peter J. Dawes, Chair

Canada-Poland Chamber of Commerce of Toronto
77 Stoneham Rd., Toronto ON M9C 4Y7
Tel: 416-621-2032; Fax: 416-621-2472
info@canada-poland.com
www.canada-poland.com

Wojciech Sniegowski, President

Canadian Armenian Business Council Inc. (CABC) / Conseil commercial canadien-arménien inc.
#302-2, 1805, rué Sauve ouest, Montréal QC H4N 3B8
Tel: 514-333-7655; Fax: 514-333-7280
info@cabc.ca
www.cabc.ca

Publications: CABC [Canadian Armenian Business Council Inc.] Business Directory

Canadian Council for the Americas (BCCC)
PO Box 1227, Oakville ON L6J 5C7
Tel: 416-367-4313; Fax: 416-595-8226
cca@iecanada.com
www.ccacanada.com

Kenneth Frankel, Chair

Canadian Council for the Americas (CCA) / Conseil Canadien pour les Amériques
#2300, 1066 West Hastings St., Vancouver BC V6E 3X2
Tel: 778-388-5206; Fax: 604-806-6112
info@cca-bc.com
www.cca-bc.com

André Nudelman, Chair
Leon Teicher, Secretary

Canadian German Chamber of Industry & Commerce Inc. / Deutsch-Kanadische Industrie- und Handelskammer
#1500, 480 University Ave., Toronto ON M5G 1V2
Tel: 416-598-3355; Fax: 416-598-1840
info.toronto@germanchamber.ca
kanada.ahk.de

Thomas Beck, President/CEO

Publications: Canadian German Headlines: CGCIC Newsletter, Membership Directory of the Canadian German Chamber of Industry & Commerce

Canadian-Croatian Chamber of Commerce
630 The East Mall, Toronto ON M9B 4B1
Tel: 416-641-2829; Fax: 416-641-2700
contactus@croat.ca
www.croat.ca

John Marion, President

Caribbean & African Chamber of Commerce of Ontario (CACCO)
PO Box 55328, Stn. Scarborough Town Centre, Toronto ON M1P 4Z7
Tel: 416-265-8603; Fax: 416-269-2081
info@cacco.ca
www.cacco.ca

Affiliation(s): Ontario Chamber of Commerce; Board of Trade
Worrick Russel, Executive Chair

Chambre de commerce Canada-Pologne
5570 Waverly Rue, Montréal QC H2T 2Y1

Chambre de commerce Canado-Tunisienne (CCCT) / Tunisian Canadian Chamber of Commerce
#806, 276, rue St-Jacques, Montréal QC H2Y 1N3
Tél: 514-847-1281; Téléc: 514-849-4910
info@cccantun.ca
www.cccantun.ca

Abdeljelil Ouanès, Président

Chambre de commerce française au canada (CCFC) / French Chamber of Commerce
#202, 1819, boul René-Lévesque ouest, Montréal QC H3H 2P5
Tél: 514-281-1246; Téléc: 514-289-9594
accueil@ccfcmtl.ca
www.ccfcmtl.ca

Florent Belleste, Directeur

Danish Canadian Chamber of Commerce
#2110, 2 Bloor St. West, Toronto ON M4W 3E2
Tel: 416-923-1811; Fax: 416-962-3668
info@dccc.ca
www.dccc.ca

Anders Fisker, Chair
Knud Westergaard, Executive Director

Indo-Canada Chamber of Commerce (ICCC) / Chambre de commerce Indo-Canada
#900, 45 Sheppard Ave. East, Toronto ON M2N 5W9
Tel: 416-224-0090; Fax: 416-224-0089
Toll-Free: 866-873-4222
iccc@iccc.org
www.iccc.org

Asha Luthra, President
Neena Gupta, Vice-President & Corp. Secretary

International Chamber of Commerce (ICC) / Chambre de Commerce Internationale
38, cours Albert 1er, Paris 75008 France
icc@iccwbo.org
www.iccwbo.org

Affiliation(s): United Nations; World Trade Organization
Dawn Chardonnal, Communications Manager
Marcus Wallenberg, Chair

Ireland-Canada Chamber of Commerce (ICCC)
121 Decarie Circle, Toronto ON M9B 3J6
Tel: 416-622-7773; Fax: 416-621-3433
main@iccto.com
www.iccto.com

Michael Power, President

Italian Chamber of Commerce of Ontario (ICCO)
1502, 80 Richmond St. West, Toronto ON M5H 2A4
Tel: 416-789-7169; Fax: 416-789-7160
info.toronto@italchambers.ca
www.italchambers.ca

Ronald J. Farano, Chair
George Visintin, President
Corrado Paina, Executive Director

Publications: Partners Magazine

Southeast Asia-Canada Business Council
5294 Imperial St., Burnaby BC V5J 1E4
Tel: 604-439-0779; Fax: 604-439-0284
info@aseancanada.com
www.aseancanada.com

The Swedish-Canadian Chamber of Commerce (SCCC)
#2120, 2 Bloor St. West, Toronto ON M4W 3E2
Tel: 416-925-8661; Fax: 416-929-8639
mglindmark@sccc.ca
www.sccc.ca

Monika G. Lindmark, Executive Director

Swiss Canadian Chamber of Commerce (Montréal) Inc. / Chambre de commerce Canado-Suisse (Montréal) Inc.
1572 Dr. Penfield Ave., Montréal QC H3G 1C4
Tel: 514-937-5822; Fax: 514-693-1032
info@cccsmtl.com
www.cccsmtl.com

Jean Serge Grisé, President

World Chambers Federation (WCF)
38 cours Albert 1er, Paris 75008 France
wcf@iccwbo.org
www.iccwbo.org/wcf
Social Media: www.youtube.com/user/03WCF

Affiliation(s): Specialized div. of International Chamber of Commerce
Anthony Parkes, Director

Chambers of Mines

Alberta Caregivers Association (ACGA)
c/o Fulton Place School, 10310 - 56th St. NW, Edmonton AB T6A 2J2
Tel: 780-453-5088; Fax: 780-465-5581
Toll-Free: 877-453-5088
office@albertacaregivers.org
www.albertacaregiversassociation.org

Peter Kossowan, Acting Chair
Giri Puligandla, Executive Director
Pat Zwartjes, Secretary
Wayne Tischer, Treasurer

Publications: Contact

Alberta Chamber of Resources
#1940, 10180 - 101 St., Edmonton AB T5J 3S4
Tel: 780-420-1030; Fax: 780-425-4623
admin@acr-alberta.com
www.acr-alberta.com

Gord Ball, President

Aquaculture Association of Canada (AAC) / Association Aquacole du Canada
16 Lobster Lane, St. Andrews NB E5B 3T6
Tel: 506-529-4766; Fax: 506-529-4609
aac@dfo-mpo.gc.ca
www.aquacultureassociation.ca

Susan Waddy, Manager, Association Office
Tim Jackson, President
Tim DeJager, Vice-President
Joy Wade, Vice-President
Shelley King, Secretary
Caroline Graham, Treasurer

Publications: Aquaculture Canada Abstracts, Aquaculture Canada Proceedings of Contributed Papers, Bulletin of the Aquaculture Association of Canada, The Watermark [a publication of the Aquaculture Association of Canada]

Asian Heritage Society of Manitoba
MB
Tel: 204-488-8059
artmiki@mts.net
www.asianheritagemanitoba.ca

Muni Mysore, Past President
Rod Cantiveros, President
Kiran Mysore, Vice-President
Harry Lee, Treasurer

Association of Filipino Canadian Accountants (AFCA)
679 Amaretto Ave., Pickering ON L1X 1M6
Tel: 416-609-8912
afcatoronto@gmail.com
www.afcatoronto.org

Edgardo Gonzales, President
Minerva Garcia, Executive Vice-President
Maria Antonio, Vice-President, External Affairs
Divinia Tupe, Vice-President, Internal Affairs
Gloria Dy, Secretary
Antonio Garcia, Treasurer
Jun Perez, Officer, Public Relations

Publications: Association of Filipino Canadian Accountants Members' Directory, Spreadsheet [a publication of the Association of Filipino Canadian Accountants]

Association of Korean Canadian Scientists & Engineers (AKCSE)
#206, 1133 Leslie St., Toronto ON M3C 2J6
Tel: 416-449-5204; Fax: 416-449-2875
info@akcse.org
www.akcse.org

Affiliation(s): Korean Federation of Science & Technology Societies (KOFST)
Bumsoo Kim, President
Oon-Doo Baik, Vice-President
Chi-Guhn Lee, Vice-President
Eugene Suk, Secretary
Wonok Park, Treasurer

Publications: AKCSE Newsletter

Bosnian Islamic Association (BIAGH)
122 North Queen St., Toronto ON M8Z 2E4
Tel: 416-233-5967; Fax: 416-237-0656
info@boscan.org
www.boscan.org

British Columbia Muslim Association (BCMA)
12300 Blundell Rd., Richmond BC V6W 1B3
Tel: 604-270-2522; Fax: 604-244-9750
bcma@shawcable.com
www.thebcma.com

Musa Ismail, President
Imtiaz Asin, Vice-President, Youth Services
Mohammed Asin Bakridi, Vice-President, Burial
Faisal Abdul Aziz, Vice-President, Education Services
VACANCY, Vice-President, Social Services
Azhar Syed, Vice-President, Religious Services
Abdul Rahiman, Vice-President, Planning & Development
David Ali, Vice-President, Public Relations & Communication
VACANCY, Vice-President, Sports & Recreation
Mohammed Ayub Khairati, General Secretary
Fareed Raza, General Treasurer

Publications: BCMA Gazette

British Columbia Muslim Association
12300 Blundell Rd., Richmond BC V6W 1B3
Tel: 604-244-9750
richmond@thebcma.com
Richmond.thebcma.com

British Columbia Muslim Association
5060 Canada Way, Burnaby BC V5E 3N2
Tel: 604-524-4499; Fax: 604-244-9750
burnaby@thebcma.com
www.bcmaburnaby.org

British Columbia Muslim Association
12407 - 72nd Ave., Surrey BC V3W 2M5
Tel: 604-596-7834; Fax: 604-244-9750
surreydelta@thebcma.com
www.thebcma.com

British Columbia Muslim Association
13585 - 62nd Ave., Surrey BC V6X 2J3
Tel: 604-597-7863
surreyeast@thebcma.com
www.thebcma.com

British Columbia Muslim Association
1120 Hwy. 33N, Kelowna BC V1X 1Z2
Tel: 250-979-1370
kelowna@thebcma.com
www.thebcma.com

British Columbia Muslim Association
4162 Welwyn St., Vancouver BC V5N 3Z2
Tel: 604-873-1787; Fax: 604-873-1787
vancouver@thebcma.com
www.thebcma.com

British Columbia Muslim Association
PO Box 8618, 2218 Quadra St., Victoria BC V8W 3S2
Tel: 250-995-1422; Fax: 250-995-1433
victoria@thebcma.com; bcmavictoria@gmail.com
www.bcmavictoria.com

British Columbia Muslim Association
#2, 2580 Cedar Park Pl., Abbotsford BC V2T 3S5
Tel: 604-302-0105
abbotsford@thebcma.com
abbotsford.thebcma.com

British Columbia Muslim Association
Islamic Centre of Nanaimo, 905 Hecate St., Nanaimo BC V9R 4K7
Tel: 250-754-3471
Nanaimo@thebcma.com
www.thebcma.com

British Columbia Muslim Association
Islamic Center, PO Box 21123, Stn. Spruceland RPO, Prince George BC V2M 7E8
Tel: 244-277-1791; Fax: 604-244-9750
princegeorge@thebcma.com; bcma.pgchapter@gmail.com
www.bcmapg.com

British Columbia Muslim Association
BC
Tel: 604-925-9991
northshore@thebcma.com
www.thebcma.com

British Columbia Society for Advancement of Korean Studies (BCSAKS)
1773 Knox Rd., Vancouver BC V6T 1S4
Tel: 604-224-1003; Fax: 604-224-1003
sslee@telus.net
www.bcsaks.com

Seong-Soo Lee, Chair
Leslie Fields, Senior Development Officer, Faculty of Education, University of British Columbia

Canada Korea Business Association (CKBA)
6038 Walker Ave., Burnaby BC V5E 3B4
Tel: 778-883-9325; Fax: 604-529-9197
melodie012@hotmail.com
www.ckba.org

Robert Fairweather, President
Jay C.H. Shin, Vice-President
John Kim, Secretary
Don Cowan, Treasurer

Canadian Caregivers Association (CCA)
#200, 440 Laurier Ave. West, Ottawa ON K1R 7X6
Tel: 613-686-6218
info@cca-acaf.ca
www.cca-acaf.ca

Canadian Chihuahua Rescue & Transport (CCRT)
PO Box 83023, 1830 Bank St., Ottawa ON K1V 1A3
Toll-Free: 877-783-7333
info@ccrt.net (General inquiries); media@ccrt (Public relations)
www.ccrt.net

Canadian Labour International Film Festival (CLiFF)
#314, 50 Cornwall St., Toronto ON M5A 4K5
info@labourfilms.ca; locations@labourfilms.ca
labourfilms.ca

Frank Saptel, Festival Founder & Director
Michele Jayakumar, Contact, CLiFF Communications & Fundraising

Canadian Meter Study Group
#903, 24 Marilyn Dr., Guelph ON N1H 8E9
rwirwin@sympatico.ca
www.postalhistorycanada.org/sg01.htm

Affiliation(s): Postal History Society of Canada
Ross W. Irwin, Contact

Publications: Canada Meter Study Group Newsletter

Cancer Advocacy Coalition of Canada (CACC)
#204, 60 St. Clair Ave. East, Toronto ON M4T 1N5
Tel: 416-538-4874; Fax: 416-538-7319
Toll-Free: 877-472-3436
info@canceradvocacy.ca
www.canceradvocacy.ca

James Gowing, Co-Chair
Darwin Kealey, Co-Chair
Kong Khoo, Vice-Chair
Pierre Major, Vice-Chair

Publications: Report Card on Cancer in Canada

Cancer Patient Education Network Canada (CPEN - Canada)
c/o Gale Turnbull, London Regional Cancer Centre, PO Box 5165, 790 Commissioners Rd. East, London ON N6A 4L6
gale.turnbull@lhsc.on.ca
www.cpencanada.org

Gale Turnbull, Co-Chair
Tamara Harth, Co-Chair

Caregivers Nova Scotia
Tower 1, #105, 7001 Mumford Rd., Halifax NS B3L 4N9
Tel: 902-421-7390; Fax: 902-421-7338
Toll-Free: 877-488-7390
info@caregiversns.org
www.caregiversns.org

Affiliation(s): Canadian Caregiver Coalition
Charlotte Cochran, Board Chair
Sharon Reashore, Executive Director
Brenda L. Sangster, Manager, Projects
Jodi Brown, Coordinator, Capital District Caregiver Support
JoAnne Connors, Coordinator, Cape Breton Support
Carrie Schell, Coordinator, South Shore Support

Publications: Caregivers Nova Scotia News

Chamber of Mineral Resources of Nova Scotia (CMRNS)
PO Box 2171, Windsor NS BON 2T0
Tel: 902-798-0187; Fax: 902-798-2141
terry.daniels@ns.sympatico.ca

Affiliation(s): Mining Association of Canada
Terry Daniels, Managing Director

Chamber of Mines of Eastern British Columbia
215 Hall St., Nelson BC V1L 5X4
Tel: 250-352-5242; Fax: 250-352-7227
chamberofminesebc@netidea.com
www.cmebc.com

Jack Denny, President
Dennis Llewellyn, Chamber Manager

East Kootenay Chamber of Mines
#201, 12 - 11th Avenue South, Cranbrook BC V1C 2P1
Tel: 250-489-2255; Fax: 250-426-8755
www.ekcm.org/chamber2

Ross Stanfield, President

Family Caregiver Centre
1509 Centre St. South, Calgary AB T2G 2E6
Tel: 403-303-6027; Fax: 403-263-9063
family.caregivercentre@calgaryhealthregion.ca
www.calgaryhealthregion.ca/programs/famcaregiver

Beth Gorchynski, Manager
Charlene Retzlaff, Resource Liaison

Publications: Journeys

Family Caregivers' Network Society (FCNS)
526 Michigan St., Victoria BC V8V 1S2
Tel: 250-384-0408; Fax: 250-361-2660
fcns@telus.net
www.fcns-caregiving.org

Barb MacLean, Executive Director
Rick Hoogendoorn, President
Carolyn Thoms, Vice-President
Irene Laing, Secretary
Yolande DeMont, Treasurer

Publications: Facilitator's Manual: Educational Activities to Support Family Caregivers, Medical Information Package, Network News [a publication of the Family Caregivers' Network Society], Resource Guide for Family Caregivers, Resource Guide for Family Caregivers

Filipino Canadian Association of London & District (FCALD)
Tel: 519-659-3652
echavia@hotmail.com
www.filipinocanadian-london.org

Billy Echavia, President
Flor Alambra, 1st Vice-President
Josie Razon, 2nd Vice-President & Coordinator, Membership
Leila Macbean, Secretary
Malene Bunag, Treasurer

Publications: Filipino Canadian Association of London & District Newsletter

Filipino Canadian Association of Vaughan (FCAV)
Vaughan ON
Tel: 905-881-4600
fcav@rogers.com
www.fcav.ca

Johnson Aben, Chair
Erlinda Insigne, President
Gloria Pasildo, Vice-President
Lily Miranda, Secretary
Mina Benesa, Treasurer
Jovel Sarmiento, Coordinator

Filipino Canadian Medical Association (FCMA)
c/o Dr. Gemma Pastolero, Laboratory, Etobicoke General Hospital, 101 Humber College Blvd., Toronto ON M9V 1R8
www.fcma.ca

Gemma C. Pastolero, President
Cesar Garcia, Vice-President
Ben Pangilinan, Secretary & CME Coordinator
Rey Robes, Treasurer

Filipino Canadian Technical Professionals Association of Manitoba, Inc. (FCTPAM)
c/o CCI Cadpower Canada Inc., #7, 1692 Dublin Ave., Winnipeg MB R3H 1AB
Tel: 204-988-9100; Fax: 204-786-3033
directors@fctpam.net
www.fctpam.net

Alexander Majul, Chair & President
Chris Santos, Vice-President
Jaime Dela Cruz, Secretary, Research & Development
Tony Parani, Treasurer
Anselmo Agustin, Director, Human Resources & Membership
Angelo Bautista, Director, Professional Recognition & Accreditation
Neil Cruz, Director, Secretariat & Communications
Mario Mance, Director, Fundraising, Cultural, Social, & Recreational
Pipo Sarmiento, Director, Skills & Technical Development Program

Filipino Students' Association of Toronto (FSAT)
PO Box 8, 12 Hart House Circle, Toronto ON M5S 3J9
fsat@utoronto.ca
fsat.sa.utoronto.ca

Benjamin Bongolan, Coordinator, Internal & University Affairs
Yasmin Tayag, Coordinator, Internal & University Affairs
Lei-Ley Hull, Coordinator, Educational & Community Affairs
Peter Pastolero, Coordinator, Social Events
Ben San Juan, Coordinator, External Affairs

Forever Young Seniors Society (FYSS)
Vancouver BC
Tel: 604-454-9907
contact@foreveryoungseniorssociety.com
www.foreveryoungseniorssociety.com

Romeo Mercado, President
Dolly Olvido, Vice-President
Angie Jimenez, Secretary
Ruben Dioquino, Treasurer
Rosalina Macuroy, Manager, Business

Publications: Forever Young Journal

Golden Horseshoe Beekeepers' Association
c/o Vince Nevidon, RR#1, Branchton ON N0B 1L0
Tel: 519-740-1416
jimhenderson93@hotmail.com; lessimonffy@mountaincable.net

Vince Nevidon, President
Joe Hadrevi, Contact, Meetings

Helping Other Parents Everywhere (HOPE)
c/o Turning Point Youth Services, 95 Wellesley St. East, Toronto ON M4Y 2X9
Tel: 905-239-3577; Toll-Free: 866-492-1299
hope@helpingotherparentseverywhere.com
www.helpingotherparentseverywhere.com

Korean Association of New Brunswick
162 Prince William St., Saint John NB E2L 2B6
Tel: 506-693-7263; Fax: 506-693-7263
yongsukca@hanmail.net

Yong Suk Jang, Contact

Korean Canadian Association of Ottawa (KCAO)
645 Somerset St. West, Ottawa ON K1R 5K3
Tel: 613-236-4720; Fax: 613-236-4720
ottawakorean@gmail.com
www.ottawakorean.com

Korean Canadian Association of Waterloo & Wellington
c/o Photo Master Kitchener Plaza, 385 Frederick St., Kitchener ON N2H 2P2
Tel: 519-744-9581
photomaster@rogers.com

Korean Canadian Cultural Association of the Greater Toronto Area (KCCA)
c/o Korean House, 1133 Leslie St., Toronto ON M3C 2J6
Tel: 416-383-0777; Fax: 416-383-1113
kcca1133@gmail.com
www.koreancentre.on.ca

Sang Hoon Lee, Contact

Korean Canadian Society of London
224 William St., London ON N6B 3B9
Tel: 519-433-2799; Fax: 519-433-5784

Sung J. Sohn, President
Joseph Park, Vice-President

Korean Community of Greater Montréal / La communauté coréenne du grand Montréal
3480, boul Décarie, 2e étage, Montréal QC H4A 3J5
Tel: 541-481-6661; Fax: 514-481-0062
montrealhanin@gmail.com
www.montrealkorean.com

Nam Soo Kwon, Contact

Korean Community of Nova Scotia
Duke Tower, #210, 5251 Duke St., Halifax NS B3J 1P3
Tel: 902-832-1764; Fax: 902-832-0950
shchoi@eastlink.ca

Korean Community of Regina
2513 Victoria Ave., Regina SK S4P 0T2
Tel: 306-525-9058; Fax: 306-522-5258
kimtkd@sasktel.net

Korean Senior Citizens Society of Toronto (KSCST)
KSCST Centre, 476 Grace St., Toronto ON M6G 3A9
Tel: 416-532-8077; Fax: 416-532-9964
www.kscst.com

Hak Hwan Koh, President
Yong Hoo Chung, Chief Director
Kil Yeo Whang, Vice-Chief Director
Kum Suk Hwang, General Manager
Sang-Im Kim, Executive Manager
Hyun-Ju Shin, Coordintor, Programs

Publications: Korean Senior Citizens Society of Toronto Newsletter

Korean Society of British Columbia for Fraternity & Culture
1320 East Hastings St., Vancouver BC V5L 1S3
Tel: 604-255-3739; Fax: 604-255-3443
koreanbc@yahoo.co.kr

J.J. Moon, President

Korean Society of Manitoba for Fraternity & Culture Inc.
#800, 150 River Ave., Winnipeg MB R3L 0A9
Tel: 204-668-7326
jslee60@yahoo.co.kr

Jong Park, Contact

Korean Students' Association of Canada (KSAC)
ksacinfo@gmail.com; ksac.sdu@gmail.com (student development)
www.ksacanada.com

JungKyu Lee, President
Patrick Lee, Vice-President
Jisoo Shin, Vice-President

Publications: Sponge & Open

Multilingual Association of Regina, Inc. (MLAR)
2144 Cornwall St., Regina SK S4P 2K7
Tel: 306-757-3171; Fax: 306-757-3172
mlar@accesscomm.ca
www.mlar.ca

Indu Jaiswal, President
Emile Carignan, Coordinator, Office

Publications: The Multilingual Association of Regina Newsletter

Newfoundland Korean Society
10 Halley Dr., St. John's NL A1A 4T2
Tel: 709-754-8666

Chung Won Cho, Contact

Niagara Korean Association
215 Garrison Rd., Fort Erie ON L2A 1M6
Tel: 905-871-2171; Fax: 905-991-8484
joe@havenmotel.ca

Chang Jo Kim, Contact

North American Association of Asian Professionals Vancouver (NAAAP)
PO Box 18518, 710 Granville St., Vancouver BC V6Z 0B3
naaap@naaap.bc.ca; communications@naaap.bc.ca;
events@naaap.bc.ca
www.naaap.bc.ca

Rudy Chung, President
Walt Woo, Vice-President
Vania Chan, Secretary
Holman Lai, Treasurer
Sharon Mah, Director, Communications

Publications: NAAAP Insight

Northern Alberta Brain Injury Society (NABIS)
Royal Alex Place, #229, 10106 - 111th Ave., Edmonton AB T5G 0B4
Tel: 780-479-1757; Fax: 780-474-4415
Toll-Free: 800-425-5552
nabis@abihelp.org
www.nabis.ab.ca

Barb Brooks, Executive Director
Barbara Baer Pillay, Manager, Volunteer & Fund Development
Louise Jensen, Manager, Operations
Mike Ryan, Manager, Programs & Coordinator, Services
Carolyn Biron, Coordinator, Information
Publications: NABIS News

Northern Alberta Brain Injury Society
PO Box 20027, 524 - 50th St., Edson AB T7E 1W4
Tel: 780-712-7560; Fax: 780-712-7567
Toll-Free: 866-712-7560
www.nabis.ab.ca

NWT & Nunavut Chamber of Mines
PO Box 2818, #103, 5102-50 Ave., Yellowknife NT X1A 2R1
Tel: 867-873-5281; Fax: 867-920-2145
info@miningnorth.com
www.miningnorth.com

Affiliation(s): Mining Association of Canada; Canadian Institute of Mining, Metallurgy & Petroleum
Tom Hoefer, Executive Director

Peretz Centre for Secular Jewish Culture
6184 Ash St., Vancouver BC V5Z 3G9
Tel: 604-325-1812; Fax: 604-325-2470
info@peretz-centre.org; peretz-centre@telus.net
www.peretz-centre.org

Affiliation(s): International Federation of Secular Humanistic Jews; Congress of Secular Jewish Organizations; Jewish Federation of Greater Vancouver
Richard Rosenberg, President
Donna Becker, Coordinator, Programs

Publications: Peretz Papers

Philippine Association of Manitoba, Inc. (PAM)
88 Juno St., Winnipeg MB R3A 1J1
Tel: 204-772-7210

St. Albert Parents' Place Association
#10A, 215 Carnegie Dr., St. Albert AB T8N 5B1
Tel: 780-459-7377; Fax: 780-459-7399
sapp@stalbertparentsplace.com
www.stalbertparentsplace.com

Publications: Parenting Resource Guide

St. Albert Stop Abuse Families Society (SAIF)
#402, 22 Sir Winston Churchill Ave., St. Albert AB T8N 1B4
Tel: 780-460-2195; Fax: 780-460-2190
info@stopabuse.ca
www.stopabuse.ca

Pam Smyth, President
Kathi Brown, Vice-President
Susan Wickett, Secretary
Don Belke, Treasurer

Publications: SAIF Notes

St. Albert Youth Community Centre
Grandin Park Plaza, #129, 22 Sir Winston Churchill Ave., St. Albert AB T8N 1B4
Tel: 780-418-0678; Fax: 780-418-1802
officeadmin@saycc.ca
www.saycc.ca

Chris Richards, Chair
Brenda O'Neill, Executive Director
Jerry Stack, Coordinator, Activity Centre
Shelley Tetrault, Coordinator, ISM & Volunteers
Linda Mason, Treasurer

Publications: The St. Albert Youth Community Centre Annual Report

Saskatoon Korean Association (SKA)
627 Wilkinson Pl., Saskatoon SK S7N 3M3
Tel: 306-966-5320; Fax: 306-966-5334
oon-doo.baik@usask.ca

Jong Soo Lee

Sholem Aleichem Community Inc. (SAC)
PO Box C105, 123 Doncaster St., Winnipeg MB R3N 2B2
Tel: 204-253-6858
hshorr@mts.net
www.mts.net/~shorr

Affiliation(s): The Congress of Secular Jewish Organizations
Henry Shorr, Contact

Publications: Sholem Aleichem Community Newsletter

Sojourn House
101 Ontario St., Toronto ON M5A 2V2
Tel: 416-864-0515
info@sojournhouse.org
www.sojournhouse.org

Rita Kohli, Program Director
Janet Sarpong, Settlement Counsellor

Publications: Sojourn House Newsletter

South East Asian Students' Association (SEASA)
#SUB 040T, Basement, University of Alberta, Edmonton AB T6G 2R3
seasa@ualberta.ca
www.ualberta.ca/~seasa

Publications: South East Asian Students' Association Newsletter

Southern Alberta Brain Injury Society (SABIS)
#137, 2723 - 37th Ave. NE, Calgary AB T1Y 5R8
Tel: 403-521-5212; Fax: 403-283-5867
Toll-Free: 866-527-2247
sabis@sabis.ab.ca
www.sabis.ab.ca

Lisa Somers, Contact, Programs & Services

Publications: Southern Alberta Brain Injury Society Newsletter, Southern Alberta Brain Injury Society Annual Report

SPEC Association for Children & Families
c/o Community Culture Center, #101, 327 - 3rd St. West, Brooks AB T1R 1B2
Tel: 403-362-5056; Fax: 403-362-5090
generalmail@spec.ab.ca
www.spec.ab.ca

Maureen Andruschak, Associate Executive Director
Debbie Piper, Coordinator

University of the Philippines Alumni Association of Toronto (UPAA Toronto)
382 Bathurst St., Toronto ON M5T 2S6
www.upaatoronto.org

Joe Zagala, President
Fred Gamboa, Vice-President
Maria Theresa Lumanlan, Secretary
Gena Baldivia, Treasurer
Rose Tijam, Officer, Public Affairs & Communications

Publications: University of the Philippines Alumni Association of Toronto Members' Diretory

Victoria Korean Community Association
PO Box 46045, Victoria BC V8T 5G7
Tel: 250-477-7811; Fax: 250-477-7825
claireyoo@shaw.ca
www.victoriahanin.com

Claire Yoo, Contact

Victoria Society for Humanistic Judaism (VSHJ)
3636 Shelbourne St., Victoria BC V8P 4H2
Tel: 250-474-7173
skobrinsky@shaw.ca

Affiliation(s): Congress of Secular Jewish Organizations; Leadership Conference of Secular & Humanistic Jews; Canadian Jewish Congress
Sharon Kobrinsky, Ceremonial Leader

Yukon Chamber of Mines (YCM)
3151B - 3rd Ave., Whitehorse YT Y1A 1G1
Tel: 867-667-2090; Fax: 867-668-7127
info@yukonminers.ca
www.yukonminers.ca

Affiliation(s): Mining Association of Canada
Mark Ayranto, President
Hugh Kitchen, Vice President

Provincial & Territorial Boards of Trade & Chambers of Commerce

Alberta Chambers of Commerce (ACC)
#1808, 10025 - 102A Ave., Edmonton AB T5J 2Z2
Tel: 780-425-4180; Fax: 780-429-1061
Toll-Free: 800-272-8854
info@abchamber.ca
www.abchamber.ca

Affiliation(s): Canadian Chamber of Commerce
Ken Kobly, President & CEO
Tim Bolton, Chair

British Columbia Chamber of Commerce
#1201, 750 West Pender St., Vancouver BC V6C 2T8
Tel: 604-683-0700; Fax: 604-683-0416
bccc@bcchamber.org
www.bcchamber.org
Social Media: www.youtube.com/user/bcchamberofcom; flickr.com/photos/43089524@N08

John Winter, President & CEO

Chambre de Commerce française au Canada
CP 4, #2006, 20 Queen St. West, Toronto ON M5H 3R3
Tél: 416-205-9820; Téléc: 416-205-9680
ccfe@bellnet.ca
www.ccife.org/canada/Toronto

Chambre de Commerce française au Canada
#101, 300, rue Métivier, Québec QC G1M 3Y9
Tél: 418-522-3434; Téléc: 418-522-0045
info@ccfcquebec.ca
www.ccfcquebec.ca

Christian Stephan, Président
Christèle Artur, Directrice administrative

Creston Chamber of Commerce
PO Box 268, 1607 Canyon St., Creston BC V0B 1G0
Tel: 250-428-4342; Fax: 250-428-9411
Toll-Free: 866-528-4342
crestonchamber@kootenay.com
www.crestonbc.com/chamber

Murray Oswald, President

Fédération des chambres de commerce du Québec
555, boul. René-Lévesque ouest, 19e étage, Montréal QC H2Z 1B1
Tél: 514-844-9571; Téléc: 514-844-0226
Ligne sans frais: 800-361-5019
info@fccq.ca
www.fccq.ca

Françoise Bertand, Présidente-directrice générale

The Manitoba Chambers of Commerce
227 Portage Ave., Winnipeg MB R3B 2A6
Tel: 204-948-0100; Fax: 204-948-0110
Toll-Free: 877-444-5222
mbchamber@mbchamber.mb.ca
www.mbchamber.mb.ca

Graham Starmer, President

New Brunswick Chamber of Commerce (NBCC)
1 ch Canada, Edmunston NB E3V 1T6
Tel: 506-737-1868; Fax: 506-737-1862
info@nbchamber.ca
www.nbchamber.ca

Judith Murray, Chair

Newfoundland & Labrador Chamber of Commerce
PO Box 352, 109 Trans Canada Hwy., Gander NL A1V 1W7
Tel: 709-651-6522; Fax: 709-256-5808
nlcc@nf.aibn.com
www.nlchamber.ca

Maureen O'Reilly, Executive Director

Northwest Territories Chamber of Commerce
NWT Commerce Place, #13, 4802 - 50th Ave., Yellowknife NT X1A 1C4
Tel: 867-920-9505; Fax: 867-873-4174
admin@nwtchamber.com
www.nwtchamber.com

Chuck Parker, President
Kathy Gray, First Vice-President
Hughie Graham, Second Vice-President
John-Eric Petersson, Secretary-Treasurer

Nova Scotia Chambers of Commerce
605 Prince Street, Truro NS B2N 5B6
Tel: 902-895-6329; Fax: 902-897-6641
info@nschamber.ca
www.nschamber.ca

Dan Fougere, President

Ontario Chamber of Commerce (OCC)
#505, 180 Dundas St. West, Toronto ON M5G 1Z8
Tel: 416-482-5222; Fax: 416-482-5879
info@occ.on.ca
www.occ.on.ca
Social Media: www.youtube.com/user/OntarioChamber; flickr.com/photos/ontariochamber

Allan O'Dette, President & CEO
Scott McCammon, Vice-President & General Manager

Ontario Gay & Lesbian Chamber of Commerce
39 River St., Toronto ON M5A 3P1
Tel: 416-646-1600; Fax: 416-646-9460
info@oglcc.com
www.oglcc.com

Ryan Tollofson, President

Prince Edward Island Chamber of Commerce
c/o Drake Truck Bodies, Riverview Crescent, RR#1, Vernon Bridge PE C0A 2E0
Tel: 902-651-2782; Fax: 902-652-2786

Allison Drake, President

Saskatchewan Chamber of Commerce
The Saskatchewan Chamber of Commerce, #1630, 1920 Broad St., Regina SK S4P 3V2
Tel: 306-352-2671; Fax: 306-781-7084
info@saskchamber.com
www.saskchamber.com

Steve McLellan, CEO

Swiss Canadian Chamber of Commerce (Ontario) Inc. (SCCC)
756 Royal York Rd., Toronto ON M8Y 2T6
Tel: 416-236-0039; Fax: 416-236-3634
sccc@swissbiz.ca
www.swissbiz.ca

Phillip Gysling, President
Patricia Keller Schläpfer, Executive Assistant

Yukon Chamber of Commerce (YCC)
#101, 307 Jarvis St., Whitehorse YT Y1A 2H3
Tel: 867-667-2000; Fax: 867-667-2001
Toll-Free: 800-661-0543
ycc@syukonchamber.com
www.yukonchamber.com

Sandy Babcock, President & CEO

Alberta

Airdrie Chamber of Commerce
PO Box 3661, Airdrie AB T4B 2B8
Tel: 403-948-4412; Fax: 403-948-3141
info@airdriechamber.ab.ca
www.airdriechamber.ab.ca

Mike Brandrick, President
Lynda Barker, Treasurer

Alberta Beach & District Chamber of Commerce
PO Box 280, Alberta Beach AB T0E 0A0
Tel: 780-924-3889; Fax: 780-924-3425
gwte@telusplanet.net

Phyllis Stark, President

Alix Chamber of Commerce
PO Box 145, Alix AB T0C 0B0
Tel: 403-747-2405; Fax: 403-747-2403
cpete@oanet.com
www.villageofalix.ca

Clarence Verveda, President

Athabasca & District Chamber of Commerce (ADCofC)
PO Box 3074, Athabasca AB T9S 2B9
Tel: 780-213-4600

Affiliation(s): Canadian Chambers of Commerce
Joanne Peckham, President
Michael Neville, Secretary

Barrhead Chamber of Commerce
PO Box 4524, Barrhead AB T7N 1A4
Tel: 403-674-2338; Fax: 403-674-5648
info@barrheadchamber.ca
www.barrheadchamber.ca

Darren Strawson, President

Bashaw Chamber of Commerce
PO Box 645, Bashaw AB T0B 0H0
bashawcc@gmail.com
www.townofbashaw.com/chamber

Peter Graham, President

Bassano & District Chamber of Commerce
PO Box 849, General Delivery, Bassano AB T0J 0B0
Tel: 403-641-3014

Tammie Rothnie, Secretary

Beaverlodge Chamber of Commerce
PO Box 303, Beaverlodge AB T0H 0C0
Tel: 780-354-8785; Fax: 780-354-2107
olsom@telusplanet.net

Keith Tourand, President
Judy Olson, Treasurer

Beiseker & District Chamber of Commerce
PO Box 277, Beiseker AB T0M 0G0
Tel: 403-947-2356; Fax: 403-947-3227

Al Henuset, Contact

Blackfalds Chamber of Commerce
PO Box 249, Blackfalds AB T0M 0J0
Tel: 403-885-2386; Fax: 403-885-2386

Curtis Pedde, President

Bluffton Chamber of Commerce
PO Box 38, RR#2, Bluffton AB T0C 0M0
Tel: 403-843-6514; Fax: 403-843-3506
lawman@telusplanet.net

Lawrence Wright, President

Bonnyville & District Chamber of Commerce
PO Box 6054, Hwy. 28 West, Bonnyville AB T9N 2G7
Tel: 780-826-3252; Fax: 780-826-4525
manager@bonnyvillechamber.ab.ca
www.bonnyvillechamber.com

Lorne Ringuette, President
Al Arbour, Vice President

Bow Island / Burdett District Chamber of Commerce
PO Box 1001, 502 Centre St., Bow Island AB T0K 0G0
Tel: 403-545-5134; Fax: 403-542-2449
info@bowislandchamber.com
www.bowislandchamber.com/

Nan Maclean, President

Ron Thomson, Vice-President

Boyle & District Chamber of Commerce
PO Box 496, Boyle AB T0A 0M0
Tel: 780-689-4646; Fax: 780-689-2250
Monica Hill, President

Bragg Creek Chamber of Commerce
PO Box 216, Bragg Creek AB T0L 0K0
Tel: 403-949-0004; Fax: 403-949-2748
office@braggcreekchamber.ca
www.braggcreekchamber.ca
Chris Tucker, President
Shannon Duncan, Secretary

Breton & District Chamber of Commerce
PO Box 364, Breton AB T0C 0P0
Tel: 780-696-2557; Fax: 780-696-2572
Glory Tornack, President

Brooks & District Chamber of Commerce
PO Box 400, #6, 403 - 2 Ave. West, Brooks AB T1R 1B4
Tel: 403-362-7641; Fax: 403-362-6893
manager@brookschamber.ab.ca
www.brookschamber.ab.ca
George Newton, President
Gillenne Bégin, Manager

Calgary Chamber of Commerce
100 - 6 Ave. SW, Calgary AB T2P 0P5
Tel: 403-750-0400; Fax: 403-266-3413
chinfo@calgarychamber.com
www.calgarychamber.com
David Sprague, President & CEO
Elizabeth Leitch, Manager, Communications

Camrose Chamber of Commerce
5402 - 48 Ave., Camrose AB T4V 0J7
Tel: 780-672-4217; Fax: 780-672-1059
camcham@telusplanet.net
www.camrosechamber.ca
Sharon Anderson, Executive Director
Diane Hutchinson, President

Cardston & District Chamber of Commerce
PO Box 1212, 490 Main St., Cardston AB T0K 0K0
Tel: 403-795-1032
Info@CardstonChamber.com
www.cardstonchamber.com/
Zenith Gaynor, President
Marian Carlson, Economic Development Officer

Caroline & District Chamber of Commerce
PO Box 90, Caroline AB T0M 0M0
Tel: 403-722-4066; Fax: 403-722-4002
ccoc@telus.net
www.carolinechamber.ca
Reg Dean, President
Deana Knight, Manager

Carstairs Chamber of Commerce
PO Box 370, Carstairs AB T0M 0N0
Tel: 403-337-3341
www.town.carstairs.ab.ca/chamber.html
Dennis Schmick, President
Karen Kneeland, Vice-President

Claresholm & District Chamber of Commerce
PO Box 1092, Claresholm AB T0L 0T0
Tel: 403-625-4229
info@claresholchamber.com
www.claresholmchamber.com
Russell Sawatsky, President

Coaldale & District Chamber of Commerce
PO Box 1117, 1401 - 20 Ave., Coaldale AB T1M 1M9
Tel: 403-345-2358; Fax: 403-345-2339
info@coaldalechamber.com
www.coaldalechamber.com
Elizabeth McLachlan, Executive Director
Leonard Fast, President

Cochrane & District Chamber of Commerce
#5, 205 - 1st St. East, Cochrane AB T4C 1X6
Tel: 403-932-6810; Fax: 403-932-6824
www.cochranechamber.ca
Adamo Cocuzzoli, President
Dawn Martin, Coordinator

Cold Lake Regional Chamber of Commerce
PO Box 454, Cold Lake AB T9M 1P1
Tel: 780-594-4747; Fax: 780-594-3711
www.coldlakechamber.ca
Rob Brassard, President
Sherri Bohme, Executive Director

Consort Chamber of Commerce
PO Box 490, 4901 - 50 Ave., Consort AB T0C 1B0
Tel: 403-577-3623; Fax: 403-577-2024
webmaster@village.consort.ab.ca
www.village.consort.ab.ca/ChamberofCommerce.htm
Peter G. Ringrose, Executive Director

Coronation Chamber of Commerce
PO Box 960, Coronation AB T0C 1C0
Tel: 403-578-4220; Fax: 403-578-3020
Jackie Morettin, President

Cremona Water Valley & District Chamber of Commerce
PO Box 356, 106 Railway Ave. West, Cremona AB T0M 0R0
Tel: 403-335-8398; Fax: 403-637-7022
vhoogenboom@aol.com
www.cremonawatervalley.com
Gabriel Grenier, President

La Crete & Area Chamber of Commerce
PO Box 1088, La Crete AB T0H 2H0
Tel: 780-928-2278; Fax: 780-928-2234
office@lacretechamber.com
www.lacretechamber.com
Larry Buhler, President
Barbara Peters, Office Manager

Crossfield Chamber of Commerce
PO Box 1490, Crossfield AB T0M 0S0
crossfieldchamber@shaw.ca
www.crossfieldchamber.com

Crowsnest Pass Chamber of Commerce
PO Box 706, Blairmore AB T0K 0E0
Tel: 403-562-7108; Fax: 403-562-7493
Toll-Free: 888-562-7108
www.crowsnest-pass.com
Affiliation(s): Alberta Chamber of Commerce
Lowry Toombs, President
Jenine Trotz, Secretary - Treasurer

Delburne & District Chamber of Commerce
PO Box 254, Delburne AB T0M 0V0
Tel: 403-749-2808; Fax: 403-749-2800
delburne@telusplanet.net
www.delburne.ca
Brenda Smith, President

Devon & District Chamber of Commerce
35 Athabasca Ave., Devon AB T9G 1G5
Tel: 780-987-5177; Fax: 780-987-5135
devoncc@telus.net
Gerry Daniel, Administrator
Wade Kosiorek, Contact

Diamond Valley Chamber of Commerce
PO Box 61, Turner Valley AB T0L 2A0
Tel: 403-652-3700; Fax: 866-855-2065
info@diamondvalleychamber.com
www.diamondvalleychamber.com
R. Williamson, President

Didsbury Chamber of Commerce
PO Box 981, 1811 - 20 St., Didsbury AB T0M 0W0
Tel: 403-335-3265; Fax: 403-335-3265
info@didsburychamber.ca
www.didsburychamber.ca
Margo Ward, President
Joelle Fournier, Office Manager

Drayton Valley & District Chamber of Commerce (DVDCC)
PO Box 5318, Drayton Valley AB T7A 1R5
Tel: 780-542-7578; Fax: 780-542-9211
chambrdv@telusplanet.net
www.dvchamber.com
Tom Campbell, President

Drumheller & District Chamber of Commerce (DDCC)
PO Box 999, 60 First Ave. West, Drumheller AB T0J 0Y0
Tel: 403-823-8100; Fax: 403-823-4469
info@drumhellerchamber.com
www.drumhellerchamber.com
Cindy Clark, President
Heather Bitz, General Manager

Eckville & District Chamber of Commerce
PO Box 609, Eckville AB T0M 0X0
Tel: 403-746-2353; Fax: 403-746-3470
eckville@telusplanet.net
www.eckvillechamber.com
Mitch Krescy, President

Edgerton & District Chamber of Commerce
PO Box 303, Edgerton AB T0B 1K0
Tel: 780-755-3947
Kim Kimball, President

Edmonton Chamber of Commerce
World Trade Centre, Sun Life Place, #700, 9990 Jasper Ave., Edmonton AB T5J 1P7
Tel: 780-426-4620; Fax: 780-424-7946
info@edmontonchamber.com
www.edmontonchamber.com
Martin Salloum, President/CEO
Kimberly Nishikaze, Contact, Communications

Edson & District Chamber of Commerce
221-55 St, Edson AB T7E 1L5
Tel: 780-723-4918; Fax: 780-723-5545
manger@edsonchamber.com
www.edsonchamber.com
Heather Kelly, Executive Director

Elk Point Chamber of Commerce
PO Box 639, Elk Point AB T0A 1A0
Tel: 780-724-4087; Fax: 780-724-4087
vbooker@stpaul.greatwest.ca
Vicki Booker, Secretary

Evansburg & Entwistle Chamber of Commerce
PO Box 598, Evansburg AB T0E 0T0
Tel: 780-727-4035; Fax: 780-727-4035
info@partnersonthepembina.com
www.partnersonthepembina.com
Maxine Lappe, President

Fairview & District Chamber of Commerce
PO Box 1034, Fairview AB T0H 1L0
Tel: 780-835-5999; Fax: 780-835-5991
executivedirector@fairviewchamber.com
www.fairviewchamber.com
Winita Mitchell, President
Kathryn Currie, Executive Director
Jasmine Adams, Contact

Falher Chamber of Commerce
PO Box 814, Falher AB T0H 1M0
Tel: 780-925-2708; Fax: 780-837-2647
patrysha@incredibleimpressions.com
Affiliation(s): Falher & Area Economic Development & Tourism
Sarah Williams, President
Aline Desaulniers, Treasurer

Foremost & District Chamber of Commerce
PO Box 272, Foremost AB T0K 0X0
Tel: 403-867-3077; Fax: 403-867-3579
cofc4mst@la.shockware.com
www.foremostalberta.com
Lorne Buis, President

Fort Macleod & District Chamber of Commerce
PO Box 178, Fort MacLeod AB T0L 0Z0
Tel: 403-553-3355
EDO@FortMacleod.com
www.fortmacleod.com/business/chamber_commerce.cfm
Emily McTighe, President

Fort McMurray Chamber of Commerce
#304, 9612 Franklin Ave., Fort McMurray AB T9H 2J9
Tel: 780-743-3100; Fax: 780-790-9757
fmcoc@telus.net
www.fortmcmurraychamber.ca
Jack Bonville, President
Diane Slater, Executive Director

Fort Saskatchewan Chamber of Commerce
PO Box 3072, 10030 - 99 Ave., Fort Saskatchewan AB T8L 2T1
Tel: 780-998-4355; Fax: 780-998-1515
chamber@fortsaskchamber.com
www.fortsaskchamber.com
Affiliation(s): Alberta Chamber of Commerce; Canadian Chamber of Commerce
Michelle Gamache, President
Janine Brisebois, Executive Director

Fort Vermilion & Area Board of Trade
PO Box 456, Fort Vermilion AB T0H 1N0
Tel: 780-927-3505
Frank Rosenberger, President

Fox Creek Chamber of Commerce
PO Box 774, Fox Creek AB T0H 1P0
Tel: 780-622-2670; Fax: 780-622-2677
fcchamb@telus.net
Bernie Hornby, President
Barb Souter, Treasurer

Rose Hearn, Secretary

Glendon & District Chamber
PO Box 300, Glendon AB T0A 1P0
Tel: 780-635-2557
Ron Mack, President

Grande Cache Chamber of Commerce
PO Box 1342, Grande Cache AB T0E 0Y0
Tel: 780-827-3790; Fax: 780-827-5698
Affiliation(s): Alberta Chamber of Commerce; Canadian Chamber of Commerce
Jean Bourdua, President

Grande Prairie & District Chamber of Commerce
#217, 11330 - 106 St., Grande Prairie AB T8V 7X9
Tel: 780-532-5340; Fax: 780-532-2926
info@gpchamber.com
www.grandeprairiechamber.com
Dan Pearcy, CEO
Karen Kluyt, Office Manager

Grimshaw Chamber of Commerce
PO Box 919, Grimshaw AB T0H 1W0
Tel: 780-332-4370; Fax: 780-332-4375
blossomb@telus.net
Theresa Bruce, President
Jenny Borys, Secretary

Hanna & District Chamber of Commerce
PO Box 2248, Hanna AB T0J 1P0
Tel: 403-854-4004; Fax: 403-854-4060
hannachamber@telus.net
www.aroundhanna.com/hannachamberofcommerce
Barb Larson, Chamber Manager

Hardisty & District Chamber of Commerce
PO Box 628, Hardisty AB T0B 1V0
Tel: 780-888-3836
ernie.ziegler@midfieldsupply.com
Rob Rondeau, President

High Level & District Chamber of Commerce
10803 - 96 St., High Level AB T0H 1Z0
Tel: 780-926-2470; Fax: 780-926-4017
hlchambr@incentre.net
www.highlevelchamber.com
Sylvia Kennedy, President
Daina French, Administrative contact

High River & District Chamber of Commerce
PO Box 5244, 149B Macleod Trail SW, High River AB T1V 1M4
Tel: 403-652-3336; Fax: 403-652-7660
hrdcc@telus.net
www.highriverchamber.com
Clair Noad, President
Lynette McCracken, Executive Director

Hinton & District Chamber of Commerce
309 Gregg Ave., Hinton AB T7V 2A7
Tel: 780-865-2777; Fax: 780-865-1062
Toll-Free: 877-446-8666
hintoncc@telus.net
www.hintonchamber.com
Janice Calihoo, Vice-President
Risa Croken, Office Manager

Hythe & District Chamber of Commerce
PO Box 404, Hythe AB T0C 2C0
Tel: 780-356-2168; Fax: 780-356-2009
chamber@hythe.ca
www.hythe.ca/chamber.html
Steve Greene, Chair

Innisfail & District Chamber of Commerce
5031 - 40th St., Innisfail AB T4G 1H8
Tel: 403-227-1177; Fax: 403-227-6749
ichamber@telusplanet.net
www.innisfailchamber.ca
Jean Barclay, President
Donna Arnold, Secretary

Irma & District Chamber of Commerce
PO Box 284, Irma AB T0B 2H0
Tel: 780-754-3996
cwilli@telusplanet.net
Claudia Williams, President

Jasper Park Chamber of Commerce
PO Box 98, 632 Connaught Dr., Jasper AB T0B 1E0
Tel: 780-852-3858; Fax: 780-852-4932
Toll-Free: 800-473-8135
info@jaspercanadianrockies.com
www.jaspercanadianrockies.com
George Andrew, President

Krista Rodger, General Manager

Kainai Chamber of Commerce
PO Box 350, Stand Off AB T0L 1Y0
Tel: 403-737-8207
chamber@bloodtribe.org
Tony Manyfingers, President
Donald Cotton, Manager

Killam & District Chamber of Commerce
PO Box 272, Killam AB T0B 2L0
Tel: 780-385-3644
Jerry Gordon, President

Lac La Biche & District Chamber of Commerce
PO Box 804, 10307, 100 St., Lac La Biche AB T0A 2C0
Tel: 780-623-2818; Fax: 780-623-7217
llbcofc@telusplanet.net
www.llbchamber.ca
Affiliation(s): Alberta Chamber of Commerce
Elaine Poulin, Executive Director
Bill Abougoush, President

Lacombe & District Chamber of Commerce
6005 - 50 Ave., Lacombe AB T4L 1K7
Tel: 403-782-4300; Fax: 403-782-4302
info@lacombechamber.ca
www.lacombechamber.ca
Faye Chomoway, Chamber Manager

Leduc Regional Chamber of Commerce
6420 - 50 St., Leduc AB T9E 7K9
Tel: 780-986-5454; Fax: 780-986-8108
info@leduc-chamber.com
www.leduc-chamber.com
Stefanie Schulz, Executive Director
Cindy Carstairs, Contact

Legal & District Chamber of Commerce
PO Box 338, General Delivery, Legal AB T0G 1L0
Tel: 780-456-3424
www.legalchamberofcommerce.com
Affiliation(s): Greater Edmonton Regional Chambers of Commerce
Frank Klassen, President
Carol Tremblay, Secretary

Lethbridge Chamber of Commerce
#200, 529 - 6 St. South, Lethbridge AB T1J 2E1
Tel: 403-327-1586; Fax: 403-327-1001
office@lethbridgechamber.com
www.lethbridgechamber.com
Jody Nilsson, General Manager
Paul G. Pharo, President

Lloydminster Chamber of Commerce
4419 - 52 Ave., Lloydminster AB T9V 0Y8
Tel: 780-875-9013; Fax: 780-875-0755
www.lloydminsterchamber.com
Pat L. Tenney, Executive Director
Peggy Bosch, President

Mallaig Chamber of Commerce
PO Box 144, Mallaig AB T0A 2K0
Tel: 780-635-3849
Tammy Bodnar, President

Mannville & District Chamber of Commerce
PO Box 54, Mannville AB T0B 2W0
Tel: 780-763-3795
Shirley J. Wosnik, President

Marwayne & District Chamber of Commerce
PO Box 183, Marwayne AB T0B 2X0
Tel: 780-847-3962; Fax: 780-847-3324
vilmar@telusplanet.net
www.village.marwayne.ab.ca
Sharon Kneen, President

Mayerthorpe & District Chamber of Commerce
PO Box 1279, Mayerthorpe AB T0E 1N0
Tel: 780-786-2444
Arnold Lotholz, Treasurer
Cynthia Eichhorn, President

McLennan Chamber of Commerce
PO Box 90, McLennan AB T0H 2L0
Tel: 780-324-3894; Fax: 780-324-3932
Bruce Brulotte, President
Sandra Thrall, Secretary

Medicine Hat & District Chamber of Commerce
413 - 6th Ave. SE, Medicine Hat AB T1A 2S7
Tel: 403-527-5214; Fax: 403-527-5182
info@medicinehatchamber.com
www.medicinehatchamber.com

Affiliation(s): Alberta Chamber of Commerce; Canadian Chamber of Commerce
Milvia Bauman, Chair
Jason Melhoff, Chair

Millet & District Chamber of Commerce
PO Box 389, Millet AB T0C 1Z0
Tel: 780-387-4534
milletchamber@canada.com
Debbie Swanson, President

Morinville & District Chamber of Commerce
PO Box 3130, Morinville AB T8R 1S1
Tel: 780-939-9462; Fax: 780-939-3087
chamber@town.morinville.ab.ca
www.morinvillechamber.com
Sheldon Fingler, President

Nanton & District Chamber of Commerce
PO Box 711, Nanton AB T0L 1R0
Tel: 403-646-2029
president@nantonchamber.com
www.nantonchamber.com
Jason Calvert, Acting President

Okotoks & District Chamber of Commerce
PO Box 1053, 14 McRae St., Okotoks AB T1S 1B1
Tel: 403-938-2848; Fax: 403-938-6649
okotokschamber@telus.net
www.okotokschamber.ca
Cathy Huth, President
Tanya McAvena, Executive Director

Olds & District Chamber of Commerce
PO Box 4210, Olds AB T4H 1P8
Tel: 403-556-7070; Fax: 403-556-1515
oldscham@telusplanet.net
www.oldsalberta.com
Debbie Packer, President
Barb Babiak, Executive Director
Paul Hildebrand, Vice-President

Onoway & District Chamber of Commerce
PO Box 723, Onoway AB T0E 1V0
Tel: 780-967-4754
tbulletin@icrossroads.com
Lyle Robinson, President

Oyen & District Chamber of Commerce
PO Box 718, Oyen AB T0J 2J0
Tel: 403-664-0406
oyenecho@telusplanet.net
Francis MacQuarrie, President

Picture Butte & District Chamber of Commerce
PO Box 540, Picture Butte AB T0K 1V0
Tel: 403-732-4302; Fax: 403-732-4703
chamber@picturebutte.ca
Wes Brouwer, President
Corrine McInnis, Office Manager

Pigeon Lake Regional Chamber of Commerce (PLRCC)
#6B Village Dr., Westerose AB T0C 2V0
Tel: 780-586-6263; Fax: 780-586-3667
plchambe@telusplanet.net
www.pigeonlakechamber.ca
Affiliation(s): Alberta Chambers of Commerce
Darlene Kobeluck, Manager
Sharon Will, President

Pincher Creek & District Chamber of Economic Development
PO Box 2287, Pincher Creek AB T0K 1W0
Tel: 403-627-5199; Fax: 403-627-5850
info@pincher-creek.com
www.pincher-creek.com
Brian Wright, President

Ponoka & District Chamber of Commerce
PO Box 4188, Ponoka AB T4J 1R6
Tel: 403-783-3888; Fax: 403-783-3888
chamber@ponoka.org
Irven Snider, Executive Manager
Judith Knutson, President

Provost & District Chamber of Commerce
PO Box 637, Provost AB T0B 3S0
Tel: 780-753-6643
chamberofcommerce@provost.ca
Anne Fraser, Contact

Rainbow Lake Chamber of Commerce
PO Box 272, Rainbow Lake AB T0H 2Y0
Tel: 780-956-3030; Fax: 780-956-3882
tschulter@rainbowcable.ca
John Watt, Mayor

Raymond Chamber of Commerce
General Delivery, Raymond AB T0K 2S0
Tel: 403-752-3057
Russell Court, President

Red Deer Chamber of Commerce
3017 Gaetz Ave., Red Deer AB T4N 5Y6
Tel: 403-347-4491; Fax: 403-343-6188
rdchamber@reddeerchamber.com
www.reddeerchamber.com
Maureen McMurtrie, President
Tim Creedon, Executive Director

Redwater & District Chamber of Commerce
c/o The Town Of Redwater Town Office, PO Box 322, 4924 - 47 St., Redwater AB T0A 2W0
Tel: 780-942-3519; Fax: 780-942-4321
Dave McRae, Project Manager
Anne Murland, Secretary
Linda Lawrence, Treasurer

Rimbey Chamber of Commerce
PO Box 87, Rimbey AB T0C 2J0
Tel: 403-843-2020; Fax: 403-843-2027
rimbeychamber@rimbey.com
Audreyann Bresnahan, President

Rocky Mountain House & District Chamber of Commerce
PO Box 1374, 5406 - 48 St., Rocky Mountain House AB T4T 1B1
Tel: 403-845-5450; Fax: 403-845-7764
Toll-Free: 800-565-3793
rmhcofc@rockychamber.org
www.rockychamber.org
Affiliation(s): AB Chamber of Commerce; Canadian Chamber of Commerce
Tammy Cote, President
Muriel Finkbeiner, Manager

St Albert Chamber of Commerce
71 St. Albert Rd., St Albert AB T8N 6L5
Tel: 780-458-2833; Fax: 780-458-6515
chamber@stalbertchamber.ca
www.stalbertchamber.ca
Joe Becigneul, Chair
Lynda Moffat, President & CEO

St Paul & District Chamber of Commerce
PO Box 887, St Paul AB T0A 3A0
Tel: 780-645-6800; Fax: 780-645-6059
Toll-Free: 888-733-8367
admin@stpaulchamber.ca
www.stpaulchamber.ca
Affiliation(s): Alberta Chambers of Commerce
Rhea Labrie, Executive Director
Doug Lamb, President

Sedgewick Chamber of Commerce
PO Box 625, Sedgewick AB T0B 4C0
Tel: 780-384-3912; Fax: 780-384-3938
Jeanette Harris, President

Sexsmith & District Chamber of Commerce
PO Box 146, Sexsmith AB T0H 3C0
Tel: 780-568-4663; Fax: 780-568-4115
chmbrtos@telusplanet.net
Freda King, President

Sherwood Park & District Chamber of Commerce
100 Ordze Ave., Sherwood Park AB T8B 1M6
Tel: 780-464-0801; Fax: 780-449-3581
Toll-Free: 866-464-0801
admin.spchamber@shaw.ca
www.sherwoodparkchamber.com
Bob Bittner, Contact, Member Services
Todd Banks, Executive Director

Slave Lake & District Chamber of Commerce
PO Box 190, Slave Lake AB T0G 2A0
Tel: 780-849-3222; Fax: 780-849-6894
sldcc@telusplanet.net
www.slavelakechamberofcommerce.ca
Fay Sand, President
Annie Aarts, Office Manager

Smoky Lake & District Chamber of Commerce
PO Box 635, Smoky Lake AB T0A 3C0
Tel: 780-656-3842; Fax: 780-451-3321
wilddeer@mcsnet.ca
Wayne Taylor, President

Spruce Grove & District Chamber of Commerce
PO Box 4210, 99 Campsite Rd., Spruce Grove AB T7X 3B4
Tel: 780-962-2561; Fax: 780-962-4417
info@sprucegrovechamber.com
www.sprucegrovechamber.com
Charlene Bell, President
Paul J. Lepine, Executive Director

Stettler Regional Board of Trade & Community Development
6606 - 50th Ave., Stettler AB T0C 2L2
Tel: 403-742-3181; Fax: 403-742-3123
Toll-Free: 877-742-9499
info@stettlerboardoftrade.com
www.stettlerboardoftrade.com
Gail Peterson, President
Keith Ryder, Executive Director

Stony Plain & District Chamber of Commerce
4815 - 44 Ave., Stony Plain AB T7Z 1V5
Tel: 780-963-4545; Fax: 780-963-4542
info@stonyplainchamber.ca
www.stonyplainchamber.ca
Graeme Dawes, President
Glen McCalpin, 1st Vice President

Strathmore & District Chamber of Commerce
PO Box 2222, Strathmore AB T1P 1K2
Tel: 403-901-3175; Fax: 403-901-1785
contactus@strathmoredistrictchamber.com
strathmoredistrictchamber.com
Robert Desjardins, President
Vi Giesbrecht, Administrative Assistance

Sundre Chamber of Commerce
PO Box 1085, Sundre AB T0M 1X0
Tel: 403-638-3245
info@sundrechamber.com
www.sundrechamber.com
Heidi Overgard, Secretary
James Eklund, President

Swan Hills Chamber of Commerce
PO Box 149, Swan Hills AB T0G 2C0
Tel: 780-333-4477; Fax: 780-333-4547
town@townofswanhills.com
Ken Pullen, President

Sylvan Lake Chamber of Commerce
4802, 48 St., Sylvan Lake AB T4S 1S6
Tel: 403-887-3048; Fax: 403-887-4944
info@sylvanlakechamber.com
www.sylvanlakechamber.com
Laurie Breeze, Administrator
Danine Weber, President

Taber & District Chamber of Commerce
4702 - 50 St., Taber AB T1G 2B6
Tel: 403-223-2265; Fax: 403-223-2291
admin@taberchamber.com
www.taberchamber.com
Louie Tams, President
Candace Karren, Manager

Thorhild Chamber of Commerce
PO Box 384, 638 - 6th Ave., Thorhild AB T0A 3J0
Tel: 780-398-2575; Fax: 780-398-2010
thorhildchamber@telus.net
John Dickey, President
Ed Cowley, Secretary

Thorsby & District Chamber of Commerce
PO Box 197, Thorsby AB T0C 2P0
Tel: 780-789-2100; Fax: 780-789-2155
jfhunter@netcom.ca
Clarence Kruger, President

Three Hills & District Chamber of Commerce
PO Box 277, Three Hills AB T0M 2A0
Tel: 780-662-4441; Fax: 780-443-7171
Timothy J. Shearlaw, President

Tofield & District Chamber of Commerce
PO Box 967, General Delivery, Tofield AB T0B 4J0
Tel: 780-661-4441; Fax: 780-662-3725
www.tofieldalberta.ca/chamber.htm
David Williamson, President

Trochu Chamber of Commerce
PO Box 607, Trochu AB T0M 2C0
Tel: 403-442-2785
Linda Hayes, President

Two Hills & District Chamber of Commerce
PO Box 547, Two Hills AB T0B 4K0
Tel: 780-657-3512; Fax: 780-657-2359
cfeir@telus.net
Robert Marsh, President

Valleyview Chamber of Commerce
PO Box 270, Valleyview AB T0H 3N0
Tel: 780-524-5150; Fax: 780-524-2727
valvadmn@telusplanet.net
www.albertafirst.com/profiles/statspack/20479.html
Gary Peterson, Town Manager
Bob Hall, Regional Manager

Vegreville & District Chamber of Commerce
Civic Bldg., PO Box 877, 5009 - 50 Ave., Vegreville AB T9C 1R9
Tel: 780-632-2771; Fax: 780-632-6958
vegchamb@telusplanet.net
www.vegrevillechamber.com
Rhonda Tkachuk, President
Elaine Kucher, General Manager

Vermilion & District Chamber of Commerce
4606 - 52nd St., Vermilion AB T9X 0A1
Tel: 780-853-6593; Fax: 780-853-1740
vermcofc@telusplanet.net
www.vermilionchamber.ca
Marlene Beattie, President

Viking Economic Development Committee (VEDC)
PO Box 369, Viking AB T0B 4N0
Tel: 780-336-3466; Fax: 780-336-2660
laura.arndt@town.viking.ab.ca
www.town.viking.ab.ca
Doug Lefsrud, Chair
Rod Krips, Town Manager

Vulcan & District Chamber of Commerce
PO Box 1161, 115 Centre St., Vulcan AB T0L 2B0
Tel: 403-485-2994; Fax: 403-485-2878
info@vulcantourism.com
www.vulcantourism.com
Brenda Weber, President

Wabamun District Chamber of Commerce Society
PO Box 29, Wabamun AB T0E 2K0
Tel: 780-892-4665
www.albertafirst.com/profiles/statspack/20590.html
Tom Harris, President

Wainwright & District Chamber of Commerce
PO Box 2997, Wainwright AB T9W 1S9
Tel: 780-842-4910; Fax: 780-842-6061
exec@wdchamber.com
www.wdchamber.com
Dave Neville, President
Marketta Fahnbulleh, Executive Director

Waterton Park Chamber of Commerce & Visitors Association
PO Box 55, Waterton Lakes National Park AB T0K 2M0
Tel: 403-859-2224; Fax: 403-859-2650
waterton.info@pc.gc.ca
www.watertonchamber.com
Rod Kretz, President

Westlock & District Chamber of Commerce
PO Box 5917, Westlock AB T7P 2P7

Wetaskiwin Chamber of Commerce (WCC)
4910 - 55A St., Wetaskiwin AB T9A 2R7
Tel: 780-352-8003; Fax: 780-352-6226
wcoc@incentre.net
www.wetaskiwinchamber.ca
Cindy Ekkel, Secretary
Harvey Loroff, Treasurer
Wayne DiLallo, President

Whitecourt & District Chamber of Commerce
PO Box 1011, 3002 - 33rd St., Whitecourt AB T7S 1N9
Tel: 780-778-5363; Fax: 780-778-2351
Toll-Free: 800-313-7383
manager@whitecourtchamber.com
www.whitecourtchamber.com
Affiliation(s): Alberta Chamber of Commerce
Pat VanderBurg, General Manager
Marc Chayer, President

Worsley Chamber of Commerce
PO Box 181, Worsley AB T0H 3W0
Tel: 780-685-3943; Fax: 780-685-2115
Doug Allen, President

British Columbia

Abbotsford Chamber of Commerce
#207, 32900 South Fraser Way, Abbotsford BC V2S 5A1
Tel: 604-859-9651; Fax: 604-850-6880
acoc@telus.net
www.abbotsfordchamber.com
James Barlow, President

Alberni Valley Chamber of Commerce
2533 Port Alberni Hwy., Port Alberni BC V9Y 8P2
Tel: 250-724-6535; Fax: 250-724-6560
avcoc@alberni.net
www.avcoc.com
Dewayne Parfitt, President
Mike Carter, Executive Director

Armstrong-Spallumcheen Chamber of Commerce
PO Box 118, 3550 Bridge St., Armstrong BC V0E 1B0
Tel: 250-546-8155; Fax: 250-546-8868
armstrong_chamber@telus.net
aschamber.com
Patti Noonan, Manager
Sandra Starke, President

Bamfield Chamber of Commerce
Bamfield BC V0R 1B0
Tel: 250-728-3006
info@bamfieldchamber.com
www.bamfieldchamber.com
Affiliation(s): Pacific Rim Tourism Association

Barriere & District Chamber of Commerce
PO Box 1190, Barriere BC V0E 1E0
Tel: 250-672-9221; Fax: 250-672-2159
info@barrieredistrict.com
www.barrieredistrict.com/
Affiliation(s): Canadian Chamber of Commerce
Lorne Richardson, Manager & Marketing Coordinator

Bowen Island Chamber of Commerce
432 Cardena Rd., Bowen Island BC V0N 1G0
Tel: 604-947-9024; Fax: 604-947-0633
info@bowenisland.org
www.bowenisland.org
Tim Rhodes, President

Burnaby Board of Trade (BBOT)
#201, 4555 Kingsway, Burnaby BC V5H 4T8
Tel: 604-412-0100; Fax: 604-412-0102
admin@bbot.ca
www.bbot.ca
Paul Holden, CEO

Burns Lake & District Chamber of Commerce
PO Box 339, Burns Lake BC V0J 1E0
Tel: 250-692-3773; Fax: 250-692-3493
bldcoc@telus.net
www.burnslakechamber.ca
Rise Johansen, President

Cache Creek Chamber of Commerce
PO Box 460, Cache Creek BC V0K 1H0
Tel: 250-457-9668; Fax: 250-457-9669
jade@coppervalleybc.ca
Gordon Daily, President

Campbell River & District Chamber of Commerce
PO Box 400, 900 Alder St., Campbell River BC V9W 5B6
Tel: 250-287-4636; Fax: 250-286-6490
admin@campbellriverchamber.ca
www.campbellriverchamber.ca
Colleen Evans, Executive Director

Castlegar & District Chamber of Commerce (CDCoC)
1995 - 6th Ave., Castlegar BC V1N 4B7
Tel: 250-365-6313; Fax: 250-365-5778
info@castlegar.com
www.castlegar.com
Kerry Hobbs, President

Chamber of Commerce of the City of Grand Forks
PO Box 1086, 1647 Central Ave., Grand Forks BC V0H 1H0
Tel: 250-442-2833; Fax: 250-442-5688
Toll-Free: 866-442-2833
www.grandforkschamber.com
David Evdokimoff, President
Cher Wyers, Manager

Chase & District Chamber of Commerce
PO Box 592, 400 Shuswap Ave., Chase BC V0E 1M0
Tel: 250-679-8432; Fax: 250-679-3120
admin@chasechamber.com
www.chasechamber.com/
Barbara Maher, President

Chemainus & District Chamber of Commerce
PO Box 575, 9796 Willow St., Chemainus BC V0R 1K0
Tel: 250-246-3944; Fax: 250-246-3251
cccoc@islandnet.com
www.chemainus.bc.ca

Chetwynd & District Chamber of Commerce
PO Box 870, Chetwynd BC V0C 1J0
Tel: 250-788-3345; Fax: 250-788-3655
chetcham@pris.bc.ca
Jackie Drake, Manager
Barb Shirley, President

Chilliwack Chamber of Commerce
#16, 45966 Yale Rd., Chilliwack BC V2P 2M3
Tel: 604-793-4323; Fax: 604-793-4303
info@chilliwackchamber.com
www.chilliwackchamber.com
Tim McAlpine, President
Sue Attrill, Chief Executive Officer

Christina Lake Chamber of Commerce
Hwy. 3 & Kimura Rd., Christina Lake BC V0H 1E2
Tel: 250-447-6161
info@christinalake.com
www.christinalake.com

Clearwater & District Chamber of Commerce
PO Box 1988, RR#1, Clearwater BC V0E 1N0
Tel: 250-674-2646; Fax: 250-674-3693
info@clearwaterbcchamber.com
www.clearwaterbcchamber.com
Sheena vanDyk

Clinton & District Chamber of Commerce
PO Box 256, Clinton BC V0K 1K0
Tel: 250-459-2640; Fax: 250-459-2627
Susan Swan, President

Cloverdale & District Chamber of Commerce
17687 - 56A Ave., Surrey BC V3S 1G4
Tel: 604-574-9802; Fax: 604-574-9122
clovcham@axion.net
www.cloverdale.bc.ca
Ben Wevers, President

Columbia Valley Chamber of Commerce (CVCC)
PO Box 1019, Invermere BC V0A 1K0
Tel: 250-342-2844; Fax: 250-342-3261
www.cvchamber.ca
Affiliation(s): British Columbia Chamber of Commerce

Comox Valley Chamber of Commerce (CVCC)
2040 Cliffe Ave., Courtenay BC V9N 2L3
Tel: 250-334-3234; Fax: 250-334-4908
Toll-Free: 888-357-4471
membership@comoxvalleychamber.com
www.comoxvalleychamber.com
Sean O'Gorman, President
Dianne Hawkins, Executive Director

Cowichan Lake District Chamber of Commerce
PO Box 824, 125C South Shore Rd., Lake Cowichan BC V0R 2G0
Tel: 250-749-3244; Fax: 250-749-0187
info@cowichanlake.ca
www.cowichanlake.ca
Affiliation(s): Canadian Chamber of Commerce
Jim Humphrey, President

Cranbrook & District Chamber of Commerce
Cranbrook & District Chamber of Commerce, PO Box 84, Cranbrook BC V1C 4H6
Tel: 250-426-5914; Toll-Free: 800-222-6174
info@cranbrookchamber.com
www.cranbrookchamber.com
Lana Kirk, President
Karin Penner, Manager

Cumberland Chamber of Commerce
PO Box 250, 2680 Dunsmuir Ave., Cumberland BC V0R 1S0
Tel: 250-336-8313; Fax: 250-336-2455
cumbcham@shaw.ca
www.cumberlandbc.org
Affiliation(s): North By Northwest Tourism Association of BC

Dawson Creek & District Chamber of Commerce
10201 - 10th St., Dawson Creek BC V1G 3T5
Tel: 250-782-4868; Fax: 250-782-2371
info@dawsoncreekchamber.ca
www.dawsoncreekchamber.ca
Affiliation(s): BC Chamber of Commerce
David Roch, President

Dease Lake & District Chamber of Commerce
PO Box 338, Dease Lake BC V0C 1L0
Tel: 250-771-3900; Fax: 250-771-3900
Lyonna Mroch, Secretary
Rich Mroch, President

Delta Chamber of Commerce
6201 - 60 Ave., Delta BC V4K 4E2
Tel: 604-946-4232; Fax: 604-946-5285
info@deltachamber.com
www.deltachamber.com
Peter Roaf, Executive Director
Greg Muirhead, President

Discovery Islands Chamber of Commerce
PO Box 190, Quathiaski Cove BC V0P 1N0
Tel: 250-285-2724; Toll-Free: 866-285-2724
chamber@discoveryislands.ca
www.discoveryislands.ca/chamber
Susan Wilson, President

Duncan-Cowichan Chamber of Commerce (DCCC)
381 Trans-Canada Hwy., Duncan BC V9L 3R5
Tel: 250-748-1111; Fax: 250-746-8222
Toll-Free: 888-303-3337
manager@duncancc.bc.ca
www.duncancc.bc.ca
Cathy Mailhot, Manager

Elkford Chamber of Commerce
PO Box 220, 4A Front St., Elkford BC V0B 1H0
Tel: 250-865-4614; Fax: 250-865-2442
Toll-Free: 877-355-9453
info@tourismelkford.ca
www.tourismelkford.ca
Susan Robitaille, Manager
Ian Benson, President

Enderby & District Chamber of Commerce
PO Box 1000, Enderby BC V0E 1V0
Tel: 250-838-6727; Fax: 250-838-0123
Toll-Free: 877-213-6509
echamber@jetstream.net
www.enderby.com/chamber

Esquimalt Chamber of Commerce
PO Box 36019, 1153 Esquimalt Rd., Victoria BC V9A 7J5
Tel: 250-704-2525; Fax: 250-380-6932
info@esquimaltchamber.com
www.esquimaltchamber.com
Ed Williams, President

Fernie Chamber of Commerce
102 Commerce Rd., Fernie BC V0B 1M5
Tel: 250-423-6868; Fax: 250-423-3811
Toll-Free: 877-433-7643
info@ferniechamber.com
www.ferniechamber.com
Affiliation(s): Economic Development Association of BC

Fort Nelson & District Chamber of Commerce
PO Box 196, 5315B - 50th Ave. South, Fort Nelson BC V0C 1R0
Tel: 250-774-2956; Fax: 250-774-2958
info@fortnelsonchamber.com
www.fortnelsonchamber.com
Geordie McLennan, President
Heather Sellors, Executive Director

Fort St. James Chamber of Commerce
PO Box 1164, Fort St James BC V0J 1P0
Tel: 250-996-7023; Fax: 250-996-7047
fsjchamb@fsjames.com
www.fortstjameschamber.com
Dennis Gladne, President
Carol Magnus, Manager

Fort St. John & District Chamber of Commerce
9325 - 100 St., Fort St John BC V1J 4N4
Tel: 250-785-6037; Fax: 250-785-7181
info@fsjchamber.com
www.fsjchamber.com
Annette Oak, Chamber Manager
Andy Ackerman, President

Gabriola Island Chamber of Commerce
PO Box 249, #3, 575 North Rd., Gabriola BC V0R 1X0
Tel: 250-247-9332; Fax: 250-247-9332
Toll-Free: 888-284-9332
info@gabriolaisland.org, manager@gabriolaisland.org
www.gabriolaisland.org
Affiliation(s): Tourism Association of Vancouver Island
Ken Wur, President

Galiano Island Chamber of Commerce
PO Box 73, Galiano BC V0N 1P0
Tel: 250-539-2233
info@galianoisland.com
www.galianoisland.com
Ken Smith, President

Gibsons & District Chamber of Commerce
PO Box 1190, #21, 900 Gibsons Way, Gibsons BC V0N 1V0
Tel: 604-886-2325; Fax: 604-886-2379
gibsonsbcchamber@telus.net
www.gibsonsbc.ca/chamber
Jeff Barringer, President
Cheryl Baron, Executive Director

Gold River Chamber of Commerce
PO Box 39, Gold River BC V0P 1G0
Tel: 250-283-7333
Gabriella Pentz, President
Craig Scott, Vice-President

Golden & District Chamber of Commerce (GDCC)
PO Box 1320, #500, 10 North Ave., Golden BC V0A 1H0
Tel: 250-344-7125; Fax: 250-344-6688
Toll-Free: 800-622-4653
info@goldenchamber.bc.ca
www.goldenchamber.bc.ca
Ruth Kowalski, Manager
Michael Dalzell, President

Greater Kamloops Chamber of Commerce
1290 Trans Canada Hwy., Kamloops BC V2C 6R3
Tel: 250-372-7722; Fax: 250-828-9500
mail@kamloopschamber.bc.ca
www.kamloopschamber.bc.ca
Leslie Brochu, President
Deb McClelland, Executive Director

Greater Langley Chamber of Commerce
#1, 5761 Glover Rd., Langley BC V3A 8M8
Tel: 604-530-6656; Fax: 604-530-7066
chamber@langleychamber.com
www.langleychamber.com
Kevin Staples, President

Greater Nanaimo Chamber of Commerce
2133 Bowen Rd., Nanaimo BC V9S 1H8
Tel: 250-756-1191; Fax: 250-756-1584
info@nanaimochamber.bc.ca
www.nanaimochamber.bc.ca
Lee Mason, CEO
Donna Hais, President
Scott Thomson, Treasurer

Greater Vernon Chamber of Commerce (GVCC)
701 Hwy. 97 South, Vernon BC V1B 3W4
Tel: 250-545-0771; Fax: 250-545-3114
info@vernonchamber.ca
www.vernonchamber.ca
Affiliation(s): Canadian Chamber of Commerce
Val Trevis, General Manager
David Fletcher, President

Greater Victoria Chamber of Commerce (GVCC)
#100, 852 Fort St., Victoria BC V8W 1H8
Tel: 250-383-7191; Fax: 250-385-3552
chamber@gvcc.org
www.victoriachamber.ca
Social Media: www.youtube.com/user/victoriachamber
Bruce Carter, CEO
Margaret Lucas, Chair
David Marshall, Treasurer

Harrison Agassiz Chamber of Commerce
PO Box 429, Harrison Hot Springs BC V0M 1K0
Tel: 604-796-1133; Fax: 604-796-3694
www.harrison.ca
Robert Reyerse, President

Hope & District Chamber of Commerce
PO Box 588, 895 - 3rd Ave., Hope BC V0X 1L0
Tel: 604-869-3111; Fax: 604-869-8208
info@hopechamber.bc.ca
www.hopechamber.bc.ca
Victor Smith, President

Houston & District Chamber of Commerce
PO Box 396, 3289 Hwy. 16, Houston BC V0J 1Z0
Tel: 250-845-7640; Fax: 250-845-3682
info@houstonchamber.ca
www.houstonchamber.ca
Troy Reitsma, President
Maureen Czirfusz, Manager

Kaslo Chamber of Commerce
PO Box 329, Kaslo BC V0G 1M0
Toll-Free: 866-276-3212
info@kaslochamber.com
www.kaslochamber.com
Gary Cockerall, President

Kelowna Chamber of Commerce
544 Harvey Ave., Kelowna BC V1Y 6C9
Tel: 250-861-3627; Fax: 250-861-3624
info@kelownachamber.org
www.kelownachamber.org
Affiliation(s): BC Chamber of Commerce
Norm LeCavalier, President

Kimberley Bavarian Society Chamber of Commerce (KBSCC)
270 Kimberley Ave., Kimberley BC V1A 3N3
Tel: 250-427-3666; Fax: 250-427-5378
Toll-Free: 866-913-3666
info@kimberleychamber.ca
www.kimberleychamber.ca
Schaun Goodeve, President

Kitimat Chamber of Commerce
PO Box 214, Kitimat BC V8C 2G7
Tel: 250-632-6294; Fax: 250-632-4685
Toll-Free: 800-664-6554
kitimatchamber@telus.net
www.visitkitimat.com
Tony Brady, President

Kitsilano Chamber of Commerce (KCC)
PO Box 34369, Stn. D, Vancouver BC V6J 4P3
Tel: 604-731-4454; Toll-Free: 877-312-1898
admin@kitsilanochamber.com
www.kitsilanochamber.com/
Thomas B. DeSchutter, President

Kootenay Lake Chamber of Commerce
PO Box 120, Crawford Bay BC V0B 1E0
Tel: 250-227-9233
info@kootenaylake.bc.ca
www.kootenaylake.bc.ca
Paul Hindson, Treasurer

Ladysmith Chamber of Commerce
PO Box 598, 441B - 1st Ave., Ladysmith BC V9G 1A4
Tel: 250-245-2112; Fax: 250-245-2124
info@ladysmithcofc.com
www.ladysmithcofc.com
Affiliation(s): Cowichan Regional Valley
Heidi Derhousoff, Manager
Brian Bancroft, President

Lake Country Chamber of Commerce
#40, 9522 Main St., Lake Country BC V4V 2L9
Tel: 250-766-5670; Fax: 250-766-0170
Toll-Free: 888-766-5670
admin@lakecountrychamber.com
www.lakecountrychamber.com
Bill Clark, President
Linda Wilson, Manager

Likely & District Chamber of Commerce
PO Box 29, Likely BC V0L 1N0
Tel: 250-790-2127; Fax: 250-790-2323
chamber@likely-bc.ca
www.likely-bc.ca

Lillooet & District Chamber of Commerce
PO Box 650, Lillooet BC V0K 1V0
Tel: 250-256-3578; Fax: 250-256-4882
deverell@telus.net
www.lillooetchamberofcommerce.com
Bob Sheridan, President

Lumby & District Chamber of Commerce
PO Box 534, Lumby BC V0E 2G0
Tel: 250-547-2300; Fax: 250-547-2300
lumbychamber@shaw.ca
www.monasheetourism.com
Stephanie Sexsmith, Manager
Bill Maltman, President

Lytton & District Chamber of Commerce
PO Box 460, Lytton BC V0K 1Z0
Tel: 250-455-2523; Fax: 250-455-6669
lyttoncc@goldtrail.com
www.coastandmountains.bc.ca/page.cfm/650
Affiliation(s): Vancouver Coast & Mountains Tourism Region
Peggy Chute, Manager
Richard Forrest, President

Mackenzie Chamber of Commerce
PO Box 880, Mackenzie BC V0J 2C0
Tel: 250-997-5459; Fax: 250-997-6117
Toll-Free: 877-622-5360
mackcoc@mackbc.com
www.mackenziechamber.bc.ca
Affiliation(s): Retail Merchants Association of BC
Margaret Grant, Manager
Amber Hancock, President

Maple Ridge Pitt Meadows Chamber of Commerce
22238 Lougheed Hwy., Maple Ridge BC V2X 2T2
Tel: 604-463-3366; Fax: 604-463-3201
carrisa@ridgemeadowschamber.com
www.ridgemeadowschamber.com
Affiliation(s): BC Chamber Executive; Canadian Chamber of Commerce; Southwestern BC Tourism
Jeff Cerpenter, President

Mayne Island Community Chamber of Commerce
PO Box 2, Mayne BC V0N 2J0
Tel: 250-539-9815
info@mayneislandchamber.ca
www.mayneislandchamber.ca
Richard Iredale, President
Joanie McCorry, Manager

McBride & District Chamber of Commerce
PO Box 2, McBride BC V0J 2E0
Tel: 250-569-3366; Fax: 250-569-2376
Toll-Free: 866-569-3366
come2mcbride@telus.net
www.mcbridebc.info
Vincent de Niet, President

Merritt & District Chamber of Commerce
PO Box 1649, 2185B Voght St., Merritt BC V1K 1B8
Tel: 250-378-5634; Fax: 250-378-6561
manager@merrittchamber.com
www.merrittchamber.com
Karen Fox, Executive Director

Mission Regional Chamber of Commerce
34033 Lougheed Hwy., Mission BC V2V 5X8
Tel: 604-826-6914; Fax: 604-826-5916
manager@missionchamber.bc.ca
www.missionchamber.bc.ca
Michelle Favero, Manager
Sean Melia, President

Nakusp & District Chamber of Commerce
PO Box 387, 92 - 6th. Ave. NW, Nakusp BC V0G 1R0
Tel: 250-265-4234; Fax: 250-265-3808
Toll-Free: 800-909-8819
nakcom@telus.net
www.nakusparrowlakes.com
Affiliation(s): Tourism British Columbia
Kim Reich, President

Nelson & District Chamber of Commerce
255 Hall St., Nelson BC V1L 5X4
Tel: 250-352-3433; Fax: 250-352-6355
Toll-Free: 877-663-5706
info@discovernelson.com
www.discovernelson.com
Affiliation(s): British Columbia Chamber of Commerce; Canadian Chamber of Commerce
Cal Renwick, President

New Westminster Chamber of Commerce
601 Queens Ave., New Westminster BC V3M 1L1
Tel: 604-521-7781; Fax: 604-521-0057
nwcc@newwestchamber.com
www.newwestchamber.com
David Brennan, Executive Director
Andrew Hopkins, President

North Shuswap Chamber of Commerce
PO Box 101, Celista BC V0E 1L0
Tel: 250-955-2113; Fax: 250-955-2113
Toll-Free: 888-955-1488
requests@northshuswapbc.com
www.northshuswapbc.com

North Vancouver Chamber of Commerce (NVCC)
#102, 124 West First St., Vancouver BC V7M 3N3
Tel: 604-987-4488; Fax: 604-987-8272
info@nvchamber.bc.ca; events@nvchamber.ca
www.nvchamber.bc.ca
Anne McMullin, President & General Manager
Stephen Joyce, Chair
Misha Wilson, Manager, Visitor Centre

Okanagan Falls Chamber of Commerce
PO Box 246, Okanagan Falls BC V0H 1R0
okfalls@img.net
Kevin Therrien, President

Osoyoos Chamber of Commerce
PO Box 277, Osoyoos BC V0H 1V0
Tel: 250-495-7142; Fax: 250-495-7132
info@osoyoochamber.bc.ca
www.osoyooschamber.bc.ca
CJ Rhodes, President

Parksville & District Chamber of Commerce
PO Box 99, 1275 East Island Hwy., Parksville BC V9P 2G3
Tel: 250-248-3613; Fax: 250-248-5210
www.parksvillechamber.com
Peter Doukakis, Executive Director
Gary Child, President

Peachland Chamber of Commerce
5812 Beach Ave., Peachland BC V0H 1X7
Tel: 250-767-2455; Fax: 250-767-2420
Toll-Free: 866-955-2455
peachlandchamber@shawcable.com
www.peachlandchamber.bc.ca
Susanne Dannenberg, Executive Director

Pemberton Chamber of Commerce
PO Box 370, Pemberton BC V0N 2L0
Tel: 604-894-6477; Fax: 604-894-5571
info@pembertonchamber.com
www.pembertonchamber.com
Affiliation(s): Vancouver Board of Trade
Paul Selina, President
Shirley Henry, Secretary Treasurer

Pender Harbour & Egmont Chamber of Commerce
PO Box 265, 1287 Madeira Park Rd., Madeira Park BC V0N 2H0
Tel: 604-883-2561; Fax: 604-883-2561
Toll-Free: 877-873-6337
chamber@penderharbour.ca
www.penderharbour.ca
Kerry Milligan, Secretary
Dave Milligan, President

Pender Island Chamber of Commerce
PO Box 123, Pender Island BC V0N 2M0
Tel: 250-629-3988; Toll-Free: 866-468-7924
travel@penderislandchamber.com
www.penderislandchamber.com

Penticton & Wine Country Chamber of Commerce
#8, 273 Power St., Penticton BC V2A 7K9
Tel: 250-492-4103; Fax: 250-492-6119
Toll-Free: 800-663-5052
admin@penticton.org
www.penticton.org
Judy Poole, Manager
Joe Morelli, President

Port Hardy & District Chamber of Commerce
PO Box 249, Port Hardy BC V0N 2P0
Tel: 250-949-7622; Fax: 250-949-6653
phcc@cablerocket.com
www.ph-chamber.bc.ca
Sandra Boyd, President

Port McNeill & District Chamber of Commerce
PO Box 129, 1594 Beach Dr., Port McNeill BC V0N 2R0
Tel: 250-956-3131; Fax: 250-956-3132
Toll-Free: 888-956-3131
pmccc@island.net
www.portmcneill.net
Gaby Wickstrom, President

Port Renfrew Chamber of Commerce
General Delivery, Port Renfrew BC V0S 1K0
Tel: 250-647-0009; Fax: 250-647-0058
prcc@portrenfrew.com
www.portrenfrewcommunity.com
Tim Cash, President
Brian Cameron, Vice-President

Powell River Chamber of Commerce
6807 Wharf St., Powell River BC V8A 2T9
Tel: 604-485-4051; Fax: 604-485-4272
office@powellriverchamber.com
www.powellriverchamber.com
Jack Barr, President

Prince George Chamber of Commerce
890 Vancouver St., Prince George BC V2L 2P5
Tel: 250-562-2454; Fax: 250-562-6510
chamber@pgchamber.bc.ca
www.pgchamber.bc.ca
Jennifer Brandle-McCall, CEO

Prince Rupert & District Chamber of Commerce (PRDCC)
PO Box 158, #100, 215 Cow Bay Rd., Prince Rupert BC V8J 1A2
Tel: 250-624-2296; Fax: 250-624-6105
Toll-Free: 800-667-1994
manager@princerupertchamber.ca
www.princerupertchamber.ca
Deb Stava, President
Maynard Angus, Vice-President
Lynne Graham, Chamber Manager

Princeton & District Chamber of Commerce
PO Box 540, Princeton BC V0X 1W0
Tel: 250-295-3103; Fax: 250-295-3255
chamber@nethop.net
www.princeton.ca
Lori Thomas, Manager

Qualicum Beach Chamber of Commerce
PO Box 159, 124 West 2nd Ave., Qualicum Beach BC V9K 1S7
Tel: 250-752-0960; Fax: 250-752-2923
chamber@qualicum.bc.ca
www.qualicum.bc.ca
Affiliation(s): Oceanside Tourism Association
Judi Ainsworth, General Manager

Queen Charlotte Islands Chamber of Commerce
PO Box 448, Port Clements BC V0T 1R0
Tel: 250-557-4565; Fax: 250-557-4565
chamber@qcislands.net
www.qcislands.net/chamber
Maggie Bell Brown, Secretary

Quesnel & District Chamber of Commerce
679B, Hwy. 97 South, Quesnel BC V2J 4C7
Tel: 250-747-0125; Fax: 250-747-0126
qchamber@quesnelbc.com
www.quesnelchamber.com
Coralee Oakes, Manager
Keith Brookes, President

Radium Hot Springs Chamber of Commerce
PO Box 225, Radium Hot Springs BC V0A 1M0
Tel: 250-347-9331; Fax: 250-347-9127
Toll-Free: 800-347-9704
info@RadiumHotSprings.com
www.RadiumHotSprings.com
Kent Kebe, Manager
Douglas McIntosh, President

Revelstoke Chamber of Commerce
PO Box 490, 204 Campbell Ave., Revelstoke BC V0E 2S0
Tel: 250-837-5345; Fax: 250-837-4223
revelstokeinfo@telus.net
revelstokechamber.com
Deenie Ottenbreit, President

Richmond Chamber of Commerce
South Tower, #101, 5811 Cooney Rd., Richmond BC V6X 3M1
Tel: 604-278-2822; Fax: 604-278-2972
rcc@richmondchamber.ca
www.richmondchamber.ca
Affiliation(s): Tourism Richmond; Sister Chamber - Kent, Washington
Carol Young, Manager, Administration & Events

Rossland Chamber of Commerce
PO Box 1385, Rossland BC V0G 1Y0
Tel: 250-362-5666; Fax: 250-362-5399
commerce@rossland.com
www.rossland.com/about
Maritza Reilly, Executive Director

Saanich Peninsula Chamber of Commerce (SPCOC)
#209, 2453 Beacon Ave., Sidney BC V8L 1X7
Tel: 250-656-3616; Fax: 250-656-7111
info@peninsulachamber.ca
www.peninsulachamber.ca
Eileen Leddy, Executive Director
Charles Hodgins, President

Salmo & District Chamber of Commerce
PO Box 400, 100 Fourth St., Salmo BC V0G 1Z0
Tel: 250-357-2596
www.salmo.net

Salmon Arm & District Chamber of Commerce (SACC)
PO Box 999, #101, 20 Hudson Ave. NE, Salmon Arm BC V1E 4P2
Tel: 250-832-6247; Fax: 250-832-8382
info@sachamber.bc.ca
www.sachamber.bc.ca
Dave Andrews, President

Salt Spring Island Chamber of Commerce
121 Lower Ganges Rd., Salt Spring Island BC V8K 2T1
Tel: 250-537-5252; Fax: 250-537-4276
Toll-Free: 866-216-2936
chamber@saltspring.com
www.saltspringtoday.com
Mafalda Hoogerdyk, President
Donna Powell, Manager

Sechelt & District Chamber of Commerce
PO Box 360, #102 - 5700 Cowrie St., Sechelt BC V0N 3A0
Tel: 604-885-0662; Fax: 604-885-0691
Toll-Free: 877-633-2963
sdcoc9@telus.net
www.secheltchamber.bc.ca
Jim Cleghorn, President
Colleen Clark, Executive Director

Seton Portage/Shalalth District Chamber of Commerce
PO Box 2067, Seton Portage BC V0N 3B0
Tel: 250-259-8312; Fax: 250-259-8213
snor@uniserve.com
Ray Klassen, Vice-President

Sicamous & District Chamber of Commerce
PO Box 346, Sicamous BC V0E 2V0
Tel: 250-836-3313; Fax: 250-836-4368
sicamouschamber@cablelan.net
www.sicamouschamber.bc.ca
Charlotte Hutchinson, President
Doreen Favel, Manager

Slocan District Chamber of Commerce
PO Box 448, New Denver BC V0G 1S0
Tel: 250-358-2544; Fax: 250-358-7998
www.slocanlake.com/chamber.html

Smithers District Chamber of Commerce
PO Box 2379, Smithers BC V0J 2N0
Tel: 250-847-5072; Fax: 250-847-3337
Toll-Free: 800-542-6673
chamber@tourismsmithers.com
www.tourismsmithers.com/chamber
Affiliation(s): Northern BC Tourism Association

Sooke Harbour Chamber of Commerce
PO Box 18, 6716 Westcoast Rd., Sooke BC V0S 1N0
Tel: 250-642-6112
info@sookeharbourchamber.com
www.sookeharbourchamber.com
Scott Gertsma, President

South Cariboo Chamber of Commerce
PO Box 2312, 100 Mile House BC V0K 2E0
Tel: 250-395-6124; Fax: 250-395-8974
manager@scariboochamber.org
www.scariboochamber.org
Affiliation(s): Canadian Chamber of Commerce
Howard McMillan, Manager
Chris Nickless, President

South Cowichan Chamber of Commerce (SCCC)
#368, 2720 Mill Bay Rd., Mill Bay BC V0R 2P1
Tel: 250-743-3566; Fax: 250-743-5332
info@southcowichanchamber.org
www.southcowichanchamber.org
Rosalie Power, Manager
Leslie Grills, President

South Okanagan Chamber Of Commerce
PO Box 460, 36205 - 93rd St., Oliver BC V0H 1T0
Tel: 250-498-6321; Fax: 250-498-3156
Toll-Free: 888-498-6321
www.sochamber.ca
Bonnie Dancey, Manager
Kenn Oldfield, President

South Shuswap Chamber of Commerce
PO Box 7, Blind Bay BC V0E 2W0
Tel: 250-675-3515; Fax: 250-675-3516
sorrentochamber@telus.net
www.southshuswapchamberofcommerce.org
Chris Emery, President
Nancy Kyle, Manager

Sparwood & District Chamber of Commerce
PO Box 1448, Aspen Dr., Sparwood BC V0B 2G0
Tel: 250-425-2423; Fax: 250-425-7130
Toll-Free: 877-485-8185
administrator@sparwoodchamber.bc.ca
www.sparwoodchamber.bc.ca
Muriel Stickney, President
Alayna Casselman, Administrator

Squamish Chamber of Commerce
Squamish Adventure Centre, #102, 38551 Loggers Lane, Squamish BC V8B 0H2
Tel: 604-815-4994; Fax: 604-815-4998
Toll-Free: 866-333-2010
info@squamishchamber.com
www.squamishchamber.com
Sameer Kajani, President
Kenny Music, Managing Director

Stewart-Hyder International Chamber of Commerce
PO Box 306, Stewart BC V0T 1W0
Tel: 250-636-9224; Fax: 250-636-2199
Toll-Free: 888-366-5999
info@stewart-hyder.com
www.stewart-hyder.com
Mary G. McKay, President
Gwen McKay, Manager

Summerland Chamber of Economic Development & Tourism (SCEDT)
PO Box 130, 15600 Hwy. 97, Summerland BC V0H 1Z0
Tel: 250-494-2686; Fax: 250-494-4039
info@summerlandchamber.com
www.summerlandchamber.com
Affiliation(s): Economic Development Association of BC; Thompson/Okanagan Tourism Association
Scott Boswell, Executive Director
Juanita Gibney, President

Surrey Board of Trade (SBOT)
#101, 14439 - 104 Ave., Surrey BC V3R 1M1
Tel: 604-581-7130; Fax: 604-588-7549
Toll-Free: 866-848-7130
info@businessinsurrey.com
www.businessinsurrey.com
Anita Huberman, CEO
Anita Huberman, Chief Executive Officer
Nigel Watkinson, President
Mary Jane Stanberg, Vice-President

Tahsis Chamber of Commerce
PO Box 278, 36 Rugged Mountain Road, Tahsis BC V0P 1X0
Tel: 204-934-6425
info@tahsischamberofcommerce.com
www.tahsischamberofcommerce.com
Corrine Dahling, President
Jude Schooner, Secretary/Treasurer

Terrace & District Chamber of Commerce
4511 Keith Ave., Terrace BC V8G 1K1
Tel: 250-635-2063; Fax: 250-635-2573
Toll-Free: 800-499-1637
executivedirector@terracechamber.com
www.terracechamber.com
Stacey Mann, Executive Director

Tofino-Long Beach Chamber of Commerce
PO Box 249, Tofino BC V0R 2Z0
Tel: 250-725-3414; Fax: 250-725-3296
info@tourismtofino.com
www.tourismtofino.com
Larry Nicolay, President

Trail & District Chamber of Commerce
#200, 1199 Bay Ave., Trail BC V1R 4A4
Tel: 250-368-3144; Fax: 250-368-6427
tcoc@netidea.com
www.trailchamber.com
Shane McIntyre, President
Pam Lewin, Executive Director

Tri-Cities Chamber of Commerce Serving Coquitlam, Port Coquitlam & Port Moody
1209 Pinetree Way, Coquitlam BC V3B 7Y3
Tel: 604-464-2716; Fax: 604-464-6796
info@tricitieschamber.com
www.tricitieschamber.com
Dennis Marsden, President

Ucluelet Chamber of Commerce (UCOC)
PO Box 428, #3, 1645 Cedar St., Ucluelet BC V0R 3A0
Tel: 250-726-4641; Fax: 250-726-4611
marny@uclueletinfo.com
www.uclueletinfo.com
Marny Saunders, General Manager

Valemount & Area Chamber of Commerce
PO Box 690, Valemount BC V0E 2Z0
Tel: 250-566-0061; Fax: 250-566-4244
www.thevalleysentinel.com/chamber
Christine Latimer, President

Vanderhoof & District Chamber of Commerce
PO Box 126, 2353 Burrard Ave., Vanderhoof BC V0J 3A0
Tel: 250-567-2124; Fax: 250-567-3316
Toll-Free: 800-752-4094
chamber@hwy16.com
www.vanderhoofchamber.com
Affiliation(s): BC Chamber of Commerce
Stuart Sinclair, President
Erin Siemens, Manager

Wells & District Chamber of Commerce
PO Box 123, Wells BC V0K 2R0
Tel: 250-994-3223; Fax: 250-994-3223
Toll-Free: 877-451-9355
marketing@wellsbc.com
www.wellsbc.com
Norma Collins, President

West Shore Chamber of Commerce
2830 Aldwynd Rd., Victoria BC V9B 3S7
Tel: 250-478-1130; Fax: 250-478-1584
chamber@westshore.bc.ca
www.westshore.bc.ca
Mike Wicks, CEO
Leiha Snow, Manager, Membership
Lucinda French, Executive Assistant

West Vancouver Chamber of Commerce
#401, 100 Park Royal, West Vancouver BC V7T 1A2
Tel: 604-926-6614; Fax: 604-925-7220
info@westvanchamber.com
www.westvanchamber.com
Leagh Gabriel, Executive Director

Westbank & District Chamber of Commerce
#4, 2375 Pamela Rd., Westbank BC V4T 2H9
Tel: 250-768-3378; Fax: 250-768-3465
Toll-Free: 866-768-3378
chamber@westbankchamber.com
www.westbankchamber.com
Broc Braconnier, President
Leah Thordarson, Manager

Whistler Chamber of Commerce
#201, 4230 Gateway Dr., Whistler BC V0N 1B4
Tel: 604-932-5922; Fax: 604-932-3755
chamber@whistlerchamber.com
www.whistlerchamber.com
Dave Davenport, Chair
Fiona Famulak, President

White Rock & South Surrey Chamber of Commerce
#101, 2430 King George Hwy., Surrey BC V4B 1H5
Tel: 604-536-6844; Fax: 604-536-4994
info@whiterockchamber.com
www.whiterockchamber.com
Affiliation(s): BC Tourism
Dan Higgins, President

Williams Lake & District Chamber of Commerce
1660 Broadway South, Williams Lake BC V2G 2W4
Tel: 250-392-5025; Fax: 250-392-4214
Toll-Free: 877-967-5253
info@williamslakechamber.com
www.williamslakechamber.com
Affiliation(s): BC Chamber of Commerce; Canadian Chamber of Commerce; Cariboo Chilcotin Coast Tourism Association
Roger Solly, President
Claudia Blair, Executive Director

Zeballos Board of Trade
PO Box 208, Zeballos BC V0P 2A0
Tel: 250-761-4261; Fax: 250-761-4188
boardoftrade@zeballos.com
www.zeballos.com
Tom Weston, President
Debra Brown, Secretary

Manitoba

Altona & District Chamber of Commerce
PO Box 329, Altona MB R0G 0B0
Tel: 204-324-8793; Fax: 204-324-1314
chamber@shopaltona.com
www.shopaltona.com
Vic Loewen, President
Susan Yakabowich, Manager

Arborg Chamber of Commerce
PO Box 415, Arborg MB R0C 0A0
Tel: 204-376-2878; Fax: 204-376-2999
Lorne Floyd, President

Ashern & District Chamber of Commerce
PO Box 582, Ashern MB R0C 0E0
Tel: 204-768-2634; Fax: 204-768-2088
info@ashern.ca
www.ashern.ca
Glen Noordenbos, President

Assiniboia Chamber of Commerce (MB) (ACC)
PO Box 42122, Stn. Ferry Road, 1867 Portage Ave., Winnipeg MB R3J 3X7
Tel: 204-774-4154; Fax: 204-774-4201
info@assiniboiacc.mb.ca
www.assiniboiacc.mb.ca
Ernie Nairn, Executive Director
Gerry Glatz, Chair
Pierre Morier, 1st Vice-Chair
Bruce MacKay, 2nd Vice-Chair
Del Halliday, Treasurer

Beausejour & District Chamber of Commerce
PO Box 224, Beausejour MB R0E 0C0
Tel: 204-268-3502; Fax: 204-268-3502
chamber@mybeausejour.com
mybeausejour.com/chamber/index.php
Carol Boychuk, Executive Director
Ken Zirk, President

Birtle & District Chamber of Commerce
PO Box 278, Birtle MB R0M 0C0
Tel: 204-842-3944
Alan Wong, Secretary
Steve Desjardins, President

Blue Water Chamber of Commerce
PO Box 11, St Georges MB R0E 1V0
Tel: 204-367-2762
Edward A Gaffray, President

Boissevain & District Chamber of Commerce
PO Box 734, Boissevain MB R0K 0E0
Tel: 204-534-6300; Fax: 204-534-6825
Ivan E.J. Strain, President
Donna Frasersik, Secretary

Brandon Chamber of Commerce
1043 Rosser Ave., Brandon MB R7A 0L5
Tel: 204-571-5340; Fax: 204-571-5347
Randy Brown, President
Marnie McGregor, General Manager

Carberry & District Chamber of Commerce
PO Box 101, Carberry MB R0K 0H0
Tel: 204-834-6616
edo@townofcarberry.ca
Christinia Steen, President
Lori Scott, Secretary

Carman & Community Chamber of Commerce
PO Box 249, Carman MB R0G 0J0
Tel: 204-750-3050
ccchamber@gmail.com
www.carmanchamberofcommerce.com
Affiliation(s): Manitoba Chamber of Commerce
Heidi Sandulak, President
Jim Hay, Secretary

Chambre de commerce de Notre Dame
PO Box 107, Notre Dame de Lourdes MB R0G 1M0
Tel: 204-248-2582; Fax: 204-248-2731
Denis Collet, President
Joey Dupasquler, Secretary

La chambre de commerce de Saint-Malo & District
CP 328, Saint-Malo MB R0A 1T0
Joël Fouasse, Co-président
Gilles Maynard, Co-président

Chambre de commerce francophone de Saint-Boniface (CCFSB) / St-Boniface chamber of Commerce
CP 204, #212, 383, boul. Provencher, Saint-Boniface MB R2H 3B4
Tél: 204-235-1406; Téléc: 204-233-1017
info@ccfsb.mb.ca
www.ccfsb.mb.ca
Alain Laurencelle, Président

Churchill Chamber of Commerce
PO Box 176, Churchill MB R0B 0E0
Tel: 204-675-2022; Toll-Free: 888-389-2327
churchillchamber@mts.net
www.churchill.ca/chamber-of-commerce/
David Daley, President
Patricia Penwarden, Secretary

Crystal City & District Chamber of Commerce
PO Box 56, Crystal City MB R0K 0N0
Tel: 204-873-2523; Fax: 204-873-2456
chamberofcommerce@crystalcitymb.ca
Sean Brooks, President
Keri Stevenson, Secretary

Cypress River Chamber of Commerce
PO Box 261, Cypress River MB R0K 0P0
Tel: 204-743-2119; Fax: 204-743-2339
www.cypressriver.ca
Jim Cassels, President

Dauphin & District Chamber of Commerce
101 - 1st Ave. NW, #B, Dauphin MB R7N 1G8
Tel: 204-622-3140; Fax: 204-622-3141
dauphinchamber@mts.net
Jason Yates, President

Deloraine & District Chamber of Commerce
PO Box 748, Deloraine MB R0M 0M0
Tel: 204-747-2842; Fax: 204-747-2856
Deb Calverley, President
Grant Cassils, Contact

Elie Chamber of Commerce
PO Box 175, Elie MB R0H 0H0
Tel: 204-353-2892; Fax: 204-353-2336
Maggy Leitgeb, Sec.-Treas.
Rick Desilets, President

Elkhorn Chamber of Commerce
PO Box 141, Elkhorn MB R0M 0N0
Tel: 204-845-2388; Fax: 204-845-2073
Kelly Martin, Secretary
Sharlean Bickerton, President

Eriksdale & District Chamber of Commerce
PO Box 434, Eriksdale MB R0C 0W0
Tel: 204-739-2641
www.eriksdale.com
Phyllis Lamb, Secretary
Cindy Kinkead, President

Falcon/West Hawk Lakes Chamber of Commerce (FWHLCC)
PO Box 187, Falcon Beach MB R0E 0N0
Tel: 204-349-3134; Fax: 204-349-3134
info@chamber-southwhiteshell.ca
www.chamber-southwhiteshell.ca
Affiliation(s): Canadian Chamber of Commerce
Bob Harbottle, President

Fisher Branch Chamber of Commerce
PO Box 566, Fisher Branch MB R0C 0Z0
Tel: 204-372-6034; Fax: 204-372-8545
fisher01@mts.net
Darcy Plett, President

Flin Flon & District Chamber of Commerce
#228, 35 Main St., Flin Flon MB R8A 1J7
Tel: 204-687-4518; Fax: 204-687-4456
flinflonchamber@mts.net
www.cityofflinflon.com/chamber
Randy Buie, President
Doug O'Brien, Secretary

Gilbert Plains & District Chamber of Commerce
PO Box 670, Gilbert Plains MB R0L 0X0
Tel: 204-548-2682; Fax: 204-548-2682
Brenda Kerns, President

Gillam Chamber of Commerce
PO Box 366, Gillam MB R0B 0L0
Tel: 204-652-5135; Fax: 204-652-5155
John Cullen, President

Grahamdale Chamber of Commerce
R.M. Of Grahamdale Administration Office, PO Box 160, 23 Government Rd., Moosehorn MB R0C 2E0
Tel: 204-768-2858; Fax: 204-768-3374
info@grahamdale.ca
www.grahamdale.ca
Karen Bittner, President

Grandview & District Chamber of Commerce
PO Box 28, Grandview MB R0L 0Y0
Tel: 204-546-2501
Linda Zazuliak, Secretary
Dennis Lukey, President

Grunthal & District Chamber of Commerce
PO Box 451, Grunthal MB R0A 0R0
Tel: 204-434-6750; Fax: 204-434-9353
leonard@emergencyvehicles.ca
Leonard Hiebert, President

Hamiota Chamber of Commerce
PO Box 403, Hamiota MB R0J 1Z0
Tel: 204-764-2884
info@hamiota.com
www.hamiota.com/business.html
Larry Oakden, President
Bonnie Michaudville, Secretary

Hartney & District Chamber of Commerce
PO Box 224, Hartney MB R0M 0X0
Tel: 204-858-2089; Fax: 204-858-2089
www.hartney.ca
Sharon Evans, Contact
Carol Thomas, President

Headingley Chamber of Commerce
5353 Portage Ave., Headingley MB R4H 1J9
Tel: 204-889-2132; Fax: 204-831-0816
dwhitermofheadingley@mts.net
www.rmofheadingley.ca/business/cofc.asp
Affiliation(s): Central Plains Development Corporation; White Horse Plains Development Corporation; Headingley Heritage Centre
Jill Ruth, President
Dave White, Executive Director

Killarney & District Chamber of Commerce
PO Box 809, Killarney MB R0K 1G0
Tel: 204-523-4202
killarneychamber@hotmail.com
Mark Witherspoon, Chair
Dale Banman, Executive Director

Lac du Bonnet & District Chamber of Commerce
PO Box 598, Lac du Bonnet MB R0E 1A0
Tel: 204-345-8194; Fax: 204-345-8194
kimbuhay@mts.net
www.lacdubonnetchamber.com
Affiliation(s): Manitoba Chambers of Commerce
Donna Tschetter, President
Kim Buhay, Manager

Landmark & Community Chamber of Commerce
PO Box 469, Landmark MB R0A 0X0
Tel: 204-355-5200
info@landmarkonline.ca
www.landmarkonline.ca
Randy Wolgemuth, President

Leaf Rapids Chamber of Commerce
PO Box 26, Leaf Rapids MB R0B 1W0
Tel: 204-473-2491; Fax: 204-473-2284
franklhd@mts.net
www.townofleafrapids.ca
Vince Cmela, Secretary

Lundar Chamber of Commerce
PO Box 26, Lundar MB R0C 1Y0
Tel: 204-762-5611; Fax: 204-762-5551
Faye Goranson, President

MacGregor Chamber of Commerce
PO Box 685, MacGregor MB R0H 0R0
Tel: 204-685-2862; Fax: 204-685-2631
www.macgregorchamber.com

Melita & District Chamber of Commerce
PO Box 666, Melita MB R0M 1L0
Tel: 204-522-3285; Fax: 204-522-3536
ccagenci@mts.net
Murray Cameron, President

Minnedosa Chamber of Commerce
PO Box 857, Minnedosa MB R0J 1E0
Tel: 204-867-2951; Fax: 204-867-3641
chamber@minnedosachamber.ca
www.minnedosachamber.ca
Don Farr, President
Callie Mashtoler, Secretary

Morden Chamber of Commerce
311 North Railway St., Morden MB R6M 1S9
Tel: 204-822-5630; Fax: 204-822-2041
www.mordenchamber.com
Cheryl Link, Manager
Carol Fehr, President

Morris & District Chamber of Commerce
PO Box 98, Morris MB R0G 1K0
Tel: 204-746-6275; Fax: 204-746-6953
Pat Eidse, President
Barbara Wiebe, Secretary

Neepawa & District Chamber of Commerce
PO Box 726, 282 Hamilton St., Neepawa MB R0J 1H0
Tel: 204-476-5292; Fax: 204-476-5231
Toll-Free: 877-633-7292
info@neepawachamber.com
www.neepawachamber.com
Dean Dietrich Vice, President
Michelle Gerrard, President

Niverville Chamber of Commerce
PO Box 157, Niverville MB R0A 1E0
Tel: 204-388-4325
chamber@niverville.com
www.niverville.com
Debbie Pearson, President
Jeannine Funk, Contact

North Interlake Chamber of Commerce
PO Box 160, 23 Government Rd., Moosehorn MB R0C 2E0
Tel: 204-768-2858; Fax: 204-768-3374
rm606@tcmsnet.com
www.grahamdale.ca
Gayle James, President
Carol Thurman, Secretary

Oakville & District Chamber of Commerce
PO Box 263, Oakville MB R0H 0Y0
Tel: 204-267-2048; Fax: 204-267-7015
bingram@mts.net
Kam Blight, President
Barb Ingram, Contact

Pansy & District United Chamber of Commerce
PO Box 34, Pansy MB R0A 1J0
Tel: 204-425-3530; Fax: 204-425-3530
Theresa Narth, Secretary
Michael Narth, President

The Pas & District Chamber of Commerce
PO Box 996, The Pas MB R9A 1L1
Tel: 204-623-7256; Fax: 204-623-2589
tpinfo@mts.net
www.thepaschamber.com
Debbie Doucette, President

Pilot Mound & District Chamber of Commerce
PO Box 356, Pilot Mound MB R0G 1P0
Tel: 204-825-2587
chamberofcommerce@pilotmound.com
www.pilotmound.com
Jill Lints, Sec.-Treas.
Carolanne Bayne, President

Pinawa Chamber of Commerce
PO Box 544, Pinawa MB R0E 1L0
Tel: 204-753-2747
chamber@granite.mb.ca
www.pinawachamber.com
Rhonda Henschell, Secretary
Marsha Sheppard, President

Piney & District Chamber of Commerce
PO Box 50, Sprague MB R0A 1Z0
Tel: 204-437-2259; Fax: 204-437-2561
Dennis Konchak, President

Plum Coulee & District Chamber of Commerce
PO Box 392, Plum Coulee MB R0G 1R0
Tel: 204-829-3419; Fax: 204-829-3436
wanderer@mts.net
June Letkeman, Secretary
June Alvinklassen, President

Portage & District Chamber of Commerce
11 - 2nd St. NE, Portage la Prairie MB R1N 1R8
Tel: 204-857-7778; Fax: 204-857-4095
info@portagechamber.com
www.portagechamber.com
Affiliation(s): Canadian Chamber of Commerce
Brent Budz, President

Rivers & District Chamber of Commerce
PO Box 795, Rivers MB R0K 1X0
Tel: 204-328-7316; Fax: 204-328-4460
mbeever@mts.net
Marlin Beener, President
Jean Young, Manager

Riverton & District Chamber of Commerce
PO Box 258, Riverton MB R0C 2R0
Tel: 204-378-2084; Fax: 204-378-2085
berniced@mts.net
www.rivertoncanada.com
Bernice Danielson, President
Karen Donnellan-Fisher, Contact

Roblin & District Chamber of Commerce
PO Box 160, Roblin MB R0L 1P0
Tel: 204-937-3194
rdcoc@mts.net
www.roblinmanitoba.com
Colin Knight, President

Rossburn & District Chamber of Commerce
PO Box 579, Rossburn MB R0J 1V0
Tel: 204-859-3334; Fax: 204-859-3313
wheatland@mts.net
Raymond Lysyshin, President
Val White, Secretary
Terence Waychyshin, First Vice President

Russell & District Chamber of Commerce
PO Box 155, Russell MB R0J 1W0
Tel: 204-773-2456
www.russellmb.com/chamber.html
Brent Havelange, President

St. Pierre Chamber of Commerce
PO Box 71, St Pierre Jolys MB R0A 1V0
Tel: 204-433-7123; Fax: 204-433-3135
st-pierre-jolys@mts.net
Sherry Stasiuk, Secretary
Luc Catellier, President

La Salle & District Chamber of Commerce
PO Box 608, La Salle MB R0G 1B0
Tel: 204-736-4555; Fax: 204-736-4363
Donna Bell, President
Ray Cormier, Treasurer

Selkirk & District Chamber of Commerce
100 Eaton Ave., Selkirk MB R1A 0W6
Tel: 204-482-7176; Fax: 204-482-5448
info@selkirkanddistrictchamber.ca
www.selkirkanddistrictchamber.ca
Kelly Lewis, President
Bev Clegg, Executive Director

Shoal Lake & District Chamber of Commerce
PO Box 547, Shoal Lake MB R0J 1Z0
Tel: 204-759-3343; Fax: 204-759-2740
nsims@simsco.mb.ca
Tara Patterson, Contact
Norman Sims, President

Somerset & District Chamber of Commerce
PO Box 353, Somerset MB R0G 2L0
Tel: 204-744-2088; Fax: 204-744-2153
Affiliation(s): Manitoba Chamber of Commerce
Jean Poiron, President
Bessette

Souris & Glenwood Chamber of Commerce
PO Box 939, Souris MB R0K 2C0
Tel: 204-483-3127; Fax: 204-483-2777
robbin2@mts.net
Affiliation(s): Manitoba Chamber of Commerce
Sande Denbow, Contact
Colleen Robbins, President

Ste Rose & District Chamber of Commerce
PO Box 688, Ste Rose du Lac MB R0L 1S0
Tel: 204-447-2196; Fax: 204-447-2692
storestarter@yahoo.ca
Trevor Gates, President
Monica Lambourne, Contact

Steinbach Chamber of Commerce
PO Box 1795, 225 Reimer Ave., Steinbach MB R5G 1N4
Tel: 204-326-9566; Fax: 204-346-6600
stbcofc@mts.net
www.steinbachchamberofcommerce.com
Paul Neustaedter, President

Stonewall & District Chamber of Commerce
PO Box 762, Stonewall MB R0C 2Z0
Tel: 204-467-8377
info@stonewallchamber.com
www.stonewallchamber.com
Don Lischka, President
Ryan Smith, Treasurer

Swan River Chamber of Commerce
PO Box 1540, Swan River MB R0L 1Z0
Tel: 204-734-3102; Fax: 204-734-4342
srcc@svcn.mb.ca
Naomi Neufeld, President

Teulon Chamber of Commerce
PO Box 235, Teulon MB R0C 3B0
Tel: 204-294-6171; Fax: 204-886-3232
president@teulonchamber.ca
Michael Ledarney, President
Debra Osbak, Secretary

Thompson Chamber of Commerce
PO Box 363, Thompson MB R8N 1N2
Tel: 204-677-4155; Fax: 204-677-3434
Toll-Free: 888-307-0103
commerce@mts.net
www.thompson.ca
Louise Hodder, President (Interim)

Treherne Chamber of Commerce
PO Box 344, Treherne MB R0G 2V0
Tel: 204-723-2774; Fax: 204-723-2719
Keith Sparling, President

Virden & District Chamber of Commerce
PO Box 899, 425 - 6th Ave. South, Virden MB R0M 2C0
Tel: 204-748-3955; Fax: 204-748-3467
virdencc@mts.net
Affiliation(s): Virden Wallace Community Development Corp.; Virden Employment Skills Centre Inc., Virden Agricultural Society; Virden Indoor Rodeo
Deke Baley, President

Wasagaming Chamber of Commerce
PO Box 222, 110 Wasagaming Dr., Wasagaming MB R0J 2H0
Tel: 204-848-2742; Fax: 204-848-7712
info@discoverclearlake.com
www.discoverclearlake.com
Debb Geiler, President
Wayne Zachedniak, Treasurer

Winkler & District Chamber of Commerce
185 Main St., Winkler MB R6W 1B4
Tel: 204-325-9758; Fax: 204-325-8290
chamber@winkleronline.com
www.winklerchamber.com
Kenneth Thomas, President
Myrna Hildebrand, Vice-President
Brenda Storey, Executive Director
Dianne Frieson, Manager

Winnipeg Chamber of Commerce (WCC) / Chambre de commerce de Winnipeg
#100, 259 Portage Ave., Winnipeg MB R3B 2A9
Tel: 204-944-8484; Fax: 204-944-8492
info@winnipeg-chamber.com
www.winnipeg-chamber.com
Social Media: www.youtube.com/wpgchamber
David Angus, President & Chief Executive Officer
Chuck Davidson, Vice-President, Policy
Karen Weiss, Vice-President, Finance & Operations
Christine Ens, Director, Membership & Marketing
Wendy Stephenson, Director, Strategic Initiatives
Stacia Franz, Coordinator, Communications
Marion Wong, Coordinator, Information

New Brunswick

Albert County Chamber of Commerce
PO Box 3051, Hillsborough NB E4H 4W5
Tel: 506-389-6002; Fax: 506-387-8331
kpower@nb.sympatico.ca
Brian Keirstead, President
Phyllis Sutherland, Secretary

Atlantic Provinces Chambers of Commerce (APCC) / Chambres de commerce des provinces de l'Atlantique
#240, 1273 Main St., Moncton NB E1C 0P4
Tel: 506-857-3980; Fax: 506-859-6131
grace@apcc.ca
www.apcc.ca
Bill Denyar, President & CEO
Valerie Roy, Vice President, Chamber and Member Services

Bath Chamber of Commerce
163A Church St., Bath NB E7J 1A7
Tel: 506-278-5213; Fax: 506-278-5963
Michael Blanchard, President
Keith Sipprell, Secretary

Bouctouche Chamber of Commerce / Chambre de commerce de Bouctouche
PO Box 338, #301, 59, boul Irving, Bouctouche NB E4S 3J6
Tel: 506-743-2411; Fax: 506-743-8991
chambouc@mon.auracom.com
Claude LeBlanc, President
Carole Léger, Staff

Campbellton Regional Chamber of Commerce / Chambre de commerce régional de Campbellton
PO Box 236, 18 Water St., Campbellton NB E3N 3G4
Tel: 506-759-7856; Fax: 506-759-7557
crcc@nbnet.nb.ca
www.campbelltonregionalchamber.ca
Affiliation(s): NB Chamber of Commerce; Atlantic Chamber of Commerce
Ginette Archambault, Secretary
Colleen Donnahee, Executive Director
Greg Davis, President

Central Carleton Chamber of Commerce
28 Palmer Rd., Waterville NB E7P 1B4
Tel: 506-375-4074
Dale Albright, President

Centreville Chamber of Commerce
PO Box 628, Centreville NB E7K 3H5
Tel: 506-276-4241; Fax: 506-276-9891
centreville.chamber@aernet.ca
Kathy Simonson, Staff
Raymond Carmichael, President

Chambre de commerce de Clair
PO Box 1025, Clair NB E7A 2J5
Tel: 506-992-6030; Fax: 506-992-6041
info@chambrecommerceclair.com
www.chambrecommerceclair.com
Marie-Josée Michaud, Présidente

Chambre de commerce de Cocagne, Notre-Dame et Grande-Digue
CP 1090, Cocagne NB E4R 1N6
Tél: 506-576-6005; Téléc: 506-576-6073
Gilles Allain, Président

Chambre de commerce de Collette
60, rue des Arbres, Collette NB E4Y 1G4
Tél: 506-622-0752; Téléc: 506-622-0477
Maurice Desroches, Président

Chambre de commerce de Kent Centre Chamber of Commerce
#2, 9235 Main St., Richibucto NB E4W 4C6
Tel: 506-523-1443; Fax: 506-523-6520
kccc@richibucto.org
Richard Thébeau, Président

Chambre de commerce de la région d'Edmundston
1, ch Canada, Edmundston NB E3V 1T6
Tél: 506-737-1866; Téléc: 506-737-1862
info@ccedmundston.com
www.ccedmundston.com
Affiliation(s): Chambre de commerce du Nouveau-Brunswick; Chambre de commerce des Provinces Atlantiques; Chambre de commerce du Canada; Chambre de commerce Internationale
Lise Couturier, Présidente

Chambre de commerce de la region de Cap-Pelé
CP 1219, Cap-Pelé NB E4N 3B1
Tél: 506-577-4560; Téléc: 506-577-8900
Marcel Doiron, Président
Stéphane Dallaire, Secrétaire

Chambre de commerce de Rogersville / Rogersville Chamber of Commerce
#5, 11101, rue Principale, Rogersville NB E4Y 2N2
Tél: 506-775-9378; Téléc: 506-775-1906
Lisa LeBlanc, Secrétaire

Yvon Doiron, Président

Chambre de Commerce de Saint Louis de Kent
#A, 83A Beauséjour, Saint-Louis-de-Kent NB E4X 1A6
Tel: 506-876-3475; Fax: 506-876-3477
René Côté, Présidente
Daniel Comeau, Secrétaire

Chambre de commerce de Saint-François
CP 378, Saint-François-de-Madawaska NB E7A 1G4
Tél: 506-992-6067; Téléc: 506-992-6049
cdecsf@nb.aibn.com
www.nbchamber.ca
Chantal Landry, Secrétaire
Luc L. Nadeau, Président

Chambre de commerce de Saint-Quentin Inc.
144D, rue Canada, Saint-Quentin NB E8A 1G7
Tél: 506-235-3666; Téléc: 506-235-1804
n6chcomm@nb.aibn.com
www.saintquentin.nb.ca
Jean-Guy R. Michaud, Président
Joyce Somers, Secrétaire

Chambre de commerce de Shippagan inc.
227, boul J.D. Gauthier, Shippagan NB E8S 3H1
Tél: 506-336-2207
chambredecommerce@shippagan.com
Donald Hachey, Président

Chambre de commerce des Iles Lamèque et Miscou inc.
CP 2075, Lamèque NB E8T 3N5
Tél: 506-344-7148
www.lameque.ca
Réginald Paulin, Président

Chambre de commerce du Grand Caraquet Inc
#214, 220, boul St-Pierre ouest, Caraquet NB E1W 1B7
Tél: 506-727-2931; Téléc: 506-727-3191
chambre@nb.aira.com
www.acadie.net
Monique Godin, Présidente
Aline Landry, Directrice générale

Chambre de commerce du Rivière-du-Portage
5898B, RR#11, Rivière-du-Portage NB E9H 1X2
Tél: 506-393-1902
jetta@nbnet.nb.ca
www.nbchamber.ca
Claude G. Savoie, Président
Alice Thibodeau, Secrétaire

Chipman Chamber of Commerce
237 Main St., Chipman NB E4E 1E5
Tel: 506-339-1821; Fax: 506-339-1823
Brian Harris, Chairman-Elect

East Restigouche Chamber of Commerce
389 Adelaide St., Dalhousie NB E8C 1B5
Tel: 506-684-5571; Fax: 506-684-4717
Paul Hayes, President

Eastern Charlotte Chamber of Commerce
#2, 21 Main St., St George NB E5C 3H9
Tel: 506-456-3951
eccc@nbnet.nb.ca
Wanda MacLean, President
Irene Wright, Secretary

Florenceville Chamber of Commerce
PO Box 601, Florenceville NB E7L 1Y7
Tel: 506-392-0900; Fax: 506-392-0900
Scott Greer, Treasurer

Fredericton Chamber of Commerce / La Chambre de Commerce de Fredericton
PO Box 275, 270 Rookwood Ave., Fredericton NB E3B 4Y9
Tel: 506-458-8006; Fax: 506-451-1119
fchamber@frederictonchamber.ca
www.frederictonchamber.ca
Andrew Steeves, President
Jennifer English, Coordinator, Research & Communications

Gagetown & Area Chamber of Commerce
76 Babbit St., Gagetown NB E5M 1C8
Tel: 506-488-3281
Nancy MacQuade, President

Grand Falls/Grand Sault & District Chamber of Commerce
#300, 81 Burgess Street, Grand Falls NB E3Y 1C6
Tel: 506-473-1905; Fax: 506-475-7755
gfcocgs@nbnet.nb.ca
Côme Ouellette, President
Linda N. Martin, Staff

Grand Manan Chamber of Commerce
1141 Rte. 776, Grand Manan NB E5G 4K9
Tel: 506-662-3442; Fax: 506-662-3593
Toll-Free: 888-525-1655
info@grandmanannb.com
www.grandmanannb.com
Joan Gallant, Staff
Theresa McFarland, President

Greater Bathurst Chamber of Commerce / Chambre de commerce du Grand Bathurst
CEI Bldg., 725 College St., Bathurst NB E2A 4B9
Tel: 506-548-8498; Fax: 506-548-2200
info@bathurstchamber.ca
www.bathurstchamber.ca
Affiliation(s): Canadian Chamber of Commerce
Danielle Gaudet, General Manager
Vilma Glidden, President
Gilles Deveaux, Treasurer

Greater Hillsborough Chamber of Commerce
PO Box 3051, Hillsborough NB E4H 4W5
Tel: 506-734-2851; Fax: 506-734-2244
Carole Coleman, Director

Greater Miramichi Chamber of Commerce
PO Box 342, Miramichi NB E1N 3A7
Tel: 506-622-5522; Fax: 506-622-5959
mirchamber@nb.aibn.com
www.miramichichamber.com
Véronique Arsenault, Executive Director
Dorothy Innes, President

Greater Moncton Chamber of Commerce (GMCC) / Chambre de commerce du Grand Moncton
#200, 1273 Main St., Moncton NB E1C 0P4
Tel: 506-857-2883; Fax: 506-857-9209
info@gmcc.nb.ca
www.gmcc.nb.ca
Valerie Roy, CEO
André Pelletier, Chair
Norm Raynard, Sec.-Treas.

Greater Sackville Chamber of Commerce
#87, 8 Main St., Sackville NB E4L 4A9
Tel: 506-364-8911; Fax: 506-364-8082
gscc@nbnet.nb.ca
www.sackvillechamber.ca
Rebecca Maclean, Staff
Lisa Smith, President
Wayne Harper, Secretary

Greater Woodstock Chamber of Commerce
#2, 220 King St., Woodstock NB E7M 1Z8
Tel: 506-325-9049; Fax: 506-328-4683
woodstockchamberofcommerce@nb.aibn.com
www.town.woodstock.nb.ca
Peter Clark, Contact
Jeanne Langille, President

Hampton Area Chamber of Commerce (HACC)
PO Box 1829, #2, 17 Centennial Rd., Hampton NB E5N 6N3
Tel: 506-832-2559; Fax: 506-832-2559
hacc@nbnet.nb.ca
www.hamptonareachamber.org
Paige Banasik, President
Gail Kilpatrick, Secretary

Kennebecasis Valley Chamber of Commerce
PO Box 4455, #8, 53C Clark Rd., Rothesay NB E2E 5X2
Tel: 506-849-2860; Fax: 506-847-0996
admin@kvbusiness.com
www.kvbusiness.com
Phil Brodersen, President
Scott Cochrane, Secretary-Treasurer
Ann-Marie O'Neill, Administrator

Mactaquac County Chamber of Commerce
PO Box 1163, Nackawic NB E6G 2N1
Tel: 506-575-9622; Fax: 506-575-2035
mccc@mactaquaccountry.com
www.mactaquaccountry.com
Melanie Sloat, President
Dora Boudreau, Secretary

Oromocto & Area Chamber of Commerce
Oromocto Mall, PO Box 20124, Oromocto NB E2V 2R6
Tel: 506-446-6043; Fax: 506-446-6925
oromotcochamber@nb.aibn.com
www.oromoctochamber.nb.ca
Lloyd Chamber, President

Perth-Andover & Area Chamber of Commerce
11640 Route 105, Kilburn NB E7H 4W3
Tel: 506-273-6375; Fax: 506-273-6915
Jeff Walters-Gray, President
Elizabeth Davenport, Secretary

River Valley Chamber of Commerce (RVCC)
PO Box 3123, Grand Bay-Westfield NB E5K 4V4
Tel: 506-738-8666; Fax: 506-738-3697
Randy Bell, Secretary
Diane Bormke, President

St. Andrews Chamber of Commerce
46 Reed Ave., St Andrews NB E5B 1A1
Tel: 506-529-3555; Fax: 506-529-8095
stachamb@nbnet.nb.ca
www.standrewsby-the-sea.ca
Dave Bennett, President
Julie Crichton, Executive Director

St. Martins & District Chamber of Commerce
229 Main St., St Martins NB E5R 1B7
Tel: 506-833-2019; Fax: 506-833-2028
fundytp@nbnet.nb.ca
Bruce Huttges, President
Brian Clark, Secretary

St. Stephen Area Chamber of Commerce
PO Box 457, 34 Milltown Blvd., St Stephen NB E3L 2X3
Tel: 506-466-7703; Fax: 506-466-7753
chamber.ststephen@nb.aibn.com
www.town.ststephen.nb.ca
Affiliation(s): Atlantic Chamber of Commerce; Canadian Chamber of Commerce
Diedre Rideout, President
Mary Gilmore, Staff

Sussex & District Chamber of Commerce
PO Box 5152, 66 Broad St., Sussex NB E4E 5L2
Tel: 506-433-1845; Fax: 506-433-1886
sdcc@nbnet.nb.ca
sdccinc.org
Affiliation(s): Atlantic Provinces Chambers of Commerce
Christine Philion, Administrative Officer
Kandy Mitton, President

Washademoak Region Chamber of Commerce
3359 Lower Cambridge, Cambridge-Narrows NB E4C 4P9
Tel: 506-488-2517; Fax: 506-488-2622
www.w-rcc.ca/frameset.html
Tom Nisbet, President
Hertha Gebhardt, Vice-President

Newfoundland and Labrador

Argentia Area Chamber of Commerce
PO Box 109, 1 O'Reilly St., Placentia NL A0B 2Y0
Tel: 709-227-0003; Fax: 709-227-0016
info@argentiachamber.org
www.argentiachamber.org
Gerry Hynes, President
Frank Collins, Director

Arnolds Cove Area Chamber of Commerce
PO Box 411, Arnolds Cove NL A0B 1A0
Tel: 709-472-4151; Fax: 709-472-4182
Gloria Warren-Slade, President
Germaine Lynch, Treasurer

Baie Verte & Area Chamber of Commerce
PO Box 578, Baie Verte NL A0K 1B0
Tel: 709-532-4204; Fax: 709-532-4252
bvachamber@nf.aibn.com
www.bvachamber.com
Shannon Lewis, President

Bay St. George Chamber of Commerce
35 Carolina Ave., Stephenville NL A2N 3P8
Tel: 709-643-5854; Fax: 709-643-6398
bsgcoc@wec-center.nl.ca
www.bsgcc.org
Sheila Hawco, Executive Director
Cynthia Downey, President

Bonavista Area Chamber of Commerce (BACC)
PO Box 280, Bonavista NL A0C 1B0
Fax: 709-468-2495
info@bacc.ca
www.bacc.ca
Diane Thorpe, Secretary

Channel Port Aux Basques Chamber of Commerce
PO Box 1389, Channel-Port-aux-Basques NL A0M 1C0
Tel: 709-695-3688; Fax: 709-695-7925
pabchamber@thezone.net
www.pabchamber.com
Gary O'Brien, Secretary
Terry Anderson, President

Clarenville Area Chamber of Commerce
292A Memorial Dr., Clarenville NL A5A 1P1
Tel: 709-466-5800; Fax: 709-466-5803
Toll-Free: 866-466-5800
info@clarenvillechamber.net
www.clarenvilleareachamber.net
Bill Farrell, President
Michelle Frye, Office Manager

Conception Bay Area Chamber of Commerce
#3, 702 Conception Bay Hwy., Conception Bay South NL A1X 3A5
Tel: 709-834-5670; Fax: 709-834-5760
info@cbachamber.com
www.cbachamber.com
Glenda Noseworthy, Managing Director
Brenda Hollohan, Secretary
David Murphy, President

Deer Lake Chamber of Commerce
6 Cresent St., Deer Lake NL A8A 1H6
Tel: 709-635-3260; Fax: 709-635-5857
s-goulding@warp.nfld.net
Affiliation(s): Newfoundland Chambers of Commerce
Todd Lee, Treasurer
Susan Goulding, Executive Director
Jim Goudie, President

Exploits Regional Chamber of Commerce
PO Box 272, 16 High St., Grand Falls-Windsor NL A2A 2J7
Tel: 709-489-7512; Fax: 709-489-7532
info@exploitschamber.com
www.exploitschamber.com
Jason Thistle, President
Ron Aucoin, Executive Director

Gander & Area Chamber of Commerce (GACC)
109 Trans Canada Hwy., Gander NL A1V 1P6
Tel: 709-256-7110; Fax: 709-256-4080
ganderchamber@ganderchamber.nf.ca
www.ganderchamber.nf.ca
Hazel Bishop, Executive Director
Pat Kearney, President

Greater Corner Brook Board of Trade
PO Box 475, 11 Confederation Dr., Corner Brook NL A2H 6E6
Tel: 709-634-5831; Fax: 709-639-9710
cbcc@thezone.net
www.gcbbt.com
Charlene Woodford, Executive Director

Irish Loop Chamber of Commerce
PO Box 6, Trepassey NL A0A 4B0
Tel: 709-432-2662; Fax: 709-438-2892
Cathy Perry, President

Labrador North Chamber of Commerce (LNCC)
PO Box 460, Stn. B, 169 Hamilton River Rd., Happy Valley-Goose Bay NL A0P 1E0
Tel: 709-896-8787; Fax: 709-896-0585
Toll-Free: 877-920-8787
admin@chamberlabrador.com
www.chamberlabrador.com
Sterling Peyton, President
Brian Fowlow, Contact

Labrador South East Chamber of Commerce
PO Box 65, Port Hope Simpson NL A0K 4E0
Tel: 709-960-0510
bfgillis@nf.sympatico.ca
Blair Gillis, President
Sharon Penney, Secretary

Labrador Straits Chamber of Commerce
PO Box 179, Forteau NL A0K 2P0
Tel: 709-931-2073; Fax: 709-931-2073
chamber@labradorstraits.net
Kinza Trimm, Executive Director

Labrador West Chamber of Commerce
PO Box 273, Labrador City NL A2V 2K5
Tel: 709-944-3723; Fax: 709-944-4699
lwc@crrstv.net
www.labradorwestchamber.ca
Patsy Ralph, Business Manager

Lewisporte & Area Chamber of Commerce
PO Box 953, Lewisporte NL A0G 3A0
Tel: 709-535-2500; Fax: 709-535-2482
lacc@superweb.ca
Cynthia Aylward, Executive Assistant

Marystown-Burin Area Chamber of Commerce
PO Box 728, Marystown NL A0E 2M0
Tel: 709-279-2080; Fax: 709-279-4492
chamber@mbacc.nf.ca
www.marystownburinchamber.com
Mike Graham, President
Kelly Pardy, Executive Director

Mount Pearl Chamber of Commerce
39 Commonwealth Ave., Mount Pearl NL A1N 1W7
Tel: 709-364-8513; Fax: 709-364-8500
info@mtpearlchamber.com
www.mtpearlchamber.com
Michelle Batterson, Executive Director

Pasadena Chamber of Commerce
c/o The Venture Centre, PO Box 149, Pasadena NL A0L 1K0
Tel: 709-686-2078; Fax: 709-686-2081
Derrick Anthony, President

St Anthony & Area Chamber of Commerce
PO Box 650, St Anthony NL A0K 4S0
Tel: 709-454-8898
stanthonyandareachamber@yahoo.ca
Kaye Strickland, Coordinator
Marshall Dean, President

Springdale & Area Chamber of Commerce
PO Box 37, 151 Main St., Springdale NL A0J 1T0
Tel: 709-673-3837; Fax: 709-673-3897
seabrightfinancial@aibn.com
Cyril Pelley, President
Glenn Seabright, Secretary

Straits-St. Barbe Chamber of Commerce
PO Box 119, Flowers Cove NL A0K 2N0
Tel: 709-456-2592; Fax: 709-456-2592
straitsstbarbe@nf.aibn.com
Maggie Chambers, Secretary
Donna Doyle, President

Northwest Territories

Baffin Regional Chamber of Commerce (BRCC)
Igluvut Bldg., 2nd Fl., PO Box 59, Iqaluit NU X0A 0H0
Tel: 867-979-4656; Fax: 867-979-2929
www.baffinchamber.ca
Hal Timar, Executive Director
Chris West, President
Frank May, Sec.-Treas.

Iqaluit Chamber of Commerce
PO Box 1107, Iqaluit NU X0A 0H0
Tel: 867-979-4095
board@icoc.nu.ca
www.icoc.nu.ca
David Fulgham, 2nd Vice-President

Kivalliq Chamber of Commerce
PO Box 147, Rankin Inlet NU X0C 0G0
Tel: 867-645-2718; Fax: 867-645-2483
krmanson@arctic.ca
Ellie Camsill, President

Kugluktuk Chamber of Commerce
PO Box 307, Kugluktuk NU X0B 0E0
Tel: 867-982-3232; Fax: 867-982-3229
coptours@polarnet.ca
Rachel Horn, President
Ruth Palmer, Office Manager

Nova Scotia

Amherst & Area Chamber of Commerce
PO Box 283, Amherst NS B4H 3Z4
Tel: 902-667-8186; Fax: 902-667-2270
info@amherstchamber.ca
www.amherstchamber.ca
David McNarin, President
Debbie Allen, Staff

Antigonish Chamber of Commerce
21B James St., Antigonish NS B2G 1R6
Tel: 902-863-6308; Fax: 902-863-2656
contact@antigonishchamber.com
www.antigonishchamber.com
Daniel Ross, President

Barrington & Area Chamber of Commerce
PO Box 110, Barrington NS B0W 1E0
Tel: 902-637-2625; Fax: 902-637-2075
bcc@auracom.com
Wendy S. McGill, President
Debra Goreham, Staff

Bridgewater & Area Chamber of Commerce
PO Box 100, 200 North St., Bridgewater NS B4V 2W8
Tel: 902-543-4263; Fax: 902-527-1156
bacc@eastlink.ca
www.bridgewaterchamber.com
Ann O'Connell, Executive Director
Sandra Statton, President
Bernice Theriault, Secretary

Brier Island Chamber of Commerce
PO Box 74, Westport NS B0V 1H0
Tel: 902-839-2347; Fax: 902-839-2006
akicita@ns.sympatico.ca
Harold Graham, President
Joan Riday, Secretary

Central Annapolis Valley Chamber of Commerce
PO Box 395, 831 Main St., Kingston NS B0P 1R0
Tel: 902-765-0344; Fax: 902-765-0141
Affiliation(s): World Trade Centre
Kenneth L. Bower, President
Melissa Robinson, Secretary

Chambre de commerce de Clare
CP 35, Pointe-de-l'Église NS B0W 1M0
Tél: 902-645-2368; Téléc: 902-645-2787
chambredecommerce@hotmail.com
www.commercedeclare.ca
Marc Robichaud, Président

Chester Municipal Chamber of Commerce
PO Box 831, #13, 4171 Hwy. 3, Chester NS B0J 1J0
Tel: 902-275-4709
info@chesterns.com
www.chesterns.com
Angela Jessome, Staff
Ben Wiper, President
Jim Barkhouse, Secretary

East Hants & District Chamber of Commerce
PO Box 1053, Lantz NS B2S 3G6
Tel: 902-883-1010; Fax: 902-883-7862
info@ehcc.ca
www.ehcc.ca
Heather Kerr, Manager
Stephen Pottie, President

Eastern Kings Chamber of Commerce (EKCC)
PO Box 314, Kentville NS B4N 3X1
Tel: 902-678-4634; Fax: 902-678-5448
ekccbob@ns.aliantzinc.ca
www.easternkingschamber.ns.ca
Bill Denyar, President
Judy Rafuse, Executive Director

Fort Simpson Chamber of Commerce
PO Box 244, Fort Simpson NT X0E 0N0
Tel: 867-695-3555; Fax: 867-695-3313
commerce@fschamber.biz
www.fschamber.biz
Duncan Canvin, President

Fort Smith Chamber of Commerce
PO Box 121, Fort Smith NT X0E 0P0
Tel: 867-872-4213; Fax: 867-872-9450
Fred Daniels, Director

Halifax Chamber of Commerce
#200, 656 Windmill Rd., Dartmouth NS B3B 1B8
Tel: 902-468-7111; Fax: 902-468-7333
info@halifaxchamber.com
www.halifaxchamber.com
Valerie Payn, President
Ian Penny, Chair

Hay River Chamber of Commerce
10K Gagnier St., Hay River NT X0E 1G1
Tel: 867-874-2565; Fax: 867-874-3631
info@hayriverchamber.com
www.hayriverchamber.com
Brian Lefebvre, President

Mahone Bay & Area Chamber of Commerce
PO Box 59, Mahone Bay NS B0J 2E0
Tel: 902-624-6151; Fax: 902-624-6152
Toll-Free: 888-624-6151
info@mahonebay.com
www.mahonebay.com
Allan O'Brien, President
Ray Morin, Secretary
Marie Raymond, Staff

Norman Wells & District Chamber of Commerce
PO Box 400, Norman Wells NT X0E 0V0
Tel: 867-587-6609; Fax: 867-587-2865

Chris Buist, Contact

Northeast Highlands Chamber of Commerce
PO Box 125, Ingonish Beach NS B0C 1L0
Tel: 902-285-2289; *Fax:* 902-285-2285
alison.roper@pc.gc.ca
www.northeasthighlands.com
Walter Lauffer, President
Mary Sue Mackinnon, Staff
Ann Hussey, Secretary

Northumberland Central Chamber of Commerce
Lower Level, Northumberland Mall, 1111 Elgin St. West, Cobourg NS K9A 5H7
Tel: 905-372-5831; *Fax:* 905-372-2411
info@cobourgchamber.com
www.cobourgchamber.com
K. Ward, Manager

Pictou County Chamber of Commerce
East River Plaza, 980 East River Rd., New Glasgow NS B2H 3S5
Tel: 902-755-3463; *Fax:* 902-755-2848
info@pictouchamber.com
www.pictouchamber.com
Faus Johnson, Executive Director
Gerald Green, President

Sheet Harbour & Area Chamber of Commerce
PO Box 239, Sheet Harbour NS B0J 3B0
Tel: 902-885-2595; *Fax:* 902-885-2708
shcoc@ns.sympatico.ca
coc.sheetharbour.ca
Myrene Keating-Owen, Secretary
Tom McInnis, President

Shelburne & Area Chamber of Commerce
PO Box 1150, Shelburne NS B0T 1W0
Tel: 902-875-0224; *Fax:* 902-875-3214
info@shelburnechamber.com
www.shelburnechamber.com
Sam Stewart, President
Ron Chute, Secretary

South Queens Chamber of Commerce
PO Box 1378, Liverpool NS B0K 1K0
Tel: 902-354-4163; *Fax:* 902-354-7388
sqchambr@atcom.com
www.southqueenschamber.com
Mark Sapp, Chair
Cheryl Beaton, Treasurer
Henry Sewuster, Chair

Springhill & Area Chamber of Commerce
PO Box 1030, Springhill NS B0M 1X0
Tel: 902-597-8462; *Fax:* 902-597-3839
audrey@surrette.com
Adrien Baillargeon, President
Carys Messinger, Secretary

Strait Area Chamber of Commerce
#2, 4 MacIntosh Ave., Port Hawkesbury NS B9A 3K5
Tel: 902-625-1588; *Fax:* 902-625-5985
straitareacoc@ns.sympatico.ca
www.straitchamber.ca
Affiliation(s): Atlantic Provinces Chamber of Commerce
Shannon MacDougall, Executive Director
Bob MacEachern, President

Sydney & Area Chamber of Commerce (SACC)
275 Charlotte Street, Sydney NS B1P 1C6
Tel: 902-564-6453; *Fax:* 902-539-7487
info@sydneyareachamber.ca
www.sydneyareachamber.ca
Anne Marie Singler, Executive Secretary

Truro & District Chamber of Commerce (TDCOC)
PO Box 54, 605 Prince St., Truro NS B2N 1G2
Tel: 902-895-6328; *Fax:* 902-897-6641
www.trurochamber.com
Tim Tucker, Executive Director
Ted Jordan, President

West Hants Chamber of Commerce
PO Box 2188, Windsor NS B0N 2T0
Tel: 902-798-5106
info@whcc.ca
www.whcc.ca
Gordon Winstone, President
Richard Cole, Vice-President

Yarmouth & Area Chamber of Commerce (YCC)
PO Box 532, #1, 342 Main St., Yarmouth NS B5A 4B4
Tel: 902-742-3074; *Fax:* 902-749-1383
info@yarmouthchamberofcommerce.com
www.yarmouthchamberofcommerce.com
Dave Hall, President
Karen Churchill, 1st Vice-President
Mike Mercier, 2nd Vice-President

Yellowknife Chamber of Commerce
#21, 4910 - 50th Ave., 3rd Fl., Yellowknife NT X1A 1C4
Tel: 867-920-4944; *Fax:* 867-920-4640
generalmanager@ykchamber.com
www.ykchamber.com
Tim Doyle, Executive Director

Ontario

Aguasabon Chamber of Commerce
PO Box 695, Terrace Bay ON P0T 2W0
Tel: 807-825-4505; *Fax:* 807-825-9664
Toll-Free: 888-445-9999
info@sncfdc.com
John Lubberdink, Chair
Robert Kirkpatrick, Director

Alliston & District Chamber of Commerce
PO Box 32, 51 Victoria St. East, Alliston ON L9R 1T9
Tel: 705-435-7921; *Fax:* 705-435-0289
Toll-Free: 888-835-3092
info@adcc.ca
www.adcc.ca
Crystal Kellard, Office Coordinator

Amherstburg Chamber of Commerce
PO Box 101, 268 Dalhousie St., Amherstburg ON N9V 2Z3
Tel: 519-736-2001; *Fax:* 519-736-9721
acoc@mnsi.net
www.amherstburgchamberofcommerce.ca
Ray Bezaire, President

Arthur & District Chamber of Commerce
PO Box 519, 146 George St., Arthur ON N0G 1A0
Tel: 519-848-5603; *Fax:* 519-848-5603
achamber@wightman.ca
Jamie Couper, President

Atikokan Chamber of Commerce
PO Box 997, Atikokan ON P0T 1C0
Tel: 807-597-1599; *Fax:* 807-597-2726
Toll-Free: 888-334-2332
info@atikokanchamber.com
www.atikokanchamber.com
Affiliation(s): Canadian Chamber of Commerce
Judi Nault, President
Nancy Jordan, Office Manager

Aurora Chamber of Commerce
#321, 6 - 14845 Yonge St., Aurora ON L4G 6H8
Tel: 905-727-7262; *Fax:* 905-841-6217
info@aurorachamber.on.ca
www.aurorachamber.on.ca
Carla Adams, Executive Director

Bancroft & District Chamber of Commerce, Tourism & Information Centre
PO Box 539, Bancroft ON K0L 1C0
Tel: 613-332-1513; *Fax:* 613-332-2119
Toll-Free: 888-443-9999
chamber@bancroftdistrict.com
www.bancroftdistrict.com
Kim Forge, General Manager

Bayfield & Area Chamber of Commerce
PO Box 2065, Bayfield ON N0M 1G0
Tel: 519-565-2499; *Toll-Free:* 800-565-2499
info@villageofbayfield.com
www.villageofbayfield.com
Janet Snider, President

Beaverton District Chamber of Commerce
PO Box 29, Beaverton ON L0K 1A0
Tel: 705-426-2051
chamber@beavertononlakesimcoe.com
www.beavertononlakesimcoe.com
Affiliation(s): Ontario Chamber of Commerce
Ted McCollum, President

Belleville & District Chamber of Commerce (BCC)
PO Box 726, 5 East Moira St., Belleville ON K8N 5B3
Tel: 613-962-4597; *Fax:* 613-962-3911
Toll-Free: 888-852-9992
info@bellevillechamber.ca
www.bellevillechamber.ca
Angela Genereaux, General Manager

Blenheim & District Chamber of Commerce
PO Box 1089, c/o 127 Malborough St. North, Blenheim ON N0P 1A0
Tel: 519-676-6555; *Fax:* 519-676-2622
Betty Russell, Admin. Secretary & Treasurer

Blind River Chamber of Commerce (BRCC)
PO Box 998, Blind River ON P0R 1B0
Tel: 705-356-2555; *Fax:* 705-356-3911
Toll-Free: 800-563-8719
chamber@brchamber.ca
www.brchamber.ca
Affiliation(s): Algoma Kinniwabi Travel Association
Betty-Ann Dunbar, President

Blue Mountains Chamber of Commerce
PO Box 477, Thornbury ON N0H 2P0
Tel: 519-599-1200; *Fax:* 519-599-3971
info@bluemountainschamber.ca
www.bluemountainschamber.ca
George Matamoros, President

Bobcaygeon & Area Chamber of Commerce
PO Box 388, 21 Canal St. East, Bobcaygeon ON K0M 1A0
Tel: 705-738-2202; *Fax:* 705-738-1534
Toll-Free: 800-318-6173
chamber@bobcaygeon.org
www.bobcaygeon.org
Affiliation(s): Kawartha Lakes Associated Chambers of Commerce
Tom Kupusa, President

Bracebridge Chamber of Commerce
#1, 1 Manitoba St., Bracebridge ON P1L 2A8
Tel: 705-645-5231; *Fax:* 705-645-7592
chamber@bracebridgechamber.com
www.bracebridgechamber.com
John Crawley, General Manager

Bradford & District Chamber of Commerce (BDCC)
PO Box 59, 100 Dissette St., Bradford ON L3Z 2A7
Tel: 905-775-3037; *Fax:* 905-775-6357
info@bradfordchamber.on.ca
Deanna Stewart, General Manager

Brighton & District Chamber of Commerce
PO Box 880, 74 Main Street, Brighton ON K0K 1H0
Tel: 613-475-2775; *Fax:* 613-475-3777
Toll-Free: 877-475-2775
info@brightonchamber.ca
www.brightonchamber.ca
George Lucas, Administrator

Brockville & District Chamber of Commerce
#1, 3 Market St. West, Brockville ON K6V 7L2
Tel: 613-342-6553; *Fax:* 613-342-6849
info@brockvillechamber.com
www.brockvillechamber.com
Sueling Ching, Executive Director

Burlington Chamber of Commerce
#201, 414 Locust St., Burlington ON L7S 1T7
Tel: 905-639-0174; *Fax:* 905-333-3956
info@burlingtonchamber.com
www.burlingtonchamber.com
Social Media: www.youtube.com/user/BurlingtonChamber
Tamar Fahmi, Chair

Caledon Chamber of Commerce
PO Box 626, Bolton ON L7E 5T5
Tel: 905-857-7393; *Fax:* 905-857-7405
Toll-Free: 888-599-9967
info@caledonchamber.com
www.caledonchamber.com
Affiliation(s): Canadian Chamber of Commerce; Ontario Chamber of Commerce
Kelly Darnley, President/CEO
Linda Bond, Chair

Caledonia Regional Chamber of Commerce
PO Box 2035, 1 Grand Trunk Lane, Caledonia ON N3W 2G6
Tel: 905-765-0377; *Fax:* 905-765-6730
crcc@mountaincable.net
www.caledonia-ontario.com
Barb Martindale, Executive Director

Cambridge Chamber of Commerce
750 Hespler Rd., Cambridge ON N3H 5L8
Tel: 519-622-2221; *Fax:* 519-622-0177
cchamber@cambridgechamber.com
www.cambridgechamber.com
Greg Durocher, General Manager

Carleton Place & District Chamber of Commerce
132 Coleman St., Carleton Place ON K7C 4M7
Tel: 613-257-1976; Fax: 613-257-8170
manager@cpchamber.com
www.cpchamber.com
Cathie McOrmond, Manager

Cayuga & District Chamber of Commerce
PO Box 118, 6 Cayuga St. North, Cayuga ON N0A 1E0
Tel: 905-772-5954; Fax: 905-772-2680
info@cayugachamber.ca
www.cayugachamber.ca
Bernadine Tompkins, President

Central Bruce Peninsula Chamber of Commerce
c/o Tourist Information Center, 2866 Hwy. 6, Wiarton ON N0H 2T0
Tel: 519-793-3178; Fax: 519-793-3296
info@centralbrucepeninsula.ca
www.centralbrucepeninsula.ca
Affiliation(s): Bruce Peninsula Tourism Association; Ontario Chamber of Commerce; Bruce County Tourism; Tobermory & District Chamber of Commerce; South Bruce Peninsula Chamber of Commerce; Sauble Beach Chamber of Commerce

Centre Wellington Chamber of Commerce
400 Tower St. South, Fergus ON N1M 2P7
Tel: 519-843-5140; Fax: 519-787-0983
Toll-Free: 877-242-6353
chamber@ferguselora.com
www.ferguselora.com
Affiliation(s): Canadian Chamber of Commerce
Deb Dalziel, General Manager

Chamber of Commerce of Brantford & Brant (BRCC)
PO Box 1294, 77 Charlotte St., Brantford ON N3T 5T6
Tel: 519-753-2617; Fax: 519-753-0921
chamber@brcc.ca
www.brcc.ca
Charlene Nicholson, Chief Executive Officer

Chatham-Kent Chamber of Commerce
54 Fourth St., Chatham ON N7M 2G2
Tel: 519-352-7540; Fax: 519-352-8741
info@chatham-kentchamber.ca
www.chatham-kentchamber.ca
G.A. (Gail) Antaya, President & CEO

Chesley & District Chamber of Commerce
PO Box 406, 112 - 1st Ave. South, Chesley ON N0G 1L0
Tel: 519-363-9837; Fax: 519-363-9838
cdcc@bmts.com
www.townofchesley.com
Stacy Charlton, Treasurer

Cobourg & District Chamber of Commerce
Northumberland Mall, 1111 Elgin St. West, Cobourg ON K9A 5H7
Tel: 905-372-5831; Fax: 905-372-2411
info@threecubed.ca
Kevin Ward, Manager

Collingwood Chamber of Commerce
PO Box 36, 25 Second St., Collingwood ON L9Y 1E4
Tel: 705-445-0221; Fax: 705-445-6858
info@collingwoodchamber.com
www.collingwoodchamber.com
Affiliation(s): Canadian Chamber of Commerce; Ontario Chamber of Commerce
David Ripley, President

Cornwall Chamber of Commerce
Commerce Court, #100, 113 Second St. East, Cornwall ON K6H 1Y5
Tel: 613-933-4004; Fax: 613-933-8466
www.cornwallchamber.com
Debbie Rioux, President

Dryden District Chamber of Commerce (DDCC)
284 Government St., Dryden ON P8N 2P3
Tel: 807-223-2622; Fax: 807-223-2626
Toll-Free: 800-667-0935
chamber@mail.drytel.net
www.drydenchamber.ca
Affiliation(s): Sunset County Travel Association; Patricia Regional Tourist Council; Kenora District Camp Owners Association
Melina Jansen, Manager
Jamie Gould, Chair

Dunnville Chamber of Commerce
PO Box 124, 231 Chestnut St., Dunnville ON N1A 2X1
Tel: 905-774-3183; Fax: 905-774-9281
chamberofcommerce@mountaincable.net
www.dunnvillechamberofcommerce.ca
Ron Speer, Office Manager

East Gwillimbury Chamber of Commerce
PO Box 199, 1590 Queensville Side Rd., Queensville ON L0G 1R0
Tel: 905-478-8447; Fax: 905-478-8786
info@egcoc.org
www.egcoc.org
Cindy Thiele, President

Eastern Ottawa Chamber of Commerce
#310, 2183 Ogilvie Rd., Gloucester ON K1J 1C8
Tel: 613-745-3578; Fax: 613-745-8575
info@easternottawa.com
www.easternottawa.com
David Brault, President

Elliot Lake & District Chamber of Commerce
PO Box 81, Elliot Lake ON P5A 2J6
Tel: 705-848-3974; Fax: 705-848-7121
elchamber@onlink.net
www.elliotlakechamber.com
Peter Seidel, President

Emo Chamber of Commerce
PO Box 476, Emo ON P0W 1E0
Tel: 807-482-1811; Fax: 807-482-1813
vennechenko@sympatico.ca
www.twspemo.on.ca/chamber.html
Colleen Vennechenko, Contact
Paul Kyro, NOACC Representative
Dave Goodman, Vice-President

Englehart & District Chamber of Commerce
PO Box 171, Englehart ON P0J 1H0
Tel: 705-544-8580; Fax: 705-544-1964
deacon@ntl.sympatico.ca
Annette Deacon, President

Espanola & District Chamber of Commerce
30 McCulloch, Espanola ON P5E 1J1
Tel: 705-869-3351; Fax: 705-869-4601
rbheale@cyberbeach.net
Rob Heale, Contact

Fenelon Falls & District Chamber of Commerce
PO Box 28, 15 Oak St., Fenelon Falls ON K0M 1N0
Tel: 705-887-3409; Fax: 705-887-6912
info@fenelonfallschamber.com
www.fenelonfallschamber.com
Sandra Barrett, President

Flamborough Chamber of Commerce (FCC)
PO Box 1030, Waterdown ON L0R 2H0
Tel: 905-689-7650; Fax: 905-689-1313
admin@flamboroughchamber.ca
www.flamboroughchamber.ca
Affiliation(s): Ontario & Canadian Chamber of Commerce
Penny Gardiner, President

Fort Frances Chamber of Commerce
474 Scott St., Fort Frances ON P9A 1H2
Tel: 807-274-5773; Fax: 807-274-8706
Toll-Free: 800-820-3678
thefort@nwonet.net
www.fortfranceschamber.com
Affiliation(s): Ontario Chamber of Commerce; Canadian Chamber of Commerce
Dawn Booth, Chamber Coordinator
Christine Denby, President

Georgina Chamber of Commerce
22937 Woodbine Ave., RR#2, Keswick ON L4P 3E9
Tel: 905-476-7870; Fax: 905-476-6700
Toll-Free: 888-436-7446
admin@georginachamber.com
www.georginachamber.com
Christine Thomas, General Manager
Dan Fellini, President

Geraldton & District Chamber of Commerce
PO Box 128, Geraldton ON P0T 1M0
Tel: 807-854-1925
ddumont42@sympatico.ca
www.gdcc-on.ca
Stephane Parent, President
Gerard Dufour, Secretary
Katherine Russwurm, NOACC Representative

Goderich & District Chamber of Commerce
56 East St., Goderich ON N7A 1N3
Tel: 519-440-0176; Fax: 519-440-0305
info@goderichchamber.ca
www.goderichchamber.ca
Laura Herman, President

Gogama Chamber of Commerce
PO Box 73, 59 Poupore St., Gogama ON P0M 1W0
Tel: 705-894-2111
gogamachamber@vianet.ca
Eija MacDonald, Chair

Grand Bend & Area Chamber of Commerce
PO Box 248, #1, 81 Crescent St., Grand Bend ON N0M 1T0
Tel: 519-238-2001; Fax: 519-238-5201
Toll-Free: 888-338-2001
info@grandbendtourism.com
www.grandbendtourism.com
Eva Miller, Manager

Gravenhurst Chamber of Commerce/Visitors Bureau
#685, 2 Muskoka Rd. North, Gravenhurst ON P1P 1N5
Tel: 705-687-4432; Fax: 705-687-4382
info@gravenhurstchamber.com
www.gravenhurstchamber.com
Rosemary King, President

Greater Arnprior Chamber of Commerce (GACC)
PO Box 213, 16 Edward St., Arnprior ON K7S 3H2
Tel: 613-623-6817; Fax: 613-623-6826
arnpriorchamberofcommerce@bellnet.ca
www.gacc.ca
Lori Martin, Administrative Assistant
Joan Carey, President

Greater Barrie Chamber of Commerce
97 Toronto St., Barrie ON L4N 1V1
Tel: 705-721-5000; Fax: 705-726-0973
chadmin@barriechamber.com
www.barriechamber.com
Sybil Goruk, Executive Director

Greater Dufferin Area Chamber of Commerce
PO Box 101, Hwy. 10, Orangeville ON L9W 2Z5
Tel: 519-941-0490; Fax: 519-941-0492
info@gdacc.ca
www.gdacc.ca
Affiliation(s): Ontario Chamber of Commerce; Canadian Chamber of Commerce
Ron Munro, President

Greater Fort Erie Chamber of Commerce
#1, 660 Garrison Rd., Fort Erie ON L2A 6E2
Tel: 905-871-3803; Fax: 905-871-1561
info@forteriechamber.com
www.forteriechamber.com
Kimberly Walpole, President
Gina Ramkissoon, Vice-President

Greater Innisfil Chamber of Commerce (GICC)
7896 Yonge St., Innisfil ON L9S 1L5
Tel: 705-431-4199; Fax: 705-431-8020
Toll-Free: 866-575-0008
info@innisfilchamber.com
www.innisfilchamber.com
Affiliation(s): Alcona Business Association; South Innisfil Business & Community Association; Cookstown Chamber of Commerce; 400 Industrial Group
David Taylor, Secretary
Heather MacDonald, President

Greater Kingston Chamber of Commerce (GKCC)
945 Princess St., Kingston ON K7L 3N6
Tel: 613-548-4453; Fax: 613-548-4743
info@kingstonchamber.on.ca
www.kingstonchamber.on.ca
John Ryce, President
David Phillips, Coordinator, New Membership

Greater Kitchener & Waterloo Chamber of Commerce
PO Box 2367, 80 Queen St. North, Kitchener ON N2H 6L4
Tel: 519-576-5000; Fax: 519-742-4760
Toll-Free: 888-672-4282
admin@greaterkwchamber.com
www.greaterkwchamber.com
Ian McLean, President & CEO

Greater Nepean Chamber of Commerce
#1175, 2720 Queensview Dr., Ottawa ON K2B 1A5
Tel: 613-828-5556; Fax: 613-828-8022
info@nepeanchamber.com
www.nepeanchamber.com
Mary Pitt, Chair
Dan Laverdure, General Manager

Greater Oshawa Chamber of Commerce
#100, 44 Richmond St. West, Oshawa ON L1G 1C7
Tel: 905-728-1683; Fax: 905-432-1259
info@oshawachamber.com
www.oshawachamber.com

Affiliation(s): Ontario Chamber of Commerce; Canadian Chamber of Commerce
Bob Malcolmson, General Manager

Greater Peterborough Chamber of Commerce (GPCC)
175 George St. North, Peterborough ON K9J 3G6
Tel: 705-748-9771; Fax: 705-743-2331
Toll-Free: 887-640-4037
info@peterboroughchamber.ca
www.peterboroughchamber.ca
Stuart Harrison, General Manager

Greater Sudbury Chamber of Commerce / Chambre de commerce du Grand Sudbury
#1, 40 Elm St., Sudbury ON P3C 1S8
Tel: 705-673-7133; Fax: 705-673-2944
cofc@sudburychamber.ca
www.sudburychamber.ca
Debbi M. Nicholson, President & CEO

Grimsby & District Chamber of Commerce
424 South Service Rd., RR#2, Grimsby ON L3M 4E8
Tel: 905-945-8319; Fax: 905-945-1615
info@grimsbychamber.com
www.grimsbychamber.com
Jinny Day, Executive Director

Guelph Chamber of Commerce (GCC)
PO Box 1268, #15, 485 Silvercreek Pkwy. North, Guelph ON N1H 6N6
Tel: 519-822-8081; Fax: 519-822-8451
chamber@guelphchamber.com
www.guelphchamber.com
Affiliation(s): Guelph Business Enterprise Centre; Guelph Partnership for Innovation
Lloyd Longfield, President and C.A.O.

Hagersville & District Chamber of Commerce
PO Box 1090, 24 Parkview Rd., Hagersville ON N0A 1H0
Tel: 905-768-3384
Brenda Moerschfelder, President

Haliburton Highlands Chamber of Commerce
PO Box 147, 5 Bobcaygeon Rd., Minden ON K0M 2K0
Tel: 705-286-7160; Fax: 705-286-6016
Toll-Free: 877-811-6111
admin@hhchamber.on.ca
www.hhchamber.on.ca
Nick Lawrence, President
Walter Schretter, Vice-President
Maria Micallef, Administrative Coordinator

Halton Hills Chamber of Commerce
328 Guelph St., Halton Hills ON L7G 4B5
Tel: 905-877-7119; Fax: 905-877-5117
info@haltonhillschamber.on.ca
www.haltonhillschamber.on.ca
Sue Walker, General Manager

Hamilton Chamber of Commerce (HCC)
555 Bay St. North, Hamilton ON L8L 1H1
Tel: 905-522-1151; Fax: 905-522-1154
hdcc@hamiltonchamber.on.ca
www.hamiltonchamber.on.ca
John Dolbec, CEO
Ruth Liebersbach, President

Hanover Chamber of Commerce
#1, 214 - 10th St., Hanover ON N4N 1N7
Tel: 519-364-5777; Fax: 519-364-6949
koelschlagel@bdo.ca

Harrow & Colchester Chamber of Commerce
PO Box 888, Harrow ON N0R 1G0
Tel: 519-974-3200; Fax: 519-974-2222
chamber@harrowchamber.ca
www.harrowchamber.ca
Ginger Cooke, President

Havelock, Belmont, Methuen Chamber of Commerce
PO Box 779, Havelock ON K0L 1Z0
Tel: 705-778-2182; Fax: 705-778-2444
info@havelockchamber.com
www.havelockchamber.com
Rae McCutcheon, Secretary

Hawkesbury Chamber of Commerce / Chambre de Commerce de Hawkesbury
PO Box 36, 2 John St., Hawkesbury ON K6A 2R4
Tel: 613-632-8066; Fax: 613-632-3324
info@hcoc.ca
www.hcoc.ca
Richard Denis, President
Sylvain Labrie, Secretary-Treasurer

Hearst, Mattice - Val Côté Chamber of Commerce
PO Box 987, 523 Hwy. 11 East, Hearst ON P0L 1N0
Tel: 705-372-2838; Fax: 705-372-2840
Toll-Free: 800-655-5769
hearstcoc@hearst.ca
www.hearstcoc.com
Ghislain Jacques, President

Ingersoll District Chamber of Commerce
132 Thames St. South, Ingersoll ON N5C 2T4
Tel: 519-485-7333; Fax: 519-485-6606
info@ingersollchamber.com
www.ingersollchamber.com
Ann Campbell, General Manager

Iroquois Falls & District Chamber of Commerce
PO Box 840, 727 Synagogue Ave., Iroquois Falls ON P0K 1G0
Tel: 705-232-4656
ifchamber@hotmail.com
www.iroquoisfallschamber.com
Elizabeth King, President

Kawartha Lakes Chamber of Commerce
Eastern Region, PO Box 537, 12 Queen St., Lakefield ON K0L 2H0
Tel: 705-652-6963; Fax: 705-652-9140
Toll-Free: 888-565-8888
info@kawarthachamber.ca
www.kawarthachamber.ca
Scott Papp, Business Administrator

Kenora & District Chamber of Commerce
PO Box 471, Kenora ON P9N 3X5
Tel: 807-467-4646; Fax: 807-468-3056
kenorachamber@kmts.ca
www.kenorachamber.com
Laurene Manson-Sillery, Chamber Manager

Kincardine & District Chamber of Commerce
PO Box 115, Kincardine ON N2Z 2Y6
Tel: 519-396-9333; Fax: 519-396-5529
kincardine.cofc@bmts.com
www.kincardinechamber.com
Jackie Pawlikowski, Office Manager

Kirkland Lake District Chamber of Commerce (KLCC)
PO Box 966, 400 Government Rd. West, Kirkland Lake ON P2N 3N1
Tel: 705-567-5444; Fax: 705-567-1666
klcofc@ntl.sympatico.ca
kirklandlakechamber.com
Affiliation(s): Ontario Chamber of Commerce
Joanne Gorzalczynski, Secretary
Jim Taylor, President

The Land of Nipigon Chamber of Commerce
PO Box 760, 22 Third Street, Nipigon ON P0T 2J0
Tel: 807-887-0740; Fax: 807-887-5117
Toll-Free: 877-596-1359
nipigonchamber@vianet.ca
www.nipigon.net
Judi Bernard, President
Rebecca Lawrence, Director

Leamington District Chamber of Commerce
PO Box 321, 21 Talbot St., Leamington ON N8H 1L1
Tel: 519-326-2721; Fax: 519-326-3204
Toll-Free: 800-250-3336
sally@leamingtonchamber.com
www.leamingtonchamber.com
Sally McDonald, General Manager

Lincoln Chamber of Commerce
4800 South Service Rd., Beamsville ON L0R 1B0
Tel: 905-563-5044; Fax: 905-563-7098
lcoc@vaxxine.com
www.lincolnchamber.ca
Cathy McNiven, General Manager

London Chamber of Commerce
#101, 244 Pall Mall St., London ON N6A 5P6
Tel: 519-432-7551; Fax: 519-432-8063
info@londonchamber.com
www.londonchamber.com
Kevin Switzer, President
Gerry MacCartney, General Manager & CEO

Longlac Chamber of Commerce
PO Box 877, 112 Hamel Ave., Longlac ON P0T 1A0
Tel: 807-876-2273; Fax: 807-876-2575
Lorraine Gagnon, Contact
Wayne Morris, President

Lucknow & District Chamber of Commerce
PO Box 313, Lucknow ON N0G 2H0
Tel: 519-528-2099

Lyndhurst Seeleys Bay & District Chamber of Commerce
PO Box 89, RR#1, Lyndhurst ON K0E 1N0
Tel: 613-387-3847
info@lyndhurstseeleysbaychamber.com
www.lyndhurstseeleysbaychamber.com
Charlie Kellington, President
Charles Shaw, Treasurer

Manitoulin Chamber of Commerce
PO Box 307, 6062 Hwy. 542, Mindemoya ON P0P 1S0
Tel: 705-377-7501; Fax: 705-377-7501
Toll-Free: 800-698-6681
office@manitoulinchamber.com
www.manitoulinchamber.com
Bob Taylor, President

Manitouwadge Chamber of Commerce
PO Box 2030, 1 Mississauga Dr., Manitouwadge ON P0T 2C0
Tel: 807-826-3227; Fax: 807-826-4592

Marathon Chamber of Commerce
PO Box 988, Marathon ON P0T 2E0
Tel: 807-229-3100; Fax: 807-229-1486
Affiliation(s): Northwestern Ontario Associated Chambers of Commerce
Bob Hancherow, Contact
George Macey, NOACC Representative

Markdale Chamber of Commerce
PO Box 177, 19 Toronto St. North, Markdale ON N0C 1H0
Tel: 519-986-4612; Fax: 519-986-4612
Toll-Free: 888-986-4612
markdalechamber@cablerocket.com
www.village.markdale.on.ca
Susan Roberts, Secretary

Maryborough Chamber of Commerce
PO Box 143, Moorefield ON N0G 2K0
Tel: 519-638-2971
dcraven@wightman.net
Dennis Craven, President

Meaford & District Chamber of Commerce (MDCC)
#1, 16 Trowbridge St. West, Meaford ON N4L 1N2
Tel: 519-538-1640; Fax: 519-538-5493
Toll-Free: 888-632-3673
info@mdcc.ca
www.mdcc.ca
Shirley Keaveney, President
Barry Altman, Manager

Milton Chamber of Commerce
#104, 251 Main St., Milton ON L9T 1P1
Tel: 905-878-0581; Fax: 905-878-4972
info@chamber.milton.on.ca
www.chamber.milton.on.ca
Sandy Martin, Executive Director

Minto Chamber of Commerce
PO Box 864, Harriston ON N0G 1Z0
Tel: 519-327-9619
info@mintochamber.on.ca
www.mintochamber.on.ca
John Burgess, President

Mount Forest District Chamber of Commerce
514 Main St. North, Mount Forest ON N0G 2L0
Tel: 519-323-4480; Fax: 519-323-1557
www.mountforest.ca
Ron Forrest, President

Muskoka Lakes Chamber of Commerce
PO Box 536, 3181 Muskoka Rd. 169, Bala ON P0C 1A0
Tel: 705-762-5663; Fax: 705-762-5664
info@muskokalakeschamber.com
www.muskokalakeschamber.com
Jane Templeton, Manager
Kailey Luker, Consultant, Event & Tourism
Tracy Owen, President
Walter Moon, Vice-President
Susan McEachern, Treasurer

Napanee & District Chamber of Commerce
Napanee Business Centre, 47 Dundas St. East, Napanee ON K7R 1H7
Tel: 613-354-6601; Fax: 613-354-6848
Toll-Free: 877-354-6601
info@napaneechamber.ca
www.napaneechamber.ca
Dan Atkinson, President

Newmarket Chamber of Commerce
470 Davis Dr., Newmarket ON L3Y 2P3
Tel: 905-898-5900; Fax: 905-853-7271
info@newmarketchamber.com
www.newmarketchamber.com
Debra Scott, President & CEO

Niagara Falls Chamber of Commerce
4056 Dorchester Rd., Niagara Falls ON L2E 6M9
Tel: 905-374-3666; Fax: 905-374-2972
info@niagarafallschamber.com
www.niagarafallschamber.com
Carolyn Bones, President
Larry Vaughan, Chair

Niagara on the Lake Chamber of Commerce
PO Box 1043, 26 Queen St., Niagara-on-the-Lake ON L0S 1J0
Tel: 905-468-1950; Fax: 905-468-4930
tourism@niagaraonthelake.com
www.niagaraonthelake.com
Janice Thomson, Executive Director

North Bay & District Chamber of Commerce
PO Box 747, 1375 Seymour St., North Bay ON P1B 8J8
Tel: 705-472-8480; Fax: 705-472-8027
Toll-Free: 888-249-8998
nbcc@northbaychamber.com
www.northbaychamber.com
Patti Alcorn-Carr, Executive Director

North Grenville Chamber of Commerce
PO Box 1047, 5 Clothier St. East, Kemptville ON K0G 1J0
Tel: 613-258-4838; Fax: 613-258-3801
info@northgrenvillechamber.com
www.northgrenvillechamber.com
Pierre Blackburn, Chair

North Perth Chamber of Commerce
580 Main St., Listowel ON N4W 1A8
Tel: 519-291-1551; Fax: 519-291-4151
info@npchamber.com
www.npchamber.com
Tami Chauvin, General Manager

Northwestern Ontario Associated Chambers of Commerce (NOACC)
#102, 200 Syndicate Ave. South, Thunder Bay ON P7E 1C9
Tel: 807-624-2626; Fax: 807-622-7752
www.noacc.ca
Affiliation(s): Ontario Chamber of Commerce
Lisa Sticca, Chair
Barry Streib, President

Oakville Chamber of Commerce
2521 Wyecroft Rd., Oakville ON L6L 6P8
Tel: 905-845-6613; Fax: 905-845-6475
inquiries@oakvillechamber.com
www.oakvillechamber.com
John Sawyer, President

Orillia & District Chamber of Commerce
150 Front St. South, Orillia ON L3V 4S7
Tel: 705-326-4424; Fax: 705-327-7841
orilinfo@orillia.com
www.orillia.com
Affiliation(s): Canadian Chamber of Commerce
Susan Lang, Managing Director

Orléans Chamber of Commerce / Chambre de commerce d'Orléans
2276A, boul St-Joseph, Orleans ON K1C 1E8
Tel: 613-824-9137; Fax: 613-824-0090
contact@orleanschamber.ca
www.orleanschamber.ca
Affiliation(s): National Capital Business Alliance
Peter Stewart, Executive Director

Oro-Medonte Chamber of Commerce
PO Box 100, 148 Line 7 South, Oro ON L0L 2X0
Tel: 705-487-7337; Fax: 705-487-0133
info@oromedontecc.com
www.oromedontecc.com
Carol Benedetti, Administrative Coordinator
Rick Dory, President
Anna Proctor, Vice-President
Bruce Chappell, Treasurer

Ottawa Chamber of Commerce (OCC)
328 Somerset St. West, Ottawa ON K2P 0J9
Tel: 613-236-3631; Fax: 613-236-7498
info@ottawachamber.ca
www.ottawachamber.ca
Erin Kelly, Executive Director
Laura Haber, Director, Events & Partnerships
Scott Williams, Director, Member Services
Kenny Leon, Manager, Communications

Owen Sound & District Chamber of Commerce
PO Box 1028, Owen Sound ON N4K 6K6
Tel: 519-376-6261; Fax: 519-376-5647
bert@oschamber.com
www.oschamber.com
David Moyer, President
Joanne Horton, Vice President

Paris Chamber of Commerce
c/o Williams Brant County Power, 65 Dundas St. East, Paris ON N3L 3H1
Tel: 519-758-5095
sinjsswint@rogers.com
www.pariscoc.ca
Tracey Palmer, President
Bryan Maude, President

Perth & District Chamber of Commerce
34 Herriott St., Perth ON K7H 1T2
Tel: 613-267-3200; Fax: 613-267-6797
Toll-Free: 888-319-3204
welcome@perthchamber.com
www.perthchamber.com
Affiliation(s): Canadian Chamber of Commerce; Ontario Chamber of Commerce
Dorothy Linden, President

Pointe-au-Baril Chamber of Commerce
PO Box 67, Pointe-au-Baril-Station ON P0G 1K0
Tel: 705-366-2331; Fax: 705-366-2331
info@pointeaubarilchamber.com
www.pointeaubarilchamber.com
Affiliation(s): Rainbow County Travel Association
Danielle Hill, President (interim)

Port Colborne-Wainfleet Chamber of Commerce
76 Main St. West, Port Colborne ON L3K 3V2
Tel: 905-834-9765; Fax: 905-834-1542
office@pcwchamber.com
www.pcwchamber.com
Donna Martens Gamm, President
Sherrie Fulbrook, Treasurer

Port Hope & District Chamber of Commerce
58 Queen St., Port Hope ON L1A 3Z9
Tel: 905-885-5519; Fax: 905-885-1142
info@porthopechamber.com
www.porthopechamber.com
Wendy Giroux, Manager

Prescott & District Chamber of Commerce
PO Box 2000, Prescott ON K0E 1T0
Tel: 613-925-2171; Fax: 613-925-4381
prescottchamber@xplornet.com
www.prescottanddistrictchamber.com
Debbie Lawless, Secretary

Prince Edward County Chamber of Tourism & Commerce (PECCTAC)
116 Main St., Picton ON K0K 2T0
Tel: 613-476-2421; Fax: 613-476-7461
Toll-Free: 800-640-4717
pec@reach.net
www.pecchamber.com
Jan Demille, Secretary/Manager

Quinte West Chamber of Commerce
97 Front St., Trenton ON K8V 4N6
Tel: 613-392-7635; Fax: 613-392-8400
Toll-Free: 800-930-3255
info@quintewestchamber.on.ca
www.quintewestchamber.on.ca
Suzanne Andrews, Manager

Rainy River & District Chamber of Commerce
PO Box 458, Rainy River ON P0W 1L0
Tel: 807-852-3343
www.rainyriver.ca/chamber
Susan Carpenter, President

Ramara & District Chamber of Commerce
PO Box 144, 2304 Highway 12, Brechin ON L0K 1B0
Tel: 705-484-2141; Fax: 705-484-0161
info@ramarachamber.com
www.ramarachamber.com
Walt Meyers, President

Red Lake Chamber of Commerce
PO Box 430, Red Lake ON P0V 2M0
Tel: 807-727-3722; Fax: 807-727-3285
redlakechamber@shaw.ca
Rob Collette, President
Cathy Quesnel-Loessl, Vice President
Everett Hobbs, Second Vice President
Yvonne Davis, Sec.-Treas.

Renfrew & Area Chamber of Commerce
161 Raglan St. South, Renfrew ON K7V 1R2
Tel: 613-432-7015; Fax: 613-432-8645
Jon Pole, President

Richmond Hill Chamber of Commerce (RHCOC)
376 Church St. South, Richmond Hill ON L4C 9V8
Tel: 905-884-1961; Fax: 905-884-1962
info@rhcoc.com
www.rhcoc.com
Affiliation(s): Toronto Board of Trade
George Simpson, Chair
Leslie Walker, CEO

Rideau Chamber of Commerce
PO Box 247, Manotick ON K4M 1A3
Tel: 613-692-6262; Fax: 613-822-4687
info@rideauchamber.com
www.rideauchamber.com
Affiliation(s): Ontario Chamber of Commerce
Salima Ismail, President

Ridgetown & District Chamber of Commerce
37 Main St. East, Ridgetown ON N0P 2C0
Tel: 519-674-0802; Fax: 519-674-0802
ridgetownchamber@sympatico.ca
www.ridgetown.com
Charlie Mitton, President
Sandra Dorner, General Manager

St Catharines-Thorold Chamber of Commerce
PO Box 940, #103, 1 St. Paul St., St Catharines ON L2R 6Z4
Tel: 905-684-2361; Fax: 905-684-2100
info@sctchamber.com
www.sctchamber.com
Nancy Diamond, Chair

St. Catherine's-Thorold Chamber of Commerce
PO Box 940, #103, 1 St. Paul St., St Catharines ON L2R 36Z4
Tel: 905-684-2361; Fax: 905-684-2100
info@scchamberofcommerce.com
www.thoroldchamber.com, www.sctchamber.com
Rob DePetris, President

St Thomas & District Chamber of Commerce
#115, 300 South Edgeware Rd., St Thomas ON N5P 4L1
Tel: 519-631-1981; Fax: 519-631-0466
mail@stthomaschamber.on.ca
www.stthomaschamber.on.ca
Affiliation(s): Ontario Chamber of Commerce; Canadian Chamber of Commerce
Bob Hammersley, President & CEO

Sarnia Lambton Chamber of Commerce
556 North Christina St., Sarnia ON N7T 5W6
Tel: 519-336-2400; Fax: 519-336-2085
info@sarnialambtonchamber.com
www.sarnialambtonchamber.com
Garry McDonald, President

Sauble Beach Chamber of Commerce
General Delivery, Sauble Beach ON N0H 2G0
Tel: 519-422-1262
info@saublebeach.com
www.saublebeach.com
Becky Knight, President
Shelley Elliott, Treasurer

Saugeen Shores Chamber Office
559 Goderich St., Port Elgin ON N0H 2C4
Tel: 519-832-2332; Fax: 519-389-3725
Toll-Free: 800-387-3456
portelgininfo@saugeenshores.ca
www.saugeenshores.ca
Gary Brown, President

Sault Ste Marie Chamber of Commerce (SSMCOC)
334 Bay St., Sault Ste Marie ON P6A 1X1
Tel: 705-949-7152; Fax: 705-759-8166
comments@ssmcoc.com
www.ssmcoc.com
Shelley Barich, General Manager

Scugog Chamber of Commerce
PO Box 1282, #G1, 181 Perry St., Port Perry ON L9L 1A7
Tel: 905-985-4971; Fax: 905-985-7698
info@scugogchamber.ca
www.scugogchamber.ca
Affiliation(s): Joint Chambers of Durham Region; Durham Network for Excellence; Tourism Durham; Tourist Association of Durham Region; Durham Home & Small Business Association

Tony Janssen, President

Simcoe & District Chamber of Commerce
95 Queensway West, Chamber Plaza, Simcoe ON N3Y 2M8
Tel: 519-426-5867; Fax: 519-428-7718
chamber@simcoechamber.on.ca
www.simcoechamber.on.ca
Yvonne Di Pietro, General Manager

Sioux Lookout Chamber of Commerce
PO Box 577, 11 First Ave. South, Sioux Lookout ON P8T 1A8
Tel: 807-737-1937; Fax: 807-737-1778
chamber@siouxlookout.com
www.siouxlookout.com
Dean Woloshuck, President
Anne Reid, Staff Contact

South Bruce Peninsula Chamber of Commerce
PO Box 68, Wiarton ON N0H 2T0
Tel: 519-534-4009
info@wiartonchamber.ca
www.sbpcc.org
Affiliation(s): Wiarton BIA
John Aiken, Treasurer

South Dundas Chamber of Commerce
PO Box 288, Morrisburg ON K0C 1X0
Tel: 613-543-3443; Fax: 613-652-4120
info@southdundaschamber.com
sdcc.southdundas.com
Ed Kingsley, President

South Huron Chamber of Commerce
PO Box 550, 414 Main St. South, Exeter ON N0M 1S6
Tel: 519-235-4520; Fax: 519-235-3141
office@shcc.on.ca
www.shcc.on.ca
Hugh McMaster, President

South Stormont Chamber of Commerce
PO Box 489, Ingleside ON K0C 1M0
Tel: 613-537-8344; Fax: 613-537-9439
info@sscc.on.ca
www.sscc.on.ca
Lesley O'Gorman, President

Southeast Georgian Bay Chamber of Commerce
PO Box 70, 99 Lone Pine Rd., Port Severn ON L0K 1S0
Tel: 705-756-4863
info@segbay.ca
www.segbay.ca
Marianne Braid, Manager

Southern Georgian Bay Chamber of Commerce / Chambre de Commerce de la Baie Georgienne Sud
208 King St., Midland ON L4R 3L9
Tel: 705-526-7884; Fax: 705-526-1744
info@sgbchamber.ca
www.southerngeorgianbay.on.ca
Denise Hayes, General Manager

Stoney Creek Chamber of Commerce
21 Mountain Ave. South, Stoney Creek ON L8G 2V5
Tel: 905-664-4000; Fax: 905-664-7228
sccc@bellnet.ca
www.chamberstoneycreek.com
David Cage, Executive Director

Stratford & District Chamber of Commerce
55 Lorne Ave. East, Stratford ON N5A 6S4
Tel: 519-273-5250; Fax: 519-273-2229
info@stratfordchamber.com
www.stratfordchamber.com
Affiliation(s): Chamber of Commerce Executives of Canada
Garry Lobsinger, General Manager

Tavistock Chamber of Commerce
PO Box 670, Tavistock ON N0B 2R0
Tel: 519-655-2277
b&croutly@rogers.com
Bob Routly, Secretary

Temagami & District Chamber of Commerce
PO Box 57, Stn. T, 7 Lakeshore Dr., Temagami ON P0H 2H0
Tel: 705-569-3344; Fax: 705-569-2834
Toll-Free: 800-661-7609
cofc@temagami.ca
www.temagamiinformation.com
Ann Richmond, Office Manager
Hendrika Krygsman, President

1,000 Islands Gananoque Chamber of Commerce
10 King St. East, Gananoque ON K7G 1E6
Tel: 613-382-3250; Fax: 613-382-1585
Toll-Free: 800-561-1595
info@1000islandschamber.com
www.1000islandsgananoque.com
Affiliation(s): Travel Media Association of Canada
Bonnie Ruddock, Operations Manager

Thunder Bay Chamber of Commerce (TBCC)
#102, 200 Syndicate Ave. South, Thunder Bay ON P7E 1C9
Tel: 807-624-2626; Fax: 807-622-7752
chamber@tb-chamber.on.ca
www.tb-chamber.on.ca
Affiliation(s): Northwestern Ontario Associated Chambers of Commerce; Ontario Chamber of Commerce; Canadian Chamber of Commerce
Harold Wilson, President
Barry Streib, NOACC Representative

Tilbury & District Chamber of Commerce
PO Box 1299, Tilbury ON N0P 2L0
Tel: 519-682-3040; Fax: 519-682-3123
tbia.dcc@pppoe.ca
Carrie Sterling, Executive Director

Tillsonburg District Chamber of Commerce
PO Box 113, Tillsonburg ON N4G 4H3
Tel: 519-842-5571; Fax: 519-842-2941
srenken@ody.ca
www.tillsonburgchamber.ca

Timmins Chamber of Commerce / Chambre de commerce de Timmins
PO Box 985, 76 McIntyre Rd., Timmins ON P4N 7H6
Tel: 705-360-1900; Fax: 705-360-1193
admin@timminschamber.on.ca
www.timminschamber.on.ca
Rob Galloway, President
Keitha Robson, Manager

Tobermory & District Chamber of Commerce
PO Box 250, 7420 Hwy. 6, Tobermory ON N0H 2R0
Tel: 519-596-2452; Fax: 519-596-2452
chamber@tobermory.org
www.tobermory.org
Affiliation(s): Central Bruce Peninsula Chamber of Commerce; South Bruce Peninsula Chamber of Commerce; Manitoulin Chamber of Commerce; Manitoulin Tourism Association; Sauble Beach Chamber of Commerce
Marilee S. Derby, Coordinator

Trent Hills & District Chamber of Commerce
PO Box 376, 51 Grand Road, Campbellford ON K0L 1L0
Tel: 705-653-1551; Fax: 705-653-1629
Toll-Free: 888-653-1556
info@trenthillschamber.ca
www.trenthillschamber.ca
Nancy Allanson, Executive Director

Tri-Town & District Chamber of Commerce
PO Box 811, 883356 Hwy. 65 East, New Liskeard ON P0J 1P0
Tel: 705-647-5771; Fax: 705-647-8633
Toll-Free: 866-947-5753
chamber@ntl.sympatico.ca
www.tritownchamber.ca
Ken Laffernier, President

Tweed Chamber of Commerce
PO Box 988, Tweed ON K0K 3J0
Tel: 613-813-2784
www.tweed-chamber.ca
Richard Rashotte, President

Upper Ottawa Valley Chamber of Commerce
PO Box 1010, 611 TV Tower Rd., Pembroke ON K8A 6Y6
Tel: 613-732-1492; Fax: 613-732-5793
manager@upperottawavalleychamber.com
www.upperottawavalleychamber.com
Lorraine MacKenzie, Executive Director
Gail Richardson, President
Richard Hale, Vice-President

Uxbridge Chamber of Commerce
#810, 2 Campbell Dr., Uxbridge ON L9P 0A3
Tel: 905-852-7683; Fax: 905-852-2517
www.uxcc.ca
Lee Ursel, Chairman

Vaughan Chamber of Commerce (VCC)
#2, 25 Edilcan Dr., Vaughan ON L4K 3S4
Tel: 905-761-1366; Fax: 905-761-1918
Toll-Free: 888-828-4426
info@vaughanchamber.ca
www.vaughanchamber.ca

Deborah Bonk, CEO

Walkerton & District Chamber of Commerce
PO Box 1344, 4 Park St., Walkerton ON N0G 2V0
Tel: 519-881-3413; Fax: 519-881-4009
Toll-Free: 888-820-9291
chamberinfo@wightman.ca
town.walkerton.on.ca/Chamber/chamber.html
Affiliation(s): Ontario Chamber of Commerce
Tracey Cassidy, Chamber Manager
Dennis Moran, President
Neil Kirstine, Vice-President

Wasaga Beach Chamber of Commerce
PO Box 394, 550 River Rd. West, Wasaga Beach ON L9Z 1A4
Tel: 705-429-2247; Fax: 705-429-1407
Toll-Free: 866-292-7242
info@wasagainfo.com
www.wasagainfo.com
Affiliation(s): Canadian Chamber of Commerce; Ontario Chamber of Commerce
Trudie McCrea, Office Manager/Special Events Coord

The Welland/Pelham Chamber of Commerce
32 East Main St., Welland ON L3B 3W3
Tel: 905-732-7515; Fax: 905-732-7175
chamber.gurix.com
Dolores Fabiano, Executive Director

West Carleton District Chamber of Commerce
PO Box 179, Carp ON K0A 1L0
Tel: 613-839-5316; Fax: 613-839-1436
rosemarylyall@hotmail.com
Rose Lyall, Secretary

West Elgin Chamber of Commerce
PO Box 276, Rodney ON N0L 2C0
Tel: 519-785-2217
secretary@westelginchamber.ca
www.westelginchamber.ca
Ted Uffen, Secretary

West Grey Chamber of Commerce
PO Box 800, 625 Garafraxa Rd. North, Durham ON N0G 1R0
Tel: 519-369-5750; Fax: 519-369-5750
info@westgreychamber.ca
www.westgreychamber.ca
Affiliation(s): Durham Business Improvement Association
Greta Kennedy, Sec.-Treas.

West Lincoln Chamber of Commerce
PO Box 555, 270 Station St., Smithville ON L0R 2A0
Tel: 905-957-1606; Fax: 905-957-4628
wloffice@westlincolnchamber.com
www.westlincolnchamber.com
Susan Wisniewski, President

Westport & Rideau Lakes Chamber of Commerce
PO Box 157, Westport ON K0G 1X0
Tel: 613-273-2929; Fax: 613-273-2929
wrlcc@rideau.net
www.westportrideaulakes.on.ca
Colin Horsfall, President

Whitby Chamber of Commerce (WCC)
128 Brock St. South, Whitby ON L1N 5Y4
Tel: 905-668-4506; Fax: 905-668-1894
info@whitbychamber.org
www.whitbychamber.org
Margot Weir, CEO

Whitchurch-Stouffville Chamber of Commerce
PO Box 1500, 6176 Main St., Stouffville ON L4A 8A4
Tel: 905-642-4227; Fax: 905-642-8966
chamber@whitchurchstouffville.ca
www.whitchurchstouffville.ca
Helene M. Johnson, President & CEO

Windsor-Essex Regional Chamber of Commerce
2575 Ouellette Place, Windsor ON N8X 1L9
Tel: 519-966-3696; Fax: 519-966-0603
info@windsorchamber.org
www.windsorchamber.org
Linda E. Smith, President
Michele Watson, Membership Coordinator

Wingham & Area Chamber of Commerce
PO Box 1360, 273 Josephine St., Wingham ON N0G 2W0
Tel: 519-357-4990; Fax: 519-357-4847
Kerri Herrfort, Manager

Woodstock District Chamber of Commerce
#3, 425 Dundas St., Woodstock ON N4S 1B8
Tel: 519-539-9411; Fax: 519-456-1611
info@woodstockchamber.on.ca
www.woodstockchamber.on.ca

Martha Dennis, General Manager

Zurich & Association District Chamber of Commerce
PO Box 189, Zurich ON N0M 2T0
Tel: 519-236-4717
www.zurich-ontario-canada.com
Phillip Knight, President
Joyce McBeath, Secretary

Prince Edward Island

Chambre de commerce acadienne et francophone de l'Ile-du-Prince-Édouard
PO Box 67, Wellington PE C0B 2E0
Tel: 902-854-3439; Fax: 902-854-3099

Greater Charlottetown Chamber of Commerce
PO Box 67, 127 Kent St., Charlottetown PE C1A 7K2
Tel: 902-628-2000; Fax: 902-368-3570
chamber@charlottetownchamber.com
www.charlottetownchamber.com
Affiliation(s): Atlantic Provinces Chamber of Commerce
Kathryn Coll, President
Kathy Hambly, Executive Director

Greater Summerside Chamber of Commerce (GSCC)
#10, 263 Harbour Dr., Summerside PE C1N 5P1
Tel: 902-436-9651; Fax: 902-436-8320
info@chamber.summerside.ca
www.chamber.summerside.ca
Bill Schurman, Executive Director
Garth Doiron, President
Heather Matheson, Secretary
Patrick McSweeney, Treasurer

Kensington & Area Chamber of Commerce
PO Box 234, Kensington PE C0B 1M0
Tel: 902-836-3209
kacc@pei.aibn.com
www.kensington.ca/chamber
Glenna Lohnes, Executive Director
George Nelson, President

South Shore Chamber of Commerce
PO Box 127, Crapaud PE C0A 1J0
Tel: 902-437-2510
www.southshorechamber.pe.ca
Marion Miller, President

Southern Kings & Queens Chamber of Commerce (SKQCC)
PO Box 1593, Montague PE C0A 1R0
Tel: 902-838-4791; Fax: 902-838-0610
Tom Rath, President
Mary Elliot, Staff

West Prince Chamber of Commerce
455 Main St., Alberton PE C0B 1B0
Tel: 902-853-4555
John Lane, President
Elmer Arsenault, Vice-President

Québec

Chambre de commerce au Coeur de la Montérégie
675, rue St-Joseph, Marieville QC J3M 1H1
Tél: 450-460-4019; Téléc: 450-460-2362
cccmonteregie@qc.aira.com
Gaétan Rozon, Président

Chambre de Commerce Bois-des-Filion - Lorraine
CP 72012, Bois-des-Filion QC J6Z 4N9
Tél: 450-471-4381
info@ccbdfl.com
www.ccbdfl.com
Danielle Dauphin, Trésorier

Chambre de commerce d'Amos-région
644, 1e rue ouest, Amos QC J9T 1V3
Tél: 819-732-8100; Téléc: 819-732-8101
www.ccar.qc.ca
Martin Veilleux, Directeur général

Chambre de commerce de Beauceville
CP 5142, Beauceville QC G5X 2P5
Tél: 418-774-1020
cdecommercebeauceville@sogetel.net
Affiliation(s): Chambre de commerce du Québec; Chambre du commerce du Canada
Julien Boudreault, Président

Chambre de commerce de Bonaventure/St-Siméon/St-Élzear
CP 5006, 119, av Port-Royal, Bonaventure QC G0C 1E0
Tél: 418-392-9832
Pierre Gallant, Vice-président

Chambre de commerce de Brandon
117, rue Pacifique, Saint-Gabriel-de-Brandon QC J0K 2N0
Tél: 450-835-2105; Téléc: 450-835-2991
Ligne sans frais: 800-363-2788
france.brisebois@qc.aira.com
Affiliation(s): Chambre de commerce du Québec
France Brisebois, Directrice générale

Chambre de Commerce de Cap-des-Rosiers
1127, boul de Cap-des-Rosiers, Cap-des-Rosiers QC G4X 6G3
Gérard O'Connor, Secrétaire

Chambre de commerce de Carleton
629, boul Perron, Carleton QC G0C 1J0
Tél: 418-364-1004
Richard Gingras, Vice-président

Chambre de commerce de Causapscal
5, rue St-Jacques sud, Causapscal QC G0J 1J0
Tél: 418-756-6048
Marthe Gagnon, Contact

Chambre de commerce de Charlevoix
658, rue Richelieu, La Malbaie QC G5A 2X1
Tél: 418-435-6187; Téléc: 418-665-0077
info@creezdesliens.com
www.creezdesliens.com
Ysabelle Lusignan, Directrice générale

Chambre de commerce de Chibougamau
#4, 600, 3e rue, Chibougamau QC G8P 1P1
Tél: 418-748-4827
Affiliation(s): Chambre de Commerce du Québec et du Canada
Louisette Tremblay, Agente de liaison

Chambre de commerce de Cowansville et région
#100B, 104, rue du Sud, Cowansville QC J2K 2X2
Tél: 450-266-1665; Téléc: 450-266-4117
cccr@qc.aira.com
www.chambre-cowansville.com
Michel Fleury, Directeur général

Chambre de commerce de Danville-Shipton
CP 599, Danville QC J0A 1A0
Tél: 819-839-2742; Téléc: 819-839-2347
info@ccdanville.com
www.ccdanville.com
Isabelle Lodge, Présidente
Martine Satre, Vice-Présidente
Pierre Picard, Trésorier
Sylvie Beauchemin, Secrétaire

Chambre de commerce de Disraéli
CP 5008, 846, av Champlain, Disraéli QC G0N 1E0
Tél: 418-449-2955; Téléc: 418-449-1669
chambcommdisraeli@tlb.sympatico.ca
www.villededisraeli.com/chambredecommerce/index.html
Louise Aubert, Présidente

Chambre de commerce de Dolbeau-Mistassini
#300, 1341, boul Wallberg, Dolbeau-Mistassini QC G8L 1H3
Tél: 418-276-6638; Téléc: 418-276-9518
info@cdcdm.com
www.cdcdm.com
André Guy, Président

Chambre de commerce de East Angus et Région
221, St-Jean Ouest, East Angus QC J0B 1R0
Tél: 819-832-4950; Téléc: 819-832-1208
info@cceastangus.com
www.cceastangus.com
Véronique Bruneau, Directrice générale

Chambre de commerce de Ferme-Neuve
125, 12e rue, Ferme-Neuve QC J0W 1C0
Tél: 819-587-2727; Téléc: 819-587-2747
c.ouellette@yahoo.ca
Céline Ouellette, Coordonnatrice

Chambre de Commerce de Fermont
CP 419, Fermont QC G0G 1J0
Tél: 418-287-3000; Téléc: 418-287-3001
chambre.commerce@diffusionfermont.ca
www.ccfermont.com
Johanne Nolin, Directrice générale

Chambre de commerce de Fleurimont
#204, 798, rue Du Conseil, Sherbrooke QC J1G 1L2
Tél: 819-565-7991; Téléc: 819-565-3160
info@ccfleurimont.com
www.ccfleurimont.com
François Desmarais, Directeur général

Chambre de commerce de Forestville
34, route 138 est, Forestville QC G0T 1E0
Tél: 418-587-6136
www.repertoire-chambres.fccq.ca

Chambre de commerce de Gatineau
#100, 45, rue de Villebois, Gatineau QC J8T 8J7
Tél: 819-243-2246; Téléc: 819-243-3346
ccgatineau@ccgatineau.ca
www.ccgatineau.ca
Karl Lavoie, Directeur général

Chambre de commerce de Hâvre-Saint-Pierre
1235, rue de la Digue, RC-1, Hâvre-Saint-Pierre QC G0G 1P0
Tél: 418-538-2576; Téléc: 418-538-3822
Richard Boudreau, Personne ressource

Chambre de commerce de Hemmingford / Hemmingford Chamber of Commerce
#6, 505, rue Frontière, Hemmingford QC J0L 1H0
Tél: 450-247-3310; Téléc: 450-247-2389
villagehford@b2b2c.ca
www.hemmingford.org

Chambre de Commerce de l'Assomption
CP 3027, 312, rue St-Jacques, L'Assomption QC J5W 4M9
Tél: 450-589-2405; Téléc: 450-589-9213
cclassomption@qc.aira.com
www.cclassomption.qc.ca
Ginette Blanchard, Directrice générale

Chambre de commerce de l'Est de la Beauce
CP 519, Saint-Prosper QC G0M 1Y0
Tél: 418-594-1219
info@ccestbeauce.com
www.ccestbeauce.com
Suzanne Lantagne, Présidente

Chambre de commerce de l'Est de Montréal
#201, 5790, av Pierre-de Coubertin, Montréal QC H1N 1R4
Tél: 514-354-5378; Téléc: 514-354-5340
info@ccemontreal.ca
www.ccemontreal.ca
Isabelle Foisy, Directrice générale

Chambre de commerce de l'Est de Portneuf
CP 4031, Pont-Rouge QC G3H 3R4
Tél: 418-873-4085; Téléc: 418-873-4599
ccep@globetrotter.net
www.portneufest.com
Chantal Trudeau, Directrice générale

Chambre de commerce de l'Ile d'Orléans (CCIO)
490, côte du Pont, Saint-Pierre-Ile-d'Orléans QC G0A 4E0
Tél: 418-828-0880; Téléc: 418-828-2335
Ligne sans frais: 866-941-9411
ccio@videotron.ca
www.cciledorleans.com
Affiliation(s): Chambre de commerce de Québec
Marie Langlois, Directrice générale

Chambre de commerce de l'Ouest-de-l'Ile de Montréal
#602, 1000, boul Saint-Jean, Pointe-Claire QC H9R 5P1
Tél: 514-697-4228; Téléc: 514-697-2562
info@wimcc.ca
www.ccoim.ca
Elizabeth Tropea, Directrice générale

Chambre de commerce de la Haute-Gaspésie
CP 6014, Sainte-Anne-des-Monts QC G4V 2Y3
Tél: 418-763-2200; Téléc: 418-763-3473
dagneau.4@globetrotter.net
www.cchg.qc.ca
Carol Dagneau, Directeur général

Chambre de commerce de la Haute-Matawinie
521, rue Brassard, Saint-Michel-des-Saints QC J0K 3B0
Tél: 450-833-1334
infocchm@satelcom.qc.ca
www.haute-matawinie.com
France Chapdelaine, Directrice générale

Chambre de Commerce de la Jacques-Cartier
4517, rte de Fossambault, RR#3, Ste-Catherine-de-la-J-Cartier QC G0A 3M0
Tél: 418-875-4103; Téléc: 418-875-2913
Stéphanie Bérard, Secrétaire

Chambre de commerce de la MRC de la Matapédia
CP 5056, 123, rue Desbiens, 4e étage, Amqui QC G5J 3S5
Tél: 418-629-5765; Téléc: 418-629-5530
www.ccmrcmatapedia.qc.ca
Affiliation(s): Fédération des Chambres de commerce du Québec

Chantal St-Pierre, Directrice générale

Chambre de commerce de la MRC de Rivière-du-Loup
298, boul. Armand-Thériault, Rivière-du-Loup QC G5R 4C2
Tél: 418-862-5243; Téléc: 418-862-5136
info@ccmrcrdl.com
www.ccmrcrdl.com
Pierre Lévesque, Directeur général

Chambre de commerce de la région d'Acton
Édifice Gauthier, 1053, rue St-André, Acton Vale QC J0H 1A0
Tél: 450-546-0123; Téléc: 450-546-2709
ccracton@cooptel.qc.ca
www.chambredecommerce.info/
Joanne Joannette, Directrice générale

Chambre de commerce de la région d'Asbestos
332, 1re av, Asbestos QC J1T 1Y9
Tél: 819-879-5768; Téléc: 819-879-5871
ccra@qc.aira.com
www.lccra.com

Chambre de commerce de la région de Berthier / D'Autray
CP 482, Berthierville QC J0K 1A0
Tél: 450-836-4689; Téléc: 450-836-4926
ccregionberthier@hotmail.com
www.ccberthier-dautray.com
Yves Rousseau, Président

Chambre de commerce de la région de Mont-Joli
#304, 1553, boul. Jacques-Cartier, Mont-Joli QC G5H 2V9
Tél: 418-775-4366; Téléc: 418-775-4366
Rémi Sénéchal, Président

Chambre de commerce de la région de Salaberry-de-Valleyfield
#400, 100, rue Sainte-Cécile, Salaberry-de-Valleyfield QC J6T 1M1
Tél: 450-373-8789; Téléc: 450-373-8642
info@ccrsv.com
www.ccrsv.com
Sylvie Villemure, Directrice générale

Chambre de commerce de la région de Weedon
280, 9e av, Weedon QC J0B 3J0
Tél: 819-560-8555; Téléc: 819-877-1111
admin@ccweedon.com
www.ccweedon.com
Affiliation(s): Chambre de Commerce du Québec
David Gauthier, Président

Chambre de commerce de Lac-Brome
CP 3654, 255-C ch Knowlton, Lac-Brome QC J0E 1V0
Tél: 450-242-2870; Téléc: 450-242-6896
Ligne sans frais: 877-242-2870
info@cclacbrome.com
www.cclacbrome.com
Joëlle Chartrand, Directrice générale

Chambre de commerce de Lévis
#225, 5700, rue JB Michaud, Lévis QC G6V 0B1
Tél: 418-837-3411; Téléc: 418-837-8497
cclevis@cclevis.ca
www.cclevis.com
Sylvie Girard, Directrice générale

Chambre de commerce de Malartic
CP 368, Malartic QC J0Y 1Z0
Tél: 819-757-2332
Dalila Dupuis, Secrétaire

Chambre de commerce de Manicouagan
#302, 67, place La Salle, Baie-Comeau QC G4Z 1K1
Tél: 418-296-2010; Téléc: 418-296-5397
info@ccmanic.qc.ca
www.ccmanic.qc.ca
Claude Théberge, Président

Chambre de commerce de Mascouche
#240, 2822-A, ch Ste-Marie, Mascouche QC J7K 1N4
Tél: 450-966-1536; Téléc: 450-966-1531
info@ccmascouche.com
www.ccmascouche.com
Manon Brunelle, Directrice générale

Chambre de commerce de Mont-Laurier
360, du Pont, Mont-Laurier QC J9L 2R4
Tél: 855-623-3642; Téléc: 819-623-5220
info@ccmont.laurier.com
www.ccmont.laurier.com
Frederic LaPointe, President
Diane Aubin, Vice-Presidente

Valeri Perron, Secretaire
Jocelyn Girouard, Administrateur
Stephanie Laucau, Administrice
Ken Piche, Administrateur
Martin Clement, Administrateur
Eric Tourangeau, Administrateur

Chambre de commerce de Montmagny
#1, 17, rue St-Jean Baptiste ouest, Montmagny QC G5V 3B4
Tél: 418-248-3111; Téléc: 418-241-5779
Francis Lemieux, Directeur général

Chambre de commerce de Nicolet
30, rue Notre-Dame, Nicolet QC J3T 1G1
Tél: 819-293-4537; Téléc: 819-293-6092
chambre@chambre-cnicolet.org
www.chambre-cnicolet.org
Mylaine Paradis, Directrice générale

Chambre de commerce de Port-Cartier
CP 82, Port-Cartier QC G5B 2G7
Tél: 418-766-8047; Téléc: 418-766-6367
popco@globetrotter.net
Yves Desrosiers, Président

Chambre de commerce de Québec
17, rue St-Louis, Québec QC G1R 3Y8
Tél: 418-692-3853; Téléc: 418-694-2286
info@ccquebec.ca
www.ccquebec.ca
Affiliation(s): Chambre de commerce du Canada; Chambre de commerce du Québec
Alain Kirouac, Vice-président exécutif et directeu

Chambre de commerce de Rawdon
3590, rue Metcalfe, Rawdon QC J0K 1S0
Tél: 450-834-2282; Téléc: 450-834-3084
ccdr@bellnet.ca
www.chambrecommercerawdon.ca
Benoit Forest, Président

Chambre de commerce de Saint-Bruno
CP 123, Saint-Bruno-de-Montarville QC J3V 4P8
Tél: 450-653-0585; Téléc: 450-653-6967
info@ccstbruno.ca
www.ccstbruno.ca
Affiliation(s): Chambre de commerce du Québec; Chambre de commerce du Canada
Jacques Laliberté, Directeur général

Chambre de commerce de Saint-Côme
1661-A rue Principale, Saint-Côme QC J0K 2B0
Tél: 450-883-2730; Téléc: 450-883-3455
info@stcomelanaudiere.com
www.stcomelanaudiere.com
Sylvain Bourque, Président

Chambre de commerce de Sainte-Adèle
100, rue Morin, Sainte-Adèle QC J8B 2P7
Tél: 450-229-2644; Téléc: 450-229-1436
chambredecommerce@sainte-adele.net
www.sainte-adele.net
Gilles Lachance, Directeur général

Chambre de Commerce de Saint-Ephrem
CP 2015, Saint-Éphrem QC G0M 1R0
Tél: 418-484-2681
info@ccstephrem.com
www.ccstephrem.com
Jean-François Busque, Président

Chambre de commerce de Ste-Julienne
1799, rte 125, Sainte-Julienne QC J0K 2T0
Tél: 819-831-3551; Téléc: 819-831-3551
Nicole Bourgie, Secrétaire

Chambre de commerce de Ste-Justine
167, rte 204, Sainte-Justine QC G0R 1Y0
Tél: 418-383-5397; Téléc: 418-383-5398
sjustine@sogetel.net
Raymonde Lachance, Trésorière

Chambre de commerce de Sept-Iles
#237, 700, boul Laure, Sept-Iles QC G4R 1Y1
Tél: 418-968-3488; Téléc: 418-968-3432
ccsi@globetrotter.net
www.ccseptiles.com
Ginette Lehoux, Directrice générale

Chambre de commerce de Sherbrooke
#402, 75, rue Wellington nord, Sherbrooke QC J1H 5A9
Tél: 819-822-6151; Téléc: 819-822-6156
info@ccsherbrooke.ca
www.ccsherbrooke.ca
Louise Bourgault, Directrice générale

Chambre de commerce de St-Côme-Linière
1614, 6e rue, Saint-Côme-Linière QC G0M 1J0
Tél: 418-685-2630; Téléc: 418-685-2630
chambredecommerce@stcomeliniere.com
www.stcomeliniere.com/c_ccommerce.php
Sylvain Bourque, Président

Chambre de commerce de St-Donat
536A, rue Principale, Saint-Donat-de-Montcalm QC J0T 2C0
Tél: 819-424-2833; Téléc: 819-424-4366
cc.st-donat@bellnet.ca
Diane Champagne, Agente de liaison

Chambre de commerce de St-Eugène-de-Guigues
CP 1013, 9, 1ere Avenue Ouest, Saint-Eugène-de-Guigues QC J0Z 3L0
Tél: 819-785-2057
Lillian Matteau, Secrétaire

Chambre de commerce de St-Frédéric
2166, rue Principale, Saint-Frédéric QC G0N 1P0
Tél: 418-426-3104; Téléc: 418-426-3357
Monique Morin-Cyr, Secrétaire
Andre Lessard, Président

Chambre de commerce de St-Georges
#310, 8585, boul Lacroix, Ville de Saint-Georges Beauce QC G5Y 5L6
Tél: 418-228-7879; Téléc: 418-228-8074
administration@ccstgeorges.com
www.ccstgeorges.com
Affiliation(s): Chambre de commerce du Québec; Chambre de commerce du Canada
Sabrina Gagné, Directrice générale

Chambre de commerce de St-Jean-de-Dieu
CP 392, Saint-Jean-de-Dieu QC G0L 3M0
Tél: 418-963-3205
Chantale Rioux, Secrétaire

Chambre de commerce de St-Jules-de-Beauce
CP 81, 213, av Roy, Saint-Jules QC G0N 1R0
Tél: 418-397-1870
Sylvain Cloutier, Président

Chambre de commerce de St-Léonard
8370, boul. Lacordaire, Saint-Léonard QC H1R 3Y6
Tél: 514-325-4232; Téléc: 514-955-8544
tmelita@citenet.net
www.ccstleonard.qc.ca
Tony De Risi, Président

Chambre de Commerce de Terrebonne
#301, 1025, montée Masson, Lachenaie QC J6W 5H9
Tél: 450-471-8779; Téléc: 450-471-5610
info@ccterrebonne.qc.ca
www.ccterrebonne.qc.ca
Affiliation(s): Chambre de commerce du Canada; Chambre de commerce du Québec; Chambre de commerce régionale de Lanaudière; Réseau canadien de centres de services aux entreprises; Centre local de développement économique des Moulins (CLDEM); Centre local d'emploi de Terrebonne; Société de développement touristique des Moulins; Conseil de développement bioalimentaire de Lanaudière.
Robert Lalancette, Directeur général

Chambre de commerce de Tring-Jonction
184, av Commerciale, Tring-Jonction QC G0N 1X0
Tél: 418-427-3320; Téléc: 418-427-1466
Danye Vachon, Secrétaire

Chambre de commerce de Valcourt et Région
CP 900, Valcourt QC J0E 2L0
Tél: 450-532-3041; Téléc: 450-532-3041
commerce@cooptel.qc.ca
Affiliation(s): Chambre de commerce régionale de l'Estrie
Ghislain D'Astous, Trésorier

Chambre de commerce de Val-d'Or
400, 3e av, Val-d'Or QC J9P 1R9
Tél: 819-825-3703; Téléc: 819-825-8599
ccvd@cablevision.qc.ca
www.ccvd.qc.ca
Alain Laplante, Président

Chambre de commerce de Villebois
3897, rue de l'Église, Villebois QC J0Z 3V0
Tél: 819-941-6302
www.villebois.qc.ca
Claude Côté, Président

Chambre de commerce de Ville-Marie
1, rue Industrielle, Ville-Marie QC J9V 1S3
Tél: 819-629-2918; Téléc: 819-622-1801
chambredecommerce-vill@cablevision.qc.ca

Anne-Marie Demers, Secrétaire

Chambre de commerce des Iles-de-la-Madeleine (CCIM)
Édifice Fernand Cyr, #103, 735, ch Principal, Cap-aux-Meules QC G4T 1G8
Tél: 418-986-4111; Téléc: 418-986-4112
info@ccim.qc.ca
www.ccim.qc.ca
Claire Gaudet, Directrice générale

Chambre de commerce du Centre-de-la-Mauricie
900, 6e Avenue, Shawinigan-Sud QC G9P 1S4
Tél: 819-536-0777; Téléc: 819-536-0039
info@cccmauricie.qc.ca
www.cccmauricie.qc.ca
Isabele Rouette, Directrice générale

Chambre de commerce du Grand Joliette
500, rue Dollard, Joliette QC J6E 4M4
Tél: 450-759-6363; Téléc: 450-759-5012
info@ccgj.qc.ca
www.ccgj.qc.ca
André Hénault, Directeur général

Chambre de commerce du Grand Paspébiac
CP 1232, 6, boul Gérard D. Lévesque est, Paspébiac QC G0C 2K0
Tél: 418-752-3330; Téléc: 418-752-3330
Roger Horth, Secrétaire

Chambre de commerce du Haut St-Maurice
547-C, rue Commerciale, La Tuque QC G9X 3A7
Tél: 819-523-9933
Hélène Langlais, Directrice générale

Chambre de commerce du Haut-Richelieu
#301, 929, boul Séminaire nord, Saint-Jean-sur-Richelieu QC J3A 1B6
Tél: 450-346-2544; Téléc: 450-346-3812
info@cchautrichelieu.qc.ca
www.cchautrichelieu.qc.ca
Marie-Josée Denis, Directrice générale

Chambre de commerce du Lac des Deux-Montagnes (Pointe-Calumet, Saint-Joseph-du-Lac, Oka & Saint-Placide)
#400, 190 - 41e av, Pointe-Calumet QC J0N 1G2
Tél: 450-472-7535; Téléc: 450-472-0229
c.c.lac2montagnes@videotron.ca
www.cclac2montagnes.com
Affiliation(s): Chambre de Commerce du Québec
Denise Lemay, Directrice générale

Chambre de commerce du Lac Robertson
CP 100, Tête-à-la-Baleine QC G0G 2W0
Tél: 418-773-2659; Téléc: 418-773-2526
Gérald Organ, Secrétaire

Chambre de commerce du Montréal métropolitain / Board of Trade of Metropolitan Montréal
Niveau plaza, #6000, 380, rue St-Antoine ouest, Montréal QC H3Y 3X7
Tél: 514-871-4000; Téléc: 514-871-1255
info@ccmm.qc.ca
www.ccmm.qc.ca
Michel Leblanc, Président et chef de la direction

Chambre de commerce du Saguenay
194, rue Price ouest, Chicoutimi QC G7J 1H1
Tél: 418-543-5941; Téléc: 418-543-5576
info@ccchic.qc.ca
www.ccchic.qc.ca
Réjean Boucher, Directeur général

Chambre de commerce du secteur de Normandin
1048, rue St-Cyrille, Normandin QC G8M 4R9
Tél: 418-274-2004; Téléc: 418-274-7171
ccnormandin@hotmail.com
www.ville.normandin.qc.ca
Denise Paquette, Directrice générale

Chambre de commerce du Transcontinental
CP 2004, Rivière-Bleue QC G0L 2B0
Tél: 418-893-2347; Téléc: 418-893-2889
cctrans@globetrotter.net
pages.globetrotter.net/cctrans
Yves Thibault, Président

Chambre de commerce Duparquet
CP 369, Duparquet QC J0Z 1W0
Tél: 819-948-2030
Jasmine Therrien, Secrétaire

Chambre de commerce East Broughton
CP 916, East Broughton QC G0N 1G0
Tél: 418-427-5761; Téléc: 418-427-4032
cceastbroughton@globetrotter.net
Annie Roy, Secrétaire

Chambre de commerce et d'entreprises de Bellechasse
225A, rue Principale, Saint-Gervais QC G0R 3C0
Tél: 418-887-4075; Téléc: 418-887-4074
info@ccbellechasse.ca
www.ccbellechasse.ca
Yvon Laflamme, Président

Chambre de commerce et d'industrie (St-Eustache / Deux-Montagnes / Ste-Marthe-sur-le-Lac)
67 A, boul. Industriel, Saint-Eustache QC J7R 5P2
Tél: 450-491-1991; Téléc: 450-491-1648
info@chambrecommerce.com
www.chambrecommerce.com
Michel Goyer, Directeur général

Chambre de commerce et d'industrie d'Abitibi-Ouest
#203, 99, 5e Av est, La Sarre QC J9Z 3A8
Tél: 819-333-9836; Téléc: 819-333-5737
ccao@ccao.qc.ca
www.ccao.qc.ca
Nathalie Aubin, Directrice générale

Chambre de commerce et d'industrie d'Argenteuil
#225, 580, rue Principale, Lachute QC J8H 1Y7
Tél: 450-562-1947; Téléc: 450-562-1896
cci.argen@qc.aira.com
www.cciargenteuil.qc.ca
Suzanne Gaudet, Directrice générale

Chambre de commerce et d'industrie de Bécancour
1045, av Nicolas Perrot, Bécancour QC G9H 3B7
Tél: 819-294-6010; Téléc: 819-294-6020
info@ccibecancour.ca
www.ccibecancour.ca
Jean-François Giroux, Président

Chambre de commerce et d'industrie de Châteauguay
#100, 15, boul Maple, Châteauguay QC J6J 3P7
Tél: 450-698-0027; Téléc: 450-698-0088
ccic@qc.aira.com
www.ccichateauguay.ca
Dorys Miousse, Directrice générale

Chambre de commerce et d'industrie de Drummond
CP 188, 234, rue Saint-Marcel, Drummondville QC J2B 6V7
Tél: 819-477-7822; Téléc: 819-477-2823
info@ccid.qc.ca
www.ccid.qc.ca
Alain Côté, Directeur général

Chambre de commerce et d'industrie de la MRC de Maskinongé
396, Ste-Élisabeth, Louiseville QC J5V 1M7
Tél: 819-228-8582; Téléc: 819-228-8989
info@cci-maskinonge.ca
www.cci-maskinonge.ca
Marc H. Plante, Directeur général

Chambre de commerce et d'Industrie de la région de Coaticook (CCIRC)
150, rue Child, Coaticook QC J1A 2B3
Tél: 819-849-4733; Téléc: 819-849-6828
ccrc@abacom.com
www.ccircoaticook.ca
Sonia Montminy, Présidente

Chambre de commerce et d'industrie de la région de Richmond
CP 3119, Richmond QC J0B 2H0
Tél: 819-826-5854; Téléc: 819-826-2813
info@ccrichmond.com
www.ccrichmond.com
Denis Cavallo, Président
Hélène Tousignant, Vice-présidente
Roger Viens, Secrétaire
Martine Plante, Trésorière
Annie Lussier, Directeur
Yvon Poirier, Directeur
Charles Mallette, Directeur

Chambre de commerce et d'industrie de la Rive-Sud
#101, 85, rue Saint-Charles ouest, Longueuil QC J4H 1C5
Tél: 450-463-2121; Téléc: 450-463-1858
info@ccirs.qc.ca
www.ccirs.qc.ca

Hélène Bergeron, Directrice générale

Chambre de commerce et d'industrie de la Vallée-du-Richelieu
#102, 230, rue Brébeuf, Beloeil QC J3G 5P3
Tél: 450-464-3733; Téléc: 450-446-4163
www.ccivr.qc.ca
Anne Durocher, Directrice générale

Chambre de commerce et d'industrie de Laval (CCIL)
#200, 1555, boul Chomedey, Laval QC H7V 3Z1
Tél: 450-682-5255; Téléc: 450-682-5735
info@ccilaval.qc.ca
www.ccilaval.qc.ca
Francine Cabral, Directrice générale

Chambre de commerce et d'industrie de Maniwaki (CCIM)
171, rue Principale sud, Maniwaki QC J9E 1Z8
Tél: 819-449-6627; Téléc: 819-449-7667
Ligne sans frais: 866-449-6728
valeried@ccimki.ca
www.ccimaniwaki.com
Claude Benoit, Président
Sophie Beaudoin, Directrice générale

Chambre de commerce et d'industrie de Mirabel
#208, 13479, boul du Curé Labelle, Mirabel QC J7J 1L2
Tél: 450-433-1944; Téléc: 450-433-5168
info@ccmirabel.com
Yves Legault, Président

Chambre de commerce et d'industrie de Montréal-Nord (CRIMN)
#006A, 6000, boul Henri-Bourassa est, Montréal-Nord QC H1G 2T6
Tél: 514-329-4453; Téléc: 514-329-5373
info@ccimn.qc.ca
www.ccimn.qc.ca
Jean C. Touchette, Directeur général

Chambre de commerce et d'industrie de Rouyn-Noranda (CCIRN)
70, Avenue du Lac, Rouyn-Noranda QC J9X 4N4
Tél: 819-797-2000; Téléc: 819-762-3091
reseau@ccirn.qc.ca
www.ccirn.qc.ca
Guy Veillet, Présidente

Chambre de commerce et d'industrie de St-Félicien
CP 34, 1209, boul Sacré-Coeur, Saint-Félicien QC G8K 2P8
Tél: 418-679-2097; Téléc: 418-679-4039
ccistfe@ville.stfelicien.qc.ca
www.chambre-sf.com
Jean-Paul Asselin, Directeur général

Chambre de commerce et d'industrie de St-Joseph-de-Beauce
165, av Taschereau, Saint-Joseph-de-Beauce QC G0S 2V0
Tél: 418-397-5980; Téléc: 418-397-5982
Marielle Bertrand, Adjointe administrative

Chambre de commerce et d'industrie de St-Laurent
#204, 935, Décarie, Saint-Laurent QC H4L 3M3
Tél: 514-333-5222; Téléc: 514-333-0937
info@ccstl.qc.ca
www.ccstl.qc.ca
Robert Petit, Directeur général

Chambre de commerce et d'industrie de Thetford Mines
81, rue Notre-Dame ouest, Thetford Mines QC G6G 1J4
Tél: 418-338-4551; Téléc: 418-335-2066
www.ccitm.com
Louis Thivierge, Directeur général

Chambre de commerce et d'industrie de Varennes (CCIV)
266, rue Ste-Anne, local B, Varennes QC J3X 1R7
Tél: 450-652-4209; Téléc: 450-652-4244
info@cciv.ca
www.cciv.ca
Carole Audet, Coordonnatrice

Chambre de commerce et d'industrie de Ville de La Baie
285, boul Grande Baie nord, La Baie QC G7B 3K4
Tél: 418-544-9861
Joanne Dubois, Directrice générale

Chambre de commerce et d'industrie des Bois-Francs et de l'Érable
122, rue de l'Acqueduc, Victoriaville QC G6P 1M3
Tél: 819-758-6371; Téléc: 819-758-4604
ccibf@ccibf.com
www.ccibf.qc.ca
Marie-France Béliveau, Directrice générale

Chambre de commerce et d'industrie du bassin de Chambly (CCIB)
929, boul. de Périgny, Chambly QC J3L 5H5
Tél: 450-658-7598; Téléc: 450-658-6477
info@ccibc.qc.ca
www.ccibc.qc.ca
Johanne Garinther, Coordonnatrice administrative

Chambre de commerce et d'industrie du secteur Roberval (CCISR)
CP 115, Roberval QC G8H 2N4
Tél: 418-275-3504; Téléc: 418-275-0851
info@ccisr.qc.ca
www.ccisr.qc.ca
Affiliation(s): Chambre de Commerce du Québec; Chambre de Commerce du Canada
Érik Simard, Directeur général

Chambre de commerce et d'industrie Lac-Saint-Jean-Est
625, rue Bergeron ouest, Alma QC G8B 1V3
Tél: 418-662-2734; Téléc: 418-669-2220
cca@qc.aira.com
www.ccilacsaintjeanest.com
Daniel Dubé, Directeur général

Chambre de commerce et d'industrie Magog-Orford
801, rue Principale Ouest, Magog QC J1X 2B4
Tél: 819-843-3494; Téléc: 819-843-4124
info@ccimo.qc.ca
www.ccimo.qc.ca
Francine Caya, Directrice générale

Chambre de commerce et d'industrie régionale de Saint-Léonard-d'Aston
#1, 370, rue Principale, Saint-Léonard-d'Aston QC J0C 1M0
Tél: 819-399-2020; Téléc: 819-399-3288
ccistl@tlb.sympatico.ca
www.ccst-leonard-daston.com
Marthe Proulx, Directrice générale

Chambre de commerce et d'industrie Sorel-Tracy métropolitain
CP 568, #112, 67, rue George, Sorel-Tracy QC J3P 1C2
Tél: 450-742-0018; Téléc: 450-742-7442
www.ccstm.qc.ca
Rachel Doyon, Directrice générale

Chambre de commerce et d'industrie St-Jérôme (CCISJ)
309, rue De Villemure, Saint-Jérôme QC J7Z 5J5
Tél: 450-431-4339; Téléc: 450-431-1677
rachel.roy@ccisj.qc.ca
www.ccisj.qc.ca
Jocelyne Légaré, Directrice générale

Chambre de commerce et d'industrie Vaudreuil-Dorion
#123, 421, av St-Charles, Vaudreuil-Dorion QC J7V 2M9
Tél: 450-424-6886; Téléc: 450-424-4989
ccvd@bellnet.ca
www.ccivd.com
Charles L. Milot, Directeur général

Chambre de commerce et d'industries de Trois-Rivières
CP 1045, 168, rue Bonaventure, Trois-Rivières QC G9A 5K4
Tél: 819-375-9628; Téléc: 819-375-9083
info@ccdtr.com
www.ccdtr.com
Claude Durand, Directrice générale

Chambre de commerce et de l'industrie du Haut St-Laurent
CP 1914, 8, rue King, Huntingdon QC J0S 1H0
Tél: 450-264-5252; Téléc: 450-264-5111
cdechsl@suroit.com
ww.cdechsl.com
Kathleen Bisson, Présidente

Chambre de commerce et de l'industrie Les Maskoutains
780, av de L'Hôtel-de-ville, Saint-Hyacinthe QC J2S 5B2
Tél: 450-773-3474; Téléc: 450-773-9339
chambre@chambrecommerce.ca
www.chambrecommerce.ca
Nicole Laverrière, Directrice générale

Chambre de commerce et de l'industrie Rimouski-Neigette
CP 1296, #101, 125, rue de l'Évêché, Rimouski QC G5L 8M2
Tél: 418-722-4494; Téléc: 418-722-8402
info@ccrimouski.com
www.ccrimouski.com
Serge Barrette, Directeur principal

Chambre de commerce et de tourisme de Gaspé
27, boul York est, Gaspé QC G4X 2K9
Tél: 418-368-8525; Téléc: 418-368-8549
info@cctgaspe.org
cctgaspe.org
Mélissa Plourde, Directrice générale

Chambre de commerce et de tourisme de la Vallée de Saint-Sauveur/Piedmont
30, rue Filion, Saint-Sauveur QC J0R 1R0
Tél: 450-227-2564; Téléc: 450-227-6480
Ligne sans frais: 877-528-2553
info@valleesaintsauveur.com
www.valleesaintsauveur.com
Pierre Urquhart, Directeur général

Chambre de commerce et de tourisme de Murdochville
CP 879, #29, 635 - 5e rue, Murdochville QC G0E 1W0
Tél: 418-784-2577; Téléc: 418-784-2597
ccmurd.roy@globetrotter.net
www.ccmurdochville.com
Francine Roy, Directrice générale

Chambre de commerce et de tourisme de St-Adolphe-d'Howard
CP 326, Saint-Adolphe-d'Howard QC J0T 2B0
Ligne sans frais: 888-710-4636
info@st-adolphe.com
www.st-adolphe.com
Albert Difruscia, Président

Chambre de commerce et de'industrie du Sud-Ouest de Montréal
#32, 410, av Lafleur, Montréal QC H8R 3H6
Tél: 514-365-4575; Téléc: 514-365-0487
www.ccisom.ca
Affiliation(s): Chambre de commerce du Canada; Fédération des Chambres de commerce du Québec
Gilles Dubien, Directeur général

Chambre de commerce gaie du Québec (CCGQ) / The Québec Gay Chamber of Commerce
#302, 249, rue St-Jacques, Montréal QC H2Y 1M6
Tél: 514-522-1885; Téléc: 514-522-9468
Ligne sans frais: 888-595-8110
info@ccgq.ca
www.ccgq.ca
Hans Janiak, Président

Chambre de commerce Haute-Yamaska et Région
650, rue Principale, Granby QC J2G 8L4
Tél: 450-372-6100; Téléc: 450-372-3161
info@chambredecommerce.org
www.chambredecommerce.org
Céline Gagnon, Directrice générale

Chambre de commerce Hemmingford—Napierville—Saint-Rémi
CP 3541, 1009, rue Notre-Dame, Saint-Rémi QC J0L 2L0
Tél: 450-615-0512; Téléc: 450-615-0612
info@ccsaint-remi.ca
www.ccsaint-remi.ca

Chambre de commerce juive / Jewish Chamber of Commerce
1, carré Cummings, Montréal QC H3W 1M6
Tél: 514-345-2645; Téléc: 514-345-2655
info@jccmontreal.com
www.jccmontreal.com
Elliot Greenstone, Coprésident
Heidi Minkoff, Coprésidente

Chambre de commerce Kamouraska-L'Islet (CCKL)
#208, 1000, 6e av, La Pocatière QC G0R 1Z0
Tél: 418-856-6227; Téléc: 418-856-6462
Ligne sans frais: 877-856-6227
cckl@qc.aira.com
www.cckl.org
Gabriel Hudon, Président

Chambre de commerce MRC du Rocher-Percé
CP 129, 35, rue Commerciale ouest, Chandler QC G0C 1K0
Tél: 418-689-6998
info@ccrocherperce.org
www.ccrocherperce.org
Sonya Cauvier, Directrice générale

Chambre de commerce Notre-Dame-du-Lac
CP 147, Notre-Dame-du-Lac QC G0L 1X0
Tél: 418-899-6987
Jean-Paul Boucher, Trésorier

Chambre de commerce Notre-Dame-du-Nord
CP 517, Notre-Dame-du-Nord QC J0Z 3B0
Tél: 819-723-2814; Téléc: 819-723-2899
Ernest Laplante, Président

Chambre de commerce Nouvelle Beauce
CP 684, #C, 700, rue Notre-Dame nord, Sainte-Marie QC G6E 2K9
Tél: 418-387-2006; Téléc: 418-387-8223
info@ccnb.ca
www.nouvellebeauce.com/site.asp
Yannick Richard, Président
Johanne Côté, Directrice

Chambre de commerce Pierre-Le Gardeur De Repentigny
#151, 534, rue Notre-Dame, Repentigny QC J6A 2T8
Tél: 450-581-3010; Téléc: 450-581-5069
info@ccrepentigny.qc.ca
www.ccrepentigny.qc.ca
Linda Mallette, Directrice générale

Chambre de commerce région de Matane
CP 518, Matane QC G4W 3P5
Tél: 418-562-9344; Téléc: 418-562-7734
info@ccmatane.com
www.ccmatane.com
Yvon Gaudet, Directeur général

Chambre de commerce région de Mégantic
6346, rue Salaberry, Lac-Mégantic QC G6B 1J3
Tél: 819-583-5392; Téléc: 819-583-5457
info@ccrmeg.com
www.ccrmeg.com
Isabelle Gagnon, Directrice générale

Chambre de commerce régionale de St-Raymond (CCRSR)
#1, 100, av St-Jacques, Saint-Raymond QC G3L 3Y1
Tél: 418-337-4049; Téléc: 418-337-8017
ccrsr@cite.net
www.ccrsr.qc.ca
Isabelle Jobin, Directrice générale

Chambre de commerce régionale de Windsor
13, rue de la Croix, Windsor QC J1S 2K3
Tél: 819-845-5646
Suzanne Grimard, Présidente

Chambre de commerce régionale des entrepreneurs de Québec (CCREQ)
#3200, 2700, boul Laurier, Sainte-Foy QC G1V 4K5
Tél: 418-651-7181; Téléc: 418-651-5248
info@cceq.ca
Yvan Lachance, Vice-président exécutif

Chambre de commerce Ste-Émélie-de-l'Énergie
CP 272, Sainte-Émélie-de-l'Énergie QC J0K 2K0
Tél: 450-886-1658
rlachance@simonlussier.com
Carmelle Tessier, Secrétaire

Chambre de commerce Saint-Lin-Laurentides
CP 3340, #101, 704, rue St-Isidore, Saint-Lin-Laurentides QC J5M 2V2
Tél: 450-439-3704; Téléc: 450-439-2066
chambrecstlin@videotron.ca
André Corbeil, Président

Chambre de commerce secteur ouest de Portneuf
CP 2006, 295, rue Gauthier, local 2, Saint-Marc-des-Carrières QC G0A 4B0
Tél: 418-268-5447; Téléc: 418-268-3532
ccsop@globetrotter.net
www.portneufouest.com
Étienne Bourré-Denis, Personne ressource

Chambre de commerce St-Félix de Valois
15, ch Joliette, Saint-Félix-de-Valois QC J0K 2M0
Tél: 450-889-8161; Téléc: 450-889-1590
ccst-flx@megacom.net
www.stfelixdevalois.qc.ca
Josée Durand, Directrice générale

Chambre de commerce St-Jean-de-Matha
1159, rte Louis-Cyr, Saint-Jean-de-Matha QC J0K 2S0
Tél: 450-886-0599; Téléc: 450-886-3123
info@chambrematha.com
www.chambrematha.com
Régis Morissette, Président

Chambre de commerce St-Martin de Beauce
CP 31, 60, 5e av ouest, Saint-Martin QC G0M 1B0
Tél: 418-382-5549
chambre@st-martin.qc.ca
www.st-martin.qc.ca
Affiliation(s): Chambre de commerce du Québec; Chambre de commerce du Canada

Chambre de commerce Vallée de la Missisquoi
858, rte de la Missisquoi, Bolton Centre QC J0E 1G0
Tél: 450-292-4217

Chambre de commerce Vallée de la Petite-Nation
185, rue Henri-Bourassa, Papineauville QC J0V 1R0
Tél: 819-427-8450; Téléc: 819-427-9849
ccvpn@videotron.ca
www.ccvpn.org
Karine Robillard, Directrice générale

Chambre de commerce Ville de Mont-Tremblant
990, rue Lauzon, Mont-Tremblant QC J8E 3J5
Tél: 819-425-8441; Téléc: 819-425-7949
info@ccdemonttremblant.com
www.ccdemonttremblant.com
Paul Bernier, Directeur général

Jeune chambre de commerce de Montréal (JCCM)
#1220, 1010, rue Sherbrooke ouest, Montréal QC H3A 2R7
Tél: 514-845-4951; Téléc: 514-845-0587
vboilard@jccm.org
www.jccm.org
Marie-Félix Gascon, Directrice générale

Jeune chambre de commerce de Québec
#249, 4600, boul Henri-Bourassa, Charlesbourg QC G1H 3A5
Tél: 418-622-6937; Téléc: 418-628-7777
jccq@jccq.qc.ca
www.jccq.qc.ca
Marie-Eve Goulet, Présidente

Regroupement des jeunes chambres de commerce du Québec (RJCCQ)
555, rue René-Lévesque Ouest, 9e étage, Montréal QC H2Z 1B1
Tél: 514-933-7595; Téléc: 514-844-0226
Ligne sans frais: 877-933-7595
info@rjccq.com
www.rjccq.com
Anthony Lacopo, Président

Saskatchewan

Assiniboia Chamber of Commerce (SK)
PO Box 1803, 110 - 4th Ave. West, Assiniboia SK S0H 0B0
Tel: 306-642-5553; Fax: 306-642-3529
aeda@assiniboia.net
Terry L. Sieffert, President
Sonia Dahlman, Treasurer
Bonnie Ruzicka, Executive Assistant

Battlefords Chamber of Commerce
PO Box 1000, North Battleford SK S9A 3E6
Tel: 306-445-6226; Fax: 306-445-6633
b.chamber@sasktel.net
www.battlefordschamber.com
Affiliation(s): Institution of Association Executives; Tourism Industry Association of Saskatchewan
Patti Acaster, President
Linda Machniak, Executive Director

Big River Chamber of Commerce
c/o Kangaroo Cottage, PO Box 351, Big River SK S0J 0E0
Tel: 306-469-2484; Fax: 306-469-2485
www.bigriver.ca
Jeanette Wicinski-Dunn, President
Linda McKenzie, Secretary

Biggar & District Chamber of Commerce
c/o Bear Hills R.D.C., PO Box 327, 117 - 3rd Ave. West, Biggar SK S0K 0M0
Tel: 306-948-2295; Fax: 306-948-5050
bearhills.rdc@sasktel.net
townofbiggar.com
Garry Faye, Co-Chair
Diane Koenders, Sec.-Treas.

Blaine Lake & District Chamber of Commerce
PO Box 178, Blaine Lake SK S0J 0J0
Tel: 306-497-2695; Fax: 306-497-2402
elhoe@sasktel.net
T.L. Bowie, President

Broadview Chamber of Commerce
PO Box 508, Broadview SK S0G 0K0
Tel: 306-696-3166
D.B. Norbeck, President
D.A. Massier, Secretary

Canora & District Chamber of Commerce
PO Box 1409, Canora SK S0A 0L0
Tel: 306-563-4123; Fax: 306-563-4124
Nick Martinuk, President
Dana Antonovitch, Secretary

Carlyle Chamber of Commerce
PO Box 365, Carlyle SK S0C 0R0
Tel: 306-453-6718; Fax: 306-453-2910
blair.andrew@andrewagencies.com
Blair Andrew, President
S. Colpitts, Secretary

Choiceland & District Chamber of Commerce
c/o Grow Plan Fertilizers Ltd., PO Box 339, 115 Railway Ave. West, Choiceland SK S0J 0M0
Tel: 306-428-2300; Fax: 306-428-2526
Frank H. Bond, President
Colleen F Digness, Secretary

Coronach Community Chamber of Commerce
PO Box 577, Coronach SK S0H 0Z0
Tel: 306-267-2077; Fax: 306-267-2047
marshalljackie@hotmail.com
Affiliation(s): Saskatchewan Chamber of Commerce
J. Marshall, President
S. Nelson, Secretary

Debden & District Chamber of Commerce
PO Box 91, Debden SK S0J 0S0
Tel: 306-724-2266; Fax: 306-724-4505
p.demers@sasktel.net
Phil Demers, President
Denis Belair, Secretary

Eastend & District Chamber of Commerce
c/o L & E Farm Sales Ltd., PO Box 534, Eastend SK S0N 0T0
Tel: 306-295-3355; Fax: 306-295-3571
Bonnie Gleim, President
Stephanie Morris, Secretary

Eatonia & District Chamber of Commerce
PO Box 370, Eatonia SK S0L 0Y0
Tel: 306-967-2506; Fax: 306-967-2267
T. Drurey, President
Anne Rhodes, Secretary

Esterhazy & District Chamber of Commerce
PO Box 778, Esterhazy SK S0A 0X0
Tel: 306-745-5405; Fax: 306-745-6797
esterhazy.ed@sasktel.net
T. Lippai, President
J. Parker, Secretary

Estevan Chamber of Commerce
322 - 4th St., Estevan SK S4A 0T8
Tel: 306-634-2828; Fax: 306-634-6729
info@estevanchamber.ca
www.estevanchamber.ca
Lynn Chipley, President
Michel Cyrenne, CEO
Kevin D'Souza, Tourism Development Coordinator
Claire Robson, Economic Development Officer

Fort Qu'Appelle & District Chamber of Commerce
c/o Mission Ridge, PO Box 1273, Fort Qu'appelle SK S0G 1S0
Tel: 306-332-5717; Fax: 306-332-1287
Denis Palmier, Secretary
K. Mattern, President

Fox Valley Chamber of Commerce
c/o Double L. Farms, PO Box 133, Fox Valley SK S0N 0V0
Tel: 306-666-4447; Fax: 306-666-4448
Lester N Lodoen, President
Delia E. Hughes, Secretary

Goodsoil & District Chamber of Commerce
PO Box 88, Main St., Goodsoil SK S0M 1A0
Tel: 306-238-2033; Fax: 306-238-4441
joan.baer@goodsoil.cu.sk.ca
Lucille Martin, President
Joan Baer, Secretary

Gravelbourg Chamber of Commerce
PO Box 85, Gravelbourg SK S0H 1X0
Tel: 306-648-3182; Fax: 306-648-2311
brouwerc@sasktel.net
G. Murray, Treasurer
Cees Brouwer, President

Greater Saskatoon Chamber of Commerce
#104, 202 - 4th Ave. North, Saskatoon SK S7K 0K1
Tel: 306-244-2151; Fax: 306-244-8366
chamber@eboardoftrade.com
www.eboardoftrade.com
Affiliation(s): Enterprise Centre; Leadership Saskatoon; Raj Manek Mentorship Program; Saskatchewan Agrivision Corporation; Saskatchewan Economic Development Authority; Saskatchewan Young Professionals & Entrepreneurs; Saskatoon Aboriginal Employment & Business Opportunities Inc., Saskatoon Air Services; Saskatoon Regional Economic Development Authority; Tourism Saskatoon; United Way of Saskatoon; Vision 2000
Kent Smith-Windsor, Executive Director
Marion Ghiglione, President

Herbert & District Chamber of Commerce
PO Box 700, Herbert SK S0H 2A0
Tel: 306-784-3475; Fax: 306-784-2801
marniescoffeeshop@sasktel.net
Kevin Braun, President
Sandra MacArthur, Secretary

Hudson Bay Chamber of Commerce
PO Box 430, Hudson Bay SK S0E 0Y0
Tel: 306-865-2288; Fax: 306-865-2177
Tonia Jones, President
Liz Johnson, Secretary

Humboldt & District Chamber of Commerce
PO Box 1440, Humboldt SK S0K 2A0
Tel: 306-682-4990; Fax: 306-682-5203
humboldtchamber@sasktel.net
www.humboldtchamber.ca
Bonnie Classen, President
Lance Stockbrugger, Vice-President

Indian Head Chamber of Commerce
PO Box 1233, Indian Head SK S0G 2K0
Tel: 306-695-2238; Fax: 306-695-2307
ihac@sasktel.net
Melanie Roth, Secretary

Kamsack & District Chamber of Commerce
PO Box 817, Kamsack SK S0A 1S0
Tel: 306-542-9694; Fax: 306-542-4396
becenko@sasktel.net
Jack Koreluik, President
Wendy Becenko, Secretary

Kelvington & District Chamber of Commerce
c/o Kelvington Radio, PO Box 667, 107 Main St., Kelvington SK S0A 1W0
Tel: 306-327-4656
Jennifer L. Crawford, President
Don Ewing, Sec.-Treas.

Kenaston & District Chamber of Commerce
PO Box 70, Kenaston SK S0G 2N0
Tel: 306-252-2236; Fax: 306-252-2089
S. Anbolt, Sec.-Treas.
Mary Lou Whittles, President

Kerrobert Chamber of Commerce
PO Box 408, Kerrobert SK S0L 1R0
Tel: 306-834-5423
kerrobert@sasktel.net
Myrna H. Kissick, President

Kindersley Chamber of Commerce
PO Box 1537, Kindersley SK S0L 1S0
Tel: 306-463-2320; Fax: 306-463-2312
kindersleychamber@sasktel.net
www.kindersleychamber.com
Richard Jones, President
Esther Redden, Office Manager

Kinistino & District Chamber of Commerce
PO Box 803, Kinistino SK S0J 1H0
Tel: 306-864-2275

Kipling Chamber of Commerce
PO Box 700, Kipling SK S0G 2S0
Tel: 306-736-8520; Fax: 306-736-2260
ssauve.mib@sasktel.net
D.G. Balon, Secretary
K. Hassler, President

Lafleche & District Chamber of Commerce
PO Box 40, 41 Main St., Lafleche SK S0H 2K0
Tel: 306-472-3252; Fax: 306-472-5958
lgs.cga@sasktel.net
L. Sutherland, President
Twyla Verhelst, Secretary

Langenburg & District Chamber of Commerce
PO Box 610, Langenburg SK S0A 2A0
Tel: 306-743-2231; Fax: 306-743-2873
R.J. Buchberger, President
Janice Fogg, Secretary

Macklin Chamber of Commerce
PO Box 642, Macklin SK S0L 2C0
Tel: 306-753-2221; Fax: 306-753-3585
macklin.coop@sasktel.net
D.J. Lysitza, President
C.A. Moss, Treasurer

Maidstone & District Chamber of Commerce
PO Box 300, Maidstone SK S0M 1M0
Tel: 306-893-2461; Fax: 306-893-4222
cheryl@elliottinsurance.ca
Cheryl D Jamieson, Secretary
Glenn Colley, President

Maple Creek Chamber of Commerce
PO Box 1766, Maple Creek SK S0N 1N0
Tel: 306-558-7055; Fax: 306-662-2422
thedailygrind@sasktel.net
Tina Cresswell, President
Wayne Litke, Secretary

Meadow Lake & District Chamber of Commerce
c/o Northwest REDA, PO Box 1168, 106 - 1st St. East, Meadow Lake SK S9X 1Y8
Tel: 306-236-4447; Fax: 306-236-1833
mltouristinfo@sasktel.net
Affiliation(s): Northwest Regional Economic Development Authority
Kirt Prete, President
Samantha L. Clarkson, Secretary

Melfort & District Chamber of Commerce
PO Box 2002, 102 Spruce Haven Rd., Melfort SK S0E 1A0
Tel: 306-752-4636; Fax: 306-752-9505
melfortchamber@sasktel.net
www.melfortchamber.com
Jim Thiessen, President
Lori Fettes, Executive Director

Melville & District Chamber of Commerce
c/o Chamber Office, PO Box 429, 420 Main St., Melville SK S0A 2P0
Tel: 306-728-4177; Fax: 306-728-5911
melvillechamber@sasktel.net
www.melvillechamber.com
Ron Walton, Manager
David Williams, President

Moose Jaw & District Chamber of Commerce
88 Saskatchewan St. East, Moose Jaw SK S6H 0V4
Tel: 306-692-6414; Fax: 306-694-6463
chamber@mjchamber.com
www.mjchamber.com
Brian Martynook, Executive Director
Darryl Pisio, President

Moosomin Chamber of Commerce
PO Box 819, Moosomin SK S0G 3N0
Tel: 306-435-2445; Fax: 306-435-3696
world_spectator@sasktel.net
www.moosomin.com/chamber
Kevin Weedmark, President
Bernie Nosterud, Sec.-Treas.

Nipawin & District Chamber of Commerce
PO Box 177, Nipawin SK S0E 1E0
Tel: 306-862-5252; Fax: 306-862-5350
info@nipawinchamber.ca
www.nipawinchamber.ca
Cindy M Murphy, Executive Director
Cliff Rose, President

Norquay & District Chamber of Commerce
PO Box 457, Norquay SK S0A 2V0
Tel: 306-594-2293; Fax: 306-594-2435
nnjohnson@sasktel.net
Nina Johnson, President
Donna Lumley, Treasurer

Outlook & District Chamber of Commerce
PO Box 431, Outlook SK S0L 2N0
Tel: 306-867-9580; Fax: 306-867-9559
www.town.outlook.sk.ca/chamber.htm
Lyle Rankin, President
Julie Haubrich, Secretary

Paradise Hill Chamber of Commerce
PO Box 118, Paradise Hill SK S0M 2G0
Tel: 306-344-2188; Fax: 306-344-4799
George H Palen, President
Sheila M Phillips, Secretary

Prince Albert Chamber of Commerce
#347, 1084 Central Ave., Prince Albert SK S6V 7P3
Tel: 306-764-6222; Fax: 306-922-4727
pachamber@sasktel.net
www.princealbertchamber.com
Affiliation(s): Canadian Chamber of Commerce; Saskatchewan Chamber of Commerce
Allan Hopkins, Chair
Lyn Brown, CEO

Radisson & District Chamber of Commerce
PO Box 397, Radisson SK S0K 3L0
Tel: 306-827-4801; Fax: 306-827-2336
Lloyd E. Lorass, President
Cheryl D. Hamilton, Secretary

Radville Chamber of Commerce
PO Box 799, Radville SK S0C 2G0
Tel: 306-869-2610; Fax: 306-869-2859
town.radville@sasktel.net
S.L. Scott, Sec.-Treas.
B.L. Loewen, President

Redvers Chamber of Commerce
PO Box 602, Redvers SK S0C 2H0
Tel: 306-452-3155; Fax: 306-452-3155
rdaycare@sasktel.net
Tricia Martel, President
Tanis Chalmers, Director

Regina & District Chamber of Commerce
2145 Albert St., Regina SK S4P 2V1
Tel: 306-757-4658; Fax: 306-757-4668
info@reginachamber.com
www.reginachamber.com
Affiliation(s): Canadian Chamber of Commerce; Saskatchewan Chamber of Commerce
John Hopkins, CEO
Fred Titanich, President

Regina Beach & District Chamber of Commerce
PO Box 606, Regina Beach SK S0G 4C0
Tel: 306-729-4596
J. Cumbers, President
D. Needham, Secretary

La Ronge & District Chamber of Commerce
PO Box 179, La Ronge SK S0J 1L0
Tel: 306-425-3056; Toll-Free: 866-527-6643
chamberofcommerce@townoflaronge.ca
B.A. Fenning, President
B.L. Bean, Secretary

Rosetown & District Chamber of Commerce
PO Box 744, Rosetown SK S0L 2V0
Tel: 306-882-1300; Fax: 306-882-1310
e2000@sasktel.net
www.rosetown.ca
Gerry Clark, Chair
Shirley Helgason, Executive Director

St. Walburg Chamber of Commerce
PO Box 501, St Walburg SK S0M 2T0
Tel: 306-248-3244; Fax: 306-248-3988
townofstwalburg@sasktel.net
www.stwalburg.com
M. Champigny, President
K. Rutherford, Treasurer

Shaunavon Chamber of Commerce
PO Box 820, Shaunavon SK S0N 2M0
Tel: 306-297-3462; Fax: 306-297-3420
www.shaunavon.com/chamber.htm
Rick Schneider, President
Penny Schreiner, Secretary

Spiritwood Chamber of Commerce
PO Box 429, Spiritwood SK S0J 2M0
Tel: 306-883-2267; Fax: 306-883-2136
B. Fee, President
Yvette McGowan, Secretary

Swift Current Chamber of Commerce
885 - 6th Ave. NE, Swift Current SK S9H 2M9
Tel: 306-773-7268; Fax: 306-773-5686
info@swiftcurrentchamber.ca
www.swiftcurrentchamber.ca
Affiliation(s): Saskatchewan Chamber of Commerce; Canadian Chamber of Commerce
Erin Kinney, President
Marianne Hawkins, Executive Director

Tisdale & District Chamber of Commerce
PO Box 219, Tisdale SK S0E 1T0
Tel: 306-873-4257; Fax: 306-873-4241
tisdalechamber@sasktel.net
A.R. Freistadt, Manager
M.R. Kinar, President

Unity & District Chamber of Commerce
PO Box 834, Unity SK S0K 4L0
Tel: 306-228-2621
T.J. Schroh, President
Christine Gerein, Treasurer

Vonda Chamber of Commerce
c/o Vonda Hometown Insurance Brokers, PO Box 285, Vonda SK S0K 4N0
Tel: 306-258-2134; Fax: 306-258-2244
rlalonde@sasktel.net
A. Bussiere, President
Robert Lalonde, Secretary

Waskesiu Chamber of Commerce
PO Box 216, Waskesiu Lake SK S0J 2Y0
Tel: 306-663-5140; Fax: 306-663-5448
wakesiuchamber@sasktel.net
www.waskesiulake.ca
G.A. Wilson, Manager
G.J.P. Bueckert, President

Watrous & District Chamber of Commerce
PO Box 906, Watrous SK S0K 4T0
Tel: 306-946-3353; Fax: 306-946-3966
E.T. Amendt, President
T. Frey, Secretary

Watson & District Chamber of Commerce
PO Box 686, Watson SK S0K 4V0
Tel: 306-287-3636; Fax: 306-287-3601
Michael Becker, President
Debbie A Schwartz, Treasurer

Weyburn Chamber of Commerce
#11, 3rd St. NE, Weyburn SK S4H 0W5
Tel: 306-842-4738; Fax: 306-842-0520
manager@weyburnchamber.com
www.weyburnchamber.com
Affiliation(s): Saskatchewan Chamber of Commerce
Brent Allen, President
Jeff Richards, Manager

Wolseley & District Chamber of Commerce
PO Box 519, Wolseley SK S0G 5H0
Tel: 306-698-2252; Fax: 306-698-2750
S. Harris, Secretary
M.M. Dunn, President

Wynyard & District Chamber of Commerce
PO Box 508, Wynyard SK S0A 4T0
Tel: 306-554-2224; Fax: 306-554-3226
E.A. Zahayko, President
D. Johannesson, Secretary

Yorkton Chamber of Commerce
PO Box 1051, Hwy. 9 South, Yorkton SK S3N 2X3
Tel: 306-783-4368; Fax: 306-786-6978
yorktonchamber@sasktel.net
www.chamber.yorkton.sk.ca
Affiliation(s): Saskatchewan Economic Developers Association
Lori Walsh, President
Guy Gendreau, Exec. Vice-President

Yukon Territory

Dawson City Chamber of Commerce
PO Box 1006, Dawson YT Y0B 1G0
Tel: 867-993-5274; Fax: 867-993-6817
dccc@dawson.net
Dina Grenon, President

St. Elias Chamber of Commerce
PO Box 5419, Haines Junction YT Y0B 1L0
Tel: 867-634-2916; Fax: 867-634-2034
kluaneridin@yknet.ca
Wade Istchenko, President

Silver Trail Chamber of Commerce
PO Box 268, Mayo YT Y0B 1M0
Tel: 867-996-2827
educate@nndfn.com
Nancy Hager, President

Southern Lakes Chamber of Commerce
PO Box 45, Carcross YT Y0B 1B0
Tel: 867-821-4372; Fax: 867-393-2436
president@southernlakeschamber.com
www.southernlakeschamber.com
Greg Kehoe, Contact

Teslin Regional Chamber of Commerce
PO Box 181, Teslin YT Y0A 1B0
Tel: 867-390-2521; Fax: 867-390-2687
wes.wirth@northwestel.net
Wes Wirth, President

Watson Lake Chamber of Commerce
PO Box 591, Watson Lake YT Y0A 1C0
Tel: 867-536-2240; Fax: 867-536-7294
wlchamberofcommerce@northwestel.net
Jennifer Anderson, Contact

Whitehorse Chamber of Commerce (WCC)
#101, 302 Steele St., Whitehorse YT Y1A 2C5
Tel: 867-667-7545; Fax: 867-667-4507
business@whitehorsechamber.ca
www.whitehorsechamber.ca
Affiliation(s): Yukon Chamber of Commerce; Tourism Industry Association of Yukon
Rick Karp, President

Credit Unions/Caisses Populaires

Credit unions and caisses populaires are owned and controlled by their members. These cooperative financial institutions are regulated at the provincial level. Credit unions, in most provinces, must engage external auditors to prepare financial statements. An annual inspection of credit unions is conducted by their provincial regulatory body.

The national trade association and central finance facility for Canadian credit unions is Credit Union Central of Canada. It is regulated under the Cooperative Credit Associations Act. In Québec, Mouvement des caisses Desjardins du Québec consists of a network of caisses. Fédération des caisses Desjardins du Québec is a cooperative which supports Mouvement des caisses Desjardins du Québec.

1st Choice Savings & Credit Union Ltd.
1320 - 3 Ave. South
Lethbridge, AB T1J 0K5
Tel: 403-320-4600; Fax: 403-329-6434
contact@1stchoicesavings.ca
www.1stchoicesavings.ca
Former Name: St. Patrick's Credit Union Ltd.; Southland Credit Union
Ownership: Public
Year Founded: 2001
Assets: $100-500 million

3M Employees' (London) Credit Union Limited
1840 Oxford St. East
London, ON N6A 4T1
Tel: 519-452-6765; Fax: 519-452-6023
cuca-corporate@mmm.com
www.3mcreditunion.com

Acadian Credit Union
PO Box 250
15089 Cabot Trail
Cheticamp, NS B0E 1H0
Tel: 902-224-2055; Fax: 902-224-3510
Toll-Free: 877-477-7724
www.acadiancreditu.ca
Social Media:
www.facebook.com/pages/Acadian-Credit-Union/144590197297;
www.twitter.com/AcadianCU
Former Name: Cheticamp Credit Union
Year Founded: 1936
Number of Employees: 12

ACE Credit Union Limited
#100, 2055 Albert St.
Regina, SK S4P 2T8
Tel: 306-337-1700; Fax: 306-337-1719
info@ace.cu.sk.ca
www.acecreditunion.com
Year Founded: 1973

Adjala Credit Union Limited
7320 St. James Lane
Colgan, ON L0G 1W0
Tel: 905-936-2761; Fax: 905-936-6391
Year Founded: 1946

Advance Savings Credit Union (ASCU)
141 Weldon St.
Moncton, NB E1C 5W1
Tel: 506-853-8881
www.advancesavings.ca
Former Name: Rexton Credit Union; Royal Credit Union; Trico Credit Union
Ownership: Member-owned
Year Founded: 2006
Assets: $50-100 million

Advantage Credit Union
PO Box 1657
118 Main St.
Melfort, SK S0E 1A0
Tel: 306-752-2744; Fax: 306-752-1919
www.advantagecu.com
Former Name: Melfort Credit Union Ltd.
Ownership: Member-owned
Year Founded: 1943

Affinity Credit Union
309 - 22nd St. East
Saskatoon, SK S7K 0G7
Tel: 306-934-4000; Fax: 306-934-5490
Toll-Free: 1-866-863-6237
questions@affinitycu.ca
www.affinitycu.com
Former Name: St. Mary's Credit Union Limited
Ownership: Member-owned
Year Founded: 1949
Assets: $1-10 billion

Agassiz Credit Union Limited
430 Stephen St.
Morden, MB R6M 1T6
Tel: 204-822-4485; Fax: 204-822-6155
Toll-Free: 1-877-822-4485
admin@agassizcu.mb.ca
www.agassizcu.mb.ca
Ownership: Member-owned

Airline Financial Credit Union Limited
#120, 5955 Airport Rd.
Mississauga, ON L4V 1R9
Tel: 905-673-7262; Fax: 905-676-8437
info@airlinecreditunion.com
www.airlinecreditunion.ca
Former Name: Airline (Malton) Credit Union Limited
Ownership: Member-owned
Year Founded: 1950
Number of Employees: 9
Assets: $10-50 million

Air-Toronto Credit Union
124 Florence Ave.
Toronto, ON M2N 1G3
Tel: 416-359-9685; Fax: 416-512-2497
Year Founded: 1959

Aldergrove Credit Union
2941 - 272nd St.
Aldergrove, BC V4W 3R3
Tel: 604-856-7724; Fax: 604-856-2565
www.aldergrovecu.ca
Former Name: Otter Farmers' Institute Credit Union
Year Founded: 1954

All Trans Financial Credit Union Limited
Administration Ctr.
#707, 3250 Bloor St. West
Toronto, ON M8X 2X9
Tel: 416-231-8400; Fax: 416-231-8296
info@alltrans.com
www.alltrans.com
Year Founded: 1993
Number of Employees: 18

L'Alliance des caisses populaires de l'Ontario limitée
PO Box 3500
1870 Bond St.
North Bay, ON P1B 4V6
Tel: 705-474-5634; Fax: 705-474-5326
support@acpol.com
www.caissealliance.com
Ownership: Member-owned.
Year Founded: 1979
Number of Employees: 240

Assets: $500m-1 billion
Revenues: $10-50 million

Alterna Savings & Credit Union Limited
400 Albert St.
Ottawa, ON K1R 5B2
Tel: 613-560-0100; Fax: 613-560-0177
Toll-Free: 877-560-0100
query@alterna.ca
www.alterna.ca
Other Contact Information: 416-252-5621 (Toronto phone)
Former Name: Civil Service Co-operative Credit Society Ltd.
Ownership: Member-owned
Year Founded: 2005
Number of Employees: 600+
Assets: $1-10 billion

Anishinabek Nation Credit Union (ANCU)
7 Shingwauk St.
Garden River, ON P6A 6Z8
Tel: 705-942-7655; Fax: 705-942-7613
Toll-Free: 866-775-2628
cu-info@ancu.ca
www.ancu.ca

Apex Credit Union Limited
Administration Office, TransCanada Centre
#210, 1440 - 52nd St. NE
Calgary, AB T2A 4T8
Tel: 403-974-8640; Fax: 403-282-3099
Toll-Free: 1-877-273-9247
www.apexcu.com
Ownership: Member-owned
Year Founded: 1940
Assets: $50-100 million

Apple Community Credit Union
406 North Cumberland St.
Thunder Bay, ON P7A 4P8
Tel: 807-345-8153; Fax: 807-343-9271
info@applecu.com
www.applecu.com
Ownership: Private

Arctic Credit Union Ltd.
800 Central Ave., 9th Fl.
Prince Albert, SK S6V 6Z2
Tel: 306-922-8252;
Former Name: Arctic Savings & Credit Union Ltd.
Year Founded: 1939

Arnstein Community Credit Union Limited
PO Box 104
Port Loring, ON P0H 1Y0
Tel: 705-757-2662; Fax: 705-757-2662
Year Founded: 1962

Assiniboine Credit Union Limited (ACU)
Corporate Office
PO Box 2, Main Stn. Main
200 Main St., 6th Fl.
Winnipeg, MB R3C 2G1
Tel: 877-958-8588; Fax: 877-958-7348
cu@assiniboine.mb.ca
www.assiniboine.mb.ca
Other Contact Information: 1-877-957-1587 (TTY Line for Hearing Impaired)
Ownership: Member-owned
Year Founded: 1943
Number of Employees: 500
Assets: $1-10 billion

Austin Credit Union
PO Box 205
24 - 2nd Ave.
Austin, MB R0H 0H0
Tel: 204-385-6140; Fax: 204-637-2204
www.austincreditunion.com
Year Founded: 1949

Auto Workers (Ajax) Credit Union Limited
PO Box 21115
290 Harwood Ave. South
Ajax, ON L1S 2J1
Tel: 905-683-0791; Fax: 905-683-6047
Year Founded: 1968

Auto Workers' Community Credit Union Limited
322 King St. West
Oshawa, ON L1J 2J9
Tel: 905-728-5187; Fax: 905-728-8727
Toll-Free: 800-268-8771
information@awccu.com
www.awccu.com
Ownership: Private. Cooperative

Year Founded: 1938
Number of Employees: 70
Revenues: $100-500 million

Battle River Credit Union Ltd.
5007 - 51 St.
Camrose, AB T4V 1S6
Tel: 780-672-1175; Fax: 780-672-5996
brcu@battlerivercreditunion.com
www.battlerivercreditunion.com
Ownership: Member-owned
Year Founded: 1949
Number of Employees: 110
Assets: $100-500 million Year End: 20080930
Revenues: $1-5 million Year End: 20080930

Bay Credit Union Limited
142 Algoma St. South
Thunder Bay, ON P7B 3B8
Tel: 807-345-7612; Fax: 807-345-8939
Toll-Free: 1-877-249-7076
info@baycreditunion.com
www.baycreditunion.com

Bay St Lawrence Credit Union
PO Box 112
3020 Bay St. Lawrence Rd.
Dingwall, NS B0C 1G0
Tel: 902-383-2003;
Year Founded: 1937
Number of Employees: 1

Bayshore Credit Union Ltd.
PO Box 878
191 North Front St.
Belleville, ON K8N 5B5
Tel: 613-966-5550; Fax: 613-966-9523
www.bayshorecu.com

Bayview Credit Union
#400, 57 King St.
Saint John, NB E2L 1G5
Tel: 506-634-1263; Fax: 506-634-1686
www.bayviewnb.com
Year Founded: 1938
Number of Employees: 115
Assets: $100-500 million

Beaubear Credit Union
PO Box 764
376 Water St.
Miramichi, NB E1V 3V4
Tel: 506-622-4532
mdaley@beaubear.creditu.net
www.beaubear.ca
Ownership: Member-owned
Year Founded: 1938
Assets: $10-50 million

Beaumont Credit Union Limited
5007 - 50th Ave.
Beaumont, AB T4X 1E7
Tel: 780-929-8561; Fax: 780-929-2999
Toll-Free: 800-307-8353
cberube@alberta-cu.com
www.beaumontcu.com
Other Contact Information: 1-800-561-7849 (Credit Card Balances); 306-566-1276 (Outside Canada)
Former Name: St Vital & Beaumont Savings & Credit Union
Year Founded: 1946

Beautiful Plains Credit Union
PO Box 99
239 Hamilton St.
Neepawa, MB R0J 1H0
Tel: 204-476-3341; Fax: 204-476-3609
info@bpcu.mb.ca
www.bpcu.mb.ca
Year Founded: 1955

Belgian-Alliance Credit Union
1177 Portage Ave.
Winnipeg, MB R3G 0T2
Tel: 204-927-0460; Fax: 204-927-0461
info@belgianalliancecu.mb.ca
www.belgianalliancecu.mb.ca
Former Name: Alliance Credit Union; Adanac Credit Union Ltd; Communicators Credit Union; Progress Vera Credit Union
Year Founded: 2001

Bengough Credit Union Ltd.
260 Main St.
Bengough, SK S0C 0K0
Tel: 306-268-2930
info@bengough.cu.sk.ca
www.bengough.cu.sk.ca
Year Founded: 1943

Bergengren Credit Union
257 Main St.
Antigonish, NS B2G 2C1
Tel: 902-863-6600; Fax: 902-863-3031
Toll-Free: 888-273-3488
info@bergengrencu.com
www.bergengrencu.com
Year Founded: 1933
Number of Employees: 51

Biggar & District Credit Union Ltd.
PO Box 670
302 Main St.
Biggar, SK S0K 0M0
Tel: 306-948-3352; Fax: 306-948-2053
www.biggarcu.com
Ownership: Member-owned

Blackville Credit Union
128 Main St.
Blackville, NB E9B 1P1
Tel: 506-843-2219; Fax: 506-843-6773
Year Founded: 1936

Bow Valley Credit Union Limited
PO Box 876
Cochrane, AB T4C 1A9
Tel: 403-932-4693; Fax: 403-932-9865
lbohn@bowvalleycu.com
www.bowvalleycu.com
Ownership: Member-owned

Brewers Warehousing Employees (Hamilton) Credit Union Limited
c/o Beer Store
673 Upper James St.
Hamilton, ON L9C 5R9
Tel: 905-574-7652; Fax: 905-574-7652

Brewers Warehousing Employees (Kitchener) Credit Union Limited
53 Filbert St.
Kitchener, ON N2H 1Y1
Tel: 519-576-7324;

Brook Street Credit Union Ltd.
Millbrook Mall
PO Box 713
2 Herald Ave., Main Level
Corner Brook, NL A2H 6G7
Tel: 709-634-4632; Toll-Free: 866-273-3488
brookstreet@brookstreet.creditu.net
www.bscu.ca
Ownership: Member-owned
Year Founded: 1963
Assets: $10-50 million

Bruno Savings & Credit Union Limited
PO Box 158
511 Main St.
Bruno, SK S0K 0S0
Tel: 306-369-2901; Fax: 306-369-2225
www.brunocu.com
Ownership: Member-owned

Buduchnist Credit Union (BCU)
2280 Bloor St. West
Toronto, ON M6S 1N9
Tel: 416-763-6883; Fax: 416-763-4512
Toll-Free: 800-461-5941
info@buduchnist.com; help@buduchnist.com (Help Desk)
www.buduchnist.com
Other Contact Information: link@buduchnist.com (BCU Link); privacyofficer@buduchnist.com (Privacy Officer)
Ownership: Member-owned
Year Founded: 1952

Bulkley Valley Credit Union
PO Box 3637
3872 - 1st Ave.
Smithers, BC V0J 2N0
Tel: 250-847-3255; Fax: 250-847-3012
infoadmin@bvcu.com
www.bvcu.com

Caisse centrale Desjardins du Québec (CCD)
#600, 1170 rue Peel
Montréal, QC H3B 0B1
Tél: 514-281-7070; Téléc: 514-281-7083
www.desjardins.com/ccd
Ownership: Cooperatively owned by the Fédération des caisses Desjardins du Québec
Year Founded: 1979

Caisse Horizon Credit Union Ltd.
PO Box 147
Girouxville, AB T0H 1S0
Tel: 780-323-4600; Fax: 780-323-4545
Toll-Free: 866-758-6466
www.powerofmembers.ca
Also Known As: Horizon Credit Union
Ownership: Member-owned
Year Founded: 1956
Number of Employees: 58
Assets: $10-50 million

Caisse populaire de Saulnierville
RR#1
Saulnierville, NS B0W 2Z0
Tél: 902-769-2574; Téléc: 902-769-3555
Year Founded: 1953

Cambrian Credit Union Ltd.
***Also listed under:** Financing & Loan Companies*
225 Broadway
Winnipeg, MB R3C 5R4
Tel: 204-925-2600; Fax: 204-231-1306
Toll-Free: 888-695-8900
ccuinfo@cambrian.mb.ca; ccuhead@cambrian.mb.ca
www.cambrian.mb.ca
Ownership: Member-owned
Year Founded: 1959
Assets: $1-10 billion

Campbell's Employees' (Toronto) Credit Union Limited
60 Birmingham St.
Toronto, ON M8V 2B8
Tel: 416-251-1117; Fax: 416-253-8669

Canada Safeway Limited Employees Savings & Credit Union
1822 - 10th Ave. SW
Calgary, AB T3C 0J8
Tel: 403-261-5681; Fax: 403-261-5748
Toll-Free: 877-723-2653
info@safewaycucalgary.com
www.safewaycucalgary.com
Ownership: Member-owned
Year Founded: 1952
Number of Employees: 10

Canadian Alternative Investment Cooperative
#111, 146 Laird Dr.
Toronto, ON M4G 3V7
Tel: 416-467-7797; Fax: 416-467-8946
Toll-Free: 866-241-2242
caic@caic.ca
www.caic.ca
Year Founded: 1984

Canadian General Tower Employees (Galt) Credit Union Limited
Cambridge Place
#117, 73 Water St. North
Cambridge, ON N1R 7L6
Tel: 519-623-2211; Fax: 519-623-2051
Ownership: Private
Number of Employees: 3

Canadian Transportation Employees' Credit Union Ltd.
PO Box 4
600 Ferguson Ave. North
Hamilton, ON L8L 4Z9
Tel: 905-523-7385; Fax: 905-523-7556
Number of Employees: 3

Carleton Pioneer Credit Union
#1, 106 Richmond St.
Woodstock, NB E7M 2N9
Tel: 506-328-8120; Fax: 506-328-3445
www.cpcu.coop
Year Founded: 1938
Number of Employees: 9

Carpathia Credit Union
952 Main St.
Winnipeg, MB R2W 3P4
Tel: 204-989-7400; Fax: 204-589-2529
info@carpathiacu.mb.ca
www.carpathiacu.mb.ca
Ownership: Member-owned
Year Founded: 1940
Assets: $100-500 million

Casera Credit Union
1300 Plessis Rd.
Winnipeg, MB R2C 2Y6
Tel: 204-958-6300; Fax: 204-222-6766
Toll-Free: 866-211-9233
www.caseracu.ca
Also Known As: Transcona Credit Union
Ownership: Member-owned
Year Founded: 1951

Cataract Savings & Credit Union Limited
7172 Dorchester Rd.
Niagara Falls, ON L2G 5V6
Tel: 905-357-5222; Fax: 905-357-9366
www.cataractsavings.on.ca
Year Founded: 1949

CBC (Nfld) Credit Union Ltd.
PO Box 12010, A Stn. A
29-31 Pippy Place
St. John's, NL A1B 3T8
Tel: 709-576-5407; Fax: 709-576-5409
cbccreditunion@cbccu.ca
www.cbccu.ca
Year Founded: 1965
Number of Employees: 3

CCB Employees' Credit Union Limited
46 Overlea Blvd.
Toronto, ON M4H 1B6
Tel: 416-424-6280; Fax: 416-701-1944
Year Founded: 1973
Number of Employees: 2
Revenues: Under $1 million

CCEC Credit Union
2250 Commercial Dr.
Vancouver, BC V5N 5P9
Tel: 604-254-4100; Fax: 604-254-6558
Toll-Free: 866-254-4100
info@ccec.bc.ca
www.ccec.bc.ca
Ownership: Cooperative
Year Founded: 1976

Central 1 Credit Union - British Columbia Region
1441 Creekside Dr.
Vancouver, BC V6J 4S7
Tel: 604-734-2511; Fax: 604-734-5055
Toll-Free: 800-661-6813
info@central1.com
www.central1.com
Former Name: Credit Union Central of British Columbia
Ownership: Member credit unions
Year Founded: 1944
Number of Employees: 500
Assets: $10-100 billion
Revenues: $100-500 million

Central 1 Credit Union - Ontario Region
2810 Matheson Blvd. East
Mississauga, ON L4W 4X7
Tel: 905-238-9400; Fax: 905-238-5008
Toll-Free: 800-661-6813
info@central1.com; customerservice@central1.com
www.ontariocreditunions.com
Other Contact Information: 905-629-5711 (Help Desk Phone)
Former Name: Credit Union Central of Ontario
Number of Employees: 125
Assets: $10-100 billion
Revenues: $100-500 million

Central Credit Union Limited
PO Box 279
512 Main St.
O'Leary, PE C0B 1V0
Tel: 902-859-2266; Fax: 902-859-3219
central.cu@central.creditu.net
www.centralcreditu.com
Ownership: Member-owned
Year Founded: 1969
Number of Employees: 17

Chinook Credit Union Ltd.
PO Box 1137
99 - 2nd St. West
Brooks, AB T1R 1B9
Tel: 403-362-4233; Fax: 403-362-4239
www.chinookcu.com
Former Name: Macleod Savings & Credit Union Ltd.
Ownership: Member-owned
Year Founded: 1941
Number of Employees: 160
Assets: $50-100 million

Church River Credit Union
305 Burnt Church Rd.
Burnt Church, NB E9G 4C8
Tel: 506-776-3247; Fax: 506-776-3247

Churchbridge Savings & Credit Union
PO Box 260
103 Vincent Ave. East
Churchbridge, SK S0A 0M0
Tel: 306-896-2544; Fax: 306-896-2325
Toll-Free: 877-890-2797
info@churchbridge.cu.sk.ca
www.churchbridgecu.ca
Year Founded: 1945

City Plus Credit Union Ltd.
Municipal Bldg.
PO Box 2100, M Stn. M
#8130, 800 MacLeod Trail SE, 5th Fl.
Calgary, AB T2P 2M5
Tel: 403-268-2626; Fax: 403-268-4886
main@cpcu.ca
www.cpcu.ca
Former Name: Calgary Civic Employees Credit Union Limited
Ownership: Private
Year Founded: 1942
Number of Employees: 5

City Savings Financial Services
6002 Yonge St.
Toronto, ON M2M 3V9
Tel: 416-225-7716; Fax: 416-225-7772
info@citysavingscu.com
www.citysavingscu.com
Former Name: City Savings & Credit Union Ltd.; The North York Municipal Employees' Credit Union
Year Founded: 1950

CN (London) Credit Union Limited
#301, 205 York St.
London, ON N6A 1B1
Tel: 519-667-2326; Fax: 519-434-5687
cncucindy@ody.ca
www.cncu.ca
Year Founded: 1945
Number of Employees: 4

CNR Employees (Lakehead Terminal) Credit Union Limited
417 Fort William Rd.
Thunder Bay, ON P7B 2Z5
Tel: 807-344-4096; Fax: 807-346-0595

Coady Credit Union
32 West Ave.
Glace Bay, NS B1A 6E9
Tel: 902-849-7610; Fax: 902-842-0911
Year Founded: 1933

Coast Capital Savings Credit Union
Corporate Head Office
15117 - 101 Ave.
Surrey, BC V3R 8P7
Tel: 604-517-7000; Fax: 604-517-7405
Toll-Free: 888-517-7000
info@coastcapitalsavings.com
www.coastcapitalsavings.com
Other Contact Information: 1-877-333-7736 (Technical Support); 604-517-7822 (Cantonese); 604-517-7823 (Mandarin); 604-517-7780 (Punjabi)
Ownership: Member-owned
Year Founded: 2000
Number of Employees: 2,000+

Coastal Community Credit Union
#21, 13 Victoria Cres.
Nanaimo, BC V9R 5B9
Tel: 250-741-3200; Fax: 250-741-3223
Toll-Free: 888-741-1010
www.cccu.ca
Other Contact Information: 1-888-741-4040 (Telephone Banking Toll-Free); 1-800-567-8111 (Lost Member Card, Canada & the USA); 1-800-567-8111 (Lost MasterCard, Canada & the USA)
Ownership: Member-owned
Year Founded: 1946
Number of Employees: 600+
Assets: $1-10 billion

Coastal Financial Credit Union
2 Collins St.
Yarmouth, NS B5A 3C3
Tel: 902-742-7322; Fax: 902-742-7476
rdoucette@coastalfinancial.ca
www.coastalfinancial.ca
Ownership: Member-owned
Year Founded: 2001
Number of Employees: 53
Assets: $50-100 million

Codroy Valley Credit Union
PO Box 29
Doyles, NL A0N 1J0
Tel: 709-955-2402; Fax: 709-955-3081
www.codroyvalleycu.com

College Hill Credit Union
c/o University of New Brunswick, McConnell Hall
PO Box 4400
#107, 19 Bailey Dr.
Fredericton, NB E3B 5A3
Tel: 506-455-3535
www.unb.ca/facilities/chcu

Columbia Valley Credit Union
PO Box 720
511 Main St.
Golden, BC V0A 1H0
Tel: 250-344-2282; Fax: 250-344-2117
Toll-Free: 888-298-1777
www.cvcu.bc.ca
Other Contact Information: 1-888-273-3488 (Online Banking Support); 1-866-344-7968 (Phone Banking)
Ownership: Member-owned
Year Founded: 1955
Assets: $100-500 million

Communication Technologies Credit Union Limited
Eaton Centre
PO Box 501
#102, 220 Yonge St.
Toronto, ON M5B 2H1
Tel: 416-598-1197; Fax: 416-598-0171
Toll-Free: 800-209-7444
member_services@comtechcu.com
www.comtechcu.com
Ownership: Member-owned
Number of Employees: 14
Assets: $50-100 million

Community Credit Union Ltd.
164 Main St.
Grunthal, MB R0A 0R0
Tel: 204-434-6338; Fax: 204-434-9074
grunthal@communitycu.mb.ca
www.communitycu.mb.ca

Community Credit Union of Cumberland Colchester Limited
PO Box 578
#201, 32 Church St.
Amherst, NS B4H 4B8
Tel: 902-667-7541; Fax: 902-667-0217
Toll-Free: 1-888-273-3488
www.communitycreditunion.ns.ca
Former Name: Amherst Credit Union; Colchester Credit Union
Ownership: Member-owned
Year Founded: 1999

Community First Credit Union Limited
289 Bay St.
Sault Ste Marie, ON P6A 1W7
Tel: 705-942-1000; Fax: 705-946-2363
www.communityfirst-cu.com
Year Founded: 1948

Community Savings Credit Union
Central City Tower
#1600, 13450 - 102nd Ave., 16th Fl.
Surrey, BC V3T 5X3
Tel: 604-654-2000; Fax: 604-586-5156
Toll-Free: 888-963-2000
www.comsavings.com
Former Name: IWA & Community Credit Union
Year Founded: 1944
Number of Employees: 500

Concentra Financial Corporate Banking
333 - 3rd Ave. North
Saskatoon, SK S7K 2M2
Toll-Free: 800-788-6311
servicecentre@concentrafinancial.ca
www.concentrafinancial.ca
Former Name: CUCORP Financial Services
Ownership: Private
Year Founded: 1997
Revenues: $1-10 billion

Conexus Credit Union
PO Box 1960, Main Stn. Main
Regina, SK S4P 4M1
Toll-Free: 800-667-7477
www.conexus.ca
Former Name: Assiniboia Credit Union Ltd.
Number of Employees: 1,000

Consolidated Credit Union
305 Water St.
Summerside, PE C1N 1C1
Tel: 902-436-9218; Fax: 902-436-7979
shickey@consolidated.creditu.net
www.consolidatedcreditu.com
Ownership: Member-owned
Assets: $100-500 million

Copperfin Credit Union
346 - 2nd St. South
Kenora, ON P9N 1G5
Tel: 807-467-4400; Fax: 807-468-3500
Toll-Free: 888-710-6664
kenora@copperfin.ca
www.copperfin.ca
Former Name: Lakewood Credit Union Ltd.
Ownership: Member-owned
Year Founded: 1954
Number of Employees: 34

Cornerstone Credit Union Ltd.
PO Box 455
1202, 100th St.
Tisdale, SK S0E 1T0
Tel: 306-873-2616; Fax: 306-873-4322
reception@cornerstone.cu.sk.ca
www.cornerstonecu.ca
Former Name: Tisdale Credit Union Ltd.
Ownership: Private. Member-owned
Year Founded: 1943
Number of Employees: 30
Assets: $100-500 million
Revenues: $1-5 million

Credit Union Atlantic (CUA)
#350, 7105 Chebucto Rd.
Halifax, NS B3L 4W8
Tel: 902-492-6500; Fax: 902-492-6501
Toll-Free: 800-474-4282
www.cua.com
Other Contact Information: 902-493-4800 (Teleservice); 1-800-963-4848 (TeleService Toll Free); 1-800-561-7849 (MasterCard Inquiries); 1-800-567-8111 (Lost MasterCards)
Year Founded: 1948
Number of Employees: 115
Assets: $100-500 million

Credit Union Central Alberta Limited
#350N, 8500 MacLeod Trail South
Calgary, AB T2H 2N1
Tel: 403-258-5900; Fax: 403-253-7720
email@albertacentral.com
www.albertacentral.com
Ownership: Owned by the credit unions of Alberta
Number of Employees: 230
Assets: $1-10 billion

Credit Union Central of Canada (CUCC)
#500, 300 The East Mall
Toronto, ON M9B 6B7
Tel: 416-232-1262; Fax: 416-232-9196
cucc@cucentral.com
www.cucentral.ca
Ownership: Owned by the provincial credit union centrals
Year Founded: 1953

Credit Union Central of Manitoba (CUCM)
#400, 317 Donald St.
Winnipeg, MB R3B 2H6
Tel: 204-985-4700; Fax: 204-957-0217
cuinfo@cucm.org
www.creditunion.mb.ca
Former Name: Cooperative Credit Society of Manitoba Ltd.
Ownership: Member-owned
Year Founded: 1950
Assets: $10-100 billion

Credit Union Central of New Brunswick (CUCNB)
663 Pinewood Rd.
Riverview, NB E1B 5R6
Tel: 506-857-8184; Toll-Free: 800-332-3320
info@cucnb.nb.ca
www.creditunion.nb.ca
Year Founded: 1950

Credit Union Central of Nova Scotia
PO Box 9200
6074 Lady Hammond Rd.
Halifax, NS B3K 5N3
Tel: 902-453-0680; Fax: 902-455-2437
Toll-Free: 800-668-2879
info@cucns.ca; humanresources@cucns.ca; communications@cucns.ca
www.ns-credit-unions.com
Year Founded: 1938

Credit Union Central of Prince Edward Island
PO Box 968
281 University Ave.
Charlottetown, PE C1A 7M4
Tel: 902-566-3350; Fax: 902-368-3534
website@cucpei.com
www.peicreditunions.com
Year Founded: 1936
Number of Employees: 200
Assets: $500m-1 billion

Creston & District Credit Union
PO Box 215
140 - 11th Ave. North
Creston, BC V0B 1G0
Tel: 250-428-5351; Fax: 250-428-5302
Toll-Free: 866-857-2802
cdcu@cdcu.com
www.cdcu.com
Ownership: Credit Union Central, BC
Year Founded: 1951

Crocus Credit Union
1016 Rosser Ave.
Brandon, MB R7A 0L6
Tel: 204-729-4800; Fax: 204-729-4818
info@crocuscu.mb.ca
www.crocuscu.mb.ca
Other Contact Information: 1-800-567-8111 (Lost ATM Cards)
Former Name: Brandon Terminal Credit Union Society Limited
Ownership: Member-owned
Year Founded: 1952

Crossroads Credit Union Ltd.
PO Box 2006
113 - 2nd Ave. East
Canora, SK S0A 0L0
Tel: 306-563-5641; Fax: 306-563-6715
Toll-Free: 877-535-1299
reception@crossroadscu.ca
www.crossroadscu.ca
Other Contact Information: Canora Branch Fax: 306-563-4834; Lost or Stolen Card, Toll-Free: 1-800-561-7849
Former Name: Canora Credit Union
Ownership: Member-owned
Year Founded: 1959
Assets: $100-500 million

Crosstown Civic Credit Union
171 Donald St.
Winnipeg, MB R3C 1M4
Tel: 204-942-1277; Fax: 204-947-3108
cu@crosstowncivic.mb.ca
www.crosstowncivic.mb.ca
Other Contact Information: 1-800-567-8111 (Lost ATM & Member Cards); 204-949-1048 (ExpressLine TeleService)
Ownership: Member-owned
Year Founded: 1943
Assets: $1-10 billion Year End: 20081231

Cut Knife Credit Union Ltd.
PO Box 308
205 Broad St.
Cut Knife, SK S0M 0N0
Tel: 306-398-2544; Fax: 306-398-2744
Mitch.Rokochy@cutknife.cu.sk.ca
Year Founded: 1960
Number of Employees: 7

Cypress Credit Union Ltd.
PO Box 1060
115 Jasper St.
Maple Creek, SK S0N 1N0
Tel: 306-662-2683; Fax: 306-662-3859
Toll-Free: 877-353-6311
www.cypresscu.sk.ca

Dauphin Plains Credit Union
PO Box 340
505 Main St. North
Dauphin, MB R7N 2V2
Tel: 204-622-4500; Fax: 204-622-4530
Toll-Free: 1-866-372-4535
info@dauphinplainscu.mb.ca
www.dauphinplainscu.mb.ca
Year Founded: 1940

Debden Credit Union Ltd.
PO Box 100
Debden, SK S0J 0S0
Tel: 306-724-8370; Fax: 306-724-2129
info@debden.cu.sk.ca
www.debdencu.com
Ownership: Member-owned
Number of Employees: 16

Desjardins Credit Union
Also listed under: *Credit Card Companies; Non-Depository Institutions*
East Tower, Whitby Mall
1615 Dundas St. East, 3rd Fl.
Whitby, ON L1N 2L1
Tel: 905-743-5790; Fax: 905-743-6156
Toll-Free: 888-283-8333
www.desjardins.com
Ownership: Member-owned
Year Founded: 2002

Desjardins Gestion d'actifs/ Desjardins Asset Management
Also listed under: *Credit Card Companies; Non-Depository Institutions*
95 St Clair Ave. West
Toronto, ON M4V 1N7

Diamond North Credit Union
PO Box 2074
Nipawin, SK S0E 1E0
Tel: 306-862-4651; Fax: 306-862-9611
Toll-Free: 877-881-2020
contactus@diamondnorthcu.com
www.diamondnorthcu.com, www.nipawincu.com
Other Contact Information: 306/862-2370 (Loans)
Year Founded: 2006
Assets: $100-500 million

Dodsland & District Credit Union Ltd.
PO Box 129
Dodsland, SK S0L 0V0
Tel: 306-356-2155; Fax: 306-356-2202
james.duncan@dodsland.cu.sk.ca
www.dodslandcreditunion.com
Year Founded: 1961
Number of Employees: 7

Dominion Credit Union
94 Commercial St.
Dominion, NS B1G 1B4
Tel: 902-849-8648; Fax: 902-842-0273
Year Founded: 1934

Domtar Newsprint Employees (Trenton) Credit Union Limited
PO Box 254
Trenton, ON K8V 5R5
Tel: 613-392-2426; Fax: 613-392-6851
ldwannamaker@sympatico.ca

DUCA Financial Services Credit Union Ltd.
5290 Yonge St.
Toronto, ON M2N 5P9
Tel: 416-223-8502; Fax: 416-223-2575
Toll-Free: 866-900-3822
duca.info@duca.com
www.duca.com
Former Name: Duca Community Credit Union Limited
Ownership: Member-owned
Year Founded: 1954
Number of Employees: 100
Assets: $500m-1 billion
Revenues: $10-50 million

Dundalk District Credit Union Limited
PO Box 340
79 Proton St. North
Dundalk, ON N0C 1B0
Tel: 519-923-2400; Fax: 519-923-2950
jmason@dundalkdistrictcreditunion.ca
www.dundalkdistrictcreditunion.ca
Year Founded: 1943
Number of Employees: 11
Assets: $10-50 million
Revenues: Under $1 million

Dunnville & District Credit Union Ltd.
208 Broad St. East
Dunnville, ON N1A 1G2
Tel: 905-774-7559; Fax: 905-774-4662
www.ddcu.com
Ownership: Member-owned
Number of Employees: 5

Dysart Credit Union Ltd.
PO Box 39
110 Main St.
Dysart, SK S0G 1H0
Tel: 306-432-2211;
Year Founded: 1960

Eagle River Credit Union
PO Box 29
8 Branch Rd.
L'Anse au Loup, NL A0K 3L0
Tel: 709-927-5524; Fax: 709-927-5759
Toll-Free: 877-377-3728
aobrien@eagleriver.creditu.net
www.eaglerivercu.com
Year Founded: 1984
Number of Employees: 40
Assets: $10-50 million
Revenues: Under $1 million

East Coast Credit Union
Admin. Office
305 Granville St.
Port Hawkesbury, NS B9A 2M5
Tel: 902-625-5610
www.eastcoastcreditu.ca
Year Founded: 2003
Number of Employees: 104
Assets: $100-500 million

East Kootenay Community Credit Union
924 Baker St.
Cranbrook, BC V1C 1A5
Tel: 250-426-6666; Fax: 250-426-0879
Toll-Free: 866-960-6666
reception@ekccu.com
www.ekccu.com
Number of Employees: 30

EasternEdge Credit Union
PO Box 2110
10 Factory Lane
St. John's, NL A1C 5H6
Tel: 709-739-2920; Fax: 709-739-3728
Toll-Free: 800-716-7283
www.easternedgecu.com
Former Name: NewTel Credit Union
Year Founded: 1976
Assets: $10-50 million

Eckville District Savings & Credit Union Ltd.
PO Box 278
Eckville, AB T0M 0X0
Tel: 403-746-2288; Fax: 403-746-3737
info@eckvillecu.com
www.eckvillecu.com
Ownership: Private
Year Founded: 1943
Number of Employees: 9

Edson Savings & Credit Union
PO Box 6118
4912 - 2nd Ave.
Edson, AB T7E 1T6
Tel: 780-723-4468; Fax: 780-723-7973
edsoncu@alberta-cu.com
www.edsoncu.com
Year Founded: 1940

Electragas Credit Union
6070 Stairs St.
Halifax, NS B3K 2E5
Tel: 902-454-6843; Fax: 902-453-5161

Electric Employees Credit Union
10 Lanceleve Cres.
Albert Bridge, NS B1K 3J3
Tel: 902-564-9707; Fax: 902-564-0956

Enderby & District Credit Union
PO Box 670
703 Mill St.
Enderby, BC V0E 1V0
Tel: 250-838-6841; Fax: 250-838-9756
info@enderbycreditunion.com
www.enderbycreditunion.com

Entegra Credit Union
Corporate Head Office
1335 Jefferson Ave.
Winnipeg, MB R2P 1S7
Tel: 204-949-7744; Fax: 204-949-5865
info@entegra.ca
www.entegra.ca
Former Name: Holy Spirit Credit Union
Year Founded: 1960
Number of Employees: 47
Assets: $100-500 million

Envision Credit Union
6470 - 201st St.
Langley, BC V2Y 2X4
Tel: 604-539-7300; Fax: 604-539-7315
www.envisionfinancial.ca
Also Known As: Envision Financial
Ownership: Member-owned
Year Founded: 1946
Number of Employees: 779
Assets: $1-10 billion
Revenues: $100-500 million

Equity Financial Services
#3, 400 Eastern Ave.
Toronto, ON M4M 1B9
Tel: 416-463-3173; Fax: 416-465-9984
Toll-Free: 1-800-263-9793
info@equityfs.ca
www.equitycreditunion.ca
Former Name: Unilever Employees Credit Union Limited; Equity Credit Union

Erickson Credit Union Limited
PO Box 100
24 Main St. West
Erickson, MB R0J 0P0
Tel: 204-636-7771; Fax: 204-636-2498
info@ericksoncu.mb.ca
www.ericksoncu.mb.ca
Ownership: Member-owned
Year Founded: 1952

Eriksdale Credit Union Limited
PO Box 99, Railway Stn. Railway
Eriksdale, MB R0C 0W0
Tel: 204-739-2137; Fax: 204-739-5409
info@eriksdalecu.mb.ca
www.eriksdalecu.mb.ca
Ownership: Member-owned
Year Founded: 1972
Number of Employees: 29

Espanola & District Credit Union Limited
91 Centre St.
Espanola, ON P5E 1S4
Tel: 705-869-3001
www.espanolacu.com
Year Founded: 1958

Estonian (Toronto) Credit Union Limited
958 Broadview Ave.
Toronto, ON M4K 2R6
Tel: 416-465-4659; Fax: 416-465-8442
Toll-Free: 866-844-3828
info@estoniancu.com
www.estoniancu.com
Year Founded: 1954
Number of Employees: 12

ETCU Financial
1 East Mall Cres.
Toronto, ON M9B 6G8
Tel: 416-622-8500; Fax: 416-622-0610
Toll-Free: 877-337-8500
www.etcu.com
Former Name: Etobicoke Teachers' Credit Union Limited
Year Founded: 1951

Ethelbert Credit Union
109 Railway Ave.
Ethelbert, MB R0L 0T0
Tel: 204-742-3529;

Fairview & District Savings & Credit Union Ltd.
PO Box 459
10300 - 110 St.
Fairview, AB T0H 1L0
Tel: 780-835-2914; Fax: 780-835-4214

Fédération des caisses Desjardins du Québec
100, av des Commandeurs
Lévis, QC G6V 7N5
Tél: 418-835-8444; Ligne sans frais: 1-866-835-8444
www.desjardins.com
Former Name: Fédération des Caisses Populaires Desjardins du Québec

Fédération des caisses populaires acadiennes ltée
CP 5554
295, boul St-Pierre ouest
Caraquet, NB E1W 1B7
Tél: 506-726-4000; Téléc: 506-726-4001
info@acadie.com
www.acadie.com
Year Founded: 1946
Number of Employees: 227

Fédération des caisses populaires de l'Ontario
214 Montreal Rd.
Ottawa, ON K1L 8L8
Tél: 613-746-3276; Téléc: 613-746-6035
Ligne sans frais: 800-423-3276

Fédération des caisses populaires du Manitoba
#200, 605 Des Meurons St.
Winnipeg, MB R2H 2R1
Tél: 204-237-8988; Téléc: 204-233-6405
federation@caisse.biz
www.caisse.biz
Ownership: Member-owned
Year Founded: 1937
Number of Employees: 240

Fiberglas Employees (Guelph) Credit Union Limited
PO Box 3603
247 York Rd.
Guelph, ON N1E 3G4
Tel: 519-824-2212; Fax: 519-824-1390
fiberglascu@bellnet.ca
Year Founded: 1953
Number of Employees: 1

Fire Services Credit Union Ltd.
1997 Avenue Rd.
Toronto, ON M5M 4A3
Tel: 416-440-1294; Fax: 416-440-4271
memberservices@firecreditunion.ca
www.firecreditunion.ca
Social Media: twitter.com/FireServicesCU
Former Name: The Fire Department Employees Credit Union Limited
Ownership: Member-owned
Year Founded: 1941

First Calgary Savings & Credit Union Limited
#200, 510 - 16th Ave. NE
Calgary, AB T2E 1K4
Tel: 403-230-2783; Fax: 403-276-6338
info@1stcalgary.com
www.1stcalgary.com
Ownership: Member-owned
Year Founded: 1987
Assets: $1-10 billion

FirstOntario Credit Union Limited
688 Queensdale Ave. East
Hamilton, ON L8V 1M1
Tel: 905-387-0770; Toll-Free: 888-283-7835
contact@firstontariocu.com
www.firstontariocu.com
Former Name: Avestel Family Savings Credit Union Limited; Family Savings & Credit Union Limited
Year Founded: 1940
Number of Employees: 300
Assets: $500m-1 billion

Flin Flon Credit Union
36 Main St.
Flin Flon, MB R8A 1J6
Tel: 204-687-6620
www.flinfloncu.mb.ca
Year Founded: 1940
Number of Employees: 3

Foam Lake Savings & Credit Union Ltd.
PO Box 160
326 Main St.
Foam Lake, SK S0A 1A0
Tel: 306-272-3385; Fax: 306-272-4948
info@foamlake.cu.sk.ca
www.foamlake.cu.sk.ca
Year Founded: 1941

Forget Credit Union Ltd.
General Delivery
Stoughton, SK S0C 0X0
Tel: 306-457-2747;
Year Founded: 1950

Fort Erie Community Credit Union Limited
1201 Garrison Rd.
Fort Erie, ON L2A 1N8
Tel: 905-994-1201; Fax: 905-994-1897
info@forteriecu.com
www.forteriecu.com

Fort York Community Credit Union Limited
Sunnyside East Wing
#207, 30 The Queensway
Toronto, ON M6R 1B5
Tel: 416-530-6474; Fax: 416-530-6763
fyinfo@fortyork.com
www.fortyork.com
Year Founded: 1950

Frontline Financial Credit Union
365 Richmond Rd.
Ottawa, ON K2A 0E7
Tel: 613-729-4312; Fax: 613-729-5075
www.911cu.com
Former Name: Ottawa Fire Fighters' Credit Union Ltd.
Year Founded: 1948

G & F Financial Group
Also listed under: *Financial Planning & Investment Management Companies; Insurance Companies*
7375 Kingsway
Burnaby, BC V3N 3B5
Tel: 604-517-5100; Fax: 604-659-4025
inquiry@gffg.com
www.gffg.com
Former Name: Gulf & Fraser Fishermen's Credit Union
Year Founded: 1941
Number of Employees: 175
Assets: $500m-1 billion
Revenues: $1-5 million

Ganaraska Financial Services Group
17 Queen St.
Port Hope, ON L1A 2Y8
Tel: 905-885-8134; Fax: 905-885-8298
info@ganaraskacu.com
www.ganaraskacu.com
Former Name: Ganaraska Credit Union
Year Founded: 1945

Glace Bay Central Credit Union
598 Main St.
Glace Bay, NS B1A 4X8
Tel: 902-849-7512; Fax: 902-842-9201
www.glacebaycentralcreditunion.com
Year Founded: 1932

Goderich Community Credit Union Limited
PO Box 66
39 St. David St.
Goderich, ON N7A 3Y5
Tel: 519-524-8366; Fax: 519-524-1329
reception@gccu.on.ca
www.gccu.on.ca
Ownership: Member-owned
Year Founded: 1954
Number of Employees: 15

Goodsoil Credit Union Limited
PO Box 88
Goodsoil, SK S0M 1A0
Tel: 306-238-2033; Fax: 306-238-4441
info@goodsoil.cu.sk.ca
www.goodsoilcu.com
Ownership: Member-owned
Year Founded: 1946
Number of Employees: 7
Assets: $10-50 million
Revenues: Under $1 million

Goodyear Employees (Bowmanville) Credit Union Limited
371 Orange Cres.
Oshawa, ON L1G 5X2
Tel: 905-623-2606; Fax: 905-432-7590
Year Founded: 1966
Number of Employees: 1

Govan Credit Union Ltd.
PO Box 280
Govan, SK S0G 1Z0
Tel: 306-484-2177; Fax: 306-484-4333
Toll-Free: 866-298-1336
govancreditunion@govan.cu.sk.ca
www.govancreditunion.ca
Year Founded: 1940

Grand Forks District Savings Credit Union
PO Box 2500
447 Market Ave.
Grand Forks, BC V0H 1H0
Tel: 250-442-5511; Fax: 250-442-5644
Toll-Free: 866-442-5511
info@gfdscu.com
www.gfdscu.com
Year Founded: 1949

Grandview Credit Union
PO Box 159
405 Main St.
Grandview, MB R0L 0Y0
Tel: 204-546-5200; Fax: 204-546-5219
info@grandviewcu.mb.ca
www.grandviewcu.mb.ca

Greater Vancouver Community Credit Union
1801 Willingdon Ave.
Burnaby, BC V5C 5R3
Tel: 604-298-3344; Fax: 604-421-8949
info@gvccu.com
www.gvccu.com

Greater Victoria Savings Credit Union
1001 Blanshard St.
Victoria, BC V8W 2H4
Tel: 250-388-4408; Fax: 250-384-4232
www.vancity.com
Year Founded: 1940

Grey Bruce Health Services Credit Union Ltd.
1939 - 8 Ave. East
Owen Sound, ON N4K 3C4
Tel: 519-376-9336; Fax: 519-376-1719
creditunion@mbts.com
Former Name: Health Centre (Owen Sound) Employees Credit Union Limited
Year Founded: 1967

GSW (Fergus) Credit Union Limited
599 Hill St. West
Fergus, ON N1M 2X1
Tel: 519-843-1616; Fax: 519-787-5533
Year Founded: 1951
Number of Employees: 2

Hald-Nor Community Credit Union Limited
PO Box 2135
22 Caithness St. East
Caledonia, ON N3W 2G6
Tel: 905-765-4071; Fax: 905-765-0485
caledonia@hald-nor.on.ca
www.hald-nor.on.ca
Ownership: Member-owned
Year Founded: 1954
Assets: $50-100 million

Halifax Civic Credit Union
6070 Lady Hammond Rd.
Halifax, NS B3K 2R6
Tel: 902-455-5489; Fax: 902-453-5491
Year Founded: 1938

Health Care Credit Union Ltd.
PO Box 5375
800 Commissioners Rd. East
London, ON N6A 4G5
Tel: 519-685-8353; Fax: 519-685-8153
creditunion@lhsc.on.ca
www.lhsc.on.ca/cr_union/
Year Founded: 1949

Healthcare & Municipal Employees Credit Union (HMECU)
209 Limeridge Rd. East
Hamilton, ON L9A 2S6
Tel: 905-575-8888; Fax: 905-575-3104
Toll-Free: 866-808-2888
www.hmecu.com
Number of Employees: 9

Heritage Credit Union
#100, 630 - 17th St.
Castlegar, BC V1N 4G7
Tel: 250-365-7232; Fax: 250-365-2913
hcu@heritagecu.ca
www.heritagecu.ca
Former Name: Castlegar Savings Credit Union
Ownership: Member-owned
Year Founded: 1948
Assets: $50-100 million

Hir-Walk Employees' (Windsor) Credit Union Limited
2072 Riverside Dr. East
Windsor, ON N8Y 4S5
Tel: 519-561-5543; Fax: 519-971-5744
hir-walker.credit@bellnet.ca
Year Founded: 1949
Number of Employees: 4

Holy Angel's & St. Anne's Parish (St Thomas) Credit Union Limited
PO Box 20125
St Thomas, ON N5P 4H4
Tel: 519-633-1710; Fax: 519-633-4024
lphoffer@bellnet.ca

Holy Name Parish (Pembroke) Credit Union Limited
667 Front St.
Pembroke, ON K8A 6J4
Tel: 613-732-3181; Fax: 613-732-1903
Ownership: Member-owned
Year Founded: 1942
Number of Employees: 3
Assets: Under $1 million
Revenues: Under $1 million

Horizon Credit Union
PO Box 1900
136 - 3rd Ave. East
Melville, SK S0A 2P0
Tel: 306-728-5425; Fax: 306-728-4520
Toll-Free: 866-522-1880
info@horizon.cu.sk.ca
www.horizon.cu.sk.ca
Other Contact Information: Telephone Banking: 306/728-1880
Former Name: Melville District Credit Union Ltd.; Aspen Prairie Credit Union Ltd.
Ownership: Co-operative. Member-owned
Year Founded: 1949
Number of Employees: 49

Hudson Bay Credit Union Ltd.
PO Box 538
208 Churchill St.
Hudson Bay, SK S0E 0Y0
Tel: 306-865-2209; Fax: 306-865-2381
info@hudsonbay.cu.sk.ca
www.hudsonbaycu.com
Year Founded: 1954
Number of Employees: 17
Assets: $10-50 million
Revenues: $1-5 million

Industrial Savings & Credit Union Ltd.
PO Box 97
Hwy 16A & 17 St.
Edmonton, AB T5J 2G9
Tel: 780-410-5502; Fax: 780-410-5391
Year Founded: 1964

Inglewood Savings & Credit Union
1328 - 9th Ave. SE
Calgary, AB T2G 0T3
Tel: 403-265-5396; Fax: 403-265-1326
manager@inglewoodcu.com
www.inglewoodcu.com
Ownership: Member-owned
Year Founded: 1938
Assets: $10-50 million

Innovation Credit Union
PO Box 638
1202 - 102nd St.
North Battleford, SK S9A 2Y7
Tel: 306-446-7000; Fax: 306-445-6086
www.innovationcu.ca
Other Contact Information: 1-866-446-7001 (North Region Toll-Free); 1-800-381-5502 (South Region Toll-Free); 306-445-6086 (North Region Fax); 306-773-0294 (South Region Fax)
Year Founded: 2007

iNova Credit Union
PO Box 8153, A Stn. A
6175 Almon St.
Halifax, NS B3K 5L9
Tel: 902-453-1145; Fax: 902-453-0370
Toll-Free: 800-665-1145
www.nspostalcreditunion.com
Former Name: Nova Scotia Postal Employees Credit Union

Integris Credit Union
1532 - 6th Ave.
Prince George, BC V2L 5B5
Tel: 250-612-3456; Fax: 250-612-3450
www.integriscu.ca
Former Name: Prince George Savings Credit Union; Nechako Valley Credit Union; Quesnel & District Credit Union
Year Founded: 2004

Interior Savings Credit Union
#300, 678 Bernard Ave.
Kelowna, BC V1Y 6P3
Tel: 250-762-4355; Fax: 250-762-9581
info@interiorsavings.com
www.interiorsavings.com
Ownership: Member-owned
Assets: $100-500 million

Island Savings Credit Union
Also listed under: *Financing & Loan Companies*
#300, 499 Canada Ave.
Duncan, BC V9L 1T7
Tel: 250-748-4728; Fax: 250-748-8831
info@iscu.com
www.iscu.com
Social Media: www.twitter.com/Island_Savings
Ownership: Member-owned
Year Founded: 1951
Number of Employees: 300
Assets: $500m-1 billion

Kawartha Credit Union Limited
PO Box 116
1054 Monaghan Rd.
Peterborough, ON K9J 6Y5
Tel: 705-743-3643; Fax: 705-749-1890
Toll-Free: 888-743-9966
info@kawarthacu.com
www.kawarthacu.com
Year Founded: 1952

Kellogg Employees Credit Union Limited
PO Box 5517
100 Kellogg Lane
London, ON N6A 4P9
Tel: 519-452-6414; Fax: 519-452-6316
kelloggcu@kelloggcu.com
www.kelloggcu.com
Year Founded: 1953
Number of Employees: 3
Revenues: $10-50 million

Kelvington Credit Union Ltd.
PO Box 459
Kelvington, SK S0A 1W0
Tel: 306-327-4728; Fax: 306-327-5100
info@kelvington.cu.sk.ca
www.kelvingtoncu.com
Year Founded: 1943

Kenaston Credit Union Ltd.
PO Box 70
607 - 3rd St.
Kenaston, SK S0G 2N0
Tel: 306-252-2160
garth.lewis@kenaston.cu.sk.ca
www.kenaston.cu.sk.ca

Kenora District Credit Union Limited
PO Box 2200
101 Park St.
Kenora, ON P9N 3X8
Tel: 807-467-4400; Fax: 807-468-6452
www.kdcu.on.ca

Kerrobert Credit Union Ltd.
PO Box 140
437 Pacific Ave.
Kerrobert, SK S0L 1R0
Tel: 306-834-2611; Fax: 306-834-5558
info@kerrobert.cu.sk.ca
www.kerrobert.cu.sk.ca
Year Founded: 1963

Khalsa Credit Union (Alberta) Limited
#604, 4656 Westwinds Dr. NE
Calgary, AB T3J 3Z5
Tel: 403-285-0707; Fax: 403-285-0771
khalsacu@telusplanet.net
www.khalsacu.ca
Year Founded: 1995
Number of Employees: 3
Assets: $1-5 million
Revenues: $1-5 million

Kingston Community Credit Union Ltd. (KCCU)
18 Market St.
Kingston, ON K7L 1W8
Tel: 613-549-3901; Fax: 613-549-6593
kccu@kccu.ca
www.kccu.ca
Social Media: www.youtube.com/user/KingstonCCU; www.facebook.com/116645398353538; twitter.com/KingstonCCU
Ownership: Member-owned

King-York Newsmen Toronto Credit Union Limited
444 Front St. West
Toronto, ON M5V 2S9
Tel: 416-585-5110; Fax: 416-585-5534
credit-union@globeandmail.ca
Ownership: Private
Year Founded: 1955
Assets: $1-5 million
Revenues: $1-5 million

Kootenay Savings Credit Union
#300, 1199 Cedar Ave.
Trail, BC V1R 4B8
Tel: 250-368-2686; Fax: 250-368-5203
info@kscu.com
www.kscu.com
Ownership: Member-owned
Year Founded: 1969
Number of Employees: 208
Assets: $500m-1 billion

Korean (Toronto) Credit Union Limited
703 Bloor St. West
Toronto, ON M6G 1L5
Tel: 416-535-4511; Fax: 416-535-9323
ktcul@rogers.com
www.koreancu.com

Korean Catholic Church Credit Union Limited
849 Don Mills Rd., 2nd Fl.
Toronto, ON M3C 1W1
Tel: 416-447-7788; Fax: 416-447-5297
kcccu@on.aibn.com

Krek Slovenian Credit Union Ltd.
747 Brown's Line
Toronto, ON M8W 3V7
Tel: 416-252-6527; Fax: 416-252-2092
main@krek.ca
www.krek.ca
Former Name: John E. Krek's Slovenian (Toronto) Credit Union Limited
Ownership: Private
Year Founded: 1953
Number of Employees: 17
Assets: $50-100 million

Ladysmith & District Credit Union
PO Box 430
330 First Ave.
Ladysmith, BC V9G 1A3
Tel: 250-245-2247; Fax: 250-245-5913
info@ldcu.ca
www.ldcu.ca
Year Founded: 1944

LaFleche Credit Union Ltd.
105 Main St.
Lafleche, SK S0H 2K0
Tel: 306-472-5215; Fax: 306-472-5545
info@lafleche.cu.sk.ca
www.laflechecu.com
Ownership: Member-owned
Year Founded: 1938

Number of Employees: 12
Assets: $10-50 million

Lake View Credit Union
800 - 102nd Ave.
Dawson Creek, BC V1G 2B2
Tel: 250-782-4871; Fax: 250-782-5828
lvcu@lakeviewcreditunion.com
www.lakeviewcreditunion.com
Ownership: Private
Number of Employees: 36

Lakeland Credit Union
PO Box 8057
5016 - 50 Ave.
Bonnyville, AB T9N 2J3
Tel: 780-826-3377; Fax: 780-826-6322
admin@lakelandcreditunion.com
www.lakelandcreditunion.com

Lambton Financial Credit Union Ltd.
1295 London Rd.
Sarnia, ON N7S 1P6
Tel: 519-542-0483; Fax: 519-542-3778
Toll-Free: 866-380-8008
www.lambtonfinancial.ca
Former Name: Polysar Lambton Credit Union Limited
Ownership: Private
Year Founded: 1947
Number of Employees: 48
Assets: $100-500 million
Revenues: $5-10 million

Landis Credit Union Ltd.
PO Box 220
Landis, SK S0K 2K0
Tel: 306-658-2152; Fax: 306-658-2153
owen.nicklin@landis.cu.sk.ca
www.landis.cu.sk.ca
Year Founded: 1942
Number of Employees: 4
Assets: $5-10 million
Revenues: Under $1 million

Lasco Employees' (Whitby) Credit Union Limited
1801 Hopkins St. South
Whitby, ON L1N 5T1
Tel: 905-668-8811; Fax: 905-668-2807

Latvian Credit Union
4 Credit Union Dr.
Toronto, ON M4A 2N8
Tel: 416-922-2551; Fax: 416-922-2758
www.kredsab.ca
Ownership: Member-owned
Number of Employees: 12

Lear Seating Canada Employees' (Kitchener) Credit Union Ltd.
PO Box 758
530 Manitou Dr.
Kitchener, ON
Tel: 519-895-3213;

Legacy Savings & Credit Union Ltd.
1940, 9 Ave.
Calgary, AB T2G 0V2
Tel: 403-265-6050; Fax: 403-265-8010
admin@legacysavings.com
www.legacysavings.com

Lethbridge Legion Savings & Credit Union Ltd.
324 Mayor Magrath Dr.
Lethbridge, AB T1J 3L7
Tel: 403-327-6417; Fax: 403-317-0122
Year Founded: 1958

Libro Financial Group
217 York St., 4th Fl.
London, ON N6A 5P9
Tel: 519-672-0124; Fax: 519-672-7831
Toll-Free: 800-361-8222
service@libro.ca
www.libro.ca
Former Name: St. Willibrod Credit Union Limited; St. Willibrod Community Credit Union Limited
Ownership: 47,000 owners
Year Founded: 1951
Number of Employees: 300
Assets: $1-10 billion
Revenues: $500m-1 billion

Lintlaw Credit Union Ltd.
PO Box 190
212 Main St.
Lintlaw, SK S0A 2H0
Tel: 306-325-2118; Fax: 306-325-4311
Year Founded: 1940

LIUNA Local 183 Credit Union Limited
#108, 1263 Wilson Ave.
Toronto, ON M3M 3G2
Tel: 416-242-6643; Fax: 416-242-7852
info@local183cu.ca
www.local183cu.ca

London Civic Employees' Credit Union Limited
343 Dundas St.
London, ON N6B 1V5
Tel: 519-661-4563; Fax: 519-663-9369
memberservices@lcecu.com
www.lcecu.com
Ownership: Private
Year Founded: 1948

London Fire Fighters' Credit Union Limited
400 Horton St. East
London, ON N6B 1L7
Tel: 519-661-5635; Fax: 519-661-5635
info@lfdcreditunion.com
www.lfdcreditunion.com
Ownership: Private
Number of Employees: 2

Luminus Financial
Also listed under: *Financial Planning & Investment Management Companies; Non-Depository Institutions*
Corporate Office
1 Yonge St.
Toronto, ON M5E 1E5
Tel: 416-366-5534; Fax: 416-366-6225
Toll-Free: 1-877-782-7639
inquiries@luminusfinancial.com
www.luminusfinancial.com
Former Name: Starnews Credit Union
Year Founded: 2011
Assets: $50-100 million

Macklin Credit Union Ltd.
PO Box 326
4809 Herald St.
Macklin, SK S0L 2C0
Tel: 306-753-2333; Fax: 306-753-2676
info@macklin.cu.sk.ca
www.macklin.cu.sk.ca
Number of Employees: 13

Main-à-Dieu Credit Union
2365 Louisbourg-Main-à-Dieu Rd.
Main-à-Dieu, NS B1C 1X2
Tel: 902-733-2555; Fax: 902-733-2301
Ownership: Member-owned
Year Founded: 1935
Number of Employees: 2
Assets: $1-5 million
Revenues: Under $1 million

Mankota Credit Union
Main St.
Mankota, SK S0H 2W0
Tel: 306-478-2284; Fax: 306-478-2277
info@mankota.cu.sk.ca
www.mankotacu.ca
Other Contact Information: Kikcaid Phone: 306-264-3822; Kincaid Office Fax: 306-264-5175
Number of Employees: 7

McMaster Savings & Credit Union Ltd.
Westdale Village
1005 King St. West
Hamilton, ON L8S 1L3
Tel: 905-522-2903; Fax: 905-522-4467
mscuwestdale@maccu.com
www.maccu.com
Ownership: Member-owned
Year Founded: 1936

Media Group Financial Credit Union Limited
369 York St.
London, ON N6A 4G1
Tel: 519-667-4505; Fax: 519-667-5522
creditunion@mediagroupfinancial.ca
www.mediagroupfinancial.ca

Me-Dian Credit Union
303 Selkirk Ave.
Winnipeg, MB R2W 2L8
Tel: 204-943-9111; Fax: 204-942-3698
www.me-diancu.mb.ca

The Medical-Dental Financial, Savings & Credit Limited
c/o Credential, Ontario Regl. Office
#200, 3430 South Service Rd.
Burlington, ON L7N 3T9
Tel: 905-632-9200; Fax: 905-632-0032

Member Savings Credit Union
55 Lakeshore Blvd. East
Toronto, ON M5E 1A4
Tel: 416-864-2461; Fax: 416-864-6858
Toll-Free: 888-560-2218
betterbanking@membersavings.ca
membersavings.ca
Year Founded: 1949
Assets: $50-100 million

MemberOne Credit Union Ltd.
PO Box 35
200 Front St. West, Concourse Level
Toronto, ON M5V 3K2
Tel: 416-344-4070; Fax: 416-344-4069
info@memberone.ca
www.memberone.ca
Former Name: WCB Credit Union Limited

Mendham-Burstall Credit Union
PO Box 69
Mendham, SK S0N 1P0
Tel: 306-628-3257; Fax: 306-628-4284
mendham@sasktel.net
Ownership: Member-owned
Assets: $10-50 million
Revenues: Under $1 million

Mennonite Savings & Credit Union (Ontario) Limited
1265 Strasburg Rd.
Kitchener, ON N2R 1S6
Tel: 519-746-1010; Fax: 519-746-1045
Toll-Free: 888-672-6728
info@mscu.com
www.mscu.com
Also Known As: Mennonite Savings & Credit Union
Ownership: Member-owned
Year Founded: 1964
Number of Employees: 145
Assets: $500m-1 billion
Revenues: $50-100 million

Meridian Credit Union
College Park
777 Bay St., 26th Fl.
Toronto, ON M5G 2C8
Tel: 416-597-4400; Fax: 416-597-5068
Toll-Free: 866-592-2226
www.meridiancu.ca
Former Name: HEPCOE Credit Union Limited
Ownership: Member-owned
Year Founded: 2005
Number of Employees: 1,000
Assets: $1-10 billion

Midale Credit Union Ltd.
PO Box 418
211 Main St.
Midale, SK S0C 1S0
Tel: 306-458-2222; Fax: 306-458-2329
www.midalecu.com

Milestone Credit Union Ltd.
PO Box 144
118 Main St.
Milestone, SK S0G 3L0
Tel: 306-436-2002; Fax: 306-436-2114
info@milestone.cu.sk.ca
Former Name: Milestone Savings & Credit Union Ltd.

Minnedosa Credit Union
PO Box 459
60 Main St.
Minnedosa, MB R0J 1E0
Tel: 204-867-6350; Fax: 204-867-6391
Toll-Free: 877-663-7228
info@minnedosacu.mb.ca
www.minnedosacu.mb.ca
Year Founded: 1947
Number of Employees: 20

Miracle Credit Union Ltd.
#22, 86 Guided Crt.
Toronto, ON M9V 4K6
Tel: 416-740-7553; Fax: 416-740-3767
miracle@on.aibn.com
www.miraclecreditunion.ca

Mitchell & District Credit Union Limited
105 Ontario Rd.
Mitchell, ON N0K 1N0
Tel: 519-348-8448; Fax: 519-348-8009
mitchell@mitchellcu.ca
www.mitchellcu.ca
Ownership: Private
Year Founded: 1960
Number of Employees: 33
Assets: $50-100 million
Revenues: $1-5 million

Molson Brewery Employees Credit Union Limited
1 Carlingview Dr.
Toronto, ON M9W 5E5
Tel: 416-675-8710; Fax: 416-213-0518
www.virtualonecu.ca
Year Founded: 1956
Number of Employees: 2

Momentum Credit Union
698 King St. East
Hamilton, ON L8M 1A3
Tel: 905-529-9445; Fax: 905-529-9016
king@MomentumCU.ca
www.momentum.ca
Number of Employees: 15

Moore Employees' Credit Union Limited
6100 Vipond Dr.
Mississauga, ON L5T 2X1
Tel: 416-241-7132
sylvia_murphy@ca.moore.com
Year Founded: 1962

Motor City Community Credit Union Limited
6701 Tecumseh Rd. East
Windsor, ON N8T 1E8
Tel: 519-944-7333; Fax: 519-944-9765
info@mcccu.com
www.mcccu.com
Ownership: Member-owned
Assets: $100-500 million

Mount Lehman Credit Union
5889 Mount Lehman Rd.
Mount Lehman, BC V4X 1V7
Tel: 604-856-7761; Fax: 604-856-1429
info@mtlehman.com
www.mtlehman.com
Other Contact Information: MemberCall: 604-856-7726
Year Founded: 1942
Number of Employees: 12

Mountain View Credit Union Ltd.
PO Box 3752
4920 - 50 Ave.
Olds, AB T4H 1P5
Tel: 403-556-3306; Fax: 403-556-1050
mvcu@mvcu.ca
www.mvcu.ca
Ownership: Member-owned
Year Founded: 1977
Number of Employees: 1977
Assets: $100-500 million

Mouvement des caisses Desjardins du Québec
Also listed under: *Financing & Loan Companies; Insurance Companies*
100, av. des Commandeurs
Lévis, QC G6V 7N5
Tél: 418-835-8444; Téléc: 418-833-5873
www.desjardins.com
Ownership: Private
Year Founded: 1901
Number of Employees: 38,000
Assets: $10-50 million

Mozart Savings & Credit Union Limited
PO Box 96
Mozart, SK S0A 2S0
Tel: 306-554-2808; Fax: 306-554-2839
mozart@sasktel.net
Year Founded: 1940
Number of Employees: 3

Municipal Employees (Chatham) Credit Union Limited
301 Delaware Ave.
Chatham, ON N7L 2W9
Tel: 519-354-9182;
Year Founded: 1954
Number of Employees: 2
Assets: $1-5 million
Revenues: Under $1 million

Nelson & District Credit Union
PO Box 350
501 Vernon St.
Nelson, BC V1L 5R2
Tel: 250-352-7207; Fax: 250-352-9663
Toll-Free: 877-352-7207
enrichingyourlife@nelsoncu.com
www.nelsoncu.com
Number of Employees: 50

New Brunswick Teachers' Association Credit Union
PO Box 752
650 Montgomery St.
Fredericton, NB E3B 5R6
Tel: 506-452-1724; Fax: 506-452-1732
Toll-Free: 800-565-5626
nbtacu@nbnet.nb.ca
www.nbtacu.nb.ca
Ownership: Private
Year Founded: 1971
Number of Employees: 12
Assets: $10-50 million

New Community Credit Union
321 - 20th St. West
Saskatoon, SK S7M 0X1
Tel: 306-653-1300; Fax: 306-653-4711
info@newcommunity.cu.sk.ca
www.newcommunitycu.com
Former Name: New Community Savings & Credit Union Ltd.
Year Founded: 1939

New Glasgow Credit Union
175 Victoria St.
New Glasgow, NS B2H 4V3
Tel: 902-752-3102; Fax: 902-755-5777

New Ross Credit Union
PO Box 32
56 Forties Rd.
New Ross, NS B0J 2M0
Tel: 902-689-2949; Fax: 902-689-2597
www.newrosscreditunion.ca
Year Founded: 1956

New Waterford Credit Union
3462 Plummer Ave.
New Waterford, NS B1H 1Z6
Tel: 902-862-6453; Fax: 902-862-9206
www.newwaterfordcreditunion.com
Year Founded: 1934
Number of Employees: 14
Assets: $10-50 million

Niverville Credit Union
PO Box 430
62 Main St.
Niverville, MB R0A 1E0
Tel: 204-388-4747; Fax: 204-388-9970
info@nivervillecu.mb.ca
www.nivervillecu.mb.ca
Year Founded: 1949

North Peace Savings & Credit Union
10344 - 100th St.
Fort St John, BC V1J 3Z1
Tel: 250-787-0361; Fax: 250-787-9704
Toll-Free: 800-561-7849
members@northpeacesavings.com
www.northpeacesavings.com
Ownership: Private
Number of Employees: 53

North Shore Credit Union
1112 Lonsdale Ave., 3rd Fl.
North Vancouver, BC V7M 2H2
Tel: 604-982-8000; Fax: 604-713-3035
Toll-Free: 880-713-6728
www.nscu.com
Year Founded: 1941

North Valley Credit Union Limited
PO Box 1389
516 Main St.
Esterhazy, SK S0A 0X0
Tel: 306-745-6615; Fax: 306-745-2858
Toll-Free: 866-533-6828
www.northvalleycu.com
Former Name: Esterhazy Credit Union Limited
Ownership: Member-owned
Year Founded: 1998
Number of Employees: 14

Northern Credit Union
Also listed under: *Financial Planning & Investment Management Companies*
681 Pine St.
Sault Ste Marie, ON P6B 3G2
Tel: 705-253-9868; Fax: 705-949-1056
www.northerncu.com
Year Founded: 1957
Assets: $500m-1 billion

Northern Lights Credit Union Limited
PO Box 876
97 Duke St.
Dryden, ON P8N 2Z5
Tel: 807-223-5358; Fax: 807-223-8650
kimf@nlcu.on.ca
www.nlcu.on.ca
Number of Employees: 57

Northern Savings Credit Union
138 Third Ave. West
Prince Rupert, BC V8J 1K8
Tel: 250-627-7571; Fax: 250-624-8297
info@northsave.com
www.northsave.com
Ownership: Member-owned

Northland Savings & Credit Union Limited
10 Cain Ave.
Kapuskasing, ON P5N 1S9
Tel: 705-335-2348; Fax: 705-337-1070
kapcu@ntl.sympatico.ca
Ownership: Member-owned
Year Founded: 1939

Northridge Savings & Credit Union Ltd.
9 Second Ave. North
Sudbury, ON P3B 3L7
Tel: 705-566-8540; Fax: 705-566-8480
www.northridgesavings.com

Oak Bank Credit Union
PO Box 217
686 Main St.
Oakbank, MB R0E 1J0
Tel: 204-444-7200; Fax: 204-444-3513
info@oakbankcu.mb.ca
www.oakbankcu.mb.ca
Year Founded: 1946

Ogema District Credit Union Ltd.
PO Box 339
Ogema, SK S0C 1Y0
Tel: 306-459-2266
info@ogema.cu.sk.ca
www.ogema.cu.sk.ca
Year Founded: 1950

OMISTA Credit Union
151 Cornhill St.
Moncton, NB E1C 6L3
Tel: 506-857-3222; Fax: 506-857-2235
cornhillstreet@omista.com
www.omista.com
Ownership: Member-owned

ONR Employees' (North Bay) Credit Union Limited
555 Oak St. East
North Bay, ON P1B 9E5
Tel: 705-472-1100; Fax: 705-472-0651
onrcu@ontc.on.ca
Year Founded: 1950

Ontario Civil Service Credit Union Limited
#1, 18 Grenville St.
Toronto, ON M4Y 3B3
Tel: 416-314-6772; Fax: 416-314-7805
Toll-Free: 888-516-6664
memberassistance@mycreditunion.ca
www.mycreditunion.ca
Ownership: Cooperative
Year Founded: 1945
Assets: $100-500 million

Revenues: $5-10 million

Ontario Educational Credit Union Limited
PO Box 360
#1, 6435 Edwards Blvd.
Mississauga, ON L5T 2P7
Tel: 905-795-1637; Fax: 905-795-0625
Toll-Free: 800-463-3602
www.oecu.on.ca
Year Founded: 1962
Number of Employees: 8

Ontario Provincial Police Association Credit Union Limited
123 Ferris Lane
Barrie, ON L4M 2Y1
Tel: 705-726-5656; Fax: 705-726-1449
Toll-Free: 800-461-4288
gd@oppacu.com
www.oppacu.com
Also Known As: O.P.P.A Credit Union
Year Founded: 1971

Osoyoos Credit Union
PO Box 360
8312 Main St.
Osoyoos, BC V0H 1V0
Tel: 250-495-6522; Fax: 250-495-3363
Toll-Free: 800-882-1966
contact@osoyooscreditunion.com
www.osoyooscreditunion.com
Ownership: Member-owned
Year Founded: 1946
Number of Employees: 20

Ottawa Police Credit Union Limited
#206, 474 Elgin St., 2nd Fl.
Ottawa, ON K2P 2J6
Tel: 613-236-1222; Fax: 613-567-3760
www.opcu.com
Former Name: Ottawa-Carleton Police Credit Union Limited
Ownership: Private.
Year Founded: 1955
Number of Employees: 5
Revenues: $10-50 million

Ottawa Women's Credit Union Limited
Co-operative House
271 Bank St.
Ottawa, ON K2P 1X5
Tel: 613-233-7711; Fax: 613-233-6413
info@owcu.on.ca
www.owcu.on.ca

PACE Savings & Credit Union Limited
#1, 8111 Jane St.
Vaughan, ON L4K 4L7
Tel: 905-738-8900; Fax: 905-738-8283
Toll-Free: 800-433-9122
pace.info@pacecu.com
www.pacecu.com
Ownership: Member-owned
Year Founded: 1984
Assets: $50-100 million
Revenues: $5-10 million

Parama Lithuanian Credit Union Limited
1573 Bloor St. West
Toronto, ON M6P 1A6
Tel: 416-532-1149; Fax: 416-532-5595
info@parama.ca
www.parama.net
Year Founded: 1952
Number of Employees: 30
Assets: $100-500 million

Pedeco (Brockville) Credit Union Limited
2337 Parkedale Ave.
Brockville, ON K6V 5W5
Tel: 613-342-4436; Fax: 613-342-6584
cmacdonald@ripnet.com
Year Founded: 1952

PenFinancial Credit Union
247 East Main St.
Welland, ON L3B 3X1
Tel: 905-735-4801; Fax: 905-735-2983
www.penfinancial.com
Former Name: St Catharines Civic Employees' Credit Union Ltd.
Year Founded: 1951
Number of Employees: 57
Assets: $100-500 million

Peterborough Community Credit Union Limited
PO Box 1600
167 Brock St.
Peterborough, ON K9J 7S4
Tel: 705-748-4481; Fax: 705-748-5520
www.pboccu.com
Year Founded: 1939

Peterborough Industrial Credit Union
890 High St.
Peterborough, ON K9J 5R2
Tel: 705-743-4651; Fax: 705-743-9889

Pierceland Credit Union Ltd.
PO Box 10
181 Main St.
Pierceland, SK S0M 2K0
Tel: 306-839-2071; Fax: 306-839-2292
info@pierceland.cu.sk.ca
Year Founded: 1941
Number of Employees: 8

Pincher Creek Credit Union Ltd.
PO Box 1660
750 Kettles St.
Pincher Creek, AB T0K 1W0
Tel: 403-627-4431; Fax: 403-627-5331
www.pinchercreek-creditunion.com
Ownership: Member-owned
Year Founded: 1944
Number of Employees: 5

Plainsview Credit Union
PO Box 150
600 Main St.
Kipling, SK S0G 2S0
Tel: 306-736-2549; Fax: 306-736-8290
info@plainsview.cu.sk.ca
www.plainsview.com

The Police Credit Union Ltd.
#303, 3650 Victoria Park Ave.
Toronto, ON M2H 3P7
Tel: 416-226-3353; Fax: 416-226-1565
Toll-Free: 800-561-2557
callcentre@tpcu.on.ca
www.tpcu.on.ca
Ownership: Member-owned
Year Founded: 1946

Porcupine Credit Union Ltd.
PO Box 189
150 McAllister Ave.
Porcupine Plain, SK S0E 1H0
Tel: 306-278-2181; Fax: 306-278-2944
info@porcupine.cu.sk.ca
www.porcupine.cu.sk.ca
Year Founded: 1946

Powell River Credit Union Financial Group
Also listed under: *Financial Planning & Investment Management Companies*
4721 Joyce Ave.
Powell River, BC V8A 3B5
Tel: 604-485-6206; Fax: 604-485-7112
Toll-Free: 800-393-6733
www.prcu.com
Year Founded: 1939
Number of Employees: 46
Assets: $100-500 million
Revenues: $5-10 million

Prairie Centre Credit Union
PO Box 940
Rosetown, SK S0L 2V0
Tel: 306-882-2693; Fax: 306-882-3326
comments@pccu.ca
www.pccu.ca
Ownership: Cooperative
Year Founded: 1993
Number of Employees: 75
Assets: $100-500 million
Revenues: $5-10 million

Prairie Diamond Credit Union
PO Box 819
123 Garfield St.
Davidson, SK S0G 1A0
Tel: 306-567-2931; Fax: 306-567-5503
info@prairiediamond.cu.sk.ca
www.affinitycu.ca
Year Founded: 1994

Prairie Pride Credit Union
PO Box 37
Alameda, SK S0C 0A0
Tel: 306-489-2131; Fax: 306-489-2188
info@prairiepride.cu.sk.ca
www.prairieepridecu.com
Former Name: Gainsborough Credit Union Ltd.
Year Founded: 2001
Number of Employees: 9

Princess Credit Union
22 Fraser Ave.
Sydney Mines, NS B1V 2B7
Tel: 902-736-9204; Fax: 902-736-2887

Progressive Credit Union
30 Hughes
Fredericton, NB E3A 2W3
Tel: 506-458-9145; Fax: 506-459-0106
www.progressivecu.nb.ca
Former Name: Capital Credit Union
Year Founded: 1949

Prosperity ONE Credit Union
44 Main St. East
Milton, ON L9T 1N3
Tel: 905-878-4168; Fax: 905-878-5500
info@prosperityone.ca
www.prosperityone.ca
Former Name: Halton Community Credit Union
Year Founded: 1957
Number of Employees: 36
Assets: $50-100 million

Province House Credit Union Ltd.
PO Box 1083
1724 Granville St.
Halifax, NS B3J 2X1
Tel: 902-424-5712; Fax: 902-424-3662
Toll-Free: 888-484-0880
info@provincehouse.com
www.provincehouse.com

Provincial Alliance Credit Union Limited
1201 Wilson Ave.
Toronto, ON M3M 1J8
Tel: 416-235-4373; Fax: 416-235-4225
Toll-Free: 877-523-7228
help@provincialalliance.com
www.provincialalliance.com
Year Founded: 1953
Number of Employees: 24

Public Service Credit Union Ltd.
403 Empire Ave.
St. John's, NL A1E 1W6
Tel: 709-579-8210; Fax: 709-579-8233
Toll-Free: 800-563-6755
pscuadmin@pscu.creditu.net
www.pscu.ca
Ownership: Cooperative
Year Founded: 1936
Number of Employees: 18
Assets: $10-50 million
Revenues: $1-5 million

Public Service Employees Credit Union
141 Weldon St.
Moncton, NB E1C 5W1
Tel: 506-853-8881; Fax: 506-856-8492
www.psecreditunion.ca

Quill Lake Credit Union Ltd.
PO Box 520
Quill Lake, SK S0A 3E0
Tel: 306-383-4155; Fax: 306-383-2622
www.quilllake.cu.sk.ca
Year Founded: 1946

QuintEssential Credit Union Limited
293 Sidney St.
Belleville, ON K8P 3Z4
Tel: 613-966-4111; Fax: 613-966-8909
info@qcu.ca
www.qcu.ca

Radville Credit Union Ltd.
PO Box 279
201 Main St.
Radville, SK S0C 2G0
Tel: 306-869-2215; Fax: 306-869-2891
info@radville.cu.sk.ca
www.radville.cu.sk.ca
Year Founded: 1943

Railway Employees' (Sarnia) Credit Union Limited
431 Russell St. South
Sarnia, ON N7T 3N1
Tel: 519-336-0093; Fax: 519-336-6945
info@recu.ca
www.recu.ca

Raymore Savings & Credit Union Ltd.
PO Box 460
121 Main St.
Raymore, SK S0A 3J0
Tel: 306-746-2160; Fax: 306-746-5811
Toll-Free: 866-612-2300
info@raymore.cu.sk.ca
www.raymorecu.com
Year Founded: 1949

RBW Employees' (Owen Sound) Credit Union Limited
2049 - 20th St.
Owen Sound, ON N4K 5R2
Tel: 519-376-8330; Fax: 519-376-1164
Number of Employees: 1

Reddy Kilowatt Credit Union Ltd.
Newfoundland Power Bldg.
PO Box 8910
50 Duffy Pl.
St. John's, NL A1B 3P6
Tel: 709-737-5624; Fax: 709-737-2937
Toll-Free: 800-409-2887
rkcu@reddykilowatt.creditu.net
www.reddyk.net
Year Founded: 1956
Number of Employees: 6

Resurrection Parish (Toronto) Credit Union Limited
3 Resurrection Rd.
Toronto, ON M9A 5G1
Tel: 416-532-3400; Fax: 416-532-4816
rpcul@rpcul.com
www.rpcul.com
Number of Employees: 13

River City Credit Union Ltd.
11715A - 108 Ave.
Edmonton, AB T5H 1B8
Tel: 780-496-3482; Fax: 780-496-3477
rivercity@alberta-cu.com
www.river-citycu.com
Former Name: Edmonton Civic Employees Credit Union Ltd.

Rochdale Credit Union Limited
943 Dundas St.
Woodstock, ON N4S 1H2
Tel: 519-539-4813; Fax: 519-539-8667
rochdale@rcu.com
www.rcu.com
Year Founded: 1942

Rocky Credit Union Ltd.
PO Box 1420
5035 - 49 St.
Rocky Mountain House, AB T4T 1B1
Tel: 403-845-2861; Fax: 403-845-7295
rockycu@alberta-cu.com
www.rockycreditunion.com
Ownership: Public
Year Founded: 1944
Number of Employees: 40
Assets: $100-500 million
Revenues: $1-5 million

Rorketon & District Credit Union
PO Box 10
691 Main St.
Rorketon, MB R0L 1R0
Tel: 204-732-2448; Fax: 204-732-2275
rorkinfo@rorketoncu.mb.ca
www.rorketoncu.mb.ca
Year Founded: 1961

Rosenort Credit Union Limited
PO Box 339
23 Main St.
Rosenort, MB R0G 1W0
Tel: 204-746-2355; Fax: 204-746-2541
Toll-Free: 800-265-7925
info@rcu.mb.ca
www.rcu.mb.ca
Year Founded: 1940
Assets: $50-100 million

Rossignol Credit Union
PO Box 310
Brooklyn, NS B0J 1H0
Tel: 902-354-2021;
Ownership: Private
Year Founded: 1937
Number of Employees: 1
Assets: $1-5 million
Revenues: Under $1 million

Royglenor Savings & Credit Union Ltd.
Royal Alexander Hospital, Community Services Centre
#174, 10240 Kingsway Ave.
Edmonton, AB T5H 3V9
Tel: 780-474-7724; Fax: 780-474-9043
www.royglenorcu.ca
Year Founded: 1956

St Gregor Credit Union Ltd.
PO Box 128
2 Main St.
St Gregor, SK S0K 3X0
Tel: 306-366-2116; Fax: 306-366-2032

St. Joseph's Credit Union
PO Box 159
3552 Hwy. 206
Petit de Grat, NS B0E 2L0
Tel: 902-226-2288; Fax: 902-226-9855
Toll-Free: 866-876-3192
www.stjosephscreditu.ca
Year Founded: 1936
Number of Employees: 12

St. Mary's Paperworkers Credit Union
75 Huron St.
Sault Ste Marie, ON P6A 5P4
Tel: 705-541-2438; Fax: 705-942-6427
baile_s@stmarys-paper.com
Ownership: Private. Closed Bond.
Year Founded: 1953
Number of Employees: 1
Assets: Under $1 million
Revenues: Under $1 million

St. Stanislaus & St. Casimir's Polish Parishes Credit Union Ltd.
220 Roncesvalles Ave.
Toronto, ON M6R 2L7
Tel: 416-537-2181; Fax: 416-536-8525
info@polcu.com
www.polcan.com
Former Name: Polish (St Catharines) Credit Union Limited
Year Founded: 1951
Number of Employees: 3

Sandhills Credit Union
PO Box 249
Leader, SK S0N 1H0
Tel: 306-628-3687; Fax: 306-628-3674
info@sandhills.cu.sk.ca
www.sandhillscu.com
Ownership: Member-owned

Sandy Lake Credit Union
PO Box 129
102 Main St.
Sandy Lake, MB R0J 1X0
Tel: 204-585-2609; Fax: 204-585-2163
slcunion@slcu.mb.ca
www.slcu.mb.ca

Sanford Credit Union
7 Mellow St.
Sanford, MB R0G 2J0
Tel: 204-736-2373; Fax: 204-736-4108
info@sanfordcu.mb.ca
www.sanfordcu.mb.ca
Year Founded: 1950

Saskatoon City Employees Credit Union
222 - 3rd Ave. North
Saskatoon, SK S7K 0J5
Tel: 306-975-3280; Fax: 306-975-7806
www.scecu.com
Social Media: twitter.com/scecu
Former Name: Saskatoon City Employee Credit Union Ltd.
Year Founded: 1947
Number of Employees: 9
Assets: $10-50 million
Revenues: $1-5 million

SaskCentral
PO Box 3030
2055 Albert St.
Regina, SK S4P 3G8
Tel: 306-566-1200; Fax: 306-566-1372
Toll-Free: 1-866-403-7499
info@saskcentral.com
www.saskcu.com
Ownership: Owned by Saskatchewan credit unions
Assets: $1-10 billion

Saugeen Community Credit Union Limited
PO Box 708
118 Queen St. South
Durham, ON N0G 1R0
Tel: 519-369-2931; Fax: 519-369-2994
durhamcu@saugeencreditunion.com
www.saugeencreditunion.com

Scarborough Hospitals Employees' Credit Union Ltd.
#504, 3050 Lawrence Ave. East
Toronto, ON M10 2T7
Tel: 416-438-2911; Fax: 416-431-8131
fran.carolyn@sympatico.ca
Year Founded: 1964

Servus Credit Union
#300, 8723 - 82 Ave.
Edmonton, AB T6C 0Y9
Tel: 780-496-2000; Fax: 780-468-5220
Toll-Free: 877-496-2151
info@servuscu.ca; careers@servuscu.ca
www.servuscu.ca
Other Contact Information: askafinancialplanner@servuscu.ca (Financial Planning); 780-450-9647 (TTY for the hearing impaired)
Ownership: Member-owned
Year Founded: 1938
Assets: $1-10 billion

Sharons Credit Union
1055 Kingsway
Vancouver, BC V5V 3C7
Tel: 604-873-6490; Fax: 604-873-6498
sharons@sharonscu.ca
www.sharons.ca
Year Founded: 1988
Number of Employees: 30
Assets: $100-500 million

Shaunavon Credit Union
399 Centre St.
Shaunavon, SK S0N 2N0
Tel: 306-297-2635; Fax: 306-297-3137
Toll-Free: 800-667-0068
contactus@myscu.ca
www.myscu.ca
Also Known As: mySCU
Ownership: Member-owned
Year Founded: 1944

Shell Employees Credit Union Limited
PO Box 100, M Stn. M
Calgary, AB T2P 2H5
Tel: 403-691-3817; Fax: 403-262-4009
shellcu@shellcu.com
www.shellcu.com
Other Contact Information: Toll Free: 1-877-582-6222 (AB only)
Ownership: Member-owned
Year Founded: 1953

Sheridan Park Credit Union Ltd.
2251 Speakman Dr.
Mississauga, ON L5K 1B2
Tel: 905-823-1263; Fax: 905-823-8661
spcu@primus.ca
www.spcu.ca

Smiths Falls Community Credit Union Limited
1 Beckwith St. North
Smiths Falls, ON K7A 2B2
Tel: 613-283-3835; Fax: 613-283-9623
Year Founded: 1951

SOC Savings & Credit Union Ltd.
Eau Claire Place I
525 - 3 Ave. SW
Calgary, AB T2P 0G4
Tel: 403-509-4078; Fax: 403-509-4299

So-Use Credit Union
2265 Bloor St. West
Toronto, ON M6S 1P1
Tel: 416-763-5575; Fax: 416-761-9604
Toll-Free: 800-322-9274
so-use.info@so-use.com
www.so-use.com
Year Founded: 1950

South Calgary Savings & Credit Union Limited
4810 - 16th St. SW
Calgary, AB T2T 4J5
Tel: 403-243-5224; Fax: 403-287-9189
Ownership: Member-owned

South Interlake Credit Union Ltd.
233 Main St.
Selkirk, MB R1A 1S1
Tel: 204-785-7625; Fax: 204-785-7649
www.sicu.mb.ca
Ownership: Member-owned
Year Founded: 1944
Number of Employees: 106
Assets: $100-500 million

Southlake Regional Health Centre Employees' Credit Union Limited
596 Davis Dr.
Newmarket, ON L0G 1V0
Tel: 905-895-4521; Fax: 905-853-2218
Former Name: York County Hospital Employees' (Newmarket) Credit Union Limited
Number of Employees: 1

Southwest Regional Credit Union
1205 Exmouth St.
Sarnia, ON N7S 1W7
Tel: 519-383-8001; Fax: 519-383-8841
info@southwestcu.com
www.southwestcu.com
Year Founded: 1989
Number of Employees: 30

Spalding Savings & Credit Union Ltd.
111 Centre St.
Spalding, SK S0K 4C0
Tel: 306-872-2050; Fax: 306-872-2100
Year Founded: 1941

Spiritwood Credit Union Ltd.
PO Box 129
Spiritwood, SK S0J 2M0
Tel: 306-883-2250; Fax: 306-883-2223
Toll-Free: 877-288-1414
contactus@spiritwood.cu.sk.ca
www.spiritwoodcu.com
Ownership: Member-owned
Year Founded: 1938

Spruce Credit Union
879 Victoria St.
Prince George, BC V2L 2K7
Tel: 250-562-5415
sprucecu@cucbc.com
www.sprucecu.bc.ca
Number of Employees: 30
Assets: $50-100 million

Squamish Credit Union
PO Box 1940
38085 - 2nd St.
Squamish, BC V0N 3G0
Tel: 604-892-8355; Fax: 604-892-8377
Toll-Free: 877-892-5288
squamishsavings.com
Ownership: Private

Stanco Credit Union Ltd.
Chevron Plaza, Room 759
500 - 5 Ave. SW
Calgary, AB T2P 0L7
Tel: 403-234-5300; Fax: 403-234-5823
info@stancocu.com
www.stancocu.com
Number of Employees: 1
Assets: $1-5 million
Revenues: Under $1 million

Starbuck Credit Union
16 Main St.
Starbuck, MB R0G 2P0
Tel: 204-735-2394; Fax: 204-735-4020
Toll-Free: 866-398-9642
info@starbuckcreditunion.com
www.starbuckcreditunion.com

Year Founded: 1940
Assets: $50-100 million

State Farm (Toronto) Credit Union Limited
333 First Commerce Dr.
Aurora, ON L4G 8A4
Tel: 905-750-4100; Fax: 905-750-4487
Year Founded: 1968

Steel Centre Credit Union
340 Prince St.
Sydney, NS B1P 5K9
Tel: 902-562-5559; Fax: 902-539-6024
www.sccu.ca
Year Founded: 1993

Steinbach Credit Union
305 Main St.
Steinbach, MB R5G 1B1
Tel: 204-326-3495; Fax: 204-326-5093
Toll-Free: 800-728-6440
scu@scu.mb.ca
www.scu.mb.ca
Ownership: Member-owned
Year Founded: 1941
Assets: $1-10 billion
Revenues: $50-100 million

Stoughton Credit Union Ltd.
PO Box 420
Stoughton, SK S0G 4T0
Tel: 306-457-2443; Fax: 306-457-2511
info@stoughton.cu.sk.ca
www.stoughtoncu.com
Year Founded: 1960
Number of Employees: 9
Assets: $10-50 million
Revenues: $1-5 million

Strathclair Credit Union
PO Box 246
Strathclair, MB R0J 2C0
Tel: 204-365-4700; Fax: 204-365-4710
info@strathclaircu.mb.ca
www.strathclaircu.mb.ca

Strathfiner Credit Union Ltd.
PO Box 1020
Edmonton, AB T5J 2M1
Tel: 780-449-8295; Fax: 780-449-8174
sfcu@datanet.ab.ca
Ownership: Member-owned. Closed bond.
Year Founded: 1954
Number of Employees: 1
Assets: $1-5 million
Revenues: Under $1 million

Sudbury Credit Union
Also listed under: *Financing & Loan Companies*
PO Box 662
1 Gribble St.
Copper Cliff, ON P0M 1N0
Tel: 705-682-0641; Fax: 705-682-1348
info@sudburycu.com
www.sudburycu.com
Former Name: Sudbury Regional Credit Union
Ownership: Member-owned
Year Founded: 1951
Assets: $100-500 million

Summerland & District Credit Union
PO Box 750
13601 Victoria Rd. North
Summerland, BC V0H 1Z0
Tel: 250-494-7181; Fax: 250-494-4261
sdcu@sdcu.com
www.sdcu.com
Year Founded: 1944
Number of Employees: 39

Sunnybrook Credit Union Limited
c/o Sunnybrook Health Sciences Centre
#CB02, 2075 Bayview Ave.
Toronto, ON M4N 3M5
Tel: 416-480-4467; Fax: 416-480-5908
info@sunnybrookcu.com
www.sunnybrookcu.com
Year Founded: 1950

SunRise Credit Union
356 South Railway St.
Boissevain, MB R0K 0E0
Tel: 204-534-2421; Fax: 204-534-6310
Former Name: Turtle Mountain Credit Union

Sunrise Credit Union Ltd.
PO Box 163
197 Broadway St.
Treherne, MB R0G 2V0
Tel: 204-723-3250; Fax: 204-723-3255
info@sunrisecu.mb.ca; treherne@sunrisecu.mb.ca
www.sunrisecu.mb.ca
Other Contact Information: Lost or Stolen Card, Toll-Free: 1-800-567-8111; MasterCard cardholder services, Toll-Free: 1-800-561-7849
Former Name: Cypress River Credit Union; Hartney Credit Union; Tiger Hills Credit Union; Turtle Mountain Credit Union; Virden Credit Union
Ownership: Member-owned
Year Founded: 2008

Sunshine Coast Credit Union
Also listed under: *Financial Planning & Investment Management Companies*
PO Box 799
985 Gibsons Way
Gibsons, BC V0N 1V0
Tel: 604-886-2122; Fax: 604-886-0797
Toll-Free: 1-866-886-2132
administration@sunshineccu.net
www.sunshineccu.com
Ownership: Member-owned
Year Founded: 1941
Number of Employees: 83
Assets: $100-500 million
Revenues: $100-500 million

Superior Credit Union Limited
318 South Syndicate Ave.
Thunder Bay, ON P7E 1E3
Tel: 807-624-2255
info@supercu.com
www.supercu.com
Year Founded: 1997

Sydenham Community Credit Union Limited
32 Front St. East
Strathroy, ON N7G 1Y4
Tel: 519-245-2530; Fax: 519-245-0167
info@sydenhamccu.on.ca
www.sydenhamccu.on.ca
Year Founded: 1957

Sydney Credit Union
PO Box 1386
95 Townsend St.
Sydney, NS B1P 6K3
Tel: 902-562-5593; Fax: 902-539-8448
sydney@sydney.creditu.net
www.sydneycreditunion.com
Ownership: Member-owned
Year Founded: 1935

Taiwanese - Canadian Toronto Credit Union Limited
Also listed under: *Financing & Loan Companies*
Metro Square
#305, 3636 Steeles Ave. East
Markham, ON L3R 1K9
Tel: 905-944-0981; Fax: 905-944-0982
Toll-Free: 866-889-8893
tcu@on.aibn.com
www.tctcu.com
Ownership: Member-owned
Year Founded: 1978
Number of Employees: 5
Assets: $5-10 million
Revenues: Under $1 million

Talka Lithuanian Credit Union Limited
830 Main St. East
Hamilton, ON L8M 1L6
Tel: 905-544-7125; Fax: 905-544-7126
www.talka.ca
Former Name: Talka Hamilton Credit Union
Year Founded: 1955

Teachers Credit Union
75 James St. South
Hamilton, ON L8P 2Y9
Tel: 905-525-8090; Fax: 905-525-7422
Toll-Free: 877-427-1281
www.teacherscu.on.ca
Former Name: Hamilton Teachers Credit Union Limited
Ownership: Private

Teachers Plus Credit Union
36 Brookshire Ct.
Bedford, NS B4A 4E9
Tel: 902-477-5664; Fax: 902-477-4108
Toll-Free: 800-565-3103
info@teachersplus.ca
www.teachersplus.ca
Former Name: Nova Scotia Teachers Credit Union
Year Founded: 1956
Number of Employees: 11
Assets: $10-50 million

Thamesville Community Credit Union
84 London Rd.
Thamesville, ON N0P 2K0
Tel: 519-692-3855; Fax: 519-692-9532
info@thamesvilleccu.ca
www.thamesvilleccu.ca
Ownership: Member-owned
Year Founded: 1955

Thorold Community Credit Union
63 Front St. South
Thorold, ON L2V 3Z3
Tel: 905-227-1106; Fax: 905-227-1109
www.thoroldcu.com

Thunder Bay Elevators Employees' Credit Union Limited
417 Fort William Rd.
Thunder Bay, ON P7B 2Z5
Tel: 807-345-2471; Fax: 807-344-0829
elevatorcreditunion@tbaytel.net
Year Founded: 1953

Toronto Catholic School Board Employees' Credit Union Ltd.
80 Sheppard Ave. East
Toronto, ON M2N 6E8
Tel: 416-229-5315; Fax: 416-512-3427
tcsbecu-info@tcsbecu.com
www.tcsbecu.com
Former Name: Metropolitan Separate School Board Employees Credit Union Limited
Ownership: Private
Year Founded: 1972
Number of Employees: 7
Assets: $10-50 million

The Toronto Electrical Utilities Credit Union Limited
14 Carlton St.
Toronto, ON M5B 1K5
Tel: 416-542-2522; Fax: 416-542-2735
teucu@teucu.com
www.teucu.com
Ownership: Member-owned
Year Founded: 1941
Number of Employees: 8

Toronto Municipal Employees' Credit Union Limited
City Hall
PO Box 30
100 Queen St. West, Main Fl.
Toronto, ON M5H 2N2
Tel: 416-392-6868; Fax: 416-392-6895
www.tmecu.com
Year Founded: 1940

Tri-Island Credit Union
PO Box 580
1 Rink Rd.
Twillingate, NL A0G 4M0
Tel: 709-884-2704; Fax: 709-884-2026
www.triislandcu.com
Year Founded: 1986
Number of Employees: 10

Turtleford Credit Union Ltd.
PO Box 370
208 Main St.
Turtleford, SK S0M 2Y0
Tel: 306-845-2105; Fax: 306-845-3035
info@turtleford.cu.sk.ca
www.turtleford.cu.sk.ca

Ukrainian (St Catharines) Credit Union Limited (USCCU)
118 Niagara St.
St Catharines, ON L2R 4L4
Tel: 905-684-5062; Fax: 905-684-3098
www.hroshi.com
Year Founded: 1946

Unigasco Credit Union Limited
40 Keil Dr. South
Chatham, ON N7M 3G8
Tel: 519-436-4590; Fax: 519-436-5451
Toll-Free: 800-592-9592
www.unigasco.com
Year Founded: 1952
Number of Employees: 23

Union Bay Credit Union
PO Box 158
313 McLeod Rd.
Union Bay, BC V0R 3B0
Tel: 250-335-2122; Fax: 250-335-2131
www.unionbaycreditunion.com
Ownership: Member-owned
Year Founded: 1944

United Employees Credit Union Limited
964 Eastern Ave.
Toronto, ON M4L 1A6
Tel: 416-461-9257; Fax: 416-461-8141
infounited@unitedcu.com
www.unitedcu.com
Year Founded: 1946
Number of Employees: 10

Unity Credit Union Ltd.
PO Box 370
120 - 2nd Ave. East
Unity, SK S0K 4L0
Tel: 306-228-2688; Fax: 306-228-2185
info@unity.cu.sk.ca
www.unity.cu.sk.ca
Year Founded: 1941
Number of Employees: 31
Assets: $50-100 million
Revenues: $1-5 million

Unity Savings & Credit Union Limited
Central Management Support Office, Bayridge Centre West
775 Strand Blvd.
Kingston, ON K7P 2S7
Tel: 613-389-9965
unityone@unitysavings.com
www.unitysavings.com
Number of Employees: 23

University Hospitals Staff Credit Union Ltd.
8440 - 112 St.
Edmonton, AB T6G 2B7
Tel: 780-407-8151; Fax: 780-407-7557
chauah@telus.net
Year Founded: 1949
Number of Employees: 3
Assets: $5-10 million
Revenues: Under $1 million

Utilities Employees' (Windsor) Credit Union Limited
4545 Rhodes Dr.
Windsor, ON N8W 5T1
Tel: 519-945-5141; Fax: 519-945-0347

Valley Credit Union
PO Box 70
5682 Hwy. #1
Waterville, NS B0P 1V0
Tel: 902-538-4510; Fax: 902-538-4529
www.valleycreditunion.com
Year Founded: 1994

Valley First Financial Group
184 Main St., 3rd Fl.
Penticton, BC V2A 8G7
Tel: 250-490-2720; Fax: 250-490-2721
Toll-Free: 800-567-8111
info@valleyfirst.com
www.valleyfirst.com
Also Known As: Valley Field Credit Union
Year Founded: 2001
Assets: $500m-1 billion

Van Tel/Safeway Credit Union
#2010, 4330 Kingsway
Burnaby, BC V5H 4G8
Tel: 604-656-6200; Fax: 604-656-6167
Toll-Free: 800-663-1557
Former Name: Van Tel Credit Union
Year Founded: 1940
Number of Employees: 70+
Assets: $100-500 million

Vancouver City Savings Credit Union
PO Box 2120, Terminal Stn. Terminal
183 Terminal Ave.
Vancouver, BC V6B 5R8
Tel: 604-877-7000; Fax: 604-877-7639
Toll-Free: 888-826-2489
vc_editor@vancity.com
www.vancity.com
Also Known As: VanCity Credit Union
Year Founded: 1946
Assets: $1-10 billion

Vanguard Credit Union
Also listed under: *Financing & Loan Companies; Investment Management*
PO Box 490
47 Main St.
Rossburn, MB R0J 1V0
Tel: 204-859-5010; Fax: 204-859-5020
contact@vanguardcu.mb.ca
www.vanguardcu.mb.ca
Ownership: Member-owned
Year Founded: 1947
Number of Employees: 92
Assets: $100-500 million
Revenues: $5-10 million

Vermilion Credit Union Ltd.
5019 - 50 Ave.
Vermilion, AB T9X 1A7
Tel: 780-853-2822; Fax: 780-853-4361
vermilion@alberta-cu.com
www.vermilioncreditunion.com

Vernon & District Credit Union
Also listed under: *Financing & Loan Companies; Investment Management*
3108 - 33rd Ave.
Vernon, BC V1T 2N7
Tel: 250-545-9251; Fax: 250-545-8166
Toll-Free: 888-339-8328
info@vdcu.com
www.vdcu.com
Ownership: Co-operative. Member-owned.
Year Founded: 1944
Number of Employees: 45
Assets: $100-500 million
Revenues: $10-50 million

Victory Community Credit Union
#102, 2100 Lawrence Ave. West
Toronto, ON M9N 3W3
Tel: 416-243-0686; Fax: 416-243-9614
creditunion@vccu.com
www.vccu.com
Year Founded: 1948
Number of Employees: 3
Assets: $5-10 million

Victory Credit Union
PO Box 340
41 Water St.
Windsor, NS B0N 2T0
Tel: 902-798-1820; Fax: 902-798-1255
www.victorycreditunion.ca
Ownership: Cooperative
Number of Employees: 30
Revenues: $10-50 million

Virtual One Credit Union Ltd.
15 Bronte College Ct.
Mississauga, ON L5B 0E7
Tel: 905-270-2223; Fax: 905-270-0902
info_cu@virtualonecu.com
www.virtualonecu.com
Year Founded: 1946
Assets: $50-100 million

Wainwright Credit Union
Administration Office
502 - 10 St.
Wainwright, AB T9W 1P4
Tel: 780-842-9184; Fax: 780-842-2855
www.wainwright-cu.com
Ownership: Member-owned
Year Founded: 1943
Number of Employees: 84
Assets: $100-500 million
Revenues: $10-50 million

Wallace Barnes Employees' Credit Union Limited
3100 Mainway Dr.
Burlington, ON L7M 1A3
Tel: 905-335-6688; Fax: 905-336-1336

Ownership: Private
Year Founded: 1943
Number of Employees: 1
Assets: Under $1 million
Revenues: Under $1 million

Westminster Savings Credit Union
Corporate Centre
#108, 960 Quayside Dr.
New Westminster, BC V3M 6G2
Tel: 604-517-0100; Fax: 604-528-3812
www.wscu.com
Ownership: Member-owned
Year Founded: 1944
Number of Employees: 357
Assets: $1-10 billion
Revenues: $50-100 million

Westoba Credit Union Limited
#C, 220 - 10th St.
Brandon, MB R7A 4E8
Tel: 204-729-2050; Fax: 204-729-8852
infowcul@westoba.com
www.westoba.com
Ownership: Member-owned
Year Founded: 1963
Number of Employees: 200
Assets: $500m-1 billion
Revenues: $10-50 million

Weyburn Credit Union Limited
PO Box 1117
205 Coteau Ave.
Weyburn, SK S4H 2L3
Tel: 306-842-6641; Fax: 306-842-6620
Toll-Free: 800-667-8842
info@weyburn.cu.sk.ca
www.weyburncu.ca
Other Contact Information: Touch Tone TeleService: 306-842-1200; Lost or stolen MemberCard or Credit Union MasterCard: 1-800-567-8111 (within Canada or Continental USA)
Ownership: Member-owned
Year Founded: 1944
Assets: $100-500 million

Weymouth Credit Union
PO Box 411
4569 Hwy. #1
Weymouth, NS B0W 3T0
Tel: 902-837-4089; Fax: 902-837-4089

Williams Lake & District Credit Union
139 North 3rd Ave.
Williams Lake, BC V2G 2A5
Tel: 250-392-4135; Fax: 250-392-4361
info@wldcu.com
www.wldcu.com
Year Founded: 1952
Number of Employees: 12

Windsor Family Credit Union
2800 Tecumseth Rd East
Windsor, ON N8W 1G4
Tel: 519-974-3100; Fax: 519-974-4077
www.wfcu.ca

Winnipeg Police Credit Union Ltd.
300 William Ave.
Winnipeg, MB R3A 1P9
Tel: 204-944-1033; Fax: 204-949-0821
Toll-Free: 866-491-7122
www.policecu.mb.ca
Year Founded: 1949

Your Credit Union Limited
14 Chamberlain Ave
Ottawa, ON K1S 1V9
Tel: 613-238-8001; Fax: 613-238-2149
Toll-Free: 800-379-7757
info@yourcu.com
www.yourcu.com
Ownership: Member-owned

Your Neighbourhood Credit Union Ltd.
5415 Tecumseh Rd. East
Windsor, ON N8T 1C5
Tel: 519-258-3890; Fax: 519-945-5933
info@yncu.com
www.yncu.com
Former Name: Windsor & Essex Educational Credit Union
Year Founded: 1953

Insurance Companies

Insurance companies are registered to conduct business under the federal Insurance Companies Act and/or corresponding provincial legislation. Life insurance companies are registered to underwrite life insurance, accident and sickness insurance and annuity business. Property and casualty insurance companies are registered to underwrite insurance other than life insurance.

Included in these listings are federally and provincially incorporated insurance companies, reinsurance companies, fraternal benefit societies and reciprocal exchanges, with the classes of insurance they offer.

*Companies marked with an * are provincially incorporated. For provincially incorporated companies not listed below, contact the government agency for each province. For further information, please see the "Government Quick Reference" guide at the beginning of Section 7, and check under "Insurance."*

Classes of insurance listed below include: Accident, Auto, Aircraft, Boiler & Machinery, Credit, Fidelity, Fire, Hail & Crop, Legal Expense, Liability, Life, Marine, Personal Accident & Sickness, Property, Reinsurance, Surety, and Theft.

Insurance Class Index

Accident
ACE INA Insurance
American Bankers Life Assurance Company of Florida
Assumption Mutual Life Insurance Company
Ayr Farmers Mutual Insurance Company
Caisse Centrale de Réassurance
Canadian Professional Sales Association
CIGNA Life Insurance Company of Canada
Connecticut General Life Insurance Co.
Continental Casualty Company
CUMIS Life Insurance Company
Desjardins Financial Security
Echelon General Insurance Company
Empire Life Insurance Company
L'Entraide assurance, compagnie mutuelle
FaithLife Financial
Federated Insurance Company of Canada
Federation Insurance Company of Canada
The Guarantee Company of North America
Industrial Alliance Pacific Insurance & Financial Services Inc.
Life Insurance Company of North America
The Nordic Insurance Company of Canada
Northbridge Insurance
Old Republic Insurance Company of Canada
Optimum Réassurance inc
Pacific Blue Cross
Peace Hills General Insurance Company
Pembridge Insurance Company
Promutuel Réassurance
Promutuel Vie inc
Québec Blue Cross
Saskatchewan Motor Club Insurance Company Ltd.
SGI CANADA Consolidated
Société de l'assurance automobile du Québec
South Easthope Mutual Insurance Co.
SSQ, Société d'assurances générales inc.
SSQ, Société d'assurance-vie inc
Tradition Mutual Insurance Company
Trillium Mutual Insurance Company
Western Financial Group Inc.
XL Reinsurance America Inc
Zurich Canada

Aircraft
ACE INA Insurance
Avemco Insurance Company
Aviation & General Insurance Company Limited
Aviva Canada Inc.
AXA General Insurance Company
AXA Insurance (Canada)
AXA Pacific Insurance Company
Berkley Canada
Caisse Centrale de Réassurance
Canadian Universities Reciprocal Insurance Exchange
Chubb Insurance Company of Canada
Continental Casualty Company
Co-operators General Insurance Company
Eagle Star Insurance Company Ltd.
Elite Insurance Company
Everest Insurance Company of Canada
Everest Reinsurance Company
GCAN Insurance Company
General Reinsurance Corporation
Global Aerospace Underwriting Managers (Canada) Limited
Great American Insurance Company
Hannover Rückversicherungs AG
Hartford Fire Insurance Company
Henderson Insurance Inc.
Johnston Meier Insurance Agencies Group
Liberty Mutual Insurance Company
Lloyd's Underwriters
Mitsui Sumitomo Insurance Co., Limited.
Old Republic Insurance Company of Canada
Omega General Insurance Company
Oxford Mutual Insurance Company
Peace Hills General Insurance Company
The Personal Insurance Company
SGI CANADA Consolidated
State Farm Canada
TD General Insurance Company
Wedgwood Insurance Limited
Western Assurance Company
Westport Insurance Corporation
XL Reinsurance America Inc.
XL Reinsurance America Inc.

Auto
ACE INA Insurance
Alberta Motor Association Insurance Co.
Algoma Insurance Group
Algoma Mutual Insurance Co.
Alliance Assurance
Allstate Insurance Company of Canada
L'ALPHA, compagnie d'assurances inc.
Alpine Insurance & Financial Inc.
The American Road Insurance Company
Astro Insurance 1000 Inc.
Atlantic Insurance Company Limited
Aviva Canada Inc.
A-WIN Insurance Network
AXA General Insurance Company
AXA Insurance (Canada)
AXA Pacific Insurance Company
Ayr Farmers Mutual Insurance Company
Bay of Quinte Mutual Insurance Co.
Belair Insurance Company Inc.
Berkley Canada
Bertie and Clinton Mutual Insurance Company
Brant Mutual Insurance Company
British Columbia Automobile Association Insurance Agency
Butler Byers Insurance Ltd.
CAA Insurance Company (Ontario)
Caisse Centrale de Réassurance
Canadian Petroleum Insurance Exchange Ltd.
Canadian Professional Sales Association
La Capitale General Insurance Inc.
Caradoc Delaware Mutual Fire Insurance Company
Carleton Mutual Insurance Company
Cavell Insurance Company Limited
Certas Direct Insurance Company
Chubb Insurance Company of Canada
CNS
Coachman Insurance Company
Coastal Community Insurance Services (2007) Ltd.
La Compagnie d'Assurance Missisquoi
Continental Casualty Company
Co-operators General Insurance Company
CorePointe Insurance Company
COSECO Insurance Company
Cowan Insurance Group Ltd.
Crowsnest Insurance Agencies Ltd.
CUMIS General Insurance Company
The CUMIS Group Limited
CUMIS Life Insurance Company
Desjardins assurances générales inc
The Dominion of Canada General Insurance Company
Dufferin Mutual Insurance Company
Dumfries Mutual Insurance Company
Eagle Star Insurance Company Ltd.
Ecclesiastical Insurance Office plc
Echelon General Insurance Company
Economical Mutual Insurance Company
Elite Insurance Company
Erie Mutual Fire Insurance Company
Everest Insurance Company of Canada
Everest Reinsurance Company
Farmers' Mutual Insurance Company (Lindsay)
Federal Insurance Company
Federated Insurance Company of Canada
Federation Insurance Company of Canada
Fenchurch General Insurance Company
First North American Insurance Company
Fundy Mutual Insurance Company
GCAN Insurance Company
General Reinsurance Corporation
Gibb's Agencies (1997) Ltd.
Glengarry Farmers' Mutual Fire Insurance Co.
Gore Mutual Insurance Company
Great American Insurance Company
Grenville Mutual Insurance Company
Grey & Bruce Mutual Insurance Co.
Le Groupe Estrie-Richelieu, compagnie d'assurance
The Guarantee Company of North America
Halwell Mutual Insurance Company
Hannover Rückversicherungs AG
Hartford Fire Insurance Company
Hay Mutual Insurance Company
Henderson Insurance Inc.
Howard Mutual Insurance Co.
Howick Mutual Insurance Company
Industrial Alliance Insurance & Financial Services Inc.
Insurance Company of Prince Edward Island
Insurance Corporation of British Columbia
JEVCO Insurance Company
Johnston Meier Insurance Agencies Group
Kent & Essex Mutual Insurance Company
Kingsway Financial Services Inc.
Kingsway General Insurance Company
Kirkham Insurance
Lambton Mutual Insurance Company
Lanark Mutual Insurance Company
Lennox & Addington Mutual Insurance Company
Liberty Mutual Insurance Company
Lloyd's Underwriters
Manitoba Public Insurance
McFarlane & Company Financial Group Limited
McKillop Mutual Insurance Company
Mennonite Mutual Insurance Co. (Alberta) Ltd.
Metro General Insurance Corp.
Middlesex Mutual Insurance Co.
Millennium Insurance Corporation
Mitsui Sumitomo Insurance Co., Limited.
Motors Insurance Corporation
Munich Reinsurance Company of Canada
The Nordic Insurance Company of Canada
Norfolk Mutual Insurance Company
North Bleinheim Mutual Insurance Co.
North Blenheim Mutual Insurance Company
North Kent Mutual Fire Insurance Company
The North Waterloo Farmers Mutual Insurance Company
Northbridge Insurance
Novex Group Insurance
Old Republic Insurance Company of Canada
Ontario Mutual Insurance Association
Ontario School Boards' Insurance Exchange
Optimum Assurance Agricole inc
Optimum Général inc
Optimum Société d'Assurance inc
Optimum West Insurance Company
Oxford Mutual Insurance Company
Pafco Insurance Company
PartnerRe SA
PC Financial Insurance Agency
Peace Hills General Insurance Company
Peel Mutual Insurance Company
The Personal General Insurance Inc.
The Personal Insurance Company
Perth Insurance Company
Pilot Insurance Company
The Portage La Prairie Mutual Insurance Company
Primmum Insurance Company
Progressive Casualty Insurance Company
Protective Insurance Company
Québec Blue Cross
RBC General Insurance Company
RBC Insurance
Royal & SunAlliance Insurance Company of Canada
Saskatchewan Auto Fund
Saskatchewan Mutual Insurance Company
Scottish & York Insurance Co. Limited
Security National Insurance Company
SGI CANADA Consolidated
Sirius America Insurance Company
Société de l'assurance automobile du Québec
South Easthope Mutual Insurance Co.
SSQ Financial Group
SSQ, Société d'assurances générales inc.
SSQ, Société d'assurance-vie inc
Stanley Mutual Insurance Company
State Farm Canada
Suecia Reinsurance Company
TD General Insurance Company
TD Home & Auto Insurance Company
Thomson Jemmett Vogelzang
Thomson-Schindle-Green Insurance & Financial Services Ltd.
The Tokio Marine & Nichido Fire Insurance Co., Ltd.

Town & Country Mutual Insurance
Townsend Farmers' Mutual Fire Insurance Company
Traders General Insurance Company
Tradition Mutual Insurance Company
Trillium Mutual Insurance Company
Unica Insurance
Unifund Assurance Company
L'Union Canadienne Compagnie d'Assurances
United General Insurance Corporation
Virginia Surety Company, Inc.
Wabisa Mutual Insurance Company
Waterloo Insurance Company
The Wawanesa Mutual Insurance Company
Wedgwood Insurance Limited
West Elgin Mutual Insurance Company
West Wawanosh Mutual Insurance Company
Western Assurance Company
Western Financial Group Inc.
Westland Insurance
Westminster Mutual Insurance Company
Westport Insurance Corporation
XL Insurance Company Limited
XL Reinsurance America Inc.
Yarmouth Mutual Fire Insurance Company
Zenith Insurance Company
Zurich Canada

Boiler & Machinery

ACE INA Insurance
Affiliated FM Insurance Company
Algoma Insurance Group
Allstate Insurance Company of Canada
The American Road Insurance Company
L'Assurance Mutuelle des Fabriques de Montréal
Atlantic Insurance Company Limited
Aviva Canada Inc.
AXA General Insurance Company
AXA Insurance (Canada)
AXA Pacific Insurance Company
Ayr Farmers Mutual Insurance Company
Bay of Quinte Mutual Insurance Co.
Belair Insurance Company Inc.
Berkley Canada
Bertie and Clinton Mutual Insurance Company
Brant Mutual Insurance Company
Caisse Centrale de Réassurance
Canadian Farm Insurance Corp.
Caradoc Delaware Mutual Fire Insurance Company
Cavell Insurance Company Limited
Chubb Insurance Company of Canada
La Compagnie d'Assurance Missisquoi
Continental Casualty Company
Co-operators General Insurance Company
CUMIS General Insurance Company
Desjardins assurances générales inc
Dufferin Mutual Insurance Company
Dumfries Mutual Insurance Company
Eagle Star Insurance Company Ltd.
Ecclesiastical Insurance Office plc
Economical Mutual Insurance Company
Elite Insurance Company
Erie Mutual Fire Insurance Company
Everest Insurance Company of Canada
Everest Reinsurance Company
Farmers' Mutual Insurance Company (Lindsay)
Federal Insurance Company
Federated Insurance Company of Canada
Federation Insurance Company of Canada
Fenchurch General Insurance Company
FM Global
Fundy Mutual Insurance Company
GCAN Insurance Company
General Reinsurance Corporation
Glengarry Farmers' Mutual Fire Insurance Co.
Grain Insurance and Guarantee Company
Great American Insurance Company
Grenville Mutual Insurance Company
Grey & Bruce Mutual Insurance Co.
Le Groupe Estrie-Richelieu, compagnie d'assurance
The Guarantee Company of North America
Halwell Mutual Insurance Company
Hannover Rückversicherungs AG
Hartford Fire Insurance Company
Howick Mutual Insurance Company
HSB BI&I
Kent & Essex Mutual Insurance Company
Lambton Mutual Insurance Company
Lanark Mutual Insurance Company
Liberty Mutual Insurance Company
Lloyd's Underwriters
Lumbermen's Underwriting Alliance
MAX Canada Insurance Company
McKillop Mutual Insurance Company
Mennonite Mutual Fire Insurance Company
Mitsui Sumitomo Insurance Co., Limited
Motors Insurance Corporation
The Nordic Insurance Company of Canada
The North Waterloo Farmers Mutual Insurance Company
Novex Group Insurance
Omega General Insurance Company
Ontario School Boards' Insurance Exchange
Oxford Mutual Insurance Company
Peace Hills General Insurance Company
Peel Mutual Insurance Company
The Personal General Insurance Inc.
The Personal Insurance Company
Promutuel Réassurance
Red River Valley Mutual Insurance Co.
Saskatchewan Mutual Insurance Company
Scottish & York Insurance Co. Limited
SGI CANADA Consolidated
South Easthope Mutual Insurance Co.
Southeastern Mutual Insurance Company
Stanley Mutual Insurance Company
State Farm Canada
TD General Insurance Company
Temple Insurance Company
Town & Country Mutual Insurance
Townsend Farmers' Mutual Fire Insurance Company
Tradition Mutual Insurance Company
Trillium Mutual Insurance Company
Virginia Surety Company, Inc.
The Wawanesa Mutual Insurance Company
West Wawanosh Mutual Insurance Company
Western Assurance Company
Western Financial Group Inc.
Westport Insurance Corporation
XL Insurance Company Limited
XL Reinsurance America Inc.
Zurich Canada

Credit

ACE INA Insurance
The American Road Insurance Company
Assurance-Vie Banque Nationale
Assurant Solutions Canada
AXA Pacific Insurance Company
Berkley Canada
Canadian Premier Life Insurance Company
CIGNA Life Insurance Company of Canada
Continental Casualty Company
CUMIS Life Insurance Company
L'Entraide assurance, compagnie mutuelle
Euler Hermes Canada
Everest Insurance Company of Canada
Everest Reinsurance Company
GCAN Insurance Company
General Reinsurance Corporation
The Guarantee Company of North America
Industrial Alliance Pacific Insurance & Financial Services Inc.
Novex Group Insurance
Omega General Insurance Company
Peace Hills General Insurance Company
Transatlantic Reinsurance Company
Westport Insurance Corporation
Zurich Canada

Fidelity

ACE INA Insurance
Affiliated FM Insurance Company
Allstate Insurance Company of Canada
Atlantic Insurance Company Limited
Aviva Canada Inc.
AXA General Insurance Company
AXA Insurance (Canada)
AXA Pacific Insurance Company
Ayr Farmers Mutual Insurance Company
Bay of Quinte Mutual Insurance Co.
Belair Insurance Company Inc.
Berkley Canada
Bertie and Clinton Mutual Insurance Company
Brant Mutual Insurance Company
Caisse Centrale de Réassurance
Canadian Farm Insurance Corp.
Cavell Insurance Company Limited
Chubb Insurance Company of Canada
La Compagnie d'Assurance Missisquoi
Continental Casualty Company
Co-operators General Insurance Company
CUMIS General Insurance Company
CUMIS Life Insurance Company
Dufferin Mutual Insurance Company
Eagle Star Insurance Company Ltd.
Ecclesiastical Insurance Office plc
Echelon General Insurance Company
Elite Insurance Company
Erie Mutual Fire Insurance Company
Everest Reinsurance Company
Farmers' Mutual Insurance Company (Lindsay)
Federal Insurance Company
Federated Insurance Company of Canada
Federation Insurance Company of Canada
GCAN Insurance Company
General Reinsurance Corporation
Glengarry Farmers' Mutual Fire Insurance Co.
Grain Insurance and Guarantee Company
Great American Insurance Company
Grenville Mutual Insurance Company
The Guarantee Company of North America
Halwell Mutual Insurance Company
Hannover Rückversicherungs AG
Hartford Fire Insurance Company
Howard Mutual Insurance Co.
Howick Mutual Insurance Company
Kent & Essex Mutual Insurance Company
Lambton Mutual Insurance Company
Liberty Mutual Insurance Company
Lloyd's Underwriters
MAX Canada Insurance Company
McKillop Mutual Insurance Company
Mitsui Sumitomo Insurance Co., Limited
The Nordic Insurance Company of Canada
The North Waterloo Farmers Mutual Insurance Company
Novex Group Insurance
Omega General Insurance Company
Oxford Mutual Insurance Company
Peace Hills General Insurance Company
Peel Mutual Insurance Company
The Personal Insurance Company
Red River Valley Mutual Insurance Co.
Saskatchewan Mutual Insurance Company
Scottish & York Insurance Co. Limited
SGI CANADA Consolidated
Sirius America Insurance Company
State Farm Canada
Suecia Reinsurance Company
Swiss Reinsurance Company Canada
TD General Insurance Company
Town & Country Mutual Insurance
Tradition Mutual Insurance Company
Trillium Mutual Insurance Company
Wabisa Mutual Insurance Company
West Elgin Mutual Insurance Company
West Wawanosh Mutual Insurance Company
Western Assurance Company
Western Financial Group Inc.
Western Surety Company
Westport Insurance Corporation
XL Reinsurance America Inc.
Zurich Canada

Fire

ACE INA Insurance
Affiliated FM Insurance Company
Alberta Motor Association Insurance Co.
Antigonish Farmers' Mutual Insurance Company
L'Assurance Mutuelle des Fabriques de Montréal
British Columbia Automobile Association Insurance Agency
Caisse Centrale de Réassurance
Carleton Mutual Insurance Company
Clare Mutual Insurance Company
La Compagnie d'Assurance Missisquoi
Co-operators General Insurance Company
CUMIS General Insurance Company
CUMIS Life Insurance Company
The Dominion of Canada General Insurance Company
Echelon General Insurance Company
Federated Insurance Company of Canada
Federation Insurance Company of Canada
Germania Mutual Insurance Company
Glengarry Farmers' Mutual Fire Insurance Co.
Gore Mutual Insurance Company
Grain Insurance and Guarantee Company
Le Groupe Estrie-Richelieu, compagnie d'assurance
The Guarantee Company of North America
Hamilton Township Mutual Insurance Company
Hartford Fire Insurance Company
The Kings Mutual Insurance Company
Lloyd's Underwriters
Mennonite Mutual Fire Insurance Company
Mennonite Mutual Insurance Co. (Alberta) Ltd.
The Mutual Fire Insurance Company of British Columbia
Norfolk Mutual Insurance Company

North Kent Mutual Fire Insurance Company
The North Waterloo Farmers Mutual Insurance Company
Ontario School Boards' Insurance Exchange
Optimum Assurance Agricole inc
Peace Hills General Insurance Company
Prince Edward Island Mutual Insurance Company
Promutuel Réassurance
RBC General Insurance Company
Red River Valley Mutual Insurance Co.
Security National Insurance Company
Southeastern Mutual Insurance Company
SSQ, Société d'assurances générales inc.
SSQ, Société d'assurance-vie inc
State Farm Canada
The Tokio Marine & Nichido Fire Insurance Co., Ltd.
The Wawanesa Mutual Insurance Company
Western Financial Group Inc.
Zurich Canada

Hail & Crop
ACE INA Insurance
Agriculture Financial Services Corporation
Astro Insurance 1000 Inc.
Aviva Canada Inc.
AXA General Insurance Company
AXA Insurance (Canada)
AXA Pacific Insurance Company
Ayr Farmers Mutual Insurance Company
Berkley Canada
Brant Mutual Insurance Company
Butler Byers Hail Insurance Ltd.
Cavell Insurance Company Limited
Clare Mutual Insurance Company
Continental Casualty Company
Co-operative Hail Insurance Company Ltd.
Co-operators General Insurance Company
Dumfries Mutual Insurance Company
Everest Insurance Company of Canada
Everest Reinsurance Company
Federation Insurance Company of Canada
GCAN Insurance Company
General Reinsurance Corporation
Great American Insurance Company
The Guarantee Company of North America
Hannover Rückversicherungs AG
Hartford Fire Insurance Company
Hay Mutual Insurance Company
Henderson Insurance Inc.
Howard Mutual Insurance Co.
Howick Mutual Insurance Company
Lambton Mutual Insurance Company
Lanark Mutual Insurance Company
Manitoba Agricultural Services Corporation - Insurance Corporate Office
McFarlane & Company Financial Group Limited
North Kent Mutual Fire Insurance Company
The North Waterloo Farmers Mutual Insurance Company
Northbridge Insurance
Optimum West Insurance Company
Oxford Mutual Insurance Company
Palliser Insurance Company Limited
Rain and Hail Insurance Corporation
Saskatchewan Crop Insurance Corporation
Saskatchewan Municipal Hail Insurance Association
Sirius America Insurance Company
Suecia Reinsurance Company
Thomson-Schindle-Green Insurance & Financial Services Ltd.
Town & Country Mutual Insurance
Townsend Farmers' Mutual Fire Insurance Company
Tradition Mutual Insurance Company
Trillium Mutual Insurance Company
West Elgin Mutual Insurance Company
Western Financial Group Inc.
Westport Insurance Corporation
XL Reinsurance America Inc.
Yarmouth Mutual Fire Insurance Company

Legal Expense
Allstate Insurance Company of Canada
Aviva Canada Inc.
AXA General Insurance Company
AXA Insurance (Canada)
AXA Pacific Insurance Company
Belair Insurance Company Inc.
Berkley Canada
CAA Insurance Company (Ontario)
Caisse Centrale de Réassurance
La Compagnie d'Assurance Missisquoi
Echelon General Insurance Company
Federation Insurance Company of Canada
Glengarry Farmers' Mutual Fire Insurance Co.
The Guarantee Company of North America
Lloyd's Underwriters
The Nordic Insurance Company of Canada
Novex Group Insurance
Omega General Insurance Company
The Portage La Prairie Mutual Insurance Company
Scottish & York Insurance Co. Limited

Liability
ACE INA Insurance
ACE INA Life Insurance
Affiliated FM Insurance Company
Algoma Insurance Group
Alliance Assurance
Allstate Insurance Company of Canada
Alpine Insurance & Financial Inc.
The American Road Insurance Company
Amherst Island Mutual Insurance Company
L'Assurance Mutuelle des Fabriques de Montréal
Astro Insurance 1000 Inc.
Atlantic Insurance Company Limited
Aviation & General Insurance Company Limited
Aviva Canada Inc.
A-WIN Insurance Network
AXA General Insurance Company
AXA Insurance (Canada)
AXA Pacific Insurance Company
Ayr Farmers Mutual Insurance Company
Bay of Quinte Mutual Insurance Co.
Belair Insurance Company Inc.
Berkley Canada
Bertie and Clinton Mutual Insurance Company
Brant Mutual Insurance Company
CAA Insurance Company (Ontario)
Caisse Centrale de Réassurance
Canadian Direct Insurance Incorporated
Canadian Farm Insurance Corp.
Canadian Lawyers Liability Assurance Society
Canadian Petroleum Insurance Exchange Ltd.
Canadian Universities Reciprocal Insurance Exchange
Canassurance Insurance Company
Caradoc Delaware Mutual Fire Insurance Company
Cavell Insurance Company Limited
Certas Direct Insurance Company
Chubb Insurance Company of Canada
CNS
La Compagnie d'Assurance Missisquoi
Continental Casualty Company
CorePointe Insurance Company
Crowsnest Insurance Agencies Ltd.
Desjardins assurances générales inc
The Dominion of Canada General Insurance Company
Dufferin Mutual Insurance Company
Dumfries Mutual Insurance Company
Eagle Star Insurance Company Ltd.
Ecclesiastical Insurance Office plc
Echelon General Insurance Company
Elite Insurance Company
Erie Mutual Fire Insurance Company
Everest Insurance Company of Canada
Everest Reinsurance Company
Farmers' Mutual Insurance Company (Lindsay)
Federal Insurance Company
Federated Insurance Company of Canada
Federation Insurance Company of Canada
Fenchurch General Insurance Company
Frank Cowan Company Limited
Fundy Mutual Insurance Company
GCAN Insurance Company
General Reinsurance Corporation
Germania Mutual Insurance Company
Glengarry Farmers' Mutual Fire Insurance Co.
Global Aerospace Underwriting Managers (Canada) Limited
Gore Mutual Insurance Company
Grain Insurance and Guarantee Company
Great American Insurance Company
Grenville Mutual Insurance Company
Grey & Bruce Mutual Insurance Co.
Le Groupe Estrie-Richelieu, compagnie d'assurance
The Guarantee Company of North America
Halwell Mutual Insurance Company
Hannover Rückversicherungs AG
Hartford Fire Insurance Company
Hay Mutual Insurance Company
Henderson Insurance Inc.
Howard Mutual Insurance Co.
Howick Mutual Insurance Company
HSB BI&I
Kent & Essex Mutual Insurance Company
The Kings Mutual Insurance Company
Kingsway General Insurance Company
Lambton Mutual Insurance Company
Lanark Mutual Insurance Company
Lawyers' Professional Indemnity Company
Legacy General Insurance Company
Lennox & Addington Mutual Insurance Company
Liberty Mutual Insurance Company
Lloyd's Underwriters
MAX Canada Insurance Company
McFarlane & Company Financial Group Limited
McKillop Mutual Insurance Company
Mennonite Mutual Insurance Co. (Alberta) Ltd.
Metro General Insurance Corp.
Middlesex Mutual Insurance Co.
Mitsui Sumitomo Insurance Co., Limited
Motors Insurance Corporation
Munich Reinsurance Company of Canada
Municipal Insurance Association of British Columbia
MUNIX Reciprocal
The Nordic Insurance Company of Canada
North Bleinheim Mutual Insurance Co.
North Blenheim Mutual Insurance Company
North Kent Mutual Fire Insurance Company
The North Waterloo Farmers Mutual Insurance Company
Northbridge Insurance
Novex Group Insurance
Old Republic Insurance Company of Canada
Omega General Insurance Company
Ontario School Boards' Insurance Exchange
Optimum Général inc
Optimum Société d'Assurance inc
Oxford Mutual Insurance Company
Peace Hills General Insurance Company
Peel Mutual Insurance Company
The Personal General Insurance Inc.
The Personal Insurance Company
Pictou Mutual Insurance Company
The Portage La Prairie Mutual Insurance Company
Premier Marine Insurance Managers Group
Prince Edward Island Mutual Insurance Company
Progressive Casualty Insurance Company
Promutuel Réassurance
Québec Blue Cross
RBC General Insurance Company
Real Estate Insurance Exchange
Red River Valley Mutual Insurance Co.
Saskatchewan Mutual Insurance Company
Scottish & York Insurance Co. Limited
SGI CANADA Consolidated
Sirius America Insurance Company
Southeastern Mutual Insurance Company
SSQ, Société d'assurances générales inc.
SSQ, Société d'assurance-vie inc
Stanley Mutual Insurance Company
State Farm Canada
Suecia Reinsurance Company
TD General Insurance Company
TD Home & Auto Insurance Company
Thomson Jemmett Vogelzang
Thomson-Schindle-Green Insurance & Financial Services Ltd.
Town & Country Mutual Insurance
Townsend Farmers' Mutual Fire Insurance Company
Tradition Mutual Insurance Company
Trans Global Insurance Company
Trillium Mutual Insurance Company
Trisura Guarantee Insurance Company
Unica Insurance
Virginia Surety Company, Inc.
Wabisa Mutual Insurance Company
The Wawanesa Mutual Insurance Company
West Elgin Mutual Insurance Company
West Wawanosh Mutual Insurance Company
Western Assurance Company
Western Financial Group Inc.
Westland Insurance
Westminster Mutual Insurance Company
Westport Insurance Corporation
XL Insurance Company Limited
XL Reinsurance America Inc.
Yarmouth Mutual Fire Insurance Company
Zenith Insurance Company
Zurich Canada

Life
ACTRA Fraternal Benefit Society
Alberta Motor Association Insurance Co.
Allianz Life Insurance Company of North America
Alpine Insurance & Financial Inc.
American Bankers Life Assurance Company of Florida
American Health & Life Insurance Company
American Income Life Insurance Company
AMEX Assurance Company

Assumption Mutual Life Insurance Company
Assurance-Vie Banque Nationale
AVie, Financial Security Advisors
BMO Life Assurance Company of Canada
British Columbia Automobile Association Insurance Agency
British Columbia Life & Casualty Company
Butler Byers Insurance Ltd.
CAA Insurance Company (Ontario)
Canada Life Financial Corporation
Canadian Premier Life Insurance Company
Canadian Professional Sales Association
Canassurance Insurance Company
La Capitale Civil Service Insurer Inc.
La Capitale Insurance & Financial Services
CIBC Life Insurance Company Limited
CIGNA Life Insurance Company of Canada
Combined Insurance Company of America
Connecticut General Life Insurance Co.
Co-operators General Insurance Company
Co-operators Life Insurance Company
Croatian Fraternal Union of America
The CUMIS Group Limited
CUMIS Life Insurance Company
Desjardins Financial Security
Empire Life Insurance Company
L'Entraide assurance, compagnie mutuelle
The Equitable Life Insurance Company of Canada
L'Excellence, Compagnie d'assurance-vie
FaithLife Financial
Foresters Life Insurance Company
GAN Assurances Vie Compagnie française d'assurances vie mixte
General American Life Insurance Company
Gerber Life Insurance Company
The Grand Orange Lodge of British America Benefit Fund
The Great-West Life Assurance Company
Independent Order of Foresters
Industrial Alliance Insurance & Financial Services Inc.
Industrial Alliance Pacific Insurance & Financial Services Inc.
Insurance Company of Prince Edward Island
Johnston Meier Insurance Agencies Group
Knights of Columbus Insurance
Life Insurance Company of North America
London Life Insurance Company
Manitoba Blue Cross
Manufacturers Life Insurance Company
Manulife Canada Ltd.
Manulife Financial
Massachusetts Mutual Life Insurance Company
McFarlane & Company Financial Group Limited
MD Life Insurance Company
Medavie Blue Cross
Munich Reinsurance Company - Canada Life
The North West Commercial Travellers' Association of Canada
Optimum Réassurance inc
The Order of United Commercial Travelers of America
Pacific Blue Cross
PartnerRe SA
Penncorp Life Insurance Company
PPI
PPI Advisory
PPI Solutions
Primerica Life Insurance Company of Canada
Principal Life Insurance Company
Promutuel Vie inc
Québec Blue Cross
RBC Insurance
RBC Life Insurance Company
RBC Travel Insurance Company
Reliable Life Insurance Company
Saskatchewan Blue Cross
SCOR Global Life Canada
Scotia Life Insurance Company
Sons of Scotland Benevolent Association
SSQ Financial Group
SSQ, Société d'assurance-vie inc
The Standard Life Assurance Company of Canada
Sun Life Assurance Company of Canada
Sun Life Financial Inc.
Supreme Council of the Royal Arcanum
La Survivance, compagnie mutuelle d'assurance vie
TD Life Insurance Company
Thomson-Schindle-Green Insurance & Financial Services Ltd.
Trans Global Life Insurance Company
Transamerica Life Canada
Ukrainian Fraternal Association of America
Ukrainian Fraternal Society of Canada
Ukrainian Mutual Benefit Association of St. Nicholas of Canada
Ukrainian National Association
L'Union-Vie, compagnie mutuelle d'assurance
United American Insurance Company
Uv Mutuelle
The Wawanesa Life Insurance Company
Wedgwood Insurance Limited
Western Financial Group Inc.
Western Life Assurance Company
XL Reinsurance America Inc.

Marine

ACE INA Insurance
Antigonish Farmers' Mutual Insurance Company
Avemco Insurance Company
Aviva Canada Inc.
Belair Insurance Company Inc.
Butler Byers Insurance Ltd.
CAA Insurance Company (Ontario)
Canadian Universities Reciprocal Insurance Exchange
Cavell Insurance Company Limited
Chubb Insurance Company of Canada
Cowan Insurance Group Ltd.
Ecclesiastical Insurance Office plc
Elite Insurance Company
Everest Insurance Company of Canada
Farmers' Mutual Insurance Company (Lindsay)
Federal Insurance Company
GCAN Insurance Company
Great American Insurance Company
Hamilton Township Mutual Insurance Company
Henderson Insurance Inc.
Intact Insurance Company of Canada
Johnston Meier Insurance Agencies Group
Lennox & Addington Mutual Insurance Company
MAX Canada Insurance Company
Northbridge Insurance
Pacific Coast Fishermen's Mutual Marine Insurance Company
Peace Hills General Insurance Company
Pembridge Insurance Company
Premier Marine Insurance Managers Group
Swiss Reinsurance Company Canada
The Tokio Marine & Nichido Fire Insurance Co., Ltd.
Trillium Mutual Insurance Company
Wedgwood Insurance Limited
Western Assurance Company
XL Reinsurance America Inc.
Zurich Canada

Personal Accident & Sickness

ACE INA Life Insurance
ACTRA Fraternal Benefit Society
Alberta Blue Cross
Alberta Motor Association Insurance Co.
Allianz Life Insurance Company of North America
Allstate Insurance Company of Canada
American Bankers Life Assurance Company of Florida
American Income Life Insurance Company
AMEX Assurance Company
Amherst Island Mutual Insurance Company
Assumption Mutual Life Insurance Company
Assurance-Vie Banque Nationale
Avemco Insurance Company
AVie, Financial Security Advisors
Aviva Canada Inc.
AXA General Insurance Company
AXA Insurance (Canada)
AXA Pacific Insurance Company
Ayr Farmers Mutual Insurance Company
Bay of Quinte Mutual Insurance Co.
Belair Insurance Company Inc.
Berkley Canada
Bertie and Clinton Mutual Insurance Company
BMO Life Assurance Company of Canada
Brant Mutual Insurance Company
British Columbia Automobile Association Insurance Agency
British Columbia Life & Casualty Company
Butler Byers Insurance Ltd.
CAA Insurance Company (Ontario)
Canadian Direct Insurance Incorporated
Canadian Farm Insurance Corp.
Canadian Premier Life Insurance Company
Canadian Professional Sales Association
Canassurance Insurance Company
La Capitale Insurance & Financial Services
Caradoc Delaware Mutual Fire Insurance Company
Cavell Insurance Company Limited
Chubb Insurance Company of Canada
CIBC Life Insurance Company Limited
CIGNA Life Insurance Company of Canada
Combined Insurance Company of America
Connecticut General Life Insurance Co.
Continental Casualty Company
Co-operators General Insurance Company
Co-operators Life Insurance Company
Croatian Fraternal Union of America
The CUMIS Group Limited
CUMIS Life Insurance Company
Desjardins Financial Security
Dufferin Mutual Insurance Company
Eagle Star Insurance Company Ltd.
Echelon General Insurance Company
Elite Insurance Company
Empire Life Insurance Company
L'Entraide assurance, compagnie mutuelle
Erie Mutual Fire Insurance Company
Everest Reinsurance Company
L'Excellence, Compagnie d'assurance-vie
FaithLife Financial
Farmers' Mutual Insurance Company (Lindsay)
Federal Insurance Company
Fenchurch General Insurance Company
First North American Insurance Company
Foresters Life Insurance Company
GCAN Insurance Company
General Reinsurance Corporation
Glengarry Farmers' Mutual Fire Insurance Co.
Global Aerospace Underwriting Managers (Canada) Limited
Gore Mutual Insurance Company
Great American Insurance Company
The Great-West Life Assurance Company
Green Shield Canada
Grenville Mutual Insurance Company
Grey & Bruce Mutual Insurance Co.
The Guarantee Company of North America
Hannover Rückversicherungs AG
Hartford Fire Insurance Company
Howard Mutual Insurance Co.
Howick Mutual Insurance Company
Independent Order of Foresters
Industrial Alliance Insurance & Financial Services Inc.
Industrial Alliance Pacific Insurance & Financial Services Inc.
Kent & Essex Mutual Insurance Company
Lambton Mutual Insurance Company
Legacy General Insurance Company
Lennox & Addington Mutual Insurance Company
Liberty Mutual Insurance Company
Life Insurance Company of North America
Lloyd's Underwriters
London Life Insurance Company
Manitoba Blue Cross
Manufacturers Life Insurance Company
Massachusetts Mutual Life Insurance Company
McKillop Mutual Insurance Company
Medavie Blue Cross
Mitsui Sumitomo Insurance Co., Limited.
Munich Reinsurance Company - Canada Life
Novex Group Insurance
Omega General Insurance Company
Ontario Blue Cross
Ontario Mutual Insurance Association
Optimum Réassurance inc
The Order of United Commercial Travelers of America
Oxford Mutual Insurance Company
Pacific Blue Cross
PartnerRe SA
Penncorp Life Insurance Company
The Personal Insurance Company
Primerica Life Insurance Company of Canada
Principal Life Insurance Company
Promutuel Vie inc
Québec Blue Cross
RBC General Insurance Company
RBC Insurance
RBC Life Insurance Company
RBC Travel Insurance Company
Reliable Life Insurance Company
Royal & SunAlliance Insurance Company of Canada
Saskatchewan Blue Cross
SCOR Global Life Canada
Scotia Life Insurance Company
SecuriCan General Insurance Company
Security National Insurance Company
The Sovereign General Insurance Company
SSQ Financial Group
SSQ, Société d'assurance-vie inc
The Standard Life Assurance Company of Canada
Suecia Reinsurance Company
Sun Life Assurance Company of Canada
Supreme Council of the Royal Arcanum
La Survivance, compagnie mutuelle d'assurance vie
TD General Insurance Company
TD Life Insurance Company
Town & Country Mutual Insurance

Townsend Farmers' Mutual Fire Insurance Company
Trans Global Insurance Company
Trans Global Life Insurance Company
Transamerica Life Canada
Transatlantic Reinsurance Company
Ukrainian Mutual Benefit Association of St. Nicholas of Canada
Ukrainian National Association
L'Union-Vie, compagnie mutuelle d'assurance
United American Insurance Company
Uv Mutuelle
Wabisa Mutual Insurance Company
The Wawanesa Life Insurance Company
West Elgin Mutual Insurance Company
West Wawanosh Mutual Insurance Company
Western Assurance Company
Western Financial Group Inc.
Western Life Assurance Company
Westport Insurance Corporation
XL Insurance Company Limited
XL Reinsurance America Inc.
Zenith Insurance Company
Zurich Canada

Property

ACE INA Insurance
Affiliated FM Insurance Company
Alberta Motor Association Insurance Co.
Algoma Insurance Group
Algoma Mutual Insurance Co.
Alliance Assurance
Allstate Insurance Company of Canada
L'ALPHA, compagnie d'assurances inc.
Alpine Insurance & Financial Inc.
The American Road Insurance Company
Amherst Island Mutual Insurance Company
Antigonish Farmers' Mutual Insurance Company
L'Assurance Mutuelle des Fabriques de Montréal
Astro Insurance 1000 Inc.
Atlantic Insurance Company Limited
Aviva Canada Inc.
A-WIN Insurance Network
AXA General Insurance Company
AXA Insurance (Canada)
AXA Pacific Insurance Company
Ayr Farmers Mutual Insurance Company
Bay of Quinte Mutual Insurance Co.
Belair Insurance Company Inc.
Berkley Canada
Bertie and Clinton Mutual Insurance Company
Brant Mutual Insurance Company
British Columbia Automobile Association Insurance Agency
Butler Byers Insurance Ltd.
CAA Insurance Company (Ontario)
Caisse Centrale de Réassurance
Canadian Direct Insurance Incorporated
Canadian Farm Insurance Corp.
Canadian Petroleum Insurance Exchange Ltd.
Canadian Professional Sales Association
Canadian Universities Reciprocal Insurance Exchange
Canassurance Insurance Company
La Capitale General Insurance Inc.
Caradoc Delaware Mutual Fire Insurance Company
Carleton Mutual Insurance Company
Cavell Insurance Company Limited
Certas Direct Insurance Company
Chicago Title Insurance Company Canada
Chubb Insurance Company of Canada
Clare Mutual Insurance Company
CNS
Coastal Community Insurance Services (2007) Ltd.
La Compagnie d'Assurance Missisquoi
Continental Casualty Company
Co-operators General Insurance Company
Co-operators Life Insurance Company
CorePointe Insurance Company
COSECO Insurance Company
Cowan Insurance Group Ltd.
Crowsnest Insurance Agencies Ltd.
CUMIS General Insurance Company
The CUMIS Group Limited
CUMIS Life Insurance Company
Desjardins assurances générales inc
The Dominion of Canada General Insurance Company
Dufferin Mutual Insurance Company
Dumfries Mutual Insurance Company
Eagle Star Insurance Company Ltd.
Ecclesiastical Insurance Office plc
Echelon General Insurance Company
Economical Mutual Insurance Company
Elite Insurance Company
Erie Mutual Fire Insurance Company
Everest Insurance Company of Canada
Everest Reinsurance Company
Farmers' Mutual Insurance Company (Lindsay)
Federal Insurance Company
Federated Insurance Company of Canada
Federation Insurance Company of Canada
Fenchurch General Insurance Company
First North American Insurance Company
FM Global
Fundy Mutual Insurance Company
GCAN Insurance Company
General Reinsurance Corporation
Germania Mutual Insurance Company
Gibb's Agencies (1997) Ltd.
Glengarry Farmers' Mutual Fire Insurance Co.
Global Aerospace Underwriting Managers (Canada) Limited
Gore Mutual Insurance Company
Grain Insurance and Guarantee Company
Great American Insurance Company
Grenville Mutual Insurance Company
Grey & Bruce Mutual Insurance Co.
Le Groupe Estrie-Richelieu, compagnie d'assurance
The Guarantee Company of North America
Halwell Mutual Insurance Company
Hannover Rückversicherungs AG
Hartford Fire Insurance Company
Hay Mutual Insurance Company
Henderson Insurance Inc.
Howard Mutual Insurance Co.
Howick Mutual Insurance Company
HSB BI&I
Industrial Alliance Insurance & Financial Services Inc.
Insurance Company of Prince Edward Island
JEVCO Insurance Company
Kent & Essex Mutual Insurance Company
The Kings Mutual Insurance Company
Kingsway Financial Services Inc.
Kingsway General Insurance Company
Kirkham Insurance
Lambton Mutual Insurance Company
Lanark Mutual Insurance Company
Legacy General Insurance Company
Lennox & Addington Mutual Insurance Company
Liberty Mutual Insurance Company
Lloyd's Underwriters
Lumbermen's Underwriting Alliance
MAX Canada Insurance Company
McFarlane & Company Financial Group Limited
McKillop Mutual Insurance Company
Mennonite Mutual Fire Insurance Company
Mennonite Mutual Insurance Co. (Alberta) Ltd.
Metro General Insurance Corp.
Middlesex Mutual Insurance Co.
Millennium Insurance Corporation
Mitsui Sumitomo Insurance Co., Limited.
Munich Reinsurance Company of Canada
MUNIX Reciprocal
The Mutual Fire Insurance Company of British Columbia
The Nordic Insurance Company of Canada
Norfolk Mutual Insurance Company
North Bleinheim Mutual Insurance Co.
North Blenheim Mutual Insurance Company
North Kent Mutual Fire Insurance Company
The North Waterloo Farmers Mutual Insurance Company
Northbridge Insurance
Novex Group Insurance
Old Republic Insurance Company of Canada
Omega General Insurance Company
Ontario Mutual Insurance Association
Ontario School Boards' Insurance Exchange
Optimum Assurance Agricole inc
Optimum Général inc
Optimum Société d'Assurance inc
Optimum West Insurance Company
Oxford Mutual Insurance Company
PartnerRe SA
PC Financial Insurance Agency
Peace Hills General Insurance Company
Peel Mutual Insurance Company
Pembridge Insurance Company
The Personal General Insurance Inc.
The Personal Insurance Company
Perth Insurance Company
Pictou Mutual Insurance Company
Pilot Insurance Company
The Portage La Prairie Mutual Insurance Company
Premier Marine Insurance Managers Group
Primmum Insurance Company
Prince Edward Island Mutual Insurance Company
Progressive Casualty Insurance Company
Promutuel Réassurance
Protective Insurance Company
RBC General Insurance Company
RBC Insurance
Red River Valley Mutual Insurance Co.
Royal & SunAlliance Insurance Company of Canada
Saskatchewan Mutual Insurance Company
Scottish & York Insurance Co. Limited
Security National Insurance Company
SGI CANADA Consolidated
Sirius America Insurance Company
South Easthope Mutual Insurance Co.
Southeastern Mutual Insurance Company
The Sovereign General Insurance Company
SSQ, Société d'assurances générales inc.
SSQ, Société d'assurance-vie inc
Stanley Mutual Insurance Company
State Farm Canada
Suecia Reinsurance Company
Swiss Reinsurance Company Canada
TD General Insurance Company
TD Home & Auto Insurance Company
Temple Insurance Company
Thomson Jemmett Vogelzang
Thomson-Schindle-Green Insurance & Financial Services Ltd.
The Tokio Marine & Nichido Fire Insurance Co., Ltd.
Town & Country Mutual Insurance
Townsend Farmers' Mutual Fire Insurance Company
Traders General Insurance Company
Tradition Mutual Insurance Company
Trans Global Insurance Company
Transatlantic Reinsurance Company
Trillium Mutual Insurance Company
Unica Insurance
Unifund Assurance Company
L'Union Canadienne Compagnie d'Assurances
Virginia Surety Company, Inc.
Wabisa Mutual Insurance Company
Waterloo Insurance Company
The Wawanesa Mutual Insurance Company
Wedgwood Insurance Limited
West Elgin Mutual Insurance Company
West Wawanosh Mutual Insurance Company
Western Assurance Company
Western Financial Group Inc.
Westland Insurance
Westminster Mutual Insurance Company
Westport Insurance Corporation
XL Insurance Company Limited
XL Reinsurance America Inc.
XL Reinsurance America Inc.
Yarmouth Mutual Fire Insurance Company
Zenith Insurance Company
Zurich Canada

Reinsurance

General American Life Insurance Company
Kingsway Financial Services Inc.
Lloyd's Underwriters
London Life Insurance Company
Munich Reinsurance Company - Canada Life
Old Republic Insurance Company of Canada
Optimum Réassurance inc
Promutuel Réassurance
RGA Life Reinsurance Company of Canada
SCOR Canada Reinsurance Company
SGI CANADA Consolidated
Suecia Reinsurance Company
Swiss Reinsurance Company Canada
The Toa Reinsurance Company of America
Transatlantic Reinsurance Company
L'Union-Vie, compagnie mutuelle d'assurance
XL Reinsurance America Inc.

Surety

ACE INA Insurance
Affiliated FM Insurance Company
Algoma Insurance Group
Allstate Insurance Company of Canada
L'ALPHA, compagnie d'assurances inc.
The American Road Insurance Company
Atlantic Insurance Company Limited
Aviva Canada Inc.
AXA General Insurance Company
AXA Insurance (Canada)
AXA Pacific Insurance Company
Belair Insurance Company Inc.
Berkley Canada
CAA Insurance Company (Ontario)
Caisse Centrale de Réassurance
Canadian Farm Insurance Corp.

Cavell Insurance Company Limited
Certas Direct Insurance Company
Chicago Title Insurance Company Canada
Chubb Insurance Company of Canada
La Compagnie d'Assurance Missisquoi
Continental Casualty Company
Co-operators General Insurance Company
CorePointe Insurance Company
Desjardins assurances générales inc
The Dominion of Canada General Insurance Company
Eagle Star Insurance Company Ltd.
Echelon General Insurance Company
Economical Mutual Insurance Company
Elite Insurance Company
Everest Insurance Company of Canada
Everest Reinsurance Company
Federal Insurance Company
Federated Insurance Company of Canada
Federation Insurance Company of Canada
Fenchurch General Insurance Company
GCAN Insurance Company
General Reinsurance Corporation
Grain Insurance and Guarantee Company
Great American Insurance Company
The Guarantee Company of North America
Hannover Rückversicherungs AG
Hartford Fire Insurance Company
Intact Insurance Company of Canada
Johnston Meier Insurance Agencies Group
Kingsway General Insurance Company
Liberty Mutual Insurance Company
Lloyd's Underwriters
McFarlane & Company Financial Group Limited
Mitsui Sumitomo Insurance Co., Limited.
The Nordic Insurance Company of Canada
Novex Group Insurance
Omega General Insurance Company
Peace Hills General Insurance Company
The Personal General Insurance Inc.
The Personal Insurance Company
Progressive Casualty Insurance Company
Promutuel Réassurance
Red River Valley Mutual Insurance Co.
Scottish & York Insurance Co. Limited
SGI CANADA Consolidated
Sirius America Insurance Company
State Farm Canada
Swiss Reinsurance Company Canada
TD General Insurance Company
Transatlantic Reinsurance Company
Trisura Guarantee Insurance Company
The Wawanesa Mutual Insurance Company
Western Assurance Company
Western Financial Group Inc.
Western Surety Company
Westport Insurance Corporation
XL Insurance Company Limited
XL Reinsurance America Inc.
XL Reinsurance America Inc.
Zurich Canada

Theft

Algoma Insurance Group
L'Assurance Mutuelle des Fabriques de Montréal
Canadian Petroleum Insurance Exchange Ltd.
La Compagnie d'Assurance Missisquoi
Co-operators General Insurance Company
CUMIS General Insurance Company
CUMIS Life Insurance Company
The Dominion of Canada General Insurance Company
Federated Insurance Company of Canada
Germania Mutual Insurance Company
Glengarry Farmers' Mutual Fire Insurance Co.
Gore Mutual Insurance Company
Grain Insurance and Guarantee Company
The Guarantee Company of North America
Hartford Fire Insurance Company
Lanark Mutual Insurance Company
Mennonite Mutual Fire Insurance Company
Munich Reinsurance Company of Canada
North Kent Mutual Fire Insurance Company
Peace Hills General Insurance Company
Prince Edward Island Mutual Insurance Company
Promutuel Réassurance
RBC General Insurance Company
Red River Valley Mutual Insurance Co.
SSQ Financial Group
SSQ, Société d'assurances générales inc.
The Wawanesa Mutual Insurance Company
Western Financial Group Inc.
Zurich Canada

Federal & Provincial Insurance Companies

ACE INA Insurance
#1400, 25 York St.
Toronto, ON M5J 2V5
Tel: 416-368-2911; Fax: 416-594-2600
www.ace-ina-canada.com
Classes of Insurance: Accident, Aircraft, Auto, Liability, Boiler & Machinery, Credit, Marine, Fidelity, Property, Fire, Surety, Hail & Crop

ACE INA Life Insurance/ Assurance-vie ACE INA
#1400, 25 York St.
Toronto, ON M5J 2V5
Tel: 416-368-2911; Fax: 416-594-2600
www.ace-ina-canada.com
Classes of Insurance: Personal Accident & Sickness, Liability

ACTRA Fraternal Benefit Society (AFBS)
1000 Yonge St.
Toronto, ON M4W 2K2
Tel: 416-967-6600; Fax: 416-967-4744
Toll-Free: 800-387-8897
benefits@actrafrat.com; finance@actrafrat.com (retirement & savings)
www.actrafrat.com
Classes of Insurance: Personal Accident & Sickness, Life

Affiliated FM Insurance Company
#500, 165 Commerce Valley Dr. West
Thornhill, ON L3T 7V8
Tel: 905-763-5555; Fax: 905-763-5556
www.affiliatedfm.ca
Classes of Insurance: Liability, Boiler & Machinery, Fidelity, Property, Fire, Surety

***Agriculture Financial Services Corporation (AFSC)**
5718 - 56 Ave.
Lacombe, AB T4J 1R5
Tel: 403-782-3000; Fax: 403-782-4226
www.afsc.ca
Classes of Insurance: Hail & Crop

***Alberta Blue Cross**
Blue Cross Place
10009 - 108th St. NW
Edmonton, AB T5J 3C5
Tel: 780-498-8000; Fax: 780-425-4627
Toll-Free: 800-661-6995
www.ab.bluecross.ca
Other Contact Information: Travel Coverage: 780/498-8550; Individual Health & Dental Plans: 780/498-8008; Group Sales: 780/498-8500
Classes of Insurance: Personal Accident & Sickness

***Alberta Motor Association Insurance Co.**
PO Box 8180, South Stn. South
Edmonton, AB T6H 5X9
Tel: 780-430-5555; Toll-Free: 800-615-5897
www.ama.ab.ca
Other Contact Information: Membership Inquiries Toll Free: 800-222-6400
Classes of Insurance: Personal Accident & Sickness, Auto, Life, Property, Fire

Algoma Insurance Group
#200, 855 Queen St. East
Sault Ste. Marie, ON P6A 2B3
Tel: 705-949-6555; Fax: 705-949-3513
info@algomains.com
www.algomains.com
Classes of Insurance: Auto, Liability, Boiler & Machinery, Property, Surety, Theft

***Algoma Mutual Insurance Co.**
131 Main St.
Thessalon, ON P0R 1L0
Tel: 705-842-3345; Fax: 705-842-3500
Toll-Free: 800-461-7260
www.amico.ca
Classes of Insurance: Auto, Property

***Alliance Assurance**
PO Box 7664
#200, 166 Broadway Blvd.
Grand Falls, NB E3Z 2J9
Tel: 506-473-9400; Fax: 506-473-9401
Toll-Free: 800-939-9400
gffax@alliance-assurance.com
www.alliance-assurance.com
Classes of Insurance: Auto, Liability, Property

Allianz Life Insurance Company of North America
#700, 2005 Sheppard Ave. East
Toronto, ON M2J 5B4
Fax: 416-502-2555
www.allianzlife.com
Classes of Insurance: Personal Accident & Sickness, Life

Allstate Insurance Company of Canada/ Allstate du Canada, Compagnie d'assurance
#100, 27 Allstate Pkwy.
Markham, ON L3R 5P8
Tel: 905-477-6900; Fax: 905-415-4831
Toll-Free: 800-255-7828
www.allstate.ca
Other Contact Information: Claims Toll-Free Numbers: 800-387-0462 (ON & USA); 800-661-1577 (BC, AB, SK, MB); 800-561-7222 (NS, NB, PE, NL); 800-463-2813 (QC)
Social Media: www.facebook.com/AllstateCanada; twitter.com/allstate
Classes of Insurance: Personal Accident & Sickness, Legal Expense, Auto, Liability, Boiler & Machinery, Fidelity, Property, Surety

***L'ALPHA, compagnie d'assurances inc.**
#119, 430, rue Saint-Georges
Drummondville, QC J2C 4H4
Tel: 819-474-7958; Fax: 819-477-6139
drummond@assurance-alpha.com
www.assurance-alpha.com
Classes of Insurance: Auto, Property, Surety

***Alpine Insurance & Financial Inc.**
#203, 1026 - 16th Ave. NW
Calgary, AB T2M 0K6
Tel: 403-270-8822; Fax: 403-270-0201
Toll-Free: 877-770-8822
calgary.info@alpineinsurance.ca
www.alpineinsurance.ca
Classes of Insurance: Auto, Liability, Life, Property

American Bankers Life Assurance Company of Florida
#2000, 5000 Yonge St., 20th Fl.
Toronto, ON M2N 7E9
Tel: 416-733-3360; Fax: 416-733-7826
Toll-Free: 800-561-3232
www.assurant.com/canada
Classes of Insurance: Accident, Personal Accident & Sickness, Life

American Health & Life Insurance Company
355 Wellington St.
London, ON N6A 3N7
Toll-Free: 800-285-8623
Classes of Insurance: Life

American Income Life Insurance Company
c/o McLean & Kerr
#2800, 130 Adelaide St. West
Toronto, ON M5H 3P5
Tel: 416-364-5371; Fax: 416-366-8571
Classes of Insurance: Personal Accident & Sickness, Life

The American Road Insurance Company
c/o CAS Accounting
#2, 1145 Nicholson Rd.
Newmarket, ON L3Y 9C3
Tel: 905-853-0858;
Classes of Insurance: Auto, Liability, Boiler & Machinery, Credit, Property, Surety

AMEX Assurance Company/ AMEX Compagnie d'Assurance
c/o Focus Group Inc.
#500, 36 King St. East
Toronto, ON M5C 1E5
Tel: 416-361-1728; Fax: 416-361-6113
Classes of Insurance: Personal Accident & Sickness, Life

***Amherst Island Mutual Insurance Company**
RR#1
Stella, ON K0H 2S0
Tel: 613-389-2012; Fax: 613-389-9986
Classes of Insurance: Personal Accident & Sickness, Liability, Property

Antigonish Farmers' Mutual Insurance Company
188 Main St.
Antigonish, NS B2G 2B9
Tel: 902-863-3544; Fax: 902-863-0664
reception@antigonish-mutual.com
www.antigonish-mutual.com
Other Contact Information: Toll Free (Maritimes only): 1-800-565-3544
Classes of Insurance: Marine, Property, Fire

Ascentus Insurance Ltd.
#800, 18 York St.
Toronto, ON M5J 2T8
Toll-Free: 888-877-1710
answers@ascentusinsurance.ca
www.ascentusinsurance.ca
Other Contact Information: Claims: 1-877-275-3698

***Assumption Mutual Life Insurance Company/ Assumption Compagnie Mutuelle d'Assurance-Vie**
Assumption Place
PO Box 160
770 Main St.
Moncton, NB E1C 8L1
Tel: 506-853-6040; Fax: 506-853-5428
Toll-Free: 800-455-7337
comments@assumption.ca; financial.services@assumption.ca
www.assumption.ca
Other Contact Information: Group Insurance, Phone: 506-869-9797; Toll Free: 1-888-869-9797; Individual Insurance, Toll-Free: 1-800-343-5622; Mortgage Loans, Phone: 506-869-9755
Classes of Insurance: Accident, Personal Accident & Sickness, Life

***L'Assurance Mutuelle des Fabriques de Montréal**
1071, rue de la Cathédrale
Montréal, QC H3B 2V4
Tel: 514-395-4969; Fax: 514-861-8921
Toll-Free: 800-567-6586
info.general@amf-mtl.com
Classes of Insurance: Liability, Boiler & Machinery, Property, Fire, Theft

***Assurance-Vie Banque Nationale/ National Bank Life Insurance Company**
1100, rue University, 11e étage
Montréal, QC H3B 2G7
Tél: 514-871-7500; Téléc: 514-394-6604
Ligne sans frais: 877-871-7500
assurances@nbc.ca
www.nbc.ca
Classes of Insurance: Personal Accident & Sickness, Life, Credit,

Assurant Solutions Canada
#2000, 5000 Yonge St., 20th Fl.
Toronto, ON M2N 7E9
Tel: 416-733-3360; Fax: 416-733-7826
Toll-Free: 800-561-3232
www.assurantsolutions.com/canada
Social Media: www.facebook.com/AssurantSolutionsSocial;
Classes of Insurance: Credit

Astro Insurance 1000 Inc.
#100, 542 - 7th St.
Lethbridge, AB T1J 2H1
Tel: 403-328-1000; Fax: 403-320-1962
astroins@astro-insurance.com
www.astro-insurance.com
Classes of Insurance: Auto, Liability, Property, Hail & Crop

***Atlantic Insurance Company Limited**
64 Commonwealth Ave.
Mount Pearl, NL A1N 1W8
Tel: 709-364-5209; Fax: 709-364-5262
Classes of Insurance: Auto, Liability, Boiler & Machinery, Fidelity, Property, Surety

Avemco Insurance Company
c/o Canadian Insurance Consultants
#401, 133 Richmond St. West
Toronto, ON M5H 2L3
Tel: 416-363-6103; Fax: 416-363-7454
Classes of Insurance: Personal Accident & Sickness, Aircraft, Marine

Aviation & General Insurance Company Limited
#201, 3650 Victoria Park Ave.
Toronto, ON M2H 3P7
Tel: 416-496-1148; Fax: 416-496-1089
Classes of Insurance: Aircraft, Liability

***AVie, Financial Security Advisors / AVie, Cabinet de conseillers en sécurité financière**
Édifice Martin-J.-Légère
CP 5554
295, boul St-Pierre ouest
Caraquet, NB E1W 1B7
Tél: 506-726-4203; Téléc: 506-726-8204
Ligne sans frais: 888-822-2343
www.acadie.com; www.assumption.ca
Classes of Insurance: Personal Accident & Sickness, Life

Aviva Canada Inc./ Aviva, Compagnie d'Assurance du Canada
2206 Eglinton Ave. East
Toronto, ON M1L 4S8
Tel: 416-288-1800; Fax: 416-288-5888
Toll-Free: 800-387-4518
www.avivacanada.com
Other Contact Information: Claims: 1-866-692-8482
Social Media: www.facebook.com/AvivaCanada; twitter.com/avivacanada
Classes of Insurance: Personal Accident & Sickness, Aircraft, Legal Expense, Auto, Liability, Boiler & Machinery, Marine, Fidelity, Property, Surety, Hail & Crop

*** A-WIN Insurance Network**
#200, 2417 - 51 Ave. SE
Calgary, AB T2C 0A2
Tel: 403-278-1050; Fax: 403-225-0515
info1@awinins.ca
www.awinins.ca
Classes of Insurance: Auto, Liability, Property

AXA Canada Inc.
#700, 2020, rue University
Montréal, QC H3A 2A5
Tel: 514-282-1914; Fax: 514-282-9588
www.axa.ca

AXA General Insurance Company/ AXA Assurances générales
#1400, 5700 Yonge St.
Toronto, ON M2M 4K2
Toll-Free: 877-292-4968
www.axa.ca
Classes of Insurance: Personal Accident & Sickness, Aircraft, Legal Expense, Auto, Liability, Boiler & Machinery, Fidelity, Property, Surety, Hail & Crop

AXA Insurance (Canada) / AXA Assurances (Canada)
#1400, 5700 Yonge St.
Toronto, ON M2M 4K2
Toll-Free: 877-292-4968
www.axa-insurance.ca; www.axa.ca; www.intactinsurance.com
Other Contact Information: After hours Emergencies & Claims: 1-800-268-8865; Life & Health Claims: 1-800-565-4550; Group Claims: 1-800-561-7251, ext. 4473
Social Media: www.facebook.com/axainsurance; twitter.com/axainsurance
Classes of Insurance: Personal Accident & Sickness, Aircraft, Legal Expense, Auto, Liability, Boiler & Machinery, Fidelity, Property, Surety, Hail & Crop

AXA Pacific Insurance Company / AXA Pacifique Compagnie d'Assurance
999 Hastings St. West, 2nd Fl.
Vancouver, BC V6C 2W2
Tel: 604-669-0595
www.axa.ca
Classes of Insurance: Personal Accident & Sickness, Aircraft, Legal Expense, Auto, Liability, Boiler & Machinery, Credit, Fidelity, Property, Surety, Hail & Crop

Ayr Farmers Mutual Insurance Company
PO Box 1170
1400 Northumberland St.
Ayr, ON N0B 1E0
Tel: 519-632-7413; Fax: 519-632-8908
Toll-Free: 800-265-8792
www.ayrmutual.com
Classes of Insurance: Accident, Personal Accident & Sickness, Auto, Liability, Boiler & Machinery, Fidelity, Property, Hail & Crop

***Bay of Quinte Mutual Insurance Co.**
PO Box 6050
13379 Loyalist Pkwy.
Picton, ON K0K 2T0
Tel: 613-476-2145; Toll-Free: 800-267-2126
info@bayofquintemutual.com
www.bayofquintemutual.com
Classes of Insurance: Personal Accident & Sickness, Auto, Liability, Boiler & Machinery, Fidelity, Property

***Belair Insurance Company Inc. / La Compagnie d'Assurance Belair Inc.**
#300, 7101, rue Jean-Talon est
Montréal, QC H1M 3T6
Tel: 514-270-9111; Toll-Free: 888-270-9111
belairdirect@belairdirect.com, belairdirect.ontario@belairdirect.com
www.belairdirect.com
Other Contact Information: 888-280-8549, 888-270-9732 (Toll Free, Auto & Home); 1-877-874-5433 (Toll Free, Travel Insurance); 877-270-9124 (Toll Free, Claims Emergency)
Classes of Insurance: Personal Accident & Sickness, Legal Expense, Auto, Liability, Boiler & Machinery, Marine, Fidelity, Property, Surety

Berkley Canada
#2610, 100 King Street W
Toronto, ON M5X 1C8
Tel: 416-304-1178; Fax: 416-304-4108
Toll-Free: 877-304-1178
info@berkleycanada.com
Classes of Insurance: Personal Accident & Sickness, Aircraft, Legal Expense, Auto, Liability, Boiler & Machinery, Credit, Fidelity, Property, Surety, Hail & Crop

***Bertie and Clinton Mutual Insurance Company**
1789 Merrittville Hwy., RR#2
Welland, ON L3B 5N5
Tel: 905-892-0606; Fax: 905-892-0365
Toll-Free: 800-263-0494
info@bertieandclinton.com
www.bertieandclinton.com
Classes of Insurance: Personal Accident & Sickness, Auto, Liability, Boiler & Machinery, Fidelity, Property

BMO Life Assurance Company of Canada
60 Yonge St.
Toronto, ON M5E 1H5
Tel: 416-596-3900; Fax: 416-596-4143
Toll-Free: 877-742-5244
www4.bmo.com
Classes of Insurance: Personal Accident & Sickness, Life

***Brant Mutual Insurance Company**
20 Holiday Dr.
Brantford, ON N3R 7J4
Tel: 519-752-0088; Fax: 519-752-7917
solutions@brantmutual.com
www.brantmutual.com
Classes of Insurance: Personal Accident & Sickness, Auto, Liability, Boiler & Machinery, Fidelity, Property, Hail & Crop

***British Columbia Automobile Association Insurance Agency**
4567 Canada Way
Burnaby, BC V5G 4T1
Tel: 604-268-5000; Fax: 604-268-5569
Toll-Free: 800-719-2224
www.bcaa.com
Other Contact Information: Claims: 604-268-5260; Toll Free, TeleCentre: 1-877-325-8888; Toll Free, BCAA Advantage Home Policy: 310-2345; Customer Contact Centre: 604-268-5555
Classes of Insurance: Personal Accident & Sickness, Auto, Life, Property, Fire

***British Columbia Life & Casualty Company**
PO Box 7000
Vancouver, BC V6B 4E1
Tel: 604-419-2000; Fax: 604-419-2990
Toll-Free: 888-275-4672
www.pbchbs.com
Classes of Insurance: Personal Accident & Sickness, Life

***Butler Byers Hail Insurance Ltd.**
PO Box 330
Saskatoon, SK S7K 3L5
Tel: 306-652-4245; Fax: 306-652-8472
Toll-Free: 800-997-4245
sbyers@butlerbyers.com
www.butlerbyers.com
Classes of Insurance: Hail & Crop

***Butler Byers Insurance Ltd.**
301 - 4th Ave. North
Saskatoon, SK S7K 2L8
Tel: 306-653-2233
www.butlerbyers.com
Classes of Insurance: Personal Accident & Sickness, Auto, Life, Marine, Property

***CAA Insurance Company (Ontario)**
60 Commerce Valley Dr. East
Thornhill, ON L3T 7P9
Tel: 905-771-3000; Fax: 905-771-3101
Toll-Free: 800-268-3750
info@caasco.ca
www.caasco.com/insurance
Other Contact Information: 877-222-3939 (Auto & Property); 800-387-2656 (Claims); 866-999-4222 (Health & Dental); 877-942-4222 (Group Life)
Classes of Insurance: Personal Accident & Sickness, Legal Expense, Auto, Liability, Life, Marine, Property, Surety

Caisse Centrale de Réassurance
#2110, 181 University Ave.
Toronto, ON M5H 3M7
Tel: 416-644-0821; Fax: 416-644-0822
info@ccr.fr
www.ccr.fr
Classes of Insurance: Accident, Aircraft, Legal Expense, Auto, Liability, Boiler & Machinery, Fidelity, Property, Fire, Surety

Canada Guaranty Mortgage Insurance Company
#400, 1 Toronto St.
Toronto, ON M5C 2V6
Tel: 416-640-8924; Fax: 416-640-8948
Toll-Free: 866-414-9109
underwriting@canadaguaranty.ca (underwriting inquiries)
www.canadaguaranty.ca
Other Contact Information: Underwriting inquiries, Toll-Free: 1-877-244-8422; Fax: 1-877-244-8448

Canadian Direct Insurance Incorporated
#600, 750 Cambie St.
Vancouver, BC V6B 0A2
Tel: 604-699-3838; Fax: 604-699-3860
Toll-Free: 888-225-5234
www.canadiandirect.com
Other Contact Information: Claims, Toll-Free Phone: 888-261-8888; Toll-Free Fax: 888-261-8880
Classes of Insurance: Personal Accident & Sickness, Liability, Property

***Canadian Farm Insurance Corp. (CFIC)**
#310, 13220 St. Albert Trail
Edmonton, AB T5L 4W1
Tel: 780-447-3276; Fax: 780-732-3607
Toll-Free: 877-909-3276
www.cdnfarmins.com
Other Contact Information: 24 hour Livestock Claims Assistance: 780-732-3692
Classes of Insurance: Personal Accident & Sickness, Liability, Boiler & Machinery, Fidelity, Property, Surety

***Canadian Lawyers Insurance Association / L'Association d'Assurance des Juristes Canadiens**
#2900, 250 Yonge St.
Toronto, ON M5B 2L7
Tel: 416-408-3721; Toll-Free: 800-268-9484
info@clia.ca
www.clia.ca

***Canadian Lawyers Liability Assurance Society (CLLAS)**
c/o Torys LLP
#3000, 79 Wellington St. West
Toronto, ON M5K 1N2
Tel: 416-865-7337; Fax: 416-865-7380
cllas.ca
Classes of Insurance: Liability

***Canadian Petroleum Insurance Exchange Ltd. (CPIX)**
#500, 717 - 7th Ave. SW
Calgary, AB T2P 0Z3
Tel: 403-261-6061; Fax: 403-261-6068
insurance@cpix.com
www.cpix.com
Classes of Insurance: Auto, Liability, Property, Theft

Canadian Premier Life Insurance Company
80 Tiverton Ct., 5th Fl.
Markham, ON L3R 0G4
Tel: 905-479-7500; Fax: 905-479-3224
www.canadianpremier.ca
Other Contact Information: Privacy Officer: 1-888-968-4155.
Classes of Insurance: Personal Accident & Sickness, Life, Credit

Canadian Professional Sales Association (CPSA)
#400, 655 Bay St.
Toronto, ON M5G 2K4
Tel: 416-408-2685; Fax: 416-408-2684
Toll-Free: 888-267-2772
www.cpsa.com
Classes of Insurance: Accident, Personal Accident & Sickness, Auto, Life, Property

***Canadian Universities Reciprocal Insurance Exchange (CURIE)**
#901, 5500 North Service Rd.
Burlington, ON L7L 6W6
Tel: 905-336-3366; Fax: 905-336-3373
Toll-Free: 888-462-8743
inquiry@curie.org
www.curie.org
Classes of Insurance: Aircraft, Liability, Marine, Property

***Canassurance Insurance Company**
c/o Ontario Blue Cross
#610, 185 The West Mall
Toronto, ON M9C 5P1
Toll-Free: 866-732-2583
www.useblue.com
Classes of Insurance: Personal Accident & Sickness, Liability, Life, Property

***La Capitale Civil Service Insurer Inc.**
625, rue Saint-Amable
Québec, QC G1R 2G5
Tel: 418-643-3884; Fax: 418-646-0370
Toll-Free: 866-227-2606
www.lacapitale.com
Classes of Insurance: Life

***La Capitale General Insurance Inc. / La Capitale assurances générales inc.**
Édifice Hector-Fabre
CP 17100
525, boul. René-Lévesque est
Québec, QC G1K 9E2
Ligne sans frais: 888-522-5260
www.lacapitale.com
Other Contact Information: Claims: 800-461-0770
Classes of Insurance: Auto, Property

***La Capitale Insurance & Financial Services / La Capitale assurances et gestion du patrimoine**
Édifice Le Delta II
#100, 2875, boul. Laurier
Québec, QC G1V 2M2
Tel: 418-644-4200; Fax: 418-644-5226
Toll-Free: 888-463-4856
collectif@lacapitale.com
www.lacapitale.com
Classes of Insurance: Personal Accident & Sickness, Life

***Caradoc Delaware Mutual Fire Insurance Company**
PO Box 460
22508 Adelaide Rd.
Mount Brydges, ON N0L 1W0
Tel: 519-264-2298; Fax: 519-264-9101
Toll-Free: 877-707-2298
info@cdmins.com
www.cdmins.com
Classes of Insurance: Personal Accident & Sickness, Auto, Liability, Boiler & Machinery, Property

***Carleton Mutual Insurance Company**
301 Main St.
Florenceville, NB E7L 3G5
Tel: 506-392-6041; Fax: 506-392-8243
Toll-Free: 800-561-1550
cmi@nb.aibn.com
www.carletonmutual.com
Classes of Insurance: Auto, Property, Fire

Cavell Insurance Company Limited
c/o D.M. Williams & Associates Ltd.
#201, 3650 Victoria Park Ave.
Toronto, ON M2H 3P7
Tel: 416-496-1148; Fax: 416-496-1089
Classes of Insurance: Personal Accident & Sickness, Auto, Liability, Boiler & Machinery, Marine, Fidelity, Property, Surety, Hail & Crop,

Certas Direct Insurance Company/ Certas Direct, compagnie d'assurances
#550, 3 Robert Speck Pkwy.
Mississauga, ON L4Z 2G5
Toll-Free: 877-818-8873
www.certas.ca
Classes of Insurance: Auto, Liability, Property, Surety

Chartis Insurance Company of Canada
145 Wellington St. West
Toronto, ON M5J 1H8
Tel: 416-596-3000; Fax: 416-877-2743
Toll-Free: 800-387-4481
askChartisCanada@chartisinsurance.com
www.chartisinsurance.com/ca
Other Contact Information: After Hours Claims: 800-235-8784; Claims Fax: 416-596-4197; Claims E-mail: newclaimsp&c@chartisinsurance.com
Social Media: www.facebook.com/112705205434853;

Chicago Title Insurance Company Canada
55 Superior Blvd.
Mississauga, ON L5T 2X9
Toll-Free: 888-868-4853
info@chicagotitle.ca; claims@ctic.ca
express.ctic.ca

Classes of Insurance: Property, Surety

Chubb Insurance Company of Canada / Chubb du Canada Compagnie d'Assurance
One Financial Place
1 Adelaide St. East
Toronto, ON M5C 2V9
Tel: 416-863-0550; Fax: 416-863-5010
feedbackCanada@chubb.com
www.chubb.com/international/canada
Social Media: www.facebook.com/ChubbInsurance; twitter.com/ChubbInsurance
Classes of Insurance: Personal Accident & Sickness, Aircraft, Auto, Liability, Boiler & Machinery, Marine, Fidelity, Property, Surety

CIBC Life Insurance Company Limited / Compagnie d'Assurance-Vie CIBC Limitée
3 Robert Speck Pkwy., 9th Fl.
Mississauga, ON L4Z 2G5
Tel: 905-306-4904; Fax: 905-306-4957
Classes of Insurance: Personal Accident & Sickness, Life

CIGNA Life Insurance Company of Canada
PO Box 14
#606, 55 Town Centre Ct.
Toronto, ON M1P 4X4
Tel: 416-290-6666; Fax: 416-290-0732
Toll-Free: 800-668-7029
www.cigna.com
Social Media: www.youtube.com/cigna; www.facebook.com/CIGNA; twitter.com/cigna
Classes of Insurance: Accident, Personal Accident & Sickness, Life, Credit

Clare Mutual Insurance Company
3300 Hwy. 1
Belliveau Cove, NS B0W 1J0
Tel: 902-837-4597; Fax: 902-837-7745
Toll-Free: 877-818-0887
www.claremutual.com
Classes of Insurance: Property, Fire, Hail & Crop

CNS
#1900, 555 Hastings St. West
Vancouver, BC V6B 4N6
Tel: 604-662-2900; Fax: 604-662-5698
Toll-Free: 800-663-1953
www.cns.ca
Classes of Insurance: Auto, Liability, Property

***Coachman Insurance Company**
802 The Queensway
Toronto, ON M8Z 1N5
Tel: 416-255-3417; Fax: 416-255-3347
Toll-Free: 800-361-2622
inquiries@coachmanins.com
www.coachmaninsurance.ca
Classes of Insurance: Auto

Coast Underwriters Limited
#1610, 200 Granville St.
Vancouver, BC V6C 1S4
Tel: 604-683-5631; Fax: 604-683-8561
www.coast-uw.com

***Coastal Community Insurance Services (2007) Ltd.**
291 4th St
Courtenay, BC V9N 1G7
Tel: 250-703-4140; Fax: 250-338-0943
www.cccu.ca/Personal
Classes of Insurance: Auto, Property

Combined Insurance Company of America / Combined Assurances
PO Box 3720, MIP Stn. MIP
7300 Warden Ave., 3rd. Fl.
Markham, ON L3R 0X3
Tel: 905-305-1922; Fax: 905-305-8600
Toll-Free: 888-234-4466
www.combined.ca
Social Media: www.facebook.com/147210245353800;
Classes of Insurance: Personal Accident & Sickness, Life

La Compagnie d'Assurance Missisquoi / The Missisquoi Insurance Company
#1400, 1 Place Ville Marie
Montréal, QC H3B 2B2
Tél: 514-875-5790; Téléc: 514-875-9769
Ligne sans frais: 800-361-7573
www.economicalinsurance.com
Classes of Insurance: Legal Expense, Auto, Liability, Boiler & Machinery, Fidelity, Property, Fire, Surety, Theft

Connecticut General Life Insurance Co. (CGLIC)
c/o CIGNA Life Insurance Company of Canada
#606, 55 Town Centre Ct.
Toronto, ON M1P 4X4
Tel: 416-290-6666; Fax: 416-290-0732
Toll-Free: 800-668-7029
www.cigna.com
Classes of Insurance: Accident, Personal Accident & Sickness, Life

Continental Casualty Company
#1500, 250 Yonge St.
Toronto, ON M5B 2L7
Tel: 416-542-7300; Fax: 416-542-7310
Toll-Free: 800-268-9399
www.cnacanada.ca
Other Contact Information: Claims Fax: 416-542-7410
Social Media: www.facebook.com/cnainsurance; twitter.com/cna_insurance
Classes of Insurance: Accident, Personal Accident & Sickness, Aircraft, Auto, Liability, Boiler & Machinery, Credit, Fidelity, Property, Surety, Hail & Crop

***Co-operative Hail Insurance Company Ltd.**
PO Box 777
2709 - 13th Ave.
Regina, SK S4P 3A8
Tel: 306-522-8891; Fax: 306-352-9130
info@coophail.com
www.coophail.com
Classes of Insurance: Hail & Crop

Co-operators General Insurance Company
130 Macdonell St.
Guelph, ON N1H 6P8
Tel: 519-824-4400; Fax: 519-823-9944
Toll-Free: 800-265-2662
service@cooperators.ca
www.cooperators.ca
Social Media: www.youtube.com/CooperatorsInsurance; www.facebook.com/TheCooperatorsInsurance; twitter.com/The_Cooperators
Classes of Insurance: Personal Accident & Sickness, Aircraft, Auto, Boiler & Machinery, Life, Fidelity, Property, Fire, Surety, Hail & Crop, Theft

Co-operators Life Insurance Company
1920 College Ave.
Regina, SK S4P 1C4
Fax: 306-347-6808
Toll-Free: 800-454-8061
service@cooperators.ca; phs_individual_life@cooperators.ca
www.cooperators.ca
Other Contact Information: Group Benefits, Toll Free: 1-800-667-8164; Fax: 306-761-7373; E-mail: group_client_services@cooperators.ca; Travel, Toll Free: 1-800-869-6747
Classes of Insurance: Personal Accident & Sickness, Life, Property

CorePointe Insurance Company (DCIC)
East Tower
#300, 2425 Matheson Blvd. East
Mississauga, ON L4W 5N7
www.corepointeinsurance.com
Classes of Insurance: Auto, Liability, Property, Surety

COSECO Insurance Company
5600 Cancross Ct.
Mississauga, ON L5R 3E9
Toll-Free: 888-394-4964
cosecoinsurance@hbgrpins.com
www.coseco.ca
Classes of Insurance: Auto, Property

***Cowan Insurance Group Ltd.**
PO Box 1510
705 Fountain St. North
Cambridge, ON N1R 5T2
Tel: 519-650-6360; Fax: 519-650-6366
Toll-Free: 866-912-6926
infocib@cowangroup.ca
www.cowangroup.ca
Classes of Insurance: Auto, Marine, Property

Croatian Fraternal Union of America
c/o Deloitte & Touche
#1400, 181 Bay St.
Toronto, ON M5J 2V1
Tel: 416-601-6150; Fax: 416-601-6590
www.croatianfraternalunion.org
Social Media: www.facebook.com/croatianfraternalunion;
Classes of Insurance: Personal Accident & Sickness, Life

Crowsnest Insurance Agencies Ltd.
PO Box 88
12731 - 20th Ave.
Blairmore, AB T0K 0E0
Tel: 403-562-8822; Fax: 403-562-8239
Toll-Free: 800-361-8658
info@crowsnestinsurance.com
crowsnestinsurance.com
Classes of Insurance: Auto, Liability, Property

CUMIS General Insurance Company
PO Box 5065
151 North Service Rd.
Burlington, ON L7R 4C2
Tel: 905-632-1221; Fax: 905-632-9412
Toll-Free: 800-263-9120
customer.service@cumis.com
www.cumis.com
Classes of Insurance: Auto, Boiler & Machinery, Fidelity, Property, Fire, Theft

The CUMIS Group Limited
PO Box 5065
151 North Service Rd.
Burlington, ON L7R 4C2
Tel: 905-632-1221; Fax: 905-632-9412
Toll-Free: 800-263-9120
customer.service@cumis.com
www.cumis.com
Classes of Insurance: Personal Accident & Sickness, Auto, Life, Property

CUMIS Life Insurance Company
PO Box 5065
151 North Service Rd.
Burlington, ON L7R 4C2
Tel: 905-632-1221; Fax: 905-632-9412
Toll-Free: 800-263-9120
customer.service@cumis.com
www.cumis.com
Classes of Insurance: Accident, Personal Accident & Sickness, Auto, Life, Credit, Fidelity, Property, Fire, Theft

***Desjardins assurances générales inc / Desjardins General Insurance Inc.**
PO Box 3500
6300, boul. de la Rive-Sud
Lévis, QC G6V 6P9
Tel: 418-835-4850; Fax: 418-835-5599
Toll-Free: 800-277-8726
www.desjardinsassurancesgenerales.com
Classes of Insurance: Auto, Liability, Boiler & Machinery, Property, Surety

***Desjardins Financial Security (DFS) / Desjardins Sécurité financière**
200, av. des Commandeurs
Lévis, QC G6V 6R2
Toll-Free: 866-838-7553
info@desjardinssecuritefinanciere.com; grouppension@dsf.ca
www.dsf-dfs.com
Classes of Insurance: Accident, Personal Accident & Sickness, Life

***Desjardins Groupe d'assurances générales inc / Desjardins General Insurance Group Inc.**
6300, boul. de la Rive-Sud
Lévis, QC G6V 6P9
Tél: 418-835-4850; Ligne sans frais: 800-463-4850
www.dgag.ca

The Dominion of Canada General Insurance Company/ Compagnie d'assurance générale dominion du Canada
165 University Ave.
Toronto, ON M5H 3B9
Tel: 416-362-7231; Fax: 416-362-9918
Toll-Free: 800-268-8447
www.thedominion.ca
Other Contact Information: After Hours Claims: 1-800-661-5522
Classes of Insurance: Auto, Liability, Property, Fire, Surety, Theft

***Dufferin Mutual Insurance Company**
712 Main St. East
Shelburne, ON L0N 1S0
Tel: 519-925-2026; Fax: 519-925-3357
Toll-Free: 800-265-9115
info@dufferinmutual.com
www.dufferinmutual.com
Social Media: twitter.com/dufferinmutual
Classes of Insurance: Personal Accident & Sickness, Auto, Liability, Boiler & Machinery, Fidelity, Property

***Dumfries Mutual Insurance Company**
12 Cambridge St.
Cambridge, ON N1R 3R7
Tel: 519-621-4660; Fax: 519-740-8732
info@dumfriesmutual.com
www.dumfriesmutual.com
Classes of Insurance: Auto, Liability, Boiler & Machinery, Property, Hail & Crop

Eagle Star Insurance Company Ltd.
c/o Focus Group Inc.
#500, 36 King St. East
Toronto, ON M5C 1E5
Tel: 416-361-1728; Fax: 416-361-6113
www.zurichinsurance.ie
Classes of Insurance: Personal Accident & Sickness, Aircraft, Auto, Liability, Boiler & Machinery, Fidelity, Property, Surety

Ecclesiastical Insurance Office plc / Société des Assurances écclésiastiques
PO Box 2004
#2200, 20 Eglinton Ave. West
Toronto, ON M4R 1K8
Tel: 416-484-4555; Fax: 416-484-6352
www.ecclesiastical.ca, www.ecclesiastical.com
Other Contact Information: After-Hours Emergency Claims: 1-888-693-2253
Social Media: www.facebook.com/ecclesiasticalgroup;
Classes of Insurance: Auto, Liability, Boiler & Machinery, Marine, Fidelity, Property

Echelon General Insurance Company / Echelon Compagnie d'Assurances Générale
#300, 2680 Matheson Blvd. East
Mississauga, ON L4W 0A5
Tel: 905-214-7880; Fax: 905-214-7893
Toll-Free: 800-324-3566
www.echelon-insurance.ca
Classes of Insurance: Accident, Personal Accident & Sickness, Legal Expense, Auto, Liability, Fidelity, Property, Fire, Surety

The Economical Insurance Group
PO Box 2000
111 Westmount St. South
Waterloo, ON N2J 4S4
Tel: 519-570-8200; Fax: 519-570-8389
Toll-Free: 800-265-2180
www.economicalinsurance.com

Economical Mutual Insurance Company
PO Box 2000
111 Westmount Rd. South
Waterloo, ON N2J 4S4
Tel: 519-570-8200; Fax: 519-570-8389
Toll-Free: 800-265-9996
www.economicalinsurance.com
Classes of Insurance: Auto, Boiler & Machinery, Property, Surety

Elite Insurance Company
2206 Eglinton Ave. East
Toronto, ON M1L 4S8
Tel: 416-288-1800; Fax: 416-288-5888
Toll-Free: 800-387-4518
www.avivacanada.com
Classes of Insurance: Personal Accident & Sickness, Aircraft, Auto, Liability, Boiler & Machinery, Marine, Fidelity, Property, Surety

***L'Entraide assurance, compagnie mutuelle / L'Entraide Assurance Mutual Company**
CP 70226, Québec-Centre Stn. Québec-Centre
520, boul. Charest est, 1er étage
Québec, QC G1K 7P5
Tél: 418-658-0663; Téléc: 418-658-5065
Ligne sans frais: 800-536-8724
service@lentraide.com
www.lentraide.com
Classes of Insurance: Accident, Personal Accident & Sickness, Life, Credit

The Equitable Life Insurance Company of Canada
PO Box 1603, Waterloo Stn. Waterloo
1 Westmount Rd. North
Waterloo, ON N2J 4C7
Tel: 519-886-5110; Fax: 519-883-7400
Toll-Free: 800-265-8878
webmaster@equitable.ca
www.equitable.ca
Other Contact Information: Automated Switchboard: 1-800-722-6615
Social Media: www.facebook.com/EquitableLife;
Classes of Insurance: Life

***Erie Mutual Fire Insurance Company**
711 Main St. East
Dunnville, ON N1A 2W5
Tel: 905-774-8566; Fax: 905-774-6468
Toll-Free: 800-263-6484
eriemutual@eriemutual.com
www.eriemutual.com
Classes of Insurance: Personal Accident & Sickness, Auto, Liability, Boiler & Machinery, Fidelity, Property

Euler Hermes Canada
#1702, 1155, boul. René-Lévesque ouest
Montréal, QC H3B 3Z7
Tel: 514-876-9656; Fax: 514-876-9658
Toll-Free: 877-509-3224
www.eulerhermes.ca
Social Media: twitter.com/ehworldwide
Classes of Insurance: Credit

Everest Insurance Company of Canada / La Compagnie d'assurance Everest du Canada
The Exchange Tower
#2520, 130 King St. West
Toronto, ON M5X 1E3
Tel: 416-862-1228; Fax: 416-366-5899
www.everestre.com
Classes of Insurance: Aircraft, Auto, Liability, Boiler & Machinery, Credit, Marine, Property, Surety, Hail & Crop

Everest Reinsurance Company
The Exchange Tower
#2520, 130 King St. West
Toronto, ON M5X 1E3
Tel: 416-862-1228; Fax: 416-366-5899
www.everestre.com
Classes of Insurance: Personal Accident & Sickness, Aircraft, Auto, Liability, Boiler & Machinery, Credit, Fidelity, Property, Surety, Hail & Crop

***L'Excellence, Compagnie d'assurance-vie / Excellence Life Insurance Company**
#202, 5055, boul. Métropolitain est
Montréal, QC H1R 1Z7
Tel: 514-327-0020; Toll-Free: 800-465-5818
service@excellence.qc.ca
www.excellence.qc.ca
Classes of Insurance: Personal Accident & Sickness, Life

FaithLife Financial
470 Weber St. North
Waterloo, ON N2J 4G4
Tel: 519-886-4610; Fax: 519-886-0350
Toll-Free: 800-563-6237
moreinfo@faithlifefinancial.ca
www.faithlifefinancial.ca
Classes of Insurance: Accident, Personal Accident & Sickness, Life

***Farmers' Mutual Insurance Company (Lindsay)**
PO Box 28
336 Angeline St. South
Lindsay, ON K9V 4R8
Tel: 705-324-2146; Fax: 705-324-3406
Toll-Free: 800-461-0310
www.farmerslindsay.com
Classes of Insurance: Personal Accident & Sickness, Auto, Liability, Boiler & Machinery, Marine, Fidelity, Property

Federal Insurance Company
One Financial Place
1 Adelaide St. East
Toronto, ON M5C 2V9
Tel: 416-863-0550; Fax: 416-863-5010
www.chubb.com/international/canada
Classes of Insurance: Personal Accident & Sickness, Auto, Liability, Boiler & Machinery, Marine, Fidelity, Property, Surety

Federated Insurance Company of Canada
717 Portage Ave.
Winnipeg, MB R3C 3C9
Tel: 204-786-6431; Fax: 204-784-6755
Toll-Free: 800-665-1934
webmaster@federated.ca
www.federated.ca
Other Contact Information: Fax Numbers: 204-783-4443 (3rd Fl.); 204-786-5707 (Claims); 204-784-6762 (Human Resources)
Classes of Insurance: Accident, Auto, Liability, Boiler & Machinery, Fidelity, Property, Fire, Surety, Theft

Federation Insurance Company of Canada/ La Fédération Compagnie d'Assurances du Canada
#1400, 1 Place Ville Marie
Montréal, QC H3B 2B2
Tel: 514-875-5790; Fax: 514-875-9769
Toll-Free: 800-361-7573
www.federation.ca
Classes of Insurance: Accident, Legal Expense, Auto, Liability, Boiler & Machinery, Fidelity, Property, Fire, Surety, Hail & Crop

***Fenchurch General Insurance Company (FGIC)**
Promontory II
#115, 2655 North Sheridan Way
Mississauga, ON L5K 2P8
Tel: 905-822-2282; Fax: 905-822-1282
info@fenchurchgeneral.com
www.fenchurchgeneral.com
Classes of Insurance: Personal Accident & Sickness, Auto, Liability, Boiler & Machinery, Property, Surety

First Canadian Title
2235 Sheridan Garden Dr.
Oakville, ON L6J 7Y5
Tel: 905-287-1000; Fax: 905-287-2400
Toll-Free: 800-307-0370
www.firstcanadiantitle.com

First North American Insurance Company
500 King St. North
Waterloo, ON N2J 4C6
Toll-Free: 800-668-0195
www.manulife.ca
Classes of Insurance: Personal Accident & Sickness, Auto, Property

FM Global
#500, 165 Commerce Valley Dr. West
Thornhill, ON L3T 7V8
Tel: 905-763-5555; Fax: 905-763-5556
www.fmglobal.com
Social Media: www.facebook.com/InsurerFMGlobal; twitter.com/FMGlobal
Classes of Insurance: Boiler & Machinery, Property

FNF Canada
2700 Superior Blvd.
Mississauga, ON L5T 2X9
Tel: 289-562-0088; Fax: 289-562-2494
Toll-Free: 877-526-3232
finance@fnf.ca; marketing@fnf.ca; hr@fnf.ca
www.fnf.ca

***Fonds d'assurance responsabilité professionnelle de la Chambre des notaires du Québec**
#1500, 1200, av. McGill College
Montréal, QC H3B 4G7
Tel: 514-871-4999; Fax: 514-879-1781
www.cdnq.org

***Fonds d'assurance responsabilité professionnelle du Barreau du Québec**
#300, 445, boul. Saint-Laurent
Montréal, QC H2Y 3T8
Tel: 514-954-3452; Fax: 514-954-3454
www.assurance-barreau.com
Other Contact Information: Toll Free: 1-800-361-8495, poste 3452

Foresters Life Insurance Company
#3, 1660 Tech Ave.
Mississauga, ON L4W 5S8
Toll-Free: 800-267-8777
clientservice@foresters.com
www.foresters.com
Social Media: www.youtube.com/user/forestersmembership; www.flickr.com/photos/forestersm; www.facebook.com/Foresters;
Classes of Insurance: Personal Accident & Sickness, Life

***Frank Cowan Company Limited**
75 Main St N
Princeton, ON N0J 1V0
Tel: 519-458-4331; Fax: 519-458-4366
Toll-Free: 800-265-4000
mail@frankcowan.com
www.frankcowan.com
Classes of Insurance: Liability

***Fundy Mutual Insurance Company**
1022 Main St.
Sussex, NB E4E 2M3
Tel: 506-432-1535; Fax: 506-433-6788
Toll-Free: 800-222-9550
info@fundymutual.com
www.fundymutual.com

Classes of Insurance: Auto, Liability, Boiler & Machinery, Property

***G & F Financial Group**
7375 Kingsway
Burnaby, BC V3N 3B5
Tel: 604-517-5100; Fax: 604-659-4025
inquiry@gffg.com
www.gffg.com

GAN Assurances Vie Compagnie française d'assurances vie mixte
c/o Clark & Partners, Attorneys
#1470, 1155, rue Metcalfe
Montréal, QC H3B 2V6
Tel: 514-286-9117; Fax: 514-286-0997
Classes of Insurance: Life

***GCAN Insurance Company (GCAN) / GCAN compagnie d'assurances**
#1000, 181 University Ave.
Toronto, ON M5H 3M7
Tel: 416-682-5300; Fax: 416-682-9213
central.office@gcan.ca
www.gcan.ca
Classes of Insurance: Personal Accident & Sickness, Aircraft, Auto, Liability, Boiler & Machinery, Credit, Marine, Fidelity, Property, Surety, Hail & Crop

General American Life Insurance Company (GALIC)
c/o RGA Life Reinsurance Company of Canada
1981, av McGill College, 13e étage
Montréal, QC H3A 3A8
Tel: 514-985-5260; Fax: 514-985-3066
Toll-Free: 800-985-4326
Classes of Insurance: Life, Reinsurance

General Reinsurance Corporation
PO Box 471
#5705, 1 First Canadian Pl.
Toronto, ON M5X 1E4
Tel: 416-869-0490; Fax: 416-360-2020
AskGenRe@genre.com
www.genre.com
Social Media: twitter.com/Gen_Re
Classes of Insurance: Personal Accident & Sickness, Aircraft, Auto, Liability, Boiler & Machinery, Credit, Fidelity, Property, Surety, Hail & Crop

Genworth Financial Mortgage Insurance Company Canada
#300, 2060 Winston Park Dr.
Oakville, ON L6H 5R7
Toll-Free: 800-511-8888
mortgage.info@genworth.com
www.genworth.ca

Gerber Life Insurance Company
PO Box 986, F Stn. F
50 Charles St. East
Toronto, ON M4Y 2T2
Toll-Free: 800-518-8884
www.gerberlife.ca
Social Media: www.facebook.com/101436288940; twitter.com/gerberlife
Classes of Insurance: Life

***Germania Mutual Insurance Company**
PO Box 30
403 Mary St.
Ayton, ON N0G 1C0
Tel: 519-665-7715; Fax: 519-665-7558
www.germaniamutual.com
Classes of Insurance: Liability, Property, Fire, Theft

***Gibb's Agencies (1997) Ltd.**
Main St.
Barons, AB T0L 0G0
Tel: 403-757-3820; Fax: 403-757-2083
Toll-Free: 888-974-4227
info@gibbsagencies.ca
www.gibbsagencies.ca
Classes of Insurance: Auto, Property

***Glengarry Farmers' Mutual Fire Insurance Co.**
PO Box 159
3720 County Rd. 34
Alexandria, ON K0C 1A0
Tel: 613-525-2557; Fax: 613-525-5162
Toll-Free: 800-263-7684
glenins@glenins.ca
www.glenins.ca
Classes of Insurance: Personal Accident & Sickness, Legal Expense, Auto, Liability, Boiler & Machinery, Fidelity, Property, Fire, Theft

Global Aerospace Underwriting Managers (Canada) Limited
#200, 100 Renfrew Dr.
Markham, ON L3R 9R6
Tel: 905-479-2244; Fax: 905-479-0751
www.global-aero.com/ca
Classes of Insurance: Personal Accident & Sickness, Aircraft, Liability, Property

Gore Mutual Insurance Company
PO Box 70, Galt Stn. Galt
252 Dundas St.
Cambridge, ON N1R 5T3
Tel: 519-623-1910; Toll-Free: 800-265-8600
www.goremutual.ca
Classes of Insurance: Personal Accident & Sickness, Auto, Liability, Property, Fire, Theft

Grain Insurance and Guarantee Company
#1240, 1 Lombard Pl.
Winnipeg, MB R3B 0V9
Tel: 204-943-0721; Fax: 204-943-6419
Toll-Free: 800-665-3351
infowinnipeg@graininsurance.com
www.graininsurance.com
Classes of Insurance: Liability, Boiler & Machinery, Fidelity, Property, Fire, Surety, Theft

The Grand Orange Lodge of British America Benefit Fund
94 Sheppard Ave. West
Toronto, ON M2N 1M5
Tel: 416-223-1690; Fax: 416-223-1324
Toll-Free: 800-565-6248
info@orange.ca
www.orangeinsurance.ca; www.grandorangelodge.ca
Classes of Insurance: Life

Great American Insurance Company
#800, 330 Bay St.
Toronto, ON M5H 2S8
Tel: 416-368-8200
www.greatamericaninsurancegroup.com
Social Media:
www.facebook.com/GreatAmericanInsuranceGroup;
Classes of Insurance: Personal Accident & Sickness, Aircraft, Auto, Liability, Boiler & Machinery, Marine, Fidelity, Property, Surety, Hail & Crop

The Great-West Life Assurance Company (GWL) / Great-West, Compagnie d'Assurance Vie
100 Osborne St. North
Winnipeg, MB R3C 3A5
Tel: 204-946-1190; Fax: 204-946-4159
Toll-Free: 800-665-5758
webmaster@gwl.ca
www.greatwestlife.com; www.grsaccess.com
Other Contact Information: TTY, Toll-Free: 1-800-990-6654
Classes of Insurance: Personal Accident & Sickness, Life

Green Shield Canada
PO Box 1606
8677 Anchor Dr.
Windsor, ON N9A 6W1
Tel: 519-739-1133; Fax: 519-739-0200
Toll-Free: 800-265-5615
www.greenshield.ca
Social Media: www.facebook.com/111841632260596;
www.youtube.com/user/GreenShieldCanada
Classes of Insurance: Personal Accident & Sickness

***Grenville Mutual Insurance Company**
PO Box 10
3005 County Rd. 21
Spencerville, ON K0E 1X0
Tel: 613-658-2013; Fax: 613-658-3374
Toll-Free: 800-267-4400
mail@grenvillemutual.com
www.grenvillemutual.com
Classes of Insurance: Personal Accident & Sickness, Auto, Liability, Boiler & Machinery, Fidelity, Property

***Grey & Bruce Mutual Insurance Co.**
517 - 10th St.
Hanover, ON N4N 1R4
Tel: 519-364-2250; Fax: 519-364-6067
Toll-Free: 800-265-5522
www.greybrucemutualinsurance.com
Classes of Insurance: Personal Accident & Sickness, Auto, Liability, Boiler & Machinery, Property

***Le Groupe Estrie-Richelieu, compagnie d'assurance (GER)**
770, rue Principale
Granby, QC J2G 2Y7
Tél: 450-378-0101; Téléc: 450-378-5189
Ligne sans frais: 800-363-8971
info@ger.qc.ca
www.ger.qc.ca
Classes of Insurance: Auto, Liability, Boiler & Machinery, Property, Fire

*** Groupe Promutuel, Fédération de sociétés mutuelles d'assurance générale**
1091, Grande Allée ouest
Québec, QC G1S 4Y7
Ligne sans frais: 866-999-2433
federation@promutuel.ca
www.promutuel.ca

The Guarantee Company of North America / La Garantie, Compagnie d'Assurance de l'Amérique du Nord
Madison Centre
#1400, 4950 Yonge St.
Toronto, ON M2N 6K1
Tel: 416-223-9580; Fax: 416-223-6577
Toll-Free: 800-260-6617
toronto@gcna.com
www.gcna.com
Classes of Insurance: Accident, Personal Accident & Sickness, Legal Expense, Auto, Liability, Boiler & Machinery, Credit, Fidelity, Property, Fire, Surety, Hail & Crop, Theft

***Halwell Mutual Insurance Company**
PO Box 60
812 Woolwich St.
Guelph, ON N1H 6J6
Tel: 519-836-2860; Fax: 519-836-2831
Toll-Free: 800-267-5706
reception@halwellmutual.com
www.halwellmutual.com
Classes of Insurance: Auto, Liability, Boiler & Machinery, Fidelity, Property

***Hamilton Township Mutual Insurance Company**
PO Box 201
1176 Division St.
Cobourg, ON K9A 4K5
Tel: 905-372-0186; Fax: 905-372-1364
Toll-Free: 800-263-3935
info@htminsurance.ca
www.htminsurance.ca
Classes of Insurance: Marine, Fire

Hannover Rückversicherungs AG
#201, 3650 Victoria Park Ave.
Toronto, ON M2H 3P7
Tel: 416-496-1148; Fax: 416-496-1089
www.hannover-rueck.de
Classes of Insurance: Personal Accident & Sickness, Aircraft, Auto, Liability, Boiler & Machinery, Fidelity, Property, Surety, Hail & Crop

Hartford Fire Insurance Company
PO Box 112
#1810, 121 King St. West
Toronto, ON M5H 3T9
Tel: 416-733-9265; Fax: 416-733-0510
Toll-Free: 888-898-8334
Classes of Insurance: Personal Accident & Sickness, Aircraft, Auto, Liability, Boiler & Machinery, Fidelity, Property, Fire, Surety, Hail & Crop, Theft

***Hay Mutual Insurance Company**
PO Box 130
37868 Zurich-Hensall Rd.
Zurich, ON N0M 2T0
Tel: 519-236-4381; Fax: 519-236-7681
Toll-Free: 877-807-3812
www.haymutual.on.ca
Classes of Insurance: Auto, Liability, Property, Hail & Crop

*** Henderson Insurance Inc.**
339 Main St. North
Moose Jaw, SK S6H 0W2
Tel: 306-694-5959; Fax: 306-693-0117
Toll-Free: 888-661-5959
hii@hendersoninsurance.ca
www.hendersoninsurance.ca
Classes of Insurance: Aircraft, Auto, Liability, Marine, Property, Hail & Crop

***Howard Mutual Insurance Co.**
PO Box 398
20 Ebenezer St. West
Ridgetown, ON N0P 2C0
Tel: 519-674-5434; Fax: 519-674-2029
howardmutual.com
Classes of Insurance: Personal Accident & Sickness, Auto, Liability, Fidelity, Property, Hail & Crop

***Howick Mutual Insurance Company**
PO Box 148
1091 Centre St.
Wroxeter, ON N0G 2X0
Tel: 519-335-3561; Fax: 519-335-6416
Toll-Free: 800-265-3033
kinglis@howickmutual.com
www.howickmutual.com
Classes of Insurance: Personal Accident & Sickness, Auto, Liability, Boiler & Machinery, Fidelity, Property, Hail & Crop

HSB BI&I
#3000, 250 Yonge St.
Toronto, ON M5B 2L7
Tel: 416-363-5491; Fax: 416-363-0538
corporate@biico.com
www.biico.com
Classes of Insurance: Liability, Boiler & Machinery, Property

Independent Order of Foresters
789 Don Mills Rd.
Toronto, ON M3C 1T9
Tel: 416-429-3000; Toll-Free: 800-828-1540
service@foresters.com; humanresources@foresters.com
www.foresters.biz
Other Contact Information: Member Benefits, Toll-Free Phone: 800-444-3043; Unity Life Policy Holders, E-mail: clientservice@unitylife.ca, Toll-Free Phone: 800-267-8777
Social Media: www.facebook.com/Foresters;
Classes of Insurance: Personal Accident & Sickness, Life

***Industrial Alliance Insurance & Financial Services Inc. / Industrielle Alliance Assurance et Services Financiers Inc.**
CP 1907, Terminus Stn. Terminus
1080, Grand Allée ouest
Québec, QC G1K 7M3
Tél: 418-684-5000; Ligne sans frais: 800-463-6236
info@inalco.com; investors@inalco.com;
accident.insurance@inalco.com
www.inalco.com
Other Contact Information: Accident Insurance, Phone: 418-684-5405, Fax: 418-684-5208
Classes of Insurance: Personal Accident & Sickness, Auto, Life, Property

Industrial Alliance Pacific Insurance & Financial Services Inc. (IAP)
PO Box 5900
2165 West Broadway
Vancouver, BC V6B 5H6
Tel: 604-734-1667; Fax: 604-734-8221
Toll-Free: 800-363-2166
intouch@iapacific.com
www.iaplife.com
Classes of Insurance: Accident, Personal Accident & Sickness, Life, Credit

***Innovative Insurance Agencies**
6351 Rideau Valley Dr. North
Ottawa, ON K4M 1B3
Fax: 613-692-0338
Toll-Free: 800-265-4275
info@innovativeinsurance.ca
www.innovativeinsurance.ca

***Insurance Company of Prince Edward Island**
14 Great George St.
Charlottetown, PE C1A 4J6
Tel: 902-368-3675; Fax: 902-626-3529
inquiries@icpei.ca
www.icpei.ca
Classes of Insurance: Auto, Life, Property

***Insurance Corporation of British Columbia (ICBC)**
151 West Esplanade
North Vancouver, BC V7M 3H9
Tel: 604-661-2800; Fax: 604-646-7400
Toll-Free: 800-663-3051
www.icbc.com
Classes of Insurance: Auto

Intact Insurance Company of Canada
700 University Ave., 15th Fl.
Toronto, ON M5G 0A1
Tel: 416-341-1464; Fax: 416-344-8030
Toll-Free: 877-341-1464
info@intact.net
www.intactinsurance.com
Classes of Insurance: Marine, Surety

JEVCO Insurance Company / La Compagnie d'Assurances JEVCO
#100, 5250, boul Décarie
Montréal, QC H3X 2H9
Tel: 514-284-9350; Fax: 514-289-9257
Toll-Free: 800-361-8500
www.jevco.ca
Other Contact Information: 24-Hour Toll-Free Claims Line: 1-866-864-1112
Classes of Insurance: Auto, Property

***Johnston Meier Insurance Agencies Group**
22367 Dewdney Trunk Road
Maple Ridge, BC V2X 3J4
Tel: 604-467-4184; Fax: 604-467-9711
Toll-Free: 888-256-4564
info@jmins.com
www.jmins.com
Classes of Insurance: Aircraft, Auto, Life, Marine, Surety

***Kent & Essex Mutual Insurance Company**
PO Box 356
10 Creek Rd.
Chatham, ON N7M 5K4
Tel: 519-352-3190; Fax: 519-352-5344
Toll-Free: 800-265-5206
info@kentesexmutual.com
www.kentessexmutual.com
Classes of Insurance: Personal Accident & Sickness, Auto, Liability, Boiler & Machinery, Fidelity, Property

The Kings Mutual Insurance Company
220 Commercial St.
Berwick, NS B0P 1E0
Tel: 902-538-3187; Fax: 902-538-7271
Toll-Free: 800-565-7220
info@kingsmutual.ns.ca
www.kingsmutual.ns.ca
Classes of Insurance: Liability, Property, Fire

Kingsway Financial Services Inc.
#400, 45 St. Clair Ave. West
Toronto, ON M4V 1K9
Tel: 416-848-1171; Fax: 416-850-5439
ir@kingsway-financial.com
www.kingsway-financial.com
Classes of Insurance: Auto, Property, Reinsurance

***Kingsway General Insurance Company**
#700, 7120 Hurontario St.
Mississauga, ON L5W 0B1
Tel: 905-677-8889; Fax: 905-677-5008
Toll-Free: 800-265-5458
kgmarketing@kingsway-general.com
www.kingsway-general.com
Classes of Insurance: Auto, Liability, Property, Surety

Kirkham Insurance
205 - 11th St. South
Lethbridge, AB T1J 4A6
Tel: 403-328-1228; Fax: 403-380-4051
Toll-Free: 800-256-2155
www.kirkhaminsurance.com
Classes of Insurance: Auto, Property

Knights of Columbus Insurance
c/o The Raymond Richer Agency
26 Davis Court
Hampton, ON L0B 1J0
Tel: 905-263-4212
www.kofc.org
Classes of Insurance: Life

***Lambton Mutual Insurance Company**
PO Box 520
7873 Confederation Line
Watford, ON N0M 2S0
Tel: 519-876-2304; Fax: 519-876-3940
Toll-Free: 800-561-4136
info@lambtonmutual.com
www.lambtonmutual.com
Classes of Insurance: Personal Accident & Sickness, Auto, Liability, Boiler & Machinery, Fidelity, Property, Hail & Crop

***Lanark Mutual Insurance Company**
96 South St., Scotch Line Rd.
Perth, ON K7H 0A2
Tel: 613-267-5554; Fax: 613-267-6793
Toll-Free: 800-267-7908
lmadmin@LanarkMutual.com; privacy@lanarkmutual.com
www.lanarkmutual.com
Classes of Insurance: Auto, Liability, Boiler & Machinery, Property, Hail & Crop, Theft

Lawyers' Professional Indemnity Company (LAWPRO)
PO Box 3
#3101, 250 Yonge St.
Toronto, ON M5B 2L7
Tel: 416-598-5800; Fax: 416-599-8341
Toll-Free: 800-410-1013
service@lawpro.ca
www.lawpro.ca
Social Media: twitter.com/LAWPRO
Classes of Insurance: Liability

Legacy General Insurance Company / Compagnie d'Assurances Générales Legacy
80 Tiverton Ct., 5th Fl.
Markham, ON L3R 0G4
Tel: 905-479-7500; Fax: 905-479-3224
www.canadianpremier.ca
Other Contact Information: Privacy Officer: 1-888-968-4155.
Classes of Insurance: Personal Accident & Sickness, Liability, Property

***Lennox & Addington Mutual Insurance Company**
PO Box 174
32 Mill St.
Napanee, ON K7R 3M3
Tel: 613-354-4810; Fax: 613-354-7112
Toll-Free: 800-267-7812
www.l-amutual.com
Classes of Insurance: Personal Accident & Sickness, Auto, Liability, Marine, Property

Liberty Mutual Insurance Company/ La Compagnie d'Assurance Liberté Mutuelle
Brookfield Place
#1000, 181 Bay St.
Toronto, ON M5J 2T3
Tel: 416-307-4353; Fax: 416-365-7281
www.libertymutual.com
Social Media: www.facebook.com/libertymutual; twitter.com/libertymutual
Classes of Insurance: Personal Accident & Sickness, Aircraft, Auto, Liability, Boiler & Machinery, Fidelity, Property, Surety

Life Insurance Company of North America (LINA)
#606, 55 Town Centre Ct.
Toronto, ON M1P 4X4
Tel: 416-290-6666; Fax: 416-290-0726
www.cigna.com
Classes of Insurance: Accident, Personal Accident & Sickness, Life

Lloyd's Underwriters
#2220, 1155, rue Metcalfe
Montréal, QC H3B 2V6
Tel: 514-861-8361; Fax: 514-861-0470
Toll-Free: 877-455-6937
info@lloyds.ca; lineage@lloyds.ca (commercial use)
www.lloyds.com
Other Contact Information: Commercial Inquiries, Phone: 514-864-5444
Classes of Insurance: Personal Accident & Sickness, Aircraft, Legal Expense, Auto, Liability, Boiler & Machinery, Fidelity, Property, Fire, Surety, Reinsurance

London Life Insurance Company / London Life, Compagnie d'Assurance-Vie
255 Dufferin Ave.
London, ON N6A 4K1
Tel: 519-432-5281
www.londonlife.com
Other Contact Information: TTY: 1-800-990-6654
Classes of Insurance: Personal Accident & Sickness, Life, Reinsurance

***The Loyalist Insurance Company**
#107, 911 Golf Links Rd.
Ancaster, ON L9K 1H9
Tel: 905-648-6767; Fax: 905-648-7220
info@loyalistinsurance.com
www.loyalistinsurance.com

Lumbermen's Underwriting Alliance
#300, 455, boul. Fénelon
Montréal, QC H9S 5T8
Toll-Free: 888-582-1905
www.lumbermensunderwriting.com
Classes of Insurance: Boiler & Machinery, Property

*** Manitoba Agricultural Services Corporation - Insurance Corporate Office (MASC)**
#400, 50 - 24th St. NW
Portage La Prairie, MB R1N 3V9
Tel: 204-239-3246; Fax: 204-239-3401
mailbox@masc.mb.ca
www.masc.mb.ca
Classes of Insurance: Hail & Crop

***Manitoba Blue Cross**
PO Box 1046
599 Empress St.
Winnipeg, MB R3C 2X7
Tel: 204-775-0151; Fax: 204-786-5965
Toll-Free: 888-873-2583
www.mb.bluecross.ca
Classes of Insurance: Personal Accident & Sickness, Life

***Manitoba Public Insurance**
PO Box 6300
Winnipeg, MB R3C 4A4
Tel: 204-985-7000; Toll-Free: 800-665-2410
www.mpi.mb.ca
Other Contact Information: TTY: 204-985-8832
Classes of Insurance: Auto

Manufacturers Life Insurance Company / La Compagnie d'Assurance-Vie Manufacturers
PO Box 1669
500 King St. North
Waterloo, ON N2J 4Z6
Toll-Free: 888-626-8543
valued_customer_centre@manulife.com
www.manulife.ca
Other Contact Information: Quebec Toll-Free: 1-888-626-8843
Classes of Insurance: Personal Accident & Sickness, Life

Manulife Canada Ltd./ Manuvie Canada Ltée
PO Box 1669
500 King St. North
Waterloo, ON N2J 4Z6
Toll-Free: 888-626-8543
valued_customer_centre@manulife.com
www.manulife.ca
Classes of Insurance: Life

Manulife Financial
500 King St. North
Waterloo, ON N2J 4C6
Toll-Free: 888-626-8543
www.manulife.ca
Other Contact Information: Québec, Toll-Free: 1-888-626-8843
Social Media: www.facebook.com/ManulifeFinancial;
Classes of Insurance: Life

Massachusetts Mutual Life Insurance Company
c/o Cassels Brock & Blackwell LLP, Scotia Plaza
#2100, 40 King St. West
Toronto, ON M5H 3C2
Tel: 416-869-5745; Fax: 416-350-6955
www.massmutual.com
Social Media: www.youtube.com/massmutual; www.facebook.com/massmutual; twitter.com/massmutual
Classes of Insurance: Personal Accident & Sickness, Life

***MAX Canada Insurance Company**
140 Foundry St.
Baden, ON N3A 2P7
Fax: 519-634-5159
Toll-Free: 877-770-7729
www.mutualaidexchange.com
Classes of Insurance: Liability, Boiler & Machinery, Marine, Fidelity, Property

McFarlane & Company Financial Group Limited
#430, 999 - 8th St. SW
Calgary, AB T2R 1J5
Tel: 403-229-0466; Fax: 403-228-9784
Toll-Free: 888-224-0466
info@mcfarlaneco.com
www.mcfarlaneco.com
Classes of Insurance: Auto, Liability, Life, Property, Surety, Hail & Crop

***McKillop Mutual Insurance Company**
PO Box 819
91 Main St. South
Seaforth, ON N0K 1W0
Tel: 519-527-0400; Fax: 519-527-2777
Toll-Free: 800-463-9204
mckillo@tcc.on.ca
www.mckillopmutual.com
Classes of Insurance: Personal Accident & Sickness, Auto, Liability, Boiler & Machinery, Fidelity, Property

MD Life Insurance Company
1870 Alta Vista Dr.
Ottawa, ON K1G 6R7
Classes of Insurance: Life

***Medavie Blue Cross**
PO Box 220
644 Main St.
Moncton, NB E1C 8L3
Tel: 506-853-1811; Fax: 506-867-4651
Toll-Free: 800-667-4511
www.medavie.bluecross.ca
Other Contact Information: Group Benefits, Atlantic Provinces & Ontario: 1-888-227-3400; Group Benefits, Québec: 1-888-588-1212
Classes of Insurance: Personal Accident & Sickness, Life

Meloche Monnex Inc.
50, Place Crémazie, 12e étage
Montréal, QC H2P 1B6
Toll-Free: 800-361-3821
www.melochemonnex.com
Other Contact Information: Claims, Toll-Free: 1-877-323-0343

***Mennonite Mutual Fire Insurance Company**
PO Box 190
Waldheim, SK S0K 4R0
Tel: 306-945-2239; Fax: 306-945-4666
mmfi@sasktel.net
www.mmfi.com
Classes of Insurance: Boiler & Machinery, Property, Fire, Theft

***Mennonite Mutual Insurance Co. (Alberta) Ltd. (MMI)**
#300, 2946 - 32nd St. NE
Calgary, AB T1Y 6J7
Tel: 403-275-6996; Fax: 403-291-6733
Toll-Free: 866-222-6996
office@mmiab.ca
www.mmiab.ca
Classes of Insurance: Auto, Liability, Property, Fire

***Metro General Insurance Corp.**
T.D. Place
PO Box 548
#700, 140 Water St.
St. John's, NL A1C 5K9
Tel: 709-726-1922; Fax: 709-726-5207
Classes of Insurance: Auto, Liability, Property

Middlesex Mutual Insurance Co.
PO Box 100
13271 Ilderton Rd.
Ilderton, ON N0M 2A0
Tel: 519-666-0075; Fax: 519-666-0079
Toll-Free: 800-851-4045
mmic@middlesexmutual.on.ca
www.middlesexmutual.on.ca
Classes of Insurance: Auto, Liability, Property

Millennium Insurance Corporation
340 Sioux Rd.
Sherwood Park, AB T8A 3X6
Tel: 780-467-1500; Fax: 780-467-0004
Toll-Free: 866-467-1245
info@millenniuminsurance.ca
www.directinsure.net
Classes of Insurance: Auto, Property

Mitsui Sumitomo Insurance Co., Limited. (MS&AD)
Chubb Insurance Company of Canada, One Financial Place
1 Adelaide St. East, 24th Fl.
Toronto, ON M5C 2V9
Tel: 416-863-0550; Fax: 416-863-5010
www.ms-ins.com/english/index.html
Classes of Insurance: Personal Accident & Sickness, Aircraft, Auto, Liability, Boiler & Machinery, Fidelity, Property, Surety

Motors Insurance Corporation
#400, 8500 Leslie St.
Thornhill, ON L3T 7M8
Toll-Free: 800-387-8095
www.gm.ca/gm/english/services/insurance/quote
Classes of Insurance: Auto, Liability, Boiler & Machinery

***Mouvement des caisses Desjardins du Québec**
100, av. des Commandeurs
Lévis, QC G6V 7N5
Tél: 418-835-8444; Téléc: 418-833-5873
www.desjardins.com

Munich Reinsurance Company - Canada Life
Munich Re Centre
390 Bay St., 26th Fl.
Toronto, ON M5H 2Y2
Tel: 416-359-2200; Fax: 416-361-0305
generalenquiries@munichre.ca
www.munichre.ca
Classes of Insurance: Personal Accident & Sickness, Life, Reinsurance

Munich Reinsurance Company of Canada
#2200, 390 Bay St.
Toronto, ON M5H 2Y2
Tel: 416-366-9206; Fax: 416-366-4330
Toll-Free: 800-444-5321
info@mroc.com
www.mroc.com
Social Media: www.facebook.com/pages/Munich-Re/112684192080056; twitter.com/munichre
Classes of Insurance: Auto, Liability, Property, Theft

***Municipal Insurance Association of British Columbia (MIA)**
#390, 1050 Homer St.
Vancouver, BC V6E 2W9
Tel: 604-683-6266; Fax: 604-683-6244
Toll-Free: 855-683-6266
info@miabc.org
www.miabc.org
Classes of Insurance: Liability

***MUNIX Reciprocal (MUNIX)**
300-8616 51 Ave.
Edmonton, AB T6E 6E6
Tel: 780-433-4431; Fax: 780-409-4314
www.auma.ca
Classes of Insurance: Liability, Property

***The Mutual Fire Insurance Company of British Columbia**
#201, 9366 - 200A St.
Langley, BC V1M 4B3
Tel: 604-881-1250; Fax: 604-881-1440
Toll-Free: 866-417-2272
info@mutualfirebc.com
www.mutualfirebc.com
Classes of Insurance: Property, Fire

***La Mutuelle d'Église de l'Inter-ouest**
180, boul. du Mont-Bleu
Gatineau, QC J8Z 3J5
Tel: 819-595-2678;

The Nordic Insurance Company of Canada
#1500A, 700 University Ave.
Toronto, ON M5G 0A1
Fax: 416-344-8011
Toll-Free: 866-302-5094
Classes of Insurance: Accident, Legal Expense, Auto, Liability, Boiler & Machinery, Fidelity, Property, Surety

***Norfolk Mutual Insurance Company**
PO Box 515
33 Park Rd.
Simcoe, ON N3Y 4L5
Tel: 519-426-1294; Fax: 519-426-7594
Toll-Free: 800-304-5573
info@norfolkmutual.com
www.norfolkmutualinsco.on.ca
Classes of Insurance: Auto, Property, Fire

***North Bleinheim Mutual Insurance Co.**
11 Baird St. North
Bright, ON N0J 1B0
Tel: 519-454-8661; Fax: 519-454-8785
Toll-Free: 800-665-6888
info@northblenheim.ca
www.northblenheim.ca
Classes of Insurance: Auto, Liability, Property

North Blenheim Mutual Insurance Company
11 Baird St. North
Bright, ON N0J 1B0
Tel: 519-454-8661; Fax: 519-454-8785
Toll-Free: 800-665-6888
info@northblenheim.com
www.northblenheim.ca
Classes of Insurance: Auto, Liability, Property

***North Kent Mutual Fire Insurance Company**
PO Box 478
29553 St. George St.
Dresden, ON N0P 1M0
Tel: 519-683-4484; Fax: 519-683-4509
Toll-Free: 888-736-4705
nkm@northkentmutual.com
www.nkmutual.com
Classes of Insurance: Auto, Liability, Property, Fire, Hail & Crop, Theft

The North Waterloo Farmers Mutual Insurance Company
100 Erb St. East
Waterloo, ON N2J 1L9
Tel: 519-886-4530; Fax: 519-746-0222
Toll-Free: 800-265-8813
insurance@nwfm.com; claims@nwfm.com
www.nwfm.com
Other Contact Information: Claims Fax: 519-746-0805
Classes of Insurance: Auto, Liability, Boiler & Machinery, Fidelity, Property, Fire, Hail & Crop

The North West Commercial Travellers' Association of Canada (NWCTA)
PO Box 336
28 Queen Elizabeth Way
Winnipeg, MB R3C 2H6
Tel: 204-284-8900; Fax: 204-284-8909
Toll-Free: 800-665-6928
nwcta@nwcta.com
www.nwcta.com
Classes of Insurance: Life

Northbridge Insurance
#700, 105 Adelaide St. West
Toronto, ON M5H 1P9
Tel: 416-350-4400; Toll-Free: 855-620-6262
info@nbfc.com
www.nbfc.com/northbridgeinsurance
Classes of Insurance: Accident, Auto, Liability, Marine, Property, Hail & Crop

Novex Group Insurance / ING Novex Compagnie d'Assurance du Canada
700 University Ave., 15th Fl.
Toronto, ON M5G 0A1
Tel: 416-341-1464; Fax: 416-344-8030
Toll-Free: 877-341-1464
info@intact.net
www.intactinsurance.com
Classes of Insurance: Personal Accident & Sickness, Legal Expense, Auto, Liability, Boiler & Machinery, Credit, Fidelity, Property, Surety

OdysseyRe - Canadian Branch
#1600, 55 University Ave.
Toronto, ON M5J 2H7
Tel: 416-862-0162; Fax: 416-367-3248
www.odysseyre.com
Classes of Insurance: Accident, Aircraft, Auto, Liability, Boiler & Machinery, Property, Fire, Surety, Hail & Crop, Reinsurance

Old Republic Insurance Company of Canada / L'Ancienne République, Compagnie d'Assurance du Ca
PO Box 557
100 King St. West
Hamilton, ON L8N 3K9
Tel: 905-523-5936; Fax: 905-523-1471
Toll-Free: 800-530-5446
service@orican.com
www.orican.com
Classes of Insurance: Accident, Aircraft, Auto, Liability, Property, Reinsurance

***Omega General Insurance Company**
#500, 36 King St. East
Toronto, ON M5C 1E5
Tel: 416-361-1728; Fax: 416-361-6113
contactus@omegageneral.com
www.omegageneral.com
Classes of Insurance: Personal Accident & Sickness, Aircraft, Legal Expense, Liability, Boiler & Machinery, Credit, Fidelity, Property, Surety

***Ontario Blue Cross**
#610, 185 The West Mall
Toronto, ON M9C 5P1
Tel: 416-626-1447; Fax: 416-626-0997
Toll-Free: 866-732-2583
bco.indhealth@ont.bluecross.ca
www.useblue.com
Classes of Insurance: Personal Accident & Sickness

***Ontario Mutual Insurance Association**
350 Pinebush Rd.
Cambridge, ON N1T 1Z6
Tel: 519-622-9220; Fax: 519-622-9227
information@omia.com
www.omia.com
Classes of Insurance: Personal Accident & Sickness, Auto, Property

***Ontario School Boards' Insurance Exchange (OSBIE)**
91 Westmount Rd.
Guelph, ON N1H 5J2
Tel: 519-767-2182; Fax: 519-767-0281
Toll-Free: 800-668-6724
info@osbie.on.ca
www.osbie.on.ca
Classes of Insurance: Auto, Liability, Boiler & Machinery, Property, Fire

***Optimum Assurance Agricole inc / Optimum Farm Insurance Inc.**
#422, 25 rue des Forges
Trois-Rivières, QC G9A 6A7
Tél: 819-373-2040; Téléc: 819-373-2801
ogi-troisrivieres-communication@optimum-general.com
www.optimum-general. com/en/oaa.home.shtml
Classes of Insurance: Auto, Property, Fire

Optimum Général inc / Optimum General Inc.
#1500, 425, boul de Maisonneuve ouest
Montréal, QC H3A 3G5
Tél: 514-288-8725; Téléc: 514-288-0760
www.optimum-general.com
Classes of Insurance: Auto, Liability, Property

*** Optimum Réassurance inc / Optimum Reassurance Inc.**
#1200, 425, boul. de Maisonneuve ouest
Montréal, QC H3A 3G5
Tél: 514-288-1900; Téléc: 514-288-8099
www.optimumre.ca
Classes of Insurance: Accident, Personal Accident & Sickness, Life, Reinsurance

***Optimum Société d'Assurance inc (OSA) / Optimum Insurance Company Inc.**
#1500, 425, boul. de Maisonneuve ouest
Montréal, QC H3A 3G5
Tél: 514-288-8711; Téléc: 514-288-8269
www.optimum-general.com/en/osa.home.shtml
Classes of Insurance: Auto, Liability, Property

***Optimum West Insurance Company**
#600, 4211 Kingsway
Burnaby, BC V5H 1Z6
Tel: 604-688-1541; Fax: 604-688-1527
ogi-vancouver-communication@optimum-general.com
www.optimum-general.com/ en/owic.home.shtml
Classes of Insurance: Auto, Property, Hail & Crop

The Order of United Commercial Travelers of America (UCT)
#300, 901 Centre St. North
Calgary, AB T2E 2P6
Tel: 403-277-0745; Fax: 403-277-6662
Toll-Free: 800-267-2371
www.uct.org
Classes of Insurance: Personal Accident & Sickness, Life

***Ordre des Architectes du Québec**
1825, boul. René-Lévesque ouest
Montréal, QC H3H 1R4
Tel: 514-937-6168; Fax: 514-933-0242
Toll-Free: 800-599-6168
info@oaq.com
www.oaq.com

***Ordre des dentistes du Québec**
625, boul. René-Lévesque ouest, 15e étage
Montréal, QC H3B 1R2
Tel: 514-875-8511; Fax: 514-393-9248
Toll-Free: 800-361-4887
www.odq.qc.ca

***Oxford Mutual Insurance Company**
PO Box 430, RR 4 Stn. RR 4
682794 Road 68
Thamesford, ON N0M 2M0
Tel: 519-285-2916; Fax: 519-285-3099
Toll-Free: 800-461-6933
mail@oxfordmutual.com
www.oxfordmutual.com
Classes of Insurance: Personal Accident & Sickness, Aircraft, Auto, Liability, Boiler & Machinery, Fidelity, Property, Hail & Crop

***Pacific Blue Cross**
PO Box 7000
4250 Canada Way
Vancouver, BC V6B 4E1
Tel: 604-419-2000; Fax: 604-419-2990
Toll-Free: 888-275-4672
www.pac.bluecross.ca
Classes of Insurance: Accident, Personal Accident & Sickness, Life

***Pacific Coast Fishermen's Mutual Marine Insurance Company**
3757 Canada Way
Burnaby, BC V5G 1G5
Tel: 604-438-4240; Fax: 604-438-5756
Toll-Free: 888-438-4242
info@mutualmarine.bc.ca
www.mutualmarine.bc.ca
Other Contact Information: Toll Free (BC only): 1-888-438-4242
Classes of Insurance: Marine

*** Pafco Insurance Company**
#100, 27 Allstate Pkwy.
Markham, ON L3R 5P8
Tel: 905-513-4000; Fax: 905-513-4026
Toll-Free: 877-216-6973
contactus@pafco.ca
www.pafco.ca
Classes of Insurance: Auto

***Palliser Insurance Company Limited**
PO Box 1358
Saskatoon, SK S7H 3N9
Tel: 306-955-4814; Fax: 306-955-1317
info@palliserinsurance.com
www.palliserinsurance.com
Classes of Insurance: Hail & Crop

PartnerRe SA
#909, 123 Front St. West
Toronto, ON M5J 2M2
Tel: 416-861-0033; Fax: 416-861-0200
www.partnerre.com
Classes of Insurance: Personal Accident & Sickness, Auto, Life, Property

PC Financial Insurance Agency
PO Box 483, A Stn. A
Windsor, ON N9A 9Z9
Toll-Free: 877-251-8652
talktous@homeauto.pcinsurance.ca
www.pcinsurance.ca
Other Contact Information: 1-877-251-8656 (Claims)
Classes of Insurance: Auto, Property

***Peace Hills General Insurance Company**
#300, 10709 Jasper Ave., 3rd Fl.
Edmonton, AB T5J 3N3
Tel: 780-424-3986; Fax: 780-424-0396
Toll-Free: 800-272-5614
phi@peacehillsinsurance.com
www.peacehillsinsurance.com
Classes of Insurance: Accident, Aircraft, Auto, Liability, Boiler & Machinery, Credit, Marine, Fidelity, Property, Fire, Surety, Theft

***Peel Maryborough Mutual Insurance Company**
PO Box 190
103 Wellington St.
Drayton, ON N0G 1P0
Tel: 519-638-3304; Fax: 519-638-3521
Toll-Free: 800-265-2473
pmmutual@pmmutual.on.ca
www.pmmutual.on.ca

***Peel Mutual Insurance Company**
103 Queen St. West
Brampton, ON L6Y 1M3
Tel: 905-451-2386; Toll-Free: 800-268-3069
info@peelmutual.com
www.peelmutual.com
Classes of Insurance: Auto, Liability, Boiler & Machinery, Fidelity, Property

***Pembridge Insurance Company**
#100, 27 Allstate Pkwy.
Markham, ON L3R 5P8
Tel: 905-513-4013; Fax: 905-513-4020
Toll-Free: 877-736-2743
contactus@pembridge.com
www.pembridge.com
Classes of Insurance: Accident, Marine, Property

Penncorp Life Insurance Company
7150 Derrycrest Dr.
Mississauga, ON L5W 0E5
Fax: 905-795-2316
Toll-Free: 800-268-2835
cs@penncorp.ca
www.penncorp.ca
Social Media: www.facebook.com/240931435964392;
Classes of Insurance: Personal Accident & Sickness, Life

***The Personal General Insurance Inc. / La Personnelle, assurances générales inc.**
PO Box 3500
6300, boul. de la Rive-Sud
Lévis, QC G6V 6P9
Tel: 418-835-9040; Fax: 418-835-5599
Toll-Free: 800-463-6416
info@lapersonnelle.com
www.lapersonnelle.com
Classes of Insurance: Auto, Liability, Boiler & Machinery, Property, Surety

The Personal Insurance Company / La Personnelle, compagnie d'assurances
PO Box 3500
6300, boul. de la Rive-Sud
Lévis, QC G6V 6P9
Toll-Free: 800-704-8980
www.thepersonal.com
Other Contact Information: 24/7 Claims Line, Toll-Free: 1-866-776-8343, TTY: 1-800-567-3232; Insurance Advice, Toll-Free: 1-888-476-8737.
Classes of Insurance: Personal Accident & Sickness, Aircraft, Auto, Liability, Boiler & Machinery, Fidelity, Property, Surety

Perth Insurance Company
#1500, 5255 Yonge St.
Toronto, ON M2N 6P4
Fax: 416-590-0556
Toll-Free: 888-307-3784
www.economicalinsurance.com
Other Contact Information: Service Centre, Toll-Free: 1-877-717-2233
Classes of Insurance: Auto, Property

Pictou Mutual Insurance Company
PO Box 130
368 Faulkland St.
Pictou, NS B0K 1H0
Tel: 902-485-4542; Fax: 902-485-5136
Toll-Free: 888-485-4542
info@pictoumutual.com
www.pictoumutual.com
Classes of Insurance: Liability, Property

*** Pilot Insurance Company**
2206 Eglinton Ave. East
Toronto, ON M1L 4S8
Tel: 416-288-1800; Fax: 416-288-5888
Toll-Free: 800-387-4518
www.avivacanada.com
Other Contact Information: Claims: 866-692-8482
Classes of Insurance: Auto, Property

*** The PMI Group, Inc. Canada**
520 Coronation Dr.
Toronto, ON M1E 5C7
Tel: 416-286-2176
www.pmicgroupinc.ca
Classes of Insurance: Credit

The Portage La Prairie Mutual Insurance Company
PO Box 340
749 Saskatchewan Ave. East
Portage La Prairie, MB R1N 3B8
Tel: 204-857-3415; Fax: 204-239-6655
Toll-Free: 800-567-7721
info@portagemutual.com
www.portagemutual.com
Other Contact Information: Claims Toll-Free Fax: 1-866-345-1770
Classes of Insurance: Legal Expense, Auto, Liability, Property

PPI
#1200, 2235 Sheppard Ave. East
Toronto, ON M2J 5B5
Tel: 416-494-7707; Fax: 416-494-0067
Toll-Free: 888-887-3892
www.ppi.ca
Classes of Insurance: Life

PPI Advisory
#1200, 2235 Sheppard Ave. East
Toronto, ON M2J 5B5
Tel: 416-494-7707; Fax: 416-494-0067
Toll-Free: 888-887-3892
www.ppiadvisory.ca
Classes of Insurance: Life

PPI Solutions
#1200, 235 Yorkland Blvd.
Toronto, ON M2J 4Y8
Tel: 647-497-9000; Fax: 416-495-7611
Toll-Free: 800-247-1312
www.ppisolutions.ca
Classes of Insurance: Life

***Premier Marine Insurance Managers Group**
#650, 625 Howe St.
Vancouver, BC V6C 2T6
Tel: 604-669-5211; Fax: 604-669-2667
www.premiermarine.com
Classes of Insurance: Liability, Marine, Property

Primerica Life Insurance Company of Canada
Plaza 5
#300, 2000 Argentia Rd.
Mississauga, ON L5N 2R7
Tel: 905-812-2900; Fax: 905-813-5310
www.primericacanada.ca
Social Media: plus.google.com/109104859117861437180; www.facebook.com/Primerica; twitter.com/primerica
Classes of Insurance: Personal Accident & Sickness, Life

Primmum Insurance Company
#400, 304 The East Mall
Toronto, ON M9B 6E2
Tel: 416-233-7590; Fax: 416-233-9171
Toll-Free: 1-866-466-5276
www.primmum.com
Other Contact Information: Toll-Free Phone, Quotes: 1-800-816-9618; Toll-Free Phone, Claims: 1-866-725-9722; Toll-Free Phone, Calgary, Edmonton, & Halifax: 1-800-268-8955
Classes of Insurance: Auto, Property

***Prince Edward Island Mutual Insurance Company**
201 Water St.
Summerside, PE C1N 1B4
Tel: 902-436-2185; Fax: 902-436-0148
Toll-Free: 800-565-5441
protect@peimutual.com
www.peimutual.com
Classes of Insurance: Liability, Property, Fire, Theft

Principal Life Insurance Company / Compagnie d'assurance-vie Principal
c/o John Milnes & Associates
1300 Bay St., 4th Fl.
Toronto, ON M5R 3K8
Tel: 416-964-0067; Fax: 416-964-3338
www.principal.com
Social Media: www.facebook.com/PrincipalFinancial; twitter.com/ThePrincipal
Classes of Insurance: Personal Accident & Sickness, Life

Progressive Casualty Insurance Company
#200, 5700 Yonge St.
Toronto, ON M2M 4K2
Tel: 416-499-6599; Fax: 416-499-7478
www.progressive.com
Social Media: www.youtube.com/progressive; plus.google.com/104375753734524612611; www.facebook.com/progressive; twitter.com/progressive
Classes of Insurance: Auto, Liability, Property, Surety

*** Promutuel Réassurance**
2000, boul. Lebourgneuf, bur.400
Québec, QC G2K 0B6
Toll-Free: 866-999-2433
federation@promutuel.ca
www.promutuel.ca
Classes of Insurance: Accident, Liability, Boiler & Machinery, Property, Fire, Surety, Theft, Reinsurance

***Promutuel Vie inc**
1091, Grande Allée ouest
Québec, QC G1S 4Y7
Tel: 418-683-1212; Fax: 418-683-2559
federation@promutuel.ca
www.promutuel.ca
Classes of Insurance: Accident, Personal Accident & Sickness, Life

Protective Insurance Company
c/o Lyndon-DFS Administrative Services Inc.
#544, 1600, boul Henri-Bourassa ouest
Toronto, ON H3M 3E2
Toll-Free: 800-838-7354
www.protective.com
Classes of Insurance: Auto, Property

***Québec Blue Cross / Croix Bleue du Québec**
#B9, 550, rue Sherbrooke ouest
Montréal, QC H3C 3S3
Tel: 514-286-8403; Fax: 514-286-8358
Toll-Free: 877-909-7686
info@qc.bluecross.ca, info@qc.croixbleue.ca
www.qc.bluecross.ca, www.qc.croixbleue.ca
Classes of Insurance: Accident, Personal Accident & Sickness, Auto, Liability, Life

***Rain and Hail Insurance Corporation**
#200, 4303 Albert St.
Regina, SK S4S 3R6
Tel: 306-584-8844; Fax: 306-584-3466
Toll-Free: 800-667-8084
regina@rainhail.com
www.rainhail.com/about/canada.htm
Classes of Insurance: Hail & Crop

RBC General Insurance Company/ Compagnie d'assurance generale RBC
6880 Financial Dr.
Mississauga, ON L5N 7Y5
Tel: 905-286-5099; Toll-Free: 800-769-2526
www.rbcinsurance.com
Classes of Insurance: Personal Accident & Sickness, Auto, Liability, Property, Fire, Theft

RBC Insurance
Tower 1
6880 Financial Dr.
Mississauga, ON L5N 7Y5
Tel: 905-949-3663; Fax: 905-813-4853
Toll-Free: 877-749-7224
www.rbcinsurance.com
Social Media: www.facebook.com/15957114910;
Classes of Insurance: Personal Accident & Sickness, Auto, Life, Property

RBC Life Insurance Company
West Tower
6880 Financial Dr.
Mississauga, ON L5N 7Y5
Tel: 905-286-5099; Toll-Free: 877-519-9501
www.rbcinsurance.com
Other Contact Information: 866-223-7113 (Toll Free, New Life Insurance Inquiries); 800-461-1413 (Toll Free, Existing Life Insurance Inquiries)
Classes of Insurance: Personal Accident & Sickness, Life

RBC Travel Insurance Company
West Tower
6880 Financial Dr., 5th Fl.
Mississauga, ON L5N 7Y5
Tel: 905-816-2561; Fax: 905-813-4719
www.rbcinsurance.com/travelinsurance/index.html
Other Contact Information: Toll Free, Trip Cancellation Insurance Claim: 800-263-8944
Classes of Insurance: Personal Accident & Sickness, Life

***Real Estate Insurance Exchange (REIX)**
#205, 4954 Richard Rd. SW
Calgary, AB T3E 6L1
Tel: 403-228-2667; Fax: 403-229-3466
Toll-Free: 877-462-7349
info@reix.ca
www.reix.ca
Classes of Insurance: Liability

***Red River Valley Mutual Insurance Co.**
PO Box 940
245 Centre Ave. East
Altona, MB R0G 0B0
Tel: 204-324-6434; Fax: 204-324-1316
Toll-Free: 800-370-2888
info@redrivermutual.com
www.redrivermutual.com
Classes of Insurance: Liability, Boiler & Machinery, Fidelity, Property, Fire, Surety, Theft

Reliable Life Insurance Company
PO Box 557
100 King St. West
Hamilton, ON L8N 3K9
Tel: 905-523-5587; Fax: 905-528-8338
Toll-Free: 800-465-0661
service@reliablelifeinsurance.com
www.reliablelifeinsurance.com
Classes of Insurance: Personal Accident & Sickness, Life

RGA Life Reinsurance Company of Canada / RGA Compagnie de réassurance-vie du Canada
#1100, 55 University Ave.
Toronto, ON M5J 2H7
Tel: 416-682-0000; Fax: 416-777-9526
Toll-Free: 800-433-4326
www.rgare.com/offices/canada
Classes of Insurance: Reinsurance

Royal & SunAlliance Insurance Company of Canada (RSA)
#800, 18 York St.
Toronto, ON M5E 1L5
Tel: 416-366-7511; Fax: 416-367-9869
Toll-Free: 800-268-8406
www.rsagroup.ca
Classes of Insurance: Personal Accident & Sickness, Auto, Property

*** Saskatchewan Auto Fund**
2260 - 11th Ave.
Regina, SK S4P 0J9
Tel: 306-751-1200; Fax: 306-565-8666
www.sgi.sk.ca
Classes of Insurance: Auto

*** Saskatchewan Blue Cross**
PO Box 4030
516, 2nd Ave. North
Saskatoon, SK S7K 3T2
Tel: 306-244-1192; Fax: 306-652-5751
Toll-Free: 800-667-6853
service@sk.bluecross.ca
www.sk.bluecross.ca
Social Media: www.facebook.com/sk.push2play;
Classes of Insurance: Personal Accident & Sickness, Life

***Saskatchewan Crop Insurance Corporation**
PO Box 3000
484 Prince William Dr.
Melville, SK S0A 2P0
Tel: 306-728-7200; Fax: 306-728-7202
Toll-Free: 888-935-0000
customer.service@scic.gov.sk.ca
www.saskcropinsurance.com
Classes of Insurance: Hail & Crop

***Saskatchewan Motor Club Insurance Company Ltd.**
200 Albert St. North
Regina, SK S4R 5E2
Tel: 306-791-4321; Fax: 306-949-4461
www.caasask.sk.ca
Classes of Insurance: Accident

***Saskatchewan Municipal Hail Insurance Association**
2100 Cornwall St.
Regina, SK S4P 2K7
Tel: 306-569-1852; Fax: 306-522-3717
Toll-Free: 877-414-7644
smhi@smhi.ca
www.smhi.ca
Classes of Insurance: Hail & Crop

Saskatchewan Mutual Insurance Company (SMI)
279 - 3 Ave. North
Saskatoon, SK S7K 2H8
Tel: 306-653-4232; Fax: 306-664-1957
Toll-Free: 800-667-3067
headoffice@saskmutual.com
www.saskmutual.com
Classes of Insurance: Auto, Liability, Boiler & Machinery, Fidelity, Property

SCOR Canada Reinsurance Company/ SCOR Canada Compagnie de Réassurance
TD Canada Trust Tower, BCE Place
PO Box 615
#5000, 161 Bay St.
Toronto, ON M5J 2S1
Tel: 416-869-3670; Fax: 416-365-9393
ca@scor.com
www.scor.com
Social Media: twitter.com/SCOR_SE
Classes of Insurance: Reinsurance

SCOR Global Life Canada/ SCOR Global Vie Canada
TD Canada Trust Tower, BCE Place, Succursale du Canada
#5000, 161 Bay St.
Toronto, ON M5J 2S1
Tel: 416-304-6536; Fax: 416-304-6574
life@scor.com
www.scor.com
Classes of Insurance: Personal Accident & Sickness, Life

Scotia Life Insurance Company/ Scotia-Vie Compagnie d'Assurance
#400, 100 Yonge St.
Toronto, ON M5H 1H1
Tel: 416-866-2017; Fax: 416-866-5400
Toll-Free: 800-387-9844
www.scotialifefinancial.com/life/index.shtml; www.scotiabank.com
Classes of Insurance: Personal Accident & Sickness, Life

***Scottish & York Insurance Co. Limited**
2206 Eglinton Ave. East
Toronto, ON M1L 4S8
Tel: 416-288-1800; Fax: 416-288-5888
Toll-Free: 800-387-4518
info@avivacanada.com
www.avivacanada.com
Classes of Insurance: Legal Expense, Auto, Liability, Boiler & Machinery, Fidelity, Property, Surety

***SecuriCan General Insurance Company**
#200, 1200 Portage Ave.
Winnipeg, MB R3G 0T5
Toll-Free: 800-431-3132
info@securican.ca
www.securican.ca
Classes of Insurance: Personal Accident & Sickness

Security National Insurance Company/ Sécurité Nationale compagnie d'assurance
50, Place Crémazie, 12e étage
Montréal, QC H2P 1B6
Toll-Free: 800-361-3821
www.melochemonnex.com
Classes of Insurance: Personal Accident & Sickness, Auto, Property, Fire

***SGI CANADA Consolidated**
2260 - 11th Ave.
Regina, SK S4P 0J9
Tel: 306-751-1200; Fax: 306-565-8666
Toll-Free: 800-667-8015
sgiinquiries@sgi.sk.ca
www.sgi.sk.ca
Social Media: www.youtube.com/SGIcommunications; www.flickr.com/photos/sgiphotos; www.facebook.com/SGIcommunity; twitter.com/SGItweets
Classes of Insurance: Accident, Aircraft, Auto, Liability, Boiler & Machinery, Fidelity, Property, Surety, Reinsurance

Sirius America Insurance Company
#1202, 80 Bloor St. West
Toronto, ON M5S 2V1
Tel: 416-928-2430; Fax: 416-928-2459
info@siriusamerica.com
www.siriusamerica.com
Classes of Insurance: Auto, Liability, Fidelity, Property, Surety, Hail & Crop

***Société de l'assurance automobile du Québec**
CP 19600, Terminus Stn. Terminus
333, boul. Jean-Lesage
Québec, QC G1K 8J6
Tél: 418-643-7620; Ligne sans frais: 800-361-7620
www.saaq.gouv.qc.ca
Other Contact Information: Montréal: 514/873-7620
Classes of Insurance: Accident, Auto

Sons of Scotland Benevolent Association
#202, 40 Eglinton Ave. East
Toronto, ON M4P 3A2
Tel: 416-482-1250; Fax: 416-482-9576
Toll-Free: 800-387-3382
info@sonsofscotland.com
www.sonsofscotland.com
Classes of Insurance: Life

***South Easthope Mutual Insurance Co.**
PO Box 33
62 Woodstock St.
Tavistock, ON N0B 2R0
Tel: 519-655-2011; Fax: 519-655-2021
Toll-Free: 800-263-9987
seins@seins.on.ca
www.seins.on.ca
Classes of Insurance: Accident, Auto, Boiler & Machinery, Property

***Southeastern Mutual Insurance Company**
378 Coverdale Rd.
Riverview, NB E1B 3J7
Tel: 506-386-9002; Fax: 506-386-3325
Toll-Free: 800-561-7223
www.semutual.nb.ca
Classes of Insurance: Liability, Boiler & Machinery, Property, Fire

The Sovereign General Insurance Company
#140, 6700 Macleod Trail SE
Calgary, AB T2H 0L3
Tel: 403-298-4200; Fax: 403-298-4217
Toll-Free: 800-661-1652
www.cooperators.ca; www.sovereigngeneral.com
Classes of Insurance: Personal Accident & Sickness, Property

***SSQ Financial Group**
PO Box 10500, Sainte-Foy Stn. Sainte-Foy
2525, boul. Laurier
Québec, QC G1V 4H6
Tel: 418-651-7000; Fax: 418-688-7791
Toll-Free: 888-900-3457
communications@ssq.ca; mutuallife@ssq.ca
www.ssq.ca
Classes of Insurance: Personal Accident & Sickness, Auto, Life, Theft

***SSQ, Société d'assurances générales inc./ SSQ General Insurance Company Inc.**
Édifice Le Delta 2
CP 10530
2515, boul. Laurier
Québec, QC G1V 0A5
Tél: 418-683-0554; Téléc: 418-683-5603
Ligne sans frais: 800-463-2343
email@ssqgenerale.com
www.ssqgenerale.com
Classes of Insurance: Accident, Auto, Liability, Property, Fire, Theft

***SSQ, Société d'assurance-vie inc/ SSQ, Life Insurance Company Inc.**
CP 10500
2525, boul. Laurier
Québec, QC G1V 4H6
Tél: 418-651-7000; Ligne sans frais: 888-900-3457
www.ssq.ca
Classes of Insurance: Accident, Personal Accident & Sickness, Auto, Liability, Life, Property, Fire

The Standard Life Assurance Company of Canada
1245, rue Sherbrooke ouest, 17e étage
Montréal, QC H3G 1G3
Tel: 514-499-6844; Fax: 514-499-4466
Toll-Free: 888-841-6633
csc@standardlife.ca; information@standardlife.ca
www.standardlife.ca
Other Contact Information: Media Inquiries, E-mail: public.relations@standardlife.ca
Classes of Insurance: Personal Accident & Sickness, Life

***Stanley Mutual Insurance Company**
32 Irishtown Rd.
Stanley, NB E6B 1B6
Tel: 506-367-2273; Fax: 506-367-3076
Toll-Free: 800-442-9714
info@stanleymutual.com
www.stanleymutual.com
Classes of Insurance: Auto, Liability, Boiler & Machinery, Property

State Farm Canada
333 First Commerce Dr.
Aurora, ON L4G 8A4
Tel: 905-750-4100
info@statefarm.com
www.statefarm.ca
Other Contact Information: Technical Help Toll-Free: 1-888-559-1922
Social Media: www.youtube.com/statefarm; www.flickr.com/photos/statefarm; www.facebook.com/statefarmcanada; twitter.com/statefarm
Classes of Insurance: Aircraft, Auto, Liability, Boiler & Machinery, Fidelity, Property, Fire, Surety

Sterling Insurance Agency Limited
800 Ouellette Ave., 9th Fl.
Windsor, ON N9A 1C7
Fax: 519-256-9730
Toll-Free: 800-354-4956
support@sterlingmutuals.com
www.sterlingmutuals.com

***Stewart Financial Services**
1282 Cornwall Rd., #B
Oakville, ON L6J 7W5
Tel: 905-845-0990; Fax: 905-845-2882
Toll-Free: 888-845-0990
drew@stewartfinancial.ca
www.stewartfinancial.ca

Stewart Title Guaranty Company
North Tower, Royal Bank Plaza
#2200, 200 Bay St.
Toronto, ON M5J 2J2
Tel: 416-307-3300; Fax: 416-307-3305
Toll-Free: 888-667-5151
inquirycda@stewart.com
www.stewart.ca

Suecia Reinsurance Company
763 Pape Ave.
Toronto, ON M4K 3T2
Tel: 416-361-0056;
Classes of Insurance: Personal Accident & Sickness, Auto, Liability, Fidelity, Property, Hail & Crop, Reinsurance

Sun Life Assurance Company of Canada
Corporate Office
150 King St. West
Toronto, ON M5H 1J9
Tel: 416-979-9966; Fax: 416-979-4853
www.sunlife.ca
Classes of Insurance: Personal Accident & Sickness, Life

Sun Life Financial Inc.
150 King St. West
Toronto, ON M5H 1J9
Tel: 416-979-9966
www.sunlife.ca
Social Media: www.youtube.com/sunlifefinancial; www.facebook.com/SLFCanada; twitter.com/sunlifecareers
Classes of Insurance: Life

Supreme Council of the Royal Arcanum
#200, 1 Hunter St. East
Hamilton, ON L8N 3R1
Toll-Free: 888-272-2686
www.royalarcanum.com
Classes of Insurance: Personal Accident & Sickness, Life

***La Survivance, compagnie mutuelle d'assurance vie**
CP 10 000
1555, rue Girouard ouest
Saint-Hyacinthe, QC J2S 7C8
Tél: 450-773-6051; Téléc: 450-773-6470
Ligne sans frais: 800-773-8404
info@lasurvivance.com
www.lasurvivance.com; www.lsmutual.com
Classes of Insurance: Personal Accident & Sickness, Life

Swiss Reinsurance Company Canada
#2200, 150 King St. West
Toronto, ON M5H 1J9
Tel: 416-408-0272; Fax: 416-408-4222
Toll-Free: 800-268-7116
www.swissre.com
Classes of Insurance: Marine, Fidelity, Property, Surety, Reinsurance

TD General Insurance Company
c/o Meloche Monnex Inc.
50, Place Crémazie, 12e étage
Montréal, QC H2P 1B6
www.tdcanadatrust.com/tdinsurance
Classes of Insurance: Personal Accident & Sickness, Aircraft, Auto, Liability, Boiler & Machinery, Fidelity, Property, Surety

TD Home & Auto Insurance Company/ Compagnie d'Assurance Habitation et Auto TD
#401, 2161 Yonge St.
Toronto, ON M4S 3A6
Toll-Free: 800-338-0218
www.tdcanadatrust.com/tdinsurance,
www.group.tdinsurance.com
Other Contact Information: 866-361-2311 (Toll Free, Client Services); 866-848-9744 (Toll Free, Claims)
Classes of Insurance: Auto, Liability, Property

TD Life Insurance Company/ TD, Compagnie d'assurance-vie
120 Adelaide St. West, 2nd Fl.
Toronto, ON M5H 1T1
Toll-Free: 877-397-4187
TD.InsuranceLifeAndHealth@td.com
www.tdcanadatrust.com /tdinsurance/life
Classes of Insurance: Personal Accident & Sickness, Life

*** Temple Insurance Company**
390 Bay St., 20nd Fl.
Toronto, ON M5H 2Y2
Tel: 416-364-2851; Fax: 416-361-1163
Toll-Free: 877-364-2851
www.templeinsurance.ca
Classes of Insurance: Boiler & Machinery, Property

***Thomson Jemmett Vogelzang**
PO Box 967
321 Concession
Kingston, ON K7K 2B9
Tel: 613-544-5313; Fax: 613-542-6839
info@insurancecentre.com; info@johnson.ca
www.insurancecentre.com
Classes of Insurance: Auto, Liability, Property

Thomson-Schindle-Green Insurance & Financial Services Ltd.
Chinook Place
#100, 623 - 4th St. SE
Medicine Hat, AB T1A 0L1
Tel: 403-526-3283; Fax: 403-526-8082
Toll-Free: 800-830-9423
tsg@tsginsurance.com
www.tsginsurance.com
Classes of Insurance: Auto, Liability, Life, Property, Hail & Crop

The Toa Reinsurance Company of America
PO Box 41
#1001, 200 King St. West
Toronto, ON M5H 3T4
Tel: 416-366-5888; Fax: 416-366-7444
info@toare.com
www.toare.com
Classes of Insurance: Reinsurance

The Tokio Marine & Nichido Fire Insurance Co., Ltd.
c/o Lombard Canada Ltd.
105 Adelaide St. West, 3rd Fl.
Toronto, ON M5H 1P9
Tel: 416-350-4400; Fax: 416-350-4417
Toll-Free: 800-268-9680
Classes of Insurance: Auto, Marine, Property, Fire

***Town & Country Mutual Insurance**
79 Caradoc St. North
Strathroy, ON N7G 2M5
Tel: 519-246-1132; Fax: 519-246-1115
Toll-Free: 888-868-5064
info@town-country-ins.ca
www.town-country-ins.ca
Classes of Insurance: Personal Accident & Sickness, Auto, Liability, Boiler & Machinery, Fidelity, Property, Hail & Crop

***Townsend Farmers' Mutual Fire Insurance Company**
First Waterford Place Plaza
PO Box 1030
Waterford, ON N0E 1Y0
Tel: 519-443-7231; Fax: 519-443-5198
Toll-Free: 888-302-6052
farmins@townsendfarmers.com
www.townsendfarmers.com
Classes of Insurance: Personal Accident & Sickness, Auto, Liability, Boiler & Machinery, Property, Hail & Crop

Traders General Insurance Company/ Compagnie d'Assurance Traders Générale
2206 Eglinton Ave. East
Toronto, ON M1L 4S8
Tel: 416-288-1800; Fax: 416-288-5888
Toll-Free: 800-387-4518
www.avivacanada.com
Classes of Insurance: Auto, Property

***Tradition Mutual Insurance Company**
PO Box 10
264 Huron Rd.
Sebringville, ON N0K 1X0
Tel: 519-393-6402; Fax: 519-393-5185
Toll-Free: 877-380-6402
www.traditionmutual.com
Classes of Insurance: Accident, Auto, Liability, Boiler & Machinery, Fidelity, Property, Hail & Crop

***Trans Global Insurance Company (TGI)**
c/o Fraser Milner Cosgrain LLP, First Canadian Place
100 King St. West, 42nd Fl.
Toronto, ON T5X 1B2
Tel: 416-862-3418; Fax: 416-863-4592
Classes of Insurance: Personal Accident & Sickness, Liability, Property

***Trans Global Life Insurance Company (TGLI)**
c/o Fraser Milner Cosgrain LLP, First Canadian Place
100 King St. West, 42nd Fl.
Toronto, ON M5X 1B2
Tel: 416-862-3418; Fax: 416-863-4592
Classes of Insurance: Personal Accident & Sickness, Life

Transamerica Life Canada
5000 Yonge St.
Toronto, ON M2N 7J8
Tel: 416-883-5000; Toll-Free: 800-846-5970
lifeservices@transamerica.ca; ipservices@transamerica.ca
www.transamerica.ca
Other Contact Information: Policy Inquiries, Phone: 416-883-5003; Fax: 416-883-5520; Toll-Free Fax: 1-800-661-7296
Classes of Insurance: Personal Accident & Sickness, Life

Transatlantic Reinsurance Company
145 Wellington St. West
Toronto, ON M5J 1H8
Tel: 416-649-5300; Fax: 416-971-8782
www.transre.com
Classes of Insurance: Personal Accident & Sickness, Credit, Property, Surety, Reinsurance

Travelers - Canada
PO Box 6
#300, 20 Queen St. West
Toronto, ON M5H 3R3
Tel: 416-360-8183; Fax: 416-360-8267
Toll-Free: 800-330-5033
www.travelerscanada.ca
Social Media: www.youtube.com/travelersinsurance; www.facebook.com/travelers; twitter.com/TRV_Insurance
Classes of Insurance: Aircraft, Auto, Liability, Boiler & Machinery, Marine, Fidelity, Property, Fire, Surety, Reinsurance

***Trillium Mutual Insurance Company**
495 Mitchell Road S
Listowel, ON N4W 0C8
Tel: 519-291-9300; Fax: 519-291-1800
Toll-Free: 800-265-3020
admin@trilliummutual.com
www.trilliummutual.com
Social Media: www.facebook.com/pages/Trillium-Mutual/196791423327;
Classes of Insurance: Accident, Auto, Liability, Boiler & Machinery, Marine, Fidelity, Property, Hail & Crop

Trisura Guarantee Insurance Company
#1100, 70 York St.
Toronto, ON M5J 1S9
Tel: 416-214-2555; Fax: 416-214-9597
info@trisura.com
www.trisura.com
Classes of Insurance: Liability, Surety

Ukrainian Fraternal Association of America (UFA)
c/o Burns Hubley
#501, 90 Allstate Pkwy.
Markham, ON L3R 6H3
Tel: 416-495-1755; Fax: 905-479-1350
Classes of Insurance: Life

Ukrainian Fraternal Society of Canada
235 McGregor St.
Winnipeg, MB R2W 4W5
Tel: 204-586-4482; Fax: 204-589-6411
Toll-Free: 800-988-8372
Classes of Insurance: Life

Ukrainian Mutual Benefit Association of St. Nicholas of Canada
804 Selkirk Ave.
Winnipeg, MB R2W 2N6
Tel: 204-582-4882; Fax: 204-586-2095
Toll-Free: 866-582-4882
umbaofsn@mts.net
www.ukrainianmutual.com
Classes of Insurance: Personal Accident & Sickness, Life

Ukrainian National Association (UNA)
Toronto, ON
www.ukrainiannationalassociation.org
Classes of Insurance: Personal Accident & Sickness, Life

***Unica Insurance**
7150 Derrycrest Drive
Mississauga, ON L5W 0E5
Tel: 905-677-9777; Fax: 905-696-1777
Toll-Free: 800-676-6967
claims@UnicaInsurance.com
www.unicainsurance.com
Classes of Insurance: Auto, Liability, Property

***Unifund Assurance Company**
PO Box 12049
10 Factory Lane
St. John's, NL A1C 6H5
Tel: 709-737-1500; Fax: 709-737-1580
Toll-Free: 888-737-1689
unifund@unifund.ca
www.unifund.ca
Classes of Insurance: Auto, Property

***L'Union Canadienne Compagnie d'Assurances**
2475, boul. Laurier
Québec, QC G1T 1C4
Tel: 418-651-3551; Toll-Free: 800-463-3382
www.unioncanadienne.com
Classes of Insurance: Auto, Property

***L'Union-Vie, compagnie mutuelle d'assurance/ The Union Life, Mutual Assurance Company**
CP 696
142, rue Hériot
Drummondville, QC J2B 6W9
Tél: 819-478-1315; Téléc: 819-474-1990
Ligne sans frais: 800-567-0988
www.uvmutuelle.ca
Classes of Insurance: Personal Accident & Sickness, Life, Reinsurance

United American Insurance Company (UA)
c/o McLean & Kerr LLP
#2800, 130 Adelaide St. West
Toronto, ON M5H 3P5
Tel: 416-369-6624; Fax: 416-366-8571
www.unitedamerican.com
Classes of Insurance: Personal Accident & Sickness, Life

***United General Insurance Corporation**
860 Prospect St.
Fredericton, NB E3B 2T8
Tel: 506-459-5120; Fax: 506-453-0882
don.dougherty@ugic.nb.ca
Classes of Insurance: Auto

***Usborne & Hibbert Mutual Fire Insurance Company**
507 Main St. South
Exeter, ON N0M 1S1
Tel: 519-235-0350; Fax: 519-235-3623
usborne@on.aibn.com
www.usborneandhibbert.ca

***Uv Mutuelle/ The International Life Insurance Company**
CP 696
142, rue Hériot
Montréal, QC J2B 6W9
Tél: 819-478-1315; Téléc: 819-474-1990
Ligne sans frais: 800-567-0988
www.uvmutuelle.ca
Classes of Insurance: Personal Accident & Sickness, Life

Virginia Surety Company, Inc. (VCS)/ Compagnie de Sûreté Virginia Inc.
#201, 3650 Victoria Park Ave.
Toronto, ON M2H 3P7

www.thewarrantygroup.com
Classes of Insurance: Auto, Liability, Boiler & Machinery, Property

***Wabisa Mutual Insurance Company**
PO Box 621
35 Talbot St. East
Jarvis, ON N0A 1J0
Tel: 519-587-4454; Fax: 519-587-5470
Toll-Free: 800-263-7280
wabisa@mountaincable.net
www.wabisa.omia.com
Classes of Insurance: Personal Accident & Sickness, Auto, Liability, Fidelity, Property

Waterloo Insurance Company
590 Riverbend Dr.
Kitchener, ON N2K 3S2
Tel: 519-570-8335; Fax: 519-570-8693
Toll-Free: 866-247-7700
www.economicalinsurance.com
Classes of Insurance: Auto, Property

The Wawanesa Life Insurance Company
#400, 200 Main St.
Winnipeg, MB R3C 1A8
Tel: 204-985-3940; Fax: 204-985-3872
Toll-Free: 888-997-9965
life@wawanesa.com; groupcustomerservice@wawanesa.com
www.wawanesalife.com
Other Contact Information: Group Phone: 204-985-3806; Fax: 204-985-5781; Toll-Free: 1-800-665-7076
Classes of Insurance: Personal Accident & Sickness, Life

The Wawanesa Mutual Insurance Company
#900, 191 Broadway
Winnipeg, MB R3C 3P1
Tel: 204-985-3923; Fax: 204-942-7724
www.wawanesa.com
Classes of Insurance: Auto, Liability, Boiler & Machinery, Property, Fire, Surety, Theft

***Wedgwood Insurance Limited**
PO Box 13370, A Stn. A
85 Thorburn Rd.
St. John's, NL A1B 4B7
Tel: 709-753-3210; Fax: 709-753-8238
Toll-Free: 888-884-4253
www.wedgwoodinsurance.com
Social Media: www.facebook.com/pages/Wedgwood-Insurance-Limited/3396852340; twitter.com/wedgwoodins
Classes of Insurance: Aircraft, Auto, Life, Marine, Property

***West Elgin Mutual Insurance Company**
PO Box 130
274 Currie Rd.
Dutton, ON N0L 1J0
Tel: 519-762-3530; Fax: 519-762-3801
Toll-Free: 800-265-7635
info@westelgin.com
www.westelgin.com
Classes of Insurance: Personal Accident & Sickness, Auto, Liability, Fidelity, Property, Hail & Crop

***West Wawanosh Mutual Insurance Company**
PO Box 130
81 Southampton St., RR#1
Dungannon, ON N0M 1R0
Tel: 519-529-7921; Fax: 519-529-3211
Toll-Free: 800-265-5595
wawains@wwmic.com
www.wwmic.com
Classes of Insurance: Personal Accident & Sickness, Auto, Liability, Boiler & Machinery, Fidelity, Property

Western Assurance Company
Sheridan Insurance Centre
#1000, 2225 Erin Mills Pkwy.
Mississauga, ON L5K 2S9
Tel: 905-403-3318; Fax: 905-403-3319
Toll-Free: 877-263-4442
www.westernassurance.ca; www.rsagroup.ca
Classes of Insurance: Personal Accident & Sickness, Aircraft, Auto, Liability, Boiler & Machinery, Marine, Fidelity, Property, Surety

***Western Financial Group Inc.**
1010 - 24 St. SE
High River, AB T1V 2A7
Tel: 403-652-2663; Fax: 403-652-2661
Toll-Free: 866-843-9378
info@westernfg.ca
www.westernfinancialgroup.net
Classes of Insurance: Accident, Personal Accident & Sickness, Auto, Liability, Boiler & Machinery, Life, Fidelity, Property, Fire, Surety, Hail & Crop, Theft

Western Life Assurance Company
1010 - 24th St. SE
High River, AB T1V 2A7
Tel: 403-652-4356; Fax: 403-652-2673
Toll-Free: 877-452-4356
info@westernlife.com
www.westernlifeassurance.net
Classes of Insurance: Personal Accident & Sickness, Life

Western Surety Company
PO Box 527
#2000, 1874 Scarth St.
Regina, SK S4P 2G8
Tel: 306-791-3735; Fax: 306-359-0929
Toll-Free: 800-475-4454
wscinfo@westernsurety.ca
www.westernsurety.ca
Classes of Insurance: Fidelity, Surety

Westland Insurance
#300, 5455 152nd St.
Surrey, BC V3S 5A5
Tel: 604-543-7788; Toll-Free: 800-899-3093
contactus@westland-insurance.com
www.westland-insurance.com
Classes of Insurance: Auto, Liability, Property

Westminster Mutual Insurance Company
14122 Belmont Rd.
Belmont, ON N0L 1B0
Tel: 519-644-1663; Fax: 519-644-0315
Toll-Free: 800-565-3523
westminster@westminstermutual.com
www.westminstermutual.com
Classes of Insurance: Auto, Liability, Property

Westport Insurance Corporation
#2200, 150 King St. West
Toronto, ON M5H 1J9
Tel: 416-408-0272; Toll-Free: 800-268-7116
www.swissre.com
Classes of Insurance: Personal Accident & Sickness, Aircraft, Auto, Liability, Boiler & Machinery, Credit, Fidelity, Property, Surety, Hail & Crop

XL Insurance Company Limited (XL)
#1802, 100 Yonge St.
Toronto, ON M5C 2W1
Tel: 416-928-5586; Fax: 416-928-8858
www.xlinsurance.com
Classes of Insurance: Personal Accident & Sickness, Auto, Liability, Boiler & Machinery, Property, Surety

XL Reinsurance America Inc.
Scotia Plaza
#1702, 100 Yonge St.
Toronto, ON M5C 2W1
Tel: 416-598-1084; Fax: 416-598-1980
www.xlre.com
Classes of Insurance: Personal Accident & Sickness, Aircraft, Auto, Liability, Boiler & Machinery, Fidelity, Property, Surety, Hail & Crop

XL Reinsurance America Inc.
#1702, 100 Yonge St.
Toronto, ON M5C 2W1
Tel: 416-598-1084; Fax: 416-598-1980
www.xlre.com
Classes of Insurance: Accident, Aircraft, Life, Marine, Property, Surety, Reinsurance

***Yarmouth Mutual Fire Insurance Company**
1229 Talbot St. East
St Thomas, ON N5P 1G8
Tel: 519-631-1572; Fax: 519-631-6058
Toll-Free: 877-792-3693
office@yarmouth-ins.com
www.yarmouth-ins.com
Classes of Insurance: Auto, Liability, Property, Hail & Crop

Zenith Insurance Company/ Compagnie d'Assurance Zenith
c/o Northbridge Financial Corporation
#700, 105 Adelaide St. West
Toronto, ON M5H 1P9
Tel: 416-350-4400; Toll-Free: 888-440-4876
inquiries@zenithinsurance.ca
www.privilege50.com
Classes of Insurance: Personal Accident & Sickness, Auto, Liability, Property

Zurich Canada
400 University Ave.
Toronto, ON M5G 1S7
Tel: 416-586-3000; Fax: 416-586-2525
Toll-Free: 800-387-5454
www.zurichcanada.com
Social Media: twitter.com/zurichcanada
Classes of Insurance: Accident, Personal Accident & Sickness, Auto, Liability, Boiler & Machinery, Credit, Marine, Fidelity, Property, Fire, Surety, Theft

Major Companies

Agriculture

AG Growth International (AGI)
1301 Kenaston Blvd.
Winnipeg, MB R3P 2P2
204-489-1855
Fax: 204-488-6929
www.aggrowth.com
Company Type: Public
Ticker Symbol: AFN / TSX
Profile: AG Growth International Inc. was created in 1996. The company is involved in the manufacturing of grain handling, conditioning, & storage equipment. Products include belt conveyors, augers, grain storage bins, & grain aeration equipment.
Gary Anderson, President & Chief Executive Officer
Steve Sommerfeld, Chief Financial Officer
204-489-1855, steve@aggrowth.com
Daniel Donner, Vice-President, Sales & Marketing
Paul Gagne, Coordinator, Logistics

Alliance Grain Traders
PO Box 30029, Regina, SK S4N 7K9
306-525-4490
Fax: 306-525-4463
ir@alliancegrain.com
Company Type: Public
Ticker Symbol: AGT / TSX
Profile: Alliance Grain Traders was created in 2007, when Agtech Income Fund, hte predecessor to alliance Grain Traders, acquired Saskcan Pulse Trading. The re-branded fund, Alliance Grain Traders Income Fund, converted to a dividend paying corporation in 2009.
Alliance Grain Traders Inc. is engaged in the purchase of lentils, peas, beans, & chickpeas from farmers & exporting them to more than 100 countreies. The corporation employs approximately 400 full-time staff.
Marad Al-Katib, President & Chief Executive Officer
Gaetan Bourassa, Chief Operating Officer
Lori Ireland, Chief Financial Officer

Asia Bio-Chem Group Corp.
#2105, 130 Adelaide St. West
Toronto, ON M5H 3P5
416-603-7500
info@asiabiochem.com
www.asiabiochem.com
Company Type: Public
Ticker Symbol: ABC / TSX
Profile: Through its wholly owned subsidiaries in China, Asia Bio-Chem Group Corp.'s business is processing corn. Cornstarch, gluten, corn germ, & fiber products are sold for the Chinese market.
Zhiping Wang, Chair, President & Chief Executive Officer
Elaine Zhao, Chief Financial Officer
Robert Wilson, Executive Vicee-President
416-603-7500, robert.wilson@asiabiochem.com

Bennett Environmental Inc.
#208, 1540 Cornwall Rd.
Oakville, ON L6J 7W5
905-339-1540
Fax: 905-339-0016
800-386-1388
info@bennettenv.com
www.bennettenv.com
Other Communications: USA Office, Phone: 978-692-9990
Company Type: Public
Ticker Symbol: BEV / TSX

Profile: The company is engaged in contaminated soil remediation.
Lawrence Haber, President & Chief Executive Officer
Fred Cranston, Chief Financial Officer

Buhler Industries Inc.
1260 Clarence Ave.
Winnipeg, MB R3T 1T2

info@buhler.com
www.buhlerindustries.com

Company Type: Public
Ticker Symbol: BUI / TSX
Profile: Buhler Industries Inc. was established in 1932. The company manufactures & distributes agricultural equipment, such as tractors, augers, fron-end loaders, & compact implements. Brand names include Versatile, Allied, & Farm King.

Yuri Ryazanov, Chief Executive Officer
Willy Janzen, Chief Financial Officer
204-654-5718, wjanzen@buhler.com

Ridley Inc.
Canadian Feed Operations
34 Terracon Pl.
Winnipeg, MB R2J 4G7

204-233-8418
Fax: 204-231-2402
www.ridleyinc.com; www.feedrite.com
Social Media:
www.facebook.com/pages/Ridley-Inc/254873578500
twitter.com/ridleyinc

Company Type: Public
Ticker Symbol: RCL / TSX
Profile: The commercial animal nutrition company manufactures & distributes animal nutrition products. Products include feeds, supplements, health products, low-moisture blocks, & animal care & livestock handling equipment. Ridley Inc. employs over 800 people in Canada & the United States.
Steve VanRoekel, President & Chief Executive Officer
Bob Frost, President, Ridley Block Operations
507-388-9400, Fax: 507-388-9559
Michael Hudspith, President, Ridley Feed Ingredients
507-388-9400, Fax: 507-388-9415
Denis Daudet, Chief Operating Officer, Canadian Feed Operations
Gordon Hildebrand, Chief Financial Officer
K. Bruce Campbell, Corporate Secretary

Sun Gro Horticulture
Waterfront Centre
PO Box 48600, #1200, 200 Burrard St.
Vancouver, BC V7X 1T2

425-641-7577
Fax: 425-641-0138
www.sungro.com

Company Type: Private
Mitchell J. Weaver, President & Chief Executive Officer
Bradley A. Wiens, Chief Financial Officer & Vice-President, Finance
425-373-3603, bradw@sungro.com

Thompsons Limited
2 Hyland Dr.
Blenheim, ON N0P 1A0

519-676-5411
Fax: 519-676-3185
800-265-5225
info@thompsonslimited.com
www.thompsonslimited.com

Company Type: Private
Profile: Thompsons Limited is a supplier of agricultural products & farm services to producers throughout Ontario, & a provider of grain handling facilities. Agricultural products include seed, fertilizer, & crop protectants. The company is also engaged in the purchasing, processing, packaging, & shipping of commercial corn, wheat, soybeans, & edible beans to both domestic & export markets.
Wes Thompson, Chief Executive Officer
Terry Koehler, Chief Financial Officer
Brad Chandler, Manager, Food Products
Ross Goldhawk, Manager, Operations
Darcy Oliphant, Manager, Trading Room

Village Farms International, Inc.
4700 - 80th St.
Delta, BC V4K 3N3

Company Type: Public
Ticker Symbol: VFF / TSX
Profile: Village Farms produces, markets, & distributes greenhouse-grown bell peppers, tomatoes, & cucumbers. Greenhouse facilities are situated in British Columbia & Texas. Products are distributed mainly to retail grocers & fresh food distributors in Canada & the United States.

Michael A. DeGiglio, Chief Executive Officer
Stephen C. Ruffini, Chief Financial Officer & Executive Vice-President

Viterra Inc.
2625 Victoria Ave.
Regina, SK S4T 7T9

866-569-4411
investor@viterra.ca
www.viterra.ca

Company Type: Public
Ticker Symbol: VT / TSX
Profile: Viterra is a global agri-business & food ingredients company. In 2012, it was announced that Glencore International plc would acquire all the issued & outstanding shared of Viterra. Glencore sources, finances, produces, & supplies metal & minerals, energy products, & agricultural products.
Mayo Schmidt, President & Chief Executive Officer
Mike Brooks, Chief Information Officer & Senior Vice-President
Rex McLennan, Chief Financial Officer
Grant Theaker, Vice-President & Treasurer
Holly Gibney, Manager, Media Relations
403-817-1088, holly.gibney@viterra.com

Business & Computer Services

20-20 Technologies
#2020, 400, boul Armand-Frappier
Laval, QC H7V 4B4

514-332-4110
Fax: 514-334-6043
866-698-2020
investor@2020.net
www.2020technologies.com
Other Communications: Support: 866-697-2020

Company Type: Public
Ticker Symbol: TWT / TSX
Profile: Established in 1987, 20-20 Technologies specializes in computer-aided design. The company provides business & manufacturing software for the furniture & interior design industries. 20-20 Technologies operates in ten countries, and has over 500 employees.
Jean-François Grou, Chief Executive Officer
Steve Perrone, Chief Financial Officer
Bernard Sanchez, Executive Vice-President, Sales & Services, Americas
André Chartier, Senior Vice-President, Product Development
Dani Knezevic, Contact, Media Relations
dani.knezevic@2020.net

Absolute Software Corporation
#1600, 1055 Dunsmuir St.
Vancouver, BC V7X 1K8

604-730-9851
Fax: 604-730-2621
800-220-0733
info@absolute.com; absolutejobs@absolute.
www.absolute.com
Other Communications: USA Headquarters, Austin, Texas, Phone: 512-600-7455

Company Type: Public
Ticker Symbol: ABT / TSX
Profile: Absolute Software Corporation provides endpoint security & management for computers & ultra-portable devices.
John Livingston, Chair & Chief Executive Officer
Rob Chase, Chief Operating Officer
Phil Gardner, Chief Technology Officer
Errol Olsen, Chief Financial Officer

ADP Canada
East Tower
3250 Bloor St. West, 16th Fl.
Toronto, ON M8X 2X9

www.adp.ca

Company Type: Private
Profile: Business outsourcing solutions are provided, including human resources management, tax & benefits administration, & payroll. In addition, ADP also offers integrated computing solutions for automobile, truck, motorcycle recreational vehicle, marine, & heavy equipment dealers.
Client service processing centres are located in the following cities: Vancouver, Calgary, Winnipeg, Toronto, & Montréal.

Aeroquest International Limited
7687 Bath Rd.
Mississauga, ON L4T 3T1

416-204-1500
866-693-9129
info@aeroquest.ca; sales@aeroquestairborn
www.aeroquest.ca

Company Type: Public
Ticker Symbol: AQL / TSX
Profile: Aeroquest International collects & interprets data about the earth's surface & resources beneath it. Through Aeroquest Airborne, the company offers geophysics surveys. Aerial geomatics surveys are provided through Aeroquest Mapcon. Geophex is engaged in the custom design & construction of geophysical sensors & instruments.
Robert Motz, President & Chief Executive Officer
Marc Beisheim, Chief Financial Officer

Apple Canada Inc.
7495 Birchmount Rd.
Markham, ON L3R 5G2

905-513-5800
Fax: 905-477-8668
www.apple.ca

Company Type: Private
Wendy Hayes, CEO & Director, Sales
Steve Jobs, President
John Hagias, Vice-President, Finance & Operations
Ayube Rahaman, Manager, Information Systems & Telecommunications
Zandra Zarris, Manager, Facilities

Axia NetMedia Corporation
Corporate Head Office
#3300, 450 - 1st St. SW
Calgary, AB T2P 5H1

403-538-4000
Fax: 403-538-4100
866-773-3348
info@axia.com; sales@axia.com; customerca
www.axia.com
Other Communications: Investor Relations: ir@axia.com
Social Media: twitter.com/axianmc
www.linkedin.com/company/339327

Company Type: Public
Ticker Symbol: AXX / TSX
Profile: The company sells services over fibre optic communications infrastructure in regions that have implemented the Axia NGN Solution. Axia's networks are in Alberta, Massachusetts, France, Spain, & Singapore.
Arthur R. Price, Chair & Chief Executive Officer
Jean-Michel Soulier, President, Axia Networks France
Peter McKeown, Chief Financial Officer
Drew McNaughton, Chief Technology Officer
Mark Blake, Vice-President, Global Business Development & Marketing
Dawn Tinling, Vice-President, Investor Relations & Communications
403-538-4074

Bridgewater Systems Corporation
Corporate Headquarters
#500, 303 Terry Fox Dr.
Ottawa, ON K2K 3J1

613-591-6655
Fax: 613-591-6656
877-943-3772
www.bridgewatersystems.com
Other Communications: USA Office, Phone: 866-652-0471

Company Type: Public
Ticker Symbol: BWC / TSX
Profile: Bridgewater Systems is a division of Amdocs. Founded in 1997, Bridgewater Systems is in the business of intelligent broadband controls. Bridgewater's products include Servce Controller (AAA), Policy Controller (PCRF, & Home Subscriber Server (HSS). Bridgewater is a TL 9000-S registered company.
Eamonn Gary, Vice-President, Strategic Programs & Advanced Technology
Gary Knee, Vice-President, Engineering & Operations
David L. Sharpley, Vice-President, Business & Products

Computer Modelling Group Ltd.
#200, 1824 Crowchild Trail NW
Calgary, AB T2M 3Y7

403-531-1300
Fax: 403-289-8502
cmgl@cmgl.ca; corp@cmgl.ca; resumes@cmgl.
www.cmgl.ca

Company Type: Public
Ticker Symbol: CMG / TSX
Profile: Computer Modelling Group Ltd. is a computer software engineering & consulting company. It serves the oil & gas industry. Sales & technical support services are situated in Calgary, Houston, London, Dubai, & Caracas.
Ken M. Dedeluk, President & Chief Executive Officer
ken.dedeluk@cmgl.ca
John Kalman, Vice-President, Finance
john.kalman@cmgl.ca
Ron Kutney, Vice-President, Canada & Eastern Hemisphere
ron.kutney@cmgl.ca
Ryan Schneider, Vice-President, Marketing
ryan.schneider@cmgl.ca

Constellation Software Inc.
#1200, 20 Adelaide St. East
Toronto, ON M5C 2T6

416-861-2279
Fax: 416-861-2287
info@csisoftware.com
www.csisoftware.com

Company Type: Public
Ticker Symbol: CSU
Profile: Constellation Software's area of expertise is the acquisition & management of industry specific software businesses. Specialized software solutions are provided to customers in more than 30 countries.
Mark Leonard, President & Chair
John Billowits, Chief Financial Officer
Bernard Anzarouth, Vice-President, Mergers & Acquisitions

CriticalControl Solutions Corporation
#1100, 840 - 7th Ave. SW
Calgary, AB T2P 3G2

403-705-7500
Fax: 403-705-7555
855-426-6368
info@criticalcontrol.com; imaging@critica
www.criticalcontrol.com
Other Communications: Document Solutions, Phone: 780-423-3100

Company Type: Public
Ticker Symbol: CCZ / TSX
Profile: CriticalControl Solutions Corporation helps industries solve data & document related challenges. The corporation provides outsourced solutions for transactional processes. CriticalControl's business information automation technology ensures secure control for sensitive information.
Alykhan Mamdani, B.Math, LLB, LLM, CMA, President & Chief Executive Officer
Bruce Byford, CA, Chief Financial Officer
Brenton Lawther, B.Sc., Chief Operating Officer
Hashu Remtulla, CMA, Vice-President & Corporate Controller

Cyberplex Inc.
#400, 1255 Bay St.
Toronto, ON M5R 2A9

416-597-8889
Fax: 416-597-2345
888-597-8889
investor@cyberplex.com
www.cyberplex.com

Company Type: Public
Ticker Symbol: CX / TSX
Geoffrey Rotstein, President/CEO
Isaac Osiel, CFO
David Katz, General Counsel/Vice President, Corporate Development

Data Group Inc.
Head Office
9195 Torbram Rd.
Brampton, ON L6S 6H2

905-791-3151
Fax: 905-791-3277
800-268-0128
webinfo@datagroup.ca
www.datagroup.ca
Other Communications: Customer Service, Phone: 877-644-5500, Fax: 888-206-6441

Company Type: Public
Ticker Symbol: DGI / TSX
Profile: Document management & marketing solutions are services offered by Data Group Inc. Sectors served include financial, manufacturing, energy, retail & consumer services, distribution, government & public services, health care, & not-for-profit. Data Group offers eco-print solutions to ensure its business is conducted in an environmentally responsible manner. The company employs more than 1,950 people across Canada.
Michael Suksi, Chief Executive Officer
Paul O'Shea, Chief Financial Officer

Enghouse Systems Limited
#800, 80 Tiverton Ct.
Markham, ON L3R 0G4

905-946-3200
Fax: 905-946-3201
info@enghouse.com; investor@enghouse.com
www.enghouse.com
Other Communications: Acquisitions, E-mail: acquire@enghouse.com

Company Type: Public
Ticker Symbol: ESL / TSX
Profile: Founded in 1984, Enghouse Systems Limited provides enterprise software solutions. The company's divisions include Enghouse Interactive, Enghouse Networks, & Enghouse Transportation.
Stephen J. Sadler, Chair/CEO
Steve Dodenhoff, President, Syntellect Division
Anthony R. Pearlman, President, Enghouse Asset Management Division
Doug Bryson, Vice-President, Finance & Administration
Todd M. May, Vice-President & General Counsel

Hartco Inc.
9393, boul Louis H. Lafontaine
Montréal, QC H1J 1Y8

514-354-3810
Fax: 514-354-1998
info@hartco.com
www.hartco.com

Company Type: Public
Ticker Symbol: HCI / TSX
Profile: Through its operating divisions, Hartco Inc. is involved in the information technology business. It serves both public & private sector organizations. Hartco has been in business since 1976.
Harry Hart, Chair & Chief Executive Officer
Patrick Waid, President & Chief Operating Officer
Harold Gervais, Chief Financial Officer & Vice-President, Finance
514-354-3810, Fax: 514-354-8989, hgervais@hartco.com
Michael Jones, Chief Information Officer

Hemisphere GPS Inc.
Corporate Headquarters, Precision Products Group
4110 - 9th St. SE
Calgary, AB T2G 3C4

403-259-3311
Fax: 403-259-8866
info@hemispheregps.com; ground@hemisphere
www.hemispheregps.com
Other Communications: Ground Agriculture Group, Hiawatha, KS, USA: 785-742-2976
Social Media: www.facebook.com/HemisphereGPS
twitter.com/hemispheregps
www.linkedin.com/company/hemisphere-gps

Company Type: Public
Ticker Symbol: HEM / TSX
Profile: Hemisphere GPS is a designer & manufacturer of GPS products for positioning, guidance, & machine control applications. Products are used in the construction, marine, & agriculture sectors. Hemisphere GPS holds several patents & intellectual property. Brand names include Outback Guidance for products used by the agricultural market.
Steven Koles, President & Chief Executive Officer
Cameron Olson, Chief Financial Officer & Senior Vice-President
Kip Pendleton, Senior Vice-President & General Manager, Agriculture
Phil Gabriel, Vice-President & General Manager, Precision Products
precision@hemispheregps.com
Lisa Smith, Vice-President, Operations
Michael Whitehead, Vice-President, Technology

Logibec Groupe Informatique Ltée
#1500, 700 Wellington St.
Montréal, QC H3C 3S4

514-766-0134
Fax: 514-766-9237
877-392-2486
marketing@logibec.com
www.logibec.com

Company Type: Public
Ticker Symbol: LGI
Profile: Logibec develops application software & implements information management systems. Management software is used by the health & social service sector. Related services include end-user training & system maintenance.
Claude Roy, Eng., MBA, President/CEO
Marc P. Brunet, Chief Financial Officer
Gilles Laporte, Sr. Vice-President, Business Development
514-762-3810
André Trudeau, Vice-President, Operations - Financial Solutions & Technical Services
Sylvain Trudeau, Vice-President, Technologies & Clinical Administrative Solutions

MacDonald, Dettwiler & Associates Ltd. (MDA Ltd.)
13800 Commerce Pkwy.
Richmond, BC V6V 2J3

604-278-3411
Fax: 604-231-2768
info@mdacorporation.com
www.mdacorporation.com
Other Communications: Investors: invest@mdacorporation.com

Company Type: Public
Ticker Symbol: MDA / TSX
Profile: Incorporated in 1969, MacDonald, Dettwiler & Associates Ltd. offers advanced information solutions to capture & process great amounts of data for business & government organizations. Products include tailored information services, complex operational systems, & electronic information products.
Daniel E. Friedmann, President & Chief Executive Officer
Anil Wirasekara, Chief Financial Officer & Executive Vice-President
Craig Thornton, General Manager, Robotics
Wendy Keyzer, Contact, MDA External Relations
604-231-2743, wendy@mdacorporation.com

Mad Catz Interactive Inc.
Brookfield Place
#2500, 181 Bay St.
Toronto, ON M5J 2T7

619-321-3545
Fax: 619-683-9829
800-831-1442
mcz@jcir.com
www.madcatz.com

Company Type: Public
Ticker Symbol: MCZ / TSX, AMEX
Profile: Mad Catz Interactive Inc. provides interactive entertainment products. The company's products are marketed under the following brands: Mad Catz, Tritton, Cyborg, Eclipse, & Saitek. Mad Catz is also involved in the development of flight simulation software through ThunderHawk Studios. Offices are located in Nrth America, Europe, & Asia.
Darren Richardson, President & Chief Executive Officer, Mad Catz, Inc.
Brian Anderson, Chief Operating Officer, Mad Catz Inc.
Allyson Evans, Chief Financial Officer, Mad Catz Inc.
Whitney Paterson, General Counsel & Vice-President, Corporate Development

March Networks Corporation
303 Terry Fox Dr.
Ottawa, ON K2K 3J1

613-591-8181
Fax: 613-591-7337
800-563-5564
info@marchnetworks.com
www.marchnetworks.com

Company Type: Public
Ticker Symbol: MN / TSX
Profile: March Networks Corporation provides IP video software & systems for risk mitigation, loss prevention, & improved security. The company's business analysis applications are used by organizations such as financial institutions, transportation authorities, & retailers. March Networks is ISO-certified.
Peter Strom, President/CEO
Kenneth Taylor, Chief Financial Officer
Cheryl Beckett, Corporate Secretary & Executive Vice-President, Legal
Peter Wilenius, Vice-President, Investor Relations & Corporate Development

McKesson Canada
8625, rte Transcanadienne
Montréal, QC H4S 1Z6

514-725-2100
Fax: 514-745-2300
communication@mckesson.ca
www.mckesson.ca

Company Type: Private
Domenic Pilla, President
Paula Keays, Vice-President/CFO
George Attar, Sr. Vice-President/CIO
Geneviève Fortier, Vice-President, Human Resources

Mediagrif Interactive Technologies Inc./ Technologies Interactives Mediagrif
Tour est
#255, 1111, rue St-Charles ouest
Longueuil, QC J4K 5G4

450-449-0102
Fax: 450-449-8725
877-677-9088
info@mediagrif.com; careers@mediagrif.com
www.mediagrif.com

Company Type: Public
Ticker Symbol: MDF / TSX
Profile: Established in 1996, Mediagrif Interactive Technologies Inc. delivers e-commerce solutions to businesses. The company employs more than 330 people.
Claude Roy, President & Chief Executive Officer
croy@mediagrif.com
Paul Bourque, Chief Financial Officer
Hélène Hallak, Senior Vice-President & General Counxel
Stéphane Anglaret, Vice-President, Technology
Eric Phaneuf, Vice-President, Business Development

Mitel Networks Corporation
Corporate Headquarters
350 Legget Dr.
Kanata, ON K2K 2W7

613-592-2122
Fax: 613-592-4784
800-267-6244
www.mitel.com

Company Type: Private
Profile: The organization provides a broad range of communications solutions, from basic business communications to tailored applications. Mitel is present in more than ninety countries.
Don Smith, Chief Executive Officer
Paul Butcher, President & Chief Operating Officer
Steve Spooner, Chief Financial Officer

NeuLion, Inc.
463 King St. West, 3rd Fl.
Toronto, ON M5V 1K4

sales@neulion.com; fansupport@neulion.com
www.neulion.com
Other Communications: Press E-mail: press@neulion.com
Social Media: www.facebook.com/neulion?v=app_4949752878
twitter.com/NeuLionIPTV

Company Type: Public
Ticker Symbol: NLN / TSX
Profile: NeuLion, Inc. was established in 2000. The company delivers live & on-demand content for any Internet-enabled device. Customers include sports, major entertainment, & news companies.
Nancy Li, President & Chief Executive Officer
Arthur J. McCarthy, Chief Financial Officer
Michael Her, Executive Vice-President, Research & Development
Ronald Nunn, Executive Vice-President, Business Operations
Roy E. Reichbach, Corporate Secretary & General Counsel

Nurun Inc.
711, rue de la Commune ouest
Montréal, QC H3C 1X6

514-392-1900
Fax: 514-392-0911
877-696-1292
montreal@nurun.com
www.nurun.com

Company Type: Private
Ticker Symbol: IFN
Profile: Nurun Inc. is a global interactive marketing agency. Working with a great range of companies & organizations, Nurun executes & measures interactive programs that use technologies.
Jacques-Hervé Roubert, President & Chief Executive Officer
Guy Lemieux, Vice-President, Finance & Administration
Bernard Robitaille, Executive Vice-President, EGovernment & NDPC
Suzanne Sauvage, Executive Vice-President & Chief Strategy Officer
Richard Shuback, Executive Vice-President & Executive Creative Director

Open Text Corporation
275 Frank Tompa Dr.
Waterloo, ON N2L 0A1

519-888-7111
Fax: 519-888-0677
800-499-6544
sales@opentext.com; support@opentext.com
www.opentext.com
Other Communications: Investors: investors@opentext.com
Social Media: www.facebook.com/opentext
twitter.com/OpenText

Company Type: Public
Ticker Symbol: OTC / TSX, NASDAQ
Profile: Founded in 1991, Open Text Corporation provides enterprise content management solutions to assist organizations manage their information assets. Approximately 4,410 are employed by Open Text Corporation.
John Shackleton, President/CEO
Paul McFeeters, Chief Financial Officer
P. Thomas Jenkins, Exec. Chair & Chief Strategy Officer
Kirk Roberts, Exec. Vice-President, Product Solutions & Marketing
Greg Secord, Director, Investor Relations
gsecord@opentext.com
Rich Maganini, Director, Corporate Communications
rmaganin@opentext.com

Oracle Corporation Canada
401 - 9th Ave. SW
Calgary, AB T2P 3C5

403-265-2622
Fax: 403-290-1836
800-363-3059
events.ca@oracle.com
www.oracle.com

Company Type: Private

Peer 1 Network Enterprises, Inc.
Also Known As: PEER 1 Hosting
#100, 555 West Hastings St.
Vancouver, BC V6B 4N5

604-683-7747
Fax: 604-683-4634
877-579-9690
investor@peer1.com
www.peer1.com
Other Communications: Sales: 866-579-9690; Support: 877-504-0091
Social Media: twitter.com/peer1

Company Type: Public
Ticker Symbol: PIX / TSX
Profile: PEER 1 Network Enterprises, Inc. is an online information technology infrastructure provider. Peer 1 has points-of-presence throughout North America & Europe.
Fabio Banducci, President & Chief Executive Officer
Gary Sherlock, Chief Financial Officer & Executive Vice-President
Ted Smith, Senior Vice-President, Operations
Jad Jebara, Vice-President, Finance & Information Technology
Ryan Murphey, Vice-President, Facilities & Data Center Operations
Rajan Sodhi, Vice-President, Marketing & Communications

Redknee Solutions Inc.
Corporate Headquarters
#500, 2560 Matheson Blvd. East
Mississauga, ON L4W 4Y9

905-626-2622
Fax: 905-625-2773
contact@redknee.com; media@redknee.com; h
www.redknee.com
Other Communications: Investors: investor_relations@redknee.com
Social Media: www.facebook.com/pages/RedkneeRKN/153720457985750
twitter.com/redkneeRKN/
www.linkedin.com/company/redknee

Company Type: Public
Ticker Symbol: RKN / TSX
Profile: Redknee Solutions provides communication software products & services.
Lucas Skoczkowski, Chief Executive Officer
David Charron, Chief Financial Officer
Vishal Kothari, Vice-President, Global Services
Nitin Singhal, Vice-President, Research & Development

Rockwell Automation Canada
135 Dundas St.
Cambridge, ON N1R 5X1

519-623-1810
Fax: 519-623-8930
ca.rockwellautomation.com

Company Type: Private
Profile: Rockwell Automation Canada offers products & solutions for businesses. Brands include Allen-Bradley & Rockwell Software.

Sandvine Corp.
408 Albert St.
Waterloo, ON N2L 3V3

519-880-2600
Fax: 519-884-9892
investor_relations@sandvine.com
www.sandvine.com
Social Media: www.facebook.com/sandvine
twitter.com/sandvine
www.linkedin.com/company/sandvine

Company Type: Public
Ticker Symbol: SVC,. TSX, London-AIM
Profile: Sandvine Corporation provides network policy control equipment & software. The company serves broadband & mobile data subscribers.
Dave Caputo, President & Chief Executive Officer
Scott Hamilton, Chief Financial Officer
Brad Siim, Chief Operating Officer & Vice-President, Engineering
Don Bowman, Chief Technology Officer
Mike Verhoeve, Vice-President & General Counsel
Jennifer Ross, Contact, Media
jross@sandvine.com
Rick Wadsworth, Contact, Investor Relations
rwadsworth@sandvine.com

SAP Canada
4120 Yonge St.
Toronto, ON M2P 2B8

416-229-0574
Fax: 416-229-0575
800-263-1337
www.sap.com

Company Type: Private

Sierra Systems Group Inc.
#2500, 1177 West Hastings St.
Vancouver, BC V6E 2K3

604-688-1371
Fax: 604-688-6482
877-688-1371
Marketing@SierraSystems.com
www.sierrasystems.com

Company Type: Private
Profile: Sierra Systems Group is an information technology & management consulting services company. Examples of the company's services include content & records management, human capital management, & finance & controlling. Sierra Systems serves the government, justice, transportation, health, energy, & financial services sectors.
Joe Campbell, President & Chief Executive Officer
Warren Beach, Chief Financial Officer & Executive Vice-President
Joe O'Leary, Chief Operating Officer
Arthur E. Stedman, Vice-President, Corporate Services

Softchoice Corporation
#200, 173 Dufferin St.
Toronto, ON M6K 3H7

416-588-9000
Fax: 416-588-9001
investor_relations@softchoice.com
www.softchoice.com

Company Type: Public
Ticker Symbol: SO / TSX
Profile: Softchoice Corporation provides technology solutions & services. Organizations & businesses are assisted with their software & hardware technology resources.
David MacDonald, President & Chief Executive Officer
David A. Long, Chief Financial Officer & Senior Vice-President, Finance
Kevin Wright, Chief Information Officer & Senior Vice-President
Steve Leslie, Senior Vice-President, Sales & Professional Services Operations

Solium Capital Inc.
Headquarters
#1500, 800 - 6th Ave. SW
Calgary, AB T2P 3G3

403-515-3910
Fax: 403-515-3919
877-380-7793
solutions@solium.com; help@solium.com
www.solium.com
Other Communications: Investors: investorrelations@solium.com

Company Type: Public
Ticker Symbol: SUM / TSX
Profile: Solium Capital is an independent provider of stock plan administration software & services. The company's technology platforms include StockVantage, Shareworks, & Transcentive. Solium Capital's headquarters is in Calgary Alberta, with regional offices in Toronto Ontario, Montréal Québec, Shelton Connecticut, Tempe Arizona, & London United Kingdom.
Michael Broadfoot, Chief Executive Officer & Managing Director
Rudi Bester, Executive Vice-President, Global Sales
Lynn Leong, Executive Vice-President, Finance & Administration
403-450-6015

SXC Health Solutions, Inc.
555 Industrial Dr.
Milton, ON L9T 5E1

905-876-4741
Fax: 905-878-8869
investors@sxc.com
www.sxc.com

Company Type: Public
Ticker Symbol: SXC / TSX, NASDAQ
Profile: SXC Health Solutions Corp. serves the healthcare benefits management industry. Healthcare information technology solutions are among the professional services provided.
Mark A. Thierer, President/CEO
Jeffrey Park, CFO & Exec. Vice-President, Finance
Mike Bennof, Exec. Vice-President, Healthcare Information Technology

John Romza, Chief Technology Officer & Exec. Vice-President, Research & Development
Cliff Berman, Sr. Vice-President, General Counsel, & Corporate Secretary
Kelly Kettlewell, Sr. Vice-President, Pharmacy Benefit Management Operations

Unisys Canada
Head Office
2001 Sheppard Ave. East
Toronto, ON M2J 4Z7

416-495-0515
www.unisys.com
Other Communications: Ottawa: 613-940-4500; Halifax: 902-422-5445
Social Media: www.facebook.com/UnisysCorp
twitter.com/UnisysCorp
www.linkedin.com/company/unisys

Company Type: Private
Profile: Unisys serves businesses & governments as a designer, builder, & manager of computing environments. The company focuses on the following areas: data center transformation & outsourcing; end user outsourcing & support services; application modernization & outsourcing; & security.
Tim Feick, President
Gregory G. Bergman, Secretary
Mary Joynt, Treasurer

Versatile Systems Inc.
#910, 355 Burrard St.
Vancouver, BC V6C 2G8

www.versatile.com

Company Type: Public
Ticker Symbol: W / TSX Venture
Profile: Versatile Systems offers information technology services & business solutions.
John Hardy, Chief Executive Officer
Fraser Atkinson, Chief Financial Officer

WebTech Wireless Inc.
Head Office
#215, 4299 Canada Way
Burnaby, BC V5G 1H3

604-434-7337
Fax: 604-287-0135
866-287-0135
info@webtechwireless.com; ir@webtechwire
www.webtechwireless.com
Other Communications: USA: 1800-530-9938; Europe: +44 (0) 1189 254966
Social Media: twitter.com/webtechwireless
www.linkedin.com/company/31591

Company Type: Public
Ticker Symbol: WEW / TSX
Profile: Vehicle fleet location based services & telematics technology are developed & manufactured by Webtech Wireless Inc.. Products include InterFleet solutions for government, Quadrant commercial fleet solutions, & NextBus passenger information services for transit fleets. The wireless solutions help to improve productivity, environmental compliance, & safety of vehicle fleets.
Scott Edmonds, President & Chief Executive Officer
Larry Juba, Chief Operating Officer
Andrew Morden, Chief Financial Officer
David Greer, Vice-President, Marketing
604-628-5194, press@webtechwireless.com

Wentworth Technologies Company
566 Arvin Ave.
Stoney Creek, ON L8E 5P1

905-643-9044
Fax: 905-643-5406
wtbvc@wtbvc.com
www.wtbvc.com

Company Type: Private

xwave Solutions
Fort William Building
PO Box 2110, 10 Factory Lane
St. John's, NL A1C 5H6

709-724-7500
Fax: 709-724-7555
877-449-9283
solutions@xwave.com
www.xwave.com

Company Type: Private
Profile: xwave Solutions is an information technology company that provides information technology professional services & advanced technology solutions. More than 700 people are employed at the following locations: Toronto, Ottawa, Montréal, Fredericton, Saint John, Moncton, Halifax, Summerside, & St. John's.
Louis Larouche, Regional Director, Québec
Jeff McGuigan, Regional Director, New Brunswick
Cecil Smith, Regional Director, Nova Scotia
June Turpin, Regional Director, Newfoundland & Labrador

Chemicals

5N Plus Inc.
Head Office
4385, rue Garand
Montréal, QC H4R 2B4

514-856-0644
Fax: 514-856-9611
info@5nplus.com
www.5nplus.com

Company Type: Public
Ticker Symbol: VNP / TSX
Profile: 5N Plus Inc. produces specialty metal & chemical products. Examples of products include bismuth, indium, germanium, compound semiconductor wafers, & inorganic chemicals. Manufacturing facilities & sales offices are located in North America, South America, Europe, & Asia.
Jacques L'Écuyer, President & Chief Executive Officer
David Langlois, Chief Financial Officer
Marc Suys, Vice-President, Corporate Affairs
Sebastian Voigt, Vice-President, Eco-Friendly Materials

Agrium Inc.
13131 Lake Fraser Dr. SE
Calgary, AB T2J 7E8

403-225-7000
Fax: 403-225-7609
877-247-4861
investor@agrium.com
www.agrium.com

Company Type: Public
Ticker Symbol: AGU / TSX, NYSE
Profile: Agrium Inc. produces & markets major agricultural nutrients throughout the world. The company also supplies specialty fertilizers across North America. In North & South America, Agrium is engaged in the retail supply of agricultural products & services.
Michael M. Wilson, B.Sc. (Chem), P.Eng., President/CEO
Richard L. Gearheard, B.S. (Accounting), CPA, Sr. Vice-President & President, Retail
Ron. A. Wilkinson, B.SC. (Chem), P.Eng., Sr. Vice-President & President, Wholesale
William (Bill) Boycott, B.Sc.Eng.(Chem), P.Eng., Vice-President & President, Agrium Advanced Technologies
Bruce G. Waterman, Sr. Vice-President/CFO
Leslie A. O'Donoghue, B.A. (Econ), LL.B., Sr. Vice-President, General Counsel & Corporate Secretary
Stephen Dyer, B.Sc. (Chem), P.Eng., Vice-President, Manufacturing

Air Liquide Canada Inc.
#1700, 1250, boul René-Lévesque ouest
Montréal, QC H3B 5E6

514-933-0303
Fax: 514-846-7700
www.ca.airliquide.com

Company Type: Private
Profile: Founded in 1902, Air Liquide is a supplier of oxygen, hydrogen, nitrogen, & other gases to industries.

AstraZeneca Canada Inc.
1004 Middlegate Rd.
Mississauga, ON L4Y 1M4

905-277-7111
Fax: 905-270-3248
800-565-5877
customer.relations1@astrazeneca.com
www.astrazeneca.ca

Company Type: Private
Mark Jones, President/CEO
Vincent Rizzi, CFO & Vice-President, Finance
Mario Tremblay, Vice-President, Sales

Atrium Innovations Inc.
1405, boul du Parc-Technologique
Québec, QC G1P 4P5

418-652-1116
Fax: 418-652-0151
www.atrium-innovations.com
Other Communications: Investors: investor.relations@atrium-innov.com
Social Media: www.facebook.com/pages/Atrium-Innovations/111312772231063
twitter.com/atrium_en_bref

Company Type: Public
Ticker Symbol: ATB / TSX
Profile: Atrium Innovations is engaged in the development & manufacture of products, which are marketed to the chemical, pharmaceutical, & nutrition industries.
Pierre Fitzgibbon, President & Chief Executive Officer
Carmen Fortino, President, North American Operations
Serge Yelle, Ph.D., Executive Vice-President, Strategy & Business Development
Mario Paradis, CA, Chief Financial Officer & Vice-President
David Torralbo, Vice-President, Legal & Corporate Affairs

BASF Canada
100 Milverton Dr., 5th Fl.
Mississauga, ON L5R 4H1

289-360-1300
Fax: 289-360-6000
866-485-2273
noc_canada-webmaster@basf-corp.com
www.basf.ca

Company Type: Private
Laurent Tainturier, President
Marc P. Muff, Director, Finance & Business Services

Baxter Corporation
#700, 4 Robert Speck Pkwy.
Mississauga, ON L4Z 3Y4

905-270-1125
Fax: 905-281-6560
800-387-8399
business_development_canada@baxter.com
www.baxter.ca

Company Type: Private
Barb Leavitt, President
Mary Parniak, Vice-President, Finance
Barbara Dawson, Director, Communications
Jim Porter, Director, Information Technology

Bioniche Life Sciences Inc.
Corporate Headquarters
PO Box 1570, 231 Dundas St. East
Belleville, ON K8N 5J2

613-966-8058
Fax: 613-966-4177
800-265-5464
info@bioniche.com; hr@bioniche.com
www.bioniche.com
Other Communications: Manufacturing, Phone: 514-697-6636, Fax: 514-697-7966

Company Type: Public
Ticker Symbol: BNC / TSX, Australia
Profile: The biopharmaceutical company specializes in discovering, developing, manufacturing, & marketing products for human & animal health. Operating divisions focus on human health, animal health, & food safety. Bioniche Life Sciences' corporate headquarters in Belleville, Ontario is also the headquarters for Bioniche Animal Health & Bioniche Food Safety.
Graeme McRae, Chair, President & Chief Executive Officer
Rick Culbert, President, Bioniche Food Safety
Andrew Grant, President, Bioniche Animal Health
Brian Ford, Chief Financial Officer
Brian.Ford@Bioniche.com
Cindy Benning, Senior Vice-President, Operations, Quality, & Regulatory Affairs
Mohamed Elrafih, Vice-President, Manufacturing Operations
Jennifer Shea, Vice-President, Communications & Investor & Government Relations
Jennifer.Shea@Bioniche.com

Canexus Corporation
#600, 801 - 7th Ave. SW
Calgary, AB T2P 3P7

403-571-7300
Fax: 403-571-7800
canexus@canexus.ca
www.canexus.ca
Other Communications: Houston: 281-875-7280; Sao Paulo, Brazil: (55) (11) 3443-746

Company Type: Public
Ticker Symbol: CUS / TSX
Profile: Canexus produces chlor-alkali & sodium chlorate products for the water treatment & pulp & paper industries. Plants are located in Canada & Brazil.
Gary L. Kubera, President & Chief Executive Officer
Richard T. McLellan, Chief Financial Officer & Senior Vice-President, Finance
Angelo Lacara, Senior Vice-President, Operations
Diane J. Pettie, General Counsel, Corporate Secretary & Vice-President

Canexus Corporation
Head Office
#600, 801 - 7th Ave. SW
Calgary, AB T2P 3P7

403-571-7300
Fax: 403-571-7800
canexus.ca
Other Communications: Houston Corporate Office: 281-875-7280

Company Type: Private
Profile: Canexus Corporation is involved in chemical manufacturing & handling. Soium chlorate & chlor-alkali products are produced for the pulp & paper & water treatment industries.

Cangene Corporation
Head Office
155 Innovation Dr.
Winnipeg, MB R3T 5Y3

204-275-4200
Fax: 204-269-7003
877-226-4363
info@cangene.com; ir@cangene.com; hr@cang
www.cangene.com
Other Communications: Service: customerservice@cangene.com

Company Type: Public
Ticker Symbol: CNJ / TSX
Profile: Cangene Corporation is a biopharmaceutical company that specializes in the development & commercialization of immune therapeutics. The company employs approximately 580 people at locations in North America. Products are sold throughout the world.
John Sedor, President & Chief Executive Officer
Michael Graham, Chief Financial Officer
Bill Bees, Senior Vice-President, Operations
Grant McClarty, Vice-President, Research & Development
John McMillan, Corporate Secretary & Vice-President, Commercial Development
Andrew Storey, Vice-President, Quality Assurance / Clinical & Regulatory Affairs

Cardiome Pharma Corp.
6190 Agronomy Rd., 6th Fl.
Vancouver, BC V6T 1Z3

604-677-6905
Fax: 604-677-6915
800-330-9928
feedback@cardiome.com; ir@cardiome.com (i
www.cardiome.com
Other Communications: Business Development, E-mail: bus-dev@cardiome.com

Company Type: Public
Ticker Symbol: COM / TSX, NASDAQ
Profile: The biopharmaceutical company is committed to the discovery, development, & commercialization of therapies to improve health.
Doug Janzen, President & Chief Executive Officer
Curtis Sikorsky, CFO
Donald A. McAfee, Ph.D., Chief Scientific Officer

Chemtrade Logistics Income Fund
#300, 155 Gordon Baker Rd.
Toronto, ON M2H 3N5

416-496-5856
Fax: 416-496-9942
investor-relations@chemtradelogistics.com
www.chemtradelogistics.com

Company Type: Public
Ticker Symbol: CHE / TSX
Profile: Chemtrade provides industrial chemicals & services to customers around the world. The company also offers industrial services, such as processing hydrogen sulphide & waste streams. In 2011, Chemtrade acquired all the businesses of Marsulex Inc.
Mark Davis, President & Chief Executive Officer
Rohit Bhardwaj, Chief Financial Officer & Vice-President, Finance
Susan Paré, Corporate Secretary
spare@chemtradelogistics.com

Dow Chemical Canada
#2100, 450 - 1st St. SW
Calgary, AB T2P 5H1

403-267-3500
Fax: 403-267-3597
800-447-4369
www.dow.com

Company Type: Private

DuPont Canada
PO Box 2200 Stn. Streetsville, , 7070 Mississauga Rd.
Mississauga, ON L5M 2H3

905-821-3300
Fax: 905-821-5057
800-387-2122
information@ca.dupont.com
www.ca.dupont.com

Company Type: Public
Ticker Symbol: DUP
Charles O. Holiday, Chairman/CEO
Michael J. Oxley, President/CFO, DuPont Canada
Yanitan G. Ho, Vice-President & Chief Information Officer, Information Technology

Enerchem International Inc.
#1950, 777 - 8th Ave. SW
Calgary, AB T2P 3R5

780-980-1682
Fax: 780-980-2610
investors@enerchem.com
www.enerchem.com

Company Type: Public
Ticker Symbol: ECH
Kenneth Bagan, President/CEO
Brian M. Zubach, CFO

GlaxoSmithKline Inc.
7333 Mississauga Rd. North
Mississauga, ON L5N 6L4

905-819-3000
Fax: 905-819-3099
800-387-7374
www.gsk.ca

Company Type: Private
Paul Lucas, President/CEO
R. Castonguay, Vice-President, Finance
Savino DiPasquale, Chief Information Officer & Vice-President, Information Technology
Maris Silnis, Manager, Health & Safety

Hanfeng Evergreen Inc.
PO Box 129, #2510, 1 First Canadian Pl.
Toronto, ON M5X 1A4

416-368-8588
Fax: 416-849-0075
info@hanfengevergreen.com
www.hanfengevergreen.com

Company Type: Public
Ticker Symbol: HF
Profile: Hanfeng Evergreen Inc.'s area of expertise is the production of slow & controlled release (S&CR) fertilizers. The company's fertilizers are used by the urban greening markets & the agricultural sectors in China & Southeast Asia. Hanfeng Evergreen has a research & development centre & production facilities in China & Southeast Asia.
Xinduo Yu, President & Chief Executive Officer
Niral Merchant, CA, Chief Financial Officer

Methanex Corporation
Waterfront Centre
#1800, 200 Burrard St.
Vancouver, BC V6C 3M1

604-661-2600
Fax: 604-661-2676
800-661-8851
invest@methanex.com; sales@methanex.com
www.methanex.com
Other Communications: Government & Public Affairs: publicaffairs@methanex.com

Company Type: Public
Ticker Symbol: MX / TSX, NASDAQ
Profile: Methanex Corporation is a producer & marketer of methanol. The company supplies major international markets.
Bruce Aitken, President & Chief Executive Officer
Ian Cameron, Chief Financial Officer & Senior Vice-President, Finance
Michael MacDonald, Senior Vice-President, Corporate Development
John Floren, Senior Vice-President, Global Marketing & Logistics
Randy Milner, Sr. Vice-President, General Counsel, & Corporate Secretary
Jason Chesko, Director, Investor Relations

Migao Corporation
#1108, 8 King St. East
Toronto, ON M5C 1B5

416-869-1108
Fax: 416-869-1101
info@migaocorp.com
www.migaocorp.com
Other Communications: Beijing, China Office, Phone: +86 10 8447 7526

Company Type: Public
Ticker Symbol: MGO / TSX
Profile: Migao Corporation is the the owner & operator of fertilizer production plants. Plants are situated across China. Products are used by Chinese domestic agricultural markets.
Liu Guocai, Chief Executive Officer
liu.guocai@migaocorp.com
Randall Smallbone, Chief Financial Officer
randall.smallbone@migaocorp.com
Jay Hussey, Vice-President, Corporate Finance
jay.hussey@migaocorp.com

Nova Chemicals Corporation
PO Box 2518, 1000 - 7th Ave. SW
Calgary, AB T2P 5C6

403-750-3600
www.novachemicals.com

Company Type: Private
Profile: Chemicals & plastics are produced by the company.
Jeffrey M. Lipton, Chief Executive Officer
Christopher D. Pappas, President/COO
Larry A. MacDonald, Sr. Vice-President/CFO
Jack S. Mustoe, Sr. Vice-President, Chief Legal Officer & Corporate Secretary
F. Peter Boer, Chair, Public Policy & Responsible Care Committee

Oncolytics Biotech Inc.
#210, 1167 Kensington Cres. NW
Calgary, AB T2N 1X7

403-670-7377
Fax: 403-283-0858
info@oncolyticsbiotech.com
www.oncolyticsbiotech.com

Company Type: Public
Ticker Symbol: ONC / TSX, NASDAQ
Profile: The biotechnology company develops oncolytic viruses as potential cancer therapeutics. Oncolytics Biotech's clinical program includes a range of human trials.

Bradley G. Thompson, Ph.D., President, Chief Executive Officer & Chair
Doug Ball, C.A., Chief Financial Officer
Matt Coffey, Ph.D., Chief Operating Officer
Karl Mettinger, M.D., Ph.D, Chief Medical Officer
George Gill, M.D., Senior Vice-President, Clinical & Regulatory Affairs

Paladin Labs Inc.
Corporate Headquarters
#600, 100, boul Alexis Nihon
Montréal, QC H4M 2P2

514-340-1112
Fax: 514-344-4675
888-376-7830
info@paladin-labs.com
www.paladin-labs.com

Company Type: Public
Ticker Symbol: PLB / TSX
Profile: The specialty pharmaceutical company acquires or in-licenses pharmaceutical products for the Canadian & world markets.
In 2011, Paladin Labs Inc. acquired Labopharm Inc.. In 2012, Paladin Labs Inc. entered into a strategic partnership, where Paladin will merge the Pharmaplan business with the pharma division of Litha Healthcare Group Limited. The partnership with Litha allows Paladin to expand in Sub-Saharan Africa.
Mark Beaudet, President & Chief Executive Officer
Samira Sakhia, CA, MBA, Chief Financial Officer
514-669-5367, Fax: 514-344-4675
Patrice Larose, Vice-President, Scientific Affairs
Michael Freeman, Vice-President, Government Affairs

Patheon Inc.
2100 Syntex Crt.
Mississauga, ON L5N 7K9

905-812-2125
Fax: 905-812-6705
info@patheon.com; investor@patheon.com
www.patheon.com
Other Communications: Research Triangle Park, NC, USA, Phone: 919-226-3200

Company Type: Public
Ticker Symbol: PTI / TSX
Profile: Patheon Inc. serves pharmaceutical & biotechnology companies by providing manufacturing services. The company's services include the manufacturing of dosage forms, such as soft gel, solid, & liquid forms. Patheon consists of development centers, manufacturing facilities, & a clinical trial material packaging facility.
James C. Mullen, Chief Executive Officer
Mark J. Kontny, Ph.D., Chief Scientific Officer & President, Global Pharmaceutical Development Services
Paul M. Garofolo, Chief Technology Officer & Executive Vice-President, PDS Global Business Operations
Stuart Grant, Chief Financial Officer & Executive Vice-President
Michael E. Lytton, General Counsel & Executive Vice-President, Corporate Development & Strategy
Wendy Wilson, Contact, Investor Relations & Corporate Communications
wendy.wilson@patheon.com

PFB Corporation
#100, 2886 Sunridge Way NE
Calgary, AB T1Y 7H9
403-569-4300
Fax: 403-569-4075
mailbox@pfbcorp.com
www.pfbcorp.com
Company Type: Public
Ticker Symbol: PFB / TSX
Profile: Through its wholly-owned subsidiaries, PFB Corporation manufactures insulating building products, based on expanded polystyrene technology. Brands of insulating building products include Plasti-Fab EPS Product Solutions, Riverbend Timber Framing, Insulspan Structural Insulating Panels Systems, Precision Craft, & Advantage ICF Systems. The company serves the construction, industrial, commercial, & residential markets throughout North America.
C. Alan Smith, President, Chief Executive Officer & Chair
Stephen P. Hardy, Chief Financial Officer & Vice-President
403-569-4303
Bruce M. Carruthers, Chief Operating Officer
William H. Smith, Q.C., Corporate Secretary

PPG Canada Inc.
2450 Bristol Way
Oakville, ON L6H 6P6
905-829-5074
Fax: 905-829-9498
www.ppg.com
Other Communications: OEM Coatings: 905-829-3592; APA: 905-829-9498
Company Type: Private
Profile: PPG Canada is a manufacturer of coatings & specialty products & services. The manufacturer serves customers in the following areas: construction, industrial markets, consumer products, & transportation markets.
Charles E. Bunch, Chair & Chief Executive Officer
Robert J. Dellinger, Chief Financial Officer & Senior Vice-President
Charles F. Kahle, Chief Technology Officer & Vice-President, Coatings Research & Development
James C. Diggs, Senior Vice-President & General Counsel
John Richter, Vice-President, Environment, Health, & Safety
Lynne D. Schmidt, Vice-President, Government & Community Affairs

QLT Inc.
887 Great Northern Way
Vancouver, BC V5T 4T5
604-707-7000
Fax: 604-707-7001
800-663-5486
corpcomm@qltinc.com
www.qltinc.com
Company Type: Public
Ticker Symbol: QLT / TSX, NASDAQ
Robert Butchofsky, President/CEO & Director
Cameron Nelson, Vice-President/CFO, Finance
Therese Hayes, Vice-President, Investor Relations & Corporate Communications

Theratechnologies Inc.
2310, boul Alfred-Nobel
Montréal, QC H4S 2B4
514-336-7800
Fax: 514-336-7242
communications@theratech.com
www.theratech.com
Company Type: Public
Ticker Symbol: TH / TSX
Profile: The pharmaceutical company is engaged in the discovery & development of therapeutic peptide products. Theratechnologies Inc.'s lead product is tesamorelin for injection.
John-Michel T. Huss, MBA, President & Chief Executive Officer
Luc Tanguay, Chief Financial Officer & Senior Executive Vice-President
Jocelyn Lafond, LL.B., LL.M., Corporate Secretary & Vice-President, Legal Affairs

Transition Therapeutics Inc.
#220, 101 College St.
Toronto, ON M5G 1L7
416-260-7770
Fax: 416-260-2886
info@transitiontherapeutics.com
www.transitiontherapeutics.com
Company Type: Public
Ticker Symbol: TTH / TSX, NASDAQ
Tony F. Cruz, Chairman & CEO
Elie Farah, Vice-President & CFO, Corporate Development

Univar Canada Ltd.
9800 Van Horne Way
Richmond, BC V6X 1W5
604-273-1441
Fax: 604-273-2046
www.univarcanada.com
Company Type: Private
Profile: Univar provides chemicals & related chemical distribution services.

Valeant Pharmaceuticals International, Inc.
Corporate Headquarters
7150 Mississauga Rd.
Mississauga, ON L5N 8M5
905-286-3000
Fax: 905-286-3050
800-556-1937
ir@valeant.com; medinfo_canada@valeant.co
Other Communications: Human Resources: recruiting@valeant.com
Company Type: Public
Ticker Symbol: VRX, TSX, NYSE
Profile: The specialty pharmaceutical company develops, manufactures, & markets pharmaceutical products. Valeant Pharmaceuticals specializes in the areas of neurology & dermatology. Products are sold in North America, Brazil, central Europe, & Australia.
J. Michael Pearson, Chair & Chief Executive Officer
Rajiv De Silva, President, Valeant Pharmaceuticals International, Inc. & COO, Specialty Pharmaceuticals
Richard K. Masterson, President, Valeant International (Barbados) SRL
Howard B. Schiller, Chief Financial Officer & Executive Vice-President
Robert Chai-Onn, Executive Vice-President, General Counsel & Corp. Secretary
Susan Hall, Ph.D., Global Head, Research & Development

Communications

Aastra Technologies Limited
155 Snow Blvd.
Concord, ON L4K 4N9
905-760-4200
Fax: 905-760-4233
investors@aastra.com
www.aastra.com
Other Communications: Media Contact: press@aastra.com
Company Type: Public
Ticker Symbol: AAH / TSX
Profile: Aastra Technologies Limited develops & delivers communications products & applications for businesses. Products include associated UC applications, high definition video communications, multimedia call center solutions, plus cordless terminals, & deskphones.
Francis N. Shen, Chair & Chief Executive Officer
Allan Brett, Chief Financial Officer
905-760-4160
Kathy Ristic, Vice-President, Investor Relations

Allstream Inc.
#1400, 200 Wellington St. West
Toronto, ON M5V 3G2
416-345-2000
855-299-7050
connect@allstream.com
www.allstream.com
Company Type: Private

Astral Media Inc.
#2700, 1800, av McGill College
Montréal, QC H3A 3J6
514-939-5000
Fax: 514-939-1515
investorrelations@corp.astral.com
www.astral.com
Social Media: www.facebook.com/pages/Astral/102750233115364?v=wall
twitter.com/astral
Company Type: Public
Ticker Symbol: ACM.A, ACM.B / TSX
Profile: Astral Media is a media company that was founded in 1961. In 2012, it was announced that Astra Media had entered into a definitive agreement with BCE Inc. for the sale of the company. BCE Inc. (Bell) will acquire Astral's pay & specialty television services, radio stations, out-of-home advertising activities, & digital media properties.
Ian Greenberg, President & Chief Executive Officer
Robert Fortier, Chief Financial Officer & Vice-President, Finance
514-939-5000, rfortier@astral.com
Alain Bergeron, Vice-President, Brand Management & Corporate Communications
514-862-8324, abergeron@bcp.ca

Bell Aliant Inc.
4 South, Maritime Centre
1505 Barrington St.
Halifax, NS B3J 3K5
877-248-3113
Fax: 877-498-2464
investors@bellaliant.ca; environment@bell
www.bellaliant.ca
Other Communications: Business Customers: aliant.business@bellaliant.ca
Social Media: www.facebook.com/BellAliant
twitter.com/bell_aliant
Company Type: Public
Ticker Symbol: BA / TSX
Profile: Bell Aliant Inc. is a regional communications provider that serves customers in Ontario, Québec, New Brunswick, Nova Scotia, Prince Edward Island, & Newfoundland & Labrador. Through its operating entities, Bell Aliant offers services such as Internet, voice, data, & video.
Karen H. Sheriff, President & Chief Executive Officer
Fred Crooks, QC, Chief Legal Officer & Executive Vice-President, Corporate Services
Glen LeBlanc, FCMA, Chief Financial Officer & Executive Vice-President
Chuck Hartlen, Senior Vice-President, Customer Experience
Rod MacGregor, Vice-President, Corporate Development & Strategy

Bell Canada
299 Queen St. West
Toronto, ON M5V 2Z5
-310-BELL
bellmediacommunications@bellmedia.ca
www.bell.ca
Company Type: Private

Bell ExpressVu
299 Queen St. West
Toronto, ON M5V 2Z5
-310-BELL
www.bell.ca
Company Type: Private

Bell Media
299 Queen St. West
Toronto, ON M5V 2Z5
416-384-8000
bellmediacommunications@bellmedia.ca
www.bellmedia.com
Company Type: Private

Bell Mobility
www.bell.ca/mobility
Company Type: Private

Canadian Satellite Communications Inc.
300 Slater St.
Ottawa, ON K1A 0C8
www.shawdirect.ca
Company Type: Private

Canadian Satellite Radio Holdings Inc.
590 King St. West, 3rd Fl.
Toronto, ON M5V 1M3
416-408-6000
Fax: 416-408-6005
investor.relations@xmradio.ca
www.xmradio.ca
Company Type: Public
Ticker Symbol: XSR / TSX
Michael Moskowitz, President & CEO
Michael Washinushi, Chief Financial Officer & Secretary/Treasurer

Cineplex Inc.
1303 Yonge St.
Toronto, ON M4T 2Y9
416-323-6600
Fax: 416-323-6603
www.cineplex.com
Company Type: Public
Ticker Symbol: CGX / TSX
Profile: Cineplex Inc. is a large motion picture exhibitor in Canada. The company owns, leases, or has a joint-venture in 130 theatres from British Columiba to Québec.
Ellis Jacob, President & Chief Executive Officer
Gord Nelson, Chief Financial Officer
416-323-6602
Jeffrey Kent, Chief Technology Officer
Dan McGrath, Executive Vice-President
Pat Marshall, Vice-President, Communications & Investor Relations
416-323-6648

Cogeco Cable Inc./ Cogeco Câble inc.
#1700, 5 Place Ville-Marie
Montréal, QC H3B 0B3

514-764-4700
Fax: 514-874-2625
Careers@cogeco.com
www.cogeco.ca

Company Type: Public
Ticker Symbol: CCA / TSX
Profile: The cable telecommunications company provides the following services: internet, telephony, audio, & analog & digital television.
Louis Audet, President & Chief Financial Officer
Pierre Gagné, Chief Financial Officer & Senior Vice-President, Finance
514-764-4756
J. François Audet, Vice-President, Telecommunications
Denis Bélanger, Vice-President, Engineering & Development
René Guimond, Vice-President, Public Affairs & Communications

Corus Entertainment Inc.
Corporate Executive Head Office
25 Dockside Dr.
Toronto, ON M5A 0B5

416-479-7000
Fax: 416-479-7006
866-537-2397
investor.relations@corusent.com
www.corusent.com
Other Communications: Calgary Office, Phone: 403-444-4244, Fax: 403-444-4242

Company Type: Public
Ticker Symbol: CJR / TSX
Profile: The media & entertainment company is engaged in the following services: television broadcasting, specialty television, pay television, specialty radio, digital audio services, advertising, children's animation, & children's book publishing. Some of the companies & brands that comprise Corus Entertainment include the following: W Network, YTV, Treehouse, TELETOON, Nelvana, & Kids Can Press.
John M. Cassaday, President/CEO
Doug Murphy, President, Nelvana, & Exec. Vice-President & General Manager, Corus Kids
Paul Robertson, President, Corus Television
Thomas C. Peddie, Sr. Vice-President/CFO
Scott Dyer, Chief Technology Officer
Gary Maavara, Vice-President & General Counsel
Tracy Ewing, Vice-President, Communications

Craig Wireless Systems Ltd.
#71, 713 Hwy. 111
Rancho Mirage, CA 92270 USA

760-346-3282
info@craigwireless.com
www.craigwireless.com

Company Type: Public
Ticker Symbol: CWG / TSX
Profile: Craig Wireless Systems & its affiliates provide telecommunications services, such as broadband internet access, hosting, business connectivity solutions, & security solutions.
T. Boyd Craig, Chief Executive Officer
Murray Banforth, Chief Financial Officer
Gary Birkland, Director, Operations

DHX Media Ltd.
1478 Queen St., 2nd Fl.
Halifax, NS B3J 2H7

902-423-0260
halifax@dhxmedia.com; info@dhxmedia.com
www.dhxmedia.com
Other Communications: Locations: toronto@dhxmedia.com; vancouver@dhxmedia.com
Social Media: www.facebook.com/dhxmedia
twitter.com/dhxmedia

Company Type: Public
Ticker Symbol: DHX / TSX
Profile: DHX Media produces, distributes, & licenses children's entertainment. W!LDBRAIN Entertainment is the company's subsidiary.
Michael Patrick Donovan, Chief Executive Officer
Steven Graham DeNure, President & Chief Operating Officer
Dana Sean Landry, Chief Financial Officer
Mark Gregory Gosine, General Counsel, Corp. Secretary, & Executive Vice-President, Legal Affairs
David A. Regan, Executive Vice-President, Corporate Development & Investor Relations
david.regan@dhxmedia.com

GLENTEL Inc.
8501 Commerce Ct.
Burnaby, BC V5A 4N3

604-415-6500
Fax: 604-415-6565
investors@glentel.com
www.glentel.com

Company Type: Public
Ticker Symbol: GLN.TO / TSX
Profile: Glentel Inc. is a provider of telecommunications services & solutions, through its retail & business operating divisions. Products & services include wireless devices, wireless engineering, & wireless asset monitoring. Locations across Canada are known as Glentel Wireless Business Centres, The Tbooth wireless / La cabine T sans fil, WIRELESS etc. / Sans fil etc., & WirelessWave / Wave Sans Fil.
Thomas E. Skidmore, President, Chief Executive Officer, & Chair
Jas Boparai, Chief Financial Officer
David M. Hartman, Vice-President, Operations, Retail Division
Daniel H. Lowndes, Vice-President, Operations, Business Division
Cary T. Skidmore, Vice-President, Marketing

IMAX Corporation
Sheridan Science & Technology Park
2525 Speakman Dr.
Mississauga, ON L5K 1B1

905-403-6500
Fax: 905-403-6450
info@imax.com
www.imax.com
Social Media: www.facebook.com/IMAX
twitter.com/IMAX

Company Type: Public
Ticker Symbol: IMX / TSX, NYSE
Profile: IMAX is an entertainment & technology company. It specializes in motion picture & sound technologies. Markets include North America, western Europe, Japan, China, & Russia. There are over 600 IMAX theatre in fifty countries.
Richard L. Gelfond, Co-Chair/Co-CEO
Greg Foster, Chair & President, Filmed Entertainment
Joseph Sparacio, CFO
Brian Bonnick, Exec. Vice-President, Technology

Manitoba Telecom Services Inc. (MTS)
PO Box 6666, 333 Main St.
Winnipeg, MB R3C 3V6

204-225-5687
Fax: 204-941-6767
800-883-2054
investor.relations@mtsallstream.com
www.mts.ca
Other Communications: French: 1-800-255-6687; TTY: 204-942-4942; Repair: 611

Company Type: Public
Ticker Symbol: MBT / TSX
Profile: Through its wholly-owned subsidiary MTS Allstream Inc., Manitoba Telecom Services Inc. provides television, voice, data, wireless, & wireline services. Both residential & business customers are served in Manitoba, while across Canada, business clients are served through a portfolio of information technology consulting & security services, as well as voice & data connectivity services. Manitoba Telecom Service Inc. employs approximately 5,500 people throughout Canada.
Pierre Blouin, Chief Executive Officer
Wayne S. Demkey, Chief Financial Officer
Ian Chadsey, Vice-President, Investor Relations
204-941-8283
Fred Riddle, Manager, Environment Programs, Wellness, & Disability Management
204-941-6521, fred.riddle@mts.ca

Mood Media Corporation
99 Sante Dr.
Concord, ON L4K 3C4

905-761-4300
info@moodmedia.com
www.moodmedia.com

Company Type: Public
Ticker Symbol: MM / TSX
Profile: Mood Media Corporation uses music, visual, & scent media to help its clients communicate to consumers. The company's principal divisions are Retail Point-of-Purchase & In-Store Media.
In 2012, Mood Media Corporation acquired DMX Holdings, Inc., a provider of multi-sensory branding services.
Lorne Abony, Chair & Chief Executive Officer
Ken Cross, Chief Executive Officer, Mood Entertainment
Mark Elfenbein, President, Mood Media North America
Steven K. Richards, President, Mood Media/Muzak
Ben Gujral, Chief Financial Officer
James Lanthier, Chief Operating Officer

Newfoundland Capital Corporation Limited
745 Windmill Rd.
Dartmouth, NS B3B 1C2

902-468-7557
Fax: 902-468-7558
ncc@ncc.ca; careers@newcapradio.com
www.ncc.ca
Other Communications: Investor Relations: investorrelations@ncc.ca

Company Type: Public
Ticker Symbol: NCC.A, NCC.B / TSX
Profile: Newfoundland Capital Corporation Limited is the owner & operator of radio stations throughout Canada. Newcap Radio is a wholly owned subsidiary of Newfoundland Capital Corporation Limited.
In addition to its involvement in radio broadcasting, Newfoundland Capital Corporation Limited also owns & operates the Glynmill Inn in Corner Brook, Newfoundland & Labrador.
Robert G. Steele, President & Chief Executive Officer
Scott G.M. Weatherby, Chief Financial Officer & Corporate Secretary
David J. Murray, Chief Operating Officer
Glendon MacBurnie, Corporate Manager, Information Services
Jeremy Hockin, Administrator, Network Systems

Quebecor Media
#600, 7400, boul. Les Galeries D'Anjou
Montréal, QC H1M 3S9

514-373-2240
877-557-2437
www.quebeor.com

Company Type: Private

Rogers Cable Communications
855 York Mills Rd.
Don Mills, ON M3B 1Z1

888-764-3771
www.rogers.com

Company Type: Private

Rogers Communications Inc.
333 Bloor St. East, 7th Fl.
Toronto, ON M4W 1G9

888-764-3771
investor.relations@rogers.com
www.rogers.com
Other Communications: TTY: 800-668-9286; Media: 416-764-2000
Social Media: www.facebook.com/Rogers
twitter.com/rogersbuzz

Company Type: Public
Ticker Symbol: RCI / TSX
Profile: The diversified communications & media company provides wireless voice & data communications services, as well as cable television, high-speed Internet, & telephony services. Through Rogers Media, magazines & trade publications, sports entertainment, television & radio broadcasteing, & televised shopping are provided.
Alan D. Horn, Chairman/Acting CEO
Philip B. Lind, CM, Vice Chairman
William W. Linton, CFO/Sr. Vice President, Finance

Rogers Media
333 Bloor Street East, 7th Fl.
Toronto, ON M4W 1G9

888-764-3771
www.rogers.com

Company Type: Private

Rogers Wireless
100 Westmorland St.
Moncton, NB E1C 0G1

416-935-5555
888-764-3771
www.rogers.com

Company Type: Private

Shaw Communications Inc.
#900, 630 - 3rd Ave. SW
Calgary, AB T2P 4L4

403-750-4500
Fax: 403-750-4501
888-472-2222
www.shaw.ca
Social Media: www.facebook.com/shaw
twitter.com/shawinfo

Company Type: Public
Ticker Symbol: SJR / TSX, NYSE
Profile: Established in 1966, the communications company provides broadband cable television, internet, digital phone, telecommunications services, & satellite direct-to-home services.

Jim Shaw, Vice-Chair/CEO
Peter J. Bissonnette, President

Steve Wilson, Sr. Vice-President/CFO
Ken C.C. Stein, Sr. Vice-President, Corporate & Regulatory Affairs
Bradley S. Shaw, Sr. Vice-President, Operations

Stratos Global Corporation
#210, 2650 Queensview Dr.
Ottawa, ON K2B 8H6
613-230-4544
Fax: 613-230-4212
877-995-9901
investor@stratosglobal.com
www.stratosglobal.com
Company Type: Private
James J. Parm, President/CEO
Paula M. McDonald, Exec. Vice-President & CFO
John M. Mackey, Chief Technology Officer

Sun Media Inc.
416-933-5696
www.sunnewsnetwork.ca
Social Media: www.facebook.com/sunnewsnetwork
twitter.com/#!/sunnewsnetwork
Company Type: Private

TELUS Corp.
TELUS Client Care
PO Box 7575, Vancouver, BC V6B 8N9
877-310-8324
ir@telus.com
www.telus.com
Other Communications: TTY: 800-855-1155; TELUS Mobility: 866-558-2273; Repair: 611
Social Media: www.facebook.com/telus
twitter.com/telus
www.linkedin.com/company/telus
Company Type: Public
Ticker Symbol: T / TSX, NYSE
Profile: Communications products include internet protocol, data, voice, & video.
Darren Entwistle, President/CEO
Robert McFarlane, Exec. Vice-President/CFO
Kevin Salvadori, Exec. Vice-President, Business Transformations & Technology Operations
Eros Spadotto, Exec. Vice-President, Technology Strategy
Janet Yale, Exec. Vice-President, Corporate Affairs

TeraGo Inc.
Corporate Headquarters
#710, 55 Commerce Valley Dr. West
Toronto, ON L3T 7V9
905-326-8711
Fax: 905-707-6212
866-837-2461
www.terago.ca
Other Communications: Technical Support: 866-837-2462
Social Media: www.facebook.com/TeraGo.Networks
twitter.com/Terago_networks
www.linkedin.com/company/terago-networks
Company Type: Public
Ticker Symbol: TGO / TSX
Profile: TeraGo Networks provides the following services to businesses in Canada: voice services, high speed internet, data networking, & internet redundancy. TeraGo owns & operates its National Wireless Network.
Bryan Boyd, President & Chief Executive Officer
Scott Browne, Chief Financial Officer
Kevin Hickey, Vice-President, Engineering & Operations
Allan Laudersmith, Vice-President, Sales
Jim Nikopoulos, General Counsel & Vice-President, Corporate Development

TVA Group Inc./ Groupe TVA
1600, boul de Maisonneuve est
Montréal, QC H2L 4P2
514-526-9251
Fax: 514-598-6085
www.tva.canoe.ca
Social Media: www.facebook.com/ReseauTVA
twitter.com/tvareseau
Company Type: Public
Ticker Symbol: TVA / TSX
Profile: The integrated communications company provides the following services: broadcasting, publishing, producing, & distributing audiovisual products. TVA Group owns French-language television stations, plus a specialty channel. It also publishes French-language magazines. The TVA Films subsidiary serves both Canada's English & French-language markets.
Pierre Dion, President & Chief Executive Officer
Denis Rozon, CA, Chief Financial Officer & Vice-President
514-598-2808

Videotron Limitée
888-433-6876
videotron.com
Company Type: Private

Construction

Aecon Group Inc.
Head Office
#800, 20 Carlson Ct.
Toronto, ON M9W 7K6
416-293-7004
Fax: 416-293-0271
877-232-2677
aecon@aecon.com
www.aecon.com
Other Communications: West Headquarters, Phone: 403-695-3085, Fax: 403-695-3094
Social Media: twitter.com/AecconGroup
Company Type: Public
Ticker Symbol: ARE
Profile: Aecon Group is a construction & infrastructure development company. It serves both public & private sector clients through the provision of engineering, financing, procurement, construction, & project management services.
John M. Beck, Chair & Chief Executive Officer
Scott C. Balfour, President/CFO
Paul P. Koenderman, Exec. Vice-President/CEO, Aecon Industrial Group
Terrance L. McKibbon, CEO, Aecon Infrastructure
R.D. (Bob) Dautovich, President, Innovative Steam Technologies
Gerard A. Kelly, Sr. Vice-President, Finance
Bruce Fleming, Vice-President & Chief Information Officer
Mike Archambault, Vice-President, Safety & Loss Control
Andy DeHaan, Vice-President, Information Technology

Badger Daylighting Ltd.
5740 - 65th Ave.
Red Deer, AB T4P 1A5
519-472-6181
Fax: 519-472-3804
800-465-4273
canadawest@badgerinc.com
www.badgerinc.com
Other Communications: Eastern Canada, Toll-Free Phone: 888-276-0546
Company Type: Public
Ticker Symbol: BAD / TSX
Profile: Badger Daylighting Ltd. provides non-destructive excavating services. The company has more than 400 hydrovac units that operate from over 80 field offices throughout Canada & the United States. Badger is employed by contractors & facility owners in the petroleum, construction, transportation, engineering, industrial, & utility industries.
Tor Wilson, President & Chief Executive Officer
Greg Kelly, CA, Chief Financial Officer & Vice-President
Derek Dillon, Vice-President, Canadian Operations
John G. Kelly, Vice-President, United States Operations

Bird Construction Inc.
5403 Eglinton Ave. West
Toronto, ON M9C 5K6
416-620-7122
Fax: 416-620-1516
investor.relations@bird.ca; corporate.inf
www.bird.ca
Company Type: Public
Ticker Symbol: BDT / TSX
Profile: The organization is a national general contractor in the residential, institutional, & industrial markets.
Tim J. Talbott, P.Eng., President & Chief Executive Officer
Stephen Entwistle, CA, Chief Financial Officer & Assistant Secretary
Jason C. Trumbla, CA, MAcc, Vice-President, Finance
Charmane L. Morrow, Corporate Secretary

Boyuan Construction Group Inc.
Boyuan Building No. 6
East Rd., Jiaxing Port
Zheijiang, PRC, 314201 China
Social Media: twitter.com/boyuangroup
Company Type: Public
Ticker Symbol: BOY / TSX
Profile: The construction company is engaged in residential, commercial, & municipal infrastructure projects. Boyuan Construction Group focuses on projects in Hainan Province, Shandong Province, & the Yangtze River Delta region of China.
Cai Liang Shou, Founder & Chair
Paul Law, CA, MBA, Chief Financial Officer
paullaw@zjboyuan.com.cn
Ren Shu, Corporate Secretary
renshu@zjboyuan.com.cnn

Calmena Energy Services Inc.
The Dome Tower
PO Box 71, #700, 333 - 7th Ave. SE
Calgary, AB T2P 2Z1
403-225-3879
Fax: 403-366-2066
www.calmena.com
Company Type: Public
Ticker Symbol: CEZ / TSX
Profile: Well construction services are provided by Calmena Energy Services Inc.. The company serves customers in Canada, the United States, Latin America, North Africa, & the Middle East.
John R. King, President & Chief Executive Officer
Peter Balkwill, Chief Financial Officer & Vice-President, Finance
Dave Brown, Vice-President, Engineering & Planning

Churchill Corporation
#400, 4954 Richard Rd. SW
Calgary, AB T3E 6L1
403-685-7777
Fax: 403-685-7770
inquiries@churchill-cuq.com
www.churchillcorporation.com
Other Communications: Investors: investor.relations@churchill-cuq.com
Company Type: Public
Ticker Symbol: CUQ / TSX
Profile: The Churchill Corporation is a provider of building construction, industrial construction, & related maintenance services. It operates in western Canada. The Churchill Corporation's business segments are as follows: Canem Systems Ltd., Stuart Olson Dominion Construction Ltd., Broda Construction Inc., Laird Electric Inc., Laird Constructors Inc., Fuller Austin (an insulation company), & Northern Industrial (an insulation company).
The company has policies, procedures, training programs, & compliance procedures in place to manage environmental issues & comply with legislation & regulations.
James C. Houck, MBA, B.Sc., President & Chief Executive Officer
403-685-7777
Daryl E. Sands, B.Comm, CA, Chief Financial Officer & Executive Vice-President
Andrew Apedoe, B.Comm., Secretary & Vice-President, Investor Relations
403-685-7775
Joette Decore, B.Sc., MBA, Vice-President, Corporate Development

Coopers Park Corporation
#900, 1095 West Pender St.
Vancouver, BC
604-662-8383
Fax: 604-662-3878
info@cooperspark.com
www.cooperspark.com
Company Type: Public
Ticker Symbol: XCP / TSX Venture
Profile: Coopers Park Corporation is a development company. Projects include residential condominiums.
Terence Hui, President & Chief Executive Officer
Dennis Au-Yeung, Chief Financial Officer
dennis.au-yeung@cooperspark.com

Cordy Oilfield Services Inc.
#1000, 1520 - 4th St. SW
Calgary, AB T2R 1H5
403-266-2067
Fax: 403-266-2087
dorr@cordy.ca
www.cordy.ca
Company Type: Public
Ticker Symbol: CKK / TSX Venture
Profile: Cordy Oilfield Services Inc. is involved in the oilfield services & construction industry.
David Mullen, Chief Executive Officer
david.mullen@cordy.ca
H. Allen Cameron, President
Matt Braaten, CA, Chief Financial Officer
matt.braaten@cordy.ca
Bob Brunt, Chief Operating Officer

Dominion Construction Company Inc.
#130, 2985 Virtual Way
Vancouver, BC V5M 4X7
604-631-1000
Fax: 604-631-1100
reception@dominionco.com
www.dominionco.com
Company Type: Private

Dennis W. Burnham, P.Eng., Director
Carl M. Stewart, President/CEO
Doug G. Allen, Vice-President, Finance

EBC Inc.
PO Box 158, 1095, rue Valet
L'Ancienne-Lorette, QC G2E 4M7

418-872-0600
Fax: 418-872-8177
ebc@ebcinc.qc.ca; ebc-mtl@ebcinc.qc.ca
www.ebcinc.qc.ca
Other Communications: Montréal Regional Office: 450-444-9333
Company Type: Private
Profile: Construction services are offered across Canada. The company has also completed a hydroelectric project in Costa Rica.
Marie-Claude Houle, P.Eng., M.B.A., President & Vice-President, Development
Jean-Serge D'Aoust, Vice-President, Construction - Building
Richard Gagné, Vice-President, Construction - Civil Works & Earthworks
Yves Gauthier, CA, CMA, Vice-President, Finance & Administration

Ellis-Don Construction Ltd.
2045 Oxford St. West
London, ON N5V 2Z7

519-455-6770
Fax: 519-455-2944
www.ellisdon.com
Company Type: Private
Geoff Smith, CEO/President
Jim King, CFO
Bruce Fleming, Vice-President/Chief Information Officer
Gerry Murphy, Chief Technology Officer
Kari Lynn Atkinson, Vice-President, Ellis Don Consulting-Health & Safety

Finning International Inc.
Park Place
#1000, 666 Burrard St.
Vancouver, BC V6C 2X8

604-691-6444
Fax: 604-691-6440
investor_relations@finning.ca
www.finning.com
Company Type: Public
Ticker Symbol: FTT / TSX
Profile: The company sells, rents, & offers customer service for Caterpillar equipment. Business is conducted in Canada, South America, & the United Kingdom.
Mike Waites, President/CEO
Dave Parker, President, Finning Canada
Andy Bone, President, Power Systems
Juan Carlos Villegas, President, Finning South America
Dave Smith, Exec. Vice-President/CFO
Tom Merinsky, Vice-President, Investor Relations & Corporate Affairs
Jeff Leigh, Vice-President, Business Processes & Systems
Bruce L. Turner, Chair, Environmental, Health & Safety Committee

Fluor Canada Ltd.
Sundance Park
55 Sunpark Plaza SE
Calgary, AB T2X 3R4

403-537-4000
Fax: 403-537-4222
www.fluor.com/canada
Company Type: Private
Alan L. Boeckmann, Chair/CEO, Fluor Corporation
Lee Richardson, Vice-President, Operations
D. Michael Steuert, Sr. Vice-President/CFO, Fluor Corporation
Lee Tashjian, Vice-President, Corporate Communications, Fluor Corporation

HONCO Inc./ HONCO Bâtiments d'Acier
1190, ch Industriel
Saint-Nicolas, QC G7A 1B1

418-831-2245
Fax: 418-831-6302
800-463-5799
honco@honco.ca; honcomtl@honco.ca (Montré
www.honco.ca
Other Communications: Montréal, Phone: 514-354-5123, Fax: 519-354-6949
Company Type: Private
Profile: Founded in 1974, HONCO Inc. designs, manufactures, & installs steel buildings. The company contributes to the commercial, industrial, & recreational construction industry.

Pomerleau
521 - 6th Ave.
Saint-Georges, QC G5Y 0H1

418-228-6688
Fax: 418-228-3524
info@pomerleau.ca
www.pomerleau.ca
Social Media: www.facebook.com/Pomerleau
twitter.com/#!/Pomerleau
www.linkedin.com/company/570096
Company Type: Private

Stuart Olson Dominion Construction Ltd.
Corporate Head Office
#400, 4954 Richard Rd. SW
Calgary, AB T3E 6L1

403-520-2767
Fax: 403-520-1250
www.sodcl.com
Social Media: twitter.com/StuartOlson_Dom
Company Type: Private
Profile: Stuart Olson Dominion is a builder & construction manager that has applied its expertise to a variety of residential, commercial, institutional, industrial, & civic projects. Division offices are located in the following places: Whitehorse Yukon, Richmond British Columbia, Kelowna British Columbia, Calgary Alberta, Edmonton Alberta, Saskatoon Saskatchewan, Regina Saskatchewan, Winnipeg Manitoba, & Thunder Bay, Ontario.
Don Pearson, P.Eng., President & Chief Operating Officer

Distribution & Retail

Alimentation Couche-Tard inc
Tour B
4204, boul Industriel
Laval, QC H7L 0E3

450-662-6632
Fax: 450-662-6640
888-999-9301
info@couche-tard.com
www.couche-tard.com
Company Type: Public
Ticker Symbol: ATD / TSX
Profile: In eastern, central, & western Canada, as well as in the United States, Alimentation Couche-Tard operates convenience stores. Some of these stores include motor fuel dispensing. In Canada, the businesses operate under the brands Couche-Tard & Mac's.
Alain Bouchard, President/CEO
Réal Plourde, Exec. Vice-President/COO
Raymond Paré, Vice-President/CFO
Isabelle Fafard, Contact, Media relations
514-865-8157

Best Buy Canada
8800 Glenlyon Parkway
Burnaby, BC V5J 5K3

866-237-8289
customerservice@bestbuycanada.ca
www.bestbuy.ca
Company Type: Private

Birks & Mayors Inc.
1240 Phillips Sq.
Montréal, QC H3B 3H4

514-397-2511
Fax: 514-397-2537
mrabinovitch@birksandmayors.com
www.birksandmayors.com
Company Type: Public
Ticker Symbol: BMJ / AMEX
Profile: Birks & Mayors Inc. designs, manufactures, & retails fine jewellery, silverware, timepieces, & gitware. Brand names include Birks, Brinkhaus, & Mayors. Retail stores are located in Canada & the United States.
Thomas A. Andruskevich, President/CEO
Michael Rabinovitch, Sr. Vice-President/CFO
Daisy Chin-Lor, Exec. Vice-President & Chief Marketing Officer
Joseph A. Keifer, III, Exec. Vice-President/COO
Jeff Morris, Corporate Controller & Group Vice-President, Accounting
Marco Pasteris, Treasurer & Group Vice-President, Finance
Miranda Melfi, Corporate Secretary & Group Vice-President, Legal Affairs
Milt Thacker, Group Vice-President & Chief Information Officer

BMTC Group Inc.
8500, Place Marien
Montréal, QC H1B 5W8

514-648-5757
Fax: 514-881-4056
info@bmtc-group.com
www.bmtc-group.com
Company Type: Public
Ticker Symbol: GBT.A / TSX
Profile: BMTC Group is a holding company. Its subsidiaries include Ameublements Tanguay Inc. & Brault et Martineau Inc. These subsidiaries are engaged in the retail sale of furniture, electronic goods, & household appliances in Québec.
Yves Des Groseillers, Chair, President & Chief Executive Officer
514-648-5757

Canada Safeway Ltd.
1020 - 64 Ave. NE
Calgary, AB T2E 7V8

403-730-3500
Fax: 403-730-3888
800-723-3929
www.safeway.com
Company Type: Private
Steve Burd, President/CEO
Robert L. Edwards, Exec. Vice President/CFO
David T. Ching, Sr. Vice-President/Chief Information Officer, Safeway Inc.

Canadian Tire Corporation, Limited
PO Box 770 Stn. K, , 2180 Yonge St.
Toronto, ON M4V 2V8

416-480-3000
Fax: 416-544-7715
866-746-7287
investor.relations@cantire.com
www.canadiantire.ca
Other Communications: Corporate Customer Relations: 800-387-8803
Social Media: www.facebook.com/Canadiantire
twitter.com/canadiantire
Company Type: Public
Ticker Symbol: CTC. CTC.a / TSX
Profile: Founded in 1922, Canadian Tire Corporation, Limited is engaged in retail, petroleum, & financial services. Canadian Tire has over 1,700 retail & gasoline outlets across Canada. Approximately 68,000 people are employed.
Stephen G. Wetmore, President & Chief Executive Officer
G. Michael Arnett, President, Canadian Tire Retail
Marco Marrone, President, Canadian Tire Financial Services, Limited
Michael B. Medline, Chief Corporate Officer & President, Diversified Businesses
Paul D. Wilson, President, Mark's Work Wearhouse, Ltd.
J. Huw Thomas, CFO & Exec. Vice-President, Finance & Administration
Patrick R. Sinnott, Exec. Vice-President, Supply Chain & Technology
Kristine Freudenthaler, Chief Information Officer & Sr. Vice-President, Information Technology
Robyn Collver, Sr. Vice-President & General Counsel
Suzanne R. Perles, Chair, Social Responsibility Committee

Canpotex Limited
PO Box 1600, #400, 111 - 2nd Ave. South
Saskatoon, SK S7K 3R7

306-931-2200
Fax: 306-653-5505
canpqlx.sasktelwebhosting.com
Company Type: Private
Steven Dechka, President/CEO
Dwayne N. Dahl, CFO/Vice President, Finance

CanWel Building Materials Group Ltd.
Corporate Office
PO Box 10377, #1100, 609 Granville St.
Vancouver, BC V7Y 1G6

604-432-1400
Fax: 604-436-6670
info@canwel.com
www.canwel.com
Company Type: Public
Ticker Symbol: CWX / TSX
Profile: CanWel Building Materials Group is involved in the distribution of building materials & related products across Canada. Its divisions are CanWelBroadLeaf & Surewood Forest Products.
Amar S. Doman, Chair & Chief Executive Officer
James Code, Chief Financial Officer
R.S. (Rob) Doman, Corporate Secretary

Cervus Equipment Corporation
Harvest Hills Business Park
#5201, 333 - 96 Ave. NE
Calgary, AB T3K OS3

403-567-0339
Fax: 403-567-0309
www.cervuscorp.com
Company Type: Public
Ticker Symbol: CVL / TSX
Profile: Cervus Equipment Corporation acquires & manages

authorized agricultural, commercial, industrial, & transportation equipment dealerships. Business is conducted in Alberta, Saskatchewan, & Manitoba. The corporation also has an investment partnership with a New Zealand based company named Agriturf Limited.
Peter Lacey, Chief Executive Officer
placey@cervuscorp.com
Randall Muth, Chief Financial Officer
rmuth@cervuscorp.com

Coast Wholesale Appliances Inc.
Corporate Headquarters
8488 Main St.
Vancouver, BC V5X 4W8
604-321-6644
Fax: 604-322-4911
888-988-8282
info@coastappliances.com; invest@coastapp
www.coastappliances.com
Other Communications: Human Resources:
coast-hr@coastappliances.com
Company Type: Public
Ticker Symbol: CWA / TSX
Profile: Coast Wholesale Appliances was founded in 1978. It supplies major household appliances & accessories to builders & developers of single-family & multi-family housing & retail customers. Operations take place in western Canada & in the Greater Toronto Area of Ontario.
Maurice Paquette, Chief Executive Officer
Jack G. Peck, Chief Financial Officer & Senior Vice-President
Stephen J. Raben, Senior Vice-President, Sales & Marketing

Coastal Contacts Inc.
#320, 2985 Virtual Way
Vancouver, BC V5M 4X2
604-669-1555
Fax: 604-669-6855
www.coastal.com
Social Media: www.facebook.com/Coastal
twitter.com/TweetCoastal
Company Type: Public
Ticker Symbol: COA / TSX, NASDAQ OMX
Profile: Coastal Contacts was founded in 2000. It is a designer, producer, & online retailer of replacement eyeglasses, sunglasses, contact lenses, & vision care accessories. Web sites include Coastal.com, Lensway.com, Lensway.se, Lenswayco,uk, ClearlyContacts.com.au, ClearlyContacts.co.nz, Contactsan.com, & Coastallens.com.
Roger Hardy, Chief Executive Officer & Founder
Gord Howie, Chief Financial Officer
Steve Bochen, Chief Opeating Officer
Peter Lee, Vice-President, Information Technology
Terry Vanderdruyk, Vice-President, Corporate Development
604-676-4498, terryv@coastalcontacts.com

Colabor Group Inc./ Groupe Colabor Inc.
1620, boul de Montarville
Boucherville, QC J4B 8P4
450-449-4911
Fax: 450-449-6180
info@colabor.com
www.colabor.com
Company Type: Public
Ticker Symbol: GCL / TSX
Profile: In 2009, Colabor Group Inc. completed the conversion of Colabor Income Fund to a corporation. The corporation is engaged in the distribution of confectionery products, refrigerated products, frozen foods, food-related products, dry goods, & beauty & care products. Products are marketed & distributed to retail & foodservice markets.
Claude Gariépy, President & Chief Executive Officer
Jack Battersby, President, Summit Distribution
Michel Loignon, Chief Financial Officer & Vice-President
Michel Delisle, Vice-President, Information Technology
Louise Laforce, Corporate Vice-President, Human Resources & Communications
Marko Potvin, Vice-President, Purchasing

Commercial Solutions Inc.
4203 - 95th St.
Edmonton, AB T6E 5R6
780-432-1611
Fax: 780-496-9172
888-522-9822
info@csinet.ca; feedback@csinet.ca
www.commercialsolutions.ca
Other Communications: Firefighting equipment sales:
fireservices@csinet.ca
Company Type: Public
Ticker Symbol: CSA / TSX
Profile: Commercial Solutions Inc. is a national, independent, industrial distributor of the following products: forestry, mining & resource management equipment, bearing & power transmission supplies, & industrial safety equipment. In addition to these products & services, Commercial Solution Inc.'s group of companies also provides Business to Business services, such as electronic fund transfers, invoicing, & electronic data interchange. Commercial Solutions is an ISO 9001-2008 certified company.
James Barker, President & Chief Executive Officer
Rozina Kassam, CA, Chief Financial Officer
William Rosser, LL.B, Corporate Secretary & Director

Costco Wholesale Canada Inc.
415 West Hunt Club
Ottawa, ON K2E 1C5
613-221-2000
Fax: 613-221-2001
www.costco.com
Company Type: Private
Jim Sinegal, CEO
Joseph P. Portera, President
Ross Hunt, Vice-President, Human Resources & Finance

Dollarama Inc.
5905 Royalmount Ave.
Montréal, QC H4P 0A1
514-737-1006
Fax: 514-940-6169
contactus@dollarama.com
www.dollarama.com
Company Type: Public
Ticker Symbol: DOL / TSX
Profile: Dollarama Inc. was founded in 1992. It sells general merchandise & seasonal products for $2 or less in close to 700 locations in ten Canadian provinces.
Larry Rossy, Chair & Chief Executive Officer
Michael Ross, CA, Chief Financial Officer & Secretary
michael.ross@dollarama.com
Stéphane Gonthier, Chief Operating Officer
Neil Rossy, Chief Merchandising Officer
Leonard Assaly, Senior Vice-President, Informaton Technology & Logistics

easyhome Ltd.
#510, 33 City Centre Dr.
Mississauga, ON L5B 2N5
905-272-2788
Fax: 905-272-9886
888-528-3279
leanne@easyhome.ca
www.easyhome.ca
Company Type: Public
Ticker Symbol: EH / TSX
Profile: easyhome Ltd. is a merchandise lease company. The company rents products, such as household furnishings, home entertainment products, electronics, appliances & computers. Customers may have the option to purchase products.
David Ingram, President & Chief Executive Officer
Steve Goertz, Chief Financial Officer & Senior Vice-President
David Maries, Senior Vice-President, Marketing & Merchandising

Futuremed Healthcare Products Corporation
Head Office & Distribution Centre
277 Basaltic Rd.
Concord, ON L4K 5V3
905-761-0068
Fax: 905-761-9929
800-387-7025
www.futuremed.ca
Company Type: Public
Ticker Symbol: FMD / TSX
Profile: Futuremed Healthcare Products Corporation is involved in the distribution of medical supplies, equipment, & specialized furniture to long-term care facilities. In Quebec, Futuremed Healthcare Products are sold under the name Dismed.
Raymond Stone, President & Chief Executive Officer
Raymond@Fmed.com
Daniel Sacks, Chief Financial Officer

GLV Inc.
#2100, 2001, av McGill College
Montréal, QC H3A 1G1
514-284-2224
Fax: 514-284-2225
courrier@glv.com
www.glv.com
Company Type: Public
Ticker Symbol: GLV / TSX
Profile: GLV Inc. supplies technological solutions & services. Processes & equipment are used in pulp & paper production & for the treatment & recycling of municipal & industrial wastewater.
Laurent Verreault, Chair/CEO
Richard Verreault, President/COO
Marc Barbeau, CA, Exec. Vice-President/CFO
William Mahoney, Sr. Vice-President, Pulp & Paper Group
Douglas Wetherbee, Vice-President, Information Technology & Business Process Optimization
Gwen Klees, Corporate Secretary & Vice-President, Legal Affairs

Groupe Deschênes Inc.
#250, 3901, rue Jarry est
Montréal, QC H1Z 2G1
514-253-3110
Fax: 514-253-3666
info@groupedeschenes.com
www.groupedeschenes.com
Company Type: Private
Profile: Subsidiaries of Deschênes Group Inc. are engaged in the distribution of the following products: electrical & industrial supplies; plumbing & heating products; refrigeration, air conditioning & ventilation products; fire protection equipment, heating controls, & related products.

Harry Winston Diamond Corporation
PO Box 4569 Stn. A, , Toronto, ON M5W 4T9
416-362-2237
Fax: 416-362-2230
hw@harrywinston.com
investor.harrywinston.com
Other Communications: Investor Relations:
investor@harrywinston.com
Company Type: Public
Ticker Symbol: HW
Profile: Harry Winston Diamond Corporation owns 40% interest in the Diavik Diamond Mine in the Northwest Territories. Rough diamonds are supplied to an international market.
The specialist diamond enterprise is also the owner of a diamond jewelry & watch retailer, known as Harry Winston Inc. Retail salons are locatedd in cities around the world, such as Tokyo, Beijing, Paris, London, & New York.
Robert A. Gannicott, Chair & Chief Executive Officer
Thomas J. O'Neill, President
Alan S. Mayne, Chief Financial Officer & Vice-President
James R.W. Pounds, Sr. Vice-President, Diamond Management
Kevin P. Marchant, Vice-President, Production
Lyle R. Hepburn, Corporate Secretary
Kelley Stamm, Manager, Investor Relations
416-205-4380

Hart Stores Inc./ Magasins Hart Inc.
900, Place Paul-Kane
Laval, QC H7C 2T2
450-661-4155
Fax: 450-661-6533
hartstoresinfo@hartstores.com
www.hartstores.com
Social Media:
www.facebook.com/group.php?gid=234174440002218
twitter.com/hartstores
ca.linkedin.com/pub/magasins-hart-stores/44/40b/665
Company Type: Public
Ticker Symbol: HIS / TSX Venture
Profile: Hart Stores Inc. operates a network of mid-sized department stores. Its stores are located in Newfoundland, Nova Scotia, New Brunswick, Québec, & Ontario. Hart Stores Inc.'s banners include Bargain Giant, Géant des Aubaines, & Hart.
Michael Hart, President/CEO
mihart@hartstores.com
Jacques Plante, CA, Vice-President/CFO
jplante@hartstores.com
Michel Lussier, Director, Store Operations
mlussier@hartstores.com
Sal Pugliese, Director, Information Technology & Internal Systems
spugliese@hartstores.com
Francine Perras, Controller & Corporate Secretary
fperras@hartstores.com

Home Hardware Stores
www.homehardware.ca
Company Type: Private

Ikea Canada LP
1065 Plains Rd. East
Burlington, ON L7T 4K1
866-866-4532
www.ikea.com
Social Media: www.facebook.com/IKEACanada
twitter.com/#!/IKEACanada
Company Type: Private

Indigo Books & Music Inc.
#500, 468 King St. West
Toronto, ON M5V 1L8
416-364-4499
Fax: 416-364-0355
800-832-9124
InvestorRelations@indigo.ca
www.chapters.indigo.ca
Other Communications: Corporate & Education: atyourservice@indigo.ca
Social Media: www.facebook.com/ChaptersIndigo
twitter.com/chaptersindigo; twitter.com/indigogreenroom
Company Type: Public
Ticker Symbol: IDG / TSX
Profile: Indigo Books & Music Inc. is a Canadian retailer of books, gifts, & specialty toys. The company is the majority shareholder of the eReading service, Kobo Inc. Stores include Indigo Books & Music, Indigo Books, Gifts, Kids, IndigoSpirit, Chapters, Coles, & The World's Biggest Bookstore. The company's online channel is indigo.ca. Indigo Books & Music also founded the Indigo Love of Reading Foundation.
Heather Reisman, Chair & Chief Executive Officer
Kay Brekken, Chief Financial Officer
Sumit Oberai, Chief Information Officer
Janet Eger, Director, Public Relations
416-342-8561, jeger@indigo.ca

Jean Coutu Group (PJC) Inc.
530, rue Bériault
Longueuil, QC J4G 1S8
450-646-9760
Fax: 450-646-0550
www.jeancoutu.com
Company Type: Public
Ticker Symbol: PJC.A /TSX
Profile: The Jean Coutu Group is engaged in pharmacy retailing. It has 396 franchised stores in Ontario, Québec, & New Brunswick, with approximately 19,000 employees. Banners include PJC Clinique, PJC Jean Coutu, PJC Santé, & PJC Santé Beauté.
François J Coutu, President & Chief Executive Officer
André Belzile, Senior Vice-President, Finance & Corporate Affairs
450-646-9760
Hélène Bisson, Vice-President, Communications
450-646-9611

Kimberley Clark Inc.
50 Burnhamthorpe Rd. West
Mississauga, ON L5B 3Y5
www.kimberly-clark.com
Company Type: Private
Profile: Kimberly-Clark supplies family & personal care products. Brands include Kleenex, Scott, Huggies, Pull-Ups, Kotex, Poise, & Depend.
Thomas J. Falk, Chair & Chief Executive Officer
Robert W. Black, Group President, Kimberly-Clark International
Mark A. Buthman, Chief Financial Officer & Senior Vice-President
Thomas J. Mielke, Chief Compliance Officer & Senior Vice-President, Law & Government Affairs

Le Château Inc.
8300 Decarie Blvd.
Montréal, QC H4P 2P5
514-738-7000
www.lechateau.com
Social Media: twitter.com/LeChateauStyle
Company Type: Public
Ticker Symbol: CTU.A / TSX
Profile: Le Château was formed in 1987. It manufactures & retails fashion apparel, accessories, & footwear for women & men. The company has more than 240 stores in Canada, two stores in the United States, plus seven stores under license in the Middle East. Le Château employs more than 3,000.
Jane Silverstone, Chair & Chief Executive Officer
Emilia Di Raddo, CA, President & Secretary
514-738-7000
Johnny Del Ciancio, CA, Vice-President, Finance
514-738-7000

Leader Auto Resources LAR Inc.
2525 Trans-Canada Highway
Pointe-Claire, QC H9R 4V6
514-694-6880
Fax: 514-694-5755
800-361-2284
www.larnet.com
Company Type: Private
Robert B. Issenman, President & CEO
roberti@larnet.com

Leon's Furniture Limited
45 Gordon Mackay Rd.
Toronto, ON M9N 3X3
416-243-7880
Fax: 416-243-7890
investors@leons.ca
www.leons.ca
Company Type: Public
Ticker Symbol: LNF / TSX
Profile: The A. Leon Company was founded in 1909 as a general merchandise store. Today, through a chain of retail facilities & franchises across Canada, Leon's Furniture Limited is engaged in the sale of home furnishings, electronics, & appliances.
Terrence T. Leon, President/CEO
Dominic Scarangella, Vice-President/CFO

Mark's Work Wearhouse Ltd.
#30, 1035 - 64 Ave. SE
Calgary, AB T2H 2J7
403-255-9220
Fax: 403-255-6005
800-663-6275
www.marks.com
Company Type: Private
Profile: Incorporated on April 12, 1977, the company operates Mark's Work Wearhouse retail stores & has granted franchises to operate Mark's stores in Canada. Stores sell a wide range of men's, women's, unisex leisure, casual & workwear clothes & footwear, healthwear & uniforms.
In Quebec, Mark's corporate & franchise stores operate under the name L'Equipeur. The company employs approximately 4,600 people. It is a wholly owned subsidiary of CTC Acquisition, a wholly owned subsidiary of Canadian Tire Corporation, Limited. Mark's was purchased by CT on Feb. 1, 2002, & is now a private company.
Paul D. Wilson, President, Mark's Work Wearhouse, Ltd.
Stephen Wetmore, President/CEO, Canadian Tire Corporation, Limited

Mitsui & Co. (Canada) Ltd.
Also Known As: Mitsui Canada
#1400, 20 Adelaide St. East
Toronto, ON M5C 2T6
416-365-3800
Fax: 416-865-1486
www.mitsui.ca
Company Type: Private
Shoei Utsuda, President/CEO, Mitsui & Co., Ltd.

Pantorama Industries Inc.
2, rue Lake
Montréal, QC H9B 3H9
514-421-1850
Fax: 514-684-3159
www.pantorama.com
Company Type: Private
Ticker Symbol: PTA
Profile: Retailing in men's & boys' clothing & accessory stores, women's clothing stores & shoe stores
Sydney Aptacker, President/CEO
Larry Wexler, Exec. Vice-President/COO
Robert Wexler, Chair

Paragon Pharmacies Limited
#8, 2604 Enterprise Way
Kelowna, BC V1X 7Y5
250-868-8400
Fax: 250-868-8402
information@paragonpharmacies.com
www.helloparagon.com
Company Type: Public
Ticker Symbol: PGN / TSX Venture
Profile: Paragon Pharmacies Limited is the owner & operator of retail pharmacies & central fill pharmacies in Manitoba, Alberta, & British Columbia.
R. Gordon Gooding, CA, Chief Executive Officer
Doug Andrews, CMA, Director, Operational Accounting
Chris Buysen, CA, Director, Finance
Edward Li, Vice-President, Operations
Mike Thomas, Vice-President, Merchandising

Parkland Fuel Corporation
Riverside Office Plaza
#236, 4919 - 59th St.
Red Deer, AB T4N 6C9
403-357-6400
Fax: 403-352-0042
corpinfo@parkland.ca
www.parkland.ca
Company Type: Public
Ticker Symbol: PKI / TSX
Profile: Parkland Fuel is engaged in the marketing & distributing of petroleum products. The company serves wholesale, retail, commercial, & home heating fuel customers. Brands include the following: Fas Gas Plus, Race Trac Gas, Bluewave Energy, Great Northern Oil, United Petroleum Products, Columbia Fuels, Neufeld Petroleum & Propane, & Island Petroleum.
Parkland Fuel has a Health, Safety, & Enviroment Department as well as HSE committees, & it developed risk mitigation programs & emergency response procedures for the hanlding of transportation fuels in a manner that is safe & healthy for employees & the environment.
Bob Espey, President & Chief Executive Officer
Mike Lambert, Chief Financial Officer & Senior Vice-President
Donna Strating, Chief Information Officer & Vice-President, Information Technology
Bob Fink, General Counsel & Corporate Secretary
Tom McMillan, Director, Corporate Communications
tom.mcmillan@parkland.ca

Reitmans (Canada) Limited
250, rue Sauvé ouest
Montréal, QC H3L 1Z2
514-384-1140
Fax: 514-385-2669
866-734-8626
info@reitmans.com
www.reitmans.ca
Social Media: www.facebook.com/Reitmans.en
Company Type: Public
Ticker Symbol: RET / TSX
Profile: Reitmans (Canada) Ltd. is the operator of clothing stores, which specialize in women's fashions & accessories. Stores are operated under the following names: Reitmans, RW & Co., Smart Set, Pennington Superstores, Addition-Elle, & Thyme Maternity. There are over 900 stores across Canada.
Jeremy H. Reitman, President
Henry Fiederer, President, Reitmans
Lesya McQueen, President, Smart Set
Suzana Vovko, President, RW & Co.
Kimberly Schumpert, President, Thyme Maternity
Isabelle Taschereau, President, Cassis
Kerry Mitchell, President, Penningtons / Addition Elle
Douglas M. Deruchie, CA, Vice-President, Finance
Diane Randolph, Vice-President & Chief Information Officer
Allen F. Rubin, Vice-President, Operations
Claude Martineau, Vice-President, Information Technology

Richelieu Hardware Ltd.
7900, boul Henri-Bourassa ouest
Montréal, QC H4S 1V4
514-336-4144
Fax: 514-832-4002
866-832-4040
info@richelieu.com; investisseurs@richeli
www.richelieu.com
Other Communications: Toll-Free (elsewhere Canada): 1-800-861-6000
Company Type: Public
Ticker Symbol: RCH / TSX
Profile: Richelieu Hardware manufactures, imports, & distributes specialty hardware & complementary products. The company serves manufacturers & retailers throughout North America. Approximately 1,500 people are employed by Richelieu.
Richard Lord, President & Chief Executive Officer
Antoine Auclair, Chief Financial Officer & Vice-President, Finance
514-832-4036

Rocky Mountain Dealerships Inc.
#301, 3345 - 8th St. SE
Calgary, AB T2G 3A4
403-265-7364
Fax: 403-214-5644
www.rockymtn.com
Company Type: Public
Ticker Symbol: RME / TSX
Profile: Rocky Mountain Dealerships Inc. has a network of full-service dealership branches that sell, rent, & lease new & used agriculture & construction equipment. Examples of brands include New Holland, Case Construction, & Case IH Agriculture. Rocky Mountain Dealerships Inc. also provides repair & maintenance services, as well as third-party finance products. Stores are located in British Columbia, Alberta, Saskatchewan, Manitoba, & the Northwest Territories.
Matt Campbell, Chief Executive Officer
Derek Stimson, President
David Ascott, Chief Financial Officer
Garrett Ganden, Chief Operating Officer

RONA inc.
220, ch du Tremblay
Boucherville, QC J4B 8H7
514-599-5900
Fax: 514-599-5161
866-283-2239
investor.relations@rona.ca
www.rona.ca
Company Type: Public
Ticker Symbol: RON / TSX
Profile: Hardware, home renovation, & gardening products are distributed & retailed by RONA inc. The company has over 950 franchise, corporate, & affiliate stores. Approximately 30,000 people are employed by RONA.
Robert Dutton, President/CEO
Claude Guévin, Exec. Vice-President/CFO
Pierre Dandoy, Exec. Vice-President, Retail Operations
Claude Bernier, Exec. Vice-President, Marketing & Customer Innovations
Daniel Ducharme, Sr. Vice-President, Information Technologies
Eva Boucher-Hartling, Director, External Communications
514-599-5114, eva.boucher-hartling@rona.ca

Sears Canada Inc.
Headquarters Building
#700, 290 Yonge St.
Toronto, ON M5B 2C3
416-362-1711
888-932-1015
home@sears.ca
www.sears.ca
Other Communications: National Customer Service Centre, Phone: 888-473-2772
Social Media: www.facebook.com/SearsCanada
twitter.com/searsca
Company Type: Public
Ticker Symbol: SCC / TSX
Profile: Sears Canada Inc. is a general merchandise retailer, as well as a catalogue publisher.
Dene L. Rogers, President/CEO
Allen Ravas, Sr. Vice-President/CFO
Dennis Singh, Sr. Vice-President, Retail Stores

Shoppers Drug Mart Corporation
243 Consumers Rd.
Toronto, ON M2J 4W8
416-493-1220
Fax: 416-491-1022
800-746-7737
investorrelations@shoppersdrugmart.ca
www.shoppersdrugmart.ca
Other Communications: Corporate Affairs: corporateaffairs@shoppersdrugmart.ca
Social Media: www.facebook.com/shoppersdrugmart
twitter.com/shopprsdrugmart
Company Type: Public
Ticker Symbol: SC / TSX
Profile: Shoppers Drug Mart Corporation licenses retail drug stores, which operate under the name Shoppers Drug Mart, & Pharmaprix in Quebec. Shoppers Home Health Care stores are also owned & operated by Shoppers Drug Mart Corporation. In addition to these retail establishments, Shoppers Drug Mart Corporation also owns a provider of pharmaceutical products & services to long-term care facilities, which operates under the name MediSystem Technologies Inc.
Jürgen Schreiber, President/CEO
George C. Halatsis, Exec. Vice-President/CFO
John Caplice, Treasurer & Sr. Vice-President, Investor Relations & Corporate Affairs
Richard Alderson, General Counsel, Secretary, & Sr. Vice-President, Legal Affairs

Sobeys Inc.
115 King St.
Stellarton, NS B0K 1S0
902-752-8371
paul.jewer@sobeys.com
www.sobeys.com
Company Type: Private
Ticker Symbol: SBY
Profile: Sobeys is a national grocery retailer. Retail banners include Sobeys, Foodland, IGA, & Price Chopper. Its two operating divisions are Thrifty Foods & Lawtons Drugs.
Bill McEwan, President & Chief Executive Officer
David Jeffs, President, Operations, Sobeys Ontario
Jason Potter, President, Operations, Sobeys Atlantic
Marc Poulin, President, Operations, Sobeys Québec
Sylvain Prud'Homme, President, Operations, Sobeys West
François Vimard, Chief Financial Officer
Karin McCaskill, Senior Vice-President, General Counsel & Secretary

Sony of Canada Ltd.
115 Gordon Baker Rd.
Toronto, ON M2H 3R6
416-499-1414
Fax: 416-497-1774
877-899-7669
general_enquiries@sony.ca
www.sony.ca
Company Type: Private
Profile: Sony of Canada Ltd. is an entertainment company that offers electronics, movies, music, & games. Examples of Sony products include BRAVIA televisions, VAIO computers, Blu-ray Disc players, Handycam Camcorders, broadcast cameras, Cyber-shot digital cameras, & IPELA security cameras.
Sony of Canada Ltd. is headquartered in Toronto. Sales offices are located in Montréal, Québec & Vancouver British Columbia. Distribution centres are situated in Whitby, Ontario & Coquitlam, British Columbia.
Douglas D. Wilson, President & Chief Operating Officer
Barry Hassler, Senior Vice-President
Candice Hayman, Contact, Public Relations
416-718-5048, Candice_hayman@sony.ca

Sterling Shoes Inc.
2580 Viscount Way
Richmond, BC V6V 1N1
604-270-6114
Fax: 604-278-7751
contact@sterlingshoes.com; marketing@ster
www.sterlingshoes.com
Social Media: www.facebook.com/mysterlingstyle
twitter.com/sterlingshoes
Company Type: Public
Ticker Symbol: SSI
Profile: Founded in 1987, Sterling Shoes is an independent retailer that offers footwear & accessories. The company operates more than 100 stores throughout Canada, including Sterling stores, Freedman stores, & Shoe Warehouse stores.
David Alves, Chief Executive Officer & President
Daniel S. Gumprich, Chief Financial Officer
604-270-6114
Sairose Kassam, Vice-President, Supply Chain
Scot Sheeler, Vice-President, Store Operations

SunOpta Inc.
2838 Bovaird Dr. West
Brampton, ON L7A 0H2
905-455-2528
Fax: 905-455-2529
foodinfo@sunopta.com; ingredients@sunopta
www.sunopta.com
Other Communications: Snacks: healthysnacks@sunopta.com
Social Media: www.linkedin.com/company/sunopta
Company Type: Public
Ticker Symbol: SOY / TSX, NASDAQ
Profile: SunOpta Inc. is focused upon sourcing, processing, & distributing healthy, environmentally responsible products. Products include natural, organic, & specialty foods. The company's SunOpta Foods is made up of the Grains & Foods Group, the Ingredients Group, the Consumer Products Group, & the International Foods Group.
SunOpta Inc. has a 66.2% ownership in Opta Minerals Inc., plus a minority ownership in Mascoma Corporation.
Steven R. Bromley, President/CEO
Murray Burke, President & Chief Technology Officer, SunOpta BioProcess Inc.
David J. Kruse, President & Chief Operating Officer, Opta Minerals Inc.
Allan G. Routh, President, SunOpta Grains & Foods Group
John H. Dietrich, Vice-President & Chief Financial Officer
Tony Tavares, Vice-President & Chief Operating Officer
Arthur J. McEvily, Vice-President, Technology
Benjamin Chhiba, Vice-President & General Counsel

The Brick Ltd.
The Brick Head Office
16930 - 114 Ave.
Edmonton, AB T5M 3S2
Fax: 514-695-9249
customercare@thebrick.com
www.thebrick.com
Other Communications: Investors, E-mail: investor@thebrick.com
Company Type: Public
Ticker Symbol: BRK / TSX
Profile: The Brick Ltd. is a publicly listed corporation, which was incorporated in September 2010. It is the successor in interest to The Brick Group Income Fund.
The Brick is a retailer of appliances, home furnishings, mattresses, & electronics. The corporation also markets warranty plans & retail credit insurance plans. The Brick operates under the following banners: The Brick, United Furniture Warehouse, The Brick Mattress Store, & Urban Brick. There are more than 200 locations, including Brick, SuperStore, franchise, mattress store, clearance, & United Furniture Warehouse locations. The company also has six distribution centres across Canada.
Vi Konkle, President & Chief Executive Officer
780-930-6300
Ken Grondin, Chief Financial Officer & President, Financial Operations, The Brick Group
780-930-6300
Richard Hannah, Chief Information Officer
Frank Talarico, Chief Distribution Officer
Jim Caldwell, Senior Vice-President, Operations
Paul Comrie, Senior Vice-President, Merchandising
Gregory Nakonechny, Corporate Secretary & Vice-President, Legal

The Home Depot
800-747-3787
www.homedepot.ca
Company Type: Private

UAP Inc.
7025, rue Ontario est
Montréal, QC H1N 2B3
514-256-5031
Fax: 514-256-8469
www.uapinc.com
Company Type: Private
Robert Hattem, President & COO
Larry Samuelson, CEO

Uni-Sélect Inc.
170, boul Industriel
Boucherville, QC J4B 2X3
450-641-2440
Fax: 450-449-4908
questions@uni-select.com; careers@unisele
www.uni-select.com
Other Communications: Investors: investorrelation@uni-select.com
Company Type: Public
Ticker Symbol: UNS / TSX
Profile: Uni-Sélect Inc. was founded in 1968. It is a wholesale distributor & marketer of heavy duty tools, equipment, replacement parts, & accessories. The company serves the North American automotive industry. Approximately 6,600 are employed by Uni-Sélect.
Richard G. Roy, FCA, President & Chief Executive Officer
Gary O'Connor, Executive Vice-President, Automotive Group Canada
Florent Jacques, Senior Vice-President, Distribution & Integration
Denis Mathieu, CA, Vice-President & Chief Financial Officer
Jean-Pierre Beaulieu, Vice-President & Chief Information Officer

Pierre Chesnay, LL.L, Secretary & Vice-President, Legal Affairs
legal@uni-select.com
Karine Vachon, Manager, Investor Relations & Communications
450-641-6972

Wajax Corporation
3280 Wharton Way
Mississauga, ON L4X 2C5
905-212-3300
Fax: 905-212-3350
ir@wajax.com
www.wajax.com
Company Type: Public
Ticker Symbol: WJX / TSX
Profile: Through its subsidiaries, Wajax is involved in the sale & parts & service support of power systems, mobile equipment, & industrial components. Wajax serves the manufacturing, natural resources, utilities, construction, & industrial processing sectors. Branches are located throughout Canada.
Neil Manning, President/CEO
nmanning@wajax.com
John J. Hamilton, Sr. Vice-President/CFO
jhamilton@wajax.com
Christopher J. Desjardins, General Counsel & Secretary

Electronics & Electrical Equipment

ARISE Technologies Corporation
65 Northland Rd.
Waterloo, ON N2V 1Y8
519-725-2244
Fax: 519-725-8907
info@arisetech.com
www.arisetech.com
Company Type: Public
Ticker Symbol: APV / TSX
Bart Tichelman, President & CEO
David Chornaby, Chief Financial Officer

Ballard Power Systems Inc.
9000 Glenlyon Pkwy.
Burnaby, BC V5J 5J8

604-454-0900
Fax: 604-412-4700
investors@ballard.com
www.ballard.com

Company Type: Public
Ticker Symbol: BLD / TSX, NASDAQ
John Sheridan, President/CEO
Dave Smith, Vice-President/CFO
Lee Craft, Vice-President, Operations
Chris Guzy, Vice-President/Chief Technology Officer
Noordin Nanji, Vice-President & Chief Customer Officer

Celestica Inc.
844 Don Mills Rd.
Toronto, ON M3C 1V7

416-448-5800
Fax: 416-448-5527
888-899-9998
contactus@celestica.com
www.celestica.com

Company Type: Public
Ticker Symbol: CLS / TSX, NYSE
Profile: Clestica Inc delivers end-to-end product lifecycle solutions. The company specializes in electronics manufacturing, engineering, & supply chain management services.
Craig Muhlhauser, President & Chief Executive Officer
Mary Gendron, Chief Information Officer & Senior Vice-President

Paul Nicoletti, Chief Financial Officer & Executive Vice-President

John Peri, Chief Operating Officer

Cinram International Income Fund
2255 Markham Rd.
Toronto, ON M1B 2W3

416-298-8190
Fax: 416-332-2403
investorrelations@cinram.com
www.cinram.com

Company Type: Public
Ticker Symbol: CRW.UN / TSX
Profile: Cinram International Inc., is an indirect, wholly-owned subsidiary ofCinram International Income Fund. The company is an independent provider of multimedia products, plus related logistics services. In 2012, Cinram International Income Fund announced a strategic partnership between it digital media subsidiary & Mobovivo, a provider of social TV technology to producers, distributors, networks, & film studios.
William Anderson, Chair, Cinram International Income Fund
Steven G. Brown, President & Chief Executive Officer
John Bell, Chief Financial Officer
David Ashton, Executive Vice-President, Manufacturing
Ben Higgins, Senior Vice-President, Business Development & Innovation

COM DEV International Ltd.
155 Sheldon Dr.
Cambridge, ON N1R 7H6

519-622-2300
Fax: 519-622-1691
investor.relations@comdev.ca
www.comdev.ca

Company Type: Public
Ticker Symbol: CDV / TSX
Profile: COM DEV International engineers & manufactures custom-designed space hardware. The space technology company serves the commercial, civil, & military space hardware market. Facilities are located in Canada, the United States, & the United Kingdom.

Dalsa Corp.
605 McMurray Rd.
Waterloo, ON N2V 2E9

519-886-6000
Fax: 519-886-0185
www.dalsa.com

Company Type: Private
Brian Doody, CEO
Wajid Ali, CFO

Descartes Systems Group Inc.
120 Randall Dr.
Waterloo, ON N2V 1C6

519-746-8110
Fax: 519-747-0082
800-419-8495
info@descartes.com
www.descartes.com
Social Media: twitter.com/descartessg
www.linkedin.com/company/descartes-systems-group

Company Type: Public
Ticker Symbol: DSG / TSX; DSGX / NASDAQ
Profile: The Descartes Systems Group provides logistics management solutions. Solutions are used by the transportation logistics, distribution, manufacturing, & retail sectors.
Arthur Mesher, Chair & Chief Executive Officer
Stephanie Ratza, CA, Chief Financial Officer
Chris Jones, Executive Vice-President, Solutions & Services
Edward J. Ryan, Executive Vice-President, Global Field Operations
J. Scott Pagan, General Counsel & Executive Vice-President, Corporate Development

DragonWave Inc.
#600, 411 Legget Dr.
Ottawa, ON K2K 3C9

613-599-9991
Fax: 613-599-4225
info@dragonwaveinc.com
www.dragonwaveinc.com
Other Communications: Technical Support: 613-271-7010

Company Type: Public
Ticker Symbol: DWI / TSX, NASDAQ
Profile: DragonWave Inc. supplies packet microwave radio systems for mobile & access networks. The systems transmit broadband voice, data, & video. The company's corporate headquarters is situated in Ottawa, with sales sites in North America, Europe, Asia, & the Middle East.
Peter Allen, President & Chief Executive Officer
Erik Boch, Chief Technical Officer & Vice-President, Engineering

Russel J. Frederick, Chief Financial Officer & Vice-President, Finance
John Lawlor, Vice-President, Corporate Relations
613-895-7000, jlawlor@dragonwaveinc.com
Alan Solheim, Vice-President, Corporate Development

Evertz Technologies Limited
5292 John Lucas Dr.
Burlington, ON L7L 5Z9

905-335-3700
Fax: 905-335-3573
877-995-3700
ir@evertz.com; sales@evertz.com
www.evertz.com
Other Communications: Customer Service: service@evertz.com

Company Type: Public
Ticker Symbol: ET / TSX
Profile: Evertz Technologies Limited is a high-technology company. It is engaged in the designing, manufacturing, & marketing of film production, post production, & broadcast equipment. This equipment is used in the film & television broadcast industry.
Romolo Magarelli, President/CEO
Douglas A DeBruin, CA, Chair & Exec. Vice-President, Administration
Anthony Gridley, CA, Chief Financial Officer & Corporate Secretary
905-335-7580
Rakesh Patel, Chief Technical Officer & Vice-President, Hardware Engineering

EXFO Inc.
400, av Godin
Québec, QC G1M 2K2

418-683-0211
Fax: 418-683-2170
800-663-3936
www.exfo.com
Other Communications: Wireline, Optical, & Datacom: 866-683-0155

Company Type: Public
Ticker Symbol: EXF / TSX; EXFO, NASDAQ
Profile: Test, measurement, & monitoring products are designed & manufactured by EXFO Inc.. The company's test & service assurance solutions are used by the global telecommunications industry.
Germain Lamonde, President, Chief Executive Officer & Chair
Pierre Plamondon, CA, Chief Financial Officer & Vice-President, Finance
Stephen Bull, Vice-President, Research & Development
Luc Gagnon, Vice-President, Telecom Manufacturing Operations & Customer Service
Vance Oliver, Manager, Investor Relations
418-683-0913, vance.oliver@EXFO.com

General Dynamics Canada
3785 Richmond Rd.
Ottawa, ON K2H 5B7

613-596-7000
Fax: 613-596-7396
info@gdcanada.com; rma.support@gdcanada.c
www.gdcanada.com
Other Communications: Calgary: 403-295-6700; Dartmouth: 902-406-3701

Company Type: Private
Profile: Established in 1948, General Dynamics Canada provides electronic systems, systems integration, plus in-service support. The company serves Canadian & international defence organizations & public security markets.
General Dynamics Canada is a part of General Dynamics C4 Systems, a business unit of General Dynamics. General Dynamics Canada is an ISO 14001/18001 certified company, which confirms successful implementation of an Environmental, Health & Safety policy.
David Ibbetson, General Manager
Tara Meinhardt, Contact, Media Inquiries
403-295-5025

Gennum Corporation
PO Box 489 Stn. A, , 4281 Harvester Rd.
Burlington, ON L7R 3Y3

905-632-2996
Fax: 905-632-2055
corporate@gennum.com
www.gennum.com
Social Media: twitter.com/GennumCorp
www.linkedin.com/company/gennum-corporation

Company Type: Public
Profile: Gennum Corporation was founded in 1973. It designs & supplies high speed analog & mixed-signal semiconductors for the video broadcast & optical communications markets. The company has been recognized for advances in high definition broadcasting. Gennum has design, research & development, & sales offices in Canada, the United States, Mexico, the United Kingdom, Germany, India, Taiwan, & Japan.
In 2012 Semtech Corporation (Nasdaq SMTC), through its indirect wholly-owned susidiary, acquired all of the issued & outstanding common shares of Gennum. Semtech Corporation is a supplier of analog & mixed-signal semiconductors.
Franz J. Fink, President & Chief Executive Officer
R. Gregory Miller, Chief Financial Officer & Senior Vice-President, Finance & Administration
Gary M. Beauchamp, Senior Vice-President, Mixed Signal & Optical Products
Chad Hutchison, Senior Vice-President, General Counsel, & Corporate Secretary
Klaus Mueller, Senior Vice-President, Global Sales
Hari Subramaniam, Vice-President, Operations

GSI Group Inc.
125 Middlesex Turnpike
Bedford, MA 01730 USA

781-266-5808
Fax: 781-266-5117
www.gsig.com

Company Type: Public
Ticker Symbol: GSIG / NASDAQ
Profile: GSI Group supplies laser scanning devices & precision motion & optical control technologies. The company serves the medical, scientific, electronics, & industrial markets.
John A. Roush, Chief Executive Officer
Jamie B. Bader, President & Group Executive, Precision Motion & Technologies Division
David Clarke, President & Group Executive, Laser Products Division
Robert J. Buckley, Chief Financial Officer

Hammond Power Solutions Inc. (HPS)
595 Southgate Dr.
Guelph, ON N1G 3W6

519-822-2441
Fax: 519-822-9701
sales@hammondpowersolutions.com
www.hammondpowersolutions.com
Other Communications: Investors: ir@hammondpowersolutions.com
Social Media: facebook.com/pages/Hammond-Power-Solutions-Inc/191136177604364
www.linkedin.com/company/133825?trk=tyah

Company Type: Public
Ticker Symbol: HPS.A / TSX
Profile: Established in 1917, Hammond Power Solutions Inc. engineers & manufactures custom & standard dry-type transformers & related magnetic products. The company's products are used by the global electrical industry.
W.G. (Bill) Hammond, Chaor/CEO
Chris R. Huether, Chief Financial Officer & Corporate Secretary

Dawn Henderson, Manager, Investor Relations & Corporate Services

Miranda Technologies Inc.
3499, rue Douglas B. Floreani
Montréal, QC H4S 2C6

514-333-1772
Fax: 514-333-9828
investorrelations@miranda.com; marketing@www.miranda.com
Other Communications: Media: pr@miranda.com; HR: humanresources@miranda.com
Social Media: www.facebook.com/mirandatechnologies twitter.com/Mirandaglobal

Company Type: Public
Ticker Symbol: MT / TSX
Profile: Miranda Technologies is a developer, manufacturer, & marketer of hardware & software. Products are used by the television broadcast, satellite, cable, & IPTV industry.

Strath Goodship, President & Chief Executive Officer
Mario Settino, Chief Financial Officer
514-333-1772
René Vachon, Exec. Vice-President, Business Development
Michel Proulx, Chief Technology Officer

MOSAID Technologies Incorporated
#203, 11 Hines Rd.
Ottawa, ON K2K 2X1

613-599-9539
Fax: 613-591-8148
communications@mosaid.com
www.mosaid.com
Other Communications: Investor Relations: ir@mosaid.com

Company Type: Private
Ticker Symbol: MSD
Profile: Founded in 1975, MOSAID Technologies Incorporated specializes in the development & licensing of patented intellectual property. Products include semiconductors, & wireless & wired communications systems.
In 2011, Sterling Partners acquired MOSAID. MOSAID's shares were then de-listed from the Toronto Stock Exchange.
John C. Lindgren, President & Chief Executive Officer
Joseph R. Brown, Chief Financial Officer
Peter B. Gillingham, Chief Technology Officer & Vice-President
Vinod Kumar, Vice-President, Business Development
Phillip Shaer, Vice-President, General Counsel, & Corporate Secretary

Research In Motion Limited
295 Phillip St.
Waterloo, ON N2L 3W8

519-888-7465
Fax: 519-888-7884
investor_relations@rim.com; help@rim.com
www.rim.com
Other Communications: Career Inquiries: careers@rim.com

Company Type: Public
Ticker Symbol: RIM / TSX
Profile: Research in Motion Limited was established in 1984. It designs, manufactures, & markets wireless solutions for the mobile communications market. The company is listed on the TSX & NASDAQ under the symbol RIM.
James Balsillie, Co-CEO
Mike Lazaridis, President/Co-CEO
Brian Bidulka, Chief Accounting Officer
Robin Bienfait, Chief Information Officer
David Yach, Chief Technology Officer, Software
Dennis Kavelman, Chief Operating Officer, Administration & Operations

Siemens Canada Limited
Canada Headquarters
1550 Appleby Lin
Burlington, ON L7L 6X7

905-319-3600
Corporate.communications.ca@siemens.com
www.siemens.ca

Company Type: Private
Profile: Siemens is a diversified company that is engaged in electronics & electrical engineering. Its business sectors include energy, healthcare, & industry. The company employs over 4,000 people across Canada.
In 2012, Siemens pursued the acquisition of RuggedCom Inc., a provider of rugged communications networking solutions for harsh environments.
Robert Hardt, President & Chief Executive Officer
Manfred Doenz, Chief Financial Officer & Executive Vice-President
Jim Graziadei, Senior Vice-President, Healthcare Sector
Michael Gross, Senior Vice-President, Industry Sector
William Smith, Senior Vice-President, Energy Sector

Sierra Wireless, Inc.
13811 Wireless Way
Richmond, BC V6V 3A4

604-231-1100
Fax: 604-231-1109
info@sierrawireless.com
www.sierrawireless.com

Company Type: Public
Ticker Symbol: SW / TSX
Profile: Sierra Wireless, Inc. specializes in wireless solutions. It provides professional services to clients who require expertise in wireless design, integration, & carrier certification.
Jason Cohenour, President/CEO
David G. McLennan, Chief Financial Officer
James B. Kirkpatrick, Chief Technology Officer
Stephen Blaine, Sr. Vice-President, Engineering
Bill Dodson, Sr. Vice-President, Operations
Sharlene Myers, Contact, Media
604-232-1445, smyers@sierrawireless.com

Vecima Networks Inc.
Corporate Headquarters
771 Vanalman Ave.
Victoria, BC V8Z 3B8

250-881-1982
Fax: 250-881-1974
888-292-8266
invest@vecima.com
www.vecima.com
Other Communications: Saskatoon Facility, Phone: 306-955-7075 7

Company Type: Public
Ticker Symbol: VCM / TSX
Profile: Vecima Networks Inc. is a designer, manufacturer, & distributor of hardware products with embedded software that supports broadband access to cable, wireless, & telephony networks. Principal markets include Broadband Wireless & Converged Wired Solutions. Vecima Networks has ISO 9001:2000 certified manufacturing operations in Saskatoon, Saskatchewan.
Surinder Kumar, Chair & Chief Executive Officer
Sumit Kumar, President
John Hanna, Chief Financial Officer
Hugh Wood, Chief Operating Officer
Mark Briggs, General Manager, Spectrum Signal Processing by Vecima

Wi-LAN Inc.
#608, 11 Holland Ave.
Ottawa, ON K1Y 4S1

613-688-4330
Fax: 613-688-4894
info@wi-lan.com; ir@wi-lan.com
www.wi-lan.com
Other Communications: Media: media@wi-lan.com

Company Type: Public
Ticker Symbol: WIN / TSX, NASDAQ
Profile: The company is a technology innovation & licensing company. Wi-LAN Inc.'s patent portfolio applies to products in the communications & consumer electronics markets.
Jim Skippen, Chair/CEO
Najmul Siddiqui, President, Wi-LAN V-chip Corp.
Shaun McEwan, Chief Financial Officer
Jung Yee, Chief Technology Officer
Bill Middleton, General Counsel & Sr. Vice-President, Licensing
Derek Nuhn, Vice-President, DSL Technologies
Andrew Parolin, Vice-President, Wireless Technologies
Tyler Burns, Director, Investor Relations & Communications
tburns@wi-lan.com

Wireless Matrix Corporation
#1A, 3751 North Fraser Way
Burnaby, BC V5J 5G4

604-439-2444
Fax: 604-439-2447
888-843-8554
invest@wirelessmatrixcorp.com
www.wirelessmatrixcorp.com

Company Type: Public
Ticker Symbol: WRX
Profile: Wireless Matrix Corporation was founded in 1991. It is engaged in the provision of software solutions to improve service fleet delivery metrics. Examples of solutions include cellular & satellite wireless data communication services & a web-based application for GPS tracking, travel reporting, & driver performance reporting.
Maria C. Izurieta, Chief Executive Officer
Mohan Rao, Chief Technology Officer
Michael Jakab, Executive Vice-President, Sales
Rick Anthony, Vice-President, Operations

Engineering & Management

Armtec Infrastructure Inc.
#3, 370 Speedvale Ave. West
Guelph, ON N1H 7M7

519-822-0210
Fax: 519-822-1160
www.armtec.com
Social Media: www.facebook.com/armtecltd twitter.com/armtecltd www.linkedin.com/company/Armtec

Company Type: Public
Ticker Symbol: ARF.UN, ARF.DB / TSX
Profile: Armtec manufactures & markets infrastructure products for industries in Canada & in selected international markets. Markets include commercial building, agricultural drainage, & natural resources.
Mark Anderson, President & Chief Executive Officer
James R. Newell, Chief Financial Officer
Carrie Boutcher, Treasurer & Vice-President, Investor Relations
519-822-0210, Fax: 519-822-8894
Thomas Cannon, Vice-President, Operations
Lisa Kissick, Vice-President, Information Technology

Bombardier Aerospace
800, rue René-Lévesque ouest
Montréal, QC A3B 1Y8

514-861-9481
Fax: 514-861-7769
www.bombardier.com/aerospace

Company Type: Private

Calian Technology Ltd.
#101, 340 Legget Dr.
Ottawa, ON K2K 1Y6

613-599-8600
Fax: 613-599-8650
877-225-4264
info@calian.com; ir@calian.com
www.calian.com

Company Type: Public
Ticker Symbol: CTY / TSX
Profile: Calian Technologies Ltd. consists of The Business & Technology Services Division & the Systems Engineering Division. The divisions provide the following services: business & technology services to industry & government; & the design, manufacturing & maintenance of systems to the communications & defence sectors.
Ray Basler, Chief Executive Officer
Kevin Ford, President, Business & Technology Services Division

Patrick Thera, President, Systems Engineering Division
Jacqueline Gauthier, Chief Financial Officer, Vice-President & Corporate Secretary

CGI Group Inc.
1130, rue Sherbrooke ouest, 7e étage
Montréal, QC H3A 2M8

514-841-3200
Fax: 514-841-3299
www.cgi.com
Social Media: www.facebook.com/cgigroup twitter.com/cgi_ir www.linkedin.com/company/cgi

Company Type: Public
Ticker Symbol: GIB / TSX, NYSE
Profile: The information technology & business process services firm is engaged in the integration & customization of technologies & software applications, as well as the management of business processes & transactions. CGI Group employs approximately 31,000.
Michael E. Roach, President/CEO
Donna Morea, President, USA Operations & India
Joseph I. Saliba, President, Europe & Australia
David Anderson, Exec. Vice-President/CFO
Luc Pinard, Exec. Vice-President & Chief Technology & Quality Officer
Daniel Rocheleau, Exec. Vice-President & Chief Business Engineering Officer
Eva Maglis, Sr. Vice-President & General Manager, Technologies & Infrastructure
John G. Campbell, Sr. Vice-President & General Manager, Communication Services Business
James Cofran, Sr. Vice-President
ehs@cgi.com
Circé Labelle, Sr. Consultant, Corporate Communications & Public Affairs

GENIVAR Inc.
1600 boul René Lévesque ouest, 16e étage
Montréal, QC H3H 1P9

514-340-0046
Fax: 514-340-1337
energy@genivar.com; environment@genivar.c
www.genivar.com
Other Communications: Municipal Infrastructure: municipalinfras@genivar.com

Company Type: Public
Ticker Symbol: GNV / TSX
Profile: GENIVAR Inc. is a large engineering company that provides a full range of consulting services. Market segments include energy, environmental, municipal infrastructure, transportation, industrial, & building. The firm employs over 5,500 employees throughout Canada & internationally.
Pierre Shoiry, President & Chief Executive Officer
pierre.shoiry@genivar.com
Alexandre L'Heureux, Chief Financial Officer
alexandre.lheureux@genivar.com
Marc Rivard, Chief Operating Officer
marc.rivard@genivar.com
Sylvain Labrèche, National Vice-President, Industrial & Telecommunications
Pierre Lacombe, National Vice-President, Energy
Carole Lauzon, Vice-President, Information Technology
Isabelle Adjahi, Director, Communications & Investor Relations
isabelle.adjahi@genivar.com

Hatch Ltd.
Sheridan Science & Technology Park
2800 Speakman Dr.
Mississauga, ON L5K 2R7

905-855-7600
Fax: 905-855-8270
webmaster@hatch.ca
www.hatch.ca

Company Type: Private
Profile: The consulting & technical design firm serves the global mining & metals, energy & infrastructure sectors.
Kurt Strobele, President/CEO
Bruce MacDonald, Director/Vice President

Jacobs Engineering Canada
PO Box 5244 Stn. A, , 205 Quarry Park Blvd. SE
Calgary, AB T2C 3E7

403-258-6411
Fax: 403-258-6614
800-869-3016
www.jacobs.com

Company Type: Private

Linamar Corporation
287 Speedvale Ave. West
Guelph, ON N1H 1C5

519-836-7550
Fax: 519-836-9175
investorrelations@linamar.com
www.linamar.com

Company Type: Public
Ticker Symbol: LNR / TSX
Profile: Highly engineered products are developed, designed, & produced by thie manufacturing company. Linamar Corporation's operating groups are as follows: Industrial, Commercial & Energy; Manufacturing; Skyjack; & Driveline Systems. The company supplies the global vehicle & mobile industrial equipment markets.
Linda Hasenfratz, Chief Execctuive Officer
Jim Jarrell, President & Chief Operating Officer
Mark Stoddart, Chief Technology Officer & Executive Vice-President, Marketing
Roger Fulton, General Counsel, Corporate Secretary, & Exec. Vice-President, Human Resources

Neo Material Technologies Inc.
Standard Life Centre
#1740, 121 King St. West
Toronto, ON M5H 3T9

416-367-8588
Fax: 416-367-5471
info@neomaterials.com
www.neomaterials.com

Company Type: Public
Ticker Symbol: NEM / TSX
Profile: Through its business divisions, Performance Materials & Magnaquench, Neo Material Technologies Inc. produces, processes, & develops zirconium, neodymium-iron-boron magnetic powders, & rare earths based engineered materials & applications. The products are used in many high technology products.
Constantine E. Karayannopoulos, BASc, MASc, PEng, President & Chief Executive Officer
Geoffrey R. Bedford, Chief Operating Officer & Executive Vice-President
Michael F. Doolan, Chief Financial Officer & Executive Vice-President, Finance
Shannon Y. Song, Executive Vice-President, Magnequench Division
Alexander D. Caldwell, Corporate Secretary & Manager, Information Systems

SNC-Lavalin Group Inc.
455, boul René-Lévesque ouest
Montréal, QC H2Z 1Z3

514-393-1000
Fax: 514-866-0795
investors@snclavalin.com
www.snclavalin.com

Company Type: Public
Ticker Symbol: SNC / TSX
Profile: The international engineering & construction organization owns infrastructure, & is engaged in the provision of operation & maintenance services. Examples of services include project financing, project management, procurement, engineering, & construction. The group is involved in sectors such as pharmaceuticals, petroleum, agrifood, the environment, transit, power, & mining.
Jacques Lamarre, O.C., Eng., President/CEO
Gilles Laramée, Exec. Vice-President/CFO
Gillian MacCormack, Vice-President, Global Public Relations
gillian.maccormack@snclavalin.com
Denis Jasmin, Vice-President, Investor Relations
denis.jasmin@snclavalin.com
Edythe A. Marcoux, Chair, Health, Safety, & Environment Committee

Stantec Inc.
10160 - 112th St.
Edmonton, AB T5K 2L6

780-917-7000
Fax: 780-917-7330
ir@stantec.com
www.stantec.com
Other Communications: Investment: communityinvestment@stantec.com
Social Media: www.facebook.com/StantecInc
twitter.com/stantec

Company Type: Public
Ticker Symbol: STN / TSX, NYSE
Profile: Stantec Inc. offers professional consulting services for infrastructure & facilities projects. The following services are provided: planning, project management, project economics, surveying & geomatics, engineering, architecture, landscape architecture, environmental science, & interior design.
Robert J. Gomes, President & Chief Executive Officer
Richard K. Allen, Chief Operating Officer & Senior Vice-President
Daniel J. Lefaivre, Chief Financial Officer & Senior Vice-President
Danny Craig, Contact, Media Relations
danny.craig@stantec.com
Crystal Verbeek, Contact, Investor Relations
crystal.verbeek@stantec.com

Finance

Accord Financial Corp.
77 Bloor St. West, 18th Fl.
Toronto, ON M5S 1M2

416-961-0007
Fax: 416-961-9443
800-231-2977
info@accordfinancial.com
www.accordfinancial.com
Other Communications: Receivables Management: 800-967-0015

Company Type: Public
Ticker Symbol: ACD / TSX
Profile: Through its subsidiaries, Accord Financial provides the following financial services to small & medium-sized businesses: record-keeping, financing, credit investigation, collection services, & guarantees.
Tom Henderson, President & Chief Executive Officer, Accord Financial Corp.
Simon Hitzig, President, Accord Financial Ltd.
Stuart Adair, Chief Financial Officer & Vice-President, Accord Financial Corp.
sadair@accordfinancial.com

AGF Management Limited
Toronto Dominion Bank Tower
PO Box 50 Stn. Toronto-Domin, , 66 Wellington St. West, 31st Fl.
Toronto, ON M5K 1E9

905-214-8203
Fax: 905-214-8243
800-268-8583
complaints@agf.com
www.agf.com
Other Communications: Toll-Free Fax: 1-888-329-4243

Company Type: Public
Ticker Symbol: AGF.B / TSX
Profile: The independent investment management firm offers products such as mutual funds, pooled funds, & mutual fun wrap programs. Assets are managed on behalf of institutional investors & private clients.
AGF Trust is a complementary business. It provides mortgages, loans & GICs through mortgage brokers & financial advisors.
Blake C. Goldring, CFA, Chair & Chief Executive Officer
Robert J. Bogart, Chief Financial Officer & Executive Vice-President
416-865-4264, bob.bogart@agf.com
Michael Clabby, Vice-President, Investor Relations & Corporate Development
416-815-6275, michael.clabby@agf.com

Alaris Royalty Corp.
#232, 2031 - 33rd Ave. SW
Calgary, AB T2T 1Z5

403-221-7304
Fax: 403-228-0906

Company Type: Public
Ticker Symbol: AD / TSX
Profile: Alaris Royalty provides alternative financing for private businesses in North America, in exchange for royalties or distributions from Private Company Partners.
Stephen King, President & Chief Executive Officer
Darren Driscoll, CA, Chief Financial Officer
Rachel Colabella, BComm, LLB, General Counsel & Corporate Secretary
Curtis Krawetz, Manager, Investor Relations
403-221-7305, Fax: 403-228-0906, ckrawetz@alarisroyalty.com

Amex Bank of Canada
PO Box 7000 Stn. B, , Willowdale, ON M2K 2R6

905-474-0870
800-869-3016
www212.americanexpress.com
Social Media: www.twitter.com/AskAmex

Company Type: Private

B2B Trust
#200, 130 Adelaide St. West
Toronto, ON M5H 3P5

416-947-7427
Fax: 416-947-9476
800-263-8349
questions@b2btrust.com
b2btrust.com

Company Type: Public
Ticker Symbol: BBT
François Desjardins, President/CEO
Diane Lafresnaye, Vice-President, Finance

Bank of America, N.A. (Canada Branch)
#2700, 200 Front St. West
Toronto, ON M5V 3L2

416-349-4100
Fax: 416-349-4278
www.bankofamerica.com

Company Type: Public
Profile: Bank of America, N.A. (Canada Branch) is a Schedule III bank that has been authorized under the Bank Act to conduct banking business in Canada. As a bank branch of a foreign institution, it operates with certain restrictions.
The bank offers financial services to Canadian individuals & corporations. Services include commercial lending, asset based lending, capital raising, foreign exchange, & cash management.

Bank of Tokyo - Mitsubishi UFJ (Canada)
#1700, South Tower, Royal Bank Plaza
Toronto, ON M5J 2J1

416-865-0220
www.bk.mufg.jp/english
Other Communications: Montréal: 514-875-9261; Vancouver: 604-691-7300

Company Type: Private
Profile: The Bank of Tokyo - Mitsubishi UFJ (Canada) operates as a Schedule II bank in Canada. As a foreign bank subsidiary, it is authorized under the Bank Act to accept deposits

BMO Financial Group
Also Known As: Bank of Montreal
First Canadian Place
100 King St. West, 18th Fl.
Toronto, ON M5X 1A1

416-867-6642
Fax: 416-867-3367
877-225-5266
feedback@bmo.com; remarque@bmo.com
www.bmo.com
Other Communications: TTY: 1-866-889-0889; Cantonese: 1-800-665-8800
Social Media: www.facebook.com/BMOcommunity
twitter.com/bmo

Company Type: Public
Ticker Symbol: BMO / TSX
Profile: Established in 1817 as Bank of Montreal, BMO Financial Group offers a wide range of financial products & services, including retail banking, investment banking, & wealth management. It trades on the TSX & NYSE under the symbol BMO.
David A. Galloway, Chair
William Downe, President & CEO
Thomas E. Flynn, Exec. VP & CFO
Simon A. Fish, Exec. VP & General Counsel
Surjit Rajpal, Exec. VP & Chief Risk Officer
Cameron Fowler, Exec. VP, Personal & Commercial Banking Canada

BMO Mortgage Corporation
100 King St. West, 28th Fl.
Toronto, ON M5X 1A1

416-867-4995
877-225-5266
feedback@bmo.com
www.bmo.com

Company Type: Private

BMO Nesbitt Burns
1 First Canadian Pl.
Toronto, ON M5X 1H3

416-359-4000
www.bmo.com

Company Type: Private

BMO Trust Company
First Canadian Place
100 King St. West, 54th Fl.
Toronto, ON M5X 1A1

855-834-2558
Other Communications: TTY: 866-889-0889

Company Type: Private
Profile: Estate & trust services are provided by BMO Trust Company. BMO Harris Private Banking is also offered through BMO Trust Company.

BNP Paribas (Canada)
1981, av McGill College
Montréal, QC H3A 2W8

514-285-6000
Fax: 514-285-6278
www.bnpparibas.ca

Company Type: Private
Anne Marie Verstraeten, President & CEO

Bridgewater Bank
#150, 926 - 5th Ave. SW
Calgary, AB T2P 0N7

403-817-7000
866-243-4301
customer.experience@bridgewaterbank.ca
bridgewaterbank.ca

Company Type: Private

Canaccord Financial Inc.
Pacific Centre
PO Box 10337, #2200, 609 Granville St.
Vancouver, BC V7Y 1H2

604-643-7300
800-382-9280
www.canaccordfinancial.com

Company Type: Public
Ticker Symbol: CF / TSX; CF. / AIM
Profile: Canaccord Financial Inc. was established in 1950. It is an independent, full-service financial services firm. Through its subsidiaries, Canaccord Financial conducts operations in the areas of wealth management & global capital markets. There are over sixty Canaccord offices throughout the world.
Paul Reynolds, President & Chief Executive Officer
Brad Kotush, CA, Chief Financial Officer & Executive Vice-President
Scott Davidson, Executive Vice-President & Global Head, Corporate Development & Strategy
416-869-3875, scott_davidson@canaccord.com

Canada Trust Company
Canada Trust Tower
161 Bay St., 35th Fl.
Toronto, ON M5J 2T2

www.tdcanadatrust.com

Company Type: Private
Profile: Deposit insurance services are offered by Canada Trust Company.

Canadian General Investments, Limited (CGI)
10 Toronto St.
Toronto, ON M5C 2B7

416-366-2931
Fax: 416-366-2729
866-443-6097
cgifund@mmainvestments.com
www.mmainvestments.com

Company Type: Public
Ticker Symbol: CGI / TSX
Profile: Founded in 1930, Canadian General Investments, Limited is a closed-end equity fund. The focus is upon medium to long-term investments in Canadian corporations. Canadian General Investments is managed by investment manager, Morgan Meighen & Associates Limited.
Jonathan A. Morgan, Chief Executive Officer & President, Canadian General Investments, Limited
jmorgan@mmainvestments.com

Canadian Imperial Bank of Commerce (CIBC)
Commerce Court
Toronto, ON M5L 1A2

416-980-2211
Fax: 416-980-5028
800-465-2422
investorrelations@cibc.com
www.cibc.com
Other Communications: French: 888-337-2422; Telex: 065-24116

Company Type: Public
Ticker Symbol: CM / TSX
Profile: The Canadian Imperial Bank of Commerce was formed in 1961. CIBC provides financial products & services through CIBC Retail Markets & CIBC World Markets. Customers include individuals & small business clients, plus corporate & institutional clients. CIBC has more than 42,000 employees worldwide, plus 1,100 branches throughout Canada.
Charles Sirois, Chair
Gerald T. McCaughey, President & CEO
Kevin Glass, Sr. Exec. VP & CFO
Tom Woods, Sr. Exec. VP & Chief Risk Officer
Victor Dodig, Sr. Exec. VP & Group Head, Wealth Mgmt.
Richard Nesbitt, Sr. Exec. VP & Group Head, Technology & Operations

Canadian Tire Bank
PO Box 3000, Welland, ON L3B 5S5

866-681-2837
www.myctfs.com

Company Type: Private

Canadian Tire Financial Services
PO Box 2000 Stn. Main, , Welland, ON L3B 5S3

905-735-7256
800-459-6415
www.ctfs.com

Company Type: Private

Canadian Western Bank Group (CWB)
Corporate Office, Canadian Western Bank Place
#3000, 10303 Jasper Ave.
Edmonton, AB T5J 3X6

780-423-8888
Fax: 780-423-8897
800-836-1886
comments@cwbank.com; InvestorRelations@cw
www.cwbankgroup.com
Other Communications: Media, E-mail: MediaEnquiries@cwbank.com
Social Media: www.facebook.com/cwbcommunity
www.twitter.com/CWBcommunity
www.linkedin.com/company/canadian-western-bank

Company Type: Public
Ticker Symbol: CWB / TSX
Profile: The federally chartered, Schedule I bank provides personal & commercial banking services across western Canada. Subsidiaries of Canadian Western Bank include Valiant Trust Company & Canadian Western Trust. These subsidiaries offer both personal & corporate trust services. Canadian Direct Insurance Inc., another of Canadian Western Bank's subsidiaries, is engaged in the provision of personal home & automobile insurance.

Larry M. Pollock, President & Chief Executive Officer
780-423-8888, larry.pollock@cwbank.com
Tracey C. Ball, FCA, Chief Financial Officer & Executive Vice-President
780-423-8855, Fax: 780-969-8326, tracey.ball@cwbank.com
Gail L. Harding, Q.C., Senior Vice-President, General Counsel & Secretary
gail.harding@cwbank.com
Darrell R. Jones, Chief Information Officer & Senior Vice-President
Kirby Hill, CFA, Director, Investor & Public Relations & External Communications
780-441-3770

Capital One Canada
PO Box 503 Stn. D, , Toronto, ON M1R 5L1

800-481-3239
www.capitalone.ca
Social Media: www.facebook.com/CapitalOneCanada

Company Type: Private
Profile: The financial services company offers Canadian credit cards. Capital One Canada has offices in Toronto & Montréal.

Carfinco Income Fund
Carfinco Financial Group Inc.
#300, 4245 - 97 St.
Edmonton, AB T6E 5Y7

780-413-7549
Fax: 780-450-1134
888-486-4356
carfinco@carfinco.com
www.carfinco.com
Other Communications: Service: customerservice@carfinco.com

Company Type: Public
Ticker Symbol: CFN / TSX
Profile: Carfinco Income Fund is a specialty finance income fund. It is involved in the provision of consumer car loans to borrowers who are unable to obtain financing through traditional sources.
Tracy A. Graf, Chief Executive Officer & Director, Carfinco Financial Group Inc.
tgraf@carfinco.com
Stephen Dykau, Chief Financial Officer
Troy S.F. Graf, Chief Operating Officer & Vice-President
Rick Hewson, Senior Vice-President, Operations

Cash Store Financial Services Inc. (CSF)
Also Known As: Cash Store Financial
Corporate Head Office
17631 - 103 Ave.
Edmonton, AB T5S 1N8

780-408-5110
Fax: 780-408-5122
information@csfinancial.ca
www.csfinancial.ca

Company Type: Public
Ticker Symbol: CSF
Profile: Cash Store Financial provides alternative financial products & services. It serves clients who seek short term loans, & operates under the following banners: Instaloans; The Cash Store.
Gordon J. Reykdal, Founder, Chair & CEO
Barret Reykdal, President & COO
Nancy Bland, Chief Financial Officer
Bill Johnson, Sr. Exec. VP
Michael Thompson, Sr. VP & Secretary

Chesswood Group Limited
4077 Chesswood Dr.
Toronto, ON M3J 2R8

416-386-3099
Fax: 416-386-3085
info@chesswoodgroup.com
www.chesswoodgroup.com
Other Communications: Investors: investorrelations@chesswoodgroup.com

Company Type: Public
Ticker Symbol: CHW / TSX
Profile: The financial services company has operating businesses in Canada & the United States.
Barry W. Shafran, B.A., CA, President & Chief Executive Officer
416-386-3099, bshafran@chesswoodgroup.com
Lisa Stevenson, MBA, CA, Director, Finance

CI Financial Corp.
2 Queen St. East, 20th Fl.
Toronto, ON M5C 3G7

416-364-1145
800-268-9374
www.cifinancial.com

Company Type: Public
Ticker Symbol: CIX / TSX
Profile: CI Financial Corp. is a diversified wealth management firm & investment fund company. CI operates primarily through Assante Wealth Management (Canada) Ltd. & CI Investments Inc.

Murray Oxby, Director, Communications
416-681-3254
Stephen A. MacPhail, President & Chief Executive Officer
Douglas J. Jamieson, Chief Financial Officer & Senior Vice-President, Finance
djamieson@ci.com
David C. Pauli, Chief Operating Officer & Executive Vice-President
Sheila A. Murray, Executive Vice-President, General Counsel, & Secretary

CIBC Mortgages
Commerce Court
Toronto, ON M5L 1A2

888-264-6843
www.cibc.com/ca/mortgages/index.html

Company Type: Private
Gerald T. McCaughey, President & CEO, Canadian Imperial Bank of Commerce

CIBC Trust Corporation
Commerce Court
25 King St. West
Toronto, ON

Fax: 416-980-7491
877-363-5620
www.cibc.com

Company Type: Private
Profile: CIBC Trust provides estate planning services.

CIBC World Markets
Brookfield Place
PO Box 500, 161 Bay St.
Toronto, ON M5J 2S8

416-594-7000
www.cibcwm.com

Company Type: Private

Citibank Canada
#1900, 123 Front St. West
Toronto, ON M5J 2M3

416-947-5500
888-638-2274
www.citi.ca

Company Type: Private

CitiGroup Finance Canada
#1400, 630 rue René-Lévesque ouest
Montréal, QC H3B 4Z9

800-995-2274
www.citifinancial.ca

Company Type: Private

Clairvest Group Inc.
Also Known As: Clairvest
#1700, 22 St. Clair Ave. East
Toronto, ON M4T 2S3

416-925-9270
Fax: 416-925-5753
www.clairvest.com

Company Type: Public
Ticker Symbol: CVG / TSX
Profile: Clarivest Group Inc. is a private equity management firm. The group invests its own capital & that of third parties in businesses with the potential to generate superior returns.
Jeff Parr, Co-Chief Executive Officer
Ken Rotman, Co-Chief Executive Officer
Daniel Cheng, Chief Financial Officer
Maria Klyuev, Director, Investor Relations & Marketing
416-925-9270, Fax: 416-925-5753, mariak@clairvest.com

Clarke Inc.
6009 Quinpool Rd., 9th Fl.
Halifax, NS B3K 5J7

902-442-3000
Fax: 902-442-0187
www.clarkeinc.com

Company Type: Public
Ticker Symbol: CKI, CKI.DB, CKI.DB.A/TSX
Profile: Clarke Inc. is an activist catalyst investment company, with several wholly-owned operating companies & divisions. The company has a diversified portfolio of investments, with operating subsidiaries as follows: Clarke Transport Inc., Clarke Road Transport Inc., Clarke IT Solutions Inc., La Traverse Rivière-du-Loup - St. Siméon Ltée., CIS Shipping International Inc., & Granby Industries.
George Armoyan, President & Chief Executive Officer
Dean M. Cull, COO, Freight Transportation Services, & President, Clarke Transport Inc. & Clarke Road Transport Inc.
John Hamblin, President, Clarke IT Solutions Inc.
Andrew Snelgrove, Chief Financial Officer
Tim Rorabeck, Corporate Vice-President & General Counsel
Matthew Towns, CFA, Vice-President, Investments

CMP Gold Trust
Dundee Place
1 Adelaide St. East, 29th Fl.
Toronto, ON M5C 2V9

416-363-5621
Fax: 416-363-5850
800-268-8186
www.cmpfunds.ca

Company Type: Public
Ticker Symbol: CMP.UN / TSX
Profile: CMP Gold Trust is a closed-end investment trust. Holders of Trust Units invest in a portfolio of precious metals & the securities of precious metals issuers & minerals issuers. The Trust is managed by Dundee Securities Ltd. & sub-advised by Ned Goodman Investment Counsel Limited.
Ned Goodman, BSc., MBA, CFA, Manager
Murray John, BSc., MBA, A.C.S.M., Manager

Counsel Corporation
PO Box 3, #700, 1 Toronto St.
Toronto, ON M5C 2V6

416-866-3000
Fax: 416-866-3061
info@counselcorp.com
www.counselcorp.com

Company Type: Public
Ticker Symbol: CXS / TSX
Profile: Founded in 1979, Counsel Corporation is a financial services company. Through its businesses, the corporation is engaged in private equity investment, residental mortgage lending, real estate finance, & distressed & surplus capital asset transactions,.
Allan Silber, Chair & Chief Executive Officer
Stephen Weintraub, Chief Financial Officer, Executive Vice-President & Secretary
416-866-3058, sweintraub@counselcorp.com
R. Adam Levy, Corporate Counsel & Sr. Vice-President, Corporate Development
Todd Thal, Director, Investor Relations

Coxe Commodity Strategy Fund
c/o BMO Nesbitt Burns Inc.
PO Box 150 Stn. 1st Cdn Pl., , 100 King St. West, 3rd Fl.
Toronto, ON M5X 1H3

866-864-7760
admin.dealerservices@bmonb.com
www.bmocm.com
Other Communications: French, Toll-Free Phone: 866-529-0017

Company Type: Public
Ticker Symbol: COX.UN / TSX
Profile: Coxe Commodity Strategy Fund is a closed-end investment fund. The investment objective of Coxe Commodity Strategy Fund is to provide long term capital growth for investors, by executing the commodity investment strategies of the chairman of Coxe Advisors LLP. The Fund's administrator is BMO Nesbitt Burns Inc.
Thomas V. Milroy, Chief Executive Officer
David Ferguson, Chief Financial Officer
Don Coxe, Portfolio Consultant

Cymbria Corporation
#500, 150 Bloor St. West
Toronto, ON M5S 2X9

416-963-9353
Fax: 416-963-5060
866-757-7207
www.edgepointwealth.com/cymbria

Company Type: Public
Ticker Symbol: CYB / TSX
Profile: Cymbria Corporation provides shareholders with long-term capital appreciation, through an investment in a portfolio of global equities & an investment in EdgePoint Wealth Management. Inc. Cymbria is managed by EdgePoint Investment Group Inc., a related party of EdgePoint Wealth Management Inc.
Geoff MacDonald, Co-CEO, Chief Investment Officer, & Founding Partner, EdgePoint Investment Group Inc.
Tye Bousada, President, Co-Chief Executive Officer, & Founding Partner, EdgePoint Investment Group Inc.
Patrick Farmer, Chief Compliance Officer, COO, & Founding Partner, EdgePoint Investment Group Inc.
Norman Tang, Director, Finance, EdgePoint Investment Group Inc.

Davis + Henderson Corporation
Also Known As: D+H
Corporate Head Office
#201, 939 Eglington Ave. East
Toronto, ON M4G 4H7

416-696-7700
Fax: 416-696-8308
888-850-6656
investorrelations@dhltd.com
www.dhltd.com

Company Type: Public
Ticker Symbol: DH / TSX
Profile: Founded in 1875, the organization supplies financial services to financial organizations, including mortgage lenders/brokers, insurance companies, governments, & regional banks.
Gerrard Schmid, Chief Executive Officer
Brian Kyle, Chief Financial Officer & Executive Vice-President
416-696-7700
Yves Denommé, Executive Vice-President, Operations

Desjardins Securities/ Valeurs mobilières Desjardins (VMD)
#300, 1170, rue Peel
Montréal, QC H3B 0A9

514-987-1749
Fax: 514-987-9593
888-987-1749
corpo.vmd.ca

Company Type: Private
Profile: Desjardins Securities is a brokerage firm that offers products & services for individual, institutional, & corporate investors. The company is a member of both the Investment Industry Regulatory Organization of Canada & the Canadian Investor Protection Fund. Desjardins Securities employs more than 950 people in Québec & Ontario.

Desjardins Trust Inc.
PO Box 34, 1, complexe Desjardins
Montréal, QC H5B 1E4

514-286-9441
Fax: 514-286-1131
800-361-6840
www.desjardins.com

Company Type: Private
Hélène Gagné, Vice-President, Communications
Monique F. Leroux, President/CEO
Jean Landry, President/COO
François Gagnon, Sr. Vice-President, Finance
Claude Dupuis, Sr. Vice-President, Technologies

DirectCash Payments Inc.
Head Office
#6, 1420 - 28th St. NE
Calgary, AB T2A 7W6

Fax: 888-777-5519
888-414-3733
investorrelations@directcash.net; sales@d
www.directcash.net
Other Communications: Customer Support: customersupport@directcash.net

Company Type: Public
Ticker Symbol: DCI / TSX
Profile: DirectCash provides debit terminals, ATMS, prepaid phone cards, & prepaid cash cards in Canada.
Jeffrey J. Smith, President & Chief Executive Officer
Brian B. Kathol, Chief Financial Officer
403-387-2103, Fax: 403-451-3003, bkathol@directcash.net
Todd Schneider, Chief Operations Officer
Joseph Xu, Chief Technology Officer
Amanda J. Galacher, Contact, Investor Relations
403-387-2158, Fax: 403-451-3058, investorrelations@directcash.net

DundeeWealth Inc.
Dundee Place
1 Adelaide St. East, 28th Fl.
Toronto, ON M5C 2V9

416-350-3250
888-292-3847
inquiries@dundeewealth.com
www.dundeewealth.com

Company Type: Public
Profile: A wholly owned subsidiary of Scotiabank, DundeeWealth is an integrated wealth management company. It offers wealth management & investment management solutions. Advisory services are offered to financial advisors, corporations, foundations, & institutions.
David Goodman, Chief Executive Officer & President
Mike O'Bee, Chief Administrative Officer
John Pereira, Chief Financial Officer & Executive Vice-President
Robert Pattillo, Executive Vice-President, Marketing & Communications
Greg Lahn, Vice-President, Wealth Management Technology Solutions

Equitable Group Inc.
Corporate Office
#700, 30 St. Clair Ave. West
Toronto, ON M4V 3A1
416-515-7000
Fax: 416-515-7001
866-407-0004
customerservice@equitabletrust.com
www.equitabletrust.com
Other Communications: Investors: investor_enquiry@equitablegroupinc.com
Company Type: Public
Ticker Symbol: ETC / TSX
Profile: Through its wholly-owned subsidiary, The Equitable Trust Company, Equitable Group Inc. offers first mortgage financing & Guaranteed Investment Certificates to depositors. The Equitable Trust Company is a federally incorporated trust company.
Andrew Moor, President & Chief Executive Officer
Kimberley Graham, Chief Compliance Officer, General Counsel, Corp. Sec., & VP
Tim Wilson, Chief Financial Officer & Vice-President

Equitable Trust Company
#700, 30 St. Clair Ave. West
Toronto, ON M4V 3A1
416-515-7000
Fax: 416-515-7001
866-407-0004
www.equitabletrust.com
Other Communications: Toll-Free Fax: 1-866-407-5859
Company Type: Private
Andrew Moore, President & CEO

FaithLife Financial
470 Weber St. North
Waterloo, ON N2J 4G4
519-886-4610
Fax: 519-886-0350
800-563-6237
moreinfo@faithlifefinancial.ca
www.faithlifefinancial.ca
Other Communications: Western Canada Region: wc.moreinfo@faithlifefinancial.ca
Social Media: www.facebook.com/FaithLifeFinancial
twitter.com/FaithLifeFin
Company Type: Private
Profile: The Christian based, member owned, not-for-profit organization offers the following financial services: investment products, income protecioin, & life insurance.
P. Wayne Musselman, Chair
Karen C. Bjerland, President & Chief Executive Officer

Fiera Sceptre Inc.
#800, 1501, av McGill College
Montréal, QC H3A 3M8
514-954-3750
Fax: 514-395-0723
800-994-9002
www.sceptre.ca
Company Type: Public
Ticker Symbol: FSZ / TSX
Profile: Fiera Sceptre is an independent, full-service, multi-product investment firm.
Jean-Guy Desjardins, Chief Executive Officer
Pierre Blanchette, Senior Vice-President, Finance
Mélanie Tardif, Contact, National Public Relations
514-843-2060

Firm Capital Mortgage Investment Corp.
1244 Caledonia Rd.
Toronto, ON M6A 2X5
416-635-0221
Fax: 416-635-1713
mortgages@firmcapital.com
www.firmcapital.com
Company Type: Public
Ticker Symbol: FC / TSX
Profile: Through its mortgage banker, Firm Capital Corporation, Firm Capital Mortgage Investment Trust is a non-bank lender. It provides residential & commercial real estate financing
Eli Dadouch, President & Chief Executive Officer
Jonathan Mair, CA, Chief Financial Officer
Edward Gilbert, Chief Operating Officer
Joseph Fried, Secretary & General Counsel
Susan DiBari, Contact, Investor Relations
sdibari@firmcapital.com

First National Financial LP
North Tower
#700, 100 University Ave.
Toronto, ON M5J 1V6
416-593-1100
Fax: 416-593-1900
800-465-0039
customer@firstnational.ca
www.firstnational.ca
Other Communications: Toll-Free Fax: 800-463-9584
Company Type: Public
Ticker Symbol: FN / TSX
Profile: First National Financial LP is a non-bank mortgage originator that provides single-family & multi-unit residential & commercial mortgage solutions.
Stephen Smith, Chair, President, & Co-Founder, First National Financial
Rob Inglis, Chief Financial Officer, First National Financial Corporation
416-593-1100, rob.inglis@firstnational.ca
Jason Ellis, Managing Director, Capital Markets
Jeremy Wedgbury, Managing Director, Commercial Mortage Origination
Scott C. McKenzie, Vice-President, Residential Mortgages
Moray Tawse, Vice-President, Mortgage Investments
Lisa White, Vice-President, Mortgage Administration
Susan J. Biggar, General Counsel

Ford Credit Canada Limited
PO Box 5005, #800, 1275 North Service Rd.
Oakville, ON L6M 3G4
905-845-2511
Fax: 866-868-1213
800-263-0582
www.fordcredit.ca
Company Type: Private
Phillippe Paillart, Chair & CEO
Charles A. Bilyeu, Vice-Chair & President

Genterra Capital Inc.
106 Avenue Rd.
Toronto, ON M5R 2H3
416-920-0500
info@genterracapital.com
www.genterracapitalinc.com
Company Type: Public
Ticker Symbol: GIC / TSX Venture
Profile: The private equity investment firm has interest in health care, real estate, & early stage venture capital.
Fred A. Litwin, President
Stanley Abramowitz, Chief Financial Officer
Mark Litwin, Vice-President

Gluskin Sheff + Associates Inc.
Bay Adelaide Centre
#5100, 333 Bay St.
Toronto, ON M5h 2R2
416-681-6000
Fax: 416-681-6060
866-681-6001
media@gluskinsheff.com; careers@gluskinsh
www.gluskinsheff.com
Other Communications: Calgary Office, Phone: 403-202-6480
Company Type: Public
Ticker Symbol: GS / TSX
Profile: Gluskin Sheff + Associates Inc. was formed in 1984. The independent, wealth management firm serves institutional investors & private clients of high net worth.
Jeremy Freedman, President & Chief Executive Officer
David R. Morris, Chief Financial Officer & Secretary
416-681-6036
Brian Ginsler, Chief Operating Officer

GMP Capital Inc.
#300, 145 King St. West
Toronto, ON M5H 1J8
416-367-8600
Fax: 416-367-8164
888-301-3244
corporatesecretary@gmpcapital.com
www.gmpcapital.com
Other Communications: Investors: investorrelations@gmpcapital.com
Company Type: Public
Ticker Symbol: GMP
Profile: GMP Capital Inc. is a Canadian independent investment dealer. Through its subsidiaries, GMP Capital is involved in the following investment areas: alternative investments, capital markets, & wealth management. Individual, corporate, & institutional investor clients are served.
Harris A. Fricker, MA, Chief Executive Officer & President
Shawn Aspden, Vice-Chair & Head, North American Institutional Equity Sales
Doug Bell, Vice-Chair & Co-Head, Investment Banking
Chris Bond, Vice-Chair & Head, Institutional Trading

Graham Income Trust
10840 - 27th St. S.E.
Calgary, AB T2Z 3R6
403-570-5000
Fax: 403-258-2807
www.graham.ca
Company Type: Private

Griffin Corporation
#801, 55 King St.
Kitchener, ON N2G 4W1
519-744-4400
Fax: 519-744-5500
www.vistahospitality.com
Company Type: Private

Guardian Capital Group Limited
PO Box 201 Stn. Commerce Cour, , #3100, 199 Bay St.
Toronto, ON M5L 1E8
416-364-8341
Fax: 416-364-2067
info@guardiancapital.com
www.guardiancapital.com
Company Type: Public
Ticker Symbol: GCG / TSX
Profile: Guardian Capital Group Limited is a diversified financial services company that was established in 1962. Through its businesses, Guardian Capital Group Limited is involved in the distribution of mutual funds, institutional & high net worth investment management, as well as other financial services.
George Mavroudis, Chief Executive Officer & President
416-364-8341
C. Verner Christensen, Chief Financial Officer & Senior Vice-President, Finance
416-947-4093

HSBC Bank Canada
885 West Georgia St.
Vancouver, BC V6C 3E9
604-685-1000
Fax: 604-641-2506
888-310-4722
hsbc_business_centre@hsbc.ca
www.hsbc.ca
Other Communications: Business: 866-808-4722; Internet Banking: 877-621-8811
Company Type: Public
Ticker Symbol: HSB / TSX
Profile: The chartered bank was established in 1981. It carries on business uner the provisions of the Bank Act.
Samuel Minzberg, Chair
Lindsay Gordon, President & CEO
Graham McIsaac, Chief Financial Officer
Mark Watkinson, Exec. VP & Regional President, Central & Eastern Canada
Margaret Willis, Exec. VP, Personal Financial Services & Wealth Mgmt.

HSBC Financial Corporation Limited
885 West Georgia St.
Vancouver, BC V6C 3E8
888-318-0271
www.hsbcfinance.ca
Other Communications: TTY: 1-866-891-9659
Company Type: Private
Profile: The company is winding down its consumer finance business, and will no longer accept new loan applications.
Walter Lubiana, President & CEO

ICICI Bank Canada
PO Box 396, Toronto, ON M3C 2S7
416-847-7979
888-424-2422
customercare.ca@icicibank.com
www.icicibank.ca
Social Media: www.facebook.com/icicibank
twitter.com/icicibank_care
www.linkedin.com/company/icici-bank
Company Type: Private

IGM Financial Inc.
447 Portage Ave.
Winnipeg, MB R3C 3B6
204-943-0361
Fax: 204-947-1659
www.igmfinancial.com
Company Type: Public
Ticker Symbol: IGM / TSX
Profile: IGM Financial Inc. is a managed asset, mutual fund, & personal financial services company. Its operating units include Investment Planning Counsel Inc., Mackenzie Financial Corporation, & Investors Group.

R. Jeffrey Orr, Chair
Charles R. Sims, Co-President & CEO
Murray J. Taylor, Co-President & CEO
Gregory D. Tretiak, Exec. VP & CFO
greg.tretiak@investorsgroup.com
Geoffrey D. Creighton, Sr. VP, General Counsel & Secretary

Investors Group Inc.
Canada Centre
#1, 447 Portage Ave.
Winnipeg, MB R3C 3B6

204-943-0361
Fax: 204-947-1659
888-746-6344
www.investorsgroup.com

Company Type: Private
Murray Taylor, President & CEO
Gregory D. Tretiak, Exec. VP & CFO
greg.tretiak@investorsgroup.com
Ron Arnst, Contact, Media Relations
204-956-3364, ron.arnst@investorsgroup.com

John Deere Credit
Customer Care
#401, 1001 Champlain Ave.
Burlington, ON L7L 5Z4

800-268-2607
www.deere.com

Company Type: Private

Jovian Capital Corporation
#920, 26 Wellington St. East
Toronto, ON M5E 1S2

204-933-5750
Fax: 204-933-5751
866-234-2552
www.joviancapital.com

Company Type: Public
Ticker Symbol: JOV / TSX
Profile: Jovian Capital Corporation acquires & grows financial services companies. The Jovian group of companies includes JovFinancial Solutions Inc., JovPortfolio Management Inc., MGI Securities Inc., MGI Securities (USA) Inc., Leon Frazer & Associates Inc., T.E. Wealth, & Hahn Investment Stewards & Company Inc.
Philip Armstrong, BA (Law) Hons, Chief Executive Officer
416-933-5752, parmstrong@joviancapital.com
Mark L. Arthur, CFA, President
marthur@joviancapital.com
J. Russell Lindsay, CA, Chief Operating Officer & Vice-President
rlindsay@joviancapital.com
Jason Mackey, CA, Chief Financial Officer & Vice-President
jmackey@joviancapital.com
Duriya Patel, BSc, LLB, General Counsel, Vice-President, & Secretary
dpatel@joviancapital.com
Don Sangster, Contact, Investor Relations
416-933-5744, Fax: 416-646-0984,
dsangster@joviancapital.com

Korea Exchange Bank of Canada
Madison Centre
#103, 4950 Yonge St.
Toronto, ON M2N 6K1

416-222-5200
Fax: 416-222-5822
kebcanada.com

Company Type: Private

Laurentian Bank of Canada
Tour Banque Laurentienne
#1660, 1981, av McGill College
Montréal, QC H3A 3K3

514-252-1846
Fax: 514-284-3916
800-522-1846
www.laurentianbank.com
Other Communications: TTY: 1-866-262-2231; Media: 514-284-4500, ext. 8232

Company Type: Public
Ticker Symbol: LB / TSX
Profile: Founded in 1846, Laurentian Bank of Canada has operations across Canada today. It serves both individuals & small & medium-sized businesses. The bank also offers services to independent financial intermediaries through B2B Trust. Laurentian Bank Securities provides full-service brokerage solutions. Approximately 4,000 people are employed by the bank.
Réjean Robitaille, President & Chief Executive Officer
Michel C. Lauzon, Chief Financial Officer & Executive Vice-President, Finance
Gladys Caron, Vice-President, Communications & Investor Relations
gladys.caron@banquelaurentienne.ca

Lloyd's Underwriters (Canada)
#2220, 1155 Metcalfe St.
Montréal, QC H3B 2V6

514-861-8361
Fax: 514-861-0470
877-455-6937
info@lloyds.ca
www.lloyds.com

Company Type: Private

Mackenzie Financial
180 Queen St. West
Toronto, ON M5V 3K1

416-922-3217
800-387-0614
service@mackenziefinancial.com
www.mackenziefinancial.com

Company Type: Private

Manulife Bank of Canada
Also Known As: Manulife Bank
PO Box 1602 Stn. Waterloo, , #500-MA, 500 King St. North
Waterloo, ON N2J 4C6

877-765-2265
Fax: 877-565-2265
manulife_bank@manulife.com; advisorbank@m
www.manulifebank.ca
Other Communications: Nova Scotia: 227 Joseph Howe Dr., Halifax, NS, B3J 2X5

Company Type: Private
Profile: Manulife Bank of Canada was established in 1993. The Schedule I federally chartered bank serves clients in all provinces & territories.

Manulife Financial Corporation
Also Known As: Manufacturers Life Insurance Company
North Tower 3
200 Bloor St. East, 2nd Fl.
Toronto, ON M4W 1E5

416-852-1189
Fax: 416-926-5410
877-308-7714
corporate_communications@manulife.com
www.manulife.ca

Company Type: Public
Ticker Symbol: MFC / TSX NYSE, Hong Kong
Profile: Manulife Financial provides financial protection services & wealth management products.
Donald A. Guloien, President & Chief Executive Officer
Michael W. Bell, Chief Financial Officer & Senior Executive Vice-President

Matrix Asset Management Inc.
PO Box 11170 Stn. Royal Centre, , #2600, 1055 West Georgia St.
Vancouver, BC V6E 3R5

604-633-1418
Fax: 604-688-9039
800-268-8244
info@matrixasset.ca
www.matrixasset.ca
Other Communications: Toronto: 416-362-3077; Montréal: 514-227-0666

Company Type: Public
Ticker Symbol: MTA / TSX
Profile: The diversified wealth & asset management company has offices throughout Canada. Matrix Asset Management's divisions are as follows: fund management operated through Matrix Funds Management, a division of GrowthWorks Capital Ltd.; venture capital & private equity operated through GrowthWorks; & institutional asset management operated through SEAMARK.
David R. Levi, Chief Executive Officer
david.levi@matrixasset.ca
David Balsdon, Chief Operating Officer
Clinton E. Matthews, Chief Financial Officer

MBNA Canada Bank
PO Box 4369 Stn. A, , Toronto, ON M5W 3P2

877-428-6060
www.mbna.ca

Company Type: Private

MCAN Mortgage Corporation
#400, 200 King St. West
Toronto, ON M5H 3T4

416-572-4880
Fax: 416-598-4142
855-213-6226
mcanexecutive@mcanmortgage.com
www.mcanmortgage.com

Company Type: Public
Ticker Symbol: MKP / TSX
Profile: MCAN Mortgage is a mortgage investment corporation. Funds are invested in a portfolio of mortgages, as well as other types of loans & investments, real estate, & marketable securities.
William Jandrisits, President & Chief Executive Officer
Tammy Oldenburg, Chief Financial Officer & Vice-President

Medwell Capital Corp.
6030 - 88 St.
Edmonton, AB T6E 6G4

780-413-7152
Fax: 780-408-3040
866-701-6033
info@medwellcapital.com
www.medwellcapital.com

Company Type: Public
Ticker Symbol: MWC / TSX Venture
Profile: Medwell Capital Corp. is an investment & advisory firm
Kevin Giese, President & Chief Executive Officer
Brent Johnston, Chief Financial Officer
Tony Hesby, Executive Vice-President
Brenda Brown, Vice-President, Clinical Operations
Randy Stroud, Vice-President, Regulatory Affairs

Mizuho Corporate Bank
#1102, 100 Yonge St.
Toronto, ON M5C 2W1

416-874-0222
www.mizuhocbk.com

Company Type: Private

Montreal Trust Company of Canada (MTCC)
Scotia Plaza
44 King St. West
Toronto, ON M5H 1H1

www.scotiabank.com

Company Type: Private
Profile: Trust services are offered.

Natcan Trust Company
1100, rue University, 10e étage
Montréal, QC H3B 2G7

514-871-7240
800-463-6643
www.nbc.ca

Company Type: Private
Louis Vachon, President & CEO, National Bank Financial Group

National Bank Financial Group
Also Known As: National Bank of Canada
Tour de la Banque Nationale
600, rue de la Gauchetière ouest
Montréal, QC H3B 4L2

514-394-5555
888-483-5628
investorrelations@nbc.ca
www.nbc.ca
Other Communications: Hearing Impaired Contact: 1-866-494-6742

Company Type: Public
Ticker Symbol: NA / TSX
Profile: Chartered under the Bank Act of Canada, the National Bank provides comprehensive financial services, including retail, commercial, corporate, international, & treasury banking services. Through its subsidiaries, National Bank Financial Group also offers security brokerage, insurance, wealth management, & mutual fund & retirement plan management. There are over 445 branches across Canada. National Bank employs approximately 19,785 people.
Louis Vachon, President & Chief Executive Officer
Ghislain Parent, Chief Financial Officer & Executive Vice-President, Finance, Risk & Treasury
514-394-6807
Jean Dagenais, Senior Vice-President, Finance, Taxation, & Investor Relations
514-394-6233
Claude Breton, Senior Director, Public Affairs
514-394-8644
Hélène Baril, Senior Director, Investor Relations
514-394-0296

Optimum Group Inc.
Head Office
#1700, 425, boul de Maisonneuve ouest
Montréal, QC

514-288-2010
Fax: 514-288-7692
www.groupe-optimum.com

Company Type: Private
Profile: The international financial group offers the following products & services: property & casualty insurance, life insurance, life reinsurance, asset management, & actuarial consulting. The company employs over 500 people.

Pacific & Western Bank of Canada
Corporate Head Office
#2002, 140 Fullarton St.
London, ON N6A 5P2

519-645-1919
Fax: 519-645-2060
866-979-1919
www.pwbank.com
Other Communications: Public, Media, & Government Relations: 866-787-9936

Company Type: Private
Profile: Pacific & Western Bank of Canada is a Schedule I domestic bank, which has been authorized under the Bank Act to accept deposits.
David R. Taylor, B.Sc. (Hons.), M.B.A., F.I.C.B., President & Chief Executive Officer
Shawn Clarke, M.Eng., P.Eng., M.B.A., Chief Information Officer & Vice-President, Corporate Development & Enterprise Risk
Barry D. Walter, B.Comm., C.A., Chief Financial Officer & Senior Vice-President
Nick Kristo, B.Comm., M.B.A., Senior Vice-President, Credit & Administration
Jonathan F.P. Taylor, B.B.A., C.H.R.P., Senior Vice-President, Human Resources & Operations

Pacific & Western Credit Corp.
#2002, 140 Fullarton St.
London, ON N6A 5P2

519-675-4201
Fax: 519-675-4241
investorrelations@pwbank.com
www.pwbank.com

Company Type: Public
Ticker Symbol: PWC / TSX
Profile: Pacific & Western Credit Corp.'s wholly owned subsidiary is the Pacific & Western Bank of Canada. Pacific & Western Bank is a Schedule I chartered bank that offers financing to corporate & government entities.
David R. Taylor, President & Chief Executive Officer
Barry D. Walter, Chief Financial Officer & Senior Vice-President
Tel Matrundola, Vice-President, Public Relations & Media
800-787-9936, telm@pwbank.com

Peoples Trust
#1400, 888 Dunsmuir St.
Vancouver, BC V6C 3K4

604-683-2881
Fax: 604-331-3469
people@peoplestrust.com
www.peoplestrust.com

Company Type: Private

Pinetree Capital Ltd.
The Exchange Tower
#2500, 130 King St. West
Toronto, ON M5X 1A9

416-941-9600
Fax: 416-941-1090
info@pinetreecapital.com; ir@pinetreecapi
www.pinetreecapital.com

Company Type: Public
Ticker Symbol: PNP/ TSX
Profile: The financial advisory, investment, & venture capital firm is focused on the small cap market. Investments are mainly in the resources sector.
Sheldon Inwentash, Chair & Chief Executive Officer
Gerry Feldman, Chief Financial Officer & Vice-President, Corporate Development
Steven Gold, Vice-President, Investments
Richard Patricio, Vice-President, Legal & Corporate Affairs
Philip Williams, Vice-President, Business Development

Power Financial Corporation
751, carré Victoria
Montréal, QC H2Y 2J3

514-286-7400
Fax: 514-286-7424
www.powerfinancial.com

Company Type: Public
Ticker Symbol: PWF
Profile: The diversified holding & management company was founded in 1940. It includes the following subsidiaries: IGM Financial Inc., Great-West Lifeco Inc., & Pargesa.
R. Jeffrey Orr, President/CEO
Philip K. Ryan, Exec. Vice-President/CFO
Edward Johnson, Sr. Vice-President, General Counsel & Secretary

President's Choice Financial
PO Box 603 Stn. Agincourt, , Toronto, ON M1S 5K9

888-723-8881
www.banking.pcfinancial.ca
Other Communications: MasterCard: 866-246-7262; Mortgages: 888-866-0866, option 3

Company Type: Private
Profile: President's Choice Financial does not have branches. Access to services is by bank machine, telephone, or Internet. President's Choice Financial services are offered by the direct banking division of CIBC.

Primary Corp.
Exchange Tower
PO Box 91, #2110, 130 King St. West
Toronto, ON M5X 1B1

416-214-9672
Fax: 416-214-5954
PYC / TSX
Other Communications: info@primarycorp.ca

Company Type: Public
Profile: Primary Corp. focuses on natural resource lending. Marret Asset Management Inc. manages Primary's investment portfolio.
Robert Pollock, MBA, President & Chief Executive Officer
David Guebert, Chief Financial Officer

RBC Capital Markets
200 Bay St.
Toronto, ON M5J 2W7

416-842-2000
www.rbccm.com

Company Type: Private

ResMor Trust Company
East Tower
#1400, 3250 Bloor St. West
Toronto, ON M8X 2X9

Fax: 866-371-0132
866-809-5800
mortgagesupport@resmor.com
www.resmor.com

Company Type: Private

Royal Bank Mortgage Corporation

www.rbcroyalbank.com/mortgages

Company Type: Private

Royal Bank of Canada (RBC)
Royal Bank Plaza
PO Box 1, 200 Bay St.
Toronto, ON M5J 2J5

416-974-5151
Fax: 416-955-7800
www.rbc.com

Company Type: Public
Ticker Symbol: RY / TSX
Profile: The Royal Bank of Canada is engaged in the following services: personal & commercial banking; corporate & investment banking; insurance; wealth management; & transaction processing services. Approximately 74,000 full and part-time staff are employed in offices in Canada, the United States, & 51 other countries.
Gordon M. Nixon, President & Chief Executive Officer
Janice Fukakusa, CFO & Chief Administrative Officer

Royal Trust Company
Royal Bank Plaza
PO Box 1, 200 Bay St.
Toronto, ON M5J 2J5

416-974-5151
Fax: 416-955-7800
www.rbc.com

Company Type: Private

Royal Trust Corporation of Canada
Royal Bank Plaza
PO Box 1, 200 Bay St.
Toronto, ON M5J 2J5

416-974-5151
Fax: 416-955-7800
www.rbc.com

Company Type: Private

Scotia Capital
Scotia Plaza
PO Box 4085 Stn. A, , 40 King St. West
Toronto, ON M5W 2X6

416-863-7411
www.gbm.scotiabank.com

Company Type: Private

Scotia Mortgage Corporation
44 King St. West
Toronto, ON M5H 1H1

416-288-4111
Fax: 416-701-7599

Company Type: Private
Jane Rowe, President & Chief Executive Officer

Scotiabank
Scotia Plaza
40 King St. West
Toronto, ON M5H 1H1

416-866-6161
Fax: 416-866-3750
800-472-6842
investor.relations@scotiabank.com
www.scotiabank.com
Other Communications: Hearing Impaired Services: 1-800-645-0288

Company Type: Public
Ticker Symbol: BNS / TSX
Profile: Scotiabank's range of services includes personal & commercial banking, corporate & investment banking services & products, as well as wealth management services. Approximately 19 million customers are served in over 55 countries. Scotiabank trades under the symbol BNS on both the Toronto & New York Stock Exchanges.
Richard E. Waugh, President & CEO
Luc A. Vanneste, Exec. VP & CFO
Sarabjit (Sabi) Marwah, Vice-Chair & COO
Stephen P. Hart, Exec. VP & Chief Credit Officer
Jeffrey C. Heath, Exec. VP & Group Treasurer

Scotiatrust
40 King St. West, 38th Fl.
Toronto, ON M5H 1H1

800-265-6978
www.scotiabank.com
Social Media: www.linkedin.com/company/scotiatrust

Company Type: Private
Profile: Scotiatrust offers estate & trust services.

SITQ
1001, rue du Square-Victoria
Montréal, QC H2Z 2B1

514-287-1852
888-599-1666
info@ivanhoecambridge.com
www.sitq.com

Company Type: Private

Société Générale (Canada)
#1800, 1501, av McGill College
Montréal, QC H3A 2M8

514-841-6000
ww2.sgcib.com/canada

Company Type: Private
Pierre Matuszewski, Chief Executive Officer

Sprott Inc.
South Tower, Royal Bank Plaza
PO Box 27, #2700, 200 Bay St.
Toronto, ON M5J 2J1

416-362-7172
Fax: 416-943-6497
888-362-7172
ir@sprott.com
www.sprottinc.com
Other Communications: Investors, Toll-Free Phone: 877-403-2310

Company Type: Public
Ticker Symbol: SII / TSX
Profile: Sprott Inc. is an independent asset management firm operating through its four business units: Sprott Asset Managemen L.P., Sprott Private Wealth L.P., Sprott Consulting L.P., & Sprott U.S. Holdings Inc..
Peter Grosskopf, Chief Executive Officer
Kevin Bambrough, President
Steven Rostowsky, CA, CFA, Chief Financial Officer
416-203-2310

Sprott Resource Lending Corp.
South Tower, Royal Bank Plaza
PO Box 90, #2750, 200 Bay St.
Toronto, ON M5J 2J2

416-362-7172
888-362-7172
www.sprottlending.com

Company Type: Public
Ticker Symbol: SIL / TSX, AMEX
A. Murray Sinclair, Chair
Peter Grosskopf, President & CEO
Jim Grosdanis, Chief Financial Officer
416-943-4698
Narinder Nagra, Chief Operating Officer

Standard Life Financial
1245 rue Sherbrooke ouest
Montréal, QC H3G 1G3

514-499-8855
Fax: 514-499-4908
information@standardlife.ca
www.standardlife.ca

Company Type: Private

State Farm Mutual Funds
333 First Commerce Drive
Aurora, ON L4G 8A4

905-750-4100
info@statefarm.com
www.statefarm.ca

Company Type: Private

State Farm Mutual Funds
333 First Commerce Drive
Aurora, ON L4G 8A4

905-750-4100
info@statefarm.com
www.statefarm.ca

Company Type: Private

State Street Bank (Canada)
State Street Financial Centre
#1500, 30 Adelaide St. East
Toronto, ON M5C 3G6

416-362-1100
Fax: 416-956-2525
888-287-8639
Montréal: 514-282-2400
www.statestreet.ca

Company Type: Private
Profile: State Street Bank (Canada) is a foreign bank branch that is categorized as a Schedule III bank in Canada. It has been authorized under the Bank Act to conduct banking business in Canada. State Street has been present in Canada since 1990, where it focuses on institutional investors.

State Street Trust Company Canada
State Street Financial Centre
#1100, 30 Adelaide St. East
Toronto, ON M5C 3G6

416-362-1100
Fax: 416-956-2525
888-287-8639
www.statestreet.ca
Other Communications: Montréal: 514-282-2400; Vancouver: 604-602-9122

Company Type: Private
Profile: Products & services are offered to institutional investors in Canada through State Street Trust Company Canada.
Kevin Drynan, Head, Sales & Relationship Management
kdrynan@statestreet.com
Jay Wiltshire, Vice-President
jay_wiltshire@ssga.com

Sumitomo Mitsui Banking of Canada
Ernst & Young Tower, Toronto Dominion Centre
PO Box 172, #1400
Toronto, ON M5K 1H6

416-368-4766
Fax: 416-367-3565
www.smbcgroup.com

Company Type: Private

Sun Life Financial Inc.
Sun Life Centre
150 King St. West
Toronto, ON M5H 1J9

416-979-9966
Fax: 416-585-7892
877-786-5433
service@sunlife.ca
www.sunlife.com
Other Communications: Investors: investor.relations@sunlife.com
Social Media: www.facebook.com/SLFCanada; www.facebook.com/BrighterLifeCA
twitter.com/brighterlifeCA; twitter.com/#!/sunlifecareers
www.linkedin.com/company/sun-life-financial

Company Type: Public
Ticker Symbol: SLF / TSX
Profile: Sun Life Financial serves both individuals & corporate customers. It offers customers a broad range of protection & wealth management products & services.
Donald A. Stewart, Chair/CEO, Sun Life
Jon A. Boscia, President, Sun Life Financial
Dean A. Connor, President, Sun Life Financial Canada
Richard P. McKenney, Exec. Vice-President/CFO
Mary De Paoli, Sr. Vice-President & Chief Marketing Officer
Christine I. Mackiw, Chief Privacy Officer & Vice-President, Records Management

TD Mortgage Corporation
#324, 8th Ave. SW
Calgary, AB T2P 2Z2

416-308-6963
Fax: 416-982-6166
www.td.com

Company Type: Private

TD Securities
TD Bank Tower
PO Box 1, 66 Wellington St. West
Toronto, ON M5K 1A2

416-307-8500
www.tdsecurities.com

Company Type: Private

Timbercreek Mortgage Investment Corporation
#500, 1000 Yonge St.
Toronto, ON M4W 2K2

416-306-9967
Fax: 416-848-9494
info@timbercreekfunds.com; careers@timber
www.timbercreekfunds.com

Company Type: Public
Ticker Symbol: TMCT / TSX
Profile: The fund acquires & maintains a portfolio of mortgage loan investments that generate stable returns, so that the fund can pay monthly distributions to shareholders.
R. Blair Tamblyn, Chief Executive Officer
Ugo Bizzarri, CFA, Chief Financial Officer
Carrie Morris, MBA, Vice-President, Corporate Governance
cmorris@timbercreek.com

TMX Group Inc.
Registered Office & Head Office, The Exchange Towe
130 King St. West
Toronto, ON M5X 1J2

416-947-4670
Fax: 416-947-4662
888-873-8392
info@tmx.com; broadcastcentre@tmx.com
www.tmx.com
Other Communications: Investor Relations: 416-947-4277; shareholder@tmx.com
Social Media: twitter.com/tmxgroup

Company Type: Public
Ticker Symbol: X
Profile: TMX Group is headquartered in Toronto. The Group also has offices in the following cities: Montréal, Calgary, Vancouver, New York, Boston, Chicago, Houston, London, & Beijing.
The following are key TMX Group companies: Toronto Stock Exchange, TSX Venture Exchange, TMX Select, Montreal Exchange, Canadian Derivatives Clearing Corporation, Natural Gas Exchange, Boston Options Exchange, Shorcan, Shorcan Energy Brokers, & Equicom. These companies offer listing markets, trading markets, clearing facilities, data products, plus other services to the financial sector around the globe.
Thomas Kloet, Chief Executive Officer
Kevan Cowan, President, TSX Markets, & Group Head, Equities
Peter Krenkel, President, NGX
Alain Miquelon, President & Chief Executive Officer, Montreal Exchange
Eric Sinclair, President, TMX Datalinx, & Group Head, Data Services
Michael Ptasznik, Chief Financial Officer, TMX Group
Brenda Hoffman, Senior Vice-President & Group Head, Information Technology, TMX Group
Sharon Pel, Senior Vice-President & Group Head, Legal & Business Affairs, TMX Group
Paul Malcolmson, Director, Investor Relations
416-947-4317, paul.malcolmson@tmx.com

Toronto-Dominion Bank
Also Known As: TD Bank Group
PO Box 1, 66 Wellington St. West
Toronto, ON M5K 1A2

416-944-6367
Fax: 416-308-1943
800-430-6095
tdshinfo@td.com
www.td.com
Other Communications: Shareholder Relations, Toll-Free: 866-756-8936

Company Type: Public
Ticker Symbol: TD / TSX
Profile: The Toronto-Dominion Bank & its subsidiaries are known collectively as TD Bank Group. The Group's four key businesses are as follows, Canadian Personal & Commercial Banking; Wealth & Insurance; U.S. Personal & Commercial Banking; & Wholesale Banking. The Toronto-Dominion Bank trades on the Toronto & New York Stock Exchanges, under the symbol TD.
W. Edmund Clark, President & Chief Executive Officer
Johnston Colleen M., CFO & Group Head, Finance
Mark Chauvin, Chief Risk Officer & Group Head, Risk Mgmt.
Mike Pedersen, Group Head, Wealth Mgmt.

Travelers Guarantee Company of Canada
PO Box 6, #300, 20 Queen St. West
Toronto, ON M5H 3R3

416-360-8183
Fax: 416-360-8267
800-330-5033
www.travelerscanada.ca

Company Type: Private

Tricon Capital Group Inc.
1067 Yonge St.
Toronto, ON M4W 2L2

416-925-7228
Fax: 416-925-5022
info@triconcapital.com
www.triconcapital.com

Company Type: Public
Ticker Symbol: TCN / TSX
Profile: Tricon Capital Group Inc. was founded in 1988. It is a residential real estate investment company. Financing is provided to operators or developers in markets in Canada & the United States.
David Berman, Chair & Chief Executive Officer
Gary Berman, President
gberman@triconcapital.com
June Alikhan, Chief Financial Officer
jalikhan@triconcapital.com
Glenn Watchorn, Chief Operating Officer

Urbana Corporation
PO Box 47, #1702, 150 King St. West
Toronto, ON M5H 1J9

416-595-9106
Fax: 416-862-2498
info@urbanacorp.com
www.urbanacorp.com

Company Type: Public
Ticker Symbol: URB / TSX
Profile: Urbana Corporation is a non-redeemable investment fund. Urbana seeks & acquires investments for capital appreciation & income.
Thomas S. Caldwell, CM, President
Jean Ponter, Chief Financial Officer
Elizabeth Naumovski, Contact, Investor Relations

West Street Capital Corporation
Brookfield Place
PO Box 762, #300, 181 Bay St.
Toronto, ON M5J 2T3

416-359-8625
Fax: 416-365-9642

Company Type: Public
Ticker Symbol: WSC / TSX Venture
Profile: West Street Capital Corporation is an investment holding company that was incorporated in 1984. Its investment portfolio consists of preferred share & debenture investments in both Canadian & foreign corporations.
Sachin G. Shah, President
416-363-9491
Mabel W.H. Wong, Vice-President, Finance
Loretta M. Corso, Corporate Secretary

Western Assurance Company
#1000, 2225 Erin Mills Parkway
Mississauga, ON L5K 2S9

905-403-3318
Fax: 905-403-3319
877-263-4442
www.rsagroup.ca, www.westernassurance.ca

Company Type: Private

Western Financial Group Inc.
1010 - 24th St.
High River, AB T1V 2A7

403-652-2663
Fax: 403-652-7037
info@westernfg.ca
www.westernfinancialgroup.ca
Other Communications: Careers: employment@westernfg.ca

Company Type: Public
Ticker Symbol: WES
Profile: Founded in 1996, Western Financial Group is a diversified financial services company serves more than 600,000 customers. Services are provided by approximately 1,500 employees.
Scott Tannas, Founder, President & Chief Executive Officer

James Savage, Executive Vice-President, Corporate Communications & Brand Marketing
403-652-2663

WestLB AG (Canada)
North Tower
#2301, 200 Bay St.
Toronto, ON M5J 2J1
416-216-5000
www.westlb.de

Company Type: Private
Profile: WestLB AG is a commercial bank that operates on a global scale. In Canada, WestLB AG (Canada) operates as a Schedule III bank that has been authorized by the Office of the Superintendent of Financial Institutions to do banking business in Canada.
The Toronto branch is a lending branch. The following industries are West LB AG's focus in Canada: metals & mining, energy, real estate, telecom, & media & entertainment.

Wilmington Capital Management Inc.
#700, 505 3rd St. SW
Calgary, AB T2P 3E6
403-800-0869
Fax: 403-800-0869
www.wilmingtoncapital.com

Company Type: Public
Ticker Symbol: WCM / TSX
Profile: The Canadian investment company holds cash & marketable securities. Wilmington Capital Management also owns land lease properties.
Joseph F. Killi, President & Chief Executive Officer
J. Francis Cooke, Treasurer
Loretta M. Corso, Corporate Secretary

Xceed Mortgage Corporation
18 King St. East, 10th Fl.
Toronto, ON M5C 1C4
416-364-7944
Fax: 888-482-6544
888-811-6660
www.xceedmortgage.com
Social Media: twitter.com/xceedmortgage

Company Type: Public
Ticker Symbol: XMC / TSX
Ivan S. Wahl, Chair
Michael R. Jones, President & CEO
Jeff Bouganim, CA, CFO & VP, Finance
Richard Wertheim, Contact, Investor & Media Relations
416-594-1600, wertheim@wertheim.ca

Zurich Insurance Company Ltd. (Canadian Branch_
Zurich Canada
400 University Ave.
Toronto, ON M5G 1S7
www.zurichcanada.com

Company Type: Private
Profile: Zurich Insurance Company provides commercial business insurance products & risk management solutions. Clients include mid-sized & large businesses & multinational corporations
Patrick Lundy, Chief Executive Officer
Nigel Ayers, Chief Financial Officer & Senior Vice-President
Gordon Thompson, General Counsel & Executive Vice-President
Bob Fellows, Senior Vice-President, Distribution, Marketing, & Communication

Fishing

Clearwater Seafoods Incorporated
757 Bedford Hwy.
Bedford, NS B4A 3Z7
902-443-0550
Fax: 902-443-8365
www.clearwater.ca
Social Media: twitter.com/Clearwatersea

Company Type: Public
Ticker Symbol: CLR / TSX
Profile: Clearwater Seafoods Incorporated supplies wild, eco-labelled seafood, including lobster, clams, scallops, crab, groundfish, & coldwater shrimp. Biologists are employed to ensure innovative & sustainable fishing practices. The company has been in business since 1976.
Ian Smith, Chief Executive Officer
Robert Wight, Chief Financial Officer
902-457-2369
Tyrone Cotie, Treasurer
902-457-8181

Food, Beverages & Tobacco

A&W Food Services of Canada Inc.
#300, 171 West Esplanade
North Vancouver, BC V7M 3K9
604-988-2141
Fax: 604-988-0553
awfranchise@aw.ca
www.aw.ca

Company Type: Private
Profile: A&W Food Services of Canada franchises A&W restaurants. The company also operates ten restaurants corporately. There are more than 730 restaurants throughout Canada. In addition to franchising & operating restaurants, A&W Root Beer in bottles & cans is marketed to retail grocers.
The company is working to reduce its environmental impact in the areas of packaging, waste, energy, water, & food.

A&W Revenue Royalties Income Fund
#300, 171 Esplanade West
North Vancouver, BC V7M 3K9
604-988-2141
Fax: 604-988-5531
investorrelations@aw.ca
www.awincomefund.ca

Company Type: Private
Ticker Symbol: AW.UN / TSX
Profile: A&W Revenue Royalties Income Fund is a limited purpose trust. It invests in A&W Trade Marks Inc., which owns the trade-marks used in the A&W restaurant business in Canada. Through its subsidiary, A&W Trade Marks Inc., A&W Revenue Royalties licences trade-marks for royalty income.
Paul F.B. Hollands, President & Chief Executive Officer, A&W Food Services of Canada Inc.
Donald T. Leslie, Chief Financial Officer
Susan Senecal, Vice-President, Operations

Andrew Peller Limited/ Andrew Peller Limitée
697 South Service Rd.
Grimsby, ON L3M 4E8
905-643-4131
Fax: 905-643-4944
info@andrewpeller.com
www.andrewpeller.com

Company Type: Public
Ticker Symbol: ADW.A, ADW.B / TSX
Profile: Andrew Peller Limited has wineries in Nova Scotia, Ontario, & British Columbia. Wines are also imported from wine regions around the world. The company's wine agencies are Grady Wine Marketing Inc. in British Columbia, & The Small Winemaker's Collection Inc. in Ontario. Andrew Peller also owns & operates more than 100 retail locations. Store names include Aisle 43, WineCountry Vintners, & Vineyards Estate Wines. Through its wholly-owned subsidiary, Global Vintners Inc., Andrew Peller also produces & markets personal winemaking products.
John E. Peller, President & Chief Executive Officer
Robert P. Van Wely, President, Winexpert & Vineco International Products
Peter B. Patchet, Chief Financial Officer & Executive Vice-President, Human Resources
peter.patchet@andrewpeller.com
Anthony M. Bristow, Chief Operating Officer
Shari A. Niles, Executive Vice-President, Marketing

Arctic Glacier Income Fund
625 Henry Ave.
Winnipeg, MB R3A 0V1
204-772-2473
Fax: 204-783-9857
888-573-9237
info@arcticglacierinc.com
www.arcticglacierinc.com

Company Type: Public
Ticker Symbol: AG / CNSX
Profile: Through its wholly-owned operating company, Arctic Glacier Inc., Arctic Glacier Income Fund produces, markets, & distributes packaged ice products. Products are marketed under the brand name, Arctic Glacier Premium Ice. Production & distribution take place throughout Canada, as well as in the western, central, & northeastern United States.
Keith W. McMahon, CA, President/CEO
Douglas A. Bailey, CA, Chief Financial Officer
Frank Larson, Exec. Vice-President, Operations
Brent Bonvarlez, Vice-President, Canadian Operating Division
Hugh A. Adams, Corporate Secretary

Bonduelle North America Inc./ Bonduelle Amerique du Nord
540, ch des Patriotes
Saint-Denis-sur-Richelieu, QC J0H 1K0
450-787-3411
Fax: 450-787-3537
humanresources@bonduelle.ca; retailsales@
www.bonduelle.ca
Other Communications: Institutional Services:
bonduellefoodservice@bonduelle.ca

Company Type: Private
Profile: Bonduelle North America processes canned & frozen vegetables, legumes, & fruit.

Boston Pizza Royalties Income Fund
5500 Parkwood Way
Richmond, BC V6V 2M4
investorrelations@bostonpizza.com
www.bpincomefund.com

Company Type: Public
Ticker Symbol: BPF.UN
Profile: Boston Pizza Royalties Income Fund is a limited purpose open-ended trust. There are 343 stores in the Royalty Pool. Units are traded on the Toronto Stock Exchange. Boston Pizza Royalties Income Fund pays unitholders a monthly distribution.
Mark Pacinda, Chief Executive Officer, Boston Pizza International Inc.
Wes Bews, Chief Financial Officer, Boston Pizza International Inc.
Jordan Holm, Vice-President, Investor Relations
604-303-6083, Fax: 604-270-4168

Canada Bread Company, Limited
Investor Relations Department
#1500, 30 St. Clair Ave. West
Toronto, ON M4V 3A2
416-926-2000
Fax: 416-926-2018
800-465-5515
Investorrelations@mapleleaf.ca
www.canadabread.ca
Other Communications: E-mail:
mapleaffoods@consumerservicesemail.com

Company Type: Public
Ticker Symbol: CBY / TSX
Profile: Canada Bread Company, Limited manufactures & markets the following products: fresh bakery products, such as bread, bagels, & sweet goods; & frozen unbaked & partially baked products, such as bread, rolls, & bagels. Brand names include New York Bakery Co., Ben's, POM, Dempster's, Tenderflake, & Olivieri. Operations are located throughout North America & in the United Kingdom.
Richard A. Lan, President/CEO
C. Barry McLean, President, Fresh Bakery
Réal Ménard, President, Canada Bread Frozen Bakery
Michael H. Vels, Chief Financial Officer
Randall Huffman, Chief Food Safety Officer
Lynda Kuhn, Sr. Vice-President, Communications & Consumer Affairs
416-926-2026

Corby Distilleries Limited
#1100, 225 King St. West
Toronto, ON M5V 3M2
416-479-2400
Fax: 416-369-9809
info@corby.ca; investors@corby.ca
www.corby.ca
Other Communications: Career Inquiries: careers@corby.ca

Company Type: Public
Ticker Symbol: CDL.A
Profile: Corby Distilleries is a marketer of distilled spirits, whiskies, & liqueurs produced in Canada. In addition, imported wines, gin, cognac, scotch, & liqueurs are marketed by the organization. Its owned brands include Wiser's Canadian whiskies & Seagram Coolers. Corby Distilleries represents international brands, such as Jameson Irish whiskey & Wyndham Estate wines, through its affiliation with Pernod Ricard.
Sales offices are located in Halifax, NS (902-445-0705), Montréal, QC (514-395-3200), Toronto, ON (416-369-1859), Edmonton, AB (780-442-9000), Regina, SK (306-586-6546), & Richmond, BC (604-276-8121).
Patrick O'Driscoll, President & Chief Executive Officer
John Leburn, Chief Financial Officer & Vice-President
Marc Valencia, General Counsel, Corporate Secretary, & Vice-President, Public Affairs
Jeff Agdern, Vice-President, Marketing
Andy Alesander, Vice-President, Sales
Jim Stanski, Vice-President, Production

Cott Corporation
6525 Viscount Rd.
Mississauga, ON L4V 1H6

905-672-1900
Fax: 905-672-7504
888-260-3776
info@cott.com; investor.relations@cott.co
www.cott.com
Other Communications: Sales: sales@cott.com; Public Info: publicaffairs@cott.com

Company Type: Public
Ticker Symbol: BCB / TSX; COT / NYSE
Profile: The beverage company focuses upon private-label products & contract manufacturing.
Jerry Fowden, Chief Executive Officer
Len Watson, Chief Information Officer
Prem Virmani, Vice-President, Technical Services

Empire Company Limited
115 King St.
Stellarton, NS B0K 1S0

902-755-4440
Fax: 902-755-6477
investor.relations@empireco.ca
www.empireco.ca

Company Type: Public
Ticker Symbol: EMP.A / TSX
Profile: The Empire Company Limited is engaged in food retailing, through its majority ownership of Sobeys Inc. Through wholly-owned companies, Empire Company is also involved in real estate. Approximately 49,000 people are employed by Empire & its related companies.
Paul D. Sobey, President & Chief Executive Officer
Bill McEwan, President & Chief Executive Officer, Sobeys Inc.
Frank C. Sobey, President, ECL Properties Limited
Stuart G. Fraser, President, Empire Theatres Limited
Paul V. Beesley, Exec. Vice-President/CFO
Stewart H. Mahoney, CFA, Vice-President, Treasury & Investor Relations
Frank C. Sobey, Vice-President, Real Estate

Export Packers Company Limited
107 Walker Dr.
Brampton, ON L6T 5K5

905-792-9700
Fax: 905-792-3569
www.exportpackers.com

Company Type: Private
Profile: Since 1937, Export Packers Company Limited has imported, exported, & marketed food commodities. The company's business segments are as follows: Fresh Seafood, Domestic Food Service, Retail, Asian Trade, & International Trading.
Jeff Rubenstein, Chief Executive Officer
Daniel LeBlanc, President & Chief Operating Officer
Brian Lampert, Chief Financial Officer
Werter Mior, Executive Vice-President, International Trading

General Mills Canada
5825 Explorer Dr.
Mississauga, ON L4W 5P6

905-212-4000
800-516-7780
www.generalmills.ca

Company Type: Private

George Weston Limited
Corporate Office
22 St. Clair Ave. East
Toronto, ON M4T 2S7

416-922-2500
Fax: 416-922-4395
investor@weston.ca; customer_service@west
www.weston.ca
Other Communications: Loblaw Companies: 905-459-2500; Weston Bakery: 416-252-7323

Company Type: Public
Ticker Symbol: WN / TSX
Profile: George Weston Limited consists of Weston Foods & Loblaws.
Weston Foods is involved in the baking & dairy industries. Operated by Loblaw Companies Limited, Loblaws is engaged in food distribution. Loblaws also offers drug store merchandise & general merchandise, as well as financial products & services.
W. Galen Weston, O.C., B.A., LL.D., President & Chair
Ralph A. Robinson, President, Weston Foods, Canada
Allan L. Leighton, President & Deputy Chair, Loblaws
Bob Vaux, Chief Financial Officer
Gordon A.M. Currie, Exec. Vice-President, General Counsel, & Secretary
Catherine Booth, Sr. Vice-President, Information Services, Loblaw
Kirk W. Mondesire, Vice-President, Corporate Systems
Walter H. Kraus, Sr. Director, Environmental Affairs
Anne L. Fraser, C.M., B.Sc., LL.D., Chair, Environmental, Health, & Safety Committee

GLG Life Tech Corporation
Corporate Headquarters
#2168, 1050 West Pender St.
Vancouver, BC V6E 3S7

604-669-2602
Fax: 604-662-8858
sales@glglifetech.com; ir@glglifetech.com
www.glglifetech.com

Company Type: Public
Ticker Symbol: GLG / TSX; GLGL / NASDAQ
Profile: GLG Life Tech Corporation is a supplier of stevia extracts, a sweetener used in food & beverages. Through its subsidiary, ANOC, GLG Life Tech Corporation markets stevia sweetened beverages & foods to serve the Chinese market.
Luke Zhang, Chair & Chief Executive Officer
Brian Meadows, Chief Financial Officer
David Bishop, Executive Vice-President, International Affairs
Sophia Luke, Vice-President, Investor Relations

High Liner Foods Incorporated
PO Box 910, 100 Battery Point
Lunenburg, NS B0J 2C0

902-634-8811
Fax: 902-634-6228
info@highlinerfoods.com
www.highlinerfoods.com
Other Communications: Investor Relations: investor@highlinerfoods.com

Company Type: Public
Ticker Symbol: HLF / TSX
Profile: High Liner Foods Incorporated specializes in processing & marketing prepared, frozen seafood products. Products are marketed under the following brands: High Liner, Sea Cuisine, Fisher Boy, Royal Sea, & Mirabel.
High Liner also sells FPI, Icelandic Seafood, Viking, Samband of Iceland, Seaside, & Seastar products to restaurants & institutions. In 2010, the company purchased the American based assets of Viking Seafoods, Inc., & in 2011 Icelandic USA, Inc. & subsidiaries of Icelandic Group hf were also purchased. High Liner Foods Incorporated serves the retail & food service markets throughout Canada, the United States, & Mexico.
Henry Earl Demone, President & Chief Executive Officer
M.P. Marino, President & Chief Operating Officer, Canadian Operations
Kelly L. Nelson, FCA, Chief Financial Officer, Executive Vice-President & Secretary
J.J. Amlinger, Vice-President, Food Service Sales & Marketing
T.L. Armstrong, Vice-President, Retail Marketing
J.J. O'Neill, Vice-President, Retail Sales
L.C. Obritsch, Vice-President, Canadian Plant Operations
Paul W. Snow, Vice-President, Procurement
G.W. LeBlanc, CA, Corporate Controller

Imvescor Restaurant Group Inc.
#400, 774 Main St.
Moncton, NB E1C 9Y3

506-853-0990
Fax: 506-853-4131
www.imvescor.ca

Company Type: Public
Ticker Symbol: IRG / TSX
Profile: Imvescor Restaurant Group owns franchised & corporate restaurants across Canada. Brands include Pizza Delight, Mikes, Scores, & Bâton Rouge.
Denis Richard, President & Chief Executive Officer
Amber Coggan-Imbeault, Chief Operating Officer, Pizza Delight
Steve Doyle, Chief Information Officer
Terry Faulconbridge, Chief Operating Officer, Mikes
Kevin Friesen, Chief Operating Officer, Scores Rotisserie
Demetri Tsigos, Chief Operating Officer, Bâton Rouge
Ming-Ming Wong, Chief Financial Officer

Lantic Inc.
5405 - 64th Ave.
Taber, AB T1G 2C4

403-223-3535
Fax: 403-223-9699
www.lantic.ca

Company Type: Private
Profile: Lantic Inc. is engaged in sugar refining, processing, distributing, & marketing.

Lassonde Industries Inc./ Industries Lassonde inc.
755, rue Principale
Rougemont, QC J0L 1M0

450-469-4926
Fax: 450-469-1366
866-552-7643
info@lassonde.com
www.lassonde.com
Other Communications: Investors, Toll-Free Phone: 800-363-6180, Fax: 450-469-1366

Company Type: Public
Ticker Symbol: LAS / TSX
Profile: Through its subsidiaries, Lassonde Industries develops, manufactures, packages, & markets food products. The following products are manufactured: fruit juices, fruit beverages, canned corn, baked beans, barbecue sauces, dipping sauces, pasta sauces, meat marinades, bruschetta topping, tapenades, & fondue bouillon.
Pierre-Paul Lassonde, Chair & Chief Executive Officer
Jean Gattuso, President & Chief Executive Officer, A. Lassonde Inc.
Jean Messier, President & Chief Executive Officer, Lassonde Specialties Inc.
Clement Pappas, Chief Executive Officer, Clement Pappas & Company, Inc.
Jocelyn Tremblay, President & Chief Executive Officer, Arista Wines Inc.
Guy Blanchette, CA, FCMA, Vice-President, Finance
Jean Tessier, Vice-President, Treasury
Caroline Lemoine, Corporate Secretary & Vice-President, Legal Affairs
Pierre Brault, Vice-President, Information Technology
Stefano Bertolli, Vice-President, Communications
Pierre Turner, Vice-President, Quality Assurance

Lilydale Inc.
Head Office
7727 - 127 Ave.
Edmonton, AB T5C 1R9

780-476-6261
Fax: 780-476-7253
800-661-5341
ContactUs@lilydale.com
www.lilydale.com
Other Communications: Lilydale Order Desk: 780-448-0990

Company Type: Private
Profile: Established in 1940, Lilydale Inc. provides poultry products across Canada. The company employs more than 2,100 people at its hatcheries & manufacturing facilities.

Liquor Stores N.A. Ltd.
#300, 10508 - 82 Ave.
Edmonton, AB T6E 2A4

780-944-9994
info@lsgp.ca; investor@lsgp.ca
www.liquorstoresgp.ca
Social Media: www.facebook.com/liquordepotAB; www.facebook.com/liquordepotBC
twitter.com/liquordepotab; twitter.com/liquordepotbc

Company Type: Public
Ticker Symbol: LIQ / TSX
Profile: Liquor Stores N.A. Ltd. is involved in the retail liquor industry. In 2010, the organization converted from an income trust to a dividend-paying corporation. The corporation has approximately 240 stores in Canada & the United States. Brand names include the Liquor Barn, Liquor Barn The Ultimate Party Source, Liqor Barn Express, the Liquor Depot, & Brown Jug
Richard J. Crook, President & Chief Executive Officer
Patrick J. de Grace, CA, Chief Financial Officer & Senior Vice-President
Scott A. Morrow, Chief Operating Officer
Craig D Corbett, General Counsel, Corporate Secretary, & Vice-President, Legal

Loblaw Companies Limited
National Head Office & Store Support Centre
1 President's Choice Circle
Brampton, ON L6Y 5S5

905-459-2500
Fax: 905-861-2206
888-495-5111
customerservice@loblaws.ca; investor@lobl
www.loblaw.ca
Other Communications: Corporate Responsibility: csr@loblaw.ca; Media: pr@loblaw.ca
Social Media: www.facebook.com/presidentschoice
twitter.com/WorthSwitching4

Company Type: Public
Ticker Symbol: L / TSX
Profile: Formed in 1956, Loblaw Companies Limited is a food distributor, as weell as a provider of general merchandise & drug store & financial products & services. The company operates the following grocery stores: Loblaws, The Real Canadian

Superstore, Atlantic Superstore, Extra Foods, Independent, No Frills, Valu-mart, Provigo, Wholesale Club, Zehrs, Club Entrepôt, Cash & Carry, & Maxi. Loblaw has over 1,000 stores throughout Canada.
Allan L. Leighton, President & Deputy Chairman
Bob Vaux, Chief Financial Officer
Dalton Philips, Chief Operating Officer
Catherine Booth, Sr. Vice-President, Information Services Department

Magnotta Winery Corporation
271 Chrislea Rd.
Vaughan, ON L4L 8N6

905-738-9463
Fax: 905-738-5551
800-461-9463
mailbox@magnotta.com
www.magnotta.com

Company Type: Private
Profile: Magnotta Winery Corporation is licensed to produce & sell wine, beer & distilled products. In 2012, the company announced the completion of its going private transaction.
Rossana Magnotta, President & Chief Executive Officer
Fulvio DeAngelis, Chief Financial Officer

Maple Leaf Foods Inc.
#1500, 30 St Clair Ave. West
Toronto, ON M4V 3A2

416-926-2000
Fax: 416-926-2018
800-268-3708
investorrelations@mapleleaf.ca
www.mapleleaf.ca
Other Communications: Media Hotline: 416-926-2020

Company Type: Public
Ticker Symbol: MFI / TSX
Profile: Maple Leaf Foods' products include fresh & prepared meats, poultry, seafood, fresh & frozen bakery goods, & animal feed. Brands include Maple Leaf, Maple Leaf Prime Naturally, Schneiders, Olivieri, POM, Shopsy's, Mitchell's Gourmet Foods, Ben's, Bon Matin, Burns, Hygrade, Chevalier, New York Bakery, & Dempsters. Products are sold to wholesale, retail, & industrial customers around the world. Maple Leaf Foods has operations in Canada, the United States, Mexico, the United Kingdom, & Asia. Approximately 19,500 people are employed.
Michael H. McCain, President & Chief Executive Officer
Kevin Golding, President, Rothsay & Elite Swine Inc.
Richard A. Lan, President/CEO, Canada Bread Company, Limited, & COO, Food Group, Maple Leaf Foods Inc.
J. Scott McCain, President/COO, Agribusiness Group, Maple Leaf Foods Inc.
C. Barry McLean, President, Canada Bread Fresh Bakery
Réal Ménard, President, Canada Bread Frozen Bakery
Richard Young, President, Maple Leaf Consumer Foods
Michael H. Vels, Chief Financial Officer
Ray Shei, Chief Information Officer
Randall Huffman, Chief Food Safety Officer
Douglas W. Dodds, Chief Strategy Officer
Nick Boland, Vice-President, Investor Relations
416-926-2005
Peter Smith, Vice-President, Corporate Engineering

McCain Foods (Canada)
107 Main St.
Florenceville, NB E7L 1B2

800-563-7437
800-387-7321
www.mccain.ca
Other Communications: Western Canada: 800-363-8516; QC: 800-363-3153

Company Type: Private
Profile: McCain Foods in Canada produces food products. Products include frozen foods, such as potato products & beverages, as well as specialty items under brand names such as Wong Wing Foods & Charcuterie la Tour Eiffel. Food products are distributed throughout Canada & internationally.
Fred Schaeffer, President & Chief Executive Officer
David Sanchez, Chief Financial Officer
Michael Campbell, Vice-President & General Counsel
Calla Farn, Vice-President, Government & Public Relations
506-392-5541

McDonald's Restaurants of Canada Ltd.
McDonald's Place
Toronto, ON M3C 3L4

416-443-1000
Fax: 416-446-3443
www.mcdonalds.ca
Other Communications: Vancouver: 604-294-2181; Montréal: 514-685-4411

Company Type: Private
Profile: McDonald's Canada consists of over 1,400 McDonald's restaurants across Canada. More than 77,000 Canadians are employed at McDonald's & its franchisees.
John Betts, President
David J. Hederson, Senior Vice-President & Chief Financial Officer
Jacques Mignault, Chief Operating Officer
Richard P. Ellis, Senior Vice-President, Communications & Public Affairs

Metro Inc.
11011, boul Maurice-Duplessis
Montréal, QC H1C 1V6

514-643-1000
Fax: 514-643-1215
finance@metro.ca
www.metro.ca

Company Type: Public
Ticker Symbol: MRUA / TSX
Profile: Metro Inc. operates food retail stores in Ontario & Québec, under the following names: Metro, Super C, A&P, Loeb, Food Basics, Marché Richelieu, AMI, Les 5 Saisons, & GEM. The company also distributes pharmaceutical products under the following banners: Brunet, Clini-Plus, The Pharmacy, & Drug Basics.
Eric R. La Flèche, President/CEO
Richard Dufresne, Sr. Vice-President/CFO & Treasurer
Simon Rivet, Secretary & Vice-President, Legal Affairs
Jacques Couture, Vice-President, Information Systems
Martin Allaire, Vice-President, Real Estate & Engineering

MRRM Inc.
2 Place Alexis Nihon
#1777, 3500, boul de Maisonneuve ouest
Montréal, QC H3Z 3C1

514-908-7777
Fax: 514-906-0220
800-361-1360
mr@mrrm.ca
www.mrrm.ca

Company Type: Public
Ticker Symbol: MRR / TSX Venture
Profile: MRRM Inc. is the parent company of MRRM (Canada) Inc.. Its two operating divisions are involved in the food industry & ship agency services. Les Aliments DAINTY Foods mills & processes rice. The company's ship agency business was acquired from the Robert Reford Company, Limited.
Terry Henderson, President & Chief Executive Officer
Lou Younan, Chief Financial Officer & Vice-President

MTY Food Group Inc./ Le Groupe MTY
3465, boul Thimens
Montréal, QC H4R 1V5

514-336-8885
Fax: 514-336-9222
info@mtygroup.com
www.mtygroup.com

Company Type: Public
Ticker Symbol: MTY / TSX
Profile: MTY Food Group is an operator & franchisor of quick service restaurants. Examples of brands include Cultures, Country Style, Jugo Juice, Mr. Sub, Vanellis, Thai Express, & Yogen Früz Canada.
Stanley Ma, Chair, President & Chief Executive Officer
Claude St-Pierre, Chief Financial Officer & Secretary
claude@mtygroup.com
Jean-Francois Dubé, Specialist, Investor Relations
450-226-8475, jfdube@mac.com

Nestlé Canada Inc.
25 Sheppard Ave. West
Toronto, ON M2N 6S8

416-512-9000
Fax: 416-218-2654
800-387-4636
corporateaffairs@ca.nestle.com
www.nestle.ca

Company Type: Private
Robert G. (Bob) Leonidas, President/CEO
William (Bill) Broughton, CFO & Sr. Vice-President

North West Company Inc.
77 Main St.
Winnipeg, MB R3C 2R1

204-943-0881
Fax: 204-934-1455
800-782-0391
nwc@northwest.ca; communitysupport@northwest.ca
www.northwest.ca
Social Media: www.facebook.com/TheNorthWestCompany
twitter.com/nwcnews
www.linkedin.com/company/45623?trk=tyah

Company Type: Public
Ticker Symbol: NWF / TSX
Profile: Through its subsidiaries, The North West Company is engaged in the retail of food & daily products & services to rual communities & urban neighbourhoods. Areas of operations include Canada, Alaska, the Caribbean, & the South Pacific.
Edward S. Kennedy, President & Chief Executive Officer
204-934-1482, Fax: 204-934-1317, ekennedy@northwest.ca
Craig T. Gilpin, Chief Operating Officer & Executive Vice-President
John King, Chief Financial Officer
204-934-1397, Fax: 204-934-1317, jking@northwest.ca
Gerry L. Mauthe, Vice-President, Information Services

Pizza Pizza Limited
500 Kipling Ave.
Toronto, ON M8Z 5E5

416-967-1010
feedback@pizzapizza.ca
www.pizzapizza.ca
Social Media: www.facebook.com/PizzaPizzaCanada
twitter.com/@pizzapizzaltd

Company Type: Private
Paul Goddard, Chief Executive Officer
Curtis Feltner, Vice-President & CFO, Finance

Pizza Pizza Royalty Income Fund
500 Kipling Ave.
Toronto, ON M8Z 5E5

416-967-1010
Fax: 416-967-9865
feedback@pizzapizza.ca
www.pizzapizza.ca
Other Communications: PZA.UN / TSX

Company Type: Public
Profile: Established in 2005, Pizza Pizza Royalty Income Fund is a limited purpose, open-ended trust. The Fund acquired trademarks & trade names used by Pizza Pizza Limited in its restaurants. The trademarks are licensed to Pizza Pizza. There are close to 700 Pizza Pizza & Pizza 73 restaurants in the royalty pool.
Paul Goddard, Chief Executive Officer, Pizza Pizza Limited
Curt Feltner, Chief Financial Officer & Vice-President, Finance, Pizza Pizza Limited
cfeltner@pizzapizza.ca
Christine D'Sylva, Director, Investor Relations, Pizza Pizza Limited
cdsylva@pizzapizza.ca

Premium Brands Holdings Corporation
7720 Alderbridge Way
Richmond, BC V6X 2A2

604-656-3100
Fax: 604-656-3170
info@premiumbrandsgroup.com
www.premiumbrandsholdings.com
Other Communications: Investors: investor@premiumbrandsgroup.com

Company Type: Public
Ticker Symbol: PBH-T
Profile: Premium Brands Holdings Corporation owns specialty food businesses with manufacturing & distribution facilities. The corporation also owns proprietary food distribution & wholesale networks. Facilities are located in Quebec, Ontario, Manitoba, Saskatchewan, Alberta, British Columbia, & Washington.
The following are some examples of Premium Brands' businesses: B&C Foods, Maximum Seafood, Direct Plus, Noble House Foods, Bread Garden Express, Kids Eat, Gloria's Catering, McSweeney's, Hempler's, Creekside Custom Foods, Quality Fast Foods, Harvest Meats, Grimm's Fine Fooks, SK Food Group, South Seas Meats, Deli Chef, & Multi-National Foods.
George Paleologou, CA, President & Chief Executive Officer
Will Kalutycz, CA, Chief Financial Officer
Douglas Goss, Q.C., General Counsel & Corporate Secretary

Rogers Sugar Inc. (RSI)
Administrative Office
4126, rue Notre-Dame est
Montréal, QC H1W 2K3

514-527-8686
Fax: 514-527-8406
infos@rogerssugar.com
www.rogerssugar.com; www.lantic.ca

Company Type: Public
Ticker Symbol: RSI / TSX
Profile: In 2008, Rogers Sugar Ltd. merged with Lantic Sugar Limited to create Lantic Inc.
In 2011, Rogers Sugar Income Fund converted into a conventional corporation named Rogers Sugar Inc.. The successor to Rogers Sugar Income Fund now owns all of the outstanding shares of Lantic Inc., plus the subordinated Lantic notes.
Lantic Inc. uses both the Lantic & Rogers trademarks. Lantic Inc. is engaged in the refining, processing, distributing, & marketing of sugar products, such as granulated sugar, sugar cubes, icing sugar, yellow & brown sugars, liquid sugars, specialty sugars, & syrups.

Edward Makin, President & Chief Executive Officer, Lantic Inc.
Daniel L. Lafrance, Chief Financial Officer & Senior Vice-President
514-940-4350, Fax: 514-527-1610

Saputo Inc.
6869, boul Métropolitain est
Montréal, QC H1P 1X8

514-328-6662
Fax: 514-328-3310
saputo@saputo.com
www.saputo.com

Company Type: Public
Ticker Symbol: SAP / TSX
Profile: Saputo Inc. is engaged in the production, commercialization, & distribution of dairy products & grocery products. The company's brands include the following: Saputo, Dairyland De Lucia, Frigo, Stella, HOP&GO!, Rondeau, Alexis de Portneuf, DuVillage de Warwick, La Paulina, Treasure Cave, Armstrong, Nutrilait, Vachon, & Ricrem. Production facilities are situated in five countries.
Lino A. Saputo, Jr., President/CEO
Dino Dello Sbarba, President/COO, Dairy Products Division (Canada)
Claude Pinard, President/COO, Bakery
Louis-Philippe Carrière, Exec. Vice-President, Finance & Administration
Pierre Leroux, Exec. Vice-President, Human Resources & Corporate Affairs
Karine Vachon, Advisor, Communications

Second Cup Ltd.
6303 Airport Rd.
Mississauga, ON L4V 1R8

905-362-1818
Fax: 905-362-1121
investor@secondcup.com
www.secondcup.com

Company Type: Public
Ticker Symbol: SCU / TSX
Profile: In 2011, the Second Cup Income Fund converted from an income trust structure to a public corporation. Second Cup Ltd. is a large specialty coffee franchisor. It operates over 350 cafés throughout Canada.
Stacey Mowbray, President & Chief Executive Officer
Robert Massion, CA, Chief Financial Officer
905-362-1824, Fax: 905-362-1121,

SIR Royalty Income Fund
#200, 5360 South Service Rd.
Burlington, ON L7L 5L1

905-681-2997
Fax: 905-681-0394
info@sircorp.com
www.sircorp.com
Other Communications: Investor Relations: ir@sircorp.com

Company Type: Public
Ticker Symbol: SRV / TSX
Profile: Trademarks related to SIR Corp.'s restaurant brands are used under a license agreement with SIR Royalty Limited Partnership. A royalty is paid by SIR Corp. to SIR Royalty Limited Partnership. SIR Royalty Income Fund has an investment in SIR Royalty Limited Partnership. The Fund receives distribution income from this investment. Distributions are paid to unitholders by the Fund on a monthly basis.
SIR Corp.'s restaurant brands include Alice Fazooli's, Jack Astor's Bar & Grill, Canyon Creek Chop House, Far Niente / Four / Petit Four, & Loose Moose Tap & Grill.
Peter Fowler, President & Chief Executive Officer, SIR Corp.
Jeff Good, Chief Financial Officer, SIR Corp.

Smucker Foods of Canada Co.
Consumer Services Department
80 Whitehall Dr.
Markham, ON L3R 0P3

800-567-1897
www.smuckers.ca

Company Type: Private
Profile: Smucker Foods of Canada manufactures & markets products such as fruit spreads, peanut butter, ice cream toppings, condiments, & shortening & oils. Brand names include Smuckers, Crisco, Robin Hood, Five Roses, Europe's Best, Bick's, Red River, & Double Fruit Spreads.
Don Twiner, President
Mark Belgya, Chief Financial Officer & Senior Vice-President
Dennis Armstrong, Senior Vice-President, Supply Chain Logistics & Operations Support

Sodexo Canada Ltd.
3350 South Service Rd.
Burlington, ON L7N 3M6

514-866-7070
877-632-8592
Canada@sodexo.com
www.sodexoca.com

Company Type: Private
Profile: Sodexo Canada provides food & facilities management. Outsourcing solutions offered include food service, grounds keeping, housekeeping, laundry services, & plant operations & maintenance.
Dean Johnson, President & Chief Executive Officer
Jon Kristjanson, Senior Vice-President, Corporate Development & Marketing

Sportscene Group Inc./ Froupe Sportscene inc.
#102, 1180, Place Nobel
Boucherville, QC J4B 5L2

450-641-3011
Fax: 450-641-9742

Company Type: Public
Ticker Symbol: SPS / TSX Venture
Profile: Sportscene Group Inc. has been in business since 1984. The company operates the chain of sports-themed resto-bars in Québec, known as La Cage aux Sport.
Sportscene is also involved in complementary activities, such as managing real estate holdings, constructing & renovating, & organizing sports-related activities.
Jean Bédard, Chair, President & Chief Executive Officer
Josée Pépin, Manager, Accounting & Disclosure

Sun-Rype Products Ltd.
1165 Ethel St.
Kelowna, BC V1Y 2W4

250-860-7973
Fax: 250-762-3611
info@sunrype.com
www.sunrype.com

Company Type: Public
Ticker Symbol: SRF / TSX
Profile: Established in 1946, Sun-Rype manufactures & markets fruit juices & fruit snacks. Products include 100% Pure Not From Concentrate Apple Juice & Fruit to Go.
Dave McAnerney, President & Chief Executive Officer
Don VanderZwaag, Chief Financial Officer & Vice-President, Finance
Bernard Bélanger, Vice-President, Sales & Marketing
Lesli Bradley, Vice-President, Operations

The Keg Royalties Income Fund
10100 Shellbridge Way
Richmond, BC V6X 2W7

604-821-6416
Fax: 604-276-0138
www.kegincomefund.com

Company Type: Public
Ticker Symbol: KEG.UN / TSX
Profile: The Keg Royalties Income Fund is an unincorporated open-ended, limited purpose trust. The Fund is the owner of The Keg Rights LP, which owns the trademarks, names, & other intellectual property used by The Keg restaurants. The Keg Royalties Income Fund licenses Keg Restaurants Ltd. to use these rights.
C.C. Woodward, Chair, The Keg Royalties Income Fund
David Aisenstat, President & Chief Executive Officer, Keg Restaurants. Ltd.
Neil Maclean, Chief Financial Officer & Executive Vice-President, Keg Restaurants Ltd.
Doug Smith, Chief Operating Officer & Executive Vice-President, Keg Restaurants Ltd.
Karyn Byrne, Manager, Investor Relations
416-646-4960, Fax: 416-695-2401, karynb@kegrestaurants.com

Tim Hortons
874 Sinclair Rd.
Oakville, ON L6K 2Y1

905-845-6511
Fax: 905-845-0265
888-601-1616
investor_relations@timhortons.com
www.timhortons.com
Other Communications: Investors, Phone: 905-339-6186
Social Media: www.facebook.com/TimHortons
twitter.com/timhortons

Company Type: Public
Ticker Symbol: THI / TSX
Profile: The first Tim Hortons restaurant was opened in 1964. Tim Hortons specialized in coffee, baked goods, & lunches. It has over 4,000 systemwide restaurants in Canada & the United States.
Tim Hortons has waste reduction strategies in an attempt to combat litter, such as the use of reusable mugs & china plates & bowls in restaurants.
Paul D. House, Executive Chair, Chief Executive Officer, & President
Scott Bonikowsky, Contact, Investor Relations
905-339-6186, bonikowsky_scott@timhortons.com

Forestry & Paper

Acadian Timber Corp.
Bentall 5
PO Box 51, #458, 550 Burrard St.
Toronto, ON V6C 2B5

604-661-9607
Fax: 604-687-3419
www.acadiantimber.com

Company Type: Public
Ticker Symbol: ADN / TSX
Profile: The timberland operator supplies primary forest products. Areas of activity are eastern Canada & the northeastern United States.
Acadian Timber complies with environmental legislation & regulations & works with government, regulators, communities, & stakeholders. The company reports regularly on its environmental performance.
Reid Carter, President & Chief Executive Officer
Brian Banfill, Chief Financial Officer & Senior Vice-President
Kevin Topolniski, Chief Forester

Ainsworth Lumber Co. Ltd.
Bentall 4
PO Box 49307, #3194, 1055 Dunsmuir St.
Vancouver, BC V7X 1L3

604-661-3200
Fax: 604-661-3201
www.ainsworthengineered.com

Company Type: Public
Ticker Symbol: ANS / TSX
Profile: Ainsworth is a forest products company that manufactures & provides engineered wood products. Products are used for industrial, commercial, & residential applications. Operations are situated in Ontario, Alberta, & British Columbia.
Jim Lake, President & Chief Operating Officer
Chris Davies, Chief Financial Officer
chris.davies@ainsworth.ca

Bowater Canadian Forest Products
156 Darrel Ave.
Thunder Bay, ON P7J 1L7

807-624-9400
info@resolutefp.com
www.resolutefp.com

Company Type: Private

Bowater Canadian Forest Products
156 Darrel Ave.
Thunder Bay, ON P7J 1L7

807-624-9400
info@resolutefp.com
www.resolutefp.com

Company Type: Private

Canfor Corporation
#100, 1700 West 75th Ave.
Vancouver, BC V6P 6G2

604-661-5241
Fax: 604-661-5435
info@canfor.cam; donations@canfor.com
www.canfor.com
Other Communications: Administration Centre: 250-962-3500;
Sales: 604-261-5111
Social Media: twitter.com/canfor_News

Company Type: Public
Ticker Symbol: CFP / TSX
Profile: Formed in 1966, Canfor Corporation is an integrated forest products company. Operations are carried out in British Columbia, Alberta, Quebec, Washington state, & North & South Carolina.
Don Kayne, President & Chief Executive Officer
Alan Nicholl, Chief Financial Officer & Senior Vice-President, Finance
David Calabrigo, Corporate Secretary & Senior Vice-President, Corporate & Legal Affairs
Mark Feldinger, Senior Vice-President, Forestry, Environment, & Energy
Wayne Guthrie, Senior Vice-President, Sales & Marketing
Patrick Elliott, Vice-President & Treasurer
604-661-5441, Patrick.Elliott@canfor.com
Christine Kennedy, Director, Public Affairs & Corporate Communications
604-862-4334, Christine.Kennedy@canfor.com

Canfor Pulp Products Inc. (CPPI)
#230, 1700 - West 75th Ave.
Vancouver, BC V6P 6G2

604-661-5241
Fax: 604-661-5235
info@canfor.ca
www.canfor.com

Company Type: Public
Ticker Symbol: CFX / TSX
Profile: In 2011, Canfor Pulp Income Fund converted from an income trust structure to a corporate structure. Canfor Pulp Products Inc. is a producer of northern softwood kraft pulp & kraft paper.
Terry Hodgins, Chief Financial Officer & Secretary
604-661-5421, terry.hodgins@canforpulp.com
Rick Remesch, Corporate Controller
604-661-5221, Rick.Remesch@canforpulp.com

Cascades Inc.
PO Box 30, 404, boul Marie-Victorin
Kingsey Falls, QC J0A 1B0

819-363-5100
Fax: 819-363-5155
info@cascades.com
www.cascades.com
Social Media: www.facebook.com/cascades
twitter.com/CascadesDD

Company Type: Public
Ticker Symbol: CAS
Profile: Cascades Inc. was founded in 1964. The company is engaged in the production, transformation, & marketing of packaging & tissue products. Products are composed mainly of recycled fibres. Cascades employs approximately 11,000 people in operations situated throughout North America & Europe.
Alain Lemaire, President & Chief Executive Officer
Suzanne Blanchet, President & Chief Executive Officer, Cascades Tissue Group
Marc-André Dépin, President & Chief Executive Officer, Norampac
Luc Langevin, President & Chief Executive Officer, Specialty Products Group
Allan Hogg, Chief Financial Officer & Vice-President
Mario Plourde, Chief Operating Officer
Robert F. Hall, Corporate Secretary & Vice-President, Legal Affairs
Hubert Bolduc, Vice-President, Communications & Public Affairs
Dominic Doré, Vice-President, Information Technology
Christian Dubé, Vice-President, Business Development
Léon Marineau, Vice-President, Environment

Catalyst Paper Corporation
3600 Lysander Lane, 2nd Fl.
Richmond, BC V7B 1C3

604-247-4400
Fax: 604-247-0551
contactus@catalystpaper.com
www.catalystpaper.com

Company Type: Public
Ticker Symbol: CTL / TSX
Richard Garneau, President/CEO
David Smales, Vice-President/CFO, Finance

Commonwealth Plywood Co. Ltd.
PO Box 90, 15, boul Labelle
Sainte-Thérèse, QC J7E 4H9

450-435-6541
Fax: 450-435-3814
info@commonwealthplywood.com
www.commonwealthplywood.com

Company Type: Private
William T. Caine, President/CEO
J. d'Orazio, Vice-President, Finance

Conifex Timber Inc.
Corporate Office
#110, 2925 Virtual Way
Vancouver, BC V5M 4X5

604-216-2949
866-301-2949
www.conifex.com
Other Communications: Prince George: 250-561-; Fort St. James: 250-996-8241

Company Type: Public
Ticker Symbol: CFF / TSX Venture
Profile: Conifex Timber Inc. & its subsidiaries are involved in the following activities: timber harvesting, reforestation, forest management, sawmilling logs into lumber & wood chips, & lumber finishing. Conifex is committed to responsible stewardship, & its work is guided by an environmental policy. The company's markets are in Canada, the United States, China, & Japan.
Ken Shields, Chair, Chief Executive Officer, & President
Kevin Horsnell, Chief Operating Officer
Yuri Lewis, Chief Financial Officer
Lorriane Ducharme, Vice-President, Human Resources & Public Relations
Kalin Uhrich, Vice-President, Fibre

Fortress Paper Ltd.
157 Chadwick Ct., 2nd Fl.
North Vancouver, BC V7M 3K2

604-904-2328
Fax: 604-988-5327
888-820-3888
info@fortresspaper.com
www.fortresspaper.com

Company Type: Public
Ticker Symbol: FTP / TSX
Profile: Established in 2006, Fortress Paper is engaged in the production of security & other specialty papers. It operates the following business segments: Pulp Segment; Security & Specialty Papers Segment; & Wallpaper Base Segment.
The company's Fortress Specialty Cellutose mill is constructing a cogeneration facility, in order to expand into the renewable energy generation sector.
Chadwick Wasilenkoff, Chief Executive Officer
604-904-2328, chadw@fortresspaper.com
Erich Sulser, Chief Financial Officer
Alfonso Ciotola, Chief Operating Officer
Kurt Loewen, Controller & Secretary

Goodfellow Inc.
225, rue Goodfellow
Delson, QC J5B 1V5

450-635-6511
Fax: 450-635-3729
800-361-6503
info@goodfellowinc.com
www.goodfellowinc.com
Other Communications: USA, Toll-Free Phone: 800-361-0625
Social Media: www.facebook.com/goodfellowinc

Company Type: Public
Ticker Symbol: GDL / TSX
Profile: Goodfellow Inc. re-manufactures, wholesales, & distributes wood & wood by-products, such as the following: dressed & rough lumber, sawn timber, composite & veneer based wood panel products, & prefinished & unfinished flooring. Customers are served in Canada & internationally.
Goodfellow Inc. has implemented an environmental policy to conduct its business in an environmentally responsible manner.
Richard Goodfellow, President & Chief Executive Officer
Pierre Lemoine, CMA, Vice-President/CFO
Luc Pothier, Vice-President, Operations
G. Douglas Goodfellow, Vice-Chair & Secretary

Hardwoods Distribution Inc. (HDI)
#306, 9440 - 202 St.
Langley, BC V1M 4A6

604-881-1988
Fax: 604-881-1995
www.hardwoods-inc.com

Company Type: Public
Ticker Symbol: HWD / TSX
Profile: In 2011, the Hardwoods Distribution Income Fund was converted to a corporation by way of a plan of arrangement. Hardwoods Distribution Inc. has a 100% ownership interest in Hardwoods Specialty Products LP & Hardwoods Specialty Products US LP.
Every distribution centre of Hardwoods Specialty Products has been certified by the Forestry Stewardship Council for Chain of Custody. Hardwoods Distribution Inc. is also a member of the Canadian Green Building Council & the US Green Building Council in support of green building initiatives.
Lance R. Blanco, President & Chief Financial Officer
Rob Brown, Chief Financial Officer
robbrown@hardwoods-inc.com
Garry W. Warner, Vice-President & Group Manager, Northwest

International Forest Products Limited
Also Known As: Interfor
Corporate Office
PO Box 49114, #3500, 1055 Dunsmuir St.
Vancouver, BC V7X 1H7

604-689-6800
Fax: 604-689-6825
info@interfor.com
www.interfor.com
Other Communications: Bellingham Washington Office, Phone: 360-788-2299

Company Type: Public
Ticker Symbol: IFP / TSX
Profile: International Forest Products Limited supplies lumber products. Operations are located in British Columbia, Washington, & Oregon.
Duncan K. Davies, President & Chief Executive Officer
John A. Horning, Chief Financial Officer, Corp. Secretary & Sr. Vice-President
Richard J. Slaco, Chief Forester & Vice-President
Stephen D. Williams, Vice-President, Finance & Administration

Kruger Inc.
3285, ch Bedford
Montréal, QC H3S 1G5

514-737-1131
Fax: 514-343-3124
www.kruger.com

Company Type: Private
Joseph Kruger II, Chair/CEO
Mario Lecaldare, Exec. Vice-President/CFO
Robert Jobin, Corporate Director, Environmental Services

Norbord Inc.
#600, 1 Toronto St.
Toronto, ON M5C 2W4

416-365-0705
Fax: 416-777-4419
info@norbord.com; sales@norbord.com
www.norbord.com

Company Type: Public
Ticker Symbol: NBD / TSX
Profile: Norbord Inc. produces wood-based panels & related products. The company has 13 operations in Canada, the United States, & Europe. Norbord employs approximately 2,030.
J. Barrie Shineton, President & Chief Executive Officer
Robin E. Lampard, Chief Financial Officer & Senior Vice-President
Peter C. Wijnbergen, Chief Operating Officer & Senior Vice-President
Nigel Banks, Senior Vice-President, Corporate Services
Michael J. Dawson, Vice-President, Sales, Marketing, & Logistics
Peter Quosai, General Manager, Environment, Health, & Safety

Sino-Forest Corporation
#1208, 90 Burnhamthorpe Rd. West
Mississauga, ON L5B 3C3

905-281-8889
Fax: 905-281-3338
info@sinoforest.com
www.sinoforest.com
Other Communications: Hong Kong, Phone: +852 2877 0078

Company Type: Public
Ticker Symbol: TRE / TSX
Profile: Sino-Forest Corporation is an owner & cultivator of forest plantation trees. The company manufactures engineered-wood products & sells standing timber & harvested logs. Operations are carried out in China. The corporation's wholly-owned subsidiary is Sino-Wood Partners, Limited in Wanchai, Hong Kong.
Allen T.Y. Chan, Chair/CEO
Kai Kit (K.K.) Poon, President
David J. Horsley, CA, CBV, Sr. Vice-President/CFO
Richard Kimel, HBA, LLB, Corporate Secretary
Louisa Wong, Sr. Manager, Investor Communications & Relations

Stella-Jones Inc.
#300, 3100 boul de la Côte-Vertu
Montréal, QC H4R 2J8

514-934-8666
Fax: 514-934-5327
ir@stella-jones.com
www.stella-jones.com
Other Communications: Human Resources Dept.: hr@stella-jones.com

Company Type: Public
Ticker Symbol: SJ / TSX
Profile: Stella-Jones specializes in the production & marketing of industrial treated wood products. Products include the following: treated wood for bridges; pressure treated railway ties; marine & foundation pilings; construction timbers; highway guardrail posts; & wood poles for electrical utilities & telecommunications companies.
Brian McManus, President/CEO
George T. Labelle, Sr. Vice-President/CFO
514-934-8665, glabelle@stella-jones.com
Doug Fox, Sr. Vice-President, Engineering & Operations
Marla Eichenbaum, Vice-President, General Counsel, & Secretary
Ian Jones, Vice-President & General Manager, Stella-Jones Canada
Gordon Murray, Vice-President, Environment & Technology, & GM, Atlantic Region

Supremex Inc.
Head Office
7213, rue Cordner
Lasalle, QC H8N 2J7
514-595-0555
Fax: 514-595-1112
investors@supremex.com; vente@supremex.co
www.supremex.com
Other Communications: Central Region:
sales.central@supremex.com
Company Type: Private
Ticker Symbol: SXP / TSX
Profile: Supremex specializes in manufacturing & marketing stock & custom envelopes & related products. Approximately 600 employees work for Supremex in manufacturing facilities aross Canada.
The company has an Enviro-logiX Program, which includes environmentally friendly bubble mailers, among other products.
Gilles Cyr, President & Chief Executive Officer
Stéphane Lavigne, Chief Financial Officer, Vice-President & Corporate Secretary
Stewart Emerson, Vice-President & General Manager, Central Region
Edward Gauer, General Manager, Western Region

Taiga Building Products Ltd.
PO Box 80329, #800, 4710 Kingsway
Burnaby, BC V5H 3X6
604-438-1471
Fax: 604-439-4242
800-663-1470
invest@taigabuilding.com
www.taigabuilding.com
Company Type: Public
Ticker Symbol: TBL / TSX
Profile: Taiga Building Products Ltd. distributes building products, such as lumber, engineered wood, mouldings, siding, flooring, & polyethylene sheeting. It is also involved in the production of treated wood, which reduces the use of timber resources. The company's customers are most often industrial manufacturers & building supply dealers.
Cam White, President & Chief Executive Officer
Trent Balog, Chief Operating Officer & Executive Vice-President, Sales & Operations
Tom Stefan, Chief Financial Officer & Vice-President, Finance & Administration
Grant Sali, Executive Vice-President, Treated Lumber, Allied Products, & Supply Management

Tembec Inc.
Head Office
#1050, 800, boul Réne-Lévesque ouest
Montréal, QC H3B 1X9
514-871-0137
Fax: 514-397-0896
info@tembec.com
www.tembec.com
Company Type: Public
Ticker Symbol: TMB / TSX
Profile: Tembec manufactures forest products such as pulp, paper, lumber, & specialty cellulose. Main operations take place in Canada & France. The company is engaged in sustainable forest management practices. It employs approximately 4,000 people.
James Lopez, President & Chief Executive Officer
Chris Black, President, Paper & High-Yield Pulp Group
Michel J. Dumas, Chief Financial Officer & Executive Vice-President
Linda Coates, Vice-President, Communications & Public Affairs
416-775-2819, linda.coates@tembec.com
Paul Dottori, Vice-President, Energy, Environment, & Technology
Patrick LeBel, Vice-President, General Counsel, & Corporate Secretary

West Fraser Timber Co. Ltd.
#501, 858 Beatty St.
Vancouver, BC V6B 1C1
604-895-2700
Fax: 604-681-6061
shareholder@westfraser.com
www.westfraser.com
Company Type: Public
Ticker Symbol: WFT / TSX
Profile: West Fraser Timber Co. Ltd. is an integrated wood products company. From facilities in Canada & the United States, the company produces the following products: plywood, lumber, wood chips, LVL, MDF, pulp, & newsprint.
Henry H. Ketcham III, Chair, President, & Chief Executive Officer
Martti Solin, CFO & Vice-President, Finance
Cindy MacDonald, Manager, Environmental Affairs

Western Forest Products Inc. (WFP)
TD Tower
PO Box 10032, #510, 700 West Georgia St.
Vancouver, BC V7Y 1A1
604-648-4500
Fax: 604-681-9584
info@westernforest.com
www.westernforest.com
Company Type: Public
Ticker Symbol: WEF / TSX
Profile: Western Forest Products is a large woodland operator & lumber producer in the coastal region of British Columbia. Activities include timber harvesting, sawmilling logs into lumber & wood chips, value-added remanufacturing, & reforestation. Customers are served in North America & around the world.
Dominic Gammiero, Chair & Chief Executive Officer
250-734-4711
Brian Cairo, Chief Financial Officer & Corporate Secretary
250-734-4710,

Weyerhaeuser Company Limited
925 West Georgia St., 5th Fl.
Vancouver, BC V6C 3L2
604-661-8000
800-525-5440
www.weyerhaeuser.com
Company Type: Private
Profile: Weyerhaeuser is part of the forest products industry. The company grows & harvests trees & produces forestry products. Businesses include cellulose fibers, newsprint & specialty papers, hardwood products, & homes. It works to conduct its business in an environmentally sustainable & socially responsible manner.
Daniel S. Fulton, President & Chief Executive Officer, Weyerhaeuser Company
Lawrence B. Burrows, President & Chief Executive Officer, Weyerhaeuser Real Estate Company
Will Holder, President, Trendmaker Homes
Michael V. McGee, President, Pardee Homes
Peter M. Orser, President, Quadrant Corporation
Alan Shapiro, President, Winchester Homes
Andy Warren, President, Maracay Homes
Heidi Biggs Brock, Vice-President, Federal & International Affairs
Christine Dean, Vice-President, Timberlands Technology
Philip C. Dennett, Vice-President, Strand Technologies
Claire S. Grace, Vice-President, Secretary, & Assistant General Counsel
Sara S. Kendall, Vice-President, Environment, Health, & Safety
Kathryn F. McAuley, Vice-President, Investor Relations
Jeffrey W. Nitta, Vice-President & Treasurer
Catherine L. Phillips, Vice-President, Sustainable Forestry
Kevin Shearer, Chief Information Officer & Vice-President, Information Technology

Holding & Other Investment

49 North Resources Inc.
#602, 224 - 4th Ave. South
Saskatoon, SK S7K 5M5
306-653-2692
Fax: 306-664-4483
ir@fnr.ca
Company Type: Public
Ticker Symbol: FNR / TSX Venture
Profile: 49 North Resources Inc. is a resource investment company that was created in 2005. Assets include shares & other securities of junior & intermediate mineral, & oil & gas exploration companies.
Tom MacNeill, BA (Econ), CGA, CFA, President & Chief Executive Officer
306-653-2692
Andrew Davidson, BComm, CA, Chief Financial Officer

ACE Aviation Holdings Inc.
5100, boul de Maisonneuve ouest
Montréal, QC H4A 3T2
514-205-7855
Fax: 514-205-7859
shareholders.actionnaires@aceaviation.com
www.aceaviation.com
Company Type: Public
Ticker Symbol: ACE.A, ACE.B / TSX
Profile: The investment holding company has an 11.11% ownership in Air Canada.
Robert A. Milton, President/CEO & Chair
Brian Dunne, Exec. Vice-President/CFO
Sydney Isaacs, Chief Legal Officer & Sr. Vice-President, Corporate Development

AGF Trust Company
PO Box 6, 1 Toronto St.
Toronto, ON M5C 2V6
866-273-9971
www.agf.com/static/en/about_agf/1790.html
Other Communications: Toll-Free Fax: 1-866-713-1187
Company Type: Private
Mario Cusarano, CA, President & CEO, AGF Trust Company
Robert J. Bogart, CPA, Exec. Vice-President & CFO, AGF Management Limited

AvenEx Energy Corp.
#300, 808 - 1st St. SW
Calgary, AB T2P 1M9
403-237-9949
Fax: 403-237-0903
www.avenexenergy.com
Company Type: Public
Ticker Symbol: AVF / TSX
Profile: In 2010, Avenir Diversified Income Trust was converted to a corporation named AvenEx Energy Corp.. The company focuses on oil & gas development & production.
William M. Gallacher, P. Eng., Chief Executive Officer
Gary H. Dundas, CMA, MBA, Chief Financial Officer & Vice-President, Finance
Grant Leslie, P. Eng., Chief Operating Officer, Oil & Gas Operations
Brad Likuski, P.Eng., Vice-President, Engineering

British Columbia Investment Management Corporation (bcIMC)
PO Box 9910, Victoria, BC V8W 9R1
250-356-0263
Fax: 250-387-7874
communications@bcimc.com
www.bcimc.com
Company Type: Public
Profile: Investment funds management, with clients including public sector pension plans, the Province of British Columbia, Crown corporations and publicly administered trust funds; pooled investment funds and segregated funds
Doug Pearce, CEO
David Woodward, Vice President, Finance & Operations
Robert des Trois Maisons, General Counsel/Vice President, Legal Affairs
Carol Iverson, Vice President, Human Resources
Lynn Hannah, Vice President, Consulting & Client Services
Sid Fattedad, Chair

Brookfield Asset Management Inc.
Brookfield Place
#300, 181 Bay St.
Toronto, ON M5J 2T3
416-363-9491
Fax: 416-365-9642
www.brookfield.com
Company Type: Public
Ticker Symbol: BAM / TSX
Profile: Brookfield Asset Management Inc. was formed in 1997. The global asset manager concentrates on property, infrastructure, & renewable power assets. The company offers clients an array of real estate advisory, property, & investment services. Brookfield Asset Management is listed on the TSX, NYSE, & Euronext Amsterdam.
Bruce Flatt, Sr. Managing Partner & CEO
Brian D. Lawson, Managing Partner & Chief Financial Officer
Joe Freedman, Sr. Managing Partner & General Counsel
Denis Couture, Sr. Vice-President, Investor Relations & Corporate & International Affairs
dcouture@brookfield.com

Brookfield Investments Corp.
Brookfield Place
PO Box 762, #300, 181 Bay St.
Toronto, ON M5J 2T3
416-363-9491
Fax: 416-956-5176
Company Type: Public
Ticker Symbol: BRN / TSX Venture
Sachin G. Shah, Vice-President & CFO

Callinan Royalties Corporation
#1110, 555 West Hastings St.
Vancouver, BC V6B 4N4
info@callinan.com; shareholder@callinan.c
www.callinan.com
Company Type: Public
Ticker Symbol: CAA / TSX Venture
Profile: Callinan Royalties Corporation is a mineral royalty company that builds a portfolio of mineral royalties. The corporation has producing royalties in Manitoba.

Roland Butler, Chief Executive Officer
709-535-3433

Tamara Edwards, Chief Financial Officer

Canada Development Investment Corporation
#302, 1240 Bay St.
Toronto, ON M5R 2A7
416-966-2221
Fax: 416-966-5485
info@cdiccei.ca
www.cdiccei.ca
Company Type: Private
Michael Carter, Exec. Vice-President
Andrew Stafl, CA, Vice-President, Finance

Canadian Real Estate Investment Trust (CREIT)
#500, 175 Bloor St. East
Toronto, ON M4W 3R8
416-628-7771
Fax: 416-628-7777
info@creit.ca
www.creit.ca
Company Type: Public
Ticker Symbol: REF / TSX
Profile: Canadian Real Estate Investment Trust is the owner of a portfolio of retail, office, & industrial properties. The trust delivers the benefits of real estates ownership to unitholders
Stephen E. Johnson, President & Chief Executive Officer
sjohnson@creit.ca
Timothy McSorley, Chief Financial Officer & Vice-President
tmcsorley@creit.ca

Capstone Infrastructure Corporation
#2930, 155 Wellington St. West
Toronto, ON M5V 3H1
416-649-1300
Fax: 416-649-1335
info@capstoneinfrastructure.com
www.capstoneinfrastructure.com
Social Media:
www.linkedin.com/company/capstone-infrastructure-corporation
Company Type: Public
Ticker Symbol: CSE / TSX
Profile: Capstone Infrastructure Corporation has a portfolio of infrastructure businesses in Canada & around the world. Investments include the following: hydro, wind, biomas, & solar power generating facilities; a 70% interest in a regulated water utility in the United Kingdom; & a 33.3% interest in a heating business in Sweden.
Michael Bernstein, President & Chief Executive Officer
Michael Smerdon, Chief Financial Officer & Executive Vice-President
Stu Miller, Executive Vice-President, General Counsel, & Corp. Secretary
Sarah Borg-Olivier, Senior Vice-President, Communications
416-649-1325, sborg-olivier@capstoneinfrastructure.com
Jens Ehlers, Senior Vice-President, Finance

CML Healthcare Inc.
Corporate Headquarters
#1, 60 Courtneypark Dr. West
Mississauga, ON L5W 0B3
905-565-0043
Fax: 905-565-2844
800-263-0801
www.cmlhealthcare.com
Company Type: Public
Ticker Symbol: CLC / TSX
Profile: CML HealthCare Inc. is a provider of laboratory testing services. It operates laboratory collection centres & medical imaging centres in Ontario.
Paul J. Bristow, President & Chief Executive Officer
Tom Weber, Chief Financial Officer & Executive Vice-President
Kent B. Nicholson, Chief Operating Officer & Executive Vice-President
Donald W. Kerr, General Manager, Laboratory Services
Kent Wentzell, General Manager, Imaging Services
Alice Dunning, Director, Corporate Communications
dunninga@cml.ca

Dundee Corporation
1 Adelaide St. East, 21st Fl.
Toronto, ON M5C 2V9
416-863-6990
Fax: 416-363-4536
investor@dundeebancorp.com
www.dundeecorporation.com
Company Type: Public
Ticker Symbol: DC.A / TSX
Profile: The asset management company is engaged in real estate & resources. Subsidiaries include Dundee Realty Corporation, Dundee Resources Limited, & Dundee Real Estate Asset Management.
Ned Goodman, President & Chief Executive Officer
416-365-5665
Lucie Presot, Chief Financial Officer & Vice-President
416-365-5157,

Exchange Income Corporation
1067 Sherwin Rd.
Winnipeg, MB R3H 0T8
204-982-1857
Fax: 204-982-1855
www.eiif.ca
Company Type: Public
Ticker Symbol: EIF / TSX
Profile: Exchange Income Corporation was established to invest in profitable companies in Canada & the United States. Cash dividends are distributed each month to shareholders. Exchange Income Corporation owns subsidiaries in the business segments of specialty manufacturing & aviation.
Michael C. Pyle, President & Chief Executive Officer
mpyle@eig.ca
Cindy Genyk, Chief Informaiton Officer
cgenyk@eig.ca
Adam S. Terwin, Chief Financial Officer
aterwin@eig.ca
Michael Rodyniuk, Chief Operating Officer, Aviation
mrod@eig.ca
Darwin R. Sparrow, Chief Operating Officer & Vice-President, Manufacturing
dsparrow@eig.ca
Michael Swistun, Director, Acquisitions
mswistun@eig.ca
David J. Patrick, Manager, Financial Reporting
Dianne M. Spencer, Manager, Compliance
dspencer@eig.ca

Fairfax Financial Holdings Limited
#800, 93 Wellington St. West
Toronto, ON M5J 2N7
416-367-4941
Fax: 416-367-4946
www.fairfax.ca
Company Type: Public
Ticker Symbol: FFH / TSX
Profile: Through its subsidiaries, the financial services holding company is involved in insurance claims management, property & casualty insurance & reinsurance, & investment management. Subsidiaries include Northbridge Financial, Crum & Forster, Falcon Insurance, First Capital, OdysseyRe, Group Re, Hamblin Watsa Investment Counsel, & MFXchange.
In 2012, 7948883 Canada Inc., a wholly owned subsidiary of Fairfax Financial Holdings Limited, acquired all the issued & outstanding shares of Prime Restaurants Inc.. Prime Restaurants' brands include Casey's, East Side Mario's, Fionn MacCool's, the Bier Markt, D'Arcy McGee's, & Paddy Flaherty's.
V. Prem Watsa, Chair/CEO
Greg Taylor, Vice-President/CFO
Ronald Schokking, Vice-President & Treasurer
David Bonham, Vice-President, Financial Reporting
Bradley Martin, Vice-President/COO & Corporate Secretary

Fonds de Solidarite F.T.Q.
8717, rue Berri
Montréal, QC H2M 2T9
514-383-3663
Fax: 514-383-2501
800-567-3663
www.fondsftq.com
Social Media: twitter.com/fondsftq
www.linkedin.com/company/fonds-de-solidarite-ftq
Company Type: Private
Yvon Bolduc, President & CEO

Freehold Royalties Ltd.
#400, 144 - 4th Ave. SW
Calgary, AB T2P 3N4
403-221-0802
Fax: 403-221-0888
888-257-1873
ir@freeholdtrust.com
www.freeholdtrust.com
Company Type: Public
Ticker Symbol: FRU / TSX
Profile: Freehold Royalties acquires & manages a portfolio of non-Crown oil & gas royalties in Canada.
David J. Sandmeyer, President & Chief Executive Officer
Joseph N. Holowisky, Chief Financail Officer & Vice-President, Finance
Karen C. Taylor, Corporate Secretary & Manager, Investor Relations
403-221-0891, ktaylor@rife.com
Garry W. Bieber, Vice-President, Production
Michael J. Okrusko, Vice-President, Land

Gendis Inc.
1370 Sony Pl.
Winnipeg, MB R3C 3C3
204-474-5200
Fax: 204-474-5201
finance@gendis.ca
www.gendis.ca
Company Type: Public
Ticker Symbol: GDS / TSX
Profile: Gendis' principal assets include investments in Veresen Inc., Osum Oilsands Corp., & real estate for lease.
James E. Cohen, President & Chief Executive Officer
Ernest B. Reinfort, Comptroller & Vice-President, Finance
N. Paul Cloutier, General Counsel, Secretary, & Vice-President

Groupe Aeroplan Inc.
Also Known As: Aimia
5100, boul de Maisonneuve ouest
Montréal, QC H3A 3T2
514-205-7315
Fax: 514-205-7578
info@aimia.com
www.aimia.com
Social Media:
www.facebook.com/pages/Aimia/195601040506049
twitter.com/AimiaInc
www.linkedin.com/company/2353423?trk=tyah
Company Type: Public
Ticker Symbol: AIM / TSX
Profile: The loyalty program, Aeroplan, is owned by Groupe Aeroplan Inc.. Members of the program earn Aeroplan Miles through the company's partners in the retial, travel, & financial sectors.
Rupert Duchesne, President & Chief Executive Officer
David L. Adams, Chief Financial Officer & Vice-President

H&R Real Estate Investment Trust
#500, 3625 Dufferin St.
Toronto, ON M3K 1N4
416-635-7520
Fax: 416-398-0040
info@hr-reit.com
www.hr-reit.com
Company Type: Public
Ticker Symbol: HR.UN / TSX
Profile: The organization is an open-ended real estate investment trust. Its portfolio include retail properties, office properties, single tenant industrial properties, & development projects.
Tom J. Hofstedter, President/CEO
Larry Froom, Chief Financial Officer
Nathan Uhr, Vice-President, Acquisitions

Humboldt Capital Corp.
#1800, 633 - 6th Ave. SW
Calgary, AB T2P 2Y5
403-269-9889
Fax: 403-269-9890
info@humboldtcapital.com
www.humboldtcapital.com
Company Type: Public
Ticker Symbol: HMB / TSX-V
Profile: Humboldt Capital Corporation is an investment company that has holdings in the resource sector. Examples of Humboldt's investments include western Canadian energy companies & international oil & gas companies.
Robert W. Lamond, Chair, President & Chief Executive Officer
Charles A. Teare, Chief Financial Officer & Executive Vice-President
D.K. Clark, Vice-President, Operations

IBI Group Inc.
230 Richmond St. West, 5th Fl.
Toronto, ON M5V 1V6
416-596-1930
Fax: 416-596-8024
www.ibigroup.com
Company Type: Public
Ticker Symbol: IBG / TSX
Profile: IBI Group provides planning, design, & other consulting services related to the development of urban land, building facilities, transportation networks, & systems technology.
Anthony Long, Chief Financial Officer

Labrador Iron Ore Royalty Corporation (LIORC)
Scotia Plaza
PO Box 4085 Stn. A, , 40 King St. West, 26th Fl.
Toronto, ON M5W 2X6
416-863-7133
Fax: 416-863-7425
investor.relations@labradorironore.com
www.labradorironore.com
Company Type: Public
Ticker Symbol: LIF / TSX

Profile: In 2010, the Labrador Iron Ore Royalty Income Fund converted to the Labrador Iron Ore Royalty Corporatio. The Canadian corporation holds an equity interest in Iron Ore Company of Canada, directly & through its wholly-woned subsidiary, Hollinger-Hanna Limited.
Bruce C. Bone, President & Chief Executive Officer
Alan R. Thomas, Chief Financial Officer
James C. McCartney, Executive Vice-President & Secretary

McVicar Industries Inc.
PO Box 19, #605, 55 University Ave.
Toronto, ON M5J 2H7
416-366-7420
Fax: 416-366-7421
info@mcvicar.ca
www.mcvicar.ca

Company Type: Public
Ticker Symbol: MCV / TSX Venture
Profile: McVicar Industries focuses on investments & acquisitions of businesses operating in China. The company's subsidiaries include Xiangshui Luyuan Chemical Co. Ltd., Zhejiang Hongbo Chemical Co. Ltd., & Hongzhou Changlong Chemical Co. Ltd..
McVicar also holds interest in Jite Technologies Inc., which manufactures terminal blocks for domestic & international customers. Jite has an office in Toronto, Ontario, as well as research & manufacturing operating in Shenzhen, China at an ISO 9001 certified facility.
Gang Chai, President & Chief Executive Officer
Winfield Ding, Chief Financial Officer

Morguard Real Estate Investment Trust
#1000, 55 City Centre Dr.
Mississauga, ON L5B 1M3
905-281-4800
Fax: 905-281-4818
investorrelations@morguardreit.com
www.morguardreit.com

Company Type: Public
Ticker Symbol: MRT.UN / TSX
Profile: The organization is an unincorporated, closed-end investment trust that was created in 1997. The Morguard Real Estate Investment Trust has a diversified portfolio of industrial, retail, & office properties across Canada.
Rai Sahi, President & Chief Executive Officer
rsahi@morguard.com
Tim Walker, Chief Financial Officer & Vice-President
Ken Moffat, Vice-President, Asset Management

NEMI Northern Energy & Mining Inc.
#200, 1095 West Pender St.
Vancouver, BC V6E 2M6
info@nemi-energy.com
www.nemi-energy.com

Company Type: Public
Ticker Symbol: NNE / CNSX
Profile: NEMI operates as a specialized merchant bank, developing its asset & equity portfolio.
Michael Cooney, Chair & Chief Executive Officer
mcooney@nemi-energy.com
Andrew Williams, Chief Financial Officer

NorTerra Inc.
Bell Tower
#1201, 10104 - 103 Ave.
Edmonton, AB T5J 0H8
780-425-6900
Fax: 780-424-1935
email@norterra.com; hrcd@norterra.com
www.norterra.com
Other Communications: Yellowknife Office: 867-669-4048
Company Type: Private
Profile: NoTerra Inc. is a management & holding company. It is owned by the Nunasi Corporation, on behalf of the Inuit of Nunavut, as well as the Inuvialuit Development Corporation, on behalf of the Inuvialuit of the Western Arctic.
The NorTerra Group of Companies is a diversified organization that offers services such as airline & marine operations & logistics management.
Mark Gardhouse, President & Chief Executive Officer
Leslie Kwasny, Vice-President, Finance
Patrick Schmidt, Vice-President, Business Development
Tanis Thomas, Corporate Secretary & Vice-President

Northampton Group Inc.
#212, 2601 Matheson Blvd. East
Mississauga, ON L4W 5A8
905-629-9992
Fax: 905-629-9636
admin@nhgi.com
www.nhgi.com

Company Type: Public
Ticker Symbol: NHG / TSX Venture
Profile: Northampton Group has ownership & management interests in hotels located in Canada & the United States.
Vinod Patel, President & Chief Executive Officer
Narendra Patel, Chief Financial Officer & Vice-President

Northfield Capital Corporation
#301, 141 Adelaide St. West
Toronto, ON M5H 3L5
416-628-5901
Fax: 416-628-5911
info@northfieldcapital.com
www.northfieldcapital.com

Company Type: Public
Ticker Symbol: NFD.A / TSX Venture
Profile: Formed in 1981, the investment company owns interests in diverse business activities. Major oil, gas, & mining holdings include GoldCorp Inc., Queenston Mining Inc., Canada Lithium Corp., Goldstone Resources Inc., & Quadra FNX Mining Ltd.
Robert D. Cudney, President & Founder
Brent J. Peters, Treasurer & Vice-President, Finance

Onex Corporation
PO Box 700, 161 Bay St.
Toronto, ON M5J 2S1
416-362-7711
Fax: 416-362-5765
info@onex.com
www.onex.com

Company Type: Public
Ticker Symbol: OCX / TSX
Profile: Through Onex Partners & ONCAP families of funds, Onex Corporation makes private equity investments. The company is also engaged in the management of alternative asset platforms, which focuses on real estate & distressed credit.
Gerald W. Schwartz, Chair/CEO
Michael Dana, President/CEO, Onex Real Estate Partners
Donald W. Lewtas, Chief Financial Officer
Andrea E. Daly, Vice-President, General Counsel, & Secretary

Power Corporation of Canada
The Secretary
751, carré Victoria
Montréal, QC H2Y 2J3
514-286-7400
Fax: 514-286-7484
www.powercorporation.com

Company Type: Public
Ticker Symbol: POW / TSX
Profile: Power Corporation of Canada was formed in 1925. The main subsidiary of this diversified international management & holding company is Power Financial Corp.
Paul Desmarais Jr., O.C., Chair/Co-CEO
André Desmarais, O.C., President/Co-CEO & Deputy Chair
Michel Plessis-Bélair, FCA, Vice-Chair
John A. Rae, Exec. Vice-President

Richards Packaging Income Fund
6095 Ordan Dr.
Mississauga, ON L4T 2M7
905-670-7760
Fax: 905-670-1961
www.richardspackaging.com
Company Type: Public
Ticker Symbol: RPI / TSX
Profile: Richards Packaging Income Fund is an indirect owner of securities of Richards Packaging Inc.. Richards Packaging is a plastic & glass container manufacturer & distributor. The company also distributes metal & plastic closures, as well as injection molded containers & packaging systems.
Gerry Glynn, Chief Executive Officer
gglynn@richardspackaging.com
David Prupas, President
president@richardspackaging.com
Enzio DiGennaro, Chief Financial Officer
edigennaro@richardspackaging.com

Senvest Capital Inc.
#2400, 1000, rue Sherbrooke ouest
Montréal, QC H3A 3G4
514-281-8082
Fax: 514-281-0166
www.senvest.com

Company Type: Public
Ticker Symbol: SEC / TSX
Profile: Senvest Capital Inc.'s subsidiaries are involved in the following sectors: asset management, merchant banking, real estate, & electronic security.
Brian Gonick, Principal & Director, Senvest International
bgonick@senvest.com
George Malikotsis, Vice-President, Finance
514-281-8082, georgem@senvest.com

Sonor Investments Limited
#2120, 130 Adelaide St. West
Toronto, ON M5H 3P5
416-369-1499
Fax: 416-369-0280

Company Type: Public
Ticker Symbol: SNIPR / TSX Venture
Profile: Sonor Investments Limited makes portfolio investments in both public & private equity & fixed income securities. Sonor's wholly owned subsidiary is Toddle Opportunities Corporation.
Michael R. Gardiner, President & Chief Executive Officer
Stephen A. Mills, Chief Financial Officer & Treasurer

TerraVest Income Fund
4901 Bruce Rd.
Vegreville, AB T9C 1C3
780-632-2040
Fax: 780-632-7694
www.terravestindustries.com
Company Type: Public
Ticker Symbol: TI.UN / TSX
Profile: The fund has investments in RJV Gas Field Services & Diamond Energy Services.
Dale Laniuk, President & Chief Executive Officer
dlaniuk@terravestindustries.com
Paul A. Casey, Chief Financial Officer
pcasey@terravestindustries.com

Tuckamore Capital Management Inc.
469 King St. West
Toronto, ON M5V 1K4
416-775-3790
irinfo@tuckamore.ca
www.tuckamore.ca
Company Type: Public
Ticker Symbol: TX / TSX
Profile: In 2011, shareholders of Newport Inc. approved a name change for the organization to Tuckamore Capital Management Inc.. Tuckamore Capital Management Inc. is a diversified fund that invests in Canadian private businesses.
Dean MacDonald, President & Chief Executive Officer
Keith Halbert, Chief Financial Officer
416-775-3796, keith@tuckamore.ca
Paul Hatcher, Chief Operating Officer
Charles P. Hutchings, Vice-President
Adrian Montgomery, Vice-President

Uranium Participation Corporation (UPC)
#402, 595 Bay St.
Toronto, ON M5G 2C2
416-979-1991
Fax: 416-979-5893
www.uraniumparticipation.com
Company Type: Public
Ticker Symbol: U / TSX
Profile: Uranium Participation Corporation was established in 2005. The investment holding company invests in uranium, either in the form of uranium oxide in concentrates or uranium hexafluoride. The manager of Uranium Participation Corporation is Denison Mines Inc.
Ron F. Hochstein, President
James R. Anderson, Chief Financial Officer
Donald C. Campbell, Vice-President, Commercial
Curt D. Steel, Vice-President, Marketing
Sheila Colman, Corporate Secretaru

Westaim Corporation
#201, 212 King St. West
Toronto, ON M5H 1K5
416-203-2253
Fax: 416-203-0734
info@westaim.com
www.westaim.com

Company Type: Public
Ticker Symbol: WED / TSX
Profile: Westaim owns 100% of JEVCO Insurance Company, which is a property & casualty insurance company.
Cameron MacDonald, Chief Executive Officer
Jeffron Sarfin, Chief Financial Officer
416-203-2253

WesternOne Equity Income Fund
Head Office
#910, 925 West Georgia St.
Vancouver, BC V6C 3L2
604-678-4042
Fax: 604-681-5969
877-278-4042
info@weq.ca
www.weq.ca

Company Type: Public
Ticker Symbol: WEQ / TSX
Profile: WesternOne Equity Income Fund is an unincorporated, open-ended trust. It invests in mainly construction &

infrastructure related businesses. The Fund's businesses are located primarily in Saskatchewan, Alberta, & British Columbia.
Darren Latoski, Chief Executive Officer
Geoff Shorten, Chief Operating Officer
Carlos Yam, Chief Financial Officer
Andrew Greig, Manager, Investor Relations
agreig@weq.ca

Westshore Terminals Investment Corporation
#1800, 1067 West Cordova St.
Vancouver, BC V6C 1C7
604-688-6764
Fax: 604-687-2601
www.westshore.com
Company Type: Public
Ticker Symbol: WTE.UN / TSX
Profile: Westshore Terminals Investment Corporation's wholly-owned subsidiary is Westshore Terminals Holdings Ltd.. Westshore Investment & Westshore Holdings derive their cash inflows from their investment in Westshore Terminals Limited Partnership. Westshore Terminals Limited Partnership operates a coal storage & loading terminal in British Columbia.
Nick Desmarais, Secretary
604-488-5214

Insurance

ACE INA Insurance
Also Known As: ACE Canada
#1400, 25 York St.
Toronto, ON M5J 2V5
416-368-2911
Fax: 416-594-2600
www.ace-ina-canada.com
Company Type: Public
Ticker Symbol: ACE
Profile: ACE Canada specializes in commercial property & casualty insurance & reinsurance. The company is owned by ACE INA Overseas Insurance Company Ltd., which is headquartered in Bermuda. The ACE Group has customers in more than 170 countries.
David Brosnan, Chief Executive Officer
Karen Barkley, President & Chief Operations Officer
Timothy J. O'Donnell, President, ACE Professional Risk
Shawn Doherty, Sr. Vice-President, CFO & Secretary, Finance
Terri Mitchell, Exec. Vice-President & COO, Life, Accident & Health Group
Ricardo Philip, Asst. Vice-President, Environmental Risk
Joe Jordan, Treasurer

Allstate Insurance Company of Canada
Corporate Head Office
#100, 27 Allstate Pkwy.
Markham, ON L3R 5P8
905-477-6900
800-255-7828
www.allstate.ca
Company Type: Private
Profile: Since 1953, the Allstate Insurance Company of Canada has provided property & casualty insurance products.

Assumption Mutual Life Insurance Company
Assumption Place
PO Box 160, 770 Main St.
Moncton, NB E1C 8L1
506-853-6040
Fax: 506-853-5428
800-455-7337
comments@assumption.ca
www.assumption.ca
Company Type: Private

Aviva Canada
2206 Eglinton Ave. East
Toronto, ON M1L 4S8
800-387-4518
www.avivacanada.com
Company Type: Private

Aviva Canada Inc.
2206 Eglinton Ave. East
Toronto, ON M1L 4S8
416-288-1800
800-387-4518
www.avivacanada.com
Company Type: Private
Profile: Property & casualty insurance group
Robin Spencer, President/CEO
Robert Merizzi, Exec. Vice President/COO, Operations & Technology
Sally Turney, Vice President, Corporate Communications

Blue Cross Company of Canada
Also Known As: Medavie Blue Cross
Blue Cross Centre
PO Box 220, 644 Main St.
Moncton, NB E1C 8L3
800-667-4511
www.medavie.bluecross.ca
Company Type: Private
Pierre-Yves Julien, President & CEO

BMO Life Assurance Company
60 Yonge St.
Toronto, ON M5E 1H5
Fax: 416-596-4143
877-742-5244
Insurance.DirectAdmin@bmo.com
www.bmo.com
Company Type: Private

Boiler Inspection & Insurance Company of Canada
Also Known As: HSB BI&I
#3000, 250 Yonge St.
Toronto, ON M5B 2L7
416-363-5491
Fax: 416-363-0538
www.biico.com
Company Type: Private
John R. Mulvihill, President & CEO

Canada Life Financial Corporation (CLFC)
330 University Ave.
Toronto, ON M5G 1R8
416-597-6981
888-252-1847
www.canadalife.com
Company Type: Public
Ticker Symbol: CL
Profile: CLFC is an diversified financial services company that provides insurance, reinsurance services, unit trusts, & wealth management products & services. Clients are both individuals & groups in Canada, the United States, the United Kingdom, Isle of Man, Ireland, & Germany.
Allen Loney, President & CEO
Paul A. Mahon, President & COO, Canada
William W. Lovatt, Exec. VP & CFO
Peter G. Munro, Exec. VP & CIO

Canada Life Insurance Co.
330 University Ave.
Toronto, ON M5G 1R8
416-597-6981
888-252-1847
www.canadalife.com
Company Type: Private

Canadian Direct Insurance
#600, 750 Cambie St.
Vancouver, BC V6B 0A2
604-699-3838
Fax: 604-699-3860
888-225-5234
www.canadiandirect.com
Other Communications: Toll-Free Fax: 1-877-515-4747
Company Type: Private
Brian Young, President & CEO
Michael Martino, Chief Financial Officer

Canadian Northern Shield Insurance Company (CNS)
#1900, 555 West Hastings St.
Vancouver, BC
www.cns.ca
Company Type: Private

Canadian Premier Life Insurance Company
80 Tiverton Crt., 5th Fl.
Markham, ON L3R 0G4
905-479-7500
www.canadianpremier.ca
Company Type: Private

Certas Direct Insurance Company
PO Box 3500, 6300, blvd de la Rive-Sud
Lévis, QC G6V 6P9
888-277-8726
www.certas.ca
Company Type: Private

Chubb Insurance Company of Canada
1 Adelaide St. East
Toronto, ON M5C 2V9
416-863-0550
Fax: 416-863-5010
www.chubb.com/international/canada
Social Media: www.facebook.com/ChubbInsurance?ref=ts
twitter.com/ChubbInsurance
Company Type: Private
Profile: Chubb Insurance Company of Canada is a global property & casualty insurance firm. The company has branch offices in the following cities: Vancouver (604-685-2113), Calgary (403-261-3881), & Montréal (514-938-4000).

Co-operators General Insurance Company
Service Quality Department
130 MacDonell St.
Guelph, ON N1H 6P8
519-824-4400
Fax: 519-823-9944
800-265-2662
service@cooperators.ca; corp_hr@cooperato
www.cooperators.ca
Other Communications: Quebec Clients, Toll-Free Phone: 1-800-363-6442
Company Type: Public
Ticker Symbol: CCS / TSX
Profile: Co-operators General Insurance Company provides home, automobile, farm, & commecial insurance services throughout Canada.
Kathy Bardswick, President/CEO
Bruce West, Sr. Vice-President/CFO
Vivien Fong, Sr. Vice-President & Chief Information Officer
Martin-Eric Tremblay, Sr. Vice-President, Insurance Operations

Commonwealth Insurance Company
#700, 105 Adelaide St. West
Toronto, ON M5H 1P9
416-350-4400
855-620-6262
www.nbfc.com
Company Type: Private
Profile: Commonwealth is a member company of Northbridge Insurance.
Fabian Richenberger, President, Northbridge Insurance

COSECO Insurance Company
5600 Cancross Crt.
Mississauga, ON L5R 3E9
888-394-4964
CosecoInsurance@hbgrpins.com
www.coseco.ca
Other Communications: Toll-Free Fax: 1-800-366-0490
Company Type: Private

Crown Life Insurance
#1900, 1874 Scarth St.
Regina, SK S4P 4B3
306-751-6900
www.canadalife.com
Company Type: Private

CUMIS General Insurance Company
The CUMIS Group Limited
PO Box 5065, 151 North Service Rd.
Burlington, ON L7R 4C2
905-632-1221
800-263-9120
customer.service@cumis.com
www.cumis.com
Company Type: Private
Profile: The CUMIS Group Limited is the holding company for the CUMIS General Insurance Company & the CUMIS Life Insurance Company. CUMIS partners with credit unions to deliver insurance products to credit union members. The CUMIS General Insurance Company was incorporated in 1980 to offer a portfolio of property & casualty insurance products.

CUMIS Life Insurance Company
The CUMIS Group Limited
PO Box 5065, 151 North Service Rd.
Burlington, ON L7R 4C2
866-772-6777
cumis_service@cooperators.ca; TeleLife@cu
www.cumis.com
Other Communications: CUMIS TeleLife: 800-263-9120, ext. 4848
Company Type: Private
Profile: CUMIS' principal companies are CUMIS Life Insurance Company & CUMIS General Insurance Company. Through partnership with CUMIS, credit unions can offer members insurance.

Desjardins Financial Security Life
200 des Commandeurs
Lévis, QC G6V 6R2
866-838-7553
www.desjardinslifeinsurance.com
Company Type: Private

Desjardins General Insurance Group
1001 E. Hallandale Beach Blvd.
Hallandale Beach, FL 33009-4429 USA
954-454-1001
Fax: 954-457-7927
800-224-7737
www.desjardinslifeinsurance.com
Company Type: Private

Dominion of Canada General Insurance
165 University Ave
Toronto, ON M5H 3B9
416-362-7231
Fax: 416-362-9918
800-268-8447
www.thedominion.ca
Company Type: Private

E-L Financial Corporation Limited
165 University Ave., 10th Fl.
Toronto, ON M5H 3B8
416-947-2578
Fax: 416-362-2592
Company Type: Public
Ticker Symbol: ELF / TSX
Profile: The investment & insurance holding company was incorporated in 1968. E-L Financial Corporation consists of the following subsidiaries: E-L Financial Services Ltd., The Dominion of Canada General Insurance Company, & The Empire Life Insurance Company.
Duncan N.R. Jackman, Chair, President, & Chief Executive Officer
Mark M. Taylor, Chief Financial Officer & Executive Vice-President
416-947-2578, Fax: 416-362-0792
Richard B. Carty, Vice-President, General Counsel, & Corporate Secretary
416-947-2578, Fax: 416-362-2592

Echelon General Insurance Company
#300, 2680 Matheson Blvd.
Mississauga, ON L4W 0A5
905-214-7880
Fax: 905-214-7893
800-324-3566
accounts@egi.ca
www.echelon-insurance.ca
Company Type: Private

Economical Mutual Insurance
PO Box 2000, 111 Westmount Rd. South
Waterloo, ON N2J 4S4
519-570-8200
Fax: 519-570-8389
800-265-9996
www.economicalinsurance.com
Company Type: Private

EGI Financial Holdings Inc.
#300, 2680 Matheson Blvd. East
Mississauga, ON L4W 0A5
905-214-7880
Fax: 905-214-8028
www.egi.ca
Company Type: Public
Ticker Symbol: EFH / TSX
Profile: EGI Financial was founded in 1997. The company is involved in the property & casualty insurance industry in Canada, the United States, & Europe. EGI Financial focuses on non-standard automobile insurance as well as other specialty insurance products.
Steve Dobronyi, Chief Executive Officer
905-214-7880
George Kalopsis, President & Chief Operating Officer, Echelon
Hemraj Singh, Chief Financial Officer & Vice-President
Michael Rocchi, Vice-President, Niche Products Division
Kathy Shulman, Contact, Investor Relations

Elite Insurance Company
Also Known As: Aviva Elite
c/o Aviva Canada Inc.
2206 Eglinton Ave. East
Toronto, ON M1L 4S8
800-387-4518
www.avivacanada.com
Social Media: www.facebook.com/AvivaCanada
twitter.com/avivacanada
www.linkedin.com/company/aviva-canada
Company Type: Private
Profile: The Elite Insurance Company is a wholly owned insurance company of Aviva Canada Inc.. Aviva Elite is an insurer of leisure & lifestyle products & services, such as mobile homes, recreational vehicles, power boats, sailboats, antique cars, & custom cars.

Empire Life Insurance
259 King St. East
Kingston, ON K7L 3A8
613-548-1881
877-548-1881
info@empire.ca
www.empire.ca
Company Type: Private

Equitable Life Insurance Company of Canada
1 Westmount Rd. North
Waterloo, ON N2J 4C7
519-886-5110
Fax: 519-883-7400
800-265-8878
headoffice@equitable.ca
www.equitable.ca
Company Type: Private
Ronald Beettam, President/CEO
Douglas Brooks, CFO/Sr. Vice President
Ravinder Singh, CIO/Vice President, Information Technology

Federated Insurance Company of Canada
717 Portage Ave.
Winnipeg, MB R3C 3C9
204-786-6431
Fax: 204-783-4443
800-665-1934
www.federated.ca
Company Type: Private

Foresters Life Insurance Company
Also Known As: Foresters Life
#3, 1660 Tech Ave.
Mississauga, ON L4W 5S8
800-267-8777
clientservice@foresters.com
www.foresters.com
Social Media: www.facebook.com/Foresters
Company Type: Private
Profile: In 2012, Unity Life of Canada, a Foresters company, changed its name to Foresters Life Insurance Company. The Canadian incorporated life insurance company offers life insurance products to Canadians. Foresters Life Insurance Company is a member of Assuris, a not for profit organization that protects Canadian policyholders if a life insurance company fails.
Anthony Poole, President & Chief Executive Officer
Ryan Jones, Contact, Media Inquiries
rjones@foresters.com

Genworth Financial Mortgage Insurance
#300, 2060 Winston Park Dr.
Oakville, ON L6H 5R7
800-511-8888
mortgage.info@genworth.com
www.genworth.ca
Company Type: Private

Genworth MI Canada Inc.
National Underwriting Centre
#300, 2060 Winston Park Dr.
Oakville, ON L6H 5R7
800-511-8888
mortgage.info@genworth.com
www.genworth.ca
Company Type: Public
Ticker Symbol: MIC / TSX
Profile: Genworth MI Canada Inc. provides mortgage default insurance in Canada through its subsidiary, Genworth Financial Mortgage Insurance Company Canada. Commonly known as Genworth Financial Canada, The Homeownership Company, it employs approximately 265 people throughout Canada.
Brian Hurley, Chair & Chief Executive Officer
905-287-5265, brian.hurley@genworth.com
Stuart Levings, Chief Operations Officer & Senior Vice-President
905-287-5478, stuart.levings@genworth.com
Philip Mayers, Chief Financial Officer & Senior Vice-President
905-287-5393, philip.mayers@genworth.com
Peter Vukanovich, Executive Vice-President, Corporate Development
905-287-5488, peter.vukanovich@genworth.com
Winsor Macdonell, Senior Vice-President, General Counsel & Secretary
905-287-5484, winsor.macdonell@genworth.com
Debbie McPherson, Senior Vice-President, Sales & Marketing
905-287-5465, debbie.mcpherson@genworth.com
Cecilia Carbonelli, Vice-President, Information Technology
905-287-5344, cecilia.carbonelli@genworth.com
Lisa Azzuolo, Director, Communications
Lisa.Azzuolo@genworth.com

Gore Mutual Insurance Company
PO Box 70, 252 Dundas St. North
Cambridge, ON N1R 5T3
519-623-1910
Fax: 800-601-9773
800-265-8600
www.goremutual.ca
Company Type: Private
Kevin McNeil, President/CEO
Lorne Motton, CFO & Secretary
Sara McLennan, Vice-President, Marketing
Richard Meertens, Vice-President, Information Services

Grain Insurance & Guarantee Company
Head Office
1240 - 1 Lombard Pl.
Winnipeg, MB R3B 0V9
204-943-0721
Fax: 204-943-6419
800-665-3351
infowinnipeg@graininsurance.com
www.graininsurance.com
Other Communications: SK: 306-757-1691; ON: 519-433-9991; Atlantic: 902-425-9228
Company Type: Private
Profile: The insurer offers standard property & casualty insurance. Grain Insurance & Guarantee also develops specialized insurance programs to meet the changing needs of diverse Canadian businesses.

Great-West Life Assurance Company
100 Osborne St. North
Winnipeg, MB R3C 3A5
204-946-1190
www.greatwestlife.com
Other Communications: TTY: 1-800-990-6654
Company Type: Public
Ticker Symbol: GWL / TSX
Profile: The insurance company serves individuals, families, businesses, & organizations. Great-West Life Assurance Company also supplies specialty general insurance & reinsurance.
D. Allen Loney, President & Chief Executive Officer
William W. Lovatt, Exec. Vice-President/CFO
Elwood C. Haas, Sr. Vice-President, Corporate Resources

Great-West Lifeco Inc.
100 Osborne St. North
Winnipeg, MB R3C 3A5
204-946-4388
Fax: 204-946-4139
contactus@gwl.ca
www.greatwestlifeco.com
Company Type: Public
Ticker Symbol: GWO / TSX
Profile: The international financial services holding company has interests in life insurance, health insurance, reinsurance. asset management, retirement, & investment services. Great-West Lifeco's companies include The Great-West Life Assurance Company, Great-West Life & Anuity Insurance Company, The Canada Life Assurance Compnay, London Life Insurance Company, & Putnam Investments. Great-West Lifeco & its companies are members of the Power Financial Corporation group of companies.
Allen Loney, President/CEO
Paul A. Mahon, President/COO, Canada
William W. Lovatt, Exec. Vice-President/CFO
Marlene Klassen, Assistant Vice-President, Communication Services

Green Shield Canada
#2100, 5140 Yonge St.
Toronto, ON M2N 6L7
416-221-7001
Fax: 416-221-0350
800-268-6613
gs.marketing@greenshield.ca
www.greenshield.ca

Company Type: Private

Guarantee Company of North America
Madison Centre
#1400, 4950 Yonge St.
Toronto, ON M2N 6K1

416-223-9580
Fax: 416-223-6577
toronto@gcna.com
www.gcna.ca

Company Type: Private
Profile: The Guarantee Company of North America is a specialty insurer. Products include contract & commercial surety, credit insurance, & fidelity insurance.
Robert A. Dempsey, President & Chief Operating Officer
rdempsey@gcna.com
Alan Rabin, Chief Financial Officer & Vice-President, Finance
arabin@gcna.com
Dean M. Basts, National Vice-President Guarantee GOLD & Vice-President, Marketing & Business Development
dbast@gcna.com
Frank Faieta, National Vice-President, Claims
ffaieta@gcna.com
Randall L. Musselman, Corporate Secretary & Vice-President, Risk Management & Government Regulation
rmusselman@gcna.com

Independent Order of Foresters
1660 Tech Ave., Suite 3
Mississauga, ON L4W 5S8

800-267-8777
clientservice@foresters.com
www.foresters.com

Company Type: Private

Industrial Alliance Insurance & Financial Services
PO Box 1907 Stn. Terminus, , 1080, Grande Allée ouest
Québec, QC G1K 7M3

418-684-5000
Fax: 418-684-5208
800-463-6236
customers@inalco.com; groupinsurance@inal
www.inalco.com
Other Communications: Public Relations: srp911@inalco.com

Company Type: Public
Ticker Symbol: IAG
Profile: Industrial Alliance Insurance & Financial Services Inc. provides a great range of financial & insurance products & services, including life & health insurance, automobile & home insurance, RRSPs, savings & retirement plans, securities, mutual & segregated funds, & mortgage loans.
Yvon Charest, President/CEO
Denis Denis, Sr. Vice-President & Chief Actuary
Jacques Carrière, Vice-President, Investor Relations

ING Canada Inc.
ING Tower
700 University Ave., 15th Fl.
Toronto, ON M5G 0A1

416-341-1464
Fax: 416-941-5320
info@ingcanada.com
www.ingcanada.com

Company Type: Private
Ticker Symbol: IIC
Profile: Through its subsidiaries, ING Canada Inc. provides the following types of insurance: property, liability, & automobile. The property & casualty insurance provider serves both individuals & businesses.
Charles Brindamour, President/CEO
Louis Gagnon, President, ING Insurance
Mark Tullis, Chief Financial Officer
Jack Ott, Sr. Vice-President & Chief Information Officer
Françoise Guénette, Secretary & Sr. Vice-President, Corporate & Legal Services

Intact Financial Corporation
700 University Ave.
Toronto, ON M5G 0A1

416-341-1464
Fax: 416-941-5320
877-341-1464
info@intact.net
www.intactfc.com
Other Communications: Toll-Free Fax: 866-933-7916

Company Type: Public
Ticker Symbol: IFC / TSX
Profile: Intact Financial Corporation provides property & casualty insurance in Canada. Products & services are marketed & distributed through Intact Insurance, belairdirect, & Grey Power.
Charles Brindamour, Chief Executive Officer
Louis Gagnon, President & Chief Operating Officer
Jean-François Blais, President, Intact Insurance
Marc Pontbriand, President, Direct to Consumers Distribution
Mark A. Tullis, Chief Financial Officer & Senior Vice-President
Claude Désilets, Chief Risk Officer & Senior Vice-President
Jack Ott, Chief Information Technology Officer & Senior Vice-President
Monika Federau, Senior Vice-President, Marketing
Françoise Guénette, Secretary & Senior Vice-President, Corporate & Legal Services

Intact Insurance Company
700 University Ave., 15th Fl.
Toronto, ON M5G 0A1

416-341-1464
Fax: 416-344-8030
877-341-1464
info@intact.net
www.intactinsurance.com
Other Communications: Personal & Business Insurance: 866-464-2424

Company Type: Private
Profile: In 2011, Intact Financial Corporation acquired AXA Canada. Intact Insurance Company joined with AXA in the provision of home, business, & automobile insurance. Intact Insurance is present throughout Canada.

James Richardson & Sons Ltd.
One Lombard Pl., 30th Fl.
Winnipeg, MB R3B 0Y1

204-953-7970
Fax: 204-942-6339
www.jrsl.ca

Company Type: Private

JEVCO Insurance Company
#100, 5250, boul Décarie
Montréal, QC H3X 2H9

514-284-9350
Fax: 514-289-9257
800-361-8500
www.jevco.ca

Company Type: Private
Profile: JEVCO Insurance Company offers the following types of personal & commercial insurance: automobile, motorcycle, all-terrain vehicle, snowmobile, property & casualty, & surety. The company has branches in the following cities: Québec, Québec (418-650-9350), Mississauga Ontario (905-277-9350), Calgary Alberta (403-255-9222), & Vancouver British-Columbia (604-608-8552).

Kingsway Financial Services Inc.
#800, 7120 Hurontario
Mississauga, ON L5W 0A9

905-696-1372
Fax: 905-696-1772
info@kingsway-financial.com
www.kingsway-financial.com

Company Type: Public
Ticker Symbol: KFS / TSX, NYSE
W. Shaun Jackson, President/CEO & Chair
Shelly Gobin, Vice-President/CFO

Lombard Canada
#700, 105 Adelaide St. West
Toronto, ON M5H 1P9

416-350-4400
855-620-6262
info@nbfc.com
www.nbfc.com

Company Type: Private

London Life Insurance Company
255 Dufferin Ave.
London, ON N6A 4K1

519-432-5281
Fax: 519-435-7077
www.londonlife.com
Other Communications: TTY Toll-Free: 1-800-990-6654

Company Type: Private
Profile: London Life Insurance Company provides financial security advice & planning for individuals, businesses, & organizations. Products include life insurance, mortgages, & group retirement plans.
D. Allen Loney, President & Chief Executive Officer
Paul A. Mahon, President & Chief Operating Officer, Canada

Manufacturer's Life Insurance
Also Known As: Manulife
PO Box 1602 Stn. Waterloo, , #500-MA, 500 King St. North
Waterloo, ON N2J 4C6

877-765-2265
Fax: 877-565-2265
manulife_bank@manulife.com

Company Type: Private

Markel Insurance Company of Canada
105 Adelaide St. West
Toronto, ON M5H 1P9

416-350-4400
855-620-6262
info@nbfc.com
www.markel.ca

Company Type: Private
Profile: Markel is a member company of Northbridge Insurance.
Fabian Richenberger, President, Northbridge Insurance

Marsh Canada Limited
Canada Headquarters
#1400, 161 Bay St.
Toronto, ON M5J 2S4

416-868-2600
canada.marsh.com

Company Type: Private
Profile: Marsh Canada is engaged in insurance broking & risk management.
Alan Garner, President & Chief Exeuctive Officer
Jim Abernethy, Chief Operating Officer

Medavie Inc.
Also Known As: Medavie Blue Cross
Blue Cross Centre
PO Box 220, 644 Main St.
Moncton, NB E1C 8L3

800-667-4511
www.medavie.bluecross.ca

Company Type: Private

Missisquoi Insurance Company
PO Box 2000, 111 Westmount Rd. South
Waterloo, ON N2J 4S4

519-570-8200
Fax: 519-570-8389
800-265-2180
www.economicalinsurance.com

Company Type: Private

Munich Reinsurance Company of Canada (MROC)
Also Known As: Munich Re
#2200, 390 Bay St.
Toronto, ON M5H 2Y2

416-366-9206
Fax: 416-366-4330
800-444-5321
www.mroc.com
Social Media:
www.facebook.com/pages/Munich-Re/112684192080056
twitter.com/munichre

Company Type: Private
Kenneth B. Irvin, President & CEO
Gary Gray, Sr. Vice-President & CFO

North Waterloo Farmers Mutual Insurance
100 Erb St. East
Waterloo, ON N2J 1L9

519-886-4530
Fax: 519-746-0222
800-265-8813
insurance@nwfm.com; claims@nwfm.com
www.nwfm.com
Other Communications: Claims: 519-746-0805

Company Type: Private
Profile: The following types of insurance are provided by North Waterloo Farmers Mutual Insurance Company: home, farm, commercial, & automobile. The company conducts business across Ontario.
Carlos Rodrigues, President & Chief Executive Officer
Les Card, Chief Financial Officer & Vice-President
Josie Gaffney, Chief Information Officer & Vice-President
Larry Nickel, Vice-President, Underwriting
Jim Zyta, Vice-President, Loss Prevention

Northbridge Financial Corporation
105 Adelaide St. West, 7th Fl.
Toronto, ON M5H 1P9

416-350-4300
Fax: 416-350-4307
investor.relations@norfin.com
www.norfin.com

Company Type: Public
Ticker Symbol: NB
Profile: Northbridge Financial Corporation provides automobile, property, general liability, & other commercial insurance products. Clients are businesses in Canada.
Mark Ram, President/CEO
Craig Pinnock, Chief Financial Officer
Innes Dey, Corporate Secretary & Vice-President, Corporate Affairs

Old Republic Insurance Company of Canada
Also Known As: Old Republic Canada
PO Box 557, 100 King St. West
Hamilton, ON L8N 3K9
905-523-5936
Fax: 905-523-1471
800-530-5446
service@orican.com
www.orican.com
Other Communications: Toll-Free Fax: 866-551-1686
Company Type: Private
Profile: The federally licensed insurance company offers long haul trucking insurance solutions to Canadians.

Pembridge Insurance Company
#100, 27 Allstate Parkway
Markham, ON L3R 5P8
905-513-4013
877-736-2743
contactus@pembridge.com
www.pembridge.com
Company Type: Private

Penncorp Life Insurance Company
7150 Derrycrest Dr.
Mississauga, ON L5W 0E5
Fax: 905-795-2316
800-268-2835
cs@penncorp.ca
www.penncorp.ca
Company Type: Private
Steven Ross, President & COO

Personal General Insurance
PO Box 3500, 6300, boul de la Rive-Sud
Lévis, QC G6V 6P9
866-704-8980
www.thepersonal.com; www.desjardins.com
Other Communications: Claims: 866-776-8343, TDD: 800-567-3232
Company Type: Private
Profile: The Personal is a subsidiary of The Desjardins Group. Personal General Insurance is a home & automobile insurer that serves the Québec market.

Personal Insurance Company
6300, boul de la Rive-Sud
Lévis, QC G6V 6P9
888-476-8737
www.thepersonal.com; www.desjardins.com
Other Communications: Customer Relations Centre: 866-704-8980
Company Type: Private
Profile: The Personal is a home & automobile insurer. One of its subsidiaries is The Personal Insurance Company, which serves the Canadian market except for Québec. The Québec market is servied by The Personal General Insurance.

Perth Insurance Company
#1500, 5255 Yonge St.
Toronto, ON M2N 6P4
Fax: 416-590-0556
888-307-3784
www.economicalinsurance.com
Other Communications: Service Centre, Phone: 877-717-2233
Company Type: Private
Profile: The Perth Insurance Company is a non-standard insurance company that serves Canadian homeowners & drivers who wish to improve their insurance records.

Pilot Insurance Company
Also Known As: Aviva Pilot
2206 Eglinton Ave. East
Toronto, ON M1L 4S8
800-387-4518
www.avivacanada.com
Other Communications: Claims, Toll-Free: 1-866-692-8482
Company Type: Private
Profile: Pilot Insurance is Aviva's property & automobile insurance arm, operating solely in Ontario.
Maurice Tulloch, President & CEO, Aviva Canada Inc.

Portage la Prairie Mutual Insurance Company
Also Known As: Portage Mutual Insurance
PO Box 340, 749 Saskatchewan Ave. East
Portage la Prairie, MB R1N 3B8
204-857-3415
Fax: 204-239-6655
800-567-7721
www.portagemutual.com
Company Type: Private
J.G. Mitchell, FCIP, CRM, President & CEO
D.G. Pedden, BA, Treasurer & CFO

Primerica Financial Services (Canada) Ltd.
Also Known As: Primerica Canada
Plaza 5
#300, 2000 Argentia Rd.
Mississauga, ON L5N 2R7
905-812-2900
Fax: 905-813-5310
www.primericacanada.ca
Company Type: Private
Glenn J. Williams, Primerica, President
Alison S. Rand, Primerica, Exec. Vice-President & CFO

Primerica Life Insurance Company of Canada
Plaza 5
#300
Mississauga, ON L5N 2R7
905-812-2900
Fax: 905-813-5310
www.primericacanada.ca
Company Type: Private
William A. Kelly, President

Primmum Insurance Company
50 Place Crémazie
Montréal, QC
866-466-5276
www.primmum.com
Other Communications: Claims: 866-725-9722
Company Type: Private
Profile: The following types of insurance are offered: home, automobile, motorcyle, & recreational vehicle.

RBC Insurance Services Inc.
West Tower
6880 Financial Dr.
Mississauga, ON L5N 7Y5
905-606-1000
877-749-7224
www.rbcinsurance.com
Other Communications: Life Insurance: 866-223-7113; Loan & Mortgage: 800-769-2323
Company Type: Private
Profile: The following types of insurance are provided by RBC Insurance: life, health, travel, home, automobile, wealth, & reinsurance. RBC Insurance has clients in Canada, the United States, & internationally.

RBC Life Insurance Company
West Tower
6880 Financial Dr.
Mississauga, ON L5N 7Y5
905-606-1000
www.rbcinsurance.com
Company Type: Private

Reliable Life Insurance Company
Also Known As: Reliable Life
PO Box 557, 100 King St. West
Hamilton, ON L8N 3K9
905-523-5587
Fax: 905-528-8338
800-465-0661
service@reliablelifeinsurance.com
www.reliablelifeinsurance.com
Company Type: Private
Profile: The Canadian federally licensed life insurance company is a specialty life insurer. Reliable Life Insurance Company manufactures & administers customized products for distributors of life, health, disability, child accident, & travel insurance.

RGA Life Reinsurance Company Canada
1981 av McGill College
Montréal, QC H3A 3A8
514-985-5260
Fax: 514-985-3066
800-985-4326
www.rgare.com
Company Type: Private

Royal & Sun Alliance Insurance Company of Canada
10 Wellington St. East
Toronto, ON M5E 1L5
416-366-7511
Fax: 416-367-9869
800-268-8406
info@royalsunalliance.ca
www.royalsunalliance.ca
Company Type: Private
Rowan Saunders, President/CEO
Philip Wilson, Vice-President, Finance
Ed Sikorski, Vice-President, Marketing & Communications
Grace Webster, Vice-President, Business Solutions

Royal & SunAlliance Canada Group
#800, 18 York St.
Toronto, ON M5J 2T8
416-366-7511
Fax: 416-367-9869
800-268-8406
www.rsagroup.ca
Company Type: Private

S&Y Insurance Company
Aviva Canada Inc.
2206 Eglinton Ave. East
Toronto, ON M1L 4S8
800-387-4518
Other Communications: Claims: 866-692-8482
Social Media: www.facebook.com/AvivaCanada
twitter.com/avivacanada
www.linkedin.com/company/aviva-canada
Company Type: Private
Profile: S&Y Insurance Company is a wholly owned company of Aviva Canada Inc.

Saskatchewan Mutual Insurance
279, 3rd Ave. North
Saskatoon, SK S7K 2H8
306-653-4232
Fax: 306-664-1957
800-667-3067
headoffice@saskmutual.com
www.saskmutual.com
Company Type: Private

Scotia Life Insurance Company
Also Known As: ScotiaLife
#400, 100 Yonge St.
Toronto, ON M5H 1H1
800-387-9844
www.scotialifefinancial.com
Company Type: Private
Profile: Scotia Life Insurance Company underwrites & sells ScotiaLife Term Insurance & ScotiaLife Accidental Death Insurance.

Scottish & York Insurance Company
Also Known As: Aviva Scottish & York
2206 Eglinton Ave. East
Toronto, ON M1L 4S8
800-387-4518
www.avivacanada.com
Company Type: Private

Security National Insurance Company
Also Known As: TD Insurance Meloche Monnex
3650 Victoria Park Ave, 9th Fl.
Toronto, ON M2H 3P7
Fax: 417-774-3196
866-337-3314
www.melochemonnex.com
Company Type: Private

SGI Canada Insurance Services Ltd.
#303, 4220 - 98 St. NW
Edmonton, AB T6E 6A1
780-822-1228
Fax: 780-435-1489
877-435-1484
inquiries.ab@sgicanada.ca
www.sgicanada.ca
Other Communications: Toll-Free Fax: 1-877-435-1489
Social Media: www.facebook.com/SGIcommunity
twitter.com/SGItweets
www.linkedin.com/company/sgi_5
Company Type: Private
Andrew R. Cartmell, President & CEO
Jeff Stepan, Chief Financial Officer

Sovereign General Insurance Company
#140, 6700 Macleod Trail SE
Calgary, AB T2H 0L3
403-298-4200
800-661-1652
www.sovereigngeneral.com
Company Type: Private
Rob Wesseling, Chief Operating Officer
416-673-5052
Herb Cline, Vice-President, Finance
493-298-4226

SSQ, Life Insurance Company
PO Box 10500 Stn. Sainte-Foy, , 2525, blvd Laurier
Québec, QC G1V 4H6
418-652-2764
888-900-3457
mutuallife@ssq.ca
www.ssq.ca
Company Type: Private

St. Paul Fire & Marine Insurance Company
PO Box 6, #300, 20 Queen St. West
Toronto, ON M5H 3R3
416-360-8183
800-330-5033
www.travelerscanada.ca
Company Type: Private
Profile: The company is part of The Travelers Companies.

Sun Life Assurance of Canada
877-786-5433
service@sunlife.ca
Social Media: www.linkedin.com/company/sun-life-financial
Company Type: Private

TD Home & Auto Insurance
2161 Yonge St.
Toronto, ON M4S 3A6
866-361-2311
www.tdinsurance.com
Other Communications: Quotes: 800-338-0218; Claims: 866-848-9744
Company Type: Private
Profile: TD Insurance products & services are available through more than 1,000 TD Canada Trust branches, the telephone, & the Internet.

TD Life Insurance
TD Insurance Customer Service
120 Adelaide St. West
Toronto, ON M5H 1T1
877-397-4191
TD.InsuranceLifeAndHealth@td.com
www.tdinsurance.com
Other Communications: New policy information: 877-397-4188
Company Type: Private
Profile: TD Life Insurance products enable clients to provide income for their family, provide for children's education, pay the outstanding balances on mortgages or other debts, set up emergency funds, pay final expenses, or provide a legacy for a charity.

Temple Insurance Company
390 Bay St., 21st Fl.
Toronto, ON M5H 2Y2
416-364-2851
Fax: 416-361-1163
877-364-2851
www.templeinsurance.ca
Company Type: Private
Roderick Hampson, Sr. Vice-President & COO
416-681-6911, rhampson@templeins.com

Traders General Insurance Company
Also Known As: Aviva Traders
c/o Aviva Canada Inc.
2206 Eglinton Ave. East
Toronto, ON M1L 4S8
800-387-4518
www.avivacanada.com
Social Media: www.facebook.com/AvivaCanada
twitter.com/avivacanada
Company Type: Private
Profile: Traders General Insurance Company is a wholly owned company of Aviva Canada Inc.. Traders delivers Aviva products & services, such as home & automobile insurance. The company serves large & mid-sized groups throughout Canada.

Trafalgar Insurance Company of Canada
#1500, 700 University Ave.
Toronto, ON M5G 0A1
trafalgarinsurance@intact.net
www.trafalgarinsurance.ca
Company Type: Private
Profile: Drivers over the age of fify are offered care & home insurance through Trafalgar Insurance Company of Canda.

Transamerica Life Canada
5000 Yonge St.
Toronto, ON M2N 7J8
416-673-9865
800-846-5970
lifeservices@transamerica.ca
www.transamerica.ca

Company Type: Private

Unifund Assurance Company
PO Box 12049, 10 Factory Lane
St. John's, NL A1C 6H5
709-737-1500
Fax: 709-737-1580
888-737-1689
unifund@unifund.ca
www.unifund.ca
Company Type: Private

Wawanesa Life Insurance Company
#400, 200 Main St.
Winnipeg, MB R3C 1A8
204-985-3940
Fax: 204-985-3872
888-997-9965
life@wawanesa.com
www.wawanesalife.com
Company Type: Private

Wawanesa Mutual Insurance Company
#700, 200 Main St.
Winnipeg, MB R3C 1A8
204-985-3811
Fax: 204-942-7257
www.wawanesa.com
Company Type: Private

Western Life Assurance
Administrative Office
PO Box 3300, 717 Portage Ave., 4th Fl.
Winnipeg, MB R3C 5S2
204-784-6900
Fax: 204-783-6913
888-647-5433
info@westernlife.com
www.westernlifeassurance.net
Other Communications: High River, AB, Head Office: 877-452-4356
Company Type: Private
Profile: The western Canadian insurance brokerage offers both individual & group insurance.

Machinery

CE Franklin Ltd.
#1800, 635 - 8th Ave. SW
Calgary, AB T2P 3M3
403-531-5600
Fax: 403-234-7698
ho-calgary@cefranklin.com
www.cefranklin.com
Company Type: Public
Ticker Symbol: CFT / TSX, NASDAQ
Profile: CE Franklin Ltd. provides products & services to the energy industry in Canada. Products include production equipment, pipes, valves, fittings, & flanges.
Michael West, President & Chief Executive Officer
Derren Newell, Chief Financial Officer
Merv Day, Senior Vice-President, Business Development
Rod Tatham, Vice-President, Operations
Kelsey Sheptak, Manager, Quality, Health, Safety, & the Environment
ksheptak@cefranklin.com

Exco Technologies Limited
Corporate Office
130 Spy Ct.
Markham, ON L3R 5H6
905-477-3065
Fax: 905-477-2449
excotech@compuserve.com
www.excocorp.com
Company Type: Public
Ticker Symbol: XTC / TSX
Profile: Exco Technologies Limited serves the automotive, die-cast, & extrusion industries by providing innovative technologies. The company employs approximately 2,100 people.
Brian A. Robbins, President & Chief Executive Officer
Lawrence C. Robbins, President, Alu-Die Division
Paul Riganelli, Chief Financial Officer & Vice-President, Finance

Husky Injection Molding Systems Ltd.
500 Queen St. South
Bolton, ON L7E 5S5
905-951-5000
Fax: 905-951-5337
888-884-8759
info@husky.ca
www.husky.ca
Company Type: Public
John Galt, President/CEO
George Halatsis, CFO & Vice-President, Finance
Bruce Catoen, Vice-President, Automated Systems

IBM Canada Ltd.
3600 Steeles Ave. East
Markham, ON L3R 9Z7
905-316-5000
Fax: 905-316-2535
800-426-4968
canada_int@vnet.ibm.com
www.ibm.com/ca/
Company Type: Private
Dan Fortin, President, IBM Canada Ltd.
Lynn Belo, CFO

Logan International Inc.
Canadian Headquarters
#850, 635 - 8th Ave. SW
Calgary, AB T2P 3M3
403-930-6810
Fax: 403-930-6811
www.loganinternationalinc.com
Company Type: Public
Ticker Symbol: LII / TSX
Profile: In 2010, Destiny Resource Services Corp. & Logan Holdings, Inc. merged. During the same year, Source Energy Tool Services Inc. & Complete Oil Tools Inc. were purchased. In 2011, Logan International Inc. purchased Scope Production Development & Kline Oilfield Services, Inc.
Logan International's Canadian business consists of Scope Production Development, Xtend Energy Services, & Logan Completion Systems. The company provides the following products: proprietary & patented products & services for production optimization in heavy oil wells; tools for horizontal drilling; & multi-zonal completion technology & conventional completion products.
David Barr, Chief Executive Officer
Robert Russell, President, Canadian Operations
Lawrence D. Keister, Chief Financial Officer & Corporate Secretary
larry.keister@loganinternational.com

Pitney Bowes Canada Ltd.
#200, 314 Harwood Ave.
Ajax, ON L1S 2J1
800-672-6937
MrBowes.Canada@pb.com
www.pitneybowes.ca
Social Media: www.facebook.com/group.php?gid=88676067555
Company Type: Private
Profile: Pitney Bowes Canada's activities focus upon mailing technology. Products include innovations that copy, scan, print, fax, insert, & seal. With Pitney Bowes' services, companies are able to manage the flow of information, mail, documents, & packages.
Deepak Chopra, President
William Checkley, Vice-President & General Manager, Pitney Bowes Management Services Canada
Jacques L'Africain, Vice-President & General Manager, Document Imaging Solutions & Customer Service
William Mackrell, Vice-President & General Manager, Marketing & Mailing Solutions
Gary Thomson, Vice-President & General Manager, Global Financial Services

Strongco Corporation
1640 Enterprise Rd.
Mississauga, ON L4W 4L4
905-565-1899
Fax: 905-565-1907
info@strongco.com
www.strongco.com
Company Type: Public
Ticker Symbol: SQP / TSX
Profile: The large multiline mobile equipment dealer sells, rents, & services equipment. Equipment is used in the following sectors: mining, oil & gas, forestry, construction, municipal, & waste management. Operations take place in Canada & the United States.
Robert Dryburgh, President & Chief Executive Officer
905-565-3802, rdryburgh@strongco.com
Stuart Welch, President, Chadwick-Baross, Inc.
J. David Wood, Chief Financial Officer & Vice-President
jdwood@strongco.com
Leonard V. Phillips, CA, Corporate Secretary & Vice-President, Administration
905-565-3840, lphillips@strongco.com
Peter Duperrouzel, Manager, Information Services

Tesco Corporation
5616 - 80th Ave. SE
Calgary, AB T2C 4N5
403-723-7902
Fax: 403-723-7826
investor@tescocorp.com
www.tescocorp.com
Other Communications: Health, Safety & Environment Team: qhse@tescocorp.com
Company Type: Public
Ticker Symbol: TESO / NASDAQ
Profile: Tesco Corporation specializes in the design, manufacture, & service of technology. The company's technology based solutions are used in the upstream energy industry.
Julio M. Quintana, President & Chief Executive Officer
Robert L. Kayl, Chief Financial Officer & Senior Vice-President
Jeff Foster, Sr. Vice-President, Operations
Keith M. Lowley, Vice-President, Manufacturing
James A. Lank, General Counsel & Corporate Secretary

Toromont Industries Ltd.
Executive Offices
PO Box 5511, 3131 Hwy. 7 West
Concord, ON L4K 1B7
416-667-5511
Fax: 416-667-5555
pjewer@toromont.com
www.toromont.com
Company Type: Public
Ticker Symbol: TIH / TSX
Profile: The company is engaged in the design, engineering, & sale of specialized equipment & other heavy equipment. Its business segments are the Equipment Group & CIMCO. The Equipment Group include rental operations. CIMCO is engage in the engineering & installation of industrial & recreational refrigeration systems.
Toromont Industries has implemented environmental practices, such as technology to recycle energy, reduce greenhouse gas emissions, & cleanse oil of contaminants.
Robert M. Ogilvie, Chair & Chief Executive Officer
Paul R. Jewer, CFO & Vice-President, Finance
Michael P. Cuddy, Vice-President & Chief Information Officer

Wenzel Downhole Tools Ltd. (WZL)
#1000, 717 - 7th Ave. SW
Calgary, AB T2P 0Z3
403-262-3050
Fax: 403-265-8154
info@wenzel-downhole.com
www.downhole.com
Other Communications: Primary Manufacturing Centre, Edmonton: 780-440-4220
Company Type: Public
Ticker Symbol: WZL / TSX
Profile: Wenzel Downhole Tools Ltds. manufactures, sells, & rents drilling tools. Products are used by companies involved in oil & gas exploration. In addition to its Canadian facilities in Alberta, Wenzel Downhole Tools also has offices in the United States & Germany.
Ken Hughes, MPA, ICD.D, Chief Executive Officer
khughes@wenzel-downhole.com
William T. Spence, CA, Chief Financial Officer
Mark Heaton, Vice-President & General Manager, Canadian Operations
mheaton@wenzel-downhole.com
Ron Patterson, Vice-President
rpatterson@wenzel-downhole.com
Tony Curtis, Contact, Health & Safety
tcurtis@wenzel-downhole.com

Westport Innovations Inc.
#101, 1750 West 75th Ave.
Vancouver, BC V6P 6G2
604-718-2000
Fax: 604-718-2001
info@westport.com
www.westport.com
Company Type: Public
Ticker Symbol: WPT / TSX, NASDAQ
David R. Demers, CEO
Elaine Wong, CFO & Vice-President, Finance
J. Michael Gallagher, Ph.D., President
Patric Ouellette, CTO & Vice-President, Research

Wolseley Canada
880 Laurentian Dr.
Burlington, ON L7N 3V6
905-335-7436
corporate.communications@wolseleyinc.ca
www.wolseleyinc.ca
Company Type: Private

Xerox Canada Inc.
5650 Yonge St.
Toronto, ON M2M 4G7
416-229-3769
Fax: 416-229-6826
800-275-9376
www.xerox.ca
Other Communications: Service: 800-275-9376
Company Type: Public
Profile: To improve work processes, Xerox Canada provides document technologies, products, & services. The company has created waste-free products, & built in waste-free facilities, as part of its continuing remanufacturing initiatives.
Anne Mulcahy, Chair/CEO
Lawrence Zimmerman, Exec. Vice-President/CFO

Manufacturing, Miscellaneous

AirBoss of America Corp.
16441 Yonge St.
Newmarket, ON L3X 2G8
905-751-1188
Fax: 905-751-1101
info@airbossofamerica.com
www.airbossofamerica.com
Company Type: Public
Ticker Symbol: BOS / TSX
Profile: The company is a developer, manufacturer, & seller of rubber compounds & specialty rubber moulded products. Products are used in the industrial, transportation, & defense industries.
R.L. (Bob) Hagerman, President & Chief Exexcutive Officer
Earl Laurie, President, AirBoss Defense Products Division
450-546-0283
Stephen W. Richards, Chief Financial Officer & Vice-President, Finance
Robert Dodd, Executive Vice-President, AirBoss Rubber Compounding
John Tomins, Vice-President, Sales & Marketing
Yvan Ambeault, Director, Manufacturing Operations, AirBoss Engineered Products

ATS Automation Tooling Systems Inc.
Building 2
730 Fountain St. North
Cambridge, ON N3H 4R7
519-653-6500
Fax: 519-653-6533
info@atsautomation.com
www.atsautomation.com
Other Communications: Investor Relations: investor@atsautomation.com
Company Type: Public
Ticker Symbol: ATA / TSX
Profile: Established in 1978, ATS Automation Tooling Systems serves the automation systems needs of companies throughout the world. ATS Automation is also involved in the solar energy industry, through its solar business in Ontario. Approximately 2,300 people are employed at ATS Automation manufacturing facilities. Manufacturing takes place in Canada, the United States, Europe, southeast Asia, & China.
Anthony Caputo, Chief Executive Officer
Maria Perrella, Chief Financial Officer
Carl Galloway, Vice-President & Treasurer

Avcorp Industries Inc.
10025 River Way
Delta, BC V4G 1M7
604-582-1137
Fax: 604-582-2620
info@avcorp.com
www.avcorp.com
Other Communications: New Business Inquiries, Phone: 604-587-4883
Company Type: Public
Ticker Symbol: AVP / TSX
Profile: Avcorp Industries is a designer & builder for aircraft companies. The company specializes in custome solutions for airframe structures. More than 500 people are employed at Avcorp Industries' facilities.
Mark van Rooij, Chief Executive Officer
Amadeep Kaler, Vice-President, Operations
Ed Merlo, Vice-President, Finance
Steven Archer, Director, Business Development

Azure Dynamics Corporation
#1210, 155 University Ave.
Toronto, ON M5H 3B7
416-367-0220
Fax: 416-367-9591
info@azuredynamics.com
www.azuredynamics.com
Company Type: Public
Ticker Symbol: AZD / TSX
Scott T. Harrison, Chief Executive Officer
Daniel P. Renzella, Sr. Vice-President & CFO, Finance

Brampton Brick Limited
225 Wanless Dr.
Brampton, ON L7A 1E9
905-840-1011
Fax: 905-840-1535
investor.relations@bramptonbrick.com
www.bramptonbrick.com
Other Communications: Sales: sales@bramptonbrick.com
Company Type: Public
Ticker Symbol: BBLA / TSX
Profile: Brampton Brick Limited manufactures clay brick, concrete masonry products, concrete interlocking paving stones, retaining walls, & enviro products. Products are used for residential construction & industrial & institutional building projects. Markets served include Ontario, Québec, & the northeastern & midwestern United States.
Universal Resource Recovery operates a waste composting facility in Welland, Ontario.

Jeffrey G. Kerbel, President & Chief Executive Officer
Trevor M. Sandler, Chief Financial Officer & Vice-President, Finance
David R. Carter, Executive Vice-President
J. Brad Duke, Vice-President, Manufacturing, Clay Brick
George Housh, Vice-President, Manufacturing, Concrete Products
Marilia Macias, Controller

Cascades Boxboard Group
1061 rue Parent
Saint-Bruno, QC J3V 6R7
450-461-8600
Fax: 450-461-8636
www.cascades.com
Company Type: Private

Cascades Specialty Products
1061 rue Parent
Saint-Bruno, QC J3V 6R7
819-478-5983
martin_taillon@cascades.com
www.cascades.com
Other Communications: 514-923-1268 (cell)
Company Type: Private

Cascades Tissue Group
77, blvd Marie-Victorin
Candiac, QC J5R 1C3
450-444-6400
Fax: 450-444-6444
800-361-4070
question@cascades.com
www.ctgebiz.cascades.com
Company Type: Private

Casco Inc.
#600, 45 The West Mall
Toronto, ON M9C 0A1
866-422-7201
customer.service@casco.ca
www.casco.ca
Company Type: Private
Profile: Casco Inc. produces food ingredients, & industrial additives. The company serves the following markets: food & beverage makers, health & personal care products, animal nutrition companies, & industrial manufacturers

CCL Industries Inc.
#500, 105 Gordon Baker Rd.
Toronto, ON M2H 3P8
416-756-8500
Fax: 416-756-8555
ccl@cclind.com
www.cclind.com
Company Type: Public
Ticker Symbol: CCL / TSX
Profile: CCL Industries Inc. is engaged in the development & provision of specialty packaging for producers of consumer brands. Products include labelling, plastic tubes, & aluminum containers. CCL serves customers in Canada, the United States, & Mexico.
Geoffrey T. Martin, President & Chief Executive Officer
Sean Washcuk, Chief Financial Officer & Senior Vice-President
416-756-8526
Janis M. Wade, Senior Vice-President, Human Resources & Corporate Communications
Bohdan I. Sirota, Senior Vice-President, General Counsel, & Secretary

Lalitha Vaidyanathan, Senior Vice-President, Finance, Information Technology, & Administration
Susan V. Snelgrove, Vice-President, Risk & Environmental Management

CGC Inc.
350 Burnhamthorpe Rd. West, 5th Fl.
Mississauga, ON L5B 3J1
905-803-5600
Fax: 905-803-5688
800-565-6607
www.cgcinc.com
Company Type: Private
Christopher Griffin, President
D. Rick Lowes, Vice-President/CFO & Treasurer

Compass Group Canada
#400, 5560 Explorer Dr.
Mississauga, ON L4W 5M3
905-568-4636
Fax: 905-568-9392
800-465-2203
www2.compass-canada.com
Company Type: Private

Creation Technologies
Headquarters
3939 North Fraser Way
Burnaby, BC V5J 5J2
604-430-4336
800-736-1271
sales@creationtech.com
www.creationtech.com
Other Communications: Investor & Media Information, Phone: 604-430-4336
Social Media: www.facebook.com/creation.technologies
twitter.com/creationtech
Company Type: Private
Profile: Creation Technologies is an EMS provider. It serves companies that require complex electronic manufacturing solutions.
Arthur Tymos, President & Chief Executive Officer
Douglas Besse, Chief Information Officer & Executive Vice-President, Global Supply Chain & Asian Operations
Darryl Catellier, Chief Architect & Leader, Business Systems
Mike Walsh, Chief Financial Officer

CVTech Group Inc./ Groupe CVTech
1975, rue Jean-Bérimens Michaud
Drummondville, QC J2C 0H2
819-479-7771
Fax: 819-479-8887
www.cvtech.ca
Company Type: Public
Ticker Symbol: CVT / TSX
Profile: Through its subsidiaries, CVTech Group designs, manufactures, & sells continuously variable power transmission systems. Thirau Ltd., one of the company's subsidiaries, is a general contracting firm that specializes in the maintenance of transmission & distribution lines, electrical power houses, & substations. CVTech employs over 1,400 employees.
André Laramée, Chief Executive Officer, M.B.A.
a.laramee@cvtech.ca
Mario Trahan, Chief Financial Officer, C.M.A.
m.trahan@cvtech.ca
Alain Charest, M.B.A., Eng., Vice-President, Vehicles Division
Alain Gagné, Vice-President, Energy Division

Day4 Energy Inc.
Corporate Headquarters, Glenwood Facility
8168 Glenwood Dr.
Burnaby, BC V3N 5E9
604-297-0444
Fax: 604-297-0445
www.day4energy.com
Other Communications: Day4 Energy Italia S.r.l., Italy, Phone: +39. 0249539100
Social Media: www.facebook.com/day4energy
twitter.com/day4energy
www.linkedin.com/company/day4-energy-inc.
Company Type: Public
Ticker Symbol: DFE / TSX
Profile: Day4 Energy Inc. was founded in 2001. The company provides solar photovoltaic products & solutions for residential, commercial, & utility scale applications. Day4Energy focuses on the following areas: solar equipment, Day4 solarSYSTEMS, solar modules, & solar projects.

Dorel Industries Inc.
#300, 1255, av Greene
Montréal, QC H3Z 2A4
514-934-3034
Fax: 514-934-9379
info@dorel.com; ir@dorel.com
www.dorel.com
Other Communications: Investor Relations Phone: 514-934-3034
Company Type: Public
Ticker Symbol: DII.A, DII.B / TSX
Profile: Established in 1962, Dorel Industries Inc. designs, manufactures, & markets juvenile products, bicycles, & home furnishings. The company has facilities in seventeen countries, & sells its products throughout the world.
Martin Schwartz, President/CEO
Hani Basile, Group President/CEO, Juvenile
Robert P. Baird, Jr., President/CEO, Recreation & Leisure
Norman Braunstein, President/CEO, Home Furnishings
Jeffrey Schwartz, Exec. Vice-President/CFO & Secretary
Alan Schwartz, Exec. Vice-President, Operations
Rick Leckner, Contact, Media & Investor Relations
514-731-0000

Dynex Power Inc.
Doddington Rd.
Lincoln
power_solutions@dynexsemi.com
www.dynexsemi.com
Other Communications: Phone: +44 (0)1522 500500; Fax: +44 (0)1522 500550
Company Type: Public
Ticker Symbol: DNX / TSX Venture
Profile: Dynex is a designer & manufacturer of bipolar semiconductors, insulated bipolar transistor modules, radiation hard silico-on-sapphire integrated circuits, & electronic assemblies. Products are used in power electronic applications. Dynex Semiconductor Ltd. holds accrediation for the Quality Management Systems standard ISO 9001:2008 & the Environmental Management Systems standard ISO 14001:2004.

Paul Taylor, President & Chief Executive Officer
Bob Lockwood, Chief Financial Officer

Electrolux Canada
5855 Terry Fox Way
Mississauga, ON L5V 3E4
904-813-7700
Fax: 905-813-2784
800-282-2886
www.electrolux.ca
Company Type: Private
Profile: Electrolux Canada is a supplier of cleaning products, such as lightweight, upright, & central vacuums.

Empire Industries Ltd.
717 Jarvis Ave.
Winnipeg, MB R2W 3B4
204-589-9300
Fax: 204-582-8057
www.empind.com
Company Type: Public
Ticker Symbol: EIL / TSX Venture
Profile: Empire Industries Ltd. is a designer & manufacturer of various industrial products & amusement park rides. The company is also engaged in erecting structural steel & offering structural & construction engineering services. Empire Industries Ltd. has a Health, Safety, & Environmental Policy, & adheres to regulations.
Some of Empire Industries Ltd.'s subsidiaries include the following: Dynamic Structures, Empire Construction Services, Empire Iron Works, George Third & Son, Hopkins Steel Works, Lemax Machine & Welding, Parr Metal Fabricators, Sorge's Welding Ltd., Somerset Engineering, Tornado Technologies Inc., & Ward Industrial Equipment.
Guy Nelson, B.Comm., MBA, Chair/CEO
416-366-7977, gnelson@empind.com
Bill Rollins, President, Tornado Technologies Inc.
Brett Third, President, George Third & Son Ltd. & Dynamic Structures
Campbell McIntyre, CA, Chief Financial Officer, Empire Industries Ltd. & President, Empire Iron Works
Trevor Heisler, Contact, Investors Relations

Enablence Technologies Inc.
Corporate Headquarters
#504, 1 St. Clair Ave. East
Toronto, ON M4T 2V7
647-729-1605
Fax: 647-729-1619
info@enablence.com
www.enablence.com
Social Media: twitter.com/enablence
www.linkedin.com/company/enablence-technologies
Company Type: Public
Ticker Symbol: ENA / TSX Venture
Profile: Enablence Technologies Inc. is a designer, manufacturer, & seller of optical components & subsytems. The company's patented technologies are used in the production of photonics components & broadband subsystems. The telecommunications access, metro, & long-haul markets are served.
Tim Thorsteinson, Chief Executive Officer
Jacob Sun, Ph.D., President, Optical Components & Subsystems Division
David Toews, Chief Financial Officer

General Donlee Canada Inc.
9 Fenmar Dr.
Toronto, ON M9L 1L5
416-743-4417
Fax: 416-746-8998
info@generaldonlee.com
www.generaldonlee.com
Other Communications: General Gear, Phone: 416-743-4410
Company Type: Public
Ticker Symbol: GDI / TSX
Profile: General Donlee manufactures precision-machined products. Products are used by power generation industries, general & commercial aerospace industries, & the military
Garen Mikirditsian, Chief Executive Officer & Chief Financial Officer
Bruce Van Nus, Chief Operating Officer
Dennis Lontok, Controller

Global Alumina Corp.
277 Park Ave., 40th Fl.
New York, NY 10172 USA
212-351-0000
info@globalalumina.com
www.globalalumina.com
Company Type: Public
Ticker Symbol: GLA / TSX, Frankfurt
Profile: Incorporated in New Brunswick in 2004, Global Alumina Corp. is involved in alumina production & sales. It is participating in a joint venture to develop a mine, an alumina refinery, & associated infrastructure in the Republic of Guinea's bauxite-rich region. Global Alumina Corp.'s wholly owned subsidiary is Global Alumina International, Ltd.
Bruce J. Wrobel, Chief Executive Officer
Graham Morrey, President
Michael J. Cella, Chief Financial Officer & Senior Vice-President
cella@globalalumina.com

GMAC of Canada
Main Mailing Dept. CA1-002-002
1908 Colonel Sam Dr.
Oshawa, ON L1H 8P7
800-463-7483
www.gm.ca
Company Type: Private

Guest-Tek Interactive Entertainment
#240, 3030-3rd Ave. NE
Calgary, AB T2A 6T7
403-509-1010
Fax: 403-509-1011
866-509-1010
info@guest-tek.com
www.guest-tek.com
Company Type: Private
Profile: Guest-Tek helps hotels organize and provide a high-speed internet system to their rooms.

H. Paulin & Co., Limited
Head Office
55 Milne Ave.
Toronto, ON M1L 4N3
416-694-3351
Fax: 416-694-1869
investor@hpaulin.com
www.hpaulin.com
Other Communications: Paulin USA Office, Phone: 216-433-7633
Company Type: Public
Ticker Symbol: PAP / TSX
Profile: H. Paulin & Co. Limited is a manufacturer & merchandiser of nuts, screws, bolts, & fluid system components. The compnay serves the automotive, industrial, & retail hardware markets. H. Paulin & Co., Limited is an ISO 9001:2000 certified company.
Richard C. Paulin, President
Murray Mateyk, Chief Financial Officer

Hammond Manufacturing Company Limited
394 Edinburgh Rd. North
Guelph, ON N1H 1E5
519-822-2960
Fax: 519-982-2898
ir@hammfg.com; sales@hammfg.com; careers@
www.hammondmfg.com
Other Communications: Datacom Sales: 877-535-3282; Electronic Sales: 519-886-7170
Company Type: Public
Ticker Symbol: HMM.A / TSX
Profile: Hammond Manufacturing Company Limited was established in 1917. Products are manufactured for the electronic & electrical products industry. Examples of products manufactured by Hammond Manufacturing include small cases, racks, outlet strips, metallic & non-metallic enclosures, electronic transformers, & surge suppressors. Facilities are located in Canada, the United States, & Europe.
Robert F. Hammond, Chair & Chief Executive Officer
Alexander Stirling, Chief Financial Officer & Secretary

Hanwei Energy Services Corp.
#902, 595 Howe St.
Vancouver, BC V6C 2T5
604-685-2239
Fax: 604-677-5579
info@hanweienergy.com
www.hanweienergy.com
Company Type: Public
Ticker Symbol: HE / TSX
Profile: Hanwei Energy Services develops, manufactures, & sells high pressure fiberglass reinforced plastic products. Products are used mainly in the global energy sector. The company owns interest in Daqing Harvest Longwall High Pressure Pipe Co. Ltd. in China.
Fulai Lang, President/CEO
Rick Yucai Huang, Chief Financial Officer
Kim Oishi, Sr. Vice-President, Financial & Business Development
416-804-9228, koishi@hanweienergy.com

Hewitt Equipment
5001 Trans-Canada Highway
Pointe-Claire, QC H9R 1B8
514-630-3100
800-363-6785
pointeclaire@hewitt.ca
www.hewitt.ca
Company Type: Private

Héroux-Devtek Inc.
Tour est
#658, 1111, rue Saint-Charles ouest
Longueuil, QC J4K 5G4
450-679-3330
ir@herouxdevtek.com
www.herouxdevtek.com
Other Communications: Aerostructure Sales: saleshda@herouxdevtek.com
Company Type: Public
Ticker Symbol: HRX
Profile: Héroux-Devtek Inc. develops, designs, manufactures, repairs, & overhauls systems & components. The company has three divisions: The Landing Gear Division; The Aerostructure Division; & The Industrial Division. Products are used in the aerospace market in both the commercial & military sectors, & in the industrial market for power generation & other machinery applications.
Héroux-Devtek requires management & employees to commit to a structured Environmental Management System.
Gilles Labbé, President & Chief Executive Officer
Réal Bélanger, Chief Financial Officer & Executive Vice-President
Stéphane Arsenault, Vice-President, Control & Information Technology
Martin Brassard, Vice-President & General Manager, Landing Gear
Gabriel Duval, Vice-President, Corporate Affairs
Michael L. Meshay, Vice-President & General Manager, Industrial Products
Richard Rosenjack, Vice-President & General Manager, Aerostructure

INSCAPE Corporation
Corporate Headquarters
67 Toll Rd.
Holland Landing, ON L9N 1H2
905-836-7676
Fax: 905-836-6000
info@inscapesolutions.com
www.inscapesolutions.com
Social Media: www.facebook.com/InscapeCorporation
twitter.com/InscapeCorp
www.linkedin.com/companies/inscape
Company Type: Public
Ticker Symbol: INQ / TSX
Profile: INSCAPE Corporation designs, manufactures, & markets office systems & storage & wall solutions for commercial workplaces. Office & production facilities are located in Canada & the United States. INSCAPE Corporation is an ISO 9001 registered company.
Rod Turgeon, President & Chief Executive Officer
Kent Smallwood, CA, Chief Financial Officer
905-836-7676, Fax: 905-836-5037

L'Oréal Canada
1500, rue University
Montréal, QC H3A 3S7
514-287-4800
www.en.loreal.ca
Company Type: Private

Lear Canada Ltd.
PO Box 9758, 530 Manitou Dr.
Kitchener, ON N2G 4C2
519-895-1600
Fax: 519-895-3248
www.lear.com
Company Type: Private
Robert E. Rossiter, President/CEO, Lear Corporation
Matthew Simoncini, CFO, Lear Corporation

Magna International Inc.
337 Magna Dr.
Aurora, ON L4G 7K1
905-726-2462
magna.IR@magna.com
www.magna.com
Social Media: www.facebook.com/MagnaInternational
twitter.com/MagnaInt
Company Type: Public
Ticker Symbol: MG / TSX, NYSE
Profile: The diversified automotive supplier designs, develops, & manufactures automotive systems, assemblies, modules, & components. Magna also engineers & assembles complete vehicles to sell to original equipment manufacturers of cars & trucks. The company's geographic segments are North America, Europe, Asia, South America, & Africa.
Siegfried Wolf, Co-CEO
Donald J. Walker, Co-CEO
Vincent J. Galifi, Exec. Vice-President/CFO
Herbert Demel, Chief Operating Officer, Vehicles & Powertrain
Tom Skudutis, Chief Operating Officer, Exteriors & Interiors
Jeffrey O. Palmer, Exec. Vice-President & Chief Legal Officer
Louis Tonelli, Vice-President, Investor Relations
Donald Resnick, Chair, Health & Safety & Environmental Committee

McCoy Corporation
#301, 9618 - 42 Ave.
Edmonton, AB T6E 5Y4
780-453-8451
Fax: 780-453-8756
888-377-0427
info@mccoyglobal.com
www.mccoyglobal.com
Other Communications: Drilling & Completions: 780-453-3277; Trailers: 866-657-2662
Company Type: Public
Ticker Symbol: MCB / TSX
Profile: McCoy Corporation serves the global energy industry. The company's two business segments are Energy Products & Services & Mobile Solutions. Operations are based in western Canada & the United States Gulf Coast.
Jim Rakievich, President & Chief Executive Officer
780-453-8707, jrakievich@mccoycorporation.ca
Milica Stolic, Chief Financial Officer
780-453-8760, mstolic@mccoycorporation.ca
Ted Redmond, Exec. Vice-President, Energy Products & Services
780-377-4002, tredmond@mccoycorporation.ca
Shawn Johns, Vice-President, Truck & Trailer Products & Services
780-465-8485, sjohns@mccoycorporation.ca
Andy McEachern, Vice-President, Trailer Manufacturing
250-487-4010, amceachern@mccoycorporation.ca
Peggy Robertson, Corporate Secretary & Vice-President, Corporate Affairs
780-453-8762, probertson@mccoycorporation.ca
Charlie Chmura, Manager, Information Technology
780-453-8752, cchmura@mccoycorporation.ca
Norma Rattray, Manager, Compliance & Financial Processes
780-377-4005, nrattray@mccoycorporation.ca
Tony Savage, Manager, Q.S.E
780-465-8479, tsavage@mccoycorporation.ca

MEG International Services Ltd. (MISL)
#1, 1850 Hartley Ave.
Coquitlam, BC V3K 7A1
604-540-6044
Fax: 604-540-6099
866-585-6044
info@ctfmeg.com; sales@ctfmeg.com; suppor
www.ctf.com
Company Type: Private
Profile: CTF MEG's magnetoencephalography instruments are operated by research & clinical institutions throughout the world. MEG International Services Ltd. provides on-site & remote services to set up & give ongoing support for MEG systems.

MEGA Brands Inc.
4505, rue Hickmore
Montréal, QC H4T 1K4
514-333-3339
800-465-6342
info_invest@megabrands.com
www.megabrands.com
Social Media: www.facebook.com/megabloks
twitter.com/megabrands
Company Type: Public
Ticker Symbol: MB / TSX
Profile: Incorporated in 1983, MEGA Brands Inc. sells construction toys, games, puzzles, arts, crafts, & stationery. Trademarks include Mega Bloks, MEGA logo, MEGA Puzzles, MEGA Games, Rose Art, & Board Dudes.
Marc Bertrand, President & Chief Executive Officer
Peter Ferrante, Chief Financial Officer & Vice-President, Finance
Mark Girgis, Corporate Secretary & Vice-President, Legal Affairs
Geneviève LeBrun, Vice-President, Marketing & Business Development

Norampac Inc.
1061 rue Parent
Saint-Bruno, QC J3V 6R7
450-461-8600
Fax: 450-461-8636
www.cascades.com
Company Type: Private

Nordion Inc.
447 March Rd.
Ottawa, ON K2K 1X8
613-592-2790
Fax: 613-592-6937
800-267-6211
investor.relations@nordion.com; service@n
www.nordion.com
Social Media: www.facebook.com/Nordion
twitter.com/NordionInc
www.linkedin.com/company/nordion
Company Type: Public
Ticker Symbol: NDN / TSX; NDZ / NYSE
Profile: Nordion Inc. provides products & services to the global health science market. Products include medial isotopes & sterilization technologies. The company employs over 500 people at its three locations.
Steve M. West, Chief Executive Officer
Peter Dans, Chief Financial Officer
Christopher Ashwood, Senior Vice-President, Corporate Services
Jill Chitra, Senior Vice-President, Quality & Regulatory Affairs
Scott McIntosh, Senior Vice-President, Operations
Tamra Benjamin, Vice-President, Public & Government Relations
Shelley Maclean, Manager, External & Internal Communications
shelley.maclean@nordion.com

Noveko International
Head Office
#1900, 1155 boul René-Lévesque ouest
Montréal, QC H3B 4V2
514-875-0606
Fax: 514-875-0660
877-874-0606
info@noveko.com; service@noveko.com
www.noveko.com
Company Type: Public
Ticker Symbol: EKO / TSX
Profile: Founded in 2002, Noveko International Inc. provides solutions for the medical & environmental fields through its wholly owned operating subsidiaries. Products include the following: filtration fabrics, air filters, antimicrobial surgical masks, antiseptic hand sanitizers, & real-time ultrasound scanners for veterinary & human medicine.
André Leroux, Chair & Chief Executive Officer
Alain Bolduc, President & Chief Operating Officer
Ginette Gagné, Chief Financial Officer & Senior Vice-President
Alain Falardeau, Senior Vice-President, Legal Affairs

Valérie Leoux, Secretary & Vice-President, Corporate Affairs
Chantal Vennat, Director, Investor Relations & Corporate Communications
cvennat@noveko.com

Novelis Inc.
191 Evans Ave.
Toronto, ON M8Z 1J5
416-506-6770
Fax: 404-814-4269
www.novelis.com
Company Type: Private

Olymel Société en Commandité
#400, 2200 ave Pratte
St-Hyacinthe, QC J2S 4B6
450-771-0400
Fax: 514-858-9000
www.olymel.com
Company Type: Private

Opta Minerals Inc.
Corporate Office
PO Box 260, 407 Parkside Dr.
Waterdown, ON L0R 2H0
905-689-7361
Fax: 905-689-3915
888-689-6661
info@optaminerals.com
www.optaminerals.com
Other Communications: Investors: investor_relations@optaminerals.com
Company Type: Public
Ticker Symbol: OPM / TSX
Profile: Opta Minerals Inc. is engaged in the recycling, manufacturing, production, & distribution of industrial minerals, specialty sands, & related products. The company's products are used mainly in the following industries: steel, foundry, roof shingle granules, loose abrasive cleaning, & municipal water filtration.
Opta Minerals production facilities are located in Ontario, Saskatchewan, Québec, Michigan, New York, Louisiana, Virginia, Maryland, South Carolina, Indiana, Ohio, Florida, & Texas, as well as France & the Slovak Republic.
David Kruse, Chief Executive Officer
Peter Fryters, Chief Financial Officer

Paterson Global Foods
333 Main St., 22nd Fl.
Winnipeg, MB R3C 4E2
204-956-2090
info@patersonglobalfoods.com
www.patersonglobalfoods.com
Company Type: Private

PolyOne Canada Inc.
#245, 5915 Airport Rd.
Mississauga, ON L4V 1T1
905-673-1213
Fax: 905-673-8369
www.polyone.com
Social Media: twitter.com/PolyOne
Company Type: Private
Stephen D. Newlin, Chair, President & CEO, PolyOne Corporation

Premier Tech Ltd.
International Corporate Office
1, av Premier
Rivière-du-Loup, QC G5R 6C1
418-867-8883
Fax: 418-862-6642
info@premiertech.com
www.premiertech.com
Company Type: Private
Ticker Symbol: PTL
Profile: Premier Tech develops, manufactures, & markets innovative solutions in the following areas: horticulture & agriculture, environmental technologies, & industrial equipment.
Bernard Bélanger, Chair & Chief Executive Officer
Jean Belanger, President & Chief Operating Officer
Christian Dollo, President, Premier Horticulture
André Noreau, President, Industrial Equipment Group
Henri Ouellet, President, Environmental Technologies Group
Martin Noël, Chief Financial Officer & Senior Vice-President
Germain Ouellet, Corporate Secretary & Senior Vice-President, Human Resources
Line C. Lamarre, Vice-President, Organizational Development
Pierre Talbot, Vice-President, Innovation

Prism Medical Ltd.
#100, 480 University Ave.
Toronto, ON M5G 1V2
416-260-2145
Fax: 416-260-9195
info@prismmedicalltd.com
www.prismmedicalltd.com
Other Communications: USA Office, Phone: 314-891-6502
Company Type: Public
Ticker Symbol: PM / TSX Venture
Profile: Prism Medical Ltd. manufactures & supplies medical equipment & related services for mobility challenged persons. Customers are in Canada, the United States, & the United Kingdom.
Stuart Meldrum, B.Sc., MBA, Chief Executive Officer
George Chiarucci, B.Sc., CA, Chief Financial Officer
gchiarucci@prismmedicalltd.com
Charley Wallace, B.A., M.B.A., Chief Operating Officer & President, Waverley Glen Division & Prism Medical USA Inc

ProSep Inc.
#630, 2015, rue Peel
Montréal, QC H3A 1T8
514-522-5550
Fax: 514-552-2643
Company Type: Public
Ticker Symbol: PRP / TSX
Profile: ProSep Inc. was formed in 1986. The company serves the upstream oil & gas industry by providing process solutions. Technologies are designed, developed, manufactured, & commercialized to separate oil, water, & gas generated by oil & gas production.
Jacques L. Drouin, President & Chief Executive Officer
Danielle Ste-Marie, Vice-President, Marketing & Communications
dste-marie@prosep.com

Reko International Group Inc.
469 Silver Creek Industrial Dr.
Lakeshore, ON N8N 4W2
519-727-3287
Fax: 519-727-6681
vpf@rekointl.com
www.rekointl.com
Social Media: www.facebook.com/group.php?gid=244989642243977
Company Type: Public
Ticker Symbol: REK / TSX Venture
Profile: In business since 1976, Reko International Group Inc. is a designer & manufacturer of customized engineering solutions. The company serves the automotive, rail, military, mining, & oil & gas sectors. Business units include Reko Manufacturing Group & Concorde Machine Tool.
Diane Reko, Chief Executive Officer
Carl A Merton, Chief Financial Officer

Royal Laser Corp.
25 Claireville Dr.
Toronto, ON M9W 5Z7
416-679-9474
Fax: 416-679-1986
info@royallaser.com
www.royallaser.com
Social Media: www.linkedin.com/company/royal-laser
Company Type: Public
Ticker Symbol: RLC
Beric Sykes, Chief Executive Officer
Niral V. Merchant, Secretary & CFO

Savaria Corporation
Corporate Office
2724, Etienne-Lenoir
Laval, QC H7R 0A3
450-681-5655
Fax: 450-628-4500
800-931-5655
www.savaria.com
Other Communications: Elevators & Lifts: 800-661-5112; Vehicles: 800-668-8705
Social Media: www.facebook.com/savariabettermobility
twitter.com/Mobilityforlife
www.linkedin.com/company/savaria-inc
Company Type: Public
Ticker Symbol: SIS / TSX
Profile: Savaria Corporation is a designer, manufacturer, & distributor of elevators, starlifts, & vertical & inclined platform lifts for residential & commercial use. The company also specializes in the conversion & adaptation of wheelchair accessible automotive vehicles. Scooters & motorized wheelchairs are also offered by Savaria.
The company's head office is located in Laval Québec, with plants in Montréal Québec, Brampton & London Ontario, Calgary Alberta, & Huizhou, China.
Marcel Bourassa, President & Chief Executive Officer
marcel.bourassa@savaria.com
Jean-Marie Bourassa, Chief Financial Officer
Hélène Bernier, CA, Vice-President, Finance
helene.bernier@savaria.com
Bill Richardson, Executive Vice-Presidemt, Elevators & Lifts
Pierre Tiernan, Executive Vice-Presidemt, Vehicles
Robert Berthiaume, Vice-President, Engineering

The Jim Pattison Group
#1800, 1067 West Cordova St.
Vancouver, BC V6C 1C7
604-688-6764
Fax: 604-687-2601
admin@jp-group.com
www.jimpattison.com
Company Type: Private

Uniprix Inc.
5000, blvd Métropolitain est
Saint-Léonard, QC H1S 3G7
514-725-1212
800-361-0845
service_clientele@uniprix.com
www.uniprix.com
Social Media: www.facebook.com/uniprix
twitter.com/#!/uniprix_inc
Company Type: Private

WaterFurnace Renewable Energy, Inc.
9000 Conservation Way
Fort Wayne, IN 46809-9794 USA
800-436-7283
www.waterfurnace.com/
Other Communications: Dealers & Suppliers, Phone: 800-934-5667
Social Media: www.facebook.com/WaterFurnaceFans
twitter.com/waterfurnace
Company Type: Public
Ticker Symbol: WFI, WFI.U / TSX
Profile: Geothermal heat pumps are designed, manufactured, & distributed by WaterFurnace Renewable Energy, Inc..
Renewable solar energy is used by the geothermal units to reduce energy consumed by buildings.
Tom Huntington, President & Chief Executive Officer
Felix Frederick Andriano, Chief Financial Officer, Treasurer, & Secretary

Winpak Ltd.
Corporate Office
100 Saulteaux Cres.
Winnipeg, MB R3J 3T3
204-889-1015
Fax: 204-888-7806
info@winpak.com
www.winpak.com
Company Type: Public
Ticker Symbol: WPK / TSX
Profile: Manufacturing & distributing packaging materials & related packaging machines are the chief activities of Winpak Ltd. Products are used to protect perishable foods & beverages, as well as in health care applications. The company's facilities are located in Canada & the United States. Its services are offered in North America, Latin America, the Pacific Rim countries, & Europe.
B.J. Berry, President & Chief Executive Officer
204-831-2216
K.P. Kuchma, chief Financial Officer & Vice-President
204-831-2254
N.L. Rozek, Vice-President, Technology

Mining

Abacus Mining & Exploration Corp.
#615, 800 West Pender St.
Vancouver, BC V6C 2V6
604-682-0301
Fax: 604-682-0307
info@amemining.com
www.amemining.com
Company Type: Public
Ticker Symbol: AME / TSX Venture
Doug Fulcher, President & CEO
Paddy Nicol, Chief Financial Officer

Aberdeen International Inc.
PO Box 75, #815, 65 Queen St. West
Toronto, ON M5H 2M5
416-861-1685
Fax: 416-861-8165
info@aberdeeninternational.ca
www.aberdeeninternational.ca
Social Media: www.facebook.com/AberdeenAAB
twitter.com/AberdeenAAB

Company Type: Public
Ticker Symbol: AAB / TSX
Profile: Aberdeen International is a resource investment corporation & merchant bank. Aberdeen focuses on private, small-cap resource companies.
George Faught, C.A., Chief Executive Officer
David Stein, President & Chief Operating Officer
416-861-5812, dstein@aberdeeninternational.ca
Ryan Ptolemy, CGA, CFA, Chief Financial Officer
Mike McAllister, Manager, Investor Relations
416-309-2134

Adanac Molybdenum Corporation
#2, 15782 Marine Dr.
White Rock, BC V4B 1E6
604-531-9639
Fax: 604-531-9634
info@adanacmoly.com
www.adanacmoly.com
Company Type: Public
Ticker Symbol: AUA / TSX Venture
Michael MacLeod, President & CEO
David Kwok, Chief Financial Officer

Adriana Resources Inc.
Corporate Office
#1000, 15 Toronto St.
Toronto, ON M5C 2E3
416-363-2200
Fax: 416-363-2202
info@adrianaresources.com
www.adrianaresources.com
Other Communications: Québec, QC Office Phone: 418-522-4580, ext. 259
Company Type: Public
Ticker Symbol: ADI / TSX Venture
Profile: Adriana Resources Inc. is focused upon its Lac Otelnuk iron ore deposit, which is situated in the Labrador Trough, Nunavik, Québec.
Allen J. Palmiere, Chief Executive Officer & President
apalmiere@adrianaresources.com
Daniel Im, Chief Financial Officer
Frank Condon, Director, Québec Operations
Connie Dos Santos, Director, Investor Relations
cdossantos@adrianaresources.com
Steven Zhang, Manager, Corporate Development

Advanced Explorations Inc. (AEI)
Simpson Tower
#2828, 401 Bay St.
Toronto, ON M5H 2Y4
416-203-0057
Fax: 416-203-0059
info@advanced-exploration.com
www.advanced-exploration.com
Social Media: twitter.com/AXI_IronOre
Company Type: Public
Ticker Symbol: AXI / TSX Venture
Profile: Advanced Explorations Inc. is engaged in the development of the Roche Bay & Tuktu Iron Ore Projects on Nunavut's Melville Peninsula.
John Gingerich, P.Geo., Chair, President, & Chief Executive Officer
Louis Nagy, CA, Chief Financial Officer
Florin Gheorghiu, Ph.D., Vice-President, Engineering & Technology
Gary Williams, Vice-President, Environmental
Joseph Chiummiento, Corporate Secretary

Afferro Mining Inc.
#3350, 1055 Dunsmuir St.
Vancouver, BC V7X 1L2
www.afferro-mining.com
Other Communications: Phone: +44 (0) 20 7257 2930
Company Type: Public
Ticker Symbol: AFF / TSX Venture
Profile: Afferro Mining's key project is the 100% owned Nkout Iron Ore Project in Cameroon.
Luis Guilherme Cabrita da Silva, President & Chief Executive Officer
Bevan John Metcalf, Chief Financial Officer
Peter Wilson, Taylor

Africo Resources Ltd.
#520, 800 West Pender St.
Vancouver, BC V6C 2V6
604-646-3225
Fax: 604-646-3226
877-648-3225
info@africoresources.com
www.africoresources.com
Company Type: Public
Ticker Symbol: ARL / TSX
Profile: Africo Resources Ltd. is engaged in the development of it Kalukundi cobalt-copper deposit in the Democratic Republic of the Congo. The Kalukundi Project developed an Environmental Management System, as part of the Health, Safety, Environment, & Community Management System, compliant with ISO 14001 standards.
Chris Theodoropoulos, Chair & Chief Executive Officer
Larry Okada, Chief Financial Officer

Agnico-Eagle Mines Limited
Executive & Registered Office
#400, 145 King St. East
Toronto, ON M5C 2Y7
416-947-1212
Fax: 416-367-4681
888-822-6714
info@agnico-eagle.com; AEM-Board@agnico-e
www.agnico-eagle.com
Company Type: Public
Ticker Symbol: AEM / TSX, NYSE
Profile: Agnico-Eagle Mines Limited is an international gold production company, which carries out exploration & development activities. Operations are conducted in Canada, the United States, Mexico, & Finland.
Sean Boyd, CA, Vice-Chair/CEO
Eberhard Scherkus, P.Eng., President/COO
David Garofalo, C.A., ICD.D, CFO & Sr. Vice-President, Finance
Daniel Racine, Ing., P. Eng., Sr. Vice-President, Operations
Jean Robitaille, Sr. Vice-President, Technical Services
David Smith, Vice-President, Investor Relations
Louise Grondin, M.Sc., Ing., P. Eng., Vice-President, Environment & Sustainable Development

Alacer Gold Corp.
#240, 10333 East Dry Creek Rd.
Englewood, CO 80112 USA
303-292-1299
Fax: 303-297-0538
www.alacergold.com
Other Communications: Australia: +61-8-9226-0625; Turkey: +90-312-472-4970
Company Type: Public
Ticker Symbol: ASR / TSX; AQG / ASX
Profile: The intermediate gold company is active in Australia & Turkey, where it has interests in gold mines & possession of a portfolio of gold & copper exploration properties.
In Australia, Alacer Gold Corp. has three operating gold mines. Two of these mines were acquired after the acquisition of Dioro Exploration NL in 2010.
In Turkey, Alacer Gold Corp.'s operating gold mine is known as Çöpler.
Edward Dowling, BSc, MSc, PhD, Chief Executive Officer
Louw Smith, BSc, BCom, MSc Mining, EMBA, AusIMM, Chief Operating Officer
Howard Stevenson, BA, BAI (Mech Eng, Hons), MBA, Chief Development Officer
Douglas Tobler, BSc (Business Administration), Chief Financial Officer
Tony James, BEng (Mining), AWASM, AusIMM, Executive Vice-President, Mine Performance
Chris Newman, BSc (Hons), AusIMM, Executive Vice-President, Exploration

Alamos Gold Inc.
#2200, 130 Adelaide St. West
Toronto, ON M5H 3P5
416-368-9932
Fax: 416-368-2934
866-788-8801
info@alamosgold.com
www.alamosgold.com
Company Type: Public
Ticker Symbol: AGI / TSX
Profile: The Canadian-based gold producer has owns & operates a mine in Mexico. The mining company also has exploration & development activities in Mexico & Turkey.
John A. McCluskey, President & Chief Executive Officer
416-368-9932
Jon Morda, Chief Financial Officer
Manley Guarducci, Chief Operating Officer & Vice-President
Ken Balleweg, Vice-President, Exploration
Jamie Porter, Vice-President, Finance
Sharon L. Fleming, Corporate Secretary
Len Harris, Committee Chair, Technical, Environmental, Social & Health & Safety

Alexco Resource Corp.
#1150, 200 Granville St.
Vancouver, BC V6C 1S4
604-633-4888
Fax: 604-633-4887
info@alexcoresource.com
www.alexcoresource.com
Other Communications: Whitehorse, YT Office, Phone: 867-633-4881
Company Type: Public
Ticker Symbol: AXR / TSX, AMEX
Profile: Alexco Resource Corp. holds several mineral properties, including the Bellekeno silver mine in the Keno Hill Silver District of the Yukon Territory. Through the company's wholly owned envrionmental services division, the Alexco Environmental Group, environmental services for mines are also offered. Services provided include remediation, reclamation, & mine closure.
Clynton R. Nauman, President & Chief Executive Officer
James Harrington, MSc, President, Alexco Envrionmental Group
Brad A. Thrall, Chief Operating Officer & Executive Vice-President
David Whittle, CA, Chief Financial Officer & Company Ethics Officer
Thomas Fudge, Senior Vice-President, Engineering & Corporate Development

Alexis Minerals Corp.
#815, 65 Queen St. West
Toronto, ON M5H 2M5
416-861-5888
Fax: 416-861-8165
info@alexisminerals.com
www.alexisminerals.com
Company Type: Public
Ticker Symbol: AMC / TSX
David M. Rigg, President & CEO
Deborah Battiston, Chief Financial Officer

Alhambra Resources Ltd.
Head Office
#3, 4015 - 1st St. SE
Calgary, AB T2G 4X7
403-228-2855
Fax: 403-228-2865
ir@alhambraresources.com
www.alhambraresources.com
Company Type: Public
Ticker Symbol: ALH / TSX Venture
Profile: The gold explorer & producer holds exploration & exploitation rights to the Uzboy Project, which is situated in northern Kazakhstan. Alhambra Resources is listed on the TSX Venture Exchange in Canada, the Over-The-Counter Market in the United States, & the Frankfurt Open Market in Germany.
John J. Komarnicki, Chair & Chief Executive Officer
403-228-2855
Donald D. McKechnie, Chief Financial Officer & Vice-President, Finance
Ihor P. Wasylkiw, P.Eng., Chief Information Officer Y Vice-President
403-508-4953
Paul Marchenko, MBA, Vice-President, Business Development

Altai Resources Inc.
#738, 2550 Victoria Park Ave.
Toronto, ON M2J 5A9
416-383-1328
Fax: 416-383-1686
info@altairesources.com
www.altairesources.com
Other Communications: Montréal Office, Phone: 514-375-0950, Fax: 514-507-3329
Company Type: Public
Ticker Symbol: ATI / TSX Venture
Profile: Altai Resources Inc. has a portfolio of gold, sulphur, oil, & gas properties located in Canada & The Philippines.
Marc-Andre Lavoie, M.Sc (Econ.), M.Phil, President & Chief Executive Officer
Geraint Lloyd, B.Sc (Hons), M.Phil, Chief Operating Officer & Vice-President, Exploration
Maria Au, MBA, CGA, Secretary-Treasurer

Altius Minerals Corporation
Kenmount Business Center
PO Box 8263 Stn. A, , #202, 66 Kenmount Rd.
St. John's, NL A1B 3N4
709-576-3440
Fax: 709-576-3441
877-576-2209
info@altiusminerals.com
www.altiusminerals.com
Other Communications: ALS / TSX

Company Type: Public
Profile: Altius Minerals Corporation is a natural resource project generation & royalty business. The company has royalty interest or equity stakes in several natural resource projects.
Brian F. Dalton, President & Chief Executive Officer
Ben Lewis, B.Comm., C.A., Chief Financial Officer
Roland W. Butler Jr., B.Sc., B. Ed., Vice-President
Chad S. Wells, B.Sc. (Honours), Corporate Secretary & Vice-President, Corporate Development
Rod Churchill, M.Sc., P.Geo., Manager, Lands & Operations

American Bonanza Gold Corp.
#1238, 200 Granville St.
Vancouver, BC V6C 1S4
604-688-7523
Fax: 604-681-0122
877-688-7523
info@americanbonanza.com
www.americanbonanza.com
Other Communications: Reno, Nevada Exploration Office, Phone: 775-824-0707
Company Type: Public
Ticker Symbol: BZA / TSX
Profile: American Bonanza Gold Corp. is involved in the exploration & development of gold mining projects in Canada & the United States. In Arizona, the company operates the Copperstone gold mine.
Brian Kirwin, President & Chief Executive Officer
Joe Chan, Chief Financial Officer & Vice-President

Amerigo Resources Ltd.
Commerce Place
#1950, 400 Burrard St.
Vancouver, BC VV6C 3A6
604-681-2802
Fax: 604-682-2802
www.amerigoresources.com
Company Type: Public
Ticker Symbol: ARG / TSX
Profile: Amerigo Resources Ltd.'s wholly-owned subsidiary is Minera Valle Central. The company specializes in the production of copper & molybdenum concentrates from tailings from an underground copper mine, known as Codelco's El Teniente mine.
Klaus M. Zeitler, President & Chief Executive Officer
Aurora G. Davidson, Chief Financial Officer
Raul Poblete, General Manager, Minera Valle Central Operations
Michael Kuta, Corporate Secretary
mk@amerigoresources.com

Andean American Gold Corp.
Westbury Corporate Centre
#101, 2275 Upper Middle Rd. East
Oakville, ON L6H 0C3
416-368-9500
Fax: 905-491-6801
866-356-4784
investors@aaggold.com
www.AAGgold.com
Company Type: Public
Ticker Symbol: AAG / TSX Venture
Profile: The exploration & mining company has gold, silver, & copper projects in Peru.
David Rae, President & Chief Executive Officer
drae@aaggold.com
Bruce Ramsden, Chief Financial Officer, Corporate Secretary & Vice-President, Finance
Jennie Ly, Corporate Controller
Linda Dorrington, Contact, Investor Relations
ldorrington@aaggold.com

Andina Minerals Inc.
Head Office
#300, 56 Temperence St.
Toronto, ON M5H 3V5
416-203-3488
Fax: 416-203-3438
info@andinaminerals.com
www.andinaminerals.com
Company Type: Public
Ticker Symbol: ADM / TSX Venture
Profile: Andina Minerals focuses upon mining exploration & development. The company owns 100% of the Volcan Gold Project, located in the Maricunga Gold Belt of Chile, as well as two other mineral properties in the primary mining regions of Chile.
George M. Bee, President & Chief Executive Officer
Bob Rose, Chief Operating Officer
Derrick Weyrauch, Chief Financial Officer
416-203-3488, ir@andinaminerals.com
Annick Chouinard, Vice-President, Exploration
Alejandro Labbé, Vice-President, Project Development

Annooraq Resources Corporation
PO Box 782103, Sandton, Gauteng, 2146 South Africa
info@anooraqresources.co.za
www.anooraqresources.com
Other Communications: Phone: +27 11 779 6800; Fax: +27 11 883 0863
Company Type: Public
Ticker Symbol: ARQ / TSX Venture, AMEX
Profile: Anooraq Resources is a platinum group metals mining, exploration, & development company. It has assets in South Africa's Bushveld Igneous Complex.
Harold Motaung, Chief Executive Officer
De Wet Schutte, Chief Financial Officer
Joel Kesler, Executive, Corporate & Business Development
joel@anooraqresources.com

AREVA Resources Canada Inc.
Main Office
PO Box 9204, 817 -45th St. West
Saskatoon, SK S7K 3X5
306-343-4500
Fax: 306-653-3883
www.arevacanada.ca
Social Media: www.facebook.com/Arevainc
twitter.com/AREVAinc
Company Type: Private
Profile: AREVA Resources Canada Inc. is engaged in the exploration & mining of Canadian uranium deposits. The company is also involved in mine decommissioning & monitoring reclaimed sites.

Asian Mineral Resources Limited (AMR)
#2500, 120 Adelaide St. West
Toronto, ON
416-360-3412
Fax: 416-367-1954
info@asianminres.com
www.asianminres.com
Other Communications: Hanoi, Vietnam Office, Phone: + 84 4 3 773 7997
Company Type: Public
Ticker Symbol: ASN / TSX Venture
Profile: Asian Mineral Resources Limited has a 90% interest in the Ban Phuc Nickel / Copper Project, which is located in northwestern Vietnam. Asian Mineral Resources also has a 90% ownership in the project company, Ban Phuc Nickel Mines LLC.
Fook Hoy Lai, BSc(Hon) Metallurgy, BSc(Hon) Economics, President & Chief Executive Officer
Paula Kember, CA, Chief Financial Officer
Steve Ennor, Assoc Dip (Met.Eng), MAusIMM, Project Development Manager & AMR Representative in Vietnam
Dinh Huu Minh, Dip Geol/Eng, PhD, MAusIMM, Exploration Manager & General Director, Ban Phuc Nickel Mines
Ian MacGregor, MA, LLB, Corporate Secretary, Corporate Secretary

ATAC Resources Ltd.
#1016, 510 West Hastings St.
Vancouver, BC V6B 1L8
604-687-2522
www.atacresources.com
Company Type: Public
Ticker Symbol: ATC / TSX Venture
Profile: The exploration company is developing its 100% owned Rackla Gold Project in the Yukon. The project contains Canada's only Carlin-Type gold discoveries. For its environmental standards, ATAC Resources has been the recipient of the Robert E. Leckie Award for Outstanding Reclamation Practices in Quartz Exploration & Mining by the Yukon Government.
Graham Downs, Chief Executive Officer
Robert C. Carne, M.Sc., P.Geo., President
Larry Donaldson, Chief Financial Officer
Ian J. Talbot, Chief Operating Officer
Glenn R. Yeadon, B.Comm., LLB., Secretary

Atlanta Gold Inc.
First Canadian Place
#5600, 100 King St. West
Toronto, ON M5X 1C9
416-777-0013
Fax: 416-777-0014
info@atgoldinc.com; generalinquiries@atgo
www.atgoldinc.com
Company Type: Public
Ticker Symbol: ATG / TSX Venture
Profile: Through its subsidiary, Atlanta Gold Corporation, Atlanta Gold Inc. has leases, options, or ownership interests in properties located in Idaho.
Warren Holmes, President & Chief Executive Officer
Bill Baird, Chief Financial Officer & Vice-President
bbaird@atlantagold.com
William Ernest Simmons, Chief Operating Officer & Vice-President, Mining

Atna Resources Ltd.
Legal Office
#3000, 1055 West Georgia St.
Vancouver, BC V6C 3R3
604-687-6575
Fax: 604-641-4949
866-687-6575
www.atna.com
Other Communications: Golden, CO, USA, Phone: 303-278-8464, Fax: 303-279-8464
Company Type: Public
Ticker Symbol: ATN / TSX
Profile: Atna Resources Ltd. is engaged in gold production & development. The company's key area of activity is the western United States. Projects are as follows: the Pinson gold mine near Winnemucca, Nevada; the Reward gold mine near Beatty, Nevada; the Briggs gold mine in Inyo County, California; & the Columbia gold project near Lincoln, Montana.
James K.B. Hesketh, M.Sc., President & Chief Executive Officer
Rodney D. Gloss, Chief Financial Officer & Vice-President
Douglas E. Stewart, Chief Operating Officer & Vice-President
William Stanley, B.Sc., MBA, Vice-President, Exploration
Valerie Kimball, Corporate Secretary & Contact, Investor Relations
vkimball@atna.com

Augusta Resource Corporation
Corporate Office
#400, 837 West Hastings St.
Vancouver, ON V6C 3N6
604-687-1717
Fax: 604-687-1715
info@augustaresource.com
www.augustaresource.com
Other Communications: Denver, CO, USA Phone: 303-300-0134
Company Type: Public
Ticker Symbol: AZC/TSX, AMEX, Frankfurt
Profile: The focus of Augusta Resource Corporation is its 100% owned Rosemont Copper Deposit, situated near Tucson, Arizona. Rosemont has a large copper & molybdenum reserve.
Gil Clausen, President & Chief Executive Officer
Rodney O. Pace, Chief Operating Officer & Executive Vice-President
Raghunath N. Reddy, Chief Financial Officer & Senior Vice-President
James A. Sturgess, Senior Vice-President, Corporate Development & Government Affairs
Katherine A. Arnold, Vice-President, Environmental & Regulatory Affairs
Letitia Cornacchia, Vice-President, Investor Relations & Corporate Communications
416-860-6310, lcornacchia@augustaresource.com
Mark G. Stevens, Vice-President, Exploration

Aura Minerals Inc.
PO Box 10434, #1950, 777 Dunsmuir St.
Vancouver, BC V7Y 1K4
604-669-4777
Fax: 604-696-0212
info@auraminerals.com
www.auraminerals.com
Company Type: Public
Ticker Symbol: ORA / TSX
Patrick G. Downey, President & CEO
Christina Cepeliauskas, Chief Financial Officer

Aurcana Corporation
#1750, 1188 West Georgia St.
Vancouver, BC V6E 4A2
604-331-9333
866-532-9333
www.aurcana.com
Company Type: Public
Ticker Symbol: AUN / TSX Venture
Profile: Aurcana Corporation is a public, junior mining company, which is listed on the TSX Venture Exchange & the OTCQX. The company owns 100% of the Shafter silver mine in Presidio County, Texas. Aurcana also has a 92% interest in the La Negra silver, copper, lead, & zinc mine, which is located in Queretaro State, Mexico.
Lenic Rodriguez, MA, President & Chief Executive Officer
Salvador Huerta, BA, Accounting & Administration, Chief Financial Officer
Nils von Fersen, PGeo, Vice-President, Exploration
Terese J. Gieselman, Corporate Secretary & Treasurer

AuRico Gold Inc.
Executive Office
#1601, 110 Yonge St.
Toronto, ON M5C 1T4

647-260-8880
Fax: 604-681-4003
647-260-8881
info@auricogold.com
www.auricogold.com
Other Communications: Halifax Office, Phone: 902-468-0614, Fax: 902-468-0631

Company Type: Public
Ticker Symbol: AUQ / TSX, NYSE
Profile: In 2011, Gammon Gold Inc. changed its corporate name to AuRico Gold.
AuRico Gold Inc. is engaged in the production of gold. The company's operating properties are located in northern Ontario, plus Chihuahua State, Sonora State, & Guanajuato State in Mexico. AuRico Gold also has exploration properties in Mexico & British Columbia.
In 2011, AurRico acquired all the issued & outstanding common shares of Northgate Minerals Corporation, a company involved in the exploration & mining of gold & copper.
René Marion, President & Chief Executive Officer
Peter MacPhail, Chief Operating Officer, Canada & Australia
Scott Perry, Chief Financial Officer & Executive Vice-President
Russell Tremayne, Chief Operating Officer & Executive Vice-President
Chris Bostwick, Senior Vice-President, Technical Services
Chris Rockingham, Vice-President, Exploration & Business Development

Aurizon Mines Ltd.
Cathedral Place
#1120, 925 West Georgia St.
Vancouver, BC V6C 3L2

604-687-6600
Fax: 604-687-3932
info@aurizon.com
www.aurizon.com
Other Communications: Quebec Office E-mail: aurizon@aurizon.qc.ca

Company Type: Public
Ticker Symbol: ARZ / TSX
Profile: Aurizon Mines Ltd. specializes in gold exploration, development, & production. Activity takes places in the Abitibi region of northwestern Quebec. The company is listed on the TSX under the symbol ARZ & on the NYSE Amex under the symbol AZK.
George Paspalas, President & Chief Executive Officer
Ian S. Walton, Chief Financial Officer & Executive Vice-President
Martin Bergeron, Vice-President, Operations
Marc Turcotte, Director, Corporate Development
Martin Demers, General Manager, Exploration
Ghislain Fournier, General Manager, Technical Operations
Jennifer North, Manager, Investor Relations
604-687-6600, Fax: 604-687-3932
Chris McLean, Corporate Controller
Julie A. Stokke Kemp, Corporate Secretary
Brian S. Moorhouse, Lead Director, Environment, Health/Safety & Sustainable Dev. Committee

Avalon Rare Metals Inc.
Corporate Headquarters
#1901, 130 Adelaide St. West
Toronto, ON M5H 3P5

416-364-4938
Fax: 416-364-5162
office@avalonraremetals.com; ir@avalonrar
www.avalonraremetals.com
Other Communications: Delta British Columbia Office, Phone: 604-940-3800

Company Type: Public
Ticker Symbol: AVL / TSX, Amex
Profile: The mineral development company is focused upon rare metals deposits in Canada. The Nechalacho Deposit, situated in the Northwest Territories, is Avalon Rare Metals' flagship project. Heavy rare earth elements are important for enabling advances in green energy technology.
Donald S. Bubar, M.Sc., P.Geo., President & Chief Executive Officer
R.J. Andersen, CA, CFP, CPA, Chief Financial Officer & Vice-President, Finance
Brian Chandler, P.Eng., Chief Operating Officer & Senior Vice-President
William Mercer, Ph.D., P.Geo., Vice-President, Exploration
Richard Pratt, Vice-President, General Counsel, & Corporate Secretary
Virginia Morgan, B.Comm, Director, Communications & Investor Relations
Ron Malashewski, P.Eng., Manager, Investor Relations

Avanti Mining Inc.
Three Bentall Centre
#2600, 595 Burrard St.
Vancouver, BC V7X 1L3

877-249-0640
www.avantimining.com
Other Communications: Denver, CO Phone: 303-565-5491

Company Type: Public
Ticker Symbol: AVT / TSX Venture
Profile: The exploration & development company's focus is the Kitsault Molybdenum Mine Project, which is situated north of Prince Rupert, British Columbia.
Craig J. Nelsen, President & Chief Executive Officer
Amjad J. Ali, Chief Financial Officer
Kenneth Collison, Senior Vice-President, Project Development
Shane Uren, Vice-President, Environmental & Permitting

Avion Gold Corporation
PO Box 67, #800, 65 Queen St. West
Toronto, ON M5H 2M5

416-309-2134
nfo@aviongoldcorp.com
www.aviongoldcorp.com
Social Media: www.facebook.com/AvionGoldCorp
twitter.com/AvionGoldAVR

Company Type: Public
Ticker Symbol: AVR / TSX
Profile: The Canadian-based gold mining company has holdings in West Africa, including the Tabakoto & Segala gold projects in Mali. Gold production started at these project in 2009. Avion Gold Corporation is working to develop its exploration properties. The public company is listed on the TSX under the symbol AVR, as well as on the OTCQX, under the symbol AVGCF.
John Begeman, P.Eng, President & Chief Executive Officer
Andrew Bradfield, Chief Operating Officer
Alex Dann, Chief Financial Officer
Brianna Davies, Corporate Secretary
Michael McAllister, Manager, Investor Relations
416-309-2134

AXMIN Inc.
#800, 120 Adelaide St. West
Toronto, ON M5H 1T1

416-368-0993
info@axmininc.com
www.axmininc.com

Company Type: Public
Ticker Symbol: AXM / TSX Venture
Profile: The exploration & development company is active in central & west Africa. AXMIN Inc.'s present projects are located in Mozambique, the Central African Republic, & Senegal.
George Roach, President & Chief Executive Officer
Janina Dusza, Chief Financial Officer
Graham Hill, Chief Operating Officer
Judith Webster, Vice-President, Investor Relations
Geoff McLoughlin, Manager, Engineering

B2Gold Corp.
PO Box 49143, #3100, 595 Burrard St.
Vancouver, BC V7X 1J1

604-681-8371
Fax: 604-681-6209
800-316-8855
investor@b2gold.com
www.b2gold.com
Social Media: twitter.com/B2GoldCorp

Company Type: Public
Ticker Symbol: BTO / TSX
Profile: Founded in 2007, B2Gold Corp. is an international gold producer that has mines in Nicaragua, plus exploration & development assets in Columbia, Uruguay, & Nicaragua. The company trades on the Toronto Stock Exchange under the symbol BTO, as well as on the OTCXQ under the symbol BGLPF.
B2Gold Corp. employs a Vice-President who specializes in offering operational health & safety, plus environmental & social assistance during all phases of mining.
Clive T. Johnson, President, Chief Executive Officer, & Director
Roger T. Richer, Executive Vice-President, General Counsel, & Secretary
Mark Corra, Chief Financial Officer & Senior Vice-President, Finance
Tom Garagan, Senior Vice-President, Exploration
George Johnson, Senior Vice-President, Operations
Dennis Stansbury, Senior Vice-President, Production & Development
Bill Lytle, Vice-President, Environmental, Health, Safety, & Permitting
Ian MacLean, Vice-President, Investor Relations
604-681-8371
Kerry Suffolk, Vice-President, Finance & Investor Relations
604-681-8371

Barrick Gold Corporation
TD Canada Trust Tower, Brookfield Place
PO Box 212, #3700, 161 Bay St.
Toronto, ON M5J 2S1

416-861-9911
Fax: 416-861-2492
800-720-7415
hr@barrick.com
www.barrick.com
Social Media: www.facebook.com/barrick.gold.corporation
twitter.com/BarrickGold

Company Type: Public
Ticker Symbol: ABX / TSX
Profile: The gold mining company explores, develops, & operates mines in five continents. It trades on the Toronto & New York stock exchanges under the symbol ABX.
Aaron Regent, President/CEO
Gregory A. Lang, Regional President, North America
Jamie C. Sokalsky, Exec. Vice-President/CFO
Peter J. Kinver, Exec. Vice-President/COO
Alexander J. Davidson, Exec. Vice-President, Exploration & Corporate Development
Vincent Borg, Sr. Vice-President, Corporate Communications
Rich Haddock, Vice-President, Environment

Bayswater Uranium Corporation
#1100, 111 Melville St.
Vancouver, BC V6E 3V6

604-687-2153
Fax: 604-669-8336
www.bayswateruranium.com

Company Type: Public
Ticker Symbol: BYU / TSX Venture
Profile: The uranium exploration & development company owns properties in Canada's Athabasca Basin, Central Mineral Belt, & Thelon Basin, & in the United States. Examples of Bayswater Uranium Corporation's projects are the Reno Creek Project & the Elkhorn/Alzada Project in Wyoming.
Mark Gelmon, CA, Chief Financial Officer
James Viellenave, BA, MA, General Manager, USA Operations
Dean Fraser, Project Manager, Labrador
Marion McGrath, Corporate Secretary

Bear Creek Mining Corporation
Corporate Head Office
#1050, 625 Howe St.
Vancouver, BC V6C 2T6

604-685-6269
Fax: 604-685-6268
info@bearcreekmining.com
www.bearcreekmining.com
Other Communications: Lima Operations Office, Phone: (511) 222-0922

Company Type: Public
Ticker Symbol: BCM / TSX Venture
Profile: Formed in 2000, Bear Creek Mining Corporation explores for mineral deposits. The company's focus is in Peru, where projects include Corani & Santa Ana. These projects contain silver & by-product base metals.
Andrew T. Swarthout, Chief Executive Officer
Marc Leduc, President & Chief Operating Officer
Steve Krause, Chief Financial Officer
Corey M. Dean, Vice-President, Legal
Lisa May, Director, Investors Relations
604-628-1111, lmay@bearcreekmining.com

Brigus Gold Corp.
Purdy's Wharf Tower II
#2001, 1969 Upper Water St.
Halifax, NS B3J 3R7

902-422-1421
Fax: 902-491-4281
866-785-0456
ir@brigusgold.com; jobs@brigusgold.com
www.brigusgold.com
Other Communications: Toronto Technical Office: 416-214-9867
Company Type: Public
Ticker Symbol: BRD / TSX, AMEX
Profile: The gold producer operates its wholly owned Black Fox Mine & Mill in the Timmins Gold District of Ontario. Brigus Gold is also advancing the Goldfields Project near Uranium City, Saskatchewan.
Wade K. Dawe, Chair, Chief Executive Officer & President
Dana Hatfield, Chief Financial Officer
Jennifer Nicholson, CA, Executive Vice-President
Howard Bird, Vice-President, Exploration
Daniel F. Gallivan, Corporate Secretary

Cameco Corporation
Investor, Corporate, & Government Relations Depart
2121 - 11 St. West
Saskatoon, SK S7M 1J3
306-956-6200
Fax: 306-956-6201
866-789-8050
www.cameco.com
Other Communications: HR: 306-956-8050; Investors: 306-956-6340
Company Type: Public
Ticker Symbol: CCO / TSX; CCJ / NYSE
Profile: Cameco is engaged in the production of uranium to generate electricity in nuclear energy plants throughout the world.
Tim S. Gitzel, President & Chief Executive Officer
Grant E. Isaac, Chief Financial Officer & Senior Vice-President
Gary M.S. Chad, Corporate Secretary & Senior Vice-President, Governance & Law
Dara Hrytzak-Lieffers, Manager, Corporate Social Responsibility
306-956-6753, Fax: 306-956-6318

Canada Zinc Metals Corp.
PO Box 11121 Stn. Royal Centre, , #2050, 1055 West Georgia St.
Vancouver, BC V6E 3P3
604-684-2181
Fax: 604-682-4768
855-684-2181
info@canadazincmetals.com
www.canadazincmetals.com
Company Type: Public
Ticker Symbol: CZX / TSX Venture
Profile: The mineral exploration company conducts operations in British Columbia. Canada Zinc Metals Corp. holds the mineral belt known as the Kechika Trough. The Kechika Region hosts base metal resources.
Peeyush Varshney, LL.B., Chair, Chief Executive Officer, & President
Praveen Varshney, CA, Chief Financial Officer
Ken MacDonald, P.Geo., Vice-President, Exploration

Canadian Salt Company Limited
Also Known As: Windsor Salt
#700, 755, boul Saint-Jean
Montréal, QC H9R 5M9
514-630-0900
Fax: 514-694-2451
www.windsorsalt.com
Company Type: Private
Wayne Corney, President
François G. Allard, Vice-President, Finance

Canadian Zinc Corporation
PO Box 11644, #1710, 650 West Georgia St.
Vancouver, BC V6B 4N9
604-688-2043
Fax: 604-688-2043
866-688-2001
www.canadianzinc.com
Other Communications: Ontario, Phone: 416-362-6686
Company Type: Public
Ticker Symbol: CZN / TSX
Profile: Canadian Zinc Corporation is listed on the Toronto Stock Exchange under the symbol CZN, on the OTCQB under the symbol CZICF, & on the Frankfurt Exchange under the symbol SRS. The junior exploration & development company's main project is the Prairie Creek Mine, a zinc, silver, & lead mine located in the Mackenzie Mountains of the Northwest Territories.
John F. Kearney, Chair, President & Chief Executive Officer
Trevor Cunningham, Chief Financial Officer, Corporate Secretary & Vice-President, Finance
Alanin Taylor, P. Geo., Chief Operating Officer & Vice-President, Exploration

CanAlaska Uranium Ltd.
#1020, 625 Howe St.
Vancouver, BC V6C 2T6
604-688-3211
Fax: 604-688-3217
info@canalaska.com
www.canalaska.com
Other Communications: Saskatoon Field Office, Phone: 306-477-1870
Company Type: Public
Ticker Symbol: CVV / TSX; CVVUF / OTCBB
Profile: CanAlaska Uranium is engaged in uramium exploration in the Athabasca Basin of Canada.
Peter Dasler, M.Sc., P.Geo., President & Chief Executive Officer
Ram Ramachandran, Chief Financial Officer
Emil Fung, Vice-President, Corporate Development
Karl Schimann, P.Geo., Vice-President, Exploration
Frances Petryshen, Corporate Secretary

Candente Copper Corp.
Commerce Place
#1650, 400 Burrard St.
Vancouver, BC V6C 3A6
604-689-1957
Fax: 604-685-1946
877-689-1964
info@candentecopper.com
www.candentecopper.com
Other Communications: Peru Office: 51 (511) 715-2001, ext. 101
Company Type: Public
Ticker Symbol: DNT / TSX, BVL
Profile: Candente Copper Corp. owns 100% of the Cañariaco Norte Copper Project in northern Peru. The company undertakes exploration in accordance with the Peruvian Ministry of Energy & Mines' General Mining Law & regulations.
Joanne C. Freeze, P.Geo., Chair & Chief Executive Officer
Sean I. Waller, P.Eng., President
Aurora Davidson, B.Sc., CGA, Chief Financial Officer
John P. Foulkes, B.Sc. (Geol), B.Ed., Vice-President, Corporate Development
Walter Spagnuolo, Manager, Investor Relations

CaNickel Mining Limited
PO Box 35, #1655, 999 West Hastings St.
Vancouver, BC V6C 2W2
778-372-1810
Fax: 604-254-8863
www.canickel.com
Company Type: Public
Ticker Symbol: CML/TSX; CMIC/Frankfurt
Profile: The junior mining company is the owner & operator of the Bucko Lake Nickel Mine near Wabowden, Manitoba. CaNickel Mining Limited also has projects in the Thompson Nickel Belt & the Sudbury Basin.
Dianmin Chen, Chief Executive Officer
dchen@canickel.com
Derek Liu, Chief Financial Officer
dliu@canickel.com
Rick Sproule, Vice-President, Geology

Capstone Mining Corp.
#900, 999 West Hastings St.
Vancouver, BC V6C 2W2
604-684-8894
Fax: 604-688-2180
866-684-8894
info@capstonemining.com
www.capstonemining.com
Company Type: Public
Ticker Symbol: CS / TSX
Profile: Capstone Mining Corp. operates a copper-silver-zinc-lead mine located in Mexico & a copper-gold-silver mine in the Yukon. Development projects are underway in British Columbia, Chile, & Australia.
In 2011, Capstone Mining acquired Far West Mining Ltd., a company engaged in the acquisition & exploration of mineral properties in Chile & Australia.
Darren M. Pylot, President & Chief Executive Officer
Richard Godfrey, Chief Financial Officer
Robert Barnes, Vice-President, Operations, Mexico
B.Sc, MBA, P.Eng
Kevin Weston, Vice-President, Operations, Canada
Cindy Burnett, Vice-President, Investor Relations
cburnett@capstonemining.com

Cardero Resource Corp.
#2300, 1177 West Hastings St.
Vancouver, BC V6E 2K3
604-408-7488
Fax: 604-408-7499
info@cardero.com
www.cardero.com
Company Type: Public
Ticker Symbol: CDU / TSX
Profile: Founded in 1999, Cardero is a mining company that works to acquire bulk commodity deposits & to bring them to production.
The company has the ability to implement a health & safety management system & an environmental management system, as well as a management plan for handling community concerns within countries & regions of operation.
Michael Hunter, President & Chief Executive Officer
Blaine Bailey, Chief Financial Officer
Keith Henderson, Executive Vice-President
Tansy O'Connor-Parsons, Senior Geochemist
Carlos Ballon, Manager, South America
Nancy Curry, Manager, Corporate Communications
Marla Ritchie, Corporate Secretary

Carpathian Gold Inc.
Corporate Office
#300, 365 Bay St.
Toronto, ON M5H 2V1
416-368-7744
Fax: 416-363-3883
info@carpathiangold.com
www.carpathiangold.com
Other Communications: Romania: (+40) 254-613-150; Brazil: (+55) 313-286-5699
Company Type: Public
Ticker Symbol: CPN / TSX
Profile: Carpathian Gold Inc. owns 100% of the Riacho dos Machados Gold Project in Brazil. The exploration & development company is also active in Romania, where it owns 100% of the Rovina Valley Au-Cu Project.
Dino Titaro, President & Chief Executive Officer
Daniel B.J. Kivari, Chief Operating Officer
Linda Prager, Chief Financial Officer
Guy Charette, Executive Vice-President, Corporate
Randall K. Ruff, Executive Vice-President, Exploration
Mike O'Brien, Manager, Investor Relations
mobrien@carpathiangold.com

Centerra Gold Inc.
#1500, 1 University Ave.
Toronto, ON M5J 2P1
416-204-1953
Fax: 416-204-1954
info@centerragold.com
www.centerragold.com
Company Type: Public
Ticker Symbol: CG / TSX
Profile: Centerra Gold Inc. is engaged in the acquisition, exploration, development, & operation of gold properties in Central Asia, the former Soviet Union, & other emerging markets.
Stephen A. Lang, President & CEO
Jeffrey S. Parr, Vice-President & CFO, Finance
John A. Ross, Vice-President, Human Resources

Century Mining Corp.
441 Peace Portal Dr.
Blaine, WA 98230 USA
360-332-4653
Fax: 360-332-4652
www.centurymining.com
Company Type: Public
Ticker Symbol: CMM / TSX Venture
Peggy Kent, Chair, President & CEO
Diana Rollo, CFO

Chesapeake Gold Corp.
#201, 1512 Yew St.
Vancouver, BC V6K 3E4
604-731-1094
Fax: 604-731-0209
chesapeake@shaw.ca
www.chesapeakegold.com
Company Type: Public
Ticker Symbol: CKG / TSX Venture
Profile: Chesapeake Gold Corp. explores for & develops precious metals projects. The company's focus is upon its 100% owned Metates gold deposit in Durango state, Mexico.
P. Randy Reifel, President & Director
Gerald L. Sneddon, Executive Vice-President, Operations
Mark Malfair, Vice-President, Exploration
Gary A. Parkison, Vice-President, Development
Bernard Poznanski, Corporate Secretary

China Gold International Resources Corp. Ltd.
One Bentall Centre
PO Box 31, #1030, 505 Burrard St.
Vancouver, BC V7X 1M5
604-609-0598
Fax: 604-688-0598
info-chinagoldintl@chinagoldintl.com
www.chinagoldintl.com
Other Communications: Investor Relations, Phone: 604-695-5032
Company Type: Public
Ticker Symbol: CGG / TSX
Profile: China Gold International Resources Corp. Ltd. is a mineral development company that operates the CSH Gold Mine, located in Inner Mongolia, as well as the Jiama Copper-Polymetallic Mine, situated in the Tibet Autonomous Region of China. The company's aim is to explore, acquire, & develop new projects in China & elsewhere.
China Gold International Resources Corp. Ltd. is listed on the Toronto Stock Exchange, under the symbol CGG, & on the Board of the Stock Exchange of Hong Kong Limited, under the symbol HKEx:2099.
Xin Song, Chief Executive Officer
Derrick Zhang, Chief Financial Officer

Jerryck Xie, Executive Vice-President & Corporate Secretary
X.D. Jiang, Vice-President, Production
Zhanming Wu, Vice-President, Business Development
Songlin Zhang, Chief Engineer

Claude Resources Inc.
#200, 224 - 4th Ave. South
Saskatoon, SK S7K 5M5
306-668-7505
Fax: 306-668-7500
claudereources@clauderesources.com
www.clauderesources.com
Social Media: www.facebook.com/clauderesources
twitter.com/clauderesource
Company Type: Public
Ticker Symbol: CRJ / TSX; CGR, NYSE Amex
Profile: Claude Resources Inc. explores for & mines gold in Canada. Projects include the Amisk Gold Project & the Seabee Gold Mine, both located in northeastern Saskatchewan. The company also owns 100% of the Madsen Gold Project in the Red Lake region of northwestern Ontario.
Neil McMillan, President & Chief Executive Officer
Rick Johnson, C.A., Chief Financial Officer & Vice-President, Finance
Brian Skanderbeg, P.Geo., Vice-President, Exploration

Cline Mining Corporation
Heritage Building, Brookfield Place
181 Bay St., 3rd Fl.
Toronto, ON M5J 2T3
416-504-7600
Fax: 416-981-7316
info@clinemining.com
www.clinemining.com
Company Type: Public
Ticker Symbol: CMK / TSX
Profile: Cline Mining Corporation is a mine development company. The company's exploration & development activities are conducted in the following regions: the United States, where metallurgical steel making coals are sought; northern Ontario, where the Cline Lake Gold Mine Property is located; & Madagascar, where exploration takes place for iron ore.
Ken Bates, President & Chief Executive Officer
Ernest M. Cleave, Chief Financial Officer & Vice-President
Dennis Mraz, Chief Operating Officer & Executive Vice-President

Colombia Crest Gold Corp.
Head Office
#300, 1055 West Hastings St.
Vancouver, BC V6E 2E9
604-684-7160
info@colombiacrestgold.com
www.colombiacrestgold.com
Company Type: Public
Ticker Symbol: CLB / TSX Venture
Profile: Colombia Crest Gold Corp. explores for & develops gold projects in Colombia. The company also has 100% ownership of the San Sim¢n project in Bolivia.
Hans J. Rasmussen, Chief Executive Officer
hans@colombiacrestgold.com
Bill Jung, Chief Financial Officer & Corporate Secretary
Walter Lienhard, Vice-President, Exploration
Gonzalo Lemuz, Country Manager, Colombia

Colossus Minerals Inc.
#401, 1 University Ave.
Toronto, ON M5J 2P1
416-643-7655
Fax: 416-643-3890
info@colossusminerals.com
www.colossusminerals.com
Other Communications: Brazil Office, Phone: 31-3223-8825
Company Type: Public
Ticker Symbol: CSI / TSX; COLUF / OTCQX
Profile: Colossus Minerals Inc. is a mining company that is active in the Carajas region of Para, Brazil, where its Serra Pelada Project is located.
Claudio Mancuso, President & Chief Executive Officer
Paulo de Tarso Serpa Fagundes, Chief Operating Officer
Alden Greenhouse, Chief Financial Officer
Augusto Kishida, PhD, Vice-President, Business Development
Graham Long, Vice-President, Exploration
Ann Wilkinson, Vice-President, Investor Relations
Lesley Duncan, Corporate Secretary

Commerce Resources Corp.
#1450, 789 West Pender St.
Vancouver, BC V6C 1H2
604-484-2700
Fax: 604-681-8240
866-484-2700
info@commerceresources.com
www.commerceresources.com
Social Media:
www.facebook.com/commerceresourcesfan?ref=ts
twitter.com/commerceresce
Company Type: Public
Ticker Symbol: CCE / TSX Venture
Profile: The exploration & development company's focus is upon British Columbia's Upper Fir Tantalum & Niobium Deposit & Québec's Eldor Rare Earth Project.
David Hodge, President
dhodge@commerceresources.com
Jody Bellefleur, Chief Financial Officer

Concordia Resource Corp.
#654, 999 Canada Pl.
Vancouver, BC V6C 3E1
604-669-6446
Fax: 604-681-3091
info@concordiaresourcecorp.com
www.concordiaresourcecorp.com
Other Communications: Western Energy Development (US Subsidiary): 775-827-3311
Company Type: Public
Ticker Symbol: CCN / TSX Venture
Profile: Concordia Resource Corp. is a junior exploration company. Development of mineral deposits in South America & Africa is the company's focus. Concordia'a exploration portfolio includes regions of the Democratic Republic of Congo, Burkina Faso, Zimbabwe, & Gabon.
Edward Flood, Chair & Chief Executive Officer
Toby Mayo, B.Sc., LL.B, President
Eduard Epshtein, CA, Chief Financial Officer
Karl Cahill, BA, Vice-President, Investor Relations
604-331-9814
John Rice, M.Sc., P. Geo., Vice-President, Exploration

Consolidated Thompson Iron Mines Ltd.
PO Box 75, #815, 65 Queen St. West
Toronto, ON M5H 2M5
416-861-5907
Fax: 416-861-8165
info@consolidatedthompson.com
www.consolidatedthompson.com
Company Type: Private
Ticker Symbol: CLM
Richard Quesnel, President & CEO
Brad Boland, Chief Financial Officer

Copper Mountain Mining Corporation
#1700, 700 West Pender St.
Vancouver, BC V6C 1G8
604-682-2992
Fax: 604-682-2993
877-451-2662
hr@cumtnop.com (human resources)
www.cumtn.com
Other Communications: Copper Mountain Mine Site, near Princeton, BC: 250-295-0123
Company Type: Public
Ticker Symbol: CUM / TSX
Profile: The resource company owns 75% of the Copper Mountain Mine, which is located south of Princeton, British Columbia.
Jim O'Rourke, P.Eng., President & Chief Executive Officer
jim@CuMtn.com
Rodney A. Shier, CA, Chief Financial Officer
rod@CuMtn.com
Peter Holbek, BSc. (Hons) M.Sc., P.Geo, Vice-President, Exploration
J. Peter Campbell, BSc., Environmental Consultant
Galina Meleger, CIM, Contact, Corporate Communication
galina@cumtn.com

Coro Mining Corp.
Corporate Head Office
#1280, 625 Howe St.
Vancouver, BC V6C 2T6
604-682-5546
Fax: 604-682-5542
investor.info@coromining.com
www.coromining.com
Company Type: Public
Ticker Symbol: COP / TSX
Profile: Coro Mining is focused on exploring for & acquiring base & precious metals projects. The company's projects are located in Argentina & Chile.
Alan Stephens, President & Chief Executive Officer
Damian Towns, Chief Financial Officer
Michael Philpot, Executive Vice-President & Secretary
604-682-5546, investor.info@coromining.com
Marcelo Cortes, Vice-President, Project Development

Corona Gold Corporation
#2100, 1 Adelaide St. East
Toronto, ON M5C 2V9
416-482-9038
Fax: 416-924-7997
info@coronagold.ca
www.coronagold.net
Company Type: Public
Ticker Symbol: CRG / TSX
Profile: Corona Gold explores & acquires mineral properties in Canada. The corporation also invests in securities of other companies with similar activities.
Murray John, Chief Executive Officer
Orest Zajcew, Chief Financial Officer

Corsa Coal Corp.
#601, 110 Yonge St.
Toronto, ON M5C 1T4
416-214-9800
855-214-9800
communication@corsacoal.com
www.corsacoal.com
Company Type: Public
Ticker Symbol: CSO / TSX Venture
Profile: Corsa Coal Corp. mines, processes, & sells metallurgical coal. The company is active in the Northern Appalachia.
Donald K. Charter, President & Chief Executive Officer
Michael Svonavec, President, Wilson Creek
Paul Caldwell, Chief Financial Officer & Corporate Secretary
Joseph Gallo, Executive Vice-President, Operation, Wilson Creek

Crew Gold
#615, 800 West Pender St.
Vancouver, BC V6C 2V6
604-681-8003
Fax: 604-662-3180
800-444-9284
Company Type: Private
John G. Bovard, President/CEO & Director
Doris Meyer, Assistant Corporate Secretary

Crocodile Gold Corp.
Corporate Office
PO Box 75, #825, 65 Queen St. West
Toronto, ON M5H 2M5
416-861-5899
Fax: 416-861-8165
info@crocgold.com
www.crocgold.com
Social Media: www.facebook.com/CrocodileGoldCorp
twitter.com/crocgold_CRK
Company Type: Public
Ticker Symbol: CRK / TSX
Profile: Crocodile Gold has gold mines in Australia's Northern Territory.
Chantal Lavoie, P.Eng., President & Chief Executive Officer
David Keough, Chief Operating Officer
Stephen Woodhead, Chief Financial Officer
Bill Nielsen, P.Geo., Vice-President, Exploration
Colinda Parent, Vice-President, Corporate Development
Brianna Davies, J.D., Corporate Secretary

Crystallex International Corporation
#1201, 18 King St. East
Toronto, ON M5C 1C4
416-203-2448
Fax: 416-203-0099
800-738-1577
info@crystallex.com
www.crystallex.com
Company Type: Public
Ticker Symbol: CRYFQ / OTCBB
Robert A. Fung, Chairman/CEO
Hemdat Sawh, CFO
William Faust, COO

Dalradian Resources Inc.
#2920, 155 Wellington St. West
Toronto, ON M5V 3H1
416-583-5600
info@dalradian.com; board@dalradian.com
www.dalradian.com
Other Communications: Omagh, Northern Ireland Office, Phone: +44 (0) 02882 246289
Company Type: Public
Ticker Symbol: DNA / TSX
Profile: Dalradian Resources is engaged in the acquisition,

exploration, & development of mineral properties. The company's wholly owned subsidiary is Dalradian Gold Limited, which has interests in Tyrone & Londonderry counties in Northern Ireland. In addition to its operations in Northern Ireland, Dalradian also hold minerals rights to land in Norway.
Patrick F.N. Anderson, Chief Executive Officer
John M. McCombe, Chief Operating Officer
Keith D. McKay, Chief Financial Officer & Corporate Secretary
Damien Stephens, Manager, Exploration
Shae-Lynn Mathers, Director, Investor Relations
416-583-5622, smathers@dalradian.com;
investor@dalradian.com

Denison Mines Corp.
Atrium on Bay
#402, 595 Bay St.
Toronto, ON M5G 2C2
416-979-1991
Fax: 416-979-5893
blazare@denisonmines.com
www.denisonmines.com

Company Type: Public
Ticker Symbol: DML / TSX, AMEX
Profile: Denison Mines Corp. is a uranium exploration & production company. Its active uranium mines are located in Canada & the United States. Denison Environmental Services (DES) was established to provide mine decommissioning, long-term care, & maintenance services to closed mining facilities.
E. Peter Farmer, Chief Executive Officer
Ron Hochstein, President/COO
James R. Anderson, Exec. Vice-President/CFO
William C. Kerr, Vice-President, Exploration
Brenda R. Lazare, Canadian Counsel & Corporate Secretary
Ian Ludgate, Manager, Denison Environmental Services (DES)
705-848-9191, Fax: 705-848-5814,
iludgate@denisonenvironmental.com

Detour Gold Corporation
North Tower, Royal Bank Plaza
PO Box 23, #2040, 200 Bay St.
Toronto, ON M5J 2J1
416-304-0800
Fax: 416-304-0184
www.detourgold.com

Company Type: Public
Ticker Symbol: DGC / TSX
Gerald Panneton, President & CEO
Jeffrey R. Mason, Chief Financial Officer

Diamonds North Resources Ltd.
#1100, 1111 Melville St.
Vancouver, BC V6E 3V6
604-689-2010
Fax: 604-484-7143
866-802-2010
info@diamondsnorth.com
www.diamondsnorthresources.com

Company Type: Public
Ticker Symbol: DDN / TSX Venture
Profile: Diamonds North Resources Ltd. is an exploration company, with diamond, gold, nickel, copper, & silver projects.
Mark Kolebaba, President & Chief Executive Officer
Michael Lee, CGA, Chief Financial Officer
Graham Gill, B.Sc., P. Geol, Vice-President, Operations
Bruce Kienlen, B.Sc., P. Geol, Vice-President, Exploration
Troy Shultz, Manager, Corporate Communications

Dianor Resources Inc./ Ressources Dianor inc.
649 - 3e av, 2e étage
Val-d'Or, QC J9P 1S7
819-825-7090
Fax: 819-825-7545
info@dianor.com
www.dianor.com

Company Type: Public
Ticker Symbol: DOR / TSX Venture
Profile: The resource company is engaged in diamond exploration on properties in the Superior Craton of Canada. One of Dianor Resources' projects is the Leadbetter Diamond Project, which is located northeast of Wawa, Ontario.
John Ryder, P.Geo., President & Chief Executive Officer
Daniel Duval, Chair & Chief Financial Officer
Thomas E. Landers, P. Eng. M.Sc., Mining Engineer

Dundee Precious Metals Inc.
Dundee Place
PO Box 195, #500, 1 Adelaide St. East
Toronto, ON M5C 2V9
416-365-5191
Fax: 416-365-9080
info@dundeeprecious.com
www.dundeeprecious.com
Other Communications: Armenia: +374 285 620 40; Bulgaria: +359 2 9301500

Company Type: Public
Ticker Symbol: DPM, DPM.WT, DPM.WT.A/TSX
Profile: Dundee Precious Metals Inc. acquires, explores, develops, & mines precious metals properties. The company is active in Armenia, Bulgaria, Serbia, & Namibia.
Jonathan Goodman, President/CEO
Stephanie Anderson, Exec. Vice-President/CFO
Laurence D. Marsland, Exec. Vice-President/COO
Adrian Goldstone, Vice-President, Environment & Sustainable Development
Sean M. Hasson, Vice-President, Exploration
James M. Small, Vice-President, Government Affairs
Lori E. Beak, Corporate Secretary & Vice-President, Investor Relations

Dynasty Metals & Mining Inc.
#270, 666 Burrard St.
Vancouver, BC V6C 2X8
604-687-0888
Fax: 604-687-0885
info@dynastymining.com
www.dynastymining.com

Company Type: Public
Ticker Symbol: DMM / TSX
Profile: The mining company is active in Ecuador, where it is engaged in the exploration & development of mineral properties. Dynasty Metals & Mining's projects include the Zaruma Gold Project, the Dynasty Copper-Gold Belt, & the Jerusalem Project.
Robert Wasjer, President & Chief Executive Officer
Nick Furber, Chief Financial Officer
Bill McCartney, Director, Business Development

East Asia Minerals Corporation
#1980, 1055 West Hastings St.
Vancouver, BC V6E 2E9
604-684-8894
Fax: 604-688-2180
patchettm@eaminerals.com
www.eaminerals.com

Company Type: Public
Ticker Symbol: EAS / TSX Venture
Profile: The mineral acquisition & exploration company has gold & copper assets in Indonesia & uranium properties in Mongolia.
Michael Hawkins, MSc., Geology, MAusIMM, President/CEO
Lionel Martin, BSc., Geology, P. Geo., Chief Operating Officer
Nick Kohlmann, Contact, Corporate Communications
416-792-8734, Kohlmann@EAminerals.com

Eastern Platinum Limited
#501, 837 West Hastings St.
Vancouver, BC V6C 3N6
604-685-6851
Fax: 604-685-6493
info@eastplats.com
www.eastplats.com
Other Communications: South Africa Office, Phone: +27 (0)11 463 0050

Company Type: Public
Ticker Symbol: ELR / TSX
Profile: Eastern Platinum Limited was established in 2003. The metals mining company has acquired platinum & rhodium deposits in South Africa.
Ian Rozier, President & Chief Executive Officer
Horng Dih Lee, Chief Financial Officer, Corp. Secretary, & Vice-President, Finance

Eastmain Resources Inc.
Corporate Office
#101, 50 Richmond St. East
Toronto, ON M5C 1N7
info@eastmain.com
www.eastmain.com
Other Communications: Exploration Office, Orangeville ON: 519-940-4870

Company Type: Public
Ticker Symbol: ER / TSX
Profile: Eastmain Resources Inc. is a gold exploration company. The company's area of operation is the Eastmain River area, in northern Québec's James Bay District. Eastmain Resources owns 100% of the Eau Clair gold deposit. Exploration projects include the Éléonore & Éléonore South properties.
Donald J. Robinson, Ph.D., P.Geo, President & Chief Executive Officer
James Bezeau, BBA, CMA, Chief Financial Officer

Catherine I. Butella, B.Sc., Manager, Exploration
Jay Goldman, BA, MBA, LLB, Corporate Secretary

Eco Oro Minerals Corp.
#1430, 333 Seymour St.
Vancouver, BC V6B 5A6
604-682-8212
Fax: 604-682-3708
info@eco-oro.com
www.eco-oro.com
Other Communications: Bucaramanga, Santander, Colombia Office: 577-634-7778

Company Type: Public
Ticker Symbol: EOM / TSX
Profile: The precious metals exploration & development company is active in northeastern Colombia, where its wholly owned Angostura gold & silver deposit is located.
Anna Stylianides, Co-Chair, President, & Chief Executive Officer
604-682-8212, anna@eco-oro.com
Paul Robertson, Chief Financial Officer
James Atherton, Corporate Secretary & Corporate Counsel

Eldorado Gold Corporation
Bentall 5
#1188, 550 Burrard St.
Vancouver, BC V6C 2B5
604-687-4018
Fax: 604-687-4026
888-353-8166
info@eldoradogold.com
www.eldoradogold.com
Other Communications: Brazil Corporate Office, Phone: 55-31-2101-3750

Company Type: Public
Ticker Symbol: ELD / TSX; EGO / NYSE
Profile: Eldorado Gold Corporation is an international company that specializes in the exploration & development of gold properties. In 2012, Eldorado Gold Corporation acquired all the issued & outstanding securities of European Goldfields Limited, a company with gold reserves in the European Union.
The gold producer now has properties in Brazil, Greece, Turkey, China, & Romania. Industry best practices are implemented in each region in an effort to minimize environmental impacts.
Paul N. Wright, President & Chief Executive Officer
Fabiana Chubbs, Chief Financial Officer
Norm S. Pitcher, Chief Operating Officer
Dawn L. Moss, Corporate Secretary & Vice-President, Administration

EMC Metals Corp.
#501, 1430 Greg St.
Sparks, NV 89431
775-355-9500
Fax: 775-355-9506
info@emcmetals.com
www.emcmetals.com

Company Type: Public
Ticker Symbol: EMC / TSX
Profile: EMC Metals owns a 100% interest in both the Springer Tungsten Mine & the Carlin Vanadium Property. Both projects are located in Nevada. The company also has a 50% earn-in right on Australia's Nyngan Scandium Project.
George Putnam, MBA Finance, President & Chief Executive Officer
Edward H. Dickinson, CPA, Chief Financial Officer
John Thompson, Vice-President, Project Development

Endeavour Silver Corp.
#301, 700 West Pender St.
Vancouver, BC V6C 1G8
604-685-9775
Fax: 604-685-9744
877-685-9775
www.edrsilver.com

Company Type: Public
Ticker Symbol: EDR / TSX, NYSE
Profile: The mid-cap silver mining company has resources in Mexico.
Bradford Cooke, M.Sc., P.Geo., Chair & Chief Executive Officer
Godfrey Walton, M.Sc., P.Geo., President & Chief Operating Officer
Dan Dickson, B.Comm., CA, Chief Financial Officer
David Howe, M.Sc. Mining Geology, Vice-President, Mexico Operations
Hugh Clarke, Contact, Investor Relations
hugh@edrsilver.com

Energold Drilling Corp.
#1100, 543 Granville St.
Vancouver, BC V6C 1X8
604-681-9501
Fax: 604-681-6813
info@energold.com
www.energold.com

Company Type: Public
Ticker Symbol: EGD / TSX Venture
Profile: The contract diamond drilling company serves the international mining sector. The driller strives to operate in an environmentally & socially sensitive manner. Canada's E3 Environmental Excellence in Exploration chose one of Energold's drill programs as a case study.
Frederick W. Davidson, President & Chief Executive Officer
Craig A. Geier, Chief Financial Officer
Jerry Huang, Manager, Investor Relations

Energy Fuels Inc.
#500, 2 Toronto St.
Toronto, ON M5C 2B6

416-214-2810
Fax: 416-214-2727
888-864-2125
investorinfo@energyfuels.com
www.energyfuels.com

Company Type: Public
Ticker Symbol: EFR / TSX
Profile: In 2012, Energy Fuels Inc. acquired Titan Uranium Inc., including the Sheep Mountain Project located in the Crooks Gap District of Wyoming. Energy Fuels' wholly owned subsidiaries now include Titan Uranium Inc., Energy Fuels Resources Corporation, & Magnum Uranium Corp.
Energy Fuels focuses upon the development & expansion of uranium & vanadium assets in the United States. The company also has exploration properties in the Athabasca Basin of Saskatchewan.
Stephen P. Antony, MBA, President & Chief Executive Officer
Jeffrey L. Vigil, Chief Financial Officer
Gary R. Steele, P.Eng., MSc., Secretary & Vice-President, Corporate Marketing
Curtis Moore, JD, MBA, Director, Communications & Legal Affairs
Frank Filas, P.Eng., Manager, Environment

Entree Gold Imc.
#1201, 1166 Alberni St.
Vancouver, BC V6E 3Z3

604-687-4777
Fax: 604-687-4770
poates@entreegold.com
www.entreegold.com

Company Type: Public
Ticker Symbol: ETG/TSX, AMEX, Frankfurt
Greg Crowe, President & CEO
Hamish Malkin, Chief Financial Officer

Erdene Resource Development Corp.
Metropolitan Place
#1480, 99 Wyse Rd.
Dartmouth, NS B3A 4S5

902-423-6419
Fax: 902-423-6432
info@erdene.com
www.erdene.com

Company Type: Public
Ticker Symbol: ERD / TSX
Profile: The diversified resource company advances gold, copper, molybdenum, coking coal, & construction aggregate projects. Erdene Resource Development's projects include the Donkin Deposit & coal exploration projects in Mongolia, the molybdenum Zuun Mod Deposit in southwestern Mongolia, plus the Altan Nar & Khuvyn Khar gold & copper prospects, which are also located in southwestern Mongolia.
Additional assets are as follows: a royalty interest in the the Galshar thermal coal project, operated by Xanadu Mines Ltd.; a royalty interest in Aggregate USA's Sparta Quarry in Georgia; & a majority interest in APM, which is a kaolin producer.
Peter C. Akerley, President & Chief Executive Officer
Kenneth W. MacDonald, Chief Financial Officer & Vice-President, Business Strategy
J.C. Cowan, Vice-President, Asia
Michael X. Gillis, Director, Operations, Mongolia
Michael MacDonald, Director, Exploration, Mongolia
D. Suzan Frazer, Corporate Secretary

Evolving Gold Corp.
#605, 1166 Alberni St.
Vancouver, BC V6E 3Z3

604-685-6375
Fax: 604-909-1163
866-604-3864
info@evolvinggold.com
www.evolvinggold.com

Company Type: Public
Ticker Symbol: EVG / TSX; EVOGF / OTCQX
Profile: Evolving Gold Corp. is a gold exploration company. It has gold properties in & adjacent to the Carlin District of northern Nevada & in Wyoming's Rattlesnake Hills.
R. Bruce Duncan, Chief Executive Officer
Chuck Jenkins, BA, CGA, Chief Financial Officer
Quinton Hennigh, Technical Advisor
Rory Quinn, Contact, Investor Relations
604-630-0792, rory@evolvinggold.com

Evraz Inc. NA Canada
7201 Ogden Dale Rd. SE
Calgary, AB T2C 2A4

403-279-3351
www.evrazna.com

Company Type: Private

Exeter Resource Corporation
AXA Place
PO Box 41, #1660, 990 West Hastings St.
Vancouver, BC V6C 2W2

604-688-9592
Fax: 604-688-9532
888-688-9592
exeter@exeterresource.com
www.exeterresource.com

Other Communications: Australia Office: 612-8920-1356; Chile Office: +562 209 0104
Social Media: www.facebook.com/group.php?gid=74215596524
Company Type: Public
Ticker Symbol: XRC/TSX; XRA/NYSE AMEX
Profile: Exeter Resource Corporation is engaged in the exploration & development of the Caspiche Project, which is located in the Maricunga Gold District of Chile.
Bryce Roxburgh, Chief Executive Officer
Cecil Bond, Chief Financial Officer
Rob Grey, Vice-President, Investor & Corporate Communications
604-688-9537, rgrey@exeterresource.com
Louis Montpellier, Legal Counsel & Vice-President, Corporate Development
Jerry Perkins, Vice-President, Development & Operations
Justin Tolman, General Manager, Chile

Farallon Mining Ltd.
#428, 800 West Pender St.
Vancouver, BC V6C 2V6

604-638-2050
Fax: 604-638-2041
www.nyrstar.com

Company Type: Private
Profile: The company mines for gold, silver, lead, copper & zinc ores.
Roland Junck, Chief Executive Officer & Director

First Majestic Silver Corp.
#1805, 925 West Georgia St.
Vancouver, BC V6C 3L2

604-688-3033
Fax: 604-639-8873
866-529-2807
info@firstmajestic.com; sales@firstmajest
www.firstmajestic.com

Company Type: Public
Ticker Symbol: FR / TSX; AG / NYSE
Profile: The silver company is focused on production in Mexico. In 2012, First Majestic Silver Corp. acquired all the issued & outstanding common share of Silvermex Resources Inc., a mining company with a portfolio of exploration & production projects in Mexico.
Keith Neumeyer, President & Chief Executive Officer
Raymond L. Polman, B.Sc (Econ), CA, Chief Financial Officer
Ramon Davila, Chief Operating Officer
Martin Palacios, MBA, CMC, Chief Information Officer

First Nickel Inc. (FNI)
#206, 120 Front St. East
Toronto, ON M5A 4L9

416-362-7050
Fax: 416-362-9050
info@firstnickel.com
www.firstnickel.com

Company Type: Public
Ticker Symbol: FNI / TSX
Profile: The mining & exploration company is active at its Lockerby Nickel & Copper Mine, which is located in northern Ontario's Sudbury Basin. First Nickel Inc. also owns other exploration properties in the Sudbury Basin, as well as in the Timmins area of northern Ontario & the Belmont region of eastern Ontario.
Thomas M. Boehlert, President & Chief Executive Officer
tboehlert@firstnickel.com
Steven Cresswell, CGA, Chief Financial Officer & Vice-President

Paul Davis, P.Geo, Vice-President, Exploration
Sean Samson, Vice-President & Head, Corporate Development

First Quantum Minerals Ltd.
#800, 543 Granville St.
Vancouver, BC V6C 1X8

604-688-6577
Fax: 604-688-3818
888-688-6577
info@fqml.com
www.first-quantum.com

Company Type: Public
Ticker Symbol: FM / TSX, London
Profile: Operations of the mining & metals company include mineral exploration, development, mining, smelting, & refining. First Quantum Minerals is engaged in copper & cobalt mining in Africa. The company also has interest in gold & cobalt production.
Philip K.R. Pascall, Chair/CEO
Philip.Pascall@fqml.com
Clive Newall, President
clive.newall@fqml.com
David E.J. Moroney, Chief Financial Officer
Christopher Lemon, General Counsel & Corporate Secretary
Sharon Loung, Contact, Corporate Communications & Investor Relations
sharon.loung@fqml.com

First Uranium Corporation
#1210, 141 Adelaide St. West
Toronto, ON M5H 3L5

416-306-3072
Fax: 416-306-3073
www.firsturanium.com

Other Communications: Westonaria, South Africa Office: +27 11 278 7006
Company Type: Public
Ticker Symbol: FIU / TSX; FUM / JSE
Profile: First Uranium Corporation is engaged in the production of gold & uranium.
Deon T. van der Mescht, President & Chief Executive Officer
Emma Oosthuizen, Chief Financial Officer & Senior Vice-President
Scot R. Sobey, Executive Vice-President
Mary Batoff, Secretary & Vice-President, Legal
mary@firsturanium.ca

Formation Metals Inc.
Head Office
#1730, 999 West Hastings St.
Vancouver, BC V6C 2W2

604-682-6229
Fax: 604-682-6205
inform@formationmetals.com
www.formationmetals.com

Other Communications: Investor Relations, Phone: 604-682-6229, ext. 6

Company Type: Public
Ticker Symbol: FCO / TSX
Profile: Formation Metals Inc.'s area of expertise is mineral exploration, mine development, & refining. The company owns 100% of the Idaho Cobalt Project & the Big Creek Hydrometallurgical Complex, also located in Idaho. Through its wholly owned subsidiaries, Formation Metals also has interests in base, precious metal, & uranium projects. Areas of activity are Canada, the United States, & Mexico.
Mari-Ann Green, B.A., B.Ed., Chair & Chief Executive Officer
J. Scott Bending, P.Geo., B.Sc., President
J. Paul Farquharson, B.B.A., C.S.C., Chief Financial Officer
W.G. (Bill) Scales, B.Sc., Executive Vice-President
E.R. (Rick) Honsinger, P.Geo., Vice-President, Corporate Communications
Mike Irish, P.Eng., M.S. Met. Eng., Manager, Metallurgy
Guy Jeske, B.Sc., P.E., General Manager, Underground Mine & Mill
Conrad Parrish, P.Eng., M.B.A., Manager, Environment
Preston Rufe, B.Sc., M Sc., P. Eng, Manager, Environment

Forsys Metals Corp.
Corporate Office
#902, 20 Adelaide St. East
Toronto, ON M5C 2T6

416-367-4242
Fax: 416-367-0598
info@forsysmetals.com
www.forsysmetals.com

Other Communications: Namibian Office, Phone: +264 (0)61 219 462

Company Type: Public
Ticker Symbol: FSY / TSX
Profile: Forsys Metals Corp. is a uranium producer. The company owns 100% of the Namibplaas Uranium Project & the Valencia Uranium Project, which are both located in Namibia, Africa.
Marcel Hilmer, Chief Executive Officer
mhilmer@forsysmetals.com

Craig Bamford, Chief Financial Officer
Johan de Bruin, M.Eng., Pr. Sci. Nat., Chief Geologist
Mark Frewin, Vice-President, Legal Affairs

Fortuna Silver Mines Inc.

#650, 200 Burrard St.
Vancouver, BC V6C 3L6

604-484-4085
Fax: 604-484-4029
866-719-8962
info@fortunasilver.com
www.fortunasilver.com

Company Type: Public
Ticker Symbol: FVI / TSX; FSM / NYSE
Profile: Fortuna is a silver & base metal producer. Areas of operation are southern Peru & Mexico.
Jorge Ganoza Durant, President & Chief Executive Officer
Luis Dario Ganoza Durant, B.Sc. Engineering, MBA, M.Sc., Chief Financial Officer
Manuel R.-C. Carlos, B.Sc. Engineering, Vice-President, Operations
Thomas I. Vehrs, Ph.D., Vice-President, Exploration

Fortune Minerals Limited

#1600, 148 Fullarton St.
London, ON N6A 5P3

519-858-8188
Fax: 519-858-8155
877-552-7726
info@fortuneminerals.com
www.fortuneminerals.com
Other Communications: Vancouver: 778-385-9610; Yellowknife: 867-669-0170

Company Type: Public
Ticker Symbol: FT / TSX
Profile: The diversified resource company has mineral deposits & exploration projects located in Canada. Projects include the Mount Klappan anthracite metallurgical coal deposit in British Columbia, & the NICO gold, colbalt, bismuth, copper deposit in the Northwest Territories.
Robin Ellis Goad, M.Sc., P.Geo., President & Chief Executive Officer
Julian B Kemp, B.B.A., C.A., Chief Financial Officer & Vice-President, Finance
Thomas R. Rinaldi, B.Sc., Vice-President, Operations
Richard P. Schryer, M.Sc., Ph.D., Director, Regulatory & Envrionmental Affairs
James P. Mucklow, M.E.Sc., P.Eng., Manager, Environment & Community Affairs
Troy D. Nazarewicz, CIM, FCSI, Manager, Investor Relations

Franco-Nevada Corporation

Exchange Tower
PO Box 467, #740, 130 King St. West
Toronto, ON M5X 1E4

416-306-6300
Fax: 416-306-6330
contact@franco-nevada.com
www.franco-nevada.com

Company Type: Public
Ticker Symbol: FNV / TSX, NYSE
Profile: Franco-Nevada Corporation has interests in large gold development & exploration projects.
David Harquail, President & Chief Executive Officer
Sandip Rana, Chief Financial Officer
416-306-6303
Stefan Axell, Manager, Investor Relations
416-306-6328

Frontera Copper Corporation

#1000, 36 Toronto St.
Toronto, ON M5C 2C5

602-667-3202
Fax: 602-424-5490
info@fronteracopper.com
www.fronteracopper.com

Company Type: Public
Ticker Symbol: FCC / TSX
Profile: Frontera Copper Corporation is a Canadian copper cathode producer. Its principal area of activity is the Piedras Verdes project in Sonora, Mexico.
Alan Edwards, President/CEO
Dave W. Peat, Vice-President/CFO
Tim J. Swendseid, Vice-President, Engineering
Rodney A. Prokop, Vice-President, Investors Relations
602-424-5483, ir@fronteracopper.com
Joseph P. Campbell, Director, Operations

Full Metal Minerals Ltd.

#1500, 409 Granville St.
Vancouver, BC V6C 1T2

604-484-7855
Fax: 604-484-7155
info@fullmetalminerals.com
www.fullmetalminerals.com

Company Type: Public
Ticker Symbol: FMM / TSX Venture
Profile: Full Metal Minerals is active in Alaska, where it explores for base & precious metals.
Michael Williams, President
Cale Moodie, Chief Financial Officer
Rob McLeod, Vice-President, Exploration
Jeff Sundar, Vice-President

Gabriel Resources Ltd.

#1501, 110 Yonge St.
Toronto, ON M5C 1T4

416-955-9200
Fax: 416-955-4661
info@gabrielresources.com
www.gabrielresources.com

Company Type: Public
Ticker Symbol: GBU / TSX
Alan Hill, President/CEO
Michael Parrett, Chair
Richard Young, Vice-President & CFO

Geomark Exploration Ltd.

Head & Registered Office
#901, 1015 - 4th St. SW
Calgary, AB T2R 1J4

403-262-1400
Fax: 403-232-1421
www.geomark.ca

Company Type: Public
Ticker Symbol: GME / TSX Venture
Profile: Geomark Exploration Ltd. explores for precious & base metals. Areas of activity includ Ontario, Nunavut, & the Northwest Territories.
G.F. Fink, President & Chief Executive Officer
M.J. Balog, Chief Operating Officer
G.E. Schultz, Chief Financial Officer, Secretary, & Vice-President, Finance

GobiMin Inc.

#1250, 120 Adelaide St. West
Toronto, ON M5H 1T1

416-915-0133
Fax: 416-915-2908
info@gobimin.com; hkoffice@gobimin.com (H
www.gobimin.com
Other Communications: Hong Kong Office, Phone: (852) 3586-0280

Company Type: Public
Ticker Symbol: GMN / TSX Venture
Profile: GobiMin Inc. is engaged in mineral exploration & development. The junior mining company is active in China's Xinjiang Uygur Autonomous Region. The company holds equity interest in the Sawayaerdun Gold Project, as well as four base metals exploration joint ventures for nickel, copper, gold, lead, & zinc.
Felipe Tan, President, Chief Executive Officer & Chair
Joyce Ko, Chief Financial Officer, Secretary, & Vice-President, Corporate Affairs

Gold-Ore Resources Ltd.

#9, 1140 - 625 Howe St.
Vancouver, BC V6C 2T6

604-687-8884
Fax: 604-629-0400
info@goldoreresources.com
www.goldoreresources.com

Company Type: Public
Ticker Symbol: GOZ / TSX
Profile: Gold-Ore Resources is a gold producing company. Its main asset is the Bjorkdal Gold Mine in Sweden.
Robert Wasylyshyn, P.Geo., President
Michael Kerfoot, Chief Financial Officer
Troy Winsor, Contact, Investor Relations
800-663-8072

Goldcorp Inc.

Park Place
#3400, 666 Burrard St.
Vancouver, BC 86C 2X8

604-696-3000
Fax: 604-696-3001
info@goldcorp.com; media@goldcorp.com
www.goldcorp.com
Other Communications: Human Resources, E-mail: hr@goldcorp.com

Company Type: Public
Ticker Symbol: G / TSX
Profile: Goldcorp Inc. is a senior gold mining company. Its development projects & operations are located throughout North & South America. The company is listed on the Toronto Stock Exchange under the symbol G and on the New York Stock Exchange under the symbol GG.
Charles A. Jeannes, President/CEO
Lindsay Hall, Exec. Vice-President/CFO
Steve Reid, Exec. Vice-President/COO
Larry Bell, Chair, Sustainability, Environment, Health, & Safety Committee

Golden Band Resources Inc.

#100, 701 Cynthia St.
Saskatoon, SK S7L 6B7

306-955-0787
Fax: 306-955-0788
info@goldenbandresources.com
www.goldenbandresources.com

Company Type: Public
Ticker Symbol: GBN / TSX Venture
Profile: The Saskatchewan-based gold explorer & producer owns 100% of the La Ronge Gold Belt properties. Golden Band Resources also owns 100% of the Jolu mill for processing.
Rob Garden, QC, President & Chief Executive Officer
Mark Thiel, CA, Chief Financial Officer, Corporate Secretary & Vice-President, Finance & Administration
Rodney Orr, P.Geol, MBA, Vice-President, Corporate Development
306-385-7123, rodney.orr@goldenbandresources.com

Golden Mineral Company

#800, 350 Indiana St.
Golden, CO 80401 USA

303-839-5060
Fax: 303-839-5907
888-696-2739
information@goldenminerals.com
www.goldenminerals.com
Other Communications: Investors: investor.relations@goldenminerals.com

Company Type: Public
Ticker Symbol: AUM / TSX, NYSE
Profile: Golden Minerals is focused on advancing the El Quevar Project in Argentina & the Velarde¤a & Chicago Mines in Mexico. In 2011, Golden Minerals Company combined with ECU Silver Mining Inc.
Jeffrey G. Clevenger, Chair, President & Chief Executive Officer
Robert P. Vogels, Chief Financial Officer & Senior Vice-President
Jerry W. Danni, Executive Vice-President
Deborah J. Friedman, Senior Vice-President, General Counsel, & Corporate Secretary

Golden Predator Corp.

888 Dunsmuir St.
Vancouver, BC V6C 3K4

604-648-4653
Fax: 604-642-0604
info@goldenpredator.com
www.goldenpredator.com

Company Type: Public
Ticker Symbol: GPD / TSX
Profile: The gold producer is active in the Yukon. Projects include Brewery Creek, Grew Creek, & Clear Creek.
William M. Sheriff, Chair & Chief Executive Officer
John Legg, BA, LLB, President
Michael G. Maslowski, BSc, CPG, Chief Operating Officer
Michael O'Brien, CA, Chief Financial Officer
Janet Lee-Sheriff, Vice-President, Communications & First Nations Relations

Golden Star Resources Ltd.

Registered Office
PO Box 20 Stn. Bay Adelaide, , #2400, 333 Bay St.
Toronto, ON M5H 2T6

303-830-9000
Fax: 303-830-9094
800-553-8436
info@gsr.com
www.gsr.com

Company Type: Public
Ticker Symbol: GSC/TSX; GSS/NYSE Amex
Profile: The gold mining company has two operating mines located on the Ashanti Gold Belt of Ghana, West Africa. Golden Star Resources conducts its activities with a long-term commitment to the environment, health, & education. Golden Star Resources Ltd. is listed on the following stock exchanges: Toronto Stock Exchange, NYSE Amex Stock Exchange, & the Ghana Stock Exchange.
Tom Mair, President & Chief Executive Officer
John Labate, Chief Financial Officer

Bruce Higson-Smith, Vice-President, Corporate Development & Investor Relations

Gran Colombia Gold
Head Office
#1100, 333 Bay St.
Toronto, ON M5H 2R2
416-360-4653
Fax: 416-360-7783
investorrelations@grancolombiagold.com
www.grancolombiagold.com
Other Communications: Bogota, D.C., Colombia: (571) 485-4747
Company Type: Public
Ticker Symbol: GCM / TSX
Profile: The company is focused upon gold & silver exploration, development, & production in Colombia. Gran Colombia Gold Corp. is also advancing its operations in Venezuela.
Maria Consuelo Araujo, President & Chief Executive Officer
Michael Davies, Chief Financial Officer
Donald East, Chief Operating Officer
Vicente Mendoza, Vice-President, Exploration
Jose R. Oro, Vice-President, Production & Corporate Development
Peter Volk, General Counsel & Secretary

Grande Cache Coal Corporation (GCC)
#1600, 800 - 5th Ave. SW
Calgary, AB T2P 3T6
403-543-7070
Fax: 403-543-7092
calgary@gccoal.com
www.gccoal.com
Other Communications: Grande Cache Office, Phone: 780-827-4646
Company Type: Public
Ticker Symbol: GCE
Profile: Created in 2000, Grande Cache Coal developed a sustainable mining operation. The corporation leases land in the Smoky River Coalfield of west-central Alberta. Metallurgical coal is exported to the world steel industry.
Grande Cache Coal established a Reserves, Safety, & Environmental Committee to assess environment, health, & safety procedures to ensure the company's compliance with regulatory requirements in the region & industry standards.
Robert H. Stan, President & Chief Executive Officer
Ian J. Bootle, Chief Financial Officer & Vice-President, Finance
Lloyd E. Metz, Vice-President, Operations & Development
Eugene H. Nagai, Vice-President, Marketing & Transportation
Tom E. Pierce, Vice-President, Business Development
Kevin R. Wade, Controller

Great Basin Gold Ltd.
#1020, 800 West Pender St.
Vancouver, BC V6C 2V6
604-684-6365
Fax: 604-684-8092
800-667-2114
info@hdgold.com
www.greatbasingold.com
Company Type: Public
Ticker Symbol: GBG / TSX, AMEX
Ferdinand Dippenaar, President/CEO
Lou Van Vuuren, Chief Financial Officer

Great Panther Silver Limited
#2100, 1177 West Hastings St.
Vancouver, BC V6E 2K3
604-608-1766
Fax: 604-608-1744
888-355-1766
info@greatpanther.com
www.greatpanther.com
Company Type: Public
Ticker Symbol: GPR/TSX; GPL/NYSE Amex
Profile: The silver mining & exploration company has wholly-owned operating mines in Mexico. Great Panther Silver Limited is also pursuing opportunities in Latin America.
Robert A. Archer, P.Geo., President & Chief Executive Officer
Charles Brown, Chief Operating Officer
Martin Carsky, CA, Chief Financial Officer & Executive Vice-President
David R. Asher, MBA, Vice-President, Technical Services
Wendy Ratcliffe, Dip. Tech. Fin. Mgt., Corporate Secretary

Great Western Minerals Group Ltd. (GWMG)
219 Robin Cres.
Saskatoon, SK S7L 6M8
306-659-4500
Fax: 306-659-4501
info@gwmg.ca
www.gwmg.ca
Company Type: Public
Ticker Symbol: GWG / TSX Venture
Profile: Great Western Minerals Group Ltd. is an integrated rare earth processor. The company holds interests in rare earth exploration & development properties. Specialty alloys are produced at Great Western Minerals Group's wholly owned subsidiaries, in the United States & the United Kingdom, & used in the aerospace, battery, & magnet sectors.
Jim Engdahl, President & Chief Executive Officer
Jim Davidson, CA, Chief Financial Officer & Vice-President, Finance
Russell Grant, Senior Vice-President, Business Development
Richard Hogan, M.Sc. Eng., Vice-President, Operations
John Pearson, M.Sc. Geo., P.Geo., Vice-President, Exploration
Brent Jellicoe, B.Sc., P.Geo., Director, International Exploration
Dwight Percy, B.Comm, Manager, Investor Relations
306-659-4516, dpercy@gwmg.ca

Guyana Goldfields Inc.
#1608, 141 Adelaide St.
Toronto, ON M5H 3L5
416-628-5936
Fax: 416-628-5935
info@guygold.com
www.guygold.com
Company Type: Public
Ticker Symbol: GUY / TSX
Profile: Guyana Goldfields Inc. explores & develops gold deposits in Guyana, South America.
Patrick Sheridan, MSc, Chief Executive Officer
Paul J. Murphy, B.Comm., CA, Chief Financial Officer & Executive Vice-President, Finance
Dan Noone, BApSci(Geol), MBA, Vice-President, Explorations
Jacqueline Wagenaar, B.MOS, Vice-President, Corporate Communications
jwagenaar@guygold.com

Homeland Energy Group Ltd.
#780, 144 Front St. West
Toronto, ON M5J 2L7
416-506-1979
Fax: 416-362-6830
info@homelandenergygroup.com
www.homelandenergygroup.com
Other Communications: Witbank, South Africa, Regional Office: (013) 656 1060/37
Company Type: Public
Ticker Symbol: HEG / TSX
Profile: Homeland Energy Group Ltd. produces coal. The Group's fully owned subsidiary is Homelnd Mining & Energy, South Africa.
Ashis Basu, Chief Executive Officer
Ajay Gupta, Chief Financial Officer
agupta@homelandenergygroup.com
Hentie Hoffmann, Chief Operating Officer & Managing Director, Homeland Mining & Energy, South Africa
hhoffmann@homelandenergygroup.com

Horizon North Logistics Inc.
#1600, 505 - 3rd St. SW
Calgary, AB T2P 3E6
403-517-4654
Fax: 403-517-4678
888-366-5558
www.horizonnorth.ca
Company Type: Public
Ticker Symbol: HNL / TSX
Profile: Horizon North Logistics Inc.'s services include northern marine transportation & logistics, mobile structures, matting solutions, & camp management & catering. Services are provided to natural resource development projects in Canada's western provinces & northern territories. Horizon North Logistics strives to conduct its business in a responsible manner that is compatible to the environment & communities where it operates. The company employs more than 1,000.
Bob German, President & Chief Executive Officer
403-517-4660, bgerman@horizonnorth.ca
Scott Matson, Chief Financial Officer & Vice-President, Finance
403-517-4662, smatson@horizonnorth.ca
William H. Anderson, Vice-President, Safety & Human Resources
banderson@horizonnorth.ca
Jan M. Campbell, Corporate Secretary

HudBay Minerals Inc.
#800, 25 York St.
Toronto, ON M5J 2V5
416-362-8181
Fax: 416-362-7844
info@hudbayminerals.com
www.hudbayminerals.com
Other Communications: Investors: investor.relations@hudbayminerals.com
Company Type: Private
Ticker Symbol: HBM / TSX
Profile: HudBay Minerals Inc. specializes in the discovery, production, & marketing of base & precious metals. Assets are located in North & South America.
In 2011, HudBay Minerals Inc. acquired Norsemont Mining Inc.. Norsemont was advancing the Constancia Copper Project in southern Peru.
David Garofalo, Chief Executive Officer & President
David S. Bryson, CFA, Chief Financial Officer & Vice-President
H. Maura Lendon, Vice-President, General Counsel, & Corporate Secretary
Brad W. Lantz, B.Sc., (Hons) Earth Sciences, Vice-President, Mining
John Vincic, Vice-President, Investor Relations & Corporate Communications
416-362-0615, john.vincic@hudbayminerals.com
M. Norman Anderson, Chair, Environmental, Health, & Safety Committee

IAMGOLD Corporation
PO Box 153, #3200, 401 Bay St.
Toronto, ON M5H 2Y4
416-360-4710
Fax: 416-360-4750
888-464-9999
info@iamgold.com
www.iamgold.com
Company Type: Public
Ticker Symbol: IMG / TSX, NYSE
Profile: The mid-tier mining company produces gold from mines on three continents. IAMGOLD also operates Niobec Inc., which produces niobium, plus development & exploration projects.
Stephen J.J. Letwin, President & Chief Executive Officer
Carol T. Banducci, Chief Financial Officer & Executive Vice-President
Robert Carreau, Senior Vice-President, Health, Safety, & Sustainability
Michael Donnelly, Senior Vice-President, Exploration
Benjamin Little, Senior Vice-President, Corporate Affairs
Bob Tait, Vice-President, Investor Relations
416-360-4743

Iberian Minerals Corp.
#500, 360 Bay St.
Toronto, ON M5H 2V6
416-815-8558
Fax: 416-815-1355
info@pgm-ventures.com
www.iberianminerals.com
Company Type: Public
Ticker Symbol: IZN / TSX Venture
Daniel Vanin, President & CEO
Leo O'Shaughnessy, Chief Financial Officer

Idaho Natural Resources Corp.
#1110, 1580 Lincoln St.
Denver, CO 80203
www.bridgeresourcescorp.com
Company Type: Public
Ticker Symbol: NEX Board / TSX Venture
Profile: In 2012, Bridge Resources Corp. sold the corporation's assets & changed the name to Idaho Natural Resources Corp.. Following this asset sale, the corporation has a carried working interest in the Idaho Acreage.
Nicholas J. Clayton, Chief Executive Officer
303-831-9022, Fax: 303-831-6366,
njc@bridgeresourcescorp.com
Robert Paradine, Chief Financial Officer

IMPACT Silver Corp.
#1100, 543 Granville St.
Vancouver, BC V6C 1X8
604-681-0172
Fax: 604-681-6813
inquiries@impactsilver.com
www.impactsilver.com
Company Type: Public
Ticker Symbol: IPT / TSX Venture
Profile: The exploration & mining company focuses on silver. Activities take place in Mexico.
Frederick W. Davidson, CA, Chief Executive Officer
Richard S. Younker, CA, CMC, Chief Financial Officer
George Gorzynski, Vice-President, Exploration
Meghan Brush, Contact, Investor Relations

Imperial Metals Corporation
#200, 580 Hornby St.
Vancouver, BC V6C 3B6
604-669-8959
Fax: 604-687-4030
info@imperialmetals.com
www.imperialmetals.com
Company Type: Public
Ticker Symbol: III / TSX
Profile: Imperial Metals Corporation explores, develops, operates, & maintains mine properties. The company's main properties are the The Mount Polley copper, gold mine & the

Huckleberry copper, molybdenum mine, which are both open pit mines in British Columbia. The Red Chris copper, gold property in British Columbia & the Sterling gold property in Nevada are under development.
J. Brian Kynoch, President
604-669-8959
Andre Deepwell, Chief Financial Officer & Corporate Secretary
Don Parsons, Chief Operating Officer
Patrick M. McAndless, Vice-President, Exploration
604-488-2665
Sabine Goetz, Contact, Shareholder Communications
604-488-2657, sgoetz@imperialmetals.com

Infinito Gold Ltd.
#600, 1100 - 1st St. SE
Calgary, AB T2G 1B1

403-444-5191
Fax: 403-444-5190
888-339-6339
info@infinitogold.com

Company Type: Public
Ticker Symbol: IG / TSX Venture
Profile: The company is engaged in gold exploration & development.
John R. Morgan, President & Chief Executive Officer
John Thomas, Vice-President, Operations

Inmet Mining Corporation
#1000, 330 Bay St.
Toronto, ON M5H 2S8

416-361-6400
Fax: 416-368-4692
ir@inmetmining.com
www.inmetmining.com

Company Type: Public
Ticker Symbol: IMN / TSX
Profile: The global mining company produces copper & zinc. Mining operations take place in Spain, Finland, & Turkey. Inmet also has a development project located in Panama.
Richard A. Ross, Chair & Chief Executive Officer
Jochen Tilk, President & Chief Operating Officer
D. James Slattery, Chief Financial Officer & Vice-President, Finance
Steve Astritis, Vice-President, General Counsel, & Secretary
Craig Ford, Vice-President, People & Environment
Flora Wood, Contact, Investor Relations
416-361-4808

Inspiration Mining Corporation
HSBC Building
#1710, 70 York St.
Toronto, ON M5J 1S9

416-842-9000
Fax: 416-865-3368
www.inspirationmining.com

Company Type: Public
Ticker Symbol: ISM/TSX; OI8/Frankfurt SE
Profile: Inspiration Mining Corporation explores for nickel, gold, copper, molybdenum, & rare earth elements. One area of activity is the company's Langmuir property near Timmins, Ontario. The company also owns a lease on contiguous lode claims, situated southwest of Salt Lake City, Utah, USA. Inspiration Mining Corporation's 100% owned subsidiary is Metal Mines Inc..
Randy Miller, Chair, Chief Executive Officer, & President
randy@inspirationmining.com
Peter Anderson, Chief Financial Officer

Inter-Citic Minerals Inc.
#501, 60 Columbia Way
Markham, ON L3R 0C9

905-479-5072
Fax: 905-479-6397
ir@inter-citic.com
www.inter-citic.com
Other Communications: Beijing, China Office, Phone: +86 10 6566 7010

Company Type: Public
Ticker Symbol: ICI / TSX; ICMTF / OCTQX
Profile: Inter-Citic Minerals Inc. is an exploration & development company. It carries out operations in the People's Republic of China, where its Dachang Gold Project is located.
James J. Moore, President & Chief Executive Officer
Lou Pasubio, CA, Chief Financial Officer & Vice-President, China
Stephen Lautens, B.A., LL.B., General Counsel, Corporate Secretary, & Vice-President, Corporate Communications
Garth A. Pierce, Vice-President, Exploration
Malcolm Swallow, P.Eng, FIMMM, C.Eng., Vice-President, Development

International Minerals Corporation
Corporate Office
#211, 7950 E. Acoma Dr.
Scottsdale, AZ 85260 USA

460-483-9932
Fax: 480-483-9926
information@intlminerals.com; IR@intlmine
www.intlminerals.com
Other Communications: Lima Peru Office, Phone: 51-1-440-1314

Company Type: Public
Ticker Symbol: IMZ / TSX
Profile: International Minerals is a silver-gold producer. The company has interests in the Pallancata silver mine & the Inmaculada gold-silver project in Peru, as well as gold projects in Ecuador & Nevada.
The company is listed on the Toronto Stock Exchange, the Swiss Stock Exchange, & the Frankfurt Stock Exchange. Its registrar & transfer agaent is Computershare Trust Company of Canada in Vancouver, British Columbia. The auditing firm is Davidson & Company, Chartered Accountants, also from Vancouver.
Stephen J. Kay, Chief Executive Officer & President
Scott M. Brunsdon, Chief Financial Officer
Nick Appleyard, Vice-President, Corporate Development
Paul Durham, Vice-President, Corporate Relations

International Tower Hill Mines Ltd. (ITH)
#2300, 1177 West Hastings St.
Vancouver, BC V6E 2K3

604-683-6332
Fax: 604-408-7499
855-208-4642
info@ithmines.com; hr@ithmines.com
www.ithmines.com
Other Communications: Englewood CO, USA: 720-881-7646; Fairbanks, AK: 907-328-2802

Company Type: Public
Ticker Symbol: ITH / TSX; THM / NYSE-A
Profile: International Tower Hill Mines Ltd. is active in Alaska, where it has a 100% interest in the Livengood Gold Project, situated north of Fairbanks. International Tower Hill Mines Ltd.'s indirect subsidiary is Tower Hill Mines (US) LLC, which manages exploration & project reviews.
James J. Komadina, President & Chief Executive Officer
Robert D. Comer, Chief Administrative Officer & General Counsel
Tom S.Q. Yip, Chief Financial Officer
Shirley Zhou, Vice-President, Corporate Communications
604-343-4799, szhou@ithmines.com
Rick Solie, Manager, Alaska Community & Media & Government Relations
907-328-2815, rsolie@ithmines.com
Marla K. Ritchie, Corporate Secretary

INV Metals
#700, 55 University Ave.
Toronto, ON M5J 2H7

416-703-8416
Fax: 416-703-8299
questions@invmetals.com
www.invmetals.com

Company Type: Public
Ticker Symbol: INV / TSX
Profile: The international mineral resource company is engaged in exploration, acquisition, & development. INV Metals has base & precious metal projects in Canada, Namibia, & Brazil.
Robert C. Bell, Chief Executive Officer
rbell@invmetals.com
Canadace MacGibbon, President & Chief Financial Officer
cmacgibbon@invmetals.com
Marcelo Schwarz, Country Manager, Brazil
Keith Webb, Country Manager, Namibia

Iron Ore Company of Canada
PO Box 1000, Labrador City, NL A2V 2L8

709-722-4200
Fax: 709-722-4265
iocrelationssi@ironore.ca
www.ironore.ca

Company Type: Private

Ivanhoe Mines Ltd.
World Trade Centre
#654, 999 Canada Pl.
Vancouver, BC V6C 3E1

604-688-5755
Fax: 604-682-2060
888-273-9999
info@ivanhoemines.com
www.ivanhoemines.com

Company Type: Public
Ticker Symbol: IVN / TSX, NYSE, NASDAQ
John Macken, President/CEO
Robert M. Friedland, Executive Chairman

Tony Giardini, CFO
Douglas J. Kirwin, Exec. Vice-President, Exploration

Ivernia Inc.
#3303, 130 Adelaide St. West
Toronto, ON M5H 3P5

416-867-9298
Fax: 416-867-9384
investor@ivernia.ca; marketing@ivernia.ca
www.ivernia.com
Other Communications: Australian Office, Phone: (08) 9267 7000

Company Type: Public
Ticker Symbol: IVW / TSX
Profile: The international metals mining compnay is engaged in exploration & development. Ivernia owns the Magellan Mine in western Australia. The company also has an earn-in agreement on the Prairie Downs Project, which is situated north of the Magellan Mine.
Alan M. De'ath, President & Chief Executive Officer
Brent Omland, Chief Financial Officer & Vice-President, Finance
416-867-9298, Fax: 416-867-9384
Rob Scargill, Executive Vice-President, Operations
D'Arcy Doherty, General Counsel & Vice-President, Legal
Richard G. Perfect, Corporate Controller

Jaguar Mining Inc.
125 North State St.
Concord, NH 03301 USA

603-224-4800
Fax: 603-228-4800
info@jaguarmining.com
www.jaguarmining.com

Company Type: Public
Ticker Symbol: JAG / TSX, NYSE
Daniel R. Titcomb, President & CEO
James Roller, Chief Financial Officer

Karnalyte Resources Inc.
Headquarters
#104, 26 Crystalridge Dr.
Okotoks, AB T1S 2C3

403-995-6560
Fax: 403-995-1678
info@karnalyte.com
www.karnalyte.com

Company Type: Public
Ticker Symbol: KRN / TSX
Profile: Karnalyte Resources explores for & develops agricultural & industrial potash & magnesium products. The company's region of activity is near Wynyard, Saskatchewan.
Robin L. Phinney, P.Eng., Chief Executive Officer
Ronald Love, CA, Chief Financial Officer & Vice-President, Finance
Julius Brinkman, Vice-President, Corporate Development
Henry Kerkhoven, MBA, PMP, Vice-President, Administration
Siu Ma, MBA, P.Eng, Vice-President, Engineering, Research, & Development

Keegan Resources Inc.
#700, 1199 West Hastings St.
Vancouver, BC V6E 3T5

604-683-8193
Fax: 604-683-8194
800-863-8655
info@keeganresources.com
www.keeganresources.com

Company Type: Public
Ticker Symbol: KGN / TSX, NYSE AMEX
Profile: Keegan Resources Inc. is a junior gold company. Its flagship project is the wholly owned Esaase Gold Project, located in Ghana, West Africa.
Shawn Wallace, Chief Executive Officer
Greg McCunn, P.Eng., MBA, Chief Financial Officer
Richard J. Haslinger, P.Eng., Vice-President, Exploration
Andrea Zaradic, P.Eng., Vice-President, Project Development
Graham Johnson, General Manager, Health, Safety, Environment, & Community

KGHM International Ltd.
Four Bentall Centre
PO Box 49185, #2414, 1055 Dunsmuir St.
Vancouver, BC V7X 1K8

604-689-8550
Fax: 604-689-8556
Other Communications: Toronto Office, Phone: 416-628-5929

Company Type: Public
Ticker Symbol: QUX / TSX
Profile: In 2012, a subsidiary of KGHM acquired all the issued & outstanding securities of Quadra FNX Mining Ltd. Quadra FNX now operates under the name KGHM International Ltd. The company focuses on copper & other metals. Operations are carried out in Canada, the United States, & Chile.

Derek White, Executive Vice-President, Corporate Development
604-699-3063
Nawojka Wachowiak, Vice-President, Investor Relations
416-642-9209, nawojka.wachowiak@quadrafnx.com

Kimber Resources Inc.
#215, 800 West Pender St.
Vancouver, BC V6C 2V6

604-669-2251
Fax: 604-669-8577
866-824-1100
info@kimberresources.com; news@kimberreso
www.kimberresources.com
Other Communications: Mexico Office, Phone: 614-410-8344, Fax: 614-423-4664

Company Type: Public
Ticker Symbol: KBR / TSX; KBX / Amex
Profile: Kimber Resources explores for gold & silver deposits in Mexico.
Gordon Cummings, CA, President & Chief Executive Officer
James Currie, P.Eng., Chief Operating Officer
Lyn Davies, CA, Chief Financial Officer
Renee Brickner, Vice-President, Investor Relations
Marius Mare, P.Geo., Vice-President, Exploration

Kinross Gold Corporation
25 York St., 17th Fl.
Toronto, ON M5J 2V5

416-365-5123
Fax: 416-363-6622
866-561-3636
info@kinross.com
www.kinross.com

Company Type: Public
Ticker Symbol: K / TSX, NYSE
Profile: Formed in 1993, Kinross Gold Corporation explores, acquires, mines, & processes gold & silver ore in North & South America.
The company aims to minimize its environmental footprint through its Guiding Principles for Corporate Responsibility & its corporate Environmental Policy.
Tye W. Burt, President/CEO
Thomas M. Boehlert, Exec. Vice-President/CFO
Tim C. Baker, Exec. Vice-President/COO
Erwyn Naidoo, Vice-President, Investor Relations
erwyn.naidoo@kinross.com
John A. Keyes, Chair, Environment, Health, & Safety Committee

Kirkland Lake Gold Inc.
Macassa Mine
PO Box 370 Stn. Main, , 1360 Government Rd. West
Kirkland Lake, ON P2N 3J1

705-567-5208
Fax: 705-568-6444
info@klgold.com
www.klgold.com

Company Type: Public
Ticker Symbol: KGI / TSX
Brian A. Hinchcliffe, President/CEO
John Thomson, Exec. Vice-President & CFO
Sandra Lee, Corporate Secretary

Kobex Minerals Inc.
#1700, 700 West Pender St.
Vancouver, BC V6C 1G8

604-688-9368
Fax: 604-688-9336
investor@kobexminerals.com
www.kobexminerals.com

Company Type: Public
Ticker Symbol: KXM / TSX Venture, Amex
Profile: In 2009, Kobex Resources Inc., IMA Exporation Inc., & International Barytex Resources Ltd. combined to create Kobex Minerals Inc.. The company works to acquire & develop mineral deposits. Kobex Minerals owns 100% of the Mel zinc, lead, barite property, which is located in the Watson Lake Mining District of the Yukon. Another property is the wholly owned Barb Property, which is situated north of Watson Lake in the Yukon.
Alfred L. Hills, President & Chief Executive Officer
Geoffrey Bach, MBA, CA, Chief Financial Officer

La Mancha Resources Inc.
Head Office
2001, rue University
Montréal, QC H3A 2A6

514-987-5115
Fax: 514-987-5119
info@lamancha.ca
www.lamancha.ca
Other Communications: Australia Head Office, Phone: +61 8 9268 4000
Social Media: www.facebook.com/lamancha.aust

Company Type: Public
Ticker Symbol: LMA / TSX
Profile: The international gold producer conducts exploration & development activities & operations in Argentina, Africa, & Australia.
Dominique Delorme, Chief Executive Officer
Nigel Tamlyn, Chief Operating Officer
Gonzague Thomasset, Chief Financial Officer
Jean-Jacques Kachrillo, Vice-President, Exploration

Labrador Iron Mines Holdings Limited (LIM)
#700, 220 Bay St.
Toronto, ON M5J 2W4

647-728-4125
Fax: 416-368-5344
info@labradorironmines.ca
www.labradorironmines.ca

Company Type: Public
Ticker Symbol: LIM / TSX
Profile: Labrador Iron Mines Limited & Schefferville Mines Inc. are wholly owned subsidiaries of Labrador Iron Mines Holdings Limited. Through these subsidiaries, Labrador Iron Mines Holdings has interests in mineral claims & licenses containing iron ore resources. Areas of activity include the Labrador Trough iron range of western Labrador & a region near the town of Schefferville, Québec.
The main office of Labrador Iron Mines Holdings is located in Toronto, with other offices in Schefferville Québec, Goose Bay Newfoundland & Labrador, & Labrador City Newfoundland & Labrador.
John F. Kearney, Chair & Chief Executive Officer
647-728-4105
Danesh K. Varma, Chief Financial Officer
Neil Steenberg, Corporate Secretary

Lake Shore Gold Corp.
Head Office
#2000, 181 University Ave.
Toronto, ON M5H 3M7

416-703-6298
Fax: 416-703-7764
info@lsgold.com
www.lsgold.com
Other Communications: Timmins, ON, Exploration Office, Phone: 705-269-4344

Company Type: Public
Ticker Symbol: LSG / TSX, NYSE Amex
Profile: Lake Shore Gold is a gold producer with properties in the Abitibi Greenstone Belt of northern Ontario & Québec. The company also has a wholly owned mill, situated on the Bell Creek Property near Timmins, Ontario.
Anthony P. Makuch, President & Chief Executive Officer
Mario Stifano, Chief Financial Officer & Vice-President
Dan Gagnon, Senior Vice-President, Operations
Eric Kallio, Vice-President, Exploration
Alasdair Federico, Corporate Secretary & General Counsel

Laramide Resources Ltd.
PO Box 99 Stn. The Exchange, , #3680, 130 King St. West
Toronto, ON M5X 1B1

416-599-7363
Fax: 416-599-4959
flora@laramide.com
www.laramide.com

Company Type: Public
Ticker Symbol: LAM / TSX; LMRXF / OTCBB
Profile: Laramide Resources Ltd. explores for & develops uranium assets. Wholly owned uranium assets are located in the United States & Australia. The company's flagship project is Westmoreland in Queensland, Australia.
Marc Henderson, President & Chief Executive Officer
Dennis Gibson, Chief Financial Officer
Greg Ferron, Vice-President, Corporate Development & Investor Relations
Peter Mullens, Vice-President, Exploration

Largo Resources Ltd.
Corporate Headquarters
#1101, 55 University Ave.
Toronto, ON M5J 2H7

416-861-9797
info@largoresources.com
www.largoresources.com
Social Media:
www.facebook.com/pages/Largo-Resources/232451330133020
twitter.com/LargoResources1

Company Type: Public
Ticker Symbol: LGO / TSX Venture
Profile: The mineral resource exploration & development company holds 100% interest in the following projects: the Currais Novos Tungsten Tailing Project in Brazil, the Campo Alegre de Lourdes Iron-Vanadium Project in Brazil, & the Northern Dancer Tungsten-Molybdenum property in the Yukon Territory. Largo Resources Ltd. also has a 90% interest in the Maracás Vanadium Project, which is located in Brazil.
Mark Brennan, President & Chief Executive Officer
John Laurie, Chief Financial Officer
Tim Mann, Chief Operating Officer
Andy Campbell, Vice-President, Exploration
Kevin Brewer, General Manager, Yukon
Kurt Menchen, General Manager, Brazil

Liberty Mines Inc.
#311A, 8925 - 51 Ave.
Edmonton, AB T6E 5J3

416-238-9736
Fax: 780-437-7898
www.libertymines.com

Company Type: Public
Ticker Symbol: LBE / TSX
Gary Nash, President & CEO
Chris Buysen, Chief Financial Officer

Lipari Energy, Inc.
849 South Hwy. 11
Manchester, KY 40962

606-599-8227
www.liparienergy.com

Company Type: Public
Ticker Symbol: LIP / TSX
Profile: Lipari Energy is a thermal coal producer. Operations & development properties are situated in the Central Appalachian region of the United States.
John Liperote, Chief Executive Officer
Richard Liperote, President
Thomas Liperote, Chief Operating Officer
Scott Warren, Chief Financial Officer
David Stetson, General Counsel

Los Andes Copper Ltd.
Commerce Place
#1950, 400 Burrard St.
Vancouver, BC V6C 3A6

604-637-2883
Fax: 604-682-2802
info@losandescopper.com
www.losandescopper.com

Company Type: Public
Ticker Symbol: LA / TSX Venture
Profile: Los Andes Copper Ltd. is an exploration & development company. It holds an interest in a copper-molybdenum deposit in Chile.
Eduardo Covarrubias, Chief Executive Officer
Aurora Davidson, Chief Financial Officer
Michael Kuta, Corporate Secretary

Lundin Mining Corporation
Corporate Head Office
PO Box 38, #1500, 150 King St. West
Toronto, ON M5H 1J9

416-342-5560
Fax: 416-348-0303
info@lundinmining.com
www.lundinmining.com
Other Communications: Operations Office in UK, Phone: +44 1444 411 900

Company Type: Public
Ticker Symbol: LUN / TSX
Profile: Lundin Mining Corporation was formed in 1994. The corporation is engaged in the exploration, mining, & production of base metal mineral resources, such as copper, nickel, zinc, & lead. Operations are located in Spain, Portugal, & Sweden. The corporation also holds a development project pipeline & an equity stake in a copper & cobalt project in the Democratic Republic of Congo.
Phil Wright, President & Chief Executive Officer
Joao Carrêlo, Chief Operating Officer & Executive Vice-President
Marie Inkster, Chief Financial Officer
416-342-5560
Neil O'Brien, Senior Vice-President, Exploration & Business Development
Peter Nicoll, Vice-President, Health, Safety, Environment, Community
Mikael Schauman, Vice-President, Marketing
Sophia Shane, Contact, Investor Relations, North America
604-689-7842

MAG Silver Corp.
#328, 550 Burrard St.
Vancouver, BC V6C 2B5

604-630-1399
Fax: 604-484-4710
info@magsilver.com
www.magsilver.com

Company Type: Public
Ticker Symbol: MAG / TSX, AMEX

Dan MacInnis, President & CEO
Frank Hallam, Chief Financial Officer

MagIndustries Corp.
372 Bay St., 8th Fl.
Toronto, ON M5H 2W9
416-368-7911
Fax: 902-257-1178
mail@magindustries.com
www.magindustries.com

Company Type: Public
Ticker Symbol: MAA / TSX
William B. Burton, President & CEO
J. Errol Farr, Chief Financial Officer

Major Drilling Group International Inc.
Corporate Office
#100, 111 St George St.
Moncton, NB E1C 1T7
506-857-8636
Fax: 506-857-9211
866-264-3986
info@majordrilling.com; sales@majordrilli
www.majordrilling.com
Other Communications: Investors: if@majordrilling.com; HR: hr@majordrilling.com

Company Type: Public
Ticker Symbol: MDI
Profile: Major Drilling Group International's drilling operations are carried out in the following areas: Canada, the United States, Central America, South America, Africa, Armenia, Indonesia, & Australia. Drilling services include geotechnical, environmental drilling, surface & underground coring, reverse circulation, water-well, shallow gas, & coal-bed methane. The company primarily serves the mining industry.
Francis P. McGuire, President & Chief Executive Officer
Denis Larocque, Chief Financial Officer
Rob Newburn, Executive Vice-President, Australian, Asian, & African Operations
Denis Despres, Vice-President, North American Operations
Kelly Johnson, Vice-President, Latin American Operations
James A. Gibson, General Counsel, Corporate Secretary, & Vice-President, Legal Affairs

Manitok Energy Inc.
#2500, 639 - 5th Ave. SW
Calgary, AB T2P 0M9
403-984-1750
Fax: 403-984-1749
info@manitok.com
www.manitokenergy.com

Company Type: Public
Ticker Symbol: MEI / TSX Venture
Profile: The oil & gas exploration & development company concentrates on conventional oil & gas reservoirs. Manitok's Energy's area of operation is the Canadian foothills.
Massimo M. Geremia, President & Chief Executive Officer
mass@manitok.com
Tim de Freitas, Ph.D., Chief Operating Officer & Vice-President, Exploration
tim@manitok.com
Robert Dion, CA, Chief Financial Officer & Vice-President, Finance
Dorothy Else, BSc., Vice-President, Land
Bob Quartero, M.Sc., P.Geol., Manager, Business Development

McEwen Mining Inc.
Bay Wellington Tower
PO Box 792, #4750, 181 Bay St.
Toronto, ON M5J 2T3
647-258-0395
Fax: 647-258-0408
866-441-0690
www.mcewenmining.com

Company Type: Public
Ticker Symbol: MUX / TSX, NYSE
Profile: In 2012, US Gold Corporation acquired Minera Andes Inc., & it was renamed McEwen Mining Inc..
McEwen Mining is engaged in the exploration, development, & production of gold. The company has assets in Nevada, Mexico, Argentina.
Robert R. McEwen, Chair & Chief Executive Officer
Perry Y. Ing, Chief Financial Officer & Vice-President

MDN Inc.
Canada Place
#680, 1010, rue de la Gauchetière ouest
Montréal, QC H3B 2N2
514-866-6500
Fax: 514-866-3799
info@mdn-mines.com
www.mdn-mines.com

Company Type: Public
Ticker Symbol: MDN / TSX
Profile: MDN Inc. is engaged in the acquisition, exploration, & development of mining properties. The company is active in Québec & Tanzania, East Africa. MDN Inc.'s wholly owned subsidiary in Tanzania is MDN Tanzania Limited.
Serge Bureau, President & Chief Executive Officer
Yves Therrien, Chief Financial Officer
Marc Boisvert, Vice-President, Exploration
Guillaume Mamias, Project Manager & Senior Geologist
Vincent Janelle, Contact, Sharholder Relations

Mega Uranium Ltd.
#2500, 130 King St. West
Toronto, ON M5X 1A9
416-643-7630
Fax: 416-941-1090
info@megauranium.com
www.megauranium.com

Company Type: Public
Ticker Symbol: MGA / TSX
Sheldon Inwentash, Chairman & CEO
Larry Goldberg, Chief Financial Officer

Melior Resources Inc.
Head Office
#2500, 120 Adelaide St.
Toronto, ON M5H 1T1
416-644-1217
investors@meliorresources.com
www.meliorresources.com

Company Type: Public
Ticker Symbol: MLR / TSX Venture
Profile: The corporation seeks investment opportunities in resource based companies.
Charles H. Entrekin, Chief Executive Officer
Rishi Tibriwal, Chief Financial Officer
416-644-1217

Mercator Minerals Ltd.
#1050, 625 Howe St.
Vancouver, BC V6C 2T6
604-694-0005
Fax: 604-558-0058
www.mercatorminerals.com
Other Communications: Mineral Park Mine: 928-565-2226
Company Type: Public
Ticker Symbol: ML / TSX
Profile: Mercator Minerals Ltd. is a molybdenum, copper, & silver producer. The company's assets include the Mineral Park Mine in Arizona, & the El Pilar & El Creston deposits in northern Mexico. In 2011, Mercator Minerals Ltd. acquired all the issued & outstanding shares of Creston Moly Corp.
Bruce McLeod, P.Eng, President & Chief Executive Officer
778-330-1290, bmcleod@mercatorminerals.com
Mark W. Dislter, CPA, Chief Financial Officer
Michael J. Broch, B.Sc. Geology, MSc. Economic Geology, Vice-President, Exploration & Valuations
Marc S. Lelanc, Corporate Secretary
David Jan, Head, Investor Relations & Communications
778-330-1295, djan@mercatorminerals.com

Metanor Resources Inc.
#2, 2872 Sullivan Rd.
Val-d'Or, QC J9P 0B9
819-825-8678
Fax: 819-825-8224
info@metanor.ca
www.metanor.ca

Company Type: Public
Ticker Symbol: MTO / TSX Venture
Profile: Metanor Resources Inc. is a gold mining company, with operations in Québec.
Serge Roy, Chief Executive Officer
Ghislain Morin, President & Chief Operating Officer
Claudine Lévesque, Chief Financial Officer
Pascal Hamelin, Vice-President, Operations
André Tremblay, Vice-President, Exploration
Diane Bournival, Corporate Secretary

Midway Gold Corp.
Point at Inverness
#280, 8310 South Valley Hwy.
Englewood, CO 80112 USA
720-979-0900
Fax: 720-979-0898
877-475-3642
infodata@midwaygold.com
www.midwaygold.com

Company Type: Public
Ticker Symbol: MDW / TSX Venture, AMEX
Profile: The precious metals company explores, builds & operates gold mines.
Daniel E. Wolfus, Chair & Chief Executive Officer
Kenneth A. Brunk, President & Chief Operating Officer
Fritz K. Schaudies, Chief Financial Officer

Richard D. Moritz, Senior Vice-President, Operations
William S. Neal, Vice-President, Geological Services
H. Thomas Williams, Vice-President, Environmental Affairs
R.J. Smith, Vice-President, Administration

Minco Silver Corporation
PO Box 11176, #2772, 1055 West Georgia St.
Vancouver, BC V6E 3R5
604-688-8002
Fax: 604-688-8030
888-288-8288
pr@mincosilver.ca
www.mincosilver.ca
Other Communications: Beijing, Peoples Republic of China Office: 86-10-8233-5198
Company Type: Public
Ticker Symbol: MSV / TSX
Profile: Minco Silver Corporation acquires & develops silver projects. The company owns a 90% interest in the Fuwan Silver Deposit, which is located in Guangdong China.
Ken Z. Cai, Chair & Chief Executive Officer
Paul Zhang, Chief Financial Officer & Vice-President, Finance
Jennifer Trevitt, Corporate Secretary

Mindoro Resources Ltd.
Registered Office
#2200, 10235 - 101 St. NW
Edmonton, AB T5J 3G1
877-413-8187
ir@mindoro.com
www.mindoro.com
Other Communications: Melbourne, Australia Office, Phone: +61 3 9614 5055
Company Type: Public
Ticker Symbol: MIO / TSX Venture
Profile: Mindoro Resources Ltd. explores for nickel, gold, & copper-gold in the mining districts of the Philippines. The company trades on the TSV Venture Exchange, the Frankfurt Stock Exchange, & the Australian Securities Exchange.
John Dugdale, B.Sc.(Hons), President & Chief Executive Officer
Tony Climie, B.Sc., P.Geol., Chief Operating Officer & Director, Exploration
Robert King, Chief Financial Officer & Vice-President, Commercial

Minefinders Corporation Ltd.
#2288, 1177 West Hastings St.
Vancouver, BC V6E 2K3
604-687-6263
Fax: 604-687-6267
866-687-6263
info@minefinders.com
www.minefinders.com
Other Communications: Exploration Office, Phone: 775-851-2202
Company Type: Public
Ticker Symbol: MFL / TSX; MFN, NYSE
Profile: Minefinders is engaged in the production of gold & silver. The company is the owner & operator of the Dolores mine in northern Mexico.
Mark H. Bailey, M.Sc. (Geo), President & Chief Executive Officer

Greg D. Smith, B.Comm, C.A., Chief Financial Officer & Vice-President, Finance
Laurence Morris, B.Sc. (Hons) Geo., B.Sc. Min. Eng., Vice-President, Operations
Tench C. Page, M.Sc. (Geo), Vice-President, Exploration
Jonathan Hackshaw, Director, Corporate Communications
604-687-6263, jon@minefinders.com

Monument Mining Limited
#910, 688 West Hastings St.
Vancouver, BC V6B 1P1
604-638-1661
Fax: 604-638-1663
www.monumentmining.com

Company Type: Public
Ticker Symbol: MMY / TSX Venture
Profile: The gold producer has properties in Malaysia.
Robert F. Baldock, CA(M), FCPA, FCMC, President & Chief Executive Officer
Cathy Zhai, B.Sc., CGA, Chief Financial Officer, Corporate Secretary & Vice-President, Finance
Zaidi Harun, B.Sc., Vice-President, Exploration, Malaysian Region
Richard Cushing, Contact, Investor Relations
rcushing@monumentmining.com

Mountain Province Diamonds Inc.
PO Box 216, #2315, 161 Bay St.
Toronto, ON M5J 2S1
416-361-3562
Fax: 416-603-8565
www.mountainprovince.com

Company Type: Public
Ticker Symbol: MPV / TSX, AMEX
Profile: Mountain Province Diamonds Inc. is engaged in diamond exploration & development. The Kennady Lake diamond project in the Northwest Territories is being developed by the company, in partnership with De Beers Canada.
Patrick Evans, B.A., B.Sc., President, Chief Executive Officer, & Director
Jennifer M. Dawson, B.B.A., Chief Financial Officer & Corporate Secretary

Nautilus Minerals Inc.
#1050, 625 Howe St.
Vancouver, BC V6C 2T6

778-785-7591
Fax: 604-688-0094
ceo@nautilusminerals.com
www.nautilusminerals.com

Company Type: Public
Ticker Symbol: NUS / TSX, London-AIM
David Heydon, President & CEO
Shontel Norgate, Secretary & CFO

Nevada Copper Corp.
#1238, 200 Granville St.
Vancouver, BC V6C 1S4

604-683-8992
Fax: 604-681-0122
877-648-8266
info@nevadacopper.com
www.nevadacopper.com
Other Communications: Yerington, Nevada Office, Phone: 885-463-3510

Company Type: Public
Ticker Symbol: NCU / TSX
Profile: Nevada Copper Corp. owns 100% of a development property in the Walker Lane mineralized belt situated in western Nevada.
Giulio Bonifacio, President & Chief Executive Officer
Joe Chan, Chief Financial Officer & Vice-President
Robert McKnight, P.Eng., Executive Vice-President
bmcknight@nevadacopper.com
Timothy M. Dyhr, Vice-President, Environment & External Relations
Greg French, CPG, M.Sc., Vice-President & Senior Project Manager
Catherine Tanaka, Corporate Secretary

Nevsun Resources Ltd.
#800, 1075 West Georgia St.
Vancouver, BC V6E 3C9

604-623-4700
Fax: 604-623-4701
888-600-2200
nevsuninfo@nevsun.com
www.nevsun.com

Company Type: Public
Ticker Symbol: NSU / TSX, AMEX
Cliff T. Davis, President & CEO
Peter Hardie, CFO

New Dawn Mining Corp.
#301, 116 Simcoe St.
Toronto, ON M5H 4E2

416-585-7890
Fax: 416-585-9801
info@newdawnmining.com
www.newdawnmining.com

Company Type: Public
Ticker Symbol: ND / TSX
Profile: The junior gold company has assets & operations in Zimbabwe. New Dawn Mining owns 100% of the Camperdown Mine, the Old Nic Mine, & the Turk & Angelus Mine, plus 85% of the Venice Mine, the Dalny Mine, & the Golden Quarry Mine.
Ian R. Saunders, President & Chief Executive Officer
Graham R. Clow, Chief Financial Officer

New Gold Inc.
South Tower, Royal Bank Plaza
#3120, 200 Bay St.
Toronto, ON M5J 2J4

416-324-6000
Fax: 416-324-9494
888-315-9715
info@newgold.com; careers@newgold.com
www.newgold.com
Other Communications: Investors: 416-324-6015; Vancouver Office: 604-696-4100

Company Type: Public
Ticker Symbol: NGD / TSX, AMEX
Profile: The intermediate gold mining company has assets in Canada, the United States, Mexico, Australia, & Chile.
Robert Gallagher, Chief Executive Officer
Basil Huxham, Exec. Vice-President/CFO
James (Jim) Currie, Vice-President, Operations
Mélanie Hennessey, Vice-President, Investor Relations
604-639-0022
Christine Marks, Contact, Media & Communications
604-639-0023, christine.marks@newgold.com

New Millennium Iron Corp.
Executive Office
1303, av Greene, 2e étage
Montréal, QC H3Z 2A7

514-935-3204
Fax: 514-935-9650
www.nmliron.com
Other Communications: Calgary, AB: 403-266-1150; St. John's NL: 709-722-5714

Company Type: Public
Ticker Symbol: NML / TSX
Profile: New Millennium Iron Corp. controls the Millennium Iron Range, which is located in the provinces of Newfoundland & Labrador & Québec. The corporation & Tata Steel Limited are working together to advance the DSO Project in the same region.
Dean Journeaux, Eng., President & Chief Executive Officer
Thiagarajan Balakrishnan, P.Geo., Chief Geologist
Mark Freedman, Chief Financial Officer
Paul Wilkinson, Senior Vice-President, Environmental & Social Affairs
Jean-Charles Bourassa, Vice-President, Mining
Ernest Dempsey, Vice-President, Investor Relations & Corporate Affairs
Cathy Dornan, Vice-President, Communications

NGEx Resources Inc.
Head Office
#2000, 885 West Georgia St.
Vancouver, BC V6C 3E8

604-689-7842
Fax: 604-689-4250
ngexresources@namdo.com
www.ngexresources.com

Company Type: Public
Ticker Symbol: NGQ / TSX
Profile: NGEx Resources Inc. is an exploration company. It is active in South America. One of NGEx Resources' projects is the Los Helados copper & gold discovery in Chile.
Wojtek Wodzicki, President & Chief Executive Officer
Wanda Lee, Chief Financial Officer
Bob Carmichael, Vice-President, Exploration

Noranda Income Fund
c/o Xstrata Canada Inc.
PO Box 403 Stn. First Canadia, , #6900, 100 King St. West
Toronto, ON M5X 1E3

416-775-1500
Fax: 416-775-1749
info@norandaincomefund.com
www.norandaincomefund.com

Company Type: Public
Ticker Symbol: NIF.UN / TSX
Profile: The Fund's main asset is CEZinc. a zinc processing facility in Salaberry-de-Valleyfield, Québec. Canadian Electrolytic Zinc Limited operates & manages the CEZ processing facility. The facility has obtained ISO 9001 & ISO 14001 certification to cover all environmental processes at the plant.
Manuel Alvarez Davila, Chief Executive Officer, Noranda Income Fund's Manager
Michael Boone, Chief Financial Officer & Vice-President, Canadian Electrolytic Zinc Limited
416-775-1561
Eva Carissimi, BSc. (Metallurgical Engineering), Vice-President, Operations of the Manager

Noront Resources Ltd.
#1100, 105 Adelaide St. West
Toronto, ON M5H 1P9

416-367-1444
Fax: 416-367-5444
investor.relations@norontresources.com
www.norontresources.com
Other Communications: Employment Inquiries: careers@norontresources.com

Company Type: Public
Ticker Symbol: NOT / TSX Venture
Profile: Noront Resources Ltd. is engaged in exploration & development operation in the James Bay Lowlands of Ontario. The company is developing the Eagle's Nest Deposit, which consists of nickel, copper, platinum, & palladium. Another focus is the Blackbird Chromite Discovery.
Wesley C. Hanson, President & Chief Executive Officer
Gregory R. Rieveley, Chief Financial Officer
Paul G. Semple, P.Eng., Chief Operating Officer
Glenn Nolan, Vice-President, Aboriginal Affairs

North American Palladium Ltd.
#2116, 130 Adelaide St. West
Toronto, ON M5H 3P5

416-360-7590
Fax: 416-360-7709
info@napalladium.com
www.napalladium.com

Company Type: Public
Ticker Symbol: PDL / TSX, AMEX
William Biggar, President/CEO
Fraser Sinclair, CFO & Vice-President, Finance
Mary Batoff, Secretary

North American Tungsten Corporation Ltd.
PO Box 19, #1640, 1188 West Georgia St.
Vancouver, BC V6E 4A2

604-684-5300
Fax: 604-684-2992
info@natungsten.com
www.northamericantungsten.com

Company Type: Public
Ticker Symbol: NTC / TSX Venture
Stephen Leahy, President & CEO
Harold schwenk, CFO

Northern Dynasty Minerals Ltd.
#1020, 800 West Pender St.
Vancouver, BC V6C 2V6

604-684-6365
Fax: 604-684-8092
info@hdgold.com
www.northerndynastyminerals.com

Company Type: Public
Ticker Symbol: NDM / TSX, AMEX
Ronald Thiessen, President & CEO
Marchand Snyman, Chief Financial Officer

Northland Resources S.A.
Scorpio Building
7A, rue Robert Stümper
Luxembourg, L-2557 Luxembourg

www.northland.eu

Company Type: Public
Ticker Symbol: NAU/TSX; NPK/Frankfurt
Profile: The mining company has a portfolio of iron ore projects in northern Finland & Sweden.
Karl-Axel Waplan, President & Chief Executive Officer
Peder Zetterberg, Chief Financial Officer
Peder Pernlöf, Chief Operating Officer & Vice-President, Procurement & Energy
Anders Antonsson, Vice-President, Investor Relations
Marguerite Manshreck-Head, Contact, Investor Relations, Canada
647-224-7882

NovaGold Resources Inc.
Granville Square
PO Box 24, #2300, 200 Granville St.
Vancouver, BC V6C 1S4

604-669-6227
Fax: 604-669-6272
866-669-6227
info@novagold.net
www.novagold.net

Company Type: Public
Ticker Symbol: NG / TSX, AMEX
Rick Van Nieuwenhuyse, President/CEO
R.J. (Don) MacDonald, CFO & Sr. Vice-President

OceanaGold Corp.
250 Collins St., Level 5
Melbourne, Victoria, 3000 Australia

info@oceanagold.com; careers@oceanagold.c
www.oceanagold.com
Other Communications: Phone: 61-3-9656-5300; Fax: 61-3-9656-5333

Company Type: Public
Ticker Symbol: OGC / TSX, ASX, NZX
Profile: The gold producer has a portfolio of exploration, development, & operating assets in the Asia Pacific region.
Michael Wilkes, Chief Executive Officer
Mark Chamberlain, Chief Financial Officer & Secretary
Mark Cadzow, Chief Operating Officer
Michael Roache, Head, Exploration

Olympus Pacific Minerals Inc.
#500, 10 King St. East
Toronto, ON M5C 1C3

416-572-2525
Fax: 416-572-4202
888-902-5522
info@olympuspacific.com
www.olympuspacific.com
Other Communications: DaNang, Son Tra District, Vietnam Office: + 84 511 394 5288
Social Media:
www.facebook.com/group.php?gid=106659006048073
www.linkedin.com/company/olympus-pacific-minerals

Company Type: Public
Ticker Symbol: OYM / TSX, Australia
Profile: The diversified gold company concentrates upon the following properties: the Bong Mieu & Phuoc Son in central Vietnam; the Bau Goldfield in eastern Malaysia; & the Capcapo in the Philippines.
John A.G. Seton, Chief Executive Officer
Jane Bell, Chief Financial Officer
Klaus Leiders, Chief Operating Officer
Peter Tiedemann, Chief Information Officer
James W. Hamilton, Vice-President, Investor Relations
Rod Murfitt, Group Manager, Exploration

Orbit Garant Drilling Inc.
3200, Jean-Jacques Cossette
Val-d'Or, QC J9P 6Y6

866-824-2707
Fax: 819-824-1595
www.orbitgarant.com

Company Type: Public
Ticker Symbol: OGD / TSX
Profile: The mineral drilling compnay provides both underground & surface drilling services. Operations are carried out in Canada & internationally. Orbit Garant Drilling Inc. employs over 1,100 people.
Eric Alexandre, CNA, President & Chief Executive Officer
eric.alexandre@orbitgarant.com
Alain Laplante, FCGA, Chief Financial Officer & Vice-President
alain.laplante@orbitgarant.com
Richard Alexandre, Director, Operations, Surface & International
Sylvain Laroche, Director, Administration
Marc Rochefort, Director, Environment & Special Projects
Ronald Thibault, Director, Operations, Underground

orex Gold Resources Inc.
#1502, 145 King St. West
Toronto, ON M5H 1J8

647-260-1500
Fax: 416-640-2011
TXG / TSX
www.torexgold.com

Company Type: Public
Profile: The mining company explores for precious metal resources, especially gold. Torex Gold Resources Inc. owns 100% of the Morelos Gold Project, which is situated in the Morelos Gold Belt near Mexico City.
Fred Stanford, PEng, President & Chief Executive Officer
647-260-1502, fred.stanford@torexgold.com
Andrew Gottwald, CA, Chief Financial Officer
Alejandro Kakarieka, Vice-President, Exploration
Gabriela Sanchez, MBA, Vice-President, Investor Relations
647-260-1503, gabriela.sanchez@torexgold.com

Orezone Gold Corporation
#201, 290 Picton Ave.
Ottawa, ON K1Z 8P8

613-241-3699
Fax: 613-241-6005
888-673-0663
www.orezone.com

Company Type: Public
Ticker Symbol: ORE / TSX
Profile: Orezone Gold Corporation is a gold exploration company. Operations are conducted in West Africa.
Ronald Neville Little, President & Chief Executive Officer
Sean Homuth, Chief Financial Officer
Pascal Marquis, Senior Vice-President, Exploration
Jow McCoy, Vice-President, Administration

Orosur Mining Inc.
#101, 50 Richmond St. East
Toronto, ON M5C 1N7

416-848-7744
Fax: 416-848-0790
info@orosur.ca
www.orosur.ca
Other Communications: Uruguay: + 598 2 601 6354; Chile: +562 9246800

Company Type: Public
Ticker Symbol: OMI / TSX Venture
Profile: The exploration company & gold producer is active in Latin America. Orosur Mining's exploration portfolio includes assets in Chile & Uruguay. It also operates a producing gold mine in Uruguay.
David Fowler, Chief Executive Officer
david.fowler@orosur.ca
Ignacio Salazar, Chief Financial Officer

Orsu Metals Corp.
1 Red Pl.
London, W1K 6PL United Kingdom

info@orsumetals.com
www.orsumetals.com
Other Communications: Phone: 44(0)20-7518-3999; Fax: 44(0)20-7518-3998

Company Type: Public
Ticker Symbol: OSU / TSX, AIM
Profile: Orsu Metals Corporation is a precious & base metals exploration & development company. It is active in the Tien Shan gold belt of the Kyrgyz Republic & the Rudny Altai copper belt in the Republic of Kazakhstan. Orsu Metals also has offices in Kyrgyzstan (+ (996) 312 626129) & Kazakhstan (+7 7273 758663).
Petro Mychalkiw, Chief Financial Officer
Alexander Yakubchuk, Chief Operating Officer
Raymond Oates, Technical Director
Tania Tchedaeva, Secretary

Orvana Minerals Corp.
#1901, 181 University Ave.
Toronto, ON M5H 3M7

416-369-1629
Fax: 416-369-1402
www.orvana.com

Company Type: Public
Ticker Symbol: ORV / TSX
Profile: The Canadian gold & copper mining & exploration company evaluates, develops, & mines precious & base metals deposits. Orvana Minerals is the owner & operator of the Don Mario gold mine in eastern Bolivia. Through its wholly owned subsidiary, Kinbauri Espa¤a S.L.U., Orvana Minerals also operates the El Valle-Boinás/Carlés copper & gold mine in northern Spain. Another Orvana asset is the Cooperwood copper project, situated in Michigan's Upper Peninsula.
Bill Williams, President & Chief Executive Officer
wcwilliams@orvana.com
Agne Ahlenius, Chief Operating Officer
Malcolm King, Chief Financial Officer & Vice-President

Osisko Mining Corporation
2140, rue St-Mathieu
Montréal, QC H3H 2J4

514-735-7131
Fax: 514-933-3290
ir@osisko.com
www.osisko.com

Company Type: Public
Ticker Symbol: OSK / TSX, Frankfurt
Sean Roosen, President & CEO
Brian A. Coates, Vice-President & CFO

Pan American Silver Corp.
Corporate Headquarters
#1500, 625 Howe St.
Vancouver, BC V6C 2T6

604-684-1175
Fax: 604-684-0147
info@panamericansilver.com
www.panamericansilver.com

Company Type: Public
Ticker Symbol: PAA / TSX NASDAQ
Profile: The silver producer was founded in 1994. Pan American Silver conducts its mining & exploration activities in Mexico, Bolivia, Peru, & Argentina.
Geoffrey A. Burns, President/CEO
Robert G. Doyle, Chief Financial Officer
Steven Busby, Chief Operating Officer
Martin Wafforn, Vice-President, Technical Services
Gonzalo Rios, Director, Environmental Affairs
Kettina Cordero, Coordinator, Investor Relations

Panoro Minerals Ltd.
#1610, 700 West Pender St.
Vancouver, BC V6C 1G8

604-684-4246
Fax: 604-684-4200
info@panoro.com
www.panoro.com
Other Communications: Lima, Peru Office: +51.1.628.5978

Company Type: Public
Ticker Symbol: PML / TSX Venture, Lima
Profile: Panoro Minerals Ltd. has a portfolio of mineral properties situated in southeastern Peru. The region is known for its copper & gold deposits.
Luquman Shaheen, M.B.A., P.Eng., P.E., President & Chief Executive Officer
Christian G. Pilon, President, Minera Panoro (Peru) S.A.C. Panoro Apurimac S.A.
David W. Huber, Chief Financial Officer
Yves Barsimantov, General Manager, Peru, & Vice-President, Operations
Luis Vela, Manager, Exploration

Parex Resources Inc.
Corporate Headquarters
#1900, 250 Second St. SW
Calgary, AB T2P 0C1

403-265-4800
Fax: 403-265-8216
info@parexresources.com
www.parexresources.com
Other Communications: Colombia: +(571) 629-1716; Trinidad/Tobago: +(868) 221-5868

Company Type: Public
Ticker Symbol: PXT / TSX
Profile: Oil & natural gas exploration & production are conducted in the Caribbean area & South America. Parex Resources has holdings onshore Trinidad & in Colombia's Llanos Basin.
Wayne K. Foo, President & Chief Executive Officer
Barry B. Larson, Chief Operating Officer & Vice-President, Operations
Kenneth G. Pinsky, Chief Financial Officer & Vice-President, Finance
403-517-1729
David R. Taylor, Vice-President, Exploration & Business Development
Michael Kruchten, Manager, Investor Relations
403-517-1733, Investor.relations@parexresources.com

PC Gold Inc.
#1200, 141 Adelaide St. West
Toronto, ON M5H 3L5

416-848-9633
Fax: 416-360-3416
www.pcgold.ca
Social Media:
www.facebook.com/pages/PC-Gold-Inc/208092952615896
twitter.com/pcgoldinc

Company Type: Public
Ticker Symbol: PKL / TSX
Profile: The gold exploration company has 100% ownership of the Pickle Crow gold mine in northwestern Ontario.
Jean-Pierre Chauvin, President & Chief Executive Officer
416-867-8567, jpchauvin@pcgold.ca
Peter J. Hooper, Chief Operating Officer
Miles Nagamatsu, Chief Financial Officer
Neil Pettigrew, M.Sc., P.Geo., Vice-President, Exploration
Shaun Drake, Corporate Secretary

Petaquilla Minerals Ltd.
#1230, 777 Hornby St.
Vancouver, BC V6Z 1S4

604-694-0021
Fax: 604-694-0063
877-694-0021
info@petaquilla.com
www.petaquilla.com

Company Type: Public
Ticker Symbol: PTQ / TSX; PTQMF / OTCBB
Profile: The gold producer is involved in acquisitions, exploration, & production. Petaquilla Minerals Ltd. is active in Panama, where its Molejon Gold Project with a surface gold processing plant are located. The company also acquired 100% of the Lomero-Poyatos Project, which is situated in the Pyrite Belt of Iberia.
Joao Manuel, Chief Executive Officer
Rodrigo Esquivel, President
Lazaro Rodriguez, Chief Operations Officer
Ezequiel Sirotinsky, Chief Financial Officer
David Kaplan, Corporate Secretary

PhosCan Chemical Corp.
#501, 1 St. Clair Ave. West
Toronto, ON M4V 1K6

416-972-9222
Fax: 416-972-0662
info@phoscan.ca
www.phoscan.ca

Company Type: Public
Ticker Symbol: FOS / TSX
Profile: PhosCan Chemical Corp. is engaged in the development of the Martison Phosphate Project, located north of Hearst, Ontario.
Stephen Case, President & Chief Executive Officer
James F. Pringle, Chief Financial Officer & Vice-President, Finance

Platinum Group Metals
Bentall Tower 5
#328, 550 Burrard St.
Vancouver, BC V6C 2B5
604-899-5450
Fax: 604-484-4710
866-899-5450
info@platinumgroupmetals.net
www.platinumgroupmetals.net
Other Communications: South Africa Office Phone: +27 (11) 782-2186
Company Type: Public
Ticker Symbol: PTM / TSX
Profile: Formed in 2000, & based in Vancouver, British Columbia & Johannesburg, South Africa, Platinum Group Metals Ltd. is engaged in the exploration, construction, & operation of mines. The company holds mineral rights in the Bushveld Igneous Complex of South Africa, in addition to two joint ventures with the government of Japan. Platinum Group Metals Ltd.'s focus is upon the development of platinum operations.
R. Michael Jones, B.A.SC., P.Eng, President, Chief Executive Officer, & Co-Founder
Peter C. Busse, P.Eng, Chief Operating Officer
Frank Hallam, B.B.A., C.A., Chief Financial Officer, Corporate Secretary, & Director
Michael Wasserfall, B.A., LLB, Corporate Counsel
Kris Begic, Vice-President, Corporate Development
Mathys Johannes Botha, Diploma, Geology, Technical Manager & Senior Geologist
Enoch Mawasha, Accounting, Manager
Len Backhouse, Mine Designer
Kamal Parbhoo, Controller

Polaris Minerals Corporation
#2740, 1055 West Georgia St.
Vancouver, BC V6E 3R5
604-915-5000
Fax: 604-915-5001
info@polarmin.com
www.polarmin.com
Company Type: Public
Ticker Symbol: PLS / TSX
Marco Romero, President & CEO
Lisa Dea, Vice-President & CFO, Finance

Polymet Mining Corp.
#390, 3600 Lysander Lane
Richmond, BC V7B 1C3
604-248-0939
Fax: 604-248-0940
info@polymetmining.com
www.polymetmining.com
Other Communications: Hoyt Lakes, MN, USA Office, Phone: 218-471-2150
Social Media: www.facebook.com/PolyMet
twitter.com/PolyMetMining
Company Type: Public
Ticker Symbol: POM / TSX, AMEX
Profile: PolyMet Mining Corp. is a mine development company. It controls 100% of the NorthMet copper, nickel, precious metals, ore project, which is located on the Mesabi Range of northeastern Minnesota. The company also owns 100% of a nearby processing facility, known as Erie Plant.
Joseph Scipioni, President, Chief Executive Officer & Chief Operating Officer
Douglas J. Newby, Chief Financial Officer
Niall Moore, Corporate Secretary & Group Controller

Potash Corporation of Saskatchewan, Inc.
#500, 122 - 1st Ave. South
Saskatoon, SK S7K 7G3
306-933-8500
800-667-0403
corporate.relations@potashcorp.com
www.potashcorp.com
Company Type: Public
Ticker Symbol: POT / TSX
Profile: Potash Corporation of Saskatchewan was created in 1975 as a Crown Corporation by the Saskatchewan government. The fertilizer enterprise produces the following plant nutrients: potash, nitrogen, & phosphate. Potash Corporation of Saskatchewan supplies the agriculture, animal nutrition, & industrial chemical markets. The company is now listed on the Toronto & New York stock exchanges under the symbol POT.
William J. Doyle, President/CEO
Garth W. Moore, President, PCS Potash
G. David Delaney, President, PCS Sales
Thomas J. Regan, Jr., President, PCS Phosphate & PCS Nitrogen
Wayne R. Brownlee, Exec. Vice-President/CFO
James F. Dietz, Exec. Vice-President/COO
Robert A. Jaspar, Sr. Vice-President, Information Technology
John R. Hunt, Vice-President, Safety, Health & Environment
Denita Stann, CA, Director, Investor Relations

Powertech Uranium Corp.
Three Bentall Centre
PO Box 49212, #3023, 595 Burrard St
Vancouver, BC V7X 1K8
604-685-9181
Fax: 604-685-9182
info@powertechuranium.com
www.powertechuranium.com
Company Type: Public
Ticker Symbol: PWE/TSX; P8A/Frankfurt
Profile: Powertech Uranium Corp. is a mineral exploration & development company. Through its subsidiary, Powertech (USA) Inc., Powertech Uranium Corp. holds the following assets: the Dewey Terrace & Aladdin Projects in Wyoming; the Dewey-Burdock Uranium Deposit in South Dakota; & the Centennial Project in Colorado.
Richard Clement, P.G., MSc., President & Chief Executive Officer
Thomas A. Doyle, Chief Financial Officer & Vice-President, Finance
Frank Lichnovsky, P.G., Chief Geologist
Richard Blubaugh, Vice-President, Health, Safety, & Environmental Resources
Jim Bonner, P.G., BSc., Vice-President, Exploration
Greg Burnett, MBA, BASc., Vice-President, Administration

Premier Gold Mines Limited
#401, 1113 Jade Crt.
Thunder Bay, ON P7B 6M7
807-346-1390
Fax: 807-346-0100
888-346-1390
info@premiergoldmines.com
www.premiergoldmines.com
Company Type: Public
Ticker Symbol: PG / TSX
Profile: The exploration company is active in Canada & the United States. Premier Gold Mines Limited's major assets are located in Ontario's Geraldton, Red Lake, & Musselwhite regions, & also in the Carlin Trend of Nevada.
In 2011, Premier Gold Mines Limited acquired ownership & control of common shares of Goldstone Resources Inc.
Ewan S. Downie, President & Chief Executive Officer
Paul Huet, Chief Operating Officer
John Seaman, Chief Financial Officer
Stephen McGibbon, Executive Vice-President, Corporate & Project Development
Steve Filipovic, Vice-President, Finance

Prodigy Gold Incorporated
#1205, 700 West Pender St.
Vancouver, BC V6C 1G8
604-688-9006
Fax: 604-688-9029
888-688-9006
ir@prodigygold.com; careers@prodigygold.c
www.prodigygold.com
Company Type: Public
Ticker Symbol: PDG / TSX Venture
Profile: Prodigy Gold is working on the Magino Mine Gold Project in Ontario.
Brian J. Maher, M.Sc., President & Chief Executive Officer
Tony Wood, B.Sc. (Hons.), CA, Chief Financial Officer & Corporate Secretary
Fred Mason, Vice-President, Operations
Tom Pollock, M.Sc. (A), P.Geo., Vice-President, Exploration

Pure Nickel Inc.
#900, 95 Wellington St.
Toronto, ON M5J 2N7
416-644-0066
Fax: 416-644-0069
info@purenickel.com
www.purenickel.com
Company Type: Public
Ticker Symbol: NIC / TSX, OTCBB
Profile: The mineral exploration company has projects in North America.
David R. McPherson, President & Chief Executive Officer
Jeffrey D. Sherman, Chief Financial Officer
Jon Findlay, Senior Geologist
Lisa Buchan, Corporate Secretary & Business Manager

Quaterra Resources Inc.
Head Office
#1100, 1199 West Hastings St.
Vancouver, BC V6E 3T5
604-681-9059
Fax: 604-641-2740
855-681-9059
info@quaterra.com
www.quaterra.com
Company Type: Public
Ticker Symbol: QTA / TSX Venture
Profile: The junior mineral exploration company conducts operations in North America.
Thomas C. Patton, B.Sc., M.Sc., Ph.D., President & Chief Executive Officer
Scott B. Hean, B.A., MBA, ICD.D, Chief Financial Officer
Charles C. Hawley, B.A., Ph.D., Vice-President, Exploration, Alaska
Eugene Spiering, B.Sc., Vice-President, Exploration

Queenston Mining Inc.
#201, 133 Richmond St. West
Toronto, ON M5H 2L3
416-364-001
info@queenston.ca
www.queenston.ca
Company Type: Public
Ticker Symbol: QMI / TSX, Frankfurt
Profile: The mineral exploration & development company has holdings in the Kirkland Lake area. Queenston Mining's assets include six 100% owned gold deposits.
Charles E. Page, B.Sc., M.Sc., P.Geo., President & Chief Executive Officer
John A. Francis, BA, CA, Chief Financial Officer
Philip Ng, M.Eng., P.Eng., Chief Operating Officer
William Mcguinty, B.Sc., P.Geo., Vice-President, Exploration
Jennifer S. McGuinty, Corporate Secretary

Rainy River Resources Ltd.
Head Office
#701, 1 Richmond St. West
Toronto, ON M5H 3W4
416-645-7280
Fax: 416-642-9312
www.rainyriverresources.com
Company Type: Public
Ticker Symbol: RR / TSX
Profile: Rainy River Resources Ltd. is a precious metals exploration company. Its main asset is the Rainy River Gold Project, which is situated in Richardson Township in northern Ontario.
Raymond W. Threlkeld, President & Chief Executive Officer
Nicholas J. Nikolakakis, MBA, Chief Financial Officer & Vice-President
Michael A. Mutchler, MBA, EJD, Chief Operating Officer & Vice-President
Gerald J. Shields, LL.B., Vice-President & General Counsel
Kerry Sparkes, M.Sc., P.Geo., Vice-President, Exploration
Kyle Stanfield, P.Eng., Vice-President, Environment & Sustainability
Indi Gopinathan, P.Eng., MBA, CMA, Director, Investor Relations
416-645-7289, igopinathan@RainyRiverResources.com

Revett Minerals Inc.
11115 East Montgomery Dr., #G
Spokane Valley, WA 99206 USA
509-921-2294
Fax: 509-891-8901
866-921-2294
revett@revettminerals.com
www.revettminerals.com
Company Type: Public
Ticker Symbol: RVM / TSX, NYSE Amex
Profile: Revett Minerals is a precious metals producer. Through its subsidiaries, Revett Minerals is the owners & operator of the Troy Mine & the Rock Creek Project in Montana.
John Shanahan, Chief Executive Officer
Ken Eickerman, Chief Financial Officer
Monique Hayes, Corporate Secretary & Director, Investor Relations

Richmont Mines Inc.
161, av Principale
Rouyn-Noranda, QC J9X 4P6
819-797-2465
Fax: 819-797-0166
info@richmont-mines.com
www.richmont-mines.com
Other Communications: Montreal Administrative Office, Phone: 514-397-1410
Company Type: Public
Ticker Symbol: RIC / TSX, AMEX
Profile: Richmont Mines Inc. specializes in gold exploration, development, & mining. Operations take place in Ontario, Quebec, & Newfoundland & Labrador.
Martin Rivard, President & Chief Executive Officer
Nicole Veilleux, CA, Financial Director
Christian Pichette, Eng., M.Sc., Vice-President, Operations
Denis Bellemare, Eng., Chief Engineer, Projects
Christine Lapointe, CA, Controller
Marcel St-Pierre, Mine Coordinator, Projects
Stéphanie Lee, Secretary

Rio Tinto Alcan
1188, rue Sherbrooke ouest
Montréal, QC H3A 3G2
514-848-8000
www.riotintoalcan.com

Company Type: Private

Rockwell Diamonds Inc.
PO Box 3011, Houghton
careers@rockwelldiamonds.com
www.rockwelldiamonds.com
Other Communications: Phone: +27(0)11 481 7200; Fax: +27(0)11 481 7235

Company Type: Public
Ticker Symbol: RDI / TSX; RDIAF / OTCBB
Profile: Rockwell Diamonds develops & operates alluvial diamond deposits. The compnay has an interest in properties in southern Africa.
James Campbell, President & Chief Executive Officer
Michael Hunt, Chief Operating Officer
Gerhard Jacobs, Chief Financial Officer
Glenn Norton, Manager, Mineral Resources

Romarco Minerals Inc.
Brookfield Place
#3630, 181 Bay St.
Toronto, ON M5J 2T3
416-367-5500
Fax: 416-367-5505
info@romarco.com
www.romarco.com

Company Type: Public
Ticker Symbol: R / TSX
Profile: The gold development company operates mainly in the United States. Romarco Minerals' flagship project is the Haile Gold Mine in South Carolina.
Diane R. Garrett, MA, Ph.D., Mineral Economics, Eng., President & Chief Executive Officer
dgarrett@romarco.com
Jim Arnold, P.E., B.Sc. Metallurgical Engineering, Chief Operating Officer & Senior Vice-President
Stanton K. Rideout, Chief Financial Officer & Senior Vice-President
Dan Symons, Vice-President, Investor Relations
416-367-5500, dsymons@romarco.com

Royal Nickel Corporation (RNC)
#1200, 220 Bay St.
Toronto, ON M5J 2W4
416-363-0649
Fax: 416-363-7826
www.royalnickel.com
Other Communications: Amos, QC Regional Office, Phone: 819-727-3777

Company Type: Public
Ticker Symbol: RNX / TSX
Profile: Royal Nickel Corporation acquires, explores, & develops base metal & platinum group metal properties. The company owns 100% of the Dumont Nickel Project, situated in the Abitibi Mining Camp near Amos, Québec.
Tyler Mitchelson, President & Chief Executive Officer
Fraser Sinclair, Chief Financial Officer
Mark Selby, Senior Vice-President, Business Development
Alger St-Jean, Vice-President, Exploration
Johnna Muinonen, Vice-President, Metallurgy
Pierre-Philippe Dupont, Manager, Sustainable Development

Rubicon Minerals Corporation
#1540, 800 West Pender St.
Vancouver, BC V6C 2V6
604-623-3333
Fax: 604-623-3355
www.rubiconminerals.com

Company Type: Public
Ticker Symbol: RMX / TSX, AMEX
David Adamson, President & CEO
Robert Lewis, Chief Financial Officer

Rusoro Mining Ltd.
#2164, 1055 Dunsmuir St.
Vancouver, BC V7X 1B1
604-632-4044
Fax: 604-632-4045
info@rusoro.com
www.rusoro.com

Company Type: Public
Ticker Symbol: RML / TSX Venture
Andre Agapov, Chief Executive Officer
Gary Warnecke, Chief Financial Officer

Sabina Gold & Silver Corp.
#202, 930 West First St.
North Vancouver, BC V7P 3N4
604-998-4175
Fax: 604-998-1051
888-648-4218
www.sabinagoldsilver.com

Company Type: Public
Ticker Symbol: SBB / SX
Profile: The precious metals company has flagship projects in Nunavut. Primary assets include the following: the Back River Gold Project; a royalty on the Hackett River silver & zinc property; & the Wishbone greenstone belt & its potential for gold discoveries.
Robert B. Pease, President & Chief Executive Officer
Elaine Bennett, Chief Financial Officer & Vice-President, Finance
Jason Hynes, Vice-President, Corporate Development
Peter Manojlovic, P.Geo, Vice-President, Exploration
Nicole Hoeller, Corporate Secretary & Vice-President, Investor Relations
nhoeller@sabinagoldsilver.com

San Gold Corporation
Lot 1, Block 12
Bissett, MB R0E 0J0
204-794-5818
info@sangoldcorp.com
www.sangoldcorp.com

Company Type: Public
Ticker Symbol: SGR / TSX
Dale Ginn, Chief Executive Officer
Gestur Kristjansson, Chief Financial Officer

Sandspring Resources Ltd.
Investor Relations
#1000, 4 King St. West
Toronto, ON M5H 1B6
416-792-7139
info@sandspringresources.com
www.sandspringresources.com

Company Type: Public
Ticker Symbol: SSP / TSX Venture
Profile: Sandspring Resources Ltd. is a junior mining company. It is focused on advancing the Toroparu Gold Deposit in the Republic of Guyana.
Rich Munson, B.A., J.D., L.L.M., Chief Executive Officer
Scott Issel, MBA, Chief Financial Officer
Greg Barnes, B.Sc., MBA, Executive Vice-President
L. Werner Claessens, Lic. Geo., P.Geo., Vice-President, Exploration

Scorpio Mining Corp.
#606, 40 University Ave.
Toronto, ON M5H 1T1
416-585-2200
Fax: 416-585-8026
scorpio@scorpiomining.com
www.scorpiomining.com

Company Type: Public
Ticker Symbol: SPM / TSX
Profile: Scorpio Mining Corporation is a silver producer. Exploring & mining activities are conducted in Mexico.
Parviz Farsangi, President & Chief Executive Officer
Hemdat Sawh, BSc, MBA, CA, Chief Financial Officer
James M. Stonehouse, MA (Geology), Vice-President, Exploration
Victoria Vargas, Vice-President, Investor Relations & Corporate Communications
416-585-2200, vvargas@scorpiomining.com

Seabridge Gold Inc.
#400, 106 Front St. East
Toronto, ON M5A 1E1
416-367-9292
Fax: 416-367-2711
info@seabridgegold.net
www.seabridgegold.net

Company Type: Public
Ticker Symbol: SEA / TSX; SA / NYSE Amex
Profile: Seabridge Gold's principal assets are the 100% owned Courageous Lake gold project in the Northwest Territories & the 100% owned KSM property near Stewart, British Columbia.
Rudi P. Fronk, President & Chief Executive Officer
Jay S. Layman, Chief Operating Officer & Executive & Vice-President
Christopher J. Reynolds, Chief Financial Officer, Corp. Secretary, & Vice-President, Finance
R. Brent Murphy, Vice-President, Environmental Affairs

Selwyn Resources Ltd.
#700, 509 Richards St.
Vancouver, BC V6B 2Z6
604-801-7240
Fax: 604-689-8355
888-989-9188
info@selwynresources.com
www.selwynresources.com

Company Type: Public
Ticker Symbol: SWN / TSX Venture
Profile: Selwyn Resources is focused upon the exploration & development of its zinc & lead properties in the Yukon.
Harlan D. Meade, President & Chief Executive Officer
David Kwong, Chief Financial Officer
Jason Dunning, M.Sc., P.Geo., Vice-President, Exploration
Justin Himmelright, Vice-President, Environment & Community Affairs
Joe Ringwald, Vice-President, Mining
Catalin Chiloflischi, Manager, Investor Communications
888-989-9188

SEMAFO Inc.
#375, 750, boul Marcel-Laurin
Montréal, QC H4M 2M4
514-744-4408
Fax: 514-744-2291
888-744-4408
info@semafo.com
www.semafo.com

Company Type: Public
Ticker Symbol: SMF / TSX, OMX
Profile: SEMAFO is a mining & gold production company. It operates gold mines in Burkina Faso, Guinea, & Niger. Exploration activities take place in West Africa.
Benoit La Salle, President & Chief Executive Officer
Martin Milette, Chief Financial Officer
Michel Crevier, Vice-President, Exploration & Mining Geology

Sherritt International Corporation
Investor Relations
1133 Yonge St.
Toronto, ON M4T 2Y7
416-924-4551
Fax: 416-924-5015
800-704-6698
info@sherritt.com; investor@sherritt.com
www.sherritt.com

Company Type: Public
Ticker Symbol: S / TSX
Profile: Sherrit International Corporation has interests in a nickel & cobalt metals business, thermal coal production, electricity generation, & oil & gas exploration, development, & production. The company conducts its operations in Canada & internationally.
Jowdat Waheed, President/CEO
Michael Garvey, Member, Environment, Health, & Safety Committee

Shore Gold Inc.
#300, 224 - 4th Ave. South
Saskatoon, SK S7K 5M5
306-664-2202
Fax: 306-664-7181
shoregold@shoregold.com
www.shoregold.com

Company Type: Public
Ticker Symbol: SGF / TSX
Profile: Shore Gold Inc. specializes in mineral exploration & development. Operations take place in Saskatchewan.
In order to fulfill its environmental responsibilities, Shore Gold has developed programs such as the Hazardous Substances & Waste Dangerous Goods Contingency Plan, the Spill Contingency Plan, the General Spill Contingency Plan, a Waste Management Policy, sampling & water quality testing of ground & surface water, & environmental inspection logs.
Kenneth E. MacNeill, President & Chief Executive Officer
Harvey Bay, Chief Financial Officer & Chief Operating Officer
George Read, Senior Vice-President, Exploration & Development
Eric Cline, Vice-President, Corporate Affairs
Pieter Du Plessis, Vice-President, Exploration
Joe Dickson, Manager, Investor Relations & Corporate Services
306-667-3505,

Silver Standard Resources Inc.
#1400, 999 West Hastings St.
Vancouver, BC V6C 2W2
604-689-3846
Fax: 604-689-3847
888-338-0046
invest@silverstandard.com
www.silverstandard.com

Company Type: Public
Ticker Symbol: SSO / TSX

Profile: Silver Standard Resources explors & operates precious metals projects. Operations take place in Canada, United States, Mexico, Argentina, Peru, & Chile. Shares are listed on the Toronto Stock Exchange under the symbol SSO & on the Nasdaq Global Market under the symbol SSRI.
R.A. Quartermain, President/Director
Ross Mitchell, Vice-President, Finance

Silver Wheaton Corp.
#3150, 666 Burrard St.
Vancouver, BC V6C 2X8
604-684-9648
Fax: 604-684-3123
800-380-8687
info@silverwheaton.com
www.silverwheaton.com
Company Type: Public
Ticker Symbol: SLW / TSX, NYSE
Profile: Silver Wheaton Corp. is engaged in silver production. The company purchases silver production from mines in Canada, the United States, Mexico, Peru, Chile, Portugal, Sweden, & Greece.
Peter Barnes, President/CEO
Gary Brown, Chief Financial Officer
Randy Smallwood, Exec. Vice-President, Corporate Development
Brad Kopp, Director, Investor Relations

Silvercorp Metals Inc.
#1378, 200 Granville St.
Vancouver, BC V6C 1S4
604-669-9397
Fax: 604-669-9387
888-224-1881
info@silvercorp.ca; investor@silvercorp.c
www.silvercorp.ca
Other Communications: China Head Office, Phone: 8610-8587-1132
Company Type: Public
Ticker Symbol: SVM, TSX, NYSE
Profile: Silvercorp Metals acquires, explores, & mines silver-related properties located in Canada & China. The company has implemented a range of employee safety measures & environmental protection measures.
Rui Feng, Ph.D., Chair/CEO
Myles J. Gao, President/COO
Maria Tang, C.A, C.P.A, Chief Financial Officer
Michael Hibbitts, B.Sc (Geology), B.Ed, P.Geo., Vice-President, Operations
Shirley Zhou, Manager, Corporate Communications

SilverCrest Mines Inc.
#501, 570 Granville St.
Vancouver, BC V6C 3P1
604-694-1730
Fax: 604-694-1761
866-691-1730
info@silvercrestmines.com
www.silvercrestmines.com
Company Type: Public
Ticker Symbol: SVL / TSX Venture
Profile: SilverCrest Mines Inc. is a precious metals producer. The company's flagship project is the 100% owned Santa Elena Mine, which is situated in the State of Sonora, Mexico.
J. Scott Drever, President
N. Eric Fier, CPG, P.Eng, Chief Operating Officer
Barney Magnusson, CA, Chief Financial Officer
Brent McFarlane, Vice-President, Operations
Jed Thomas, Vice-President, Exploration
Bernard Poznanski, B.Sc., LLB, LLM, Corporate Secretary

Sirocco Mining Inc.
Corporate Office
#2000, 885 West Georgia St.
Vancouver, BC V6C 3E8
604-689-7842
Fax: 604-689-4250
siroccomining@namdo.com
www.siroccomining.com
Other Communications: Santiago, Chile Office, Phone: 56-2-597 5901
Company Type: Public
Ticker Symbol: AAM / TSX Venture
Profile: Sirocco Mining Inc. produces iodine from its Aguas Blancas mine in northern Chile. The company also has exploration interests in West Africa & Brazil.
Richard P. Clark, President & Chief Executive Officer
Lawrence Simon Jackson, President
Alessandro Bitelli, Chief Financial Officer
Kevin Ross, Chief Operating Officer
Brendan Pidcock, Vice-President, Mining
Kathy Love, Corporate Secretary

SouthGobi Resources Ltd.
#654, 999 Canada Pl.
Vancouver, BC V6C 3E1
604-681-6799
Fax: 604-688-8391
info-southgobi@southgobi.com
www.southgobi.com
Other Communications: SouthGobi Resources (Hong Kong) Limited; +852-2156-7029
Company Type: Public
Ticker Symbol: SGQ / TSX, Hong Kong
Profile: SouthGobi Resources has metallurgical & thermal coal deposits in the South Gobi Region of Mongolia. The company's flagship coal mine is known as Ovoot Tolgoi. Coal is produced & sold to customers in China.
Alexander Molyneux, President & Chief Executive Officer
Curtis Church, Chief Operating Officer
Matthew O'Kane, Chief Financial Officer
David Bartel, Vice-President, External Affairs & Investor Relations
Jess Harding, Vice-President, Evaluations & Project Development
Tony Pearson, Vice-President, Corporate Development

Spanish Mountain Gold Ltd.
Head Office
#920, 1055 West Hastings St.
Vancouver, BC V6E 2E9
604-601-3651
Fax: 604-681-6866
855-772-6397
info@spanishmountaingold.com
www.spanishmountaingold.com
Company Type: Public
Ticker Symbol: SPA / TSX Venture
Profile: Spanish Mountain Gold's flagship project is located in south central British Columbia.
Brian Groves, President & Chief Executive Officer
Morris Beattie, Chief Operating Officer
Larry Yau, Chief Financial Officer
Judy Stoeterau, Vice-President, Geology

Sprott Resource Corp.
Royal Bank Plaza
200 Bay St.
Toronto, ON M5J 2J2
416-977-7333
Fax: 416-977-7555
info@sprottresource.com
www.sprottresource.com
Company Type: Public
Ticker Symbol: SCP / TSX
Kevin Bambrough, President/CEO
Stephen Austin, Chief Financial Officer

St. Andrew Goldfields Ltd.
Corporate Head Office
#801, 20 Adlaide St. East
Toronto, ON M5C 2T6
416-815-9855
Fax: 416-815-9437
info@standrewgoldfields.com
www.standrewgoldfields.com
Other Communications: Regional Exploration Office, Matheson, ON: 705-273-3030
Company Type: Public
Ticker Symbol: SAS / TSX
Profile: The gold mining & exploration company conducts operations in the Timmins mining district in northeastern Ontario.

Jacques Perron, P.Eng, President & Chief Executive Officer
Ben Au, CA, Chief Financial Officer & Vice-President, Finance & Administration
Duncan Middlemiss, P.Eng, Vice-President & General Manager, East Timmins Operations
Linda Weinzetti, Corporate Secretary
Suzette N. Ramcharan, Contact, Investor Relations
investor@sasgoldmines.com

Starcore International Mines Ltd.
PO Box 113, #750, 580 Hornby St.
Vancouver, BC V6C 3B6
604-602-4935
Fax: 604-602-4936
866-602-4935
info@starcore.com
www.starcore.com
Company Type: Public
Ticker Symbol: SAM / TSX
Profile: The mining company acquires & develops gold & silver properties. Starcore International Mines is active in Mexico.
Robert Eadie, President & Chief Executive Officer
Gary Arca, CA, Chief Financial Officer
David Gunning, P.Eng., Chief Operating Officer

Cory Kent, LLB, Corporate Secretary

Starfield Resources Inc.
PO Box 8, #900, 120 Adelaide St. West
Toronto, ON M5H 1T1
416-860-0400
Fax: 416-860-0822
info@starfieldres.com
www.starfieldres.com
Company Type: Public
Ticker Symbol: SRU / TSX
Profile: The exploration & development company is active in Nunavut at it Ferguson Lake nickel, copper, cobalt, platinum, palladium property. Starfield Resources also has assets in Montana, California, & Nevada.
The company funded the development of an energy efficient & environmentally friendly hydrometallurgical flow sheet to recover metals from massive sulphides.
Philip S. Martin, President & Chief Executive Officer
pmartin@starfield res.com
Michal G. Moran, Director, Engineering
Raymond Irwin, Vice-President, Exploration
Fred Mason, Vice-President, Operations

Stonegate Agricom Ltd.
PO Box 118, #2010, 401 Bay St.
Toronto, ON M5H 2Y4
416-864-0303
Fax: 416-860-0813
www.stonegateagricom.com
Company Type: Public
Ticker Symbol: ST / TSX
Profile: Stonegate Agricom Ltd. acquires & develops agricultural nutrient projects. Projects include the Mantaro Phosphate Project in Peru & the Paris Hills Phosphate Project in Idaho.
Mark N.J. Ashcroft, M.Sc., P.Eng., President & Chief Executive Officer
Germaine Coombs, Chief Financial Officer & Vice-President
Wayne Cheveldayoff, Vice-President, Investor Relations
416-864-0303, wcheveldayoff@stonegateagricom.com
Lorna D. MacGillivray, LL.B., Vice-President, Secretary, & General Counsel
William A. Napier, Vice-President, Safety, Sustainability, Health, & the Environment
Kenneth L. Norris, P.Eng., Vice-President, Project Development

Stornoway Diamond Corp.
#800, 625 Howe St.
Vancouver, BC V6C 2T6
604-331-2259
Fax: 604-689-5041
info@stornowaydiamonds.com
www.stornowaydiamonds.com
Company Type: Public
Ticker Symbol: SWY / TSX
Eira Thomas, Chief Financial Officer
Zara Boldt, Chief Financial Officer

Strateco Resources Inc.
1225, rue Gay-Lussac
Boucherville, QC J4B 7K1
450-641-0775
Fax: 450-641-1601
866-774-7722
info@stratecoinc.com
www.stratecoinc.com
Company Type: Public
Ticker Symbol: RSC / TSX
Profile: Strateco Resources Inc.'s main project is the wholly owned Matoush uranium property, which is situated in the Otish Mountains in Québec.
Guy Hébert, President & Chief Executive Officer
Yvon Robert, Chief Financial Officer, Treasurer, & Vice-President, Finance
Jonathan Lafontaine, Chief Geologist
Jean-Pierre Lachance, Executive Vice-President, Exploration
Pierre H. Terreault, Vice-President, Operations & Engineering
Gabriel R. Maurice, Director, Human Resources & Health & Safety
Caroline Hardy, Manager, Environment

Strategic Metals Ltd.
#1016, 510 West Hastings St.
Vancouver, BC V6B 1L8
604-688-2568
888-688-2522
www.strategicmetalsltd.com
Company Type: Public
Ticker Symbol: SMD / TSX Venture
Profile: Strategic Metals Ltd. is an exploration company, with properties & royalty interests in the Yukon. The company also owns shares of the following resource companies: Silver Range Resources, ATAC Resources Ltd., Wolverine Minerals Corp., & Rockhaven Resources Ltd.

W. Douglas Eaton, Chief Executive Officer
Larry B. Donaldson, Chief Financial Officer
Ian J. Talbot, B.Sc., LL.B, Chief Operating Officer
Richard Drechsler, Contact, Corporate Communications
rdrechsler@strategicmetalsltd.com

Strathmore Minerals Corp.
#700, 1620 Dickson Ave
Kelowna, BC V1Y 9Y2

800-647-3303
info@strathmoreminerals.com
www.strathmoreminerals.com

Company Type: Public
Ticker Symbol: STM / TSX
Profile: Strathmore Minerals is a resource company engaged in the acquisition, exploration & development of uranium properties in the United States. The company's property portfolio is located primarily in New Mexico & Wyoming. Common shares are listed on the TSX under the symbol STM & trade on the OTCQX International electronic trading system in the United States under the symbol STJKF.
David Miller, Chief Executive Officer
Steven Khan, MBA, CFA, President
Patrick Groening, B.Comm. (Hon), CA, CPA, Chief Financial Officer
John DeJoia, P. Geol., Senior Vice-President, New Mexico Operations
James Crouch, BSc, Vice-President, Wyoming Operations
Juan Velasquez, MBA, Vice-President, Government, Regulatory, & Environmental Affairs
Craig Christy, MA, Corporate Secretary & Contact, Investor Relations

Sulliden Gold Corporation Ltd.
1250, boul René Levesque ouest
Montréal, QC H3B 5E9

416-861-5805
Fax: 416-861-8165
contact@sulliden.com; careers@sulliden.co
www.sulliden.com
Other Communications: Lima, Peru Office, Phone: (51-1) 651-2500
Social Media:
www.facebook.com/group.php?gid=119885398026454
twitter.com/Sullidengold
www.linkedin.com/company/2399027

Company Type: Public
Ticker Symbol: SUE / TSX, BVL
Profile: The precious metals company is engaged in the exploration & development of its 100% owned Shahuindo Gold & Silver Project, which is situated in northern Peru.
Peter Tagliamonte, P.Eng., MBA, President & Chief Executive Officer
Denis C. Arsenault, CA, Chief Financial Officer
Stéphane Amireault, MScA., P.Eng., Vice-President, Exploration

Joe Milbourne, FAusIMM, Vice-President, Operations & Technical Services
G. Scott Moore, MBA, Vice-President, Corporate Development
Caroline Arsenault, Manager, Investor Relations
Javier Fernández Concha Stucker, General Manager, Peru
Patrick Gleeson, Corporate Secretary

Sunridge Gold Corp.
Executive Office
#1490, 1075 West Georgia St.
Vancouver, BC V6E 3C9

604-688-9478
Fax: 604-688-9458
info@sunridgegold.com
www.sunridgegold.com
Other Communications: White Rock Corporate Office: 604-536-2711, Fax: 604-536-2788

Company Type: Public
Ticker Symbol: SGC / TSX Venture
Profile: Sunridge Gold Corp. is a mineral exploration & development company. The company's focus is the Asmara Project in Eritrea & exploration properties in Madagascar.
Michael Hopley, President & Chief Executive Officer
Scott Ansell, Vice-President, Project Development
Greg Davis, Vice-President, Business Development
604-688-1263, Fax: 604-688-9458, greg@sunridgegold.com
Dave Daoud, Manager, Exploration

Taseko Mines Limited
1040 West Georgia St., 15th Fl.
Vancouver, BC V6E 4H1

778-373-4533
Fax: 778-373-4534
877-441-4533
Investor@tasekomines.com
www.tasekomines.com
Social Media:
www.facebook.com/pages/Taseko/129461390453642
twitter.com/tasekomines

Company Type: Public
Ticker Symbol: TKO
Profile: Taseko Mines Limited is a mineral exploration & mining company. The company is engaged in the following main projects in British Columbia: the New Prosperity gold-copper project; the Gibraltar open pit copper mine; the wholly owned Aley niobium project; & the Harmony gold prospect.
Russell Hallbauer, President/CEO & Director
Peter Mitchell, Chief Financial Officer
John McManus, Vice-President, Operations
Brian Battison, Vice-President, Corporate Affairs
Brian Bergot, Contact, Investor Relations
778-373-4545, brianbergot@hdgold.com

Teck Highland Valley Copper
Bentall 5
#3300, 550 Burrard St.
Vancouver, BC V6C 0B3

604-699-4000
Fax: 604-699-4750
info@teck.com
www.teck.com
Social Media: twitter.com/#!/teckresources
www.linkedin.com/company/teck-resources-limited

Company Type: Private

Teck Resources Limited
Bentall 5
#3300, 550 Burrard St.
Vancouver, BC V6C 0B3

604-699-4000
Fax: 604-699-4750
info@teck.com
www.teck.com
Social Media: twitter.com/teckresources
www.linkedin.com/company/teck-resources-limited

Company Type: Public
Ticker Symbol: TCK / TSX
Profile: The resource company has business units focused on zinc, copper, stealmaking coal, & energy. Teck is building parnerships to confront sustainability challenges in the regions where it operates & globally. The company is committed to increasing awareness of the global health issue of zinc deficiency. Shares are listed on the Toronto & New York stock exchanges.
Donald R. Lindsay, President/CEO
Ronald A. Millos, CA, CFO & Sr. Vice-President, Finance
G. Leonard Manuel, Sr. Vice-President & General Counsel
Gregory A. Waller, Vice-President, Investor Relations & Strategic Analysis
John F.H. Thompson, Vice-President, Technology
Michel P. Filion, Vice-President, Environment, Health, & Safety

Thompson Creek Metals Company Inc.
#2101, 885 West Georgia St.
Vancouver, BC V6C 3E8

604-681-9930
Fax: 604-630-2090
info@tcrk.com
www.thompsoncreekmetals.com

Company Type: Public
Ticker Symbol: TCM / TSX; TC / NYSE
Profile: The molybdenum producer owns the Thompson Creek open-pit molybdenum mine & mill in Idaho, a metallurgical roasting facility in Pennsylvania, as well as 75% of northern British Columbia's Endako open-pit mine, mill, & roasting facility. Thompson Creek Metals Company is exploring on properties in northern British Columbia, the Yukon, & Nunavut.
Kevin Loughrey, Chair/CEO
Pamela L. Saxton, Chief Financial Officer & Vice-President, Finance
Kenneth W. Collison, Chief Operating Officer
Dale Huffman, Vice-President, General Counsel, & Secretary
Wayne Cheveldayoff, Director, Investor Relations
wcheveldayoff@tcrk.com

Timmins Gold Corp.
#1900, 570 Granville St.
Vancouver, BC V6C 3P1

604-682-4002
Fax: 604-682-4003
info@timminsgold.com
www.timminsgold.com

Company Type: Public
Ticker Symbol: TMM/TSX; TGD/NYSE Amex
Profile: Timmins Gold Corp.'s wholly owned San Francisco Gold Mine is situated in Sonora, Mexico.
Bruce Bragagnolo, LLB, Chief Executive Officer
604-682-4002, Fax: 604-682-4003, Bruce@timminsgold.com
Arturo Bonillas, P.Eng., President
Arturo@timminsgold.com
Miguel Angel Soto, Geo. Eng., Chief Operating Officer
Colin Sutherland, CA, Chief Financial Officer
Alex Peter Tsakumis, BA, Vice-President, Corporate Development

Treasury Metals Incorporated
The Exchange Tower
PO Box 99, #3680, 130 King St. West
Toronto, ON M5X 1B1

416-214-4654
Fax: 416-599-4959
info@treasurymetals.com
www.treasurymetals.com

Company Type: Public
Ticker Symbol: TML / TSX
Profile: The mineral exploration & development company is focused on the acquisition of gold projects in the Americas. Treasury Metals' main asset is the Goliath Gold Project, which is situated in the Kenora Mining District near Dryden, Ontario. Another of the company's operations is the Goldcliff Project, which is located in the Manitou Straits Fault Zone, south of Dryden, Ontario.
Martin Walter, MBA, B.Sc. (Geology), President & Chief Executive Officer
martin@treasurymetals.com
Dennis Gibson, CGA, Chief Financial Officer
Norm Bush, B.Sc. Mech Eng., Vice-President, Goliath Gold Project
Greg Ferron, B.Com., Vice-President, Corporate Development
greg@treasurymetals.com
John Chulick, MBA, B.Sc. Geology, Head, Exploration

Trevali Mining Corporation
#2300, 1177 West Hastings St.
Vancouver, BC V6E 2K3

604-488-1661
Fax: 604-408-7499
info@trevali.com
www.trevali.com

Company Type: Public
Ticker Symbol: TV / TSX, Frankfurt
Profile: Trevali Mining Corporation has two zinc, lead, silver, & copper deposits in northern New Brunswick & in Peru. Through its wholly owned subsidary, Trevali Renewable Energy Inc., the Trevali Mining Corporation is upgrading its hydroelectric generating facility & transmission lines, in order to supply power to mining operations & sell surplus power to the Peruvian National Energy Grid.
Mark Cruise, President & Chief Executive Officer
Anna Ladd, Chief Financial Officer
Paul Keller, P.Eng., Vice-President, Operations
Steve Stakiw, Manager, Corporate Communications
604-638-5623, sstakiw@trevali.com

TVI Pacific Inc.
Head Office
#2000, 736 - 6th Ave. SW
Calgary, AB T2P 3T7

403-265-4356
Fax: 403-264-7028
tvi-info@tvipacific.com
www.tvipacific.com
Social Media: www.facebook.com/tvipacific
twitter.com/tvipacific

Company Type: Public
Ticker Symbol: TVI / TSX
Profile: TVI Pacific Inc. is engaged in the exploration for, acquisition, development, & production of resources in the Philippines. Interests include the copper & zinc producing Canatuan mine, the Balabag silver & gold project, & an offshore Philippine oil property.
Clifford M. James, Chair, President & Chief Executive Officer
Patrick Hanna, Chief Financial Officer & Vice-President, Finance & Administration
Rhonda Bennetto, Vice-President, Investor & Corporate Relations
403-265-4356, rhonda.bennetto@tvipacific.com

Tyhee Gold Corp.
#401, 675 West Hastings St.
Vancouver, BC V6B 1N2

604-681-2877
Fax: 604-681-2879
info@tyhee.com
www.tyhee.com

Company Type: Public
Ticker Symbol: TDC / TSX Venture
Profile: Tyhee Gold Corp. is developing the Yellowknife Gold Project in the Northwest Territories.
Brian K. Briggs, P.Eng., Chief Executive Officer
Harjinder S. Gill, CGA, Chief Financial Officer
Val Pratico, B.Sc., P.Geol., Chief Geologist, Chief Geologist, Yellowknife Gold Project
Hugh R. Wilson, Vice-President, Environment & Community Affairs, Tyhee NWT Corp.
Cory Kent, Corporate Secretary

U.S. Silver Corporation
Corporate Office
PO Box 136, #2702, 401 Bay St.
Toronto, ON M5H 2Y4

416-907-5501
Fax: 647-722-9652
info@us-silver.com
www.us-silver.com

Company Type: Public
Ticker Symbol: USA / TSX; USSIF / OTCQX
Profile: Through its wholly owned subsidiaries, U.S. Silver owns or operates silver, lead, & copper mines located in Shoshone County, Idaho. The company has developed a set of practices & procedures to protect the environment & has a history of regulatory compliance.
Gordon E. Pridham, Executive Chair & Chief Executive Officer
Christopher J. Hopkins, Chief Financial Officer
Steve Long, Chief Operating Officer
Heather Foster, Manager, Investor Relations

UEX Corporation
#1007, 808 Nelson St.
Vancouver, BC V6Z 2H2

604-669-2349
Fax: 604-669-1240
info@uex-corporation.com
www.uex-corporation.com

Company Type: Public
Ticker Symbol: UEX / TSX
Profile: Formed in 2002, UEX Corporation is engaged in uranium exploration & development. The company is active in northern Saskatchewan's Athabasca Basin.
Graham C. Thody, President & Chief Executive Officer
Ed Boney, CA, Chief Financial Officer
R. Sierd Eriks, P.Geo., Vice-President, Exploration
Nan H. Lee, M.Sc., P.Eng., Vice-President, Project Development

Ur-Energy Inc.
#279, 1128 Clapp Lane
Manotick, ON K4M 1A3

613-692-7704
Fax: 613-692-3234
www.ur-energy.com

Company Type: Public
Ticker Symbol: URE / TSX, AMEX
W. William Boberg, President & CEO
Roger Smith, Chief Financial Officer

Uranium One Inc.
Bay Adelaide Centre
#1710, 333 Bay St.
Toronto, ON M5H 2R2

647-788-8500
Fax: 647-788-8501
www.uranium1.com
Other Communications: Human Resources: 647-788-8500

Company Type: Public
Ticker Symbol: UUU / TSX
Profile: The uranium producer's assets are located in the United States, Australia, & Kazakhstan.
Chris Sattler, Chief Executive Officer
Vadim Jivov, President
Graham du Preez, Chief Financial Officer & Executive Vice-President
Steve Magnuson, Chief Operating Officer & Executive Vice-President
Alexander Boytsov, Executive Vice-President, Exploration
Dmitry Shulga, Executive Vice-President, Government Affairs
Thys Heyns, Senior Vice-President, New Business & Technical Services
Anton Jivov, Director, Corporate Development & Investor Relations
647-788-8461, anton.jivov@uranium1.com

Vale Canada

www.vale.com

Company Type: Private

Victoria Gold Corp.
Corporate Office
#303, 80 Richmond St. West
Toronto, ON M5H 2A4

416-866-8800
Fax: 416-866-8801
www.vitgoldcorp.com
Other Communications: Vancouver: 604-682-5122; Whitehorse: 867-393-4653

Company Type: Public
Ticker Symbol: VIT / TSX Venture
Profile: The gold company is engaged in acquisitions, exploration, & project development. Victoria Gold Corp.'s flagship project is the Eagle Gold Deposit, which is located on the Dublin Gulch property in the Yukon. The company continues to explore in the Yukon & Nevada.
John McConnell, President & Chief Executive Officer
Marty Rendall, Chief Financial Officer
Kelly Arychuk, Vice-President, Mine Support Services
Mark Ayranto, Vice-President, Yukon
John Goyman, Vice-President, Nevada Projects

Victory Nickel Inc.
Victory Building
80 Richmond St. West, 18th Fl.
Toronto, ON M5H 2A4

416-363-8527
Fax: 416-626-0890
admin@victorynickel.ca
www.victorynickel.ca

Company Type: Public
Ticker Symbol: NI / TSX
Profile: Victory Nickel Inc. is a nickel producer, with properties in Manitoba & northwestern Québec. The company also owns shares in Prophecy Coal Corp., Prophecy Platinum Corp., Wallbridge Mining Company Limited, & Miocene Metals Limited.
René Galipeau, CGA, Vice-Chair & Chief Executive Officer
Steve Harapiak, President & Chief Operating Officer
Alison J. Sutcliffe, CA, Chief Financial Officer & Vice-President, Finance
Paul L. Jones, B.Sc., P.Geo, Vice-President, Exploration
David Mchaina, Ph.D., P.Eng., Vice-President, Environment & Sustainable Development
Sean Stokes, Corporate Secretary & Vice-President, Public Affairs

Virginia Energy Resources Inc.
#611, 675 West Hastings St.
Vancouver, BC V6B 1N2

604-669-4799
Fax: 604-669-2543
www.virginiaenergyresources.com

Company Type: Public
Ticker Symbol: VAE / TSX Venture
Profile: The uranium exploration & development company holds a 29% stake in a uranium project in Virginia. Virginia Energy Resources is also engaged in exploration projects in the Otish Basin of Québec & the Athabasca Basin of Saskatchewan.
Walter Coles, President & Chief Executive Officer
Karen A. Allan, CMA, Chief Financial Officer
Michael Cathro, M.Sc., P.Geo., Vice-President, Exploration
Tony Perri, Manager, Investor Relations

Virginia Mines Inc./ Mines Virginia inc.
#200, 116, rue Saint-Pierre
Québec, QC G1K 4A7

418-694-9832
Fax: 418-694-9120
800-476-1853
info@minesvirginia.com
www.minesvirginia.com

Company Type: Public
Ticker Symbol: VGQ / TSX
Profile: Virginia Mines Inc. is an active mining exploration company in northern Quebec.
Andre Gaumond, President
Robin Villeneuve, Chief Financial Officer
Paul Archer, Vice-President, Exploration
Amélie Laliberté, Contact, Investor Relations

Vista Gold Corp.
Waterfront Centre
PO Box 48600, #900, 200 Burrard St.
Vancouver, BC V7X 1T2

720-981-1185
Fax: 720-981-1186
www.vistagold.com

Company Type: Public
Ticker Symbol: VGZ / TSX, AMEX
Michael Richings, President/CEO
Gregory Marlier, Chief Financial Officer

Volta Resources Inc.
Head Office
#602, 67 Yonge St.
Toronto, ON M5E 1J8

416-867-2299
Fax: 416-867-2298
questions@voltaresources.com
www.voltaresources.com
Other Communications: Ghana: +233 (0) 302 772 708; Burkina Faso: +226 50 50 43 84

Company Type: Public
Ticker Symbol: VTR / TSX
Profile: The mineral company is engaged in the acquisition & exploration of gold properties in West Africa. Volta Resources' flagship project is the Kiaka Gold Project in Burkina Faso.
Kevin Bullock, P.Eng., President & Chief Executive Officer
kbullock@voltaresources.com
Victor King, Chief Operations Officer
Alan Rootenberg, Chief Financial Officer & Secretary
Guy Franceschi, Vice-President, Exploration

Wallbridge Mining Company Limited
129 Fielding Rd.
Lively, ON P3Y 1L7

705-682-9297
Fax: 888-316-4156
info@wallbridgemining.com
www.wallbridgemining.com

Company Type: Public
Ticker Symbol: WM / TSX
Profile: Wallbridge Mining Company is engaged in the discovery & development of mineral resources, such as nickel, gold, copper, platinum, & palladium. The company conducts operations in North America. Its main area of activity is Sudbury, Ontario.
Alar Soever, Chief Executive Officer
Marz Kord, Mining Eng., President
Mary Montgomery, CA, Chief Financial Officer
Joshua Bailey, M.Sc., P.Geo, Vice-President, Corporate Development
jbailey@wallbridgemining.com
H.J. (James) Blake, Q.C., LL.M, Corporate Secretary
Michael Weirmeir, Manager, Land

Wesdome Gold Mines Ltd.
Head Office
#1305, 8 King St. East
Toronto, ON M5C 1B5

416-360-3743
Fax: 416-360-7620
info@wesdome.com; invest@wesdome.com
www.wesdome.com

Company Type: Public
Ticker Symbol: WDO / TSX
Profile: Wesdome Gold Mines Ltd. is the owner of the Mishi & Eagle River gold mining operations in Wawa, Ontario & the Kiena mining complex, situated in Val d-Or, Québec.
Donovan Pollitt, P.Eng., CFA, Chief Executive Officer
Brian Ma, Chief Financial Officer

Western Copper & Gold Corporation
Corporate Head Office
#2050, 1111 West Georgia St.
Vancouver, BC V6E 4M3

604-684-9497
Fax: 604-669-2926
888-966-9995
info@westerncopperandgold.com
www.westerncopperandgold.com

Company Type: Public
Ticker Symbol: WRN / TSX
Profile: The exploration & development company has gold, copper, & molybdenum resources & reserves. The company is active in the Yukon, where it owns 100% of the Casino Project.
Dale Corman, B.Sc., P.Eng., Chair & Chief Executive Officer
Paul West-Sells, President & Chief Operating Officer
Julien François, Chief Financial Officer & Vice-President, Finance
Cameron Brown, Vice-President, Engineering
Julie Kim Pelly, Manager, Corporate Communications & Investor Relations

Western Potash Corp.
#1818, 701 West Georgia St.
Vancouver, BC

604-689-9378
Fax: 604-689-8199
info@westernpotash.com
www.westernpotash.com
Other Communications: Regina, SK: 306-924-9378; London, UK: +44(0)203.159.5263

Company Type: Public
Ticker Symbol: WPX / TSX

Profile: Western Potash Corp. is engaged in the development of its potash mineral properties in western Canada.
Dean Pekeski, Executive Vice-President
dean@westernpotash.com
Richard Lock, Project Director
John Costigan, Vice-President, Corporate Development
jcostigan@westernpotash.com
Limin Sun, Vice-President, International Relations
David Thornley-Hall, Corporate Secretary
david@westernpotash.com

WesternZagros Resources Ltd.
Head Office
#600, 440 - 2nd Ave. SW
Calgary, AB T2P 5E9
403-693-7017
investorrelations@westernzagros.com
www.westernzagros.com

Company Type: Public
Ticker Symbol: WZR / TSX Venture
Profile: The natural resources company is engaged in the acquisition of properties to explore for, develop, & produce crude oil & natural gas. WesternZagros is active in Iraq.
Simon Hatfield, Chief Executive Officer
Greg Stevenson, Chief Financial Officer
403-693-7007
Tony Kraljic, Vice-President, Business Development
Ian McIntosh, Vice-President, Kurdistan Business Unit
Mike Tinkler, Vice-President, Exploration & Reservoir Development
David Reeve, General Manager, Petroleum Engineering
Lisa Harriman, Manager, Investor Relations
403-693-7017

White Tiger Gold Ltd.
111 Buckingham Palace Rd., 3rd Fl.
London, SW1W0SR UK
info@whitetigergold.com
www.whitetigergold.com
Other Communications: Phone: 44 7833445961

Company Type: Public
Ticker Symbol: WTG / TSX
Profile: The exploration & mining company develops mineral resources in Canada, Peru, & the Russian Federation. White Tiger Gold's operations include the Lamaque Mine in Val D'Or Québec, the San Juan Gold Mine in Peru, & a gold operation in Siberia.
Daniel Major, Chief Executive Officer
Sergey Chalykh, Chief Financial Officer
Andrey Shchetinin, Corporate Secretary

Whitecap Resources Inc.
#500, 222 - 3rd Ave. SW
Calgary, AB T2P 0B4
403-266-0767
Fax: 403-266-6975
info@wcap.ca
www.wcap.ca

Company Type: Public
Ticker Symbol: WCP / TSX
Profile: The oil company's core operating areas include the Valhalla North Property in Alberta, the Pembina Property in Alberta, the Fosterton Property in Saskatchewan, & the West Central Sask Property.
Grant Fagerheim, President & Chief Executive Officer
Thanh Kang, Chief Financial Officer & Vice-President
Joel Armstrong, Vice-President, Production & Operations
Darin Dunlop, Vice-President, Engineering
Gary Lebsack, Vice-President, Land
Dave Mombourquette, Vice-President, Business Development

Wildcat Silver Corporation
#400, 837 West Hastings St.
Vancouver, BC V6C 3N6
604-484-3597
Fax: 604-687-1715
info@wildcatsilver.com
www.wildcatsilver.com

Company Type: Public
Ticker Symbol: WS / TSX
Profile: Wildcat Silver Corporation is a mineral exploration company. The company has 80% ownership of a silver project located in Santa Cruz County, Arizona.
Christopher M. Jones, President & Chief Executive Officer
Paul J. Ireland, Chief Financial Officer
Letitia Cornacchia, Vice-President, Investor Relations & Corporate Communications
416-860-6310, lcornacchia@wildcatsilver.com
Gregory F. Lucero, Vice-President, Sustainable Development
William J. Pennstrom, Vice-President, Technical Services

Xinergy Ltd.
#400, 8351 East Walker Springs Lane
Knoxville, TN 37923
865-474-7000
nfo@xinergycorp.com; investor@xinergycorp
www.xinergycorp.com

Company Type: Public
Ticker Symbol: XRG / TSX
Profile: Through its wholly owned subsidiary, Xinergy Corp. & its subsidiaries, Xinergy Ltd. mines for coal. Areas of operation include Virginia, West Virginia, & Kentucky. Xinergy sells thermal coal to industrial companies & electric utilities in the southeastern United States.
Jon E. Nix, Chief Executive Officer
Gregory L. Mason, President
Michael R. Castle, Chief Financial Officer
Jack R. Hagewood, Vice-President, Mining Operations, North
William R. Snodgrass, Vice-President, Mining Operations, South
Chris Halouma, Director, Investor Relations

Yamana Gold Inc.
North Tower, Royal Bank Plaza
#2200, 200 Bay St.
Toronto, ON M5J 2J3
416-815-0220
Fax: 416-815-0021
investor@yamana.com
www.yamana.com

Company Type: Public
Ticker Symbol: YRI / TSX; AUY / NYSE
Profile: Yamana Gold Inc. began operations in 2003. It is engaged in the exploration & production of gold, copper, & other precious metals. Development projects & operating mines are located in Mexico, Central America, Brazil, & Argentina.
Peter Marrone, Chair/CEO
Antenor Silva, President
Charles Main, CFO & Sr. Vice-President, Finance
Ludovico Costa, Sr. Vice-President/COO
Evandro Cintra, Sr. Vice-President, Technical Services
Jodi Peake, Vice-President, Public & Investor Relations
Ana Lucia Martins, Vice-President, Safety, Health, Environment, & Community

Yangarra Resources Ltd. (YGR)
#1530, 715 - 5th Ave. SW
Calgary, AB T2P 2X6
403-262-9558
Fax: 403-262-8281
info@yangarra.ca
www.yangarra.ca

Company Type: Public
Ticker Symbol: YGR / TSX Venture
Profile: The junior oil & gas company is engaged in exploration, development, & production in central Alberta.
Jim Evaskevich, President & Chief Executive Officer
Michael d'Entremont, Chief Operating Officer
James Glessing, CA, Chief Financial Officer
Grant Evaskevich, MBA, Vice-President, Corporate Development
Ron Gardiner, P.Geol., Vice-President, Exploration
Gordan Bowerman, Chair, Health & Safety Committee

Yukon - Nevada Gold Corp.
#490, 688 West Hastings St.
Vancouver, BC V6B 1P1
604-688-9427
Fax: 604-688-9426
yngc@yngc.ca
www.yukon-nevadagold.com

Company Type: Public
Ticker Symbol: YNG / TSX, Frankfurt
Graham Dickson, President & CEO
Shaun Heinrichs, Chief Financial Officer (acting)

Oil & Gas

Advantage Oil & Gas Ltd.
Canterra Tower
#700, 400 - 3rd Ave. SW
Calgary, AB T2P 4H2
403-718-8000
Fax: 403-718-8300
866-393-0393
ir@advantageog.com; hr@advantageog.com
www.advantageog.com

Company Type: Public
Ticker Symbol: AAV / TSX, NYSE
Profile: The intermediate oil & natural gas corporation has properties in western Canada, including the Montney natural gas resource at Glacier, Alberta.
Andy J. Mah, Chief Executive Officer
Kelly I. Drader, President & Chief Financial Officer
Patrick J. Cairns, Senior Vice-President
Neil Bokenfohr, Vice-President, Exploitation
Weldon Kary, Vice-President, Geosciences & Land

Africa Oil Corp.
#2000, 885 West Georgia St.
Vancouver, BC V6C 3E8
604-689-7842
Fax: 604-689-4250
africaoilcorp@namdo.com
www.africaoilcorp.com

Company Type: Public
Ticker Symbol: AOI / TSX Venture
Profile: The oil & gas company has assets in Ethiopia, Kenya, & Mail. Through its equity interest in Horn Petroleum Corporation, Africa Oil Corp. also has assets in Somalia.
Keith C. Hill, President & Chief Executive Officer
Ian Gibbs, Chief Financial Officer
James Phillips, Chief Operating Officer
David Grellman, Vice-President, Operations

Aker Kvaerner Canada Inc.
1818 Cornwall Ave.
Vancouver, BC V6J 1C7
604-734-1200
Fax: 604-734-0340
www.akersolutions.com

Company Type: Private

Akita Drilling Ltd.
#900, 311 - 6 Ave. SW
Calgary, AB T2P 3H2
403-292-7979
Fax: 403-292-7990
akitainfo@akita-drilling.com
www.akita-drilling.com

Company Type: Public
Ticker Symbol: AKT / TSX
Profile: Akita Drilling Ltd. serves the oil & gas industry by providing contract drilling services. Western Canada, Canada's northern territories, & Alaska are the principal areas of activity.
Karl A. Ruud, President & Chief Executive Officer
Murray J. Roth, Chief Financial Officer & Vice-President, Finance
403-292-7950
Lou C. Klaver, P.Eng., Vice-President, Engineering
Craig W. Kushner, Corporate Secretary & Administrator, Human Resources

Alberta Oilsands Inc. (AOS)
#800, 350 - 7th Ave. SW
Calgary, AB T2P 3N9
403-263-6700
Fax: 403-263-6702
info@aboilsands.ca; community@aboilsands.
www.aboilsands.ca
Other Communications: Community Relations, Phone: 403-444-6490

Company Type: Public
Ticker Symbol: AOS / TSX Venture
Profile: Alberta Oilsands Inc. explores for & develops bitumen. The company's area of operation is northeastern Alberta's Athabasca oil sands.
Michael Lee, P.Eng., President & Chief Executive Officer
403-232-3371, mlee@aboilsands.ca
Andrew Constantinidis, MBA, Vice-President, Finance & Business Development
Claes T.S. Palmgren, P.Eng., Vice-President, Engineering - Resource Development
Ian Walker, P.Eng., Vice-President, Exploration

Alter NRG Corp.
#700, 910 - 7th Ave. SW
Calgary, AB T2P 3N8
403-806-3875
Fax: 403-806-3701
info@alternrg.ca
www.alternrg.ca

Company Type: Public
Ticker Symbol: NRG / TSX
Mark Montemurro, President & CEO
Daniel Hay, Chief Financial Officer

Americas Petrogas Inc.
3911, Trasimene Cres SW
Calgary, AB T3E 7J6
403-685-1888
Fax: 403-685-1880
info@americaspetrogas.com
www.americaspetrogas.com
Other Communications: Argentina Office, Phone: +54 11 4121 5600

Company Type: Public
Ticker Symbol: BOE / TSX Venture

Profile: Americas Petrogas Inc. has both conventional & unconventional shale oil & gas & tight sands oil & gas interests. The company is active in Argentina's Neuquen Basin.
Barclay Hambrook, P. Eng., MBA, President & Chief Executive Officer
403-685-1888, inquiries@americaspetrogas.com
Gustavo Diez, P. Eng., MBA, Chief Geophysicist
Douglas Yee, Chief Financial Officer
Guimar Vaca Coca, Managing Director, Argentina

Anderson Energy Ltd.
#700, 555 - 4th Ave. SW
Calgary, AB T2P 3E7

403-262-6307
Fax: 403-261-2792
info@andersonenergy.ca
www.andersonenergy.ca

Company Type: Public
Ticker Symbol: AXL / TSX
Brian H. Dau, President/CEO
M. Darlene Wong, Vice-President & CFO, Finance

Angle Energy Inc.
#700, 324 - 8th Ave. SW
Calgary, AB T2P 2Z2

403-263-4534
Fax: 403-263-4179
invest@angleenergy.com; careers@angleener
www.angleenergy.com
Company Type: Public
Ticker Symbol: NGL / TSX
Profile: Angle Energy Inc. was incorporated in 2004. The oil & gas exploration & development company is focused on assets in the Western Canadian Sedimentary Basin.
Angle Energy works to protect the environment through project planning, energy conservatoin, & waste minimization & management.
Gregg Fischbuch, Chief Executive Officer
Heather Christie-Burns, President & Chief Operating Officer
Stuart Symon, Chief Financial Officer, Corporate Secretary & Vice-President, Finance
Matthew Mazuryk, Vice-President, Engineering
Elizabeth More, Vice-President, Exploration
Glen Richardson, Vice-President, Land

Antrim Energy Inc.
Bankers Hall, Hollinsworth Building
#610, 301 - 8th Ave. SW
Calgary, AB T2P 1C5

403-264-5111
Fax: 403-264-5113
info@antriumenergy.com
www.antriumenergy.com
Other Communications: London, UK Office, Phone: +44 (0) 1 483 307 530
Company Type: Public
Ticker Symbol: AEN / TSX, London
Profile: Antrim Energy is an oil & gas exploration & production company. The company's operations are as follows: onshore operations in Argentina; offshore operations in the North Sea, United Kingdom; offshore Ireland; & interests in Tanzania.
Stephen E. Greer, President & Chief Executive Officer
greer@antrimenergy.com
Douglas B. Olson, Chief Financial Officer
olson@antrimenergy.com
Kerry Fulton, Vice-President, Operations
Scott Berry, Manager, Investor Relations
berry@antrimenergy.com

Apache Canada Ltd.
700 - 9 Ave. SW
Calgary, AB T2P 3V4

403-261-1200
Fax: 403-266-5987
www.apachecorp.com
Company Type: Private
John A. Crum, President, North America

ARC Resources Ltd.
#1200, 308 - 4th Ave. SW
Calgary, AB T2P 0H7

403-503-8600
Fax: 403-503-8607
888-272-4900
ir@arcresources.com
www.arcresources.com
Social Media: www.facebook.com/arcresources
twitter.com/arcresources
www.linkedin.com/company/61848?trk=tyah
Company Type: Public
Ticker Symbol: ARX / TSX
Profile: ARC resources is a conventional oil & gas company. ARC was formed in 1996.
John P. Dielwart, B.Sc., P.Eng., Chief Executive Officer
Steven W. Sinclair, B. Comm., CA, Chief Financial Officer & Senior Vice-President, Finance
Myron M. Stadnyk, P.Eng., Chief Operating Officer & Senior Vice-President
Terry Gill, B.PE., Senior Vice-President, Corporate Services
Cameron S. Kramer, P.Eng., Senior Vice-President, Capital Markets
Al Roberts, Vice-President, Production

Arcan Resources Ltd.
#2500, 308 - 4th Ave. SW
Calgary, AB T2P 0H7

403-262-0321
Fax: 403-262-4636
www.arcanres.com

Company Type: Public
Ticker Symbol: ARN / TSX Venture
Profile: Arcan Resources Ltd. acquires & develops petroleum & natural gas resources. The company carries out its operations in the Western Sedimentary Basin of Canada.

Ed Gilmet, P. Geoph., President & Chief Executive Officer
egilmet@arcanres.com
Douglas Penner, CA, CIA, CFA, Chief Financial Officer & Executive Vice-President
dpenner@arcanres.com
Andy Fisher, B.Comm. PLM, Executive Vice-President & Committee Member, Reserves / Health Safety & Environment
Kyle Baumgardner, P.Eng., Vice-President, Production
Kevin Gunning, P.Eng., Vice-President, Engineering
Thanos Natras, P. Geol., Vice-President, Exploration

Argosy Energy Inc.
#2100, 500 - 4th Ave. SW
Calgary, AB T2P 2V6

403-269-8846
Fax: 403-269-8366
investor@argosyenergy.com
www.argosyenergy.com

Company Type: Public
Ticker Symbol: GSY / TSX
Profile: Argosy Energy Inc. was formed in 2008. The company explores for & produces crude oil & natural gas in Alberta.
Peter Salamon, President & Chief Executive Officer
Tom Dalton, Chief Financial Officer & Vice-President, Finance
Ray Dobek, Executive Vice-President, Exploration
Rick Campbell, Vice-President, Engineering & Business Development
Norm George, Vice-President, Production & Operations

Arsenal Energy Inc.
#1900, 639 - 5th Ave. SW
Calgary, AB T2P 0M9

403-262-4854
Fax: 403-265-6877
info@arsenalenergy.com
www.arsenalenergy.com

Company Type: Public
Ticker Symbol: AEI / TSX
Profile: The energy exploration & production company has properties in Canada & the United States.
Tony van Winkoop, President & Chief Executive Officer
J. Paul Lawrence, Chief Financial Officer & Vice-President, Finance
Ron Forth, P.Eng., Vice-President, Engineering
Gjoa Taylor, Vice-President, Land

Athabasca Oil Sands Corp. (AOSC)
Bow Valley Square 4
#2000, 250 - 6th Ave. SW
Calgary, AB T2P 3H7

403-237-8227
info@aosc.com; ir@aosc.com
Other Communications: Career Information, E-mail: careers@aosc.com

Company Type: Public
Ticker Symbol: ATH / TSX
Profile: Athabasca Oil Sands Corp. was incorporated in 2006. The oil company is engaged in the development of oilsands resources in northern Alberta's Athabasca region.
The company promotes sustainable development through applying in situ technologies.
Sveinung Svarte, MBA, MSc., President & Chief Executive Officer

Baja Mining Corp.
#2350, 1177 West Hastings St.
Vancouver, BC V6E 2K3

604-685-2323
Fax: 604-629-5228
info@bajamining.com
www.bajamining.com

Company Type: Public
Ticker Symbol: BAJ / TSX
John Greenslade, Chief Executive Officer
Rowland Wallenius, Chief Financial Officer

Bankers Petroleum Ltd.
Bow Valley Square III
#1700, 255 - 5th Ave. SW
Calgary, AB TPP 3G6

403-513-2699
Fax: 403-228-9506
888-797-7170
investorrelations@bankerspetroleum.com
www.bankerspetroleum.com

Company Type: Public
Ticker Symbol: BNK / TSX, London-AIM
Profile: The company focuses on oil & gas exploration & production in Albania.
Abdel F. Badwi, President & Chief Executive Officer
Douglas C. Urch, B.Comm., CMA, Chief Financial Officer & Executive Vice-President, Finance

Baytex Energy Corp.
East Tower, Centennial Place
2800. 520 - 3rd Ave. SW
Calgary, AB T2P 0R3

587-952-3000
Fax: 587-952-3029
800-524-5521
helpdesk@baytex.ab.ca; investor@baytex.ab
www.baytex.ab.ca
Other Communications: Investor Relations, Phone: 587-952-3000
Social Media: twitter.com/BaytexEnergy
Company Type: Public
Ticker Symbol: BTE / TSX, NYSE
Profile: Baytex Energy specializes in the acquisition, development, & production of oil & natural gas. The area of operation is the Western Canadian Sedimentary Basin, in addition to a growing presence in the United States.
Anthony W. Marino, President & Chief Executive Officer
587-952-3100
W. Derek Aylesworth, Chief Financial Officer
587-952-3120
Marty L. Proctor, Chief Operating Officer
Randal J. Best, Sr. Vice-President, Corporate Development
Steve Brownridge, Vice-President, Heavy Oil
Brian Ector, Vice-President, Investor Relations
587-952-3237
Brett J. McDonald, Vice-President, Land
Mark F. Smith, Vice-President, Conventional Oil & Gas

Bellatrix Exploration Ltd.
#2300, 530 - 8th Ave. SW
Calgary, AB T2P 3S8

403-266-8670
Fax: 403-264-8163
general.info@bellatrixexp.com
www.bellatrixexploration.com
Other Communications: Investor Relations: 1-800-663-8072
Company Type: Public
Ticker Symbol: BXE / TSX
Profile: The oil & gas company operates in British Columbia, Alberta, & Saskatchewan.
Raymond G. Smith, P.Eng., President & Chief Executive Officer
Edward J. Brown, C.A., Chief Financial Officer & Vice-President, Finance
Ving Y. Woo, P.Eng., Chief Operating Officer & Vice-President, Engineering
Tim A. Blair, Vice-President, Land
Russell G. Oicle, P. Geol., Vice-President, Exploration
Garrett K. Ulmer, P.Eng.., Vice-President, Engineering

Birchcliff Energy Ltd.
#500, 630 - 4th Ave. SW
Calgary, AB T2P 0J9

403-261-6401
Fax: 403-261-6424
866-566-2923
info@birchcliffenergy.com
www.birchcliffenergy.com

Company Type: Public
Ticker Symbol: BIR / TSX
Profile: The intermediate oil & gas company is involved in exploration, development, & production.
A. Jeffery Tonken, President & Chief Executive Officer
jtonken@birchcliffenergy.com
Myles R. Bosman, Chief Operating Officer & Vice-President, Exploration
mbosman@birchcliffenergy.com
Bruno P. Geremia, Chief Financial Officer & Vice-President
bgeremia@birchcliffenergy.com

BlackPearl Resources Inc.
#700, 444 - 7th Ave. SW
Calgary, AB T2P 0X8

403-215-8313
Fax: 403-262-5123
info@blackpearlresources.ca
www.blackpearlresources.ca

Company Type: Public
Ticker Symbol: PXX / TSX
Profile: BlackPearl Resources Inc. operates in western Canada, where it has heavy oil & oil sands assets.
John Festival, President & Chief Executive Officer
festival@pxx.ca
Don Cook, Chief Financial Officer
don.cook@pxx.ca
Chris Hogue, Vice-President, Operations
Ed Sobel, Vice-President, Exploration

BNK Petroleum Inc.
#350, 760 Paseo Camarillo
Camarillo, CA 93010

805-484-3613
Fax: 805-484-9649
investorrelations@bnkpetroleum.com
www.bnkpetroleum.com

Company Type: Public
Ticker Symbol: BKX / TSX
Profile: The company is focused on the exploration for & production of oil & gas. Through its subsidiaries & affiliates, BNK Petroleum Inc. is the owner & operator of shale gas properties located in the United States, Spain, Poland, & Germany.
Wolf E. Regener, Chief Executive Officer
Warren Nelson, Chief Financial Officer & Vice-President
James M. Hill, Vice-President, New Ventures
Martin Robert, Vice-President, Engineering & Operations
Steven M. Warshauer, Ph.D., Vice-President, Exploration
Mark A. Shemaria, Manager, Health, Safety, & Environment

Bonavista Energy Corporation
#1500, 525 - 8th Ave. SW
Calgary, AB T2P 1G1

403-213-4300
Fax: 403-262-5184
inv_rel@bonavistaenergy.com
www.bonavistaenergy.com

Company Type: Public
Ticker Symbol: BNP / TSX
Profile: Bonavista Energy is an oil & gas company that was formed in 1997.
Keith MacPhail, Chief Executive Officer
Jason E. Skehar, President & Chief Operating Officer
Glenn A. Hamilton, Chief Financial Officer & Senior Vice-President
Ronald J. Poelzer, Executive Vice-President
Scott H. Hanson, Vice-President, Production
Cam Deller, Contact, Investor Relations

Bonnett's Energy Corp.
Corporate Head Office
Box 1, Site 33, RR#2
Grande Prairie, AB T8V 2Z9

780-513-3400
Fax: 780-532-9266
info@bonnettsenergy.com
www.bonnettsenergy.com
Other Communications: Calgary Office, Phone: 403-264-3010

Company Type: Public
Ticker Symbol: BT / TSX
Profile: The diversified corporation supplies wireline, fishing, frac-flowback & testing, & swabbing services. Operations take place in the Western Canadian Sedimentary Basin.
Murray Toews, Chief Executive Officer
David Ross, Chief Financial Officer
Troy Tews, Vice-President, Operations

Bonterra Energy Corp.
#901, 1015 - 4th St. SW
Calgary, AB T2R 1J4

403-262-5307
Fax: 403-265-7488
info@bonterraenergy.com
www.bonterraenergy.com

Company Type: Public
Ticker Symbol: BNE / TSX
Profile: Bonterra Energy Corp. is engaged in acquiring, exploring, & developing oil & natural gas properties. Activities are conducted in Saskatchewan, Alberta, & British Columbia.
George F. Fink, President & Chief Executive Officer
Robb D. Thompson, Chief Financial Officer & Secretary
Randy M. Jarock, Chief Operating Officer
Kirsten Lankester, Manager, Investor Relations

Brownstone Energy Inc.
The Exchange Tower
#2500, 130 King St. West
Toronto, ON M5X 1A9

416-941-8900
Fax: 416-941-1090
info@brownstoneenergy.com; ir@brownstonee
www.brownstoneenergy.com
Other Communications: Media: media@brownstoneenergy.com; Calgary: 403-984-3112

Company Type: Public
Ticker Symbol: BWN / TSX Venture
Profile: Brownstone Energy Inc. has interests in oil & gas exploration projects. Examples of operations include off-shore Israel & the Llanos Basin in Colombia.
Sheldon Inwentash, Chair & Chief Executive Officer
Jonathan Schroeder, President & Chief Operating Officer
schroeder@brownstoneenergy.com
Gerry Feldman, Chief Financial Officer
Feldman@brownstoneenergy.com
Richard Patricio, Vice-President, Legal & Corporate Affairs
Brian Balazs, Director, Exploration

Bucking Horse Energy Inc.
Corporate Office
#900, 609 West Hastings St.
Vancouver, BC V6B 4W4

604-331-3398
Fax: 604-688-4712
www.buckinghorseenergy.com

Company Type: Public
Ticker Symbol: BUC / TSX
Profile: Bucking Horse Energy is an oil & gas exploration, development, & production company.
Gordon Nielsen, Chair, President & Chief Executive Officer
Dean Willows, Chief Financial Officer, Corporate Secretary, & Treasurer

C&C Energia Ltd.
#1250, 555 - 4th Ave. SW
Calgary, AB T2P 3E7

403-262-6046
Fax: 403-262-6076
investor.relations@ccenergialtd.com
www.ccenergialtd.com
Other Communications: Columbia Office, Phone: +571-235-0007

Company Type: Public
Ticker Symbol: CZE / TSX
Profile: Formed in 2005 as a private company named C&C Energy Canada Ltd, C&C Energia Ltd. is now a public, independent oil & gas company. It is engaged in the exploration for, acquisition, development, & production of oil resources. The corporation's area of activity is Columbia. C&C Energia Ltd.'s subsidiary is rupo C&C Energia (Barbados) Ltd.
Richard A. Walls, Ph.D., President & Chief Executive Officer
Kenneth D. Hillier, CA, Chief Financial Officer
Randy P. McLeod, P.Eng., Chief Operating Officer
Tomas Villamil, Ph.D., P.Doc, Executive Vice-President, Exploration
Tyler Rimbey, MEc., Vice-President, Business Development
Victor Hugo Franco, P.Emg, General Manager, Columbia
Jennifer Dugdale, CA, Controller
Daniel McLeod, Corporate Secretary

Calfrac Well Services Ltd.
Corporate Headquarters
411 - 8th Ave. SW
Calgary, AB T2P 1E3

403-266-6000
Fax: 403-266-7381
866-770-3722
info@calfrac.com
www.calfrac.com

Company Type: Public
Ticker Symbol: CFW / TSX
Profile: Calfrac Well Services Ltd. is engaged in the provision of oilfield services, such as cementing, fracturing, & well stimulation services. Operations are situated in western Canada, the United States, Mexico, Argentina, & Russia.
Douglas R. Ramsay, Chief Executive Officer
Laura A. Cillis, Chief Financial Officer & Sr. Vice-President, Finance
Gordon A. Dibb, Chief Operating Officer
Dwight M. Bobier, Technical Services, Sr. Vice-Presidemt
Stephen T. Dadge, Sr. Vice-President, Corporate Services
Mark Paslawski, Vice-President, General Counsel, & Corporate Secretary

Calvalley Petroleum Inc.
#700, 600 - 6th Ave. SW
Calgary, AB T2P 0S5

403-297-0490
Fax: 403-297-0499
inquiries@calvalleypetroleum.com
www.calvalleypetroleum.com
Other Communications: Investors: investorrelations@calvalleypetroleum.com

Company Type: Public
Ticker Symbol: CVI.A / TSX
Profile: Calvalley Petroleum's area of expertise is acquiring, exploring, & developing oil & gas properties. Activity takes place in The Republic of Yemen & The Republic of Ethiopia.
Edmund M. Shimoon, Chief Executive Officer
Bill Cummins, Chief Financial Officer
Memet Kont, Chief Operating Officer
Grant Harms, Vice-President, Engineering & Operations
Terry McCoy, Vice-President, Exploration

Canacol Energy Ltd.
Eighth Avenue Place
#4500, 525 - Eighth Ave. SW
Calgary, AB T2P 1G1

403-561-1648
800-554-3590
ir@canacolenergy.com
www.canacolenergy.com
Other Communications: Colombia: +571.621.1747; Brazil: +55.21.2103.7617

Company Type: Public
Ticker Symbol: CNE / TSX; CNEC / BVC
Profile: The oil & gas company has operations in Colombia & Ecuador.
Charle Gamba, President & Chief Executive Officer
George Gramatke, Chief Financial Officer
Mark Holliday, Chief Operating Officer
Mark Teare, Vice-President, Exploration
Anthony Zaidi, General Counsel & Vice-President, Business Development
Rafael Rozo, Country Manager, Colombia

Canada Energy Partners Inc.
Head Office
#1500, 885 West Georgia St.
Vancouver, BC V6C 3E8

604-909-1154
Fax: 604-488-0319
info@canadaenergypartners.com
www.canadaenergypartners.com
Other Communications: Operations Office, Baton Rouge, LA, USA: 225-388-9900

Company Type: Public
Ticker Symbol: CE / TSX Venture
Profile: Canada Energy Partners Inc. was incorporated in 2006. The natural gas exporation & development company conducts operations in northeastern British Columbia
Benjamin M. Jones, President & Chief Executive Officer
Eileen Au, Corporate Secretary

Canadian Energy Services & Technology Corp. (CESTC)
#900, 715 - 5th Ave. SW
Calgary, AB T2P 2X6

403-269-2800
Fax: 403-266-5708
888-785-6695
info@ceslp.ca
www.canadianenergyservices.com

Company Type: Public
Ticker Symbol: CEU / TSX
Profile: Canadian Energy Services & Technology Corp. is involved in the design & implementation of drilling fluid systems. The company serves the oil & natural gas industry in western Canada & in the United States through its subsidiary, AES Drilling Fluids, LLC.
Thomas Simons, President & Chief Executive Officer
tsimons@ceslp.ca
Craig F. Nieboer, CA, Chief Financial Officer
cnieboer@ceslp.ca
Kenneth E. Zinger, Chief Operating Officer
Scott R. Cochlan, Corporate Secretary

Canadian Natural Resources Limited
#2500, 855 - 2nd St. SW
Calgary, AB T2P 4J8

403-517-6700
Fax: 403-517-7370
ir@cnrl.com
www.cnrl.com
Other Communications: Investor Relations, Phone: 403-514-7777

Company Type: Public
Ticker Symbol: CNQ / TSX

Profile: Canadian Natural Resources Limited is an independent oil & natural gaz producer. It is engaged in the exploration, development, & production of oil & natural gas. Operations are carried out in western Canada, the North Sea, & offshore west Africa.
Steve W. Laut, President/COO
Douglas A. Proll, CFO & Sr. Vice-President, Finance
Tim S. McKay, Sr. Vice-President, Operations
Steve C. Suche, Vice-President, Information & Corporate Services
Corey B. Bieber, Vice-President, Finance & Investor Relations
William R. Clapperton, Vice-President, Regulatory, Stakeholder & Environmental Affairs

Canadian Oil Sands Limited
First Canadian Centre
#2500, 350 - 7th Ave. SW
Calgary, AB T2P 3N9
403-218-6200
Fax: 403-218-6201
invest@cdnoilsands.com
www.cdnoilsands.com
Company Type: Public
Ticker Symbol: COS / TSX
Profile: In 2011, Canadian Oil Sands converted from a Trust to a corporation. The corporation offers an investment opportunity in the oil sands, through its interest in the Syncrude Project. Syncrude has operated since 1978.
Marcel R. Coutu, President & Chief Executive Officer
Siren Fisekci, Vice-President, Investor & Corporate Relations
Alison Trollope, Manager, Investor Relations

Canadian Phoenix Resources Corp.
#3300, 205 - 5th Ave. SW
Calgary, AB T2P 2V7
403-920-0040
Fax: 403-920-0043
www.canadian-phoenix.com
Other Communications: CXP / TSX Venture
Company Type: Public
Profile: The junior oil & gas company is engaged in exploration, development, & production. Canadian Phoenix Resources Corp.'s operations are in western Canada.
Michael Atkinson, President & Chief Executive Officer
604-689-1428
John Downes, Chief Financial Officer
604-488-5415

Canadian Spirit Resources Inc. (CSRI)
Ford Tower
#1950, 633 - 6th Ave. SW
Calgary, AB T2P 2Y5
403-539-5005
Fax: 403-262-4177
info@csri.ca
www.csri.ca
Company Type: Public
Ticker Symbol: SPI / TSX Venture
Profile: The natural resources company focuses on opportunities in the unconventional gas sector.
Alfred Sorensen, Chief Executive Officer
alfred.sorensen@csri.ca
Phillip D.C. Geiger, B.Sc., P.Eng., President & Chief Operating Officer
Dean G. Hill, BComm, CA, Chief Financial Officer & Vice-President, Finance
Paul A. Smolarchuk, B.Sc., P.Eng., Vice-President, Engineering & Operations

Canadian Tire Petroleum
866-217-1106
gasplus.canadiantire.ca
Other Communications: www.youtube.com/canadiantire
Social Media: www.facebook.com/Canadiantire
twitter.com/#!/canadiantire
Company Type: Private

Candax Energy Inc.
#2700, 130 Adelaide St. West
Toronto, ON M5H 3P5
416-368-9137
Fax: 416-364-5400
www.candax.com
Company Type: Public
Ticker Symbol: CAX / TSX
Michael Wood, President & CEO
Hywel R.R. John, Chief Financial Officer

CanElson Drilling Inc.
#700, 808 - 4th Ave. SW
Calgary, AB T2P 3E8
403-266-3922
Fax: 403-266-3968
info@canelsondrilling.com; hr@canelsondri
Other Communications: Nisku Office: 780-979-0747; Carlyle Office: 306-453-2506
Social Media: www.canelsondrilling.com
Company Type: Public
Ticker Symbol: CDI / TSX
Profile: CanElson Drilling provides services to the oil & gas industry. Drilling takes place in the Western Canadian Sedimentary Basin, the Permian Basin in western Texas, North Dakota, & the Ebano-Panuco-Cacalilao field near Tampico, Mexico.
In 2012, the company entered into an amalgamation agreement to acquire all the issued & outstanding securities of CanGas Solutions Ltd.
W. Randy Hawkings, President & Chief Executive Officer
Robert Skilnick, Chief Financial Officer
Derrick Big Eagle, Vice-President, Business Development
Ryan Hawkings, Vice-President, Operations
Lawrence Kolasa, Vice-President, Rig Construction

Canoro Resources Ltd.
#1620, 400 Burrard St.
Vancouver, BC V6C 3A6
604-408-8538
Fax: 604-683-3205
info@canoro.com
www.canoro.com
Company Type: Public
Ticker Symbol: CNS / TSX Venture
Profile: The junior natural resources company develops & produces oil & gas in northeastern India.
Jelena Djordjevic Lausevic, Chief Executive Officer

Canyon Services Group Inc.
#1600, 510 - 5th St. SW
Calgary, AB T2P 3S2
403-355-2300
Fax: 403-355-2211
investor@canyontech.ca
www.canyontech.ca
Company Type: Public
Ticker Symbol: FRC / TSX
Profile: Fracturing & chemical stimulation services are provided to oil & natural gas exploration & production companies throughout the Western Canadian Sedimentary Basin. Canyon Services Group Inc.'s wholly owned subsidiary is Canyon Technical Services Ltd.
Brad Fedora, President & Chief Executive Officer, Canyon Technical Services Ltd.
Barry O'Brien, Chief Financial Officer, Canyon Technical Services Ltd.
403-290-2478, Fax: 403-355-2211

Caspian Energy Inc.
56 Temperance St., 4th Fl.
Toronto, ON M5H 3V5
416-947-1087
Fax: 416-366-8179
Company Type: Public
Ticker Symbol: CEK / TSX
John Pollock, President

Cathedral Energy Services Ltd.
Head Office (Drilling + Completions
6030 - 3rd St. SE
Calgary, AB T2H 1K2
403-265-2560
Fax: 403-262-4682
866-276-8201
info@cathedralenergyservices.com
www.cathedralenergyservices.com
Other Communications: Investors: investors@cathedralenergyservices.com
Company Type: Public
Ticker Symbol: CET.TO / TSX
Profile: Cathedral Energy Services provides drilling & completions services. The company employs more than 850 people. Cathedral Energy works to meet its social, environmental, & ethical responsibilities.
Mark Bentsen, President & Chief Executive Officer
Scott MacFarlane, Chief Financial Officer
Randy Pustanyk, Vice-President, Operations
John Ruzicki, Vice-President
Ken Sawatzky, CRSP, Manager, Corporate Safety & Loss Control
Paul Zamora, Manager, Health, Safety, & Environment - USA Operations
970-523-5104, Fax: 970-523-2086,

Caza Oil & Gas, Inc.
#200, 10077 Grogan's Mill Rd.
The Woodlands, TX 77380
281-363-4442
Fax: 281-363-4454
info@CazaPetro.com
www.cazapetro.com
Company Type: Public
Ticker Symbol: CAZ / TSX, AIM
Profile: Caza Oil & Gas, Inc. is an exploration, appraisal, development, & production company. Through its subsidiary, Caza Petroleum, Inc., Caza Oil & Gas is active in the Texas & Louisiana Gulf Coast & in Permian Basin of western Texas & southeastern New Mexico.
W. Michael Ford, Chief Executive Officer
James Michael Markgraf, Chief Financial Officer & Vice-President, Finance
Richard Ronald Albro, Secretary & Vice-President, Land
Anthony Bryan Sam, Vice-President, Operations

Celtic Exploration Ltd.
West Tower
#600, 321 Sixth Ave. SW
Calgary, AB T2P 3H3
403-201-9153
Fax: 403-201-9163
invest@celticex.com
www.celticex.com
Company Type: Public
Ticker Symbol: CLT / TSX
Profile: Celtic Exploration Ltd. specializes in the exploration for & production of oil & gas.
David J. Wilson, President & Chief Executive Officer
403-201-5340
Sadiq H. Lalani, Chief Financial Officer & Vice-President, Finance
403-215-5310
Alan G. Franks, Vice-President, Operations
Michael R. Shea, Vice-President, Land
Michael R. Shea, Vice-President, Land

Cenovus Energy
Head Office
PO Box 766, 421 - 7 Ave. SW
Calgary, AB T2P 0M5
403-766-2000
Fax: 403-766-7600
877-766-2066
Integrity.Helpline@cenovus.com
www.cenovus.com
Other Communications: Emergencies: 1-877-458-8080
Social Media: www.facebook.com/Cenovus
twitter.com/cenovus
www.linkedin.com/company/cenovus-energy
Company Type: Public
Ticker Symbol: CVE / TSX
Profile: The Canadian oil company employs mores than 3,500 staff. Cenovus Energy oversees the following operations: a natural gas & oil production situated in southern Alberta & across Alberta; & an oil sands projects located in northern Alberta. Cenovus also has 50 percent ownership in two refineries in Roxana, Illinois & Borger, Texas.
Cenovus Energy employs environmental specialists to analyze land for drilling activities & to develop a plan to reclaim the land.
Brian Ferguson, Chief Executive Officer & President
John Brannan, Chief Operating Officer & Executive Vice-President
Ivor Ruste, Chief Financial Officer & Executive Vice-President
Harbir Chhina, Executive Vice-President, Oil Sands
Kerry Dyte, Executive Vice-President, Legal, Corporate Secretarial, & Internal Audit
Judy Fairburn, Executive Vice-President, Environment & Strategic Planning
Sheila McIntosh, Executive Vice-President, Communications & Stakeholder Relations
Don Swystun, Executive Vice-President, Refining, Marketing, Transportation, & Development

Cequence Energy Ltd.
#3100, 525 - 8th Ave. SW
Calgary, AB T2P 1G1
403-229-3050
Fax: 403-229-0603
info@cequence-energy.com
www.cequence-energy.com
Company Type: Public
Ticker Symbol: CQE / TSX
Profile: In western Canada, Cequence Energy Ltd. is engaged in the acquisition, exploration, development, & production of natural gas & crude oil.
Paul Wanklyn, President & Chief Executive Officer
Howard Crone, P.Eng, Executive Vice-President & Chief Operating Officer

David Gillis, CA, Chief Financial Officer & Vice-President, Finance
James R. Jackson, P.Eng, CFA, Vice-President, Engineering
Christopher C. Soby, Vice-President, Land

CGX Energy Inc.
#1010, 130 Adelaide St. West
Toronto, ON
416-364-5569
Fax: 416-364-5400
info@cgxenergy.com
www.cgxenergy.ca
Company Type: Public
Ticker Symbol: OYL / TSX Venture
Profile: The oil & gas exploration company is active in the Guyana - Suriname Basin. CGX Energy is also pursuing the Equatorial Atlantic Margin Play.
Stephen Hermeston, President & Chief Executive Officer
shermeston@cgxenergy.com
Tralisa Maraj, Chief Financial Officer
Michael Stockinger, Chief Operating Officer
Dewi Jones, Executive Vice-President, Exploration
John Clarke, Vice-President, Business Development
Charlotte May, Corporate Secretary & Manager, Communications
416-364-3353, cmay@cgxenergy.com

Changfeng Energy Inc.
#1612, 25 Adelaide St. East
Toronto, ON M5C 3A1
416-362-5032
Fax: 416-362-2393
info@changfengenergy.com
www.changfengenergy.com
Social Media: www.facebook.com/changfengenergy
twitter.com/tsxv_cfy
Company Type: Public
Ticker Symbol: CFY / TSX Venture
Profile: The natural gas service provider has operations in southern China. Changfeng Energy serves residential, commercial, & industrial customers in Hainan & Hunan Provinces.
Huajun Lin, Chair, President & Chief Executive Officer
Kevin Ming Zhang, Chief Financial Officer
kevin@changfengenergy.com
Ann S.Y. Lin, Corporate Secretary
ann@changfengenergy.com

Charger Energy Corp.
#2500, 500 - 4th Ave. SW
Calgary, AB T2P 2V6
403-457-1612
Fax: 403-457-1613
info@chargerenergy.com
www.chargerenergy.com
Company Type: Public
Ticker Symbol: CHX / TSX Venture
Profile: In 2012, Charger Energy, Seaview Energy, Silverback Energy, & Sirius Energy combined to form Charger Energy Corp.. The crude oil & natural gas company has assets in the Ghost Pine & the Halkirk-Provost regions of east central Alberta & in the Wapiti & Peace River Arch areas of northwestern Alberta.
Tom Buchanan, Chair & Chief Executive Officer
Dan O'Byrne, President & Chief Operating Officer
Mark Walker, Chief Financial Officer & Vice-President, Finance
Kelly Cowan, Vice-President, Corporate Development & Land
John Milford, Vice-President, Exploration & Development
Dan Fournier, General Counsel & Corporate Secretary

Chinook Energy Inc.
#700, 700 - 2nd St. SW
Calgary, AB T2P 2W1
403-261-6883
Fax: 403-266-1814
info@chinookenergyinc.com; resumes@chinoo
www.chinookenergyinc.com
Company Type: Public
Ticker Symbol: CKE / TSX
Profile: Chinook Energy Inc. is an oil & gas exploration & development company. It has assets in western Canada as well as onshore & offshore Tunisia in North Africa.
Matthew Brister, President & Chief Executive Officer
L. Geoffrey Barlow, Chief Financial Officer & Vice-President, Finance
Roy Smitshoek, Chief Operating Officer, International
P. Grant Wierzba, Chief Operating Officer & Vice-President, Production
Tom Lindskog, Vice-President, Exploration

Compton Petroleum Corporation
East Tower, Fifth Avenue Place
#3300, 425 - 1st St. SW
Calgary, AB T2P 3L8
403-237-9400
Fax: 403-237-9410
investorinfo@comptonpetroleum.com
www.comptonpetroleum.com
Company Type: Public
Ticker Symbol: CMT / TSX
Profile: Compton Petroleum Corporation explores for, develops, & produces natural gas, natural gas liquids, & crude oil. Activities are carried out in western Canada's sedimentary basin.
Ernest G. Sapieha, CA, President/CEO
Norman G. Knecht, CA, CFO & Vice-President, Finance
Murray Stodalka, P.Eng., Vice-President, Operations & Engineering
Tim Millar, LL.B., Vice-President, General Counsel, & Corporate Secretary
D. Monea, Manager, Government & Media Communications
J. Kendrick, Manager, Environmental, Health & Safety

Connacher Oil & Gas Limited
#900, 332 - 6th Ave. SW
Calgary, AB T2P 0B2
403-538-6201
Fax: 403-538-6225
inquiries@connacheroil.com
www.connacheroil.com
Company Type: Public
Ticker Symbol: CLL / TSX
Profile: Connacher Oil & Gas Limited is involved in the exploration, development, & production of oil & natural gas. The company's operations are carried out in western Canada, where its principal asset is oil sands leases in the Great Divide & Halfway Creek regions near Fort McMurray, Alberta. It is also the owner & operator of a refinery in Montana.
Richard A. (Dick) Gusella, President/CEO
Peter D. Sametz, Exec. Vice-President/COO
Richard R. (Rick) Kines, Chief Financial Officer & Vice-President, Finance
Steve Marston, Vice-President, Exploration
Grant D. Ukrainetz, Vice-President, Corporate Development
Charles W. Berard, Chair, Health, Safety, & Environment Committee

Conoco Phillips Canada
Gulf Canada Square
PO Box 130 Stn. M, , 401 - 9 Ave. SW
Calgary, AB T2P 2H7
403-233-4000
Fax: 403-233-5143
www.conocophillips.ca
Company Type: Private
Matt Fox, President

Corridor Resources Inc.
Head Office
#301, 5475 Spring Garden Rd.
Halifax, NS B3J 3T2
902-429-4511
Fax: 902-429-0209
888-429-4511
info@corridor.ca
www.corridor.ca
Other Communications: Penobsquis, New Brunswick, Field Office, Phone: 506-433-3066
Company Type: Public
Ticker Symbol: CDH / TSX
Profile: Corridor Resources Inc. is a junior resource company, which is engaged in the exploration & development of oil & gas properties. Activities are carried out onshore in Prince Edward Island, New Brunswick, & Québec, & offshore in the Gulf of St. Lawrence.
Phillip R. Knoll, President & Chief Executive Officer
Paul Durling, Chief Geophysicist
Lisette F. Hachery, Chief Financial Officer
Don LeBlanc, Chief Reservoir / Production Engineer
Tom Martel, Chief Geologist
Dena Murphy, Manager, Health, Safety, & Environment

Crescent Point Energy Corp.
East Tower, Suncor
#2800, 111 - 5th Ave. SW
Calgary, AB T2P 3Y6
403-693-0020
Fax: 403-693-0070
888-693-0020
ir@crescentpointenergy.com
www.crescentpointenergy.com
Other Communications: Freehold Royalty, Phone: 403-513-1128
Company Type: Public
Ticker Symbol: CPG / TSX
Profile: Formed in 1994, Crescent Point Energy Corp. is an oil & gas producer. The company is engaged in acquisition or reserves & production in western Canada.
Scott Saxberg, President & Chief Executive Officer
Greg Tisdale, Chief Financial Officer
Dave Balutis, Vice-President, Exploration
Brad Borggard, Vice-President, Corporate Planning
Derek Christie, Vice-President, Geosciences
Ken Lamont, Treasurer & Vice-President, Finance
Tamara MacDonald, Vice-President, Land
Neil Smith, Vice-President, Engineering & Business Development
Trent Stangl, Vice-President, Marketing & Investor Relations
Mark Eade, Corporate Secretary

Crew Energy Inc.
#1400, 425 First St. SW
Calgary, AB T2P 3L8
403-266-2088
Fax: 403-266-6259
investor@crewenergy.com
www.crewenergy.com
Company Type: Public
Ticker Symbol: CR / TSX
Profile: The junior oil & natural gas producer carries out its activities in northeastern British Columbia & central Alberta.
Dale O. Shwed, President/CEO
John G. Leach, CFO & Sr. Vice-President, Finance
Ken Truscott, Sr. Vice-President, Business Development & Land
Shawn Van Spankeren, Controller & Vice-President, Finance
Dale Kuzyk, Manager, Production & Operations
Rosanna Dardano, Office Manager

Crocotta Energy Inc.
Head Office
#700, 639 - 5th Ave. SW
Calgary, AB T2P 0M9
403-538-3737
Fax: 403-538-3735
info@crocotta.ca
www.crocotta.ca
Company Type: Public
Ticker Symbol: CTA / TSX
Profile: The junior oil & natural gas company is engaged in exploration, acquisition, development & production activities in western Canada.
Robert J. Zakresky, President & Chief Executive Officer
Nolan Chicoine, MPAcc, CA, Chief Financial Officer & Vice-President, Finance
Terry L. Trudeau, P.Eng., Chief Operating Officer & Vice-President, Operations
Weldon Dueck, B.Sc., P.Eng., Vice-President, Business Development
Helmut R. Eckert, P.Land, Vice-President, Land

CWC Well Services Corp.
Bow Valley Square III
#755, 255 - 5th Ave. SW
Calgary, AB T2P 3G6
403-264-2177
Fax: 403-264-2842
877-341-3933
info@cwcwellservices.com
www.cwcwellservices.com
Social Media:
www.facebook.com/pages/CWC-Well-Services-Corp/122409711 146882
www.linkedin.com/company/1613347
Company Type: Public
Ticker Symbol: CWC / TSX Venture
Profile: The well servicing company operates in the Western Canadian Sedimentary Basin. Services include coil tubing, well testing, & snubbing. Operations centers are located in Red Deer, Grande Prairie, Lloydminster, Provost, Brooks, & Weyburn.
Duncan Au, CA, CFA, President & Chief Executive Officer
Kevin Howell, Chief Financial Officer
Rick Dawson, Vice-President, Business Development
Darwin McIntyre, Vice-President, Operations (Eastern)
Layne Wilk, Vice-President, Operations (Central)

Dejour Energy Inc.
World Trade Centre
#598, 999 Canada Pl.
Vancouver, BC V6C 3E1
604-638-5050
Fax: 604-638-5051
866-888-8230
investor@dejour.com
www.dejour.com
Other Communications: Dejour Energy (Alberta) Ltd., Phone: 403-266-3825
Company Type: Public
Ticker Symbol: DEJ / TSX, AMEX
Profile: The independent oil & natural gas exploration &

production company conducts its operations in the Peace River Arch & Piceance Basin regions of North America. Dejour Energy Inc.'s wholly owned subsidiaries include Dejour Energy (Alberta) Ltd. & Dejour Energy (USA) Corp.
Robert L. Hodgkinson, Co-Chair & Chief Executive Officer
Mathew Wong, CA, CFA, CPA, Chief Financial Officer
Phil Bretzlof, BA, LLB, Vice-President & General Counsel

Delphi Energy Corp.
Head Office
#300, 500 - 4th Ave. SW
Calgary, AB T2P 2V6
403-265-6171
Fax: 403-265-6207
info@delphienergy.ca
www.delphienergy.ca

Company Type: Public
Ticker Symbol: DEE / TSX
Profile: Delphi Energy is engaged in the exploration for & the development & production of oil & natural gas. Operations take place in western Canada.
David J. Reid, President & Chief Executive Officer
Brian P. Kohlhammer, Chief Financial Officer & Senior Vice-President
Tony Angelidis, P.Geol., Senior Vice-President, Exploration
Rob Hume, P.Eng., Senior Vice-President, Engineering

Devon Canada Corporation
#2000, 400 - 3rd Ave. SW
Calgary, AB T2P 4H2
403-232-7100
Fax: 403-232-7221
www.devonenergy.com
Company Type: Public
Ticker Symbol: DVN
John Richels, President/CEO
Jeff A. Agosta, Sr. Vice-President, Finance
Janice A. Dobbs, Corporate Secretary

Direct Energy Marketing Ltd.
37 Dufflaw Rd.
Toronto, ON M6A 2W2
866-203-1016
www.directenergy.com
Company Type: Private

Dundee Energy Limited
Dundee Place
#2800, 1 Adelaide St. East
Toronto, ON M5C 2V9
416-863-6990
Fax: 416-363-4536
dundee-energy@dundee-energy.com
www.dundee-energy.com
Other Communications: Calgary Office, Phone: 403-264-4985, Fax: 403-262-8299

Company Type: Public
Ticker Symbol: DEN / TSX
Profile: The oil & natural gas company is engaged in exploration, development, production & marketing. Dundee Energy Limited has interests in Ontario & Spain. Through a preferred share investment, the company also has exploration & evaluation programs for oil & natural gas offshore Tunisia.
Jaffar Khan, President & Chief Executive Officer
David Bhumgara, CA, CA-IT, Chief Financial Officer
Lucie Presot, CMA, Vice-President

Eaglewood Energy Inc.
Corporate Office
602, 304 - 8th Ave. SW
Calgary, AB T2P 1C2
403-264-6944
Fax: 403-266-6441
info@eaglewoodenergy.ca
www.eaglewoodenergy.ca
Other Communications: Australia: +61 2 4929 0500; Papua New Guinea: +675 321 0530
Social Media: twitter.com/eaglewoodenergy
Company Type: Public
Ticker Symbol: EWD / TSX Venture
Profile: The oil & gas exploration company has exploration licenses in Papua New Guinea. Eaglewood Energy's corporate office is located in Calgary, Alberta, its operating office in in Port Moresby, Papua New Guinea, & the technical office is in Newcastle, Australia.
Brad Hurtubise, Chief Executive Officer
bhurtubise@eaglewoodenergy.ca
Michael McGowan, President & Chief Operating Officer
mmcgowan@eaglewoodenergy.ca
Diana Moes, Chief Financial Officer & Controller
dmoes@eaglewoodenergy.ca
Bruce Apana, Country Manager, Papua New Guinea
Bapana@eaglewoodenergy.com.pg
Ray Antony, Chair, Environmental Health & Safety Committee

Enbridge Gas Distribution
Fifth Avenue Place
#3000, 425 - 1st St. S.W.
Calgary, AB T2P 3L8
403-508-6563
Fax: 888-711-1211
877-362-7434
customercare@enbridge.com
www.enbridge.com
Company Type: Private

Enbridge Inc.
Fifth Avenue Place
#3000, 425 - 1st St. SW
Calgary, AB T2P 3L8
403-231-3900
Fax: 403-231-3920
investor.relations@enbridge.com
www.enbridge.com
Other Communications: Human Resources, E-mail: enbridgecareers@enbridge.com
Company Type: Public
Ticker Symbol: ENB / TSX, NYSE
Profile: Enbridge Inc. is engaged in the following businesses: natural gas pipelines, crude oil & liquids pipelines, & natural gas distribution. The company's pipeline system is located in Canada & the United States. International activity includes energy projects & renewable energy.
In 2011, Enbridge, through Canadain Acquireco, acquired all the outstanding common shares of Tonbridge Power Inc.
Patrick D. Daniel, President/CEO
J. Richard Bird, Exec. Vice-President/CFO, Corporate Development
Bonnie D. DuPont, Group Vice-President, Corporate Resources
David T. Robottom, Group Vice-President, Corporate Law
Vern Yu, Vice-President, Investor Relations & Enterprise Risk
James J. Blanchard, Chair, Corporate Social Responsibility Committee
Karen Radford, Executive Vice-President, People & Partners
Janet A. Holder, Executive Vice-President, Western Access

Enbridge Pipelines
Fifth Avenue Place
#3000, 425 - 1st St. SW
Calgary, AB T2P 3L8
403-508-6563
Fax: 888-711-1211
877-362-7434
customercare@enbridge.com
www.enbridge.com

Company Type: Private

EnCana Corporation
PO Box 2850, #1800, 855 - 2nd St. SW
Calgary, AB T2P 2S5
403-645-2000
Fax: 403-645-3400
888-568-6322
corpcomm@encana.com
www.encana.com
Other Communications: Investors: investor.relations@encana.com
Social Media: www.facebook.com/Encana
twitter.com/encanacorp
Company Type: Public
Ticker Symbol: ECA / TSX
Profile: The company is engaged in producing natural gas, oil, & natural gas liquied. Common shares trade on the Toronto & New York stock exchanges under the symbol ECA.
Randy Eresman, President/CEO
Brian Ferguson, CA, Exec. Vice-President/CFO
Sheila McIntosh, Exec. Vice-President, Corporate Communications
Hayward Walls, Exec. Vice-President, Corporate Services

Enerplus Corp.
The Dome Tower
#3000, 333 - 7th Ave. SW
Calgary, AB T2P 2Z1
403-298-2200
Fax: 403-298-2211
877-319-6462
investorrelations@enerplus.com
www.enerplus.com
Other Communications: Media: 403-298-1293; HR E-mail: humanresources@enerplus.com
Company Type: Public
Ticker Symbol: ERF / TSX
Profile: Enerplus Resources Fund has a portfolio of oil & natural gas producing properties. Properties are situated in western Canada & the United States.
Gordon J. Kerr, B.Comm., C.A., President/CEO
Robert J. Waters, MBA, C.A., Sr. Vice-President/CFO
Garry A. Tanner, MBA, Exec. Vice-President/COO
Jo-Anne M. Caza, Vice-President, Investor Relations & Corporate Communications
Lyonel G. Kawa, Vice-President, Information Services
Daniel M. Stevens, Vice-President, Development Services

Enhanced Oil Resources, Inc.
#610, One Riverway
Houston, TX 77056
832-485-8500
Fax: 832-485-8506
888-990-3551
www.enhancedoilres.com
Company Type: Public
Ticker Symbol: EOR / TSX Venture
Profile: Through enhanced oil recovery & infill drilling projects, it is the goal of Enhanced Oil Resources Inc. to increase crude oil & natural gas production.
Barry D. Lasker, President & Chief Executive Officer
W. Kyle Willis, Chief Financial Officer, Treasurer & Vice-President
Donald J. Currie, Contact, Investor Relations
604-488-1514, Fax: 604-844-7572,
dcurrie@enhancedoilres.com

Enseco Energy Services Corp.
#500, 1111 - 11 Ave. SW
Calgary, AB T2R
403-806-0088
Fax: 403-806-0084
www.enseco.ca
Company Type: Public
Ticker Symbol: ENS / TSX Venture
David Hawkins, President & CEO
Aly Musani, Senior Vice-President & CFO

Ensign Energy Services Inc.
#1000, 400 - 5th Ave. SW
Calgary, AB T2P 0L6
403-262-1361
Fax: 403-266-3596
info@ensignenergy.com
www.ensignenergy.com
Company Type: Public
Ticker Symbol: ESI / TSX
Profile: Ensign Energy Services Inc. is a service contractor that provides oilfield services throughout the world to the oil & natural gas industry. Some of Ensign Energy Services's principal operating subsidiaries include Arctic Ensign Drilling Ltd., Big Sky Drilling Inc., Encore Coring & Drilling Inc., Opsco Energy Industries Ltd., Rockwell Servicing Inc., & Gwich'in Ensign Oilfield Services Inc.
Robert H. Geddes, President & Chief Operating Officer
Glenn Dagenais, Chief Financial Officer & Executive Vice-President, Finance
403-262-1361
Ed Kautz, Exec. Vice-President, United States & International Operations
Rob Wilman, Vice-President, Health, Safety, & Environment
Suzanne Davies, Associate Corporate Secretary & In-house Legal Counsel

Epsilon Energy Ltd.
Canadian Head Office
#9, 150 Jardin Dr.
Concord, ON L4K 3P9
905-738-7877
Fax: 905-669-8220
866-545-6555
Information@epsilonenergyltd.com
www.epsilonenergyltd.com
Other Communications: Investors Relations: Information@epsilonenergyltd.com
Company Type: Public
Ticker Symbol: EPS / TSX
Profile: Established in 2005, Epsilon Energy Ltd. is involved in the exploration & production of natural gas reserves. The company has participating interests & production sharing agreements in North America & Africa.
Zoran Arandjelovic, Executive Chair, President, Chief Executive Officer
Ramik Arandjelovic, Chief Operating Officer
ramik@epsilonenergyltd.com
Daniel J. Ward, Vice-President, Exploration

Equal Energy Ltd.
Head Office
#2700, 500 - 4th Ave. SW
Calgary, AB T2P 2V6

403-263-0262
Fax: 403-294-1197
877-263-0262
info@equalenergy.ca
www.equalenergy.ca
Other Communications: Oklahoma City Operations Office, Phone: 405-242-6000

Company Type: P
Ticker Symbol: EQU / TSX, NYSE
Profile: The oil & gas exploration & production company has producing properties in Alberta & Oklahoma.
Don Klapko, President & Chief Executive Officer
Dell Chapman, Chief Financial Officer & Senior Vice-President
John F. Reader, Chief Operating Officer & Senior Vice-President

Terry Fullerton, Senior Vice-President, Exploration
Peter Letizia, Vice-President, Production

Essential Energy Services Ltd.
Livingston Place West
#1100, 250 - 2nd St. SW
Calgary, AB T2P 0C1

403-263-6778
Fax: 403-263-6737
service@essentialenergy.ca
www.essentialenergy.ca
Other Communications: Investor Relations: 403-513-7272
Social Media: www.facebook.com/pages/Essential-Energy-Services/105659136177052
twitter.com/essentialpeople

Company Type: Public
Ticker Symbol: ESN / TSX
Profile: Essential Energy Services Ltd. offers oilfield services to oil & gas producers in western Canada. In 2011, Essential Energy Services acquired Technicoil Corporation to strengthen the company's position as a coil tubing well service provider.
Garnet K. Amundson, President & Chief Executive Officer
Jeff B. Newman, Chief Financial Officer
Karen Perasalo, Contact, Investor Relations

Exall Energy Corporation
#400, 715 - 5th Ave. SW
Calgary, AB T2P 2X6

403-237-7820
Fax: 403-262-4723
info@exall.com
www.exall.com
Other Communications: Toronto Office, Phone: 416-368-3949

Company Type: Public
Ticker Symbol: EE / TSX
Profile: The junior oil & gas company has properties in Alberta.
Roger N. Dueck, President & Chief Executive Officer
Warren F.E. Coles, Chief Financial Officer & Vice-President, Finance
Glen Kerr, P.Eng., Chief Operating Officer
Janet MacKenzie, P.Geol., Vice-President, Exploration
Dee A. Dueck, Controller

Fairborne Energy Ltd.
#3400, 450 - 1st St. SW
Calgary, AB T2P 5H1

403-290-7750
Fax: 403-290-7724
info@fairborne-energy.com
www.fairborne-energy.com

Company Type: Public
Ticker Symbol: FEL / TSX
Profile: Fairborne Energy Ltd. develops oil & gas properties. The company's main operating areas are as follows: Central Alberta; West Pembina/Brazeau; Columbia/Harlech; Deep Basin; Peace River Arch in Alberta; & Sinclair in southwestern Manitoba. The company has implemented a comprehensive health, safety, & environmental program.
Steven R. VanSickle, President/CEO
svansickle@fairborne-energy.com
Aaron G. Grandberg, Chief Financial Officer
agrandberg@fairborne-energy.com
David L. Summers, Chief Operating Officer
dsummers@fairborne-energy.com
David S. Cymbalisty, Vice-President, Engineering
Tom Park, Vice-President, Marketing
David E.T. Pyke, Vice-President, Land & Contracts

Falcon Oil & Gas Ltd.
#1400, 1875 Lawrence St.
Denver, CO

303-898-1800
Fax: 303-572-8927
info@falconoilandgas.com
www.falconoilandgas.com

Company Type: Public
Ticker Symbol: FO / TSX Venture
Marc A. Bruner, Chairman, President & CEO
Evan Wasoff, Chief Financial Officer

Flint Energy Services Ltd.
#700, 300 - 5th Ave. SW
Calgary, AB T2P 3C4

403-218-7100
Fax: 403-215-5481
www.flint-energy.com

Company Type: Public
Ticker Symbol: FES / TSX
Profile: In 2012, Flint Energy Service Ltd. was acquired by URS Corporation. Flint provides integrated products & services for the oil & gas industry. The company has approximately 10,000 employees.
W.J. (Bill) Lingard, President & Chief Executive Officer
Paul M. Boechler, Chief Financial Officer & Executive Vice-President
Wayne Shaw, Chief Operating Officer
Glen Greenshields, Senior Vice-President, Production Services
Guy Cocquyt, Vice-President, Communications
403-218-7195, gcocquyt@flintenergy.com
Brad McFarlane, Vice-President, Environment, Health & Safety

Gastar Exploration Ltd.
#1080, 1331 Lamar St.
Houston, TX 77010 USA

713-739-1800
Fax: 713-739-0458
ir@gastar.com
www.gastar.com

Company Type: Public
Ticker Symbol: YGA / AMEX
J. Russell Porter, President & CEO
Michael Gerlich, Chief Financial Officer

Gibson Energy Inc.
Head Office
#1700, 440 - 2nd Ave. SW
Calgary, AB T2P 5E9

403-206-4000
Fax: 403-206-4001
www.gibsons.com
Social Media: www.facebook.com/gibsonenergy

Company Type: Public
Ticker Symbol: GEI / TSX
Profile: Gibson Energy Inc. is a midstream energy company that is engaged in the following activities: crude oil transportation; blending & processing hydrocarbons; marketing & distributing crude oil & refined products; & providing water disposal & oilfield waste management services.
In 2011, Gibson Energy Inc. & Palko Environmental Ltd. entered into an arrangement agreement, providing for the acquisition by Gibson of all the issued & outstanding common shares of Palko.
A. Stewart Hanlon, President & Chief Executive Officer
Richard G. Taylor, Chief Financial Officer & Executive Vice-President
Rodney J. Bantle, Senior Vice-President, Transportation
Richard M. Wise, Senior Vice-President, Operations
Ken Hall, Vice-President, Investor Relations & Communications
403-781-2899, ken.hall@gibsons.com

Guide Exploration Ltd.
Also Known As: Guidex
West Tower, Livingston Place
#400, 250 - 2nd St. SW
Calgary, AB T2P 0C1

403-261-6012
Fax: 403-262-5561
888-598-1330
information@guidex.ca
www.guidex.ca

Company Type: Public
Ticker Symbol: GO / TSX
Profile: In 2011, Galleon Energy Inc. changed its name to Guide Exploration Ltd.. The intermediate oil & natural gas company works in western Canada.
Bill Andrew, P.Eng., President & Chief Executive Officer
403-261-9287, steves@galleonenergy.com
Dale A. Miller, P.Eng., President
Shivon M. Crabtree, CMA, Chief Financial Officer & Vice-President, Finance
Jim Iverson, P.Geol., Vice-President, Exploration
Dale Orton, P.Eng., Vice-President, Operations & Engineering

William Tang Kong, P.Eng., Vice-President, Corporate Development

Harvest Operations Corp.
Calgary Place
#2100, 330 - 5th Ave. SW
Calgary, AB T2P 0L4

403-265-1178
Fax: 403-265-3490
Information@harvestenergy.ca
www.harvestenergy.ca

Company Type: Private
Ticker Symbol: HTE / TSX
John Zahary, President/CEO
Robert Fotheringham, CFO

Heritage Oil Corporation
#2000, 633 - 6th Ave. SW
Calgary, AB T2P 2Y5

403-234-9974
Fax: 403-261-1941
info@heritageoilcorp.com
www.heritageoilplc.com

Company Type: Public
Ticker Symbol: HOC / TSX
Profile: Heritage Oil Corporation is a junior oil & gas exploration & production company that was formed in 1996. Areas of activity include Africa, the Middle East, & Russia.
Tony Buckingham, Chief Executive Officer
Paul Atherton, Chief Financial Officer
Cathy Hume, Contact, Investor Relations
416-868-1079

High Arctic Energy Services Inc.
8112 Edgar Idustrial Dr.
Red Deer, AB T4P 3R2

403-340-9825
Fax: 403-340-1047
800-668-7143
reception@haes.ca
www.haes.ca

Company Type: Public
Ticker Symbol: HWO / TSX
Profile: Through its subsidiaries, High Arctic Energy Services specializes in providing oilfield equipment & services. Operations are carried out in western Canada & in Papua New Guinea.
Bruce Thiessen, Chief Executive Officer
Robert Morin, Chief Financial Officer
403-340-9825, robert.morin@haes.ca
Dennis Sykora, Executive Vice-President & General Counsel
Dan Beaulieu, Vice-President, Canadian Operations
Kevin Doran, Vice-President, International Operations

Husky Energy Inc.
PO Box 6525 Stn. D, , 707 - 8 Ave. SW
Calgary, AB T2P 3G7

403-298-6111
Fax: 403-298-7464
investor.relations@huskyenergy.ca
www.huskyenergy.ca

Company Type: Public
Ticker Symbol: HSE / TSX
Profile: Husky Energy Inc. is engaged in the exploration & development of crude oil & natural gas, as well as the production, transportation & marketing of petroleum products. The company has upstream, midstream, & downstream business segments, & operates globally. Husky Energy works to meet & exceed regulatory requirements to reduce its impact to land, habitat, air, & water.
John C.S. Lau, President/CEO
Alister Cowan, Vice-President/CFO
Robert J. Peabody, Chief Operating Officer, Operations & Refining
James D. Girgulis, Corporate Secretary & Vice-President, Legal
Patrick Aherne, Manager, Investor Relations

Hyduke Energy Services Inc.
Head Office
609 - 21 Ave.
Nisku, AB T9E 7X9

780-955-0355
Fax: 780-955-0368
www.hyduke.com

Company Type: Public
Ticker Symbol: HYD / TSX
Profile: The oilfield services company specializes in the manufacture, repair, & distribution of oilfield equipment & supplies. Drilling rigs & well service equipment are also inspected & certified. Hyduke Energy Services serves the drilling & well service industries in Canada & internationally.
Gordon R. McCormack, President & Chief Executive Officer
Veronica Dutchak, CA, Chief Financial Officer

Hyperion Exploration Corp.
Calgary Place II
#2010, 355 - 4th Ave. SW
Calgary, AB T2P 0J1

403-930-0700
Fax: 403-266-4911
info@hyperionexploration.com
www.hyperionexploration.com

Company Type: Public
Ticker Symbol: HYX / TSX Venture
Profile: Hyperion Exploration is a junior oil & gas company. It resulted from the recapitalization of Triple 8 Energy Ltd. in 2010. Hyperion Exploration's operations are in Alberta's Buck Lake, Chip Lake, North Pembina, Niton, & Garrington regions, as well as in British Columbia's Paradise area.
Trevor Spagrud, P.Eng, President & Chief Executive Officer
403-930-0701, tspagrud@hyperionexploration.com
Doug Bailey, Chief Financial Officer
403-930-0703, dbailey@hyperionexploration.com
Larry Hammond, P.Eng, Chief Operating Officer
Tim Gee, P.Eng, Vice-President, Engineering
Ryan Heath, Vice-President, Land & Business Development

Imperial Oil Limited
PO Box 2480 Stn. M, , 237 Fourth Ave. SW
Calgary, AB T2P 3M9

800-567-3776
Fax: 800-367-0585
investor.relations@esso.ca
www.imperialoil.ca
Other Communications: Key to the Hwy Help Centre: 1-877-359-9792

Company Type: Public
Ticker Symbol: IMO / TSX
Profile: The company is a producer of crude oil & natural gas. Imperial Oil also refines & markets petroleum products. The company aims to minimize its impact on the air, land, & water by investing in research & technology & adhering to detailed management systmes.
B.H. (Bruce) March, President/CEO & Chair
P.A. (Paul) Smith, Treasurer & Sr. Vice-President, Finance & Administration
B.W. (Brian) Livingston, Vice-President, General Counsel & Corporate Secretary
R.L. (Randy) Broiles, Sr. Vice-President, Resources Division

Imperial Oil Resources

www.imperialoil.ca

Company Type: Private

Insignia Energy Ltd.
#2300, 500 - 4th Ave. SW
Calgary, AB T2P 2V6

403-536-8132
Fax: 403-514-6940
info@insigniaenergy.ca
www.insigniaenergy.ca

Company Type: Public
Ticker Symbol: ISN / TSX
Profile: Insignia Energy Ltd. is an oil & natural gas exploration, development, & production company. The company works in western Canada.
Jeffrey D. Newcommon, President & Chief Executive Officer
Glen Fischer, Chief Operating Officer & Professional Engineer
Danny Geremia, Chief Financial Officer & Vice-President, Finance
Steven J. Mackay, Vice-President, Exploration

Inter Pipeline Fund
#2600, 237 - 4th Ave. SW
Calgary, AB T2P 4K3

403-290-6000
Fax: 403-290-6092
866-716-7473
investorrelations@interpipelinefund.com
www.interpipelinefund.com

Company Type: Public
Ticker Symbol: IPL.UN / TSX
Profile: Inter Pipeline Fund was created in 1997. It is involved in natural gas liquids extraction, petroleum storage, & tranportation.

David W. Fesyk, President/CEO, Pipeline Management Inc.
William A. van Yzerloo, CFO, Pipeline Management Inc.
James J. Madro, Vice-President, Operations

InterOil Corp.
#420, 25025 I-45 North
The Woodlands, TX 77380 USA

281-292-1800
Fax: 281-292-0888
www.interoil.com

Company Type: Public
Ticker Symbol: IOC / NYSE
Phil E. Mulacek, Chairman & Chief Executive Officer

IROC Energy Services Corporation
Head Office
#8113, 49th Ave. Close
Red Deer, AB T4P 2V5

403-346-9710
Fax: 403-346-9770
877-346-9710
mail@iroccorp.com; investorrelations@iroc
www.iroccorp.com
Other Communications: Calgary Corporate Office, Phone: 403-263-1110

Company Type: Public
Ticker Symbol: ISC / TSX Venture
Profile: Through the IROC Energy Services Partnership, the IROC Energy Services Corporation provides products, services, & equipment to the oil & gas industry. IROC Energy Services Partnership operates under the following business names: Aero Rental Services, Eagle Well Servicing, & Helix Coil Services.
Thomas Alford, President & Chief Executive Officer
Ryan Michaluk, CA CMA, Chief Financial Officer
Timothy J. Sebastian, General Counsel & Vice-President, Corporate Development

Ithaca Energy Inc.
#1600, 311 - 6th Ave. SW
Calgary, AB T2P 3H2

403-263-0050
Fax: 403-234-7722
info@ithacaenergy.com
www.ithacaenergy.com

Company Type: Public
Ticker Symbol: IAE / TSX
Profile: Ithaca Energy is involved in the exploration, development, & production of oil & gas. The company is active in the United Kingdom's Continental Shelf.
Iain McKendrick, Chief Executive Officer
imckendrick@ithacaenergy.com
Graham Forbes, Chief Financial Officer
gforbes@ithacaenergy.com

Ivanhoe Energy Inc.
#654, 999 Canada Pl.
Vancouver, BC V6C 3E1

604-688-8323
Fax: 604-682-2060
info@ivanhoeenergy.com
www.ivanhoeenergy.com

Company Type: Public
Ticker Symbol: IE / TSX, NASDAQ
Joseph Gasca, President/CEO
W. Gordon Lancaster, CFO

Junex Inc.
#200, 2795, boul Laurier
Québec, QC G1V 4M7

418-654-9661
Fax: 418-654-9662
junex@junex.ca
www.junex.ca

Company Type: Public
Ticker Symbol: JNX / TSX Venture
Profile: Founded in 1999, Junex is engaged in oil & gas exploration in Québec. The junior oil & gas company holds exploration rights on lands in the Appalachian basin, the St. Lawrence lowlands, & on Anticosti Island.
Jean-Yves Lavoie, Eng., Chief Executive Officer & Co-Founder
Peter Dorrins, Eng., President & Chief Operations Officer
Dave Pépin, MBA, Chief Financial Officer & Vice-President, Corporate Affairs
Mathieu Lavoie, Eng., Vice-President, Operations
Jean-Sébastien Marcil, Eng., Manager, Exploration

Kinder Morgan Canada
#2700, 300 - 5th Ave.
Calgary, AB T2P 5J2

403-514-6400
Fax: 403-514-6401
800-535-7219
info@kindermorgan.com
www.kindermorgan.com

Company Type: Public
Ian Anderson, President

Kodiak Oil & Gas Corp.
#250, 1625 Broadway
Denver, CO 80202 USA

303-592-8075
Fax: 303-592-8071
kodiakland@kodiakog.com; resumes@kodiakog
www.kodiakog.com

Company Type: Public
Ticker Symbol: KOG / NYSE
Profile: The independent energy company focuses on the exploration, acquisition, & production of crude oil & natural gas. Operating areas include North Dakota & Montana's Williston Basin & Wyoming's Green River Basin & Vermillion Basin.
Lynn A. Peterson, President & Chief Executive Officer
James E. Catlin, Chair, Chief Operating Officer, & Secretary
James P. Henderson, Chief Financial Officer

Legacy Oil + Gas Inc.
#4400, 525 - 8th Ave. SW
Calgary, AB T2P 1G1

403-441-2300
Fax: 403-441-2017
info@legacyoilandgas.com
www.legacyoilandgas.com
Other Communications: Accounts Payable Inquiries: legacy_acct@legacyoilandgas.com

Company Type: Public
Ticker Symbol: LEG / TSX
Profile: Legacy Oil + Gas Inc. is an intermediate oil & natural gas company. Light oil opportunities in western Canada are of interest to the company.
Trent J. Yanko, President & Chief Executive Officer
Matt Janisch, Chief Financial Officer & Vice-President
Curt W. Labelle, Vice-President, Production
Dale C.J. Mennis, Vice-President, Land
Mark Oliver, Vice-President, Exploration
Bill Wee, Vice-President, Operations

LNG Energy Ltd.
#250, 1075 West Georgia St.
Vancouver, BC V6E 3C9

778-373-0103
Fax: 604-639-4670
info@LNGEnergyltd.com
www.lngenergyltd.com
Other Communications: Calgary Office Phone: 403-457-3398, Fax: 403-457-3352

Company Type: Public
Ticker Symbol: LNG / TSX Venture
Profile: LNG Energy Ltd. develops oil & gas reserves in Bulgaria, Papua New Guinea, & Poland. The company also owns 100% of BWB Exploration, LLC, which holds oil & gas leases in Alabama & Mississippi.
David Afseth, President & Chief Executive Officer
Danny Lee, Chief Financial Officer
Weldon Beauchamp, Vice-President, Exploration
Trevor Tjostheim, Vice-President, Operations

Mart Resources, Inc.
#310, 1167 Kensington Rd. NW
Calgary, AB T2N 1X7

403-270-1841
Fax: 403-521-0443
info@martresources.com
www.martresources.com

Company Type: Public
Ticker Symbol: MMT / TSX Venture
David J. Halpin, Secretary & CFO

MEG Energy Corp. (MEG)
520 - 3rd Ave SW, 11th Fl.
Calgary, AB T2P 0R3

403-770-0446
Fax: 403-264-1711
info@megenergy.com; invest@megenergy.com
www.megenergy.com
Other Communications: Media, E-mail: media@megenergy.com

Company Type: Public
Profile: The Canadian oil sands company focuses upon sustainable in situ development & production. The area of activity is Alberta's Southern Athabasca oil sands region. MEG Energy Corp. also owns interests in Stonefell Terminal & Access Pipeline.
The company strives to meet environmental regulations & look beyond compliance, by implementing technology & environmental programs to mitigate impacts on land, air, water, & wildlife.
William McCaffrey, President, Chief Executive Officer, & Director

Dale Hohm, Chief Financial Officer
Grant Boyd, Senior Vice-President, Resource Management - Growth Properties
Jamey Fitzgibbon, Senior Vice-President, Resource Management - Christina Lake & Special Projects
Richard Sendall, Senior Vice-President, Strategy & Government Relations
Chi-Tak Yee, Senior Vice-President, Reservoir & Geosciences
John Rogers, Vice-President, Investor Relations
Don Sutherland, Vice-President, Regulatory & Community Relations
Brad Bellows, Director, External Relations
403-212-8705

Helen Kelly, Director, Investor Relations
403-767-6206
Tara McCool, Director, Community Investment & Communications
403-767-1485, communityinvestment@megenergy.com
Rory O'Connor, Manager, Community Relations
403-775-1853, communityrelations@megenergy.com

MGM Energy Corp.
#4100, 350 - 7th Ave. SW
Calgary, AB T2P 3N9
403-781-7800
Fax: 403-781-7801
info@mgmenergy.com
www.mgmenergy.com

Company Type: Public
Ticker Symbol: MGX / TSX
Clay Riddell, Chief Executive Officer
Rick Miller, Chief Financial Officer

Midway Energy Ltd.
Corporate Headquarters
#210, 4838 Richard Rd. SW
Calgary, AB T3E 6L1
403-216-2705
Fax: 403-290-0587
nfo@midwayenergy.com
www.midwayenergy.com

Company Type: Public
Ticker Symbol: MEL / TSX
Profile: The oil & natural gas company is active in Alberta's Garrington & Swan Hills regions.
M. Scott Ratushny, Chair & Chief Executive Officer
Shane Peet, P.Eng, Chief Operating Officer
Douglas K. Smith, CA, Chief Financial Officer
Craig Kolochuk, B.Comm., PLM, Manager, Land
Todd Lemieux, P.Eng., Manager, Operations

Murphy Oil Company
PO Box 2721 Stn. M, , #4000, 520 - 3rd Ave. SW
Calgary, AB T2P 0R3
870-862-6411
webmaster@murphyoilcorp.com
www.murphyoilcorp.com

Company Type: Private

Nexen Inc.
801 - 7 Ave. SW
Calgary, AB T2P 3P7
403-699-4000
Fax: 403-699-5800
ir@nexeninc.com
www.nexeninc.com

Company Type: Public
Ticker Symbol: NXY / TSX
Profile: The independent, global oil & gas company carries out operations in western Canada, The United Kingdom North Sea, the Gulf of Mexico, offshore West Africa, & the Middle East. Nexen Inc. is listed on both the Toronto & New York stock exchanges.
Marvin Romanow, President/CEO
Kevin Reinhart, Sr. Vice-President/CFO
Tim Thomas, Sr. Vice-President, Canadian Oil & Gas
Kim McKenzie, Vice-President & Chief Information Officer
Barry Jackson, Chair, Health, Safety, Environment, & Social Responsibility

Niko Resources Ltd.
#4600, 400 - 3rd Ave. SW
Calgary, AB T2P 4H2
403-262-1020
Fax: 403-263-2686
niko@nikoresources.com
www.nikoresources.com

Company Type: Public
Ticker Symbol: NKO / TSX
Profile: Niko Resources Ltd. is engaged in the exploration for & production of oil & natural gas. Operations are conducted in Bangladesh, India, Kurdistan Iraq, Indonesia, Pakistan, Madagascar, & Trinidad.
Edward S. Sampson, Chair, President & Chief Executive Officer
Murray E. Hesje, Chief Financial Officer & Vice-President, Finance

NiMin Energy Corp.
#100, 1160 Eugenia Pl.
Carpinteria, CA 93013 USA
805-566-2900
Fax: 805-566-2917
www.niminenergy.com

Company Type: Public
Ticker Symbol: NNN / TSX; NEYYF / OTCBB
Profile: The oil & gas exploration & production company is active in the San Joaquin Basin of California & in the Bighorn Basin of Wyoming.
Clarence Cottman, Chair & Chief Executive Officer
Jonathan Wimbish, CFA, Chief Financial Officer
jwimbish@niminenergy.com
Scott Dobson, Chief Operating Officer

North American Energy Partners Inc. (NAEP)
Zone 3, Acheson Industrial Area
#2, 53016 Hwy. 60
Acheson, AB T7X 5A7
780-960-7171
Fax: 780-960-7103
IR@nacg.ca
www.nacg.ca
Other Communications: Calgary Executive Office, Phone: 403-767-4825

Company Type: Public
Ticker Symbol: NOA / TSX, NYSE
Profile: North American Energy Partners Inc. is the corporate parent of North American Construction Group Inc. The following services are provided by North American Energy Partners Inc.: pipeline, piling, heavy construction, & mining. Large oil, natural gas, & resource companies are the main recipients of these services. The principal area of activity is the Canadian oil sands.

Rod Ruston, President & Chief Executive Officer
Peter Dodd, Chief Financial Officer
Bernie Robert, Vice-President, Corporate Affairs & Business Strategy
Bob Harris, Vice-President, Human Resources, Health, Safety, & the Environment
Miles Safranovich, Vice-President, General Construction Group
Chris Yellowega, Vice-President, Heavy Construction & Mining
Kevin Rowand, Director, Strategic Planning & Investor Relations
780-969-5528, Fax: 780-969-5599, krowand@nacg.ca

Northern Star Mining Corp.
153A, rue Perreault
Val d'Or, QC J9P 2H1
819-825-8088
Fax: 819-825-1199
info@nsmgold.com
www.nsmgold.com

Company Type: Public
Ticker Symbol: NSM / TSX Venture
Michel David, Chair, President & CEO
Jonathan Awde, Chief Financial Officer

Novus Energy Inc.
#5200, 150 - 6th Ave. SW
Calgary, AB T2P 3Y7
403-263-4310
Fax: 403-263-4368
info@novusenergy.ca
www.novusenergy.ca

Company Type: Public
Ticker Symbol: NVS / TSX Venture
Profile: Novus Energy Inc. is a junior oil & gas company that targets light oil resource plays. Core properties include Dodsland in southwestern Saskatchewan & Wapiti in Alberta.
Hugh G. Ross, BA, President & Chief Executive Officer
Ketan Panchmatia, B.Mgt., C.M.A., Chief Financial Officer & Vice-President, Finance
Julian Din, B.Comm., MBA, Vice-President, Business Development
Greg Groten, B.Sc., P.Geoph., Vice-President, Exploration
Jack Lane, P.Eng., Vice-President, Operations

NuVista Energy Ltd.
#700, 311 - 6th Ave. SW
Calgary, AB T2P 3H2
403-538-8500
Fax: 403-538-8505
inv_rel@nuvistaenergy.com
www.nuvistaenergy.com

Company Type: Public
Ticker Symbol: NVA / TSX
Profile: Nuvista Energy is a Canadian oil & gas company, which acquires, explores, & develops oil & gas properties. The company is active in the Western Canadian Sedimentary Basin.
Alex G. Verge, President/CEO
Robert F. Froese, CFO & Vice-President, Finance
D. Chris McDavid, Vice-President, Operations
Dan B. McKinnon, Vice-President, Engineering
Glenn A. Hamilton, Corporate Secretary
Keith A. MacPhail, Chair, Board of Directors & Member, Reserves Committee

Open Range Energy Corp.
#1100, 645 - 7th Ave. SW
Calgary, AB T2P 4G8
403-262-2936
Fax: 403-262-3924
info@openrangeenergy.com
www.openrangeenergy.com

Company Type: Public
Ticker Symbol: ONR / TSX
Profile: The energy company has operations in west central Alberta's Deep Basin.
A. Scott Dawson, P.Eng., President & Chief Executive Officer
Mark Munro, Chief Financial Officer & Vice-President
Gerald R. Costigan, P.Geol., Executive Vice-President
James L. Beninger, B.Comm., Vice-President, Land
David M. Griffith, B.Geoph., Vice-President, Exploration

Pace Oil & Gas Ltd.
West Tower, Livingston Place
#1700, 250 - 2nd St. SW
Calgary, AB T2P 0C1
403-303-8500
Fax: 403-264-0085
info@paceoil.ca; ir@paceoil.ca; resumes@p
www.paceoil.ca

Company Type: Public
Ticker Symbol: PCE / TSX; PACEF / OTC
Profile: The intermediate oil company has a portfolio of opportunities in the Western Canadian Sedimentary Basin.
Fred Woods, President & Cbief Executive Officer
fwoods@paceoil.ca
Todd Brown, Chief Operating Officer & Vice-President
tbrown@paceoil.ca
Chad Kalmakoff, Chief Financial Officer & Vice-President, Finance
ckalmakoff@paceoil.ca
Volker Braun, Vice-President, Exploration
Colin Merrick, Vice-President, Human Resources, Investor Relations, & Administration
Martin Saizew, Vice-President, Engineering
George Swerdan, Vice-President, Production & Operations

Pacific Northern Gas Ltd. (PNG)
#950, 1185 West Georgia St.
Vancouver, BC V6E 4E6
604-691-5680
Fax: 604-697-6210
info@png.ca
www.png.ca

Company Type: Public
Ticker Symbol: PNG / TSX
Profile: Pacific Northern Gas Ltd. is the owner & operator of natural gas transmission & distribution systems. Service is provided to communities & industrial facilities from north of Prince George to Kitimat & Prince Rupert in British Columbia. Pacific Northern Gas (N.E.) is a subsidiary of Pacific Northern Gas Ltd. It provides gas distribution services in the areas of Tumbler Ridge, Fort St. John, & Dawson Creek, British Columbia.
Janet Kennedy, Vice-President, Finance
Kevin R. Teitge, Treasurer & Vice-President, Corporate Development
604-691-5689
Greg B. Weeres, P.Eng., Vice-President, Engineering & Operations
Craig P. Donohue, Director, Regulatory Affairs & Gas Supply

Pacific Rubiales Energy
Canada Office
#1100, 333 Bay St.
Toronto, ON M5H 2R2
416-362-7735
Fax: 416-360-7783
www.petrorubiales.com
Other Communications: Columbia Corporate Office, Phone: +57 1 756-0080

Company Type: Public
Ticker Symbol: PRE / TSX
Profile: Pacific Rubiales Energy is engaged in oil & gas exploration. It owns 100% of Pacific Stratus & Meta Petroleum Limited, which are Colombian oil & gas operators.
Ronald Pantin, Chief Executive Officer
Jose Francisco Arata, President
Carlos Perez, Chief Financial Officer
Luis Pacheco, Sr. Vice-President, Planning
Luis Andres Rojas, Sr. Vice-President, Production
Peter Volk, General Counsel & Secretary

Painted Pony Petroleum Ltd.
#300, 602 - 12th Ave. SW
Calgary, AB T2R 1J3
403-475-0440
Fax: 403-238-1487
866-975-0440
info@paintedpony.ca
www.paintedpony.ca
Company Type: Public
Ticker Symbol: PPY / TSX Venture
Profile: The public resource company is engaged in exploration, drilling, & production in western Canada.
Patrick R. Ward, P.Geol., President & Chief Executive Officer
Joan E. Dunne, B.Comm, C.A., Chief Financial Officer & Vice-President, Finance
Bruce G. Hall, P.Land, Vice-President, Corporate Development
James S. Thomson, P.Land, Vice-President, Land

Pan Orient Energy Corp.
#1505, 505 - 3rd St. SW
Calgary, AB T2P 3E6
403-294-1770
Fax: 403-294-1780
www.panorient.ca
Company Type: Public
Ticker Symbol: POE / TSX-V
Profile: The junior oil & natural gas company has principal properties located in the following regions: on-shore Thailand; onshore Indonesia; & the Canadian oil sands.
Jeff Chisholm, B.Sc, Chief Executive Officer & Director
Bill Ostlund, CA, Chief Financial Officer & Corporate Secretary
bill@panorient.ca

Paramount Resources Ltd.
Bankers Hall West
#4700, 888 - 3rd St. SW
Calgary, AB T2P 5C5
403-290-3600
Fax: 403-262-7994
info@paramountres.com
www.paramountres.com
Company Type: Public
Ticker Symbol: POU / TSX
Profile: The oil & natural gas exploration, development, & production company carries out its operations in western Canada. In 2011, Paramount Resources Ltd. completed the acquisition of ProspEx Resources Ltd.
C.H. (Clay) Riddell, Chair & Chief Executive Officer
J.H.T. (Jim) Riddell, President & Chief Operating Officer
B.K. (Bernie) Lee, Chief Financial Officer
E.M. (Mitch) Shier, Corporate Secretary

Pason Systems Corp.
6130 - 3 St. SE
Calgary, AB T2H 1K4
403-301-3400
Fax: 403-301-3499
877-255-3158
InvestorRelations@pason.com; Sales@pason.
www.pason.com
Other Communications: Technical Support Centre, E-mail: TechSupport@pason.com
Company Type: Public
Ticker Symbol: PSI / TSX
Profile: Pason Systems Inc. specializes in the design & manufacture of data management systems. These systems are used by the oilfield industry on land based & offshore drilling & service rigs. Operations are located in Canada, the United States, Mexico, South America, & Australia.
James Hill, President/CEO
Greg Lindsay, President & General Manager, Pason USA Corp.
Jim Glasspoole, Chief Financial Officer
Robert Rodda, Chief Operating Officer
Joe Seeman, Manager, Manufacturing
David White, Manager, Research & Development

Peak Energy Services
#900, 222 - 3rd Ave. SW
Calgary, AB T2P 0B4
403-543-7325
Fax: 403-543-7335
800-661-3803
www.peak-energy.com
Company Type: Private
Profile: Peak Energy Services became a wholly owned subsidiary of Clean Harbors Industrial Services Canada, Inc. in 2011, after Clean Harbors acquired all the issued & outstanding common shares of Peak Energy. The diversified energy services company serves the conventional & unconventional oil & natural gas industry in Canada & the United States by offering rental equipment. Peak Energy Services also provides water technology solutions throughout North America.
Alan S. McKim, Chair, President, & Chief Executive Officer, Clean Harbors, Inc.

Pembina NGL Corporation
#2100, 250 - 2nd St. SW
Calgary, AB T2P 0C1
403-296-2233
Fax: 403-294-0111
investor-relations@pembina.com
www.pembina.com
Company Type: Public
Ticker Symbol: PVE / TSX, NYSE
Profile: In 2012, Pembina Pipeline Corporation acquired Provident Energy Ltd.. Provident amalgamated with a wholly owned subsidiary of Pembina, & it is continued under the name, Pembina NGL Corporation. As a result of this acquisition, Pembina has a greater & more diversified portfolio of energy businesses.
Scott Burrows, Senior Manager, Corporate Development & Planning
403-231-7500
Shawn Davis, Manager, Communications & Public Affairs
403-231-7500

Pembina Pipeline Corporation
#3800, 525 - 8th Ave. SW
Calgary, AB T2P 1G1
403-231-7500
Fax: 403-237-0254
888-428-3222
investor-relations@pembina.com; community
www.pembina.com
Other Communications: Media: 403-231-7500; Land: landrequests@pembina.com
Company Type: Public
Ticker Symbol: PPI / TSX
Profile: In 2010, Pembina converted from an income trust to a corporation. Pembina Pipeline Corporation is an energy transportation & service provider that has over 8,500 kilometres of pipeline. Areas of activity are British Columbia & Alberta
Robert B. Michaleski, Chief Executive Officer
Michael Dilger, President & Chief Operating Officer
Peter Robertson, Chief Financial Officer & Vice-President, Finance
Glenys Hermanutz, Vice-President, Corporate Affairs
James Watkinson, Vice-President, General Counsel, & Secretary
Allan Charlesworth, Senior Manager, Integrity & Technical Services

Pengrowth Energy Corporation
#2100, 222 - 3rd Ave. SW
Calgary, AB T2P 0B4
403-233-0224
Fax: 403-265-6251
800-223-4122
investorrelations@pengrowth.com
www.pengrowth.com
Other Communications: Investor Relations: 888-744-1111; Media: 403-213-3764
Social Media: twitter.com/Pengrowth
Company Type: Public
Ticker Symbol: PGF / TSX; PGH / NYSE
Profile: The corporation is an intermediate producer of oil & natural gas. Pengrowth's main area of activity is the Western Canadian Sedimentary Basin.
In 2012, Pengrowth Energy Corporation & NAL Energy Corporation entered into an arrangement agreement that provides for the strategic combination of Pengrowth & NAL.
Derek Evans, President & Chief Executive Officer
Christopher Webster, Chief Financial Officer
James Causgrove, Senior Vice-President, Operations & Engineering
Steve De Maio, Vice-President, In-Situ Development & Operations
Andrew Grasby, Vice-President, General Counsel, & Corporate Secretary
Dean Evans, Treasurer

Penn West Petroleum Ltd.
Also Known As: Penn West Exploration
Penn West Plaza
#200, 207 - 9th Ave. SW
Calgary, AB T2P 1K3
403-777-2500
Fax: 403-777-2699
866-693-2707
investor_relations@pennwest.com
www.pennwest.com
Other Communications: Investor Relations, Toll-Free: 888-770-2633
Company Type: Public
Ticker Symbol: PWT / TSX; PWE / NYSE
Profile: Penn West is engaged in the production of oil & natural gas. Operations are conducted in western Canada.
Murray Nunns, President & Chief Executive Officer
403-218-8939, murray.nunns@pennwest.com
Hilary Foulkes, Executive Vice-President & Chief Operating Officer
Todd H. Takeyasu, Chief Financial Officer & Executive Vice-President
S. Keith Luft, General Counsel & Senior Vice-President, Stakeholder Relations
Gregg Gegunde, Senior Vice-President, Production
Bob Shepherd, Senior Vice-President, Enhanced Oil Recovery & Cordova Joint Venture

Perpetual Energy Inc.
#3200, 605 - 5th Ave. SW
Calgary, AB T2P 3H5
403-269-4400
Fax: 403-269-4444
800-811-5522
info@perpetualenergyinc.com
www.perpetualenergyinc.com
Other Communications: Human Resources: careers@perpetualenergyinc.com
Company Type: Public
Ticker Symbol: PMT / TSX
Profile: Established in 2010, Perpetual Energy Inc. operates as an independent natural gas company. Perpetual Energy's field offices are located in Athabasca, Alberta (780-675-9252), Viking, Alberta (780-336-3391), & Drayton Valley, Alberta (780-542-4700).
Susan L. Riddell Rose, President & Chief Executive Officer
Cameron R. Sebastian, Chief Financial Officer & Vice-President, Finance
Jeffrey R. Green, Vice-President, Corporate & Engineering Services
Gary C. Jackson, Vice-President, Land & Acquisitions
Linda L. McKean, Vice-President, South / West Business Unit
R. William Thornton, Vice-President, Enhanced Recovery & North Business Unit

Petroamerica Oil Corp. (PTA)
#700, 520 - 5th Ave. SW
Calgary, AB T2P 3R7
403-237-8300
Fax: 403-237-9738
www.petroamericaoilcorp.co
Company Type: Public
Ticker Symbol: PTA / Venture
Profile: The oil exploration & production company has operations in Colombia.
Nelson Navarrete, President & Chief Executive Officer
Colin Wagner, Chief Financial Officer
Ralph Gillcrist, Vice-President, Exploration
Pat Klassen, Vice-President, Administration

PetroBakken Energy Ltd.
#2800, 525 - 8th Ave. SW
Calgary, AB T2P 1G1
403-268-7800
Fax: 403-218-6075
ir@petrobakken.com
www.petrobakken.com
Other Communications: Careers, E-mail: resumes@petrobakken.com
Company Type: Public
Ticker Symbol: PBN / TSX
Profile: PetroBakken Energy was created in 2009. During the same year, it acquired TriStar Oil & Gas Ltd.
The oil exploration & production company has light oil assests in southeast Saskatchewan, as well as Cardium potential in central Alberta. The company is also exploring natural gas development opportunities in the Horn River & Montney regions of northeastern British Columbia.
John D. Wright, President & Chief Executive Officer
Peter D. Scott, Chief Financial Officer & Senior Vice-President
R. Gregg Smith, Chief Operating Officer & Senior Vice-President
Lawrence Fisher, Vice-President, Land
Peter Hawkes, Vice-President, Exploration
William A. Kanters, Vice-President, Capital Markets
Doreen Scheidt, Controller
Andrea Hatzinikolas, Corporate Secretary

Petrobank Energy & Resources Ltd.
#1900,111 - 5th Ave. SW
Calgary, AB T2P 3Y6
403-750-4400
Fax: 403-266-5794
ir@petrobank.com
www.petrobank.com
Other Communications: Careers: resumes@petrobank.com
Company Type: Public
Ticker Symbol: PBG / TSX
Profile: The company is engaged in the acquisition, exploration, & development of natural gas & oil properties. Operations are

carried out in western Canada.
Petrobank Energy & Resources Ltd. has wholly-owned subsidiaries named Whitesand Insitu Inc. & Archon Technologies. Petrobank also has a 59% ownership in PetroBakken Energy Ltd.
John D. Wright, President/CEO
Corey C. Ruttan, Sr. Vice-President/CFO
R. Gregg Smith, Sr. Vice-President/COO, Canada
Chris J. Bloomer, Sr. Vice-President/COO, Heavy Oil
Richard Press, Vice-Presient, Land & Contracts
Andrew D. Grasby, Corporate Secretary

Petrolifera Petroleum Limited
#900, 332 - 6th Ave. SW
Calgary, AB T2P 0B2

403-538-6201
Fax: 403-538-6225
inquiries@petrolifera.ca
www.petrolifera.ca

Company Type: Private
Profile: The oil & natural gas exploration & production company is active in Peru, Argentina, & Columbia. Connacher Oil & Gas Limited owns part of Petrolifera's shares.
Gary D. Wine, President/COO
Kristen Bibby, CA, CFO & Vice-President, Finance
Jennifer Kennedy, Corporate Secretary
Robert Erlich, International Geologist
Donald D. Barkwell, Chair, Reserves Committee

Petromanas Energy Inc.
Life Plaza
#1720, 734 - 7th Ave. SW
Calgary, AB T2P 3P8

403-457-4400
info@petromanas.com
www.petromanas.com

Company Type: Public
Ticker Symbol: PMI / TSX Venture
Profile: The oil & gas company is engaged in exploration & development activites in Albania's Berati thrust belt.
Glenn McNamara, Chief Executive Officer
Bill Cummins, Chief Financial Officer
Hamid Mozayani, Chief Operating Officer
Steve Farner, Vice-President, Exploration

Petrowest Corporation
Head Office
#204, 10605 Westside Dr.
Grande Prairie, AB T8V 8E6

780-830-0881
Fax: 780-830-0882
888-830-0881
info@petro-west.com
www.petro-west.com
Other Communications: Calgary: 403-237-0881; Fort McMurray: 780-743-0486

Company Type: Public
Ticker Symbol: PRW / TSX
Profile: Pre-drilling & post-completion services are provided by Petrowest Corporation. The company works in the northern area of the Western Canadian Sedimentary Basin.
Rick Quigley, Chief Executive Officer
Lloyd A. Wiggins, CA, Chief Financial Officer

PEYTO Exploration & Development Corp.
#1500, 250 - 2nd St. SW
Calgary, AB T2P 0C1

403-261-6081
Fax: 403-451-4100
info@peyto.com
www.peyto.com

Company Type: Public
Ticker Symbol: PEY / TSX
Profile: PEYTO Exploration & Development is engaged in the exploration for & the production of unconventional natural gas in Alberta's Deep Basin.
Darren Gee, President & Chief Executive Officer
Scott Robinson, Chief Operating Officer & Executive Vice-President
Kathy Turgeon, Chief Financial Officer & Vice-President
Tim Louie, Vice-President, Land
David Thomas, Vice-President, Exploration

PHX Energy Services Corp.
#1400, 240 - 2nd St. SW
Calgary, AB T2P 0C1

403-543-4466
Fax: 403-543-4485
investor@phxtech.com
www.phxtech.com

Company Type: Public
Ticker Symbol: PHX / TSX
Profile: PHX Energy Services' Canadian operations are carried out through Phoenix Technology Service LP. American operations are conducted through PHX Energy Services' wholly owned subsidiary, Phoenix Technology Services USA Inc.. PHX Energy Services also has sales offices in Peru, Colombia, Albania, & Russia.
John M. Hooks, President & Chief Executive Officer
Cameron M. Ritchie, CA, Chief Financial Officer & Sennior Vice-President, Finance
Mike Buker, Sr. Vice-President, Business Development
Craig Brown, Vice-President, Operations

Precision Drilling Corporation
#800, 525 - 8th Ave. SW
Calgary, AB T2P 1G1

403-716-4500
Fax: 403-264-0251
info@precisiondrilling.com
www.precisiondrilling.com

Company Type: Public
Ticker Symbol: PD / TSX; PDS / NYSE
Profile: The oilfield services company provides drilling, well servicing, & strategic support services to customers.
Kevin A. Neveu, Chief Executive Officer
Gene C. Stahl, President, Canadian Operations
Carey Ford, Vice-President, Finance & Investor Relations
403-716-4575, Fax: 403-716-4755
David W. Wehlmann, Exec. Vice-President, Investor Relations
Joanne L. Alexander, Vice-President, General Counsel, & Corporate Secretary

Progress Energy Resources Corp.
#1200, 205 - 5th Ave. SW
Calgary, AB T2P 2V7

403-216-2510
Fax: 403-216-2514
ir@progressenergy.com
www.progressenergy.com

Company Type: Public
Ticker Symbol: PRQ / TSX
Profile: Progress Energy Resources Corp. is a natural gas & crude oil exploration & production organization.
Michael R. Culbert, President/CEO
403-539-1820
Art MacNichol, CFO & Vice-President, Finance
Gary Miller, Vice-President, Operations
Greg Kist, Vice-President, Investor Relations & Marketing
403-539-1809
Cindy Rutherford, Vice-President, Land
Jim Stannard, Vice-President, Engineering

ProspEx Resources Ltd.
#2500, 255 - 5th Ave. SW
Calgary, AB T2P

403-268-3940
Fax: 403-268-3987
www.psx.ca

Company Type: Public
Ticker Symbol: PSX

Pure Energy Services Ltd.
#300, 1010 - 1st St. SW
Calgary, AB T2R 1K4

403-262-4000
Fax: 403-237-9728
kdelaney@pure-energy.ca
www.pure-energy.ca

Company Type: Public
Ticker Symbol: PSV / TSX
Profile: The oilfield services company conducts production & completion related services in western Canada & in the United States. Pure Energy Services' wholly owned subsidiary in the United States is Pure Energy Services (USA), Inc.
Kevin Delaney, Chair & Chief Executive Officer
Bradley Gabel, President
Ruger Niers, President, Pure Energy Services (USA), Inc.
Christopher N. Martin, Chief Financial Officer & Vice-President, Finance
Ian Buchanan, Corporate Counsel & Senior Vice-President

Questerre Energy
Guiness House
#1580, 727 - 7th Ave. SW
Calgary, AB T2P 0Z5

403-777-1185
Fax: 403-777-1578
info@questerre.com
www.questerre.com

Company Type: Public
Ticker Symbol: QEC / TSX
Michael R. Binnion, President & CEO

RMP Energy Inc.
Head Office
#1200, 500 - 4th Ave. SW
Calgary, AB T2P 2V6

403-930-6300
Fax: 403-930-6301
www.rmpenergyinc.com
Other Communications: Investors: 403-930-6304; Stettler Field Office: 403-742-5200

Company Type: Public
Ticker Symbol: RMP / TSX
Profile: The junior, upstream oil & gas company has assets in the Big Muddy area of southeastern Saskatchewan & in the Pine Creek, Waskahigan, & Kaybob regions of west central Alberta.
John W. Ferguson, President & Chief Executive Officer
403-930-6303, john.ferguson@rmpenergyinc.com
Dean J.W. Bernhard, Chief Financial Officer & Vice-President, Finance
403-930-6304, dean.bernhard@rmpenergyinc.com
Brent W. DesBrisay, Vice-President, Geosciences
Jonathan L. Grimwood, Vice-President, Exploration
Ross E. MacDonald, Vice-President, Engineering
R. Bruce McFarlane, Vice-President, Business Development

Rock Energy Inc.
Corporate Office
#800, 607 - 8th Ave. SW
Calgary, AB T2P 0A7

403-218-4380
Fax: 403-234-0598
info@rockenergy.ca
www.rockenergy.ca

Company Type: Public
Ticker Symbol: RE / TSX
Profile: Rock Energy Inc. is focused upon heavy oil exploration & development in its Plains & southwest Saskatchewan regions. The company is a member of the Canadian Association of Petroleum Producers & is committed to the association's Steward of Excellence Program.
Allen J. Bey, President & Chief Executive Officer
John H. Van de Pol, President & Chief Financial Officer
Jeff Campbell, Chief Operating Officer & Senior Vice-President
Bryan P. Dozzi, Vice-President, Business Development

Savanna Energy Services Corp.
#800, 311 - 6th Ave. SW
Calgary, AB T2P 3H2

403-503-9990
Fax: 403-503-0654
877-568-2344
info@savannaenergy.com
www.savannaenergy.com
Social Media: SVY / TSX

Company Type: Public
Ticker Symbol: SVY
Profile: Drilling & well servicing are provided by Savanna Energy Services. Operations take place in Canada, the United States, & Australia.
Ken Mullen, President & Chief Executive Officer
Darcy Draudson, Chief Financial Officer
Chris Oddy, Chief Operating Officer & Vice-President, Operations
Steve Ross, Chief Information Officer & General Manager, Technical Services
Lori Connell, Corporate Secretary
Tom Morris, Manager, Corporate Health, Safety, & Environment

Second Wave Petroleum Inc.
#1400, 202 - 6th Ave. SW
Calgary, AB T2P 2R9

403-451-0165
Fax: 403-451-0166
info@secondwavepetroleum.com
www.secondwavepetroleum.com

Company Type: Public
Ticker Symbol: SCS / TSX
Profile: The junior oil & gas company operates in Western Canada. Second Wave Petroleum's focus is on crude oil & natural gas production in the Judy Creek region of Alberta.
Colin B. Witwer, President & Chief Executive Officer
Randy L. Denecky, Chief Financial Officer & Vice-President, Finance
Randy Bergmann, Vice-President, Land
Douglas Hibbs, Vice-President, Exploration
Devery Neumann, Vice-President, Operations

Secure Energy Services Inc.
Bow Valley Square 2
#1900, 205 - 5th Ave. SW
Calgary, AB T2P 2V7

403-984-6100
Fax: 403-984-6101
info@secure-energy.ca
www.secure-energy.ca

Company Type: Public
Ticker Symbol: SES / TSX
Profile: The energy services company provides specialized services to upstream oil & natural gas compnaies. Secure Energy Services' two divisions are the Processing, Recovery & Disposal Division & the Drilling Division. Operations are carried out in the Western Canadian Sedimentary Basin.
Rene Amirault, Chair, President, & Chief Executive Officer
George Wadsworth, President, Drilling Services Division
Nick Wieler, Chief Financial Officer
Gary Perras, Vice-President, Operations
Dan Steinke, Vice-President, Business Development

ShaMaran Petroleum Corp.
#2000, 885 West Georgia St.
Vancouver, BC V6C 3E8
604-689-7842
Fax: 604-689-4250
www.shamaranpetroleum.com
Company Type: Public
Ticker Symbol: SNM / TSX Venture
Profile: The oil exploration & development company is focused upon projects in Kurdistan. The Canadian oil & gas company is listed on the TSX Venture Exchange & on the NASDAQ OMX First North.
Pradeep Kabra, President & Chief Executive Officer
Brenden Johnstone, Chief Financial Officer

ShawCor Ltd.
25 Bethridge Rd.
Toronto, ON M9W 1M7
416-743-7111
Fax: 416-743-7199
www.shawcor.com
Company Type: Public
Ticker Symbol: SCL.A, SCL.B / TSX
Profile: ShawCor Ltd. is a provider of technology-based products & services for the pipeline & pipe services market, as well as the petrochemical & industrial market. Facilities are located in over twenty countries.
William P. Buckley, President & Chief Executive Officer
Gary S. Love, Chief Financial Officer & Vice-President, Finance
glove@shawcor.com
D.R. Ewert, Corporate Secretary

Sinopec Daylight Energy
East Tower, Sun Life Plaza
#2700, 112 - 4th Ave. SW
Calgary, AB T2P 0H3
403-266-6900
Fax: 403-266-6988
877-266-6901
ir@daylightenergy.com; careers@daylighten
www.daylightenergy.com
Other Communications: Investors, Phone: 403-536-4664
Company Type: Public
Ticker Symbol: DAYDB / TSX
Profile: Sinopec Daylight Energy Ltd. is a wholly owned indirect subsidiary of Sinopec International Petroleum Exploration & Production Corporation. The oil & natural gas company has operations in Alberta's Deep Basin & in northeastern British Columbia.
Anthony Lambert, President & Chief Executive Officer
alambert@daylightenergy.com
Stacy Knull, Chief Operating Officer & Vice-President
Steve Nielsen, Chief Financial Officer & Vice-President
snielsen@daylightenergy.com
Cam Proctor, Chief Legal Officer & Corporate Secretary

Sonde Resources Corp.
Head Office
#3200, 500 - 4th Ave. SW
Calgary, AB T2P 2V6
403-294-1411
Fax: 403-216-8551
www.sonderesources.com
Other Communications: Drumheller, AB: 403-823-9232; Tunis, Tunisia: +216-7196-1039
Company Type: Public
Ticker Symbol: SOQ / TSX, NYSE Amex LLC
Profile: Sonde Resources Corp. explores for & produces oil & natural gas. Operations are located in western Canada & offshore North Africa.
Jack W. Schanck, President & Chief Executive Officer
Toufic Nassif, President, Sonde North Africa
William Dirks, Chief Operating Officer
Kurt Nelson, CPA, Chief Financial Officer
Garry Mann, M.Sc., P.Biol., General Manager, Health, Safety, & Environment
Ed Chau, Manager, Exploration
Randell D. Pryor, Manager, Drilling & Completions

Southern Pacific Resource Corp.
#1700, 205 - 5 Ave. SW
Calgary, AB T2P 2V7
403-269-5243
Fax: 403-269-5273
info@shpacific.com
www.shpacific.com
Company Type: Public
Ticker Symbol: STP / TSX
Profile: Southern Pacific Resource Corp. explores, develops, & produces in-situ thermal heavy oil & bitumen. The company is active in Alberta's Athabasca oil sands & in Senlac, Saskatchewan.
In 2010, Southern Pacific Resource Corp. acquired all the issued securities of North Peace Energy Corp.. A highlight of North Peace Energy's assets included working interest in the Peace River oil sands region.
Byron Lutes, P.Eng., President & Chief Executive Officer
403-269-1529, blutes@shpacific.com
Howard Bolinger, CA, Chief Financial Officer
403-269-2640, hbolinger@shpacific.com
Ron Clarke, Chief Operating Officer
Glenn Miller, Land & Regulatory Affairs, Vice-President

Sterling Resources Ltd.
Corporate Office
#1450, 736 - 6th Ave. SW
Calgary, AB T2P 3T7
403-237-9256
Fax: 403-215-9279
info@sterling-resources.com
www.sterling-resources.com
Company Type: Public
Ticker Symbol: SLG / TSX Venture
Profile: The oil & gas company has assets in the United Kingdom, France, the Netherlands, & Romania.
Mike Azancot, President & Chief Executive Officer
mike.azancot@sterling-resources.com
David Blewden, Chief Financial Officer
david.blewden@sterling-resources.com
John Rapach, Chief Operating Officer
David A. Findlater, Vice-President, Exploration
George Kesteven, Manager, Corporate & Investor Relations
george.kesteven@sterling-resources.com

Storm Resources Ltd.
#800, 205 - 5th Ave. SW
Calgary, AB T2P 2V7
403-817-6145
Fax: 403-817-6146
www.stormresourcesltd.com
Company Type: Public
Ticker Symbol: SRX / TSX Venture
Profile: Storm Resources Ltd. is a junior exploration & production company that commenced operations in 2010. The company focuses upon exploring for, acquiring, & developing oil & natural gas reserves in the Grande Prairie region of northwestern Alberta & the Horn River Basin & Umbach areas of northeastern British Columbia. In 2012, Storm Resources Ltd. acquired Bellamont Exploration Ltd..
Brian Lavergne, President & Chief Executive Officer
Donald G. McLean, Chief Financial Officer
Robert S. Tiberio, Chief Operating Officer
Carol Knudsen, Manager, Corporate Affairs

Strad Emergy Services Ltd.
#1200, 440 - 2nd Ave. SW
Calgary, AB T2P 5E9
403-232-6900
Fax: 403-232-6901
866-967-8723
Other Communications: Denver, CO Office, Toll-Free Phone: 877-337-8723
Company Type: Public
Ticker Symbol: SDY / TSX
Profile: The energy services company provides oilfield solutions to the natural gas & oil industry. An example of Strad Energy Services' work is the provision of drilling related oilfield equipment.
Henry van der Sloot, CA, CFA, Chief Executive Officer
403-249-7336, Fax: 403-232-6901,
hvandersloot@stradenergy.com
Andy Pernal, CA, President & Chief Financial Officer
403-775-9202, Fax: 403-232-6901, apernal@stradenergy.com
Rob Gramdfield, Chief Operating Officer

Suncor Energy Inc.
PO Box 2844, 150 - 6 Ave. SW
Calgary, AB T2P 3E3
403-269-8000
Fax: 403-403-2963
866-786-2671
info@suncor.com; invest@suncor.com
www.suncor.com
Other Communications: Media Relations: media@suncor.com
Company Type: Public
Ticker Symbol: SU / TSX
Profile: Suncor Energy Inc. is engaged in natural gas production in western Canada, with a focus on the oil sands. Refinement & marketing operations are carried out in Ontario & Colorado. The company also invests in renewable energy, especially ethanol production & wind power.
Rick L. George, President/CEO
Kenneth Alley, Sr. Vice-President/CFO
Steve Williams, Chief Operating Officer
Sue Lee, Sr. Vice-Presidemt, Human Resources & Communications
Terry Hopwood, Sr. Vice-President & General Counsel
Gord Lambert, Vice-President, Sustainable Development

SunCor Energy Products
PO Box 2844, 150 - 6th Ave. S.W.
Calgary, AB T2P 3E3
800-558-9071
invest@suncor.com
Company Type: Private

Sure Emergy Inc.
#1100, 606 - 4th St. SW
Calgary, AB T2P 1T1
403-410-3100
Fax: 403-410-3111
info@sureenergyinc.com
www.sureenergyinc.com
Company Type: Public
Ticker Symbol: SHR / TSX
Profile: Sure Energy Inc. was formed in 2006, when Clear Energy Inc. & NAV Energy Trust merged. Sure Energy is a junior natural gas & oil exploration company, with operations in Alberta & Saskatchewan.
Jeffrey S. Boyce, Chair & Chief Executive Officer
Chris Baker, B.Sc.Hons, President & Chief Operating Officer
Lance Wirth, B.Comm., Chief Financial Officer & Vice-President, Finance
Tom Banks, P.Eng., Vice-President, Engineering
Rob Sheedy, B.Comm., Vice-President, Land

Surge Energy Inc.
#2100, 635 - 8th Ave. SW
Calgary, AB T2P 3M3
403-930-1010
Fax: 403-930-1011
info@surgeenergy.ca; hr@surgeenergy.ca
www.surgeenergy.ca
Other Communications: Investor Relations: invest@surgeenergy.ca
Company Type: Public
Ticker Symbol: SGY / TSX
Profile: The oil & gas company conducts operations in Manitoba, Alberta, & North Dakota.
Dan O'Neill, President & Chief Executive Officer
doneil@surgeenergy.ca
Dan Brown, Chief Operating Officer
Max Lof, Chief Financial Officer
mlof@surgeenergy.ca
Malcolm Adams, Vice-President, Corporate Development
Kevin Angus, Vice-President, Exploration
Margaret Elekes, Vice-President, Land
Tee Ong, Vice-President, Engineering

Suroco Energy Inc.
#810, 940 - 6th Ave. SW
Calgary, AB T2P 3T1
403-232-6784
Fax: 403-232-6747
www.suroco.com
Company Type: Public
Ticker Symbol: SRN / TSX Venture
Profile: The junior oil & gas company is engaged in the exploration for, & the development, production, & sale of crude oil, natural gas, & natural gas liquids. Suroco Energy is active in Colombia.
Alastair Hill, President & Chief Executive Officer
Travis Doupe, Chief Financial Officer & Vice-President, Finance

Syncrude Canada Ltd.
PO Box 4023 Stn. Main, , 9911 MacDonald Ave.
Fort McMurray, AB T9H 3H5
780-790-5911
Fax: 780-790-6215
800-667-9494
info@syncrude.com
www.syncrude.com
Company Type: Private
Profile: Crude petroleum & natural gas extraction
Tom Katinas, President/CEO
Phil Lachambre, CFO & Exec. Vice-President
Donald Thompson, Corporate Secretary & General Manager, Environment, Health & Safety

Talisman Energy Inc.
#2000, 888 - 3rd St. SW
Calgary, AB T2P 5C5
403-237-1234
Fax: 403-237-1902
tlm@talisman-energy.com
www.talisman-energy.com
Company Type: Public
Ticker Symbol: TLM / RSX, NYSE
Profile: Talisman Eenergy carries out its operations as an oil & gas producer in Canada. The company's subsidiaries have operations in the United States, Trinidad & Tobago, North Africa, the North Sea, Southeast Asia, & Australia.
John A. Manzoni, President/CEO
Scott Thomson, CFO/Exec. Vice-President, Finance
Robert M. Redgate, Exec. Vice-President, Corporate Services
Robert Rooney, General Counsel & Exec. Vice-President, Legal
John T. Hart, Exec. Vice-President, Exploration

Tamarack Valley Energy Ltd.
#1800, 407 - 2nd St. SW
Calgary, AB T2P 2Y3
403-263-4440
Fax: 403-263-5551
operations@tamarackvalley.ca
www.tamarackvalley.ca
Other Communications: Investors: investorrelations@tamarackvalley.ca
Company Type: Public
Ticker Symbol: TBE / TSX Venture
Profile: Tamarack Valley Energy Ltd. is an oil & gas company with operations in the Western Canadian Sedimentary Basin. Assets are located in the following places: the Garrington/Harmattan, Buck Lake, Lochend, Foley Lake, & the Quaich areas of Alberta; Wilder in northeastern British Columbia; southeast of Lloydminster in Saskatchewan.
Brian Schmidt, President & Chief Executive Officer
Ron Hozjan, Chief Financial Officer & Vice-President, Finance
Ken Cruikshank, Vice-President, Land
Niels Gundesen, Vice-President, Engineering
Kevin Screen, Vice-President, Production & Operations

Terra Energy Corp.
#970, 333 - 7th Ave. SW
Calgary, AB T2P 2Z1
403-699-7777
Fax: 403-264-7189
info@terraenergy.ca
www.terraenergy.ca
Company Type: Public
Ticker Symbol: TT / TSX
Profile: Terra Energy Corp. is a junior oil & natural gas exploration & production company. Operations are conducted in the Peace River Arch area of Alberta & northeastern British Columbia.
Cas H. Morel, President & Chief Executive Officer
Bud K. Love, Chief Financial Officer & Vice-President, Finance
403-699-7751, Fax: 403-264-7189, blove@terraenergy.ca
Berk Sumen, Manager, Corporate Affairs
403-699-7769, Fax: 403-264-7189

Tesla Exploration Ltd.
4500 - 8A St. NE
Calgary, AB T2E 6J7
Fax: 403-216-0989
emailus@teslaexploration.com; jobs@teslae
www.teslaexploration.com
Other Communications: Safety: safetydept@teslaexploration.com
Company Type: Public
Ticker Symbol: TXL / TSX
Profile: Established in 2000, Telsa Exploration Ltd. serves the oil & gas exploration industry. Tesla Exploration Ltd. is engaged in geophysical & related services in Canada. The company also provides these services internationally, through the following wholly owned subsidiaries: Tesla Exploration International Ltd.; Tesla Exploration Trinidad Ltd.; Tesla Exploration Inc. in the United States; & Tesla Offshore LLC, which is also in the United States.
Richard Habiak, Chief Executive Officer
403-216-0990
Stuart Craven, Chief Financial Officer
403-692-4602
Milt Tetzlaff, Senior Vice-President, Canadian Operations
tetzlaffm@teslaexploration.com
Eric C. Mikkelborg, Vice-President, Marketing
mikkelborge@teslaexploration.com
Ron Seabrook, Vice-President, Health, Safety, & Environment
seabrookr@teslaexploration.com
Todd Jones, Manager, Corporate Information Technology
jonest@teslaexploration.com

Tourmaline Oil Corp.
#3700, 250 - 6th Ave. SW
Calgary, AB T2P 3H7
403-266-5992
Fax: 403-266-5952
info@tourmalineoil.com
www.tourmalineoil.com
Company Type: Public
Ticker Symbol: TOU / TSX
Profile: Formed in 2008, Tourmaline Oil Corp. is an intermediate crude oil & natural gas exploration & production company. The company's operations are conducted in the Western Canadian Sedimentary Basin.
In 2011, Tourmaline Oil Corp. acquired Cinch Energy Corp.
Michael L. Rose, President & Chief Executive Officer
rose@tourmalineoil.com
Stanley M. Nowek, Chief Operating Officer & Vice-President, Operations
Brian G. Robinson, Chief Financial Officer & Vice-President, Finance
robinson@tourmalineoil.com
Robert N. Yurkovich, Executive Vice-President, Exploration
Drew E. Tumbach, Vice-President, Land & Contracts
W. Scott Kirker, General Counsel & Secretary
kirker@tourmalineoil.com

TranAtlantic Petroleum Ltd.
Corporate Office
PO Box 246, 16803 Dallas Pkwy.
Addison, TS 75001-0246 USA
214-220-4323
Fax: 214-265-4798
www.transatlanticpetroleum.com
Other Communications: Istanbul, Turkey: 90-212-317-25-00; Bulgaria: +3592 963 3244
Company Type: Public
Ticker Symbol: TNP / TSX, AMEX
Profile: TransAtlantic Petroleum Ltd. is involved in acquiring, exploring for, developing, & producing oil & natural gas. The company's interests are in Turkey, Bulgaria, & Romania.
Malone Mitchell, Chair & Chief Executive Officer
Wil F. Saqueton, Chief Financial Officer & Vice-President
Mustafa Yavuz, Chief Operating Officer
Jeff Mecom, Vice-President, Legal
Chad Potter, Vice-President, Financial & Investor Relations

TransCanada PipeLines Limited (TCPL)
PO Box 1000 Stn. M, , 450 - 1st St. SW
Calgary, AB T2P 4K5
403-920-2000
Fax: 403-920-2200
800-661-3805
communications@transcanada.com
www.transcanada.com
Other Communications: Investors: investor_relations@transcanada.com
Company Type: Public
Ticker Symbol: TCA / TSX
Profile: Incorporated in 1951, the energy infrastructure company is focused on natural gas pipelines, oil pipelines, & energy.
Harold N. Kvisle, President/CEO
Russell K. Girling, President, Pipelines
Gregory A. Lohnesg, Exec. Vice-President/CFO
Sarah E. Raiss, Exec. Vice-President, Corporate Services
Sean McMaster, General Counsel & Exec. Vice-President, Corporate
Dennis McConaghy, Exec. Vice-President, Pipeline Strategy & Development

TransGlobe Energy Corporation
Head Office
#2300, 250 - 5th Ave. SW
Calgary, AB T2P OR4
403-264-9888
Fax: 403-770-8855
contact@trans-globe.com; careers@trans-gl
www.trans-globe.com
Other Communications: Investors: investor.relations@trans-globe.com
Company Type: Public
Ticker Symbol: TGL / TSX; TGA / NASDAQ
Profile: TransGlobe Energy acquires, explores, & develops oil & gas properties. The Alberta-based oil & gas exploration & development company focuses its production activities in Egypt & Yemen.
Ross G. Clarkson, P.Geol., ICD.D, President & Chief Executive Officer
David C. Ferguson, CA, Chief Financial Officer & Vice-President, Finance
Lloyd W. Herrick, P.Eng, ICD.D, Chief Operating Officer & Vice-President
Albert E. Gress, CPA, Vice-President, Business Development
Scott Koyich, Contact, Investor Relations
403-264-9888

Trican Well Service Ltd.
#2900, 645 - 7th Ave. SW
Calgary, AB T2P 4G8
403-266-0202
Fax: 403-237-7716
877-787-4226
www.trican.ca
Other Communications: Investors: 403-476-6767; R&D Centre: 403-723-3688
Company Type: Public
Ticker Symbol: TCW / TSX
Profile: Trican Well Service Ltd. is an international pressure pumping company. It provides products, equipment, & services, which are employed in the exploration & development of oil & gas reserves. The company conducts its operations in Canada, the United States, Russia, Kazakhstan, & Algeria.
Dale Dusterhoft, Chief Executive Officer
ddusterhoft@trican.ca
Michael Baldwin, Chief Financial Officer & Vice-President, Finance
mbaldwin@trican.ca
Donald R. Luft, Chief Operating Officer & Senior Vice-President, Operations
Robert Cox, Vice-President, Canadian Geographic Region
Bonita Croft, General Counsel, Corporate Secretary, & Vice-President, Legal
Steven Redmond, Vice-President, Human Resources, Health, Safety, & the Environment

Trilogy Energy Corp.
#1400, 332 - 6th Ave. SW
Calgary, AB T2P 0B2
403-290-2900
Fax: 403-263-8915
info_@trilogyenergy.com
www.trilogyenergy.com
Company Type: Public
Ticker Symbol: TET / TSX
Profile: In 2010, Trilogy converted from an income trust to a corporate structure. The Canadian energy corporation is engaged in the development & production of crude oil, natural gas, & natural gas liquids.
J.H.T. (Jim) Riddell, Chief Executive Officer
J.B. (John) Williams, President & Chief Operating Officer
Michael Kohut, Chief Financial Officer

Trinidad Drilling Ltd.
#2500, 700 - 9th Ave. SW
Calgary, AB T2P 3V4
403-265-6525
Fax: 403-265-4168
info@trinidaddrilling.com
www.trinidaddrilling.com
Company Type: Public
Ticker Symbol: TDG / TSX
Profile: The company specializes in drilling, well servicing, & barge drilling operations within the North American oil & gas industry. Trinidad Drilling Ltd.incorporates environmental protection measures into its procedures for site inspections, products, equipment, & waste disposal.
Lyle C. Whitmarsh, President/CEO
Brent J. Conway, Chief Financial Officer
Lisa Ciulka, Director, Investor Relations
403-294-4401, lciulka@trinidaddrilling.com

TriOil Resources Ltd.
355 - 4th Ave. SW, 10th Fl.
Calgary, AB T2P 0J1
403-265-4115
investor@trioilresources.com
www.trioilresources.com
Company Type: Public
Ticker Symbol: TOL / TSX Venture
Profile: The junior oil company carries out its operations in western Canada. TriOil Resources Ltd. is targeting opportunities in Alberta's Dunvegan & Cardium regions.
Russell J. Tripp, LLB, P.Land, President & Chief Executive Officer

Cheryne Lowe, CA, MPAcc., Chief Financial Officer & Vice-President, Finance
Craig Haavardsrud, B.Comm., Vice-President, Business Development & Land
Andrew Z. Wiacek, M.Sc., P. Geoph., Vice-President, Exploration
Shaun Wyzykoski, P.Eng., Vice-President, Engineering

Twin Butte Energy Ltd.
#410, 396 - 11 Ave. SW
Calgary, AB T2R 0C5
403-215-2045
Fax: 403-215-2055
www.twinbutteenergy.com
Company Type: Public
Ticker Symbol: TBE / TSX
Profile: Twin Butte Energy is a junior oil & gas company. The company is active in the greater Lloydminster area of Alberta & Saskatchewan.
Jim Saunders, President & Chief Executive Officer
Bruce W. Hall, Chief Operating Officer
Alan Steele, Chief Financial Officer & Vice-President, Finance
Neil Cathcart, Vice-President, Exploration
Preston Kraft, Vice-President, Engineering

Ultra Petroleum Corp.
Investor Relations
#1200, 363 North Sam Houston Pkwy. East
Houston, TX 77060
281-876-0120
Fax: 281-876-2831
info@ultrapetroleum.com
www.ultrapetroleum.com
Other Communications: Shareholder Inquires: InvestorCentreCA@computershare.com
Company Type: Public
Ticker Symbol: UPL / NYSE
Profile: Incorporated in British Columbia in 1979, Ultra Petroleum Corp. is engaged in the exploration & development of oil & gas properties in the Green River Basin of Wyoming. The company's registrar & transfer agent is Computershare Investor Services Inc. in Vancouver (service@computershare.com).
Michael D. Watford, President/CEO & Chair
Marshall D. Smith, Chief Financial Officer
William R. (Bill) Picquet, Vice-President, Operations, Rocky Mountains
Kelly L. Whitley, Manager, Investor Relations

Ultramar Ltd.
2200, av McGill College
Montréal, QC H3A 3L3
514-499-6111
800-363-6949
publicaffairs@ultramar.ca
www.ultramar.ca
Other Communications: Customer Service, E-mail: customer@ultramar.ca
Company Type: Private
Profile: Ultramar Ltd. is engaged in the provision of clean-burning, environmentally sound petroleum fuels at the industrial, commercial, & retail levels in North America. The company has a network of service stations, including car washes & stores, located throughout eastern Ontario, Québec, & the Atlantic provinces. Ultramar Ltd. also provides home heating & air conditioning services.
Jean Bernier, President

Union Gas Limited
PO Box 2001, 50 Keil Dr. North
Chatham, ON N7M 5M1
519-352-3100
Fax: 519-436-4566
888-774-3111
customerrelations@uniongas.com
www.uniongas.com
Company Type: Public
Ticker Symbol: UNG / TSX
Profile: The natural gas storage, transmission, & distribution company provides services in northern, southwestern, & eastern Ontario to commercial, industrial, & residential customers. In Quebec, Ontario, & the United States, Union Gas Limited also offers natural gas storage & transportation services to other utilities.
Julie A. Dill, President
John Patrick Reddy, Chief Financial Officer & Group Vice-President
Steve Baker, Vice-President, Business Development, Storage & Transmission
sbaker@uniongas.com
Mel Ydreos, Vice-President, Marketing & Customer Care
Andrea Stass, Manager, External Communications & Media Relations
519-436-5490

UPI Energy LP
#200, #105 Silvercreek Pkwy. North
Guelph, ON N1H 8M1
519-821-2667
Fax: 519-821-4919
800-396-2667
info@upi.on.ca; customers@upi.on.ca
www.upienergylp.com
Other Communications: Business Opportunities: busops@upi.on.ca
Company Type: Public
Profile: UPI Energy LP provides environmentally friendly energy products & related services. Examples of products & services offered to farms & businesses include gasolines, diesel fuels, propane, & lubricants. The company serves consumers & motorists in rural Ontario.
Robert P. Sicard, President & Chief Executive Officer

Valener Inc.
1717, rue du Havre
Montréal, QC H2K 2X3
514-598-6220
Fax: 514-521-8168
888-598-6220
info@valener.com; investors@valener.com
www.valener.com
Other Communications: Media Relations: communications@valener.com
Company Type: Public
Ticker Symbol: VNR / TSX
Profile: Valener is engaged in the production, storage, transportation, & distribution of energy. It owns an economic interest in Gaz Métro.
The company favours clean energy sources. It owns a stake in the Seigneurie de Beaupré wind power projects, situated northeast of Québec City.
Pierre Monahan, Chair
Caroline Warren, Senior Advisor, Investor Relations
514-598-3324
Audrey Giguère, Advisor, Media & Public Relations
514-598-3449

Valeura Energy Inc.
Bow Valley Square 1
#1200, 202 - 6th Ave. SW
Calgary, AB T2P 2R9
403-237-7102
www.valeuraenergy.com
Company Type: Public
Ticker Symbol: VLE / TSX
Profile: Valeura Energy Inc. is an explorer, developer, & producer of petroleum & natural gas. Operations take place in western Canada & Turkey.
Jim McFarland, B.Sc., M.Sc., P.Eng., Chief Financial Officer
Steve Bjornson, B.Comm., CA, Chief Financial Officer
403-930-1151, Fax: 403-237-7103, sbjornson@valeuraenergy.com
Lyle Martinson, B.Sc., P.Eng., Vice-Preident, Operations
Donald Shepherd, B.Sc., P.Eng., Vice-Preident, Engineering

Vast Exploration Inc.
#1100, 505 - 3rd St. SW
Calgary, AB T2P 3E6
403-263-3000
Fax: 403-263-3041
info@vastexploration.com
www.vastexploration.com
Company Type: Public
Ticker Symbol: VST / TSX Venture
Profile: The independent oil & gas company is engaged in exploration & development. Vast Exploration's principal asset is the Qara Dagh Block, which is situated in Iraq's Kurdistan region.
Sig Slotboom, President & Chief Executive Officer
Deborah Battiston, Chief Financial Officer
Neil Said, Corporate Secretary

Veresen Inc.
Livingston Place
222 - 3rd Ave. SW
Calgary, AB T2P 0B4
403-296-0140
Fax: 403-213-3648
investor-relations@vereseninc.com
www.vereseninc.com
Other Communications: Investors, Phone: 403-213-3633
Company Type: Public
Ticker Symbol: VSN
Profile: Veresen Inc. is engaged in the following businesses: a pipeline business, with interests in the Alliance Pipeline & the Alberta Ethane Gathering System; a midstream business, with interest in an extraction facility near Chicago, Illinois; & a power business, with renewable & gas-fired facilities & development projects as well as district energy systems & waste heat power facilities.
Stephen H. White, Chief Executive Officer & President
Keith O'Regan, Chief Operating Officer & Senior Vice-President
Richard G. Weech, Chief Financial Officer & Senior Vice-President, Finance
David I. Holm, Executive Vice-President, Corporate & Business Development
Kevan S. King, Senior Vice-President, General Counsel, & Secretary

Vermilion Energy Inc.
#3500, 520 - 3rd Ave. SW
Calgary, AB T2P 0R3
403-269-4884
Fax: 403-476-8100
866-895-8101
investor_relations@vermilionenergy.com
www.vermilionenergy.com
Other Communications: Community Investment, E-mail: community@vermilionenergy.com
Company Type: Public
Ticker Symbol: VET / TSX
Profile: Vermilion Energy Inc. specializes in the acquisition, exploration, development & optimization of oil & natural gas producing properties. Activities take place in western Canada, western Europe, & Australia.
Lorenzo Donadeo, P.Eng., President & Chief Executive Officer
Curtis W. Hicks, Chief Financial Officer & Executive Vice-President
Dean Morrison, CFA, Director, Investor Relations

Vero Energy Inc.
#900, 520 - 3rd Ave. SW
Calgary, AB T2P 0R3
403-218-2063
Fax: 403-218-2064
866-709-8376
general.info@veroenergy.ca
www.veroenergy.ca
Company Type: Public
Ticker Symbol: VRO / TSX
Profile: Established in 2005, Vero Energy Inc. specializes in oil & natural gas exploration, development, & production. The company is active in western Canada.
Douglas J. Bartole, P Eng., President & cChief Executive Officer
Gerry Gilewicz, Chief Financial Officer & Vice-President, Finance
403-693-3170
R.S. (Bob) Bachynski, Vice-President, Land
Shane Manchester, Vice-President, Operations
Kevin Yakiwchuk, Vice-President, Exploration

Waldron Energy Corporation
#2410, 520 - 3rd Ave. SW
Calgary, AB T2P 0R3
403-532-6700
Fax: 403-532-3993
info@waldronenergy.ca
www.waldronenergy.ca
Company Type: Public
Ticker Symbol: WDN / TSX
Profile: Waldron Energy explores for, develops & produces petroleum & natural gas. The company's core area of operation is central Alberta.
Ernest G. Saphieha, CA, President & Chief Executive Officer
esapieha@waldronenergy.ca
Dean J. Schultz, CA, Chief Financial Officer & Vice-President, Finance
dschultz@waldronenergy.ca
Byron E. Lissel, P.Geol., Vice-President, Exploration
Murray J. Stodalka, P.Eng, Executive Vice-President, Engineering & Operations
mstodalka@waldronenergy.ca

Westcoast Energy Inc
Legal Department
PO Box 11162, #1100, 1055 West Georgia St.
Vancouver, BC V6E 3R5
604-691-5500
www.spectraenergy.com
Company Type: Public
Ticker Symbol: W / TSX
Profile: Westcoast is an indirect subsidiary of Spectra Energy Corp. Spectra Energy Corp. is a natural gas infrastructure company engaged in gathering & processing, transmission & storage, & distribution.
Gregory L. Ebel, President & Chief Executive Officer
Douglas P. Bloom, President, Spectra Energy Transmission West
Julie A. Dill, President, Union Gas Limited
Dorothy M. Ables, Chief Administrative Officer
John R. Arensdorf, Chief Communications Officer
Alan N. Harris, Chief Development & Operations Officer

John Patrick Reddy, Chief Financial Officer

Western Energy Service Corp.
#900, 606 - 4th St. SW
Calgary, AB T2P 1T1

403-984-5916
Fax: 403-984-5917
info@wesc.ca
www.wesc.ca

Company Type: Public
Ticker Symbol: WRG / TSX
Profile: Western Energy Services Corp. provides contract drilling services & well servicing for oil companies. In 2011, Western Energy Services Corp. acquired Stoneham Drilling Trust. Stoneham Drilling Corporation is now a Western company that provides drilling services in the United States. Western Energy Services' wholly owned subsidiary, Horizon Drilling Inc. offers services in Canada. Well servicing is handled by another of Western Energy Services' wholly owned subsidiaries, Matrix Well Servicing Inc.
Dale E. Tremblay, Chief Executive Officer
403-984-5929, dtremblay@wesc.ca
Alex MacAusland, President & Chief Operating Officer
403-984-5392, amacausland@wesc.ca
Jeffrey K. Bowers, Chief Financial Officer & Vice-President, Finance
403-984-5333, jbowers@wesc.ca

WestFire Energy Ltd.
#1400, 440 - 2nd Ave. SW
Calgary, AB T2P 5E9

403-261-6955
Fax: 403-261-9658
info@westfireenergy.com; investors@westfi
www.westfireenergy.com
Other Communications: Career Information:
careers@westfireenergy.com

Company Type: Public
Ticker Symbol: WFE / TSX
Profile: WestFire Energy Ltd. is a junior oil & natural gas company. Areas of activity include Alberta & west central Saskatchewan.
Lowell Jackson, President & Chief Executive Officer
Jeffrey W. Holmgren, Chief Financial Officer & Vice-President, Finance

Winstar Resources Ltd.
#845, 401 - 9th Ave. SW
Calgary, AB T2P 3C5

403-205-3722
Fax: 403-205-2722
800-875-1217
info@winstar.ca
www.winstar.ca

Company Type: Public
Ticker Symbol: WIX / TSX
Profile: Winstar Resources Ltd. is an oil & gas exploration & development company. Operations are carried out in Canada, Romania, Hungary, & Tunisia.
Charles de Mestral, BSc, MSc Geology, Chief Executive Officer
cdemestral@winstar-resources.ch
David Monachello, President
dmonachello@winstar.ca
Jerrad Blanchard, Chief Financial Officer
jblanchard@winstar.ca

Xtreme Coil Drilling Corp.
#770, 340 - 12th Ave. SW
Calgary, AB T2R 1L5

403-262-9500
Fax: 403-262-9522
ir@xtremecoil.com
www.xtremecoil.com
Social Media:
www.facebook.com/XtremeDrillCoilSvces?sk=app_20051197667 8729
www.linkedin.com/company/637062

Company Type: Public
Ticker Symbol: XDC / TSX
Profile: Xtrene Drilling & Coil Services is the brand name for Xtreme Coil Drilling Corp. & its subsidiaries. The company designs, builds, & operates coiled tubing well service units & drilling rigs.
Thomas D. Wood, Chair & Chief Executive Officer
Matthew S. Porter, Chief Financial Officer

Yoho Resources Inc.
#750, 736 - 6th Ave. SW
Calgary, AB T2P 3T7

403-537-1771
Fax: 403-537-1775
info@yohoresources.ca; investor@yohoresou
www.yohoresources.ca

Company Type: Public
Ticker Symbol: YO / TSX Venture
Profile: The junior oil & natural gas company has operations in the Western Canadian Sedimentary Basin. Core areas of activity include the Peace River Arch region of northern Alberta, west central Alberta, & northeastern British Columbia.
Brian A. McLachlan, President & Chief Executive Officer
Barry Stobo, Chief Operating Officer & Vice-President, Engineering
Wendy Woolsey, Chief Operating Officer & Vice-President, Finance
Clark Drader, Vice-President, Land

Zargon Oil & Gas Ltd.
Corporate Office
#700, 333 - 5th Ave. SW
Calgary, AB T2P 3B6

403-264-9992
Fax: 403-265-3026
855-464-9992
zargon@zargon.ca
www.zargon.ca
Other Communications: Investor Relations:
investor-relations@zargon.ca

Company Type: Public
Ticker Symbol: ZAR / TSX
Profile: Zargon is involved in oil & natural gas exploration, development, & production. The organization is active in the western Canadian & Williston sedimentary basins.
Craig H. Hansen, President & Chief Executive Officer
J.B. Dranchuk, Chief Financial Officer & Vice-President, Finance
R.J. (Randy) Doetzel, Vice-President, Operations
Robert T. Moriyama, Vice-President, Enhanced Recovery
Tracy Howard, Corporate Secretary
403-218-7329

ZCL Composites Inc.
6907 - 36 St.
Edmonton, AB T6B 2Z6

Fax: 780-466-6126
800-661-8265
ir@zcl.com
www.zcl.com

Company Type: Public
Ticker Symbol: ZCL / TSX
Profile: ZCL Composites Inc. designs, manufactures & distributes fiberglass tank systems. The environmentally friendly liquid handling solutions are used by the petroleum industry.
Venence (Ven) Côté, President/CEO
Darin R. Coutu, Chief Financial Officer
darin.coutu@zcl.com

Zedi Inc.
Head Office
902 - 11th Ave. SW
Calgary, AB T2R 0E7

403-444-1100
Fax: 403-444-1101
investors@zedi.ca; contactsales@zedi.ca
www.zedi.ca
Other Communications: General Support: support@zedi.ca

Company Type: Public
Ticker Symbol: ZED / TSX Venture
Profile: Integrated services, applications, & technology are provided to oil & gas producers. Zedi Inc. operates in twenty-five countries.
Matthew Heffernan, President & Chief Executive Officer
Grant Exner, Chief Financial Officer
Clement Gaudet, Chief Operations Officer
Tokunosuke Ito, Chief Technology Officer
Debra Deane, Vice-President, Operations & Investor Relations

Printing & Publishing

Canadian Bank Note Company, Limited
145 Richmond Rd.
Ottawa, ON K1Z 1A1

613-722-3421
Fax: 613-722-2548
headoffice@cbnco.com
www.cbnco.com

Company Type: Private
Douglas R. Arends, Chair
Ronald G. Arends, President/CEO
Charles R. Lavoie, CFO & Exec. Vice President
Michel Perras, Vice President/Treasurer/Corporate Controller

FP Newspapers Inc. (FPI)
PO Box 11583, #2900, 650 West Georgia St.
Vancouver, BC V6B 4N8

204-697-7425
Fax: 204-663-2028
www.fpnewspapers.com

Company Type: Public
Profile: Incorporated in 2010, FP Newspapers Inc. carried on the business previously held by FP Newspapers Income Fund. FPI owns securities of FP Canadian Newspapers Limited Partnership. The Partnership owns the Brandon Sun & the Winnipeg Free Press & their related businesses, The Carillon in Steinbach, Manitoba & its related commercial printing operations, plus the Canstar Community News division. The Canstar division publishes eight community & special interest newspapers in the Winnipeg area. The businesses employ approximately 570 people.
Daniel Koshowski, Chief Financial Officer
Glenn Buffie, Publisher, The Carillon, & General Manager, Derksen Printers
Bob Cox, Publisher, Winnipeg Free Press
Eric Lawson, Publisher, Brandon Sun

Glacier Media Inc.
1970 Alberta St.
Vancouver, BC V5Y 3X4

604-872-8565
Fax: 604-879-1483
info@glaciermedia.ca
www.glaciermedia.ca
Other Communications: Investor Relations:
investors@glaciermedia.ca

Company Type: Public
Ticker Symbol: GVC / TSX
Profile: Glacier Media Inc. provides information & related services through print, electronic, & online media.
The Business & Professional Information Group consists of organizations such as CD-Pharma, Eco Log, Specialty Technical Publishers, & Fundata.
The Newspaper & Trade Information Group is comprised of newspapers such as the Prince George Citizen, The Kamloops Daily News, & the Estevan Mercury. Trade information group publications include The Western Producer, The Daily Oil Bulletin, New Technology Magazine, Business in Vancouver, Canadian Cattlemen, & The Northern Miner.
Jonathon J.L. Kennedy, President & Chief Executive Officer
Bruce Creighton, President, Business Information Group
Chris Heming, President, Specialty Technical Publishers
Janny Vincent, President & Chief Executive Officer, Fundata
Orest Smysniuk, Chief Financial Officer
Paul Hecht, Vice-President, Digital Media

GVIC Communications Corp.
275 - 4th Ave. West
Vancouver, BC V5Y 1G8

604-708-3264
Fax: 604-879-1483

Company Type: Public
Ticker Symbol: GCT / TSX
Profile: GVIC Communications is an information communications company. Information is provided through print, electronic, & online media. The company's core businesses are local newspapers, trade information, & business & porfessional information markets.
In 2011, GVIC Communications Corp., through its affiliates, completed the acquisition of Postmedia Network Inc.'s community newspapers in British Columbia, the Times Colonist, related digital media assets, plus certain real estate assets.
Jonathon J.L. Kennedy, Chief Executive Officer
Orest Smysnuik, CA, Chief Financial Officer
604-708-3264

Harlequin Enterprises Limited
225 Duncan Mills Rd.
Toronto, ON M3B 3K9

888-432-4879
CustomerService@Harlequin.com
www.harlequin.com
Other Communications: Corporate Information:
public_relations@harlequin.ca

Company Type: Private
Profile: Harlequin is a publisher of books for women. Over 100 titles are published each month in several languages to serve an international market.

McGraw-Hill Ryerson Limited
300 Water St.
Whitby, ON L1N 9B6

800-245-2914
Fax: 800-463-5885
800-565-5758
cs_queries@mcgrawhill.ca
www.mcgrawhill.ca

Company Type: Public
Ticker Symbol: MHR / TSX
Profile: McGraw-Hill Ryerson publishes & distributes educational, technical, & professional materials in both print & digital formats.
David Swail, President & Chief Executive Officer
Patrick Ferrier, President, Higher Education Division

Nancy Gerrish, President, Elementary & Secondary Division
Claudio Pascucci, President, Professional Division
Gordon Dyer, Chief Financial Officer, Exec. Vice-President& Sec.-Treasurer
Marshall I. Morris, Executive Vice-President, Customer Satisfaction
Clive Powell, Executive Vice-President, Editorial, Production, & Design

MDC Partners
45 Hazelton Ave.
Toronto, ON M5R 2E3

416-960-9000
Fax: 416-960-9555
www.mdc-partners.com

Company Type: Public
Ticker Symbol: MDZA / TSX, NASDAQ
Miles S. Nadal, CEO/Chair
Glenn Gibson, CFO

Metroland Media Group Ltd.
Head Office
3125 Wolfedale Rd.
Mississauga, ON L5C 1W1

905-279-0440
Fax: 905-279-5103
www.metroland.com
Other Communications: Print/Corp. Sales: 416-493-1300; Digital Media: 905-265-4499

Company Type: Private
Profile: The media group provides business & community information through newspapers & advertising venues, plus Internet & web publishing.

Pollard Banknote Limited (PBL)
1499 Buffalo Pl.
Winnipeg, MB R3T 1L7

204-474-2323
Fax: 204-453-1375
winnipeg@pollardbanknote.com
www.pollardbanknote.com

Company Type: Public
Ticker Symbol: PBL / TSX
Profile: Pollard Banknote Limited is a lottery vendor & supplier to the charitable gaming industry. The company manufactures instant tickets, pull tab tickets, & bingo paper. Other activities include warehousing, distributing, & marketing.
Gordon Pollard, Co-Chief Executive Officer
John Pollard, Co-Chief Executive Officer
Riva Richard, General Counsel & Executive Vice-President, Legal Affairs
Robert Rose, Executive Vice-President, Finance
Donald Sawatzky, Executive Vice-President, Sales & Marketing
Robert Stewart, Executive Vice-President, Manufacturing
Jennifer Westbury, Executive Vice-President, Sales & Marketing

Quebecor Inc.
612, rue Saint-Jacques
Montréal, QC H3C 4M8

514-877-9777
Fax: 514-954-0052
webmaster@quebecor.com
www.quebecor.com

Company Type: Public
Ticker Symbol: QBR.A, QBR.B / TSX
Profile: Quebecor Inc. is a holding company that has a 54,7% interest in Quebecor Media Inc. Quebecor Media is a large media group with over 16,000 employees.
Pierre Karl Péladeau, President & Chief Executive Officer
Jean-François Pruneau, Chief Financial Officer
514-380-4144, jean-francois.pruneau@quebecor.com

St. Joseph Communications
50 MacIntosh Boul.
Concord, ON L4K 4P3

905-660-3111
communications@stjoseph.com
www.stjoseph.com
Social Media: www.facebook.com/313897708631041
twitter.com/chasethisnow
www.linkedin.com/company/st.-joseph-communications

Company Type: Private
Profile: The company was founded in 1956 as a basement-run printing business, & now offers marketing & communications services in print, photography, & other media forms. They operate through the following three divisions: St. Joseph Content, St. Joseph Print, & St. Joseph Media.
Gaetano Gagliano, Honorary Chair & Founder
Tony Gagliano, Exec. Chair & CEO
Frank Gagliano, Vice-Chair
John Gagliano, President, St. Joseph Print
Douglas Knight, President, St. Joseph Media
Doug Templeton, President, St. Joseph Content
Tim Zahavich, Chief Financial Officer
Martin Byrne, Chief Technology/Innovation Officer

Thomson Reuters
#400, 333 Bay St.
Toronto, ON M5H 2R2

416-360-8700
investor.relations@thomsonreuters.com
www.thomsonreuters.com
Other Communications: Financial Services & Media, Phone: 416-687-7500
Social Media: www.facebook.com/thomsonreuters
twitter.com/thomsonreuters
www.linkedin.com/company/thomson-reuters_1400

Company Type: Public
Ticker Symbol: TRI / TSX, NYSE
Profile: Thomson Reuters provides intelligent information for businesses & professionals.
Thomas H. Glocer, CEO
Daleo Robert D., Exec. Vice-President/CFO
Gustav Carlson, Exec. Vice-President & Chief Marketing Officer
James Powell, Exec. Vice-President & Chief Technology Officer
Deirdre Stanley, Exec. Vice-President & General Counsel

Torstar Corporation
Corporate Office
1 Yonge St.
Toronto, ON M5E 1P9

416-869-4010
Fax: 416-869-4183
torstar@thestar.ca
www.torstar.com

Company Type: Public
Ticker Symbol: TS.B / TSX
Profile: The media & book publishing company includes the following businesses: Star Media Group, which features the Toronto Star & digital properties such as toronto.com & thestar.com; Metroland Media Group, which publishes community & daily newspapers throughout Ontario; & Harlequin Enterprises, which publishes books for women.
David Holland, President & Chief Executive Officer
Donna Hayes, Chief Executive Officer & Publisher, Harlequin Enterprises Limited
Ian Oliver, President, Media Group Ltd.
Tomer Strolight, President, Torstar Digital, & Vice-President, Digital Media, Toronto Star, & Star Media Group
Lorenzo DeMarchi, Chief Financial Officer & Executive Vice-President
416-869-4776, Fax: 416-869-4183
Marie Beyette, Vice President, General Counsel & Corporate Secretary

Transcontinental Inc.
#3315, 1, Place Ville Marie
Montréal, QC H3B 3N2

514-954-4000
Fax: 514-954-4016
info@transcontinental.ca
www.transcontinental.com

Company Type: Public
Ticker Symbol: TCL / TSX
Profile: The company is engaged in the printing & publishing of consumer magazines & community newspapers, as well as direct marketing, & distribution of advertising material. Transcontinental Inc. has worked to address environmental issues, by programs such as the implementation of the Transcontinental Paper Purchasing Policy.
François Olivier, President & Chief Executive Officer
Brian Reid, President, Transcontinental Printing
Natalie Larivière, President, Transcontinental Media
Benoit Huard, Chief Financial Officer & Vice-President
Jean Denault, Corporate Vice-President, Procurement & Technology
Jennifer F. McCaughey, Senior Director, Investor Relations & Financial Communications
514-954-4000, Fax: 514-954-4016,
jennifer.mccaughey@transcontinental.ca
Nessa Prendergast, Director, Media Relations
nessa.prendergast@transcontinental.ca

Yellow Media Inc.
Ile des Soeurs
16, Place du Commerce
Montréal, QC H3E 2A5

514-934-2611
800-361-6010
ir.info@ypg.com
www.ypg.com
Other Communications: Yellow Pages Group: 877-909-9356; Canpages: 800-634-1476
Social Media: www.facebook.com/yellowpagesgroup
twitter.com/yellowpages_ca

Company Type: Public
Ticker Symbol: YLO / TSX
Profile: Yellow Media owns & operates properties & publications such as the Yellow Pages print directories, YellowPages.ca, Canada411.ca, & RedFlagDeals.com. The company is also involved in digital advertising through Mediative. Yellow Media employs approximately 3,300 people.
Marc P. Tellier, President & Chief Executive Officer
Ginette Maillé, Chief Financial Officer
François D. Ramsay, Senior Vice-President, General Counsel, & Secretary
Hind Ounis, Director, Communications
514-934-2097, hind.ounis@ypg.com
Anne-Sophie Roy, Treasurer
514-934-2828, anne-sophie.roy@ypg.com

ZoomerMedia Limited
#105, 550 Queen St. East
Toronto, ON M5A 1V2

416-607-7738
Fax: 416-648-0835
www.zoomermedia.ca

Company Type: Public
Ticker Symbol: ZUM / TSX Venture
Profile: Formed in 1991, ZoomerMedia Limited is a multimedia company that serves the interests of persons 45 years of age & older. The company offers the following services: television, radio, magazines, internet, & trade shows. Examples of ZoomerMedia's television properties include Vision TV, ONE, & Joytv. Radio properties include CFMZ-FM Toronto, CFMX-FM Cobourg, & CFZM-AM 740 Toronto. ZoomerMedia also publishes Zoomer Magazine. An example of the company's online content is www.50plus.com. ZoomerMedia's trade show division produces the Zoomer Show.
Moses Znaimer, Chief Executive Officer
George Kempff, Chief Financial Officer & Vice-President
g.kempff@zoomermedia.ca
Leanne Wright, Vice-President, Communications
leanne@zoomers.ca

Real Estate

Allied Hotel Properties Inc.
#300, 515 West Pender St.
Vancouver, BC V6B 6H5

604-669-5335
Fax: 604-682-8131
info@alliedhotels.com
www.alliedhotels.com

Company Type: Public
Ticker Symbol: AHP / TSX
Profile: The hotel company owns first class business hotels in major Canadian centres. Allied Hotel Properties Inc.'s principal hotel properties are the Toronto Don Valley Hotel & Suites & the Crowne Plaza Chateau Lacombe Hotel in Edmonton, Alberta.
Peter Y.L. Eng, Chair & Chief Executive Officer
Michael F. Chan, President & Chief Financial Officer

Allied Properties Real Estate Investment Trust
255 Adelaide St. West
Toronto, ON M5H 1X9

416-977-9002
Fax: 416-977-9053
info@alliedpropertiesreit.com
www.alliedpropertiesreit.com

Company Type: Public
Ticker Symbol: AP / TSX
Profile: Allied Properties Real Estate Investment Trust is the owner of urban office properties. The organization plans to continue the acquisition of Class I & other office properties. Target markets are in Victoria, Vancouver, Edmonton, Calgary, Winnipeg, Kitchener, Toronto, Ottawa, Montréal, & Québec.
Michael R. Emory, President & Chief Executive Officer
Thomas G. Burns, Chief Operating Officer & Executive Vice-President
Peter E. Sweeney, Chief Financial Officer & Vice-President
Wayne L. Jacobs, Executive Vice-President
Jennifer L. Irwin, Vice-President, Human Resources & Communications

Altus Group Limited
Head Office
#500, 33 Yonge St.
Toronto, ON M5E 1G4

416-641-9500
Fax: 416-641-9501
877-953-9948
info@altusgroup.com
www.altusgroup.com

Company Type: Public
Ticker Symbol: AIF.CS / TSX
Profile: Altus Group offers real estate consulting & advisory services. The organization's business units are as follows: Research, Valuation, & Advisory; Realty Tax Consulting; Cost Consulting & Project Management; ARGUS Software; & Geomatics. Altus has offices in fourteen countries.

Stuart Smith, Executive Chair & Chief Executive Officer
Angelo Bartolini, Chief Financial Officer
Sayla Nordin, Vice-President, Investor Relations & Corporate Communications

Amica Mature Lifestyles Inc.
Executive Offices
1111 Melville St., 10th Fl.
Vancouver, BC V6E 3V6
604-608-6777
Fax: 604-608-6717
877-447-4827
mail@amica.ca
www.amica.ca
Other Communications: Toronto Office, Phone: 416-408-0076, Fax: 416-408-0068

Company Type: Public
Ticker Symbol: ACC / TSX
Profile: Amica Mature Lifestyles Inc. is a designer, developer, manager, & marketer of seniors' retirement residences & services. Amica has locations in Ontario & British Columbia.
Samir A. Manji, President, Chief Executive Officer, & Chair
Arthur J. Ayres, Chief Financial Officer
Colin R. Halliwell, Chief Operating Officer
Claudia L. Salgado, Vice-President, Design & Construction
Alyssa Barry, Manager, Investor Communications
604-639-2171, a.barry@amica.ca

Boardwalk Real Estate Income Trust
#200, 1501 - 1st St. SW
Calgary, AB T2R 0W1
403-531-9255
Fax: 403-261-9267
www.boardwalkreit.com

Company Type: Public
Ticker Symbol: BEI.UN / TSX
Profile: The open-ended real estate investment trust owns & operates multi-family communities. Boardwalk REIT's portfolio is concentrated in British Columbia, Alberta, Saskatchewan, Ontario, & Quebec.
Sam Kolias, Chair & Chief Executive Officer
403-206-6789, Fax: 403-261-9270
William Wong, CFO & Sr. Vice-President, Finance
Michael Guyette, Vice-President, Technology

BPO Properties Ltd.
Brookfield Place
PO Box 770, #330, 181 Bay St.
Toronto, ON M5J 2T3
416-359-8555
Fax: 416-359-8596
info@bpoproperties.com
www.bpoproperties.com

Company Type: Public
Ticker Symbol: BPP / TSX
Profile: The Canadian commercial real estate company is engaged in the ownership, development, & management of office properties. BPO Properties has endeavoured to develop several environmental initiatives in its properties, such as energy savings programs, environmentally sensitive fittings & finishes, & recycling.
Jan Sucharda, President & Chief Executive Officer
Bryan Davis, Chief Financial Officer & Senior Vice-President
416-956-5170, bryan.davis@brookfield.com
Deborah R. Rogers, Senior Vice-President, Legal Counsel, & Secretary
Matthew Cherry, Director, Investor Relations & Communications
416-359-8593, matthew.cherry@brookfield.com

Brookfield Office Properties
Brookfield Place
#330, 181 Bay St.
Toronto, ON M5J 2T3
416-369-2300
Fax: 416-369-2301
melissa.coley@brookfieldproperties.com
www.brookfieldproperties.com

Company Type: Public
Ticker Symbol: BPO / TSX
Profile: The corporation owns, develops, & manages office properties. Brookfield's portfolio includes the following places: Bankers Hall in Calgary, BCE Place in Toronto, World Financial Center in New York, & Bank of America Plaza in Los Angeles. The company is working towards developing properties that are sustainable & environmentally friendly, by ensuring that all future developments are built to a Leadership in Energy & Environmental Design (LEED) Gold standard.
Richard B. Clark, Chief Executive Officer
Steve Douglas, President
Tom Farley, President/CEO, Canadian Commercial Operations
Dennis Friedrich, President/CEO, U.S. Commercial Operations
Alan Norris, President/CEO, Residential Operations
Bryan Davis, Chief Financial Officer
Jan Jan, Chief Operating Officer, Canadian Commercial Operations
Melissa Coley, Vice-President, Investor Relations & Communications

Brookfield Real Estate Services Inc.
39 Wynford Dr.
Toronto, ON M3C 3K5
416-510-5800
Fax: 416-446-0050
info@brookfieldresinc.com
www.brookfieldresinc.com

Company Type: Public
Ticker Symbol: BRE / TSX
Profile: Brookfield Real Estate Services is involved in the provision of services to residential real estate brokers & their realtors. Cash flow is generated from franchise royalties & service fees from brokers & agents who operate under the following brand names: Johnston & Daniel; Royal LePage; & Via Capitale Real Estate Network.
Philip Soper, President & Chief Executive
416-386-6000, philsoper@brookfieldres.com
Kevin Cash, Chief Financial Officer
416-510-5634, kevin.cash@brookfieldrps.com
Tammy Gilmer, Director, Public Relations & Global Communications, Real Estate
416-510-5783, tgilmer@brookfieldres.com

BTB Real Estate Investment Trust/ Fonds de placement immobilier BTB
Also Known As: BTB REIT
#300, 2155, rue Crescent
Montréal, QC H3G 2C1
514-286-0188
www.btbreit.com
Social Media: twitter.com/btbreit

Company Type: Public
Ticker Symbol: BTB / TSX Venture
Profile: The real estate investment trust invests in a portfolio of industrial, commercial, office, & retail properties. BTB Real Estate Investment Trust's properties are located predominantly in Québec.
Michael Léonard, Chief Executive Officer & President
mleonard@btbreit.com
Benoit Cyr, Chief Financial Officer & Vice-President
Daniel G. Oana, Vice-President, Leasing
Georges A. Renaud, Vice-President, Property Management

Calloway Real Estate Investment Trust
#200, 700 Applewood Cres.
Vaughan, ON L4K 5X3
905-326-6400
Fax: 905-326-0783
investorrelations@callowayreit.com
www.callowayreit.com

Company Type: Public
Ticker Symbol: CWT / TSX
Profile: Calloway REIT is an unincorporated, open-end real estate investment trust. It focuses on owning & developing high quality retail properties. Its portfolio consists of leaseable area throughout Canada.
Simon Nyilassy, President & Chief Executive Officer
snyilassy@callowayreit.com
Bart Munn, Chief Financial Officer
bmunn@callowayreit.com
Rudy Gobin, Exec. Vice-President & Strategy Officer
rgobin@callowayreit.com

Canadian Apartment Properties REIT (CAP REIT)
Also Known As: Canadian Apartment Properties Real Estate Investment Trust
#401, 11 Church St.
Toronto, ON M5E 1W1
416-861-9404
Fax: 416-861-9209
rentals@capreit.net
www.caprent.com
Social Media: www.facebook.com/caprent
twitter.com/caprent

Company Type: Public
Ticker Symbol: CAR.UN / TSX
Profile: Canadian Apartment Properties Real Estate Investment Trust is an investmen trust that owns freehold interests in multi-unit residential properties, such as townhouses & apartment buildings. Properties are situated in or near major Canadian urban centres.
Tom Schwartz, President & Chief Executive Officer
416-861-9404, Fax: 416-861-9209, t.schwartz@capreit.net
Maria Amaral, Chief Accounting Officer
Scott Cryer, Chief Financial Officer
Mark Kenney, Chief Operating Officer
Robert Sestito, Chief Information Systems Officer & Vice-President, Information Technology
Trish MacPherson, Vice-President, Sales & Marketing
Corinne Pruzanski, General Counsel & Corporate Secretary

Chartwell Seniors Housing REIT
Also Known As: Chartwell Seniors Housing Real Estate Investment Trust
#700, 100 Milverton Dr.
Mississauga, ON L5R 4H1
905-501-9219
Fax: 905-501-9107
www.chartwellreit.ca

Company Type: Public
Ticker Symbol: CSH.UN / TSX
Stephen Suske, Vice-Chair & Co-CEO
Vlad Volodarski, Chief Financial Officer

Cominar Real Estate Investment Trust
455, rue du Marais
Québec, QC G1M 3A2
418-681-8151
Fax: 418-681-2946
info@cominar.com
www.cominar.com

Company Type: Public
Ticker Symbol: CUF / TSX
Profile: Cominar is a large, diversified real estate investment trust. It ownscommercial property in Québec. The real estate investment trust also has a portfolio of properties in the Atlantic provinces, Ontario, & western Canada.
Michel Dallaire, President & Chief Executive Officer
mdallaire@cominar.com
Michel Berthelot, CA, Chief Financial Officer & Executive Vice-President
mberthelot@cominar.com
Alain Dallaire, Exec. Vice-President, Operations
alaind@cominar.com
Michel Paquet, Secretary & Exec. Vice-President, Legal Affairs
mpaquet@cominar.com
Louis Bolduc, Vice-President, Montreal Construction
Robert Larivière, Vice-President, Quebec Construction

Consolidated HCI Holdings Corporation
#3, 100 Strada Dr.
Woodbridge, ON L4L 5V7
905-851-7741
Fax: 416-253-5074
ewdl@sympatico.ca

Company Type: Public
Ticker Symbol: CXA / TSX
Profile: Consolidated HCI Holdings Corporation is an Ontario-based real estate & development company.
Stanley Goldfarb, Chief Executive Officer
Arnold J. Resnick, Chief Financial Officer

Crombie Real Estate Investment Trust
115 King St.
Stellarton, NS B0K 1S0
902-755-8100
Fax: 902-752-5136
investing@crombie.ca
www.crombiereit.ca

Company Type: Public
Ticker Symbol: CRR.UN / TSX
Profile: Crombie REIT is an open-ended real estate investment trust. It owns & manages properties in eight provinces. Crombie's portfolio consists of retail, office, & mixed-use properties.
Donald E. Clow, President & Chief Executive Officer
Glenn R. Hynes, Chief Fiancial Officer & Secretary
Scott R. MacLean, Senior Vice-President, Operations

Dundee Real Estate Investment Trust
State Street Financial Centre
#1600, 30 Adelaide St. East
Toronto, ON M5C 3H1
416-365-3535
Fax: 416-365-6565
info@dundeereit.com
www.dundeereit.com

Company Type: Public
Ticker Symbol: D.UN / TSX
Profile: Dundee REIT is an unincorporated, open-ended real estate investment trust. It owns industrial & office assets throughout Canada.
In 2012, Dundee REIT acquired Whiterock Real Estate Investment Trust, a provider of office, retail, & industrial properties in Canada.
Michael J. Cooper, Vice-Chair & Chief Executive Officer
Mario Barrafato, Chief Financial Officer & Senior Vice-President
Peter A. Crossgrove, Chair, Governance & Environmental Committee

Extendicare Real Estate Investment Trust
#700, 3000 Steeles Ave. East
Markham, ON L3R 9W2
905-470-4000
Fax: 905-470-5588
hgould@extendicare.com
www.extendicare.com

Company Type: Public
Ticker Symbol: EXE / TSX
Profile: Extendicare Real Estate Investment Trust was established in 2006. Through its wholly owned subsidiaries, Extendicare REIT owns & operates health care centers with post-acute & long-term senior care services.
In Canada, Extendicare's wholly owned subsidiary is Extendicare (Canada) Inc.. Home health care services are provided through Extendicare (Canada) Inc.'s ParaMed Home Health Care division.
Timothy L. Lukenda, President/CEO
Paul Tuttle, President
Douglas J. Harris, Sr. Vice-President/CFO
djharris@extendicare.com
Jillian E. Fountain, Secretary

First Capital Realty Inc.
#400, 85 Hanna Ave.
Toronto, ON M6K 3S3
416-504-4114
Fax: 416-941-1655
investor.relations@firstcapitalrealty.ca
www.firstcapitalrealty.ca
Other Communications: HR: HumanResources@firstcapitalrealty.ca

Company Type: Public
Ticker Symbol: FCR / TSX
Profile: First Capital Realty Inc. owns, develops, & operates shopping centres, anchored by supermarkets & drug stores. Properties are located mainly in metropolitan areas.
Dori J. Segal, President & Chief Executive Officer
Karen H. Weaver, Chief Financial Officer & Executive Vice-President
Maryanne McDougald, LEED AP, Vice-President, Property Management
Roger J. Chouinard, General Counsel

FirstService Corporation
FirstService Building
#4000, 1140 Bay St.
Toronto, ON M5S 2B4
416-960-9500
Fax: 416-960-5333
info@firstservice.com
www.firstservice.com

Company Type: Public
Ticker Symbol: FSV / TSX, NASDAQ
Profile: FirstService Corporation is involved in residential property management, property improvement services, & commerical real estate.
Jay S. Hennick, Founder & Chief Executive Officer
D. Scott Patterson, President & Chief Operating Officer
John B. Friedrichsen, Chief Financial Officer & Senior Vice-President
Elias Mulamoottil, Senior Vice-President, Strategy & Corporate Development
Douglas G. Cooke, Vice-President, Corporate Controller, & Secretary

Gazit America Inc.
Corporate Office
#303, 109 Atlantic Ave.
Toronto, ON M6K 1X4
416-447-6400
Fax: 416-447-6488
investor.relations@gazitamerica.com
www.gazitamerica.com
Other Communications: HR: HumanResources@gazitamerica.com

Company Type: Public
Ticker Symbol: GAA / TSX
Profile: Gazit America is engaged in the acquisition, development, & operation of health care retail, medical office, & mixed-use properties. The company has interest in properties in London, Cambridge, Kitchener, Mississuga, Toronto, & Ottawa Ontario, Longueuil & Montréal Québec, & Calgary & Edmonton Alberta.
Gail Mifsud, Chief Executive Officer
Lenis W. Quan, Chief Financial Officer

Genesis Land Development Corp.
#200, 3115 - 12 St. NE
Calgary, AB T2E 7J2
403-265-8079
Fax: 403-266-0746
800-341-7211
genesis@genesisland.com
www.genesisland.com

Company Type: Public
Ticker Symbol: GDC / TSX
Profile: The community development company operates in British Columbia & Alberta. Most of the land is situated in & around Calgary. Activities include land development, single-family & multi-family home building, & commercial development & leasing.
Jeff Blair, Chief Executive Officer
Simon Fletcher, Chief Financial Officer

Halmont Properties Corporation
#400, 51 Yonge St.
Toronto, ON M5E 1J1
416-956-5140
Fax: 416-203-9931

Company Type: Public
Ticker Symbol: HHC / TSX Venture
Profile: Halmont Properties Corporation invests directly in real estate & securities of companies with real estate interests.
Edward C. Kress, President & Chief Executive Officer
Anthony E. Rubin, Chief Financial Officer

Holloway Lodging Real Estate Investment Trust
Also Known As: Holloway Lodging REIT
#202, 117 Kearney Lake Rd.
Halifax, NS B3M 4N9
902-404-3499
Fax: 902-457-3277
investorrelations@hlreit.com
www.hlreit.com

Company Type: Public
Ticker Symbol: HLR / TSX
W. Glenn Squires, President/CEO
Tracey C. Sherren, Secretary/CFO

Homburg Invest Inc.
#600, 1741 Brunswick St.
Halifax, NS B3J 3X8
902-468-3395
Fax: 902-468-2457
www.homburginvest.com

Company Type: Public
Ticker Symbol: HII / TSX
Profile: The company is the owner, developer, & operator of residential & commercial real estate, including townhouses, apartments, offices, & retail properties. Properties are located in Canada, the United States, Germany, & The Netherlands.
Richard Homburg, Chair/CEO
J. Richard Stolle, President/COO
Ashley Phillips, President, Canadian Operations
James Miles, CA, CFO & Vice-President, Finance

Huntingdon Capital Corp.
#2000, 5000 Miller Rd.
Richmond, BC V7B 1K6
604-249-5100
Fax: 604-249-5101
nfo@huntingdoncapital.com
www.huntingdoncapital.com

Company Type: Public
Ticker Symbol: HNT / TSX
Profile: In 2011, Huntingdon Real Estate Investment Trust converted from an income trust to a corporation. The Huntingdom Capital Corp. (formerly 0918070 B.C. Ltd.) became the successor reporting issuer.
Huntingdon Capital Corp. is a real estate operating company. It is the owner & manager of a portfolio of retail, office, industrial & aviation-related facilities. Huntingdon Capital's corporate office is located in Richmond, British Columbia, with regional offices in the Northwest Territories, Saskatchewan, Manitoba, & Ontario.
Zachary R. George, President & Chief Executive Officer
604-249-5119, zgeorge@huntingdoncapital.com
Sandeep Manak, CA, Chief Financial Officer
Azim Lalani, CA, CBV, Director, Finance

Imperial Equities Inc.
Scotia Place
#2151, 10060 Jasper Ave.
Edmonton, AB T5J 3R8
780-424-7227
Fax: 780-425-6379
www.imperialequities.com
Other Communications: Pharmaceutical: 780-484-2287; Real Estate: 780-424-7227

Company Type: Public
Ticker Symbol: IEI / TSX Venture
Profile: Through its wholly owned subsidiary, Imperial Distributors Canada Inc., Imperial Equities Inc. is involved in the distribution of pharmaceutical products to both retail & institutional customers. The company is also engaged in the real estate sector, with industrial & commercial properties in Alberta.
Sine Chadi, President & Chief Executive Officer
sine@imperialequities.com
Wendy Fair, CMA, Chief Financial Officer
wendyf@imperialequities.com

InnVest Real Estate Investment Trust
Also Known As: InnVest REIT
5090 Explorer Dr., 7th Fl.
Mississauga, ON L4W 4T9
905-206-7100
Fax: 905-206-7114
877-209-3429
investor@innvestreit.com
www.innvestreit.com

Company Type: Public
Ticker Symbol: INN.UN
Profile: InnVest Real Estate Investment Trust holds a portfolio of hotels. InnVest's hotels are managed by the following companies; Delta Hotels Limited, Westmont Hospitality Management Canada Limited, Hilton Canada Co., & Fairmont Hotels & Resorts.
InVest also owns retail & office real estate, plus a retirement home. These interests are adjacent to owned hotels.
Kenneth D. Gibson, President/CEO
Tamara L. Lawson, Chief Financial Officer & Secretary

InterRent Real Estate Investment Trust
Also Known As: InterRent REIT
#207, 485 Bank St.
Ottawa, ON K2P 1Z2
613-569-5699
Fax: 888-696-5698
info@interrentreit.com; investorinfo@inte
www.interrentreit.com

Company Type: Public
Ticker Symbol: IIP.UN / TSX
Profile: InterRent Real Estate Investment Trust works to increase unitholder value by acquiring & owning multi-residential properties.
Mike McGahan, Chief Executive Officer
mmcgahan@interrentreit.com
Curt Millar, CA, Chief Financial Officer
cmillar@interrentreit.com

Ivanhoe Cambridge
Centre CDP Capital
#C-500, 1001 square Victoria
Montréal, QC H2Z 2B5
514-841-7600
Fax: 514-841-7762
communications@ivanhoecambridge.com
www.ivanhoecambridge.com

Company Type: Private
Kim D. McInnes, President/CEO
Gervais Levasseur, CFO & Exec. Vice-President

Killam Properties Inc.
#100, 3700 Kempt Rd.
Halifax, NS B3K 4X8
902-453-9000
Fax: 902-455-4525
fredericton@killamproperties.com
www.killamproperties.com
Social Media: www.facebook.com/killamproperties
twitter.com/KillamTweets

Company Type: Public
Ticker Symbol: KMP / TSX
Profile: Killam Properties Inc. is a large residential landlord. The company owns, develops, & operates multi-family apartments & manufactured home communities.
Environmental intiatives at Killam's properties include the increasing use of solar power, reducing heating costs with outdoor controllers, & reducing water consumption with water saving kits.
Philip D. Fraser, President & Chief Executive Officer
Robert Richardson, Chief Financial Officer & Executive Vice-President
Ruth Buckle-McIntosh, Vice-President, Property Management
Keith Foster, Vice-President, Finance
Dale Noseworthy, Vice-President, Investor Relations & Corporate Planning
902-442-0388, dnoseworthy@killamproperties.com

Lakeview Hotel Real Estate Investment Trust
Also Known As: Lakeview Hotel REIT
#600, 185 Carlton St.
Winnipeg, MB R3C 3J1
204-947-1161
Fax: 204-957-1697
investorrelations@lakeviewhotels.com
www.lakeviewreit.com
Company Type: Public
Ticker Symbol: LHRUN / TSX Venture
Keith Levit, Chief Executive Officer
Rudy Beyer, Chief Financial Officer

Lanesborough Real Estate Investment Trust (LREIT)
Also Known As: Lanesborough REIT
c/o Shelter Canadian Properties Limited
2600, Seven Evergreen Pl.
Winnipeg, MB R3L 2T3
204-475-9090
Fax: 204-452-5505
info@lreit.com
www.lreit.com
Company Type: Public
Ticker Symbol: LRT / TSX
Profile: Lanesborough Real Estate Investment Trust aims to provide unitholders with stable cash distributions by investing in a diversified portfolio of real estate properties.
Arni C. Thorsteinson, Chief Executive Officer
Kenneth J. Dando, Chief Financial Officer & Secretary

Madison Pacific Properties Inc.
389 West 6th Ave.
Vancouver, BC V5Y 1L1
604-732-6540
Fax: 604-732-6550
reception@madisonpacific.ca
www.madisonpacific.ca
Company Type: Public
Ticker Symbol: MPC / TSX
Profile: Madison Pacific Properties Inc. is a real estate investment & development company. Its properties include rentable industrial & commercial space.
In 2011, Madison Pacific Properties Inc. acquired the shares of MP Western Properties Inc.. The shares were acquired for investment purposes.
Alan Firth, President & Chief Executive Officer
Bill Ramsey, Chief Financial Officer & Secretary

Mainstreet Equity Corp.
305 - 10 Ave. SE
Calgary, AB T2G OW2
403-215-6060
Fax: 403-266-8867
mainstreet@mainst.biz
www.mainst.biz
Social Media: www.facebook.com/MainstreetEquity
twitter.com/mainst_apts
Company Type: Public
Ticker Symbol: MEQ / TSX
Profile: Mainstreet Equity is engaged in the acquisition & renting of apartments. Business is conducted in Abootsford & Surrey British Columbia, Calgary & Edmonton Alberta, Saskatoon Saskatchewan, & Toronto & Mississauga Ontario.
Bob Dhillon, President & Chief Executive Officer
Johnny Lam, Chief Financial Officer
Lizaine Wheeler, Senior Vice-President, Operations
Michael Guidolin, Vice-President, Capital Expenditures & Maintenance

Melcor Developments Ltd.
#900, 10310 Jasper Ave.
Edmonton, AB T5J 1Y8
780-423-6931
Fax: 780-426-1796
info@melcor.ca
www.melcor.ca
Other Communications: Investor Relations: ir@melcor.ca
Company Type: Public
Ticker Symbol: MRD / TSX
Profile: Melcor Developments Ltd. is a real estate development company that was established in 1923. It acquires land to develop & sell for multi-family sites, residential communities, & commercial sites. The organization is also the owner, developer, & manager of commercial income properties & golf courses.
Ralph B. Young, President & Chief Executive Officer
780-423-6931
Jonathan Chia, CA, Chief Financial Officer & Vice-President, Finance
780-423-6931, Fax: 780-426-1796, jchia@melcor.ca
Brian Baler, Chief Operating Officer

MI Developments Inc. (MID)
455 Magna Dr.
Aurora, ON L4G 7A9
905-713-6322
Fax: 905-713-6332
ir@midevelopments.com
www.midevelopments.com
Company Type: Public
Ticker Symbol: MIM / TSX, NYSE
Profile: The real estate company is the owner, leaser, developer, & manager of industrial & commercial properties. MI Developments Inc.'s real estate properties are located in North America & Europe. The company also holds a controlling interest in Magna Entertainment Corp.
Dennis Mills, Chief Executive Officer
Richard J. Smith, Exec. Vice-President/CFO
905-726-7507
Don Cameron, Chief Operating Officer
Richard J. Crofts, General Counsel, Secretary, & Exec. Vice-President, Corporate Development

Morguard Corporation
#1000, 55 City Centre Dr.
Mississauga, ON L5B 1M3
905-281-3800
Fax: 905-281-5890
info@morguard.com
www.morguard.com
Other Communications: Head Office: headoffice@morguard.com
Company Type: Public
Ticker Symbol: MRC / TSX
Profile: Morguard Corporation is a real estate & property management company. Through its investment in Morguard REIT, the corporation has a diversified portfolio of residential, office, retail, & industrial properties owned or under management. Through Morguard Investments Limited & Morguard Residential, management services to institutional & other investors for residential & commercial real estate are offered.
K. (Rai) Sahi, Chair/CEO, Morguard Corporation & President/CEO, Morguard REIT
rsahi@morguard.com
Antony K. Stephens, President, Morguard Financial
tstephens@morguard.com
Stephen Taylor, President/COO, Morguard Investments
staylor@morguard.com
Paul Miatello, Chief Financial Officer
905-281-3800, pmiatello@morguard.com
Frank M. Munsters, Vice-President, Credit & Banking
fmunsters@morguard.com
Beverley G. Flynn, General Counsel & Secretary
bflynn@morguard.com

Morguard Investments Limited
#800, 55 City Centre Dr.
Mississauga, ON L5B 1M3
905-281-3800
Fax: 905-281-1800
info@morguard.com
www.morguard.com
Company Type: Private
Profile: The real estate company has a diversified portfolio of properties that it owns or mananges. Properties include residential, retail, office, & industrial.

Mountain China Resorts (Holding) Limited (MCR)
Park Place
#1700, 666 Burrard St.
Vancouver, BC V6C 2X8
info@melcochinaresorts.com
www.mountainchinaresorts.com
Other Communications: Investors:
investor_relations@mountainchinaresorts.com
Company Type: Public
Ticker Symbol: MCG / TSX Vemture
Profile: Mountain China Resorts (Holding) Limited develops ski resorts in China.
Zhenhua Mao, Chief Executive Officer
Gang Han, Chief Financial Officer
Patrick Cao Yue, Executive Vice-President, Corporate Development

Northern Property Real Estate Investment Trust (NPREIT)
#110, 6131 - 6th St. SE
Calgary, AB T2H 1L9
403-531-0720
Fax: 403-531-0727
info@npreit.com
www.npreit.com
Company Type: Public
Ticker Symbol: NPR / TSX
Profile: Northern Property Real Estate Investment Trust is an unincorporated, open-end real estate investment trust. The Trust invests in mainly residential income-producing properties. Commercial buildings & executive suites are also owned by the Trust. Properties are situated in Newfoundland & Labrador, Alberta, northeastern British Columbia, Nunavut & the Northwest Territories.
B. James Britton, President/CEO
Todd Cook, Chief Financial Officer
Richard Anda, Vice-President, Operations
Alan Vaughab, Vice-President, Business Development

Partners Real Estate Investment Trust
Also Known As: Partners REIT
#200, 710 Redbrick St.
Victoria, BC V8T 5J3
250-592-3395
Fax: 250-940-5501
877-772-8836
www.partnersreit.com
Company Type: Public
Ticker Symbol: PARUN / TSX Venture
Profile: Partners REIT is an open-end real estate investment trust. The real estate investment trust owns retail properties situated in British Columbia, Alberta, Manitoba, Ontario, & Québec.
Adam Grant, Chief Executive Officer
Patrick Miniutti, President & Chief Operating Officer
250-940-5530, patrick.miniutti@partnersreit.com
Dionne Barnes, Chief Financial Officer
Jay Lin, Manager, Acquisitions & Assets

Plazacorp Retail Properties Ltd.
Head Office
#200, 527 Queen St.
Fredericton, NB E3B 1B8
506-451-1826
Fax: 506-451-1802
info@plaza.ca
www.plaza.ca
Other Communications: Montréal Office: 514-457-7007; Halifax Office: 902-468-8688
Company Type: Public
Ticker Symbol: PLZ / TSX Venture
Profile: Plazacorp Retail Properties Ltd. is engaged in the acquisition, development, & re-development of enclosed mall shopping centres & strip plazas. Operations take place in Ontario, Québec, & Atlantic Canada.
Michael Zakuta, President & Chief Executive Officer
Floriana Cipollone, Chief Financial Officer
416-848-4583,
Lynda Savoie, Treasurer
506-444-6449, lynda.savoie@plaza.ca

Primaris Retail Real Estate Investment Trust
#900, 1 Adelaide St. West
Toronto, ON M5C 2V9
416-642-7800
info@primarisreit.com
www.primarisreit.com
Company Type: Public
Ticker Symbol: PMZ / TSX
Profile: The open-ended real estate investment trust owns Canadian mid-market retail centres. Centres are located in major cities & in shopping malls in secondary cities.
John Morrison, President & Chief Executive Officer
Louis Forbes, Chief Financial Officer & Executive Vice-President
416-642-7810, lforbes@primarisreit.com
Devon Jones, Secretary & Vice-President, Legal

Pure Industrial Real Estate Trust
#910, 925 West Georgia St.
Vancouver, BC V6C 3L6
604-681-5959
Fax: 604-681-5969
888-681-5959
info@piret.cac
www.piret.ca
Company Type: Public
Ticker Symbol: AAR.UN / TSX Venture
Profile: Pure Industrial Real Estate Trust is an open-ended, unincorporated trust. Its purpose is to acquire, own, & operate a portfolio of income producing industrial properties throughout Canada.
Stephen Evans, Co-Chief Executive Officer
Darren T. Latoski, Co-Chief Executive Officer
Scott Hayes, Chief Operating Officer
shayes@piret.ca
Francis Tam, Chief Financial Officer
Andrew Greig, Director, Investor Relations
agreig@piret.ca

Realex Properties
1200 - 4th St. SW
Calgary, AB T2P 1T1
403-264-5889
Fax: 403-264-5892
realex@realex.org
www.realexproperties.ca

Company Type: Private
Marc Sardachuk, President/CEO
Mark Suchan, CFO

RioCan Real Estate Investment Trust
RioCan Yonge Eglinton Centre
PO Box 2386, #500, 2300 Yonge St.
Toronto, ON M4P 1E4
416-866-3033
Fax: 416-866-3020
800-465-2733
inquiries@riocan.com; investments@riocan.
www.riocan.com
Other Communications: HR: recruiting@riocan.com; Investors: ir@riocan.com

Company Type: Public
Ticker Symbol: REI / TSX
Profile: The Trust owns a portfolio of retail properties throughout Canada. RioCan manages neighbourhood shopping centres that are anchored by supermarkets.
Edward Sonshine, Q.C., President/CEO
Frederic A. Waks, Exec. Vice-President/COO
Raghunath Davloor, Sr. Vice-President/CFO
Michael Connolly, Vice-President, Construction
Debra Chan, Director, Investor Relations
416-864-6483, dchan@riocan.com

Royal Host Inc.
CIBC Building
#1108, 1809 Barrington St.
Halifax, NS B3J 3K8
902-470-4500
Fax: 902-470-4501
investorinfo@royalhost.com
www.royalhost.com

Company Type: Public
Ticker Symbol: RYL / TSX
Profile: The hospitality company is engaged in hotel ownership, franchising, & investment. Royal Host Inc. hotels are situated in five provinces & territories. The hotels operate under brands such as Super 8, Hilton, Holiday Inn, & Country Inns & Suites. Royal Host is also the owner & operator of the Travelodge Canada franchise business.
John A. Carnella, President & Chief Executive Officer
Michael McFeters, Chief Financial Officer

Scott's Real Estate Investment Trust
Also Known As: Scott's REIT
Canada Trust Tower, Brookfield Place
PO Box 222, #2300, 161 Bay St.
Toronto, ON M5J 2S1
416-361-9665
Fax: 416-361-6018
info@scottsreit.com; ir@scottsreit.com (i
www.scottsreit.com
Other Communications: Investor Relations, Phone: 416-361-9953

Company Type: Public
Ticker Symbol: SRQ / TSX
Profile: Scott's Real Estate Investment Trust owns small box retail properties & quick service restaurants in eight provinces. The organization works to provide unitholders with stable monthly cash distributions.
John I. Bitove, Chair & Chief Executive Officer
Teresa Neto, Chief Financial Officer
teresa.neto@scottsreit.com
Kevin Salsberg, Chief Operating Officer

Stoneset Equity Development Corp.
PO Box 16099, 815 - 17th Ave. SW
Calgary, AB T2T 5H7
info@stonesetgreen.com
www.stonesetgreen.com

Company Type: Public
Ticker Symbol: SQC / CNSX
Profile: In 2010, SEL amalgamated with Aqueous Capital Corp. to create Stoneset Equity Development Corp.. Stoneset Equity Development Corp. carries on business in Alberta as a real estate investment company & property developer.
Tony Argento, Contact
tony@stonesetequities.com

Temple Real Estate Investment Trust (TREIT)
Also Known As: Temple REIT
c/o Shelter Canadian Properties Limited
2600 Seven Evergreen Pl.
Winnipeg, MB R3L 2T3
204-475-9090
Fax: 204-452-5505
info@treit.ca
www.treit.ca

Company Type: Public
Ticker Symbol: TR.UN / TSX Venture
Profile: Temple Real Estate Investment Trust invests in a portfolio of hotel properties & related assets in order to provide unitholders with stable cash distributions.
Arni Thorsteinson, CFA, Chief Executive Officer
arni@scpl.com
Richard N. Blair, CA, Chief Operating Officer & Senior Vice-President
rnblair@scpl.com
Larry Beeston, CA, FCCI, Senior Manager, Financial Reporting
lbeeston@scpl.com
William S. Robertson, CA, Manager, Financial Reporting - Commercial & Hotel Properties
wrobertson@scpl.com
Gino Romagnoli, Manager, Investor Relations
gromagnoli@scpl.com

Wall Financial Corporation
#3502, 1088 Burrard St.
Vancouver, BC V6Z 2R9
604-893-7131
Fax: 604-893-7179

Company Type: Public
Ticker Symbol: WFC / TSX
Profile: The corporation is engaged in the following activities: real estate development; investment in properties; management of residential rental apartments & hotel properties; & development & construction of residential housing for resale.
Bruno Wall, President
603-893-7131
Darcee Wise, Executive Vice-President & Secretary
Joanne Liu, Vice-President, Finance

Services, Miscellaneous

AEterna Zentaris Inc.
1405, boul du Parc Technologique
Québec, QC G1P 4P5
418-652-8525
Fax: 418-948-0881
aeternazentaris@aeternazentaris.com
www.aeternazentaris.com

Company Type: Public
Ticker Symbol: AEZ / TSX, NASDAQ
David J. Mazzo, President & CEO
Dennis Turpin, Vice-President & CFO

Aramark Canada
811 Islington Ave.
Toronto, ON M8Z 5W8
416-255-1331
Fax: 416-255-4706
www.aramark.com

Company Type: Private

Arbor Memorial Services Inc.
2 Jane St.
Toronto, ON M6S 4W8
416-763-4531
Fax: 416-763-4821
www.arbormemorial.com

Company Type: Public
Ticker Symbol: ABO / TSX
Profile: Arbor Memorial Services Inc. is the owner of the following: reception centres, funeral homes, crematoria, & cemeteries. Services are available in all Canadian provinces, except Prince Edward Island & Newfoundland & Labrador.
Brian D. Snowdon, President & Chief Executive Officer
bsnowdon@arbormemorial.com
Laurel L. Ancheta, Chief Financial Officer & Vice-President
lancheta@arbormemorial.com
Michael Scanlan, Sr. Vice-President, Marketing, Operations, Construction, & Development
Gary R. Carmichael, Chief Privacy Officer & Vice-President, Government & Corporate Affairs
carmichg@arbormemorial.com
Mike Ayres, Vice-President, Information Services
Brian Zenkovich, Chair, Environmental Committee

Black Diamond Group Limited
#200, 715 - 5th Ave. SW
Calgary, AB T2P 2X6
403-206-4747
Fax: 403-264-9281
www.blackdiamondlimited.com

Company Type: Public
Ticker Symbol: BDI / TSX
Profile: Black Diamond Group was founded in 2003. The corporation provides modular buildings, workforce accommodations, & energy services. The three operating divisions are Black Diamond Camps & Logistics, Black Diamond Energy Services, & BOXX Modular.
Trevor Haynes, President & Chief Executive Officer
Michael Burnyeat, Chief Financial Officer & Executive Vice-President
Steven Stein, Chief Operating Officer & Executive Vice-President
Glen Clark, Senior Vice-President, Business Development
Paul de Rosenroll, Senior Vice-President, Corporate Servies & HSE
Toby LaBrie, Vice-President & Controller

Boyd Group Income Fund
3570 Portage Ave.
Winnipeg, MB R3K 0Z8
204-895-1244
Fax: 204-895-1283
info@boydgroup.com
www.boydgroup.com

Company Type: Public
Ticker Symbol: BYD.UN / TSX
Profile: The Boyd Group Income Fund is an unincorporated, open-ended mutual fund trust. It was formed to acquire & hold investments, including a majority interest in The Boyd Group Inc. & its subsidiaries. Boyd Group Inc. operates collision repair centres throughout North America. Boyd Group Income Fund pays monthly distributions to unitholders of record on or around the last business day of the month.
Brock Bulbuck, President & Chief Executive Officer
bulbuck@boydgroup.com
Dan Dott, Chief Financial Officer & Vice-President
dan.dott@boydgroup.com

Canlan Ice Sports Corp.
Western Corporate office
6501 Sprott St.
Burnaby, BC V5B 3B8
604-736-9152
Fax: 604-736-9170
iwu@icesports.com
www.canlanicesports.com
Other Communications: Eastern Corporate Office (Toronto), Phone: 416-661-4423

Company Type: Public
Ticker Symbol: ICE / TSX
Profile: Canlan Ice Sports develops, owns, & operates multi-purpose recreation & entertainment facilities in Canada & the United States. The company's flagship facility is Canlan Ice Sports - Burnaby 8 Rinks, located in Burnaby, British Columbia. Canlan Ice Sports also offers programs such as Canlan Sports Camps, Hockey Academy, Canlan Classic Tournaments, & Skating Academy.
Joey St-Aubin, President & Chief Executive Officer
Michael F. Gellard, Chief Financial Officer & Senior Vice-President
Paul Dillon, Vice-President, Sales, Marketing, & Service
Mark Faubert, Senior Vice-President, Operations

Centric Health Corporation
#2100, 20 Eglinton Ave. West
Toronto, ON M4R 1K8
416-927-8400
Fax: 416-927-8405
info@centrichealth.ca
www.centrichealth.ca

Company Type: Public
Ticker Symbol: CHH / TSX
Profile: Centric Health Corporation is a diversified healthcare services company. Operations include medical assessments, specialty pharmacy services, surgical centres, physiotherapy, rehabilitation & disability management, homecare, & the provision of home medical equipment.
Daniel P. Carriere, President & Chief Executive Officer
Tina Bishai, President, Active Health Eldercare Division
Ron Lowe, President, LifeMark Health
Peter Walkey, Chief Financial Officer
416-619-9417, peter.walkey@centrichealth.ca

CIBT Education Group Inc.
International Head Office
#1200, 777 West Broadway
Vancouver, BC V5Z 4J7
604-871-9909
Fax: 604-871-9919
888-865-0901
info@cibt.net
www.cibt.net
Company Type: Public
Ticker Symbol: MBA / TSX, NYSE Amex
Profile: The education management company is the owner & operator of language, business, & technical colleges. CIBT Education Group's subsidiaries include Sprott-Shaw Degree College, Sprott-Shaw Community College, King George International College, & the CIBT School of Business China. These subsidiaries enable the CIT Education Group to offer Western & Chinese accredited business & management degrees, plus programs in college preparation, information technology, English language training, English teacher certification, automotive maintenance, hotel management, & tourism.
Toby Chu, Vice-Chair, President, & Chief Executive Officer
Dennis Huang, Chief Financial Officer

Cineplex Entertainment LP
1303 Yonge St.
Toronto, ON M4T 2Y9
800-333-0061
www.cineplex.com
Company Type: Private

ClubLink Enterprises Limited
15675 Dufferin St.
King City, ON L7B 1K5
905-841-3730
Fax: 905-841-1134
800-661-1818
memberservices@clublink.ca; jobs@clublink
www.clublink.ca
Other Communications: Investor Relations: invest@clublink.ca
Company Type: Public
Ticker Symbol: CLK / TSX
Profile: ClubLink owns, develops, & operates member golf clubs, daily fee golf clubs, & resorts. The organization's trademark is "ClubLink One Membership More Golf". ClubLink is also involved in tourism, rail, & port operations. The "White Pass & Yukon Route" extends from Skagway, Alaska to Whitehorse, Yukon. The company operates three docks for cruise ships.
K. (Rai) Sahi, President & Chief Executive Officer
Robert Visentin, Chief Financial Officer
905-841-5360, rvisentin@clublink.ca
John Gordon, Director, Communications
905-841-5364, jgordon@clublink.ca

Compass Group Canada
#400, 5560 Explorer Dr.
Mississauga, ON L4W 5M3
905-568-4636
Fax: 905-568-9392
905-568-9392
info@compass-canada.com
www.compass-canada.com
Company Type: Private
Jack MacDonald, CEO
Stephen Kelly, CFO

Extendicare (Canada) Inc. (ECI)
3000 Steeles Ave. East
Markham, ON L3R 9W2
905-470-4000
www.extendicarecanada.com
Company Type: Private
Profile: Extendicare (Canada) Inc. operates senior care facilities. Through its ParaMed Home Health Care division, home health care services are also provided.

Gamehost Inc.
#400, 4406 - 50 Ave.
Red Deer, AB T4N 3Z5
403-346-4545
Fax: 403-340-0683
877-703-4545
info@gamehost.ca
www.gamehost.ca
Company Type: Public
Ticker Symbol: GH, GH.DB / TSX
Profile: The corporation was established under the laws of the Province of Alberta. Gamehost Inc. is involved in the hotel & gaming business. Operations include the Great Northern Casino, Boomtown Casino, & Service Plus Inns & Suites hotel in Alberta. The company also has a 91% controlling interest in Deerfoot Inn & Casino in Calgary.
David J. Will, Chief Executive Officer
Darcy J Will, President
djwill@gamehost.ca
Craig M. Thomas, CMA, Chief Financial Officer
Elston J. Noren, Chief Operations Officer

Garda World Security Corporation
1390, rue Barré
Montréal, QC H3C 1N4
514-281-2811
Fax: 514-281-2860
800-859-1599
info@garda.ca
www.gardaglobal.com
Social Media: www.facebook.com/pages/Garda/241299323038
www.linkedin.com/company/32924
Company Type: Public
Ticker Symbol: GW / TSX
Profile: Garda World Security Corporation's areas of expertise are global risk consulting, cash logistics, investigation, & physical security services. The firm's operations are located in Canada, the United States, Latin America, Europe, Africa, the Middle East, & Asia.
Stéphan Crétier, President & Chief Executive Officer
Marc-André Aubé, P. Eng, MBA, CFA, Chief Operating Officer, Security Solutions
Guy Côté, Chief Security Officer & Vice-President
Patrick Prince, Chief Financial Officer & Senior Vice-President
Patrice Boily, Senior Vice-President
Nathalie de Champlain, Vice-President, Marketing & Communications

GDI Distinction Group Inc.
Corporate Headquarters
695 - 90e av
Montréal, QC H8R 3A4
514-368-1504
Fax: 514-368-1691
montreal.info@gdiservices.ca
www.gdiservices.ca
Company Type: Private
Ticker Symbol: GD
Profile: Through its subsidiaries, GDI provides mechanical maintenance & industrial janitorial services to the commercial real estate industry. It employs more than 9,500 people. GDI's environmental stewardship has been certified EcoLogo.
In 2012, Distinction Group Inc.'s common shares were delisted from the Toronto Stock Exchange, & the company became a private organization.
Claude Bigras, Chief Executive Officer
Réal Paré, President
real.pare@gdiservices.ca
Jocelyn Trottier, CA, CMA, Chief Financial Officer & Executive Vice-Presidnet
jocelyn.trottier@gdiservices.ca

Granville Pacific Capital Corp.
8382 - 156th St.
Surrey, BC V3S 3R7
604-597-7931
Fax: 604-596-3641
info@hhtotalcare.com
Company Type: Public
Ticker Symbol: GE / TSX Venture
Profile: Granville Pacific Capital Corp. was incorporated in 1998. The company focuses on the provision of housing & care for the elderly. Wholly owned subsidiaries include Bear Creek Lodge Ltd. & Evergreen Cottage Corp..
Hendrik Van Ryk, Chief Executive Officer
Andre Van Ryk, Chief Financial Officer

Great Canadian Gaming Corporation
#200, 13775 Commerce Pkwy.
Richmond, BC V6V 2V4
604-303-1000
Fax: 604-279-8605
info@gcgaming.com
www.gcgaming.com
Company Type: Public
Ticker Symbol: GC / TSX
Profile: Great Canadian Gaming Corporation is a gaming & entertainment operator. Operations include entertainment facilities, such as casinos, racetracks, & show theatres. Business is conducted in Nova Scotia, Ontario, British Columbia, & Washington State.
Ross J. McLeod, Chair/CEO
Milton Woensdregt, Chief Financial Officer
Vincent Trudel, Chief Operating Officer
Howard Blank, Vice-President, Media, Entertainment, & Responsible Gaming
hblank@gcgaming.com
Nathan Sellyn, Director, Investor Relations & Corporate Development

HSE Integrated Ltd.
#1000, 630 - 6th Ave. SW
Calgary, AB T2P 0S8
403-266-1833
Fax: 403-266-1834
888-346-8260
information@hseintegrated.com
www.hseintegrated.com
Other Communications: Careers: recruiting@hseintegrated.com
Company Type: Public
Ticker Symbol: HSL / TSX
Profile: HSE Integrated Ltd. supplies onsite health, safety, & environmental services. The company has locations in British Columbia, Alberta, Saskatchewan, Ontario, New Brunswick, Nova Scotia, Newfoundland & Labrador, Michigan, & Texas. In 2012, HSE Integrated Ltd. completed the acquisition of the business assets of the Flint Safety Unit of Flint Field Services Ltd., a subsidiary of Flint Energy Services Ltd.
Thomas Hickey, Chief Executive Officer
Lori McLeod-Hill, Chief Financial Officer
Glenn R. Roberts, Chief Operating Officer

IMRIS Inc.
#100, 1370 Sony Pl.
Winnipeg, MB R3T 1N5
204-480-7070
Fax: 204-480-7071
888-304-0114
info@imris.com
www.imris.com
Other Communications: USA: 952-358-7040; Europe & Middle East: +49 0911 580 80 30
Company Type: Public
Ticker Symbol: IM / TSX, NASDAQ
Profile: IMRIS Inc. provides image guided therapy solutions to clinicians during interventional or surgical procedures, through its VISIUS Surgical Theatre. The cardiovascular, neurosurgical, & cerebrovascular markets are served by VISIUS Surgical Theatres.
David Graves, Chair & Chief Executive Officer
Kelly McNeill, Chief Financial Officer & Executive Vice-President, Finance & Administration
Meir Dahan, Executive Vice-President, Research & Development
Mark Reade, Executive Vice-President, Global Sales
Brad Woods, Director, Investor Relations & Corporate Communications
204-480-7094, bwoods@imris.com

Intermap Technologies Corporation
#400, 8310 South Valley Hwy.
Englewood, CO 80112 USA
303-708-0955
Fax: 303-708-0952
info@intermap.com
www.intermap.com
Company Type: Public
Ticker Symbol: IMP / TSX
Brian Bullock, Chair, President & CEO
Richard Mohr, Senior Vice-President & CFO

K-Bro Linen Inc.
15023 - 123 Ave.
Edmonton, AB T5V 1J7
780-453-5218
Fax: 780-455-6676
inquiries@k-brolinen.com
www.k-brolinen.com
Company Type: Public
Ticker Symbol: KBL / TSX
Profile: K-Bro Linen Inc. is involved in the operation of laundry & linen processing facilities. It serves industrial & commercial sectors, such as hospitality & healthcare. Processing facilities are located in Montréal, Québec, Toronto, Calgary, Edmonton, Vancouver, & Victoria. Brands include Les Buanderies Dextraze, Buanderie HMR, K-Bro Linen Systems Inc.
Linda McCurdy, President & Chief Executive Officer
Christopher T.J. Burrows, Chief Financial Officer & Vice-President

LAB Research Inc.
445, boul Armand-Frappier
Laval, QC H4V 4B3
450-973-2240
Fax: 450-973-2259
ir@labresearch.com
www.labresearch.com
Company Type: Public
Ticker Symbol: LRI / TSX
Luc Mainville, CEO
Louise Bussieres, Chief Financial Officer

Leisureworld Senior Care Corporation
#200, 302 Town Centre Blvd.
Markham, ON L3R 0E8
905-477-4006
Fax: 905-415-7623
855-895-3801
info@leisureworld.ca; investors@leisurewo
www.leisureworld.ca
Other Communications: Investor, Phone: 416-447-4740, ext. 232
Company Type: Public
Ticker Symbol: LW / TSX
Profile: Leisureworld Senior Care Corporation is a licensed long-term care provider, with operations in Ontario. The corporation owns 26 long-term care homes, 3 retirement residences, & one independent living residence. Subsidiaries include Ontario Long Term Care & Preferred Health Care Services
David Cutler, Chief Executive Officer
Manny DiFilippo, Chief Financial Officer
Paul Rushforth, Chief Operating Officer
Lisa Egan, Vice-President, Communications
Daniel Neufeld, Vice-President, Information Systems

Lions Gate Entertainment Corp.
#2200, 1055 West Hastings St.
Vancouver, BC V6E 2E9
604-983-5555
Fax: 604-983-5554
pwilkes@lgf.com
www.lgf.com
Company Type: Public
Ticker Symbol: LGF / NYSE
Profile: Lions Gate Entertainment Corp. is a developer, producer, & distributor of television, motion picture, family entertainment, home entertainment, video-on-demand, & digitally delivered content. The company is made up of the following operating divisions: Motion Pictures, Television, Animation, & Studio Facilities.
Jon Feltheimer, Co-Chair/CEO
Steve Beeks, President/Co-COO
Joe Drake, President, Motion Picture Group & Co-COO
Kevin Beggs, President, Television Programming & Production
Jim Keegan, Chief Financial Officer
Wayne Levin, General Counsel & Exec. Vice-President, Corporate Operations
Peter D. Wilkes, Contact, Lionsgate Investor & Corporate Inquiries
pwilkes@lionsgate.com

Medical Facilities Corporation (MFC)
Bay Adelaide Centre
#3400, 333 Bay St.
Toronto, ON M5H 2S7
416-848-7380
877-402-7162
medicalfacilitiescorp.ca
Company Type: Public
Ticker Symbol: DR / TSX
Profile: Medical Facilities Corporation owns controlling interests in four specialty surgical hospitals in Oklahoma & South Dakota. The corporation also owns interests in an ambulatory surgery center, located in California. The specialty surgical hospitals derive revenue from fees charged for use of the facilities.
Donald Schellpfeffer, Chief Executive Officer
Larry Teuber, President
Michael Salter, CA, CPA, Chief Financial Officer

MFC Industrial Ltd. (MFC)
#1620, 400 Burrard St.
Vancouver, BC V6C 3A6
604-683-8286
Fax: 604-683-3205
www.mfcindustrial.com
Company Type: Public
Ticker Symbol: MIL / NYSE
Profile: In 2011, Terra Nova Royalty Corporation changed its name to MFC Industrial Ltd.. The global commodity supply chain company sources & delivers materials & commodities to clients. MFC Industrial Ltd. specializes in the financing & risk management business areas.
Michael Smith, Chair & Chief Executive Officer
Rene Randall, Contact, Corporate Information
rrandall@bmgmt.com

Morneau Shepell Ltd.
Tower One
#700, 895 Don Mills Rd.
Toronto, ON M3C 1W3
416-445-2700
Fax: 416-445-7989
info@morneaushepell.com
www.morneaushepell.com
Other Communications: Media: media@morneaushepell.com
Social Media: twitter.com/Morneau_Shepell
Company Type: Public
Ticker Symbol: MSI / TSX
Profile: Morneau Shepell offers human resource consulting & outsourcing services. The company has more than 2,500 employees to provide services to organization in Canada & around the world.
Alan Torrie, President & Chief Executive Officer
René Beaudoin, Chief Information Officer
Pierre Chamberland, Chief Operating Officer & Executive Vice-President, Administrative Solutions
Scott Milligan, Chief Financial Officer & Executive Vice-President

Lorraine Coady, Executive Vice-President, Human Resources & Organizational Development
Karen Seward, Executive Vice-President, Business Development & Marketing
Lynn Korbak, General Counsel & Corporate Secretary

New Look Eyewear Inc.
#3438, 1, Place Ville-Marie
Montréal, QC H3B 3N6
418-624-6100
Fax: 418-624-4040
800-463-5665
www.newlook.ca
Company Type: Public
Ticker Symbol: BCI / TSX
Profile: In 2010, Benvest New Look Income Fund was converted into a corporation named New Look Eyewear Inc.. The eye care organization operates laboratories & stores in eastern Canada.
Martial Gagné, President
Jean-Luc Deschamps, Chief Financial Officer & Senior Vice-President
514-904-5665
Claire Boulanger, Vice-President, Real Estate & Development
Mario Pageau, Vice-President, Optical Products & Services

Newalta Corporation
211 - 11th Ave. SW
Calgary, AB T2R 0C6
403-806-7000
Fax: 403-806-7348
800-774-8466
info@newalta.com
www.newalta.com
Other Communications: Service, E-mail: customerservice@newalta.com
Company Type: Public
Ticker Symbol: NAL / TSX
Profile: Newalta Corporation is involved in the product recovery business in order to reduce the environmental impact of industrial waste. The corporation has 85 facilities throughout Canada & employs approximately 2,000 people.
Alan P. Cadotte, President & Chief Executive Officer
Michael Borys, Chief Financial Officer & Executive Vice-President
Peter Dugandzic, Executive Vice-President
Criag Wilkie, Executive Vice-President
Doug Pecharsky, Senior Vice-President, Onsite Operations
Took Whiteley, General Counsel & Senior Vice-President, Business Development
Linda Dietsche, Vice-President, Finance
Harry Wells, Vice-President, Technical Development
Andre Cyr, Executive Director, Information Technology
Robbin Dawe, Executive Director, Technical Development
Stephen Lewis, Executive Director, Corporate Communications & Community Relations
Cam MacNaughton, Executive Director, Treasury
Anne Plasterer, Executive Director, Investor Relations
Rhonda Rudnitski, Executive Director, Environment, Health, & Saftey

Park Lawn Corporation
57 Linelle St.
Toronto, ON M2N 2J4
416-231-1462
Fax: 416-233-8155
www.parklawnlp.ca
Social Media: www.facebook.com/ParkLawnLP
twitter.com/#!/Park_Lawn_LP
www.linkedin.com/company/park-lawn-limited-partnership
Company Type: Public
Ticker Symbol: PLC / TSX Venture
Profile: In 2011, Park Lawn Income Trust converted from an income trust to a corporation. Park Lawn Corporation indirectly holds six cemeteries in the Greater Toronto Area of Ontario, plus Services Memorables Harmonia Inc. located in Quebec City. The corporation also has an interest in Bloorpark Developments Inc.
Frank Mills, Chief Executive Officer
416-231-1462
Larry Boland, Chief Financial Officer, Treasurer, & Secretary

Points International Ltd.
171 John St., 5th Fl.
Toronto, ON M5T 1X3
416-595-0000
Fax: 016-595-6444
info@points.com
www.points.com
Social Media: www.facebook.com/pointsfans
twitter.com/pointsadvisor
Company Type: Public
Ticker Symbol: PTS / TSX
Profile: Points International Ltd. owns & operates the loyalty reward management program platform, www.Points.com. The platform permits users to redeem, exchange, & trade miles & rewards.
Robert MacLean, Chief Executive Officer
Anthony Lam, Chief Financial Officer

Progressive Waste Solutions Ltd.
Corporate Office
400 Applewood Cres., 2nd Fl.
Vaughan, ON L4K 0C3
905-532-7510
Fax: 905-532-7580
corporate.communications@progressivewaste
www.progressivewaste.com
Company Type: Public
Ticker Symbol: BIN / TSX, NYSE
Profile: Progressive Waste Solutions Ltd. is a full-service waste management company. It offers non-hazardous solid waste collection & landfill disposal services. The company serves residential, municipal, commercial, & industrial customers located in six Canadian provinces & the District of Columbia in the United States. Brand BFI Canada, Waste Services, & IESI.
Joseph Quarin, Vice-Chair & Chief Executive Officer
William P. Hulligan, President & Chief Operating Officer
Thomas J. Cowee, Chief Financial Officer & Vice-President
Izzie Abrams, Vice-President, Corporate Development & Government Relations
Chaya Cooperberg, Vice-President, Investor Relations & Corporate Communications
905-532-7517, chaya.cooperberg@progressivewaste.com

Pulse Seismic Inc.
Head Office
#2400, 639 - 5th Ave. SW
Calgary, AB T2P 0M9
403-237-5559
Fax: 403-531-0688
877-460-5559
info@pulseseismic.com
www.pulseseismic.com
Company Type: Public
Ticker Symbol: PSD / TSX
Profile: Pulse Seismic Inc. is engaged in the acquisition, marketing, & licensing of 2D & 3D seismic data. The company's data library covers key areas in the Northwest Territories, Yukon, northeastern British Columbia, Alberta, Saskatchewan, Manitoba, & Montana. Pulse Seismic serves the western Canadian energy sector.
Douglas Cutts, President & Chief Executive Officer
Brent Gale, Chief Operating Officer & Senior Vice-President
Pamela Wicks, Chief Financial Officer & Vice-President, Finance

Norman Hall, Corporate Secretary

Pure Technologies Ltd.
#300, 705 - 11th Ave. SW
Calgary, AB T2R 0E3
403-266-6794
Fax: 403-266-6570
855-280-7873
www.puretechnologiesltd.com
Other Communications: Investor Relations, Phone: 403-266-6794
Social Media: twitter.com/PTLNews
www.linkedin.com/company/573861
Company Type: Public
Ticker Symbol: PUR / TSX
Profile: The asset management technology & service company developed technologies for inspecting, monitoring, & managing critical infrastructure throughout the world. Physical infratructure include buildings, bridges, & water & hydrocarbon pipelines.
Peter O. Paulson, Chief Executive Officer & Chief Technology Officer
John F. Elliott, P.Eng., President & Chief Operating Officer
Karen Keebler, CA, Chief Financial Officer & Corporate Secretary

Superior Plus Corp.
#1400, 840 - 7th Ave. SW
Calgary, AB T2P 3G2
403-218-2970
Fax: 403-218-2973
866-490-7587
info@superiorplus.com
www.superiorplus.ca

Company Type: Public
Ticker Symbol: SPB / TSX
Profile: Superior Plus Corp. consists of the following businesses: Specialty Chemical, including manufacturing & selling; Energy Services, involving the distribution of propane & distillates; & Construction Products Distribution.
Luc Desjardins, President & Chief Executive Officer
Douglas Elliott, President, Superior Propane
Greg L. McCamus, President, U.S. Refined Fuels & Superior Energy Management
Paul S. Timmons, President, Specialty Chemicals
Paul J. Vanderberg, President, Construction Products Distribution
Wayne M. Bingham, Chief Financial Officer & Executive Vice-President
403-218-2951, Fax: 403-218-2973, wbingham@superiorplus.com
Eric McFadden, Executive Vice-President, Business Development
Dave Tims, Senior Vice-President, Commodity Portfolio Management
Jay Bachman, Treasurer & Vice-President, Investor Relations
403-218-2957, Fax: 403-218-2973, jbachman@superiorplus.com

YM BioSciences Inc.
Building 11
#400, 5045 Orbitor Dr.
Mississauga, ON L4W 4Y4
905-629-9761
Fax: 905-629-4959
ir@ymbiosciences.com
www.ymbiosciences.com

Company Type: Public
Ticker Symbol: YM / TSX, AMEX
David G.P. Allan, Chairman & CEO

Steel & Metal

ADF Group Inc.
300, rue Henry-Bessemer
Terrebonne, QC J6Y 1T3
450-965-1911
Fax: 450-965-8558
800-965-8558
infos@adfgroup.com
www.adfgroup.com

Company Type: Public
Ticker Symbol: DRX / TSX
Profile: ADF Group Inc. specializes in the design, engineering, fabrication, & installation of steel superstructures, architectural, & miscellaneous metals. The company serves the non-residential construction market.
Jean Paschini, Chair & Chief Executive Officer
Pierre Paschini, P.Eng., President & Chief Operating Officer
Jean-François Boursier, Chief Financial Officer
Kathleen Ryffranck, Director, Public Relations

Bri-Chem Corp.
#15, 53016 Hwy. 60
Acheson, AB T7X 5A7
780-455-8667
Fax: 780-451-4420
info@brichem.com; ir@brichem.com; hr@bric
www.brichem.com

Company Type: Public
Ticker Symbol: BRY / TSX
Profile: Bri-Chem Corp. was formed in 1985. Its divisions are the Drilling Fluid Division & the Steel Pipe Division. The Drilling Fluid Division supplies drilling fluids to the oil & gas industry, while the Steel Pipe Division manuafactures & provides steel pipe for the energy industry.
Don Caron, Chief Executive Officer
Trent Abraham, President, Fluids Division
Neil Rasmussen, President, Steel Division
Jason Theiss, CA, Chief Financial Officer
jtheiss@brichem.com

Canam Group Inc.
270, ch du Tremblay
Boucherville, QC J4B 5X9
450-641-4000
Fax: 450-641-4001
infocanamcanada@canam.ws
www.canamgroup.ws
Other Communications: Shareholders: infoinvestors@canamgroup.ws
Social Media: www.facebook.com/groupecanam
twitter.com/GroupeCanam
www.linkedin.com/company/66983?trk=tyah

Company Type: Public
Ticker Symbol: CAM / TSX
Profile: Canam Group Inc. is engaged in the design & fabrication of construction products & solutions. The company operates over twenty-five engineering offices & manufacturing plants in Canada, the United States, Romania, India, & China.
Marc Dutil, President & Chief Executive Officer
Sam Blatchford, President, Canam Steel Corporation
Mario Bernard, Chief Manufacturing Officer & Executive Vice-President
Charles Pinel, Chief Financial Officer & Vice-President
François Bégin, Vice-President, Communications
francois.begin@canamgroup.ws
Michael Burnet, Vice-President, Purchasing
Louis Guertin, Secretary & Vice-President, Legal Affairs

Essar Steel Algoma
105 West St.
Sault Ste. Marie, ON P6A 7B4
705-945-2351
Fax: 705-945-2203
www.algoma.com

Company Type: Private

Martinrea International Inc.
3210 Langstaff Rd.
Vaughan, ON L4K 5B2
289-982-3000
info@martinrea.com; HR@martinrea.com
www.martinrea.com
Other Communications: Investor Information: Investor@martinrea.com

Company Type: Public
Ticker Symbol: MRE
Profile: Martinrea International Inc. specializes in the production of metal parts, assemblies & modules, & fluid management systems. The company supplies the automotive industry & other industrial sectors. Divisions are located in Canada, the United States, Mexico, & Europe.
Fred Jaekel, Chief Executive Officer
Nick Orlando, President/CFO

Russel Metals Inc.
#210, 1900 Minnesota Ct.
Mississauga, ON L5N 3C9
905-816-5178
Fax: 905-819-7409
info@russelmetals.com
www.russelmetals.com
Other Communications: Investor Relations Phone: 905-816-5178
Company Type: Public
Ticker Symbol: RUS
Profile: The metal processor & distributor operates in North America. The company implemented environmental standards & an ongoing audit process.
Edward (Bud) M. Siegel, President & Chief Executive Officer
Brian R. Hedges, Chief Operating Officer & Executive Vice-President
Marion E. Britton, Vice-President & Chief Financial Officer
Lesley M.S. Coleman, Vice President, Controller, & Assistant Secretary
Maureen A. Kelly, Vice-President, Information Systems

Timminco Limited
Sun Life Financial Tower
#2401, 150 King St. West
Toronto, ON M5H 1J9
416-364-5171
Fax: 416-364-3451
info@timminco.com
www.timminco.com

Company Type: Public
Ticker Symbol: TIM
Heinz C. Schimmelbusch, Chairman/CEO
Robert J. Dietrich, CFO & Exec. Vice-President, Finance

Tree Island Wire Income Fund
3933 Boundary Rd.
Richmond, BC V6V 1T8
604-524-3744
Fax: 604-524-2657
800-663-0955
www.treeisland.com
Company Type: Public
Ticker Symbol: TIL / TSX
Profile: Tree Island Wire Income Fund is an unincorporated open ended limited purpose trust. It owns Tree Island Industries Ltd.. The company serves the following industries: residential construction, commercial construction, industrial, & agriculture. Products include the following: bright, galvanized, & stainless steel wire; fabricated wire products, such as fencing; stucco; engineered structural mesh; & bulk, packaged, & collated nails.
Daniel McAtee, President/CEO
Brian Irving, Vice-President, Finance
BIrving@treeisland.com
Dale Derischebourg, Vice-President, Global Supply Chain
Stephen Ogden, Vice-President, Engineering & Technology
Ken Stuttaford, Vice-President, Sales & Marketing

Velan Inc.
7007, ch de la Côte-de-Liesse
Montréal, QC H4T 1G2
514-748-7743
Fax: 514-748-8635
sales@velan.com
www.velan.com
Company Type: Public
Ticker Symbol: VLN / TSX
Profile: Velan Inc. manufactures industrial steel valves. Manufacturing plants are located in Canada, the United States, Europe, & Asia. Velan valves are used in numerous industries, such as oil & gas, chemical & petrochemical, pulp & paper, mining, & power generation. The company also offers aftermarket services.
A.K. Velan, Chief Executive Officer
Tom C. Velan, President
John Ball, Chief Financial Officer
jball@velanvalve.com
Tracy Fairchild, Manager, Communications

Vicwest Inc.
1296 South Service Rd. West
Oakville, ON L6L 5T7
905-925-2252
Fax: 905-825-1090
IR@vicwestinc.com
www.vicwestinc.com
Company Type: Public
Ticker Symbol: VIC / TSX
Profile: Vicwest Inc. manufactures & distributes building construction products, as well as steel containment products for agricultural grain, fertilizer, & liquid storage.
Colin Osborne, President & Chief Executive Officer
905-469-5700
Kent Harris, Chief Financial Officer
905-469-5706, Fax: 905-825-1090
André Granger, Vice-President & General Manager, Westeel
Emile Mabro, P.Eng., MBA, Vice-President & General Manager, Vicwest Building Products

Yalian Steel Corporation
Canada Office
#1010, 1055 West Hastings St.
Vancouver, BC V6E 2E9
604-696-6388
Fax: 604-648-8100
info@yaliansteel.com
www.yaliansteel.com
Company Type: Public
Ticker Symbol: YL / TSX Venture
Profile: Yalian Steel Corporation produces Longitudinally Submerged Arc Welded steel pipe. The corporation serves the energy transportation infrastructure market.
In addition to its office in Vancouver, British Columbia, Yalian Steel also has a facility located in China at the following address: No. 66 Shuangtang Road West, Weiyang District, Yangzhou, Jiangsu, China 225008.
Xia Xu, Chief Executive Officer
Helen Lu, Chief Financial Officer

Textiles, Apparel & Leather

Bauer Performance Sports Ltd.
100 Domain Dr.
Exter, NH 03833

603-610-5805
Fax: 603-292-1505
investors@bauerperformancesports.com
www.bauerperformancesports.com
Other Communications: Media Inquiries: media@bauerperformancesports.com

Company Type: Public
Ticker Symbol: BAU / TSX
Profile: Bauer Performance Sports develops & manufactures ice hockey, roller hockey, & lacrosse equipment, plus related apparel. Brands include Bauer Hockey, Mission Roller Hockey, & Maverik Lacrosse.
Kevin Davis, President & Chief Executive Officer
Amir Rosenthal, Chief Financial Officer
Paul Gibson, Executive Vice-President, Product Creation & Supply Chain
Paul Dachsteiner, Vice-Presidemt, Information Services

Danier Leather Inc.
Customer Service
2650 St. Clair Ave. West
Toronto, ON M6N 1M2

416-762-8175
Fax: 416-762-4570
877-932-6437
customerservice@danier.com; marketing@dan
www.danier.com
Other Communications: French Services: 877-532-6437; Careers: jobs@danier.com

Company Type: Public
Ticker Symbol: DL / TSX
Profile: Danier Leather specializes in the design, manufacture, distribution, & retail of leather apparel & accessories. PRoducts are available at more than 90 stores with the Danier brand name.
Jeffrey Wortsman, President & Chief Executive Officer
leather@danier.com
Bryan Tatoff, Chief Financial Officer
bryan@danier.com
Guia Lopez, Chief Sourcing Officer
guial@danier.com
Cris Ruivo, Vice-President, Store Operations
crisr@danier.com

Gildan Activewear Inc.
600, boul de Maisonneuve ouest, 33 étage
Montréal, QC H3A 3J2

514-735-2023
Fax: 514-735-6810
866-755-2023
info@gildan.com; investors@gildan.com
www.gildan.com
Other Communications: Customer Service, Toll-Free: 800-668-8337, ext. 4115

Company Type: Public
Ticker Symbol: GIL / TSX, NYSE
Profile: Gildan Activewear manufactures & markets activewear, athletic socks, & underwear. The company serves both North American & international markets.
Glenn J. Chamandy, President & Chief Executive Officer
Michael R. Hoffman, President, Gildan Activewear SRL
Laurence G. Sellyn, Exec. Vice-President/Chief Financial & Administrative Officer, Finance
514-343-8805, lsellyn@gildan.com
Benito Masi, Executive Vice-President, Manufacturing
Georges Sam Yu Sum, Executive Vice-President, Operations
Sophie Argiriou, Director, Investor Communications
514-343-8815, sargiriou@gildan.com
Geneviève Gosselin, Director, Corporate Communications
514-343-8814, ggosselin@gildan.com

Intertape Polymer Group Inc.
999, boul Cavendish, 2e étage
Montréal, QC H4M 2X5

514-731-7591
Fax: 514-731-5039
info@intertapeipg.com
www.intertapepolymer.com

Company Type: Public
Ticker Symbol: ITP / TSX
Melbourne F. Yull, Chair/CEO
Jim Bob Carpenter, President, Woven Products Procurement
Victor DiTommaso, CFO
James A. Jackson, Vice-President/Chief Information Officer

Warnaco of Canada
20600 Clark Graham Ave.
Baie-D'Urfé, QC H9X 4B6

514-457-5554
Fax: 514-457-5558
800-465-4764
www.warnaco.com

Company Type: Private

Transportation & Travel

407 ETR
Customer Service Centre
6300 Steeles Ave. West
Woodbridge, ON L4H 1J1

Fax: 905-264-5315
888-407-0407
www.407etr.com

Company Type: Private
Profile: 407 ETR is an toll highway that stretches from Burlington to Pickering, Ontario.
Jose Tamariz, President & Chief Executive Officer
Robert Ives, Chief Information Officer
Mike Miller, Chief Customer Operations Officer
Louis-M. St-Maurice, Chief Financial Officer

Air Canada
7373, boul Côte-Vertu ouest
Montréal, QC H4S 1Z3

514-422-5000
Fax: 514-422-5909
888-247-2262
shareholders.actionnaires@aircanada.ca
www.aircanada.com
Social Media: www.facebook.com/aircanada
twitter.com/aircanada

Company Type: Public
Ticker Symbol: AC / TSX
Profile: The Canadian-based international air carrier provides scheduled & chartered air transportation for both passengers & cargo. Air Canada serves over 180 destinations on five continents.
Calin Rovinescu, President/CEO
Michael Rousseau, Exec. Vice-President/CFO
Bill Bredt, Exec. Vice-President/COO
Lise Fournel, Chief Information Officer & Sr. Vice-President, E-Commerce
Alan D. Butterfield, Vice-President, Air Canada Maintenance & Engineering

Algoma Central Corporation
Executive Office
#600, 63 Church St.
St Catharines, ON L2R 3C4

905-687-7888
Fax: 905-687-7840
www.algonet.com
Other Communications: Sault Ste. Marie Head Office, Phone: 705-946-7200

Company Type: Public
Ticker Symbol: ALC / TSX
Profile: Algoma Central Corporation is a Canadian-flag ship owner on the Great Lakes - St. Lawrence Waterway. The company owns both dry-bulk carriers & product tankers. As well as the operation of vessels, ship & diesel engine repair & fabrication are part of Algoma Central's operations.
In addition to shipping, Algoma Central Corporation also owns Algoma Central Hotels & Algoma Central Properties Inc.. These businesses own & manage commercial real estate properties in St Catharines, Waterloo, & Sault Ste. Marie.
Greg D. Wight, FCA, President & Chief Executive Officer
905-687-7850
Peter D. Winkley, CA, Chief Financial Officer & Vice-President, Finance
905-687-7897
Al J. Vanagas, C.E.T., Sr. Vice-President, Technical
Wayne A. Smith, Sr. Vice-President, Commercial
William S. Vaughan, B.C.L., Secretary
Radcliffe R. Latimer, Member, Environmental, Health, & Safety Committee

AutoCanada Inc.
#200, 15505 Yellowhead Trail
Edmonton, AB T5H 1E5

780-732-3135
Fax: 780-447-0651
www.autocan.ca
Social Media: www.facebook.com/autocan
twitter.com/autocanada

Company Type: Public
Ticker Symbol: ACQ / TSX
Profile: AutoCanada is an automobile dealership group. It operates franchised dealerships in Nova Scotia, New Brunswick, Ontario, Manitoba, Alberta, & British Columbia.
Patrick J. (Pat) Priestner, Chief Executive Officer
Tom Orysiuk, President
780-732-3135, president@autocan.ca
Stephen R.E. Rose, General Counsel, Secretary, & Exeuctive Vice-President, Corporate Services
Jeff Christie, CA, Vice-President, Finance
780-732-7164, jchristie@autocan.ca

Automodular Corporation
Head Office
#6, 225 Salem Rd. South
Ajax, ON L1Z 0B1

905-619-4200
Fax: 905-619-9466
info@Automodular.com; hr@Automodular.net
www.automodular.com
Other Communications: Investors: invest@Automodular.com

Company Type: Public
Ticker Symbol: AM / TSX
Profile: Automodular Corporation is engaged in automotive parts sequencing & sub-assembly. Components & modules are installed in vehicles made by North American Original Equipment Manufacturers in Canada.
Christopher S. Nutt, President & Chief Executive Officer
Melinda Diebel, Chief Financial Officer & Vice-President, Finance
Travis Doyle, Vice-President, Program Launches
James Gazo, Vice-President, Operations
Diane C. Erlingher, Corporate Secretary
derlingher@automodular.com

Bombardier Inc.
800, boul René-Lévesque ouest
Montréal, QC H3B 1Y8

514-861-9481
Fax: 514-861-7769
investors@bombardier.com
www.bombardier.com

Company Type: Public
Ticker Symbol: BBD.A, BBD.B / TSX
Profile: Bombardier Inc. manufactures transportation solutions, such as rail equipment & commercial aircraft. Bombardier is listed as an index component to the Dow Jones Sustainability World & North America indexes.
Pierre Beaudoin, President & Chief Executive Officer
Guy C. Hachey, President/COO, Bombardier Aerospace
André Navarri, President/COO, Bombardier Transportation
Pierre Alary, Sr. Vice-President/CFO
John Paul Macdonald, Sr. Vice-President, Human Resources & Public Affairs
André Bérard, Chair, Finance & Risk Management Committe

CAE Inc.
8585, ch de Côte-de-Liesse
Montréal, QC H4T 1G6

514-341-6780
Fax: 514-341-7699
866-999-6223
investor.relations@cae.com; media.relatio
www.cae.com
Other Communications: Military Customers: militarycustomerservices@cae.com

Company Type: Public
Ticker Symbol: CAE / TSX, NYSE
Profile: CAE Inc. serves the civil aviation & defense forces, through the provision of simulation & modelling technologies, as well as integrated training solutions. The company's civil aviation & military training centres are located throughout the world.
CAE Inc. has been granted the BOMA Go Green plan certification, & has implemented environmental programs such as the management of residual materials, recycling, pollution prevention, & residue exchange.
Marc Parent, President & Chief Executive Officer
Martin Gagné, Group President, Military Simulation Products, Training, & Services
Jeff Roberts, Group President, Civil Simulation Products, Training, & Services
Stéphane Lefebvre, Chief Financial Officer & Vice-President, Finance
Andrew Arnovitz, Vice-President, Investor Relations & Strategy
514-734-5760, andrew.arnovitz@cae.com
Nathalie Bourque, Vice-President, Public Affairs & Global Communications
514-734-5788, nathalie.bourque@cae.com

Canadian Helicopters Group Inc./ Hélicoptères Canadiens
Also Known As: CH Group
1215, montee Pilon
Les Cèdres, QC J7T 1G1
450-452-3000
Fax: 450-452-3057
www.canadianhelicopters.ca

Company Type: Public
Ticker Symbol: CHL / TSX
Profile: Helicopter transportation & related support services are provided by Canadian Helicopters Group. The Group operates under the following brands: CHL (Canadian Helicopters Limited) & HNZ Global. Fixed primary operations are located in Canada, southeast Asia, Australia, & New Zealand. Canadian Helicopters also provides demand support operations in Antarctica & Afghanistan.
Don Wall, CPA, President & Chief Executive Officer
Robert Lafleur, Chief Financial Officer & Vice-President
Mark Olson, MBA, Vice-President, Operations
Ed Bergnach, Vice-President & Director, Maintenance
Walter Heneghan, Vice-President, Safety & Quality

Canadian National Railway Company (CN)
935, rue de la Gauchetière ouest
Montréal, QC H3B 2M9
514-399-6591
Fax: 514-399-4296
888-888-5909
CNON@cn.ca (ON); CNSKMB@cn.ca (SK & MB)
www.cn.ca
Other Communications: BC: CNBC@cn.ca; CNPQATL@cn.ca (QC & Maritimes)
Social Media: www.facebook.com/CNrail
www.linkedin.com/company/cn

Company Type: Public
Ticker Symbol: CNR / TSX
Profile: Crossing the North American continent with approximately 20,600 route miles of track, the Canadian National Railway Company serves ports on the Atlantic, Pacific, & Gulf coasts. The company employs approximately 21,967 people across Canada & the United States.
E. Hunter Harrison, President/CEO
Claude Mongeau, Exec. Vice-President/CFO
Sean Finn, Chief Legal Officers & Exec. Vice-President, Corporate Services
Fred Grigsby, Sr. Vice-President & Chief Information Officer
Jim Bright, Vice-President, Information Technology
Paul C. Millwe, Chief Safety & Officer, Transportation

Canadian Pacific Railway Limited (CP)
Gulf Canada Square
#500, 401 - 9th Ave. SW
Calgary, AB T2P 4Z4
403-319-7000
888-333-6370
investor@cpr.ca
www.cpr.ca
Other Communications: Sales inquiries & rates: 1-877-277-7283
Company Type: Public
Ticker Symbol: CP / TSX, NYSE
Profile: The transcontinental carrier operates in North America. Canadian Pacific provides freight transportation services, supply chain expertise, & logistics solutions. The company incorporates technology & environmental practices for safety & efiiciency.
Fred J. Green, President & Chief Executive Officer
Kathryn McQuade, Exec. Vice-President/CFO
Brock Winter, Sr. Vice-President, Operations
Janet Weiss, Assistant Vice-President, Investor Relations
Michael W. Wright, Chair, Health, Safety, Security & Environment Committee

Cargojet Inc.
#5&6, 350 Britannia Rd. East
Mississauga, ON L4Z 1X9
905-501-7373
Fax: 905-501-8228
www.cargojet.com
Other Communications: Human Resources: hr@cargojet.com
Social Media: cs@cargojet.com (customer service)
Company Type: Public
Ticker Symbol: CJT / TSX
Profile: Cargojet provides overnight air cargo services across North America.
Ajay K. Virmani, President & Chief Executive Officer
Jamie Porteous, Executive Vice-President, Sales & Service
jporteous@cargojet.com
Roger Arbour, Vice-President, National Accounts & Network Planning
rarbour@cargojet.com
Pauline Dhillon, Vice-President, Marketing, Public & Government Relations
pdhillon@cargojet.com
Gord Johnston, Vice-President, International & Strategic Alliances
gjohnston@cargojet.com

Chorus Aviation Inc.
First Canadian Place
PO Box 50, #6100, 2011 King St. West
Toronto, ON M5X 1B8
902-873-5094
Fax: 902-873-2098
investorsinfo@flyjazz.ca
www.chorusaviation.ca
Company Type: Public
Ticker Symbol: CHR.B / TSX
Profile: Incorporated in September 2010, Chorus Aviation is the successor to Jazz Air Income Fund. Jazz Aviation LP is wholly owned by Chorus Aviation.
Joseph D. Randell, Chief Executive Officer & President
Rick Flynn, Chief Financial Officer
Barbara Snowdon, General Counsel & Corporate Secretary
Scott Tapson, Vice-President, Business Development

Contrans Group Inc.
PO Box 1669, 1179 Ridgeway Rd.
Woodstock, ON N4S 0A9
519-421-4600
info@contrans.ca
www.contrans.ca
Company Type: Public
Ticker Symbol: CSS / TSX
Profile: Through its subsidiaries, Contrans Group Inc. provides freight transportation services. Shippers are offered van, flatbed, liquid tank, dry tank, & dump trailing equipment services. The company employs approximately 1,000.
Stan G. Dunford, Chair & Chief Executive Officer
Gregory W. Rumble, President & Chief Operating Officer
Jamie Clark, Chief Financial Officer & Vice-President, Finance
Todd Jenereaux, Vice-President, Corporate Development
Norman McDonough, Risk & Compliance, Vice-President
Jamie Miller, Secretary-Treasurer
Tom Masterson, Corporate Controller
Darren Levine, Director, Information Technology

Discovery Air Inc.
PO Box 1530, 126 Bristol Ave.
Yellowknife, NT X1A 2P2
Fax: 867-873-5350
867-873-5351
www.discoveryair.com
Other Communications: 866-903-3247
Social Media: www.facebook.com/pages/Discovery-Air/325565460607?ref=ts
Company Type: Public
Ticker Symbol: DA / TSX
Profile: Incorporated in 2004, Discovery Air Inc. created an alliance of aviation companies to provide safe, professional air transportation in selected niche markets. The following are Discovery Air's subsidiaries: Discovery Air Technical Services, Great Slave Helicopters Ltd., Discovery Mining Services, Air Tindi, Discovery Air Fire Services, Top Aces, & Discovery Air Innovation.
David A. Jennings, President & Chief Executive Officer
Richard H.L. Jankura, Chief Financial Officer
R. Shawn Clarke, Chief Operating Officer
Chuck Parker, Exec. Vice-President, Northern Operations
Tammie L. Ashton, Vice-President & General Counsel
Wade MacBain, Director, Investor Relations
519-951-3580, wadem@discoveryair.com

Ford Motor Company of Canada, Limited
PO Box 2000, The Canadian Rd.
Oakville, ON L6J 5E4
Fax: 905-845-7016
800-565-3673
www.ford.ca
Company Type: Private
David Mondragon, President/CEO

Global Railway Industries Ltd.
155, boul Montréal-Toronto
Lachine, QC H8S 1B4
514-634-3139
Fax: 514-634-3932
info@globalrailway.com
www.globalrailway.com
Company Type: Public
Ticker Symbol: GBI.H / NEX
Profile: Founded in 1997, Global Railway Industries Ltd. is a designer, manufacturer, & marketer of railway equipment. The company is also engaged in remanufacturing locomotives & repairing rail cars. Global Railway Industries Ltd.'s products are provided through its operating subsidiaries: CAD Railway Industries Ltd. in Lachine, Quebec & Prime Railway Services in Courtice, Ontario. The rail product company employs approximately 265 to serve the North American railway industry.
Fausto Levy, President & Chief Executive Officer
flevy@cadrail.ca
Ross Corcoran, Chief Financial Officer & Vice-President
rcorcoran@cadrail.ca
William (Bill) Sturtz, Chief Operating Officer
Peter Spence, Secretary

Groupe Robert/ Robert Group
20, boul Marie-Victorin
Boucherville, QC J4B 1V5
514-521-1011
800-361-8281
information@robert.ca
www.robert.ca
Company Type: Private
Barry Normet, Regional Vice President
416-642-3731, bnormet@travelers.com

Honda Canada Inc.
715 Milner Ave.
Toronto, ON M1B 2K8
416-284-8110
Fax: 416-286-1322
888-946-6329
www.honda.ca
Company Type: Private
Shigeru Takagi, President/CEO & Secretary
T. Moriya, Vice-President, Finance & Administration

Imperial Parking Corporation
Also Known As: Impark
#300, 601 West Cordova St.
Vancouver, BC V6B 1G1
604-681-7311
866-277-5501
www2.impark.com
Other Communications: Payment Notices: 800-315-7275; Monthly Parking: 877-909-6199
Social Media: twitter.com/impark
Company Type: Private
Profile: Imperial Parking Corporation operates parking facilities in Canada & the United States.
Allan Copping, Chief Executive Officer
acopping@impark.com
Gordon Craig, Chief Operating Officer
Milan Zivkovic, Chief Information Officer
Julian Jones, Senior Vice-President, Business Development
Nicola-Jane NcNeill, Corporate Secretary & Vice-President, Legal Affairs

International Road Dynamics Inc. (IRD)
Corporate Office
702 - 43rd St. East
Saskatoon, SK S7K 3T9
306-653-6600
Fax: 306-242-5599
877-444-4473
info@irdinc.com; Customer.Service@irdinc.
www.irdinc.com
Other Communications: Investors: irdir@irdinc.com; Career: jobs@irdinc.com
Social Media: www.facebook.com/InternationalRoadDynamics
twitter.com/IRDInc1
www.linkedin.com/company/ird_3
Company Type: Public
Ticker Symbol: IRD / TSX
Profile: The highway traffic management technology company focuses on supplying products to the Intelligent Transportation Systems industry. International Road Dynamics' systems are used to manage & protect highway infrastructures.
The management system of the Canadian corporate office is registered to ISO 9001:2008, under QMI-SAI Global's registration program.
Terry Bergan, Chief Executive Officer
Randy Hanson, Chief Operating Officer & Executive Vice-President
Francine Senecal-Lepage, Contact, Investor Relations
306-653-6603, Fax: 306-653-6609

Logistec Corporation
#1500, 360, rue Saint-Jacques
Montréal, QC H2Y 1P5
514-844-9381
Fax: 514-843-5217
corp@logistec.com
www.logistec.com
Company Type: Public
Ticker Symbol: LGT / TSX
Profile: Logistec Corporation & its subsidiaries serve the marine & industrial sectors. Cargo-handling services are offered at port terminals situated in eastern Canada & the United States, & on the Great Lakes. Other services include agency services to

foreign ship-owners & operators at Canadian ports, marine transportation services, & on-site decontamination services.
Madeleine Paquin, President & Chief Executive Officer
Jean-Claude Dugas, CA, Vice-President, Finance
jdugas@logistec.com
Ingrid Stefancic, LL.B., Vice-President, Corporate & Legal Services
Nicole Paquin, Vice-President, Information Systems

Magellan Aerospace Corporation
3160 Derry Rd. East
Mississauga, ON L4T 1A9
905-677-1889
Fax: 905-677-5658
info@magellanaerospace.com
www.magellanaerospace.com

Company Type: Public
Ticker Symbol: MAL / TSX
Profile: Magellan is engaged in designing, engineering, & manufacturing aeroengine & aerostructure assemblies & components. The company serves the aerospace & military markets. Operating units are located in Canada, the United States, & the United Kingdom.
James S. Butyniec, President & Chief Executive Officer
John B. Dekker, Corporate Secretary & Vice-President, Finance
Larry A. Winegarden, Vice-President, Corporate Strategy
Daniel R. Zanatta, Vice-President, MArketing & Contracts

Mercedes-Benz Canada Inc.
98 Vanderhoof Ave.
Toronto, ON M4G 4C9
800-387-0100
www.mercedes-benz.ca

Company Type: Private
Marcus W. Breitschwerdt, President/CEO
Harald H. Henn, Vice-President/CFO
John Westcott, Chief Information Officer

Mullen Group
#121A, 31 Southridge Dr.
Okotoks, AB T1S 2N3
403-995-5200
Fax: 403-995-5296
866-995-7711
IR@mullen-group.com
www.mullen-group.com

Company Type: Public
Ticker Symbol: MTL / TSX
Profile: Mullen Group serves western Canada's oil & natural gas industry by providing specialized transportation & related services. The company also provides management & financial services as well as technology & systems support to the independently operated businesses that it owns.
Murray K. Mullen, Chair & Chief Executive Officer
Stephen H. Lockwood, President & Co-Chief Executive Officer
P. Stephen Clark, Chief Financial Officer

NAV Canada
PO Box 3411 Stn. D, , 77 Metcalfe St.
Ottawa, ON K1P 5L6
613-563-5588
Fax: 613-563-3426
800-876-4693
service@navcanada.ca
www.navcanada.ca

Company Type: Private
John W. Crichton, President/CEO
Nick Geer, Chair
Neil R. Wilson, Vice President/General Counsel/Corp. Secretary

New Flyer Industries Inc.
711 Kernaghan Ave.
Winnipeg, MB R2C 3T4
204-224-1251
Fax: 204-224-6652
investor@newflyer.com
www.newflyer.com

Company Type: Public
Ticker Symbol: NFI / TSX
Profile: The company manufactures heavy-duty transit vehicles. New Flyer Industries' operations are located in Winnipeg Manitoba, Crookston Minnesota, & St. Cloud Minnesota. All facilities are ISO 9001, ISO 14001, & OHSAS 18001 certified.
Paul Soubry, President & Chief Executive Officer
Glenn Asham, Chief Financial Officer
204-224-1251
Paul Smith, Executive Vice-President, Sales & Marketing
Paul_Smith@newflyer.com

Nissan Canada Inc.
5290 Orbitor Dr.
Mississauga, ON L4W 4Z5
Fax: 905-629-6553
800-387-0122
information.centre@nissancanada.com
www.nissan.ca

Company Type: Private
Mark McNabb, Sr. Vice President, Sales & Marketing/Nissan North America

Northstar Aerospace Inc.
Northstar Aerospace (Canada) Inc., Milton Plant
180 Market Dr.
Milton, ON L9T 3H5
905-875-4000
Fax: 905-875-4087
infomilton@nsaero.com; infowindsor@nsaero
www.nsaero.com

Company Type: Public
Ticker Symbol: NAS / TSX
Profile: Northstar Aerospace Inc. manufactures flight critical gears & transmissions. Products include rotocraft drive systems, helicopter gears & transmissions, & accessory gearbox assemblies. Maintenance & repair of components & transmissions are also provided.
Glenn Hess, President & Chief Executive Officer
Peter Jackson, President, Canadian Operations
Craig Yuen, Chief Financial Officer, Senior Vice-President, & Officer, Strategy
cyuen@nsaero.com
David G. Anderson, General Counsel
Scott Crego, Director, Information Technology
Scott Langdon, Contact, Media Relations
slangdon@nsaero.com

Phoenix Oilfield Hauling Inc.
Corporate Office
#480, 700 - 4th Ave. SW
Calgary, AB T2P 3J4
403-262-9151
Fax: 403-262-9195
800-529-0076
www.phoenixhauling.com
Other Communications: Nisku Office: 780-955-8840; Grande Prairie: 780-513-6495

Company Type: Public
Ticker Symbol: PHN / TSX Venture
Profile: Specialized transportation of materials & equipment for the oil & gas industry is provided by Phoenix Oilfield Hauling. The company operates in the Western Canadian Sedimentary Basin as well as in & around the states of Pennsylvania & Texas. Phoenix Oilfield Hauling also rents equipment, such as pickers, tanks, matts, light towers, & other equipment needed for oilfield operations.
Bharat Mahajan, CA, Chief Financial Officer & Vice-President, Finance
bmahajan@phoenixhauling.com

Porter Aviation Holdings
Billy Bishop Toronto City Airport
Toronto, ON M5V 1A1
416-203-8100
Fax: 416-203-8150
media@flyporter.com
www.flyporter.com

Company Type: Private

Purolator Courier Ltd.
5995 Avebury Rd.
Mississauga, ON L5R 3T8
888-744-7123
www.purolator.com
Other Communications: TTY: 1-800 561-7876; Technical: 1-800-459-5599

Company Type: Private
Profile: The courier company has facilities throughout Canada. Purolator also provides international delivery services.
William A. Henderson, President & Chief Executive Officer
Sheldon Bell, President, Purolator Freight
Shawn Klerer, Chief Financial Officer & Senior Vice-President
Brian R. Meagher, Senior Vice-President, Sales, Marketing, & Customer Service

Rolls-Royce Canada Ltd.
9500, ch de Côte-de-Liesse
Montréal, QC H8T 1A2
514-636-0964
Fax: 514-636-9969
www.rolls-royce.com
Other Communications: Coquitlam, Phone: 604-942-1100

Company Type: Private
Profile: Canadian operations consist of engineering, repair, & overhaul within the diversified aerospace, industrial engine, & energy businesses. Facilities are situated in Montréal, Quebec & Vancouver, British Columbia. Customers include airlines, government bodies, & corporate operators around the world.
Michel Toutant, President & Chief Operating Officer
William T. Powers III, Chief Financial Officer & Executive Vice-President
Mia K. Walton, Senior Vice-President, Corporate Communications

Student Transportation Inc. (STI)
#6, 160 Saunders Rd.
Barrie, ON L4N 9A4
705-721-2626
Fax: 705-721-2627
888-942-2250
info@ridesta.com; invest@rideSTA.com
www.ridesta.com
Other Communications: USA Corporate Office, Phone: 732-280-4200

Company Type: Public
Ticker Symbol: STB / TSX
Profile: Founded in 1997, Student Transportation Inc. is a provider of school bus transportation services. The company operates over 8,500 vehicles throughoutCanada & the United States.
Denis J. Gallagher, Chief Executive Officer
Patrick Vaughan, Chief Operating Officer
Patrick J. Walker, Chief Financial Officer & Executive Vice-President
Christopher J. Harwood, Senior Vice-President, Canadian Operations
Keith P. Engelbert, Director, Investor Relations

Transat A.T. Inc.
#600, 300, rue Léo-Pariseau
Montréal, QC H2X 4C2
514-987-1616
Fax: 514-987-8035
800-387-2672
info@transat.com; investorrelations@trans
www.transat.com
Other Communications: Customers: customerrelations@transat.com

Company Type: Public
Ticker Symbol: TRZ / TSX
Profile: Transat A.T. is an integrated tour operator, which organizes & markets holiday travel. Tour operators are based in Canada & France.
Jean-Marc Eustache, Chair, President, & Chief Executive Officer

Philippe Sureau, President, Distribution
Lina De Cesare, President, Tour Operators
Nelson Gentiletti, Executive Vice-President, Tour Operations
Michel Lemay, Chief Brand Officer & Vice-President, Communications & Corporate Affairs
514-987-1660, philan@transat.com
Denis Pétrin, Chief Financial Officer
514-987-1660, investorrelations@transat.com
Lina De Cesare, Chair, Sustainable Tourism Executive Committee

TransForce Inc. Fund
#500, 8801 Trans-Canada Hwy.
Montréal, QC H4S 1Z6
514-331-4000
Fax: 514-337-4200
administration@transforce.ca
www.transforcecompany.com

Company Type: Public
Ticker Symbol: TFI / TSX
Profile: TransForce provides trucking & transportation logistics services. The company operates across Canada & the United States.
Alain Bédard, Chair, President & Chief Executive Officer
abedard@transforcecompany.com
Salvatore Vitale, CA, Chief Financial Officer
Johanne Dean, Vice-President, Marketing & Communications
Chantal Martel, LL.B., Vice-President, Insurance & Compliance
Josiane-M. Langlois, LL.M., Corporate Secretary & Vice-President, Legal Affairs

Trimac Transportation Ltd.
Head Office
PO Box 3500, #1700, 800 - 5th Ave. SW
Calgary, AB T2P 5A3
403-298-5100
Fax: 403-298-5258
info@trimac.com
www.trimac.com

Company Type: Public
Ticker Symbol: TMA / TSX
Profile: Trimac Transportation was extablished in 1945. The company provides bulk trucking service throughout Canada. Through its National Tank Services division, Trimac is involved in

repairing, maintaining, & cleaning the Trimac fleet & the fleets of commercial customers.
Bulk Plus Logistics is Trimac's wholly-owned subsidiary. It provides third party transportation logistics services. Areas of operation are Canada & the United States.
Trimac's Environmental Protection Policy has been in place since 1990 & is reviewed annually.
Edward V. Malysa, President & Chief Operating Officer
Scott D. Calver, Chief Financial Officer & Vice-President

Vector Aerospace
Corporate Head Office
#2100, 2 Bloor St. West
Toronto, ON M4W 3E2

416-925-1143
Fax: 416-925-7214
info@vectoraerospace.com
www.vectoraerospace.com

Company Type: Private
Profile: In 2011, a subsidiary of Eurocopter Holding SAS paid for common shares of Vector, & Vector became part of the EADS/Eurocopter group of companies. Vector ceased to be a reporting issuer, under the securities laws of Ontario, British Columbia, Alberta, Saskatchewan, Manitoba, Québec, New Brunswick, Nova Scotia, Prince Edward Island, & Newfoundland & Labrador.
Vector Aerospace supports various types of turbine engines, dynamic components, structures, & avionics. Customers include commercial & private operators, government agencies, & defense departments.
Declan O'Shea, President & Chief Executive Officer
Paul Cockell, President, Helicopter Services - North America
Fabrice Dumas, President, SECA
Jeff Poirier, President, Engine Services - Atlantic
Randal L. Levine, Chief Financial Officer & Senior Vice-President
Brian Thompson, Senior Vice-President, Global Engine Services

Vitran Corporation Inc.
#701, 185 The West Mall
Toronto, ON M9C 5L5

416-596-7664
Fax: 416-596-8039
webmaster@vitran.com
www.vitran.com

Company Type: Public
Ticker Symbol: VTN / TSX, NASDAQ
Profile: Vitran Corporation provides freight surface transportation & related logistics services in Canada & the United States. Services include logistics, less-than-truckload, & truckload services.
Richard E. Gaetz, President/CEO
Steve Cook, President, Frontier Transport Inc.
Mike Glodziak, President, Canadian & US Logistics
Dave Kimack, President, Vitran Express Inc.
Mark Kosovec, President, PJAX Inc.
Anthony Trichilo, President, Vitran Express Canada Inc.
Sean P. Washchuk, CFO & Vice-President, Finance

Wescast Industries Inc.
150 Savannah Oaks Dr.
Brantford, ON N3T 5V7

519-750-0000
Fax: 519-720-1629
investor.relations@wescast.com
www.wescast.com
Other Communications: Human Resources: recruitment@wescast.com

Company Type: Public
Ticker Symbol: WCS.A / TSX
Profile: Wescast Industries designs, casts, machines, assembles, & supplies exhaust system components for passenger car & light trucks. The company's markets are in North America, South America, Europe, Asia, Africa, & Australia.
Wescast strives to implement plans for the prevention of pollution, in its efforts to meet or exceed environmental requirements.
Wescast employs approximately 2,000 people in production facilities & sales & design centres, located in Canada, the United States, Germany, Hungary, China, & Japan.
Edward G. Frackowiak, Chair & Chief Executive Officer
Teresa Fortney, Chief Financial Officer
Rick Legate, Chief Operating Officer
Jay McNaughton, Vice-President, Sales & Innovation
Blair Alton, Director, Sales, North America
blair.alton@wescast.com

WestJet Airlines Ltd.
22 Aerial Pl. NE
Calgary, AB T2E 3J1

403-444-2600
Fax: 403-444-2261
888-937-8538
investor_relations@westjet.com; media@wes
www.westjet.com
Other Communications: TTY: 877-952-0100; Group: 877-952-4696; Invest: 877-493-7853
Social Media: www.facebook.com/westjet
www.twitter.com/westjet

Company Type: Public
Ticker Symbol: WJA / TSX
Profile: Scheduled passenger airline transportation to cities in North America & the Caribbean is provided by WestJet Airlines.
Sean Durfy, President/CEO
Vito Culmone, CFO & Exec. Vice-President, Finance
Hugh Dunleavy, Exec. Vice-President, Commercial Distribution
Ken McKenzie, Exec. Vice-President, Operations
Bob Cummings, Exec. Vice-President, Guest Experience & Marketing

World Point Terminals Inc.
#110, 1981, av McGill College
Montréal, QC H3A 3C1

403-261-3700
www.wpo.ca

Company Type: Private
Profile: World Point Terminals Inc. & its subsidiaries are involved in the ownership & operation of oil terminaling facilities. The facilities tranship crude oil, refined petroleum, & other liquid products. Bulk storage is also offered. Liquid bulk storage & terminal facilities are situated in North America, the Bahamas, & the Netherlands.
Bernard A. Roy, President/CEO
Steven G. Twele, Chief Financial Officer
Paul F. Little, Secretary

Zongshen PEM Power Systems Inc. (ZPP)
#588, 580 Hornby St.
Vancouver, BC V6C 3B6

604-687-7908
Fax: 604-677-7008
info@zongshenpem.com
www.zongshenpem.com
Other Communications: Zongshen Industrial Group, China +86.023.66372196

Company Type: Public
Ticker Symbol: ZPP / TSX
Profile: Zongshen PEM Power Systems Inc. is a manufacturer of environmentally friendly gas motorbikes, electric motorcycles, electric bicycles, & other e-vehicles.
Zongshen Zuo, Chair & Chief Executive Officer
Yao Li, President
Michael Cheung, Chief Financial Officer & Vice-President, Business Development & Investor Relations
mcheung@zongshenpem.com

Utilities

Algonquin Power & Utilities Corp.
2845 Bristol Circle
Oakville, ON L6H 7H7

905-465-4500
Fax: 905-465-4514
apif@algonquinpower.com
www.algonquinpower.com

Company Type: Public
Ticker Symbol: AQN / TSX
Profile: Algonquin Power & Utilities Corp. is a renewable energy & regulated utility company. Its operating subsidiaries are Algonquin Power Company & Liberty Utilities. Through these subsidiaries, Algonquin Power & Utilities Corp. invests in sustainable utility distribution businesses as well as hydroelectric, wind, & solar power facilities.
Ian Robertson, Chief Executive Officer
David Pasieka, President, Liberty Utilities
Mike Snow, President, Algonquin Power Company
David Bronicheski, Chief Financial Officer
Linda Beairsto, General Counsel & Corporate Secretary
Kelly Castledine, Contact, Investor Relations

AltaGas Ltd.
#1700, 355 - 4th Ave. SW
Calgary, AB T2P 0J1

403-691-7575
Fax: 403-691-7576
888-890-2715
www.altagas.ca
Other Communications: Investors: 403-691-7100; Media Relations: 403-691-9873

Company Type: Public
Ticker Symbol: ALA, ALA.PR.A, ALA.R/TSX
Profile: AltaGas is a business involved in power, natural gas, & regulated utilities. It will focus on renewable energy sources.
David W. Cornhill, B.Sc.(Hons), MBA, Chair/CEO
Richard M. Alexander, BBM, CFA, CMA, President/COO
David Wright, B.Sc., M.Sc., LLB, Exec. Vice-President, Strategy & Corporate Development
Deborah S. Stein, CFO & Vice-President, Finance
James (Jim) Bracken, CA, Sr. Vice-President, Major Projects
Gregory A. Aarssen, B.Sc.(Hons), MBA, LLB, Vice-President, Corporate Affairs
Denis C. Fonteyne, Chair, Environment Occupational Health & Safety Committee

AltaLink Management Ltd.
2811 - 3rd Ave. SE
Calgary, AB T2A 7W7

403-267-3400
866-451-7817
www.altalink.ca
Social Media: www.facebook.com/altalinktransmission
twitter.com/Altalink

Company Type: Private
Profile: AltaLink is a regulated electricity transmission company in Alberta. Electricity is generated from hydro, thermal energy, & wind power & transported through transmission lines to substations. Electricity is then deliverd to homes & businesses via distribution lines. The company employs over 600 people.
Leanne Niblock, Manager, Communications
Leanne.Niblock@AltaLink.ca

Alterra Power Corp.
#600, 888 Dunsmuir St.
Vancouver, BC V6C 3K4

604-669-4999
Fax: 604-682-3727
877-669-4999
info@alterrapower.ca
www.alterrapower.ca
Social Media: twitter.com/#%21/Alterra_Power
www.linkedin.com/company/alterra-power-corp-

Company Type: Public
Ticker Symbol: AXY / TSX
Profile: In 2011, Magma Energy Corp. & Plutonic Power Corp. merged to create Alterra Power Corp.. The renewable energy company operates power plants & projects in British Columbia, Nevada, Chile, Peru, Iceland, & Italy. In British Columbia, Alterra Power has a wind farm & run of river hydro facilities.
John Carson, Chief Executive Officer
Catherine Hickson, Chief Geologist & Vice-President, Exploration
Bruce Ripley, Chief Operating Officer
Peter Wong, Chief Financial Officer
Rupert Legge, LL.B., Corporate Secretary & Executive Vice-President, Legal
Asgeir Margeirsson, Vice-President, Geothermal
Paul Rapp, Vice-President, Wind Power
Jay Sutton, Vice-President, Hydro Power

ATCO Ltd.
ATCO Centre
#1400, 909 - 11th Ave. SW
Calgary, AB T2R 1N6

403-292-7500
Fax: 403-292-7623
investorrelations@atco.com; mediarelation
www.atco.ca

Company Type: Public
Ticker Symbol: ACO / TSX
Profile: ATCO Ltd. employs over 8,800 people. The company delivers business solutions with companies engaged in the following: utilities, including natural gas & electricity transmission & distribution; energy, including power generation & liquids extraction; logistics & structures, included manufacturing & noise abatement; & technologies.
Nancy C. Southern, President & Chief Executive Officer
B.R. (Brian) Bale, Chief Financial Officer & Senior Vice-Presidnent
403-292-7502
S.W. Kiefer, Chief Operating Officer, Energy & Utilities
A.M. Skiffington, Chief Information Officer & Vice-President
C.J. Ackroyd, Vice-President, Marketing & Communications
C.L. Gareau, Vice-President & Treasurer
R.C. Neumann, Vice-President & Controller

Atlantic Power Corporation
#215, 10451 Shellbridge Way
Richmond, BC V6X 2W8

250-586-7788
www.atlanticpower.com
Other Communications: Toronto Office, Phone: 416-773-7400

Company Type: Public
Ticker Symbol: ATP / TSX

Profile: Atlantic Power Corporation is a power & infrastructure company that trades on the TSX under the symbol ATP, & on the New York Stock Exchange, under the symbol AT. The company's portfolio of assets are located in Canada & the United States. Electricity from Atlantic Power's generation projects are sold to utilities & commercial customers.
In 2011, Atlantic Power acquired Capital Power Income L.P..
Barry Welch, President & Chief Executive Officer
Paul Rapisarda, Executive Vice-President, Commercial Development

Atlantic Power Preferred Equity Ltd.
#215, 10451 Shellbridge Way
Richmond, BC V6X 2W8
250-586-7788
info@atlanticpower.com
www.atlanticpower.com
Company Type: Public
Ticker Symbol: AZP.PR.A
Profile: In 2012, CPI Preferred Equity Ltd., a subsidiary of Atlantic Power Corporation, announced that it had changed its name to Atlantic Power Preferred Equity Ltd.. The corporation is listed on the TSX under the symbols, AZP.PR.A & AZP.PR.B.
Atlantic Power Preferred Equity Ltd. is an indirect, wholly-owned subsidiary of Atlantic Power Corporation. The subsidiary operates as a holding company. Atlantic Power Preferred Equity Ltd. directly holds Atlantic Power's business & power generation assets in British Coloumbia, & indirectly holds certain of Atlantic Power's business & power generation assets in the United States.
Barry Welch, President & Chief Executive Officer, Atlantic Power Corporation
Amanda Wagemaker, Contact, Investor Relations
617-977-2700

Atomic Energy of Canada Limited/ Énergie atomique du Canada Ltée (AECL)
Head Office, Chalk River Laboratories
Chalk River, ON K0J 1J0
613-584-3311
800-364-6989
librarycr@aecl.ca (Library)
www.aecl.ca
Other Communications: Public Requests for Information: 1-866-513-2325
Company Type: Private
Profile: Established in 1952, AECL is a nuclear technology & services company. It provides services to utilities in Canada & throughout the world.
AECL's head office in Mississauga provides the following services: nuclear service initiatives; the development, manufacturing, & testing of commercial products; engineering; the management & support of nuclear projects; commercial operations; & international sales & marketing.
Atomic Energy of Canada Limited is also responsible for the management & operation of laboratories, including the Chalk River Laboratories, the Whiteshell Laboratories, & the Underground Research Laboratory.
Hugh MacDiarmid, President & Chief Executive Officer
George Bothwell, Senior Vice-President, External Relations & Communications
Anthony (Tony) De Vuono, Senior Vice-President & Chief Technology Officer
Kent Harris, Senior Vice-President & Chief Financial Officer
Allan A. Hawryluk, Senior Vice-President, Strategic Contracting
Jonathan Lundy, Senior Vice-President, General Counsel & Corporate Secretary
Pilkington William, Senior Vice-President, Operations
Ala Alizadeh, Vice-President, Marketing & Business Development
Earnest (Hank) Drumhiller, Vice-President & General Manager, Operations (RTO) & Chief Nuclear Officer
Steve Halpenny, Vice-President, Finance, Nuclear Laboratories
William Kupferschmidt, Vice-President & General Manager, Research & Development
Joseph Lau, Vice-President, Engineering & Technical Delivery
Joan Miller, Vice-President & General Manager, Waste Management & Decommissioning
Ian Trotman, Vice-President, Project Management & Engineering Services

BCE Inc.
Also Known As: Bell Canada
Building A
1 Carrefour Alexander-Graham-Bell
Montréal, QC H3B 3B3
514-870-4619
Fax: 514-766-5735
888-932-6666
bcecomms@bce.ca
www.bce.ca
Other Communications: Investors: investor.relations@bce.ca
Company Type: Public
Ticker Symbol: BCE / TSX
Profile: Formed in 1970, BCE Inc. is a communications company that provides broadband wireless & wireline communication services. Clients include both residents & businesses across Canada.
Bell Media is a multimedia company, with assets in television, radio, & digital media.
George Cope, CEO
Stephen Wetmore, President, National Markets
Siim Vanaselja, CFO
Eugene Roman, Group President, Systems & Technology

Boralex Inc.
36, rue Lajeunesse
Kingsey Falls, QC J0A 1B0
819-363-5860
Fax: 819-363-5866
info@boralex.com
www.boralex.com
Other Communications: Communications Dept., Phone: 514-985-1353, Fax: 514-284-9895
Company Type: Public
Ticker Symbol: BLX, BLX.DB / TSX
Profile: Boralex Inc. is a power producer. It focuses on the following power generation types: hydroelectric, thermal, wind, & solar. The company has more than 200 employees.
Patrick Lemaire, President & Chief Executive Officer
Jean-François Thibodeau, Chief Financial Officer & Vice-President
Sylvain Aird, Corporate Secretary & Vice-President, Legal Affairs
Patricia Lemaire, Director, Public Affairs & Communications

Brookfield Renewable Energy Partners L.P. (BREP)
c/o Brookfield Asset Management, Brookfield Pl.
#300, 181 Bay St.
Toronto, ON M5J 2T3
888-327-2722
enquiries@brookfieldrenewable.com
www.brookfieldrenewable.com
Company Type: Public
Ticker Symbol: BEP.UN / TSX
Profile: In November 2011, Brookfield Renewable Power Fund merged with Brookfield Asset Management Inc.'s wind & hydro assets in Canada, the United States, & Brazil.
The combined organization, Brookfield Renewable Energy Partners L.P., is concentrated largely in hydro power projects. Wind projects make up the balance. The company also holds development projects. The portfolio is diversified across river systems & power markets in Canada, the United States, & Brazil. Brookfield Asset Management (TSX: BAM.A, NYSE: BAM) owns, directly & indirectly, about 68% of Brookfield Renewable on a fully-exchanged basis.
Richard Legault, Chief Executive Officer
Ben Vaughan, President & Chief Operating Officer
Sachin Shah, Chief Financial Officer
Zev Korman, Director, Investor Relations & Communications
416-359-1955, zev.korman@brookfield.com

Brookfield Renewable Power Ltd.
888-327-2722
enquiries@brookfieldrenewable.com
brookfieldrenewable.com
Company Type: Private

Canadian Utilities Limited
Investor Relations
#1500, 909 - 11th Ave. SW
Calgary, AB T2R 1N6
403-292-7500
Fax: 403-292-7532
investorrelations@atco.com
www.canadian-utilities.com
Company Type: Public
Ticker Symbol: CU / TSX
Profile: Part of the ATCO Group of Companies, Canadian Utilities Limited is engaged in natural gas & electricity transmission & distribution, as well as technology, logistics, & energy services. Canadian Utilities Limited employs over 6,700 people.
Nancy C. Southern, President/CEO
Karen M. Watson, Sr. Vice-President/CFO
Siegfried W. Kiefer, Chief Information Officer & Managing Director, Utilities
Susan R. Werth, Sr. Vice-President & Chief Administration Officer

Capital Power Corporation
Corporate Head Office
#1200, 10423 - 101 St. NW
Edmonton, AB T5H 0E9
780-392-5100
info@capitalpower.com
www.capitalpower.com
Social Media: www.facebook.com/capitalpowercommunity
twitter.com/capitalpower
www.linkedin.com/company/capital-power-corporation
Company Type: Public
Ticker Symbol: CPX / TSX
Profile: Capital Power Corporation is a power producer. The company has sixteen facilities throughout North America. Capital Power is also developing wind generation projects in Ontario, Alberta, & British Columbia.
Brian Vaasjo, President & Chief Executive Officer
Stuart Lee, Chief Financial Officer & Senior Vice-President, Finance
Peter Arnold, Senior Vice-President, Human Resources & Health, Safety & the Environment
B. Kathryn Chisholm, Q.C., Senior Vice-President, Legal, Regulatory, Government Affairs
Darcy Trufyn, Senior Vice-President, Construction & Engineering
Allan Danroth, Vice-President, Planning, Business Transformation, & Information Svs.

Centra Gas Manitoba Inc.
Manitoba Hydro Corporate Head Office
PO Box 815 Stn. Main, , Winnipeg, MB R3C 2P4
888-624-9376
customerservice@hydro.mb.ca
www.hydro.mb.ca
Other Communications: TTY Toll-Free: 855-287-6809
Company Type: Private
Profile: Centra Gas Manitoba Inc. distributes natural gas to residential & commercial customers in Manitoba.

China Wind Power International Corp.
Corporate Office
#502, 110 Yonge St.
Toronto, ON M5C 1T4
www.chinawindpowerinternational.com
Social Media: www.facebook.com/ChinaWindPower
twitter.com/chinawindpower
Company Type: Public
Ticker Symbol: CNW / TSX Venture
Profile: China Wind Power International Corp. is an independent wind power producer, with operations in China. The company indirectly holds rights for wind energy development in Du Mon County, Heilongjiang Province.
Jun Liu, Chief Executive Officer
Wendell Zhang, Chief Financial Officer
416-916-4205, Fax: 416-916-5463, wzhang@chinawindpowerinternational.com
Zhijie Song, Chief Engineer
Walter Huang, Senior Vice-President

CU Inc.
Corporate Head Office
#1600, 909 - 11 Ave. SW
Calgary, AB T2R 1N6
403-292-7500
Fax: 403-292-7523
www.canadian-utilities.com
Company Type: Public
Ticker Symbol: CIU / TSX
Profile: A wholly owned subsidiary of Canadian Utilities Limited, CU Inc. is involved in natural gas & electricity transmission & distribution, as well as power generation. The corporation employs more than 4,300 people.
N.C. Southern, Chair, President & Chief Executive Officer
B.R. (Brian) Bale, Chief Financial Officer & Senior Vice-President
403-292-7502

Emera Incorporated
1223 Lower Water St.
Halifax, NS B3J 3S8
902-450-0507
Fax: 902-428-6112
888-450-0507
investors@emera.com
www.emera.com
Other Communications: Investor Services, Toll-Free Phone: 800-358-1995
Company Type: Public
Ticker Symbol: EMA / TSX
Profile: The holding company is involved in the energy sector. Emera Inc.'s investments include Bangor Hydro-Electric Company, Nova Scotia Power Inc., Emera Energy, Emera Utility Services, Bayside Power, Maritimes & Northeast Pipeline, ATlantic Hydrogen Inc., Emera New Brunswick, Emera

Newfoundland & Labrador, Barbados Light & Power Co., & Grand Bahama Power Ltd.
Christopher Huskilson, President/CEO
Rob Bennett, President/CEO, Nova Scotia Power Inc.
Robert Hanf, President/COO, Bangor Hydro Electric Company
Robin McAdam, President, Brunswick Pipeline Company Ltd.
Nancy Tower, F.C.A., Chief Financial Officer
902-429-6991, nancy.tower@emera.com
Wayne Crawley,, CA, Vice-President, Corporate Strategy & Development
James Spurr, General Counsel & Vice-President, Government Relations
Jennifer Nicholson, CA, Director, Investor Relations & Strategic Development
902-428-6347, jennifer.nicholson@emera.com

Enbridge Income Fund Holdings Inc.
Fifth Avenue Place
#3000, 425 - 1st St. SW
Calgary, AB T2P 3L8

403-231-3900
Fax: 403-231-3920
866-859-5957
webmaster@enbridgeincomefund.com
www.enbridgeincomefund.com
Other Communications: Corporate Communications, Toll-Free Phone: 888-992-0997

Company Type: Public
Ticker Symbol: ENF / TSX
Profile: Through its investment in Enbridge Income Fund, Enbridge Income Fund Holdings Inc. holds energy infrastructure assets. These assets include the following: a 100% interest in the pipelines that comprise the Saskatchewan System; a 50% interest in the Canadian segment of the Alliance Pipeline; & interests in renewable & alternative power generation capacity. The manager of Enbridge Income Fund Holdings Inc. is Enbridge Management Services Inc.
John K. Whelen, President
Colin K. Gruending, Chief Financial Officer
Darren Yaworsky, Treasurer
Debra J. Poon, Corporate Secretary
Teri Majer, Manager, Investor Relations
403-508-3185, teri.majer@enbridge.com
Jennifer Varey, Director, Corporate Communications
403-508-6563, jennifer.varey@enbridge.com

EnerCare Inc.
PO Box 4645 Stn. A, , Toronto, ON M5W 7A3

416-649-1890
Fax: 866-521-8882
866-449-4423
rentalinfo@enercare.ca; connections.care@www.enercare.ca
Other Communications: New Business: metersales@enercare.ca

Company Type: Public
Ticker Symbol: ECI / TSX
Profile: EnerCare Inc. is the owner of approximately 1.2 million installed water heaters & other assets, which are rented mainly to residential customers in Ontario. The company also owns EnerCare Connections, a sub-metering company. EnerCare Connections has metering contracts for apartment & condominium suites, primarily in Ontario & Alberta.
John MacDonald, President & Chief Executive Officer
Evelyn Sutherland, Chief Financial Officer
John Toffoletto, General Counsel, Corporate Secretary, & Senior Vice-President
Tom Cooper, Vice-President, Sales & Marketing

ENMAX Corporation
141 - 50 Ave. SE
Calgary, AB T2G 4S7

403-514-3000
Fax: 403-310-2010
877-571-7111
customercare@enmax.com
www.enmax.com

Company Type: Public
Profile: ENMAX Corporation provides electricity & natural gas energy services in Alberta.
Gary Holden, President/CEO
David Halford, CFO & Exec. Vice-President, Finance

Ensource Corp.
3240 Mavis Rd.
Mississauga, ON L5C 3K1

905-273-9050
Fax: 905-566-2737
info@enersource.com; account-info@enersou
www.enersource.com

Company Type: Private
Profile: The energy provider serves both residential & commercial customers in Mississauga, Ontario. Emersource also offers conservation programs.

Craig Fleming, President & Chief Executive Officer
Dan Pastoric, Chief Operating Officer & Executive Vice-President
Norm Wolff, Chief Financial Officer & Executive Vice-President
Raymond Rauber, Vice-President, Engineering & Operations
Karen Ras, Director, Corporate Relations
905-283-4275, Fax: 647-401-3942, publicaffairs@enersource.com

Epcor Utilities
#2000, 10423 - 101 St. NW
Edmonton, AB T5H 0E8

780-412-3414
www.epcor.com

Company Type: Private

Etrion Corporation
rue du Stand 60-62
Geneva

info@etrion.com
www.etrion.com
Other Communications: Phone: +41 22 715 20 90; Fax: +41 22 715 20 99

Company Type: Public
Ticker Symbol: ETX / TSX
Profile: The independent power producer owns & operates solar photovoltaic power plants in Italy.
Marco Anotonio Northland, Chief Executive Officer
Garrett Soden, Chief Financial Officer
Robert Eriksson, Contact, Investor Relations
reriksson@etrion.com

Fortis Inc.
Fortis Building
PO Box 8837, #1201, 139 Water St.
St. John's, NL A1B 3T2

709-737-2800
Fax: 709-737-5307
investorrelations@fortisinc.com
www.fortisinc.com

Company Type: Public
Ticker Symbol: FTS / TSX
Profile: Fortis Inc. is an international distribution utility holding company, which serves gas & electricity customers. The company also owns hotels & commercial real estate in Canada.
H. Stanley Marshall, President/CEO
Barry V. Perry, CFO & Vice-President, Finance
Ronald W. McCabe, General Counsel & Corporate Secretary

FortisAlberta Inc.
320 - 17th Ave. SW
Calgary, AB T2S 2V1

403-514-4000
Fax: 403-514-4001
866-717-3113
www.fortisalberta.com

Company Type: Private
Profile: FortisAlberta provides power to various communities in Alberta. It is affiliated with the Fortis Family of Companies.
Nipa Chakravarti, Vice-President, Customer Service
Karl W. Smith, President and CEO

FortisBC Energy Inc.
16705 Fraser Highway
Surrey, BC V4N 0E8

604-576-7000
800-773-7001
www.fortisbc.com

Company Type: Private

FortisBC Inc.
16705 Fraser Hwy.
Surrey, BC V4N 0E8

604-576-7000
800-773-7001
electricity.customerservice@fortisbc.com
www.fortisbc.com
Other Communications: Natural gas: 888-224-2710; Electricity: 866-436-7847

Company Type: Private
Profile: FortisBC delivers energy to homes, institutions, & businesses in British Columbia. The company employs approximately 2,300 people. In 2011, FortisBC & Terasen Gas began sharing the name, FortisBC.
John Walker, President & Chief Executive Officer
Michele Leeners, Chief Financial Officer & Vice-President, Finance
Michael Mulcahy, Executive Vice-President, Customer & Corporate Services
Roger Dall'Antonia, Vice-President, Strategic Planning, Corp. Dev., & Regulatory Affairs
Doyle Sam, Vice-President, Engineering & Generation
Douglas Stout, Vice-President, Energy Solutions & External Relations

Gaz Métro inc
1717, rue du Havre
Montréal, QC H2K 2X3

514-598-3444
Fax: 514-598-3144
800-361-4005
info@gazmetro.com
www.gazmetro.com

Company Type: Private
Sophie Brochu, President/CEO
Pierre Despars, Vice-President, Finance & Corporate Affairs
Stéphanie-Hélène Leclerc, Contact, Public & Governmental Affairs
E. Morin, Director, Engineering, Geomatics & Technology
J.-P. Noël, Director, Regulatory Matters, Rates & Environment

Innergex Renewable Energy Inc.
#1255, 1111, rue Saint-Charles ouest
Longueuil, QC J4K 5G4

450-928-2550
Fax: 450-928-2544
info@innergex.com
www.innergex.com
Other Communications: Vancouver Office, Phone: 604-633-9990, Fax: 604-633-9991

Company Type: Public
Ticker Symbol: INE / TSX
Profile: Innergex Renewable Energy develops & operates renewable power generating facilities. Operations are carried out in British Columbia, Ontario, Québec, & Idaho, USA. The company focuses upon the wind power, solar power, & hydroelectric sectors.
Michel Letellier, MBA, President & Chief Executive Officer
Jean Perron, Chief Financial Officer & Vice-President
Michèle Beauchamp, LL.B., LL.M.., Corporate Secretary & Vice-President, Legal Affairs
Guy Dufort, Vice-President, Public Affairs
Peter Grover, Eng., Vice-President, Project Management
Jean Trudel, MBA, Vice-President, Finance & Investor Relations

Just Energy
First Canadian Place
PO Box 355, #2630, 100 King St. West
Toronto, ON M5X 1E1

866-587-8674
Fax: 888-548-7690
877-488-7809
www.justenergy.com
Other Communications: Investors, Phone: 416-367-2998
Social Media: www.facebook.com/justenergygroup
twitter.com/JustEnergyGroup
www.linkedin.com/company/just-energy_2

Company Type: Public
Ticker Symbol: JE / TSX
Profile: The independent energy supplier sells electricity & natural gas to residential & commercial customers throughout Canada & the United States. Through National Home Services, high efficiency & tankless water heaters, furnaces, & air conditioners are sold & rented. Wheat-based ethanol is produced & sold through Terra Grain Fuels.
Green products are offered through Just Energy's JustGreen & JustClean programs. JustGreen products are sourced from renewable sources such as wind, biomass, or run of the river hydro. JustClean products allow some customers to offset their carbon footprint.
Ken Hartwick, CA, Chief Executive Officer & President
905-795-3557
Beth Summers, CA, Chief Financial Officer
905-795-4206
Gord Potter, Executive Vice-President, Regulatory & Legal Affairs
905-795-4214, gpotter@justenergy.com

Keyera Corp.
West Tower, Sun Life Plaza
#600, 144 - 4 Ave. SW
Calgary, AB T2P 3N4

403-205-8300
Fax: 403-205-8318
ir@keyera.com; hr@keyera.com
www.keyera.com

Company Type: Public
Ticker Symbol: KEY / TSX
Profile: Keyera is engaged in natural gas gathering & processing. The company also transports, stores, & markets natural gas liquids. Activities are conducted in the Western Canada Sedimentary Basin.
Jim V. Bertram, President & Chief Executive Officer
Dean Setoguchi, Chief Financial Officer & Vice-President
Graham Balzun, Vice-President, Engineering & Corporate Responsibility

Ron Daniels, Manager, Manager, Information Technology
403-205-7635
Tanis Fiss, Manager, Financial Communications
Murray Selle, Manager, Health & Safety
Rod Sikora, Manager, Environment
403-205-8335
W. John Cobb, Director, Investor Relations
403-205-7670, Fax: 403-205-7670

Maritime Electric
c/o Island Customer Service Centre
PO Box 1328, 180 Kent St.
Charlottetown, PE C1A 7N2

Fax: 902-629-3630
800-670-1012
customerservice@maritimeelectric.com
www.maritimeelectric.com

Company Type: Public
Profile: Maritime Electric operates according to the Electric Power Act & the Renewable Energy Act to deliver electricity on Prince Edward Island.
Fred J. O'Brien, President & Chief Executive Officer
J. William Geldert, CFO, Corporate Secretary, & Vice-President, Finance & Administration
John D. Gaudet, Vice-President, Corporate Planning & Energy Supply
Kim A. Griffin, Manager, Corporate Communications & Public Affairs
Gil A. Jubainville, Manager, Information Technology

MAXIM Power Corp.
#1210, 715 - 5th Ave. SW
Calgary, AB T2P 2X6

403-263-3021
Fax: 403-263-9125
maxim@maximpowercorp.com
www.maximpowercorp.com
Other Communications: Investor Relations: investors@maximpowercorp.com

Company Type: Public
Ticker Symbol: MXG / TSX
Profile: MAXIM Power Corp. is an independent power producer. The company is involved in the acquisition, development, ownership, & operation of environmentally responsible power projects. Its assets include coal & natural gas powered generators in western Canada, the United States, & France.
John R. Bobenic, President & Chief Executie Officer
403-750-9300
Xavier Embroise, President, COMAX France S.A.S.
Michael R. Mayder, Chief Financial Officer & Vice-President, Finance
403-750-9311
Kim Karran, Vice-President, Corporate Development
Jamie Urquhart, Vice-President, Operations

Nevada Geothermal Power Inc. (NGP)
840, 1140 West Pender St.
Vancouver, BC V6E 4G1

604-688-1553
Fax: 604-688-5926
866-688-0808
info@nevadageothermal.com
www.nevadageothermal.com
Other Communications: Investor Relations, Phone: 604-638-8784

Company Type: Public
Ticker Symbol: NGP / TSX Venture
Profile: Nevada Geothermal Power Inc. is the operator of the Faulkner 1 geothermal plant in Nevada. The company owns leasehold interests in the following properties: New Truckhaven in California; Crump Geyser, in Oregon; & Pumpernickel Valley, North Valley, Blue Mountain, & Edna Mountain in Nevada.
Brian D. Fairbank, B.A.Sc., P. Eng., President & Chief Executive Officer
Andrew T. Studley, P. Eng, CPA, MBA, Chief Financial Officer & Secretary
Max Walenciak, P. Eng, Senior Vice-President, Development & Plant Operations
Stuart D. Johnson, Vice-President, Resource Development
Kim Niggemann, Vice-President, Resource Operations & External Affairs

Newfoundland Power Inc.
PO Box 8910, 55 Kenmout Rd.
St. John's, NL A1B 3P6

709-737-2802
Fax: 709-737-2903
800-663-2802
contactus@newfoundlandpower.com
www.newfoundlandpower.com
Other Communications: Emergencies: 1-888-491-5066 or 1-800-474-5711

Company Type: Private
Profile: Newfoundland Power Inc. is engaged in the operation of an integrated generation, transmission, & distribution system. Safe, reliable electricity is supplied to the island portion of Newfoundland & Labrador.
Earl Ludlow, President & Chief Executive Officer
Peter Alteen, Vice-President, Regulation & Planning
Jocelyn Perry, Chief Financial Officer & Vice-President, Finance
Gary Smith, Vice-President, Customer Operations & Engineering

Peter Collins, Manager, Customer Relations & Information Technology

Northland Power Inc.
30 St Clair Ave. West, 17th Fl.
Toronto, ON M4V 3A1

416-962-6262
Fax: 416-962-6266
investorrelations@northlandpower.ca
www.northlandpower.ca

Company Type: Public
Ticker Symbol: NPI / TSX
Profile: Northland Power Inc. is engaged in the development of wind, solar, run-of-river hydro projects, & additional power generation opportunities. The company's assets include facilities that produce electricity form natural gas & renewable resources such as biomass, solar, & wind.
John W. Brace, Chief Executive Officer
Paul J. Bradley, Chief Financial Officer
Barb Bokla, Manager, Investor Relations
647-288-1438

Nova Scotia Power Inc. (NSPI)
PO Box 910, Halifax, NS B3J 2W5

902-450-0507
Fax: 902-428-6112
800-428-6230
investors@emera.com
www.nspower.ca
Other Communications: TTY: 1-800-565-6051

Company Type: Public
Ticker Symbol: NSI
Profile: Nova Scotia Power Inc. is engaged in the generation, transmission, & distribution of electric power across Nova Scotia.

Rob Bennett, President & Chief Executive Officer
Robin McAdam, Executive Vice-President, Strategic Business & Custome Services
René Gallant, Vice-President, Regulatory Affairs
Claudette Porter, Vice-President, Finance & Information Technology
Mark Savory, Vice-President, Technical & Construction Services

Primary Energy Recycling Corporation
#202, 2215 So. York Rd.
Oak Brook, IL 60523 USA

630-230-1313
investorinfo@primaryenergy.com
www.primaryenergyrecycling.com

Company Type: Public
Ticker Symbol: PRI / TSX
Profile: Primary Energy Recycling Corporation is involved in capturing & recycling recoverable heat & byproduct fuels from industrial & electric generation processes. Recovered materials are then converted into economical electricity & thermal energy. The company is the indirect owner & operator of four recycled energy projects, & it also has a 50% interest in a pulverized coal facility.
John Prunkl, President & Chief Executive Officer
Mike Alverson, Chief Financial Officer

Ram Power, Corp.
#200, 9460 Double R. Blvd.
Reno, NV 89521

775-398-3700
Fax: 775-828-0904
info@ram-power.com
www.ram-power.com
Social Media: www.facebook.com/pages/Ram-Power-Corp/365229206828708
www.linkedin.com/company/ram-power-corp.

Company Type: Public
Ticker Symbol: RPG / TSX
Profile: Ram Power is a renewable energy company that was founded in 2008. The company acquires, explores, develops, & operates geothermal properties. Projects are located in Canada, the United States, & Latin America.
Shuman Moore, President & Chief Executive Officer
Selby F. Little, Chief Financial Officer
Gordon Alter, Vice-President & General Counsel

Toronto Hydro Corporation
14 Carlton St.
Toronto, ON M5B 1K5

416-542-3100
Fax: 416-542-3452
contactus@torontohydro.com
www.torontohydro.com

Company Type: Private
David S. O'Brien, President/CEO
David Dobbin, President, Toronto Hydro Telecom
Jean-Sebastien Couillard, CFO
Blair H. Peberdy, Vice-President, Communications & Public Affairs
Anthony M. Haines, President
Ave Lethbridge, Vice-President, Organizational Effectiveness
Lawrence Wilde, Vice-President and General Counsel

TransAlta Corporation
PO Box 1900 Stn. M, , 110 - 12 Ave. SW
Calgary, AB T2P 2M1

403-267-7110
Fax: 403-267-2559
877-700-9288
www.transalta.com
Other Communications: Investor Relations, Toll-Free Phone: 800-387-3598

Company Type: Public
Ticker Symbol: TA / TSX, MYSE
Profile: TansAlta Corporation is engaged in coal & gas-fired generation. The company carries out its activities in Canada, the United States, Mexico, & Australia.
The company works to limit enviromental impact by focusing growth on renewable generation methods. It meets ISO 14001 standards.
Stephen G. Snyder, President/CEO
Brian Burden, Exec. Vice-President/CFO
William D.A. Bridge, Exec. Vice-President, Generation Technology & Procurement
Dawn Farrell, Exec. Vice-President, Commercial Operations & Development
Mike Williams, Exec. Vice-President, Human Resources, Information Technology & Communication
Ken Stickland, Exec. Vice-President, Legal, SD, & Environmental Health & Safety

TransCanada Corporation
450 - 1 St. SW
Calgary, AB T2P 5H1

403-920-2000
Fax: 403-920-2200
800-661-3805
communications@transcanada.com
www.transcanada.com
Other Communications: Communications/Media Relations: 1-800-608-7859
Social Media: twitter.com/transcanada

Company Type: Public
Ticker Symbol: TRP / TSX
Profile: TransCanada is engaged in the development & operation of energy infrastructure, including nautral gas & oil pipelines, power generation, & gas storage facilities in North America. Common shares trade on the Toronto & New York stock exchanges.
Russ Girling, President & Chief Executive Officer
Alexander J. Pourbaix, President, Energy
Russell K. Girling, President, Pipelines
Gregory A. Lohnes, Exec. Vice-President/CFO
Sarah E. Raiss, Exec. Vice-President, Corporate Services
Sean McMaster, General Counsel & Exec. Vice-President, Corporate
Don Wishart, Exec. Vice-President, Operations & Engineering

Western Wind Energy Corp.
HSBC Building
#1326, 885 West Georgia St.
Vancouver, BC V6C 3E8

604-685-9463
Fax: 604-685-9441
866-765-0826
investorrelations@westernwindenergy.com
www.westernwindenergy.com
Other Communications: California Office, Phone: 661-822-1418

Company Type: Public
Ticker Symbol: WND / TSX Venture
Profile: Western Wind Energy Corp. is a renewable energy production company. It directly owns more than 165 MW of wind & solar capacity in production in Arizona & California. The company also owns development assets for wind & solar energy in Arizona, California, Ontario, & the Commonwealth of Puerto Rico.
Western Wind Energy Corp. trades on the TSX Venture Exchange, & also in the United States on the OTCQX under the symbol "WNDEF".

Jeffrey J. Ciachurski, President & Chief Executive Officer
Kevin Craig, CA, Chief Financial Officer
Steve R. Mendoza, Chief Engineer & Executive Vice-President
T. Alana Steele, Chief Operating Officer & General Counsel

Stock Exchanges

Canadian National Stock Exchange (CNSX)
c/o CNSX Markets Inc.
220 Bay St., 9th Fl.
Toronto, ON M5J 2W4
Tel: 416-572-2000; Fax: 416-572-4160
www.cnsx.ca
Former Name: Canadian Trading & Quotation System Inc.
Also Known As: CNSX
Year Founded: 2004

Canadian Unlisted Board Inc.
The Exchange Tower, Trading Services, Toronto Stock Exchange
130 King St. West
Toronto, ON M5X 1J2
Tel: 416-947-4705; Fax: 416-947-4280
cubadmin@cub.ca
www.cub.ca
Also Known As: CUB
Year Founded: 2000

ICE Futures Canada, Inc.
Commodity Exchange Tower
#400, 360 Main St.
Winnipeg, MB R3C 3Z4
Tel: 204-925-5000; Fax: 204-943-5448
www.theice.com
Other Contact Information: 204-925-5017 (Phone, ICE Clear Canada)
Former Name: Winnipeg Commodity Exchange Inc.
Ownership: Wholly owned subsidiary of IntercontinentalExchange (ICE), Atlanta, GA, USA
Year Founded: 1887

Montréal Exchange Inc. (MX)/ Bourse de Montréal Inc.
Tour de la Bourse
CP 61
800, carré Victoria
Montréal, QC H4Z 1A9
Tél: 514-871-2424; Téléc: 514-871-3514
Ligne sans frais: 800-361-5353
info@m-x.ca; communications@m-x.ca; finances@m-x.ca; legal@m-x.ca
www.m-x.ca
Other Contact Information: 00.800.36.15.35.35 (Toll-free from Great Britain & France); rh@m-x.ca (HR); marketdata@m-x.ca (Market Data); reg@m-x.ca (Regulation / Registration)
Also Known As: MX
Year Founded: 1874

Natural Gas Exchange Inc. (NGX)
#2330, 140 - 4 St. SW
Calgary, AB T2P 3N3
Tel: 403-974-1700; Fax: 403-974-1719
Clearing@ngx.com; Marketing@ngx.com
www.ngx.com
Other Contact Information: Ops@ngx.com (NGX Help Desk & Operations)
Also Known As: NGX
Ownership: Wholly owned by TMX Group Inc., Toronto, ON.
Year Founded: 1994

NEX Board
PO Box 11633
#2700, 650 West Georgia St.
Vancouver, BC V6B 4N9
Tel: 604-689-3334; Fax: 604-844-7502
Toll-Free: 866-344-5639
nex@tsxventure.com
www.tsx.com/en/nex
Also Known As: NEX
Year Founded: 2003

TMX Group Limited
PO Box 450
130 King St. West, 3rd Fl.
Toronto, ON M5X 1J2
Tel: 416-947-4670; Fax: 416-947-4662
Toll-Free: 888-873-8392
info@tmx.com (TMX); information@tsxventure.com (TSX Venture)
www.tmx.com; www.abetterexchange.com
Other Contact Information: Couriered deliveries to TMX Group Inc.: c/o Plus One Inc., First Canadian Place, 77 Adelaide St. West, Toronto, ON, M5X 1A4
Social Media: www.facebook.com/tmxmoney; twitter.com/TMXGroup
Former Name: TMX Group Inc.; TSX Group Inc.
Also Known As: TSX-X
Ownership: Owned by Maple Group Acquisition Corp.

The Toronto Stock Exchange (TSX)
The Exchange Tower
PO Box 450
130 King St. West , 3rd Fl.
Toronto, ON M5X 1J2
Tel: 416-947-4670; Fax: 416-947-4770
Toll-Free: 888-873-8392
info@tsx.com; listedissuers@tsx.com; issuersupport@tsxconnect.com
www.tsx.com
Other Contact Information: marketregs@tsx.com (Investor Services); disclosure@tsx.com (Compliance & disclosure); queries@tsxdatalinx.com (TSX Datalinx)
Also Known As: TSX
Ownership: Subsidiary of TMX Group Inc., Toronto, ON
Year Founded: 1861

TSX Venture Exchange
PO Box 450
130 King St. West, 3rd Fl.
Toronto, ON M5X 1J2
Tel: 416-365-2200; Fax: 416-365-2224
Toll-Free: 877-421-2369
information@tsxventure.com
www.tsxventure.com
Other Contact Information: 888-873-8392 (Toll-Free, Business Development); complianceanddisclosure@tsxventure.com (E-mail, Concerns regarding listed issuers)
Former Name: Canadian Venture Exchange
Ownership: Subsidiary of TMX Group Inc., Toronto, ON

Trust Companies

Trust companies are regulated under the federal Trust and Loan Companies Act and operate under either provincial or federal legislation. The business of trust companies includes activities like those of a bank, plus fiduciary functions.

AGF Trust Company
Toronto-Dominion Centre
66 Wellington St. West, 31st Fl.
Toronto, ON M5K 1E9
Tel: 416-216-5353; Toll-Free: 800-244-8457
trust@agf.com
www.agf.com/mortgages
Ownership: Wholly owned subsidiary of AGF Management Limited.
Year Founded: 1988

All Nations Trust Company
#208, 345 Yellowhead Hwy.
Kamloops, BC V2H 1H1
Tel: 250-828-9770; Fax: 250-372-2585
Toll-Free: 800-663-2959
antco@antco.bc.ca
www.antco.bc.ca
Ownership: Private
Year Founded: 1984
Number of Employees: 13

B2B Trust
130 Adelaide St. West
Toronto, ON M5H 3P5
Tel: 416-947-7427; Fax: 416-947-9476
Toll-Free: 800-263-8349
www.b2b-trust.com
Former Name: Sun Life Trust Company
Ownership: Private. Subsidiary of Laurentian Bank of Canada, Montréal, QC.
Year Founded: 1991
Number of Employees: 258
Assets: $1-10 billion
Revenues: $50-100 million

The Bank of Nova Scotia Trust Company
Scotia Plaza
44 King St. West
Toronto, ON M5H 1H1
Tel: 416-866-6161; Fax: 416-866-3750
Also Known As: Scotiatrust
Ownership: Private. Subsidiary of Bank of Nova Scotia
Year Founded: 1993
Number of Employees: 450

BMO Trust Company
55 Bloor St. West, 12th Fl.
Toronto, ON M4W 3N5
Tel: 416-867-6784
AATinvestmentservices@bmo.com
www.advisorsadvantagetrust.com
Former Name: The Trust Company of Bank of Montréal
Also Known As: Advisor's Advantage Trust
Ownership: Wholly owned subsidiary of Bank of Montréal. Member of BMO Financial Group.

BNY Trust Company of Canada
#1101, 4 King St. West
Toronto, ON M5H 1B6
www.bankofny.com
Ownership: Wholly owned subsidiary of the Bank of New York Company Inc.
Year Founded: 2001

The Canada Trust Company
Toronto Dominion Centre
PO Box 1, TD Centre Stn. TD Centre
55 King St. West, 12th Fl.
Toronto, ON M5K 1A2
Toll-Free: 888-222-3456
www.tdcanadatrust.com
Year Founded: 1855

Canadian Western Trust Co. (CWT)
#600, 750 Cambie St.
Vancouver, BC V6B 0A2
Tel: 604-685-2081; Fax: 604-669-6069
Toll-Free: 800-663-1124
informationservices@cwt.ca
www.cwt.ca
Ownership: Wholly owned subsidiary of Canadian Western Bank

CIBC Mellon Trust Company
320 Bay St., 4th Fl.
Toronto, ON M5H 4A6
Tel: 416-643-5000; Fax: 416-643-6409
www.cibcmellon.com
Ownership: Parent companies are Canadian Imperial Bank of Commerce & Mellon Financial Corporation
Year Founded: 1978
Number of Employees: 350
Assets: $500m-1 billion

CIBC Trust Corporation
#900, 55 Yonge St.
Toronto, ON M5E 1J4
Toll-Free: 800-465-3863
www.cibc.com

Citizens Trust Company
#401, 815 West Hastings St.
Vancouver, BC V6B 1B4
Tel: 604-682-7171; Fax: 604-708-7790
Toll-Free: 800-663-1435
www.citizensbank.ca

Clarica Trustco Company
PO Box 1601, Waterloo Stn. Waterloo
227 King St. South
Waterloo, ON N2J 4C5
Toll-Free: 888-864-5463
service@clarica.com
www.clarica.ca
Former Name: Mutual Trust Co.
Ownership: Subsidiary of Sun Life Assurance Company of Canada
Year Founded: 1918

Community Trust Company
2271 Bloor St. West
Toronto, ON M6S 1P1
Tel: 416-763-2291; Fax: 416-763-2444
officepresident@communitytrust.ca
Ownership: Private
Year Founded: 1975

Computershare Trust Company of Canada
100 University Ave., 11th Fl.
Toronto, ON M5J 2Y1
Tél: 416-263-9200; Téléc: 416-263-9261
Ligne sans frais: 800-663-9097
www.computershare.com
Former Name: Montreal Trust
Ownership: Public. Listed on the Australian Stock Exchange
Year Founded: 2000
Number of Employees: 1,400
Revenues: $1-5 million

The Effort Trust Company
240 Main St. East
Hamilton, ON L8N 1H5
Tel: 905-528-8956; Fax: 905-528-8182
www.efforttrust.ca
Ownership: Private. Wholly owned subsidiary of Effort Corporation.
Year Founded: 1978
Number of Employees: 100
Assets: $100-500 million
Revenues: $10-50 million

The Equitable Trust Company
#700, 30 St. Clair Ave. West
Toronto, ON M4V 3A1
Tel: 416-515-7000; Fax: 416-515-7001
mortgage@equitabletrust.com
www.equitabletrust.com
Ownership: Wholly owned subsidiary of Equitable Group Inc.
Year Founded: 1970

Equity Transfer & Trust Company
#400, 200 University Ave.
Toronto, ON M5H 4H1
Tel: 416-361-0152; Fax: 416-361-0470
Toll-Free: 866-393-4891
info@equitytransfer.com, trustservices@equitytransfer.com
www.equitytransfer.com
Other Contact Information: newbusiness@equitytransfer.com (New Business); investor@equitytransfer.com (Investor Inquiries); clientservices@equitytransfer.com (Client Services)
Ownership: Wholly owned subsidiary of Grey Horse Capital Corporation.
Year Founded: 1990

Fiduciary Trust Company of Canada
Also listed under: *Financial Planning & Investment Management Companies*
#3000, 350 Seventh Ave. SW
Calgary, AB T2P 3N9
Tel: 403-543-3950; Fax: 403-543-3955
Toll-Free: 800-574-3822
www.fiduciarytrust.ca
Former Name: Bissett & Associates Investment Management Ltd.
Year Founded: 1982

Home Trust Company
Also listed under: *Credit Card Companies*
#2300, 145 King St. West
Toronto, ON M5H 1J8
Tel: 416-360-4663; Fax: 416-360-0401
Toll-Free: 800-990-7881
inquiry@hometrust.ca
www.hometrust.ca
Ownership: Public. Principal subsidiary of Home Capital Group Inc.
Year Founded: 1977
Number of Employees: 296
Assets: $1-10 billion
Revenues: $100-500 million

HSBC Trust Company (Canada)
620, 885 West Georgia St.
Vancouver, BC V6C 3E9
Tel: 604-641-1122; Fax: 604-641-1138
Toll-Free: 888-887-3388
www.hsbc.ca
Ownership: Private. Wholly owned subsidiary of HSBC Bank Canada
Year Founded: 1972
Number of Employees: 28

IBT Trust Company (Canada)
PO Box 231, First Canadian Place Stn. First Canadian Place
#2800, 100 King St. West
Toronto, ON M5X 1C8
Tel: 416-363-6427; Fax: 416-861-8989
www.ibtco.com
Other Contact Information: 416-861-8983 (Sales phone)
Ownership: Subsidiary of Investors Bank & Trust, Boston, MA
Year Founded: 1993

Industrial Alliance Trust Inc.
1080, Grande Allée ouest
Québec, QC G1K 7M3
Tel: 418-684-5000
www.inalco.com
Former Name: Industrial-Alliance Trust Company
Year Founded: 2000

Investors Group Trust Co. Ltd./ La Compagnie de Fiducie du Groupe Investors Ltée
One Canada Centre
447 Portage Ave.
Winnipeg, MB R3C 3B6
Tel: 204-943-0361; Fax: 204-949-1340
Toll-Free: 888-746-6344
www.investorsgroup.com
Ownership: Subsidiary of Investors Group Inc.
Year Founded: 1968

Laurentian Trust of Canada Inc.
1981, av. McGill College
Montréal, QC H3A 3K3
Tel: 514-284-4500; Fax: 514-284-3396
mail@laurentianbank.ca
www.laurentianbank.com
Ownership: Private. Wholly owned subsidiary of the Laurentian Bank of Canada.
Year Founded: 1939
Assets: $500m-1 billion
Revenues: $10-50 million

LBC Trust
130 Adelaide St. West
Toronto, ON M5H 3P5
Toll-Free: 800-522-1846
www.laurentianbank.ca
Ownership: Wholly owned subsidiary of Laurentian Bank

Legacy Private Trust
PO Box 1
#800, 1 Toronto St.
Toronto, ON M5C 2V6
Tel: 416-868-0001; Fax: 416-868-6541
rlw@legacyprivatetrust.com
www.legacyprivatetrust.com
Other Contact Information: 416-868-4205 (Corporate Secretary Phone)
Ownership: Private
Year Founded: 2002

Maple Trust Company/ Compagnie Maple Trust
TD Waterhouse Tower, Toronto-Dominion Centre
PO Box 349
#3500, 79 Wellington St. West
Toronto, ON M5K 1K7
Tel: 416-350-7400; Fax: 416-350-7441
Toll-Free: 800-307-8341
MTDepositServices@mapletrust.com
www.mapletrust.com
Other Contact Information: 416-350-7488 (Client Services Hotline); 416-350-7498 (Client Services Fax); MTMortgageAdministration@mapletrust.com (Mortgage Email)
Former Name: London Trust and Savings Corporation
Ownership: Private. Member of the Scotiabank Group.
Year Founded: 1999
Assets: $1-10 billion

Mennonite Trust Limited
PO Box 40
3005 Central Ave.
Waldheim, SK S0K 4R0
Tel: 306-945-2080; Fax: 306-945-2225
mtl@sasktel.ca
www.mennonitetrust.com
Year Founded: 1917

M.R.S. Trust Company
#2100, 777 Bay St.
Toronto, ON M5G 2N4
Tel: 416-964-0028; Fax: 416-413-1723
Toll-Free: 800-387-2087
accounthelp@mrs.com
www.mackenziefinancial.com
Other Contact Information: mortgages@mrs.com (Email MRS Mortgages); 888-677-5363 (Mortgage Toll-Free); 416-926-0570 (Mortgage Information Phone)
Former Name: Mackenzie Trust Company
Also Known As: MRS Trust
Ownership: Subsidiary of Mackenzie Financial Corporation.
Year Founded: 1979

NATCAN Trust Company
National Bank
1100, rue University, 12e étage
Montréal, QC H3B 2G7
Tel: 514-871-7633; Fax: 514-871-7580
Toll-Free: 800-235-5566
Ownership: Wholly owned by National Bank Acquisition Holding Inc.

National Bank Trust/ Trust Banque National
1100, rue University, 10e étage
Montréal, QC H3B 2G7
Tel: 514-871-7240; Toll-Free: 800-463-6643
www.nbc.ca

Northern Trust Company, Canada
PO Box 526
#1510, 145 King St. West
Toronto, ON M5H 1J8
Tel: 416-365-7161; Fax: 416-365-9484
www.ntrs.com
Ownership: Subsidiary of Northern Trust Company, Chicago, USA
Number of Employees: 31

Oak Trust Company
One London Place
#1770, 255 Queens Ave.
London, ON N6A 5R8
Tel: 519-433-6629; Fax: 519-433-6652
Toll-Free: 866-973-6631
www.oaktrust.ca
Other Contact Information: 519-979-2338 (Windsor/Essex Phone)
Year Founded: 2004

Olympia Trust Company
#2300, 125 - 9th Ave. SW
Calgary, AB T2G 0P6
Tel: 403-261-0900; Fax: 403-265-1455
Toll-Free: 800-727-4493
info@olympiatrust.com
www.olympiatrust.com
Ownership: Wholly owned subsidiary of Olympia Financial Group Inc.

Pacific Corporate Trust Company
510 Burrard St., 2nd Fl.
Vancouver, BC V6C 3B9
Tel: 604-689-9853; Fax: 604-689-8144
pacific@pctc.com
www.pctc.com
Former Name: Pacific Corporate Services Limited
Ownership: Private
Year Founded: 1981

Peace Hills Trust Company
Samson Mall, Samson Cree Nation Reserve
PO Box 60
Hobbema, AB T0C 1N0
Tel: 780-585-3013; Fax: 780-585-2216
pht@peacehills.com
www.peacehills.com
Ownership: Private
Year Founded: 1981
Number of Employees: 120
Assets: $100-500 million
Revenues: $10-50 million

Peoples Trust Company
Also listed under: *Financing & Loan Companies*
888 Dunsmuir St., 14th Fl.
Vancouver, BC V6C 3K4
Tel: 604-683-2881; Fax: 604-331-3469
people@peoplestrust.com
www.peoplestrust.com
Ownership: Private
Year Founded: 1985

RBC Dexia Investor Services Trust
Royal Trust Tower, Toronto Dominion Centre
77 King St. West, 35th Fl.
Toronto, ON M5W 1P9
Tel: 416-955-5907
www.rbcdexia-is.com
Ownership: Wholly owned subsidiary of RBC Dexia Investor Services
Year Founded: 2006

ResMor Trust Company
Also listed under: *Financing & Loan Companies*

#400, 555 - 4th Ave. SW
Calgary, AB T2P 3E7
Tel: 403-539-4920; Fax: 403-539-4921
Toll-Free: 866-333-7030
www.resmor.com

Former Name: Equisure Trust Company
Ownership: Private. Wholly owned subsidiary of Ally Financial, Inc.
Year Founded: 1964
Number of Employees: 195
Assets: $100-500 million
Revenues: $10-50 million

The Royal Trust Company
Also listed under: *Financial Planning & Investment Management Companies*
Royal Bank
1, Place Ville-Marie, 6e étage sud
Montréal, QC H3B 2B2
Tel: 514-874-7222; Toll-Free: 800-668-1990
tradvtor@rbc.com (East), tradvcal@rbc.com (West)
www.rbc.com
Other Contact Information: 866-553-5585 (Eastern Canada Toll Free); 888-299-5290 (Western Canada Toll Free); 866-474-4344 (Québec Toll Free); tradvmtl@rbc.com (Québec Email)
Ownership: Part of RBC Financial Group.
Year Founded: 1899

Standard Life Trust Company
1245, rue Sherbrooke ouest
Montréal, QC H3G 1G3
Toll-Free: 888-841-6633
www.standardlife.ca

Former Name: Bonaventure Trust Company of Canada
Ownership: Private
Year Founded: 1825

State Street Bank & Trust Company - Canada
Also listed under: *Foreign Banks: Schedule III*
#1100, 30 Adelaide St. East
Toronto, ON M5C 3G6
Tel: 416-362-1100; Fax: 416-956-2525
Toll-Free: 888-287-8639
www.statestreet.com

Former Name: State Street Trust Company Canada
Ownership: State Street Corporation
Year Founded: 1990
Number of Employees: 700

Sun Life Financial Trust Inc.
PO Box 1601, Waterloo Stn. Waterloo
227 King St. South
Waterloo, ON N2J 4C5
Toll-Free: 877-786-5433
www.sunlife.com

Trimark Trust/ Fiducie Trimark
#900, 5140 Yonge St.
Toronto, ON M2N 6X7
Tel: 416-590-0036; Toll-Free: 800-631-7008
inquiries@aimtrimark.com
www.aimtrimark.com

Former Name: Bayshore Trust
Ownership: AIM Trimark Investments, Toronto, ON.
Year Founded: 1977

The Trust Company of London Life
One Canada Centre
447 Portage Ave.
Winnipeg, MB R3C 3B6
Tel: 204-956-8470;

Valiant Trust Company
#600, 750 Cambie St.
Vancouver, BC V6B 0A2
Tel: 604-699-4880; Fax: 604-681-3067
Toll-Free: 877-699-4880
inquiries@valianttrust.com
www.valianttrust.com

Ownership: Subsidiary of Canadian Western Bank

Western Pacific Trust Company
#500, 1130 West Pender St.
Vancouver, BC V6E 4A4
Tel: 604-683-0455; Fax: 604-669-6978
www.westernpacifictrust.com

Ownership: Public
Year Founded: 1964

SECTION 6
EDUCATION

Arranged by province, and each province includes the following categories. Each category is further arranged by specific subcategories, as applicable to each province.

Government Agencies

School Boards/Districts/Divisions
Public; Protestant; Catholic; French; School Authorities

Schools: Specialized
Charter; First Nations; Hearing Impaired; Distance Education; Special Education

Schools: Independent & Private

Universities & Colleges

Post Secondary/Technical

Alberta

Government Agencies

Edmonton: Alberta Enterprise & Advanced Education
Communications Branch, Phipps-McKinnon Bldg.
10020 - 101A Ave., 7th Fl., Edmonton, AB T5J 3G2, Canada
Tel: 780-422-5400; *Toll-Free:* 310-0000
eae.alberta.ca
Hon. Stephen Khan, Minister, 780-427-2025, fax: 780-427-5582

School Boards/Districts/Divisions

Public

Airdrie: Rocky View School Division #41
2651 Chinook Winds Dr., Airdrie, AB T4B 0B4, Canada
Tel: 403-945-4000; *Fax:* 403-945-4001
www.rockyview.ab.ca
Enrollment: 16000
Sylvia Eggerer, Chair
seggerer@rockyview.ab.ca

Athabasca: Aspen View Regional Division #19
3600 - 48 Ave., Athabasca, AB T9S 1M8, Canada
Tel: 780-675-7080; *Fax:* 780-675-3660
Toll-Free: 1-888-488-0288
aspenview@aspenview.org
www.aspenview.org
Grades: Kindergarten - 12
Paul Ponich, Board Chair, 780-525-2288
paul.ponich@aspenview.org
Derm Madden, Superintendent, Schools
derm.madden@aspenview.org
Bernie Giacobbo, Associate Superintendent
bernie.giacobbo@aspenview.org
Brian LeMessurier, Associate Superintendent
brian.lemessurier@aspenview.org
Mark Francis, Director, Education Initiatives
mark.francis@aspenview.org
Dave Holler, Director, Business Services
dave.holler@aspenview.org

Barrhead: Pembina Hills Regional Division #7
5310 - 49 St., Barrhead, AB T7N 1P3, Canada
Tel: 780-674-8500; *Fax:* 780-674-3262
info@phrd.ab.ca
www.phrd.ab.ca
Enrollment: 4355
Richard Harvey, Superintendent

Bonnyville: Northern Lights School Division #69
6005 - 50 Ave., Bonnyville, AB T9N 2L4, Canada
Tel: 780-826-3145; *Fax:* 780-826-4600
www.nlsd.ab.ca
twitter.com/nlsd69
www.youtube.com/user/NLSDTV
Number of Schools: 22 *Grades:* K.-12 *Enrollment:* 5885 *Note:* This division is an amalgamation of the Lac La Biche School Division and the Lakeland Public School District.
Roger Nippard, Superintendent, Schools
roger.nippard@nlsd.ab.ca

Brooks: Grasslands Regional Division #6
Also known as: Grasslands Public Schools
745 - 2nd Ave. East, Brooks, AB T1R 1L2, Canada
Tel: 403-793-6700; *Fax:* 403-362-8225
www.grasslands.ab.ca
Number of Schools: 13 schools; 7 Hutterite colony schools
Grades: Kindergarten - 12; Alternative Ed.
Susan Chomistek, Superintendent
Scott Brandt, Assistant Superintendent
David Steele, Deputy Superintendent
David Steele, Deputy Superintendent
Shane Harahus, Director, Finance
Michael Nielsen, Director, Technology
Alan Kloepper, Manager, Facilities & Maintenance

Calgary: Calgary Board of Education
515 Macleod Trail SE, Calgary, AB T2G 2L9, Canada
Tel: 403-294-8255
www.cbe.ab.ca
Other Information: Trustees: 403-294-8487; Aboriginal Education: 403-777-8970
Number of Schools: 128 elementary; 26 junior high; 24 ele./middle/high; 16 senior high schools; 14 unique settings
Grades: Kindergarten - 12; Continuing Ed. *Enrollment:* 102376
Naomi Johnson, Chief Superintendent, Schools, 403-294-8100
David Stevenson, Deputy Chief Superintendent, Schools, 403-294-8100
Deborah Meyers, Chief Financial Officer, Business & Finance Services, 403-294-8392
Frank Coppinger, Superintendent, Facilities & Environment Servicess, 403-214-1119
Cathy Faber, Superintendent, Learning Innovation, 403-294-8154
John G. Johnston, Superintendent, Human Resources, 403-294-8189
Deborah Lewis, Superintendent, Learning Support, 403-294-8118
Diane Yee, Director, Area I, 403-777-8710
Susan Church, Director, Area II, 403-777-8720
Darlene Selby, Director, Area III, 403-777-6233
Jim Langley, Director, Area IV, 403-777-8750
Jane Rogerson, Director, Area V, 403-777-8780

Calgary: Francophone Regional Authority (South) (FRA)
#230, 6940 Fisher Rd. SE, Calgary, AB T2H 0W3, Canada
Tel: 403-686-6998; *Fax:* 403-686-2914
Toll-Free: 1-877-245-7686
Number of Schools: 13 *Enrollment:* 2008
Anne-Marie Bocher, Chair, 403-686-6998
Diane Boutin, Chair
403-685-9881

Camrose: Battle River Regional Division #31
5402 - 48A Ave., Camrose, AB T4V 0L3, Canada
Tel: 780-672-6131; *Fax:* 780-672-6137
Toll-Free: 1-800-262-4869
www.brrd.ab.ca
Enrollment: 6700
Cheryl Smith, Board Chair, 780-678-3265
csmith@brsd.ab.ca
Dr. Larry Payne, Superintendent, Schools, 780-672-4718, ext. 5227
LPayne@brsd.ab.ca
Ray Bosh, Deputy Superintendent, Sc, 780-672-4718, ext. 5011
RBosh@brsd.ab.ca
Rick Jarret, Assistant Superintendent,, 780-672-4718, ext. 5238
RJarrett@brsd.ab.ca
Bill Schulte, Assistant Superintendent,, 780-672-4718, ext. 5229
Greg Friend, Director, Personnel, 780-672-4718, ext. 5247
GFriend@brsd.ab.ca
Brenda Johnson, Director, Transportation, 780-672-4718, ext. 5245
BJohnson@brsd.ab.ca
Maureen Parker, Director, Curriculum, 780-672-4718, ext. 5223
MParker@brsd.ab.ca
Percy Roberts, Director, Maintenance & O, 780-672-4718, ext. 5246
PRoberts@brsd.ab.ca
Diane Hutchinson, Coordinator, Communicatio, 780-672-4718, ext. 5248
DHutchinson@brsd.ab.ca

Canmore: Canadian Rockies Public Schools
618 - 7th St., Canmore, AB T1W 2H5, Canada
Tel: 403-609-6072; *Fax:* 403-609-6071
hr@crps.ab.ca (Human Resources)
www.crps.ab.ca
Number of Schools: 6 *Grades:* Kindergarten - 12 *Enrollment:* 2042
Brian Callaghan, Superintendent, Schools
D. MacKenzie, Secretary-Treasurer

Cardston: Westwind School Division #74
P.O. Box 10
445 Main St., Cardston, AB T0K 0K0, Canada
Tel: 403-653-4991; *Fax:* 403-653-4641
Toll-Free: 800-655-4991
www.westwind.ab.ca
Grades: Pre-K.-12 *Enrollment:* 4249
Ken Summerfeldt, Supt.
Dexter Durfey, Sec.-Treas.
Lance Miller, Chair., 403-634-4770

Claresholm: Livingstone Range School Division #68
P.O. Box 69
5202 - 5 St. East, Claresholm, AB T0L 0T0, Canada
Tel: 403-625-3356; *Fax:* 403-325-2424
Toll-Free: 800-310-6579
centraloffice@lrsd.ab.ca
www.lrsd.ab.ca
Grades: Pre.-12 *Enrollment:* 3845
Ellie Elliot, Supt. of Schools

Dunmore: Prairie Rose Regional Division #8
P.O. Box 204
918 - 2 Ave., Dunmore, AB T0J 1A0, Canada
Tel: 403-527-5516; *Fax:* 403-528-2264
www.prrd.ab.ca
Number of Schools: 17 public schools, 15 colony schools, 1 outreach *Enrollment:* 3380 *Number of Employees:* 645
Doug Nicholls, Superintendent of Schools
Brian Andjelic, Deputy Superintendent
Brad Volkman, Assistant Superintendent
Patricia Cocks, Secretary-Treasurer
Jeff Swanson, Assistant Secretary-Treasurer
Donna Balas, Director of Inclusion
Kerry Watson, Coordination of Student Service - Primary Programming
Val Miller, Transportation Supervisor
Lyle Roberts, Director of Technology
Brian Frey, Maintenance Supervisor

Edmonton: Edmonton School District #7
Centre for Education
One Kingsway Ave., Edmonton, AB T5H 4G9, Canada
Tel: 780-429-8000; *Fax:* 780-429-8318
info@epsb.ca
www.epsb.ca
www.facebook.com/EdmontonPublicSchools
twitter.com/EPSBNews
www.linkedin.com/company/edmonton-public-schools
www.YouTube.com/EdPublicSchools
Number of Schools: 197 *Enrollment:* 80767 *Number of Employees:* 7593
Edgar Schmidt, Superintendent, Schools

Edmonton: Greater North Central Francophone Education Region No.2
Conseil scolaire Centre-Nord
#322, 8627 - 91st St. (Marie-Anne-Gaboury St.), Edmonton, AB T6C 3N1, Canada
Tel: 780-468-6440; *Fax:* 780-440-1631
Toll-Free: 1-800-248-6886
conseil@centrenord.ab.ca
www.centrenord.ab.ca
twitter.com/CSCNInfo
Number of Schools: 14 *Grades:* K - 12 *Enrollment:* 2400
Paul Dumont, President
pdumont@centrenord.ab.ca
Henrie Lemire, Superintendent
hlemire@centrenord.ab.ca
Nicole Bugeaud, Associate Superintendent
nbugeaud@centrenord.ab.ca
Josée Devaney, Secretary-Treasurer
jdevaney@centrenord.ab.ca
Jean-Marc Cloutier, Director, Technological Services, 780-432-4654
jmcloutier@centrenord.ab.ca
Denise Lauzon Dempsey, Coordinator, Transportation
dldempsey@centrenord.ab.ca
Denise Lavallée, Coordinator, Communications
dlavallee@centrenord.ab.ca
Suzanne Amyotte, Associate, Human Ressources & Finance
samyotte@centrenord.ab.ca

Edson: Grande Yellowhead Public School Division No. 77
3656 - 1st Ave., Edson, AB T7E 1S8, Canada
Tel: 780-723-2414; *Fax:* 780-723-2414
Toll-Free: 1-800-723-2564
escgyrd@gyrd.ab.ca
www.gyrd.ab.ca
Number of Schools: 18 *Grades:* Elementary - Secondary
Enrollment: 5000 *Number of Employees:* 800
Dean Lindquist, Superintendent, Schools, 780-723-4471, ext. 103
deanlind@gyrd.ab.ca
Cory Gray, Deputy Superintendent, Leadership & Human Resources, 780-723-4471, ext. 106
corygray@gyrd.ab.ca
Ed Latka, Assistant Superintendent, Business Services, 780-723-4471, ext. 102
edlatk@gyrd.ab.ca
Nancy Spencer-Poitras, Assistant Superintendent, Learning Services, 780-723-4471, ext. 116
nancspen@gyrd.ab.ca
Ken Baluch, Director, Facility Services, 780-723-4471, ext. 119
kenbalu@gyrd.ab.ca
Leigh McDonald, Director, Transportation Services, 780-723-4471, ext. 121
leigmcdo@gyrd.ab.ca
Kathleen Gardiner, Manager, Financial Services, 780-723-4471, ext. 112
kathgard@gyrd.ab.ca
Nikki Gilks, Manager, Communications, 780-723-4471, ext. 142
nikkgilk@gyrd.ab.ca
Jody Beck, Supervisor, Learning Services - Student Programs, 780-723-4471
jodybeck@gyrd.ab.ca

Kurt Scobie, Supervisor, Learning Services - Special Programs, 780-865-5692
kurtscob@gyrd.ab.ca
Sharon Styles, Supervisor, Learning Services - Curriculum & Instruction, 780-723-4471
sharstyl@gyrd.ab.ca

Fort McMurray: Fort McMurray Public School District
District Office, Clearwater Public Education Cent
231 Hardin St., Fort McMurray, AB T9H 2G2, Canada
Tel: 780-799-7900
www.fortmcmurraypsd.sharpschool.com
Number of Schools: 9 elementary schools; 3 high schools *Grades:* ECS - 12
Jeff Thompson, Board Chair, 780-743-3798, fax: 780-743-4542
Paula.Ogonoski@fmpsd.ab.ca
Dennis Parsons, Superintendent, Schools, 780-799-7903
Dennis.Parsons@fmpsd.ab.ca
Allan Kallal, Associate Superintendent, Business & Finance, 780-799-7908
Allan.Kallal@fmpsd.ab.ca
Phil Meagher, Associate Superintendent, Education & Administration, 780-799-7909
Phil.Meagher@fmpsd.ab.ca
Amgad Rushdy, Associate Superintendent, Human Resources & Administration, 780-799-7902
Amgad.Rushdy@fmpsd.ab.ca
Dr. Brenda Sautner, Director, Special Education, 780-792-5656
Brenda.Sautner@fmpsd.ab.ca
Leslie Ann Booker, Coordinator, Early Childhood Programs, 780-799-7928
Leslie.Booker@fmpsd.ab.ca
Ray Campbell, Coordinator, Education - Curriculum, 780-799-7925
Ray.Campbell@fmpsd.ab.ca
Lyndel Donald, Coordinator, Special Education Staffing, 780-788-8008
Lyndel.Donald@fmpsd.ab.ca
Malcolm Fedoretz, Coordinator, Student Information Systems, 780-799-7928
Malcolm.Fedoretz@fmpsd.ab.ca
Myrna Matheson, Coordinator, Literacy, 780-799-7906
Myrna.Matheson@fmpsd.ab.ca
Paula Ogonoski, Coordinator, Communications, 780-788-8009
Paula.Ogonoski@fmpsd.ab.ca
Ali Syed, Coordinator, Educational Technology, 780-799-7923
Ali.Syed@fmpsd.ab.ca
Lori Weinberger, Coordinator, District Numeracy, 780-788-8007
Lori.Weinberger@fmpsd.ab.ca

Fort Vermilion: Fort Vermilion School Division No. 52
P.O. Box 1
5213 River Rd., Fort Vermilion, AB T0H 1N0, Canada
Tel: 780-927-3766; *Fax:* 780-927-4625
info@fvsd.ab.ca
www.fvsd.ab.ca
Number of Schools: 15 & 4 Learning Stores *Grades:* Kindergarten - 12 *Enrollment:* 3355
Roger Clarke, Superintendent, Schools, 780-927-3766
rogerc@fvsd.ab.ca
Rick Cusson, Assistant Superintendent, Operations, 780-927-3766
rickc@fvsd.ab.ca
Kathryn Kirby, Assistant Superintendent, Teaching & Learning, 780-927-3766
kathrynk@fvsd.ab.ca
Bill Driedger, Assistant Superintendent, Teaching & Learning, 780-927-3766
billd@fvsd.ab.ca
Dan Dyck, Manager, Maintenance, 780-928-3013
dand@fvsd.ab.ca
Peter Braun, Manager, Transportation & Safety, 780-928-3860
peterb@fvsd.ab.ca
Norman Buhler, Secretary-Treasurer, 780-927-3766
normanb@fvsd.ab.ca

Grande Prairie: Grande Prairie School District
10213 - 99 St., Grande Prairie, AB T8V 2H3, Canada
Tel: 780-532-4491; *Fax:* 780-539-4265
www.gppsd.ab.ca
www.facebook.com/162375753809463
Number of Schools: 14 *Grades:* Kindergarten - 12 *Enrollment:* 6300
Karen Prokopowich, Chair, 780-532-1575
Carol Ann MacDonald, Superintendent
carolann.macdonald@gppsd.ab.ca
Alexander McDonald, Assistant Superintendent, Human Resources & Technology
sandy.mcdonald@gppsd.ab.ca
Nick Radujko, Assistant Superintendent, Curriculum
nick.radujko@gppsd.ab.ca
James Robinson, Assistant Superintendent, Student Services
james.robinson@gppsd.ab.ca
Barry Bodner, Director, Operations
barry.bodner@gppsd.ab.ca
Angela DesBarres, Director, Instruction
angela.desbarres@gppsd.ab.ca
Kimberly Frykas, Director, Education Technology
kimberly.frykas@gppsd.ab.ca
Justin Vickers, Director, Information Technology
justin.vickers@gppsd.ab.ca
Wade Webb, Director, Finance
wade.webb@gppsd.ab.ca
Lorna Nordhagen, Manager, Human Resources
lorna.nordhagen@gppsd.ab.ca

Grande Prairie: Peace Wapiti Public School Division #76
8611A - 108 St., Grande Prairie, AB T8V 4C5, Canada
Tel: 780-532-8133; *Fax:* 780-532-4234
www.pwsd76.ab.ca
Enrollment: 5600
Sheldon Rowe, Superintendent

Hanna: Prairie Land Regional Division #25
P.O. Box 1400
Hanna, AB T0J 1P0, Canada
Tel: 403-854-4481; *Fax:* 403-854-2803
Toll-Free: 800-601-3898
lana.campbell@plrd.ab.ca
www.plrd.ab.ca
Enrollment: 1625
Wes Neumeier, Superintendent
wes.neumeier@plrd.ab.ca

High Prairie: High Prairie School Division #48
P.O. Box 870
High Prairie, AB T0G 1E0, Canada
Tel: 780-523-3337; *Fax:* 780-523-4639
Toll-Free: 877-523-3337
www.hpsd48.ab.ca
Enrollment: 3600
Laura Poloz, Superintendent
lpoloz@hpsd48.ab.ca

High River: Foothills School Division
P.O. Box 5700
120 - 5th Ave. West, High River, AB T1V 1M7, Canada
Tel: 403-652-3001; *Fax:* 403-652-4204
www.fsd38.ab.ca
Number of Schools: 27 *Grades:* Kindergarten - 12; French Immersion
Doug Gardner, Chair, 403-652-7842
gardnerd@fsd38.ab.ca
Denise Rose, Chief Executive Officer & Superintendent, Schools, 403-652-6522
Del Litke, Deputy Superintendent
Louise Ascah, Manager, Communications, 403-652-6522

Innisfail: Chinook's Edge School Division #73
4904 - 50 St., Innisfail, AB T4G 1W4, Canada
Tel: 403-227-7070; *Fax:* 403-227-3652
Toll-Free: 800-561-9229
division.office@chinooksedge.ab.ca
www.chinooksedge.ab.ca
Enrollment: 11000

Lethbridge: Lethbridge School District #51
433 - 15 St. South, Lethbridge, AB T1J 2Z5, Canada
Tel: 403-380-5300; *Fax:* 403-327-4387
www.lethsd.ab.ca
Grades: K-12 *Enrollment:* 8000
Gary Bartlett, Chair

Lethbridge: Palliser Regional Division #26
#101, 3305 - 18 Ave. North, Lethbridge, AB T1H 5S1, Canada
Tel: 403-328-4111; *Fax:* 403-380-6890
Toll-Free: 877-667-1234
www.pallisersd.ab.ca
Enrollment: 6300
Kevin Gietz, Superintendent

Lloydminster: Lloydminster School Division #99
5017 - 46 St., Lloydminster, AB T9V 1R4, Canada
Tel: 780-875-5541; *Fax:* 780-875-7829
www.lpsd.ca
Grades: K.-12 *Enrollment:* 3862
Dr. Michael Diachuk, Dir.
michael.diachuk@lpsd.ca
Walter Hardy, Supt. of Admin., 780-808-2523
walter.hardy@lpsd.ca

Medicine Hat: Medicine Hat School District #76
601 - 1 Ave. SW, Medicine Hat, AB T1A 4Y7, Canada
Tel: 403-528-6700; *Fax:* 403-529-5339
www.sd76.ab.ca
Grades: K.-12 *Enrollment:* 6275
Linda Rossler, Supt. of Schools
Jerry Labossiere, Sec.-Treas.

Morinville: Sturgeon School Division #24
9820 - 104 St., Morinville, AB T8R 1L8, Canada
Tel: 780-939-4341; *Fax:* 780-939-5520
www.sturgeon.ab.ca
Number of Schools: 16 *Grades:* Kindergarten - 12 *Enrollment:* 5000 *Note:* Including a school on the Morinville Hutterite Colony & a school operated in conjunction with the Oak Hill Boys' Ranch, plus 3 outreach learning centres
Dr. Michèle Dick, Superintendent, 780-939-4341
mdick@sturgeon.ab.ca
Wolfgang Jeske, Director, Curriculum & Instruction

Nisku: Black Gold Regional Division #18
1101 - 5 St., 3rd Fl., Nisku, AB T9E 7N3, Canada
Tel: 780-955-6025; *Fax:* 780-955-6050
www.blackgold.ab.ca
Grades: Junior Kindergarten - Secondary
Barb Martinson, Chair, Board of Education
barb.martinson@blackgold.ca
Stuart Evans, Superintendent, 780-955-6026
stuart.evans@blackgold.ca
Neil Fenske, Associate Superintendent, 780-955-6028
neil.fenske@blackgold.ca
Dennis Nosyk, Associate Superintendent, 780-955-6032
dennis.nosyk@blackgold.ca
Dianne Butler, Director, Student Services, 780-955-6037
dianne.butler@blackgold.ca
Peter Balding, Administrator, Division Technology, 780-955-6037
dianne.butler@blackgold.ca
Dan Borys, Manager, Operations & Maintenance, 780-955-6068
dan.borys@blackgold.ca
Laurel Kvarnberg, Manager, Finance, 780-955-6059
laurel.kvarnberg@blackgold.ca
Sue Timmermans, Manager, Transportation, 780-955-6034
sue.timmermans@blackgold.ca
Warren Watson, Manager, Projects, 780-955-6062
warren.watson@blackgold.ca

Peace River: Northland School Division #61
P.O. Box 1400
9809 - 77 Ave., Peace River, AB T8S 1V2, Canada
Tel: 780-624-2060; *Fax:* 780-624-5914
Toll-Free: 800-362-1360
central.office@northland61.ab.ca
www.northland61.ab.ca
Grades: K.-12 *Enrollment:* 2600
Donald Tessier, Supt., ext. 6102
don.tessier@northland61.ab.ca
Dennis Walsh, Dir. of Finance, ext. 6141
dennis.walsh@northland61.ab.ca
Delores Pruden, Coordinator, Aboriginal Programs, ext. 6161

Peace River: Peace River School Division #10
10018 - 101 St., Peace River, AB T8S 2A5, Canada
Tel: 780-624-3601; *Fax:* 780-624-5941
peaceriversd@prsd.ab.ca
www.prsd.ab.ca
Enrollment: 3100
Nan Bartlett, Chair

Ponoka: Wolf Creek School Division #72
6000 Hwy. 2A, Ponoka, AB T4J 1P6, Canada
Tel: 403-783-3473; *Fax:* 403-783-3483
info@wolfcreek.ab.ca
www.wolfcreek.ab.ca
Grades: K.-12 *Enrollment:* 7500
Larry Jacobs, Supt.
ljacobs@wolfcreek.ab.ca
Joe Henderson, Sec.-Treas., 403-783-5441, ext. 1229
jhenderson@wolfcreek.ab.ca
Lorrie Jess, Chair

Red Deer: Red Deer School District #104
4747 - 53 St., Red Deer, AB T4N 2E6, Canada
Tel: 403-343-1405; *Fax:* 403-347-8190
info@rdpsd.ab.ca
www.rdpsd.ab.ca
Enrollment: 9000
Don Falk, Superintendent

Rocky Mountain House: Wild Rose School Division #66
4912 - 43 St., Rocky Mountain House, AB T4T 1P4, Canada
Tel: 403-845-3376; *Fax:* 403-845-3850
www.wrsd.ca

Grades: K.-12 *Enrollment:* 5469
Brian Celli, Supt.
brian.celli@wrsd.ca
Gordon Majeran, Sec.-Treas.
gordon.majeran@wrsd.ca
Keith Warren, Chair
keith.warren@wrsd.ca

***Sherwood Park:* Elk Island Public Schools Regional Division #14**
683 Wye Rd., Sherwood Park, AB T8B 1N2, Canada
Tel: 780-464-3477; *Fax:* 780-417-8181
Toll-Free: 800-905-3477
communications@ei.educ.ab.ca
www.ei.educ.ab.ca
Enrollment: 16200

***St Isidore:* Conseil scolaire du Nord-Ouest No. 1**
P.O. Box 1220
St Isidore, AB T0H 3B0, Canada
Tél: 780-624-8855; *Téléc:* 780-624-8554
Ligne sans frais: 866-624-8855
conseil@csno.ab.ca
www.csno.ab.ca
Enrollment: 279

***St Paul:* St. Paul Education Regional Division #1**
4313 - 48th Ave., St Paul, AB T0A 3A3, Canada
Tel: 780-645-3323; *Fax:* 780-645-5789
www.stpauleducation.ab.ca
Number of Schools: 18 (including 5 kindergarten to grade 12 schools, 2 Hutterite colonies, 2 outreach schools *Grades:* Kindergarten - 12 *Enrollment:* 3988 *Number of Employees:* 270 teaching staff; 346 support staff
Darrell Younghans, Chair, 780-943-2460
Glen Brodziak, Superintendent, 780-645-3323
Patricia Gervais, Assistant Superintendent, 780-645-3323
Patrick Rivard, Assistant Superintendent, 780-645-3323
Glenda Bristow, Coordinator, Program, 780-645-3323
Janice Muench, Coordinator, Special Education, 780-645-3323
Jean Champagne, Secretary-Treasurer, 780-645-3323

***St-Paul:* Conseil scolaire Centre-Est**
P.O. Box 249
4537, av. 50, St-Paul, AB T0A 3A0, Canada
Tél: 780-645-3888; *Téléc:* 780-645-2045
Ligne sans frais: 866-645-9556
www.centreest.ca
Number of Schools: 4 *Grades:* Pre-12 *Enrollment:* 493

***Stettler:* Clearview School Division #71**
P.O. Box 1720
5031 - 50 St., Stettler, AB T0C 2L0, Canada
Tel: 403-742-3331; *Fax:* 403-742-1388
www.clearview.ab.ca
Number of Schools: 12 *Grades:* K - 12 *Enrollment:* 2462
John Bailey, Superintendent, Schools
jbailey@clearview.ab.ca

***Stony Plain:* Parkland School Division #70**
4603 - 48 St., Stony Plain, AB T7Z 2A8, Canada
Tel: 780-963-4010; *Fax:* 780-963-4169
www.psd70.ab.ca
Enrollment: 9454

***Strathmore:* Golden Hills School Division #75**
435A Hwy. #1, Strathmore, AB T1P 1J4, Canada
Tel: 403-934-5121; *Fax:* 403-934-5125
Toll-Free: 1-800-320-3739
www.ghsd75.ca
Grades: ECS - 12
Dave Price, Chair, 403-651-5317
Bevan Daverne, Superintendent, Schools
Edwin Holt, Associate Superintendent, Schools
Dr. Kandace Jordan, Associate Superintendent, Schools
Michael Kuystermans, Manager, Financial Services, 403-934-5121, ext. 2022
Don Hartman, Manager, Facilities & Maintenance, 403-934-5121, ext. 2053
Ken MacLean, Supervisor, Transportation, 877-442-4340
Tahra Sabir, Secretary-Treasurer, 403-934-5121, ext. 2024

***Taber:* Horizon School Division #67**
6302 - 56 St., Taber, AB T1G 1Z9, Canada
Tel: 403-223-3547; *Fax:* 403-223-2999
www.horizon.ab.ca
Enrollment: 3500
Marie Logan, Chair

***Wainwright:* Buffalo Trail Public Schools Regional Division No. 28**
Central Office
1041 - 10A St., Wainwright, AB T9W 2R4, Canada
Tel: 780-842-6144; *Fax:* 780-842-3255
central_office@btps.ca
www.btps.ca
Number of Schools: 19 (including 7 Hutterite Colony schools, 1 outreach site, 1 distance learning site) *Grades:* Kindergarten - 12 *Enrollment:* 4500 *Number of Employees:* 281 FTE teachers + 236 support staff
Darcy Eddleston, Chair, 780-745-2370
darcy.eddleston@btps.ca
Bob Allen, Superintendent, Schools, 780-842-6144
superintendent@btps.ca
Brad Romanchuk, Assistant Superintendent, Human Resources, 780-842-6144
brad.romanchuk@btps.ca
Lisa Blackstock, Assistant Superintendent, Learning Services, 780-842-6144
lisa.blackstock@btps.ca
Bob Brown, Secretary-Treasurer, 780-806-2050
bob.brown@btps.ca
Daryl Hoey, Director, Technology, 780-806-2065
daryl.hoey@btps.ca
Randy Huxley, Director, Facilities, 780-806-2064
randy.huxley@btps.ca
Chrysti Mannix, Director, Transportation, 780-806-2051
chrysti.mannix@btps.ca
Shannon Melin, Director, Human Resources, 780-806-2062
shannon.melin@btps.ca
Crystal Tower, Director, Student Services, 780-806-2056
crystal.tower@btps.ca
Hugh Forrester, Curriculum Lead, 780-872-1885
hugh.forrester@btps.ca

***Wetaskiwin:* Wetaskiwin Regional Division #11**
***Also known as:* Wetaskiwin Regional Public Schools**
5515 - 47A Ave., Wetaskiwin, AB T9A 3S3, Canada
Tel: 780-352-6018; *Fax:* 780-352-7886
wrps@wrps.ab.ca
www.wrps.ab.ca
Grades: Pre-K.-12 *Enrollment:* 4081
Terry Pearson, Supt.
Sherri Senger, Dir., Bus. Services
Robert Reimer, Chair

***Whitecourt:* Northern Gateway Regional Division #10**
P.O. Box 840
4104 Kepler St., Whitecourt, AB T7S 1M8, Canada
Tel: 780-778-2800; *Fax:* 780-778-6719
Toll-Free: 800-262-8674
www.ngrd.ab.ca
Grades: K.-12 *Enrollment:* 5300
Kevin Andrea, Supt.
Mike Gramatovich, Sec.-Treas.
mgramatovich@ngrd.ab.ca

Protestant

***St Albert:* St. Albert Protestant Separate School District #6**
60 Sir Winston Churchill Ave., St Albert, AB T8N 0G4, Canada
Tel: 780-460-3712; *Fax:* 780-460-7686
www.spschools.org
Enrollment: 6600
Barry Wowk, Superintendent

Catholic

***Bonnyville:* Lakeland Roman Catholic Separate School District #150**
4810 - 46 St., Bonnyville, AB T9N 1B5, Canada
Tel: 780-826-3764; *Fax:* 780-826-7576
www.lcsd150.ab.ca
Enrollment: 2200
Bernadette Provost, Superintendent

***Calgary:* Calgary Catholic School District**
Catholic School Centre
1000 - 5th Ave. SW, Calgary, AB T2P 4T9, Canada
Tel: 403-500-2000
communications@cssd.ab.ca; trustees@cssd.ab.ca
www.cssd.ab.ca
Other Information: Communications: 403-500-2763; Trustees: 403-500-2761
Number of Schools: 52 elementary; 34 ele./junior high; 9 sen. high; 6 junior high; 2 congregated special education *Grades:* Kindergarten - 12 *Enrollment:* 45066 *Number of Employees:* 3,143 instructional staff; 1,202 support staff; 314 caretaking staff; 144 exempt staff; 9 senior off
Dr. Lucy Miller, EdD, Chief Superintendent
John Deausy, Superintendent, Finance & Business, & Secretary-Treasurer
Craig Foley, Superintendent, Human Resources
Judy MacKay, Superintendent, Specialized Schools/Instruction/Religious Ed.
Dr. Andra McGinn, Superintendent, Area A Schools
Luba Diduch, Superintendent, Area B Schools
Mark Rawlek, Superintendent, Area C Schools
Gary Strother, Superintendent, Area D Schools & Information Technology
Michael Barbero, Superintendent, Area E Schools & Support Services
Tania Younker, Director, Communications, 403-500-2763, fax: 403-500-2927
communications@cssd.ab.ca

***Edmonton:* Edmonton Catholic School District #7**
9807 - 106 St., Edmonton, AB T5K 1C2, Canada
Tel: 780-441-6000; *Fax:* 780-425-8759
Toll-Free: 888-441-6010
info@ecsd.net
www.ecsd.net
www.facebook.com/EdmontonCatholicSchoolDistrict
twitter.com/EdmCathSchools
www.youtube.com/user/EdmontonCatholic?feature=mhee#p/u
Number of Schools: 87 *Grades:* K - 12 *Enrollment:* 34616
Number of Employees: 3005

***Fort McMurray:* Fort McMurray Roman Catholic Board of Education**
Fort McMurray Catholic Education Centre
9809 Main St., Fort McMurray, AB T9H 1T7, Canada
Tel: 780-799-5700; *Fax:* 780-799-5706
district@fmcsd.ab.ca
www.fmcsd.ab.ca
Other Information: Service Support Centre, Phone: 780-799-5714
Number of Schools: 9 *Grades:* Kindergarten - 12; French Immersion *Enrollment:* 4300 *Number of Employees:* 260 teachers; 160 support staff
Geraldine Carbery, Chair
Kim Jenkins, Superintendent, Schools, 780-799-5799, ext. 5001
kjenkins@fmcsd.ab.ca
George McGuigan, Deputy Superintendent, 780-799-5799, ext. 5020
gmcguigan@fmcsd.ab.ca
Francois Gagnon, Associate Superintendent, Business & Finance, 780-799-5700
fgagnon@fmcsd.ab.ca
Norena Hart, Director, Facilities, 780-799-5714
NHart@fmcsd.ab.ca
Monica Mankowski, Director, Student Services, 780-799-5799, ext. 5041
mmankowski@fmcsd.ab.ca
Kathleen Murray House, Director, School Based Administration, & Mentor Principal, 780-799-5799, ext. 5001
kmurphy@fmcsd.ab.ca
Betty-Lou Cahill, Coordinator, Human Resources, 780-799-5799, ext. 5021
BCahill@fmcsd.ab.ca

***Grande Prairie:* Grande Prairie & District Catholic Schools**
Catholic Education Centre
9902 - 101 St., Grande Prairie, AB T8V 2P4, Canada
Tel: 780-532-3013; *Fax:* 780-532-3430
Toll-Free: 1-800-661-2568
cec@gpcsd.ca (Catholic Ed. Ctr.); support@gpcsd.ca (Tech Support)
www.gpcsd.ca
Other Information: Transportation & Maintenance, Phone: 780-513-1220
Number of Schools: 12 *Grades:* JK - 12; French Immersion; Outreach *Enrollment:* 3900 *Number of Employees:* 400
Karl Germann, Superintendent, Schools, 780-532-3013
Ed Buckle, Assistant Superintendent, Human Resources, 780-532-3013, ext. 121
Marlene Stefura, Assistant Superintendent, Curriculum & Assessment, 780-532-3013, ext. 122
Bryan Turner, Associate Superintendent, Business Operations, 780-532-3013, ext. 123
Pauline Ruel-Wyant, Director, Student Services, 780-532-3013, ext. 403
Clint Carrell, Administrator, Information Systems, 780-532-3013, ext. 300
John Dooley, Supervisor, Maintenance, 780-513-1220
Randy Lester, Supervisor, Transportation & Custodians, 780-513-1220

Leduc: St. Thomas Aquinas Roman Catholic Separate Regional Division #38
4906 - 50th Ave., Leduc, AB T9E 6W9, Canada
Tel: 780-986-2500; *Fax:* 780-986-8620
Toll-Free: 1-800-583-0688
feedback@starcatholic.ab.ca
www.faithinyourfuture.ca
Number of Schools: 9 schools; 1 outreach centre *Grades:* Kindergarten - 12; Catholicism *Enrollment:* 2500 *Number of Employees:* 140 full-time teachers; 100 support staff
Maria Lentz, Board Chair
Jamie McNamara, Superintendent, Schools
Troy Davies, Assistant Superintendent
Jeanne Fontaine, Secretary-Treasurer
Tara-Ann Drexler, Coordinator, Transportation, & Accounting Clerk
Marilyn Kunitz, Coordinator, Student Services
Pius MacLean, Coordinator, Curriculum & Instruction
Michael Marien, Coordinator, Faith Life & Curriculum
David Scribner, Coordinator, Facilites
Dan Svitich, Coordinator, Information Technology
Susan Baudin, Officer, Human Resouces & Payroll

Lethbridge: Holy Spirit Roman Catholic Separate Regional Division #4
620 - 12B St. North, Lethbridge, AB T1H 2L7, Canada
Tel: 403-327-9555; *Fax:* 403-327-9595
www.holyspirit.ab.ca
Enrollment: 4400
Christopher Smeaton, Superintendent

Lloydminster: Lloydminster Roman Catholic Separate School Division #89
6611B - 39th St., Lloydminster, AB T9V 2Z4, Canada
Tel: 780-808-8585; *Fax:* 780-808-8787
information@lcsd.ca
www.lcsd.ca
Grades: K.-12
Doug Robertson, Dir.
Tom Schinold, Supt. of Admin.
tschinold@lcsd.ca

Medicine Hat: Medicine Hat Catholic Separate School Regional Division #20
1251 - 1 Ave. SW, Medicine Hat, AB T1A 8B4, Canada
Tel: 403-527-2292; *Fax:* 403-529-0917
Toll-Free: 866-864-0013
www.mhcbe.ab.ca
Grades: Pre-K.-12 *Enrollment:* 2800
David Leahy, Supt. of Schools

Okotoks: Christ the Redeemer Catholic Separate Regional Division #3
1 McRae St., Okotoks, AB T1S 1B3, Canada
Tel: 403-938-2659; *Fax:* 403-938-4575
Toll-Free: 800-737-9383
info@redeemer.ab.ca
www.redeemer.ab.ca
Number of Schools: 17 *Grades:* K - 12 *Enrollment:* 6200
Mary Stengler, Chair, Board of Trustees
mstengler@redeemer.ab.ca

Peace River: Holy Family Catholic Regional Division #37
10307 - 99 St., Peace River, AB T8S 1R5, Canada
Tel: 780-624-3956; *Fax:* 780-624-1154
Toll-Free: 800-285-8712
www.hfcrd.ab.ca
Enrollment: 2000
Betty Turpin, Superintendent

Red Deer: Red Deer Catholic Regional Division #39
5210 - 61 St., Red Deer, AB T4N 6N8, Canada
Tel: 403-343-1055; *Fax:* 403-347-6410
info@rdcrd.ab.ca
www.rdcrd.ab.ca
www.facebook.com/317027491725647
twitter.com/RDCatholic
Number of Schools: 18 *Enrollment:* 7300
V. Paul Mason, Superintendent

Sherwood Park: Elk Island Catholic Separate Regional Division #41
160 Festival Way, Sherwood Park, AB T8A 5Z2, Canada
Tel: 780-467-8896; *Fax:* 780-467-5469
eics@eics.ab.ca
www.eics.ab.ca
Number of Schools: 16 *Grades:* K - 12 *Enrollment:* 5200
Michael Hauptman, Superintendent, Schools
michaelh@eics.ab.ca

Spruce Grove: Evergreen Catholic Separate Regional Division No. 2
Holy Trinity Church
P.O. Box 4265
200 Boundry Rd., 2nd Fl., Spruce Grove, AB T7X 3B4, Canada
Tel: 780-962-5627; *Fax:* 780-962-4664
Toll-Free: 1-800-825-7152
www.ecsrd.ca
Number of Schools: 9 *Grades:* ECS - 12 *Enrollment:* 3481
Gerald Bernakevitch, Board Chair
Dr. Cindi Vaselenak, Superintendent
Michael Hauptman, Deputy Superintendent
Sime Fatovic, Director, Facilities & Technology
Sheila Shumate, Director, Student Services
Karen Koester, Coordinator, Religious Education
Marlene Fehr, Treasurer
Al Brettnell, Network Administrator

St Albert: Greater St. Albert Catholic Schools
6 St. Vital Ave., St Albert, AB T8N 1K2, Canada
Tel: 780-459-7711; *Fax:* 780-458-3213
www.gsacrd.ab.ca
Number of Schools: 17 *Grades:* Kindergarten - 12 *Enrollment:* 6251 *Number of Employees:* 666 staff in schools; 48 staff in division operations
David Keohane, Superintendent
dkeohane@gsacrd.ab.ca
Steve Bayus, Deputy Superintendent
sbayus@gsacrd.ab.ca
David Quick, Assistant Superintendent, Learning Services
dquick@gsacrd.ab.ca
Colleen McClure, Interim Associate Superintendent, Student Services
cmcclure@gsacrd.ab.ca
Calvin Wait, Director, Facilities
cwait@gsacrd.ab.ca
Lydia Yeomans, Division Principal
lyeomans@gsacrd.ab.ca
Deb Schlag, Secretary-Treasurer
dschlag@gsacrd.ab.ca

Wainwright: East Central Alberta Catholic Separate School Regional Division #16
1018 - 1st Ave., Wainwright, AB T9W 1G9, Canada
Tel: 780-842-3992; *Fax:* 780-842-5322
reception@ecacs16.ab.ca
www.ecacs16.ab.ca
Number of Schools: 8 *Grades:* K - 12 *Enrollment:* 3000
Valerie Burgardt, Acting Superintendent, Schools
valerie.burgardt@ecacs16.ab.ca

Whitecourt: Living Waters Catholic Regional Division #42
P.O. Box 1949
4204 Kepler St., Whitecourt, AB T7S 1P6, Canada
Tel: 780-778-5666; *Fax:* 780-778-2727
Toll-Free: 888-434-7348
www.livingwaters.ab.ca
Grades: Pre.-12 *Enrollment:* 1723

First Nations

Brownvale: Duncan's First Nation Education
P.O. Box 148
Brownvale, AB T0H 0L0, Canada
Tel: 780-597-3777; *Fax:* 780-597-3920
www.duncansfn.ca
Note: Duncan's First Nation is a small band situated southwest of Peace River, Alberta. A Child Development Centre offers daycare & a head start program. The head start program, for children from age three to five, includes a Cree language & cultural program. School buses transport Duncan's First Nation students to Berwyn, Grimshaw, & Peace River to enter a public school system.
Don Testawich, Chief, Duncan's First Nation

Chard: Chipewyan Prairie Dene First Nation Education Authority
General Delivery, Chard, AB T0P 1G0, Canada
Tel: 780-559-2259; *Fax:* 780-559-2213
Number of Schools: 1

Chateh: Dene Tha' First Nation Education Department
P.O. Box 120
Chateh, AB T0H 0S0, Canada
Tel: 780-321-3886; *Fax:* 780-321-3775
Toll-Free: 877-336-3842
info@denetha.ca
www.denetha.ca
Number of Schools: 1 *Grades:* Jr. Kindergarten-10; Dene language *Enrollment:* 450 *Note:* (Dene Tha' Community School). The Dene Tha' First Nation Education Department oversees education, counselling, transportation, & accommodation for Dene Tha' First Nation band members. Through its association with the North Peace Tribal Council, the Dene Tha' First Nation Education Department also directs post-secondary student services.
Adrienne Beaulieu, Coordinator, Post-Secondary Student Services, 780-926-2786, fax: 780-926-6652
Adrienne.Beaulieu@denetha.ca
Debbie Ahkimnachie, Clerk, Education Program, 780-321-3405
Debbie.Ahkimnachie@denetha.ca

Duffield: Paul Band Education Authority
P.O. Box 89
Duffield, AB T0E 0N0, Canada
Tel: 780-892-2025; *Fax:* 780-892-2019
directorrbird@pfneducation.ca
Grades: K.-12

Enoch: Kitaskinaw Education Authority
P.O. Box 90
Enoch, AB T7X 3Y3, Canada
Tel: 780-470-5657
Number of Schools: 1 *Grades:* Nursery - 9 *Note:* Kitaskinaw School. The Kitaskinaw Education Authority oversees education for the Enoch Cree Nation.

Fort Vermilion: Tallcree First Nation School Division
P.O. Box 310
Fort Vermilion, AB T0H 1N0, Canada
Tel: 780-927-3803
tallcreesd@gmail.com
Number of Schools: 2 *Grades:* K4 - 6 *Enrollment:* 100 *Note:* Chief Tallcree North School & Chief Tallcree South School
Vic Dikaitis, Director, Education

Goodfish Lake: Whitefish Lake Education Authority
P.O. Box 274
Goodfish Lake, AB T0A 1R0, Canada
Tel: 780-636-7000; *Fax:* 780-636-3101
Grades: K.-9

Hobbema: Kisipatnahk School Society
P.O. Box 1290
Hobbema, AB T0C 1N0, Canada
Tel: 780-585-3978; *Fax:* 780-585-3799
Number of Schools: 1 *Grades:* Pre.-6 *Enrollment:* 177

Hobbema: Nipisihkopahk Education Authority
P.O. Box 658
Hobbema, AB T0C 1N0, Canada
Tel: 780-585-2211; *Fax:* 780-585-3857
Toll-Free: 800-843-7359
www.scnea.com
Number of Schools: 4 *Grades:* 1-12

John D'Or Prairie: Little Red River Board of Education
P.O. Box 90
John D'Or Prairie, AB T0H 3X0, Canada
Tel: 780-759-3780; *Fax:* 780-759-3848
www.lrrbe.ab.ca
Number of Schools: 3 *Grades:* Kindergarten - 12; Special Ed. *Enrollment:* 1050 *Note:* (Jean Baptiste Sewepagaham School; John D'Or Prairie School; & Sister Gloria School). Number of Employees: 110+. The Little Red River Board of Education administers the provision of educational programming for First nation students of the Little Red River Cree Nation. Cultural programming is part of the students' education. The Board also offers adult upgrading & trades training.
Gloria Cardinal, Director, Education
glocardinal@gmail.com
Leah Blesse, Financial Controller

Lac La Biche: Beaver Lake Education Authority
P.O. Box 5000
Lac La Biche, AB T0A 2C0, Canada
Tel: 780-623-4549; *Fax:* 780-623-4523
amiskcommunityschool@yahoo.ca
www.beaverlakecreenation.ca
Other Information: Amisk Community School, Phone: 780-623-4548; Fax: 780-623-4659
Number of Schools: 1 *Grades:* Early Childhood Svs.-Jr. Secondary *Note:* The Beaver Lake Education Authority operates the Amisk Community School. The school is led by a nine member management team which is supervised by the Beaver Lake Cree Nation Band Council Education Portfolio Holder.
Councillor Germaine Anderson, Beaver Lake Cree Nation Council Education Portfolio Holder

Morinville: Alexander First Nation Education Authority
P.O. Box 3449
Morinville, AB T8R 1S3, Canada
Tel: 780-939-3868; Fax: 780-939-3991
Note: The Alexander First Nation Education Authority operates the Kipohtakaw Education Centre.
Raymond Soetaert, Principal, Kipohtakaw Education Centre

Morley: Stoney Education Authority
P.O. Box 238
Morley, AB T0L 1N0, Canada
Tel: 403-881-2743; Fax: 403-881-4252
www.stoneynation.com
Number of Schools: 3 Grades: Kindergarten - 12; Stoney language Enrollment: 1100 Note: (Morley Community School; Ta Otha Community School; & Chief Jacob Bearspaw School). The Stoney Education Authority, located west of Calgary, Alberta, provides education to members of the Stoney Nakoda First Nation. Education includes cultural programs.
Nadeem Altaf, Administrator, Education, 403-881-2776

Rocky Mountain House: Sunchild First Nation Band Education Authority
P.O. Box 1149
Rocky Mountain House, AB T4T 1A8, Canada
Tel: 403-989-3476; Fax: 403-989-3614
Number of Schools: 1 Grades: Kindergarten - 12 Note: Sunchild First Nation School. Number of Employees: 50+ full-time & part-time personnel
Caroline Bigchild, Chair
Nelson Daychief, Director, Education
administrator@sunchildschool.com

Saddle Lake: Saddle Lake Education Authority
P.O. Box 130
Saddle Lake, AB T0A 3T0, Canada
Tel: 780-726-7609; Fax: 780-726-4069
Toll-Free: 800-668-0243
www.saddlelake.ca/Saddlelake1.html
Grades: 1-12
Debra Cardinal, Director
dcardinal@saddlelake.ca

Siksika: Siksika Board of Education
P.O. Box 1099
Siksika, AB T0J 3W0, Canada
Tel: 403-734-5220; Fax: 403-734-2505
www.siksikaboardofeducation.com
Number of Schools: 4 Grades: Pre.-12
Harvina Red Crow, Chairperson
redcrowh@siksikaboardofeducation.com

Stand Off: Kainaiwa Board of Education
P.O. Box 240
Stand Off, AB T0L 1Y0, Canada
Tel: 403-737-3966; Fax: 403-737-2361
kainaied.ca
Grades: 7-12

Tsuu T'ina Sarcee: Tsuu T'ina Nation Board of Education
#250, 9911 Chiila Blvd. SW, Tsuu T'ina Sarcee, AB T2W 6H6, Canada
Tel: 403-238-5484
www.tsuutina.ca
Number of Schools: 3 Grades: K4 - 12; Adult Upgrading Enrollment: 299 Note: (Chiila Elementary School; Tsuu T'ina Junior Senior High School; & Tsuu T'ina Bullhead Adult Education Centre)

Valleyview: Sturgeon Lake First Nation, Band #154, Education Authority
P.O. Box 5
Valleyview, AB T0H 3N0, Canada
Tel: 780-524-4590
Number of Schools: 1 Grades: Kindergarten - 12 Enrollment: 230 Note: Sturgeon Lake School

Wabasca: Bigstone Cree Nation Education Authority
P.O. Box 870
Wabasca, AB T0G 2K0, Canada
Tel: 780-891-3825; Fax: 780-891-3021
Toll-Free: 1-800-661-3891
www.bigstone.ca
Number of Schools: 1 Grades: Elementary Enrollment: 247 Note: Oski Pasikoniwew Kamik, also known as the Bigstone Community School
P. Ray Peters, Director, Education
ray.peters@bigstone.ca
Priscilla Auger, Counsellor, Post-Secondary Education, 877-458-2447, fax: 866-801-3021
priscilla.auger@bigstone.ca

Independent & Private Schools

Didsbury: Koinonia Christian Schools
c/o Koinonia Christian Education Society
P.O. Box 1405
#107, 1001 - 20th Ave., Didsbury, AB T0M 0W0, Canada
Tel: 403-335-9587; Fax: 403-335-9513
kces@koinoniaschools.com
www.koinoniaschools.com
Note: Koinona Christian Schools is a system of 9 evangelical, non-denominational schools in Alberta.
Vern Rand, Superintendent
vern.rand@koinonia.ca
Garry Anderson, Associate Superintendent
garryka@gmail.com
Judy Nelson, Business Administrator
jnelson@koinoniaschools.com

Schools: Specialized

Charter

Androssan: New Horizons School
53145 Range Rd., Androssan, AB T8E 2M8, Canada
Tel: 780-467-6409; Fax: 780-417-1786
administration@newhorizons.ab.ca
www.newhorizons.ab.ca
Grades: K-9 Enrollment: 160

Calgary: Almadina Language Charter Academy
225 - 28 St. SE, Calgary, AB T2A 5K4, Canada
Tel: 403-543-5078; Fax: 403-543-5079
www.esl-almadina.com
Grades: 1-9 Enrollment: 600
Keith Jones, Superintendent
kjones@esl-almadina.com
Janice LeDuc, Secretary-Treasurer
jleduc@esl-almadina.com
Faduma Omar, Board Secretary
fomar@esl-almadina.com

Calgary: Calgary Arts Academy Society
4931 Grove Hill Rd. SW, Calgary, AB T3E 4G4, Canada
Tel: 403-532-3020; Fax: 403-217-0965
info@calgaryartsacademy.com
www.calgaryartsacademy.com
Enrollment: 279

Calgary: Calgary Girls' School - Lakeview Campus
6304 Larkspur Way SW, Calgary, AB T3E 5P7, Canada
Tel: 403-220-0745; Fax: 403-217-1371
www.calgarygirlsschool.com
Grades: 4-9 Enrollment: 460 Note: Bel Aire Campus: 1011 Beverley Blvd. SW, (403) 253-3785.
Caroline Parker, Principal
Campuses
Calgary Girls' School - Bel Aire Campus
1011 Beverley Blvd. SW, Calgary, AB T2V 2C4, Canada
Tel: 403-253-3785; Fax: 403-253-0430
www.calgarygirlsschool.com
Grades: 4-9 Note: Lakeview Campus: 6304 Larkspur Way SW, (403) 220-0745.

Calgary: Calgary Science School (CSS)
5915 Lewis Dr. SW, Calgary, AB T3E 5Z4
Tel: 403-282-2890; Fax: 403-282-2896
www.calgaryscienceschool.com
Grades: 4-9 Enrollment: 600 Number of Employees: 34 teaching staff Note: Calgary Science School opened in 1999. The charter shcool focuses on authentic inquiry-based learning.
Garry McKinnon, Superintendent, 403-282-2890, ext. 232
Darrell Lonsberry, Principal, 403-282-2890, ext. 122
Phil Butterfield, Assistant Principal, 403-282-2890, ext. 116
Scott Petronech, Assistant Principal & Educational Technologist

Calgary: Foundations for the Future Charter Academy (FFCA)
FFCA Central Office
#240, 688 Heritage Dr. SE, Calgary, AB T2H 1M6
Tel: 403-520-3206; Fax: 403-520-3209
www.ffca-calgary.com
Grades: Kindergarten - 12 Note: Campuses include the Southeast Elementary Campus, the Southwest Elementary Campus, the South Middle School Campus, the Northwest Elementary Campus, the Northeast Elementary Campus, the North Middle School Campus, & the High School Campus.
Jay Pritchard, Superintendent
Ken Dewald, Director, Facilities
Cathy McCauley, Coordinator, School Development
Lorie Skaper-Burtch, Coordinator, Instruction

Calgary: Westmount Charter School Society
728 - 32 St. NW, Calgary, AB T2N 2V9, Canada
Tel: 403-217-0426; Fax: 403-217-0252
admin@westmountcharter.com
www.westmountcharter.com
Grades: K-12 Enrollment: 880

Edmonton: Aurora Charter School
12245 - 131 St., Edmonton, AB T5L 1M8
Tel: 780-454-1855; Fax: 780-454-8104
aurorasc@auroraschool.com
www.auroraschool.com
Grades: Kindergarten - 9 Enrollment: 450
Don Wilson, Board Chair
Dale Bischoff, Superintendent
Ian Gray, Principal
igray@auroraschool.com
Janet Rockwood, Assistant Principal
jrockwood@auroraschool.com
Georgia Foster, Registrar
gfoster@auroraschool.com

Edmonton: Boyle Street Education Centre
10312 - 105 Ave., Edmonton, AB T5J 1E6, Canada
Tel: 780-428-1420; Fax: 780-429-1428
info@bsec.ab.ca
www.bsec.ab.ca
Grades: 7-12 Enrollment: 105

Edmonton: Suzuki Charter School Society
10720 - 54 St., Edmonton, AB T6A 2H9
Tel: 780-468-2598; Fax: 780-463-8630
www.suzukischool.ca
Grades: Preschool - 6 Note: The charter school provides academics, enriched with music based on the Suzuki Approach.
Lee Lucente, Superintendent
lucentel@suzukischool.ca
Karen Spencer, Principal
spencerk@suzukischool.ca
Dale Szalacsi, Assistant Principal
szalacsid@suzukischool.ca
Heather Christison, Secretary-Treasurer
christison@suzukischool.ca

Medicine Hat: Centre for Academic & Personal Excellence Institute - CAPE
830A Balmoral St. SE, Medicine Hat, AB T1A 0W9, Canada
Tel: 403-528-2983; Fax: 403-528-3048
tdininno@capeisgreat.org
www.capeisgreat.org
Grades: 1-9 Enrollment: 135

Stony Plain: Mother Earth's Children's Charter School Society (MECCS)
P.O. Box 11
Site 504, RR#5, Stony Plain, AB T7Z 1X5, Canada
Tel: 780-892-7531; Fax: 780-848-2395
admin@meccs.org
www.meccs.org
Erin Danforth, Principal
edanforth@meccs.org

First Nations

Brocket: Peigan Band
P.O. Box 130
Brocket, AB T0K 0H0, Canada
Tel: 403-965-3910; Fax: 403-965-3713
Grades: K - 12

Cadotte Lake: Woodland Cree First Nation Cadotte Lake School
General Delivery, Cadotte Lake, AB T0H 0N0
Tel: 780-629-3767
Grades: Kindergarten - 12

Chard: Chipewyan Prairie Dene High School (CPDHS)
Chipewyan Prairie Education Multi-Plex
General Delivery, Chard, AB T0P 1G0
Tel: 780-559-2478
Grades: Secondary Enrollment: 30 Note: The band operated high school is situated south of Fort McMurray, Alberta, where it provides education for the Chipewyan Prairie Dene First Nation.

Chateh: Dene Tha' Community School (DTCS)
P.O. Box 120
Chateh, AB T0H 0S0
Tel: 780-321-3775; Fax: 780-321-3886
Toll-Free: 877-336-3842
info@denetha.ca
www.denetha.ca

Grades: Jr. Kindergarten-10; Dene language *Enrollment:* 450
Note: Dene Tha' Community School provides education that follows Alberta's kindergarten to grade 10 curriculum, as well as programs such as an early literacy program, a special education program, & Dene language & culture programs.
Lori Aliche, Principal, 780-321-3940, fax: 780-926-0500
Virginia Alarcon, Vice-Principal, Junior High, 780-321-3940, fax: 780-926-1412
Rosalie Metchooyeah, Elder, 780-321-3940
Hayley Natannah, Office Manager, 780-321-3940
Hayley.Natannah@denetha.ca
Ann Austin, Librarian, 780-321-3940
Helen Metchooyeah, Instructor, Dene Language, 780-321-3940
Tyler Metchooyeah, Instructor, Dene, 780-321-3940
Shane Providence-Toho, Instructor, Dene, 780-321-3940

Cold Lake: LeGeoff School
P.O. Box 1769
Cold Lake, AB T9M 1P4
Tel: 780-594-7183; *Fax:* 780-594-3577
clfns.com
Grades: K-9 *Enrollment:* 96 *Number of Employees:* 13 *Note:* LeGeoff School is federally administered & funded by the Department of Indian Affairs. The school employs seven federally funded teachers & six Cold Lake First Nations funded positions.
Maryanne Bushore, Principal, 780-594-3733, fax: 780-594-5845
maryannebushore@kinusoo.ca

Driftpile: Driftpile Community School
P.O. Box 240
Driftpile, AB T0G 0V0, Canada
Tel: 780-355-3615; *Fax:* 780-355-2135
www.driftpilecreenation.com
Grades: K-4, K-5 - 8; Cree language *Enrollment:* 75 *Note:* Driftpile Community School offers a full academic program, as well as a Cree language & cultural program with traditional music, folklore, & crafts.
Daisy McGee, Principal
Josephine Willier, Secretary
Janice Chalifoux, Family School Wellness Worker
Leonard Isadore, Contact, Cultural Appreciation

Enoch: Kitaskinaw School
P.O. Box 90
Enoch, AB T7X 3Y3
Tel: 780-470-5657; *Fax:* 780-470-5687
Grades: Nursery - 9 *Note:* Kitaskinaw School is part of the Kitaskinaw Education Authority. The school educates members of the Enoch Cree Nation.

Fox Lake: Jean Baptiste Sewepagaham School
P.O. Box 270
Fox Lake, AB TOH 1R0
Tel: 780-659-3820
Grades: K - 12; Cree language *Enrollment:* 600 *Note:* Jean Baptiste Sewepagaham School is one of three schools in the Little Red River Board of Education. The school serves members of the Little Red River Cree Nation, located approximately 125 kilometres east of High Level, Alberta.

Frog Lake: Frog Lake Chief Napeweaw Comprehensive School
General Delivery, Frog Lake, AB T0A 1M0, Canada
Tel: 780-943-3918; *Fax:* 780-943-2336
www.froglake.ca/education_authority.html
Grades: Pre.-12; Special Ed.

Garden River: Sister Gloria School
P.O. Box 90
Garden River, AB TOH 4G0
Tel: 780-659-3644; *Fax:* 780-659-3890
Note: The Little Red River Board of Education consists of three schools, including Sister Gloria School. Sister Gloria School provides education to First Nation students of the Little Red River Cree Nation. The Alberta community is situated approximately 125 kilometres east of High Level.
Garry Wilson, Principal
wilson_garry@hotmail.com

Glenevis: Alexis Nakota Sioux First Nation School
P.O. Box 27
Glenevis, AB T0E 0X0, Canada
Tel: 780-967-4878
www.alexised.ca
Grades: Elementary - Junior Secondary

Goodfish Lake: Whitefish Lake First Nation #128 Pakan Elementary & Junior High School
P.O. Box 274
Goodfish Lake, AB T0A 1R0
Tel: 780-636-2525
www.wfl128.ca

Grades: Kindergarten - 9
Dale Steinhauer, Board Chair
Nav Atwal, Principal
Velma Memnook, School Liaison & Counsellor
Georgina Halfe, Cree Instructor

Hobbema: Meskanahk Ka-Nipa-Wit School
***Also known as:* Montana School**
P.O. Box 129
Hobbema, AB T0C 1N0, Canada
Tel: 780-585-2799; *Fax:* 780-585-2264
Grades: K.-9

Hobbema: Miyo Wahkohtowin Community Education Authority
P.O. Box 248
Hobbema, AB T0C 1N0, Canada
Tel: 780-585-2118; *Fax:* 780-585-2116
www.miyo.ca
Number of Schools: 3 *Grades:* Pre.-9 *Note:* A First Nations-managed education system that operates three schools: Ermineskin Elementary, Junior Senior High, & Ehpewapahk schools for the Ermineskin Cree Nation in Alberta.
Brian Wildcat, Director, Education
brian_wildcat@miyo.ca
Sanila Mehal, Director, Student Services
sanila_mehal@miyo.ca
Peter Kerr, Financial Controller
peter_kerr@miyo.ca

John D'Or Prairie: John D'Or Prairie School
P.O. Box 120
John D'Or Prairie, AB T0H 3X0
Tel: 780-759-3772
www.lrrbe.ab.ca
Note: John D'Or Prairie School is part of the Little Red River Board of Education. Education is provided to the Little Red River Cree Nation, located approximately 865 kilometres north of Edmonton, Alberta.

Kehewin: Kehewin High School Community Education Centre
P.O. Box 30
Kehewin, AB T0A 1C0, Canada
Tel: 780-826-6200; *Fax:* 780-826-5919
tcef.ca
Grades: K-12
Linda Gadwa, Principal
linda.gadwa@tcef.ca

Kinuso: Swan River First Nation School
P.O. Box 120
Kinuso, AB T0G 1K0
Tel: 780-775-2177; *Fax:* 780-775-2155
Grades: 7 - 12 *Enrollment:* 100 *Note:* The Swan River First Nation School operates on the Swan River First Nation Reserve in Kinuso, Alberta.

Lac La Biche: Amisk Community School
P.O. Box 5000
Lac La Biche, AB T0A 2C0
Tel: 780-623-4548; *Fax:* 780-623-4659
www.beaverlakecreenation.ca
Grades: Early Childhood Svs.-Jr. Secondary *Note:* Operated by the Beaver Lake Education Authority, the Amisk Community School provides education to the Beaver Lake Cree Nation.

Lac La Biche: Heart Lake Kohls School
P.O. Box 1619
Lac La Biche, AB T0A 2C0, Canada
Tel: 780-623-2330; *Fax:* 780-623-3505
tcef.ca/our-schools/kohls-school
Grades: Pre.-12
Flo Kanhair, Principal
flo.kanhai@tcef.ca

Longview: Chief Jacob Bearspaw School
P.O. Box 116
100 Center St. SW, Longview, AB T0L 1H0
Tel: 403-558-2480; *Fax:* 403-558-3618
www.stoney-nation.com
Note: Chief Jacob Bearspaw School, located on the Eden Valley Reserve in Alberta, is part of the Stoney Education Authority.
Bill Shade, Principal

Morley: Morley Community School
P.O. Box 238
Morley, Morley, AB T0L 1N0
Tel: 403-881-2755; *Fax:* 403-881-2333
www.stoney-nation.com
Grades: K4 - 12; Stoney language *Note:* The Stoney Education Authority oversees the Morley Community School. The First Nations school serves members of the Nakoda First Nation, situated west of Calgary, Alberta.

Rocky Mountain House: O'chiese Education Authority
P.O. Box 337
Rocky Mountain House, AB T4T 1A3, Canada
Tel: 403-989-3911; *Fax:* 403-989-2122
ochiese.ca/education/education
Grades: K-12
Lara Jollymore, Principal
lara.jollymore@ochieseeducation.ca

Rocky Mountain House: Sunchild First Nation School
P.O. Box 1149
Rocky Mountain House, AB T4T 1A8
Tel: 403-989-3476; *Fax:* 403-989-3614
www.sunchildschool.com
Grades: Kindergarten - 12 *Note:* The Sunchild First Nation School is part of the Sunchild First Nation Band Education Authority.
Martin Sacher, Principal
sacher@sccyber.net
Susan Collicutt, Vice-Principal
collicutts@yahoo.ca

Tsuu T'ina Sarcee: Chiila Elementary School
#250, 991 Chiila Blvd. SW, Tsuu T'ina Sarcee, AB T2W 6H6
Tel: 403-238-5484
www.tsuutina.ca
Grades: K4 - 5 *Note:* Chiila Elementary School is part of the Tsuu T'ina Nation Board of Education.

Tsuu T'ina Sarcee: Tsuu T'ina Junior Senior High School
#250, 991 Chiila Blvd. SW, Tsuu T'ina Sarcee, AB T2W 6H6
Tel: 403-251-9555; *Fax:* 403-251-9833
www.tsuutina.ca
Grades: 6 - 12 *Note:* The Tsuu T'ina Nation Board of Education oversees the operations of the Tsuu T'ina Junior Senior High School.

Valleyview: Sturgeon Lake School
P.O. Box 5
Valleyview, AB T0H 3N0
Tel: 780-524-4590; *Fax:* 780-524-3696
Grades: Kindergarten - 12 *Enrollment:* 230 *Note:* The Sturgeon Lake School is part of the Sturgeon Lake First Nation, Band #154, Education Authority. The First Nation school serves the Sturgeon Lake Cree Nation.

Wabasca: Bigstone Cree Nation Community School Oski Pasikoniwew Kamik
P.O. Box 930
Wabasca, AB T0G 2K0
Tel: 780-891-3830; *Fax:* 780-891-3831
www.bigstone.ca
Grades: Preschool - 6 *Enrollment:* 247 *Note:* The Bigstone Community School operates under the direction of the Bigstone Cree Nation Education Authority. The school strives to maintain traditional values as its educational foundation.

Independent & Private Schools

Three Hills: Prairie Bible Institute (PBI)
P.O. Box 4000
330 - 5th Ave. Northeast, Three Hills, AB T0M 2N0
Tel: 403-443-5511; *Fax:* 403-443-5540
presidentsoffice@prairie.edu
www.prairie.edu
www.facebook.com/PrairieColleges
twitter.com/prairiecolleges
www.youtube.com/user/PrairieColleges
Number of Employees: 45 employees
Mark Maxwell, President
mark.maxwell@prairie.edu
Peter Mal, Dean, 4034435511, ext. 3054
Peter.Mal@prairie.edu

Schools
Prairie Christian Academy (PCA) Elementary School
P.O. Box 68
1025 - 4th St. N, Three Hills, AB T0M 2A0
Tel: 403-443-4210
pcainfo@ghsd75.ca
www.pca3hills.ca
www.facebook.com/group.php?gid=2260682242
twitter.com/pca3hills
Grades: K.-6 *Enrollment:* 300 *Note:* Prairie Christian Academy (PCA) is a non-denominational, Christian school for Preschool to Grade 12 students.

Prairie Christian Academy (PCA) Secondary School
P.O. Box 68
Three Hills, AB T0M 2A0, Canada
Tel: 403-443-4220
pcainfo@ghsd75.ca
pca.ghsd75.ca

Grades: 7-12

Servant Magazine
Tel: 800-221-8532
servant@prairie.edu

Schools: Independent & Private

Catholic

***Calgary:* Clear Water Academy**
2521 Dieppe Ave. SW, Calgary, AB T3E 7J9, Canada
Tel: 403-217-8448; *Fax:* 403-217-8043
administration@clearwateracademy.com
www.clearwateracademy.com
Grades: Pre.-12 *Note:* An independent Catholic school.
Paul Hudec, Principal

***Vermilion:* St. Jerome's Catholic School**
4820 - 46th St., Vermilion, AB T9X 1G2
Tel: 780-853-5251; *Fax:* 780-853-4343
stjschool.org
Grades: Elementary

Special Education

***Calgary:* Foothills Academy**
745 - 37 St. NW, Calgary, AB T2N 4T1, Canada
Tel: 403-270-9400; *Fax:* 403-270-9438
info@foothillsacademy.org
www.foothillsacademy.org
www.facebook.com/pages/Foothills-Academy/333239973359586
www.linkedin.com/groups?gid=3112702&trk=hb_side_g
Grades: 1-12; Special Ed.

***Edmonton:* Edmonton Academy**
10231 - 120 St., Edmonton, AB T5K 2A4, Canada
Tel: 780-482-5449; *Fax:* 780-482-0902
lizrich@telusplanet.net
www.edmontonacademy.com
Grades: 7-12 *Note:* Founded in 1983; provides specialized teaching for students with learning disabilities.
Liz Richards, Executive Director

***Edmonton:* Elves Child Development Centre**
10825 - 142 St., Edmonton, AB T5N 3Y7, Canada
Tel: 780-454-5310; *Fax:* 780-454-5889
elvessoc@telusplanet.net
www.elves-society.com
Grades: Pre.-12 *Note:* The Elves Special Needs Society offers programs for pre-school and older children, youth and adults who are severely developmentally delayed and/or medically fragile, as well as outreach to students unable to attend school for extended periods of time.
Cristina Molina, Executive Director

***Edmonton:* John Howard Society of Edmonton Alternative Learning Program**
10523 - 100 Ave., 2nd Fl., Edmonton, AB T5J 0A8, Canada
Tel: 780-423-4878; *Fax:* 780-425-0008
info@johnhoward.ab.ca
www.johnhoward.ab.ca
www.facebook.com/JohnHowardSocietyOfAlberta
twitter.com/johnhowardab
Grades: To Gr. 9 *Note:* The Edmonton John Howard Society's Adult Transition Learning Centre offers courses to clients at every stage of learning, including: literacy, GED & college preparation, language arts, math & computer basics, personal development, & life skills (addictions, anger management, mental health; all aspects of employment preparation). The Centre is located at 10010 105th St., Suite 401, in Edmonton.

Independent & Private Schools

***Airdrie:* Airdrie Koinonia Christian School (AKCS)**
2104 Yankee Valley Blvd. SW, Airdrie, AB T4B 0R7, Canada
Tel: 403-948-5100; *Fax:* 403-948-5563
secretary@akcs.com
www.akcs.com
Grades: Pre.-12 *Enrollment:* 300 *Number of Employees:* 36
Earl Driedger, Principal

***Banff:* Banff Mountain Academy**
P.O. Box 369 Main
1 Mount Norquay, Banff, AB T1L 1A5, Canada
Tel: 403-760-4101
Grades: 9-12 *Enrollment:* 40 *Note:* Banff Mountain Academy is a residential, co-educational school. It offers a flexible program for athletes.

***Bow Island:* Cherry Coulee Christian Academy (CCCA)**
P.O. Box 10370
Bow Island, AB T0K 0G0, Canada
Tel: 403-545-2107; *Fax:* 403-545-2944
cherrycoulee@shaw.ca
www.cherrycoulee.ca
Grades: K-9
Kim Dolan, Administrator

***Brant:* Brant Christian School**
P.O. Box 130
Brant, AB T0L 0L0, Canada
Tel: 403-684-3752; *Fax:* 403-684-3894
www.brantchristianschool.com
Grades: Kindergarten - 12
Corry Brown, Principal
Susan McLean, Librarian

***Brooks:* Newell Christian School (NCS)**
P.O. Box 100
Brooks, AB T1R 1B2, Canada
Tel: 403-378-4448; *Fax:* 403-378-3991
www.newellchristianschool.com
Grades: Kindergarten - 9 *Note:* The Alberta curriculum is taught from a Christian perspective.
Dale Rempel, Chair
Ron Cousins, Principal

***Calgary:* Akiva Academy**
140 Haddon Rd. SW, Calgary, AB T2V 2Y3, Canada
Tel: 403-258-1312; *Fax:* 403-258-3812
office@akiva.ca
www.akiva.ca
Grades: Pre.-6
Jemmie Silver, Principal

***Calgary:* Banbury Crossroads Private School**
#201, 2451 Dieppe Ave. SW, Calgary, AB T3E 7K1, Canada
Tel: 403-270-7787; *Fax:* 403-270-7486
general@banburycrossroads.com
www.banburycrossroads.com
Note: Banbury Crossroads Private School offers education to children aged 3 to 18.
Diane Swiatek, Principal
Karen Harrison, Vice Principal

***Calgary:* Bearspaw Christian School (BCS)**
15001 - 69 St. NW, Calgary, AB T3R 1C5, Canada
Tel: 403-295-2566; *Fax:* 403-275-8170
info@bearspawschool.com
www.bearspawschool.com
www.facebook.com/BearspawChristianSchool
Number of Schools: 1 *Grades:* J.K. - 12 *Enrollment:* 600
Number of Employees: 90
Kelly Blake, President & CEO
kblake@bearspawschool.com
Judy Huffman, Principal
jhuffman@bearspawschool.com
Jennifer Lockhart, Vice Principal, Elementary
jlockhart@bearspawschool.com
Lara Melashenko, Vice Principal, Secondary
lmelashenko@bearspawschool.com

***Calgary:* Bethel Christian Academy**
2220 - 39th Ave. NE, Calgary, AB T2E 5T4, Canada
Tel: 403-735-3335; *Fax:* 403-219-3059
tbetts@encountergod.org
www.encountergod.org
Grades: Kindergarten - 12

***Calgary:* Calgary Academy**
9400 - 17th Ave. SW, Calgary, AB T3H 4A6, Canada
Tel: 403-686-6444; *Fax:* 403-240-3427
info@calgaryacademy.com; careers@calgaryacademy.com (Employment)
www.calgaryacademy.com
Grades: 2 - 12 *Enrollment:* 625
Peter Istvanffy, President/CEO
Joanne Endacott, Director, Admissions
jendacott@calgaryacademy.com

***Calgary:* Calgary Chinese Alliance School**
Calgary Chinese Alliance Church
150 Beddington Blvd. NE, Calgary, AB T3K 2E2, Canada
Tel: 403-274-6925; *Fax:* 403-275-7799
Grades: 10 - 12 *Enrollment:* 500
Alex Hung, President
Mimi Fong, Principal
mimiefong@hotmail.com

***Calgary:* Calgary Chinese Private School**
599 Northmount Dr. NW, Calgary, AB T2K 3J6, Canada
Tel: 403-264-2233; *Fax:* 403-263-3895
Grades: 10 - 12 *Note:* The Calgary Chinese Private School works to maintain Chinese heritage & culture in the community.

***Calgary:* Calgary Christian School**
North Bldg.
5029 - 26th Ave. SW, Calgary, AB T3E 0R5, Canada
Tel: 403-242-2896; *Fax:* 403-242-6682
www.calgarychristianschool.com
Grades: Preschool - 12 *Note:* Calgary Christian School has an elementary campus & a secondary campus.
Scott Hickling, Executive Director
Harry Fritschy, Principal, Elementary
Gwen Uittenbosch, Principal, Secondary
Glenda Jullion, Vice Principal, Elementary
Jason Kupery, Vice Principal, Secondary

***Calgary:* Calgary French & International School (CFIS)**
700 - 77th St. SW, Calgary, AB T3H 5R1, Canada
Tel: 403-240-1500; *Fax:* 403-249-5899
inquiries@cfis.com
www.cfis.com
Grades: Preschool - 12 *Note:* Calgary French & International School offers French Immersion education.
John McVicar, Chair & President
societyboard@cfis.com
Dr. Richard Slevinsky, Headmaster, 403-240-1500, ext. 130
rslevinsky@cfis.com
Michele Gariépy, Vice Principal, Junior High School
mgariepy@cfis.com
Cecile Triggle, Vice Principal, Elementary School, 403-240-1500, ext. 210
ctriggle@cfis.com
Janice Jalving, Director, Child Care Centre, 403-246-4708
childcare@cfis.com
Katharine Ray, Officer, Admissions, 403-240-1500, ext. 329
kray@cfis.com

***Calgary:* Calgary Islamic Private School (CIS)**
2612 - 37th Ave. NE, Calgary, AB T1Y 5L2, Canada
Tel: 403-248-2773
www.calgaryislamicschool.com
Grades: Kindergarten - 9 *Enrollment:* 490 *Note:* Calgary Islamic School offers the regular curriculum, as well as a Quran recitation & memorization curriculum, an Arabic language curriculum, an Islamic Studies curriculum.

***Calgary:* Calgary Italian School**
Centro Linguistico e culturale italiano di Calgar
416 - 1st Ave. NE, Calgary, AB T2E 0B4, Canada
Tel: 403-264-6349
clcic@shaw.ca
italianschoolcalgary.com
Grades: K-12 *Enrollment:* 196 *Number of Employees:* 12 teachers *Note:* A total of 13 courses (9 courses for children and 4 for adults).

***Calgary:* Calgary Jewish Academy (CJA)**
6700 Kootenay St. SW, Calgary, AB T2V 1P7, Canada
Tel: 403-253-3992; *Fax:* 403-255-0842
info@cja.ab.ca
www.cja.ab.ca
Grades: Preschool - 9
Ben Karmel, Principal
KarmelB@cja.ab.ca
Barbara Dare, Associate Principal, Alberta Curriculum
dareb@cja.ab.ca
Shoshana Kirmayer, Associate Principal, Judaic Studies
kirmayers@cja.ab.ca

***Calgary:* Calgary Quest School**
c/o Spruce Cliff Elementary
3405 Spruce Dr. SW, Calgary, AB T3C 0A5, Canada
Tel: 403-253-0003; *Fax:* 403-253-0025
info@calgaryquestschool.com
www.calgaryquestschool.com
Note: Calgary Quest School offers a program for children with special challenges.
Kathy Peron, Chair

***Calgary:* Calgary Waldorf School**
515 Cougar Ridge Dr. SW, Calgary, AB T3H 5G9, Canada
Tel: 403-287-1868; *Fax:* 403-287-3414
info@calgarywaldorf.org
www.calgarywaldorf.org
Grades: Preschool - 9 *Note:* Calgary Waldorf School offers a Parent-and-Tot program.
Cathie Foote, School Administrator
Kathleen Brunetta, Pedagogical Administrator
Dinah Clark, Financial Administrator

Laureen Loree, Principal
Sandra Langlois, Manager, Admissions & Facility

***Calgary:* The Chinese Academy**
John G. Diefenbaker Senior High School
6620 - 4th St. NW, Calgary, AB T2K 1C2, Canada
Tel: 403-777-7663; *Fax:* 403-777-7669
admin@chineseacademy.ca; chineseacademy@telus.net
www.chineseacademy.ca
Grades: Kindergarten - 12 *Enrollment:* 1925 *Note:* Kindergarten, Level 1, begins for children aged 3.5 years at the Sir John A. Macdonald Junior High School, 6600 - 4th St. NW in Calgary. The goal of the school is to promote Chinese language & culture. Cantonese & Mandarin classes, as well as Chinese as a Second Language for beginners in Cantonese & Mandarin.
Martina Lui, President
Judy Fung, School Superintendent
Elaine Chan, BSc., M.A. (Ed. Admin.), Principal

***Calgary:* Chinook Winds Adventist Academy (CWAA)**
10101 - 2nd Ave. SW, Calgary, AB T3B 5T2, Canada
Tel: 403-286-5686; *Fax:* 403-247-1623
cwaa2@cwaa.net
www.cwaa.net
Grades: Kindergarten - 12 *Note:* The Seventh-day Adventist school also features music, outdoor education, Bible instruction, & mission trips for senior high students.
Murray McLeod, BA, Principal
Marilyn Kelloway, BEd., Vice Principal
Samuel Millen, MDiv., Chaplain

***Calgary:* Community Connections School**
225 - 37 St. NW, Calgary, AB T2N 4N6, Canada
Tel: 403-283-6361; *Fax:* 403-283-5741
Grades: 1-12

***Calgary:* Delta West Academy**
414 - 11A St. NE, Calgary, AB T2E 4P3, Canada
Tel: 403-290-0767; *Fax:* 403-290-0768
info@deltawestacademy.ca
www.deltawestacademy.ca
Grades: Pre.-12; Special Ed.
Denise Dutchuk-Smith, B.A., B.Ed., Head of School
ddutchuk-smith@deltawestacademy.ca

***Calgary:* Eastside Christian Academy (ECA)**
1320 Abbeydale Dr. SE, Calgary, AB T2A 7L8
Tel: 403-569-1003; *Fax:* 403-569-7557
admin@ecaab.ca
eastsidechristianacademy.ca
www.facebook.com/122526574470804
Number of Schools: 1
Frank Moody, Principal
drmoody52@hotmail.com
Marie Poulin, Career Counsellor
mpoulin@shaw.ca

***Calgary:* Edge School for Athletes**
33055 Township Rd. 250, Calgary, AB T3Z 1L4
Tel: 403-246-6432; *Fax:* 403-217-8463
info@edgeschool.com
www.edgeschool.com
www.facebook.com/edgeschool
twitter.com/edgeschool
Grades: 5-12 *Note:* The school prepares student-athletes for university.
Cameron Hodgson, Chief Executive Officer & Principal, 403-246-6432, ext. 105
chodgson@edgeschool.com
Pat McLaughlin, Executive Director, Edge Foundation & Business Operations, 403-246-6432, ext. 111
pmclaughlin@edgeschool.com
Anne McCaffrey, Director, Admissions, 403-246-6432, ext. 111
amccaffrey@edgeschool.com
Lauren Ritchie, Director, Marketing & Communications, 403-246-6432, ext. 439
lritchie@edgeschool.com

***Calgary:* Educere International College**
#1500, 910 - 7 Ave. SW, Calgary, AB T2P 3N8, Canada
Tel: 403-232-8551
Note: Founded in 1962, the school offers the opportunity to acquire English & learn about business & culture in North America.

***Calgary:* Equilibrium International Educational Institute**
707 - 14 St. NW, Calgary, AB T2N 2A4, Canada
Tel: 403-283-1111; *Fax:* 403-270-7786
school@equilibrium.ab.ca
www.equilibrium.ab.ca
Grades: 10-12

***Calgary:* German Language School**
German Canadian Club
#204, 2333 18 Ave NE, Calgary, AB T2E 8T6, Canada
Tel: 403-288-2255; *Fax:* 403-286-8457
info@germancanadianclub.com
www.germancanadianclub.com

***Calgary:* Glenmore Christian Academy**
16520 - 24th St., Calgary, AB T2Y 4W2, Canada
Tel: 403-254-9050; *Fax:* 403-256-9695
www.gcaschool.ca
Grades: Pre.-9; Special Ed.
Derrick Mohamed, Intermediate Principal
Gwen Uittenbosch, Elementary Principal

***Calgary:* Greek Community School**
1 Tamarac Cres. SW, Calgary, AB T3C 3B7, Canada
Tel: 403-246-4553; *Fax:* 403-246-8191
school@calgaryhellenic.com
Grades: 1-12

***Calgary:* Heritage Christian Academy**
2003 McKnight Blvd. NE, Calgary, AB T2E 6L2, Canada
Tel: 403-219-3201; *Fax:* 403-219-3210
ibelong@hcacalgary.com
www.hcacalgary.com
Grades: Pre.-12 *Enrollment:* 500
LaVerne Pue, Principal

***Calgary:* International School of Excellence (ISE)**
3915 - 34th St. NE, Calgary, AB T1Y 6Z8
Tel: 403-234-0453; *Fax:* 403-250-2401
isoe@telus.net
www.isoe-online.com
Grades: Early Childhood Services - 12 *Note:* The International School of Excellence was incorporated in 2002. The private school serves a diverse community & follows the Alberta curriculum.
Jean Fevry, Founder
Kassem Hammoud, Vice-Principal & Head, Arabic Language Department
Jennifer Berriault, Head, Junior & Senior High Schools
Jean Reimer, Head, Elementary School

***Calgary:* Janus Academy**
2223 Spiller Rd. SE, Calgary, AB T2G 4G9
Tel: 403-262-3333
contact@janusacademy.org
www.janusacademy.org
Other Information: Jr. High & High School Site, Phone: 403-228-5559
Grades: 1-12; Special Education *Enrollment:* 44 *Note:* Janus Academy strives to enhance the lives of children with autism. The program is accredited by both Alberta Education & The Association of Independent Schools & Colleges. Janus Academy is a registered charity.
Ian Menzies, President, 403-668-6176
ian@janusacademy.org
Alice Woolley, Vice-President & Secretary
alice@janusacademy.org
Stacey Oliver, Principal
Paige McNeill, Program Director, Elementary School
Koren Trnka, Program Director, Junior & Senior High School

***Calgary:* Lycée Louis Pasteur**
4099, boul Garrison sud-ouest, Calgary, AB T2T 6G2, Canada
Tél: 403-243-5420; *Téléc:* 403-287-2245
office@lycee.ca
www.lycee.ca
Grades: Mat./Prim.
Benjamin Orillon, Chef d'établissement

***Calgary:* Master's Academy & College**
4414 Crowchild Trail SW, Calgary, AB T2T 5J4
Tel: 403-242-7034
Academy@masters.ab.ca; College@masters.ab.ca
Other Information: Academy (K-6): 403-242-7034, ext 200; College (7-12): ext. 260
www.facebook.com/MastersAcademyCollege
Grades: Kindergarten - 12 *Note:* Master's Academy & College, established in 1997, is known as a school of Profound Learning. Instruction & guidance is provided from a Christian perspective. Master's Academy features Kindergarten to grade 6, & Master's College includes grades 7 to 12.
Tom Rudmik, Founder & Chief Executive Officer
Paul Graham, Chief Operating Officer
Lynda Dyck, Academy Principal
Peter Muller, College Principal
Susan McAllister, College Vice-Principal
Doreen Grey, Coordinator, Research & Development

***Calgary:* Menno Simons Christian School**
7000 Elkton Dr. SW, Calgary, AB T3H 4Y7, Canada
Tel: 403-531-0745; *Fax:* 403-531-0747
office@mennosimons.ab.ca
www.mennosimonschristianschool.ca
Grades: Pre.-9
Byron Thiessen, Principal

***Calgary:* Montessori School of Calgary**
2201 Cliff St. SW, Calgary, AB T2S 2G4, Canada
Tel: 403-229-1011
www.montessorischoolofcalgary.com
Grades: Preschool / Elementary *Enrollment:* 100 *Note:* The children at the Montessori School of Calgary range in age from 2.5 to 12. Both the Montessori program & the Alberta Programme of Studies are followed.
Sandy Moser, Principal
sandy.moser@msofc.ca

***Calgary:* Mountain View Academy (MVA)**
#B4, 2452 Battleford Ave. SW, Calgary, AB T3E 7K9, Canada
Tel: 403-217-4346; *Fax:* 403-249-4312
www.mountainviewacademy.ca
Grades: Preschool - 12
Jitka Smuszko, Director
Lenka Popplestone, Principal
Colleen Ryan, Vice Principal
Jane Lizotte, Assistant Principal

***Calgary:* Renfrew Educational Services**
Main School & Administrative Centre
2050 - 21st St. NE, Calgary, AB T2E 6S5, Canada
Tel: 403-291-5038; *Fax:* 403-291-2499
renfrew@renfreweducation.org
www.renfreweducation.org
Grades: Preschool - Elementary *Enrollment:* 700 *Note:* Renfrew Educational Services offers specialized educational programs for preschool & elementary students. The not-for-profit society also develops programs for children with special needs.
Tom Buchanan, Chair
Janice McTighe, Executive Director
Kim LaCourse, Associate Executive Director
Cathy Gable, Director, Community Services
Mary lou Hill, Director, Education
Bruce Monnery, Director, Finance & Administration

***Calgary:* River Valley School**
3127 Bowwood Dr. NW, Calgary, AB T3B 2E7
Tel: 403-246-2275; *Fax:* 403-686-7631
info@rivervalleyschool.ca
www.rivervalleyschool.ca
www.facebook.com/287475947950915
twitter.com/rvssocial
www.linkedin.com/pub/erin-corbett/42/655/4b0
www.flickr.com/photos/69513039@N07
Grades: JK-6 *Enrollment:* 200
Erin Corbett, Head of School

***Calgary:* Rundle College Academy**
4330 - 16 St. SW, Calgary, AB T2T 4H9
Tel: 403-250-2965; *Fax:* 403-250-2914
delcastilho@rundle.ab.ca
www.rundle.ab.ca/academy
Grades: 4-12 *Note:* Rundle College Academy offers a program for students with learning disabilities.
Jason Rogers, Contact
rogers@rundle.ab.ca

***Calgary:* Rundle College Elementary School**
2634 - 12 Ave. NW, Calgary, AB T2N 1K6, Canada
Tel: 403-282-8411; *Fax:* 403-282-4460
johnston@rundle.ab.ca
www.rundle.ab.ca/elementary
Grades: Pre.-6
Nicola Spencer, Director of Admissions
spencer@rundle.ab.ca

***Calgary:* Rundle College Junior High School**
7375 - 17 Ave. SW, Calgary, AB T3H 3W5, Canada
Tel: 403-250-7180; *Fax:* 403-250-7184
baird@rundle.ab.ca
www.rundle.ab.ca/high
Grades: 7-9
Dave Hauk, Superintendent/Headmaster
hauk@rundle.ab.ca
Wayne Schneider, Principal
schneider@rundle.ab.ca

***Calgary:* Rundle College Senior High School**
7375 - 17 Ave. SW, Calgary, AB T3H 3W5, Canada
Tel: 403-250-7180; *Fax:* 403-250-7184
bridal@rundle.ab.ca
www.rundle.ab.ca

Grades: 7-12
Mr. Hauk, Headmaster
hauk@rundle.ab.ca

Calgary: St. John Bosco Private School
712 Fortalice Cres. SE, Calgary, AB T2A 2E1, Canada
Tel: 403-248-3664; *Fax:* 403-273-8012
stjohnbosco@shaw.ca
www.stjohnboscoprivateschool.com
Grades: Pre.-9

Calgary: Third Academy
B4 Bldg., Currie Barracks
2452 Battleford Ave. SW, Calgary, AB T3E 7K1, Canada
Tel: 403-288-5335; *Toll-Free:* 1-877-508-5335
info@thirdacademy.com
www.thirdacademy.com
Grades: 1 - 12 *Note:* The Third Academy offers an Individualized Program Plan for students with special needs to remediate of compensate for their learning disorder. There is a Calgary North location, a Calgary South location, & a Red Deer location.
Jitka Smuszko, Chair
Dr. S. Lal Mattu, CEO & Founder
Sunil Mattu, LLB (Hons) Law, BEd, Chief Operating Officer
David Lambe, Vice President, Business & Community Relations.
Kathleen Colmant, Coordinator, Special Events
Rehana Mattu, BEd, Master Teacher
Liz Wray, Registrar

Calgary: The Timothy Centre for Scholarship
P.O. Box 49096
7740 - 18th St. SE, Calgary, AB T2C 3W5, Canada
Tel: 403-230-0702
info@timothycentre.com
www.timothycentre.com
Grades: Kindergarten - 12 *Note:* The Timothy Centre for Scholarship offers a classical Christian education for Calgary homeschoolers.
Laurel Roberts, Principal

Calgary: Trinity Christian School (TCS)
#100, 295 Midpark Way SE, Calgary, AB T2X 2A8, Canada
Tel: 403-254-6682; *Fax:* 403-254-9843
trinity@tcskids.com
www.tcskids.com
Other Information: 403-254-6716 (Phone, Business Office)
Grades: Kindergarten - 9
Merle Rayner, Chair
James Sijpheer, Principal
james.sijpheer@tcskids.com
George Graffunder, Vice Principal
ggraffunder@tcskids.com
Tania Spears, Manager, Business
Sandy Stasko, Coordinator, Resources

Calgary: Truth Academy
615 Northmount Dr. NW, Calgary, AB T2K 3J6, Canada
Tel: 403-282-0238; *Fax:* 403-289-8356
Grades: Preschool - 12

Calgary: Webber Academy
1515 - 93rd St. SW, Calgary, AB T3H 4A8, Canada
Tel: 403-277-4700; *Fax:* 403-277-2770
www.webberacademy.ca
Grades: Junior Kindergarten - 12 *Note:* Webber Academy is a coeducational, non-denominational university preparatory school.
Dr. Neil Webber, Head of School
nwebber@webberacademy.ca
Barbara Webber, Vice-President, Administration
bwebber@webberacademy.ca
Dianne Lever, Contact, Admissions
admissions@webberacademy.ca

Calgary: West Island College (WIC)
7410 Blackfoot Trail SE, Calgary, AB T2H 1M5, Canada
Tel: 403-255-5300; *Fax:* 403-252-1434
office@westislandcollege.ab.ca
www.westislandcollege.ab.ca
Other Information: admissions@westislandcollege.ab.ca (E-mail, Admissions)
Grades: 7 - 12 *Note:* West Island College provides pre-university training. Programs include English & French communication skills & the arts.
Carol Grant-Watt, Head of School, 403-255-5300, ext. 238
Boyd Belisle, Head, Junior School, 403-255-5300, ext. 277
Claire Allen, Director, International Studies, 403-255-5300, ext. 302
Scott Bennett, Director, Faculty Development, 403-255-5300, ext. 501
Roland Chalifoux, Director, Programme Studies, 403-255-5300, ext. 237
Todd Larsen, Director, Co-Curricular Programmes, 403-255-5300, ext. 231
Murray Marran, Director, Admissions & Bursar, 403-255-5300, ext. 285
Pierre Poitras, Director, Technology, 403-255-5300, ext. 260
Malcolm Rennie, Director, Post-Secondary Placement, 403-255-5300, ext. 286

Canmore: Mountain Gate Community School
P.O. Box 8287
Canmore, AB T1W 2V1, Canada
Tel: 403-609-2105; *Fax:* 403-609-8355
Grades: 1 - 6

Cardston: Red Crow Community College (RCCC)
P.O. Box 1258
Cardston, AB T0K 0K0, Canada
Tel: 403-737-2400; *Fax:* 403-737-2101
Toll-Free: 866-937-2400
nealshade@redcrowcollege.com
www.redcrowcollege.com
Note: Mi'Kai'sto Red Crow Community College is a post-secondary institution whcih offers Diploma, Degree and Masters programs. The College partners with Mount Royal, Lethbridge Community College, SAIT, the University of Lethbridge, & the University of Calgary.
Dr. Marie Smallface-Marule, President

Champion: Hope Christian School (HSC)
P.O. Box 235
320 - 3rd Ave. North, Champion, AB T0L 0R0
Tel: 403-897-3019; *Toll-Free:* 1-877-897-3131
secretary@hopechristianschool.ca
www.hopechristianschool.ca
Other Information: Home School Office, Phone: 403-897-3799
Grades: 1-12 *Note:* Hope Christian School was established in 1981. It is owned & operated by the Evangelical Free Church of Champion, Alberta. The school offers day school on campus, home education, & HSC online learning.
Dale Anger, Principal & Administrator
Mayruth Guenter, Manager, Day School Office
Sherrill Losey, Manager, Homeschool Office
Marie Greenhalgh, Administrator, Online School Office
Tim Hill, School & Church Pastor

Coaldale: Coaldale Christian School
2008 - 8 St., Coaldale, AB T1M 1L1, Canada
Tel: 403-345-4055; *Fax:* 403-345-6436
ccsoffic@telusplanet.net
www.coaldalechristianschool.com
Grades: Pre.-12; Special Ed.
Joop Harthoorn, Principal

Cold Lake: Lakeland Christian Academy
P.O. Box 8397
Cold Lake, AB T9M 1N2
Tel: 780-639-2077; *Fax:* 780-639-4151
www.hlvc.org/lca
Grades: Kindergarten - 12 *Note:* The school offers an individualized academic program & an emphasis on moral values.
Allan Amesman, Contact

Cold Lake: Trinity Christian School
5731 - 50th Ave., Cold Lake, AB T9M 1T1, Canada
Tel: 780-594-2205; *Fax:* 780-594-3737
trinity@cablerocket.com
Grades: Preschool - 12
Richard Schienbein, Principal

Devon: Devon Christian School
P.O. Box 5390
Hwy. 60 & Miquelon Ave., Devon, AB T9G 1Y1, Canada
Tel: 780-987-4157; *Fax:* 780-987-4156
dcs@devonchristianschool.ca
www.devonchristianschool.ca
Grades: Pre.-9

Edmonton: Columbus Academy
6770 - 129 Ave., Edmonton, AB T5C 1V7
Tel: 780-440-0708; *Fax:* 780-440-0760
www.boscohomes.ca
Grades: 7-12 *Note:* The school is a special education, private school in Alberta. Students are referred from social service agencies, surrounding school jurisdictions, & parents.

Edmonton: Concordia University College of Alberta University & College Entrance Program
7128 Ada Blvd., Edmonton, AB T5B 4E4, Canada
Tel: 780-479-8481; *Fax:* 780-378-8460
Toll-Free: 866-479-5200
ucep@concordia.ab.ca
concordia.ab.ca/academic-upgrading
www.facebook.com/Concordia.University.College
twitter.com/cuca_edmonton
www.youtube.com/user/ConcordiaEdmonton
Grades: 10-12

Edmonton: Coralwood Adventist Academy
12218 - 135 St. NW, Edmonton, AB T5L 1X1, Canada
Tel: 780-454-2173; *Fax:* 780-455-6946
office@coralwood.org
www.coralwood.org
Grades: Pre.-12
Michelle Northam, Principal
mdnortham@yahoo.com

Edmonton: Dante Alighieri Society School of Italian Language and Culture
c/o Archbishop O'Leary High School
8760 - 132 Ave., Edmonton, AB T5E 0X8, Canada
Tel: 780-474-1787; *Fax:* 780-451-0669
aristidem@shaw.ca
www.ladanteedmonton.org
Enrollment: 192 *Number of Employees:* 13 teachers *Note:* Courses are offered for both children and adults.
Aristide Melchionna, Principal

Edmonton: Edmonton Bible Heritage Christian School
13054 - 112 St. NW, Edmonton, AB T5E 6E6
Tel: 780-454-3672; *Fax:* 780-488-3672
Grades: 1-9 *Note:* The school offers a home education program & a home education blended program.

Edmonton: Edmonton Islamic Academy
14525 - 127 St., Edmonton, AB T6V 0B3, Canada
Tel: 780-454-4573; *Fax:* 780-454-3498
eia@islamicschool.ca
www.islamicacademy.ca
Grades: K.-9 *Enrollment:* 700
Abdullah A. Omar, Principal

Edmonton: Edmonton Menorah Academy
10735 McQueen Rd. NW, Edmonton, AB T5N 3L1, Canada
Tel: 780-451-1848; *Fax:* 780-451-2254
ema613@yahoo.ca
Grades: Pre.-9

Edmonton: Faith Lutheran School
11515 - 36 St., Edmonton, AB T5W 2A9, Canada
Tel: 780-496-9302; *Fax:* 780-496-3556
Grades: Pre.-9

Edmonton: German Language School Society of Edmonton
c/o Rio Terrace School
7608 - 154 St., Edmonton, AB T5R 1R7, Canada
Tel: 780-435-7540
kerstin.buelow@shaw.ca
www.germanschooledmonton.org
Grades: 10-12
Judith Meyers, Administrator
judith.meyers@gmx.de

Edmonton: Gil Vicente School
8830 - 132 Ave., Edmonton, AB T5E 0X8, Canada
Tel: 780-474-7242
cpereira@gsacrd.ab.ca
Grades: 10-12

Edmonton: Headway School Society of Alberta
3530 - 91 St., Edmonton, AB T6E 6P1, Canada
Tel: 780-461-7683; *Fax:* 780-485-0507
headway@telusplanet.net
www.members.shaw.ca/worman/
Grades: Pre.-12

Edmonton: Ivan Franko School of Ukrainian Studies (IFSUS)
10611 - 110 Ave., Edmonton, AB T5H 2W9
Tel: 780-439-2320; *Fax:* 780-439-0989
Note: The school teaches Ukrainian courses.
Liliya Sukhy, Director, 780-476-7529
lsukhy@hotmail.com

Edmonton: **Meadowlark Christian School**
9825 - 158 St., Edmonton, AB T5P 2X4, Canada
Tel: 780-483-6476; *Fax:* 780-487-8992
meadowlarkChristian@epsb.ca
www.k-9christian.com
Grades: Pre.-9
Darren Sweeney, Principal

Edmonton: **Parkland Immanuel Christian School**
21304 - 35 Ave. NW, Edmonton, AB T6M 2P6, Canada
Tel: 780-444-6443; *Fax:* 780-444-6448
info@parklandimmanuel.ca
www.parklandimmanuel.ca
Grades: Pre.-12

Edmonton: **Phoenix Academy**
6770 - 129 Ave., Edmonton, AB T5C 1V7, Canada
Tel: 780-440-0708; *Fax:* 780-440-0760
Grades: K.-12 *Note:* School for students who struggle with behavioural disorders and learning disabilities

Edmonton: **Progressive Academy**
13212 - 106 Ave., Edmonton, AB T5N 1A3, Canada
Tel: 780-455-8344; *Fax:* 780-455-1425
info@progressiveacademy.ca
www.progressiveacademy.ca
Grades: Junior Kindergarten - 12 *Note:* The school offers small classes & the flexibility for students to progress through grades at an irregular pace. Progressive Academy is licensed by Applied Scholastics International & accredited by Alberta Education.

Edmonton: **St. George's Hellenic Language School**
10831 - 124 St., Edmonton, AB T5M 0H4, Canada
Tel: 780-452-1455; *Fax:* 780-452-1455
Grades: 10-12

Edmonton: **Solomon College**
#228, 10621 - 100 Ave., Edmonton, AB T5J 0B3, Canada
Tel: 780-431-1515; *Fax:* 780-431-1644
info@solomoncollege.ca
www.solomoncollege.ca
Grades: 10-12

Edmonton: **Tempo School**
5603 - 148 St., Edmonton, AB T6H 4T7, Canada
Tel: 780-434-1190; *Fax:* 780-430-6209
admin@tempooschool.org
www.temposchool.org
Grades: Pre.-12 *Enrollment:* 380
P. Mitchell, Headmaster

Edmonton: **Victory Christian School (VCS)**
11520 Ellerslie Rd., Edmonton, AB T6W 1A2, Canada
Tel: 780-988-5433; *Fax:* 780-988-5280
info@victorychristianschool.ca
www.victorychristianschool.ca
Grades: Preschool - 12 *Enrollment:* 120 *Note:* Victory Christian School's preschool offers curriculum suited to the developmental stages of four year old children.

Edson: **Yellowhead Koinonia Christian School**
430 - 72 St., Edson, AB T7E 1N3
Tel: 780-723-3850; *Fax:* 780-723-7566
office@ykcschool.com
www.ykcschool.com
Grades: Pre-kindergarten - 12 *Note:* The independent Christian school serves Edson & the surrounding area.
Henry Fousert, Board Chair
Jason Rand, Administrator
Glenda Ferguson, Home School Coordinator (West)
Bobbie Luymeson, Home School Coordinator (East)

Fort McMurray: **Fort McMurray Christian School**
190 Tamarack Way, Fort McMurray, AB T9K 1A1
Tel: 780-743-1079; *Fax:* 780-743-1379
www.fortmcmurraychristianschool.ca
Grades: Kindergarten - 8 *Note:* The Fort McMurray Christian School is an interdenominational Christian school that is affiliated with the Association of Independent Schools & Colleges in Alberta as well as Christian Schools International.
J. Champion, Principal
Joseph.Champion@fmpsd.ab.ca

Grande Prairie: **Grande Prairie Christian School**
8202 - 110 St., Grande Prairie, AB T8W 1M3, Canada
Tel: 780-539-4566; *Fax:* 780-539-4748
diana.krahn@gppsd.ab.ca
www.gppsd.ab.ca/school/gpchristian
Grades: Pre.-12 *Enrollment:* 220
John Bueckert, Principal

Grande Prairie: **Hillcrest Christian School**
10306 - 102 St., Grande Prairie, AB T8V 2W3, Canada
Tel: 780-539-9161; *Fax:* 780-532-6932
Grades: Pre.-12

High Level: **High Level Christian Academy**
P.O. Box 1100
10701 - 100 Ave., High Level, AB T0H 1Z0, Canada
Tel: 780-926-2360; *Fax:* 780-926-3245
hlca@telusplanet.net
www.highlevelchristianacademy.ca
Grades: Pre.-12
Vera Bartlett, Vice Principal

Joussard: **North Country School**
1, Joussard, AB T0G 1J0, Canada
Tel: 780-776-2215
Grades: Kindergarten - 12

Kingman: **Cornerstone Christian Academy**
P.O. Box 99
Kingman, AB T0B 2M0, Canada
Tel: 780-672-7197; *Fax:* 780-608-1420
sioanidis@brsd.ab.ca
www.brsd.ab.ca/school/cornerstonekingman
Grades: Pre.-12; Special Ed. *Note:* Core subjects are taught; Bible Studies.
Steve Ioanidis, Principal

Lacombe: **Central Alberta Christian High School (CACHS)**
22 Eagle Rd., Lacombe, AB T4L 1G7, Canada
Tel: 403-782-4535; *Fax:* 403-782-5425
office@cachs.ca
www.cachs.ca
www.facebook.com/167864616645517
Grades: 10-12 *Enrollment:* 108 *Number of Employees:* 8 teaching staff; 7 support staff
Beatrice Vriend, Development Director
bvriend@cachs.ca
Mel Brandsma, Principal
mbrandsma@cachs.ca
Wendy Barnes, Business Administrator
wbarnes@cachs.ca
Peter Hoekstra, Vice Principal
phoekstra@cachs.ca

Lacombe: **College Heights Christian School (CHCS)**
5201 College Ave., Lacombe, AB T4L 1Z6
Tel: 403-782-6212
office@collegeheightschristianschool.ca
www.collegeheightschristianschool.ca
Grades: Early chilhood services - 9 *Note:* Operated by the Seventh-day Adventist Church, the College Heights Christian School offers a spiritually oriented education.
Shelley Hulin, Principal
Stephen Reasor, Chaplain & Bible Teacher

Lacombe: **Lacombe Christian School**
5206 - 58 St., Lacombe, AB T4L 1G9, Canada
Tel: 403-782-6531; *Fax:* 403-782-5760
office@lacs.ca
www.lacs.ca
Grades: Pre.-9
M. Folkerts, Principal
mfolkerts@lacs.ca

Lacombe: **Parkview Adventist Academy**
5505 College Ave., Lacombe, AB T4L 2E7, Canada
Tel: 403-782-3381; *Fax:* 403-782-7308
www.paa.ca
Grades: 10-12 *Note:* Christian boarding school affiliated with Canadian University College

Leduc: **Covenant Christian School**
P.O. Box 3827 Main
49257, RR#250, Leduc, AB T9E 6M7, Canada
Tel: 780-986-8353; *Fax:* 780-986-8360
www.covenantchristian.ca
Grades: 1-9; Special Ed. *Enrollment:* 165 *Note:* Christ-centered education within a curriculum of core subjects.
Gayle Monsma, Principal
gayle.monsma@blackgold.ca

Lethbridge: **Immanuel Christian Elementary School**
2010 - 5 Ave. North, Lethbridge, AB T1H 0N5, Canada
Tel: 403-317-7860; *Fax:* 403-317-7862
icesoffice@gmail.com
ices.icssa.ca
Grades: Pre.-6
Jay Visser, Principal
jvisser@immanuelcs.ca

Lethbridge: **Immanuel Christian High School**
802 - 6 Ave. North, Lethbridge, AB T1H 0S1, Canada
Tel: 403-328-4783; *Fax:* 403-327-6333
ichs.icssa.ca
Grades: 7-12
Rob van Spronsen, Principal
rob.vanspronsen@gmail.com

Linden: **Kneehill Christian School**
P.O. Box 370
Linden, AB T0M 1J0
Tel: 403-546-3781; *Fax:* 403-546-3181
Grades: 1-9

Medicine Hat: **Cornerstone Christian School**
2566 Southview Dr. SE, Medicine Hat, AB T1B 1R2
Tel: 403-529-6169; *Fax:* 403-529-6165
www.cornerstonechristianschool.ca
twitter.com/CCSMedHat
Elaine Rowan, Principal

Medicine Hat: **Medicine Hat Christian School**
68 Rice Dr. SE, Medicine Hat, AB T1B 3X2, Canada
Tel: 403-526-3246; *Fax:* 403-528-9048
mhcs@shockware.com
www.pcce.ca/medhat.htm
Grades: K.-9 *Enrollment:* 195
Shade Holmes, Principal

Monarch: **Calvin Christian School**
P.O. Box 40
Monarch, AB T0L 1M0, Canada
Tel: 403-381-3030; *Fax:* 403-381-4241
office@ccschool.ca

Monarch: **Providence Christian School**
P.O. Box 240
Monarch, AB T0L 1M0, Canada
Tel: 403-381-4418; *Fax:* 403-381-4418
admin@pcsmonarch.com
www.pcsmonarch.com
Grades: Preschool - 12
Chris Heikoop, Principal

Morinville: **Morinville Christian School**
10515 - 100 Ave., Morinville, AB T8R 1A2, Canada
Tel: 780-939-2987
mcfs@telus.net
www.morinvillechristian.com
Lou Brunelle, Director, School

Neerlandia: **Covenant Canadian Reformed School**
P.O. Box 67
Neerlandia, AB T0G 1R0, Canada
Tel: 780-674-4774; *Fax:* 780-401-3295
ccrs@xplornet.com
www.ccrs.110mb.com
Grades: Pre.-12; Special Ed. *Enrollment:* 170 *Note:* Students are members of the Canadian Reformed or United Reformed churchesLocation: 3030 Township Rd. 615A, Neerlandia.
Harry VanDelden, Principal

Okotoks: **Edison School**
Box 2, Site 11, RR#2, Okotoks, AB T1S 1A2
Tel: 403-938-7670; *Fax:* 403-938-7224
office@edisonschool.ca
www.edisonschool.ca
Grades: Kindergarten - 12 *Enrollment:* 185 *Note:* Edison School is a fully accredited private school.

Okotoks: **Strathcona-Tweedsmuir School**
RR#2, Okotoks, AB T1S 1A2, Canada
Tel: 403-938-4431; *Fax:* 403-938-8343
advancement@sts.ab.ca
www.sts.ab.ca
Grades: 1-12

Olds: **Olds Koinonia Christian School**
P.O. Box 4039
Olds, AB T4H 1P7, Canada
Tel: 403-556-4038; *Fax:* 403-556-8770
www.oldskoinonia.com
Grades: K-12 *Enrollment:* 300
Dwayne Brown, Administrator/Principal
dwaynebrown@chinooksedge.ab.ca

Ponoka: **Ponoka Christian School**
6300 - 50 St., Ponoka, AB T4J 1V3, Canada
Tel: 403-783-6563; *Fax:* 403-783-6687
ponxsch@telus.net
www.ponokachristianschool.com
Grades: Pre.-9
Robert Morris, Principal

Ponoka: **Woodlands Adventist School**
P.O. Box 16
Site 2, RR#3, Ponoka, AB T4J 1R3, Canada
Tel: 403-783-2640; *Fax:* 403-783-2878
woodlands22.adventistschoolconnect.org
Grades: Pre.-9
Andrea Gray, Principal
andrea.a.gray@gmail.com

Purple Springs: **Tween Valley Christian School**
P.O. Box 96
Purple Springs, AB T0K 1X0, Canada
Tel: 403-223-9571; *Fax:* 403-224-9594
tvcs.principal@hotmail.com
Grades: 1 - 12

Raymond: **Mennonite School**
P.O. Box 768
Raymond, AB T0K 2S0, Canada
Tel: 403-756-2277

Red Deer: **Destiny Christian School**
P.O. Box 30
Site 4, RR#4, Red Deer, AB T4N 5E4, Canada
Tel: 403-343-6510; *Fax:* 403-343-1963
info@destinyschool.ca
www.destinyschool.ca
Grades: Pre.-9
Glenn Mullen, Principal
Marjorie Mullen, Principal

Red Deer: **Koinonia Christian School of Red Deer**
6014 - 57 Ave., Red Deer, AB T4N 4S9, Canada
Tel: 403-346-1818; *Fax:* 403-347-3013
info@koinonia.ca
www.koinonia.ca
Grades: Pre.-12
Vern Rand, Principal

Red Deer: **Parkland School Special Education**
6016 - 45 Ave., Red Deer, AB T4N 3M4, Canada
Tel: 403-347-3911; *Fax:* 403-342-2677
prkland@shaw.ca
www.parklandschool.org
Grades: Special Ed.
Monica Lawes, Principal

Red Deer: **South Side Christian School**
P.O. Box 219
Red Deer, AB T4N 5E8, Canada
Tel: 403-886-2266; *Fax:* 403-886-5026
www.southsidechristianschool.ca
Grades: Pre.-10 *Note:* Affiliated with the Seventh-day Adventist Church

Rimbey: **Rimbey Christian School**
P.O. Box 90
4522 - 54th Ave., Rimbey, AB T0C 2J0, Canada
Tel: 403-843-4790; *Fax:* 403-843-3904
office@rimbeychristianschool.com
www.rimbeychristianschool.com
Grades: Kindergarten - 9 *Enrollment:* 84 *Note:* The Alberta Provincial Program of Studies is taught from a Christian perspective.
Tambourine Simpson, Principal
principal@rimbeychristianschool.com

Rocky Mountain House: **Rocky Christian School (RCS)**
5204 - 54 Ave., Rocky Mountain House, AB T4T 1S5, Canada
Tel: 403-845-3516; *Fax:* 403-845-4370
office@rockycs.com
www.rockycs.com
Grades: Kindergarten - 9 *Enrollment:* 105 *Note:* The interdenominational school provides a Biblically based curriculum, which reflects Alberta Learning requirements.
Dave Simmelink, Chair
Rob Duiker, Principal

Saddle Lake: **Saddle Lake Full Gospel School**
P.O. Box 69
Saddle Lake, AB T0A 3T0, Canada
Tel: 780-636-3736; *Fax:* 780-636-3994
Grades: 1-12

Siksika: **Old Sun Community College**
P.O. Box 1250
Siksika, AB T0J 3W0, Canada
Tel: 403-734-3862; *Fax:* 403-734-5363
admin@oldsuncollege.net
www.oldsuncollege.net
Grades: College
Amelia Clark, B.A., M.A., President/Post-Secondary Director, 403-734-3862, ext. 222
amelia@oldsuncollege.net

Slave Lake: **Slave Lake Koinonia Christian**
P.O. Box 1548
328 - 2 St. NE, Slave Lake, AB T0G 2A0, Canada
Tel: 780-849-5400; *Fax:* 780-849-5460
koinonia@telusplanet.net
www.slkoinoniacs.ca
Grades: 1-12
Sandra Sergeant, Principal

Spirit River: **Northern Lights School**
Box 19, Site 4, RR#1, Spirit River, AB T0H 3G0, Canada
Tel: 780-351-2242; *Fax:* 780-351-2280
Grades: 1 - 9 *Note:* The Northern Lights Church of God in Christ Mennonite congregation operates the Northern Lights School.

Spruce Grove: **Harvest Baptist Academy**
26404 Hwy. 16 West, Spruce Grove, AB T7X 3H5, Canada
Tel: 780-960-0235; *Fax:* 780-960-9235
Toll-Free: 888-960-0235
www.newtestamentbaptist.ca
Grades: Pre.-12
Brian Coldwell, Pastor
bcoldwell@newtestamentbaptist.ca

Spruce Grove: **Living Waters Christian Academy**
5 Grove Dr. West, Spruce Grove, AB T7X 3X8, Canada
Tel: 780-962-3331; *Fax:* 780-962-3958
www.lwca.ab.ca
Grades: Pre.-12
Keith Penner, Principal
kpenner@lwca.ab.ca
Savaya Hofsink, Community Resource Director
savaya.hofsink@lwca.ab.ca

St Paul: **Blue Quills First Nations College (BQFNC)**
P.O. Box 279
3 Airport Rd. North, St Paul, AB T0A 3A0, Canada
Tel: 780-645-4455; *Fax:* 780-645-5215
Toll-Free: 1-888-645-4455
www.bluequills.ca
Dr. Leona Makokis, BAdm, BEd, MA, EdD, President
Bernadine Houle-Steinhauer, BA, PRdip, Director, Special Projects
Dr. Patricia Makokis, EdD, Director, Curriculum Development
Dr. Halia Boychuk, BEd, MA, PhD, Coordinator, University Transfer
Sherri Chisan, BMgmt, MA, Coordinator, Leadership & Management
Sharon Steinhauer, BSW, RSW, Coordinator, Social Work Diploma
Lena Lapatrack, Registrar
registrar@bluequills.ca

Stony Plain: **St. Matthew Lutheran School**
5014 - 53 Ave., Stony Plain, AB T7Z 1R8, Canada
Tel: 780-963-2715; *Fax:* 780-963-7324
school@st-matthew.com
Grades: Pre.-9
Glen Schmitke, Principal
glen@st-matthew.com

Sundre: **Olds Mountain View Christian School**
Box 2, Site 8, RR#2, Sundre, AB T4H 1P3, Canada
Tel: 403-556-1551; *Fax:* 403-556-5936
principal@omvcs.ca
www.omvcs.ca
Grades: K-12

Post Secondary/Technical

Calgary: **Columbia College**
802 Manning Rd. NE, Calgary, AB T2E 7N8, Canada
Tel: 403-235-9300; *Fax:* 403-272-3805
columbia@columbia.ab.ca
www.columbia.ab.ca
Grades: 10-12; Special Ed. *Note:* Adult education & continuing education. Professional programmes (business management, dental assisting, paramedic, health care aide, practical nurse); ESL; bridging programmes/university preparation; academic upgrading. ISO 9001:2000 certified.

Universities & Colleges

First Nations

Edmonton: **Yellowhead Tribal College**
#304, 17304 - 105 Ave., Edmonton, AB T5S 1G4, Canada
Tel: 780-484-0303; *Fax:* 780-481-7275
ytced.ab.ca

Hobbema: **Maskwachees Cultural College**
P.O. Box 960
2 Saddleback Rd. North, Hobbema, AB T0C 1N0, Canada
Tel: 780-585-3925; *Fax:* 780-585-2080
Toll-Free: 866-585-3925
info@maskwachees.ca
www.maskwachees.ca

Universities

Athabasca: **Athabasca University**
1 University Dr., Athabasca, AB T9S 3A3, Canada
Tel: 780-675-6100; *Fax:* 780-675-6437
Toll-Free: 800-788-9041
www.athabascau.ca
www.facebook.com/Athabasca.University
www.twitter.com/AthabascaU
www.youtube.com/user/AthabascaUniversity
Full Time Equivalency: 39700 *Note:* An open university offering any student access to university-level study.
James D'Arcy, Registrar, 780-675-6302, fax: 780-675-6174
registrar@athabascau.ca
Dr Frits Pannekoek, President
auprez@athabascau.ca
Dr Margaret Haughey, Vice-Pres., Academic
mhaughey@athabascau.ca
Dr Ray Block, Vice-Pres., Finance/Admin.
Lori Van Rooijen, Vice-Pres., Advancement
Brian Stewart, Chief Information Officer
brians@athabascau.ca
Greg Wiens, Dir., Facilities/Services
gregw@athabascau.ca
David Hrenewich, Dir., Computing Services
daveh@athabascau.ca
Elizabeth Munroe, Assoc. Dir., Human Resources
Steve Schafer, Dir., Library Services
steves@athabascau.ca

Schools

Centre for Global & Social Analysis
Dr David Gregory, Chair
davidg@athabascau.ca

Centre for Distance Education
Dr Mohamed Ally, Director
mohameda@athabascau.ca

Centre for Innovative Management
Kay Devine, Director
kay_devine@mba.athabascau.ca

Centre for Language & Literature
Kathy Williams, Chair
kathyw@athabascau.ca

Centre for Science
Dr Norman Temple, Chair
normant@athabascau.ca

Centre for Nursing & Health Studies
Dr Donna Romyn, Dean, Health Disciplines
dromyn@athabascau.ca

Centre for Psychology
Dr Cheryl Kier, Chair
cherylk@athabascau.ca

Centre for State & Legal Studies
Dr Evelyn Ellerman, Co-Chair
evelyne@athabascau.ca
Dr Alvin Finkel, Co-Chair
alvinf@athabascau.ca

Centre for Work & Community Studies
Dr Lynda Ross, Chair
lyndar@athabascau.ca

Centre for Learning Accreditation
Dr Dianne Conrad, Director
diannec@athabascau.ca

Centre of Computing & Information Systems
Dr Kinshuk, Director
kinshuk@athabascau.ca

Centre for World Indigenous Knowledge
Dr Tracey Lindberg, Director
traceyl@athabascau.ca

Centre for Integrated Studies
Dr Mike Gismondi, Director
mikeg@athabascau.ca

Centre for Graduate Education in Applied Psychology
Dr Sandra Collins, Director
sandrac@athabascau.ca

Publications
The Voice Magazine
Note: Published by the Athabasca University Students' Union
Tamra Ross, Editor-In-Chief
voice@voicemagazine.org

Calgary: The University of Calgary
2500 University Dr. NW, Calgary, AB T2N 1N4, Canada
Tel: 403-220-5110; *Fax:* 403-282-8413
www.ucalgary.ca

Full Time Equivalency: 24141
Joanne Cuthbertson, Chancellor
Jack Perraton, Chair
Harvey P. Weingarten, B.Sc., M.Sc., M.Phil., Ph, President & Vice-Chancellor
David B. Johnston, B.A., M.A., Registrar
Alan Harrison, Vice-President & Provost
Jonathan (Jake) Gebert, Interim Vice-President
Dennis R. Salahub, B.Sc., Ph.D., F.R.S.C., Vice-President
Dr. Ann Davies, Director
Rhonda M. Williams, B.A. (Hons.), Director
Roman Cooney, B.A., M.C.S., Vice-President

Faculties
Continuing Education
Dr. Scott McLean, Ph.D., Director

Education
Dr. Dennis Sumara, B.Ed., M.Ed., Ph.D., Dean

Engineering
M. Elizabeth Cannon, P.Eng, FCAE, FRSC, Dean

Environmental Design
Prof. Loraine Fowlow, Dean

Fine Arts
Ann E. Calvert, B.A., Dip.Ed., M.Ed., Ph., Dean

Graduate Studies & Assoc. Vice-President, Graduate & Post-Degree Progams
Dr. Fred Hall, Ph.D., Dean

Humanities
Dan Maher, Interim Dean

Law
Alastair R. Lucas, Q.C., Dean

Medicine
Dr. Tom Feasby, M.D., B.Sc., Dean

Nursing
Dianne Tapp, M.N., Ph.D., Dean

Kinesiology
Dr. Wayne Giles, Ph.D., Dean

Science
Dr. J.S. Murphree, B.Sc., Ph.D., Dean

Social Sciences
Dr. Kevin McQuillan, B.A., M.A., Ph.D., Dean

Social Work
Gayla Rogers, B.A., B.SW., R.SW., Ph.D., Dean

Communication & Culture
Wisdom Tettey, B.A. (Hons.), M.A., Ph.D., Interim Dean

Haskayne School of Business
Leonard Waverman, Dean

Publications
Alumni Magazine

The Gauntlet

Edmonton: University of Alberta
114 St. - 89 Ave., Edmonton, AB T6G 2E1, Canada
Tel: 780-492-3111
www.ualberta.ca

Full Time Equivalency: 36962
Linda Hughes, Chancellor
Dr. Indira Samarasekera, O.C., President & Vice-Chancellor
Brian Heidecker, Chair
Carl Amrhein, Ph.D., Provist & Vice-President
P. Clark, M.A., Vice-President
Sandra Conn, Vice-President
D. Hickey, P.Eng., Vice-President
Lee Elliott, Director
C. Byrne, M.B.A., Vice-Provost & Registrar
M. Craige, C.P.P., Director
T. Anderson, Director
K. Adams, Director
Frank Robinson, Interim Vice-Provost & Dean
L. Babiuk, Ph.D., Vice-President

Faculties
Agriculture, Forestry & Home Economics
John Kennelly, Ph.D., Dean

Arts
C. Skidmore, Ph.D., Interim Dean

Business
M. Percy, Ph.D., Dean

Education
Fern Snart, Ph.D., Dean

Engineering
D. Lynch, Ph.D., Dean

Extension
K. Campbell, Ph.D., Dean

Graduate Studies & Research
M. Shirvani, Ph.D., Dean

Law
P. Bryden, B.A., B.C.L., LL.M., Dean

Medicine & Dentistry
Philip Baker, D.M., FRCOG, Dean

Nursing
Dr. Anita Molzahn, Ph.D., Dean

Pharmacy & Pharmaceutical Sciences
F. Pasutto, Ph.D., Dean

Physical Education & Recreation
M. Mahon, Ph.D., Dean

Rehabilitation Medicine
M. Ferguson-Pell, Ph.D., Dean

School of Native Studies
E. Beilawski, Ph.D., Dean

Science
G. Taylor, Ph.D., Dean

Campus Saint-Jean
M. Arnal, Ph.D., Dean

Campuses
Augustana Faculty
R. Epp

St. Joseph's College
University of Alberta
11325 - 89 Ave., Edmonton, AB T6G 2J5, Canada
Tel: 780-492-7681; *Fax:* 780-492-8145
stjosephs.ualberta.ca
Note: The College, located at the University of Alberta, was established by the Roman Catholic Archdiocese of Edmonton. It offers courses in Christian theology & philosophy.
Fr. Terry Kersch, President
terry.kersch@ualberta.ca
Brian Maraj, Academic Dean
brian.maraj@ualberta.ca

St. Stephen's College
University of Alberta Campus
8810 - 112 St., Edmonton, AB T6G 1J6, Canada
Tel: 780-439-7311; *Fax:* 780-433-8875
Toll-Free: 1-800-661-4956
st.stephens@ualberta.ca
www.ualberta.ca/st.stephens/
www.facebook.com/pages/St-Stephens-College/301735949851204?ref=ts

Earle Sharam, Dean
esharam@ualberta.ca
Shelley Westermann, Registrar
westerma@ualberta.ca

New Trail
c/o Alumni Association
430 Athabasca Hall, Edmonton, AB T6G 2E8, Canada

Folio

Lethbridge: University of Lethbridge
4401 University Dr., Lethbridge, AB T1K 3M4, Canada
Tel: 403-329-2111; *Fax:* 403-329-2097
inquiries@uleth.ca
www.uleth.ca

Full Time Equivalency: 8000
Bill Cade, Ph.D., President & Vice-Chancellor
Chris Horbachewski, Vice-President
Seamus O'Shea, Vice-President
Andrew Hakin, Vice-President
Dennis Fitzpatrick, Vice-President
Daryl Schacher, Manager
Annette Bright, Manager
Nancy Walker, Vice-President

Faculties
Arts & Science
Chris Nicol, Dean

Education
Jane O'Dea, Dean

Fine Arts
Dr. Desmond Rochfort, Dean

Management
Murray Lindsay, Dean

Schools
Graduate Studies
Dr. Jo-Anne Fiske, Dean

Health Sciences
Christopher Hosgood, Dean

Publications
The Meliorist
Note: Student newspaper at the University of Lethbridge

Colleges

Calgary: Alberta College of Art & Design (ACAD)
1407 - 14 Ave. NW, Calgary, AB T2N 4R3, Canada
Tel: 403-284-7600; *Fax:* 403-289-6682
registrar@acad.ca
www.acad.ca
www.facebook.com/AlbertaCollegeofArtandDesign
twitter.com/acadonline
www.youtube.com/acadonline

Full Time Equivalency: 1115
Dr. Daniel Doz, President & CEO
Marc Scholes, Dean of Undergraduate Studies
marc.scholes@acad.ca

Calgary: Ambrose University College
150 Ambrose Circle SW, Calgary, AB T3H 0L5, Canada
Tel: 403-410-2000; *Fax:* 403-571-2556
Toll-Free: 800-461-1222
reception@ambrose.edu
www.ambrose.edu
facebook.com/ambroseuc
twitter.com/ambroseuc

Full Time Equivalency: 700 *Note:* Formerly Alliance University College/Nazarene University College
Gordon T. Smith, President
Riley Coulter, Chancellor

Calgary: Bow Valley College
332 - 6 Ave. SE, Calgary, AB T2G 4S6, Canada
Tel: 403-410-1400; *Fax:* 403-297-4887
Toll-Free: 1-866-428-2669
info@bowvalleycollege.ca
www.bowvalleycollege.ca
TTY: 403-410-1412
www.facebook.com/bowvalleycollege
twitter.com/BowValley
www.flickr.com/photos/bowvalleycollege

Sharon Carry, President & CEO
Katherine Cormack, Director, Marketing, Communications & Recruitment
kcormack@bowvalleycollege.ca
Val Hoey, Director, Development

Calgary: DeVry Institute of Technology
2700 - 3rd Ave. SE, Calgary, AB T2A 7W4, Canada
Tel: 403-235-3450; *Toll-Free:* 800-363-5558
www.devry.ca

Calgary: St. Mary's University College
14500 Bannister Rd. SE, Calgary, AB T2X 1Z4, Canada
Tel: 403-531-9130; *Fax:* 403-531-9136
admissions@stmu.ca
www.stmu.ab.ca
twitter.com/StMarysUC

Note: The post-secondary institution operates in the tradition of Catholic scholarship in Canada. Liberal arts & sciences are taught.
Most Rev. Frederick Henry, DD, Chancellor
Dr. Terrence Downey, Vice-Chancellor & President, 403-254-3701
Tamara Acheson, Registrar, 403-254-3732

Edmonton: Concordia University College of Alberta
7128 Ada Blvd., Edmonton, AB T5B 4E4, Canada
Tel: 780-479-8481; *Fax:* 780-474-1033
Toll-Free: 866-479-5200
info@concordia.ab.ca
www.concordia.ab.ca
www.facebook.com/Concordia.University.College
twitter.com/CUCA_Edmonton
www.youtube.com/user/ConcordiaEdmonton

Full Time Equivalency: 1700
Dr. Gerald Krispin, President
Dr. Richard Willie, Vice-President Academic & Provost

Patricia Warmington, Vice-President, Advancement
Jerry Reglin, Vice-President, Finance
Judy Kruse, Registrar

Edmonton: Grant MacEwan Community College
P.O. Box 1796
Edmonton, AB T5J 2P2, Canada
Tel: 780-497-5712; *Fax:* 780-497-5720
Toll-Free: 1-888-497-4622
info@macewan.ca
www.gmcc.ab.ca/
www.facebook.com/GrantMacEwanUniversity
twitter.com/macewanu
www.youtube.com/macewanchannel
Full Time Equivalency: 40791 *Note:* Enrolment figure includes full-time & part-time students
Dr. David Atkinson, President

Edmonton: The King's University College
9125 - 50 St., Edmonton, AB T6B 2H3, Canada
Tel: 780-465-3500; *Fax:* 780-465-3534
Toll-Free: 800-661-8582
www.kingsu.ca
Full Time Equivalency: 652
Dr. Harry J. Fernhout, President

Edmonton: NorQuest College
Downtown Campus, Main Bldg.
10215 - 108 St., Edmonton, AB T5J 1L6, Canada
Tel: 780-644-6000; *Fax:* 780-644-6013
Toll-Free: 1-866-534-7218
info@norquest.ca
www.norquest.ca
www.facebook.com/pages/NorQuest-College/144418728949989
twitter.com/NorQuest
www.linkedin.com/company/36492
www.youtube.com/NorQuestVids
Full Time Equivalency: 10800

Edmonton: Taylor University College & Seminary
11525 - 23 Ave., Edmonton, AB T6J 4T3, Canada
Tel: 780-431-5200; *Fax:* 780-436-9416
Toll-Free: 800-567-4988
info@taylor-edu.ca
www.taylor-edu.ca
www.facebook.com/TaylorUpdates
David Williams, President
Craig Weston, Registrar
Terry Opperman, Director, Student Development
Tom Berekoff, Vice President of Development

Fort McMurray: Keyano College
8115 Franklin Ave., Fort McMurray, AB T9H 2H7, Canada
Tel: 780-791-4800; *Fax:* 780-791-1555
Toll-Free: 800-251-1408
www.keyanoc.ab.ca
www.facebook.com/keyanocollege
www.twitter.com/keyanocollege
www.youtube.com/user/keyanocollege
Full Time Equivalency: 1200 *Note:* 5000 part-time enrollment
Kevin F. Nagel, President
Al Adibi, Vice-President, Finance & Administration
Marylea Jarvis, Vice-President, Instruction

Janvier Learning Center
P.O. Box 85
Janvier, AB T0P 1G0, Canada
Tel: 780-559-2047; *Fax:* 780-559-2999

Campuses
Gregoire Lake Learning Centre
General Delivery, Arzac, AB, Canada
Tel: 780-334-2559; *Fax:* 780-334-2559

Conklin Learning Centre
245 Northland Dr., Conklin, AB, Canada
Tel: 780-559-2434; *Fax:* 780-559-2048

Fort McKay Learning Centre
General Delivery, Fort McKay, AB T0P 1C0, Canada
Tel: 780-828-4433; *Fax:* 780-828-4434

Grande Prairie: Grande Prairie Regional College
10726 - 106 Ave., Grande Prairie, AB T8V 4C4, Canada
Tel: 780-539-2944; *Fax:* 780-539-2832
Toll-Free: 888-539-4772
studentinfo@gprc.ab.ca
www.gprc.ab.ca
Full Time Equivalency: 2000
Don Gnatiuk, President
dgnatiuk@gprc.ab.ca
Susan Bansgrove, Vice-President, Academics & Research
sbansgrove@gprc.ab.ca

Fairview Campus
11235 - 98 Ave., Fairview, AB T0H 1L0, Canada
Tel: 780-835-6600; *Fax:* 780-835-6788
Marg McCuaig-Boyd, Vice President
mmccuaig-boyd@gprc.ab.ca

Lac La Biche: Portage College
P.O. Box 417
Lac La Biche, AB T0A 2C0, Canada
Tel: 780-623-5551; *Fax:* 780-623-5639
info@portagecollege.ca
www.portagecollege.ca
Note: Business Career; Human Services; Native Arts & Culture; Health & Wellness; Trades & Technical; Academic Upgrading programs
William (Bill) Persley, President

Lacombe: Canadian University College
5415 College Ave., Lacombe, AB T4L 2E5, Canada
Tel: 403-782-3381; *Toll-Free:* 800-661-8129
info@cauc.ca
www.cauc.ca
www.facebook.com/pages/Canadian-University-College/447452
96545
www.youtube.com/cucvideos
Full Time Equivalency: 400
Mark Haynal, President, 403-782-3381, ext. 4147
mhaynal@cauc.ca

Lethbridge: Lethbridge College
3000 College Dr. South, Lethbridge, AB T1K 1L6, Canada
Tel: 403-320-3200; *Fax:* 403-320-1461
Toll-Free: 800-572-0103
info@lethbridgecollege.ab.ca
www.lethbridgecollege.ab.ca
www.facebook.com/LethbridgeCollege
www.twitter.com/LethCollege
www.youtube.com/lethbridgecollege
Full Time Equivalency: 7200
Peter Leclaire, B.A, MBA, President, 403-320-3209
president@lethbridgecollege.ca

Claresholm Campus
5202 - 5th St. East, Claresholm, AB, Canada
Tel: 403-625-4231
christina.burrows@lethbridgecollege.ca

Campuses
Crowsnest Pass Campus
MDM Community Centre
2802 - 222 St., Bellevue, AB, Canada
Tel: 403-562-2853
c.frier@lethbridgecollege.ca

Fort Macleod Campus
521 - 26th St., Fort Macleod, AB, Canada
Tel: 403-553-4788
roberta.macivor@lethbridgecollege.ca

Pincher Creek Campus
Co-Op Ranchland Mall
1300 Hewetson Ave., Pincher Creek, AB, Canada
Tel: 403-627-4478
shelley.ingram@lethbridgecollege.ca

Lakeshore Campus
Lethbridge Correctional Centre
Coaldale Rd., Lethbridge, AB T1J 3Z3, Canada
Tel: 403-317-7544; *Fax:* 403-320-5281
d.kitaguchi@lethbridgecollege.ca

Olds: Olds College
4500 - 50th St., Olds, AB T4H 1R6, Canada
Tel: 403-556-8281; *Fax:* 403-556-4711
Toll-Free: 1-800-661-6537
info@oldscollege.ca; library@oldscollege.ca
www.oldscollege.ca
Other Information: Continuing Education: 403-507-7956; Registrar: 403-556-8281
Full Time Equivalency: 1309 *Note:* Olds College features the following schools: School of Agriculture, Business & Technology; School of Animal Science; School of Applied Arts & Career Studies; School of Horticulture; School of Land Sciences; School of Innovation; & Continuing Education.
Bill Quinney, Chair
H.J. (Tom) Thompson, President/CEO

Campuses
Calgary Campus
640 - 14th Ave. SE, Calgary, AB T2G 1E8

Slave Lake: Northern Lakes College
1201 Main St. SE, Slave Lake, AB T0G 2A3, Canada
Tel: 780-849-8600; *Fax:* 780-849-2570
Toll-Free: 1-866-652-3456
info@northernlakescollege.ca;
webmaster@northernlakescollege.ca
www.northernlakescollege.ca
Other Information: Grouard Phone: 780-751-3200; Library (Slave Lake): 780-849-8670
www.facebook.com/NorthernLakesCollege
www.twitter.com/Your_Future
Note: Distance learning is an important part of the college education. Northern Lakes College reaches full-time & part-time students in 30 rural communities in north central Alberta.
Trevor W. Gladue, Chair
Rick Neidig, President/CEO, 780-751-3260

Grouard Campus
P.O. Box 3000
Grouard, AB T0G 1C0, Canada
Tel: 780-849-8600; *Fax:* 780-751-3355

Vermilion: Lakeland College
Also known as: Alberta/Saskatchewan Interprovincial Coll.
Vermillion Campus
5707 College Dr., Vermilion, AB T9X 1K5, Canada
Tel: 780-853-8400; *Fax:* 780-853-7355
Toll-Free: 1-800-661-6490
admissions@lakelandc.ab.ca
www.lakelandcollege.ca
www.facebook.com/pages/Lakeland-College-Canada/31034183
894
twitter.com/LakelandCollege
www.linkedin.com/company/lakeland-college-canada
www.youtube.com/user/LakelandCollegeAB
Full Time Equivalency: 7000
Glenn Charlesworth, President & CEO

Campuses
Lloyminster Campus
P.O. Box 6600
2602 - 59 Ave., Lloydminster, SK S9V 1Z3, Canada
Tel: 780-871-5700; *Fax:* 780-875-5136
Toll-Free: 1-800-661-6490

Emergency Training School
5704 - 47 College Dr., Vermilion, AB T9X 1K4, Canada
Tel: 780-853-5800; *Fax:* 780-853-3008
Toll-Free: 1-888-863-2387
infofire@lakelandcollege.ca

Post Secondary/Technical

Independent & Private Schools

Sylvan Lake: Lighthouse Christian School (LCA)
PO Box 1078, RR#1, Sylvan Lake, AB T4S 1X6
Tel: 403-887-2166; *Fax:* 403-887-5729
www.lighthousechristianacademy.com
www.facebook.com/group.php?gid=133384233375987
Grades: Kindergarten - 12 *Note:* Private education is offered in a Christian community setting.
Evan McKay, Board Chair
Leland Makaroff, Principal, 250-474-5311
info@lighthousechristianacademy.com
Sharon Ocello, Vice-Principal

Colleges

Calgary: Mount Royal College
Lincoln Park Campus
4825 Mount Royal Gate SW, Calgary, AB T3E 6K6, Canada
Tel: 403-440-6111; *Fax:* 403-440-5938
Toll-Free: 1-877-440-5001
externalrelations@mtroyal.ca; international@mtroyal.ca
www.mtroyal.ca
www.facebook.com/MountRoyal4U?ref=ts
twitter.com/mountroyal4u
www.youtube.com/user/MountRoyal4U
Enrollment: 11992 *Note:* Sixty-eight credit programs are offered by the college.
Richard Shaw, Chair
Dr. David Docherty, President, 403-440-6393, fax: 403-440-6040
president@mtroyal.ca
Dr. Robin Fisher, Provost & Vice-President, Academic

Sprinkbank Campus
143 MacLaurin Dr., Springbank, AB
Tel: 403-288-9551;

Paul Tigchelaar, B.Sc., B.Ed., M.Ed., Principal
Grace Lo-Voo, B.Sc., M.Ed., Vice Principal
Dan Dowber, H.R. Management Diploma o, Director, Development
Elsy TerMaat, B.A., Business Administrator

Edmonton: Grant MacEwan University
P.O. Box 1796
Edmonton, AB T5J 2P2, Canada
Toll-Free: 888-497-4622
info@macewan.ca
www.macewan.ca
www.facebook.com/GrantMacEwanUniversity
twitter.com/macewanu
www.youtube.com/macewanchannel
Dr. David Atkinson, President
atkinsond@macewan.ca

Campuses
Alberta College Campus
10050 MacDonald Dr., Edmonton, AB T5J 0S3, Canada
Tel: 780-497-5040

Centre for the Arts & Communications
10045 - 156 St., Edmonton, AB T5P 2P7, Canada
Tel: 780-497-4340

City Centre Campus
10700 - 104 Ave., Edmonton, AB T5J 4S2, Canada
Tel: 780-497-5040; *Fax:* 780-497-5001

South Campus
7319 - 29 Ave., Edmonton, AB T6K 2P1, Canada
Tel: 780-497-4040

Publications
The Intercamp
The Interpreter
c/o Students' Association
P.O. Box 1796
Edmonton, AB T5J 2P2, Canada
The MacEwan Journalist
10700 - 104 St, Edmonton, AB T5J 4S2, Canada
Fax: 780-497-5630

Fort McMurray: Keyano College
8115 Franklin Ave., Fort McMurray, AB T9H 2H7, Canada
Tel: 780-791-4800; *Fax:* 780-791-1555
Toll-Free: 1-800-251-1408
registrar@keyano.ca
www.keyano.ca
www.facebook.com/keyanocollege
www.twitter.com/keyanocollege
www.youtube.com/user/keyanocollege
Dr. Kevin Nagel, President

Publications
Student Connection

Lethbridge: Lethbridge Community College
3000 College Dr. South, Lethbridge, AB T1K 1L6, Canada
Tel: 403-320-3200; *Fax:* 403-320-1461
Toll-Free: 1-800-572-0103
info@lethbridgecollege.ca
www.lethbridgecollege.ca
www.facebook.com/LethbridgeCollege
www.twitter.com/LethCollege
www.youtube.com/lethbridgecollege
Enrollment: 4100
Peter Leclaire, BA, MBA, President/CEO
president@lethbridgecollege.ca

Campuses
Claresholm Campus
P.O. Box 2049
5202-5th St. East, Claresholm, AB T0L 0T0, Canada
Tel: 403-625-4231
christina.burrows@lethbridgecollege.ca

Crowsnest Pass Campus
MDM Community Centre
P.O. Box 1349
2802 - 222 St., Bellevue, AB T0K 0E0, Canada
Tel: 403-562-2853
c.frier@lethbridgecollege.ca

Fort Macleod Campus
P.O. Box 2539
521 - 26th St., Fort Macleod, AB T0L 0Z0, Canada
Tel: 403-553-4788
roberta.macivor@lethbridgecollege.ca

Pincher Creek Campus
Co-Op Ranchland Mall
P.O. Box 1206
1300 Hewetson Ave., Pincher Creek, AB T0K 1W0, Canada
Tel: 403-627-4478
shelley.ingram@lethbridgecollege.ca

Lakeshore Campus
Lethbridge Correctional Centre
Coaldale Rd., Lethbridge, AB T1J 3Z3, Canada
Tel: 403-317-7544; *Fax:* 403-320-5281
d.kitaguchi@lethbridgecollege.ca

Medicine Hat: Medicine Hat College
299 College Dr. SE, Medicine Hat, AB T1A 3Y6, Canada
Tel: 403-529-3811; *Fax:* 403-504-3517
Toll-Free: 866-282-8394
info@mhc.ab.ca
www.mhc.ab.ca
www.facebook.com/MHCollege
twitter.com/mhcollege
www.youtube.com/mhcca
Ralph Weeks, Ph.D., President
weeks@mhc.ab.ca

Campuses
Brooks Campus
200 Horticultural Rd. East, Brooks, AB T1R 1E5, Canada
Tel: 403-362-1677; *Fax:* 403-362-1474

Publications
Express This

Red Deer: Red Deer College
P.O. Box 5005
100 College Blvd., Red Deer, AB T4N 5H5, Canada
Tel: 403-342-3300; *Fax:* 403-340-8940
inquire@rdc.ab.ca
www.rdc.ab.ca
www.facebook.com/RedDeerCollege?sk=app_21310458208813
6
www.twitter.com/RedDeerCollege
Joel Ward, President

Publications
Bricklayer

Post Secondary/Technical

Banff: The Banff Centre
Also known as: Centre for Mountain Culture
P.O. Box 1020
107 Tunnel Mountain Dr., Banff, AB T1L 1H5, Canada
Tel: 403-762-6100; *Fax:* 403-762-6444
www.banffcentre.ca
Other Information: Telex: Artsbanff 03-826657
www.facebook.com/thebanffcentre
www.twitter.com/thebanffcentre
www.youtube.com/thebanffcentre
Mary E. Hofstetter, President/CEO
Jeff Melanson, President

Calgary: Enform
5055 - 11 St. NE, Calgary, AB T2E 8Y3, Canada
Tel: 403-516-8000; *Fax:* 403-516-8166
Toll-Free: 800-667-5557
customerservice@enform.ca
www.enform.ca
Note: Enform provides training for the oil and gas industry.
Cameron MacGillvray, President/CEO

Calgary: The Southern Alberta Institute of Technology
Also known as: SAIT
1301 - 16th Ave. NW, Calgary, AB T2M 0L4, Canada
Tel: 403-284-7248; *Fax:* 403-284-7112
Toll-Free: 1-877-284-7248
advising@sait.ca
www.sait.ca
Note: Canada's premier technical institute by 2010
Irene Lewis, President & CEO

Publications
The Emery Weal

Edmonton: European School of Esthetics MediSpa & Laser Training Centre
6724 - 75 St., Edmonton, AB T6E 6T9, Canada
Tel: 780-466-5271; *Toll-Free:* 877-422-5271
info@dreamcareer.ca
www.dreamcareer.ca
www.facebook.com/EIEMediSpa
twitter.com/EIEMediSpa
Note: Esthetics
Linda Malito, General Manager

Edmonton: The Northern Alberta Institute of Technology
11762 - 106 St., Edmonton, AB T5G 2R1, Canada
Tel: 780-471-7400; *Fax:* 780-471-8583
president@nait.ca
www.nait.ca

Campuses
Fairview Campus
P.O. Box 3000
11235 - 98 Ave., Fairview, AB T0H 1L0, Canada
Fax: 780-835-6698
Toll-Free: 1-888-999-7882

Grande Prairie Campus
10632 - 102 Ave., Grande Prairie, AB T8V 6J8, Canada
Fax: 780-539-2081

High Level Campus
P.O. Box 810
10901 - 93 St., High Level, AB T0H 1Z0, Canada
Fax: 780-926-2264

Peace River Campus
P.O. Box 3500
8106 - 99 Ave., Peace River, AB T8S 1V9, Canada
Fax: 780-624-4532

St. Albert Campus
506B St. Albert Rd., St Albert, AB T8N 5Z1, Canada
Fax: 780-458-6495

Publications
The Nugget

Edmonton: Reeves College
#620, 10310 Jasper Ave, Edmonton, AB T5J 2W4
Toll-Free: 1-800-670-4512
www.reevescollege.ca
www.facebook.com/ReevesCollege
twitter.com/ReevesCollege
www.youtube.com/ReevesCollege
Note: Reeves College delivers vocational training licensed under the Private Vocational Schools Act. Programs are offered in the areas of business, legal, health care, & art & design. The college has five campus locations across Alberta.

Grande Prairie: Mayfair College
#305, 9804 - 100 Ave., Grande Prairie, AB T8V 0T8, Canada
Tel: 780-539-5090; *Fax:* 780-539-7089
www.mayfaircareers.com
Note: Computer training.

Red Deer: Academy of Professional Hair Design (APHD)
4929 - 49 St., Red Deer, AB T4N 1Z1, Canada
Tel: 403-347-2018; *Fax:* 403-342-4244
aphd@telus.net
www.academyofprofessionalhairdesign.com
www.facebook.com/AcademyofProfessionalHairDesign
Note: Esthetics, hair design.

British Columbia

Government Agencies

Victoria: Ministry of Advanced Education
P.O. Box 9059 Prov Govt
Victoria, BC V8W 9E2, Canada
Fax: 250-356-2598
Toll-Free: 1-888-664-225
AVED.Minister@gov.bc.ca
www.gov.bc.ca/aved
TTY: 604-775-0303
Hon. Naomi Yamamoto, Minister
Cheryl Wenezenki-Yolland, Acting Deputy Minister, 250-356-0179, fax: 250-952-0260
AVED.DeputyMinister@gov.bc.ca

Victoria: Ministry of Education (BCED)
Parliament Bldgs.
P.O. Box 9146 Prov Govt
Victoria, BC V8V 9H1
Tel: 250-356-5963; *Fax:* 250-356-5945
Toll-Free: 888-879-1166
www.gov.bc.ca/bced
Hon. George Abbott, Minister, 250-387-1977, fax: 250-387-3200
educ.minister@gov.bc.ca

School Boards/Districts/Divisions

Public

***Abbotsford:* Abbotsford School District #34**
2790 Tims St., Abbotsford, BC V2T 4M7
Tel: 604-859-4891; *Fax:* 604-852-8587
info@sd34.bc.ca
www.sd34.bc.ca
Other Information: Facilities, Phone: 604-852-9494; Fax: 604-852-4876
www.facebook.com/AbbotsfordSchoolDistrict
twitter.com/AbbotsfordSD34
Number of Schools: 46 *Grades:* K-12 *Enrollment:* 19000
Number of Employees: 2,100
Kevin Godden, Superintendent, 604-859-4891, ext. 1230
kevin_godden@sd34.bc.ca
Ray Velestuk, Secretary-Treasurer, 604-859-4891, ext. 1241
ray_velestuk@sd34.bc.ca
Greg Sharpe, Director, Instruction/Curriculum, 604-504-4613, ext. 1816
greg_sharpe@sd34.bc.ca
Vacant , Director, Finance, 604-859-4891, ext. 1287
Marnie Wright, Director, Human Resources, 604.859.4891, ext. 1249
marnie_wright@sd34.bc.ca
Dave Stephen, Manager, Communications, 604-859-4891, ext. 1206
dave_stephen@sd34.bc.ca

***Ashcroft:* Gold Trail School District #74**
P.O. Box 250
400 Hollis Rd., Ashcroft, BC V0K 1A0, Canada
Tel: 250-453-9101; *Fax:* 250-453-2425
www.sd74.bc.ca
Number of Schools: 12 *Grades:* Kindergarten - Secondary
Enrollment: 1800 *Number of Employees:* 150 teachers & support staff
Valerie Adrian, Chair
vadrian@gw.sd74.bc.ca
Alison Sidow, Superintendent, Education, 250-453-9101, ext. 208
asidow@gw.sd74.bc.ca
Teresa Downs, District Principal, 250-453-9101, ext. 234
tdowns@gw.sd74.bc.ca
Marianne Munro, Manager, Information Technology, 250-453-9101, ext. 222
mmunro@gw.sd74.bc.ca
Patrice Barth, District Teacher, Learner Support, 250-453-9101, ext. 210
pbarth@gw.sd74.bc.ca
Wendy Blaskovic, District Resource Teacher, Trades, 250-453-9101, ext. 235
wblaskovic@gw.sd74.bc.ca
Lynda Minnabarriet, Secretary-Treasurer, 250-453-9101, ext. 200
lminnab@gw.sd74.bc.ca

***Burnaby:* Burnaby School District #41**
5325 Kincaid St., Burnaby, BC V5G 1W2
Tel: 604-664-8441; *Fax:* 604-664-8382
www.sd41.bc.ca
Number of Schools: 40 elementary schools (including 7 community schools); 8 secondary *Grades:* Kindergarten - 12; Continuing Ed. *Enrollment:* 24000 *Number of Employees:* 4000+
Diana Mumford, Chair, 604-434-9757
Heather Hart, Acting Superintendent, Schools, 604-664-7051
heather.hart@sd41.bc.ca
Kevin Kaardal, Assistant Superintendent, 604-664-8377
kevin.kaardal@sd41.bc.ca
Gina Niccoli-Moen, Assistant Superintendent, 604-664-8365
Gina.Niccoli-Moen@sd41.bc.ca
Doug Berardine, Director, Employee Relations, 604-664-8362
doug.berardine@sd41.bc.ca
Bonda Bitzer, Director, Human Resources, 604-664-8353
Bonda.Bitzer@sd41.bc.ca
Phil Shepherd, Director, Facility Services, 604-664-8383
phil.shepherd@sd41.bc.ca
Greg Frank, Secretary-Treasurer, 604-664-8387
Greg.Frank@sd41.bc.ca

***Campbell River:* Campbell River School District #72**
425 Pinecrest Rd., Campbell River, BC V9W 3P2
Tel: 250-830-2300; *Fax:* 250-287-2616
www.sd72.bc.ca
Number of Schools: 15 elementary schools; 2 middle schools; 2 secondary schools *Grades:* Kindergarten-12; Continuing Ed; ESL *Enrollment:* 5874 *Number of Employees:* 750
Tom Longridge, Superintendent, Schools, 250-830-2398
Jim Ansell, Assistant Superintendent, Schools, 250-830-2398
Nevenka Fair, Director, Instructional Programs, 250-830-2339
Sheila Johnsrude, Director, Student Services, 250-286-4400, ext. 2253
Diane Rhenisch, Director, Leadership Support, 250-830-2327
Yves Vachon, Manager, Human Resources, 250-830-2310
Geoff Wilson, Manager, Information Technology, 250-830-2390
Steve Woods, Manager, Operations, 250-830-2334
Greg Johnson, District Principal, Aboriginal Education, 250-923-4902, ext. 2216
Sean Toal, District Principal, Robron Centre, 250-923-4918
Lyle Boyce, Secretary-Treasurer, 250-830-2302
Ruth Kine, District Teacher Librarian, 250-830-2322

***Chilliwack:* Chilliwack School District #33**
8430 Cessna Dr., Chilliwack, BC V2P 7K4
Tel: 604-792-1321; *Fax:* 604-792-9665
www.sd33.bc.ca
Number of Schools: 20 elementary schools; 6 middle schools; 3 secondary schools; 4 alternative schools *Grades:* K.-12; Adult Ed. *Enrollment:* 14003
Louise Piper, Chair
Evelyn Novak, Superintendent
Maureen Carradice, Sec.-Treas.
Brenda Point, District VP, Aboriginal Education, 604-703-1762, fax: 604-703-1774

***Coquitlam:* Coquitlam School District #43**
550 Poirier St., Coquitlam, BC V3J 6A7
Tel: 604-939-9201; *Fax:* 604-939-7828
information@sd43.bc.ca
www.sd43.bc.ca
Number of Schools: 45 elementary schools; 1 elementary-junior secondary school; 13 middle schools; 12 secondary schools *Grades:* K.-12 *Enrollment:* 33131
Melissa Hyndes, Chair
mhyndes@sd43.bc.ca
Tom Grant, Supt.
tgrant@sd43.bc.ca
Rick Humphreys, Sec.-Treas.
rhumphreys@sd43.bc.ca

***Courtenay:* Comox Valley School District #71**
607 Cumberland Rd., Courtenay, BC V9N 7G5
Tel: 250-334-5500; *Fax:* 250-334-4472
info@sd71.bc.ca; hr@sd71.bc.ca (employment inquiries)
www.sd71.bc.ca
www.facebook.com/SchoolDistrict71
twitter.com/ComoxValleySD71
plus.google.com/112750829425460904312
Number of Schools: 15 elementary schools; 1 elementary-secondary school; 3 middle schools; 31 secondary schools *Grades:* K.-12 *Enrollment:* 9959
Tom Weber, Chair, 250-218-7095
Tom.Weber@sd71.bc.ca
Sherry Elwood, Supt.
Russell Horswill, Sec.-Treas.
Russell.Horswill@sd71.bc.ca
Bruce Carlos, District Principal, Aboriginal Education
Bruce.Carlos@sd71.bc.ca

***Cranbrook:* Southeast Kootenay School District #5**
940 Industrial Rd. No. 1, Cranbrook, BC V1C 4C6
Tel: 250-426-4201; *Fax:* 250-489-5460
www.sd5.bc.ca
Enrollment: 6204
Bill Gook, Superintendent
bill.gook@sd5.bc.ca
Robert Norum, Sec.-Treas.
Doug McPhee, Aboriginal Education Contact, 250-489-3480
doug.mcphee@sd5.bc.ca

***Dawson Creek:* Peace River South School District #59**
11600, 7th St., Dawson Creek, BC V1G 4R8, Canada
Tel: 250-782-8571; *Fax:* 250-782-3204
www.sd59.bc.ca
Enrollment: 4855
Kathy Sawchuk, Superintendent
Gerry Slykhuis, Sec.-Treas.
Cammy-Jo Plummer, Aboriginal Education Contact

***Dease Lake:* Stikine School District #87**
P.O. Box 190
Dease Lake, BC V0C 1L0, Canada
Tel: 250-771-4440; *Fax:* 250-771-4441
Number of Schools: 4 elementary schools; 3 high schools; 1 alternative school *Grades:* Kindergarten - 12; Alternative Ed.
Enrollment: 260 *Number of Employees:* 71
Bryan Ennis, Superintendent, Schools
bennis@sd87.bc.ca

***Delta:* Delta School District #37**
4585 Harvest Dr., Delta, BC V4K 5B4
Tel: 604-946-4101; *Fax:* 604-952-5375
web.deltasd.bc.ca
Number of Schools: 24 elementary schools; 7 secondary schools *Grades:* K.-12; Adult Ed. *Enrollment:* 15800
Dale Saip, Chair, 604-612-8833
dsaip@deltasd.bc.ca
Diane Turner, Supt., 604-952-5340, fax: 604-952-5379
dturner@deltasd.bc.ca
Joe Strain, Sec.-Treas., 604-952-5354
jstrain@deltasd.bc.ca
Kathy Guild, Special Programs Branch, 604-952-5323, fax: 604-946-7803
kguild@deltasd.bc.ca
Tracey Nelson, Contact, 604-952-5340
tnelson@deltasd.bc.ca

***Duncan:* Cowichan Valley School District #79**
2557 Beverly St., Duncan, BC V9L 2X3
Tel: 250-748-0321; *Fax:* 250-748-6591
www.sd79.bc.ca
Enrollment: 9801
Joe Rhodes, Superintendent
jrhodes@sd79.bc.ca
Robert Harper, Secretary-Treasurer
Denise Augustine, Aboriginal Education Contact, 250-748-0321, ext. 247, fax: 250-748-0739
daugusti@sd79.bc.ca

***Fort Nelson:* Fort Nelson School District #81**
P.O. Box 87
5104 Airport Dr., Fort Nelson, BC V0C 1R0
Tel: 250-774-2591; *Fax:* 250-774-2598
www.sd81.bc.ca
Number of Schools: 5 *Grades:* Kindergarten - 12 *Enrollment:* 889 *Number of Employees:* 100
Linda Dolen, Chair
ldolen@sd81.bc.ca
Diana Samchuck, Superintendent
dsamchuck@sd81.bc.ca
Ray Irwin, Director, Instruction
rirwin@sd81.bc.ca
Patti Burt, District Vice Principal, Technology / Distributed Learning
pburt@sd81.bc.ca
Margaret-Anne Hall, Secretary-Treasurer
mhall@sd81.bc.ca
Darryl Low, Supervisor, Maintenance
dlow@sd81.bc.ca

***Fort St John:* Peace River North School District #60**
10112 - 105 Ave., Fort St John, BC V1J 4S4, Canada
Tel: 250-262-6000; *Fax:* 250-262-6048
www.prn.bc.ca
Enrollment: 5792
Larry Espe, Superintendent
lespe@prn.bc.ca
Doug Boyd, Sec.-Treas.
Brenda Paul, Aboriginal Education Contact, 250-785-8324, fax: 250-785-0846

***Gibsons:* Sunshine Coast School District #46**
P.O. Box 220
494 South Fletcher Rd., Gibsons, BC V0N 1V0, Canada
Tel: 604-886-8811; *Fax:* 604-886-4652
Questions@sd46.bc.ca; board@sd46.bc.ca
www.sd46.bc.ca
Number of Schools: 9 elementary schools; 4 secondary schools *Grades:* Kindergarten - 12; Alternative Ed. *Enrollment:* 3600
Silas White, Chair
silas@nightwoodeditions.com
Deborah Palmer, Superintendent, Schools
dpalmer@sd46.bc.ca
Tom Hierck, Assistant Superintendent
thierck@sd46.bc.ca
Debbie Amaral, District Principal, Student Support Services
damaral@sd46.bc.ca
Kerry Mahlman, District Principal, Aboriginal Programs & Svs. & Partnerships
cmahlman@sd46.bc.ca
Maurice Arduin, Manager, Facilities & Transportation
marduin@sd46.bc.ca
Diane Ready, Secretary-Treasurer
dready@sd46.bc.ca
Tara Sweet, Officer, Human Resources
hr@sd46.bc.ca

Gold River: **Vancouver Island West School District #84**
P.O. Box 100
2 Hwy. 28, Gold River, BC V0P 1G0, Canada
Tel: 250-283-2241; *Fax:* 250-283-7352
www.sd84.bc.ca
Number of Schools: 5 *Grades:* Kindergarten - 12 *Enrollment:* 466
Jessie Smith, Chair
Lawrence Tarasoff, Superintendent, Schools, & Secretary-Treasurer
Annie James, Administrator, Human Resources

Grand Forks: **Boundary School District #51**
P.O. Box 640
1021 Central Ave., Grand Forks, BC V0H 1H0
Tel: 250-442-8258; *Fax:* 250-442-8800
info@sd51.bc.ca
www.sd51.bc.ca
Grades: Kindergarten - 12; Alternate Ed.
Teresa Rezansoff, Board Chair, 250-442-2240
teresa.rezansoff@sd51.bc.ca
Michael Strukoff, Superintendent, Schools
michael.strukoff@sd51.bc.ca
Jeanette Hanlon, Secretary-Treasurer
jeanette.hanlon@sd51.bc.ca
Maxine Ruzicka, Director, Instruction
maxine.ruzicka@sd51.bc.ca
Dean Higashi, Manager, Operations
dean.higashi@sd51.bc.ca
John Popoff, Manager, Technology
john.popoff@sd51.bc.ca

Hagensborg: **Central Coast School District #49**
PO Bag 130, Hagensborg, BC V0T 1H0
Tel: 250-982-2691; *Fax:* 250-982-2319
www.sd49.bc.ca
Number of Schools: 5 *Grades:* Kindergarten - 12 *Enrollment:* 200
Robyn Willis, Chair, Board of Trustees
rwillis@sd49.bc.ca
Denise Perry, CEO, Superintendent of Schools, & Secretary-Treasurer
dperry@sd49.bc.ca
Sheldon Lee, CMA, Director, Business Operations
Sheldon.Lee.SDBOC@telus.net
Lela Walkus, Coordinator, Aboriginal Studies
lwalkus@sd49.bc.ca
Jeremy Baillie, Principal, Sir Alexander Mackenzie Secondary School
jbaillie@sd49.bc.ca
Nam Nguyen, Principal, Bella Coola Elementary School
nnguyen@sd49.bc.ca
Erin Chapman, District Librarian
echapman@sd49.bc.ca
Debbie Gibson, Comptroller
dgibson@sd49.bc.ca
Mark Chatham, Lead Hand, Maintenance
mchatham@sd49.bc.ca
Stephen Sheppard, Lead Hand, Transportation
ssheppard@sd49.bc.ca

Hope: **Fraser Cascade School District #78**
650 Kawkawa Lake Rd., Hope, BC V0X 1L4
Tel: 604-869-2411; *Fax:* 604-869-7400
www.sd78.bc.ca
Other Information: Agassiz Phone: 604-796-2225
Number of Schools: 12 *Grades:* Kindergarten - 12
Linda McMullan, Chair
Dr. Karen Nelson, Superintendent, Schools
Dr. Scott Benwell, Assistant Superintendent
Natalie Lowe-Zucchet, CA, Secretary-Treasurer
Donna Barner, Speech Pathologist
Dan Landrath, Supervisor, Transportation
Mike Repstock, Supervisor, Maintenance
Pat Marsh, Assistant, First Nations Education

Invermere: **Rocky Mountain School District #6**
P.O. Box 430
620, 4th St., Invermere, BC V0A 1K0, Canada
Tel: 250-342-9243; *Fax:* 250-342-6966
www.sd6.bc.ca
Enrollment: 3823
Paul Carriere, Superintendent
pcarriere@sd6.bc.ca
Cameron Dow, Sec.-Treas.

Kamloops: **Kamloops-Thompson School District #73**
1383 - 9 Ave., Kamloops, BC V2C 3X7
Tel: 250-374-0679; *Fax:* 250-372-1183
www.sd73.bc.ca
Enrollment: 15087
Dr. Terry Sullivan, Superintendent
tsullivan@sd73.bc.ca
Jim Sheldon, Sec.-Treas.
Debora Draney, Aboriginal Education Principal, 250-374-0679

Kelowna: **Central Okanagan School District #23**
1940 Underhill St., Kelowna, BC V1X 5X7
Tel: 250-860-8888; *Fax:* 250-860-9799
www.sd23.bc.ca
Grades: Kindergarten - 12; Alternate Ed.
Rolli Cacchioni, Chair, 250-470-3216, fax: 250-860-9799
board@sd23.bc.ca
Hugh Gloster, Superintendent, 250-470-3256, fax: 250-860-9799
hgloster@sd23.bc.ca
Terry Lee Beaudry, Assistant Superintendent, 250-470-3225, fax: 250-870-5025
tbeaudry@sd23.bc.ca
Norm Bradley, Co-Director, Instruction K-12, 250-470-3271, fax: 250-870-5053
gthomson@sd23.bc.ca
Jim Colquhoun, Director, Human Resources - Labour Relations, 250-470-3237, fax: 250-870-5088
jcolquho@sd23.bc.ca
Alan Cumbers, Director, Operations, 250-491-4001, fax: 250-870-5094
acumbers@sd23.bc.ca
Ross Dumontet, Director, Instruction - Human Resources, 250-470-3237, fax: 250-870-5088
rdumonte@sd23.bc.ca
Lisa McCullough, Co-Director, Instruction K-12, 250-470-3210, fax: 250-870-5021
bbrowns@sd23.bc.ca
Peter Molloy, Director, Student Support Services, 250-470-3267, fax: 250-470-3272
berickso@sd23.bc.ca
Jon Rever, Co-Director, Instruction K-12, 250-860-9729, ext. 4688, fax: 250-870-5086
lgradidg@sd23.bc.ca
Eileen Sadlowski, Director, Finance, 250-470-3224, fax: 250-470-3274
esadlows@sd23.bc.ca
Clara Sulz, Co-Director, Instruction K-12, 250-470-3217, fax: 250-870-5027
lpaziuk@sd23.bc.ca

Langley: **Langley School District #35**
4875 - 222 St., Langley, BC V3A 3Z7
Tel: 604-534-7891; *Fax:* 604-533-1115
www.sd35.bc.ca
Enrollment: 18000
Cheryle Beaumont, Superintendent
cbeaumont@sd35.bc.ca
Peter Greenwood, Sec.-Treas.
Dave Coutu, Aboriginal Program Administrator, 604-534-7891, fax: 604-532-1458
dcoutu@sd35.bc.ca

Maple Ridge: **Maple Ridge School District #42**
22225 Brown Ave., Maple Ridge, BC V2X 8N6
Tel: 604-463-4200; *Fax:* 604-463-4181
www.sd42.ca
Grades: K.-12 *Enrollment:* 15559
Jan Unwin, Supt.
junwin@sd42.ca
Wayne Jefferson, Sec.-Treas.
wjefferson@sd42.ca
Doug Hoey, Principal, Aboriginal Education, 604-466-6265
dhoey@sd42.ca

Merritt: **Nicola-Similkameen School District #58**
P.O. Box 4100 Main
1550 Chapman St., Merritt, BC V1K 1B8
Tel: 250-378-5161; *Fax:* 250-378-6263
www.sd58.bc.ca
Grades: K.-12 *Enrollment:* 2500
Dr Robert Peacock, Supt.
rpeacock@sd58.bc.ca
H. Bruce Tisdale, Sec.-Treas.
btisdale@sd58.bc.ca
Shelley Oppenheim-Lacerte, Principal, Aboriginal Education, ext. 1111
so-lacerte@sd58.bc.ca

Mission: **Mission School District #75**
33046 - 4 Ave., Mission, BC V2V 1S5
Tel: 604-826-6286; *Fax:* 604-826-4517
www.mpsd.ca
Grades: Pre-K.-12 *Enrollment:* 6311
Frank Dunham, Supt.
frank.dunham@mpsd.ca
Roy Daykin, Sec.-Treas.
roy.daykin@mpsd.ca
Colleen Hannah, Aboriginal Education Contact, 604-826-3103, fax: 604-820-2850
colleen.hannah@sd75.mission.bc.ca

Nakusp: **Arrow Lakes School District #10**
P.O. Box 340
98 - 6th Ave. NW, Nakusp, BC V0G 1R0
Tel: 250-265-3638; *Fax:* 250-265-3701
sdchanges@sd10.bc.ca
www.public.bcelearner.ca
Grades: Kindergarten - 12 *Enrollment:* 589
Walter Posnikoff, District Superintendent & Secretary-Treasurer, 250-265-3638, ext. 25, fax: 250-265-3701
George Harding, District Facilitator & Coordinator, Instruction & Programs, 250-265-3638, fax: 250-265-3081
gharding@sd10.bc.ca
Alistair Skey, Manager, District Technology, 250-265-3638, ext. 26, fax: 250-265-3701
askey@sd10.bc.ca
Natalie Verigin, District Financial Comptroller, 250-265-3638, fax: 250-265-3701
nverigin@sd10.bc.ca

Nanaimo: **Nanaimo-Ladysmith District #68**
395 Wakesiah Ave., Nanaimo, BC V9R 3K6
Tel: 250-754-5521; *Fax:* 250-741-5248
info@sd68.bc.ca
www.sd68.bc.ca
facebook.com/pages/Nanaimo-Ladysmith-School-District/259438914072
twitter.com/sd68bc
Number of Schools: 40 *Grades:* Pre-K.-12 *Enrollment:* 14000
Michael J. Munro, Supt./CEO
mmunro@sd68.bc.ca
J. David Green, Sec.-Treas., 250-754-5521
dgreen@sd68.bc.ca
Stella Bates, District Principal, Aboriginal Education, 250-741-5318
sbates@sd68.bc.ca

Nelson: **Kootenay Lake School District #8**
570 Johnstone Rd., Nelson, BC V1L 6J2
Tel: 250-352-6681; *Fax:* 250-352-6686
www.sd8.bc.ca
Grades: K-12 *Enrollment:* 6113
Pat Dooley, Superintendent
Monica Schulte, Sec.-Treas.
Nancy Cobra, Aboriginal Education Co-ordinator, 250-428-2217, fax: 250-428-4990
ncobra@sd8.bc.ca

New Aiyansh: **Nisga'a School District #92**
P.O. Box 240
5201 Tait Ave., New Aiyansh, BC V0J 1A0
Tel: 250-633-2228; *Fax:* 250-633-2401
www.nisgaa.bc.ca
Grades: K.-12 *Enrollment:* 480
Keith Spencer, Supt., ext. 1102
kspencer@nisgaa.bc.ca
Bruce Matthews, Sec.-Treas., ext. 1104, fax: 250-633-2425
bmatthews@nisgaa.bc.ca
Tina Jules, Aboriginal Education Contact, ext. 1107
tjules@nisgaa.bc.ca
S. Grandison, Contact, ext. 1107
sgrandison@nisgaa.ca

New Westminster: **New Westminster School District #40**
1001 Columbia St., New Westminster, BC V3M 1C4
Tel: 604-517-6240; *Fax:* 604-517-6390
district.sd40.bc.ca
Grades: K.-12 *Enrollment:* 6095
John Woudzia, Supt., 604-517-6328
rbennett@sd40.bc.ca
Brian Sommerfeldt, Sec.-Treas., 604-517-6320
bsommerfeldt@sd40.bc.ca
Bertha Lansdowne, Aboriginal Education Contact, 604-517-6316, fax: 604-517-6204
blansdow@sd40.bc.ca

North Vancouver: **North Vancouver School District #44**
721 Chesterfield Ave., North Vancouver, BC V7M 2M5, Canada
Tel: 604-903-3444; *Fax:* 604-903-3445
www.nvsd44.bc.ca
Grades: K.-12 *Enrollment:* 16917
John Lewis, Supt., 604-903-3449, fax: 604-903-3448
jlewis@nvsd44.bc.ca
Irene Young, Sec.-Treas.
iyoung@nvsd44.bc.ca

Brad Baker, Aboriginal Education Contact, 604-903-3463, fax: 604-903-3778
bbaker@nvsd44.bc.ca

Oliver: Okanagan Similkameen School District #53
P.O. Box 1770
35061, 101 St., Oliver, BC V0H 1T0, Canada
Tel: 250-498-3481; *Fax:* 250-498-4070
www.sd53.bc.ca
Enrollment: 2800
Juleen McElgunn, Superintendent
jmcelgunn@sd53.bc.ca
Richard Goodwein, Sec.-Treas.
Jim Insley, Asst. Superintendent, 250-498-3481, ext. 117

Parksville: Qualicum School District #69
P.O. Box 430
Parksville, BC V9P 2G5, Canada
Tel: 250-248-4241; *Fax:* 250-248-5767
www.sd69.bc.ca
Enrollment: 5322
Candice Morgan, Superintendent
cmorgan@sd69.bc.ca
Bernice Hannam, Sec.-Treas.
Rosie McLeod-Shannon, Aboriginal Education Contact, 250-954-3024, fax: 250-954-3027

Penticton: Okanagan Skaha School District #67
425 Jermyn Ave., Penticton, BC V2A 1Z4, Canada
Tel: 250-770-7700; *Fax:* 250-770-7730
sd67@summer.com
www.sd67.bc.ca
Number of Schools: 18 *Enrollment:* 6300 *Number of Employees:* 800
Wendy Hyer, Superintendent, 250-770-7700, ext. 6182
whyer@summer.com
Ron Shongrunden, Sec.-Treas., 250-770-7706
rs@summer.com
Kathy Pierre, Aboriginal Education Contact, 250-770-7703, fax: 250-770-7732

Port Alberni: Alberni School District #70
4690 Roger St., Port Alberni, BC V9Y 3Z4
Tel: 250-723-3565; *Fax:* 250-723-0318
www.sd70.bc.ca
Grades: Kindergarten - Secondary
Cam Pinkerton, Superintendent, 250-720-2770
cpinkerton@sd70.bc.ca
Jerry Linning, Secretary-Treasurer, 250-720-2756
jlinning@sd70.bc.ca
Jack Hitchings, Director, Instruction & IT, 250-720-2779

Port Hardy: Vancouver Island North School District #85
Administration Office
P.O. Box 90
6975 Rupert St., Port Hardy, BC V0N 2P0, Canada
Tel: 250-949-6618; *Fax:* 250-949-8792
msalski@sd85.bc.ca
www.sd85.bc.ca
Number of Schools: 12 *Grades:* Kindergarten - 12 *Enrollment:* 1550
Kathy Bedard, Superintendent, Schools, & Chief Executive Officer, 250-949-6618, ext. 2236
kbedard@sd85.bc.ca
John Martin, Secretary-Treasurer, 250-949-6618, ext. 2222
jmartin@sd85.bc.ca
Katherine McIntosh, Director, Instruction (Curriculum), 250-949-6618, ext. 2234
kmcintosh@sd85.bc.ca
Kaleb Child, District Principal, FN Programs, Initiatives, & Assessment, 250-949-6618, ext. 2233
kchild@sd85.bc.ca
Wally Wright, District Principal, Special Programs, 250-949-6618, ext. 2229
wwright@sd85.bc.ca
Wendy Glos, Speech-Language Pathologist, 250-949-6618, ext. 2244
wglos@sd85.bc.ca
Jennifer Holme, District Teacher. Literacy & Early Learning, 250-949-6618, ext. 2228
jholme@sd85.bc.ca
Charleen Purdy, District Counsellor, Elementary Schools, 250-949-6618, ext. 2251
cpurdy@sd85.bc.ca
Randy Ball, Manager, Operations & Maintenance, 250-949-8155, ext. 229

Powell River: Powell River School District #47
4351 Ontario Ave., Powell River, BC V8A 1V3, Canada
Tel: 604-485-6271; *Fax:* 604-485-6435
Enrollment: 2500
Jay Yule, Superintendent
jyule@sd47.bc.ca
Steve Hopkins, Sec.-Treas.
Wayne Pielle, Aboriginal Education Contact, 604-485-6271, fax: 250-483-3127
wpielle@sd47.bc.ca

Prince George: Prince George School District #57
2100 Ferry Ave., Prince George, BC V2L 4R5, Canada
Tel: 250-561-6800; *Fax:* 250-561-6801
sd57@sd57.bc.ca
www.sd57.bc.ca
Enrollment: 15260
Brian Pepper, Superintendent
bpepper@sd57.bc.ca
Bryan Mix, Sec.-Treas.
Charlotte Henay, Aboriginal Education Contact, 250-561-6800, ext. ext.315, fax: 250-561-6820

Prince Rupert: Prince Rupert School District #52
634 - 6 Ave. East, Prince Rupert, BC V8J 1X1, Canada
Tel: 250-624-6717; *Fax:* 250-624-6517
Enrollment: 2937
Lynn Hauptman, Superintendent
Cam McIntyre, Sec.-Treas.
Debbie Leighton-Stephens, Aboriginal Education Contact, 250-627-1536, ext. ext.221, fax: 250-624-6572
debbiels@sd52.bc.ca

Queen Charlotte: Haida Gwaii / Queen Charlotte School District #50
P.O. Box 69
107 - 3rd Ave., Queen Charlotte, BC V0T 1S0, Canada
Tel: 250-559-8471; *Fax:* 250-559-8849
Toll-Free: 1-888-771-3131
trustees@sd50.bc.ca
www.sd50.bc.ca
Number of Schools: 6 *Grades:* Elementary-Secondary; Aboriginal Ed
Wayne Wilson, Chair, 250-559-4760, fax: 250-559-4773
Angus Wilson, Superintendent, Schools
Ken Campbell, Secretary-Treasurer
Tawni Davidson, Coordinator, Early Learning
Alison Gear, Coordinator, Early Learning
Joanne Yovanovich, Principal, Aboriginal Education

Quesnel: Quesnel School District #28
401 North Star Rd., Quesnel, BC V2J 5K2, Canada
Tel: 250-992-8802; *Fax:* 250-992-7652
www.sd28.bc.ca
Enrollment: 4360
Sue-Ellen Miller, Superintendent
Teri Stoneman, Sec.-Treas.
Holly Toews, Aboriginal Education Contact

Revelstoke: Revelstoke School District #19
P.O. Box Bag 5800
1121 Vernon Ave., Revelstoke, BC V0E 2S0, Canada
Tel: 250-837-2101; *Fax:* 250-837-9335
www.sd19.bc.ca
Enrollment: 1200
Anne Cooper, Superintendent
acooper@sd19.bc.ca
Barbara Ross, Sec.-Treas.
Shan Jorgenson-Adam, Aboriginal Education Contact, 250-837-2101, fax: 250-837-9335

Richmond: Conseil scolaire francophone de la C.-B. (S.D. #93)
French Education Authority of British Columbia
#180, 10200 Shellbridge Way, Richmond, BC V6X 2W7, Canada
Tél: 604-214-2600; *Téléc:* 604-214-9881
info@csf.bc.ca
www.csf.bc.ca
Number of Schools: 28 écoles primaires; 16 écoles secondaires
Enrollment: 4703 *Number of Employees:* 260 enseignants du primaire; 100 enseignants du secondaire
Marie Bourgeois, President
Pierre Claveau, Director, Public Relations, 604-214-2617
pclaveau@csf.bc.ca

Richmond: Richmond School District #38
7811 Granville Ave., Richmond, BC V6Y 3E3, Canada
Tel: 604-668-6000; *Fax:* 604-668-6006
www.sd38.bc.ca
Enrollment: 23092
Monica Pamer, Superintendent
Mark De Mello, Sec.-Treas.
Mike Akiwenzie, Aboriginal Education Contact, 604-668-6068, fax: 604-668-6697

Saanichton: Saanich School District #63
2125 Keating Cross Rd., Saanichton, BC V8M 2A5, Canada
Tel: 250-652-7300; *Fax:* 250-652-6421
www.sd63.bc.ca
Enrollment: 9081
Dr. Keven Elder, Superintendent
kelder@sd63.bc.ca
Joan Axford, Sec.-Treas.
jaxford@sd63.bc.ca
Sheila Austin, Aboriginal Education Contact, 250-652-7331, fax: 250-652-7361
saustin@sd63.bc.ca

Salmon Arm: North Okanagan-Shuswap School District #83
P.O. Box 129
220 Shuswap St. NE, Salmon Arm, BC V1E 4N2, Canada
Tel: 250-832-2157; *Fax:* 250-832-9428
supt@sd83.bc.ca
www.sd83.bc.ca
Grades: K.-12 *Enrollment:* 6723
Doug Pearson, Supt.
supt@sd83.bc.ca
Bruce Hunt, Sec.-Treas., 250-804-7830
bhunt@sd83.bc.ca
Irene LaPierre, Principal, Aboriginal Education, 250-832-8223, fax: 250-832-4456
ilapierr@sd83.bc.ca

Salt Spring Island: Gulf Islands School District #64
112 Rainbow Rd., Salt Spring Island, BC V8K 2K3
Tel: 250-537-5548; *Fax:* 250-537-4200
dfennell@sd64.bc.ca (Executive Assistant, Dawne Fennell)
www.sd64.bc.ca
Number of Schools: 10 *Grades:* Kindergarten-12; International Ed.
May McKenzie, Chair, 250-539-2530
mayonmayne@shaw.ca
Jeff Hopkins, Superintendent
jhopkins@sd64.bc.ca
Sheila Miller, Director, Instruction, 250-537-9441, ext. 206
sheilamiller@sd64.bc.ca
Linda Underwood, Director, Human Resources
lunderwood@sd64.bc.ca
Rob Scotvold, Secretary-Treasurer
rscotvold@sd64.bc.ca
Dr. Holly Smith, District Psychologist, 250-537-9441
hsmith@sd64.bc.ca

Smithers: Bulkley Valley School District #54
P.O. Box 758
1235 Montreal St., Smithers, BC V0J 2N0
Tel: 250-877-6820; *Fax:* 250-877-6835
info@sd54.bc.ca; contact-sd54@sd54.bc.ca
www.sd54.bc.ca
Number of Schools: 7 elementary; 2 secondary *Grades:* Elementary - Secondary
Les Kearns, Board Chair, 250-845-7859
Beverly Young, Superintendent, Schools
Chris van der Mark, Assistant Superintendent
Steven Richards, Secretary-Treasurer
Toni Perreault, Administrator, Human Resources
Barb Guillon, Administrator, Payroll
Ed Hildebrandt, Supervisor, Operations

Squamish: Howe Sound School District #48
P.O. Box 250
37866 Second Ave., Squamish, BC V8B 0A2
Tel: 604-892-5228; *Fax:* 604-892-1038
tfarina@sd48.bc.ca
www.sd48.bc.ca
Enrollment: 4536
Dr. Rick Erickson, Superintendent
ricke@sd48.bc.ca
John Hetherington, Sec.-Treas.
jhetherington@sd48.bc.ca
Juanita Coltman, Aboriginal Education Administrator
jcoltman@sd48.bc.ca

Surrey: Surrey School District #36
14225 - 56th Ave., Surrey, BC V3X 3A3, Canada
Tel: 604-596-7733; *Fax:* 604-596-4197
www.sd36.bc.ca
Number of Schools: 99 elementary schools; 19 secondary schools; 5 student learning centres; 4 adult education centres
Grades: Kindergarten - 12; Adult Education *Enrollment:* 67293
Number of Employees: 8,700 (including approximately 5,000 teachers)
Laurae McNally, Chair, 604-531-1091, fax: 604-542-2613
mcnally_laurae@sd36.bc.ca
Mike McKay, Superintendent, Schools, 604-596-7733, ext. 469
Sharon Cohen, Deputy Superintendent, 604-596-7733, ext. 469
Rick Fabbro, Assistant Superintendent, 604-596-7733, ext. 470

Alan Jones, Assistant Superintendent, 604-596-7733, ext. 471
John Ormond, Assistant Superintendent, 604-596-7733, ext. 478
David Paul, Assistant Superintendent, 604-596-7733, ext. 471
Rick Ryan, Assistant Superintendent, 604-596-7733, ext. 470
Brett Raycroft, District Principal, 604-596-7733, ext. 435
Wayne D. Noye, Secretary-Treasurer, 604-596-7733, ext. 416

Terrace: Coast Mountains School District #82
3211 Kenney St., Terrace, BC V8G 3E9
Tel: 250-635-4931; *Fax:* 888-290-4786
Toll-Free: 855-635-4931
www.cmsd.bc.ca

Number of Schools: 12 elementary schools; 2 elementary-secondary schools; 2 jr.-sec. schools; 5 secondary schools *Grades:* K.-12; Adult Ed. *Enrollment:* 5380
Art Erasmus, Chair, 250-635-0258
art.erasmus@cmsd.bc.ca
Nancy Wells, Supt., 250-638-4407
nancy.wells@cmsd.bc.ca
Alanna Cameron, Sec.-Treas., 250-638-4434
alanna.cameron@cmsd.bc.ca
Cheryl Sebastian, Aboriginal Education Contact, 250-638-4464, fax: 888-231-2913
cheryl.sebastian@cmsd.bc.ca

Trail: Kootenay-Columbia School District #20
#120, 1290 Esplanade, Trail, BC V1R 4T2, Canada
Tel: 250-368-6434; *Fax:* 250-364-2470
Toll-Free: 888-316-3338
www.sd20.bc.ca

Enrollment: 4926
Greg Luterbach, Superintendent
gluterbach@sd20.bc.ca
Kim Morris, Sec.-Treas.
Christine Marsh, Aboriginal Education Program Coordinator, 250-364-1275, ext. 241

Vancouver: Vancouver School District #39
1580 West Broadway Ave., Vancouver, BC V6J 5K8, Canada
Tel: 604-713-5000; *Fax:* 604-713-5049
info@vsb.bc.ca
www.vsb.bc.ca

Grades: K.-12 *Enrollment:* 59182
Steve Cardwell, Supt., 604-713-5100, fax: 604-713-5412
scardwell@vsb.bc.ca
Brenda Ng, Sec.-Treas., 604-713-5080, fax: 604-713-5049
bng@vsb.bc.ca
Debra Martel, Aboriginal Education Contact, 604-713-5682, fax: 604-713-5076
dmartel@vsb.bc.ca

Vanderhoof: Nechako Lakes School District #91
P.O. Box 129
153 Connaught St. East, Vanderhoof, BC V0J 3A0
Tel: 250-567-2284; *Fax:* 250-567-4639
www.sd91.bc.ca

Grades: K.-12 *Enrollment:* 5500
Ray LeMoigne, Supt.
rlemoigne@mail.sd91.bc.ca
Sterling Olson, Sec.-Treas.
solson@mail.sd91.bc.ca
Libby McDiarmid, Aboriginal Education Contact, 250-567-2284, fax: 250-567-4639

Vernon: Vernon School District #22
1401 - 15 St., Vernon, BC V1T 8S8, Canada
Tel: 250-542-3331; *Fax:* 250-549-9200
district_web@sd22.bc.ca
www.sd22.bc.ca

Grades: Pre-K.-12 *Enrollment:* 9047
Bev Rundell, Supt., 250-549-9226
brundell@sd22.bc.ca
Randy Hoffman, Sec.-Treas., 250-549-9205
rhoffman@sd22.bc.ca
Sandra Lynxleg, Aboriginal Education Contact, 250-542-3331
slynxleg@sd22.bc.ca

Victoria: Greater Victoria School District #61
556 Boleskine Rd., Victoria, BC V8Z 1E8
Tel: 250-475-3212; *Fax:* 250-475-6161
Trustees@sd61.bc.ca
www.sd61.bc.ca
Other Information: Alternative Ed., Phone: 250-360-4321; Continuing Ed: 250-360-4332

Number of Schools: 26 elementary schools; 10 middle schools; 7 secondary schools *Grades:* Kindergarten - 12; Continuing Ed. *Enrollment:* 20000
Tom Ferris, Board Chair, 250-889-0689
tferris@sd61.bc.ca
John Gaiptman, Superintendent, Schools
Sherri Bell, Associate Superintendent
Pat Duncan, Associate Superintendent
Chris Harvey, Associate Superintendent
Deborah Courville, District Principal
Ted Pennell, Director, Information Technology
Jim Soles, Supervisor, Building Projects
Ross Walker, Supervisor, Construction
George Ambeault, Secretary-Treasurer

Victoria: Sooke School District #62
3143 Jacklin Rd., Victoria, BC V9B 5R1, Canada
Tel: 250-474-9800; *Fax:* 250-474-9825
info@sd62.bc.ca
www.sd62.bc.ca

Enrollment: 8500
Jim Cambridge, Superintendent
jcambridge@sd62.bc.ca
David Lockyer, Sec.-Treas.
Kathleen King-Hunt, Aboriginal Education Contact, 250-474-9879, fax: 250-474-9825

West Vancouver: West Vancouver School District #45
1075 - 21st St., West Vancouver, BC V7V 4A9, Canada
Tel: 604-981-1000; *Fax:* 604-981-1001
info@sd45.bc.ca
www.sd45.bc.ca

Grades: K.-12 *Enrollment:* 6758
Geoff Jopson, Supt., 604-981-1034
gjopson@sd45.bc.ca
Ellen Forsyth, Sec.-Treas., 604-981-1048
eforsyth@sd45.bc.ca
Jody Langlois, Aboriginal Education Contact, 604-981-1095, fax: 604-981-1096
jlanglois@sd45.bc.ca

Williams Lake: Cariboo-Chilcotin School District #27
School Administration Office
350 - 2nd Ave. North, Williams Lake, BC V2G 1Z9
Tel: 250-398-3833; *Fax:* 250-392-3600
www.sd27.bc.ca

Grades: Kindergarten - 12; Adult Education *Enrollment:* 6800
Number of Employees: 1000+
Wayne Rodier, Chair, 250-305-7981
wayne.rodier@sd27.bc.ca
Diane Wright, Superintendent, Schools, 250-398-3824, fax: 250-392-3600
diane.wright@sd27.bc.ca
Harj Manhas, Assistant Superintendent, 250-398-3810, fax: 250-398-7871
harjinder.manhas@sd27.bc.ca
Mark Wintjes, Director, Instruction for Human Resources
mark.wintjes@sd27.bc.ca
Doug Gorcak, Manager, Facilities & Transportation, 250-398-3877, fax: 250-392-2202
doug.gorcak@sd27.bc.ca
Ken Matieshen, District Principal, Information Technology, 250-305-7955
Bonnie Roller, Secretary-Treasurer, 250-398-3801, fax: 250-392-3600
bonnie.roller@sd27.bc.ca

Schools: Specialized

Hearing Impaired

Burnaby: BC Provincial School for the Deaf
c/o Burnaby South Secondary School
5455 Rumble St., Burnaby, BC V5J 2B7, Canada
Tel: 604-664-8560; *Fax:* 604-664-8561
TTY: 604-664-8563

Grades: 1-12 *Enrollment:* 75
M. Henderson, Principal

Distance Education

Chilliwack: Fraser Valley Distance Education
49520 Prairie Central Rd., Chilliwack, BC V2P 6H3, Canada
Tel: 604-794-7310; *Fax:* 604-795-8480
Toll-Free: 800-663-3381
www.fvdes.com

Grades: K.-12 *Enrollment:* 537
Trish Williams, Principal
twilliams@fvdes.com

Courtenay: North Island Distance Education
2505 Smith Rd., Courtenay, BC V9J 1T6, Canada
Tel: 250-898-8999; *Fax:* 250-898-8883
Toll-Free: 800-663-7925
principal@nides.bc.ca
www.nides.bc.ca

Grades: K.-12 *Enrollment:* 466
Sheila Shanahan, Principal
sshanahan@nides.bc.ca

Creston: SelfDesign Learning Community
P.O. Box 747
Creston, BC V0B 1G0, Canada
Tel: 604-224-3640; *Fax:* 604-224-3662
info@selfdesign.org
www.selfdesign.org

Grades: K. *Enrollment:* 652
Brent Cameron, Principal
brentcameron@selfdesign.org

Fort St John: Northern BC Distance Education
10511 - 99 Ave., Fort St John, BC V1J 1V6, Canada
Tel: 250-261-5660; *Fax:* 250-785-1188
Toll-Free: 800-663-9511
info@nbcdes.com
www.des.prn.bc.ca

Grades: K.-12 *Enrollment:* 228
Randy Pauls, Principal

Grindrod: Christian Homelearner's eStreams
P.O. Box 162
Grindrod, BC V0E 1Y0, Canada
Tel: 877-777-1547; *Fax:* 877-777-1547
info@estreams.ca
www.estreams.ca

Grades: K.-12
H. Hunt, Principal

Kelowna: Heritage Christian Online School
905 Badke Rd., Kelowna, BC V1X 5Z5, Canada
Tel: 250-862-2376; *Fax:* 250-762-9277
Toll-Free: 877-862-2375
info@onlineschool.ca
www.onlineschool.ca

Grades: K.-12 *Enrollment:* 864
Greg Bitgood, Superintendent

Merritt: South Central Interior Distance Education School
P.O. Box 4700 Main
2475 Merritt Ave., Merritt, BC V1K 1B8, Canada
Tel: 250-378-4245; *Fax:* 250-378-1447
Toll-Free: 800-663-3536
www.scides.com

Grades: K.-12 *Enrollment:* 137
Al Mackay-Smith, Principal, 800-663-3536, ext. 1200

Nelson: Distance Education School of the Kootenays
811 Stanley St., Nelson, BC V1L 1N8, Canada
Tel: 250-354-4311; *Fax:* 250-505-7007
Toll-Free: 800-663-4614
www.desk.bc.ca

Grades: K-12
Dan Dalgaard, Principal

Prince George: Central Interior Distance Education
P.O. Box 7400
1270 - 2nd Ave., Prince George, BC V2L 3B3, Canada
Tel: 250-563-1818; *Fax:* 250-563-1150
Toll-Free: 800-661-7515
www.cides.sd57.bc.ca

Grades: K.-12 *Enrollment:* 188
Steve Fleck, Principal

Salmon Arm: Anchor Academy International and BC Certified Distributed Learning
P.O. Box 3015
7201 Hurst Rd., Salmon Arm, BC V1E 4R8, Canada
Tel: 250-832-2754; *Fax:* 250-832-4379
Toll-Free: 888-917-3783
anchor@ark.net
www.ark.net
www.facebook.com/pages/Anchor-Academy/180829665299141

Grades: K.-12 *Enrollment:* 595
Howard Hunt, Principal & Missions Coordinator

Surrey: Traditional Learning Academy (DL)
6225C - 136 St., Surrey, BC V3X 1H3, Canada
Tel: 604-572-3441; *Fax:* 604-572-7832
Toll-Free: 866-576-3001
principal@schoolathome.ca
www.schoolathome.ca

Grades: K.-12 *Enrollment:* 334
Karen Gledhill, Principal

Terrace: North Coast Distance Education
P.O. Box 5000
3211 Kenney St., Terrace, BC V8G 5K2, Canada
Tel: 250-635-7944; *Fax:* 250-638-2399
Toll-Free: 800-663-3865
www.ncdes.ca

Grades: K.-12 *Enrollment:* 220

Cindy Sousa, Principal
Cindy.Sousa@cmsd.bc.ca

Vancouver: Vancouver Learning Network
Also known as: Greater Vancouver Distance Education
530 East 41st Ave., Vancouver, BC V5W 1P3, Canada
Tel: 604-713-5520; *Fax:* 604-713-5528
vln@vsb.bc.ca
www.gvdes.com
Grades: K.-12 *Enrollment:* 578
Cindy Gauthier, Principal
cgauthier@gvdes.com

Victoria: South Island Distance Education
4575 Wilkinson Rd., Victoria, BC V8Z 7E8, Canada
Tel: 250-704-4979; *Fax:* 250-479-9870
Toll-Free: 800-663-7610
sides@sides.ca
www.sides.sd63.bc.ca
Grades: K.-12 *Enrollment:* 626
Kevin White, Principal

Schools: Independent & Private

Catholic

Burnaby: Holy Cross Elementary
1450 Delta Ave., Burnaby, BC V5B 3G2, Canada
Tel: 604-299-3530; *Fax:* 604-299-3534
hcoffice@telus.net
www.holycrosselementary.ca
Grades: K.-7 *Enrollment:* 224
Dino Alberti, Principal

North Vancouver: Holy Trinity Elementary School
128 - 27 St. West, North Vancouver, BC V7N 2H1, Canada
Tel: 604-987-4454; *Fax:* 604-987-0360
holyt@telus.net
www.holytschool.org; www.holytrinityparish.ca
Grades: K.-7 *Enrollment:* 233
Kevin Smith, Principal

Penticton: Holy Cross Elementary School
1298 Main St., Penticton, BC V2A 5G2, Canada
Tel: 250-492-4480; *Fax:* 250-490-4602
www.holyc.com
Grades: K.-7 *Enrollment:* 145
Jeff Brophy, Principal

Port Coquitlam: Archbishop Carney Regional Secondary School
1335 Dominion Ave., Port Coquitlam, BC V3B 8G7, Canada
Tel: 604-942-7465; *Fax:* 604-942-5289
admin@acrss.org
www.acrss.org
Grades: 8-12 *Enrollment:* 720
Lorraine Paruzzolo, Principal
paruzzol@acrss.org

Powell River: Assumption Catholic School
7091 Glacier St., Powell River, BC V8A 1R8, Canada
Tel: 604-485-9894; *Fax:* 604-485-7984
assump.office@shaw.ca
www.assumpschool.com
Grades: K.-9 *Enrollment:* 186 *Note:* Accredited by the B.C. Min. of Education. Curriculum includes math, sciences, social studies, physical education, languages, music, art, drama, & relgion.
Mimi Richardson, Principal

Surrey: Cloverdale Catholic School
17511 - 59th Ave., Surrey, BC V3S 1P3, Canada
Tel: 604-574-5151; *Fax:* 604-574-5160
office@ccsunited.ca
ccsunited.ca
Grades: Preschool; K.-7 *Enrollment:* 245
Jason Borkowski, Principal

Vancouver: Corpus Christi School
6344 Nanaimo St., Vancouver, BC V5P 4K7, Canada
Tel: 604-321-1117; *Fax:* 604-321-1410
mkcc@telus.net
www.corpuschristi-school.ca
Grades: K.-7 *Enrollment:* 241
Rosa Natola, Principal

French

Vancouver: L'Ecole Française Internationale de Vancouver
French International School of Vancouver
3657, rue Fromme, Vancouver, BC V7K 2E6
Tél: 604-924-2457; *Téléc:* 604-924-4483
info@efiv.org; administration@efiv.org
www.efiv.org
twitter.com/EFIVANCOUVER
www.flickr.com/photos/efivancouver
Grades: Pre.-8 *Enrollment:* 143
Gérard Martinez, Principal
principal@efiv.org

First Nations

Bella Coola: Acwsalcta Band School
P.O. Box 778
Bella Coola, BC V0T 1C0, Canada
Tel: 250-799-5911; *Fax:* 250-799-5576
www.acwsalcta.ca
Grades: K.-12 *Enrollment:* 136 *Note:* Acwsalcta School promotes the teaching of Nuxalk cultural skills and values, and promote the use of twenty-first-century technology.
Gerry Tetrault, Principal

Iskut: Klappan Independent Day School
P.O. Box 60
Iskut, BC V0J 1K0
Tel: 250-234-3561; *Fax:* 250-234-3562
www.bced.gov.bc.ca
Grades: K.-9 *Enrollment:* 41 *Note:* Serving students of Iskut First Nation.
Carolyn Ann Doody, Principal
carolyn_ann_doody@hotmail.com

Merritt: Lower Nicola Band School
181 Nawishaskin Lane, Merritt, BC V1K 1N2, Canada
Tel: 250-378-5157; *Fax:* 250-378-6188
www.lnib.net
Grades: K.-6 *Enrollment:* 34 *Note:* As an independent school, the Band School follows the BC Curriculum. Their teachers not only have their BC Teaching Certificates, but have knowledge and deep appreciation of First Nations cultures.
Angie Sterling, Principal
asterling@lnib.net

Special Education

Kelowna: Venture Academy
#101, 1865 Dilworth Dr., Kelowna, BC V1Y 9T1
Tel: 250-491-4593; *Fax:* 250-491-0251
Toll-Free: 866-762-2211
info@ventureacademy.ca
www.ventureacademy.ca
Grades: 7-12 *Note:* A therapeutic program & boarding school for troubled teens; also has locations in Alberta & Ontario
Gordon Hay, B.G.S., Executive Director & Founder

Maple Ridge: James Cameron School
P.O. Box 157 Del Ctr.
20245 Dewdney Trunk Rd., Maple Ridge, BC V2X 7G1, Canada
Tel: 604-465-8444; *Fax:* 604-465-4561
jcsadmin@jcs.bc.ca
www.jcs.bc.ca
www.facebook.com/pages/James-Cameron-School/285177034850085
Grades: 2-7 *Enrollment:* 54
Olive Wagstaff, Principal

Vancouver: Eaton Arrowsmith School
c/o University of British Columbia
#204, 6190 Agronomy Rd., Vancouver, BC V6T 1Z3
Tel: 604-264-8327; *Fax:* 604-222-8327
info@eatonarrowsmithschool.com
www.eatonarrowsmithschool.com
www.facebook.com/eatonarrowsmithschool
twitter.com/eatonarrowsmith
Grades: K.-12 *Enrollment:* 100
Howard Eaton, Director
Simon Hayes, Principal

Campuses
Victoria Campus
#200, 3200 Shelbourne St., Victoria, BC V8P 5G8
Tel: 250-370-0046; *Fax:* 250-370-0034
victoria@eatonarrowsmithschool.com
Jason Cruickshank, Principal

Surrey/White Rock Campus
1538 Foster St., 3rd Fl., White Rock, BC V4B 3X7
Tel: 604-264-8327; *Fax:* 604-222-8327
info@eatonarrowsmithschool.com
Luciana Holmes, Principal

Independent & Private Schools

100 Mile House: Cariboo Christian School
P.O. Box 670
550 Exeter Truck Rd., 100 Mile House, BC V0K 2E0, Canada
Tel: 250-395-4637
Grades: Kindergarten - 9

Abbotsford: Abbotsford Christian School
35011 Old Clayburn Rd., Abbotsford, BC V2S 7L7, Canada
Tel: 604-850-5730; *Fax:* 604-850-6978
administration@abbotsfordchristian.com
www.abbotsfordchristian.com
Grades: K.-12 *Enrollment:* 1014
Daryl Verbeek, Executive Director

Abbotsford: Cornerstone Christian School
P.O. Box 520 Main
3970 Gladwin Rd., Abbotsford, BC V2T 6Z7, Canada
Tel: 604-859-7867; *Fax:* 604-859-7860
admin@cornerstoneschool.ca
www.cornerstoneschool.ca
Grades: K.-12 *Enrollment:* 176
M. Dana, Principal

Abbotsford: Dasmesh Punjabi School
33094 South Fraser Way, Abbotsford, BC V2S 2A9, Canada
Tel: 604-852-8986; *Fax:* 604-852-8924
www.dasmeshschool.com
Grades: K.-10 *Enrollment:* 397
Dalip Singh Gill, Principal

Abbotsford: Mennonite Educational Institute (MEI)
4081 Clearbrook Rd., Abbotsford, BC V4X 2M8, Canada
Tel: 604-859-3700; *Fax:* 604-859-9206
www.meisoc.com
Grades: Preschool - 12 *Enrollment:* 1774 *Note:* The British Columbia curriculum is taught from a Biblical perspective.
Tim Regehr, President
Peter Froese, Superintendent
Ernest Janzen, Principal, Elementary
Dave Loewen, Principal, Chilliwack
David Neufeld, Principal, Secondary
dneufeld@meisoc.com
Heather Smith, Principal, Middle
Jeff Gamache, Vice Principal, Elementary
Rick Thiessen, Vice Principal, Secondary
rthiessen@meisoc.com
Grant Wardle, Vice Principal, Middle
Mr. M. Friesen, Business Adminstrator

Abbotsford: St. James School
2767 Townline Rd., Abbotsford, BC V2T 5E1, Canada
Tel: 604-852-1788; *Fax:* 604-850-5376
Grades: K.-7 *Enrollment:* 219
J. Lindenbach, Principal
principal.stjames@shaw.ca

Abbotsford: St. John Brebeuf
2747 Townline Rd., Abbotsford, BC V2T 5E1, Canada
Tel: 604-855-0571; *Fax:* 604-855-0572
www.stjohnbrebeuf.ca
Grades: 8-12 *Enrollment:* 347
Ted Brennan, Principal
tbrennan@stjohnbrebeuf.ca

Abbotsford: Valley Christian School (VCS)
32721 Cherry Ave., Abbotsford, BC V2V 2T8, Canada
Tel: 604-826-1388; *Fax:* 604-826-2744
info@valleychristianschool.ca
www.valleychristianschool.ca
Grades: Preschool - 9 *Note:* The preschool program works with children, ages three & four. A home school program is supported by the interdenominational school.
Ken Keis, Chair, Board of Directors
Bill Humphreys, Principal
Bob Barclay, Business Administrator

Agassiz: Agassiz Christian School
7571 Morrow Rd., Agassiz, BC V0M 1A2, Canada
Tel: 604-796-9310; *Fax:* 604-796-9519
office@agassizchristianschool.com
www.agassizchristianschool.com
Grades: K.-7 *Enrollment:* 58
J. Zuidhof, Principal

Agassiz: Seabird College
P.O. Box 650
2895 Chowat Rd., Agassiz, BC V0M 1A0, Canada
Tel: 604-796-2177; *Fax:* 604-796-3729
www.seabirdisland.ca
www.facebook.com/pages/Seabird-Island-Band/147393798735724
twitter.com/SeabirdIsland
Enrollment: 162
Dianne Parkinson, Contact
dianneparkinson@seabirdisland.ca

Ahousat: Maaqtusiis School
General Delivery, Ahousat, BC V0R 1A0, Canada
Tel: 250-670-9555; *Fax:* 250-670-9543
Grades: K.-12 *Enrollment:* 217
Rebecca Atleo, Principal

Aldergrove: Fraser Valley Adventist Academy (FVAA)
26026 - 48th Ave., Aldergrove, BC V4W 1J2, Canada
Tel: 604-607-3822; *Fax:* 604-856-1002
fvaa@fvaa.net
www.edline.net/pages/Fraser_Valley_Adventist
Grades: K.-12 *Enrollment:* 175
Karen Wallace, Principal, ext. 332
Janet Brock, Vice Principal, ext. 319
Jean Septembre, Registrar, ext. 319

Alert Bay: T'lisalagi'lakw School
P.O. Box 50
Alert Bay, BC V0N 1A0, Canada
Tel: 250-974-5591; *Fax:* 250-974-2475
WayneP@namgis.bc.ca
Grades: K.-11 *Enrollment:* 66
G. Alfred, Principal

Armstrong: North Okanagan Junior Academy
4699 South Grandview Flats Rd., Armstrong, BC V0E 1B5, Canada
Tel: 250-546-8330; *Fax:* 250-546-8343
info@noja.ca
www.noja.ca
Note: The Academy is operated by the Seventh-day Adventist Church.
Marilyn Ilchuk, B.Sc., Principal
marilynilchuk@aol.com
Sharon Trussell, B.Sc., M.A., Vice Principal
shrbet@shaw.ca
Cameron Koronko, Pastor
koronkoc@hotmail.com

Bowen Island: Island Pacific School
P.O. Box 128
671 Carter Rd., Bowen Island, BC V0N 1G0, Canada
Tel: 604-947-9311; *Fax:* 604-947-9366
info@go.islandpacific.org
www.islandpacific.org
www.facebook.com/islandpacificschool
www.facebook.com/islandpacificschool
www.youtube.com/user/islandpacificschool
Grades: 6-9 *Enrollment:* 52 *Note:* Core program elements include inquiry-based learning within the IB Middle Years Program; special classes in reasoning, philosophy and ethics; hiking, sailing and kayaking expeditions; a grade 9 Masterworks program that requires student to complete, (and publicly defend), a 15-30 page independent research project; monthly community service activities; and a House system that requires, among other things, that students clean the school.
Dr. Ted Spear, Principal

Burnaby: Deer Lake SDA School
5550 Gilpin St., Burnaby, BC V5G 2H6, Canada
Tel: 604-434-5844; *Fax:* 604-434-5845
office@deerlakeschool.ca
www.deerlakeschool.ca
Grades: K.-10 *Enrollment:* 192
Caren Erickson, Principal

Burnaby: John Knox Christian School
8260 - 13 Ave., Burnaby, BC V3N 2G5, Canada
Tel: 604-522-1410; *Fax:* 604-522-4606
admin@johnknoxbc.org
johnknoxbc.org
Grades: K.-7 *Enrollment:* 310
A. Ferguson, Principal

Burnaby: Kenneth Gordon School
7855 Meadow Ave., Burnaby, BC V3N 2V8, Canada
Tel: 604-524-5224; *Fax:* 604-524-8297
Grades: Elem. Ungraded *Enrollment:* 85
Eithne Harrison, Principal
joniharrison@shaw.ca

Burnaby: Our Lady of Mercy School
7481 - 10 Ave., Burnaby, BC V3N 2S1, Canada
Tel: 604-526-7121; *Fax:* 604-520-3194
office@ourladyofmercy.ca
www.ourladyofmercy.ca
Grades: K.-7 *Enrollment:* 240
Neva Grout, Principal

Burnaby: St. Francis de Sales School
6656 Balmoral St., Burnaby, BC V5E 1J1, Canada
Tel: 604-435-5311; *Fax:* 604-434-4798
office@sfdsschool.ca
www.sfdsschool.ca
Grades: K.-7 *Enrollment:* 217 *Note:* St. Francis de Sales is a Catholic school located in the Highgate region of South Burnaby.
Irene Wihak, Principal

Burnaby: St. Helen's School
3894 Triumph St., Burnaby, BC V5C 1Y7, Canada
Tel: 604-299-2234; *Fax:* 604-299-3565
sthelens@telus.net
Grades: K.-7 *Enrollment:* 352
Waldemar Sambor, Principal

Burnaby: St. Michaels School
9387 Holmes St., Burnaby, BC V3N 4C3, Canada
Tel: 604-526-9768; *Fax:* 604-540-9799
ckennedy@cisva.bc.ca
Grades: K.-7 *Enrollment:* 216
C. Kennedy, Principal

Burnaby: St. Thomas More Collegiate
7450 - 12 Ave., Burnaby, BC V3N 2K1, Canada
Tel: 604-521-1801; *Fax:* 604-520-0725
www.stmc.bc.ca
Grades: 8-12 *Enrollment:* 666
D. Hall, Principal
principal@stmc.bc.ca

Burnaby: Vancouver Christian School, Carver Christian High School
7650 Sapperton Ave., Burnaby, BC V3N 4E1
Tel: 604-523-1580; *Fax:* 604-523-9646
www.vancouverchristian.org; www.carverchristian.org
Grades: 9 - 12

Campbell River: Campbell River Christian School (CRCS)
250 South Dogwood St., Campbell River, BC V9W 6Y7, Canada
Tel: 250-287-4266; *Fax:* 250-287-3130
office@crcs.bc.ca
www.crcs.bc.ca
www.facebook.com/crcs.bc.ca
Grades: Kindergarten - 12
Neil Steinke, Principal
ns-admin-crcs@uniserve.com

Chemainus: St. Joseph's School
9735 Elm St., Chemainus, BC V0R 1K0, Canada
Tel: 250-246-3191; *Fax:* 250-246-2921
sjc@cisdv.bc.ca
Grades: K.-7 *Enrollment:* 115
B. Cleary, Principal

Chetwynd: Peace Christian School
P.O. Box 2050
5124, 46th Ave., Chetwynd, BC V0C 1J0, Canada
Tel: 250-788-2044; *Fax:* 250-788-2579
pcs@persona.ca
Grades: K.-10 *Enrollment:* 74
S. Lee, Principal

Chilliwack: Highroad Academy
46641 Chilliwack Central Rd., Chilliwack, BC V2P 1K3, Canada
Tel: 604-792-4680; *Fax:* 604-792-2465
info@highroadacademy.com
www.highroadacademy.com
Grades: K.-12 *Enrollment:* 430
Dave Shinness, Principal
dshinness@highroadacademy.com

Chilliwack: John Calvin School
4268 Stewart Rd., Chilliwack, BC V2R 5G3, Canada
Tel: 604-823-6814; *Fax:* 604-823-6791
office@jcss.ca
www.jcss.ca
Grades: K.-7 *Enrollment:* 170
Pieter H. Torenvliet, Principal

Chilliwack: Mount Cheam Christian School
48988 Yale Rd. East, Chilliwack, BC V2P 6H4, Canada
Tel: 604-794-3072; *Fax:* 604-794-3078
office@mccsbc.com
Grades: Kindergarten - 12 *Enrollment:* 360
Adrian Stoutjesdyk, B.Ed. M.Ed., Principal

Chilliwack: St. Mary's School
8909 Mary St., Chilliwack, BC V2P 4J4, Canada
Tel: 604-792-7715; *Fax:* 604-792-7031
principalstmary@telus.net
Grades: K.-7 *Enrollment:* 183
M. McDermott, Principal

Chilliwack: Timothy Christian School
50420 Castleman Rd., Chilliwack, BC V2P 6H4, Canada
Tel: 604-794-7114; *Fax:* 604-794-3520
Grades: Kindergarten - 12 *Enrollment:* 367
Doug Stam, Principal

Chilliwack: Unity Christian School, Elementary Campus (UCS)
Elementary Campus
P.O. Box 371
9750 McNaught Rd., Chilliwack, BC V2P 6J4, Canada
Tel: 604-792-4171; *Fax:* 604-792-0640
elementary@unitychristian.ca; general@unitychristian.ca
www.unitychristian.ca
Grades: Preschool - 6 *Note:* A Christ-centered education is provided by Unity Christian School.
Ed Noot, Principal
Jeanette Berkenbosch, Vice Principal

Chilliwack: Unity Christian School, Secondary Campus (UCS)
Secondary Campus
P.O. Box 371
50950 Hack-Brown Rd., Chilliwack, BC V2P 6J4
Tel: 604-794-7797; *Fax:* 604-794-7667
general@unitychristian.ca
www.unitychristian.ca
Grades: 7 - 12 *Note:* Unity Christian School offers a Christ-centered education.

Cobble Hill: Evergreen Independent School
P.O. Box 166
3515 Watson Ave., Cobble Hill, BC V0R 1L0, Canada
Tel: 250-743-2433; *Fax:* 250-743-2570
evergreen@evergreenbc.net
www.evergreenbc.net
Grades: K.-6 *Enrollment:* 63
J. Ovans, Principal

Comox: Comox Valley Christian School
P.O. Box 425
2085 Wallace Ave., Comox, BC V9M 1W4, Canada
Tel: 250-339-1200; *Fax:* 250-339-1215
office@cvchristian.com
www.cvchristian.com
Grades: K.-9 *Enrollment:* 112
R. Janzen, Principal

Coquitlam: Coquitlam College
516 Brookmere Ave., Coquitlam, BC V3J 1W9, Canada
Tel: 604-939-6633; *Fax:* 604-939-0336
admiss@coquitlamcollege.com
www.coquitlamcollege.com
Grades: 11-12 *Enrollment:* 85
W. Eckford, Principal

Coquitlam: Eagle Ridge Montessori Elementary
2541 Quay Pl., Coquitlam, BC V3S 3H7, Canada
Tel: 604-461-1223; *Fax:* 604-461-1228
info@childrenofintegrity.com
www.childrenofintegrity.com
Grades: K.-6 *Enrollment:* 38
V. Lawrie, Principal

Coquitlam: Mediated Learning Academy
550 Thompson Ave., Coquitlam, BC V3J 3Z8, Canada
Tel: 604-937-3641; *Fax:* 604-931-5155
info@mediatedlearningacademy.org
www.mediatedlearningacademy.org
Grades: K.-12 *Enrollment:* 84 *Note:* The Mediated Learning Academy is a new and innovative educational facility for children to learn through Mediated Learning Experience and "brain-based" teaching.
Kathleen Jeffrey, Principal

Coquitlam: Our Lady of Fatima School
315 Walker St., Coquitlam, BC V3K 4C7, Canada
Tel: 604-936-4228; *Fax:* 604-936-4403
info@fatimaschool.ca
www.fatimaschool.ca

Grades: K.-7 *Enrollment:* 388
Maria Katsionis, Principal

Coquitlam: Queen of All Saints Elementary School (QAS)
1405 Como Lake Ave., Coquitlam, BC V3J 3P4, Canada
Tel: 604-931-9071; *Fax:* 604-931-9089
queenofallsaintsschool@shawcable.com
www.queenofallsaintsschool.ca
Grades: Kindergarten - 7 *Note:* Queen of All Saints Elementary School was established by the Roman Catholic Archdiocese of Vancouver. The school belongs to All Saints Parish.
Oscar Pozzolo, Principal
Mrs. J. Sussex, Vice Principal
Father Tien Tran, Pastor

Coquitlam: Traditional Learning Academy (TLA)
1189 Rochester Ave., Coquitlam, BC V3K 2X3, Canada
Tel: 604-931-7265; *Fax:* 604-931-3432
tlaoffice@traditionallearning.com
www.traditionallearning.com
Other Information: tlaprincipal@traditionallearning.com (E-mail, Principal)
Note: Traditional Learning Academy encourages students to know the Catholic faith.
Allan Garneau, Administrator

Cranbrook: Kootenay Christian Academy (KCA)
1200 Kootenay St. North, Cranbrook, BC V1C 5X1
Tel: 250-426-0166; *Fax:* 250-426-0186
office@kcacademy.ca; preschool@kcacademy.ca
www.kcacademy.ca
Other Information: KCA Preschool, Phone: 250-489-3426
Grades: Preschool - 9; Special Education *Note:* The Kootenay Christian Academy is an independent, non-denominational school. Operated by the Cranbrook Christian Society, the school offers a biblically directed education. Kootenay Christian Academy is accredited by the British Columbia Ministry of Education, & it follows British Columbia's curriculum guidelines.
Dave Heidt, Chair
Larry Schalk, Secretary
Bob Conroy, Treasurer

Cranbrook: St. Mary's Catholic Independent School
1701 - 5 St. South, Cranbrook, BC V1C 1K1
Tel: 250-426-5017; *Fax:* 250-426-5076
jmacneil@cintek.com
Grades: K.-6 *Enrollment:* 143
J. Macneil, Principal

Dawson Creek: Mountain Christian School (MCS)
11501 - 17th St., Dawson Creek, BC V1G 4S7, Canada
Tel: 250-782-9528; *Fax:* 250-782-3888
mcs@shawcable.com
www.mcsed.ca
Grades: Kindergarten - 12 *Enrollment:* 94
Trevor Ragan, Principal

Dawson Creek: Notre Dame School
925 - 104th Ave., Dawson Creek, BC V1G 2H8
Tel: 250-782-4923; *Fax:* 250-782-4388
www.notredamedc.org/notre-dame-school
Grades: Kindergarten - 7 *Enrollment:* 150 *Note:* Notre Dame School provides a Catholic education.
Mrs. Terri Haynal, Principal
Kathy Lear, Principal

Dawson Creek: Ron Pettigrew Christian School
1761 - 110th Ave., Dawson Creek, BC V1G 4X4
Tel: 250-782-4580; *Fax:* 250-782-9805
rpcs@pris.ca
www.rpschool.ca
Grades: K - 12 *Enrollment:* 75
Phyllis Roch, Principal

Delta: Delta Christian School
4789 - 53 St., Delta, BC V4K 2Y9, Canada
Tel: 604-946-2514; *Fax:* 604-946-2589
Info@deltachristianschool.org
deltachristianschool.org
Grades: K.-7 *Enrollment:* 169
G. de Vos, Principal

Delta: Immaculate Conception School
8840 - 119 St., Delta, BC V4C 6M4, Canada
Tel: 604-596-6116; *Fax:* 604-596-4338
immaculate_conception_school@hotmail.com
www.icdelta.com
Grades: K.-7 *Enrollment:* 473
Maurice Jacob, Principal
Fr. Patrick Tepoorten, Pastor

Delta: Sacred Heart School
P.O. Box 10 Main
3900 Arthur Dr., Delta, BC V4K 3N5, Canada
Tel: 604-946-2611; *Fax:* 604-946-0598
office@shsdelta.org
www.shsdelta.net
Grades: K.-7 *Enrollment:* 400
Wendell MacCormack, Principal

Duncan: Duncan Christian School
495 Beech Ave., Duncan, BC V9L 3J8, Canada
Tel: 250-746-3654; *Fax:* 250-746-3615
office@duncanchristianschool.ca
Grades: K.-12 *Enrollment:* 276
Kevin Visscher, Principal

Duncan: Island Oak High School
P.O. Box 873 Main
5814 Banks Rd., Duncan, BC V9L 3Y2, Canada
Tel: 250-701-0400; *Fax:* 250-701-0410
mail@islandoak.org
islandoak.org
Grades: 9-12 *Enrollment:* 36
Gary Ward, Principal

Duncan: Queen Margaret's School (QMS)
660 Brownsey Ave., Duncan, BC V9L 1C2, Canada
Tel: 250-746-4185; *Fax:* 250-746-4187
admissions@qms.bc.ca
www.qms.bc.ca
Grades: Junior Kindergarten - 12 *Note:* Queen Margaret's School consists of a coeducational junior school for students from junior kindergarten to grade seven. The school also consists of an All-Girls High School, which offers a university preparatory program. An English as a Second Language Program is available for beginner & advanced students.
Leigh Taylor, Chair
Wilma Jamieson, Head of School
wjamieson@qms.bc.ca
Sharon Klein, Deputy Head, Education & Senior School Principal
sklein@qms.bc.ca
Susan Cruikshank, Junior School Principal
scruikshank@qms.bc.ca
Celina Mason, Director, Residential Life & Student Support
cmason@qms.bc.ca
Julie Scurr, Director, Finance & Privacy Officer
jascurr@qms.bc.ca
Courtney Gillan, Executive Director, Admissions & Advancement
cgillan@qms.bc.ca

Duncan: Queen of Angels Catholic School
2085 Maple Bay Rd., Duncan, BC V9L 5L9, Canada
Tel: 250-746-5919; *Fax:* 250-746-8689
qa@cisdv.bc.ca
www.queenofangels.ca
Grades: Pre-K - 9
Tina Campagne, Chair, Local School Council
Art Therrien, Principal
Ciaran McLaverty, Vice Principal
Lana Durand, Coordinator, Special Education
Denika Osmond, Secretary

Duncan: Sunrise Waldorf School
4344 Peters Rd., Duncan, BC V9L 6M3, Canada
Tel: 250-743-7253; *Fax:* 250-743-7245
mail@sunrisewaldorfschool.org
www.sunrisewaldorfschool.org
Grades: K.-8 *Enrollment:* 162
J. Canty, Principal

Fernie: Fernie Academy
P.O. Box 2677
Fernie, BC V0B 1M0, Canada
Tel: 250-423-0212; *Fax:* 250-423-4799
www.thefernieacademy.ca
Grades: K.-12 *Enrollment:* 97
J. Sombrowski, Principal
jsombrowski@fernieacademy.com

Fort Nelson: Chalo School
Mile 293, RR#1, Fort Nelson, BC V0C 1R0, Canada
Tel: 250-774-7651; *Fax:* 250-774-7655
chaloschool@gmail.com
www.chaloschool.bc.ca
Grades: Preschool - 12 *Enrollment:* 200 *Note:* Fort Nelson First Nation owns & operates Chalo School.
Colette Duperreault-Young, Principal
chaloschool@gmail.com

Fort St James: Nak'albun Elementary School
P.O. Box 1390
Fort St James, BC V0J 1P0, Canada
Tel: 250-996-8441; *Fax:* 250-996-2229
www.nakalbun.com
Grades: Kindergarten - 7 *Enrollment:* 60 *Note:* The elementary school is operated under the jurisdiction of Nak'azdli Band.
Rick Aucoin, Principal
nkbprincipal@fsjames.com

Fort St John: Christian Life School
8923 - 112th Ave., Fort St John, BC V1J 5H8
Tel: 250-785-1437; *Fax:* 250-785-4852
office@christianlifeschool.ca
www.christianlifeschool.ca
Grades: Kindergarten - 12; Christianity
Steve Brousson, Chair, 250-785-1437

Fort St John: Maccabee Christian School
P.O. Box 6051 Main
Fort St John, BC V1J 4H6, Canada
Tel: 250-772-5010; *Fax:* 250-772-5009
F. Roscher, Principal

Fort Ware: Aatse Davie School
P.O. Box 79
Fort Ware, BC V0J 3B0, Canada
Tel: 250-471-2002; *Fax:* 250-471-2080
aatse@pris.bc.ca
www.kwadacha.com
Grades: K.-12 *Enrollment:* 84 *Note:* The school serves the Kwadacha First Nation. In addition to the standard humanities & sciences curriculum, classes in the Tsek'ene language are taught.
Andreas Rohrbach, Principal

Houston: Houston Christian School
P.O. Box 237
2161 Caledonia Ave., Houston, BC V0J 1Z0
Tel: 250-845-7736; *Fax:* 250-845-7738
hcschool@houstonchristianschool.ca
www.houstonchristianschool.ca
Grades: K.-12 *Enrollment:* 131
John Siebenga, Principal

Kamloops: Kamloops Christian School
750 Cottonwood Ave., Kamloops, BC V2B 3X2
Tel: 250-376-6900; *Fax:* 250-376-6904
www.kamcs.org
www.facebook.com/KamloopsChristianSchool
twitter.com/KCS_Kamloops
Grades: K.-12
Gordon Hohensee, Principal
gordonh@kamcs.org

Kamloops: Our Lady of Perpetual Help School
235 Poplar St., Kamloops, BC V2B 4B9
Tel: 250-376-2343; *Fax:* 250-376-2361
rose@olphschool.ca
www.olphschool.ca
Grades: K.-7 *Enrollment:* 181
Rose Nowicki, Principal
rose@olphschool.ca

Kamloops: St. Ann's Academy
205 Columbia St., Kamloops, BC V2C 2S7
Tel: 250-372-5452; *Fax:* 250-372-5257
admin@st-anns.ca
st-anns.ca
Grades: K.-12 *Enrollment:* 480
S. Chisholm, Principal
principal@stannsacademy.bc.ca

Kelowna: Aberdeen Hall Preparatory School
950 Academy Way, Kelowna, BC V1V 3A4
Tel: 250-491-1270; *Fax:* 250-491-1289
info@aberdeenhall.com; admissions@aberdeenhall.com
www.aberdeenhall.com
www.facebook.com/AberdeenHallPS
twitter.com/aberdeenhallPS
Grades: Pre.-12 *Enrollment:* 320
Christopher H. Grieve, Head of School

Kelowna: First Lutheran Christian School
4091 Lakeshore Rd., Kelowna, BC V1W 1V7, Canada
Tel: 250-764-3111; *Fax:* 250-764-3129
school@firstlutheran.ca
Grades: K.-6 *Enrollment:* 64
T. Hennig, Principal
thennig@firstlutheran.ca

***Kelowna:* Heritage Christian School**
907 Badke Rd., Kelowna, BC V1X 5Z5
Tel: 250-862-2377; *Fax:* 250-862-4943
office@heritagechristian.ca
www.heritagechristian.ca
Grades: K.-12 *Enrollment:* 308
Greg Bitgood, Principal
gbitgood@heritagechristian.ca

***Kelowna:* Immaculata Catholic Regional High School**
1493 K.L.O. Rd., Kelowna, BC V1W 3N8
Tel: 250-762-2730; *Fax:* 250-861-3028
secretary@immaculatakelowna.ca
www.immaculatakelowna.ca
twitter.com/IRHS_Athletics
Grades: Secondary; Religious Education *Enrollment:* 350
Number of Employees: 26 (14 teachers)
Rob Plaxton, B.Ed. M.Ed., Principal
Lois Ehman, B.Ed. M.Ed., Vice-Principal
lehman@immaculatakelowna.ca
Fr. Pat Monette, Chaplain
Mary Gallagher, B.Ed, Coordinator, Religious Education
mgallagher@immaculatakelowna.ca
Chris Schmidt, B.Ed., Librarian
cschmidt@immaculatakelowna.ca
Nadine Casorso, Librarian
ncasorso@immaculatakelowna.ca

***Kelowna:* Kelowna Christian School**
2870 Benvoulin Rd., Kelowna, BC V1W 2E3
Tel: 250-861-3238; *Fax:* 250-861-4844
Grades: K.-12 *Enrollment:* 802
Tyler Bishop, Principal, Middle/High School, 250-861-3238, ext. 302
Scott Campbell, Principal, Elementary School, 250-861-5432
Darren Lewis, Vice-Principal, Middle/High School, 250-861-3238, ext. 308

***Kelowna:* Kelowna Christian School**
2870 Benvoulin Rd., Kelowna, BC V1W 2E3, Canada
Tel: 250-861-3238; *Fax:* 250-861-4844
kcschool.ca
Grades: K.-9 *Enrollment:* 195
Dave Shinness, Head of School, 250-861-3238
dave.shinness@kelownachristian.ca

***Kelowna:* Kelowna Waldorf School**
429 Collett Rd., Kelowna, BC V1W 1K6
Tel: 250-764-4130; *Fax:* 250-764-4139
info@kelownawaldorf.org
www.kelownawaldorf.org
Grades: K.-7
Cindy Taylor, Principal
cindy.taylor@kelownawaldorf.org

Campuses
Cameron House
2339 Richter St., Kelowna, BC V1Y 2P3
Tel: 250-763-6794
cameronhouse@kelownawaldorf.org
Note: Offers parent & child programs, as well as an introduction to Waldorf education.

***Kelowna:* Okanagan Adventist Academy**
1035 Hollywood Rd. South, Kelowna, BC V1X 4N3
Tel: 250-860-5305; *Fax:* 250-868-9703
www.okaa.ca
Grades: JK-12 *Enrollment:* 135 *Note:* Operated by the Seventh-day Adventist Church.
Don Straub, Principal

***Kelowna:* St. Joseph Elementary School**
839 Sutherland Ave., Kelowna, BC V1Y 5X4
Tel: 250-763-3371; *Fax:* 250-763-2740
school@stjosephkelowna.ca
www.stjosephkelowna.ca
Grades: K.-7 *Enrollment:* 316
R. Smith, Principal

***Kelowna:* Vedanta Academy**
1180 Houghton Rd., Kelowna, BC V1X 2C9, Canada
Tel: 250-868-8816; *Fax:* 250-868-8836
www.vedantaacademy.com
Grades: Kindergarten - 12
C. Belliveau, Principal

***Kispiox:* Kispiox Elementary-Junior Secondary School**
1439 Mary Blackwater Dr., Kispiox, BC V0J 1Y4
Tel: 250-842-6148; *Fax:* 250-842-5799
Grades: K.-7 *Enrollment:* 85
Reinhold Steinbeisser, Principal
RSteinbeisser@kispioxschool.ca

***Kitimat:* St. Anthony's School**
1750 Nalabila Blvd., Kitimat, BC V8C 1E6
Tel: 250-632-6313; *Fax:* 250-632-6317
stanthonys@citywest.ca
www.stanthonysschoolkitimat.com
www.facebook.com/groups/151699398219872
Grades: K.-7 *Enrollment:* 150 *Number of Employees:* 13 teachers
Katja Groves, Principal

***Ladysmith:* Stu"ate Lelum Secondary School**
P.O. Box 730
Ladysmith, BC V9G 1A5, Canada
Tel: 250-245-3522; *Fax:* 250-245-8263
len.merriman@cfnation.com
Grades: GA *Enrollment:* 76
L. Merriman, Principal

***Langley:* Aldergrove Christian Academy**
4057 - 248 St., Langley, BC V4W 1E3, Canada
Tel: 604-856-2577
academy@rosbc.com
www.rosbc.com/christianschool.html
Grades: Kindergarten - 12; Religious ed. *Note:* The Aldergrove Christian Academy was established in 1992.
David Strauss, Principal & Executive Director, Rose of Sharon Ministries

***Langley:* Credo Christian Schools**
21846 - 52 Ave., Langley, BC V2Y 2M7, Canada
Tel: 604-530-5396; *Fax:* 604-530-8965
www.credochs.com
Grades: K.-12 *Enrollment:* 470
H. Moes, Principal, 604-530-1941
h.moes@credochs.com

***Langley:* King's School**
The King's Centre
21783 - 76B Ave., Langley, BC V0X 1T0, Canada
Tel: 604-888-0969; *Fax:* 604-888-0977
school@tkc.com
www.thekingsschool.org
Grades: K.-12 *Enrollment:* 141
P. Thomas, Principal

***Langley:* Langley Christian School**
22702 48th Ave., Langley, BC V2Z 2T6, Canada
Tel: 604-533-2222; *Fax:* 604-533-7276
elem@langleychristian.com
Grades: K.-12 *Enrollment:* 813
Henry Vanderveen, Superintendent
superintendent@langleychristian.com

***Langley:* Langley Montessori School**
21488 Old Yale Rd., Langley, BC V3A 4M8
Tel: 604-532-5667; *Fax:* 604-532-5634
info@langleymontessorischool.com
www.langleymontessorischool.com
Other Information: Early Learning Centre Phone: 604-533-5664
Grades: Preschool-7
Ursula Hodgson, Principal
admin@langleymontessorischool.com

***Langley:* St. Catherines School**
20244 - 32 Ave., Langley, BC V2Z 2E1, Canada
Tel: 604-534-6564; *Fax:* 604-534-4871
www.stcatherines.ca
Grades: K.-7 *Enrollment:* 229
A. Castellon, Principal
acastellon@stcatherines.ca

***Langley:* Whytecliff Agile Learning Centre-Langley**
20561 Logan Ave., Langley, BC V3A 7R3, Canada
Tel: 604-532-1268; *Fax:* 604-532-1269
whytecliffiangley@focusbc.org
www.focusbc.org
Grades: 8-11 *Enrollment:* 49 *Note:* Whytecliff Agile Learning Centres are provincially accredited, independent schools for boys and girls, aged 12-19, who face personal or behavioural challenges. Many of the students have dropped out of school, been excluded or expelled.
A. Butler, Principal
abutler@focusbc.org

Whytecliff Agile Learning Centre-Burnaby
3450 Boundary Rd., Burnaby, BC V5M 4A5
Tel: 604-438-4451; *Fax:* 604-438-5572
whytecliffburnaby@focusbc.org
Grades: 8-11

***Lantzville:* Aspengrove School**
7660 Clark Dr., Lantzville, BC V0R 2H0, Canada
Tel: 250-390-2201; *Fax:* 250-390-2281
cgrunlund@aspengroveschool.ca
aspengroveschool.ca
Grades: K.-12 *Enrollment:* 190 *Note:* Accredited International Baccalaureate programs for primary and middle years; core academic subjects, as well as performing arts, physical and outdoor education, community service.
Zinda Fitzgerald, Head of School

***Lax Kw'Alaams:* Coast Tsimshian Academy**
11 Lagaic St., Lax Kw'Alaams, BC V0V 1H0, Canada
Tel: 604-625-3207; *Fax:* 604-625-3425
ctahome@tsimshianacademy.com
Grades: K.-12 *Enrollment:* 152
S. Campbell, Principal

***Lillooet:* Fountainview Academy**
P.O. Box 500
7615 Lytton-Lillooet Hwy., Lillooet, BC V0K 1V0, Canada
Tel: 250-256-5400; *Fax:* 250-256-5499
info@fountainview.ca
fountainviewacademy.ca
fountainviewacademy.ca/blog
Grades: 10-12 *Enrollment:* 87 *Number of Employees:* 9 administrators; 9 teachers; 10 student life; 3 industry; 4 maintenance; 2 cafeteria; 5 media dept.
Baird Corrigan, Principal
bcorrigan@fountainview.ca

***Lister:* Bountiful Elementary - Secondary School**
P.O. Box 226
1070 JRB Rd., Lister, BC V0B 1Y0
Tel: 250-428-4679; *Fax:* 250-428-4789
bountifulschool@gmail.com
www.bountifulschool.org
Grades: Kindergarten - 12 *Note:* Bountiful Elementary - Secondary School prrovides education for members of the FLDS faith.
Merrill R. Palmer, Principal

***Lister:* Mormon Hills Elementary Secondary School**
P.O. Box 725
Lister, BC V0B 1Y0, Canada
Tel: 250-428-4800; *Fax:* 250-428-4810
mormonhillsschool@yahoo.ca
Grades: Kindergarten - 11 *Enrollment:* 191
Jeff Banman, Principal

***Lytton:* Stein Valley Nlakapamux School**
PO Bag 300, Lytton, BC V0K 1Z0, Canada
Tel: 250-455-2522; *Fax:* 250-455-2512
steinvalleyschool@yahoo.com
Grades: K.-12 *Enrollment:* 109
C. Holmes, Principal

***Mansons Landing:* Linnaea School**
P.O. Box 98
Mansons Landing, BC V0P 1K0, Canada
Tel: 250-935-6747; *Fax:* 250-935-6413
Grades: K.-8 *Enrollment:* 57
Christine Robinson, Principal

***Maple Ridge:* Maple Ridge Christian School**
12140 - 203 St., Maple Ridge, BC V2X 2S5, Canada
Tel: 604-465-4442; *Fax:* 604-465-1685
y.cramer@mrcs.ca
www.mrcs.ca
Grades: K.-12 *Enrollment:* 322
R. Roxburgh, Principal

***Maple Ridge:* Meadowridge School**
12224 - 240th St., Maple Ridge, BC V4R 1N1, Canada
Tel: 604-467-4444; *Fax:* 604-467-4989
www.meadowridge.bc.ca
Grades: K.-12 *Enrollment:* 450
H. Burke, Principal
hburke@meadowridge.bc.ca

***Maple Ridge:* St. Patrick's School**
22589 - 121 Ave., Maple Ridge, BC V2X 3T5, Canada
Tel: 604-467-1571; *Fax:* 604-467-2686
Grades: K.-7 *Enrollment:* 214
Irene Wihak, Principal
iwihak@cisva.bc.ca

***Mill Bay:* Brentwood College School**
2735 Mount Baker Rd., Mill Bay, BC V0R 2P1, Canada
Tel: 250-743-5521; *Fax:* 250-743-2911
admissions@brentwood.bc.ca
www.brentwood.bc.ca
Grades: 9 - 12 *Note:* Brentwood College School is a co-educational university prep school.

Andrea Pennells, Head, Brentwood College School
amp@brentwood.bc.ca
John Allpress, Deputy Head, Advancement
allpress@brentwood.bc.ca
Marius Felix, Assistant Head, Campus Life
marius.felix@brentwood.bc.ca
John Garvey, Assistant Head, Administration
garveyj@brentwood.bc.ca
Clayton Johnston, Director, Admissions
clayton.johnston@brentwood.bc.ca
Dave McCarthy, Director, Academics
mccarthd@brentwood.bc.ca
Gerry Pennells, Director, University Planning
pennells@brentwood.bc.ca

***Nanaimo:* Malaspina International High School**
900 Fifth St., Nanaimo, BC V9R 5S5, Canada
Tel: 250-740-6317; *Fax:* 250-740-6470
highschool@viu.ca
Grades: 10-12 *Enrollment:* 121
T. Lewis, Principal

***Nanaimo:* Nanaimo Christian School (NCS)**
198 Holland Rd., Nanaimo, BC V9R 6W2, Canada
Tel: 250-754-4512; *Fax:* 250-754-4271
inquiries.ncs@shaw.ca
www.nanaimochristianschool.ca
Grades: Preschool - 12
John Reems, Principal
Brian De Schiffart, Vice Principal
Sue De Schiffart, Coordinator, Special Education

***Nanoose Bay:* Beacon Christian School**
2210 Morello Rd., Nanoose Bay, BC V9P 9A9, Canada
Tel: 250-468-9433; *Fax:* 250-468-7748
Grades: K - 8 *Enrollment:* 12
Barbara Judd, Principal

***Nelson:* Nelson Waldorf School**
P.O. Box 165 Main
Nelson, BC V1L 5P9
Tel: 250-352-6919; *Fax:* 250-352-6887
info@nelsonwaldorf.org
www.nelsonwaldorf.org
Grades: Kindergarten - 8 *Note:* The school offers Waldorf education to children in the West Kootenay area.
Beverley Barcham, General Administrator & Principal
Lisa Bramson, Coordinator, Special Needs
Diana Finley, Coordinator, Social Inclusion
Andromeda Drake, Bookkeeper

***Nelson:* St. Joseph's School**
523 Mill St., Nelson, BC V1L 4S2
Tel: 250-352-3041; *Fax:* 250-352-9188
office@stjosephnelson.ca
www.stjosephnelson.ca
Grades: K.-6 *Enrollment:* 122
L. Luck, Principal

***New Westminster:* Purpose Independent Secondary School**
Also known as: Purpose Young Adult Learning Centre
40 Begbie St., New Westminster, BC V3M 3L9, Canada
Tel: 604-526-2522; *Fax:* 604-526-6546
info@purposesociety.org
www.purposesociety.org/purpose
Grades: 10 - 12 *Note:* The program at The Purpose School is designed for students, aged fifteen to nineteen, who are unable to succeed in the traditional school system. A Purpose Secondary School education leads to a Standard Dogwood Diploma.
Phill Esau, Principal

***New Westminster:* Urban Academy**
101 Third St., New Westminster, BC V3L 2P9
Tel: 604-524-2211; *Fax:* 604-524-2711
admin@urbanacademy.ca
www.urbanacademy.ca
www.facebook.com/278963742167615
Grades: JK-12 *Enrollment:* 115
Michael Bouchard, B.A., M.A., Head of School

***North Vancouver:* Bodwell High School**
955 Harbourside Dr., North Vancouver, BC V7P 3S4, Canada
Tel: 604-924-5056; *Fax:* 604-924-5058
www.bodwell.edu/highschool
Grades: 8 - 12 *Note:* Bodwell High School is a co-educational day & boarding school.
Stephen Smith, B.A., Dip. Ed., M.A., M.E, Principal
Cathy Lee, B.S.Sc., M.S.W., Director, Admissions

***North Vancouver:* Brockton School**
3467 Duval Rd., North Vancouver, BC V7J 3E8
Tel: 604-929-9201; *Fax:* 604-929-9501
info@brocktonschool.com
www.brocktonschool.com
Grades: K.-11 *Enrollment:* 140
Alison Wall, B.A. (Hons.), M.Sc., Head of School

***North Vancouver:* L'École française internationale de Vancouver**
French International School of Vancouver
4343 Starlight Way, North Vancouver, BC V7N 3N8, Canada
Tél: 604-924-2457; *Téléc:* 604-924-4483
info@efiv.org
www.efiv.org
Grades: Mat./Prim. *Enrollment:* 125 *Note:* Programme du Ministère de l'Éducation Nationale Français, enrichi par des cours d'histoire, de géographie et des cultures du Canada.
Jérémy Harrison, Directeur (par intérim)

***North Vancouver:* Lions Gate Christian Academy (LGCA)**
925 Harbourside Dr., North Vancouver, BC V7P 3S1
Tel: 604-984-8226; *Fax:* 604-984-8254
lgca@lionsgateca.org
www.lionsgateca.org
Grades: Kindergarten - 12 *Enrollment:* 250 *Note:* Established in 1994, the school offers Christian education for students on the North Shore of British Columbia. The British Columbia curriculum of the Ministry of Education is provided by the Lions Gate Christian Academy.
Terry Kooy, Principal
tkooy@lionsgateca.org

***North Vancouver:* St. Edmund's School**
535 Mahon Ave., North Vancouver, BC V7M 2R7, Canada
Tel: 604-988-7364; *Fax:* 604-988-7350
www.stedmunds.ca
Grades: K.-7 *Enrollment:* 204
Michael Field, Principal
mfield@stedmunds.ca

***North Vancouver:* St. Pius X Elementary School**
1150 Mount Seymour Rd., North Vancouver, BC V7G 1R6, Canada
Tel: 604-929-0345; *Fax:* 604-929-5051
stpiusxschool@telus.net
Grades: K.-7 *Enrollment:* 227
Fabio Battisti, Principal

***North Vancouver:* St. Thomas Aquinas School**
541 Keith Rd. West, North Vancouver, BC V7M 1M5, Canada
Tel: 604-987-4431; *Fax:* 604-987-7816
office@aquinas.org
www.aquinas.org
Grades: 8-12 *Enrollment:* 601
F. Dragojevich, Principal
dragojevich@aquinas.org

***North Vancouver:* Vancouver Waldorf School**
2725 St. Christophers Rd. North, North Vancouver, BC V7K 2B6, Canada
Tel: 604-985-7435; *Fax:* 604-985-4948
reception@vws.ca
www.vws.ca
Other Information: board@vws.ca (E-mail, Board of Trustees)
Grades: Preschool - 12 *Note:* Vancouver Waldorf School integrates the movement arts & artistic activities throughout the curriculum.
Rea Gill, Administrator
Robert Adams, Administrator, High School
Mary Paradis, Director, Development
Fiona Thatcher, Director, Admissions, 604-985-7435, ext. 200
admissions@vws.ca

***Oliver:* Sen Pok Chin**
#2 McKinney Rd., Oliver, BC V0H 1T0, Canada
Tel: 250-498-2019; *Fax:* 250-498-3096
office@senpokchin.com
www.senpokchin.com
Grades: K.-7 *Enrollment:* 36
R. Laurie, Principal
principal@senpokchin.com

***Penticton:* Penticton Community Christian School**
P.O. Box 910 Main
Penticton, BC V2A 6J9, Canada
Tel: 250-493-5233; *Fax:* 250-276-4124
office@pentictonchristianschool.ca
www.pentictonchristianschool.ca
Grades: K.-12 *Enrollment:* 54
K. Boehmer, Principal
kboehmer@pentictonchristianschool.ca

***Port Alberni:* Haahuupayak School**
6000 Santu Dr., Port Alberni, BC V9Y 7M2, Canada
Tel: 250-724-5542; *Fax:* 250-724-7335
ha-ak-sap@hotmail.com
www.haahuupayak.com
Grades: K.-6 *Enrollment:* 79
Tricia McAuley, Principal

***Port Alberni:* Port Alberni Christian School**
4283 Glenside Rd., Port Alberni, BC V9Y 5W9, Canada
Tel: 250-723-2700; *Fax:* 250-723-5799
Grades: K.-7 *Enrollment:* 36
M. Walker, Principal

***Port Coquitlam:* British Columbia Christian Academy**
1019 Fernwood Ave., Port Coquitlam, BC V3B 5A8, Canada
Tel: 604-941-8426; *Fax:* 604-945-6455
admissions@bcchristianacademy.ca
www.bcchristianacademy.ca
Grades: Preschool - 12 *Note:* British Columbia Christian Academy is an interdenominational Christian school.
Mr. I. Jarvie, Head Principal
ijarvie@bcchristianacademy.ca
Mr. T. Bryerton, Elementary Principal
tbryerton@bcchristianacademy.ca
Ms. T. Cota, Director, Preschool, Out Of School, Daycare
tcota@bcchristianacademy.ca
Mr. D. Dowell, Director, Foreign Studies & Continuing Education
ddowell@bcchristianacademy.ca
Ms. Tko, Librarian
library@bcchristianacademy.ca

***Port Coquitlam:* Hope Lutheran Elementary**
3151 York St., Port Coquitlam, BC V3B 4A7, Canada
Tel: 604-942-5322; *Fax:* 604-942-5311
info@hopelcs.ca
www.hopelcs.ca
www.facebook.com/hopelcs
twitter.com/hopelcs
Grades: K.-11 *Enrollment:* 190
Mike Schiemann, Principal

***Port Coquitlam:* Our Lady of the Assumption School**
2255 Fraser Ave., Port Coquitlam, BC V3B 6G8, Canada
Tel: 604-942-5522; *Fax:* 604-942-8313
info@assumptionschool.com
www.assumptionschool.com
Grades: K.-7 *Enrollment:* 244
J. Brophy, Principal

***Port Hardy:* Avalon Adventist Junior Academy**
P.O. Box 974
Port Hardy, BC V0N 2P0, Canada
Tel: 250-949-8243; *Fax:* 250-949-6770
avalonacad@hotmail.com
www.aaja.ca
Grades: Kindergarten - 10
Clifford Wood, Principal
wagonwoody2003@yahoo.ca
Jenny Hilton, Secretary

***Port Hardy:* Gwa'sala-'Nakwaxda'xw School**
P.O. Box 1799
Port Hardy, BC V0N 2P0, Canada
Tel: 250-949-7743; *Fax:* 250-949-7422
www.gwanak.bc.ca
Grades: K.-7 *Enrollment:* 82 *Note:* Independent First Nation's school
Barry Prong, Principal

***Prince George:* Cedars Christian School**
701 North Nechako Rd., Prince George, BC V2K 1A2
Tel: 250-564-0707; *Fax:* 250-564-0729
www.cedars.bc.ca
Grades: Preschool - 12 *Note:* Cedars Christian School is a non-denominational school.
Judy Serup, Chair

***Prince George:* Immaculate Conception School**
3285 Cathedral Ave., Prince George, BC V2N 5R2
Tel: 250-964-4362; *Fax:* 250-964-9465
iconceptoffice@shawcable.com
www.icschool.ca
Grades: K.-7
Donncha O'Callaghan, Principal

***Prince George:* Sacred Heart School**
785 Patricia Blvd., Prince George, BC V2L 3V5
Tel: 250-563-5201; *Fax:* 250-563-5201
shspg@netbistro.com
www.shspg.com
www.facebook.com/127658757272916
Grades: K.-7 *Enrollment:* 104 *Number of Employees:* 9

Rebecca Gilbert, Principal
principal@shspg.com

***Prince George:* St. Mary's School**
1088 Gillett St., Prince George, BC V2M 2V3
Tel: 250-563-7502; *Fax:* 250-563-7818
coachbrent@stmaryspg.org
www.stmaryspg.org
Grades: K.-7 *Enrollment:* 199
Brent Arsenault, Principal
coachbrent@stmaryspg.org

***Prince George:* Westside Academy**
3791 Hwy. 16 West, Prince George, BC V2N 5P8
Tel: 250-964-9600
office@westsideacademy.ca
www.westsideacademy.ca
Grades: K - 12 *Note:* Westside Academy is a ministry of Westside Family Fellowship.
Donna Rosenbaum, High School Principal
drosenbaum@westsideacademy.ca
Sherry Breck, Elementary Principal
sbreck@westsideacademy.ca

***Prince Rupert:* Annunciation School**
627 - 5 Ave. West, Prince Rupert, BC V8J 1V1
Tel: 250-624-5873; *Fax:* 250-627-4486
www.annunciationpr.ca
Grades: K.-7
Laura Lowther, Principal

***Quesnel:* North Cariboo Christian School (NCCS)**
2876 Red Bluff Rd., Quesnel, BC V2J 6C7
Tel: 250-747-4417; *Fax:* 250-747-4410
office@nccschool.ca
www.nccschool.ca
Grades: K - 9 *Enrollment:* 63 *Note:* The North Cariboo Christian School is a non-denominational school.
John Hengen, Principal

***Quesnel:* St. Ann's School**
150 Sutherland Ave., Quesnel, BC V2J 2J5
Tel: 250-992-6237; *Fax:* 250-992-6234
office.stanns@shawcable.com;
principal.stanns@shawcable.com
www.stannsschool.ca
Grades: K.-7 *Enrollment:* 71
R. Nieman, Principal

***Richmond:* BC Muslim School**
12300 Blundell Rd., Richmond, BC V6W 1B3, Canada
Tel: 604-270-2511; *Fax:* 604-270-2679
admin@bcmuslimschool.ca
www.bcmuslimschool.ca
Grades: Kindergarten - 7 *Note:* BC Muslim School offers an accredited Arabic program.
Farida Wahab, Principal

***Richmond:* Choice School**
Main Campus
20451 Westminster Hwy. North, Richmond, BC V6V 1B3, Canada
Tel: 604-273-2418; *Fax:* 604-273-2419
info@choiceschool.org
www.choiceschool.org
Grades: Pre-Kindergarten - 8 *Note:* Choice School offers gifted education to talented & gifted children.
Ken Affolder, Principal

***Richmond:* Cornerstone Christian Academy**
7890 No. 5 Rd., Richmond, BC V6Y 2V2
Tel: 604-303-9181; *Fax:* 604-303-9187
cca@cebccanada.com
cornerstonechristianacademy.ca
Grades: Pre. K-7 *Enrollment:* 141 *Note:* Associated with the Cornerstone Evangelical Baptist Church located on the same property.
W. Kushnir, Principal

***Richmond:* Richmond Christian School (RCS) Elementary School Campus**
5240 Woodwards Rd., Richmond, BC V7E 1H1, Canada
Tel: 604-272-5720; *Fax:* 604-272-7370
info@richmondchristian.ca
www.richmondchristian.ca
Grades: Preschool - 5 *Enrollment:* 400 *Note:* The Richmond Christian Elementary School is an independent school, which offers a Christ-centered curriculum.
Richard Macdonald, Chair
Roger Grose, Systems & Elementary Campus Principal
Hugh Mawby, Vice Principal, Elementary Campus
Aza Nakagawa, Business Manager
Darlene Neufeld, Coordinator, Educational Support Services
Judy Sawatsky, Secretary, Elementary Campus & Admissions

***Richmond:* Richmond Christian School (RCS) Middle School Campus**
10200 No. 5 Rd., Richmond, BC V7A 4E5
Tel: 604-274-1122; *Fax:* 604-274-1128
info@richmondchristian.ca
www.richmondchristian.ca
Grades: 6 - 8 *Enrollment:* 200 *Note:* The Richmond Christian Middle School provides a Christ-centred community for students.

***Richmond:* Richmond Christian School (RCSS) Secondary School Campus**
10260 No. 5 Rd., Richmond, BC V7A 4E5
Tel: 604-274-1122; *Fax:* 604-274-1128
info@richmondchristian.ca
www.richmondchristian.ca
Grades: 9 - 12 *Enrollment:* 233 *Note:* The Richmond Christian Secondary School is an independent school, where students grow academically, physically, & spiritually.

***Richmond:* Richmond Jewish Day School (RJDS)**
8760 No. 5 Rd., Richmond, BC V6Y 2V4, Canada
Tel: 604-275-3393; *Fax:* 604-275-9322
www.rjds.ca
Grades: Preschool - 7 *Note:* Richmond Jewish Day School incorporates Hebrew & Judaic studies with the British Columbia curriculum.
Shay Kell, Co-President, Board of Directors
Sara Levine, Co-President, Board of Directors
Abba Brodt, Principal
abrodt@rjds.ca
Mary Jane Brown, Business Manager
mjbrown@rjds.ca
Malki Moshkovitz, Counsellor
mmoshkovitz@rjds.ca
Kelly Koyanagi, Administrative Assistant
kkoyanag@rjds.ca

***Richmond:* St. Joseph the Worker School**
4451 Williams Rd., Richmond, BC V7E 1J7, Canada
Tel: 604-277-1115; *Fax:* 604-272-5214
office@stjo.richmond.bc.ca
Grades: K.-7 *Enrollment:* 222
M. Jacob, Principal

***Richmond:* St. Paul's School**
8251 St. Alban's Rd., Richmond, BC V6Y 2L2, Canada
Tel: 604-277-4487; *Fax:* 604-277-1810
principal@stpaulschool.ca
www.stpaulschool.ca
Grades: K.-7 *Enrollment:* 241
Nicole Regush, Principal

***Salmon Arm:* King's Christian School**
350B - 30th St. NE, Salmon Arm, BC V1E 1J2, Canada
Tel: 250-832-5200; *Fax:* 250-832-5201
info@kingschristianschool.com
www.kingschristianschool.com
www.facebook.com/KCSOkanagan
twitter.com/KCSOkanagan
Grades: K.-12 *Enrollment:* 214
Dan Demeter, Principal

***Shawnigan Lake:* Dwight International School**
2371 East Shawnigan Lake Rd., Shawnigan Lake, BC V0R 2W5
Tel: 250-929-0506
info@dwightinternational.org
dwightinternational.com
www.facebook.com/dwightcanada
twitter.com/dwightcanada
www.linkedin.com/company/dwight-school-canada
Grades: 6-12
Jerry Salvador, Head of School
Christine Bater, Contact, Admissions Office
admissions@dwightinternational.org

***Shawnigan Lake:* Shawnigan Lake School**
RR#1, 1975 Renfrew Rd., Shawnigan Lake, BC V0R 2W0, Canada
Tel: 250-743-5516; *Fax:* 250-743-6200
info@sls.bc.ca
Grades: 8-12 *Enrollment:* 444
D. Robertson, Principal

***Sicamous:* Eagle River Secondary School**
518 Main St., Sicamous, BC V0E 2V0
Tel: 250-836-2831; *Fax:* 250-836-2664
ers@sd83.bc.ca
www.ers.sd83.bc.ca
Grades: Secondary

***Smithers:* Bulkley Valley Christian School (BVCS)**
P.O. Box 3635
3575 - 14th Ave., Smithers, BC V0J 2N0
Tel: 250-847-4238; *Fax:* 250-847-3564
www.bvcs.ca
Other Information: 250-857-9833 (Elementary); 250-847-4238 (Distributed Learning)
Grades: Elementary / Secondary *Note:* Bulkley Valley Christian School offers an program for international students.
Klaas Kort, Principal
Hugo VanderHoek, Vice Principal
Glenda Posthuma, Business Adminstrator, 250-847-4238
John Buikema, Director, Development

***Smithers:* Ebenezer Canadian Reformed School**
P.O. Box 3700
1685 Lower Viewmount Rd., Smithers, BC V0J 2N0, Canada
Tel: 250-847-3492; *Fax:* 250-847-3912
ebenezer@bulkley.net
Grades: K.-12 *Enrollment:* 133
D. Stoffels, Principal

***Smithers:* Moricetown Elementary School**
#2, 205 Beaver Rd., RR#1, Smithers, BC V0J 2N1
Tel: 250-847-3166; *Fax:* 250-877-5092
www.moricetown.ca
Grades: Elementary *Enrollment:* 49

***Smithers:* St. Joseph's School**
P.O. Box 454
4054 Broadway Ave., Smithers, BC V0J 2N0
Tel: 250-847-9414; *Fax:* 250-847-9402
stjosephs@telus.net
Grades: K.-7 *Enrollment:* 191
S. Forbrigger, Principal

***South Hazelton:* Gitsegukla Elementary School**
21 Seymour Ave., RR#1, South Hazelton, BC V0J 2R0, Canada
Tel: 250-849-5739; *Fax:* 250-849-5276
www.gitsegukla.org
Grades: K.-7 *Enrollment:* 60
Tuskasa Sakata, Principal

***Surrey:* Bibleway Christian Academy (BCA)**
18603 - 60th Ave., Surrey, BC V3S 7P4, Canada
Tel: 604-576-8188; *Fax:* 604-576-1370
www.biblewayacademy.org
Grades: Kindergarten - 9
Julius Briner, President
Randall Timmermans, Principal

***Surrey:* Cornerstone Montessori School**
14724 - 84 Ave., Surrey, BC V3S 2M5, Canada
Tel: 604-599-9918; *Fax:* 604-597-0468
corstone@telus.net
Grades: K.-7 *Enrollment:* 121
Rita Gausman, Principal

***Surrey:* Diamond Elementary**
18620, Hwy. 10, Surrey, BC V3S 1G1, Canada
Tel: 604-576-1146; *Fax:* 604-574-9831
diamondschool@shawlink.ca
Grades: K.-7 *Enrollment:* 159
Douglas Smith, Principal

***Surrey:* Heritage Christian School**
3487 King George Hwy., Surrey, BC V4P 1B7, Canada
Tel: 604-536-5967; *Fax:* 604-536-6073
Grades: K.-12 *Enrollment:* 198
T. Bryerton, Principal

***Surrey:* Holy Cross Regional High School**
16193 - 88 Ave., Surrey, BC V4N 1G3, Canada
Tel: 604-581-3023; *Fax:* 604-583-4795
office@holycross.bc.ca
www.holycross.bc.ca
Grades: 8-12 *Enrollment:* 797
Robert Dejulius, Principal

***Surrey:* Iqra School**
14590 - 116A Ave., Surrey, BC V3R 2V1
Tel: 604-583-7530; *Fax:* 604-583-7510
info@iqraschool.com
www.iqraschool.com
Grades: K.-8 *Enrollment:* 340
Faisal Ali, Principal

***Surrey:* Khalsa School (Surrey)**
6933 - 124th St., Surrey, BC V3W 3W6, Canada
Tel: 604-591-2248; *Fax:* 604-591-3396
kssinfo@khalsaschool.ca
www.khalsaschoolcanada.com
Grades: K.-10 *Enrollment:* 1468

J. Bhatia, Principal
jsbhatia@khalsaschool.ca

Surrey: Our Lady of Good Counsel School
10504 - 139 St., Surrey, BC V3T 4L5, Canada
Tel: 604-581-3154; *Fax:* 604-588-1633
olgcprincipal@shaw.ca
www.ourladyofgoodcounselschool.ca
Grades: K.-7 *Enrollment:* 245
G. Wright, Principal

Surrey: Pacific Academy
10238 - 168 St., Surrey, BC V4N 1Z4, Canada
Tel: 604-581-5353; *Fax:* 604-581-0087
contact@pacificacademy.net
www.pacificacademy.net
www.facebook.com/groups/154091321343008/
Grades: K.-12 *Enrollment:* 1450 *Note:* Private Christian School
Paul Horban, Head of School

Surrey: Regent Christian Academy (RCA)
15100 - 66A Ave., Surrey, BC V3S 2A6, Canada
Tel: 604-599-8171; *Fax:* 604-599-8175
www.regent.bc.ca
Grades: Preschool - 13 *Enrollment:* 550 *Note:* Regent Christian Academy is a coeducational school, which offers primary, middle, high school, English as a Second Language, & international programs.
Paul Johnson, Principal
Linda Mehus-Barber, Administrator, Middle Division
Allan Visser, Administrator, International Division
Amanda Whone, Administrator, Primary Division
Maureen Sayler, Registrar & Secretary

Surrey: Relevant Schools' Society
Relevant High School
18620 Hwy. #10, Surrey, BC V3S 1G1, Canada
Tel: 604-574-4736; *Fax:* 604-574-9831
relevantschool@shawlink.ca
www.relevanthighschool.ca
Grades: 8 - 12 *Note:* Relevant High School is coeducational, non-denominational secondary school.

Surrey: Relevant Schools' Society
Diamond Elementary School
18620 Hwy. #10, Surrey, BC V3S 1G1
Tel: 604-576-1146; *Fax:* 604-574-9831
diamondschool@shawlink.ca
www.relevanthighschool.ca
Grades: Kindergarten - 7

Surrey: Roots & Wings Montessori Place
5438 - 152nd St., Surrey, BC V3S 5J9, Canada
Tel: 604-574-5399; *Fax:* 604-574-5319
info@rootsandwingsbc.com
www.rootsandwingsbc.com
Grades: Preschool - Elementary *Note:* Primary Montessori programs are offered for children between the ages of 2.5 & 5. The senior program at the school is designed for students from age 9 to 12.

Surrey: St. Bernadette School
13130 - 65B Ave., Surrey, BC V3W 9M1, Canada
Tel: 604-596-1101; *Fax:* 604-596-1550
kkozack@cisva.bc.ca
Grades: K.-7 *Enrollment:* 227
K. Kozack, Principal

Surrey: Southridge Senior School
2656 - 160 St., Surrey, BC V3S 0B7, Canada
Tel: 604-535-5056; *Fax:* 604-535-3676
Grades: 8-12 *Enrollment:* 260
M. Ayotte, Head of Senior School
mayotte@southridge.bc.ca

Surrey: Star of the Sea School
15024 - 24 Ave., Surrey, BC V4A 2H8, Canada
Tel: 604-531-6316; *Fax:* 604-531-0171
www.starofthesea.bc.ca/school
Grades: K.-7 *Enrollment:* 316
L. Balsevich, Principal
lbalsevich@starofthesea.bc.ca

Surrey: Surrey Christian High School
9115 160 St., Surrey, BC V4N 2X7, Canada
Tel: 604-581-2474; *Fax:* 604-581-5211
info@surreychristian.com
Grades: K.-12 *Enrollment:* 454
D. de Groot, Principal

Surrey: Surrey Christian School
9115 - 160 St., Surrey, BC V4N 2X7, Canada
Tel: 604-581-2474; *Fax:* 604-581-5211
info@surreychristian.com
www.surreychristian.com
www.facebook.com/SurreyChristianSchool
twitter.com/surreychristian
www.youtube.com/user/SurreyChristianFilms
Grades: K.-8 *Enrollment:* 608
A. Stegeman, Principal

Surrey: White Rock Christian Academy
2265 - 152 St., Surrey, BC V4A 4P1, Canada
Tel: 604-531-9186; *Fax:* 604-531-1727
wrca@wrca.bc.ca
wrca.bc.ca
Grades: K.-12 *Enrollment:* 308
Stephen Hardy, Principal

Surrey: William of Orange Christian School
P.O. Box 34090
17790 Hwy. 10, Surrey, BC V3S 8C4, Canada
Tel: 604-576-2144; *Fax:* 604-576-0975
admin@wofo.org
www.faithwebsites.com/credochs/wohome.cfm
Grades: K.-7 *Enrollment:* 106
J. Siebenga, Principal

Surrey: Zion Lutheran Christian Church & School
***Also known as:* Cloverdale Christian School**
5950 - 179 St., Surrey, BC V3S 4J9, Canada
Tel: 604-576-6313; *Fax:* 604-576-1399
www.cloverdalechristianschool.ca/school
Grades: K.-9 *Enrollment:* 162
D. Davis, Principal

Terrace: Centennial Christian School
3608 Sparks St., Terrace, BC V8G 2V6
Tel: 250-635-6173; *Fax:* 250-635-9385
office@centennialchristian.ca
www.centennialchristian.ca
Grades: K - 12
Edgars Veldman, Principal
Mrs. Petras, Vice Principal

Terrace: Veritas Catholic School
4836 Straume Ave., Terrace, BC V8G 4G3
Tel: 250-635-3035; *Fax:* 250-635-7588
veritas.class@telus.net
www.veritascatholicschool.com
Grades: Kindergarten - 7 *Enrollment:* 200
Colleen LeBlanc, Chair
Glen Palahicky, Principal
veritas.principal@telus.net
Isabel DeMedeiros, Secretary

Trail: St. Michael's Elementary School
1329 - 4 Ave., Trail, BC V1R 1S3
Tel: 250-368-6151; *Fax:* 250-368-9962
Grades: K.-7 *Enrollment:* 179
D. Nowicki, Principal

Tsawwassen: Southpointe Academy
1900 - 56 St., Tsawwassen, BC V4L 2B1, Canada
Tel: 604-948-8826; *Fax:* 604-948-8853
info@spacademy.ca
www.southpointeacademy.ca
Grades: K.-12 *Enrollment:* 425
Bruce Griffioen, Headmaster
bruce.griffioen@spacademy.ca

Vancouver: Blessed Sacrament School
École Saint Sacrement
3020 Heather St., Vancouver, BC V5Z 3K3, Canada
Tel: 604-876-7211; *Fax:* 604-876-7280
admin@ess.vancouver.bc.ca
moodle.ess.vancouver.bc.ca/moodle
Grades: Kindergarten - 7
Michael Yaptinchay, Director
michael.yaptinchay@ess.vancouver.bc.ca

Vancouver: Canadian College International
#200, 1050 Alberni St., Vancouver, BC V6E 1A3, Canada
Tel: 604-688-9366; *Fax:* 604-688-9322
study@canadiancollege.com
www.canadiancollege.com
Enrollment: 300
Jim Clark, President & Owner
jim.clark@canadiancollege.com
Jeff Carter, Director, Academic
jeff.carter@canadiancollege.com
Cindy Kwon, Director, Marketing
cindy.kwon@canadiancollege.com

Vancouver: Century High School (CHS)
#300, 1788 West Broadway, Vancouver, BC V6J 1Y1, Canada
Tel: 604-730-8138; *Fax:* 604-731-9542
admission@centuryhighschool.ca
www.centuryhighschool.ca
Grades: 8 - 12

Vancouver: Columbia College
#500, 555 Seymour St., Vancouver, BC V6B 6J9, Canada
Tel: 604-683-8360; *Fax:* 604-682-7191
admin@columbiacollege.ca
www.columbiacollege.ca
Enrollment: 57 *Note:* A liberal arts college offering 1st & 2nd year university transfer courses, associate degrees, university preparation programmes, adult secondary school completion, & English language instruction geared to international students.
Dr. Trevor Toone, Principal

Vancouver: Core Education & Fine Arts (CEFA)
2946 Commercial Dr., Vancouver, BC V5N 4C9
Tel: 604-879-2332; *Fax:* 604-879-2330
vancouver@cefa.ca
www.cefa.ca
www.facebook.com/167143796669678
twitter.com/cefakids
cefakids.wordpress.com
Grades: Pre.-K.
Natacha V. Beim, Founder

Campuses

Abbotsford Campus
1785 Clearbrook Rd., Abbotsford, BC V2T 5X5
Tel: 604-853-2332; *Fax:* 604-608-3585
abbotsford@cefa.ca
cefaabbotsford.wordpress.com

Burnaby - Canada Way Campus
4970 Canada Way, Burnaby, BC V5G 1M4
Tel: 604-299-2373; *Fax:* 604-299-2378
canadaway@cefa.ca

Burnaby - Kingsway Campus
4021 Kingsway, Burnaby, BC V5H 1Y9
Tel: 604-568-8808
kingsway@cefa.ca

Calgary - Chinook Campus
5728 - 1 St. SW, Calgary, AB T2H 0E2
Tel: 403-319-2332
calgary-chinook@cefa.ca

Coquitlam Campus
3380 David Ave., Coquitlam, BC V3E 3G8
Tel: 604-315-6020
coquitlam@cefa.ca
Note: Opening Spring 2013

Langley Campus
#100, 19950 - 88th Ave. East, Langley, BC V1M 0A5
Tel: 604-881-2332; *Fax:* 604-881-2338
langley@cefa.ca

New Westminster Campus
725 Carnarvon St., New Westminster, BC V3M 1E6
Tel: 604-777-0053
newwestminster@cefa.ca

North Vancouver Campus
#402, 935 Marine Dr., North Vancouver, BC V7P 1S3
Tel: 604-929-2332; *Fax:* 604-929-2303
newwestminster@cefa.ca

Richmond Campus
#160, 10811 No. 4 Rd., Richmond, BC V7A 2Z5
Tel: 604-275-2332; *Fax:* 604-288-5065

West Vancouver Campus
2008 Park Royal South, West Vancouver, BC V7T 2W4
Tel: 604-913-7713; *Fax:* 604-913-7714

White Rock Campus
15300 Croydon Dr., South Surrey, BC V3S 0Z5
Tel: 778-294-2646; *Fax:* 604-608-2585
cefawhiterock.wordpress.com

Vancouver: Crofton House School
3200 - 41 Ave. West, Vancouver, BC V6N 3E1, Canada
Tel: 604-263-3255; *Fax:* 604-263-4941
www.croftonhouse.ca
Grades: Elem./Sec.; girls *Enrollment:* 667
Patricia J. Dawson, Head of School
pdawson@croftonhouse.ca

***Vancouver:* Fraser Academy**
2294 - 10 Ave. West, Vancouver, BC V6K 2H8, Canada
Tel: 604-736-5575; *Fax:* 604-736-5578
www.fraseracademy.ca
www.facebook.com/fraseracademy
www.twitter.com/fraseracademy
www.youtube.com/fraseracademyschool
Grades: 1-12 *Enrollment:* 188
E. Nesling, Principal

***Vancouver:* Immaculate Conception School Vancouver**
3745 - 28 Ave. West, Vancouver, BC V6S 1S6, Canada
Tel: 604-224-5012; *Fax:* 604-224-3721
www.icschoolvancouver.com
Grades: K.-7 *Enrollment:* 196
C. Riviere, Principal

***Vancouver:* Khalsa School (Vancouver)**
5987 Prince Albert St., Vancouver, BC V5W 3E2, Canada
Tel: 604-321-1226; *Fax:* 604-321-2709
Toll-Free: 866-933-2248
Grades: K.-7 *Enrollment:* 207
Amar Dhaliwal, Principal

***Vancouver:* King David High School**
5718 Willow St., Vancouver, BC V5Z 4S9, Canada
Tel: 604-263-9700; *Fax:* 604-263-4848
kdhs.org
Grades: 8-12 *Enrollment:* 140 *Note:* King David High School (KDHS) is a pluralistic, community, co-educational, Jewish high school in the Oakridge district of Vancouver.
Russ Klein, Head of School
rklein@kdhs.org

***Vancouver:* Little Flower Academy**
4195 Alexandra St., Vancouver, BC V6J 4C6, Canada
Tel: 604-738-9016; *Fax:* 604-738-5749
lfa@lfabc.com
www.lfabc.org
Grades: 8-12 *Enrollment:* 469
M. DeFreitas, Principal

***Toronto:* Language Studies Canada Toronto (LSC)**
#400, 124 Eglinton Ave. West, Toronto, ON M4R 2G8, Canada
Tel: 416-488-2200; *Fax:* 416-488-2225
toronto@lsc-canada.com
www.lsc-canada.com
www.facebook.com/ec.english.language.centres
twitter.com/ecenglish
www.youtube.com/user/ecwebteam
David S. Diplock, Director

***Vancouver:* LSC Vancouver**
#200, 570 Dusmuir St., Vancouver, BC V6B 1Y1, Canada
Tel: 604-683-1199; *Fax:* 604-683-6088
vancouver@lsc-canada.com

LSC Montréal
#401, 1610 St. Catherine West., Montréal, QC H3H 2S2, Canada
Tel: 514-939-9911; *Fax:* 514-939-2223
montreal@lsc-canada.com

***Vancouver:* Madrona School Society**
2050 West 10th Ave., Vancouver, BC V6J 2B3
Tel: 604-732-9965
www.madronaschool.com
Grades: 1-9 *Enrollment:* 25
Eric D'Donnell, Director, 778-991-5545
eric@madronaschool.com
Judy O'Donnell, Principal
judy@madronaschool.com

***Vancouver:* Notre Dame Regional Secondary School**
2855 Parker St., Vancouver, BC V5K 2T8, Canada
Tel: 604-255-5454; *Fax:* 604-255-2115
www.ndrs.ca
Grades: 8 - 12 *Enrollment:* 620 *Note:* Notre Dame Regional Secondary School is a Catholic school.
Mr. R. DesLauriers, Principal
Mr. R. Gabriele, Vice Principal
Mr. G. Oswald, Vice Principal
Mrs. M. Grant, Manager, Office

***Vancouver:* Our Lady of Perpetual Help School**
2550 Camosun St., Vancouver, BC V6R 3W6, Canada
Tel: 604-228-8811; *Fax:* 604-224-6822
Grades: K.-7 *Enrollment:* 406
Lora Clarke, Acting Principal

***Vancouver:* Our Lady of Sorrows School**
575 Slocan St., Vancouver, BC V5K 3X5, Canada
Tel: 604-253-2434; *Fax:* 604-253-1523
ourladyofsorrows1@telus.net
www.ourladyofsorrows.ca
Grades: K.-7 *Enrollment:* 231
P. Balletta, Principal

***Vancouver:* Pacific Spirit School**
Jericho Hill Centre
4196 West 4th Ave., Vancouver, BC V6J 4J5, Canada
Tel: 604-222-1900; *Fax:* 604-222-1934
info@pacificspiritschool.org
www.pacificspiritschool.org
Grades: K.-7 *Enrollment:* 227 *Note:* Formerly Life Song School, Pacific Spirit School is the flagship for the New Learning Society, which promotes and supports the growth of the whole child.
Ingrid Price, Ph.D., Executive Director

***Vancouver:* Pattison High School**
981 Nelson St., Vancouver, BC V6Z 3B6
Tel: 604-608-8788; *Fax:* 604-608-8789
info@pattisonhighschool.ca
www.pattisonhighschool.ca
www.facebook.com/pattison.high
twitter.com/pattisonhigh
www.youtube.com/user/pattisonhigh
Grades: 8-12 *Enrollment:* 170
Ken Davies, Principal
principal@pattisonhighschool.ca

***Vancouver:* Royal Canadian College**
8610 Ash St., Vancouver, BC V6P 3M2, Canada
Tel: 604-738-2221; *Fax:* 604-738-2282
info@royalcanadiancollege.com
www.royalcanadiancollege.com
Grades: 8-12 *Enrollment:* 52
Leon King, President

***Vancouver:* St. Andrew's School**
450 - 47th Ave. East, Vancouver, BC V5W 2B4, Canada
Tel: 604-325-6317; *Fax:* 604-325-0920
Grades: K.-7 *Enrollment:* 227
M. Mailley, Principal

***Vancouver:* St. Anthony of Padua**
1370 - 73rd Ave. West, Vancouver, BC V6P 3E8, Canada
Tel: 604-261-4043; *Fax:* 604-261-4036
office@stanthonyofpaduaschool.ca
www.stanthonyofpaduaschool.ca
Grades: K.-7 *Enrollment:* 209
C. Kraemer, Principal

***Vancouver:* St. Augustine's School**
2145 - 8 Ave. West, Vancouver, BC V6K 2A5, Canada
Tel: 604-731-8024; *Fax:* 604-739-1712
info@faithandfoundation.com
www.faithandfoundation.com
Grades: K.-7 *Enrollment:* 224
Catherine Oberndorf, Principal

***Vancouver:* St. Francis of Assisi School**
870 Victoria Dr., Vancouver, BC V5L 4E7, Canada
Tel: 604-253-7311; *Fax:* 604-253-7375
sfaprincipal@telus.net
Grades: K.-7 *Enrollment:* 191
Joan Sandberg, Principal

***Vancouver:* St. Francis Xavier School**
428 Great Northern Way, Vancouver, BC V5T 4S5, Canada
Tel: 604-254-2714; *Fax:* 604-254-2514
admin@sfxschool.ca
www.sfxschool.ca
Grades: K.-7 *Enrollment:* 327
B. Krivuzoff, Principal

***Vancouver:* St. George's School**
4175 - 29 Ave. West, Vancouver, BC V6S 1V1, Canada
Tel: 604-224-1304; *Fax:* 604-224-7066
sradmin@stgeorges.bc.ca
www.stgeorges.bc.ca
Grades: 1-12 *Enrollment:* 1123 *Note:* Day and boarding school for boys
Nigel Toy, Headmaster

***Vancouver:* St. John's International**
1885 West Broadway, Vancouver, BC V6J 1Y5, Canada
Tel: 604-683-4572; *Fax:* 604-683-4679
info@stjohnsis.com
www.stjohnsis.com
Grades: 8-12 *Enrollment:* 76

***Vancouver:* St. John's School**
2215 - 10 Ave. West, Vancouver, BC V6K 2J1, Canada
Tel: 604-732-4434; *Fax:* 604-732-1074
info@stjohns.bc.ca
www.stjohns.bc.ca
Grades: K.-12 *Enrollment:* 342 *Note:* University prep school
S. Hutchison, Headmaster
shutchison@stjohns.bc.ca

***Vancouver:* St. Joseph's School**
3261 Fleming St., Vancouver, BC V5N 3V6, Canada
Tel: 604-872-5715; *Fax:* 604-872-5700
stjosephsvancouver@telus.net
www.stjoesschool-vancouver.org
Grades: K.-7 *Enrollment:* 210
Dierdre O'Callaghan, Principal

***Vancouver:* St. Jude's School**
2953 - 15 Ave. East, Vancouver, BC V5M 2K7, Canada
Tel: 604-434-1633; *Fax:* 604-434-8677
stjude@shawcable.com
Grades: K.-7 *Enrollment:* 221
M. Perry, Principal

***Vancouver:* St. Mary's School**
5239 Joyce St., Vancouver, BC V5R 4G8, Canada
Tel: 604-437-1312; *Fax:* 604-437-1193
Grades: K.-7 *Enrollment:* 230
K. Smith, Principal
ksmith@cisva.bc.ca

***Vancouver:* St. Patrick Regional Secondary School**
115 - 11 Ave. East, Vancouver, BC V5T 2C1, Canada
Tel: 604-874-6422; *Fax:* 604-874-5176
administration@stpats.bc.ca
Grades: 8-12 *Enrollment:* 501
J. Bevacqua, Principal
jbevacqua@stpats.bc.ca

***Vancouver:* St. Patrick's Elementary School**
2850 Quebec St., Vancouver, BC V5T 3A9, Canada
Tel: 604-879-4411; *Fax:* 604-879-3737
Grades: K.-7 *Enrollment:* 249
M. Boreham, Principal
mboreham@shaw.ca

***Vancouver:* Stratford Hall**
3000 Commercial Dr., Vancouver, BC V5N 4E2, Canada
Tel: 604-436-0608; *Fax:* 604-436-0616
info@stratfordhall.ca
www.stratfordhall.ca
Grades: K.-12 *Enrollment:* 370
J. McConnell, Principal

***Vancouver:* Torah High School - Vancouver**
Schara Tzedeck Synagogue
3476 Oak St., Vancouver, BC V6H 2L8
Tel: 604-736-7607; *Fax:* 604-730-1621
info@vncsy.com
vancouver.torahhigh.ca
Grades: 8-12 *Note:* Torah High offers courses in Religious Studies, Hebrew Language, Philosophy, Political Science, Nutrition, Arts & Interdisciplinary Studies for students attending public or private secondary schools. Classes take place on Monday nights in King David High School.
Rabbi Stephen Berger, Director, Education
rabbiberger@vncsy.com

***Vancouver:* Vancouver Christian School (VCS)**
3496 Mons Dr., Vancouver, BC V5M 3E6, Canada
Tel: 604-435-3113; *Fax:* 604-430-1591
office@vancouverchristian.org
www.vancouverchristian.org
Other Information: 604-523-1580 (Phone, Carver Christian High School)
Grades: Kindergarten - 12 *Note:* Vancouver Christian School is an independent, interdenominational school. Grades nine to twelve are offered at Carver Christian High School.
Mrs. E. Freestone, Principal
Mrs. Wiebe, Vice Principal, Kindergarten - Grade 5
Miss Wong, Vice Principal, Grades 6 to 8

***Vancouver:* Vancouver College**
5400 Cartier St., Vancouver, BC V6M 3A5, Canada
Tel: 604-261-4285; *Fax:* 604-261-2284
info@vc.bc.ca
www.vc.bc.ca
Grades: Kindergarten - 12 *Enrollment:* 1000 *Note:* Vancouver College consists of an elementary school, a middle school, & a senior school.
John McFarland, Principal
jmcfarland@vc.bc.ca
Mary-Joy Derouin, Assistant Principal, Senior School
Michel DesLauriers, Assistant Principal, Middle School

Barbara Seppelt, Assistant Principal, Elementary School
Kelly Lattimer, Business Manager
Ronith Cogswell, Athletic Director & Communications Officer
Mr. Kim Findlay, Chief Development Officer
Rev. John Horgan, Chaplain
Margaret Vossen, Registrar
Wade Anderson, Department Head, Physical Education
Monica Beck, Department Head, Student Services
Henry Budai, Department Head, Second Languages
Anne Field, Department Head, English
Br. Charles Gattone, Department Head, Religion
Marilia Marghetti, Department Head, Sciences
Enzo Nardi, Department Head, Mathematics
Larry Olson, Department Head, Applied / Fine Arts
Lilian Vernier, Department Head, Social Studies

Vancouver: Vancouver Hebrew Academy
1545 West 62nd Ave., Vancouver, BC V6P 2E8, Canada
Tel: 604-266-1245; *Fax:* 604-264-0648
vha@vhebrewacademy.com
www.vhebrewacademy.com
Grades: Preschool - 10 *Note:* Vancouver Hebrew Academy is an Orthodox Jewish school which offers Judaic & general studies.
Rabbi Don Pacht, Head of School
Patricia Haslop, Principal
Nancy Scambler, Administrative Secretary

Vancouver: Vancouver Montessori School
8650 Barnard St., Vancouver, BC V6P 5G5, Canada
Tel: 604-261-0315
www.vancouvermontessorischool.com
Grades: Preschool - Elementary *Note:* Preschool (Casa) programs are available for three to six year old children. Elementary classes are offered for children from age six to twelve.
Prasannata Runkel, Principal
Roni (Bamendine) Jones, Administrator, School Operations
Chrystle Williams, Registrar & Administration Assistant

Vancouver: Vancouver Talmud Torah School (VTT)
998 West 26th Ave., Vancouver, BC V5Z 2G1, Canada
Tel: 604-736-7307; *Fax:* 604-736-9754
info@talmudtorah.com
sites.google.com/a/vttschool.ca/vtt1/Home
Grades: Preschool - 7 *Enrollment:* 500 *Note:* Vancouver Talmud Torah School is a Jewish day school.
Cathy Lowenstein, B.Ed., M.Ed., Principal
Janice St. Helene, Vice Principal, General Studies
Judith Wolfman, Vice Principal, Judaic Studies
Adam Gelmon, Director, Admissions & School-Wide Programs
Gaby Lutrin, Director, Preschool
Mark Maibauer, Director, Operations
Jessica Neville, Director, Student Services
Jennifer Shecter-Balin, Director, Communications

Vancouver: West Coast Christian School (WCCS)
15 North Renfrew St., Vancouver, BC V5K 3N6, Canada
Tel: 604-255-2990; *Fax:* 604-255-2103
principal@westcoastchristianschool.ca
www.westcoastchristianschool.ca
Grades: Kindergarten - 12 *Enrollment:* 100 *Note:* The school is a ministry of West Coast Christian Fellowship. It offers a Christian approach to learning.
David Ferguson, Principal
Julie Shettler, Administrative Assistant

Vancouver: West Point Grey Academy (WPGA)
4125 West 8th Ave., Vancouver, BC V6R 4P9, Canada
Tel: 604-222-8750; *Fax:* 604-222-8756
admissions@wpga.ca
www.wpga.ca
Other Information: 604-224-1332 (Phone, Senior School)
Grades: Preschool - 12 *Enrollment:* 905 *Note:* West Point Grey Academy demonstrates a belief in Humanism in its community of Renaissance learners. The pre-kindergarten class is for four year old children.
Robert Standerwick, Chair
boardchair@wpga.ca
Clive S.K. Austin, Headmaster
headmaster@wpga.ca
Stephen Anthony, Head, Senior School
headmaster@wpga.ca

Vancouver: Westside Montessori Academy
3075 Slocan St., Vancouver, BC V5M 3E4
Tel: 604-434-9611
info@westsidemontessoriacademy.ca
www.westsidemontessoriacademy.ca
Grades: Pre.-4 *Enrollment:* 85
Sarah Gatiss, Principal, Preschool/Director, Administration
Andrea Nardi, Principal, Elementary

Vancouver: York House School
4176 Alexandra St., Vancouver, BC V6J 2V6, Canada
Tel: 604-736-6551; *Fax:* 604-736-6530
info@yorkhouse.ca
www.yorkhouse.ca
Grades: K.-12 *Enrollment:* 598
G. Ruddy, Principal

Vanderhoof: Northside Christian School
3337 Voth Rd., Vanderhoof, BC V0J 3A2
Tel: 250-567-9335; *Fax:* 250-567-9332
info@thenorthsideschool.ca
www.thenorthsideschool.ca
www.twitter.com/NCS_Vanderhoo
Grades: 1 - 12 *Enrollment:* 67
Michael Shenk, Principal

Vanderhoof: Rainbow Christian School
P.O. Box 710
2994 Burrard Ave., Vanderhoof, BC V0J 3A0
Tel: 250-567-3127; *Fax:* 250-567-3167
rcschool@telus.net
Grades: PreK - 8 *Enrollment:* 84 *Note:* The day school offers a Christ-centered learning environment.

Vanderhoof: St. Joseph's School
P.O. Box 1429
Vanderhoof, BC V0J 3A0
Tel: 250-567-2794; *Fax:* 250-567-2333
Grades: K.-7 *Enrollment:* 92
G. Gillis, Principal

Vernon: Pleasant Valley Christian Academy
1802 - 45th Ave., Vernon, BC V1T 3M7
Tel: 250-545-7852; *Fax:* 250-545-9230
pvadmin@shaw.ca
Grades: K.-9 *Enrollment:* 30 *Note:* Affiliated with the Seventh-day Adventist Church
R. Tiller, Principal

Vernon: St. James School
2700 - 28 Ave., Vernon, BC V1T 1V7
Tel: 250-542-4081; *Fax:* 250-542-5696
principalsjs@shaw.ca
Grades: K.-7 *Enrollment:* 106
G. Higginson, Principal

Vernon: Vernon Christian School
Elementary Campus
6890 Pleasant Valley Rd., Vernon, BC V1B 3R5
Tel: 250-545-7345; *Fax:* 250-545-0254
info@vcs.ca
www.vcs.ca
www.facebook.com/pages/Vernon-Christian-School/1723235761 27694
twitter.com/myvcs
www.youtube.com/user/vernonchristian
Grades: Kindergarten - 12 *Enrollment:* 350 *Note:* Vernon Christian School is an interdenominational school. The school's secondary campus is located at 6920 Pleasant Valley Road.
Karen Wiseman, Chair
kwiseman@vcs.ca
Steve Onsorge, Lead Principal / Principal Elementary Campus
sonsorge@vcs.ca
Matt Driediger, Principal, Secondary Campus
mdriediger@vcs.ca
Andy Overend, Vice-Principal, Elementary Campus
aoverend@vcs.ca
Brad Martens, Vice-Principal, Secondary Campus
bmartens@vcs.ca

Victoria: Christ Church Cathedral School (CCCS)
Cathedral Memorial Hall
912 Vancouver St., Victoria, BC V8V 3V7, Canada
Tel: 250-383-5125; *Fax:* 250-383-5128
cathedralschool@cathedralschool.ca (office)
www.cathedralschool.ca
Grades: Kindergarten - 8 *Enrollment:* 155 *Note:* Christ Church Cathedral School is an Anglican school attached to a cathedral.
Mary Hendy, President
Charles Peacock, Head of School
head@cathedralschool.ca
Tobi Blue, Assistant Head, Elementary Grades
Marylee McKeown, Assistant Head, Middle & Intermediate Grades

Victoria: Glenlyon Norfolk School
801 Bank St., Victoria, BC V8S 4A8, Canada
Tel: 250-370-6800; *Fax:* 250-370-6840
gns@mygns.ca
www.glenlyonnorfolk.bc.ca
Grades: K.-12 *Enrollment:* 643
Simon Bruce-Lockhart, Head of School

Victoria: Lakeview Christian School
729 Cordova Bay Rd., Victoria, BC V8Y 1P7
Tel: 250-658-5082; *Fax:* 250-658-5072
www.lakeviewchristianschool.ca
Grades: Preschool - 9 *Note:* The Lakeview Christian School is affiliated with other Seventh-day Adventist Christian schools to provide Christian education.
Erin Sutherland, Board Chair
Agnes Oosterhof, Principal

Victoria: Lighthouse Christian Academy
1289 Parkdale Dr., Victoria, BC V9B 4G9, Canada
Tel: 250-474-5311; *Fax:* 250-474-5021
info@lighthousechristianacademy.com
www.lighthousechristianacademy.com
www.facebook.com/133384233375987
Grades: K.-9 *Enrollment:* 70
Leland Makaroff, Principal

Victoria: Maria Montessori Academy
1841 Fairburn Dr., Victoria, BC V8N 1P8, Canada
Tel: 250-479-4746; *Fax:* 250-744-1925
mma@montessori.bc.ca
www.montessori.bc.ca
Grades: K.-7 *Enrollment:* 95
B. McDermitt, Principal

Victoria: Pacific Christian School
654 Agnes St., Victoria, BC V8Z 2E7, Canada
Tel: 250-479-9365; *Fax:* 250-479-3685
www.pacificchristian.ca
Grades: K.-12 *Enrollment:* 1000
B. Helmus, Principal
bhelmus@pacificchristian.ca

Victoria: St. Andrew's Regional High School
880 Mckenzie Ave., Victoria, BC V8X 3G5, Canada
Tel: 250-479-1414; *Fax:* 250-479-5356
sarhs@cisdv.bc.ca
www.standrewshigh.ca
Grades: 8-12 *Enrollment:* 469
W. Jamieson, Principal

Victoria: St. Andrew's School
1002 Pandora Ave., Victoria, BC V8V 3P5, Canada
Tel: 250-382-3815; *Fax:* 250-385-3830
kpollard@cisdv.bc.ca
Grades: K.-7 *Enrollment:* 188
K. Pollard, Principal

Victoria: St. Joseph's Catholic School
757 Burnside Rd. West, Victoria, BC V8Z 1M9, Canada
Tel: 250-479-1232; *Fax:* 250-479-1907
sdicastri@cisdv.bc.ca
Grades: K.-7 *Enrollment:* 203
S. Di Castri, Principal

Victoria: St. Margaret's School
1080 Lucas Ave., Victoria, BC V8X 3P7, Canada
Tel: 250-479-7171; *Fax:* 250-479-8976
stmarg@stmarg.ca
www.stmarg.ca
Grades: K.-12 *Enrollment:* 325
Mary Cameron, Principal, Senior School
mcameron@stmarg.ca
Megan Hedderick, Principal, Junior School
mhedderick@stmarg.ca

Victoria: St. Michael's University School (Junior)
820 Victoria Ave., Victoria, BC V8S 4N3, Canada
Tel: 250-598-3922; *Fax:* 250-592-0783
nrichards@smus.ca
www.smus.ca
Grades: K.-5 *Enrollment:* 160 *Note:* University prep boarding school
Nancy Richards, Principal

Victoria: St. Michael's University School (Middle)
3400 Richmond Rd., Victoria, BC V8P 4P5, Canada
Tel: 250-592-3549; *Fax:* 250-592-3942
www.smus.bc.ca
Grades: 6-8 *Enrollment:* 204
X. Abrioux, Principal
xabrioux@smus.bc.ca

Victoria: St. Michael's University School (Senior)
3400 Richmond Rd., Victoria, BC V8P 4P5, Canada
Tel: 250-592-2411; *Fax:* 250-592-2812
www.smus.bc.ca
Grades: 9-12 *Enrollment:* 573
K. Roth, Principal
kathy.roth@smus.bc.ca

Victoria: St. Patrick's School
2368 Trent St., Victoria, BC V8R 4Z3, Canada
Tel: 250-592-6713; *Fax:* 250-592-6717
Grades: K.-7 *Enrollment:* 355
P. McKenna, Principal

Victoria: Selkirk Montessori School
2970 Jutland Rd., Victoria, BC V8T 5K2, Canada
Tel: 250-384-3414; *Fax:* 250-384-3449
office@selkirkmontessori.ca
www.selkirkmontessori.ca
Grades: K. *Enrollment:* 202
G. Henry, Interim Academic Head

Victoria: West-Mont School
4075 Metchosin Rd., Victoria, BC V9C 4A4, Canada
Tel: 250-474-2626; *Fax:* 250-478-8944
info@west-mont.ca
www.west-mont.ca
Grades: Preschool - 7 *Note:* West-Mont School provides a Montessori preschool to grade three. For students in grades four to seven, an enriched British Columbia curriculum is offered. The school is operated by the Western Communities Montessori Society.
Bruce Laurie, Principal
Cory Meausette, Vice Principal
Barbara Kennelly, Manager, Business
bkennelly@west-mont.ca
Barb Lewis, Head, Admissions
admissions@west-mont.ca

Waglisla: Bella Bella Community School (BBCS)
General Delivery, Waglisla, BC V0T 1Z0, Canada
Tel: 250-957-2391; *Fax:* 250-957-2691
Brendah@bellabella.net
www.bellabella.ca
Grades: Nursery - Secondary
Brenda Humchitt, Principal
Jason Cobey, Vice Principal
Frances Brown, Head, Heiltsuk Language Program

West Vancouver: The Anna Wyman School of Dance Arts
1457 Marine Dr., West Vancouver, BC V7T 1B8
Tel: 604-926-6535; *Fax:* 604-926-6912
info@annawyman.com
www.annawyman.com
Enrollment: 300 *Number of Employees:* 12 faculty members
Note: The school of dance features two large studios.
Anna Wyman, Founder & Artistic Director
Neil Wortley, Founder, Co-Director, & Stage Manager

West Vancouver: Collingwood School
Morven Campus
70 Morven Dr., West Vancouver, BC V7S 1B2, Canada
Tel: 604-925-3331; *Fax:* 604-925-3862
jonna.mcguinness@collingwood.org
www.collingwood.org
Grades: K.-12 *Enrollment:* 1196
R. Wright, Principal

West Vancouver: Mulgrave School
2330 Cypress Lane, West Vancouver, BC V7S 3H9, Canada
Tel: 604-922-3223; *Fax:* 604-922-3328
info@mulgrave.com
www.mulgrave.com
Grades: Kindergarten - 12 *Note:* The coeducational, non-denominational school is an IB World School.
Donald Kirkwood, Chair
Tony Macoun, Head of School
tmacoun@mulgrave.com
Derek Muzyka, Head, Finance
dmuzyka@mulgrave.com
Graham Gilley, Director, Educational Technology
ggilley@mulgrave.com
Martin Jones, Director, Summer Camp Programmes
mjones@mulgrave.com
Luke Lawson, Director, University Counselling
Tony Macoun, Director, Advancement
tmacoun@mulgrave.com
Mark Steffens, Director, Community Relations
msteffens@mulgrave.com
Lesley Tetiker, Director, Admissions
ltetiker@mulgrave.com

West Vancouver: St. Anthony's School
595 Keith Rd., West Vancouver, BC V7T 1L8, Canada
Tel: 604-922-0011; *Fax:* 604-922-3196
office@saswv.ca
www.saswv.ca
Grades: K.-7 *Enrollment:* 204
Laila Maravillas, Principal
principal@saswv.ca

Westbank: Our Lady of Lourdes Elementary School
2547 Hebert Rd., Westbank, BC V4T 2J6, Canada
Tel: 250-768-9008; *Fax:* 250-768-0168
adminolol@telus.net
www.ourladyoflourdeswestbank.com
Grades: K.-7 *Enrollment:* 132
M. Manton, Principal

Westbank: Sensisyusten House of Learning
1920 Quail Lane, Westbank, BC V4T 2H3
Tel: 250-768-2802; *Fax:* 250-768-5462
school@wfn.ca
Grades: K.-6 *Enrollment:* 36
R. Howardson, Principal

Whistler: Whistler Secondary Community School
8000 Alpine Way, Whistler, BC V0N 1B8
Tel: 604-905-2581; *Fax:* 604-905-2583
www.whistlersecondary.bc.ca
Grades: Secondary
Bev Oakley, Principal
boakley@sd48.bc.ca

Williams Lake: Cariboo Adventist Academy
1405 South Lakeside Dr., Williams Lake, BC V2G 3A7
Tel: 250-392-4741
cacademy@yahoo.com
an681g.adventistschoolconnect.org
Grades: Kindergarten - 12 *Note:* The Cariboo Adventist Academy is operated by the Seventh-day Adventist Church.

Williams Lake: Maranatha Christian School
1278 Lakeview Cres., Williams Lake, BC V2G 1A3, Canada
Tel: 250-392-7410; *Fax:* 250-392-7409
maranatha@wlefc.org
Grades: K.-12 *Enrollment:* 155
C. Klaue, Principal

Williams Lake: Sacred Heart Catholic School
455 Pigeon Ave., Williams Lake, BC V2G 4R5, Canada
Tel: 250-398-7770; *Fax:* 250-398-7725
principal.shcs@telus.net
Grades: K.-7 *Enrollment:* 84
Donna Ameerali, Principal

Universities & Colleges

Universities

Abbotsford: Summit Pacific College
P.O. Box 1700
35235 Straiton Rd., Abbotsford, BC V2S 7E7, Canada
Tel: 604-853-7491; *Fax:* 604-853-8951
Toll-Free: 1-800-976-8388
www.summitpacific.ca
Note: Formerly Western Pentecostal Bible College

Burnaby: Simon Fraser University
8888 University Dr., Burnaby, BC V5A 1S6, Canada
Tel: 604-291-3111
www.sfu.ca
Full Time Equivalency: 30313
Dr. Brandt C. Louie, Chancellor
Dr. Michael Stevenson, B.A., M.A, Ph.D., President & Vice-Chancellor
Dr. Jon Driver, Vice-President
Pat Hibbitts, B.A., M.B.A., Vice-President
Mario Pinto, Vice-President
William Krane, B.A., M.A., Ph.D., Assoc. Vice-President
Kate Ross, Registrar
Lynn Copeland, B.Sc., M.A., M.L.S., University Librarian & Dean
R. Szczotko, Manager
Biff Savoie, B.A., Director
Gregg Macdonald, B.A., M.A., Executive Director
Warren Gill, B.A., M.A., Ph.D., Vice-President
Joe Weinberg, Assoc. Vice-President
Judith Osborne, LL.B., M.A., LL.M., Vice-President
Joanne Curry, B.Sc., Ph.D., Executive Director
Cathy Daminato, Vice-President

__Faculties__
Applied Sciences
Brian Lewis, B.A., M.A., Ph.D., Dean
Arts
John T. Pierce, B.A., M.A., Ph.D., Dean
Business Administration
Daniel Shapiro, B.A., M.A., Ph.D., Dean
Continuing Studies
John Labrie, Ph.D., Dean
Education
Paul Shaker, B.A., M.A., Ph.D., Dean
Graduate Studies
Wade Parkhouse, B.P.E., M.P.E., Ph.D., Dean
Health Sciences
David MacLean, Ph.D., Dean
Science
Michael Plischke, B.Sc., M.Phil., Ph.D., Dean

__Publications__
Alumni Journal
c/o Simon Fraser University
8888 University Dr., Burnaby, BC V5A 1S6, Canada
The Peak

Kamloops: Thompson Rivers University
P.O. Box 3010
900 McGill Rd., Kamloops, BC V2C 5N3, Canada
Tel: 250-828-5000; *Fax:* 250-828-5086
Toll-Free: 800-663-1663
admissions@tru.ca
www.tru.ca
Full Time Equivalency: 7632 *Note:* With distance-learning, enrolment figures swell to over 25,000 students.
The Hon Nancy Greene Raine, Chancellor
Dr Roger H. Barnsley, Interim President & Vice-chancellor, 250-828-5001
president@tru.ca
Dr Ulrich Scheck, Provost & Vice-Pres., Academic, 250-377-6126
uscheck@tru.ca
Cliff Neufeld, Vice-Pres., Admin. & Finance, 250-828-5012
Christopher Seguin, Vice-Pres., Advancement, 250-574-0474
cseguin@tru.ca
Judith Murray, Vice-Pres., Open Learning, 250-828-5007
judithmurray@tru.ca

__Faculties__
Arts
Tel: 250-371-5566; *Fax:* 250-371-5510
baadvising@tru.ca
Dr Michael Mehta, Dean, 250-852-7275
mmehta@tru.ca
Science
Dr Tom Dickinson, Dean, 250-852-7137
tdickinson@tru.ca
Human, Social, & Educational Development
Dr. Charles F. Webber, Dean, 250-828-5249
cwebber@tru.ca
Law
Chris Axworthy, QC, Dean, 250-852-7267
caxworthy@tru.ca

__Schools__
Business & Economics (SoBE)
Dr. Murray Young, Dean, 250-828-5217
myoung@tru.ca
Nursing
Barbara Paterson, Dean, 250-852-7288
bpaterson@tru.ca
Tourism
Harold Richins, Dean, 250-852-7138
hrichins@tru.ca
Trades & Technology
Lindsay Langill, Dean, 250-828-5110
lblangill@tru.ca

__Campuses__
100 Mile House Centre
P.O. Box 2109
485 South Birch Ave., 100 Mile House, BC V0K 2E0, Canada
Tel: 250-395-3115; *Fax:* 250-395-2894
Robin Bercowski, Coordinator
rbercowski@tru.ca
Ashcroft/Cache Creek Centre
P.O. Box 1419
310 Railway Ave., Ashcroft, BC V0K 1A0, Canada
Tel: 250-453-9999; *Fax:* 250-453-2518
Sloane Hammond, Coordinator
shammond@tru.ca
Barriere Centre
629 Barriere Town Rd., Barriere, BC V0E 1E0, Canada
Tel: 250-672-9875; *Fax:* 250-672-9875
Susan Ross, Coordinator
sross@tru.ca

Clearwater Centre
Also known as: North Thompson Community Skills Centre
751 Clearwater Village Rd., RR#1, Clearwater, BC V0E 1N0, Canada
Tel: 250-674-3530; *Fax:* 250-674-3540
Sylvia Arduini, Coordinator
sarduini@tru.ca

Lillooet Centre
P.O. Box 339
#10, 155 Main St., Lillooet, BC V0K 1V0, Canada
Tel: 250-256-4296; *Fax:* 250-256-4278
Jane Bryson, Coordinator
jbryson@tru.ca

Williams Lake Campus
1250 Western Ave., Williams Lake, BC V2G 1H7, Canada
Tel: 250-392-8000; *Fax:* 250-392-4984
Toll-Free: 800-663-4936
wlmain@tru.ca

Open Learning Division
P.O. Box 3010
900McGill Rd., Kamloops, BC V2C 5N3, Canada
Tel: 250-852-7000; *Fax:* 250-852-6405
Toll-Free: 1-800-663-1663
student@tru.ca

Publications
The Omega
Tel: 250-372-1272; *Fax:* 250-372-5331
theomega.ca
Sadie Cox, Editor-In-Chief
editorofomega@gmail.com

Langley: The Associated Canadian Theological Schools of Trinity Western University
Also known as: ACTS
7600 Glover Rd., Langley, BC V2Y 1Y1, Canada
Tel: 604-888-6045; *Fax:* 604-513-2045
acts@twu.ca

Langley: Canadian Baptist Seminary
7600 Glover Rd., Langley, BC V2Y 1Y1, Canada
Tel: 604-513-2015; *Fax:* 604-513-2078
canadianbaptistseminary.com
Full Time Equivalency: 23 *Note:* This institution is one of six seminaries representative of other denominations forming a consortium called Associated Canadian Theological Seminaries (ACTS). It is located on the Trinity Western University campus.

Langley: Canadian Pentecostal Seminary
Fosmark Bldg.
7600 Glover Rd., Langley, BC V2Y 1Y1, Canada
Tel: 604-513-2161; *Fax:* 604-513-2078
cps@twu.ca
canadianpentecostalseminary.ca
Note: This institution is in partnership with Trinity Western University, and with five other denominations, to form ACTS, the Associated Canadian Theological Schools. It is located on the Trinity Western U. campus.

Langley: Canadian Theological Seminary
7600 Glover Rd., Langley, BC V2Y 1Y1, Canada
Tel: 604-888-7511

Langley: Mennonite Brethren Biblical Seminary - BC
Also known as: MB Biblical Seminary
7600 Glover Rd., Langley, BC V2Y 1Y1, Canada
Tel: 604-513-2133
mbbsbc@twu.ca
www.mbseminary.ca
Bruce L. Guenther, President

Mennonite Brethren Biblical Seminary - MB
Also known as: MB Biblical Seminary
500 Shaftesbury Blvd., Winnipeg, BC R3P 2N2, Canada
Tel: 877-231-4570
winnipeg@mbseminary.ca

Langley: Northwest Baptist Seminary
P.O. Box 790
Langley, BC V1M 2S2, Canada
Tel: 604-888-3310

Langley: Trinity Western University
7600 Glover Rd., Langley, BC V2Y 1Y1, Canada
Tel: 604-888-7511; *Fax:* 604-513-2061
admissions@twu.ca
www.twu.ca
www.facebook.com/trinitywestern
twitter.com/TrinityWestern
Full Time Equivalency: 2510
Dr Jonathan S. Raymond, President
president@twu.ca
Paul Weme, Vice-Pres., Strategic Advancement
paul.weme@twu.ca
David Coons, Vice-Pres., Developemnt
Jim Poulsen, Vice-Pres., Finance
poulsen@twu.ca
Joan van Dyck, Vice-Pres., University Communications
joan.vandyck@twu.ca
Alma Barranco-Mendoza, Exec. Dir., Information Technology
alma.barranco@twu.ca
Janis Ryder, Exec. Dir., Human Resources
janis.ryder@twu.ca
Scott Henderson, Dir., University Enterprises
scott.henderson@twu.ca
Grant McMillan, Registrar, 604-513-2070, fax: 604-513-2096
registrar@twu.ca

Faculties
Natural & Applied Sciences
Dr Ka Yin Leung, Dean
kayin.leung@twu.ca

Humanities & Social Sciences
Dr Robert K. Burkinshaw, Dean
burkinsh@twu.ca

Professional Studies & Performing Arts
David Squires, Dean
david.squires@twu.ca

Schools
Graduate Studies
Tel: 604-513-2019; *Fax:* 604-513-2064
Toll-Free: 888-468-6898
gradadmissions@twu.ca
Dr William R. Acton, Interim Dean
william.acton@twu.ca

Business
Andrea Soberg, Dean, 604-513-2137, fax: 604-513-2042
andreas@twu.ca

Education
Dr Kimberly Franklin, Dean, 604-513-2105
kimberly.franklin@twu.ca

Human Kinetics
Dr Blair Whitmarsh, Dean, 604-513-2121, ext. 2114
whitmars@twu.ca

Nursing
Dr Landa Terblanche, Dean, 604-888-7511, ext. 3268, fax: 604-513-2012
landa.terblanche@twu.ca

Affiliations
Associated Canadian Theological Seminaries of Trinity Western University (ACTS)
Also known as: ACTS Seminaries
7600 Glover Rd., Langley, BC V2Y 1Y1, Canada
Tel: 604-513-2044; *Fax:* 604-513-2078
acts@twu.ca
acts.twu.ca
Dr John W. Auxier, Acting President & Dean
auxier@twu.ca

Canadian Baptist Seminary
7600 Glover Rd., Langley, BC V2Y 1Y1, Canada
Tel: 604-513-2015; *Fax:* 604-513-2078
canadianbaptistseminary.com
Dr Ed Stuckey, Interim President
estuckey@journeycentre.ca
Cal Netterfield, D.Min., Vice-Pres., Development, ext. 3805
cal.netterfield@twu.ca
Dr Daryl Busby, Dean, ext. 3833
daryl@twu.ca
Wendell Phillips, Registrar, ext. 3807
phillips@twu.ca

Canadian Pentecostal Seminary
7600 Glover Rd., Langley, BC V2Y 1Y1, Canada
Tel: 604-513-2161; *Fax:* 604-513-2078
cps@twu.ca
canadianpentecostalseminary.ca
Dr. Jim Lucas, President
jim@clcc.ca
Dr Joanne Pepper, Dean

Northwest Baptist Seminary
7600 Glover Rd., Langley, BC V2Y 1Y1, Canada
Tel: 604-888-7592; *Fax:* 604-637-3212
www.nbseminary.ca
Dr Larry Perkins, President, ext. 3861
Loren Warkentin, Registrar, ext. 3866

Trinity Western Seminary
7600 Glover Rd., Langley, BC V2Y 1Y1, Canada
Tel: 604-513-2044; *Fax:* 604-513-2078
Dr John Auxier, Acting-President

Pacific Summit College
P.O. Box 1700
35235 Straiton Rd., Abbotsford, BC V2S 7E7, Canada
Tel: 604-853-7491; *Fax:* 604-853-8951
Toll-Free: 800-976-8388
pr@summitpacific.ca
www.summitpacific.ca
Note: Formerly Western Pentecostal Bible College
Dr Dave Demchuk, President
ddemchuk@summitpacific.ca
Melody Deeley, Registrar
registrar@summitpacific.ca

North Vancouver: Capilano University
Lynmour Campus
2055 Purcell Way, North Vancouver, BC V7J 3H5, Canada
Tel: 604-986-1911; *Fax:* 604-984-4985
www.capilanou.ca
TTY: 604-990-7848
Full Time Equivalency: 14500
Peter Ufford, Chancellor
Dr. Kris Bulcroft, President/Vice-Chancellor, 604-984-4925
kbulcrof@capilanou.ca
Cindy Turner, VP, Finance & Administration, 604-984-4937
cturner@capilanou.ca
Dr Jacalyn Snodgrass, VP, Education - Academic & Arts Programs, 604-984-1740
jsnodgra@capilanou.ca
Catherine Vertesi, VP, Education - Mgmt. & International Programs, 604-990-7894
cvertesi@capilanou.ca
Dr Patrick Donahoe, VP, Student and Institutional Support, 604-984-4975
pdonahoe@capilanou.ca
Mike Arbogast, VP, Human Resources, 604-984-4991
marbogas@capilanou.ca
Cheryl Helm, Acting Registrar, 604-983-7506
chelm@capilanou.ca

Faculties
Arts & Science
Dr Robert Campbell, Dean, 604-984-4976
robertc@capilanou.ca

Business
Graham Fane, Dean, 604-984-4988
gfane@capilanou.ca

Fine & Applied Arts
Jennifer Moore, Dean, 604-990-7801
jmoore2@capilanou.ca

Health & Education
Jean Bennett, Dean, 604-990-7982
jbennett@capilanou.ca

Tourism & Outdoor Recreation
Dr Chris Bottrill, Dean, 604-983-7586
cbottril@capilanou.ca

Campuses
Squamish
P.O. Box 1538
1150 Carson Pl., Squamish, BC V8B 0B1, Canada
Tel: 604-892-5322; *Fax:* 604-892-9274
squamish@capilanou.ca

Sunshine Coast
P.O. Box 1609
5627 Inlet Ave., Sechelt, BC V0N 3A0, Canada
Tel: 604-885-9310; *Fax:* 604-885-9350

Publications
Capilano Courier

Prince George: University of Northern British Columbia (UNBC)
3333 University Way, Prince George, BC V2N 4Z9, Canada
Tel: 250-960-5555; *Fax:* 250-960-5794
www.unbc.ca
Full Time Equivalency: 3675
Dr. George Iwama, President
Nancy Black, Acting University Librarian
Dr. Mark R.T. Dale, Vice-President
John DeGrace, University Secretariat & Registrar
Eileen Bray, Vice-President
John DeGrace, Registrar
Dr. Gail Fondahl, Vice-President
Rob van Adrichem, Director

Faculties
Arts, Social & Health Sciences
Dr. John Young, Acting Dean

Graduate Programs
Dr. Ian Hartley, Dean

Science & Management
Dr. William McGill, Dean

Publications
Over the Edge
Note: Student newspaper at the University of Northern British Columbia

Vancouver: University of British Columbia
2329 West Mall, Vancouver, BC V6T 1Z4, Canada
Tel: 604-822-2211
www.ubc.ca
Other Information: Telex: 04-51233

Full Time Equivalency: 48610
Bill Levine, Chair
Sarah Morgan-Silvester, Chancellor
Dr Stephen J. Toope, President & Vice-Chancellor, 604-822-8300, ext. 604-822-50
presidents.office@ubc.ca
Dr David H. Farrar, Provost & Vice-Pres., Academic, 604-822-4948
david.farrar@ubc.ca
Pierre Ouillet, Vice-Pres., Finance, Resources & Operations, 604-822-6317
carolina.cerna@ubc.ca
Barbara Miles, Vice-Pres., Development & Alumni Engagement, 604-822-1585
barbara.miles@ubc.ca
Stephen Owen, Vice-Pres., External, Legal & Community Relations, 604-822-5017
Dr John Hepburn, Vice-Pres., Research & International, 604-822-1995
vpr@exchange.ubc.ca
Brian D. Sullivan, Vice-Pres., Students, 604-822-3955
vpstudents@exchange.ubc.ca
James Ridge, Assoc. Vice-Pres. & Registrar, 604-822-3265
james.ridge@ubc.ca

Faculties
Applied Science
www.apsc.ubc.ca
Dr Tyseer Aboulnasr, Dean, 604-822-6413, fax: 604-822-7006
info@apsc.ubc.ca

Arts
www.arts.ubc.ca
Dr Gage Averill, Dean, 604-822-3751
mtw@mail.arts.ubc.ca

Dentistry
www.dentistry.ubc.ca
Dr Charles Shuler, Dean, 604-822-0738, fax: 604-822-4532
foddo@interchange.ubc.ca

Education
www.educ.ubc.ca
Dr Jon shapiro, Interim Dean, 604-822-5214, fax: 604-822-6501
jon.shapiro@ubc.ca

Forestry
www.forestry.ubc.ca
Dr John Innes, Dean, 604-822-3542
john.innes@ubc.ca

Graduate Studies
www.grad.ubc.ca
Barbara Evans, Dean, 604-827-5547
barbara.evans@ubc.ca

Land & Food Systems
www.landfood.ubc.ca
Murray B. Isman, Dean, 604-822-1219, fax: 604-822-6394
dean.landfood@ubc.ca

Law
www.law.ubc.ca
Mary Ann Bobinski, Dean, 604-822-6335
deansoffice@law.ubc.ca

Medicine
www.med.ubc.ca
Dr Gavin Stuart, Dean, 604-822-2421, fax: 604-822-6061
fomdo_reception@medd.med.ubc.ca

Pharmaceutical Sciences
www.pharmacy.ubc.ca
Robert Sindelar, Dean, 604-822-2343, fax: 604-822-3035
sindelar@interchange. ubc.ca

Sciences
www.science.ubc.ca
Dr Simon Peacock, Dean, 604-822-3336, fax: 604-822-5558
scidean@science.ubc.ca

Schools
Architecture & Landscape Architecture
Tel: 604-822-2779; *Fax:* 604-822-3808
arch1@interchange.ubc.ca; larc@interchange.ubc.ca
www.sala.ubc.ca
Leslie Van Duzer, Director
vanduzer@interchange.ubc.ca

Audiology & Speech Sciences
Tel: 604-822-5591; *Fax:* 604-822-6569
inquiry@audiospeech.ubc.ca
www.audiospeech.ubc.ca
Valter Ciocca, Director
director@audiospeech.ubc.ca

Community & Regional Planning
Tel: 604-822-3276; *Fax:* 604-822-3787
www.scarp.ubc.ca
Dr Penny Gurstein, Director
gurstein@interchange.ubc.ca

Continuing Studies
Tel: 604-822-1444; *Fax:* 604-822-1599
www.cstudies.ubc.ca
Dr Judith Plessis, Executive Director

Human Kinetics
Tel: 604-822-3838; *Fax:* 604-822-6842
www.hkin.educ.ubc.ca
Dr Robert E.C. Sparks, Director
robert.sparks@ubc.ca

Library, Archival & Information Studies
Tel: 604-822-2404; *Fax:* 604-822-6006
slais@interchange.ubc.ca
www.slais.ubc.ca
Terry Eastwood, Interim Director
eastwood@interchange.ubc.ca

Music
Tel: 604-822-3113; *Fax:* 604-822-4884
www.music.ubc.ca
Dr Richard Kurth, Director
richard.kurth@ubc.ca

Nursing
Tel: 604-822-7417; *Fax:* 604-822-7466
www.nursing.ubc.ca
Dr Sally Thorne, Director
sally.thorne@nursing.ubc.ca

Population & public Health
Tel: 604-822-2772; *Fax:* 604-822-4994
www.spph.ubc.ca
Dr Martin Schechter, Director
martin.schechter@ubc.ca

Journalism
Tel: 604-822-6688; *Fax:* 604-822-6707
journal@interchange.ubc.ca
www.journalism.ubc.ca
Dr Mary Lynn Young, Director

Social Work
Tel: 604-822-2255; *Fax:* 604-822-8656
www.socialwork.ubc.ca
Dr Kwong-leung Tang, Director
kltang@interchange.ubc.ca

Sauder School of Business
Tel: 604-822-8868; *Fax:* 604-822-8468
www.sauder.ubc.ca
Dr Daniel Muzyka, Dean
daniel.muzyka@sauder.ubc.ca

Environmental Health
Tel: 604-822-9595; *Fax:* 604-822-9588
soeh@interchange.ubc.ca
www.soeh.ubc.ca
Christie Hurrell, Exeuctive Director
hurrell@interchange.ubc.ca

College of Health Disciplines
Tel: 604-822-5571; *Fax:* 604-822-2495
chd@interchange.ubc.ca
www.health-disciplines.ubc.ca
Louise Nasmith, Principal
louise.nasmith@ubc.ca

College of Interdisciplinary Studies
www.cfis.ubc.ca
Michael Burgess, Principal, 604-827-5262
cfis.principal@ubc.ca

Campuses
UBC Okanagan Campus
3333 University Way, Kelowna, BC V1V 1V7, Canada
Tel: 250-807-8000; *Toll-Free:* 866-596-0767
askme@ubc
www.ubc.ca/okanagan

UBC Robson Square Campus
800 Robson St., Vancouver, BC V6Z 3B7
Tel: 604-822-3333; *Fax:* 604-822-0070
robson.info@ubc.ca
www.robsonsquare.ubc.ca

Great Northern Way Campus
577 Great Northern Way, Vancouver, BC V5T 1E1
Tel: 778-370-1001; *Fax:* 778-370-1045
admin@gnwc.ca
www.gnwc.ca

Affiliations
Regent College
5800 University Blvd., Vancouver, BC V6T 2E4, Canada
Tel: 604-224-3245; *Fax:* 604-224-3097
Toll-Free: 1-800-663-8664
admissions@regent-college.edu; registrar@regent-college.edu
www.regent-college.edu
Other Information: Regent Bookstore, Toll Free: 1-800-334-3279
Dr Rod J.K. Wilson, President
presidentsoffice@regent-college.edu

St. Mark's College
5935 Iona Dr., Vancouver, BC V6T 1J7, Canada
Tel: 604-822-4463; *Fax:* 604-822-4659
stmarks@stmarkscollege.ca
www.stmarkscollege.ca
Dr. J. Stapleton, Interim Principal
Dr. Marjorie Budnikas, Registrar
registrar@stmarkscollege.ca

Carey Theological College
5920 Iona Dr., Vancouver, BC V6T 1J6
Tel: 604-224-4308; *Fax:* 604-224-5014
info@careytheologicalcollege.ca
www.careycentre.com

Vancouver School of Theology
6000 Iona Dr., Vancouver, BC V6T 1L4
Tel: 604-822-0824; *Fax:* 604-822-9212
possibilities@vst.edu
www.vst.edu

Publications
Perspectives
perspectives.ubc.ca
Note: An English-Chinese bilingual student paper
KaGeen Cheung, Editor-In-Chief
editor@perspectives.ubc.ca

Discorder Magazine
discorder.ca/discorder-magazine
Jordie Yow, Editor-In-Chief
editor.discorder@gmail.com

The Graduate Magazine
Note: Published by the Graduate Student Society

The Point
thepoint@rec.ubc.ca
www.thepoint.ubc.ca
Note: Focusing on recreational activities, health and lifestyle news

The Thunderbird
thethunderbird.ca
Note: A student publication of the Graduate School of Journalism

The Ubyssey
ubyssey.ca
Justin McElroy, Coordinating Editor
coordinating@ubyssey.ca

Trek Magazine
www.alumni.ubc.ca/trekmagazine/index.php
Note: Published by UBC Alumni Affairs

Chris Petty, Editor
chris.petty@ubc.ca

Victoria: Royal Roads University
2005 Sooke Rd., Victoria, BC V9B 5Y2, Canada
Tel: 250-391-2511; *Fax:* 250-391-2500
Toll-Free: 1-800-788-8028
info@royalroads.ca .ca
www.royalroads.ca
www.facebook.com/royalroadsu
twitter.com/royalroads

Full Time Equivalency: 4130 *Note:* Royal Roads University offers: Doctoral degrees in Social Sciences; Masters degrees in Arts, Business Admin., Science; Bachelor degrees in Arts, Commerce, Science; Graduate Certificates; Graduate Diplomas.
Peter Robinson, Chair & Chancellor
Dr Allan Cahoon, President & Vice-Chancellor, 250-391-2517
allan.cahoon@royalroads.ca
Thomas Chase, Vice-Pres., Academic & Provost, 250-391-2545
thomas.chase@royalroads.ca
Dan Tulip, Vice-Pres. & CFO, 250-391-2521
dan.tulip@royalroads.ca
Cyndi McLeod, Vice-Pres., Marketing, Recruitment & Business Development, 250-391-2516
cyndi.mcleod@royalroads.ca
Steve Grundy, Registrar, CIO & Assoc. Vice-Pres., Program Development, 250-391-2606
steve.grundy@royalroads.ca

Victoria: University of Victoria
P.O. Box 1700 CSC
Victoria, BC V8W 2Y2, Canada
Tel: 250-721-7211; *Fax:* 250-721-7212
www.uvic.ca

Full Time Equivalency: 16961
Murray Farmer, B.A., Chancellor
David H. Turpin, B.Sc., Ph.D., President
James L. Cassels, B.A., LL.B., LL.M., Vice-President
Gayle Gorrill, B.B.A., C.A., C.B.V., Vice-President
Julia Eastman, B.A., M.A., Ph.D., University Secretary
Vacant, Administrative Registrar
Bruce Kilpatrick, B.A., Director
J. Howard Brunt, B.A., A.D.N., M.Sc.N., Ph, Vice-President
Valerie Kuehne, B.Sc.N., M.Ed., M.A., Ph., Vice-President

Faculties

Business
Ali Dastmalchian, B.Sc., M.Sc., Ph.D., Dean

Continuing Studies
Maureen MacDonald, B.A., LL.B., M.B.A., D.Ph, Dean

Education
Ted Riecken, B.A., M.Ed., Ph.D., Dean

Engineering
Thomas Tiedje, B.Sc., M.Sc., Ph.D., Dean

Fine Arts
Sarah Blackstone, B.A., M.A., Ph.D., Dean

Graduate Studies
Aaron H. Devor, B.A., M.A., Ph.D., Dean

Human & Social Development
Mary Ellen Purkis, B.S.N., M.Sc., Ph.D., Dean

Humanities
Andrew Rippin, B.A., M.A., Ph.D., Dean

Law
Donna Greschner, B.Comm., LL.B., Dean

Science
Tom Pedersen, B.Sc., Ph.D., Dean

Social Sciences
Peter Keller, B.A., M.A., Ph.D., Dean

Publications

The Martlet
Note: Independent weekly student newspaper at the University of Victoria

The Ring
Note: The University of Victoria's monthly newspaper

Standard
Note: The University of Victoria's monthly newspaper

The UVic Torch
P.O. Box 3060
3775 Haro Rd, Victoria, BC V8W 3R4, Canada
Fax: 250-721-8955

Note: Alumni magazine

Colleges

Castlegar: Selkirk College
Castlegar Campus
301 Frank Beinder Way, Castlegar, BC V1N 4L3, Canada
Tel: 250-365-7292; *Fax:* 250-365-6568
Toll-Free: 1-888-953-1133
www.selkirk.ca
www.facebook.com/SelkirkCollege
twitter.com/FrankenSmarter
www.youtube.com/selkirkcollege

Note: The regional community college consists of the following schools: Kootenay School of the Arts; School of Adult Basic Education & Transitional Training; School of Business & Aviation; School of Digital Media & Music; School of Health & Human Services; School of Hospitality & Tourism; School of Industry & Trades Training; School of Renewable Resources; School of University Arts & Sciences; & Selkirk International.
Christian Schadendorf, Chair
Angus Graeme, President

Campuses

Grand Forks Campus
P.O. Box 968
486 - 72nd Ave., Grand Forks, BC V0H 1H0, Canada
Tel: 250-442-2704; *Fax:* 250-442-2877

Kaslo Centre
P.O. Box 1149
421 Front St., Kaslo, BC V0G 1M0, Canada
Tel: 250-353-2618; *Fax:* 250-353-7121

Kootenay School of the Arts (KSA) Campus
606 Victoria St., Nelson, BC V1L 4K9
Tel: 250-352-2821; *Fax:* 250-352-1625
Toll-Free: 1-877-552-2821

Nakusp Centre
P.O. Box 720
311 Broadway, Nakusp, BC V0H 1R0, Canada
Tel: 250-265-4077; *Fax:* 250-265-3195
Other Information: Adult Basic Education: 250-265-3640

Silver King Campus
2001 Silver King Rd., Nelson, BC V1L 1C8, Canada
Tel: 250-352-6601; *Fax:* 250-352-3180
Toll-Free: 1-866-301-6601

Tenth Street Campus
820 Tenth St., Nelson, BC V1L 3C7, Canada
Tel: 250-352-6601; *Fax:* 250-352-5716
Toll-Free: 1-866-301-6601

Trail Campus
900 Helena St., Trail, BC V1R 4S6, Canada
Tel: 250-368-5236; *Fax:* 250-368-4983

Cranbrook: College of the Rockies
P.O. Box 8500
2700 College Way, Cranbrook, BC V1C 5L7, Canada
Tel: 250-489-2751; *Fax:* 250-489-1790
Toll-Free: 1-877-489-2687
ask@cotr.bc.ca
www.cotr.bc.ca
www.facebook.com/COTR1
twitter.com/cotr_updates
www.linkedin.com/company/561622
www.youtube.com/cotr1

Full Time Equivalency: 2100
Dr. Nicholas Rubidge, President

Campuses

Creston Campus
P.O. Box 1978
301-16th Ave., Creston, BC V0B 1G0, Canada
Tel: 250-428-5332; *Fax:* 250-428-4314
Toll-Free: 1-877-489-2687
creston@cotr.bc.ca
www.cotr.bc.ca/creston/

Kathy Tompkins, Manager
ktompkins@cotr.bc.ca

Invermere Campus
#2, 1535 - 14th St., RR#4, Invermere, BC V0A 1K4, Canada
Tel: 250-342-3210; *Fax:* 250-342-9221
Toll-Free: 1-877-489-2687
invermere@cotr.bc.ca
www.cotr.bc.ca/invermere/
www.facebook.com/168647829825291
twitter.com/COTRinvermere

Fernie Campus
P.O. Box 1770
342-3rd Ave., Fernie, BC V0B 1M0, Canada
Tel: 250-423-4691; *Fax:* 250-423-3932
Toll-Free: 1-866-423-4691
fernie@cotr.bc.ca
www.cotr.bc.ca/fernie/

Golden Campus
P.O. Box 376
1305 South 9th St., Golden, BC V0A 1H0, Canada
Tel: 250-344-5901; *Fax:* 250-344-5745
Toll-Free: 1-877-489-2687
golden@cotr.bc.ca
www.cotr.bc.ca/golden/
www.facebook.com/cotrgolden
twitter.com/COTR_Golden

Kimberley Campus
1850 Warren Ave., Kimberley, BC V1A 1S1, Canada
Tel: 250-427-7116; *Fax:* 250-427-3034
Toll-Free: 1-877-489-2687
kimberley@cotr.bc.ca
www.cotr.bc.ca/kimberley
www.facebook.com/COTRConEd

Dawson Creek: Northern Lights College
Regional Administration
11401 - 8th St., Dawson Creek, BC V1G 4G2, Canada
Tel: 250-782-5251; *Fax:* 250-782-5233
Toll-Free: 1-866-463-6652
appinfo@nlc.bc.ca; webmaster@nlc.bc.ca
www.nlc.bc.ca
www.facebook.com/NLCollege?sk=wall
twitter.com/NLCinthenews

Kate O'Neil, Board Chair
D. Jean Valgardson, CEO
jvalgardson@nlc.bc.ca

Campuses

Atlin Campus
Also known as: Atlin Learning Centre
P.O. Box 29
Atlin, BC V0W 1A0
Tel: 250-651-7762; *Fax:* 250-651-7730
Toll-Free: 1-866-463-6652

Note: The campus offers continuing education in academic & pre-professional studies, development & upgrading, distance education, & industrial & workforce training.
Richard Macdonald, Chair
Roger Grose, Systems Principal
Bob White, Principal, Secondary Campus
Henry Au, Vice Principal, Secondary Campus
Aza Nakagawa, Business Manager
Blondie Enns, Secretary, High School

Chetwynd Campus
P.O. Box 1180
5132 - 50th St., Chetwynd, BC V0C 1J0, Canada
Tel: 250-788-2248; *Fax:* 250-788-9706
Toll-Free: 1-866-463-6652

Note: Programs offered include applied business technology, teacher assistant training, social services worker training, forestry, hospitality & tourism operations, continuing education, adult basic education, university transfer, & adult special education.
Donna Merry, Campus Administrator
dmerry@nlc.bc.ca

Dawson Creek Campus
11401 - 8 St., Dawson Creek, BC V1G 4G2, Canada
Tel: 250-782-5251; *Fax:* 250-784-7563
Toll-Free: 1-866-463-6652

Note: The campus features technical, academic, trades, & vocational programs.
Lorelee Friesen, Dean of Students

Dease Lake Campus
P.O. Box 220
Commercial Dr., Lot 10, Dease Lake, BC V0C 1L0
Tel: 250-771-5500; *Fax:* 250-771-5510
Toll-Free: 1-866-463-6652

Note: The campus serves full-time & part-time vocational and continuing education students in Atlin, Telegraph Creek, Lower Post, Iskut, & Good Hope Lake.
Tiffany Scobie, Head of School, 905-565-8707, ext. 10
tscobie@rotherglen.com
Laura Rossi, Office Manager, 905-565-8707, ext. 10
lrossi@rotherglen.com

Fort Nelson Campus
P.O. Box 860
5201 Simpson Trail, Fort Nelson, BC V0C 1R0, Canada
Tel: 250-774-2741; *Fax:* 250-774-2750
Toll-Free: 1-866-463-6652

Note: Continuing education programs are provided.
Laurie Dolan, Campus Administrator
ldolan@nlc.bc.ca

Fort St. John Campus
P.O. Box 1000
9820 - 120 St., Fort St John, BC V1J 6K1, Canada
Tel: 250-785-6981; *Fax:* 250-785-1294
Toll-Free: 1-866-463-6652
Note: Academic, apprenticeship, career/technical, vocational, & international students students are served by the Fort St. John campus.
Kathy Handley, Campus Administrator
khandley@nlc.bc.ca

Tumbler Ridge Campus
P.O. Box 180
180 Southgate, Tumbler Ridge, BC V0C 2W0
Tel: 250-242-5591; *Fax:* 250-242-3109
Toll-Free: 1-866-463-6652
Note: Adult basic education is offered in Tumbler Ridge.
Donna Merry, Administrator
dmerry@nlc.bc.ca

Kelowna: Okanagan University College
North Kelowna Campus
1000 KLO Rd., Kelowna, BC V1V 1V7, Canada
Tel: 250-762-5445; *Fax:* 250-470-6004
www.okanagan.bc.ca
Jim Hamilton, President, 250-862-5403
jhamilton@okanagan.bc.ca

Salmon Arms Campus
2552 Trans Canada Hwy. NE, Salmon Arm, BC V1E 4N3, Canada
Tel: 250-832-2126; *Toll-Free:* 888-831-0341

Vernon Campus
7000 College Way, Vernon, BC V1B 2N5, Canada
Tel: 250-545-7291; *Toll-Free:* 800-289-8993

Penticton Campus
583 Duncan Ave. West, Penticton, BC V2A 8E1, Canada
Tel: 250-492-4305; *Toll-Free:* 866-510-8899

Publications
The Phoenix

Langley: Trinity Western Seminary
7600 Glover Rd., Langley, BC V2Y 1Y1, Canada
Tel: 604-513-2019; *Fax:* 604-513-2045
www.acts.twu.ca

Publications
Mars' Hill
Note: Official student newspaper of Trinity Western University

Nanaimo: Vancouver Island University
Nanaimo Campus
900 - 5th St., Nanaimo, BC V9R 5S5, Canada
Tel: 250-753-3245; *Toll-Free:* 888-920-2221
info@viu.ca
www.viu.ca
www.facebook.com/LoveWhereYouLearn
twitter.com/VIUniversity
www.linkedin.com/companies/vancouver-island-university
www.youtube.com/user/viuchannel
Full Time Equivalency: 19124
Dr. Ralph Nilson, President, 250-740-6102
ralph.nilson@viu.ca

Cowichan Campus
2011 University Way, Duncan, BC V9L 0C7, Canada
Tel: 250-746-3500
www.cc.viu.ca

Campuses
Parksville-Qualicum Campus
100 Jensen Ave. East, Parksville, BC V9P 2G3, Canada
Tel: 250-248-2096; *Fax:* 250-248-9792
pqcampus@viu.ca
www.viu.ca/parksville

Powell River Campus
100 - 7085 Nootka St., Powell River, BC V8A 3C6, Canada
Tel: 604-485-2878; *Fax:* 604-485-2868
Toll-Free: 877-888-8890
pr.viu.ca

Prince George: College of New Caledonia
3330 - 22 Ave., Prince George, BC V2N 1P8, Canada
Tel: 250-562-2131; *Fax:* 250-561-5861
Toll-Free: 1-800-371-811
askcnc@cnc.bc.ca
www.cnc.bc.ca/
www.facebook.com/CollegeOfNewCaledonia
twitter.com/CNC_BC_CA
Full Time Equivalency: 5000
John Bowman, President
bowmanj@cnc.bc.ca

Lakes District Campus
P.O. Box 5000
Burns Lake, BC V0J 1E0, Canada
Tel: 250-692-1715; *Fax:* 250-692-1750
Toll-Free: 1-866-692-1943
lksdist@cnc.bc.ca
Joan Ragsdale, Regional Director

Campuses
Mackenzie Campus
P.O. Box 2110
Mackenzie, BC V0J 2C0, Canada
Tel: 250-997-7201; *Fax:* 250-997-3779
Toll-Free: 1-877-997-4333
cncmackenzie@cnc.bc.ca
Tanya Helton, Interim Regional Director

Nechako Campus
3231 Hospital Rd., Vanderhoof, BC V0J 3A2, Canada
Tel: 250-567-3200; *Fax:* 250-567-3217
nechako@cnc.bc.ca
Maureen Mallais, Regional Director

Fort St. James Campus
179 Douglas, Fort St. James, BC V0J 1P0, Canada
Tel: 250-996-7019; *Fax:* 250-996-7014
cncfsj@cnc.bc.ca
Maureen Mallais, Regional Director

Quesnel Campus
100 Campus Way, Quesnel, BC V2J 7K1, Canada
Tel: 250-991-7500; *Fax:* 250-991-7502
Toll-Free: 1-866-680-7550
quesnel@cnc.bc.ca
Doug Larsen, Regional Director

Fraser Lake Learning Centre
298 McMillan Ave., Fraser Lake, BC V0J 1S0, Canada
Tel: 250-699-6249; *Fax:* 250-699-6247
cncfl@cnc.bc.ca

John A. Brink Trades & Technology Centre
1727 W. Central, Prince George, BC V2N 1P8, Canada
Tel: 250-561-5804;

Nicholson Campus
2211 Nicholson Ave. South, Prince George, BC V2N 1P8, Canada
Tel: 250-562-2131

Valemount Learning Centre
P.O. Box 789
Valemount, BC V0E 2Z0, Canada
Tel: 250-566-4601; *Fax:* 250-566-4602
valemount@cnc.bc.ca

Surrey: Kwantlen Polytechnic University
12666 - 72nd Ave., Surrey, BC V3W 2M8, Canada
Tel: 604-599-2100; *Fax:* 604-599-2068
facilities@kwantlen.ca
www.kwantlen.ca
www.facebook.com/kwantlenU
twitter.com/kwantlenu
Full Time Equivalency: 11590
Alan R. Davis, President & Vice Chancellor, 604-599-2078

Terrace: Northwest Community College
College Services
5331 McConnell Ave., Terrace, BC V8G 4X2, Canada
Tel: 250-635-6511; *Fax:* 250-635-5432
Toll-Free: 1-877-277-2288
www.nwcc.bc.ca
Stephanie Forsyth, President

Campuses
Hazelton Campus
P.O. Box 338
4815 Swannell Dr., Hazelton, BC V0J 1Y0, Canada
Tel: 250-842-5291; *Fax:* 250-842-5813
www.nwcc.bc.ca

Houston Campus
P.O. Box 1277
3221 - 14 St. West, Houston, BC V0J 1Z0, Canada
Tel: 250-845-7266; *Fax:* 250-845-5629
www.nwcc.bc.ca

Kitimat Campus
606 Mountainview Sq., Kitimat, BC V8C 2N2, Canada
Tel: 250-632-4766; *Fax:* 250-632-5069
www.nwcc.bc.ca

Prince Rupert Campus
353 - 5th St., Prince Rupert, BC V8J 3L6, Canada
Tel: 250-624-6054; *Fax:* 250-624-3923
www.nwcc.bc.ca

Queen Charlotte City Campus
P.O. Box 67
138 Bay St., Queen Charlotte Village, BC V0T 1S0, Canada
Tel: 250-559-8222; *Fax:* 250-559-8219
www.nwcc.bc.ca

Smithers Campus
P.O. Box 3606
3966 - 2nd Ave., Smithers, BC V0J 2N0, Canada
Tel: 250-847-4461; *Fax:* 250-847-4568
www.nwcc.bc.ca

Stewart Campus
P.O. Box 919
Stewart, BC V0T 1W0, Canada
Tel: 250-636-9184; *Fax:* 250-636-2770
www.nwcc.bc.ca

Terrace Campus
5331 McConnell Ave., Terrace, BC V8G 4X2, Canada
Tel: 250-635-6511; *Fax:* 250-638-5432

Masset Campus
P.O. Box 559
1730 Hodges, Masset, BC V0T 1M0, Canada
Tel: 250-626-3670; *Fax:* 250-626-3680
www.nwcc.bc.ca

Vancouver Island: North Island College
Toll-Free: 800-715-0914
questions@nic.bc.ca
www.northislandcollege.ca
www.facebook.com/pages/North-Island-College/327464742944
Full Time Equivalency: 8253
Dr. Lou Dryden, President
Susan Toresdahl, Director

Campuses
Campbell River Campus
1685 South Dogwood St., Campbell River, BC V9W 8C1, Canada
Tel: 250-923-9700; *Fax:* 250-923-9703

Comox Valley Campus
2300 Ryan Rd., Courtenay, BC V9N 8N6, Canada
Tel: 250-334-5000; *Fax:* 250-334-5018

Port Alberni Campus
3699 Roger St., Port Alberni, BC V9Y 8E3, Canada
Tel: 250-724-8711; *Fax:* 250-724-8700

Mount Waddington Regional Campus
P.O. Box 901
9300 Trustee Rd., Port Hardy, BC V0N 2P0, Canada
Tel: 250-949-7912; *Fax:* 250-949-2617

Vigar Vocational Centre
2780 Vigar Rd., Campbell River, BC V9W 6A3, Canada
Tel: 250-923-9794; *Fax:* 250-830-0816

Tebo Vocational Centre
4781 Tebo Ave., Port Alberni, BC V9Y 6X7, Canada
Tel: 250-724-8738; *Fax:* 250-723-4573

Ucluelet Centre
P.O. Box 198
#10, 1636 Penninsula Rd., Ucluelet, BC V0R 3A0, Canada
Tel: 250-726-2697; *Fax:* 250-726-2698

Victoria: Camosun College
Lansdowne Campus
3100 Foul Bay Rd., Victoria, BC V8P 5J2, Canada
Tel: 250-370-3000; *Fax:* 250-370-3551
Toll-Free: 877-554-7555
info@camosun.bc.ca
www.camosun.bc.ca/
www.facebook.com/CamosunCollege
twitter.com/camosun
youtube.com/user/mycamosun
Full Time Equivalency: 20000 *Number of Employees:* 1000
Kathryn Laurin, President

Interurban Campus
4461 Interurban Rd., Victoria, BC V9E 2C1, Canada

Victoria: Lester B. Pearson College of the Pacific
Also known as: Pearson UWC
650 Pearson College Dr., Victoria, BC V9C 4H7, Canada
Tel: 250-391-2411; *Fax:* 250-391-2412
admin@pearsoncollege.ca
www.pearsoncollege.ca
www.facebook.com/PearsonUWC
twitter.com/PCUWC
www.linkedin.com/groups?gid=49277&home=
www.youtube.com/user/PearsonUWC
Full Time Equivalency: 200
David B. Hawley, College Director

Post Secondary/Technical

Universities

Abbotsford: University of the Fraser Valley
33844 King Rd., Abbotsford, BC V2S 7M8, Canada
Tel: 604-504-7441; *Fax:* 604-855-7614
Toll-Free: 888-504-7441
info@ufv.ca
www.ucfv.ca
Enrollment: 10000
Dr Brian Minter, Chancellor
Dr Mark Evered, President & Vice-Chancellor, 604-864-4608, fax: 604-853-7341
jill.smith@ufv.ca
Dr Brian Minter, Chancellor
Dr Eric Davis, Provost & Vice-Pres., Academic, 604-864-4642
eric.davis@ufv.ca
Eleanor Busse-Klassen, Exec. Ass't to Vice-Pres., Administration
eleanor.busse@ufv.ca
Bill Cooke, Registrar, ext. 2820
bill.cooke@ufv.ca

Faculties
Arts
Dr Jacqueline Nolte
jacqueline.nolte@ufv.ca
Science
Ora Stein, Interim Dean
ora.steyn@ufv.ca
Professional Studies
Dr Rosetta Khalideen, Dean
rosetta.khalideen@ufv.ca
Trades & Technology
Harv McCullough, Dean
harv.mccullough@ufv.ca
Access & Continuing Studies
Dr Karen Evans
karen.evans@ufv.ca

Schools
Graduate Studies
Yvon Dandurand, Assoc. Vice-President
yvon.dandurand@ufv.ca

Campuses
Chilliwack Campus
45635 Yale Rd., Chilliwack, BC V2P 6T4, Canada
Tel: 604-792-0025; *Fax:* 604-792-2388
Chilliwack, Trades & Tech Centre
Canada Education Park
5579 Tyson Rd., Chilliwack, BC V2R 0H9, Canada
Fax: 604-824-7931
Toll-Free: 888-504-7441
UFV Aerospace Centre
Abbotsford Airport
30645 Firecat Ave., Abbotsford, BC V2T 6H5, Canada
Fax: 604-852-7399
Toll-Free: 888-504-7441
aerospace@ufv.ca
Hope Centre
1250 7th Ave., Hope, BC V0X 1L4, Canada
Tel: 604-869-9991; *Fax:* 604-869-7431
Mission Campus
Heritage Park Centre
33700 Prentis Ave., Mission, BC V2V 7B1, Canada
Tel: 604-557-7603; *Fax:* 604-826-0681
Abbotsford, Marshall Rd. Annex
34194 Marshall Rd., Abbotsford, BC V2S 5E4
Tel: 604-851-6324
UFV India Office
SD College Chandigarh
Sector 32C, Chandigarth, UT, India
ufv.india@ufv.ca
www.ufv.ca/chandigarh
Other Information: (0)172 500 1048

Publications
The Cascade
ufvcascade.ca

Nanaimo: Vancouver Island University
900 Fifth St., Nanaimo, BC V9R 5S5, Canada
Tel: 250-753-3245; *Fax:* 250-740-6473
Toll-Free: 888-920-2221
info@viu.ca
www.viu.ca
Enrollment: 18000 *Note:* VIU offers a variety of certificate, diploma, and degree programs.
Chief Shawn A. Atleo, Chancellor
Dr Ralph Nilson, President & Vice-chancellor, 250-740-6101, fax: 250-740-6555
president@viu.ca
Pat Eager, Vice-Pres., Admin. & Finance
ralph.nilson@viu.ca
David Witty, Vice-Pres., Academic & Provost
david.witty@viu.ca
Fred Jacklin, Registrar, 250-753-3245, ext. 2283
david.witty@viu.ca

Campuses
Cowichan Campus
222 Cowichan Way, Duncan, BC V9L 6P4, Canada
Tel: 250-746-3500; *Fax:* 250-746-3529
Parksville-Qualicum Centre
100 Jensen Ave. East, Parksville, BC V9P 2G3, Canada
Tel: 250-248-2096; *Fax:* 250-248-9792
pqcampus@viu.ca
Powell River Campus
3960 Selkirk Ave., Powell River, BC V8A 3C6, Canada
Tel: 604-485-2878; *Fax:* 604-485-2868
Toll-Free: 877-888-8890

Publications
Navigator
editor@thenav.ca
thenav.mala.bc.ca

Surrey: Kwantlen Polytechnic University
12666 - 72 Ave., Surrey, BC V3W 2M8, Canada
Tel: 604-599-2100; *Fax:* 604-599-2068
switchboard@kwantlen.ca
www.kwantlen.bc.ca
Enrollment: 17000
Arvinder Singh Bubber, Chancellor
David W. Atkinson, President & Vice-Chancellor, 604-599-2078, fax: 604-599-2235
sandy.kuzyk@kwantlen.ca
Judith McGillivray, Provost & Vice-Pres., Academic, 604-599-2363
judith.mcgillivray@kwantlen.ca
Robert Hensley, Registrar, 604-599-2018
robert.hensley@kwantlen.ca

Faculties
Humanities
Dr Mazen Guirguis, Dean, 604-599-2672
humanities.dean@kwantlen.ca
Social Sciences
Dr Robert Adamoski, Dean, 604-599-3068, fax: 604-599-2966
robert.adamoski@kwantlen.ca
Design
Barbara Duggan, Dean, 604-599-2525
barbara.duggan@kwantlen.ca
Community & Health Studies
Jean Nicolson-Church, Interim Dean, 604-599-2266
jean.nicolson-church@kwantlen.ca
Academic & Career Advancement
Dr Arthur Coren, Interim Dean, 604-599-3252
arthur.coren@kwantlen.ca
Trades & Technology
Wayne Tebb, Dean, 604-599-6101
wayne.tebb@kwantlen.ca
Science, Mathematics & Applied Sciences
Dr Brian G. Carr, Dean, 604-599-2244, fax: 604-599-2435
brian.carr@kwantlen.ca
Business
Dr Arthur Coren, Dean, 604-599-3252
arthur.coren@kwantlen.ca

Schools
Horticulture
David Davidson, Assoc. Dean, 604-599-3254
horticulture@kwantlen.ca

Campuses
Surrey Campus
12666 - 72 Ave., Surrey, BC V3T 5H8, Canada
Fax: 604-599-2068
Richmond Campus
8771 Lansdowne Rd., Richmond, BC V6X 3V8, Canada
Fax: 604-599-2578
Cloverdale Campus
5500 - 180 St., Surrey, BC V3S 4K5, Canada
Langley Campus
20901 Langley Bypass, Langley, BC V3A 8G9, Canada
Fax: 604-599-3242

Publications
Kwantlen Chronicle
www.kwantlenchronicle.ca

Colleges

Kelowna: Okanagan College
1000 KLO Rd., Kelowna, BC V1Y 4X8, Canada
Tel: 250-762-5445; *Toll-Free:* 877-755-2266
www.okanagan.bc.ca
Enrollment: 4850
Jim Hamilton, President

Campuses
Penticton Campus
583 Duncan Ave. West, Penticton, BC V2A 8E1, Canada
Fax: 250-492-4305
Toll-Free: 866-510-8899
Donna Lomas, Regional Dean
Salmon Arm Campus
P.O. Box 189
Salmon Arm, BC V1E 4N3, Canada
Tel: 250-832-2126; *Fax:* 250-804-8850
Toll-Free: 888-831-0341
Lynda Wilson, Regional Dean
Kalamalka Campus
7000 College Way, Vernon, BC V1B 2N5, Canada
Fax: 250-545-3277
Tony Sellars, Regional Dean
South Kelowna Campus
1000 KLO Rd., Kelowna, BC V1Y 4X8, Canada
Heather Schneider, Regional Dean

New Westminster: Douglas College
P.O. Box 2503
700 Royal Ave., New Westminster, BC V3M 2Z4, Canada
Tel: 604-527-5400; *Fax:* 604-527-5095
ce-tg_registration@douglascollege.ca
www.douglas.bc.ca
www.facebook.com/douglascollege
twitter.com/douglascollege/
www.youtube.com/user/DouglasCollegeVideo
Enrollment: 7000
Susan R. Witter, President
David Lam Campus
1250 Pinetree Way, Coquitlam, BC V3B 7X3, Canada

Publications
Other Press

North Vancouver: Capilano University
Also known as: Capilano College
2055 Purcell Way, North Vancouver, BC V7J 3H5, Canada
Tel: 604-986-1911; *Fax:* 604-984-4985
www.capcollege.bc.ca
TTY: 604-990-7848
Enrollment: 5537
Dr. Kris Bulcroft, President, Vice-Chancellor

Publications
Capilano Courier

Prince George: College of New Caledonia
3330 - 22nd Ave., Prince George, BC V2N 1P8, Canada
Tel: 250-562-2131; *Fax:* 250-561-5816
Toll-Free: 1-800-371-811
askcnc@cnc.bc.ca
www.cnc.bc.ca
Enrollment: 5250

John Bowman, President, 250-561-5825
Bruce Sutherland, Chair

Campuses
Lakes District Campus
Also known as: Burns Lake
P.O. Box 5000
545 Hwy. 16 West, Burns Lake, BC V0J 1E0, Canada
Tel: 250-692-1700; *Fax:* 250-692-1750
Toll-Free: 866-692-1943
lksdist@cnc.bc.ca
Joan Ragsdale, Director, 250-692-1715
ragsdale@cnc.bc.ca

Mackenzie Campus
P.O. Box 2110
540 Mackenzie Blvd., Mackenzie, BC V0J 2C0, Canada
Tel: 250-997-7200; *Fax:* 250-997-3779
cncmackenzie@cnc.bc.ca
Carole L'Herault, Director, 250-997-7203
lherault@cnc.bc.ca

Quesnel Campus
100 Campus Way, Quesnel, BC V2J 7K1, Canada
Tel: 250-991-7500; *Fax:* 250-991-7502
Toll-Free: 866-680-7523
quesnel@cnc.bc.ca
Lynda Williams, Associate Director, 250-991-7622
williamsl2@cnc.bc.ca

Nechako Campus
3231 Hospital Rd., Vanderhoof, BC V0J 3A2, Canada
Tel: 250-567-3200; *Fax:* 250-567-3217
nechako@cnc.bc.ca
Maureen Mallais, Director, 250-567-3200
mallais@cnc.bc.ca

Fort St. James Campus
P.O. Box 1557
179 Douglas St., Fort St. James, BC V0J 1P0
Tel: 250-996-7019; *Fax:* 250-996-7014
cncfsj@cnc.bc.ca
Ann McCormick, Campus Supervisor
mccormicka@cnc.bc.ca

Valemount Campus
P.O. Box 789
99 Gorse St., Valemount, BC V0E 2Z0, Canada
Tel: 250-566-4601; *Fax:* 250-566-4602
Toll-Free: 888-690-4422
valemount@cnc.bc.ca
Sandra Craig, Program Clerk
craigs@cnc.bc.ca

Fraser Lake Campus
298 McMillan Ave., Fraser Lake, BC V0J 1S0
Tel: 250-699-6249; *Fax:* 250-699-6247
cncfl@cnc.bc.ca
Wendy Galvin, Program Assistant
galvinw@cnc.bc.ca

Publications
The Confluence

cncsn@cnc.bc.ca

Vancouver: Langara College
100 West 49th Ave., Vancouver, BC V5Y 2Z6, Canada
Tel: 604-323-5511; *Fax:* 604-323-5555
geninfo@langara.bc.ca
www.langara.bc.ca
Enrollment: 12218
Korena Jang, Manager, Executive & Board Operations

Publications
Gleaner

The Voice

Vancouver: Vancouver Community College
1155 East Broadway, Vancouver, BC V5T 4V5, Canada
Tel: 604-871-7000; *Fax:* 604-871-7100
www.vcc.ca
Dale Dorn, President
L. Martin, Vice-President
Alan Davis, Vice-President
Peter Legg, Interim Vice-President

Campuses
City Centre Campus
250 West Pender St., Vancouver, BC V6B 1S9, Canada
Fax: 604-443-8588

King Edward Campus
1155 East Broadway, Vancouver, BC V5T 4V5, Canada
Fax: 604-871-7100

Publications
The Gleaner

V.C.C. Voice
100 - 49th Ave. West, Vancouver, BC V5Y 2Z6, Canada

Victoria: Camosun College
Lansdowne Campus
3100 Foul Bay Rd., Victoria, BC V8P 5J2, Canada
Tel: 250-370-3000; *Fax:* 250-370-3551
Toll-Free: 877-554-7555
camosun.ca
www.facebook.com/CamosunCollege
twitter.com/camosun
youtube.com/user/mycamosun
Kathryn Laurin, President, 250-370-3410

Campuses
Interurban Campus
4461 Interurban Rd., RR#3, Victoria, BC V9E 2C1, Canada
Fax: 250-370-3750

Publications
Nexus

Post Secondary/Technical

Burnaby: BC Institute of Technology
3700 Willingdon Ave., Burnaby, BC V5G 3H2, Canada
Tel: 604-434-1610; *Fax:* 604-431-6917
Toll-Free: 866-434-1610
www.bcit.ca
Dr. Tony Knowles, President
Marshall Heinekey, Acting Vice President
Dr. Verna Magee-Shepherd, Vice President

Campuses
Burnaby Campus
3700 Willingdon Ave., Burnaby, BC V5G 3H2, Canada

Aircraft Technology Campus
5301 Airport Rd. South, Richmond, BC V7B 1B5, Canada

Downtown Campus
555 Seymour St., Vancouver, BC V6B 3H6, Canada

Marine Campus
265 West Esplanade, North Vancouver, BC V7M 1A5, Canada

Publications
Great Northern Way Campus
555 Great Northern Way, Vancouver, BC V5T 1E2, Canada

Burnaby: CDI College of Business, Technology, & Health Care (CDI)
Collège CDI de la Technologie et de la Santé
Headquarters
#101, 4603 Kingsway, Burnaby, BC V5H 4M4
Toll-Free: 1-800-675-4392
www.cdicollege.com
www.facebook.com/CDICollege
twitter.com/CDICollege
www.youtube.com/CDICareerCollege
Note: Graduates of the college are trained to work in the business, technology, & healthcare sectors.
Bohdan J. Bilan, Vice President

Campuses
Victoria Campus
950 Kings Rd., Victoria, BC V8T 1W6

Vancouver Campus
#200, 789 Pender St., Vancouver, BC V6C 1H2

Burnaby Campus
#500, 5021 Kingsway, Burnaby, BC V5H 4M4

Surrey Campus
#100, 11125 - 124th St., Surrey, BC V3V 4V2
Tel: 604-585-8585

Abbotsford Campus
31838 Fraser Way South, Abbotsford, BC V2T 1V3

Richmond Campus
#100, 4351 No 3 Rd., Richmond, BC V6X 3A7

Calgary City Centre Campus
Trimac House
#100, 800 - 5th Ave. SW, Calgary, AB T2P 3T6
Tel: 888-707-0573

Calgary North Campus
#100, 403 - 33rd St. NE, Calgary, AB T2A 1X5

Calgary South Campus
Midnapore Mall
#200, 240 Midpark Way SE, Calgary, AB T2X 1N4

Edmonton City Centre Campus
P.O. Box 30
9939 Jasper Ave., Edmonton, AB T5J 2W8

Edmonton North Campus
#104, 9450 - 137th Ave., Edmonton, AB T5E 6C2

Edmonton South Campus
#2, 810 Saddleback Rd. NW, Edmonton, AB T6J 4W4

Edmonton West Campus
176 Mayfield Common, Edmonton, AB T5P 4B3

Winnipeg Campus
280 Main St., Winnipeg, MB R3C 1A9

Scarborough Campus
2131 Lawrence Ave. East, 3rd Fl., Toronto, ON M1R 3A3

Mississauga Campus
#280, 33 City Centre Dr., Mississauga, ON L5B 2N5

Hamilton Campus
#104, 14 Hughson St. South, Hamilton, ON L8N 2A1

North York Campus
#33, 4950 Yonge St., North York, ON M2N 6K1

Ajax Campus
#E100, 100 Westney Rd. South, Ajax, ON L1S 7H3

Toronto Campus
2 Bloor St. East, 16th Fl., Toronto, ON M4W 1A1
Bohdan J. Bilan, Vice-President, Academics

Montréal Campus
#700, 416, boul de Maisonneuve ouest, Montréal, QC H3A 1L2

Laval Campus
#400, 3, place Laval, Laval, QC H7N 1A2, Canada
Martin Gascon, Directeur

Québec City Campus
#20, 905, av Honore-Mercier, Quebec, QC G1R 5M6

Pointe-Claire Campus
1000, boul Saint-Jean, Pointe-Claire, QC H9R 5P1

Longueuil Campus
Complexe St-Charles
#120, 1111, rue St-Charles ouest, Longueuil, QC J4K 5G4

Burnaby: Jennings Institute for Performing Artists Inc.
1870 Sperling Ave., Burnaby, BC V5B 4K5
Tel: 604-420-3213; *Fax:* 604-420-3210
forperfomingartists@hotmail.com
Note: Established in 1974, the institute is a not-for-profit college engaged in training artists of all ages.

Burnaby: Nicola Valley Institute of Technology - Vancouver Campus (NVIT)
#200, 4355 Mathissi Place, Burnaby, BC V5G 4S8, Canada
Tel: 604-602-9555; *Fax:* 604-602-3400
info@nvit.bc.ca
www.nvit.bc.ca

Burnaby: Pacific Vocational College (PVC)
4064 McConnell Dr., Burnaby, BC V5A 3A8
Tel: 604-421-5255; *Fax:* 604-421-7445
admin@pacificvocationalcollege.ca
www.pacificvocationalcollege.ca
Note: Technical training is offered through the following programs: plumbing, sprinklerfitting, steamfitting, gasfitting, & cross connection control.
Robert F. Bradbury, President

Burnaby: ProCare Institute Inc.
#240, 4411 Hastings St., Burnaby, BC V5C 2K1
Tel: 604-291-0030; *Fax:* 604-291-0003
Toll-Free: 1-800-282-0030
procare@telus.net
www.procare.ca
Note: ProCare Institute is a private post-secondary education institution that was founded in 1987. It is registered with & accredited by the Private Career Training Institutions Agency of British Columbia. The institute offers the Health Care Assistant program, which prepares students for work in the long-term care sector.

Courtenay: Comox Valley Beauty School
911 McPhee Ave., Courtenay, BC V9N 3A1
Tel: 250-338-9982

Kelowna: Fine-Art Bartending School - Kelowna
Invue Building
#202, 2040 Springfield Rd., Kelowna, BC V1Y 9N7
Tel: 250-863-6392
www.fineartbartending.com
Note: Since 1973, Fine Art Bartending has provided bartending training & certification. Subjects include mixology, beer & wine service, responsible alcohol service, & customer service. Fine Art Bartending is a Registered Private Trade School with Human Resources & Skills Development Canada.

Kelowna: Kelowna College of Professional Counselling (KCPC)
#101, 251 Lawrence Ave., Kelowna, BC V1Y 6L2
Tel: 250-717-0412; *Fax:* 250-717-0427
Toll-Free: 1-855-888-5272
www.counsellortraining.com
Note: The Kelowna College of Professional Counselling is accrdited by the Private Career Training Institutions Agency. Students may earn a Diploma of Applied Psychology & Counselling.
Phillip R. Hay, Executive Director & Registrar
Tristyn Hay, Director, Student Services
Libby Stowers, Ph.D., Director, Program
Ilona Sobczak, Financial Officer

Langley: New Directions - Langley
#5566, 204 St., Langley, BC V3A 1Z5
Tel: 604-530-0535; *Fax:* 604-532-0561
newdir_elsa@telus.net
www.elsanet.org
Note: New Directions in Langley, British Columbia is an English Language Services for Adults (ELSA) school.
Kate Collins, Coordinator, ELSA

Langley: RCABC (Roofing Contractors Association of British Columbia) Roofing Institut
9734 - 201st St., Langley, BC V1M 3E8
Tel: 604-882-9734; *Fax:* 604-882-9684
www.rcabc.org
Note: Instruction is delivered to the roofing & construction-related industries of British Columbia. Apprenticeship training is provided in the architectural sheet metal & the roof, damp, & waterproofing sectors.
Ivan van Spronsen, Executive. Vice-President
Barbara Porth, Manager, Administrative Services

Maple Creek: RSH International College of Cosmetology
11922 - 227th St., Maple Creek, BC V2X-6J2, Canada
Tel: 604-467-0222
www.hairdressing.ca
www.facebook.com/groups/4792886444
twitter.com/instructor6
Note: Hairstyling courses

Maple Ridge: Ridge Meadows College
20575 Thorne Ave., Maple Ridge, BC V2X 9A6
Tel: 604-466-6555; *Fax:* 604-463-5437
rmc@sd42.ca
www.rmcollege.ca
Note: The fully accredited private college offers certificate programs. General interest courses are available, as well as trades programs, such as Forklift Operator & Building Service Worker.

Campuses
Arthur Peake Centre
23125 - 116th Ave., Maple Ridge, BC V2X 3M6, Canada
Fax: 604-467-4143

Thomas Haney Centre
23000C - 116th Ave., Maple Ridge, BC V2X 0T8, Canada
Fax: 604-463-5437

Merritt: Nicola Valley Institute of Technology
4155 Belshaw St., Merritt, BC V1K 1R1, Canada
Tel: 250-378-3300; *Fax:* 250-378-3332
Toll-Free: 1-877-682-330
info@nvit.bc.ca
www.nvit.bc.ca
Enrollment: 800 *Note:* Certificate & diploma programs, adult basic education, collaborative degrees & on-campus, in-community & online delivery
Ken Tourand, Director
ktourand@nvit.bc.ca
John Chenoweth, MA, Dean of Community Education & Applied Programs
jchenoweth@nvit.bc.ca

New Westminster: Hilltop Academy
#440, 604 Columbia St., New Westminster, BC V3M 1A5
Tel: 604-553-0505; *Fax:* 604-357-1133
info@hilltopacademy.ca
www.hilltopacademy.ca
Note: The academy offers a fitness leadership diploma program. Graduates become BC Recreation & Park Association registered weight trainers, personal trainers, & group fitness instructors. The academy is a partner of the American Council on Exercise, so students are able to become ACE certified personal trainers.

New Westminster: Justice Institute of B.C.
715 McBride Blvd., New Westminster, BC V3L 5T4, Canada
Tel: 604-525-5422; *Fax:* 604-528-5518
Toll-Free: 1-88-865-7764
infodesk@jibc.ca
www.jibc.ca
www.facebook.com/justiceinstitute
twitter.com/JIBCnews
www.linkedin.com/company/justice-institute-of-british-columbia
www.youtube.com/user/JusticeInstitute
Jack McGee, President

Campuses
Chilliwack Campus
5470 Dieppe St., Chilliwack, BC V2R 5Y8, Canada
Tel: 604-847-0881; *Fax:* 604-847-0134

Vancouver
555 Great Northern WayFl., Vancouver, BC V5T 1E2, Canada
Tel: 604-528-5801; *Fax:* 604-638-0137

Maple Ridge Campus
13500 - 256 St., Maple Ridge, BC V4R 1C9, Canada
Tel: 604-462-1000; *Fax:* 604-462-9149
Toll-Free: 1-888-844-0445

Okanagan Campus
825 Walrod St., Kelowna, BC V1Y 2S4, Canada
Tel: 250-469-6020; *Fax:* 250-469-6022

Victoria Campus
810 Fort St., Victoria, BC V8W 1H8, Canada
Tel: 250-405-3500; *Fax:* 250-405-3505

Fire & Safety Training Centre
13500 - 256 St., Maple Ridge, BC V4R 1C9, Canada
Tel: 604-462-1000; *Fax:* 604-462-9149
Toll-Free: 1-888-844-0445
fire@jibc.ca
www.facebook.com/JIBC.FSD
Note: Courses offered on marine & industrial firefighting, emergency response to incidents involving hazardous materials, fire service training from recruit to chief officer.
Dan Murphy, Manager

Port Coquitlam: Sprott-Shaw Community College
#200, 1405 Broadway St., Port Coquitlam, BC V3C 6L6
Tel: 604-552-9711
www.sprottshaw.com
www.facebook.com/sprottshaw
twitter.com/sprottshaw
www.flickr.com/photos/sprottshaw/collections
Note: Trades programs are offered at the Port Coquitlam location.

Port Moody: Western Montessori Teachers' College
#108, 135 Balmoral Dr., Port Moody, BC V3H 1X7, Canada
Tel: 604-461-7132; *Toll-Free:* 1-888-832-4030
wmtcbc@telus.net
www.westernmontessori.ca

Campuses
AB Office
P.O. Box 1120
Bragg Creek, AB T0L 0K0, Canada
Tel: 403-949-2238; *Fax:* 403-949-2238
WMTCab@telus.net

Prince George: ABC Safety & First Aid Training Services
#215, 1990 Ogilvie St., Prince George, BC V2N 6C5
Tel: 250-960-1112
www.abcsoffirstaid.ca
Note: Training is provided in all areas of first aid training & safety. Instructors for ABC Safety & First Aid Training Services are certified by WorkSafe BC & EMP Canada.
Robbin Worthington, Manager
Melanie Funk, Evaluator & Instructor
Christine Hale, Evaluator & Instructor

Revelstoke: Canadian Avalanche Association
P.O. Box 2759
110 MacKenzie Ave., Revelstoke, BC V0E 2S0
Tel: 250-837-2141; *Fax:* 250-366-2094
canav@avalanche.ca
www.avalanche.ca
Note: The Canadian Avalanche Association offers an Industry Training Program for avalanche workers. The Industry Training Program is a fully bonded, private, post-secondary educational institution that teaches over 500 student each year across Canada.
Joe Obad, Executive Director, 250-837-2435
jobad@avalanche.ca
Bridget Daughney, Manager, Industry Training Program, 250-837-2435, ext. 223
itpadmin@avalanche.ca

Surrey: Automotive Training Centre - Surrey (ATC)
12160 - 88th Ave, Surrey, BC V3W 3J2
Tel: 604-635-2222; *Fax:* 604-635-2223
Toll-Free: 1-888-546-2886
www.autotrainingcentre.com
Note: The Automotive Training Centre provides instruction for careers as an automotive service technician, an automotive diesel technician, a refinishing prep technician, an automotive service consultant, & a business manager, as well as jobs in sales & leasing.

Surrey: Stenberg College
#750, 13450 - 102nd Ave., Surrey, BC V3T 5X3, Canada
Tel: 604-580-2772; *Fax:* 604-580-2774
Toll-Free: 1-866-580-2772
www.stenbergcollege.com
Note: Resident care attendant; community support worker; nursing unit clerk, medical office assistant; institutional aid; veterinary assistant; practical nursing program; automotive technician
Jeremy Sabell, President

Surrey: West Coast College of Health Care
#204, 9648 - 128 St., Surrey, BC V3T 2X9
Tel: 604-951-6644; *Toll-Free:* 1-800-807-8558
admin@westcoastcollege.com
www.westcoastcollege.com
www.facebook.com/pages/West-Coast-College/173782172655449
Note: West Coast College of Health Care provides health & human services training. Programs include instruction to become a medical laboratory assistant, a pharmacy technician, & a veterinary assistant. The college is accredited by the Private Career Training Institutions Agency of British Columbia.

Vancouver: Academy of Learning - Vancouver
#302, 2555 Commercial Dr., Vancouver, BC V5N 4C1
Tel: 604-876-8600; *Fax:* 604-876-4333
aolritu@shawlink.ca (Admissions)
www.academyoflearning.com
Note: The Academy of Learning offers certificate & diploma programs in fields such as accounting, business, customer service, health care, home inspection, hospitality, information technology, office administration, & web design.

Vancouver: Blanche Macdonald Centre
City Square
#100, 555 West 12th Ave., Vancouver, BC V5Z 3X7
Tel: 604-685-0347
info@blanchemacdonald.com
www.blanchemacdonald.com
Note: Since 1960, the Blanche Macdonald Centre has provided training in the areas of fashion design & merchandising, makeup artistry, hair design, nail technology, & spa therapy.
Lise Graham, Managing Director
lise@blanchemacdonald.com
Barbara Johnston, Managing Director
barb@blanchemacdonald.com
Jaye Wong Klippenstein, Director, International Marketing
jaye@blanchemacdonald.com

Vancouver: BM Chan International Cosmetology College
3012 Kingsway, Vancouver, BC V5R 5J7
Tel: 604-437-3109
info@bmchan.com
www.bmchan.com
Note: Established in 1985, the accredited cosmetology college provides training & diploma courses in hair design, medical esthetics, & nail technology.
Monita Chan, Founder & Managing Director

Vancouver: Canadian College of English Language
#450, 1050 Alberni St., Vancouver, BC V6E 1A3
Tel: 604-688-9366
www.canada-english.com

Note: An English certificate & diploma are offered, as well as English for business lessons, & English tutoring.
Jim Clark, Chair & Owner
Lane Clark, Chief Executive Officer
Jay Ariken, Chief Operating Officer & Academic Director
Jeremy Clark, Chief Information Officer

Vancouver: Canadian Electrolysis College Ltd. (CEC)
#265, 1651 Commercial Dr., Vancouver, BC V5L 3Y3
Tel: 604-319-2515
info@canadianelectrolysiscollege.ca
www.canadianelectrolysiscollege.ca
Note: Opened in 1986, the Canadian Electrolysis College provides state of the art training for professional electrologists, featuring both theory & practical instruction. Graduates receive a diploma & are able to apply for membership uin The Association of Professional Electrologists of BC & the Federation of Canadian Electrolysis Associations.
Athena Martins, RE, CCE, CPE, Contact

Vancouver: Canadian Institute of Gemmology (CIG)
P.O. Box 57010
Vancouver, BC V5K 5G6
Tel: 604-530-8569; *Toll-Free:* 1-800-294-2211
info@cigem.ca
www.cigem.ca
Note: The institute provides the opportunity to learn about gems, diamonds, & jewellery. Examples of courses include introductory gemmology, advanced gemmology, & appraisal.

Vancouver: Canadian Tourism College (CTC)
#501, 1755 West Broadway, Vancouver, BC V6J 4S5
Tel: 604-736-8000; *Fax:* 604-731-9819
Toll-Free: 1-877-731-9810
www.tourismcollege.com
www.facebook.com/ctcfans
twitter.com/tourismcollege1
www.youtube.com/user/tourismcollegeCTC
Note: The Canadian Tourism College was established in 1980 to offer hospitality & tourism education in British Columbia. The college is fully accredited college by the Private Career Training Institutions Agency of British Columbia.

Vancouver: Emily Carr Institute of Art & Design
1399 Johnston St., Vancouver, BC V6H 3R9, Canada
Tel: 604-844-3800; *Fax:* 604-844-3801
Toll-Free: 1-800-832-7788
www.eciad.ca
Enrollment: 1173
Dr. Ronald Burnett, President

Vancouver: Erickson College International
2021 Columbia St., Vancouver, BC V5Y 3C9
Tel: 604-879-5600; *Fax:* 604-879-7234
Toll-Free: 1-800-665-6949
info@erickson.edu
www.erickson.edu
Note: Erickson College offers certified professional coach training.
Lawrence McGinnis, LLB, Executive Director
corporate@erickson.edu
Talyaa Vardar, Head, Corporate Development
talyaa@erickson.edu

Vancouver: Eurocentres Vancouver
#250, 815 West Hastings St., Vancouver, BC V6C 1B4
Tel: 604-688-7942; *Fax:* 604-688-7985
info@languagecanada.com
www.languagecanada.com
www.facebook.com/eurocentres.canada.schools
twitter.com/eurocentrescan
www.flickr.com/people/eurocentrescanada
Note: Eurocentres Vancouver provides instruction in English as a Second Language to international students.

Vancouver: Gateway College
395 West Broadway, Vancouver, BC V5Y 1A7
Tel: 604-738-0285; *Fax:* 604-738-0994
info@gwcollege.ca
www.gwcollege.ca
Other Information: Admissions Office, Phone: 604-738-0994
Note: Founded in 1986, the college offers programs that lead to careers such as a health care assistant, a long-term care aide, a nursing assistant, & a dementia professional. Red Cross emergency first aid training is also available.
Gateway College is a member of the following organizations: Private Career Training Institutes Agency, British Columbia Career Colleges Association, British Columbia Education Quality Assurance, National Association of Career Colleges, BC Care, & the Better Business Bureau.

Vancouver: Granville Business College
#725, 570 Dunsmuir St., Vancouver, BC V6B 1Y1
Tel: 604-683-8850; *Fax:* 604-682-7115
Toll-Free: 1-800-661-9885
vetassistant@telus.net
www.vet-assistant.com
Note: Granville Business College is accredited by the Private Career Training Institutions Agency. Since 1993, the college has prepared students to work as veterinary office assistants in the animal health care sector.

Vancouver: MTI Community College - Vancouver
541 Seymour St.., Vancouver, BC V6B 3K3, Canada
Tel: 604-682-6020; *Fax:* 604-682-6468
Toll-Free: 1-866-682-6020
vancouver@mticc.com
www.metrocollege.net
www.facebook.com/mticc
www.twitter.com/MTI_College
ca.linkedin.com/in/mticareercollege
Note: ECCE; Residential Care; Long Term Care Aide; Community Support Worker; Internet Development; MCSE

Campuses
Surrey Campus
10072 King George Blvd., Surrey, BC V3T 2W4, Canada
Tel: 604-583-6020; *Fax:* 604-583-6019
surrey@mticc.com

Coquitlam Campus
#405, 2963 Glen Dr., Coquitlam, BC V3B 2P7, Canada
Tel: 604-464-8718; *Fax:* 604-942-6355
coquitlam@mticc.com

Burnaby Campus
#200, 4980 Kingsway, Burnaby, BC V5H 4K7, Canada
Tel: 604-437-6030; *Fax:* 604-437-6036
burnaby@mticc.com

Chilliwack Campus
#107, 7491 Vedder Rd., Chilliwack, BC V2R 4E7, Canada
Tel: 604-824-6081; *Fax:* 604-824-6084
chilliwack@mticc.com

Abbotsford Campus
#308, 2777 Gladwin Rd., Abbotsford, BC V2T 4V1, Canada
Tel: 604-864-8920; *Fax:* 604-864-8947
abbotsford@mticc.com

Vancouver: Native Education College (NEC)
285 East 5th Ave., Vancouver, BC V5T 1H2
Tel: 604-873-3772; *Fax:* 604-873-9152
Info@NECVancouver.org
www.necvancouver.org
Note: The college opened in 1967 to offer developmental, vocational, & applied academic programs to Aboriginal adult students. The non-profit society is governed by a Board of Directors.
Keith Henry, Chair

Vancouver: Pacific Gateway International College (PGIC)
1155 Robson St., 3rd Fl., Vancouver, BC V6E 1B5, Canada
Tel: 604-687-3595; *Fax:* 604-687-3586
info@pgicvancouver.com
pgic.ca
www.facebook.com/pages/PGIC-Vancouver/181044735269225

Toronto Campus
2040 Yonge St., 3rd Fl., Toronto, ON M4S 1Z9, Canada
Tel: 416-977-9800; *Fax:* 416-977-9801
info@pgicvancouver.com

Vancouver: Rhodes Wellness College
#280, 1125 Howe St., Vancouver, BC V6Z 2K8
Tel: 604-708-4416; *Fax:* 604-708-4418
Toll-Free: 1-877-708-4416
admin@rhodescollege.ca; admissions@rhodescollege.ca
www.rhodescollege.ca
Note: Since 1996, Rhodes Wellness College has offered coaching, counselling, & wellness training to certify professional life coaches & counsellors.
Bea Rhodes, B.A., M.Ed., Founder & President, 604-708-4416, ext. 26
bea@rhodescollege.ca
Brendan Stitchman, R.P.C., Director, Training, 604-708-4416, ext. 31
brendan@rhodescollege.ca
Denise Stroude, R.P.C., Director, Admissions, 604-708-4416, ext. 23
denise@rhodescollege.ca
Kim Waters, Office Manager
kim@rhodescollege.ca

Vancouver: Vancouver School of Theology
6000 Iona Dr., Vancouver, BC V6T 1L4, Canada
Tel: 604-822-9031; *Fax:* 604-822-9212
Toll-Free: 1-866-822-9031
possibilities@vst.edu
www.vst.edu
Note: Multi-denominational graduate school educating leaders for the church, service agencies & businesses
Rev. Dr. Wendy Fletcher, Principal

Vancouver: Western Imperial College of Canada
#201, 2460 Commercial Dr., Vancouver, BC V5N 4B9
Tel: 604-872-1236
wiccbc.tripod.com
Note: The college was established by ESL International in association with Aspen University. Western Imperial College of Canada offers Masters programs in Business Management & Information Technology. Imperial College is registered with the Private Post-Secondary Education Commission of British Columbia.
Jay Ariken, Dean

Victoria: Academy of Excellence
303 Goldstream Ave., Victoria, BC V9B 2W4
Tel: 250-386-7843; *Fax:* 250-386-0090
excellence@telus.net
www.academyofexcellencevictoria.com
Note: Established in 1963, the Academy of Excellence offers career training in hair design & spa therapy.
Lorie Chadsey, Director & Esthetic / Spa Therapy Instructor
Tina Kelly, Registrar
Danielle St. Jacques Rand, Registrar
Greg Abbott, Manager, Hair Design Education

Victoria: Aveda Institute
1400 Douglas St., Victoria, BC V8W 2G1
Tel: 250-386-7985; *Fax:* 250-386-7945
Toll-Free: 1-800-391-7873
info@avedainstitutevictoria.ca
www.avedainstitutevictoria.ca
Note: Founded in 1978, the Aveda Institute offers Private Career Training Institutions Agency accredited programs leading to careers in hair styling or cosmetology.
Paul Da Costa, Founder, Aveda Institute Victoria
Roxana Barlow, Director

Victoria: BC School of Art Therapy
125 Skinner St., Victoria, BC V9A 6X4
Tel: 250-598-6434; *Fax:* 250-598-6449
info@bcsat.com
www.bcsat.com
Note: The School of Art Therapy offers a post-master's certifcate & a post-bachelor's diploma. The organization is a registered charity.
Barbara M. Klassen, President
Lucille Proulx, Executive Director
Michelle Winkel, Registrar & Practicum Coordinator

Victoria: Canadian Acupressure College
256 Linden Ave., Victoria, BC V8V 4E5
Tel: 250-388-7475; *Fax:* 250-388-7498
Toll-Free: 1-877-909-2244
cai@islandnet.com
www.acupressureshiatsuschool.com
Note: The Canadian Acupressure College is a member of the Health Action Network Society, Association of Holistic Practitioners, & Natural Health Practitioners of Canada. The college is registered by the Private Career Training Institutions Agency of British Columbia.
Since 1994, the Canadian Acupressure College has developed health practitioners who use acupressure for human & social change.
Kathy de Bucy, Founder, Administrator & Director

Victoria: Canadian College of Performing Arts
1701 Elgin Rd., Victoria, BC V8R 5L7, Canada
Tel: 250-595-9970; *Fax:* 250-595-0779
admin@ccpacanada.com
www.ccpacanada.com
Enrollment: 65 *Note:* Two, 1-year extensive training programs in acting, voice, dance & career management

Victoria: Lester B. Pearson United World College
650 Pearson College Dr., Victoria, BC V9C 4H7, Canada
Tel: 250-391-2411; *Fax:* 250-391-2412
www.pearsoncollege.ca
www.facebook.com/PearsonUWC
twitter.com/PCUWC
www.youtube.com/user/PearsonUWC
David Hawley, Director
dhawley@pearsoncollege.ca

Victoria: Western Academy of Photography
755A Queens Ave., Victoria, BC V8T 1M2
Tel: 250-383-1522; *Fax:* 250-383-1534
Toll-Free: 1-866-889-1235
infowaop@shaw.ca
www.westernacademyofphotography.com
www.facebook.com/group.php?gid=123708291001707
Note: Western Academy of Photography offers training in professional photography, photojournalism, & journalism.

West Vancouver: Vancouver Art Therapy Institute
#350, 1425 Marine Dr., West Vancouver, BC V7T 1B9, Canada
Tel: 604-681-8284; *Fax:* 604-926-5728
vatimail@telus.net
www.vati.bc.ca

Manitoba

Government Agencies

Winnipeg: Manitoba Advanced Education & Literacy
Legislative Bldg.
#156, 450 Broadway, Winnipeg, MB R3C 0V8, Canada
Tel: 204-945-0825; *Fax:* 204-948-2216
www.edu.gov.mb.ca/ael
Hon. Diane McGifford, Minister
Dwight Botting, Acting Deputy Minister

Winnipeg: Manitoba Education & Literacy
#168, 450 Broadway, Winnipeg, MB R3C 0Y8, Canada
Tel: 204-945-3720; *Fax:* 204-945-1291
minedu@leg.gov.mb.ca
www.edu.gov.mb.ca
Note: Includes the ministries of Education, Advanced Education & Literacy, & Entrepreneurship, Training & Trade
Hon. Nancy Allan, Minister, Education
Hon. Erin Selby, Minister, Advanced Education & Literacy, 204-945-0825, fax: 204-948-2216
minaed@leg.gov.mb.ca
Hon. Peter Bjornson, Minister, Entrepreneurship, Training & Trade, 204-945-0067, fax: 204-945-4882
minett@leg.gov.mb.ca

School Boards/Districts/Divisions

Public

Altona: Border Land School Division
P.O. Box 390
120 - 9th St. NW, Altona, MB R0G 0B0, Canada
Tel: 204-324-6491; *Fax:* 204-324-1664
Toll-Free: 1-866-324-6491
www.borderland.ca
Other Information: Transportation Office: 204-427-2091; Maintenance: 204-324-9536
Grades: Kindergarten - 12; French Immersion
Krista Curry, Chief Executive Officer / Superintendent, 204-324-6491, ext. 1010, fax: 204-324-1664
Carol Braun, Assistant Superintendent, 204-324-6491, ext. 1011, fax: 204-324-1664
Anne Malyon, Secretary-Treasurer, 204-324-6491, ext. 1012, fax: 204-324-1664
Todd Nichols, Coordinator, Transportation, 204-427-2091, ext. 1510, fax: 204-427-2531
Julie Weber, Coordinator, Student Services, 204-427-2091, ext. 1013, fax: 204-427-2531

Beausejour: Sunrise School Division
Sunrise Education Center
P.O. Box 1206
344 Second St. North, Beausejour, MB R0E 0C0, Canada
Tel: 204-268-6500; *Fax:* 204-268-6545
Toll-Free: 1-866-444-5559
kwold@sunrisesd.ca (Kathy Wold, Reception)
www.sunrisesd.ca
Other Information: Transportation, Phone: 204-444-2498; Business, Fax: 204-268-4149
Number of Schools: 24 *Grades:* Kindergarten - 12; Adult Education
Don Nichol, Chair, 204-348-2818
dnichol@sunrisesd.ca
Wayne Leckie, Superintendent & Chief Executive Officer, 204-268-6507
wleckie@sunrisesd.ca
Paul Barnard, Assistant Superintendent, People Services, 204-268-6538
pbarnard@sunrisesd.ca
Paul Magnan, Assistant Superintendent, Student Learning, 204-268-6517
pmagnan@sunrisesd.ca
Lesley Eblie Trudel, Division Principal, Student Support Programs, 204-268-6535
leblie@sunrisesd.ca
Joan Badger, Leader, Middle Years & ICt Program, 204-268-6543
jbadger@sunrisesd.ca
Karen David, Leader, Early Years Program, 204-268-6527
kdavid@sunrisesd.ca
Kevin Doell, Leader, Music Program, 204-444-2473
kdoell@sunrisesd.ca
Marie Josee Morneau, Leader, Senior Years Program, 204-268-6532
mjmorneau@sunrisesd.ca
Fran King, Manager, Purchasing, 204-268-6531
fking@sunrisesd.ca
Roger Hardman, Secretary-Treasurer, 204-268-6514
rhardman@sunrisesd.ca

Birtle: Park West School Division
P.O. Box 68
1126 St. Claire St., Birtle, MB R0M 0C0, Canada
Tel: 204-842-2100; *Fax:* 204-842-2110
Toll-Free: 877-418-5320
cbonner@pwsd.ca
www.pwsd.ca
Enrollment: 1800
Joe Arruda, Chief Executive Officer

Brandon: Brandon School Division
Administration Office
1031 - 6th St., Brandon, MB R7A 4K5, Canada
Tel: 204-729-3100; *Fax:* 204-727-2217
info@brandonsd.mb.ca
www.brandonsd.mb.ca
Grades: K.-12; French Immersion *Enrollment:* 7200
George Buri, Chair, 204-727-3156
buri.george@brandonsd.mb.ca
Dr. Donna Michaels, Chief Executive Officer & Superintendent of Schools
michaels.donna@brandonsd.mb.ca
Greg Malazdrewicz, Associate Superintendent
malazdrewicz.greg@brandonsd.mb.ca
Gerald F. Barnes, Secretary-Treasurer
barnes.gerald@brandonsd.mb.ca

Carman: Prairie Rose School Division
45 Main St. South, Carman, MB R0G 0J0, Canada
Tel: 204-745-2003; *Fax:* 204-745-3699
Toll-Free: 866-745-3699
prsd@prsdmb.ca
www.prsdmb.ca
Enrollment: 2278
Bruce Wood, Superintendent

Dauphin: Mountain View School Division
P.O. Box 715
Dauphin, MB R7N 3B3, Canada
Tel: 204-638-3001; *Fax:* 204-638-7250
www.mvsd.ca
Grades: K.-12 *Enrollment:* 3300
Jack Sullivan, Superintendent
jsullivan@mvsd.ca
Bart Michaleski, Secretary-Treasurer, 204-638-3001
michale@mvsd.ca

Eriksdale: Lakeshore School Division
P.O. Box 100
Eriksdale, MB R0C 0W0, Canada
Tel: 204-739-2101; *Fax:* 204-739-2145
admin@lakeshoresd.mb.ca
www.lakeshoresd.mb.ca
Enrollment: 1304
Janet Martell, Superintendent

Flin Flon: Flin Flon School Division
9 Terrace Ave., Flin Flon, MB R8A 1S2, Canada
Tel: 204-681-3413; *Fax:* 204-681-3417
www.ffsd.mb.ca
Number of Schools: 3 elementary schools; 2 secondary schools *Grades:* Kindergarten - 12; Alternative Ed. *Enrollment:* 1378
Murray Skeavington, Chair
Blaine Veitch, Superintendent
bveitch@ffsd.mb.ca
Dean Grove, Assistant Superintendent
dgrove@ffsd.mb.ca
Heather Fleming, Secretary-Treasurer
Bruce Fidler, Supervisor, Maintenance
bfidler@ffsd.mb.ca

Gimli: Evergreen School Division
Education Support Centre
P.O. Box 1200
140 Centre Ave. West, Gimli, MB R0C 1B0, Canada
Tel: 204-642-6260; *Fax:* 204-642-7273
info@esd.mb.ca
www.esd.mb.ca
Number of Schools: 8 *Grades:* Kindergarten - 12; Continuing Ed. *Enrollment:* 1671 *Number of Employees:* 273
Ruth Ann Furgala, Chair, 204-378-2901
rfurgala@esd.mb.ca
Paul Cuthbert, Superintendent & Chief Executive Officer, 204-642-6278
pcuthbert@esd.mb.ca
Roza Gray, Assistant Superintendent, 204-642-6267
rgray@esd.mb.ca
Daniel Howe, Director, Operations, 204-642-6269
dhowe@esd.mb.ca
Fay Cassidy, Coordinator, Student Services, 204-642-6279
fcassidy@esd.mb.ca
Brenda Chapman, Officer, Safety, 204-641-1365
bchapman@esd.mb.ca
Charlie Grieve, Secretary-Treasurer, 204-642-6266
cgrieve@esd.mb.ca

Gladstone: Pine Creek School Division
P.O. Box 420
Gladstone, MB R0J 0T0, Canada
Tel: 204-385-2216; *Fax:* 204-385-2825
pcsddo@pinecreeksd.mb.ca
www.pinecreeksd.mb.ca
Enrollment: 1200
Brian Gouriluk, Superintendent
bgouriluk@pinecreeksd.mb.ca

Killarney: Turtle Mountain School Division
P.O. Box 280
435 Williams Ave., Killarney, MB R0K 1G0, Canada
Tel: 204-523-7531; *Fax:* 204-523-7269
dbo@tmsd.mb.ca
www.tmsd.mb.ca
Number of Schools: 4 Hutterian schools; 1 elementary / middle school; 2 K - 12 schools; 2 adult ed *Grades:* Kindergarten - 12; Continuing Ed.
Neil Finch, Superintendent
Tanya Edgar, Assistant Superintendent, Student Services
Kathy Siatecki, Secretary-Treasurer

Lorette: Division Scolaire franco-manitobaine (DSFM)
P.O. Box 204
1263, ch Dawson, Lorette, MB R0A 0Y0
Tél: 204-878-9399; *Téléc:* 204-878-9407
Ligne sans frais: 800-699-3736
dsfm@dsfm.mb.ca
www.dsfm.mb.ca
Number of Schools: 24 écoles francophones; 1 Centre d'apprentissage franco-manitobain *Grades:* K.-12
Bernard Lesage, Président
bernard.lesage@atrium.ca
Denis Ferre, Supt.

Lorette: Seine River School Division
475A Senez St., Lorette, MB R0A 0Y0, Canada
Tel: 204-878-4713; *Fax:* 204-878-4717
www.srsd.mb.ca
Enrollment: 3500
Michael Borgfjord, Superintendent

McCreary: Turtle River School Division
P.O. Box 309
808 Burrows Rd., McCreary, MB R0J 1B0, Canada
Tel: 204-835-2067; *Fax:* 204-835-2426
trsd32.mb.ca
Number of Schools: 7 *Grades:* Kindergarten - 12 *Enrollment:* 771 *Number of Employees:* 63 teachers; 52 support staff
Allan Trotter, Chair, Board of Trustees
Bev Szymesko, Superintendent, Student Services
bevs@trsd32.mb.ca
Richard Bidzinski, Secretary-Treasurer
Richard@trsd32.mb.ca
Dean Bluhm, Supervisor, Transportation & Maintenance
deanb@trsd32.mb.ca
Shannon Desjardins, Accountant
shannon@trsd32.mb.ca
Helen Sommer, Speech / Language Pathologist
helen@trsd32.mb.ca
Jeff Fudge, Information & Communication Technology Technician
jeff@trsd32.mb.ca

Melita: Southwest Horizon School Division
P.O. Box 370
Melita, MB R0M 1L0, Canada
Tel: 204-483-5533; _Fax:_ 204-483-5535
www.shmb.ca
Enrollment: 1793
Brad Kyle, Superintendent

Minnedosa: Rolling River School Division
P.O. Box 1170
Minnedosa, MB R0J 1E0, Canada
Tel: 204-867-2754; _Fax:_ 204-867-2037
rrsd@rrsd.mb.ca
www.rrsd.mb.ca
Enrollment: 1882
Reg Klassen, Superintendent
rklassen@rrsd.mb.ca

Morden: Western School Division
75 Thornhill St., #4, Morden, MB R6M 1P2, Canada
Tel: 204-822-4448; _Fax:_ 204-822-4262
divoff@westernsd.mb.ca
www.westernsd.mb.ca
Grades: K.-12 _Enrollment:_ 1600
Stephen Ross, Supt.
sross@westernsd.mb.ca
Carl Pedersen, Sec.-Treas.
cpedersen@westernsd.mb.ca
Dr David McAndrew, Chair
dmcandrew@westernsd.mb.ca

Morris: Red River Valley School Division
P.O. Box 400
233 Main St., Morris, MB R0G 1K0, Canada
Tel: 204-746-2317; _Fax:_ 204-746-2785
rrvsd@rrvsd.ca
www.rrvsd.ca
Enrollment: 2196
Pauline Lafond-Bouchard, Superintendent & CEO
plbouchard@rrsvd.ca

Neepawa: Beautiful Plains School Division
P.O. Box 700
Neepawa, MB R0J 1H0, Canada
Tel: 204-476-2388; _Fax:_ 204-476-3606
bpsd@bpsd.mb.ca
www.bpsd.mb.ca
Grades: K.-3; Special Ed. _Enrollment:_ 1500
Jason Young, Superintendent
jyoung@bpsd.mb.ca
Gord Olmstead, Secretary-Treasurer
golmstead@bpsd.mb.ca
Melanie Burnett, Coordinator, Student Services
mburnett@bpsd.mb.ca
Melanie Nordstrom, Coordinator, Technology
mordstrom@bpsd.mb.ca
Jennifer Donais, Speech Language Pathologist
jdonais@bpsd.mb.ca

Pinawa: Whiteshell School District
20 Vanier Dr., Pinawa, MB R0E 1L0, Canada
Tel: 204-753-8366; _Fax:_ 204-753-2237
www.sdwhiteshell.mb.ca
Grades: K.-12 _Enrollment:_ 206
Bob Derousie, Supt./CEO
derousie@sdwhiteshell.mb.ca
Jenny Petersen, Sec.-Treas.

Portage la Prairie: Portage la Prairie School Division
535 - 3 St. NW, Portage la Prairie, MB R1N 2C4, Canada
Tel: 204-857-8756; _Fax:_ 204-239-5998
www.plpsd.mb.ca
Enrollment: 3486
Hazen Barrett, Superintendent

Selkirk: Lord Selkirk School Division
LSSD Board Office
205 Mercy St., Selkirk, MB R1A 2C8, Canada
Tel: 204-482-5942; _Fax:_ 204-482-3000
Toll-Free: 866-433-5942
lssd.boardoffice@lssd.ca
www.lssd.ca
Grades: K.-12 _Enrollment:_ 5000 _Note:_ The schools celebrate the heritage and culture of the region - including the Brokenhead Ojibway Nation, the Scottish pioneers, the French Canadian voyageurs and the Ukrainian settlers.
Scott Kwasnitza, Supt./CEO
Bruce Cairns, Sec. Treas.

Steinbach: Hanover School Division
5 Chrysler Gate, Steinbach, MB R5G 0E2, Canada
Tel: 204-326-6471; _Fax:_ 204-326-9901
hsdadmin@hsd.ca
www.hsd.ca
Enrollment: 7400
Ken Klassen, Superintendent

Stonewall: Interlake School Division
192 - 2nd Ave. North, Stonewall, MB R0C 2Z0, Canada
Tel: 204-467-5100; _Fax:_ 204-467-8334
www.isd21.mb.ca
Enrollment: 3040
Ross Metcalfe, Superintendent
rmetcalfe@isd21.mb.ca

Swan Lake: Prairie Spirit School Division
P.O. Box 130
15 Lorne Ave., Swan Lake, MB R0G 2S0, Canada
Tel: 204-825-2721; _Fax:_ 204-825-2725
prspirit@mts.net
www.prairiespirit.mb.ca
Enrollment: 2479
Don Hurton, Superintendent

Swan River: Swan Valley School Division
John Kastrukoff Building
1481 - 3rd St. North, Swan River, MB R0L 1Z0, Canada
Tel: 204-734-4531
www.svsd.ca
Number of Schools: 9 _Grades:_ JK - 12; French Immersion
Bryon Fried, Chair
M. Marquis-Forster, Superintendent
R. Rausch, Secretary-Treasurer
D. Coulthart, Supervisor, Transportation
L. Delaurier, Supervisor, Maintenance
D. Burnside, Coordinator, Student Services

The Pas: Kelsey School Division
P.O. Box 4700
322 Edwards Ave., The Pas, MB R9A 1R4, Canada
Tel: 204-623-6421; _Fax:_ 204-623-7704
www.ksd.mb.ca
Enrollment: 1733
Doug Long, Superintendent
douglong@ksd.mb.ca

Thompson: Mystery Lake School District
408 Thompson Dr. North, Thompson, MB R8N 0C5, Canada
Tel: 204-677-6150; _Fax:_ 204-677-9528
sdml@mysterynet.mb.ca
www.mysterynet.mb.ca
Grades: K.-12 _Enrollment:_ 3000
Beverly Hammond, Supt./CEO
Arnie Assoignon, Sec.-Treas.
aassoignon@mysterynet.mb.ca

Virden: Fort la Bosse School Division
P.O. Box 1420
523 - 9th Ave. South, Virden, MB R0M 2C0, Canada
Tel: 204-748-2692; _Fax:_ 204-748-2436
flbsd@flbsd.mb.ca
www.flbsd.mb.ca
Number of Schools: 11 _Grades:_ Kindergarten - 12 _Enrollment:_ 1400
Gary E. Draper, Chair
Barry Pitz, Superintendent
Vaughn Wilson, Supervisor, Operations
Kent Reid, Secretary-Treasurer
Judy Dandridge, Coordinator, Student Services
Dr. Robert Paulet, School Psychologist

Winkler: Garden Valley School Division
P.O. Box 1330
750 Triple E Blvd., Winkler, MB R6W 4B3, Canada
Tel: 204-325-8335; _Fax:_ 204-325-4132
gvsd@gvsd.ca
www.gvsd.ca
Grades: Kindergarten - Secondary _Enrollment:_ 4100
Hilda Froese, Board Chair
Vern Reimer, Chief Executive Officer & Superintendent of Schools
Todd Monster, Assistant Superintendent
Debra Loewen, Assistant Superintendent, Student Services
Jenn Sager Hlady, Manager, Human Resources
Ken Bergen, Supervisor, Operations
Abe Wiebe, Supervisor, Capital Projects
James Reimer, Coordinator, Technology
Terry Penner, Secretary-Treasurer

Winnipeg: Frontier School Division
30 Speers Rd., Winnipeg, MB R2J 1L9, Canada
Tel: 204-775-9741; _Fax:_ 204-775-9940
frontier@frontiersd.mb.ca
www.frontiersd.mb.ca
Number of Schools: 41 _Enrollment:_ 6869
Linda Ballantyne, Chair
Gordon Shead, Chief Superintendent
Bradley Hampson, Assistant Superintendent, Technology
Don McCaskill, Assistant Superintendent, Senior Years & Careers Program
Arnold Dysart, Superintendent, Area 1
Karen Crozier, Superintendent, Area 2
Cam Giavedoni, Superintendent, Area 3
Catherine Fidierchuk, Superintendent, Area 4
David Swanson, Superintendent, Area 5
Lena McAlinden, Director, Human Resources
Gerald Cattani, Secretary-Treasurer

Winnipeg: Louis Riel School Division
900 St. Mary's Rd., Winnipeg, MB R2M 3R3, Canada
Tel: 204-257-7827; _Fax:_ 204-256-8553
www.lrsd.net
Grades: K.-12 _Enrollment:_ 14464 _Note:_ The is an amalgamation of the St. Boniface and St. Vital School Divisions.
Terry D. Borys, Supt./CEO

Winnipeg: Pembina Trails School Division
181 Henlow Bay, Winnipeg, MB R3Y 1M7, Canada
Tel: 204-488-1757; _Fax:_ 204-487-3667
ptsdwebinfo@pembinatrails.ca
www.pembinatrails.ca
Enrollment: 13385
Lawrence Lussier, Superintendent

Winnipeg: River East Transcona School Division
Administration Offices
589 Roch St., Winnipeg, MB R2K 2P7, Canada
Tel: 204-667-7130; _Fax:_ 204-661-5618
www.retsd.mb.ca
Enrollment: 17000
Dennis Pottage, Superintendent

Winnipeg: St. James-Assiniboia School Division
2574 Portage Ave., Winnipeg, MB R3J 0H8, Canada
Tel: 204-888-7951; _Fax:_ 204-831-0859
inquiries@sjsd.net; mnachtigall@sjsd.net (administration & board)
www.sjsd.net
Other Information: Continuing Ed., Phone: 204-832-9637; Intl. Program: 204-837-1331
Number of Schools: 15 early years schools; 6 middle years schools; 5 senior years schools _Grades:_ Kindergarten - Senior 4
Bruce Chegus, Chair, 204-888-9498
bchegus@sjsd.net
Ron K. Weston, Chief Superintendent
Brett J. Lough, Assistant Superintendent, Administration, Planning & Research
Greg Mutter, Assistant Superintendent, Personnel & Human Resources
Tanis C.M. Pshebniski, Assistant Superintendent, Program & Curriculum
Dennis G. Dart, Manager, Facilities & Maintenance
Carrol A. Harvey, Manager, Human Resources (MANTE & excluded)
Cindy Labaty, Manager, Human Resources (CUPE)
P. Elsworth, Officer, Information
pelsworth@sjsd.net
B. Neufeld, Officer, Purchasing
bneufeld@sjsd.net
Michael J. Friesen, Secretary-Treasurer

Winnipeg: Seven Oaks School Division
830 Powers St., Winnipeg, MB R2V 4E7, Canada
Tel: 204-586-8061; _Fax:_ 204-589-2504
communitybeginshere@7oaks.org
www.7oaks.org
Enrollment: 8950
Brian O'Leary, Superintendent

Winnipeg: Winnipeg School Division
1577 Wall St. East, Winnipeg, MB R3E 2S5, Canada
Tel: 204-775-0231; _Fax:_ 204-772-6464
adminofc@wsd1.org
ww.wsd1.org
Grades: Pre-K.-12 _Enrollment:_ 32000
Pauline Clarke, Chief Supt.
pclarke@wsd1.org
Rene Appelmans, Sec.-Treas.
rappelmans@wsd1.org
Val Georges, Dir., Aboriginal Ed., 204-788-0203, fax: 204-772-3911
vgeorges@wsd1.org

First Nations

***Ebb & Flow:* Ebb & Flow Eduction Authority**
P.O. Box 160
Ebb & Flow, MB R0L 0R0
Tel: 204-448-2438; *Fax:* 204-448-2393
eandf@mts.net
Number of Schools: 1 *Grades:* Elementary - Secondary *Note:* Ebb & Flow School. The Ebb & Flow Eduction Authority serves the Ebb & Flow First Nation in Manitoba
Arlene Mousseau, Director, Education

***Gods River:* Amos Okemow Memorial Education Authority**
Building 1D
103, Gods River, MB R0B 0N0, Canada
Tel: 204-366-2070; *Fax:* 204-366-2105
Grades: Kindergarten - 9 *Enrollment:* 170 *Note:* The Amos Okemow Memorial Education Authority serves the Manto Sipi Cree Nation through operation of the Amos Okemow Memorial School. To continue their secondary school education, students must leave the community.
A. Jane Tuesday, Director, Education
ajanet25@hotmail.com
Alan Pogson, Principal

***Oxford House:* Oxford House First Nation Board of Education**
General Delivery, Oxford House, MB R0B 1C0
Tel: 204-538-2051
Number of Schools: 2 *Grades:* Elementary - S4 *Enrollment:* 675 *Note:* Oxford House Elementary School & 1972 Memorial High School. The Oxford House First Nation Board of Education serves the Bunibonibee Cree Nation of Oxford House, which is situated 600 km north of Winnipeg, Manitoba.
Alvin Grieves, Director, Education, Oxford House First Nation Board of Ed.
argrieves@hotmail.com

***Pelican Rapids:* Sapotaweyak Education Authority**
General Delivery, Pelican Rapids, MB R0L 1L0
Tel: 204-587-2045; *Fax:* 204-587-2341
Number of Schools: 1 *Grades:* Nursery - 12 *Enrollment:* 350 *Number of Employees:* 50 *Note:* Neil Dennis Kematch Memorial School. The Sapotaweyak Education Authority is responsible for the provision of education for the Sapotaweyak Cree Nation, near the towns of Swan River & The Pas in Manitoba.
Diane Genaille, Director, Education
school@ndkms.com

***Pine Falls:* Sagkeeng Education Authority**
P.O. Box 1610
Pine Falls, MB R0E 1M0, Canada
Tel: 204-367-2287; *Fax:* 204-367-4315
Toll-Free: 1-866-878-2911
Number of Schools: 3 *Grades:* Elementary - Secondary *Note:* Anicinabe Community School; Sagkeeng Junior High School; & Sagkeeng Anicinabe High School
Eva Courchene, Education Director
Alan Courchene, Principal, Sagkeeng Anicinabe High School, 204-367-2243, fax: 204-367-4566
Rick Fewchuck, Principal, Anicinabe Community School, 204-367-2285, fax: 204-367-9205
Claude Guimond, Principal, Sagkeeng Junior High School, 204-367-2588, fax: 204-367-9231

***Winnipeg:* Southeast Tribal Division for Schools Inc.**
#301, 208 Edmonton St., Winnipeg, MB R3C 1R7
Tel: 204-943-7412; *Fax:* 204-947-8386

Schools: Specialized

First Nations

***Beulah:* Chan Kagha Otina Dakota Wayawa Tipi School**
P.O. Box 40
Beulah, MB R0M 0B0, Canada
Tel: 204-568-4757; *Fax:* 204-568-4762
www.frontiersd.mb.ca
Grades: birdtailschool@gmail.ca *Enrollment:* 130 *Note:* The Chan Kagha Otina Dakota Wayawa Tipi School serves the Birdtail Sioux Dakota Nation. It is part of Manitoba's Frontier School Division.
Karen Crozier, Superintendent, Frontier School Division (Dauphin Area), 204-638-6839
jacqueline_birdtail@yahoo.ca
Michael Gamblin, Principal

***Birch River:* Chief Charles Thomas Audy Memorial School**
P.O. Box 307
Birch River, MB R0L 0E0, Canada
Tel: 204-236-4783; *Fax:* 204-236-4779
Grades: Nursery - 8 *Note:* Chief Charles Thomas Audy Memorial School serves the Wuskwi Sipihk First Nation.

***Bloodvein:* Miskooseepi School**
General Delivery, Bloodvein, MB R0C 0J0
Tel: 204-395-2012; *Fax:* 204-395-2189
Grades: Pre.-9
Stella Keller, Director, Education
Irene Rupp, Principal

***Camperville:* Pine Creek Indian Day School**
P.O. Box 130
973 Duck Bay Rd., Camperville, MB R0L 0J0
Tel: 204-524-2318; *Fax:* 204-524-2177
Grades: Pre.-11

***Crane River:* Donald Ahmo School**
P.O. Box 91
Crane River, MB R0L 0M0, Canada
Tel: 204-732-2548; *Fax:* 204-732-2753
Note: The Donald Ahmo School is a band-operated First Nation school which serves the O-Chi-Chak-Ko-Sipi First Nation in Crane River, Manitoba.
Peter McKay, Director, Education & Principal
mckay_pj@hotmail.com

***Cross Lake:* Mikisew Middle School**
P.O. Box 128
Cross Lake, MB R0B 0J0, Canada
Tel: 204-676-3030; *Fax:* 204-676-2798
www.mfnerc.org
Grades: 5-8
Peter McKay, Director of Education
pmckay@clea.mb.ca
Greg Halcrow, Principal

***Cross Lake:* Otter Nelson River School**
P.O. Box 38
Cross Lake, MB R0B 0J0
Tel: 204-676-2050; *Fax:* 204-676-2464
crosslakeeducation.homestead.com/ONR.html
Grades: Pre.-12 *Enrollment:* 1200
Peter McKay, Director, Education
pmckay@clea.mb.ca
Clarence Haney, Principal
chaney@clea.mb.ca

***Dakota Tipi:* Dakota Tipi School**
2000A Dakota Dr., Dakota Tipi, MB R1N 3P1, Canada
Tel: 204-857-7190
Enrollment: 60 *Note:* Located outside the city of Portage La Prairie, Manitoba, the Dakota Tipi School is a First Nations band operated school. The school serves the Dakota Tipi First Nation.

***Dominion City:* Ginew School**
Lot 60, Dominion City, MB R0A 2R0
Tel: 204-427-2490
Grades: Pre.-8 *Enrollment:* 121

***Easterville:* Chemawawin School**
P.O. Box 10
Easterville, MB R0C 0V0, Canada
Tel: 204-329-2115; *Fax:* 204-329-2214
Note: Located on the southern shore of Cedar Lake, 300 kilometres north of Winnipeg, Manitoba, the Chemawawin School provides education to the Chemawawin Cree Nation.
Melvin George, Director, Education
Amie Martin, Principal
amiemd@gmail.com

***Ebb & Flow:* Ebb & Flow School**
P.O. Box 160
Ebb & Flow, MB R0L 0R0, Canada
Tel: 204-448-2012; *Fax:* 204-448-2393
eandf@mts.net
Grades: Elementary - Secondary *Note:* The Ebb & Flow School is a band-operated school in Manitoba which provides education to the Ebb & Flow First Nation.
Paul Monchka, Principal

***Edwin:* Dakota Plains School**
P.O. Box 120
Edwin, MB R0H 0G0, Canada
Tel: 204-252-2895; *Fax:* 204-252-2188
Grades: Elementary *Note:* The Dakota Plains School serves the Dakota Plains Wahpeton Nation.
Donald R. Smoke, Director, Education

***Elphinstone:* Keeseekoowenin School**
P.O. Box 129
Elphinstone, MB R0J 0N0
Tel: 204-625-2062; *Fax:* 204-625-2418
keesee@mts.net
Grades: Pre.-8
Barry Bone, Director, Education
Derrick Campbell, Principal

***Fairford:* Pinaymootang School**
Fairford Reserve
Fairford, MB R0C 0X0, Canada
Tel: 204-659-2045; *Fax:* 204-659-2270
Grades: Pre.-12

***Fisher River:* Charles Sinclair School**
P.O. Box 109
Fisher River, MB R0C 1S0, Canada
Tel: 204-645-2206; *Fax:* 204-645-2614
www.csschool.mb.ca
Note: Part of the Fisher River Board of Education, Charles Sinclair School provides education to the Fisher River Cree Nation.
Davin Dumas, Principal, 204-645-2206, fax: 204-645-2614
davin@csschool.mb.ca
Jennifer Garson, Vice-Principal, 204-645-2206, fax: 204-645-2614
jennifer@csschool.mb.ca

***Garden Lake:* Kistiganwacheeng Elementary School**
General Delivery, Garden Lake, MB R0B 0T0, Canada
Tel: 204-456-2391; *Fax:* 204-456-2350
kistiganwacheengelementaryschool@knet.ca
Grades: K-6
Ernie McDougall, Director of Education
ernest.mcdougall@ghfn.ca

***Gillam:* Fox Lake Native Spiritual School**
P.O. Box 279
Gillam, MB R0B 0L0
Tel: 204-486-2307; *Fax:* 204-486-2606
Grades: K.-8

***God's Lake Narrows:* God's Lake Narrows First Nation School**
P.O. Box 284
God's Lake Narrows, MB R0B 0M0
Tel: 204-335-2003; *Fax:* 204-335-2440
www.glns.ca
Grades: Pre.-9 *Enrollment:* 400

***Gods River:* Amos Okemow Memorial School**
Building 1D
103, Gods River, MB R0B 0N0
Tel: 204-366-2312; *Fax:* 204-366-2105
Toll-Free: 866-896-4255
Grades: Kindergarten - 9 *Enrollment:* 170 *Note:* Under the direction of the Amos Okemow Memorial Education Authority, the Amos Okemow Memorial School serves the Manto Sipi Cree Nation. Students must leave the community to continue their secondary school education.

***Griswold:* Sioux Valley School**
P.O. Box 99
Griswold, MB R0M 0S0, Canada
Tel: 204-855-2536; *Fax:* 204-855-3204
kcnabess@hotmail.com
Grades: Pre.-12
Kevin Nabess, Principal, Director of Education

***Gypsumville:* Dauphin River School**
P.O. Box 140
Gypsumville, MB R0C 1J0, Canada
Tel: 204-659-5268; *Fax:* 204-659-5790
Grades: Elementary *Note:* Dauphin River First Nation is located at the junction of Dauphin River & Lake Winnipeg. A Dauphin River Mature Student Program is also available.

***Gypsumville:* Lake St. Martin School**
P.O. Box 2020
Gypsumville, MB R0C 1J0, Canada
Tel: 204-659-2699; *Fax:* 204-659-5739
Grades: Nursery - 9 *Enrollment:* 120 *Note:* The Lake St. Martin School provides elementary education to the Lake St. Martin First Nation in Manitoba's Interlake Region.
Roselyn Beardy, Principal

***Gypsumville:* Little Saskatchewan H.A.G.M.E. School**
P.O. Box 5050
Gypsumville, MB R0C 1J0, Canada
Tel: 204-659-2672; *Fax:* 204-659-5763
saskatchewanlittle@yahoo.ca
Grades: JK-10

Jerry Sumner, Director, Education
Pat Anderson, Principal

Hodgson: Lawrence Sinclair Memorial School
P.O. Box 359
Hodgson, MB R0C 1N0, Canada
Tel: 204-394-2314; *Fax:* 204-394-2431
lawrencesinclairmemorialschool@hotmail.com
Grades: Nursery - 10 *Note:* Lawrence Sinclair Memorial School is a band operated school which serves members of the Kinonjeoshtegon First Nation.
Adeline Traverse, Principal

Island Lake: Garden Hill First Nations High School
General Delivery, Island Lake, MB R0B 0T0, Canada
Tel: 204-456-2886; *Fax:* 204-456-2894
Grades: 7-12

Lac Brochet: Petit Casimir Memorial School
General Delivery, Lac Brochet, MB R0B 2E0
pcms@gmail.com
www.pcmschool.ca
Grades: Kindergarten - 8 *Note:* Petit Casimir Memorial School is a Northlands Dene First Nation School. The Dene culture, heritage, & language are integrated in education.
Gerard Butt, Principal
Pierre Bernier, Vice-Principal

Marius: Isaac Beaulieu Memorial School
P.O. Box 108
Marius, MB R0H 0T0
Tel: 204-843-2407; *Fax:* 204-843-2269
trustssaints.ca/ibms-newsletter.htm
Grades: Pre.-12
George Beaulieu, Director, Education
george_beaulieu@msn.com
Colleen West, Principal
colleen_62@yahoo.com

Nelson House: Nisichawayasihk Neyo Ohtinwak
General Delivery, Nelson House, MB R0B 1A0, Canada
Tel: 204-484-2095; *Fax:* 204-484-2257
Grades: 9-12
William Elvis Thomas, Director of Education

Nelson House: Otetiskewin Kiskinwamahtowekamik
General Delivery, Nelson House, MB R0B 1A0, Canada
Tel: 204-484-2242; *Fax:* 204-484-2002
Grades: Pre.-8

O'Hanly: Little Black River School
General Delivery, O'Hanly, MB R0E 1K0, Canada
Tel: 204-367-8298; *Fax:* 204-367-2266
Grades: Kindergarten - 12 *Enrollment:* 242 *Note:* Members of the Little Black River First Nation are educated at the Little Black River School in O'Hanley, Manitoba. The First Nation community is situated approximately 150 kilometres north of Winnipeg.
Sheldon Kent, Chief

Opaskwayak: Joe A. Ross School
P.O. Box 10160
136 Waller Rd., Opaskwayak, MB R0B 2J0
Tel: 204-623-4286; *Fax:* 204-623-4442
www.joeaross-school.ca
Grades: Pre.-6
Bev Fontaine, Director, Education
bfontaine@opaseducation.ca
Karon McGillivary, Principal
karon.mcgillivary@opased.com

Oxford House: 1972 Memorial High School
General Delivery, Oxford House, MB R0B 1C0, Canada
Tel: 204-538-2020; *Fax:* 204-538-2075
Toll-Free: 1-888-377-8520
www.ohboe.ca
Other Information: Oxford House First Nation Bd. of Ed., Phone: 204-538-2051
Grades: 7 - S4 *Enrollment:* 225 *Note:* Under the Oxford House First Nation Board of Education, the 1972 Memorial High School serves the Bunibonibee Cree Nation of Oxford House.
Alvin Grieves, Director, Education, Oxford House First Nation Board of Ed.
argrieves@hotmail.com
Lawrence Einarsson, Principal
l.einarsson@hotmail.com

Oxford House: Oxford House Elementary School
General Delivery, Oxford House, MB R0B 1C0, Canada
Tel: 204-538-2318; *Fax:* 204-538-2782
Toll-Free: 1-888-377-8520
www.ohboe.ca
Other Information: Oxford House First Nation Bd. of Ed., Phone: 204-538-2051
Grades: Elementary *Enrollment:* 450 *Note:* Under the Oxford House First Nation Board of Education, the Oxford House Elementary School serves the Bunibonibee Cree Nation of Oxford House.
Alvin Grieves, Director, Education, Oxford House First Nation Board of Ed.
argrieves@hotmail.com
Wilfred Wood, Principal
wilfred.wood@ohboe.ca

Peguis First Nation: Peguis Central School
P.O. Box 609
Peguis First Nation, MB R0C 3J0, Canada
Tel: 204-645-2359; *Fax:* 204-645-2189
Toll-Free: 866-552-0166
www.peguisfirstnation.ca/peguiscentralschool.html
Grades: 6-12

Pelican Rapids: Neil Dennis Kematch Memorial School (NDKMS)
General Delivery, Pelican Rapids, MB R0L 1L0, Canada
Tel: 204-587-2045; *Fax:* 204-587-2341
school@ndkms.com
www.ndkms.com
Grades: Nursery - 12 *Enrollment:* 350 *Note:* The Neil Dennis Kematch Memorial School serves the citizens of Sapotaweyak Cree First Nation in a community located approximately 120 kilometres north of Swan River, Manitoba. The school is administered by the Sapotaweyak Education Authority.
Lorna Carter, Principal
principal@ndkms.com

Pine Falls: Anicinabe Community School
P.O. Box 219
Pine Falls, MB R0E 1M0
Tel: 204-367-2285; *Fax:* 204-367-9205
Note: Anicinabe Community School serves the Sagkeeng First Nation. It operates under the direction of the Sagkeeng Education Authority.
Rick Fewchuck, Principal

Pine Falls: Sagkeeng Anicinabe High School
P.O. Box 1610
Pine Falls, MB R0E 1M0
Tel: 204-367-2243; *Fax:* 204-367-4566
Grades: Secondary *Note:* The Sagkeeng Education Authority operates the Sagkeeng Anicinabe High School, which educates secondary school students of the Sagkeeng First Nation.
Alan Courchene, Principal

Pine Falls: Sagkeeng Junior High School
P.O. Box 1610
Pine Falls, MB R0E 1M0
Tel: 204-367-2588; *Fax:* 204-367-9231
Note: Sagkeeng Junior High School serves the Sagkeeng First Nation. The school operates under the Sagkeeng Education Authority.
Claude Guimond, Principal

Pipestone: Wambdi Iyotaka School
P.O. Box 146
Pipestone, MB R0M 1T0, Canada
Tel: 204-854-2975; *Fax:* 204-854-2933
Note: The Wambdi Iyotaka School serves members of the Canupawakpa Dakota Nation in Manitoba.
Anna Bone, Principal

Portage la Prairie: Long Plain School
P.O. Box 430
Portage la Prairie, MB R1N 3B7
Tel: 204-252-2326; *Fax:* 204-252-2786
Grades: Pre.-9
Liz Merrick, Director, Education
Morris Pelletier, Principal
morris_john22@hotmail.com

Pukatawagan: Sakastew School
P.O. Box 319
Pukatawagan, MB R0B 1G0, Canada
Tel: 204-553-2163; *Fax:* 204-553-2225
doriscastel@hotmail.com
Grades: K.-12
Doris Castel, Principal
Jackie Ferlund, Director of Education
ferlandjackie@hotmail.com

Red Sucker Lake: Red Sucker Lake School
General Delivery, Red Sucker Lake, MB R0B 1H0
Tel: 204-469-5302; *Fax:* 204-469-5436
Grades: Pre.-12
Leonard McDougall, Director, Education
Wesley Harper, Principal

Scanterbury: Sergeant Tommy Prince School
P.O. Box 179
Scanterbury, MB R0E 1W0
Tel: 204-766-2636; *Fax:* 204-766-2809
Grades: K.-12
Wendell Sinclair, Director, Education
wsinclair@stpschool.ca
Marie Zahorodny, Principal
stpadmin@stpschool.ca

Shamattawa: Abraham Beardy Memorial School
General Delivery, Shamattawa, MB R0B 1K0, Canada
Tel: 204-565-2022; *Fax:* 204-565-2122
Grades: Kindergarten - 10 *Enrollment:* 350 *Note:* Abraham Beardy Memorial School serves the Cree First Nation of Shamattawa. To attend grades 11 & 12, students must enroll in educational institutions outside the community.
Ron Miles, Director, Education
Roberto Romero, Principal
r_romero@hotmail.com

Shortdale: Chief Clifford Lynxleg Anishinabe School
General Delivery, Shortdale, MB R0L 1W0, Canada
Tel: 204-546-2641; *Fax:* 204-546-3120
Enrollment: 60 *Number of Employees:* 13 *Note:* Chief Clifford Lynxleg Anishinabe School is located on the Tootinawaziibeeng (Valley River) Reserve, where it provides education to the Tootinaowaziibeeng First Nation.
Stan Furman, Director, Education, & Principal
cclas@live.ca
Willo-Dawn Lynxleg, Secretary

Split Lake: Chief Sam Cook Mahmuwee Education Centre
General Delivery, Split Lake, MB R0B 1P0, Canada
Tel: 204-342-2134; *Fax:* 204-342-2139
Grades: Nursery - 12 *Note:* Chief Sam Cook Mahmuwee Education Centre serves the Tataskweyak Cree Nation. The Tataskweyak reserve is located approximately 150 kilometres northeast of Thompson, Manitoba.
Alfred Beardy, Director, Education
Dan Beardy, Principal, Grades 7 - 12
Thelma Spence, Principal, Nursery - Grade 6
Blake Symons, Principal, Middle Years

St Theresa Point: St. Theresa Point School
General Delivery, St Theresa Point, MB R0B 1J0, Canada
Tel: 204-462-2600; *Fax:* 204-462-2341
Grades: K.-12

Swan Lake: Indian Springs School
P.O. Box 145
Swan Lake, MB R0G 2S0
Tel: 204-836-2332; *Fax:* 204-836-2317
Toll-Free: 866-786-7841
isprings@mts.net
www.swanlakefirstnation.ca/iss.html
Grades: Pre.-8
Donovan Mann, Principal & Director, Education

Tadoule Lake: Peter Yassie Memorial School
General Delivery, Tadoule Lake, MB R0B 2C0
Tel: 204-684-2279; *Fax:* 204-684-2130
Note: Peter Yassie Memorial School is a Sayisi Dene First Nation school.
Betty Bickell, Director, Education
Lawrence Berger, Principal
bergerlawrence@hotmail.com

Vogar: Lake Manitoba School
P.O. Box 1250
Vogar, MB R0C 3C0, Canada
Tel: 204-768-2728; *Fax:* 204-768-2194
Grades: Nursery - 8 *Note:* Lake Manitoba School provides education to the Lake Manitoba First Nation.
Freda Missayabit, Principal

Wasagamack: George Knott School
P.O. Box 82
Wasagamack, MB R0B 1Z0
Tel: 204-457-2485; *Fax:* 204-457-2273
Grades: Pre.-12
Percy Harper, Director, Education
Adam Knott, Principal

Waywayseecappo: Waywayseecappo Community School
P.O. Box 9
Waywayseecappo, MB R0J 1S0, Canada
Tel: 204-859-2811; *Fax:* 204-859-2992
wayway school@yahoo.ca
Grades: Nursery - 8 *Enrollment:* 457 *Number of Employees:* 21 teachers; 6 teacher assistants; 8 bus drivers; 3 custodians *Note:*

The Waywayseecappo Community School is a band operated elementary school, which provides education to members of Manitoba's Waywayseecappo First Nation. The First Nation community is situated approximately thirty-four kilometres east of Russell. Secondary school students from Waywayseecappo First Nation are transported to Russell's Major Pratt School.
Patrick Anderson, Principal

***York Landing:* George Saunders Memorial School**
General Delivery, York Landing, MB R0B 2B0, Canada
Tel: 204-341-2118; *Fax:* 204-341-2235
gsmschool@hotmail.com
Grades: K.-8 *Enrollment:* 107

Hearing Impaired

***Winnipeg:* Manitoba School for the Deaf**
242 Stradford St., Winnipeg, MB R2Y 2C9
Tel: 204-945-8934; *Fax:* 204-945-1767
principal@msd.ca
www.msd.ca
TTY: 204-945-8934
Grades: JK-12
Kathy Melnyk, Principal
kmelnyk@msd.ca

Special Education

***Brandon:* Child & Adolescent Treatment Centre (CATC)**
1240 - 10th St., Brandon, MB R7A 7L6
Tel: 204-727-3445; *Fax:* 204-727-3451
Toll-Free: 866-403-5459
www.brandonrha.mb.ca/en/Mental_Health/CATC
Other Information: After Hours Phone: 204-571-7278
Grades: 4-12 *Note:* The CATC provides mental health services to children, including a day program, Crisis Stabilization Unit, Early Intervention Services, & educational services
Brian Schoonbaert, CEO, Brandon Regional Health Authority, 204-578-2301
schoonbaertb@brandonrha.mb.ca
Jayne Troop, VP, Community Services & Long-Term Care, 204-578-2304
troopj@brandonrha.mb.ca
Doreen Lawrence, Executive Assistant, 204-578-2300
lawrenced@brandonrha.mb.ca

***Portage la Prairie:* Gladys Cook Educational Centre**
P.O. Box 1342
2 River Rd., Portage la Prairie, MB R1N 3A9
Tel: 204-239-3029; *Fax:* 204-239-3025
Grades: 1-12

***St Norbert:* Behavioural Health Foundation**
P.O. Box 250
35 av de la Digue, St Norbert, MB R3V 1L6, Canada
Tel: 204-269-3430; *Fax:* 204-269-8049
info@bhf.ca
www.bhf.ca/index.html
Grades: K-S4 *Note:* The Behavioural Health Foundation provides long term residential addictions treatment programming for men, women, teens and family units experiencing a variety of addiction problems and co-occurring mental health concerns.
Christy Nichols, Contact, 204-269-3430
christyn@bhf.ca

***Winnipeg:* Manitoba Youth Centre**
170 Doncaster St., Winnipeg, MB R3N 1X9, Canada
Tel: 204-475-2010; *Fax:* 204-945-3112
Note: The Manitoba Youth Centre is a correctional facility for Manitoba youth charged as young offenders.

***Winnipeg:* Marymound School**
442 Scotia St., Winnipeg, MB R2V 1X4, Canada
Tel: 204-336-5285; *Fax:* 204-338-4690
school@marymound.com
www.marymound.com/wp/marymound-school
Grades: Elem.-11
Mark Miles, Principal

***Winnipeg:* St. Amant School**
440 River Rd., Winnipeg, MB R2M 3Z9, Canada
Tel: 204-256-4301; *Fax:* 204-257-4349
www.stamant.mb.ca
Grades: K.-12

Schools: Independent & Private

Protestant

***Austin:* Edrans Christian School**
P.O. Box 1
RR #1, Austin, MB R0H 0C0, Canada
Tel: 204-466-2865; *Fax:* 204-466-2994
www.echurchnet.ca
Grades: K.-12
Dwight Kinley, Contact

***Stonewall:* Faith Academy - Stonewall Campus**
P.O. Box 1669
539 - 4th Ave. South, Stonewall, MB R0C 2Z0, Canada
Tel: 204-467-5833; *Fax:* 204-467-5833
www.faithacademy.ca
Grades: K.-8
Bill Cavey, Executive Director
FA_ceo@shaw.ca

***Winnipeg:* Faith Academy - Winnipeg Campus**
437 Matheson Ave., Winnipeg, MB R2W 0E1, Canada
Tel: 204-582-3400; *Fax:* 204-582-2616
www.faithacademy.ca
Grades: K.-12 *Enrollment:* 520 *Note:* Faith Academy is a conservative, evangelical, Christian, revival-based educational institution open to any Manitoba student willing and able to follow the established school guide. Winnipeg Middle School located at 600 Jefferson Ave., (204) 338-6150; Pritchard Campus located at 220 Pritchard Ave., (204) 589-6885.
Bill Cavey, Executive Director
FA_ceo@shaw.ca

Catholic

***Winnipeg:* Holy Cross School**
300 Dubuc St., Winnipeg, MB R2H 1E4, Canada
Tel: 204-237-4936; *Fax:* 204-237-7433
Grades: K.-8 *Enrollment:* 159
John Talaga, Principal

Independent & Private Schools

***Altona:* Sunflower Valley Christian School**
P.O. Box 2484
Altona, MB R0G 0B0, Canada
Tel: 204-324-1564; *Fax:* 204-327-5505
Grades: 1-9

***Arborg:* Interlake Mennonite Fellowship School**
P.O. Box 388
Arborg, MB R0C 0A0, Canada
Tel: 204-364-2328
Grades: 1-12

***Arborg:* Lake Centre Mennonite Fellowship School**
P.O. Box 838
Arborg, MB R0C 0A0, Canada
Tel: 204-364-2201; *Fax:* 204-364-2272
Grades: K.-9

***Arborg:* Morweena Christian School (MCS)**
P.O. Box 1030
Arborg, MB R0C 0A0, Canada
Tel: 204-364-2466; *Fax:* 204-364-3117
info@morweenaschool.org
www.morweenaschool.org
Grades: Kindergarten - 12 *Enrollment:* 135
Tim Reimer, Principal

***Austin:* Austin Christian Academy**
P.O. Box 460
Austin, MB R0H 0C0, Canada
Tel: 204-637-2303; *Fax:* 204-637-2529
Grades: Kindergarten - 12 *Enrollment:* 50

***Austin:* Austin Mennonite School**
P.O. Box 267
Austin, MB R0H 0C0, Canada
Tel: 204-637-2008
Grades: 1 - 12

***Austin:* Pine Creek School**
Pine Creek Colony
P.O. Box 370
Austin, MB R0H 0C0, Canada
Tel: 204-466-2925; *Fax:* 204-466-2698
Grades: K.-10

***Austin:* Pine Creek School**
P.O. Box 74
Austin, MB ROH OCO, Canada
Tel: 204-385-3025
Grades: K.-10

***Beausejour:* Willow Grove School**
P.O. Box 59
Beausejour, MB R0E 0C0
Tel: 204-268-4035; *Fax:* 204-268-9452
Grades: 1-9

***Birnie:* Shady Oak Christian School**
P.O. Box 14
Birnie, MB R0J 0J0, Canada
Tel: 204-966-3477; *Fax:* 204-966-3479
www.shadyoak.net
Grades: 1-9

***Brandon:* Christian Heritage School**
Heritage Campus
2025 - 26 St., Brandon, MB R7B 3Y2
Tel: 204-725-3209; *Fax:* 204-728-9641
office@chsbrandon.ca
www.chsbrandon.ca
Grades: K.-8 *Enrollment:* 135
Bryce Neufeld, President, Christian Heritage School Society
Bryan Schroeder, Principal
principal@chsbrandon.ca

***Carman:* Dufferin Christian School**
P.O. Box 1450
Carman, MB R0G 0J0
Tel: 204-745-2278; *Fax:* 204-745-3441
office@dufferinchristian.ca
www.dufferinchristian.ca
Grades: K.-12
Arie Veenendaal, Chair
arieveenendaal@dufferinchristian.ca
Andy Huisman, Principal
andyhuisman@dufferinchristian.ca

***Cartwright:* Cartwright Community Independent School (CCIS)**
P.O. Box 419
Cartwright, MB R0K 0L0, Canada
Tel: 204-529-2357; *Fax:* 204-529-2455
Grades: 12 (Senior 4)

***Cartwright:* Rock Lake School**
P.O. Box 69
Cartwright, MB R0K 0L0, Canada
Tel: 204-529-2349; *Fax:* 204-529-2184
Grades: 1 - 9

***Elie:* Huron Christian Academy**
Elie, MB R0H 0H0, Canada
Tel: 204-353-4120
Grades: 1-12

***Elie:* Milltown Academy**
P.O. Box 250
Elie, MB R0H 0H0, Canada
Tel: 204-353-4111; *Fax:* 204-353-2224
Grades: Kindergarten - 12

***Elm Creek:* Wingham HB School**
P.O. Box 45
RR #1, Elm Creek, MB R0G 0N0, Canada
Tel: 204-436-3231; *Fax:* 204-436-3230
winghamhbschool.com
Grades: K.-12
James Waldner, Principal
james@winghamhbschool.com

Der Wingham Bote
winghamhbschool.com/student_work.html

***Elma:* Riverside School**
P.O. Box 136
Elma, MB R0E 0Z0, Canada
Tel: 204-348-2686; *Fax:* 204-348-7181
Grades: 1 - 9

***Elma:* Twin Rivers Country School**
P.O. Box 30
Elma, MB R0E 0Z0, Canada
Tel: 204-426-5611; *Fax:* 204-426-5611
Grades: 1 - 9

***Fairford:* Interlake Christian Academy**
Fairford, MB R0C 0X0, Canada
Tel: 204-659-5359
Grades: 1-10

***Grandview:* Poplar Grove School**
P.O. Box 70
Grandview, MB R0L 0Y0, Canada
Tel: 204-546-2691
Grades: 1-9

***Gretna:* Mennonite Collegiate Institute**
P.O. Box 250
Gretna, MB R0G 0V0
Tel: 204-327-5891; *Fax:* 204-327-5872
Toll-Free: 877-624-2583
info@mciblues.net
www.mciblues.net
Grades: 9-12 *Enrollment:* 155
Darryl Loewen, Principal
darrylloewen@mciblues.net

***Grunthal:* Mennonite Christian Academy**
P.O. Box 149
Grunthal, MB R0A 0R0
Tel: 204-434-9315
Grades: K.-12

***Hodgson:* Hodgson Christian Academy**
P.O. Box 220
Hodgson, MB R0C 1N0, Canada
Tel: 204-372-8483
Grades: 1-12

***Horndean:* Horndean Christian Day School**
P.O. Box 79
Horndean, MB R0G 0Z0, Canada
Tel: 204-829-3354
Grades: 1-10

***Kenville:* Riverdale School**
RR#1, Kenville, MB R0L 0Z0, Canada
Tel: 204-539-2660
Grades: 1 - 9

***Kenville:* Solid Rock Christian School**
P.O. Box 1239
Kenville, MB R0L 1Z0, Canada
Tel: 204-734-2651
Grades: K.-12

***Killarney:* Lakeside Christian School**
P.O. Box 894
Killarney, MB R0K 1G0
Tel: 204-523-8240; *Fax:* 204-523-8351
ics@mts.net
Grades: K.-10
Nancy Reimer, Principal

***Kleefeld:* New Hope Christian School**
P.O. Box 120
Kleefeld, MB R0A 0V0, Canada
Tel: 204-377-4204
Grades: 1 - 12

***Kleefeld:* Wild Rose School**
P.O. Box 167
Kleefeld, MB R0A 0V0
Tel: 204-377-4778; *Fax:* 204-377-4778
Grades: 1-9

***Kola:* Kola Community School**
P.O. Box 312
Kola, MB R0M 1B0, Canada
Tel: 204-556-2347; *Fax:* 204-556-2425
kola.flbsd.mb.ca
Grades: K.-9 *Number of Employees:* 4 teachers; 3 administrative; 2 custodial; 1 bus driver *Note:* Kola School is a Grade One to Grade Nine School within Fort La Bosse School Division. They offer complete programming in 3 combined classrooms with the following divisions: Grade One to Grade Three, Grade Four to Grade Six, and Grade Seven to Grade Nine.
Lance Barrate, Principal, 204-748-1605

***Lorette:* Daystar Christian Academy**
PO Box 5, Group 100, RR#2, Lorette, MB R0A 0Y0
Tel: 204-878-3044
Grades: 1-12

***MacGregor:* H.B. Community Baker Colony School**
P.O. Box 40
MacGregor, MB R0H 0R0, Canada
Tel: 204-252-2178; *Fax:* 204-252-2381
Grades: K.-12

***Minnedosa:* Odanah Colony School**
P.O. Box 990
Minnedosa, MB R0J 1E0, Canada
Tel: 204-867-5074; *Fax:* 204-867-2037
Grades: K.-12

***Neepawa:* Living Hope School**
P.O. Box 2158
Neepawa, MB R0J 1H0, Canada
Tel: 204-966-3274
Grades: 3-12

***Pine Falls:* Christian Faith Academy**
P.O. Box 130
Pine Falls, MB R0E 1M0, Canada
Tel: 204-367-2056; *Fax:* 204-367-2056
Grades: 1 - 12

***Pine River:* Pine River School**
P.O. Box 242
Pine River, MB R0L 1M0, Canada
Tel: 204-263-2617; *Fax:* 204-263-2184
Grades: K.-9

***Plum Coulee:* Christ Full Gospel Academy**
P.O. Box 107
75 Elm St., Plum Coulee, MB R0G 1R0, Canada
Tel: 204-829-3506; *Fax:* 204-829-7937
cfgf@mts.net
www.christfullgospel.org/main/academy.html
Other Information: 204-829-7937 (Phone, Pastor's study)
Grades: Kindergarten - 12 *Note:* Christ Full Gospel Academy uses the Accelerated Christian Education curriculum.

***Plum Coulee:* Prairie Mennonite School**
P.O. Box 50
Plum Coulee, MB R0G 1R0
Tel: 204-829-3336
Grades: K.-12

***Portage la Prairie:* Airport Colony School**
P.O. Box 967
Portage la Prairie, MB R1N 3C4, Canada
Tel: 204-274-2412
Grades: K.-12 *Note:* Location: NE 2-13-8 W, MacDonald, MB.

***Portage la Prairie:* Lighthouse Christian School**
P.O. Box 1360
Portage la Prairie, MB R1N 3N9, Canada
Tel: 204-428-5332; *Fax:* 204-428-5386
Grades: K.-12

***Portage la Prairie:* Westpark School**
P.O. Box 91
2375 Saskatchewan Ave. West, Portage la Prairie, MB R1N 3B2, Canada
Tel: 204-857-3726
office@westparkschool.com
www.westparkschool.com
www.facebook.com/westparkschool
Grades: K.-12 (Senior 1 - 4) *Enrollment:* 220 *Note:* The school is a ministry of Portage Alliance Church.
Lydia Stoesz, B.Ed., M.Div, Principal
Merrill Friesen, B.Ed., Interim Principal

***Roblin:* Parkland Christian School**
P.O. Box 480
Roblin, MB R0L 1P0, Canada
Tel: 204-937-2870
Grades: 1-9

***Rosenort:* Prairie View School**
P.O. Box 117
112 River Rd. North, Rosenort, MB R0G 1W0, Canada
Tel: 204-746-8837; *Fax:* 204-746-8517
Grades: 1 - 9

***Sinclair:* Stony Creek School**
P.O. Box 5
Sinclair, MB R0M 2A0, Canada
Tel: 204-662-4431; *Fax:* 204-662-4539
Grades: 1-9

***Sperling:* Silverwinds School**
P.O. Box 130
Sperling, MB R0G 2M0, Canada
Tel: 204-626-3378; *Fax:* 204-626-3397
Grades: K.-12

***Ste. Anne:* Greenland School**
P.O. Box 224
RR#1, Ste. Anne, MB R5H 1R1, Canada
Tel: 204-355-4922; *Fax:* 204-355-9280
Grades: 1-9

***Steinbach:* Church of God Sunrise Academy**
P.O. Box 3368
Steinbach, MB R5G 1P6, Canada
Tel: 204-434-6643; *Fax:* 204-326-6681
Grades: K.-12

***Steinbach:* Country View School**
P.O. Box 3910
Steinbach, MB R5G 1P9, Canada
Tel: 204-326-1481; *Fax:* 204-326-4788
Number of Schools: 1 *Grades:* 2-9 *Enrollment:* 22 *Number of Employees:* 2
Phyllis Wohlgemuth, Principal, 306-326-4968
Tim Wiebe, Vice-Principal, 306-326-1413, fax: 204-392-3288

***Steinbach:* Steinbach Christian Academy**
P.O. Box 20629
Steinbach, MB R5G 1S1, Canada
Tel: 204-326-5553
Grades: K.-12

***Steinbach:* Steinbach Christian High School**
50 Pth 12 North, Steinbach, MB R5G 1T4, Canada
Tel: 204-326-3537; *Fax:* 204-326-5164
schs@schs.ca
www.schs.ca
Grades: 7-12 *Enrollment:* 161 *Note:* Christian High School with Mennonite affiliation

***Stonewall:* Northern Shield Academy**
P.O. Box 1039
Stonewall, MB R0C 2Z0, Canada
Tel: 204-467-5547; *Fax:* 204-467-2571
Grades: 6 - 12 *Enrollment:* 50 *Note:* This is a private Christian school.

***Stuartburn:* Border View Christian Day School**
P.O. Box 103
Stuartburn, MB R0A 2B0, Canada
Tel: 204-427-2932
Grades: 1-10

***Swan River:* Community Bible Fellowship Christian School**
P.O. Box 1630
Swan River, MB R0L 1Z0, Canada
Tel: 204-734-2174; *Fax:* 204-734-5706
Grades: K.-8

***Wawanesa:* Green Acres Colony High School**
P.O. Box 190
Wawanesa, MB R0K 2G0, Canada
Tel: 204-824-2340; *Fax:* 204-824-2112
Grades: 9-12

***Winkler:* Grace Valley Mennonite Academy**
P.O. Box 839
Winkler, MB R6W 4A9, Canada
Tel: 204-829-3301; *Fax:* 204-829-3038
Grades: 1-12

***Winkler:* Schoenweise Christian School**
P.O. Box 663
Group 11, Winkler, MB R6W 4A1, Canada
Tel: 204-325-5401
Grades: 1-11

***Winkler:* Valley Mennonite Academy**
6 720 Norquay Dr., Winkler, MB R6W 4A1, Canada
Tel: 204-325-8172; *Fax:* 204-331-3199
Grades: Kindergarten - 12 *Enrollment:* 134 *Note:* Two private schools are operated by the Valley Mennonite Academy.

***Winnipeg:* Al-Hijra Islamic School (AOS)**
410 Desalaberry Ave., Winnipeg, MB R2L 0Y7
Tel: 204-489-1300; *Fax:* 204-489-1323
ais123@mts.net
www.alhijra.ca
Grades: Kindergarten - 9 *Enrollment:* 185 *Note:* Established in 1996, teaching at Al-Hijra Islamic School includes Arabic, Quranic, & Islamic studies.
Abdo El-Tassi, Board Chair
Abed Moussa, Principal
Khadijah Abdulkader, Arabid & Islam Teacher
Fouad Elmazini, Arabid & Islam Teacher

***Winnipeg:* Balmoral Hall School**
630 Westminster Ave., Winnipeg, MB R3C 3S1, Canada
Tel: 204-784-1600
www.balmoralhall.com
TTY: 1-866-373-2611
Grades: Nursery - 5 *Note:* Balmoral Hall School specializes in education for girls. It also offers a child care program for girls, aged 2 & 3.
Corrine Scott, Chair
Dr. Linda Schwartz, Head
Tina Alto, Director, Advancement, 204-784-1600
Pamela McGhie, Director, Admissions, 204-784-1621

Winnipeg: Beautiful Savior Lutheran School (BSLS)
52 Birchdale Ave., Winnipeg, MB R2H 1R9, Canada
Tel: 204-984-9600; *Fax:* 204-984-9607
admin@bsls.ca; admissions@bsls.ca; preschool@bsls.ca
www.bsls.ca
Grades: Nursery - 8 *Note:* Beautiful Savior Lutheran School also offers a daycare program & before & after school care.
Jennifer McCrea, Principal
Heather Burnett, Director, Child Care Services

Winnipeg: Calvin Christian School
Collegiate Campus
706 Day St., Winnipeg, MB R2C 1B6, Canada
Tel: 204-222-7910; *Fax:* 204-222-8511
www.calvinchristian.mb.ca
Other Information: 204-338-7981 (Elementary phone); 204-339-3280 (Elementary fax)
Grades: Kindergarten - 12
Rob Booy, Chair & Staff Liaison
David Taylor, Principal, Collegiate Campus
Hank Vande Kraats, Principal, Elementary Campus
Rod Harris, Vice Principal, Collegiate Campus
Maureen Vaags-Nyhof, Vice Principal, Elementary Campus

Winnipeg: Christ the King School
12 Lennox Ave., Winnipeg, MB R2M 1A6, Canada
Tel: 204-257-0027; *Fax:* 204-257-2129
www.ctkschool.ca
Grades: Junior Kindergarten - 8
Brian Steeves, Chair
Maria Coutu, Principal
Mrs. S. Finnigan, Accountant
Ms. S. Barnert, Administrative Secretary

Winnipeg: The Collegiate at the University of Winnipeg
515 Portage Ave., Winnipeg, MB R3B 2E9, Canada
Tel: 204-786-9221; *Fax:* 204-775-1942
collegiate@uwinnipeg.ca
www.uwinnipeg.ca/index/collegiate-index
Grades: 9 - 12 *Note:* The independent secondary school is a division of The University of Winnipeg.
Rick Martin, Dean, 204-786-9843
rc.martin@uwinnipeg.ca
Heather Singer, Associate Dean, 204-786-9258
h.singer@uwinnipeg.ca
Michael West, Associate Dean, 204-786-9392
m.west@uwinnipeg.ca
Tara Days, Registrar & Office Manager, 204-786-9901
t.dias@uwinnipeg.ca

Winnipeg: Gray Academy of Jewish Education
A100, 123 Doncaster St., Winnipeg, MB R3N 2B4, Canada
Tel: 204-477-7410; *Fax:* 204-477-7474
info@grayacademy.ca
www.grayacademy.ca
Grades: K.-12 *Note:* The largest independent Jewish day school in Western Canada. Co-educational. General subjects & Jewish studies programmes.
Rory Paul, Head of School

Winnipeg: Holy Ghost School
319 Selkirk Ave., Winnipeg, MB R2W 2L8
Tel: 204-582-1053; *Fax:* 204-582-4870
schooloffice@holyghost.ca
www.holyghostschool.ca
Grades: K.-8
Rev. Maciej Pajak, O.M.I., Pastor
David Hood, Principal

Winnipeg: Immaculate Heart of Mary School
650 Flora Ave., Winnipeg, MB R2W 2S5
Tel: 204-582-5698; *Fax:* 204-586-6698
ihms.mb.ca
Other Information: Alternate Phone: 204-589-2709
Grades: JK-8
Mike Mager, Chair
Rod Picklyk, Principal

Winnipeg: Immanuel Christian School
215 Rougeau Ave., Winnipeg, MB R2C 3Z9
Tel: 204-661-8937; *Fax:* 204-669-7013
office@immanuelchristian.ca
www.immanuelchristian.ca
Grades: K.-12 *Enrollment:* 181
Rob Dewitt, Chair
Peter Veenendaal, Principal

Winnipeg: Islamic Academy of Manitoba
Académie islamique du Manitoba
340 Provencher Blvd., Winnipeg, MB R2H 0G7, Canada
Tel: 204-231-4441; *Fax:* 204-231-3240
www.miaonline.org
www.facebook.com/pages/MIA-2011-2013/210028615746389
Grades: K.-6 *Note:* Program & instruction Arabic, English & French. Daily Qur'an studies.
Dr. Taib Soufi, Principal

Winnipeg: The King's School
851 Panet Rd., Winnipeg, MB R2K 4C9, Canada
Tel: 204-989-6581; *Fax:* 204-989-6584
www.thekingsschool.ca
Grades: Kindergarten - 12 *Enrollment:* 250 *Note:* The King's School is a co-educational school, which is a ministry of Gateway Christian Community Church.
Peter Todd, BA (Hons), PGCE, Principal

Winnipeg: The Laureate Academy
100 Villa Maria Pl., Winnipeg, MB R3V 1A9, Canada
Tel: 204-831-7107; *Fax:* 204-885-3217
www.laureateacademy.com
Grades: Kindergarten - 12

Winnipeg: Linden Christian School
877 Wilkes Ave., Winnipeg, MB R3P 1B8
Tel: 204-989-6730; *Fax:* 204-487-7068
www.lindenchristian.org
Grades: K.-12 *Enrollment:* 800
Gerry Bettig, Chair
Robert Charach, Principal
rcharach@lindenchristian.org

Winnipeg: Mennonite Brethren Collegiate Institute
180 Riverton Ave., Winnipeg, MB R2L 2E8
Tel: 204-667-8210; *Fax:* 204-661-5091
mbci.mb.ca
Grades: 6-12
Ken Opalko, Assistant Principal, Middle School
Fred Pauls, Assistant Principal, High School

Winnipeg: Montessori Learning Centre (MLC)
Asland School
170 Ashland Ave., Winnipeg, MB R3L 1L1, Canada
Tel: 204-475-1039; *Fax:* 204-452-4643
mlcmont@mts.net
www.mlcwinnipeg.ca
Grades: Preschool - Kindergarten *Note:* The Centre's preschool program is designed for children from age 3 to 5.

Winnipeg: Oholei Torah School
2095 Sinclair St., Winnipeg, MB R2V 3K2, Canada
Tel: 204-339-8737; *Fax:* 204-586-0487
rabbialtein@chabadwinnipeg.org
Grades: Gr. N.-8 *Enrollment:* 13

Winnipeg: Ohr Hatorah School
620 Brock St., Winnipeg, MB R3N 0Z4, Canada
Tel: 204-489-1147; *Fax:* 204-489-5899
Grades: Gr. N.-4

Winnipeg: Our Lady of Victory School
249 Arnold Ave., Winnipeg, MB R3L 0W4, Canada
Tel: 204-452-7632; *Fax:* 204-453-3081
olv@shawbiz.ca
www.victoryedu.com
Grades: Pre K.-8 *Enrollment:* 117
A. Cap, Principal

Winnipeg: Red River Valley Junior Academy (RRVJA)
56 Grey St., Winnipeg, MB R2L 1V3, Canada
Tel: 204-667-2383; *Fax:* 204-667-1396
info@rrvja.ca
www.rrvja.ca
Other Information: info@rrvja.ca
Grades: Junior Kindergarten - 10 *Note:* Red River Valley Junior Academy is owned & operated by the Seventh Day Adventist Church.
Ian Mighty, M.A., B.Ed., PBCE, Admin., Principal
imight@rrvja.ca
Daniel NcGuire, B.Ed., Vice Principal & Middle Years Specialist
dmcguire@rrvja.ca
Lora Troop, Administrative Assistant
ltoop@rrvja.ca

Winnipeg: St. Aidan's Christian School
418 Aberdeen Ave., Winnipeg, MB R2W 1V7, Canada
Tel: 204-586-6792; *Fax:* 204-582-4729
Grades: K.-8 *Enrollment:* 30

Winnipeg: St. Alphonsus School
343 Munroe Ave., Winnipeg, MB R2K 1H2, Canada
Tel: 204-667-6271; *Fax:* 204-663-4187
info@stalphonsusschool.ca
www.stalphonsusschool.ca
Grades: K.-8 *Enrollment:* 230

Winnipeg: St. Boniface Diocesan High School
282 Dubuc St., Winnipeg, MB R2H 1E4, Canada
Tel: 204-987-1560; *Fax:* 204-237-9891
admin@sbdhs.net
www.sbdhs.net
Grades: S1-S4 *Enrollment:* 150
Jeff Beaudin, Principal

Winnipeg: St. Charles Interparochial School
331 St. Charles St., Winnipeg, MB R3K 1T6, Canada
Tel: 204-837-1520; *Fax:* 204-837-2326
sec@stccs.ca
www.stccs.ca
Grades: K.-8 *Enrollment:* 206
Dr. Penny Parzyjagla, Principal

Winnipeg: St. Edward's School
836 Arlington St., Winnipeg, MB R3E 2E4, Canada
Tel: 204-774-8773; *Fax:* 204-775-0011
www.stedwards.ca
Grades: K.-6 *Enrollment:* 191
Linda Doyle, Principal
lindadoyle@mts.net

Winnipeg: St. Emile School
552 St. Anne's Rd., Winnipeg, MB R2M 3G4, Canada
Tel: 204-989-5020; *Fax:* 204-989-5026
www.stemileschool.ca
Grades: K.-8 *Enrollment:* 236

Winnipeg: St. Gerard School
40 Foster St., Winnipeg, MB R2L 1V7, Canada
Tel: 204-667-4862; *Fax:* 204-668-7932
stgerard@shaw.ca
Grades: Gr. N.-8 *Enrollment:* 240

Winnipeg: St. Ignatius School
239 Harrow St., Winnipeg, MB R3M 2Y3, Canada
Tel: 204-475-1386; *Fax:* 204-475-3961
school@stignatius.mb.ca
www.stignatius.mb.ca
Grades: K.-8 *Enrollment:* 245
G. Palahicky, Principal

Winnipeg: St. John Brebeuf School
605 Renfrew St., Winnipeg, MB R3N 1J8, Canada
Tel: 204-489-2115; *Fax:* 204-928-7455
schooloffice@sjbcommunity.ca
www.sjbcommunity.ca/school
Grades: K.-8 *Enrollment:* 221

Winnipeg: St. John's-Ravenscourt School
400 South Dr., Winnipeg, MB R3T 3K5, Canada
Tel: 204-477-2485; *Fax:* 204-477-2429
info@sjr.mb.ca
www.sjr.mb.ca
Grades: K.-12 *Enrollment:* 780

Winnipeg: St. Joseph the Worker School
505 Brewster St., Winnipeg, MB R2C 2W6, Canada
Tel: 204-222-1841; *Fax:* 204-222-1769
stjoesch@mts.net
www.stjosephtheworkerschool.ca
Grades: K.-6 *Enrollment:* 129
Brian Hargrave, Principal

Winnipeg: St. Mary's Academy
550 Wellington Cres., Winnipeg, MB R3M 0C1, Canada
Tel: 204-477-0244; *Fax:* 204-453-2417
www.stmarysacademy.mb.ca
Grades: 7-12 *Enrollment:* 550

Winnipeg: St. Mary's Montessori School Inc.
150 Pacific Ave., Winnipeg, MB R3B 3K8, Canada
Tel: 204-956-1622; *Fax:* 204-956-7088
Grades: Gr. N.-K. *Enrollment:* 74

Winnipeg: St. Maurice School
1639 Pembina Hwy., Winnipeg, MB R3T 2G6, Canada
Tel: 204-453-4020; *Fax:* 204-452-4050
admin@stmaurice.mb.ca
www.stmaurice.mb.ca
Grades: K.-12 *Enrollment:* 585
G. Caligiuri, Principal

***Winnipeg:* St. Paul's High School**
2200 Grant Ave., Winnipeg, MB R3P 0P8, Canada
Tel: 204-831-2300; *Fax:* 204-831-2340
contact-us@stpauls.mb.ca
www.stpauls.mb.ca
Grades: 9-12 *Enrollment:* 582 *Note:* Jesuit University prep school for boys
Tom Lussier, Principal

***Winnipeg:* Southeast College**
1301 Lee Blvd., Winnipeg, MB R3T 5W8, Canada
Tel: 204-261-3551; *Fax:* 204-269-7880
ilinklater@secollege.ca
www.secollege.ca
Grades: S1-S4
Irene Linklater, Principal

***Winnipeg:* Springs Christian Academy**
#1, 595 Lagimodiere Blvd., Winnipeg, MB R2J 3X2, Canada
Tel: 204-235-0863; *Fax:* 204-235-0390
www.springschurch.com/sca
Grades: K.-12 *Enrollment:* 689 *Note:* Affiliated with Springs Church
Darcy Bayne, Principal

***Winnipeg:* Twelve Tribes School**
89 East Gate, Winnipeg, MB R3C 2C2, Canada
Tel: 204-779-1118
Grades: 1 - 8

***Winnipeg:* Westgate Mennonite Collegiate**
86 West Gate, Winnipeg, MB R3C 2E1, Canada
Tel: 204-775-7111; *Fax:* 204-786-1651
www.westgatemennonite.ca
Grades: 7 - 12 *Enrollment:* 315 *Note:* The Christian school is based upon the Anabaptist Mennonite tradition.
Bob Hummelt, Principal

***Winnipeg:* Winnipeg Mennonite Elementary & Middle School**
250 Bedson St., Winnipeg, MB R3K 1R7
Tel: 204-885-1032; *Fax:* 204-897-4068
wmems@wmems.ca; bedson.office@wmems.ca
www.wmems.ca
Grades: K.-8 *Enrollment:* 400
John Sawatzky, Principal
john.sawatzky@wmems.ca

Schools
Winnipeg Mennonite Elementary School - Agassiz
26 Agassiz Dr., Winnipeg, MB R3T 2K7
Tel: 204-261-9637; *Fax:* 204-275-5181
agassiz.office@wmems.ca
Grades: K.-6
David Stoesz, Principal
david.stoesz@wmems.ca

***Winnipeg:* Winnipeg Montessori School Inc.**
1525 Willson Pl., Winnipeg, MB R3T 4H1, Canada
Tel: 204-452-3315; *Fax:* 204-452-3315
Grades: K.

***Winnipeg:* Winnipeg South Academy**
870 Scotland Ave., Winnipeg, MB R3M 1X8
Tel: 204-452-6547
info@kiddiekampus.ca
www.kiddiekampus.ca
Grades: Junior Kindergarten - 3 *Note:* Founded in 1990, Winnipeg South Academy is a private school that offers an extension of the Montessori philosophy.
Gayle Lavigne, Founder
Susan Kiburn, Head of School
Suzanne Van Cauwenberghe, Principal

Universities & Colleges

Universities

***Brandon:* Brandon University**
270 - 18th St., Brandon, MB R7A 6A9, Canada
Tel: 204-728-9520; *Fax:* 204-726-4573
www.brandonu.ca
Full Time Equivalency: 2625
Dr. Deborah C. Poff, Pres./Vice-Chancellor
president@brandonu.ca
Scott J.B. Lamont, Vice-Pres., Admin./Finance
lamont@brandonu.ca
Dr. Scott Grills, Vice-Pres., Academic
grillss@brandonu.ca
Bruce Strang, Dean, Arts
artsdean@brandonu.ca
Dr Cam Symons, Dean, Education
symonsc@Brandonu.ca
Dr W. Dean Care, Dean, Health Studies
cared@brandonu.ca
Dr Austin F. Gulliver, Dean, Science
gulliver@brandonu.ca
Dr. Lawrence VanBeek, Registrar, 204-727-7310
vanbeekl@brandonu.ca

Faculties
Arts
S. Grills, Dean

Education
Jerrie Storie, Acting Dean

Science
Dr. Austin Gulliver, Acting Dean

Student & International Affairs
Dr. Janet Wright, Dean

Schools
Health Studies
L. Ross, Dean

Music
G. Carruthers, Dean

Publications
Quill

***Winnipeg:* Canadian Mennonite University**
500 Shaftsbury Blvd., Winnipeg, MB R3P 2N2, Canada
Tel: 204-487-3300; *Fax:* 204-487-3858
Toll-Free: 877-231-4570
info@cmu.ca
www.cmu.ca
Full Time Equivalency: 1600
Gerald Gerbrandt, President
ggerbrandt@cmu.ca
Earl Davey, Vice-Pres., Academic
edavey@cmu.ca
Wesley Toews, Registrar & Assistant VP
wtoews@cmu.ca
Gordon Matties, Dean, Humanities & Sciences
gmatties@cmu.ca
Dietrich Bartel, Dean, School of Music
dbartel@cmu.ca
Paul Redekop, Dean, Social Sciences
p.redekop@uwinnipeg.ca
Paul Kroeker, Dean, International Programs
pkroeker@cmu.ca
Ruth Taronno, Assoc. Vice-Pres., MSC
rtaronno@cmu.ca

***Winnipeg:* Prairie Theatre Exchange**
300-393 Portage Ave., #Y, Winnipeg, MB R3B 2H6, Canada
Tel: 204-942-7291; *Fax:* 204-942-1774
www.pte.mb.ca

***Winnipeg:* Salvation Army William & Catherine Booth University College**
Also known as: Booth College; Booth University College
447 Webb Pl., Winnipeg, MB R3B 2P2, Canada
Tel: 204-947-6701; *Fax:* 204-942-3856
Toll-Free: 877-942-6684
admissions@boothcollege.ca
www.boothcollege.ca
Full Time Equivalency: 500 *Note:* Enrollment number includes on-campus and distance students.

***Winnipeg:* University College**
#203, 220 Dysart Rd., Winnipeg, MB R3T 2M8, Canada
Tel: 204-474-9751; *Fax:* 204-261-0021
ucsecr@cc.umanitoba.ca
umanitoba.ca/colleges/uc/
Note: Affiliated with the University of Manitoba

***Winnipeg:* University of Manitoba**
134 Services Building
97 Dafoe Rd., Winnipeg, MB R3T 2N2, Canada
Tel: 204-474-8880
www.umanitoba.ca
Full Time Equivalency: 29932
William Norrie, C.M., O.M., Q.C., B.A., L, Chancellor
Dr. David T. Barnard, B.Sc., M.Sc., Ph.D., Dip., President & Vice-Chancellor
Bob Raeburn, B.Sc., Executive Assistant to the President
Deborah J. McCallum, B.Sc., Vice-President
Digvir Jayas, Ph.D., Vice-President
Joanne C. Keselman, B.A., M.A., Ph.D., Vice-President
P. Dueck, Director
Alan Simms, B.Comm.(Hons.), L.L.B., Assoc. Vice-President
Peter Cattini, B.Sc.(Hons.), Ph.D., Assoc. Vice-President
David R. Morphy, B.A., M.A., Ph.D., Vice-Provost
Karen R. Grant, B.A., M.A., Ph.D., Vice-Provost
Richard A. Lobdell, B.A., M.A., Ph.D., Vice-Provost
Terry Voss, B.Comm. (Hons.), C.H.R.P., Exec. Director
Karen Adams, B.A., M.L.S., Director
John G. Alho, B.A.(Hons.), Assoc. Vice-President
B. Hanchard, Manager
Peter A. Cattini, B.Sc., Ph.D., Assoc. Vice-President
Elaine V. Goldie, Cert.Ed., Vice-President
Gerry Miller, B.Sc., Exec. Director
A. Simms, L.L.B., Exec. Director
James S. Gardner, B.Sc., M.Sc., Ph.D., Exec. Director
Jeffrey M. Leclerc, B.Ed., University Secretary

Faculties
Agricultural & Food Sciences
Michael Trevan, Dean

Architecture
Richard Perron, Acting Dean

Arts
Richard Sigurdson, Dean

Continuing Education
A. Percival, Dean

Dentistry
Anthony Iacopino, Dean

Education
John Wiens, Dean

Engineering
Douglas Ruth, Dean

Environment
Clayton H. Riddell, Dean

Graduate Studies
Jay Doering, Dean

Human Ecology
Gustaaf P. Sevenhuysen, Dean

I.H. Asper School of Business
Glenn Feltham, Dean

Law
Chris Axworthy, Q.C., Dean

Medicine
Dean Sandham, Dean

Music
Edmund Dawe, Dean

Nursing
Ruth Anne Kinsman, Dean

Pharmacy
David M. Collins, Dean

Physical Education & Recreation Studies
Dr. Jane Watkinson, Dean

Science
Mark Whitmore, Dean

Social Work
Harvy Frankel, Dean

University 1
Christine Blais, Dean

Schools
Agriculture
Mervyn K. Pritchard, Director

Art
Prof. Celia Rabinovitch, Director

Dental Hygiene
Salme Lavigne, Director

Extended Education Division
Anne Percival, Director

Medical Rehabilitation
Emily Etcheverry, Director

St. John's College
92 Dysart Rd., Winnipeg, MB R3T 2M5, Canada
Tel: 204-474-8531; *Fax:* 204-474-7610
Toll-Free: 1-800-432-1960
umanitoba.ca/colleges/st_johns
Note: Affiliated with the Anglican Church of Canada, St. John's College is located on the University of Manitoba campus.
Dr. Chris Trott, Warden & Vice-Chancellor
trottcg@cc.umanitoba.ca
Sherry Peters, Registrar
sherry.peters@ad.umanitoba.ca

St. Paul's College
70 Dysart Rd., Winnipeg, MB R3T 2M6, Canada
Tel: 204-474-8575
stpauls@umanitoba.ca
www.umanitoba.ca/stpauls
www.facebook.com/pages/St-Pauls-College-U-of-M/1887800445 07028
Note: The Roman Catholic College is located on the University of Manitoba campus.
Denic C. Bracken, Rector
bracken@cc.umanitoba.ca
Christine Butterill, Dean of Studies
butteri@cc.umanitoba.ca

University College
University of Manitoba
#203, 220 Dysart Rd., Winnipeg, MB R3T 2N2, Canada
Tel: 204-474-6839; *Fax:* 204-261-0021
Toll-Free: 800-432-1960
fmajor@cc.umanitoba.ca
umanitoba.ca/colleges/uc
Dr. Richard Sigurdson, B.A., M.A. Ph.D., Acting Provost

Booth Bible College
447 Webb Pl., Winnipeg, MB R3B 2P2, Canada
Tel: 204-947-6701; *Fax:* 204-942-3856
Toll-Free: 877-942-6684
admissions@boothuc.ca
www.boothuc.ca
www.facebook.com/BoothUniversityCollege
www.twitter.com/boothuc
Dr. Donald Burke, President, 204-924-4868
president@boothcollege.ca
Denise Young, BBA, MPA, Director, College Admin., 204-924-4864
dyoung@boothcollege.ca
Deborah Knight, Financial Coordinator, 204-924-4853
dknight@boothcollege.ca

Prairie Theatre Exchange
300-393 Portage Ave., #Y, Winnipeg, MB R3B 2H6, Canada
Tel: 204-942-7291; *Fax:* 204-942-1774
education@pte.mb.ca
www.pte.mb.ca
twitter.com/PrairieTheatre
Robert Metcalfe, Artistic Director
ad@pte.mb.ca

Publications
Alumni Journal
180 Dafoe Rd, Winnipeg, MB R3T 2N2, Canada

The Gradzette

The Manitoban

Winnipeg: University of Winnipeg
515 Portage Ave., Winnipeg, MB R3B 2E9, Canada
Tel: 204-786-7811
www.uwinnipeg.ca
Full Time Equivalency: 9460
Robert Silver, Chancellor
Lloyd Axworthy, President & Vice-Chancellor, 204-786-9214
president@uwinnipeg.ca
John Corlett, Vice-Pres., Academic, 204-786-9120
j.corlett@uwinnipeg.ca
Bill Balan, Vice-Pres., Finance & Administration, 204-786-9229
b.balan@uwinnipeg.ca
Laurel Repski, Vice-Pres., Human Resources, 204-789-1451
l.repski@uwinnipeg.ca
Neil Besner, Vice-Pres., Students & International, 204-786-8656
n.besner@uwinnipeg.ca

Faculties
Arts
David Fitzpatrick, Dean, 204-786-9943
d.fitzpatrick@uwinnipeg.ca

Business & Economics
Michael Benarroch, Dean, 204-786-9268
m.benarroch@uwinnipeg.ca

Education
Ken Mccluskey, Dean, 204-786-9470
k.mccluskey@uwinnipeg.ca

Science
Rodney Hanley, Dean, 204-786-9862
r.hanley@uwinnipeg.ca

Theology
Dr James Christie, Dean, 204-786-9247
j.christie@uwinnipeg.ca

Affiliations
Menno Simons College
520 Portage Ave., Winnipeg, MB R3C 0G2, Canada
Tel: 204-953-3855; *Fax:* 207-783-3699
msc@uwinnipeg.ca
mscollege.ca
www.facebook.com/mennosimonscollege
Note: A college of the Canadian Mennonite University, maintaining an affiliation with the University of Winnipeg. It is located on the campus of the U. of W.
Dr. Earl Davey, Vice-President, Academic (CMU), 204-953-3873
e.davey@uwinnipeg.ca
Dr. Paul Redekop, Dean, MSC/Faculty of Social Sciences (CMU), 204-953-3858
p.redekop@uwinnipeg.ca

Publications
The Uniter
Tel: 204-786-9790; *Fax:* 204-786-9497
uniter@uniter.ca
uniter.ca

Colleges

Brandon: Assiniboine Community College
1430 Victoria Ave. East, Brandon, MB R7A 2A9, Canada
Tel: 204-725-8700; *Fax:* 204-725-8740
Toll-Free: 1-800-862-6307
info@assiniboine.net
www.assiniboine.net
facebook.com/accmanitoba
twitter.com/accmb
youtube.com/user/accmanitoba
Full Time Equivalency: 2500
Joel Ward, President
wardj@assiniboine.net
Karen Barclay, Associate Registrar
barclay@assiniboine.net

Campuses
Parkland Campus
520 Whitmore Ave. East, Dauphin, MB R7N 2V5, Canada
Tel: 204-622-2222; *Fax:* 800-482-2933
parklandinfo@assiniboine.net

Victoria Avenue East Campus
1430 Victoria Ave. East, Brandon, MB R7A 2A9, Canada
Tel: 204-725-8700; *Fax:* 204-725-8740
Toll-Free: 1-800-862-6307
info@assiniboine.net

North Hill Campus
1035 - 1st St. North, Brandon, MB R7A 2Y1, Canada
Fax: 204-725-8740
trades@assiniboine.net, mica@assiniboine.net

Adult Collegiate
725 Rosser Ave., Brandon, MB R7A 0K8, Canada
Tel: 204-725-8735; *Fax:* 204-725-8740
adultcollegiate@assiniboine.net

Brandon: Manitoba Emergency Services College
1601 Vanhorne Ave. East, Brandon, MB R7A 7K2, Canada
Tel: 204-726-6855; *Fax:* 204-726-6847
Toll-Free: 1-888-253-1488
firecomm@gov.mb.ca
www.firecomm.gov.mb.ca/mesc.html
Note: The college is a broad-based emergency services training organizationwhich offers a full-time program for those interested in a career in the EMS field.
Rick Negrich, 204-945-3330

The Pas: University College of the North (UCN)
P.O. Box 3000
436 - 7 St. East, The Pas, MB R9A 1M7, Canada
Tel: 204-627-8500; *Fax:* 204-623-7316
Toll-Free: 866-627-8500
admissions@ucn.ca
www.ucn.ca
www.facebook.com/345539599541
Full Time Equivalency: 3500
Denise K. Henning, President & Vice-Chancellor
Carol Girling, Registrar & Director, Enrolment Services, 204-627-8553
cgirling@ucn.ca

Thompson Campus (UCN)
504 Princeton Dr., The Pas, MB R8N 0A5, Canada
Tel: 204-677-6450; *Toll-Free:* 866-677-6450

Winnipeg: Red River College of Applied Arts, Science & Technology
Notre Dame Campus
2055 Notre Dame Ave., Winnipeg, MB R3H 0J9, Canada
Tel: 204-632-3960; *Toll-Free:* 1-888-515-7722
register@rrc.mb.ca; cde@rrc.mb.ca; intled@rrc.mb.ca
www.rrc.mb.ca
www.facebook.com/redrivercollege
twitter.com/rrc
www.youtube.com/redrivercollege
Full Time Equivalency: 32000
Al Morin, Chair
Stephanie Forsyth, President/CEO
sgforsyth@rrc.ca

Campuses
Interlake Campus
P.O. Box 304
825 Manitoba Ave., Selkirk, MB R1A 1T0
Tel: 204-642-5496; *Fax:* 204-642-4189
gimli@rrc.mb.ca

Portage Campus
32 - 5th St. SE, Portage la Prairie, MB R1N 1J2
Tel: 204-856-1914; *Fax:* 204-856-1915
portage@rrc.mb.ca

Steinbach Campus
#2, 385 Loewen Blvd., Steinbach, MB R5G 0B3
Tel: 204-320-2500; *Fax:* 204-346-0178
steinbach@rrc.mb.ca
Note: The Steinbach Campus has community learning centres in Steinbach (204-320-2500) and in St. Pierre (204-433-7404).

Winkler Campus
#100, 561 Main St., Winkler, MB R6W 1E8
Tel: 204-325-9672; *Fax:* 204-325-4947
winkler@rrc.mb.ca; winklerlearningcentre@rrc.mb.ca
Other Information: Winkler Community Learning Centre, Phone: 204-325-4997

Peguis-Fisher River Campus
P.O. Box 598
Peguis, MB R0C 3J0
Tel: 204-645-4179;

Winnipeg: St. Andrew's College
29 Dysart Rd., Winnipeg, MB R3T 2M7, Canada
Tel: 204-474-8895; *Fax:* 204-474-7624
st_andrews@umanitoba.ca
www.umanitoba.ca/colleges/st_andrews
Note: Affiliated with the University of Manitoba, St. Andrew's College is an institution of the Ukrainian Orthodox Church of Canada. It works to promote spiritual, academic, cultural, & moral leadership.
His Eminence John Stinka, Chancellor
V. Rev. Fr. Roman Bozyk, Chair, Dean of Theology, Acting Principal, & Registrar

Winnipeg: Université de Saint-Boniface
200, av de la Cathédrale, Winnipeg, MB R2H 0H7, Canada
Tél: 204-233-0210; *Téléc:* 204-237-3240
Ligne sans frais: 1-888-233-5112
info@ustboniface.mb.ca
www.ustboniface.mb.ca
Raymonde Gagné, B.A., Cert.Ed., M.B.A., Rectrice
rgagne@ustboniface.mb.ca

Faculties
Arts
André Samson, Dean

School of Translation

School of Business Administration

Science
André Samson, Dean

School of Scoial Work

Technical & Professional Programs
Charlotte Walkty

Education
Stéfan Delaquis, Dean

École technique et professionnelle
c/o Collège universitaire de Saint-Boniface
200, av de la Cathédrale, Saint-Boniface, MB R2H 0H7, Canada
Tél: 204-233-0210; *Téléc:* 204-237-3240
Ligne sans frais: 1-888-233-5112
sci@ustboniface.mb.ca
www.ustboniface.mb.ca
Raymonde Gagné, Rectrice

Post Secondary/Technical

Post Secondary/Technical

Dauphin: Academy of Learning
Village Mall
P.O. Box 603
1430 Main St. South, Dauphin, MB R7N 2V4, Canada
Tel: 204-622-9999; *Fax:* 204-622-9998
academyoflearning@wcgwave.ca
www.academyoflearning.com
Note: Computer & business training; other locations in Brandon, Steinbach, Swan River, Winnipeg - North, Winnipeg - South

Otterburne: Providence University College
10 College Cres., Otterburne, MB R0A 1G0, Canada
Tel: 204-433-7488; *Fax:* 204-433-7158
Toll-Free: 800-668-7768
info@prov.ca
www.prov.ca
Enrollment: 717 *Note:* Institution for Christian higher education

Winnipeg: Anokiiwin Training Institute
105-260 St. Mary Ave., Winnipeg, MB R3C 0M6, Canada
Tel: 204-925-2790; *Fax:* 204-943-0023
learn@anokiiwin.com
www.anokiiwin.com
Note: Aboriginally owned and operated training company committed to providing culturally sensitive, high quality training to First Nation communinities.

Campuses
Thompson Campus
79 Selkirk Ave., Thompson, MB R8N 0M5, Canada
Tel: 204-778-5937; *Fax:* 204-677-5813
learn@anokiiwin.com
www.anokiiwin.com/learn
Note: Aboriginally owned and operated training company committed to providing culturally sensitive, high quality training to First Nation communinities.

Winnipeg: Canadian School of Floral Art
569 St. Mary's Rd., Winnipeg, MB R2M 3L6, Canada
Tel: 204-233-2426; *Fax:* 204-237-7301

Winnipeg: Mid-Ocean School of Media Arts (MOSMA)
1588 Erin St., Winnipeg, MB R3E 2T1, Canada
Tel: 204-775-3308; *Fax:* 204-775-9231
info@midoceanschool.ca
www.midoceanschool.ca
Note: Audio engineer, audio in media

Winnipeg: National Screen Institute
#400, 141 Bannatyne Ave., Winnipeg, MB R3B 0R3, Canada
Tel: 204-956-7800; *Fax:* 204-956-5811
Toll-Free: 800-952-9307
info@nsi-canada.ca
www.nsi-canada.ca
Note: Professional training & development for Canadian film & television writers, directors & producers
Susan Millican, CEO
Glynis Corkal, Manager
Paul Moreau, Director

Winnipeg: Panache Model & Talent Management & School
#106, 897 Corydon Ave., Winnipeg, MB R3M 0W7, Canada
Tel: 204-982-6150; *Fax:* 204-474-2687
www.panachemanagement.com
Note: Models training

Winnipeg: Patal Vocational School
264 Portage Ave., Winnipeg, MB R3C 0B6
Tel: 204-944-8202; *Fax:* 204-944-8207
Toll-Free: 1-877-829-8071
www.patalvoc.com
Note: Patal Vocational School has operated since 1986 as a registered private vocational school. Patal delivers diploma programs to students in areas such as culinary arts, network management, & office assistance.
Amelia Knoedler, Contact
aknoedler@patalvocational.mb.ca

Winnipeg: Professional Transport Driver Training School
300 Oak Point Hwy., Winnipeg, MB R2R 1V1, Canada
Tel: 204-925-1580; *Fax:* 204-925-1587
Toll-Free: 1-888-883-7483
learn@transportdriver.com
www.transportdriver.com
Note: Class 1 air brake licence training
Tim McArthur, General Manager
tim@transportdriver.com

Campuses
Brandon Branch
1731 B Middleton Ave., Brandon, MB R7A 1A7, Canada
Tel: 204-729-0240; *Toll-Free:* 1-888-883-7483
Darrell Wonnick, Manager

Winnipeg: Reimer Express Driver Training Institute Inc.
50 Milner St., Winnipeg, MB R2X 2X3, Canada
Tel: 204-958-5100; *Fax:* 204-958-3034
wayne.hartle@reimerexpress.com
Note: Class 1S driver training.
Wayne Hartle, Manager

Winnipeg: Robertson College
265 Notre Dame Ave., Winnipeg, MB R3B 1N9, Canada
Tel: 204-800-7919; *Fax:* 204-926-8320
Toll-Free: 1-877-880-8789
info@robertsoncollege.com
www.robertsoncollege.com
www.facebook.com/OfficialRobertsonCollege
www.twitter.com/RobertsonColleg
www.youtube.com/RobertsonCollege
Wayne Palendat, Registrar

Campuses
Calgary Campus
#300, 417 - 14th St. NW, Calgary, AB T2N 2A1, Canada
Tel: 403-331-8233; *Fax:* 403-263-8176
Toll-Free: 1-866-920-0070
CalgaryInfo@RobertsonCollege.com

Brandon Campus
Town Centre
800 Rosser Ave., Brandon, MB R7A 6N5, Canada
Tel: 204-725-7200; *Fax:* 204-725-7218
Toll-Free: 1-877-757-7575
Info@RobertsonCollegeBrandon.com

Winnipeg: Winnipeg Technical College
130 Henlow Bay, Winnipeg, MB R3Y 1G4, Canada
Tel: 204-989-6500; *Fax:* 204-488-4152
www.wtc.mb.ca
www.facebook.com/winnipegtechnicalcollege?ref=ts
twitter.com/@WpgTechCollege
Enrollment: 1200
Dave Thorlakson, Director

New Brunswick

Government Agencies

Fredericton: Department of Education & Early Childhood Development
P.O. Box 6000
Place 2000, Fredericton, NB E3B 5H1
Tel: 506-453-3678; *Fax:* 506-457-4810
edcommunication@gnb.ca
www.gnb.ca/education
Hon. Jody Carr, Minister
jody.carr@gnb.ca

Fredericton: Department of Post-Secondary Education & Training (asp)
Chestnut Complex
P.O. Box 6000
Fredericton, NB E3B 5H1, Canada
Tel: 506-453-2597; *Fax:* 506-453-3618
dpetlinfo@gnb.ca
www.gnb.ca/post-secondarysp
Margaret-Ann Blaney, Minister
Barbara Leger, Manager
Félixine Thériault, Administrator

School Boards/Districts/Divisions

Public

Campbellton: District Scolaire #5
Also known as: L'Etoile du Nord
21, rue King, Campbellton, NB E3N 1C5
Tel: 506-789-2255; *Fax:* 506-789-4840
carmelle.gallant@gnb.ca
district5.nbed.nb.ca
Enrollment: 4900
Jean-Guy Levesque, Dir. gén.
jean-guy.levesque@gnb.ca

Dalhousie: School District #15
464 Montgomery St., Dalhousie, NB E8C 2A6, Canada
Tel: 506-684-7557; *Fax:* 506-684-7552
Toll-Free: 888-950-1515
district15@gnb.ca
www.district15.nbed.nb.ca
Enrollment: 3982
Nancy Boucher, Director, Education
John McLaughlin, Superintendent
john.mclaughlin@gnb.ca

Dieppe: District Scolaire #1 (District scolaire francophone Sud)
425, rue Champlain, Dieppe, NB E1A 1P2
Tel: 506-856-3333; *Fax:* 506-856-3254
Toll-Free: 888-268-9088
district1.nbed.nb.ca
www.facebook.com/154467881271905
twitter.com/ds01transport
www.youtube.com/user/districtscolaire01
Number of Schools: 35 écoles *Enrollment:* 13000
Gerald Richard, Dir. Gén.
gerald.richard@gnb.ca
Diane Albert-Ouellette, Dir. exéc. de l'apprentissage
diane.albert-ouellette@gnb.ca
Monique Boudreau, Dir. exéc. de l'apprentissage
monique.boudreau2@gnb.ca

Edmundston: District Scolaire #3 (District scolaire francophone du Nord-Ouest)
298, rue Martin, Edmundston, NB E3V 5E5, Canada
Tel: 506-737-4567; *Fax:* 506-737-4568
www.district3.nbed.nb.ca
www.facebook.com/263366697014308
twitter.com/District_sc3
Enrollment: 5948
Bertrand Beaulieu, Dir. gén.
bertrand.beaulieu@gnb.ca
Luc Caron, Dir. éxéc. à l'apprentissage
Eric Konopka, Principal, 780-559-2478

Fredericton: School District #18
P.O. Box 10
1135 Prospect St., Fredericton, NB E3B 4Y4, Canada
Tel: 506-453-5454; *Fax:* 506-444-5264
www.district18.nbed.nb.ca
Enrollment: 12000
Dianne Wilkins, Director, Education
dianne.wilkins@gnb.ca
Alex Dingwall, Superintendent
alex.dingwall@gnb.ca

Miramichi: School District #16
78 Henderson St., Miramichi, NB E1N 2R7, Canada
Tel: 506-778-6075; *Fax:* 506-778-6090
www.district16.nbed.nb.ca
Enrollment: 8100
Richard Walsh, Director, Education
richard.walsh@gnb.ca
Laurie Keoughan, Superintendent
laurie.keoughan@gnb.ca

Moncton: School District #2
1077 St. George Blvd., Moncton, NB E1E 4C9, Canada
Tel: 506-856-3222; *Fax:* 506-856-3224
www.district2.nbed.nb.ca
Enrollment: 16000
Gregg Ingersoll, Director, Education
Gregg.Ingersoll@gnb.ca
Karen Branscombe, Superintendent
karen.branscombe@gnb.ca

Oromocto: School District #17
17 Miramichi Rd., Oromocto, NB E2V 2P6, Canada
Tel: 506-357-4010; *Fax:* 506-357-4011
Enrollment: 5200
David McTimoney, Superintendent
Rick Demmings, Director, Education

Richibucto: District Scolaire #11
10, rue Commerciale, Richibucto, NB E4W 3X6
Tél: 506-523-7655; *Téléc:* 506-523-7659
Ligne sans frais: 866-523-7655
district11.nbed.nb.ca
www.facebook.com/districtscolaire11
twitter.com/DS11NB
Number of Schools: 20 écoles *Enrollment:* 5294 *Number of Employees:* 800
Monique Boudreau, Dir. gén. par intérim
Yolande McLaughlin, Dir. de l'éducation
yolande.mclaughlin@gnb.ca

Rothesay: **School District #6**
70B Hampton Rd., Rothesay, NB E2E 5Y2, Canada
Tel: 506-847-6262; *Fax:* 506-847-6211
www.district6.nbed.nb.ca
Enrollment: 10200
Andrew Hopper, Director, Education
andrew.hopper@gnb.ca
Zoë Watson, Superintendent
zoe.watson@gnb.ca

Saint John: **School District #8**
490 Woodward Ave., Saint John, NB E2K 5N3, Canada
Tel: 506-658-5300; *Fax:* 506-658-5399
www.district8.nbed.nb.ca
Enrollment: 13000
Susan Tipper, Superintendent
susan.tipper@gnb.ca
Beverly MacDonald, Director, Education
bev.macdonald@gnb.ca

St Stephen: **School District #10**
11 School St., St Stephen, NB E3L 2N4, Canada
Tel: 506-466-7300; *Fax:* 506-466-7309
d10webadmin@gnb.ca
www.district10.nbed.nb.ca
Enrollment: 4340
Jenny MacDougall, Director, Education
Jenny.MacDougall@gnb.ca
Zoe Watson, Superintendent
Zoe.Watson@gnb.ca

Tracadie-Sheila: **District Scolaire #9 de la Péninsule acadienne**
Également connu sous le nom de: District scolaire Nord-Est
P.O. Box 3668 Bureau chef
3376, rue Principale, Tracadie-Sheila, NB E1X 1G5
Tél: 506-394-3400; *Téléc:* 506-394-3455
www.district9.nbed.nb.ca
Number of Schools: 22 écoles *Enrollment:* 7412
Solange Haché, Dir. gén.
Robert Roy-Boudreau, Dir., Pédagogique

Woodstock: **School District #14**
138 Chapel St., Woodstock, NB E7M 1H3, Canada
Tel: 506-325-4432; *Fax:* 506-325-4490
www.district14.nbed.nb.ca
Enrollment: 8511
Loree Kaye, Director, Education
loree.kaye@gnb.ca
Lisa Gallagher, Superintendent
lisa.gallagher@gnb.ca

Schools: Specialized

First Nations

Burnt Church: **Burnt Church School**
Also known as: Esgenoôpetitj School
626 Bayview Dr., Burnt Church, NB E9G 2A8, Canada
Tel: 506-776-1206; *Fax:* 506-776-1226
lflanagan@burntchurchschool.ca
burntchurchschool.ca
Grades: Kindergarten - 8 *Enrollment:* 120 *Note:* The Burnt Church School, located northeast of the City of Miramichi, is part of School District #16. The school serves the Burnt Church First Nation.
Robert Bowes, Principal

Eel Ground: **Eel Ground First Nation School**
55 Church St., Eel Ground, NB E1V 4E6, Canada
Tel: 506-627-4615; *Fax:* 506-627-4624
www.eelgroundschool.ca
Grades: Kindergarten - 8; Mi'kmaq Language *Note:* Eel Ground First Nation School operates as part of School District #16 in Miramichi, New Brunswick. The school provides education to the Eel Ground First Nation, a Mi'kmaq community in northeastern New Brunswick.
Donald Donahue, Principal

Eel River Bar: **Eel River Bar First Nation Pre-School**
Eel River Bar First Nation
P.O. Box 4007
#201, 11 Main St., Eel River Bar, NB E8C 1A1, Canada
Tel: 506-684-6307; *Fax:* 506-684-6282
Grades: Pre-School (K4) *Note:* Eel River Bar First Nation Pre-School is a First Nations band operated school in a Mi'kmaq village on New Brunswick's north shore.
Priscilla Pictou, Principal

Elsipogtog: **Elsipogotg School**
356 Big Cove Rd., Elsipogtog, NB E4W 2S6, Canada
Tel: 506-523-8240; *Fax:* 506-523-8235
www.elsipogtogschool.ca
Grades: Kindergarten - 8 *Note:* Part of Miramichi, New Brunswick's School District #16, the Elsipogtog School provides education to the Elsipogtog First Nation.
Levi Sock, Superintendent
Ivan Augustine, Principal
Stan Drillen, Vice-Principal
Laurie Donovan, Program Coordinator, Resources
lauried@elsipogtogschool.ca

Fredericton: **Chief Harold Sappier Memorial Elementary School**
c/o St. Mary's Maliseet First Nation
305 Maliseet Dr., Fredericton, NB E3A 5R8, Canada
Tel: 506-462-9683; *Fax:* 506-462-9686
chsmesjf@nb.aibn.com
www.firstnationhelp.com/stmarys
Grades: K4 - K5; 1 - 5; Maliseet Language *Note:* In addition to providing elementary education beginning with kindergarten, the Chief Harold Sappier Memorial Elementary School provides education about the Maliseet language & culture.
Allison Brooks, Principal
Judith Fullarton, Office Manager

Fredericton: **Wulastukw Elementary School**
Kingsclear First Nation
712 Church St., Fredericton, NB E3E 1K8
Tel: 506-363-3019; *Fax:* 506-363-4051
www.firstnationhelp.com/wulastukw
Grades: K4; 1-5
Sarah Sacobie, Contact
sacobie_sarah@hotmail.com

Red Bank: **Metepenagiag - Red Bank School**
1926 MicMac Rd., Red Bank, NB E9E 1B3, Canada
Tel: 506-836-6160; *Fax:* 506-836-2787
metdu@nbnet.nb.ca
metepenagiagschool.ca
Grades: K4; 1-6
Robert Bowes, Principal
rrbowes@yahoo.ca
Mindy Ward-Wayne, Administrative Assistant

Tobique First Nation: **Mah-Sos School**
270 Main St., Tobique First Nation, NB E7H 2Y8
Tel: 506-273-5407; *Fax:* 506-273-5436
w8liftr@hotmail.com
www.firstnationhelp.com/mahsos
Grades: K4; 1-5
Paula Pirie, Principal

Woodstock First Nation: **Woodstock First Nation Pre-School**
6 Eagles Nest Dr., Woodstock First Nation, NB E7M 4J3
Tel: 506-328-4332; *Fax:* 506-328-2420
Note: The school serves Woodstock First Nation.
Janet Paul, Principal
June Tomah, Principal

Schools: Independent & Private

Independent & Private Schools

Fredericton: **Devon Park Christian School**
P.O. Box 3510 B
145 Clark St., Fredericton, NB E3A 5J8
Tel: 506-458-9379; *Fax:* 506-458-8702
dpcs@dpcs.ca
www.dpcs.ca
twitter.com/MeetDPCS
Grades: K.-12 *Enrollment:* 180
Jonathan McAloon, Principal
j.mcaloon@dpcs.ca

Moncton: **Moncton Christian Academy (MCA)**
945 St. George Blvd., Moncton, NB E1E 2C9, Canada
Tel: 506-855-5403; *Fax:* 506-857-9016
www.monctonchristianacademy.com
Grades: Kindergarten - 12 *Enrollment:* 120 *Note:* Moncton Christian Academy is an interdenominational school.
Willie Brownlee, Administrator
Esther Flanagan, Assistant

Plaster Rock: **Apostolic Christian School**
123 Main St., Plaster Rock, NB E7G 2H2
Tel: 506-356-8690; *Fax:* 506-356-9996
Grades: K.-12
Sanford Goodine, Principal

Rothesay: **Rothesay Netherwood School (RNS)**
40 College Hill Rd., Rothesay, NB E2E 5H1, Canada
Tel: 506-847-8224; *Fax:* 506-848-0851
education@rns.cc; admission@rns.cc; bursar@rns.cc; alumni@rns.cc
www.rns.cc
Grades: 6 - 12 *Note:* Rothesay Netherwood School is a day & boarding school.
Sylvia MacVey, Chair
Paul G. Kitchen, Head of School, 506-848-0863
kitchenp@rns.cc
Paul McLellan, Director, Senior School & Assistant Head of School, 506-848-0864
mclellanp@rns.cc
Dean Van Doleweerd, Director, Middle School & Assistant Head of School, 506-847-8224
vandoleweerdd@rns.cc
Jayne Fillman, Director, Admission, 506-848-0859
fillmanj@rns.cc
David Keeping, Director, Finance & Operations, 506-848-0855
keepingd@rns.cc
Linda MacDonald, Director, Residential Life, 506-848-8224
macdonaldl@rns.cc
Geoffrey McCullogh, Director, Athletics, 506-848-0852
mcculloghg@rns.cc
Brian Murray, Director, Student Life, 506-848-0876
murrayb@rns.cc
Tammy Earle, Head, Information Technology & Coordinator IB Diploma, 506-848-1739
earlet@rns.cc

Rothesay: **Touchstone Community School**
68A Hampton Rd., Rothesay, NB E2E 5L5
Tel: 506-847-2673; *Fax:* 506-849-9582
info@tcsweb.ca
www.touchstonecommunityschool.ca
Grades: Pre.-5 *Enrollment:* 80
Jeff McAloon, Principal
Angela Prosser, Head, Academics

Rothesay: **Valley Christian Academy (VCA)**
P.O. Box 4722
30 Vincent Rd., Rothesay, NB E2E 5X4, Canada
Tel: 506-848-6373; *Fax:* 506-848-6379
www.valleychristianacademy.com
Grades: Preschool - 9 *Note:* Valley Christian Academy is a ministry of Rothesay Baptist Church. The preschool accepts children as young as three years of age.
Barry Todd, Principal
principal@bellaliant.com

Somerville: **Somerville Christian Academy**
2608, rte 103, Somerville, NB E7P 3A9, Canada
Tel: 506-375-4327; *Fax:* 506-375-4406
Grades: K.-5 *Enrollment:* 63
Angela Mabey, Principal

Sussex: **Sussex Christian School**
45 Chapman Dr., Sussex, NB E4E 1M4, Canada
Tel: 506-433-4005; *Fax:* 506-433-3402
info@sussexchristianschool.ca
www.sussexchristianschool.ca
Grades: Jr. K.-12 *Enrollment:* 67
Marsha Boyd-Mitchell, Principal

Universities & Colleges

Universities

Fredericton: **Maritime College of Forest Technology**
Hugh John Flemming Forestry Centre
1350 Regent St., Fredericton, NB E3C 2G6, Canada
Tel: 506-458-0653; *Fax:* 506-458-0652
info@mcft.ca
www.mcft.ca
Full Time Equivalency: 150

Fredericton: **St. Thomas University**
51 Dineen Dr., Fredericton, NB E3B 5G3, Canada
Tel: 506-452-0640; *Fax:* 506-450-9615
www.stu.ca
twitter.com/StThomasU
Most Rev. Faber MacDonald, B.Comm., Chancellor
Dawn Russell, President & Vice-Chancellor, 506-452-0537, fax: 506-452-0633
president@stu.ca
Barry Craig, Ph.D., Vice-President, 506-452-0531
vpacademic@stu.ca
Lily Fraser, Vice-President, 506-452-0533
vpfa@stu.ca
Karen Preston, Registrar, 506-452-0400
preston@stu.ca

Kathryn Monti, Director of Admissions, 506-452-0603
monti@stu.ca
Jacqueline Cormier, Alumni Affairs Officer
jcormier@stu.ca
Fr. Peter Wetmore, Chaplain, 506-452-0643

Publications
Aquinian

Fredericton: University of New Brunswick
P.O. Box 4400 A
Fredericton, NB E3B 5A3, Canada
Tel: 506-453-4666; *Fax:* 506-453-5158
trudya@unb.ca
www.unb.ca
www.facebook.com/uofnb
twitter.com/unb
www.youtube.com/unbtube

Full Time Equivalency: 11000 *Number of Employees:* 3000
Dr. H.E.A. (Eddy) Campbell, President & Vice-Chancellor
Dr. Anthony (Tony) Secco, Vice-President
Daniel V. Murray, C.A., B.Comm., Vice-President, Fredericton, Academic
dmurray@unb.ca
Dr. David Burns, Vice-President, Research
S. Strople, B.A., M.A., University Secretary
sstrople@unb.ca
David Hinton, B.Sc., M.Sc., Registrar
hinton@unb.ca
Bob Skillen, Vice-President, Advancement

Faculties
Arts
James Murray, B.A., M.A., Ph.D., Dean
arts@unb.ca

Arts (Saint John)
Robert MacKinnon, B.A., M.A., Ph.D., Dean

Business (Saint John)
Shelley Rinehart, B.A., M.B.A., Ph.D., Dean

Business Administration
Daniel Coleman, B.A., Ph.D., Dean
fadmin@unb.ca

Computer Science
Virendra Bhavsar, B.Eng., M.Tech., Ph.D., Dean

Education
Sharon Rich, Ed.D., M.Ed., B.A., Dean
educ@unb.ca

Engineering
David Coleman, B.Sc.E., Ph.D., P.Eng., M, Dean
deaneng@unb.ca

Forestry & Environmental Management
D. MacLean, B.Sc., Ph.D., Dean
forem@unb.ca

Kinesiology
Terry Haggerty, B.A., B.P.H.E., Dip.Educ., Dean
cls@unb.ca

Law
Philip Bryden, B.A., B.C.L., L.L.M., Dean
law@unb.ca

Nursing
C.H. Gibson, B.N., M.Sc.N., Ph.D., Dean
nursing@unb.ca

School of Graduate Studies
Gwendolyn Davies, B.A., M.A., Ph.D., Cert.E, Dean
gradschl@unb.ca

Science
A.R. Sharp, B.Sc., M.Sc., Ph.D., Dean
science@unb.ca

Science, Applied Science & Engineering (Saint John)
Deborah MacLatchy, B.Sc., Ph.D., Dean
sci-eng@unbsj.ca

Campuses
Renaissance College
P.O. Box 4400
811 Charlotte St., Fredericton, NB E3B 5A3, Canada
Tel: 506-447-3092; *Fax:* 506-447-3274
www.facebook.com/RenaissanceCollege
Pierre Zundel, Dean

Saint John Campus
Saint John
P.O. Box 5050
100 Tucker Park Rd., Saint John, NB E2L 4L5, Canada
Tel: 506-648-5500; *Fax:* 506-648-5528
K.E. Hamer, Vice-President

Affiliations
Maritime College of Forest Technology
1350 Regent St., Fredericton, NB E3C 2G6, Canada
Tel: 506-458-0199; *Fax:* 506-458-0679
info@mcft.ca
www.mcft.ca
www.facebook.com/268728173163393
www.youtube.com/user/MCFTVIDEOS
Robert A. Whitney, Acting Executive Director
rwhitney@mcft.ca
Jason A. Thibodeau, MFRS, Recruitment Officer
jthibodeau@mcft.ca

Publications
Baron (St. John campus)

Brunswickan

Fredericton: Yorkville University
1149 Smythe St., Fredericton, NB E3B 3H4, Canada
Fax: 506-454-1221
Toll-Free: 866-838-6542
www.yorkvilleu.ca
Rick Davey, President

Education
Dorothy MacKeracher, Ph.D, Dean

Faculties
Behavioural Sciences
John McLaughlin, Ed.D, Dean

Business
Wiktor Askanas, Ph.D, Dean

Moncton: Université de Moncton
Campus de Moncton
Moncton, NB E1A 3E9, Canada
Tél: 506-858-4000; *Téléc:* 506-858-4544
Ligne sans frais: 1-800-363-8336
info@umoncton.ca
www.umoncton.ca

Note: Une institution d'enseignement exclusivement de langue française; campus: Edmunston, Moncton et Shippagan
Louis R. Comeau, C.M., Chancelier
Yvon Fontaine, Recteur et Vice-Chancelier
recteur@umoncton.ca
Lynne Castonguay, Secrétaire générale
Nassir El-Jabi, Vice-recteur à l'administration et aux ressources humaines
eljabin@umoncton.ca
Linda Schofield, Dir. gén.
schofil@umoncton.ca
Daniel Godbout, Directeur
godboud@umoncton.ca
Roger Boulay, Directeur
boulayr@umoncton.ca
vacant, Bibliothécaire en chef
Janique Léger, Directrice
legerja@umoncton.ca
Rhéal Belliveau, Directeur
bellivr@umoncton.ca
Paul-Emile Benoit, Directeur
benoitpe@umoncton.ca
Thérèse Thériault, Directrice
theriat@umoncton.ca
Gaston LeBlanc, Doyen
Isabelle McKee-Allain, Doyenne
chiassz@umoncton.ca
Andrew Boghen, Doyen
Anne Lowe, Doyenne
Charles Bourque, Doyen
Lise Caron, Doyenne
Marie-France Albert, Doyenne
Paul Chiasson, Doyen
Régina Robichaud, Directrice
Sylvie Robichaud-Ekstrand, Directrice
Paul Bourque, Directeur
Normand Gionet, Directeur
Paul Albert, Vice-recteur
Jocelyne Roy-Vienneau, Vice-rectrice
Normand Gionet, Doyen (par intérim)
Nasser Baccouche, Directeur
Zénon Chiasson, Directeur
chiassz@umoncton.ca
Terrance J. LeBlanc, Director
leblanct@umoncton.ca
Marc Boudreau, Directeur
boudrema@umoncton.ca
Neil Boucher, Vice-recteur à l'enseignement et à la recherche
bouchen@umoncton.ca

Campus d'Edmundston
165, boul Hébert, Edmundston, NB E3V 2S8, Canada
Tél: 506-737-5051

Campuses
Campus de Shippagan
218, boul J.-D.-Gauthier, Shippagan, NB E8S 1P6, Canada
Tél: 506-336-3400

Publications
Le Front

Sackville: Mount Allison University
62 York St., Sackville, NB E4L 1E2, Canada
Tel: 506-364-2269; *Fax:* 506-364-2263
regoffice@mta.ca
www.mta.ca
www.twitter.com/mountallison
www.youtube.com/MountAllison
Peter Mansbridge, Chancellor
Robert M. Campbell, President & Vice-Chancellor, 506-364-2300, fax: 506-364-2299
rcampbell@mta.ca
Brian G. Johnston, Chair
John F. Read, Vice-President
John David Stewart, Vice-President
Dr. Hans vanderLeest, Dean
deanofarts@mta.ca
Paul Berry, Dean
deanofsocialsciences@mta.ca
Chris Parker, Registrar
Charles W. F. Hunter, Associate Vice-President
Dr. Jeff Ollerhead, Dean
deanofscience@mta.ca

Publications
Argosy Weekly

Colleges

Bathurst: Collège communautaire du Nouveau-Brunswick
P.O. Box 700
725, rue du Collège, Bathurst, NB E2A 3Z6, Canada
Tél: 506-547-2063; *Téléc:* 506-547-2741
Ligne sans frais: 1-855-676-2262
www.facebook.com/CCNB.officielle
Liane Roy, Directeur général

Campus de Dieppe
505, rue du Collège, Dieppe, NB E1A 7H9, Canada
Tél: 506-856-2200; *Téléc:* 506-856-2847
Ligne sans frais: 1-800-561-7162
Claude Allard, Directeur
claude.allard@gnb.ca

Campuses
Campus de Campbellton
P.O. Box 309
47, av Village, Campbellton, NB E3N 3G7, Canada
Tél: 506-789-2377; *Téléc:* 506-789-2433
Ligne sans frais: 1-888-648-4111

Campus de Bathhurst
P.O. Box 266
725, rue du Collège, Bathurst, NB E2A 3Z2, Canada
Tél: 506-547-2145; *Téléc:* 506-547-7674
Ligne sans frais: 1-800-552-5483

Campus d'Edmundston
P.O. Box 70
35, rue du 15-Août, Edmundston, NB E3V 3K7, Canada
Tél: 506-735-2500; *Téléc:* 506-735-2717
Ligne sans frais: 1-888-695-2262

Campus de la Péninsule acadienne
232 A, avenue de l'Église, Shippagan, NB E8S 1J2, Canada
Tél: 506-336-3073; *Téléc:* 506-336-3075
Ligne sans frais: 1-866-299-9900

Post Secondary/Technical

Post Secondary/Technical

Fredericton: Atlantic Business College (ABC)
1115 Regent St., Fredericton, NB E3B 3Z2, Canada
Tel: 506-450-1408; *Fax:* 506-450-8388
Toll-Free: 1-800-983-2929
atlantic@abc.nb.ca
www.abc.nb.ca
www.facebook.com/AtlanticBusinessCollege?ref=ts
twitter.com/ABCFredericton

Note: Day school programs, continuing education courses, corporate training; also in Moncton.
Jacqueline Devine, Principal

Fredericton: **Maritime College of Forest Technology (MCFT)**
1350 Regent St., Fredericton, NB E3C 2G6, Canada
Tel: 506-458-0199; *Fax:* 506-458-0652
hflinn@mcft.ca
mcft.ca
Note: Established 1946. Identical francophone program offered at the Bathurst, NB campus. A minimum 12-month pre-admission apprenticeship in woods work or forestry is required. In addition to course work, students are required to work a minimum 12-week practicum.
J.S. Hoyt, Director

Fredericton: **New Brunswick Community Colleges Collèges communautaires du Nouveau-Brunswick**
284 Smythe St., Fredericton, NB E3B 3C9, Canada
Tel: 506-462-5012; *Toll-Free:* 888-796-6222
collegeworks@nbcc.ca
www.nbcc.ca

Campuses
New Brunswick Community College (Bathurst)
Collège communautaire du Nouveau-Brunswick (Bathurst)
P.O. Box 266
725, rue du Collège, Bathurst, NB E2A 3Z2, Canada
Tél: 506-547-2145; *Téléc:* 506-547-7674
Ligne sans frais: 1-800-552-5483
Jeanne A. Comeau, Principal
jeanne.a.comeau@gnb.ca

New Brunswick Community College (Edmundston)
Collège communautaire du Nouveau-Brunswick (Edmundston)
P.O. Box 70
35, rue du 15-Août, Edmundston, NB E3V 3K7, Canada
Tel: 506-735-2500; *Fax:* 506-735-2717
Toll-Free: 1-888-695-2262
Richard Doiron, Principal
richard.doiron@gnb.ca

New Brunswick Community College (Miramichi)
Collège communautaire du Nouveau-Brunswick (Miramichi)
P.O. Box 1053
80 University Ave., Miramichi, NB E1N 3W4, Canada
Tel: 506-778-6000; *Fax:* 506-778-6001
Toll-Free: 877-773-6222
nbcc.miramichi@nbcc.ca
Karen White-O'Connell, Principal

New Brunswick Community College (Moncton)
Collège communautaire du Nouveau-Brunswick (Moncton)
1234 Mountain Rd., Moncton, NB E1C 8H9, Canada
Tel: 506-856-2220; *Fax:* 506-856-3288
Toll-Free: 1-888-664-1477
student.services@nbcc.ca
Full Time Equivalency: 3500
Darren Ros, Principal
darren.rose@gnb.ca

New Brunswick Community College (St. Andrews)
Collège communautaire du Nouveau-Brunswick (St. Andrews)
99 Augustus St., St Andrews, NB E5B 2E9, Canada
Tel: 506-529-5024; *Fax:* 506-529-5078
webinquiries@nbcc.ca
Diane Burt, Principal
diane.burt@gnb.ca

New Brunswick Community College (Saint John)
Collège communautaire du Nouveau-Brunswick (Saint John)
P.O. Box 2270
950 Grandview Ave., Saint John, NB E2L 3V1, Canada
Tel: 506-658-6600; *Fax:* 506-658-6792
Toll-Free: 800-416-4080
studentservices.nbccsj@nbcc.ca
Annette Albert, Principal
annette.albert@gnb.ca

New Brunswick Community College (Woodstock)
Collège communautaire du Nouveau-Brunswick (Woodstock)
100 Broadway St., Woodstock, NB E7M 5C5, Canada
Tel: 506-325-4400; *Fax:* 506-328-8426
studentservices.nbccwood@nbcc.ca
Joy Dion, Principal
joy.dion@gnb.ca

New Brunswick Community College (Péninsule acadienne)
Collège communautaire du Nouveau-Brunswick (Péninsule acad
232A, avenue de l'Église, Shippagan, NB E8S 1J2, Canada
Tél: 506-336-3073; *Téléc:* 506-336-3075
Ligne sans frais: 1-866-299-9900
Thérèse Finn-McGraw, Principal
therese.finn-mcgraw@gnb.ca

New Brunswick Community College (Fredericton)
Collège communautaire du Nouveau-Brunswick (Fredericton)
26 Duffie Dr., Fredericton, NB E3B 0R6, Canada
Tel: 506-453-3641; *Fax:* 506-453-7944
nbccfrederictoncampus@nbcc.ca
Bronwen Cunningham, Principal
bronwen.cunningham@gnb.ca

New Brunswick Community College (Campbellton)
Collège communautaire du Nouveau-Brunswick (Campbellton)
P.O. Box 309
47, avenue Village, Campbellton, NB E3N 3G7, Canada
Tél: 506-789-2377; *Téléc:* 506-789-2433
Ligne sans frais: 888-648-4110

New Brunswick Community College (Dieppe)
Collège communautaire du Nouveau-Brunswick (Dieppe)
505, rue du Collège, Dieppe, NB E1A 6X2, Canada
Tél: 506-856-2200; *Téléc:* 506-856-2847
Ligne sans frais: 800-561-7162

Newfoundland & Labrador

Government Agencies

St. John's: **Department of Education**
Confederation Bldg., West Block
P.O. Box 8700
100 Prince Philip Dr., 3rd Fl., St. John's, NL A1B 4J6, Canada
Tel: 709-729-5097; *Fax:* 709-729-5896
education@gov.nl.ca
www.ed.gov.nl.ca/edu
Hon. Clyde Jackman, Minister, 709-729-5040, fax: 709-729-0414

School Boards/Districts/Divisions

Public

Corner Brook: **Western School District**
P.O. Box 368
10 Wellington St., Corner Brook, NL A2H 6G9, Canada
Tel: 709-637-4000; *Fax:* 709-634-1828
www.wnlsd.ca
Grades: K.-12 *Enrollment:* 14737 *Note:* This district is an amalgation of school districts 2, 3, and 4.
Ross Elliott, PhD, Dir., 709-634-8349
Donald Brown, Chair

Gander: **Nova Central - School District 3**
203 Elizabeth Dr., Gander, NL A1V 1H6, Canada
Tel: 709-256-2547; *Fax:* 709-651-3044
info@ncsd.ca
www.ncsd.ca
Number of Schools: 65 *Enrollment:* 13000
John George, Chair
johngeorge@ncsd.ca

Happy Valley-Goose Bay: **Labrador - School district 1**
P.O. Box 1810 B
16 Strathcona St., Happy Valley-Goose Bay, NL A0P 1E0, Canada
Tel: 709-896-2431; *Fax:* 709-896-9638
www.lsb.ca
Grades: K-12 *Enrollment:* 5000
Bruce Vey, Director, Education
bvey@lsb.ca

Happy Valley-Goose Bay: **Labrador District School Board**
P.O. Box 1810 B
16 Strathcona, Happy Valley-Goose Bay, NL A0P 1E0, Canada
Tel: 709-896-2431; *Fax:* 709-896-9638
bpardy@lsb.ca
www.lsb.ca
Cindy Fleet, Director

Regional Office (Lab.West)
669 Tamarack Dr., Labrador City, NL A2V 2V2, Canada
Tel: 709-944-7628; *Fax:* 709-944-3480
sthibeau@lsb.ca
www.lsb.ca

St. Jean: **Conseil scolaire francophone provincial de Terre-Neuve-et-Labrador**
#212, 65, ch Ridge, St. Jean, NL A1B 4P5, Canada
Tél: 709-722-6324; *Téléc:* 709-722-6325
Ligne sans frais: 888-794-6324
www.csfp.nf.ca
Dr. Ahmed Derradji-Aouat, Président du Conseil

St. John's: **Eastern - School District 4**
#601 Atlantic Place
P.O. Box 64-66
215 Water St., St. John's, NL A1C 6C9
Tel: 709-758-2372; *Fax:* 709-758-2706
www.esdnl.ca
twitter.com/ESDNLCA
Number of Schools: 119 schools *Number of Employees:* 4200 teaching and support staff
Ford Rice, Dir. of Education

Schools: Specialized

First Nations

Conne River: **Se't A'newey Kina'magino'kuom School**
Also known as: St. Anne's School
Miawpukek Mi'kamawey Mawi'omi
P.O. Box 10
Conne River, NL A0H 1J0
Tel: 709-882-2470
Note: The Miawpukek Mi'kmaw Mawi'omi of Conne River operate the Se't A'newey Kina'magino'kuom school. The curriculum, prescribed by the province of Newfoundland & Larador, is provided to members of the community from preschool children to elders. The school also offers a Mi'kmaq studies program that includes the language & spiritual & cultural teachings of the Mi'kmaq

Natuashish: **Mushuau Innu Natuashish**
P.O. Box 189
Natuashish, NL A0P 1A0, Canada
Tel: 709-478-8971; *Fax:* 709-478-8989
www.mymsm.ca
Grades: K.-12
Dave Jackman, Principal
Mary Jane Edmunds, Community Director of Education

Schools: Independent & Private

Independent & Private Schools

Churchill Falls: **Eric G. Lambert All-Grade School**
P.O. Box 40
Churchill Falls, NL A0R 1A0, Canada
Tel: 709-925-3371; *Fax:* 709-925-3364
www.ericglambert.ca
Grades: K.-12 *Enrollment:* 156
Adrian Clarke, Principal
aclarke@nlh.nf.ca

St. John's: **Lakecrest - St. John's Independent School**
58 Patrick St., St. John's, NL A1E 2S7, Canada
Tel: 709-738-1212; *Fax:* 709-738-1701
rpittman@lakecrest.ca
www.lakecrest.ca
Grades: K.-9 *Enrollment:* 129
Ron Pellerin, Principal

St. John's: **St. Bonaventure's College**
Bonaventure Ave., St. John's, NL A1C 6B3, Canada
Tel: 709-726-0024; *Fax:* 709-726-0148
principal@stbonaventurescollege.ca
www.stbonaventurescollege.ca/
Grades: K.-12 *Enrollment:* 325 *Note:* Catholic school in the Jesuit tradition
Cecil Critch, Principal
ccritch@stbonaventurescollege.ca

Universities & Colleges

Universities

St. John's: **Memorial University of Newfoundland**
P.O. Box 4200
230 Elizabeth Ave., St. John's, NL A1C 5S7, Canada
Tel: 709-737-8000; *Fax:* 709-737-4569
www.mun.ca
Full Time Equivalency: 17300
The Hon. Edward Roberts, O.N.L., B.A., LL.B., LL.D, Official Visitor
Gen. Rick Hillier, Chancellor

Dr. H.E.A. Campbell, Acting President & Vice-Chancellor
Dr. Chris Loomis, Vice-President
vpacad@mun.ca
Kent Decker, B.Comm. (Hons.), C.A., Vice-President
kdecker@mun.ca
Christopher W. Loomis, B.Sc., M.Sc., Ph.D., Vice-President
cwloomis@mun.ca
Glenn Collins, B.Sc., B.Ed., M.Sc., Registrar
gcollins@mun.ca
Deborah Collis, Acting Director
dcollis@mun.ca
Robert E. Simmonds, QC, Chair
Wilf Nicholls, B.Sc., Ph.D., Director
John Hanchar, Ph.D., Director
Charles Randell, P.Eng., B.Eng., M.A.Sc.,, President/CEO
Bill Morrissey, B.A.(Ed.), M.Ed., Director
Kenneth M. LeDez, M.B., Ch.B., F.R.C.T.C., Director
Graham Mowbray, B.Sc., Director
Peter Cornish, B.Sc., M.A., Ph.D., Director
Karen Hollett, B.A., L.L.B., Director
Martin Lovelace, B.A., M.A., Ph.D., Director
Bonnie Simmons, B.Comm., M.B.A., Director
David King, B.Comm., M.B.A., C.A., President & CEO
Lisa Hollett, B.A., M.I.R., Director
James A. Tuck, A.B., Ph.D., F.R.S.C., Director
Ron Sparkes, Ed.D., Interim Director
Richard H. Ellis, B.A., M.L.S., University Librarian
rhellis@mun.ca
Heather Wareham, B.A., Archivist
Peter Pope, B.A., M.A., Ph.D., Director
B.J. Veitch, B.Eng., M.Eng., L.Tech.,, Director
Ian Fleming, Ph.D., Director
Barbara Cox, B.A., Director
Norman Lee, B.M.S., M.D., C.C.F.P., Director
Sheila Devine, B.A., B.Ed., LL.B., Director
Robert Sheppard, B.Eng., M.B.A., M.Eng., P, Director
Victoria Collins, B.A., Director
Darrell Miles, P.Eng., Director
L. Husa, M.V.Dr., Director
Susan Vaughan, B.A., M.B.A., Director
Georgina Hedges, M.D., Acting Chair
Michael Collins, M.Sc., M.Ed., Ph.D., Assoc. Vice-President
collinsm@mun.ca
Penny Blackwood, B.Sc., M.Sc., Ph.D., Director
Paul Chancey, B.Sc., B.Comm., Director
Gerald Pocius, B.Sc., M.A., Ph.D., Director
Robert Shea, B.A., B.S.W., M.Ed., R.S., Director
Keith Storey, B.A., M.A., Ph.D., Director
Christine Burke, B.Comm., M.B.A., Director
J. Beal (Britain), B.A.(Hons.), Ph.D., Director
Anthony B. Dickinson, B.Sc., B.Ed., M.Sc., M.A., Acting Exec. Director
James Feehan, B.A., M.Sc., Ph.D., Director
Claude Horlick, B.Comm., Director
Bruce Belbin, B.A., B.Ed., M.Ed., Director
Dr. Lilly Walker, B.A., M.A., Ph.D., Dean
lwalker@mun.ca
Robert Greenwood, B.A.(Hons.), M.A., Ph.D., Director

Faculties
Arts
Reeta Tremblay, Ph.D., Dean

Business Administration
Gary Gorman, B.B.A., M.B.A., Ph.D., Dean

Education
Alice Collins, B.A., B.Ed., M.A., Ph.D., Dean

Engineering & Applied Science
Ray Gosine, B.Eng., Ph.D., P.Eng., Dean

Graduate Studies
Chet Jablonski, B.Sc., Ph.D., F.C.I.C., Dean

Medicine
James Rourke, M.D., C.C.F.P. (EM), F.C., Dean

Science
Robert Lucas, B.Sc., M.Sc., D.Phil., F., Dean

Schools
Division of Lifelong Learning
Doreen Whalen, Dip. A.A., C.T.T., B.Voc., Director

Distance Education & Learning Technologies
Anne Marie Vaughan, B.A., B.Ed., M.Ed., M.A., Director

Human Kinetics & Recreation
Mary Bluechardt, B.P.H.D., M.Sc., Ph.D., Director

Marine Institute
Glenn Blackwood, B.Sc. (Hon.), M.A., Executive Director

Music
Tom Gordon, B.A., B.Mus., M.A., Ph.D., Director

Nursing
Sandra LeFort, B.A., B.N., M.N., Ph.D., Director

Pharmacy
Linda Hensman, B.Sc.(Pharm.), S.U.N.Y.,, Director

Social Work
Shelly Birnie-Lefcovitch, B.A., M.S.W., Ph.D., Director

Affiliations
Fisheries & Marine Institute of Memorial University of Newfoundland
P.O. Box 4920
St. John's, NL A1C 5R3, Canada
Tel: 709-778-0200; *Fax:* 709-778-0672
Toll-Free: 1-800-563-5799
public.relations@mi.mun.ca; admissions@mi.mun.ca
www.mi.mun.ca
Other Information: Registrar, Phone: 709-778-0492
Glenn Blackwood, Executive Director
Carey Bonnell, Head, MI School of Fisheries

Harlow Campus Trust
The Maltings, St. John's Walk, Market St., Old Harl, Essex, England
hcampus@hcampus.inty.net
www.mun.ca/harlow
Other Information: Phone: (0)1279-455900; Fax: (0)1279-455921
Sandra Wright, General Manager

Queen's College
c/o The Provost, Faculty of Theology
#3000, 210 Prince Philip Dr., St. John's, NL A1B 3R6, Canada
Tel: 709-753-0116; *Fax:* 709-753-1214
Toll-Free: 1-877-753-0116
queens@mun.ca
www.mun.ca/queens
The Rev. Dr. William Bellamy, Provost & Vice-Chancellor & Associate Professor
wbellamy@mun.ca

Sir Wilfred Grenfell College
1 University Dr., Corner Brook, NL A2H 6P9, Canada
Tel: 709-637-6200
info@swgc.mun.ca; helpdesk@swgc.mun.ca;
webadmin@swgc.mun.ca
www.swgc.mun.ca
www.facebook.com/grenfellcampus
www.twitter.com/grenfellcampus
www.youtube.com/grenfellcampus
Note: The College features the following divisions: Arts, Fine Arts, Science, & Social Science.
E. Holly Pike, Ph.D., Acting Principal, 709-637-6200, ext. 6231
hpike@swgc.mun.ca

Publications
The Muse

Colleges

***Stephenville:* College of the North Atlantic**
P.O. Box 5400
Stephenville, NL A2N 2Z6, Canada
Tel: 709-643-7701; *Fax:* 709-643-7808
Toll-Free: 888-982-2268
info@cna.nl.ca
www.cna.nl.ca
www.facebook.com/CNANewfoundlandLabrador
twitter.com/cna_news
www.youtube.com/user/CNamarketing
Full Time Equivalency: 20000
Ann Marrie Vaughan, President, 709-643-7701, fax: 709-643-7808
John Hutchings, Vice-Pres., Finance & Administration, 709-643-7704
Cyril Organ, Vice-Pres., Academic & Learner Services, 709-643-7732
Corinne Dunne, Vice-Pres., Development/College Advancement, 709-758-7652
Greg Chaytor, Vice-Pres., Qatar Project, 709-643-7702
Linda Dunne, Registrar, 709-643-0827, fax: 709-643-7843

Schools
Academics
Brenda Tobin, Dean, 709-292-5636, fax: 709-643-0518

Applied Arts
Brenda Tobin, Dean, 709-292-5636, fax: 709-489-0518

Business
Mary Vaughan, Dean, 709-649-7970, fax: 709-643-8454

Engineering Technology
Arthur Leung, Dean, 709-758-7100, fax: 709-758-7126

Health Sciences
Jane Gamberg, Dean, 709-758-7624, fax: 709-758-7634

Industrial Trades
Norris Eaton, Dean, 709-637-8523, fax: 709-634-8767

Information Technology
Mary Vaughan, Dean, 709-649-7970, fax: 709-643-8454

Tourism & Natural Resources
Brent Howell, Dean, 709-637-8608, fax: 709-634-2126

Campuses
Baie-Verte Campus
1 Terra Nova Rd., Baie Verte, NL A0K 1B0, Canada
Tel: 709-532-8066; *Fax:* 709-532-4624
Emily Foster, Campus Administrator, 709-532-8066, fax: 709-532-4624
emily.foster@cna.nl.ca

Bay St. George Campus - Headquarters
DSB Fowlow Bldg.
P.O. Box 5400
432 Massachussetts Dr., Stephenville, NL A2N 2Z6, Canada
Tel: 709-643-7838; *Fax:* 709-643-7734
Chris Dohaney, Campus Administrator, 709-643-7916, fax: 709-643-7827
chris.dohaney@cna.nl.ca

Bonavista Campus
P.O. Box 670
301 Confederation Dr., Bonavista, NL A0C 1B0, Canada
Tel: 709-468-2610; *Fax:* 709-468-2004
Marilyn Coles-Hayley, Campus Administrator, 709-468-1700, fax: 709-468-2004
marilyn.hayley@cna.nl.ca

Burin Campus
P.O. Box 370
105 Main St., Burin Bay, NL A0E 1G0, Canada
Tel: 709-891-5600; *Fax:* 709-891-2256
Toll-Free: 800-838-0976
ask.burin@cna.nl.ca
Mike Graham, Campus Administrator, 709-891-5602, fax: 709-891-2256
mike.graham@cna.nl.ca

Carbonear Campus
4 Pike's Lane, Carbonear, NL A1Y 1A7, Canada
Tel: 709-596-6139; *Fax:* 709-596-2688
Gary Myrden, Campus Administrator, 709-596-6139, fax: 709-596-2688
gary.myrden@cna.nl.ca

Clarenville Campus
69 Pleasant St., Clarenville, NL A5A 1V9, Canada
Tel: 709-466-6900; *Fax:* 709-466-2771
Maisie Caines, Campus Administrator, 709-466-6931, fax: 709-466-2771
maisie.caines@cna.nl.ca

Corner Brook Campus
P.O. Box 822
41 O'Connell Dr., Corner Brook, NL A2H 6H6, Canada
Tel: 709-637-8530; *Fax:* 709-634-2126
Chad Simms, Campus Administrator, 709-637-8549, fax: 709-634-2126
chad.simms@cna.nl.ca

Gander Campus
P.O. Box 395
1 Magee Rd., Gander, NL A1V 1W8, Canada
Tel: 709-651-4800; *Fax:* 709-651-3376
Bob Dwyer, Campus Administrator, 709-651-4803, fax: 709-651-3376
bob.dwyer@cna.nl.ca

Grand Falls-Windsor Campus
P.O. Box 413
5 Cromer Ave., Grand Falls-Windsor, NL A2A 1X3, Canada
Tel: 709-292-5600; *Fax:* 709-489-4180
Joan Pynn, Campus Administrator, 709-292-5625, fax: 709-489-5765
joan.pynn@cna.nl.ca

Happy Valley Campus
P.O. Box 1720 B
219 Hamilton River Rd., Happy Valley-Goose Bay, NL A0P 1E0, Canada
Tel: 709-896-6300; *Fax:* 709-896-3733
Paul Motty, Campus Administrator, 709-896-6312, fax: 709-896-9533
paul.motty@cna.nl.ca

Labrador West Campus
1 Campbell Dr., Labrador City, NL A2V 2Y1, Canada
Tel: 709-944-7210; *Fax:* 709-944-6581

Richard Sawyer, Campus Administrator, 709-944-6814, fax: 709-944-5413
richard.sawyer@cna.nl.ca

Placentia Campus
P.O. Box 190
1 Roosevelt Ave., Placentia, NL A0B 2Y0, Canada
Tel: 709-227-2037; *Fax:* 709-227-7185
Darrell Clarke, Campus Administrator, 709-227-2037, fax: 709-227-7185
darrell.clarke@cna.nl.ca

Port-aux-Basques Campus
P.O. Box 760
59 Grand Bay Rd., Port-aux-Basques, NL A0M 1C0, Canada
Tel: 709-695-3582; *Fax:* 709-695-2963
Mr Jan Peddle, Campus Administrator, 709-695-3582, fax: 709-695-2963
jan.peddle@cna.nl.ca

Prince Philip Drive Campus - St. John's
P.O. Box 1693
1 Prince Philip Dr., St. John's, NL A1C 5P7, Canada
Tel: 709-758-7284; *Fax:* 709-758-7304
Trudy Barnes, Campus Administrator, 709-758-7418, fax: 709-758-7235
trudy.barnes@cna.nl.ca

Ridge Road Campus
P.O. Box 1150
St. John's, NL A1C 6L8
Tel: 709-758-7000; *Fax:* 709-758-7059
John Oates, Campus Administrator, 709-758-7517, fax: 709-758-7126
john.oates@cna.nl.ca

Seal Cove Campus
P.O. Box 19003 Seal Cove
1670 Conception Bay Highway, Conception Bay South, NL A1X 5C7, Canada
Tel: 709-744-2047; *Fax:* 709-744-3929
Chris Patey, Campus Administrator, 709-744-1041, fax: 709-744-3929
chris.patey@cna.nl.ca

St. Anthony Campus
P.O. Box 550
83-93 East St., St Anthony, NL A0K 4S0, Canada
Tel: 709-454-3559; *Fax:* 709-454-8808
Fred Russell, Campus Administrator, 709-454-2884, fax: 709-454-8808
frederick.russell@cna.nl.ca

Qatar Campus
P.O. Box 24449
Doha, Qatar
Other Information: 974-495-2222

The Troubadour
Tel: 709-643-7746
the.troubador@cna.nl.ca
www.cna.nl.ca/troubadour

Post Secondary/Technical

Post Secondary/Technical

Badger: Central Training Academy
P.O. Box 400
6 Third Ave., Badger, NL A0H 1A0
Tel: 709-539-5150; *Fax:* 709-539-5145
Toll-Free: 1-800-563-5153
www.centraltraining.ca
Note: The Academy has state-of-the-art heavy equipment for national accredited training. The hands-on program also provides instruction for excavating, land clearing, road, building, grading, & the maintenance of machinery.

Conception Bay South: Woodford Training Centre Inc.
P.O. Box 17145 Kelligrews
4 Woodgrove Acres, Conception Bay South, NL A1X 3H1, Canada
Tel: 709-834-7000; *Fax:* 709-834-9663
info@woodfordtraining.com
www.woodfordtraining.com
Note: Cosmetology & barbering
Sharon Woodford

Corner Brook: Academy Canada - Corner Brook Campus
2 University Dr., Corner Brook, NL A2H 5G4, Canada
Tel: 709-637-2100; *Fax:* 709-637-2123
Toll-Free: 1-800-561-8000
www.academycanada.com
www.facebook.com/AcademyCanada
www.twitter.com/academycanada
M.A.Ed. Michael Barrett, President

Campuses
St. John's Campus
#167, 169 Kenmount Rd., St. John's, NL A1B 3P9, Canada
Tel: 709-739-6767; *Fax:* 709-739-6797

Trades College
#37, 45 Harding Rd., St. John's, NL A1C 5R4, Canada
Tel: 709-722-9151; *Fax:* 709-722-9197

Gander: Gander Flight Training Aerospace
P.O. Box 355
70 C. L. Dobbin Dr., Gander, NL A1V 1W7, Canada
Tel: 709-256-7484; *Fax:* 709-256-7953
Toll-Free: 1-877-438-2359
admin@gft.ca
www.gft.ca
Patrick White, President & CEO

Grand Falls-Windsor: Corona Training Institute
P.O. Box 819
60 Hardy Ave., Grand Falls-Windsor, NL A2A 2P7, Canada
Tel: 709-489-7825; *Fax:* 709-489-5001
Toll-Free: 1-888-926-7662
admin@coronacollege.com
www.coronacollege.com
Number of Employees: 14
Bernice Walker, President & CEO

Holyrood: Boilermakers Industrial Training Centre
P.O. Box 250
Holyrood, NL A0A 2R0, Canada
Tel: 709-229-7958; *Fax:* 709-229-7300
Tom Welsh

Holyrood: Operating Engineers College (OEC)
P.O. Box 389 Salmonier Line
Holyrood, NL A0A 2R0, Canada
Tel: 709-229-6464; *Fax:* 709-229-6469
Toll-Free: 888-229-6468
oec@oecollege.com
www.oecollege.com

Lewisporte: DieTrac Technical Institute
P.O. Box 970
82 Premier Dr., Lewisporte, NL A0G 3A0, Canada
Tel: 709-535-0550; *Fax:* 709-535-6101
studentservices@dietrac.com
www.dietrac.com

Mount Pearl: Iron Workers Education & Training Co. Inc.
Donavans Industrial Park
38 Sagona Ave., Mount Pearl, NL A1N 4R3, Canada
Tel: 709-747-2158; *Fax:* 709-747-1042
info@ironworkerslocal764.com
www.ironworkerslocal764.com
Note: This program follows the Provincial Plan of Training. The Ironworker Generalist Program offers the student both theory and practical exposure to all aspects of the Ironworker trade including structural erection and dismantling, reinforcing, post-tensioning, rigging, and cranes.
Lawrence R. Hawco, President, Training Coordinator

Paradise: Carpenters Millwrights College Inc.
P.O. Box 3040
89 McNamara Dr., Paradise, NL A1L 3W2, Canada
Tel: 709-364-5586; *Fax:* 709-364-5587
kpower@nlrc.ca
www.nlrc.ca

St. John's: Association for New Canadians (ANC)
P.O. Box 2031 C
St. John's, NL A1C 5R6
Tel: 709-726-6848; *Fax:* 709-726-6841
linc@nfld.net
www.ancnl.ca
Note: The Association for New Canadians is a non-profit organization that offers an ESL Training Centre to support the integration of immigrants & refugees.

St. John's: Graduate Centre of Applied Technology
P.O. Box 6345 C
275 Duckworth St., St. John's, NL A1C 6J9, Canada
Tel: 709-722-8580; *Fax:* 709-722-8318
Toll-Free: 1-800-563-1393
Cal Burton

St. John's: Judy Knee Dance Studio
27 Mayor Ave., St. John's, NL A1C 4N4, Canada
Tel: 709-579-3233
judy@judyknee.com
judyknee.com
Judy Knee, Owner

St. John's: Keyin College
303 Thorburn Rd., St. John's, NL A1B 4G3, Canada
Tel: 709-579-1061; *Fax:* 709-579-6002
Toll-Free: 1-800-563-8989
www.keyin.com
twitter.com/KeyinCollege
Note: Industry-directed education
Gwen Tucker, Founder

Campuses
Carbonear Campus
81 LeMarchant St., Carbonear, NL A1Y 1A9, Canada
Tel: 709-596-6472; *Fax:* 709-596-0217
Toll-Free: 800-563-8989
dpenney@keyin.ca
Ken Drover, Principal

Clarenville Campus
240A Memorial Dr., Clarenville, NL A5A 1N9, Canada
Tel: 709-466-7115; *Fax:* 709-466-1290
pdrover@keyin.ca
Paula Benson, Principal

Fortune Adult Learning Centre Campus
8 Benson St., Fortune, NL A0E 1P0, Canada
Tel: 709-279-5090; *Fax:* 709-279-5091
Toll-Free: 1-800-563-8989
wlewis@keyin.ca

Gander Campus
175 Airport Blvd., Gander, NL A1V 1K6, Canada
Tel: 709-651-8560; *Fax:* 709-651-8565
Toll-Free: 1-800-563-8989
thayden@keyincentral.nf.ca
Elise Babstock, Principal

Grand Falls-Windsor Campus
60 Hardy Ave., Grand Falls-Windsor, NL A2A 2P8, Canada
Tel: 709-489-8560; *Fax:* 709-489-8565
Toll-Free: 1-800-563-8989
thayden@keyincentral.nf.ca
Bill Hanlon, Principal

Lamaline Adult Learning Centre Campus
GLADA Bldg.
P.O. Box 39
Lamaline, NL A0E 2C0, Canada
Tel: 709-279-5090; *Fax:* 709-279-5091
Toll-Free: 1-800-563-8989
wlewis@keyin.ca

Lewisporte Adult Learning Centre Campus
139 Main St., Lewisporte, NL A0G 3A0, Canada
Tel: 709-535-3946; *Fax:* 709-535-3946
Toll-Free: 1-800-563-8989
thayden@keyincentral.nf.ca
Brian Caravan, Principal

Marystown Campus
P.O. Box 1327
814 Ville Marie Dr., Marystown, NL A0E 2M0, Canada
Tel: 709-279-8090; *Fax:* 709-279-5091
Toll-Free: 1-800-563-8989
wlewis@keyin.ca
Marc Coady, Principal

St. John's Campus
P.O. Box 13609 A
44 Austin St., St. John's, NL A1B 4G1, Canada
Tel: 709-579-1061; *Fax:* 709-579-6002
Toll-Free: 1-800-563-8989
jim@keyin.com

St. Lawrence Adult Learning Centre
P.O. Box 1327
414 Ville Marie Dr., Marystown, NL A0E 2M0, Canada
Tel: 709-279-5090; *Fax:* 709-279-5091
Toll-Free: 1-800-563-8989
wlewis@keyin.ca

Lawn Adult Learning Centre
P.O. Box 1327
414 Ville Marie Dr., Marystown, NL A0E 2M0, Canada
Tel: 709-279-5090; *Fax:* 709-279-5091
Toll-Free: 1-800-563-8989
wlewis@keyin.ca

St. John's: LeMoine's School of Hair Design
P.O. Box 5744
St. John's, NL A1C 5X3, Canada
Tel: 709-576-2148; *Fax:* 709-579-1134
lemoines@nl.rogers.com
www.lemoines.com
Note: Hair dressing and esthetics school.
Verna LeMoine, Executive Director

St. John's: T&R Goldshield Institute
300 Topsail Rd., St. John's, NL A1E 2B5, Canada
Tel: 709-697-2038
Don Ross

St.John's: United Association of Journeymen & Apprentices of the Plumbing & Pipefitting (UA)
P.O. Box 8583 A
48 Sagona Ave., St.John's, NL A1B 3P2, Canada
Tel: 709-747-0364; *Fax:* 709-747-2861
www.ualocal740.ca
Note: Official name: "United Association of Journeymen & Apprentices of the Plumbing and Pipefitting Industry of the United States and Canada".
Betty Shea, Organizer, 709-7472248
bshea@ualocal740.ca

Northwest Territories

Government Agencies

Yellowknife: Department of Education, Culture & Employment
P.O. Box 1320
Yellowknife, NT X1A 2L9, Canada
Tel: 867-669-2344; *Fax:* 867-873-0481
www.ece.gov.nt.ca
Hon. Jackson Lafferty, Minister
jackson_lafferty@gov.nt.ca

School Boards/Districts/Divisions

Public

Fort Simpson: Dehcho Divisional Education Council
P.O. Box 376
Fort Simpson, NT X0E 0N0, Canada
Tel: 867-695-7300; *Fax:* 867-695-7348
www.dehcho.nt.ca
Terry Jaffray, Superintendent

Fort Smith: South Slave Divisional Education Council
P.O. Box 510
Fort Smith, NT X0E 0P0, Canada
Tel: 867-872-5701; *Fax:* 867-872-2150
www.ssdec.nt.ca
Curtis Brown, Superintendent
cbrown@ssdec.nt.ca
Michael Kenny, Public Affairs Coordinator
mkenny@ssdec.nt.ca

Inuvik: Beaufort Delta Divisional Education Council
c/o Bag Service No. 12, Inuvik, NT X0E 0T0, Canada
Tel: 867-777-7136; *Fax:* 867-777-2469
www.bdec.nt.ca
Grades: Kindergarten - 12 *Enrollment:* 1800
Roy Cole, Superintendent, Schools, 867-777-7332
roy_cole@bdec.learnnet.nt.ca
Gayle Strikes With A Gun, Assistant Superintendent, 867-777-7176
gaylestrikeswithagun@bdec.learnnet.nt.ca
Grey Storey, Supervisor, Schools, 867-777-7131
greg_storey@bdec.learnnet.nt.ca
Austin Abbott, Coordinator, Skills Programs, 867-777-7367
austin_abbott@bdec.learnnet.nt.ca
Camellia Gray, Coordinator, Public Affairs, 867-777-7322
camellia_gray@bdec.learnnet.nt.ca
Liz Hansen, Coordinator, Gwich'in Aboriginal Language & Culture, 867-777-7101
liz_hansen@bdec.learnnet.nt.ca
Rose Marie Kirby, Coordinator, Inuvialuit Aboriginal Language & Culture, 867-777-7371
rosemarie_kirby@bdec.learnnet.nt.ca

Norman Wells: Sahtu Divisional Education Council
P.O. Box 64
Norman Wells, NT X0E 0V0, Canada
Tel: 867-587-3450
info@sahtudec.ca
www.sahtudec.ca
Seamus Quigg, Superintendent

Rae Edzo: Tłı̨chǫ Community Services Agency
Bag Service #5, Rae Edzo, NT X0E 0Y0, Canada
Tel: 867-392-3000; *Fax:* 867-392-3001
tcsa@tlicho.net
www.tlicho.ca
Lucy Lafferty, Superintendent

Yellowknife: Commission scolaire francophone des Territoires du Nord-Ouest
Également connu sous le nom de: Commission scolaire francophone TNO
P.O. Box 1980
207 - 4915, rue 48, Yellowknife, NT X1A 2P5, Canada
Tél: 867-873-6555; *Téléc:* 867-873-5644
csftno@gov.nt.ca
www.csftno.com
Number of Schools: 2 *Grades:* K.-12
Philippe Brûlot, Directeur général

Yellowknife: Yellowknife Catholic Schools
5124 - 49 St., Yellowknife, NT X1A 2P4, Canada
Tel: 867-766-7400; *Fax:* 867-766-7401
www.ycs.nt.ca
Grades: K.-12 *Enrollment:* 1450
Claudia Parker, Supt.
Mike Huvenaars, Asst. Supt., Business
Dianne Lafferty, Coordinator, Aboriginal Ed.

Yellowknife: Yellowknife Education District No. 1
P.O. Box 788
5402 - 50th Ave., Yellowknife, NT X1A 2N6, Canada
Tel: 867-766-5050; *Fax:* 867-873-5051
yk1@yk1.nt.ca
www.yk1.nt.ca/#Scene_1
Grades: K.-12 *Enrollment:* 2000
Metro Huculak, Supt./CEO, 867-766-5064
metro.huculak@yk1.nt.ca
Metro Huculak, Supt./CEO, 867-766-5064
metro.huculak@yk1.nt.ca
Myrna Pokiak, Coordinator, Aboriginal Ed., 867-766-5054
myrna.pokiak@yk1.nt.ca

Universities & Colleges

Colleges

Inuvik: Aurora College
P.O. Box 1290
Inuvik, NT X0E 0P0, Canada
Tel: 867-777-7800; *Fax:* 867-777-2850
Toll-Free: 1-866-287-2655
www.auroracollege.nt.ca
Maurice Evans, President

Campuses
Aurora Campus
P.O. Box 1008
87 Gwich'in Rd., Inuvik, NT X0E 0T0, Canada
Tel: 867-777-7800; *Fax:* 867-777-2850
Toll-Free: 1-866-287-2655
Doug Robertson, Director
drobertson@auroracollege.nt.ca

Thebacha Campus
P.O. Box 600
50 Conibear Cres., Fort Smith, NT X0E 0P0, Canada
Tel: 867-872-7500; *Fax:* 867-872-4511
Toll-Free: 1-866-266-4966
Faye Heron, Director
fheron@auroracollege.nt.ca

Yellowknife/North Shore Campus
P.O. Box 9700
5004 - 54th St., Yellowknife, NT X1A 2R3, Canada
Tel: 867-920-3030; *Fax:* 867-920-4350
Toll-Free: 1-866-291-4856
Sarah Wright, Campus Director

Nova Scotia

Government Agencies

Halifax: Department of Education
P.O. Box 578
2021 Brunswick St., Halifax, NS B3J 2S9, Canada
Tel: 902-424-5168; *Fax:* 902-424-0511
Toll-Free: 888-825-7770
www.ednet.ns.ca
Hon. Ramona Jennex, Minister, 902-681-3741, fax: 902-681-6261
ramonajennexmla@bellaliant.com

School Boards/Districts/Divisions

Public

Berwick: Annapolis Valley Regional School Board
P.O. Box 340
121 Orchard St., Berwick, NS B0P 1E0, Canada
Tel: 902-538-4600; *Fax:* 902-538-4630
Toll-Free: 1-800-850-3887
communications@avrsb.ednet.ns.ca
www.avrsb.ca
Grades: Elementary - Secondary *Enrollment:* 16000
Margo Tait, Superintendent, Schools, 902-538-4606, fax: 902-538-4634
superintendent@avrsb.ednet.ns.ca
Erica Weatherbie, Director, Human Resources, 902-538-4610, fax: 902-538-4635
erica.weatherbie@avrsb.ca
Stuart Jamieson, Director, Finance & Operations, 902-538-4607, fax: 902-538-4657
stuart.jamieson@avrsb.ca
Dave Jones, Director, Programs & Services, 902-538-4611, fax: 902-538-4630
dave.jones@avrsb.ca

Bridgewater: South Shore Regional School Board
130 North Park St., Bridgewater, NS B4V 4G9, Canada
Tel: 902-543-2468; *Fax:* 902-541-3051
Toll-Free: 888-252-2217
tsmith@ssrsb.ca
www.ssrsb.ca
Enrollment: 7400
Elliott Payzant, Chair
Nancy Pynch-Worthylake, Superintendent
npynch-worthylake@ssrsb.ca

Dartmouth: Halifax Regional School Board
90 Alderney Dr., Dartmouth, NS B2Y 4S8, Canada
Tel: 902-464-2000
www.hrsb.ns.ca
Number of Schools: 85 elementary schools; 28 junior high schools; 15 senior high schools; 9 K-9 schools *Grades:* Primary - 12 *Enrollment:* 52000 *Number of Employees:* 8,000 (including 3,478 teachers & school administrators)
Irvine Carvery, Chair, 902-464-2000, ext. 4445
icarvery@hrsb.ns.ca
Carole Olsen, Superintendent
Geoff Cainen, Director, Program
Mike Christie, Director, Human Resource Services
Charles Clattenburg, Director, Operations Services
Danielle McNeil-Hessian, Director, School Administration
Richard Morris, Director, Financial Services
Heather Chandler, Coordinator, Diversity Management
Gerard Costard, Coordinator, Information Technology
Doug Hadley, Coordinator, Communications
Kim Matheson, Coordinator, Policy & Research
Tracey O'Kroneg, Coordinator, Human Resource Services
Jim Gunn, Corporate Secretary

Port Hastings: Strait Regional School Board
16 Cemetery Rd., Port Hastings, NS B9A 1K6, Canada
Tel: 902-625-2191; *Fax:* 902-625-2281
Toll-Free: 1-800-650-4448
srsb@srsb.ca
srsb.ca
twitter.com/straitrsb
Number of Schools: 24 *Grades:* Primary - 12 *Enrollment:* 6765
Number of Employees: 1010
Mary Jess MacDonald, Chair
Ford Rice, Superintendent, Schools, 902-625-7065
ford.rice@srsb.ca
William J. Cormier, Director, Finance, 902-625-7050
william.cormier@srsb.ca
Terry Doyle, Director, Operations, 902-747-3647
terry.doyle@srsb.ca
Sherman England, Director, Human Resources, 902-625-7081

Monica Williams, Director, Programs & Student Services, 902-625-7083
monica.williams@srsb.ca

Saulnierville: Conseil scolaire acadien provincial
P.O. Box 88
Saulnierville, NS B0W 2Z0, Canada
Tél: 902-769-5458; *Téléc:* 902-769-5459
Ligne sans frais: 888-533-2727
csap.ednet.ns.ca
Enrollment: 4059 *Note:* Adresse civique: 9248, rte 1, La Butte, Meteghan River, N-É.
Darrell Samson, Directeur général
Audrée-Maude Goud, Secrétaire du Conseil
goudam@csap.ednet.ns.ca

Sydney: Cape Breton-Victoria Regional School Board
275 George St., Sydney, NS B1P 1J7, Canada
Tel: 902-564-8293; *Fax:* 902-564-0123
Number of Schools: 61 *Grades:* Elementary - Secondary; Adult Ed. *Enrollment:* 16006
Lorne Green, Chair
Ed Davis, Superintendent
Charles Sheppard, Coordinator, School Services

Truro: Chignecto-Central Regional School Board
60 Lorne St., Truro, NS B2N 3K3, Canada
Tel: 902-897-8900; *Fax:* 902-897-8989
Toll-Free: 800-770-0008
www.ccrsb.ednet.ns.ca
Enrollment: 25722
Gary G. Clarke, Superintendent
Trudy Thompson, Chair, 902-261-2084

Yarmouth: Tri-County Regional School Board
79 Water St., Yarmouth, NS B5A 1L4, Canada
Tel: 902-749-5696; *Fax:* 902-749-5697
Toll-Free: 1-800-915-0113
www.tcrsb.ca
Number of Schools: 30 *Grades:* Primary - 12
Faye Haley, Chair
Lisa Doucet, Superintendent, Schools, 902-749-5682
ldoucet@tcrsb.ca
Trevor Cunningham, Director, Programs & Student Services, 902-749-5675
tcunning@tcrsb.ca
Gerry Purdy, Director, Human Resources, 902-749-5684
gpurdy@tcrsb.ca
Steve Stoddart, Director, Operations, 902-749-5691
sstoddar@tcrsb.ca
Wade Tattrie, Director, Finance, 902-541-3009
wtattrie@ssrsb.ca
Steve Adams, Manager, Transportation, 902-749-2804
Mark Albert, Manager, Technology Services, 902-749-5689
mark.albert@tcrsb.ca
Dave Buckland, Coordinator, Monitoring & Evaluation, 902-749-5814
dbuckland@tcrsb.ca
Craig Crosby, Coordinator, Property Services, 902-749-2827
ccrosby@tcrsb.ca
Jason Curtis, Coordinator, Information Systems, 902-749-5186
jcurtis@tcrsb.ca
Lisa Doucet, Coordinator, Student Services, 902-749-5196
ldoucet@tcrsb.ca
Steven Gaudet, Coordinator, French Programs, 902-749-5680
sgaudet@tcrsb.ca
Gerry Pitman, Coordinator, Community Learning, 902-749-5679
gpitman@tcrsb.ca
Gerry Randell, Coordinator, Programs 7 - 12, 902-749-5197
grandell@tcrsb.ca
Gerry Stockman, Coordinator, Programs P - 6, 902-749-2826
kstockman@tcrsb.ca

First Nations

Eskasoni: Eskasoni First Nation School Board
P.O. Box 7959
4645 Shore Rd., Eskasoni, NS B1W 1B8
Tel: 902-379-2507; *Fax:* 902-379-2273
eskasoni@schoolbd.ca
www.eskasonischoolbd.com
Number of Schools: 1 *Grades:* Day Care - Secondary; Mi'kmaq *Enrollment:* 1249 *Note:* Eskasoni Ksite'taqnk Day Care; Eskasoni Unama'ki Training & Education Centre; Eskasoni Elementary & Middle School, & Chief Allison Bernard Memorial High School. Number of Employees: 175. Situated on eastern Cape Breton Island, Eskasoni First Nation is a large Mi'kmaq community. Education in the community is directed by the Eskasoni First Nation School Board, which is overseen by the Eskasoni Band Council.
John F. Toney, Chair
Patricia Marshall, Director, Education, 902-379-2507, fax: 902-379-2273
Patrick Johnson, Director, Mi'kmaq Student Services at Cape Breton University, 902-379-2507, fax: 902-379-2273
Terry Lynn Marshall, Contact, Finance, 902-379-2507, fax: 902-379-2273
terrylynnmarshall@schoolbd.ca
Barbara Sylliboy, Contact, Language, 902-379-2507, fax: 902-379-2273
barbsylliboy@schoolbd.ca
Belinda Stevens, Clerk, Post-Secondary Program, 902-379-2507, fax: 902-379-2273
belindastevens@schoolbd.ca

Schools: Specialized

First Nations

Chapel Island: Mi'kmaway School
P.O. Box 538
RR#1, Richmond County, Chapel Island, NS B0E 3B0, Canada
Tel: 902-535-2307; *Fax:* 902-535-3428
mikmawey@auracom.com
www.kinu.ns.ca/chapel
Grades: Primary - 6; Mi'kmaq language *Enrollment:* 73 *Note:* The Mi'kmaway School is administered by the Potlotek Board of Education. The school serves the Chapel Island First Nation.
Nancy MacLeod, Director, Potlotek Education Office, fax: 902-535-3164
nmacleod@potlotek.ca

Eskasoni: Chief Allison Bernard Memorial High School
Also known as: Eskasoni High School
P.O. Box 7969
4673 Shore Rd., Eskasoni, NS B1W 1B8, Canada
Tel: 902-379-3000; *Fax:* 902-379-3011
www.eskasonischoolbd.com
Grades: 10 - 12; Mi'kmaq language & culture *Enrollment:* 200 *Note:* Chief Allison Bernard Memorial High School operates under the direction of the Eskasoni First Nation School Board. The First Nation secondary school is situated in the Mi'kmaq community of Eskasoni in Cape Breton Island. Chief Allison Bernard Memorial High School follows the Nova Scotia Curriculum Guide & also offers Mi'kmaq studies.
John Googoo, Principal
johndgoogoo@hotmail.com
Newell Johnson, Vice-Principal

Eskasoni: Eskasoni Elementary & Middle School
P.O. Box 7970
4675 Shore Rd., Eskasoni, NS B1W 1B8, Canada
Tel: 902-379-2825; *Fax:* 902-379-2886
eems@eskasonischool.ca
www.eskasonischool.ca
Grades: Kindergarten - 9; Mi'kmaq language *Note:* Eskasoni Elementary & Middle School is a Mi'kmaq First Nation school, which operates under the direction of the Eskasoni First Nation School Board. Mi'kmaq immersion classes are offered from kindergarten to grade 3.
Philomena Moore, Principal
philmoore46@hotmail.com
Cameron Frost, Vice-Principal

Eskasoni: Eskasoni Ksite'taqnk Day Care
c/o Eskasoni First Nation School Board
P.O. Box 7959
4645 Shore Rd., Eskasoni, NS B1W 1B8
Tel: 902-379-2017
www.eskasonischoolbd.com
Grades: Pre-School *Number of Employees:* 1 coordinator, 6 early childhood educators; 1 cook / day care worker *Note:* The Eskasoni Ksite'taqnk Day Care operates under the administration of the Eskasoni First Nation School Board. The day care offers a Mi'kmaq educational program, taught in the Mi'kmaq language.
Miranda Bernard, Contact

Eskasoni: Eskasoni Unama'ki Training & Education Centre (TEC)
P.O. Box 7010
Eskasoni, NS B1L 1A1, Canada
Tel: 902-379-2758; *Fax:* 902-379-2586
www.unamakitec.ca
Grades: Adult & Alternative Education *Enrollment:* 75 *Number of Employees:* 1 principal; 1 teaching vice-principal; 5 teachers; 1 guidance counsellor; 1 secretary *Note:* Activities of the Unama'ki Training & Education Centre are guided by the Eskasoni First Nation School Board.
Michelle Marshall-Johnson, Principal
Joanne MacDonald, Vice-Principal

Micmac: Indian Brook Education Center
Shubenacadie First Nation Administration
General Delivery, Micmac, NS B0N 1W0
Tel: 902-758-3564; *Fax:* 902-758-2017
www.indianbrook.ca
Other Information: Education: 902-758-2049, ext. 229; Pre-Kindergarten: 902-758-3788
Note: The Indian Brook Education Center is part of the Mi'kmaq First Nation community.

Sydney: Membertou Elementary School
45 Maillard St., Sydney, NS B1S 2P5
Tel: 902-562-2205; *Fax:* 902-562-4561
www.membertouschool.ca
Grades: Primary - 6 *Note:* Membertou Elementary School's staff consists of a Mi'kmaw language teacher. The school follows the curriculum guidelines established by the Nova Scotia Department of Education.
Sharon Bernard, M.Ed, B.Ed, BACS, Principal
sbernard@membertouschool.ca
Lucy Joe, M.Ed, B.Ed, BA, Vice-Principal
ljoe@membertouschool.ca

Trenton: Pictou Landing First Nation School
P.O. Box 116
Site 6, RR#2, Trenton, NS B0K 1X0
Tel: 902-755-9954; *Fax:* 902-752-4916
schooladmin@pictoulandingschool.ca
www.pictoulandingschool.ca
Grades: 1-6 *Note:* The Pictou Landing First Nation School works in partnership with the Pictou Landing First Nation community, its Elders, & parents to provide an education that includes the Mi'kmaw language & culture.
Irene Endicott, Principal

Wagmatcook: Wagmatcookewey School
P.O. Box 30018
Wagmatcook, NS B0E 3N0, Canada
Tel: 902-295-3491
Grades: Primary - 12; Mi'kmaq Studies *Note:* Located on the Wagmatcook First Nation Reserve in Cape Breton, Nova Scotia, the Wagmatcookewey School provides education to Mi'Kmaq First Nation students.
Wayne Morris, Principal

Whycocmagh: We'koqma'q Mikmaw School Secondary Education
80 Reservation Rd., Whycocmagh, NS B0E 3M0, Canada
Tel: 902-756-9000; *Fax:* 902-756-2017
admin@wfns.ca
wfns.ca
Grades: 7-12
John Leonard, Principal
Lisa Lunney, Vice-Principal

Whycocomagh: We'koqma'q Elementary School
P.O. Box 209
15 Reservation Rd., Whycocomagh, NS B0E 3M0, Canada
Tel: 902-756-9000; *Fax:* 902-756-2171
Grades: K.-6

Special Education

Halifax: Atlantic Provinces Special Education Authority (APSEA)
5940 South St., Halifax, NS B3H 1S6, Canada
Tel: 902-424-8500; *Fax:* 902-424-0543
apsea@apsea.ca
www.apsea.ca
Note: The Atlantic Provinces Special Education Authority (APSEA) is an interprovincial cooperative agency established in 1975 by joint agreement among the Ministers of Education of New Brunswick, Newfoundland, Nova Scotia, and Prince Edward Island.
Bertram R. Tulk, Supt., 902-424-7765, fax: 902-424-5819
tulkb@apsea.ca

Schools: Independent & Private

Independent & Private Schools

Bedford: Sandy Lake Academy
435 Hammond's Plains Rd., Bedford, NS B4B 1Y2, Canada
Tel: 902-835-8548; *Fax:* 902-835-9752
principal@sandylakeacademy.ca
www.sandylakeacademy.ca
www.facebook.com/SandyLakeAcademy
twitter.com/SandyLakeAcdmy
Grades: Pre.-12 *Enrollment:* 76 *Note:* A Seventh-day Adventist Christian School
Chris Dupuis, Principal

Guysborough: Chedabucto Education Centre / Guysborough Academy
P.O. Box 19
27 Green St., Guysborough, NS B0H 1N0
Tel: 902-533-2288; *Fax:* 902-533-3554
cecga.srsb.ca
Other Information: Alternate Phone: 902-533-4006
Grades: K-12 *Enrollment:* 296

Halifax: Armbrae Academy
1400 Oxford St., Halifax, NS B3H 3Y8, Canada
Tel: 902-423-7920; *Fax:* 902-423-9731
office@armbrae.ns.ca
www.armbrae.ns.ca
Grades: Pre.-12 *Enrollment:* 245
Gary O'Meara, Headmaster
omeara@armbrae.ednet.ns.ca

Halifax: Halifax Christian Academy
114 Downs Ave., Halifax, NS B3N 1Y6, Canada
Tel: 902-475-1441; *Fax:* 902-477-4922
office@halifaxchristianacademy.ca
www.halifaxchristianacademy.ca
Grades: Pre.-12 *Enrollment:* 243
Jo-an Dennis, Principal

Halifax: Halifax Grammar School
945 Tower Rd., Halifax, NS B3H 2Y2, Canada
Tel: 902-423-9312; *Fax:* 902-423-9315
info@hgs.ns.ca
www.hgs.ns.ca
Grades: Pre.-12 *Enrollment:* 410
Blayne Addley, Headmaster

Halifax: Maritime Muslim Academy
6225 Chebucto Rd., Halifax, NS B3L 1K7, Canada
Tel: 902-429-9067; *Fax:* 902-429-0136
www.maritimemuslimacademy.ca/
Grades: Pre.-12; Islamic studies; Arabic *Enrollment:* 78
Dr. Hadi Salah, Principal

Halifax: Sacred Heart School of Halifax
5820 Spring Garden Rd., Halifax, NS B3H 1X8, Canada
Tel: 902-422-4459; *Fax:* 902-423-7691
admin@shsh.ca
www.sacredheartschool.ns.ca
Grades: Pre.-12 *Enrollment:* 444
Patricia Donnelly, Headmistress
pdonnelly@sacredheartschool.ns.ca

Halifax: Shambhala School
5450 Russell St., Halifax, NS B3K 1W9, Canada
Tel: 902-454-6100; *Fax:* 902-454-6157
director@shambhalaschool.org
www.shambhalaschool.org
Grades: Preschool - 12 *Enrollment:* 160 *Note:* This is a non-denominational school, which offers an enriched curriculum.
Steve Mustain, Director

Lower Sackville: Newbridge Academy
409 Glendale Dr., Lower Sackville, NS B4C 2T6
Tel: 902-252-3339; *Fax:* 902-252-3108
info@newbridgeacademy.ca
www.newbridgeacademy.ca
Grades: Pre.-12 *Enrollment:* 140
Travor MacEachern, CEO/Chair
Jason Wolfe, Headmaster
jason.wolfe@newbridgeacademy.ca

Lunenburg: Class Afloat - West Island College International
P.O. Box 10
97 Kaulbach St., Lunenburg, NS B0J 2C0
Tel: 902-634-1895; *Fax:* 902-634-7155
info@classafloat.com; transcripts@classafloat.com
www.classafloat.com
www.facebook.com/classafloat
twitter.com/classafloat
Grades: 10-Univ. *Enrollment:* 60 *Note:* Students at Class Afloat sail the world on a classic tall ship, which they themselves sail, while engaged in academic study. Courses are available at the following levels of study: grade 11, 12, & first-year university.
David Jones, President

Tantallon: Crossroads Academy
15 French Village Station Rd., Tantallon, NS B3Z 1H3, Canada
Tel: 902-826-1805; *Fax:* 902-826-1867
ca@crossroadsacademy.ca
www.crossroadsacademy.ca
Grades: Pre.-6
Sylvia Luffman, Principal

Truro: Colchester Christian Academy
P.O. Box 393
15 Elm St., Truro, NS B2N 5C5, Canada
Tel: 902-895-6520; *Fax:* 902-893-3727
Grades: Pre.-12 *Enrollment:* 132
Steve Vanderkwaak, Principal

Tusket: Living Waters Christian Academy
P.O. Box 175
Tusket, NS B0W 3M0, Canada
Tel: 902-648-2676; *Fax:* 902-648-2676
Grades: Pre.-9 *Enrollment:* 44
Mardee Nickerson, Acting Principal

Windsor: King's-Edgehill School
33 King's-Edgehill Lane, Windsor, NS B0N 2T0, Canada
Tel: 902-798-2278; *Fax:* 902-798-2105
admissions@kes.ns.ca
www.kes.ns.ca
www.facebook.com/kingsedgehill
twitter.com/kingsedgehill
www.youtube.com/kingsedgehill
Grades: 1-12 *Enrollment:* 282
David R. Penaluna, Headmaster

Wolfville: Landmark East School
708 Main St., Wolfville, NS B4P 1G4
Tel: 902-542-2237; *Fax:* 902-542-4147
Toll-Free: 800-565-5887
admissions@landmarkeast.org
www.landmarkeast.org
Grades: 3-12 *Enrollment:* 55 *Note:* The international school serves students with learning disabilities. Landmark East has an overall student-teacher ratio of 3:1.
Jim Sotvedt, Chair
Peter Coll, Headmaster
pcoll@landmarkeast.org
Glen Currie, Director, Students
gcurrie@landmarkeast.org
Wendy Harris, Head, Academics
wharris@landmarkeast.org

Universities & Colleges

Universities

Antigonish: St. Francis Xavier University
P.O. Box 5000
Antigonish, NS B2G 2W5, Canada
Tel: 902-867-2219; *Fax:* 902-867-2329
admit@stfx.ca
www.stfx.ca
Other Information: Admissions: 902-867-2219
www.facebook.com/stfxuniversity
twitter.com/stfxuniversity
www.youtube.com/user/stfxbox
Full Time Equivalency: 4200 *Note:* The university is primarily an undergraduate university, offering education in the arts, science, business & information systems, & applied programs.
Sean E. Riley, Ph.D., President
sriley@stfx.ca
Dr. Mary B. McGillivray, Vice-President, Academic & Provost
Peter Fardy, Vice-President, University Advancement
Ramsay Duff, Vice-President, Finance & Operations
Mary Coyle, Vice-President & Director, Coady International Institute
Danny McInnis, Acting Registrar
John Blackwell, Director, Research Grants
Lynne Murphy, Librarian

Faculties
Arts
Dr. Steve Baldner, Dean
Science
Dr. William Marshall, Dean
Students
Joe MacDonald, Dean

Schools
Coady International Institute
Mary Coyle, Director
mcoyle@stfx.ca
Enterprise Development Centre
Sue McNeil, Interim Director

Halifax: Atlantic School of Theology
660 Francklyn St., Halifax, NS B3H 3B5, Canada
Tel: 902-423-6939; *Fax:* 902-492-4048
www.astheology.ns.ca
Full Time Equivalency: 150
The Rev. Canon Eric Beresford, President, 902-423-6801
Rev. Dr. David MacLachlan, Academic Dean & Registrar, 902-496-7941
David Myatt, Chief Admin. Officer, 902-496-7946
Joyce Thomson, Library Director, 902-496-7948

Halifax: Dalhousie University
Henry Hicks Academic Administration Bldg.
P.O. Box 15000
6299 South St., Halifax, NS B3H 4R2, Canada
Tel: 902-494-2211; *Fax:* 902-494-1630
communications.marketing@dal.ca
www.dal.ca
Full Time Equivalency: 16000 *Note:* Dalhousie University is a comprehensive teaching & research university located in Atlantic Canada. Dalhousie places special emphasis on Ocean Studies & Health Studies & has a growing involvement in Advanced Technical Studies.
Dr Fred Fountain, Chancellor
Dr Tom Traves, Vice-Chancellor & President, 902-494-2511, fax: 902-494-1658
tom.traves@dal.ca
Dr Carolyn Watters, Acting Vice-Pres., Academic & Provost, 902-494-2586
carolyn.watters@dal.ca
Ken Burt, Vice-Pres., Finance & Admin., 902-494-3862
ken.burt@dal.ca
Floyd Dykeman, Vice-Pres., External, 902-494-2238
floyd.dykeman@dal.ca
Dr Bonnie Neuman, Vice-Pres., Student Services, 902-494-8021
bonnie.neuman@dal.ca
Dr Martha Crago, Vice-Pres., Research, 902-494-8075, fax: 902-494-1595
martha.crago@dal.ca

Faculties
Architecture & Planning
Tel: 902-494-3971; *Fax:* 902-423-6672
arch.office@dal.ca
Christine Macy, Dean
Arts & Social Sciences
Tel: 902-494-1440; *Fax:* 902-494-1957
fass@dal.ca
Dr Robert Summerby-Murray, Dean
Computer Science
Tel: 902-494-2093; *Fax:* 902-492-1517
inquiries@cs.dal.ca
Dr Michael Shephard, Dean
Dentistry
Tel: 902-494-2824; *Fax:* 902-494-2527
Dr Thomas Boran, Dean
thomas.boran@dal.ca
Engineering
Tel: 902-494-6217; *Fax:* 902-429-3011
Dr L. Joshua Leon, Dean
joshua.leon@dal.ca
Graduate Studies
Tel: 902-494-2485; *Fax:* 902-494-8797
Sunny Marche, Acting Dean
sunny.marche@dal.ca
Health Professions
Tel: 902-494-3327; *Fax:* 902-494-1966
Dr William G. Webster, Dean
will.webster@dal.ca
Management
Tel: 902-494-2582; *Fax:* 902-494-1195
Peggy Cunningham, Dean
managementdean@dal.ca
Medicine
Tel: 902-494-6592; *Fax:* 902-494-7119
Dr Thomas J. Marrie, Dean
dean.medicine@dal.ca
Science
Tel: 902-494-3540; *Fax:* 902-494-1123
science@dal.ca
Chris Moore, Dean

Schools
Atlantic Health Promotion Research Centre
Tel: 902-494-2240; *Fax:* 902-494-3594
ahprc@dal.ca
Sandra J. Crowell, Managing Director
Business Administration
Tel: 902-494-7080; *Fax:* 902-494-1107
Dr Greg Hebb, Director
gregory.hebb@dal.ca

Canadian Institute of Fisheries Technology
Tel: 902-494-6030; *Fax:* 902-494-0219
cift@dal.ca
Dr Tom Gill, Director

Centre for Foreign Policy Studies
Tel: 902-494-3769; *Fax:* 902-494-3825
centre@dal.ca
David R. Black, Director

College of Continuing Education
Tel: 902-494-2526; *Fax:* 902-494-3662
ducceinf@dal.ca
Andrew Cochrane, Dean

College of Pharmacy
Tel: 902-494-2378; *Fax:* 902-494-1396
pharmacy@dal.ca
Rita Caldwell, Director

Dental Hygiene
Nancy Neish, Director, 902-494-8864
nancy.neish@dal.ca

Division of Medical Education
Tel: 902-494-1845; *Fax:* 902-494-2278
dme@dal.ca
Dr. Frank Blye, Director

Health & Human Performance
Tel: 902-494-2152; *Fax:* 902-494-5120
hahp@dal.ca
Dr Fred McGinn, Interim Director

Health Administration
Tel: 902-494-7097; *Fax:* 902-494-6849
healthadmin@dal.ca
Dr Joseph M. Byrne, Director

Human Communication Disorders
Tel: 902-494-7052; *Fax:* 902-494-5151
hucd@dal.ca
Dr. Joy Armson, Director

Information Management
Tel: 902-494-3656; *Fax:* 902-494-2451
sim@dal.ca
Fiona Black, Director

International Research & Development
Tel: 902-494-2038; *Fax:* 902-494-1216
ird@dal.ca
Pat Rodee, Director

Neuroscience Institute
Tel: 902-494-1251; *Fax:* 902-494-2050
neurosci@dal.ca
Dr Alan Fine, Director

Nursing
Tel: 902-494-2535; *Fax:* 902-494-3487
nursing@dal.ca
Dr. Patricia Sullivan, Director

Occupational Therapy
Tel: 902-494-8804; *Fax:* 902-494-1229
occupational.therapy@dal.ca
Dr Fazley Siddiq, Director

Physiotherapy
Tel: 902-494-2524; *Fax:* 902-494-1941
physiotherapy@dal.ca
Dr Sandy Rennie, Director

Public Administration
Tel: 902-494-3742; *Fax:* 902-494-7023
dalmpa@dal.ca

Resource & Environmental Studies
Tel: 902-494-3632; *Fax:* 902-494-3728
sres@dal.ca
Dr. Peter Duinker, Director

Schulich School of Law
Tel: 902-494-3495; *Fax:* 902-494-1316
Kim R. Brooks, Dean
lawdean@dal.ca

Social Work
Tel: 902-494-3760; *Fax:* 902-494-6709
social.work@dal.ca
Dr. Wanda Thomas Bernard, Director

Transition Year Program
Prof. Patricia Doyle-Bedwell, Director, 902-494-8810, fax: 902-494-2135
patricia.doyle.bedwell@dal.ca

Affiliations
Nova Scotia Agricultural College
P.O. Box 550
Truro, NS B2N 5E3, Canada
Tel: 902-893-6600
reg@nsac.ca
www.nsac.ns.ca
Full Time Equivalency: 900 *Note:* NSAC has the following academic departments: Business & Social Sciences, Engineering, Environmental Sciences, & Plant & Animal Sciences; as well as, these academic units: Continuing & Distance Education, Research.
Carol Goodwin, Chair
Dr. Bernie Macdonald, Co-President & VP, Admin.
Dr. Leslie MacLaren, Co-President & VP, Academic

University of King's College
6350 Coburg Rd., Halifax, NS B3H 2A1, Canada
Tel: 902-422-1271; *Fax:* 902-423-3357
www.ukings.ns.ca
Full Time Equivalency: 1170
The Hon. Michael A. Meighen, QC, Chancellor
Dr William Barker, President & Vice-Chancellor, ext. 121
Elizabeth Yeo, Registrar, ext. 122
elizabeth.yeo@ukings.ns.ca

Publications
Dalhousie Gazette
6136 University Ave., Halifax, NS B3H 4J2
Tel: 902-128-0
www.dalgazette.com
Josh Boyter, Editor-In-Chief
editor.dalgazatte.com

Halifax: Mount Saint Vincent University
166 Bedford Hwy., Halifax, NS B3M 2J6, Canada
Tel: 902-457-6117; *Fax:* 902-457-6498
www.msvu.ca
Full Time Equivalency: 4900
Kathryn E. Laurin, M.Mus., President & Vice-Chancellor
Donna Woolcott, Vice-President
Brigitte MacInnes, Registrar
Amanda Whitewood, C.M.A., C.H.E., Vice-President
Sr. Donna Geernaert, Chancellor

Faculties
Arts & Sciences
Susan Mumm, Ph.D., Dean

Education
Jim Sharpe, Ph.D., Dean

Professional Studies
Mary Lyon, Ph.D., Dean

Publications
Jargon

Picaro

Halifax: NSCAD University
5163 Duke St., Halifax, NS B3J 3J6, Canada
Tel: 902-444-9600; *Fax:* 902-425-2420
admiss@nscad.ca
www.nscad.ca
Full Time Equivalency: 1025
Prof. David B. Smith, President
Kenn Gardner Honeychurch, Sr. Vice-President
Peter Flemming, Vice-President
Dr. Laurelle LeVert, Registrar & Director
Deborah Carver, Executive Director

Halifax: Saint Mary's University
923 Robie St., Halifax, NS B3H 3C3, Canada
Tel: 902-420-5400
public.affairs@smu.ca; webmaster@smu.ca; helpdesk@smu.ca
www.smu.ca
Other Information: Students Closure/Cancellation Hotline: 902-491-6263
www.facebook.com/smuhalifax
twitter.com/SMUHalifaxNews
Full Time Equivalency: 8500 *Note:* Offering a wide range of both undergraduate & graduate programs, Saint Mary's University has a student-faculty ratio of 21-1.
Most Rev. Terrence Prendergast, Chancellor
Most Rev. Claude Champagne, Vice-Chancellor
Dr. J. Colin Dodds, President
Gabrielle Morrison, Vice-President, Administration
Dr. Terry Murphy, Vice-President, Academic & Research

Faculties
Arts
Dr. Esther Enns, Dean

Commerce
Dr. David Wicks, Dean

Continuing Education
Betty MacDonald, Director
betty.macdonald@smu.ca

Graduate Studies & Research
Dr. Kevin Vessey, Dean

Science
Dr. Malcolm Butler, Dean

Pointe-de-L'Église: Université Sainte-Anne
1695, Route 1, Pointe-de-L'Église, NS B0W 1M0, Canada
Tél: 902-769-2114; *Téléc:* 902-769-2930
Ligne sans frais: 1-888-338-8337
www.usainteanne.ca
facebook.com/usainteanne
twitter.com/usainteanne
www.youtube.com/user/usainteannecom/videos
Note: La seule institution d'enseignement post-secondaire de langue française en Nouvelle-Écosse. Programmes: administration des affaires, éducation, sciences humaines, science pures, programmes professionnels. Campus: Pointe-de-L'Église, Halifax, Petit-de-Grat, Saint-Joseph-du Moine, et Tusket
Kenneth Deveau, Vice-recteur à l'enseignement et recherche
Murielle Comeau, Registraire
Éric Tufts, Vice-recteur (Administrations)
Hughie Batherson, Vice-recteur (Affaires étudiantes)
Allister Surette, Vice-recteur (Développement & partenariats)

Campuses
Campus de Halifax
1589, rue Walnut, Halifax, NS B3H 3S1, Canada
Tel: 902-424-2630; *Fax:* 902-424-3607
Daniel Lamy, Directeur
Daniel.Lamy@usainteanne.ca

Campus de Petit-de-Grat
3433, rte 206, Petit-de-Grat, NS B0E 2L0, Canada
Tel: 902-226-3900; *Fax:* 902-226-3919
Philippe Haché, Directeur
philippe.hache@usainteanne.ca

Campus de Saint-Joseph-du-Moine
12521, Cabot Trail, St-Joseph-du-Moine, NS B0E 3A0, Canada
Tel: 902-244-4100; *Fax:* 902-224-4119
René Aucoin, Directeur
Rene.Aucoin@usainteanne.ca

Campus de Tusket
1 Slocumb Cres., Tusket, NS B0W 3M0, Canada
Tel: 902-648-3524; *Fax:* 902-648-3525
Marie-Germaine Chartrand, Directrice
mariegermaine.chartrand@usainteanne.ca

Sydney: Cape Breton University
P.O. Box 5300
1250 Grand Lake Rd., Sydney, NS B1P 6L2, Canada
Tel: 902-539-5300; *Fax:* 902-562-0119
Toll-Free: 888-959-9995
welcome@cbu.ca; registrar@cbu.ca
www.capebretonu.ca
Full Time Equivalency: 3110 *Note:* The university is also home to Unama'ki College which offers Mi'kmaw programs and services, such as teacher training, court worker certification, business, Mi'kmaw language, health careers, and natural resources. Email: mci@cbu.ca
Annette Verschuren, Chancellor
H. John Harker, President & Vice-Chancellor, 902-563-1333
john_harker@cbu.ca
Gordon MacInnis, Vice-Pres., Finance & Operations, 902-563-1128
gordon_macinnis@cbu.ca
Robert Baily, Vice-Pres., Academic & Research, 902-563-1980
robert_bailey@cbu.ca
Roger Winn, Vice-Pres., Academic
roger_winn@cbu.ca
Brown Keith, Vice-Pres., External, 902-563-1859
keith_brown@cbu.ca
Dr Ross McCurdy, COO, 902-563-1392
ross_mccurdy@cbu.ca
Debbie Rudderham, CIO, 902-563-1446
debbie_rudderham@cbu.ca
Alexis Manley, Registrar/VP, Student Services, 902-563-1650
registrar@cbu.ca

Faculties
Arts & Social Studies
Dr Roderick Nicholls, Dean, 902-563-1354
rod_nicholls@cbu.ca

Science & Technology
Dr Allen Britten, Dean, 902-563-1262
allen_britten@cbu.ca

Schools
Shannon School of Business
John MacKinnon, Dean, 902-563-1221
john_mackinnon@cbu.ca

School of Professional & Graduate Studies
Robert Baily, Interim Dean, 902-563-1304
brenda_leloup@cbu.ca

Publications
Caper Times
Suzanne MacNeil, Editor-In-Chief, 902-563-1473
editor@capertimes.ca

The 60th Meridian

Wolfville: Acadia Divinity College
31 Horton Ave., Wolfville, NS B4P 2R6, Canada
Tel: 902-585-2210; *Fax:* 902-585-2233
Toll-Free: 866-875-8975
adc.acadiau.ca
Full Time Equivalency: 160
Dr Harry G. Gardner, President/Dean, Theology
Dr Bruce Fawcett, Academic Dean/Dir., Doctoral Studies
Shawna Peverill, Registrar, 902-585-2216

Wolfville: Acadia University
15 University Ave., Wolfville, NS B4P 2R6, Canada
Tel: 902-542-2201; *Fax:* 902-585-1072
Toll-Free: 877-585-1121
agi@acadiau.ca
www.acadiau.ca
www.facebook.com/acadiauniversity
twitter.com/acadiau
www.youtube.com/user/AcadiaWebmaster
Full Time Equivalency: 3620
Ray Ivany, Pres./Vice-Chancellor, 902-585-1218, fax: 902.585.1077
president@acadiau.ca
Dr. Tom Herman, Vice-Pres., Academic, ext. 1357
Dr Akivah Starkman, Vice-Pres., Admin.
Rosemary Jotcham, Registrar
Scott Roberts, Exec. Dir., Communications & Public Affairs, 902-585-1705

Faculties
Arts
Robert Perrins, B.A., M.A., Ph.D., Dean, ext. 1782

Professional Studies
Dr Heather Hemming, B.Sc., M.Sc., D.P.E., Dean, ext. 1133

Pure & Applied Science
Dr Peter Williams, B.Sc., M.Sc., Ph.D., Dean, ext. 1472

Theology
Dr Harry Gardner, B.A., B.D., Th.M., Ph.D., Dean, ext. 2212

Schools
Business Administration
Dr Ian Hutchinson, Director, ext. 1205

Computer Science
Dr Daniel Silver, Director, ext. 1331

Education
Dr. Ann Vibert, Director, ext. 1229

Engineering
Andrew Mitchell, Dip.Eng., B.Eng., M.A.Sc., Director, ext. 1206

Music
Dr Jeff Hennessy, Director, ext. 1512

Nutrition & Dietetics
Barb Anderson, Director, ext. 1346

Recreation, Management & Kinesiology
Dr Rene Murphy, Director, ext. 1559

Publications
The Athenaeum
Note: The official student newspaper
Tim Hansen, Editor-in-Chief

Colleges

Halifax: Nova Scotia Community College (NSCC)
P.O. Box 220
Halifax, NS B3J 2M4, Canada
Tel: 902-491-4911; *Fax:* 902-491-3514
Toll-Free: 1-866-679-6722
admissions@nscc.ca
www.nscc.ca
Other Information: Toll Free Fax: 1-866-329-6722
TTY: 1-866-288-7034
Note: The college has the following institutes: The Aviation Institute, located in the Halifax Regional Municipality at Shearwater, the Centre of Geographic Sciences in Lawrencetown, & the Nautical Institute in Port Hawkesbury & the School of Fisheries at Pictou.
Sandra Greer, Chair
Joan McArthur-Blair, President, 902-491-6701, fax: 902-491-4825
Ronald Farrell, Dean, Trades & Technology
Ken Jones, Dean, Business Development
Judith Limkilde, Dean, Health & Human Services
Claudine Lowry, Dean, Organizational Learning
George MacDonald, Dean, Access
Bruce Tawse, Dean, Applied Arts & New Media
Bill Walsh, Dean, Business

Campuses
Akerley Campus
21 Woodlawn Rd., Dartmouth, NS B3W 2R7, Canada
Tel: 902-491-4940; *Fax:* 902-491-4903
akerley.info@nscc.ca
Other Information: Centre for Student Success, Phone: 902-491-4940
Enrollment: 4000
Graham MacDermott, Principal

Cumberland Campus Community Learning Centre
147 Albion St. South, Amherst, NS B4H 2X2, Canada
Tel: 902-661-3180; *Fax:* 902-661-3170

Annapolis Valley Campus & Centre of Geographic Sciences (COGS)
50 Elliott Rd., Lawrencetown, NS B0S 1M0
Tel: 902-825-3491; *Fax:* 902-825-2285
avc.info@nscc.ca
Other Information: Centre for Student Success, Phone: 902-825-2930
Enrollment: 900
Jim Stanley, Principal

Burridge Campus
372 Pleasant St., Yarmouth, NS B5A 2L2, Canada
Tel: 902-742-0760; *Fax:* 902-749-2402
burridge.info@nscc.ca
Other Information: Centre for Student Success, Phone: 902-742-0760
Enrollment: 950
Marcel Cottreau, Principal

Cumberland Campus
P.O. Box 550
1 Main St., Springhill, NS B0M 1X0, Canada
Tel: 902-597-3737; *Fax:* 902-597-8548
cumberland.info@nscc.ca
Other Information: Centre for Student Success, Phone: 902-597-4101
Enrollment: 400
Shelley Carter-Rose, Principal

Aviation Institute - Dartmouth Gate
#100, 375 Pleasant St., Dartmouth, NS B2Y 4N4, Canada
Tel: 902-491-4937; *Fax:* 902-491-4989

Institute of Technology Campus
P.O. Box 2210
5685 Leeds St., Halifax, NS B3J 3C4, Canada
Tel: 902-491-6722; *Fax:* 902-491-4800
it.info@nscc.ca
Other Information: Centre for Student Success, Phone: 902-491-4752
Enrollment: 5200
Daurene Lewis, Principal

Kingstec Campus
236 Belcher St., Kentville, NS B4N 0A6, Canada
Tel: 902-678-7341; *Fax:* 902-679-4381
kingstec.info@nscc.ca
Other Information: Centre for Student Success, Phone: 902-679-7361
Enrollment: 1750
Don Bureaux, Principal

Lunenburg Campus
75 High St., Bridgewater, NS B4V 1V8, Canada
Tel: 902-543-4608; *Fax:* 902-543-0190
lunenburg.info@nscc.ca

Nautical Institute
226 Reeves St., Port Hawkesbury, NS B9A 2A2, Canada
Tel: 902-625-4228; *Fax:* 902-625-0193
Craig Collins, Principal

Marconi Campus
P.O. Box 1042
1240 Grand Lake Rd., Sydney, NS B1P 6J7, Canada
Tel: 902-563-2450; *Fax:* 902-563-3440
marconi.info@nscc.ca
Other Information: Centre for Student Success, Phone: 902-563-2464
Enrollment: 2300
Dave MacLean, Principal

NSCC Online Learning
P.O. Box 1153
5685 Leeds St., Halifax, NS B3J 2X1, Canada
Tel: 902-491-6774; *Fax:* 902-491-4835
Toll-Free: 1-877-491-6774
online.learning@nscc.ca

Pictou Campus
P.O. Box 820
39 Acadia Ave., Stellarton, NS B0K 1S0, Canada
Tel: 902-752-2002; *Fax:* 902-752-5446
pictou.info@nscc.ca
Other Information: Centre for Student Success, Phone: 902-755-7299
Enrollment: 1675
Dave Freckelton, Principal

Shelburne Campus
P.O. Box 760
1575 Lake Rd., Shelburne, NS B0T 1W0, Canada
Tel: 902-875-8640; *Fax:* 902-875-3797
shelburne.info@nscc.ca
Other Information: Centre for Student Success, Phone: 902-875-8640
Enrollment: 350
Marcel Cottreau, Principal

Strait Area Campus
226 Reeves St., Port Hawkesbury, NS B9A 2A2, Canada
Tel: 902-625-4017; *Fax:* 902-625-0193
strait.info@nscc.ca
Other Information: Centre for Student Success, Phone: 902-625-4017
Enrollment: 800 *Note:* The Nautical Institute is located on the Strait Area Campus.
Bert Lewis, Principal

Truro Campus
36 Arthur St., Truro, NS B2N 1X5, Canada
Tel: 902-893-5385; *Fax:* 902-893-5610
truro.info@nscc.ca
www.truro.nscc.ca
Other Information: Centre for Student Success, Phone: 902-893-5346
Enrollment: 1300
Kevin Quinlan, Principal

Waterfront Campus
80 Mawiomi Pl., Dartmouth, NS B2Y 0A5
Tel: 902-491-1100; *Fax:* 902-491-1795
waterfront.info@nscc.ca
Other Information: Centre for Student Success, Phone: 902-491-1793
Enrollment: 4300
Cathy MacLean, Principal

Halifax: University of King's College
6350 Coburg Rd., Halifax, NS B3H 2A1, Canada
Tel: 902-422-1271; *Fax:* 902-423-3357
www.ukings.ns.ca
Full Time Equivalency: 1100

Publications
Watch
Note: Student newspaper at University of King's College

Post Secondary/Technical

Post Secondary/Technical

Bedford: C.L. Douglas - Centre for Computer Studies
1142 Bedford Hwy., Bedford, NS B4A 1B8, Canada
Tel: 902-835-8880; *Fax:* 902-835-6751
info@cldouglas.com
www.cldouglas.com
Note: Computer software, network management training.
Paul Cudmore

Halifax: Maritime Conservatory of Performing Arts
6199 Chebucto Rd., Halifax, NS B3L 1K7, Canada
Tel: 902-423-6995; *Fax:* 902-423-6029
admin@maritimeconservatory.com
www.maritimeconservatory.com
Cheryl McCarthy, Dean, School of Music
cheryl.mcpa@gmail.com
Barbara Dearborn, Dean, School of Dance
bjdearborn@hotmail.com

Halifax: **Success College**
800 Sackville Dr., Halifax, NS B4E 1R8, Canada
Toll-Free: 1-800-352-0094
successcollege.ca
www.facebook.com/pages/Success-College/191535104191456
www.twitter.com/Success_NS
www.linkedin.com/company/1169863
www.youtube.com/user/SuccessCollegeNS
Note: Work-related programs.
Hazel Matthews

Hubbards: **Atlantic Home Building & Renovation Sector Council**
P.O. Box 337
Hubbards, NS B0J 1T0
Toll-Free: 1-800-565-2151
info@ahbrsc.com
www.ahbrsc.com
Note: The Atlantic Home Building & Renovation Sector Council has provided courses to over 7,000 builders, carpenters, renovators, designers, inspectors, labourers, & sub-trade workers.
Michael Montgomery, Executive Director, 902-240-1133

North Sydney: **Mactech Distance Education**
P.O. Box 457
North Sydney, NS B2A 3M3, Canada
Fax: 902-794-1414
Toll-Free: 1-888-622-8324
administration@HomeEd.com
www.homeed.com
www.facebook.com/group.php?gid=39322797586
twitter.com/Mactech_HomeEd
www.youtube.com/user/MactechDistanceEd
Note: Distance education
Heather Sophocleous, Vice-President of Operations
hsophocleous@HomeEd.com

St. Ann's: **The Gaelic College/Colaisde Na Gàidhlig**
P.O. Box 80
51779 Cabot Trail, St. Ann's, NS B0C 1H0, Canada
Tel: 902-295-3411; *Fax:* 902-295-2912
info@gaeliccollege.edu
www.gaeliccollege.edu
www.facebook.com/GaelicCollege
twitter.com/GaelicCollege
youtube.com/user/gaeliccollege
Number of Schools: 1

Truro: **Institute for Human Services Education**
#1, 60 Lorne St., 2nd Fl., Truro, NS B2N 3K3, Canada
Tel: 902-893-3342; *Fax:* 902-895-4487
admin@inst-hse.ca
www.inst-hse.ca
Note: Early Childhood Education Diploma, Public School Program Assistants Certificate, Special Education Diploma, Youth Worker Diploma
Kimberly Elliott, B.Comm., Executive Director
Anna MacDonell, CDSA IV, B.A., M.Ed., Program Director
Debbie Connolly, CDSA IV, BBA, Student Services Coordinator

Nunavut

Government Agencies

Iqaluit: **Nunavut - Department of Education**
Sivummut Building, 2nd Fl.
P.O. Box 1000 910
Iqaluit, NU X0A 0H0, Canada
Tél: 867-975-5600; *Téléc:* 867-975-5605
www.edu.gov.nu.ca
Hon. Eva Aariak, Minister

School Boards/Districts/Divisions

Public

Arctic Bay: **Arctic Bay District Education Authority**
P.O. Box 90
Arctic Bay, NU X0A 0A0, Canada
Tel: 867-439-8843
Grades: Kindergarten - 12

Arviat: **Arviat District Education Authority**
P.O. Box 180
Arviat, NU X0C 0E0, Canada
Tel: 867-857-2885; *Fax:* 867-857-2622

Baker Lake: **Baker Lake District Education Authority**
P.O. Box 119
Baker Lake, NU X0C 0A0, Canada
Tel: 867-793-4657; *Fax:* 867-793-4659

Baker Lake: **Kivalliq School Operations**
P.O. Box 90
Baker Lake, NU X0C 0A0, Canada
Tel: 867-793-2803; *Fax:* 867-793-2996
kivalliq.edu.nu.ca

Cambridge Bay: **Cambridge Bay District Education Authority**
Also known as: Ikaluktutiak District Education Authority
P.O. Box 9
Cambridge Bay, NU X0B 0C0, Canada
Tel: 867-983-2510; *Fax:* 867-983-2515
Karen Wilford, Chair

Cape Dorset: **Cape Dorset District Education Authority**
P.O. Box 210
Cape Dorset, NU X0A 0C0, Canada
Tel: 867-897-8826
Grades: Kindergarten - 12; Inuktitut

Chesterfield Inlet: **Chesterfield Inlet District Education Authority**
Victor Sammurtok School
P.O. Box 6
Chesterfield Inlet, NU X0C 0B0, Canada
Tel: 867-898-9007; *Fax:* 867-898-9143
www.vsschool.ca/contact.htm
Solomon Autut, Chair
Allan Pitcher, Principal, Victor Sammurtok School
apitcher@kivalliq.edu.nu.ca

Clyde River: **Clyde River District Education Authority**
General Delivery, Clyde River, NU X0A 0E0, Canada
Tel: 867-924-6309; *Fax:* 867-924-6247
Jacob Jaypoody

Coral Harbour: **Coral Harbour District Education Authority**
Coral Harbour, NU
Tel: 867-925-8637
Other Information: Alternate Phone: 867-925-9923
Dino Bruce, Chair

Gjoa Haven: **Gjoa Haven District Education Authority**
General Delivery, Gjoa Haven, NU X0E 1J0, Canada
Tel: 867-360-7414; *Fax:* 867-360-7314
Raymond Kamookak, Chair

Grise Fiord: **Grise Fiord District Education Authority**
General Delivery, Grise Fiord, NU X0A 0J0, Canada
Tel: 867-980-9921

Hall Beach: **Hall Beach District Education Authority**
P.O. Box 83
Hall Beach, NU X0A 0K0, Canada
Tel: 867-928-8839
Grades: Kindergarten - 12

Igloolik: **Igloolik District Education Authority**
P.O. Box 150
Igloolik, NU X0A 0L0, Canada
Tel: 867-934-8909; *Fax:* 867-934-8571
Lucasi Ivvalu, Chair

Iqaluit: **Apex District Education Authority**
P.O. Box 1420
Iqaluit, NU X0A 0H0, Canada
Tel: 867-979-6597

Iqaluit: **La Commission scolaire francophone du Nunavut**
P.O. Box 11008
Iqaluit, NU X0A 1H0, Canada
Tél: 867-979-5849; *Téléc:* 867-979-5878
info.ecoletrois-soleils@csfn.ca
www.trois-soleils.ca
Martine St-Louis, Directrice

Iqaluit: **Iqaluit District Education Authority**
P.O. Box 235
Iqaluit, NU X0A 0H0, Canada
Tel: 867-979-5314; *Fax:* 867-979-0330
ssherman@qikiqtani.edu.nu.ca
iqaluitdistricteducationauthority.com
Sabrina Sherman, Administrator

Kimmirut: **Kimmirut District Education Authority**
General Delivery, Kimmirut, NU X0A 0N0, Canada
Tel: 867-939-2221; *Fax:* 867-939-2334
Pudloo Akavak, Chair

Kugaaruk: **Kugaaruk District Education Authority**
c/o Kugaaruk Iliniarvik
P.O. Box 53
Kugaaruk, NU X0B 1K0, Canada
Tel: 867-769-6211; *Fax:* 867-769-6116
Remi Krikort, Chair

Kugluktuk: **Kitikmeot School Operations**
P.O. Box 287
Kugluktuk, NU X0B 0E0, Canada
Tel: 867-982-7220; *Fax:* 867-982-3054
kitikmeot.edu.nu.ca

Kugluktuk: **Kugluktuk District Education Authority**
P.O. Box 273
Kugluktuk, NU X0B 0E0, Canada
Tel: 867-982-5001; *Fax:* 867-982-5706
Simon Kuliktana, Chair

Pangnirtung: **Pangnirtung District Education Authority**
P.O. Box 54
Pangnirtung, NU X0A 0R0, Canada
Tel: 867-473-8810; *Fax:* 867-473-8718
Tim Evic, Chair

Pond Inlet: **Pond Inlet District Education Authority**
General Delivery, Pond Inlet, NU X0A 0S0, Canada
Tel: 867-899-8779; *Fax:* 867-899-8780
Norman Simonie, Chair

Pond Inlet: **Qikiqtani School Operations**
P.O. Box 429
Pond Inlet, NU X0A 0S0, Canada
Tel: 867-899-7350; *Fax:* 867-899-7334
qikiqtani.edu.nu.ca
Trudy Pettigrew, Executive Director

Qikiqtarjuaq: **Qikiqtarjuaq District Education Authority**
P.O. Box 7
Qikiqtarjuaq, NU X0A 0B0, Canada
Tel: 867-927-8938; *Fax:* 867-927-8067
Toomasie Newkingnak, Chair

Rankin Inlet: **Rankin Inlet District Education Authority**
PO Bag 002, Rankin Inlet, NU X0C 0G0, Canada
Tel: 867-645-2642; *Fax:* 867-645-2209
Darrin Nichol, Chair

Repulse Bay: **Repulse Bay District Education Authority**
P.O. Box 105
Repulse Bay, NU X0C 0H0, Canada
Tel: 867-462-4045; *Fax:* 867-462-4232
Elizabeth Kidlapik, Chair

Resolute Bay: **Resolute Bay District Education Authority**
P.O. Box 120
Resolute Bay, NU X0A 0V0, Canada
Tel: 867-252-3888; *Fax:* 867-252-3690
Zipporah K. Aronsen, Chair

Sanikiluaq: **Sanikiluaq District Education Authority**
General Delivery, Sanikiluaq, NU X0A 0W0, Canada
Tel: 867-266-8816; *Fax:* 867-266-8843
Lucassie Arragutainaq, Chair

Taloyoak: **Taloyoak District Education Authority**
c/o Netsilik Ilihakvik
P.O. Box 9
Taloyoak, NU X0B 1B0, Canada
Tel: 867-561-6706; *Fax:* 867-561-5036
Johnny Kootook, Chair

Whale Cove: **Whale Cove District Education Authority**
P.O. Box 90
Whale Cove, NU X0C 0J0, Canada
Tel: 867-896-9300; *Fax:* 867-896-9005
Grades: K.-12 *Enrollment:* 110
Imelda Angotialuk, Chair

Post Secondary/Technical

Post Secondary/Technical

Arviat: **Nunavut Arctic College**
Head Office
P.O. Box 230
Arviat, NU X0C 0E0, Canada
Tel: 867-857-8608; *Fax:* 867-857-8623
Toll-Free: 866-988-4636
www.arcticcollege.ca

Michael Shouldice, President
Linda Pemik, Director, Academic Affairs, 867-857-8603, fax: 867-857-8623
linda.pemik@arcticcollege.ca
Penny Dominix-Nadeau, Registrar, 866-979-7222, fax: 867-979-7103
penny.dominix-nadeau@arcticcollege.ca

Campuses
Kitikmeot Campus - Cambridge Bay
P.O. Box 54
Cambridge Bay, NU X0B 0C0, Canada
Tel: 867-983-4107; *Fax:* 867-983-4106
Toll-Free: 866-988-4636
Fiona Buchan-Corey, Director
Kivalliq Campus - Rankin Inlet
P.O. Box 002
Rankin Inlet, NU X0C 0G0, Canada
Tel: 867-645-5500; *Fax:* 867-645-2387
Mike Shouldice, Director, 866-988-4636, fax: 867-645-2387
Nunatta Campus - Iqaluit
P.O. Box 600
Iqaluit, NU X0A 0H0, Canada
Tel: 867-979-7200; *Fax:* 867-979-7102
Peesee Pitsiulak-Stephens, Director, 867-979-7216, fax: 867-979-7102

Ontario

Government Agencies

Toronto: **Ministry of Education**
Mowat Block, 14th Fl.
900 Bay St., Toronto, ON M7A 1L2
Tel: 416-325-2929; *Fax:* 416-325-6348
Toll-Free: 1-800-387-5514
info@edu.gov.on.ca
www.edu.gov.on.ca
TTY: 1-800-325-3408
twitter.com/OntarioEDU
www.youtube.com/user/OntarioEDU

Number of Employees: 1700 *Note:* The ministry administers the system of publicly funded elementary and secondary school education in Ontario.
Laurel Broten, Minister
Marie-Lison Fougère, Director, 416-325-2660

Campuses
Barrie
20 Rose St., 2nd Fl., Barrie, ON L4M 2T2, Canada
Fax: 705-725-7635
Toll-Free: 800-471-0713
London
#207, 217 York St., London, ON N6A 5P9, Canada
Fax: 519-667-9769
Toll-Free: 800-265-4221
North Bay/Sudbury
#211, 447 McKeown Ave., North Bay, ON P1B 9S9, Canada
Fax: 705-497-6896
Toll-Free: 800-461-9570
Ottawa
#504, 1580 Merivale Rd., Nepean, ON K2G 4B5, Canada
Fax: 613-225-2881
Toll-Free: 800-267-1067
Thunder Bay
#336, 435 James St. South, Thunder Bay, ON P7E 6S9, Canada
Fax: 807-475-1550
Toll-Free: 800-465-5020
Toronto & Area
880 Bay St., 2nd Fl., Toronto, ON M7A 1N3, Canada
Fax: 416-325-4190
Toll-Free: 800-268-5755

Toronto: **Ministry of Training, Colleges & Universities**
Mowat Block
900 Bay St. 14th Fl., Toronto, ON M7A 1N2, Canada
Tel: 416-325-2929; *Fax:* 416-325-6348
information.met@ontario.ca
www.tcu.gov.on.ca
TTY: 1-800-263-289

School Boards/Districts/Divisions

Public

Aurora: **York Region District School Board**
The Education Centre
60 Wellington St. West, Aurora, ON L4G 3H2, Canada
Tel: 905-727-3141; *Fax:* 905-727-1931
feedback@yrdsb.edu.on.ca
www.yrdsb.edu.on.ca

Grades: Pre-K.-12 *Enrollment:* 112000
Ken Thurston, Dir.
ken.thurston@yrdsb.edu.on.ca
Bruce Richardson, Assoc. Dir., Bus. Services
bruce.richardson@yrdsb.edu.on.ca
Diane Giangrande, Chair, 905-770-0826
diane.giangrande@yrdsb.edu.on.ca

Belleville: **Hastings & Prince Edward District School Board**
156 Ann St., Belleville, ON K8N 1N9, Canada
Tel: 613-966-1170; *Fax:* 613-966-6023
Toll-Free: 800-267-4350
information@hpedsb.on.ca
www.hpedsb.on.ca

Grades: JK-12 *Enrollment:* 15700
Kathy Soule, Director, Education
Carl Pitman, Chair

Brantford: **Grand Erie District School Board**
Education Centre
349 Erie Ave., Brantford, ON N3T 5V3, Canada
Tel: 519-756-6301; *Fax:* 519-756-9181
Toll-Free: 1-888-548-8878
www.granderie.ca

Number of Schools: 64 elementary schools; 18 secondary schools *Grades:* JK - 12; Special Ed; Continuing Ed. *Enrollment:* 28226
Jane Angus, Chair, 519-753-2530
jane.angus@granderie.ca
Jim Wibberley, Director, Education, & Secretary, 519-756-6301, ext. 281137
Sharon Bell, Manager, Human Resources, 519-756-6301, ext. 281289
Kevin Holly, Manager, Information Technology Services, 519-754-0696, ext. 287033
Kathy Kirby, Manager, Business Services, 519-754-0696, ext. 281123
Phil Kuckyt, Manager, Transportation Services, 519-751-7532, ext. 282202
Michael Tancredi, Manager, Facilities Services, 519-751-7532, ext. 281161
Wayne Hobbs, Executive Supervisor, Student Support Services, 519-754-0696, ext. 287237
Jamie Gunn, Treasurer, 519-756-6301, ext. 281142

Brockville: **Upper Canada District School Board**
Administration Building
225 Central Ave. West, Brockville, ON K6V 5X1, Canada
Tel: 613-342-0371; *Toll-Free:* 1-800-267-7131
inquiries@ucdsb.on.ca
www.ucdsb.on.ca

Number of Schools: 100 elementary & secondary schools (alternative & continuing ed) *Grades:* K-12; Alternative Ed; Continuing Ed *Enrollment:* 30825 *Number of Employees:* 5000
David K. Thomas, Director, Education, 613-342-0371, ext. 1234, fax: 613-342-6084
david.thomas@ucdsb.on.ca
Ian Carswell, Associate Director, 613-342-0371, ext. 1397, fax: 613-342-0277
ian.carswell@ucdsb.on.ca
David Coombs, Superintendent, School Effectiveness, 613-933-5256, ext. 4279, fax: 613-933-5275
david.coombs@ucdsb.on.ca
Susan Edwards, Superintendent, Student Engagement, 877-485-1211
susan.edwards@ucdsb.on.ca
Rick Gales, Superintendent, Business, 613-342-0371, ext. 1255, fax: 613-343-0277
rick.gales@ucdsb.on.ca
Ted Kennedy, Superintendent, School Operations, 613-258-9393, ext. 2551, fax: 613-258-6321
ted.kennedy@ucdsb.on.ca
Linda Lumsden, Superintendent, School Effectiveness, 613-342-0371, ext. 1414, fax: 613-342-6084
linda.lumsden@ucdsb.on.ca
Charlotte Patterson, Superintendent, Human Resources, 613-342-0371, ext. 1240, fax: 613-342-0277
charlotte.patterson@ucdsb.on.ca
Jeremy Hobbs, Chief Information & Facilities Officer, 613-342-0371, ext. 1126, fax: 613-498-0291
jeremy.hobbs@ucdsb.on.ca
Terry Davies, Officer, Accountability & Alignment, 613-342-0371, ext. 1274, fax: 613-342-6084
terry.davies@ucdsb.on.ca
Terry Simzer, Manager, Communications, 613-342-0371, ext. 1119, fax: 613-342-0277
terry.simzer@ucdsb.on.ca
Frances Boomhouwer, Trustee Liaison, 613-342-0371, ext. 1279, fax: 613-342-6084
frances.boomhouwer@ucdsb.on.ca

Burlington: **Halton District School Board**
J.W. Singleton Education Centre
P.O. Box 5005 LCD 1
2050 Guelph Line, Burlington, ON L7R 3Z2, Canada
Tel: 905-335-3663; *Fax:* 905-335-9802
inquiry@haltonbus.ca (student transportation)
www.hdsb.ca
Other Information: Special Ed. Ctr., Student Svs., & Programs, Phone: 905-631-6120

Number of Schools: 80 elementary schools; 17 secondary schools *Grades:* Elementary - Secondary *Enrollment:* 54000 *Number of Employees:* 3,244 teachers; 1,350 non-teaching & support staff; 181 principals & vice-principals
Bruce Jones, Chair, 905-257-5926, fax: 905-257-5923
jonesbr@hdsb.ca
David Euale, Director, Education, fax: 905-335-4447
director@hdsb.ca
Ruth Peden, Acting Associate Director, Education, 905-335-3663, ext. 3352, fax: 905-335-4447
pedenr@hdsb.ca
Marnie Denton, Manager, Communication Services, fax: 905-335-4447
dentonm@hdsb.ca
Gail Gortmaker, Manager, Director's Office, fax: 905-335-4447
gortmakerg@hdsb.ca
Suzanne Muir, Coordinator, Diversity, 905-631-6120, ext. 434, fax: 905-335-4447
muirs@hdsb.ca
Jacki Oxley, Liaison, School & Community, fax: 905-335-4447
oxleyj@hdsb.ca

Chesley: **Bluewater District School Board**
P.O. Box 190
351 - 1st Ave. North, Chesley, ON N0G 1L0, Canada
Tel: 519-363-2014; *Fax:* 519-370-2909
Toll-Free: 1-800-661-7509
communications@bwdsb.on.ca
www.bwdsb.on.ca

Grades: Elementary - Secondary; Special Ed. *Enrollment:* 19454
Jennifer Yenssen, Chair
Mary Ann Alton, Director, Education
Brenda Booth, Treasurer & Superintendent, Business
Marnie Coke, Superintendent, Elementary Education
Alana Murray, Superintendent, Secondary Education
Jean Stephenson, Superintendent, Student Success
Lori Wilder, Superintendent, Student Services
Jacqui Traverse-Thomas, Principal, Program
Richard Thomas, Coordinator, Communications

Fort Frances: **Rainy River District School Board**
522 Second St. East, Fort Frances, ON P9A 1N4, Canada
Tel: 807-274-9855; *Fax:* 807-274-5078
Toll-Free: 800-214-1753
www.rrdsb.com

Enrollment: 3080
Heather Campbell, Director, Education
Dan Belluz, Chair

Guelph: **Upper Grand District School Board**
Main Office
500 Victoria Rd. North, Guelph, ON N1E 6K2
Tel: 519-822-4420; *Fax:* 519-822-4487
Toll-Free: 800-321-4025
inquiry@ugdsb.on.ca
www.ugdsb.on.ca

Number of Schools: 60 elementary schools; 11 secondary schools *Grades:* JK-12; Continuing Ed. *Enrollment:* 32000
Bob Borden, Chair, 519-822-4420, ext. 735
bob.borden@ugdsb.on.ca
Martha Rogers, Director, Education, & Secretary-Treasurer

***Hamilton:* Hamilton-Wentworth District School Board**
P.O. Box 2558
100 Main St. West, Hamilton, ON L8N 3L1, Canada
Tel: 905-527-5092; *Fax:* 905-521-2536
www.hwdsb.on.ca
Enrollment: 50000
John Malloy, Director, Education
Jessica Brennan, Chair

***Kenora:* Keewatin-Patricia District School Board**
100 First Ave. West, Kenora, ON P9N 3Z7, Canada
Tel: 807-468-5571; *Fax:* 807-468-3857
Toll-Free: 877-275-7771
www.kpdsb.on.ca
Enrollment: 7000
Larry Hope, Director, Education
David Penney, Chair

***Kingston:* Limestone District School Board**
P.O. Box Bag 610
220 Portsmouth Ave., Kingston, ON K7L 4X4, Canada
Tel: 613-544-6920; *Fax:* 613-544-6804
Toll-Free: 800-267-0935
inq@limestone.on.ca
www.limestone.on.ca
Other Information: Automated: 613-544-6925
TTY: 613-548-0279
Grades: JK-12 *Enrollment:* 22000
Brenda Hunter, Director, Education
Helen Chadwick, Chair

***Kitchener:* Waterloo Region District School Board**
51 Ardelt Ave., Kitchener, ON N2C 2R5, Canada
Tel: 519-570-0003; *Fax:* 519-742-1364
www.wrdsb.on.ca
Grades: Pre-K.-12 *Enrollment:* 60000
Linda Fabi, Dir., ext. 4222
Colin Harrington, Chair, ext. 4224

***Lindsay:* Trillium Lakelands District School Board**
Corporate Office
P.O. Box 420
300 County Rd. 36, Lindsay, ON K9V 4S4, Canada
Tel: 705-324-6776; *Fax:* 705-328-2036
Toll-Free: 1-888-526-5552
info@tldsb.on.ca
www.tldsb.on.ca
Other Information: Bracebridge Office, Phone: 705-645-8704; Haliburton: 705-457-1980
Number of Schools: 41 elementary schools; 7 secondary schools; 6 education centres *Grades:* K-12; French Immersion; Adult Ed. *Enrollment:* 18000 *Number of Employees:* 1,216 elementary school staff; 626 secondary school staff
Larry Hope, Director, Education, 705-324-6776
Bruce Barrett, Superintendent, Secondary School Improvement/Student Success, 705-324-6776
Kevin Cutler, Superintendent, Special Education, 705-645-8704
Bob Kaye, Superintendent, Business, 705-324-6776
Dianna Scates, Superintendent, ICT & Secondary Operations, 705-324-6776
Gale Sherin, Superintendent, Elementary School Improvement, 705-324-6776
Andrea Gillespie, District Principal, Elementary School Improvement, 705-645-8704
Greg Ingram, District Principal, Secondary School Improvement, 705-324-6776
Shelley Woon, District Principal, Special Education, 705-324-6776
Earl Manners, Administrator, Human Resources, 705-324-6776
Jeanne Pengelly, Officer, Communications, 888-526-5552, ext. 22129
jeanne.pengelly@tldsb.on.ca

***London:* Thames Valley District School Board**
P.O. Box 5888
1250 Dundas St., London, ON N5W 5P2, Canada
Tel: 519-452-2000; *Fax:* 519-452-2395
info@tvdsb.on.ca
www.tvdsb.ca
Number of Schools: 148 elementary schools; 32 secondary schools *Grades:* JK - 12; Adult Ed.; Alternative Ed. *Enrollment:* 76864 *Number of Employees:* 4,920 teachers; 297 principals & vice-principals; 2,645 support staff
Bill Tucker, Director, Education & Secretary, 519-452-2000, ext. 20001
Karen Dalton, Executive Superintendent, Operations, 519-452-2000, ext. 20083
Laura Elliott, Executive Superintendent, Program Services, 519-452-2000, ext. 20380
Brian Greene, Executive Superintendent, Business Services, & Treasurer, 519-452-2000, ext. 20343
Michael Sereda, Executive Superintendent, Human Resources, 519-452-2000, ext. 20254
C. Bourbonnais Macdonald, Superintendent, Education - Operations Services, 519-452-2000, ext. 20376
Karen Edgar, Superintendent, Education - Operations Svs. / Program Svs., 519-452-2000, ext. 20275
Lynne Griffith-Jones, Superintendent, Education - HR Services / Operations Services, 519-452-2000, ext. 20250
Scott Hughes, Superintendent, Education - Operations Svs. / Program Svs., 519-452-2000, ext. 20082
Marion Moynihan, Superintendent, Education - Operations Services, 519-452-2000, ext. 20075
Valerie Neilsen, Superintendent, Education - Operations Svs. / Program Svs., 519-452-2000, ext. 20387
Mary Ellen Smith, Superintendent, Education - Operations Services, 519-452-2000, ext. 20251
Barbara Sonier, Superintendent, Education - Operations Services, 519-452-2000, ext. 20078
Paul Tufts, Superintendent, Education - Operations Services, 519-452-2000, ext. 20073
Karen Wilkinson, Superintendent, Education - Operations Services, 519-452-2000, ext. 20501

***Marathon:* Superior-Greenstone District School Board**
P.O. Box A
12 Hemlo Dr., Marathon, ON P0T 2E0, Canada
Tel: 807-229-0436; *Fax:* 807-229-1471
boardoffice@sgdsb.on.ca
www.sgdsb.on.ca
Number of Schools: 17 *Grades:* Elementary - Secondary *Enrollment:* 1612 *Number of Employees:* 131
David Tamblyn, Director of Education, 807-229-0436, ext. 232
dtamblyn@sgdsb.on.ca
Nancy Petrick, Superintendent of Education, 807-229-0436, ext. 231
npetrick@sgdsb.on.ca
Cathy Tsubouchi, Superintendent of Business, & Treasurer, 807-229-0436, ext. 229
ctsubouchi@sgdsb.on.ca

***Midhurst:* Simcoe County District School Board**
1170 Hwy. 26, Midhurst, ON L0L 1X0, Canada
Tel: 705-728-7570; *Fax:* 705-728-2265
Toll-Free: 1-877-728-1187
www.scdsb.on.ca
Number of Schools: 87 Elementary; 17 Secondary; 6 Adult Learning Centres *Enrollment:* 50000
Kathi Wallace, Director, Education, 705-734-6363, ext. 11223
Brad Saunders, Chair
Anita Simpson, Superintendent, Education, Area 1, 705-734-6363, ext. 11357
Stephen Blake, Superintendent, Education, Area 2, 705-734-6363, ext. 11208
Kathy Bailey, Superintendent, Education, Area 3A, 705-734-6363, ext. 11397
Phyllis Hili, Superintendent, Education, Area 3B, 705-734-6363, ext. 11244
Paula Murphy, Superintendent, Education, Area 4, 705-734-6363, ext. 11811
Paul Sloan, Superintendent, Education, Area 5, 705-734-6363, ext. 11638

***Mississauga:* Peel District School Board**
5650 Hurontario St., Mississauga, ON L5R 1C6, Canada
Tel: 905-890-1099; *Fax:* 905-890-6747
Toll-Free: 800-668-1146
communications@peelsb.com
www.peel.edu.on.ca
Enrollment: 150000
Tony Pontes, Director, Education
Janet McDougald, Chair

***Nepean:* Ottawa-Carleton District School Board**
133 Greenbank Rd., Nepean, ON K2H 6L3, Canada
Tel: 613-721-1820; *Fax:* 613-820-6968
www.ocdsb.edu.on.ca
Enrollment: 72436
Cathy Curry, Chair
Dr. Lyall M. Thompson, Director, Education

***North Bay:* Near North District School Board**
P.O. Box 3110
963 Airport Rd., North Bay, ON P1B 8H1, Canada
Tel: 705-472-8170; *Fax:* 705-472-9927
Toll-Free: 800-278-4922
info@nearnorthschools.ca
www.nearnorthschools.ca
Grades: Pre-K.-12 *Enrollment:* 4895
Heli Vail, Dir., ext. 5050
vailh@nearnorthschools.ca
Al Bottomley, Chair, 705-384-5267
bottomleya@nearnorthschools.ca

***Pembroke:* Renfrew County District School Board**
1270 Pembroke St. West, Pembroke, ON K8A 4G4, Canada
Tel: 613-735-0151; *Fax:* 613-735-6315
www.renfrew.edu.on.ca
Enrollment: 10537
Roger Clarke, Director, Education
Roy C. Reiche, Chair

***Peterborough:* Kawartha Pine Ridge District School Board**
P.O. Box 7190
1994 Fisher Dr., Peterborough, ON K9J 7A1, Canada
Tel: 705-742-9773; *Fax:* 705-742-7801
Toll-Free: 877-741-4577
kpr_info@kprdsb.ca
www.kprschools.ca
Enrollment: 31327 *Number of Employees:* 2065 teachers; 1383 administrative staff
W.R. (Rusty) Hick, Director, Education
Diane Lloyd, Chair

***Sarnia:* Lambton Kent District School Board**
P.O. Box 2091
200 Wellington St., Sarnia, ON N7T 7L2, Canada
Tel: 519-336-1500; *Fax:* 519-336-0992
Toll-Free: 800-754-7125
www.lkdsb.net
Enrollment: 24000
Jim Costello, Director
Carmen McGregor, Chair

***Sault Ste Marie:* Algoma District School Board**
Central Board Office, Education Centre
644 Albert St. East, Sault Ste Marie, ON P6A 2K7, Canada
Tel: 705-945-7111; *Toll-Free:* 1-888-393-3639
vanders@adsb.on.ca (Susan Vandermolen)
www.adsb.on.ca
Other Information: Northern Office: 705-856-2309; Eastern Office: 705-848-3661
Grades: Kindergarten - 12; Adult Education
Mario Turco, Director, Education
Wanda McQueen, Chair

***Seaforth:* Avon Maitland District School Board**
62 Chalk St. North, Seaforth, ON N0K 1W0, Canada
Tel: 519-527-0111; *Fax:* 519-527-0222
Toll-Free: 1-800-592-5437
info@fc.amdsb.ca
www.avonmaitland.on.ca
Grades: JK - Secondary; Continuing Ed. *Enrollment:* 17000
Jenny Versteeg, Chair, Board of Trustees, 519-335-3623
jennvers@fc.amdsb.ca
Chuck Reid, Director, Education & Secretary of the Board, 519-527-0111, ext. 106
chucreid@fc.amdsb.ca
Mike Ash, Superintendent, Education - School Operations, 519-527-0111, ext. 113
Janet Baird-Jackson, Superintendent, Business, 519-527-0111, ext. 206
Jodie Baker, Superintendent, Education - Learning Services, 519-527-0111, ext. 109
Ted Doherty, Superintendent, Education - Human Resources, 519-527-0111, ext. 208
Patricia Stanley, Superintendent, Education - Curriculum & Assessment, 519-527-0111, ext. 116
Steve Howe, Manager, Communications, 519-527-0111, ext. 132

***St Catharines:* District School Board of Niagara**
191 Carleton St., St Catharines, ON L2R 7P4
Tel: 905-641-1550
inquiries@dsbn.org
www.dsbn.edu.on.ca
Other Information: Free Local Phone: 905-563-0909
www.facebook.com/DSBNiagara
twitter.com/d_s_b_n
Number of Schools: 95 elementary schools; 20 secondary schools *Enrollment:* 38000
Kevin Maves, Chair
Warren Hoshizaki, Director, Education

***Sudbury:* Rainbow District School Board**
69 Young St., Sudbury, ON P3E 3G5, Canada
Tel: 705-674-3171; *Fax:* 705-647-9112
Toll-Free: 866-421-2661
www.rainbowschools.ca
Enrollment: 14762
Norm Blaseg, Director, Education
Tyler Campbell, Chair

***Thunder Bay:* Lakehead District School Board**
The Jim McCuaig Education Centre
2135 Sills St., Thunder Bay, ON P7E 5T2, Canada
Tel: 807-625-5100; *Fax:* 807-622-0961
www.lakeheadschools.ca
Enrollment: 10906
Catherine Siemieniuk, Director, Education
Deborah Massaro, Chair

***Timmins:* District School Board Ontario North East**
P.O. Box 1020
Timmins, ON P4N 7H7
Tel: 705-360-1151; *Fax:* 705-268-7100
Toll-Free: 800-381-7280
comments@dsb1.edu.on.ca
www.dsb1.edu.on.ca
Number of Schools: 30 elementary schools; 10 secondary schools; 2 alternative schools *Grades:* K.-Sec.; Adult Ed. *Enrollment:* 8105
Doug Shearer, Chair
doug.shearer@dsb1.edu.on.ca
Linda Knight, Director, Education

***Toronto:* Toronto District School Board**
5050 Yonge St., Toronto, ON M2N 5N8, Canada
Tel: 416-397-3000
communications@tdsb.on.ca
www.tdsb.on.ca
Other Information: Public Affairs, Phone: 416-395-2721
www.facebook.com/toronto.dsb?ref=ts
twitter.com/TDSB
www.youtube.com/user/TDSBOfficial
Number of Schools: 565 *Grades:* K - 12; Adult Ed.; French Immersion *Enrollment:* 260000 *Number of Employees:* 37,000
Chris Spence, Director, Education
chris.spence@tdsb.on.ca
Chris Bolton, Chair, 416-397-3100
chris@chrisbolton.ca
Leila Girdhar-Hill, Superintendent, Region WR01, 416-394-2036
Leila.Girdhar@tdsb.on.ca
Anne Seymour, Superintendent, Region WR02, 416-394-2034
Anne.Seymour@tdsb.on.ca
Jeff Hainbuch, Superintendent, Region WR03, 416-394-2034
Jeff.Hainbuch@tdsb.on.ca
Susan Winter, Superintendent, Region WR04, 416-394-2038
Susan.Winter@tdsb.on.ca
Glenford Duffus, Superintendent, Region WR05, 416-394-2030
Glenford.Duffus@tdsb.on.ca
Jane Phillips-Long, Superintendent, Region WR06, 416-394-2042
Jane.Phillips-Long@tdsb.on.ca
Curtis Ennis, Superintendent, Region WR07, 416-394-2044
Curtis.Ennis@tdsb.on.ca
Ian Allison, Superintendent, Region WR08, 416-394-2048
Ian.Allison@tdsb.on.ca
Beth Butcher, Superintendent, Region WR09, 416-394-2050
Beth.Butcher@tdsb.on.ca
Mike Gallagher, Superintendent, Region WR10, 416-394-2048
Mike.Gallagher@tdsb.on.ca
Roula Anastasakos, Superintendent, Region ER11, 416-396-9196
Roula.Anastasakos@tdsb.on.ca
Nadira Persaud, Superintendent, Region ER12, 416-396-9186
Nadira.Persaud@tdsb.on.ca
Kerry-Lynn Stadnyk, Superintendent, Region ER13, 416-396-9188
Kerry-Lynn.Stadnyk@tdsb.on.ca
John Chasty, Superintendent, Region ER14, 416-394-2032
john.chasty@tdsb.on.ca
Kathleen Meighan, Superintendent, Region ER15, 416-396-9174
Kathleen.Meighan@tdsb.on.ca
Rauda Dickinson, Superintendent, Region ER16, 416-396-9186
Rauda.Dickinson@tdsb.on.ca
Sue Pfeffer, Superintendent, Region ER17, 416-396-9172
Sue.Pfeffer@tdsb.on.ca
Peter Chang, Superintendent, Region ER18, 416-396-9180
p.chang@tdsb.on.ca
Colleen Russell, Superintendent, Region ER19, 416-396-9178
Colleen.Russell@tdsb.on.ca
Uton Robinson, Superintendent, Region ER20, 416-396-9190
Uton.Robinson@tdsb.on.ca
Anne Kerr, Superintendent, Region SE5, 416-396-9194
Anne.Kerr@tdsb.on.ca
Johanne Messner, Superintendent, Region NE6, 416-396-9182
johanne.messner@tdsb.on.ca
Sandy Spyropoulos, Superintendent, Region NE3, 416-396-9176
sandy.spyropoulos@tdsb.on.ca

***Whitby:* Durham District School Board**
400 Taunton Rd. East, Whitby, ON L1R 2K6, Canada
Tel: 905-666-5500; *Fax:* 905-666-6474
Toll-Free: 1-800-265-3968
douglas_karen@durham.edu.on.ca (Executive Assistant to Director)
www.durham.edu.on.ca
Other Information: Trustees' Administrative Assistant, Phone: 905-666-6363
TTY: 905-666-6943
Number of Schools: 109 elementary schools; 26 secondary schools & learning centres *Grades:* K - 12; Special Ed.; Continuing Ed. *Enrollment:* 69086 *Number of Employees:* 2,760 elementary teachers; 1,663 secondary teachers *Note:* In addition to its teachers, the school board also employs 208 elementary administrators, 77 secondary administrators, & 2,665 educational services staff (including educational assistants, clerical, custodial, maintenance, & lunchroom supervisors).
Martyn Beckett, Director, Education, 905-666-5500, fax: 905-666-6318
beckett_martyn@durham.edu.on.ca
Luigia Ayotte, Superintendent, Education (Programs), 905-666-5500, fax: 905-666-6946
ayotte_luigia@durham.edu.on.ca
John Beatty, Superintendent, Education (Brock, Uxbridge, & Scugog), 905-666-6905
beatty_john@durham.edu.on.ca
John Bowyer, Superintendent, Education (Whitby), 905-666-6373
bowyer_john@durham.edu.on.ca
Doug Crichton, Superintendent, Education (Special Education), 905-666-6371
crichton_doug@durham.edu.on.ca
Janet Edwards, Superintendent, Education (Ajax), 905-666-6379
edwards_janet@durham.edu.on.ca
Ed Hodgins, Superintendent, Education & Business, & Treasurer, 905-666-6402, fax: 905-666-6969
hodgins_ed@durham.edu.on.ca
Mark Joel, Superintendent, Education (Ops, Transportation & Leadership), 905-666-5500, fax: 905-666-6376
joel_mark@durham.edu.on.ca
Jeannine Joubert, Superintendent, Education (Oshawa), 905-666-6369
joubert_jeannine@durham.edu.on.ca
Lisa Millar, Superintendent, Education (Pickering), 905-666-6486
millar_lisa@durham.edu.on.ca
Lou Vavougios, Superintendent, Education (Employee Services), 905-666-6332, fax: 905-666-6908
vavougios_lou@durham.edu.on.ca
David Visser, Superintendent, Education (Facilities Services), 905-666-6426, fax: 905-666-6439
visser_david@durham.edu.on.ca
Denise Gilbert, Executive Director, Schoolhouse Playcare Centres, 905-666-6487
gilbert_denise@durham.edu.on.ca
Andrea Pidwerbecki, Manager, Communications, 905-666-6313
pidwerbecki_andrea@durham.edu.on.ca

***Windsor:* Greater Essex County District School Board**
P.O. Box 210
451 Park St. West, Windsor, ON N9A 6K1, Canada
Tel: 519-255-3200
www.gecdsb.on.ca
Other Information: Adult & Continuing Education, Phone: 519-253-5006
Number of Schools: 61 elementary schools; 16 secondary schools; 5 agency schools *Grades:* Jr Kindergarten-12; Alternative Ed. *Enrollment:* 35350
Warren Kennedy, Director, Education, 519-255-3200, ext. 10250
Penny Allen, Superintendent, Business, 519-255-3200, ext. 10210
Paul Antaya, Superintendent, Secondary Schools, 519-255-3200, ext. 10254
Clara Howitt, Superintendent, Program & Instructional Services, 519-255-3200, ext. 10255
John Howitt, Superintendent, Operations & Information Technology, 519-255-3200, ext. 10253
Heather Liffiton, Superintendent, Education, 519-255-3200, ext. 10251
Terry Lyons, Superintendent, Accommodations & Safe Schools, 519-255-3200, ext. 10223
Donne Petryshyn, Superintendent, Human Resources, 519-255-3200, ext. 10264
Sharon Pyke, Superintendent, Special Education, 519-255-3200, ext. 10222
Mary Guthrie, Chief Information Officer, 519-255-3200, ext. 10260

Catholic

***Aurora:* York Catholic District School Board**
320 Bloomington Rd. West, Aurora, ON L4G 0M1, Canada
Tel: 905-713-1211; *Fax:* 905-713-1272
www.ycdsb.ca
Grades: Pre-K.-12 *Enrollment:* 54580
Susan LaRosa, Dir.
susan.larosa@ycdsb.ca
John Sabo, Assoc. Dir./Board Treas., ext. 12300
john.sabo@ycdsb.ca
Elizabeth Crowe, Chair
elizabeth.crowe@ycdsb.ca

***Barrie:* Simcoe Muskoka Catholic District School Board**
46 Alliance Blvd., Barrie, ON L4M 5K3, Canada
Tel: 705-722-3555; *Fax:* 705-722-6534
www.smcdsb.on.ca
Enrollment: 22000
Michael. O'Keefe, Director, Education
John Grisé, Chair

***Brantford:* Brant Haldimand Norfolk Catholic District School Board**
P.O. Box 217
322 Fairview Dr., Brantford, ON N3T 5M8, Canada
Tel: 519-756-6505; *Fax:* 519-756-9913
webmaster@bhncdsb.ca
www.bhncdsb.edu.on.ca
Number of Schools: 31 Catholic elementary schools; 3 Catholic secondary schools *Grades:* Elementary - Secondary; Special Ed. *Enrollment:* 10653 *Number of Employees:* 700+ teachers; 300+ non-academic staff
June Szeman, Chair, 519-753-9198
jszeman@bhncdsb.ca
Cathy Horgan, Director, Education & Secretary, 519-756-6505, ext. 223
William Chopp, Superintendent, Education, 519-756-6505, ext. 244
Patricia (Trish) Kings, Superintendent, Education, 519-756-6505, ext. 242
Chris Roehrig, Superintendent, Education, 519-756-6505, ext. 240
Wally Easton, Associate Director, Corporate Services, & Treasurer, 519-756-6505, ext. 272
Mary Gallo, Principal, Secondary Program, 519-756-6505, ext. 251
Terre Slaght, Principal, Special Education Program, 519-759-8862, ext. 402
Leslie Telfer, Principal, School Effectiveness, 519-756-6505, ext. 264
Maureen Wills, Principal, Elementary Program, 519-756-6505, ext. 256
Tony Castagna, Manager, Information Technology, 519-758-5924, ext. 342
Paula Dunn, Manager, Human Resources, 519-756-6505, ext. 235
Phillip Kuckyt, Manager, Transportation Services, 519-751-7532, ext. 28220
Pat Petrella, Manager, Finance, 519-756-6505, ext. 228
Don Zelem, Manager, Facilities & Construction Projects, 519-759-3555, ext. 15
Tracey Austin, Coordinator, Communications & Community Relations, 519-756-6505, ext. 234
taustin@bhncdsb.ca

***Burlington:* Halton Catholic District School Board**
Education Center
802 Drury Lane, Burlington, ON L7R 2Y2, Canada
Tel: 905-632-6300; *Fax:* 905-333-4661
Toll-Free: 1-800-741-8382
comments@hcdsb.org; communications@hcdsb.org; business@hcdsb.org
www.haltonrc.edu.on.ca
Other Information: Special Education Services, E-mail: speced@hcdsb.org
Number of Schools: 40 elementary schools; 8 secondary schools; 2 continuing education centres *Grades:* Elementary-Secondary; Continuing Ed *Enrollment:* 29000
Michael Pautler, Director, Education, 905-632-6314, ext. 110, fax: 905-333-4661
director@hcdsb.org
Erica vanRoosmalen, Chief Officer, Research & Development Services, 905-632-6314, ext. 367
Joseph O'Hara, Executive Officer, Human Resources, 905-632-6314, ext. 104
Giacomo Corbacio, Superintendent, Facilities Services, 905-632-6314, ext. 170
Jacqueline Herman, Superintendent, Education, 905-632-6314, ext. 161

John Langill, Superintendent, School Services, 905-632-6314, ext. 183
Richard MacDonald, Superintendent, Curriculum Services, 905-632-6314, ext. 122
Fiammetta Mazzetti, Superintendent, Education, 905-632-6314, ext. 216
Paul McMahon, Superintendent, Business Services, 905-632-6314, ext. 130
Suzanne Rossini, Superintendent, Special Education Services, 905-632-6314, ext. 128
James Rowles, Superintendent, Education, 905-632-6314, ext. 180
Mary Tessari, Superintendent, Education, Staff Dev. & Faith Formation Svs., 905-632-6314, ext. 118
Wayne Elshof, Senior Administrator, Information Technology, 905-632-6314, ext. 550
Scott Bland, Administrator, Planning Services, 905-632-6314, ext. 107
Christopher Jewell, Administrator, Communication Services, 905-632-6314, ext. 157

Dublin: Huron-Perth Catholic District School Board
P.O. Box 70
87 Mill St., Dublin, ON N0K 1E0, Canada
Tel: 519-345-2440; *Fax:* 519-345-2449
www.hpcdsb.edu.on.ca

Enrollment: 1753
Martha Dutrizac, Director, Education
Mike Miller, Chair

Dubreuilville: Conseil des écoles séparées catholiques de Dubreuilville
P.O. Box 69
149, av du Parc, Dubreuilville, ON P0S 1B0, Canada
Tél: 705-884-2309; *Téléc:* 705-884-2062
www.dubreuilville.ca

Enrollment: 138
Guy Pelletier, Président du Conseil

Fort Frances: Northwest Catholic District School Board
555 Flinders Ave., Fort Frances, ON P9A 3L2, Canada
Tel: 807-274-2931; *Fax:* 807-274-8792
www.tncdsb.on.ca

Enrollment: 1434
Mary-Catherine Kelly, Director, Education
Anne-Marie Fitzgerald, Chair
amfitzgerald@tncdsb.on.ca

Guelph: Wellington Catholic District School Board
75 Woolwich St., Guelph, ON N1H 6N6, Canada
Tel: 519-821-4600; *Fax:* 519-824-3088
andrew_duszczyszyn@wellingtoncssb.edu.on.ca
www.wellingtoncssb.edu.on.ca

Grades: Pre-K.-12 *Enrollment:* 61000
Don Drone, Dir., 519-821-4640, fax: 519-837-4156
ddrone@wellingtoncdsb.ca
Dan Duszczyszyn, Supt. of Corp. Services/Treas., fax: 519-837-4154
dduszczyszyn@wellingtoncdsb.ca
Rev Dennis J. Noon, Chair, 519-824-3951, fax: 519-824-1920
dnoon@dionet.ca

Hamilton: Hamilton-Wentworth Catholic District School Board
P.O. Box 2012
90 Mulberry St., Hamilton, ON L8N 3R9, Canada
Tel: 905-525-2930; *Fax:* 905-525-1724
www.hwcdsb.edu.on.ca/
Other Information: Summer fax: 905-525-2914

Grades: K-12 *Enrollment:* 30000
Patricia Amos, Director, Education, 905-525-2930, ext. 2180
Patrick J. Daly, Chair, 905-525-2930, ext. 2162

Hanover: Bruce-Grey Catholic District School Board
799 - 16th Ave., Hanover, ON N4N 3A1, Canada
Tel: 519-364-5820; *Fax:* 519-364-5882
bruce_grey@bgcdsb.org
www.bgcdsb.org
www.facebook.com/185958928107172
twitter.com/BGCDSB

Number of Schools: 13 *Grades:* Kindergarten-12; Religious Ed.; ESL *Enrollment:* 3524
Norman Bethune, Chair, 519-376-8315
Bruce MacPherson, Director, Education
Gerald Casey, Superintendent, Education
Catherine Montreuil, Superintendent, Education
Cathy Colton, Superintendent, Business
Jim Aitken, Supervisor, Maintenance
Joyce Benninger, Supervisor, Payroll & Health & Safety
Doreen Schultz, Coordinator, Community Relations & Outreach
Ann-Marie Deas, Social Worker
Alecia Lantz, Financial Analyst
Brenda Leahy, Speech Language Pathologist
Catherine Penner, Psychometrist

Kemptville: Catholic District School Board of Eastern Ontario
c/o Kemptville Board Office
P.O. Box 2222
2755 Hwy. 43, Kemptville, ON K0G 1J0, Canada
Tel: 613-258-7757; *Fax:* 613-258-7134
Toll-Free: 1-800-443-4562
mail@cdsbeo.on.ca
www.cdsbeo.on.ca
Other Information: Western Ed. Ctr.: 613-283-5007; Eastern Ed. Ctr.: 613-933-1720

Number of Schools: 40 elementary schools; 10 secondary schools *Grades:* Elementary - Secondary *Enrollment:* 15000
Number of Employees: 850 teachers; 450 support staff
Ronald Eamer, Chair, 613-931-2369
Ronald.Eamer@cdsbeo.on.ca
Dr. Donaleen Hawes, Superintendent, Education, 613-283-5007, ext. 234, fax: 613-283-5783
Donaleen.Hawes@cdsbeo.on.ca
Mark Musca, Superintendent, Human Resources, 613-258-7757, fax: 613-258-3610
Mark.Musca@cdsbeo.on.ca
Marg Shea-Lawrence, Superintendent, Religious & Family Life Education, 613-258-7757, ext. 207, fax: 613-258-3610
Marg.Shea@cdsbeo.on.ca
Bernie Kehoe, Manager, Plant & Maintenance, 613-258-7757, ext. 227, fax: 613-258-3610
Bernie.Kehoe@cdsbeo.on.ca
Nicole Makinson, Manager, Transportation & Assessment, 613-258-7757, ext. 107, fax: 613-258-3610
Nicole.Makinson@cdsbeo.on.ca
Bonnie Norton, Manager, Finance, 613-258-7757, ext. 238, fax: 613-258-3610
Bonnie.Norton@cdsbeo.on.ca
James Proulx, Manager, ICT Services, 613-258-7757, ext. 555, fax: 613-258-3610
James.Proulx@cdsbeo.on.ca
Sheila Farris, Supervising Principal, Student Success Initiative, 613-283-5007, fax: 613-283-5783
Sheila.Farris@cdsbeo.on.ca
Tom Jordan, Principal, Special Education, 613-283-5007, ext. 205, fax: 613-283-5783
Tom.Jordan@cdsbeo.on.ca
Jim Roberts, Principal, Religious Education, 613-258-7757, ext. 246, fax: 613-258-3610
jim.roberts@cdsbeo.on.ca
Charlotte Rouleau, Principal, Curriculum, 613-933-1720, ext. 377, fax: 613-933-7966
charlotte.rouleau@cdsbeo.on.ca

Kenora: Kenora Catholic District School Board
200 First St. North, Kenora, ON P9N 2K4, Canada
Tel: 807-468-9851; *Fax:* 807-468-8094
mcunningham@kcdsb.on.ca
www.kcdsb.on.ca

Enrollment: 1475
Phyllis Eikre, Director, Education
Darryl Michaluk, Chair

Kitchener: Waterloo Catholic District School Board
P.O. Box 91116
35 Weber St. W, #A, Kitchener, ON N2G 4G2, Canada
Tel: 519-578-3660; *Fax:* 519-578-5291
info@wcdsb.ca
www.wcdsb.ca

Grades: Pre-K.-12 *Enrollment:* 40000
Roger Lawler, Dir.
roger.lawler@wcdsb.ca
Shesh Maharaj, CFO
shesh.maharaj@wcdsb.ca
Wayne Buchholtz, Chair

L'Orignal: Conseil scolaire de district catholique de l'Est ontarien
875, ch de comté 17, L'Orignal, ON K0B 1K0, Canada
Tél: 613-675-4691; *Téléc:* 613-675-2921
Ligne sans frais: 800-204-4098
bur-central@csdceo.on.ca
www.csdceo.ca

Enrollment: 3718
Céline Cadieux, Directrice de l'éducation/Sec.
Michel Pilon, Président du Conseil

London: London District Catholic School Board
Catholic Education Centre
P.O. Box 5474
5200 Wellington Rd. South, London, ON N6A 4X5, Canada
Tel: 519-663-2088
communications@ldcsb.on.ca
www.ldcsb.on.ca
Number of Schools: 48 elementary schools; 8 secondary schools *Grades:* Jr Kindergarten - 12; Continuing Ed
Enrollment: 21000
Bill Hall, Chair, Board of Trustees
Wilma de Rond, Director, Education, & Secretary-Treasurer, 519-663-2088, ext. 40002, fax: 519-663-9250
w.derond@ldcsb.on.ca
Terry Grand, Superintendent, Education
Vince MacDonald, Superintendent, Education
John Mombourquette, Superintendent, Education
Tamara Nugent, Superintendent, Education
Sharon Wright-Evans, Superintendent, Education

Mississauga: Dufferin-Peel Catholic District School Board
40 Matheson Blvd. West, Mississauga, ON L5R 1C5
Tel: 905-890-1221; *Toll-Free:* 800-387-9501
www.dpcdsb.org
Other Information: Staff Directory: 905-890-0708
twitter.com/DPCDSBSchools

Number of Schools: 120 elementary schools; 26 secondary schools *Grades:* K.-12; Adult Ed. *Enrollment:* 85334
John B. Kostoff, Director of Education
Arthur Peters, Chair

Napanee: Algonquin & Lakeshore Catholic District School Board
151 Dairy Ave., Napanee, ON K7R 4B2, Canada
Tel: 613-354-2255; *Toll-Free:* 1-800-581-1116
info@alcdsb.on.ca
www.alcdsb.on.ca
Other Information: info@alcdsb.on

Grades: Elementary - Secondary *Enrollment:* 12397
Jody DiRocco, Director, Education, 613-354-6257, ext. 448
dricco@alcdsb.on.ca
Bob Koubsky, Superintendent, Finance & Business Services, 613-354-6257, ext. 436
koubsky@alcdsb.on.ca
Louise Lannan, Coodinator, Curriculum & Staff Development, 613-354-6257, ext. 402
lannan@alcdsb.on.ca

Nepean: Ottawa-Carleton Catholic District School Board
570 Hunt Club Rd. West, Nepean, ON K2G 3R4, Canada
Tel: 613-224-2222; *Fax:* 613-224-5063
www.occdsb.on.ca

Enrollment: 39000
Julian Hanlon, Director, Education & Sec.-Treas.
Gordon Butler, Chair

North Bay: Conseil scolaire catholique Franco-Nord
681-C, rue Chippewa ouest, North Bay, ON P1B 6G8, Canada
Tél: 705-472-1702; *Téléc:* 705-474-3824
information@franco-nord.ca
www.franco-nord.edu.on.ca

Enrollment: 3400
Cynthia Roveda, Directrice de l'éducation/Sec.-trésorière
Ronald Demers, Président du Conseil

North Bay: Nipissing-Parry Sound Catholic District School Board (NPSC)
Elementary & Secondary
1000 High St., North Bay, ON P1B 6S6, Canada
Tel: 705-472-1201; *Fax:* 705-472-0507
contact@npsc.ca
www.npsc.ca
twitter.com/npsc_schools

Number of Schools: 13
Anna Marie Bitonti, Director of Education
Joanne Bénard, Superintendent of Education
Paula Mann, Superintendent of Education
Grace Barnhardt, Superintendent of Business & Treasurer

Oshawa: Durham Catholic District School Board
650 Rossland Rd. West, Oshawa, ON L1J 7C4
Tel: 905-576-6150; *Fax:* 905-721-8239
Toll-Free: 877-482-0722
www.dcdsb.ca

Number of Schools: 39 elementary schools; 7 secondary schools *Enrollment:* 23885
Jim McCafferty, Chair, 905-839-8454
Paul Pulla, Director, Education

Ottawa: Conseil des écoles catholiques du Centre-Est
4000, rue Labelle, Ottawa, ON K1J 1A1, Canada
Tél: 613-744-2555; *Téléc:* 613-746-3081
Ligne sans frais: 888-230-5131
ecolecatholique@ecolecatholique.ca
www.ceclf.edu.on.ca

Enrollment: 18000

Diane Doré, Présidente du Conseil
Bernard Roy, Directeur de l'éducation/Sec.-trésorier

Pembroke: Renfrew County Catholic District School Board
499 Pembroke St. West, Pembroke, ON K8A 5P1, Canada
Tel: 613-735-1031; *Fax:* 613-735-2649
Toll-Free: 800-267-0191
www.rccdsb.edu.on.ca

Enrollment: 5000
Michele Arbour, Director
Bob Schreader, Chair

Peterborough: Peterborough Victoria Northumberland & Clarington Catholic District School B
1355 Lansdowne St. West, Peterborough, ON K9J 7M3, Canada
Tel: 705-748-4861; *Fax:* 705-748-9734
Toll-Free: 800-461-8009
www.pvnccdsb.on.ca

Enrollment: 14678
John Mackle, Director, Education & Secretary-Treasurer
David Bernier, Chair

Sault Ste Marie: Huron-Superior Catholic District School Board
90 Ontario Ave., Sault Ste Marie, ON P6B 6G7, Canada
Tel: 705-945-5400; *Fax:* 705-945-5575
Toll-Free: 800-267-0754
www.hscdsb.on.ca

Enrollment: 6795
John Stadnyk, Director, Education
Marchy Bruni, Chair

Sudbury: Conseil scolaire catholique du Nouvel-Ontario
201, rue Jogues, Sudbury, ON P3C 5L7, Canada
Tél: 705-673-5626; *Téléc:* 705-669-1270
Ligne sans frais: 800-259-5567
info@nouvelon.ca
www.nouvelon.ca

Enrollment: 7500
Marcel Montpellier, Président du Conseil
Lyse-Anne Papineau, Directrice de l'éducation

Sudbury: Sudbury Catholic District School Board
Catholic Education Centre
165A D'Youville St., Sudbury, ON P3C 5E7, Canada
Tel: 705-673-5620; *Fax:* 705-673-6670
employment@sudburycatholicschools.ca
www.scdsb.edu.on.ca
Other Information: Transportation, Phone: 705-521-1234
Number of Schools: 20 elementary schools; 5 secondary schools *Grades:* JK - 12; French Immersion; Adult Ed
Enrollment: 6595
Catherine McCullough, Director, Education, & Secretary of the Board, 705-673-5620, ext. 242, fax: 705-688-1781
Catherine.McCullough@sudburycatholicschools.ca
Rossella Bagnato, Superintendent, Special Education & Academic Programs, 705-673-5620, ext. 238, fax: 705-688-1781
Rossella.Bagnato@sudburycatholicschools.ca
Dennis Bazinet, Superintendent, Business & Finance, 705-673-5620, ext. 238, fax: 705-688-1781
Dennis.Bazinet@sudburycatholicschools.ca
Jean McHarg, Superintendent, Programs (K-12), 705-673-5620, ext. 238, fax: 705-688-1781
Jean.McHarg@sudburycatholicschools.ca
Roland Muzzatti, Superintendent, Student Success & 7-12 Schools, 705-673-5620, ext. 238, fax: 705-688-1781
Roland.Muzzatti@sudburycatholicschools.ca
Suzanne Dubien, Senior Manager, Human Resources, 705-673-5620, ext. 312
Denis Faucher, Manager, Facility Services, 705-673-5620, ext. 415
Gerry Robillard, Manager, Information Management Services, 705-673-5620, ext. 371
Gina Tullio, Coordinator, Outreach & Media Relations, 705-673-5620, ext. 244

Terrace Bay: Superior North Catholic District School Board
P.O. Box 610
21 Simcoe Plaza, Terrace Bay, ON P0T 2W0, Canada
Tel: 807-825-3209; *Fax:* 807-825-3885
BoardOffice@sncdsb.on.ca; Board@sncdsb.on.ca
www.sncdsb.on.ca
Number of Schools: 9 Elementary Catholic schools *Grades:* Elementary; Religious Program
Valerie Pichette, Director, Education
vpichette@sncdsb.on.ca
Mary Anne Baker, Superintendent, Education
mbaker@sncdsb.on.ca
Sherry Bortolotti, Superintendent, School Effectiveness
sbortolotti@sncdsb.on.ca
Scott Adams, Manager, Finance
sadams@sncdsb.on.ca
Dan Bourgeault, Manager, Operations
dbourgeault@sncdsb.on.ca
Laureen Kay, Officer, Payroll & Human Resources, 807-825-3209, ext. 25, fax: 807-825-3885
lkay@sncdsb.on.ca
Maria Lapenskie, Officer, Transportation
mlapenskie@sncdsb.on.ca

Thunder Bay: Conseil scolaire de district catholique des Aurores boréales
175, rue High nord, Thunder Bay, ON P7A 8C7, Canada
Tél: 807-344-2266; *Téléc:* 807-344-3734
Ligne sans frais: 800-367-0874
info@csdcab.on.ca
www.csdcab.on.ca

Enrollment: 652
Sylvianne Mauro, Directrice de l'éducation
Angèle Brunelle, Présidente du Conseil

Thunder Bay: Thunder Bay Catholic District School Board
Catholic Education Centre
459 Victoria Ave. West, Thunder Bay, ON P7C 0A4, Canada
Tel: 807-625-1555
jsheriff@tbcdsb.on.ca (Jocelynne Sheriff, Executive Assistant)
www.tbcdsb.on.ca
Number of Schools: 16 elementary schools; 3 senior elementary schools; 2 secondary schools *Grades:* Jr. Kindergarten-12; Alternative Ed *Enrollment:* 8606 *Number of Employees:* 366 elementary teachers; 194 secondary teachers; 283 non-teaching staff
John De Faveri, Director, Education, 807-625-1567, fax: 807-623-2167
jdefaver@tbcdsb.on.ca
Tom Mustapic, Associate Director & Superintendent, Business & Corporate Svs, 807-625-1508, fax: 807-625-1583
tmustapi@tbcdsb.on.ca
Rob Kruse, Superintendent, Education (St. Ignatius HS & St. Patrick HS), 807-625-1590, fax: 807-625-1560
dsebesta@tbcdsb.on.ca
Joan Powell, Superintendent, Education - Special Education & JK-8 Schools, 807-625-1573, fax: 807-625-1560
jpowell@tbcdsb.on.ca
David Bragnalo, Officer, Education, 807-625-1585, fax: 807-625-1560
dbragnal@tbcdsb.on.ca
Michael Thompson, Officer, Communications, 807-625-1587, fax: 807-623-2187
mthompso@tbcdsb.on.ca
Garry Grgurich, Manager, Employee Services, 807-625-1577, fax: 807-625-8601
jwillis@tbcdsb.on.ca

Timmins: Conseil des écoles séparées catholiques de Foleyet
52, pl Theodore, Timmins, ON P4N 7P6, Canada
Tél: 705-267-3521; *Téléc:* 705-267-3691
www.afocsc.org

Enrollment: 15
Lisa Côté, Sec.-Treas.
Suzanne Roch, Chair

Timmins: Conseil scolaire catholique de district des Grandes Rivières
896, promenade Riverside, Timmins, ON P4N 3W2, Canada
Tél: 705-267-1421; *Téléc:* 705-267-7247
www.cscdgr.on.ca

Enrollment: 2668
Isabelle Charbonneau, Présidente du Conseil
charbonneau@cscdgr.on.ca
Lorraine Presley, Directrice de l'éducation

Timmins: Northeastern Catholic District School Board
101 Spruce St. North, Timmins, ON P4N 6M9, Canada
Tel: 705-268-7443; *Fax:* 705-267-3590
Toll-Free: 877-422-9322
www.ncdsb.on.ca

Grades: Pre-K.-12 *Enrollment:* 2373
Glenn Sheculski, Dir., fax: 705-268-7499
gsheculski@ncdsb.on.ca
Tricia Stefanic Weltz, Supt., fax: 705-266-9144
tricia.weltz@ncdsb.on.ca

Toronto: Conseil scolaire de district catholique Centre-Sud
110, av Drewry, Toronto, ON M2M 1C8, Canada
Tél: 416-397-6564; *Téléc:* 416-397-6576
Ligne sans frais: 800-274-3764
commentaires@csdccs.edu.on.ca
www.csdccs.edu.on.ca

Enrollment: 12000
Réjean Sirois, Directeur de l'éducation/Sec.-trésorier
Mikale-Andrée Joly, Directrice des communications stratégiques

Toronto: Toronto Catholic District School Board
80 Sheppard Ave. East, Toronto, ON M2N 6E8, Canada
Tel: 416-222-8282; *Fax:* 416-229-5345
webmaster@tcdsb.org; helpdesk@tcdsb.org (technical difficulties)
www.tcdsb.org
Other Information: Public Relations, Phone: 416-222-8282, ext. 5314
Number of Schools: 168 elementary schools; 31 secondary schools; 2 combined elementary and secondary *Grades:* Kindergarten - 12; Adult Education *Enrollment:* 93054 *Number of Employees:* 5,997 teachers; 2,806 support & academic staff; 356 principals & vps; 202 administrative personnel
Ann Perron, Director, Education, 416-222-8282, ext. 2296
ann.perron@tcdsb.org
Angela Gauthier, Associate Director, Academic Services, 416-222-8282, ext. 2641
angela.gauthier@tcdsb.org
Sandra Pessione, Associate Director, Business Services, CFO, & Treasurer, 416-222-8282, ext. 2641
sandra.pessione@tcdsb.org
Angelo Sangiorgio, Associate Director, Planning & Facilities, 416-222-8282, ext. 2349
Josie DiGiovanni, Superintendent, Curriculum & Accountability & Staff Dev., 416-222-8282, ext. 2490
josie.digiovanni@tcdsb.org
Lori DiMarco, Superintendent, Schools - Area 4ountability & Staff Dev., 416-222-8282, ext. 2267
lori.dimarco@tcdsb.org
Richard Francki, Superintendent, Facilities Services, 416-222-8282, ext. 2349
richard.francki@tcdsb.org
Geoffrey Grant, Superintendent, Schools - Area 8, 416-222-8282, ext. 2730
geoffrey.grant@tcdsb.org
Patrick Keyes, Superintendent, Student Success, Equity & Inclusive Education, 416-222-8282, ext. 5370
patrick.keyes@tcdsb.org
Rory McGuckin, Superintendent, Safe Schools & Parent & Community Engagement, 416-222-8282
rory.mcguckin@tcdsb.org
Michael McMorrow, Superintendent, Schools - Area 6, 416-222-8282, ext. 5371
michael.mcmorrow@tcdsb.org
Josie Nespolo, Superintendent, Schools - Area 2, 416-222-8282, ext. 2732
josephine.nespolo@tcdsb.org
Loretta Notten, Superintendent, Schools - Area 1, 416-222-8282, ext. 2732
loretta.notten@tcdsb.org
Anthony Petitti, Superintendent, Schools - Area 7, 416-222-8282, ext. 2730
anthony.petitti@tcdsb.org
Frank Piddisi, Superintendent, Special Services & Parent Engagement, 416-222-8282, ext. 2486
frank.piddisi@tcdsb.org
Gary Poole, Superintendent, Human Resources, 416-222-8282, ext. 2304
gary.poole@tcdsb.org
Vidyia Rego, Superintendent, Business Services, 416-222-8282, ext. 2257
vidyia.rego@tcdsb.org
Jim Saraco, Superintendent, Schools - Area 5, 416-222-8282, ext. 5371
jim.saraco@tcdsb.org
Doug Yack, Superintendent, Schools - Area 3, 416-222-8282, ext. 2267
douglas.yack@tcdsb.org
Barbara McMorrow, Executive Corporate Secretary & Board Liaison Officer, 416-222-8282, ext. 2080
barbara.mcmorrow@tcdsb.org
Mary Jo Dieghan, Coordinator, Communications, 416-222-8282, ext. 5314
maryjo.deighan@tcdsb.org; commdept@tcdsb.org

Wallaceburg: St. Clair Catholic District School Board
Catholic Education Centre
420 Creek St., Wallaceburg, ON N8A 4C4, Canada
Tel: 519-627-6762; *Fax:* 519-627-8230
Toll-Free: 1-866-336-6139
media@st-clair.net
www.st-clair.ne
Number of Schools: 29 elementary schools; 3 secondary schools *Grades:* Elementary - Secondary *Number of Employees:* 1100+
Anita Labadie, Chair, 519-360-9254
Paul Wubben, Director, Education, Chief Executive Officer, & Secretary, 519-627-6762, ext. 241
James McKenzie, Associate Director & Treasurer
Deb Crawford, Superintendent, Education
Dr. Frank Leddy, Superintendent, Education
Ann Sutton, Superintendent, Education
Steven Mitchell, Chief Information Officer
Carol Ann Bélanger, Assistant Superintendent, Catholic Curriculum
Lisa Demers, Principal, Special Education
Cindy Waddick, Leader, Elementary Chaplaincy
cindy.waddick@st-clair.net
Karen Dolson, Manager, Planning Services
Bruce Hannah, Manager, Facility Services
Amy Janssens, Manager, Financial Services
Todd Lozon, Supervisor, Communications & Community Relations, 519-627-6762, ext. 243
todd.lozon@st-clair.net

Welland: Niagara Catholic District School Board
427 Rice Rd., Welland, ON L3C 7C1, Canada
Tel: 905-735-0240; *Fax:* 905-734-8828
info@ncdsb.com
www.niagararc.com
Grades: Pre-K.-12 *Enrollment:* 25000
John Crocco, Dir./Sec.-Treas., ext. 220
john.crocco@ncdsb.com
Kathy Burtnik, Chair

Windsor: Conseil scolaire de district des écoles catholiques du Sud-Ouest
7515, promenade Forest Glade, Windsor, ON N8T 3P5, Canada
Tél: 519-948-9227; *Téléc:* 519-948-1091
Ligne sans frais: 888-768-2219
www.csdecso.on.ca
Enrollment: 1412
Janine Griffore, Directrice générale

Windsor: Windsor-Essex Catholic District School Board
1325 California Ave., Windsor, ON N9B 3Y6, Canada
Tel: 519-253-2481; *Fax:* 519-253-8397
www.wecdsb.on.ca
Grades: Pre-K.-12 *Enrollment:* 27518
Joseph Berthiaume, Dir., ext. 1201
joseph_berthiaume@wecdsb.on.ca
Mario Iatonna, Supt. of Business, ext. 1211
mario_iatonna@wecdsb.on.ca
Fred Alexander, Chair, 519-735-8664
fred_alexander@wecdsb.on.ca

French

North Bay: Conseil scolaire public du Nord-Est de l'Ontario
310 , av Algonquin, North Bay, ON P1B 9T5, Canada
Tél: 705-472-3443; *Téléc:* 705-472-5757
Ligne sans frais: 888-591-5656
information@csdne.edu.on.ca
www.csdne.edu.on.ca
Enrollment: 1725 *Note:* Timmins: 111, av Wilson, (705) 264-1119.
Roch Gallien, Directeur de l'éducation
Robert Poirier, Président du Conseil

Ottawa: Conseil des écoles publiques de l'Est de l'Ontario
2445, boul Saint-Laurent, Ottawa, ON K1G 6C3, Canada
Tél: 613-747-3802; *Téléc:* 613-747-3810
Ligne sans frais: 888-332-3736
www.cepeo.on.ca
Rachid El Keurti, Directeur exécutif
rachid.elkeurti@cepeo.on.ca
Georges Orfal, Président du Conseil
georges.orfali@cepeo.on.ca

Sudbury: Conseil scolaire public Grand Nord de l'Ontario
296, rue Van Horne, Sudbury, ON P3B 1H9, Canada
Tél: 705-671-1533; *Téléc:* 705-671-1720
Ligne sans frais: 800-465-5993
www.cspgno.ca
Enrollment: 902
Pierre Riopel, Directeur général (par intérim)
Jean-Marc Aubin, Président

Toronto: Conseil scolaire de district du Centre-Sud-Ouest
116, Cornelius Pkwy., Toronto, ON M6L 2K5, Canada
Tél: 416-614-0844; *Téléc:* 416-397-2012
Ligne sans frais: 888-538-1702
www.csdcso.on.ca
Enrollment: 7700
Jean-Luc Bernard, Directeur de l'éducation
Ronald Marion, Président du Conseil

School Authorities

Armstrong: Northern District School Area Board
P.O. Box 98
1 Hwy. 527, Armstrong, ON P0T 1A0, Canada
Tel: 807-583-2010; *Fax:* 807-583-2614
Grades: Pre-K.-8 *Enrollment:* 123
Fred Porter, Supervisory Officer, 807-475-6989
Yolanda Wanakamik, Chair

Hornepayne: Hornepayne Roman Catholic Separate School Board
P.O. Box 430
200 Front St., Hornepayne, ON P0M 1Z0, Canada
Tel: 807-868-2010; *Fax:* 807-868-3026
Enrollment: 86
Julie Roy, Sec.
Carol MacEachern, Chair

Madawaska: Murchison & Lyell District School Area Board
c/o G. Breshnahan, Major Lake Rd.
P.O. Box 10
Madawaska, ON K0J 2C0, Canada
Tel: 613-637-1349; *Fax:* 613-637-1349
esip.edu.gov.on.ca/english/profiles/board_directory.asp?ID=B15229
Grades: Pre-K.-8 *Enrollment:* 21
Elaine Hare, Vice-Chair/Trustee

Mine Centre: Mine Centre District Area School Board
P.O. Box 128
Mine Centre, ON P0W 1H0, Canada
Tel: 807-599-2836; *Fax:* 807-599-2815
esip.edu.gov.on.ca/english/profiles/board_directory.asp?ID=B15172
Grades: Pre-K.-8 *Enrollment:* 84
Sheila McMillen, Sec.-Treas.
Genevieve Bliss, Chair

Moose Factory: Moose Factory Island District School Area Board
P.O. Box 160
Moose Factory, ON P0L 1W0, Canada
Tel: 705-658-4571; *Fax:* 705-658-4768
esip.edu.gov.on.ca/english/profiles/board_directory.asp?ID=B15199
Grades: Pre-K.-8 *Enrollment:* 362
Brenda J. Chilton-Jeffries, Sec.-Treas.
Irene Hunter, Chair

Moosonee: James Bay Lowlands Secondary School Board
P.O. Box 157
1 Keewatin Dr., Moosonee, ON P0L 1Y0, Canada
Tel: 705-336-2903; *Fax:* 705-336-0234
Enrollment: 179
Charles Faries, Adm.
Bernice Morrison, Chair

Moosonee: Moosonee District School Area Board
P.O. Box 250
Moosonee, ON P0L 1Y0, Canada
Tel: 705-336-2300; *Fax:* 705-336-0334
esip.edu.gov.on.ca/english/profiles/board_directory.asp?ID=B15202
Grades: Pre-K.-8 *Enrollment:* 328
Barbara Faries, Sec.-Treas.
Dianne Wynne, Chair

Moosonee: Moosonee Roman Catholic Separate School Board
P.O. Box 340
Moosonee, ON P0L 1Y0, Canada
Tel: 705-336-2605; *Fax:* 705-336-2881
esip.edu.gov.on.ca/english/profiles/board_directory.asp?ID=B16063
Grades: Pre-K-8 *Enrollment:* 109
Kathy Hallett, Supervisory Officer

Oshawa: Campbell Children's School Authority
600 Towline Rd. South, Oshawa, ON L1H 7K6, Canada
Tel: 905-576-8403; *Fax:* 905-576-4414
ccs@grtc.ca
Grades: Specialized programs *Note:* Campbell Children's School serves students from the local district school boards with communication or multiple disabilities.
Lynda Schuler, Chair

Ottawa: Ottawa Children's Treatment Centre School Authority
395 Smyth Rd., Ottawa, ON K2H 8L2, Canada
Tel: 613-737-0871; *Fax:* 613-523-5167
Enrollment: 23
Neil Wilson, Chair

Parry Sound: Parry Sound Roman Catholic Separate School Board
#203, 60 James St., Parry Sound, ON P2A 1T5, Canada
Tel: 705-746-6231; *Fax:* 705-746-7568
Enrollment: 208
Brian McLeod, Chair

Penetanguishene: The Protestant Separate School Board of the Town of Penetanguishene
P.O. Box 107
2 Poyntz St., Penetanguishene, ON L9M 1M2, Canada
Tel: 705-549-6422; *Fax:* 705-549-2768
pssbp@bellnet.ca
www.pssbp.com
Number of Schools: 1 *Enrollment:* 234
June Merkley, Supervisory Officer
junemerkley@bellnet.ca
Sally Baker, Comptroller
sallybaker@bellnet.ca

Red Lake: Red Lake Area Combined Roman Catholic Separate School Board
P.O. Box 888
54 Discovery Rd., Red Lake, ON P0V 2M0, Canada
Tel: 807-727-3470; *Fax:* 807-727-3211
Enrollment: 119
Nora Kolmel, Secretary
Vaughan Blab, Chair

St Catharines: Niagara Children's Centre
567 Glenridge Ave., St Catharines, ON L2T 4C2, Canada
Tel: 905-688-3550; *Fax:* 905-688-1055
Toll-Free: 800-896-5496
info@niagarachildrenscentre.com
niagarachildrenscentre.com
Enrollment: 84 *Note:* A non-profit, charitable organization aiming to provide programs and services to enable children and youth with physical or communicative challenges to maximize their independence.
Oksana Fisher, CEO

Timmins: Missarenda District School Area Board
869 Denise St., Timmins, ON P6N 7M5, Canada
Tel: 705-268-6217; *Fax:* 705-268-6217
esip.edu.gov.on.ca/english/profiles/board_directory.asp?ID=B15180
Enrollment: 3
Jody Charette, Sec.
Lise Anglehart, Chair

Toronto: Bloorview School Authority
150 Kilgour Rd., Toronto, ON M4G 1R8, Canada
Tel: 416-424-3831; *Fax:* 416-425-2981
school@bloorview.ca
www.bloorviewschool.ca
Note: Bloorview School Authority provides school programs to children & youth with special needs.
Rachee Allen, Trustee
Dr. Doug Biggar, Trustee
Earl Campbell, Trustee
Mary Campbell, Trustee
Brenda Keleher, Trustee
James McCarron, Trustee
Richard Volpe, Trustee

Waterloo: KidsAbility School Authority Board
500 Hallmark Dr., Waterloo, ON N2K 3P5, Canada
Tel: 519-886-8886; *Fax:* 519-885-6222
www.kidsability.ca
Note: KidsAbility School Authority Board serves children with a wide range of special needs. Programs & services include a kindergarten program, individual education plans, composite classes, communication classes, & language classes.
Justin Heimpel, Chair
Linda Rogers, Principal & Secretary to the Board
Joanne Cotter, Secretary-Treasurer

Windsor: John McGivney Children's Centre School Authority
3945 Matchette Rd., Windsor, ON N9C 4C2, Canada
Tel: 519-252-7281; *Fax:* 519-252-5873
www.jmccentre.ca
Note: The John McGivney Children's Centre School Authority governs the John McGivney Children's Centre School, formerly known as the Children's Rehabilitation Centre School. The school provides a post trauma / post operative rehabilitation program for students from ages four to twenty-one, who live in Windsor / Essex County.
Carolyn Tavolieri, Chair
Adelina Irvine, Vice-Chair
Dr. Brenda Roberts-Santarossa, Secretary
Karen McConnell, Treasurer

First Nations

Attawapiskat: Attawapiskat First Nation Education Authority
General Delivery, Attawapiskat, ON P0L 1A0, Canada
Tel: 705-997-2114; *Fax:* 705-997-2357
psinfo@afnea.com; recruit@afnea.com (Recruitment)
www.afnea.com
Number of Schools: 2 *Grades:* Junior Kindergarten-12; Special Ed. *Enrollment:* 800 *Note:* J.R. Nakogee School & Vezina Secondary School
John B. Nakogee, Director, Education
Andrew Hirst, Chair

Big Trout Lake: Kitchenuhmaykoosib Education Authority
General Delivery, Big Trout Lake, ON P0V 1G0, Canada
Tel: 807-537-2553; *Fax:* 807-537-2316
kifirstnation@knet.ca
www.bigtroutlake.firstnation.ca
Number of Schools: 1 *Grades:* Junior Kindergarten-11; Special Ed. *Enrollment:* 275 *Note:* Aglace Chapman Education Centre. Number of Employees: 30. The Kitchenuhmaykoosib Education Authority serves the Kitchenuhmaykoosib Inninnuwug First Nation, formerly known as Big Trout Lake First Nation, located north of Thunder Bay, Ontario. Secondary programs are also available through computer, radio, & television.

Christian Island: Beausoleil First Nation Education Authority
Administration Building
1 O'Gema St., Main Level, Christian Island, ON L0K 1C0, Canada
Tel: 705-247-2051; *Fax:* 705-247-2239
n.assance@beausoleil-education.ca
www.beausoleil-education.ca
Number of Schools: 1 *Grades:* Junior Kindergarten - 8; Special Ed *Note:* The Beausoleil First Nation Education Authority serves the Chippewas of the Beausoleil First Nation by operating the Christian Island Elementary School. For secondary education, students attend high schools in the Simcoe County District School Board or the Simcoe Muskoka Catholic School Board.
Amanda Monague, Director, Education
ed.dir@beausoleil-education.ca
Angela Johnson, Principal, Christian Island Elementary School
a.johnson@beausoleil-education.ca
Angela Haskill, Coordinator, Adult Education

Constance Lake: Constance Lake First Nation Education Authority
P.O. Box 4000
Constance Lake, ON P0L 1B0, Canada
Tel: 705-463-4511; *Fax:* 705-463-2222
www.clfn.on.ca
Number of Schools: 1 *Grades:* Daycare - JK - 12; Adult Education *Enrollment:* 257 *Note:* Mamawmatawa Holistic Education Center. Located in the District of Cochrane, the Constance Lake First Nation Education Authority provides education to community members of Cree & Ojibway ancestry. The Constance Lake First Nation Education Authority is supported by the Matawa Education Department in Thunder Bay, Ontario.
Ronnie Martin, President, Board of Diretors
Ron Wesley, Councillor (Education, Day care, Finance, & Administration)
Ken Neegan, Administrator, Education
Veronica Ramadan, Manager, Finance
Lizzie Sutherland, Librarian & Secretary

Cornwall: Ahkwesahsne Mohawk Board of Education
P.O. Box 819
169 International Rd., Cornwall, ON K6H 5T7, Canada
Tel: 613-933-0409; *Fax:* 613-933-9262
www.akwesasne.ca
Grades: Pre-Kindergarten-8; Alternative Ed. *Note:* The Ahkwesahsne Mohawk Board of Education operates three elementary schools. Since the Ahkwesahsne Mohawk Board of Education does not have a secondary school, there is an agreement with the Upper Canada Public School Board to provide secondary education.
Barry M. Montour, Director, Education, 613-933-0409
bmontour@akwesasne.ca
Deborah Terrance, Associate Director
Lillian Macias, Coordinator, Curriculum, 613-933-3366
Val Mitchell, Coordinator, Alternative Education Program, 613-575-1969
Sandra Rourke, Coordinator, Student Services
Norma Sunday, Coordinator, Post Secondary Program
Alice King, Supervisor, Head Start Program
Dwayne Thomas, Supervisor, Transportation
Gerald Thompson, Supervisor, Operation & Maintenance
Anneke Fischer-Fey, Psychometrist, 613-932-3366

Deer Lake: Deer Lake Education Authority
P.O. Box 69
Deer Lake, ON P0V 1N0
Tel: 807-775-2055; *Fax:* 807-751-9225
www.deerlake.firstnation.ca
TTY: 1-888-751-9225
Number of Schools: 1 *Grades:* K4 - K5; 1 - 9; Special Education *Note:* Deer Lake School. The Deer Lake Education Authority oversees education for the Deer Lake First Nation, an Oji-Cree community situated about 180 kilometres north of Red Lake, Ontario. Deer Lake School provides education to grade nine. The Authority coordinates the enrollment & boarding for students who leave the reserve for schooling beyond ninth grade, in places such as Ear Falls, Sioux Lookout, Red Lake, Thunder Bay, & Winnipeg.
Leonard Mamakeesic, Director, Education

Dinorwic: Wabigoon Lake Ojibway Nation Education Authority
P.O. Box 24
Site 112, Dinorwic, ON P0V 1P0, Canada
Tel: 807-938-6684; *Fax:* 807-938-1166
Number of Schools: 1 *Grades:* Junior Kindergarten - 8 *Note:* Wabsnki-Penasi School. Elementary education is provided in a school operated by the Wabigoon Lake Ojibway Nation. Secondary school students are bused to nearby Dryden, Ontario.

Eabamet Lake: Eabametoong (Fort Hope) First Nation Education Authority
P.O. Box 294
Eabamet Lake, ON P0T 1L0, Canada
Tel: 807-242-1305; *Fax:* 807-242-1313
efnea64@gmail.com
www.eabametoong.firstnation.ca
Other Information: Education Coordinator, Phone: 807-242-1305, ext. 24
Number of Schools: 1 *Grades:* Kindergarten - 10; Special Ed. *Enrollment:* 380 *Note:* John C. Yesno Education Centre. Number of Employees: 25 teachers; 10 teaching assistants & tutor escorts; 3 counsellors. Eabametoong (Fort Hope) is a fly-in Ojibwe First Nations community located approximately 360 kilometres northeast of Thunder Bay, Ontario. The Eabametoong (Fort Hope) First Nation Education Authority consists of a Board of Directors & a head office staff. The Matawa Education Department in Thunder, Bay, Ontario supports the education authority.
Sharon Allan, Education Coordinator, Eabametoong First Nation
sharon-nate@hotmail.com

Fort Albany: Mundo Peetabeck Education Authority
P.O. Box 31
Fort Albany, ON P0L 1H0, Canada
Tel: 705-278-3390; *Fax:* 705-278-1049
Grades: Elem. *Enrollment:* 150
Nicole Gillies, Administrator

Fort Severn: Wasaho Education Authority
General Delivery, Fort Severn, ON P0V 1W0, Canada
Tel: 807-478-9548; *Fax:* 807-478-2573
Number of Schools: 1 *Enrollment:* 120 *Note:* The Wasaho Education Authority provides education to members of the Fort Severn First Nation. The Fort Severn First Nation Reserve is situated in northern Ontario, near the mouth of the Severn River.

Heron Bay: Pic River First Nation Education Authority
General Delivery, Heron Bay, ON P0T 1R0, Canada
Tel: 807-229-1749; *Fax:* 807-229-1944
Grades: Elem. *Enrollment:* 94
Cindy Fisher, Education Director
cfisher@picriver.com

Kasabonika: Sineonokway Education Authority
P.O. Box 33
Kasabonika, ON P0V 1Y0, Canada
Tel: 807-535-1117; *Fax:* 807-535-1152
Grades: Elem. *Enrollment:* 250

Kashechewan: Hishkoonikun Education Authority (HEA)
P.O. Box 210
Kashechewan, ON P0L 1S0, Canada
Tel: 705-275-4538; *Fax:* 705-275-4515
Toll-Free: 1-800-433-4863
www.kashechewan.firstnation.ca/kfn/education
Number of Schools: 1 elementary; 1 secondary *Grades:* JK-12 *Enrollment:* 500 *Number of Employees:* 77 employees
Leo Metatawabin, Chair

Keewaywin: Keewaywin First Nation
P.O. Box 90
Keewaywin, ON P0V 3G0, Canada
Tel: 807-771-1210; *Fax:* 807-771-1053
Toll-Free: 866-437-9505
David Thompson, Chief
Chris Kakegamic, Director, Education

Kejick: Shoal Lake Chief & Council: Education Authority
General Delivery, Kejick, ON P0X 1E0, Canada
Tel: 807-733-2315; *Fax:* 807-733-3115
Grades: Elem. *Enrollment:* 50
Kelvin Redsky, Administrator

Kenora: Northwest Angle #33 Education Authority
P.O. Box 1490
Kenora, ON P9N 3X7, Canada
Tel: 807-733-2200; *Fax:* 807-733-3148
www.akrc.on.ca
Grades: Elem. *Enrollment:* 16
Josephine Sandy, Education Counsellor

Kingfisher: Kingfisher Lake Education Authority
P.O. Box 57
Kingfisher, ON P0V 1Z0, Canada
Tel: 807-532-2067; *Fax:* 807-532-2063
www.kingfisherlake.ca
Grades: Elem. *Enrollment:* 100
Solomon Mamakwa, Dir.

Lac Seul: Lac Seul Education Authority
P.O. Box 100 Hudson
Lac Seul, ON P0V 2A0, Canada
Tel: 807-582-3503
Grades: Elem./Sec. *Enrollment:* 97
Karen Ningewance, Chair
Richard Morris, Dir.

Longlac: Long Lake #58 & Ginoogaming First Nations Education Authority
P.O. Box 89
Longlac, ON P0T 2A0
Tel: 807-876-4914
Number of Schools: 2 *Grades:* JK-12; Special Ed; Ojibway language *Enrollment:* 173 *Note:* Migizsi Wazisin Elementary School & Nimiki Migizsi Secondary School. Number of Employees: 24 teachers, board administrative personnel, support staff, & custodial personnel. The Long Lake #58 & Ginoogaming First Nations Education Authority consists of three board members from Long Lake #58 First Nation & three board members from Ginoogaming First Nation (formerly the Long Lake #77 First Nation). Both First Nations are members of Matawa First Nations, so that educational support services for the Long Lake #58 & Ginoogaming First Nations Education Authority are provided by the Matawa Education Department in Thunder Bay, Ontario.
Claire Onabigon, Director, Education, 807-876-1270
conabigo@lakeheadu.ca
Fred Simoniatis, Principal

M'Chigeeng: West Bay Board of Education
22 Bebonang St., M'Chigeeng, ON P0P 1G0, Canada
Tel: 705-377-5611; *Fax:* 705-377-5080
Grades: Elem. *Enrollment:* 180
Melvina Corbiere, Education Coordinator

MacDiarmid: Rocky Bay First Nation Education Authority
General Delivery
MacDiarmid, ON P0T 2B0, Canada
Tel: 807-885-3401; *Fax:* 807-885-3231
Grades: Elem. *Enrollment:* 41

Migisi Sahgaigan: Migisi Sah Gai Gun Education Authority
P.O. Box 1005
Migisi Sahgaigan, ON P0V 3H0, Canada
Tel: 807-755-5350; *Fax:* 807-755-5696
Grades: Elem. *Enrollment:* 44
Leonard Gardner, Dir.

Mishkeegogamang: Mishkeegogamang Education Authority
General Delivery, Mishkeegogamang, ON P0V 2H0
Tel: 807-928-2299; *Fax:* 807-928-2494
Grades: Elem./Sec.; 3 schools *Enrollment:* 255
Ida Mackuck, Education Coordinator
Isabe Skunk, Secretary

Morson: Big Grassy River (Mishkosiimiiniiziibig) Education Authority
P.O. Box 453
Beach Rd., Morson, ON P0W 1J0, Canada
Tel: 807-488-5916; *Fax:* 807-488-5345
biggrassy.ca/education
Number of Schools: 1 *Grades:* Jr. Kindergarten - 8; Special Ed. *Enrollment:* 61 *Note:* Pegamigaabo Elementary School

Muncey: Chippewas of the Thames First Nation Board of Education
330 Chippewa Rd., Muncey, ON N0L 1Y0, Canada
Tel: 519-289-0621; *Fax:* 519-289-0633
www.chippewa-ed.on.ca
Number of Schools: 1 elementary school *Grades:* Elementary
Note: Antler River Elementary School
Kristin Hendrick, Council Liaison
Joanne Henry, Coordinator, Eucation Administration
joann.henry@chippewa-ed.on.ca
Jody Joseph, Contact, Post-Secondary Program & Guidance, 519-289-0621, fax: 519-289-0633
postsecondary@chippewa-ed.on.ca
Starr McGahey-Albert, Contact, Education Finance
postsecondary@chippewa-ed.on.ca

Muskrat Dam: Muskrat Dam First Nation Education Authority
P.O. Box 140
Muskrat Dam, ON P0V 3B0, Canada
Tel: 807-471-2524; *Fax:* 807-471-2649
Other Information: Whasa Distant Education Centre, Phone: 807-471-2619
Number of Schools: 1 *Grades:* Junior Kindergarten - 8 *Note:* Samson Beardy Memorial School. The Muskrat Dam First Nation community is situated approximately 370 kilometres north of Sioux Lookout. Oji-Cee & English are spoken. The community features an elementary school, plus the Wahsa Distance Education Centre to support secondary & post-secondary students attending schools in towns & cities.
Vernon Morris, Chief, Muskrat Dam First Nation

North Spirit Lake: North Spirit Lake Education Authority
General Delivery, North Spirit Lake, ON P0V 2G0, Canada
Tel: 807-776-0001; *Fax:* 807-776-0003
Number of Schools: 1 *Grades:* Elem. *Enrollment:* 60
Luke Rae, Dir.

Ogoki Post: Marten Falls (Ogoki) First Nation Education Authority
Education Administration Office
General Delivery, Ogoki Post, ON P0T 2L0, Canada
Tel: 807-349-2628; *Fax:* 807-349-2511
Number of Schools: 1 *Grades:* Kindergarten - 8 *Note:* Henry Coaster Memorial School. The Marten Falls (Ogoki) First Nation Education Authority offers elementary education in the Cree-Ojibwe community. Members of the First Nation board in Thunder Bay, Ontario to attend secondary school. The Matawa Education Department provides educational support services to the Marten Falls (Ogoki) First Nation Education Authority.

Pawitik: Whitefish Bay: Northwest Angle Education Authority
General Delivery, Pawitik, ON P0X 1L0, Canada
Tel: 807-226-5411; *Fax:* 807-226-5389
Grades: Elem./Sec. *Enrollment:* 300
Isobel White, Dir.

Peawanuck: Weenusk First Nation Education Services
P.O. Box 1
Peawanuck, ON P0L 2H0, Canada
Tel: 705-473-2554; *Fax:* 705-473-2503
Grades: Elem. *Enrollment:* 60
Abraham Hunter Sr., Chair
George Hunter, Dir.

Pikangikum: Pikangikum Education Authority
c/o Eenchokay Birchstick School
General Delivery, Pikangikum, ON P0V 2L0, Canada
Tel: 807-773-1093; *Fax:* 807-773-1014
Number of Schools: 1 *Grades:* Elem./Sec. *Enrollment:* 520
Number of Employees: 60 teachers
Charlie Pascal, Dir.
George Suggashie, Chair

Rama: Chippewas of Rama First Nation Chief & Council
#200, 5884 Rama Rd., Rama, ON L3V 6H6, Canada
Tel: 705-325-3611; *Fax:* 705-325-0879
Toll-Free: 866-854-2121
cherylm@ramafirstnation.ca
www.mnjikaning.ca
Note: The Chippewas of Rama First Nation Chief & Council are responsible for education & career planning.
Sharon Stinson Henry, Chief
chief@ramafirstnation.ca

Sandy Lake: Sandy Lake Board of Education
P.O. Box 8
Sandy Lake, ON P0V 1V0, Canada
Tel: 807-774-1135; *Fax:* 807-774-1166
www.sandylake.firstnation.ca
Number of Schools: 3 *Grades:* Kindergarten - 10; Adult Ed. *Enrollment:* 514 *Note:* Thomas Fiddler Memorial Elementary School; Thomas Fiddler Memorial High School; Gabbius Goodman Memorial Adult Learning Centre). The Sandy Lake Board of Education oversees the management of schools which serve students of Sandy Lake First Nation.
Christina Meekis, Director, Education
Troy Kakepetum, Assistant Director, Education
Russell Kakepetum, Band Councillor, Education Portfolio
Florance Ballentyne, Officer, Finance

Sarnia: Aamjiwnaang First Nation Education Administration
978 Tashmoo Ave., Sarnia, ON N7T 7H5, Canada
Tel: 519-336-8410; *Fax:* 519-336-0382
www.aamjiwnaang.ca
Note: Formerly Chippewas of Sarnia, the community of Aamjiwnaang First Nation is located in the city limits of Sarnia, Ontario.
Jodi Branton, Coordinator, Education Services, 519-336-0382, ext. 247
Diane Aiken, Assistant, Education Services, 519-336-0382, ext. 246

Sioux Lookout: Windigo Education Authority
P.O. Box 299
160 Alcona Dr., Sioux Lookout, ON P8T 1A3, Canada
Tel: 807-737-1064; *Fax:* 807-737-3452
wea@windigo.on.ca
www.windigoeducation.on.ca
Number of Schools: 4 *Grades:* JK-8; Aboriginal language & culture *Enrollment:* 445 *Note:* Windigo Education Authority consists of the following First Nation members: Bearskin Lake First Nation, Cat Lake First Nation, Sachigo Lake First Nation, & Slate Falls Nation. The language of each First Nation community is Ojibway or Oji-Cree.
Lana Bighead, Education Coordinator, Bimaychikamah School, 807-737-5701, fax: 807-347-1299
James Chapman, Education Coordinator, Martin McKay Memorial School, 807-595-2527, fax: 807-595-1119
Vince Ostberg, Education Coordinator, Michikan Lake School, 807-363-1011, fax: 807-363-2519
Marie Stewart, Education Coordinator, Titotay Memorial School, 807-347-2102, fax: 807-347-2057

Sioux Narrows: Northwest Angle #37 Education Authority
P.O. Box 267
Sioux Narrows, ON P0X 1N0, Canada
Tel: 807-226-5353; *Fax:* 807-226-1164

Southwold: Onyota'aka Kalthuny Nihtsla Tehatilihutakwas (OKT) Education Authority
2315 Keystone Pl., Southwold, ON N0L 2G0, Canada
Tel: 519-652-1580; *Fax:* 519-652-3219
Grades: Elem. *Enrollment:* 185
Neil Cornelius, Chair
Lynda Doxtator, Education Adm.

Thunder Bay: Matawa Education Department
c/o Matawa First Nations Management
233 South Court St., Thunder Bay, ON P7B 2X9, Canada
Tel: 807-344-4575; *Fax:* 807-344-2977
Toll-Free: 1-800-463-2249
learningcentre@matawa.on.ca
www.education.matawa.on.ca
Number of Schools: 9 *Grades:* JK - Secondary; Adult Education
Note: Johnny Therriault School, Aroland First Nation; Mamawmatawa Holistic Education Centre, Constance Lake First Nation; John C. Yesno Education Centre, Eabametoong First Nation; Nibinamik Education Centre, Nibinamik First Nation; Migizi Wazisin Elementary School, Long Lake #58 First Nation; Henry Coaster Memorial School, Marten Falls First Nation; Nimiki Migizi Secondary School, Ginoogaming First Nation; Neskantaga Education Centre, Neskantaga First Nation; & Simon Jacob Memorial Education Centre, Webequie First Nation). The Matawa Education Department delivers educational support services to local education authorities. Education is provided at local Matawa First Nation schools in a culturally appropriate environment to meet the diverse needs of students. Post-secondary student support services, as well as alternative learning & adult education & training are also offered.
Murray L. Wavoose, Manager, Education Department
mwaboose@matawa.on.ca
Georgette O'Nabigon, Coordinator, Post Secondary Program
gonabigon@matawa.on.ca
Steve Chase, Developer, E-Learning
schase@matawa.on.ca

Tyendinaga Mohawk Territory: Tyendinaga Mohawk Education, Culture, & Language Department
Administration Building
13 Old York Rd., Tyendinaga Mohawk Territory, ON K0K 1X0, Canada
Tel: 613-396-3424; *Fax:* 613-396-3627
Note: Educational programs available for the Mohawks of the Bay of Quinte include the Eksa'okon:'a Child Care Centre, the Tahatikonhsotontie Head Start Program, a Post-Secondary Education Program, a Native Student Liaison Program, an Employment & Training Program, the Ka:nhiote Public Library, & Mohawk Bus Lines. Mohawk language & cultural instruction is part of Tahatikonhsotontie Head Start, an early childhood education program.
Tracey Gazley, Manager, Tahatikonhsotontie Head Start Program, 613-396-6716
traceyg@mbq-tmt.org
Cheryl Lavigne, Manager, Day Care (Eksa'okon:'a Child Care Centre), 613-967-4401
daycare@tyendinaga.net
Bruce Maracle, Manager, Mohawk Bus Lines, 613-396-2000
Karen Lewis, Librarian, Ka:nhiote Public Library, 613-967-6264
karenl@tyendinaga.net
Patti Brinklow, Coordinator, Post-Secondary Education, 613-396-3424, ext. 119
pattig@mbq-tmt.org
Betty Maracle, Teacher, Culture, 613-396-6716
bettym@mbq-tmt.org
Melissa Maracle, Teacher, Mohawk Language
Sandra Sero, Counsellor, Employment & Training Program, 613-968-1122, ext. 141
sandys@mbq-tmt.org

Wallaceburg: Walpole Island Elementary School
RR#3, Wallaceburg, ON N8A 4K9, Canada
Tel: 519-627-0712; *Fax:* 519-627-8596
Grades: Junior Kindergarten - 8 *Note:* The Walpole Island Elementary School is a First Nation operated school which serves members of the Walpole Island First Nation community. School employees are required to have knowledge & understanding of the Anishinaabeg culture. The education program is administered by the Walpole Island First Nation Board of Education. For secondary education, students from Walpole Island First Nation are transported to the nearby communities of Sarnia, Chatham, & Wallaceburg.

Wallaceburg: Walpole Island First Nation Board of Education
RR#3, Wallaceburg, ON N8A 4K9
Tel: 519-627-1481; *Fax:* 519-627-0440
Number of Schools: 1 *Grades:* Junior Kindergarten - 8 *Note:* Walpole Island Elementary School. Secondary school students from the Walpole Island First Nation community are transported to Chatham, Sarnia, & Wallaceburg to attend school.
Joseph Gilbert, Chief
Bill Tooshkenig, Chair
Cynthia Williams, Officer, Human Resources
cynthia.williams@wifn.org

***Weagamow Lake:* North Caribou Lake First Nation Education Authority**
P.O. Box 155
Weagamow Lake, ON P0V 2Y0, Canada
Tel: 807-469-1254; *Fax:* 807-469-1351
northcariboulakefirstnation@knet.ca
Grades: Elem. *Enrollment:* 136
Saul Williams, Education Director

***Webequie:* Webequie First Nation Education Authority**
P.O. Box 102
Webequie, ON P0T 3A0
Tel: 807-353-9942; *Fax:* 807-353-9966
info@webequie.ca; webequieeducation@knet.ca
Number of Schools: 1 *Grades:* K-10; Native Language; Special Ed. *Enrollment:* 200 *Note:* Simon Jacob Memorial Education Centre. The Webequie First Nation Education Authority is located in a Oji-Cree community on the Winisk River in northern Ontario. The education authority receives educational support services from the Matawa Education Department in Thunder Bay, Ontario. Programs include special education, native education, distance education, & post-secondary education support services.
Ennis Jacob, Director, Education
ennisjacob@hotmail.com
Paul Quisses, Administrator, Finance

***Whitedog:* Wabaseemoong Education Authority**
General Delivery, Whitedog, ON P0X 1P0, Canada
Tel: 807-927-2062; *Fax:* 807-927-2176
Number of Schools: 1 *Grades:* JK - 12; Cultural activities *Enrollment:* 300 *Note:* Wabaseemoong School. The Wabaseemoong Education Authority oversees education in the Wabaseemoong First Nation community located approximately 100 kilometres northwest of Kenora, Ontario.

***Wiarton:* Chippewas of Nawash Unceded First Nation Board of Education**
6 Harbour Rd., RR#5, Cape Croker Reserve, Wiarton, ON N0H 2T0, Canada
Tel: 519-534-0882; *Fax:* 519-534-5138
www.nawash.ca
Number of Schools: 1 *Note:* The board of education serves the Chippewas of Nawash Unceded First Nation band members of the Neyaashiinigmiing Indian Reserve No. 27. The reserve is situated on the eastern shore of the Saugeen (Bruce) Peninsula in Ontario, approximately 26 kilometres from Wiarton. The Chippewas of Nawash Unceded First Nation Board of Education strives to offer a culturally & community based education, based upon traditional values.
Pamela J. Keeshig, Chair & Curriculum & Program Development Portfolio Holder
Judy Nadjiwan, Education Administrator, 519-534-0882
nawashed.administrator@gbtel.ca
Jennifer Linklater, Coordinator, Nawash Post-Secondary Education Program
nawashed.postsec@gbtel.ca
Lisa Pedoniquotte, Education Counsellor, Secondary Student Services Program
nawashed.edcounsellor@gbtel.ca
Vanessa M. Keeshig, Contact, Administrative Support
nawashed.vkeeshig@gbtel.ca

***Wikwemikong:* Wikwemikong Board of Education**
34 Henry St, Wikwemikong, ON P0P 2J0, Canada
Tel: 705-859-3834; *Fax:* 705-859-2407
info@wbe-education.ca
www.wbe-education.ca
Number of Schools: 7 schools *Grades:* Elem./Sec. *Enrollment:* 486
Dominic Beaudry, B.A., B.Ed., M.A., Education Director

***Wunnummin Lake:* Wunnumin Lake Education Authority**
P.O. Box 105
Wunnummin Lake, ON P0V 2Z0, Canada
Tel: 807-442-2559; *Fax:* 807-442-2627
www.wunnumin.ca
Grades: Elem. *Enrollment:* 146
Samuel Mamokwa, Chair
Sam Mamakwa, Director
samm@wunnumin.ca

Schools: Specialized

First Nations

Neskantaga First Nation Education Centre
P.O. Box 106
Lansdowne House, , ON P0T 1Z0
Tel: 807-479-1170; *Fax:* 807-479-1178
www.education.matawa.on.ca
Grades: JK - 9; Native culture & language *Note:* The Neskantaga First Nation Education Centre is situated in a community approximately 180 kilometres north of Pickle Lake in northern Ontario. The elementary school is a Matawa First Nations community school which receives educational support services from the Matawa Education Department.
Tony Sakanee, Member, Matawa Regional Committee on Education
tonysakanee@hotmail.com

***Aroland:* Johnny Therriault Memorial School**
c/o Aroland First Nation
P.O. Box 40
Aroland, ON P0T 1B0
Tel: 807-329-5470; *Fax:* 807-329-5472
www.education.matawa.on.ca
Grades: Junior Kindergarten - 9 *Enrollment:* 120 *Note:* The Johnny Therriault School serves the Aroland First Nation School, which is located approximately 350 kilometres northeast of Thunder Bay, Ontario. The school is supported by the Matawa Education Department. Tuition agreements are in place with the Superior-Greenstone District School Board, so that Aroland First Nation students can attend grades 10 to 12 in the communities of Nakina & Geraldton.
Sam Kashkeesh, Chief, Aroland First Nation
Patricia Magiskan, Member, Matawa Regional Committee on Education
Stephanie Ash, Communications Officer, Aroland First Nation, 807-767-4443

***Attawapiskat:* J.R. Nakogee Elementary School**
***Also known as:* Attawapiskat First Nation Elementary**
P.O. Box 15
Attawapiskat, ON P0L 1A0
Tel: 705-997-2114; *Fax:* 705-997-2357
www.afnea.com
Grades: Junior Kindergarten - 8; Special Ed *Note:* J.R. Nakogee Elementary School is located in the Ontario Cree fly-in only community of Attawapiskat. It is part of the Attawapiskat First Nation Education Authority.

***Attawapiskat:* Vezina Secondary School**
P.O. Box 15
Attawapiskat, ON P0L 1A0
Tel: 705-997-2117; *Fax:* 705-997-2357
www.afnea.com
Grades: 9 - 12 *Note:* Attawapiskat First Nation Education Authority operates the high school on the west coast of James Bay.

***Bearskin Lake:* Michikan Lake School**
P.O. Box 78
Bearskin Lake, ON P0V 1E0
Tel: 807-363-1011; *Fax:* 807-363-2519
Grades: JK-8; Aboriginal language & culture *Enrollment:* 100 *Note:* Operations of the Michikan Lake School are overseen by the Windigo Education Authority. The school provides elementary education to young people of the Bearskin Lake First Nation. The First Nation community is located about 425 kilometres north of Sioux Lookout, Ontario.
Dennis Myran, Principal, 807-363-2570, fax: 807-363-1078

***Big Trout Lake:* Aglace Chapman Education Centre**
P.O. Box 168
Big Trout Lake, ON P0V 1G0, Canada
Tel: 807-537-2264; *Fax:* 807-537-1067
www.aglacechapmaneducationcentre.myknet.org
Grades: Junior Kindergarten-11; Special Ed. *Enrollment:* 275 *Note:* The Kitchenuhmaykoosib Education Authority oversees operations of the Aglace Chapman Education Centre. The centre is located about 270 air miles north of Sioux Lookout, Ontario, where it provides education to the Kitchenuhmaykoosib Inninnuwug First Nation.

***Cat Lake:* Titotay Memorial School**
P.O. Box 80
Cat Lake, ON P0V 1J0
Tel: 807-347-2102; *Fax:* 807-347-2057
www.titotayschool.myknet.org; www.windigoeducation.on.ca
Grades: JK-8; Aboriginal language & culture *Enrollment:* 120 *Note:* The Titotay Memorial School is one of four schools within the Windigo Education Authority. The First Nation School provides elementary education to members of the Cat Lake First Nation. The school is situated about 180 kilometres north of Sioux Lookout, Ontario.
Ruby Keesiquayash, Principal, 807-347-2102, fax: 807-347-2057

***Christian Island:* Christian Island Elementary School**
67 Kate Kegwin St., Christian Island, ON L0K 1C0
Tel: 705-247-2011
l.monague@beausoleil-education.ca
ASSISTANT)
WWW.BEAUSOLEIL-EDUCATION.CA
Grades: Junior Kindergarten - 8; Special Ed *Note:* Under the Beausoleil First Nation Education Authority, the Christian Island Elementary School provides education to the Chippewas of the Beausoleil First Nation.
Mike Lucas, Principal
m.lucas@beausoleil-education.ca
Sylvia Norton-Sutherland, Native Student Advisor

***Constance Lake:* Mamawmatawa Holistic Education Center**
P.O. Box 4000
Constance Lake, ON P0L 1B0
Tel: 705-463-1199; *Fax:* 705-463-2077
www.clfn.on.ca
Grades: Daycare - JK - 12; Adult Education *Enrollment:* 257 *Note:* The Mamawmatawa Holistic Education Center educates members of the Constance Lake First Nation, who live west of Hearst, Ontario. The school operates under the direction of the Constance Lake First Nation Education Authority.
Zandra Bear-Lowen, Principal
Karen Wesley, Administrator, Daycare
Pamela Dalcourt, Teacher, Literacy Resources
Judy Hewitt, Teacher, Special Education
Florrie Sutherland, Teacher, Native Language
Vivian Bird, Counsellor, Attendance & Guidance
Linda Chum, Counsellor, Child & Youth
Leo Grezla, Counsellor, Guidance
Susan Sutherland, Contact, Adult Education, ILC, & Co-op

***Deer Lake:* Deer Lake School**
P.O. Box 69
Deer Lake, ON P0V 1N0, Canada
Tel: 807-775-2055; *Fax:* 807-775-2148
Toll-Free: 1-888-751-9225
www.dls.firstnationschools.ca
Grades: K4 - K5; 1 - 9; Special Education *Note:* The Deer Lake School also offers native language instruction.
Leonard Mamakeesic, Director, Education
Elizabeth Rae, Finance Officer
Loretta Cameron, Teacher, Special Education
Victoria Meekis, Senior Instructor, Native Language

***Dinorwic:* Wabsnki-Penasi School**
P.O. Box 24
Site 112, Dinorwic, ON P0V 1P0
Tel: 807-938-6684; *Fax:* 807-938-1166
Grades: Junior Kindergarten - 8 *Note:* The First Nation elementary school is part of the Wabigoon Lake Ojibway Nation Education Authority. For secondary school education, students are transported thirty kilometres west to Dryden, Ontario.

***Fort Hope:* John C. Yesno Education Centre**
P.O. Box 297
Fort Hope, ON P0T 1L0, Canada
Tel: 807-242-8421; *Fax:* 807-242-1592
Grades: Kindergarten - 10; Special Ed. *Enrollment:* 380 *Note:* The John C. Yesno Education Centre serves the Eabametoong First Nation. The Ojibwe First Nations community is located on the north shore of northern Ontario's Eabamet Lake. Eabametoong First Nation students, continuing their education beyond tenth grade, attend schools in Thunder Bay, Sault Ste. Marie, & Sioux Lookout.

***Fort Severn:* Wasaho First Nations School**
P.O. Box 165
Fort Severn, ON P0V 1W0
Tel: 807-478-9548; *Fax:* 807-478-2573
Enrollment: 120 *Note:* The Wasaho First Nations School is part of the Wasaho Education Authority. The school serves members of the Fort Severn First Nation in northern Ontario.

***Longlac:* Migizi Wazisin Elementary School**
P.O. Box 240
Martin Rd., Longlac, ON P0T 2A0
Tel: 807-876-4482; *Fax:* 807-876-4128
www.education.matawa.on.ca
Grades: JK - 7; Special Ed; Native language *Note:* The Migizi Wazisin Elementary School is located in Long Lake #58 First Nation, an Anishinaabe (Ojibway) First Nation near Geraldton, Ontario. It serves students from both the Long Lake #58 First Nation & the Ginoogaming First Nation. Operations of the elementary school are administered by the Long Lake #58 & Ginoogaming First Nations Education Authority.

***Longlac:* Nimiki Migizi Secondary School**
P.O. Box 360
100 Balsam St., Longlac, ON P0T 2A0
Tel: 807-876-1270; *Fax:* 807-876-4151
www.education.matawa.on.ca; www.ginoogaming.ca
Grades: 8 - 12; Ojibway language *Note:* The Nimiki Migizi Secondary School is located in the Ginoogaming First Nation, which is an Anishnawbe (Ojibway) First Nation near Geraldton, Ontario. The high school serves students from both the Ginoogaming First Nation & Long Lake #58 First Nation. Nimiki Migizi Secondary School operates with support from the Long Lake #58 & Ginoogaming First Nations Education Authority.

***Mobert:* Netamisakomik Education Centre**
P.O. Box 615
Mobert, ON P0M 2J0, Canada
Tel: 807-822-2011; *Fax:* 807-822-2710
www.picmobert.ca
Grades: JK-8
Jacky Craig, Principal
principal@picmobert.ca

***Muskrat Dam:* Samson Beardy Memorial School**
P.O. Box 43
Muskrat Dam, ON P0V 3B0
Tel: 807-471-2524; *Fax:* 807-471-2649
Grades: Junior Kindergarten - 8 *Note:* The Samson Beardy Memorial School is a First Nation operated school administered by the Muskrat Dam First Nation Education Authority. Secondary & post-secondary students attend schools outside the remote First Nation community.

***Nordegg:* Ta Otha Community School**
P.O. Box 39
Nordegg, ON T0M 2H0
Tel: 403-721-3989; *Fax:* 403-721-2174
www.stoney-nation.com
Note: The Ta Otha School is part of the Stoney Education Authority. The school serves members of the Stoney Nakoda First Nation.

***Ogoki Post:* Henry Coaster Memorial School**
General Delivery, Ogoki Post, ON P0T 2L0
Tel: 807-349-2509; *Fax:* 807-349-2511
www.education.matawa.on.ca
Grades: Junior Kindergarten - 8 *Enrollment:* 90 *Note:* Henry Coaster Memorial School is located in Marten Falls Nation, on the north side of the Albany River in northern Ontario. The First Nation school offers traditional culture & language programming. The elementary school operates with support from the Marten Falls (Ogoki) First Nation Education Authority.

***Ohsweken:* Six Nations of the Grand River**
P.O. Box 5000
1695 Chiefswood Rd., Ohsweken, ON N0A 1M0, Canada
Tel: 519-445-2201; *Fax:* 519-445-4208
www.sixnations.ca
Grades: Elem.; 5 schools *Enrollment:* 1328
Kathy Knott

***Sachigo Lake:* Martin McKay Memorial School**
P.O. Box 51
Sachigo Lake, ON P0V 2P0, Canada
Tel: 807-595-2526; *Fax:* 807-595-1305
Grades: JK-8; Aboriginal language & culture *Enrollment:* 100 *Note:* The Martin McKay Memorial School serves students of the Sachigo Lake First Nation. The First Nation community is situated approximately 150 kilometres west of Big Trout Lake, Ontario. Activities of the Sachigo Lake First Nation school are administered by the Windigo Education Authority.
Bob Salvisburg, Principal, 807-595-2526, fax: 807-595-1305

***Sarnia:* Aamjiwnaang Junior Kindergarten (Aamjiwnaang Binoojiinyag Kino Maagewgamgoon**
1900 Virgil Ave., Sarnia, ON N7T 8A7
Tel: 519-344-4132; *Fax:* 519-344-6956
Grades: Junior Kindergarten *Note:* Under the Aamjiwnaang First Nation Education Administration, education is offered to members of the Aamjiwnaang First Nation.
Kim Henry, Principal
Muriel Joseph-Plain, Supervisor, 519-344-5831

***Sault St. Marie:* Batchewana Learning Centre**
15 Jean Ave., Sault St. Marie, ON P6B 4B1, Canada
Tel: 705-759-7285; *Fax:* 705-759-9982
Toll-Free: 1-866-339-3370
colleen@batchewana.ca
www.batchewana.ca
Elaine McDonagh, Education Director/Principal

***Slate Falls:* Bimaychikamah School**
General Delivery, Slate Falls, ON P0V 3C0
Grades: JK-8; Aboriginal language & culture *Enrollment:* 42 *Note:* Education for members of the Slate Falls Nation is provided by the Bimaychikamah School. The elementary school is situated in the Slate Falls Nation community north of Sioux Lookout, Ontario. Operations of Bimaychikamah School are overseen by the Windigo Education Authority.
Susan Deley, Principal, 807-737-5701, fax: 807-347-1299

***Summer Beaver:* Nibinamik First Nation Education Centre**
General Delivery, Summer Beaver, ON P0T 3B0
Tel: 807-593-2195; *Fax:* 807-593-2198
Grades: JK - 10; Native Language *Note:* The Nibinamik First Nation Education Centre is a Matawa First Nations community school which receives educational support services from the Matawa Education Department. The Nibinamik First Nation is located approximately 185 kilometres northwest of Pickle Lake in northern Ontario.

***Whitedog:* Wabaseenmoong School**
General Delivery, Whitedog, ON P0X 1P0, Canada
Tel: 807-927-2062; *Fax:* 807-927-2176
Grades: JK - 12; Alternative Education *Enrollment:* 300 *Note:* Elementary & secondary education is provided to Wabaseemoong First Nation students living in a community situated about 100 kilometres northwest of Kenora, Ontario. The school focuses upon academics as well as cultural education. School activities are overseen by the Wabaseemoong Education Authority.
Ron R. McDonald, Principal, 807-927-2000, ext. 264

***Wiarton:* Cape Croker Elementary School**
***Also known as:* Chippewas of Nawash Elementary School**
17 School Rd., RR#5, Wiarton, ON N0H 2T0
Tel: 519-534-0719; *Fax:* 519-534-1592
www.nawash.ca
Grades: Pre-Kindergarten - 8 *Note:* Part of the Chippewas of Nawash Unceded First Nation Board of Education, the Cape Croker Elementary School provides a culturally-based education, which includes the history of the Anishnabek, band sovereignty, & communication & language arts in Anishinaabemowin & English.
Judy Nadjiwan, Education Administrator, Board of Education, 519-534-0882
nawashed.administrator@gbtel.ca
Debra Chegahno, Principal, Cape Croker Elementary School, 519-534-0719, fax: 519-534-1592
nawashed.principal@gbtel.ca
Juanita Pheasant, Ojibway Language Resource Teacher

Hearing Impaired

***Belleville:* The Sir James Whitney School**
350 Dundas St. West, Belleville, ON K8P 1B2
Tel: 613-967-2823; *Toll-Free:* 800-501-6240
www.psbnet.ca/eng/schools/sjw
TTY: 613-967-2823
Linda Ritchie, Principal

***Brantford:* The W. Ross Macdonald School**
350 Brant Ave., Brantford, ON N3T 3J9
Tel: 519-759-0730; *Toll-Free:* 866-618-9092
www.psbnet.ca/eng/schools/wross
Enrollment: 217
Donald Neale, Principal, Blind/Low Vision Program
Martha Martino, Principal, Deafblind Programs
Elizabeth Dunton, Principal, Resource Services

***London:* The Robarts School**
1515 Cheapside St., London, ON N5V 3N9
Tel: 519-453-4400
www.psbnet.ca/eng/schools/robarts
TTY: 519-453-4400
Jacqueline Raulin, Chair
jtraulin06@yahoo.ca
Antony McLetchie, Principal

***Milton:* The Ernest C. Drury School**
255 Ontario St., Milton, ON L9T 2M5
Tel: 905-878-2851
www.psbnet.ca/eng/schools/ecd
TTY: 905-878-7195
Jeanne Leonard, Principal, Elementary Program
Antony McLetchie, Principal, Secondary Program

Special Education

***Belleville:* Sagonaska Demonstration School**
350 Dundas St. West, Belleville, ON K8P 1B2
Tel: 613-967-2830
www.psbnet.ca/eng/schools/sagonaska

***London:* Amethyst Demonstration School**
1515 Cheapside St., London, ON N5Y 4V9
Tel: 519-453-4400
www.psbnet.ca/eng/schools/amethyst
John Barry, Principal

***Milton:* Trillium Demonstration School**
347 Ontario St. South, Milton, ON L9T 3X9
Tel: 905-878-2851
www.psbnet.ca/eng/schools/trillium
TTY: 905-878-7195
Desiree Smith, Principal

***Ottawa:* Centre Jules-Léger**
281, av Lanark, Ottawa, ON K1Z 6R8, Canada
Tél: 613-761-9300; *Téléc:* 613-761-9301
www.centrejulesleger.com
Other Information: ATS: 613-761-9302
Note: Services aux enfants (et leurs familles) en difficultés d'apprentissage, avec ou sans déficit d'attention/hyperactivité, qui sont sourds ou malentendant, qui sont aveugles ou en basse vision, ou qui sont sourds et aveugles.
Lillian Patry, Surintendante

Schools: Independent & Private

Catholic

***Mississauga:* Holy Name of Mary College School**
2241 Mississauga Rd., Mississauga, ON L5H 2K8
Tel: 905-891-1890; *Fax:* 905-891-2082
office@hnmcs.ca; admissions@hnmcs.ca
www.holynameofmarycollegeschool.com
Grades: 5-12; Girls
Margaret DeCourcy, President
decourcy@hnmcs.ca
Marilena Tesoro, Principal
tesoro@hnmcs.ca

***Mississauga:* Lumen Veritatis Academy**
225 Broadway St., Mississauga, ON L5M 1H9
Tel: 905-813-9215
lumenveritatis.ca
www.facebook.com/lumenveritatisacademy
twitter.com/lvablog
Grades: JK-8 *Enrollment:* 75
Greg La Chimea, Principal
Alma Grace Crowe, Vice-Principal, Streetsville Campus
Campuses
Thornhill Campus
191 Wade Gate, Thornhill, ON L4J 5Y4
Tel: 905-597-4933

***Richmond Hill:* Holy Trinity School**
c/o The Head of School
11300 Bayview Ave., Richmond Hill, ON L4S 1L4, Canada
Tel: 905-737-1114; *Fax:* 905-737-5187
Toll-Free: 866-727-7580
Grades: Elem./Sec. *Enrollment:* 694
George Rutherford, Head of School

French

***Mississauga:* Mississauga Christian French School (MCFS)**
1245 Eglinton Ave. West, Mississauga, ON L5V 2M4
Tel: 905-567-4032
principal@mcfschool.ca
www.mcfschool.ca
Grades: Pre.-8 *Enrollment:* 120
Sandra Gerges, Principal

First Nations

***Deer Lake:* David Meekis Memorial School**
***Also known as:* Deer Lake First Nation School**
P.O. Box 69
Deer Lake, ON P0V 1N0, Canada
Tel: 807-775-2055; *Fax:* 807-775-2148
www.dls.firstnationschools.ca
Grades: Sec. *Enrollment:* 236
Leonard Mamakeesic, Education Director

***Pikangikum:* Eenchokay Birchstick School**
General Delivery, Pikangikum, ON P0V 2L0, Canada
Tel: 807-773-5561; *Fax:* 807-773-5958
Grades: K./Elem./Sec. *Enrollment:* 166 *Note:* Serving students of the Pikangikum First Nation.
Jonah Strang, Chief, Pikangikum First Nation, 807-773-5578

Special Education

***Burlington:* Woodview Learning Centre**
69 Flatt Rd., Burlington, ON L7R 3X5
Tel: 905-689-4727; *Fax:* 905-689-2474
wcc@woodview.ca
www.woodview.ca
www.facebook.com/225044664274074
twitter.com/WoodviewWLC
Grades: K.-9 *Enrollment:* 12 *Note:* The Learning Centre provides individualized learning strategies for students with Autism.
Cindy I'Anson, Executive Director

Campuses
Brantford Office
643 Park Rd. North, Brantford, ON N3T 5L8
Tel: 519-752-5308; *Fax:* 519-752-9102
general@woodview.ca

Hamilton Office
Also known as: Mischa Weisz Centre for Autism Services
1900 Main St. West, Hamilton, ON L8S 4R8
Tel: 905-527-9771; *Fax:* 905-522-4690
wcc@woodview.ca

***Mississauga:* Good Samaritan School for Exceptional Learners**
Also known as: Good Samaritan Private School
6341 Mississauga Rd., Mississauga, ON L5N 1A7
Tel: 905-219-9969
gsschool@gsschool.ca
www.gsschool.ca
Grades: JK-12; Adult Ed. *Enrollment:* 300
Mary Ashun, Principal

***Ottawa:* Académie de la Capitale**
#200, 1010 Morrison Dr., Ottawa, ON K2H 8K7
Tel: 613-721-3872; *Fax:* 613-721-8189
info@acadecap.org
www.acadecap.org
www.facebook.com/175529857687
twitter.com/Acadecap
Grades: Pre.-12
Lucy Lalonde, Director

***Ottawa:* Astolot Educational Centre**
#203, 1187 Bank St., Ottawa, ON K1S 3X7
Tel: 613-260-5996
astolot@rogers.com
www.astolot.com
Jennifer Cowan, M.Ed., Owner/Director

***Peterborough:* Arrowsmith School Peterborough**
366 Parkhill Rd. East, Peterborough, ON K9L 1C3
Tel: 705-741-4800; *Fax:* 705-741-1832
peterborough@arrowsmithprogram.ca
www.arrowsmithschool.org/arrowsmithschool-peterborough
www.facebook.com/arrowsmithprogram
Grades: 1-12 *Enrollment:* 40
Jill Marcinkowski, Program Director

***Richmond Hill:* Academy for Gifted Children**
Also known as: P.A.C.E.
12 Bond Cres., Richmond Hill, ON L4E 3K2, Canada
Tel: 905-773-0997; *Fax:* 905-773-4722
www.pace.on.ca
Grades: Elem./Sec. *Enrollment:* 284 *Note:* P.A.C.E. - Programming for Academic & Creative Excellence. A non-denominational, co-ed, private day school, with programmes focussing on basic skills, with a strong emphasis on math & science, accelerated learning & individual instruction.
Barbara Rosenberg, Founder & Principal

***St Catharines:* Pinehurst School**
10 Seymour Ave., St Catharines, ON L2P 1A4
Tel: 905-641-0993; *Fax:* 905-641-0399
explore@pinehurst.on.ca
www.pinehurst.on.ca
Grades: 7-12 *Enrollment:* 40
Dave Bird, Principal

***Toronto:* Arrowsmith School Toronto**
245 St. Clair Ave. West, Toronto, ON M4V 1R3
Tel: 416-963-4962; *Fax:* 416-963-5017
reception@arrowsmithschool.org
www.arrowsmithschool.org
www.facebook.com/arrowsmithprogram
Grades: 1-12 *Enrollment:* 75
Barbara Arrowsmith Young, Director

***Toronto:* Brighton School**
240 The Donway West, Toronto, ON M3B 2V8
Tel: 416-932-8273; *Fax:* 416-850-5493
contactus@brightonschool.ca
www.brightonschool.ca
twitter.com/brighton_school
Grades: 1-12 *Enrollment:* 60

***Toronto:* Don Valley Academy**
#408, 4576 Yonge St., Toronto, ON M2N 6N4
Tel: 416-223-7561; *Fax:* 416-223-0065
www.donvalleyacademy.com
www.facebook.com/donvalleyacademy
Grades: 9-12 *Enrollment:* 30 *Note:* Don Valley Academy provides personalized education for gifted students, as well as those with learning difficulties.
Alex J. Evans, Principal

***Toronto:* Finding The Way Learning Centre & Bright Start Academy (FTW)**
#102 & 202, 2950 Keele St., Toronto, ON M3M 2H2
Tel: 647-347-6122; *Fax:* 647-347-6153
info@brightstartacademy.info
www.brightstartacademy.info
Grades: Pre.-9 *Note:* The Academy offers a behaviour & education program for children with autism & learning difficulties.
Allie Offman, Executive Director

***Toronto:* Kohai Educational Centre**
41 Roehampton Ave., Toronto, ON M4P 1P9
Tel: 416-489-3636; *Fax:* 416-489-3662
kohai@bellnet.ca
www.kohai.ca
Note: Programs & education for students with genetic disorders, behaviour problems, & language disorders.
Barbara Brown, Principal

***Toronto:* Shoore Centre for Learning**
801 Eglinton Ave. West, Toronto, ON M5N 1E3
Tel: 416-781-4754; *Fax:* 416-781-0163
info@shoorecentre.com
www.shoorecentre.com
www.facebook.com/222318484489159
twitter.com/ShooreCentre
www.youtube.com/user/ShooreCentre
Michael I. Shoore, B.Sc., M.Ed., Director
michael@shoorecentre.com
Tamara Shoore, Principal
tammy@shoorecentre.com

***Toronto:* Tikvat Hayim School**
c/o Beth Tikvah Synagogue
3080 Bayview Ave., Toronto, ON M2N 5L3
Tel: 416-221-3433
Note: The school offers programs every Sunday for children with learning disabilities, aged 5-12.
Dr. Zeev Greenberg, Principal

***Toronto:* The YMCA Academy**
Also known as: The Academy
15 Breadalbane St., 3rd Fl., Toronto, ON M4Y 1C2
Tel: 416-928-0124; *Fax:* 416-928-0212
reception@ymcaacademy.org
www.ymcaacademy.org
www.facebook.com/ymcaacademy
twitter.com/ymcaacademy
www.youtube.com/user/YMCAAcademy
Grades: Secondary *Note:* The YMCA Academy is a high school for students with learning disabilities, located in downtown Toronto.
Don Adams, Head of School, 416-928-0124, ext. 31401
don.adams@ymcagta.org
Nicole Klement, Assistant Head of School, 416-928-0124, ext. 31411
nicole.klement@ymcagta.org

***Toronto:* Zareinu Educational Centre of Metropolitan Toronto**
Administration Office
#301, 4630 Dufferin St., Toronto, ON M3H 5S4
Tel: 416-661-1800; *Fax:* 416-661-1801
info@zareinu.org
zareinu.org
Grades: Pre.-12 *Note:* Zareinu Educational Centre is a treatment centre & Jewish day school for children with physical & developmental disabilities.
Dr. Mitchell Parker, Principal & Clinical Director

Campuses
School Office
#108, 7026 Bathurst St., Thornhill, ON L4J 8K3
Tel: 905-738-5542; *Fax:* 905-738-8047
Phyllis Resnick, Contact, School Administration
Sarah Weitz, Contact, School Administration

***Utopia:* Renaissance Academy**
8058 - 8th Line, Utopia, ON L0M 1T0
Tel: 705-423-9688; *Fax:* 705-423-9788
www.renaissanceacademy.ca
Grades: K.-12
Giancarlo Marchi, Head of School
gmarchi@renaissanceacademy.ca

Independent & Private Schools

***Ajax:* Faithway Baptist Church School**
1964 Salem Rd., Ajax, ON L1T 4V3, Canada
Tel: 905-686-0951; *Fax:* 905-686-1450
faithway@faithway.org
Grades: K./Elem./Sec. *Enrollment:* 65
L. Homan

***Ajax:* Montessori Learning Centre of Ajax**
Also known as: 849179 Ontario Inc.
250 Bayly St. West, Ajax, ON L1S 3V4, Canada
Tel: 905-428-3122
www.montessorilearningcentreofajax.ca
Grades: Preschool / Elementary *Note:* Montessori Learning Centre of Ajax offers a toddler program for children from 18 months to 3 years, as well as a Casa program for 3 to 6 year old children. Elementary education is provided for children from age 6 to 12.
Camilla Graziani, Principal

***Ajax:* Pickering Christian School**
162 Rossland Rd. East, Ajax, ON L1T 4V2, Canada
Tel: 905-427-3120; *Fax:* 905-427-0211
office@pickeringcs.on.ca
www.pickeringcs.on.ca
Grades: Elem. *Enrollment:* 219
Dr. Paul Douglas Ogborne, Principal

***Ajax:* Wasdell Centre for Innovative Learning**
85 Kings Cres., Ajax, ON L1S 2M4
Tel: 905-426-3241; *Fax:* 905-426-2921
Toll-Free: 888-525-2385
www.wasdellcentre.org
Grades: Pre.-12 *Enrollment:* 55
Elizabeth Moxley-Paquette, Principal/Director
e.moxley-paquette@wasdellcentre.org

***Alliston:* Alliston Community Christian School**
4428 Adjala-Tecumseth Townline, RR#4, Alliston, ON L9R 1V4, Canada
Tel: 705-434-2227; *Fax:* 705-435-0126
www.allistonccs.ca
Grades: K./Elem. *Enrollment:* 113
Lillian Parasol, Principal

***Ancaster:* Hamilton District Christian High School**
92 Glancaster Rd., RR#1, Ancaster, ON L9G 3K9, Canada
Tel: 905-648-6655; *Fax:* 905-648-3139
info@hdch.org
www.hdch.org
www.facebook.com/HDCH.info
www.twitter.com/HDCH_Info
Grades: Sec. *Enrollment:* 600
George VanKampen, Principal

***Aurora:* Aurora Montessori School & Private School**
330 Industrial Pkwy. North, Aurora, ON L4G 4C3, Canada
Tel: 905-841-0065; *Fax:* 905-841-2022
info@auroramontessori.com;
admissions@auroramontessori.com
www.auroramontessori.com
Grades: 1-8 *Note:* Aurora Montessori School & Private School also offers a toddler program for children from ages 18 months to 3 years. Casa programs are for children from ages 2.5 to 6 years.
Brenda Glashan, Principal

***Aurora:* Foundations Private School**
81 Industrial Pkwy. North, Aurora, ON L4G 4C4, Canada
Tel: 905-713-1141; *Fax:* 905-713-6340
www.foundationsps.com
Grades: JK-8 *Enrollment:* 159
Ellen Powers, Principal
powers@greatschool.ca

***Aurora:* St. Andrew's College**
15800 Yonge St. North, Aurora, ON L4G 3H7, Canada
Tel: 905-727-3178; *Fax:* 905-841-6911
info@sac.on.ca
www.sac.on.ca
Grades: 6-12 *Enrollment:* 560 *Note:* All-boys boarding and day school
Kevin McHenry, Headmaster

Aylmer: Immanuel Christian School Society
75 Caverly Rd., Aylmer, ON N5H 2P6
Tel: 519-773-8476; *Fax:* 519-773-8315
info@immanuelchristianschool.net; info@icsaylmer.ca
www.immanuelchristianschool.net
www.facebook.com/150239838428877
twitter.com/ICSAylmer
Grades: K./Elem.
Keith Cameron, Principal
k.cameron@immanuelchristianschool.net

Aylmer: Mount Salem Christian School (MSCS)
c/o Evangelical Mennonite Church
6576 Springfield Rd., RR#6, Aylmer, ON N5H 2R5, Canada
Tel: 519-765-3555; *Fax:* 519-765-3879
mscsch@amtelecom.net
www.mountsalemchristianschool.ca
Grades: Junior Kindergarten - 12 *Note:* Mount Salem Christian School is an interdenominational school, using a BEKA curriculum.
Judy Wiebe, Principal

Aylmer: Old Colony Christian School
P.O. Box 127
Aylmer, ON N5H 2R8, Canada
Tel: 519-765-1138
Grades: Elem./Sec. *Enrollment:* 288
Anna Ens

Baden, Region of Waterloo: Canadian Independent College (CIC)
3601 Sandhills Rd., Baden, Region of Waterloo, ON N3A 3B9
Tel: 519-634-9255; *Fax:* 519-634-9355
info@cicbaden.ca
www.cicbaden.ca
Grades: 6-12 *Enrollment:* 115 *Note:* The CIC has a sister campus in Accra, Ghana.
Dr. Heather Bohez, B.Sc., N.D.

Bancroft: Bancroft Christian Academy
P.O. Box 657
160 South Baptiste Lake Rd., Bancroft, ON K0L 1C0, Canada
Tel: 613-332-3670
Grades: Elementary / Secondary

Barrie: Heritage Christian Academy
79 Ardagh Rd., Barrie, ON L4N 9B6, Canada
Tel: 705-733-0112; *Fax:* 705-733-2054
Grades: JK.-12 *Enrollment:* 75
Pastor Brett Pennell, Principal

Barrie: Kempenfelt Bay School
576 Bryne Dr., Barrie, ON L4N 9P6
Tel: 705-739-4731; *Fax:* 705-739-3678
www.kempenfeltbayschool.com
www.facebook.com/153567748086397
Grades: JK-8 *Enrollment:* 175
Graham Hookey, Head of School
Diane Fitzgerald, Director, Academics & School Life

Barrie: Timothy Christian School
750 Essa Rd., Barrie, ON L4N 9E9, Canada
Tel: 705-726-6621; *Fax:* 705-726-8571
tcsgen@timothychristianschool.ca
www.timothychristianschool.ca
Grades: Junior Kindergarten - 8 *Note:* Timothy Christian School is an interdenominational school.
Kevin Eisses, Chair
Andrew Straatsma, Principal
Brenda Goodnough, Vice Principal
Ina VanHouten, Director, Development

Beamsville: Great Lakes Christian College
4875 King St., Beamsville, ON L0R 1B0, Canada
Tel: 905-563-5374; *Fax:* 905-563-0818
www.glchs.on.ca
Grades: Sec. *Enrollment:* 130
Don Rose, President
drose@glchs.on.ca

Belleville: Albert College
160 Dundas St. West, Belleville, ON K8P 1A6, Canada
Tel: 613-968-5726; *Fax:* 613-968-9651
info@albertcollege.ca
www.albertc.on.ca
Grades: Elem./Sec. *Enrollment:* 298
Heather Kidd, Director, Admission
hkidd@albertc.on.ca

Belleville: Belleville District Christian School (BCS)
18 Christian School Rd., RR#5, Belleville, ON K8N 4Z5, Canada
Tel: 613-962-7849; *Fax:* 613-962-6440
bellevillechristianschool@yahoo.com
www.bellevillechristianschool.ca
Grades: Junior Kindergarten - 8
Jennifer Richmond, Principal

Belleville: Quinte Christian High School (QCHS)
138 Wallbridge-Loyalist Rd., Belleville, ON K8N 4Z2, Canada
Tel: 613-968-7870; *Fax:* 613-968-7970
admin@qchs.ca; finance@qchs.ca
www.qchs.ca
Grades: Secondary
Johan Cooke, Principal

Bloomingdale: Koinonia Christian Academy
850 Sawmill Rd., Bloomingdale, ON N0B 1K0, Canada
Tel: 519-744-7447; *Fax:* 519-744-6745
kcf@kcf.org
www.kcf.org
www.facebook.com/koinoniacf
www.twitter.com/kcf_org
Enrollment: 157
David J. Champion
dave.champion@kcf.org

Bolton: Countryside Montessori Private School
1 Loring Dr., Bolton, ON L7E 1Y1, Canada
Tel: 905-951-3359; *Fax:* 905-951-3920
Enrollment: 257

Bowmanville: Durham Christian Academy
RR#3, Bowmanville, ON L1J 3K4
Tel: 905-697-2351; *Fax:* 905-697-6495
durhamca@rogers.com
www.durhamca.ca
Grades: JK-8
Carol Dempsey, Principal

Bowmanville: Durham Christian High School
340 West Scugog Lane, Bowmanville, ON L1C 3K2
Tel: 905-623-5940; *Fax:* 905-623-6258
office@dchs.com
www.dchs.com
www.facebook.com/185439688168242
Grades: Sec.
Fred Spoelstra, Principal
principal@dchs.com

Bowmanville: Knox Christian School
410 North Scugog Ct., Bowmanville, ON L1C 3K2
Tel: 905-623-5871
office@knoxchristian.com
www.knoxchristian.com
Grades: K./Elem. *Enrollment:* 150
Terry Vanleeuwen, Principal
principal@knoxchristian.com

Brampton: Brampton-Georgetown Montessori School (BGMS)
1030 Queen St. West, Brampton, ON L6X 0B2, Canada
Tel: 905-457-2496
info@bgmschool.com
www.bgmschool.com
Grades: Casa / Elementary *Note:* Brampton-Georgetown Montessori School provides programs for children from ages 2.5 to 11.

Brampton: Canada Christian Academy
22 Abbey Rd., Brampton, ON L6W 2T8, Canada
Tel: 905-789-5841; *Fax:* 905-789-0645
www.canadachristianacademy.com
Grades: Junior Kindergarten - 12 *Enrollment:* 100

Brampton: Har Tikvah Congregational School
P.O. Box 36023
9893 Torbram Rd., Brampton, ON L6S 6A3
Tel: 905-792-7589; *Fax:* 905-792-7589
info@hartikvah.org
www.hartikvah.org

Brampton: John Knox Christian School
82 McLaughlin Rd. South, Brampton, ON L6Y 2C7
Tel: 905-451-3236; *Fax:* 905-451-3448
bramptonjkcs.org
Grades: JK-8 *Enrollment:* 300
Garry Zondervan, Principal
gzondervan@bramptonjkcs.org

Brampton: Khalsa Community School
69 Maitland St., Brampton, ON L6S 3B5, Canada
Tel: 905-791-1750; *Fax:* 905-458-9133
khalsacommunityschool@hotmail.com
www.khalsacommunityschool.com
Grades: K.-8 *Enrollment:* 187

Brampton: Khalsa Montessori School
#2, 4535 Ebenezer Rd., Brampton, ON L6P 2P7
Tel: 905-913-0801
www.kmschool.org
www.facebook.com/theKMSchool
twitter.com/theKMSchool
Harpeet Singh, Principal

Brampton: Rowntree Montessori Schools - RMS Academy
3 Sunforest Dr., Brampton, ON L6Z 2Z2
Tel: 905-790-3838; *Fax:* 905-790-5686
admin@rowntreemontessori.com
rowntreemontessori.com
Grades: K.-10 *Enrollment:* 100
J. Essaye, Managing Director
D. Zebeljan, Principal

Campuses

Bramalea Campus
93 Autumn Blvd., Brampton, ON L6T 2W1
Tel: 905-793-2196; *Fax:* 905-790-9083
rowntreemontessori.com/campuses/bramalea
Grades: Pre.-SK; Toddler
S. Verma, Principal

Central Park Campus
502 Central Park Dr., Brampton, ON L6S 2C8
Tel: 905-793-6231; *Fax:* 905-793-9020
rowntreemontessori.com/campuses/central-park
Grades: Pre.-SK; Toddler
M. Penrice, Principal

Downtown Campus
4 Elizabeth St. North, Brampton, ON L6X 1S2
Tel: 905-457-7439; *Fax:* 905-457-2518
rowntreemontessori.com/campuses/downtown
Grades: Pre.-SK; Toddler
T. Rivard, Principal

Brampton: Tall Pines School
8525 Torbram Rd., Brampton, ON L6T 5K4, Canada
Tel: 905-458-6770; *Fax:* 905-458-7967
registrar@tallpinesschool.com
www.tallpinesschool.com
Number of Schools: Montessori programs, Traditional Private School *Grades:* K.-9 *Enrollment:* 519 *Note:* Private Montessori and Progressive school
Elizabeth Szekeres, Registrar, 905-458-6770, ext. 228
eszekeres@insidetps.com

Brantford: Braemar House School
36 Baxter St., Brantford, ON N3R 2V8, Canada
Tel: 519-753-2929; *Fax:* 519-753-1235
admin@braemarhouseschool.ca
www.braemarhouseschool.ca
Grades: Junior Kindergarten - 8 *Enrollment:* 92 *Note:* Braemar House School also offers a Montessori Casa program.
Annette Minutillo, Executive Director

Brantford: Brantford Christian Collegiate
Friendship House
P.O. Box 28116
452 Grey St., Brantford, ON N3R 7X5, Canada
Tel: 519-753-4900
Grades: 9 - 12
Jeff Gillmore, Principal
Rev. Ron Humphries, Faculty Member

Brantford: Brantford Christian School (BCS)
7 Calvin St., Brantford, ON N3S 3E4, Canada
Tel: 519-752-0433; *Fax:* 519-752-6088
www.bcsbrantford.ca
Grades: Junior Kindergarten - 8
Walter Hartholt, Principal
whartholt@bcsbrantford.ca
Heather Murray, Vice Principal
hmurray@bcsbrantford.ca
Audrey Reitsma, Vice Principal
areitsma@bcsbrantford.ca

Brantford: Central Baptist Academy (CBA)
300 Fairview Dr., Brantford, ON N3R 2X6, Canada
Tel: 519-754-4806; *Fax:* 519-754-4201
cbaoffice@centralbaptistbrantford.com
www.centralbaptistbrantford.com
Grades: Junior Kindergarten - 8

Rev. Minne Bouma, Principal

***Brantford:* Montessori House of Children**
85 Charlotte St., Brantford, ON N3T 2X2, Canada
Tel: 519-759-7290; *Fax:* 519-759-6774
mails@montessorihouseofchildren.com
www.montessorihouseofchildren.com
Other Information: admissions@montessorihouseofchildren.com (Admission inquiries)
Note: Brantford's Montessori House of Children provides programs for children from 2.5 to 9 years of age.
Nahida Hamam, Principal

***Breslau:* St. John's-Kilmarnock School**
P.O. Box 179
2201 Shantz Station Rd., Breslau, ON N0B 1M0, Canada
Tel: 519-648-2183; *Fax:* 519-648-2186
info@sjkschool.org
www.sjkschool.org
Grades: Jr. K.-12 *Enrollment:* 505
Ian Hornsby

***Breslau:* Woodland Christian High School**
1058 Spitzig Rd., Breslau, ON N0B 1M0
Tel: 519-648-2114; *Fax:* 519-648-3402
office@woodland.on.ca
www.woodland.on.ca
www.facebook.com/WoodlandCHS
twitter.com/@woodlandchs
www.linkedin.com/company/woodland-christian-high-school
www.youtube.com/user/WoodlandCHSVideos
Grades: Sec. *Enrollment:* 194
John VanPelt, Principal

***Burlington:* Burlington Christian Academy (BCA)**
521 North Service Rd. West, Burlington, ON L7P 5C3, Canada
Tel: 905-639-7364; *Fax:* 905-639-1657
office@onlyatbccs.com
onlyatbca.com
Grades: JK - 8 *Enrollment:* 130
Gord McNeice, Principal
Heather Crossing, Vice Principal (Part-time)
Jessica Purdy, Vice Principal (Part-time)
Jann Schlett, Coordinator, Advancement & Recruitment

***Burlington:* Fairview Glen Montessori**
3508 Commerce Ct., Burlington, ON L7N 3L7
Tel: 905-634-0781
info@fairviewglen.com
www.fairviewglen.com
Grades: Pre.-6 *Enrollment:* 125
Tammy-Leigh Sage, Director

***Burlington:* Halton Waldorf School (HWS)**
2193 Orchard Rd., Burlington, ON L7R 3X5, Canada
Tel: 905-331-4387; *Fax:* 905-331-3231
enrollment@haltonwaldorf.com
www.waldorfschool.net
Grades: Preschool - 8 *Enrollment:* 160 *Note:* The school provides Waldorf education.

***Burlington:* John Calvin Christian School**
607 Dynes Rd., Burlington, ON L7N 2V4
Tel: 905-634-8015; *Fax:* 905-634-9772
jcss@on.aibn.com
Grades: K./Elem. *Enrollment:* 72
Jason Heemskerk, Principal

***Burlington:* Niagara Montessori School**
3132 South Dr., Burlington, ON L7N 1H7, Canada
Tel: 905-632-2374; *Fax:* 905-632-9959
Grades: Preschool - Kindergarten *Note:* The Montessori School offers programs for children from age 2.5 to 6.
Jacqueline Gaskin, Principal

***Burlington:* Trinity Christian School**
2170 Itabashi Way, Burlington, ON L7M 5B3, Canada
Tel: 905-634-3052; *Fax:* 905-634-9382
trinity@tcsonline.ca
www.tcsonline.ca
Grades: Junior Kindergarten - 8
Juliette Lamb, Chair
Rick Schenk, Principal
principal@tcsonline.ca
Sara Flokstra, Vice Principal
Cheri VanderBrook, Bookkeeper

***Caledon:* Brampton Christian School (BCS)**
12480 Hurontario St., Caledon, ON L7C 2B6, Canada
Tel: 905-846-3771; *Fax:* 905-843-2929
admin@bramptoncs.org
www.bramptoncs.org
Grades: Elementary/Junior High/Senior High
R. Andrews, Principal
randrews@bramptoncs.org
A. Cabral, Division Head, Senior High
afcabral@bramptoncs.org
C. Doggart, Division Head, Elementary
cdoggart@bramptoncs.org
J. Miller, Division Head, Junior High
jmiller@bramptoncs.org

***Caledon:* King's College School**
16379 The Gore Rd., Caledon, ON L7E 0X4
Tel: 905-880-7645; *Fax:* 905-880-9439
info@kingscollegeschool.ca
www.kingscollegeschool.ca
www.facebook.com/132101376817812
twitter.com/kingscollschool
Grades: 3-12
Barbara H. Lord, Headmistress

***Cambridge:* Cambridge Christian School (CCS)**
229 Myers Rd., Cambridge, ON N1R 7H3, Canada
Tel: 519-623-2261; *Fax:* 519-623-4042
cc2@bellnet.ca
www.cambridgechristianschool.com
Grades: Kindergarten - 8
Derek Frank, Chair
Jules de Jager, Principal
ccsprincipal@bellnet.ca

***Cambridge:* Temple Baptist Christian Academy**
400 Holiday Inn Dr., Cambridge, ON N3C 3T1, Canada
Tel: 519-658-9001; *Fax:* 519-658-9426
academy@tbca.ca
www.tbca.ca
Grades: Jr. K-8 *Enrollment:* 267
Evelyn Hewitt, Principal

***Campbellville:* Hitherfield Preparatory School**
2439 - 10th Side Rd., Campbellville, ON L0P 1B0, Canada
Tel: 905-854-0890; *Fax:* 905-854-3155
Grades: Elem./Sec. *Enrollment:* 115
Ann J. Scott, Principal, 9058540890, ext. 102, fax: 9058543155

***Carp:* Venta Preparatory School**
2013 Old Carp Rd., Carp, ON K0A 1L0, Canada
Tel: 613-839-2175; *Fax:* 613-839-1956
info@ventapreparatoryschool.com
www.ventapreparatoryschool.com
Grades: 1 - 10 *Note:* Venta Preparatory School is a day & boarding school. The maximum class size is twelve students.
Marilyn Mansfield, Principal, 613-839-2175, ext. 223
Sean Hopper, Dean, Students, 613-839-2175, ext. 225
Shaun Quinn, Director, Studies, 613-839-2175, ext. 224
Tracey Quinn, Director, Enrollment, 613-839-2175, ext. 240

***Chatham:* Chatham Christian High School (CCHS)**
475 Keil Dr. South, Chatham, ON N7M 6L8
Tel: 519-352-4980; *Fax:* 519-352-4041
office@chathamchristian.ca
www.chathamchristian.ca
Grades: 9-12 *Enrollment:* 140
Jessica Brooks, Vice-Principal
JessicaBrooks@chathamchristian.ca

***Chatham:* Chatham Christian School**
475 Keil Dr. South, Chatham, ON N7M 6L8
Tel: 519-352-4980; *Fax:* 519-352-4041
office@chathamchristian.ca
www.chathamchristian.ca
Grades: JK-8 *Enrollment:* 300
Marvin Bierling, Head Administrator
marvinbierling@chathamchristian.ca

***Chatham:* Eben-Ezer Christian School**
485 McNaughton Ave. East, Chatham, ON N7L 2H2
Tel: 519-354-1142; *Fax:* 519-354-2159
eecs@eecschatham.com; board@eecschatham.com
eecschatham.com
Grades: Elem.
R. Vanderveen, Chair
Carlos Bos, Principal

***Clinton:* Huron Christian School**
87 Percival St., Clinton, ON N0M 1L0
Tel: 519-482-7851; *Fax:* 519-482-7448
office@clintonchristian.ca
www.huronchristianschool.ca
Grades: K.-8
Heather VanDorp, Chair
Nick Geleynse, Principal
principal@clintonchristian.ca

***Cobourg:* Northumberland Christian School**
8861 Danforth Rd., RR#5, Cobourg, ON K9A 4J8, Canada
Tel: 905-372-8766; *Fax:* 905-372-6299
ncsoffice@bellnet.ca
www.northumberlandchristianschool.com
Grades: Junior Kindergarten - 8 *Note:* Northumberland Christian School is an interdenominational school.
Cindy Warr

***Cookstown:* Thor College**
4073 - 4th Line Innisfil, Cookstown, ON L0L 1L0
Tel: 705-458-9705
www.thorcollege.ca
Grades: Preschool - 12
W.H. Madden, BA, BPHE, BEd, Director
Michael J. Madden, Headmaster

***Copetown:* Rehoboth Christian School - Copetown (RCS)**
P.O. Box 70
198 Inksetter Rd., Copetown, ON L0R 1J0, Canada
Tel: 905-627-5977; *Fax:* 905-628-4422
office@rehoboth.on.ca
www.rehoboth.on.ca
Grades: Kindergarten - 12 *Note:* Rehoboth Free Reformed Christian School Society of Copetown owns & operates the school. Education is provided with a Reformed Christian view.
Dick Naves, High School Vice Principal
dnaves@rehoboth.on.ca
Herman den Hollander, Elementary Vice Principal
hdenhollander@rehoboth.on.ca

***Cornwall:* Islamic Institute Al-Rashid**
18345 County Rd. 2, RR#1, Cornwall, ON K6H 5R5
Tel: 613-931-2895
contact@alrashid.ca; edu@alrashid.ca (Secular Education Dept.)
www.alrashid.ca
Grades: Elem./Sec.
M. Mazhar Alam, Principal

***Deep River:* The Deep River Science Academy (DRSA)**
20 Forest Ave., Deep River, ON K0J 1P0, Canada
Tel: 613-584-4541
info@drsa.ca
www.drsa.ca
Grades: Secondary *Note:* The Deep River Science Academy partners with Atomic Energy of Canada, Ltd. to offer science camps. Students must have completed a grade 10 or higher science high school credit. Hhigh school credits are awarded.

***Drayton:* Community Christian School (CCS)**
P.O. Box 141
35 High St., Drayton, ON N0G 1P0, Canada
Tel: 519-638-2935; *Fax:* 519-638-3373
ccsdray@bellnet.ca
www.ccsdray.org
Grades: Junior Kindergarten - 8

***Dundas:* Calvin Christian School - Dundas**
542 Ofield Rd. North, Dundas, ON L9H 5E2, Canada
Tel: 905-627-1411; *Fax:* 905-627-8004
www.dccs.ca
Grades: Kindergarten - 8 *Enrollment:* 180
Rick Dykstra, Principal
rdykstra@dccs.ca
Mrs. I. Vos, Coordinator, Curriculum
ivos@dccs.ca
Corrie Zandstra, Administrator, Office
office@dccs.ca

***Dunnville:* Attercliffe Canadian Reformed Elementary School**
75785 Canborough Rd., RR#1, Dunnville, ON N1A 2W1, Canada
Tel: 905-774-9009
Grades: Kindergarten - 8 *Note:* This is a coducational school.
Ed Slaa, Principal

***Dunnville:* Dunnville Christian School**
37 Robinson Rd., RR#1, Dunnville, ON N1A 2W1, Canada
Tel: 905-774-5142; *Fax:* 905-774-5519
www.dunnvillechristianschool.ca
www.facebook.com/groups/2413644356
Grades: K./Elem. *Enrollment:* 100
Ralph De Boer, Chair
info@dunnvillechristianschool.ca
Joyce Koornneef, Principal
principal@dunnvillechristianschool.ca

***Embrun:* Canada eSchool**
P.O. Box 277
921 Notre-Dame St., Embrun, ON K0A 1W0
Tel: 613-443-9522; *Fax:* 613-482-4504
info@myeschool.ca
www.canadaeschool.ca
www.facebook.com/142423952478564
twitter.com/Canada_eSchool
Grades: 9-12 *Enrollment:* 1340 *Note:* Canada eSchool supplements students' education with eLearning technology, accessible anywhere in the world.
Carl J. Frizell, Principal

***Etobicoke:* Al-Ashraf Islamic School**
23 Brydon Dr., Etobicoke, ON M9W 4M7, Canada
Tel: 416-740-1495
Grades: Elem./Sec. *Enrollment:* 157
Riyad Khan, Principal

***Etobicoke:* Alderwood Toronto Private School**
26 Fieldway Rd., Etobicoke, ON M8Z 3L2
Tel: 416-239-2100
info@alderwoodtoronto.ca
alderwoodtoronto.com
Grades: Pre.-8
Sheileen Krone, Principal

***Etobicoke:* Humbervale Montessori School Inc.**
1447 Royal York Rd., Etobicoke, ON M9P 3V8
Tel: 416-244-4001
humbervalemontessori.ca
Grades: Pre.-JK *Enrollment:* 85
Andrea Heitz, Principal

***Etobicoke:* Kingsley Primary School**
516 The Kingsway, Etobicoke, ON M9A 3W6
Tel: 416-233-0150; *Fax:* 416-233-5971
kingsleyschool@bellnet.ca
www.kingsleyschool.ca
www.facebook.com/kingsleyprimaryschool
Grades: K./Elem.
Mark Huttram, Chair
Julie Middleton, Principal
Louisa Florio, Principal-Elect

***Etobicoke:* Kingsway College School**
4600 Dundas St. West, Etobicoke, ON M9A 1A5
Tel: 416-234-5073; *Fax:* 416-234-8386
office@kcs.on.ca; admissions@kcs.on.ca
www.kcs.on.ca
www.facebook.com/KCSMatters
twitter.com/KCSMatters
www.linkedin.com/groups?home=&gid=4030878
www.youtube.com/KCSMatters
Grades: Elem. *Enrollment:* 309
Derek Logan, Head of School

***Etobicoke:* Madresatul Banaat Almuslimaat Muslim Girl's School**
10 Vulcan St., Etobicoke, ON M9W 1L2
Tel: 416-244-8600; *Fax:* 416-244-0059
www.muslimgirlsschool.com
Grades: 6-12; Girls *Enrollment:* 152 *Note:* Alhamdulillah, Madresatul Banaat Almuslimaat, the first Muslim girls school in Toronto, Ontario, Canada, is a registered, non-profit, charitable organization duly approved and accredited by the Ontario Ministry of Education and Waqf Lillahi Taala.
S. Ataullah Qadri, President/Principal

Schools
Madresatul Atfaal Almuslimeen
Muslim Children's School
Grades: JK.-5; Boys and Girls *Note:* The school now provides primary education from JK to grade 5, for boys and girls at the same location (under the same management) as Madresatul Banaat Almuslimaat's, at their junior school.

***Etobicoke:* Olivet New Church School**
279 Burnhamthorpe Rd., Etobicoke, ON M9B 1Z6
Tel: 416-239-3054; *Fax:* 416-239-4935
contact@olivetnewchurch.org
www.olivetnewchurch.org
Grades: JK-6 *Enrollment:* 50
Rev. James Cooper, Pastor

***Etobicoke:* Richmond Hill Christian Academy**
Administration
96 Antioch Dr., Etobicoke, ON M9B 5V4, Canada
Tel: 416-621-4100; *Fax:* 416-621-0930
rhca@rogers.com
www.rhcaweb.ca
Other Information: 905-770-4055 (Phone, RHCA Campus); 905-770-6255 (Fax, Campus)
Grades: Junior Kindergarten - 8 *Enrollment:* 339 *Note:* Richmond Hill Christian Academy is a non-denominational school, which is a member of the Association of Christian Schools International. The A Beka curriculum is used. Its campus is located at 9711 Bayview Avenue in Richmond Hill.
Brian R. Hayes, B.Com., C.F.A., Administrator
Madeline J. Hayes, B.A., M.Ed., Principal

***Fergus:* Emmanuel Christian High School**
8037 Wellington Rd. 19, RR#3, Fergus, ON N1M 2W4
Tel: 519-843-3029; *Fax:* 519-843-4711
echs@bellnet.ca
www.echs.ca
Grades: Elem./Sec.
Henk Nobel, Principal
henk_nobel@bellnet.ca

***Fergus:* Maranatha Christian School**
8037 Wellington Rd. 19, RR#3 Garafraxia St., Fergus, ON N1M 2W4
Tel: 519-843-3029; *Fax:* 519-843-4711
info@mcsfergus.ca; maranatha@bellnet.ca
mcsfergus.ca
Grades: Elem. *Enrollment:* 175
R. Hoeksema, Principal

***Fort Erie:* Niagara Christian Community of Schools (NCC)**
2619 Niagara Pkwy., Fort Erie, ON L2A 5M4, Canada
Tel: 905-871-6980; *Fax:* 905-871-9260
ncc@niagaracc.com
www.niagaracc.com
Grades: Junior Kindergarten - 12
Kevin Bayne, Principal, Secondary School
kbayne@niagaracc.com
Cari Dean, Principal, Elementary School & Middle School
cdean@niagaracc.com
Mark Thiessen, Principal, Secondary School
mthiess@niagaracc.com
Tom Auld, Director, Student Life
tomauld@niagaracc.com
Vivian Pengelly, Business Administrator
vivianp@niagaracc.com

***Fort Frances:* Lac La Croix Elementary & High School**
P.O. Box 640
Fort Frances, ON P9A 3M9
Tel: 807-485-2402; *Fax:* 807-485-2558
Grades: Elem./9-12

***Fort Frances:* Seven Generations Education Institute School**
P.O. Box 297
Fort Frances, ON P9A 3M6, Canada
Tel: 807-274-2796; *Fax:* 807-274-8761
www.7generations.org/
Dan Bird

***Fruitland:* John Knox Christian School**
795 Hwy. #8, Fruitland, ON L8E 5J3, Canada
Tel: 905-643-2460; *Fax:* 905-643-5875
www.nace.ca
Grades: K./Elem. *Enrollment:* 185 *Note:* The Niagara Ass'n for Christian Education (NACE).
Bonnie Desjardins, Principal
bdesjardins@nace.ca

***Georgetown:* Halton Hills Christian School**
11643 Trafalgar Rd., Georgetown, ON L7G 4S4, Canada
Tel: 905-877-4221; *Fax:* 905-877-1483
office@haltonhillschristianschool.org
www.haltonhillschristianschool.org
Grades: K./Elem. *Enrollment:* 228 *Note:* Formerly known as Georgetown District Christian School
Marianne Vangoor, Principal

***Grassy Narrows:* Sakatcheway-Anishinabe**
P.O. Box 213
General Delivery, Grassy Narrows, ON P0X 1B0, Canada
Tel: 807-925-2626; *Fax:* 807-925-2855

***Guelph:* Elora Road Christian School (ERCS)**
5696 Wellington Rd.7, RR #5, Guelph, ON N1H 6J2, Canada
Tel: 519-824-1890; *Fax:* 519-821-3518
school@ercf.ca
www.eloraroad.ca
Grades: JK-8 *Enrollment:* 99
Amanda McAlpine, Vice Principal

***Guelph:* Guelph Community Christian School**
286 Water St., Guelph, ON N1G 1B8, Canada
Tel: 519-824-8860; *Fax:* 519-824-2105
info@guelphccs.ca
www.guelphccs.ca
Grades: K./Elem. *Enrollment:* 188
Bob Moore, M.Ed., Principal

***Guelph:* Resurrection Christian Academy**
400 Speedvale Ave. East, Guelph, ON N1E 1N9
Tel: 519-836-5395
www.rcaflames.com
www.facebook.com/groups/139369669490620
Grades: K./Elem.
Sue Warren, Director & Co-Founder

***Haliburton:* St. Peter's ACHS College School**
#21, 4252 County Rd., Haliburton, ON K0M 1S0
Tel: 705-457-8887
achscanada@gmail.com
achscanada.com
Grades: 1-8; Boys
Peter Thyrring, Headmaster

***Hamilton:* Calvin Christian School (CCS)**
547 West 5th St., Hamilton, ON L9C 3P7, Canada
Tel: 905-388-2645; *Fax:* 905-388-2769
www.ccshamilton.ca
Grades: Junior Kindergarten - 8 *Enrollment:* 450
Ted Postma, Principal

***Hamilton:* Columbia International College of Canada**
1003 Main St. West, Hamilton, ON L8S 4P3, Canada
Tel: 905-572-7883; *Fax:* 905-572-9332
columbia@cic-totalcare.com
www.cic-totalcare.com
Grades: Sec. *Enrollment:* 1285
Ron Rambarran, Principal

***Hamilton:* Guido de Bres Christian High School**
P.O. Box 30013
1576 Upper James St., Hamilton, ON L9B 1K0, Canada
Tel: 905-574-4011; *Fax:* 905-574-8662
office@guidodebres.org
www.guidodebres.org
Grades: Sec. *Enrollment:* 400
J.G. Vandooren, Principal

***Hamilton:* Hamilton Hebrew Academy Zichron Meir School**
60 Dow Ave., Hamilton, ON L8S 1W4, Canada
Tel: 905-528-0330; *Fax:* 905-528-0544
school@hamiltonhebrewacademy.ca
www.hamiltonhebrewacademy.ca
Grades: Elem. *Enrollment:* 132
Daniel Green, Dean
dean@hamiltonhebrewacademy.ca

***Hamilton:* Hamilton Hebrew High / Midrasha (H3)**
60 Dow Ave., Hamilton, ON L8S 1W4
Tel: 905-528-0039; *Fax:* 905-528-7360
info@hhhmidrasha.ca
hhhmidrasha.ca
Grades: 8-12 *Note:* Hamilton Hebrew High offers secondary school students extra Ontario Secondary School credits with a Jewish perspective.
Yaakov Morel, Director
yaakov@hhhmidrasha.ca
Gord Garshowitz, Educational Coordinator, 905-906-6900
gord@hhhmidrasha.ca

***Hamilton:* Hillfield Strathallan College**
299 Fennell Ave. West, Hamilton, ON L9C 1G3
Tel: 905-389-1367; *Fax:* 905-389-6366
www.hsc.on.ca
www.facebook.com/hillfieldstrathallancollege
twitter.com/HillStrath
www.youtube.com/officialHSC
Grades: JK-12 *Enrollment:* 1000
Marc Ayotte, Head, College

***Hamilton:* Islamic School of Hamilton (ISH)**
1545 Stonechurch Rd. East, Hamilton, ON L8W 3P8, Canada
Tel: 905-383-7786; *Fax:* 905-667-4797
Enrollment: 170 *Note:* The school also teaches the Arabic language, Quran, & Islam Studies.
Zakir Patel, Principal

***Hamilton:* Southern Ontario College**
430 York Blvd., Hamilton, ON L8R 3K8, Canada
Tel: 905-546-1500; *Fax:* 905-538-5494
info@mysoc.ca
www.mysoc.ca

Grades: Sec. *Enrollment:* 181 *Note:* International Secondary School specializing in ESL and University prep.
Brian Inglis, Director

Hamilton: Timothy Canadian Reformed School
430 East 25th St., Hamilton, ON L8V 3B4, Canada
Tel: 905-385-3953; *Fax:* 905-385-8073
Grades: Kindergarten - 8 *Note:* The school is affiliated with the Canadian Reformed Church.
Hendrik Plug, Principal

Hawkesville: Countryside Christian School
3745 Hergott Rd., Hawkesville, ON N0B 1X0, Canada
Tel: 519-699-5793; *Fax:* 519-699-4576
Grades: K./Elem./Sec.
Howard Lichty, Contact

Jarvis: Jarvis Community Christian School
149 Talbot St. East, Jarvis, ON N0A 1J0
Tel: 519-587-4444; *Fax:* 519-587-2985
info@jdcs.ca
www.jccs.ca
Grades: K.-8 *Enrollment:* 129
Doug Osborn, Principal
principal@jdcs.ca

Jordan Station: Heritage Christian School
P.O. Box 400
2850 Fourth Ave., Jordan Station, ON L0R 1S0, Canada
Tel: 905-562-7303; *Fax:* 905-562-0020
Grades: Elem./Sec. *Enrollment:* 501
Ben Harsvoort, Principal

Jordan Station: Jordan Christian School
P.O. Box 69
4171 - 15 St. South, Jordan Station, ON L0R 1S0, Canada
Tel: 905-562-4023; *Fax:* 905-562-4024
jcsecr@talkwireless.ca
www.jordanchristianschool.ca
Enrollment: 132
Mark Fintelman

Kasabonika Lake: Chief Simeon McKay Education Centre
P.O. Box 120
Kasabonika Lake, ON P0V 1Y0, Canada
Tel: 807-535-2574; *Fax:* 807-535-1108

King: The Country Day School (CDS)
13415 Dufferin St., King, ON L7B 1K5, Canada
Tel: 905-833-1220; *Fax:* 905-833-1350
www.cds.on.ca
Grades: Junior Kindergarten - 12 *Note:* The co-educational school is non-denominational.
Paul C. Duckett, Headmaster
David Huckvale, Director, Admission

King City: St. Thomas of Villanova College School
P.O. Box 133
2480 15th Sideroad, King City, ON L7B 1A4, Canada
Tel: 905-833-1909; *Fax:* 905-833-1915
www.villanovacollege.net
Grades: 5-12 *Enrollment:* 450
Paul Paradiso

Kingston: Kingston Christian School
1212 Woodbine Rd., Kingston, ON K7L 4V2
Tel: 613-384-9572; *Fax:* 613-384-9580
kcs@kingston.jkl.net
www.kingstonchristianschool.ca
Grades: K./Elem.
Karl Reid, Contact

Kingsville: Old Colony Christian Academy
Kingsville Campus
1521 County Rd. 4 West, RR#2, Kingsville, ON N9Y 2E5, Canada
Tel: 519-733-8308; *Fax:* 519-733-2167
Grades: Elem./Sec. *Enrollment:* 194
Peter Klassen

Kitchener: Carmel New Church School
40 Chapel Hill Dr., Kitchener, ON N2R 1N2
Tel: 519-748-5802
secretary@carmelnewchurch.org
www.carmelnewchurch.org/school.html
Grades: JK-10
Brad Heinrichs, Pastor/Principal
pastor@carmelnewchurch.org

Kitchener: Fellowship Christian School
1780 Glasgow St., Kitchener, ON N2N 0A7
Tel: 519-746-0008; *Fax:* 519-746-4206
fcsprincipal@execulink.com
www.kwfcs.com
Grades: Elem.
Trevor Long, Principal

Kitchener: Laurentian Hills Christian School
11 Laurentian Dr., Kitchener, ON N2E 1C1
Tel: 519-576-6700; *Fax:* 519-576-2583
Grades: JK-8
Ian Timmerman, Principal

Kitchener: Rockway Mennonite Collegiate Inc.
110 Doon Rd., Kitchener, ON N2G 3C8, Canada
Tel: 519-743-5209; *Fax:* 519-743-5935
www.rockway.on.ca
Grades: 7 - 12 *Enrollment:* 350 *Note:* Rockway Mennonite Collegiate is an inspected & accredited private school, with students from Mennonite congregations & Christian denominations.
Gloria Eby, Chair
Betsy Petker, Principal
Dennis Wikerd, Assistant Principal
Tom Bileski, Director, Community Relations
Bernie Burnett, Director, Development
Barry Bishop, Business Manager

Kitchener: St. Jude's School Inc.
888 Trillum Dr., Kitchener, ON N2R 1K4, Canada
Tel: 519-888-0807; *Fax:* 519-884-0316
www.stjudes.com
Grades: 1-12 *Enrollment:* 172 *Note:* Founded in 1980 for students with learning difficulties. Also offers an after-hours Tutoring School and Second Language School

Kitchener: Sunshine Montessori School
10 Boniface Ave., Kitchener, ON N2C 1L9, Canada
Tel: 519-744-1423; *Fax:* 519-744-9929
admin@sunshinemontessori.on.ca
www.sunshinemontessori.on.ca
Grades: Jr. K.-8 *Enrollment:* 209
Roshmina Shamji, Principal/Administrator

Kleinburg: Kleinburg Christian Academy (KCA)
6950 Nashville Rd., Kleinburg, ON L0J 1C0, Canada
Tel: 905-893-7211
ccs.behosted.ca
Grades: Junior Kindergarten - 8
LeeAnn Major, Principal

Lakefield: Lakefield College School
4391 County Rd. 29, Lakefield, ON K0L 2H0, Canada
Tel: 705-652-3324; *Fax:* 705-652-6320
www.lcs.on.ca
Grades: Elem./Sec. *Enrollment:* 321 *Note:* Founded 1879; co-ed boarding and day school, for grades 9-12 and 7-12 respectively; core academics, athletics, and co-curricular arts programmes.
David Thompson, Head of School
Kathy Green, Board Secretary
kgreen@lcs.on.ca

Laurel: Dufferin Area Christian School
General Delivery, Laurel, ON L0N 1L0
Tel: 519-941-4368; *Fax:* 519-941-3748
dacs@on.aibn.com
Grades: Elem.
Nick Mans, Principal

Leamington: United Mennonite Educational Institute (UMEI)
614 Mersea Rd. 6, RR#5, Leamington, ON N8H 3V8, Canada
Tel: 519-326-7448; *Fax:* 519-326-0278
umei@mnsi.net
www.umei.on.ca
Grades: 9 - 12 *Note:* United Mennonite Educational Institute is a secondary school which provides an education that incorporates an Anabaptist / Mennonite world view.
Victor J. Winter, Principal
umeiadmi@mnsi.net
Jane Klassen, Secretary

Lindsay: Heritage Christian School
159 Colborne St. West, Lindsay, ON K9V 5Z8, Canada
Tel: 705-324-8363; *Fax:* 705-324-8363
hcs_office@bellnet.ca
Grades: K./Elem. *Enrollment:* 102
John Frederick

Listowel: Listowel Christian School
P.O. Box 151
6020 Line 87, Listowel, ON N4W 3H2
Tel: 519-291-3086; *Fax:* 519-291-3086
lcs@cyg.net
www.listowelchristianschool.ca
Grades: JK-8
Garth Bierma, Principal

London: Al-Taqwa Islamic Schools
Elementary School
35 Jim Ashton St., London, ON N5V 3H4, Canada
Tel: 519-951-1414; *Fax:* 519-951-1092
Toll-Free: 866-812-9127
ischool@altaqwa.org
www.altaqwa.org
Grades: Elem./Sec. *Enrollment:* 163 *Note:* The elementary school is located at 35 Jim Ashton St.; the secondary school is located at 1697 Trafalgar St., (519) 452-3366, secondary@altaqwa.org.
Siham Kaloti, Principal

London: Covenant Christian School
7 Howard Ave., London, ON N6P 1B3
Tel: 519-203-0266
info@ccslondon.org
www.ccslondon.org
Grades: K.-8 *Enrollment:* 80
William Dokter, Chair
board@ccslondon.org
Shawn Wolski, Principal
principal@ccslondon.org

London: London Christian Academy (LCA)
85 Charles St., London, ON N6H 1H1, Canada
Tel: 519-473-3332; *Fax:* 519-473-9843
www.londonchristianacademy.ca
Grades: Junior Kindergarten - 8 *Note:* London Christian Academy is an interdenominational, Christian school.
Glen Smeltzer, Chair
chairman@londonchristianacademy.ca
Ron Hesman, Principal
principal@londonchristianacademy.ca
Steve Gaunt, Vice Principal
sgaunt@londonchristianacademy.ca

London: London Christian Elementary School
202 Clarke Rd., London, ON N5W 5E4, Canada
Tel: 519-455-0360; *Fax:* 519-455-6717
info@londonchristian.ca
www.londonchristian.ca
Grades: JK-8 *Enrollment:* 200
Mary Haven, Principal
mhaven@londonchristian.ca

London: London Community Hebrew Day School
536 Huron St., London, ON N6A 2M2
Tel: 519-439-8419; *Fax:* 519-439-0404
info@lchds.ca; lchds@rogers.com
www.lchds.ca
www.facebook.com/130138960416975
Grades: K./Elem.
Carol Marcus, Chair
Rachelle Frydman, Principal

London: London District Christian Secondary School
24 Braesyde Ave., London, ON N5W 1V3, Canada
Tel: 519-455-4360; *Fax:* 519-455-4364
office@ldcss.ca
www.ldcss.ca
Grades: Sec. *Enrollment:* 360
Dwayne Bulthuis, Principal
dbulthuis@ldcss.ca

London: London Islamic School
151 Oxford St. West, London, ON N6H 1S3, Canada
Tel: 519-679-9920; *Fax:* 519-679-6842
www.londonislamicschool.com
Grades: K.-8 *Enrollment:* 187
Patricia Zabian, Principal

London: London Waldorf School
7 Beaufort St., London, ON N6G 1A5
Tel: 519-858-8862
info@londonwaldorf.ca
www.londonwaldorf.ca
www.facebook.com/122238667810381
twitter.com/londonwaldorf
londonwaldorf.wordpress.com
Grades: Pre.-8 *Enrollment:* 109
Peter von Holtzendorff, Contact

London: Matthews Hall Private School
1370 Oxford St. West, London, ON N6H 1W2
Tel: 519-471-1506; *Fax:* 519-471-8647
matthewshall.on.ca
Grades: JK-8
Patricia A. Doig, Head of School
Janet Frame, Associate Head
frame.j@matthewshall.ca
Suzanne Fratschko Elliott, Director, Advancement
elliott.s@matthewshall.ca

London: Montessori Academy of London
711 Waterloo St., London, ON N6A 3W1
Tel: 519-433-9121; *Fax:* 519-433-8941
reception@montessori.on.ca
montessori.on.ca
Grades: Pre.-8 *Enrollment:* 375 *Note:* The Montessori Academy of London also offers a toddler program for children from 18 to 30 months & a Casa program, for children from ages 2.5 to 6.
Margaret Whitley, Director
mwhitley@montessori.on.ca
Chandra Peretic, Coordinator, Communications & Administration
Kristen Crouse, Coordinator, Elementary & Junior High
kcrouse@montessori.on.ca
Marianne Rutledge, Coordinator, Admissions
registrar@montessori.on.ca
Kathy Work-Schlattman, Coordinator, Casa
kwork@montessori.on.ca
Shonagh Stevenson-Ramsay, Directress, Toddler Program
sstevenson@montessori.on.ca
Walter Iwanowski, Controller
wki@montessori.on.ca

Lucknow: Lucknow & District Christian School
37521 Amberley Rd., Lucknow, ON N0G 2H0
Tel: 519-528-2016; *Fax:* 519-528-2095
Grades: K./Elem.
Lawrence Uyl

Markham: J. Addison School
2 Valleywood Dr., Markham, ON L3R 8H3
Tel: 905-477-4999; *Fax:* 905-477-4380
info@addisonschool.com
www.addisonschool.com
www.facebook.com/150702185027644
Grades: Pre.-Sec.
Bill Macdonald, Supervising Principal
bmacdonald@addisonschool.com

Markham: Learning Has No Limits (LHNL)
#2669, 2 Bur Oak Ave., Markham, ON L6B 1K9
Tel: 905-265-7553
admin@learninghasnolimits.com
www.learninghasnolimits.com
Grades: 9-12

Campuses
Markham Campus
#2705, 2 Bur Oak Ave., Markham, ON L6B 1K9
Tel: 905-265-7553
Note: School located in the former Keen Minds Inc. building

Woodbridge Campus
7971 Kipling Ave., Woodbridge, ON L4L 1Z3
Tel: 905-265-7553
Note: School located inside the Faith Apostolic Church

Markham: Peoples Christian Academy (PCA)
245 Renfrew Dr., Markham, ON L3R 6G3
Tel: 416-733-2010
info@pca.ca
www.pca.ca
www.facebook.com/181436515199705
Grades: Pre.-12 *Enrollment:* 350
Rev. Reg Andrews, B.A., B.Ed., M.A.

Markham: Royal Cachet Montessori School
9921 Woodbine Ave., Markham, ON L6C 1H7
Tel: 905-888-7700; *Fax:* 905-888-6200
info@rcmschool.ca
www.rcmschool.ca
Grades: Pre.-3 *Enrollment:* 110
Kathy Bobotsis, Director

Markham: Somerset Academy
7700 Brimley Rd., Markham, ON L3R 0E5, Canada
Tel: 905-940-8990; *Fax:* 905-940-8992
administration@somersetacademy.ca
www.somersetacademy.ca
Grades: Jr. K.-8 *Enrollment:* 172
Cathy Barogianis, Principal

Markham: Town Centre Montessori Private Schools (TCMPS)
Main Campus
155 Clayton Dr., Markham, ON L3R 7P3, Canada
Tel: 905-470-1200; *Fax:* 905-470-0184
admin@tcmps.com
www.tcmps.com
Other Information: 905-474-3434 (Phone, Preschool & Grade 1)
Grades: Preschool - 8 *Note:* The preschool program accepts children as young as two years of age.
Marianne Vanderlugt, Principal

Markham: Town Centre Private High School (TCPHS)
155 Clayton Dr., Markham, ON L3R 7P3
Tel: 905-470-1200; *Fax:* 905-470-1721
www.tcphs.com
Grades: 9 - 12 *Note:* This is a coeducational school which provides university bound & advanced placement courses.

Markham: Trillium School
4277 - 14th Ave., Markham, ON L3R 0J2, Canada
Tel: 905-946-1181; *Fax:* 905-946-8267
info@trilliumschool.ca
www.trilliumschool.ca
Grades: Preschool - 8 *Note:* Trillium School is a coeducational, non-denominational school. It features a pre-Casa program for toddlers & a Casa program.
Lily Moon, Principal
lmoon@trilliumschool.ca

Markham: Wesley Christian Academy
22 Heritage Rd., Markham, ON L3P 1M4, Canada
Tel: 905-201-8461; *Fax:* 905-201-6438
office@wesleychristianacademy.com
www.wesleychristianacademy.com
Grades: Senior Kindergarten - 8 *Note:* Wesley Christian Academy offers an academic program within the context of Christian principles.

Markham: Wishing Well Montessori School
#30, 455 Cochrane Dr., Markham, ON L3R 9R4
Tel: 905-470-9751
www.wishingwellschools.com
www.facebook.com/207952285907957
Grades: K./Elem.
Anthony Mauriell, Principal

Metcalfe: Community Christian School
2681 Glen St., Metcalfe, ON K0A 2P0, Canada
Tel: 613-821-3669; *Fax:* 613-821-6135
info@communitychristianschool.ca
www.communitychristianschool.ca
Grades: Elem. *Enrollment:* 77
Rick Dykstra, Principal
rick.dykstra@communitychristianschool.ca

Millgrove: Covenant Christian School
P.O. Box 2
497 Millgrove Side Rd., Millgrove, ON L0R 1V0, Canada
Tel: 905-689-3191; *Fax:* 905-689-0191
covenantchristianschool@bellnet.ca
Grades: Elem. *Enrollment:* 119
Tracy Jelsma, Principal

Milverton: Fair Haven Christian Day School
4184 Line 61, RR#1, Milverton, ON N0K 1M0, Canada
Tel: 519-595-4568
Grades: K.-10
Howard Bean, Principal, 519-462-2220
Melvin Roes, Bishop, 519-273-1515

Mississauga: ABC Montessori
305 Matheson Blvd. East, Mississauga, ON L4Z 1X8
Tel: 905-568-8989; *Fax:* 905-568-0958
abcmontessori@bellnet.ca
www.abcmontessori.com
Grades: Pre-5 *Enrollment:* 140
Raj Vekaria, Principal

Campuses
Cawthra Casa Campus
4300 Cawthra Rd., Mississauga, ON L4Z 1V8
Tel: 905-281-2595; *Fax:* 905-568-0958
Mari Ang, Principal

Matheson Casa & Toddler Campus
285 Matheson Blvd. East, Mississauga, ON L4Z 1X8
Tel: 905-568-1716; *Fax:* 905-568-0958
Rick Kordts, Campus Administrator

Mississauga: Bet Sefer Solel
2399 Folkway Dr., Mississauga, ON L5L 2M6
Tel: 905-820-5915; *Fax:* 905-820-1956
info@solel.ca
www.solel.ca/betsefersolel.html
Note: Bet Sefer Solel is a Reform Jewish school.
Rabbi Lawrence Englander
Ted Greenberg, President
Arliene Botnick, B.A., M.Ed., Director, Education
amora@solel.ca

Mississauga: Bronte College of Canada
88 Bronte College Ct., Mississauga, ON L5B 1M9, Canada
Tel: 905-270-7788; *Fax:* 905-270-7828
info@brontecollege.ca; admissions@brontecollege.ca
www.brontecollege.ca
Grades: 9 - 12 *Note:* Bronte College of Canada is a co-educational, international day & boarding school. The school also offers University of Guelph & Bronte College first year university courses, an advanced placement program, & English as a Second Language (ESL).

Mississauga: Froebel Education Centre
1576 Dundas St. West, Mississauga, ON L5C 1E5, Canada
Tel: 905-277-9371; *Fax:* 905-277-9402
office@froebel.com
www.froebel.com
Grades: K.-8 *Enrollment:* 89 *Note:* Education based on the principle's of Friedrich Froebel: working in partnership with the child's family, tranformation of creative play into creative work, & making connections with others, the world & God.
Barbara E. Corbett, B.A., Ed.D., Director, Education

Mississauga: Grade Learning
#20, 5225 Orbitor Dr., Mississauga, ON L4W 4Y8
Tel: 905-624-9661; *Fax:* 905-629-0079
Toll-Free: 800-208-3826
office@gradelearning.ca
gradelearning.ca
www.facebook.com/gradelearning
twitter.com/gradelearning
www.linkedin.com/company/grade-learning
www.youtube.com/gradelearning
Grades: 9-12
Margaret Prophet, Program Director

Campuses
Barrie Campus
#6, 250 Bayview Dr., Barrie, ON L4N 4Y8
Tel: 705-739-6619; *Fax:* 705-739-1236
barrie@gradelearning.ca

Brampton West Campus
#202, 37 George St. North, Brampton, ON L6X 1R5
Tel: 905-861-9554; *Fax:* 905-861-9797
bramptonwest@gradelearning.ca

Downsview Campus
#15, 1126 Finch Ave. West, Downsview, ON M3J 3J6
Tel: 416-667-1500; *Fax:* 416-667-1502
downsview@gradelearning.ca

Etobicoke Campus
#502, 1243 Islington Ave., Etobicoke, ON M8X 1Y9
Tel: 416-231-0333; *Fax:* 416-231-0023
etobicoke@gradelearning.ca

Kingston Campus
#200, 1020 Bayridge Dr., Kingston, ON K7P 2S2
Tel: 613-389-1361; *Fax:* 613-389-7571
kingston@gradelearning.ca

Kitchener Campus
1378 Weber St. East, Kitchener, ON N2A 1C4
Tel: 519-745-8798; *Fax:* 519-745-2720
kitchener@gradelearning.ca

Markham Campus
#100, 25 Royal Crest Ct., Markham, ON L3R 9X4
Tel: 905-471-9166; *Fax:* 905-474-2226
markham@gradelearning.ca

Mississauga West Campus
#101, 2227 South Millway, Mississauga, ON L5L 3R6
Tel: 905-821-0112; *Fax:* 905-821-0113
mississaugawest@gradelearning.ca

North York Campus
#7B, 3200 Dufferin St., Toronto, ON M6A 3B2
Tel: 416-781-7667; *Fax:* 416-781-3560
northyork@gradelearning.ca

Orangeville Campus
#100, 14 Stewart Ct., Orangeville, ON L9W 3Z9
Tel: 519-940-4498; *Fax:* 519-940-9628
orangeville@gradelearning.ca

Orillia Campus
#4B, 575 West St. South, Orillia, ON L4V 7N6
Tel: 705-327-3459; *Fax:* 705-327-2458
orillia@gradelearning.ca

Oshawa Campus
#1J, 57 Simcoe St. South, Oshawa, ON L1H 4G4
Tel: 905-433-1033; *Fax:* 866-817-2392
oshawa@gradelearning.ca

Ottawa Campus
#10-12, 1300 - 340 Albert St., Ottawa, ON K1R 7Y6
Tel: 613-721-6777; *Fax:* 800-410-2023
ottawa@gradelearning.ca

Owen Sound Campus
#1, 1450 - 1st Ave., Owen Sound, ON N4K 6W2
Tel: 519-371-2675; *Fax:* 519-371-2770
owensound@gradelearning.ca

Peterborough Campus
#300, 425 Water St., Peterborough, ON K9H 3L9
Tel: 705-748-2111; *Fax:* 866-817-2392
peterborough@gradelearning.ca

Rexdale Campus
#109-110, 557 Dixon Rd., Toronto, ON M9W 6K1
Tel: 416-244-4433; *Fax:* 416-244-8076
rexdale@gradelearning.ca

Richmond Hill Campus
#13-14, 1455 - 16th Ave., Richmind Hill, ON L4B 4W5
Tel: 905-886-6500; *Fax:* 416-781-3560
richmondhill@gradelearning.ca

Scarborough East Campus
#207, 2425 Eglinton Ave. East, Toronto, ON M1K 5G8
Tel: 416-755-8547; *Fax:* 866-817-2392
scarborougheast@gradelearning.ca

Stoney Creek Campus
#303, 800 Queenston Rd., Stoney Creek, ON L8G 1A7
Tel: 905-662-5325; *Fax:* 905-662-3728
stoneycreek@gradelearning.ca

Sudbury Campus
Sudbury, ON
Tel: 705-524-1158; *Fax:* 800-410-2023
sudbury@gradelearning.ca
Note: Contact for location information.

Toronto Central Campus
#902, 2300 Yonge St., Toronto, ON M4P 2W6
Tel: 416-482-2272; *Fax:* 416-482-2270
torontocentral@gradelearning.ca

Weston Campus
#12, 2007 Lawrence Ave. West, Toronto, ON M9N 3V1
Tel: 416-243-2272; *Fax:* 416-243-2262
weston@gradelearning.ca

Windsor Campus
1215 Walker Rd., Windsor, ON N8Y 2N9
Tel: 519-968-1776; *Fax:* 519-419-3176
windsor@gradelearning.ca

Woodbridge Campus
#10, 4140 Steeles Ave., Woodbridge, ON L4L 4V3
Tel: 905-850-3719; *Fax:* 905-850-2981
woodbridge@gradelearning.ca

***Mississauga:* IQRA Islamic School**
5751 Coopers Ave., Mississauga, ON L4Z 1R9, Canada
Tel: 905-507-6688; *Fax:* 905-507-9243
iqraislamicschool@gmail.com
www.iqraislamicschool.com
Enrollment: 150
Ghzala Khan

***Mississauga:* ISNA Elementary School**
1525 Sherway Dr., Mississauga, ON L4X 1C5
Tel: 905-272-4303; *Fax:* 905-272-4311
elementary@isnaschools.com
elementary.isnaschools.com
Grades: K./Elem.
Obaid Yarkhan, Principal

***Mississauga:* ISNA High School**
2200 South Sheridan Way, Mississauga, ON L5J 2M4
Tel: 905-403-8406; *Fax:* 905-403-9463
high.isnaschools.com
Grades: 9-12
S.A. Rasoul, Principal

***Mississauga:* Kendellhurst Academy**
175 Queen St. South, Mississauga, ON L5M 1L2
Tel: 905-567-1070; *Fax:* 905-821-0891
info@kendellhurst.com
www.kendellhurst.com
Grades: Pre.-6 *Enrollment:* 150
Paula Carrasco, Director
Campuses
Oakville Campus
#11 & 12, 2460 Neyagawa Blvd., Oakville, ON L6H 7P4
Tel: 905-257-2030

***Mississauga:* Lynn-Rose Heights Private School**
7215 Millcreek Dr., Mississauga, ON L5N 3R3
Tel: 905-567-3553; *Fax:* 905-567-5318
lynnroseinfo@lynnroseheights.net
www.lynnroseheights.net
Grades: Pre.-8 *Enrollment:* 300

***Mississauga:* Meadow Green Academy**
649 Queensway West, Mississauga, ON L5B 1C2
Tel: 905-273-3344
mgainfo@meadowgreenacademy.ca
meadowgreenacademy.ca
twitter.com/MeadowGreenAc
Grades: Pre.-3 *Enrollment:* 150
Georganne M. MacKenzie, Director
Campuses
Senior Campus
1884 Lakeshore Rd. West, Mississauga, ON L5J 1J7
Tel: 905-273-3344
Grades: 4-8

***Mississauga:* Mentor College**
Main Campus
40 Forest Ave., Mississauga, ON L5G 1L1, Canada
Tel: 905-271-3393; *Fax:* 905-271-8367
40forest@mentorcollege.edu (Main campus)
www.mentorcollege.edu
Other Information: 56cayuga@mentorcollege.edu (E-mail, Primary campus)
Grades: Junior Kindergarten - 12
Ken Philbrook, Director

***Mississauga:* Mississauga Christian Academy (MCA)**
Gananoque Campus
2720 Gananoque Dr., Mississauga, ON L5N 2R2, Canada
Tel: 905-826-4114; *Fax:* 905-567-5874
office@mississaugachristianacademy.com
www.mississaugachristianacademy.com
Grades: Junior Kindergarten - 8 *Note:* The Mississauga Christian Academy also operates a licensed day care.

***Mississauga:* Northstar Montessori Private School**
4900 Tomken Rd., Mississauga, ON L4W 1J8, Canada
Tel: 905-890-7827; *Fax:* 905-890-6771
www.northstarmontessori.com
www.facebook.com/NorthstarMontessoriPrivateSchool
www.twitter.com/NorthstarMontes
Grades: Preschool / Elementary *Note:* Northstar Montessori offers the following programs: toddlers, pre-Casa, primary, & elementary. Ages of children range from 18 months to 12 years.
Virginia Ramirez, Principal
Sherry Gosal, Vice Principal
Rick Ramirez, Manager, Business
Rose Sta. Ana, Office Administrator

***Mississauga:* Peel Montessori School**
964 Meadow Wood Rd., Mississauga, ON L5J 2S6
Tel: 905-823-6522; *Fax:* 905-823-5397
info@peelmontessori.com
peelmontessori.com
Grades: JK-6 *Enrollment:* 100
Santina Cowdrey, Founding Principal

***Mississauga:* Philopateer Christian College**
6341 Mississauga Rd., Mississauga, ON L5N 1A5
Tel: 905-814-5181
www.pccnet.ca
Grades: Pre.-12 *Enrollment:* 300
Mary Ashun, Principal

***Mississauga:* Rotherglen School**
Gooderham Estate Campus
929 Old Derry Rd., Mississauga, ON L5W 1A1
Tel: 905-565-8707; *Fax:* 905-565-0485
www.rotherglen.com
Grades: Preschool - 8 *Note:* The Casa program is designed for children from age three to five. Rotherglen school has over 1,200 students who attend the school's four campuses.

***Mississauga:* Rotherglen School**
Erin Mills Campus
3553 South Common Ct., Mississauga, ON L5L 2B3
Tel: 905-820-9445; *Fax:* 905-569-1569
www.rotherglen.com
Grades: Preschool - 6 *Note:* The Erin Mills campus provides a Montessori program for its students, from Casa to grade six.

***Mississauga:* St. Jude's Academy**
6670 Campobello Rd., Mississauga, ON L5N 2L8
Tel: 905-814-0202; *Fax:* 905-814-0299
info@stjudesacademy.com
www.stjudesacademy.com
Grades: Pre.-8 *Enrollment:* 115
Aaron Sawatsky, Head of School

***Mississauga:* Sherwood Heights School**
3065 Glen Erin Dr., Mississauga, ON L5L 1J3, Canada
Tel: 905-569-8999; *Fax:* 905-569-9034
info@sherwoodheights.com
www.sherwoodheights.com
Grades: Elem. *Enrollment:* 206
Anthony H. Mutlak

***Mississauga:* Sommerville Manor Private School**
1135 Central Pkwy. West, Mississauga, ON L5C 3J2, Canada
Tel: 905-277-1085; *Fax:* 905-277-3801
info@sommervillemanor.com
www.sommervillemanor.com
Grades: K.-8 *Enrollment:* 283
Winefride Johnson

***Mississauga:* Springfield Preparatory School**
1444 Dundas Cres., Mississauga, ON L5C 1E9, Canada
Tel: 905-273-9717; *Fax:* 905-273-9717
info@springfieldprep.ca
www.springfieldprep.ca
Grades: Jr. K.-6 *Enrollment:* 66
Janet Murphy

***Mississauga:* Star Academy**
1587 Cormack Cres., Mississauga, ON L5E 2P8
Tel: 905-891-1555; *Fax:* 905-891-1696
info@staracademy.ca
www.staracademy.ca
twitter.com/myStarAcademy
Grades: JK-8 *Enrollment:* 95
Belinda Bernardo, Principal

***Mississauga:* TEAM School**
Also known as: Tutorial & Educ. Assistance in Mississauga
275 Rudar Rd., Mississauga, ON L5A 1S2, Canada
Tel: 905-279-7200; *Fax:* 905-279-1561
www.teamschool.com
Grades: K./Elem./Spec. Ed. *Enrollment:* 299
Chuck MacDonald, Principal

***Mississauga:* Toronto Ability School**
1146 Clarkson Rd. North, Mississauga, ON L5J 2W2, Canada
Tel: 905-855-3800
Grades: Preschool - 8

***Mississauga:* White Oaks Montessori School Ltd.**
Vanier Campus
1200 Vanier Dr., Mississauga, ON L5H 4C7, Canada
Tel: 905-278-4454; *Fax:* 905-278-5184
admin@woms.ca
www.woms.ca
Other Information: 905-855-2321 (Phone, Clarkson Campus)
Grades: Preschool - Elementary *Note:* White Oaks Montessori School is a fully accredited Canadian Council of Montessori Administrators school. The youngest children are offered toddler programs. Casa programs are provided for children from age three to five. The Clarkson Campus is located at the following address: 1338 Clarkson Road North, Mississauga.
Barbara S. Ward, AMI, Founder & Chief Administrative Officer
Irene Stathoukos, BSc., AMI, Principal
Daniel Ward, Information Technologist

***Mount Hope:* Grandview Adventist Academy**
3975 Hwy. 6, Mount Hope, ON L0R 1W0, Canada
Tel: 905-679-4492; *Fax:* 905-679-4492
info@grandviewschool.ca
www.grandviewschool.ca
Grades: Elem./Sec. *Enrollment:* 58
Gisela I. Hoelzel

***Nepean:* Ottawa Islamic School**
10 Coral Ave., Nepean, ON K2E 5Z6, Canada
Tel: 613-727-5066; *Fax:* 613-727-8486
info@ottawaislamicschool.org
www.ottawaislamicschool.org
Grades: JK-12 *Enrollment:* 246
Mohamed Sheik Ahmed (Dalmar, Principal

Nepean: **Rambam Day School**
25 Esquimault Ave., Nepean, ON K2H 6Z5, Canada
Tel: 613-820-9484; *Fax:* 613-820-0029
www.rambam.ca
Other Information: 613-820-9484, ext. 348 (Phone, Admissions & Judaica)
Grades: Preschool - 8 *Note:* The RAMBAM Day School offers general & Judaic studies, in Hebrew, French, & English.
Rabbi Dovid Hayes, Executive Director, 613-820-9484, ext. 350
Chana Hayes, Principal & Head, Judaica
Susan Spence, Vice Principal & Head, General Studies
Rabbi Yaakov Wilschanski, Educational Director, 613-820-9484, ext. 351

Nepean: **Redeemer Christian High School (RCHS)**
82 Colonnade Rd. North, Nepean, ON K2E 7L2, Canada
Tel: 613-723-9262; *Fax:* 613-723-9321
info@rchs.on.ca
www.rchs.on.ca
www.facebook.com/RedeemerChristianHighSchool
Grades: 9 - 12 *Note:* Redeemer Christian High School offers a Christ-centered education. The school also provides programs for students with learning disabilities.
Chuck Schoenmaker, Principal
principal@rchs.on.ca
J. David Naftel, B.Ed., B.Sc., Vice Principal
dnaftel@rchs.on.ca

Nestor Falls: **Mikinaak Onigaming School**
P.O. Box 160
Nestor Falls, ON P0X 1K0, Canada
Tel: 807-484-2162; *Fax:* 807-484-2737
Grades: Junior Kindergarten - 12 *Enrollment:* 100 *Note:* Mikinaak Onigaming School is a band operated school, providing education for the Ojibways of Onigaming First Nation.
Owen Zoccole, Director, Education

Newmarket: **Holland Marsh District Christian School**
18955 Dufferin St., RR#2, Newmarket, ON L3Y 4V9
Tel: 905-775-3701; *Fax:* 905-775-2395
hmdcs@hmdcs.ca
www.hmdcs.ca
Grades: K./Elem. *Enrollment:* 220
Rod Berg, Principal

Newmarket: **Newmarket & District Christian Academy (NDCA)**
P.O. Box 297
221 Carlson Dr., Newmarket, ON L3Y 4X1, Canada
Tel: 905-895-1199; *Fax:* 905-895-4353
ndca@rogers.com
www.ndca.ca
Grades: Kindergarten - 8
Steve Klassen, Chair
Jane MacLachlan, Principal

Newmarket: **Or Hadash Religious School**
#5, 451 Botsford St., Newmarket, ON L3Y 1T2
Tel: 905-898-2220
info@orhadash.org
www.orhadash.org
Len Bates, President
len@orhadash.org
Mark Klady, Contact
markklady@rogers.com

Newmarket: **Pickering College**
16945 Bayview Ave., Newmarket, ON L3Y 4X2, Canada
Tel: 905-895-1700; *Fax:* 905-895-9076
Toll-Free: 877-895-1700
info@pickeringcollege.on.ca
www.pickeringcollege.on.ca
Grades: Jr. K.-University Prep *Enrollment:* 415 *Note:* Day and Boarding School
Peter C. Sturrup, Headmaster

Niagara Falls: **Niagara Community Church School**
9527 McLeod St., RR#2, Niagara Falls, ON L2E 6S5, Canada
Tel: 905-357-9519
Grades: Kindergarten - 8
Chris Schmoll, Principal

Nobleton: **The Montessori Country School**
Nobleton Campus
P.O. Box 455
6185 - 15th Sideroad, Nobleton, ON L0G 1N0, Canada
Tel: 905-859-4739; *Fax:* 905-859-5696
Toll-Free: 1-866-557-2272
admin@mcs-nobleton.com
www.montessoricountryschool.ca
Grades: Preschool / Elementary *Note:* The Montessori Country School offers a toddler program, a Casa program, & an elementary program. Children range in age from 12 months to 12 years.
Jack Rice, Director, Education
Joanne Hastie, Director, Curriculum & Instruction
Gregory Dixon, Administrator

North York: **Scarborough Christian School**
95 Jonesville Cres., North York, ON M4A 1H2, Canada
Tel: 416-750-7515; *Fax:* 905-750-7720
info@scarboroughchristianschool.com
www.scarboroughchristianschool.com
Grades: K./Elem./Sec. *Enrollment:* 276
Martin D. Sandford, Principal

Norwich: **Rehoboth Christian School - Norwich**
P.O. Box 220
43 Main St. East, Norwich, ON N0J 1P0, Canada
Tel: 519-863-2403; *Fax:* 519-863-3984
office@rcsnorwich.com
Grades: Kindergarten - 12 *Enrollment:* 600
J. Heikoop, Principal
Martien Vanderspek, Vice Principal
mvanterspek@nor-del.com

Oakville: **Al-Falah Islamic School**
391 Burnhamthorpe Rd. East, Oakville, ON L6H 7B4, Canada
Tel: 905-257-5782; *Fax:* 905-257-0848
office@al-falah.org
www.al-falah.org
Grades: Elem. *Enrollment:* 215 *Note:* Accredited by the Ontario Min. of Education; curriculum also includes programmes in the arts, computers, physicial education, Arabic language, & Quran studies.
Nafees Khan, Principal

Oakville: **Appleby College**
540 Lakeshore Rd. West, Oakville, ON L6K 3P1, Canada
Tel: 905-845-4681; *Fax:* 905-845-9828
info@appleby.on.ca
www.appleby.on.ca
Grades: Elem./Sec. *Enrollment:* 740 *Note:* Independent, co-educational school for boarding & day students in Grandes 7 through 12.
Guy S. McLean, Principal

Oakville: **Chisholm Educational Centre**
Also known as: Chisholm Academy
1484 Cornwall Rd., Oakville, ON L6J 7W5, Canada
Tel: 905-844-3240
www.chisholmcentre.com
Grades: Secondary / Post Secondary *Note:* Chisholm Educational Centre consists of the Academy High School & the Collegiate.
Dr. Howard Bernstein, C. Psych., Executive Director
Dr. Shirley Bryntwick, C. Psych., Director, Professional Services
Frances Hatcher, Dip. Math., Post Grad. Ed, Head, Chisholm Collegiate
C. David Jowett, M.Ed., Principal, Chisholm Academy
Sylvia Moyssakos, M.Sc.Ed., O.C.T., Head, Tutorial & Remedial Services
Karen Boyd, Manager, Office

Oakville: **Clanmore Montessori School**
2463 Lakeshore Rd. East, Oakville, ON L6J 1M7
Tel: 905-337-8283; *Fax:* 905-842-2898
info@clanmore.ca
www.clanmore.ca
www.facebook.com/Clanmore
twitter.com/ClanmoreMontess
foursquare.com/clanmoremontess
Grades: Pre.-8 *Enrollment:* 110
Elaine Delsnyder, Coordinator, Casa Program
Grace Kidney, Coordinator, Elementary Program
Susan Fielden, Office Administration, 905-842-2200, ext. 233

Oakville: **Dearcroft Montessori School & West Wind Montessori Jr. High**
1167 Lakeshore Rd. East, Oakville, ON L6J 1L3
Tel: 905-844-2114; *Fax:* 905-844-3529
dearcroft@primus.ca
Grades: JK-8
Gordon Phippen, Principal/Director

Oakville: **Fern Hill School**
Oakville Campus
3300 Ninth Line Rd., Oakville, ON L6H 7A8, Canada
Tel: 905-257-0022
admissions@fernhillschool.com
oakville.fernhillschool.com
Grades: Elem. *Note:* Co-educational.
Joanne McLean, Co-Director & Founder
Deb Bell, Head of School, Primary Division
Robin Grout Ogden, Head of School, Junior/Intermediate Division

Campuses
Burlington Campus
801 North Service Rd., Burlington, ON L7P 5B8
Tel: 905-634-8652
enrol@fernhillschool.com
burlington.fernhillschool.com
Grades: Pre.-8 *Enrollment:* 180
Derrick Muntwyler, Assistant Head of School
dmuntwyler@fernhillschool.com

Oakville: **Glenburnie School**
2035 Upper Middle Rd. East, Oakville, ON L6J 7G6, Canada
Tel: 905-338-6236; *Fax:* 905-338-2654
admin@glenburnieschool.com
www.glenburnieschool.com
Grades: K./Elem. *Enrollment:* 361
Melissa Leduc, Principal
mleduc@glenburnieschool.com

Oakville: **John Knox Christian School**
2232 Sheridan Garden Dr., Oakville, ON L6J 7T1
Tel: 905-829-8048; *Fax:* 905-829-8056
info@jkcs-oakville.org
www.jkcs-oakville.org
Grades: Elem. *Enrollment:* 395
George Petrusma, Principal
gpetrusma@jkcs-oakville.org

Oakville: **King's Christian Collegiate**
528 Burnhamthorpe Rd. West, Oakville, ON L6M 4K6, Canada
Tel: 905-257-5464; *Fax:* 905-257-5463
office@kingschristian.net
www.kingschristian.net
Grades: 9-12 *Enrollment:* 470 *Note:* An independent government-inspected and approved Christian high school.
John De Boer, 905-257-5464, ext. 505
jdeboer@kingschristian.net

Oakville: **MacLachlan College**
337 Trafalgar Rd., Oakville, ON L6J 3H3
Tel: 905-844-0372; *Fax:* 905-844-9369
admissions@maclachlan.ca
www.maclachlan.ca
www.facebook.com/MacLachlanCollege
www.youtube.com/maclachlanc
Grades: Pre.-12 *Enrollment:* 300
Michael Piening, Head of School

Oakville: **Oakville Christian School (OCS)**
112 Third Line, Oakville, ON L6L 3Z6, Canada
Tel: 905-825-1247
ocsadmissions@ocsonline.org
www.ocsonline.org
Grades: Junior Kindergarten - 8 *Enrollment:* 245
Jeff Kennedy, Principal

Oakville: **Rotherglen School**
Oakville Elementary Campus
2050 Neyagawa Blvd., Oakville, ON L6H 6R2, Canada
Tel: 905-849-1897; *Fax:* 905-849-1354
www.rotherglen.com
Grades: 1 - 8 *Note:* The school features the Rotherglen Education in Active Leadership initiative for its grade eight students. Over 1,200 students attend Rotherglen School's four campuses in Oakville & Mississauga.
Tracey Du Preez, Coordinator, Admissions
tdupreez@rotherglen.com

Oakville: **Rotherglen School**
Oakville Primary Campus
2045 Sixth Line, Oakville, ON L6H 1X9
Tel: 905-338-3528; *Fax:* 905-338-9599
www.rotherglen.com
Grades: Preschool - 1 *Note:* The Casa program is designed for children as young as three years of age. The school includes students from age three to six.

Oakville: **St. Mildred's-Lightbourn School**
1080 Linbrook Rd., Oakville, ON L6J 2L1, Canada
Tel: 905-845-2386; *Fax:* 905-845-4799
info@smls.on.ca
www.smls.on.ca
Grades: Jr. K.-12 *Enrollment:* 600 *Note:* All-girls school
Dorothy Byers, Head of School
dbyers@smls.on.ca
Karen Hansen-Cowper, Head of Senior School
khansencowper@smls.on.ca
Irene McRae, Head of Junior School
imcrae@smls.on.ca

Sally Dobie, Director, Advancement
sdobie@smls.on.ca
Donna Cossitt, Coordinator, Admissions
dcossitt@smls.on.ca

Oakville: Shaarei-Beth El Religious School
186 Morrison Rd., Oakville, ON L6J 4J4
Tel: 905-849-6000; *Fax:* 905-849-1134
office@sbe.ca
www.sbe.ca

Grades: Pre.-12
Cheryl Wise, Educator, 905-849-6000, ext. 15
educator@sbe.ca

Oakville: Wildwood Academy
2250 Sheridan Garden Dr., Oakville, ON L6J 7T1
Tel: 905-829-4226; *Fax:* 905-829-2318
wildwoodadmin.wix.com/wildwood-academy
www.facebook.com/WildwoodAcademy

Grades: 2-8 *Enrollment:* 60
Kim Ewing, Co-Director
Michelle Quick, Co-Director

Orangeville: Hillcrest School
7A Little York St., Orangeville, ON L9W 1L8
Tel: 519-941-5591

Grades: K./Elem./Sec.
Gail P. Hooper, Principal

Orangeville: The Maples Independent Country School
RR#4, Orangeville, ON L9W 2Z1, Canada
Tel: 519-942-3310; *Fax:* 519-942-8041
info@TheMaplesSchool.com
www.themaplesschool.com

Grades: Preschool - 8 *Enrollment:* 120

Orillia: Orillia Christian School
P.O. Box 862
505 Gill St., Orillia, ON L3V 6K8, Canada
Tel: 705-326-0532; *Fax:* 705-327-9856
www.ocswebsite.com

Grades: K./Elem. *Enrollment:* 120
Bill Freeman

Oshawa: College Park Elementary School
220 Townline Rd. North, Oshawa, ON L1K 2J6, Canada
Tel: 905-723-0163; *Fax:* 905-723-2984
www.cpes.ca

Grades: K.-8 *Enrollment:* 200
Daniel Carley, Principal
dancarley@yahoo.com

Oshawa: Immanuel Christian School
849 Rossland Rd. West, Oshawa, ON L1J 8R5
Tel: 905-728-9071; *Fax:* 905-728-0604
www.immanuelschool.ca
www.facebook.com/169017956538053

Grades: K./Elem.
Jasper Hoogendam, Principal

Oshawa: Kingsway College
1200 Leland Rd., Oshawa, ON L1K 2H4
Tel: 905-433-1144; *Fax:* 905-433-1156
admissions@kingswaycollege.on.ca;
alumni@kingswaycollege.on.ca
www.kingswaycollege.on.ca
Other Information: Records Fax: 905-433-8078
www.facebook.com/groups/kingswaycollege
twitter.com/kingswayc
www.youtube.com/user/KingswayCollege

Grades: 9-12
Scott Bowes, President, 905-433-1144, ext. 217
bowess@kingswaycollege.on.ca
Jeremy O'Dell, Vice-President, Finance, 905-433-1144, ext. 214

Ottawa: Abraar School
P.O. Box 332
1568 Merivale Rd., Ottawa, ON K2G 5Y7, Canada
Tel: 613-820-0044; *Fax:* 613-820-1495
info@abraarschool.com
www.abraarschool.com

Grades: Elem. *Enrollment:* 212 *Note:* Islamic school. Location: 1085 Grenon Ave., Ottawa.
Moussa Ouarou, Principal

Ottawa: Ashbury College
362 Mariposa Ave., Ottawa, ON K1M 0T3
Tel: 613-749-5954; *Fax:* 613-749-9724
info@ashbury.ca
www.ashbury.ca
www.facebook.com/pages/Ashbury-College/9869212766
twitter.com/ashburycollege
www.linkedin.com/groups?gid=1353977
www.youtube.com/user/ashburycollege

Grades: 4-12 *Enrollment:* 100
Tam Mathews, Headmaster
Brian Storosko, Head, Junior School
Tim Putt, Head, Senior School

Ottawa: Bishop Hamilton Montessori School
2199 Regency Terrace, Ottawa, ON K2C 1H2
Tel: 613-596-4013; *Fax:* 613-596-4971
bhswest@bhsmontessori.ca
www.bhsmontessori.ca

Grades: Pre.-8 *Enrollment:* 222 *Note:* Bishop Hamilton School is a Christian Montessori school for children from ages 18 months to 14 years.
Heather Smith, Chair
Renette Sasouni, Director

Ottawa: Counterpoint Academy Inc.
149 King George St., Ottawa, ON K1K 1V2, Canada
Tel: 613-748-1052; *Fax:* 613-748-8234
www.counterpointacademy.com

Grades: K.-6 *Enrollment:* 163 *Note:* Enriched curriculum, including early literacy, spelling/phonics/grammar, writing skills, math, science, English & French language arts, public speaking, art, music, drama, computers, & physical education. Counterpoint Academy West: 35 Beaufort Dr., Kanata, (613) 271-6356 (Ms. C. Kim, B.A., B.Ed., Principal & Registrar). Day care centres at both locations.
Laura W. Tilson, B.A., B.Ed., M.Ed., Principal

Ottawa: Elmwood School
Rockcliffe Park
261 Buena Vista Rd., Ottawa, ON K1M 0V9
Tel: 613-749-6761
communications@elmwood.ca
www.elmwood.ca
www.facebook.com/ElmwoodSchool
twitter.com/ElmwoodDotCa
pinterest.com/elmwoodschool

Grades: JK-12; girls *Enrollment:* 564
Cheryl Boughton, Headmistress

Ottawa: Fern Hill School (Ottawa) Inc.
50 Vaughan St., Ottawa, ON K1M 1X1, Canada
Tel: 613-746-0255; *Fax:* 613-746-7514
www.fernhillottawa.com

Grades: Pre./K./Elem. *Enrollment:* 99 *Note:* Enriched academic programme; before/after school care & after school programmes; Extended French programme.
Elizabeth Milligan, Principal
principal@fernhillottawa.com

Ottawa: Joan of Arc Academy
2221 Elmira Dr., Ottawa, ON K2C 1H3
Tel: 613-728-6364; *Fax:* 613-728-2935
administration@joanofarcacademy.com
joanofarcacademy.com
www.facebook.com/pages/Joan-of-Arc-Academy/183912149161
twitter.com/JoAAcademy

Grades: K.-8; Girls

Ottawa: Life Christian Academy
1080B St Pierre St., Ottawa, ON K1C 1L3
Tel: 613-834-6588; *Fax:* 613-834-6588
www.lifechristianacademy.ca
www.facebook.com/LifeChristianAcademy
twitter.com/LCA_AVC

Grades: Elem./Sec.
Mike Karpishka, Principal

Ottawa: Lycée Claudel
1635, prom Riverside, Ottawa, ON K1G 0E5, Canada
Tél: 613-733-8522; *Téléc:* 613-733-3782
www.claudel.org

Grades: Mat./Prim./Sec. *Enrollment:* 887
Joëlle Émorine, Proviseure
proviseure@claudel.org

Ottawa: Ottawa Christian School
255 Tartan Dr., Ottawa, ON K2M 1N4, Canada
Tel: 613-825-3000; *Fax:* 613-825-4008
info@ocschool.org
www.ocschool.org
www.facebook.com/pages/Ottawa-Christian-School/123631987687122

Grades: K.-8 *Enrollment:* 194
Paul Triemstra, Principal

Ottawa: Ottawa Languages Institute Ltd.
1990 Leslie Ave., Ottawa, ON K1H 5M3, Canada
Tel: 613-521-3331; *Fax:* 613-521-6482

Grades: Sec.
Tin S. Yap

Ottawa: Ottawa Montessori School l'École Montessori d'Ottawa
335 Lindsay St., Ottawa, ON K1G 0L6, Canada
Tel: 613-521-5185; *Fax:* 613-521-6796
info@ottawamontessori.com
www.ottawamontessori.com

Grades: Pre.-8 *Enrollment:* 320
Pat Gere, Director

Ottawa: Parsifal Waldorf School
1644 Bank St., Ottawa, ON K1V 7Y6, Canada
Tel: 613-733-2668; *Fax:* 613-733-6774

Grades: K./Elem.
Rachel Montgomery

Ottawa: St-Laurent Academy Académie St-Laurent
641 Sladen Ave., Ottawa, ON K1K 2S8
Tel: 613-842-8047; *Fax:* 613-842-9956
admin@st-laurentacademy.com;
admissions@st-laurentacademy.com
www.st-laurentacademy.com

Grades: Pre.-8 *Enrollment:* 200
Susan Kelly, Principal
principal@st-laurentacademy.com

Ottawa: Torah High School - Ottawa
21 Nadolny Sachs Private, Ottawa, ON K2A 1R9
Tel: 613-262-6279; *Fax:* 613-798-9839
torahhighottawa.weebly.com
www.facebook.com/TorahHighOttawa

Grades: 8-12 *Note:* Torah High offers courses in Religious Studies, Hebrew Language, Philosophy, Political Science, Nutrition, Arts & Interdisciplinary Studies for students attending public or private secondary schools. The school is located at 261 Centrepointe Dr., Ottawa, ON K2G 5Y6.
Rabbi Yehuda Simes, Dean & Co-Founder
Bram Bregman, Executive Director & Co-Founder
bram@ncsy.ca

Ottawa: Turnbull School
1132 Fisher Ave., Ottawa, ON K1Z 6P7, Canada
Tel: 613-729-9940; *Fax:* 613-729-1636
admin@turnbull.ca
www.turnbull.ca

Grades: Junior Kindergarten - 8
Mary Ann S. Turnbull, B.Sc. (Psychology), Director
Gareth Reid, Principal
Buddy Clinch, Vice Principal, Junior School
Craig Dunn, Vice Principal, Senior School
Liz Doran, Head, Academic Studies (Primary Division)
Christine Ferris, Head, Academic Studies (Senior Division)
Katie Horton, Head, Academic Studies (Junior Division)
Jane Minty, Head, School Life
Sally Swan, Head, Community Service
Joyce Walker-Steed, Registrar
jwalker-steed@turnbull.ca

Ottawa: Westboro Academy Académie Westboro
200 Brewer Way, Ottawa, ON K1S 5R2, Canada
Tel: 613-737-9543
Westboro@WestboroAcademy.com
www.westboroacademy.com

Grades: Junior Kindergarten - 8 *Note:* Westboro Academy is a coeducational school, which offers an enriched bilingual education.
Marcel Papineau, Principal

Owen Sound: Riverforest Montessori School
1595 - 3rd Ave. West, Owen Sound, ON N4K 4R2, Canada
Tel: 519-371-2313; *Fax:* 519-371-1178
riverforestmontessori@hotmail.com
www.riverforestmontessori.com

Grades: Preschool - 6 *Note:* The Casa program is offered for children from age 2.5 to 6.

Owen Sound: Timothy Christian School (TCS)
1735 - 4th Ave. West, Owen Sound, ON N4K 4X7, Canada
Tel: 519-371-9151; *Fax:* 519-371-8607
timothy@timothycs.org
www.timothycs.org

Grades: Junior Kindergarten - 8
Matthew Bittel, Principal
Kendra VanSchepen, Bookkeeper

Pawitik: Baibombeh Anishinabe School
Whitefish Bay First Nation
General Delivery, Pawitik, ON P0X 1L0, Canada
Tel: 807-226-5698; *Fax:* 807-226-1089
bbbschool@hotmail.com; bbbschool@kmts.ca
www.kmts.ca/~baibombe
Grades: Junior Kindergarten - 12 *Note:* Baibombeh Anishinabe School is a band operated Ojibway school.

Peterborough: Grace Christian Academy
575 Centreline, Peterborough, ON K9J 7Y4, Canada
Tel: 705-745-4400; *Fax:* 705-745-5427
Grades: K./Elem. *Enrollment:* 92
Kim T. Bolton

Peterborough: Rhema Christian School
29 County Rd. 4, Peterborough, ON K9L 1B8, Canada
Tel: 705-743-1400; *Fax:* 705-743-1415
office@rhema.ca
www.rhema.ca
Grades: Junior Kindergarten - 8 *Note:* Rhema Christian School is a day school which offers a Christ-centered education.
Joel Slofstra, Principal
Joanne Brethour, Business Administrator
Rena Ridley, Office Administrator

Pickering: Blaisdale Montessori School
415 Toynevale Rd., Pickering, ON L1W 2G9, Canada
Tel: 905-509-5005; *Fax:* 905-509-1959
info@blaisdale.com
www.blaisdale.com
Grades: Toddler/Casa/Elementary/Renaissance *Note:* Blaisdale Montessori School offers programs for ages 12 months to 14 years, including pre-toddler.
Heather Wilson, Principal & Administrator, 905-509-5005, ext. 107
hwilson@blaisdale.com

Campuses

Bowmanville Campus
80 Rhonda Blvd., Bowmanville, ON L1C 3Y9
Tel: 905-697-3064
www.blaisdale.com/bowmanville.html

Milner Campus
231 Milner Ave., Toronto, ON M1S 5E3
Tel: 416-289-2273
www.blaisdale.com/milner-scarb.html

Oshawa Campus
1037 Simcoe St. North, Oshawa, ON L1G 4W3
Tel: 905-721-1933
www.blaisdale.com/oshawa-ajax.html
Other Information: Alternate Phone: 416-607-6297

Rotherglen Campus
403 Kingston Rd., Ajax, ON L1S 6L7
Tel: 905-683-5005
www.blaisdale.com/rotherglen-ajax.html

Village Campus
56 Old Kingston Rd., Ajax, ON L1T 2Z7
Tel: 905-427-5006
www.blaisdale.com/viillage-ajax.html

Westney Campus
20 O'Brien Ct., Ajax, ON L1S 7J8
Tel: 905-426-5665
www.blaisdale.com/westney-ajax.html

Whitby Campus
200 Byron St. South, Ajax, ON L1N 4P6
Tel: 905-665-1516
www.blaisdale.com/whitby-whitby.html

Pickering: Montessori Learning Centre of Pickering (MLCP)
401 Kingston Rd., Pickering, ON L1V 1A3, Canada
Tel: 905-509-1722; *Fax:* 905-509-8283
info@montessorilearningcentre.com
www.mlcp.ca
Grades: Preschool / Elementary *Enrollment:* 240 *Note:* Montessori Learning Centre of Pickering provides the following programs: infants, pre-Casa, Casa, & elementary.

Picton: Sonrise Christian Academy
P.O. Box 845
58 Johnson St., Picton, ON K0K 2T0, Canada
Tel: 613-476-7883; *Fax:* 613-476-4202
office@sonrisechristianacademy.com
www.sonrisechristianacademy.com
Grades: Elem. *Enrollment:* 62
Julie Scrivens, Principal

Port Hope: Trinity College School (TCS)
55 Deblaquire St. North, Port Hope, ON L1A 4K7, Canada
Tel: 905-885-3217; *Fax:* 905-885-9690
info@tcs.on.ca; communications@tcs.on.ca;
admissions@tcs.on.ca
www.tcs.on.ca
Grades: 5 - 12 *Enrollment:* 600 *Note:* The school is a coeducational boarding / day school. The senior school has approximately 500 students. Over 100 students attend the junior school.
Stuart K.C. Grainger, Headmaster
Jeffrey Prince, Secretary

Prince Albert: Scugog Christian School
P.O. Box 3308
14480 Old Simcoe Rd., Prince Albert, ON L9L 1C3, Canada
Tel: 905-985-3741; *Fax:* 905-985-7153
scugogchristianschool@powergate.ca
www.scugogchristianschool.com
Grades: K.-8 *Enrollment:* 53
Grace van Niejenhuis, Principal

Richmond Hill: Beit Rayim Hebrew School
Ross Doan Public School
101 Weldrick Rd. West, Richmond Hill, ON L4C 3T9
Tel: 905-889-0276; *Fax:* 905-889-4413
school@beitrayim.org
www.beitrayim.org
Note: Beit Rayim Hebrew School is an egalitarian Conservative Jewish school. Classes meet two days a week: Sunday mornings & Thursday afternoons. The school will soon be moving to the Joseph & Wolf Lebovic Jewish Community Campus.
Kevin Knopman, Principal
principalkevin@beitrayim.org
Steffi Goodfield, Director & Team Leader
Grace Tetelbaun, School Administrator

Richmond Hill: Century Montessori School
Regent Campus
71 Regent St., Richmond Hill, ON L4C 9Y1, Canada
Tel: 905-737-9494; *Fax:* 905-737-1014
Info@CenturyMontessori.com
www.centurymontessori.com
Grades: Casa / PresSchool - 8 *Note:* Century Montessori School offers education for children from age 2.5 to grade 8.

Richmond Hill: Chabad Romano Sunday Hebrew School
Silver Pines Public School
112 Stave Cres., Richmond Hill, ON L4C 9J2
Tel: 905-303-1880; *Fax:* 905-303-1008
www.chabadrc.org
Rabbi Shlomo Vorovitch, Director, Education
sv@chabadrc.org

Richmond Hill: Discovery Academy
10030 Yonge St., Richmond Hill, ON L4C 1T8
Tel: 416-302-4085; *Fax:* 888-778-0492
diacademyonline@gmail.com
www.diacademy.ca
Other Information: Dayschool Phone: 647-727-1737
Grades: 6-12
Marina Blumin, Ph.D., Headmistress

Richmond Hill: Richland Academy
11570 Yonge St., Richmond Hill, ON L4E 3N7
Tel: 905-224-5600; *Fax:* 905-224-4080
info@richlandacademy.ca
www.richlandacademy.ca
Grades: Pre.-6 *Enrollment:* 115
Marlina Oliveira, Head of School
moliveira@richlandacademy.ca

Richmond Hill: Richmond Hill Montessori & Elementary School (RHMS)
Hillsview Campus
118 Hillsview Dr., Richmond Hill, ON L4C 1T2, Canada
Tel: 905-508-2228; *Fax:* 905-508-2229
reception@rhms.org
www.rhms.org
Grades: Preschool - 8 *Note:* The school's preschool program is Montessori based. The junior program includes three & four year old children. The senior program is designed for children who are four & five year olds.
Walter Ribeiro, Director
w.ribeiro@rhms.org
Janet Darbey, Principal, Hillsview Campus
jdarbey@rhms.org
Anita Gonzalez, Principal, 16th Avenue Campus
agonzalez@rhms.org
Dino D'Amato, Vice Principal, Hillsview Campus
ddamato@rhms.org
Rose Chitiz, Administrator
rchitiz@rhms.org
Catherine Evans, Administrator
cevans@rhms.org
Sarah Salvatore, Administrator
ssalvatore@rhms.org
Claude Rodrigues, Contact, Purchasing & Finance
crodrigues@rhms.org

Richmond Hill: Toronto Montessori Schools (TMS)
Also known as: TMS School
8569 Bayview Ave., Richmond Hill, ON L4B 3M7
Tel: 905-889-6882; *Fax:* 905-886-6516
admissions@tmsschool.ca; advancement@tmsschool.ca
www.tmsschool.ca
Other Information: tmshr@tmsschool.ca (E-mail, Human Resources)
Grades: Pre.-12 *Enrollment:* 750

Campuses

Elgin Mills Campus
500 Elgin Mills Rd. East, Richmond Hill, ON L4C 5G1
Tel: 905-889-6882; *Fax:* 905-886-6516

Rosseau: Rosseau Lake College (RLC)
1967 Bright St., Rosseau, ON P0C 1J0, Canada
Tel: 705-732-4351; *Fax:* 705-732-6319
Toll-Free: 800-265-0569
info@rlc.on.ca; advancement@rlc.on.ca; admissions@rlc.on.ca
www.rosseaulakecollege.com
Enrollment: 150 *Note:* Rosseau Lake College is a coeducational day & boarding school. The average class size is twelve.
Graham Hookey, Head of School

Sandy Lake: Thomas Fiddler Memorial Elementary School
P.O. Box 8
Sandy Lake, ON P0V 1V0, Canada
Tel: 807-744-4491; *Fax:* 807-774-1324
www.sandylake.firstnation.ca
Grades: Kindergarten - 6; Special Ed. *Enrollment:* 390 *Number of Employees:* 53 *Note:* The Thomas Fiddler Memorial Elementary School is part of the Sandy Lake Board of Education. The elementary school educates members of Sandy Lake First Nation. From kindergarten to grade four, Thomas Fiddler Memorial Elementary School provides a native immersion program.
Rose Yesno, Principal
roseyesno@hotmail.com
Doreen Fiddler, Social Counsellor
Andrew Mamakeesic, Social Counsellor

Sandy Lake: Thomas Fiddler Memorial High School
P.O. Box 8
Sandy Lake, ON P0V 1V0
Tel: 807-774-1229; *Fax:* 807-774-1228
www.sandylake.firstnation.ca
Grades: 7 - 10 *Enrollment:* 124 *Note:* The activities of Thomas Fiddler Memorial High School are overseen by the Sandy Lake Board of Education. The secondary school serves students of the Sandy Lake First Nation.

Sarnia: Sarnia Christian School
1273 Exmouth St., Sarnia, ON N7S 1W9, Canada
Tel: 519-383-7750; *Fax:* 519-383-6304
info@sarniachristian.com
www.sarniachristian.com
Grades: K.-8 *Enrollment:* 164
Len Smit, Principal
len.smit@sarniachristian.com

Sarnia: Temple Christian Academy
1410 Quinn Dr., Sarnia, ON N7T 7H4, Canada
Tel: 519-542-9563; *Fax:* 519-542-9889
office@templechristianacademy.ca
www.templechristianacademy.ca
Grades: Jr. K.-8 *Enrollment:* 84
P. Wes Harding, Principal

Scarborough: Islamic Foundation School
441 Nugget Ave., Scarborough, ON M1V 5E1, Canada
Tel: 416-321-0909; *Fax:* 416-321-1995
info@islamicfoundation.ca
www.islamicfoundation.ca
Number of Schools: 1 academic school; 4 religious schools
Grades: Elem. *Enrollment:* 327
Yahya Qurechi, Principal, 416-754-7752, ext. 242
Yousuf Siddiqui, Vice Principal, 416-754-7752, ext. 241

Schools
Full-Time Hifz School
441 Nugget Ave., Scarborough, ON M1V 5E1, Canada
Tel: 416-321-0909; *Fax:* 416-321-1995
shahtoronto@gmail.com
www.islamicfoundation.ca
Grades: Religious Education

Evening Madressah
441 Nugget Ave., Scarborough, ON M1V 5E1, Canada
Tel: 416-321-0909; *Fax:* 416-321-1995
yingar@islamicfoundation.ca
www.islamicfoundation.ca
Grades: Religious Education
Qani Yunus Ingar, Principal, 416-321-0909, ext. 226

Sunday School
Islamic Foundation
441 Nugget Ave., Scarborough, ON M1V 5E1, Canada
Tel: 416-321-0909; *Fax:* 416-321-1995
yingar@islamicfoundation.ca
www.islamicfoundation.ca
Grades: Religious Education

Summer Hifz & Summer School
Islamic Foundation
441 Nugget Ave., Scarborough, ON M1V 5E1, Canada
Tel: 416-321-0909; *Fax:* 416-321-1995
ukhan@islamicfoundation.ca
www.islamicfoundation.ca
Grades: Religious Education
Uzma Khan, Administrative Assistant, 416-321-3776, ext. 231
ukhan@islamicfoundation.ca

Scarborough: Madinatul-Uloom Academy - Primary School & Boys Campus
670 Progress Ave, Scarborough, ON M1H 3A4, Canada
Tel: 416-332-9428; *Fax:* 416-332-0470
info@mua.ca
www.mua.ca
Grades: Elem.-Sec.; Boys *Enrollment:* 358
Nilofar Asif, Principal

Schools
Madinatul-Uloom - Girls Campus
700 Progress Ave., Scarborough, ON M1H 2Z7
Tel: 416-332-1810; *Fax:* 416-332-0470
Grades: Elem.; Girls

Scarborough: Salaheddin Islamic School
741 Kennedy Rd., Scarborough, ON M1K 2C6, Canada
Tel: 416-264-9495
Grades: Elem. *Enrollment:* 185
Laila Maarouf

Scarborough: Whitefield Christian Schools
5808 Finch Ave. East, Scarborough, ON M1B 4Y6
Tel: 416-297-1212; *Fax:* 416-291-4632
wcs@bellnet.ca
whitefieldchristianschools.ca
Grades: Elem.

Sebringville: Stratford District Christian School
130 Huron Rd., RR#1, Sebringville, ON N0K 1X0, Canada
Tel: 519-393-5675; *Fax:* 519-393-6306
Grades: K./Elem. *Enrollment:* 90
Edward J. Petrusma

Simcoe: Bethel Baptist Christian School
P.O. Box 752
4059 Hwy. #3 East, Simcoe, ON N3Y 4T2, Canada
Tel: 519-426-8421; *Fax:* 519-426-8426
www.bethelsimcoe.addr.com/school.html
Grades: Junior Kindergarten - 12
Dr. Michael Glowacki, Principal

Sioux Lookout: New Life Christian Academy
P.O. Box 697
28 - 1st Ave., Sioux Lookout, ON P8T 1B1, Canada
Tel: 807-737-0020; *Fax:* 807-737-4281

Sioux Lookout: Pelican Falls First Nation High School
P.O. Box 4127
Sioux Lookout, ON P8T 1J9, Canada
Tel: 807-737-1110; *Fax:* 807-737-1449
Toll-Free: 1-800-378-911
www.nnec.on.ca/pffnhs/
Grades: Sec. *Enrollment:* 143
Desta Buswa, Principal

Sioux Lookout: Wahsa Distance Education Centre
P.O. Box 1118
74 Front St., Sioux Lookout, ON P8T 1B7, Canada
Tel: 807-737-1488; *Fax:* 807-737-1732
Grades: 9 - 12 *Enrollment:* 950 *Note:* The Wahsa Distance Education Centre allows students in northern Ontario communities across the Sioux Lookout District to complete their secondary school education at home. Courses & services are developed in consultation with First Nation communities. The Centre is operated by the Northern Nishnawbe Education Council.
Norma Kejick

Smithville: Covenant Christian School
6470 Regional Rd. #14, Smithville, ON L0R 2A0, Canada
Tel: 905-957-7796; *Fax:* 905-957-7794
www.nace.ca
Grades: Elem. *Enrollment:* 226 *Note:* The Niagara Ass'n for Christian Education (NACE).
Sid Bakker, Principal
sbakker@nace.ca

Smithville: John Calvin Private School
P.O. Box 280
320 Station St., Smithville, ON L0R 2A0, Canada
Tel: 905-957-2341; *Fax:* 905-957-2342
Grades: K./Elem.
Frank C. Ludwig, Principal

Smithville: Smithville Christian High School
P.O. Box 40
6488 Smithville Rd., Smithville, ON L0R 2A0, Canada
Tel: 905-957-3255; *Fax:* 905-957-3431
office@smithvillechristian.ca
www.smithvillechristian.ca
www.facebook.com/smithvillechristian
twitter.com/smthvllechrstn
www.smithvillechristian.blogspot.com
www.youtube.com/smithCHSchool
Grades: Sec. *Enrollment:* 224
Ted Harris, Administrator
Marlene Bergsma, Contact

St Catharines: Beacon Christian School
300 Scott St., St Catharines, ON L2N 1J3
Tel: 905-937-7411
mail@beaconchristian.org
www.beaconchristian.org
www.facebook.com/pages/Beacon-Christian-School/139816026123900
twitter.com/BeaconChristian
Grades: JK-8 *Note:* Beacon Christian School is an independent, interdenominational school.
Ralph Pot, Principal
rpot@beaconchristian.org

St Catharines: Beyond Montessori School
St. George's Anglican Church
P.O. Box 647
83 Church St., St Catharines, ON L0S 1E0
Tel: 905-937-0700
info@beyondmontessori.com
www.beyondmontessori.com
www.facebook.com/208151271840
twitter.com/BMontessoriStC
beyondmontessori.wordpress.com
Grades: Pre.-3 *Enrollment:* 50
Natasha Secord, Head of School

St Catharines: Grey Gables School
1 Dexter St., St Catharines, ON L2S 2L4, Canada
Tel: 905-685-4577; *Fax:* 905-685-5102
Grades: K./Elem./Sec. *Enrollment:* 176
Kathleen Miller

St Catharines: Ridley College
P.O. Box 3013
2 Ridley Rd., St Catharines, ON L2R 7C3, Canada
Tel: 905-684-1889; *Fax:* 905-684-8875
admission@ridleycollege.com
www.ridley.on.ca
www.facebook.com/pages/Ridley-College/145690058823243
twitter.com/Ridley_College
www.youtube.com/RidleyCollege1889
Enrollment: 607 *Note:* Ridley College is a university preparatory school, which features both a lower school & an uppper school. Boarding is available. Over 30% of students are international students.
George C. Hendrie, President, Board Chair
Ed Kidd, Headmaster
ed_kidd@ridleycollege.com
Stephen Clarke, Deputy Headmaster, 905-684-1889, ext. 2205
stephen_clarke@ridleycollege.com
Jim Parke, Director, Finance & Operations
jim_parke@ridleycollege.com
Andrew T. Weller, Dean of Admissions, 905-684-1889, ext. 2298
andrew_t_weller@ridleycollege.com
Margaret Lech, Assistant Headmaster, Student Affairs
margaret_lech@ridleycollege.com
James Milligan, Assistant Head, Lower School
jim_milligan@ridleycollege.com

St Catharines: St Catharines Montessori School
238 Geneva St., St Catharines, ON L2R 4P8, Canada
Tel: 905-684-6110
stcathmontessori@hotmail.com
Grades: K./Elem.
Susan Bowslaugh

St Catharines: Wheatley School of Montessori Education Inc.
497 Scott St., St Catharines, ON L2M 3X3, Canada
Tel: 905-641-3012; *Fax:* 905-641-1443
mail@wheatleyschool.com
www.wheatleyschool.com
Grades: Preschool - 8 *Note:* The coeducational, non-denominational school provides Montessori programs for children from preschool to grade four. The Wheatley School's preschool program accepts children as young as two years of age. For upper elementary students in grades five to eight, a traditional, enriched program is offered.
Eda Varalli, Principal

St Thomas: Faith Christian Academy
345 Fairview Ave., St Thomas, ON N5R 6M7
Tel: 519-633-0943; *Fax:* 519-633-6848
www.faithchristianacademy.ca
Grades: JK-8
Barry E. Pearce, Principal
bpearce@path2faith.com

St Thomas: St. Thomas Community School
77 Fairview Ave., St Thomas, ON N5R 4X7, Canada
Tel: 519-633-0690; *Fax:* 519-633-0019
info@stthomaschristian.org
www.stthomaschristian.org
Grades: Jr. K.-8 *Enrollment:* 789
John Lunshof

Stittsville: Ottawa Waldorf School
1 Goulbourn St., Stittsville, ON K2S 1N9, Canada
Tel: 613-836-1547; *Fax:* 613-831-4447
ottawawaldorf@bellnet.ca
www.waldorf.cyberus.ca
Grades: K./Elem. *Enrollment:* 91
Karen Ann McKinna

Stouffville: The Progressive Montessori Academy
6411 Main St., Stouffville, ON L4A 1G4
Tel: 416-220-8070
www.thepma.ca
Grades: Pre.-6 *Enrollment:* 40
Lubna Jaffer, Principal
ljaffer@thepma.ca

Stouffville: Stouffville Christian School
12485 Tenth Line, Stouffville, ON L4A 7X3, Canada
Tel: 905-640-3297; *Fax:* 905-640-7845
stouffville_cs@bellnet.ca
www.stouffvillechristianschool.org
Grades: Jr. K.-8 *Enrollment:* 70
Jake Vriend, Principal

Strathroy: Strathroy Community Christian School
7880 Walkers Dr., RR#2, Strathroy, ON N7G 3H4, Canada
Tel: 519-245-1934; *Fax:* 519-245-4424
sccs@sympatico.ca
www.sccs.ca
Grades: Jr. K.-8 *Enrollment:* 200
Henry Wiersema

Thornhill: Associated Hebrew Schools of Toronto — The Kamin Education Centre
300 Atkinson Ave., Thornhill, ON L4J 8A2, Canada
Tel: 905-889-3998; *Fax:* 905-889-5183
www.associatedhebrewschools.com
Grades: K./Elem. *Enrollment:* 1415 *Note:* Bet Hayeled: Eynat Katz, Vice Principal; Brenda Dzalov, Preschool Coordinator.
Sandy Rabinowitz, Principal
srabinowitz@ahschools.com

Thornhill: Central Montessori Schools (CMS)
72 Steels Ave. West, Thornhill, ON L4J 1A1, Canada
Tel: 416-889-0012; *Fax:* 905-889-0422
www.cmschool.net
Grades: Toddlers - 8 *Enrollment:* 900 *Note:* Central Montessori Schools are co-educational, non-denominational schools. The

early childhood education program is designed for children from 18 months to 2.5 years.
Deborah Sharp, Principal

Campuses
Florence Campus
157 Florence Ave., Toronto, ON M2N 1G5
Tel: 416-222-5097; *Fax:* 416-222-0584

Sheppard Campus
200 Sheppard Ave. East, Toronto, ON M2N 3A9
Tel: 416-222-5940; *Fax:* 416-222-2546

Willowdale Campus
157 Willowdale Ave., Toronto, ON M2N 4Y3
Tel: 416-250-1022; *Fax:* 416-250-5191

York Mills Campus
18 Coldwater Rd., Toronto, ON M2N 1Y7
Tel: 416-510-1200; *Fax:* 416-510-1230

Thornhill: Chabad of Markham Hebrew School
83 Green Lane, Thornhill, ON L3T 6K6
Tel: 905-886-0420; *Fax:* 905-886-0421
www.chabadmarkham.org
www.facebook.com/pages/Chabad-of-Markham/267334146633060
Grades: K.-9
Rabbi M. Gitlin, Hebrew School & Youth Director
rabbig@on.aibn.com

Thornhill: Everest Academy
130 Racco Pkwy., Thornhill, ON L4J 8X9
Tel: 905-881-3335; *Fax:* 905-756-1111
info@everestacademies.com;
admissions@everestacademies.com
www.everestacademies.com
Grades: 1-12
Tim Sim, Principal

Thornhill: Jewish Youth Network Hebrew School (JYN)
#5, 8700 Bathurst St., Thornhill, ON L4J 9J8
Tel: 905-889-7582
www.jewishyouth.ca
www.facebook.com/JewishYouth
Grades: 1-7
Chani Nachlas, Director

Thornhill: Joe Dwek Ohr HaEmet Sephardic School
7026 Bathurst St., Thornhill, ON L4J 8K3
Tel: 905-669-7653; *Fax:* 905-669-5138
www.orhaemet.com
Note: Orthodox & Sephardic Jewish education for children aged 4 & 5.
Sarah Wasserman, Principal
s.wasserman@ohrhaemet.com

Thornhill: The Leo Baeck Day School North Campus
36 Atkinson Ave., Thornhill, ON L4J 8C9
Tel: 905-709-3636; *Fax:* 905-709-1999
info@leobaeck.ca
www.leobaeck.ca
www.facebook.com/leobaeckdayschool
twitter.com/LeoBaeckNorth
Grades: Preschool - 8 *Note:* The Leo Baeck Day School is a Reform Jewish day school. Students experience Judaism from a Reform perspective.
Laurie Davis, President
board@leobaeck.ca
Eric Petersiel, RJE, Head of School
epetersiel@leobaeck.ca
Robyn Buchmam, Director, Admission
rbuchman@leobaeck.ca
Yvette Burke, B.A., B.Ed., M.Ed., Principal
yburke@leobaeck.ca

Campuses
South Campus
1950 Bathurst St., Toronto, ON M5P 3K9
Tel: 416-787-9899; *Fax:* 416-787-9893
twitter.com/LeoBaeckSouth
Ron Mintz, Prinicpal
rmintz@leobaeck.ca

Thornhill: Ner Israel Yeshiva College
250 Bathurst Glen Dr., Thornhill, ON L4J 8A7, Canada
Tel: 905-731-1224; *Fax:* 905-731-2104
Note: The college provides undergraduate & graduate religious degrees.

Thornhill: Netivot HaTorah Day School
18 Atkinson Ave., Thornhill, ON L4J 8C8, Canada
Tel: 905-771-1234; *Fax:* 905-771-1807
webregistration@netivothatorah.com
www.netivot.com
Grades: Elementary *Enrollment:* 600 *Note:* Netivot HaTorah is an orthodox Jewish school. Its program includes Judaic & general studies.
Dr. Reuven Stern, Head of School
rstern@netivothatorah.com
Rabbi Elliott Diamond, Vice-Principal, Judaic Studies
ediamond@netivothatorah.com
Robyn Shiner, Vice-Principal, General Studies
rshiner@netivothatorah.com
Eileen Goldstein, Director, ECE Department
egoldstein@netivothatorah.com
Alan Steinfeld, Director, Development
asteinfeld@netivothatorah.com
Carol Weir, Director, Podolski NESS Department
cweir@netivothatorah.com

Thornhill: Northwood Academy Montessori Plus Centre St. Campus
86 Centre St., Thornhill, ON L4J 1E9
Tel: 416-492-7812; *Fax:* 416-492-7812
info@northwoodmontessori.ca
www.northwoodmontessori.ca
Grades: Pre.-K. *Enrollment:* 50
Heather Spear, Principal

Campuses
Finch Campus
Tri-Congregational Church
1080 Finch Ave. East, Toronto, ON M2J 2X2
Tel: 416-492-7812; *Fax:* 905-881-8394

Gallanough Campus
Gallanough Resource Centre
1 Brooke St., Thornhill, ON L4J 2K2
Tel: 416-492-7812; *Fax:* 416-492-7812

Madawaska Campus
Newton Baptist Church
53 Madawaska Ave., Toronto, ON M2M 2R2
Tel: 416-492-7812; *Fax:* 416-492-7812

Markham Campus
Markham Community Church
9329 McCowan Rd., Markham, ON L3P 3J3
Tel: 416-492-7812; *Fax:* 416-492-7812

St. Agnes Campus
St. Agnes School
280 Otonabee Ave., Toronto, ON M2M 2T2
Tel: 416-492-7812; *Fax:* 416-492-7812

Thornhill: Temple Har Zion Religious School
7360 Bayview Ave., Thornhill, ON L3T 2R7
Tel: 905-889-2252; *Fax:* 905-889-2258
information@templeharzion.com
www.templeharzion.com/education.html
www.facebook.com/templeharzion
twitter.com/templeharzion
www.youtube.com/user/TempleHarZion
Grades: K.-10
Susan Sermer, Director, Education
susansermer@templeharzion.com

Thornhill: Temple Kol Ami Religious School
36 Atkinson Ave., Thornhill, ON L4J 8C9
Tel: 416-578-0809; *Fax:* 905-695-9232
templekolami.ca
Grades: Elem.
Judy Silver, Director, Education
educator@templekolami.ca
Brenda Gottlieb, Administrator
brenda@templekolami.ca

Thornhill: Torah 4 Teens
#5, 8700 Bathurst St., Thornhill, ON L4J 9J8
Tel: 905-889-7582; *Fax:* 416-661-5477
www.jewishyouth.ca
Note: Torah 4 Teens offers secondary school students approved high school & pre-university courses about the Torah.

Thornhill: Torah High School - Toronto
7000 Bathurst St., Thornhill, ON L4J 7L1
Tel: 905-761-6279; *Fax:* 905-761-9115
toronto.torahhigh.org
www.facebook.com/TorahHigh
twitter.com/TorahHigh
www.youtube.com/ncsytube
Grades: 8-12 *Note:* Torah High offers courses in Religious Studies, Hebrew Language, Philosophy, Political Science, Nutrition, Arts & Interdisciplinary Studies for students attending public or private secondary schools. The school has seven locations in Toronto.

Thornhill: Toronto Waldorf School (TWS)
9100 Bathurst St., Thornhill, ON L4J 8C7, Canada
Tel: 905-881-1611; *Fax:* 905-881-6710
www.torontowaldorfschool.com
Grades: Preschool - Secondary
Bill Harlow, Chair
Michèle Andrews, Administrative Director
Katharina Dannenberg, High School Administrator
Natalie Semenov, Financial Administrator
Darlene Gregoire, Manager, Business
Paul Sheardown, Manager, Facilities
Aileen Stewart, Coordinator, Admissions

Thorold: Grand River Academy of Christian Education
29 Claremont St., Thorold, ON L2V 1R4, Canada
Tel: 905-227-7507
Grades: Elem./Sec. *Enrollment:* 125
Terrence Edwards

Thunder Bay: Thunder Bay Christian School (TBCS)
37 Cooper Rd., Thunder Bay, ON P7C 4V1, Canada
Tel: 807-939-1209; *Fax:* 807-939-2843
tbcs@tbaytel.net
www.tbaychristianschool.ca
Grades: Junior Kindergarten - 10 *Enrollment:* 165 *Note:* Thunder Bay Christian School is an interdenominational school operated by parents.
Bea Hayen, Principal

Toronto: The Abelard School
203 College St., Toronto, ON M5T 1P9
Tel: 416-944-0661; *Fax:* 416-944-8902
info@abelardschool.org
www.abelardschool.org
Grades: 9-12 *Enrollment:* 55
Mark Young, Principal

Toronto: Academy c60
1650 Ave. Rd, 2nd Fl., Toronto, ON M5M 2Y1
Tel: 647-352-6060; *Fax:* 647-342-3563
learn@academyc60.com
www.academyc60.com
Grades: 9-12
Leslie Zulauf, Founder & Executive Director
David Beger, Co-Founder & Principal

Toronto: Adath Israel Religious School
37 Southbourne Ave., Toronto, ON M3H 1A4
Tel: 416-635-5340; *Fax:* 416-635-1629
info@adathisrael.com
www.adathisrael.com
Grades: Pre.-Sec.; Adult Ed.
Rabbi Steven Saltzman, Senior Rabbi, 416-635-5340, ext. 302
rabbi@adathisrael.com
Bernie Rabinovitch, Executive Director, 416-635-5340, ext. 317
bernie@adathisrael.com
Cantor A. Eliezer Kirshblum, M.Sc., Educational Director
Linda Schwartz, School Administrator, 416-635-5354
linda@adathisrael.com
Wendy Steinberg-Himmel, Director, Preschool Program
wendy@adathisrael.com

Toronto: AGBU Zaroukian School
930 Progress Ave., Toronto, ON M1G 3T5, Canada
Tel: 416-439-3900; *Fax:* 416-431-2510
school.agbutoronto.ca
Grades: Pre.-5 *Enrollment:* 66
Orysia Perun, Principal

Toronto: Ahavat Yisrael Hebrew School
54 Glen Park Ave., Toronto, ON M6B 2C2
Tel: 416-781-8088
contact@ahavatyisrael.ca
www.ahavatyisraelhebrewschool.com
Grades: JK-7 *Note:* Sunday morning classes for junior kindergarten-grade 7 are held in Ventura Park Middle School, Stephen Lewis Secondary School, & Bais Yaakov Elementary School, 10:00 am-12:30 pm. Tuesday evening classes for grades 1-6 are held in Stephen Lewis Secondary School, 6:00-7:30 pm.
Leslie Shapiro, Principal & Director, Education

Toronto: Alathena International Academy
1065 McNicoll Ave., Toronto, ON M1W 3W6
Tel: 416-756-3338
alathena.com
Grades: 9-12
Simon Huynh, Director

Campuses
Richmond Hill Campus
#201, 650 Hwy. 7, Richmond Hill, ON L4B 1G7
Tel: 905-763-8788

Toronto: ARS Armenian Private School
45 Hallcrown Pl., Toronto, ON M2J 4Y4, Canada
Tel: 416-491-2675; *Fax:* 416-491-8559
www.arsdayschool.ca
Grades: K.-12 *Enrollment:* 363
Armen Martirossian, Principal

Toronto: Associated Hebrew Schools of Toronto
Hurwich Education Centre
252 Finch Ave. West, Toronto, ON M2R 1M9, Canada
Tel: 416-494-7666; *Fax:* 416-494-2925
www.associatedhebrewschools.com
Grades: K.-8 *Enrollment:* 1700 *Note:* A community day school with a focus on Torah-values & high academic standards. Locations in Toronto & Thornhill.
Dr. Mark Smiley, Director, Education
msmiley@ahschools.com

Toronto: Bais Chaya Mushka Preschool
4375 Chesswood Dr., Toronto, ON M3J 2C2
Tel: 416-398-9532; *Fax:* 416-398-3903
Grades: Pre./Elem. *Note:* Orthodox Jewish education for girls.
Rabbi Nochum Sosover, Director

Toronto: Bais Yaakov Elementary School
15 Saranac Blvd., Toronto, ON M6A 2G4, Canada
Tel: 416-256-4436; *Fax:* 416-783-4688
Grades: Pre-school - 8 *Enrollment:* 400 *Note:* Bais Yaakov Elementary School is a school for girls.
Magda Simon, Principal, 416-783-6181
Devorah Drebin, Junior High Principal, 416-783-6181

Toronto: Bannockburn School
12 Bannockburn Ave., Toronto, ON M5M 2M8, Canada
Tel: 416-789-7855; *Fax:* 416-789-7963
bannockburn@bannockburn.ca
www.bannockburn.ca
Grades: Toddler / Preschool / Elementary *Note:* Bannockburn School offers Montessori education.
Adalove Gorrie, Principal, Elementary Program, 416-789-7855, ext. 303
agorrie@bannockburn.ca
Terry Gorrie, Director, Business, 416-789-7855, ext. 302
tgorrie@bannockburn.ca

Toronto: Bayview Glen
275 Duncan Mill Rd., Toronto, ON M3B 3H9, Canada
Tel: 416-443-1030; *Fax:* 416-443-1032
jmaxwell@bayviewglen.ca
www.bvg.on.ca
Grades: Preschool - 12 *Enrollment:* 1011 *Note:* Preschool education at Bayview Glen starts at age 2. The school includes lower school, prep school, & upper school.
Eileen Daunt, Head
Vince Haines, Director, Finance
vhaines@bayviewglen.ca
Dara Kahane, Director, Summer Camp
darak@bayviewglen.ca
Judy Maxwell, Director, Admissions
jmaxwell@bayviewglen.ca

Toronto: Beth Jacob High School
410 Lawrence Ave. West, Toronto, ON M5M 1C2, Canada
Tel: 416-787-4949; *Fax:* 416-787-0453
Grades: Secondary *Note:* Beth Jacob High School is a school for Orthodox Jewish girls.

Toronto: Beth Radom Jumpin' for Judaism
Also known as: J4J
Beth Radom Congregation
18 Reiner Rd., Toronto, ON M3H 2K9
Tel: 416-636-3451; *Fax:* 416-636-1042
info@bethradomj4j.com
www.bethradomj4j.com
Note: Programs at J4J include small group turorials, classroom activities, & family education. Classes also meet at Toronto Waldorf School; please see website for more detials.

Toronto: Beth Sholom Hebrew School
1445 Eglinton Ave. West, Toronto, ON M6C 2E6
Tel: 416-783-6103; *Fax:* 416-783-9923
www.bethsholom.net/hebrew-school.htm
Grades: JK-7
Karen L. Goodis, Principal, 416-783-6103, ext. 225
karen@bethsholom.net

Toronto: Beth Torah Hebrews' Cool
47 Glenbrook Ave., Toronto, ON M6B 2L7
Tel: 416-782-4495; *Fax:* 416-782-4496
hebrewschool@bethtorah.ca
www.bethtorah.ca
Grades: 1-6 *Note:* A one-day-a-week program teaching children about the Torah, Israel, Hebrew & Jewish tradition.

Toronto: Beth Tzedec Congregational School
1700 Bathurst St., Toronto, ON M5P 3K3
Tel: 416-781-3514; *Fax:* 416-781-0150
www.beth-tzedec.org
Grades: JK-7 *Note:* Classes in Conservative Judaism are held on Sunday mornings & Wednesday evenings. For more information please see the website, or contact the school office.
Ron Polster, Contact, School Office
rpolster@beth-tzedec.org

Toronto: Bialik Hebrew Day School
2760 Bathurst St., Toronto, ON M6B 3A1, Canada
Tel: 416-783-3346; *Fax:* 416-785-8287
www.bialik.ca
Grades: Junior kindergarten - 8 *Enrollment:* 800
Sonia Shron, Executive Director
sshron@bialik.ca
Shana Harris, Head
sharris@bialik.ca
Benjamin Cohen, Principal, General Studies
bcohen@bialik.ca
Anita Eckhaus, Vice Principal, Elementary Division
aeckhaus@bialik.ca
Amy Platt, Vice Principal, Primary
aplatt@bialik.ca
Beverley Young, Vice Principal, Senior Division
beverley_young@bialik.on.ca

Toronto: The Bishop Strachan School (BSS)
298 Lonsdale Rd., Toronto, ON M4V 1X2, Canada
Tel: 416-483-4325; *Fax:* 416-481-5632
strachan@bss.on.ca
www.bss.on.ca
Grades: Junior Kindergarten - 12 *Note:* The Bishop Strachan School educates girls.
Kate Berghuis, Chair, Board of Governors
Sarah Kavanagh, Chair, Board of Trustees
Deryn Lavell, Head of School
Catherine Hart, Director, Admissions
admissions@bss.on.ca
Rachel Yeager, Director, Marketing & Communications
ryeager@bss.on.ca ca

Toronto: Blyth Academy
146 Yorkville Ave., Toronto, ON M5R 1C2
Tel: 416-960-3552; *Fax:* 416-960-9506
Toll-Free: 866-960-3552
info@blytheducation.com; blythadmissions@blytheducation.com
www.blytheducation.com

Campuses
Barrie Campus
11 Victoria St., Barrie, ON L4N 6T3
Tel: 705-719-9595

Burlington Campus
952 Century Dr., Burlington, ON L7L 5P2
Tel: 905-637-0346
Alex MacKinnon, Principal

Lawrence Park Campus
3284 Yonge St., Toronto, ON M4N 3M7
Tel: 416-488-9301; *Fax:* 416-916-9060

Port Credit Campus
1470 Hurontario St., Mississauga, ON L5G 3G4
Tel: 905-990-2855; *Fax:* 905-990-3155

Thornhill Campus
300 John St., Toronto, ON L3T 5W4
Tel: 905-889-8081; *Fax:* 905-889-4797

Whitby Campus
209 Dundas St. East, Whitby, ON L1N 7H8
Tel: 905-666-3773;

Toronto: Bnei Akiva Schools
45 Canyon Ave., Toronto, ON M3H 3S4, Canada
Tel: 416-630-5434; *Fax:* 416-638-7905
www.bneiakivaschools.org
Grades: 9-12 *Enrollment:* 283 *Note:* Bnei Akiva Schools serves the Jewish community.
Jeff Shumacher, President
Frank Samuels, Principal, General Studies
Rabbi Scot A. Berman, Headmaster
Jay Shiel, Director, Operations
Jerry Solomon, MSW, Director, Development

Toronto: Bond Academy
1500 Birchmount Rd., Toronto, ON M1P 2G5
Tel: 416-266-8878; *Fax:* 416-266-3898
www.bondacademy.ca
Grades: K./Elem./Sec. *Enrollment:* 450
John Healey, Principal, Elementary
johnh@web.bondacademy.ca
Jeffrey Farber, Principal, Secondary
jfarber@web.bondacademy.ca

Toronto: Bond International College
1500 Birchmount Rd., Toronto, ON M1P 2G5, Canada
Tel: 416-266-8878; *Fax:* 416-266-3898
info@bondcollege.com
www.bondcollege.com
Grades: Secondary *Note:* Bond International College prepares international students for colleges & universities in Canada, the United States, the United Kingdom, & Australia.
Jeffrey Farber, Principal

Toronto: Branksome Hall
10 Elm Ave., Toronto, ON M4W 1N4, Canada
Tel: 416-920-9741; *Fax:* 416-920-5390
attendance@branksome.on.ca
www.branksome.on.ca
Grades: Junior Kindergarten - 12 *Note:* Branksome Hall is an independent day & boarding school for girls & an International Baccalaureate (IB) World School.
Karen Murton, Principal
kmurton@branksome.on.ca
Sarah Craig, Head, Junior School
scraig@branksome.on.ca
Karrie Weinstock, Head, Senior / Middle School & Admissions
kweinstock@branksome.on.ca
Terence Carty, Director, Information Technology
tcarty@branksome.on.ca
Joanne Colwell, Director, Student Life
jcolwell@branksome.on.ca
Julia Drake, Director, Communications & Marketing
jdrake@branksome.on.ca
Rosemary Evans, Director, Academic Studies
revans@branksome.on.ca
Judy Gordon, Director, Finance & Administration
jgordon@branksome.on.ca
Nanci Smith, Director, Residence & Athletics
nsmith@branksome.on.ca

Toronto: Cambridge International College of Canada (CICC)
35 Ourland Ave., Toronto, ON M8Z 4E1, Canada
Tel: 416-252-9195
Grades: Secondary *Note:* The school for foreign students specializes in TOEFL / ESL & preparation courses for university.

Toronto: Cathedral Christian Academy
c/o The Prayer Palace Ministries
1111 Arrow Rd., Toronto, ON M9N 3B3, Canada
Tel: 416-241-1100; *Fax:* 416-241-4404
www.ccaschool.ca
Grades: JK - 12

Toronto: Centre for Jewish Living & Learning Religious School
Also known as: Lomdim
120 Old Colony Rd., Toronto, ON M2I 2K2
Tel: 416-449-3880; *Fax:* 416-449-9831
reception@templeemanuel.ca
www.templeemanuel.ca
Note: The school offers progressive Jewish learning for children.
Robin Leszner, Director, Education
robin@templeemanuel.ca

Toronto: Children's Garden Junior School (CGS)
670 Eglinton Ave. East, Toronto, ON M4G 2K4, Canada
Tel: 416-423-5017; *Fax:* 416-423-0727
info@cgsschool.com
www.childrensgardenschool.com
Grades: Pre- K - 3
Marie Bates, Principal & Founder, 416-423-5017, ext. 24
marie@cgsschool.com
Zandee Toovey, Executive Assistant, 416-423-5017, ext. 44
ztoovey@cgsschool.com

Toronto: Children's Garden Nursery School
1847 Bayview Ave., Toronto, ON M4G 3E4
Tel: 416-488-4298; *Fax:* 416-488-6499
info@childrensgarden.ca
www.childrensgarden.ca
Grades: Pre-K. *Enrollment:* 140
Pauline Foulkes, Director

Toronto: La Citadelle International Academy of Arts & Science
15 Mallow Rd., Toronto, ON M3B 1G2
Tel: 416-385-9685; *Fax:* 416-385-9685
info@lacitadelleacademy.com
www.lacitadelleacademy.com
Grades: Pre.-12 *Enrollment:* 230
Alfred Abouchar, Headmaster
Faye Tabbara, Coordinator, Administration & Admission
admin@lacitadelleacademy.com

Toronto: City Academy
3080 Yonge St., Toronto, ON M4N 3N1, Canada
Tel: 416-482-2521; *Fax:* 416-482-2496
info@cityacademy.ca
www.cityacademy.ca
Grades: Sec. *Enrollment:* 230
Sheila Dever, Principal

Toronto: Community Hebrew Academy of Toronto (CHAT)
Also known as: TanenbaumCHAT
Wallenberg Campus
200 Wilmington Ave., Toronto, ON M3H 5J8, Canada
Tel: 416-636-5984; *Fax:* 416-636-7717
info@tanenbaumchat.org
tanenbaumchat.org
www.facebook.com/TanenbaumCHAT1
twitter.com/TanenbaumCHAT; twitter.com/TCWallenberg
Grades: Sec. *Enrollment:* 800 *Note:* Co-educational high school of the Greater Toronto Jewish community. Campuses in Toronto & Vaughan. Programmes include core subjects & Jewish studies. The Wallenberg Campus is for students living south of Steeles Ave. in Toronto.
Paul Shaviv, M.A., M.Phil., Director, Education
Helen Fox, B.A., Principal
Carly Reed, Coordinator, Admissions
creed@tanenbaumchat.org

Campuses
Kimel Family Education Centre
Joseph & Wolf Lebovic Jewish Community Campus
9600 Bathurst St., Vaughan, ON L6A 3Z8
Tel: 905-787-8772; *Fax:* 905-787-8773
Note: The Kimel Family Education is for students living north of Steeles Ave. in Vaughan.
Jonathan Levy, Principal
Jill Garazi, Coordinator, Admissions
jgarazi@tanenbaumchat.org

Toronto: Cornerstone Montessori Prep School (CMPS)
177 Beverley St., Toronto, ON M5T 1Y7
Tel: 416-977-1204
www.cornerstoneprep.ca
Grades: Pre.-12 *Enrollment:* 130
Dr. Stephanie Ling, Ph.D., Principal

Campuses
Don Mills Campus
33 Mallard Rd., Toronto, ON M3B 1S4
Tel: 647-977-5584

Toronto: Crawford Adventist Academy
531 Finch Ave. West, Toronto, ON M2R 3X2, Canada
Tel: 416-633-0090; *Fax:* 416-633-0467
info@tadsb.com
Grades: K./Elem./Sec. *Enrollment:* 500
Norman Brown, Supervising Principal

Toronto: Crescent School
2365 Bayview Ave., Toronto, ON M2L 1A2, Canada
Tel: 416-449-2556; *Fax:* 416-449-7950
info@crescentschool.org
www.crescentschool.org
Grades: 3 - 12 *Note:* Crescent School is a day school for boys.
Geoff Roberts, Headmaster
Mark Hord, Head, Middle School
Ross MacDonald, Head, Lower School
Christopher White, Director, Admissions

Toronto: Crestwood Preparatory College
217 Brookbanks Dr., Toronto, ON M3A 2T7, Canada
Tel: 416-391-1441; *Fax:* 416-444-0949
www.crestwood.on.ca
www.facebook.com/pages/Crestwood-Preparatory-College/1091 25222250
Grades: Elem./Sec. *Enrollment:* 391
Vince Pagano, Principal

Toronto: Crestwood School
411 Lawrence Ave. East, Toronto, ON M3C 1N9
Tel: 416-444-5858; *Fax:* 416-444-2127
Grades: Elem.
Dalia Eisen, Contact
dalia.eisen@crestwood.on.ca

Toronto: Danforth Jewish Circle Children's Jewish Studies Programme (DJC)
#125, 283 Danforth Ave., Toronto, ON M4K 1N2
Tel: 416-580-1233
info@djctoronto.com
djctoronto.com/explore/children.php
Grades: JK-7 *Note:* Jewish studies program emphasizing arts, music, culture, & film.

Toronto: Darchei Noam Hebrew School
864 Sheppard Ave. West, Toronto, ON M3H 2T5
Tel: 416-638-4783; *Fax:* 416-638-5852
caroldn@bellnet.ca
sites.google.com/site/youthandfamilyatdn
Grades: JK-6
Jennifer Katz, Director, Youth Education & Programming
educator.darcheinoam@gmail.com

Toronto: David & Esther Freiman Childhood Education Centre
4588 Bathurst St., Toronto, ON M2R 1W6
Tel: 416-638-1881; *Fax:* 416-636-5813
Note: Non-denominational education for children aged 18 months to 5 years.

Toronto: De La Salle College
131 Farnham Ave., Toronto, ON M4V 1H7, Canada
Tel: 416-969-8771; *Fax:* 416-969-9175
info@delasalle.toronto.on.ca
www.delasalleoaklands.ca
Grades: Elem./Sec. *Enrollment:* 578

Toronto: Downtown Jewish Community School (DJCS)
Miles Nadal Jewish Community Centre
750 Spadina Ave., Toronto, ON M5S 2J2
Tel: 416-924-6212; *Fax:* 416-924-0442
djcs.org
www.facebook.com/downtownjewishcommunityschool
Grades: JK-7
Naomi Azrieli, Chair
Joan Schoenfeld, Founder & Principal

Toronto: Dr. Abraham Shore She'Arim Hebrew Day School
4588 Bathurst St., Toronto, ON M2R 1W6, Canada
Tel: 416-633-8247; *Fax:* 416-633-4783
info@shearim.ca
Grades: Elem./Spec. Ed.

Toronto: Dr. Eric Jackman Institute of Child Study
45 Walmer Rd., Toronto, ON M5R 2X2, Canada
Tel: 416-934-4509; *Fax:* 416-978-6485
Grades: Elem. *Enrollment:* 176
Janette Pelletier, Director
Elizabeth Morley, Principal

Toronto: The Dragon Academy
35 Prince Arthur Ave., Toronto, ON M5R 1B2
Tel: 416-323-3243; *Fax:* 416-323-7780
info@dragonacademy.org
www.dragonacademy.org
www.facebook.com/151620228237983
twitter.com/dragonacademy
Grades: 7-12 *Enrollment:* 75
Meg Fox, Ph.D., Founding Principal

Toronto: Eitz Chaim Schools - Administrative/Patricia Branch
475 Patricia Ave., Toronto, ON M2R 2N1
Tel: 416-225-1187; *Fax:* 416-225-3732
patricia@eitzchaim.com
Grades: 1-8 *Enrollment:* 800 *Note:* This branch houses the boys school & administrative offices.
Elias Levy, Executive Director
Rabbi Pliner, Dean

Campuses
Spring Farm Branch
80 York Hill Blvd., Thornhill, ON L4J 2P6
Tel: 905-764-6633; *Fax:* 905-764-9577
spring@eitzchaim.com
Grades: Pre.-8 *Note:* This branch houses the girls school.

Viewmount Branch
1 Viewmount Ave., Toronto, ON M5B 1T2
Tel: 416-789-4366; *Fax:* 416-785-1384
view@eitzchaim.com
Grades: Pre.-8 *Note:* This branch houses the girls school (grades 1-8); preschool, JK & SK are mixed

Toronto: Ellesmere Montessori School
37 Marchington Circle, Toronto, ON M1R 3M6
Tel: 416-447-1059; *Fax:* 416-447-1059
info@ellesmeremontessori.ca
www.ellesmeremontessori.ca
Grades: K./Elem.

Toronto: Ellington Montessori
2102 Lawrence Ave. East, Toronto, ON M1R 2Z9
Tel: 416-759-8363; *Fax:* 416-759-2162
ellingtonmontessorischool@on.aibn.com
www.ellingtonmontessori.ca
Grades: Elem. *Note:* Located in the lower level of Wexford United Church.
Deborah Renwick, Principal

Toronto: Fieldstone Day School
2999 Dufferin St., Toronto, ON M6B 3T4, Canada
Tel: 416-487-7381; *Fax:* 416-487-8190
office@fieldstonedayschool.org
www.fieldstonedayschool.org
Grades: K.-12 *Enrollment:* 244 *Note:* Enriched curriculum.
Melissa Volekaert, Head of Lower School
mvol@fieldstonedayschool.org
Sue Johnson, Ass't Head of Lower School
sjohnson@fieldstonedayschool.org

Toronto: Gan Netivot
470 Glencairn Ave., Toronto, ON M5N 1V8
Tel: 416-789-3213
Grades: Pre.-JK; Orthodox

Toronto: German International School Toronto
585 Cranbrooke Ave., Toronto, ON M6A 2X9
Tel: 416-922-6413; *Fax:* 416-922-6413
www.gistonline.ca
www.facebook.com/175972742449216
www.linkedin.com/company/german-international-school-toronto
Grades: Pre.-8 *Enrollment:* 54 *Note:* German International School Toronto offers students a curriculum that blends German & Ontario educational standards.
Dr. Christian von Twickel, Chair & President
Arnd Rupp, Principal

Toronto: The Giles School
L'École Giles
80 Scarsdale Rd., Toronto, ON M3C 2C3, Canada
Tel: 416-446-0825; *Fax:* 416-446-0846
info@gilesschool.ca
www.gilesschool.ca
Grades: Pre-Kindergarten - 12 *Note:* The Giles School is a co-educational school which offers an enriched French immersion program. Students are introduced to a third language in grade one.
Kemp Rickett, Headmaster
kemp_rickett@gilesschool.ca
Sue Vijh, Deputy Headmaster
sue_vijh@gilesschool.ca
Harry Giles, Director, Education
Rosine Dika Balotoken, Manager, Administration
rosine_dika@gilesschool.ca
Bob Spencer, Manager, Special Projects
rgspencer@rogers.com

Toronto: Gradale Academy
159 Roxborough Dr., Toronto, ON M4W 1X7
Tel: 416-923-9009
www.gradaleacademy.com
Grades: Pre.-3 *Enrollment:* 60 *Note:* Gradale Academy also offers classes outdoors at Evergreen Brick Works in Toronto.
Michelle Gradish, Founder & Head of School

Toronto: Great Lakes College of Toronto (GLCT)
Toronto Campus
323 Keele St., Toronto, ON M6P 2K6, Canada
Tel: 416-763-4121; *Fax:* 416-763-5225
query@glctschool.com
www.glctschool.com
Grades: 10 - 12 *Note:* The school is an international high school, which offers a pre-university program. English as a Second Language courses are also provided.
Tom Tidey, B.A., M.Ed., Principal

Schools
Beijing Office - Great Lakes College of Toronto
QianHe Housing Estate, Bldg. 3
#608, 108 - 4th Ring Rd. E, ChaoYang District, Beijing 100029, China
glctbjoffice@yahoo.cn
www.glctschool.com; www.glctschool.com.cn
Other Information: Tel: 010-84833541 / 84833542; Fax: 010-84833540
Grades: 10 - 12

The Canadian Trillium College - Quanzhou (CTC)
#7 High School, 46 Tian Hou Rd., Quanzhou City, China
www.ctc-school.com
Other Information: Tel: 011-86-595-2203068; Fax: 011-86-595-220-2528
Grades: Middle *Enrollment:* 150 *Note:* CTC is a private Canadian School that offers an Ontario Secondary School curriculum to students in China. After passing their Chinese Middle School program and completing the necessary Ontario Secondary School courses students may be granted an Ontario Secondary School Diploma (OSSD). The granting of an OSSD is based on the total educational experience the student has acquired over their entire educational history in China
Dr. Ernest Smith, Principal
ernest.smith2@sympatico.ca

The Canadian Trillium College - Jinhau (CTC)
Jinhua City, Zhejiang Province, China
www.jh-school.com
Grades: Middle *Enrollment:* 250

The Canadian Trillium College - Shanghai (CTC)
261 Huang Yang Rd., Shanghai City, Pudong District 201206, China
zhaosheng@shphschool.com
www.shphschool.com/xxgk.htm
Other Information: Tel: 021-50310791
Enrollment: 100 *Note:* Bilingual school.

***Toronto:* Greenwood College School**
443 Mount Pleasant Rd., Toronto, ON M4S 2L8
Tel: 416-482-9811; *Fax:* 416-482-9188
www.greenwoodcollege.com
www.facebook.com/138629896185229
twitter.com/chiefthegrizzly
www.linkedin.com/company/501131
www.youtube.com/user/greenwoodcollege
Richard Wernham, Chair
Allan Hardy, B.A., B.Ed., M.A.T., Principal
allan.hardy@greenwoodcollege.com

***Toronto:* Guildwood Village Montessori School (GVMS)**
Montessori Village & Education Centre
297 Old Kingston Rd., Toronto, ON M1C 1B4
Tel: 416-266-0424
www.gvmontessori.ca
Grades: Pre.-8 *Enrollment:* 75
Elisa Bourdon, Principal
edeblasibourdon@rogers.com

***Toronto:* Havergal College**
1451 Avenue Rd., Toronto, ON M5N 2H9, Canada
Tel: 416-483-3843; *Fax:* 416-483-6796
www.havergal.on.ca
Grades: K./Elem./Sec. *Enrollment:* 956 *Note:* University-preparatory day and boarding school for girls.
Dr. Susan R. Groesbeck, Principal

***Toronto:* Hawthorn School for Girls**
101 Scarsdale Rd., Toronto, ON M3B 2R2, Canada
Tel: 416-444-3054; *Fax:* 416-449-2891
www.hawthornschool.com
Grades: Elem./Sec. *Enrollment:* 222
Eliza Trotter, School Head

***Toronto:* High Park Centennial Montessori School**
35 High Park Gdns., Toronto, ON M6R 1S8, Canada
Tel: 416-763-6097; *Fax:* 416-763-0380
Grades: K./Elem. *Enrollment:* 332
Tracy Grisdale

***Toronto:* High Park Day School**
#202, 2150 Bloor St. West, Toronto, ON M6S 1M8
Tel: 416-762-4447
info@highparkdayschool.com
highparkdayschool.com
www.facebook.com/highpark.dayschool
twitter.com/HighParkDS
Grades: 1-8 *Enrollment:* 13
Amanda Dervaitis, Founder & Director
amanda@highparkdayschool.com
Aaron Downey, Teacher & Curriculum Coordinator
aaron@highparkdayschool.com

***Toronto:* Holy Blossom Preschool**
Holy Blossom Temple
1950 Bathurst St., Toronto, ON M5V 2R3
Tel: 416-789-3291; *Fax:* 416-789-9697
templemail@holyblossom.org
www.holyblossom.org/study-limud/preschool
www.facebook.com/pages/Holy-Blossom-Temple/98017462501
twitter.com/holyblossom
www.linkedin.com/groups?gid=4507427
www.youtube.com/user/holyblossomtemple
Grades: Preschool
Pamela Hamovitch, Principal, Nursery School
phamovitch@holyblossom.org

***Toronto:* Humberside Montessori School**
121 Kennedy Ave., Toronto, ON M6S 2X8
Tel: 416-762-8888; *Fax:* 416-766-1211
www.humbersidemontessori.ca
Grades: Elem./Ungraded
Felix Bednarski, Director & Owner
Molly Galle, Director & Owner

***Toronto:* Imperial College of Toronto**
20 Queen Elizabeth Blvd., Toronto, ON M8Z 1L8
Tel: 416-251-4970; *Fax:* 416-251-0259
info@imperialcollege.org
www.imperialcollege.org
Grades: Sec.
Eileen Crichton, Principal

***Toronto:* The Japanese School of Toronto Shokokai Inc.**
c/o McMurrich Junior Public Shool
115 Winnona Dr., Toronto, ON M6G 3S8, Canada
Tel: 416-656-4822; *Fax:* 416-658-8931
www.torontohoshuko.ca
Note: This is a Japanese Saturday school

***Toronto:* The Jewish Heritage School at Congregation Habonim**
5 Glen Park Ave., Toronto, ON M6B 4J2
Tel: 416-782-2682
info@jewishheritageschool.com
jewishheritageschool.wordpress.com
Grades: 1-6 *Note:* The school offers Judaic & Hebrew language studies, & Jewish music class.
Yodfat S. Mandil, Principal
habonimprincipal@gmail.com
Cathy Rechtshaffen, Registrar
habonimschool@gmail.com

***Toronto:* Junior Academy**
2454 Bayview Ave., Toronto, ON M2L 1A6, Canada
Tel: 416-425-4567; *Fax:* 416-425-7379
www.junioracademy.com
Grades: Kindergarten - 8
Pat Kendall, B.A., Graduate Diploma in, Administrator
Dianne Johnson, Principal
Julie Stewart, Vice Principal
Cathy Hibbert, Director, Physical Education
Susan Jones, Director, Middle School
Kris Potter, Director, Student Affairs

***Toronto:* Kesher School**
729 St. Clair Ave. West, Toronto, ON M6C 1B2
Tel: 647-444-7291
kesher.school@gmail.com
kesherschool.weebly.com
Grades: JK-2
Mika Gang, Principal

***Toronto:* The Laurel School**
44 Upjohn Rd., Toronto, ON M3B 2W1
Tel: 416-510-2500
info@laurelschool.ca
www.laurelschool.ca
Grades: Pre.-6 *Enrollment:* 70
Mary Kindos, Principal

***Toronto:* Leonardo Da Vinci Academy of Arts & Sciences**
100 Allanhurst Dr., Toronto, ON M9A 4K4
Tel: 416-247-6137; *Fax:* 416-247-6138
Toll-Free: 877-218-0079
ldva@ldva.on.ca
www.ldva.on.ca
Grades: Pre.-8
Salvatore Ritacca, President & Co-Founder
sr@ldva.on.ca
Dom Tassielli, Treasurer & Co-Founder
dt@ldva.on.ca

***Toronto:* The Linden School**
10 Rosehill Ave., Toronto, ON M4T 1G5, Canada
Tel: 416-966-4406
www.lindenschool.ca
Grades: 1 - 12 *Note:* The Linden School provides education for girls.
Alana Bell, BA (Honours) (English), M, Co-Principal
Dawn Chan, B.Sc. (Biology), M.Sc. (S, Co-Principal
Ina Székely, B.A., M.A., B.Ed., Co-Principal
Kate Raven, B.A. (Honours), Post-Grad, Coordinator, Communications

***Toronto:* Little Feet Little Faces**
183 Avenue Rd., Toronto, ON M5R 2J2
Tel: 416-923-8882; *Fax:* 416-923-8802
arts@littlefeetlittlefaces.com
www.littlefeetlittlefaces.com
Grades: Pre.-SK *Enrollment:* 55 *Note:* A private licensed daycare following the Ontario academic curriculum, with an emphasis on the arts.
Ingrid Rea, Creative Director

***Toronto:* Lycée Français de Toronto**
2327, rue Dufferin, Toronto, ON M6E 3S5, Canada
Tél: 416-924-1789; *Téléc:* 416-924-9078
samia.farahat@lft.ca
www.lft.ca
Grades: Prim./Sec. *Enrollment:* 340
M. Dominique Duthel, Proviseur

***Toronto:* The Mabin School**
50 Poplar Plains Rd., Toronto, ON M4V 2M8, Canada
Tel: 416-964-9594; *Fax:* 416-964-3643
admissions@mabin.com
www.mabin.com
Grades: Junior Kindergarten - 6 *Note:* The Mabin School provides a full day, non-denominational program for girls & boys.
Lynn Seligman, Principal

***Toronto:* Maria Montessori School**
125 Brentcliffe Rd., Toronto, ON M4G 3Y7
Tel: 416-423-9123; *Fax:* 416-423-7819
www.mariamontessori.ca
Grades: Elem.
James Brand, Head of School

***Toronto:* McDonald International Academy**
920 Yonge St., 2nd Fl., Toronto, ON M4W 3C7, Canada
Tel: 416-322-1502; *Fax:* 416-322-5775
mia@mcdonaldacademy.com
www.mcdonaldacademy.com
Enrollment: 753
Fraser Rose

***Toronto:* Metropolitan Preparatory Academy**
49 Mobile Dr., Toronto, ON M4A 1H5, Canada
Tel: 416-285-0870; *Fax:* 416-285-0873
www.metroprep.com
Grades: 6 - 12 *Note:* Metropolitan Preparatory Academy offers a middle & high school program for university-oriented students.
William Wayne McKelvey, Hons. B.A., M.A., Dip. Ed, Principal
Debra McKelvey-Cleveland, Vice Principal & Head, Guidance
dmckelvey@MetroPrep.com
Jason Van Allen, Administrator, Information Technology
jvanallen@metroprep.com

***Toronto:* Miles Nadal Jewish Community Centre Nursery School**
750 Spadina Ave., Toronto, ON M5S 2J2
Tel: 416-924-6211; *Fax:* 416-924-0442
mnjccnurseryschool.com
Grades: Preschool *Note:* Non-denominational education for children aged 2 1/2 - 5 years.
Cathy Indig, Director, Early Childhood Education
cathyi@mnjcc.org

***Toronto:* Montcrest School**
4 Montcrest Blvd., Toronto, ON M4K 1J7, Canada
Tel: 416-469-2008; *Fax:* 416-469-0934
info@montcrest.on.ca
www.montcrest.on.ca
Grades: Junior Kindergarten - 8 *Enrollment:* 300 *Note:* Montcrest School is a co-educational, nondenominational school. The school also offers special education classes for students with learning disabilities.
Stephen Beatty, Head of School

***Toronto:* Montessori Jewish Day School**
55 Yeomans Rd., Toronto, ON M3H 3J7
Tel: 416-784-5071
adminmjds@mjds.ca
www.mjds.ca
www.facebook.com/133140750091854
Grades: Pre.-8 *Enrollment:* 115

Regina Lulka, Head of School
regina@mjds.ca
Matti Shorr, Director, Administration

Toronto: Morris Winchevsky School: Toronto's Secular Jewish Community School
The Winchevsky Centre
585 Cranbrooke Ave., Toronto, ON M6A 2X9
Tel: 416-789-5502; *Fax:* 416-789-5981
info@mwstoronto.org; info@winchevskycentre.org
www.mwstoronto.org
www.facebook.com/167027090018410
Grades: K.-8 *Note:* The school caters to secular, non-traditional, mixed culture, & unaffiliated families.
David Lipovitch, Director, Education
dlipovitch@tsjcs.com

Toronto: MPS Etobicoke (MPS)
Also known as: Mississauga Private School
30 Barrhead Cres., Toronto, ON M9W 3Z7, Canada
Tel: 416-745-1328; *Fax:* 416-745-4168
mpsinfo@rogers.com
www.mpsontario.com
Grades: Junior Kindergarten - 12
Gabrielle Bush, Director

Toronto: National Ballet School (NBS)
400 Jarvis St., Toronto, ON M4Y 2G6, Canada
Tel: 416-964-3780; *Fax:* 416-964-5133
Toll-Free: 1-800-387-0785
careers@nbs-enb.ca
www.nbs-enb.ca
www.facebook.com/NBSENB
twitter.com/NBS_ENB
www.youtube.com/nbsenb
Note: The school offers elite ballet training, academic instruction, & residential care.
Troy Maxwell, Chair
Grant Troop, Executive Director & Co-Chief Executive Officer
Mavis Staines, Artistic Director & Co-Chief Executive Officer

Toronto: Northmount School
26 Mallard Rd., Toronto, ON M3B 1S3, Canada
Tel: 416-449-8823; *Fax:* 416-449-1244
Lolita.Pereira@northmount.com
www.northmount.com
Grades: Junior Kindergarten - 8 *Note:* Northmount School specializes in the education of boys.
Dr. Carmen Mombourquette, Head of School

Toronto: Oraynu Children's School
St. Andrews Junior High School
131 Fenn Ave., Toronto, ON M2P 1X7
Tel: 416-385-3910
info@oraynu.org
www.oraynu.org/school
www.facebook.com/Oraynu
Grades: K.-7 *Note:* The school is part of the Oraynu Congregation for Humanistic Judaism.
Steven Shabes, Director, Education
stevenshabes@yahoo.com
Roby Sadler, Contact

Toronto: P.T. Montessori School
280 Culford Rd., Toronto, ON M6L 2V3, Canada
Tel: 416-242-3725
Grades: Elem. *Enrollment:* 51
Linda Harrison, Administrator

Toronto: People's Christian Academy
374 Sheppard Ave. East, Toronto, ON M2N 3B6, Canada
Tel: 416-222-3341; *Fax:* 416-222-3344
info@pca.ca
www.pca.ca
Grades: Jr. K.-12 *Enrollment:* 808
Rev. Reg Andrews, Director, Operations & Ministry

Toronto: The Prestige School
44 Appian Dr., Toronto, ON M2J 2P9
Tel: 416-250-0648; *Fax:* 416-250-5873
prestige@prestigeschool.com
www.prestigeschool.com
Grades: JK-12 *Enrollment:* 150
Olga Margold, Principal

Campuses
Richmond Hill Campus
11 Headdon Game, Richmond Hill, ON L4C 9W9
Tel: 905-780-6565
Grades: Pre.-6

Toronto: Prince Edward Montessori School
2850 Bloor St. West, Toronto, ON M8X 1B2
Tel: 416-234-9127
info@princeedwardmontessori.com
www.princeedwardmontessori.com
Grades: Pre.-SK *Enrollment:* 96
Bozena Nowicka-Lipa, Principal

Campuses
Mississauga Campus
12 Peter St. South, Mississauga, ON L5H 0A1
Tel: 905-891-6912

Toronto: Queensway Christian College School (QCC)
1536 The Queensway, Toronto, ON M8Z 1T5, Canada
Tel: 416-255-6033; *Fax:* 416-255-7389
www.qccollege.com
Grades: Junior Kindergarten - 12 *Note:* Queensway Christian College os a non-denominational Christian school, which consists of a high school, a middle school, & a junior school.
David Broomer, Executive Director
John Allardyce, Supervising Principal
Tim Bramer, Elementary Vice Principal
Sue Broomer, Secretary

Toronto: Robbins Hebrew Academy
Administration House
3072 Bayview Ave., Toronto, ON M2N 5L3
Tel: 416-224-8737; *Fax:* 416-225-9108
info@rhacademy.ca
www.rhacademy.ca
www.facebook.com/RobbinsHebrewAcademy
Grades: Pre.-8 *Enrollment:* 600 *Note:* Robbins Hebrew Academy is a Conservative Jewish day school.
Claire Sumerlus, Head of School
csumerlus@rhacademy.ca
Michele Viner, Director, Admissions
mviner@rhacademy.ca

Campuses
Bathurst Campus
1700 Bathurst St., Toronto, ON M5P 2K3
Tel: 416-781-5658; *Fax:* 416-787-9632
Valerie Turner, Principal
vturner@rhacademy.ca

Bayview Campus
3080 Bayview Ave., Toronto, ON M2N 5L3
Tel: 416-225-1143; *Fax:* 416-225-0659
Silvia Eilath, Principal
seilath@rhacademy.ca

Toronto: The Rosedale Day School
#426, 131 Bloor St. West, Toronto, ON M5S 1R1
Tel: 416-923-4726; *Fax:* 416-923-7379
office@rds-on.com
www.rds-on.com
Grades: JK-8 *Enrollment:* 115
James Lee, Head of School

Toronto: Royal St. George's College
120 Howland Ave., Toronto, ON M5R 3B5
Tel: 416-533-9481; *Fax:* 416-533-0028
contactus@rsgc.on.ca
www.rsgc.on.ca
www.facebook.com/RSGC1
twitter.com/RoyalSGC
www.youtube.com/user/royalsgc
Grades: Elem./Sec.; Boys *Enrollment:* 426
Stephen Beatty, Headmaster
sbeatty@rsgc.on.ca
Paul O'Leary, Assistant Headmaster & Head of Senior School
poleary@rsgc.on.ca
Catherine Kirkland, Head of Junior School
ckirkland@rsgc.on.ca

Toronto: St. Clement's School
21 St. Clement's Ave., Toronto, ON M4R 1G8, Canada
Tel: 416-483-4835; *Fax:* 416-483-8242
admissions@scs.on.ca
www.scs.on.ca/
Grades: 1-12 *Enrollment:* 450 *Note:* All-girl's school affiliated with the Anglican church
Patricia Parisi, Principal

Toronto: St. Michael's College School
1515 Bathurst St., Toronto, ON M5P 3H4, Canada
Tel: 416-653-3180; *Fax:* 416-653-7704
info@smcsmail.com; privacyofficer@smcsmail.com (privacy officer)
www.stmichaelscollegeschool.com
Grades: 7-12 *Enrollment:* 1100 *Note:* St. Michael's College School provides Catholic, Liberal Arts eductaion for young men.
Fr. Tim Scott, C.S.B., Chair, Board of Directors
Rev. John Malo, C.S.B., Superior
Fr. Joseph Redican, C.S.B., President, 416-653-3180, ext. 174
Terence Sheridan, Principal, 416-653-3180, ext. 139
Emile John, Vice-Principal, 416-653-3180, ext. 156
David Lee, Vice-Principal
Kimberley Bailey, Director, Advancement, 416-653-3180, ext. 118
Michael De Pellegrin, Director, Communications, 416-653-3180, ext. 292
Fr. John Malo, C.S.B., Director, Pastoral Care, 416-653-3180, ext. 229
Greg Paolini, Director, Admissions, 416-653-3180, ext. 195
Fr. John Reddy, C.S.B., Director, Faith Development, 416-653-3180, ext. 217
Bill Smith, Director, Plant, 416-653-3180, ext. 129
Gino Saccone, Corporate Controller, 416-653-3180, ext. 239

Toronto: Sathya Sai School of Canada
#4, 505 Ellesmere Rd., Toronto, ON M1R 4E5
Tel: 416-297-7970; *Fax:* 416-297-0945
info@sathyasaischool.ca
www.sathyasaischool.ca
Grades: JK-6 *Enrollment:* 160 *Note:* Sathya Sai School seeks to promote the five human values of Truth, Right Conduct, Peace, Love, & Non-violence in students through education of character, along with academics.
Revathi Chennabathni, Ph.D., Principal
principal@sathyasaischool.ca

Toronto: School of Liberal Arts (SOLA)
#200, 36 Eglinton Ave. West, Toronto, ON M4R 1A1, Canada
Tel: 416-489-7652; *Fax:* 416-489-2074
www.solaprep.com
Grades: Sec. *Enrollment:* 251 *Note:* University Preparatory School
David L. Ferguson

Toronto: Shmuel Zahavy Cheder Chabad of Toronto
#203, 900 Alness St., Toronto, ON M3J 2H6, Canada
Tel: 416-663-1972; *Fax:* 416-650-9404
www.chederchabad.com
Note: Students at Shmuel Zahavy Cheder Chabad of Toronto also receive education in Torah scholarship & classic Jewish values.
Rabbi Yona Shur, Director
Rabbi Baruch Zaltzman, Principal

Toronto: Sidney Ledson School Ltd.
#107, 220 Duncan Mill Rd., Toronto, ON M3B 3J5, Canada
Tel: 416-447-5355; *Fax:* 416-447-5283
www.sidneyledsoninstitute.com
Grades: K./Elem. *Enrollment:* 50
Sidney Ledson

Toronto: Signet Christian School
95 Jonesville Cres., Toronto, ON M4A 1H2
Tel: 416-750-7515; *Fax:* 416-750-7720
info@signetschool.ca
www.signetschool.ca
www.facebook.com/124533100975300
Grades: JK-12 *Enrollment:* 80
Martin D. Sandford, Principal

Toronto: Sterling Hall School of Toronto (SHS)
99 Cartwright Ave., Toronto, ON M6A 1V4, Canada
Tel: 416-785-3410; *Fax:* 416-785-6616
shsadmin@sterlinghall.com
www.sterlinghall.com
Grades: Junior Kindergarten - 8 *Enrollment:* 300 *Note:* Sterling Hall School of Toronto educates boys.
Ian Robinson, Principal
Claire Reed, Director, Admissions
admissions@sterlinghall.com

Toronto: Sunnybrook School
469 Merton St., Toronto, ON M4S 1B4, Canada
Tel: 416-487-5308; *Fax:* 416-487-5381
sbmail@sunnybrookschool.com
www.sunnybrookschool.com
Grades: Jr. K.-6 *Enrollment:* 134
Dr. Irene Davy, Ph.D., Director

Toronto: Temple Sinai Hebrew & Religious School
210 Wilson Ave., Toronto, ON M5M 3B1
Tel: 416-487-3281; *Fax:* 416-487-5499
templesinai.net/study
Grades: Pre./Elem. *Note:* The Temple Sinai Congregation of Toronto also offers a nursery program.
Ira Schweitzer, Director, Education
ira@templesinai.net
Charlotte Koven, Principal, Hebrew & Religious Schools
charlotte@templesinai.net

Bibi Golberg, Principal, Nursery
bibi@templesinai.net

Toronto: Three Fishes Christian Elementary School
Miracle Family Temple
1100 Bellamy Rd. North, Toronto, ON M1H 1H2, Canada
Tel: 416-284-9003
3fishes@threefishes.org
www.threefishes.org

Grades: Junior Kindergarten - 8 *Note:* Three Fishes Christian Elementary School offers a Christ-centered & academically demanding program.
Laurel Ann Mirams, Principal
dmirams@sympatico.ca

Toronto: Tiferes Bais Yaakov
Also known as: Daniel T. Gordon High School for Girls
85 Stormont Ave., Toronto, ON M5N 2C3
Tel: 416-785-4044; *Fax:* 416-785-4046
secretary@tiferesbaisyaakov.com
tiferesbaisyaakov.com

Grades: Secondary; Girls *Note:* Tiferes Bais Yaakov is an Orthodox Jewish high school for girls.
Rabbi Yitzchak Feigenbaum, Principal
rabbif@tiferesbaisyaakov.com
Malka Meckler, Principal, General Studies
Adina Ribacoff, Principal, Judaic Studies

Toronto: Timothy Christian School (Rexdale) (TCS)
28 Elmhurst Dr., Toronto, ON M9W 2J5, Canada
Tel: 416-741-5770; *Fax:* 416-741-3359
www.timothycs.com

Grades: Junior Kindergarten - 8 *Enrollment:* 100 *Note:* Timothy Christian School in Rexdale offers a Christ-centred education.
Margareth Lise, Principal
Bobbie Van Ysseldyk, Finance Administrator & Administrative Assistant

Toronto: Toronto Cheder School
3995 Bathurst St., Toronto, ON M3H 5V3, Canada
Tel: 416-636-2987

Enrollment: 200 *Note:* Toronto Cheder School is an Orthodox school for boys.
Rabbi D. Engel, Principal

Toronto: Toronto French Montessori
432 Sheppard Ave. East, Toronto, ON M2N 3B7
Tel: 416-250-9952; *Fax:* 416-250-9952
info@torontofrenchmontessori.com
www.torontofrenchmontessori.com
www.facebook.com/119316424792686

Grades: Pre.-8 *Enrollment:* 90
Marie Mousa
principal@torontofrenchmontessori.com

Campuses
Cummer Campus
53 Cummer Ave., Toronto, ON M2M 2E5

Toronto: Toronto French School (TFS)
Toronto Campus
306 Lawrence Ave. East, Toronto, ON M4N 1T7, Canada
Tel: 416-484-6533; *Fax:* 416-488-3090
admissions@tfs.ca
www.tfs.ca

Grades: Preschool - 12 *Note:* Toronto French School is a co-educational, non-denominational school, which offers bilingual education.
Lena Sarkissian, Chair
board@tfs.ca
John Godfrey, Headmaster
Alain Delaune, Principal, Mississauga School
Heidi Gollert, Principal, Senior School
Mirna Hafez, Principal, Junior School

Toronto: The Toronto Heschel School
819 Sheppard Ave. West, Toronto, ON M3H 2T3, Canada
Tel: 416-635-1876; *Fax:* 416-635-1800
info@torontoheschel.org
www.torontoheschel.org

Grades: Junior Kindergarten - 8 *Enrollment:* 300 *Note:* The Jewish day school combines the teaching of Judaism with a general studies curriculum.
Ashira Gobrin, Board Co-Chair
Ken Kraft, Board Co-Chair
Mark Abramsohn, Executive Director
Gail Baker, Head of School & Principal
Rav Eliot Feldman, Vice Principal
Greg Beiles, Director, Curriculum & Training

Toronto: Toronto New School
519 Jarvis St., Toronto, ON M4Y 2H7
Tel: 416-960-1867

Grades: 9-12
Ewa Kasinska, Head of School

Toronto: Toronto Prep School
#200, 250 Davisville Ave., Toronto, ON M4S 1H2
Tel: 416-545-1020; *Fax:* 416-545-1456
www.torontoprepschool.com

Grades: 7-12 *Enrollment:* 185
Steve Tsimikalis, B.A., B.Ed., M.E.S., Principal
stsimikalis@torontoprepschool.com

Toronto: University of Toronto Schools (UTS)
371 Bloor St. West, Toronto, ON M5S 2R7, Canada
Tel: 416-978-3212; *Fax:* 416-978-6775
info@utschools.ca
www.utschools.ca
Other Information: 416-946-7995 (Phone, Admissions); 416-978-7325 (Student Services)

Grades: 7 - 12 *Enrollment:* 640 *Note:* UTS is a coeducational school, affiliated with the University of Toronto.
Robert E. Lord, Chair
UTSBoard@utschools.ca
Michaele Robertson, Principal

Toronto: Upper Canada College (UCC)
200 Lonsdale Rd., Toronto, ON M4V 1W6, Canada
Tel: 416-488-1125; *Fax:* 416-484-8611
admission@ucc.on.ca; administration@ucc.on.ca
www.ucc.on.ca
Other Information: 416-488-1125, ext. 2313 (Phone, Office of Advancement)

Grades: Senior Kindergarten - 12 *Note:* The Preparatory School has over 400 boys from Senior Kindergarten to grade seven. The Upper School offers a five year secondary education.
Andy Burgess, Chair, Board of Governors
andyburgess64@gmail.com
Jim Power, Principal, 416-488-1125, ext. 4010
Steve Griffin, Head, Upper School
David Matthews, Asst. Head, University Relations & Sec., Board of Governors, 416-488-1125, ext. 2260
dmatthews@ucc.on.ca
Andrea Aster, Associate Director, Marketing & Communications 416-488-1125, ext. 3355

Toronto: Voice Intermediate School
Bldg. 32
#300, 55 Mill St., Toronto, ON M5A 3C4
Tel: 416-691-4639; *Fax:* 416-691-3722
vis@voiceintermediate.com
www.voiceintermediate.com

Grades: 4-8 *Enrollment:* 85
Marie Lardino, B.A., B.Ed., M.Ed., Founder & Principal

Toronto: Waldorf Academy
250 Madison Ave., Toronto, ON M4V 2W6
Tel: 416-962-6447; *Fax:* 416-975-5513
info@waldorfacademy.org
waldorfacademy.org
www.facebook.com/121407927910549
twitter.com/WALDORFtoronto

Grades: Pre.-8 *Enrollment:* 240
Dean Husseini, Director
Sara Anderson, Enrollment
admissions@waldorfacademy.org

Toronto: Willowdale Christian School
60 Hilda Ave., Toronto, ON M2M 1V5
Tel: 416-222-1711; *Fax:* 416-222-1939
office@willowdalechristianschool.org
www.willowdalechristianschool.org

Grades: K.-8
Justin De Moor, Principal

Toronto: WillowWood School
55 Scarsdale Rd., Toronto, ON M3B 2R3
Tel: 416-444-7644; *Fax:* 416-444-1801
info@willowwoodschool.ca
www.willowwoodschool.ca

Grades: Elem./Sec./Spec. Ed. *Enrollment:* 250
Joy Kurtz, Principal
joykurtz@willowwoodschool.ca

Toronto: Yeshiva Bnei Zion of Bobov
44 Champlain Blvd., Toronto, ON M3H 2Z1, Canada
Tel: 416-633-6332; *Fax:* 416-633-6704

Grades: JK-8; Boys
Rabbi Shlomo Tzvi Frank, Director, Education
schloime.frank@gmail.com

Toronto: Yeshiva Darchei Torah
18 Champlain Blvd., Toronto, ON M3H 2Z1
Tel: 416-782-7974; *Fax:* 416-782-7811
darchei.ca

Grades: Secondary *Note:* Yeshiva Darchei Torah is an Orthodox Jewish high school for boys, with Jewish & secular programs.
Rabbi Eliezer Breitowitz, Rosh Yeshiva
breitowitz@darchei.ca
Ron Roberto, English Principal
ronrob17@yahoo.com
Jeff Toledano, Executive Director
toledano@darchei.ca

Toronto: Yeshiva Yesodei Hatorah
77 Glen Rush Blvd., Toronto, ON M5N 2T8
Tel: 416-787-1101; *Fax:* 416-787-9044
yesodeihat@gmail.com

Grades: Pre.-8; Boys *Enrollment:* 450
Rabbi M. Bornstein, Principal

Toronto: Yeshivas Nachalas Zvi
475 Lawrence Ave. West, Toronto, ON M5M 1C6, Canada
Tel: 416-782-8912; *Fax:* 416-782-8517

Grades: 8-12; Religious Orthodox, Boys *Enrollment:* 75
Bruce Graham

Toronto: The York School
1320 Yonge St., Toronto, ON M4T 1X2, Canada
Tel: 416-926-1325; *Fax:* 416-926-9592
info@yorkschool.com
www.yorkschool.com
Other Information: 416-646-5275 (Phone, Admissions)
www.facebook.com/pages/The-York-School/144875382199807
twitter.com/theyorkschool
www.linkedin.com/company/the-york-school

Grades: JK - 12 *Enrollment:* 593 *Note:* The York School is co-educational & non-denominational. It is an International Baccalaureate World School, which offers PYP, MYP, & Diploma programs.
Jason Hanson, Chair
Conor Jones, Head of School, 416-646-5271
Susan Charron, Principal, Lower School, 416-646-5273
susan_charron@tys.on.ca
David Hamilton, Principal, Upper School, 416-646-5272
david_hamilton@tys.on.ca
Helen Gin, Principal, Middle School
Conor Jones, Director, Admission
Robin Kester, Director, Advancement
Annette Whiteley, Director, Business & Finance

Toronto: The Yorkland School (TYS)
255 Yorkland Blvd., Toronto, ON M2J 1S3, Canada
Tel: 416-491-7667; *Fax:* 416-491-3806
admin@yorkland.on.ca
www.yorkland.on.ca

Grades: 7 - 12 *Note:* The Yorkland School is the middle & upper school division of the North Toronto Christian School, The school is commited to Biblical principles & values. The Yorkland School helps its students achieve both academically & athletically.
Kevin Ko, Principal

Trenton: Trenton Christian School
340 Second Dug Hill Rd., Trenton, ON K8V 5P7, Canada
Tel: 613-392-3600; *Fax:* 613-392-6316
office@trentonchristianschool.com
www.trentonchristianschool.com

Grades: Junior Kindergarten - 8
Linda Wikkerink, Chair
Allen Bron, Principal
Laurie Tuckey, Vice Principal
Mrs. K. Whitley, Director, Development

Unionville: Unionville Montessori School (UMS)
9302 Kennedy Rd., Unionville, ON L6C 1N6, Canada
Tel: 905-474-9888; *Fax:* 905-474-5767
www.unionvillemontessori.com

Grades: Preschool - 8 *Note:* Unionville Montessori School is a coeducational, non-denominational school. The Casa program is available for children from age two to six.
Kevin R. McCarthy, Principal
B.A, B.Sc., M.Ed.

Unionville: Yip's Music & Montessori Elementary School
100 Lee Ave., Unionville, ON L3R 8G2
Tel: 905-948-9477
www.yips.com
Other Information: Administration Phone: 905-752-0275, ext. 2100
www.facebook.com/YipsCanada
twitter.com/YipsCanada
www.youtube.com/user/kenny72ca

Grades: Pre.-8
Katherine Kwok, Chief Administrator
katherine@yips.com

Christian Bayly, Principal, Unionville Campus
christian@yips.com

Campuses
Markham Campus
#19, 28 Crown Steel Dr., Markham, ON L3R 0A1
Tel: 905-513-0955
Elsa Lee, Principal
elsa@yips.com

Thornhill Campus
#8, 8100 Yonge St., Thornhill, ON L4J 1W3
Tel: 905-881-9333
Amy Or, Principal
amy.or@yips.com

Utterson: Muskoka Christian School
P.O. Box 150
2483 Old Muskoka Rd., Utterson, ON P0B 1M0, Canada
Tel: 705-385-2847; *Fax:* 705-385-1756
mcs@muskoka.com
www.muskokachristianschool.com
Grades: Junior Kindergarten - 8 *Note:* The school is owned and operated by the Muskoka Association for Christian Education.
Lauralyn Mercer, Principal

Vaughan: Casa Dei Bambini Montessori School
#4-6, 661 Chrislea Rd., Vaughan, ON L4L 8A3
Tel: 905-851-8837; *Fax:* 905-851-8837
info@casadeibambini.ca
www.casadeibambini.ca
www.facebook.com/191392617592230
Grades: Pre.-K. *Enrollment:* 75
Francesca Davide, Director

Vaughan: Community Hebrew Academy of Toronto (CHAT)
Also known as: Kimel Centre
Vaughan Campus
9600 Bathurst St., Vaughan, ON L4A 3Z8, Canada
Tel: 905-787-8772; *Fax:* 905-787-8773
info@tanenbaumchat.org
www.chat-edu.ca
Grades: Sec. *Enrollment:* 600
Paul Shaviv, M.A., M.Phil., Director, Education

Vaughan: Kachol Lavan - The Centre for Hebrew & Israel Studies
Administration
Schwartz/Reisman Centre
#240, 9600 Bathurst St., Vaughan, ON L6A 3Z8
Tel: 905-303-5025
info@kachol-lavan.com
www.kachol-lavan.com
Note: Kachol-Lavan holds classes at the following schools: Leo Baek School, Thornhill Woods Public School, Bialik Hebrew Day School, & the University of Toronto. Please see website for more details.
Ariel Zaltzman, Director, Education
ariel@kachol-lavan.com

Vaughan: RoyalCrest Academy
9500 Dufferin St., Vaughan, ON L6A 1S2
Tel: 905-303-7557; *Fax:* 905-303-7107
admin@royalcrestacademy.com
www.royalcrestacademy.com
Grades: Pre.-8 *Enrollment:* 250
Michelle Johnson, Director, Admissions
Sharon Levy, Principal

Vaughn: As-Sadiq Islamic School
9000 Bathurst St., Vaughn, ON L4J 8A7, Canada
Tel: 905-695-1588; *Fax:* 905-695-1590
www.as-sadiqschool.com
Enrollment: 165
William Lahey

Wallaceburg: Wallaceburg Christian Private School (WCS)
693 Albert St., Wallaceburg, ON N8A 1Y8, Canada
Tel: 519-627-6013; *Fax:* 519-627-5051
admin@wallaceburgchristianschool.com
www.wallaceburgchristianschool.com
Grades: Junior Kindergarten - 8 *Note:* The school is a member of the Ontario Alliance of Christian Schools & Christian Schools International. It is independent of the Ministry of Education, although the school is registerd with the Ministry.
Andy J. Alblas, Principal

Waterloo: Kitchener Waterloo Bilingual School
600 Erb St. West, Waterloo, ON N2L 2Z4
Tel: 519-886-6510
kitchenerwaterloobilingualschool.org
Grades: JK-8
Michel Poinot
mpoinot@kitchenerwaterloobilingualschool.org

Waterloo: Kitchener-Waterloo Montessori School
194 Allen St. East, Waterloo, ON N2J 1K1
Tel: 519-742-1051; *Fax:* 519-742-1051
www.kwmontessorischool.com
Grades: K./Elem.

Campuses
Kitchener Location
527 Bridgeport Rd. East, Kitchener, ON N2K 1N6
Tel: 519-742-1051; *Fax:* 519-742-1051
Grades: K./Elem.

Webequie: Simon Jacob Memorial Education Centre
P.O. Box 265
Webequie, ON P0T 3A0, Canada
Tel: 807-353-6491; *Fax:* 807-353-1306
www.education.matawa.on.ca
Grades: K-10; Native Language; Special Ed. *Note:* The Simon Jacob Memorial Education Centre serves members of the Webequie First Nation, in a community about 540 kilometres northeast of Thunder Bay, Ontario. The education centre operates on a schedule, which is sensitive to the Webequie First Nation culture. The school is administered by the Webequie First Nation Education Authority.
Mary Gardiner, Principal
Stephanie Jones, Teacher, Special Education
Lois Whitehead, Instuctor, Native Language

Wellandport: Robert Land Academy
6726 South Chippawa Rd., RR#3, Wellandport, ON L0R 2J0, Canada
Tel: 905-386-6203; *Fax:* 905-386-6607
www.robertlandacademy.com
Grades: 6 - 12 *Enrollment:* 165 *Note:* Robert Land Academy is a highly structured military boarding school, which provides education for previously under-achieving boys with potential.
Major (retired) G. Scott Bowman, Founder & Headmaster

Wheatley: Old Colony Christian Academy
21311 Campbell Rd., RR#1, Wheatley, ON N0P 2P0, Canada
Tel: 519-825-9188; *Fax:* 519-825-9122
Grades: Elem. *Enrollment:* 252
Abe Thiessen

Whitby: Trafalgar Castle School
401 Reynolds St., Whitby, ON L1N 3W9, Canada
Tel: 905-668-3358; *Fax:* 905-668-4136
www.trafalgarcastle.ca
www.facebook.com/Trafalgarcastle
twitter.com/trafalgarcastle
Grades: 6 - 12 *Note:* The day & boarding school educates young women.
Adam De Pencier, Head of School
depencier.adam@trafalgarcastle.ca
Gillian Martin, Vice Principal, School Life, 905-668-3358, ext. 228
martin.gillian@trafalgarcastle.ca
Tim Southwell, Vice Principal, Academics, 905-668-3358, ext. 229
southwell.tim@trafalgarcastle.ca
Marguerita Dykstra, Director, Finance, 905-668-3358, ext. 232
dykstra.marguerita@trafalgarcastle.ca
Sharon Magor, Director, Marketing & Development
magor.sharon@trafalgarcastle.ca

Whitby: Whitby Montessori & Elementary School
95 Taunton Rd. East, Whitby, ON L1R 3L3, Canada
Tel: 905-430-8201
Grades: Preschool - Elementary *Note:* Whitby Montessori & Elementary School educates children from age thirteen months to fourteen years.
Cathy Barber, Principal

Williamsburg: Timothy Christian School
P.O. Box 179
12600 County Rd. 18, Williamsburg, ON K0C 2H0, Canada
Tel: 613-535-2687; *Fax:* 613-535-1074
www.tcswilliamsburg.ca
Grades: Junior Kindergarten - 8 *Enrollment:* 130
Gary Postma, Principal
Principal@tcswilliamsburg.ca
Truusje Berkelaar, Administrative Assistant
office@tcswilliamsburg.ca

Windsor: Académie Ste. Cécile International School
925 Cousineau Rd., Windsor, ON N9G 1V8, Canada
Tél: 519-969-1291; *Téléc:* 519-969-7953
info@stececile.ca
www.stececile.ca
Grades: Pre./Elem./Sec. *Enrollment:* 250 *Note:* Affiliated with the Univ. of Windsor. Programmes include the Ontario Sec. School Programme, the International Bacc. Programme, Advanced Placement; emphasis on music, dance, art, & performing arts, as well as programmes in technology; ESL, FSL & TOEFL courses; summer school.
Thérèse H. Gadoury, Principal

Windsor: An-Noor Private School
1480 Janette Ave., Windsor, ON N8X 1Z4, Canada
Tel: 519-966-4422; *Fax:* 519-966-5233
www.wiao.org
www.facebook.com/windsormosque
Grades: JK-8 *Enrollment:* 158 *Note:* Provides students with an academic and Islamic education.
Amney Behiry, Principal
amneybehiry@cogeco.ca

Windsor: First Lutheran Christian Academy
3850 Locke St., Windsor, ON N9G 1S1, Canada
Tel: 519-250-7888; *Fax:* 519-250-7715
flca@mnsi.net
www.flca.ca
Enrollment: 201
Suzanne Eberhard, Principal
Rev. Gilvan L.C. de Azevedo, Pastor

Windsor: Maranatha Christian Academy
939 Northwood St., Windsor, ON N9E 1A2
Tel: 519-966-7424; *Fax:* 519-966-9519
www.maranathachristian.ca
Grades: JK-12
Amy Kulik, Principal
akulik@maranathachristian.ca

Windsor: Windsor Christian Fellowship Academy
4490 - 7th Concession, RR#1, Windsor, ON N9A 6J3, Canada
Tel: 519-972-5977; *Fax:* 519-972-0075
www.wcf.ca
www.facebook.com/WindsorChristianFellowship
twitter.com/wincf/wcf-pastors
Grades: Elem. *Enrollment:* 81
Patti Banks

Woodbridge: Credo Christian Private School
8260 Huntington Rd., RR#1, Woodbridge, ON L4L 1A5, Canada
Tel: 905-851-1620; *Fax:* 905-851-1620
office@credochristianschool.com
credochristianschool.com
Grades: K.-8
L.P. Maat, Principal
G. Vanluik, Principal's Relief

Woodbridge: King Heights Academy
28 Roytec Rd., Woodbridge, ON L4L 8E4
Tel: 905-652-1234; *Fax:* 905-652-9000
info@kingheightsacademy.com
kingheightsacademy.com
Grades: JK-6 *Enrollment:* 150
Elsa Norberto, Director

Woodbridge: Maple Leaf Montessori Schools Inc.
8286 Islington Ave., Woodbridge, ON L4L 1W8, Canada
Tel: 905-856-3359
info@mlmontessori.org
www.mlmontessori.org
Grades: Elementary *Enrollment:* 178
Johanna Madeley, Administrator & Co-founder
johanna@mlmontessori.org
Michael Madeley, Principal
michael@mlmontessori.org

Woodbridge: Toronto District Christian High School
377 Woodbridge Ave., Woodbridge, ON L4L 2V7, Canada
Tel: 905-851-1772; *Fax:* 905-851-9992
info@tdchristian.ca
www.tdchristian.ca
Grades: Secondary
William Groot, Principal
principal@tdchristian.ca
Tim Bentum, Vice Principal, Admissions & Students
bentum@tdchristian.ca
Tim Buwalda, Coordinator, Communications
buwalda@tdchristian.ca
Meg Cate, Financial Administrator
cate@tdchristian.ca

Wunnummin Lake: Lydia Lois Beardy Memorial School
P.O. Box 108
General Delivery, Wunnummin Lake, ON P0V 2Z0
Tel: 807-442-2575; *Fax:* 807-442-2640
llbms.firstnationschools.ca
Grades: Elem./Sec.

Wyoming: John Knox Christian School of Wyoming
4738 Confederation Line, Wyoming, ON N0N 1T0
Tel: 519-845-3112; *Fax:* 519-845-1404
www.wyomingjkcs.com
Grades: K./Elem.
Ymko Boersma, Principal

Universities & Colleges

Universities

Guelph: University of Guelph
50 Stone Rd. East, Guelph, ON N1G 2W1, Canada
Tel: 519-824-4120; *Fax:* 519-767-1693
www.uoguelph.ca
www.facebook.com/uofguelph
twitter.com/uofg
www.youtube.com/uofguelph
Full Time Equivalency: 19408
Pamela Wallin, O.C., S.O.M., Chancellor
chancellor@uoguelph.ca
Alastair J.S. Summerlee, President & Vice-Chancellor
president@uoguelph.ca
Maureen Mancuso, Provost & Vice-President (Academic)
Don O'Leary, Vice-President (Finance & Administration)
Martha Harley, Asst. Vice-President (Human Resources)
Brenda Whiteside, Assoc. Vice-President (Student Affairs)
Serge Desmarais, Assoc. Vice-President (Academic)
Michael Ridley, Chief Librarian & Chief Information Officer

Faculties
Arts
Donald Bruce, Dean
Biological Science
Dr. Michael J. Emes, Dean
Environmental Sciences
Josef Ackerman, Dean
Graduate Studies
Isobel Heathcote, Dean
Management & Economics
Julia Christensen Hughes, Dean
Ontario Agricultural College
Robert J. Gordon, Dean
Ontario Veterinary College
Dr. Elizabeth Stone, Dean
Physical & Engineering Science
Anthony Vannelli, Dean
Social & Applied Human Sciences
Kerry Daly, Dean

Schools
College d'Alfred
Marcel Couture, Acting Director
Engineering
Richard Zynter, Acting Director
Environmental Design & Rural Development
Robert Brown, Acting Director
Fine Arts & Music
John Kissick, Director
Hospitality & Tourism Management
Marion Joppe, Director
Kemptville College
Michael Goss, Director
Ridgetown College
Ron Pitblado, Acting Director
School of English & Theatre Studies
David Murray, Acting Director

Publications
At Guelph
Guelph Peak
The Ontarion

Hamilton: McMaster University
1280 Main St. West, Hamilton, ON L8S 4L8, Canada
Tel: 905-525-9140; *Fax:* 905-521-9183
www.mcmaster.ca
Full Time Equivalency: 23325
Lynton (Red) Wilson, Chancellor, ext. 24340
Peter George, President & Vice-Chancellor, ext. 24340
Engineering
David S. Wilkinson, Dean
Graduate Studies
F.L. Hall, Dean
Health Sciences
John G. Kelton, Dean
Humanities
Suzanne Crosta, Dean
Science
John P. Capone, Dean
Social Sciences
Charlotte A.B. Yates, Dean

Schools
DeGroote School of Business
Paul Bates, Dean
Arts & Science Program
Gary Warner, Director
Indigenous Studies Program
Dawn Martin-Hill, Director
Institute on Globalization & the Human Condition
Robert O'Brien, Director

Affiliations
McMaster Divinity College
1280 Main St. West, Hamilton, ON L8S 4K1, Canada
Tel: 905-525-9140; *Fax:* 090-577-4782
divinity@mcmaster.ca
www.macdiv.ca
www.facebook.com/pages/McMaster-Divinity-College/12129417 4658731
twitter.com/McMasterDiv
Full Time Equivalency: 300
Stanley E. Porter, Principal & Dean
Bill Marshall, Director, Finance, 905-525-9140, ext. 24685
marshaw@mcmaster.ca
Dr. Phil Zylla, Academic Dean, 905-525-9140, ext. 20104
zyllap@mcmaster.ca

Publications
Community Report
McMaster Times
vanraay@mcmaster.ca
Note: Alumni magazine.
McMaster Update
c/o Office of Public Relations, Room 111, Chester
1280 Main St. West, Hamilton, ON L8S 4L9, Canada
Tel: 905-525-9140
update@mcmaster.ca

Hearst: Université de Hearst
P.O. Box 580
60, 9e Rue, Hearst, ON P0L 1N0, Canada
Tél: 705-372-1781; *Ligne sans frais:* 1-800-887-1781
info_gen@uhearst.ca
www.uhearst.ca
www.facebook.com/uhearst
Raymond Tremblay, B.A., B.Sc., M.A., Ph.D., Recteur
Pierre Ouellette, B.A., M.A., Vice-recteur
Manon Cyr, B.A., M.B.A., Secrétaire générale
Kapuskasing
7, av Aurora, Kapuskasing, ON P5N 1J6, Canada
Tél: 705-335-8561; *Ligne sans frais:* 1-866-335-8561

Campuses
Timmins
395, boul Thériault, Timmins, ON P4N 0A8, Canada
Tél: 705-267-2144; *Ligne sans frais:* 1-866-467-2144

Kingston: Queen's University
99 University Ave., Kingston, ON K7L 3N6, Canada
Tel: 613-533-2000; *Fax:* 613-533-6300
www.queensu.ca
Full Time Equivalency: 21607
David A. Dodge, Chancellor
Dr. Tom Williams, B.Sc., M.A., Ph.D., Principal & Vice-Chancellor
Leora Jackson, B.Sc.H, Rector
Sean Conway, B.A., Vice-Principal
Bill Bryck, Vice-Principal
Jo-Anne Brady, B.A., M.B.A., University Registrar
Georgina Moore, B.A., Secretary of the Senate, University & Board
Richard P. Seres, B.Comm., Director
Peggy Watkin, Secretary of the University Council
Mike Stefano, Director
Chris Tabor, Bookstore Manager
Dr. Patrick Deane, Ph.D., Vice-Principal
Dr. Kerry Rowe, B.Sc., B.E., Ph.D., D.Eng, Vice-Principal
Roderick Morrison, B.A., M.B.A., M.I.R., Vice-Principal

Faculties
Applied Science
Dr. K. Woodhouse, Ph.D., P.Eng., Dean
Arts & Science
Dr. A. MacLean, Ph.D., C.Psych., Dean
Business
Dr. David Saunders, Ph.D., Dean
Education
Dr. Rosa Bruno-Jofré, Ph.D., Dean
Graduate Studies & Research
Dr. J. Deakin, Ph.D., Dean
Health Sciences
Dr. David M.C. Walker, M.D., F.R.C.P.(C), Dean
Law
William F. Flanagan, J.D., D.E.A., LL.M., Dean

Schools
Centre for International Relations
Charles Pentland, B.A., M.A., Ph.D., Director
English
Amanda Marshall, Acting Co-Chair
Barbara Yates, Acting Co-Chair
Institute of Intergovernmental Relations
Sean Conway, Director
Music
Gordon E. Smith, A.R.C.T., B.A., M.A., Ph., Director
Nursing
Cynthia Baker, M.N., Ph.D., Director
Physical & Health Education
Janice Deakin, B.A., B.P.H.E., M.Sc., Director
Policy Studies
Arthur Sweetman, B.Eng., M.A., Ph.D., Director
Rehabilitation Therapy
Sandra J. Olney, B.Sc., Ph.D., M.Ed., Director
Theological College
Jean Stairs, Mus.Bac., M.Div., D.Min., Principal
Urban & Regional Planning
Hok-Lin Leung, B.Arch., M.C.P., M.Sc., P, Director
Computing
James Cordy, B.Sc., M.Sc., Ph.D., P.En, Director

Publications
antiThesis
Golden Words
Queen's Alumni Review
79 Stuart St, Kingston, ON K7L 3N6, Canada
Fax: 613-545-6777
Queen's Journal

Kingston: Royal Military College of Canada
Collège militaire royal du Canada
P.O. Box 17000 Forces
Kingston, ON K7K 7B4, Canada
Tel: 613-541-6000; *Fax:* 613-542-3565
Toll-Free: 1-866-762-2672
liaison@rmc.ca; transcripts@rmc.ca; webmaster@rmc.ca
www.rmc.ca
Other Information: Undergraduate Programs: 613-541-6000, ext. 6797
Note: Individuals must be a Canadian citizen in possession of the necessary academic qualifications. Applicants must also be one of the following: an MOC ((Military Occupation Classification) qualified member of the Canadian Forces; an applicant for the Regular Officer Training Plan (ROTP) or the Reserve Entry Training Plan (RETP); an employee of the Department of National Defence; or the spouse of a member of the Canadian Forces.
Dr. Joel Sokolsky, BA, MA, PhD, Principal
principals.office@rmc.ca
BGen Don Macnamara, Chair
MGen Pierre Forgues, Vice-Chair
Colonel J.G.B. Ouellette, CD, Director, Cadets
Major Raymond Stouffer, CD, BA, MA, PhD, Registrar, 613-541-6000, ext. 6302

Faculties
Arts
J.J. Sokolsky, BA, MA, PhD, Dean
sokolsky-j@rmc.ca
Continuing Studies
M.A. Hennessy, BA, MA, PhD., Dean
hennessy-m@rmc.ca

Engineering
Dr. John A. Stewart, Dean
stewart_j@rmc.ca

Graduate Studies & Research
Dr. B.J. Fugère, Dean
fugere-j@rmc.ca

Science
Dr. Richard Marsden, Dean
marsden-r@rmc.ca

London: Brescia University College
1285 Western Rd., London, ON N6G 1H2, Canada
Tel: 519-432-8353; *Fax:* 519-858-5137
brescia@uwo.ca
www.brescia.uwo.ca
Full Time Equivalency: 1005 *Note:* A women's university affiliated with the University of Western Ontario

London: King's University College
266 Epworth Ave., London, ON N6A 2M3, Canada
Tel: 519-433-3491; *Fax:* 519-433-2227
Toll-Free: 1-800-265-4406
kings@uwo.ca
www.uwo.ca/kings
www.facebook.com/kingsatwestern
twitter.com/KUCatUWO
www.youtube.com/kingsatuwo
Full Time Equivalency: 3650

London: University of Western Ontario
#2, 1151 Richmond St., London, ON N6A 5B8, Canada
Tel: 519-661-2111
www.uwo.ca
Full Time Equivalency: 25000
Dr. Amit Chakma, President & Vice-Chancellor
Frank Angeletti, Vice-Chair
Fred Longstaffe, Provost & Vice-President
Gitta Kulczycki, Vice-President
Ted Garrard, Vice-President
Ted Hewitt, Vice-President
Irene Birrell, Secretary
Valerie Smith, Director
G. Blazak, Director
D. Jones, Director
G.E. Hutchinson, Director
Therese Quigley, Director
S. Grindrod, Assoc. Vice-President
J. Schroeder, Director
Joyce Garnett, Director
V. Smith, Director
R. Moore, Director
Susan Hoddinott, Director
S. Bantock, Director
Michael Mics, Manager
D. Estok, Director
Alan Weedon, Vice-Provost
Carole A. Orchard, Director
Roma Harris, Vice-Provost & Registrar
Tyrrel de Langley, Director
D. Dawson, Director
Alex Navarre, Director
Steve Alb, Director
F. Bauer, Ombudsman
Michele Noble, Chair
John Thompson, Chancellor

Faculties
Arts & Humanities

Education
Julia O'Sullivan, Dean

Engineering
Amit Chakma, Dean

Graduate Studies
Alan C. Weedon, Dean

Health Sciences
William James Weese, Dean

Information & Media Studies
Dr. Thomas Carmichael, Dean

Law
Ian Holloway, Dean

Medicine & Dentistry
Carol Herbert, Dean

Music
Robert Wood, Dean

Richard Ivey School of Business
Carol Stephenson, Dean

Science
David M. Wardlaw, Dean

Social Science
Brian Timney, Dean

Schools
Applied Electrostatics Research Centre
I. Inculet, Director

Boundary Layer Wind Tunnel Laboratory
A.G. Davenport, Director

Canadian Centre for Activity & Aging
Clara Fitzgerald, Director

Centre for Cognitive Science
Z.W. Pylyshyn, Director

Centre for Health & Well-Being
W. Avison, Director

Centre for Interdisciplinary Studies in Chemical Physics
M. Stillman, Director

Centre for Mass Media Studies
A.M. Osler, Director

Centre for Research & Teaching of Canadian Native Languages
R. Darnell, Director

Centre for Studies in Family Medicine
M. Stewart, Director

Centre for the Study of International Economic Relations
J. Whalley, Director

Centre for the Study of Theory & Criticism
T. Rajan, Director

Centre for Textual Scholarship
R.J. Shroyer, Director

Centre for Women's Studies & Feminist Research
Katherine McKenna, Director

Chemical Reactor Engineering Centre
H. de Lasa, Director

Continuing Studies
Kim Miller, Acting Director

Geotechnical Research Centre
K. Lo, Director

International Centre for Olympic Studies
R. Barney, Director

John P. Robarts Research Institute
M. Poznansky, Director
poznansky@admin.rri.uwo.ca

London Museum of Archaeology
Robert Pearce, Director

National Centre for Management Research & Development
K. Hardy, Director

National Tax Centre
T.W. Edgar, Director

Population Studies Centre
Rajulton Fernando, Director

Research Centre in Tribology
W.K. Wan, Director

Surface Science Western
Leo Lau, Director

Affiliations
Brescia University College
1285 Western Rd., London, ON N6G 1H2, Canada
Tel: 519-432-8553; *Fax:* 519-679-6489
www.brescia.uwo.ca
www.facebook.com/BresciaUniversityCollege
twitter.com/bresciauc
www.linkedin.com/company/brescia-university-college
www.youtube.com/bresciauc
Dr. Colleen Hanycz, Principal, 519-432-8353, ext. 28263
chanycz@uwo.ca
Dr John B. Mitchell, Academic Dean, 519-432-8353, ext. 28263
jbmitche@uwo.ca
Marianne Simm, Registrar & Director, Student Affairs, 519-432-8353, ext. 28266
msimm@uwo.ca

King's University College
266 Epworth Ave., London, ON N6A 2M3, Canada
Tel: 519-433-3491; *Fax:* 519-433-2227
Toll-Free: 800-265-4406
kings@uwo.ca
www.kings.uwo.ca
www.facebook.com/kingsatwestern
twitter.com/kucatuwo
Dr. David Sylvester, Principal
Sauro Camiletti, Academic Dean
academic.dean@uwo.ca
Marilyn Mason, Registrar
mmason@uwo.ca

Huron University College
1349 Western Rd., London, ON N6G 1H3, Canada
Tel: 519-438-7224; *Fax:* 519-438-3938
www.huronuc.on.ca
www.facebook.com/101245552822
twitter.com/huronatwestern
Dr. Stephen McClatchie, Principal
smcclatchie@huron.uwo.ca

Publications
Alumni Gazette

The Gazette
Rm. 244, University Community Centre
London, ON N6A 3K7, Canada
Fax: 519-661-3816

Western Alumni Gazette
#11, Alumni Hall, University of Western Ontario
Richmond St. N, London, ON N6A 5B9, Canada
Fax: 519-661-3948

Western News

North Bay: Nipissing University
P.O. Box 5002
100 College Dr., North Bay, ON P1B 8L7, Canada
Tel: 705-474-3450; *Fax:* 705-474-1947
nuinfo@nipissingu.ca
www.nipissingu.ca
www.facebook.com/NipissingU
twitter.com/NipissingU
www.youtube.com/user/nipissinguniversity
Full Time Equivalency: 4800
David Brian Liddle, Chancellor
Vicky Paine-Mantha, Interim President & Vice-Chancellor
Peter Gavan, Chair
Richard Onley, Vice-Pres., Finance & Administration, ext. 4289
Dr. Harley d'Entremont, Vice-Pres., Academic & Research, ext. 4565
Bob Keech, Vice-Pres., Operations
Laurie McLaren, Exec. Dir., Aboriginal Initiatives
Jamie Graham, Registrar & Institutional Analyst

Faculties
Applied & Professional Studies
Rick Vanderlee, Dean
rickv@nipissingu.ca

Arts & Science
Dr. Craig Cooper, Dean, ext. 4290
craigc@nipissingu.ca

Schulich School of Education
Dr. Sharon Rich, Dean
sharonr@nipissingu.ca

Campuses
Brantford
50 Wellington St., Brantford, ON N3T 2L6
Tel: 519-752-1524; *Fax:* 519-752-8372
brant@nipissingu.ca.
Dr Maria Cantalini-Williams, Interim Assoc. Dean
mariac@nipissingu.ca

Muskoka
125 Wellington St., Bracebridge, ON P1L 1E2
Tel: 705-645-2921; *Fax:* 705-645-2922
muskoka@nipissingu.ca
Jan Lucy, Campus Administrator
janl@nipissingu.ca

Oshawa: University of Ontario Institute of Technology (UOIT)
2000 Simcoe St. North, Oshawa, ON L1H 7K4, Canada
Tel: 905-721-8668; *Fax:* 905-721-3178
admissions@uoit.ca
www.uoit.ca
Full Time Equivalency: 6500
Hon. Perrin Beatty, B.A., Chancellor
Dr. Ronald Bordessa, B.A., Ph.D, L.L.D. (Hons.), President & Vice-Chancellor, 905-721-8668, ext. 3212
ron.bordessa@uoit.ca

Richard Marceau, B.Eng., M.Sc.A., Ph.D., F, Provost, 905-721-8668, ext. 3147, fax: 905-721-3210
richard.marceau@uoit.ca
MaryLynn West-Moynes, B.Sc. (Hons.), M.A., Vice-President, External Relations, 905-721-8668, ext. 3135
marylynn.west-moynes@uoit.ca
Ralph Aprile, B.Tech., M.B.A., Vice-President, Facilities & Ancillary Services, 905-721-8668, ext. 3024
ralph.aprile@dc-uoit.ca
Tom Austin, B.A., C.M.A., Vice-President, Finance & CFO, 905-721-8668, ext. 3796
tom.austin@uoit.ca
Margaret Greenley, B.Ed., M.A., Vice-President, Student Affairs, 905-721-8668, ext. 2340
margaret.greenley@uoit.ca
Pamela Drayson, B.A., M.A., Ph.D., Chief Librarian, 905-721-8668, ext. 2348
pamela.drayson@uoit.ca
Victoria Choy, B.A. (Hons.), M.A., Registrar, 905-721-8668, ext. 2988
victoria.choy@uoit.ca

Faculties
Business & Information Technology
www.businessandit.uoit.ca
Pamela Ritchie, B.A., M.Sc., Ph.D., Dean, 905-721-8668, ext. 3160
pamela.ritchie@uoit.ca

Criminology, Justice, & Policy Studies (Social Sciences & Humanities)
www.criminologyandjustice.uoit.ca/
Nawal Ammar, B.Sc. (Hons.), M.Sc., Ph., Dean, 905-721-8668, ext. 3159
nawal.ammar@uoit.ca

Education
kim.mitchell@uoit.ca (Receptionist, Faculty of Education)
education.uoit.ca
Jim Greenlaw, B.A., B.Ed., M.A.(T), Ph., Dean, 905.721.8668, ext. 3158
jim.greenlaw@uoit.ca

Energy Systems & Nuclear Science
admissions@uoit.ca
nuclear.uoit.ca
George Bereznai, B.Eng., M.Eng., Ph.D., Dean, 905-721-8668, ext. 3142
george.bereznai@uoit.ca

Engineering & Applied Science
engineering@uoit.ca
www.engineering.uoit.ca
George Bereznai, B.Eng., M.Eng., Ph.D., Dean, 905-721-8668, ext. 3142
george.bereznai@uoit.ca

Health Sciences
viven.ricard@uoit.ca
www.healthsciences.uoit.ca
Mary Bluechardt, E.M.T., B.PHE, M.Sc., Ph., Dean, 905-721-8668, ext. 2518
mary.bluechardt@uoit.ca

Science
facultyofscience@uoit.ca
www.science.uoit.ca
Deborah Saucier, Ph.D., Dean, 905-721-8668, ext. 3235
deborah.saucier@uoit.ca

Office of Graduate Studies
gradstudies@uoit.ca
gradstudies.uoit.ca/
Brian Campbell, Dean, 905-721-8668, ext. 2650
brian.campbell@uoit.ca

Ottawa: Carleton University
1125 Colonel By Dr., Ottawa, ON K1S 5B6, Canada
Tel: 613-520-7400; *Fax:* 613-520-7858
info@carleton.ca
www.carleton.ca

Grades: 25200
Herb Gray, Chancellor
Dr. Roseann O'Reilly Runte, President & Vice-Chancellor, 613-520-3801
presidents_office@carleton.ca
Peter Ricketts, Provost & Vice-President, 613-520-3884
provost@carleton.ca
Duncan Watt, Vice-Pres., Finance & Administration, 613-520-3804
duncan_watt@carleton.ca
Kimberly Matheson, Vice-Pres., Research & International, 613-520-7838
vpri@carleton.ca
Gisele Samson-Verreault, Chair, 613-520-3811
governors@carleton.ca
Suzanne Blanchard, Registrar, 613-520-2874, fax: 613-520-4410
registrar@carleton.ca

Faculties
Arts & Social Sciences
John Osborne, Dean, 613-520-2355, fax: 613-520-4481
fassod@carleton.ca

Engineering & Design
Dr Rafik Goubran, Dean, 613-520-5790, fax: 613-520-7481
info_engdesign@carleton.ca

Graduate & Postdoctoral Affairs
John Shepard, Dean, 613-520-2525, fax: 613-520-4049
graduate_studies@carleton.ca

Public Affairs
John ApSimon, Interim Dean, 613-520-3741, fax: 613-520-3742
odfpa@carleton.ca

Science
Malcolm Butler, Dean, 613-520-4388, fax: 613-520-4389
odscience@carleton.ca

Azrieli School of Architecture & Urbanism
Sheryl Boyle, Director, 613-520-2855, fax: 613-520-2849
architecture@carleton.ca

Schools
School for Studies in Art & Culture
Brian Foss, Director, 613-520-2600, ext. 3791, fax: 613-520-3575
brian_foss@carleton.ca

Linguistics & Language Studies
Lynne Young, Acting Director, 613-520-6612, fax: 613-520-6641
slals@carleton.ca

Sprott School of Business
Dr. Jerry Tomberlin, Dean, 613-520-2388, fax: 613-520-4427
info@sprott.carleton.ca

Canadian Studies
André Loiselle, Director, 613-520-2366, fax: 613-520-3903
canadian_studies@carleton.ca

Computer Science
Dr Douglas Howe, Director, 613-520-4333, fax: 613-520-4334
howescs.carleton.ca

Technology, Society, Environment Studies
Dr. John Buschek, Chair, 613-520-4483
john_buschek@carleton.ca

Industrial Design
Thomas Garvey, Director, 613-520-5672, fax: 613-520-4465
diane_smyth@carleton.ca

Information Technology
Dr Anthony Whitehead, Director, 613-520-5644, fax: 613-520-6623
info@bitdegree.ca

Journalism & Communication
Christopher Waddell, Director, 613-520-7404, fax: 613-520-6690
journalism@carleton.ca

Norman Paterson School of International Affairs
Bryan Henderson, Director, 613-520-6655, fax: 613-520-2889
international_affairs@carleton.ca

Public Policy & Administration
Dr. Susan Phillips, Director, 613-520-2547, fax: 613-520-2551
sppa@carleton.ca

Social Work
Hugh Shewell, Director, 613-520-5601, fax: 613-520-7496
karen_spencer@carleton.ca

Mathematics & Statistics
Yiqiang Zhao, Director, 613-520-3531
ms-dir@math.carleton.ca

Institute for Comparative Studies in Literature, Art & Culture
Paul Théberge, Director, 613-520-2177
icslac@carleton.ca

Institute of African Studies
Blair Rutherford, Director, 613-520-2600, ext. 2220, fax: 613-520-2363
african_studies@carleton.ca

Institute of Cognitive Science
Dr Jo-Anne Lefevre, Director, 613-520-2368, fax: 613-520-3985
jo-anne_lefevre@carleton.ca

Institute of Interdisciplinary Studies
Fran Cherry, Director, 613-520-2368, fax: 613-520-3985
iis@carleton.ca

Pauline Jewett Institute of Women's & Gender Studies
Katharine Kelly, Director, 613-520-6645, fax: 613-520-2622
womens_studies@carleton.ca

Institute of Criminology & Criminal Justice
Joanna Pozzulo, Director, 613-520-2588, fax: 613-520-6654
criminology@carleton.ca

Institute of European, Russian & Eurasian Studies
Dr Jeff Sahadeo, Director, 613-520-2888, fax: 613-520-7501
jeff_sahadeo@carleton.ca

Institute of Political Economy
Prof Janet Siltanen, Director, 613-520-7414, fax: 613-520-2154
political_economy@carleton.ca

Institute of Biochemistry
John Vierula, Director, 613-520-2478, fax: 613-520-3539
biochem@carleton.ca

Institute of Environmental Science
Dr Frederick A. Michel, Director, 613-520-2600, ext. 4461, fax: 613-520-3422
environmentalscience@carelton.ca

Integrated Science Institute
Pam Wolff, Director, 613-520-2600, ext. 4461, fax: 613-520-3422
integratedscience@carleton.ca

Publications
Carleton University Magazine
Tel: 613-520-3636; *Fax:* 613-520-3587
advancement@carleton.ca
magazine.carleton.ca
Fateema Sayani, Editor
fateema_sayani@carleton.ca

The Charlatan
Tel: 613-520-6680
charlatan@charlatan.ca
www.charlatan.ca
Note: An independent student newspaper since 1945
Julia Johnson, Editor-In-Chief
editor@charlatan.ca

Ottawa: Dominican University College
Collège Universitaire Dominicain
96 Empress Ave., Ottawa, ON K1R 7G3, Canada
Tel: 613-233-5696; *Fax:* 613-233-6064
info@dominicancollege.ca
www.collegedominicain.ca

Full Time Equivalency: 110
Yvon Pomerleau, O.P., Chancellor
Gabor Csepregi, President & Regent of Studies
Michel Gourges, O.P., Vice-President
Peter Foy, Sec.-Treas.
Francis Peddle, Master of Studies
Daniel Cadrin, Chair, Institute of Pastoral Studies
Marie-Thérèse Nadeau, C.N.D., Dean, Faculty of Theology
Jean-François Méthot, Dean, Philosophy

Ottawa: Saint Paul University
Université Saint-Paul
223 Main St., Ottawa, ON K1S 1C4, Canada
Tel: 613-236-1393; *Fax:* 613-782-3005
Toll-Free: 1-800-637-6859
info@ustpaul.ca; studentservices@ustpaul.ca;
bookstore@ustpaul.ca
www.ustpaul.ca
www.facebook.com/143697609023948
www.youtube.com/user/uspottawa

Rev. Dale Schlitt, Rector
Prof. Achiel Peelman, Acting Vice-Rector, Academic
Prof. Chantal Beauvais, Vice-Rector, Administration
Rev. Andrea Spatafora, Dean, Faculty of Theology

Canon Law
Anne Asselin, Dean

Faculties
Human Sciences
Karlijn Demasure, Dean

Philosophy

Theology
Andrea Spatafora, Dean

Ottawa: University of Ottawa
Université d'Ottawa

75 Laurier Ave. East, Ottawa, ON K1N 6N5, Canada
Tel: 613-562-5700; *Fax:* 613-562-5103
Toll-Free: 1-877-868-8292
www.uottawa.ca

Full Time Equivalency: 35548
Huguette Labelle, O.C., B.Sc.N.Ed., B.Ed.,, Chancellor
Allan Rock, B.A., P.C., President & Vice-Chancellor
François Hule, Vice-President, Academic & Provost
Sylvie Lauzon, B.Sc., M.Sc., Ph.D., Assoc. Vice-President
Victor Simon, B.A., M.A., Vice-President
Louis de Melo, B.A., C.M.A., Vice-President
Pierre Mercier, B.A., M.A., Ph.D., Assoc. Vice-President
Pamela Harrod, Secretary
François Chapleau, B.Sc., M.Sc., Ph.D., Registrar & Assoc. Vice-President
Leslie Weir, B.A., M.L.S., Chief Librarian
Lyse Huot, B.A., Director
Kathryn Prud'homme, B.A., LL.B., Legal Counsel
Mona Nemer, Vice-President
Nicolas Georganas, Ph.D., F.I.E.E., F.R.S.Ca, Assoc. Vice-President
Adele Reinhart, B.A., M.A., Ph.D., Assoc. Vice-President
Paul Boult, B.A., Director

Faculties
Management
Micheál J. Kelly, A.B., M.A., Ph.D., Dean

Arts
Antoni Lewkowicz, B.A., M.A., Ph.D., Dean

Education
Marie Josée Berger, B.Ed., M.Ed. Ph.D., Dean

Engineering
Claude Laguë, Dean

Health Sciences
Denis Prud'homme, B.Sc., M.Sc., PR.D., M.D., Dean

Law, Common Law Section
Bruce Feldthusen, Dean

Law, Civil Law Section
Sébastien Grammond, Dean

Medicine
Jacques Bradwejn, Dean

Science
André Lalonde, B.Sc., M.Sc., Ph.D., Dean

Social Sciences
Catherine M. Lee, Ph.D., Acting Dean

Graduate Studies & Postdoctoral
Gary Slater, B.Sc., M.Sc., Ph.D., Dean

Publications
Tabaret Magazine

The Fulcrum

La Rotonde

Peterborough: Trent University

1600 West Bank Dr., Peterborough, ON K9J 7B8, Canada
Tel: 705-748-1011; *Fax:* 705-748-1246
Toll-Free: 1-888-739-8885
www.trentu.ca

Full Time Equivalency: 7475
David L. Morton, B.A., M.B.A., LL.D., Chair
Tom Jackson, O.C., LL.D (Hon.), Chancellor
Dr. Steven E. Franklin, Ph.D., President & Vice-Chancellor
Don F. O'Leary, B.B.A., Vice-President
Colin Taylor, M.A., Ph.D., Dean
Dianne Lister, Vice-President
Christopher Michael, B.A., LL.B., Registrar
Julie E. Smith, LL.B., Secretary of the Senate
Leonard Conolly, M.A., Ph.D.., Principal
Michael Peterman, A.B., M.A., Ph.D., Principal
Stephen Brown, M.A., Ph.D., F.S.A., Master
A.A. Krüger, STAATSEXAMEN, Principal
Ian Storey, M.A., Ph.D., Head
Dr. Jocelyn Aubrey, Assoc. Dean of Arts & Science
Garth Brownscombe, B.A., CGA, Director
Lorraine Hayes, B.Sc., Manager
Don Cumming, B.A., Senior Director
Bill Byrick, B.A., Director
D'Arcy Legros, Bookstore Manager
Dr. Christine McKinnon, B.A. (Hons.), B.Phil., D., Vice-President
James Parker, B.A., M.A., Ph.D., Assoc. Vice-President
David Poole, B.Sc., M.Sc., Ph.D., Associate Dean

Publications
Arthur

St Catharines: Brock University

500 Glenridge Ave., St Catharines, ON L2S 3A1, Canada
Tel: 905-688-5550; *Fax:* 905-688-2789
www.brocku.ca

Full Time Equivalency: 17493
Dr Ned Goodman, Chancellor
Dr Jack N. Lightstone, President & Vice-Chancellor
Dr Murray Knuttila, Provost/Vice-Pres., Academic
Steven Pillar, Vice-Pres., Finance/Admin.
David Petis, Vice-Pres., Advancement
Ian Brindle, Vice-Pres., Research
Barb Anderson, Registrar, ext. 3566
bdavis@brocku.ca

Faculties
Business
Barbara Sainty, Interim Dean, ext. 3182
bsainty@brocku.ca

Education
James Heap, Dean, ext. 5190
jheap@brocku.ca

Humanities
Rosemary Hale, Dean, ext. 4562
rhale@brocku.ca

Social Sciences
Thomas Dunk, Dean, ext. 3426
tdunk@brocku.ca

Mathematics & Sciences
Richard Cheel, Interim Dean, ext. 3421
dean.fms@brocku.ca

Applied Health Sciences
John Corlett, Dean, ext. 3385
john.corlett@brocku.ca

Graduate Studies
Marilyn Rose, Dean, ext. 5152
mrose@brocku.ca

Publications
Brock Press
Katherine Gottli, Editor-In-Chief, ext. 3269
editor@brockpress.com

Sudbury: Huntington University

935 Ramsey Lake Rd., Sudbury, ON P3E 2C6, Canada
Tel: 705-673-4126; *Fax:* 705-673-6917
Toll-Free: 800-461-6366
www.huntingtonu.ca

Note: Liberal Arts University specializing in Communication Studies, Ethics, Gerontology, Religious studies and Theology.

Sudbury: Laurentian University of Sudbury
Université Laurentienne de Sudbury

935 Ramsey Lake Rd., Sudbury, ON P3E 2C6, Canada
Tel: 705-675-1151; *Fax:* 705-675-4891
Toll-Free: 800-461-4030
admissions@laurentian.ca
www.laurentian.ca

Full Time Equivalency: 8270 *Note:* Teaching is in French & English. Certain faculties offer parallel programs in both languages.
Dominic Giroux, MBA, President
Susan Silverton, Ph.D., M.D., Vice-President
Harley d'Entremont, M.A., Ph.D., Vice-President
R. Bertoli, Director
D. Mayer, M.Sc., Assoc. Vice-President
R. Smith, B.Sc., Registrar
L. Bonin, B.A., M.L.S., Director
Gerry Labelle, B.Comm., C.A., Director

Faculties
Humanities & Social Sciences
Donald Dennie, B.A., M.A., Ph.D., Dean

Management
Huguette Blanco, M.B.A., Ph.D., Dean

Professional Schools
Anne-Marie Mawhiney, B.A., B.S.W., M.S.W., Ph., Dean

Sciences & Engineering
R. Haq, B.Sc., M.Sc., Ph.D., Dean

Schools
Commerce & Administration
Ozhand Ganjavi, M.M.Sc., Ph.D., Director

Education (English)
John Lundy, Ed.D., Director

Education (French)
Serge Demers, Ph.D., Director

Engineering
Anis Farah, Ph.D., Director

Graduate Studies
Paul Colilli, M.A., Ph.D., Director

Human Kinetics
Roger Couture, M.A., Ph.D., Director

Nursing
Sharolyn Mossey, M.Sc.N., Director

Social Work
Duncan Matheson, M.S.W., Ph.D., Director

Sports Administration
K. Lefroy, B.Ed., M.Ed., Ed.D., Director

Affiliations
University of Sudbury
Université de Sudbury
935 Ramsey Lake Rd., Sudbury, ON P3E 2C6, Canada
Tel: 705-673-5661; *Fax:* 705-673-4912
usudreg@usudbury.ca; usudburyalumni@usudbury.ca (Alumni)
www.usudbury.com
Other Information: Registrar, E-mail: registrar@usudbury.ca
Note: Founded in 1913 as Collège du Sacré-Coeur, the University of Sudbury operates in the Jesuit tradition. The bilingual university is committed to the English, French, & First Nations cultures. Courses include Religious Studies, Philosophy, Communications, French-Canadian Folklore, & Native Studies.
André Lacroix, Q.C., LL.D., Chancellor
Robert L. Fabbro, LL.B., Chair, Board of Regents
Dr. Pierre Zundel, Ph.D., President & Vice-Chancellor
pzundel@usudbury.ca
Sylvie Renault, H.B.Com., Registrar & Director, Recruitment & Communications
srenault@usudbury.ca
Shelley R. Machum, B.Com., C.A., Treasurer & Director, Administrative Services
smachum@usudbury.ca
Gerry Copeman, B.A., S.T.B., B.Th., Director, Spiritual Services
gcopeman@usudbury.ca
Paul Laverdure, Ph.D., Director, Library Services
plaverdure@usudbury.ca
Rachel Haliburton, Chair, Philosophy
rhaliburton@usudbury.ca
Jack Laughlin, Chair, Religious Studies
jlaughlin@usudbury.ca
Roger Spielmann, Chair, Native Studies
rspielmann@usudbury.ca
Pierre Brideau, Manager, Facilities & Security
pbrideau@usudbury.ca

Huntington University
935 Ramsey Lake Rd., Sudbury, ON P3E 2C6, Canada
Tel: 705-673-4126; *Fax:* 705-673-6917
Toll-Free: 800-461-6366
huntingtonu.ca
Dr. Kevin McCormick, President & Vice-Chancellor
kmccormick@huntingtonu.ca

Thorneloe University at Laurentian University
935 Ramsey Lake Rd., Sudbury, ON P3E 2C6, Canada
Tel: 705-673-1730; *Fax:* 705-673-4979
Toll-Free: 1-866-846-7635
smoores@laurentian.ca (Susan Moores, Administrative Secretary)
www.thorneloe.laurentian.ca
Note: Affiliated with the Anglican Church, Thorneloe University features the departments of Religious Studies, Classical Studies, Theatre Arts, & Women's Studies.
The Rev. Dr. Robert A. Derrenbacker, PhD., President, Provost, & Chaplain
rderrenbacker@laurentian.ca
Dr. Ian Maclennan, Registrar
imaclennan@laurentian.ca
Markus Rukkila, Dean
David Macdonald, Coordinator, Distance Education & Learning Technologies, 705-673-1730, ext. 33, fax: 705-673-4979
dmacdonald@laurentian.ca
Janine Moutsatsos, Librarian
jmoutsatsos@laurentian.ca

Publications
Lambda

L'Original déchaîné

Sudbury: Thorneloe University
935 Ramsey Lake Rd., Sudbury, ON P3E 2C6, Canada
Tel: 705-673-1730; *Fax:* 705-673-4979
Toll-Free: 866-846-7635
info@thorneloe.ca
www.thorneloe.ca
www.facebook.com/ThorneloeUni
twitter.com/ThorneloeUni

Sudbury: University of Sudbury
Ramsey Lake Rd, Sudbury, ON P3E 2C6, Canada
Tel: 705-673-5661
usudreg@usudbury.ca
www.usudbury.ca
www.facebook.com/260336550720945
twitter.com/UofSudbury
www.linkedin.com/groups?gid=4419839&trk=hb_side_g

Faculties
Folklore et ethnologie

Études journalistiques

Indigenous Studies

Philosophy

Religious Studies

Thunder Bay: Lakehead University
955 Oliver Rd., Thunder Bay, ON P7B 5E1, Canada
Tel: 807-343-8110; *Fax:* 807-343-8023
www.lakeheadu.ca

Full Time Equivalency: 8050
L.G. Everett, Chancellor
Frederick F. Gilbert, President & Vice-Chancellor
K. Roche, Registrar & Secretary of Senate
A.E. Deighton, University Librarian
R. Blais, Controller
G. Wojda, Director
J. Podd, Director
J. Smith, Director
C. Calvert, Director
K.L. Clarke, Director
T. Warden, Director
L. Hayes, Vice-President
E.G. Walsh, Executive Director
M. Pawlowski, Vice-President
B. Sabourin, Vice-Provost
E. Abaya, Director
B. Moore, Director
S. Jafri, Director
R. Wang, Vice-President

Faculties
Business Administration
B. Dadgostar, Dean

Education
J. O'Sullivan, Dean

Engineering
H.T. Saliba, Dean

Forestry & the Forest Environment
U. Runesson, Dean

Graduate & International Studies
P. Hicks, Dean

Northern Ontario School of Medicine
J. Lanphear, West Campus Dean

Professional Schools
I. Newhouse, Dean

Science & Environmental Studies
A.P. Dean, Dean

Schools
Kinesiology
J. Farrell, Director

Nursing
K. Poole, Director

Outdoor Recreation
B. Cuthbertson, Director

Social Work
D. Tranter, Director

Publications
The Argus

Toronto: Emmanuel College
75 Queen's Park Cres. East, Toronto, ON M5S 1K7, Canada
Tel: 416-585-4539; *Fax:* 416-585-4516
ec.office@utoronto.ca
www.vicu.utoronto.ca/emmanuel.htm

Full Time Equivalency: 173 *Note:* Theological college affiliated with the United Church of Canada

Toronto: Innis College
2 Sussex Ave., Toronto, ON M5S 1J6, Canada
Tel: 416-978-2513; *Fax:* 416-978-5503
www.utoronto.ca/innis/

Full Time Equivalency: 1480 *Note:* Constituent college of the University of Toronto
Janet Paterson, Principal, 416-978-2510
principal.innis@utoronto.ca
Donald Boere, Assistant Principal & Registrar, 416-978-2513
donald.boere@utoronto.ca

Toronto: Knox College
59 St. George St., Toronto, ON M5S 2E6, Canada
Tel: 416-978-4500; *Fax:* 416-971-2133
knox.college@utoronto.ca
www.utoronto.ca/knox/

Note: Theological college at the University of Toronto affiliated with the Presbyterian Church in Canada

Toronto: Massey College
4 Devonshire Pl., Toronto, ON M5S 2E1, Canada
Tel: 416-978-2895; *Fax:* 416-946-7890
porter@masseycollege.ca
masseycollege.ca

Full Time Equivalency: 130

Toronto: Ontario College of Art & Design (OCAD)
100 McCaul St., Toronto, ON M5T 1W1, Canada
Tel: 416-977-6000; *Fax:* 416-977-0235
www.ocad.ca

Full Time Equivalency: 3467
Sara Diamond, President
Dr. Sarah McKinnon, Vice-President
Peter Caldwell, Vice-President
Josephine Polera, Director
Simone Jones, Asst. Dean
Dr. Anthony Cahalan, Dean
Blake Fitzpatrick, Dean
Wendy Coburn, Asst. Dean
Steve Quinlan, Asst. Dean
Peter Fraser, Director
Colleen Reid, Asst. Dean
Rosemary Donegan, Asst. Dean
Jill Patrick, Director
Alastair MacLeod, Director
Christine Swiderski, Exhibitions Coordinator
Cindy Ball, Director
Marian Ruston, Manager
Jan Sage, Director
Nicky Davis, Director
Peter Lashko, Director
Ted Rickard, Manager
Sarah Mulholand, Coordinator
Laura Matthews, Director
Charles Reeve, Curator
Lance Straun, Manager
Dr. Kathryn Shailer, Dean
Vladimir Spicanovic, Asst. Dean
Doreen Balabanoff, Asst. Dean

Toronto: Ryerson University
350 Victoria St., Toronto, ON M5B 2K3, Canada
Tel: 416-979-5000
inquire@ryerson.ca
www.ryerson.ca

Full Time Equivalency: 25600
Peter Lukasiewicz, Chair
G. Raymond Chang, Chancellor
Sheldon Levy, President & Vice-Chancellor
Sheldon Levy, Provost & Vice-President
Michael Dewson, Vice-Provost
Dr. Linda Grayson, Vice-President
Keith Alnwick, Registrar
Janice Winton, Executive Director
Marion Creery, Sr. Director
Renée Lemieux, Sr. Director
Shirley Lewchuk, Secretary of the Board of Governors
Ian Marlatt, Sr. Director
Peter Lukasiewicz, Vice-Chair
Dr. Anastasios (Tas) Venetsanopoulos, Vice-President
Judith Sandys, Assoc. Vice-President

Faculties
Arts
Dr. Carla Cassidy, Dean

Business
Dr. Ken Jones, Ph.D., Dean

Communication & Design
Dr. Daniel Doz, Dean

Community Services
Dr. Usha George, Ph.D., Dean

Engineering & Applied Science
Dr. Mohamed Lachemi, Interim Dean

Engineering & Applied Science, Research, Development & New Science Programs
Steven Liss, Assoc. Dean

Engineering & Applied Science, Undergraduate Programs & Student Affairs
Zouheir Fawaz, Assoc. Dean

The G. Raymond Chang School of Continuing Education
Anita Shilton, Dean

Graduate Studies

Publications
The Eyeopener

The Ryerson Rambler
350 Victoria St, Toronto, ON M5B 2K3, Canada

Ryersonian

NightViews

Toronto: University of Guelph Humber
207 Humber College Blvd., Toronto, ON M9W 5L7, Canada
Tel: 416-798-1331; *Fax:* 416-798-1991
info@guelphhumber.ca
www.guelphhumber.ca

Dr. John Walsh, Vice-Provost, Chief Academic & Executive Officer
Dalia Smith, Librarian
dalia.smith@guelphhumber.ca
Jock Phippen, Manager, Registrarial Services
jock.phippen@guelphhumber.ca
Gabrielle Bernardi-Dengo, Manager, Finance & Administration Services
gabrielle.bernardi-dengo@guelphhumber.ca

Toronto: University of Toronto
91 Charles St. West, Toronto, ON M5S 1K7, Canada
Tel: 416-585-4524
www.utoronto.ca

Full Time Equivalency: 45009
The Hon. David Peterson, Chancellor
Dr. David Naylor, President
Cheryl Misak, Vice-President & Provost
Edith Hillan, Vice-Provost
John Challis, Assoc. Provost & Vice-President
Safwat Zaky, Vice-Provost
Rivi Frankle, Asst. Vice-President & Chief Operations Officer
Angela Hildyard, Vice-President
Catherine J. Riggall, Vice-President
Tim McTiernan, Asst. Vice-President, Research & Executive Director
Joan E. Foley, University Ombudsperson
Karel Swift, University Registrar & Director
Avon McFarlane, Acting Asst. Vice-President
Catharine Whiteside, Vice-Provost
Robert Steiner, Asst. Vice-President
Jonathan Freedman, Deputy Provost
John F. (Jack) Petch, Chair of the Governing Council
Sheila Brown, CFO
Judith Wolfson, Vice-President

Faculties
Applied Science & Engineering
Prof. Cristina Amon, Dean

John H. Daniels Faculty of Architecture, Landscape & Design
Richard M. Sommer, Dean

Arts & Science
Meric Gertler, Dean

Dentistry
Daniel Haas, Dean

Forestry
Dr. Sandy Smith, Dean

Information Studies
Dr. Ross Seamus, Dean

Law
Mayo Moran, Dean

Rotman School of Management
Roger L. Martin, Dean

Medicine
Catharine Whiteside, MD, PhD, FRCP (C), Dean

Music
Don McLean, Dean

Lawrence S. Bloomberg Faculty of Nursing
Sioban Nelson, Dean

Ontario Institute for Studies in Education (OISE)
Also known as: Faculty of Education
Julia O'Sullivan, Dean

Leslie Dan Faculty of Pharmacy
Henry J. Mann, PharmD, FASHP, FCCP, FCCM, Dean

Physical Education & Health
Ira Jacobs, Dean

School of Graduate Studies
Brian Corman, AB, AM, PhD, Dean

Factor-Inwentash Social Work
Faye Wishna, Dean

University College
15 King's College Circle, Toronto, ON M5S 3H7, Canada
Tel: 416-978-3170; *Fax:* 416-978-6019
Donald Ainslie, Principal, 416-978-7516, fax: 416-978-8854
uc.principal@utoronto.ca

Schools

Asian Institute
Joseph Wong, Director

Canadian Institute for Theoretical Astrophysics
Norm Murray, Director

Centre for Comparative Literature
Neil ten Kortenaar, Director

Centre for Environmental Studies
Donald Jackson, Interim Director

Centre for European, Russian, & Eurasian Studies
Randall Hansen, Director

Centre for Industrial Relations
Anil Verma, Director

Centre for Medieval Studies
John Magee, Director

Centre for Reformation & Renaissance Studies
Lynne Magnusson, Director

Centre for South Asian Studies
Rita Birla, Director

Centre for the Study of Pain
Bonnie Stevens, RN, PhD, Director

Centre for Urban & Community Studies
David Hulchanski, Director

Centre of Criminology
Anthony Doob, Acting Director

Coalition for Research in Women's Health
Heather Maclean, Director

Computing in the Humanities & Social Sciences
Chris Leowski, Director

David Dunlap Observatory
Note: Sold to Metrus Development in 2008, operated by The Royal Astronomical Society of Canada

Fields Institute for Research in Mathematical Sciences
Note: Sold to Metrus Development in 2008, operated by The Royal Astronomical Society of Canada
Edward Bierstone, Director

Frank Iacobucci Centre for Italian Canadian Studies
Note: Sold to Metrus Development in 2008, operated by The Royal Astronomical Society of Canada
Salvatore Bancheri, Acting Director

Graduate Centre for Study of Drama
Note: Sold to Metrus Development in 2008, operated by The Royal Astronomical Society of Canada
Prof. Stephen Johnson, Director

Institute for Aerospace Studies
Note: Sold to Metrus Development in 2008, operated by The Royal Astronomical Society of Canada
D.W. Zingg, Director

Institute for History & Philosophy of Science & Technology
Note: Sold to Metrus Development in 2008, operated by The Royal Astronomical Society of Canada
Craig Fraser, Director

Institute for Human Development, Life Course & Aging
Note: Sold to Metrus Development in 2008, operated by The Royal Astronomical Society of Canada
L. McDonald, Director

Institute for Women's Studies & Gender Studies
Note: Sold to Metrus Development in 2008, operated by The Royal Astronomical Society of Canada
Bonnie McElhinny, Director

Institute of Biomaterials & Biomedical Engineering
Note: Sold to Metrus Development in 2008, operated by The Royal Astronomical Society of Canada
Paul Santerre, Director

Institute of Child Study
Note: Sold to Metrus Development in 2008, operated by The Royal Astronomical Society of Canada
Kang Lee, Director

Institute of Medical Science
Note: Sold to Metrus Development in 2008, operated by The Royal Astronomical Society of Canada
Allan S. Kaplan, Director

Knowledge Media Design Institute
Note: Sold to Metrus Development in 2008, operated by The Royal Astronomical Society of Canada
Andrew Clement, Director

Masters of Mathematical Finance
Note: Sold to Metrus Development in 2008, operated by The Royal Astronomical Society of Canada
Luis Seco, Director

McLuhan Program in Culture & Technology
Also known as: Coach House
Note: Sold to Metrus Development in 2008, operated by The Royal Astronomical Society of Canada
Dr. Dominique Scheffel-Dunand, Director

Munk School of Global Affairs
Prof. Janice Gross Stein, Director

Museum Studies Program
Note: Sold to Metrus Development in 2008, operated by The Royal Astronomical Society of Canada
John Fleming, Interim Director

Pontifical Institute of Medieval Studies
Note: Sold to Metrus Development in 2008, operated by The Royal Astronomical Society of Canada
James K. McConica, Director

Toronto School of Theology
Note: Sold to Metrus Development in 2008, operated by The Royal Astronomical Society of Canada
Alan Hayes, Director

Transitional Year Program
Note: Sold to Metrus Development in 2008, operated by The Royal Astronomical Society of Canada
Rhonda Love, Director

U of T Joint Program in Transportation
Note: Sold to Metrus Development in 2008, operated by The Royal Astronomical Society of Canada
Eric Miller, Director

Affiliations

University of Toronto Mississauga
Also known as: Erindale College
3359 Mississauga Rd., Mississauga, ON L5L 1C6, Canada
Tel: 905-569-4455
hrserv.utm@utoronto.ca (human resources)
www.utm.utoronto.ca
Other Information: Admissions, Phone: 905-828-5400; Public Affairs: 905-828-5214
Full Time Equivalency: 11430 *Note:* The University of Toronto Mississauga provides undergraduate education to approximately 11,000 students & graduate studies to about 430 graduate students. With 14 academic departments, the school employs 700 faculty & staff.
Professor Hargurdeep Saini, Vice-President & Principal
Lynda Collins, Director, Human Resources, 905-828-5210
lynda.collins@utoronto.ca

Massey College
4 Devonshire Pl., Toronto, ON M5S 2E1, Canada
Tel: 416-978-2895; *Fax:* 416-978-1759
porter@masseycollege.ca
www.masseycollege.ca
John Fraser, Master/CAO, 416-978-2549
Danylo Dzwonyk, Registrar, 416-978-2891
ddzwonyk@masseycollege.ca
Anna Luengo, College Administrator, 416-978-6606
annaluengo@masseycollege.ca

New College
300 Huron St., Toronto, ON M5S 2Z3, Canada
Tel: 416-978-2460; *Fax:* 416-978-0554
newcollege.registrar@utoronto.ca
www.newcollege.utoronto.ca
www.facebook.com/192175714169723
www.twitter.com/newcollegeUofT
Prof. Yves Roberge, Principal, 416-978-2461, fax: 416-978-4345
nc.principal@utoronto.ca
Prof. June Larkin, Vice-Principal, 416-978-8282
june.larkin@utoronto.ca

University of Toronto Scarborough
1265 Military Trail, Toronto, ON M1C 1A4, Canada
Tel: 416-287-8872
stuaff@utsc.utoronto.ca (student affairs)
www.utsc.utoronto.ca
Full Time Equivalency: 10131 *Number of Employees:* 189 academic staff & librarians; 373 non-academic staff *Note:* Number of Programs: 242
Professor Franco J. Vaccarino, Vice-President, U of T, & Principal, U of T Scarborough
Professor Rick Halpern, Vice-Principal & Dean, Academic
deanadmin@utsc.utoronto.ca
Professor Malcolm Campbell, MA (Oxon), PhD, Vice-Principal, Research
vpresearch@utsc.utoronto.ca
Tom Nowers, Dean, Student Affairs
Professor William Gough, Vice-Dean, Graduate Education & Program Development
Professor John Scherk, Vice-Dean, Undergraduate
Lesley Lewis, Assistant Dean
Andrew Arifuzzaman, Chief Strategy Officer
Kim McLean, Chief Administrative Officer
Georgette Zinaty, Executive Director, Development & Alumni Relations
gzinaty@utsc.utoronto.ca
Kim Burbine Richard, Director, Human Resource Services
Rita Pearsall, Director, Enrollment Services
Professor John Bassili, Chair, Department of Psychology
Professor William Bowen, Chair, Department of Humanities
Professor Donald Cormack, Chair, Department of Physical & Environmental Sciences
Professor Vassos Hadzilacos, Chair, Department of Computer & Mathematical Sciences
Professor Michael Krashinsky, Chair, Department of Management
Professor Ted Relph, Chair, Department of Social Sciences
Professor Greg Vanlerberghe, Chair, Department of Biological Sciences

University College
15 King's College Circle, Toronto, ON M5S 3H7, Canada
Tel: 416-978-3170; *Fax:* 416-978-6019
uc.registrar@utoronto.ca
www.uc.utoronto.ca

Woodsworth College
119 St George St., Toronto, ON M5S 1A9, Canada
Tel: 416-978-4444; *Fax:* 416-978-4088
www.wdw.utoronto.ca
twitter.com/WWCollege
Joseph R. Desloges, Principal
Mary Choi, CAO
Cheryl Shook, Registrar

St. Michael's College
81 St. Mary St., Toronto, ON M4S 1J4, Canada
Tel: 416-926-1300
stmikes.utoronto.ca
Note: Fully federated with the University of Toronto, St. Michael's College has a large Faculty of Theology. It also features the Canadian Catholic Bioethics Institute & the Pontifical Institute of Mediaeval Studies.
Anne Anderson, President
Domenico Pietropaolo, Principal

Trinity College in the University of Toronto
6 Hoskin Ave., Toronto, ON M5S 1H8, Canada
Tel: 416-978-2522; *Fax:* 416-978-2797
deanofstudents@trinity.utoronto.ca; chaplain@trinity.utoronto.ca
www.trinity.utoronto.ca
Other Information: Bursar's Office, E-mail: fees@trinity.utoronto.ca
Full Time Equivalency: 1840 *Note:* Trinity College educates approximately 1,700 undergraduate students in the Faculty of Arts & Science, plus 140 students in the Faculty of Divinity. Founded in 1851, it is Canada's oldest Anglican theological school.

The Hon. Bill Graham, Chancellor
Professor Andy Orchard, Provost & Vice-Chancellor, 416-978-2689
provost@trinity.utoronto.ca
Bruce Bowden, B.A., M.A., Ph.D. (Tor.), Registrar & Director, Student Services, 416-978-2687, fax: 416-978-2831
bowden@trinity.utoronto.ca; registrar@trinity.utoronto.ca
Linda W. Corman, A.B. (Vassar), M.A. (Chi., College Librarian, 416-978-4398, fax: 416-978-2797
linda.corman@utoronto.ca
Jill Willard, Officer, Personnel
jwillard@trinity.utoronto.ca

Victoria University
73 Queen's Park Cres. East, Toronto, ON M5S 1K7, Canada
Tel: 416-585-4524; *Fax:* 416-585-4584
www.vicu.utoronto.ca
www.facebook.com/vicu.utoronto
twitter.com/VicCollege_UofT

Paul W. Gooch, President, 416-585-4511
vic.president@utoronto.ca
Susan McDonald, Registrar, 416-585-4405
s.mcdonald@utoronto.ca
Kelly Castle, Dean of Students, 416-585-4495
jason.hunter@utoronto.ca

Emmanuel College
75 Queen's Park Cres. East, Toronto, ON M5S 1K7, Canada
Tel: 416-585-4539; *Fax:* 416-585-4516
ec.office@utoronto.ca
www.emmanuel.utoronto.ca

Mark G. Toulouse, Principal
Wanda Chin, Registrar, 416-585-4538, fax: 416-585-4516
wanda.chin@utoronto.ca

Knox College
59 St George St., Toronto, ON M5S 2E6, Canada
Tel: 416-978-4500; *Fax:* 416-971-2133
knox.college@utoronto.ca
www.knox.utoronto.ca

Rev. Dr. J. Dorcas Gordon, Principal, 416-978-4503
jd.gordon@utoronto.ca
Rev. John Henderson, Director, Academic Programs
knox.academicdirector@utoronto.ca

Wycliffe College
5 Hoskin Ave., Toronto, ON M5S 1H7, Canada
Tel: 416-979-3535; *Fax:* 416-946-3545
registrar@wycliffe.utoronto.ca
www.wycliffecollege.ca

Rev. Dr. George Sumner, Principal

Regis College
100 Wellesley St. West, Toronto, ON M5S 2Z5, Canada
Tel: 416-922-5474; *Fax:* 416-922-2898
inquiries@regiscollege.ca
www.regiscollege.ca

Note: Regis is a Roman Catholic college in the Jesuit tradition. It is a federated college of the University of Toronto.
Very Reverend Adolfo Nicolas, S.J., Chancellor , Ecclesiastical Faculty
Joseph G. Schner, S.J., President & Rector

Elliott Allen Institute for Theology & Ecology
81 St. Mary's St., Toronto, ON M5S 1J4, Canada
Tel: 416-926-1300; *Fax:* 416-926-7294
eaite.contact@utoronto.ca
stmikes.utoronto.ca/theology/eaite
Other Information: ext. 3408

Dr. Dennis Patrick O'Hara, Director, 416-926-1300, ext. 3408

Publications

The Bulletin
Dept. of Public Affairs
21 King's College Circle, Toronto, ON M5S 1A1, Canada

The Newspaper
#245, 1 Spadina Cres, Toronto, ON M5S 1A1, Canada
Fax: 416-593-0552

The Toike Oike

University of Toronto Magazine
Dept. of Public Affairs
21 King's College Circle, Toronto, ON M5S 1A1, Canada
Fax: 416-978-7430

Varsity

Toronto: Victoria University
73 Queen's Park Cres., Toronto, ON M5S 1K7, Canada
Tel: 416-585-4508; *Fax:* 416-585-4459
vic.registrar@utoronto.ca
www.vicu.utoronto.ca

Full Time Equivalency: 2300 *Note:* Although the university is located within the University of Toronto campus, it has its own independent administration, faculty and governing body.

Toronto: Woodsworth College
119 Saint George St., Toronto, ON M5S 1A9, Canada
Tel: 416-978-4444; *Fax:* 416-978-6111
wdwregistrar@utoronto.ca
wdw.utoronto.ca

Full Time Equivalency: 6000

Toronto: Wycliffe College
5 Hoskin Ave., Toronto, ON M5S 1H7, Canada
Tel: 416-979-3535; *Fax:* 416-946-3545
www.wycliffecollege.ca

Note: Seminary at the University of Toronto affiliated with the Anglican Church of Canada

Toronto: York University
4700 Keele St., Toronto, ON M3J 1P3, Canada
Tel: 416-736-2100; *Fax:* 416-736-5700
www.yorku.ca

Full Time Equivalency: 45890
Marshall Cohen, Chair of the Board
Roland (Roy) McMurty, O.C., O.O., B.A., LL.B., Chancellor
Mahmoud Shoukri, B.Sc., M.Eng., Ph.D., President & Vice-Chancellor
S.M. Embleton, B.Sc., M.Sc., Ph.D., Vice-President
John Lennox, Assoc. Vice-President
G. Brewer, Vice-President
S. Shapson, B.Sc., M.A., Ph.D., Vice-President
H.I. Lewis, B.A., M.A., LL.B., University Secretary & General Counsel
Sylvia Schippke, Asst. Vice-President
Trudy Pound-Curtis, CFO & Asst. Vice-President
Michael Graham, Asst. Vice-President
P. Cantor, B.A., L.L.B., F.I.C.B., Chair
N. White, Director
Luana Jursza, CIO & Executive Director
Norman Ahmet, Asst. Vice-President
B. Purves, President
B. Miller, Director
J. Meikle, Director
P. Murray, B.P.H.E., M.Sc., Director
R. Woodhouse, Academic Director
T. Mohammed, B.Sc., M.Sc., P.Eng., Director
P. Monk, Director/Curator
M. Scheepers, B.A., Director
J. Briggs, Director
B. Bellissimo, Director
R. Thompson, B.A., Director
P. Yu, B.Sc., Director
K. Irani, B.E., P.Eng., Director
D.L. Glass, B.A., B.Ed., M.E.D., Director
E.S. Spence, Director
B. Abner, B.A., M.A., Assoc. Vice-President
M. Chan, Director
Robert J. Tiffin, Vice-President
C. Archer, University Librarian
N. Gouda, Director
Calum MacKechnie, Director
K. Swartz, B.A., B.S.W., M.S.W., Director
Joanne Duklas, University Registrar
B. Brown, Director
S. MacDonald, Director
R.A. Webb, Assoc. Vice-President
A. Shubert, Assoc. Vice-President
A. Wickens, Asst. Vice-President
S. Spence, Director
B. Woodward, Director
R. Faverin, Director
Suzanne MacDonald, Assoc. Vice-President

Faculties

Arts
Bob Drummond, Dean

Joseph E. Atkinson College
Rhonda Lenton, Dean

Education
Paul Axelrod, Dean

Environmental Studies
David Morley, Dean

Fine Arts
Phillip Silver, B.A., Dean

Glendon College
K. McRoberts, B.A., M.A., Ph.D., Principal

Graduate Studies
Ronald Pearlman, Dean

Health
Harvey Skinner, Dean

Law School, Osgoode Hall
Patrick Monahan, Dean

Schulich School of Business
Dezsö J. Horvath, Dean

Science & Engineering
Nick Cercone, Dean

Schools

Canadian Centre for German & European Studies
Kurt Huebner, Acting Director

Centre for Applied Sustainability
D.V.J. Bell, B.A., A.M., Ph.D., Director

Centre for Atmospheric Chemistry
G.W. Harris, B.Sc., Ph.D., Director

Centre for International & Security Studies
D.B. Dewitt, B.A., M.A., Ph.D., Director

Centre for Jewish Studies
M. Lockshin, Director

Centre for Practical Ethics
Shirley Katz, Acting Director

Centre for Public Law & Public Policy
Bruce Ryder, Director

Centre for Refugee Studies
Susan McGrath, Director

Centre for Research in Earth & Space Science
G.G. Shepherd, B.Sc., M.Sc., Ph.D., F.R., Director

Centre for Research in Mass Spectrometry
M. Siu, Director

Centre for Research on Latin America & the Caribbean
Viviana Patroni, Director

Centre for Research on Work & Society
N. Pupo, Director

Centre for Vision Research
J. Tsotsos, B.A., M.Sc., Ph.D., Director

Institute for Research & Innovation in Sustainability
David Wheeler, Director

Institute for Research on Learning Technologies
Ron Owston, Director

Institute for Social Research
M.D. Ornstein, B.Sc., Ph.D., Director

Jack & Mae Nathanson Centre for the Study of Organized Crime & Corruption
M. Beare, B.A., M.A., M.P.H.L., Ph., Director

La Marsh Centre for Research on Violence & Conflict Resolution
Anne Marie Wall, Acting Director

Robarts Centre for Canadian Studies
S. Feldman, Director

York Centre for Asian Research
P. Vandergeest, Director

York Centre for Feminist Research
V. Agnew, Director

York Institute for Health Research
M. Rioux, Director

Campuses

Glendon Campus
2275 Bayview Ave., Toronto, ON M4N 3M6, Canada

Publications

Atkinsonian

Excalibur

Lexicon

MacMedia (McLaughlin College)

Obiter Dicta (Osgoode Hall)

The Pro Tem (Glendon College)

Waterloo: Conrad Grebel University College
140 Westmount Rd. North, Waterloo, ON N2L 3G6, Canada
Tel: 519-885-0220; *Fax:* 519-885-0014
congreb@uwaterloo.ca
grebel.uwaterloo.ca

Full Time Equivalency: 3894

Waterloo: University of Waterloo
200 University Ave. West, Waterloo, ON N2L 3G1, Canada
Tel: 519-888-4567; *Fax:* 519-884-8009
www.uwaterloo.ca/

Full Time Equivalency: 26457
V. Prem Watsa, Chancellor
Bob Harding, Chair

D.L. Johnston, C.C., A.B., L.L.B., President & Vice-Chancellor
Bruce Mitchell, B.Sc., M.Sc., Ph.D., Vice-President
Meg Beckell, B.A., M.B.A., Vice-President
W.B. Mitchell, B.A., M.A., Ph.D., Associate Provost
P.D. Guild, B.A., M.A., D.Phil., Vice-President
A.C. Scott, B.A., Associate Provost
D.E. Huber, B.B.A., C.M.A., Vice-President
L.H.P. Claxton, B.A., B.L.S., M.L.S., Secretary of the University
K.A. Lavigne, B.A., Registrar
G. Cuthbert Brandt, B.A., M.A., Ph.D., Associate Vice-President
J.D. Walker, B.A., M.A.Sc., Director
J.A. George, B.Sc., M.Sc., Ph.D., F.R., Vice-President, University Research & Associate Provost

Faculties

Applied Health Sciences
R.C. Mannell, B.A., M.P.E., Ph.D., Dean

Arts
Ken Coates, Dean

Engineering
A.S. Sedra, B.Sc., M.A.Sc., Ph.D., Dean

Environmental Studies
H.S. (Deep) Saini, B.Sc., M.Sc., Ph.D., Dean

Graduate Studies
R. Bird, B.Sc., M.Sc., Ph.D., Dean

Mathematics
T.F. Coleman, Ph.D., Dean

Science
Terry McMahon, Dean

Affiliations

Conrad Grebel University College
140 Westmount Rd. North, Waterloo, ON N2L 3G6, Canada
Tel: 519-885-0220; *Fax:* 519-885-0014
congreb@uwaterloo.ca
uwaterloo.ca/grebel
facebook.com/ConradGrebel
twitter.com/Conrad_Grebel
www.linkedin.com/groups?home=&gid=1582077&trk=anet_ug_hm
www.youtube.com/user/ConradGrebelUC
Susan Schultz Huxman, Principal, 519-885-0220, ext. 24237
E. Paul Penner, Dir., Operations, 519-885-0220, ext. 24231
eppenner@uwaterloo.ca
Dr James Pankratz, Academic Dean, 519-885-0220, ext. 24232
pankratz@uwaterloo.ca

Renison University College
240 Westmount Rd. North, Waterloo, ON N2L 3G4, Canada
Tel: 519-884-4404; *Fax:* 519-884-5135
uwaterloo.ca/renison
www.facebook.com/RenisonUniversityCollege
twitter.com/renisoncollege
www.youtube.com/user/renisonvideo
Note: College programs lead to a Bachelor of Arts or an Honours Bachelor of Social Work degree of the University of Waterloo.
John Crossley, B.A., M.A., Ph.D., Principal

St. Jerome's University
290 Westmount Rd. North, Waterloo, ON N2L 3G3, Canada
Tel: 519-884-8110; *Fax:* 519-884-5759
www.sju.ca
www.facebook.com/stjeromesuniversity?ref=ts
twitter.com/StJeromesUni
Full Time Equivalency: 1019 *Number of Employees:* 28 faculty; 23 staff *Note:* Federated with the University of Waterloo, St. Jerome's University is a public Catholic university. Education in the Arts & Mathematics is provided.
Jim Beingessner, Chancellor
Dr. Katherine Bergman, President & Vice-Chancellor, 519-884-8111, ext. 28253
kbergman@uwaterloo.ca

St. Paul's United College
University of Waterloo
190 Westmount Rd. North, Waterloo, ON N2L 3G5, Canada
Tel: 519-885-1460; *Fax:* 519-885-6364
stpauls@uwaterloo.ca
www.stpauls.uwaterloo.ca
www.facebook.com/StPaulsUniversityCollege
twitter.com/UWStPauls
www.youtube.com/uwstpauls
Note: The residential teaching institution is affiliated with the University of Waterloo. It features the international development program.
Dr. Bob Rosehart, Chair
Graham Brown, Principal
ggbrown@uwaterloo.ca
Peter Frick, Academic Dean
pfrick@uwaterloo.ca

Rod McAllister, Dean of Students
rjmcallister@uwaterloo.ca

Publications

Imprint
Note: Student newspaper at the University of Waterloo

UW Gazette
Note: Newspaper published by the Office of Information and Public Affairs

Waterloo: Wilfrid Laurier University
75 University Ave. West, Waterloo, ON N2L 3C5, Canada
Tel: 519-884-0710; *Fax:* 519-886-9351
www.wlu.ca

Full Time Equivalency: 12239
Dr. Max Blouw, President
Dr. Deborah MacLatchy, Vice-President
dmaclatchy@wlu.ca
Jim Butler, Vice-President
jbutler@wlu.ca
Ray Darling, Registrar
rdarling@wlu.ca
Robert Donelson, Vice-President
rdonelson@wlu.ca
Sharon Brown, University Librarian
sbrown@wlu.ca

Faculties

Arts
Dr. David Docherty, Dean

Brantford Campus
73 George St., Brantford, ON N3T 2Y3, Canada
Tel: 519-756-8228; *Fax:* 519-759-2172
Dr. Bruce Arai, Dean
barai@wlu.ca

Graduate Studies & Research
73 George St., Brantford, ON N3T 2Y3, Canada
Tel: 519-756-8228; *Fax:* 519-759-2172
Dr. Joan Norris, Dean

Music
73 George St., Brantford, ON N3T 2Y3, Canada
Tel: 519-756-8228; *Fax:* 519-759-2172
Charles Morrison, Dean
cdmorris@wlv.ca

School of Business & Economics
73 George St., Brantford, ON N3T 2Y3, Canada
Tel: 519-756-8228; *Fax:* 519-759-2172
Ginny Dybenko, Dean
gdybenko@wlv.ca

Science
73 George St., Brantford, ON N3T 2Y3, Canada
Tel: 519-756-8228; *Fax:* 519-759-2172
Dr. Peter Tiidus, Acting Dean
ptiidus@wlv.ca

Social Work
73 George St., Brantford, ON N3T 2Y3, Canada
Tel: 519-756-8228; *Fax:* 519-759-2172
Lesley Cooper, Dean

Waterloo Lutheran Seminary
73 George St., Brantford, ON N3T 2Y3, Canada
Tel: 519-756-8228; *Fax:* 519-759-2172
Dr. David Pfrimmer, Principal-Dean
dpfrimmer@wlu.ca

Publications

The Cord Weekly
Note: Student newspaper at Wilfrid Laurier University

Windsor: Iona College
208 Sunset Ave., Windsor, ON N9B 3A7, Canada
Tel: 519-253-3000; *Fax:* 519-973-7050
office@ionacollege.edu
www.ionacollege.edu
Note: Affiliate College to the University of Windsor, affiliated with the United Church of Canada designed to promote theological educaion, social justice and Chaplaincy.
Rev. Dr. BoJeong Kim, Principal & Chaplain Emeritus
principal@ionacollege.edu
Rev. Dr. Lloyd Smith, Chancellor
Dr. Norman King, Director, School of Theology
theology@ionacollege.edu

Windsor: University of Windsor
401 Sunset Ave., Windsor, ON N9B 3P4, Canada
Tel: 519-253-3000
www.uwindsor.ca
www.facebook.com/uwindsor
www.twitter.com/uwindsor
www.linkedin.com/groups?gid=38761&trk=hb_side_g
www.youtube.com/uwindsor
Full Time Equivalency: 15700 *Number of Employees:* 524 faculty
Amanda Gellman, Vice-President, University Advancement

Faculties

Arts & Social Sciences
Robert Orr, Acting Dean

Education
Dr. Clinton Beckford, Dean

Engineering
Dr. Mehrdad Saif, Dean

Graduate Studies & Research
Dr. Patricia Weir, Dean

Human Kinetics
Dr. Michael A. Khan, Dean

Law
Camilla Cameron, Dean

Nursing
Dr. Linda Patrick, RN, BScN, MA, MSc, PhD, Dean

Odette School of Business
Dr. Allan Conway, Dean

Science
Dr. Marlys Koschinsky, Dean

Schools

Athletics & Recreational Services
Gord Grace, Head

Biological Sciences
William Crosby, Head

Chemistry & Biochemistry
Douglas Stephan, Head

Civil & Environmental Engineering
Ram Balachandar, B.E., Ph.D., P.Eng., Head

Classical & Modern Languages
Dietmar Lage, B.A., M.A., Ph.D., Head

Communication Studies
James Wittebols, Head

Dramatic Art
Lionel Walsh, Head

Earth Sciences
Ihsan Al-Aasm, Head

Economics, Mathematics & Statistics
Ronald Meng, Head

Electrical & Computer Engineering
Maher Sid-Ahmed, Head

English
Karl Jirgens, Head

History
Christina Simmons, Head

Industrial & Manufacturing Systems Engineering
Leo Oriet, Head

Intelligent Manufacturing Systems
Hoda ElMaraghy, B.Eng., M.Eng., Ph.D., Head
Waguih ElMaraghy, B.Eng., M.Eng., Ph.D., Head

Languages, Literatures, Cultures
Dietmar Lage, Head

Mechanical, Automotive & Materials Engineering
Robert Gaspar, B.A.Sc., M.A.Sc., Ph.D., Head

Philosophy
Jeffrey Noonan, Head

Physics
Gordon Drake, B.Sc., M.Sc., Ph.D., Head

Political Science
Tom Najem, Head

Psychology
Shelagh Towson, B.A., M.A., Ph.D., Head

Social Work
Brent Angell, Head

Sociology & Anthropology
Lynne Phillips, B.A., M.A., Ph.D., Head
Student Health Services
Maria Blass, M.D., Head
Visual Arts
Brenda Pelkey, Head
Women's Studies
Anne Forrest, Head

Affiliations
Assumption University
2629 Riverside Dr. West, Windsor, ON N9B 1B4, Canada
Tel: 519-973-7033; *Fax:* 519-973-7089
cbertrand@assumptionu.ca
www.assumptionu.ca

Most Rev. Ronald P. Fabbro, C.S.B., D.D.Bishop of Lon, Chancellor
Fr William A. Riefel, C.S.B., Treas./Dir., Operations
Dr. Lois Smedick, Chair
Rev. Dr. Paul Rennick, C.S.B., Pres./Vice-Chancellor
Dr Anne Snowdon, Dir., Centre for Religion & Culture
Anne Shore, Prog. Dir., Dept. of Theology

Canterbury College
2500 University Ave. West, Windsor, ON N9B 3Y1, Canada
Tel: 519-971-3646; *Fax:* 519-971-3645
canter@uwindsor.ca
www.uwindsor.ca/canterbury
Note: Canterbury College offers the following courses: Doctor of Ministry Degree (in affiliation with Ashland Theological Seminary at Ashland University); certificate courses for the Anglican Community of Deacons & interested lay people; & professional courses for the community.
Dr. Gordon W.F. Drake, Principal
Crystal Martens, Head of College
Brenda Smith, Coordinator, Residence Admissions
brsmith@uwindsor.ca

Iona College
208 Sunset Ave., Windsor, ON N9B 3A7, Canada
Tel: 519-973-7039

Publications
The Lance

The Uniter

Colleges

Barrie: Georgian College
One Georgian Dr., Barrie, ON L4M 3X9, Canada
Tel: 705-728-1968; *Fax:* 705-722-5123
inquire@georgianc.on.ca
www.georgianc.on.ca
www.facebook.com/georgiancollege
www.twitter.com/georgiancollege
www.georgianc.on.ca/linkedin
www.youtube.com/user/georgianvideos

Full Time Equivalency: 9000
Brian Tamblyn, President

Campuses
South Georgian Bay Campus
499 Ragian St., Collingwood, ON L9Y 3Z1, Canada
Tel: 705-445-2961; *Fax:* 705-445-1218

Midland Campus
649 Prospect Blvd., Midland, ON L4R 4L3, Canada
Tel: 705-526-3666; *Fax:* 705-526-5124

Muskoka Campus
111 Wellington St., Bracebridge, ON P1L 1E2, Canada
Tel: 705-646-7629; *Fax:* 705-646-2120

Orangeville Campus
22 Centennial Rd., Orangeville, ON L9W 1P8, Canada
Tel: 519-940-0331; *Fax:* 519-941-0905

Orillia Campus
P.O. Box 2316
825 Memorial Ave., Orillia, ON L3V 6S2, Canada
Tel: 705-325-2740; *Fax:* 705-325-3690

Owen Sound Campus
1450 - 8th St. East, Owen Sound, ON N4K 5R4, Canada
Tel: 519-376-0840; *Fax:* 519-376-5395

Marine Training & Research Centre
2193 Barber Dr., Port Colborne, ON L3K 5X7, Canada
Tel: 905-834-5513; *Toll-Free:* 1-866-468-3229
marinetraining.ca
www.facebook.com/GLIMTRC
www.youtube.com/marineeducation

Publications
The Georgian Eye

Belleville: Loyalist College of Applied Arts & Technology
P.O. Box 4200
375 Wallbridge-Loyalist Rd., Belleville, ON K8N 5B9, Canada
Tel: 613-969-1913; *Fax:* 613-962-1376
Toll-Free: 888-569-2547
www.loyalistcollege.com
www.facebook.com/loyalistcollege
twitter.com/loyalistcollege

Jeff MacNab, Registrar, ext. 2366
jmacnab@loyalistc.on.ca
Aatos Lehtila, Dean, ext. ext-2332

Hamilton: Mohawk College
P.O. Box 2034
Hamilton, ON L8N 3T2, Canada
Tel: 905-575-1212; *Fax:* 905-575-2378
www.mohawkcollege.ca
www.facebook.com/mohawkcollege
www.mohawkcollege.ca/social-media/twitter.html
www.linkedin.com/company/20545
www.youtube.com/mohawkcollege

Full Time Equivalency: 13000
Rob MacIsaac, President, 905-575-2253, fax: 905-575-2313
Cheryl Jensen, Vice President, Academic
Karen Moore, Chief Financial Officer

Campuses
Brantford Campus
411 Elgin St., Brantford, ON N3T 5V2, Canada
Tel: 519-759-7200; *Fax:* 519-758-6043

Fennell Campus
135 Fennell Ave. West, Hamilton, ON L9C 1E9, Canada
Tel: 905-575-1212; *Fax:* 905-575-2378

Mohawk - McMaster Institute for Applied Health Sciences
1400 Main St. West, Hamilton, ON L8S 1C7, Canada
Tel: 905-540-4247; *Fax:* 905-528-8242

Skilled Trades & Apprenticeship Research, Resources & Training (STARRT)
481 Barton St. East, Stoney Creek, ON L8E 2L7, Canada
Tel: 905-575-1212; *Fax:* 905-575-2549

Wentworth Campus
196 Wentworth St. North, Hamilton, ON L8L 5V7, Canada
Tel: 905-575-2424; *Fax:* 905-523-8504

Publications
The Satellite

Kingston: St. Lawrence College
Also known as: Collège Saint-Laurent
Kingston Campus
100 Portsmouth Ave., Kingston, ON K7L 5A6, Canada
Tel: 613-544-5400; *Fax:* 613-545-3923
Toll-Free: 866-276-6601
dreamit@sl.on.ca
www.sl.on.ca
www.facebook.com/stlawrencecollege.ca
www.twitter.com/whatsinsideslc
www.youtube.com/aboutslc

Full Time Equivalency: 6500
Chris Whitaker, President & CEO
Glenn Vollebregt, Sr. Vice-Pres., Finance & Administration, ext. 1591
Gordon MacDougall, Vice-Pres., Student Services & External Affairs, ext. 1298
Lorraine Carter, Vice-Pres., Academic, ext. 1446

Campuses
Brockville Campus
2288 Parkedale Ave., Brockville, ON K6V 5X3, Canada
Tel: 613-345-0660; *Fax:* 613-345-2231
Toll-Free: 888-622-8880

Beverlie Dietze, Campus Dean, ext. 3260
bdietze@sl.on.ca

Cornwall Campus
2 St. Lawrence Dr., Cornwall, ON K6H 4Z1, Canada
Tel: 613-933-6080; *Fax:* 613-937-1523

Don Fairweather, Campus Dean, ext. 2223
dfairweather@sl.on.ca

Kitchener: Conestoga College Institute of Technology & Advanced Learning
299 Doon Valley Dr., Kitchener, ON N2G 4M4, Canada
Tel: 519-748-5220; *Fax:* 519-748-3505
www.conestogac.on.ca/
TTY: 1-866-463-4484
www.facebook.com/ConnectWithConestoga
www.twitter.com/ConestogaC
www.youtube.com/user/conestogapolytechnic

Full Time Equivalency: 6900
Dr. John W. Tibbits, President
jtibbits@conestogac.on.ca

Cambridge Campus
850 Fountain St. South, Cambridge, ON N3H 0A8, Canada
Tel: 519-748-5220

Campuses
Guelph Campus
460 Speedvale Ave. West, Guelph, ON N1H 6N6, Canada
Tel: 519-824-9390;

Waterloo Campus
108 University Ave. East, Waterloo, ON N2J 2W2, Canada
Tel: 519-885-0300

Cambridge Downtown Campus
#402, 150 Main St., Cambridge, ON N1R 6P9, Canada
Tel: 519-623-4890

Ingersoll Skills Training Centre
420 Thomas St., Ingersoll, ON N5C 3J7, Canada
Tel: 519-485-5666; *Fax:* 519-485-5558

Stratford Campus
130 Youngs St., Stratford, ON N5A 1J7, Canada
Tel: 519-271-5700

Publications
Spoke

London: Fanshawe College
P.O. Box 7005
1001 Fanshawe College Blvd., London, ON N5Y 5R6, Canada
Tel: 519-452-4430; *Fax:* 519-452-4420
www.fanshawec.ca
www.facebook.com/fanshaweapplicants
www.twitter.com/fanshawecollege
www.youtube.com/myfanshawe

Full Time Equivalency: 15000
Dr. Howard W. Rundle, President
hrundle@fanshawec.ca
Janice Lamoureux, Registrar
jlamoureux@fanshawec.ca

Centre for Applied Transportation Technologies
Z Bldg.
1764 Oxford St. East, London, ON N5V 3R6, Canada
Tel: 519-452-4430; *Fax:* 519-452-4420

Campuses
Downtown London Campus
Citi Plaza Mall
#114, 355 Wellington St., London, ON N6A 3N7, Canada
Tel: 519-667-2392

James N. Allan Campus (Simcoe)
P.O. Box 10
634 Ireland Rd., Simcoe, ON N3Y 4K8, Canada
Tel: 519-426-8260; *Fax:* 519-428-3112

St. Thomas/Elgin Campus
120 Bill Martyn Pkwy., St Thomas, ON N5R 6A7, Canada
Tel: 519-633-2030; *Fax:* 519-633-0043

Woodstock Campus
369 Finkle St., Woodstock, ON N4V 1A3, Canada
Tel: 519-421-0144; *Fax:* 519-539-3870

Tillsonburg Campus
The Livingston Centre
90 Tillson Ave., Tillsonburg, ON N4G 3A1, Canada
Tel: 519-842-9008; *Fax:* 519-688-1846
Toll-Free: .

Publications
The Interrobang

North Bay: Canadore College of Applied Arts & Technology
P.O. Box 5001
100 College Dr., North Bay, ON P1B 8K9, Canada
Tel: 705-474-7600; *Fax:* 705-474-2384
info@canadorec.on.ca
www.canadorec.on.ca
www.facebook.com/canadorecollege
twitter.com/canadorecollege
www.youtube.com/user/CanadoreLiaison
Full Time Equivalency: 3500
Barbara Taylor, President & CEO

Commerce Court Campus
60 Commerce Cres., North Bay, ON, Canada
Tel: 705-474-7600; *Fax:* 705-474-2384

Campuses
Aviation Campus
55 Aviation Ave., North Bay, ON, Canada
Tel: 705-474-7600; *Fax:* 705-474-2384

West Parry Sound Campus
1 College Dr., Parry Sound, ON, Canada
Tel: 705-746-9222;

Oakville: Sheridan College Institute of Technology & Advanced Learning
P.O. Box 2250 Main
Oakville, ON L6H 7T7, Canada
Tel: 905-845-9430
infosheridan@sheridaninstitute.ca
www.sheridancollege.ca
www.facebook.com/sheridaninstitute
twitter.com/sheridancollege
www.youtube.com/user/SheridanInstitute
Full Time Equivalency: 14472 *Note:* The polytechnic institute offers pre-apprenticeship & apprenticeship training, one-year certificate & graduate certificates, two & three-year diplomas, & Bachelor's degrees in applied areas of study. Collaborative degree progrmas are provided through partnerships with the following universities: Brock University, University of Toronto at Mississauga, & York University.
Dr. Jeff Zabudsky, President/CEO
jeff.zabudsky@sheridanc.on.ca

Trafalgar Road Campus
1430 Trafalgar Rd., Oakville, ON L6H 2L1, Canada
Tel: 905-845-9430

Campuses
Davis Campus
7899 McLaughlin Rd., Brampton, ON L6V 5H9, Canada
Tel: 905-459-7533

Skills Training Centre
407 Iroquois Shore Rd., Oakville, ON L6H 1M3, Canada
Tel: 905-845-9430

Hazel McCallum (Mississauga) Campus
4180 Duke of York Blvd., Mississuaga, ON L5B 0G5, Canada
Tel: 905-845-9430

Oshawa: Durham College
P.O. Box 385
2000 Simcoe St. North, Oshawa, ON L1H 7L7, Canada
Tel: 905-721-2000; *Fax:* 905-721-3113
registrarsoffice@durhamcollege.ca
www.durhamcollege.ca
www.facebook.com/durhamcollege
twitter.com/durhamcollege
www.youtube.com/durhamcollege
Full Time Equivalency: 6000 *Number of Employees:* 715 full-time; 400 part-time
Don Lovisa, President
Ralph Aprile, Vice-President, Facilities & Ancillary Services
Ruth MacKay, Director, Institutional Research & Government Relations
David Chambers, President, Foundation & Vice-President, Advancement
Judy Robinson, Vice-President, Academic
Margaret Greenley, Vice-President, Student Affairs
Donna MacFarlane, Vice-President, Communications & Marketing
Ken Robb, Vice-President, Human Resources
Gerry Pinkney, Vice-President, Information Technology Services

Whitby Campus
1610 Champlain Ave., Whitby, ON L1N 6A7, Canada
Tel: 905-721-3300
whitbyregistrarsoffice@durhamcollege.ca

Publications
The Chronicle
P.O. Box 385
Oshawa, ON L1H 7L7, Canada
Fax: 905-436-9774

Ottawa: Algonquin College of Applied Arts & Technology
1385 Woodroffe Ave., Ottawa, ON K2G 1V8, Canada
Tel: 613-727-4723; *Fax:* 613-727-7743
www.algonquincollege.com/
Full Time Equivalency: 16000
Kent MacDonald, President

Faculties
Technology & Trades
Chris Janzen, Dean

Health, Public Safety & Community Studies
Barbara Foulds, Dean

Arts, Media & Design
Russell Mills, Dean

School of Business
Karen Davies, Dean

School of Hospitality & Tourism
Michel Savard, Dean

Centre for Continuing & Online Learning
Linda Rees, Dean

Perth Campus
7 Craig St., Perth, ON K7H 1X7, Canada
Tel: 613-267-2859

Campuses
Pembroke Campus
315 Pembroke St. East, Pembroke, ON K8A 3K2, Canada
Tel: 613-735-4700

Peterborough: Sir Sandford Fleming College
Sutherland Campus
599 Brealey Dr., Peterborough, ON K9J 7B1, Canada
Tel: 705-749-5530; *Fax:* 705-749-5507
Toll-Free: 1-866-353-6464
info@flemingc.on.ca
flemingcollege.ca
facebook.com/flemingcollege
twitter.com/flemingcollege
Full Time Equivalency: 3500 *Note:* The College consists of the following schools: School of Business & Technology; School of Environmental & Natural Resource Sciences; School of Health & Wellness; School of Interdisciplinary Studies; School of Law, Justice & Community Services; School of Continuing Education & Skilled Trades; & the Haliburton School of The Arts.
Murray Rodd, Chair
Tony Tilly, Ph.D., President

Campuses
Cobourg Campus
1005 Elgin St. West, Cobourg, ON K9A 5J4
Tel: 905-372-6865; *Fax:* 905-372-8570
Note: The Cobourg Campus offers academic upgrading & part time studies, as well as esthetician studies.

Frost Campus
P.O. Box 8000
200 Albert St. South, Lindsay, ON K9V 5E6, Canada
Tel: 705-324-9144; *Fax:* 705-878-9312
Note: The Frost Campus features Fleming College's School of Environmental & Natural Resource Sciences, The Centre for Alternative Wastewater Treatment, The Centre for Heavy Equipment Technology, & The Geomatics Institute.

Haliburton Campus
P.O. Box 839
297 College Dr., Haliburton, ON K0M 1S0, Canada
Tel: 705-457-1680; *Fax:* 705-457-2255
Note: The Haliburton Campus features the Haliburton School of The Arts & Fleming's Ecotourism & Adventure Tourism Management program.

McRae Campus
P.O. Box 4350
555 Bonnacord St., Peterborough, ON K9J 7B1
Tel: 705-749-5530; *Fax:* 705-741-3279
Note: This campus offers specialized programs in skilled trades, apprenticeships, & several part-time studies.
Michael N. Durisin, Chair
Dr. Glenn Zederayko, Head of Schools
Ann Bianco-Harvey, Director, Marketing & Communications
webmaster@torontomontessori.ca; editor@torontomontessori.ca
Silvana Fazzari, Director, Admissions, 905-889-6882, ext. 230
Sharron Cooper, Registrar, 905-889-6882, ext. 254

Sarnia: Lambton College of Applied Arts & Technology
South Building - Main Campus
1457 London Rd., Sarnia, ON N7S 6K4, Canada
Tel: 519-542-7751; *Fax:* 519-541-2418
nfo@lambtoncollege.ca
www.lambton.on.ca
www.facebook.com/lambtoncollege.ca?v=wall
twitter.com/lambtoncollege
www.linkedin.com/company/443242
Full Time Equivalency: 2500
Catherine Holden, Registrar, 519-542-7751, ext. 3310
cathie@lambton.on.ca
Tony Hanlon, President

Toronto Campus
New Campus
400 - 265 Yorkland Blvd., Sarnia, ON M2J 1S5, Canada
Tel: 416-485-2098; *Fax:* 416-485-3505
toronto@lambtoncollege.ca

Publications
Lion's Tale

Sault Ste Marie: Sault College of Applied Arts & Technology
443 Northern Ave., Sault Ste Marie, ON P6A 5L3, Canada
Tel: 705-759-2554; *Fax:* 705-759-3273
Toll-Free: 1-800-461-2260
studentrecruitment@saultcollege.ca; registrar@saultcollege.ca
www.saultcollege.ca
www.facebook.com/SaultCollege?v=wall
twitter.com/SaultCollege
Full Time Equivalency: 6000 *Note:* The College offers education & training to full-time & part-time students in post-secondary, apprenticeship, adult retraining, continuing education, & contract training programs. Specializes in Environmental Studies, Nursing & Aviation.
Joe Nardi, Chair
Dr. Ron Common, President
Max S. Liedke, Sec.-Treas.
Jason Bird, Director

Sault Ste. Marie: Algoma University College
1520 Queen St. East, Sault Ste. Marie, ON P6A 2G4, Canada
Tel: 705-949-2301; *Fax:* 705-949-6583
Toll-Free: 888-254-6628
info@algomau.ca
www.algomau.ca
www.facebook.com/algomau
www.twitter.com/algomau
Full Time Equivalency: 1207
Dr Richard Myers, President
Dr. Arthur H. Perlini, Academic Dean, ext. 4116
dean@algomau.ca
David Marasco, Registrar, ext. 4218
registrar@algomau.ca

Brampton Campus
#102/3 24 Queen St. East, Brampton, ON L6V 1A3, Canada
Tel: 905-451-0100; *Fax:* 905-451-0102
brampton@algomau.ca

Campuses
Timmins Campus
P.O. Box 3211
4715 Hwy. 101 East, Timmins, ON L6V 1A3, Canada
Tel: 705-949-2301
timmins@algomau.ca

St. Thomas Campus
50 Wellington St., St Thomas, ON N5R 3M2, Canada
Tel: 519-633-6501
info@algomau.ca

Sudbury: Cambrian College of Applied Arts & Technology
1400 Barrydowne Rd., Sudbury, ON P3A 3V8, Canada
Tel: 705-566-8101; *Fax:* 705-524-7334
Toll-Free: 800-461-7145
info@cambriancollege.ca
www.cambriancollege.ca
www.facebook.com/cambriancollege
www.twitter.com/CambrianCollege
www.youtube.com/user/CambrianCollege?gl=CA&hl=en
Full Time Equivalency: 4500
Sylvia Barnard, President

Manitoulin Campus
7 Water St., Little Current, ON POP 1KO, Canada
Tel: 705-368-3194; *Fax:* 705-368-3496

Campuses
Espanola Campus
#101, 91 Tudhope St., Espanola, ON P5E 1S6, Canada
Tel: 705-869-4113; *Fax:* 705-869-3071

Publications
The Shield

Sudbury: Collège Boréal
21, boul Lasalle, Sudbury, ON P3A 6B1
Tél: 705-560-6673; *Ligne sans frais:* 1-800-361-6673
info@collegeboreal.ca
www.collegeboreal.ca
Note: Collège Boréal is a francophone Collège of Applied Arts & Technologies. Its main campus is in Sudbury, Ontario, with six other campuses located in Toronto, Timmins, West Nipissing, Hearst, Kapuskasing, & New Liskeard.
Denis Hubert, President
Daniel Giroux, Vice-President, Teaching

Thunder Bay: Confederation College
P.O. Box 398
1450 Nakina Dr., Thunder Bay, ON P7C 4W1, Canada
Tel: 807-475-6110; *Fax:* 807-623-4512
Toll-Free: 800-465-5493
www.confederationc.on.ca
www.facebook.com/confederation
www.twitter.com/confederation
www.youtube.com/confederationcollege
Full Time Equivalency: 4160
Patricia Lang, President, 807-475-6350
plang@confederationc.on.ca
Brian Campbell, Director, Resource Development, 807-475-6582
campbell@confederationc.on.ca

Dryden Campus
100 Casimir Ave., Dryden, ON P8N 3L4, Canada
Tel: 807-223-3035; *Fax:* 807-223-5460

Campuses
Greenstone Campus (Geraldton)
P.O. Box 368
300 Beamish Ave., Geraldton, ON P0T 1M0, Canada
Tel: 807-854-0652; *Fax:* 807-854-0809

Lake of the Woods Campus (Kenora)
P.O. Box 1370
900 Golf Course Rd., Kenora, ON P9N 3X7, Canada
Tel: 807-468-3121; *Fax:* 807-468-3601

Northshore Campus (Marathon)
P.O. Box 520
14 Hemio Dr., Marathon, ON P0T 2E0, Canada
Tel: 807-229-2464; *Fax:* 807-229-3393

Rainy River District Campus (Fort Frances)
440 McIrvine Rd., Fort Frances, ON P9A 3T8, Canada
Tel: 807-274-5395; *Fax:* 807-274-2462

Red Lake Campus
P.O. Box 328
104 Howe St., Red Lake, ON P0V 2M0, Canada
Tel: 807-727-2604; *Fax:* 807-727-2144

Sioux Lookout Campus
70 Wellington St., Sioux Lookout, ON P8T 1B1, Canada
Tel: 807-737-2851; *Fax:* 807-737-2436

Wawa Campus
3 Maple St., Wawa, ON P0S 1K0, Canada
Tel: 705-856-0713; *Fax:* 705-856-0443

Publications
Opus

Polar Press

Talon

Toronto: Centennial College of Applied Arts & Technology
P.O. Box 631 A
Toronto, ON M1K 5E9, Canada
Tel: 416-289-5300; *Fax:* 416-439-7358
Toll-Free: 800-268-4419
success@centennialcollege.ca
www.centennialcollege.ca
www.facebook.com/centennialcollege
www.twitter.com/centennialc
www.youtube.com/centennialcollege
Full Time Equivalency: 40000
Ann Buller, President
abuller@centennialcollege.ca

Ashtonbee Campus
75 Ashtonbee Rd., Toronto, ON M1L 4N4, Canada

Campuses
Centre for Creative Communications
951 Carlaw Ave., Toronto, ON M4K 3M2, Canada

Midland Campus
1450 Midland Ave., Scarborough, ON M1P 4Z8, Canada

Pickering Learning Site
1340 Pickering Pkwy., Pickering, ON L1V 4E2, Canada

Progress Campus
941 Progress Ave., Toronto, ON M1G 3T8, Canada

Residence and Conference Centre
940 Progress Ave., Toronto, ON M1G 3T8, Canada

Morningside Campus
755 Morningside Ave., Toronto, ON M1C 5J9, Canada

Toronto: George Brown College
P.O. Box 1015 B
Toronto, ON M5T 2T9, Canada
Tel: 416-415-2000; *Fax:* 416-415-4493
Toll-Free: 800-265-2002
info@georgebrown.ca
www.georgebrown.ca
TTY: 1-877-515-5559
Full Time Equivalency: 15000
Anne Sado, President
asado@georgebrown.ca

Casa Loma Campus
160 Kendal Ave., Toronto, ON M5R 1M3, Canada

Campuses
Financial Services and Business
290 Adelaide St. East, Toronto, ON M5A 1N1, Canada

Hospitality & Tourism Centre
300 Adelaide St. East, Toronto, ON M5A 1N1, Canada

School of Design
230 Richmond St. East, Toronto, ON M5A 1P4, Canada

Ryerson University
99 Gerrard St. East, Toronto, ON M5B 2K8, Canada

St. James Campus
200 King St. East, Toronto, ON M5A 3W8, Canada

Waterfront Campus
51 Dockside Dr., Toronto, ON M5A 0B6, Canada

Affiliations
The Yorkville School of Makeup and Aesthetics
70 Yorkville Ave., Toronto, ON M5R 1B9, Canada

Young Centre for the Performing Arts
50 Tankhouse Lane, Toronto, ON M5A 3C4, Canada

Publications
Dialog Newspaper

Toronto: Humber Institute of Technology & Advanced Learning
North Campus
205 Humber College Blvd., Toronto, ON M9W 5L7, Canada
Tel: 416-675-3111; *Fax:* 416-675-2427
enquiry@humber.ca
www.humber.ca
www.facebook.com/humbercollege
twitter.com/humbercollege
youtube.com/humberlive
Full Time Equivalency: 15000
Michael Hatton, Vice-President, Academic, ext. 4510
michael.hatton@humber.ca
John Mason, Vice-President, Student & Corporate Services, ext. 5041
john.mason@humber.ca
Rani K. Dhaliwal, Vice-President, Finance & Administrative Services, ext. 5062
rani.dhaliwal@humber.ca
Chris Whitaker, President & CEO, ext. 5070

Lakeshore Campus
3199 Lakeshore Blvd. West, Toronto, ON M8V 1K8, Canada
Fax: 416-252-8842
Enrollment: 5000

Sailing & Powerboating Centre (SPC)
Humber Bay Park Rd. West, Toronto, ON M8V 3X7, Canada
Tel: 416-252-7291; *Fax:* 416-252-5393
sailing@humber.ca
www.humber.ca/sailing

Transportation Training Centre (TTC)
55 Woodbine Downs Blvd., Toronto, ON M9W 6N5, Canada
Tel: 416-798-0300; *Fax:* 416-798-0307
humber.ca/trucking

Orangeville Campus
Alder Street Recreation Complex
275 Alder St., Orangeville, ON L9W 5A9, Canada
Fax: 416-798-0307

Publications
Etcetera

Toronto: New College
300 Huron St., Toronto, ON M5S 3J6, Canada
Tel: 416-978-2460; *Fax:* 416-978-0554
newcollege.registrar@utoronto.ca
www.newcollege.utoronto.ca/site6.aspx
Full Time Equivalency: 4300

Toronto: Seneca College of Applied Arts & Technology
Newnham Campus
1750 Finch Ave. East, Toronto, ON M2J 2X5, Canada
Tel: 416-491-5050; *Fax:* 416-493-3958
admissions@senecac.on.ca
www.senecac.on.ca
www.facebook.com/senecacollege
twitter.com/Seneca_College
www.youtube.com/user/VideoSeneca
Note: The polytechnic educational institution consists of the following faculties: Faculty of Applied Arts & Health Sciences; Faculty of Applied Science & Engineering Technology; Faculty of Business; Faculty of Information Arts & Technology; Faculty of Continuing Education & Training; & Faculty of Workforce Skills Development
Bill Hogarth, B.A., M.Ed, Chair
David Agnew, President
president@senecac.on.ca

Campuses
Buttonville Campus
Hangers 6, 7, & 8, Buttonville Airport
P.O. Box 190
2833 - 16th Ave., Markham, ON L3R 0P8, Canada
Tel: 416-491-5050; *Fax:* 905-477-8103

Jane Campus
21 Beverley Hills Dr., Toronto, ON M3L 1A2, Canada
Tel: 416-491-5050; *Fax:* 416-235-0462

King Campus
13990 Dufferin St., King City, ON L7B 1B3, Canada
Tel: 905-833-3333
Other Information: King Campus Library, Circulation: 416-491-5050, ext. 5108

Markham Campus
8 The Seneca Way, Markham, ON L3R 5Y1, Canada
Tel: 416-491-5050

Seneca @ York Campus
70 The Pond Rd., Toronto, ON M3J 3M6, Canada
Tel: 416-491-5050
Other Information: Student Services: 416-491-5050, ext. 3000

Newmarket Campus
Weston Produce Plaza
#3, 16655 Yonge St., Newmarket, ON L3X 1V6, Canada
Tel: 905-898-6199

Yorkgate Campus
1 York Gate Blvd., Toronto, ON M3N 3A1, Canada
Tel: 416-491-5050;

Scarborough Campus
3660 Midland Ave. 2nd Fl., Scarborough, ON M1V 0B8, Canada
Tel: 416-293-3722

Vaughan Campus
1490 Major Mackenzie Dr. West, #D5, Vaughan, ON L6A 4H6, Canada
Tel: 905-417-1781

Welland: Niagara College
Welland Campus
300 Woodlawn Rd., Welland, ON L3C 7L3, Canada
Tel: 905-735-2211; *Fax:* 905-736-6020
infocentre@niagaracollege.ca
www.niagarac.on.ca
Other Information: Grimsby Phone: 905-563-3254
www.facebook.com/niagaracollege
twitter.com/Niagara_College
www.youtube.com/user/niagaracollegecanada
Full Time Equivalency: 6300 *Note:* Niagara College offers over 90 post-secondary diploma & graduate certificate programs,

skills & apprenticeship training programs, plus two bachelor degree programs.
Jim Ryan, Chair
Dan Patterson, President, 905-641-2252, ext. 4040
dpatterson@niagaracollege.ca

Campuses
Maid of the Mist Campus
Also known as: Tourism Industry Development Centre
5881 Dunn St., Niagara Falls, ON L2G 2N9, Canada
Tel: 905-374-7454

Niagara-on-the-Lake Campus
135 Taylor Rd., Niagara-on-the-Lake, ON L0S 1J0, Canada
Tel: 905-641-2252

Windsor: St. Clair College
South Campus
2000 Talbot Rd. West, Windsor, ON N9A 6S4, Canada
Tel: 519-966-1656; *Fax:* 519-972-3811
Toll-Free: 1-800-387-0524
info@stclaircollege.ca
www.stclaircollege.ca
www.facebook.com/StClairCollege
www.twitter.com/stclaircollege
www.youtube.com/stclairmarketing
Full Time Equivalency: 5000 *Note:* The College consists of the following schools of specialization: School of Liberal Arts & Sciences; School of Business & Information Technology; School of Academic Studies; School of Community Studies; School of Media, Art & Design; School of Engineering Technologies; School of Health Sciences; & School of Skilled Trades.
Vince Marcotte, Chair
John A. Strasser, Ph.D., President, 519-972-2701
jstrasser@stclaircollege.ca
Sherry Sharon, Registrar, 519-972-2727, ext. 4260
ssharon@stclaircollege.ca

Campuses
Thames Campus
1001 Grand Ave. West, Chatham, ON N7M 5W4, Canada
Tel: 519-354-9100; *Fax:* 519-354-6941
Note: The campus provides specialized training from the Schools of Business & Technology, & Health & Community Studies.

Wallaceburg Campus - James A. Burgess Skills Centre
920 Elgin St., Wallaceburg, ON N8A 3E1, Canada
Tel: 519-627-8336; *Fax:* 519-627-5950
Note: The campus features the Technical Industry Education Partnership.

St. Clair Centre for the Arts
201 Riverside Dr. West, Windsor, ON N9A 5K4
Tel: 519-252-8311; *Fax:* 519-973-4976
Enrollment: 500 *Note:* The campus features the School of Media, Art & Design.
Ed Noot, Principal
Mike Campbell, Vice Principal & Counsellor

Post Secondary/Technical

Independent & Private Schools

Toronto: Outward Bound Canada
Centre for Green Cities
#404, 550 Bayview Ave., Toronto, ON M4W 3X8, Canada
Tel: 705-382-5454; *Fax:* 705-382-5959
Toll-Free: 1-888-688-9273
info@outwardbound.ca
www.outwardbound.ca
www.facebook.com/outwardboundcanada?ref=ts
twitter.com/OutwardBoundCan
www.linkedin.com/company/outward-bound-canada
www.youtube.com/user/OutwardBoundCanada
Enrollment: 440
Sarah Wiley, Executive Director
sarah_wiley@outwardbound.ca

Post Secondary/Technical

Northern Ontario School of Medicine
Tel: 807-766-7300; *Toll-Free:* 1-800-461-8777
www.nosm.ca
www.facebook.com/thenosm
twitter.com/nosmtweets
www.youtube.com/user/NOSMtv/feed
Note: 4-year MD program
Dominic Giroux, Chair
Roger Strasser, Dean, CEO & Secretary

Campuses
East Campus (NORMED)
935 Ramsey Lake Rd., Sudbury, ON P3E 2C6, Canada
Tel: 705-675-4883; *Fax:* 705-675-4858
Note: Associated with Laurentian University.

West Campus (NORMED)
955 Oliver Rd., Thunder Bay, ON P7B 5E1, Canada
Tel: 807-766-7300; *Fax:* 807-766-7370
Note: Associated with Lakehead University.

Alfred: Collège d'Alfred de l'Université de Guelph
31, rue St-Paul, CP 580, Alfred, ON K0B 1A0, Canada
Tél: 613-679-2218; *Téléc:* 613-679-2423
www.alfredc.uoguelph.ca
Note: Agriculture, horticulture, techniques de diététique, développement international, techniques soins vétérinaires
Dr. Renée Bergeron, Ph.D., Directrice

Ancaster: Redeemer University College
777 Garner Rd. East, Ancaster, ON L9K 1J4, Canada
Tel: 905-648-2131; *Fax:* 905-648-2134
www.redeemer.ca
www.facebook.com/redeemer
twitter.com/RedeemerUC
www.youtube.com/redeemeruc#p/a/u/1/U073KL05ktl
Enrollment: 816
Justin D. Cooper, Ph.D., President
Jacob P. Ellens, Ph.D., Vice-President
William van Staalduinen, M.A., Vice-President
Ineke VanBruinessen, C.G.A., Senior Director
Marian Ryks-Szelekovszky, M.Ed., Senior Director, Admissions & Student Services
Mark Van Beveren, M.B.A., Media & Public Relations Director
Doug Loney, Ph.D., Dean
Doug Needham, Ph.D., Dean

Publications
The Crown

Belleville: Loyalist College
P.O. Box 4200
376 Wallbridge-Loyalist Rd., Belleville, ON K8N 5B9, Canada
Tel: 613-969-1913; *Fax:* 613-962-1376
Toll-Free: 888-569-2547
liaison@loyalistc.on.ca
www.loyalistcollege.com
TTY: 613-962-0633
www.facebook.com/loyalistcollege
twitter.com/loyalistcollege
Douglas A.L. Auld, President

Publications
The Pioneer

Brantford: Medical Radiation Technology
c/o Ontario Association of Medical Radiation Tech
P.O. Box 1054
Brantford, ON N3T 5S7, Canada
Tel: 519-753-6037; *Fax:* 519-753-6408
Toll-Free: 1-800-387-467
inquiries@oamrt.on.ca
www.oamrt.on.ca

Burlington: Charles Sturt University, Ontario
Bay Area Learning Centre
860 Harrington Ct., Burlington, ON L7N 3N4, Canada
Tel: 905-333-4955; *Fax:* 905-333-6562
canada@csu.edu.au
www.charlessturt.ca
Number of Employees: 20 academic staff; 8 faculty advisors; 2 adminsitrative staff *Note:* 1-year teacher education program
Dr. Will Letts, Head of School, 905-333-4955, ext. 55105, fax: 905-333-6562
wletts@csu.edu.au

Burlington: HBI College (HBI)
#26, 460 Brant St., Burlington, ON L7R 4B6, Canada
Tel: 905-637-3415; *Fax:* 905-637-2843
Toll-Free: 1-855-949-9909
info@hbicollege.com
www.hbicollege.com
Note: Administrative & computer programs.

Brampton Campus (HBI)
#314, 7700 Hurontario St., Brampton, ON L6Y 4M3, Canada
Toll-Free: 1-855-949-9909

Concord: RCC College of Technology
2000 Steeles Ave. West, Concord, ON L4K 4N1, Canada
Tel: 905-669-0544; *Fax:* 905-669-0551
Toll-Free: 1-800-83865428
www.rcc.on.ca
Note: Electronics & computer networks engineering technology training & programs
Dr. Rick Davey, President

School of Engineering Technology & Computing
2000 Steeles Ave. West, Concord, ON L4K 4N1, Canada
Fax: 905-695-1389
Toll-Free: 866-838-6542
www.rccsetc.ca
www.facebook.com/SETCCanada
twitter.com/SETCCanada
www.youtube.com/user/rccit?feature=mhum
Rick Davey, President

Schools
Academy of Design
2000 Steeles Ave. West, Concord, ON L4K 4N1, Canada
Tel: 905-669-0544; *Fax:* 905-669-0551
Toll-Free: 1-866-838-6542
www.aodt.ca
www.facebook.com/AcademyOfDesignToronto
twitter.com/TorontoAOD
www.youtube.com/user/AcademyToronto
Note: Fashion design, fashion marketing, interior design, graphic media.

Toronto Film School
2000 Steeles Ave. West, Concord, ON L4K 4N1, Canada
Tel: 905-669-0544; *Fax:* 905-669-0551
Toll-Free: 1-800-83865428
www.torontofilmschool.ca
www.facebook.com/TorontoFilmSchool
twitter.com/TorontoFilmS
www.youtube.com/user/TorontoFilmS1

Davisville Campus
1835 Yonge St., 2nd Fl., Toronto, ON M4S 1X8, Canada
Tel: 905-669-0544; *Fax:* 905-669-0551

Campuses
Dundas Campus
#704, 10 Dundas St. East, Toronto, ON M5B 2G9, Canada
Tel: 647-288-8496; *Fax:* 647-644-1903

Dundas: Dundas Valley School of Art (DVSA)
21 Ogilvie St., Dundas, ON L9H 2S1, Canada
Tel: 905-628-6357; *Fax:* 905-628-1087
dvsa@cogeco.net
www.dvsa.ca
Arthur Greenblatt, Director

Guelph: Ontario Agricultural College
OAC Dean's Office, Univ. of Guelph
103 Johnston Hall, Guelph, ON N1G 2W1, Canada
Tel: 519-824-4120; *Fax:* 519-766-1423
oacinfo@uoguelph.ca
www.oac.uoguelph.ca
Heather Renwick, Executive Assistant, 519-824-4120, ext. ext.56513
hrenwick@oac.uoguelph.ca
Dr. Craig J. Pearson, Dean, 519-824-4120, ext. ext.52285
cpearson@uoguelph.ca

Hamilton: Canadian Institute for NDE
135 Fennell Ave. West, Hamilton, ON L8N 3T2, Canada
Tel: 905-387-1655; *Fax:* 905-574-6080
info@cinde.ca
www.cinde.ca
Note: Nondestructive testing/nondestructive examination
Douglas Marshall, Managing Director

Hamilton: Grand Health Academy
760 King St. East, Hamilton, ON L8M 1A6
Tel: 905-577-7707; *Fax:* 905-577-7738
www.grandhealthacademy.com
www.facebook.com/grandhealthacademy
twitter.com/GHA_school
Note: Established in 1992, Grand Health Academy offers programs that prepare students to become personal support workers, food service workers, pharmacy assistants, & rehabilitation assistants.

Hamilton: Luba Mera School of Aesthetics & Cosmetology
370 Main St. East, Hamilton, ON L8N 1J6, Canada
Tel: 905-522-3883; *Toll-Free:* 1-888-809-5559
institute@lubamera.com
www.lubamera.com
www.facebook.com/LubaMeraInstitute
Note: Aesthetics training.

Hamilton: Medical Laboratory Technology
The Canadian Society for Medical Laboratory Scien
P.O. Box 2830
Hamilton, ON L8N 3N8, Canada
Tel: 905-528-8642; *Fax:* 905-528-4968
kurtd@csmls.org
www.csmls.org
Kurt H. Davis, Executive Director

***London:* AlphaLogic Career College**
280 King Edward Ave., London, ON N5Z 3V3
Tel: 519-858-0010; *Fax:* 519-858-0089
info@alphalogic.net
www.alphalogic.net
Note: Since 1995, the private career college has offered diploma programs, industry standard certifications, & courses in the areas of customer service, network administration, desktop support, & medical office & automotive specialties.
Jerry S. Vandergoot, President
Kerry Cruickshank, Director, Student Services

***London:* Elegance Schools Inc.**
219 Oxford St. West, London, ON N6H 1S5, Canada
Tel: 519-434-1181; *Fax:* 519-434-1182
www.eleganceschools.on.ca
Note: Esthetics & electrolysis.
Lisa Hakim, Director

***London:* St. Peter's Seminary**
1040 Waterloo St. North, London, ON N6A 3Y1, Canada
Tel: 519-432-1824; *Fax:* 519-432-0964
stpeters@uwo.ca
www.stpetersseminary.ca
Rev. W.T. McGrattan, B.E.Sc., M.Div., S.T.L., Rector
Rev. T.F. O'Connor, M.A., M.T.S., M.Th., Spiritual Director
Rev. Brian Dunn, Dean
Rev. John Comiskey, B.A., M.Div., H.E.L., H.E, Vice Rector & Registrar
Gabriella Catolino, D.M.C., M.Div., Executive Director

***London:* Westervelt College**
1060 Wellington Rd., London, ON N6E 3W5
Tel: 226-289-2108; *Toll-Free:* 1-877-668-2001
Info@WesterveltCollege.com
www.westervelt.ca
Note: Westervelt College opened in 1885. The college has faculties of healthcare, business, law, service, & technology.

***Mississauga:* Credit Institute of Canada**
#216C, 219 Dufferin St., Mississauga, ON M6K 3J1, Canada
Tel: 905-572-2615; *Fax:* 905-572-2619
www.creditedu.org
E. Keith Devolin, President & Dean
Geoff Wilkinson, General Manager

***Mississauga:* The Investment Funds Institute of Canada (IFSE)**
#601, 50 Burnhamthorpe Rd. West, Mississauga, ON L5B 3C2, Canada
Tel: 416-865-1237; *Toll-Free:* 1-888-865-2437
ifse@ifse.ca
www.ifse.ca
Keith Costello, Managing Director

Campuses
Québec Branch
#1800, 1010, rue Sherbrooke ouest, Montréal, QC H3A 2R7, Canada
Fax: 514-985-5113

***Niagara Falls:* Niagara Parks School of Horticulture**
P.O. Box 150
Niagara Falls, ON L2E 6T2, Canada
Tel: 905-356-8554; *Fax:* 905-356-5488
schoolofhorticulture@niagaraparks.com
www.niagaraparks.com/school-of-horticulture
Enrollment: 30
R. Stoner, Contact, 905-356-8554, ext. 226
rstoner@niagaraparks.com

***North Bay:* Canadore College of Applied Arts & Technology**
P.O. Box 5001
100 College Dr., North Bay, ON P1B 8K9, Canada
Tel: 705-474-7600; *Fax:* 705-474-2384
info@canadorec.on.ca
www.canadorec.on.ca
Enrollment: 2977
Barbara Taylor, President

***Norwood:* Eastern Ontario Fire Academy**
P.O. Box 460
36 Industrial Dr., Norwood, ON K0L 2V0
Tel: 705-639-2121; *Fax:* 905-426-3032
eofa@oafc.on.ca
www.eofa.ca

***Ohsweken:* Six Nations Polytechnic**
P.O. Box 700
Ohsweken, ON N0A 1M0, Canada
Tel: 519-445-0023; *Fax:* 519-445-4416
president@snpolytechnic.com
www.snpolytechnic.com

Rebecca Jamieson, President

***Ottawa:* Algonquin Careers Academy**
1830 Bank St., Ottawa, ON K1V 7Y6
Tel: 613-722-7811; *Fax:* 613-722-4494
Toll-Free: 1-888-722-7818
www.algonquinacademy.com
www.facebook.com/AlgonquinCareersAcademy?sk=wall
Note: Since 1981, the Algonquin Careers Academy has offered programs in areas such as travel counselling, personal support work, medical lab assistance, medical office assistance, health & fitness promotion, & accounting.

***Ottawa:* Canadian Police College (CPC)**
Collège canadien de police
P.O. Box 8900
1 Sandridge Rd., Ottawa, ON K1G 3J2, Canada
Tel: 613-993-9500; *Fax:* 613-990-9738
cpc-ccp@rcmp-grc.gc.ca
www.cpc.gc.ca
www.facebook.com/262605970429119
twitter.com/cpc1976ccp
www.youtube.com/user/CanPoliceCollege?feature=mhee
Cal Corley, Director general
cal.corley@rcmp-grc.gc.ca

Campuses
Canadian Police College West
Collège canadien de police
1101 Calais Cres., Chilliwack, BC V2R 5S7, Canada
Tel: 604-703-7500; *Fax:* 604-703-2517
Number of Employees: 300 instructors
Sue Gadsby, Contact
susan.gadsby@rcmp-grc.gc.ca

***Ottawa:* La Cité collégiale**
801, promenade de l'Aviation, Ottawa, ON K1K 4R3, Canada
Tél: 613-742-2483; *Téléc:* 613-742-2481
Ligne sans frais: 1-800-267-2483
info@lacitec.on.ca
www.lacitecollegiale.com
www.facebook.com/lacitecollegiale.on
twitter.com/citecollegiale
www.youtube.com/user/LaCitecollegiale
Enrollment: 3500
Andrée Lortie, Président

Campus Alphonse-Desjardins
Centre des métiers Minto
8865, North Service Rd., Orléans, ON, Canada
Ligne sans frais: 1-800-267-2483

Campuses
Campus de Hawkesbury
570, rue Kitchener, Hawkesbury, ON K6A 2P3, Canada
Ligne sans frais: 1-800-267-2483

Campus de Pembroke
412, rue Pembroke ouest, Pembroke, ON K8A 5N6, Canada
Ligne sans frais: 1-800-267-2483

***Ottawa:* Ican College of Computers and Healthcare**
1825 Woodward Dr., Ottawa, ON K2C 0P9, Canada
Tel: 613-224-6211; *Fax:* 613-224-2739
www.icancollege.com
www.facebook.com/367056359972043
Nicki Wilmore, President
nicki@Icancollege.com

***Ottawa:* International Academy Health Education Centre**
380 Forest St., Ottawa, ON K2B 8E6, Canada
Tel: 613-820-0318; *Fax:* 613-820-7478
Toll-Free: 800-267-8732
info@intlacademy.com
www.intlacademy.com
Note: Nutrition; herbs; iridology; reflexology; aromatherapy; homeopathy; shiatsu/accupressure; massage
Dorothy Marshall, Ph.D., N.D., C.H.H.P., N., Executive Director

***Ottawa:* International Academy of Natural Health Sciences**
380 Forest St., Ottawa, ON K2B 8E6, Canada
Tel: 613-820-0318; *Fax:* 613-820-7478
Toll-Free: 1-800-267-8732
naturalhealth@intlacademy.com
www.intlacademy.com
Note: Nutrition; herbs; iridology; reflexology

***Ottawa:* Ottawa School of Art**
35 George St., Ottawa, ON K1N 8W5, Canada
Tel: 613-241-7471; *Fax:* 613-241-4391
info@artottawa.ca
www.artottawa.ca
Note: Fine arts training.

Jeff Stellick, Executive Director

***Ottawa:* Pères Montfortains (Residence des étudiants)**
463 Riverdale Ave., Ottawa, ON K1S 1S1, Canada
Tél: 613-731-2271
Cor Kauffman, s.m.m., Superior

***Ottawa:* Versailles Academy of Make-Up Arts, Esthetics, Hair**
#1, 1930 Bank St., Ottawa, ON K1V 7Z8
Tel: 613-521-4155; *Fax:* 613-521-6945
info@versaillesacademy.com
www.versaillesacademy.com
Note: Since 1981, the private career college has trained students for work in the cosmetic, hairstyling, & esthetic fields.

***Ottawa:* Willis College of Business & Technology**
85 O'Connor St., Ottawa, ON K1P 5M6, Canada
Tel: 613-233-1128; *Fax:* 613-233-9286
Toll-Free: 877-233-1128
inquiries@ottawa.williscollege.com
www.williscollege.com
www.facebook.com/pages/Willis-College/161733597204726
www.twitter.com/williscollege
www.youtube.com/williscollege
Note: E-business & IT training.
Rima Aristocrat, President/CEO

Smith Falls Campus
25 William St. West, Smith Falls, ON K7A 1N2, Canada
Tel: 613-283-1905; *Fax:* 613-283-1333
inquires@smithsfalls.williscollege.com

Campuses
Cobourg Campus
1111 Elgin St. West, Cobourg, ON K9A 5H7, Canada
Tel: 905-372-8978; *Fax:* 905-372-5189
Toll-Free: 877-762-9979

***Owen Sound:* Creative Career Systems Academy**
114 Drive-In Cres., RR#5, Owen Sound, ON N4K 5N7, Canada
Tel: 519-376-7396; *Fax:* 519-376-6772
info@CCSAcademy.com
www.ccsacademy.com
www.twitter.com/ccsacademy
Note: Health care aide program.

***Richmond Hill:* Academy of Learning - Richmond Hill**
10235 Yonge St., Richmond Hill, ON L4C 3B4
Tel: 905-508-5791; *Fax:* 905-508-9409
aolrichmondhill1@rogers.com
www.academyoflearning.com
Note: The career & business college offers more than thirty certificate & diploma programs.

***Ridgetown:* Ridgetown College - University of Guelph**
120 Main. St. East, Ridgetown, ON N0P 2C0, Canada
Tel: 519-674-1500; *Fax:* 519-674-1515
www.ridgetownc.uoguelph.ca
Ken McEwan, Interim Director
J.M. Brooks, Executive Officer
jbrooks@ridgetownc.uoguelph.ca

***Scarborough:* CJ Health Care College - Scarborough Campus**
#413, 1371 Neilson Rd., Scarborough, ON M1B 4Z8, Canada
Tel: 416-283-8252; *Fax:* 416-283-3796
admin.scar@cjcollege.com
www.cjcollege.com
Note: Health care related program.
Altheia Jordan, Manager

Campuses
Etobicoke Campus
702 Pape Ave., Toronto, ON M4K 3S7, Canada
Tel: 416-422-5627; *Fax:* 416-422-5628

***Scarborough:* St. Augustine's Seminary of Toronto**
2661 Kingston Rd., Scarborough, ON M1M 1M3, Canada
Tel: 416-261-7207; *Fax:* 416-261-2529
tehil@web.net
www.staugustines.on.ca
Enrollment: 95
Rev. Msgr. A. Robert Nusca, B.A., M.Div., S.T.B., S.S, Rector
Rev. Robert J. Barringer, C.S.B., Dean

Sudbury: **Transport Canada Training Institute**
2565 Kingsway Blvd., Sudbury, ON P3B 2G1, Canada
Tel: 705-521-1157; *Fax:* 705-521-1156
Toll-Free: 1-800-805-0662
headoffice@ttcc.ca
www.ttcc.ca
www.facebook.com/transporttraining
Note: 23 locations around Ontario, Nova Scotia and New Brunswick.

Timmins: **Northern College**
P.O. Box 3211
Hwy. 101 East, South Porcupine, Timmins, ON P4N 8R6
Tel: 705-235-3211; *Fax:* 705-235-7279
Toll-Free: 1-866-736-587
info@northern.on.ca
www.northernc.on.ca
www.facebook.com/northernc
twitter.com/northernc_on_ca
Enrollment: 1489
Fred Gibbons, President
Dave McGirr, Chair

Campuses
Haileybury Campus
640 Latchford St., Haileybury, ON P0J 1K0
Tel: 705-672-3376; *Fax:* 705-672-2014

Kirkland Lake Campus
140 Government Rd. East, Kirkland Lake, ON P2N 3L8, Canada
Tel: 705-567-9291; *Fax:* 705-568-8186

Porcupine Campus
P.O. Box 3211
4715 Highway 101 East, South Porcupine, ON P0N 1H0, Canada
Tel: 705-235-3211

Moosonee Campus
First Ave. Box 130, Moosonee, ON P0L 1Y0
Tel: 705-336-2913

Toronto: **Automotive Training Centres - Toronto Centre**
152 Norseman St., Toronto, ON M8Z 2R4, Canada
Tel: 416-231-7227; *Fax:* 416-231-2753
Toll-Free: 1-800-458-7473
toronto@autotrainingcentre.com
www.autotrainingcentre.com
Note: Private college specializing in automotive training

Campuses
Montreal Campus
7555, boul Henri-Bourassa, Montréal, QC H1E 1N9, Canada
Tel: 514-725-6026; *Fax:* 514-725-1630
Toll-Free: 1-877-725-6026
Montreal@AutoTraiingCentre.com

Surrey Campus
12160 - 88th Ave., Surrey, BC V3W 3J2, Canada
Tel: 604-635-2222; *Fax:* 604-635-2223
Toll-Free: 1-888-546-2886
Surry@AutoTrainingCentre.com

Toronto: **Canadian Academy of Floral Art (CAFA) L'Académie canadienne d'art floral**
72 Northdale Rd., Toronto, ON M2L 2M1
Tel: 519-836-5495; *Fax:* 519-836-7529
Toll-Free: 800-698-0113
www.cafachat.com
www.cafachat.com
www.facebook.com/group.php?gid=113431802003393
Note: Floral designers who become members of the Canadian Academy of Floral Art are permitted to add the initials CAFA after their name.

Toronto: **Canadian Business College**
Head Office
2 Bloor St. West, 22nd Fl., Toronto, ON M4W 3E2
Tel: 416-925-9929; *Fax:* 416-925-9220
www.cbstraining.com
www.facebook.com/cbstraining
twitter.com/cbstraining
www.youtube.com/watch?v=ylidYvYAVxc
Note: Courses are offered in the areas of business, information technology, digital media, law, health, community service, & child care. The Canadian Business College is registered with the Government of Canada's Human Resources Development Canada,

Toronto: **Canadian Churches' Forum for Global Ministries**
Toronto School of Theology
47 Queen's Park Cres. East, Toronto, ON M5S 2C3, Canada
Tel: 416-924-9351; *Fax:* 416-978-7821
director@ccforum.ca
www.ccforum.ca
Note: Cross cultural orientation programs for church related personnel & volunteers involved in global mission & ministry

Toronto: **The Canadian College of Naturopathic Medicine**
1255 Sheppard Ave. East, Toronto, ON M2K 1E2, Canada
Tel: 416-498-1255; *Fax:* 416-498-1576
Toll-Free: 1-866-241-226
info@ccnm.edu
www.ccnm.edu
Note: Naturopathic medical education, research & clinical practice; 4,500+ hours of classroom & clinical training
Nicholas De Groot, Dean
Bob Bernhardt, President & CEO

Toronto: **Canadian Institute of Health Care & Business**
#303, 7 Hayden St., Toronto, ON M4Y 2P2, Canada
Tel: 416-925-4417; *Fax:* 416-646-2054
Note: Personal Support Worker; Live-in Caregiver; Travel & Tourism; Pharmacy Technician

Toronto: **Canadian Jewellers Association (CJA)**
#600, 27 Queen St. East, Toronto, ON M5C 2M6, Canada
Tel: 416-368-7616; *Fax:* 416-368-1986
Toll-Free: 1-800-580-0942
www.canadianjewellers.com
Note: Programs include Jewellery Education Training System (JETS), and the Accredited Appraiser Program.
Maria Garcia, Manager, Education Services

Toronto: **Canadian Law Enforcement Training College**
#2, 4646 Dufferin St., Toronto, ON M3H 5S4, Canada
Tel: 416-480-1545
info@policefoundations.org
www.policefoundations.org
twitter.com/cdnlawenforce
Note: Police & law enforcement courses

Toronto: **Canadian Memorial Chiropractic College**
6100 Leslie St., Toronto, ON M2H 3J1, Canada
Tel: 416-482-2340; *Fax:* 416-482-9745
Toll-Free: 800-463-2923
communications@cmcc.ca
www.cmcc.ca
Note: Undergraduate and graduate Chiropratic College.
Jean A. Moss, D.C., M.B.A., President
president@cmcc.ca

Toronto: **Canadian School of Private Investigation & Security Ltd.**
2828 Dufferin St., Toronto, ON M6B 3S3, Canada
Tel: 416-785-5701; *Fax:* 416-785-6064
efranco@CSPIS.com
www.cspis.com
Note: Private investigation, paralegal, security, law enforcement & police foundations training.
Carl Franco, President & Founder

Toronto: **Canadian Securities Institute (CSI)**
200 Wellington St. West, 15th Fl., Toronto, ON M5V 3C7, Canada
Tel: 416-364-9130; *Fax:* 866-866-2660
Toll-Free: 1-866-866-2601
customer_support@csi.ca
www.csi.ca
www.facebook.com/csiglobal
twitter.com/CSIGlobalEd
www.linkedin.com/groups?gid=3720042
csiblog.csi.ca

Campuses
Montréal Office
#400, 625, boul René-Lévesque ouest, Montréal, QC H3B 1R2, Canada
Fax: 866-866-2660
Toll-Free: 1-866-866-2601

Toronto: **The Certified General Accountants Association of Ontario**
240 Eglinton Ave. East, Toronto, ON M4P 1K8, Canada
Tel: 416-322-6520; *Fax:* 416-322-5594
Toll-Free: 1-800-668-1454
info@cga-ontario.org
www.cga-ontario.org/
www.facebook.com/cga
twitter.com/CGA_Ontario
www.linkedin.com/company/cga-ontario

Toronto: **CMS Training**
205 Richmond St. West, Toronto, ON M5V 1V3, Canada
Tel: 416-971-4267; *Fax:* 416-971-6750
info@cms.ca
www.cmstraining.ca
Note: Home study in computer programming

Toronto: **Complections College of Makeup Art & Design**
110 Lombard St., Toronto, ON M5C 1M3
Tel: 416-968-6739; *Fax:* 416-968-7340
www.complectionsmake-up.com
www.facebook.com/ComplectionsMakeup?sid=a
twitter.com/Complections
www.youtube.com/user/ComplectionsMakeup
Note: Complections, the International Academy of Make-up Artistry offers instruction that leads to a career in makeup artistry.
Pamela Earle, President, Complections International Academy

Toronto: **Frontier College**
35 Jackes Ave., Toronto, ON M4T 1E2, Canada
Fax: 416-323-3522
Toll-Free: 1-800-555-6523
information@frontiercollege.ca
www.frontiercollege.ca
www.facebook.com/137772832974312
twitter.com/FrontierCollege
www.youtube.com/user/frontiercollege
Note: Volunteer-based, literacy organization.
Sherry Campbell, President & CEO

Toronto: **The Glenn Gould School of the Royal Conservatory of Music**
90 Croatia St., Toronto, ON M6H 1K9, Canada
Tel: 416-408-2824; *Fax:* 416-408-3096
glenngouldschool@rcmusic.ca
rcmusic.ca/glenn-gould-school
Enrollment: 130 *Note:* Professional training in music performance & pedagogy at the bachelor & graduate levels
Rennie Regehr, Dean

Toronto: **Global Village - Toronto**
#202, 180 Bloor St. West, Toronto, ON M5S 2V6, Canada
Tel: 416-968-1405; *Fax:* 416-968-6667
toronto@gvenglish.com
www.gvenglish.com
www.facebook.com/GlobalVillageToronto
twitter.com/GVECMarketing
www.youtube.com/user/readyforielts
www.flickr.com/photos/gvenglish
Geneviève Bouchard, Director
Chris Pink, Contact
cpink@gvenglish@com

Campuses
Global Village - Calgary
North-West Travellers Building
#200, 515 - 1st Str. SE, Calgary, AB T2G 2G6, Canada
Tel: 403-543-7300; *Fax:* 403-543-7309
calgary@gvenglish.com
www.facebook.com/GlobalVillageCalgary

Global Village - Vancouver
888 Cambie St., Vancouver, BC V6B 2P6, Canada
Tel: 604-684-2112; *Fax:* 604-684-2124
vancouver@gvenglish.com
www.facebook.com/GlobalVillageVancouver
www.gvenglish.com/videos/gvvancouver01.html
Paul Maher, President/CEO

Global Village - Victoria
#200, 1290 Broad St., Victoria, BC V8W 2A5, Canada
Tel: 250-384-2199; *Fax:* 250-384-2123
victoria@gvenglish.com
www.facebook.com/gvvictoria
www.youtube.com/gvvictoria

***Toronto:* Institute of Technical Trades Ltd.**
749 Warden Ave., Toronto, ON M1L 4A8, Canada
Tel: 416-750-1950; *Fax:* 416-750-4702
Toll-Free: 1-800-461-4981
info@instituteoftechnicaltrades.com
www.instituteoftechnicaltrades.com
Note: Welding & CNC machine setup operation.

***Toronto:* International Institute of Travel (iitravel)**
Admissions & Registration
#402, 120 Carlton St., Toronto, ON M5A 4K2, Canada
Tel: 416-924-2271; *Fax:* 416-924-9632
www.iitravel.com
Note: Travel & tourism training including "Learning at Seas Seminars".

***Toronto:* Marvel Beauty Schools**
25 Yorkville Ave., 2nd Fl., Toronto, ON M4W 1L1, Canada
Tel: 416-923-0993; *Fax:* 416-640-4490
Toll-Free: 1-800-661-6096
info@marvelschools.com
www.marvelschools.com
Note: Skin care & hairstyling

The School of Make-Up Art
25 Yorkville Ave., 3rd Fl., Toronto, ON M4W 1L1, Canada
Tel: 416-340-1300; *Fax:* 416-640-4491
info@schoolofmakeupart.com

Schools
Pebec School of Esthetics
496 Dundas St., London, ON N6B 1W6, Canada
Tel: 519-432-7162; *Fax:* 416-640-5950
info@pebec.com

***Toronto:* Medix School - Toronto Campus**
Head Office
#300, 700 Lawrence Ave. West, Toronto, ON M6A 3B4, Canada
Tel: 866-981-0683; *Fax:* 416-630-9790
Toll-Free: 1-866-962-7685
www.medixschool.ca
Note: Health care programs
Randy Henry, President

Campuses
Brantford Campus
39 King George Rd., Brantford, ON N3R 5K2, Canada
Tel: 519-752-4859; *Fax:* 519-752-2217

Kitchener Campus
#14, 248 Stirling Ave., Kitchener, ON N2G 4L1, Canada
Tel: 519-895-0013; *Fax:* 519-772-0107
Toll-Free: 800-695-2414

London Campus
1299 Oxford St. East, London, ON N5Y 4W5, Canada
Tel: 519-659-4822; *Fax:* 519-659-2516
Toll-Free: 800-695-2414

Scarborough Campus
#205, 2130 Lawrence Avenue East, Scarborough, ON M1R 3A6, Canada
Tel: 866-981-0684; *Fax:* 416-701-0855
Toll-Free: 866-981-0684

Brampton Campus
13 Queen St. East, Brampton, ON L6W 2A7, Canada
Fax: 905-487-1162
Toll-Free: 866-981-3295

***Toronto:* National Institute of Broadcasting (NIB)**
1498 Yonge St., Toronto, ON M4T 1Z6, Canada
Tel: 416-922-2556; *Fax:* 416-922-5470
Toll-Free: 1-800-216-6247
www.nibbroadcasttraining.com
Note: Radio & television broadcast training.
Mona Matteo, President

***Toronto:* New Skills College of Health, Business, & Technology**
720 Midland Ave., Toronto, ON M1K 4C9
Tel: 416-269-2666; *Fax:* 416-266-3898
www.newskillscollege.ca
Note: The New Skills College is a member of the Ontario Association of Career Colleges. The college provides training for health care personnel. Examples of programs include training for food handlers, personal attendants, & medical office assistants.
Julia Li, President, 416-266-8878
Paul Preikschas, Program Manager, 416-269-2666, ext. 221

***Toronto:* Ontario Institute for Studies in Education**
252 Bloor St. West, Toronto, ON M5S 1V6, Canada
Tel: 416-923-6641; *Fax:* 416-926-4725
www.oise.utoronto.ca
Jane Gaskell, Dean

***Toronto:* The RCM Community School at The Royal Conservatory of Music**
90 Croatia St., Toronto, ON M6H 1K9, Canada
Tel: 416-408-2825; *Fax:* 416-408-3096
communityschool@rcmusic.ca
www.rcmusic.ca
Enrollment: 6000 *Note:* Music lessons for people of all ages & levels of ability; recognized for its Early Childhood Education programs & its commitment to life-long learning

***Toronto:* Regency Dental Hygiene Academy Inc.**
#400, 481 University Ave., Toronto, ON M5G 2E9, Canada
Tel: 416-341-0100; *Fax:* 416-341-0747
Toll-Free: 1-866-666-0481
info@regencydha.ca
www.regencydha.com
www.facebook.com/121627584576269
twitter.com/#%21/RegencyDHA

***Toronto:* Rets PLC Training**
2084 Danforth Ave., Toronto, ON M4C 1J9, Canada
Tel: 416-698-5287; *Fax:* 416-689-5288
Note: PLC automation; engineering technology; government regulated & approved.

***Toronto:* The Royal Conservatory of Music**
McMaster Hall
273 Bloor St. West, Toronto, ON M5S 1W2
Tel: 416-408-2825; *Fax:* 866-263-4447
Toll-Free: 1-800-461-6058
conservatoryschool@rcmusic.ca;
candidateservices@rcmusic.ca
www.rcmusic.ca
Other Information: TELUS Centre for Performance & Learning, Phone: 416-408-0208
www.facebook.com/theroyalconservatory
twitter.com/the_rcm
www.youtube.com/rcmusic
Note: The Royal Conservatory was founded in 1886. The Conservatory's core programs are as follows: The Royal Conservatory School; The Glenn Gould School; the Young Artists Performance Academy; Learning Through the Arts; The Frederick Harris Music Co., Limited; & Examinations. Every year, approximately 600,000 people from across Canada participate in music education programs offered by The Royal Conservatory.
Michael Foulkes, Chair
Michael M. Koerner, Chancellor
Peter Simon, President
Tony Flynn, Chief Administrative Officer
Krista O'Donnell, Chief Development Officer
Mervon Mehta, Executive Director, Performing Arts
Angela Elster, Vice-President, Academic
Karen Leiter, Vice-President, Marketing & Communication

***Toronto:* Shiatsu School of Canada Inc.**
547 College St., Toronto, ON M6G 1A9, Canada
Tel: 416-323-1818; *Fax:* 416-323-1681
Toll-Free: 1-800-263-1703
info@shiatsucanada.com
www.shiatsucanada.com
Note: 2,200-hour program has the highest standard in the world outside of Japan
Enza Ierullo, Director

***Toronto:* The Society of Management Accountants of Ontario**
#1100, 25 York St., Toronto, ON M5J 2V5, Canada
Tel: 416-977-7741; *Fax:* 416-977-6079
Toll-Free: 1-800-387-299
info@cmaontario.org
www.cma-canada.org/ontario/default.asp
Merv Hillier, FCMA, C. Dir., President & CEO

***Toronto:* Sutherland Chan School & Teaching Clinic**
#400, 330 Dupont St., Toronto, ON M5R 1V9, Canada
Tel: 416-924-1107; *Fax:* 416-924-9413
admissions@sutherland-chan.com
www.sutherland-chan.com
www.facebook.com/127460549809
twitter.com/SutherlandChan
Note: Massage therapy.
Grace Chan, President
Carol Oya, Admissions & Student Services Coordinator

***Toronto:* Toronto Art Therapy Institute**
#103, 66 Portland St., Toronto, ON M5V 2M6, Canada
Tel: 416-924-6221; *Fax:* 416-924-0156
www.tati.on.ca
Gilda Grossman, M.S.W., R.S.W., R.C.A.T., Director

***Toronto:* Toronto Baptist Seminary & Bible College**
130 Gerrard St. East, Toronto, ON M5A 3T4, Canada
Tel: 416-925-3263; *Fax:* 416-925-8305
www.tbs.edu
www.facebook.com/pages/Toronto-Baptist-Seminary/176191542436733
twitter.com/tbsedu
Dr. Glendon G. Thompson, President

***Toronto:* Toronto Institute of Pharmaceutical Technology**
#800, 55 Town Centre Ct., Toronto, ON M1P 4X4, Canada
Tel: 416-296-8860; *Fax:* 416-296-7077
info@tipt.com
www.tipt.com
www.facebook.com/TIPTechnology
www.twitter.com/TIPTechnology
Alexander MacGregor, President & Dean

***Toronto:* Townshend College of Business & Computers Inc.**
#714, Victoria St., Toronto, ON M5C 1Y2
Tel: 416-642-0567; *Fax:* 416-642-0567
canada@kkjgroup.ca
www.townshendcollege.com
Note: Founded in 1992, Townshend College provides courses in computerized accounting, e-commerce design & development, computer programming, business, office administration, & technology.

***Toronto:* Travel Training Career Centre Ltd.**
#201, 16 Spadina Rd., Toronto, ON M5R 2S7, Canada
Tel: 416-481-2265; *Fax:* 416-487-5428
info@travelcollege.ca
www.travelcollege.ca
www.facebook.com/TravelCollegeCanada
Note: Travel & tourism industry courses, customer service.
Louise Blazik, Founder & Director

***Toronto:* Tyndale University College & Seminary**
25 Ballyconnor Ct., Toronto, ON M2M 4B3, Canada
Tel: 416-226-6380; *Fax:* 416-226-6746
Toll-Free: 1-877-896-3253
contact@tyndale.ca
www.tyndale.ca
Note: A Christian College and Seminary whose mission is to educate and equip Christians to serve the world with passion for Jesus Christ.
Archie McLean, Chair
Dr. Brian C. Stiller, President
The Hon. Jake Epp, Chancellor

***Waterloo:* Shad International**
8 Young St. East, Waterloo, ON N2J 2L3, Canada
Tel: 519-884-8844; *Fax:* 519-884-8191
info@shad.ca
www.shad.ca
Grades: 10-12 *Note:* Four week summer enrichment program for students in grades 11 or 12, secondaire V or CEGEP I for Quebec students, or the international equivalent. The program includes the sciences, technology, and entrepreneurship. Shad Valley is held on campus at 10 leading universities across Canada. Students live in residence at each university for the month of July.
Barry Bisson, President
barry@shad.ca
Mary Dever, National Director of Development
mary@shad.ca

Prince Edward Island

Government Agencies

***Summerside:* Department of Education & Early Childhood Development**
Holman Centre
#101, 250 Water St., Summerside, PE C1N 1B6, Canada
Tel: 902-438-4130; *Fax:* 902-438-4062
www.gov.pe.ca/eecd
Other Information: Charlottetown Phone: 902-368-4600
Hon. J. Alan McIsaac, Minister, 902-438-4876, fax: 902-438-4150
jamcisaac@gov.pe.ca

School Boards/Districts/Divisions

Public

Abram Village: French Language School Board of Prince Edward Island
La Commission scolaire de langue française de l'Ie-du-Prin
P.O. Box 124
1596 rte. 124, Abram Village, PE C0B 2E0, Canada
Tel: 902-854-2975; *Fax:* 902-854-2981
cslf@edu.pe.ca
www.edu.pe.ca/cslf
Number of Schools: 6 *Grades:* 1 - 12
Robert Maddix, Chair
Gilles Benoit, Chief Executive Officer
gjbenoit@edu.pe.ca
Paul Cyr, Director, Instruction
pacyr@edu.pe.ca
Louise Gallant, Director, Accounting
lzgallant@edu.pe.ca
Brad Samson, Director, Administration
blsamson@edu.pe.ca
Michel Gagnon, Manager, Information Systemes & Communications
mgagnon@edu.pe.ca
Élise Milligan, Secretary
emmilligan@edu.pe.ca

Charlottetown: Eastern School District
P.O. Box 8600
234 Shakespeare Dr., Charlottetown, PE C1A 8V7, Canada
Tel: 902-368-6990; *Fax:* 902-368-6960
www.edu.pe.ca/esd
twitter.com/ESDNLCA
Number of Schools: 36 *Enrollment:* 14309
Cindy MacLean, Superintendent
cjmaclean@edu.pe.ca
Ronald Lee, Vice-Chair
John Cummings, Director, Corporate Services
jacummings@edu.pe.ca
Bob Andrews, Director, School Development
rgandrews@edu.pe.ca
David MacDonald, Secretary

Summerside: Western School Board
272 MacEwen Rd., Summerside, PE C1N 2P7, Canada
Tel: 902-888-8400; *Fax:* 902-888-8449
www.edu.pe.ca/wsb
Grades: K.-12 *Enrollment:* 6244
Gary Doucette, Chair

Schools: Specialized

First Nations

Lennox Island: John J. Sark Memorial School
P.O. Box 124
Lennox Island, PE C0B 1P0, Canada
Tel: 902-831-2777; *Fax:* 902-831-3065
www.lennoxisland.com/lennoxcommunity/Education.html
Grades: K.-6 *Enrollment:* 50 *Number of Employees:* 10 *Note:* Curriculum includes Mi'kmaq language & culture.
Neil Forbes, Education Director
neil.forbes@lennoxisland.com

Schools: Independent & Private

Independent & Private Schools

Charlottetown: Fair Isle Adventist School
20 Lapthorne Ave., Charlottetown, PE C1A 2M2, Canada
Tel: 902-894-9301
Grades: 1-9; Seventh-day Adventist *Enrollment:* 7
Deanna Fall, Principal

Charlottetown: Full Circle Co-operative
219 Kent St., Charlottetown, PE C1A 1P1, Canada
Tel: 902-628-6174
principal@fullcircleschoolonline.net
Grades: 5-12 *Enrollment:* 15
Scott Davidson, B.A., B.Ed., Principal

Charlottetown: Grace Christian Academy
50 Kirkdale Rd., Charlottetown, PE C1E 1N6, Canada
Tel: 902-628-1668; *Fax:* 902-628-1668
gbc@gracechristianschool.ca
www.gracechristianschool.ca
Number of Schools: 1 *Grades:* K.-12 *Enrollment:* 131 *Number of Employees:* 14

Charlottetown: Grace Christian School
50 Kirkdale Rd., Charlottetown, PE C1E 1N6, Canada
Tel: 902-628-1668; *Fax:* 902-628-1668
gbc@gracechristianschool.ca
www.gracechristianschool.ca
Grades: K.-12 *Enrollment:* 190 *Note:* A ministry of Grace Baptist Church
Jason Biech, Principal
principal@gracechristianschool.ca

Charlottetown: Immanuel Christian School
7 Trafalgar St., Charlottetown, PE C1A 3Z2, Canada
Tel: 902-628-6465; *Fax:* 902-628-1831
icsprincipal@eastlink.ca
www.immanuelchristianschool.ca
Grades: K-9 *Enrollment:* 28
Matthew Mann, Principal

Universities & Colleges

Universities

Charlottetown: University of Prince Edward Island
550 University Ave., Charlottetown, PE C1A 4P3, Canada
Tel: 902-566-0439; *Fax:* 902-566-0420
www.upei.ca
Full Time Equivalency: 3500
H. Wade MacLaughlan, B.B.A., LL.B., LL.M., President & Vice-Chancellor
William G. (Bill Andrew, Chancellor
Fred Hyndman, Chair of the Board
Alan Buchannan, B.A., M.A., Registrar & University Secretary
Dr. Rosemary Herbert, Ph.D., Acting Vice-President
Roger Cook, Purchasing Agent
Kevin Rogers, Manager
Kevin Lewis, B.B.A., M.B.A., Chief Development Officer
Gary Bradshaw, Vice-President
Katherine Schultz, Vice-President
Mark Leggott, B.Sc., M.Sc, M.L.I.S., University Librarian

Faculties
Arts
Richard Kurial, B.A., M.A., Ph.D., Dean
Business Administration
Roberta MacDonald, B.A., Dean
Education
J. Tim Goddard, Ph.D., Dean
Nursing
Dr. Kim Critchley, Dean
Science
Christian Lacroix, B.Sc., M.Sc., Dean
Veterinary Medicine
Dr. Donald L. Reynolds, Dean

Publications
The Cadre
Panther Prints
X-Press

Post Secondary/Technical

Post Secondary/Technical

Charlottetown: Holland College of Applied Arts & Technology
Montgomery Hall
305 Kent St., 1st Fl., Charlottetown, PE C1A 4Z1, Canada
Tel: 902-629-4217; *Fax:* 902-629-4239
Toll-Free: 800-446-5265
info@hollandcollege.com
www.hollandc.pe.ca
Dr. Brian McMillan, President

Campuses
Atlantic Police Academy
P.O. Box 156
Slemon Park, PE C0A 2A0, Canada
Fax: 902-888-6725

Marine Training Centre
100 Water St., Summerside, PE C1N 1A9, Canada
Fax: 902-888-6404

Royalty Centre
40 Enman Cres., Charlottetown, PE C1E 1E6, Canada
Fax: 902-566-9323

Souris Centre
Main St. Plaza
P.O. Box 429
Souris, PE C0B 2B0, Canada
Fax: 902-687-3543

East Prince Centre
223 Water St., Summerside, PE C1N 1B4, Canada
Fax: 902-888-6402

Montague Centre
Montague, PE C0A 1R0, Canada
Fax: 902-838-3518

Atlantic Technology Centre
140 Weymouth St., Charlottetown, PE C1A 4Z1, Canada

Culinary Institute of Canada
4 Sydney St., Charlottetown, PE C1A 1E9, Canada
Fax: 902-894-6801
Toll-Free: 877-475-2844

Tourism & Culinary Centre
4 Sydney St., Charlottetown, PE C1A 1E9, Canada
Fax: 902-894-6801
Toll-Free: 877-475-2844

Charlottetown Centre
140 Weymouth St., Charlottetown, PE C1A 4Z1, Canada
Fax: 902-566-9505

Georgetown Centre
117 Kent St., Georgetown, PE C0A 1L0, Canada
Fax: 902-652-2424

Atlantic Technology Centre
140 Weymouth St., Charlottetown, PE C1A 4Z1, Canada

Assessment & Counselling Service
140 Weymouth St., Charlottetown, PE C1A AZ1, Canada
Fax: 902-566-9639
Toll-Free: 800-446-5265

Publications
The Surveyor

Summerside: The College of Piping & Celtic Performing Arts of Canada
619 Water St. East, Summerside, PE C1N 4H8, Canada
Tel: 902-436-5377; *Fax:* 902-436-4930
Toll-Free: 1-877-224-7473
info@collegeofpiping.com
www.collegeofpiping.com
Scott MacAulay, Director

Québec

Government Agencies

Québec: Ministère de l'Éducation, du Loisir et du Sport
Renseignement generaux
1035, rue De La Chevrotière, 28e étage, Québec, QC G1R 5A5, Canada
Tél: 418-643-7095; *Téléc:* 418-646-6561
Ligne sans frais: 866-747-6626
www.mels.gouv.qc.ca
twitter.com/MELSQuebec
Michelle Courchesne, Ministre
Martine Dubé, Contact
rensgen@mels.gouv.qc.ca

Campuses
Directions régionales 1 & 11: Bas St-Laurent/Gaspésie-Iles-de-la-Madeleine
337, rue Moreault, bureau 2.04, 2e étage, Rimouski, QC G5L 0A5, Canada
Tel: 418-727-3600; *Fax:* 418-727-3557
dr-01@mels.gouv.qc.ca
Gérard Bédard, Directeur régional

Direction régionale 2: Saguenay—Lac-Saint-Jean
2220, rue Saint-David, Jonquière, QC G7X 0L3, Canada
Tel: 418-695-7982; *Fax:* 418-695-7990
dr-02@mels.gouv.qc.ca
François Paquette, Directeur régional

Directions régionales 3 & 12: Capitale-Nationale et Chaudière-Appalaches
1020, rte de l'Église, 3e étage, Québec, QC G1V 3V9, Canada
Tel: 418-643-7934; *Fax:* 418-643-0972
dr-03-mels.gouv.qc.ca
Marie-Sylvie Descôteau, Directrice régionale

Directions régionales 4 & 17: Mauricie et Centre-du-Québec
Édifice Capitanal
#213, 100, rue Laviolette, Trois-Rivières, QC G9A 5S9, Canada
Tel: 819-371-6711; *Fax:* 819-371-6075
dr-04@mels.gouv.qc.ca
Claude Lamarre, Directeur régional

Direction régionale 5: Estrie
#3.05, 200, rue Belvédère nord, Sherbrooke, QC J1H 4A9, Canada
Tel: 819-820-3382; *Fax:* 819-820-3947
dr-05@mels.gouv.qc.ca
Diane Lamothe, Directrice régionale

Direction régionale 6: Montréal
600, rue Fullum, 10e étage, Montréal, QC H2K 4L1, Canada
Tel: 514-873-4630; *Fax:* 514-873-0620
dr-063@mels.gouv.qc.ca
Gilles Lamirande, Directeur régional

Direction régionale 7: Outaouais
170, rue de l'Hôtel-de-Ville, 4e étage, Gatineau, QC J8X 4C2, Canada
Tel: 819-772-3382; *Fax:* 819-772-3955
dr-07@mels.gouv.qc.ca
Hélène Audet, Directrice régionale

Directions régionales 8 & 10: Abitibi-Témiscamingue et Nord-du-Québec
215, boul Rideau, 1er étage, Rouyn-Noranda, QC J9X 5Y6, Canada
Tel: 819-763-3001; *Fax:* 819-763-3017
dr-08@mels.gouv.qc.ca
Louise Bilodeau, Directrice régionale (par intérim)

Direction régionale 9: Côte-Nord (Services adm. et gén.)
Édifice Paul-Provencher
#1.812, 625, boul Laflèche, Baie-Comeau, QC G5C 1C5, Canada
Tel: 418-295-4400; *Fax:* 418-295-4467
dr09-bc@mels.gouv.qc.ca
Lucy de Mendonça, Directrice régionale

Direction régionale 9: Côte-Nord (Services éducatifs)
#201, 106, rue Napoléon, Sept-Iles, QC G4R 3L7, Canada
Tel: 418-964-8420; *Fax:* 418-964-8504
dr09-si@mels.gouv.qc.ca
Lucy de Mendoça, Directrice régionale

Directions régionales 13, 14 et 15: Laval, Lanaudière, et Laurentides
#200, 300, rue Sicard, Sainte-Thérèse, QC J7E 3X5, Canada
Tel: 450-430-3611; *Fax:* 450-430-4005
dr-061@mels.gouv.qc.ca
Lauraine Langlois, Directrice régionale

Direction régionale 16: Montérégie
Édifice Montval
201, place Charles-Le Moyne, 6e étage, Longueuil, QC J4K 2T5, Canada
Tel: 450-928-7438; *Fax:* 450-928-7451
dr-062@mels.gouv.qc.ca
Francis Culée, Directeur régional

School Boards/Districts/Divisions

Public

***Aylmer:* Commission scolaire Western Québec**
Western Québec School Board
15, rue Katimavik, Aylmer, QC J9J 0E9, Canada
Tél: 819-684-2336; *Téléc:* 819-684-1328
Ligne sans frais: 800-363-9111
wqsb@wqsb.qc.ca
www.wqsb.qc.ca
Michael Dawson, Directeur général

***Châteauguay:* Commission scolaire New Frontiers**
New Frontiers School Board
219, rue McLeod, Châteauguay, QC J6J 2H4, Canada
Tél: 450-691-1440; *Téléc:* 450-699-8327
secgen@nfsb.qc.ca
www.csnewfrontiers.qc.ca
Wayne Goldthorp, Directeur général

***Dorval:* Commission scolaire Lester-B.-Pearson**
Lester B. Pearson School Board
1925, av Brookdale, Dorval, QC H9P 2Y7, Canada
Tél: 514-422-3000
info@lbpsb.qc.ca
www.lbpsb.qc.ca
Robert T. Mills, Directeur général

***Magog:* Commission scolaire Eastern Townships**
Eastern Townships School Board
#205, 101, rue Du Moulin, Magog, QC J1X 6H8, Canada
Tél: 819-868-3100; *Téléc:* 819-868-2286
priests@etsb.qc.ca
www.etsb.qc.ca
Chantal C. Beaulieu, Directrice générale

***Montréal:* Commission scolaire English-Montréal**
English Montréal School Board
6000, av Fielding, Montréal, QC H3X 1T4, Canada
Tél: 514-483-7200; *Téléc:* 514-483-7324
webmaster@emsb.qc.ca
www.emsb.qc.ca
Robert Stocker, Directeur général

***New Carlisle:* Commission scolaire Eastern Shores**
Eastern Shores School Board
40, rue Mount Sorrel, New Carlisle, QC G0C 1Z0, Canada
Tél: 418-752-2247; *Téléc:* 418-752-6447
info@essb.qc.ca
www.essb.qc.ca
Howard Miller, Directeur général
howard.miller@essb.qc.ca

***Québec:* Commission scolaire Central Québec**
Central Québec School Board
2046, ch Saint-Louis, Québec, QC G1T 1P4, Canada
Tél: 418-688-8730; *Téléc:* 418-682-5891
Ligne sans frais: 800-249-5573
cqsb@cqsb.qc.ca
www.cqsb.qc.ca
M. Stewart, Directeur général

***Rosemère:* Commission scolaire Sir-Wilfrid-Laurier**
Sir Wilfrid Laurier School Board
235, montée Lesage, Rosemère, QC J7A 4Y6, Canada
Tél: 450-621-5600; *Téléc:* 450-621-7929
Ligne sans frais: 866-621-5600
www.swlauriersb.qc.ca
Anne-Marie Lepage, Directrice générale

***Saint-Lambert:* Commission scolaire Riverside**
Riverside School Board
299, boul Sir Wilfrid-Laurier, Saint-Lambert, QC J4R 2V7, Canada
Tél: 450-672-4010; *Téléc:* 450-465-8809
rsb@rsb.qc.ca
www.rsb.qc.ca
Stephen Lessard, Directeur général
slessard@rsb.qc.ca

French

***Alma:* Commission scolaire du Lac-Saint-Jean**
350, boul Champlain sud, Alma, QC G8B 5W2, Canada
Tél: 418-669-6000; *Téléc:* 418-669-6351
www.cslacst-jean.qc.ca
Eric Blackburn, Directeur général
dglstjean@cslacst-jean.qc.ca

***Amos:* Commission scolaire Harricana**
341, rue Principale nord, Amos, QC J9T 2L8, Canada
Tél: 819-732-6561; *Téléc:* 819-732-1623
communications@csharricana.qc.ca
www.csharricana.qc.ca
Guy Baril, Directeur général

***Amqui:* Commission scolaire des Monts-et-Marées**
93, rue du Parc, Amqui, QC G5J 2L8, Canada
Tél: 418-629-6200; *Téléc:* 418-629-6234
www.csmm.qc.ca
Note: Centre de services de Matane: 530, av Saint-Jérôme, 418-566-2500.
Pierre Berthelet, Directeur général

***Baie-Comeau:* Commission scolaire de l'Estuaire**
771, boul Joliet, Baie-Comeau, QC G5C 1P3, Canada
Tél: 418-589-0806; *Téléc:* 418-589-2711
Ligne sans frais: 877-589-0806
www.csestuaire.qc.ca
Alain Ouellet, Directeur général

***Beauharnois:* Commission scolaire de la Vallée-des-Tisserands**
630, rue Ellice, Beauharnois, QC J6N 3S1, Canada
Tél: 450-225-2788; *Téléc:* 450-225-0691
Ligne sans frais: 877-225-2788
info@csvt.qc.ca
www.csvt.qc.ca
Carole Houle, Directrice générale
dg@csvt.qc.ca

***Beauport:* Commission scolaire des Premières-Seigneuries**
643, av du Cénacle, Beauport, QC G1E 1B3, Canada
Tél: 418-666-4666; *Téléc:* 418-666-9783
sic@csdps.qc.ca
www.csdps.qc.ca
www.facebook.com/136523216368423
Serge Pelletier, Directeur général

***Bonaventure:* Commission scolaire René-Lévesque**
145, av Louisbourg, Bonaventure, QC G0C 1E0, Canada
Tél: 418-534-3003; *Téléc:* 418-534-3220
www.cs-renelevesque.qc.ca
Chantal Bourdages, Directrice générale

***Cabano:* Commission scolaire du Fleuve-et-des-Lacs**
14, rue du Vieux-Chemin, Cabano, QC G0L 1E0, Canada
Tél: 418-854-2370; *Téléc:* 418-854-2715
info@csfl.qc.ca
www.csfl.qc.ca
Serge Pelletier, Directeur général

***Chibougamau:* Commission scolaire de la Baie-James**
596, 4e rue, Chibougamau, QC G8P 1S3, Canada
Tél: 418-748-7621; *Téléc:* 418-748-2440
www.csbj.qc.ca
Michèle Perron, Directrice générale

***Chicoutimi:* Commission scolaire des Rives-du-Saguenay**
36, rue Jacques-Cartier est, Chicoutimi, QC G7H 1W2, Canada
Tél: 418-698-5000; *Téléc:* 418-698-5262
www.csrsaguenay.qc.ca
Note: Centre de services La Baie: 3111, rue Mgr Dufour, La Baie, 418-544-3307. Service informatique: 475, rue Lafontaine, Chicoutimi, 418-541-7799.
Yvon Pelletier, Directeur général

***Donnacona:* Commission scolaire de Portneuf**
310, rue de l'Église, Donnacona, QC G3M 1Z8, Canada
Tél: 418-285-2600; *Téléc:* 418-285-2738
www.csportneuf.qc.ca
Jean-Pierre Soucy, Directeur général
jeanpsoucy@csdp.qc.ca

***Drummondville:* Commission scolaire des Chênes**
P.O. Box 846
457, rue des Écoles, Drummondville, QC J2B 6X1, Canada
Tél: 819-478-6700; *Téléc:* 819-478-6777
commentaires@csdeschenes.qc.ca
www.csdeschenes.qc.ca
Yvan Aubé, Directeur général

***East Angus:* Commission scolaire des Hauts-Cantons**
308, rue Palmer, East Angus, QC J0B 1R0, Canada
Tél: 819-832-4953; *Téléc:* 819-832-4863
www.cshc.qc.ca
Bernard Lacroix, Directeur général

***Gaspé:* Commission scolaire des Chic-Chocs**
102, rue Jacques-Cartier, Gaspé, QC G4X 2S9, Canada
Tél: 418-368-3499; *Téléc:* 418-368-6531
commission.scolaire@cschic-chocs.net
www.cschic-chocs.net
Jean Letarte, Directeur général

***Gatineau:* Commission scolaire au Coeur-des-Vallées**
582, rue MacLaren est, Gatineau, QC J8L 2W2, Canada
Tél: 819-986-8511; *Téléc:* 819-986-9283
Ligne sans frais: 800-958-9966
info@cscv.qc.ca
www.cscv.qc.ca
Maurice Groulx, Directeur général

***Gatineau:* Commission scolaire des Draveurs**
200, boul Maloney est, Gatineau, QC J8P 1K3, Canada
Tél: 819-663-9221; *Téléc:* 819-663-6176
reception@csdraveurs.qc.ca
www.csdraveurs.qc.ca
François Jetté, Directeur général
dg@csdraveurs.qc.ca

***Gatineau:* Commission scolaire des Portages-de-l'Outaouais**
225, rue St-Rédempteur, Gatineau, QC J8X 2T3, Canada
Tél: 819-771-4548; *Téléc:* 819-771-6964
www.cspo.qc.ca
Jean-Claude Bouchard, Directeur général
dgcspo@cspo.qc.ca

Granby: **Commission scolaire du Val-des-Cerfs**
P.O. Box 9000
55, rue Court, Granby, QC J2G 9H7, Canada
Tél: 450-372-0221; *Téléc:* 450-372-3150
descerfs@csvdc.qc.ca
www.csvdc.qc.ca
André Messier, Directeur général

Havre-Saint-Pierre: **Commission scolaire de la Moyenne-Côte-Nord**
1235, rue de la Digue, Havre-Saint-Pierre, QC G0G 1P0, Canada
Tél: 418-538-3044; *Téléc:* 418-538-3268
www.csmcn.qc.ca
Marius Richard, Directeur général

Jonquière: **Commission scolaire De La Jonquière**
P.O. Box 1600
3644, rue St-Jules, Jonquière, QC G7X 7X4, Canada
Tél: 418-542-7551; *Téléc:* 418-542-1505
info@csjonquiere.qc.ca
www.csjonquiere.qc.ca
Raynald Thibeault, Directeur général

L'Étang-du-Nord: **Commission scolaire des Iles**
1419, ch de l'Étang-du-Nord, L'Étang-du-Nord, QC G4T 3B9, Canada
Tél: 418-986-5511; *Téléc:* 418-986-3552
info@csdesiles.qc.ca
www.csdesiles.qc.ca
Diane Arsenault, Directrice générale

La Malbaie: **Commission scolaire de Charlevoix**
575, boul de Comporté, La Malbaie, QC G5A 1T5, Canada
Tél: 418-665-3765; *Téléc:* 418-665-6805
www.cscharlevoix.qc.ca
Robert Labbé, Directeur général
robert.labbe@cscharlevoix.qc.ca

La Prairie: **Commission scolaire des Grandes-Seigneuries**
50, boul Taschereau, La Prairie, QC J5R 4V3, Canada
Tél: 514-380-8899; *Téléc:* 514-380-8345
www.csdgs.qc.ca
Michelle Fournier, Directrice générale
directiongenerale@csdgs.qc.ca

La Sarre: **Commission scolaire du Lac-Abitibi**
500, rue Principale, La Sarre, QC J9Z 2A2, Canada
Tél: 819-333-5411; *Téléc:* 819-333-3044
www.csdla.qc.ca
Huguette Théberge, Directrice générale

Laval: **Commission scolaire de Laval**
955, boul Saint-Martin ouest, Laval, QC H7S 1M5, Canada
Tél: 450-662-7000; *Téléc:* 450-625-2042
www2.cslaval.qc.ca
Claude Sabourin, Directeur général
directiongenerale@cslaval.qc.ca

Longueuil: **Commission scolaire Marie-Victorin**
13, rue St-Laurent est, Longueuil, QC J4H 4B7, Canada
Tél: 450-670-0730; *Téléc:* 450-670-0902
info@csmv.qc.ca
www.csmv.qc.ca
André Byette, Directeur général

Magog: **Commission scolaire des Sommets**
449, rue Percy, Magog, QC J1X 1B5, Canada
Tél: 819-847-1610; *Téléc:* 819-847-2065
Ligne sans frais: 888-847-1610
info@csdessommets.qc.ca
www.csdessommets.qc.ca
Christian Provencher, Directeur général

Maniwaki: **Commission scolaire des Hauts-Bois-de-l'Outaouais**
331, rue du Couvent, Maniwaki, QC J9E 1H5, Canada
Tél: 819-449-7866; *Téléc:* 819-449-2636
Ligne sans frais: 888-831-9606
info@cshbo.qc.ca
www.cshbo.qc.ca
Harold Sylvain, Directeur général
Charles Millar
charles.millar@schbo.qc.ca

Mont-Laurier: **Commission scolaire Pierre-Neveu**
525, rue de la Madone, Mont-Laurier, QC J9L 1S4, Canada
Tél: 819-623-4310; *Téléc:* 819-623-7979
Ligne sans frais: 866-334-4114
cspn@cspn.qc.ca
www.cspn.qc.ca
Normand Bélanger, Directeur général
belanger.normand@cspn.qc.ca

Montmagny: **Commission scolaire de la Côte-du-Sud**
157, rue Saint-Louis, Montmagny, QC G5V 4N3, Canada
Tél: 418-248-1001
info@cscotesud.qc.ca
www.cscotesud.qc.ca
Jocelyn Carrier, Directeur général

Montréal: **Commission scolaire de la Pointe-de-l'Ile**
550, 53e av, Montréal, QC H1A 2T7, Canada
Tél: 514-642-9520; *Téléc:* 514-642-1590
www.cspi.qc.ca
Antonio Bernardelli, Directeur général

Montréal: **Commission scolaire de Montréal**
3737, rue Sherbrooke est, Montréal, QC H1X 3B3, Canada
Tél: 514-596-6000; *Téléc:* 514-596-7570
info@csdm.qc.ca
www.csdm.qc.ca
Gilles Petitclerc, Directeur général

Nicolet: **Commission scolaire de la Riveraine**
375, rue de Monseigneur-Brunault, Nicolet, QC J3T 1Y6, Canada
Tél: 819-293-5821; *Téléc:* 819-293-8691
csdlrweb@admin.csriveraine.qc.ca
www.csriveraine.qc.ca
Jean-René Dubois, Directeur général

Québec: **Commission scolaire de la Capitale**
1900, rue Côté, Québec, QC G1N 3Y5, Canada
Tél: 418-686-4040; *Téléc:* 418-686-4032
adm2@cscapitale.qc.ca
www.cscapitale.qc.ca
Berthe Bernatchez, Directrice générale
Christine Spychala, Secrétaire de gestion
Spychala.Christine@cscapitale.qc.ca

Québec: **Commission scolaire des Découvreurs**
945, av Wolfe, Québec, QC G1V 4E2, Canada
Tél: 418-652-2121; *Téléc:* 418-652-2146
www.csdecou.qc.ca
Reynald Deraspe, Directeur général
dirgen@csdecou.qc.ca

Repentigny: **Commission scolaire des Affluents**
80, rue Jean-Baptiste-Meilleur, Repentigny, QC J6A 6C5, Canada
Tél: 450-492-9400; *Téléc:* 450-492-3720
info@csaffluents.qc.ca
www.csaffluents.qc.ca
Thomas Duzyk, Directeur général
thomas.duzyk@dg.csaffluents.qc.ca

Rimouski: **Commission scolaire des Phares**
435, av Rouleau, Rimouski, QC G5L 8V4, Canada
Tél: 418-723-5927; *Téléc:* 418-724-3350
dgphares@csphares.qc.ca
www.csphares.qc.ca
Jacques Poirier, Directeur général
jpoirier@csphares.qc.ca

Rivière-du-Loup: **Commission scolaire de Kamouraska—Rivière-du-Loup**
464, rue Lafontaine, Rivière-du-Loup, QC G5R 3C2, Canada
Tél: 418-868-8201; *Téléc:* 418-862-0964
web.cskamloup.qc.ca
Yvan Tardif, Directeur général

Roberval: **Commission scolaire du Pays-des-Bleuets**
828, boul Saint-Joseph, Roberval, QC G8H 2L5, Canada
Tél: 418-275-4136; *Téléc:* 418-275-6217
www.cspaysbleuets.qc.ca
Note: Secteur Dolbeau-Mistassini: 1950, boul Sacré-Coeur, Dolbeau-Mistassini, 418-276-2012.
Serge Bergeron, Directeur général

Rouyn-Noranda: **Commission scolaire de Rouyn-Noranda**
P.O. Box 908
70, rue des Oblats est, Rouyn-Noranda, QC J9X 5C9, Canada
Tél: 819-762-8161; *Téléc:* 819-764-7170
dgcsrn@csrn.qc.ca
www.csrn.qc.ca
Richard Gauthier, Directeur général

Saint-Eustache: **Commission scolaire de la Seigneurie-des-Mille-Iles**
430, boul Arthur-Sauvé, Saint-Eustache, QC J7R 6V6, Canada
Tél: 450-974-7000
www.cssmi.qc.ca
Jean-François Lachance, Directeur général

Saint-Félix-de-Valois: **Commission scolaire des Samares**
4671, rue Principale, Saint-Félix-de-Valois, QC J0K 2M0, Canada
Tél: 450-758-3500; *Téléc:* 450-889-8604
sg@cssamares.qc.ca
www.cssamares.qc.ca
Richard Fiset, Directeur général

Saint-Hyacinthe: **Commission scolaire de Saint-Hyacinthe**
2255, av Sainte-Anne, Saint-Hyacinthe, QC J2S 5H7, Canada
Tél: 450-773-8401; *Téléc:* 450-773-3262
webcorp.cssh.qc.ca
Yvan Gauthier, Directeur général
yvan.gauthier@cssh.qc.ca

Saint-Jean-sur-Richelieu: **Commission scolaire des Hautes-Rivières**
210, rue Notre-Dame, Saint-Jean-sur-Richelieu, QC J3B 6N3, Canada
Tél: 450-359-6411; *Téléc:* 450-359-4623
casegen@csdhr.qc.ca
www.csdhr.qc.ca
Mme Claude Boivin, Directrice générale

Saint-Jérôme: **Commission scolaire de la Rivière-du-Nord**
995, rue Labelle, Saint-Jérôme, QC J7Z 5N7, Canada
Tél: 450-438-3131; *Téléc:* 450-436-5277
csrdn@csrdn.qc.ca
www.csrdn.qc.ca
Note: Centre administratif II: 795, rue Melançon, 450-438-3131.
Lise Allaire, Directrice générale

Saint-Laurent: **Commission scolaire Marguerite-Bourgeoys**
1100, boul de la Côte-Vertu, Saint-Laurent, QC H4L 4V1, Canada
Tél: 514-855-4500; *Téléc:* 514-855-4749
www.csmb.qc.ca
www.facebook.com/csmbourgeoys
twitter.com//csmbourgeoys
www.linkedin.com/company/commission-scolaire-marguerite-bourgeoys
Number of Schools: 87 primaire; 12 secondaire; 6 FP; 6 FGA
Number of Employees: 8500
Yves Sylvain, Directeur général
Jean-Michel Nahas, Contact
jean-michelnahas@csmb.qc.ca

Saint-Romuald: **Commission scolaire des Navigateurs**
1860, 1e rue, Saint-Romuald, QC G6W 5M6, Canada
Tél: 418-839-0500; *Téléc:* 418-839-0536
dg@csnavigateurs.qc.ca
www.csdn.qc.ca
Joanne Plourde, Directrice générale

Sainte-Agathe-des-Monts: **Commission scolaire des Laurentides**
13, rue Saint-Antoine, Sainte-Agathe-des-Monts, QC J8C 2C3, Canada
Tél: 819-326-0333; *Téléc:* 819-326-2121
beattiej@cslaurentides.qc.ca
www.cslaurentides.qc.ca
Claude Pouliot, Directeur général

Sept-Iles: **Commission scolaire du Fer**
30, rue Comeau, Sept-Iles, QC G4R 4N2, Canada
Tél: 418-968-9901; *Téléc:* 418-962-7760
www.csdufer.qc.ca
Robert Smith, Directeur général

Sept-Iles: **Commission scolaire du Littoral**
789, rue Beaulieu, Sept-Iles, QC G4R 1P8, Canada
Tél: 418-962-5559; *Téléc:* 418-968-2942
Ligne sans frais: 877-745-7226
www.csdulittoral.qc.ca
Lucy de Mendonça, Administratrice
dglittoral@csdulittoral.qc.ca

Shawinigan: **Commission scolaire de l'Énergie**
P.O. Box 580
2072, rue Gignac, Shawinigan, QC G9N 6V7, Canada
Tél: 819-539-6971; *Téléc:* 819-539-7797
cse@csenergie.qc.ca
www.csenergie.qc.ca
Denis Lemaire, Directeur général

Sherbrooke: **Commission scolaire de la Région-de-Sherbrooke**
2955, boul de l'Université, Sherbrooke, QC J1K 2Y3, Canada
Tél: 819-822-5540; *Téléc:* 819-822-5530
www.csrs.qc.ca
Claude St-Cyr, Directeur général

Sorel-Tracy: **Commission scolaire de Sorel-Tracy**
41, av de l'Hôtel-Dieu, Sorel-Tracy, QC J3P 1L1, Canada
Tél: 450-746-3990; *Téléc:* 450-746-4474
www.cs-soreltracy.qc.ca
Jean Morin, Directeur général
dgen@cs-soreltracy.qc.ca

St-Bruno-de-Montarville: **Commission scolaire des Patriotes**
1740, rue Roberval, St-Bruno-de-Montarville, QC J3V 3R3, Canada
Tél: 450-441-2919; *Téléc:* 450-441-0838
courriel@csp.qc.ca
www.csp.qc.ca
www.facebook.com/Commissionscolairedespatriotes
twitter.com/cspatriotes
Number of Schools: 65 *Enrollment:* 30479 *Number of Employees:* 4 505
Normande Lemieux, Directrice générale

St-Georges: **Commission scolaire de la Beauce-Etchemin**
1925, 118e rue, St-Georges, QC G5Y 7R7, Canada
Tél: 418-228-5541; *Téléc:* 418-228-5549
secretariat.general@csbe.qc.ca
www.csbe.qc.ca
Normand Lessard, Directeur général

Thetford Mines: **Commission scolaire des Appalaches**
650, rue Lapierre, Thetford Mines, QC G6G 7P1, Canada
Tél: 418-338-7800; *Téléc:* 418-338-7845
ghebert@csappalaches.qc.ca
www.csappalaches.qc.ca
Camil Turmel, Directeur général

Trois-Rivières: **Commission scolaire du Chemin-du-Roy**
1515, rue Ste-Marguerite, Trois-Rivières, QC G9A 5E7, Canada
Tél: 819-379-6565; *Téléc:* 819-379-2068
info@csduroy.qc.ca
www.csduroy.qc.ca
Michel Morin, Directeur général
dgduroy@csduroy.qc.ca

Val-d'Or: **Commission scolaire de l'Or-et-des-Bois**
799, boul Forest, Val-d'Or, QC J9P 2L4, Canada
Tél: 819-825-4220; *Téléc:* 819-825-5305
info@csob.qc.ca
www.csob.qc.ca
Jean Denommé, Directeur général

Vaudreuil-Dorion: **Commission scolaire des Trois-Lacs**
400, av St-Charles, Vaudreuil-Dorion, QC J7V 6B1, Canada
Tél: 514-477-7000
dgenerale@cstrois-lacs.qc.ca
www.cstrois-lacs.qc.ca
Sophie Proulx, Directrice générale

Victoriaville: **Commission scolaire des Bois-Francs**
40, boul Bois-Francs nord, Victoriaville, QC G6P 6S5, Canada
Tél: 819-758-6453; *Téléc:* 819-758-4925
info@csbf.qc.ca
www.csbf.qc.ca
François Labbé, Directeur général

Ville-Marie: **Commission scolaire du Lac-Témiscamingue**
2, rue Maisonneuve, Ville-Marie, QC J9V 1V4, Canada
Tél: 819-629-2472; *Téléc:* 819-629-2791
courrier@cslactem.qc.ca
www.cslactem.qc.ca
Éric Larivière, Directeur général
eric.lariviere@cslactem.qc.ca

First Nations

Lac-Simon: **Conseil de l'Éducation du Lac-Simon**
1013, av Amikwiche, Lac-Simon, QC J0Y 3M0, Canada
Tél: 819-736-2121
Grades: Elem./Sec.

Mistissini: **Commission scolaire Crie Cree School Board**
203, rue Principale, Mistissini, QC G0W 1C0, Canada
Tél: 418-923-2764; *Téléc:* 418-923-2072
www.cscree.qc.ca
Abraham Jolly, Directeur général
ajolly@cscree.qc.ca

Saint-Laurent: **Commission scolaire Kativik Kativik School Board**
#400, 9800, boul Cavendish, Saint-Laurent, QC H4M 2V9, Canada
Tél: 514-482-8220; *Téléc:* 514-482-8496
www.kativik.qc.ca
Annie Grenier, Directrice générale

Schools: Cégep

Cégep

Baie-Comeau: **Cégep de Baie-Comeau**
537, boul Blanche, Baie-Comeau, QC G5C 2B2, Canada
Tél: 418-589-5707; *Téléc:* 418-589-9842
Ligne sans frais: 1-800-463-2030
fraduval@cegep-baie-comeau.qc.ca
www.cegep-baie-comeau.qc.ca
www.facebook.com/cegepbaiecomeau
twitter.com0cegepbaiecomeau
Grades: Préuniv., Techniques, Form. cont.
Danielle Delorme, Directrice générale

Publications
D.E.C. express

Chicoutimi: **Cégep de Chicoutimi**
534, rue Jacques-Cartier est, Chicoutimi, QC G7H 1Z6, Canada
Tél: 418-549-9520; *Téléc:* 418-549-1315
dirgene@cegep-chicoutimi.qc.ca
www.cegep-chicoutimi.qc.ca
Grades: Préuniv., Techniques, Form. cont.
Pierre Boulianne, Président

Publications
La Grenouille
Le Nénu phare

Drummondville: **Cégep de Drummondville**
960, rue St-Georges, Drummondville, QC J2C 6A2, Canada
Tél: 819-478-4671; *Téléc:* 819-474-6859
communications@cdrummond.qc.ca
www.cdrummond.qc.ca
Grades: Préuniv., Techniques *Enrollment:* 1900
Annie Durocher, Présidente

Publications
Mouton Noir

Gaspé: **Cégep de la Gaspésie et des Iles**
96, rue Jacques-Cartier, Gaspé, QC G4X 2S8, Canada
Tél: 418-368-2201; *Téléc:* 418-328-7069
Ligne sans frais: 1-888-368-2201
infogaspe@cgaspesie.qc.ca
www.cgaspesie.qc.ca
www.facebook.com/cegep.gaspesie.iles
twitter.com/cegepgim
Grades: Préuniv., Techniques, Form. cont. *Enrollment:* 1140
Roland Auger, Directeur général

Campus de Carleton-sur-Mer
776, boul Perron, Carleton-sur-Mer, QC G0C 1J0, Canada
Tél: 418-364-3341; *Téléc:* 416-364-7938
Ligne sans frais: 1-866-424-3341

Campuses
Campus des Iles-de-la-madeleine
15, ch de la Piscine, L'Étang-du-Nord, QC G4T 3X4, Canada
Tél: 418-986-5187; *Téléc:* 416-986-6788

École des pêches et de l'aquaculture du Québec
P.O. Box 220
167, La Frande-Allée est, Grande-Rivière, QC G0C 1V0, Canada
Tél: 418-385-2241; *Téléc:* 418-385-2888

Gatineau: **Cégep de l'Outaouais**
Campus Gabrielle-Roy
333, boul de la Cité-des-Jeunes, Gatineau, QC J8Y 6M4, Canada
Tél: 819-770-4012; *Téléc:* 819-770-8167
www.cegepoutaouais.qc.ca
Enrollment: 4418
Marielle Poirier, Directrice générale
dirgen@cegepoutaouais.qc.ca

Campus Félix-Leclerc
820, bou. de la Gappe, Gatineau, QC J8T 7T7, Canada
Tél: 819-770-4012; *Téléc:* 819- 24-3900

Campuses
Campus Louis-Reboul
125, boul Sacré-Coeur, Gatineau, QC J8X 1C5, Canada
Tél: 819-770-4012; *Téléc:* 819-777-7594

Publications
La Brise
L'Entremetteur

Granby: **Cégep de Granby Haute-Yamaska**
P.O. Box 7000
235, rue St-Jacques, Granby, QC J2G 9H7, Canada
Tél: 450-372-6614; *Téléc:* 450-372-6565
lfalvarez@cegepgranby.qc.ca
www.cegepgranby.qc.ca
www.facebook.com/CegepGranby
twitter.com/CegepGranby
www.youtube.com/CegepdeGranby
Sylvain Lambert, Directrice générale

Publications
de Fouille-moi

Jonquière: **Cégep de Jonquière**
2505, rue St-Hubert, Jonquière, QC G7X 7W2, Canada
Tél: 418-547-2191; *Téléc:* 418-547-3359
cegep@cjonquiere.qc.ca
www.cjonquiere.qc.ca
www.facebook.com/cegepjonq
www.youtube.com/user/cegepdejonquiere
Guylaine Desgagnés, Directeur général
guylaine.proulx@cjonquiere.qc.ca

Publications
La Pige

La Pocatière: **Cégep de La Pocatière**
140, 4e av, La Pocatière, QC G0R 1Z0, Canada
Tél: 418-856-1525; *Téléc:* 418-856-4589
information@cegeplapocatiere.qc.ca
www.cegeplapocatiere.qc.ca
www.facebook.com/cegeplapocatiere
twitter.com/cegeplapoc
Enrollment: 900
Claude Harvey, Directeur général

Publications
Le Nordet

Lasalle: **Cégep André-Laurendeau**
1111, rue Lapierre, Lasalle, QC H8N 2J4, Canada
Tél: 514-364-3320; *Téléc:* 514-364-7130
www.claurendeau.qc.ca
Grades: Préuniv., Tech., Form. continue *Enrollment:* 5000
Hervé Pilon, Directeur général

Publications
Vox-Populi

Lévis: **Cégep de Lévis-Lauzon**
205, rte Mgr Bourget, Lévis, QC G6V 6Z9, Canada
Tél: 418-833-5110; *Téléc:* 418-833-7323
cll.qc.ca
www.facebook.com/cegeplevislauzon
twitter.com/ComLevisLauzon
Enrollment: 2885
Guy Demers, Directeur général

Publications
Le Forcep

Matane: **Cégep de Matane**
616, av St-Rédempteur, Matane, QC G4W 1L1, Canada
Tél: 418-562-1240; *Téléc:* 418-566-2115
Ligne sans frais: 1-800-463-4299
information@cegep-matane.qc.ca
www.cegep-matane.qc.ca
www.facebook.com/cegepdematane
twitter.com/cegepmatane
www.youtube.com/cegepdematane
Émery Béland, Directeur général

Publications
La Criée

Montréal: **Cégep de Saint-Laurent**
625, av Ste-Croix, Montréal, QC H4L 3X7, Canada
Tél: 514-747-6521; *Téléc:* 514-748-1249
info@cegep-st-laurent.qc.ca
www.cegep-st-laurent.qc.ca
www.facebook.com/137132236299536
Enrollment: 2500

Paul-Émile Bourque, Directeur général
pebourque@cegep-st-laurent.qc.ca

Publications
La Minerve

Montréal: Cégep du Vieux Montréal
255, rue Ontario est, Montréal, QC H2X 1X6, Canada
Tél: 514-982-3437; *Téléc:* 514-982-3400
gestionnairew3@cvm.qc.ca
www.cvm.qc.ca
Enrollment: 6000
Jacques Roussil, Directeur général
jroussil@cvm.qc.ca

Publications
Le République

Montréal: Cégep Marie-Victorin
7000, rue Marie-Victorin, Montréal, QC H1G 2J6, Canada
Tél: 514-325-0150; *Téléc:* 514-328-3830
promotion@collegemv.qc.ca
www.collegemv.qc.ca
www.facebook.com/cegepmarievictorin
twitter.com/cegepmarievic
www.linkedin.com/company/c-gep-marie-victorin
youtube.com/cegepmarievictorin
Enrollment: 3082
Nicole Rouillier, Directrice générale

Québec: Cégep de Sainte-Foy
2410, ch Ste-Foy, Québec, QC G1V 1T3, Canada
Tél: 418-659-6600; *Téléc:* 418-659-4563
info@cegep-ste-foy.qc.ca
www.cegep-ste-foy.qc.ca
www.facebook.com/cegepsaintefoy
www.twitter.com/cegepsaintefoy
www.youtube.com/user/cegepdesaintefoy
Grades: Préuniv., Techniques, Form. cont. *Enrollment:* 8000
Denis Juneau, Directeur général

Publications
Éclosion

Québec: Cégep François-Xavier-Garneau
1660, boul de l'Entente, Québec, QC G1S 4S3, Canada
Tél: 418-688-8310; *Téléc:* 418-681-9384
communications@cegepgarneau.ca
www.cegep-fxg.qc.ca
www.facebook.com/CegepGarneau
twitter.com/cegepgarneau
www.youtube.com/CollegeGarneau
Grades: Préuniv., Bacc. int'l, Tech. *Enrollment:* 9000
Denise Trudeau, Directeur général

Publications
La Crise

Québec: Cégep Limoilou
1300, 8e av, Québec, QC G1J 5L5, Canada
Tél: 418-647-6600; *Téléc:* 418-647-6798
info@climoilou.qc.ca
www.climoilou.qc.ca
Enrollment: 4470
Line Beaulieu, Directrice général

Campus de Charlesbourg
7600, av 3e est, Québec, QC G1H 7L4, Canada
Tél: 418-647-6600; *Téléc:* 418-624-3714

Publications
L'Interdit

Repentigny: Cégep régional de Lanaudière
781, rue Notre-Dame, Repentigny, QC J5Y 1B4, Canada
Tél: 450-470-0911; *Téléc:* 450-581-1567
infocom@collanaud.qc.ca
www.collanaud.qc.ca
Denis Caron, Directeur général

Campuses
L'Assomption
180, rue Dorval, L'Assomption, QC J5W 6C1, Canada
Fax: 450-589-8926

Joliette
20, rue Saint-Charles sud, Joliette, QC J6E 4T1, Canada
Fax: 450-759-4468

Terrebonne
2505, boul des Entreprises, Terrebonne, QC J6X 5S5, Canada

Publications
L'Alinéa

Rimouski: Cégep de Rimouski
60, rue de l'Évêché ouest, Rimouski, QC G5L 4H6, Canada
Tél: 418-723-1880; *Téléc:* 418-724-4961
Ligne sans frais: 1-800-463-0617
infoscol@cegep-rimouski.qc.ca
www.cegep-rimouski.qc.ca
www.facebook.com/pages/C%C3%A9gep-de-Rimouski/216198528401766
twitter.com/cegeprimouski
Enrollment: 4000
Jean-Pierre Villeneuve, Directeur général

Publications
Le Calvaire

Rivière-du-Loup: Cégep de Rivière-du-Loup
80, rue Frontenac, Rivière-du-Loup, QC G5R 1R1, Canada
Tél: 418-862-6903; *Téléc:* 418-862-4959
sercom@cegep-rdl.qc.ca
www.cegep-rdl.qc.ca
www.facebook.com/cegeprdl
twitter.com/cegeprdl
www.youtube.com/user/cgrdl
Grades: Préuniv., Techniques, Form. cont. *Enrollment:* 2200
André Morin, Directeur général

Publications
L'Ulcère

Rouyn-Noranda: Cégep de l'Abitibi-Témiscamingue
425, boul du Collège, Rouyn-Noranda, QC J9X 5E5, Canada
Tél: 819-762-0931; *Téléc:* 819-762-2071
Ligne sans frais: 1-866-234-3728
cegepat.qc.ca
www.facebook.com/CegepAbitibiTemiscamingue
twitter.com/cegepat
Grades: Préuniv., Techniques, Form. cont. *Enrollment:* 2400
Daniel Marcotte, Directeur général
daniel.marcotte@cegepat.qc.ca

Publications
Le Profane

Saint-Félicien: Cégep de St-Félicien
P.O. Box 7300
1105, boul Hamel, Saint-Félicien, QC G8K 2R8, Canada
Tél: 418-679-5412; *Téléc:* 418-679-0238
info@cegepstfe.ca
www.cstfelicien.qc.ca
www.facebook.com/cegepstfe
twitter.com/cstfelicien
www.youtube.com/cegepstfe
Grades: Préuniv., Techniques *Enrollment:* 1000
Louis Lefebvre, Directeur général
bmaurino@cegepstfe.ca

Publications
Le Sentier

Saint-Hyacinthe: Cégep de Saint-Hyacinthe
3000, av Boullé, Saint-Hyacinthe, QC J2S 1H9, Canada
Tél: 450-773-6800; *Téléc:* 450-773-9971
info@cegepsth.qc.ca
www.cegepsth.qc.ca
Grades: Préuniv., Techniques, Form. cont. *Enrollment:* 3200
Roger Sylvestre, Directeur général

Publications
L'Électic

Saint-Jean-sur-Richelieu: Cégep Saint-Jean-sur-Richelieu
P.O. Box 1018
30, boul du Séminaire, Saint-Jean-sur-Richelieu, QC J3B 7B1, Canada
Tél: 450-347-5301; *Téléc:* 450-347-3329
communications@cstjean.qc.ca
www.cstjean.qc.ca
www.facebook.com/278415881842
Grades: Préuniv., Techniques, Form. cont. *Enrollment:* 3600
Chantal Denis, Directrice générale

Publications
L'Hermes

Saint-Jérôme: Cégep de Saint-Jérôme
455, rue Fournier, Saint-Jérôme, QC J7Z 4V2, Canada
Tél: 450-436-1580; *Téléc:* 450-436-1756
info@cstj.qc.ca
cstj.qc.ca
www.facebook.com/cstj1
Enrollment: 3300
Francine Paquette, Directeur général

Sainte-Anne-de-Bellevue: Cégep John Abbott College
21275, rue Lakeshore, Sainte-Anne-de-Bellevue, QC H9X 3L9, Canada
Tél: 514-457-6610; *Téléc:* 514-457-4730
admissions@johnabbott.qc.ca
www.johnabbott.qc.ca
twitter.com/JACNews
Enrollment: 7600
Ginette Sheehy, Directeur général
ginette.sheehy@johnabbott.qc.ca

Publications
Bandersnatch

Sept-Iles: Cégep de Sept-Iles
175, rue De La Vérendrye, Sept-Iles, QC G4R 5B7, Canada
Tél: 418-962-9848; *Téléc:* 418-962-2458
communications@cegep-sept-iles.qc.ca
www.cegep-sept-iles.qc.ca
www.facebook.com/cegepdeseptiles
twitter.com/Cegep_7iles
www.youtube.com/watch?v=KAaoUV_QSSQ
Donald Bhérer, Directeur général
donald.bherer@cegep-sept-iles.qc.ca

Publications
D'Épiderme

Sherbrooke: Cégep de Sherbrooke
475, rue du Cégep, Sherbrooke, QC J1E 4K1, Canada
Tél: 819-564-6350; *Téléc:* 819-564-1579
communications@cegepsherbrooke.qc.ca
www.cegepsherbrooke.qc.ca
www.facebook.com/cegepsherbrooke
twitter.com/cegepsherbrooke
Grades: Préuniv., Techniques, Form. cont. *Enrollment:* 6000
Sylvain Saint-Cyr, Directeur général

Publications
in Extremis

Sherbrooke: Champlain Regional College
P.O. Box 5000
1301, boul Portland, Sherbrooke, QC J1J 1S2, Canada
Tél: 819-564-3600; *Téléc:* 819-564-2639
www.crc-sher.qc.ca
Kenneth Robertson, Directeur général
krobertson@champlaincollege.qc.ca

Campuses
Campus Lennoxville
P.O. Box 5003
2580 College St., Lennoxville, QC J1M 0C8, Canada
Tel: 819-564-3666; *Fax:* 819-564-5171
admissions@crc-lennox.qc.ca
www.crc-lennox.qc.ca

Campus St. Lambert
900, av Riverside, Saint-Lambert, QC J4P 3P2, Canada
Tel: 450-672-7360; *Fax:* 450-672-9299
InfoCenter@champlaincollege.qc.ca
www.champlainonline.com

Campus St. Lawrence
790, rue Nérée-Tremblay, Sainte-Foy, QC G1V 4K2, Canada
Tel: 418-656-6921; *Fax:* 418-656-6925
slccegep@slc.qc.ca
www.slc.qc.ca

Sorel-Tracy: Cégep de Sorel-Tracy
3000, boul Tracy, Sorel-Tracy, QC J3R 5B9, Canada
Tél: 450-742-6651; *Téléc:* 450-742-1878
info@cegep-sorel-tracy.qc.ca
www.cegep-sorel-tracy.qc.ca
www.facebook.com/group.php?gid=2511302018
twitter.com/cegepsoreltracy
www.youtube.com/user/cegepsoreltracy
Grades: Préuniv., Techniques, Form. cont.
Fabienne Desroches, Directrice générale, 450-742-6651, ext. 2102
fabienne.desroches@cegepst.qc.ca

Publications
L'Exemplaire

***St-Georges:* Cégep Beauce-Appalaches**
1055, 116e rue, St-Georges, QC G5Y 3G1, Canada
Tél: 418-228-8896; *Téléc:* 418-228-0562
Ligne sans frais: 1-800-893-5111
info@cegepba.qc.ca
www.cegepba.qc.ca
Enrollment: 1424
Charles Garneau, Directeur général
cgarneau@cegepbceapp.qc.ca

***Thetford Mines:* Cégep de Thetford**
671, boul Frontenac ouest, Thetford Mines, QC G6G 1N1, Canada
Tél: 418-338-8591; *Téléc:* 418-338-3498
www.cegep-ra.qc.ca
Enrollment: 1000
Christine Demers, Directeur général

***Trois-Rivières:* Cégep de Trois-Rivières**
P.O. Box 97
3500, rue De Courval, Trois-Rivières, QC G9A 5E6, Canada
Tél: 819-376-1721; *Téléc:* 819-693-8023
infoprog@cegeptr.qc.ca
www.cegeptr.qc.ca
Grades: Préuniv., Techniques, Form. cont. *Enrollment:* 9475
Raymond Robert Tremblay, Directeur général

Publications
La Gifle

***Victoriaville:* Cégep de Victoriaville**
475, rue Notre-Dame est, Victoriaville, QC G6P 4B3, Canada
Tél: 819-758-6401; *Téléc:* 819-758-6026
Ligne sans frais: 1-888-284-9476
information@cgpvicto.qc.ca
www.cgpvicto.qc.ca
www.facebook.com/CGPVICTO
www.linkedin.com/company/cegep-de-victoriaville
www.youtube.com/user/melissagosselin1
Vincent Guay, Directeur général
guay.vincent@cgpvicto.qc.ca

Publications
La Réplique

Schools: Specialized

First Nations

***Betsiamites:* École Nussim du conseil de bande de Betsiamites**
P.O. Box 70
4, rue Pulis, Betsiamites, QC G0H 1B0, Canada
Tél: 418-567-2215; *Téléc:* 418-567-8010
Grades: K./Elem.

***Côte-Nord-du-Golfe-du-Saint-Lau:* École Olamen du Conseil des Montagnais (La Romaine)**
P.O. Box 222
Côte-Nord-du-Golfe-du-Saint-Lau, QC G0G 1M0, Canada
Tél: 418-229-2450
Grades: K./Elem./Sec.

***Kawawachikamach:* École Jimmy Sandy Memorial**
P.O. Box 5152
Kawawachikamach, QC G0G 2Z0, Canada
Tél: 418-585-3811; *Téléc:* 418-585-3347
Grades: Prim.

***Malioténam:* École Tshishteshinu du conseil des Montagnais de Sept-Iles et Maliotenam**
P.O. Box 430 Moise
Maliotênam, QC G0G 2B0, Canada
Tél: 418-927-2956; *Téléc:* 418-927-3127
Grades: K./Elem.

***Manawan:* École Otapi**
470, rue Otapi, Manawan, QC J0K 1M0, Canada
Tél: 819-971-1379
Grades: Sec.

***Manawan:* École Simon P. Ottawa**
150, rue Wapoc, Manawan, QC J0K 1M0, Canada
Tél: 819-971-8817; *Téléc:* 819-871-8872
Grades: K./Elem./Sec.

***Mashteuiatsh:* École Amishk**
225, Uapileu, Mashteuiatsh, QC G0W 2H0, Canada
Tél: 418-275-2473; *Téléc:* 418-275-0002
Grades: K./Elem. *Enrollment:* 300

***Mashteuiatsh:* École secondaire Kassinu Mamu**
1711, rue Amishk, Mashteuiatsh, QC G0W 2H0, Canada
Tél: 418-275-2473
kassinumamu@monecole-myschool.com
www.monecole-myschool.com/kassinumamu/
Grades: Sec.

***Natashquan:* École Uauitshitun Natashquan**
132, Tettaut, Natashquan, QC G0G 2E0, Canada
Tél: 418-726-3368
uauitshitun@monecole-myschool.com
www.monecole-myschool.com/uauitshitun
Grades: K./Elem./Sec.

***Obedjiwan:* École primaire Niska**
70, rue Niska, Obedjiwan, QC G0W 3B0, Canada
Tél: 819-974-8842
Grades: K./Elem.
Francine Gagnon Awashish, Directrice

***Obedjiwan:* École secondaire Mikisiw**
92, rue Tcikatnaw, Obedjiwan, QC G0W 3B0, Canada
Tél: 819-974-1221
Grades: Sec.

***Pessamit:* École secondaire Uashkaikan du conseil de bande de Betsiamites**
63, rue Messek, Pessamit, QC G0H 1B0, Canada
Tél: 418-567-2271
Grades: Sec.

***Pikogan:* École Mikwan**
P.O. Box 36
RR#4, Pikogan, QC J9T 3A3, Canada
Tél: 819-732-5213
Grades: Gr. K./Elem.

***Sept-Iles:* École Johnny-Pilot du conseil des Montagnais de Sept-Iles et Maliotenam**
P.O. Box 8000
100, Pashin, Sept-Iles, QC G4R 5V2, Canada
Tél: 418-962-5777; *Téléc:* 418-961-2666
Grades: K./Elem.

***Sept-Iles:* École Manikanetish du conseil des Montagnais de Sept-Iles et Maliotenam**
P.O. Box 8000
1, rue Ukuiass, Sept-Iles, QC G4R 2N5, Canada
Tél: 418-968-1550; *Téléc:* 418-962-6509
Grades: Sec.

***St-Augustin:* École Pakuashipi**
P.O. Box 68
52, rue Pakua, St-Augustin, QC G0G 2R0, Canada
Tél: 418-947-2729; *Téléc:* 418-947-2209
pakuashipi@yahoo.ca
www.monecole-myschool.com/pakuashipi/home.html
Grades: Gr. K./Elem./Sec.

***Weymontachie:* École secondaire Waratinak**
P.O. Box 222 B
Weymontachie, QC G0X 3R0, Canada
Tél: 819-666-2232
www.monecole-myschool.com/waratinak
Nicole Potvin, Directrice

***Weymontaci:* École primaire Seskitin**
P.O. Box 39 A
Weymontaci, QC G0X 3R0, Canada
Tél: 819-666-2226
ericniquay@hotmail.com
www.monecole-myschool.com/seskitin
Grades: Elem.
Viviane Chilton, Directrice

Schools: Independent & Private

Catholic

***Anjou:* Le Collège d'Anjou**
11 000, Renaude Lapointe, Anjou, QC H1J 2V7, Canada
Tél: 514-322-8111; *Téléc:* 514-322-8112
info@collegedanjou.qc.ca
www.collegedanjou.qc.ca
www.facebook.com/132529583479406
Grades: Sec.
Luc Plante, Directeur général
Denis de Villers, Directeur des services pédagogiques

***Ayer's Cliff:* Collège Servite**
470, rue Main, Ayer's Cliff, QC J0B 1C0, Canada
Tél: 819-838-4221; *Téléc:* 819-838-4222
courrier@collegeservite.ca
www.collegeservite.ca
Grades: Sec.; Pens. & Ext. *Note:* Confessionnelle catholique.
Carl Morissette, Directeur général
cmorissette@cnds.qc.ca
François Leblanc, Directeur du service aux élèves
fleblanc@cnds.qc.ca

***Baie-Comeau:* École secondaire Jean-Paul II**
20, av de Ramezay, Baie-Comeau, QC G4Z 1B2, Canada
Tél: 418-296-6212; *Téléc:* 418-296-3654
admjpii@globetrotter.net
www.jpii.ca
Grades: Sec.
Dorsay Talaï, Directrice générale

***Coaticook:* Collège Rivier**
343, rue St-Jacques nord, Coaticook, QC J1A 2R2, Canada
Tél: 819-849-4833; *Téléc:* 819-849-3621
crivier@crivier.qc.ca
www.crivier.qc.ca
Grades: Sec.; Pens. & Ext. *Enrollment:* 250 *Note:* École catholique, privée et mixte.
Benoit Hélie, Directeur général

***Dolbeau-Mistassini:* Juvénat Saint-Jean**
200, boul Wallberg, Dolbeau-Mistassini, QC G8L 6A5, Canada
Tél: 418-276-3340; *Téléc:* 418-276-1757
juvenatstjean@hotmail.com
www.juvenatstjean.ca
Grades: Sec.; Pens. & Ext.
Marc Tremblay, Directeur général

***Grenville-sur-la-Rouge:* Séminaire du Sacré-Coeur**
2738, rte 148, Grenville-sur-la-Rouge, QC J0V 1B0, Canada
Tél: 819-242-0957; *Téléc:* 819-242-4089
administration@seminairedusacrecoeur.qc.ca
www.seminairedusacrecoeur.qc.ca
Grades: Sec.; Pens. & Ext.
Richard Dupuis, Directeur

***Lan-Saint-Jean:* Séminaire Marie-Reine-du-Clergé**
1569, rte 169 Métabetchouan-Lac-à-la-Croix, Lan-Saint-Jean, QC G8G 1A8, Canada
Tél: 418-349-2816; *Téléc:* 418-349-8055
direction@smrc.qc.ca
www.smrc.qc.ca
Grades: Sec.; Pens. & Ext.
Jacques Ménard, Directeur général

***Lévis:* École Sainte-Famille (Fraternité St-Pie X) inc.**
10425, boul de la Rive-Sud, Lévis, QC G6V 7M5, Canada
Tél: 418-837-3028; *Téléc:* 418-837-7070
www.sspx.ca/fr/Quebec/L-Ecolle_Sainte_Famille
Grades: Prim./Sec.
Vincent d'André, Directeur

***Montréal:* Collège de Montréal**
1931, rue Sherbrooke ouest, Montréal, QC H3H 1E3, Canada
Tél: 514-933-7397; *Téléc:* 514-933-3225
cdm@college-montreal.qc.ca
www.college-montreal.qc.ca
Grades: Sec. *Note:* École catholique privée.
Jacques Giguère, Directeur général

***Montréal:* École Augustin Roscelli inc.**
11960, boul de l'Acadie, Montréal, QC H3M 2T7, Canada
Tél: 514-334-0057; *Téléc:* 514-334-4060
info@ecoleaugustinroscelli.com
www.ecoleaugustinroscelli.com
Grades: Mat./Prim. *Note:* École Catholique, privée, mixte.
Sr. Rosa Rossi, Soeur Supérieure

***Montréal:* École Marie-Clarac**
3530, boul Gouin est, Montréal, QC H1H 1B7, Canada
Tél: 514-322-1161; *Téléc:* 514-322-4364
dcormier@marie-clarac.qc.ca
www.ecolemarie-clarac.qc.ca
Grades: Mat./Prim./Sec.; mixte; filles *Enrollment:* 1300 *Note:* Garderie et préscolaire/primaire (mixte); secondaire (filles); dirigée par les Soeurs de Charité de Sainte-Marie.
Sr. Martine Côté, Directrice générale

***Montréal:* École Saint-Joseph (1985) inc.**
4080, rue De Lorimier, Montréal, QC H2K 3X7, Canada
Tél: 514-526-8288; *Téléc:* 514-526-5498
secretariat@stjoseph.qc.ca
www.stjoseph.qc.ca
Grades: Mat./Prim.
Marc Tremblay, Directeur général
mtremblay@stjoseph.qc.ca

***Montréal:* External Mont-Jésus-Marie**
2755, ch de la Côte-Ste-Catherine, Montréal, QC H3T 1B5, Canada
Tél: 514-272-1035
www.montjesusmarie.com
Grades: Mat./Prim.
Sylvie Gagné, Directrice générale

***Montréal:* Pensionnat du Saint-Nom-de-Marie**
628, ch de la Côte Ste-Catherine, Montréal, QC H2V 2C5, Canada
Tél: 514-735-5261; *Téléc:* 514-735-5266
admission@psnm.qc.ca
www.psnm.qc.ca
Grades: Sec.; filles; Pens. & Ext. *Enrollment:* 1020
Sr. Kathleen Caissy, Directrice
kcaissy@psnm.qc.ca

***Montréal:* The Sacred Heart School of Montreal**
3635, av Atwater, Montréal, QC H3H 1Y4, Canada
Tel: 514-937-2845; *Fax:* 514-937-8214
admissions@sacredheart.qc.ca
www.sacredheart.qc.ca
Grades: Sec.; Girls; Eng.; Res & Day *Note:* One of Canada's oldest, independent Catholic schools for girls.
Mr. Shawn O'Donnell, Head of School

***Québec:* Collège Jésus-Marie de Sillery**
2047, ch St-Louis, Québec, QC G1T 1P3, Canada
Tél: 418-687-9250; *Téléc:* 418-687-9847
dir.gen@cjmds.qc.ca
www.cjmds.qc.ca
Grades: Prim./Sec.; filles; Pens. & Ext. *Note:* Dirigé par la Congrégation des Religieuses de Jésus-Marie; programme enrichi au primaire, programme d'éducation internationale au secondaire.
Sr. Odile Fortin, Directrice

***Québec:* Collège Saint-Charles-Garnier**
1150, boul René-Lévesque ouest, Québec, QC G1S 1V7, Canada
Tél: 418-681-0107; *Téléc:* 418-681-9631
cscg@collegegarnier.qc.ca
www.collegegarnier.qc.ca
Grades: Sec. *Note:* Propriétaire du Collège des Jésuites.
Mario Gagnon, Directeur général
mgagnon@collegegarnier.qc.ca

***Québec:* Externat Saint-Coeur de Marie**
30, av des Cascades, Québec, QC G1E 2J8, Canada
Tél: 418-663-0605; *Téléc:* 418-663-9484
richard.morin@pscm.qc.ca
www.pscm.qc.ca
Grades: Prim.; Pens. & Ext. *Enrollment:* 411
Richard Morin, Directeur général

***Rosemère:* Externat Sacré-Coeur**
535, rue Lefrançois, Rosemère, QC J7A 4R5, Canada
Tél: 450-621-6720; *Téléc:* 450-621-1525
courrier@externat.qc.ca
www.externat.qc.ca
Grades: Sec. *Enrollment:* 1000
Denyse Hébert, Directrice générale

***Saint-Augustin-de-Desmaures:* Séminaire Saint-François**
4900, rue Saint-Félix, Saint-Augustin-de-Desmaures, QC G3A 1X3, Canada
Tél: 418-872-0611; *Téléc:* 418-872-5845
l.lessard@ss-f.com
www.ss-f.com
Grades: Sec.; Pens. & Ext.
Père Jean-Marc Boulé, Directeur général/Directeur des élèves
jmb@ss-f.com

***Saint-Hyacinthe:* École secondaire Saint-Joseph de Saint-Hyacinthe**
2875, av Bourdages nord, Saint-Hyacinthe, QC J2S 5S3, Canada
Tél: 450-774-3775; *Téléc:* 450-774-6340
www.essj.qc.ca
Grades: Sec.; Pens. & Ext.
Simone Leblanc, Directrice général

***Saint-Laurent:* École bilingue Notre-Dame de Sion**
1775, boul Décarie, Saint-Laurent, QC H4L 3N5, Canada
Tél: 514-747-3895; *Téléc:* 514-747-5492
cnicolet@ebnds.ca
www.ebnds.ca
Grades: Mat./Prim.; Fr./Angl.
Véronique Lemieux-Boyer, Directrice générale

***Saint-Michel-de-Bellechasse:* Collège Dina-Bélanger**
1, rue St-Georges, Saint-Michel-de-Bellechasse, QC G0R 3S0, Canada
Tél: 418-884-2360; *Téléc:* 418-884-3274
colldb@globetrotter.net
www.collegedina-belanger.qc.ca
Grades: Sec.; Pens. & Ext. *Enrollment:* 300 *Note:* Dirigé par les Relgieuses de Jésus-Marie.
Sr Yvette Rioux, Directrice générale

***Sherbrooke:* Collège du Sacré-Coeur**
155, rue Belvédère nord, Sherbrooke, QC J1H 4A7, Canada
Tél: 819-569-9457; *Téléc:* 819-820-0636
info@cscoeur.ca
www.college-sacre-coeur.qc.ca
Grades: Sec.; filles *Enrollment:* 500
Daniel Léveillé, Directeur général

***St-Bruno-de-Montarville:* Séminaire Sainte-Trinité**
1475, ch des Vingt, St-Bruno-de-Montarville, QC J3V 4P6, Canada
Tél: 450-653-2409; *Téléc:* 450-441-4786
secretariat@ste-trinite.qc.ca
www.ste-trinite.qc.ca
Grades: Sec.
Guy Saumure, Directeur général

***Trois-Rivières:* Séminaire Saint-Joseph**
858, rue Laviolette, Trois-Rivières, QC G9A 5S3, Canada
Tél: 819-376-4459; *Téléc:* 819-378-0607
andrem@ssj.qc.ca
www.ssj.qc.ca
Grades: Sec.; garçons; Pens. & Ext.
Michel Trépanier, Directeur général

Special Education

***Montréal:* L'École à Pas de Géant (Montréal)**
Giant Steps School (Montréal)
5460, av Connaught, Montréal, QC H4V 1X7, Canada
Tél: 514-935-1911
info@giantstepsmontreal.com
giantstepsmontreal.com
Grades: Mat./Prim./Sec; Éd. spéc. *Note:* Favoriser l'éducation et l'insertion scolaire et sociale des jeunes autistes.
Pierre Martin, Président, Conseil d'administration

***Montréal:* École orale de Montréal pour les sourds inc.**
Montreal Oral School for the Deaf Inc.
4670, rue Sainte-Catherine ouest, Montréal, QC H3Z 1S5, Canada
Tél: 514-488-4946; *Téléc:* 514-488-0802
info@montrealoralschool.com
www.montrealoralschool.com
Grades: Mat./Prim.; Éd. spéc. *Note:* Mission: enseigner aux enfants sourds à parler & à communiquer verbalement. Programmes d'études et programmes d'intégration; services cliniques; counseling.
Martha Pérusse, Directrice

***Montréal:* École Peter Hall inc.**
Peter Hall School
Campus Côte-Vertu & Centre administratif
840, boul de la Côte-Vertu, Montréal, QC H4L 1Y4, Canada
Tél: 514-747-4075; *Téléc:* 514-747-0164
cote-vertu@peterhall.qc.ca
www.peterhall.qc.ca
Grades: Mat./Prim./Sec.; Fr./Angl.;Éd.Spec. *Note:* Services éducatifs pour des élèves de 4 à 21 ans présentant une déficience intellectuelle. Campus Ouimet: 1200, rue Ouimet, St-Laurent, 514-748-1050, courriel: ouimet@peterhall.qc.ca.
Jean Laliberté, Directeur général

***Saint-Laurent:* Summit School**
École le Sommet
1750, rue Deguire, Saint-Laurent, QC H4L 1M7, Canada
Tel: 514-744-2867; *Fax:* 514-744-6410
admin@summit-school.com
www.summit-schol.com
Grades: Pre./Elem./Sec.; Spec. Ed.; Eng. *Enrollment:* 450 *Note:* Educational services for special needs students, from ages 4 to 21, with developmental disabilities such as autism, behavioral disturbances and other associated problems.
Lucy Orsini, Registrar

Independent & Private Schools

***Baie-d'Urfé:* École internationale allemande Alexander von Humboldt inc. (AvH)**
Alexander von Humboldt German International School Inc.
216, rue Victoria, Baie-d'Urfé, QC H9X 2H9, Canada
Tél: 514-457-2886; *Téléc:* 514-457-2885
avh@avh.montreal.qc.ca
www.avh.montreal.qc.ca
Grades: Mat./Prim./Sec.; Deutsche/Fr./Eng. *Note:* Environnement multilingue: allemand, anglais, français; sciences naturelles & sociales; arts; Dipl. d'études sec. du Québec & bacc. allemand international; Deutsches Sprachdiplom der Kultusministerkonferenz.
Dr. Jörg Klinkert, Directeur

***Beauceville:* École Jésus-Marie de Beauceville**
670, 9e av est, Beauceville, QC G5X 3P6, Canada
Tél: 418-774-3709; *Téléc:* 418-774-5749
secretariat@ejm.qc.ca
ww.ejm.qc.ca
Grades: Sec.; Pens. & Ext. *Enrollment:* 80
Monique Lambert, Directrice générale

***Boisbriand:* L'Académie des jeunes filles Beth Tziril**
241, av Beth Halevy, Boisbriand, QC J7E 4H4, Canada
Tél: 450-419-4085; *Téléc:* 418-434-5440
cpetash@yahoo.com
Grades: Mat./Prim./Sec.
Abraham Halpern, Directeur

***Boucherville:* École Les Trois Saisons**
570, boul de Mortagne, Boucherville, QC J4B 5E4, Canada
Tél: 450-641-2000
3saisons@biz.videotron.ca
Grades: Prim.
Monique Mathieu, Directrice générale

***Brossard:* Académie Marie-Laurier**
Marie-Laurier Academy
1555, av Stravinski, Brossard, QC J4X 2H5, Canada
Tél: 450-923-2787; *Téléc:* 450-923-2291
academie@marielaurier.com
www.marielaurier.com
Grades: Mat./Prim./Sec.; Fr./Angl. *Note:* Enseignement bilingue.
Monique Bergeron, Directrice

***Châteauguay:* Collège Héritage de Châteauguay inc.**
P.O. Box 80036
270, boul d'Youville, Châteauguay, QC J6J 5X2, Canada
Tél: 450-692-5578
www.collegeheritage.ca
Grades: Prim./Sec. *Enrollment:* 570
Jean-Guy Brais, Directeur

***Chicoutimi:* École Apostolique de Chicoutimi (2A3)**
913, rue Jacques-Cartier est, Chicoutimi, QC G7H 2A3, Canada
Tél: 418-549-1055; *Téléc:* 418-639-8609
accueil@soeursantoniennes.org
www.soeursantoniennes.org
Grades: Prim.
France Croussette, Supérieure générale

***Chicoutimi:* Le Lycée du Saguenay**
658, rue Racine est, Chicoutimi, QC G7H 1V1, Canada
Tél: 418-543-4448; *Téléc:* 418-543-1716
Grades: Sec.
Jean-François Gagné, Directeur

***Chicoutimi:* Séminaire de Chicoutimi**
679, rue Chabanel, Chicoutimi, QC G7H 1Z7, Canada
Tél: 418-549-0190; *Téléc:* 418-549-1524
Lycee.seminaire@lycee-sdec.qc.ca
www.sdec.qc.ca
www.facebook.com/sdec.qc.ca
Grades: Sec.
Marcel Bergeron, Directeur

***Compton:* École primaire Des Arbrisseaux**
6288, rte Louis-S.-St-Laurent, Compton, QC J0B 1L0, Canada
Tél: 819-835-9503; *Téléc:* 819-835-9506
direction@arbrisseaux.qc.ca
www.arbrisseaux.qc.ca
Grades: Prim.; Pens. & Ext.
Brigitte Raymond, Directrice

***Côte Saint-Luc:* L'Académie Hébraïque Inc.**
Hebrew Academy
5700, av Kellert, Côte Saint-Luc, QC H4W 1T4, Canada
Tél: 514-489-5321; *Téléc:* 514-489-8607
www.ha-mtl.org

Grades: Mat./Prim./Sec.; Angl./Fr.
Linda Lehrer, Directrice
director@ha-montreal.org

***Dollard-des-Ormeaux:* Collège de l'Ouest de l'Ile West Island College**
851, rue Tecumseh, Dollard-des-Ormeaux, QC H9B 2L2, Canada
Tél: 514-683-4660; *Téléc:* 514-683-1702
office@westislandcollege.qc.ca
www.westislandcollege.qc.ca
Grades: Sec.; Fr./Angl.
Martin Bailly, Directeur des services éducatifs

***Dollard-des-Ormeaux:* Emmanuel Christian School École chrétienne Emmanuel**
4698, boul St-Jean, Dollard-des-Ormeaux, QC H9H 4S5, Canada
Tel: 514-696-6430; *Fax:* 514-696-3687
ladirection@emmanuelchristianschool.qc.ca
www.emmanuelchristianschool.qc.ca
Grades: Pre./Elem./Sec.; Eng./Fr. *Enrollment:* 300 *Note:* A Christian education, with instruction in English & French.
Jack Bauer, Director

***Dollard-des-Ormeaux:* Hebrew Foundation School École de formation hébraïque**
2, rue Hope, Dollard-des-Ormeaux, QC H9A 2V5, Canada
Tel: 514-684-6270; *Fax:* 514-684-1998
hebrewfoundation@gmail.com
206.132.176.122/BJEC_HebrewFoundation/index.php
Grades: Pre./Elem.; Eng./Fr. *Note:* Programmes include M.E.L.S. French Immersion, traditional Jewish subjects, as well as the standard curriculum, dance & visual arts; instruction in English, French & Hebrew.
Rabbi Achiya Delouya, Head of School

***Dollard-des-Ormeaux:* The Learning Tree L'Arbre de Connaissance**
16, rue Séville, Dollard-des-Ormeaux, QC H9B 2V5
Tel: 514-683-8426; *Fax:* 514-683-8426
info@thelearningtree.ca
www.thelearningtree.ca
Grades: Preschool & Pre-Kindergarten *Enrollment:* 160
Linda McPherson, Director

***Dorval:* Queen of Angels Academy**
100, boul Bouchard, Dorval, QC H9S 1A7, Canada
Tel: 514-636-0900; *Fax:* 514-633-8969
www.qaa.qc.ca
Other Information: Admissions: 514-636-0900 x 268
Grades: Sec.; Girls; Eng.
Mary Reynolds, Principal
reynolds.m@qaa.qc.ca

***Drummondville:* Collège Saint-Bernard**
25, av des Frères, Drummondville, QC J2B 6A2, Canada
Tél: 819-478-3330; *Téléc:* 819-478-2582
csb@csb.qc.ca
www.csb.qc.ca
Grades: Prim./Sec.; Pens. & Ext.
Alexandre Cusson, Directeur général

***Gatineau:* Collège Saint-Alexandre**
2425, rue Saint-Louis, Gatineau, QC J8V 1E7, Canada
Tél: 819-561-3812; *Téléc:* 819-561-5205
www.college-stalexandre.qc.ca
Grades: Sec.
Mario Vachon, Directeur général
mario.vachon@i-alex.qc.ca

***Gatineau:* Collège Saint-Joseph de Hull**
174, rue Notre-Dame-de-l'Ile, Gatineau, QC J8X 3T4, Canada
Tél: 819-776-3123; *Téléc:* 819-776-0992
direction@collegestjoseph.ca
www.collegestjoseph.ca
Grades: Sec.; filles
Sandra Beauchamp, Directrice générale

***Gatineau:* École Montessori de l'Outaouais inc.**
161, rue Principale, Gatineau, QC J9H 7H4, Canada
Tél: 819-682-3299; *Téléc:* 819-682-7484
info.montessori@videotron.ca
www.montessori-outaouais.qc.ca
Grades: Mat./Prim.
Paul Dumetz, Directeur

***Granby:* Collège Mont-Sacré-Coeur**
210, rue Denison est, Granby, QC J2G 8E3, Canada
Tél: 450-372-6882; *Téléc:* 450-372-9219
info@college-msc.qc.ca
www.college-msc.qc.ca
Grades: Sec. *Enrollment:* 870 *Note:* Programme Exploration; Programme sports instensifs; Programme anglais intensif.
Claude Lacroix, S.C., Directeur général

***Granby:* École secondaire du Verbe Divin**
P.O. Box 786
1021, rue Cowie, Granby, QC J2G 8W8, Canada
Tél: 450-378-1074; *Téléc:* 450-378-4566
pedagogie@verbedivin.com
www.verbedivin.com
Grades: Sec. *Note:* Programmes - Immersion anglaise; Sports-Élite; Arts-Élite; Voyages; Programme Découverte.
Pierre Labbé, Directeur

***Joliette:* Académie Antoine Manseau**
P.O. Box 410
20, rue St-Charles-Borromée sud, Joliette, QC J6E 3Z9, Canada
Tél: 450-753-4271; *Téléc:* 450-753-3661
courrier@amanseau.qc.ca
www.amanseau.qc.ca
www.youtube.com/watch?v=A_XF9g_7CCM
Grades: Sec.
Christian Paul Carrière, Directeur général

***Joliette:* École les Mélèzes**
393, rue de Lanaudière, Joliette, QC J6E 3L9, Canada
Tél: 450-752-4433; *Téléc:* 450-752-4337
info@lesmelezes.qc.ca
www.lesmelezes.qc.ca
Grades: Mat./Prim.; filles; Pens. & Ext.
Renée Champagne, Directrice générale

***Kirkland:* Académie Marie-Claire**
18190, boul Elkas, Kirkland, QC H9J 3Y4, Canada
Tél: 514-697-9995; *Téléc:* 514-697-5575
www.academiemarie-claire.qc.ca
Grades: Mat./Prim. *Note:* 1ère année à 6ème année. Enseignement bilingue.
Marie-Claire Martin, Directrice
mmartin@amcca.ca

***Kirkland:* Kuper Academy**
#2 & #4, 2975, rue Edmond, Kirkland, QC H9H 5K5, Canada
Tel: 514-426-3007; *Fax:* 514-426-0377
admissions@kuperacademy.ca
www.kuperacademy.ca
Grades: K./Prim./Sec.; Eng. *Note:* Liberal arts, mathematics, sciences, social sciences, & creative & performing arts.
Joan Salette, Director

***L'Assomption:* Collège de l'Assomption**
270, boul de l'Ange-Gardien, L'Assomption, QC J5W 1R7, Canada
Tél: 450-589-5621; *Téléc:* 450-589-2910
dirgen@classomption.qc.ca
www.classomption.qc.ca
Grades: Sec.
Robert Corriveau, Directeur général

***La Pocatière:* Collège de Sainte-Anne-de-la-Pocatière**
100, 4e av, La Pocatière, QC G0R 1Z0, Canada
Tél: 418-856-3012; *Téléc:* 418-856-5611
info@leadercsa.com
www.leadercsa.com
Grades: Sec.; Pens. & Ext. *Enrollment:* 600 *Note:* Le programme Leader est offert.
Martine Dubé, Directrice générale

***La Prairie:* Collège Jean de la Mennais**
870, ch de St-Jean, La Prairie, QC J5R 2L5, Canada
Tél: 450-659-7657; *Téléc:* 450-659-3717
administration@jeandelamennais.qc.ca
www.jeandelamennais.qc.ca
Grades: Prim./Sec. *Enrollment:* 1400
Serge Courtemanche, Directeur général

***Laval:* Académie Lavalloise**
5290, boul des Laurentides Auteuil, Laval, QC H7K 2J8, Canada
Tél: 450-628-1430; *Téléc:* 450-628-1431
info@academielavalloise.com
www.academielavalloise.com
Grades: Mat./Prim. *Enrollment:* 300
David C. Zakaïb, Directeur
david.zakaib@academielavalloise.com

***Laval:* Collège Laval**
275, rue Laval, Laval, QC H7C 1W8, Canada
Tél: 450-661-7714; *Téléc:* 450-661-7146
secretariat@collegelaval.ca
www.collegelaval.ca
Grades: Sec. *Note:* Centre sportif, salle de théâtre, laboratoires informatiques, bibliothèque.
Richard Roy, Directeur

***Laval:* Collège Letendre**
1000, boul de l'Avenir, Laval, QC H7N 6J6, Canada
Tél: 450-688-9933; *Téléc:* 450-688-3591
info@collegeletendre.qc.ca
www.collegeletendre.com
Grades: Sec.
Yves Legault, Directeur

***Laval:* École Charles-Perrault (Laval)**
1750, boul de la Concorde est, Laval, QC H7G 2E7, Canada
Tél: 450-975-2233; *Téléc:* 450-975-2248
direction@charles-perrault-laval.com
www.ecolecharlesperrault.com/laval/
Grades: Mat./Prim./Sec. *Enrollment:* 380
Denis Faber, Directeur général (Pierrefonds)

***Laval:* École Démosthène**
1565, boul Saint-Martin ouest, Laval, QC H7S 1N1, Canada
Tél: 450-972-1800; *Téléc:* 450-972-1345
Grades: Mat./Prim. *Enrollment:* 218 *Note:* École privée de la communauté greque orthodoxe de Laval; formation générale; langues d'enseignement: française, greque.
Liza Henry, Directrice

***Laval:* École Notre-Dame de Nareg**
555, 67E Av, Laval, QC H7V 2M3, Canada
Tél: 450-680-1168
naregvarjaran@hotmail.com
Grades: Mat./Prim.
L'Abbé Paul Kazandjian, Directeur

***Lévis:* Juvénat Notre-Dame du Saint-Laurent**
30, rue du Juvénat, Lévis, QC G6V 6P5, Canada
Tél: 418-839-9592; *Téléc:* 418-839-5605
juvenat@jnd.qc.ca
www.jnd.qc.ca
Grades: Sec.
Claude Gélinas, Directeur général
cgelinas@jnd.qc.ca

***Longueuil:* Collège Charles-Lemoyne inc. Administration générale/Campus Longueuil**
901, ch Tiffin, Longueuil, QC J4P 3G6, Canada
Tél: 514-875-0505; *Téléc:* 450-463-4494
college@cclemoyne.edu
www.cclemoyne.edu
Grades: Sec. *Enrollment:* 2700 *Note:* Campus Longueuil II: 2301, boul Fernand-Lafontaine; Campus Ville de Sainte-Catherine: 125, place Charles-Lemoyne.
Réjean Palardy, Directeur général

***Longueuil:* Collège Français - Primaire Longueuil**
1391, rue Beauregard, Longueuil, QC J4K 2M3, Canada
Tél: 514-495-2581; *Téléc:* 514-279-5131
info@collegefrancais.ca
www.collegefrancais.ca
Grades: Mat./Prim.

***Longueuil:* Collège Notre-Dame-de-Lourdes**
845, ch Tiffin, Longueuil, QC J4P 3G5, Canada
Tél: 450-670-4740; *Téléc:* 450-670-2800
collegendl@ndl.qc.ca
www.ndl.qc.ca
Grades: Sec. *Enrollment:* 950
Lucie D'Amour, Directrice générale

***Mont-Saint-Hilaire:* Collège Saint-Hilaire inc.**
800, rue Rouillard, Mont-Saint-Hilaire, QC J3G 4S6, Canada
Tél: 450-467-7001; *Téléc:* 450-467-9040
info@csh.qc.ca
www.csh.qc.ca
Grades: Sec. *Enrollment:* 600
Diane Lavoie, Directrice générale

***Montebello:* Sedbergh School École Sedbergh**
810, Côte Azélie, Montebello, QC J0V 1L0, Canada
Tel: 819-423-5523; *Fax:* 819-423-5769
admissions@sedbergh.com
www.sedberghschool.ca
Grades: Elem./Sec.; Eng.; Res. & Day *Enrollment:* 80 *Note:* A co-educational boarding school, with a focus on academics, athletics & outdoor programs, & environmental education.
Andrew Blair, Headmaster

***Montréal:* Académie Beth Rivkah**
5001, rue Vézina, Montréal, QC H3W 1C2, Canada
Tél: 514-731-3681; *Téléc:* 514-342-4956
info@bethrivkah.com
www.bethrivkah.com
Grades: Mat./Prim./Sec.; filles *Enrollment:* 500 *Note:* Une école pour filles juives, fondée en 1956 par le Rebbe Menachem Schneerson de Loubavitch.
Rabbin Leib Kramer, Directeur

Montréal: Académie Kells
Kells Academy
6865, boul Maisonneuve ouest, Montréal, QC H4B 1T1, Canada
Tél: 514-485-8565; *Téléc:* 514-485-8505
kadmin@kells.ca
www.kells.ca
Grades: Prim./Sec.; Fr./Angl.; Éd. spéc. *Note:* École mixte. Enseignement bilingue.
Irene Woods, Directrice

Montréal: Académie Louis-Pasteur
7220, rue Marie-Victorin, Montréal, QC H1G 2J5, Canada
Tél: 514-322-6123; *Téléc:* 514-322-6787
info@academielouispasteur.com
www.academielouispasteur.com
Grades: Mat./Prim. *Note:* École primaire privée qui accueille des enfants de la maternelle à la 6e année.
Gisèle Bisaillon, Directrice générale

Montréal: Académie Michèle-Provost inc.
1517, av des Pins ouest, Montréal, QC H3G 1B3, Canada
Tél: 514-934-0596; *Téléc:* 514-934-2390
info@academiemicheleprovost.qc.ca
www.academiemicheleprovost.qc.ca
www.facebook.com/AcademieMicheleProvost
Grades: Prim./Sec.; Pens. & Ext.
Michèle Provost, Directrice

Montréal: Académie Saint-Louis de France
4430, rue Bélanger est, Montréal, QC H1T 1B3, Canada
Tél: 514-725-0340; *Téléc:* 514-725-1460
pascal.foucault@academiesldf.ca
academiestlouisdefrance.googlepages.com
Grades: Mat./Prim.
Pascal Foucault, Directeur

Montréal: Centennial Academy
L'Académie Centennale
3641, av Prud'homme, Montréal, QC H4A 3H6, Canada
Tel: 514-486-5533; *Fax:* 514-486-1401
aburgos@centennial.qc.ca
www.centennial.qc.ca
Grades: Sec.; Eng.
Angéla Burgos, Directrice

Montréal: Centre d'intégration scolaire inc.
6361, 6e av, Montréal, QC H1Y 2R7, Canada
Tél: 514-374-8490; *Téléc:* 514-374-3978
pallard@cisi.qc.ca
www.cisi.qc.ca
Grades: Prim./Sec.; Éd. spéc.
Patrice Allard, Directeur général

Montréal: Centre François-Michelle
10095, rue Meunier, Montréal, QC H3L 2Z1, Canada
Tel: 514-381-4418; *Fax:* 514-381-2895
dsormany@francois-michelle.qc.ca
www.francois-michelle.qc.ca
Grades: Mat./Prim./Sec.; Éd. spéc.
Danielle Sormany, Directrice générale

Montréal: Collège Beaubois
4901, rue du Collège Beaubois, Montréal, QC H8Y 3T4, Canada
Tél: 514-684-7642; *Téléc:* 514-684-3011
info@collegebeaubois.qc.ca
www.collegebeaubois.qc.ca
Grades: Mat./Prim./Sec.
Daniel Trottier, Directeur général

Montréal: Collège Charlemagne inc.
5000, rue Pilon, Montréal, QC H9K 1G4, Canada
Tél: 514-626-7060; *Téléc:* 514-626-1654
admin@collegecharlemagne.com
www.collegecharlemagne.com
Grades: Mat./Prim./Sec.
Julie Beaudet, Directrice générale
jbeaudet@collegecharlemagne.com
Claudette Bélanger, Registraire
cbelanger@collegecharlemagne.com

Montréal: Collège Français - Secondaire Montréal
185, av Fairmount ouest, Montréal, QC H2T 2M6, Canada
Tél: 514-495-2581; *Téléc:* 514-279-2823
info@collegefrancais.ca
www.collegefrancais.ca
Grades: Sec.; Pens. & Ext.
Colette Portal, Directrice

Montréal: Collège international Marie de France
4635, ch Queen Mary, Montréal, QC H3W 1W3, Canada
Tél: 514-737-1177; *Téléc:* 514-737-0789
college@mariedefrance.qc.ca
www.mariedefrance.qc.ca
Grades: Mat./Prim./Sec. *Enrollment:* 1800
Brigitte Peytier, Directrice générale

Montréal: Collège Jean-Eudes
3535, boul Rosemont, Montréal, QC H1X 1K7, Canada
Tél: 514-376-5740; *Téléc:* 514-376-4325
info@jeaneudes.qc.ca
www.jeaneudes.qc.ca
www.facebook.com/collegejeaneudes
Grades: Sec. *Enrollment:* 1700
Réginald Lavertu, Président

Montréal: Collège Mont-Royal
2165, rue Baldwin, Montréal, QC H1L 5A7, Canada
Tél: 514-351-7851; *Téléc:* 514-351-3124
mradm@collegemont-royal.qc.ca
www.collegemont-royal.qc.ca
Grades: Sec.
Anne-Marie Blais, Directrice générale

Montréal: Collège Mont-Saint-Louis
1700, boul Henri-Bourassa est, Montréal, QC H2C 1J3, Canada
Tél: 514-382-1560; *Téléc:* 514-382-5886
jldesrosiers@msl.qc.ca
www.msl.qc.ca
Grades: Sec.
André Lacroix, Directeur général
alacroix@msl.qc.ca

Montréal: Collège Notre-Dame
3791, ch Queen Mary, Montréal, QC H3V 1A8, Canada
Tél: 514-739-3371; *Téléc:* 514-739-4833
info@collegenotre-dame.qc.ca
www.collegenotre-dame.qc.ca
Grades: Sec.; Pens. & Ext.
Yvon Lafrenière, Directeur général

Montréal: College Prep International
7475, rue Sherbrooke ouest, Montréal, QC H4B 1S3, Canada
Tel: 514-489-7287; *Fax:* 514-489-7280
info@prepinternational.com
www.prepinternational.com
Grades: Elem./Sec.; Eng. *Note:* A private, non-sectarian & co-educational school.
Ursulene T. Mora, CEO

Montréal: Collège rabbinique du Canada
6405, av Westbury, Montréal, QC H3W 2X5, Canada
Tél: 514-735-2201; *Téléc:* 514-345-0275
Grades: Mat./Prim./Sec.; garçons *Enrollment:* 350 *Note:* École juive orthodoxe.
Linda Rosenblum, Directrice

Montréal: Collège Rachel
5030, rue Jeanne-Mance, Montréal, QC H2V 4J8, Canada
Tél: 514-287-1944; *Téléc:* 514-287-7523
collegerachel@qc.aira.com
www.collegerachel.qc.ca
Grades: Sec. *Enrollment:* 250
Véronique Geoffrion, Directrice générale

Montréal: Collège Regina Assumpta
1750, rue Sauriol est, Montréal, QC H2C 1X4, Canada
Tél: 514-382-4121; *Téléc:* 514-387-7825
info@reginaassumpta.qc.ca
www.reginaassumpta.qc.ca
Grades: Sec. *Enrollment:* 2200 *Note:* Programme de musique; danse; centre culturel & sportif; chapelle.
Pierre Carle, Directeur général

Montréal: Collège Reine-Marie
9300, boul Saint-Michel, Montréal, QC H1Z 3H1, Canada
Tél: 514-382-0484; *Téléc:* 514-858-1401
secretariat@reine-marie.qc.ca
www.reine-marie.qc.ca
Grades: Sec.; filles *Enrollment:* 500
Johanne Kenyon, Directrice générale

Montréal: Collège Sainte-Anne de Lachine
1250, boul St-Joseph, Montréal, QC H8S 2M8, Canada
Tél: 514-637-3571; *Téléc:* 514-637-8906
lariviered@college-sainte-anne.qc.ca
www.college-sainte-anne.qc.ca
Grades: Sec.
Ugo Cavenaghi, M.Éd., M.B.A., Directeur général
cavenaghiu@college-sainte-anne.qc.ca

Montréal: Collège Sainte-Marcelline
9155, boul Gouin ouest, Montréal, QC H4K 1C3, Canada
Tél: 514-334-9651; *Téléc:* 514-334-0210
information@college.marcelline.qc.ca
college.marcelline.qc.ca
Grades: Mat./Prim/Sec. *Note:* Enseignement préscolaire et primaire pour garçons et filles; et l'enseignement secondaire pour filles.
Sr. Marielle Dion, Directrice

Montréal: Collège St-Jean-Vianney
12630, boul Gouin est, Montréal, QC H1C 1B9, Canada
Tél: 514-648-3821; *Téléc:* 514-648-8401
college@st-jean-vianney.qc.ca
www.st-jean-vianney.qc.ca
Grades: Sec. *Enrollment:* 1350
Yves Lacroix, Directeur général

Montréal: Collège Ville-Marie
2850, rue Sherbrooke est, Montréal, QC H2K 1H3, Canada
Tél: 514-525-2516; *Téléc:* 514-525-7675
college@cvmarie.qc.ca
www.cvmarie.qc.ca
Grades: Sec. *Note:* Programme d'Éducation internationale.
Hélène Sirois, Directrice générale

Montréal: L'école Ali Ibn Abi Talib
1610, rue de Beauharnois ouest, Montréal, QC H4N 1J5, Canada
Tél: 514-744-0801; *Téléc:* 514-387-3457
info@ecoleali.com
www.ecoleali.com
Grades: Mat./Prim./Sec.
Bilal Jundi, Directeur

Montréal: L'École arménienne Sourp Hagop
3400, rue Nadon, Montréal, QC H4J 1P5, Canada
Tél: 514-332-1373; *Téléc:* 514-332-8303
direction@sourphagop.com
www.sourphagop.com
Grades: Mat./Prim./Sec. *Enrollment:* 700
Hagop Boulgarian, Directeur

Montréal: École au Jardin Bleu inc.
1690, rue Sauvé est, Montréal, QC H2C 2A8, Canada
Tél: 514-388-4949; *Téléc:* 514-388-1970
ecole@ecoleaujardinbleu.ca
www.ecoleaujardinbleu.ca
Grades: Mat./Prim. *Note:* École privée française d'allégeance catholique.
Nicole Auclair Normand, Directrice

Montréal: École Charles-Perrault (Pierrefonds)
106, rue Cartier, Montréal, QC H8Y 1G8, Canada
Tél: 514-684-5043; *Téléc:* 514-684-5048
info@ecolecharlesperrault.com
www.ecolecharlesperrault.com/pierrefonds/
Grades: Mat./Prim.
Denis Faber, Directeur général

Montréal: L'École des Premières Lettres
5155, av de Gaspé, Montréal, QC H2T 2A1, Canada
Tél: 514-272-2229; *Téléc:* 514-272-3330
info@premiereslettres.com
www.premiereslettres.com
Grades: Mat./Prim.
Anne Deguilhem, Directrice
adeguilhem@premiereslettres.com

Montréal: École Maïmonide
Campus Jacob Safra
1900, rue Bourdon, Montréal, QC H4M 2X7, Canada
Tél: 514-744-5300; *Téléc:* 514-744-4838
admin@maimonide.ca
www.maimonide.ca
Grades: Mat./Prim./Sec. *Note:* École de la communauté Sépharade de Montréal. Campus Parkhaven: 5615, rue Parkhaven, Côte Saint-Luc, 514-488-9224 (Michelle Serano, Directrice).
Lucienne Azoulay, Directrice générale

Montréal: École Montessori de Montréal
1505, rue Serre, Montréal, QC H8N 1N3
Tél: 514-363-6603; *Téléc:* 514-363-0942
www.ecolemontessorimontreal.com
Grades: Pre.-6 *Enrollment:* 265
Anne Mansour, Directrice
annemansour@bellnet.ca

Montréal: École Montessori International
10025, boul. de l'Acadie, Montréal, QC H4N 2S1
Tél: 514-331-1244
montessori_international@qc.aira.com
www.montessoriinternational.ca

Grades: Pre.-6 *Enrollment:* 250
Jeanette Kechichian, Directrice

Campuses
Pavillon Blainville
325, ch du Bas-de-Ste-Thérèse, Blainville, QC H4N 2S1
Tel: 450-965-7878
jgaron@emiblainville.com

Montréal: École Montessori Ville-Marie inc.
6520, boul Gouin ouest, Montréal, QC H4K 1B2, Canada
Tél: 514-335-6688; *Téléc:* 514-333-8988
emvm76@hotmail.com
ecolemontessorivillemarie.org
Grades: Mat./Prim. *Note:* Campus Saint-Laurent: 760, rue St-Germain; Campus Laval-Duvernay: 755, rue Roland-Forget. Enseignement bilingue.
Claudette Debbané, Directrice

Montréal: École Pasteur
12345, av de la Miséricorde, Montréal, QC H4J 2E8, Canada
Tél: 514-331-0850; *Téléc:* 514-331-2312
www.ecolepasteur.qc.ca
Grades: Mat./Prim./Sec. *Enrollment:* 800
Volta Ramirez, Directeur général

Montréal: École première Mesifta du Canada
2355, av Ekers, Montréal, QC H3S 1C6, Canada
Tél: 514-738-1738
eelbaz@myway.com
Grades: Mat./Prim./Sec. *Note:* École juive.
Rabbin Chesky Buchinger, Directeur général

Montréal: École primaire Socrates
Socrates School
5777, av Wilderton, Montréal, QC H3S 2K8, Canada
Tél: 514-738-2421; *Téléc:* 514-906-0764
www.hcm-chm.org
Grades: Mat./Prim. *Note:* Langues d'enseignement: française, greque et anglaise.
Chris Adamopoulos, Directeur général
chis.adamopoulos@hcm-chm.org

Montréal: École Rudolf Steiner de Montréal
4855, av Kensington, Montréal, QC H3X 3S6, Canada
Tél: 514-481-5686; *Téléc:* 514-481-5072
info@ersm.org
www.ersm.org
Grades: Mat./Prim./Sec. *Note:* Pédagogie Waldorf.
Anne Lange, Directrice

Montréal: École secondaire Duval
260, boul Henri-Bourassa est, Montréal, QC H3L 1B8, Canada
Tél: 514-382-6070; *Téléc:* 514-382-7207
info@ecoleduval.com
www.ecoleduval.com
Grades: Sec. *Note:* École sec. pour élèves qui ont abandonné leurs études régulières mais désirent obtenir leur diplôme dans les plus brefs délais, ou qui désirent satisfaire aux préalables d'un programme ou suivre un cours pour l'admission au collégial; cours individualisés ou cours de groupe.
Jacques Duval, Directeur

Montréal: École secondaire Jeanne-Normandin
690, boul Crémazie est, Montréal, QC H2P 1E9, Canada
Tél: 514-381-3945; *Téléc:* 514-381-1695
mtremblay@jeanne-normandin.qc.ca
www.jeanne-normandin.qc.ca
Grades: Sec.; filles
Marie Robert, Directrice générale

Montréal: Les écoles communautaires Skver
1235, av Ducharme, Montréal, QC H2V 1E2, Canada
Tél: 514-274-6133; *Téléc:* 514-274-1468
Grades: Mat./Prim./Sec.; Fr./Eng.
Ruth Bensimhon, Directrice
bensimhon@btmtl.ca

Montréal: Écoles musulmanes de Montréal
Campus Secondaire
2255, boul Cavendish, Montréal, QC H4B 2L7, Canada
Tél: 514-484-5084; *Téléc:* 514-484-5439
info@emms.ca
www.emms.ca
Grades: Prim./Sec. *Note:* Campus Primaire: 7445, av Chester, (514) 484-8845 (Radjouh Idriss, directeur).
Fouzi Belaiboud, Directeur, Campus Secondaire

Montréal: Greaves Adventist Academy
2330, av West Hill, Montréal, QC H4B 2S3, Canada
Tel: 514-486-5092; *Fax:* 514-486-0515
www.greavesadventistacademy.com
Grades: Pre./Elem./Sec.; Eng.

Montréal: Jewish People's Schools & Peretz Schools Inc.
Les Écoles juives populaires et Les Écoles Peretz inc.
Also known as: JPPS-Bialik
Head Office
6502, ch Kildare, Montréal, QC H4W 3B8, Canada
Tel: 514-731-2944; *Fax:* 514-731-0343
info@jppsbialik.ca
www.jppsbialik.ca
Grades: Pre./Elem./Sec.; Eng./Fr. *Note:* One educational system retaining the names of both founding schools, united in 1971. JPPS-Bialik is a Jewish day school system in Montréal, comprising: Bialik High School, 6500, ch Kildare, 514-481-2736; JPPS Elementary School, 5170, av Van Horne, 514-731-6456; and JPPS Children's Centre, 7950 ch Wavell, 514-488-1232. Instruction in English, French & Hebrew, with language programmes in French, Hebrew, Yiddish; mathematics, sciences & technology, Judaic Studies, Social Sciences, Arts; athletics; library.
Arnold Cohen, President
Elaine Wisenthal Milech, Principal, Bialik High School
Ms. Randy Zucker, Director, JPPS Children's Centre
Adina Matas, Principal/Educational Director, JPPS

Montréal: Lower Canada College
4090, av Royale, Montréal, QC H4A 2M5, Canada
Tel: 514-482-9916; *Fax:* 514-482-0195
admin@lcc.ca
www.lcc.ca
Grades: K-11; Eng./Fr.
Christopher J. Shannon, Headmaster

Montréal: Loyola High School
7272, rue Sherbrooke ouest, Montréal, QC H4B 1R2, Canada
Tel: 514-486-1101; *Fax:* 514-486-7266
admin@loyola.ca
www.loyola.ca
Grades: Sec.; Boys; Eng.
Éric McLean, Directeur

Montréal: Orchard House
Maison Orchard
5565, ch Côte-Saint-Antoine, Montréal, QC H4A 1R3
Tel: 514-483-6556
admin@orchard-house.ca
www.orchard-house.ca
www.facebook.com/Orchard.House.Preschools
www.youtube.com/user/OrchardHouseMontreal
Yasmine Ghandour, Founder

Campuses
Pointe-Claire Campus
159, Place Frontenac, Montréal, QC H9R 4Z7
Tel: 514-630-3993
Stefanie Havas, Director

Montréal: Pensionnat Notre-Dame-des-Anges
5680, boul Rosemont, Montréal, QC H1T 2H2, Canada
Tél: 514-254-6447; *Téléc:* 514-254-6261
pnda@pnda.qc.ca
www.pnda.qc.ca/
Grades: Prim.
France Mailloux, Directrice générale

Montréal: The Priory School inc.
3120 The Boulevard, Montréal, QC H3Y 1R9, Canada
Tel: 514-935-5966; *Fax:* 514-935-1428
info@priory.qc.ca
www.priory.qc.ca
Grades: Pre./Elem.; Eng.
John Marinelli, Directeur

Montréal: St. George's School of Montreal
École St-Georges de Montréal
3100, The Boulevard, Montréal, QC H3Y 1R9, Canada
Tel: 514-937-9289; *Fax:* 514-933-3621
www.stgeorges.qc.ca
Grades: Pre./Elem./Sec.; Eng. *Note:* A co-educational, non-denominational school.
James A. Officer, Head of School
james.officer@stgeorges.qc.ca

Montréal: Solomon Schechter Academy
Académie Solomon Schechter
5555, ch de la Côte-St-Luc, Montréal, QC H3X 2C9, Canada
Tel: 514-485-0866; *Fax:* 514-485-2267
info@solomonschechter.ca
www.ssa.koumbit.org
Grades: Pre./Prim.; Eng./Fr. *Note:* Committed to the values of Conservative Judaism; affiliated with the Shaare Zion Synagogue. Pre-Kindergarten to Gr. 6. Instruction in English, French & Hebrew.

Dr. Shimshon Hamerman, B.A., M.Sc., Ph.D., Principal

Montréal: Trafalgar School for Girls
3495, rue Simpson, Montréal, QC H3G 2J7, Canada
Tel: 514-935-2644; *Fax:* 514-935-2359
admissions@trafalgar.qc.ca
www.trafalgar.qc.ca/
Grades: Sec.; Girls; Eng.
Geoffrey Dowd, Director
gd@trafalgar.qc.ca

Montréal: United Talmud Torahs of Montréal
Talmud Torahs Unis de Montréal
Herzliah High School, Snowdon Campus
4840, av Saint-Kevin, Montréal, QC H3W 1P2, Canada
Tél: 514-739-2294; *Téléc:* 514-739-2296
www.herzliahsnowdon.qc.ca
Grades: Pre./Elem./Sec.; Eng./Fr. *Note:* Instruction in Hebrew, French & English; college preparatory programme; Judaic Studies; athletics; arts; library.
Linda Leiberman, Campus Director
lleiberman@utt.qc.ca

Montréal: Villa Maria
4245, boul Décarie, Montréal, QC H4A 3K4, Canada
Tel: 514-484-4950; *Fax:* 514-484-4492
secretariat@villamaria.qc.ca
www.villamaria.qc.ca
Grades: Sec.; Girls; Eng./Fr. *Enrollment:* 600 *Note:* Committed to students' proficiency in French & English; programmes include languages; arts (visual arts, drama, music); mathematics & sciences; technology; social sciences; ethics & religious culture; physical education & health.
Claire Drolet, Director General

Montréal: Villa Sainte-Marcelline
815, av Upper Belmont, Montréal, QC H3Y 1K5, Canada
Tél: 514-488-2528
info@villa.marcelline.qc.ca
villa.marcelline.qc.ca
Grades: Mat./Prim./Sec.; filles
Monique Pierre-Louis, Présidente

Montréal: Yeshiva Gedola Merkaz Hatorah
Section anglaise
6155, ch Deacon, Montréal, QC H3S 2P4, Canada
Tel: 514-735-6611; *Fax:* 513-343-0083
mainoffice@yeshivagedola.org
www.yeshivagedola.com
Grades: Pre./Elem./Sec.; Eng./Fr.
Rabbi Moshe Glustein, Directeur

Montréal-Nord: Centre Académique Fournier
10339, av du Parc-Georges, Montréal-Nord, QC H1H 4Y4, Canada
Tél: 514-321-2642; *Téléc:* 514-321-0278
paola.gravino@academiefournier.qc.ca
www.academiefournier.qc.ca
Grades: Prim./Sec.; Éd. spéc.
Paola Gravino, Directrice générale
paola.gravino@academiefournier.qc.ca

Montréal-Nord: École Michelet
10550, av Pelletier, Montréal-Nord, QC H1H 3R5, Canada
Tél: 514-321-9551; *Téléc:* 514-321-9111
michelet@qc.aira.com
www.ecolemichelet.com
Grades: Prim.
Lucienne Mortier, Directrice

Nicolet: Collège Notre-Dame-de-l'Assomption
225, rue St-Jean-Baptiste, Nicolet, QC J3T 0A2, Canada
Tél: 819-293-4500; *Téléc:* 819-293-2099
snault@cnda.qc.ca
www.cnda.qc.ca
Grades: Sec.; Pens. & Ext. *Note:* École privée mixte.
Robert Cyr, Directeur général

Outremont: Belz Community School
École communautaire Belz
Also known as: Belz Girls School
1495, av Ducharme, Outremont, QC H2V 1E8, Canada
Tel: 514-271-0611; *Fax:* 514-271-9329
belz@belzschool.org
Grades: Pre./Elem./Sec.; Fr./Eng.; girls *Note:* Belz Boys School: 6508, Durocher, Outremont, (514) 270-5086.
Helen Liberman, Principal

Outremont: Beth Jacob School Inc.
École Beth Jacob inc.
1750, av Glendale, Outremont, QC H2V 1B3, Canada
Tel: 514-739-3614; *Fax:* 514-739-0172
bjdrh@hotmail.com
Grades: Pre./Elem./Sec.; Eng./Fr.; Girls

Rabbin S. Aisenstark, Directeur

***Outremont:* Collège Stanislas**
780, boul Dollard, Outremont, QC H2V 3G5, Canada
Tél: 514-273-9521; *Téléc:* 514-273-3409
direction@stanislas.qc.ca
www.stanislas.qc.ca
Grades: Mat./Prim./Sec./Coll. *Enrollment:* 2150
Henri-Laurent Brusa, Directeur général

***Outremont:* École Buissonnière, centre de formation artistique inc.**
215, av de l'Épée, Outremont, QC H2V 3T3, Canada
Tél: 514-272-4739; *Téléc:* 514-907-5094
infos@ecolebuissonniere.ca
www.ecolebuissonniere.ca
Grades: Mat./Prim. *Note:* Intégration des arts aux programmes du Min. de l'Éducation; arts plastiques, musique, danse, art dramatique.
Hélène Bourduas, Directrice générale

***Québec:* Académie Saint-Louis (Québec)**
1500, rue de La Rive-Boisée sud, Québec, QC G2C 2B3, Canada
Tél: 418-845-5121; *Téléc:* 418-845-5244
www.aslouis.qc.ca
Grades: Sec. *Enrollment:* 800 *Note:* Programmes: Concentration Langues; Études-Sports: Hockey, Golf, Natation, Football, Cheerleading, et Soccer féminin.
Jocelyn Lee, Directeur général

***Québec:* Centre Psycho-Pédagogique de Québec inc. (École Saint-François)**
1000, rue du Joli-Bois, Québec, QC G1V 3Z6, Canada
Tél: 418-650-1171; *Téléc:* 418-650-1145
adm@cppq.qc.ca
www.cppq.qc.ca
Grades: Prim./Sec./; Éd. spéc. *Enrollment:* 200 *Note:* Favoriser l'intégration sociale de filles et garçons présentant des difficultés d'adaptation scolaire.
Jean-Marie Guay, Directeur

***Québec:* Collège de Champigny**
1400, rte de l'Aéroport, Québec, QC G2G 1G6, Canada
Tél: 418-872-0508; *Téléc:* 418-872-1002
www.collegedechampigny.com
www.facebook.com/collegedechampigny
twitter.com/ColldeChampigny
www.youtube.com/watch?v=hOer5eHEdKo&feature=youtu.be
Grades: Sec.
Guy Bouchard, Directeur général
guy.bouchard@collegedechampigny.com

***Québec:* L'École des Ursulines de Québec et de Loretteville**
P.O. Box 820
4, rue du Parloir, Québec, QC G1R 4S7, Canada
Tél: 418-692-2612; *Téléc:* 418-692-1240
secrectariat_euq@ursulinesquebec.com
www.ursulinesquebec.com
Grades: Prim./Sec.; filles; Pens. & Ext. *Enrollment:* 580 *Note:* Loretteville: 63, rue Racine, (418) 842-2949.
Serge Goyette, Directeur

***Québec:* École Montessori de Québec inc.**
1265, av Du Buisson, Québec, QC G1T 2C4, Canada
Tél: 418-688-7646; *Téléc:* 418-687-5282
montessori_qc@yahoo.ca
www.montessori-qc.net
Grades: Mat./Prim.
Benoît Dubuc, Directeur

***Québec:* École Saint-Louis-de-Gonzague**
980, rue Richelieu, Québec, QC G1R 1L5, Canada
Tél: 418-692-1072; *Téléc:* 418-692-5965
secretariat@eslg.qc.ca
www.eslg.qc.ca
Grades: Prim.; garçons *Enrollment:* 300 *Note:* Programme d'éducation internationale.
Patrick L'Heureux, Directeur général
dirgen@eslg.qc.ca

***Québec:* École secondaire François-Bourrin**
50, av des Cascades, Québec, QC G1E 6B3, Canada
Tél: 418-661-6978; *Téléc:* 418-661-4778
efb@fbourrin.qc.ca
www.fbourrin.qc.ca
Grades: Sec.
M. Magella Beaulieu, Directeur général

***Québec:* Externat Saint-Jean-Eudes**
650, av du Bourg-Royal, Québec, QC G2L 1M8, Canada
Tél: 418-627-1550; *Téléc:* 418-627-0770
info@sje.qc.ca
www.sje.qc.ca
Grades: Sec.
Édouard Malenfant, Directeur général

***Québec:* Externat St-Jean-Berchmans**
2303, ch Saint-Louis, Québec, QC G1T 1R5, Canada
Tél: 418-687-5871; *Téléc:* 418-687-5886
sec@externatsjb.com
www.externatsjb.com
Grades: Mat./Prim.
Alain Roy, Directeur général

***Québec:* Institut St-Joseph**
Pavillon Saint-Vallier
900, av. Joffre, Québec, QC G1S 4Z3, Canada
Tél: 418-688-0736; *Téléc:* 418-688-0737
www.st-joseph.qc.ca
www.facebook.com/institutstjoseph
Grades: Mat./Prim.
Jean-Guy Lussier, Directeur général

***Québec:* Le Petit Séminaire de Québec**
6, rue de la Vielle-Université, Québec, QC G1R 5X8, Canada
Tél: 418-694-1020; *Téléc:* 418-694-1072
admission@psq.qc.ca
www.psq.qc.ca
Grades: Sec.
Réjean Lemay, Directeur général

***Québec:* Séminaire des Pères Maristes**
2315, ch Saint-Louis, Québec, QC G1T 1R5, Canada
Tél: 418-651-4944; *Téléc:* 418-651-6841
spmecole@spmaristes.qc.ca
www.spmaristes.qc.ca
Grades: Sec.
Jean-François Bussières, Directeur général
jfbussieres@spmaristes.qc.ca

***Rawdon:* Collège Champagneur**
3713, rue Queen, Rawdon, QC J0K 1S0, Canada
Tél: 450-834-5401; *Téléc:* 450-834-6500
secretariat@champagneur.qc.ca
www.champagneur.qc.ca
Grades: Sec.; Pens. & Ext. *Note:* Privée mixte.
Sylvain Brabant, Directeur

***Rawdon:* École et Pensionnat Marie-Anne**
4567, rue du Mont-Pontbriand, Rawdon, QC J0K 1S0, Canada
Tél: 450-834-4668; *Téléc:* 450-834-2800
ema@intermonde.net
www.ecolemarieanne.qc.ca
Grades: Mat./Prim.; Pens. & Ext.
Carole Lalancette, Directrice

***Repentigny:* Académie François-Labelle**
1227, rue Notre-Dame, Repentigny, QC J5Y 3H2, Canada
Tél: 450-582-2020; *Téléc:* 450-582-9732
afl@classomption.qc.ca
www.academiefrancoislabelle.qc.ca
Grades: Mat./Prim.
Michèle Beaudry, Directrice générale

***Repentigny:* Centre Académique de Lanaudière**
930, boul L'Assomption, Repentigny, QC J6A 5H5, Canada
Tél: 450-654-5026
drn@lecadl.com
www.lecadl.com
Grades: Mat./Prim.
Denise Normandin, Directrice

***Rigaud:* Collège Bourget**
65, rue St-Pierre, Rigaud, QC J0P 1P0, Canada
Tél: 450-451-0815; *Téléc:* 450-451-4171
dg@collegebourget.qc.ca
www.collegebourget.qc.ca
Grades: Prim./Sec.; Pens. & Ext.
Jean-Marc St-Jacques, c.s.v., Directeur général

***Rivière-du-Loup:* Collège Notre-Dame**
P.O. Box 820
56, rue Saint-Henri, Rivière-du-Loup, QC G5R 3Z5, Canada
Tél: 418-862-8257; *Téléc:* 418-862-8495
info@collegenotredame.ca
collegenotredame.ca
Grades: Sec.
Abbé Fernand Chouinard, Directeur général

***Saint-Augustin-de-Desmaures:* Collège Saint-Augustin**
4950, rue Lionel-Groulx, Saint-Augustin-de-Desmaures, QC G3A 1V2, Canada
Tél: 418-872-0954; *Téléc:* 418-872-8249
Grades: Sec.; Pens. & Ext.
Charles Fournier, Directeur

***Saint-Bruno-de-Montarville:* Pensionnat des Sacrés-Coeurs**
1575, ch des Vingt, Saint-Bruno-de-Montarville, QC J3V 4P6, Canada
Tél: 450-653-3681; *Téléc:* 450-653-0816
info@psscc.qc.ca
www.pssc.qc.ca
Grades: Mat./Prim.; Pens. & Ext.
Guy Saumure, Directeur général

***Saint-Gabriel-de-Valcartier:* École secondaire Mont-Saint-Sacrement**
200, boul St-Sacrement, Saint-Gabriel-de-Valcartier, QC G0A 4S0, Canada
Tél: 418-844-3771; *Téléc:* 418-844-2926
secretariat@mss.qc.ca
www.mss.qc.ca
Grades: Sec. *Note:* Programme Baccalauréat international; Programme Magellan.
Pierre Lantier, Directeur général

***Saint-Guillaume:* Juvénat Saint-Louis-Marie**
96, rue Saint-Jean-Baptiste, Saint-Guillaume, QC J0C 1L0, Canada
Tél: 819-396-2076; *Téléc:* 819-396-3331
info@juvenat.ca
www.juvenat.ca
Grades: Sec.; Pens. & Ext.
Martin Girard, Directeur

***Saint-Hyacinthe:* Collège Antoine-Girouard**
700, rue Girouard est, Saint-Hyacinthe, QC J2S 2Y2, Canada
Tél: 514-773-4334; *Téléc:* 450-773-8011
admin@antoine-girouard.qc.ca
www.antoine-girouard.qc.ca
Grades: Sec.
M. Dominique Lestage, Directeur général

***Saint-Hyacinthe:* Collège Saint-Maurice**
630, rue Girouard ouest, Saint-Hyacinthe, QC J2S 2Y3, Canada
Tél: 450-773-7478; *Téléc:* 450-773-1413
info.college@csm.qc.ca
www.csm.qc.ca
Grades: Sec.; filles; Pens. & Ext. *Note:* École secondaire pour filles; Programme d'éducation internationale.
Jean-Pierre Jeannotte, Directeur général

***Saint-Hyacinthe:* La Petite Académie**
1090, av Pratte, Saint-Hyacinthe, QC J2S 4B6, Canada
Tél: 450-771-0644; *Téléc:* 450-771-7242
info@lapetiteacademie.qc.ca
www.lapetiteacademie.qc.ca
Grades: Mat./Prim.
Lise Thiboutot, Directrice générale

***Saint-Jacques:* Collège Esther-Blondin**
101, rue Ste-Anne, Saint-Jacques, QC J0K 2R0, Canada
Tél: 450-839-3672; *Téléc:* 450-839-3951
admin@collegeblondin.qc.ca
www.collegeblondin.qc.ca
Grades: Sec.; Pens. & Ext. *Enrollment:* 1100 *Note:* Membre, Soc. des établissements du bacc. international du Québec, et Org. du bacc. international; le collège est reconnu École Verte Brundtland.
Julie Pothier, Directrice générale

***Saint-Jean-sur-Richelieu:* École secondaire Marcellin-Champagnat**
14, ch des Patriotes est, Saint-Jean-sur-Richelieu, QC J2X 5P9, Canada
Tél: 450-347-5343; *Téléc:* 450-347-2423
webmaster@esmc.qc.ca
www.esmc.qc.ca
Grades: Sec.
F. Jacques Bélisle, Directeur général

***Saint-Jérôme:* Académie Lafontaine**
2171, boul Maurice, Saint-Jérôme, QC J7Y 4M7, Canada
Tél: 450-431-3733; *Téléc:* 450-431-7390
info@academielafontaine.qc.ca
www.academielafontaine.qc.ca
Grades: Mat./Prim./Sec. *Note:* Camps du jour; piscine; cantine.
Claude Potvin, Directeur général

***Saint-Lambert:* Collège Durocher Saint-Lambert**
Pavillon Durocher
857, rue Riverside, Saint-Lambert, QC J4P 1C2, Canada
Tél: 450-465-7213; *Téléc:* 450-465-0860
johanne.tremblay@cdsl.qc.ca
www.cdsl.qc.ca
Grades: Sec. *Enrollment:* 2230 *Note:* Pavillon Saint-Lambert: 375, rue Riverside, 450-671-5585.
Carmen Poirier, Directrice générale

***Saint-Laurent:* École Alex Manoogian**
755, rue Manoogian, Saint-Laurent, QC H4N 1Z5, Canada
Tél: 514-744-5636; *Téléc:* 514-744-2785
armenque@qc.aira.com
www.alexmanoogian.qc.ca
Grades: Mat./Prim./Sec.; Fr./Eng./Armenian *Enrollment:* 550 *Note:* La première école arménienne au Canada; école privée.
Dr. Robert Marc Kechayan, Directeur

***Saint-Laurent:* École Vanguard Québec ltée (École primaire interculturelle)**
Vanguard Québec School
1150, rue Deguire, Saint-Laurent, QC H4L 1M2, Canada
Tél: 514-747-3711; *Téléc:* 514-747-2831
cccaputo@vanguardquebec.qc.ca
www.vanguardquebec.qc.ca
Grades: Prim./Sec.; Fr./Angl.; Éd. spéc. *Note:* Services adaptés à des élèves présantant des difficultés graves d'apprentissage. École Vanguard Primaire Interculturelle: 1150, rue Deguire, (514) 747-3711 (Denise Bédard, directrice). École Vanguard Secondaire Francophone: 83, boul des Prairies, Laval, (450) 972-6268 (François Papineau, directeur). École Vanguard Secondaire Interculturelle: 175, rue Metcalfe, (514) 932-9770 (Maryse Bessette, directrice).
Carolyn Coffin-Caputo, Directrice générale, 514-747-5500

***Saint-Laurent:* Education Plus**
1275, rue Hodge, Saint-Laurent, QC H4N 2B1, Canada
Tel: 514-733-9600; *Fax:* 514-733-3060
www.edplus.ca
Grades: Grs. 10 & 11 *Enrollment:* 40 *Note:* Relationship-based education, flexible structure, informal environment; Life Skills courses; drama; arts; English & French language skills.
James Watts, Director
j.watts@sympatico.ca

***Sainte-Thérèse:* Académie Ste-Thérèse**
Campus Ste-Thérèse
425, rue Blainville est, Sainte-Thérèse, QC J7E 1N7, Canada
Tél: 450-434-1130; *Téléc:* 450-434-0010
infostetherese@academie.ste-therese.com
www.academie.ste-therese.com
Grades: Mat./Prim./Sec.; Pens. & Ext. *Note:* Campus Rosemère: 1, ch des Écoliers, Rosemère, 450-434-1130.
Rose De Angelis, Directrice générale

***Sept-Iles:* Institut d'enseignement de Sept-Iles inc.**
737, av Gamache, Sept-Iles, QC G4R 2J8, Canada
Tél: 418-962-9104; *Téléc:* 418-962-8561
www.annuairefeep.com
Grades: Sec. *Enrollment:* 236
Richard Savignac, Directeur général

***Shawinigan:* Séminaire Sainte-Marie**
5655, boul des Hêtres, Shawinigan, QC G9N 4V9, Canada
Tél: 819-539-5493; *Téléc:* 819-539-1749
apsssm@ssm1950.qc.ca
www.seminairestemarie.com
Grades: Prim./Sec.
Marc St-Onge, Directeur général

***Sherbrooke:* Bishop's College School, Inc. (BCS)**
P.O. Box 5001 Lennoxville
80, ch Moulton Hill, Sherbrooke, QC J1M 1Z8, Canada
Tel: 819-566-0227; *Fax:* 819-822-8917
admissions@bishopscollegeschool.com
www.bishopscollegeschool.com
Grades: 7-12 *Note:* Bishop's College School is a bilingual boarding & day school.
Ian Watt, Headmaster, 819-566-0227, ext. 201
Charles de Sainte Marie, Director, Development, 819-566-0227, ext. 203
François de Sainte Marie, Director, Finance & Operations, 819-566-0227, ext. 205
Valerie Scullion, Director, Admissions, 819-566-0227, ext. 248

***Sherbrooke:* Collège du Mont-Sainte-Anne**
2100, ch Ste-Catherine, Sherbrooke, QC J1N 3V5, Canada
Tél: 819-823-3003; *Téléc:* 819-569-9636
Ligne sans frais: 877-823-3003
msa@collegemsa.qc.ca
www.college-mont-sainte-anne.qc.ca
Grades: Sec.; garçons; Pens. & Ext.
André Ricard, Directeur général

***Sherbrooke:* Collège Mont Notre-Dame de Sherbrooke inc.**
114, rue de la Cathédrale, Sherbrooke, QC J1H 4M1, Canada
Tél: 819-563-4104; *Téléc:* 819-563-8689
cmnd@mont-notre-dame.qc.ca
www.mont-notre-dame.qc.ca
Grades: Mat./Prim./Sec; filles *Note:* Programme d'éducation international; école de musique; école de danse; Espagnol; sports.
Richard Custeau, Directeur général

***Sherbrooke:* École Plein Soleil (Association coopérative)**
300, rue de Montréal, Sherbrooke, QC J1H 1E5, Canada
Tél: 819-569-8359; *Téléc:* 819-569-3979
info@pleinsoleil.qc.ca
www.pleinsoleil.qc.ca
Grades: Mat./Prim. *Note:* Programme d'éducation internationale.
Marie-Josée Mayrand, Directrice générale
mjmayrand@pleinsoleil.qc.ca

***Sherbrooke:* École secondaire de Bromptonville**
125, rue du Frère-Théode, Sherbrooke, QC J1C 0S3, Canada
Tél: 819-846-2738; *Téléc:* 819-846-4808
esb@esb-fsc.ca
www.esb.bromptonville.qc.ca
Grades: Sec.; garçons; Pens. & Ext.
Fr. Jean-Guy Beaulieu, Directeur général
dirgen@esb-fsc.ca

***Sherbrooke:* Séminaire de Sherbrooke**
195, rue Marquette, Sherbrooke, QC J1H 1L6, Canada
Tél: 819-563-2050; *Téléc:* 819-562-8261
courrier@seminaire-sherbrooke.qc.ca
www.seminaire-sherbrooke.qc.ca
Grades: Sec. *Note:* Secondaire et collégial; formation continue.
André Métras, Recteur-Directeur général

***Sherbrooke:* Séminaire Salésien**
135, rue Don Bosco nord, Sherbrooke, QC J1L 1E5, Canada
Tél: 819-566-2222; *Téléc:* 819-566-6969
salesien@seminairesalesien.org
www.seminairesalesien.org
Grades: Sec.
Raymond Lepage, Directeur

***St-Augustin-de-Desmaures:* Réseau VISION**
Également connu sous le nom de: Écoles VISION Schools
Maître Franchiseur Vision inc.
4920, rue Pierre-Georges-Roy, St-Augustin-de-Desmaures, QC G3A 1V7, Canada
Tél: 418-653-3547; *Téléc:* 418-653-6435
Ligne sans frais: 866-553-3547
info@visionschools.com
www.visionschools.com
Grades: Mat./Prim./Sec. *Note:* Le réseau regroupe huit écoles VISION (immersion) et deux écoles Once Upon a Time (préscolaire; apprentissage de l'anglais ou de l'espagnol).
Richard Dumais, Président

***Stanstead:* Stanstead College**
450, rue Dufferin, Stanstead, QC J0B 3E0, Canada
Tel: 819-876-2223; *Fax:* 819-876-5891
admissions@stansteadcollege.com
www.stansteadcollege.com
www.facebook.com/pages/Stanstead-College/78975058390
twitter.com/stansteadcolleg
Grades: Sec.; Eng.; Res. & Day *Enrollment:* 200 *Note:* Co-educational; curriculum/instruction in English, with programmes in French, arts, music, drama; athletics.
Michael T. Wolfe, Headmaster, 819-876-7891, ext. 230
michael.wolfe@stansteadcollege.com

***Terrebonne:* Collège Saint-Sacrement**
901, rue St-Louis, Terrebonne, QC J6W 1K1, Canada
Tél: 450-471-6615; *Téléc:* 450-471-5904
css@collegesaintsacrement.qc.ca
www.collegesaintsacrement.qc.ca
Grades: Sec.
Luc St-Louis, Directeur général
lst-louis@collegesaintsacrement.qc.ca

***Trois-Rivières:* Collège Marie-de-l'Incarnation**
725, rue Hart, Trois-Rivières, QC G9A 5S3, Canada
Tél: 819-379-3223; *Téléc:* 819-379-3226
ecole@cmitr.qc.ca
www.cmitr.qc.ca
Grades: Mat./Prim./Sec.; Pens. & Ext. *Note:* École pour filles; école de musique.
Martine Talbot, Directrice, Services éducatifs du secondaire
martine.talbot@cmitr.qc.ca
Carolyne Gagnon, Directrice, Services éducatifs du préscolaire & du primaire
carolyne.gagnon@cmitr.qc.ca

***Trois-Rivières:* Institut secondaire Keranna (1992) inc.**
6205, boul des Chenaux, Trois-Rivières, QC G9A 5S3, Canada
Tél: 819-378-4833; *Téléc:* 819-378-2417
keranna@keranna.qc.ca
keranna.qc.ca
Grades: Sec.; filles; Pens. & Ext.
Julie L'Heureux, Directrice générale

***Trois-Rivières:* Val Marie**
88, ch du Passage, Trois-Rivières, QC G8T 2M3, Canada
Tél: 819-379-8040; *Téléc:* 819-378-8559
secretariat@ecolevalmarie.qc.ca
www.ecolevalmarie.qc.ca
Grades: Mat./Prim.; Pens. & Ext.
France Vadeboncoeur, Directrice générale

***Val-Morin:* Académie Laurentienne**
1200, 14e av, Val-Morin, QC J0T 2R0, Canada
Tél: 819-322-2913; *Téléc:* 819-322-7086
info@al.qc.ca
www.academielaurentienne.com
Grades: Prim./Sec.; Pens. & Ext. *Note:* Programmes académiques et sportifs; installations sportives: piscines, palestre, gymnase double; terrains de jeux, de tennis; centre équestre.
Guy Richard, Directeur
richard.guy@al.qc.ca

***Varennes:* Centre Éducatif Chante Plume**
104, boul de la Marine, Varennes, QC J3X 1Z5, Canada
Tél: 450-652-6869; *Téléc:* 450-652-5773
varennes@visionschools.com
varennes.visionschools.com
Grades: Mat./Prim.
Colette Cardin, Directrice

***Varennes:* Collège Saint-Paul**
235, rue Sainte-Anne, Varennes, QC J3X 1P9, Canada
Tél: 450-652-2941; *Téléc:* 450-652-4461
reception@college-st-paul.qc.ca
www.college-st-paul.qc.ca
Grades: Sec. *Note:* Programme de formation générale; Programme d'éducation internationale.
André Langevin, Directeur général

***Vaudreuil-Dorion:* Éco-lita Trilingue**
1255, boul André-Chartrand, Vaudreuil-Dorion, QC J7V 0B7
Tél: 450-510-5454; *Téléc:* 450-510-0927
info@ecolita.ca
www.ecolita.ca
Grades: Pre.-6 *Enrollment:* 100
Michelle Vaudrin, Direction, fondatrice et directrice pédagogique

***Victoriaville:* Collège Clarétain**
663, rue Gamache, Victoriaville, QC G6R 0W3, Canada
Tél: 819-752-4571; *Téléc:* 819-752-4572
administration@collegeclaretain.com
www.collegeclaretain.com
Grades: Sec.; Pens. & Ext. *Note:* École privée mixte.
Jean-Roch Gagné, Directeur général

***Waterville:* Collège François-Delaplace**
365, rue Compton est, Waterville, QC J0B 3H0, Canada
Tél: 819-837-2882; *Téléc:* 819-837-0625
dir@college-francois-delaplace.qc.ca
www.college-francois-delaplace.qc.ca
Grades: Sec.; filles *Note:* École Verte Brundtland; école secondaire privée pour filles (pensionnaires & externes).
Josée Hamel, Directrice générale

***Westmount:* The Akiva School**
450, av Kensington, Westmount, QC H3Y 3A2, Canada
Tel: 514-939-2430; *Fax:* 514-939-2432
suzanna@akivaschool.com
www.akivaschool.com
Grades: Pre-K./Gr. 6; Eng./Fr./Hebrew *Note:* Jewish community school; programmes include English Language Arts, Français, Judaic Studies, Music, Mathematics, Art, Media & Technology, Physical Education, & Ethics & Religious Cultures.
Frances Levy, Head of School

***Westmount:* Miss Edgar's & Miss Cramp's School (ECS)**
525, av Mount Pleasant, Westmount, QC H3Y 3H6, Canada
Tel: 514-935-6357; *Fax:* 514-935-1099
www.ecs.qc.ca

Grades: Pre./Elem./Sec.; Girls; Eng. *Enrollment:* 344 *Note:* University-preparatory programme, to Gr. 11; French Immersion junior school; arts, athletics, math, sciences, languages, citizenship education; extended day programme; library.
Katherine Nikidis, B.Ed., MHSc, Head of School
nikidisk@ecs.qc.ca

Westmount: Selwyn House
École Selwyn House
95, ch Côte-St-Antoine, Westmount, QC H3Y 2H8, Canada
Tel: 514-931-9481; *Fax:* 514-931-6118
admission@selwyn.ca
www.selwyn.ca
Grades: Pre./Elem./Sec.; Eng.; Boys *Enrollment:* 570
Hal Hannford, Headmaster

Westmount: The Study
3233, The Boulevard, Westmount, QC H3Y 1S4, Canada
Tel: 514-935-9352; *Fax:* 514-935-1721
info@thestudy.qc.ca
www.thestudy.qc.ca
www.facebook.com/pages/SOGA-Network/157775784348963
twitter.com/thestudyschool
www.youtube.com/thestudyschool
Grades: Pre./Elem./Sec.; Eng.; Girls *Note:* Committed to best practices in education, with a focus on proficiency in both English & French, academics & athletics. The school is the first in Québec to introduce a Mandarin language program at the primary level.
Nancy Sweer, Head of School, 514-935-9352, ext. 226
nsweer@thestudy.qc.ca

Universities & Colleges

Universities

Gatineau: Université du Québec en Outaouais
Pavillion Alexandre-Taché
283, boul Alexandre-Taché, Gatineau, QC J9A 1L8, Canada
Tél: 819-595-3900; *Téléc:* 819-595-3924
Ligne sans frais: 1-800-567-1283
questions@uqo.ca
www.uqo.ca
www.facebook.com/sharer.php?u=http://uqo.ca/accueil&t=
twitter.com/share?url=http://uqo.ca/accueil&text=
Full Time Equivalency: 5200

Campus Saint-Jérôme
5, rue Saint-Joseph, Saint-Jérôme, QC J7Z 0B7, Canada
Tél: 450-530-7616; *Téléc:* 800-567-1283

Publications
Le Canard Déchaine

Le Virus

Laval: Institut Armand-Frappier
531, boul des Prairies, Laval, QC H7V 1B7, Canada
Tél: 450-687-5010; *Téléc:* 450-686-5501
info@iaf.inrs.ca
www.iaf.inrs.ca
www.facebook.com/UniversiteINRS
www.twitter.com/U_INRS
www.youtube.com/user/MyINRS

Montréal: Concordia University
Université Concordia
Sir George Williams Campus
1455, boul de Maisonneuve ouest, Montréal, QC H3G 1M8, Canada
Tel: 514-848-2424
www.concordia.ca
Full Time Equivalency: 44000
Judith Woodsworth, President & Vice-Chancellor
David Graham, Provost & Vice-President, Academic
Kathy Assayag, Vice-President, Advancement and Alumni Relations
Bram Freedman, Vice-President, External Relations and Secretary-General
Patrick Kelley, CFO
Louise Dandurand, Vice-President, Research and Graduate Studies
Michael Di Grappa, Vice-President, Services
Philippe Beauregard, CCO

Faculties
Arts & Science
Dr. David Graham, Dean

Engineering & Computer Science
Nabil Esmail, Dean

Fine Arts
Catherine Wild, Dean

Graduate Studies & Research
Elizabeth Saccà, Dean

John Molson School of Business (JMSB)
Jerry Tomberlin, Dean

Campuses
Loyola Campus
7141, rue Sherbrooke ouest, Montréal, QC H4B 1R6, Canada

Sir George Williams Campus
1455, boul de Maisonneuve ouest, Montréal, QC H3G 1M8, Canada

Publications
Concordia University Magazine
Office of Alumni Affairs
#BC-101, 1455, boul de Maisonneuve ouest, Montréal, QC H3G 1M8, Canada
Fax: 514-848-2826

The Concordian

The Link

The Sting

Thursday Report

CAS

Montréal: École de technologie supérieure
1100, rue Notre-Dame ouest, Montréal, QC H3C 1K3, Canada
Tél: 514-396-8800; *Téléc:* 514-396-8950
Ligne sans frais: 1-888-394-7888
admission@etsmtl.ca
www.etsmtl.ca
www.facebook.com/etsmtl
twitter.com/etsmtl
www.youtube.com/user/etsmtl
Full Time Equivalency: 4800

Publications
Le Jets

Montréal: HEC Montréal
Également connu sous le nom de: École des Hautes Études Commerciales
Université de Montréal
3000, ch de la Côte-Sainte-Catherine, Montréal, QC H3T 2A7, Canada
Tél: 514-340-6000; *Téléc:* 514-340-6411
webmestre@hec.ca
www.hec.ca
Full Time Equivalency: 12000 *Note:* HEC Montréal est la première école de gestion au Canada. Affaires internationales; finance; gestion des opérations/logistique; gestion des ressources humaines; management; marketing; méthodes quantitatives de gestion; sciences comptables; technologies de l'information; économie appliquée. Édifice Decelles: 5255, av Decelles. Campus Laval: 2572, boul Daniel-Johnson, (450) 973-7741. Campus Longueuil: 101, place Charles-Lemoyne, (450) 651-5458. Bureau international à Paris: 15, rue du Louvre, 75001 Paris, 33(0)1 42 33 43 40.
Michel Patry, Directeur

Montréal: McGill University
845, rue Sherbrooke ouest, Montréal, QC H3A 2T5, Canada
Tel: 514-398-4455; *Fax:* 514-398-4455
www.mcgill.ca
Full Time Equivalency: 32510
Arnold Steinberg, Chancellor
Robert Rabinovitch, Ph.D., M.A., B.Com., Chair of Board
Heather Munroe-Blum, O.C. Ph.D. FRSC, Principal & Vice-Chancellor
Anthony C. Masi, Provost
Morty Yalovsky, Vice-Principal
Sylvia Franke, CIO
Denis Therien, Vice-Principal
Johanne Pelletier, Secretary General
Sylvia Franke, Registrar & Exec. Director
Jennifer Robinson, Assoc. Vice-Principal
Kim Bartlett, Director
Howard Tontini, Director
Ann Dowsett Johnston, Vice-Principal

Faculties
Agricultural & Environmental Sciences
Chandra A. Madramootoo, B.Sc., M.Sc., Ph.D., Dean

Arts
John Galaty, Dean

Centre for Continuing Education
Robin Eley, Director

Dentistry
James Percy Lund, B.D.S., Ph.D., Dean

Education
Dr. Roger Slee, Dean

Engineering
Pierre Christophe, Dean

Graduate & Post-Doctoral Studies
Dr. James Nemes, Dean

Law
Prof. Nicholas Kasirer, Dean

Management
Peter Todd, Dean

Medicine
Abraham Fuks, B.Sc., M.D., C.M., Dean

Music
Don McLean, Dean

Religious Studies
B. Barry Levy, B.A., B.R.E., M.A., Ph.D., Dean

Science
Martin Grant, Dean

Schools
Architecture
David Covo, B.Sc.Arch., M.B.Arch., O., Director

Communication Sciences & Disorders
Dr. Shari R. Baum, Director

Computer Science
Sue Whitesides, Director

Dietetics & Human Nutrition
Dr. Kristine G. Koski, Director

International Executive Institute
Peter Todd, Director

Library & Information Studies
France Bouthillier, Director

Nursing
Dr. Hélène Ezer, Acting Director

Physical & Occupational Therapy
Dr. Maureen J. Simmonds, Director

Social Work
Dr. Wendy Thomson, Director

Urban Planning
David Brown, Director

Affiliations
Macdonald Campus
21111, ch Bord-du-Lac, Sainte-Anne-de-Bellevue, QC H9X 3V9, Canada
Tel: 514-398-7707; *Fax:* 514-398-7766
info.macdonald@mcgill.ca
www.mcgill.ca/macdonald/
Note: Established in 1905, Macdonald College began as Canada's foremost institution for agricultural education. In 1972, it became the Macdonald Campus of McGill University & is the home of the University's Faculty of Agricultural & Environmental Sciences, the McGill School of Environment, & the School of Dietetics & Human Nutrition. Programmes leading to the degree of B.Sc.(Agr.), as well as graduate programs in agriculture, food, natural sciences, applied economics, environment, & engineering are offered.

The Montreal Diocesan Theological College
3475, rue University, Montréal, QC H3A 2A8, Canada
Tel: 514-849-3004; *Fax:* 514-849-4113
info@dio-mdtc.ca
www.dio-mdtc.ca
Note: An Anglican theological college founded in 1873. Affiliated with McGill Univ. & l'Univ. de Montréal. Degree courses: B.Th., Dip.Min, M.Div. Advanced degrees, offered through McGill: S.T.M, M.A., Ph.D. Distance education courses leading to the Cert. in Theology, or Licentiate in Theology also available.
The Rev. Canon John Simons, Principal

The Presbyterian College, Montréal
Collège Presbytérien, Montréal
3495, rue University, Montréal, QC H3A 2A8, Canada
Tél: 514-288-5256; *Téléc:* 514-288-8072
info@presbyteriancollege.ca
www.presbyteriancollege.ca
Note: Founded in 1867 & affiliated with McGill Univ.
J. Vink, 514-288-5256, ext. 200

Royal Victoria College
3425, rue University, Montréal, QC H3A 2A8, Canada
Tel: 514-398-6378; *Fax:* 514-398-4445
housing.residences@mcgill.ca
www.mcgill.ca/students/housing/downtown-undergrad/residences/rvc

Full Time Equivalency: 266 Note: Royal Victoria College is McGill's only all women's residence.

The United Theological College
Le Séminaire Uni
3521, rue University, Montréal, QC H3A 2A9, Canada
Tel: 514-849-2042; Toll-Free: 888-849-2042
admin@utc.ca
www.utc.ca

Note: A college of the United Church of Canada, committed to the training of persons, regardless of race, economic status, sexual orientation & gender identity, for various Christian ministries. Instruction in English & French is offered.
Philip L. Joudrey, M.Div., D.Min., Principal
pjoudrey@utc.ca
Alyson Huntly, Dip.Min., M.T.S., Ph.D., Director, Studies
ahuntly@utc.ca

Publications
Debit Memo

The Faucet

The McGill News
c/o Graduates' Society
3605 Mountain St, Montréal, QC H3G 2M1, Canada
Fax: 514-398-7338

The Reporter

The Tablet

Montréal: Télé-Université (Montréal)
100, rue Sherbrooke ouest, Montréal, QC H2X 3P2, Canada
Tél: 514-843-2015; Téléc: 514-843-2160
Ligne sans frais: 1-800-665-4333
nfo@teluq.ca
www.teluq.uquebec.ca
www.teluq.uquebec.ca/facebook
twitter.com/teluq

Full Time Equivalency: 20000

Montréal: The United Theological College Le Séminaire Uni
3521, rue University, Montréal, QC H3A 2A9, Canada
Tel: 514-849-2042; Fax: 514-849-8634
Toll-Free: 888-849-2042
admin@utc.ca
www.utc.ca

Montréal: Université de Montréal
Pavillon J-A.-DeSève
P.O. Box 6205
2332, boul Édouard-Montpetit, Montréal, QC H3C 3T5, Canada
Tél: 514-343-7076; Téléc: 514-343-5788
www.umontreal.ca

Full Time Equivalency: 55000 Note: Facultés: Aménagement; Arts/Sciences; Droit; Éducation permanente; Études supérieures/postdoctorales; Médecine; Médecine dentaire; Médecine vétérinaire; Musique; Pharmacie; Sciences de l'éducation; Sciences infirmières; Théologie; Kinésiologie; Optometrie; Santé publique. Campus régionaux: Terrebonne; Ville de Laval; Longueuil; Québec.
Guy Breton, Recteur, 514-343-6776
guy.breton@umontreal.ca

Affiliations
École Polytechnique de Montréal
Également connu sous le nom de: Polytechnique Montréal
P.O. Box 6079 Centre-ville
Montréal, QC H3C 3A7, Canada
Tél: 514-340-4711
www.polymtl.ca

Full Time Equivalency: 4000 Note: Fondée en 1873, Le Polytechnique est une école d'ingénierie de classe internationale; programmes au baccalauréat, cycles supérieurs, formation continue; recherche; l'École se trouve à 2900, boul Édouard-Montpetit, Campus de l'Univ. de Montréal, 2500 ch de Polytechnique.
Christophe Guy, ing., Ph.D., MACG, Directeur général

HEC Montréal
Également connu sous le nom de: École des Hautes Études Commerciales
3000, ch de la Côte-Sainte-Catherine, Montréal, QC H3T 2A7, Canada
Tél: 514-340-6000; Téléc: 514-340-6411
www.hec.ca

Michel Patry, Directeur

Circuit
Presses de l'Université de Montréal
P.O. Box 6128 Centre-ville
Montréal, QC H3C 3J7
Tel: 514-343-6388; Fax: 514-343-5727
info@revuecircuit.ca
www.pum.umontreal.ca; www.revuecircuit.ca

Note: Circuit, créée en 1989, publie des articles sur la musique contemporaine québécoise et internationale. Trois fois par année.
Jonathan Goldman, Rédacteur en chef

Études françaises
Presses de l'Université de Montréal
P.O. Box 6128 Centre-ville
Montréal, QC H3C 3J7
Tel: 514-343-6933; Fax: 514-343-2232
www.pum.umontreal.ca

Note: Fondée en 1965; littératures de langue française, québécoises et internationales; critique et théorie. Trois fois par année.
Francis Gingras, Directeur

Pigeon Dissident
#A-2412, 3200, rue Jean-Brillant, Montréal, QC H3T 1N8
Tel: 514-343-6111; Fax: 514-343-5929
info@pigeondissident.com
www.pigeondissident.com

Note: Le journal des étudiants de la Faculté de droit, l'Université de Montréal. Six fois par année.
Takwa Souissi, Rédactrice en chef

Quartier Libre
P.O. Box 6128 Centre-ville
2350, boul Édouard-Montpetit, Montréal, QC H3C 3J7
Tel: 514-343-7630; Fax: 514-343-7744
quartierlibre@hotmail.com
www.ql.umontreal.ca

Note: Quartier Libre est le journal des étudiants de l'Université de Montréal, publié par Les Publications du Quartier Libre, une corporation sans but lucratif créée par des étudiants en 1992. Le version papier (bimensuel) est distribué gratuitement sur tout le campus de l'UM et dans ses environs.
Mikaëlle Monfort, Directrice
monfortmikaelle@hotmail.com

Montréal: Université du Québec à Montréal (UQAM)
P.O. Box 8888 Centre-Ville
Montréal, QC H3C 3P8, Canada
Tél: 514-987-3000
general@uqam.ca
www.uqam.ca
www.facebook.com/uqam1
twitter.com/uqam

Campus de Lanaudière
Pavillon D
#D106, 2700, boul des Entreprises, Terrebonne, QC J6X 4J8, Canada
Tél: 450-654-8768; Téléc: 450-477-8712
Ligne sans frais: 1-800-361-4567
lanaudiere@uqam.ca

Amar Belhal, Coordonnateur, 450 662-1340
belhal.amar@uqam.ca

Campuses
Campus de Laval
#A1950, 475, boul de l'Avenir, Laval, QC H7N 5H9, Canada
Tél: 450-662-1300; Téléc: 450-662-1244
laval@uqam.ca

Campus de l'Ouest-de-l'île
#A-215, 3501, boul Saint-Charles, Kirkland, QC H9H 4S3, Canada
Tél: 514-428-1181; Téléc: 514-428-1292
ouestdel'ile@uqam.ca

Chantal Boucher, Coordonnatrice, 514 987-3000, ext. 2176
boucher.chantal@uqam.ca

Campus de Longueuil
#2050, 150, Place Charles-Le Moyne, Longueuil, QC J4K 0A8, Canada
Tél: 514-987-3063; Téléc: 514-987-4648
Ligne sans frais: 1-800-363-9290
longueuil@uqam.ca

Publications
L'Action

Journal U.Q.A.M

Le Temporel

Transactions

Unité

Uquam

Suites

Québec: École nationale d'administration publique
555, boul Charest est, Québec, QC G1K 9E5, Canada
Tél: 418-641-3000; Téléc: 418-641-3060
info@enap.ca
www.enap.ca
www.facebook.com/ENAP.CA?ref=nf
twitter.com/#%21/@Info_ENAP

Full Time Equivalency: 1832 Note: Campus: Québec, Montréal, Gatineau, Saguenay, Trois-Rivières

Québec: Institut national de la recherche scientifique (INRS)
490, rue de la Couronne, Québec, QC G1K 9A9, Canada
Tél: 418-654-4677; Téléc: 418-654-2525
Ligne sans frais: 877-326-5762
www.inrs.ca
www.facebook.com/UniversiteINRS
www.twitter.com/U_INRS
www.youtube.com/user/MyINRS

Québec: Université du Québec
475, rue du Parvis, Québec, QC G1K 9H7, Canada
Tél: 418-657-3551; Téléc: 418-657-2132
cscuq@uqss.uquebec.ca
www.uquebec.ca

Guy Massicotte, Directeur
Pierre Moreau, Président
Michel Quimper, Secrétaire général
Serge Cabana, Directeur
Pierre Chenard, Directeur

Affiliations
Université du Québec en Abitibi-Témiscamingue
445, boul de l'Université, Rouyn-Noranda, QC J9X 5E4, Canada
Tél: 819-762-0971; Téléc: 819-797-4727
www.uqat.ca

Johanne Jean, Rectrice
Jean Turgeon, Secrétaire général

Université du Québec à Chicoutimi
555, boul de l'Université, Chicoutimi, QC G7H 2B1, Canada
Tél: 418-545-5011; Téléc: 418-545-5012
www.uqac.ca

Martin Gauthier, Recteur

Université du Québec en Outaouais
Pavillion Alexandre-Taché
P.O. Box 1250 Hull
283, boul Alexandre-Taché, Gatineau, QC J8X 3X7, Canada
Tél: 819-595-3900; Téléc: 819-595-3924
Ligne sans frais: 800-567-1283
dcr@uqo.ca
www.uqo.ca

Daniel-Marc Dubé, Président

Université du Québec à Montréal
P.O. Box 8888 Centre-Ville
Montréal, QC H3C 3P8, Canada
Tél: 514-987-3000
general@uqam.ca
www.uqam.ca
Other Information: Urgence: 514-987-3131

Claude Corbo, Recteur

Université du Québec à Rimouski
P.O. Box 3300
300, allée des Ursulines, Rimouski, QC G5L 3A1, Canada
Tél: 418-723-1986; Téléc: 418-724-1525
Ligne sans frais: 800-511-3382
uqar@uqar.qc.ca
www.uqar.ca

Jean-Pierre Ouellet, Recteur, 418-724-1410
recteur@uqar.ca

Université du Québec à Trois-Rivières
P.O. Box 500 Bureau-chef
3351, boul des Forges, Trois-Rivières, QC G9A 5H7, Canada
Tél: 819-376-5011; Téléc: 819-376-5210
Ligne sans frais: 800-365-0922
www.uqtr.ca

Ghislain Bourque, Recteur

École nationale d'administration publique
555, boul Charest est, Québec, QC G1K 9E5, Canada
Tél: 418-641-3000; *Téléc:* 418-641-3055
www.enap.ca
Marcel Proulx, Directeur général

École de technologie supérieure
1100, rue Notre-Dame ouest, Montréal, QC H3C 1K3, Canada
Tél: 514-396-8800; *Téléc:* 514-396-8950
www.etsmtl.ca
Yves Beauchamp, Directeur général

Institut Armand-Frappier
531, boul des Prairies, Laval, QC H7V 1B7, Canada
Tél: 450-687-5010; *Téléc:* 450-686-5501
www.iaf.inrs.ca
Charles M. Dozois, Directeur, 450 687-5010
charles.dozois@iaf.inrs.ca

Institut national de la recherche scientifique (INRS)
490, rue de la Couronne, Québec, QC G1K 9A9, Canada
Tél: 418-654-4677; *Téléc:* 418-654-2525
Daniel Coderre, Directeur général
daniel.coderre@adm.inrs.ca

Télé-université
P.O. Box 4800 Terminus
455, rue du Parvis, Québec, QC G1K 9H5, Canada
Tél: 418-657-2747; *Téléc:* 418-657-2094
Ligne sans frais: 888-843-4333
info@teluq.ca
www.teluq.uquebec.ca
Louise Bertrand, Directrice générale

Télé-Université (Montréal)
100 rue Sherbrooke ouest, Montréal, QC H2X 3P2, Canada
Tél: 514-843-2015; *Téléc:* 514-843-2160

Québec: Université Laval
2325, rue de l'Université, Québec, QC G1V 0A6, Canada
Tél: 418-656-3333; *Téléc:* 418-656-5216
Ligne sans frais: 1-877-785-2825
renseignements@ulaval.ca
www.ulaval.ca
www.facebook.com/ulaval.ca
twitter.com/universitelaval

Full Time Equivalency: 38500 *Number of Employees:* 1,509 professors *Note:* Première université francophone d'Amerique, ouverte sur le monde et animée d'une culture de l'exigence, l'Université Laval contribue au développement de la société par la formation de personnes compétentes, responsables et promotrice de changement, par l'avancement et le partage des connaissances, dans un environnement dynamique de recherche et de création
Denis Brière, Recteur

Campuses
Service des communications
Pavillon Alphonse-Desjardins.
#3577, Université de Laval, Laval, QC G1K 7P4, Canada
Fax: 418-656-2809
Richard Fournier, Directeur

Publications
Au Fil des Evénements
#214, Tour des Arts, Québec, QC G1K 7P4, Canada
Fax: 418-529-0649

Impact Campus

Rimouski: Université du Québec à Rimouski
P.O. Box 3300 A
300, allée des Ursulines, Rimouski, QC G5L 3A1, Canada
Tél: 418-723-1986; *Téléc:* 418-724-1525
Ligne sans frais: 1-800-511-3382
uqar@uqar.qc.ca
www.uqar.ca
www.facebook.com/accueil.uqar
www.twitter.com/UQAR

Campus de Lévis
1595, boul Alphonse-Desjardins, Lévis, QC G6V 0A6, Canada
Tél: 418-833-8800; *Téléc:* 418-833-1113
Ligne sans frais: 1-800-463-4712
campus_levis@uqar.ca

Publications
U.Q.A.R. Information

Uquarium

Rouyn-Noranda: Université du Québec en Abitibi-Témiscamingue
445, boul de l'Université, Rouyn-Noranda, QC J9X 5E4, Canada
Tél: 819-762-0971; *Téléc:* 819-797-4727
information@uqat.ca
www.uqat.ca
www.facebook.com/uqat.ca
www.youtube.com/uqatinformation

Publications
Le Voyeur

Sherbrooke: Bishop's University
2600, rue College, Sherbrooke, QC J1M 1Z7, Canada
Tel: 819-822-9600; *Fax:* 819-822-9661
businessoffice@ubishops.ca
www.ubishops.ca
www.facebook.com/bishops
twitter.com/ubishops
www.youtube.com/user/bishopsuniversity

Full Time Equivalency: 2263
Michael Goldbloom, Principal/Vice-Chancellor, ext. 2611
principal@ubishops.ca
Michael Goldbloom, Principal & Vice-Chancellor
Yves Jodoin, Registrar/Sec.-General, ext. 2676
yves.jodoin@ubishops.ca

Sherbrooke: Université Bishop's
P.O. Box 5000
2600 College St., Sherbrooke, QC J1M 1Z7, Canada
Tél: 819-822-9600; *Téléc:* 819-822-9661
Ligne sans frais: 1-800-567-279
liaison@ubishops.ca
www.ubishops.ca

Full Time Equivalency: 2206
Scott Griffin, B.A., D.C.L., Chancellor
Philip Matthews, B.A., LL.B., President of Corporation
Yves Jodoin, B.A., B.Sp. Adm., M.B.A., Registrar
Joan Stadelman, B.Sc., M.Sc., Vice-President of Corporation
Sam Elkas, Chair
Robert Poupart, B.A., B.Ph., M.Ps., D.Ps., Principal & Vice-Chancellor
Mark McLaughlin, B.B.A., C.A., Vice-Principal
Tony Addona, B.Sc., Dip.Ed., M.Sc., Director
Cathy Beauchamp, B.A., Dip.Ed., M.A., Ph.D, Director
Hans Rouleau, B.A., Liaison Coordinator
Damien Roy, B.A., Director
Suzanne Meeson, B.B.A., Continuing Education Coordinator
Pam McPhail, B.A., Director
Matt McBrine, B.A., Alumni Relations Coordinator
Patricia MacAulay, Manager
Jonathan Rittenhouse, B.A., M.A., Ph.D., Vice-Principal

Faculties
Business Administration
W. Robson, B.Com., M.B.A., Dean

Humanities
Stephen Sheeran, B.A., M.A., Dean

Natural Sciences & Mathematics
Brad Willms, B.Math, M.M. Ph.D., Dean

Social Sciences
Andrew Johnson, B.A., M.A., Ph.D., Dean

Student Affairs
Bruce Stevenson, B.A., Dip.Ed., M.Ed., Dean

Williams School of Business
Sylvie Béquet, M.Sc., Dean

Publications
The Campus

Sherbrooke: Université de Sherbrooke
2500, boul de l'Université, Sherbrooke, QC J1K 2R1, Canada
Tél: 819-821-7686
information@usherbrooke.ca
www.usherbrooke.ca

Denis Marceau, Vice-recteur
Edwin Bourget, Vice-recteur
Jean Desclos, Vice-recteur
Martin Buteau, Vice-recteur
Roger Noël, Doyen
Bruno-Marie Béchard, Recteur
Luce Samoisette, Rectrice adjointe et vice-rectrice à l'administration
Daniel Proulx, Doyen
Céline Garant, Doyenne
Paul Deshaies, Doyen
Linda Bellalite, Doyenne
Dr. Réjean Hébert, Doyen
Donald Thomas, Doyen
Gérard Lachiver, Doyen
Marc Dumas, Doyen
Sylvie Belzile, Directrice
Jacques Labrecque, Directeur
Christian Gagnon, Directeur
Serge Cabana, Directeur
Renald Mercier, Directeur
René Alarie, Directeur
Luc Bédard, Directeur
Pierre Lemieux, Directeur
France Myette, Registraire
Lise Grenier, Directrice
Gilles Bilodeau, Directeur
Daniel Dupont, Directeur
Mario Laforest, Directeur
Michèle Desrochers, Directrice
Denis Marceau, Directeur (par interim)
Serge Fortier, Directeur
François Dubé, Directeur (par intérim)

Publications
Bilan

La Sagace

Liaison

Sommets
2500, boul de l'Université, Sherbrooke, QC J1K 2R1, Canada
Fax: 819-821-7900

Trois-Rivières: Université du Québec à Trois-Rivières
P.O. Box 500
3351, boul des Forges, Trois-Rivières, QC G9A 5H7, Canada
Tél: 819-376-5011; *Téléc:* 819-376-5210
Ligne sans frais: 1-800-365-0922
communications@uqtr.ca
www.uqtr.ca
www.facebook.com/uqtr.ca
twitter.com/InformationUQTR
www.flickr.com/photos/comuqtr

Full Time Equivalency: 11000

Publications
En Tete

Le Voyeur

Colleges

La Pocatière: Institut de technologie agroalimentaire
Campus de La Pocatière
401, rue Poiré, La Pocatière, QC G0R 1Z0, Canada
Tél: 418-856-1110; *Téléc:* 418-856-1719
scitalp@mapaq.gouv.qc.ca
www.ita.qc.ca

Full Time Equivalency: 1000 *Note:* Spécialisé en agroalimentaire; Campus de Saint-Hyacinthe: 3230, rue Sicotte, (450) 778-6504; Collège Macdonald, Univ. McGill.
Rosaire Ouellet, Directeur général

Campuses
Campus de Saint-Hyacinthe
P.O. Box 70
3230, rue Sicotte, Saint-Hyacinthe, QC J2S 7B3, Canada
Tel: 450-778-6504; *Fax:* 450-778-6536
ita.st.hyacinthe@mapaq.gouv.qc.ca
www.ita.qc.ca

Montréal: École Polytechnique de Montréal
Également connu sous le nom de: Polytechnique de Montréal
Université de Montréal
2900, boul Édouard-Montpetit, Montréal, QC H3T 1J4, Canada
Tél: 514-340-4711
www.polymtl.ca

Full Time Equivalency: 4000 *Note:* Fondée en 1873, le Polytechnique est une école d'ingénierie de classes internationale; programmes au baccalauréat, cycles supérieures, formation continue; recherche. Adresse postale: CP 6079, succ. Centre-ville, Montréal, QC H3C 3A7.

Publications
Le Polyscope

Montréal: HEC Montréal
Également connu sous le nom de: École des Hautes Études Commerciales
3000, ch de la Côte-Sainte-Catherine, Montréal, QC H3T 2A7, Canada
Tél: 514-340-6000; *Téléc:* 514-340-6411
webmestre@hec.ca
www.hec.ca
Grades: Bacc., MBA, LL.M., M.Sc., Ph.D. *Full Time Equivalency:* 12000 *Note:* La première école de gestion au Canada, fondée en 1907

Publications
Le Caducée
#310, 3333 Queen Mary Rd, Montréal, QC H3V 1A2, Canada
Fax: 514-340-6508

L'Intérêt

Montréal: Institut de tourisme et d'hôtellerie du Québec
3535, rue Saint-Denis, Montréal, QC H2X 3P1, Canada
Tél: 514-282-5111; *Téléc:* 514-282-5126
Ligne sans frais: 1-800-361-5111
info@ithq.qc.ca
www.ithq.qc.ca
www.facebook.com/ecoleITHQ
twitter.com/ITHQ
Lucille Daoust, Directrice

Montréal: The Montreal Diocesan Theological College
3475, rue University, Montréal, QC H3A 2A8, Canada
Tel: 514-849-3004; *Fax:* 514-849-4113
info@dio-mdtc.ca
www.dio-mdtc.ca

Québec: Direction générale du Conservatoire de musique et d'art dramatique du Québec
225, Grande Allée est, Bloc C, 3e étage, Québec, QC G1R 5G5, Canada
Tél: 418-380-2327; *Téléc:* 418-380-2328
info@conservatoire.gouv.qc.ca
www.conservatoire.gouv.qc.ca
twitter.com/ConservatoireQc
www.youtube.com/my_videos?feature=mhee

Campuses
Conservatoire de musique de Saguenay
202, rue Jacques-Cartier est, Chicoutimi, QC G7H 6R8, Canada
Tel: 418-698-3505; *Fax:* 418-698-3521
CMS@conservatoire.gouv.qc.ca
Régis Rousseau, Directeur

Conservatoire de musique de Gatineau
430, boul Alexandre-Taché, Gatineau, QC J9A 1M7, Canada
Tel: 819-772-3283; *Fax:* 819-772-3346
CMG@conservatoire.gouv.qc.ca
Marc Landry, Directeur

Conservatoire de musique de Montréal
4750, av Henri-Julien, 1e étage, Montréal, QC H2T 2C8, Canada
Tel: 514-873-4031; *Fax:* 514-873-4601
CMM@conservatoire.gouv.qc.ca
Manon Lafrance, Directrice
manon.lafrance@conservatoire.gouv.qc.ca

Conservatoire de musique de Québec
270, rue St-Amable, Québec, QC G1R 5G1, Canada
Tel: 418-643-2190; *Fax:* 418-644-9658
CMQ@conservatoire.gouv.qc.ca
Louis Dallaire, Directeur
louis.dallaire@conservatoire.gouv.qc.ca

Conservatoire de musique de Rimouski
22, rue Sainte-Marie, Rimouski, QC G5L 4E2, Canada
Tel: 418-727-3706; *Fax:* 418-727-3818
CMR@conservatoire.gouv.qc.ca
Benoît Plourde, Directeur
benoit.plourde@conservatoire.gouv.qc.ca

Conservatoire de musique de Trois-Rivières
587, rue Radisson, Trois-Rivières, QC G9A 2C8, Canada
Tel: 819-371-6748; *Fax:* 819-371-6955
CMT@conservatoire.gouv.qc.ca
Johanne Pothier, Directrice
johanne.pothier@conservatoire.gouv.qc.ca

Conservatoire de musique de Val-d'Or
88, rue Allard, Val-d'Or, QC J9P 2Y1, Canada
Tel: 819-354-4585; *Fax:* 819-354-4297
CMV@conservatoire.gouv.qc.ca
Jean Saint-Jules, Directeur
jean.st-jules@conservatoire.gouv.qc.ca

Conservatoire d'art dramatique de Montréal
4750, av Henri-Julien, 1e étage, Montréal, SK H2T 2C8, Canada
Tel: 514-873-4283; *Fax:* 514-864-2771
CADM@conservatoire.gouv.qc.ca
Benoit Dagenais, Directeur
benoit.dagenais@conservatoire.gouv.qc.ca

Conservatoire d'art dramatique de Québec
31, rue Mont-Carmel, Québec, QC G1R 4A6, Canada
Tel: 418-643-2139; *Fax:* 418-646-9255
CADQ@conservatoire.gouv.qc.ca
André Jean, Directeur
andre.jean@conservatoire.gouv.qc.ca

Cégep

Alma: Collège d'Alma
675, boul Auger ouest, Alma, QC G8B 2B7, Canada
Tél: 418-668-2387; *Téléc:* 418-668-7336
college@calma.qc.ca
www.calma.qc.ca
www.facebook.com/CollegedAlma
twitter.com/collegealma
www.youtube.com/user/CollegeAlma
Grades: Préuniv., Techniques, Form. cont.
Jean Paradis, Directeur générale

Publications
Le Majeur

Gatineau: Heritage College
325, boul Cité des Jeunes, Gatineau, QC J8Y 6T3, Canada
Tel: 819-778-2270; *Fax:* 819-778-7364
www.cegep-heritage.qc.ca
www.youtube.com/user/heritagecollegevideo
Full Time Equivalency: 1387 *Note:* Career Programs (Nursing; Early Childhood Ed.; New Media & Publication Design; Electronics; Computer Science); Pre-University Programs: Liberal Arts, Sciences, Commerce, Social Sciences, Visual Arts; Continuing Ed.: French as a Second Language; Distance Education; Corporate Training.
Louise Brunet, Director General
dg@cegep-heritage.qc.ca

Laval: Collège Montmorency
475, boul de l'Avenir, Laval, QC H7N 5H9, Canada
Tél: 450-975-6100; *Téléc:* 450-975-6116
www.cmontmorency.qc.ca
Denyse Blanchet, Directrice générale

Publications
Le Zèle

Lévis: Collège de Lévis
9, rue Monseigneur Gosselin, Lévis, QC G6V 5K1, Canada
Tél: 418-833-1249; *Téléc:* 418-833-1974
info@collegedelevis.qc.ca
www.collegedelevis.qc.ca
Grades: Sec.
Michelle Soucy, Directeur 1er cycle (1re et 2e secondaire)
msoucy@collegedelevis.qc.ca
Mélanie Champagne, Directrice de 2e cycle (3e, 4e et 5e secondaire)
mchampagne@collegedelevis.qc.ca

Publications
Le Script

Longueuil: Collège Édouard-Montpetit
945, ch de Chambly, Longueuil, QC J4H 3M6, Canada
Tél: 450-679-2631; *Téléc:* 450-679-5570
communications@college-em.qc.ca
www.college-em.qc.ca
www.facebook.com/CollegeEdouardM
twitter.com/collegeedouardm
Number of Employees: 1000
Serge Brasset, Directeur général

Publications
Le Motdit

Montréal: Collège Ahuntsic
9155, rue St-Hubert, Montréal, QC H2M 1Y8, Canada
Tél: 514-389-5921; *Téléc:* 514-389-5762
information@collegeahuntsic.qc.ca
www.collegeahuntsic.qc.ca
www.facebook.com/collegeahuntsic
twitter.com/CollegeAhuntsic
twitter.com/CollegeAhuntsic
Full Time Equivalency: 10100
Roch Tremblay, Directeur général

Publications
L'Attribut

Le Misanthrope

Montréal: Collège Dawson
3040, rue Sherbrooke ouest, Montréal, QC H3Z 1A4, Canada
Tél: 514-931-8731; *Téléc:* 514-931-5181
www.dawsoncollege.qc.ca
www.facebook.com/dawsoncollege
twitter.com/mydawsoncollege
Full Time Equivalency: 10000
Richard Filion, Director General
rfilion@dawsoncollege.qc.ca

Publications
Plant

Montréal: Collège de Bois-de-Boulogne
10555, av de Bois-de-Boulogne, Montréal, QC H4N 1L4, Canada
Tél: 514-332-3000; *Téléc:* 514-332-5857
info@bdeb.qc.ca
www.bdeb.qc.ca
www.facebook.com/college.de.bois.de.boulogne
twitter.com/CollegeBdeB
www.linkedin.com/company/coll-ge-de-bois-de-boulogne
Grades: Préuniv., Techniques, Form. cont.
Maurice Piché, Directeur général
maurice.piche@bdeb.qc.ca

Publications
L'Infomane

Montréal: Collège de Maisonneuve
3800, rue Sherbrooke est, Montréal, QC H1X 2A2, Canada
Tél: 514-254-7131; *Téléc:* 514-253-7637
communic@cmaisonneuve.qc.ca
www.cmaisonneuve.qc.ca
Grades: Préuniv., Techniques *Full Time Equivalency:* 3398
Pierre Harrison, Directeur général

Publications
Le Trait d'Union

Montréal: Collège de Rosemont
6400, 16e av, Montréal, QC H1X 2S9, Canada
Tél: 514-376-1620
www.crosemont.qc.ca
Patricia Hanigan, Directrice générale

Publications
République étudiante

Montréal: Collège Jean-de-Brébeuf inc.
3200, ch Côte Ste-Catherine, Montréal, QC H3T 1C1, Canada
Tél: 514-342-9342; *Téléc:* 514-342-6607
diradm@brebeuf.qc.ca
www.brebeuf.qc.ca
www.facebook.com/372651986136536
twitter.com/CollegeBrebeuf
www.youtube.com/user/collbrebeuf
Grades: Sec., Collégial
Michel April, Directeur générale

Publications
Le Grafitti

Saint-Laurent: Vanier College
821, av Ste-Croix, Saint-Laurent, QC H4L 3X9, Canada
Tel: 514-744-7500; *Fax:* 514-744-7505
info@vaniercollege.qc.ca
www.vaniercollege.qc.ca
www.facebook.com/pages/Vanier-College/164180234895
www.twitter.com/vaniercollege
www.linkedin.com/groups?mostPopular=&gid=3295473
www.youtube.com/user/vaniercollege
Full Time Equivalency: 6700 *Note:* An English Cégep.
Gilbert Héroux, Dir. gén.
dg@vaniercollege.qc.ca
Martine Gauthier, Dean
academicdean@vaniercollege.qc.ca

Faculties
Careers & Technical Programs
Michael Sendbuehler, Dean
sendbuem@vaniercollege.qc.ca
Science & General Studies
Eric Lozowy, Dean
lozowye@vaniercollege.qc.ca
Social Sciences, Commerce, Arts & Letters
Odette Côtè, Dean
coteo@vaniercollege.qc.ca

Publications
The Echo
Vanier Phoenix
The Vanier Vandoo

Sainte-Geneviève: Cégep Gérald-Godin
15615, boul Gouin ouest, Sainte-Geneviève, QC H9H 5K8, Canada
Tél: 514-626-2666; *Téléc:* 514-626-6866
information@cgodin.qc.ca
www.cgodin.qc.ca
www.facebook.com/cegepgeraldgodin
twitter.com/geraldgodin
Full Time Equivalency: 1200
Christian Roy, Directeur général
c.roy@cgodin.qc.ca

Sainte-Thérèse: Le Collège Lionel-Groulx
100, rue Duquet, Sainte-Thérèse, QC J7E 3G6, Canada
Tél: 450-430-3120; *Téléc:* 450-971-7883
info@clg.qc.ca
www.clg.qc.ca
www.facebook.com/collegelionelgroulx
twitter.com/clionelgroulx
Grades: Préuniv., Techniques, Form. cont. *Full Time Equivalency:* 4109
Monique Laurin, Directrice générale

Publications
L'Écorché

Salaberry-de-Valleyfield: Collège de Valleyfield
169, rue Champlain, Salaberry-de-Valleyfield, QC J6T 1X6, Canada
Tél: 450-373-9441; *Téléc:* 450-377-7719
courrier@colval.qc.ca
www.colval.qc.ca
Guy Laperrière, Directeur général

Publications
Pars ailleurs

Shawinigan: Collège Shawinigan
P.O. Box 610
2263, av du Collège, Shawinigan, QC G9N 6V8, Canada
Tél: 819-539-6401; *Téléc:* 819-539-8819
information@collegeshawinigan.qc.ca
www.collegeshawinigan.qc.ca
www.facebook.com/collegeshawinigan?ref=profile
Full Time Equivalency: 1500
Jean Lefebvre, Directeur général par intérim

Publications
Journal l'actif

Post Secondary/Technical

Post Secondary/Technical

Brossard: Academy of Arts & Design
Académie des arts et de design
7305, Marie-Victorin, 2e étage, Brossard, QC J4W 1A6, Canada
Tel: 514-875-9777; *Toll-Free:* 800-268-9777
www.aadmtl.com
Note: Fashion Design, Fashion Merchandising, Interior Design, Advertising & Web Design, Animation Design. Instruction in French & English.
Serge Landry, Directeur général

Drummondville: Collège Ellis
235, rue Moisan, Drummondville, QC J2C 1W9, Canada
Tél: 819-477-3113; *Téléc:* 819-477-4556
www.ellis.qc.ca
Note: Les installations du Pensionnat de Drummondville passent au Collège Ellis en 2006. Campus Trois-Rivières: 90, rue Dorval, (819) 691-2600.
Alain Scalzo, Directeur général

Montréal: Les Ateliers de danse moderne de Montréal
#211, 372, rue Ste-Catherine ouest, Montréal, QC H3B 1A2, Canada
Tél: 514-866-9814; *Téléc:* 514-866-5887
info@edcmtl.com
www.ladmmi.com
www.facebook.com/EcoleDeDanseContemporaineDeMontreal
twitter.com/edcmtl
Christine Bouchard, Directrice générale

Montréal: Collège André-Gasset
1001 Crémazie est, Montréal, QC H2M 1M3, Canada
Tél: 514-381-4293; *Téléc:* 514-381-7421
inform@grasset.qc.ca
www.grasset.qc.ca
www.facebook.com/CollegeAndreGrasset
Number of Employees: 75 professeurs; 40 l'enseignement technique; 60 personnel professionnel et administratif
Régent-Yves Desjardins, Président

Montréal: Collège d'enseignement en immobilier inc.
255, boul Crémazie est, Montréal, QC H2M 1M2, Canada
Tél: 514-905-1551; *Téléc:* 514-904-1453
info@enseignementimmobilier.com
www.enseignementimmobilier.com
www.facebook.com/CollegeCEI
Shirley Soulard, Directeur général

Montréal: Collège d'informatique Marsan
#400, boul de Pie-IX, Montréal, QC H1V 2C8, Canada
Tél: 514-525-3030; *Téléc:* 514-525-3314
info@collegemarsan.qc.ca
www.collegemarsan.qc.ca
www.facebook.com/pages/College-MARSAN/110908012260197
Carlos Richer, Directeur général

Montréal: Collège de photographie Marsan
1001, boul de Maisonneuve est, 9e étage, Montréal, QC H2L 4P9, Canada
Tél: 514-525-2352; *Téléc:* 514-525-3314
info@collegemarsan.qc.ca
www.collegemarsan.qc.ca
Michel Proulx, Directeur pédagogique photographie

Montréal: College Inter Dec
#8000, 2000, rue Sainte-Catherine ouest, Montréal, QC H3H 2T2
Tel: 514-939-4444; *Toll-Free:* 1-877-341-4445
interdec@collegeinterdec.com
www.collegeinterdec.com
Note: Founded in 1983, Inter-Dec College is associated with LaSalle International. Fields of study include beauty, interior design, & digital arts.

Montréal: Collège Jean-de-Brébeuf
3200, ch de la côte Ste-Catherine, Montréal, QC H3T 1C1
Tél: 514-342-9342
www.brebeuf.qc.ca
Michel April, Directeur général
dirgen@brebeuf.qc.ca
France Lavoie, Directrice des ressources financières
Jacques Lemaire, Directeur des études au collégial

Montréal: Collège LaSalle
Lasalle College
2000, rue Sainte-Catherine ouest, Montréal, QC H3H 2T2, Canada
Tél: 514-939-2006; *Téléc:* 514-939-2015
Ligne sans frais: 800-363-3541
admission@clasalle.com
www.lasallecollege.com
www.facebook.com/collegelasalle
twitter.com/LaSalleCollege
www.youtube.com/lasallecollege
Jacques Marchand, Directeur général

Montréal: Collège Salette
418, rue Sherbrooke est, 3e étage, Montréal, QC H2L 1J6
Tél: 514-388-5725; *Téléc:* 514-388-5957
info@collegesalette.qc.ca
www.collegesalette.qc.ca
Note: Established in 1942, Collège Salette is a design school that offers programs in graphic design, web design & interactive media, & illustration advertising.

Montréal: L'École du Show-Business (ESB)
7093. av du Parc, Montréal, QC H3N 1X7
Tél: 514-271-2244; *Ligne sans frais:* 1-877-271-2244
info@ecoledushowbusiness.com
www.ecoledushowbusiness.com
twitter.com/EcoleShowBizz
www.youtube.com/user/EcoleShowBizz#p/u
Note: Since 1999, the school has taught theatre trades. Programs include writing techniques, the production of advertising, scenography & set design, production of stage costumes, organizing an event, production techniques for cultural & corporate events, management of film & stage sets, web design techniques, & marketing & export of a product or service.

Montréal: École nationale de cirque
National Circus School
8181, 2e av, Montréal, QC H1Z 4N9, Canada
Tél: 514-982-0859; *Téléc:* 514-982-6025
Ligne sans frais: 8002670859
info@enc.qc.ca
www.enc.qc.ca
Marc Lalonde, Directeur général

Montréal: École nationale de l'humour
2120, rue Sherbrooke est, 7e étage, Montréal, QC H2K 1C3, Canada
Tél: 514-849-7876; *Téléc:* 514-849-3307
humour@enh.qc.ca
www.enh.qc.ca
Note: Formation professionnelle aux humoristes & aux auteurs. Reconnue par le Min. de l'Éducation, du Loisir & du Sport du Québec.
Louise Richer, Directrice générale

Montréal: L'École supérieure de ballet du Québec
4816, rue Rivard, Montréal, QC H2J 2N6
Tél: 514-849-4929; *Téléc:* 514-849-6107
info@esbq.ca
www.esbq.ca
www.facebook.com/ecolesuperieuredeballetduquebec
twitter.com/ecole_sup
Alix Laurent, Directeur général, 514-849-4929, ext. 224
Anik Bissonnette, Directrice artistique, 514-849-4929, ext. 221
Beverley Aitchison, Directrice associée aux programmes de formation, 514-849-4929, ext. 223
Claudine Balaux, Registraire et responsable, vie étudiante, 514-849-4929, ext. 225
Lili Marin, Responsable, communications et marketinge, 514-849-4929, ext. 249

Montréal: Herzing College
www.herzing.ca
Note: Information technology programs (programming, networking, database management & microprocessor technology), healthcare & legal.

Winnipeg Campus
723 Portage Ave., Winnipeg, MB R3G 0M8, Canada
Tel: 204-775-8175; *Fax:* 204-783-8107
info@wpg.herzing.edu
Bill Riches, President

Campuses
Montréal Campus
1616, boul René-Lévesque ouest, Montréal, QC H3H 1P8
Tél: 450-686-7494; *Téléc:* 450-933-6182
Ligne sans frais: 800-818-9688
info@mtl.herzing.edu
www.herzing.ca/montreal
www.facebook.com/herzingmontreal
Note: Founded in 1968, Herzing College Montreal prepares studens for careers in business, technology, & design.
Hayat Telmat Drinali, Campus President

Toronto Campus
Eaton Centre Galleria Offices
#202, 220 Yonge St., Toronto, ON M5B 2H1, Canada
Tel: 416-599-6996; *Fax:* 416-599-0192
info@tor.herzing.edu
www.facebook.com/herzingtoronto
George Hood, Campus President

Ottawa Campus
P.O. Box 225
1200. boul St. Laurent, Ottawa, ON K1K 3B8
Tel: 613-742-8099; *Fax:* 613-742-8336
info@otw.herzing.edu
www.facebook.com/herzingottawa
Michael McAllister, Campus President

***Montréal:* Institut supérieur d'informatique (ISI)**
#100, 255, boul Crémazie est, Montréal, QC H2M 1M2
Tél: 514-842-2426; *Téléc:* 514-842-2084
info@isi-mtl.com
www.isi-mtl.com
www.facebook.com/isimtl
twitter.com/isimtl
www.youtube.com/user/isimtl
Note: Training is offered in networks & telecommunications, programming & internet technologies, integration of information systems, integration of websites, & IP telphony.

***Montréal:* Institut Teccart**
3030, rue Hochelaga, Montréal, QC H1W 1G2
Tel: 514-526-2501; *Fax:* 514-526-9192
Toll-Free: 1-866-832-2278
www.teccart.qc.ca
Note: Programs are offered inthe areas of arts, design, & technology.

***Montréal:* The International College of Spiritual & Psychic Sciences**
P.O. Box 1387 H
1974, boul de Maisonneuve ouest, Montréal, QC H3G 2N3, Canada
Tél: 514-937-8359; *Téléc:* 514-937-5380
info@iiihs.org
www.iiihs.org
Dr. Marilyn Zwaig Rossner, Ph.D., Dean
mrossner@iiihs.org

***Montréal:* National Theatre School of Canada (NTS) École nationale de théâtre du Canada**
5030, rue St-Denis, Montréal, QC H2J 2L8, Canada
Tel: 514-842-7954; *Fax:* 514-842-5661
Toll-Free: 1-866-547-732
info@ent-nts.ca
www.ent-nts.qc.ca
www.facebook.com/entnts.montreal
www.youtube.com/user/ENTNTSMontreal
Enrollment: 160 *Number of Employees:* 25 *Note:* Offers training in acting, playwriting, directing, set & costume design & technical production in both English & French.
Simon Brault, O.C., Chief Executive Officer
Irena Malyholowka, Director, Communications
irenam@ent-nts.ca

***Montréal:* Trebas Institute Institut Trebas**
#600, 550, rue Sherbrooke ouest, Montréal, QC H3A 1B9, Canada
Tel: 514-845-4141; *Fax:* 514-845-2581
Toll-Free: 866-587-3227
infomtl@trebas.com
www.trebas.com
Enrollment: 300
David P. Leonard, Président
Martin Morissette, Directeur les études

Campuses
Toronto
2340 Dundas St. West, 2nd Fl., Toronto, ON M6P 4A9, Canada
Tel: 416-966-3066; *Fax:* 416-966-0030
info@trebas.com
www.trebas.com
Enrollment: 300 *Note:* Audio Engineering & Production/DJ Arts, Entertainment Management, Film/Television Production
Peter Di Santo, Director

***Outremont:* École de Musique Vincent d'Indy**
628, ch Côte Ste-Catherine, Outremont, QC H2V 2C5, Canada
Tél: 514-735-5261; *Téléc:* 514-735-5266
info@isdm-mode.com
www.emvi.qc.ca
Yves Petit, Directrice générale

***Québec:* Collège Mérici**
755, Grande Allée ouest, Québec, QC G1S 1C1, Canada
Tél: 418-683-1591; *Téléc:* 418-682-8938
Ligne sans frais: 800-208-1463
information@college-merici.qc.ca
merici.ca
www.facebook.com/collegemerici
twitter.com/CollegeMerici
Enrollment: 1200 *Note:* Le Collège Mérici est un établissement d'enseignement collégial privé accueillant environ 1200 étudiants.
Nicole Blodeau, Directeur général

***Québec:* Collège radio télévision de Québec inc.**
751, côte d'Abraham, Québec, QC G1R 1A2, Canada
Tél: 418-647-2095; *Téléc:* 418-522-5456
info@crtq.net
www.crtq.net
Christian Lavoie, Dir.

***Québec:* L'École de danse de Québec**
Centre de production artistique et culturelle Aly
#214, 310, boul Langelier, Québec, QC G1K 5N3
Tél: 418-649-4715; *Téléc:* 418-649-4702
reception@ledq.qc.ca; secteurprofessionnel@ledq.qc.ca
www.ledq.qc.ca
Steve Huot, Directeur général, 418-649-4715
shuot@ledq.qc.ca
Lyne Binette, Directrice de la formation professionnelle, 418-649-4715, ext. 225
lbinette@ledq.qc.ca
Joëlle Turcotte, Directrice de l'école loisir, 418-649-4715, ext. 230
jturcotte@ledq.qc.ca
Natalie Lavallée, Responsable des communications, 418-649-4715, ext. 222
nlavallee@ledq.qc.ca
Jean-Pierre Parent, Responsable des services financiers, 418-649-4715, ext. 224
jpparent@ledq.qc.ca

***Saint-Hubert:* Académie de l'Entrepreneurship Québécois inc.**
4619, rue de Niverville, Saint-Hubert, QC J3Y 9G6, Canada
Tél: 450-676-5826; *Téléc:* 450-676-2261
Ligne sans frais: 888-676-5826
info@academieentrepreneurship.com
www.academieentrepreneurship.com
Johanne Bouchard

***Trois-Rivières:* Collège Laflèche**
1687, boul du Carmel, Trois-Rivières, QC G8Z 3R8, Canada
Tél: 819-375-7346; *Téléc:* 819-375-7347
college@clafleche.qc.ca
www.clafleche.qc.ca
Note: Le seul établissement collégial privé en Mauricie et au Centre-du-Québec à offrir à la fois des programmes préuniversitaires et techniques.
Julie Anne Trottier, Directeur général

***Verdun:* Collège de l'immobilier du Québec**
600, ch du Golf, Verdun, QC H3E 1A8, Canada
Tél: 514-762-1862; *Téléc:* 514-762-4975
francine.forget@cigm.qc.ca
www.collegeimmobilier.com
Francine Forget, Directrice générale

***Ville Mont-Royal:* Collège Technique de Montréal**
#204, 5490 Royalmount, Ville Mont-Royal, QC H4P 1H7, Canada
Tél: 514-932-6444; *Téléc:* 514-932-6448
info@mtccollege.com
www.mtccollege.com

***Westmount:* International Career School Canada ICS Canada**
#610, 245 Victoria Ave., Westmount, QC H3Z 2M6, Canada
Tel: 514-482-6951; *Fax:* 514-482-6868
Toll-Free: 1-888-427-2400
info@icslearn.ca
www.icslearn.ca
Enrollment: 12875 *Note:* At-home training in 50 career fields.
Connie C. Dempsey, Chief Academic Officer

***Westmount:* Marianopolis College**
4873, ave Westmount, Westmount, QC H3Y 1K9, Canada
Tel: 514-931-8792; *Fax:* 514-931-8790
admissions@marianopolis.edu
www.marianopolis.edu
Len Even, Director General
DGsOffice@marianopolis.edu

Publications
The Papercut
students.marianopolis.edu/papercut
Note: "The Papercut" is an independent newspaper published monthly by student volunteers at Marianopolis College. Founded in 1974 and published on a monthly basis.

Saskatchewan

Government Agencies

***Regina:* Saskatchewan Advanced Education & Employment**
2220 College Ave., Regina, SK S4P 4V9, Canada
Tel: 306-787-6030; *Fax:* 306-798-2045
Toll-Free: 1-888-775-327
www.aee.gov.sk.ca

***Regina:* Saskatchewan Education**
Communciations Branch
2220 College Ave., 5th Fl., Regina, SK S4P 4V9, Canada
Tel: 306-787-5589; *Fax:* 306-798-2045
linquir@gov.sk.ca
www.education.gov.sk.ca
Hon. Russ Marchuk, Minister, 306-787-7360, fax: 306-798-0263
minister.edu@gov.sk.ca

Campuses
Southern Region
1831 College Ave., 3rd Fl., Regina, SK S4P 4V5, Canada
Tel: 306-787-6075; *Fax:* 306-787-6139
Boris Okrainetz, Regional Director

Central Region
112 - 3rd Ave. North, 8th Fl., Saskatoon, SK S7K 2H6, Canada
Tel: 306-933-5028; *Fax:* 306-933-7469
Patricia Kovacs, Regional Director

Northern Region
P.O. Box 5000
La Ronge, SK S0J 1L0, Canada
Tel: 306-425-4382; *Fax:* 306-425-4383
Daryl Arnott, Regional Director

School Boards/Districts/Divisions

Public

***Creighton:* Creighton School Division #111**
P.O. Box 158
325 Main St., Creighton, SK S0P 0A0, Canada
Tel: 306-688-5138; *Fax:* 306-688-5740
creightonschool.com
Enrollment: 394
Bob Smith, Director
Shirley Owen, Sec.-Treas.

***Englefeld:* Engelfeld Protestant Separate School Division #132**
P.O. Box 100
Englefeld, SK S0K 1N0, Canada
Tel: 306-287-3568; *Fax:* 306-287-3569
www.englefeld.ca
Enrollment: 107
Jim Martin, Sec.-Treas.
Harvey Bowers, Dir.

***Ile-a-la-Crosse:* Ile a la Crosse School Division #112**
P.O. Box 89
Ile-a-la-Crosse, SK S0M 1C0, Canada
Tel: 306-833-2141; *Fax:* 306-833-2104
Enrollment: 469
Christine Arnett, Sec.-Treas.
carnett@icsd.ca
Lon Borgerson, Director, Education
lborgerson@icsd.ca

***La Ronge:* Northern Lights School Division #113**
Bag Service #6500, La Ronge, SK S0J 1L0, Canada
Tel: 306-425-3302; *Fax:* 306-425-3377
centraloffice@nlsd113.net
www.nlsd113.com
Grades: K.-12 *Enrollment:* 4168
Ralph Pilz, Dir.
ralphpilz@nlsd113.net
Charlie McCloud, Sec.-Treas.
charliemccloud@nlsd113.net
Julius Park, First Nations/Metis Education Consultant
juliuspark@nlsd113.net

***Langian:* Horizon School Division #205**
P.O. Box 100
110 main st., Langian, SK S0K 2M0, Canada
Tel: 306-365-4888; *Fax:* 306-365-2808
Toll-Free: 877-365-4888
www.hzsd.ca
Enrollment: 6992
Marc Danylchuk, Director, Education
Philip Benson, Sec.-Treas.

Melfort: North East School Division #200
P.O. Box 6000
402 Main St., Melfort, SK S0E 1A0, Canada
Tel: 306-752-5741; *Fax:* 306-752-1933
Toll-Free: 888-752-5741
www.nesd.ca

Grades: Pre-K.-12 *Enrollment:* 5317
Don Rempel, Dir.
Ralph Paquin, Supt. of Bus. Admin., 306-752-1211, fax: 306-752-4580

Melville: St. Henry's Roman Catholic Separate School Division #5
P.O. Box 1930
633 Main St., Melville, SK S0A 2P0, Canada
Tel: 306-728-4426; *Fax:* 306-728-2351
Enrollment: 309 *Note:* This division amalgamated with Yorkton RCSSD #86, St. Theodore RCSSD #138 Melville Rural RCSSD #217 and Yorkton Rural RCSSD #216 to form the new Christ the Teacher Roman Catholic Separate School Division #212.
Brian Boechler, Dir.
Wilfred Hotsko, Sec.-Treas.

Moose Jaw: Holy Trinity Roman Catholic Separate School Division #22
P.O. Box 1087
502 - 6 Ave. NE, Moose Jaw, SK S6H 4P8, Canada
Tel: 306-694-5333; *Fax:* 306-692-2238
www.htcsd.ca

Enrollment: 2080
Celeste York, Director, Education
Gerry Gieni, Sec.-Treas.

Moose Jaw: Prairie South School Division #210
15 Thatcher Dr. East, Moose Jaw, SK S6J 1L8, Canada
Tel: 306-694-1200; *Fax:* 306-694-4955
Toll-Free: 877-434-1200
www.prairiesouth.ca

Enrollment: 6931
Brenda Edwards, Director, Education
Gordon Stewart, Chair

North Battleford: Living Sky School Division #202
509 Pioneer Ave., North Battleford, SK S9A 4A5, Canada
Tel: 306-937-7702; *Fax:* 306-445-4332
office@lskysd.ca
www.lskysd.ca
www.facebook.com/lskysd
twitter.com/SD202

Grades: K.-12 *Enrollment:* 5550
Randy Fox, Director of Education, 306-937-7930
randy.fox@lskysd.ca
Lonny Darroch, Chief Financial Officer, 306-937-7924
lonny.darroch@lskysd.ca

North Battleford: North West Roman Catholic Separate School Division #16
9301 - 19 Ave., North Battleford, SK S9A 3N5, Canada
Tel: 306-445-6158; *Fax:* 306-445-3993
loccsd@loccsd.ca
www.loccsd.ca

Grades: Pre-K.-12 *Enrollment:* 1968 *Note:* This school division is an amalgamation of 4 boards: North Battleford RCSSD#16, Wilkie St. George RCSSD#85, Unity RCSSD#88 and Spiritwood RCSSD#82.
Herb Sutton, Dir.
h.sutton@loccsd.ca
Guy Denton, Supt. of Admin.
g.denton@loccsd.ca

Prince Albert: Prince Albert Roman Catholic Separate School Division #6
118 - 11 St. East, Prince Albert, SK S6V 1A1, Canada
Tel: 306-953-7500; *Fax:* 306-763-1723
info@cec.pacsd6.sk.ca
www.pacsd6.sk.ca

Enrollment: 3121
Tim Jelinski, Director, Education
Don Orr, Sec.-Treas.

Prince Albert: Saskatchewan Rivers School Division #119
545 - 11 St. East, Prince Albert, SK S6V 1B1, Canada
Tel: 306-764-1571; *Fax:* 306-763-4460
www.srsd119.ca

Enrollment: 9200
Robert Bratvold, Director, Education
Dennis Moniuk, Superintendent, Business Administration

Regina: Division scolaire francophone #310
#200, 3850 Hillsdale St., Regina, SK S4S 7J5, Canada
Tel: 306-757-7541; *Fax:* 306-757-2040
dsf.regina@dsf.sk.ca

Enrollment: 1095
Denis Ferré, Dir.
Lise Gareau, Sec.-Treas.

Regina: Prairie Valley School Division #208
P.O. Box 1937
3080 Albert St. North, Regina, SK S4P 3E1, Canada
Tel: 306-949-3366; *Fax:* 306-543-1771
reception@pvsd.ca
www.pvsd.ca

Enrollment: 8292
Ben J. Grebinski, Director
Michael Back, Sec.-Treas.

Regina: Regina Roman Catholic Separate School Division #81
2160 Cameron St., Regina, SK S4T 2V6, Canada
Tel: 306-791-7200; *Fax:* 306-347-7699
rcs@rcs.sk.ca
www.rcsd.ca

Grades: K-12 *Enrollment:* 10000
Gwen Keith, Director
Curt Van Parys, Sec.-Treas.

Regina: Regina School Division #4
1600 - 4 Ave., Regina, SK S4R 8C8, Canada
Tel: 306-523-3000; *Fax:* 306-532-3031
info@rbe.sk.ca
www.rbe.sk.ca

Enrollment: 20678
Don Hoium, Director
Debra Burnett, Sec.-Treas.

Rosetown: Sun West School Division #207
P.O. Box 700
Rosetown, SK S0L 2V0, Canada
Tel: 306-882-2677; *Fax:* 306-882-3366
Toll-Free: 1-866-375-2677
info@sunwestsd.ca
www.sunwestsd.ca

Number of Schools: 14 kindergarten to grade 12 schools; 15 Hutterite colony schools; 7 elem.; 3 sec.; 1 distance ed *Grades:* Kindergarten - 12 *Enrollment:* 4500
Guy G. Tétrault, Director, Education
Tony Baldwin, Superintendent, Education
Shari Martin, Superintendent, Education
Tracy Dollansky, Superintendent, Education
Shelley Hengen, Superintendent, Education
Ryan Smith, Superintendent, Business
Roxan Foursha, Officer, Communications
Janine Walker, Officer, Human Resources
Doug Klassen, Supervisor, Technology
Earl McKnight, Supervisor, Transportation
Rob Minion, Supervisor, Facilities
Rhonda Saathoff, Supervisor, Business

Saskatoon: Greater Saskatoon Catholic Schools
420 - 22nd St. East, Saskatoon, SK S7K 1X3, Canada
Tel: 306-659-7000
info@gscs.sk.ca
www.scs.sk.ca
Other Information: Learning Services, Phone: 306-659-2010; HR Services: 306-659-2012

Number of Schools: 37 elementary schools; 6 secondary schools; 2 associate schools *Grades:* K-12; French, Cree, & Ukrainian *Enrollment:* 15000 *Number of Employees:* 1900+ *Note:* Co-manager of Humboldt Collegiate Institute, with Horizon School Division
Diane Boyko, Board Chair, 306-382-2832
DLBoyko@gscs.sk.ca
Beverley Hanson, Director, Education, 306-659-7001
Darryl Bazylak, Superintendent, Education, 306-659-7040
Al Boutin, Superintendent, Human Resource Services, 306-659-7048
Greg Chatlain, Superintendent, Education, 306-659-7090
Dr. Donald Lloyd, Superintendent, Administrative Services, 306-659-7021
Gordon Martell, Superintendent, Education, 306-659-7056
John McAuliffe, Superintendent, Education, 306-659-7044
Joanne Weninger, Superintendent, Education, 306-659-7041
Donella Hoffman, Consultant, Communications, 306-659-7077
dhoffman@gscs.sk.ca

Saskatoon: Saskatoon School Division #13
310 - 21st St. East, Saskatoon, SK S7K 1M7, Canada
Tel: 306-683-8200; *Fax:* 306-657-3900
totht@spsd.sk.ca
www.spsd.sk.ca

Enrollment: 20000
George Rathwell, Director, Education
Garry Benning, Chief Financial Officer

Swift Current: Chinook School Division No. 211
P.O. Box 1809
2100 Gladstone St. E, Swift Current, SK S9H 4J8, Canada
Tel: 306-778-9200; *Fax:* 306-773-8011
Toll-Free: 1-877-321-9200
info@chinooksd.ca
www.chinooksd.ca

Number of Schools: 59 schools *Enrollment:* 6200 *Number of Employees:* 1125 teachers and administrative staff
Randy Beler, Chair
Liam Choo-Foo, Director of Education
Rod Quintin, Sec.-Treas.

Turtleford: Northwest School Division #203
P.O. Box 280
Turtleford, SK S0M 2Y0, Canada
Tel: 306-845-2150; *Fax:* 306-845-3392
www.nwsd.ca

Enrollment: 4910
Glen Winkler, Director, Education
Greg Gerwing, Sec.-Treas.

Viscount: St. Alphonse Roman Catholic Separate School Division #2
P.O. Box 71
Viscount, SK S0K 4M0, Canada
Tel: 306-944-4446; *Fax:* 306-944-4446

Enrollment: 21
Joseph Kammermayer, Dir.
Mary Comeault, Sec.-Treas.

Warman: Prairie Spirit School Division #206
P.O. Box 809
121 Klassen St. East, Warman, SK S0K 4S0, Canada
Tel: 306-683-2800; *Fax:* 306-934-8221
www.spiritsd.ca

Enrollment: 8787
Evelyn Novak, Director, Education
Jim Shields, Superintendent

Weyburn: Holy Family R.C.S.S.D. #140
110 Souris Ave., 3rd Fl., Weyburn, SK S4H 2Z8, Canada
Tel: 306-842-7025; *Fax:* 306-842-7033
www.holyfamilyrcssd.ca

Enrollment: 981
Shelley Rowein, Director, Education
Bruno Tuchscherer, Chair

Weyburn: South East Cornerstone School Division #209
80A - 18 St. NE, Weyburn, SK S4H 2W4, Canada
Tel: 306-848-0080; *Fax:* 306-848-4747
Toll-Free: 888-938-0080
contactus@cornerstonesd.ca
www.cornerstonesd.ca

Enrollment: 7862
Marc Casavant, Director, Education
Lionel Diederichs, Chief Financial Officer

Yorkton: Christ the Teacher Roman Catholic Separate School Division No. 212
45A Palliser Way, Yorkton, SK S3N 4C5, Canada
Tel: 306-783-8787; *Fax:* 306-783-4992
www.christtheteacher.ca
Grades: Pre-K.-12 *Enrollment:* 1800 *Note:* This division is an amalgamation of St. Henry's RCSSD #5, Yorkton RCSSD #86, St. Theodore RCSSD #138, Melville Rural RCSSD #217 and Yorkton Rural RCSSD #216.
Angie Rogalski, Chair
Darrell Zaba, Director
Wilfred Hotsko, Sec.-Treas.

Yorkton: Good Spirit School Division #204
Fairview Education Centre
63 King St. East, Yorkton, SK S3N 0T7, Canada
Tel: 306-786-5500; *Fax:* 306-783-0355
Toll-Free: 1-866-390-0773
feedback@mail.gssd.ca
www.gssd.ca
Other Information: GSSD Distance Learning Center, Toll-Free Phone: 1-877-988-1122

Number of Schools: 28 *Grades:* Junior Kindergarten - 12 *Enrollment:* 5935
Raymond Sass, Chair
Dwayne Reeve, Director, Education
Juanita Brown, Superintendent, Instruction & Learning
Susan Maserek, Superintendent, Schools
Quintin Robertson, Superintendent, Student Services
Alan Sharp, Superintendent, Program Development
Sherry Todosichuk, Superintendent, Business Administration

Protestant

***Englefeld:* Englefeld Protestant Separate School District #132**
Englefeld School
P.O. Box 100
Englefeld, SK S0K 1N0, Canada
Tel: 306-287-3568; *Fax:* 306-287-3569
www.englefeld.ca/School
Carol Sommer, President, Englefeld School Community Council

Schools: Specialized

Special Education

***Pilot Butte:* Ranch Ehrio Society**
P.O. Box 570
Pilot Butte, SK S0G 3Z0, Canada
Tel: 306-781-1800; *Fax:* 306-757-0599
inquiries@ranchehrlo.ca
www.ehrlo.com
www.facebook.com/RanchEhrlo
Grades: K.-12 *Enrollment:* 192 *Note:* The Ranch is a residental school for children, youth, and young adults, who are experiencing social, psychological, mental, psychiatric, and/or physical disabilities, through the provision of holistic, psycho-social therapies.
Marion MacIver, President

Buckland Campus
P.O. Box 1892
Prince Albert, SK S6V 6J9, Canada
Tel: 306-764-4511; *Fax:* 306-764-0042

Campuses
Corman Park Campus
P.O. Box 500
Martensville, SK S0K 2T0, Canada
Tel: 306-659-3100; *Fax:* 306-956-2570

***Regina:* Cornwall Alternative School**
40 Dixon Cres., Regina, SK S4N 1V4, Canada
Tel: 306-522-0044; *Fax:* 306-359-0720
Grades: 7-10 *Enrollment:* 39
Eunice Cameron, Principal

***Saskatoon:* Radius Community Centre for Education & Employment**
P.O. Box 1812
611 - 1st Ave. North, Bay 1, Saskatoon, SK S7K 1X7, Canada
Tel: 306-665-0362; *Fax:* 306-665-5579
info@radiuscentre.com
www.radiuscentre.com
Gail McKenzie-Wilcox, Principal

Schools: Independent & Private

Independent & Private Schools

***Battleford:* Heritage Christian School**
P.O. Box 490
11 - 20th St. West, Battleford, SK S0M 0E0, Canada
Tel: 306-446-3188; *Fax:* 306-446-3187
heritage@lskysd.ca
www.heritagechristianschool.lskysd.ca
Grades: K.-12; Days only *Enrollment:* 59
Jeremy Verity, Principal

***Caronport:* Caronport High School (CHS)**
c/o Briercrest College & Seminary
510 College Dr., Caronport, SK S0H 0S0, Canada
Tel: 306-756-3200
info@briercrest.ca
www.briercrest.ca/chs
Grades: 9 - 12
Deborah Ike, Principal
deborahi@briercrest.ca
David Frostad, Vice Principal
dfrostad@briercrest.ca
George Willatt, Vice Principal
gwillatt@briercrest.ca
Vi Thiessen, Office Administrator
vthiessen@briercrest.ca

***Moose Jaw:* Cornerstone Christian School (CCS)**
43 Iroquois St. East, Moose Jaw, SK S6H 4S9
Tel: 306-693-2937; *Fax:* 306-694-1880
office@ccsmj.ca
www.ccsmj.ca
www.facebook.com/CornerstoneChristianSchoolAlumni
Grades: Kindergarten - 12 *Note:* The school is recognized by the Government of Saskatchewan as an Associate School. It is responsible to the local public school, the Prairie South School Division #210.
Ashley Taylor, Board Chair

***Outlook:* Lutheran Collegiate Bible Institute**
P.O. Box 459
Outlook, SK S0L 2N0, Canada
Tel: 306-867-8971; *Fax:* 306-867-9947
office@lcbi.sk.ca
www.lcbi.sk.ca
www.facebook.com/pages/LCBI-High-School/10150089137100296
twitter.com/LCBINews
Grades: 10-12; Residential only
Philip Guebert, Principal

***Pilot Butte:* Schaller School**
P.O. Box 570
Pilot Butte, SK S0G 3Z0, Canada
Tel: 306-781-1838; *Fax:* 306-757-0599
Grades: K.-12 *Enrollment:* 190
Marion MacIver, Principal

***Prince Albert:* Rivier Academy**
1405 Bishop Pascal Pl., Prince Albert, SK S6V 5J1, Canada
Tel: 306-764-6289; *Fax:* 306-763-1442
rivier.academy_rivier@sasksschools.ca
www.sasksschools.ca/~rivier
Grades: 7 - 12 *Note:* An associate school of the Prince Albert Roman Catholic School Division 6, Rivier Academy is an independent, Catholic high school for young women. It provides a full course, as prescribed by Saskatchewan Learning.
Sr. Mary Woodward, Principal
Claude Jalbert, Vice Principal

***Regina:* Harvest City Christian Academy**
Harvest City Church
2202 - 8th Ave. North, Regina, SK S4R 7T9, Canada
Tel: 306-569-1935; *Fax:* 306-359-9047
hcc.office@harvestcity.sk.ca
www.harvestcity.sk.ca
Grades: K.-12 (Non-Denom.); Day only *Enrollment:* 172
Todd Harrison, Principal

***Regina:* Luther College High School**
1500 Royal St., Regina, SK S4T 5A5, Canada
Tel: 306-791-9150
www.facebook.com/LCHSRegina
Grades: 9-12
Brian Hills, Principal
bryan.hillis@luthercollege.edu

***Regina:* Regina Christian School (RCS)**
2505 - 23rd Ave., Regina, SK S4S 7K7, Canada
Tel: 306-775-0919; *Fax:* 306-775-3070
office@reginachristianschool.org
www.reginachristianschool.org
Other Information: development@reginachristianschool.org (E-mail, Development)
Grades: Preschool - 12 *Enrollment:* 504 *Note:* The interdenominational school's academic program is offered with an evangelical Christian view.
Darryl Brown, Board Chair
Rod Rilling, B.Ed., B.A. (Hons), Principal
principal@reginachristianschool.org
Krista Munson, B.Ed., B.A., Vice Principal
krista.munson@rbe.sk.ca
Doreen Brace, B.Ed., Learning Leader & Resource Teacher
doreen.brace@rbe.sk.ca

***Regina:* Regina Huda School**
40 Sheppard St., Regina, SK S4R 3M6, Canada
Tel: 306-565-1988
www.hudaschool.regina.sk.ca
Grades: Preschool - 12 *Note:* Regina Huda School strives to preserve the Islamic identity, by offering Islamic & Arabic studies for the Muslim community.
Dr. Ayman Aboguddah, Board President
aboguddah@gmail.com
Twila Wilson, Principal
twila.wilson@rbe.sk.ca
Diane Szabo, School Secretary
secretary@hudaschool.regina.sk.ca

***Rosthern:* Rosthern Junior College**
410 - 6th Ave., Rosthern, SK S0K 3R0, Canada
Tel: 306-232-4222; *Fax:* 306-232-5250
office@rjc.sk.ca
www.rjc.sk.ca
Grades: 10 - 12 *Note:* The Christian secondary school operates within a Mennonite school community, for students of any faith. Completion of enriched courses leads to a Saskatchewan senior matriculation.
Gail Schellenberg, Principal
Lloyd Schmidt, Academic Coordinator
Holly Epp, Dean, Women
Matt Love, Dean, Men
Kathy Powley, Dean, Women
Graeme Rinholm, Dean, Men
Dave Feick, Contact, Admissions & Relations
Dave Feick, Contact, Admissions

***Saskatoon:* Christian Centre Academy (CCA)**
102 Pinehouse Dr., Saskatoon, SK S7K 5H7, Canada
Tel: 306-242-7141
academy@christiancentre.ca
www.christiancentre.ca/academy
Grades: Kindergarten - 12 *Note:* The Accelerated Christian Education curriculum is used from kindergarten to grade 9 at the Christian Centre Academy. From grade 10 to 12, Saskatchewan Association of Independent Church Schools materials are used.

***Saskatoon:* Saskatoon Christian School**
Site 510, Box 8, RR#5, Saskatoon, SK S7K 3J8, Canada
Tel: 306-343-1494; *Fax:* 306-343-0366
ssce@saskatoonchristianschool.ca
www.saskatoonchristianschool.ca
Grades: K.-12; Day only
Doug Wiebe, Principal
wiebedo@spsd.sk.ca

***Wilcox:* Athol Murray College of Notre Dame**
P.O. Box 100
49 Main St., Wilcox, SK S0G 5E0, Canada
Tel: 306-732-2080; *Fax:* 306-732-4409
info@notredame.ca
www.notredame.sk.ca
Grades: 9-12 *Enrollment:* 350 *Note:* Athol Murray College of Notre Dame is an international coeducational & residential college preparatory school. It is dedicated to Catholic Christian education.
Rob Palmarin, B.Ed., M.Th., President, 306-732-1230
Bob Baumuller, B.Ed., Director, Student Services, 306-732-1221
Dave Kenney, B.A., M.Ed., Director, Admissions, MarComm, & Alumni Relations, 306-732-2080, ext. 221
Hugh Lambert, B.Ed, B.Sc., Director, Academics, 306-732-2080, ext. 143

Universities & Colleges

Universities

***Caronport:* Briercrest College & Seminary**
510 College Dr., Caronport, SK S0H 0S0, Canada
Tel: 306-756-3200; *Fax:* 306-756-5500
Toll-Free: 800-667-5199
info@briercrest.ca
www.briercrest.ca
Full Time Equivalency: 640 *Note:* The institution also operates the Caronport High School.

***Regina:* Campion College**
University of Regina
3737 Wascana Pkwy., Regina, SK S4S 0A2, Canada
Tel: 306-586-4242; *Fax:* 306-359-1200
Toll-Free: 800-667-7282
campion.college@uregina.ca
www.campioncollege.sk.ca
Full Time Equivalency: 1000

***Regina:* First Nations University of Canada**
1 First Nations Way, Regina, SK S4S 7K2, Canada
Tel: 306-790-5950; *Fax:* 306-790-5999
www.firstnationsuniversity.ca
Full Time Equivalency: 760

***Regina:* Luther College**
University of Regina Campus
Regina, SK S4S 0A2, Canada
Tel: 306-585-5333; *Fax:* 306-585-2949
Toll-Free: 800-588-4378
www.luthercollege.edu
Full Time Equivalency: 1000 *Note:* While administratively independent, Luther is academically integrated with the University of Regina.

***Regina:* The University of Regina**
3737 Wascana Pkwy., Regina, SK S4S 0A2, Canada
Tel: 306-585-4402; *Fax:* 306-585-4997
communications@uregina.ca
www.uregina.ca
Full Time Equivalency: 11554
Lt. Gov. The Ho L.M. Haverstock, Visitor
Garth Fredrickson, Chairman
William F. Ready, Chancellor

Dr. Vianne Timmins, B.A., B.Ed., M.Ed., Ph.D., President & Vice-Chancellor
Dr. Gary Boire, Ph.D., Vice-President
Dave Button, M.Sc., P.Eng., P.M.P., Vice-President
Annette Revet, B.Sc.(Hons.), MBA, University Secretary
Barbara Pollock, B.A., B.Ed., Vice-President
Bev Liski, Registrar
Dr. Lynn Wells, B.A. (Hons.), M.A., Ph.D., Assoc. Vice-President
John D. Smith, Assoc. Vice-President
Allan Cahoon, B.A., M.Sc., Ph.D., Vice-President
Kelly Kummerfield, B.Admin., Assoc. Vice-President
Nelson Wagner, Assoc. Vice-President
Dale Schoffer, Assoc. Vice-President

Faculties
Arts
Dr. Lynn Wells, B.A. (Hons.), M.A., Ph.D., Acting Dean

Business Administration
Dr. Anne Lavack, Ph.D, Dean

Education
Dr. James McNinch, B.A., Ph.D., Dean

Engineering
Dr. Paitoon Tontiwachwuthikul, B.A., B.Eng. (Hons.), M.E, Dean

Fine Arts
Dr. Sheila Petty, B.A. (Hons.), L ès L, M è, Dean

Graduate Studies & Research
Dr. Rodney A. Kelln, B.Sc. (Hons.), Ph.D., Dean

Kinesiology & Health Studies
Dr. Craig Chamberlin, B.P.E., M.P.E., Ph.D., Dean

Science
Dr. Brien Maguire, B.Sc., M.Sc., Ph.D., Dean

Social Work
Dr. David Schantz, Ph.D., Dean

Schools
Canadian Plains Research Center
Dr. Polo Diaz, Ph.D., Executive Director

Centre for Continuing Education/Conservatory of Performing Arts
Dr. Harvey King, Ph.D., Director

Counselling Services
Dr. Brian Sveinson, B.A., M.A., Ph.D., Director

Graduate School of Business
Anne Lavack, B.Sc., M.B.A., Ph.D., Director

Graduate School of Public Policy
Dr. Michael Atkinson, B.A., M.A., Ph.D., Executive Director

School of Journalism
Mitch Diamantopoulos, B.A. Hons., M.A., Department Head

Affiliations
Campion College
c/o University of Regina
3737 Wascana Pkwy., Regina, SK S4S 0A2, Canada
Tel: 306-586-4242; *Fax:* 306-359-1200
Toll-Free: 1-800-667-7282
campion.college@uregina.ca
www.campioncollege.sk.ca
Enrollment: 1000 *Number of Employees:* 21 full-time professors; 12 full-time staff members; 1 campus minister
Fr. Benjamin Fiore, SJ, Ph.D., President, 306-359-1212
benjamin.fiore@uregina.ca
Fred Marcia, Exec. Dir., Administrative Services, 306-359-1231
fred.marcia@uregina.ca
Joanne Kozlowski, Dir., Admissions & Communications, 306-359-1244
joanne.kozlowski@uregina.ca
Kenneth Yanko, Dir. Facilities & Operations, 306-359-1249
ken.yanko@uregina.ca
Stephanie Molloy, Dir., Pastoral Studies, 306-359-1235
stephanie.molloy@uregina.ca
Frank Obrigewitsch, Dean, 306-359-1237
frank.obrigewitsch@uregina.ca
Nancy McNeill, Coordinator, Library, 306-359-1233
nancy.mcNeill@uregina.ca
Deborah Morrison, Registrar, 306-359-1226
deborah.morrison@uregina.ca

First Nations University of Canada
1 First Nations Way, Regina, SK S4S 7K2, Canada
Tel: 306-790-5950; *Fax:* 306-790-5999
tpelletier@firstnationsuniversity.ca (Communications)
www.firstnationsuniversity.ca
Other Information: Human Resources, E-mail: mseveright@firstnationsuniversity.ca
Enrollment: 2190 *Note:* At the First Nations University of Canada, students have the opportunity to learn in an environment of First Nations languages, traditions, & values.
Dr. Shauneen Pete, President, 306-790-5950, ext. 2105
spete@firstnationsuniversity.ca
Dr. Herman Michell, Vice-President, Academic
Joely BigEagle, Chair
Tina Pelletier, Officer, Communications

Gabriel Dumont Institute (GDI)
917 - 22nd St. West, Saskatoon, SK S7M 0R9, Canada
Tel: 306-242-6070; *Fax:* 306-242-0002
Toll-Free: 877-488-6888
general@gdi.gdins.org
www.gdins.org
www.facebook.com/gabrieldumontinstitute
Note: The Institute is designated as the official education arm of the Métis Nation-Saskatchewan (MN-S).

Luther College
c/o University of Regina
Regina, SK S4S 0A2, Canada
Tel: 306-585-5333
www.luthercollege.edu
Bruce Perlson, President, 306-585-5024
bruce.perlson@luthercollege.edu
Mark Duke, Dir. of Finance, 306-585-5023
mark.duke@luthercollege.edu
Mary Vetter, Academic Dean, 306-585-5036
mary.vetter@luthercollege.edu

Publications
The Carillon

Cityside
Regina, SK S4S 0A2, Canada

Saskatoon: College of Emmanuel & St. Chad
Also known as: University of Emmanuel College
114 Seminary Cres., Saskatoon, SK S7N 0X3, Canada
Tel: 306-975-3753; *Fax:* 306-934-2683
emmanuel.stchad@usask.ca
www.usask.ca/stu/emmanuel

Saskatoon: Lutheran Theological Seminary
114 Seminary Cres., Saskatoon, SK S7N 0X3, Canada
Tel: 306-966-7850; *Fax:* 306-966-7852
lutheran.seminary@usask.ca
www.usask.ca/stu/luther
Full Time Equivalency: 142 *Note:* Theological college at the University of Saskatchewan affiliated with the Evangelical Lutheran Church in Canada

Saskatoon: St. Thomas More College
1437 College Dr., Saskatoon, SK S7N 0W6, Canada
Tel: 306-966-8900; *Fax:* 306-966-8904
Toll-Free: 800-667-2019
http://www.facebook.com/stmcollege/
stmcollege.ca
www.facebook.com/stmcollege
twitter.com/stm1936
www.youtube.com/stm1936
Full Time Equivalency: 2294

Saskatoon: University of Saskatchewan
105 Admin. Place, Saskatoon, SK S7N 5A2, Canada
Tel: 306-966-4343; *Fax:* 306-966-4530
www.usask.ca
Full Time Equivalency: 15228
The Hon. G. Barnhart, Lt. Governor of Saskatche, Visitor
Dr. Vera Pezer, Ph.D., Chancellor
Art Dumont, B.E.(ME), Chair
R.P. MacKinnon, Q.C., B.A., LL.B., LL.M., President
Dr. Brett Fairbairn, B.A. (Hons.), D.Phil., Provost & Vice-President
Richard Florizone, B.Sc., M.Sc., Ph.D., Vice-President
L. Pennock, B.A., M.A., Ph.D., University Secretary
Kelly McInnes, B.Sc., B.Ed., Registrar
L. Kennedy, B. Comm., C.A., Assoc. Vice-President & Controller
Karen Chad, Ph.D., Acting Vice-President
R. Bunt, B.Sc., M.Sc., Ph.D., Assoc. Vice-President
D. Hannah, B.Ed., M.Ed. Ph.D., Assoc. Vice-President
Jim Germida, B.S., M.S., Ph.D., Vice-Provost
Barb Daigle, B.Comm., M.B.A., C.H.R.P., Assoc. Vice-President

Faculties
Agriculture
Dr. G.J. Scoles, B.Sc., M.Sc., Ph.D., Acting Dean

Arts & Science
J. Dillon, A.R.C.T., B.Sc., M.Sc., P, Dean

Commerce
G.E. Isaac, B.A., M.A., Ph.D., Dean

Dentistry
G. Uswak, Dean

Education
C. Reynolds, B.A., M.A., Ph.D., Dean

Engineering
J.A. Kozinski, B.S., M.Eng., Ph.D., Dean

Extension
W. Archer, B.A., B.Ed., M.A., Ph.D., Dean

Graduate Studies & Research
L. Martz, B.Sc., M.Sc., Ph.D., Dean

Kinesiology
Carol Rodgers, Ph.D., B.P.E., M.H.K., Dean

Law
B. Cotter, B.Comm., LL.B., LL.M., Dean

Medicine
W. Albritton, M.D., Ph.D., FRCPC, Dean

Nursing
L. Butler, B.S.N., M.N., Ph.D., Dean

Pharmacy & Nutrition
D.K.J. Gorecki, B.S.P., Ph.D., Dean

Physical Therapy & Interprofessional Health Sciences Education
E.L. Harrison, Assoc. Dean

Veterinary Medicine
C. Rhodes, B.Sc., D.V.M., M.Sc., Dean

Schools
Physical Therapy
A. Busch, B.P.T., M.Sc., Ph.D., Director

Affiliations
Briercrest Bible College & Biblical Seminary
510 College Dr., Caronport, SK S0H 0S0, Canada
Tel: 306-756-3200; *Fax:* 306-756-5500
info@briercrest.ca
www.briercrest.ca
Dr Dwayne Uglem, President
Glenn Werner, Chair

College of Emmanuel & St. Chad
114 Seminary Cres., Saskatoon, SK S7N 0X3, Canada
Tel: 306-975-3753; *Fax:* 306-934-2683
www.usask.ca/stu/emmanuel
The Rev Derek Hoskin, Chancellor
Rev. Dr Bill Richards, Vice-Chancellor
The Rt. Rev Greg Kerr-Wilson, President
The Rt. Rev. Dr Jane Alexander, Vice-President
Colleen Walker, Registrar
colleen.walker@usask.ca

Gabriel Dumont College
McLean Hall
#2, Wiggins Rd., Saskatoon, SK S7M 5E6, Canada
Tel: 306-934-4941; *Fax:* 306-242-0002
www.gdins.org/GDC.shtml
Geordy McCaffrey, Executive Director, 306-657-2231
geordy.mccaffrey_dti@sasktel.net

Lutheran Theological Seminary
114 Seminary Cres., Saskatoon, SK S7N 0X3, Canada
Tel: 306-966-7850; *Fax:* 306-966-7852
Kevin Ogilvie, President
Gordon Jensen, Dean of Studies
Susan Avant, Registrar
Debbie Thiessen, Office Manager

St. Andrew's College
1121 College Dr., Saskatoon, SK S7N 0W3, Canada
Tel: 306-966-8970; *Fax:* 306-966-8981
Toll-Free: 1-877-644-8970
standrews.registrar@usask.ca
www.usask.ca/stu/standrews
Note: The College is a theological school of The United Church of Canada.
Vic Wiebe, Chair
vbwiebe@sasktel.net
Laura Balas, Acting Principal, 306-966-8975
laura.balas@usask.ca

St. Peter's College
P.O. Box 40
Muenster, SK S0K 2Y0, Canada
Tel: 306-682-7888; *Fax:* 306-682-4402
spc@stpeters.sk.ca
www.stpeterscollege.ca
Note: Affiliated with the University of Saskatchewan, the College provides Arts & Science, Agriculture, & Commerce courses to first and second year students.
Robert Harasymchuk, President
Grant McConnell, Coordinator, Fine Arts, Conexus Community Art Gallery
Barbara Langhorst, Coordinator, Humanities, Academic Centre for Excellence

St. Thomas More College (STM)
1437 College Dr., Saskatoon, SK S7N 0W6, Canada
Tel: 306-966-8900; *Fax:* 306-966-8904
Toll-Free: 1-800-667-2019
info@stmcollege.ca
www.stmcollege.ca
Enrollment: 2000 *Note:* St. Thomas More College is a Catholic, liberal arts college, federated with the University of Saskatchewan. The college has 31 full-time tenure track faculty, 3 full-time term faculty, & 42 sessional faculty.
Dr. Terrence Downey, President, 306-966-8927
tdowney@stmcollege.ca
Carl Still, Dean & Associate Professor, 306-966-8950
cstill@stmcollege.ca
Patricia McDougall, Associate Dean & Associate Professor, 306-966-8919
pmcdougall@stmcollege.ca
Derrin Raffey, Chief Financial Officer & Director, Administration, 306-966-8912
draffey@stmcollege.ca
Dianne Anton, Development Officer, 306-966-8918
danton@stmcollege.ca
Donna Brockmeyer, Director, Library, 306-966-8962
dbrockmeyer@stmcollege.ca
Kathie Jeffrey, Manager, Human Resources, 306-966-6467
kjeffrey@stmcollege.ca
Kerry Stefaniuk, Manager, Accounting, 306-966-2191
kstefaniuk@stmcollege.ca
Stacy Stillwell, Manager, Information Technology, 306-966-8920
sstillwell@stmcollege.ca
Richard Medernach, Coordinator, Student Services, 306-966-8946
rmedernach@stmcollege.ca
Gertrude Rompre, Special Advisor to the President on Mission Education, 306-966-8929
grompre@stmcollege.ca

Publications
The Green & White
234 Kirk Hall, Saskatoon, SK S7N 0W0, Canada
Fax: 306-966-8717

The Sheaf

Colleges

***Saskatoon:* Gabriel Dumont Institute**
#2, 604 - 22nd St. West, Saskatoon, SK S7M 5W1, Canada
Tel: 306-934-4941; *Fax:* 306-244-0252
Toll-Free: 888-344-0445
general@gdi.gdins.org
www.gdins.org
Note: Has partnerships with University of Saskatchewan & University of Regina; Educational arm of the Métis Nation-Saskatchewan

***Saskatoon:* Horizon College & Seminary**
***Also known as:* Central Pentecostal College**
1303 Jackson Ave., Saskatoon, SK S7H 2M9, Canada
Tel: 306-374-6655; *Fax:* 306-373-6968
inquiries@horizon.edu
www.horizon.edu

Post Secondary/Technical

Post Secondary/Technical

***Air Ronge:* Northlands College**
P.O. Box 1000
Air Ronge, SK S0J 3G0, Canada
Tel: 306-425-4480; *Fax:* 306-425-3002
Toll-Free: 1-888-311-1185
www.northlandscollege.sk.ca
Note: Program Centers are located in La Ronge (306-425-4353), Buffalo Narrows (306-235-1765), & Creighton (306-688-8838).
Kelvin (Toby) Greschnern, CEO, 306-425-4273

La Ronge Campus
P.O. Box 509
La Ronge, SK S0J 1L0, Canada
Tel: 306-425-4353; *Fax:* 306-425-2696

Campuses
Buffalo Narrows Campus
P.O. Box 190
Buffalo Narrows, SK S0M 0J0, Canada
Tel: 306-235-1765; *Fax:* 306-235-4346

***Humboldt:* Carlton Trail Regional College**
P.O. Box 720
623 - 7 St., Humboldt, SK S0K 2A0, Canada
Tel: 306-682-2623; *Fax:* 306-682-3101
Toll-Free: 1-800-667-2623
humboldt@ctrc.sk.ca
www.ctrc.sk.ca/ctrc/
Number of Schools: 4 campuses
Rob Barber, CEO

***Kindersley:* Great Plains College**
Toll-Free: 866-296-2472
info@greatplainscollege.ca
www.greatplainscollege.ca
www.facebook.com/home.php?#!/greatplainscollege?ref=ts
David Keast, CEO/President

Campuses
Kindersley Campus
P.O. Box 488
514 Main St., Kindersley, SK S0L 1S0, Canada
Tel: 306-463-6431; *Fax:* 306-463-1161
kindersley.office@greatplainscollege.ca

Swift Current Campus
P.O. Box 5000
129 - 2 Ave. NE, Swift Current, SK S9H 4G3, Canada
Tel: 306-773-1531; *Fax:* 306-773-2384
swiftcurrent.office@greatplainscollege.ca

Warman Campus
P.O. Box 1001
201 Central St., Warman, SK S0K 4S0, Canada
Tel: 306-242-5377; *Fax:* 306-242-8662
warman.office@greatplainscollege.ca

Biggar Program Centre
P.O. Box 700
701 Dominion St., Biggar, SK S0K 0MO, Canada
Tel: 306-948-3363; *Fax:* 306-948-2094
biggar.office@greatplainscollege.ca

Gravelbourg Program Centre
P.O. Box 652
7 Arthabasca St., Gravelbourg, SK S0H 1X0, Canada
Tel: 306-648-3244; *Fax:* 306-648-2983
gravelbourg.office@greatplainscollege.ca

Maple Creek Program Centre
P.O. Box 1738
20 Pacific Ave., Maple Creek, SK S0N 1N0, Canada
Tel: 306-662-3829; *Fax:* 306-662-3849
maplecreek.office@greatplainscollege.ca

Nekaneet Program Centre
P.O. Box 548
Maple Creek, SK S0N 1N0, Canada
Tel: 306-662-3660; *Fax:* 306-662-4160

Outlook Program Centre
P.O. Box 1237
104 Saskatchewan Ave., Outlook, SK S0L 2N0, Canada
Tel: 306-867-8857; *Fax:* 306-867-8722
outlook.office@greatplainscollege.ca

Outlook Program Centre
P.O. Box 1237
104 Saskatchewan Ave., Outlook, SK S0L 2N0, Canada
Tel: 306-867-8857; *Fax:* 306-867-8722
outlook.office@greatplainscollege.ca

Macklin Training Centre
#1, 4801 Herald St., Macklin, SK S0L 2C0, Canada
Tel: 306-753-2143

Shaunavon Training Centre
499 Centre St., Shaunavon, SK S0N 2M0, Canada
Tel: 306-297-3462

***Melville:* Parkland Regional College Administration Office**
P.O. Box 790
200 Block 9th Ave. East, Melville, SK S0A 2P0, Canada
Tel: 306-728-4471; *Fax:* 306-728-2576
www.parklandcollege.sk.ca
Number of Schools: 5 main campuses; 2 training centres
Fay Myers, CEO

***Nipawin:* Cumberland College**
P.O. Box 2225
503 - 2nd St. East, Nipawin, SK S0E 1E0, Canada
Tel: 306-862-9833; *Fax:* 306-862-4940
www.cumberlandcollege.sk.ca
Valerie Mushinski, CEO
vmushinski@cumberlandcollege.sk.ca

Campuses
Nipawin Campus
P.O. Box 2225
501 - 6th St. East, Nipawin, SK S0E 1E0, Canada
Tel: 306-862-9833; *Fax:* 306-862-4940
crc.nipawin@cumberlandcollege.sk.ca

Melfort Campus
P.O. Box 2320
400 Burns Ave. East, Melfort, SK S0E 1A0, Canada
Tel: 306-752-2786; *Fax:* 306-752-3484
crc.melfort@cumberlandcollege.sk.ca

Hudson Bay Campus
P.O. Box 207
501 Prince St., Hudson Bay, SK S0E 0Y0, Canada
Tel: 306-865-2175; *Fax:* 306-865-2314
crc.hudsonbay@cumberlandcollege.sk.ca

Tisdale Campus
800 - 101 St., Tisdale, SK S0E 1T0, Canada
Tel: 306-873-2525; *Fax:* 306-873-4450
tisdale@cumberlandcollege.sk.ca

***North Battleford:* North West Regional College**
10702 Diefenbaker Dr., North Battleford, SK S9A 4A8, Canada
Tel: 306-937-5100; *Fax:* 306-445-1575
www.nwrc.sk.ca
Enrollment: 823
Bryan Nylander, CEO

***Regina:* INtouch Career Advancement Training**
Office of the Registrar
633 Park St., Regina, SK S4N 5N1, Canada
Tel: 306-781-0360; *Fax:* 306-781-0369
info@intouchcareercollege.com
www.intouchcareercollege.com
Note: Academic upgrading, employment preparation, computer education & business programs
Donna Singer, Principal
dsinger@intouchcareercollege.com

***Saskatoon:* Academy of Fashion Design**
218-B Ave. B South, Saskatoon, SK S7M 1M4, Canada
Tel: 306-978-9088; *Fax:* 306-933-9362
Toll-Free: 1-877-978-9088
fashiondesign@sasktel.net
www.aofdesign.com
Heather J. Brigidear, Program Coordinator

***Saskatoon:* McKay Career Training Inc.**
133 - 3rd Ave. North, Saskatoon, SK S7K 2H4, Canada
Tel: 306-955-2622; *Fax:* 306-955-1601
www.mckaycareertraining.ca
Note: Medical & veterinary office assistant, graphic art/electronic prepress, multi media, massage therapy.
Gordon McKay

***Saskatoon:* Redhouse College of Animation**
#1, 505 - 23rd St. East, Saskatoon, SK S7K 4K7, Canada
Tel: 306-668-0013
info@redhousecollege.com
redhouse.sasktelwebhosting.com
Note: Three year animation program which includes basic animation principles and the process of writing, directing, and animating ones own film.
Gord Groat, Principal & Manager

***Saskatoon:* Saskatchewan Indian Institute of Technologies**
c/o Asimakaniseekan Askiy Reserve
#118, 335 Packham Ave., Saskatoon, SK S7N 4S1, Canada
Tel: 306-244-4444; *Fax:* 306-244-1391
Toll-Free: 800-667-9704
www.siit.sk.ca
Ray Ahenakew, Acting President
Paul Ledoux, Registrar
Darlene Arcand, Director, Admission

***Saskatoon:* Saskatchewan Institute of Applied Science & Technology (SIAST)**
Administrative Offices, S.J. Cohen Centre
#400, 119 4th Ave. South, Saskatoon, SK S7K 5X2, Canada
Tel: 306-933-7331; *Toll-Free:* 866-467-4278
askaquestion@siast.sk.ca
www.siast.sk.ca
www.facebook.com/SIAST
twitter.com/SIAST
www.youtube.com/siasttv

Campuses
SIAST Kelsey Campus
P.O. Box 1520
1130 Idylwyld Dr., Saskatoon, SK S7K 3R5, Canada
Tel: 306-659-4300
HR.Kelsey@siast.sk.ca
Gerry Bonsal, Director

SIAST Palliser Campus
P.O. Box 1420
600 Saskatchewan St., Moose Jaw, SK S6H 4R4, Canada
Tel: 306-691-8200
Don Shanner, Director

SIAST Wascana Campus
P.O. Box 556
4500 Wascana Pkwy., Regina, SK S4P 3A3, Canada
Tel: 306-775-7300
Noel Selinger, Director

SIAST Woodland Campus
P.O. Box 3003
1100 - 15 St. East, Prince Albert, SK S6V 6G1, Canada
Tel: 306-765-1500
Larry Fladager, Director

***Saskatoon:* Saskatoon Business College**
221 - 3rd Ave. North, Saskatoon, SK S7K 2H7, Canada
Tel: 306-244-6333; *Fax:* 306-652-4888
Toll-Free: 1-800-679-7711
www.saskbusinesscollege.com
twitter.com/sbccollege
Note: Business, health care, computer courses

***Saskatoon:* Universal Career College**
1202A Quebec Ave., Saskatoon, SK S7K 1V2, Canada
Tel: 306-373-8700; *Fax:* 306-373-8708
www.uccsaskatoon.ca
Note: Office & business management, travel & tourism
Laurette McCaig, Manager

***Saskatoon:* Western Academy Broadcasting College**
1222 Alberta Ave., Saskatoon, SK S7K 4E5, Canada
Tel: 306-665-1771; *Fax:* 306-244-1219
wabc@shaw.ca
www.wabcwesternacademy.com
Don Scott, Manager

***Weyburn:* Southeast Regional College**
Administrative Offices
P.O. Box 1565
Weyburn, SK S4H 0T1, Canada
Tel: 306-848-2500; *Fax:* 306-848-2524
www.southeastcollege.org
Number of Schools: 7 centres & campuses
Graham Mickleborough, President

Yukon Territory

Government Agencies

***Whitehorse:* Department of Education**
P.O. Box 2703
1000 Lewes Blvd., Whitehorse, YT Y1A 2C6, Canada
Tel: 867-667-5141; *Fax:* 867-393-6254
Toll-Free: 800-661-0408
contact.education@gov.yk.ca
www.education.gov.yk.ca
Hon. Scott Kent, Minister

School Boards/Districts/Divisions

Public

***Whitehorse:* Yukon Francophone School Board**
P.O. Box 3983
3151C - 3rd Ave., Whitehorse, YT Y1A 5M6, Canada
Tel: 867-667-8680; *Fax:* 867-393-6946
Toll-Free: 800-661-0408
Grades: Pre-K.-12 *Enrollment:* 165 *Note:* The board operates the Yukon's only French first language school, École Émilie-Tremblay.
André Bourcier, President

Universities & Colleges

Colleges

***Whitehorse:* Yukon College**
P.O. Box 2799
500 College Dr., Whitehorse, YT Y1A 5K4, Canada
Tel: 867-668-8800; *Fax:* 867-668-8890
Toll-Free: 800-661-0504
www.yukoncollege.yk.ca
www.facebook.com/yukoncollege
www.twitter.com/yukoncollege
Terry Weninger, President
Karen Barnes, Vice-President (Education & Training)
Wayne Coghill, Director, Administrative Services
Jock Bryce, Director, Human Resources

Overseas Schools/Programs

***Accra:* Canadian Independent College (CIC) Ghana Campus**
Airport Residential Area
No. Z 26 Patrice Lumumba Rd., Accra, Ghana
business@cicbaden.ca; tutor@cicbaden.ca
www.ghanacic.com
Other Information: Main Phone: 233-302-760-571
www.facebook.com/GhanaCIC
twitter.com/GhanaCIC
Note: Sister campus to the CIC in Baden, Region of Waterloo, Canada.

***Belleville*: AFNORTH International School**
P.O. Box 5053 Stn Forces
Belleville, ON K8N 5W6
canada@afnorth-is.com
www.afnorth-is.com/canadian-section
Other Information: Canada Phone: 011-31-45-527-8201; Fax: 011-31-45-527-8277
Enrollment: 1000 *Note:* The AFNORTH International School was founded in September 1967 & educates children of nearby NATO personnel. It is located at Ferdinand Bolstraat 1, Brunssum, The Netherlands, 6445 EE.
Dr. Uwe Bettscheider, International Director
Shannon Tipping, Principal

***Bermuda:* Hamilton: Mount Saint Agnes Academy**
P.O. Box 1004
19 Dundonald St. West, Hamilton, Bermuda
Tel: 441-292-4134; *Fax:* 441-295-7265
msaoffice@msa.bm
www.msa.bm
Grades: K.-Sec. *Note:* The school has been preliminarily accredited with Alberta Education since the 2010-2011 school year.
Garry Madeiros, Chair
Sue Moench, Principal
smoench@msa.bm

***Canada:* Maple: Canadian College Italy - The Renaissance**
Canadian Head Office
59 Macamo Crt., Maple, ON L6A 1G1, Canada
Tel: 905-508-7108; *Fax:* 905-508-5480
Toll-Free: 800-422-0548
cciren@rogers.com; cciren@tin.it
www.canadiancollegeitaly.com
Other Information: Int'l Phone: 39-(0872)-71-49-69; Fax: 39-(0872)-450-28
www.facebook.com/110636132290645
www.youtube.com/user/TheRenaissanceSchool
Grades: Secondary *Enrollment:* 115 *Note:* CCI is the first private school in Italy to offer a Canadian high school program. Students may enroll for a single semester or for up to three academic years (two semesters per year). CCI is accredited by the province of Ontario, & is a member of the European Council of International Schools (ECIS). It is located at Via Cavour 13, Lanciano (CH), Italy 66034.
Marisa DiCarlo D'Alessandro, Founder
George Rutherford, Head of School

***Canada:* New Westminster: Canadian Secondary Wenzhou No. 22 School**
School District No. 40 Business Company
1001 Columbia St., 2nd Fl., New Westminster, BC V3M 1C4, Canada
Tel: 604-517-6157; *Fax:* 604-517-6162
business_services@sd40.bc.ca
www.sd40.bc.ca/sd40bc/offshoreschool.htm
Grades: 10-12 *Note:* Canadian Secondary Wenzhou No. 22 School is certified by the British Columbia Ministry of Education. It is located in Wenzhou, Zhejiang Province, China.
Gregory Batt, Principal
Tom Harris, Offshore Representative, 604-936-7382
tomharris@shaw.ca

***Canada:* Vancouver: Dalian Maple Leaf International School**
#400 - 601 Broadway West, Vancouver, BC V5Z 4C2, Canada
Tel: 604-675-6910; *Fax:* 604-675-6911
helen@mapleleafschools.com
www.mapleleafschools.com
Grades: 9-12 *Enrollment:* 1616 *Note:* Maple Leaf Educational Systems is a Chinese firm that currently operates 12 schools in China enrolling approximately 5,000 students. Maple Leafs High Schools (Grade 10-12) programs and its Foreign Nationals Schools (K-9) are taught in English by British Columbia, Canada certified teachers. These programs are inspected and certified by British Columbia's Ministry of Eductation. Grade 12 graduates receive both the Chinese and British Columbia graduation certificates
Howard Ballock, Director

***Canada:* Vancouver: Maple Leaf Educational Systems**
Vancouver Office
#400, 601 West Broadway, Vancouver, BC V5Z 4C2, Canada
Tel: 604-675-6910; *Fax:* 604-675-6911
info@mapleleafschools.com
www.mapleleafschools.com
Other Information: China Phone: 86-411-8790-6822; Fax: 86-411-8790-6811
Number of Schools: 24 *Grades:* Pre.-12 *Enrollment:* 10500
Note: Maple Leaf Educational Systems was founded in 1995, with the goal of blending Eastern & Western educational practices. Maple Leaf schools offer Canadian & Chinese accreditation & diplomas. The Chinese Office can be contacted at: Jinshitan National Holiday Resort, No. 9 Central St., Dalian, China 116650.

***Canada:* Coquitlam: Sino Bright School**
Vancouver Campus
1100 Winslow Ave., Coquitlam, BC V3J 2G3, Canada
Tel: 778-688-6849; *Fax:* 778-883-6849
www.schoolbj.com
Other Information: Beijing Phone: 10-65537171; 10-65538727
Grades: 9-12 *Note:* Sino Bright School is certified by the British Columbia Ministry of Education, & operates the following five campuses: Vancouver, Beijing, Shanghai, QingDao, & XiAn.
Iris Chan, Principal
iris@schoolbj.com
Bob Albiston, Offshore Representative
balbiston@gmail.com

***China:* Jiangmen City: Boren Sino - Canadian School**
65 Shuanglong Ave., Jiangmen City, China
academics@borenschool.com
en.borenschool.com
Other Information: Tel: 86-750-321-8848,3217848; Fax: 86-750-321-9003
Note: Boren Sino-Canadian School is a privately-funded education initiative with authorization from the Ministries of Education in the provinces of Guangdong, The People's Republic of China, and Ontario, Canada. As such, it adheres strictly to curricular requirements and grants education credits in the pursuit of high school diplomas in both countries. The Chinese curriculum is designed to prepare students for national academic examinations qualifying students for university and college entrance. At the same time, the Ontario curriculum of the school is both demanding and exciting and requires a high level of aptitude and dedication
William D. Walter, Principal

***China:* Changchun City, Jilin Province: Canada Changchun Shiyi Secondary School**
2666 Jingyang Rd., Changchun City, Jilin Province, China
normanxu_83@hotmail.com
www.cc11.net/canada/shownew.asp?46.html
Other Information: Phone: 0431-87662985 13204309767 18655182062
Grades: Secondary *Note:* Canada Changchun Shiyi Secondary School is certified by the British Columbia Ministry of Education.
Tim Krysko, Principal
Rodger Lindstrom, Offshore Representative
rlindstrom@shaw.ca

China: Haikou, Hainan Province: Canada Hainan Secondary School
Hainan ISIP Experimental School
Xiuying National High Tech Zone, Haikou, Hainan Province, China

www.canadahainanss.com
Other Information: Phone: 86-898-68612170; Fax: 86-898-68631818
Grades: Secondary *Note:* Canada Hainan Secondary School is certified by the British Columbia Ministry of Education.
Chris Davidson, Canadian Principal
canvan123@yahoo.com
Yao Yuqin, Chinese Principal
susanyyq@163.com
Wu Yongxing, Foreign Affairs & External Liaison
della020@163.com
Brian Roodnick, Offshore Representative
roodnick@shaw.ca

China: Hefei, Anhui Province: Canada Hefei No. 1 Secondary School
Hefei, Anhui Province, China
Grades: Secondary *Note:* Canada Hefei No. 1 Secondary School is certified by the British Columbia Ministry of Education.
Monica Francis, Principal
Rodger Lindstrom, Offshore Representative
rlindstrom@shaw.ca

China: Kunming, Yunnan Province: Canada Kunming No. 10 Secondary School
Kunming, Yunnan Province, China
Grades: Secondary *Note:* Canada Kunming No. 10 Secondary School is certified by the British Columbia Ministry of Education.
Kyle Chong, Principal
Rodger Lindstrom, Offshore Representative
rlindstrom@shaw.ca

China: Langfang, Hebei Province: Canada Langfang Secondary School
Langfang, Hebei Province, China
Grades: Secondary *Note:* Canada Langfang Secondary School is certified by the British Columbia Ministry of Education.
Corri Gallicano, Principal
Rodger Lindstrom, Offshore Representative

China: Qingdao, Shandong Province: Canada Qingdao Secondary School
Qingdao No.9 Middle School
Qingdao, Shandong Province, China

Tel: 778-893-8566
info@cess.ca
www.csee.ca/18201.html
Grades: Secondary *Note:* Canada Qingdao Secondary School is certified by the British Columbia Ministry of Education.
Yvan Zebroff, Principal
Brian Fichter, Offshore Representative, 604-574-8294
fichter.brian@gmail.com

China: Tai'an, Shandong Province: Canada Shandong Secondary School
Shandong Taishan Middle School
Tai'an, Shandong Province, China

Tel: 778-893-8566
info@cess.ca
www.csee.ca/14422.html
Grades: Secondary *Note:* Canada Shandong Secondary School is certified by the British Columbia Ministry of Education.
Lynne Haley, Principal
Brian Fichter, Offshore Representative, 604-574-8294
fichter.brian@gmail.com

China: Weifang, Shandong Province: Canada Weifang No. 1 Secondary School
High Tech Zone
East Baotong St., Weifang, Shandong Province, China
Grades: Secondary *Note:* Canada Weifang No. 1 Secondary School is certified by the British Columbia Ministry of Education.
Tim Newman, Principal, 604-760-7564
timnewman@shaw.ca
Rodger Lindstrom, Offshore Representative
rlindstrom@shaw.ca

China: Zibo, Shandong Province: Canada Zibo No. 11 Secondary School
119 Liuquan Rd., Zhangdian District, Zibo, Shandong Province, China

www.zb11.net
Grades: 10-12 *Enrollment:* 65 *Note:* Canada Zibo No. 11 Secondary School is certified by the British Columbia Ministry of Education.
John Linehan, Principal, 604-760-7564
linehanjw@gmail.com
Rodger Lindstrom, Offshore Representative
rlindstrom@shaw.ca

China: Nanjing: Canadian International Academy Sino-Canadian Campus of Liaoning Province Shiyan High School
32 QingDao Rd., Nanjing, China

www.njisedu.cn
Other Information: Tel: 011-86-25-8320-8201; Fax: 011-86-25-8323-3866
Grades: 9-12 *Note:* Canadian international school in China, located in Yingkou
Rudy Maharaj
rudymaharaj@rogers.com

China: Yongchuan District, Chongqing: Chongqing Maple Leaf International School
777 Maple Leaf Rd., Xuefu Ave., Yongchuan District, Chongqing, China

info@mapleleafschools.com
www.mapleleafschools.com
Other Information: Phone: 023-4957-2957; Fax: 023-49566111
Grades: 10-12 *Note:* Chongqing Maple Leaf International School is certified by the British Columbia Ministry of Education.
Dave Brecht, Ph.D., Principal
dbrecht@mapleleaf.net.cn
George Watson, Superintendent, BC Program, 604-675-6910
georgewatson.mapleleaf@gmail.com

China: Guangdong Province: Clifford School
Also known as: Clifford Experimental School
Clifford Estates
Panyu, Guangzhou, Guangdong Province, China

www.clifford-school.cn
Other Information: Phones: 86-20-8471-1441, 86-20-3477-4263
Grades: K.-Sec. *Note:* Clifford School is accredited by the Province of Manitoba.
Donna Everitt, Coordinator, International Education, 204-945-1126, fax: 204-957-1793

China: Dalian, Liaoning Province: Dalian Maple Leaf Foreign Nationals School
104 Shengli Rd., Xigang District, Dalian, Liaoning Province, China

info@mapleleafschools.com
www.mapleleafschools.com
Other Information: Phone: 86-411-8238-7757; Fax: 86-411-8239-6922
Grades: K.-9 *Note:* Dalian Maple Leaf Foreign Nationals School is certified by the British Columbia Ministry of Education.
Mark Wilkins, Principal
mwilkins@mapleleaf.net.cn
George Watson, Superintendent, BC Program, 604-675-6910
georgewatson.mapleleaf@gmail.com

China: Ranghulu District, Daqing: Daqing Secondary School
284 Shengli Rd., Ranghulu District, Daqing, China
Grades: Sec. *Enrollment:* 12000 *Number of Employees:* 964 staff

China: Shanghai: Grand Canadian Academy (Hongkou) (GCA)
No. 88, Hongguan Rd., Shanghai, China

www.gcahighschool.ca/sh_hongkou
Other Information: Phone: 86-021-65038661
Grades: 10-12 *Note:* Grand Canadian Academy (Hongkou) is certified by the British Columbia Ministry of Education.
Geoff Nicki, Principal
Brian Fichter, Offshore Representative, 604-574-8294
fichter.brian@gmail.com

China: Tongxiang, Zhejiang Province: Grand Canadian Academy (Jiaxing) (GCA)
288 Zhenxing Donglu, Tongxiang, Zhejiang Province, China

www.gcahighschool.ca/jiaxing
Other Information: Phone & Fax: 573-8810-7576; Alt. Phone: 573-8810-7658
Grades: 10-12 *Enrollment:* 96 *Note:* Grand Canadian Academy (Jiaxing) is certified by the British Columbia Ministry of Education. Correspondence for GCA (Jiaxing) may be sent to: Grand Canadian Academy (Asia) Limited, #200, 100 Park Royal, West Vancouver, BC, Canada V7T 1A2
Kelly Wu, Project Coordinator
kwu@firstasiaacademy.com
Mary Xu, Program Liaison
xuxy008@yahoo.com.cn

China: Tianjin: Harbor View School
#71, 3rd Avenue South, Tianjin, China

highschool@harviewschool.com
www.chinatefl.com/tianjin/teach/tjbhxyzy.htm#3
Other Information: Tel: 86-022-66226888-5800; Fax: 86-022-66226486
Grades: K.-12 *Note:* Harbor View School is a private-run boarding school owned & managed by Home World Corporation, & certified with the Ministry of Education of Ontario. The school, founded in 2000 & licensed as a private school in 2001, is approved by the Tianjin Education Committee.

China: Guangzhou, Guangdong Province: Huamei-Bond International College
Huamei Rd., Tianhe District, Guangzhou, Guangdong Province, China

wasdurhamsecondary@hotmail.com
www.hm163.com/englishvesion
Other Information: Phone: 020-87210372; Alternate Phone: 020-87210083
Grades: K.-12 *Note:* Huamei-Bond International College (HBIC) is operated jointly by Bond International College (Toronto) & Huamei International School (China). HBIC is accredited by & inspected by the Ontario Ministry of Education, Canada. The school offers Ontario secondary school academic courses as well as a Chinese high school curriculum leading to an Ontario Secondary School Diploma & a Chinese High School Diploma. With these two diplomas, graduates can apply directly to universities in China or overseas.
Robert McDonnell, Principal

China: Nanjing, Jiangsu Province: Nanjing Foreign Language School British Columbia (NFLS BC)
Nanjing, Jiangsu Province, China
Grades: Secondary *Note:* Nanjing Foreign Language School British Columbia is certified by the British Columbia Ministry of Education.
Charles Dillion, Principal
Bill Gook, Offshore Representative
bill.gook@gmail.com

China: Nanjing, Jiangsu Province: Nanjing-Bond International College
Nanjing No. 13 High School
#14, Xijia Datang, Xuanwu District, Nanjing, Jiangsu Province, China

bond13z@yahoo.com.cn
bond.nj13z.cn
Other Information: Phone: 011-86-25-8326-9911; Fax: 011-86-25-8326-9927
Grades: Secondary *Note:* The school is operated jointly by Bond International College in Ontario, & Nanjing No. 13 High School in China. Students who recieve their diploma from Nanjing-Bond International College may apply directly to overseas universities.
Michael Boniface, Principal
michael_boniface@yahoo.ca
Tu Guifang, Chinese Principal

China: Shenzhen, Guangdong Province: Oxstand-Bond International College
2040 Buxin Rd., Luohu District, Shenzhen, Guangdong Province, China

enquiry@oxstand.com.cn
oxstand.com.cn/ciep/index.html
Other Information: Phone: 011-86-755-2581-4853; Fax: 011-86-755-2581-3921
Grades: Mid./Sec. *Note:* Graduates of Oxtand's Canadian International Education Program receive Ontario Secondary School diplomas.
Anthony Mauriell, Principal
ciepprincipal@oxstand.com.cn

China: Longkou: Shandong Canada China Donghai School
Donghai Development Zone
Longkou, China

donghaischool@sina.cn
Other Information: Tel: 011-86-535-8606000; Fax: 011-86-535-8606002
Lisette Martineau-Garcia, Principal

China: Xuhui District, Shanghai: Shanghai Nanyang Model High School
Xuhui District, Shanghai, China
Grades: Secondary *Note:* Shanghai Nanyang Model High School was founded in 1901, making it one of China's oldest modern schools. It is certified by the British Columbia Ministry of Education.
Greg Corry, Principal
Tom Harris, Offshore Representative, 604-936-7382
tomharris@shaw.ca

China: Minhang District, Shanghai: Shanghai United International School (SUIS)
Minhang District, Shanghai, China
www.suis.com.cn
Grades: Elem.-Sec. *Note:* Shanghai United International School offers primary & secondary courses certified by the British Columbia Ministry of Education.
John (Jack) Orchard, Principal
Brian Butcher, Offshore Representative
bdbutcher@telus.net

China: Shenzhen City, Futian District: Shenzhen Foreign Language School
Jingtian North, Futian District, Shenzhen City, Futian District, China
office@swis.cn
www.sfls.net.cn
Other Information: Phone: 086-0755-8654-1221; 086-0755-8654-1223
Grades: 9-12

China: Wujiang City, Jiangsu Province: Sino-Canada High School
Wujiang City, Jiangsu Province, China
www.sinocanadahighschool.com
Other Information: Phone: 86-512-6326-1000
Grades: 10-12 *Enrollment:* 1500 *Note:* Sino-Canada High School is certified by the British Columbia Ministry of Education.
Mark Butcher, Principal
Dr. Betty Boult, Offshore Representative, 604-689-8260
blboult@shaw.ca

China: Jiangsu: Suzhou Industrial Park Foreign Language School
Suzhou Industrial Park
Jiangsu, China
Note: The school is a British Columbia Certified School.
Pat McManus, Principal
Denis Therrien, Offshore Representative
denistherrien45@gmail.com

China: Tianjin: Tianjin (TEDA) Maple Leaf International School
71 - 3rd Ave., Tianjin, China
gjwalrus@msn.com; info@mapleleafschools.com
www.mapleleafschools.com/ML_Tianjin_International
Other Information: Phone: 86-22-6200-1920; Fax: 86-22-6622-6088
Grades: 10-12 *Note:* Tianjin (TEDA) Maple Leaf International School is certified by the British Columbia Ministry of Education.
Ryan Waurynchuk, Principal/Vice Head Master
George Watson, Superintendent, BC Program, 604-675-6910
georgewatson.mapleleaf@gmail.com

China: Wuhan: Wuhan Maple Leaf Foreign National School
East Lake Hi-Tech Development Zone
1018 Minzu Rd., Wuhan, China
info@mapleleafschools.com
www.mapleleafschools.com/ML_Wuhan_Foreign_Nationals
Other Information: Phone: 86-027-8192-5705; Fax: 86-027-8192-5704
Grades: K.-9 *Note:* Wuhan Maple Leaf Foreign National School is certified by the British Columbia Ministry of Education.
Darrell Goss, Principal
dgoss@mapleleaf.net.ca
George Watson, Superintendent, BC Program, 604-675-6910
georgewatson.mapleleaf@gmail.com

China: Wuhan: Wuhan Maple Leaf International School
East Lake Hi-Tech Development Zone
1018 Minzu Rd., Wuhan, China
info@mapleleafschools.com
www.mapleleafschools.com/ML_Wuhan_International
Other Information: Phone: 86-027-8192-5705; Fax: 86-027-8192-5788
Grades: 10-12 *Note:* Wuhan Maple Leaf International School is certified by the British Columbia Ministry of Education.
Darrell Goss, Principal
dgoss@mapleleaf.net.cn
George Watson, Superintendent, BC Program, 604-675-6910
georgewatson.mapleleaf@gmail.com

China: Yizhuang, Beijing: Yang Guang Qing International School of Beijing
Beijing Economic & Development Zone
2 Tian Bao North St., Yizhuang, Beijing, China
bjetownschool@gmail.com; ctychat@139.com
www.bdaschool.com
Other Information: Phone: 010-67872277; Fax: 010-67871129
Enrollment: 2000 *Note:* Yang Guang Qing International School of Beijing is accredited by the Province of Manitoba.
Donna Everitt, Coordinator, International Education, 204-945-1126, fax: 204-957-1793

China: WuQing District, Tianjin: Yinghua-Bond International College
Yong Yang West Rd., WuQing District, Tianjin, China
www.bondschoolsinternational.com
Other Information: Phone: 011-86-22-5961-1023; Fax: 011-86-22-5961-1166
Stephen Pelland, Principal
srpelland@hotmail.com

China: Zhenjiang, Jiangsu Province: Zhenjiang Maple Leaf International School
Zhenjiang, Jiangsu Province, China
info@mapleleafschools.com
www.mapleleafschools.com
Grades: 10-12 *Note:* Zhenjiang Maple Leaf International School is certified by the British Columbia Ministry of Education.
Ewan Hunt, Principal
George Watson, Superintendent, BC Program, 604-675-6910
georgewatson.mapleleaf@gmail.com

Egypt: El Sherouk City, Cairo: British Columbia Canadian International School (BCCIS)
P.O. Box 98
5th Settlement Section, 34 Suez Rd. Entrance, El Sherouk City, Cairo, Egypt
www.bccis.net
Other Information: Phone: 202-26300323; Fax: 202-26300445
Grades: K.-12 *Note:* BCCIS is certified by the British Columbia Ministry of Education.
Collette Ellis-Toddington, Principal
c.ellistoddington@bccis.net
Margaret Compo, Offshore Representative
mdcompo@yahoo.ca

Egypt: Zone 4, New Greater Cairo: Canadian International School of Egypt
El Tagamosa El Khames, Zone 4, New Greater Cairo, Egypt
cise-egypt.com
Other Information: Phone: 011-202-010-4482; Fax: 011-202-617-4500
Note: CISE is a Junior Kindergarten to Grade Twelve International School in Cairo (Kattameya - New Cairo) approved by the Egyptian Ministry of Education & licensed as a Canadian School by the Ontario Ministry of Education. Its administration & over 85% of its teachers are trained and licensed (certified) in Canada. The school uses a Canadian curriculum, teaching & classroom management techniques & Canadian learning materials (text books, computer software & audio-visual aids). The school opened its doors in September 2002.
Melanie Seifert, Principal
mseifert@cise-eg.com

Egypt: 6th of October City, Giza: Heritage International School
Al-Yasmine Greenland, Second Touristic Village
P.O. Box 38-12568
6th of October City, Giza, Egypt
info@heritageinternationalschool.com
www.heritageinternationalschool.com
Other Information: Phone: 202-38377251/2/4; Fax: 202-38377253
www.facebook.com/218640688193402
twitter.com/heritageegypt
Grades: SK-12 *Note:* Heritage International School is certified by both the Ministries of Education of Egypt & the Province of Manitoba, in Canada.
Mostafa Awara, Chair
Richard Strongman, School Head Principal
Bill Parent, Elementary Principal
Ruth Suderman, Secondary Principal
Donna Everitt, Coordinator, International Education, 204-945-1126, fax: 204-957-1793

Ghana: Accra: Canadian Independent College of Ghana (CIC)
Airport Residential Area
#Z-26 Patrice Lumumba Rd., Accra, Ghana
business@cicbaden.ca; tutor@cicbaden.ca
www.heritageinternationalschool.com
Other Information: Phone: 233-302-760-571
www.facebook.com/GhanaCIC
twitter.com/GhanaCIC
Grades: Pre.-Sec. *Note:* Canadian Independent College of Ghana is accredited by the Province of Manitoba.
Dr. Heather Bohez, B.Sc., N.D., Director
Donna Everitt, Coordinator, International Education, 204-945-1126, fax: 204-957-1793

Hong Kong: Aberdeen: Canadian International School of Hong Kong
36 Nam Long Shan Rd., Aberdeen, Hong Kong
schoolinfo@cdnis.edu.hk
www.cdnis.edu.hk
Other Information: Phone: 011-852-2525-7088; Fax: 011-852-2525-7579
Grades: K.-Sec. *Enrollment:* 1332
John Jalsavec, Principal

Hong Kong: Quarry Bay: Delia School of Canada Elementary Section
Tai Fung Rd., Taikoo Shing, Quarry Bay, Hong Kong
Tel: 365-805-08; *Fax:* 251-382-40
e.office@delia.edu.hk
www.delia.edu.hk
Grades: Pre.-6 *Note:* Delia School of Canada is a private school. Delia School of Canada is a member of the Delia Group of Schools. It follows the curriculum offered in Ontario. Delia School of Canada is accredited with the Ministry of Education in Ontario & registered with the Hong Kong Education and Manpower Bureau. The school meets the appropriate regulations put forth by the Education Department of Ontario & the Hong Kong Education & Manpower Bureau. Delia School of Canada was established in 1987.
P. Lee, Principal
T. Vienneau, Head Teacher, Elementary Section
t.vienneau@delia.edu.hk

Campuses
Secondary Section
Tai Fung Rd., Taikoo Shing, Quarry Bay, Hong Kong
Tel: 365-803-38; *Fax:* 288-578-24
s.office@delia.edu.hk
Grades: 7-12
P. Farrell, Head Teacher, Secondary Section

Hong Kong: New Territories: Renaissance College
5 Hang Ming St., New Territories, Hong Kong
admissions@rchk.edu.hk
www.renaissance.edu.hk
Other Information: Phone: 852-3556-3556; Fax: 852-3556-3446
Harry Brown, Principal

India: Bangalore 560 092: Canadian International School
14/1 Kodighalli Main Rd., Sahakar Nagar, Bangalore 560 092, India
Tel: 091-803-4384; *Fax:* 091-803-4364
info@cisb.org.in
Enrollment: 212 *Note:* Provides a learning experience to mainly expatriate and Indian students, representing over 25 nationalities from Pre indergarten to Grade 12. The school is accredited by

the International Baccalaureate Organization and Ontario Ministry of Education, and is a member of the Council of International Schools
Brian Tinker, Principal

Japan: Tokyo: Canadian International School Tokyo
Admissions Office
5-8-20 Kitashinagawa, Shinagawa-ku, Tokyo, Japan

study@cisjapan.net
cisjapan.net
Other Information: Phone: 03-5793-1392; Fax: 03-5793-3559
Grades: Pre.-12 *Note:* The Canadian International School Tokyo was founded in 1999, & is accredited with the Prince Edward Island Department of Education.
Ian A.M. Robertson, Principal

Japan: Saitama, Tokyo: Columbia International School of Japan
153 Matsugo, Tokorozawa, Saitama, Tokyo 359-0027, Japan
Tel: 042-946-1911; *Fax:* 042-946-1955
office@columbia-ca.co.jp; admissions@columbia-ca.co.jp
columbia-ca.co.jp
Enrollment: 280 *Note:* Prepares students for the post secondary education overseas with a world recognized & accepted Ontario Secondary School Diploma (grade 12) of Canada. CIS admits students regardless of their nationality or ethnic origin. CIS is accredited & annually inspected by the Ontario Ministry of Education, & follows the Ontario curriculum.
Barrie McCliggott, Principal

Japan: Tosa City, Kochi Prefecture: Meitoku Gijuku School
Ryu Campus
564 Ryu Usa Cho, Tosa City, Kochi Prefecture, Japan

info@meitoku-gijuku.ed.jp
www.meitoku-gijuku.ed.jp
Other Information: Phone: 088-828-6688; Fax: 088-856-3060
Grades: Secondary *Note:* Meitoku Gijuku School is accredited by the Province of Manitoba.
Satoshi Takahashi, Director, Public Admissions
takahashi@meitoku-gijuku.ed.jp
Donna Everitt, Coordinator, International Education, 204-945-1126, fax: 204-957-1793

Kowloon: Kowloon City: Christian Alliance P.C. Lau Memorial International School (CAIS)
Kowloon Campus
2 Fu Ning St., Kowloon City, Kowloon

info@cais.edu.hk
www.cais.edu.hk
Other Information: Phone: 852-2713-3733; Fax: 852-2760-4324
www.facebook.com/CAIS.HK
Grades: 4-12 *Enrollment:* 600 *Note:* CAIS is one of 15 schools owned & operated by the Kowloon Tong Church of the Chinese Christian & Missionary Alliance (KTAC) in Hong Kong. It has been accredited by Alberta Education since 2007.

Campuses
Lai Yiu Campus
Lai Yiu Estate
Wah Yiu Rd., Lai King, New Territories

lyoffice@cais.edu.hk
Other Information: Phone: 852-2778-3370; Fax: 852-2778-3326
Grades: K.-3

Macao: Taipa: The International School of Macao (TIS)
Block K, Macau University of Science & Technology
Avenida Wai Long, Taipa, Macao

tis@tis.edu.mo
www.tis.edu.mo
Other Information: Phone: 853-2853-3700; Fax: 853-2853-3702
www.facebook.com/117917438263544
Note: TIS has been accredited with Alberta Education since 2006.
Howard Stribbell, Head of Schools

Malaysia: Petaling Jaya, Selanger Darul E: Canadian International Matriculation Programme
Sunway College
P.O. Box 46150
No. 5 Jalan Kolej, Bandar Sunway, Petaling Jaya, Selanger Darul E, Malaysia

info@sunway.edu.my
sunway.edu.my/college/cimp
Other Information: Phone: 6-03-5638-7176/7491-8622; Fax: 6-03-5638-7177/5635-8633
www.facebook.com/SunwayCollegeKL
twitter.com/sunwayu
www.youtube.com/sunwayedu
Note: CIMP is an Ontario Curriculum, developed according to the requirements of the Ontario Ministry of Education, Canada. It is identical to the programme offered in Ontario, which upon completion, students will receive the Ontario Secondary School Diploma (OSSD). Establised in 1990, the Canadian International Matriculation Programme (CIMP) has grown to become the largest Canadian Matriculation programme in the world
John Futa, Director, Programme

Malaysia: Petaling Jaya, Selangor: Sunway International School (SIS)
***Also known as:* Sunway University College**
#3 Jalan Universiti, Jalan Kolej, Bandar Sunway, Petaling Jaya, Selangor, Malaysia

infosis@sunway.edu.my
www.sis.sunway.edu.my
Other Information: Phone: 011-603-7491-8623, ext. 8124; Fax: 011-603-5635-8630
Grades: 7-11 *Note:* The only school in Malaysia offering the Ontario curriculum for grades 7-11. SIS opened in 2008.
John Futa, Principal
johnfuta@sunway.edu.my

Malaysia: Selangor: Taylor's College International Canadian Pre-University
No. 1, Jalan SS15/8, 47500 Subang Jaya, Selangor, Malaysia

admission@taylors.edu.my
www.taylors.edu.my/en/college/programmes/pre-u/cpu
Other Information: Phone: 603-5636-2641; Fax: 603-5634-5209
www.facebook.com/166519953397649
www.youtube.com/user/taylorspreu
Enrollment: 490 *Note:* For over three decades, Taylor's University College has been recognised as Malaysia's leading private college of higher learning. International Canadian Pre-University (ICPU) programme: Students choose this programme for its flexibility & wide-ranging subjects. Accepted for university entry internationally, ICPU students at Taylor's University College are constantly exposed to the latest developments in education & the global experiences provided by a team of qualified Malaysian & Canadian lecturers
James Leonard, Principal
james.leonard@taylors.edu.my

Mexico: Acueducto Providencia, Guadalaj: Canadian School Guadalajara
Montevideo 3306, Acueducto Providencia, Guadalaj, Mexico

www.canadianschool.com.mx
Other Information: Phones: 3610-17-06; 3641-64-52
www.facebook.com/176388335730456
Grades: Elementary *Note:* The school has preliminary accreditation with Alberta Education for the 2012-2013 school year.
Sandra Beltrán, Director
s.beltran@canadianschool.com.mx

Netherlands Antilles: St. Maarten: Caribbean International Academy (CIA)
P.O. Box 5454
Cupecoy, Tigris Rd., #4, Simpson Bay, St. Maarten, Netherlands Antilles

admission@carib-international.net
www.carib-international.net
Other Information: Phone: 011-721-545-3871; Fax: 011-721-545-3872
Note: The CIA opened in 2003, & the Principal & 80% of the teachers have been certified by the Ontario College of Teachers.
Jake Johnston, Principal
principal@carib-international.net; principalcia@hotmail.com

Qatar: Doha: Hayat Universal School Qatar (HUBS)
Muaither Bldg. 55, Area 53
P.O. Box 6124
Muaither St., Doha, Qatar

info.qa@hayatschool.com
www.hayatschool.com
Other Information: Phone: 4468-7171: Fax: 4469-3352
Grades: Pre.-12 *Note:* Hayat Universal School Qatar is certified by the British Columbia Ministry of Education.
Mike Munro, Principal
Keith Forshaw, Offshore Representative
keithforshaw@shaw.ca

Qatar: Doha: Qatar Canadian School (QCS)
P.O. Box 24359
Doha, Qatar

qcs@cna-qatar.edu.qa
www.qcs.edu.qa
Other Information: Phone: 974-4421-7553/4; Fax: 974-4421-7556
Grades: K.-10 *Note:* The school has preliminary accreditation with Alberta Education for the 2011-2012 school year. The campus is located in the Landmark Mall area.
Mike O'Leary, Principal

Rep. Of Trinidad & Tobago: Chaguanas: Trillium International School
Liberty Centre
Hakim Juman St., Chaguanas, Rep. Of Trinidad & Tob
Tel: 868-665-2641; *Fax:* 868-665-6174
trilliumtt.com
Note: A private school, established in 2002, offering the Ontario Ministry of Education Curriculum to Kindergarten, Elementary and Secondary Students. Located in the Borough of Chaguanas, in Trinidad & Tobago.
Linford Carrabon, Chair
Betty Anne Craig, Principal

Singapore: Canadian International School Lakeside Campus
7 Jurong West St. 41, , Singapore

www.cis.edu.sg
Other Information: Phone: 65-6467-1732; Fax: 65-6467-1729
www.facebook.com/CIS.edu.sg
twitter.com/cissingapore
Number of Schools: 2 *Enrollment:* 2500 *Note:* Accredited by the Ontario Ministry of Education, and the International Baccalaureate programmes. Their graduates receive the Ontario Secondary Diploma or the IB Diploma, both of which are recognized around the world by major universities. Associate member in the Council of International Schools (CIS).
Glenn Odland, Head of School

Campuses
Tanjong Katong Campus
371 Tanjong Katong Rd., Singapore 437128, Singapore

Other Information: Phone: 65-6345-1573; Fax: 65-6345-4057

South Korea: Sungnam-si, Gyeonggi-do: BIS Canada
200 Gumgok-dong, Bundang-gu, Sungnam-si, Gyeonggi-do, South Korea

info@biscanada.org
www.biscanada.org
Other Information: Phone: 031-8022-7114; Fax: 031-8022-7115
Grades: Pre.-10 *Note:* BIS Canada is certified by the British Columbia Ministry of Education, & was founded in 2008.
Dong Young Seo, CEO/Director
Larry Simpson, B.Ed., Principal
lsimpson@biscanada.org
Judy Chapman, Offshore Representative
chapman@experienceabbotsford.com

South Korea: Seoul: British Columbia Collegiate Canada
Seoul, South Korea

www.bced.gov.bc.ca
Note: British Columbia Collegiate Canada is certified by the British Columbia Ministry of Education.
Scott Reid, Principal
Dave Maljaars, Offshore Representative
dmecs@aebc.com

South Korea: Nam-Gu, Incheon: Canada Maple International School (CMIS)
400-1 Mun-hak Dong, Nam-Gu, Incheon, South Korea
Tel: 032-715-8000; *Fax:* 032-715-8080
info@cmis.kr
www.cmis.kr
www.facebook.com/271476482896372
cafe.naver.com/cmis.cafe
Grades: Secondary *Note:* Canada Maple International School is accredited by the Province of Manitoba.
Joe B.H. Chang, Chief Director
Keith Warner, Principal
Donna Everitt, Coordinator, International Education, 204-945-1126, fax: 204-957-1793

South Korea: Sokcho, Gangwondo Province: SIS Canada (CISS)
#802, 38 Gyodong, Sokcho, Gangwondo Province, South Korea
ciss.kr
Other Information: Phone: 82-33-637-8817; Fax: 82-33-637-8815
twitter.com/siscanada2
blog.naver.com/sis8817
Grades: 9-12 *Note:* SIS Canada is certified by the British Columbia Ministry of Education. The Parent Information Line is 10-7338-0599.
Sheila Johnsrude, B.Ed, M.Ed, Principal
Dr. Harry Janzen, Offshore Representative
Harry.janzen@viu.ca

Switzerland: Neuchâtel: Neuchâtel Jr. College
P.O. Box 2002
Crêt-Taconnet, 4, Neuchâtel, Switzerland
Tel: 416-368-8169; *Fax:* 416-368-0956
admissions@neuchatel.org
www.njc.ch/school
www.facebook.com/neuchateljuniorcollege
twitter.com/njcsuisse
www.linkedin.com/company/neuch-tel-junior-college
www.youtube.com/user/NJCNeuchatel
Grades: 12 & AP *Enrollment:* 90 *Note:* Member of the Canadian Association of Independent Schools (CAIS). Neuchâtel Junior College is a Swiss non-profit foundation of the Ville de Neuchâtel. As such, NJC has a governing council comprising two Boards of Governors, one in Switzerland (Le Conseil de Fondation), & the other in Canada. The members of the Conseil are appointed by the Neuchâtel City Council & come largely from the fields of education & business. The Canadian Board members are alumni of NJC &/or parents of recent students. The Boards are responsible for the selection of the Principal, the financial operation of the College, & the general direction of NJC's curricular & extra-curricular programs. All members of both Boards act on a volunteer basis.
Bill Boyer, Head of School
Dayle Leishman, Director of Canadian Operations
Brenda Neil, Director of Admission
admissions@neuchatel.org

Affiliations
Canadian Head Office
#1310, 44 Victoria St., Toronto, ON M5C 1Y2
Tel: 416-368-8169; *Fax:* 416-368-0956
Toll-Free: 800-263-2923
Note: The Canadian Head Office is responsible for admissions, alumni publications, events & records, & fundraising.
Dale Leishman, Director, Canadian Operations
dleishman@neuchatel.org
Brenda Neil, Director, Admission
admissions@neuchatel.org
Barbara Sutton, Director, Advancement
advancement@neuchatel.org

Thailand: Phasicharoen, Bangkok: British Columbia International School Bangkok (BCISB)
606 Kalaprapruek Rd., Bangwa, Phasicharoen, Bangkok, Thailand
www.bcisb.net
Other Information: Phone: 662-802-1188, 802-2550; Fax: 662-802-2551, 802-1055#0
www.facebook.com/169194296453823
twitter.com/bcisb
Grades: Elem./Sec. *Note:* BCISB is certified by the British Columbia Ministry of Education.
Gerry Morgan, Principal
gerryrmorgan@shaw.ca
Rodger Lindstrom, Offshore Representative
rlindstrom@shaw.ca

Thailand: Nongkhaem District, Bangkok: Lertlah Schools
45, Soi Phetkasem 77, Nongkangploo, Nongkhaem District, Bangkok, Thailand
information@lertlah.com
www.lertlah.com
Other Information: Phone: 02-809-9081-5; Fax: 02-809-9898
Number of Schools: 3 *Grades:* K.-9 *Enrollment:* 3000 *Note:* Lertlah Schools operates three campuses: Petchkasem Road, Kanchanaphisek Road, & Kaset-Navamin Road. All three are accredited by the Province of Manitoba.
Donna Everitt, Coordinator, International Education, 204-945-1126, fax: 204-957-1793

Trinidad: Petit Valley: Maple Leaf International School
Alyce Heights Dr., Alyce Glen, Petit Valley, Trinidad
Tel: 868-632-9578; *Fax:* 868-633-3068
mlis@tstt.net.tt
www.mapleleaf-school.com
Other Information: Alternate Phone: 868-633-3173
Grades: K - Sec.; Intl. Ed. *Enrollment:* 509 *Note:* Maple Leaf International School opened on September 5, 1994 & offers a Canadian International Education Program in Port of Spain, Trinidad. The curriculum follows the guidelines established by the Province of Ontario Ministry of Education, offering advanced level courses leading to university & college entrance.
William Hargreaves, Principal
Al Tatem, Ontario Agent

United Arab Emirates: Abu Dhabi: Canadian International School (CIS)
P.O. Box 3976
Khalifa A City, Abu Dhabi, United Arab Emirates
admin@cisabudhabi.com
www.cisabudhabi.com
Other Information: Phone: 971-2-556-4206; Fax: 971-2-556-4207
Grades: K.-12 *Enrollment:* 500 *Note:* The school has been accredited with Alberta Education preliminarily since 2009, & fully since the 2011-2012 school year.
Darcy Reynolds, Principal

United Arab Emirates: Abu Dhabi: The Sheikh Zayed Private Academy for Girls
P.O. Box 42989
Abu Dhabi, United Arab Emirates
www.szpag.com
Other Information: Phone: 02-4469777; Fax: 02-4430110
Grades: K.-12; Girls *Note:* The Sheikh Zayed Private Academy for Girls is based in Abu Dhabi, & offers a holistic, international education programme based on the Canadian Curriculum.
Sheryl Cowcill, Head, Elementary School

West Indes: Antigua: Island Academy
Oliver's Estate
P.O. Box W1884
Off Buckley's Main Rd., Antigua, West Indes
Tel: 268-460-1094
admin@islandacademy.com
www.islandacademy.com
Grades: K.-11 *Note:* Accredited with the Ontario Ministry of Education (allowing the school to offer the Ontario Secondary School Diploma). Island Academy opened its doors to students in September, 2001 at Piccadilly, Antigua. It is located off Buckley's Main Road.
Paul Sudolski, Chair/Treasurer
Dr. Ronan Matthew, Headmaster
rmatthew@islandacademy.com

SECTION 7
GOVERNMENT
FEDERAL & PROVINCIAL

Listings in this section are as current as possible at time of publication. For appointments made and results of elections held after publication, please refer to Canada's Information Resource Centre (CIRC), if your library subscribes to this online database.

Government Quick Reference Guide

ABORIGINAL AFFAIRS

Aboriginal Affairs & Northern Development Canada, 10 Wellington St., North Tower, Gatineau, QC K1A 0H4
819-997-0380, Fax: 866-817-3977, 800-567-9604, infopubs@aadnc-aandc.gc.ca
Canadian Heritage, 15 Eddy St., Gatineau, QC K1A 0M5
819-997-0055, 866-811-0055, info@pch.gc.ca
Office of Intergovernmental Affairs, c/o Privy Council Office, #1000, 85 Slater St., Ottawa, ON K1A 0A3
613-957-5153, Fax: 613-957-5043, info@pco-bcp.gc.ca
Saskatchewan Government Relations, 1855 Victoria Ave., Regina, SK S4P 3T2
306-787-8885
Specific Claims Tribunal Canada, #400, 427 Laurier Ave. West, PO Box 31, Ottawa, ON K1R 7Y2
613-947-0751, Fax: 613-943-0586, info@sct-trp.ca

British Columbia
British Columbia Ministry of Aboriginal Relations & Reconciliation, 2957 Jutland Rd., PO Box 9100 Prov Govt,Victoria, BC V8W 9B1
250-387-6121, 800-663-7867, abrinfo@gov.bc.ca

Manitoba
Manitoba Aboriginal & Northern Affairs, Legislative Bldg, 344-450 Broadway, Winnipeg, MB R3C OV8
204-945-3719, Fax: 204-945-8374, anaweb@gov.mb.ca
Aboriginal Affairs Secretariat, #200, 500 Portage Ave., Winnipeg, MB R3C 3X1
204-945-2510, Fax: 204-945-3689

New Brunswick
Aboriginal Affairs Secretariat, Kings Place, #237, 440 King St., PO Box 6000, Fredericton, NB E3B 5H8
506-462-5177, Fax: 506-444-5142, aboriginalaffairssecretariat@gnb.ca

Northwest Territories
Department of Aboriginal Affairs & Intergovernmental Relations, 4910 - 52nd St., PO Box 1320, Yellowknife, NT X1A 2L9
867-873-7143, Fax: 867-873-0233, 877-838-8194, nancy_gardiner@gov.nt.ca

Nunavut
Department of Culture, Language, Elders & Youth, PO Box 1000 800,Iqaluit, NU X0A 0H0
867-975-5500, Fax: 867-975-5504, 866-934-2035

Ontario
Ontario Ministry of Aboriginal Affairs, 160 Bloor St. East, 4th & 9th Fl., Toronto, ON M7A 2E6
416-326-4740, Fax: 416-326-4017

Quebec
Secrétariat aux affaires autochtones, 905, av Honoré-Mercier, 1er étage, Québec, QC G1R 5M6
418-643-3166, Fax: 418-646-4918

ACTS & REGULATIONS

Justice Canada, East Memorial Bldg., 284 Wellington St., Ottawa, ON K1A 0H8
613-957-4222, Fax: 613-954-0811, webadmin@justice.gc.ca

New Brunswick
Justice Services Division, Centennial Building, PO Box 6000, Fredericton, NB E3B 5H1
506-453-2458, Fax: 506-453-3651, general.comments@gnb.ca

Newfoundland & Labrador
Newfoundland & Labrador Department of Justice, Confederation Bldg., East Block, 4th Fl., PO Box 8700, St. John's, NL A1B 4J6
709-729-2869, Fax: 709-729-0469, justice@gov.nl.ca
Newfoundland & Labrador Department of Transportation & Works, Confederation Bldg., West Block, 6th Fl., PO Box 8700, St. John's, NL A1B 4J6
709-729-3679, Fax: 709-729-4285, twminister@gov.nl.ca

Northwest Territories
Department of Justice, Courthouse, 4903 - 49th St., 6th Fl., PO Box 1320, Yellowknife, NT X1A 2L9
867-920-6197

Nova Scotia
Department of Service Nova Scotia & Municipal Relations, 1505 Barrington St., PO Box 216, Halifax, NS B3J 3K5
902-424-5200, Fax: 902-424-0581, 800-670-4357, askus@gov.ns.ca

Ontario
Ontario Ministry of the Attorney General, McMurtry-Scott Bldg., 720 Bay St., 11th Fl., Toronto, ON M5G 2K1
416-326-2220, Fax: 416-326-4007, 800-518-7901

Quebec
Les Publications du Québec, #500, 1000 rte de l'Église, Québec, QC G1V 3V9
418-643-5150, Fax: 418-643-6177, 800-463-2100, publicationsduquebec@cspq.gouv.qc.ca

Yukon Territory
Yukon Justice, Andrew Philipsen Law Centre, 2134 Second Ave., PO Box 2703, Whitehorse, YT Y1A 2C6
867-667-3033, Fax: 867-393-5790, jus.msb@gov.yk.ca

AGRICULTURE

See Also: Land Resources
Agriculture & Agri-Food Canada, 1341 Baseline Rd., Ottawa, ON K1A 0C5
613-773-1000, Fax: 613-773-2772, 866-345-7972, info@agr.gc.ca
Canadian Grain Commission, #600, 303 Main St., Winnipeg, MB R3C 3G8
204-983-2770, Fax: 204-983-2751, 800-853-6705, contact@grainscanada.gc.ca
Canadian Wheat Board, 423 Main St., PO Box 816 Main,Winnipeg, MB R3C 2P5
204-983-0239, Fax: 204-983-3841, 800-275-4292, questions@cwb.ca; farmerservice@cwb.ca
Farm Products Council of Canada, Building 59, Central Experimental Farm, 960 Carling Ave., Ottawa, ON K1A 0C6
613-759-1555, Fax: 613-759-1566, fpcc-cpac@agr.gc.ca
Plant Biotechnology Institute, 110 Gymnasium Pl., Saskatoon, SK S7N 0W9
306-975-5248, Fax: 306-975-4839, pbi-info@nrc-cnrc.gc.ca

Alberta
Agricultural Products Marketing Council, JG O'Donoghue Bldg., 7000 - 113 St., 3rd Fl., Edmonton, AB T6H 5T6
780-427-2164, Fax: 780-422-9690
Alberta Agriculture & Rural Development, JG O'Donoghue Bldg., #100A, 7000 - 113th St., Edmonton, AB T6H 5T6
780-427-2727, -310-3276, duke@gov.ab.ca

British Columbia
British Columbia Ministry of Agriculture, PO Box 9120 Prov Govt,Victoria, BC V8W 9E2
250-387-5121

Manitoba
Agricultural Societies, 1129 Queens Ave., Brandon, MB R7A 1L9
204-726-6195, Fax: 204-726-6260
Manitoba Agriculture, Food & Rural Initiatives, Legislative Bldg., 165-450 Broadway, Winnipeg, MB R3C 0V8
204-945-3722, Fax: 204-945-3470, minagr@leg.gov.mb.ca
Food Development Centre, 810 Phillips St., PO Box 1240, Portage la Prairie, MB R1N 3J9
204-239-3150, Fax: 204-239-3180, 800-870-1044

New Brunswick
New Brunswick Department of Agriculture, Aquaculture & Fisheries, Agricultural Research Station (Experimental Farm), PO Box 6000, Fredericton, NB E3B 5H1
506-453-2666, Fax: 506-453-7170, DAAF-MAAP@gnb.ca

Newfoundland & Labrador
Agrifoods Development, Provincial Agriculture Bldg., Brookfield Rd., PO Box 8700, St. John's, NL A1B 4J6
709-729-6588, Fax: 709-729-2674

Northwest Territories
Department of Environment & Natural Resources, PO Box 1320, Yellowknife, NT X1A 2L9

Nova Scotia
Department of Agriculture, 1741 Brunswick St., 3rd Fl., PO Box 2223, Halifax, NS B3J 3C4
902-424-4560, Fax: 902-424-4671

Ontario
Ontario Ministry of Agriculture, Food & Rural Affairs, Ontario Government Bldg., 1 Stone Rd. West, Guelph, ON N1G 4Y2
519-826-3100, 888-466-2372

Prince Edward Island
Prince Edward Island Department of Agriculture & Forestry, Jones Bldg., 11 Kent St., PO Box 2000, Charlottetown, PE C1A 7N8
902-368-4880, Fax: 902-368-4857

Quebec
Ministère de l'Agriculture, des Pêcheries et de l'Alimentation, 200, ch Sainte-Foy, Québec, QC G1R 4X6
418-380-2110, 888-222-6272

Saskatchewan
Saskatchewan Agriculture, Walter Scott Bldg., 3085 Albert St., Regina, SK S4S 0B1
866-457-2377, aginfo@gov.sk.ca

AGRICULTURE & FOOD

Agriculture & Agri-Food Canada, 1341 Baseline Rd., Ottawa, ON K1A 0C5
613-773-1000, Fax: 613-773-2772, 866-345-7972, info@agr.gc.ca
Agriculture Policy & Regulatory Division, Jones Bldg., 11 Kent St., 5th Fl., Charlottetown, PE C1A 7N8
Market & Industry Services Branch, Tower 5, 1341 Baseline Rd., Ottawa, ON K1A 0C5
613-759-1000, Fax: 613-773-1711
Plant Biotechnology Institute, 110 Gymnasium Pl., Saskatoon, SK S7N 0W9
306-975-5248, Fax: 306-975-4839, pbi-info@nrc-cnrc.gc.ca
Research Branch, Tower 5, 1341 Baseline Rd., Ottawa, ON K1A 0C5
613-759-1000, Fax: 613-773-1866
Soil, Plant & Feed Laboratory, Brookfield Rd., PO Box 8700, St. John's, NL A1B 4J6
709-729-6738, Fax: 709-729-6734
Strategic Policy Branch, Tower 7, 1341 Baseline Rd., Ottawa, ON K1A 0C5
613-759-1000, Fax: 613-773-2111

Alberta
Agricultural Products Marketing Council, JG O'Donoghue Bldg., 7000 - 113 St., 3rd Fl., Edmonton, AB T6H 5T6
780-427-2164, Fax: 780-422-9690
Alberta Agriculture & Rural Development, JG O'Donoghue Bldg., #100A, 7000 - 113th St., Edmonton, AB T6H 5T6
780-427-2727, -310-3276, duke@gov.ab.ca
Alberta Livestock & Meat Agency, Ellwood Office Park South, #101, 1003 Ellwood Rd. SW, Edmonton, AB T6X 0B3
780-638-1699, Fax: 780-638-6495, info@almaltd.ca
Irrigation Council, Provincial Bldg., 200 - 5 Ave. South, 3rd Fl., Lethbridge, AB T1J 4L1
403-381-5176, Fax: 403-382-4406

British Columbia
Agricultural Land Commission, #133, 4940 Canada Way, Burnaby, BC V5G 4K6
604-660-7000, Fax: 604-660-7033, ALCBurnaby@Victoria1.gov.bc.ca
British Columbia Ministry of Agriculture, PO Box 9120 Prov Govt,Victoria, BC V8W 9E2
250-387-5121

Manitoba
Agricultural Societies, 1129 Queens Ave., Brandon, MB R7A 1L9
204-726-6195, Fax: 204-726-6260
Manitoba Agriculture, Food & Rural Initiatives, Legislative Bldg., 165-450 Broadway, Winnipeg, MB R3C 0V8
204-945-3722, Fax: 204-945-3470, minagr@leg.gov.mb.ca
Farm Lands Ownership Board, #812, Norquay Bldg., 401 York Ave., Winnipeg, MB R3C 0P8
204-945-3149, Fax: 204-945-1489, 800-282-8069, robert.mckenzie@gov.mb.ca
Farm Machinery Board, Norquay Bldg., #812, 401 York Ave., Winnipeg, MB R3C 0P8
204-945-3856, Fax: 204-948-2844, randy.ozunko@gov.mb.ca
Manitoba Agricultural Services Corporation, #100, 1525 First St. South, Brandon, MB R7A 7A1
204-726-6850, Fax: 204-726-6849, mailbox@masc.mb.ca

New Brunswick
New Brunswick Farm Products Commission, c/o Department of Agriculture, Aquaculture & Fisheries, PO Box 6000, Fredericton, NB E3B 5H1
506-453-3647, Fax: 506-444-5969

Newfoundland & Labrador
Agrifoods Development, Provincial Agriculture Bldg., Brookfield Rd., PO Box 8700, St. John's, NL A1B 4J6
709-729-6588, Fax: 709-729-2674
Newfoundland & Labrador Department of Natural Resources, Natural Resources Bldg., 50 Elizabeth Ave., 7th Fl., PO Box 8700, St. John's, NL A1B 4J6
709-729-2920, Fax: 709-729-0059

Nova Scotia
Department of Agriculture, 1741 Brunswick St., 3rd Fl., PO Box 2223, Halifax, NS B3J 3C4
902-424-4560, Fax: 902-424-4671

Ontario
AGRICORP, 1 Stone Rd. West, 3rd Fl., PO Box 3660 Central, Guelph, ON N1H 8M4
Fax: 519-826-4118, 888-247-4999, cac@agricorp.com
Agricultural Research Institute of Ontario, 1 Stone Rd. West, 2nd Fl., Guelph, ON N1G 4Y2
519-826-4199, Fax: 519-826-4211
Agriculture, Food & Rural Affairs Tribunal, 1 Stone Rd. West, 2nd Fl., Guelph, ON N1G 4Y2
519-826-3433, Fax: 519-826-4232, appeals.tribunal@omafra.gov.on.ca
Ontario Ministry of Agriculture, Food & Rural Affairs, Ontario Government Bldg., 1 Stone Rd. West, Guelph, ON N1G 4Y2
519-826-3100, 888-466-2372

Prince Edward Island
Agricultural Insurance Corporation, 29 Indigo Cres., PO Box 1600, Charlottetown, PE C1A 7N3
902-368-4842, Fax: 902-368-6677
BIO FOOD TECH, 101 Belvedere Ave., PO Box 2000, Charlottetown, PE C1A 7N8
902-368-5548, Fax: 902-368-5549, 877-368-5548, biofoodtech@biofoodtech.ca

Prince Edward Island Department of Agriculture & Forestry, Jones Bldg., 11 Kent St., PO Box 2000, Charlottetown, PE C1A 7N8
902-368-4880, Fax: 902-368-4857

Quebec

Ministère de l'Agriculture, des Pêcheries et de l'Alimentation, 200, ch Sainte-Foy, Québec, QC G1R 4X6
418-380-2110, 888-222-6272

Commission de protection du territoire agricole du Québec, 200, ch Ste-Foy, 2e étage, Québec, QC G1R 4X6
418-643-3314, Fax: 418-643-2261, 800-667-5294, info@cptaq.gouv.qc.ca

Régie des marchés agricoles et alimentaires du Québec, 201, boul Crémazie est, 5e étage, Montréal, QC H2M 1L3
514-873-4024, Fax: 514-873-3984

Saskatchewan

Saskatchewan Agriculture, Walter Scott Bldg., 3085 Albert St., Regina, SK S4S 0B1
866-457-2377, aginfo@gov.sk.ca

Saskatchewan Crop Insurance Corporation, 484 Prince William Dr., PO Box 3000, Melville, SK S0A 2P0
306-728-7200, Fax: 306-728-7202, 888-935-0000, customer.service@scic.gov.sk.ca

Yukon Territory

Yukon Environment, PO Box 2703, Whitehorse, YT Y1A 2C6
867-667-5652, Fax: 867-393-7197, environment.yukon@gov.yk.ca

AIR POLLUTION

See Also: Environment

Prince Edward Island

Administrative Services Division, Jones Bldg., 11 Kent St., 4th Fl., PO Box 2000, Charlottetown, PE C1A 7N8
902-368-5000, Fax: 902-368-5830

Clean Energy Division, Centre West Building, 10035 - 108 St., 8th Fl., Edmonton, AB T5J 3E1

Environmental Stewardship Branch, 351 boul St-Joseph, Gatineau, QC K1A 0H3
819-997-1575, Fax: 819-953-9452

Integrated Environmental Policy Division, 77 Wellesley St. West, 11th Fl., Toronto, ON M7A 2T5
416-314-6338, Fax: 416-314-6346

International Joint Commission, 234 Laurier Ave. West, 22nd Fl., Ottawa, ON K1P 6K6
613-947-1420, Fax: 613-993-5583, beckhoffb@ottawa.ijc.org

Springdale, 200 Main St., Springdale, NL A0J 1T0
709-673-4218, Fax: 709-673-4232

Alberta

Alberta Environment & Sustainable Resource Development, Oxbridge Place, 9820 - 106 St., Main Fl., Edmonton, AB T5K 2J6
780-427-2700, Fax: 780-422-4086, -310-0000, env.infocent@gov.ab.ca; srd.infocent@gov.ab.ca

British Columbia

British Columbia Ministry of Environment, PO Box 9339 Prov Govt,Victoria, BC V8W 9M1
250-387-1161, Fax: 250-387-5669, envmail@gov.bc.ca

Manitoba

Manitoba Conservation & Water Stewardship, 200 Saulteaux Cres., Winnipeg, MB R3J 3W3
800-214-6497, mws@gov.mb.ca

New Brunswick

Community Planning & Environmental Protection Division, Marysville Place, PO Box 6000, Fredericton, NB E3B 5H1
506-444-5119, Fax: 506-457-7333, elg/egl-info@gnb.ca

New Brunswick Department of Environment & Local Government, Marysville Place, PO Box 6000, Fredericton, NB E3B 5H1
506-453-2690, Fax: 506-457-4994, elg/egl-info@gnb.ca

New Brunswick Department of Natural Resources, Hugh John Flemming Forestry Centre, PO Box 6000, Fredericton, NB E3B 5H1
506-453-3826, Fax: 506-444-4367, dnrweb@gnb.ca

Partnerships & Innovation Division, Marysville Place, PO Box 6000, Fredericton, NB E3B 5H1
506-453-2862, Fax: 506-453-2265, elg/egl-info@gnb.ca

Newfoundland & Labrador

Newfoundland & Labrador Department of Environment & Conservation, Confederation Bldg., West Block, 4th Fl., PO Box 8700, St. John's, NL A1B 4J6
709-729-2664, Fax: 709-729-6639, 800-563-6181, info@gov.nl.ca

Northwest Territories

Department of Environment & Natural Resources, PO Box 1320, Yellowknife, NT X1A 2L9

Nova Scotia

Department of Environment, 5151 Terminal Rd., 5th Fl., PO Box 442, Halifax, NS B3J 2P8
902-424-3600, Fax: 902-424-0503, 877-936-8476

Nunavut

Department of Environment, PO Box 1000 1300,Iqaluit, NU X0A 0H0
867-975-7700, Fax: 867-975-7742, environment@gov.nu.ca

Ontario

Ontario Ministry of Environment, 135 St. Clair Ave. West, Toronto, ON M4V 1P5
416-325-4000, Fax: 416-325-3159, 800-565-4923

Prince Edward Island

Prince Edward Island Department of Environment, Labour & Justice, Shaw Bldg. South, 95 Rochford St., 4th Fl., PO Box 2000, Charlottetown, PE C1A 7N8
902-620-3774, Fax: 902-368-4242, rrryder@gov.pe.ca

Quebec

Ministère du Développement durable, de l'Environnement, de la Faune, et des Parcs, Édifice Marie-Guyart, 675, boul René-Lévesque est, 29e étage, Québec, QC G1R 5V7
418-521-3830, Fax: 418-646-5974, 800-561-1616, info@mddep.gouv.qc.ca

Saskatchewan

Saskatchewan Environment, 3211 Albert St., 2nd Fl., Regina, SK S4S 5W6
306-787-2584, Fax: 306-787-9544, 800-567-4224, Centre.Inquiry@gov.sk.ca

Yukon Territory

Yukon Environment, PO Box 2703, Whitehorse, YT Y1A 2C6
867-667-5652, Fax: 867-393-7197, environment.yukon@gov.yk.ca

AIRPORTS & AVIATION

See Also: Transportation

Canadian Air Transport Security Authority, 99 Bank St., 13th Fl., Ottawa, ON K1P 6B9
Fax: 613-990-1295, 888-294-2202

Institute for Aerospace Research, 1200 Montreal Rd., Ottawa, ON K1A 0R6
613-990-0765, Fax: 613-952-7214

Transport Canada, Place de Ville, 330 Sparks St., Tower C, Ottawa, ON K1A 0N5
613-990-2309, Fax: 613-954-4731, 866-995-9737

Transportation Appeal Tribunal of Canada, #1201, 333 Laurier Ave. West, 12th Fl., Ottawa, ON K1A 0N5
613-990-6906, Fax: 613-990-9153, info@tatc.gc.ca

Newfoundland & Labrador

Newfoundland & Labrador Department of Transportation & Works, Confederation Bldg., West Block, 6th Fl., PO Box 8700, St. John's, NL A1B 4J6
709-729-3679, Fax: 709-729-4285, twminister@gov.nl.ca

Northwest Territories

Airports, YK Centre, 4922 - 28th St., 4th fl., PO Box 1320, Yellowknife, NT X1A 2L9
867-873-7725, Fax: 867-873-0297

Department of Transportation, Lahm Ridge Bldg., 4501 50 Ave., PO Box 1320, Yellowknife, NT X1A 2L9
867-920-3460, Fax: 867-873-0363

Nunavut

Department of Community & Government Services, W.G. Brown Bldg., 4th Fl., PO Box 1000 700,Iqaluit, NU X0A 0H0
867-975-5400, Fax: 867-975-5305

Ontario

Ontario Ministry of Transportation, Ferguson Block, 77 Wellesley St. West, 3rd Fl., Toronto, ON M7A 1Z8
416-235-4686, Fax: 905-704-2001, 800-268-4686

Saskatchewan

Saskatchewan Highways & Infrastructure, Victoria Tower, 1855 Victoria Ave., Regina, SK S4P 3T2
306-787-4800, communications@highways.gov.sk.ca

Yukon Territory

Yukon Highways & Public Works, PO Box 2703, Whitehorse, YT Y1A 2C6
867-393-7193, Fax: 867-393-6218, 800-661-0408, hpw-info@gov.yk.ca

APPRENTICESHIP PROGRAMS

Canadian Council of Directors of Apprenticeship, 140 Promenade du Portage, 5th Fl, Phase IV, Gatineau, QC K1A 0J9
819-953-7443, Fax: 819-994-0202, redseal-sceaurouge@hrsdc-rhdcc.gc.ca

Alberta

Community, Learner & Industry Connections Division, Phipps-McKinnon Bldg., 10020 - 101A Ave., 5th Fl., Edmonton, AB T5J 3G2

Alberta Enterprise & Advanced Education, Legislature Bldg., #324, 10800 - 97 Ave., Edmonton, AB T5K 2B6
780-422-5400, -310-0000

New Brunswick

New Brunswick Department of Post-Secondary Education, Training, & Labour, Chestnut Complex, PO Box 6000, Fredericton, NB E3B 5H1
506-453-2597, Fax: 506-453-3618, dpetlinfo@gnb.ca

Northwest Territories

Northwest Territories Apprenticeship, Trade & Occupations Certification Board, PO Box 1320, Yellowknife, NT X1A 2L9
867-873-7357, Fax: 867-873-0200

Prince Edward Island

SkillsPEI, Atlantic Technology Centre, #212, 90 University Ave., Charlottetown, PE C1A 4K9
902-368-4260, Fax: 902-368-6340, 877-491-4766

Quebec

Conseil consultatif du travail et de la main d'oeuvre, #9.400, 500, boul René-Lévesque ouest, Montréal, QC H2Z 1W7
514-873-2880, Fax: 514-873-1129, cctm@cctm.gouv.qc.ca

Saskatchewan

Saskatchewan Advanced Education, 1945 Hamilton St., Regina, SK S4P 2C8
306-787-9478, aeeinquiry@gov.sk.ca

Yukon Territory

Yukon Education, PO Box 2703, Whitehorse, YT Y1A 2C6
867-667-5141, Fax: 867-393-6254, contact.education@gov.yk.ca

ARCTIC & NORTHERN AFFAIRS

Aboriginal Affairs & Northern Development Canada, 10 Wellington St., North Tower, Gatineau, QC K1A 0H4
819-997-0380, Fax: 866-817-3977, 800-567-9604, infopubs@aadnc-aandc.gc.ca

Canadian Polar Commission, Constitution Square, #1710, 360 Albert St., Ottawa, ON K1R 7X7
613-943-8605, Fax: 613-943-8607, 888-765-2701, mail@polarcom.gc.ca

Polar Continental Shelf Program, #487, 615 Booth St., Ottawa, ON K1A 0E4
613-947-1650, Fax: 613-947-1611, pcsp@nrcan-rncan.gc.ca

British Columbia

Northern Development Initiative Trust, #301, 1268 Fifth Ave., Prince George, BC V2L 3L2
250-561-2525, Fax: 250-561-2563, info@northerndevelopment.bc.ca

Manitoba

Manitoba Aboriginal & Northern Affairs, Legislative Bldg, 344-450 Broadway, Winnipeg, MB R3C 0V8
204-945-3719, Fax: 204-945-8374, anaweb@gov.mb.ca

Northwest Territories

Department of Environment & Natural Resources, PO Box 1320, Yellowknife, NT X1A 2L9

Nunavut

Department of Executive & Intergovernmental Affairs, 1084 Aeroplex bldg., PO Box 1000 200,Iqaluit, NU X0A 0H0
867-975-6000, Fax: 867-975-6099

Ontario

Ontario Ministry of Northern Development & Mines, 159 Cedar St., Sudbury, ON P3E 6A5
Fax: 416-327-0651, 888-415-9845

Northern Development Division, Roberta Bondar Place, #200, 70 Foster Dr., Sault Ste Marie, ON P6A 6V8
705-945-5900, Fax: 705-945-5931, 800-461-2287

Yukon Territory

Yukon Economic Development, PO Box 2703, Whitehorse, YT Y1A 2C6
867-393-7191, Fax: 867-393-6412, 800-661-0408, ecdev@gov.yk.ca

ARTS & CULTURE

Canada Council for the Arts, 350 Albert St., PO Box 1047, Ottawa, ON K1P 5V8
613-566-4414, Fax: 613-566-4390, 800-263-5588

Canada Place Corporation, 504 - 999 Canada Place, Vancouver, BC V6C 3E1
604-775-7200, Fax: 604-775-6251, admin@canadaplace.ca

Canada Science & Technology Museum Corporation, PO Box 9724 T,Ottawa, ON K1G 5A3
613-991-6090, Fax: 613-990-3636, info@technomuses.ca

Canadian Artists & Producers Professional Relations Tribunal, C.D. Howe Bldg., 240 Sparks St., 1st Fl., West Tower, Ottawa, ON K1A 1A1
613-996-4052, Fax: 613-947-4125, 800-263-ARTS, info@capprt-tcrpap.gc.ca

Canadian Broadcasting Corporation, 181 Queen St., PO Box 3220 C,Ottawa, ON K1Y 1E4
613-288-6033, liaison@radio-canada.ca

Canadian Heritage, 15 Eddy St., Gatineau, QC K1A 0M5
819-997-0055, 866-811-0055, info@pch.gc.ca

Canadian Museum of Civilization Corporation, 100 Laurier St., Gatineau, QC K1A 0M8
819-776-7000, 800-555-5621

Canadian Museum of Nature, PO Box 3443 D,Ottawa, ON K1P 6P4
613-566-4700, Fax: 613-364-4021, 800-263-4433
Conexus Arts Centre, 200A Lakeshore Dr., Regina, SK S4S 7L3
306-565-4500, 800-667-8497, cac.admin@conexusartscentre.ca
Library of Parliament, Parliamentary Buildings, Ottawa, ON K1A 0A9
613-992-4793, 866-599-4999, info@parl.gc.ca
National Arts Centre, 53 Elgin St., PO Box 1534 B,Ottawa, ON K1P 5W1
613-947-7000, Fax: 613-996-9578, 866-850-2787, info@nac-cna.ca
National Film Board of Canada, 3155, rue Côte de Liesse, CP 1600 Centre-ville,Saint-Laurent, QC H4N 2N4
514-283-9000, Fax: 514-283-7564, 800-267-7710
National Gallery of Canada, 380 Sussex Dr., PO Box 427 A,Ottawa, ON K1N 9N4
613-990-1985, Fax: 613-993-4385, 800-319-2787, info@gallery.ca; info@beaux-arts.ca
Parks Canada, 25 Eddy St., Gatineau, QC K1A 0M5
613-860-1251, 888-773-8888, information@pc.gc.ca
Provincial Capital Commission, 4607 Dewdney Ave., Regina, SK S4T 1B7
306-787-9261
Telefilm Canada, #500, 360, rue Saint-Jacques, Montréal, QC H2Y 1P5
514-283-6363, Fax: 514-283-2365, 800-567-0890, info@telefilm.gc.ca

British Columbia

British Columbia Ministry of Social Development, PO Box 9058 Prov Govt,Victoria, BC V8W 9E1
Islands Trust, #200, 1627 Fort St., Victoria, BC V8R 1H8
250-405-5151, Fax: 250-405-5155, information@islandstrust.bc.ca

Manitoba

Communications Services Manitoba, 155 Carlton St., 10th Fl., Winnipeg, MB R3C 3H8
204-945-3765, Fax: 204-948-2147,
Manitoba Culture, Heritage & Tourism, Legislative Building, #118, 450 Broadway Ave., Winnipeg, MB R3C 0V8
204-945-3729, Fax: 204-945-5223, mincht@leg.gov.mb.ca
Heritage Grants Advisory Council, 213 Notre Dame Ave., 3rd Fl., Winnipeg, MB R3B 1N3
204-945-2213, Fax: 204-948-2086
Le Centre Culturel franco-manitobain/Franco-Manitoban Cultural Centre, 340, boul Provencher, St Boniface, MB R2H 0G7
204-233-8972, Fax: 204-233-3324, ccfm@ccfm.mb.ca
Manitoba Arts Council, #525, 93 Lombard Ave., Winnipeg, MB R3B 3B1
204-945-2237, Fax: 204-945-5925, 866-994-2787, info@artscouncil.mb.ca
Manitoba Centennial Centre Corporation, 555 Main St., Winnipeg, MB R3B 1C3
204-956-1360, Fax: 204-944-1390
Manitoba Film Classification Board, #216, 301 Weston St., Winnipeg, MB R3E 3H4
204-945-8962, Fax: 204-945-0890, 866-612-2399, mfcb@gov.mb.ca
Manitoba Heritage Council, 213 Notre Dame Ave., Main Fl., Winnipeg, MB R3B 1N3
204-945-2118, Fax: 204-948-2384, hrb@gov.mb.ca
Manitoba Museum, 190 Rupert Ave., Winnipeg, MB R3B 0N2
204-956-2830, Fax: 204-942-3679, info@manitobamuseum.mb.ca
Multiculturalism Secretariat, 213 Notre Dame Ave., 4th Fl., Winnipeg, MB R3B 1N3
204-945-1156, Fax: 204-948-2323

New Brunswick

New Brunswick Arts Board, 61 Carleton St., Fredericton, NB E3B 3T2
506-444-4444, Fax: 506-444-5543, 866-460-2787
New Brunswick Department of Social Development, Sartain MacDonald Bldg., 551 King St., PO Box 6000, Fredericton, NB E3B 5H1
506-453-2001, Fax: 506-453-7478, sd-ds@gnb.ca

Newfoundland & Labrador

Newfoundland & Labrador Department of Tourism, Culture, & Recreation, Confederation Bldg., West Block, 2nd Fl., PO Box 8700, St. John's, NL A1B 4J6
709-729-0862, Fax: 709-729-0870, tcrinfo@gov.nl.ca
Provincial Information & Library Resources Board, 48 St. George's Ave, Stephenville, NL A2H 1K9
709-643-0900, Fax: 709-643-0925

Northwest Territories

Department of Education, Culture & Employment, PO Box 1320, Yellowknife, NT X1A 2L9
867-669-2399, Fax: 867-873-0431, 866-606-5627
NWT Arts Council, PO Box 1320 Main, Yellowknife, NT X1A 2L9
867-920-6370, Fax: 867-873-0205

Nova Scotia

Culture Division, #601, 1800 Argyle St., PO Box 456, Halifax, NS B3J 2R5
902-424-4510, Fax: 902-424-0710, culture@gov.ns.ca
Department of Education, Trade Mart Bldg., #402-2021 Brunswick St., PO Box 578, Halifax, NS B3J 2S9
902-424-5168, Fax: 902-424-0680
Film Nova Scotia, Collins Bank Bldg., 1869 Upper Water St., 3rd Fl., Halifax, NS B3J 1S9
902-424-7177, Fax: 902-424-0617, 888-360-2111
Nova Scotia Tourism Partnership Council, World Trade & Convention Centre, #603, 1800 Argyle St., Halifax, NS B3J 3N8
902-424-0048, Fax: 902-424-0723

Nunavut

Department of Culture, Language, Elders & Youth, PO Box 1000 800,Iqaluit, NU X0A 0H0
867-975-5500, Fax: 867-975-5504, 866-934-2035

Ontario

Ontario Heritage Trust, 10 Adelaide St. East, Toronto, ON M5C 1J3
416-325-5000, Fax: 416-325-5071
Ontario Library Service - North, 334 Regent St., Sudbury, ON P3C 4E2
705-675-6467, Fax: 705-675-2285, 800-461-6348
Ontario Media Development Corporation, South Tower, #501, 175 Bloor St. East, Toronto, ON M4W 3R8
416-314-6858, Fax: 416-314-6876, mail@omdc.on.ca
Ontario Northland, 555 Oak St. East, North Bay, ON P1B 8L3
705-472-4500, Fax: 705-472-4267, 800-363-7512, info@ontarionorthland.ca
Ontario Place Corporation, 955 Lake Shore Blvd. West, Toronto, ON M6K 3B9
416-314-9900, Fax: 416-314-9992
Ontario Tourism Marketing Partnership Corporation, #900,10 Dundas St. East, Toronto, ON M7A 2A1
416-212-0757, Fax: 416-325-6004, 800-668-2746
Ontario Trillium Foundation, 800 Bay St., 5th Fl., Toronto, ON M5S 3A9
416-963-4927, Fax: 416-963-8781, 800-263-2887, trillium@trilliumfoundation.org
Ottawa Convention Centre, 55 Colonel By Dr., Ottawa, ON K1N 9J2
613-563-1984, Fax: 613-563-7646
Royal Ontario Museum, 100 Queen's Park Cres., Toronto, ON M5S 2C6
416-586-5549, Fax: 416-586-5685, info@rom.on.ca
Southern Ontario Library Service, #902, 111 Peter St., Toronto, ON M5V 2H1
416-961-1669, Fax: 416-961-5122, 800-387-5765
Ontario Ministry of Tourism & Culture, Hearst Block, 900 Bay St., 9th Fl., Toronto, ON M7A 2E1
416-326-9326, Fax: 416-314-7854, 800-668-2746

Prince Edward Island

Prince Edward Island Department of Community Services & Seniors, Jones Bldg., 11 Kent St., 2nd Fl., PO Box 2000, Charlottetown, PE C1A 7N8
902-620-3777, Fax: 902-368-4740, 866-594-3777

Quebec

Bibliothèque et Archives nationales du Québec (BAnQ), 475, boul De Maisonneuve est, Montréal, QC H2L 5C4
514-873-1100, Fax: 514-873-9312, 800-363-9028
Commission des biens culturels du Québec, Bloc A-RC, 225, Grande Allée est, Québec, QC G1R 5G5
418-643-8378, Fax: 418-643-8591, info@cbcq.gouv.qc.ca
Conseil des arts et des lettres du Québec, 79, boul René-Lévesque est, 3e étage, Québec, QC G1R 5N5
418-643-1707, Fax: 418-643-4558, 800-897-1707, info@calq.gouv.qc.ca
Conseil des relations interculturelles, #10.04, 500, boul René-Lévesque ouest, Montréal, QC H2Z 1W7
514-873-5634, Fax: 514-873-3469, info@conseilinterculturel.gouv.qc.ca
Ministère de la Culture, des Communications & de la Condition féminine, 225, Grande Allée est, Québec, QC G1R 5G5
888-380-8882
Curateur public du Québec, 600, boul René-Lévesque ouest, Montréal, QC H3B 4W9
514-873-4074, Fax: 514-873-5033, 800-363-9020
Musée d'art contemporain de Montréal, 185, rue Ste-Catherine ouest, Montréal, QC H2X 3X5
514-847-6226, Fax: 514-847-6290, info@macm.org
Musée de la civilisation, 85, rue Dalhousie, CP 155 B,Québec, QC G1K 7A6
418-643-2158, Fax: 418-646-9705, 866-710-8031, mcqweb@mcq.org
Musée national des beaux-arts du Québec, Parc des Champs-de-Bataille, 1, av Wolfe-Montcalm, Québec, QC G1R 5H3
418-643-2150, Fax: 418-646-3330, 866-220-2150, webmestre@mnba.qc.ca
Régie du cinéma, #100, 390, rue Notre-Dame ouest, Montréal, QC H2Y 1T9
514-873-2371, Fax: 514-873-8874, 800-463-2463, regieducinema@rcq.gouv.qc.ca
Secrétariat à la politique linguistique, 225 Grande-Allée est, 4e étage, Québec, QC G1R 5G5
418-643-4248, Fax: 418-646-7832, info@spl.gouv.qc.ca
Société de développement des entreprises culturelles, #800, 215, rue Saint-Jacques, Montréal, QC H2Y 1M6
514-841-2200, Fax: 514-841-8606, 800-363-0401, info@sodec.gouv.qc.ca
Société de la Place des Arts de Montréal, 260, boul de Maisonneuve ouest, Montréal, QC H2X 1Y9
514-285-4200, Fax: 514-285-1968, info@pda.qc.ca
Société de télédiffusion du Québec (Télé-Québec), 1000, rue Fullum, Montréal, QC H2K 3L7
514-521-2424, Fax: 514-873-2601, 800-361-4362, info@telequebec.tv
Société du Grand Théâtre de Québec, 269, boul René-Lévesque est, Québec, QC G1R 2B3
418-643-8111, gtq@grandtheatre.qc.ca

Saskatchewan

Saskatchewan Archives Board, University of Regina, 3303 Hillsdale St., PO Box 1665, Regina, SK S4P 3C6
306-787-4068, Fax: 306-787-1197, info.regina@archives.gov.sk.ca
Saskatchewan Film & Video Classification Board, #500, 1919 Saskatchewan Dr., Regina, SK S4P 4H2
306-787-5550, Fax: 306-787-9779, 888-374-4636

Yukon Territory

Yukon Tourism & Culture, 100 Hanson St., Whitehorse, YT Y1A 2C6
867-667-5036, Fax: 867-667-3546,

ASSESSMENT

British Columbia

British Columbia Environmental Assessment Office, 836 Yates St., 1st Fl., PO Box 9426 Prov Govt,Victoria, BC V8W 9V1
250-356-7479, Fax: 250-356-6448, eaoinfo@gov.bc.ca

AUDITORS-GENERAL

Auditor General of Canada, 240 Sparks St., Ottawa, ON K1A 0G6
613-995-3708, Fax: 613-957-0474, 888-761-5953, communications@oag-bvg.gc.ca; infomedia@oag-bvg.gc.ca

Alberta

Alberta Office of the Auditor General, 9925 - 109 St., 8th Fl., Edmonton, AB T5K 2J8
780-427-4222, Fax: 780-422-9555, info@oag.ab.ca

British Columbia

Office of the Auditor General, PO Box 9036 Prov Govt,Victoria, BC V8W 9A2
250-419-6100, Fax: 250-387-1230

Manitoba

Office of the Auditor General, #500, 330 Portage Ave., Winnipeg, MB R3C 0C4
204-945-3790, Fax: 204-945-2169, oag.contact@oag.mb.ca

New Brunswick

Office of the Auditor General, HSBC Place, 520 King St., 6th Fl., Fredericton, NB E3B 6G3
506-453-2243, Fax: 506-453-3067

Newfoundland & Labrador

Office of the Auditor General, PO Box 8700, St. John's, NL A1B 4J6
709-729-2695, Fax: 709-729-5970, oagmail@oag.nl.ca

Nova Scotia

Office of the Auditor General, #302, 1888 Brunswick St., Halifax, NS B3J 3J8
902-424-5907, Fax: 902-424-4350

Ontario

Office of the Auditor General, Atrium on Bay, #1530, 20 Dundas St. West, PO Box 105, Toronto, ON M5G 2C2
416-327-2381, Fax: 416-327-9862, comments@auditor.on.ca

Prince Edward Island

Office of the Auditor General, Shaw Bldg., 105 Rochford St. North, 2nd Fl., Charlottetown, PE C1A 7N8
902-368-4520, Fax: 902-368-4598, www.assembly.pe.ca

Quebec

Vérificateur général du Québec, 750, boulevard Charest est, 3e étage, Québec, QC G1K 9J6
418-691-5900, Fax: 418-644-4460, verificateur.general@vgq.gouv.qc.ca

Saskatchewan

Provincial Auditor Saskatchewan, #1500, 1920 Broad St., Regina, SK S4P 3V2
306-787-6398, Fax: 306-787-6383, info@auditor.sk.ca

AUTOMOBILE INSURANCE

See Also: Insurance (Life, Fire Property)

Alberta
Alberta Automobile Insurance Rate Board, Canadian Western Bank Place, #2440, 10303 Jasper Ave., Edmonton, AB T5J 3N6
780-427-5428, Fax: 780-638-4254, -310-0000, airb@gov.ab.ca
British Columbia
Insurance Corporation of British Columbia, 151 West Esplanade, North Vancouver, BC V7M 3H9
604-661-2800, 800-663-3051
Manitoba
Manitoba Public Insurance, #B100, 234 Donald St., PO Box 6300, Winnipeg, MB R3C 4A4
204-985-7000, Fax: 204-985-3525, 800-665-2410
Northwest Territories
Department of Finance, Arthur Laing Building, 5th Fl., 5003 - 49th St., PO Box 1320, Yellowknife, NT X1A 2L9
867-873-7117, Fax: 867-873-0414
Nova Scotia
Nova Scotia Utility & Review Board, Summit Place, 1601 Lower Water St., 3rd Fl., Halifax, NS B3J 3P6
902-424-4448, Fax: 902-424-3919, uarb.board@gov.ns.ca
Ontario
Financial Services Commission of Ontario, New York City Ctr., 5160 Yonge St., 17th Fl., PO Box 85, Toronto, ON M2N 6L9
416-250-7250, Fax: 416-590-7070, 800-668-0128
Quebec
Société de l'assurance automobile du Québec, 333, boul Jean-Lesage, CP 19600 Terminus, Québec, QC G1K 8J6
418-643-7620, Fax: 418-644-0339, 800-361-7620, courrier@saaq.gouv.qc.ca
Saskatchewan
Saskatchewan Government Insurance, 2260 - 11th Ave., Regina, SK S4P 0J9
306-751-1200, Fax: 306-787-7477, 800-667-8015, sgiinquiries@sgi.sk.ca
Yukon Territory
Yukon Justice, Andrew Philipsen Law Centre, 2134 Second Ave., PO Box 2703, Whitehorse, YT Y1A 2C6
867-667-3033, Fax: 867-393-5790, jus.msb@gov.yk.ca

BANKING & FINANCIAL INSTITUTIONS

Bank of Canada, 234 Wellington St., Ottawa, ON K1A 0G9
613-782-7902, Fax: 613-782-7713, 800-303-1282, info@bankofcanada.ca; communications@bankofcanada.ca (Media)
Business Development Bank of Canada, #400, 5, Place Ville-Marie, Montréal, QC H3B 5E7
514-283-5904, Fax: 514-283-5626, 877-232-2269
Canada Deposit Insurance Corporation, 50 O'Connor St., 17th Floor, PO Box 2340 D,Ottawa, ON K1P 5W5
Fax: 613-996-6095, 800-461-2342, info@cdic.ca; info@sadc.ca
Finance Canada, L'esplanade Laurier, 140 O'Connor St., Ottawa, ON K1A 0G5
613-992-1573, Fax: 613-943-0938, finpub@fin.gc.ca
Financial Consumer Agency of Canada, 427 Laurier Ave. West, 6th Fl., Ottawa, ON K1R 1B9
Fax: 613-941-1436, info@fcac-acfc.gc.ca
Office of the Superintendent of Financial Institutions, Kent Square, 255 Albert St., Ottawa, ON K1A 0H2
613-990-7788, Fax: 613-990-5591, 800-385-8647, information@osfi-bsif.gc.ca
Provincial-Local Finance Division, College Park, 777 Bay St., 10th Fl., Toronto, ON M5G 2C8
416-327-0264, Fax: 416-325-7644
Treasury & Risk Management, Terrace Building, 9515 - 107 St., 3rd Fl., Edmonton, AB T5K 2C3
Alberta
ATB Financial, 9888 Jasper Ave., Edmonton, AB T5J 1P1
403-245-8110, 800-332-8383
Credit Union Deposit Guarantee Corporation, #2000, 10104 - 103 St., Edmonton, AB T5J 0H8
780-428-6680, Fax: 780-428-7571, 800-661-0351, mail@cudgc.ab.ca
Alberta Treasury Board & Finance, Oxbridge Place, 9820 - 106 St., 5th Fl., Edmonton, AB T5K 2J6
780-415-4519, -310-000
British Columbia
British Columbia Ministry of Finance, PO Box 9417 Prov Govt,Victoria, BC V8W 9V1
877-388-4440, CTBTaxQuestions@gov.bc.ca (tax inquiries)
Financial Institutions Commission, #1200, 13450 - 102 Ave., Surrey, BC V3T 5X3
604-953-5300, Fax: 604-953-5301, 866-206-3030, FICOM@ficombc.ca; HR@ficombc.ca
Manitoba
Credit Union Deposit Guarantee Corporation, #390, 200 Graham Ave., Winnipeg, MB R3C 4L5
204-942-8480, Fax: 204-947-1723, 800-697-4447, mail@cudgc.com
Financial Institutions Regulation Branch, #1115, 405 Broadway, Winnipeg, MB R3C 3L6
204-945-2542, Fax: 204-948-2268
Newfoundland & Labrador
Credit Union Deposit Guarantee Corporation, PO Box 340, Marystown, NL A0E 2M0
709-279-0170, Fax: 709-279-0177, 877-279-0170
Northwest Territories
Department of Finance, Arthur Laing Building, 5th Fl., 5003 - 49th St., PO Box 1320, Yellowknife, NT X1A 2L9
867-873-7117, Fax: 867-873-0414
Nunavut
Nunavut Business Credit Corporation, Parnaivak Bldg., #100, PO Box 2548, Iqaluit, NU X0A 0H0
867-975-7891, Fax: 867-975-7897, 800-758-0038, credit@nbcc.nu.ca
Ontario
Deposit Insurance Corporation of Ontario, #700, 4711 Yonge St., Toronto, ON M2N 6K8
416-325-9444, Fax: 416-325-9722, 800-268-6653
Ontario Ministry of Finance, Frost Bldg. South, 7 Queen's Park Cres., 7th Fl., Toronto, ON M7A 1Y7
Fax: 866-888-3850, 866-668-8297, financecommunications.fin@ontario.ca
Financial Services Commission of Ontario, New York City Ctr., 5160 Yonge St., 17th Fl., PO Box 85, Toronto, ON M2N 6L9
416-250-7250, Fax: 416-590-7070, 800-668-0128
Quebec
Registraire des entreprises, 787, boul Lebourgneuf, Québec, QC G2J 1C3
418-644-4545, Fax: 418-528-5703, 877-644-4545, registre@servicesquebec.gouv.qc.ca
Saskatchewan
Saskatchewan Finance, 2350 Albert St., Regina, SK S4P 4A6
306-787-6768, Fax: 306-787-0241, communications@finance.gov.sk.ca
Saskatchewan Financial Services Commission, #601, 1919 Saskatchewan Dr., Regina, SK S4P 4H2
306-787-5645, Fax: 306-787-5899
Yukon Territory
Yukon Finance, PO Box 2703, Whitehorse, YT Y1A 2C6
867-667-5343, Fax: 867-393-6217, fininfo@gov.yk.ca

BILINGUALISM

Canadian Heritage, 15 Eddy St., Gatineau, QC K1A 0M5
819-997-0055, 866-811-0055, info@pch.gc.ca
Office of the Commissioner of Official Languages, 344 Slater St., 3rd fl., Ottawa, ON K1A 0T8
613-996-6368, Fax: 613-993-5082, 877-996-6368
Manitoba
Le Centre Culturel franco-manitobain/Franco-Manitoban Cultural Centre, 340, boul Provencher, St Boniface, MB R2H 0G7
204-233-8972, Fax: 204-233-3324, ccfm@ccfm.mb.ca
Northwest Territories
Office of the Languages Commissioner, Laing Bldg., 5003 - 49 St., Yellowknife, NT X1A 2P4
867-873-7034, Fax: 867-873-0357, 800-661-0889, langcom@gov.nt.ca
Nunavut
Department of Culture, Language, Elders & Youth, PO Box 1000 800,Iqaluit, NU X0A 0H0
867-975-5500, Fax: 867-975-5504, 866-934-2035
Ontario
Office of Francophone Affairs, #200, 777 Bay St., Toronto, ON M7A 0A2
416-325-4949, Fax: 416-325-4980, 800-268-7507, ofa@ontario.ca
Quebec
Secrétariat à la politique linguistique, 225 Grande-Allée est, 4e étage, Québec, QC G1R 5G5
418-643-4248, Fax: 418-646-7832, info@spl.gouv.qc.ca

BIOTECHNOLOGY

Biotechnology Research Institute, 6100, av Royalmount, Montréal, QC H4P 2R2
514-496-6100, Fax: 514-496-1928, bri-info@cnrc-nrc.gc.ca
Plant Biotechnology Institute, 110 Gymnasium Pl., Saskatoon, SK S7N 0W9
306-975-5248, Fax: 306-975-4839, pbi-info@nrc-cnrc.gc.ca

BOARDS OF REVIEW

Canada Industrial Relations Board, 240 Sparks St., 4th Fl. West, Ottawa, ON K1A 0X8
Fax: 613-941-4461, 800-575-9696, info@cirb-ccri.gc.ca
Canadian International Trade Tribunal, Standard Life Centre, 333 Laurier Ave. West, 15 Floor, Ottawa, ON K1A 0G7
613-990-2452, Fax: 613-990-2439, secretary@citt-tcce.gc.ca
Canadian Nuclear Safety Commission, 280 Slater St., PO Box 1046 B,Ottawa, ON K1P 5S9
613-995-5894, Fax: 613-995-5086, 800-668-5284
Commission for Public Complaints Against the Royal Canadian Mounted Police, National Intake Office, PO Box 88689, Surrey, BC V3W 0X1
Fax: 613-952-8045, 800-665-6878, org@cpc-cpp.gc.ca
Committee on the Status of Endangered Wildlife in Canada, c/o Canadian Wildlife Service, 351 St. Joseph Blvd, 4th Fl., Gatineau, QC K1A 0H3
819-953-3215, Fax: 819-994-3684, cosewic/cosepac@ec.gc.ca
Immigration & Refugee Board of Canada, Canada Bldg, 344 Slater St., 12th Fl., Ottawa, ON K1A 0K1
613-995-6486, Fax: 613-943-1550, contact@irb-cisr.gc.ca
Mackenzie Valley Environmental Impact Review Board, 200 Scotia Centre, #5102, 50th Ave., PO Box 938, Yellowknife, NT X1A 2N7
867-766-7050, Fax: 867-766-7074, 866-912-3472
Merchant Seamen Compensation Board, Secretary, Merchant Seamen Compensation Board, Phase II, Place du Portage, 10th Fl., Ottawa, ON K1A 0J2
819-953-8001, Fax: 819-994-5368
National Energy Board, 444 - 7 Ave. SW, Calgary, AB T2P 0X8
403-292-4800, Fax: 403-292-5503, 800-899-1265, info@neb-one.gc.ca
Nunavut Impact Review Board, PO Box 1360, Cambridge Bay, NU X0B 0C0
867-983-4600, Fax: 867-983-2594, 866-233-3033, info@nirb.ca
Nunavut Water Board, PO Box 119, Gjoa Haven, NU X0B 1J0
867-360-6338, Fax: 867-360-6369
Patented Medicine Prices Review Board, Standard Life Centre, #1400, 333 Laurier Ave. West, PO Box L40, Ottawa, ON K1P 1C1
613-954-8299, Fax: 613-952-7626, 877-861-2350, pmprb@pmprb-cepmb.gc.ca
Porcupine Caribou Management Board, PO Box 31723, Whitehorse, YT Y1A 6L3
867-633-4780, Fax: 867-393-3904, pcmb@taiga.net
Public Service Staffing Tribunal, 240 Sparks St., 6th Fl., Ottawa, ON K1A 0A5
613-949-6516, Fax: 613-949-6551, 866-637-4491, info@psst-tdfp.gc.ca
Royal Canadian Mounted Police External Review Committee, PO Box 1159 B, Ottawa, ON K1P 5R2
613-998-2134, Fax: 613-990-8969, org@erc-cee.gc.ca
Rural & Co-operatives Secretariat, Tower 7, 1341 Baseline Rd., Ottawa, ON K1A 0C5
613-759-1000, Fax: 613-773-2727
Security Intelligence Review Committee, Jackson Bldg., 122 Bank St., 4th Fl., PO Box 2430 D,Ottawa, ON K1P 5W5
613-990-8441, Fax: 613-990-5230, ellardm@sirc-csars.gc.ca
Veterans Review & Appeal Board, Daniel J. MacDonald Bldg., 161 Grafton St., PO Box 9900, Charlottetown, PE C1A 8V7
902-566-8751, Fax: 902-566-7850, 800-450-8006, vrab_tacra@vac-acc.gc.ca
Alberta
Alberta Review Board, Oxford Tower, 10235 - 101 St., 11th Fl., Edmonton, AB T5J 3E9
780-422-5994, Fax: 780-427-1762
British Columbia
British Columbia Review Board, #1020, 510 Burrard St., Vancouver, BC V6C 3A8
604-660-8789, Fax: 604-660-8809, 877-305-2277
Manitoba
Manitoba Review Board, 408 York Ave., 2nd Fl., Winnipeg, MB R3C 0P9
204-945-4438, Fax: 204-945-5751
Northwest Territories
Legal Services Board of the Northwest Territories, PO Box 1320, Yellowknife, NT X1A 2L9
867-873-7450, Fax: 867-873-5320
Territorial Board of Revision, #400, 5201 - 50th Ave., PO Box 1320, Yellowknife, NT X1A 2L9
867-873-7125, Fax: 867-873-0609
Ontario
Animal Care Review Board, 77 Grenville St., 8th Fl., Toronto, ON M5S 1B3
416-314-3509, Fax: 416-314-3518
Medical Eligibility Committee, 370 Select Dr., PO Box 168, Kingston, ON K7M 8T4
613-548-6405
Ontario Municipal Board & Board of Negotiation, 655 Bay St., 15th Fl., Toronto, ON M5G 1E5
416-326-6800, Fax: 416-326-5370, 866-887-8820

Ontario Review Board, 151 Bloor St. West, 10th Fl., Toronto, ON M5S 2T5
416-327-8866, Fax: 416-327-8867

Quebec

Bureau d'audiences publiques sur l'environnement, Édifice Lomer-Gouin, #2.10, 575, rue Saint-Amable, Québec, QC G1R 6A6
418-643-7447, Fax: 418-643-9474, 800-463-4732, communication@bape.gouv.qc.ca

Saskatchewan

Public & Private Rights Board, #323, 3085 Albert St., Regina, SK S4S 0B1
306-787-4071, Fax: 306-787-0088

Saskatchewan Film & Video Classification Board, #500, 1919 Saskatchewan Dr., Regina, SK S4P 4H2
306-787-5550, Fax: 306-787-9779, 888-374-4636

Surface Rights Board of Arbitration, 113 - 2nd Ave. East, PO Box 1597, Kindersley, SK S0L 1S0
306-463-5447, Fax: 306-463-5449, surfacerightsboard@gov.sk.ca

BROADCASTING

Canadian Broadcasting Corporation, 181 Queen St., PO Box 3220 C,Ottawa, ON K1Y 1E4
613-288-6033, liaison@radio-canada.ca

Canadian Radio-Television & Telecommunications Commission, Central Building, 1, Promenade du Portage, Les Terrasses de la Chaudière, Gatineau, QC J8X 4B1
819-997-0313, Fax: 819-994-0218, 877-249-2782

Knowledge Network Corporation, 4355 Mathissi Pl., Burnaby, BC V5G 4S8
604-431-3222, Fax: 604-431-3387, 877-456-6988, info@knowledge.ca; hr@knowledge.ca (employment information)

Alberta

Alberta Public Affairs Bureau, Park Plaza, 10611 - 98 Ave., 6th Fl., Edmonton, AB T5K 2P7
780-427-2754, Fax: 780-422-4168, -310-0000

Manitoba

News Media Services, Legislative Bldg., #29, 450 Broadway Ave., Winnipeg, MB R3C 0V8
204-945-3746, Fax: 204-945-3988, nmservices@leg.gov.mb.ca

Nova Scotia

Communications Nova Scotia, 1723 Hollis St., 3rd Fl., PO Box 608, Halifax, NS B3J 2R7
902-424-7690, Fax: 902-424-0515

Quebec

Société de télédiffusion du Québec (Télé-Québec), 1000, rue Fullum, Montréal, QC H2K 3L7
514-521-2424, Fax: 514-873-2601, 800-361-4362, info@telequebec.tv

BUDGET PLANNING

British Columbia

Provincial Treasury, PO Box 9414 Prov Govt,Victoria, BC V8V 9V1
250-387-4541, Fax: 250-356-3041

New Brunswick

Budget & Financial Management, Centennial Bldg., #250, 670 King St., PO Box 6000, Fredericton, NB E3B 5H1
506-453-2808, Fax: 506-444-4499

Northwest Territories

Department of Finance, Arthur Laing Building, 5th Fl., 5003 - 49th St., PO Box 1320, Yellowknife, NT X1A 2L9
867-873-7117, Fax: 867-873-0414

Financial Management Board Secretariat, c/o Secretary of the FMB / Comptroller General, 5003 - 49 St., PO Box 1320, Yellowknife, NT X1A 2L9

Nova Scotia

Department of Finance, Provincial Bldg., 1723 Hollis St., 7th Fl., PO Box 187, Halifax, NS B3J 2N3
902-424-5554, Fax: 902-424-0635, FinanceWeb@gov.ns.ca

Nunavut

Department of Finance, Bldg. 1079, 1st Fl., PO Box 1000 330,Iqaluit, NU X0A 0H0
867-975-5800, Fax: 867-975-5805

BUSINESS & FINANCE

Atlantic Canada Opportunities Agency, Blue Cross Centre, 644 Main St., 3rd Fl., PO Box 6051, Moncton, NB E1C 9J8
506-851-2271, Fax: 506-851-7403, 800-561-7862, information@acoa-apeca.gc.ca

Auditor General of Canada, 240 Sparks St., Ottawa, ON K1A 0G6
613-995-3708, Fax: 613-957-0474, 888-761-5953, communications@oag-bvg.gc.ca; infomedia@oag-bvg.gc.ca

Bank of Canada, 234 Wellington St., Ottawa, ON K1A 0G9
613-782-7902, Fax: 613-782-7713, 800-303-1282, info@bankofcanada.ca; communications@bankofcanada.ca (Media)

Business Development Bank of Canada, #400, 5, Place Ville-Marie, Montréal, QC H3B 5E7
514-283-5904, Fax: 514-283-5626, 877-232-2269

Calgary, #2403, 308-4th Ave. SW, Calgary, AB T2P 0H7
403-817-6700, Fax: 403-817-6701,

Canada Business Network, 235 Queen St., Ottawa, ON K1A 0H5
888-576-4444

Canada Deposit Insurance Corporation, 50 O'Connor St., 17th Floor, PO Box 2340 D,Ottawa, ON K1P 5W5
Fax: 613-996-6095, 800-461-2342, info@cdic.ca; info@sadc.ca

Canada Economic Development for Québec Regions, Édifice Dominion Square, #900, 1255, rue Peel, Montréal, QC H3B 2T9
514-283-6412, Fax: 514-283-3302, 866-385-6412

Canada Mortgage & Housing Corporation, 700 Montreal Rd., Ottawa, ON K1A 0P7
613-748-2000, Fax: 613-748-2098, 800-668-2642, chic@cmhc-schl.gc.ca

Canada Pension Plan Investment Board, #2600, 1 Queen St. East, PO Box 101, Toronto, ON M5C 2W5
416-868-4075, Fax: 416-868-8689, 866-557-9510, csr@cppib.ca

Canada Revenue Agency, 875 Heron Rd., Ottawa, ON K1A 0L5
800-267-6999

Canada Savings Bonds, #900, 110 Yonge St., Toronto, ON M5C 1T4
416-952-1252, Fax: 416-952-1270, 800-575-5151, csb@csb.gc.ca

Canadian Commercial Corporation, 50 O'Connor St., 11th Fl., Ottawa, ON K1A 0S6
613-996-0034, Fax: 613-995-2121, 800-748-8191

Canadian International Development Agency, 200, Promenade du Portage, Gatineau, QC K1A 0G4
819-997-5456, Fax: 819-953-6088, 800-230-6349, info@acdi-cida.gc.ca

Competition Bureau, Place du Portage, Phase I, 50 Victoria Street, Ottawa, ON K1A 0C9
819-997-4282, Fax: 819-997-0324, 800-348-5358

Competition Tribunal, Thomas D'Arcy McGee Bldg., #600, 90 Sparks St., Ottawa, ON K1P 5B4
613-957-3172, Fax: 613-957-3170, tribunal@ct-tc.gc.ca

Corporate Services Branch, c/o Department of Advanced Education & Skills, PO Box 8700, St. John's, NL A1B 4J6

Electronic Commerce Branch, 300 Slater St., Ottawa, ON K1A 0C8
613-954-5031, Fax: 613-954-2340, 800-328-6189

Enterprise Cape Breton Corporation, Silicon Island, 70 Crescent St., Sydney, NS B1S 2Z7
902-564-3600, Fax: 902-564-3825, 800-705-3926, information@ecbc-secb.gc.ca

Export Development Canada, 151 Slater St., Ottawa, ON K1A 1K3
613-598-2500, Fax: 613-598-3811, 800-267-8510

Farm Credit Canada, 1800 Hamilton St., PO Box 4320, Regina, SK S4P 4L3
306-780-8100, Fax: 306-780-8919, 888-332-3301, csc@fcc-fac.ca

Finance Canada, L'esplanade Laurier, 140 O'Connor St., Ottawa, ON K1A 0G5
613-992-1573, Fax: 613-943-0938, finpub@fin.gc.ca

Financial & Corporate Services Division, Telus Plaza NT, 10025 Jasper Ave., 19th Fl., Edmonton, AB T5J 1S6

Office of the Superintendent of Financial Institutions, Kent Square, 255 Albert St., Ottawa, ON K1A 0H2
613-990-7788, Fax: 613-990-5591, 800-385-8647, information@osfi-bsif.gc.ca

Financial Transactions & Reports Analysis Centre of Canada, 234 Laurier Ave. West, 24th Fl., Ottawa, ON K1P 1H7
Fax: 613-943-7931, 866-346-8722, guidelines-lignesdirectrices@fintrac-canafe.gc.ca

Foreign Affairs & International Trade Canada, 125 Sussex Dr., Ottawa, ON K1A 0G2
613-944-4000, Fax: 613-996-9709, 800-267-8376, enqserv@international.gc.ca

Freshwater Fish Marketing Corporation, 1199 Plessis Rd., Winnipeg, MB R2C 3L4
204-983-6601, Fax: 204-983-6497, sandi.cain@freshwaterfish.com

HR Ontario, Whitney Block, #5320, 99 Wellesley St. West, Toronto, ON M7A 1N3
416-212-2057, Fax: 416-325-6317

Industry Canada, C.D. Howe Building, 235 Queen St., Ottawa, ON K1A 0H5
613-954-5031, Fax: 613-954-2340, 800-328-6189, info@ic.gc.ca

Internal Administrative Services Division, 400 University Ave., 14th Fl., Toronto, ON M7A 1T7
416-326-7586, Fax: 416-326-5809

Législation & enquêtes, 3800, rue de Marly, Secteur 5-1-9, Québec, QC G1X 4A5
418-652-6844, Fax: 418-643-9381

National Round Table on the Environment & Economy, #200, 344 Slater St., Ottawa, ON K1R 7Y3
613-992-7189, Fax: 613-992-7385, info@nrtee-trnee.ca

North American Free Trade Agreement (NAFTA) Secretariat, Canadian Section, #705, 90 Sparks St., Ottawa, ON K1P 5B4
613-992-9388, Fax: 613-992-9392, webmaster@nafta-alena.gc.ca

Public Sector Pension Investment Board, #200, 440 Laurier Ave. West, Ottawa, ON K1R 7X6
613-782-3095, Fax: 613-782-6864, info@investpsp.ca

Royal Canadian Mint, 320 Sussex Dr., Ottawa, ON K1A 0G8
613-993-3500, Fax: 613-993-4092, 800-267-1871

Statistics Canada, R.H. Coats Bldg., Tunney's Pasture, 150 Tunney's Pasture Driveway, Ottawa, ON K1A 0T6
613-951-8116, Fax: 877-287-4369, 800-263-1136, infostats@statcan.ca

Treasury & Risk Management, Terrace Building, 9515 - 107 St., 3rd Fl., Edmonton, AB T5K 2C3

Treasury Board of Canada, 140 O'Connor St., Ottawa, ON K1A 0R5
613-957-2400, Fax: 613-941-4000, 877-636-0656

Western Economic Diversification Canada, Canada Place, #1500, 9700 Jasper Ave. NW, Edmonton, AB T5J 4H7
780-495-4164, Fax: 780-495-4557, 888-338-9378

Alberta

Agricultural Products Marketing Council, JG O'Donoghue Bldg., 7000 - 113 St., 3rd Fl., Edmonton, AB T6H 5T6
780-427-2164, Fax: 780-422-9690

Alberta Automobile Insurance Rate Board, Canadian Western Bank Place, #2440, 10303 Jasper Ave., Edmonton, AB T5J 3N6
780-427-5428, Fax: 780-638-4254, -310-0000, airb@gov.ab.ca

Alberta Capital Finance Authority, Canadian Western Bank Place, #2450, 10303 Jasper Ave., Edmonton, AB T5J 3N6
780-427-9711, Fax: 780-422-2175, webacfa@gov.ab.ca

Alberta Securities Commission, #600, 250 - 5th St. SW, Calgary, AB T2P 0R4
403-297-6454, Fax: 403-297-6156, 877-355-0585, inquiries@asc.ca; media@asc.ca; complaints@asc.ca

ATB Financial, 9888 Jasper Ave., Edmonton, AB T5J 1P1
403-245-8110, 800-332-8383

Alberta Office of the Auditor General, 9925 - 109 St., 8th Fl., Edmonton, AB T5K 2J8
780-427-4222, Fax: 780-422-9555, info@oag.ab.ca

Credit Union Deposit Guarantee Corporation, #2000, 10104 - 103 St., Edmonton, AB T5J 0H8
780-428-6680, Fax: 780-428-7571, 800-661-0351, mail@cudgc.ab.ca

Intergovernmental Relations, Commerce Place, 10155 - 102 St., 12th Fl., Edmonton, AB T5J 4G8
780-427-6543, Fax: 780-427-0939

Alberta Treasury Board & Finance, Oxbridge Place, 9820 - 106 St., 5th Fl., Edmonton, AB T5K 2J6
780-415-4519, -310-000

British Columbia

Auditor Certification Board, PO Box 9431 Prov Govt, Victoria, BC V8W 9V3
250-356-8658, Fax: 250-356-9422, Kelly.Fitzsimonds@gov.bc.ca

Office of the Auditor General, PO Box 9036 Prov Govt,Victoria, BC V8W 9A2
250-419-6100, Fax: 250-387-1230

British Columbia Innovation Council, 1188 West Georgia St., 9th Fl., Vancouver, BC V6E 4A2
604-683-2724, Fax: 604-683-6567, 800-665-7222, info@bcic.ca

British Columbia Ministry of Finance, PO Box 9417 Prov Govt,Victoria, BC V8W 9V1
877-388-4440, CTBTaxQuestions@gov.bc.ca (tax inquiries)

British Columbia Ministry of Social Development, PO Box 9058 Prov Govt,Victoria, BC V8W 9E1

British Columbia Pension Corporation, 2995 Jutland Rd., PO Box 9460, Victoria, BC V8W 9V8
250-387-1002, Fax: 250-953-0429, 800-663-8823, PensionCorp@pensionsbc.ca; Retired.Members@pensionsbc.ca

British Columbia Securities Commission, Pacific Centre, 701 West Georgia St., 12th Fl., PO Box 10142, Vancouver, BC V7Y 1L2
604-899-6500, Fax: 604-899-6506, 800-373-6393, inquiries@bcsc.bc.ca

Crown Agencies Resource Office, PO Box 9469 Prov Govt, Victoria, BC V8V 9V8
250-387-8770, Fax: 250-387-9061, CAS@gov.bc.ca

Financial Institutions Commission, #1200, 13450 - 102 Ave., Surrey, BC V3T 5X3
604-953-5300, Fax: 604-953-5301, 866-206-3030, FICOM@ficombc.ca; HR@ficombc.ca
Insurance Corporation of British Columbia, 151 West Esplanade, North Vancouver, BC V7M 3H9
604-661-2800, 800-663-3051
Insurance Council of British Columbia, #300, 1040 West Georgia St., PO Box 7, Vancouver, BC V6E 4H1
604-688-0321, Fax: 604-662-7767, 877-688-0321
Office of the Superintendent of Motor Vehicles, PO Box 9254 Prov Govt,Victoria, BC V8W 9J2
250-387-7747, Fax: 250-387-4891, OSMV.Mailbox@gov.bc.ca
Public Sector Employers' Council Secretariat, #210, 880 Douglas St., PO Box 9400 Prov Govt, Victoria, BC V8V 9V1
250-387-0842, Fax: 250-387-6258
Timber Export Advisory Committee, PO Box 9514 Prov Govt, Victoria, BC V8W 9C2
250-387-8916, Fax: 250-387-5050

Manitoba

Office of the Auditor General, #500, 330 Portage Ave., Winnipeg, MB R3C 0C4
204-945-3790, Fax: 204-945-2169, oag.contact@oag.mb.ca
Claimant Adviser Office, #200, 330 Portage Ave., Winnipeg, MB R3C 0C4
204-945-7413, Fax: 204-948-3157,
Communities Economic Development Fund, #100, 23 Station Rd., Thompson, MB R8N 0N6
204-778-4138, Fax: 204-778-4313, 800-561-4315
Comptroller Division, #715, 401 York Ave., Winnipeg, MB R3C 0P8
204-945-4920, Fax: 204-945-2394
Credit Union Deposit Guarantee Corporation, #390, 200 Graham Ave., Winnipeg, MB R3C 4L5
204-942-8480, Fax: 204-947-1723, 800-697-4447, mail@cudgc.com
Crown Corporations Council, #1130, 444 St. Mary Ave., Winnipeg, MB R3C 3T1
204-949-5270, Fax: 204-949-5283, crowncc@mts.net
Manitoba Development Corporation, #555, 155 Carlton St., Winnipeg, MB R3C 3H8
204-945-7626, Fax: 204-945-1193
Manitoba Entrepreneurship, Training & Trade, #1000, 259 Portage Ave, Winnipeg, MB R3B 3P4
204-945-2475, Fax: 204-945-3977, minctt@leg.gov.mb.ca
Federal-Provincial Relations & Research Division, #910, 386 Broadway, Winnipeg, MB R3C 3R6
204-945-3757, Fax: 204-945-5051
Manitoba Finance, #109, Legislative Bldg., Winnipeg, MB R3C 0V8
204-945-3754, Fax: 204-945-8316, minfin@leg.gov.mb.ca
Heritage Grants Advisory Council, 213 Notre Dame Ave., 3rd Fl., Winnipeg, MB R3B 1N3
204-945-2213, Fax: 204-948-2086
Manitoba Public Insurance, #B100, 234 Donald St., PO Box 6300, Winnipeg, MB R3C 4A4
204-985-7000, Fax: 204-985-3525, 800-665-2410
Manitoba Local Government, #301, 450 Broadway Ave., Winnipeg, MB R3C 0V8
Fax: 204-945-1383, mnia@leg.gov.mb.ca
Manitoba Agricultural Services Corporation, #100, 1525 First St. South, Brandon, MB R7A 7A1
204-726-6850, Fax: 204-726-6849, mailbox@masc.mb.ca
Manitoba Bureau of Statistics, #824, 155 Carlton St., Winnipeg, MB R3C 3H9
204-945-2406, Fax: 204-945-0695
Manitoba Round Table for Sustainable Development, #160, 123 Main St., Winnipeg, MB R3C 1A5
204-945-1869, Fax: 204-948-2357, mrtsd@gov.mb.ca
Manitoba Securities Commission, #500, 400 St. Mary Ave., Winnipeg, MB R3C 4K5
204-945-2548, Fax: 204-945-0330, 800-655-5244, securities@gov.mb.ca
Pension Commission of Manitoba, #1004, 401 York Ave., Winnipeg, MB R3C 0P8
204-945-2740, Fax: 204-948-2375, pensions@gov.mb.ca
Manitoba Treasury Board Secretariat, #200, 386 Broadway, Winnipeg, MB R3C 3R6
204-945-4150, Fax: 204-948-4878

New Brunswick

Office of the Auditor General, HSBC Place, 520 King St., 6th Fl., Fredericton, NB E3B 6G3
506-453-2243, Fax: 506-453-3067
Communications Division, Centennial Bldg., PO Box 6000, Fredericton, NB E3B 5H1
506-453-8607, Fax: 506-453-3993
Office of the Comptroller, Centennial Bldg., 670 King St., Fredericton, NB E3B 1G1
506-453-2565, Fax: 506-453-2917, wwwooc@gnb.ca
Finance & Administration, Centennial Bldg., #375, 670 King St., PO Box 6000, Fredericton, NB E3B 5H1
506-453-2451, Fax: 506-444-4724
New Brunswick Department of Economic Development, Centennial Building, PO Box 6000, Fredericton, NB E3B 5H1
506-453-3707, Fax: 506-453-3993, 800-665-1800, tradenb@gnb.ca
New Brunswick Department of Finance, 670 King St., PO Box 6000, Fredericton, NB E3B 5H1
506-453-2451, Fax: 506-457-4989, wwwfin@gnb.ca
New Brunswick Department of Government Services, Marysville Place, 20 McGloin St., Fredericton, NB E3A 5T8
506-453-6100, Fax: 506-462-5049
New Brunswick Farm Products Commission, c/o Department of Agriculture, Aquaculture & Fisheries, PO Box 6000, Fredericton, NB E3B 5H1
506-453-3647, Fax: 506-444-5969
New Brunswick Investment Management Corporation, York Tower, #581, 440 King St., Fredericton, NB E3B 5H8
506-444-5800, Fax: 506-444-5025, comments@nbimc.com
New Brunswick Lotteries & Gaming Corporation, Centennial Bldg., 670 King St., PO Box 6000, Fredericton, NB E3B 5H1
506-444-3468, Fax: 506-444-5818
Regional Development Corporation, RDC Bldg., 836 Churchill Row, PO Box 428, Fredericton, NB E3B 5R4
506-453-2277, Fax: 506-453-7988

Newfoundland & Labrador

Office of the Auditor General, PO Box 8700, St. John's, NL A1B 4J6
709-729-2695, Fax: 709-729-5970, oagmail@oag.nl.ca
Credit Union Deposit Guarantee Corporation, PO Box 340, Marystown, NL A0E 2M0
709-279-0170, Fax: 709-279-0177, 877-279-0170
Newfoundland & Labrador Department of Finance, Confederation Bldg., PO Box 8700, St. John's, NL A1B 4J6
709-729-6165, Fax: 709-729-2070, finance@gov.nl.ca
Newfoundland & Labrador Department of Innovation, Business, & Rural Development, Confederation Bldg., West Block, PO Box 8700, St. John's, NL A1B 4J6
709-729-7000, Fax: 709-729-0654, intrd@gov.nl.ca
Newfoundland & Labrador Municipal Financing Corporation, Confederation Bldg., PO Box 8700, St. John's, NL A1B 4J6
709-729-6686, Fax: 709-729-2095

Northwest Territories

Department of Finance, Arthur Laing Building, 5th Fl., 5003 - 49th St., PO Box 1320, Yellowknife, NT X1A 2L9
867-873-7117, Fax: 867-873-0414
Department of Public Works & Services, PO Box 1320, Yellowknife, NT X1A 2L9
Financial Management Board Secretariat, c/o Secretary of the FMB / Comptroller General, 5003 - 49 St., PO Box 1320, Yellowknife, NT X1A 2L9

Nova Scotia

Office of the Auditor General, #302, 1888 Brunswick St., Halifax, NS B3J 3J8
902-424-5907, Fax: 902-424-4350
Department of Economic & Rural Development & Tourism, Centennial Building, #600, 1660 Hollis St., PO Box 2311, Halifax, NS B3J 1V7
902-424-0377, Fax: 902-424-0500, comm@gov.ns.ca
Department of Finance, Provincial Bldg., 1723 Hollis St., 7th Fl., PO Box 187, Halifax, NS B3J 2N3
902-424-5554, Fax: 902-424-0635, FinanceWeb@gov.ns.ca
Nova Scotia Business Inc., World Trade & Convention Centre, #701, 1800 Argyle St., PO Box 2374, Halifax, NS B3J 3N8
902-424-6650, Fax: 902-424-5739, 800-260-6682, info@nsbi.ca

Nunavut

Department of Finance, Bldg. 1079, 1st Fl., PO Box 1000 330,Iqaluit, NU X0A 0H0
867-975-5800, Fax: 867-975-5805
Legal Registries, Brown Bldg., 1st Fl., PO Box 1000 570,Iqaluit, NU X0A 0H0
Fax: 867-975-6594

Ontario

Advertising Review Board, Macdonald Block, #M2-56, 900 Bay St., 2nd Fl., Toronto, ON M7A 1N3
416-327-2183, Fax: 416-327-2179
Agriculture, Food & Rural Affairs Tribunal, 1 Stone Rd. West, 2nd Fl., Guelph, ON N1G 4Y2
519-826-3433, Fax: 519-826-4232, appeals.tribunal@omafra.gov.on.ca
Office of the Auditor General, Atrium on Bay, #1530, 20 Dundas St. West, PO Box 105, Toronto, ON M5G 2C2
416-327-2381, Fax: 416-327-9862, comments@auditor.on.ca
Ontario Ministry of Consumer Services, Mowat Block, 900 Bay St., 6th Fl., Toronto, ON M7A 1L2
416-327-8300, Fax: 416-326-1947, 866-665-0662, infomcs@ontario.ca
Deposit Insurance Corporation of Ontario, #700, 4711 Yonge St., Toronto, ON M2N 6K8
416-325-9444, Fax: 416-325-9722, 800-268-6653
Ontario Ministry of Economic Development & Innovation, Hearst Block, 900 Bay St., 8th Fl., Toronto, ON M7A 2E1
416-325-6666, Fax: 416-325-6688, 866-668-4249, info@edt.gov.on.ca
Ontario Ministry of Finance, Frost Bldg. South, 7 Queen's Park Cres., 7th Fl., Toronto, ON M7A 1Y7
Fax: 866-888-3850, 866-668-8297, financecommunications.fin@ontario.ca
Financial Services Commission of Ontario, New York City Ctr., 5160 Yonge St., 17th Fl., PO Box 85, Toronto, ON M2N 6L9
416-250-7250, Fax: 416-590-7070, 800-668-0128
Ontario Ministry of Government Services, Whitney Block, #4320, 99 Wellesley St. West, 4th Fl., Toronto, ON M7A 1W3
416-326-1234, Fax: 416-327-3790, 800-268-1142
Grain Financial Protection Board, 1 Stone Rd. West, 1st Fl. Northeast, PO Box 3660 Central, Guelph, ON N1H 8M4
519-826-3949, Fax: 519-826-3367
Licence Appeal Tribunal, 20 Dundas St. West, 5th Fl., Toronto, ON M5G 2C2
416-314-4260, Fax: 416-314-4270, 800-255-2214
Liquor Control Board of Ontario, 55 Lake Shore Blvd. East, Toronto, ON M5E 1A4
416-365-5900, Fax: 416-864-2476, 800-668-5226, infoline@lcbo.com
Livestock Financial Protection Board, 1 Stone Rd. West, 5th Fl. Northwest, Guelph, ON N1G 4Y2
519-826-3886, Fax: 519-826-4375
Metro Toronto Convention Centre Corporation, 255 Front St. West, Toronto, ON M5V 2W6
416-585-8120, Fax: 416-585-8198, info@mtccc.com; sales@mtccc.com
Normal Farm Practices Protection Board, 1 Stone Rd. West, 3rd Fl., Guelph, ON N1G 4Y2
Fax: 519-826-3259, 877-424-1300
Ontario Electricity Financial Corporation, #1400, 1 Dundas St. West, Toronto, ON M7A 1Y7
416-325-8000, Fax: 416-325-8005
Ontario Farm Products Marketing Commission, 1 Stone Rd. West, 5th Fl. Southwest, Guelph, ON N1G 4Y2
519-826-4220, Fax: 519-826-3400
Ontario Financing Authority, #1400, 1 Dundas St. West, Toronto, ON M7A 1Y7
416-325-8000, Fax: 416-325-8005
Ontario Food Terminal Board, 165 The Queensway, Toronto, ON M8Y 1H8
416-259-5479, Fax: 416-259-4303
Ontario Place Corporation, 955 Lake Shore Blvd. West, Toronto, ON M6K 3B9
416-314-9900, Fax: 416-314-9992
Ontario Securities Commission, #1903, 20 Queen St. West, PO Box 55, Toronto, ON M5H 3S8
416-597-0681, Fax: 416-593-8241
Ottawa Convention Centre, 55 Colonel By Dr., Ottawa, ON K1N 9J2
613-563-1984, Fax: 613-563-7646
Pay Equity Commission, #300, 180 Dundas St. West, Toronto, ON M7A 2S6
416-314-1896, Fax: 416-314-8741, 800-387-8813
Stadium Corporation of Ontario Ltd., 33 King St. West, 6th Fl., Oshawa, ON L1H 8H5
416-314-5158, Fax: 905-433-6688

Prince Edward Island

Agricultural Insurance Corporation, 29 Indigo Cres., PO Box 1600, Charlottetown, PE C1A 7N3
902-368-4842, Fax: 902-368-6677
Charlottetown Area Development Corporation, 4 Pownal St., PO Box 786, Charlottetown, PE C1A 7L9
902-892-5341, Fax: 902-368-1935
Office of the Auditor General, Shaw Bldg., 105 Rochford St. North, 2nd Fl., Charlottetown, PE C1A 7N8
902-368-4520, Fax: 902-368-4598, www.assembly.pe.ca
Prince Edward Island Department of Innovation & Advanced Learning, Shaw Bldg., 105 Rochford St., 5th Fl., PO Box 2000, Charlottetown, PE C1A 7N8
902-368-4240, Fax: 902-368-4242
Prince Edward Island Lending Agency, Homburg Financial Tower, 98 Fitzroy St., 2nd Fl., Charlottetown, PE C1A 1R7
902-368-6200, Fax: 902-368-6201

Quebec

Ministère des Finances et de l'Économie, Édifice Gérard-D.-Lévesque, 12, rue Saint-Louis, Québec, QC G1R 5L3
418-528-9323, Fax: 418-646-1631, info@finances.gouv.qc.ca

Fonds de la recherche en santé du Québec, #800, 500, rue Sherbrooke ouest, Montréal, QC H3A 3C6
514-873-2114, Fax: 514-873-8768

Innovatech Québec, #410, 888, rue St-Jean, Québec, QC G1R 5H6
418-528-9770, Fax: 418-528-9783, 866-605-1676

Le Protecteur du Citoyen, #1.25, 525, boul René-Lévesque est, Québec, QC G1R 5Y4
418-643-2688, Fax: 418-643-8759, 800-463-5070, protecteur@protecteurducitoyen.qc.ca

Registraire des entreprises, 787, boul Lebourgneuf, Québec, QC G2J 1C3
418-644-4545, Fax: 418-528-5703, 877-644-4545, registre@servicesquebec.gouv.qc.ca

Ministère des Relations internationales, Édifice Hector-Fabre, 525, boul Réne-Lévesque est, Québec, QC G1R 5R9
418-649-2300, Fax: 418-649-2656

Revenu Québec, Direction des relations publiques/Communications, 3800, rue de Marly, Québec, QC G1X 4A5
418-652-6831, Fax: 418-646-0167

Société du Centre des congrès de Québec, 1000, boul René-Lévesque est, Québec, QC G1R 5T8
418-644-4000, Fax: 418-644-6455, 888-679-4000

Secrétariat du Conseil du trésor, 875, Grande Allée est, 5e étage, secteur 500, Québec, QC G1R 5R8
418-643-1529, Fax: 418-643-9226, 866-552-5158, communication@sct.gouv.qc.ca

Vérificateur général du Québec, 750, boulevard Charest est, 3e étage, Québec, QC G1K 9J6
418-691-5900, Fax: 418-644-4460, verificateur.general@vgq.gouv.qc.ca

Saskatchewan

Board of Revenue Commissioners, #480, 2151 Scarth St., Regina, SK S4P 2H8
306-787-6221, Fax: 306-787-1610

Crown Investments Corporation of Saskatchewan, #400, 2400 College Ave., Regina, SK S4P 1C8
306-787-6851, Fax: 306-787-8125

Energy & Resources, #300, 2103 - 11th Ave., Regina, SK S4P 3Z8
306-787-2528

Provincial Auditor Saskatchewan, #1500, 1920 Broad St., Regina, SK S4P 3V2
306-787-6398, Fax: 306-787-6383, info@auditor.sk.ca

Saskatchewan Crop Insurance Corporation, 484 Prince William Dr., PO Box 3000, Melville, SK S0A 2P0
306-728-7200, Fax: 306-728-7202, 888-935-0000, customer.service@scic.gov.sk.ca

Saskatchewan Development Fund Corporation, #400, 2400 College Ave., Regina, SK S4P 1C8
306-787-1645, Fax: 306-787-8125

Saskatchewan Finance, 2350 Albert St., Regina, SK S4P 4A6
306-787-6768, Fax: 306-787-0241, communications@finance.gov.sk.ca

Saskatchewan Financial Services Commission, #601, 1919 Saskatchewan Dr., Regina, SK S4P 4H2
306-787-5645, Fax: 306-787-5899

Saskatchewan Government Insurance, 2260 - 11th Ave., Regina, SK S4P 0J9
306-751-1200, Fax: 306-787-7477, 800-667-8015, sgiinquiries@sgi.sk.ca

Yukon Territory

Yukon Finance, PO Box 2703, Whitehorse, YT Y1A 2C6
867-667-5343, Fax: 867-393-6217, fininfo@gov.yk.ca

Yukon Lottery Commission, 312 Wood St., Whitehorse, YT Y1A 2E6
867-633-7890, Fax: 867-668-7561, lotteriesyukon@gov.yk.ca

BUSINESS DEVELOPMENT

See Also: Industry; Science & Technology

Atlantic Canada Opportunities Agency, Blue Cross Centre, 644 Main St., 3rd Fl., PO Box 6051, Moncton, NB E1C 9J8
506-851-2271, Fax: 506-851-7403, 800-561-7862, information@acoa-apeca.gc.ca

Business Development Bank of Canada, #400, 5, Place Ville-Marie, Montréal, QC H3B 5E7
514-283-5904, Fax: 514-283-5626, 877-232-2269

Canada Business Network, 235 Queen St., Ottawa, ON K1A 0H5
888-576-4444

Canada Economic Development for Québec Regions, Édifice Dominion Square, #900, 1255, rue Peel, Montréal, QC H3B 2T9
514-283-6412, Fax: 514-283-3302, 866-385-6412

Enterprise Cape Breton Corporation, Silicon Island, 70 Crescent St., Sydney, NS B1S 2Z7
902-564-3600, Fax: 902-564-3825, 800-705-3926, information@ecbc-secb.gc.ca

Export Development Canada, 151 Slater St., Ottawa, ON K1A 1K3
613-598-2500, Fax: 613-598-3811, 800-267-8510

Industry Canada, C.D. Howe Building, 235 Queen St., Ottawa, ON K1A 0H5
613-954-5031, Fax: 613-954-2340, 800-328-6189, info@ic.gc.ca

Market & Industry Services Branch, Tower 5, 1341 Baseline Rd., Ottawa, ON K1A 0C5
613-759-1000, Fax: 613-773-1711

Western Economic Diversification Canada, Canada Place, #1500, 9700 Jasper Ave. NW, Edmonton, AB T5J 4H7
780-495-4164, Fax: 780-495-4557, 888-338-9378

British Columbia

British Columbia Innovation Council, 1188 West Georgia St., 9th Fl., Vancouver, BC V6E 4A2
604-683-2724, Fax: 604-683-6567, 800-665-7222, info@bcic.ca

British Columbia Ministry of Jobs, Tourism, & Skills Training (& Responsible for Labour), PO Box 9071 Prov Govt,Victoria, BC V8W 9E2
EnquiryBC@gov.bc.ca; GCPE.JTI.Media.Requests@gov.bc.ca

British Columbia Ministry of Social Development, PO Box 9058 Prov Govt,Victoria, BC V8W 9E1

Northern Development Initiative Trust, #301, 1268 Fifth Ave., Prince George, BC V2L 3L2
250-561-2525, Fax: 250-561-2563, info@northerndevelopment.bc.ca

Manitoba

Manitoba Development Corporation, #555, 155 Carlton St., Winnipeg, MB R3C 3H8
204-945-7626, Fax: 204-945-1193

Manitoba Entrepreneurship, Training & Trade, #1000, 259 Portage Ave, Winnipeg, MB R3B 3P4
204-945-2475, Fax: 204-945-3977, minctt@leg.gov.mb.ca

New Brunswick

New Brunswick Department of Economic Development, Centennial Building, PO Box 6000, Fredericton, NB E3B 5H1
506-453-3707, Fax: 506-453-3993, 800-665-1800, tradenb@gnb.ca

Regional Development Corporation, RDC Bldg., 836 Churchill Row, PO Box 428, Fredericton, NB E3B 5R4
506-453-2277, Fax: 506-453-7988

Newfoundland & Labrador

Newfoundland & Labrador Department of Innovation, Business, & Rural Development, Confederation Bldg., West Block, PO Box 8700, St. John's, NL A1B 4J6
709-729-7000, Fax: 709-729-0654, intrd@gov.nl.ca

Northwest Territories

Department of Industry, Tourism & Investment, PO Box 1320, Yellowknife, NT X1A 2L9
Fax: 867-873-0306, info@iti.ca

Nova Scotia

Department of Economic & Rural Development & Tourism, Centennial Building, #600, 1660 Hollis St., PO Box 2311, Halifax, NS B3J 1V7
902-424-0377, Fax: 902-424-0500, comm@gov.ns.ca

InNOVACorp, #1400, 1801 Hollis St., Halifax, NS B3J 3N4
902-424-8670, Fax: 902-424-4679, 800-565-7051, communications@innovacorp.ca

Nova Scotia Business Inc., World Trade & Convention Centre, #701, 1800 Argyle St., PO Box 2374, Halifax, NS B3J 3N8
902-424-6650, Fax: 902-424-5739, 800-260-6682, info@nsbi.ca

Trade Centre Limited, 1800 Argyle St., PO Box 955, Halifax, NS B3J 2V9
902-421-8686, Fax: 902-422-2922

Nunavut

Department of Economic Development & Transportation, Bldg. 1104 A, Inuksugait Plaza, PO Box 1000 1500,Iqaluit, NU X0A 0H0
867-975-7800, Fax: 867-975-7870, 888-975-5999, edt@gov.nu.ca

Ontario

Ontario Ministry of Consumer Services, Mowat Block, 900 Bay St., 6th Fl., Toronto, ON M7A 1L2
416-327-8300, Fax: 416-326-1947, 866-665-0662, infomcs@ontario.ca

Ontario Ministry of Economic Development & Innovation, Hearst Block, 900 Bay St., 8th Fl., Toronto, ON M7A 2E1
416-325-6666, Fax: 416-325-6688, 866-668-4249, info@edt.gov.on.ca

Northern Development Division, Roberta Bondar Place, #200, 70 Foster Dr., Sault Ste Marie, ON P6A 6V8
705-945-5900, Fax: 705-945-5931, 800-461-2287

Prince Edward Island

Charlottetown Area Development Corporation, 4 Pownal St., PO Box 786, Charlottetown, PE C1A 7L9
902-892-5341, Fax: 902-368-1935

Innovation PEI, 94 Euston St., PO Box 910, Charlottetown, PE C1A 7L9
902-368-6300, Fax: 902-368-6301, 800-563-3734

Prince Edward Island Department of Innovation & Advanced Learning, Shaw Bldg., 105 Rochford St., 5th Fl., PO Box 2000, Charlottetown, PE C1A 7N8
902-368-4240, Fax: 902-368-4242

Prince Edward Island Lending Agency, Homburg Financial Tower, 98 Fitzroy St., 2nd Fl., Charlottetown, PE C1A 1R7
902-368-6200, Fax: 902-368-6201

Quebec

Ministère du Développement économique, de l'Innovation et de l'Exportation, 710, place D'Youville, 3e étage, Québec, QC G1R 4Y4
418-691-5950, Fax: 418-644-0118, 866-680-1884

Saskatchewan

Energy & Resources, #300, 2103 - 11th Ave., Regina, SK S4P 3Z8
306-787-2528

Enterprise Saskatchewan, #200, 3085 Albert St., Regina, SK S4S 0B1
306-787-4484, Fax: 306-798-0629, invest@gov.sk.ca

Yukon Territory

Yukon Development Corporation, #2 Miles Canyon Rd., PO Box 5920, Whitehorse, YT Y1A 6S7
867-393-5337, Fax: 867-393-5401

Yukon Economic Development, PO Box 2703, Whitehorse, YT Y1A 2C6
867-393-7191, Fax: 867-393-6412, 800-661-0408, ecdev@gov.yk.ca

BUSINESS REGULATIONS

Canada Revenue Agency, 875 Heron Rd., Ottawa, ON K1A 0L5
800-267-6999

Consumer & Commercial Affairs Branch, PO Box 8700, St. John's, NL A1B 4J6
709-729-2570, Fax: 709-729-4151, gsinfo@gov.nl.ca

Industry Canada, C.D. Howe Building, 235 Queen St., Ottawa, ON K1A 0H5
613-954-5031, Fax: 613-954-2340, 800-328-6189, info@ic.gc.ca

Alberta

Strategic Planning & Financial Services, Commerce Place, 10155 - 102 St., 13th Fl., Edmonton, AB T5J 4G8
780-422-8545

British Columbia

Corporate & Ministry Support Services, PO Box 9415 Prov Govt,Victoria, BC V8W 9V1

Manitoba

Companies Office, #1010, 405 Broadway, Winnipeg, MB R3C 3L6
204-945-2500, Fax: 204-945-1459, companies@gov.mb.ca

Nova Scotia

Nova Scotia Business Inc., World Trade & Convention Centre, #701, 1800 Argyle St., PO Box 2374, Halifax, NS B3J 3N8
902-424-6650, Fax: 902-424-5739, 800-260-6682, info@nsbi.ca

Nunavut

Department of Finance, Bldg. 1079, 1st Fl., PO Box 1000 330,Iqaluit, NU X0A 0H0
867-975-5800, Fax: 867-975-5805

Ontario

ServiceOntario, College Park, 777 Bay St., 15th fl., Toronto, ON M7A 2J3
416-326-1234, Fax: 416-326-1313, 800-267-8097

Quebec

Registraire des entreprises, 787, boul Lebourgneuf, Québec, QC G2J 1C3
418-644-4545, Fax: 418-528-5703, 877-644-4545, registre@servicesquebec.gouv.qc.ca

CABINETS & EXECUTIVE COUNCILS

See Also: Government (General Information); Parliament

The Canadian Ministry, Information Service, Parliament of Canada, Ottawa, ON K1A 0A9
613-992-4793, 866-599-4999, info@parl.gc.ca

Alberta

Executive Council, Legislature Building, 10800 - 97 Ave., Edmonton, AB T5K 2B6
780-427-2711, -310-0000

British Columbia

Executive Council of the Government of British Columbia, Cabinet Operations, 617 Government St., 1st Fl., PO Box 9487 Prov Govt,Victoria, BC V8W 9W6

Manitoba

Executive Council, Legislative Building, 450 Broadway Ave., Winnipeg, MB R3C 0V8

New Brunswick

Executive Council, Centennial Building, PO Box 6000, Fredericton, NB E3B 5H1
506-444-4417, Fax: 506-453-2266, Executivecounciloffice@gnb.ca

Newfoundland & Labrador
Executive Council, c/o Communications Branch, East Block, Confederation Building, 10th Fl., St. John's, NL A1B 4J6
info@gov.nl.ca
Northwest Territories
Executive Council, PO Box 1320, Yellowknife, NT X1A 2L9
executive@gov.nt.ca
Nova Scotia
Executive Council, One Government Place, 1700 Granville St., 5th Fl., PO Box 2125, Halifax, NS B3J 3B7
902-424-5970, Fax: 902-424-0667, execounc@gov.ns.ca
Nunavut
Executive Council, Legislative Bldg., 2nd Fl., Box 2410, Iqaluit, NU X0A 0H0
867-975-5090, Fax: 867-975-5095
Ontario
Executive Council, Whitney Block, Queen's Park, 99 Wellesley St. West, 6th Fl., Toronto, ON M7A 1A1
416-325-5721, Fax: 416-314-1551
Prince Edward Island
Executive Council, Shaw Bldg., 5th Fl., PO Box 2000, Charlottetown, PE C1A 7N8
902-368-4502, Fax: 902-368-6118
Quebec
Ministère du Conseil exécutif, 875, Grande Allée est, Québec, QC G1R 4Y8
418-646-3021, Fax: 418-528-9242
Saskatchewan
Executive Council, Communications Services, Executive Council, #130, 3085 Albert St., Regina, SK S4S 0B1
306-787-6276, Fax: 306-787-6123, commserv@gov.sk.ca
Yukon Territory
Executive Council, #2071, 2nd Ave., Whitehorse, YT Y1A 2C6
867-667-5393, Fax: 867-393-6214, eco@gov.yk.ca

CANADIANS & SOCIETY

Aboriginal Affairs & Northern Development Canada, 10 Wellington St., North Tower, Gatineau, QC K1A 0H4
819-997-0380, Fax: 866-817-3977, 800-567-9604, infopubs@aadnc-aandc.gc.ca
Beverly & Qamanirjuaq Caribou Management Board, Secretariat, PO Box 629, Stonewall, MB R0C 2Z0
204-467-2438, caribounews@arctic-caribou.com
British Columbia Treaty Commission, #700, 1111 Melville St., Vancouver, BC V6E 3V6
604-482-9200, Fax: 604-482-9222, 800-665-8330, info@bctreaty.net
Canada Council for the Arts, 350 Albert St., PO Box 1047, Ottawa, ON K1P 5V8
613-566-4414, Fax: 613-566-4390, 800-263-5588
Canada Lands Company Ltd., #1200, 1 University Ave., Toronto, ON M5J 2P1
416-952-6111, Fax: 416-952-6115, 888-252-5263
Canadian Heritage, 15 Eddy St., Gatineau, QC K1A 0M5
819-997-0055, 866-811-0055, info@pch.gc.ca
Canadian Human Rights Commission, 344 Slater St., 8th Fl., Ottawa, ON K1A 1E1
613-995-1151, Fax: 613-996-9661, 888-214-1090
Canadian Human Rights Tribunal, 160 Elgin St., 11th Fl., Ottawa, ON K1A 1J4
613-995-1707, Fax: 613-995-3484, registrar@chrt-tcdp.gc.ca
Canadian Race Relations Foundation, #701, 4576 Yonge St., Toronto, ON M2N 6N4
416-952-3500, Fax: 416-952-3326, 888-240-4936
Citizenship & Immigration Canada, Jean Edmonds, South Tower, 365 Laurier Ave. West, Ottawa, ON K1A 1L1
613-954-9019, Fax: 613-954-2221, 888-242-2100
First Nations Tax Commission, #321, 345 Yellowhead Hwy, Kamloops, BC V2H 1H1
250-828-9857, Fax: 250-828-9858, mailkamloops@fntc.ca
Foreign Affairs & International Trade Canada, 125 Sussex Dr., Ottawa, ON K1A 0G2
613-944-4000, Fax: 613-996-9709, 800-267-8376, enqserv@international.gc.ca
Government of Canada, c/o Canada Enquiry Centre, Service Canada, Ottawa, ON K1A 0J9
613-941-1827, 800-622-6232, canadasite@canada.gc.ca
Historic Sites & Monuments Board of Canada, Terrasses de la Chaudière, 25 Eddy St., Gatineau, QC K1A 0M5
Fax: 819-934-1115, 855-283-8730, hsmbc-clmhc@pc.gc.ca
Human Resources & Skills Development Canada, 140 Promenade du Portage, Gatineau, QC K1A 0J9
Immigration & Refugee Board of Canada, Canada Bldg, 344 Slater St., 12th Fl., Ottawa, ON K1A 0K1
613-995-6486, Fax: 613-943-1550, contact@irb-cisr.gc.ca
National Battlefields Commission, 390, av de Bernières, Québec, QC G1R 2L7
418-648-3506, Fax: 418-648-3638, information@ccbn-nbc.gc.ca
National Capital Commission, #202, 40 Elgin St., Ottawa, ON K1P 1C7
613-239-5000, Fax: 613-239-5063, 800-465-1867, info@ncc-ccn.ca; contracts-contrats@ncc-ccn.ca (Contracting)
National Round Table on the Environment & Economy, #200, 344 Slater St., Ottawa, ON K1R 7Y3
613-992-7189, Fax: 613-992-7385, info@nrtee-trnee.ca
National Seniors Council, Place Vanier, Tower B, 355 North River Rd. 14th Fl., PO Box 4, Ottawa, ON K1A 0K9
Fax: 613-946-8871, 800-622-6232, nsc-cna@hrsdc-rhdcc.gc.ca
Nunavut Impact Review Board, PO Box 1360, Cambridge Bay, NU X0B 0C0
867-983-4600, Fax: 867-983-2594, 866-233-3033, info@nirb.ca
Nunavut Planning Commission, PO Box 2101, Cambridge Bay, NU X0B 0C0
867-983-4625, Fax: 867-983-4626
Nunavut Water Board, PO Box 119, Gjoa Haven, NU X0B 1J0
867-360-6338, Fax: 867-360-6369
Office of the Prime Minister, Conservative Party of Canada / Conservative Research Bureau, Langevin Block, 80 Wellington St., Ottawa, ON K1A 0A2
613-992-4211, Fax: 613-995-0101, pm@pm.gc.ca
Office of the Commissioner of Official Languages, 344 Slater St., 3rd fl., Ottawa, ON K1A 0T8
613-996-6368, Fax: 613-993-5082, 877-996-6368
Passport Canada, Le 70 Crémazie, 70 Crémazie St., Gatineau, QC K1A 0G3
Fax: 819-953-5856, 800-567-6868
Porcupine Caribou Management Board, PO Box 31723, Whitehorse, YT Y1A 6L3
867-633-4780, Fax: 867-393-3904, pcmb@taiga.net
Privacy Commissioner of Canada, Tower B, Place de Ville, 112 Kent St., 3rd Fl., Ottawa, ON K1A 1H3
613-947-1698, Fax: 613-947-6850, 800-282-1376
Secteur du Québec de la Force terrestre, Montréal, QC
514-252-2777
Social Sciences & Humanities Research Council of Canada, Constitution Sq., 350 Albert St., PO Box 1610 B,Ottawa, ON K1P 6G4
613-992-0691, Fax: 613-992-1787, info@sshrc.ca
Specific Claims Tribunal Canada, #400, 427 Laurier Ave. West, PO Box 31, Ottawa, ON K1R 7Y2
613-947-0751, Fax: 613-943-0586, info@sct-trp.ca
Status of Women Canada, 123 Slater St., 10th Fl., Ottawa, ON K1P 1H9
613-995-7835, Fax: 613-947-0761, 866-902-2719, infonational@swc-cfc.gc.ca
Veterans Affairs Canada, 161 Grafton St., PO Box 7700, Charlottetown, PE C1A 8M9
902-566-8888, 866-522-2111, information@vac-acc.gc.ca
Veterans Review & Appeal Board, Daniel J. MacDonald Bldg., 161 Grafton St., PO Box 9900, Charlottetown, PE C1A 8V7
902-566-8751, Fax: 902-566-7850, 800-450-8006, vrab_tacra@vac-acc.gc.ca
Alberta
Alberta Sport, Recreation, Parks, & Wildlife Foundation, Standard Life Centre, #903, 10405 Jasper Ave., 9th Fl., Edmonton, AB T5J 4R7
780-415-1167, Fax: 780-415-0308, -310-0000
Alberta Health, PO Box 1360 Main,Edmonton, AB T5J 2N3
780-427-7164, Fax: 780-427-1171, -310-0000
Labour Relations Board, Labour Building, 10808 - 99 Ave., 5th Fl., Edmonton, AB T5K 0G5
780-422-5926, Fax: 780-422-0970, 800-463-2572, alrbinfo@lab.gov.ab.ca
Premier's Council on the Status of Persons with Disabilities, HSBC Building, 10055 - 106 St., 11th Fl., Edmonton, AB T5J 1G3
780-422-1095, 800-272-8841, pcspd@gov.ab.ca
Seniors Advisory Council for Alberta, Standard Life Centre, #600, 10405 Jasper Ave., 6th Fl., Edmonton, AB T5J 4R7
780-422-2321, Fax: 780-422-8762, -310-0000, saca@gov.ab.ca
Alberta Seniors, Communications, Standard Life Centre, 10405 Jasper Ave., 3rd Fl., Edmonton, AB T5J 4R7
780-415-9950, Fax: 780-644-1227, 866-477-8589, seniors.communications@gov.ab.ca
Alberta Tourism, Parks, & Recreation, Communications Branch, Commerce Place, 10155 - 102 St., 6th Fl., Edmonton, AB T5J 4L6
780-644-5589, TPR.Communications@gov.ab.ca
British Columbia
British Columbia Ministry of Children & Family Development, PO Box 9770 Prov Govt,Victoria, BC V8W 9S5
250-387-7027, Fax: 250-356-3007, 877-387-7027, MCF.CorrespondenceManagement@gov.bc.ca
British Columbia Ministry of Community, Sport, & Cultural Development, PO Box 9490 Prov Govt,Victoria, BC V8W 9N7
Local Government, PO Box 9490 Prov Govt,Victoria, BC V8W 9N7
250-356-6575, Fax: 250-387-7973
Native Economic Development Advisory Board, c/o Director, Economic Initiatives, PO Box 9100 Prov Govt, Victoria, BC V8W 9B1
250-387-2536, Fax: 250-356-9467
Manitoba
Manitoba Aboriginal & Northern Affairs, Legislative Bldg, 344-450 Broadway, Winnipeg, MB R3C 0V8
204-945-3719, Fax: 204-945-8374, anaweb@gov.mb.ca
Aboriginal Affairs Secretariat, #200, 500 Portage Ave., Winnipeg, MB R3C 3X1
204-945-2510, Fax: 204-945-3689
Communications Services Manitoba, 155 Carlton St., 10th Fl., Winnipeg, MB R3C 3H8
204-945-3765, Fax: 204-948-2147
Communities Economic Development Fund, #100, 23 Station Rd., Thompson, MB R8N 0N6
204-778-4138, Fax: 204-778-4313, 800-561-4315
Manitoba Culture, Heritage & Tourism, Legislative Building, #118, 450 Broadway Ave., Winnipeg, MB R3C 0V8
204-945-3729, Fax: 204-945-5223, mincht@leg.gov.mb.ca
Manitoba Family Services & Labour, #219, 114 Garry St., Winnipeg, MB R3C 4V6
204-945-3242, Fax: 204-945-2156, minfam@leg.gov.mb.ca
Manitoba Healthy Living, Seniors & Consumer Affairs, #822, 155 Carlton St., Winnipeg, MB R3C 3H8
204-945-6565, Fax: 204-948-2514, 800-665-6565, seniors@gov.mb.ca
Heritage Grants Advisory Council, 213 Notre Dame Ave., 3rd Fl., Winnipeg, MB R3B 1N3
204-945-2213, Fax: 204-948-2086
Manitoba Human Rights Commission, 175 Hargrave St., 7th Fl., Winnipeg, MB R3C 3R8
204-945-3007, Fax: 204-945-1292, 888-884-8681, hrc@gov.mb.ca
Le Centre Culturel franco-manitobain/Franco-Manitoban Cultural Centre, 340, boul Provencher, St Boniface, MB R2H 0G7
204-233-8972, Fax: 204-233-3324, ccfm@ccfm.mb.ca
Manitoba Centennial Centre Corporation, 555 Main St., Winnipeg, MB R3B 1C3
204-956-1360, Fax: 204-944-1390
Manitoba Film Classification Board, #216, 301 Weston St., Winnipeg, MB R3E 3H4
204-945-8962, Fax: 204-945-0890, 866-612-2399, mfcb@gov.mb.ca
Manitoba Heritage Council, 213 Notre Dame Ave., Main Fl., Winnipeg, MB R3B 1N3
204-945-2118, Fax: 204-948-2384, hrb@gov.mb.ca
Multiculturalism Secretariat, 213 Notre Dame Ave., 4th Fl., Winnipeg, MB R3B 1N3
204-945-1156, Fax: 204-948-2323
Public Health & Primary Health Care, 300 Carlton St., 2nd Floor, Winnipeg, MB R3B 3M9
New Brunswick
Premier's Council on the Status of Disabled Persons, Kings Place, #648, 440 King St., Fredericton, NB E3B 5H8
506-444-3000, Fax: 506-444-3001, 800-442-4412, pcsdp@gnb.ca
New Brunswick Human Rights Commission, PO Box 6000, Fredericton, NB E3B 5H1
506-453-2301, Fax: 506-453-2653, 888-471-2233, hrc.cdp@gnb.ca
Intergovernmental Affairs Division, Centennial Bldg., #274, 670 King St., PO Box 6000, Fredericton, NB E3B 5H1
506-457-7275, Fax: 506-453-2995, iga@gnb.ca
New Brunswick Department of Health, PO Box 5100, Fredericton, NB E3B 5G8
506-457-4800, Fax: 506-453-5243, dh-ms@dh-ms.ca
New Brunswick Department of Social Development, Sartain MacDonald Bldg., 551 King St., PO Box 6000, Fredericton, NB E3B 5H1
506-453-2001, Fax: 506-453-7478, sd-ds@gnb.ca
Regional Development Corporation, RDC Bldg., 836 Churchill Row, PO Box 428, Fredericton, NB E3B 5R4
506-453-2277, Fax: 506-453-7988
New Brunswick Advisory Council on Youth, Frederick Square, #130, 77 Westmorland St., PO Box 6000, Fredericton, NB E3B 5H1
506-453-3271, Fax: 506-444-4413, 888-830-5588, nbacy-ccjnb@gnb.ca
Newfoundland & Labrador
C.A. Pippy Park Commission, Mount Scio House, 15 Mount Scio Rd., St. John's, NL A1B 3T2
709-737-3655, Fax: 709-737-3303, info@pippypark.com
Newfoundland & Labrador Human Rights Commission, PO Box 8700, St. John's, NL A1B 4J6
709-729-2709, Fax: 709-729-0790, 800-563-5808, humanrights@mail.gov.nl.ca

Newfoundland & Labrador Department of Advanced Education & Skills, Confederation Building, West Block, 3rd Fl., PO Box 8700, St. John's, NL A1B 4J6
709-729-2480, aesweb@gov.nl.ca
Newfoundland & Labrador Department of Tourism, Culture, & Recreation, Confederation Bldg., West Block, 2nd Fl., PO Box 8700, St. John's, NL A1B 4J6
709-729-0862, Fax: 709-729-0870, tcrinfo@gov.nl.ca
Provincial Advisory Council on the Status of Women, #103, 15 Hallett Cres., St. John's, NL A1B 4C4
709-753-7270, Fax: 709-753-2606, 877-753-7270, info@pacsw.ca

Northwest Territories

Department of Aboriginal Affairs & Intergovernmental Relations, 4910 - 52nd St., PO Box 1320, Yellowknife, NT X1A 2L9
867-873-7143, Fax: 867-873-0233, 877-838-8194, nancy_gardiner@gov.nt.ca
Department of Municipal & Community Affairs, PO Box 1320, Yellowknife, NT X1A 2L9
867-873-7118, Fax: 867-873-0309
Office of the Languages Commissioner, Laing Bldg., 5003 - 49 St., Yellowknife, NT X1A 2P4
867-873-7034, Fax: 867-873-0357, 800-661-0889, langcom@gov.nt.ca
Status of Women Council of the Northwest Territories, PO Box 1320, Yellowknife, NT X1A 2L9
867-920-6177, Fax: 867-873-0285, 888-234-4485, council@statusofwomen.nt.ca

Nova Scotia

Department of Community Services, Nelson Place, 5675 Spring Garden Rd., 8th Fl., PO Box 696, Halifax, NS B3J 2T7
902-424-4304, Fax: 902-428-0618
Nova Scotia Human Rights Commission, Joseph Howe Bldg., 1690 Hollis St., 6th Fl., Halifax, NS B3J 3C4
902-424-4111, Fax: 902-424-0596, hrcinquiries@gov.ns.ca
Nova Scotia Advisory Commission on AIDS, Dennis Bldg., 1740 Granville St., 6th Fl., Halifax, NS B3J 1X5
902-424-5730, Fax: 902-424-4727, AIDS@gov.ns.ca
Nova Scotia Disabled Persons Commission, Dartmouth Professional Center, #104, 277 Pleasant St., Dartmouth, NS B2Y 4B7
902-424-8280, Fax: 902-424-0592, 800-565-8280
Pay Equity Commission, 5151 Terminal Rd., 6th Fl., PO Box 697, Halifax, NS B3J 2T8
902-424-2385, Fax: 902-424-0575
Seniors' Secretariat, Dennis Bldg., 1740 Granville St., 4th Fl., PO Box 2065, Halifax, NS B3J 2Z1
902-424-0065, Fax: 902-424-0561, 800-670-0065, seniors@gov.ns.ca
Department of Service Nova Scotia & Municipal Relations, 1505 Barrington St., PO Box 216, Halifax, NS B3J 3K5
902-424-5200, Fax: 902-424-0581, 800-670-4357, askus@gov.ns.ca
Nova Scotia Advisory Council on the Status of Women, 1700 Granville St., PO Box 943, Halifax, NS B3J 2V9
902-424-7660, women@gov.ns.ca

Ontario

Ontario Ministry of Aboriginal Affairs, 160 Bloor St. East, 4th & 9th Fl., Toronto, ON M7A 2E6
416-326-4740, Fax: 416-326-4017
Citizenship & Immigration Division, 400 University Ave., 3rd Fl., Toronto, ON M7A 2R9
416-314-7541, Fax: 416-314-7599
Ontario Ministry of Citizenship & Immigration, 400 University Ave., 6th Fl., Toronto, ON M7A 2R9
416-327-2422, Fax: 416-314-4965, 800-267-7329
Ontario Ministry of Community & Social Services, Hepburn Block, 80 Grosvenor St., 6th Fl., Toronto, ON M7A 1E9
416-325-5666, Fax: 416-325-5172, 888-789-4199
Office of Francophone Affairs, #200, 777 Bay St., Toronto, ON M7A 0A2
416-325-4949, Fax: 416-325-4980, 800-268-7507, ofa@ontario.ca
Ontario Ministry of Government Services, Whitney Block, #4320, 99 Wellesley St. West, 4th Fl., Toronto, ON M7A 1W3
416-326-1234, Fax: 416-327-3790, 800-268-1142
Ontario Human Rights Commission, 180 Dundas St. West, 7th Fl., Toronto, ON M7A 2R9
416-326-9511, Fax: 416-314-4494, 800-387-9080
Information & Privacy Commissioner of Ontario, #1400, 2 Bloor St. East, Toronto, ON M4W 1A8
416-326-3333, Fax: 416-325-9195, 800-387-0073, info@ipc.on.ca
Ontario Heritage Trust, 10 Adelaide St. East, Toronto, ON M5C 1J3
416-325-5000, Fax: 416-325-5071
Ontario Northland, 555 Oak St. East, North Bay, ON P1B 8L3
705-472-4500, Fax: 705-472-4267, 800-363-7512, info@ontarionorthland.ca
Royal Ontario Museum, 100 Queen's Park Cres., Toronto, ON M5S 2C6
416-586-5549, Fax: 416-586-5685, info@rom.on.ca
Social Benefits Tribunal, 1075 Bay St., 7th Fl., Toronto, ON M5S 2B1
416-326-0978, Fax: 416-325-5135, 800-753-3895
Ontario Women's Directorate, 777 Bay St., 6th Fl., Toronto, ON M7A 2J4
416-314-0300, Fax: 416-314-0247, 866-510-5902, owd@ontario.ca

Prince Edward Island

Prince Edward Island Human Rights Commission, 53 Water St., PO Box 2000, Charlottetown, PE C1A 7N8
902-368-4180, Fax: 902-368-4236, 800-237-5031
Prince Edward Island Department of Community Services & Seniors, Jones Bldg., 11 Kent St., 2nd Fl., PO Box 2000, Charlottetown, PE C1A 7N8
902-620-3777, Fax: 902-368-4740, 866-594-3777

Quebec

Secrétariat aux affaires autochtones, 905, av Honoré-Mercier, 1er étage, Québec, QC G1R 5M6
418-643-3166, Fax: 418-646-4918
Commission administrative des régimes de retraite et d'assurances (Québec), 475, rue Saint-Amable, Québec, QC G1R 5X3
418-643-4881, Fax: 418-644-3839, 800-463-5533
Commission des biens culturels du Québec, Bloc A-RC, 225, Grande Allée est, Québec, QC G1R 5G5
418-643-8378, Fax: 418-643-8591, info@cbcq.gouv.qc.ca
Conseil des arts et des lettres du Québec, 79, boul René-Lévesque est, 3e étage, Québec, QC G1R 5N5
418-643-1707, Fax: 418-643-4558, 800-897-1707, info@calq.gouv.qc.ca
Conseil des relations interculturelles, #10.04, 500, boul René-Lévesque ouest, Montréal, QC H2Z 1W7
514-873-5634, Fax: 514-873-3469, info@conseilinterculturel.gouv.qc.ca
Ministère de la Culture, des Communications & de la Condition féminine, 225, Grande Allée est, Québec, QC G1R 5G5
888-380-8882
Curateur public du Québec, 600, boul René-Lévesque ouest, Montréal, QC H3B 4W9
514-873-4074, Fax: 514-873-5033, 800-363-9020
Ministère de l'Emploi et de la Solidarité sociale, 425, rue St-Amable, 4e étage, Québec, QC G1R 4Z1
418-643-4721, 888-643-4721
Fonds québécois de la recherche sur la société et la culture, #470, 140, Grande Allée est, Québec, QC G1R 5M8
418-643-7582, Fax: 418-644-5248, fqrsc@fqrsc.gouv.qc.ca
Ministère de l'Immigration et des Communautés culturelles, Édifice Gérald-Godin, 360, rue McGill, Montréal, QC H2Y 2E9
514-864-9191, Fax: 514-864-2899, 877-864-9191
Office des personnes handicapées du Québec, 309, rue Brock, Drummondville, QC J2B 1C5
Fax: 819-475-8753, 800-567-1465, michael.magner@ophq.gouv.qc.ca
Ministère des Relations internationales, Édifice Hector-Fabre, 525, boul Réne-Lévesque est, Québec, QC G1R 5R9
418-649-2300, Fax: 418-649-2656
Ministère de la Santé et des Services sociaux, Direction des communications, 1075, ch Sainte-Foy, 16e étage, Québec, QC G1S 2M1
418-643-9395, Fax: 418-643-4768, regisseur.web@msss.gouv.qc.ca
Secrétariat aux affaires intergouvernementales canadiennes, 875, Grande Allée est, 3e étage, Québec, QC G1R 4Y8
418-643-4011, Fax: 418-528-0052
Secrétariat à la politique linguistique, 225 Grande-Allée est, 4e étage, Québec, QC G1R 5G5
418-643-4248, Fax: 418-646-7832, info@spl.gouv.qc.ca
Société de développement des entreprises culturelles, #800, 215, rue Saint-Jacques, Montréal, QC H2Y 1M6
514-841-2200, Fax: 514-841-8606, 800-363-0401, info@sodec.gouv.qc.ca
Tribunal administratif du Québec, 575, rue Saint-Amable, Québec, QC G1R 5R4
418-643-3418, Fax: 418-643-5335

Saskatchewan

Government Services, 1920 Rose St., Regina, SK S4P 0A9
306-787-6911, Fax: 306-787-1061, GSReception@gs.gov.sk.ca
Information & Privacy Commissioner of Saskatchewan, #503, 1801 Hamilton St., Regina, SK S4P 4B4
306-787-8350, Fax: 306-798-1603, 877-748-2298, webmaster@oipc.sk.ca
Saskatchewan Human Rights Commission, Saskatoon Office, Sturdy Stone Bdg., #816, 122 - 3 Ave. North, 8th Fl., Saskatoon, SK S7K 2H6
306-933-5952, Fax: 306-933-7863, 800-667-9249, shrc@gov.sk.ca
Saskatchewan Social Services, 1920 Broad St., Regina, SK S4P 3V6
306-787-3700, 866-221-5200, socialservicesinquiry@gov.sk.ca

Yukon Territory

Yukon Community Services, PO Box 2703, Whitehorse, YT Y1A 2C6
867-667-5811, Fax: 867-393-6295, 800-661-0408, inquiry@gov.yk.ca
Yukon Health & Social Services, PO Box 2703, Whitehorse, YT Y1A 2C6
867-667-3673, Fax: 867-667-3096, hss@gov.yk.ca
Yukon Women's Directorate, #1, 404 Hason St., Whitehorse, YT Y1A 1Y8
867-667-3030, Fax: 867-393-6270
Yukon Human Rights Commission, #101, 9010 Quartz St., Whitehorse, YT Y1A 2Z5
867-667-6226, Fax: 867-667-2662, 800-661-0535, humanrights@yhrc.yk.ca

CAREER PLANNING

New Brunswick

Labour & Planning Division, Chestnut Complex, PO Box 6000, Fredericton, NB E3B 5H1
506-453-8202, Fax: 506-453-3038, dpetlinfo@gnb.ca

Ontario

Ontario Ministry of Training, Colleges & Universities, Mowat Block, 900 Bay St., 14th Fl., Toronto, ON M7A 1L2
416-325-2929, Fax: 416-325-6348, 800-387-5514, information.met@ontario.ca

Saskatchewan

Saskatchewan Education, 2220 College Ave., Regina, SK S4P 4V9
linquiry@gov.sk.ca

CENSORSHIP (MEDIA)

Canadian Broadcasting Corporation, 181 Queen St., PO Box 3220 C,Ottawa, ON K1Y 1E4
613-288-6033, liaison@radio-canada.ca
Canadian Radio-Television & Telecommunications Commission, Central Building, 1, Promenade du Portage, Les Terrasses de la Chaudière, Gatineau, QC J8X 4B1
819-997-0313, Fax: 819-994-0218, 877-249-2782

Manitoba

Manitoba Film Classification Board, #216, 301 Weston St., Winnipeg, MB R3E 3H4
204-945-8962, Fax: 204-945-0890, 866-612-2399, mfcb@gov.mb.ca

Nunavut

Department of Community & Government Services, W.G. Brown Bldg., 4th Fl., PO Box 1000 700,Iqaluit, NU X0A 0H0
867-975-5400, Fax: 867-975-5305

Quebec

Régie du cinéma, #100, 390, rue Notre-Dame ouest, Montréal, QC H2Y 1T9
514-873-2371, Fax: 514-873-8874, 800-463-2463, regieducinema@rcq.gouv.qc.ca

Saskatchewan

Saskatchewan Film & Video Classification Board, #500, 1919 Saskatchewan Dr., Regina, SK S4P 4H2
306-787-5550, Fax: 306-787-9779, 888-374-4636

CHEMICALS

Institute for Chemical Process & Environmental Technology, Bldg. M-12, 1200 Montreal Rd., Ottawa, ON K1A 0R6
613-993-4041, Fax: 613-957-8231

CHILD WELFARE

See Also: Day Care Services

Prince Edward Island

Children's Secretariat, c/o Sarah Henry, Education & Early Childhood Development, 161 St. Peters Rd., PO Box 2000, Charlottetown, PE C1A 7N8
Office of the Child & Youth Advocate, Peace Hills Trust Tower, #805, 10011 - 109 St., Edmonton, AB T5J 3S8
780-422-6056, Fax: 780-644-8833, 800-661-3446

New Brunswick

Program Design & Quality Management, Sartain MacDonald Bldg., #4007, 551 King St., PO Box 6000, Fredericton, NB E3B 5H1
506-453-2181, Fax: 506-453-3829

Northwest Territories

Department of Health & Social Services, Centre Square Tower, PO Box 1320, Yellowknife, NT X1A 2L9
Fax: 867-873-0266

Nunavut

Department of Health & Social Services, PO Box 1000 1000,Iqaluit, NU X0A 0H0
867-975-5700, Fax: 867-975-5705

Ontario

Ontario Ministry of Children & Youth Services, 56 Wellesley St. West, 14th Fl., Toronto, ON M5S 2G3
Fax: 416-325-5191, 866-821-7770

CITIZENSHIP
Immigration & Refugee Board of Canada, Canada Bldg, 344 Slater St., 12th Fl., Ottawa, ON K1A 0K1
613-995-6486, Fax: 613-943-1550, contact@irb-cisr.gc.ca
Manitoba
Manitoba Education, #168, Legislative Bldg., 450 Broadway, Winnipeg, MB R3C 0V8
204-945-3720, Fax: 204-945-1291, minedu@leg.gov.mb.ca
Ontario
Ontario Ministry of Citizenship & Immigration, 400 University Ave., 6th Fl., Toronto, ON M7A 2R9
416-327-2422, Fax: 416-314-4965, 800-267-7329

CLIMATE & WEATHER
Canadian Hurricane Centre, 45 Alderney Dr., 16th Fl., Dartmouth, NS B2Y 2N6
902-426-7231, Fax: 902-426-6348, 15th.reception@ec.gc.ca
Canadian Space Agency, John H. Chapman Space Centre, 6767, rte de l'Aéroport, Saint-Hubert, QC J3Y 8Y9
450-926-4800, Fax: 450-926-4352, promo@asc-csa.gc.ca

CLIMATE CHANGE
Climate Change Impacts & Adaptation Division, 601, rue Booth, Ottawa, ON K1A 0E8
613-992-8302, Fax: 613-947-0126, adaptation@nrcan.gc.ca
Springdale, 200 Main St., Springdale, NL A0J 1T0
709-673-4218, Fax: 709-673-4232
Quebec
Ministère du Développement durable, de l'Environnement, de la Faune, et des Parcs, Édifice Marie-Guyart, 675, boul René-Lévesque est, 29e étage, Québec, QC G1R 5V7
418-521-3830, Fax: 418-646-5974, 800-561-1616, info@mddep.gouv.qc.ca

COAL
See Also: Energy
Alberta
Energy Resources Conservation Board, #1000, 250 - 5 Ave. SW, Calgary, AB T2P 0R4
403-297-8311, Fax: 403-297-7336, 855-297-8311, inquiries@ercb.ca; infoservices@ercb.ca; ADR@ercb.ca
Ontario
Ontario Power Generation, 700 University Ave., Toronto, ON M5G 1X6
416-592-2555, 877-592-2555, webmaster@opg.com
Saskatchewan
Saskatchewan Power Corporation (SaskPower), 2025 Victoria Ave., Regina, SK S4P 0S1
306-566-3306, Fax: 800-757-6937, 888-757-6937

COMMUNICATIONS
See: Telecommunications
Canada Post Corporation, Corporate Secretariat, 2701 Riverside Dr., Ottawa, ON K1A 0B1
866-607-6301
Canadian Broadcasting Corporation, 181 Queen St., PO Box 3220 C,Ottawa, ON K1Y 1E4
613-288-6033, liaison@radio-canada.ca
Canadian Radio-Television & Telecommunications Commission, Central Building, 1, Promenade du Portage, Les Terrasses de la Chaudière, Gatineau, QC J8X 4B1
819-997-0313, Fax: 819-994-0218, 877-249-2782
Communications, 1919 Saskatchewan Dr., 4th Fl., Regina, SK S4P 4H2
306-787-0346, Fax: 306-798-0033
Communications Research Centre Canada, 3701 Carling Ave., PO Box 11490 H, Ottawa, ON K2H 8S2
613-991-3313, Fax: 613-998-5355, info@crc.gc.ca
Institute for Information Technology, Bldg. M-50, 1200 Montreal Rd., Ottawa, ON K1A 0R6
613-991-3373, Fax: 613-952-0074, 877-672-2672
Spectrum, Information Technologies & Telecommunications, Journal Tower North, 300 Slater St., 20th Fl., Ottawa, ON K1A 0C8
613-998-0368, Fax: 613-952-1203
Alberta
Alberta Public Affairs Bureau, Park Plaza, 10611 - 98 Ave., 6th Fl., Edmonton, AB T5K 2P7
780-427-2754, Fax: 780-422-4168, -310-0000
Manitoba
Communications Services Manitoba, 155 Carlton St., 10th Fl., Winnipeg, MB R3C 3H8
204-945-3765, Fax: 204-948-2147
News Media Services, Legislative Bldg., #29, 450 Broadway Ave., Winnipeg, MB R3C 0V8
204-945-3746, Fax: 204-945-3988, nmservices@leg.gov.mb.ca
Manitoba Telecom Services Inc., 333 Main St., PO Box 6666, Winnipeg, MB R3C 3V6
204-941-4111, Fax: 204-772-6391
New Brunswick
Justice Services Division, Centennial Building, PO Box 6000, Fredericton, NB E3B 5H1
506-453-2458, Fax: 506-453-3651, general.comments@gnb.ca
Northern Development Division, Harbourview Place, #400, 275 Main St., Bathurst, NB E2A 1A9
506-547-2227, Fax: 506-547-2269
Ontario
Ontario Library Service - North, 334 Regent St., Sudbury, ON P3C 4E2
705-675-6467, Fax: 705-675-2285, 800-461-6348
Quebec
Ministère de la Culture, des Communications & de la Condition féminine, 225, Grande Allée est, Québec, QC G1R 5G5
888-380-8882,
Saskatchewan
Saskatchewan Telecommunications (SaskTel), 2121 Saskatchewan Dr., 7th Fl., Regina, SK S4P 4C3
306-777-3737, 800-727-5835, corporate.comments@sasktel.sk.ca

COMMUNITY & MUNICIPAL DEVELOPMENT
Atlantic Canada Opportunities Agency, Blue Cross Centre, 644 Main St., 3rd Fl., PO Box 6051, Moncton, NB E1C 9J8
506-851-2271, Fax: 506-851-7403, 800-561-7862, information@acoa-apeca.gc.ca
Canada Economic Development for Québec Regions, Édifice Dominion Square, #900, 1255, rue Peel, Montréal, QC H3B 2T9
514-283-6412, Fax: 514-283-3302, 866-385-6412
Canadian Tourism Commission, Four Bentall Centre, #1400, 1055 Dunsmuir St., PO Box 49230, Vancouver, BC V7X 1L2
604-638-8300
Saskatchewan Government Relations, 1855 Victoria Ave., Regina, SK S4P 3T2
306-787-8885
Western Economic Diversification Canada, Canada Place, #1500, 9700 Jasper Ave. NW, Edmonton, AB T5J 4H7
780-495-4164, Fax: 780-495-4557, 888-338-9378
Alberta
Alberta Tourism, Parks, & Recreation, Communications Branch, Commerce Place, 10155 - 102 St., 6th Fl., Edmonton, AB T5J 4L6
780-644-5589, TPR.Communications@gov.ab.ca
British Columbia
Local Government, PO Box 9490 Prov Govt,Victoria, BC V8W 9N7
250-356-6575, Fax: 250-387-7973
Manitoba
Manitoba Aboriginal & Northern Affairs, Legislative Bldg, 344-450 Broadway, Winnipeg, MB R3C 0V8
204-945-3719, Fax: 204-945-8374, anaweb@gov.mb.ca
Provincial-Municipal Support Services, #508, 800 Portage Ave., Winnipeg, MB R3G 0N4
New Brunswick
Regional Development Corporation, RDC Bldg., 836 Churchill Row, PO Box 428, Fredericton, NB E3B 5R4
506-453-2277, Fax: 506-453-7988
Newfoundland & Labrador
Newfoundland & Labrador Department of Health & Community Services, West Block, Confederation Bldg., PO Box 8700, St. John's, NL A1B 4J6
709-729-5021, Fax: 709-729-5824, healthinfo@gov.nl.ca
Northwest Territories
Department of Municipal & Community Affairs, PO Box 1320, Yellowknife, NT X1A 2L9
867-873-7118, Fax: 867-873-0309
Nova Scotia
Department of Service Nova Scotia & Municipal Relations, 1505 Barrington St., PO Box 216, Halifax, NS B3J 3K5
902-424-5200, Fax: 902-424-0581, 800-670-4357, askus@gov.ns.ca
Nunavut
Department of Community & Government Services, W.G. Brown Bldg., 4th Fl., PO Box 1000 700,Iqaluit, NU X0A 0H0
867-975-5400, Fax: 867-975-5305
Ontario
Ontario Ministry of Municipal Affairs & Housing, College Park, 777 Bay St., 17th Fl., Toronto, ON M5G 2E5
416-585-7041, Fax: 416-585-6470, 866-220-2290, mininfo@ontario.ca
Prince Edward Island
SkillsPEI, Atlantic Technology Centre, #212, 90 University Ave., Charlottetown, PE C1A 4K9
902-368-4260, Fax: 902-368-6340, 877-491-4766
Quebec
Ministère des Affaires municipales, des Régions et de l'Occupation du territoire, Aile Chaveau, 10, rue Pierre-Olivier-Chauveau, 3e étage, Québec, QC G1R 4J3
418-691-2019, Fax: 418-643-7385, communications@mamrot.gouv.qc.ca
Ministère du Développement économique, de l'Innovation et de l'Exportation, 710, place D'Youville, 3e étage, Québec, QC G1R 4Y4
418-691-5950, Fax: 418-644-0118, 866-680-1884
Saskatchewan
Enterprise Saskatchewan, #200, 3085 Albert St., Regina, SK S4S 0B1
306-787-4484, Fax: 306-798-0629, invest@gov.sk.ca

COMMUNITY FINANCING
Atlantic Canada Opportunities Agency, Blue Cross Centre, 644 Main St., 3rd Fl., PO Box 6051, Moncton, NB E1C 9J8
506-851-2271, Fax: 506-851-7403, 800-561-7862, information@acoa-apeca.gc.ca
Business Development Bank of Canada, #400, 5, Place Ville-Marie, Montréal, QC H3B 5E7
514-283-5904, Fax: 514-283-5626, 877-232-2269
Canada Economic Development for Québec Regions, Édifice Dominion Square, #900, 1255, rue Peel, Montréal, QC H3B 2T9
514-283-6412, Fax: 514-283-3302, 866-385-6412
Canada Savings Bonds, #900, 110 Yonge St., Toronto, ON M5C 1T4
416-952-1252, Fax: 416-952-1270, 800-575-5151, csb@csb.gc.ca
Finance Canada, L'esplanade Laurier, 140 O'Connor St., Ottawa, ON K1A 0G5
613-992-1573, Fax: 613-943-0938, finpub@fin.gc.ca
Provincial-Local Finance Division, College Park, 777 Bay St., 10th Fl., Toronto, ON M5G 2C8
416-327-0264, Fax: 416-325-7644
Western Economic Diversification Canada, Canada Place, #1500, 9700 Jasper Ave. NW, Edmonton, AB T5J 4H7
780-495-4164, Fax: 780-495-4557, 888-338-9378
Alberta
Alberta Capital Finance Authority, Canadian Western Bank Place, #2450, 10303 Jasper Ave., Edmonton, AB T5J 3N6
780-427-9711, Fax: 780-422-2175, webacfa@gov.ab.ca
Manitoba
Communities Economic Development Fund, #100, 23 Station Rd., Thompson, MB R8N 0N6
204-778-4138, Fax: 204-778-4313, 800-561-4315
Provincial-Municipal Support Services, #508, 800 Portage Ave., Winnipeg, MB R3G 0N4
Newfoundland & Labrador
Newfoundland & Labrador Municipal Financing Corporation, Confederation Bldg., PO Box 8700, St. John's, NL A1B 4J6
709-729-6686, Fax: 709-729-2095
Nova Scotia
Nova Scotia Municipal Finance Corporation, Maritime Centre, 1505 Barrington St., 10th Fl. South, PO Box 850 M, Halifax, NS B3J 2V2
902-424-4590, Fax: 902-424-0525
Prince Edward Island
SkillsPEI, Atlantic Technology Centre, #212, 90 University Ave., Charlottetown, PE C1A 4K9
902-368-4260, Fax: 902-368-6340, 877-491-4766
Quebec
Ministère des Affaires municipales, des Régions et de l'Occupation du territoire, Aile Chaveau, 10, rue Pierre-Olivier-Chauveau, 3e étage, Québec, QC G1R 4J3
418-691-2019, Fax: 418-643-7385, communications@mamrot.gouv.qc.ca
Yukon Territory
Yukon Economic Development, PO Box 2703, Whitehorse, YT Y1A 2C6
867-393-7191, Fax: 867-393-6412, 800-661-0408, ecdev@gov.yk.ca

COMMUNITY SERVICES
Alberta
Alberta Tourism, Parks, & Recreation, Communications Branch, Commerce Place, 10155 - 102 St., 6th Fl., Edmonton, AB T5J 4L6
780-644-5589, TPR.Communications@gov.ab.ca
British Columbia
British Columbia Ministry of Community, Sport, & Cultural Development, PO Box 9490 Prov Govt,Victoria, BC V8W 9N7
Manitoba
Local Government Development Division, 59 Elizabeth Dr., PO Box 33, Thompson, MB R8N 1X4
204-677-6794, Fax: 204-677-6525

New Brunswick
New Brunswick Department of Social Development, Sartain MacDonald Bldg., 551 King St., PO Box 6000, Fredericton, NB E3B 5H1
506-453-2001, Fax: 506-453-7478, sd-ds@gnb.ca
Newfoundland & Labrador
Newfoundland & Labrador Department of Health & Community Services, West Block, Confederation Bldg., PO Box 8700, St. John's, NL A1B 4J6
709-729-5021, Fax: 709-729-5824, healthinfo@gov.nl.ca
Northwest Territories
Department of Municipal & Community Affairs, PO Box 1320, Yellowknife, NT X1A 2L9
867-873-7118, Fax: 867-873-0309
Nova Scotia
Department of Community Services, Nelson Place, 5675 Spring Garden Rd., 8th Fl., PO Box 696, Halifax, NS B3J 2T7
902-424-4304, Fax: 902-428-0618
Nunavut
Department of Community & Government Services, W.G. Brown Bldg., 4th Fl., PO Box 1000 700,Iqaluit, NU X0A 0H0
867-975-5400, Fax: 867-975-5305
Ontario
Ontario Ministry of Community & Social Services, Hepburn Block, 80 Grosvenor St., 6th Fl., Toronto, ON M7A 1E9
416-325-5666, Fax: 416-325-5172, 888-789-4199
Prince Edward Island
Prince Edward Island Department of Community Services & Seniors, Jones Bldg., 11 Kent St., 2nd Fl., PO Box 2000, Charlottetown, PE C1A 7N8
902-620-3777, Fax: 902-368-4740, 866-594-3777
Saskatchewan
Saskatchewan Social Services, 1920 Broad St., Regina, SK S4P 3V6
306-787-3700, 866-221-5200, socialservicesinquiry@gov.sk.ca
Yukon Territory
Yukon Community Services, PO Box 2703, Whitehorse, YT Y1A 2C6
867-667-5811, Fax: 867-393-6295, 800-661-0408, inquiry@gov.yk.ca

CONFLICT OF INTEREST

Office of the Conflict of Interest & Ethics Commissioner, Commissioner's Office, 66 Slater St., 22nd Fl., Ottawa, ON K1A 0A6
613-995-0721, Fax: 613-995-7308, ciec-ccie@parl.gc.ca
Alberta
Alberta Office of the Ethics Commissioner, #1250, 9925 - 109 St. NW, Edmonton, AB T5K 2J8
780-422-2273, Fax: 780-422-2261, generalinfo@ethicscommissioner.ab.ca
British Columbia
Office of the Conflict of Interest Commissioner, #101, 431 Menzies St., Victoria, BC V8V 1X4
250-356-0750, Fax: 250-356-6580, conflictofinterest@coibc.ca
Ontario
Office of the Integrity Commissioner, #2101, 2 Bloor St. East, Toronto, ON M4W 1A8
416-314-8983, Fax: 416-314-8987, integrity.mail@oico.on.ca

CONSERVATION & ECOLOGY

See Also: Heritage Resources; Natural Resources
Arctic Goose, c/o Prairie & Northern Region, CWS, #200, 4999 - 98 Ave., Edmonton, AB T6B 2X3
780-951-8652, Fax: 780-495-2615, agjv@ec.gc.ca
Black Duck, Environment Canada, Canadian Wildlife Service, 335 River Rd., Ottawa, ON K1A 0H3
613-949-8254
Canadian Heritage, 15 Eddy St., Gatineau, QC K1A 0M5
819-997-0055, 866-811-0055, info@pch.gc.ca
Canadian Polar Commission, Constitution Square, #1710, 360 Albert St., Ottawa, ON K1R 7X7
613-943-8605, Fax: 613-943-8607, 888-765-2701, mail@polarcom.gc.ca
Canadian Wildlife Service, 351, boul St-Joseph, Gatineau, QC K1A 0H3
819-997-1301, Fax: 819-953-7177
Commission for Environmental Cooperation, Secretariat, #200, 393, rue St-Jacques ouest, Montréal, QC H2Y 1N9
514-350-4300, Fax: 514-350-4314, info@cec.org
Eastern Habitat, c/o Environment Canada, Canadian Wildlife Service, 335 River Rd., Ottawa, ON K1A 0H3
613-949-8264
Environment Canada, 10 Wellington St., Gatineau, QC K1A 0H3
819-997-2800, Fax: 819-994-1412, 800-668-6767, enviroinfo@ec.gc.ca
Fisheries Resource Conservation Council, PO Box 2001 D, Ottawa, ON K1P 5W3
613-998-0433, Fax: 613-998-1146, info@frcc-ccrh.ca
Forestry Division, Petroleum Plaza ST, 9915 - 108 St. 11th Fl., Edmonton, AB T5K 2G8
Integrated Environmental Policy Division, 77 Wellesley St. West, 11th Fl., Toronto, ON M7A 2T5
416-314-6338, Fax: 416-314-6346
Land Use Secretariat, Centre West Building, 10035 - 108 St., Edmonton, AB T5J 3E1
780-644-7972, Fax: 780-644-1034, luf@gov.ab.ca
Natural Resources Canada, 580 Booth St., Ottawa, ON K1A 0E4
613-995-0947, Fax: 613-992-7211
North American Bird Conservation Initiative, Canadian Wildlife Service, 351, boul St-Joseph, 3e étage, Gatineau, QC K1A 0H3
819-994-0512, Fax: 819-994-4445, nabci@ec.gc.ca
North American Waterfowl Management Plan, NAWCC (Canada) Secretariat, Place Vincent Massey, 351 St. Joseph Blvd., 7th Fl., Gatineau, QC K1A 0H3
819-934-6034, Fax: 819-934-6017, nawmp@ec.gc.ca
Pacific Coast, c/o Environment Canada, Canadian Wildlife Service, #201, 401 Burrard St., Vancouver, BC V6C 3S5
604-940-4703
Parks Canada, 25 Eddy St., Gatineau, QC K1A 0M5
613-860-1251, 888-773-8888, information@pc.gc.ca
Prairie Habitat, c/o Prairie & Northern Region, CWS, #200, 4999 - 98 Ave., Edmonton, AB T6B 2X3
780-951-8652, phjv@ec.gc.ca
Wascana Centre Authority, 2900 Wascana Dr., PO Box 7111, Regina, SK S4P 3S7
306-522-3661, Fax: 306-565-2742, wca@wascana.ca
Alberta
Alberta Environmental Appeals Board, Peace Hills Trust Tower, #306, 10011 - 109 St., Edmonton, AB T5J 3S8
780-427-6207, Fax: 780-427-4693
Alberta Used Oil Management Association, Empire Building, #1008, 10080 Jasper Ave., Edmonton, AB T5J 1V9
780-414-1510, Fax: 780-414-1519, 866-414-1510, reception@usedoilrecycling.ca
Beverage Container Management Board, #750, 10707 - 100 Ave., Edmonton, AB T5J 3M1
780-424-3193, Fax: 780-428-4620, 888-424-7671
Alberta Environment & Sustainable Resource Development, Oxbridge Place, 9820 - 106 St., Main Fl., Edmonton, AB T5K 2J6
780-427-2700, Fax: 780-422-4086, -310-0000, env.infocent@gov.ab.ca; srd.infocent@gov.ab.ca
Natural Resources Conservation Board, Sterling Place, 9940 - 106 St., Edmonton, AB T5K 2N2
780-422-1977, Fax: 780-427-0607, 866-383-6722, info@nrcb.gov.ab.ca
Special Areas Board, Special Areas Board Administration, 212 - 2nd Ave. West, PO Box 820, Hanna, AB T0J 1P0
403-854-5600, Fax: 403-854-5527, specarea@telus.net
British Columbia
British Columbia Assessment Authority, #400, 3450 Uptown Blvd., Victoria, BC V8Z 0B9
250-595-6211, Fax: 250-595-6222, info@bcassessment.ca
British Columbia Ministry of Environment, PO Box 9339 Prov Govt,Victoria, BC V8W 9M1
250-387-1161, Fax: 250-387-5669, envmail@gov.bc.ca
Environmental Appeal Board, 747 Fort St., 4th Fl., PO Box 9425 Prov Govt, Victoria, BC V8W 3E9
250-387-3464, Fax: 250-356-9923, eabinfo@gov.bc.ca
Environmental Stewardship Division, PO Box 9339 Prov Govt,Victoria, BC V8W 9M1
250-356-0121, Fax: 250-387-5669
Forest Practices Board, 1675 Douglas St., 3rd Fl., PO Box 9905 Prov Govt, Victoria, BC V8W 9R1
250-213-4700, Fax: 250-213-4725, 800-994-5899, fpboard@gov.bc.ca
North Area, 1011 - 4 Ave., 5th Fl., Prince George, BC V2L 3H9
250-565-6100
Manitoba
Clean Environment Commission, #305, 155 Carlton St., Winnipeg, MB R3C 3H8
204-945-0594, Fax: 204-945-0090
Manitoba Conservation & Water Stewardship, 200 Saulteaux Cres., Winnipeg, MB R3J 3W3
800-214-6497, mws@gov.mb.ca
Ecological Reserves Advisory Committee, c/o Manitoba Conservation, Parks & Natural Areas Branch, 200 Saulteaux Cres., Winnipeg, MB R3J 3W3
204-945-4148, Fax: 204-945-0012, hhernandez@gov.mb.ca
Manitoba Conservation Districts Commission, Secretariat c/o Planning & Coordination Branch, 123 Main St., PO Box 20000, Neepawa, MB R0J 1H0
204-476-7033, Fax: 204-476-7539, whildebran@gov.mb.ca
New Brunswick
New Brunswick Department of Environment & Local Government, Marysville Place, PO Box 6000, Fredericton, NB E3B 5H1
506-453-2690, Fax: 506-457-4994, elg/egl-info@gnb.ca
Newfoundland & Labrador
Newfoundland & Labrador Department of Environment & Conservation, Confederation Bldg., West Block, 4th Fl., PO Box 8700, St. John's, NL A1B 4J6
709-729-2664, Fax: 709-729-6639, 800-563-6181, info@gov.nl.ca
Northwest Territories
Department of Environment & Natural Resources, PO Box 1320, Yellowknife, NT X1A 2L9
Nova Scotia
Department of Natural Resources, Founder's Square, 1701 Hollis St., 3rd Fl., PO Box 698, Halifax, NS B3J 2T9
902-424-5935, Fax: 902-424-0594, 800-565-2224
Ontario
Ontario Ministry of Environment, 135 St. Clair Ave. West, Toronto, ON M4V 1P5
416-325-4000, Fax: 416-325-3159, 800-565-4923
Ontario Ministry of Natural Resources, Whitney Block, #6630, 99 Wellesley St. West, 6th Fl., Toronto, ON M7A 1W3
800-667-1940
Niagara Escarpment Commission, 232 Guelph St., Georgetown, ON L7G 4B1
905-877-5191, Fax: 905-873-7452
Prince Edward Island
Environmental Advisory Council, PO Box 2000, Charlottetown, PE C1A 7N8
Prince Edward Island Department of Environment, Labour & Justice, Shaw Bldg. South, 95 Rochford St., 4th Fl., PO Box 2000, Charlottetown, PE C1A 7N8
902-620-3774, Fax: 902-368-4242, rrryder@gov.pe.ca
Prince Edward Island Department of Tourism & Culture, PO Box 2000, Charlottetown, PE C1A 7N8
902-368-5540, Fax: 902-368-5277, tpswitch@gov.pe.ca
Quebec
Comité consultatif de l'environnement Kativik, CP 930, Kuujjuaq, QC J0M 1C0
819-964-2961, Fax: 819-964-0694
Ministère du Développement durable, de l'Environnement, de la Faune, et des Parcs, Édifice Marie-Guyart, 675, boul René-Lévesque est, 29e étage, Québec, QC G1R 5V7
418-521-3830, Fax: 418-646-5974, 800-561-1616, info@mddep.gouv.qc.ca
Fondation de la faune du Québec, Place Iberville II, #420, 1175, av Lavigerie, Québec, QC G1V 4P1
418-644-7926, Fax: 418-643-7655, 877-639-0742, ffq@fondationdelafaune.qc.ca
Société de développement de la Baie James, 110, boul Matagami, CP 970, Matagami, QC J0Y 2A0
819-739-4717, Fax: 819-739-4329, mat@sdbj.gouv.qc.ca
Société québécoise de récupération et de recyclage, #200, 420, boul Charest est, Québec, QC G1K 8M4
418-643-0394, Fax: 418-643-6507, 866-523-8290, info@recyc-quebec.gouv.qc.ca
Saskatchewan
Saskatchewan Assessment Management Agency, #200, 2201 - 11th Ave., Regina, SK S4P 0J8
306-924-8000, Fax: 306-924-8070, 800-667-7262, info.request@sama.sk.ca
Saskatchewan Conservation Data Centre, 3211 Albert St., Regina, SK S4S 5W6
306-787-9038, Fax: 306-787-9544
Saskatchewan Environment, 3211 Albert St., 2nd Fl., Regina, SK S4S 5W6
306-787-2584, Fax: 306-787-9544, 800-567-4224, Centre.Inquiry@gov.sk.ca
Saskatchewan Watershed Authority, 111 Fairford St. East, Moose Jaw, SK S6H 7X9
306-694-3900, Fax: 306-694-3944, comm@swa.ca
Yukon Territory
Alsek Renewable Resource Council, PO Box 2077, Haines Junction, YT Y0B 1L0
867-634-2524, Fax: 867-634-2527
Carmacks Renewable Resource Council, PO Box 122, Carmacks, YT Y0B 1C0
867-863-6838, Fax: 867-863-6429, carmacksrrc@northwestel.net
Dawson District Renewable Resource Council, PO Box 1380, Dawson City, YT Y0B 1G0
867-993-6976, Fax: 867-993-6093, dawsonrrc@northwestel.net
Yukon Environment, PO Box 2703, Whitehorse, YT Y1A 2C6
867-667-5652, Fax: 867-393-7197, environment.yukon@gov.yk.ca
Mayo District Renewable Resources Council, PO Box 249, Mayo, YT Y0B 1M0
867-996-2942, Fax: 867-996-2948, mayorrc@yknet.yk.ca

North Yukon Renewable Resources Council, PO Box 80, Old Crow, YT Y0B 1N0
867-966-3034, Fax: 867-966-3036, vgrrc@yknet.yk.ca
Selkirk Renewable Resources Council, PO Box 32, Pelly Crossing, YT Y0B 1P0
867-537-3937, Fax: 867-537-3939, selkirkrrc@yknet.yk.ca
Teslin Renewable Resource Council, PO Box 186, Teslin, YT Y0A 1B0
867-390-2323, Fax: 867-390-2919, teslinrrc@northwestel.net
Yukon Land Use Planning Council, #201, 307 Jarvis St., Whitehorse, YT Y1A 2H3
867-667-7397, Fax: 867-667-4624, ylupc@planyukon.ca

CONSTRUCTION

Northwest Territories

Asset Management Division, Stuart M. Hodgson Bldg., 5009 - 49th St., 3rd Fl., Yellowknife, NT X1A 2L9
Canada Mortgage & Housing Corporation, 700 Montreal Rd., Ottawa, ON K1A 0P7
613-748-2000, Fax: 613-748-2098, 800-668-2642, chic@cmhc-schl.gc.ca
Corporate Marketing Division, Marysville Place, 20 McGloin St., Fredericton, NB E3A 5T8
506-453-6100, Fax: 506-462-5049
Defence Construction Canada, Constitution Square, 350 Albert St., 19th Fl., Ottawa, ON K1A 0K3
613-998-9548, Fax: 613-998-1061, 800-514-3555, info@dcc-cdc.gc.ca
Infrastructure Canada, 180 Kent St., Ottawa, ON K1P 0B6
613-948-1148, 877-250-7154, info@infc.gc.ca
Institute for Research in Construction, Bldg. M-24, 1500 Montreal Rd., Ottawa, ON K1A 0R6
613-993-2607, Fax: 613-952-7673, Irc.Client-Services@nrc-cnrc.gc.ca
Policy & Corporate Services Division, Twin Atria Building, 4999 - 98 Ave., 3rd Fl., Edmonton, AB T6B 2X3

Alberta

Alberta Infrastructure, Infrastructure Building, 6950 - 113 St., Edmonton, AB T6H 5V7
780-415-0507, Fax: 780-427-2187, -310-0000, Infra.Contact.Us.m@gov.ab.ca

Manitoba

Construction & Maintenance Branch, #1610, 215 Garry St., Winnipeg, MB R3C 3Z1
Fax: 204-945-3841

Newfoundland & Labrador

Newfoundland & Labrador Department of Transportation & Works, Confederation Bldg., West Block, 6th Fl., PO Box 8700, St. John's, NL A1B 4J6
709-729-3679, Fax: 709-729-4285, twminister@gov.nl.ca

Nunavut

Department of Community & Government Services, W.G. Brown Bldg., 4th Fl., PO Box 1000 700,Iqaluit, NU X0A 0H0
867-975-5400, Fax: 867-975-5305

Ontario

Building Code Commission, 777 Bay St., 2nd Fl., Toronto, ON M5G 2E5
416-585-6666, Fax: 416-585-7531
Building Materials Evaluation Commission, 777 Bay St., 2nd Fl., Toronto, ON M5G 2E5
416-585-4234, Fax: 416-585-7531

Quebec

Commission de la construction du Québec, 3530, rue Jean-Talon ouest, Montréal, QC H3R 2G3
514-341-7740, Fax: 514-341-6354, 888-842-8282
Régie du bâtiment du Québec, 545, boul Crémazie est, 4e étage, Montréal, QC H2M 2V2
514-873-0976, Fax: 514-864-2903, 800-361-0761, crc@rbq.gouv.qc.ca

CONSUMER PROTECTION

See Also: Public Safety

Newfoundland & Labrador

Consumer & Commercial Affairs Branch, PO Box 8700, St. John's, NL A1B 4J6
709-729-2570, Fax: 709-729-4151, gsinfo@gov.nl.ca
Consumer Services & Information Development, Berska Bldg., 2nd Fl., 307 Black St., Whitehorse, YT
Fax: 867-393-6943
Financial Consumer Agency of Canada, 427 Laurier Ave. West, 6th Fl., Ottawa, ON K1R 1B9
Fax: 613-941-1436, info@fcac-acfc.gc.ca
HR Ontario, Whitney Block, #5320, 99 Wellesley St. West, Toronto, ON M7A 1N3
416-212-2057, Fax: 416-325-6317

Alberta

Registry Services, Telus Plaza South, 10020 - 100 St., 29th Fl., Edmonton, AB T5J 0N3

Nova Scotia

Department of Service Nova Scotia & Municipal Relations, 1505 Barrington St., PO Box 216, Halifax, NS B3J 3K5
902-424-5200, Fax: 902-424-0581, 800-670-4357, askus@gov.ns.ca

Nunavut

Department of Community & Government Services, W.G. Brown Bldg., 4th Fl., PO Box 1000 700,Iqaluit, NU X0A 0H0
867-975-5400, Fax: 867-975-5305

CORONERS

British Columbia

Coroners Service of British Columbia, Metrotower II, #800, 4720 Kingsway, Burnaby, BC V5H 4N2
604-660-7745, Fax: 604-660-7766, BC.CorSer@gov.bc.ca

Manitoba

Office of the Chief Medical Examiner, #210, 1 Wesley Ave., Winnipeg, MB R3C 4C6
204-945-2088, Fax: 204-945-2442, 800-282-9069

Nova Scotia

Office of the Chief Medical Examiner, Halifax Insurance Bldg., #701, 5670 Spring Garden Rd., Halifax, NS B3J 1H7
902-424-2722, Fax: 902-424-0607

Nunavut

Office of the Chief Coroner, PO Box 1000 590, Iqaluit, NU X0A 0H0

Quebec

Bureau du coroner, Édifice le Delta 2, #390, 2875, boul Laurier, Québec, QC G1V 5B1
418-643-1845, Fax: 418-643-6174, 866-312-7051, clientele.coroner@msp.gouv.qc.ca

CORRECTIONAL SERVICES

Alberta

Corporate Services Division (Solicitor General), John E. Brownlee Building, 10365 - 97 St., 9th Fl., Edmonton, AB T5J 3W7
Office of the Correctional Investigator, PO Box 3421 D,Ottawa, ON K1P 6L4
Fax: 613-990-9091, 877-885-8848, org@oci-bec.gc.ca
Correctional Service Canada, 340 Laurier Ave. West, Ottawa, ON K1A 0P9
613-992-5891, Fax: 613-943-1630

British Columbia

Corrections Branch, PO Box 9278 Prov Govt,Victoria, BC V8W 9J7
250-387-5059, Fax: 250-387-5698

Manitoba

Corrections Division, #810, 405 Broadway Ave., Winnipeg, MB R3C 3L6
204-945-7291

Nunavut

Baffin Correctional Centre, 1550 Federal Rd., PO Box 368, Iqaluit, NU X0A 0H0
867-979-8100, Fax: 867-979-4646

Saskatchewan

Saskatchewan Corrections & Policing, 1874 Scarth St., Regina, SK S4P 4B3
306-787-7872, communicationsCPSP@gov.sk.ca

CRIMES COMPENSATION

Communications Branch, 284 Wellington St., Ottawa, ON K1A 0H8
Fax: 613-941-2329,

Alberta

Criminal Injuries Review Board, #1502, 10025 - 102A Ave., Edmonton, AB T5J 2Z2
780-427-7330, Fax: 780-427-7347, cirb@gov.ab.ca

Manitoba

Compensation for Victims of Crime, 1410 - 405 Broadway, Winnipeg, MB R3C 3L6
204-945-0899, Fax: 204-948-3071, 800-262-9344

Northwest Territories

Victims Assistance Committee, c/o Community Justice Division, PO Box 1320, Yellowknife, NT X1A 2L9
867-920-6911, Fax: 867-873-0199

Ontario

Criminal Injuries Compensation Board, 439 University Ave., 4th Fl., Toronto, ON M5G 1Y8
416-326-2900, Fax: 416-326-2883, 800-372-7463, info.cicb@ontario.ca
Office for Victims of Crime, 700 Bay St., 3rd Fl., Toronto, ON M5G 1Z6
416-326-1682, Fax: 416-326-4497, 887-435-7661
Victims & Vulnerable Persons Division, 18 King St. E, 7th Fl., Toronto, ON M5C 1C4
416-325-3265, Fax: 416-212-1091

CULTURE & HERITAGE

See: Arts & Culture

Aboriginal Affairs & Northern Development Canada, 10 Wellington St., North Tower, Gatineau, QC K1A 0H4
819-997-0380, Fax: 866-817-3977, 800-567-9604, infopubs@aadnc-aandc.gc.ca
Office of African Nova Scotian Affairs, #604, 5670 Spring Garden Rd., PO Box 2691, Halifax, NS B3J 1H6
902-424-5555, Fax: 902-424-7189, 866-580-2672, ansa_newsletter@gov.ns.ca
Canadian Heritage, 15 Eddy St., Gatineau, QC K1A 0M5
819-997-0055, 866-811-0055, info@pch.gc.ca
Cultural Planning & Development, 1919 Saskatchewan Dr., 2nd Fl., Regina, SK S4P 4H2
306-787-5877, Fax: 306-798-3177
Culture & Heritage Division, PO Box 310, Igloolik, NU X0A 0L0
867-975-2046, Fax: 867-934-2047, cleypermits@gov.nu.ca
Office of Gaelic Affairs, Johnston Building, 1672 Granville St., 2nd Fl., PO Box 186, Halifax, NS B3J 2N2
902-424-4298, Fax: 902-424-0171, 888-842-3542, gaelicinfo@gov.ns.ca; fiosgaidhlig@gov.ns.ca
Historic Sites & Monuments Board of Canada, Terrasses de la Chaudière, 25 Eddy St., Gatineau, QC K1A 0M5
Fax: 819-934-1115, 855-283-8730, hsmbc-clmhc@pc.gc.ca
Housing, Seniors & Corporate Support, Jones Bldg., 11 Kent St., 2nd Fl., PO Box 2000, Charlottetown, PE C1A 7N8
Fax: 902-894-0242
Provincial Capital Commission, 4607 Dewdney Ave., Regina, SK S4T 1B7
306-787-9261
Saskatchewan Parks, Culture, & Sport, 1919 Saskatchewan Dr., 4th Fl., Regina, SK S4P 4H2
306-787-5729, Fax: 306-798-0033, 800-205-7070, info@tpcs.gov.sk.ca
Wascana Centre Authority, 2900 Wascana Dr., PO Box 7111, Regina, SK S4P 3S7
306-522-3661, Fax: 306-565-2742, wca@wascana.ca

Alberta

Alberta Sport, Recreation, Parks, & Wildlife Foundation, Standard Life Centre, #903, 10405 Jasper Ave., 9th Fl., Edmonton, AB T5J 4R7
780-415-1167, Fax: 780-415-0308, -310-0000
Alberta International & Intergovernmental Relations, Commerce Place, 10155 - 102 St., 12th Fl., Edmonton, AB T5J 4G8
780-422-1510, -310-0000

British Columbia

British Columbia Ministry of Community, Sport, & Cultural Development, PO Box 9490 Prov Govt,Victoria, BC V8W 9N7

Manitoba

Manitoba Culture, Heritage & Tourism, Legislative Building, #118, 450 Broadway Ave., Winnipeg, MB R3C 0V8
204-945-3729, Fax: 204-945-5223, minchtt@leg.gov.mb.ca
Manitoba Heritage Council, 213 Notre Dame Ave., Main Fl., Winnipeg, MB R3B 1N3
204-945-2118, Fax: 204-948-2384, hrb@gov.mb.ca

New Brunswick

New Brunswick Department of Culture, Tourism, & Healthy Living, Centennial Building, PO Box 6000, Fredericton, NB E3B 5H1
506-444-5205, Fax: 506-457-4984, taponlinedirectory@gnb.ca

Newfoundland & Labrador

Newfoundland & Labrador Department of Tourism, Culture, & Recreation, Confederation Bldg., West Block, 2nd Fl., PO Box 8700, St. John's, NL A1B 4J6
709-729-0862, Fax: 709-729-0870, tcrinfo@gov.nl.ca

Northwest Territories

Department of Aboriginal Affairs & Intergovernmental Relations, 4910 - 52nd St., PO Box 1320, Yellowknife, NT X1A 2L9
867-873-7143, Fax: 867-873-0233, 877-838-8194, nancy_gardiner@gov.nt.ca
Department of Education, Culture & Employment, PO Box 1320, Yellowknife, NT X1A 2L9
867-669-2399, Fax: 867-873-0431, 866-606-5627

Nova Scotia

Culture Division, #601, 1800 Argyle St., PO Box 456, Halifax, NS B3J 2R5
902-424-4510, Fax: 902-424-0710, culture@gov.ns.ca

Ontario

Ontario Trillium Foundation, 800 Bay St., 5th Fl., Toronto, ON M5S 3A9
416-963-4927, Fax: 416-963-8781, 800-263-2887, trillium@trilliumfoundation.org

Saskatchewan

Government Services, 1920 Rose St., Regina, SK S4P 0A9
306-787-6911, Fax: 306-787-1061, GSReception@gs.gov.sk.ca

CURRENCY

Bank of Canada, 234 Wellington St., Ottawa, ON K1A 0G9
613-782-7902, Fax: 613-782-7713, 800-303-1282, info@bankofcanada.ca; communications@bankofcanada.ca (Media)

Royal Canadian Mint, 320 Sussex Dr., Ottawa, ON K1A 0G8
613-993-3500, Fax: 613-993-4092, 800-267-1871

CUSTOMS

Canada Border Services Agency, Headquarters, 191 Laurier Ave. West, Ottawa, ON K1A 0L8
800-461-9999, Contact@cbsa.gc.ca; communications@ps.gc.ca (Public Safety)

DAIRY INDUSTRY

Canadian Dairy Commission, Central Experimental Farm, NCC Driveway, Bldg. 55, 960 Carling Ave., Ottawa, ON K1A 0Z2
613-792-2000, Fax: 613-792-2009, cdc-ccl@cdc-ccl.gc.ca

Manitoba

Manitoba Milk Prices Review Commission, c/o Boards, Commissions & Legislation Branch, #812, 401 York Ave., Winnipeg, MB R3C 0P8
204-945-3854, Fax: 204-948-2844, randy.ozunko@gov.mb.ca

Prince Edward Island

Prince Edward Island Department of Agriculture & Forestry, Jones Bldg., 11 Kent St., PO Box 2000, Charlottetown, PE C1A 7N8
902-368-4880, Fax: 902-368-4857,

DANGEROUS GOODS & HAZARDOUS MATERIALS

See Also: Occupational Safety; Waste Management

Prince Edward Island

Administrative Services Division, Jones Bldg., 11 Kent St., 4th Fl., PO Box 2000, Charlottetown, PE C1A 7N8
902-368-5000, Fax: 902-368-5830

Government Services Branch, PO Box 8700, St. John's, NL A1B 4J6

Hazardous Materials Information Review Commission, 427 Laurier Ave. West, 7th Fl., Ottawa, ON K1A 1M3
613-993-4331, Fax: 613-993-4686, hmirc-ccrmd@hc-sc.gc.ca

British Columbia

British Columbia Ministry of Transportation & Infrastructure, PO Box 9850 Prov Govt,Victoria, BC V8W 9T5
250-387-3198, Fax: 250-356-7706

Northwest Territories

Department of Transportation, Lahm Ridge Bldg., 4501 50 Ave., PO Box 1320, Yellowknife, NT X1A 2L9
867-920-3460, Fax: 867-873-0363

Nova Scotia

Department of Transportation & Infrastructure Renewal, Johnston Bldg., 1672 Granville St., 2nd Fl., PO Box 186, Halifax, NS B3J 2N2
902-424-2297, Fax: 902-424-0532, tpwpaff@gov.ns.ca

Ontario

Ontario Ministry of Transportation, Ferguson Block, 77 Wellesley St. West, 3rd Fl., Toronto, ON M7A 1Z8
416-235-4686, Fax: 905-704-2001, 800-268-4686

Prince Edward Island

Prince Edward Island Department of Transportation & Infrastructure Renewal, Jones Bldg., 11 Kent St., 3rd Fl., PO Box 2000, Charlottetown, PE C1A 7N8
902-368-5100, Fax: 902-368-5395

Quebec

Ministère du Développement durable, de l'Environnement, de la Faune, et des Parcs, Édifice Marie-Guyart, 675, boul René-Lévesque est, 29e étage, Québec, QC G1R 5V7
418-521-3830, Fax: 418-646-5974, 800-561-1616, info@mddep.gouv.qc.ca

Saskatchewan

Saskatchewan Highways & Infrastructure, Victoria Tower, 1855 Victoria Ave., Regina, SK S4P 3T2
306-787-4800, communications@highways.gov.sk.ca

Yukon Territory

Yukon Highways & Public Works, PO Box 2703, Whitehorse, YT Y1A 2C6
867-393-7193, Fax: 867-393-6218, 800-661-0408, hpw-info@gov.yk.ca

DAY CARE SERVICES

See Also: Child Welfare

Ontario

Ontario Ministry of Children & Youth Services, 56 Wellesley St. West, 14th Fl., Toronto, ON M5S 2G3
Fax: 416-325-5191, 866-821-7770

DEBT MANAGEMENT

Finance Canada, L'esplanade Laurier, 140 O'Connor St., Ottawa, ON K1A 0G5
613-992-1573, Fax: 613-943-0938, finpub@fin.gc.ca

British Columbia

Provincial Treasury, PO Box 9414 Prov Govt,Victoria, BC V8V 9V1
250-387-4541, Fax: 250-356-3041

New Brunswick

Treasury, Centennial Bldg., #376, 670 King St., PO Box 6000, Fredericton, NB E3B 5H1
506-453-3952, Fax: 506-453-2053

DEFENCE

See Also: Emergency Response; Public Safety

Canadian Forces Grievance Board, 60 Queen St., 10th Fl., Ottawa, ON K1P 5Y7
613-996-8529, Fax: 613-996-6491, 877-276-4193

Defence Construction Canada, Constitution Square, 350 Albert St., 19th Fl., Ottawa, ON K1A 0K3
613-998-9548, Fax: 613-998-1061, 800-514-3555, info@dcc-cdc.gc.ca

Defence Research & Development Canada, 305 Rideau St., Ottawa, ON K1A 0K2
613-992-7237, info@drdc-rddc.gc.ca

Military Police Complaints Commission, 270 Albert St., 10th Fl., Ottawa, ON K1P 5G8
613-947-5625, Fax: 613-947-5713, 800-632-0566, commission@mpcc-cppm.gc.ca

National Defence Canada, Major-General George R. Pearkes Bldg., 101 Colonel By Dr., Ottawa, ON K1A 0K2
613-995-2534, Fax: 613-992-4739, 800-856-8488

DISABLED PERSONS SERVICES

Canadian Human Rights Commission, 344 Slater St., 8th Fl., Ottawa, ON K1A 1E1
613-995-1151, Fax: 613-996-9661, 888-214-1090

Health System Strategy & Policy Division, Hepburn Block, 80 Grosvenor St., 8th Fl., Toronto, ON M7A 1R3
416-327-8295, Fax: 416-327-5109

Transportation Development Centre, Tour Ouest, Complexe Guy-Favreau, 800, boul René-Lévesque ouest, 6e étage, Montréal, QC H3B 1X9
514-283-0000, Fax: 514-283-7158, tdccdt@tc.gc.ca

Alberta

Persons with Developmental Disabilities Community Boards, c/o PDD Program Branch, Peace Hills Trust Tower, 10011 - 109 St., 4th Fl., Edmonton, AB T5J 3S8
780-427-1177, Fax: 780-427-1220, 800-310-0000, PDDinfo@gov.ab.ca

Premier's Council on the Status of Persons with Disabilities, HSBC Building, 10055 - 106 St., 11th Fl., Edmonton, AB T5J 1G3
780-422-1095, 800-272-8841, pcspd@gov.ab.ca

Alberta Seniors, Communications, Standard Life Centre, 10405 Jasper Ave., 3rd Fl., Edmonton, AB T5J 4R7
780-415-9950, Fax: 780-644-1227, 866-477-8589, seniors.communications@gov.ab.ca

Manitoba

Disabilities Issues Office, #630, 240 Graham Ave., Winnipeg, MB R3C 0J7
204-945-7613, Fax: 204-948-2896, dio@gov.mb.ca

New Brunswick

Premier's Council on the Status of Disabled Persons, Kings Place, #648, 440 King St., Fredericton, NB E3B 5H8
506-444-3000, Fax: 506-444-3001, 800-442-4412, pcsdp@gnb.ca

Nova Scotia

Nova Scotia Disabled Persons Commission, Dartmouth Professional Center, #104, 277 Pleasant St., Dartmouth, NS B2Y 4B7
902-424-8280, Fax: 902-424-0592, 800-565-8280

Nunavut

Department of Culture, Language, Elders & Youth, PO Box 1000 800,Iqaluit, NU X0A 0H0
867-975-5500, Fax: 867-975-5504, 866-934-2035,

Quebec

Office des personnes handicapées du Québec, 309, rue Brock, Drummondville, QC J2B 1C5
Fax: 819-475-8753, 800-567-1465, michael.magner@ophq.gouv.qc.ca

DISCRIMINATION & EMPLOYMENT EQUITY

Canadian Human Rights Commission, 344 Slater St., 8th Fl., Ottawa, ON K1A 1E1
613-995-1151, Fax: 613-996-9661, 888-214-1090

Canadian Human Rights Tribunal, 160 Elgin St., 11th Fl., Ottawa, ON K1A 1J4
613-995-1707, Fax: 613-995-3484, registrar@chrt-tcdp.gc.ca

Alberta

Labour Relations Board, Labour Building, 10808 - 99 Ave., 5th Fl., Edmonton, AB T5K 0G5
780-422-5926, Fax: 780-422-0970, 800-463-2572, alrbinfo@lab.gov.ab.ca

British Columbia

British Columbia Human Rights Tribunal, #1170, 605 Robson St., Vancouver, BC V6B 5J3
604-775-2000, Fax: 604-775-2020, 888-440-8844, BCHumanRightsTribunal@gov.bc.ca

Manitoba

Manitoba Human Rights Commission, 175 Hargrave St., 7th Fl., Winnipeg, MB R3C 3R8
204-945-3007, Fax: 204-945-1292, 888-884-8681, hrc@gov.mb.ca

New Brunswick

New Brunswick Human Rights Commission, PO Box 6000, Fredericton, NB E3B 5H1
506-453-2301, Fax: 506-453-2653, 888-471-2233, hrc.cdp@gnb.ca

Newfoundland & Labrador

Newfoundland & Labrador Human Rights Commission, PO Box 8700, St. John's, NL A1B 4J6
709-729-2709, Fax: 709-729-0790, 800-563-5808, humanrights@mail.gov.nl.ca

Nova Scotia

Nova Scotia Human Rights Commission, Joseph Howe Bldg., 1690 Hollis St., 6th Fl., Halifax, NS B3J 3C4
902-424-4111, Fax: 902-424-0596, hrcinquiries@gov.ns.ca

Ontario

Ontario Human Rights Commission, 180 Dundas St. West, 7th Fl., Toronto, ON M7A 2R9
416-326-9511, Fax: 416-314-4494, 800-387-9080

Prince Edward Island

Prince Edward Island Human Rights Commission, 53 Water St., PO Box 2000, Charlottetown, PE C1A 7N8
902-368-4180, Fax: 902-368-4236, 800-237-5031

Quebec

Commission de l'équité salariale, 200, ch Ste-Foy, 4e étage, Québec, QC G1R 6A1
418-528-8765, Fax: 418-528-6999, 888-528-8765, equite.salariale@ces.gouv.qc.ca

Saskatchewan

Saskatchewan Human Rights Commission, Saskatoon Office, Sturdy Stone Bdg., #816, 122 - 3 Ave. North, 8th Fl., Saskatoon, SK S7K 2H6
306-933-5952, Fax: 306-933-7863, 800-667-9249, shrc@gov.sk.ca

Yukon Territory

Yukon Human Rights Commission, #101, 9010 Quartz St., Whitehorse, YT Y1A 2Z5
867-667-6226, Fax: 867-667-2662, 800-661-0535, humanrights@yhrc.yk.ca

DIVORCE

Justice Canada, East Memorial Bldg., 284 Wellington St., Ottawa, ON K1A 0H8
613-957-4222, Fax: 613-954-0811, webadmin@justice.gc.ca

DRIVERS' LICENCES

Nova Scotia

Registry of Motor Vehicles, 1505 Barrington St., 8th Fl. North, PO Box 1652, Halifax, NS B3J 2Z3
902-424-7801, Fax: 902-424-0772, 800-898-7668

Alberta

Strategic Planning & Financial Services, Commerce Place, 10155 - 102 St., 13th Fl., Edmonton, AB T5J 4G8
780-422-8545

British Columbia

British Columbia Ministry of Transportation & Infrastructure, PO Box 9850 Prov Govt,Victoria, BC V8W 9T5
250-387-3198, Fax: 250-356-7706

Manitoba

Manitoba Infrastructure & Transportation, Legislative Building, #203, 450 Broadway Ave., Winnipeg, MB R3C 0V8
204-945-3723, Fax: 204-945-7610

Northwest Territories

Road Licensing & Safety, 4510 - 50 Ave., 1st fl., PO Box 1320, Yellowknife, NT X1A 2L9
867-873-7972, Fax: 867-873-0120

Ontario

Licence Appeal Tribunal, 20 Dundas St. West, 5th Fl., Toronto, ON M5G 2C2
416-314-4260, Fax: 416-314-4270, 800-255-2214

Ontario Ministry of Transportation, Ferguson Block, 77 Wellesley St. West, 3rd Fl., Toronto, ON M7A 1Z8
416-235-4686, Fax: 905-704-2001, 800-268-4686

Prince Edward Island
Prince Edward Island Department of Transportation & Infrastructure Renewal, Jones Bldg., 11 Kent St., 3rd Fl., PO Box 2000, Charlottetown, PE C1A 7N8
902-368-5100, Fax: 902-368-5395

Quebec
Société de l'assurance automobile du Québec, 333, boul Jean-Lesage, CP 19600 Terminus, Québec, QC G1K 8J6
418-643-7620, Fax: 418-644-0339, 800-361-7620, courrier@saaq.gouv.qc.ca

Saskatchewan
Saskatchewan Government Insurance, 2260 - 11th Ave., Regina, SK S4P 0J9
306-751-1200, Fax: 306-787-7477, 800-667-8015, sgiinquiries@sgi.sk.ca

Yukon Territory
Driver Control Board, 2130 Second Ave., 3rd Fl., PO Box 2703, Whitehorse, YT Y1A 2C6
867-667-5111, Fax: 867-667-3609, dcb@gov.yk.ca

DRUGS & ALCOHOL

See Also: Liquor Control
Canadian Centre on Substance Abuse, #500, 75 Albert St., Ottawa, ON K1P 5E7
613-235-4048, Fax: 613-235-8101, info@ccsa.ca
Provincial Secretary, Legislative Building, #28, 2405 Legislative Dr., Regina, SK S4S 0B3
306-787-1636, Fax: 306-787-0012,

Alberta
Alberta Health Services, Corporate Office, North Tower, Seventh Street Plaza, 10030 - 107th St. NW, 14th Fl., Edmonton, AB T5J 3E4
780-342-2000, Fax: 780-342-2060, 888-342-2471, ahsb.admin@albertahealthservices.ca

British Columbia
British Columbia Ministry of Health, 1515 Blanshard St., Victoria, BC V8W 3C8
800-663-7100, hlth.health@gov.bc.ca

Quebec
Bureau des projets Centres hospitaliers universitaires de Montréal, CHUM, CUSM et CHU Sainte-Justine, #10.049, 2021, rue Union, Montréal, QC H3A 2S9
514-864-9883, Fax: 514-873-7362, info.construction3chu@msss.gouv.qc.ca
Ministère de la Santé et des Services sociaux, Direction des communications, 1075, ch Sainte-Foy, 16e étage, Québec, QC G1S 2M1
418-643-9395, Fax: 418-643-4768, regisseur.web@msss.gouv.qc.ca

ECONOMIC DEVELOPMENT

See: Business Development

New Brunswick
Invest NB, HSBC Place, PO Box 6000, Fredericton, NB E3B 5H1
Summerside Regional Development Corporation Ltd., 268 Water St., Summerside, PE C1N 1B6
902-436-2246, Fax: 902-436-9269, acroken@srdcpei.com

New Brunswick
New Brunswick Department of Economic Development, Centennial Building, PO Box 6000, Fredericton, NB E3B 5H1
506-453-3707, Fax: 506-453-3993, 800-665-1800, tradenb@gnb.ca

Prince Edward Island
Innovation PEI, 94 Euston St., PO Box 910, Charlottetown, PE C1A 7L9
902-368-6300, Fax: 902-368-6301, 800-563-3734

EDUCATION

Canada School of Public Service, 373 Sussex Dr., Ottawa, ON K1N 6Z2
819-953-5400, Fax: 819-953-7953, 866-703-9598, info@csps-efpc.gc.ca
Canadian Council of Directors of Apprenticeship, 140 Promenade du Portage, 5th Fl, Phase IV, Gatineau, QC K1A 0J9
819-953-7443, Fax: 819-994-0202, redseal-sceaurouge@hrsdc-rhdcc.gc.ca
Canadian Forces College, Toronto, ON
416-482-6800
Canadian Police College, PO Box 8900, Ottawa, ON K1G 3J2
613-993-9500, Fax: 613-990-9738, cpc-ccp@rcmp-grc.gc.ca
Children's Secretariat, c/o Sarah Henry, Education & Early Childhood Development, 161 St. Peters Rd., PO Box 2000, Charlottetown, PE C1A 7N8
Prince Edward Island Athletic Association, #101, 250 Water St., Summerside, PE C1N 1B6
902-438-4846, Fax: 902-438-4884
RCMP Training Academy, 6101 Dewdney Ave., Regina, SK S4P 3J7
306-780-5002, Fax: 306-780-7940
Royal Military College, Kingston, ON
613-541-6000

Alberta
Alberta Apprenticeship & Industry Training Board, Commerce Place, 10155 - 102nd St., 10th Fl., Edmonton, AB T5J 4L5
780-427-8765, Fax: 780-422-7376, -310-0000
Alberta Council on Admissions & Transfer, Commerce Place, 10155 - 102 St., 11th Fl., Edmonton, AB T5J 4L5
780-422-9021, Fax: 780-422-3688, -310-0000, acat@gov.ab.ca
Alberta Enterprise Corporation Board, Alberta Enterprise Corporation, #1100, 10830 Jasper Ave., Edmonton, AB T5J 2B3
780-392-3901
Alberta Innovates - Technology Futures, 250 Karl Clark Rd., Edmonton, AB T6N 1E4
780-450-5111, Fax: 780-450-5333, referral@albertainnovates.ca
Campus Alberta Quality Council, Commerce Place, 10155 - 102 St., 11th Fl., Edmonton, AB T5J 4L5
780-427-8921, Fax: 780-427-4185, caqc@gov.ab.ca
Community, Learner & Industry Connections Division, Phipps-McKinnon Bldg., 10020 - 101A Ave., 5th Fl., Edmonton, AB T5J 3G2
Council on Alberta Teaching Standards, 10044 - 108 St., Edmonton, AB T5J 5E6
780-427-2045, Fax: 780-422-4199
Alberta Education, Commerce Place, 10155 - 102 St., 7th Fl., Edmonton, AB T5J 4L5
780-427-7219, Fax: 780-427-0591, -310-0000
Alberta Enterprise & Advanced Education, Legislature Bldg., #324, 10800 - 97 Ave., Edmonton, AB T5K 2B6
780-422-5400, -310-0000

British Columbia
Auditor Certification Board, PO Box 9431 Prov Govt, Victoria, BC V8W 9V3
250-356-8658, Fax: 250-356-9422, Kelly.Fitzsimonds@gov.bc.ca
British Columbia Ministry of Advanced Education, Innovation, & Technology (& Responsible for Multiculturalism), PO Box 9059 Prov Govt,Victoria, BC V8W 9E2
250-952-6508, Fax: 250-356-6942
British Columbia Ministry of Education, PO Box 9161 Prov Govt,Victoria, BC V8W 9H3
888-879-1166, EDUC.Correspondence@gov.bc.ca
Degree Quality Assessment Board, Degree Quality Assessment Board Secretariat, PO Box 9177 Prov Govt, Victoria, BC V8W 9H8
250-387-5163, DQABsecretariat@gov.bc.ca
Leading Edge Endowment Fund Board, 1188 West Georgia St., 9th Fl., Vancouver, BC V6E 4A2
604-438-3220, contact@leefbc.ca
Private Career Training Institutions Agency, #300, 5172 Kingsway, Burnaby, BC V5H 2E8
604-660-4400, Fax: 604-660-3312, 800-661-7441, info@pctia.bc.ca

Manitoba
Manitoba Advanced Education & Literacy, Legislative Building, #162, 450 Broadway Ave., Winnipeg, MB R3C 0V8
204-945-0825, Fax: 204-948-2216, minaed@leg.gov.mb.ca
Division du Bureau de l'éducation française, #509, 1181 av Portage, Winnipeg, MB R3C 0T3
204-945-6916, Fax: 204-945-1625
Manitoba Education, #168, Legislative Bldg., 450 Broadway, Winnipeg, MB R3C 0V8
204-945-3720, Fax: 204-945-1291, minedu@leg.gov.mb.ca
Manitoba Education, Research & Learning Information Networks, #100 - 135 Innovation Dr., University of Manitoba, Winnipeg, MB R3T 6A8
204-474-7800, Fax: 204-474-7830, 800-430-6404
Public Schools Finance Board, #506, 1181 Portage Ave., Winnipeg, MB R3G 0T3
204-945-6628, Fax: 204-948-2001
School Programs Division, #5, 1567 Dublin Ave, Winnipeg, MB R3E 3J5
204-945-7934, Fax: 204-945-8303

New Brunswick
New Brunswick Department of Education & Early Childhood Development, Place 2000, PO Box 6000, Fredericton, NB E3B 5H1
506-453-3678, Fax: 506-453-3325, edcommunication@gnb.ca
New Brunswick Department of Post-Secondary Education, Training, & Labour, Chestnut Complex, PO Box 6000, Fredericton, NB E3B 5H1
506-453-2597, Fax: 506-453-3618, dpetlinfo@gnb.ca

Newfoundland & Labrador
Newfoundland & Labrador Department of Education, West Block, Confederation Bldg., 100 Prince Philip Dr., 3rd Fl., PO Box 8700, St. John's, NL A1B 4J6
709-729-5097, Fax: 709-729-5896, education@gov.nl.ca

Northwest Territories
Aurora Research Institute, 191 MacKenzie Rd., PO Box 1450, Inuvik, NT X0E 0T0
867-777-3298, Fax: 867-777-4264, webmaster@nwtresearch.com
Department of Education, Culture & Employment, PO Box 1320, Yellowknife, NT X1A 2L9
867-669-2399, Fax: 867-873-0431, 866-606-5627

Nova Scotia
Council of Atlantic Ministers of Education & Training, PO Box 2044, Halifax, NS B3J 2Z1
902-424-5352, Fax: 902-424-8976, camet_camef@cap-cpma.ca
Department of Education, Trade Mart Bldg., #402-2021 Brunswick St., PO Box 578, Halifax, NS B3J 2S9
902-424-5168, Fax: 902-424-0680
Nova Scotia Apprenticeship Board, 2021 Brunswick St., PO Box 578, Halifax, NS B3J 2S9
902-424-0872, Fax: 902-424-0488, 800-494-5651, bedgoomm@gov.ns.ca

Nunavut
Department of Education, Sivummut Bldg., 2nd Fl., PO Box 1000 910,Iqaluit, NU X0A 0H0
867-975-5600, Fax: 867-975-5605

Ontario
Academic & Experience Requirements Committee of the Association of Ontario Land Surveyors, 1043 McNicoll Ave., Toronto, ON M1W 3W6
416-491-9020, Fax: 416-491-2576
College of Veterinarians of Ontario, 2106 Gordon St., Guelph, ON N1L 1G6
519-824-5600, Fax: 519-824-6497, 800-424-2856, inquiries@cvo.org
Ontario Ministry of Education, Mowat Block, 900 Bay St., 22nd. Fl., Toronto, ON M7A 1L2
416-325-2929, Fax: 416-325-2934, 800-387-5514, info@edu.gov.on.ca
Elementary/Secondary Business & Finance Division, Mowat Block, 900 Bay St., 20th fl., Toronto, ON M7A 1L2
416-325-6127, Fax: 416-325-9560
Learning & Curriculum Division, Mowat Block, 900 Bay st., 22nd fl., Toronto, ON M7A 1L2
416-325-2135, Fax: 416-327-1182
Ontario Graduate Scholarship Program Selection Board, 189 Red River Rd., 4th Fl., PO Box 4500, Thunder Bay, ON P7B 6G9
807-343-7257, Fax: 807-343-7278, 800-465-3957
Ontario Student Assistance Appeal Board, Mowat Block, 900 Bay St., 7th Fl., Toronto, ON M7A 1L2
416-314-0714, Fax: 416-325-3096
Post-secondary Education Quality Assessment Board, #1511, 2 Carlton St., Toronto, ON M5B 1J3
416-212-1230, Fax: 416-212-6620
Ontario Ministry of Training, Colleges & Universities, Mowat Block, 900 Bay St., 14th Fl., Toronto, ON M7A 1L2
416-325-2929, Fax: 416-325-6348, 800-387-5514, information.met@ontario.ca

Prince Edward Island
Prince Edward Island Department of Education & Early Childhood Development, Holman Centre, #101, 250 Water St., Summerside, PE C1N 1B6
902-438-4130, Fax: 902-438-4062

Quebec
Comité-conseil sur les programmes d'études, 1035, de la Chevrotière, 17e étage, Québec, QC G1R 5A5
418-646-0133, Fax: 418-643-0056, ccpe@mels.gouv.qc.ca
Commission consultative de l'enseignement privé, 1035, rue de la Chevrotière, 14e étage, Québec, QC G1R 5A5
418-646-1249, Fax: 418-643-7752, commission.consultative@mels.gouv.qc.ca
Commission d'évaluation de l'enseignement collégial, 800, place d'Youville, 18e étage, Québec, QC G1R 5P4
418-643-9938, Fax: 418-643-9019, info@ceec.gouv.qc.ca
Commission de l'éducation en langue anglaise, 600, rue Fullum, 9e étage, Montréal, QC H2K 4L1
514-873-5656, Fax: 514-864-4181, cela-abee@mels.gouv.qc.ca
Conseil supérieur de l'éducation, #180, 1175, av Lavigerie, Québec, QC G1V 5B2
418-643-3850, Fax: 418-644-2530, panorama@cse.gouv.qc.ca
Ministère de l'Éducation, du Loisir et du Sport, 1035, rue De La Chevrotière, 28e étage, Québec, QC G1R 5A5
418-643-7095, Fax: 418-646-6561, 866-747-6626

Saskatchewan
Saskatchewan Advanced Education, 1945 Hamilton St., Regina, SK S4P 2C8
306-787-9478, aeeinquiry@gov.sk.ca
Saskatchewan Education, 2220 College Ave., Regina, SK S4P 4V9
linquiry@gov.sk.ca
Saskatchewan Research Council, #125, 15 Innovation Blvd., Saskatoon, SK S7N 2X8
306-933-5400, Fax: 306-933-7446, info@src.sk.ca
Yukon Territory
Yukon Education, PO Box 2703, Whitehorse, YT Y1A 2C6
867-667-5141, Fax: 867-393-6254, contact.education@gov.yk.ca

EDUCATION & TRAINING

Human Resources & Skills Development Canada, 140 Promenade du Portage, Gatineau, QC K1A 0J9
Department of Labour & Advanced Education, 5151 Terminal Rd., 6th Fl., PO Box 697, Halifax, NS B3J 2T8
902-424-5301, Fax: 902-424-0575
Alberta
Alberta Human Services, Office of the Minister, Legislature Building, #224, 10800 - 97 Ave., Edmonton, AB T5K 2B6
780-644-5135, 866-644-5135
British Columbia
British Columbia Ministry of Citizens' Services & Open Government, PO Box 9594 Prov Govt,Victoria, BC V8W 9E2
250-952-7623, Fax: 250-952-7628, 800-663-7867, EnquiryBC@gov.bc.ca
Private Career Training Institutions Agency, #300, 5172 Kingsway, Burnaby, BC V5H 2E8
604-660-4400, Fax: 604-660-3312, 800-661-7441, info@pctia.bc.ca
New Brunswick
New Brunswick Department of Post-Secondary Education, Training, & Labour, Chestnut Complex, PO Box 6000, Fredericton, NB E3B 5H1
506-453-2597, Fax: 506-453-3618, dpetlinfo@gnb.ca
Northwest Territories
Department of Education, Culture & Employment, PO Box 1320, Yellowknife, NT X1A 2L9
867-669-2399, Fax: 867-873-0431, 866-606-5627
Ontario
Ontario Ministry of Labour, 400 University Ave., 14th Fl., Toronto, ON M7A 1T7
416-326-7160, 800-531-5551
Saskatchewan
Saskatchewan Advanced Education, 1945 Hamilton St., Regina, SK S4P 2C8
306-787-9478, aeeinquiry@gov.sk.ca

ELECTED OFFICIALS & CONSTITUENCIES

Fortieth Provincial Parliament - Ontario, Clerk's Office, #104, Legislative Building, Queen's Park, Toronto, ON M7A 1A2
416-325-7500, Fax: 416-325-7489, tourbookings@ontla.ola.org
Forty-first Parliament - Canada, House of Commons, Parliament Buildings, Ottawa, AB K1A 0A6
Alberta
Twenty-eighth Legislature - Alberta, Legislature Bldg., 10800 - 97 Ave., Edmonton, AB T5K 2B6
780-427-2826, laocommunications@assembly.ab.ca
British Columbia
Thirty-ninth Legislature - British Columbia, Parliament Buildings, Victoria, BC V8V 1X4
250-387-3785, Fax: 250-387-0942, ClerkHouse@leg.bc.ca
Manitoba
Fortieth Legislature - Manitoba, Legislative Building, 450 Broadway Ave., Winnipeg, MB R3C 0V8
204-945-3636, Fax: 204-948-2507, clerkla@leg.gov.mb.ca
New Brunswick
Fifty-seventh Legislative Assembly - New Brunswick, Centre Block, Legislative Building, 706 Queen St., PO Box 6000, Fredericton, NB E3B 5H1
506-453-2506, Fax: 506-453-7154, wwwleg@gnb.ca
Newfoundland & Labrador
Forty-seventh House of Assembly - Newfoundland & Labrador, Confederation Building, PO Box 8700, St. John's, NL A1B 4J6
709-729-3405, ClerkHOA@gov.nl.ca
Northwest Territories
Seventeenth Legislature - Northwest Territories, PO Box 1320, Yellowknife, NT X1A 2L9
867-669-2200, Fax: 867-920-4735, 800-661-0784
Nova Scotia
Sixty-first Assembly - Nova Scotia, Province House, 1726 Hollis St., Halifax, NS B3J 2Y3
902-424-4661, Fax: 902-424-0574
Nunavut
Third Legislature - Nunavut, PO Box 1200, Iqaluit, NU X0A 0H0
Prince Edward Island
Sixty-fourth General Assembly - Prince Edward Island, Province House, 165 Richmond St., 1st Fl., PO Box 2000, Charlottetown, PE C1A 7N8
902-368-5970, Fax: 902-368-5175, 877-315-5518
Quebec
Trente-neuvième assemblée nationale, Hôtel du Parlement, 1045, rue des Parlementaires, Québec, QC G1A 1A4
418-643-7239, Fax: 418-646-4271, 866-337-8837
Saskatchewan
Twenty-seventh Legislature - Saskatchewan, 2405 Legislative Dr., Regina, SK S4S 0B3
Yukon Territory
Thirty-third Legislative Assembly - Yukon Territory, Yukon Legislative Assembly Office, 2071 Second Ave., PO Box 2703, Whitehorse, YT Y1A 2C6
867-667-5498

ELECTIONS

Elections Canada, The Jackson Bldg., 257 Slater St., Ottawa, ON K1A 0M6
613-993-2975, Fax: 613-954-8584, 800-463-6868
Alberta
Alberta Office of the Chief Electoral Officer / Elections Alberta, 11510 Kingsway Ave., 1st Fl., Edmonton, AB T5G 2Y5
780-427-7191, Fax: 780-422-2900, info@electionsalberta.ab.ca
British Columbia
Elections British Columbia, PO Box 9275 Prov Govt,Victoria, BC V8W 9J6
250-387-5305, Fax: 250-387-3578, 800-661-8683, electionsbc@elections.bc.ca
Manitoba
Elections Manitoba, #120, 200 Vaughan St., Winnipeg, MB R3C 1T5
204-945-3225, Fax: 204-945-6011, 866-628-6837, election@elections.mb.ca
New Brunswick
Office of the Chief Electoral Officer, PO Box 6000, Fredericton, NB E3B 5H1
506-453-2218, Fax: 506-457-4926, 800-308-2922
Newfoundland & Labrador
Office of the Chief Electoral Officer, 39 Hallett Cr., St. John's, NL A1B 4C4
709-729-0712, Fax: 709-729-0679, 877-729-7987, enl@gov.nl.ca
Northwest Territories
Elections NWT/Plebiscite Office, YK Centre East, #7, 4915-48th St., 3rd Fl., Yellowknife, NT X1A 3S4
867-920-6999, Fax: 867-873-0366, 800-661-0796, electionsnwt@gov.nt.ca
Nova Scotia
Elections Nova Scotia, #6-7037 Mumford Rd., PO Box 2246, Halifax, NS B3J 2J1
902-424-8584, Fax: 902-424-6622, 800-565-1504, elections@gov.ns.ca
Nunavut
Nunavut Legislative Assembly, 926 Federal Rd., PO Box 1200, Iqaluit, NU X0A 0H0
867-975-5000, Fax: 867-975-5190, 877-334-7266, leginfo@assembly.nu.ca
Ontario
Elections Ontario, 51 Rolark Dr., Toronto, ON M1R 3B1
416-326-6300, Fax: 416-326-6200, 888-668-8683, info@elections.on.ca
Prince Edward Island
Elections Prince Edward Island, J. Angus MacLean Bldg., 94 Great George St., 1st Fl., PO Box 774, Charlottetown, PE C1A 7L3
902-368-5895, Fax: 902-368-6500, 888-234-8783
Quebec
Directeur général des Élections du Québec, Édifice René-Lévesque, 3460, rue de La Pérade, Québec, QC G1X 3Y5
418-528-0422, Fax: 418-643-7291, 888-353-2846, info@electionsquebec.qc.ca
Saskatchewan
Elections Saskatchewan, 1702 Park St., Regina, SK S4N 6B2
306-787-4000, Fax: 306-787-4052, 877-958-8683, info@elections.sk.ca

EMERGENCY MEASURES

Environment Canada, 10 Wellington St., Gatineau, QC K1A 0H3
819-997-2800, Fax: 819-994-1412, 800-668-6767, enviroinfo@ec.gc.ca
National Search & Rescue Secretariat, #400, 275 Slater St., Ottawa, ON K1A 0K2
613-992-0054, Fax: 613-996-3746, 800-727-9414, inquiry@nss.gc.ca
Public Safety Canada, 269 Laurier Ave. West, Ottawa, ON K1A 0P8
613-944-4875, Fax: 613-954-5186, 800-830-3118, communications@ps.gc.ca
Alberta
Alberta Environment & Sustainable Resource Development, Oxbridge Place, 9820 - 106 St., Main Fl., Edmonton, AB T5K 2J6
780-427-2700, Fax: 780-422-4086, -310-0000, env.infocent@gov.ab.ca; srd.infocent@gov.ab.ca
British Columbia
British Columbia Provincial Emergency Program, Block A, #200, 2261 Keating Cross Rd., Saanichton, BC V8M 2A5
250-952-4913, Fax: 250-952-4888, 888-257-4777
Manitoba
Emergency Measures Organization, 405 Broadway Ave., 15th Floor, Winnipeg, MB R3C 3L6
204-945-4772, Fax: 204-945-4929, 888-267-8298, emo@gov.mb.ca
Nova Scotia
Nova Scotia Emergency Management Office, PO Box 2581, Halifax, NS B3J 3N5
902-424-5620, Fax: 902-424-5376, 866-424-5620, emo@gov.ns.ca
Nunavut
Nunavut Emergency Management, PO Box 1000 700,Iqaluit, NU X0A 0H0
867-975-5403, Fax: 867-979-4221, 800-693-1666
Yukon Territory
Emergency Measures Organization, Combined Services Bldg., 2nd Fl., 60 Norseman Rd, Airport, Whitehorse, YT Y1A 2C6
867-667-5220, Fax: 867-393-6266, 800-661-0408, emo.yukon@gov.yk.ca

EMPLOYMENT

Alberta
Alberta Human Services, Office of the Minister, Legislature Building, #224, 10800 - 97 Ave., Edmonton, AB T5K 2B6
780-644-5135, 866-644-5135
Manitoba
Manitoba Immigration & Multiculturalism, Legislative Building, 317, 450 Broadway Ave., Winnipeg, MB R3C 0V8
204-945-4079, Fax: 204-945-8312, minlab@leg.gov.mb.ca
New Brunswick
Office of Human Resources, Centennial Bldg, #345, 670 King St., PO Box 6000, Fredericton, NB E3B 5H1
506-453-2264, Fax: 506-453-7195
Newfoundland & Labrador
Newfoundland & Labrador Department of Advanced Education & Skills, Confederation Building, West Block, 3rd Fl., PO Box 8700, St. John's, NL A1B 4J6
709-729-2480, aesweb@gov.nl.ca
Northwest Territories
Department of Human Resources, PO Box 1320, Yellowknife, NT X1A 2L9
867-920-3409, Fax: 867-873-0306, 866-475-8162
Nunavut
Department of Human Resources, PO Box 1000 400,Iqaluit, NU X0A 1H0
Fax: 867-975-6216, 888-668-9993, gnhr@gov.nu.ca
Quebec
Ministère de l'Emploi et de la Solidarité sociale, 425, rue St-Amable, 4e étage, Québec, QC G1R 4Z1
418-643-4721, 888-643-4721
Emploi-Québec, 425, rue St-Amable, #RC 175, Québec, QC G1R 4Z1
418-643-4721, 888-643-4721
Ministère du Travail, 200, ch Sainte-Foy, 5e étage, Québec, QC G1R 5S1
418-644-4545, Fax: 418-528-0559, 800-643-4817
Saskatchewan
Saskatchewan Advanced Education, 1945 Hamilton St., Regina, SK S4P 2C8
306-787-9478, aeeinquiry@gov.sk.ca

EMPLOYMENT INSURANCE

Canada Employment Insurance Commission, 140, Promenade du Portage, Phase IV, Gatineau, QC K1A 0J9
800-206-7218
Saskatchewan
Saskatchewan Labour Relations & Workplace Safety, #300, 1870 Albert St., Regina, SK S4P 4W1
306-787-7404, webmaster@lab.gov.sk.ca

ENERGY

See Also: Natural Resources

Canadian Nuclear Safety Commission, 280 Slater St., PO Box 1046 B,Ottawa, ON K1P 5S9
613-995-5894, Fax: 613-995-5086, 800-668-5284

CANMET Energy Technology Centre-Devon, 1 Oil Patch Dr., #A202, PO Box 1280, Devon, AB T9G 1A8
780-987-8614, Fax: 780-987-8690, hamza@nrcan.gc.ca

CANMET Energy Technology Centre-Ottawa, 1 Haanel Dr., Nepean, ON K1A 1M1
613-996-8201, Fax: 613-995-9584

CANMET Energy Technology Centre-Varennes, 1615, boul Lionel-Boulet, CP 4800, Varennes, QC J3X 1S6
450-652-4621, Fax: 450-652-0999, 800-322-8122, canmetenergy.nrcan.gc.ca

Chalk River Laboratories, NRC Canadian Neutron Beam Centre, Building 459, Station 18, Chalk River, ON K0J 1J0
613-584-8293, 800-364-6989

Energy Solutions Centre, 206A Lowe St., 1st Fl., Whitehorse, YT Y1A 1W6
867-393-7063, Fax: 867-393-7061, esc@gov.yk.ca

Indian Oil & Gas Canada, #100, 9911 Chiila Blvd., Tsuu T'ina (Sarcee), AB T2W 6H6
403-292-5625, Fax: 403-292-5618, ContactIOGC@inac-ainc.gc.ca

Lands, Minerals & Petroleum Division, Hugh John Flemming Forestry Centre, PO Box 6000, Fredericton, NB E3B 5H1
506-453-2684, Fax: 506-453-2930, dnrweb@gnb.ca

National Energy Board, 444 - 7 Ave. SW, Calgary, AB T2P 0X8
403-292-4800, Fax: 403-292-5503, 800-899-1265, info@neb-one.gc.ca

Office of Climate Change, Energy Efficiency & Emissions Trading, PO Box 8700, St. John's, NL A1B 4J6
709-729-1210, Fax: 709-729-1119, climatechange@gov.nl.ca

Office of Energy Research & Development, 580 Booth St., 14th Fl., Ottawa, ON K1A 0E4
613-947-1421, Fax: 613-995-6146

Petroleum Products Division, Stuart M. Hodgson, 5009 - 49th St., 1st Fl., Yellowknife, NT X1A 2L9
867-920-3447, Fax: 867-873-0100

Yukon Energy Corporation, 2 Miles Canyon Rd., PO Box 5920, Whitehorse, YT Y1A 6S7
867-393-5300, 866-926-3749, communications@yukonenergy.ca

Alberta

Energy Resources Conservation Board, #1000, 250 - 5 Ave. SW, Calgary, AB T2P 0R4
403-297-8311, Fax: 403-297-7336, 855-297-8311, inquiries@ercb.ca; infoservices@ercb.ca; ADR@ercb.ca

Alberta Energy, North Petroleum Plaza, 9945 - 108 St., Edmonton, AB T5K 2G6
780-427-8050, Fax: 780-422-0698, -310-0000, Library.Energy@gov.ab.ca

British Columbia

British Columbia Hydro, 6911 Southpoint Dr., Burnaby, BC V3N 4X8
604-224-9376, 800-224-9376

British Columbia Ministry of Energy, Mines, & Natural Gas (& Responsible for Housing), PO Box 9053 Prov Govt,Victoria, BC V8W 9E2

British Columbia Utilities Commission, 900 Howe St., 6th Fl., PO Box 250, Vancouver, BC V6Z 2N3
604-660-4700, Fax: 604-660-1102, 800-663-1385, commission.secretary@bcuc.com

Oil & Gas Commission, #100, 10003 - 110 Ave., Fort St John, BC V1J 6M7
250-794-5200, Fax: 250-794-5375

Powerex Corp., #1400, 666 Burrard St., Vancouver, BC V6C 2X8
604-891-5000, Fax: 604-891-6060, 800-220-4907, Brian.Moghadam@powerex.com

Powertech Labs Inc., 12388 - 88 Ave., Surrey, BC V8W 7R7
604-590-7500, Fax: 604-590-6611

Manitoba

Manitoba Hydro, 360 Portage Ave., PO Box 815 Main,Winnipeg, MB R3C 2P4
204-474-3311, publicaffairs@hydro.mb.ca

New Brunswick

New Brunswick Department of Energy, Brunswick Square, #100M, 1 Germain St., Saint John, NB E2L 4V1
506-658-3180, Fax: 506-643-2919, DOEweb@gnb.ca

New Brunswick Department of Natural Resources, Hugh John Flemming Forestry Centre, PO Box 6000, Fredericton, NB E3B 5H1
506-453-3826, Fax: 506-444-4367, dnrweb@gnb.ca

Newfoundland & Labrador

Canada - Newfoundland & Labrador Offshore Petroleum Board, TD Place, 140 Water St., 5th Fl., St. John's, NL A1C 6H6
709-778-1400, Fax: 709-778-1473, information@cnlopb.nl.ca

Churchill Falls (Labrador) Corporation Limited, Hydro Place, 500 Columbus Dr., PO Box 12500, St. John's, NL A1B 4K7
709-737-1859, Fax: 709-737-1816

Newfoundland & Labrador Hydro, Hydro Place, Columbus Dr., PO Box 12400, St. John's, NL A1B 4K7
709-737-1400, Fax: 709-737-1800, hydro@nlh.nl.ca

Newfoundland & Labrador Board of Commissioners of Public Utilities, PO Box 21040, St. John's, NL A1A 5B2
709-726-8600, Fax: 709-726-9604, 866-782-0006, ito@pub.nf.ca

Twin Falls Power Corporation, PO Box 12500, St. John's, NL A1B 3T5

Northwest Territories

Department of Environment & Natural Resources, PO Box 1320, Yellowknife, NT X1A 2L9

Northwest Territories Power Corporation, 4 Capital Dr., Hay River, NT X0E 1G2
867-874-5200, Fax: 867-874-5251, info@ntpc.com

Nova Scotia

Canada - Nova Scotia Offshore Petroleum Board, TD Centre, 1791 Barrington St., 18th Fl., Halifax, NS B3J 3K9
902-422-5588, Fax: 902-422-1799, postmaster@cnsopb.ns.ca

Department of Energy, Bank of Montreal Bldg., #400, 5151 George St., PO Box 2664, Halifax, NS B3J 3P7
902-424-4575, Fax: 902-424-0528, energyinfo@gov.ns.ca

Nova Scotia Utility & Review Board, Summit Place, 1601 Lower Water St., 3rd Fl., PO Box 1692 M,Halifax, NS B3J 3S3
902-424-4448, Fax: 902-424-3919, uarb.board@gov.ns.ca

Ontario

Ontario Ministry of Energy, Hearst Block, 900 Bay St., 4th Fl., Toronto, ON M7A 2E1
416-327-6758, Fax: 416-325-8440, 888-668-4636, write2us@ontario.ca

Ontario Ministry of Environment, 135 St. Clair Ave. West, Toronto, ON M4V 1P5
416-325-4000, Fax: 416-325-3159, 800-565-4923

Hydro One Inc., North Tower, 483 Bay St., Toronto, ON M5G 2P5
416-345-5000, 877-955-1155, customercommunications@HydroOne.com

Independent Electricity System Operator, PO Box 4474 A,Toronto, ON M5W 4E5
905-403-6900, Fax: 905-403-6921, 888-448-7777, customer.relations@ieso.ca

Ontario Energy Board, #2700, 2300 Yonge St., Toronto, ON M4P 1E4
416-481-1967, Fax: 416-440-7656, 888-632-6273

Ontario Power Authority, #1600, 120 Adelaide St. West, Toronto, ON M5H 1T1
416-967-7474, Fax: 416-967-1947, 800-797-9604, info@powerauthority.on.ca

Ontario Power Generation, 700 University Ave., Toronto, ON M5G 1X6
416-592-2555, 877-592-2555, webmaster@opg.com

Prince Edward Island

Prince Edward Island Department of Environment, Labour & Justice, Shaw Bldg. South, 95 Rochford St., 4th Fl., PO Box 2000, Charlottetown, PE C1A 7N8
902-620-3774, Fax: 902-368-4242, rrryder@gov.pe.ca

Prince Edward Island Energy Corporation, Jones Bldg., 11 Kent St., 4th Fl., PO Box 2000, Charlottetown, PE C1A 7N8

Quebec

Agence de l'efficacité énergétique, 5700, 4e av ouest, Québec, QC G1H 6R1
418-627-6379, Fax: 418-643-5828, 877-727-6655, efficaciteenergetique@mrnf.gouv.qc.ca

Hydro-Québec, 75, boul René-Lévesque ouest, Montréal, QC H2Z 1A4
514-289-2211

Régie de l'énergie, Tour de la Bourse, #2.55, 800, Place Victoria, Montréal, QC H4Z 1A2
514-873-2452, Fax: 514-873-2070, 888-873-2452, secretariat@regie-energie.qc.ca

Société d'énergie de la Baie-James, 888, de Maisonneuve est, 6e étage, Montréal, QC H2L 5B2
514-286-2020

Saskatchewan

Energy & Resources, #300, 2103 - 11th Ave., Regina, SK S4P 3Z8
306-787-2528

Saskatchewan Power Corporation (SaskPower), 2025 Victoria Ave., Regina, SK S4P 0S1
306-566-3306, Fax: 800-757-6937, 888-757-6937

SaskEnergy Incorporated, 1777 Victoria Ave., Regina, SK S4P 4K5
306-777-9225, 800-567-8899

Yukon Territory

Yukon Energy, Mines & Resources, PO Box 2703, Whitehorse, YT Y1A 2C6
867-667-3130, Fax: 867-456-3965, 800-661-0408, emr@gov.yk.ca

ENGINEERING & CONSULTING

Canadian Environmental Assessment Agency, Place Bell Canada, 160 Elgin St., 22nd Fl., Ottawa, ON K1A 0H3
613-957-0700, Fax: 613-957-0862, 866-582-1884, info@ceaa-acee.gc.ca

Defence Construction Canada, Constitution Square, 350 Albert St., 19th Fl., Ottawa, ON K1A 0K3
613-998-9548, Fax: 613-998-1061, 800-514-3555, info@dcc-cdc.gc.ca

Natural Sciences & Engineering Research Council of Canada, Constitution Square, Tower II, 350 Albert St., Ottawa, ON K1A 1H5
613-995-4273, Fax: 613-943-1624, marie-josee.duval@nserc-crsng.gc.ca

British Columbia

Transportation Policy & Programs Department, PO Box 9850 Prov Govt,Victoria, BC V8W 9T5
250-387-5062, Fax: 250-387-6431

Manitoba

Manitoba Infrastructure & Transportation, Legislative Building, #203, 450 Broadway Ave., Winnipeg, MB R3C 0V8
204-945-3723, Fax: 204-945-7610

Northwest Territories

Highways & Marine, 4510 - 50 Ave., 2nd fl., PO Box 1320, Yellowknife, NT X1A 2L9
867-920-8771, Fax: 867-873-0288

Saskatchewan

Saskatchewan Highways & Infrastructure, Victoria Tower, 1855 Victoria Ave., Regina, SK S4P 3T2
306-787-4800, communications@highways.gov.sk.ca

ENVIRONMENT

Commissioner of the Environment & Sustainable Development, 240 Sparks St., Ottawa, ON K1A 0G6
613-995-3708, Fax: 613-957-0474, petitions@oag-bvg.gc.ca

Environment Canada, 10 Wellington St., Gatineau, QC K1A 0H3
819-997-2800, Fax: 819-994-1412, 800-668-6767, enviroinfo@ec.gc.ca

British Columbia Environmental Assessment Office, 836 Yates St., 1st Fl., PO Box 9426 Prov Govt,Victoria, BC V8W 9V1
250-356-7479, Fax: 250-356-6448, eaoinfo@gov.bc.ca

National Laboratory for Environmental Testing, Environment Canada, 867 Lakeshore Rd., PO Box 5050, Burlington, ON L7R 4A6
905-336-4563, Fax: 905-336-6404

National Round Table on the Environment & Economy, #200, 344 Slater St., Ottawa, ON K1R 7Y3
613-992-7189, Fax: 613-992-7385, info@nrtee-trnee.ca

Alberta

Alberta Environment & Sustainable Resource Development, Oxbridge Place, 9820 - 106 St., Main Fl., Edmonton, AB T5K 2J6
780-427-2700, Fax: 780-422-4086, -310-0000, env.infocent@gov.ab.ca; srd.infocent@gov.ab.ca

British Columbia

British Columbia Ministry of Environment, PO Box 9339 Prov Govt,Victoria, BC V8W 9M1
250-387-1161, Fax: 250-387-5669, envmail@gov.bc.ca

Manitoba

Manitoba Conservation & Water Stewardship, 200 Saulteaux Cres., Winnipeg, MB R3J 3W3
800-214-6497, mws@gov.mb.ca

New Brunswick

New Brunswick Department of Environment & Local Government, Marysville Place, PO Box 6000, Fredericton, NB E3B 5H1
506-453-2690, Fax: 506-457-4994, elg/egl-info@gnb.ca

Newfoundland & Labrador

Newfoundland & Labrador Department of Environment & Conservation, Confederation Bldg., West Block, 4th Fl., PO Box 8700, St. John's, NL A1B 4J6
709-729-2664, Fax: 709-729-6639, 800-563-6181, info@gov.nl.ca

Northwest Territories

Department of Environment & Natural Resources, PO Box 1320, Yellowknife, NT X1A 2L9

Nova Scotia

Department of Environment, 5151 Terminal Rd., 5th Fl., PO Box 442, Halifax, NS B3J 2P8
902-424-3600, Fax: 902-424-0503, 877-936-8476

Nunavut

Department of Environment, PO Box 1000 1300,Iqaluit, NU X0A 0H0
867-975-7700, Fax: 867-975-7742, environment@gov.nu.ca

Ontario
Ontario Ministry of Environment, 135 St. Clair Ave. West, Toronto, ON M4V 1P5
416-325-4000, Fax: 416-325-3159, 800-565-4923
Environmental Commissioner of Ontario, #605, 1075 Bay St., Toronto, ON M5S 2B1
416-325-3377, Fax: 416-325-3370, 800-701-6454, commissioner@eco.on.ca
Prince Edward Island
Prince Edward Island Department of Environment, Labour & Justice, Shaw Bldg. South, 95 Rochford St., 4th Fl., PO Box 2000, Charlottetown, PE C1A 7N8
902-620-3774, Fax: 902-368-4242, rrryder@gov.pe.ca
Quebec
Bureau d'audiences publiques sur l'environnement, Édifice Lomer-Gouin, #2.10, 575, rue Saint-Amable, Québec, QC G1R 6A6
418-643-7447, Fax: 418-643-9474, 800-463-4732, communication@bape.gouv.qc.ca
Ministère du Développement durable, de l'Environnement, de la Faune, et des Parcs, Édifice Marie-Guyart, 675, boul René-Lévesque est, 29e étage, Québec, QC G1R 5V7
418-521-3830, Fax: 418-646-5974, 800-561-1616, info@mddep.gouv.qc.ca
Saskatchewan
Saskatchewan Environment, 3211 Albert St., 2nd Fl., Regina, SK S4S 5W6
306-787-2584, Fax: 306-787-9544, 800-567-4224, Centre.Inquiry@gov.sk.ca

ENVIRONMENT DEPARTMENTS/MINISTRIES

Environment Canada, 10 Wellington St., Gatineau, QC K1A 0H3
819-997-2800, Fax: 819-994-1412, 800-668-6767, enviroinfo@ec.gc.ca
Alberta
Alberta Environment & Sustainable Resource Development, Oxbridge Place, 9820 - 106 St., Main Fl., Edmonton, AB T5K 2J6
780-427-2700, Fax: 780-422-4086, -310-0000, env.infocent@gov.ab.ca; srd.infocent@gov.ab.ca
British Columbia
British Columbia Ministry of Environment, PO Box 9339 Prov Govt,Victoria, BC V8W 9M1
250-387-1161, Fax: 250-387-5669, envmail@gov.bc.ca
Manitoba
Manitoba Conservation & Water Stewardship, 200 Saulteaux Cres., Winnipeg, MB R3J 3W3
800-214-6497, mws@gov.mb.ca
New Brunswick
New Brunswick Department of Environment & Local Government, Marysville Place, PO Box 6000, Fredericton, NB E3B 5H1
506-453-2690, Fax: 506-457-4994, elg/egl-info@gnb.ca
Newfoundland & Labrador
Newfoundland & Labrador Department of Environment & Conservation, Confederation Bldg., West Block, 4th Fl., PO Box 8700, St. John's, NL A1B 4J6
709-729-2664, Fax: 709-729-6639, 800-563-6181, info@gov.nl.ca
Northwest Territories
Department of Environment & Natural Resources, PO Box 1320, Yellowknife, NT X1A 2L9
Nova Scotia
Department of Environment, 5151 Terminal Rd., 5th Fl., PO Box 442, Halifax, NS B3J 2P8
902-424-3600, Fax: 902-424-0503, 877-936-8476
Nunavut
Department of Environment, PO Box 1000 1300,Iqaluit, NU X0A 0H0
867-975-7700, Fax: 867-975-7742, environment@gov.nu.ca
Ontario
Ontario Ministry of Environment, 135 St. Clair Ave. West, Toronto, ON M4V 1P5
416-325-4000, Fax: 416-325-3159, 800-565-4923
Prince Edward Island
Prince Edward Island Department of Environment, Labour & Justice, Shaw Bldg. South, 95 Rochford St., 4th Fl., PO Box 2000, Charlottetown, PE C1A 7N8
902-620-3774, Fax: 902-368-4242, rrryder@gov.pe.ca
Quebec
Ministère du Développement durable, de l'Environnement, de la Faune, et des Parcs, Édifice Marie-Guyart, 675, boul René-Lévesque est, 29e étage, Québec, QC G1R 5V7
418-521-3830, Fax: 418-646-5974, 800-561-1616, info@mddep.gouv.qc.ca
Saskatchewan
Saskatchewan Environment, 3211 Albert St., 2nd Fl., Regina, SK S4S 5W6
306-787-2584, Fax: 306-787-9544, 800-567-4224, Centre.Inquiry@gov.sk.ca
Yukon Territory
Yukon Environment, PO Box 2703, Whitehorse, YT Y1A 2C6
867-667-5652, Fax: 867-393-7197, environment.yukon@gov.yk.ca

ENVIRONMENTAL ASSESSMENT

Canadian Environmental Assessment Agency, Place Bell Canada, 160 Elgin St., 22nd Fl., Ottawa, ON K1A 0H3
613-957-0700, Fax: 613-957-0862, 866-582-1884, info@ceaa-acee.gc.ca
Environmental Assessment Branch, 3211 Albert St., 4th Fl., Regina, SK S4S 5W6
306-787-6132, Fax: 306-787-0930
British Columbia Environmental Assessment Office, 836 Yates St., 1st Fl., PO Box 9426 Prov Govt,Victoria, BC V8W 9V1
250-356-7479, Fax: 250-356-6448, eaoinfo@gov.bc.ca
Land & Environment Division, Jones Bldg., 11 Kent St., 3rd Fl., PO Box 2000, Charlottetown, PE C1A 7N8
902-368-5221, Fax: 902-368-5395
National Laboratory for Environmental Testing, Environment Canada, 867 Lakeshore Rd., PO Box 5050, Burlington, ON L7R 4A6
905-336-4563, Fax: 905-336-6404
Port aux Basques, Provincial Bldg., Main St., PO Box 478, Port Aux Basques, NL A0M 1C0
709-695-2835, Fax: 709-695-2393
New Brunswick
Community Planning & Environmental Protection Division, Marysville Place, PO Box 6000, Fredericton, NB E3B 5H1
506-444-5119, Fax: 506-457-7333, elg/egl-info@gnb.ca

ENVIRONMENTAL HEALTH

British Columbia
British Columbia Environmental Assessment Office, 836 Yates St., 1st Fl., PO Box 9426 Prov Govt,Victoria, BC V8W 9V1
250-356-7479, Fax: 250-356-6448, eaoinfo@gov.bc.ca

EROSION CONTROL

Prince Edward Island
Agriculture Policy & Regulatory Division, Jones Bldg., 11 Kent St., 5th Fl., Charlottetown, PE C1A 7N8
Research Branch, Tower 5, 1341 Baseline Rd., Ottawa, ON K1A 0C5
613-759-1000, Fax: 613-773-1866
Quebec
Commission de protection du territoire agricole du Québec, 200, ch Ste-Foy, 2e étage, Québec, QC G1R 4X6
418-643-3314, Fax: 418-643-2261, 800-667-5294, info@cptaq.gouv.qc.ca
Saskatchewan
Saskatchewan Agriculture, Walter Scott Bldg., 3085 Albert St., Regina, SK S4S 0B1
866-457-2377, aginfo@gov.sk.ca

EXPORT DEVELOPMENT

Business Development Bank of Canada, #400, 5, Place Ville-Marie, Montréal, QC H3B 5E7
514-283-5904, Fax: 514-283-5626, 877-232-2269
Canadian Trade Commissioner Service, c/o Foreign Affairs & International Trade, 125 Sussex Dr., Ottawa, ON K1A 0G2
613-944-9991, Fax: 613-996-9709, 888-306-9991, enqserv@international.gc.ca
Export Development Canada, 151 Slater St., Ottawa, ON K1A 1K3
613-598-2500, Fax: 613-598-3811, 800-267-8510
Industry Canada, C.D. Howe Building, 235 Queen St., Ottawa, ON K1A 0H5
613-954-5031, Fax: 613-954-2340, 800-328-6189, info@ic.gc.ca
Western Economic Diversification Canada, Canada Place, #1500, 9700 Jasper Ave. NW, Edmonton, AB T5J 4H7
780-495-4164, Fax: 780-495-4557, 888-338-9378
New Brunswick
New Brunswick Department of Economic Development, Centennial Building, PO Box 6000, Fredericton, NB E3B 5H1
506-453-3707, Fax: 506-453-3993, 800-665-1800, tradenb@gnb.ca
Northern Development Division, Harbourview Place, #400, 275 Main St., Bathurst, NB E2A 1A9
506-547-2227, Fax: 506-547-2269
Ontario
Ontario Ministry of Economic Development & Innovation, Hearst Block, 900 Bay St., 8th Fl., Toronto, ON M7A 2E1
416-325-6666, Fax: 416-325-6688, 866-668-4249, info@edt.gov.on.ca
Saskatchewan
Energy & Resources, #300, 2103 - 11th Ave., Regina, SK S4P 3Z8
306-787-2528

EXPROPRIATION

Canada Lands Company Ltd., #1200, 1 University Ave., Toronto, ON M5J 2P1
416-952-6111, Fax: 416-952-6115, 888-252-5263
Justice Canada, East Memorial Bldg., 284 Wellington St., Ottawa, ON K1A 0H8
613-957-4222, Fax: 613-954-0811, webadmin@justice.gc.ca
National Defence Canada, Major-General George R. Pearkes Bldg., 101 Colonel By Dr., Ottawa, ON K1A 0K2
613-995-2534, Fax: 613-992-4739, 800-856-8488
Alberta
Land Compensation Board, 1229 - 91 St. SW, Edmonton, AB T6X 1E9
srb.lcb@gov.ab.ca
Manitoba
Manitoba Land Value Appraisal Commission, 800 Portage Ave., Winnipeg, MB R3G 0N4
204-945-2941, Fax: 204-948-2235
Quebec
Ministère de la Justice, Édifice Louis-Philippe-Pigeon, 1200, rte de l'Église, Québec, QC G1V 4M1
418-643-5140, 866-536-5140, informations@justice.gouv.qc.ca
Ministère des Transports, 700, boul René-Lévesque est, 28e étage, Québec, QC G1R 5H1
418-643-6980, Fax: 418-643-2033, 888-355-0511, communications@mtq.gouv.qc.ca
Saskatchewan
Public & Private Rights Board, #323, 3085 Albert St., Regina, SK S4S 0B1
306-787-4071, Fax: 306-787-0088

FAMILY BENEFITS

See Also: Income Security; Social Services
British Columbia
British Columbia Ministry of Children & Family Development, PO Box 9770 Prov Govt,Victoria, BC V8W 9S5
250-387-7027, Fax: 250-356-3007, 877-387-7027, MCF.CorrespondenceManagement@gov.bc.ca
Manitoba
Manitoba Family Services & Labour, #219, 114 Garry St., Winnipeg, MB R3C 4V6
204-945-3242, Fax: 204-945-2156, minfam@leg.gov.mb.ca
New Brunswick
New Brunswick Department of Social Development, Sartain MacDonald Bldg., 551 King St., PO Box 6000, Fredericton, NB E3B 5H1
506-453-2001, Fax: 506-453-7478, sd-ds@gnb.ca
Newfoundland & Labrador
Newfoundland & Labrador Department of Advanced Education & Skills, Confederation Building, West Block, 3rd Fl., PO Box 8700, St. John's, NL A1B 4J6
709-729-2480, aesweb@gov.nl.ca
Northwest Territories
Department of Education, Culture & Employment, PO Box 1320, Yellowknife, NT X1A 2L9
867-669-2399, Fax: 867-873-0431, 866-606-5627
Quebec
Ministère de l'Emploi et de la Solidarité sociale, 425, rue St-Amable, 4e étage, Québec, QC G1R 4Z1
418-643-4721, 888-643-4721
Ministère de la Famille, 425, rue Saint-Amable, 1er étage, Québec, QC G1R 4Z1
877-216-6202

FEDERAL-PROVINCIAL AFFAIRS

Canadian Intergovernmental Conference Secretariat, 222 Queen St., 10th Fl., PO Box 488 A,Ottawa, ON K1N 8V5
613-995-2341, Fax: 613-996-6091, info@scics.gc.ca
Office of Intergovernmental Affairs, c/o Privy Council Office, #1000, 85 Slater St., Ottawa, ON K1A 0A3
613-957-5153, Fax: 613-957-5043, info@pco-bcp.gc.ca
Alberta
Alberta International & Intergovernmental Relations, Commerce Place, 10155 - 102 St., 12th Fl., Edmonton, AB T5J 4G8
780-422-1510, -310-0000
British Columbia
Intergovernmental Relations Secretariat, PO Box 9333 Prov Govt,Victoria, BC V8W 9N3
250-387-0752, Fax: 250-387-1920, igrs@gov.bc.ca; protocol@gov.bc.ca
New Brunswick
Intergovernmental Affairs Division, Centennial Bldg., #274, 670 King St., PO Box 6000, Fredericton, NB E3B 5H1
506-457-7275, Fax: 506-453-2995, iga@gnb.ca

Newfoundland & Labrador
Intergovernmental & Aboriginal Affairs Secretariat, Confederation Bldg., East Block, 7th Fl., PO Box 8700, St. John's, NL A1B 4J6
709-729-3164, Fax: 709-729-5038, iga@gov.nl.ca
Northwest Territories
Department of Aboriginal Affairs & Intergovernmental Relations, 4910 - 52nd St., PO Box 1320, Yellowknife, NT X1A 2L9
867-873-7143, Fax: 867-873-0233, 877-838-8194, nancy_gardiner@gov.nt.ca
Nova Scotia
Department of Intergovernmental Affairs, Duke Tower, 5251 Duke St., 5th Fl., PO Box 1617, Halifax, NS B3J 2Y3
Fax: 902-424-0728, iga@gov.ns.ca
Nunavut
Department of Executive & Intergovernmental Affairs, 1084 Aeroplex bldg., PO Box 1000 200,Iqaluit, NU X0A 0H0
867-975-6000, Fax: 867-975-6099
Ontario
Ontario Ministry of Intergovernmental Affairs, 77 Wellesley St. West, Toronto, ON M7A 1N3
416-325-4800, Fax: 416-325-4787
Quebec
Secrétariat aux affaires intergouvernementales canadiennes, 875, Grande Allée est, 3e étage, Québec, QC G1R 4Y8
418-643-4011, Fax: 418-528-0052

FILM PRODUCTION & COLLECTIONS

Canadian Broadcasting Corporation, 181 Queen St., PO Box 3220 C,Ottawa, ON K1Y 1E4
613-288-6033, liaison@radio-canada.ca
National Film Board of Canada, 3155, rue Côte de Liesse, CP 1600 Centre-ville,Saint-Laurent, QC H4N 2N4
514-283-9000, Fax: 514-283-7564, 800-267-7710
Telefilm Canada, #500, 360, rue Saint-Jacques, Montréal, QC H2Y 1P5
514-283-6363, Fax: 514-283-2365, 800-567-0890, info@telefilm.gc.ca
Manitoba
Manitoba Film & Sound Recording Development Corporation, #410, 93 Lombard Ave., Winnipeg, MB R3B 3B1
204-947-2040, Fax: 204-956-5261, carole@mbfilmsound.mb.ca
Newfoundland & Labrador
Newfoundland & Labrador Film Development Corporation, 12 King's Bridge Rd., St. John's, NL A1C 3K3
709-738-3456, Fax: 709-739-1680, 877-738-3456, info@nlfdc.ca
Nova Scotia
Film Nova Scotia, Collins Bank Bldg., 1869 Upper Water St., 3rd Fl., Halifax, NS B3J 1S9
902-424-7177, Fax: 902-424-0617, 888-360-2111
Ontario
Ontario Media Development Corporation, South Tower, #501, 175 Bloor St. East, Toronto, ON M4W 3R8
416-314-6858, Fax: 416-314-6876, mail@omdc.on.ca

FINANCE

See Also: Banking & Financial Institutions
Finance Canada, L'esplanade Laurier, 140 O'Connor St., Ottawa, ON K1A 0G5
613-992-1573, Fax: 613-943-0938, finpub@fin.gc.ca
Prince Edward Island Department of Finance, Energy & Municipal Affairs, Shaw Bldg., 95 Rochford St. South, 2nd Fl., PO Box 2000, Charlottetown, PE C1A 7N8
902-368-4000, Fax: 902-368-5544
Alberta
Alberta Treasury Board & Finance, Oxbridge Place, 9820 - 106 St., 5th Fl., Edmonton, AB T5K 2J6
780-415-4519, -310-000
British Columbia
British Columbia Ministry of Finance, PO Box 9417 Prov Govt,Victoria, BC V8W 9V1
877-388-4440, CTBTaxQuestions@gov.bc.ca (tax inquiries)
Manitoba
Manitoba Finance, #109, Legislative Bldg., Winnipeg, MB R3C 0V8
204-945-3754, Fax: 204-945-8316, minfin@leg.gov.mb.ca
New Brunswick
New Brunswick Department of Finance, 670 King St., PO Box 6000, Fredericton, NB E3B 5H1
506-453-2451, Fax: 506-457-4989, wwwfin@gnb.ca
Newfoundland & Labrador
Newfoundland & Labrador Department of Finance, Confederation Bldg., PO Box 8700, St. John's, NL A1B 4J6
709-729-6165, Fax: 709-729-2070, finance@gov.nl.ca
Northwest Territories
Department of Finance, Arthur Laing Building, 5th Fl., 5003 - 49th St., PO Box 1320, Yellowknife, NT X1A 2L9
867-873-7117, Fax: 867-873-0414
Nova Scotia
Department of Finance, Provincial Bldg., 1723 Hollis St., 7th Fl., PO Box 187, Halifax, NS B3J 2N3
902-424-5554, Fax: 902-424-0635, FinanceWeb@gov.ns.ca
Nunavut
Department of Finance, Bldg. 1079, 1st Fl., PO Box 1000 330,Iqaluit, NU X0A 0H0
867-975-5800, Fax: 867-975-5805
Ontario
Ontario Ministry of Finance, Frost Bldg. South, 7 Queen's Park Cres., 7th Fl., Toronto, ON M7A 1Y7
Fax: 866-888-3850, 866-668-8297, financecommunications.fin@ontario.ca
Quebec
Ministère des Finances et de l'Économie, Édifice Gérard-D.-Lévesque, 12, rue Saint-Louis, Québec, QC G1R 5L3
418-528-9323, Fax: 418-646-1631, info@finances.gouv.qc.ca
Saskatchewan
Saskatchewan Finance, 2350 Albert St., Regina, SK S4P 4A6
306-787-6768, Fax: 306-787-0241, communications@finance.gov.sk.ca
Yukon Territory
Yukon Finance, PO Box 2703, Whitehorse, YT Y1A 2C6
867-667-5343, Fax: 867-393-6217, fininfo@gov.yk.ca

FINANCING & LOANS

See Also: Investment
Business Development Bank of Canada, #400, 5, Place Ville-Marie, Montréal, QC H3B 5E7
514-283-5904, Fax: 514-283-5626, 877-232-2269
Canada Mortgage & Housing Corporation, 700 Montreal Rd., Ottawa, ON K1A 0P7
613-748-2000, Fax: 613-748-2098, 800-668-2642, chic@cmhc-schl.gc.ca
Farm Credit Canada, 1800 Hamilton St., PO Box 4320, Regina, SK S4P 4L3
306-780-8100, Fax: 306-780-8919, 888-332-3301, csc@fcc-fac.ca
Alberta
Alberta Capital Finance Authority, Canadian Western Bank Place, #2450, 10303 Jasper Ave., Edmonton, AB T5J 3N6
780-427-9711, Fax: 780-422-2175, webacfa@gov.ab.ca
ATB Financial, 9888 Jasper Ave., Edmonton, AB T5J 1P1
403-245-8110, 800-332-8383
British Columbia
Provincial Treasury, PO Box 9414 Prov Govt,Victoria, BC V8V 9V1
250-387-4541, Fax: 250-356-3041
Manitoba
Manitoba Agricultural Services Corporation, #100, 1525 First St. South, Brandon, MB R7A 7A1
204-726-6850, Fax: 204-726-6849, mailbox@masc.mb.ca
New Brunswick
New Brunswick Department of Economic Development, Centennial Building, PO Box 6000, Fredericton, NB E3B 5H1
506-453-3707, Fax: 506-453-3993, 800-665-1800, tradenb@gnb.ca
Newfoundland & Labrador
Newfoundland & Labrador Department of Finance, Confederation Bldg., PO Box 8700, St. John's, NL A1B 4J6
709-729-6165, Fax: 709-729-2070, finance@gov.nl.ca
Northwest Territories
Department of Industry, Tourism & Investment, PO Box 1320, Yellowknife, NT X1A 2L9
Fax: 867-873-0306, info@iti.ca
Nova Scotia
Nova Scotia Farm Loan Board, PO Box 550, Truro, NS B2N 5E3
902-893-6506, Fax: 902-895-7693, flb@gov.ns.ca
Nunavut
Nunavut Business Credit Corporation, Parnaivak Bldg., #100, PO Box 2548, Iqaluit, NU X0A 0H0
867-975-7891, Fax: 867-975-7897, 800-758-0038, credit@nbcc.nu.ca
Ontario
Ontario Electricity Financial Corporation, #1400, 1 Dundas St. West, Toronto, ON M7A 1Y7
416-325-8000, Fax: 416-325-8005
Ontario Financing Authority, #1400, 1 Dundas St. West, Toronto, ON M7A 1Y7
416-325-8000, Fax: 416-325-8005
Prince Edward Island
Prince Edward Island Lending Agency, Homburg Financial Tower, 98 Fitzroy St., 2nd Fl., Charlottetown, PE C1A 1R7
902-368-6200, Fax: 902-368-6201
Quebec
La financière agricole de Québec, 1400, boul de la Rive-Sud, Saint-Romuald, QC G6W 8K7
418-838-5602, Fax: 418-833-3871, 800-749-3646, financiereagricole@fadq.qc.ca
Yukon Territory
Yukon Economic Development, PO Box 2703, Whitehorse, YT Y1A 2C6
867-393-7191, Fax: 867-393-6412, 800-661-0408, ecdev@gov.yk.ca

FIRE PREVENTION

British Columbia
Emergency Management BC, PO Box 9223 Prov Govt,Victoria, BC V8W 9J1
250-953-4002, Fax: 250-953-4081, BC.CorSer@gov.bc.ca (Coroner); OFC@gov.bc.ca (Fire Commissioner)
Manitoba
Office of the Fire Commissioner, #508, 401 York Ave., Winnipeg, MB R3C 0P8
204-945-3322, Fax: 204-948-2089, 800-282-8069, firecomm@gov.mb.ca
Newfoundland & Labrador
Eastern Waste Management Commission, #200, 120 Lemarchant Rd., St. John's, NL A1C 2H2
709-579-7960, Fax: 709-579-5392, info@easternwaste.ca
Northwest Territories
Department of Municipal & Community Affairs, PO Box 1320, Yellowknife, NT X1A 2L9
867-873-7118, Fax: 867-873-0309
Nunavut
Nunavut Emergency Management, PO Box 1000 700,Iqaluit, NU X0A 0H0
867-975-5403, Fax: 867-979-4221, 800-693-1666
Ontario
Fire Safety Commission, Place Nouveau Bldg., 5775 Yonge St., 7th Fl., Toronto, ON M2M 4J1
416-325-3100, Fax: 416-314-1217
Quebec
Commissariat des incendies, 455, rue Dupont, Québec, QC G1K 6N2
418-529-5706, Fax: 418-529-9922, cdelage@notarius.net
Yukon Territory
Fire Marshal's Office, 91790 Alaska Hwy., Whitehorse, YT Y1A 5X7
867-667-5811, Fax: 867-667-3165, inquiry@gov.yk.ca

FIREARMS

Canada Firearms Program, Ottawa, ON K1A 0R2
Fax: 613-825-0297, 800-731-4000, cfp-pcaf@rcmp-grc.gc.ca
British Columbia
British Columbia Ministry of Justice, PO Box 9044 Prov Govt,Victoria, BC V8W 9E2

FISHERIES

Fisheries & Oceans Canada, 200 Kent St., Ottawa, ON K1A 0E6
613-993-0999, Fax: 613-990-1866, info@dfo-mpo.gc.ca
Fisheries Resource Conservation Council, PO Box 2001 D, Ottawa, ON K1P 5W3
613-998-0433, Fax: 613-998-1146, info@frcc-ccrh.ca
Freshwater Fish Marketing Corporation, 1199 Plessis Rd., Winnipeg, MB R2C 3L4
204-983-6601, Fax: 204-983-6497, sandi.cain@freshwaterfish.com
Gulf Fisheries Centre, 343, av Université, 5th Fl., Moncton, NB E1C 9B6
506-851-3886, Fax: 506-851-7732
British Columbia
British Columbia Ministry of Agriculture, PO Box 9120 Prov Govt,Victoria, BC V8W 9E2
250-387-5121
Parks & Protected Areas Division, PO Box 9339 Prov Govt,Victoria, BC V8W 9M9
Fax: 250-953-3414
New Brunswick
New Brunswick Department of Agriculture, Aquaculture & Fisheries, Agricultural Research Station (Experimental Farm), PO Box 6000, Fredericton, NB E3B 5H1
506-453-2666, Fax: 506-453-7170, DAAF-MAAP@gnb.ca
Newfoundland & Labrador
Newfoundland & Labrador Department of Fisheries & Aquaculture, Petten Bldg., 30 Strawberry Marsh Rd., PO Box 8700, St. John's, NL A1B 4J6
709-729-3723, Fax: 709-729-6082, fisheries@gov.nl.ca
Northwest Territories
Department of Environment & Natural Resources, PO Box 1320, Yellowknife, NT X1A 2L9

Nova Scotia

Fisheries & Aquaculture Loan Board, 1741 Brunswick St., 3rd Fl., PO Box 2223, Halifax, NS B3J 3C4
902-424-0318, Fax: 902-424-3502

Department of Fisheries & Aquaculture, 1741 Brunswick St., 3rd Fl., PO Box 2223, Halifax, NS B3J 3C4
902-424-4560, Fax: 902-424-4671

Ontario

Ontario Fish & Wildlife Heritage Commission, Robinson Pl., 300 Water St., PO Box 7000, Peterborough, ON K9J 8M5
705-755-1905, Fax: 705-755-1900

Prince Edward Island

Prince Edward Island Department of Agriculture & Forestry, Jones Bldg., 11 Kent St., PO Box 2000, Charlottetown, PE C1A 7N8
902-368-4880, Fax: 902-368-4857

FISHERIES & WILDLIFE

Arctic Goose, c/o Prairie & Northern Region, CWS, #200, 4999 - 98 Ave., Edmonton, AB T6B 2X3
780-951-8652, Fax: 780-495-2615, agjv@ec.gc.ca

Beverly & Qamanirjuaq Caribou Management Board, Secretariat, PO Box 629, Stonewall, MB R0C 2Z0
204-467-2438, caribounews@arctic-caribou.com

Black Duck, Environment Canada, Canadian Wildlife Service, 335 River Rd., Ottawa, ON K1A 0H3
613-949-8254

Canadian Wildlife Service, 351, boul St-Joseph, Gatineau, QC K1A 0H3
819-997-1301, Fax: 819-953-7177

Committee on the Status of Endangered Wildlife in Canada, c/o Canadian Wildlife Service, 351 St. Joseph Blvd, 4th Fl., Gatineau, QC K1A 0H3
819-953-3215, Fax: 819-994-3684, cosewic/cosepac@ec.gc.ca

Eastern Habitat, c/o Environment Canada, Canadian Wildlife Service, 335 River Rd., Ottawa, ON K1A 0H3
613-949-8264

Fisheries & Oceans Canada, 200 Kent St., Ottawa, ON K1A 0E6
613-993-0999, Fax: 613-990-1866, info@dfo-mpo.gc.ca

Natural Resources Canada, 580 Booth St., Ottawa, ON K1A 0E4
613-995-0947, Fax: 613-992-7211

North American Bird Conservation Initiative, Canadian Wildlife Service, 351, boul St-Joseph, 3e étage, Gatineau, QC K1A 0H3
819-994-0512, Fax: 819-994-4445, nabci@ec.gc.ca

North American Waterfowl Management Plan, NAWCC (Canada) Secretariat, Place Vincent Massey, 351 St. Joseph Blvd., 7th Fl., Gatineau, QC K1A 0H3
819-934-6034, Fax: 819-934-6017, nawmp@ec.gc.ca

Pacific Coast, c/o Environment Canada, Canadian Wildlife Service, #201, 401 Burrard St., Vancouver, BC V6C 3S5
604-940-4703

Porcupine Caribou Management Board, PO Box 31723, Whitehorse, YT Y1A 6L3
867-633-4780, Fax: 867-393-3904, pcmb@taiga.net

Prairie Habitat, c/o Prairie & Northern Region, CWS, #200, 4999 - 98 Ave., Edmonton, AB T6B 2X3
780-951-8652, phjv@ec.gc.ca

Alberta

Alberta Environment & Sustainable Resource Development, Oxbridge Place, 9820 - 106 St., Main Fl., Edmonton, AB T5K 2J6
780-427-2700, Fax: 780-422-4086, -310-0000, env.infocent@gov.ab.ca; srd.infocent@gov.ab.ca

British Columbia

British Columbia Ministry of Environment, PO Box 9339 Prov Govt,Victoria, BC V8W 9M1
250-387-1161, Fax: 250-387-5669, envmail@gov.bc.ca

Manitoba

Endangered Species Advisory Committee, 200 Saulteaux Cres., PO Box 24, Winnipeg, MB R3J 3W3
204-945-7465, Fax: 204-945-3077

Manitoba Habitat Heritage Corporation, #200, 1555 St. James St., Winnipeg, MB R3H 1B5
204-784-4350, Fax: 204-784-7359, mhhc@mhhc.mb.ca

New Brunswick

New Brunswick Department of Agriculture, Aquaculture & Fisheries, Agricultural Research Station (Experimental Farm), PO Box 6000, Fredericton, NB E3B 5H1
506-453-2666, Fax: 506-453-7170, DAAF-MAAP@gnb.ca

Newfoundland & Labrador

Forestry Services, Fortis Bldg., PO Box 2006, Corner Brook, NL A2H 6J8
709-637-2284, Fax: 709-634-4378

Newfoundland & Labrador Department of Fisheries & Aquaculture, Petten Bldg., 30 Strawberry Marsh Rd., PO Box 8700, St. John's, NL A1B 4J6
709-729-3723, Fax: 709-729-6082, fisheries@gov.nl.ca

Northwest Territories

Department of Environment & Natural Resources, PO Box 1320, Yellowknife, NT X1A 2L9

Nova Scotia

Department of Natural Resources, Founder's Square, 1701 Hollis St., 3rd Fl., PO Box 698, Halifax, NS B3J 2T9
902-424-5935, Fax: 902-424-0594, 800-565-2224

Ontario

Ontario Ministry of Natural Resources, Whitney Block, #6630, 99 Wellesley St. West, 6th Fl., Toronto, ON M7A 1W3
800-667-1940

Prince Edward Island

Prince Edward Island Department of Environment, Labour & Justice, Shaw Bldg. South, 95 Rochford St., 4th Fl., PO Box 2000, Charlottetown, PE C1A 7N8
902-620-3774, Fax: 902-368-4242, rrryder@gov.pe.ca

Prince Edward Island Department of Tourism & Culture, PO Box 2000, Charlottetown, PE C1A 7N8
902-368-5540, Fax: 902-368-5277, tpswitch@gov.pe.ca

Quebec

Ministère de l'Agriculture, des Pêcheries et de l'Alimentation, 200, ch Sainte-Foy, Québec, QC G1R 4X6
418-380-2110, 888-222-6272

Yukon Territory

Yukon Environment, PO Box 2703, Whitehorse, YT Y1A 2C6
867-667-5652, Fax: 867-393-7197, environment.yukon@gov.yk.ca

Yukon Fish & Wildlife Management Board, 106 Main St., 2nd Fl., Whitehorse, YT Y1A 5P7
867-667-3754, Fax: 867-393-6947, officemanager@yfwmb.ca

FOOD

See: Agriculture; Nutrition

Prince Edward Island

BIO FOOD TECH, 101 Belvedere Ave., PO Box 2000, Charlottetown, PE C1A 7N8
902-368-5548, Fax: 902-368-5549, 877-368-5548, biofoodtech@biofoodtech.ca

FOREST RESOURCES

Northwest Territories

Forest Management Division, PO Box 7, Fort Smith, NT X0E 0P0
Fax: 867-874-2077, forestmanagement.enr.gov.nt/

Forestry Division, Petroleum Plaza ST, 9915 - 108 St. 11th Fl., Edmonton, AB T5K 2G8

Alberta

Alberta Innovates - Bio Solutions, Phipps McKinnon Bldg., 10020 - 101A Ave., Edmonton, AB T5J 3G2
780-427-1956, Fax: 780-427-3252, 877-828-0444, bio@albertainnovates.ca

British Columbia

British Columbia Ministry of Forests, Lands & Natural Resource Operations, PO Box 9352 Prov Govt,Victoria, BC V8W 9M1
250-387-4809, 877-855-3222, FLNRO.MediaRequests@gov.bc.ca

Newfoundland & Labrador

Forestry Services, Fortis Bldg., PO Box 2006, Corner Brook, NL A2H 6J8
709-637-2284, Fax: 709-634-4378

Nova Scotia

NS Primary Forest Products Marketing Board, #804, 45 Alderney Dr., Dartmouth, NS B2Y 2N6
902-424-7598, Fax: 902-424-6965

Nunavut

Department of Environment, PO Box 1000 1300,Iqaluit, NU X0A 0H0
867-975-7700, Fax: 867-975-7742, environment@gov.nu.ca

Ontario

Algonquin Forestry Authority - Huntsville, 222 Main St. West, Huntsville, ON P1H 1Y1
705-789-9647, Fax: 705-789-3353, info@algonquinforestry.on.ca

Algonquin Forestry Authority - Pembroke, Victoria Centre, 84 Isabella St., 2nd Fl., Pembroke, ON K8A 5S5
613-735-0173, Fax: 613-735-4192, info@algonquinforestry.on.ca

Policy Division, #6540, 99 Wellesley St. West, Toronto, ON M7A 1W3
Fax: 416-314-1994, 800-667-1940

Quebec

Forêt Québec, 880, ch Ste-Foy, #RC 120, Québec, QC G1S 4X4
418-627-8652, Fax: 418-528-1278, foretquebec@mrnf.gouv.qc.ca

Yukon Territory

Yukon Energy, Mines & Resources, PO Box 2703, Whitehorse, YT Y1A 2C6
867-667-3130, Fax: 867-456-3965, 800-661-0408, emr@gov.yk.ca

Yukon Environment, PO Box 2703, Whitehorse, YT Y1A 2C6
867-667-5652, Fax: 867-393-7197, environment.yukon@gov.yk.ca

FORESTRY & PAPER

Alberta

Forestry Division, Petroleum Plaza ST, 9915 - 108 St. 11th Fl., Edmonton, AB T5K 2G8

Natural Resources Canada, 580 Booth St., Ottawa, ON K1A 0E4
613-995-0947, Fax: 613-992-7211

Policy Coordination Division, Herald Bldg., PO Box 2006, Corner Brook, NL A2H 6J8
709-729-3752, Fax: 709-729-3374

Alberta

Alberta Innovates - Bio Solutions, Phipps McKinnon Bldg., 10020 - 101A Ave., Edmonton, AB T5J 3G2
780-427-1956, Fax: 780-427-3252, 877-828-0444, bio@albertainnovates.ca

British Columbia

British Columbia Ministry of Forests, Lands & Natural Resource Operations, PO Box 9352 Prov Govt,Victoria, BC V8W 9M1
250-387-4809, 877-855-3222, FLNRO.MediaRequests@gov.bc.ca

Forest Practices Board, 1675 Douglas St., 3rd Fl., PO Box 9905 Prov Govt, Victoria, BC V8W 9R1
250-213-4700, Fax: 250-213-4725, 800-994-5899, fpboard@gov.bc.ca

Timber Export Advisory Committee, PO Box 9514 Prov Govt, Victoria, BC V8W 9C2
250-387-8916, Fax: 250-387-5050

Newfoundland & Labrador

Forestry Services, Fortis Bldg., PO Box 2006, Corner Brook, NL A2H 6J8
709-637-2284, Fax: 709-634-4378

Newfoundland & Labrador Department of Natural Resources, Natural Resources Bldg., 50 Elizabeth Ave., 7th Fl., PO Box 8700, St. John's, NL A1B 4J6
709-729-2920, Fax: 709-729-0059

Nova Scotia

Department of Natural Resources, Founder's Square, 1701 Hollis St., 3rd Fl., PO Box 698, Halifax, NS B3J 2T9
902-424-5935, Fax: 902-424-0594, 800-565-2224

Ontario

Algonquin Forestry Authority - Huntsville, 222 Main St. West, Huntsville, ON P1H 1Y1
705-789-9647, Fax: 705-789-3353, info@algonquinforestry.on.ca

Algonquin Forestry Authority - Pembroke, Victoria Centre, 84 Isabella St., 2nd Fl., Pembroke, ON K8A 5S5
613-735-0173, Fax: 613-735-4192, info@algonquinforestry.on.ca

Ontario Ministry of Natural Resources, Whitney Block, #6630, 99 Wellesley St. West, 6th Fl., Toronto, ON M7A 1W3
800-667-1940

Quebec

Ministère du Développement durable, de l'Environnement, de la Faune, et des Parcs, Édifice Marie-Guyart, 675, boul René-Lévesque est, 29e étage, Québec, QC G1R 5V7
418-521-3830, Fax: 418-646-5974, 800-561-1616, info@mddep.gouv.qc.ca

Saskatchewan

Saskatchewan Environment, 3211 Albert St., 2nd Fl., Regina, SK S4S 5W6
306-787-2584, Fax: 306-787-9544, 800-567-4224, Centre.Inquiry@gov.sk.ca

Yukon Territory

Yukon Environment, PO Box 2703, Whitehorse, YT Y1A 2C6
867-667-5652, Fax: 867-393-7197, environment.yukon@gov.yk.ca

GEOLOGICAL SERVICES

Geological Survey of Canada, 601 Booth St., Ottawa, ON K1A 0E8
613-996-3919, Fax: 613-943-8742, esic@nrcan.gc.ca

Mapping Services Branch - Geomatics Canada, 615 Booth St., Ottawa, ON K1A 0E9
613-995-4945, Fax: 613-995-8737

Northwest Territories Geoscience Office, 4601 B - 52 Ave., PO Box 1500, Yellowknife, NT X1A 2R3
867-669-2636, Fax: 867-669-2725, ntgo@gov.nt.ca

Ontario Geological Survey, Willet Green Miller Centre, 933 Ramsey Lake Rd., Level B6, Sudbury, ON P3E 6B5
705-670-5758, Fax: 705-670-5818, 888-415-9845

Alberta
Energy Resources Conservation Board, #1000, 250 - 5 Ave. SW, Calgary, AB T2P 0R4
403-297-8311, Fax: 403-297-7336, 855-297-8311, inquiries@ercb.ca; infoservices@ercb.ca; ADR@ercb.ca

British Columbia
British Columbia Ministry of Energy, Mines, & Natural Gas (& Responsible for Housing), PO Box 9053 Prov Govt,Victoria, BC V8W 9E2

Nova Scotia
Geomatics Centre, 160 Willow St., Amherst, NS B4H 3W5
902-667-7231, Fax: 902-667-6008, 800-798-0706, geoinfo@gov.ns.ca

GOVERNMENT

Aboriginal Affairs & Northern Development Canada, 10 Wellington St., North Tower, Gatineau, QC K1A 0H4
819-997-0380, Fax: 866-817-3977, 800-567-9604, infopubs@aadnc-aandc.gc.ca

Auditor General of Canada, 240 Sparks St., Ottawa, ON K1A 0G6
613-995-3708, Fax: 613-957-0474, 888-761-5953, communications@oag-bvg.gc.ca; infomedia@oag-bvg.gc.ca

Bank of Canada, 234 Wellington St., Ottawa, ON K1A 0G9
613-782-7902, Fax: 613-782-7713, 800-303-1282, info@bankofcanada.ca; communications@bankofcanada.ca (Media)

British Columbia Treaty Commission, #700, 1111 Melville St., Vancouver, BC V6E 3V6
604-482-9200, Fax: 604-482-9222, 800-665-8330, info@bctreaty.net

Business Development Bank of Canada, #400, 5, Place Ville-Marie, Montréal, QC H3B 5E7
514-283-5904, Fax: 514-283-5626, 877-232-2269

Canada Economic Development for Québec Regions, Édifice Dominion Square, #900, 1255, rue Peel, Montréal, QC H3B 2T9
514-283-6412, Fax: 514-283-3302, 866-385-6412

Canada Lands Company Ltd., #1200, 1 University Ave., Toronto, ON M5J 2P1
416-952-6111, Fax: 416-952-6115, 888-252-5263

Canada Revenue Agency, 875 Heron Rd., Ottawa, ON K1A 0L5
800-267-6999

Canadian Intergovernmental Conference Secretariat, 222 Queen St., 10th Fl., PO Box 488 A,Ottawa, ON K1N 8V5
613-995-2341, Fax: 613-996-6091, info@scics.gc.ca

Canadian Nuclear Safety Commission, 280 Slater St., PO Box 1046 B,Ottawa, ON K1P 5S9
613-995-5894, Fax: 613-995-5086, 800-668-5284

Corporate Services Division, Marysville Place, PO Box 6000, Fredericton, NB E3B 5H1
506-453-3742, Fax: 506-444-4400, Reception.Marysville@gnb.ca

Defence Construction Canada, Constitution Square, 350 Albert St., 19th Fl., Ottawa, ON K1A 0K3
613-998-9548, Fax: 613-998-1061, 800-514-3555, info@dcc-cdc.gc.ca

Elections Canada, The Jackson Bldg., 257 Slater St., Ottawa, ON K1A 0M6
613-993-2975, Fax: 613-954-8584, 800-463-6868

Finance Canada, L'esplanade Laurier, 140 O'Connor St., Ottawa, ON K1A 0G5
613-992-1573, Fax: 613-943-0938, finpub@fin.gc.ca

First Nations Tax Commission, #321, 345 Yellowhead Hwy, Kamloops, BC V2H 1H1
250-828-9857, Fax: 250-828-9858, mailkamloops@fntc.ca

Foreign Affairs & International Trade Canada, 125 Sussex Dr., Ottawa, ON K1A 0G2
613-944-4000, Fax: 613-996-9709, 800-267-8376, enqserv@international.gc.ca

Fortieth Provincial Parliament - Ontario, Clerk's Office, #104, Legislative Building, Queen's Park, Toronto, ON M7A 1A2
416-325-7500, Fax: 416-325-7489, tourbookings@ontla.ola.org

Forty-first Parliament - Canada, House of Commons, Parliament Buildings, Ottawa, AB K1A 0A6

Government of Canada, c/o Canada Enquiry Centre, Service Canada, Ottawa, ON K1A 0J9
613-941-1827, 800-622-6232, canadasite@canada.gc.ca

Governor General & Commander-in-Chief of Canada, Rideau Hall, 1 Sussex Dr., Ottawa, ON K1A 0A1
613-993-8200, Fax: 613-998-8760, 800-465-6890, info@gg.ca

House of Commons, Canada, House of Commons, Centre Block, Parliament Buildings, 111 Wellington St., Ottawa, ON K1A 0A6
613-992-4793, 866-599-4999, info@parl.gc.ca

Industry Canada, C.D. Howe Building, 235 Queen St., Ottawa, ON K1A 0H5
613-954-5031, Fax: 613-954-2340, 800-328-6189, info@ic.gc.ca

International Development Research Centre, 150 Kent St., PO Box 8500, Ottawa, ON K1G 3H9
613-236-6163, Fax: 613-238-7230, info@idrc.ca

Justice Canada, East Memorial Bldg., 284 Wellington St., Ottawa, ON K1A 0H8
613-957-4222, Fax: 613-954-0811, webadmin@justice.gc.ca

National Defence Canada, Major-General George R. Pearkes Bldg., 101 Colonel By Dr., Ottawa, ON K1A 0K2
613-995-2534, Fax: 613-992-4739, 800-856-8488

North American Free Trade Agreement (NAFTA) Secretariat, Canadian Section, #705, 90 Sparks St., Ottawa, ON K1P 5B4
613-992-9388, Fax: 613-992-9392, webmaster@nafta-alena.gc.ca

Nunavut Impact Review Board, PO Box 1360, Cambridge Bay, NU X0B 0C0
867-983-4600, Fax: 867-983-2594, 866-233-3033, info@nirb.ca

Nunavut Planning Commission, PO Box 2101, Cambridge Bay, NU X0B 0C0
867-983-4625, Fax: 867-983-4626

Office of Intergovernmental Affairs, c/o Privy Council Office, #1000, 85 Slater St., Ottawa, ON K1A 0A3
613-957-5153, Fax: 613-957-5043, info@pco-bcp.gc.ca

Office of Protocol, 125 Sussex Dr., Ottawa, ON K1A 0G2
613-996-8683, Fax: 613-943-1075

Office of the Leader, Bloc Québécois, Centre Block, Ottawa, ON K1A 0A6
613-992-6779, Fax: 613-954-2121

Office of the Leader, Green Party of Canada, Confederation Building,, #518, 244 Wellington St., Ottawa, ON K1A 0A6
613-996-1119, Fax: 613-996-0850, 866-868-3447, leader@greenparty.ca; info@greenparty.ca

Office of the Leader, Official Opposition, New Democratic Party / New Democratic Party Research Bureau, 111 Wellington St., Ottawa, ON K1A 0A6
613-995-7224, Fax: 613-995-4565

Office of the Prime Minister, Conservative Party of Canada / Conservative Research Bureau, Langevin Block, 80 Wellington St., Ottawa, ON K1A 0A2
613-992-4211, Fax: 613-995-0101, pm@pm.gc.ca

Office of the Commissioner of Official Languages, 344 Slater St., 3rd fl., Ottawa, ON K1A 0T8
613-996-6368, Fax: 613-993-5082, 877-996-6368

Privy Council Office, #1000, 85 Sparks St., Ottawa, ON K1A 0A3
613-957-5153, Fax: 613-997-5043, info@pco-bcp.gc.ca

Public Service Commission, West Tower, 300 Laurier Ave. West, Ottawa, ON K1A 0M7
613-992-9562, Fax: 613-992-9352, infocom@psc-cfp.gc.ca

Public Service Staffing Tribunal, 240 Sparks St., 6th Fl., Ottawa, ON K1A 0A5
613-949-6516, Fax: 613-949-6551, 866-637-4491, info@psst-tdfp.gc.ca

Public Works & Government Services Canada, Place du Portage, Phase III, 11, rue Laurier, Ottawa, ON K1A 0S5
questions@tpsgc-pwgsc.gc.ca

Royal Canadian Mint, 320 Sussex Dr., Ottawa, ON K1A 0G8
613-993-3500, Fax: 613-993-4092, 800-267-1871

Senate of Canada, Ottawa, QC K1A 0A4
866-599-4999

Statistics Canada, R.H. Coats Bldg., Tunney's Pasture, 150 Tunney's Pasture Driveway, Ottawa, ON K1A 0T6
613-951-8116, Fax: 877-287-4369, 800-263-1136, infostats@statcan.ca

The Canadian Ministry, Information Service, Parliament of Canada, Ottawa, ON K1A 0A9
613-992-4793, 866-599-4999, info@parl.gc.ca

Treasury Board of Canada, 140 O'Connor St., Ottawa, ON K1A 0R5
613-957-2400, Fax: 613-941-4000, 877-636-0656

Alberta

Alberta Apprenticeship & Industry Training Board, Commerce Place, 10155 - 102nd St., 10th Fl., Edmonton, AB T5J 4L5
780-427-8765, Fax: 780-422-7376, -310-0000

Alberta Pensions Services Corporation, 5103 Windermere Blvd. SW, Edmonton, AB T6W 0S9
780-427-2782, 800-661-8198, memberservices@apsc.ca; employerservices@apsc.ca; pay@apsc.ca

Alberta Review Board, Oxford Tower, 10235 - 101 St., 11th Fl., Edmonton, AB T5J 3E9
780-422-5994, Fax: 780-427-1762

Alberta Office of the Auditor General, 9925 - 109 St., 8th Fl., Edmonton, AB T5K 2J8
780-427-4222, Fax: 780-422-9555, info@oag.ab.ca

Alberta Office of the Chief Electoral Officer / Elections Alberta, 11510 Kingsway Ave., 1st Fl., Edmonton, AB T5G 2Y5
780-427-7191, Fax: 780-422-2900, info@electionsalberta.ab.ca

Alberta Office of the Ethics Commissioner, #1250, 9925 - 109 St. NW, Edmonton, AB T5K 2J8
780-422-2273, Fax: 780-422-2261, generalinfo@ethicscommissioner.ab.ca

Executive Council, Legislature Building, 10800 - 97 Ave., Edmonton, AB T5K 2B6
780-427-2711, -310-0000

Government of Alberta, PO Box 1333, Edmonton, AB T5J 2N2
780-427-2711, Fax: 780-422-2852, -310-0000

Alberta Office of the Information & Privacy Commissioner, Office of the Information & Privacy Commissioner (Edmonton), #410, 9925 - 109 St., 4th Fl., Edmonton, AB T5K 2J8
780-422-6860, Fax: 780-422-5682, 888-878-4044, generalinfo@oipc.ab.ca

Alberta Infrastructure, Infrastructure Building, 6950 - 113 St., Edmonton, AB T6H 5V7
780-415-0507, Fax: 780-427-2187, -310-0000, Infra.Contact.Us.m@gov.ab.ca

Alberta International & Intergovernmental Relations, Commerce Place, 10155 - 102 St., 12th Fl., Edmonton, AB T5J 4G8
780-422-1510, -310-0000

Legislative Assembly of Alberta, Legislature Annex, 9718 - 107 St., Edmonton, AB T5K 1E4
780-427-2826, Fax: 780-427-1623, laocommunications@assembly.ab.ca

Office of the Lieutenant Governor, Office of the Lieutenant Governor of AB, Legislature Bldg., 10800 - 97 Ave., 3rd Fl., Edmonton, AB T5K 2B6
780-427-7243, Fax: 780-422-5134, ltgov@gov.ab.ca

Alberta Municipal Affairs, Communications Branch, Commerce Place, 10155 - 102 St., 18th Fl., Edmonton, AB T5J 4L4
780-427-2732, Fax: 780-422-1419, comments@gov.ab.ca

Alberta Office of the Ombudsman, Canadian Western Bank Building, #2800, 10303 Jasper Ave. NW, 28th Fl., Edmonton, AB T5J 5C3
780-427-2756, Fax: 780-427-2759, 888-455-2756, info@ombudsman.ab.ca

Office of the Premier, Office of the Premier, Legislature Building, #307, 10800 - 97 Ave., Edmonton, AB T5K 2B6
780-427-2251, Fax: 780-427-1349, -310-0000

Alberta Public Affairs Bureau, Park Plaza, 10611 - 98 Ave., 6th Fl., Edmonton, AB T5K 2P7
780-427-2754, Fax: 780-422-4168, -310-0000

Registry Services, Telus Plaza South, 10020 - 100 St., 29th Fl., Edmonton, AB T5J 0N3

Special Areas Board, Special Areas Board Administration, 212 - 2nd Ave. West, PO Box 820, Hanna, AB T0J 1P0
403-854-5600, Fax: 403-854-5527, specarea@telus.net

Alberta Treasury Board & Finance, Oxbridge Place, 9820 - 106 St., 5th Fl., Edmonton, AB T5K 2J6
780-415-4519, -310-000

Twenty-eighth Legislature - Alberta, Legislature Bldg., 10800 - 97 Ave., Edmonton, AB T5K 2B6
780-427-2826, laocommunications@assembly.ab.ca

British Columbia

Agricultural Land Commission, #133, 4940 Canada Way, Burnaby, BC V5G 4K6
604-660-7000, Fax: 604-660-7033, ALCBurnaby@Victoria1.gov.bc.ca

Office of the Auditor General, PO Box 9036 Prov Govt,Victoria, BC V8W 9A2
250-419-6100, Fax: 250-387-1230

BC Legislative Assembly & Independent Offices, Clerk's Office, #221, Parliament Bldgs., Victoria, BC V8V 1X4
250-387-3785, Fax: 250-387-0942, ClerkHouse@leg.bc.ca

British Columbia Assessment Authority, #400, 3450 Uptown Blvd., Victoria, BC V8Z 0B9
250-595-6211, Fax: 250-595-6222, info@bcassessment.ca

British Columbia Public Service Agency, #4, 810 Blanshard St., PO Box 9404 Prov Govt,Victoria, BC V8W 9V1
250-387-0518, Fax: 250-356-7074

British Columbia Utilities Commission, 900 Howe St., 6th Fl., PO Box 250, Vancouver, BC V6Z 2N3
604-660-4700, Fax: 604-660-1102, 800-663-1385, commission.secretary@bcuc.com

Office of the Conflict of Interest Commissioner, #101, 431 Menzies St., Victoria, BC V8V 1X4
250-356-0750, Fax: 250-356-6580, conflictofinterest@coibc.ca

Court Services Branch, PO Box 9249 Prov Govt,Victoria, BC V8W 9J2
250-356-1550, Fax: 250-356-8152

Crown Agencies Resource Office, PO Box 9469 Prov Govt, Victoria, BC V8V 9V8
250-387-8770, Fax: 250-387-9061, CAS@gov.bc.ca

Elections British Columbia, PO Box 9275 Prov Govt,Victoria, BC V8W 9J6
250-387-5305, Fax: 250-387-3578, 800-661-8683, electionsbc@elections.bc.ca

Executive Council of the Government of British Columbia, Cabinet Operations, 617 Government St., 1st Fl., PO Box 9487 Prov Govt,Victoria, BC V8W 9W6

Government of British Columbia, Parliament Bldgs., Victoria, BC V8V 1X4
250-387-6121, 800-663-7867

Office of the Information & Privacy Commissioner for British Columbia, 947 Fort St., 4th Fl., PO Box 9038 Prov Govt,Victoria, BC V8W 9A4
250-387-5629, Fax: 250-387-1696, 800-663-7867, info@oipc.bc.ca
Office of the Lieutenant Governor, Government House, 1401 Rockland Ave., Victoria, BC V8S 1V9
250-387-2080, Fax: 250-387-2078, ghinfo@gov.bc.ca
Office of the Ombudsperson, 947 Fort St., 2nd Fl., PO Box 9039 Prov Govt,Victoria, BC V8W 9A5
250-387-5855, Fax: 250-387-0198, 800-567-3247, systems@bcombudsperson.ca (Information technology inquiries)
Office of the Premier, West Annex, Parliament Bldgs., PO Box 9041 Prov Govt,Victoria, BC V8W 9E1
250-387-1715, Fax: 250-387-0087, premier@gov.bc.ca
Thirty-ninth Legislature - British Columbia, Parliament Buildings, Victoria, BC V8V 1X4
250-387-3785, Fax: 250-387-0942, ClerkHouse@leg.bc.ca

Manitoba

Aboriginal Affairs Secretariat, #200, 500 Portage Ave., Winnipeg, MB R3C 3X1
204-945-2510, Fax: 204-945-3689
Office of the Auditor General, #500, 330 Portage Ave., Winnipeg, MB R3C 0C4
204-945-3790, Fax: 204-945-2169, oag.contact@oag.mb.ca
Board of Electrical Examiners, #500, 401 York Ave, Winnipeg, MB R3C 0P8
204-945-3507, terry.rieger@gov.mb.ca
Civil Service Commission Board, #935, 155 Carlton St., Winnipeg, MB R3C 3H8
204-945-1435, Fax: 204-945-1486
Manitoba Civil Service Commission, #935, 155 Carlton St., Winnipeg, MB R3C 3H8
204-945-2332, Fax: 204-945-1486, 800-282-8069, cschrp@gov.mb.ca
Crown Corporations Council, #1130, 444 St. Mary Ave., Winnipeg, MB R3C 3T1
204-949-5270, Fax: 204-949-5283, crowncc@mts.net
Elections Manitoba, #120, 200 Vaughan St., Winnipeg, MB R3C 1T5
204-945-3225, Fax: 204-945-6011, 866-628-6837, election@elections.mb.ca
Executive Council, Legislative Building, 450 Broadway Ave., Winnipeg, MB R3C 0V8
Federal-Provincial Relations & Research Division, #910, 386 Broadway, Winnipeg, MB R3C 3R6
204-945-3757, Fax: 204-945-5051
Fortieth Legislature - Manitoba, Legislative Building, 450 Broadway Ave., Winnipeg, MB R3C 0V8
204-945-3636, Fax: 204-948-2507, clerkla@leg.gov.mb.ca
Government of Manitoba, Legislative Building, Rm. 237, Winnipeg, MB R3C 0V8
204-945-3636, Fax: 204-948-2507, clerkla@leg.gov.mb.ca
Office of the Lieutenant Governor, Legislative Building, #235, 450 Broadway Ave., Winnipeg, MB R3C 0V8
204-945-2753, Fax: 204-945-4329, ltgov@leg.gov.mb.ca
Local Government Development Division, 59 Elizabeth Dr., PO Box 33, Thompson, MB R8N 1X4
204-677-6794, Fax: 204-677-6525
Manitoba Local Government, #301, 450 Broadway Ave., Winnipeg, MB R3C 0V8
Fax: 204-945-1383, mnia@leg.gov.mb.ca
Manitoba Land Value Appraisal Commission, 800 Portage Ave., Winnipeg, MB R3G 0N4
204-945-2941, Fax: 204-948-2235
Manitoba Legislative Assembly, c/o Clerk's Office, Legislative Bldg., #237, 450 Broadway, Winnipeg, MB R3C 0V8
204-945-3636, Fax: 204-948-2507, clerkla@leg.gov.mb.ca
Manitoba Municipal Board, #1144, 363 Broadway, Winnipeg, MB R3C 3N9
204-945-2941, Fax: 204-948-2235
News Media Services, Legislative Bldg., #29, 450 Broadway Ave., Winnipeg, MB R3C 0V8
204-945-3746, Fax: 204-945-3988, nmservices@leg.gov.mb.ca
Manitoba Office of the Ombudsman, 750 - 500 Portage Ave., Winnipeg, MB R3C 3X1
204-982-9130, Fax: 204-942-7803, 800-665-0531, ombudsma@ombudsman.mb.ca
Office of the Premier, Legislative Building, #204, 450 Broadway Ave., Winnipeg, MB R3C 0V8
204-945-3714, Fax: 204-949-1484, premier@leg.gov.mb.ca
Provincial-Municipal Support Services, #508, 800 Portage Ave., Winnipeg, MB R3G 0N4
Residential Tenancies Commission, #1650, 155 Carlton St., Winnipeg, MB R3C 3H8
204-945-2028, Fax: 204-945-5453, 800-782-8403, rtc@gov.mb.ca
Manitoba Treasury Board Secretariat, #200, 386 Broadway, Winnipeg, MB R3C 3R6
204-945-4150, Fax: 204-948-4878

New Brunswick

Office of the Auditor General, HSBC Place, 520 King St., 6th Fl., Fredericton, NB E3B 6G3
506-453-2243, Fax: 506-453-3067
Communications Division, Centennial Bldg., PO Box 6000, Fredericton, NB E3B 5H1
506-453-8607, Fax: 506-453-3993,
Office of the Comptroller, Centennial Bldg., 670 King St., Fredericton, NB E3B 1G1
506-453-2565, Fax: 506-453-2917, wwwooc@gnb.ca
Office of the Chief Electoral Officer, PO Box 6000, Fredericton, NB E3B 5H1
506-453-2218, Fax: 506-457-4926, 800-308-2922
Executive Council, Centennial Building, PO Box 6000, Fredericton, NB E3B 5H1
506-444-4417, Fax: 506-453-2266, Executivecounciloffice@gnb.ca
Fifty-seventh Legislative Assembly - New Brunswick, Centre Block, Legislative Building, 706 Queen St., PO Box 6000, Fredericton, NB E3B 5H1
506-453-2506, Fax: 506-453-7154, wwwleg@gnb.ca
Finance & Administration, Centennial Bldg., #375, 670 King St., PO Box 6000, Fredericton, NB E3B 5H1
506-453-2451, Fax: 506-444-4724
Government of New Brunswick, PO Box 6000, Fredericton, NB E3B 5H1
Intergovernmental Affairs Division, Centennial Bldg., #274, 670 King St., PO Box 6000, Fredericton, NB E3B 5H1
506-457-7275, Fax: 506-453-2995, iga@gnb.ca
Legislative Assembly of New Brunswick, Centre Block, Legislative Building, 706 Queen St., PO Box 6000, Fredericton, NB E3B 5H1
506-453-2506, Fax: 506-453-7154, wwwleg@gnb.ca
New Brunswick Department of Government Services, Marysville Place, 20 McGloin St., Fredericton, NB E3A 5T8
506-453-6100, Fax: 506-462-5049
Office of the Lieutenant-Governor, Government House, 51 Woodstock Rd., PO Box 6000, Fredericton, NB E3B 5H1
506-453-2505, Fax: 506-444-5280, LTgov@gnb.ca
Office of the Ombudsman, 767 Brunswick St., PO Box 6000, Fredericton, NB E3B 5H1
506-453-2789, Fax: 506-453-5599, 800-465-1100, nbombud@gnb.ca
Office of the Premier, Centennial Bldg., 670 King St., PO Box 6000, Fredericton, NB E3B 5H1
506-453-2144, Fax: 506-453-7407, premier@gnb.ca

Newfoundland & Labrador

Office of the Auditor General, PO Box 8700, St. John's, NL A1B 4J6
709-729-2695, Fax: 709-729-5970, oagmail@oag.nl.ca
Office of the Chief Electoral Officer, 39 Hallett Cr., St. John's, NL A1B 4C4
709-729-0712, Fax: 709-729-0679, 877-729-7987, enl@gov.nl.ca
Executive Council, c/o Communications Branch, East Block, Confederation Building, 10th Fl., St. John's, NL A1B 4J6
info@gov.nl.ca
Forty-seventh House of Assembly - Newfoundland & Labrador, Confederation Building, PO Box 8700, St. John's, NL A1B 4J6
709-729-3405, ClerkHOA@gov.nl.ca
Government of Newfoundland & Labrador, Confederation Bldg., St. John's, NL A1B 4J6
info@gov.nl.ca
House of Assembly, c/o Clerk's Office, Confederation Bldg., PO Box 8700, St. John's, NL A1B 4J6
709-729-3405, Fax: 709-729-4820
Office of the Lieutenant Governor, Government House, Military Rd., PO Box 5517, St. John's, NL A1C 5W4
709-729-4494, Fax: 709-729-2234, governmenthouse@gov.nl.ca
Newfoundland & Labrador Department of Municipal Affairs, West Block, Main Fl., Confederation Bldg., PO Box 8700, St. John's, NL A1B 4J6
709-729-3046, Fax: 709-729-0943, mainfo@gov.nl.ca
Newfoundland & Labrador Department of Service NL, PO Box 8700, St. John's, NL A1B 4J6
709-729-4834, gsinfo@gov.nl.ca
Newfoundland & Labrador Municipal Financing Corporation, Confederation Bldg., PO Box 8700, St. John's, NL A1B 4J6
709-729-6686, Fax: 709-729-2095
Office of the Premier, East Block, Confederation Bldg., PO Box 8700, St. John's, NL A1B 4J6
709-729-3570, Fax: 709-729-5875, premier@gov.nl.ca

Northwest Territories

Office of the Commissioner, #803 Northwest Tower, PO Box 1320, Yellowknife, NT X1A 2L9
867-873-7400, Fax: 867-873-0223, 888-270-3318, commissioner@gov.nt.ca
Department of Aboriginal Affairs & Intergovernmental Relations, 4910 - 52nd St., PO Box 1320, Yellowknife, NT X1A 2L9
867-873-7143, Fax: 867-873-0233, 877-838-8194, nancy_gardiner@gov.nt.ca
Department of Public Works & Services, PO Box 1320, Yellowknife, NT X1A 2L9
Executive Council, PO Box 1320, Yellowknife, NT X1A 2L9
executive@gov.nt.ca
Financial Management Board Secretariat, c/o Secretary of the FMB / Comptroller General, 5003 - 49 St., PO Box 1320, Yellowknife, NT X1A 2L9
Government of the Northwest Territories, PO Box 1320, Yellowknife, NT X1A 2L9
NWT Legislative Assembly, c/o Clerk's Office, PO Box 1320, Yellowknife, NT X1A 2L9
867-669-2299, Fax: 867-920-4735, 800-661-0784
Office of the Premier, Legislative Assembly Bldg., PO Box 1320, Yellowknife, NT X1A 2L9
867-669-2311, Fax: 867-873-0385, premier@gov.nt.ca
Seventeenth Legislature - Northwest Territories, PO Box 1320, Yellowknife, NT X1A 2L9
867-669-2200, Fax: 867-920-4735, 800-661-0784

Nova Scotia

Office of the Auditor General, #302, 1888 Brunswick St., Halifax, NS B3J 3J8
902-424-5907, Fax: 902-424-4350
Council of Atlantic Premiers, Council Secretariat, #1006, 5161 George St., PO Box 2044, Halifax, NS B3J 2Z1
902-424-7590, Fax: 902-424-8976, info@cap-cpma.ca
Crown Land Information Management Centre, Founders Square, #501, 1701 Hollis St., PO Box 698, Halifax, NS B3J 2T9
902-424-3171
Elections Nova Scotia, #6-7037 Mumford Rd., PO Box 2246, Halifax, NS B3J 2J1
902-424-8584, Fax: 902-424-6622, 800-565-1504, elections@gov.ns.ca
Executive Council, One Government Place, 1700 Granville St., 5th Fl., PO Box 2125, Halifax, NS B3J 3B7
902-424-5970, Fax: 902-424-0667, execounc@gov.ns.ca
Government of Nova Scotia, Province House, 1726 Hollis St., Halifax, NS B3J 2T3
Legislative House of Assembly, c/o Clerk's Office, Province House, 1st Fl., PO Box 1617, Halifax, NS B3J 2Y3
902-424-5978, Fax: 902-424-0632
Office of the Lieutenant Governor, Government House, 1451 Barrington St., Halifax, NS B3J 1Z2
902-424-7001, Fax: 902-424-0537, lgoffice@gov.ns.ca
Office of the Ombudsman, #700, 5670 Spring Garden Rd., PO Box 2152, Halifax, NS B3J 3B7
902-424-6780, Fax: 902-424-6675, 800-670-1111, ombudsman@gov.ns.ca
Office of the Premier, One Government Place, 1700 Granville St., 7th Fl., PO Box 726, Halifax, NS B3J 2T3
902-424-6600, Fax: 902-424-7648, 800-267-1993, premier@gov.ns.ca
Department of Service Nova Scotia & Municipal Relations, 1505 Barrington St., PO Box 216, Halifax, NS B3J 3K5
902-424-5200, Fax: 902-424-0581, 800-670-4357, askus@gov.ns.ca
Sixty-first Assembly - Nova Scotia, Province House, 1726 Hollis St., Halifax, NS B3J 2Y3
902-424-4661, Fax: 902-424-0574
Nova Scotia Treasury & Policy Board, 1700 Granville St., 5th Fl., PO Box 1617, Halifax, NS B3J 2Y3
902-424-8910, Fax: 902-424-7638, TBenquiries@gov.ns.ca
Nova Scotia Utility & Review Board, Summit Place, 1601 Lower Water St., 3rd Fl., PO Box 1692 M,Halifax, NS B3J 3S3
902-424-4448, Fax: 902-424-3919, uarb.board@gov.ns.ca

Nunavut

Department of Community & Government Services, W.G. Brown Bldg., 4th Fl., PO Box 1000 700,Iqaluit, NU X0A 0H0
867-975-5400, Fax: 867-975-5305
Department of Culture, Language, Elders & Youth, PO Box 1000 800,Iqaluit, NU X0A 0H0
867-975-5500, Fax: 867-975-5504, 866-934-2035
Department of Education, Sivummut Bldg., 2nd Fl., PO Box 1000 910,Iqaluit, NU X0A 0H0
867-975-5600, Fax: 867-975-5605
Department of Environment, PO Box 1000 1300,Iqaluit, NU X0A 0H0
867-975-7700, Fax: 867-975-7742, environment@gov.nu.ca
Department of Executive & Intergovernmental Affairs, 1084 Aeroplex bldg., PO Box 1000 200,Iqaluit, NU X0A 0H0
867-975-6000, Fax: 867-975-6099
Department of Finance, Bldg. 1079, 1st Fl., PO Box 1000 330,Iqaluit, NU X0A 0H0
867-975-5800, Fax: 867-975-5805
Department of Health & Social Services, PO Box 1000 1000,Iqaluit, NU X0A 0H0
867-975-5700, Fax: 867-975-5705

Department of Human Resources, PO Box 1000 400,Iqaluit, NU X0A 1H0
Fax: 867-975-6216, 888-668-9993, gnhr@gov.nu.ca
Department of Justice, Sivummut, 1st Fl., PO Box 1000 500,Iqaluit, NU X0A 0H0
867-975-6170, Fax: 867-975-6195, justice@gov.nu.ca
Nunavut Emergency Management, PO Box 1000 700,Iqaluit, NU X0A 0H0
867-975-5403, Fax: 867-979-4221, 800-693-1666
Executive Council, Legislative Bldg., 2nd Fl., Box 2410, Iqaluit, NU X0A 0H0
867-975-5090, Fax: 867-975-5095
Government of Nunavut, PO Box 1200, Iqaluit, NU X0A 0H0
888-252-9869, info@gov.nu.ca
Nunavut Legislative Assembly, 926 Federal Rd., PO Box 1200, Iqaluit, NU X0A 0H0
867-975-5000, Fax: 867-975-5190, 877-334-7266, leginfo@assembly.nu.ca
Office of the Commissioner, PO Box 2379, Iqaluit, NU X0A 0H0
867-975-5120, Fax: 867-975-5123, nunavutcommissioner@gov.nu.ca
Office of the Premier, Legislative Assembly Bldg., 2nd Fl., PO Box 2410, Iqaluit, NU X0A 0H0
867-975-5050, Fax: 867-975-5051
Third Legislature - Nunavut, PO Box 1200, Iqaluit, NU X0A 0H0

Ontario

Office of the Auditor General, Atrium on Bay, #1530, 20 Dundas St. West, PO Box 105, Toronto, ON M5G 2C2
416-327-2381, Fax: 416-327-9862, comments@auditor.on.ca
Cancer Care Ontario, 620 University Ave., 15th Fl., Toronto, ON M5G 2L7
416-971-9800, Fax: 416-971-6888
Elections Ontario, 51 Rolark Dr., Toronto, ON M1R 3B1
416-326-6300, Fax: 416-326-6200, 888-668-8683, info@elections.on.ca
Executive Council, Whitney Block, Queen's Park, 99 Wellesley St. West, 6th Fl., Toronto, ON M7A 1A1
416-325-5721, Fax: 416-314-1551
Government of Ontario, Queen's Park, Toronto, ON M7A 1A2
416-326-1234, 800-267-8097
Office of the Integrity Commissioner, #2101, 2 Bloor St. East, Toronto, ON M4W 1A8
416-314-8983, Fax: 416-314-8987, integrity.mail@oico.on.ca
Ontario Ministry of Intergovernmental Affairs, 77 Wellesley St. West, Toronto, ON M7A 1N3
416-325-4800, Fax: 416-325-4787
Office of the Lieutenant Governor, Room 131, Legislative Bldg., Queen's Park, Toronto, ON M7A 1A1
416-325-7780, Fax: 416-325-7787, ltgov@gov.on.ca
Ontario Ministry of Municipal Affairs & Housing, College Park, 777 Bay St., 17th Fl., Toronto, ON M5G 2E5
416-585-7041, Fax: 416-585-6470, 866-220-2290, mininfo@ontario.ca
Office of the Ombudsman, Bell Trinity Sq., South Tower, 483 Bay St., 10th Fl., Toronto, ON M5G 2C9
416-586-3300, Fax: 416-586-3485, 800-263-1830, info@ombudsman.on.ca
Ontario Legislative Assembly, c/o Clerk's Office, #104, Legislative Bldg., Queen's Park, Toronto, ON M7A 1A2
416-325-7500, Fax: 416-325-7489, assemblyinternet@ontla.ola.org
Ontario Mental Health Foundation, 441 Jarvis St., 2nd Fl., Toronto, ON M4Y 2G8
416-920-7721, Fax: 416-920-0026, grants@omhf.on.ca
Ontario Northland, 555 Oak St. East, North Bay, ON P1B 8L3
705-472-4500, Fax: 705-472-4267, 800-363-7512, info@ontarionorthland.ca
Ontario Pension Board, Sun Life Bldg., #2200, 200 King St. West, Toronto, ON M5H 3X6
416-364-8558, Fax: 416-364-7578, 800-668-6203, office.services@opb.on.ca
Office of the Premier, Legislative Bldg., #281, 1 Queen's Park Cres. South, Toronto, ON M7A 1A1
416-325-1941, Fax: 416-325-3745

Prince Edward Island

Elections Prince Edward Island, J. Angus MacLean Bldg., 94 Great George St., 1st Fl., PO Box 774, Charlottetown, PE C1A 7L3
902-368-5895, Fax: 902-368-6500, 888-234-8783
Executive Council, Shaw Bldg., 5th Fl., PO Box 2000, Charlottetown, PE C1A 7N8
902-368-4502, Fax: 902-368-6118
Government of Prince Edward Island, Island Information Service, PO Box 2000, Charlottetown, PE C1A 7N8
902-368-4000, island@gov.pe.ca
Office of the Premier, Shaw Bldg., 95 Rochford St. South, 5th Fl., PO Box 2000, Charlottetown, PE C1A 7N8
902-368-4501, Fax: 902-368-6118
Prince Edward Island Legislative Assembly, Province House, 165 Richmond St., 1st Fl., PO Box 2000, Charlottetown, PE C1A 7N8
902-368-5970, Fax: 902-368-5175, 877-315-5518, legislativelibrary@assembly.pe.ca
Sixty-fourth General Assembly - Prince Edward Island, Province House, 165 Richmond St., 1st Fl., PO Box 2000, Charlottetown, PE C1A 7N8
902-368-5970, Fax: 902-368-5175, 877-315-5518

Quebec

Ministère des Affaires municipales, des Régions et de l'Occupation du territoire, Aile Chaveau, 10, rue Pierre-Olivier-Chauveau, 3e étage, Québec, QC G1R 4J3
418-691-2019, Fax: 418-643-7385, communications@mamrot.gouv.qc.ca
Bureau du coroner, Édifice le Delta 2, #390, 2875, boul Laurier, Québec, QC G1V 5B1
418-643-1845, Fax: 418-643-6174, 866-312-7051, clientele.coroner@msp.gouv.qc.ca
Centre de recherche industrielle du Québec, 333, rue Franquet, Québec, QC G1P 4C7
418-659-1550, Fax: 418-652-2251, 800-667-2386, infocriq@criq.qc.ca
Comité de déontologie policière, Tour du Saint-Laurent, #A-200, 2525, boul Laurier, 2e étage, Québec, QC G1V 4Z6
418-646-1936, Fax: 418-528-0987, comite.deontologie@msp.gouv.qc.ca
Commissaire à la déontologie policière, #1-40, 1200, rte de l'Église, Québec, QC G1V 4Y9
418-643-7897, Fax: 418-528-9473, 877-237-7897, deontologie-policiere.quebec@msp.gouv.qc.ca
Commissariat des incendies, 455, rue Dupont, Québec, QC G1K 6N2
418-529-5706, Fax: 418-529-9922, cdelage@notarius.net
Commission de la fonction publique (Québec), 800, Place d'Youville, 7e étage, Québec, QC G1R 3P4
418-643-1425, Fax: 418-643-7264, 800-432-0432, cfp@cfp.gouv.qc.ca
Commission québecoise des libérations conditionnelles, #1.32A, 300, boul Jean-Lesage, Québec, QC G1K 8K6
418-646-8300, Fax: 418-643-7217, cqlc@msp.gouv.qc.ca
Ministère du Conseil exécutif, 875, Grande Allée est, Québec, QC G1R 4Y8
418-646-3021, Fax: 418-528-9242
Direction générale de la Sûreté du Québec, 1701, rue Parthenais, Montréal, QC H2K 3S7
514-598-4141, Fax: 514-598-4242
Commission des droits de la personne et des droits de la jeunesse, 360, rue St-Jacques, 2e étage, Montréal, QC H2Y 1P5
514-873-5146, Fax: 514-873-6032, 800-361-6477, accueil@cdpdj.qc.ca
Ministère du Développement économique, de l'Innovation et de l'Exportation, 710, place D'Youville, 3e étage, Québec, QC G1R 4Y4
418-691-5950, Fax: 418-644-0118, 866-680-1884
Commission de la fonction publique, 800, place D'Youville, 7e étage, Québec, QC G1R 3P4
418-643-1425, Fax: 418-643-7264, 800-432-0432, cfp@cfp.gouv.qc.ca
Gouvernement du Québec, Hôtel du Parlement, 1045, rue des Parlementaires, Québec, QC G1A 1A3
418-643-7239, Fax: 418-646-4271, 866-337-8837
Ministère de l'Immigration et des Communautés culturelles, Édifice Gérald-Godin, 360, rue McGill, Montréal, QC H2Y 2E9
514-864-9191, Fax: 514-864-2899, 877-864-9191
L'Assemblée nationale, Hôtel du Parlement, 1045, rue des Parlementaires, Québec, QC G1A 1A3
418-643-7239, Fax: 418-646-4271, 866-337-8837, responsable.contenu@assnat.qc.ca
Cabinet du Lieutenant-gouverneur, Édifice André-Laurendeau, 1050, rue des Parlementaires R.C., Québec, QC G1A 1A1
418-643-5385, Fax: 418-644-4677, 866-791-0766
Cabinet du premier ministre, Édifice Honoré-Mercier, 835, boul René-Lévesque est, 3e étage, Québec, QC G1A 1B4
418-643-5321, Fax: 418-643-3924
Ministère des Relations internationales, Édifice Hector-Fabre, 525, boul Réne-Lévesque est, Québec, QC G1R 5R9
418-649-2300, Fax: 418-649-2656
Ministère des Ressources naturelles, 880, ch Sainte-Foy, Québec, QC G1S 4X4
418-627-8600, Fax: 418-644-6513, 866-248-6936, services.clientele@mrnf.gouv.qc.ca
Régie des alcools, des courses et des jeux, 560, boul Charest est, Québec, QC G1K 3J3
418-643-7667, Fax: 418-643-5971, 800-363-0320
Secrétariat aux affaires intergouvernementales canadiennes, 875, Grande Allée est, 3e étage, Québec, QC G1R 4Y8
418-643-4011, Fax: 418-528-0052
Trente-neuvième assemblée nationale, Hôtel du Parlement, 1045, rue des Parlementaires, Québec, QC G1A 1A4
418-643-7239, Fax: 418-646-4271, 866-337-8837
École nationale de police du Québec, 350, rue Marguerite-d'Youville, Nicolet, QC J3T 1X4
819-293-8631, Fax: 819-293-8630, courriel@enpq.qc.ca
Directeur général des Élections du Québec, Édifice René-Lévesque, 3460, rue de La Pérade, Québec, QC G1X 3Y5
418-528-0422, Fax: 418-643-7291, 888-353-2846, info@electionsquebec.qc.ca

Saskatchewan

Board of Revenue Commissioners, #480, 2151 Scarth St., Regina, SK S4P 2H8
306-787-6221, Fax: 306-787-1610
Elections Saskatchewan, 1702 Park St., Regina, SK S4N 6B2
306-787-4000, Fax: 306-787-4052, 877-958-8683, info@elections.sk.ca
Executive Council, Communications Services, Executive Council, #130, 3085 Albert St., Regina, SK S4S 0B1
306-787-6276, Fax: 306-787-6123, commserv@gov.sk.ca
Government of Saskatchewan, Regina, SK S4S 0B3
Government Services, 1920 Rose St., Regina, SK S4P 0A9
306-787-6911, Fax: 306-787-1061, GSReception@gs.gov.sk.ca
Legislative Assembly of Saskatchewan, Office of the Clerk, Legislative Building, #239, 2405 Legislative Dr., Regina, SK S4S 0B3
info@legassembly.sk.ca
Office of the Lieutenant Governor, Government House, 4607 Dewdney Ave., Regina, SK S4T 1B7
306-787-4070, Fax: 306-787-7716, lgo@ltgov.sk.ca
Office of the Premier, Legislative Building, #226, 2405 Legislative Dr., Regina, SK S4S 0B3
306-787-9433, Fax: 306-787-0885,
Ombudsman Saskatchewan, #150, 2401 Saskatchewan Dr., Regina, SK S4P 4H8
306-787-6211, Fax: 306-787-9090, 800-667-7180, ombreg@ombudsman.sk.ca
Provincial Auditor Saskatchewan, #1500, 1920 Broad St., Regina, SK S4P 3V2
306-787-6398, Fax: 306-787-6383, info@auditor.sk.ca
Saskatchewan Development Fund Corporation, #400, 2400 College Ave., Regina, SK S4P 1C8
306-787-1645, Fax: 306-787-8125
Twenty-seventh Legislature - Saskatchewan, 2405 Legislative Dr., Regina, SK S4S 0B3

Yukon Territory

Office of the Commissioner, Closeleigh Manor, 1098 First Ave., Whitehorse, YT Y1A 0C1
867-667-5121, Fax: 867-393-6201, commissioner@gov.yk.ca
Executive Council, #2071, 2nd Ave., Whitehorse, YT Y1A 2C6
867-667-5393, Fax: 867-393-6214, eco@gov.yk.ca
Government of the Yukon Territory, PO Box 2703, Whitehorse, YT Y1A 2C6
867-667-5811, 800-661-0408
Office of the Premier, 2071 Second Ave., PO Box 2703, Whitehorse, YT Y1A 1B2
867-667-8660, Fax: 867-393-6252, premier@gov.yk.ca
Yukon Public Service Commission, Yukon Government Administration Building, #2071-2nd Ave., PO Box 2703, Whitehorse, YT Y1A 2C6
867-667-5653, Fax: 867-667-5755, 800-661-0408, PSCWebsite@gov.yk.ca
Thirty-third Legislative Assembly - Yukon Territory, Yukon Legislative Assembly Office, 2071 Second Ave., PO Box 2703, Whitehorse, YT Y1A 2C6
867-667-5498
Yukon Legislative Assembly, PO Box 2703, Whitehorse, YT Y1A 2C6
867-667-5498, Fax: 867-393-6280, yla@gov.yk.ca

GOVERNMENT (GENERAL INFORMATION)

Aboriginal Affairs & Northern Development Canada, 10 Wellington St., North Tower, Gatineau, QC K1A 0H4
819-997-0380, Fax: 866-817-3977, 800-567-9604, infopubs@aadnc-aandc.gc.ca
Auditor General of Canada, 240 Sparks St., Ottawa, ON K1A 0G6
613-995-3708, Fax: 613-957-0474, 888-761-5953, communications@oag-bvg.gc.ca; infomedia@oag-bvg.gc.ca
Canada Business Network, 235 Queen St., Ottawa, ON K1A 0H5
888-576-4444
Citizenship & Immigration Canada, Jean Edmonds, South Tower, 365 Laurier Ave. West, Ottawa, ON K1A 1L1
613-954-9019, Fax: 613-954-2221, 888-242-2100
Communications & Consultations Branch, Tower 7, 1341 Baseline Rd., Ottawa, ON K1A 0C7
613-759-1000, Fax: 613-773-2772
Communications Branch, 284 Wellington St., Ottawa, ON K1A 0H8
Fax: 613-941-2329

Consultations & Communications Branch, East Tower, 140 O'Connor St., 19th Fl., Ottawa, ON K1A 0G5
613-992-1573, finpub@fin.gc.ca
Correctional Service Canada, 340 Laurier Ave. West, Ottawa, ON K1A 0P9
613-992-5891, Fax: 613-943-1630
Environment Canada, 10 Wellington St., Gatineau, QC K1A 0H3
819-997-2800, Fax: 819-994-1412, 800-668-6767, enviroinfo@ec.gc.ca
Fisheries & Oceans Canada, 200 Kent St., Ottawa, ON K1A 0E6
613-993-0999, Fax: 613-990-1866, info@dfo-mpo.gc.ca
Foreign Affairs & International Trade Canada, 125 Sussex Dr., Ottawa, ON K1A 0G2
613-944-4000, Fax: 613-996-9709, 800-267-8376, enqserv@international.gc.ca
Health Canada, Tunney's Pasture, Ottawa, ON K1A 0K9
613-957-2991, Fax: 613-941-5366, 866-225-0709, info@hc-sc.gc.ca
House of Commons, Canada, House of Commons, Centre Block, Parliament Buildings, 111 Wellington St., Ottawa, ON K1A 0A6
613-992-4793, 866-599-4999, info@parl.gc.ca
Human Resources & Skills Development Canada, 140 Promenade du Portage, Gatineau, QC K1A 0J9
Industry Canada, C.D. Howe Building, 235 Queen St., Ottawa, ON K1A 0H5
613-954-5031, Fax: 613-954-2340, 800-328-6189, info@ic.gc.ca
National Defence Canada, Major-General George R. Pearkes Bldg., 101 Colonel By Dr., Ottawa, ON K1A 0K2
613-995-2534, Fax: 613-992-4739, 800-856-8488
Office of the Prime Minister, Conservative Party of Canada / Conservative Research Bureau, Langevin Block, 80 Wellington St., Ottawa, ON K1A 0A2
613-992-4211, Fax: 613-995-0101, pm@pm.gc.ca
Service Canada, 140, Promenade du Portage, Gatineau, QC K1A 0J9
800-622-6232
Statistics Canada, R.H. Coats Bldg., Tunney's Pasture, 150 Tunney's Pasture Driveway, Ottawa, ON K1A 0T6
613-951-8116, Fax: 877-287-4369, 800-263-1136, infostats@statcan.ca
Transport Canada, Place de Ville, 330 Sparks St., Tower C, Ottawa, ON K1A 0N5
613-990-2309, Fax: 613-954-4731, 866-995-9737
Treasury Board of Canada, 140 O'Connor St., Ottawa, ON K1A 0R5
613-957-2400, Fax: 613-941-4000, 877-636-0656
Veterans Affairs Canada, 161 Grafton St., PO Box 7700, Charlottetown, PE C1A 8M9
902-566-8888, 866-522-2111, information@vac-acc.gc.ca

Alberta

Alberta Public Affairs Bureau, Park Plaza, 10611 - 98 Ave., 6th Fl., Edmonton, AB T5K 2P7
780-427-2754, Fax: 780-422-4168, -310-0000
Service Alberta, Government of Alberta, PO Box 1333, Edmonton, AB T5J 2N2
780-427-4088, -310-0000, service.alberta@gov.ab.ca

Newfoundland & Labrador

Newfoundland & Labrador Department of Service NL, PO Box 8700, St. John's, NL A1B 4J6
709-729-4834, gsinfo@gov.nl.ca

Nova Scotia

Department of Service Nova Scotia & Municipal Relations, 1505 Barrington St., PO Box 216, Halifax, NS B3J 3K5
902-424-5200, Fax: 902-424-0581, 800-670-4357, askus@gov.ns.ca

Nunavut

Department of Executive & Intergovernmental Affairs, 1084 Aeroplex bldg., PO Box 1000 200,Iqaluit, NU X0A 0H0
867-975-6000, Fax: 867-975-6099

Ontario

ServiceOntario, College Park, 777 Bay St., 15th fl., Toronto, ON M7A 2J3
416-326-1234, Fax: 416-326-1313, 800-267-8097

Quebec

Services Québec, Bureau de la qualité, 800, place D'Youville, 20e étage, Québec, QC G1R 3P4
418-644-4545, 877-644-4545

Yukon Territory

Government Inquiry Office, Yukon Government Administration Building, 2071 Second Ave., PO Box 2703, Whitehorse, YT Y1A 2C6
867-667-5811, information@gov.yk.ca

GRANTS & SUBSIDIES

See Also: Student Aid

Atlantic Canada Opportunities Agency, Blue Cross Centre, 644 Main St., 3rd Fl., PO Box 6051, Moncton, NB E1C 9J8
506-851-2271, Fax: 506-851-7403, 800-561-7862, information@acoa-apeca.gc.ca
Business Development Bank of Canada, #400, 5, Place Ville-Marie, Montréal, QC H3B 5E7
514-283-5904, Fax: 514-283-5626, 877-232-2269
Canada Council for the Arts, 350 Albert St., PO Box 1047, Ottawa, ON K1P 5V8
613-566-4414, Fax: 613-566-4390, 800-263-5588
Canada Economic Development for Québec Regions, Édifice Dominion Square, #900, 1255, rue Peel, Montréal, QC H3B 2T9
514-283-6412, Fax: 514-283-3302, 866-385-6412
Canada Mortgage & Housing Corporation, 700 Montreal Rd., Ottawa, ON K1A 0P7
613-748-2000, Fax: 613-748-2098, 800-668-2642, chic@cmhc-schl.gc.ca
Canadian Institutes of Health Research, 160 Elgin St., 9th Fl., Ottawa, ON K1A 0W9
613-941-2672, Fax: 613-954-1800, 888-603-4178, info@cihr-irsc.gc.ca
International Development Research Centre, 150 Kent St., PO Box 8500, Ottawa, ON K1G 3H9
613-236-6163, Fax: 613-238-7230, info@idrc.ca
National Film Board of Canada, 3155, rue Côte de Liesse, CP 1600 Centre-ville,Saint-Laurent, QC H4N 2N4
514-283-9000, Fax: 514-283-7564, 800-267-7710
Natural Sciences & Engineering Research Council of Canada, Constitution Square, Tower II, 350 Albert St., Ottawa, ON K1A 1H5
613-995-4273, Fax: 613-943-1624, marie-josee.duval@nserc-crsng.gc.ca
Western Economic Diversification Canada, Canada Place, #1500, 9700 Jasper Ave. NW, Edmonton, AB T5J 4H7
780-495-4164, Fax: 780-495-4557, 888-338-9378

Alberta

Local Government Services Division, Commerce Place, 10155 - 102 St., 17th Fl., Edmonton, AB T5J 4L4

Newfoundland & Labrador

Newfoundland & Labrador Municipal Financing Corporation, Confederation Bldg., PO Box 8700, St. John's, NL A1B 4J6
709-729-6686, Fax: 709-729-2095

Nova Scotia

Department of Finance, Provincial Bldg., 1723 Hollis St., 7th Fl., PO Box 187, Halifax, NS B3J 2N3
902-424-5554, Fax: 902-424-0635, FinanceWeb@gov.ns.ca

Saskatchewan

Energy & Resources, #300, 2103 - 11th Ave., Regina, SK S4P 3Z8
306-787-2528

HAZARDOUS MATERIALS

Hazardous Materials Information Review Commission, 427 Laurier Ave. West, 7th Fl., Ottawa, ON K1A 1M3
613-993-4331, Fax: 613-993-4686, hmirc-ccrmd@hc-sc.gc.ca
Institute for Chemical Process & Environmental Technology, Bldg. M-12, 1200 Montreal Rd., Ottawa, ON K1A 0R6
613-993-4041, Fax: 613-957-8231
Low-Level Radioactive Waste Management Office, #200, 1900 City Park Dr., Ottawa, ON K1J 1A3
613-998-9442, Fax: 613-952-0760, 800-377-5995, info@llrwmo.org

British Columbia

British Columbia Provincial Emergency Program, Block A, #200, 2261 Keating Cross Rd., Saanichton, BC V8M 2A5
250-952-4913, Fax: 250-952-4888, 888-257-4777

Manitoba

Emergency Measures Organization, 405 Broadway Ave., 15th Floor, Winnipeg, MB R3C 3L6
204-945-4772, Fax: 204-945-4929, 888-267-8298, emo@gov.mb.ca

Ontario

Ontario Ministry of Environment, 135 St. Clair Ave. West, Toronto, ON M4V 1P5
416-325-4000, Fax: 416-325-3159, 800-565-4923
Pesticides Advisory Committee, 135 St. Clair Ave. West, 15th Fl., Toronto, ON M4V 1P5
416-314-9230, Fax: 416-314-9237

HEALTH

New Brunswick

Addiction, Mental Health, Primary Health Care & Extra Mural Services Division, HSBC Place, 520 King St., 5th Fl., PO Box 5100, Fredericton, NB E3B 5G8
506-457-4800, Fax: 506-453-5243, Health.Sante@gnb.ca
Canadian Centre for Occupational Health & Safety, 135 Hunter St. East, Hamilton, ON L8N 1M5
905-572-2981, Fax: 905-572-2206, 800-668-4284
Canadian Centre on Substance Abuse, #500, 75 Albert St., Ottawa, ON K1P 5E7
613-235-4048, Fax: 613-235-8101, info@ccsa.ca
Canadian Food Inspection Agency, 1400 Merivale Rd., Ottawa, ON K1A 0Y9
613-225-2342, Fax: 613-228-6601, 800-442-2342
Children's Secretariat, c/o Sarah Henry, Education & Early Childhood Development, 161 St. Peters Rd., PO Box 2000, Charlottetown, PE C1A 7N8
Communications Branch, HSBC Place, 520 King St., 5th Fl., PO Box 5100, Fredericton, NB E3B 6G3
506-457-2356, Fax: 506-444-4697, Health.Sante@gnb.ca
Financial & Corporate Services Division, Telus Plaza NT, 10025 Jasper Ave., 19th Fl., Edmonton, AB T5J 1S6
Hazardous Materials Information Review Commission, 427 Laurier Ave. West, 7th Fl., Ottawa, ON K1A 1M3
613-993-4331, Fax: 613-993-4686, hmirc-ccrmd@hc-sc.gc.ca
Health Canada, Tunney's Pasture, Ottawa, ON K1A 0K9
613-957-2991, Fax: 613-941-5366, 866-225-0709, info@hc-sc.gc.ca
Health PEI, 16 Garfield St., PO Box 2000, Charlottetown, PE C1A 7N8
902-368-6130, Fax: 902-368-6136, healthinput@gov.pe.ca
Health Services Information & Information Technology Cluster, 56 Wellesley St. West, 10th Fl., Toronto, ON M5S 2S3
416-314-4243, Fax: 416-314-0289
Health System Strategy & Policy Division, Hepburn Block, 80 Grosvenor St., 8th Fl., Toronto, ON M7A 1R3
416-327-8295, Fax: 416-327-5109
Health Workforce Division, Telus Plaza NT, 10025 Jasper Ave., 10th Fl., Edmonton, AB T5J 1S6
National Seniors Council, Place Vanier, Tower B, 355 North River Rd. 14th Fl., PO Box 4, Ottawa, ON K1A 0K9
Fax: 613-946-8871, 800-622-6232, nsc-cna@hrsdc-rhdcc.gc.ca
Patented Medicine Prices Review Board, Standard Life Centre, #1400, 333 Laurier Ave. West, PO Box L40, Ottawa, ON K1P 1C1
613-954-8299, Fax: 613-952-7626, 877-861-2350, pmprb@pmprb-cepmb.gc.ca
Public Health Agency of Canada, 130 Colonnade Rd., Ottawa, ON K1A 0K9
Ste-Anne's Hospital, 305 boul des Anciens-Combattants, Sainte-Anne-de-Bellevue, QC H9X 1Y9
514-457-3440, 800-361-9287, steanne@vac-acc.gc.ca

Alberta

Alberta Health Services, Corporate Office, North Tower, Seventh Street Plaza, 10030 - 107th St. NW, 14th Fl., Edmonton, AB T5J 3E4
780-342-2000, Fax: 780-342-2060, 888-342-2471, ahsb.admin@albertahealthservices.ca
Health Quality Council of Alberta, #210, 811 - 14 St. NW, Calgary, AB T2N 2A4
403-297-8162, Fax: 403-297-8258, info@hqca.ca
Alberta Health, PO Box 1360 Main,Edmonton, AB T5J 2N3
780-427-7164, Fax: 780-427-1171, -310-0000
Occupational Health & Safety Council, Labour Building, 10808 - 99 Ave., 9th Fl., Edmonton, AB T5K 0G5
780-415-8690, 866-415-8690
Office of the Chief Medical Officer of Health, Telus Plaza NT, 10025 Jasper Ave., 24th Fl., Edmonton, AB T5J 1S6
780-427-5263
Premier's Council on the Status of Persons with Disabilities, HSBC Building, 10055 - 106 St., 11th Fl., Edmonton, AB T5J 1G3
780-422-1095, 800-272-8841, pcspd@gov.ab.ca
Seniors Advisory Council for Alberta, Standard Life Centre, #600, 10405 Jasper Ave., 6th Fl., Edmonton, AB T5J 4R7
780-422-2321, Fax: 780-422-8762, -310-0000, saca@gov.ab.ca
Alberta Seniors, Communications, Standard Life Centre, 10405 Jasper Ave., 3rd Fl., Edmonton, AB T5J 4R7
780-415-9950, Fax: 780-644-1227, 866-477-8589, seniors.communications@gov.ab.ca

British Columbia

British Columbia Ministry of Health, 1515 Blanshard St., Victoria, BC V8W 3C8
800-663-7100, hlth.health@gov.bc.ca

Manitoba

Addictions Foundation of Manitoba, 1031 Portage Ave., Winnipeg, MB R3G 0R8
204-944-6200, Fax: 204-786-7768, library@afm.mb.ca
Manitoba Health, #100, 300 Carlton St., Winnipeg, MB R3B 3M9
204-786-7191, minhlt@leg.gov.mb.ca
Manitoba Council on Aging, #822, 155 Carlton St., Winnipeg, MB R3C 3H8
204-945-6565, Fax: 204-948-2514, 800-665-6565
Manitoba Drug Standards & Therapeutics Committee, #1014, 300 Carlton St., Winnipeg, MB R3B 3M9
204-786-7317, Fax: 204-942-2030
Office of the Chief Medical Examiner, #210, 1 Wesley Ave., Winnipeg, MB R3C 4C6
204-945-2088, Fax: 204-945-2442, 800-282-9069,
Public Health & Primary Health Care, 300 Carlton St., 2nd Floor, Winnipeg, MB R3B 3M9

New Brunswick
Premier's Council on the Status of Disabled Persons, Kings Place, #648, 440 King St., Fredericton, NB E3B 5H8
506-444-3000, Fax: 506-444-3001, 800-442-4412, pcsdp@gnb.ca
New Brunswick Department of Culture, Tourism, & Healthy Living, Centennial Building, PO Box 6000, Fredericton, NB E3B 5H1
506-444-5205, Fax: 506-457-4984, taponlinedirectory@gnb.ca
New Brunswick Department of Health, PO Box 5100, Fredericton, NB E3B 5G8
506-457-4800, Fax: 506-453-5243, dh-ms@dh-ms.ca
Workplace Health, Safety & Compensation Commission of New Brunswick, 1 Portland St., PO Box 160, Saint John, NB E2L 3X9
506-632-2200, 800-222-9775, communications@ws-ts.nb.ca

Newfoundland & Labrador
Newfoundland & Labrador Department of Health & Community Services, West Block, Confederation Bldg., PO Box 8700, St. John's, NL A1B 4J6
709-729-5021, Fax: 709-729-5824, healthinfo@gov.nl.ca
Newfoundland & Labrador Health Boards Associations, Beothuck Bldg., 20 Crosbie Pl., 2nd Fl., St. John's, NL A1B 3Y8
709-364-7701, Fax: 709-364-6460

Northwest Territories
Department of Health & Social Services, Centre Square Tower, PO Box 1320, Yellowknife, NT X1A 2L9
Fax: 867-873-0266

Nova Scotia
Department of Health & Wellness, Joseph Howe Bldg., 1690 Hollis St., 4th Fl., PO Box 488, Halifax, NS B3J 2R8
902-424-5818, Fax: 902-424-0730, 800-387-6665, DoHweb@gov.ns.ca
Nova Scotia Advisory Commission on AIDS, Dennis Bldg., 1740 Granville St., 6th Fl., Halifax, NS B3J 1X5
902-424-5730, Fax: 902-424-4727, AIDS@gov.ns.ca
Office of the Chief Medical Examiner, Halifax Insurance Bldg., #701, 5670 Spring Garden Rd., Halifax, NS B3J 1H7
902-424-2722, Fax: 902-424-0607

Nunavut
Department of Culture, Language, Elders & Youth, PO Box 1000 800,Iqaluit, NU X0A 0H0
867-975-5500, Fax: 867-975-5504, 866-934-2035
Department of Health & Social Services, PO Box 1000 1000,Iqaluit, NU X0A 0H0
867-975-5700, Fax: 867-975-5705
Office of the Chief Coroner, PO Box 1000 590, Iqaluit, NU X0A 0H0

Ontario
Cancer Care Ontario, 620 University Ave., 15th Fl., Toronto, ON M5G 2L7
416-971-9800, Fax: 416-971-6888
Consent & Capacity Board, 151 Bloor St. West, 10th Fl., Toronto, ON M5S 2T5
416-327-4142, Fax: 416-924-8873, 866-777-7391
Ontario Ministry of Health & Long-Term Care, Hepburn Block, 80 Grosvenor St., 10th Fl, Toronto, ON M7A 2C4
416-327-4327, 800-268-1153
Health Boards Secretariat, 151 Bloor St. West, 9th Fl., Toronto, ON M5S 2T5
416-327-8512, Fax: 416-327-8524, 866-282-2179
Medical Eligibility Committee, 370 Select Dr., PO Box 168, Kingston, ON K7M 8T4
613-548-6405
Ontario Mental Health Foundation, 441 Jarvis St., 2nd Fl., Toronto, ON M4Y 2G8
416-920-7721, Fax: 416-920-0026, grants@omhf.on.ca
Ontario Review Board, 151 Bloor St. West, 10th Fl., Toronto, ON M5S 2T5
416-327-8866, Fax: 416-327-8867
Pesticides Advisory Committee, 135 St. Clair Ave. West, 15th Fl., Toronto, ON M4V 1P5
416-314-9230, Fax: 416-314-9237
Trillium Gift of Life Network, #900, 522 University Ave., Toronto, ON M5G 1W7
416-363-4001, Fax: 416-363-4002, 800-263-2833

Prince Edward Island
BIO FOOD TECH, 101 Belvedere Ave., PO Box 2000, Charlottetown, PE C1A 7N8
902-368-5548, Fax: 902-368-5549, 877-368-5548, biofoodtech@biofoodtech.ca
Prince Edward Island Department of Health & Wellness, 105 Rochford St. North, 4th Fl., PO Box 2000, Charlottetown, PE C1A 7N8
902-368-6414, Fax: 902-368-4121

Quebec
Agence d'évaluation des technologies et des modes d'intervention en santé, #10.083, 2021, av Union, Montréal, QC H3A 2S9
514-873-2563, Fax: 514-873-1369
Bureau des projets Centres hospitaliers universitaires de Montréal, CHUM, CUSM et CHU Sainte-Justine, #10.049, 2021, rue Union, Montréal, QC H3A 2S9
514-864-9883, Fax: 514-873-7362, info.construction3chu@msss.gouv.qc.ca
Bureau du coroner, Édifice le Delta 2, #390, 2875, boul Laurier, Québec, QC G1V 5B1
418-643-1845, Fax: 418-643-6174, 866-312-7051, clientele.coroner@msp.gouv.qc.ca
Commissaire à la santé et du bien-être, #700, 1020, rte de l'Église, Québec, QC G1V 3V9
418-643-3040, Fax: 418-644-0654, csbe@csbe.gouv.qc.ca
Commission de la santé et de la sécurité du travail, 425, rue du Pont, CP 4900 Terminus, Québec, QC G1K 7S6
418-266-4000, Fax: 418-266-4015, 888-999-2778
Conseil du médicament, #100, 1195, av Lavigerie, 1er étage, Québec, QC G1V 4N3
418-644-8103, Fax: 418-644-8120, cdm@cdm.gouv.qc.ca
Corporation d'hébergement du Québec, 2535, boul Laurier, 5e étage, Québec, QC G1V 4M3
418-644-3600, Fax: 418-644-3609, clientele.sante@siq.gouv.qc.ca
Fonds de la recherche en santé du Québec, #800, 500, rue Sherbrooke ouest, Montréal, QC H3A 3C6
514-873-2114, Fax: 514-873-8768
Institut national de santé publique du Québec, 945, av Wolfe, Québec, QC G1V 5B3
418-650-5115, Fax: 418-646-9328, info@inspq.qc.ca
Régie de l'assurance maladie du Québec, 1125, Grande Allée ouest, Québec, QC G1S 1E7
418-646-4636
Commission de la santé et de la sécurité du travail du Québec, 524, rue Bourdages, CP 1200 Terminus postal,Québec, QC G1K 7E2
418-266-4850, Fax: 418-266-4669, 866-302-2778
Ministère de la Santé et des Services sociaux, Direction des communications, 1075, ch Sainte-Foy, 16e étage, Québec, QC G1S 2M1
418-643-9395, Fax: 418-643-4768, regisseur.web@msss.gouv.qc.ca
Secrétariat à l'accès aux services en langue anglaise et aux communautés ethnoculturelles, #1.03, 201 boul Crémazie est, 1er étage, Montréal, QC H2M 1L2
514-873-5163, Fax: 514-873-9876
Urgences-santé Québec, 3232, rue Bélanger, Montréal, QC H1Y 3H5
514-723-5600, info@urgences-sante.qc.ca

Saskatchewan
Health Quality Council, 241, 111 Research Dr., Saskatoon, SK S7N 3R2
306-668-8810, Fax: 306-668-8820, info@hqc.sk.ca
Saskatchewan Health, T.C. Douglas Bldg., 3475 Albert St., Regina, SK S4S 6X6
306-787-0146, 800-667-7766, info@health.gov.sk.ca

Yukon Territory
Yukon Health & Social Services, PO Box 2703, Whitehorse, YT Y1A 2C6
867-667-3673, Fax: 867-667-3096, hss@gov.yk.ca

HEALTH & SAFETY

Canadian Centre for Occupational Health & Safety, 135 Hunter St. East, Hamilton, ON L8N 1M5
905-572-2981, Fax: 905-572-2206, 800-668-4284
Canadian Coast Guard, Centennial Towers, #6S018, 200 Kent St., Ottawa, ON K1A 0E6
613-993-0999, Fax: 613-990-1866, info@dfo-mpo.gc.ca
Canadian Environmental Assessment Agency, Place Bell Canada, 160 Elgin St., 22nd Fl., Ottawa, ON K1A 0H3
613-957-0700, Fax: 613-957-0862, 866-582-1884, info@ceaa-acee.gc.ca
Canadian Food Inspection Agency, 1400 Merivale Rd., Ottawa, ON K1A 0Y9
613-225-2342, Fax: 613-228-6601, 800-442-2342
Canadian Food Inspection Agency, 1400 Merivale Rd., Ottawa, ON K1A 0Y9
613-225-2342, Fax: 613-228-6601, 800-442-2342
Hazardous Materials Information Review Commission, 427 Laurier Ave. West, 7th Fl., Ottawa, ON K1A 1M3
613-993-4331, Fax: 613-993-4686, hmirc-ccrmd@hc-sc.gc.ca
Health Canada, Tunney's Pasture, Ottawa, ON K1A 0K9
613-957-2991, Fax: 613-941-5366, 866-225-0709, info@hc-sc.gc.ca
Human Resources & Skills Development Canada, 140 Promenade du Portage, Gatineau, QC K1A 0J9
Department of Labour & Advanced Education, 5151 Terminal Rd., 6th Fl., PO Box 697, Halifax, NS B3J 2T8
902-424-5301, Fax: 902-424-0575
National Defence Canada, Major-General George R. Pearkes Bldg., 101 Colonel By Dr., Ottawa, ON K1A 0K2
613-995-2534, Fax: 613-992-4739, 800-856-8488
Policy & Corporate Services Division, Twin Atria Building, 4999 - 98 Ave., 3rd Fl., Edmonton, AB T6B 2X3
Public Safety Canada, 269 Laurier Ave. West, Ottawa, ON K1A 0P8
613-944-4875, Fax: 613-954-5186, 800-830-3118, communications@ps.gc.ca
Transportation Safety Board of Canada, 200 Promenade du Portage, 4th Fl., Ottawa, ON K1A 1K8
819-994-3741, Fax: 819-997-2239, 800-387-3557
Workers' Compensation Board, 9912 - 107 St., Edmonton, AB T5J 2S5
780-498-3999, Fax: 780-427-5863, 866-922-9221

Alberta
Alberta Health, PO Box 1360 Main,Edmonton, AB T5J 2N3
780-427-7164, Fax: 780-427-1171, -310-0000
Alberta Human Services, Office of the Minister, Legislature Building, #224, 10800 - 97 Ave., Edmonton, AB T5K 2B6
780-644-5135, 866-644-5135
Occupational Health & Safety Council, Labour Building, 10808 - 99 Ave., 9th Fl., Edmonton, AB T5K 0G5
780-415-8690, 866-415-8690
Transportation Safety Board, North Office, Twin Atria Building, 4999 - 98 Ave., Main Fl., Edmonton, AB T6B 2X3
780-427-7178, Fax: 780-422-9739, -310-0000

British Columbia
British Columbia Ministry of Citizens' Services & Open Government, PO Box 9594 Prov Govt,Victoria, BC V8W 9E2
250-952-7623, Fax: 250-952-7628, 800-663-7867, EnquiryBC@gov.bc.ca
British Columbia Ministry of Health, 1515 Blanshard St., Victoria, BC V8W 3C8
800-663-7100, hlth.health@gov.bc.ca
British Columbia Provincial Emergency Program, Block A, #200, 2261 Keating Cross Rd., Saanichton, BC V8M 2A5
250-952-4913, Fax: 250-952-4888, 888-257-4777
Workers' Compensation Board of British Columbia, PO Box 5350 Terminal,Vancouver, BC V6B 5L5
604-276-3100, Fax: 604-276-3247, 888-621-7233

Manitoba
Advisory Council on Workplace Safety & Health, #200, 401 York Ave., Winnipeg, MB R3C 0P8
204-945-3446, Fax: 204-945-4556
Emergency Measures Organization, 405 Broadway Ave., 15th Floor, Winnipeg, MB R3C 3L6
204-945-4772, Fax: 204-945-4929, 888-267-8298, emo@gov.mb.ca
Manitoba Health, #100, 300 Carlton St., Winnipeg, MB R3B 3M9
204-786-7191, minhlt@leg.gov.mb.ca
Manitoba Immigration & Multiculturalism, Legislative Building, 317, 450 Broadway Ave., Winnipeg, MB R3C 0V8
204-945-4079, Fax: 204-945-8312, minlab@leg.gov.mb.ca

New Brunswick
New Brunswick Department of Health, PO Box 5100, Fredericton, NB E3B 5G8
506-457-4800, Fax: 506-453-5243, dh-ms@dh-ms.ca
New Brunswick Department of Post-Secondary Education, Training, & Labour, Chestnut Complex, PO Box 6000, Fredericton, NB E3B 5H1
506-453-2597, Fax: 506-453-3618, dpetlinfo@gnb.ca
Workplace Health, Safety & Compensation Commission of New Brunswick, 1 Portland St., PO Box 160, Saint John, NB E2L 3X9
506-632-2200, 800-222-9775, communications@ws-ts.nb.ca

Newfoundland & Labrador
Newfoundland & Labrador Department of Environment & Conservation, Confederation Bldg., West Block, 4th Fl., PO Box 8700, St. John's, NL A1B 4J6
709-729-2664, Fax: 709-729-6639, 800-563-6181, info@gov.nl.ca
Newfoundland & Labrador Department of Health & Community Services, West Block, Confederation Bldg., PO Box 8700, St. John's, NL A1B 4J6
709-729-5021, Fax: 709-729-5824, healthinfo@gov.nl.ca
Newfoundland & Labrador Workplace Health, Safety & Compensation Commission, 146 - 148 Forest Rd., PO Box 9000, St. John's, NL A1A 3B8
709-778-1000, Fax: 709-738-1714, 800-563-9000, general.inquiries@whscc.nl.ca

Northwest Territories
Department of Health & Social Services, Centre Square Tower, PO Box 1320, Yellowknife, NT X1A 2L9
Fax: 867-873-0266

Northwest Territories & Nunavut Workers' Safety & Compensation Commission, Centre Square Tower, 5022 - 49th St., 5th Fl., PO Box 8888, Yellowknife, NT X1A 2R3
867-920-3888, Fax: 867-873-4596, 800-661-0792

Nova Scotia

Nova Scotia Emergency Management Office, PO Box 2581, Halifax, NS B3J 3N5
902-424-5620, Fax: 902-424-5376, 866-424-5620, emo@gov.ns.ca

Department of Health & Wellness, Joseph Howe Bldg., 1690 Hollis St., 4th Fl., PO Box 488, Halifax, NS B3J 2R8
902-424-5818, Fax: 902-424-0730, 800-387-6665, DoHweb@gov.ns.ca

Ontario

Ontario Ministry of Government Services, Whitney Block, #4320, 99 Wellesley St. West, 4th Fl., Toronto, ON M7A 1W3
416-326-1234, Fax: 416-327-3790, 800-268-1142

Ontario Ministry of Health & Long-Term Care, Hepburn Block, 80 Grosvenor St., 10th Fl, Toronto, ON M7A 2C4
416-327-4327, 800-268-1153

Ontario Ministry of Labour, 400 University Ave., 14th Fl., Toronto, ON M7A 1T7
416-326-7160, 800-531-5551

Road User Safety Division, Bldg A, #191, 1201 Wilson Ave., Downsview, ON M3M 1J8
416-235-2999, Fax: 416-235-4153

Prince Edward Island

Prince Edward Island Department of Health & Wellness, 105 Rochford St. North, 4th Fl., PO Box 2000, Charlottetown, PE C1A 7N8
902-368-6414, Fax: 902-368-4121

Prince Edward Island Workers Compensation Board, 14 Weymouth St., PO Box 757, Charlottetown, PE C1A 7L7
902-368-5680, Fax: 902-368-5696, 800-237-5049

Quebec

Commission de la santé et de la sécurité du travail du Québec, 524, rue Bourdages, CP 1200 Terminus postal,Québec, QC G1K 7E2
418-266-4850, Fax: 418-266-4669, 866-302-2778

Ministère de la Santé et des Services sociaux, Direction des communications, 1075, ch Sainte-Foy, 16e étage, Québec, QC G1S 2M1
418-643-9395, Fax: 418-643-4768, regisseur.web@msss.gouv.qc.ca

Ministère de la Sécurité publique, Tour des Laurentides, 2525, boul Laurier, 5e étage, Québec, QC G1V 2L2
418-643-2112, Fax: 418-646-6168, 866-644-6826

Ministère du Travail, 200, ch Sainte-Foy, 5e étage, Québec, QC G1R 5S1
418-644-4545, Fax: 418-528-0559, 800-643-4817

Saskatchewan

Saskatchewan Health, T.C. Douglas Bldg., 3475 Albert St., Regina, SK S4S 6X6
306-787-0146, 800-667-7766, info@health.gov.sk.ca

Saskatchewan Labour Relations & Workplace Safety, #300, 1870 Albert St., Regina, SK S4P 4W1
306-787-7404, webmaster@lab.gov.sk.ca

Yukon Territory

Emergency Measures Organization, Combined Services Bldg., 2nd Fl., 60 Norseman Rd, Airport, Whitehorse, YT Y1A 2C6
867-667-5220, Fax: 867-393-6266, 800-661-0408, emo.yukon@gov.yk.ca

Yukon Health & Social Services, PO Box 2703, Whitehorse, YT Y1A 2C6
867-667-3673, Fax: 867-667-3096, hss@gov.yk.ca

Yukon Workers' Compensation Health & Safety Board, 401 Strickland St., Whitehorse, YT Y1A 5N8
867-667-5645, Fax: 867-393-6279, 800-661-0443, worksafe@gov.yk.ca

HEALTH CARE INSURANCE

Health Canada, Tunney's Pasture, Ottawa, ON K1A 0K9
613-957-2991, Fax: 613-941-5366, 866-225-0709, info@hc-sc.gc.ca

Health Services Information & Information Technology Cluster, 56 Wellesley St. West, 10th Fl., Toronto, ON M5S 2S3
416-314-4243, Fax: 416-314-0289

Health Workforce Division, Telus Plaza NT, 10025 Jasper Ave., 10th Fl., Edmonton, AB T5J 1S6

British Columbia

Medical Services Commission, 1515 Blanshard St., 3rd Fl., Victoria, BC V8W 3C8
250-952-3073, Fax: 250-952-3131

Newfoundland & Labrador

Newfoundland & Labrador Department of Health & Community Services, West Block, Confederation Bldg., PO Box 8700, St. John's, NL A1B 4J6
709-729-5021, Fax: 709-729-5824, healthinfo@gov.nl.ca

Northwest Territories

Department of Health & Social Services, Centre Square Tower, PO Box 1320, Yellowknife, NT X1A 2L9
Fax: 867-873-0266

Nunavut

Department of Health & Social Services, PO Box 1000 1000,Iqaluit, NU X0A 0H0
867-975-5700, Fax: 867-975-5705

Prince Edward Island

Prince Edward Island Department of Health & Wellness, 105 Rochford St. North, 4th Fl., PO Box 2000, Charlottetown, PE C1A 7N8
902-368-6414, Fax: 902-368-4121

Quebec

Régie de l'assurance maladie du Québec, 1125, Grande Allée ouest, Québec, QC G1S 1E7
418-646-4636

HEALTH SERVICES

See Also: Health Care Insurance; Occupational Safety

Canadian Centre for Occupational Health & Safety, 135 Hunter St. East, Hamilton, ON L8N 1M5
905-572-2981, Fax: 905-572-2206, 800-668-4284

Canadian Institutes of Health Research, 160 Elgin St., 9th Fl., Ottawa, ON K1A 0W9
613-941-2672, Fax: 613-954-1800, 888-603-4178, info@cihr-irsc.gc.ca

Health Canada, Tunney's Pasture, Ottawa, ON K1A 0K9
613-957-2991, Fax: 613-941-5366, 866-225-0709, info@hc-sc.gc.ca

Health PEI, 16 Garfield St., PO Box 2000, Charlottetown, PE C1A 7N8
902-368-6130, Fax: 902-368-6136, healthinput@gov.pe.ca

Health Services Information & Information Technology Cluster, 56 Wellesley St. West, 10th Fl., Toronto, ON M5S 2S3
416-314-4243, Fax: 416-314-0289

Ste-Anne's Hospital, 305 boul des Anciens-Combattants, Sainte-Anne-de-Bellevue, QC H9X 1Y9
514-457-3440, 800-361-9287, steanne@vac-acc.gc.ca

Alberta

Alberta Health, PO Box 1360 Main,Edmonton, AB T5J 2N3
780-427-7164, Fax: 780-427-1171, -310-0000

British Columbia

British Columbia Ministry of Health, 1515 Blanshard St., Victoria, BC V8W 3C8
800-663-7100, hlth.health@gov.bc.ca

Medical Services Commission, 1515 Blanshard St., 3rd Fl., Victoria, BC V8W 3C8
250-952-3073, Fax: 250-952-3131

Manitoba

Manitoba Health, #100, 300 Carlton St., Winnipeg, MB R3B 3M9
204-786-7191, minhlt@leg.gov.mb.ca

Manitoba Healthy Child Office, #219, 114 Garry St., Winnipeg, MB R3C 1G1
204-945-2266, 888-848-0140, healthychild@gov.mb.ca

Manitoba Health Appeal Board, #4011, 300 Carlton St., Winnipeg, MB R3B 3M9
204-788-6704, Fax: 204-948-2024, 866-744-3257

New Brunswick

New Brunswick Department of Health, PO Box 5100, Fredericton, NB E3B 5G8
506-457-4800, Fax: 506-453-5243, dh-ms@dh-ms.ca

Newfoundland & Labrador

Newfoundland & Labrador Department of Health & Community Services, West Block, Confederation Bldg., PO Box 8700, St. John's, NL A1B 4J6
709-729-5021, Fax: 709-729-5824, healthinfo@gov.nl.ca

Northwest Territories

Department of Health & Social Services, Centre Square Tower, PO Box 1320, Yellowknife, NT X1A 2L9
Fax: 867-873-0266

Nova Scotia

Department of Health & Wellness, Joseph Howe Bldg., 1690 Hollis St., 4th Fl., PO Box 488, Halifax, NS B3J 2R8
902-424-5818, Fax: 902-424-0730, 800-387-6665, DoHweb@gov.ns.ca

Nunavut

Department of Health & Social Services, PO Box 1000 1000,Iqaluit, NU X0A 0H0
867-975-5700, Fax: 867-975-5705

Prince Edward Island

Prince Edward Island Department of Health & Wellness, 105 Rochford St. North, 4th Fl., PO Box 2000, Charlottetown, PE C1A 7N8
902-368-6414, Fax: 902-368-4121

Quebec

Institut national de santé publique du Québec, 945, av Wolfe, Québec, QC G1V 5B3
418-650-5115, Fax: 418-646-9328, info@inspq.qc.ca

Ministère de la Santé et des Services sociaux, Direction des communications, 1075, ch Sainte-Foy, 16e étage, Québec, QC G1S 2M1
418-643-9395, Fax: 418-643-4768, regisseur.web@msss.gouv.qc.ca

Saskatchewan

Saskatchewan Health, T.C. Douglas Bldg., 3475 Albert St., Regina, SK S4S 6X6
306-787-0146, 800-667-7766, info@health.gov.sk.ca

HERITAGE RESOURCES

See Also: Land Resources; Parks

Canadian Heritage, 15 Eddy St., Gatineau, QC K1A 0M5
819-997-0055, 866-811-0055, info@pch.gc.ca

Child & Family Services Division, Jones Bldg., 11 Kent St., 2nd Fl., PO Box 2000, Charlottetown, PE C1A 7N8
902-368-5294

Culture & Heritage Division, PO Box 310, Igloolik, NU X0A 0L0
867-975-2046, Fax: 867-934-2047, cleypermits@gov.nu.ca

Parks Canada, 25 Eddy St., Gatineau, QC K1A 0M5
613-860-1251, 888-773-8888, information@pc.gc.ca

Provincial Capital Commission, 4607 Dewdney Ave., Regina, SK S4T 1B7
306-787-9261

Manitoba

Manitoba Culture, Heritage & Tourism, Legislative Building, #118, 450 Broadway Ave., Winnipeg, MB R3C 0V8
204-945-3729, Fax: 204-945-5223, mincht@leg.gov.mb.ca

Heritage Grants Advisory Council, 213 Notre Dame Ave., 3rd Fl., Winnipeg, MB R3B 1N3
204-945-2213, Fax: 204-948-2086

Manitoba Heritage Council, 213 Notre Dame Ave., Main Fl., Winnipeg, MB R3B 1N3
204-945-2118, Fax: 204-948-2384, hrb@gov.mb.ca

Nova Scotia

Heritage Division, 1747 Summer St., Halifax, NS B3H 3A6
902-424-7344, Fax: 902-424-0560, 800-632-1114, heritage@gov.ns.ca

Nunavut

Department of Culture, Language, Elders & Youth, PO Box 1000 800,Iqaluit, NU X0A 0H0
867-975-5500, Fax: 867-975-5504, 866-934-2035

Ontario

Conservation Review Board, 400 University Ave. 4th Fl., Toronto, ON M7A 2R9
416-314-7137, Fax: 416-314-7175, conservation.review.board@ontario.ca

Ontario Heritage Trust, 10 Adelaide St. East, Toronto, ON M5C 1J3
416-325-5000, Fax: 416-325-5071

Quebec

Commission des biens culturels du Québec, Bloc A-RC, 225, Grande Allée est, Québec, QC G1R 5G5
418-643-8378, Fax: 418-643-8591, info@cbcq.gouv.qc.ca

Saskatchewan

Saskatchewan Archives Board, University of Regina, 3303 Hillsdale St., PO Box 1665, Regina, SK S4P 3C6
306-787-4068, Fax: 306-787-1197, info.regina@archives.gov.sk.ca

Yukon Territory

Yukon Tourism & Culture, 100 Hanson St., Whitehorse, YT Y1A 2C6
867-667-5036, Fax: 867-667-3546

HISTORY & ARCHIVES

Canada Council for the Arts, 350 Albert St., PO Box 1047, Ottawa, ON K1P 5V8
613-566-4414, Fax: 613-566-4390, 800-263-5588

Library & Archives Canada, 395 Wellington St., Ottawa, ON K1A 0N4
613-996-5115, Fax: 613-995-6274, 866-578-7777

Library of Parliament, Parliamentary Buildings, Ottawa, ON K1A 0A9
613-992-4793, 866-599-4999, info@parl.gc.ca

Alberta

Recreation & Sport Development Division, Standard Life Centre, 10405 Jasper Ave., 9th Fl., Edmonton, AB T5J 4R7

Nova Scotia

Culture Division, #601, 1800 Argyle St., PO Box 456, Halifax, NS B3J 2R5
902-424-4510, Fax: 902-424-0710, culture@gov.ns.ca

Ontario

Information, Privacy & Archives Division, 134 Ian Macdonald Blvd., Toronto, ON M7A 2C5
416-327-1600, Fax: 416-327-1999, 800-668-9933

Quebec

Bibliothèque et Archives nationales du Québec (BAnQ), 475, boul De Maisonneuve est, Montréal, QC H2L 5C4
514-873-1100, Fax: 514-873-9312, 800-363-9028

Saskatchewan
Saskatchewan Archives Board, University of Regina, 3303 Hillsdale St., PO Box 1665, Regina, SK S4P 3C6
306-787-4068, Fax: 306-787-1197, info.regina@archives.gov.sk.ca

HOSPITALS
See Also: Health Care Insurance

Alberta
Alberta Health, PO Box 1360 Main,Edmonton, AB T5J 2N3
780-427-7164, Fax: 780-427-1171, -310-0000

British Columbia
British Columbia Ministry of Health, 1515 Blanshard St., Victoria, BC V8W 3C8
800-663-7100, hlth.health@gov.bc.ca

Hospital Appeal Board, 747 Fort St., 4th Fl., PO Box 9425 Prov Govt, Victoria, BC V8W 9V1
250-387-3464, Fax: 250-356-9923, 800-663-7867, hab@gov.bc.ca

Northwest Territories
Department of Health & Social Services, Centre Square Tower, PO Box 1320, Yellowknife, NT X1A 2L9
Fax: 867-873-0266

Nunavut
Department of Health & Social Services, PO Box 1000 1000,Iqaluit, NU X0A 0H0
867-975-5700, Fax: 867-975-5705

Prince Edward Island
Prince Edward Island Department of Health & Wellness, 105 Rochford St. North, 4th Fl., PO Box 2000, Charlottetown, PE C1A 7N8
902-368-6414, Fax: 902-368-4121

Quebec
Ministère de la Santé et des Services sociaux, Direction des communications, 1075, ch Sainte-Foy, 16e étage, Québec, QC G1S 2M1
418-643-9395, Fax: 418-643-4768, regisseur.web@msss.gouv.qc.ca

HOUSING

Canada Mortgage & Housing Corporation, 700 Montreal Rd., Ottawa, ON K1A 0P7
613-748-2000, Fax: 613-748-2098, 800-668-2642, chic@cmhc-schl.gc.ca

British Columbia
Local Government, PO Box 9490 Prov Govt,Victoria, BC V8W 9N7
250-356-6575, Fax: 250-387-7973

Manitoba
Manitoba Housing Authority - Public Housing, #2100, 185 Smith St., Winnipeg, MB R3C 3G4
204-945-4663, Fax: 204-948-2013, 800-661-4663

New Brunswick
New Brunswick Department of Social Development, Sartain MacDonald Bldg., 551 King St., PO Box 6000, Fredericton, NB E3B 5H1
506-453-2001, Fax: 506-453-7478, sd-ds@gnb.ca

Newfoundland & Labrador
Newfoundland & Labrador Housing Corporation, Sir Brian Dunfield Bldg., 2 Canada Dr., PO Box 220, St. John's, NL A1C 5J2
709-724-3000, Fax: 709-724-3250

Northwest Territories
Northwest Territories Housing Corporation, Scotia Centre, 5102 50th Ave., PO Box 2100, Yellowknife, NT X1A 2P6
867-873-7853, Fax: 867-873-9426

Nova Scotia
Department of Service Nova Scotia & Municipal Relations, 1505 Barrington St., PO Box 216, Halifax, NS B3J 3K5
902-424-5200, Fax: 902-424-0581, 800-670-4357, askus@gov.ns.ca

Nunavut
Department of Community & Government Services, W.G. Brown Bldg., 4th Fl., PO Box 1000 700,Iqaluit, NU X0A 0H0
867-975-5400, Fax: 867-975-5305

Nunavut Housing Corporation, PO Box 480, Arviat, NU X0C 0E0
867-857-3000, Fax: 867-857-3040,

Quebec
Société d'habitation du Québec, Aile St-Amable, 1054, rue Louis-Alexandre-Taschereau, 3e étage, Québec, QC G1R 5E7
418-643-4035, Fax: 418-643-2533, 800-463-4315

Yukon Territory
Yukon Housing Corporation, 410H Jarvis St., PO Box 2703, Whitehorse, YT Y1A 2H5
867-667-5759, Fax: 867-667-3664, 800-661-0408, ykhouse@housing.yk.ca

HUMAN RIGHTS
See Also: Boards of Review

Canadian Human Rights Commission, 344 Slater St., 8th Fl., Ottawa, ON K1A 1E1
613-995-1151, Fax: 613-996-9661, 888-214-1090

Canadian Human Rights Tribunal, 160 Elgin St., 11th Fl., Ottawa, ON K1A 1J4
613-995-1707, Fax: 613-995-3484, registrar@chrt-tcdp.gc.ca

British Columbia
British Columbia Human Rights Tribunal, #1170, 605 Robson St., Vancouver, BC V6B 5J3
604-775-2000, Fax: 604-775-2020, 888-440-8844, BCHumanRightsTribunal@gov.bc.ca

Manitoba
Manitoba Human Rights Commission, 175 Hargrave St., 7th Fl., Winnipeg, MB R3C 3R8
204-945-3007, Fax: 204-945-1292, 888-884-8681, hrc@gov.mb.ca

New Brunswick
New Brunswick Human Rights Commission, PO Box 6000, Fredericton, NB E3B 5H1
506-453-2301, Fax: 506-453-2653, 888-471-2233, hrc.cdp@gnb.ca

Newfoundland & Labrador
Newfoundland & Labrador Human Rights Commission, PO Box 8700, St. John's, NL A1B 4J6
709-729-2709, Fax: 709-729-0790, 800-563-5808, humanrights@mail.gov.nl.ca

Nova Scotia
Nova Scotia Human Rights Commission, Joseph Howe Bldg., 1690 Hollis St., 6th Fl., Halifax, NS B3J 3C4
902-424-4111, Fax: 902-424-0596, hrcinquiries@gov.ns.ca

Ontario
Ontario Human Rights Commission, 180 Dundas St. West, 7th Fl., Toronto, ON M7A 2R9
416-326-9511, Fax: 416-314-4494, 800-387-9080

Prince Edward Island
Prince Edward Island Human Rights Commission, 53 Water St., PO Box 2000, Charlottetown, PE C1A 7N8
902-368-4180, Fax: 902-368-4236, 800-237-5031

Quebec
Commission des droits de la personne et des droits de la jeunesse, 360, rue St-Jacques, 2e étage, Montréal, QC H2Y 1P5
514-873-5146, Fax: 514-873-6032, 800-361-6477, accueil@cdpdj.qc.ca

Saskatchewan
Saskatchewan Human Rights Commission, Saskatoon Office, Sturdy Stone Bdg., #816, 122 - 3 Ave. North, 8th Fl., Saskatoon, SK S7K 2H6
306-933-5952, Fax: 306-933-7863, 800-667-9249, shrc@gov.sk.ca

Yukon Territory
Yukon Human Rights Board of Adjudication, #202, 407 Black St., Whitehorse, YT Y1A 2N2
867-667-5412, Fax: 867-633-6952, beyondwords@northwestel.net

Yukon Human Rights Commission, #101, 9010 Quartz St., Whitehorse, YT Y1A 2Z5
867-667-6226, Fax: 867-667-2662, 800-661-0535, humanrights@yhrc.yk.ca

HYDRO, ELECTRIC POWER

National Energy Board, 444 - 7 Ave. SW, Calgary, AB T2P 0X8
403-292-4800, Fax: 403-292-5503, 800-899-1265, info@neb-one.gc.ca

Yukon Energy Corporation, 2 Miles Canyon Rd., PO Box 5920, Whitehorse, YT Y1A 6S7
867-393-5300, 866-926-3749, communications@yukonenergy.ca

Alberta
Energy Resources Conservation Board, #1000, 250 - 5 Ave. SW, Calgary, AB T2P 0R4
403-297-8311, Fax: 403-297-7336, 855-297-8311, inquiries@ercb.ca; infoservices@ercb.ca; ADR@ercb.ca

British Columbia
British Columbia Hydro, 6911 Southpoint Dr., Burnaby, BC V3N 4X8
604-224-9376, 800-224-9376

Powertech Labs Inc., 12388 - 88 Ave., Surrey, BC V8W 7R7
604-590-7500, Fax: 604-590-6611

Manitoba
Manitoba Hydro, 360 Portage Ave., PO Box 815 Main,Winnipeg, MB R3C 2P4
204-474-3311, publicaffairs@hydro.mb.ca

Newfoundland & Labrador
Churchill Falls (Labrador) Corporation Limited, Hydro Place, 500 Columbus Dr., PO Box 12500, St. John's, NL A1B 4K7
709-737-1859, Fax: 709-737-1816

Newfoundland & Labrador Hydro, Hydro Place, Columbus Dr., PO Box 12400, St. John's, NL A1B 4K7
709-737-1400, Fax: 709-737-1800, hydro@nlh.nl.ca

Twin Falls Power Corporation, PO Box 12500, St. John's, NL A1B 3T5

Northwest Territories
Northwest Territories Power Corporation, 4 Capital Dr., Hay River, NT X0E 1G2
867-874-5200, Fax: 867-874-5251, info@ntpc.com

Nova Scotia
Nova Scotia Utility & Review Board, Summit Place, 1601 Lower Water St., 3rd Fl., PO Box 1692 M,Halifax, NS B3J 3S3
902-424-4448, Fax: 902-424-3919, uarb.board@gov.ns.ca

Ontario
Hydro One Inc., North Tower, 483 Bay St., Toronto, ON M5G 2P5
416-345-5000, 877-955-1155, customercommunications@HydroOne.com

Independent Electricity System Operator, PO Box 4474 A,Toronto, ON M5W 4E5
905-403-6900, Fax: 905-403-6921, 888-448-7777, customer.relations@ieso.ca

Ontario Power Authority, #1600, 120 Adelaide St. West, Toronto, ON M5H 1T1
416-967-7474, Fax: 416-967-1947, 800-797-9604, info@powerauthority.on.ca

Ontario Power Generation, 700 University Ave., Toronto, ON M5G 1X6
416-592-2555, 877-592-2555, webmaster@opg.com

Quebec
Hydro-Québec, 75, boul René-Lévesque ouest, Montréal, QC H2Z 1A4
514-289-2211

Société d'énergie de la Baie-James, 888, de Maisonneuve est, 6e étage, Montréal, QC H2L 5B2
514-286-2020

Saskatchewan
Saskatchewan Power Corporation (SaskPower), 2025 Victoria Ave., Regina, SK S4P 0S1
306-566-3306, Fax: 800-757-6937, 888-757-6937,

IMMIGRATION
See Also: Citizenship

Citizenship & Immigration Canada, Jean Edmonds, South Tower, 365 Laurier Ave. West, Ottawa, ON K1A 1L1
613-954-9019, Fax: 613-954-2221, 888-242-2100

Immigration & Refugee Board of Canada, Canada Bldg, 344 Slater St., 12th Fl., Ottawa, ON K1A 0K1
613-995-6486, Fax: 613-943-1550, contact@irb-cisr.gc.ca

Passport Canada, Le 70 Crémazie, 70 Crémazie St., Gatineau, QC K1A 0G3
Fax: 819-953-5856, 800-567-6868

Prince Edward Island
Island Investment Development Inc., 94 Euston St., 2nd Fl., Charlottetown, PE C1A 7M8
902-620-3628, Fax: 902-368-5886, peinominee@gov.pe.ca

IMPORTS
See Also: Trade

Canada Border Services Agency, Headquarters, 191 Laurier Ave. West, Ottawa, ON K1A 0L8
800-461-9999, Contact@cbsa.gc.ca; communications@ps.gc.ca (Public Safety)

Canadian International Trade Tribunal, Standard Life Centre, 333 Laurier Ave. West, 15 Floor, Ottawa, ON K1A 0G7
613-990-2452, Fax: 613-990-2439, secretary@citt-tcce.gc.ca

North American Free Trade Agreement (NAFTA) Secretariat, Canadian Section, #705, 90 Sparks St., Ottawa, ON K1P 5B4
613-992-9388, Fax: 613-992-9392, webmaster@nafta-alena.gc.ca

New Brunswick
Corporate Services Division, Centennial Building, PO Box 6000, Fredericton, NB E3B 5H1
506-453-3707, Fax: 506-453-5428

Quebec
Revenu Québec, Direction des relations publiques/Communications, 3800, rue de Marly, Québec, QC G1X 4A5
418-652-6831, Fax: 418-646-0167

INCOME SECURITY
See Also: Social Services

Ontario
Ontario Ministry of Community & Social Services, Hepburn Block, 80 Grosvenor St., 6th Fl., Toronto, ON M7A 1E9
416-325-5666, Fax: 416-325-5172, 888-789-4199

Yukon Territory
Yukon Health & Social Services, PO Box 2703, Whitehorse, YT Y1A 2C6
867-667-3673, Fax: 867-667-3096, hss@gov.yk.ca

INCORPORATION OF COMPANIES & ASSOCIATIONS

Alberta
Strategic Planning & Financial Services, Commerce Place, 10155 - 102 St., 13th Fl., Edmonton, AB T5J 4G8
780-422-8545

Northwest Territories
Department of Justice, Courthouse, 4903 - 49th St., 6th Fl., PO Box 1320, Yellowknife, NT X1A 2L9
867-920-6197

Nova Scotia
Department of Economic & Rural Development & Tourism, Centennial Building, #600, 1660 Hollis St., PO Box 2311, Halifax, NS B3J 1V7
902-424-0377, Fax: 902-424-0500, comm@gov.ns.ca
Registry of Joint Stock Companies, Maritime Centre, 1505 Barrington St., 9th Fl., Halifax, NS B3J 3K5
902-424-7770, Fax: 902-424-4633, 800-225-8227, joint-stock@gov.ns.ca

Nunavut
Legal Registries, Brown Bldg., 1st Fl., PO Box 1000 570,Iqaluit, NU X0A 0H0
Fax: 867-975-6594

Ontario
ServiceOntario, College Park, 777 Bay St., 15th fl., Toronto, ON M7A 2J3
416-326-1234, Fax: 416-326-1313, 800-267-8097

Quebec
Registraire des entreprises, 787, boul Lebourgneuf, Québec, QC G2J 1C3
418-644-4545, Fax: 418-528-5703, 877-644-4545, registre@servicesquebec.gouv.qc.ca

Yukon Territory
Yukon Community Services, PO Box 2703, Whitehorse, YT Y1A 2C6
867-667-5811, Fax: 867-393-6295, 800-661-0408, inquiry@gov.yk.ca

INDUSTRY

See Also: Business Development
Agriculture & Agri-Food Canada, 1341 Baseline Rd., Ottawa, ON K1A 0C5
613-773-1000, Fax: 613-773-2772, 866-345-7972, info@agr.gc.ca
Atlantic Canada Opportunities Agency, Blue Cross Centre, 644 Main St., 3rd Fl., PO Box 6051, Moncton, NB E1C 9J8
506-851-2271, Fax: 506-851-7403, 800-561-7862, information@acoa-apeca.gc.ca
Canada Mortgage & Housing Corporation, 700 Montreal Rd., Ottawa, ON K1A 0P7
613-748-2000, Fax: 613-748-2098, 800-668-2642, chic@cmhc-schl.gc.ca
Canadian Dairy Commission, Central Experimental Farm, NCC Driveway, Bldg. 55, 960 Carling Ave., Ottawa, ON K1A 0Z2
613-792-2000, Fax: 613-792-2009, cdc-ccl@cdc-ccl.gc.ca
Canadian Food Inspection Agency, 1400 Merivale Rd., Ottawa, ON K1A 0Y9
613-225-2342, Fax: 613-228-6601, 800-442-2342
Canadian Grain Commission, #600, 303 Main St., Winnipeg, MB R3C 3G8
204-983-2770, Fax: 204-983-2751, 800-853-6705, contact@grainscanada.gc.ca
Canadian International Development Agency, 200, Promenade du Portage, Gatineau, QC K1A 0G4
819-997-5456, Fax: 819-953-6088, 800-230-6349, info@acdi-cida.gc.ca
Canadian International Trade Tribunal, Standard Life Centre, 333 Laurier Ave. West, 15 Floor, Ottawa, ON K1A 0G7
613-990-2452, Fax: 613-990-2439, secretary@citt-tcce.gc.ca
Canadian Nuclear Safety Commission, 280 Slater St., PO Box 1046 B,Ottawa, ON K1P 5S9
613-995-5894, Fax: 613-995-5086, 800-668-5284
Canadian Radio-Television & Telecommunications Commission, Central Building, 1, Promenade du Portage, Les Terrasses de la Chaudière, Gatineau, QC J8X 4B1
819-997-0313, Fax: 819-994-0218, 877-249-2782
Canadian Space Agency, John H. Chapman Space Centre, 6767, rte de l'Aéroport, Saint-Hubert, QC J3Y 8Y9
450-926-4800, Fax: 450-926-4352, promo@asc-csa.gc.ca
Canadian Tourism Commission, #1400, 1055 Dunsmuir St., PO Box 49230, Vancouver, BC V7X 1L2
604-638-8300
Canadian Wheat Board, 423 Main St., PO Box 816 Main,Winnipeg, MB R3C 2P5
204-983-0239, Fax: 204-983-3841, 800-275-4292, questions@cwb.ca; farmerservice@cwb.ca
Centre for Surface Transportation Technology, 2320 Lester Rd., Ottawa, ON K1V 1S2
613-998-9639, Fax: 613-957-0831, inquiries.cstt@nrc-cnrc.gc.ca
Communications Research Centre Canada, 3701 Carling Ave., PO Box 11490 H, Ottawa, ON K2H 8S2
613-991-3313, Fax: 613-998-5355, info@crc.gc.ca
Competition Bureau, Place du Portage, Phase I, 50 Victoria Street, Ottawa, ON K1A 0C9
819-997-4282, Fax: 819-997-0324, 800-348-5358,
Competition Tribunal, Thomas D'Arcy McGee Bldg., #600, 90 Sparks St., Ottawa, ON K1P 5B4
613-957-3172, Fax: 613-957-3170, tribunal@ct-tc.gc.ca
Defence Construction Canada, Constitution Square, 350 Albert St., 19th Fl., Ottawa, ON K1A 0K3
613-998-9548, Fax: 613-998-1061, 800-514-3555, info@dcc-cdc.gc.ca
Enterprise Cape Breton Corporation, Silicon Island, 70 Crescent St., Sydney, NS B1S 2Z7
902-564-3600, Fax: 902-564-3825, 800-705-3926, information@ecbc-secb.gc.ca
Environmental Sciences & Standards Division, 135 St. Clair Ave. West, 14th Fl., Toronto, ON M4V 1P5
416-314-6357, Fax: 416-314-6358
Export Development Canada, 151 Slater St., Ottawa, ON K1A 1K3
613-598-2500, Fax: 613-598-3811, 800-267-8510
Farm Credit Canada, 1800 Hamilton St., PO Box 4320, Regina, SK S4P 4L3
306-780-8100, Fax: 306-780-8919, 888-332-3301, csc@fcc-fac.ca
Farm Products Council of Canada, Building 59, Central Experimental Farm, 960 Carling Ave., Ottawa, ON K1A 0C6
613-759-1555, Fax: 613-759-1566, fpcc-cpac@agr.gc.ca
Office of the Superintendent of Financial Institutions, Kent Square, 255 Albert St., Ottawa, ON K1A 0H2
613-990-7788, Fax: 613-990-5591, 800-385-8647, information@osfi-bsif.gc.ca
Fisheries & Oceans Canada, 200 Kent St., Ottawa, ON K1A 0E6
613-993-0999, Fax: 613-990-1866, info@dfo-mpo.gc.ca
Foreign Affairs & International Trade Canada, 125 Sussex Dr., Ottawa, ON K1A 0G2
613-944-4000, Fax: 613-996-9709, 800-267-8376, enqserv@international.gc.ca
Freshwater Fish Marketing Corporation, 1199 Plessis Rd., Winnipeg, MB R2C 3L4
204-983-6601, Fax: 204-983-6497, sandi.cain@freshwaterfish.com
Hazardous Materials Information Review Commission, 427 Laurier Ave. West, 7th Fl., Ottawa, ON K1A 1M3
613-993-4331, Fax: 613-993-4686, hmirc-ccrmd@hc-sc.gc.ca
Health System Strategy & Policy Division, Hepburn Block, 80 Grosvenor St., 8th Fl., Toronto, ON M7A 1R3
416-327-8295, Fax: 416-327-5109
Housing, Seniors & Corporate Support, Jones Bldg., 11 Kent St., 2nd Fl., PO Box 2000, Charlottetown, PE C1A 7N8
Fax: 902-894-0242
Indian Oil & Gas Canada, #100, 9911 Chiila Blvd., Tsuu T'ina (Sarcee), AB T2W 6H6
403-292-5625, Fax: 403-292-5618, ContactIOGC@inac-ainc.gc.ca
Industry Canada, C.D. Howe Building, 235 Queen St., Ottawa, ON K1A 0H5
613-954-5031, Fax: 613-954-2340, 800-328-6189, info@ic.gc.ca
Institute for Aerospace Research, 1200 Montreal Rd., Ottawa, ON K1A 0R6
613-990-0765, Fax: 613-952-7214
Institute for Information Technology, Bldg. M-50, 1200 Montreal Rd., Ottawa, ON K1A 0R6
613-991-3373, Fax: 613-952-0074, 877-672-2672
National Energy Board, 444 - 7 Ave. SW, Calgary, AB T2P 0X8
403-292-4800, Fax: 403-292-5503, 800-899-1265, info@neb-one.gc.ca
National Film Board of Canada, 3155, rue Côte de Liesse, CP 1600 Centre-ville,Saint-Laurent, QC H4N 2N4
514-283-9000, Fax: 514-283-7564, 800-267-7710
National Research Council Canada, Bldg. M-58, 1200 Montreal Rd., Ottawa, ON K1A 0R6
613-993-9101, Fax: 613-952-7928, 877-672-2672, info@nrc-cnrc.ca
National Round Table on the Environment & Economy, #200, 344 Slater St., Ottawa, ON K1R 7Y3
613-992-7189, Fax: 613-992-7385, info@nrtee-trnee.ca
Natural Resources Canada, 580 Booth St., Ottawa, ON K1A 0E4
613-995-0947, Fax: 613-992-7211
Natural Sciences & Engineering Research Council of Canada, Constitution Square, Tower II, 350 Albert St., Ottawa, ON K1A 1H5
613-995-4273, Fax: 613-943-1624, marie-josee.duval@nserc-crsng.gc.ca
North American Free Trade Agreement (NAFTA) Secretariat, Canadian Section, #705, 90 Sparks St., Ottawa, ON K1P 5B4
613-992-9388, Fax: 613-992-9392, webmaster@nafta-alena.gc.ca
Office of the Conflict of Interest & Ethics Commissioner, Commissioner's Office, 66 Slater St., 22nd Fl., Ottawa, ON K1A 0A6
613-995-0721, Fax: 613-995-7308, ciec-ccie@parl.gc.ca
Parks, PO Box 2703 V-4, Whitehorse, YT Y1A 2C6
867-667-5648, Fax: 867-393-6223, 800-661-0408, yukon.parks@gov.yk.ca
Patented Medicine Prices Review Board, Standard Life Centre, #1400, 333 Laurier Ave. West, PO Box L40, Ottawa, ON K1P 1C1
613-954-8299, Fax: 613-952-7626, 877-861-2350, pmprb@pmprb-cepmb.gc.ca
Spectrum, Information Technologies & Telecommunications, Journal Tower North, 300 Slater St., 20th Fl., Ottawa, ON K1A 0C8
613-998-0368, Fax: 613-952-1203
Standards Council of Canada, #200, 270 Albert St., Ottawa, ON K1P 6N7
613-238-3222, Fax: 613-569-7808, info@scc.ca
Telefilm Canada, #500, 360, rue Saint-Jacques, Montréal, QC H2Y 1P5
514-283-6363, Fax: 514-283-2365, 800-567-0890, info@telefilm.gc.ca
Western Economic Diversification Canada, Canada Place, #1500, 9700 Jasper Ave. NW, Edmonton, AB T5J 4H7
780-495-4164, Fax: 780-495-4557, 888-338-9378

Alberta
Alberta Agriculture & Rural Development, JG O'Donoghue Bldg., #100A, 7000 - 113th St., Edmonton, AB T6H 5T6
780-427-2727, -310-3276, duke@gov.ab.ca
Alberta Grains Council, JG O'Donoghue Bldg., 7000 - 113 St., 3rd Fl., Edmonton, AB T6H 5T6
780-427-7329, Fax: 780-422-9690
Alberta Innovates - Energy & Environmental Solutions, AMEC Place, #2540, 801 - 6th Ave. SW, Calgary, AB T2P 3W2
403-297-7089, ees@albertainnovates.ca
Alberta Livestock & Meat Agency, Ellwood Office Park South, #101, 1003 Ellwood Rd. SW, Edmonton, AB T6X 0B3
780-638-1699, Fax: 780-638-6495, info@almaltd.ca
Community, Learner & Industry Connections Division, Phipps-McKinnon Bldg., 10020 - 101A Ave., 5th Fl., Edmonton, AB T5J 3G2
Energy Resources Conservation Board, #1000, 250 - 5 Ave. SW, Calgary, AB T2P 0R4
403-297-8311, Fax: 403-297-7336, 855-297-8311, inquiries@ercb.ca; infoservices@ercb.ca; ADR@ercb.ca
Alberta Energy, North Petroleum Plaza, 9945 - 108 St., Edmonton, AB T5K 2G6
780-427-8050, Fax: 780-422-0698, -310-0000, Library.Energy@gov.ab.ca
Alberta Environment & Sustainable Resource Development, Oxbridge Place, 9820 - 106 St., Main Fl., Edmonton, AB T5K 2J6
780-427-2700, Fax: 780-422-4086, -310-0000, env.infocent@gov.ab.ca; srd.infocent@gov.ab.ca
Intergovernmental Relations, Commerce Place, 10155 - 102 St., 12th Fl., Edmonton, AB T5J 4G8
780-427-6543, Fax: 780-427-0939
Land Compensation Board, 1229 - 91 St. SW, Edmonton, AB T6X 1E9
srb.lcb@gov.ab.ca

British Columbia
Agricultural Land Commission, #133, 4940 Canada Way, Burnaby, BC V5G 4K6
604-660-7000, Fax: 604-660-7033, ALCBurnaby@Victoria1.gov.bc.ca
British Columbia Farm Industry Review Board, 780 Blanshard St., PO Box 9129 Prov Govt, Victoria, BC V8W 9B5
250-356-8945, Fax: 250-356-5131, firb@gov.bc.ca
British Columbia Hydro, 6911 Southpoint Dr., Burnaby, BC V3N 4X8
604-224-9376, 800-224-9376
British Columbia Ministry of Agriculture, PO Box 9120 Prov Govt,Victoria, BC V8W 9E2
250-387-5121
British Columbia Ministry of Citizens' Services & Open Government, PO Box 9594 Prov Govt,Victoria, BC V8W 9E2
250-952-7623, Fax: 250-952-7628, 800-663-7867, EnquiryBC@gov.bc.ca
British Columbia Ministry of Energy, Mines, & Natural Gas (& Responsible for Housing), PO Box 9053 Prov Govt,Victoria, BC V8W 9E2

British Columbia Ministry of Forests, Lands & Natural Resource Operations, PO Box 9352 Prov Govt,Victoria, BC V8W 9M1
250-387-4809, 877-855-3222, FLNRO.MediaRequests@gov.bc.ca

British Columbia Ministry of Jobs, Tourism, & Skills Training (& Responsible for Labour), PO Box 9071 Prov Govt,Victoria, BC V8W 9E2
EnquiryBC@gov.bc.ca; GCPE.JTI.Media.Requests@gov.bc.ca

British Columbia Utilities Commission, 900 Howe St., 6th Fl., PO Box 250, Vancouver, BC V6Z 2N3
604-660-4700, Fax: 604-660-1102, 800-663-1385, commission.secretary@bcuc.com

Financial Institutions Commission, #1200, 13450 - 102 Ave., Surrey, BC V3T 5X3
604-953-5300, Fax: 604-953-5301, 866-206-3030, FICOM@ficombc.ca; HR@ficombc.ca

Forest Practices Board, 1675 Douglas St., 3rd Fl., PO Box 9905 Prov Govt, Victoria, BC V8W 9R1
250-213-4700, Fax: 250-213-4725, 800-994-5899, fpboard@gov.bc.ca

Insurance Council of British Columbia, #300, 1040 West Georgia St., PO Box 7, Vancouver, BC V6E 4H1
604-688-0321, Fax: 604-662-7767, 877-688-0321

Oil & Gas Commission, #100, 10003 - 110 Ave., Fort St John, BC V1J 6M7
250-794-5200, Fax: 250-794-5375

Real Estate Council of British Columbia, #900, 750 West Pender St., Vancouver, BC V6C 2T8
604-683-9664, Fax: 604-683-9017, 877-683-9664, info@recbc.ca

Manitoba

Manitoba Aboriginal & Northern Affairs, Legislative Bldg, 344-450 Broadway, Winnipeg, MB R3C 0V8
204-945-3719, Fax: 204-945-8374, anaweb@gov.mb.ca

Advisory Council on Workplace Safety & Health, #200, 401 York Ave., Winnipeg, MB R3C 0P8
204-945-3446, Fax: 204-945-4556

Agricultural Societies, 1129 Queens Ave., Brandon, MB R7A 1L9
204-726-6195, Fax: 204-726-6260,

Manitoba Agriculture, Food & Rural Initiatives, Legislative Bldg., 165-450 Broadway, Winnipeg, MB R3C 0V8
204-945-3722, Fax: 204-945-3470, minagr@leg.gov.mb.ca

Community & Economic Development Committee of Cabinet Secretariat, #648, 155 Carlton St., Winnipeg, MB R3C 3H8
204-945-8221, Fax: 204-945-8229

Crown Corporations Council, #1130, 444 St. Mary Ave., Winnipeg, MB R3C 3T1
204-949-5270, Fax: 204-949-5283, crowncc@mts.net

Manitoba Development Corporation, #555, 155 Carlton St., Winnipeg, MB R3C 3H8
204-945-7626, Fax: 204-945-1193

Manitoba Education, #168, Legislative Bldg., 450 Broadway, Winnipeg, MB R3C 0V8
204-945-3720, Fax: 204-945-1291, minedu@leg.gov.mb.ca

Manitoba Entrepreneurship, Training & Trade, #1000, 259 Portage Ave, Winnipeg, MB R3B 3P4
204-945-2475, Fax: 204-945-3977, minctt@leg.gov.mb.ca

Farm Lands Ownership Board, #812, Norquay Bldg., 401 York Ave., Winnipeg, MB R3C 0P8
204-945-3149, Fax: 204-945-1489, 800-282-8069, robert.mckenzie@gov.mb.ca

Farm Machinery Board, Norquay Bldg., #812, 401 York Ave., Winnipeg, MB R3C 0P8
204-945-3856, Fax: 204-948-2844, randy.ozunko@gov.mb.ca

Manitoba Hydro, 360 Portage Ave., PO Box 815 Main,Winnipeg, MB R3C 2P4
204-474-3311, publicaffairs@hydro.mb.ca

Manitoba Immigration & Multiculturalism, Legislative Building, 317, 450 Broadway Ave., Winnipeg, MB R3C 0V8
204-945-4079, Fax: 204-945-8312, minlab@leg.gov.mb.ca

Manitoba Lotteries Corporation, 830 Empress St., Winnipeg, MB R3G 3H3
204-957-2500, Fax: 204-957-3991, 800-265-2912, communications@casinosofwinnipeg.com

Manitoba Agricultural Services Corporation, #100, 1525 First St. South, Brandon, MB R7A 7A1
204-726-6850, Fax: 204-726-6849, mailbox@masc.mb.ca

Manitoba Bureau of Statistics, #824, 155 Carlton St., Winnipeg, MB R3C 3H9
204-945-2406, Fax: 204-945-0695

Manitoba Habitat Heritage Corporation, #200, 1555 St. James St., Winnipeg, MB R3H 1B5
204-784-4350, Fax: 204-784-7359, mhhc@mhhc.mb.ca

Manitoba Labour Board, A.A. Heaps Bldg., #402, 258 Portage Ave., Winnipeg, MB R3C 0B6
204-945-3783, Fax: 204-945-1296, mlb@gov.mb.ca

Manitoba Minimum Wage Board, 614 - 401 York Ave., Winnipeg, MB R3C 0P8
204-945-4889, Fax: 204-948-2085, mw@gov.mb.ca

Public Utilities Board, #400, 330 Portage Ave., Winnipeg, MB R3C 0C4
204-945-2638, Fax: 204-945-2643, 866-854-3698, publicutilities@gov.mb.ca

Taxicab Board, #200, 301 Weston St., Winnipeg, MB R3E 3H4
Fax: 204-948-2315

Tourism Secretariat, 155 Carlton St., 7th Fl., Winnipeg, MB R3C 3H8
800-665-0040

Manitoba Workers' Compensation Board, 333 Broadway Ave., Winnipeg, MB R3C 4W3
204-954-4321, Fax: 204-954-4999, 800-362-3340, wcb@wcb.mb.ca

New Brunswick

Communications Division, Centennial Bldg., PO Box 6000, Fredericton, NB E3B 5H1
506-453-8607, Fax: 506-453-3993

Corporate Services Division, Centennial Building, PO Box 6000, Fredericton, NB E3B 5H1
506-453-3707, Fax: 506-453-5428

New Brunswick Department of Agriculture, Aquaculture & Fisheries, Agricultural Research Station (Experimental Farm), PO Box 6000, Fredericton, NB E3B 5H1
506-453-2666, Fax: 506-453-7170, DAAF-MAAP@gnb.ca

New Brunswick Department of Environment & Local Government, Marysville Place, PO Box 6000, Fredericton, NB E3B 5H1
506-453-2690, Fax: 506-457-4994, elg/egl-info@gnb.ca

New Brunswick Department of Natural Resources, Hugh John Flemming Forestry Centre, PO Box 6000, Fredericton, NB E3B 5H1
506-453-3826, Fax: 506-444-4367, dnrweb@gnb.ca

New Brunswick Department of Social Development, Sartain MacDonald Bldg., 551 King St., PO Box 6000, Fredericton, NB E3B 5H1
506-453-2001, Fax: 506-453-7478, sd-ds@gnb.ca

New Brunswick Farm Products Commission, c/o Department of Agriculture, Aquaculture & Fisheries, PO Box 6000, Fredericton, NB E3B 5H1
506-453-3647, Fax: 506-444-5969

New Brunswick Industrial Development Board, Centennial Building, PO Box 6000, Fredericton, NB E3B 5H1
506-453-4200, Fax: 506-457-7282

New Brunswick Liquor Corporation, 170 Wilsey Rd., PO Box 20787, Fredericton, NB E3B 5B8
506-452-6826, Fax: 506-462-2024, info@anbl.com

Regional Development Corporation, RDC Bldg., 836 Churchill Row, PO Box 428, Fredericton, NB E3B 5R4
506-453-2277, Fax: 506-453-7988

New Brunswick Research & Productivity Council, 921 College Hill Rd., Fredericton, NB E3B 6Z9
506-452-1212, Fax: 506-452-1395, info@rpc.ca

Workplace Health, Safety & Compensation Commission of New Brunswick, 1 Portland St., PO Box 160, Saint John, NB E2L 3X9
506-632-2200, 800-222-9775, communications@ws-ts.nb.ca

Newfoundland & Labrador

Newfoundland & Labrador Housing Corporation, Sir Brian Dunfield Bldg., 2 Canada Dr., PO Box 220, St. John's, NL A1C 5J2
709-724-3000, Fax: 709-724-3250

Newfoundland & Labrador Hydro, Hydro Place, Columbus Dr., PO Box 12400, St. John's, NL A1B 4K7
709-737-1400, Fax: 709-737-1800, hydro@nlh.nl.ca

Labour Relations Board, Beothuck Bldg., 20 Crosbie Pl., 5th Fl., PO Box 8700, St. John's, NL A1B 4J6
709-729-2707, Fax: 709-729-5738, lrb@gov.nl.ca

Newfoundland & Labrador Department of Fisheries & Aquaculture, Petten Bldg., 30 Strawberry Marsh Rd., PO Box 8700, St. John's, NL A1B 4J6
709-729-3723, Fax: 709-729-6082, fisheries@gov.nl.ca

Newfoundland & Labrador Department of Natural Resources, Natural Resources Bldg., 50 Elizabeth Ave., 7th Fl., PO Box 8700, St. John's, NL A1B 4J6
709-729-2920, Fax: 709-729-0059

Newfoundland & Labrador Liquor Corporation, 90 Kenmount Rd., PO Box 8750 A, St. John's, NL A1B 3V1
709-724-1100, Fax: 709-754-0321, info@nfliquor.com

Newfoundland & Labrador Municipal Financing Corporation, Confederation Bldg., PO Box 8700, St. John's, NL A1B 4J6
709-729-6686, Fax: 709-729-2095

Professional Fish Harvesters Certification Board, 368 Hamilton Ave., PO Box 8541, St. John's, NL A1B 3P2
709-722-8170, Fax: 709-722-8201, pfh@pfhcb.com

Newfoundland & Labrador Board of Commissioners of Public Utilities, PO Box 21040, St. John's, NL A1A 5B2
709-726-8600, Fax: 709-726-9604, 866-782-0006, ito@pub.nf.ca

Northwest Territories

Department of Environment & Natural Resources, PO Box 1320, Yellowknife, NT X1A 2L9

Department of Industry, Tourism & Investment, PO Box 1320, Yellowknife, NT X1A 2L9
Fax: 867-873-0306, info@iti.ca

Highways & Marine, 4510 - 50 Ave., 2nd fl., PO Box 1320, Yellowknife, NT X1A 2L9
867-920-8771, Fax: 867-873-0288

Northwest Territories Housing Corporation, Scotia Centre, 5102 50th Ave., PO Box 2100, Yellowknife, NT X1A 2P6
867-873-7853, Fax: 867-873-9426

Northwest Territories Liquor Commission, #201, 31 Capital Dr., Hay River, NT X0E 1G2
867-874-2100, Fax: 867-874-2180

Northwest Territories Liquor Licensing & Enforcement, #210, 31 Capital Dr., Hay River, NT X0E 1G2
867-874-2906, Fax: 867-874-6011

Northwest Territories Liquor Licensing Board, #210, 31 Capital Dr., Hay River, NT X0E 1G2
867-874-2906, Fax: 867-874-6011, delilah_st-arneault@gov.nt.ca

Northwest Territories Power Corporation, 4 Capital Dr., Hay River, NT X0E 1G2
867-874-5200, Fax: 867-874-5251, info@ntpc.com

Nova Scotia

Department of Agriculture, 1741 Brunswick St., 3rd Fl., PO Box 2223, Halifax, NS B3J 3C4
902-424-4560, Fax: 902-424-4671

Crane Operators Appeal Board, 5151 Terminal Rd., 7th Fl., PO Box 697, Halifax, NS B3J 2T8
902-424-8595, Fax: 902-424-0217, fernanfs@gov.ns.ca

Department of Economic & Rural Development & Tourism, Centennial Building, #600, 1660 Hollis St., PO Box 2311, Halifax, NS B3J 1V7
902-424-0377, Fax: 902-424-0500, comm@gov.ns.ca

Film Nova Scotia, Collins Bank Bldg., 1869 Upper Water St., 3rd Fl., Halifax, NS B3J 1S9
902-424-7177, Fax: 902-424-0617, 888-360-2111

InNOVACorp, #1400, 1801 Hollis St., Halifax, NS B3J 3N4
902-424-8670, Fax: 902-424-4679, 800-565-7051, communications@innovacorp.ca

Nova Scotia Liquor Corporation, Bayers Lake Business Park, 93 Chain Lake Dr., Halifax, NS B3S 1A3
902-450-6752, 800-567-5874

Department of Natural Resources, Founder's Square, 1701 Hollis St., 3rd Fl., PO Box 698, Halifax, NS B3J 2T9
902-424-5935, Fax: 902-424-0594, 800-565-2224

Nova Scotia Farm Loan Board, PO Box 550, Truro, NS B2N 5E3
902-893-6506, Fax: 902-895-7693, flb@gov.ns.ca

Trade Centre Limited, 1800 Argyle St., PO Box 955, Halifax, NS B3J 2V9
902-421-8686, Fax: 902-422-2922,

Nova Scotia Utility & Review Board, Summit Place, 1601 Lower Water St., 3rd Fl., PO Box 1692 M,Halifax, NS B3J 3S3
902-424-4448, Fax: 902-424-3919, uarb.board@gov.ns.ca

Waterfront Development Corporation Ltd., 1751 Lower Water St., 2nd Fl., Halifax, NS B3J 1S5
902-422-6591, Fax: 902-422-7582, info@wdcl.ca

Nunavut

Department of Economic Development & Transportation, Bldg. 1104 A, Inuksugait Plaza, PO Box 1000 1500,Iqaluit, NU X0A 0H0
867-975-7800, Fax: 867-975-7870, 888-975-5999, edt@gov.nu.ca

Nunavut Liquor Licensing Board, Bag 002, Rankin Inlet, NU X0C 0G0
Fax: 867-645-3327

Ontario

AGRICORP, 1 Stone Rd. West, 3rd Fl., PO Box 3660 Central, Guelph, ON N1H 8M4
Fax: 519-826-4118, 888-247-4999, cac@agricorp.com

Agricultural Research Institute of Ontario, 1 Stone Rd. West, 2nd Fl., Guelph, ON N1G 4Y2
519-826-4199, Fax: 519-826-4211

Ontario Ministry of Agriculture, Food & Rural Affairs, Ontario Government Bldg., 1 Stone Rd. West, Guelph, ON N1G 4Y2
519-826-3100, 888-466-2372

Building Code Commission, 777 Bay St., 2nd Fl., Toronto, ON M5G 2E5
416-585-6666, Fax: 416-585-7531

Building Materials Evaluation Commission, 777 Bay St., 2nd Fl., Toronto, ON M5G 2E5
416-585-4234, Fax: 416-585-7531

Ontario Ministry of Consumer Services, Mowat Block, 900 Bay St., 6th Fl., Toronto, ON M7A 1L2
416-327-8300, Fax: 416-326-1947, 866-665-0662, infomcs@ontario.ca

Corporate Services Division, Hearst Block, 900 Bay St., 7th fl., Toronto, ON M7A 2E1
416-325-6486, Fax: 416-325-6392

Ontario Ministry of Economic Development & Innovation, Hearst Block, 900 Bay St., 8th Fl., Toronto, ON M7A 2E1
416-325-6666, Fax: 416-325-6688, 866-668-4249, info@edt.gov.on.ca

Ontario Ministry of Environment, 135 St. Clair Ave. West, Toronto, ON M4V 1P5
416-325-4000, Fax: 416-325-3159, 800-565-4923
Environmental Commissioner of Ontario, #605, 1075 Bay St., Toronto, ON M5S 2B1
416-325-3377, Fax: 416-325-3370, 800-701-6454, commissioner@eco.on.ca
Ontario Ministry of Government Services, Whitney Block, #4320, 99 Wellesley St. West, 4th Fl., Toronto, ON M7A 1W3
416-326-1234, Fax: 416-327-3790, 800-268-1142
Hydro One Inc., North Tower, 483 Bay St., Toronto, ON M5G 2P5
416-345-5000, 877-955-1155, customercommunications@HydroOne.com
Independent Electricity System Operator, PO Box 4474 A,Toronto, ON M5W 4E5
905-403-6900, Fax: 905-403-6921, 888-448-7777, customer.relations@ieso.ca
Ontario Ministry of Labour, 400 University Ave., 14th Fl., Toronto, ON M7A 1T7
416-326-7160, 800-531-5551
Ontario Ministry of Municipal Affairs & Housing, College Park, 777 Bay St., 17th Fl., Toronto, ON M5G 2E5
416-585-7041, Fax: 416-585-6470, 866-220-2290, mininfo@ontario.ca
Ontario Ministry of Natural Resources, Whitney Block, #6630, 99 Wellesley St. West, 6th Fl., Toronto, ON M7A 1W3
800-667-1940
Ontario Ministry of Northern Development & Mines, 159 Cedar St., Sudbury, ON P3E 6A5
Fax: 416-327-0651, 888-415-9845
Office of the Employer Advisor, #704, 151 Bloor St. West., Toronto, ON M5S 1S4
416-327-0020, Fax: 416-327-0726, 800-387-0774
Ontario Media Development Corporation, South Tower, #501, 175 Bloor St. East, Toronto, ON M4W 3R8
416-314-6858, Fax: 416-314-6876, mail@omdc.on.ca
Ontario Power Generation, 700 University Ave., Toronto, ON M5G 1X6
416-592-2555, 877-592-2555, webmaster@opg.com
ServiceOntario, College Park, 777 Bay St., 15th fl., Toronto, ON M7A 2J3
416-326-1234, Fax: 416-326-1313, 800-267-8097
Ontario Ministry of Tourism & Culture, Hearst Block, 900 Bay St., 9th Fl., Toronto, ON M7A 2E1
416-326-9326, Fax: 416-314-7854, 800-668-2746
Workplace Safety & Insurance Board, 200 Front St. West, Ground Fl., Toronto, ON M5V 3J1
416-344-1000, Fax: 416-344-4684, 800-387-0750

Prince Edward Island

Advisory Council on the Status of Women, Sherwood Business Centre, 161 St. Peter's Rd., Main Level, PO Box 2000, Charlottetown, PE C1A 7N8
902-368-4510, Fax: 902-368-3269, peistatusofwomen@eastlink.ca
Agricultural Insurance Corporation, 29 Indigo Cres., PO Box 1600, Charlottetown, PE C1A 7N3
902-368-4842, Fax: 902-368-6677
Anne of Green Gables Licensing Authority Inc., 94 Euston, PO Box 910, Charlottetown, PE C1A 7L9
902-569-7787, Fax: 902-368-6301, kobaker@gov.pe.ca; aggla@bellnet.ca
BIO FOOD TECH, 101 Belvedere Ave., PO Box 2000, Charlottetown, PE C1A 7N8
902-368-5548, Fax: 902-368-5549, 877-368-5548, biofoodtech@biofoodtech.ca
Charlottetown Area Development Corporation, 4 Pownal St., PO Box 786, Charlottetown, PE C1A 7L9
902-892-5341, Fax: 902-368-1935
Grain Elevators Corporation, 7 Gerald McCarville Dr., PO Box 250, Kensington, PE C0B 1M0
902-836-8935, Fax: 902-836-8926
Innovation PEI, 94 Euston St., PO Box 910, Charlottetown, PE C1A 7L9
902-368-6300, Fax: 902-368-6301, 800-563-3734
Prince Edward Island Department of Agriculture & Forestry, Jones Bldg., 11 Kent St., PO Box 2000, Charlottetown, PE C1A 7N8
902-368-4880, Fax: 902-368-4857
Prince Edward Island Department of Innovation & Advanced Learning, Shaw Bldg., 105 Rochford St., 5th Fl., PO Box 2000, Charlottetown, PE C1A 7N8
902-368-4240, Fax: 902-368-4242
Prince Edward Island Department of Tourism & Culture, PO Box 2000, Charlottetown, PE C1A 7N8
902-368-5540, Fax: 902-368-5277, tpswitch@gov.pe.ca
Prince Edward Island Department of Transportation & Infrastructure Renewal, Jones Bldg., 11 Kent St., 3rd Fl., PO Box 2000, Charlottetown, PE C1A 7N8
902-368-5100, Fax: 902-368-5395
Prince Edward Island Liquor Control Commission, 3 Garfield St., PO Box 967, Charlottetown, PE C1A 7M4
902-368-5710, Fax: 902-368-5735
Prince Edward Island Workers Compensation Board, 14 Weymouth St., PO Box 757, Charlottetown, PE C1A 7L7
902-368-5680, Fax: 902-368-5696, 800-237-5049
SkillsPEI, Atlantic Technology Centre, #212, 90 University Ave., Charlottetown, PE C1A 4K9
902-368-4260, Fax: 902-368-6340, 877-491-4766

Quebec

Agence de l'efficacité énergétique, 5700, 4e av ouest, Québec, QC G1H 6R1
418-627-6379, Fax: 418-643-5828, 877-727-6655, efficaciteenergetique@mrnf.gouv.qc.ca
Ministère de l'Agriculture, des Pêcheries et de l'Alimentation, 200, ch Sainte-Foy, Québec, QC G1R 4X6
418-380-2110, 888-222-6272
Centre de recherche industrielle du Québec, 333, rue Franquet, Québec, QC G1P 4C7
418-659-1550, Fax: 418-652-2251, 800-667-2386, infocriq@criq.qc.ca
Comité conjoint de chasse, de pêche et de piégeage, #C220, 383 rue Saint-Jacques, Montréal, QC H2Y 1N9
514-284-2151, Fax: 514-284-0039, infohftcc@cccpp-hftcc.com
Commission de protection du territoire agricole du Québec, 200, ch Ste-Foy, 2e étage, Québec, QC G1R 4X6
418-643-3314, Fax: 418-643-2261, 800-667-5294, info@cptaq.gouv.qc.ca
Conseil consultatif du travail et de la main d'oeuvre, #9.400, 500, boul René-Lévesque ouest, Montréal, QC H2Z 1W7
514-873-2880, Fax: 514-873-1129, cctm@cctm.gouv.qc.ca
Ministère de la Culture, des Communications & de la Condition féminine, 225, Grande Allée est, Québec, QC G1R 5G5
888-380-8882
Ministère du Développement durable, de l'Environnement, de la Faune, et des Parcs, Édifice Marie-Guyart, 675, boul René-Lévesque est, 29e étage, Québec, QC G1R 5V7
418-521-3830, Fax: 418-646-5974, 800-561-1616, info@mddep.gouv.qc.ca
Ministère du Développement économique, de l'Innovation et de l'Exportation, 710, place D'Youville, 3e étage, Québec, QC G1R 4Y4
418-691-5950, Fax: 418-644-0118, 866-680-1884
Hydro-Québec, 75, boul René-Lévesque ouest, Montréal, QC H2Z 1A4
514-289-2211
Innovatech Québec, #410, 888, rue St-Jean, Québec, QC G1R 5H6
418-528-9770, Fax: 418-528-9783, 866-605-1676
La financière agricole de Québec, 1400, boul de la Rive-Sud, Saint-Romuald, QC G6W 8K7
418-838-5602, Fax: 418-833-3871, 800-749-3646, financiereagricole@fadq.qc.ca
Régie des marchés agricoles et alimentaires du Québec, 201, boul Crémazie est, 5e étage, Montréal, QC H2M 1L3
514-873-4024, Fax: 514-873-3984
Régie du bâtiment du Québec, 545, boul Crémazie est, 4e étage, Montréal, QC H2M 2V2
514-873-0976, Fax: 514-864-2903, 800-361-0761, crc@rbq.gouv.qc.ca
Société d'habitation du Québec, Aile St-Amable, 1054, rue Louis-Alexandre-Taschereau, 3e étage, Québec, QC G1R 5E7
418-643-4035, Fax: 418-643-2533, 800-463-4315
Société de développement des entreprises culturelles, #800, 215, rue Saint-Jacques, Montréal, QC H2Y 1M6
514-841-2200, Fax: 514-841-8606, 800-363-0401, info@sodec.gouv.qc.ca
Société québécoise de récupération et de recyclage, #200, 420, boul Charest est, Québec, QC G1K 8M4
418-643-0394, Fax: 418-643-6507, 866-523-8290, info@recyc-quebec.gouv.qc.ca
Ministère du Tourisme, #400, 900, boul René-Lévesque est, Québec, QC G1R 2B5
418-643-5959, Fax: 418-646-8723, 800-482-2433

Saskatchewan

Agri-Food Council, #302, 3085 Albert St., Regina, SK S4S 0B1
306-787-5978, Fax: 306-787-5134, corey.ruud@gov.sk.ca
Crown Investments Corporation of Saskatchewan, #400, 2400 College Ave., Regina, SK S4P 1C8
306-787-6851, Fax: 306-787-8125
Energy & Resources, #300, 2103 - 11th Ave., Regina, SK S4P 3Z8
306-787-2528
Farm Stress Unit, #125, 3085 Albert St., Regina, SK S4S 0B1
306-787-5196, Fax: 306-798-3042, 800-667-4442
Labour Relations Board, #1600, 1920 Broad St., Regina, SK S4P 3V2
306-787-2406, Fax: 306-787-2664
Prairie Agricultural Machinery Institute, Hwy 5 West, PO Box 1150, Humboldt, SK S0K 2A0
306-682-2555, Fax: 306-682-5080, 800-567-7264, humboldt@pami.ca
Saskatchewan Agriculture, Walter Scott Bldg., 3085 Albert St., Regina, SK S4S 0B1
866-457-2377, aginfo@gov.sk.ca
Saskatchewan Crop Insurance Corporation, 484 Prince William Dr., PO Box 3000, Melville, SK S0A 2P0
306-728-7200, Fax: 306-728-7202, 888-935-0000, customer.service@scic.gov.sk.ca
Saskatchewan Environment, 3211 Albert St., 2nd Fl., Regina, SK S4S 5W6
306-787-2584, Fax: 306-787-9544, 800-567-4224, Centre.Inquiry@gov.sk.ca
Saskatchewan Lands Appeal Board, #202, 3085 Albert St., Regina, SK S4S 0B1
306-787-4693, Fax: 306-787-1315, Donald.Brooks@gov.sk.ca
Saskatchewan Liquor & Gaming Authority, 2500 Victoria Ave., PO Box 5054, Regina, SK S4P 3M3
306-787-4213, inquiry@slga.gov.sk.ca
Saskatchewan Power Corporation (SaskPower), 2025 Victoria Ave., Regina, SK S4P 0S1
306-566-3306, Fax: 800-757-6937, 888-757-6937
Saskatchewan Water Corporation (SaskWater), #200, 111 Fairford St. East, Moose Jaw, SK S6H 1C8
Fax: 306-694-3207, 888-230-1111, comm@saskwater.com; customerservice@saskwater.com
Saskatchewan Workers' Compensation Board, #200, 1881 Scarth St., Regina, SK S4P 4L1
306-787-4370, Fax: 306-787-4311, 800-667-7590, internet_clientsvc@wcbsask.com
Saskatchewan Workers' Compensation Board, #200, 1881 Scarth St., Regina, SK S4P 4L1
306-787-4370, Fax: 306-787-7582, 800-667-7590, internet_clientsvc@wcbsask.com
SaskEnergy Incorporated, 1777 Victoria Ave., Regina, SK S4P 4K5
306-777-9225, 800-567-8899

Yukon Territory

Yukon Development Corporation, #2 Miles Canyon Rd., PO Box 5920, Whitehorse, YT Y1A 6S7
867-393-5337, Fax: 867-393-5401
Yukon Economic Development, PO Box 2703, Whitehorse, YT Y1A 2C6
867-393-7191, Fax: 867-393-6412, 800-661-0408, ecdev@gov.yk.ca
Yukon Environment, PO Box 2703, Whitehorse, YT Y1A 2C6
867-667-5652, Fax: 867-393-7197, environment.yukon@gov.yk.ca
Yukon Housing Corporation, 410H Jarvis St., PO Box 2703, Whitehorse, YT Y1A 2H5
867-667-5759, Fax: 867-667-3664, 800-661-0408, ykhouse@housing.yk.ca
Yukon Liquor Corporation, 9031 Quartz Rd., Whitehorse, YT Y1A 4P9
867-667-5245, Fax: 867-393-6306, yukon.liquor@gov.yk.ca
Yukon Tourism & Culture, 100 Hanson St., Whitehorse, YT Y1A 2C6
867-667-5036, Fax: 867-667-3546

INDUSTRY & TRADE

Atlantic Canada Opportunities Agency, Blue Cross Centre, 644 Main St., 3rd Fl., PO Box 6051, Moncton, NB E1C 9J8
506-851-2271, Fax: 506-851-7403, 800-561-7862, information@acoa-apeca.gc.ca
Business Development Bank of Canada, #400, 5, Place Ville-Marie, Montréal, QC H3B 5E7
514-283-5904, Fax: 514-283-5626, 877-232-2269
Corporate Services Division, PO Box 2000, Charlottetown, PE C1A 7N8
Defence Construction Canada, Constitution Square, 350 Albert St., 19th Fl., Ottawa, ON K1A 0K3
613-998-9548, Fax: 613-998-1061, 800-514-3555, info@dcc-cdc.gc.ca
Export Development Canada, 151 Slater St., Ottawa, ON K1A 1K3
613-598-2500, Fax: 613-598-3811, 800-267-8510
Foreign Affairs & International Trade Canada, 125 Sussex Dr., Ottawa, ON K1A 0G2
613-944-4000, Fax: 613-996-9709, 800-267-8376, enqserv@international.gc.ca
Industrial Materials Institute, 75, boul de Mortagne, Boucherville, QC J4B 6Y4
450-641-5000, Fax: 450-641-5101, Imi-Info@cnrc-nrc.gc.ca
Industry Canada, C.D. Howe Building, 235 Queen St., Ottawa, ON K1A 0H5
613-954-5031, Fax: 613-954-2340, 800-328-6189, info@ic.gc.ca

Institute for Research in Construction, Bldg. M-24, 1500 Montreal Rd., Ottawa, ON K1A 0R6
613-993-2607, Fax: 613-952-7673, Irc.Client-Services@nrc-cnrc.gc.ca

London - Centre for Automotive Materials & Manufacturing, 800 Collip Circle, London, ON N6G 4X8
519-430-7166, Fax: 519-430-7064, John.Lyons@nrc-cnrc.gc.ca

Market & Industry Services Branch, Tower 5, 1341 Baseline Rd., Ottawa, ON K1A 0C5
613-759-1000, Fax: 613-773-1711

Standards Council of Canada, #200, 270 Albert St., Ottawa, ON K1P 6N7
613-238-3222, Fax: 613-569-7808, info@scc.ca

Western Economic Diversification Canada, Canada Place, #1500, 9700 Jasper Ave. NW, Edmonton, AB T5J 4H7
780-495-4164, Fax: 780-495-4557, 888-338-9378

British Columbia

Timber Export Advisory Committee, PO Box 9514 Prov Govt, Victoria, BC V8W 9C2
250-387-8916, Fax: 250-387-5050

Manitoba

Manitoba Entrepreneurship, Training & Trade, #1000, 259 Portage Ave, Winnipeg, MB R3B 3P4
204-945-2475, Fax: 204-945-3977, minctt@leg.gov.mb.ca

New Brunswick

New Brunswick Department of Economic Development, Centennial Building, PO Box 6000, Fredericton, NB E3B 5H1
506-453-3707, Fax: 506-453-3993, 800-665-1800, tradenb@gnb.ca

New Brunswick Industrial Development Board, Centennial Building, PO Box 6000, Fredericton, NB E3B 5H1
506-453-4200, Fax: 506-457-7282

Regional Development Corporation, RDC Bldg., 836 Churchill Row, PO Box 428, Fredericton, NB E3B 5R4
506-453-2277, Fax: 506-453-7988

Northwest Territories

Department of Environment & Natural Resources, PO Box 1320, Yellowknife, NT X1A 2L9

Nova Scotia

Department of Agriculture, 1741 Brunswick St., 3rd Fl., PO Box 2223, Halifax, NS B3J 3C4
902-424-4560, Fax: 902-424-4671

Department of Economic & Rural Development & Tourism, Centennial Building, #600, 1660 Hollis St., PO Box 2311, Halifax, NS B3J 1V7
902-424-0377, Fax: 902-424-0500, comm@gov.ns.ca

Pay Equity Commission, 5151 Terminal Rd., 6th Fl., PO Box 697, Halifax, NS B3J 2T8
902-424-2385, Fax: 902-424-0575

Workers' Compensation Board of Nova Scotia, 5668 South St., PO Box 1150, Halifax, NS B3J 2Y2
902-491-8999, Fax: 902-491-8002, 800-870-3331, info@wcb.gov.ns.ca

Ontario

Ontario Ministry of Economic Development & Innovation, Hearst Block, 900 Bay St., 8th Fl., Toronto, ON M7A 2E1
416-325-6666, Fax: 416-325-6688, 866-668-4249, info@edt.gov.on.ca

Ontario Ministry of Northern Development & Mines, 159 Cedar St., Sudbury, ON P3E 6A5
Fax: 416-327-0651, 888-415-9845

Prince Edward Island

Prince Edward Island Department of Innovation & Advanced Learning, Shaw Bldg., 105 Rochford St., 5th Fl., PO Box 2000, Charlottetown, PE C1A 7N8
902-368-4240, Fax: 902-368-4242,

Quebec

Commission des lésions professionnelles, #700, 900, Place d'Youville, Québec, QC G1R 3P7
418-644-7777, Fax: 418-644-6443, 800-463-1591

Innovatech Québec, #410, 888, rue St-Jean, Québec, QC G1R 5H6
418-528-9770, Fax: 418-528-9783, 866-605-1676

Saskatchewan

Energy & Resources, #300, 2103 - 11th Ave., Regina, SK S4P 3Z8
306-787-2528

Yukon Territory

Yukon Development Corporation, #2 Miles Canyon Rd., PO Box 5920, Whitehorse, YT Y1A 6S7
867-393-5337, Fax: 867-393-5401

INFORMATION & PRIVACY COMMISSIONER

Office of the Information Commissioner of Canada, Place de Ville, Tower B, 112 Kent St., 7th Fl., Ottawa, ON K1A 1H3
613-995-2410, Fax: 613-947-7294, 800-267-0441, general@oic-ci.gc.ca

Privacy Commissioner of Canada, Tower B, Place de Ville, 112 Kent St., 3rd Fl., Ottawa, ON K1A 1H3
613-947-1698, Fax: 613-947-6850, 800-282-1376

Ontario

Information & Privacy Commissioner of Ontario, #1400, 2 Bloor St. East, Toronto, ON M4W 1A8
416-326-3333, Fax: 416-325-9195, 800-387-0073, info@ipc.on.ca

Saskatchewan

Information & Privacy Commissioner of Saskatchewan, #503, 1801 Hamilton St., Regina, SK S4P 4B4
306-787-8350, Fax: 306-798-1603, 877-748-2298, webmaster@oipc.sk.ca

INFORMATION RESOURCES

Industry Canada, C.D. Howe Building, 235 Queen St., Ottawa, ON K1A 0H5
613-954-5031, Fax: 613-954-2340, 800-328-6189, info@ic.gc.ca

Mapping Services Branch - Geomatics Canada, 615 Booth St., Ottawa, ON K1A 0E9
613-995-4945, Fax: 613-995-8737

Public Works & Government Services Canada, Place du Portage, Phase III, 11, rue Laurier, Ottawa, ON K1A 0S5
questions@tpsgc-pwgsc.gc.ca

Statistics Canada, R.H. Coats Bldg., Tunney's Pasture, 150 Tunney's Pasture Driveway, Ottawa, ON K1A 0T6
613-951-8116, Fax: 877-287-4369, 800-263-1136, infostats@statcan.ca

Nova Scotia

Geomatics Centre, 160 Willow St., Amherst, NS B4H 3W5
902-667-7231, Fax: 902-667-6008, 800-798-0706, geoinfo@gov.ns.ca

Ontario

Ontario Geographic Names Board, Robinson Place, 300 Water St., 2nd Fl., PO Box 7000, Peterborough, ON K9J 8M5
705-755-2134

Science & Information Resources Division, Roberta Bondar Pl., #400, 70 Foster Dr., Sault Ste Marie, ON P6A 6V5
705-755-2000, Fax: 705-755-2802, 800-667-1940

Saskatchewan

Saskatchewan Conservation Data Centre, 3211 Albert St., Regina, SK S4S 5W6
306-787-9038, Fax: 306-787-9544

INSURANCE (LIFE, FIRE, PROPERTY)

See Also: Automobile Insurance; Health Care Insurance

Alberta

Budget & Fiscal Planning, Terrace Building, 9515 - 107 St., 4th Fl., Edmonton, AB T5K 2C3

Canada Deposit Insurance Corporation, 50 O'Connor St., 17th Floor, PO Box 2340 D,Ottawa, ON K1P 5W5
Fax: 613-996-6095, 800-461-2342, info@cdic.ca; info@sadc.ca

Office of the Superintendent of Financial Institutions, Kent Square, 255 Albert St., Ottawa, ON K1A 0H2
613-990-7788, Fax: 613-990-5591, 800-385-8647, information@osfi-bsif.gc.ca

British Columbia

Insurance Council of British Columbia, #300, 1040 West Georgia St., PO Box 7, Vancouver, BC V6E 4H1
604-688-0321, Fax: 604-662-7767, 877-688-0321

Manitoba

Financial Institutions Regulation Branch, #1115, 405 Broadway, Winnipeg, MB R3C 3L6
204-945-2542, Fax: 204-948-2268

Manitoba Public Insurance, #B100, 234 Donald St., PO Box 6300, Winnipeg, MB R3C 4A4
204-985-7000, Fax: 204-985-3525, 800-665-2410

Manitoba Agricultural Services Corporation, #100, 1525 First St. South, Brandon, MB R7A 7A1
204-726-6850, Fax: 204-726-6849, mailbox@masc.mb.ca

Northwest Territories

Department of Finance, Arthur Laing Building, 5th Fl., 5003 - 49th St., PO Box 1320, Yellowknife, NT X1A 2L9
867-873-7117, Fax: 867-873-0414

Nova Scotia

Nova Scotia Utility & Review Board, Summit Place, 1601 Lower Water St., 3rd Fl., Halifax, NS B3J 3P6
902-424-4448, Fax: 902-424-3919, uarb.board@gov.ns.ca

Ontario

Deposit Insurance Corporation of Ontario, #700, 4711 Yonge St., Toronto, ON M2N 6K8
416-325-9444, Fax: 416-325-9722, 800-268-6653

Financial Services Commission of Ontario, New York City Ctr., 5160 Yonge St., 17th Fl., PO Box 85, Toronto, ON M2N 6L9
416-250-7250, Fax: 416-590-7070, 800-668-0128

Prince Edward Island

Agricultural Insurance Corporation, 29 Indigo Cres., PO Box 1600, Charlottetown, PE C1A 7N3
902-368-4842, Fax: 902-368-6677

Quebec

Commission administrative des régimes de retraite et d'assurances (Québec), 475, rue Saint-Amable, Québec, QC G1R 5X3
418-643-4881, Fax: 418-644-3839, 800-463-5533

Saskatchewan

Saskatchewan Crop Insurance Corporation, 484 Prince William Dr., PO Box 3000, Melville, SK S0A 2P0
306-728-7200, Fax: 306-728-7202, 888-935-0000, customer.service@scic.gov.sk.ca

Saskatchewan Financial Services Commission, #601, 1919 Saskatchewan Dr., Regina, SK S4P 4H2
306-787-5645, Fax: 306-787-5899

Saskatchewan Government Insurance, 2260 - 11th Ave., Regina, SK S4P 0J9
306-751-1200, Fax: 306-787-7477, 800-667-8015, sgiinquiries@sgi.sk.ca

INTELLECTUAL PROPERTY

London - Centre for Automotive Materials & Manufacturing, 800 Collip Circle, London, ON N6G 4X8
519-430-7166, Fax: 519-430-7064, John.Lyons@nrc-cnrc.gc.ca

INTERGOVERNMENTAL AFFAIRS

See: Federal-Provincial Affairs; International Affairs

Canadian Tourism Commission, Four Bentall Centre, #1400, 1055 Dunsmuir St., PO Box 49230, Vancouver, BC V7X 1L2
604-638-8300

INTERNATIONAL AFFAIRS

See Also: Trade

Canadian International Development Agency, 200, Promenade du Portage, Gatineau, QC K1A 0G4
819-997-5456, Fax: 819-953-6088, 800-230-6349, info@acdi-cida.gc.ca

Canadian International Trade Tribunal, Standard Life Centre, 333 Laurier Ave. West, 15 Floor, Ottawa, ON K1A 0G7
613-990-2452, Fax: 613-990-2439, secretary@citt-tcce.gc.ca

Canadian Tourism Commission, Four Bentall Centre, #1400, 1055 Dunsmuir St., PO Box 49230, Vancouver, BC V7X 1L2
604-638-8300

Foreign Affairs & International Trade Canada, 125 Sussex Dr., Ottawa, ON K1A 0G2
613-944-4000, Fax: 613-996-9709, 800-267-8376, enqserv@international.gc.ca

International Development Research Centre, 150 Kent St., PO Box 8500, Ottawa, ON K1G 3H9
613-236-6163, Fax: 613-238-7230, info@idrc.ca

National Defence Canada, Major-General George R. Pearkes Bldg., 101 Colonel By Dr., Ottawa, ON K1A 0K2
613-995-2534, Fax: 613-992-4739, 800-856-8488

Alberta

Alberta International & Intergovernmental Relations, Commerce Place, 10155 - 102 St., 12th Fl., Edmonton, AB T5J 4G8
780-422-1510, -310-0000

British Columbia

Intergovernmental Relations Secretariat, PO Box 9333 Prov Govt,Victoria, BC V8W 9N3
250-387-0752, Fax: 250-387-1920, igrs@gov.bc.ca; protocol@gov.bc.ca

Manitoba

Manitoba Local Government, #301, 450 Broadway Ave., Winnipeg, MB R3C 0V8
Fax: 204-945-1383, mnia@leg.gov.mb.ca

New Brunswick

Intergovernmental Affairs Division, Centennial Bldg., #274, 670 King St., PO Box 6000, Fredericton, NB E3B 5H1
506-457-7275, Fax: 506-453-2995, iga@gnb.ca

Ontario

Ontario Ministry of Intergovernmental Affairs, 77 Wellesley St. West, Toronto, ON M7A 1N3
416-325-4800, Fax: 416-325-4787

Quebec

Ministère des Relations internationales, Édifice Hector-Fabre, 525, boul Réne-Lévesque est, Québec, QC G1R 5R9
418-649-2300, Fax: 418-649-2656

INTERNATIONAL AID

Canadian International Development Agency, 200, Promenade du Portage, Gatineau, QC K1A 0G4
819-997-5456, Fax: 819-953-6088, 800-230-6349, info@acdi-cida.gc.ca

International Development Research Centre, 150 Kent St., PO Box 8500, Ottawa, ON K1G 3H9
613-236-6163, Fax: 613-238-7230, info@idrc.ca

INVESTMENT

See Also: Business Development; Industry

Canada Economic Development for Québec Regions, Édifice Dominion Square, #900, 1255, rue Peel, Montréal, QC H3B 2T9
514-283-6412, Fax: 514-283-3302, 866-385-6412

Canada Pension Plan Investment Board, #2600, 1 Queen St. East, PO Box 101, Toronto, ON M5C 2W5
416-868-4075, Fax: 416-868-8689, 866-557-9510, csr@cppib.ca

Canada Savings Bonds, #900, 110 Yonge St., Toronto, ON M5C 1T4
416-952-1252, Fax: 416-952-1270, 800-575-5151, csb@csb.gc.ca

Finance Canada, L'esplanade Laurier, 140 O'Connor St., Ottawa, ON K1A 0G5
613-992-1573, Fax: 613-943-0938, finpub@fin.gc.ca

Industry Canada, C.D. Howe Building, 235 Queen St., Ottawa, ON K1A 0H5
613-954-5031, Fax: 613-954-2340, 800-328-6189, info@ic.gc.ca

Public Sector Pension Investment Board, #200, 440 Laurier Ave. West, Ottawa, ON K1R 7X6
613-782-3095, Fax: 613-782-6864, info@investpsp.ca

Tax & Revenue Administration, Sir Frederick W. Haultain Building, 9811 - 109 St., 2nd Fl., Edmonton, AB T5K 2L5
780-427-3044

Alberta

Intergovernmental Relations, Commerce Place, 10155 - 102 St., 12th Fl., Edmonton, AB T5J 4G8
780-427-6543, Fax: 780-427-0939

British Columbia

Forestry Innovation Investment Ltd., #1200, 1130 West Pender St., Vancouver, BC V6E 4A4
604-685-7507, Fax: 604-685-5373, info@bcfii.ca

Labour Market & Immigration Division, PO Box 9213, Vancouver, BC V8W 9J1
250-953-3585, Fax: 250-356-0033

New Brunswick

Corporate Services Division, Centennial Building, PO Box 6000, Fredericton, NB E3B 5H1
506-453-3707, Fax: 506-453-5428

New Brunswick Investment Management Corporation, York Tower, #581, 440 King St., Fredericton, NB E3B 5H8
506-444-5800, Fax: 506-444-5025, comments@nbimc.com

Northwest Territories

Department of Industry, Tourism & Investment, PO Box 1320, Yellowknife, NT X1A 2L9
Fax: 867-873-0306, info@iti.ca

Nova Scotia

InNOVACorp, #1400, 1801 Hollis St., Halifax, NS B3J 3N4
902-424-8670, Fax: 902-424-4679, 800-565-7051, communications@innovacorp.ca

Prince Edward Island

Charlottetown Area Development Corporation, 4 Pownal St., PO Box 786, Charlottetown, PE C1A 7L9
902-892-5341, Fax: 902-368-1935

Prince Edward Island Lending Agency, Homburg Financial Tower, 98 Fitzroy St., 2nd Fl., Charlottetown, PE C1A 1R7
902-368-6200, Fax: 902-368-6201

JUSTICE DEPARTMENTS

Justice Canada, East Memorial Bldg., 284 Wellington St., Ottawa, ON K1A 0H8
613-957-4222, Fax: 613-954-0811, webadmin@justice.gc.ca

Alberta

Alberta Justice & Solicitor General, Communications, Bowker Building, 9833 - 109 St., 3rd Fl., Edmonton, AB T5K 2E8
780-427-2745, 800-310-0000,

British Columbia

British Columbia Ministry of Justice, PO Box 9044 Prov Govt,Victoria, BC V8W 9E2

Manitoba

Manitoba Justice, Legislative Building, #104, 405 Broadway Ave., Winnipeg, MB R3C 3L6
204-945-3728, Fax: 204-945-2517, minjus@gov.mb.ca

Newfoundland & Labrador

Newfoundland & Labrador Department of Justice, Confederation Bldg., East Block, 4th Fl., PO Box 8700, St. John's, NL A1B 4J6
709-729-2869, Fax: 709-729-0469, justice@gov.nl.ca

Northwest Territories

Department of Justice, Courthouse, 4903 - 49th St., 6th Fl., PO Box 1320, Yellowknife, NT X1A 2L9
867-920-6197

Nova Scotia

Department of Justice, 5151 Terminal Rd., 4th Fl., PO Box 7, Halifax, NS B3J 2L6
902-424-4030, Fax: 902-424-0510, justweb@gov.ns.ca

Nunavut

Department of Justice, Sivummut, 1st Fl., PO Box 1000 500,Iqaluit, NU X0A 0H0
867-975-6170, Fax: 867-975-6195, justice@gov.nu.ca

Ontario

Ontario Ministry of the Attorney General, McMurtry-Scott Bldg., 720 Bay St., 11th Fl., Toronto, ON M5G 2K1
416-326-2220, Fax: 416-326-4007, 800-518-7901

Quebec

Ministère de la Justice, Édifice Louis-Philippe-Pigeon, 1200, rte de l'Église, Québec, QC G1V 4M1
418-643-5140, 866-536-5140, informations@justice.gouv.qc.ca

Saskatchewan

Saskatchewan Justice & Attorney General, 1874 Scarth St., Regina, SK S4P 4B3
306-787-8971, communications@justice.gov.sk.ca

Yukon Territory

Yukon Justice, Andrew Philipsen Law Centre, 2134 Second Ave., PO Box 2703, Whitehorse, YT Y1A 2C6
867-667-3033, Fax: 867-393-5790, jus.msb@gov.yk.ca

LABOUR

Canada Industrial Relations Board, 240 Sparks St., 4th Fl. West, Ottawa, ON K1A 0X8
Fax: 613-941-4461, 800-575-9696, info@cirb-ccri.gc.ca

Canadian Artists & Producers Professional Relations Tribunal, C.D. Howe Bldg., 240 Sparks St., 1st Fl., West Tower, Ottawa, ON K1A 1A1
613-996-4052, Fax: 613-947-4125, 800-263-ARTS, info@capprt-tcrpap.gc.ca

Canadian Council of Directors of Apprenticeship, 140 Promenade du Portage, 5th Fl, Phase IV, Gatineau, QC K1A 0J9
819-953-7443, Fax: 819-994-0202, redseal-sceaurouge@hrsdc-rhdcc.gc.ca

Commission des relations du travail, 900, boul René-Lévesque est, 5e étage, Québec, QC G1R 6C9
418-643-3208, Fax: 418-643-8946, 866-864-3646, crtm@crt.gouv.qc.ca

Corporate Services Branch, c/o Department of Advanced Education & Skills, PO Box 8700, St. John's, NL A1B 4J6

Human Resources & Skills Development Canada, 140 Promenade du Portage, Gatineau, QC K1A 0J9

Internal Administrative Services Division, 400 University Ave., 14th Fl., Toronto, ON M7A 1T7
416-326-7586, Fax: 416-326-5809

Department of Labour & Advanced Education, 5151 Terminal Rd., 6th Fl., PO Box 697, Halifax, NS B3J 2T8
902-424-5301, Fax: 902-424-0575

Labour & Planning Division, Chestnut Complex, PO Box 6000, Fredericton, NB E3B 5H1
506-453-8202, Fax: 506-453-3038, dpetlinfo@gnb.ca

Merchant Seamen Compensation Board, Secretary, Merchant Seamen Compensation Board, Phase II, Place du Portage, 10th Fl., Ottawa, ON K1A 0J2
819-953-8001, Fax: 819-994-5368

National Joint Council, C.D. Howe Bldg., 240 Sparks St. West, 7th Fl., PO Box 1525 B,Ottawa, ON K1P 5V2
613-990-1805, Fax: 613-990-7071, email.courrier@njc-cnm.gc.ca

Operations Division, 400 University Ave., 14th Fl., Toronto, ON M7A 1T7
416-326-7606, Fax: 416-212-4455

Public Service Commission, West Tower, 300 Laurier Ave. West, Ottawa, ON K1A 0M7
613-992-9562, Fax: 613-992-9352, infocom@psc-cfp.gc.ca

Public Service Labour Relations Board, CD Howe Building, 240 Sparks St., 6th Fl., PO Box 1525 B, Ottawa, ON K1P 5V2
613-990-1800, Fax: 613-990-1849, 866-931-3454, mail.courrier@pslrb-crtfp.gc.ca

Public Service Staffing Tribunal, 240 Sparks St., 6th Fl., Ottawa, ON K1A 0A5
613-949-6516, Fax: 613-949-6551, 866-637-4491, info@psst-tdfp.gc.ca

Workers' Compensation Appeals Tribunal, #1002, 5670 Spring Garden Rd., Halifax, NS B3J 1H6
902-424-2250, Fax: 902-424-2321, 800-274-8281

Alberta

Alberta Apprenticeship & Industry Training Board, Commerce Place, 10155 - 102nd St., 10th Fl., Edmonton, AB T5J 4L5
780-427-8765, Fax: 780-422-7376, -310-0000

Community, Learner & Industry Connections Division, Phipps-McKinnon Bldg., 10020 - 101A Ave., 5th Fl., Edmonton, AB T5J 3G2

Health Quality Council of Alberta, #210, 811 - 14 St. NW, Calgary, AB T2N 2A4
403-297-8162, Fax: 403-297-8258, info@hqca.ca

Alberta Human Services, Office of the Minister, Legislature Building, #224, 10800 - 97 Ave., Edmonton, AB T5K 2B6
780-644-5135, 866-644-5135

Labour Relations Board, Labour Building, 10808 - 99 Ave., 5th Fl., Edmonton, AB T5K 0G5
780-422-5926, Fax: 780-422-0970, 800-463-2572, alrbinfo@lab.gov.ab.ca

Occupational Health & Safety Council, Labour Building, 10808 - 99 Ave., 9th Fl., Edmonton, AB T5K 0G5
780-415-8690, 866-415-8690

British Columbia

British Columbia Labour Relations Board, Oceanic Plaza, #600, 1066 West Hastings St., Vancouver, BC V6E 3X1
604-660-1300, Fax: 604-660-1892, information@lrb.bc.ca

British Columbia Ministry of Citizens' Services & Open Government, PO Box 9594 Prov Govt,Victoria, BC V8W 9E2
250-952-7623, Fax: 250-952-7628, 800-663-7867, EnquiryBC@gov.bc.ca

Employment Standards Tribunal, Oceanic Plaza, #650, 1066 West Hastings St., Vancouver, BC V6E 3X1
604-775-3512, Fax: 604-775-3372, registrar.est@bcest.bc.ca

Workers' Compensation Appeal Tribunal, #150, 4600 Jacombs Rd., Richmond, BC V6V 3B1
604-664-7800, Fax: 604-664-7898, 800-663-2782

Workers' Compensation Board of British Columbia, PO Box 5350 Terminal,Vancouver, BC V6B 5L5
604-276-3100, Fax: 604-276-3247, 888-621-7233

Manitoba

Advisory Council on Workplace Safety & Health, #200, 401 York Ave., Winnipeg, MB R3C 0P8
204-945-3446, Fax: 204-945-4556

Board of Electrical Examiners, #500, 401 York Ave, Winnipeg, MB R3C 0P8
204-945-3507, terry.rieger@gov.mb.ca

Civil Service Commission Board, #935, 155 Carlton St., Winnipeg, MB R3C 3H8
204-945-1435, Fax: 204-945-1486

Manitoba Civil Service Commission, #935, 155 Carlton St., Winnipeg, MB R3C 3H8
204-945-2332, Fax: 204-945-1486, 800-282-8069, cschrp@gov.mb.ca

Manitoba Education, #168, Legislative Bldg., 450 Broadway, Winnipeg, MB R3C 0V8
204-945-3720, Fax: 204-945-1291, minedu@leg.gov.mb.ca

Manitoba Immigration & Multiculturalism, Legislative Building, 317, 450 Broadway Ave., Winnipeg, MB R3C 0V8
204-945-4079, Fax: 204-945-8312, minlab@leg.gov.mb.ca

Manitoba Labour Board, A.A. Heaps Bldg., #402, 258 Portage Ave., Winnipeg, MB R3C 0B6
204-945-3783, Fax: 204-945-1296, mlb@gov.mb.ca

Manitoba Minimum Wage Board, 614 - 401 York Ave., Winnipeg, MB R3C 0P8
204-945-4889, Fax: 204-948-2085, mw@gov.mb.ca

Pension Commission of Manitoba, #1004, 401 York Ave., Winnipeg, MB R3C 0P8
204-945-2740, Fax: 204-948-2375, pensions@gov.mb.ca

Manitoba Workers' Compensation Board, 333 Broadway Ave., Winnipeg, MB R3C 4W3
204-954-4321, Fax: 204-954-4999, 800-362-3340, wcb@wcb.mb.ca

New Brunswick

New Brunswick Department of Post-Secondary Education, Training, & Labour, Chestnut Complex, PO Box 6000, Fredericton, NB E3B 5H1
506-453-2597, Fax: 506-453-3618, dpetlinfo@gnb.ca

Workplace Health, Safety & Compensation Commission of New Brunswick, 1 Portland St., PO Box 160, Saint John, NB E2L 3X9
506-632-2200, 800-222-9775, communications@ws-ts.nb.ca

Newfoundland & Labrador

Labour Relations Board, Beothuck Bldg., 20 Crosbie Pl., 5th Fl., PO Box 8700, St. John's, NL A1B 4J6
709-729-2707, Fax: 709-729-5738, lrb@gov.nl.ca

Newfoundland & Labrador Department of Advanced Education & Skills, Confederation Building, West Block, 3rd Fl., PO Box 8700, St. John's, NL A1B 4J6
709-729-2480, aesweb@gov.nl.ca

Newfoundland & Labrador Workplace Health, Safety & Compensation Commission, 146 - 148 Forest Rd., PO Box 9000, St. John's, NL A1A 3B8
709-778-1000, Fax: 709-738-1714, 800-563-9000, general.inquiries@whscc.nl.ca

Northwest Territories

Department of Education, Culture & Employment, PO Box 1320, Yellowknife, NT X1A 2L9
867-669-2399, Fax: 867-873-0431, 866-606-5627

Northwest Territories Apprenticeship, Trade & Occupations Certification Board, PO Box 1320, Yellowknife, NT X1A 2L9
867-873-7357, Fax: 867-873-0200
Northwest Territories & Nunavut Workers' Safety & Compensation Commission, Centre Square Tower, 5022 - 49th St., 5th Fl., PO Box 8888, Yellowknife, NT X1A 2R3
867-920-3888, Fax: 867-873-4596, 800-661-0792

Nova Scotia

Nova Scotia Advisory Board on Colleges & Universities, 2021 Brunswick St., PO Box 2086 M, Halifax, NS B3J 3B7
Fax: 902-424-0651
Pay Equity Commission, 5151 Terminal Rd., 6th Fl., PO Box 697, Halifax, NS B3J 2T8
902-424-2385, Fax: 902-424-0575
Workers' Advisers Program, #502, 5670 Spring Garden Rd., PO Box 1063, Halifax, NS B3J 2X1
902-424-5050, Fax: 902-424-0530, 800-774-4712
Workers' Compensation Board of Nova Scotia, 5668 South St., PO Box 1150, Halifax, NS B3J 2Y2
902-491-8999, Fax: 902-491-8002, 800-870-3331, info@wcb.gov.ns.ca

Nunavut

Department of Human Resources, PO Box 1000 400,Iqaluit, NU X0A 1H0
Fax: 867-975-6216, 888-668-9993, gnhr@gov.nu.ca

Ontario

Ontario Ministry of Education, Mowat Block, 900 Bay St., 22nd. Fl., Toronto, ON M7A 1L2
416-325-2929, Fax: 416-325-2934, 800-387-5514, info@edu.gov.on.ca
Ontario Ministry of Labour, 400 University Ave., 14th Fl., Toronto, ON M7A 1T7
416-326-7160, 800-531-5551
Office of the Employer Advisor, #704, 151 Bloor St. West., Toronto, ON M5S 1S4
416-327-0020, Fax: 416-327-0726, 800-387-0774
Office of the Worker Advisor, #1300, 123 Edward St., Toronto, ON M5G 1E2
416-325-8570, Fax: 416-325-4830, 800-435-8980
Ontario Labour Relations Board, 505 University Ave., 2nd Fl., Toronto, ON M5G 2P1
416-326-7500, Fax: 416-326-7531, 877-339-3335
Pay Equity Commission, #300, 180 Dundas St. West, Toronto, ON M7A 2S6
416-314-1896, Fax: 416-314-8741, 800-387-8813
Ontario Ministry of Training, Colleges & Universities, Mowat Block, 900 Bay St., 14th Fl., Toronto, ON M7A 1L2
416-325-2929, Fax: 416-325-6348, 800-387-5514, information.met@ontario.ca
Workplace Safety & Insurance Board, 200 Front St. West, Ground Fl., Toronto, ON M5V 3J1
416-344-1000, Fax: 416-344-4684, 800-387-0750

Prince Edward Island

Advisory Council on the Status of Women, Sherwood Business Centre, 161 St. Peter's Rd., Main Level, PO Box 2000, Charlottetown, PE C1A 7N8
902-368-4510, Fax: 902-368-3269, peistatusofwomen@eastlink.ca
Prince Edward Island Workers Compensation Board, 14 Weymouth St., PO Box 757, Charlottetown, PE C1A 7L7
902-368-5680, Fax: 902-368-5696, 800-237-5049
Workers Compensation Appeal Tribunal, 161 St. Peters Rd., 1st Fl., PO Box 2000, Charlottetown, PE C1A 7N8

Quebec

Commission de l'équité salariale, 200, ch Ste-Foy, 4e étage, Québec, QC G1R 6A1
418-528-8765, Fax: 418-528-6999, 888-528-8765, equite.salariale@ces.gouv.qc.ca
Commission de la construction du Québec, 3530, rue Jean-Talon ouest, Montréal, QC H3R 2G3
514-341-7740, Fax: 514-341-6354, 888-842-8282
Commission des lésions professionnelles, #700, 900, Place d'Youville, Québec, QC G1R 3P7
418-644-7777, Fax: 418-644-6443, 800-463-1591
Commission des normes du travail, Hall Est, 400, boul Jean-Lesage, 7e étage, Québec, QC G1K 8W1
418-644-0817, Fax: 418-643-5132, 800-563-9058
Conseil consultatif du travail et de la main d'oeuvre, #9.400, 500, boul René-Lévesque ouest, Montréal, QC H2Z 1W7
514-873-2880, Fax: 514-873-1129, cctm@cctm.gouv.qc.ca
Conseil des services essentiels du Québec, #9.100, 500, boul René-Lévesque ouest, 9e étage, CP 38, Montréal, QC H2Z 1W7
514-873-7246, Fax: 514-873-3839, 800-337-7246, info@cses.gouv.qc.ca
Office des professions du Québec, 800, place D'Youville, 10e étage, Québec, QC G1R 5Z3
418-643-6912, Fax: 418-643-0973, 800-643-6912, courrier@opq.gouv.qc.ca
Régie du bâtiment du Québec, 545, boul Crémazie est, 4e étage, Montréal, QC H2M 2V2
514-873-0976, Fax: 514-864-2903, 800-361-0761, crc@rbq.gouv.qc.ca
Commission de la santé et de la sécurité du travail du Québec, 524, rue Bourdages, CP 1200 Terminus postal,Québec, QC G1K 7E2
418-266-4850, Fax: 418-266-4669, 866-302-2778
Ministère du Travail, 200, ch Sainte-Foy, 5e étage, Québec, QC G1R 5S1
418-644-4545, Fax: 418-528-0559, 800-643-4817

Saskatchewan

Labour Relations Board, #1600, 1920 Broad St., Regina, SK S4P 3V2
306-787-2406, Fax: 306-787-2664
Minimum Wage Board, #400, 1870 Albert St., Regina, SK S4P 4W1
Office of the Worker's Advocate, #300, 1870 Albert St., Regina, SK S4P 4W1
306-787-2456, Fax: 306-787-0249, 877-787-2456
Saskatchewan Education, 2220 College Ave., Regina, SK S4P 4V9
linquiry@gov.sk.ca
Saskatchewan Labour Relations & Workplace Safety, #300, 1870 Albert St., Regina, SK S4P 4W1
306-787-7404, webmaster@lab.gov.sk.ca
Saskatchewan Workers' Compensation Board, #200, 1881 Scarth St., Regina, SK S4P 4L1
306-787-4370, Fax: 306-787-4311, 800-667-7590, internet_clientsvc@wcbsask.com
Saskatchewan Workers' Compensation Board, #200, 1881 Scarth St., Regina, SK S4P 4L1
306-787-4370, Fax: 306-787-7582, 800-667-7590, internet_clientsvc@wcbsask.com

Yukon Territory

Yukon Public Service Commission, Yukon Government Administration Building, #2071-2nd Ave., PO Box 2703, Whitehorse, YT Y1A 2C6
867-667-5653, Fax: 867-667-5755, 800-661-0408, PSCWebsite@gov.yk.ca
Yukon Workers' Compensation Health & Safety Board, 401 Strickland St., Whitehorse, YT Y1A 5N8
867-667-5645, Fax: 867-393-6279, 800-661-0443, worksafe@gov.yk.ca

LAND RESOURCES

See Also: Agriculture; Forest Resources; Parks

Canada Lands Company Ltd., #1200, 1 University Ave., Toronto, ON M5J 2P1
416-952-6111, Fax: 416-952-6115, 888-252-5263
Land Use Secretariat, Centre West Building, 10035 - 108 St., Edmonton, AB T5J 3E1
780-644-7972, Fax: 780-644-1034, luf@gov.ab.ca
Natural Resources Canada, 580 Booth St., Ottawa, ON K1A 0E4
613-995-0947, Fax: 613-992-7211
Parks Canada, 25 Eddy St., Gatineau, QC K1A 0M5
613-860-1251, 888-773-8888, information@pc.gc.ca

Alberta

Special Areas Board, Special Areas Board Administration, 212 - 2nd Ave. West, PO Box 820, Hanna, AB T0J 1P0
403-854-5600, Fax: 403-854-5527, specarea@telus.net

British Columbia

Strategic Industry Partnerships Division, PO Box 9120 Prov Govt,Victoria, BC V8W 9B4
250-356-1122, Fax: 250-356-7279

Manitoba

Farm Lands Ownership Board, #812, Norquay Bldg., 401 York Ave., Winnipeg, MB R3C 0P8
204-945-3149, Fax: 204-945-1489, 800-282-8069, robert.mckenzie@gov.mb.ca
Manitoba Conservation Districts Commission, Secretariat c/o Planning & Coordination Branch, 123 Main St., PO Box 20000, Neepawa, MB R0J 1H0
204-476-7033, Fax: 204-476-7539, whildebran@gov.mb.ca
Manitoba Land Value Appraisal Commission, 800 Portage Ave., Winnipeg, MB R3G 0N4
204-945-2941, Fax: 204-948-2235

Northwest Territories

Department of Environment & Natural Resources, PO Box 1320, Yellowknife, NT X1A 2L9
Department of Municipal & Community Affairs, PO Box 1320, Yellowknife, NT X1A 2L9
867-873-7118, Fax: 867-873-0309

Nunavut

Department of Environment, PO Box 1000 1300,Iqaluit, NU X0A 0H0
867-975-7700, Fax: 867-975-7742, environment@gov.nu.ca

Prince Edward Island

Prince Edward Island Department of Environment, Labour & Justice, Shaw Bldg. South, 95 Rochford St., 4th Fl., PO Box 2000, Charlottetown, PE C1A 7N8
902-620-3774, Fax: 902-368-4242, rryder@gov.pe.ca

Quebec

Commission de protection du territoire agricole du Québec, 200, ch Ste-Foy, 2e étage, Québec, QC G1R 4X6
418-643-3314, Fax: 418-643-2261, 800-667-5294, info@cptaq.gouv.qc.ca
Foncier Québec, 5700, 4e av ouest, Québec, QC G1H 6R1
418-643-3582, Fax: 418-528-8721, 866-226-0977, assistance.clientele@mrnf.registrefoncier.gouv.qc.ca
Territoire, #A313, 5700, 4e av ouest, Québec, QC G1H 6R1
418-627-6256, Fax: 418-528-2075

Saskatchewan

Saskatchewan Lands Appeal Board, #202, 3085 Albert St., Regina, SK S4S 0B1
306-787-4693, Fax: 306-787-1315, Donald.Brooks@gov.sk.ca

Yukon Territory

Yukon Land Use Planning Council, #201, 307 Jarvis St., Whitehorse, YT Y1A 2H3
867-667-7397, Fax: 867-667-4624, ylupc@planyukon.ca

LAND TITLES

See Also: Real Estate

Canada Lands Company Ltd., #1200, 1 University Ave., Toronto, ON M5J 2P1
416-952-6111, Fax: 416-952-6115, 888-252-5263
Consumer & Commercial Affairs Branch, PO Box 8700, St. John's, NL A1B 4J6
709-729-2570, Fax: 709-729-4151, gsinfo@gov.nl.ca

British Columbia

British Columbia Assessment Authority, #400, 3450 Uptown Blvd., Victoria, BC V8Z 0B9
250-595-6211, Fax: 250-595-6222, info@bcassessment.ca

Nova Scotia

Registry of Deeds, PO Box 2205, Halifax, NS B3J 3C4
Fax: 902-424-5872

Nunavut

Legal Registries, Brown Bldg., 1st Fl., PO Box 1000 570,Iqaluit, NU X0A 0H0
Fax: 867-975-6594

LANDLORD & TENANT REGULATIONS

Alberta

Alberta Justice & Solicitor General, Communications, Bowker Building, 9833 - 109 St., 3rd Fl., Edmonton, AB T5K 2E8
780-427-2745, 800-310-0000

Northwest Territories

Northwest Territories Housing Corporation, Scotia Centre, 5102 50th Ave., PO Box 2100, Yellowknife, NT X1A 2P6
867-873-7853, Fax: 867-873-9426

Nunavut

Nunavut Housing Corporation, PO Box 480, Arviat, NU X0C 0E0
867-857-3000, Fax: 867-857-3040

Prince Edward Island

Prince Edward Island Regulatory & Appeals Commission, National Bank Tower, #501, 134 Kent St., PO Box 577, Charlottetown, PE C1A 7L1
902-892-3501, Fax: 902-566-4076, 800-501-6268, info@irac.pe.ca

Quebec

Régie du logement du Québec, Pyramide Ouest, #2095, 5199, rue Sherbrooke est, Montréal, QC H1T 3X1
514-873-2245, Fax: 514-864-8077, 800-683-2245

Saskatchewan

Provincial Mediation Board, #120, 2151 Scarth St., Regina, SK S4P 2H8
306-787-5387, Fax: 306-787-5574, 877-787-5408

LANDS & SOILS

Aboriginal Affairs & Northern Development Canada, 10 Wellington St., North Tower, Gatineau, QC K1A 0H4
819-997-0380, Fax: 866-817-3977, 800-567-9604, infopubs@aadnc-aandc.gc.ca
Agriculture & Agri-Food Canada, 1341 Baseline Rd., Ottawa, ON K1A 0C5
613-773-1000, Fax: 613-773-2772, 866-345-7972, info@agr.gc.ca
Canada Centre for Remote Sensing - Geomatics Canada, 588 Booth St., Ottawa, ON K1A 0Y7
613-995-0947, Fax: 613-947-1382
Natural Resources Canada, 580 Booth St., Ottawa, ON K1A 0E4
613-995-0947, Fax: 613-992-7211
Soil, Plant & Feed Laboratory, Brookfield Rd., PO Box 8700, St. John's, NL A1B 4J6
709-729-6738, Fax: 709-729-6734

Alberta
Irrigation Council, Provincial Bldg., 200 - 5 Ave. South, 3rd Fl., Lethbridge, AB T1J 4L1
403-381-5176, Fax: 403-382-4406
Land Compensation Board, 1229 - 91 St. SW, Edmonton, AB T6X 1E9
srb.lcb@gov.ab.ca
British Columbia
British Columbia Ministry of Environment, PO Box 9339 Prov Govt,Victoria, BC V8W 9M1
250-387-1161, Fax: 250-387-5669, envmail@gov.bc.ca
Forest Practices Board, 1675 Douglas St., 3rd Fl., PO Box 9905 Prov Govt, Victoria, BC V8W 9R1
250-213-4700, Fax: 250-213-4725, 800-994-5899, fpboard@gov.bc.ca
Timber Export Advisory Committee, PO Box 9514 Prov Govt, Victoria, BC V8W 9C2
250-387-8916, Fax: 250-387-5050
New Brunswick
New Brunswick Department of Environment & Local Government, Marysville Place, PO Box 6000, Fredericton, NB E3B 5H1
506-453-2690, Fax: 506-457-4994, elg/egl-info@gnb.ca
New Brunswick Department of Natural Resources, Hugh John Flemming Forestry Centre, PO Box 6000, Fredericton, NB E3B 5H1
506-453-3826, Fax: 506-444-4367, dnrweb@gnb.ca
Newfoundland & Labrador
Newfoundland & Labrador Department of Service NL, PO Box 8700, St. John's, NL A1B 4J6
709-729-4834, gsinfo@gov.nl.ca
Northwest Territories
Department of Environment & Natural Resources, PO Box 1320, Yellowknife, NT X1A 2L9
Nova Scotia
Department of Natural Resources, Founder's Square, 1701 Hollis St., 3rd Fl., PO Box 698, Halifax, NS B3J 2T9
902-424-5935, Fax: 902-424-0594, 800-565-2224
Prince Edward Island
Prince Edward Island Department of Environment, Labour & Justice, Shaw Bldg. South, 95 Rochford St., 4th Fl., PO Box 2000, Charlottetown, PE C1A 7N8
902-620-3774, Fax: 902-368-4242, rrryder@gov.pe.ca
Prince Edward Island Department of Tourism & Culture, PO Box 2000, Charlottetown, PE C1A 7N8
902-368-5540, Fax: 902-368-5277, tpswitch@gov.pe.ca
Quebec
Ministère du Développement durable, de l'Environnement, de la Faune, et des Parcs, Édifice Marie-Guyart, 675, boul René-Lévesque est, 29e étage, Québec, QC G1R 5V7
418-521-3830, Fax: 418-646-5974, 800-561-1616, info@mddep.gouv.qc.ca
Territoire, #A313, 5700, 4e av ouest, Québec, QC G1H 6R1
418-627-6256, Fax: 418-528-2075
Saskatchewan
Saskatchewan Assessment Management Agency, #200, 2201 - 11th Ave., Regina, SK S4P 0J8
306-924-8000, Fax: 306-924-8070, 800-667-7262, info.request@sama.sk.ca
Yukon Territory
Carmacks Renewable Resource Council, PO Box 122, Carmacks, YT Y0B 1C0
867-863-6838, Fax: 867-863-6429, carmacksrrc@northwestel.net
Yukon Environment, PO Box 2703, Whitehorse, YT Y1A 2C6
867-667-5652, Fax: 867-393-7197, environment.yukon@gov.yk.ca
Selkirk Renewable Resources Council, PO Box 32, Pelly Crossing, YT Y0B 1P0
867-537-3937, Fax: 867-537-3939, selkirkrrc@yknet.yk.ca
Yukon Land Use Planning Council, #201, 307 Jarvis St., Whitehorse, YT Y1A 2H3
867-667-7397, Fax: 867-667-4624, ylupc@planyukon.ca

LAW & JUSTICE

Auditor General of Canada, 240 Sparks St., Ottawa, ON K1A 0G6
613-995-3708, Fax: 613-957-0474, 888-761-5953, communications@oag-bvg.gc.ca; infomedia@oag-bvg.gc.ca
Canadian Forces Grievance Board, 60 Queen St., 10th Fl., Ottawa, ON K1P 5Y7
613-996-8529, Fax: 613-996-6491, 877-276-4193
Canadian Human Rights Commission, 344 Slater St., 8th Fl., Ottawa, ON K1A 1E1
613-995-1151, Fax: 613-996-9661, 888-214-1090
Canadian Human Rights Tribunal, 160 Elgin St., 11th Fl., Ottawa, ON K1A 1J4
613-995-1707, Fax: 613-995-3484, registrar@chrt-tcdp.gc.ca
Canadian International Trade Tribunal, Standard Life Centre, 333 Laurier Ave. West, 15 Floor, Ottawa, ON K1A 0G7
613-990-2452, Fax: 613-990-2439, secretary@citt-tcce.gc.ca
Canadian Judicial Council, 150 Metcalfe St., 15th Fl., Ottawa, ON K1A 0W8
613-288-1566, Fax: 613-288-1575, info@cjc-ccm.gc.ca
Canadian Police College, PO Box 8900, Ottawa, ON K1G 3J2
613-993-9500, Fax: 613-990-9738, cpc-ccp@rcmp-grc.gc.ca
Canadian Radio-Television & Telecommunications Commission, Central Building, 1, Promenade du Portage, Les Terrasses de la Chaudière, Gatineau, QC J8X 4B1
819-997-0313, Fax: 819-994-0218, 877-249-2782
Canadian Security Intelligence Service, PO Box 9732 T,Ottawa, ON K1G 4G4
613-993-9620, Fax: 613-231-0612
Commission for Public Complaints Against the Royal Canadian Mounted Police, National Intake Office, PO Box 88689, Surrey, BC V3W 0X1
Fax: 613-952-8045, 800-665-6878, org@cpc-cpp.gc.ca
Copyright Board of Canada, #800, 56 Sparks St., Ottawa, ON K1A 0C9
613-952-8621, Fax: 613-952-8630, secretariat@cb-cda.gc.ca
Office of the Correctional Investigator, PO Box 3421 D,Ottawa, ON K1P 6L4
Fax: 613-990-9091, 877-885-8848, org@oci-bec.gc.ca
Correctional Service Canada, 340 Laurier Ave. West, Ottawa, ON K1A 0P9
613-992-5891, Fax: 613-943-1630
Defence Research & Development Canada, 305 Rideau St., Ottawa, ON K1A 0K2
613-992-7237, info@drdc-rddc.gc.ca
Environmental Sciences & Standards Division, 135 St. Clair Ave. West, 14th Fl., Toronto, ON M4V 1P5
416-314-6357, Fax: 416-314-6358
Office of the Commissioner for Federal Judicial Affairs, 99 Metcalfe St., 8th Fl., Ottawa, ON K1A 1E3
613-995-5140, Fax: 613-995-5615, 877-583-4266
Financial Transactions & Reports Analysis Centre of Canada, 234 Laurier Ave. West, 24th Fl., Ottawa, ON K1P 1H7
Fax: 613-943-7931, 866-346-8722, guidelines-lignesdirectrices@fintrac-canafe.gc.ca
Housing, Seniors & Corporate Support, Jones Bldg., 11 Kent St., 2nd Fl., PO Box 2000, Charlottetown, PE C1A 7N8
Fax: 902-894-0242
Immigration & Refugee Board of Canada, Canada Bldg, 344 Slater St., 12th Fl., Ottawa, ON K1A 0K1
613-995-6486, Fax: 613-943-1550, contact@irb-cisr.gc.ca
International Joint Commission, 234 Laurier Ave. West, 22nd Fl., Ottawa, ON K1P 6K6
613-947-1420, Fax: 613-993-5583, beckhoffb@ottawa.ijc.org
Justice Canada, East Memorial Bldg., 284 Wellington St., Ottawa, ON K1A 0H8
613-957-4222, Fax: 613-954-0811, webadmin@justice.gc.ca
Legal Services Division, Bowker Building, 9833 - 109 St., 2nd Fl., Edmonton, AB T5K 2E8
780-422-0500
Législation & enquêtes, 3800, rue de Marly, Secteur 5-1-9, Québec, QC G1X 4A5
418-652-6844, Fax: 418-643-9381
Military Police Complaints Commission, 270 Albert St., 10th Fl., Ottawa, ON K1P 5G8
613-947-5625, Fax: 613-947-5713, 800-632-0566, commission@mpcc-cppm.gc.ca
National Parole Board, 410 Laurier Ave. West, Ottawa, ON K1A 0R1
613-954-7474, Fax: 613-995-4380, 800-874-2652, info@npb-cnlc.gc.ca
Office of the Conflict of Interest & Ethics Commissioner, Commissioner's Office, 66 Slater St., 22nd Fl., Ottawa, ON K1A 0A6
613-995-0721, Fax: 613-995-7308, ciec-ccie@parl.gc.ca
Passport Canada, Le 70 Crémazie, 70 Crémazie St., Gatineau, QC K1A 0G3
Fax: 819-953-5856, 800-567-6868
Privacy Commissioner of Canada, Tower B, Place de Ville, 112 Kent St., 3rd Fl., Ottawa, ON K1A 1H3
613-947-1698, Fax: 613-947-6850, 800-282-1376
RCMP Training Academy, 6101 Dewdney Ave., Regina, SK S4P 3J7
306-780-5002, Fax: 306-780-7940
Royal Canadian Mounted Police, 1200 Vanier Pkwy., Ottawa, ON K1A 0R2
613-993-7267, Fax: 613-993-0260
Royal Canadian Mounted Police External Review Committee, PO Box 1159 B, Ottawa, ON K1P 5R2
613-998-2134, Fax: 613-990-8969, org@erc-cee.gc.ca
Security Intelligence Review Committee, Jackson Bldg., 122 Bank St., 4th Fl., PO Box 2430 D,Ottawa, ON K1P 5W5
613-990-8441, Fax: 613-990-5230, ellardm@sirc-csars.gc.ca
Transportation Appeal Tribunal of Canada, #1201, 333 Laurier Ave. West, 12th Fl., Ottawa, ON K1A 0N5
613-990-6906, Fax: 613-990-9153, info@tatc.gc.ca
Transportation Safety Board of Canada, 200 Promenade du Portage, 4th Fl., Ottawa, ON K1A 1K8
819-994-3741, Fax: 819-997-2239, 800-387-3557
Veterans Review & Appeal Board, Daniel J. MacDonald Bldg., 161 Grafton St., PO Box 9900, Charlottetown, PE C1A 8V7
902-566-8751, Fax: 902-566-7850, 800-450-8006, vrab_tacra@vac-acc.gc.ca
Workers' Compensation Appeals Tribunal, #1002, 5670 Spring Garden Rd., Halifax, NS B3J 1H6
902-424-2250, Fax: 902-424-2321, 800-274-8281
Alberta
Alberta Review Board, Oxford Tower, 10235 - 101 St., 11th Fl., Edmonton, AB T5J 3E9
780-422-5994, Fax: 780-427-1762
Criminal Injuries Review Board, #1502, 10025 - 102A Ave., Edmonton, AB T5J 2Z2
780-427-7330, Fax: 780-427-7347, cirb@gov.ab.ca
Alberta Office of the Ethics Commissioner, #1250, 9925 - 109 St. NW, Edmonton, AB T5K 2J8
780-422-2273, Fax: 780-422-2261, generalinfo@ethicscommissioner.ab.ca
Alberta Justice & Solicitor General, Communications, Bowker Building, 9833 - 109 St., 3rd Fl., Edmonton, AB T5K 2E8
780-427-2745, 800-310-0000
Land Compensation Board, 1229 - 91 St. SW, Edmonton, AB T6X 1E9
srb.lcb@gov.ab.ca
Law Enforcement Review Board, City Centre Place, #1502, 10025 - 102A Ave., Edmonton, AB T5J 2Z2
780-422-9376, Fax: 780-422-4782, lerb@gov.ab.ca
Alberta Office of the Ombudsman, Canadian Western Bank Building, #2800, 10303 Jasper Ave. NW, 28th Fl., Edmonton, AB T5J 5C3
780-427-2756, Fax: 780-427-2759, 888-455-2756, info@ombudsman.ab.ca
Public Security Division, John E. Brownlee Building, 10365 - 97 St., 10th Fl., Edmonton, AB T5J 3W7
Registry Services, Telus Plaza South, 10020 - 100 St., 29th Fl., Edmonton, AB T5J 0N3
British Columbia
British Columbia Ministry of Justice, PO Box 9044 Prov Govt,Victoria, BC V8W 9E2
British Columbia Office of the Police Complaint Commissioner, #501, 947 Fort St., PO Box 9895 Prov Govt, Victoria, BC V8W 9T8
250-356-7458, Fax: 250-356-6503, 877-999-8707, info@opcc.bc.ca
British Columbia Review Board, #1020, 510 Burrard St., Vancouver, BC V6C 3A8
604-660-8789, Fax: 604-660-8809, 877-305-2277
Office of the Conflict of Interest Commissioner, #101, 431 Menzies St., Victoria, BC V8V 1X4
250-356-0750, Fax: 250-356-6580, conflictofinterest@coibc.ca
Court Services Branch, PO Box 9249 Prov Govt,Victoria, BC V8W 9J2
250-356-1550, Fax: 250-356-8152
Judicial Council of British Columbia, Pacific Centre, #602, 700 West Georgia St., PO Box 10287, Vancouver, BC V7Y 1E8
604-660-2864, Fax: 604-660-1108, info@provincialcourt.bc.ca
Legal Services Society, #400, 510 Burrard St., Vancouver, BC V6C 3A8
604-601-6000
Office of the Ombudsperson, 947 Fort St., 2nd Fl., PO Box 9039 Prov Govt,Victoria, BC V8W 9A5
250-387-5855, Fax: 250-387-0198, 800-567-3247, systems@bcombudsperson.ca (Information technology inquiries)
Office of the Representative for Children & Youth, #201, 546 Yates St., Victoria, BC V8W 1K8
250-356-6710, Fax: 250-356-0837, 800-476-3933, rcy@rcybc.ca
Public Guardian & Trustee of British Columbia, #700, 808 West Hastings St., Vancouver, BC V6C 3L3
604-660-4444, Fax: 604-660-0374, 800-663-7867, mail@trustee.bc.ca
Manitoba
Advisory Council on Workplace Safety & Health, #200, 401 York Ave., Winnipeg, MB R3C 0P8
204-945-3446, Fax: 204-945-4556
Office of the Auditor General, #500, 330 Portage Ave., Winnipeg, MB R3C 0C4
204-945-3790, Fax: 204-945-2169, oag.contact@oag.mb.ca
Automobile Injury Compensation Appeal Commission, #301, 428 Portage Ave.., Winnipeg, MB R3C 0E2
204-945-4155, Fax: 204-948-2402, autoinjury@gov.mb.ca
Compensation for Victims of Crime, 1410 - 405 Broadway, Winnipeg, MB R3C 3L6
204-945-0899, Fax: 204-948-3071, 800-262-9344

Comptroller Division, #715, 401 York Ave., Winnipeg, MB R3C 0P8
204-945-4920, Fax: 204-945-2394
Highway Traffic Board/Motor Transport Board, #200, 301 Weston St., Winnipeg, MB R3E 3H4
204-945-8912, Fax: 204-783-6529
Manitoba Human Rights Commission, 175 Hargrave St., 7th Fl., Winnipeg, MB R3C 3R8
204-945-3007, Fax: 204-945-1292, 888-884-8681, hrc@gov.mb.ca
Manitoba Justice, Legislative Building, #104, 405 Broadway Ave., Winnipeg, MB R3C 3L6
204-945-3728, Fax: 204-945-2517, minjus@gov.mb.ca
Law Enforcement Review Agency, #420, 155 Carlton St., Winnipeg, MB R3C 3H8
204-945-8667, Fax: 204-948-1014, 800-282-8069, lera@gov.mb.ca
Law Reform Commission, #432, 405 Broadway, Winnipeg, MB R3C 3L6
204-945-2896, Fax: 204-948-2184, lawreform@gov.mb.ca
Legal Aid Manitoba, 402 - 294 Portage Ave., Winnipeg, MB R3C 0B9
204-985-8500, Fax: 204-944-8582, 800-261-2960, info@legalaid.mb.ca
License Suspension Appeal Board/Medical Review Committee, #200, 301 Weston St., Winnipeg, MB R3E 3H4
204-945-7350, Fax: 204-948-2682
Manitoba Film Classification Board, #216, 301 Weston St., Winnipeg, MB R3E 3H4
204-945-8962, Fax: 204-945-0890, 866-612-2399, mfcb@gov.mb.ca
Manitoba Labour Board, A.A. Heaps Bldg., #402, 258 Portage Ave., Winnipeg, MB R3C 0B6
204-945-3783, Fax: 204-945-1296, mlb@gov.mb.ca
Manitoba Land Value Appraisal Commission, 800 Portage Ave., Winnipeg, MB R3G 0N4
204-945-2941, Fax: 204-948-2235
Manitoba Liquor Control Commission, 1555 Buffalo Pl., PO Box 1023, Winnipeg, MB R3C 2X1
204-284-2501, Fax: 204-475-7666, info@mlcc.mb.ca
Manitoba Minimum Wage Board, 614 - 401 York Ave., Winnipeg, MB R3C 0P8
204-945-4889, Fax: 204-948-2085, mw@gov.mb.ca
Manitoba Review Board, 408 York Ave., 2nd Fl., Winnipeg, MB R3C 0P9
204-945-4438, Fax: 204-945-5751
Manitoba Securities Commission, #500, 400 St. Mary Ave., Winnipeg, MB R3C 4K5
204-945-2548, Fax: 204-945-0330, 800-655-5244, securities@gov.mb.ca
Office of the Chief Medical Examiner, #210, 1 Wesley Ave., Winnipeg, MB R3C 4C6
204-945-2088, Fax: 204-945-2442, 800-282-9069
Office of the Fire Commissioner, #508, 401 York Ave., Winnipeg, MB R3C 0P8
204-945-3322, Fax: 204-948-2089, 800-282-8069, firecomm@gov.mb.ca
Office of the Public Trustee, #500, 155 Carlton St., Winnipeg, MB R3C 5R9
204-945-2700, Fax: 204-948-2251, publictrustee@gov.mb.ca
Manitoba Office of the Ombudsman, 750 - 500 Portage Ave., Winnipeg, MB R3C 3X1
204-982-9130, Fax: 204-942-7803, 800-665-0531, ombudsma@ombudsman.mb.ca
Residential Tenancies Commission, #1650, 155 Carlton St., Winnipeg, MB R3C 3H8
204-945-2028, Fax: 204-945-5453, 800-782-8403, rtc@gov.mb.ca
Manitoba Workers' Compensation Board, 333 Broadway Ave., Winnipeg, MB R3C 4W3
204-954-4321, Fax: 204-954-4999, 800-362-3340, wcb@wcb.mb.ca

New Brunswick

New Brunswick Human Rights Commission, PO Box 6000, Fredericton, NB E3B 5H1
506-453-2301, Fax: 506-453-2653, 888-471-2233, hrc.cdp@gnb.ca
New Brunswick Department of Public Safety, 364 Argyle St., PO Box 6000, Fredericton, NB E3B 5H1
506-453-3992, Fax: 506-453-3870, DPS-MSP.Information@gnb.ca
New Brunswick Liquor Corporation, 170 Wilsey Rd., PO Box 20787, Fredericton, NB E3B 5B8
506-452-6826, Fax: 506-462-2024, info@anbl.com
Office of the Ombudsman, 767 Brunswick St., PO Box 6000, Fredericton, NB E3B 5H1
506-453-2789, Fax: 506-453-5599, 800-465-1100, nbombud@gnb.ca
New Brunswick Police Commission, Fredericton City Centre, #202, 435 King St., Fredericton, NB E3B 1E5
506-453-2069, Fax: 506-457-3542, nbpc@gnb.ca
Workplace Health, Safety & Compensation Commission of New Brunswick, 1 Portland St., PO Box 160, Saint John, NB E2L 3X9
506-632-2200, 800-222-9775, communications@ws-ts.nb.ca

Newfoundland & Labrador

Newfoundland & Labrador Human Rights Commission, PO Box 8700, St. John's, NL A1B 4J6
709-729-2709, Fax: 709-729-0790, 800-563-5808, humanrights@mail.gov.nl.ca
Newfoundland & Labrador Department of Justice, Confederation Bldg., East Block, 4th Fl., PO Box 8700, St. John's, NL A1B 4J6
709-729-2869, Fax: 709-729-0469, justice@gov.nl.ca
Newfoundland & Labrador Legal Aid Commission, #300, 251 Empire Ave., PO Box 399 C, St. John's, NL A1C 5J9
709-753-7863, Fax: 709-753-6226, 800-563-9911, nlac@legalaid.nl.ca
Royal Newfoundland Constabulary Public Complaints Commission, Bally Rou Place, #E-160, 280 Torbay Rd., St. John's, NL A1A 3W8
709-729-0950, Fax: 709-729-1302, rnccomplaintscommission@gov.nl.ca

Northwest Territories

Assessment Appeal Tribunal of the Northwest Territories, #400, 5201 - 50th Ave., PO Box 1320, Yellowknife, NT X1A 2L9
867-873-7125, Fax: 867-873-0609,
Department of Justice, Courthouse, 4903 - 49th St., 6th Fl., PO Box 1320, Yellowknife, NT X1A 2L9
867-920-6197
Judicial Council, PO Box 550, Yellowknife, NT X1A 2N4
867-873-7105, Fax: 867-873-0287
Legal Services Board of the Northwest Territories, PO Box 1320, Yellowknife, NT X1A 2L9
867-873-7450, Fax: 867-873-5320
Northwest Territories Liquor Commission, #201, 31 Capital Dr., Hay River, NT X0E 1G2
867-874-2100, Fax: 867-874-2180
Northwest Territories Liquor Licensing & Enforcement, #210, 31 Capital Dr., Hay River, NT X0E 1G2
867-874-2906, Fax: 867-874-6011
Northwest Territories Liquor Licensing Board, #210, 31 Capital Dr., Hay River, NT X0E 1G2
867-874-2906, Fax: 867-874-6011, delilah_st-arneault@gov.nt.ca
Territorial Board of Revision, #400, 5201 - 50th Ave., PO Box 1320, Yellowknife, NT X1A 2L9
867-873-7125, Fax: 867-873-0609
Victims Assistance Committee, c/o Community Justice Division, PO Box 1320, Yellowknife, NT X1A 2L9
867-920-6911, Fax: 867-873-0199
Northwest Territories & Nunavut Workers' Safety & Compensation Commission, Centre Square Tower, 5022 - 49th St., 5th Fl., PO Box 8888, Yellowknife, NT X1A 2R3
867-920-3888, Fax: 867-873-4596, 800-661-0792

Nova Scotia

Nova Scotia Human Rights Commission, Joseph Howe Bldg., 1690 Hollis St., 6th Fl., Halifax, NS B3J 3C4
902-424-4111, Fax: 902-424-0596, hrcinquiries@gov.ns.ca
Department of Justice, 5151 Terminal Rd., 4th Fl., PO Box 7, Halifax, NS B3J 2L6
902-424-4030, Fax: 902-424-0510, justweb@gov.ns.ca
Nova Scotia Legal Aid Commission, #102, 137 Chain Lake Dr., Halifax, NS B3S 1B3
902-420-6573, Fax: 902-420-3471, nsla.exec@ns.sympatico.ca
Nova Scotia Police Commission, #300, 1601 Lower Water St., PO Box 1573, Halifax, NS B3J 2Y3
902-424-3246, Fax: 902-424-3919, uarb.polcom@gov.ns.ca
Office of the Chief Medical Examiner, Halifax Insurance Bldg., #701, 5670 Spring Garden Rd., Halifax, NS B3J 1H7
902-424-2722, Fax: 902-424-0607
Office of the Ombudsman, #700, 5670 Spring Garden Rd., PO Box 2152, Halifax, NS B3J 3B7
902-424-6780, Fax: 902-424-6675, 800-670-1111, ombudsman@gov.ns.ca
Pay Equity Commission, 5151 Terminal Rd., 6th Fl., PO Box 697, Halifax, NS B3J 2T8
902-424-2385, Fax: 902-424-0575
Workers' Compensation Board of Nova Scotia, 5668 South St., PO Box 1150, Halifax, NS B3J 2Y2
902-491-8999, Fax: 902-491-8002, 800-870-3331, info@wcb.gov.ns.ca

Nunavut

Baffin Correctional Centre, 1550 Federal Rd., PO Box 368, Iqaluit, NU X0A 0H0
867-979-8100, Fax: 867-979-4646
Department of Justice, Sivummut, 1st Fl., PO Box 1000 500,Iqaluit, NU X0A 0H0
867-975-6170, Fax: 867-975-6195, justice@gov.nu.ca
Legal Registries, Brown Bldg., 1st Fl., PO Box 1000 570,Iqaluit, NU X0A 0H0
Fax: 867-975-6594
Legal Services Board of Nunavut, PO Box 125, Gjoa Haven, NU X0A 0H0
Fax: 867-360-6112
Nunavut Liquor Licensing Board, Bag 002, Rankin Inlet, NU X0C 0G0
Fax: 867-645-3327
Office of the Chief Coroner, PO Box 1000 590, Iqaluit, NU X0A 0H0
Young Offenders, 1548 Federal Rd., PO Box 1439, Iqaluit, NU X0A 0H0
867-979-4452, Fax: 867-979-5506

Ontario

Alcohol & Gaming Commission of Ontario, 90 Sheppard Ave. East, Toronto, ON M2N 0A4
416-326-8700, Fax: 416-326-5555, 800-522-2876
Assessment Review Board, Eaton Tower, #1500, 655 Bay St., Toronto, ON M5G 1E5
416-212-6349, Fax: 416-314-3717, 866-448-2248, assessment.review.board@ontario.ca
Association of Ontario Land Surveyors, 1043 McNicoll Ave., Toronto, ON M1W 3W6
416-491-9020, Fax: 416-491-2576
Ontario Ministry of the Attorney General, McMurtry-Scott Bldg., 720 Bay St., 11th Fl., Toronto, ON M5G 2K1
416-326-2220, Fax: 416-326-4007, 800-518-7901
Chief Inquiry Officer - Expropriations Act, McMurtry-Scott Bldg., 720 Bay St., 8th Fl., Toronto, ON M7A 2S9
416-314-2226
Ontario Ministry of Community Safety & Correctional Services, George Drew Bldg., 25 Grosvenor St., 18th Fl., Toronto, ON M7A 1Y6
416-326-5000, Fax: 416-326-0498, 866-517-0571, mcscs.feedback@ontario.ca
Criminal Injuries Compensation Board, 439 University Ave., 4th Fl., Toronto, ON M5G 1Y8
416-326-2900, Fax: 416-326-2883, 800-372-7463, info.cicb@ontario.ca
Ontario Human Rights Commission, 180 Dundas St. West, 7th Fl., Toronto, ON M7A 2R9
416-326-9511, Fax: 416-314-4494, 800-387-9080
Information & Privacy Commissioner of Ontario, #1400, 2 Bloor St. East, Toronto, ON M4W 1A8
416-326-3333, Fax: 416-325-9195, 800-387-0073, info@ipc.on.ca
Office of the Integrity Commissioner, #2101, 2 Bloor St. East, Toronto, ON M4W 1A8
416-314-8983, Fax: 416-314-8987, integrity.mail@oico.on.ca
Judicial Appointments Advisory Committee, McMurtry-Scott Bldg., 720 Bay St., 3rd Fl., Toronto, ON M7A 2S9
416-326-4060, Fax: 416-212-7316
Legal Aid Ontario, #404, 375 University Ave., Toronto, ON M5G 2G1
416-979-1446, Fax: 416-979-8669, 800-668-8258, info@lao.on.ca
Licence Appeal Tribunal, 20 Dundas St. West, 5th Fl., Toronto, ON M5G 2C2
416-314-4260, Fax: 416-314-4270, 800-255-2214
Liquor Control Board of Ontario, 55 Lake Shore Blvd. East, Toronto, ON M5E 1A4
416-365-5900, Fax: 416-864-2476, 800-668-5226, infoline@lcbo.com
Office for Victims of Crime, 700 Bay St., 3rd Fl., Toronto, ON M5G 1Z6
416-326-1682, Fax: 416-326-4497, 887-435-7661
Office of the Ombudsman, Bell Trinity Sq., South Tower, 483 Bay St., 10th Fl., Toronto, ON M5G 2C9
416-586-3300, Fax: 416-586-3485, 800-263-1830, info@ombudsman.on.ca
Ontario Civilian Police Commission, 250 Dundas St. West, 6th Fl., Toronto, ON M7A 2T3
416-314-3004, Fax: 416-314-0198, 888-515-5005
Ontario Labour Relations Board, 505 University Ave., 2nd Fl., Toronto, ON M5G 2P1
416-326-7500, Fax: 416-326-7531, 877-339-3335
Ontario Municipal Board & Board of Negotiation, 655 Bay St., 15th Fl., Toronto, ON M5G 1E5
416-326-6800, Fax: 416-326-5370, 866-887-8820
Ontario Parole Board, #1803, 415 Yonge St., Toronto, ON M5B 2E7
416-325-4480, Fax: 416-325-4485, 888-579-2888
Ontario Police Arbitration Commission, George Drew Bldg., 25 Grosvenor St., 1st Fl., Toronto, ON M7A 1Y6
416-314-3520, Fax: 416-314-3522
Ontario Review Board, 151 Bloor St. West, 10th Fl., Toronto, ON M5S 2T5
416-327-8866, Fax: 416-327-8867
OPSEU Pension Trust, #1200, 1 Adelaide St. East, Toronto, ON M5C 3A7
416-681-6161, Fax: 416-681-6175, 800-637-0024

Road User Safety Division, Bldg A, #191, 1201 Wilson Ave., Downsview, ON M3M 1J8
416-235-2999, Fax: 416-235-4153
ServiceOntario, College Park, 777 Bay St., 15th fl., Toronto, ON M7A 2J3
416-326-1234, Fax: 416-326-1313, 800-267-8097
Social Benefits Tribunal, 1075 Bay St., 7th Fl., Toronto, ON M5S 2B1
416-326-0978, Fax: 416-325-5135, 800-753-3895
Workplace Safety & Insurance Board, 200 Front St. West, Ground Fl., Toronto, ON M5V 3J1
416-344-1000, Fax: 416-344-4684, 800-387-0750

Prince Edward Island

Advisory Council on the Status of Women, Sherwood Business Centre, 161 St. Peter's Rd., Main Level, PO Box 2000, Charlottetown, PE C1A 7N8
902-368-4510, Fax: 902-368-3269, peistatusofwomen@eastlink.ca
Prince Edward Island Human Rights Commission, 53 Water St., PO Box 2000, Charlottetown, PE C1A 7N8
902-368-4180, Fax: 902-368-4236, 800-237-5031
Office of the Auditor General, Shaw Bldg., 105 Rochford St. North, 2nd Fl., Charlottetown, PE C1A 7N8
902-368-4520, Fax: 902-368-4598, www.assembly.pe.ca
Prince Edward Island Liquor Control Commission, 3 Garfield St., PO Box 967, Charlottetown, PE C1A 7M4
902-368-5710, Fax: 902-368-5735
Prince Edward Island Workers Compensation Board, 14 Weymouth St., PO Box 757, Charlottetown, PE C1A 7L7
902-368-5680, Fax: 902-368-5696, 800-237-5049
Prince Edward Island Regulatory & Appeals Commission, National Bank Tower, #501, 134 Kent St., PO Box 577, Charlottetown, PE C1A 7L1
902-892-3501, Fax: 902-566-4076, 800-501-6268, info@irac.pe.ca
Workers Compensation Appeal Tribunal, 161 St. Peters Rd., 1st Fl., PO Box 2000, Charlottetown, PE C1A 7N8

Quebec

Bureau du coroner, Édifice le Delta 2, #390, 2875, boul Laurier, Québec, QC G1V 5B1
418-643-1845, Fax: 418-643-6174, 866-312-7051, clientele.coroner@msp.gouv.qc.ca
Comité de déontologie policière, Tour du Saint-Laurent, #A-200, 2525, boul Laurier, 2e étage, Québec, QC G1V 4Z6
418-646-1936, Fax: 418-528-0987, comite.deontologie@msp.gouv.qc.ca
Commissaire à la déontologie policière, #1-40, 1200, rte de l'Église, Québec, QC G1V 4Y9
418-643-7897, Fax: 418-528-9473, 877-237-7897, deontologie-policiere.quebec@msp.gouv.qc.ca
Commissariat des incendies, 455, rue Dupont, Québec, QC G1K 6N2
418-529-5706, Fax: 418-529-9922, cdelage@notarius.net
Commission des lésions professionnelles, #700, 900, Place d'Youville, Québec, QC G1R 3P7
418-644-7777, Fax: 418-644-6443, 800-463-1591
Commission des services juridiques, Tour de l'Est, #1404, 2, Complexe Desjardins, Montréal, QC H5B 1B3
514-873-3562, Fax: 514-873-8762, info@csj.qc.ca
Commission québecoise des libérations conditionnelles, #1.32A, 300, boul Jean-Lesage, Québec, QC G1K 8K6
418-646-8300, Fax: 418-643-7217, cqlc@msp.gouv.qc.ca
Conseil de la justice administrative, #RC-01, 575, rue Saint-Amable, Québec, QC G1R 2G4
418-644-6279, Fax: 418-528-8471, 888-848-2581, courrier@cja.gouv.qc.ca
Conseil de la magistrature, #5.12, 300, boul Jean-Lesage, Québec, QC G1K 8K6
418-644-2196, Fax: 418-528-1581, information@cm.gouv.qc.ca
Direction générale de la Sûreté du Québec, 1701, rue Parthenais, Montréal, QC H2K 3S7
514-598-4141, Fax: 514-598-4242
Commission des droits de la personne et des droits de la jeunesse, 360, rue St-Jacques, 2e étage, Montréal, QC H2Y 1P5
514-873-5146, Fax: 514-873-6032, 800-361-6477, accueil@cdpdj.qc.ca
Fonds d'aide aux recours collectifs, #10.30, 1, rue Notre-Dame est, Montréal, QC H2Y 1B6
514-393-2087, Fax: 514-864-2998, farc@justice.gouv.qc.ca
Ministère de la Justice, Édifice Louis-Philippe-Pigeon, 1200, rte de l'Église, Québec, QC G1V 4M1
418-643-5140, 866-536-5140, informations@justice.gouv.qc.ca
Le Protecteur du Citoyen, #1.25, 525, boul René-Lévesque est, Québec, QC G1R 5Y4
418-643-2688, Fax: 418-643-8759, 800-463-5070, protecteur@protecteurducitoyen.qc.ca
Registraire des entreprises, 787, boul Lebourgneuf, Québec, QC G2J 1C3
418-644-4545, Fax: 418-528-5703, 877-644-4545, registre@servicesquebec.gouv.qc.ca
Régie des alcools, des courses et des jeux, 560, boul Charest est, Québec, QC G1K 3J3
418-643-7667, Fax: 418-643-5971, 800-363-0320
Société québécoise d'information juridique, 715, carré Victoria, 8e étage, Montréal, QC H2Y 2H7
514-842-8741, Fax: 514-844-8984, 800-363-6718, info@soquij.qc.ca
Ministère de la Sécurité publique, Tour des Laurentides, 2525, boul Laurier, 5e étage, Québec, QC G1V 2L2
418-643-2112, Fax: 418-646-6168, 866-644-6826
Tribunal administratif du Québec, 575, rue Saint-Amable, Québec, QC G1R 5R4
418-643-3418, Fax: 418-643-5335
Vérificateur général du Québec, 750, boulevard Charest est, 3e étage, Québec, QC G1K 9J6
418-691-5900, Fax: 418-644-4460, verificateur.general@vgq.gouv.qc.ca
École nationale de police du Québec, 350, rue Marguerite-d'Youville, Nicolet, QC J3T 1X4
819-293-8631, Fax: 819-293-8630, courriel@enpq.qc.ca

Saskatchewan

Agricultural Implements Board, #202, 3085 Albert St., Regina, SK S4S 0B1
306-787-4693, Fax: 306-787-1315
Information & Privacy Commissioner of Saskatchewan, #503, 1801 Hamilton St., Regina, SK S4P 4B4
306-787-8350, Fax: 306-798-1603, 877-748-2298, webmaster@oipc.sk.ca
Law Reform Commission of Saskatchewan, c/o University of Saskatchewan, College of Law, #209, 15 Campus Drive, Saskatoon, SK S7N 5A6
306-966-1625, Fax: 306-966-5900, director.research@sasklawreform.com
Ombudsman Saskatchewan, #150, 2401 Saskatchewan Dr., Regina, SK S4P 4H8
306-787-6211, Fax: 306-787-9090, 800-667-7180, ombreg@ombudsman.sk.ca
Provincial Mediation Board, #120, 2151 Scarth St., Regina, SK S4P 2H8
306-787-5387, Fax: 306-787-5574, 877-787-5408
Public & Private Rights Board, #323, 3085 Albert St., Regina, SK S4S 0B1
306-787-4071, Fax: 306-787-0088
Saskatchewan Film & Video Classification Board, #500, 1919 Saskatchewan Dr., Regina, SK S4P 4H2
306-787-5550, Fax: 306-787-9779, 888-374-4636
Saskatchewan Financial Services Commission, #601, 1919 Saskatchewan Dr., Regina, SK S4P 4H2
306-787-5645, Fax: 306-787-5899
Saskatchewan Human Rights Commission, Saskatoon Office, Sturdy Stone Bdg., #816, 122 - 3 Ave. North, 8th Fl., Saskatoon, SK S7K 2H6
306-933-5952, Fax: 306-933-7863, 800-667-9249, shrc@gov.sk.ca
Saskatchewan Justice & Attorney General, 1874 Scarth St., Regina, SK S4P 4B3
306-787-8971, communications@justice.gov.sk.ca
Saskatchewan Legal Aid Commission, #502, 201 - 21 St. East, Saskatoon, SK S7K 0B8
306-933-5300, Fax: 306-933-6764, 800-667-3764
Saskatchewan Liquor & Gaming Authority, 2500 Victoria Ave., PO Box 5054, Regina, SK S4P 3M3
306-787-4213, inquiry@slga.gov.sk.ca
Saskatchewan Public Complaints Commission, #300, 1919 Saskatchewan Dr., Regina, SK S4P 4H2
306-787-6519, Fax: 306-787-6528, 866-256-6194
Saskatchewan Workers' Compensation Board, #200, 1881 Scarth St., Regina, SK S4P 4L1
306-787-4370, Fax: 306-787-4311, 800-667-7590, internet_clientsvc@wcbsask.com
Surface Rights Board of Arbitration, 113 - 2nd Ave. East, PO Box 1597, Kindersley, SK S0L 1S0
306-463-5447, Fax: 306-463-5449, surfacerightsboard@gov.sk.ca

Yukon Territory

Driver Control Board, 2130 Second Ave., 3rd Fl., PO Box 2703, Whitehorse, YT Y1A 2C6
867-667-5111, Fax: 867-667-3609, dcb@gov.yk.ca
Law Society of Yukon - Discipline Committee, #202, 302 Steele St., Whitehorse, YT Y1A 3W8
867-668-4231, Fax: 867-667-7556, lsy@yknet.yk.ca
Law Society of Yukon - Executive, #202, 302 Steele St., Whitehorse, YT Y1A 2C5
867-668-4231, Fax: 867-667-7556, info@lawsocietyyukon.com
Yukon Liquor Corporation, 9031 Quartz Rd., Whitehorse, YT Y1A 4P9
867-667-5245, Fax: 867-393-6306, yukon.liquor@gov.yk.ca
Yukon Workers' Compensation Health & Safety Board, 401 Strickland St., Whitehorse, YT Y1A 5N8
867-667-5645, Fax: 867-393-6279, 800-661-0443, worksafe@gov.yk.ca
Yukon Human Rights Board of Adjudication, #202, 407 Black St., Whitehorse, YT Y1A 2N2
867-667-5412, Fax: 867-633-6952, beyondwords@northwestel.net
Yukon Human Rights Commission, #101, 9010 Quartz St., Whitehorse, YT Y1A 2Z5
867-667-6226, Fax: 867-667-2662, 800-661-0535, humanrights@yhrc.yk.ca
Yukon Judicial Council, PO Box 31222, Whitehorse, YT Y1A 5P7
867-667-5438, Fax: 867-393-6400, courtservices@gov.yk.ca
Yukon Law Foundation, PO Box 31789, Whitehorse, YT Y1A 6L3
867-668-4231, Fax: 867-667-7556, lsy@yknet.yk.ca
Yukon Legal Services Society/Legal Aid, #203, 2131 - 2nd Ave., Whitehorse, YT Y1A 1C3
867-667-5210, Fax: 867-667-8649, 800-661-0408, legalaid@yknet.yk.ca

LEGAL & REGULATORY

Canadian Coast Guard, Centennial Towers, #6S018, 200 Kent St., Ottawa, ON K1A 0E6
613-993-0999, Fax: 613-990-1866, info@dfo-mpo.gc.ca
Commission for Environmental Cooperation, Secretariat, #200, 393, rue St-Jacques ouest, Montréal, QC H2Y 1N9
514-350-4300, Fax: 514-350-4314, info@cec.org
Institute for National Measurement Standards, Bldg. M-36, 1500 Montreal Rd., Ottawa, ON K1A 0R6
613-998-7018, Fax: 613-954-1473, alexandra.shaw@nrc-cnrc.gc.ca
Standards Council of Canada, #200, 270 Albert St., Ottawa, ON K1P 6N7
613-238-3222, Fax: 613-569-7808, info@scc.ca
Standards Council of Canada, #200, 270 Albert Street, Ottawa, ON K1P 6N7
613-238-3222, Fax: 613-569-7808, info@scc.ca

New Brunswick

Community Planning & Environmental Protection Division, Marysville Place, PO Box 6000, Fredericton, NB E3B 5H1
506-444-5119, Fax: 506-457-7333, elg/egl-info@gnb.ca

Northwest Territories

Assessment Appeal Tribunal of the Northwest Territories, #400, 5201 - 50th Ave., PO Box 1320, Yellowknife, NT X1A 2L9
867-873-7125, Fax: 867-873-0609

Nova Scotia

Crane Operators Appeal Board, 5151 Terminal Rd., 7th Fl., PO Box 697, Halifax, NS B3J 2T8
902-424-8595, Fax: 902-424-0217, fernanfs@gov.ns.ca
Pay Equity Commission, 5151 Terminal Rd., 6th Fl., PO Box 697, Halifax, NS B3J 2T8
902-424-2385, Fax: 902-424-0575
Workers' Advisers Program, #502, 5670 Spring Garden Rd., PO Box 1063, Halifax, NS B3J 2X1
902-424-5050, Fax: 902-424-0530, 800-774-4712
Workers' Compensation Board of Nova Scotia, 5668 South St., PO Box 1150, Halifax, NS B3J 2Y2
902-491-8999, Fax: 902-491-8002, 800-870-3331, info@wcb.gov.ns.ca

Ontario

Ontario Ministry of Community Safety & Correctional Services, George Drew Bldg., 25 Grosvenor St., 18th Fl., Toronto, ON M7A 1Y6
416-326-5000, Fax: 416-326-0498, 866-517-0571, mcscs.feedback@ontario.ca
Environmental Commissioner of Ontario, #605, 1075 Bay St., Toronto, ON M5S 2B1
416-325-3377, Fax: 416-325-3370, 800-701-6454, commissioner@eco.on.ca
Environmental Review Tribunal, #1500, 655 Bay St., Toronto, ON M5G 1E5
416-212-6349, Fax: 416-314-4506, 866-448-2248, erttribunalsecretary@ontario.ca
Road User Safety Division, Bldg A, #191, 1201 Wilson Ave., Downsview, ON M3M 1J8
416-235-2999, Fax: 416-235-4153

Prince Edward Island

Prince Edward Island Regulatory & Appeals Commission, National Bank Tower, #501, 134 Kent St., PO Box 577, Charlottetown, PE C1A 7L1
902-892-3501, Fax: 902-566-4076, 800-501-6268, info@irac.pe.ca

LEGAL AID SERVICES

Alberta
Court Services Division, Bowker Building, 9833 - 109 St., 5th Fl., Edmonton, AB T5K 2E8
780-427-4992, Fax: 780-422-6613
New Brunswick Legal Aid Services Commission, #501, 500 Beaverbrook Ct., Fredericton, NB E3B 5X4
506-444-2776, Fax: 506-444-2290, info@legalaid.nb.ca

British Columbia
Legal Services Society, #400, 510 Burrard St., Vancouver, BC V6C 3A8
604-601-6000

Manitoba
Legal Aid Manitoba, 402 - 294 Portage Ave., Winnipeg, MB R3C 0B9
204-985-8500, Fax: 204-944-8582, 800-261-2960, info@legalaid.mb.ca

New Brunswick
New Brunswick Department of Justice & Attorney General, Centennial Building, PO Box 6000, Fredericton, NB E3B 5H1
506-462-5100, Fax: 506-453-3651, justice.comments@gnb.ca

Newfoundland & Labrador
Newfoundland & Labrador Legal Aid Commission, #300, 251 Empire Ave., PO Box 399 C, St. John's, NL A1C 5J9
709-753-7863, Fax: 709-753-6226, 800-563-9911, nlac@legalaid.nl.ca

Northwest Territories
Legal Services Board of the Northwest Territories, PO Box 1320, Yellowknife, NT X1A 2L9
867-873-7450, Fax: 867-873-5320

Nova Scotia
Nova Scotia Legal Aid Commission, #102, 137 Chain Lake Dr., Halifax, NS B3S 1B3
902-420-6573, Fax: 902-420-3471, nsla.exec@ns.sympatico.ca

Ontario
Legal Aid Ontario, #404, 375 University Ave., Toronto, ON M5G 2G1
416-979-1446, Fax: 416-979-8669, 800-668-8258, info@lao.on.ca

Quebec
Fonds d'aide aux recours collectifs, #10.30, 1, rue Notre-Dame est, Montréal, QC H2Y 1B6
514-393-2087, Fax: 514-864-2998, farc@justice.gouv.qc.ca

Saskatchewan
Saskatchewan Legal Aid Commission, #502, 201 - 21 St. East, Saskatoon, SK S7K 0B8
306-933-5300, Fax: 306-933-6764, 800-667-3764

Yukon Territory
Yukon Legal Services Society/Legal Aid, #203, 2131 - 2nd Ave., Whitehorse, YT Y1A 1C3
867-667-5210, Fax: 867-667-8649, 800-661-0408, legalaid@yknet.yk.ca

LEGISLATIVE ASSEMBLIES/NATIONAL ASSEMBLIES/HO

See Also: uses
House of Commons, Canada, House of Commons, Centre Block, Parliament Buildings, 111 Wellington St., Ottawa, ON K1A 0A6
613-992-4793, 866-599-4999, info@parl.gc.ca

Alberta
Legislative Assembly of Alberta, Legislature Annex, 9718 - 107 St., Edmonton, AB T5K 1E4
780-427-2826, Fax: 780-427-1623, laocommunications@assembly.ab.ca

British Columbia
BC Legislative Assembly & Independent Offices, Clerk's Office, #221, Parliament Bldgs., Victoria, BC V8V 1X4
250-387-3785, Fax: 250-387-0942, ClerkHouse@leg.bc.ca

Manitoba
Manitoba Legislative Assembly, c/o Clerk's Office, Legislative Bldg., #237, 450 Broadway, Winnipeg, MB R3C 0V8
204-945-3636, Fax: 204-948-2507, clerkla@leg.gov.mb.ca

New Brunswick
Legislative Assembly of New Brunswick, Centre Block, Legislative Building, 706 Queen St., PO Box 6000, Fredericton, NB E3B 5H1
506-453-2506, Fax: 506-453-7154, wwwleg@gnb.ca

Newfoundland & Labrador
House of Assembly, c/o Clerk's Office, Confederation Bldg., PO Box 8700, St. John's, NL A1B 4J6
709-729-3405, Fax: 709-729-4820

Northwest Territories
NWT Legislative Assembly, c/o Clerk's Office, PO Box 1320, Yellowknife, NT X1A 2L9
867-669-2299, Fax: 867-920-4735, 800-661-0784

Nova Scotia
Legislative House of Assembly, c/o Clerk's Office, Province House, 1st Fl., PO Box 1617, Halifax, NS B3J 2Y3
902-424-5978, Fax: 902-424-0632

Nunavut
Nunavut Legislative Assembly, 926 Federal Rd., PO Box 1200, Iqaluit, NU X0A 0H0
867-975-5000, Fax: 867-975-5190, 877-334-7266, leginfo@assembly.nu.ca

Ontario
Ontario Legislative Assembly, c/o Clerk's Office, #104, Legislative Bldg., Queen's Park, Toronto, ON M7A 1A2
416-325-7500, Fax: 416-325-7489, assemblyinternet@ontla.ola.org

Prince Edward Island
Prince Edward Island Legislative Assembly, Province House, 165 Richmond St., 1st Fl., PO Box 2000, Charlottetown, PE C1A 7N8
902-368-5970, Fax: 902-368-5175, 877-315-5518, legislativelibrary@assembly.pe.ca

Quebec
L'Assemblée nationale, Hôtel du Parlement, 1045, rue des Parlementaires, Québec, QC G1A 1A3
418-643-7239, Fax: 418-646-4271, 866-337-8837, responsable.contenu@assnat.qc.ca

Saskatchewan
Legislative Assembly of Saskatchewan, Office of the Clerk, Legislative Building, #239, 2405 Legislative Dr., Regina, SK S4S 0B3
info@legassembly.sk.ca

Yukon Territory
Yukon Legislative Assembly, PO Box 2703, Whitehorse, YT Y1A 2C6
867-667-5498, Fax: 867-393-6280, yla@gov.yk.ca

LEISURE CRAFT & VEHICLE REGULATIONS

Nova Scotia
Registry of Motor Vehicles, 1505 Barrington St., 8th Fl. North, PO Box 1652, Halifax, NS B3J 2Z3
902-424-7801, Fax: 902-424-0772, 800-898-7668

Alberta
Strategic Planning & Financial Services, Commerce Place, 10155 - 102 St., 13th Fl., Edmonton, AB T5J 4G8
780-422-8545

Northwest Territories
Road Licensing & Safety, 4510 - 50 Ave., 1st fl., PO Box 1320, Yellowknife, NT X1A 2L9
867-873-7972, Fax: 867-873-0120

Nova Scotia
Department of Transportation & Infrastructure Renewal, Johnston Bldg., 1672 Granville St., 2nd Fl., PO Box 186, Halifax, NS B3J 2N2
902-424-2297, Fax: 902-424-0532, tpwpaff@gov.ns.ca

Ontario
Ontario Ministry of Transportation, Ferguson Block, 77 Wellesley St. West, 3rd Fl., Toronto, ON M7A 1Z8
416-235-4686, Fax: 905-704-2001, 800-268-4686

Quebec
Ministère des Transports, 700, boul René-Lévesque est, 28e étage, Québec, QC G1R 5H1
418-643-6980, Fax: 418-643-2033, 888-355-0511, communications@mtq.gouv.qc.ca

Saskatchewan
Saskatchewan Government Insurance, 2260 - 11th Ave., Regina, SK S4P 0J9
306-751-1200, Fax: 306-787-7477, 800-667-8015, sgiinquiries@sgi.sk.ca

LIBRARIES

Library & Archives Canada, 395 Wellington St., Ottawa, ON K1A 0N4
613-996-5115, Fax: 613-995-6274, 866-578-7777
Library of Parliament, Parliamentary Buildings, Ottawa, ON K1A 0A9
613-992-4793, 866-599-4999, info@parl.gc.ca

New Brunswick
Legislative Assembly of New Brunswick, Centre Block, Legislative Building, 706 Queen St., PO Box 6000, Fredericton, NB E3B 5H1
506-453-2506, Fax: 506-453-7154, wwwleg@gnb.ca

Newfoundland & Labrador
Provincial Information & Library Resources Board, 48 St. George's Ave, Stephenville, NL A2H 1K9
709-643-0900, Fax: 709-643-0925

Nova Scotia
Legislative House of Assembly, c/o Clerk's Office, Province House, 1st Fl., PO Box 1617, Halifax, NS B3J 2Y3
902-424-5978, Fax: 902-424-0632

Nunavut
Department of Culture, Language, Elders & Youth, PO Box 1000 800,Iqaluit, NU X0A 0H0
867-975-5500, Fax: 867-975-5504, 866-934-2035

Ontario
Ontario Library Service - North, 334 Regent St., Sudbury, ON P3C 4E2
705-675-6467, Fax: 705-675-2285, 800-461-6348
Southern Ontario Library Service, #902, 111 Peter St., Toronto, ON M5V 2H1
416-961-1669, Fax: 416-961-5122, 800-387-5765

Quebec
Bibliothèque et Archives nationales du Québec (BAnQ), 475, boul De Maisonneuve est, Montréal, QC H2L 5C4
514-873-1100, Fax: 514-873-9312, 800-363-9028

LIQUOR CONTROL

See Also: Drugs & Alcohol

British Columbia
Liquor Distribution Branch, 3200 East Broadway, Vancouver, BC V5M 1Z6
604-252-3000, Fax: 604-252-3026

Manitoba
Manitoba Liquor Control Commission, 1555 Buffalo Pl., PO Box 1023, Winnipeg, MB R3C 2X1
204-284-2501, Fax: 204-475-7666, info@mlcc.mb.ca

New Brunswick
New Brunswick Liquor Corporation, 170 Wilsey Rd., PO Box 20787, Fredericton, NB E3B 5B8
506-452-6826, Fax: 506-462-2024, info@anbl.com

Newfoundland & Labrador
Newfoundland & Labrador Liquor Corporation, 90 Kenmount Rd., PO Box 8750 A, St. John's, NL A1B 3V1
709-724-1100, Fax: 709-754-0321, info@nfliquor.com

Northwest Territories
Northwest Territories Liquor Commission, #201, 31 Capital Dr., Hay River, NT X0E 1G2
867-874-2100, Fax: 867-874-2180
Northwest Territories Liquor Licensing & Enforcement, #210, 31 Capital Dr., Hay River, NT X0E 1G2
867-874-2906, Fax: 867-874-6011
Northwest Territories Liquor Licensing Board, #210, 31 Capital Dr., Hay River, NT X0E 1G2
867-874-2906, Fax: 867-874-6011, delilah_st-arneault@gov.nt.ca

Nova Scotia
Nova Scotia Liquor Corporation, Bayers Lake Business Park, 93 Chain Lake Dr., Halifax, NS B3S 1A3
902-450-6752, 800-567-5874

Nunavut
Nunavut Liquor Licensing Board, Bag 002, Rankin Inlet, NU X0C 0G0
Fax: 867-645-3327

Ontario
Alcohol & Gaming Commission of Ontario, 90 Sheppard Ave. East, Toronto, ON M2N 0A4
416-326-8700, Fax: 416-326-5555, 800-522-2876,
Liquor Control Board of Ontario, 55 Lake Shore Blvd. East, Toronto, ON M5E 1A4
416-365-5900, Fax: 416-864-2476, 800-668-5226, infoline@lcbo.com

Prince Edward Island
Prince Edward Island Liquor Control Commission, 3 Garfield St., PO Box 967, Charlottetown, PE C1A 7M4
902-368-5710, Fax: 902-368-5735

Quebec
Régie des alcools, des courses et des jeux, 560, boul Charest est, Québec, QC G1K 3J3
418-643-7667, Fax: 418-643-5971, 800-363-0320

Saskatchewan
Saskatchewan Liquor & Gaming Authority, 2500 Victoria Ave., PO Box 5054, Regina, SK S4P 3M3
306-787-4213, inquiry@slga.gov.sk.ca

Yukon Territory
Yukon Liquor Corporation, 9031 Quartz Rd., Whitehorse, YT Y1A 4P9
867-667-5245, Fax: 867-393-6306, yukon.liquor@gov.yk.ca

LOTTERIES & GAMING

British Columbia
British Columbia Lottery Corporation, 74 West Seymour St., Kamloops, BC V2C 1E2
250-828-5500, Fax: 250-828-5631, 866-815-0222

Manitoba
Manitoba Lotteries Corporation, 830 Empress St., Winnipeg, MB R3G 3H3
204-957-2500, Fax: 204-957-3991, 800-265-2912, communications@casinosofwinnipeg.com

Manitoba Gaming Control Commission, #800, 215 Garry St., Winnipeg, MB R3C 3P3
204-954-9400, Fax: 204-954-9450, 800-782-0363, information@mgcc.mb.ca

New Brunswick

New Brunswick Lotteries & Gaming Corporation, Centennial Bldg., 670 King St., PO Box 6000, Fredericton, NB E3B 5H1
506-444-3468, Fax: 506-444-5818

Newfoundland & Labrador

Newfoundland & Labrador Department of Service NL, PO Box 8700, St. John's, NL A1B 4J6
709-729-4834, gsinfo@gov.nl.ca

Nunavut

Department of Community & Government Services, W.G. Brown Bldg., 4th Fl., PO Box 1000 700,Iqaluit, NU X0A 0H0
867-975-5400, Fax: 867-975-5305

Ontario

Alcohol & Gaming Commission of Ontario, 90 Sheppard Ave. East, Toronto, ON M2N 0A4
416-326-8700, Fax: 416-326-5555, 800-522-2876

Ontario Lottery & Gaming Corporation, Roberta Bondar Pl., #800, 70 Foster Dr., Sault Ste Marie, ON P6A 6V2
705-946-6464, Fax: 416-224-7000, 800-387-0098

Quebec

Régie des alcools, des courses et des jeux, 560, boul Charest est, Québec, QC G1K 3J3
418-643-7667, Fax: 418-643-5971, 800-363-0320

Saskatchewan

Saskatchewan Liquor & Gaming Authority, 2500 Victoria Ave., PO Box 5054, Regina, SK S4P 3M3
306-787-4213, inquiry@slga.gov.sk.ca

Yukon Territory

Yukon Lottery Commission, 312 Wood St., Whitehorse, YT Y1A 2E6
867-633-7890, Fax: 867-668-7561, lotteriesyukon@gov.yk.ca

MAPS, CHARTS & AERIAL PHOTOGRAPHS

Canada Centre for Remote Sensing - Geomatics Canada, 588 Booth St., Ottawa, ON K1A 0Y7
613-995-0947, Fax: 613-947-1382

Mapping Services Branch - Geomatics Canada, 615 Booth St., Ottawa, ON K1A 0E9
613-995-4945, Fax: 613-995-8737

Nova Scotia

Geomatics Centre, 160 Willow St., Amherst, NS B4H 3W5
902-667-7231, Fax: 902-667-6008, 800-798-0706, geoinfo@gov.ns.ca

Ontario

Association of Ontario Land Surveyors, 1043 McNicoll Ave., Toronto, ON M1W 3W6
416-491-9020, Fax: 416-491-2576

MARINE NAVIGATION

Atlantic Pilotage Authority, Cogswell Tower, #910, 2000 Barrington St., Halifax, NS B3J 3K1
902-426-2550, Fax: 902-426-4004, 877-272-3477, dispatch@atlanticpilotage.com

Great Lakes Pilotage Authority, 202 Pitt St., 2nd fl., PO Box 95, Cornwall, ON K6H 5R9
613-933-2991, Fax: 613-932-3793, administration@glpa-apgl.com

Pacific Pilotage Authority Canada, #1000, 1130 Pender St. West, Vancouver, BC V6E 4A4
604-666-6771, Fax: 604-666-1647, info@ppa.gc.ca

St. Lawrence Seaway Management Corporation, 202 Pitt St., Cornwall, ON K6J 3P7
613-932-5170, Fax: 613-932-7286, marketing@seaway.ca

MINERALS & MINING

New Brunswick

Lands, Minerals & Petroleum Division, Hugh John Flemming Forestry Centre, PO Box 6000, Fredericton, NB E3B 5H1
506-453-2684, Fax: 506-453-2930, dnrweb@gnb.ca

Resource Development Policy Division, Petroleum Plaza NT, 9945 - 108 St., Edmonton, AB T5K 2G6

British Columbia

Mines & Mineral Resources, PO Box 9319 Prov Govt,Victoria, BC V8W 9N3

Manitoba

Mining Board, #360, 1395 Ellice Ave., Winnipeg, MB R3G 3P2
204-489-0018

Northwest Territories

Department of Industry, Tourism & Investment, PO Box 1320, Yellowknife, NT X1A 2L9
Fax: 867-873-0306, info@iti.ca

Nova Scotia

Department of Energy, Bank of Montreal Bldg., #400, 5151 George St., PO Box 2664, Halifax, NS B3J 3P7
902-424-4575, Fax: 902-424-0528, energyinfo@gov.ns.ca

Nunavut

Department of Environment, PO Box 1000 1300,Iqaluit, NU X0A 0H0
867-975-7700, Fax: 867-975-7742, environment@gov.nu.ca

Ontario

Mines & Minerals Division, Willet Green Miller Centre, 933 Ramsey Lake Rd., Sudbury, ON P3E 6B5
705-670-5755, Fax: 705-670-5818, 888-415-9845

Quebec

Mines, Centre de service des Mines, 1685, boul Wilfrid Hamel ouest, 1er étage, Québec, QC G1N 3Y7
418-627-6278, Fax: 418-644-8960, 800-363-7233, service.mines@mrnf.gouv.qc.ca

Énergie, #B401, 5700, 4e av ouest, Québec, QC G1H 6R1
418-627-6377, Fax: 418-643-0701

Saskatchewan

Energy & Resources, #300, 2103 - 11th Ave., Regina, SK S4P 3Z8
306-787-2528

Yukon Territory

Yukon Energy, Mines & Resources, PO Box 2703, Whitehorse, YT Y1A 2C6
867-667-3130, Fax: 867-456-3965, 800-661-0408, emr@gov.yk.ca

MINES & MINERALS

CANMET Mineral Technology Branch, 555 Booth St., Ottawa, ON K1A 0G1

Lands, Minerals & Petroleum Division, Hugh John Flemming Forestry Centre, PO Box 6000, Fredericton, NB E3B 5H1
506-453-2684, Fax: 506-453-2930, dnrweb@gnb.ca

Resource Development Policy Division, Petroleum Plaza NT, 9945 - 108 St., Edmonton, AB T5K 2G6

Alberta

Alberta Sport, Recreation, Parks, & Wildlife Foundation, Standard Life Centre, #903, 10405 Jasper Ave., 9th Fl., Edmonton, AB T5J 4R7
780-415-1167, Fax: 780-415-0308, -310-0000

British Columbia

British Columbia Ministry of Energy, Mines, & Natural Gas (& Responsible for Housing), PO Box 9053 Prov Govt,Victoria, BC V8W 9E2

Manitoba

Mining Board, #360, 1395 Ellice Ave., Winnipeg, MB R3G 3P2
204-489-0018

Northwest Territories

Department of Environment & Natural Resources, PO Box 1320, Yellowknife, NT X1A 2L9

Ontario

Mines & Minerals Division, Willet Green Miller Centre, 933 Ramsey Lake Rd., Sudbury, ON P3E 6B5
705-670-5755, Fax: 705-670-5818, 888-415-9845

Ontario Ministry of Northern Development & Mines, 159 Cedar St., Sudbury, ON P3E 6A5
Fax: 416-327-0651, 888-415-9845

Quebec

Mines, Centre de service des Mines, 1685, boul Wilfrid Hamel ouest, 1er étage, Québec, QC G1N 3Y7
418-627-6278, Fax: 418-644-8960, 800-363-7233, service.mines@mrnf.gouv.qc.ca

MINIMUM WAGES

See Also: Labour

British Columbia

British Columbia Ministry of Citizens' Services & Open Government, PO Box 9594 Prov Govt,Victoria, BC V8W 9E2
250-952-7623, Fax: 250-952-7628, 800-663-7867, EnquiryBC@gov.bc.ca

Quebec

Commission des normes du travail, Hall Est, 400, boul Jean-Lesage, 7e étage, Québec, QC G1K 8W1
418-644-0817, Fax: 418-643-5132, 800-563-9058

Saskatchewan

Minimum Wage Board, #400, 1870 Albert St., Regina, SK S4P 4W1

MULTICULTURALISM

Canadian Race Relations Foundation, #701, 4576 Yonge St., Toronto, ON M2N 6N4
416-952-3500, Fax: 416-952-3326, 888-240-4936

British Columbia

Multicultural Advisory Council of BC, Multiculturalism & Inclusive Communities Office, 605 Robson St., 5th Fl., Vancouver, BC V6B 5J3
604-660-2203, Fax: 604-775-0670

Manitoba

Manitoba Ethnocultural Advisory & Advocacy Council, 215 Notre Dame Ave. 4th Fl., Winnipeg, MB R3B 1N3
204-945-2339, Fax: 204-948-2323, 800-665-8332, meaac@gov.mb.ca

Multiculturalism Secretariat, 213 Notre Dame Ave., 4th Fl., Winnipeg, MB R3B 1N3
204-945-1156, Fax: 204-948-2323

Northwest Territories

Department of Education, Culture & Employment, PO Box 1320, Yellowknife, NT X1A 2L9
867-669-2399, Fax: 867-873-0431, 866-606-5627

Nova Scotia

Department of Communities, Culture & Heritage, World Trade & Convention Centre, 1800 Argyle St., 6th Fl., PO Box 456, Halifax, NS B3J 3N8
902-424-4510, Fax: 902-424-0710, culture@gov.ns.ca

Prince Edward Island

Prince Edward Island Department of Education & Early Childhood Development, Holman Centre, #101, 250 Water St., Summerside, PE C1N 1B6
902-438-4130, Fax: 902-438-4062

Quebec

Conseil des relations interculturelles, #10.04, 500, boul René-Lévesque ouest, Montréal, QC H2Z 1W7
514-873-5634, Fax: 514-873-3469, info@conseilinterculturel.gouv.qc.ca

Ministère de la Culture, des Communications & de la Condition féminine, 225, Grande Allée est, Québec, QC G1R 5G5
888-380-8882

MUNICIPAL & RURAL AFFAIRS

Aboriginal Affairs & Northern Development Canada, 10 Wellington St., North Tower, Gatineau, QC K1A 0H4
819-997-0380, Fax: 866-817-3977, 800-567-9604, infopubs@aadnc-aandc.gc.ca

Canada Economic Development for Québec Regions, Édifice Dominion Square, #900, 1255, rue Peel, Montréal, QC H3B 2T9
514-283-6412, Fax: 514-283-3302, 866-385-6412,

Canada Mortgage & Housing Corporation, 700 Montreal Rd., Ottawa, ON K1A 0P7
613-748-2000, Fax: 613-748-2098, 800-668-2642, chic@cmhc-schl.gc.ca

Mackenzie Valley Environmental Impact Review Board, 200 Scotia Centre, #5102, 50th Ave., PO Box 938, Yellowknife, NT X1A 2N7
867-766-7050, Fax: 867-766-7074, 866-912-3472

Nunavut Impact Review Board, PO Box 1360, Cambridge Bay, NU X0B 0C0
867-983-4600, Fax: 867-983-2594, 866-233-3033, info@nirb.ca

Nunavut Planning Commission, PO Box 2101, Cambridge Bay, NU X0B 0C0
867-983-4625, Fax: 867-983-4626

Saskatchewan Government Relations, 1855 Victoria Ave., Regina, SK S4P 3T2
306-787-8885

Alberta

Alberta Agriculture & Rural Development, JG O'Donoghue Bldg., #100A, 7000 - 113th St., Edmonton, AB T6H 5T6
780-427-2727, -310-3276, duke@gov.ab.ca

Alberta Municipal Affairs, Communications Branch, Commerce Place, 10155 - 102 St., 18th Fl., Edmonton, AB T5J 4L4
780-427-2732, Fax: 780-422-1419, comments@gov.ab.ca

Municipal Government Board, Commerce Place, 10155 - 102 St., 15th Fl., Edmonton, AB T5J 4L4
780-427-4864, Fax: 780-427-0986, -310-0000, mgbmail@gov.ab.ca

Alberta Tourism, Parks, & Recreation, Communications Branch, Commerce Place, 10155 - 102 St., 6th Fl., Edmonton, AB T5J 4L6
780-644-5589, TPR.Communications@gov.ab.ca

British Columbia

Local Government, PO Box 9490 Prov Govt,Victoria, BC V8W 9N7
250-356-6575, Fax: 250-387-7973

Manitoba

Manitoba Aboriginal & Northern Affairs, Legislative Bldg, 344-450 Broadway, Winnipeg, MB R3C OV8
204-945-3719, Fax: 204-945-8374, anaweb@gov.mb.ca

Manitoba Local Government, #301, 450 Broadway Ave., Winnipeg, MB R3C 0V8
Fax: 204-945-1383, mnia@leg.gov.mb.ca

Manitoba Municipal Board, #1144, 363 Broadway, Winnipeg, MB R3C 3N9
204-945-2941, Fax: 204-948-2235

New Brunswick
New Brunswick Department of Health, PO Box 5100, Fredericton, NB E3B 5G8
506-457-4800, Fax: 506-453-5243, dh-ms@dh-ms.ca
Regional Development Corporation, RDC Bldg., 836 Churchill Row, PO Box 428, Fredericton, NB E3B 5R4
506-453-2277, Fax: 506-453-7988
Newfoundland & Labrador
Newfoundland & Labrador Department of Health & Community Services, West Block, Confederation Bldg., PO Box 8700, St. John's, NL A1B 4J6
709-729-5021, Fax: 709-729-5824, healthinfo@gov.nl.ca
Newfoundland & Labrador Department of Municipal Affairs, West Block, Main Fl., Confederation Bldg., PO Box 8700, St. John's, NL A1B 4J6
709-729-3046, Fax: 709-729-0943, mainfo@gov.nl.ca
Northwest Territories
Department of Municipal & Community Affairs, PO Box 1320, Yellowknife, NT X1A 2L9
867-873-7118, Fax: 867-873-0309
Nova Scotia
Department of Service Nova Scotia & Municipal Relations, 1505 Barrington St., PO Box 216, Halifax, NS B3J 3K5
902-424-5200, Fax: 902-424-0581, 800-670-4357, askus@gov.ns.ca
Department of Transportation & Infrastructure Renewal, Johnston Bldg., 1672 Granville St., 2nd Fl., PO Box 186, Halifax, NS B3J 2N2
902-424-2297, Fax: 902-424-0532, tpwpaff@gov.ns.ca
Ontario
Ontario Ministry of Agriculture, Food & Rural Affairs, Ontario Government Bldg., 1 Stone Rd. West, Guelph, ON N1G 4Y2
519-826-3100, 888-466-2372
Ontario Ministry of Municipal Affairs & Housing, College Park, 777 Bay St., 17th Fl., Toronto, ON M5G 2E5
416-585-7041, Fax: 416-585-6470, 866-220-2290, mininfo@ontario.ca
Ontario Ministry of Northern Development & Mines, 159 Cedar St., Sudbury, ON P3E 6A5
Fax: 416-327-0651, 888-415-9845
Northern Development Division, Roberta Bondar Place, #200, 70 Foster Dr., Sault Ste Marie, ON P6A 6V8
705-945-5900, Fax: 705-945-5931, 800-461-2287
Prince Edward Island
Prince Edward Island Department of Transportation & Infrastructure Renewal, Jones Bldg., 11 Kent St., 3rd Fl., PO Box 2000, Charlottetown, PE C1A 7N8
902-368-5100, Fax: 902-368-5395
Quebec
Ministère des Affaires municipales, des Régions et de l'Occupation du territoire, Aile Chaveau, 10, rue Pierre-Olivier-Chauveau, 3e étage, Québec, QC G1R 4J3
418-691-2019, Fax: 418-643-7385, communications@mamrot.gouv.qc.ca
Comité consultatif de l'environnement Kativik, CP 930, Kuujjuaq, QC J0M 1C0
819-964-2961, Fax: 819-964-0694
Commission municipale du Québec, Mezzanine, aile Chauveau, 10, rue Pierre-Olivier-Chauveau, Québec, QC G1R 4J3
418-691-2014, Fax: 418-644-4676, 866-353-6767, cmq@mamr.gouv.qc.ca
Ministère du Développement économique, de l'Innovation et de l'Exportation, 710, place D'Youville, 3e étage, Québec, QC G1R 4Y4
418-691-5950, Fax: 418-644-0118, 866-680-1884
Yukon Territory
Yukon Community Services, PO Box 2703, Whitehorse, YT Y1A 2C6
867-667-5811, Fax: 867-393-6295, 800-661-0408, inquiry@gov.yk.ca

MUNICIPAL AFFAIRS

Prince Edward Island
Prince Edward Island Department of Finance, Energy & Municipal Affairs, Shaw Bldg., 95 Rochford St. South, 2nd Fl., PO Box 2000, Charlottetown, PE C1A 7N8
902-368-4000, Fax: 902-368-5544
Alberta
Alberta Municipal Affairs, Communications Branch, Commerce Place, 10155 - 102 St., 18th Fl., Edmonton, AB T5J 4L4
780-427-2732, Fax: 780-422-1419, comments@gov.ab.ca
British Columbia
Local Government, PO Box 9490 Prov Govt,Victoria, BC V8W 9N7
250-356-6575, Fax: 250-387-7973
Manitoba
Manitoba Aboriginal & Northern Affairs, Legislative Bldg, 344-450 Broadway, Winnipeg, MB R3C 0V8
204-945-3719, Fax: 204-945-8374, anaweb@gov.mb.ca
Local Government Development Division, 59 Elizabeth Dr., PO Box 33, Thompson, MB R8N 1X4
204-677-6794, Fax: 204-677-6525
Manitoba Local Government, #301, 450 Broadway Ave., Winnipeg, MB R3C 0V8
Fax: 204-945-1383, mnia@leg.gov.mb.ca
Manitoba Municipal Board, #1144, 363 Broadway, Winnipeg, MB R3C 3N9
204-945-2941, Fax: 204-948-2235
Provincial-Municipal Support Services, #508, 800 Portage Ave., Winnipeg, MB R3G 0N4
New Brunswick
Regional Development Corporation, RDC Bldg., 836 Churchill Row, PO Box 428, Fredericton, NB E3B 5R4
506-453-2277, Fax: 506-453-7988
Newfoundland & Labrador
Newfoundland & Labrador Department of Municipal Affairs, West Block, Main Fl., Confederation Bldg., PO Box 8700, St. John's, NL A1B 4J6
709-729-3046, Fax: 709-729-0943, mainfo@gov.nl.ca
Newfoundland & Labrador Municipal Financing Corporation, Confederation Bldg., PO Box 8700, St. John's, NL A1B 4J6
709-729-6686, Fax: 709-729-2095,
Northwest Territories
Department of Municipal & Community Affairs, PO Box 1320, Yellowknife, NT X1A 2L9
867-873-7118, Fax: 867-873-0309
Nova Scotia
Nova Scotia Municipal Finance Corporation, Maritime Centre, 1505 Barrington St., 10th Fl. South, PO Box 850 M, Halifax, NS B3J 2V2
902-424-4590, Fax: 902-424-0525
Department of Service Nova Scotia & Municipal Relations, 1505 Barrington St., PO Box 216, Halifax, NS B3J 3K5
902-424-5200, Fax: 902-424-0581, 800-670-4357, askus@gov.ns.ca
Nunavut
Department of Community & Government Services, W.G. Brown Bldg., 4th Fl., PO Box 1000 700,Iqaluit, NU X0A 0H0
867-975-5400, Fax: 867-975-5305
Ontario
Ontario Ministry of Municipal Affairs & Housing, College Park, 777 Bay St., 17th Fl., Toronto, ON M5G 2E5
416-585-7041, Fax: 416-585-6470, 866-220-2290, mininfo@ontario.ca
Prince Edward Island
Prince Edward Island Department of Community Services & Seniors, Jones Bldg., 11 Kent St., 2nd Fl., PO Box 2000, Charlottetown, PE C1A 7N8
902-620-3777, Fax: 902-368-4740, 866-594-3777
Quebec
Ministère des Affaires municipales, des Régions et de l'Occupation du territoire, Aile Chaveau, 10, rue Pierre-Olivier-Chauveau, 3e étage, Québec, QC G1R 4J3
418-691-2019, Fax: 418-643-7385, communications@mamrot.gouv.qc.ca

MUSEUMS

Canada Science & Technology Museum Corporation, PO Box 9724 T,Ottawa, ON K1G 5A3
613-991-6090, Fax: 613-990-3636, info@technomuses.ca
Canadian Heritage, 15 Eddy St., Gatineau, QC K1A 0M5
819-997-0055, 866-811-0055, info@pch.gc.ca
Canadian Museum of Civilization Corporation, 100 Laurier St., Gatineau, QC K1A 0M8
819-776-7000, 800-555-5621
Canadian Museum of Nature, PO Box 3443 D,Ottawa, ON K1P 6P4
613-566-4700, Fax: 613-364-4021, 800-263-4433
Canadian War Museum, 1 Vimy Pl., Ottawa, ON K1A 0M8
819-776-7000, 800-555-5621
National Gallery of Canada, 380 Sussex Dr., PO Box 427 A,Ottawa, ON K1N 9N4
613-990-1985, Fax: 613-993-4385, 800-319-2787, info@gallery.ca; info@beaux-arts.ca
Western Development Museum, Curatorial Centre, 2935 Melville St,, Saskatoon, SK S7J 5A6
306-934-1400, Fax: 306-934-4467, 800-363-6345, info@wdm.ca; curatorial@wdm.ca
Alberta
Recreation & Sport Development Division, Standard Life Centre, 10405 Jasper Ave., 9th Fl., Edmonton, AB T5J 4R7
Manitoba
Manitoba Museum, 190 Rupert Ave., Winnipeg, MB R3B 0N2
204-956-2830, Fax: 204-942-3679, info@manitobamuseum.mb.ca
Newfoundland & Labrador
Newfoundland & Labrador Department of Fisheries & Aquaculture, Petten Bldg., 30 Strawberry Marsh Rd., PO Box 8700, St. John's, NL A1B 4J6
709-729-3723, Fax: 709-729-6082, fisheries@gov.nl.ca
Nova Scotia
Culture Division, #601, 1800 Argyle St., PO Box 456, Halifax, NS B3J 2R5
902-424-4510, Fax: 902-424-0710, culture@gov.ns.ca
Ontario
Royal Ontario Museum, 100 Queen's Park Cres., Toronto, ON M5S 2C6
416-586-5549, Fax: 416-586-5685, info@rom.on.ca
Quebec
Ministère de la Culture, des Communications & de la Condition féminine, 225, Grande Allée est, Québec, QC G1R 5G5
888-380-8882
Musée d'art contemporain de Montréal, 185, rue Ste-Catherine ouest, Montréal, QC H2X 3X5
514-847-6226, Fax: 514-847-6290, info@macm.org
Musée de la civilisation, 85, rue Dalhousie, CP 155 B,Québec, QC G1K 7A6
418-643-2158, Fax: 418-646-9705, 866-710-8031, mcqweb@mcq.org
Musée national des beaux-arts du Québec, Parc des Champs-de-Bataille, 1, av Wolfe-Montcalm, Québec, QC G1R 5H3
418-643-2150, Fax: 418-646-3330, 866-220-2150, webmestre@mnba.qc.ca
Yukon Territory
Yukon Tourism & Culture, 100 Hanson St., Whitehorse, YT Y1A 2C6
867-667-5036, Fax: 867-667-3546

NATIVE PEOPLES & NORTHERN AFFAIRS

British Columbia
North Area, 1011 - 4 Ave., 5th Fl., Prince George, BC V2L 3H9
250-565-6100
New Brunswick
Aboriginal Affairs Secretariat, Kings Place, #237, 440 King St., PO Box 6000, Fredericton, NB E3B 5H8
506-462-5177, Fax: 506-444-5142, aboriginalaffairssecretariat@gnb.ca
Yukon Territory
Yukon Development Corporation, #2 Miles Canyon Rd., PO Box 5920, Whitehorse, YT Y1A 6S7
867-393-5337, Fax: 867-393-5401
Yukon Land Use Planning Council, #201, 307 Jarvis St., Whitehorse, YT Y1A 2H3
867-667-7397, Fax: 867-667-4624, ylupc@planyukon.ca

NATURAL RESOURCES

Canadian Museum of Nature, PO Box 3443 D,Ottawa, ON K1P 6P4
613-566-4700, Fax: 613-364-4021, 800-263-4433
Fish & Wildlife Division, Petroleum Plaza ST, 9915 - 108 St., 11th Fl., Edmonton, AB T5K 2G8
Natural Resources Canada, 580 Booth St., Ottawa, ON K1A 0E4
613-995-0947, Fax: 613-992-7211
Wascana Centre Authority, 2900 Wascana Dr., PO Box 7111, Regina, SK S4P 3S7
306-522-3661, Fax: 306-565-2742, wca@wascana.ca
Alberta
Natural Resources Conservation Board, Sterling Place, 9940 - 106 St., Edmonton, AB T5K 2N2
780-422-1977, Fax: 780-427-0607, 866-383-6722, info@nrcb.gov.ab.ca
British Columbia
British Columbia Ministry of Energy, Mines, & Natural Gas (& Responsible for Housing), PO Box 9053 Prov Govt,Victoria, BC V8W 9E2
British Columbia Ministry of Environment, PO Box 9339 Prov Govt,Victoria, BC V8W 9M1
250-387-1161, Fax: 250-387-5669, envmail@gov.bc.ca
British Columbia Ministry of Forests, Lands & Natural Resource Operations, PO Box 9352 Prov Govt,Victoria, BC V8W 9M1
250-387-4809, 877-855-3222, FLNRO.MediaRequests@gov.bc.ca
Manitoba
Manitoba Conservation & Water Stewardship, 200 Saulteaux Cres., Winnipeg, MB R3J 3W3
800-214-6497, mws@gov.mb.ca
Manitoba Conservation Districts Commission, Secretariat c/o Planning & Coordination Branch, 123 Main St., PO Box 20000, Neepawa, MB R0J 1H0
204-476-7033, Fax: 204-476-7539, whildebran@gov.mb.ca

New Brunswick
New Brunswick Department of Natural Resources, Hugh John Flemming Forestry Centre, PO Box 6000, Fredericton, NB E3B 5H1
506-453-3826, Fax: 506-444-4367, dnrweb@gnb.ca
Newfoundland & Labrador
Newfoundland & Labrador Department of Natural Resources, Natural Resources Bldg., 50 Elizabeth Ave., 7th Fl., PO Box 8700, St. John's, NL A1B 4J6
709-729-2920, Fax: 709-729-0059
Northwest Territories
Department of Environment & Natural Resources, PO Box 1320, Yellowknife, NT X1A 2L9
Nova Scotia
Department of Natural Resources, Founder's Square, 1701 Hollis St., 3rd Fl., PO Box 698, Halifax, NS B3J 2T9
902-424-5935, Fax: 902-424-0594, 800-565-2224
Nunavut
Department of Environment, PO Box 1000 1300,Iqaluit, NU X0A 0H0
867-975-7700, Fax: 867-975-7742, environment@gov.nu.ca
Ontario
Ontario Ministry of Natural Resources, Whitney Block, #6630, 99 Wellesley St. West, 6th Fl., Toronto, ON M7A 1W3
800-667-1940
Ontario Ministry of Northern Development & Mines, 159 Cedar St., Sudbury, ON P3E 6A5
Fax: 416-327-0651, 888-415-9845
Prince Edward Island
Prince Edward Island Department of Agriculture & Forestry, Jones Bldg., 11 Kent St., PO Box 2000, Charlottetown, PE C1A 7N8
902-368-4880, Fax: 902-368-4857
Prince Edward Island Department of Environment, Labour & Justice, Shaw Bldg. South, 95 Rochford St., 4th Fl., PO Box 2000, Charlottetown, PE C1A 7N8
902-620-3774, Fax: 902-368-4242, rrryder@gov.pe.ca
Quebec
Ministère du Développement durable, de l'Environnement, de la Faune, et des Parcs, Édifice Marie-Guyart, 675, boul René-Lévesque est, 29e étage, Québec, QC G1R 5V7
418-521-3830, Fax: 418-646-5974, 800-561-1616, info@mddep.gouv.qc.ca
Ministère des Ressources naturelles, 880, ch Sainte-Foy, Québec, QC G1S 4X4
418-627-8600, Fax: 418-644-6513, 866-248-6936, services.clientele@mrnf.gouv.qc.ca
Saskatchewan
Energy & Resources, #300, 2103 - 11th Ave., Regina, SK S4P 3Z8
306-787-2528
Saskatchewan Environment, 3211 Albert St., 2nd Fl., Regina, SK S4S 5W6
306-787-2584, Fax: 306-787-9544, 800-567-4224, Centre.Inquiry@gov.sk.ca
Yukon Territory
Yukon Energy, Mines & Resources, PO Box 2703, Whitehorse, YT Y1A 2C6
867-667-3130, Fax: 867-456-3965, 800-661-0408, emr@gov.yk.ca
Yukon Environment, PO Box 2703, Whitehorse, YT Y1A 2C6
867-667-5652, Fax: 867-393-7197, environment.yukon@gov.yk.ca

NUCLEAR ENERGY
Canadian Nuclear Safety Commission, 280 Slater St., PO Box 1046 B,Ottawa, ON K1P 5S9
613-995-5894, Fax: 613-995-5086, 800-668-5284
Alberta
Alberta Energy, North Petroleum Plaza, 9945 - 108 St., Edmonton, AB T5K 2G6
780-427-8050, Fax: 780-422-0698, -310-0000, Library.Energy@gov.ab.ca
Ontario
Ontario Power Generation, 700 University Ave., Toronto, ON M5G 1X6
416-592-2555, 877-592-2555, webmaster@opg.com
Quebec
Hydro-Québec, 75, boul René-Lévesque ouest, Montréal, QC H2Z 1A4
514-289-2211

NUTRITION
New Brunswick
Communications Branch, HSBC Place, 520 King St., 5th Fl., PO Box 5100, Fredericton, NB E3B 6G3
506-457-2356, Fax: 506-444-4697, Health.Sante@gnb.ca
Health Workforce Division, Telus Plaza NT, 10025 Jasper Ave., 10th Fl., Edmonton, AB T5J 1S6
Research Branch, Tower 5, 1341 Baseline Rd., Ottawa, ON K1A 0C5
613-759-1000, Fax: 613-773-1866
Manitoba
Manitoba Healthy Child Office, #219, 114 Garry St., Winnipeg, MB R3C 1G1
204-945-2266, 888-848-0140, healthychild@gov.mb.ca
Public Health & Primary Health Care, 300 Carlton St., 2nd Floor, Winnipeg, MB R3B 3M9
Newfoundland & Labrador
Newfoundland & Labrador Department of Health & Community Services, West Block, Confederation Bldg., PO Box 8700, St. John's, NL A1B 4J6
709-729-5021, Fax: 709-729-5824, healthinfo@gov.nl.ca
Northwest Territories
Department of Health & Social Services, Centre Square Tower, PO Box 1320, Yellowknife, NT X1A 2L9
Fax: 867-873-0266
Nunavut
Department of Health & Social Services, PO Box 1000 1000,Iqaluit, NU X0A 0H0
867-975-5700, Fax: 867-975-5705
Ontario
Ontario Ministry of Health & Long-Term Care, Hepburn Block, 80 Grosvenor St., 10th Fl, Toronto, ON M7A 2C4
416-327-4327, 800-268-1153
Prince Edward Island
Prince Edward Island Department of Health & Wellness, 105 Rochford St. North, 4th Fl., PO Box 2000, Charlottetown, PE C1A 7N8
902-368-6414, Fax: 902-368-4121
Quebec
Ministère de la Santé et des Services sociaux, Direction des communications, 1075, ch Sainte-Foy, 16e étage, Québec, QC G1S 2M1
418-643-9395, Fax: 418-643-4768, regisseur.web@msss.gouv.qc.ca
Saskatchewan
Saskatchewan Health, T.C. Douglas Bldg., 3475 Albert St., Regina, SK S4S 6X6
306-787-0146, 800-667-7766, info@health.gov.sk.ca

OCCUPATIONAL SAFETY
See Also: Dangerous Goods & Hazardous Materials
Canadian Centre for Occupational Health & Safety, 135 Hunter St. East, Hamilton, ON L8N 1M5
905-572-2981, Fax: 905-572-2206, 800-668-4284
Occupational Health & Safety Branch, PO Box 8700, St. John's, NL A1B 4J6
Alberta
Occupational Health & Safety Council, Labour Building, 10808 - 99 Ave., 9th Fl., Edmonton, AB T5K 0G5
780-415-8690, 866-415-8690
Workplace Standards Division, Labour Building, 10808 - 99 Ave., 9th Fl., Edmonton, AB T5K 0G5
780-644-1500, Fax: 780-422-0014
British Columbia
British Columbia Ministry of Citizens' Services & Open Government, PO Box 9594 Prov Govt,Victoria, BC V8W 9E2
250-952-7623, Fax: 250-952-7628, 800-663-7867, EnquiryBC@gov.bc.ca
Workers' Compensation Board of British Columbia, PO Box 5350 Terminal,Vancouver, BC V6B 5L5
604-276-3100, Fax: 604-276-3247, 888-621-7233
Manitoba
Advisory Council on Workplace Safety & Health, #200, 401 York Ave., Winnipeg, MB R3C 0P8
204-945-3446, Fax: 204-945-4556
New Brunswick
Workplace Health, Safety & Compensation Commission of New Brunswick, 1 Portland St., PO Box 160, Saint John, NB E2L 3X9
506-632-2200, 800-222-9775, communications@ws-ts.nb.ca
Newfoundland & Labrador
Newfoundland & Labrador Workplace Health, Safety & Compensation Commission, 146 - 148 Forest Rd., PO Box 9000, St. John's, NL A1A 3B8
709-778-1000, Fax: 709-738-1714, 800-563-9000, general.inquiries@whscc.nl.ca
Northwest Territories
Northwest Territories & Nunavut Workers' Safety & Compensation Commission, Centre Square Tower, 5022 - 49th St., 5th Fl., PO Box 8888, Yellowknife, NT X1A 2R3
867-920-3888, Fax: 867-873-4596, 800-661-0792
Nova Scotia
Workers' Compensation Board of Nova Scotia, 5668 South St., PO Box 1150, Halifax, NS B3J 2Y2
902-491-8999, Fax: 902-491-8002, 800-870-3331, info@wcb.gov.ns.ca
Ontario
Workplace Safety & Insurance Board, 200 Front St. West, Ground Fl., Toronto, ON M5V 3J1
416-344-1000, Fax: 416-344-4684, 800-387-0750
Prince Edward Island
Prince Edward Island Workers Compensation Board, 14 Weymouth St., PO Box 757, Charlottetown, PE C1A 7L7
902-368-5680, Fax: 902-368-5696, 800-237-5049
Quebec
Commission des lésions professionnelles, #700, 900, Place d'Youville, Québec, QC G1R 3P7
418-644-7777, Fax: 418-644-6443, 800-463-1591
Commission de la santé et de la sécurité du travail du Québec, 524, rue Bourdages, CP 1200 Terminus postal,Québec, QC G1K 7E2
418-266-4850, Fax: 418-266-4669, 866-302-2778
Saskatchewan
Office of the Worker's Advocate, #300, 1870 Albert St., Regina, SK S4P 4W1
306-787-2456, Fax: 306-787-0249, 877-787-2456
Saskatchewan Workers' Compensation Board, #200, 1881 Scarth St., Regina, SK S4P 4L1
306-787-4370, Fax: 306-787-4311, 800-667-7590, internet_clientsvc@wcbsask.com
Yukon Territory
Yukon Workers' Compensation Health & Safety Board, 401 Strickland St., Whitehorse, YT Y1A 5N8
867-667-5645, Fax: 867-393-6279, 800-661-0443, worksafe@gov.yk.ca

OCCUPATIONAL TRAINING
Canada School of Public Service, 373 Sussex Dr., Ottawa, ON K1N 6Z2
819-953-5400, Fax: 819-953-7953, 866-703-9598, info@csps-efpc.gc.ca
Income, Employment, & Youth Services Branch, c/o Department of Advanced Education & Skills, PO Box 8700, St. John's, NL A1B 4J6
709-729-5151
Alberta
Community, Learner & Industry Connections Division, Phipps-McKinnon Bldg., 10020 - 101A Ave., 5th Fl., Edmonton, AB T5J 3G2
British Columbia
British Columbia Ministry of Citizens' Services & Open Government, PO Box 9594 Prov Govt,Victoria, BC V8W 9E2
250-952-7623, Fax: 250-952-7628, 800-663-7867, EnquiryBC@gov.bc.ca
Manitoba
Manitoba Advanced Education & Literacy, Legislative Building, #162, 450 Broadway Ave., Winnipeg, MB R3C 0V8
204-945-0825, Fax: 204-948-2216, minaed@leg.gov.mb.ca
New Brunswick
New Brunswick Department of Post-Secondary Education, Training, & Labour, Chestnut Complex, PO Box 6000, Fredericton, NB E3B 5H1
506-453-2597, Fax: 506-453-3618, dpetlinfo@gnb.ca
Office of Human Resources, Centennial Bldg, #345, 670 King St., PO Box 6000, Fredericton, NB E3B 5H1
506-453-2264, Fax: 506-453-7195
Ontario
Ontario Ministry of Training, Colleges & Universities, Mowat Block, 900 Bay St., 14th Fl., Toronto, ON M7A 1L2
416-325-2929, Fax: 416-325-6348, 800-387-5514, information.met@ontario.ca
Quebec
École nationale de police du Québec, 350, rue Marguerite-d'Youville, Nicolet, QC J3T 1X4
819-293-8631, Fax: 819-293-8630, courriel@enpq.qc.ca
École nationale des pompiers du Québec, #3.08, 2800, boul Saint-Martin ouest, Laval, QC H7T 2S9
450-680-6800, Fax: 450-680-6818, 866-680-3677

OCEANOGRAPHY
Bayfield Institute, 867 Lakeshore Rd., PO Box 5050, Burlington, ON L7R 4A6
905-336-6240
Bedford Institute of Oceanography, 1 Challenger Dr., PO Box 1006, Dartmouth, NS B2Y 4A2
902-426-3492, Fax: 902-426-8484
Fisheries & Oceans Canada, 200 Kent St., Ottawa, ON K1A 0E6
613-993-0999, Fax: 613-990-1866, info@dfo-mpo.gc.ca
Institut Maurice-Lamontagne, 850, rte de le Mer, CP 1000, Mont-Joli, QC G5H 3Z4
418-775-0555, Fax: 418-775-0730
Institute for Marine Biosciences, 1411 Oxford St., Halifax, NS B3H 3Z1
902-426-8332, Fax: 902-426-9413, communications.imb@nrc-cnrc.gc.ca

Institute for Ocean Technology, Kerwin Pl. & Arctic Ave., PO Box 12093, St. John's, NL A1B 3T5
709-772-4939, Fax: 709-772-2462, Noel.Murphy@nrc-cnrc.gc.ca
Institute of Ocean Sciences, 9860 West Saanich Rd., PO Box 6000, Sidney, BC V8L 4B2
250-363-6517, Fax: 250-363-6390

OIL & NATURAL GAS RESOURCES

See Also: Energy; Natural Resources
Indian Oil & Gas Canada, #100, 9911 Chiila Blvd., Tsuu T'ina (Sarcee), AB T2W 6H6
403-292-5625, Fax: 403-292-5618, ContactIOGC@inac-ainc.gc.ca
Lands, Minerals & Petroleum Division, Hugh John Flemming Forestry Centre, PO Box 6000, Fredericton, NB E3B 5H1
506-453-2684, Fax: 506-453-2930, dnrweb@gnb.ca
National Energy Board, 444 - 7 Ave. SW, Calgary, AB T2P 0X8
403-292-4800, Fax: 403-292-5503, 800-899-1265, info@neb-one.gc.ca
Oil & Gas Mineral Resources, #300, 211 Main St., Whitehorse, YT Y1A 2B2
867-667-5087, Fax: 867-393-6262, oilandgas@gov.yk.ca
Petroleum Products Division, Stuart M. Hodgson, 5009 - 49th St., 1st Fl., Yellowknife, NT X1A 2L9
867-920-3447, Fax: 867-873-0100

Alberta
Energy Resources Conservation Board, #1000, 250 - 5 Ave. SW, Calgary, AB T2P 0R4
403-297-8311, Fax: 403-297-7336, 855-297-8311, inquiries@ercb.ca; infoservices@ercb.ca; ADR@ercb.ca
Alberta Energy, North Petroleum Plaza, 9945 - 108 St., Edmonton, AB T5K 2G6
780-427-8050, Fax: 780-422-0698, -310-0000, Library.Energy@gov.ab.ca

British Columbia
British Columbia Ministry of Energy, Mines, & Natural Gas (& Responsible for Housing), PO Box 9053 Prov Govt,Victoria, BC V8W 9E2
British Columbia Utilities Commission, 900 Howe St., 6th Fl., PO Box 250, Vancouver, BC V6Z 2N3
604-660-4700, Fax: 604-660-1102, 800-663-1385, commission.secretary@bcuc.com
Oil & Gas Commission, #100, 10003 - 110 Ave., Fort St John, BC V1J 6M7
250-794-5200, Fax: 250-794-5375

Manitoba
Surface Rights Board, #360, 1395 Ellice Ave., Winnipeg, MB R3G 3P2
204-945-0731, Fax: 204-948-2578, 800-282-8069, bmiskimmin@gov.mb.ca

Newfoundland & Labrador
Canada - Newfoundland & Labrador Offshore Petroleum Board, TD Place, 140 Water St., 5th Fl., St. John's, NL A1C 6H6
709-778-1400, Fax: 709-778-1473, information@cnlopb.nl.ca

Nova Scotia
Canada - Nova Scotia Offshore Petroleum Board, TD Centre, 1791 Barrington St., 18th Fl., Halifax, NS B3J 3K9
902-422-5588, Fax: 902-422-1799, postmaster@cnsopb.ns.ca
Nova Scotia Utility & Review Board, Summit Place, 1601 Lower Water St., 3rd Fl., PO Box 1692 M,Halifax, NS B3J 3S3
902-424-4448, Fax: 902-424-3919, uarb.board@gov.ns.ca

Nunavut
Department of Environment, PO Box 1000 1300,Iqaluit, NU X0A 0H0
867-975-7700, Fax: 867-975-7742, environment@gov.nu.ca

Ontario
Ontario Ministry of Natural Resources, Whitney Block, #6630, 99 Wellesley St. West, 6th Fl., Toronto, ON M7A 1W3
800-667-1940

Saskatchewan
SaskEnergy Incorporated, 1777 Victoria Ave., Regina, SK S4P 4K5
306-777-9225, 800-567-8899

OIL SPILLS

Canadian Coast Guard, Centennial Towers, #6S018, 200 Kent St., Ottawa, ON K1A 0E6
613-993-0999, Fax: 613-990-1866, info@dfo-mpo.gc.ca

Newfoundland & Labrador
Canada - Newfoundland & Labrador Offshore Petroleum Board, TD Place, 140 Water St., 5th Fl., St. John's, NL A1C 6H6
709-778-1400, Fax: 709-778-1473, information@cnlopb.nl.ca

OMBUDSMEN

Office of the Correctional Investigator, PO Box 3421 D,Ottawa, ON K1P 6L4
Fax: 613-990-9091, 877-885-8848, org@oci-bec.gc.ca
Office of the Commissioner of Official Languages, 344 Slater St., 3rd fl., Ottawa, ON K1A 0T8
613-996-6368, Fax: 613-993-5082, 877-996-6368
Privacy Commissioner of Canada, Tower B, Place de Ville, 112 Kent St., 3rd Fl., Ottawa, ON K1A 1H3
613-947-1698, Fax: 613-947-6850, 800-282-1376

Alberta
Alberta Office of the Ombudsman, Canadian Western Bank Building, #2800, 10303 Jasper Ave. NW, 28th Fl., Edmonton, AB T5J 5C3
780-427-2756, Fax: 780-427-2759, 888-455-2756, info@ombudsman.ab.ca

British Columbia
Office of the Ombudsperson, 947 Fort St., 2nd Fl., PO Box 9039 Prov Govt,Victoria, BC V8W 9A5
250-387-5855, Fax: 250-387-0198, 800-567-3247, systems@bcombudsperson.ca (Information technology inquiries)

Manitoba
Manitoba Office of the Ombudsman, 750 - 500 Portage Ave., Winnipeg, MB R3C 3X1
204-982-9130, Fax: 204-942-7803, 800-665-0531, ombudsma@ombudsman.mb.ca

New Brunswick
Office of the Ombudsman, 767 Brunswick St., PO Box 6000, Fredericton, NB E3B 5H1
506-453-2789, Fax: 506-453-5599, 800-465-1100, nbombud@gnb.ca

Nova Scotia
Office of the Ombudsman, #700, 5670 Spring Garden Rd., PO Box 2152, Halifax, NS B3J 3B7
902-424-6780, Fax: 902-424-6675, 800-670-1111, ombudsman@gov.ns.ca

Ontario
Office of the Ombudsman, Bell Trinity Sq., South Tower, 483 Bay St., 10th Fl., Toronto, ON M5G 2C9
416-586-3300, Fax: 416-586-3485, 800-263-1830, info@ombudsman.on.ca

Quebec
Le Protecteur du Citoyen, #1.25, 525, boul René-Lévesque est, Québec, QC G1R 5Y4
418-643-2688, Fax: 418-643-8759, 800-463-5070, protecteur@protecteurducitoyen.qc.ca

Saskatchewan
Ombudsman Saskatchewan, #150, 2401 Saskatchewan Dr., Regina, SK S4P 4H8
306-787-6211, Fax: 306-787-9090, 800-667-7180, ombreg@ombudsman.sk.ca

PARKS

See Also: Land Resources

Saskatchewan
Saskatchewan Parks, Culture, & Sport, 1919 Saskatchewan Dr., 4th Fl., Regina, SK S4P 4H2
306-787-5729, Fax: 306-798-0033, 800-205-7070, info@tpcs.gov.sk.ca

PARKS & RECREATION

Auyuittuq National Park of Canada, PO Box 353, Pangnirtung, NU X0A 0R0
867-473-2500, Fax: 867-473-8612, nunavut.info@pc.gc.ca
Canadian Heritage, 15 Eddy St., Gatineau, QC K1A 0M5
819-997-0055, 866-811-0055, info@pch.gc.ca
Corporate Services Division, PO Box 2000, Charlottetown, PE C1A 7N8
Historic Sites & Monuments Board of Canada, Terrasses de la Chaudière, 25 Eddy St., Gatineau, QC K1A 0M5
Fax: 819-934-1115, 855-283-8730, hsmbc-clmhc@pc.gc.ca
Parks, PO Box 2703 V-4, Whitehorse, YT Y1A 2C6
867-667-5648, Fax: 867-393-6223, 800-661-0408, yukon.parks@gov.yk.ca
Parks Canada, 25 Eddy St., Gatineau, QC K1A 0M5
613-860-1251, 888-773-8888, information@pc.gc.ca
Saskatchewan Parks, Culture, & Sport, 1919 Saskatchewan Dr., 4th Fl., Regina, SK S4P 4H2
306-787-5729, Fax: 306-798-0033, 800-205-7070, info@tpcs.gov.sk.ca

Alberta
Alberta Sport, Recreation, Parks, & Wildlife Foundation, Standard Life Centre, #903, 10405 Jasper Ave., 9th Fl., Edmonton, AB T5J 4R7
780-415-1167, Fax: 780-415-0308, -310-0000
Parks Division, Oxbridge Place, 9820 - 106 St., 2nd Fl., Edmonton, AB T5K 2J6
780-427-3582, Fax: 780-427-5980, 866-427-3582
Special Areas Board, Special Areas Board Administration, 212 - 2nd Ave. West, PO Box 820, Hanna, AB T0J 1P0
403-854-5600, Fax: 403-854-5527, specarea@telus.net

British Columbia
British Columbia Ministry of Environment, PO Box 9339 Prov Govt,Victoria, BC V8W 9M1
250-387-1161, Fax: 250-387-5669, envmail@gov.bc.ca

Manitoba
Ecological Reserves Advisory Committee, c/o Manitoba Conservation, Parks & Natural Areas Branch, 200 Saulteaux Cres., Winnipeg, MB R3J 3W3
204-945-4148, Fax: 204-945-0012, hhernandez@gov.mb.ca
Manitoba Entrepreneurship, Training & Trade, #1000, 259 Portage Ave, Winnipeg, MB R3B 3P4
204-945-2475, Fax: 204-945-3977, minctt@leg.gov.mb.ca

New Brunswick
New Brunswick Department of Culture, Tourism, & Healthy Living, Centennial Building, PO Box 6000, Fredericton, NB E3B 5H1
506-444-5205, Fax: 506-457-4984, taponlinedirectory@gnb.ca

Newfoundland & Labrador
Newfoundland & Labrador Department of Tourism, Culture, & Recreation, Confederation Bldg., West Block, 2nd Fl., PO Box 8700, St. John's, NL A1B 4J6
709-729-0862, Fax: 709-729-0870, tcrinfo@gov.nl.ca

Northwest Territories
Department of Environment & Natural Resources, PO Box 1320, Yellowknife, NT X1A 2L9

Nova Scotia
Department of Economic & Rural Development & Tourism, Centennial Building, #600, 1660 Hollis St., PO Box 2311, Halifax, NS B3J 1V7
902-424-0377, Fax: 902-424-0500, comm@gov.ns.ca

Nunavut
Department of Environment, PO Box 1000 1300,Iqaluit, NU X0A 0H0
867-975-7700, Fax: 867-975-7742, environment@gov.nu.ca

Ontario
Ontario Ministry of Economic Development & Innovation, Hearst Block, 900 Bay St., 8th Fl., Toronto, ON M7A 2E1
416-325-6666, Fax: 416-325-6688, 866-668-4249, info@edt.gov.on.ca

Prince Edward Island
Prince Edward Island Department of Innovation & Advanced Learning, Shaw Bldg., 105 Rochford St., 5th Fl., PO Box 2000, Charlottetown, PE C1A 7N8
902-368-4240, Fax: 902-368-4242
Prince Edward Island Department of Tourism & Culture, PO Box 2000, Charlottetown, PE C1A 7N8
902-368-5540, Fax: 902-368-5277, tpswitch@gov.pe.ca

Quebec
Ministère du Développement durable, de l'Environnement, de la Faune, et des Parcs, Édifice Marie-Guyart, 675, boul René-Lévesque est, 29e étage, Québec, QC G1R 5V7
418-521-3830, Fax: 418-646-5974, 800-561-1616, info@mddep.gouv.qc.ca
Société des établissements en plein air du Québec, Place de la Cité, Tour Cominar, #250, 2640, boul Laurier, 2e étage, Québec, QC G1V 5C2
418-890-6527, Fax: 418-528-6025, 800-665-6527, inforeservation@sepaq.com

Yukon Territory
Yukon Tourism & Culture, 100 Hanson St., Whitehorse, YT Y1A 2C6
867-667-5036, Fax: 867-667-3546

PARLIAMENT

See Also: Government (General Information; Protocol (State)
Forty-first Parliament - Canada, House of Commons, Parliament Buildings, Ottawa, AB K1A 0A6
Library of Parliament, Parliamentary Buildings, Ottawa, ON K1A 0A9
613-992-4793, 866-599-4999, info@parl.gc.ca
Office of the Leader, Bloc Québécois, Centre Block, Ottawa, ON K1A 0A6
613-992-6779, Fax: 613-954-2121
Office of the Leader, Green Party of Canada, Confederation Building,, #518, 244 Wellington St., Ottawa, ON K1A 0A6
613-996-1119, Fax: 613-996-0850, 866-868-3447, leader@greenparty.ca; info@greenparty.ca
Office of the Leader, Official Opposition, New Democratic Party / New Democratic Party Research Bureau, 111 Wellington St., Ottawa, ON K1A 0A6
613-995-7224, Fax: 613-995-4565
Office of the Prime Minister, Conservative Party of Canada / Conservative Research Bureau, Langevin Block, 80 Wellington St., Ottawa, ON K1A 0A2
613-992-4211, Fax: 613-995-0101, pm@pm.gc.ca
Privy Council Office, #1000, 85 Sparks St., Ottawa, ON K1A 0A3
613-957-5153, Fax: 613-997-5043, info@pco-bcp.gc.ca

The Canadian Ministry, Information Service, Parliament of Canada, Ottawa, ON K1A 0A9
613-992-4793, 866-599-4999, info@parl.gc.ca

Alberta

Legislative Assembly of Alberta, Legislature Annex, 9718 - 107 St., Edmonton, AB T5K 1E4
780-427-2826, Fax: 780-427-1623, laocommunications@assembly.ab.ca

British Columbia

BC Legislative Assembly & Independent Offices, Clerk's Office, #221, Parliament Bldgs., Victoria, BC V8V 1X4
250-387-3785, Fax: 250-387-0942, ClerkHouse@leg.bc.ca

Manitoba

Manitoba Legislative Assembly, c/o Clerk's Office, Legislative Bldg., #237, 450 Broadway, Winnipeg, MB R3C 0V8
204-945-3636, Fax: 204-948-2507, clerkla@leg.gov.mb.ca

New Brunswick

Legislative Assembly of New Brunswick, Centre Block, Legislative Building, 706 Queen St., PO Box 6000, Fredericton, NB E3B 5H1
506-453-2506, Fax: 506-453-7154, wwwleg@gnb.ca

Northwest Territories

NWT Legislative Assembly, c/o Clerk's Office, PO Box 1320, Yellowknife, NT X1A 2L9
867-669-2299, Fax: 867-920-4735, 800-661-0784

Nova Scotia

Legislative House of Assembly, c/o Clerk's Office, Province House, 1st Fl., PO Box 1617, Halifax, NS B3J 2Y3
902-424-5978, Fax: 902-424-0632,

Nunavut

Nunavut Legislative Assembly, 926 Federal Rd., PO Box 1200, Iqaluit, NU X0A 0H0
867-975-5000, Fax: 867-975-5190, 877-334-7266, leginfo@assembly.nu.ca

Ontario

Ontario Legislative Assembly, c/o Clerk's Office, #104, Legislative Bldg., Queen's Park, Toronto, ON M7A 1A2
416-325-7500, Fax: 416-325-7489, assemblyinternet@ontla.ola.org

Prince Edward Island

Prince Edward Island Legislative Assembly, Province House, 165 Richmond St., 1st Fl., PO Box 2000, Charlottetown, PE C1A 7N8
902-368-5970, Fax: 902-368-5175, 877-315-5518, legislativelibrary@assembly.pe.ca

Quebec

L'Assemblée nationale, Hôtel du Parlement, 1045, rue des Parlementaires, Québec, QC G1A 1A3
418-643-7239, Fax: 418-646-4271, 866-337-8837, responsable.contenu@assnat.qc.ca

Saskatchewan

Legislative Assembly of Saskatchewan, Office of the Clerk, Legislative Building, #239, 2405 Legislative Dr., Regina, SK S4S 0B3
info@legassembly.sk.ca

Yukon Territory

Yukon Legislative Assembly, PO Box 2703, Whitehorse, YT Y1A 2C6
867-667-5498, Fax: 867-393-6280, yla@gov.yk.ca

PAROLE BOARDS

See Also: Correctional Services

Alberta

Criminal Justice Division, Bowker Building, 9833 - 109 St., 2nd Fl., Edmonton, AB T5K 2E8

National Parole Board, 410 Laurier Ave. West, Ottawa, ON K1A 0R1
613-954-7474, Fax: 613-995-4380, 800-874-2652, info@npb-cnlc.gc.ca

Manitoba

Corrections Division, #810, 405 Broadway Ave., Winnipeg, MB R3C 3L6
204-945-7291

New Brunswick

New Brunswick Department of Public Safety, 364 Argyle St., PO Box 6000, Fredericton, NB E3B 5H1
506-453-3992, Fax: 506-453-3870, DPS-MSP.Information@gnb.ca

Ontario

Ontario Parole Board, #1803, 415 Yonge St., Toronto, ON M5B 2E7
416-325-4480, Fax: 416-325-4485, 888-579-2888

Quebec

Commission québecoise des libérations conditionnelles, #1.32A, 300, boul Jean-Lesage, Québec, QC G1K 8K6
418-646-8300, Fax: 418-643-7217, cqlc@msp.gouv.qc.ca

PASSPORT INFORMATION

See Also: Citizenship; Immigration

Passport Canada, Le 70 Crémazie, 70 Crémazie St., Gatineau, QC K1A 0G3
Fax: 819-953-5856, 800-567-6868

PATENTS & COPYRIGHT

Copyright Board of Canada, #800, 56 Sparks St., Ottawa, ON K1A 0C9
613-952-8621, Fax: 613-952-8630, secretariat@cb-cda.gc.ca

PAY EQUITY

Human Resources & Skills Development Canada, 140 Promenade du Portage, Gatineau, QC K1A 0J9

British Columbia

British Columbia Ministry of Citizens' Services & Open Government, PO Box 9594 Prov Govt,Victoria, BC V8W 9E2
250-952-7623, Fax: 250-952-7628, 800-663-7867, EnquiryBC@gov.bc.ca

Employment Standards Tribunal, Oceanic Plaza, #650, 1066 West Hastings St., Vancouver, BC V6E 3X1
604-775-3512, Fax: 604-775-3372, registrar.est@bcest.bc.ca

New Brunswick

Office of Human Resources, Centennial Bldg, #345, 670 King St., PO Box 6000, Fredericton, NB E3B 5H1
506-453-2264, Fax: 506-453-7195

Nova Scotia

Pay Equity Commission, 5151 Terminal Rd., 6th Fl., PO Box 697, Halifax, NS B3J 2T8
902-424-2385, Fax: 902-424-0575

Ontario

Pay Equity Commission, #300, 180 Dundas St. West, Toronto, ON M7A 2S6
416-314-1896, Fax: 416-314-8741, 800-387-8813

Prince Edward Island

Workers Compensation Appeal Tribunal, 161 St. Peters Rd., 1st Fl., PO Box 2000, Charlottetown, PE C1A 7N8

Quebec

Commission de l'équité salariale, 200, ch Ste-Foy, 4e étage, Québec, QC G1R 6A1
418-528-8765, Fax: 418-528-6999, 888-528-8765, equite.salariale@ces.gouv.qc.ca

PENSIONS

Canada Pension Plan Investment Board, #2600, 1 Queen St. East, PO Box 101, Toronto, ON M5C 2W5
416-868-4075, Fax: 416-868-8689, 866-557-9510, csr@cppib.ca

Finance Canada, L'esplanade Laurier, 140 O'Connor St., Ottawa, ON K1A 0G5
613-992-1573, Fax: 613-943-0938, finpub@fin.gc.ca

Office of the Superintendent of Financial Institutions, Kent Square, 255 Albert St., Ottawa, ON K1A 0H2
613-990-7788, Fax: 613-990-5591, 800-385-8647, information@osfi-bsif.gc.ca

Office of the Commissioner of Review Tribunals, PO Box 8250 T, Ottawa, ON K1G 5S5
613-954-1313, Fax: 613-946-1588, 800-363-0076, info@ocrt-bctr.gc.ca

Pension Appeals Board, PO Box 8567 T, Ottawa, ON K1G 3H9
613-995-0612, Fax: 613-995-6834, 888-640-8001, info@pab-cap.gc.ca

Public Sector Pension Investment Board, #200, 440 Laurier Ave. West, Ottawa, ON K1R 7X6
613-782-3095, Fax: 613-782-6864, info@investpsp.ca

Veterans Review & Appeal Board, Daniel J. MacDonald Bldg., 161 Grafton St., PO Box 9900, Charlottetown, PE C1A 8V7
902-566-8751, Fax: 902-566-7850, 800-450-8006, vrab_tacra@vac-acc.gc.ca

Alberta

Alberta Pensions Services Corporation, 5103 Windermere Blvd. SW, Edmonton, AB T6W 0S9
780-427-2782, 800-661-8198, memberservices@apsc.ca; employerservices@apsc.ca; pay@apsc.ca

British Columbia

British Columbia Pension Corporation, 2995 Jutland Rd., PO Box 9460, Victoria, BC V8W 9V8
250-387-1002, Fax: 250-953-0429, 800-663-8823, PensionCorp@pensionsbc.ca; Retired.Members@pensionsbc.ca

Manitoba

Pension Commission of Manitoba, #1004, 401 York Ave., Winnipeg, MB R3C 0P8
204-945-2740, Fax: 204-948-2375, pensions@gov.mb.ca

Teachers' Retirement Allowances Fund Board, #330 Johnston Terminal, 35 Forks Market Rd., Winnipeg, MB R3C 4S8
204-949-0048, Fax: 204-944-0361

Ontario

Financial Services Commission of Ontario, New York City Ctr., 5160 Yonge St., 17th Fl., PO Box 85, Toronto, ON M2N 6L9
416-250-7250, Fax: 416-590-7070, 800-668-0128

Ontario Pension Board, Sun Life Bldg., #2200, 200 King St. West, Toronto, ON M5H 3X6
416-364-8558, Fax: 416-364-7578, 800-668-6203, office.services@opb.on.ca

OPSEU Pension Trust, #1200, 1 Adelaide St. East, Toronto, ON M5C 3A7
416-681-6161, Fax: 416-681-6175, 800-637-0024

Quebec

Commission administrative des régimes de retraite et d'assurances (Québec), 475, rue Saint-Amable, Québec, QC G1R 5X3
418-643-4881, Fax: 418-644-3839, 800-463-5533

Saskatchewan

Crown Investments Corporation of Saskatchewan, #400, 2400 College Ave., Regina, SK S4P 1C8
306-787-6851, Fax: 306-787-8125

Saskatchewan Financial Services Commission, #601, 1919 Saskatchewan Dr., Regina, SK S4P 4H2
306-787-5645, Fax: 306-787-5899

PERFORMING ARTS

See: Arts & Culture

Saskatchewan

Conexus Arts Centre, 200A Lakeshore Dr., Regina, SK S4S 7L3
306-565-4500, 800-667-8497, cac.admin@conexusartscentre.ca

PESTICIDES, HERBICIDES

Farm Financial Programs Branch, Tower 7, 1341 Baseline Rd., Ottawa, ON K1A 0C5
613-759-1000, Fax: 613-773-2121

Pest Management Regulatory Agency, 2720 Riverside Dr., Ottawa, ON K1A 0K9
613-736-3401, Fax: 613-736-3798

Port aux Basques, Provincial Bldg., Main St., PO Box 478, Port Aux Basques, NL A0M 1C0
709-695-2835, Fax: 709-695-2393

New Brunswick

Community Planning & Environmental Protection Division, Marysville Place, PO Box 6000, Fredericton, NB E3B 5H1
506-444-5119, Fax: 506-457-7333, elg/egl-info@gnb.ca

Ontario

Pesticides Advisory Committee, 135 St. Clair Ave. West, 15th Fl., Toronto, ON M4V 1P5
416-314-9230, Fax: 416-314-9237

PIPELINES

New Brunswick

Lands, Minerals & Petroleum Division, Hugh John Flemming Forestry Centre, PO Box 6000, Fredericton, NB E3B 5H1
506-453-2684, Fax: 506-453-2930, dnrweb@gnb.ca

National Energy Board, 444 - 7 Ave. SW, Calgary, AB T2P 0X8
403-292-4800, Fax: 403-292-5503, 800-899-1265, info@neb-one.gc.ca

Alberta

Energy Resources Conservation Board, #1000, 250 - 5 Ave. SW, Calgary, AB T2P 0R4
403-297-8311, Fax: 403-297-7336, 855-297-8311, inquiries@ercb.ca; infoservices@ercb.ca; ADR@ercb.ca

Alberta Energy, North Petroleum Plaza, 9945 - 108 St., Edmonton, AB T5K 2G6
780-427-8050, Fax: 780-422-0698, -310-0000, Library.Energy@gov.ab.ca

British Columbia

British Columbia Hydro, 6911 Southpoint Dr., Burnaby, BC V3N 4X8
604-224-9376, 800-224-9376

Northwest Territories

Department of Environment & Natural Resources, PO Box 1320, Yellowknife, NT X1A 2L9

Nova Scotia

Department of Energy, Bank of Montreal Bldg., #400, 5151 George St., PO Box 2664, Halifax, NS B3J 3P7
902-424-4575, Fax: 902-424-0528, energyinfo@gov.ns.ca

Nova Scotia Utility & Review Board, Summit Place, 1601 Lower Water St., 3rd Fl., PO Box 1692 M,Halifax, NS B3J 3S3
902-424-4448, Fax: 902-424-3919, uarb.board@gov.ns.ca

Saskatchewan

SaskEnergy Incorporated, 1777 Victoria Ave., Regina, SK S4P 4K5
306-777-9225, 800-567-8899

POLICING SERVICES

Royal Canadian Mounted Police, 1200 Vanier Pkwy., Ottawa, ON K1A 0R2
613-993-7267, Fax: 613-993-0260

Alberta

Public Security Division, John E. Brownlee Building, 10365 - 97 St., 10th Fl., Edmonton, AB T5J 3W7

Manitoba
Manitoba Justice, Legislative Building, #104, 405 Broadway Ave., Winnipeg, MB R3C 3L6
204-945-3728, Fax: 204-945-2517, minjus@gov.mb.ca
Law Enforcement Review Agency, #420, 155 Carlton St., Winnipeg, MB R3C 3H8
204-945-8667, Fax: 204-948-1014, 800-282-8069, lera@gov.mb.ca
New Brunswick
New Brunswick Police Commission, Fredericton City Centre, #202, 435 King St., Fredericton, NB E3B 1E5
506-453-2069, Fax: 506-457-3542, nbpc@gnb.ca
Newfoundland & Labrador
Royal Newfoundland Constabulary Public Complaints Commission, Bally Rou Place, #E-160, 280 Torbay Rd., St. John's, NL A1A 3W8
709-729-0950, Fax: 709-729-1302, rnccomplaintscommission@gov.nl.ca
Nova Scotia
Nova Scotia Police Commission, #300, 1601 Lower Water St., PO Box 1573, Halifax, NS B3J 2Y3
902-424-3246, Fax: 902-424-3919, uarb.polcom@gov.ns.ca
Nunavut
Department of Justice, Sivummut, 1st Fl., PO Box 1000 500,Iqaluit, NU X0A 0H0
867-975-6170, Fax: 867-975-6195, justice@gov.nu.ca
Quebec
Direction générale de la Sûreté du Québec, 1701, rue Parthenais, Montréal, QC H2K 3S7
514-598-4141, Fax: 514-598-4242
Saskatchewan
Saskatchewan Public Complaints Commission, #300, 1919 Saskatchewan Dr., Regina, SK S4P 4H2
306-787-6519, Fax: 306-787-6528, 866-256-6194
Yukon Territory
Yukon Justice, Andrew Philipsen Law Centre, 2134 Second Ave., PO Box 2703, Whitehorse, YT Y1A 2C6
867-667-3033, Fax: 867-393-5790, jus.msb@gov.yk.ca

POLITICS & SOCIETY

Auditor General of Canada, 240 Sparks St., Ottawa, ON K1A 0G6
613-995-3708, Fax: 613-957-0474, 888-761-5953, communications@oag-bvg.gc.ca; infomedia@oag-bvg.gc.ca
Canadian International Development Agency, 200, Promenade du Portage, Gatineau, QC K1A 0G4
819-997-5456, Fax: 819-953-6088, 800-230-6349, info@acdi-cida.gc.ca
Commission for Environmental Cooperation, Secretariat, #200, 393, rue St-Jacques ouest, Montréal, QC H2Y 1N9
514-350-4300, Fax: 514-350-4314, info@cec.org
Finance Canada, L'esplanade Laurier, 140 O'Connor St., Ottawa, ON K1A 0G5
613-992-1573, Fax: 613-943-0938, finpub@fin.gc.ca
Foreign Affairs & International Trade Canada, 125 Sussex Dr., Ottawa, ON K1A 0G2
613-944-4000, Fax: 613-996-9709, 800-267-8376, enqserv@international.gc.ca
Government Services Branch, PO Box 8700, St. John's, NL A1B 4J6
International Development Research Centre, 150 Kent St., PO Box 8500, Ottawa, ON K1G 3H9
613-236-6163, Fax: 613-238-7230, info@idrc.ca
International Joint Commission, 234 Laurier Ave. West, 22nd Fl., Ottawa, ON K1P 6K6
613-947-1420, Fax: 613-993-5583, beckhoffb@ottawa.ijc.org
National Capital Commission, #202, 40 Elgin St., Ottawa, ON K1P 1C7
613-239-5000, Fax: 613-239-5063, 800-465-1867, info@ncc-ccn.ca; contracts-contrats@ncc-ccn.ca (Contracting)
National Defence Canada, Major-General George R. Pearkes Bldg., 101 Colonel By Dr., Ottawa, ON K1A 0K2
613-995-2534, Fax: 613-992-4739, 800-856-8488
National Round Table on the Environment & Economy, #200, 344 Slater St., Ottawa, ON K1R 7Y3
613-992-7189, Fax: 613-992-7385, info@nrtee-trnee.ca
Public Safety Canada, 269 Laurier Ave. West, Ottawa, ON K1A 0P8
613-944-4875, Fax: 613-954-5186, 800-830-3118, communications@ps.gc.ca
Public Works & Government Services Canada, Place du Portage, Phase III, 11, rue Laurier, Ottawa, ON K1A 0S5
questions@tpsgc-pwgsc.gc.ca
Strategic Policy Branch, Tower 7, 1341 Baseline Rd., Ottawa, ON K1A 0C5
613-759-1000, Fax: 613-773-2111

Alberta
Alberta International & Intergovernmental Relations, Commerce Place, 10155 - 102 St., 12th Fl., Edmonton, AB T5J 4G8
780-422-1510, -310-0000
Alberta Public Affairs Bureau, Park Plaza, 10611 - 98 Ave., 6th Fl., Edmonton, AB T5K 2P7
780-427-2754, Fax: 780-422-4168, -310-0000
British Columbia
British Columbia Ministry of Community, Sport, & Cultural Development, PO Box 9490 Prov Govt,Victoria, BC V8W 9N7
Manitoba
Manitoba Round Table for Sustainable Development, #160, 123 Main St., Winnipeg, MB R3C 1A5
204-945-1869, Fax: 204-948-2357, mrtsd@gov.mb.ca
New Brunswick
New Brunswick Department of Government Services, Marysville Place, 20 McGloin St., Fredericton, NB E3A 5T8
506-453-6100, Fax: 506-462-5049
Newfoundland & Labrador
Newfoundland & Labrador Department of Service NL, PO Box 8700, St. John's, NL A1B 4J6
709-729-4834, gsinfo@gov.nl.ca
Newfoundland & Labrador Department of Transportation & Works, Confederation Bldg., West Block, 6th Fl., PO Box 8700, St. John's, NL A1B 4J6
709-729-3679, Fax: 709-729-4285, twminister@gov.nl.ca
Northwest Territories
Department of Aboriginal Affairs & Intergovernmental Relations, 4910 - 52nd St., PO Box 1320, Yellowknife, NT X1A 2L9
867-873-7143, Fax: 867-873-0233, 877-838-8194, nancy_gardiner@gov.nt.ca
Department of Public Works & Services, PO Box 1320, Yellowknife, NT X1A 2L9
Nova Scotia
Nova Scotia Emergency Management Office, PO Box 2581, Halifax, NS B3J 3N5
902-424-5620, Fax: 902-424-5376, 866-424-5620, emo@gov.ns.ca
Ontario
Environmental Commissioner of Ontario, #605, 1075 Bay St., Toronto, ON M5S 2B1
416-325-3377, Fax: 416-325-3370, 800-701-6454, commissioner@eco.on.ca
Environmental Review Tribunal, #1500, 655 Bay St., Toronto, ON M5G 1E5
416-212-6349, Fax: 416-314-4506, 866-448-2248, erttribunalsecretary@ontario.ca
Prince Edward Island
Prince Edward Island Department of Health & Wellness, 105 Rochford St. North, 4th Fl., PO Box 2000, Charlottetown, PE C1A 7N8
902-368-6414, Fax: 902-368-4121
Saskatchewan
Government Services, 1920 Rose St., Regina, SK S4P 0A9
306-787-6911, Fax: 306-787-1061, GSReception@gs.gov.sk.ca
Yukon Territory
Emergency Measures Organization, Combined Services Bldg., 2nd Fl., 60 Norseman Rd, Airport, Whitehorse, YT Y1A 2C6
867-667-5220, Fax: 867-393-6266, 800-661-0408, emo.yukon@gov.yk.ca

POPULATION

See Also: Statistics
Statistics Canada, R.H. Coats Bldg., Tunney's Pasture, 150 Tunney's Pasture Driveway, Ottawa, ON K1A 0T6
613-951-8116, Fax: 877-287-4369, 800-263-1136, infostats@statcan.ca
Alberta
Registry Services, Telus Plaza South, 10020 - 100 St., 29th Fl., Edmonton, AB T5J 0N3
Manitoba
Manitoba Bureau of Statistics, #824, 155 Carlton St., Winnipeg, MB R3C 3H9
204-945-2406, Fax: 204-945-0695,
Nunavut
Department of Executive & Intergovernmental Affairs, 1084 Aeroplex bldg., PO Box 1000 200,Iqaluit, NU X0A 0H0
867-975-6000, Fax: 867-975-6099

POSTAL SERVICE

Canada Post Corporation, Corporate Secretariat, 2701 Riverside Dr., Ottawa, ON K1A 0B1
866-607-6301

PREMIERS & LEADERS

See Also: Cabinets & Executive Councils; Government (General Info)

Office of the Prime Minister, Conservative Party of Canada / Conservative Research Bureau, Langevin Block, 80 Wellington St., Ottawa, ON K1A 0A2
613-992-4211, Fax: 613-995-0101, pm@pm.gc.ca
Alberta
Office of the Premier, Office of the Premier, Legislature Building, #307, 10800 - 97 Ave., Edmonton, AB T5K 2B6
780-427-2251, Fax: 780-427-1349, -310-0000
British Columbia
Office of the Premier, West Annex, Parliament Bldgs., PO Box 9041 Prov Govt,Victoria, BC V8W 9E1
250-387-1715, Fax: 250-387-0087, premier@gov.bc.ca
Manitoba
Office of the Premier, Legislative Building, #204, 450 Broadway Ave., Winnipeg, MB R3C 0V8
204-945-3714, Fax: 204-949-1484, premier@leg.gov.mb.ca
New Brunswick
Office of the Premier, Centennial Bldg., 670 King St., PO Box 6000, Fredericton, NB E3B 5H1
506-453-2144, Fax: 506-453-7407, premier@gnb.ca
Newfoundland & Labrador
Office of the Premier, East Block, Confederation Bldg., PO Box 8700, St. John's, NL A1B 4J6
709-729-3570, Fax: 709-729-5875, premier@gov.nl.ca
Northwest Territories
Office of the Premier, Legislative Assembly Bldg., PO Box 1320, Yellowknife, NT X1A 2L9
867-669-2311, Fax: 867-873-0385, premier@gov.nt.ca
Nova Scotia
Office of the Premier, One Government Place, 1700 Granville St., 7th Fl., PO Box 726, Halifax, NS B3J 2T3
902-424-6600, Fax: 902-424-7648, 800-267-1993, premier@gov.ns.ca
Nunavut
Office of the Premier, Legislative Assembly Bldg., 2nd Fl., PO Box 2410, Iqaluit, NU X0A 0H0
867-975-5050, Fax: 867-975-5051
Ontario
Office of the Premier, Legislative Bldg., #281, 1 Queen's Park Cres. South, Toronto, ON M7A 1A1
416-325-1941, Fax: 416-325-3745
Prince Edward Island
Office of the Premier, Shaw Bldg., 95 Rochford St. South, 5th Fl., PO Box 2000, Charlottetown, PE C1A 7N8
902-368-4501, Fax: 902-368-6118
Quebec
Cabinet du premier ministre, Édifice Honoré-Mercier, 835, boul René-Lévesque est, 3e étage, Québec, QC G1A 1B4
418-643-5321, Fax: 418-643-3924
Saskatchewan
Office of the Premier, Legislative Building, #226, 2405 Legislative Dr., Regina, SK S4S 0B3
306-787-9433, Fax: 306-787-0885
Yukon Territory
Office of the Premier, 2071 Second Ave., PO Box 2703, Whitehorse, YT Y1A 1B2
867-667-8660, Fax: 867-393-6252, premier@gov.yk.ca

PROPERTY ASSESSMENT

New Brunswick
Assessment & Plannning Appeal Board, City Centre, PO Box 6000, Fredericton, NB E3B 5H1
506-453-2126, Fax: 506-444-4881, lg/gl-info@gnb.ca
Alberta
Registry Services, Telus Plaza South, 10020 - 100 St., 29th Fl., Edmonton, AB T5J 0N3
British Columbia
British Columbia Assessment Authority, #400, 3450 Uptown Blvd., Victoria, BC V8Z 0B9
250-595-6211, Fax: 250-595-6222, info@bcassessment.ca
Newfoundland & Labrador
Newfoundland & Labrador Department of Municipal Affairs, West Block, Main Fl., Confederation Bldg., PO Box 8700, St. John's, NL A1B 4J6
709-729-3046, Fax: 709-729-0943, mainfo@gov.nl.ca
Northwest Territories
Assessment Appeal Tribunal of the Northwest Territories, #400, 5201 - 50th Ave., PO Box 1320, Yellowknife, NT X1A 2L9
867-873-7125, Fax: 867-873-0609
Prince Edward Island
Prince Edward Island Regulatory & Appeals Commission, National Bank Tower, #501, 134 Kent St., PO Box 577, Charlottetown, PE C1A 7L1
902-892-3501, Fax: 902-566-4076, 800-501-6268, info@irac.pe.ca

Saskatchewan
Saskatchewan Assessment Management Agency, #200, 2201 - 11th Ave., Regina, SK S4P 0J8
306-924-8000, Fax: 306-924-8070, 800-667-7262, info.request@sama.sk.ca

PROTOCOL (STATE)
See Also: Parliament
Governor General & Commander-in-Chief of Canada, Rideau Hall, 1 Sussex Dr., Ottawa, ON K1A 0A1
613-993-8200, Fax: 613-998-8760, 800-465-6890, info@gg.ca
Office of Protocol, 125 Sussex Dr., Ottawa, ON K1A 0G2
613-996-8683, Fax: 613-943-1075
Prince Edward Island
Office of the Lieutenant Governor, Government House, PO Box 846, Charlottetown, PE C1A 7L9
902-368-5480, Fax: 902-368-5481,

PUBLIC SAFETY
See Also: Occupational Safety
Canadian Coast Guard, Centennial Towers, #6S018, 200 Kent St., Ottawa, ON K1A 0E6
613-993-0999, Fax: 613-990-1866, info@dfo-mpo.gc.ca
Canadian Security Intelligence Service, PO Box 9732 T,Ottawa, ON K1G 4G4
613-993-9620, Fax: 613-231-0612
Canadian Transportation Agency, Les Terrasses de la Chaudière, 15, rue Eddy, Gatineau, QC J8X 4B3
Fax: 819-997-6727, 888-222-2592, info@otc-cta.gc.ca
Communications Security Establishment, 1500 Bronson Ave., PO Box 9703 Terminal, Ottawa, ON K1A OK2
613-991-7600, Fax: 613-991-8514
National Defence Canada, Major-General George R. Pearkes Bldg., 101 Colonel By Dr., Ottawa, ON K1A 0K2
613-995-2534, Fax: 613-992-4739, 800-856-8488
Office of the Communications Security Establishment Commissioner, PO Box 1984 B, Ottawa, ON K1P 5R5
613-992-3044
Public Safety Canada, 269 Laurier Ave. West, Ottawa, ON K1A 0P8
613-944-4875, Fax: 613-954-5186, 800-830-3118, communications@ps.gc.ca
Royal Canadian Mounted Police, 1200 Vanier Pkwy., Ottawa, ON K1A 0R2
613-993-7267, Fax: 613-993-0260
Alberta
Public Security Division, John E. Brownlee Building, 10365 - 97 St., 10th Fl., Edmonton, AB T5J 3W7
New Brunswick
New Brunswick Department of Public Safety, 364 Argyle St., PO Box 6000, Fredericton, NB E3B 5H1
506-453-3992, Fax: 506-453-3870, DPS-MSP.Information@gnb.ca
Northwest Territories
Department of Justice, Courthouse, 4903 - 49th St., 6th Fl., PO Box 1320, Yellowknife, NT X1A 2L9
867-920-6197
Nunavut
Department of Justice, Sivummut, 1st Fl., PO Box 1000 500,Iqaluit, NU X0A 0H0
867-975-6170, Fax: 867-975-6195, justice@gov.nu.ca
Quebec
Ministère de la Sécurité publique, Tour des Laurentides, 2525, boul Laurier, 5e étage, Québec, QC G1V 2L2
418-643-2112, Fax: 418-646-6168, 866-644-6826
Saskatchewan
Saskatchewan Corrections & Policing, 1874 Scarth St., Regina, SK S4P 4B3
306-787-7872, communicationsCPSP@gov.sk.ca

PUBLIC SERVICES
Canada Deposit Insurance Corporation, 50 O'Connor St., 17th Floor, PO Box 2340 D,Ottawa, ON K1P 5W5
Fax: 613-996-6095, 800-461-2342, info@cdic.ca; info@sadc.ca
Canada Post Corporation, Corporate Secretariat, 2701 Riverside Dr., Ottawa, ON K1A 0B1
866-607-6301
Canadian Broadcasting Corporation, 181 Queen St., PO Box 3220 C,Ottawa, ON K1Y 1E4
613-288-6033, liaison@radio-canada.ca
Canadian Centre for Occupational Health & Safety, 135 Hunter St. East, Hamilton, ON L8N 1M5
905-572-2981, Fax: 905-572-2206, 800-668-4284
Canadian Coast Guard, Centennial Towers, #6S018, 200 Kent St., Ottawa, ON K1A 0E6
613-993-0999, Fax: 613-990-1866, info@dfo-mpo.gc.ca
Canadian Security Intelligence Service, PO Box 9732 T,Ottawa, ON K1G 4G4
613-993-9620, Fax: 613-231-0612
Citizenship & Immigration Canada, Jean Edmonds, South Tower, 365 Laurier Ave. West, Ottawa, ON K1A 1L1
613-954-9019, Fax: 613-954-2221, 888-242-2100
Commission for Public Complaints Against the Royal Canadian Mounted Police, National Intake Office, PO Box 88689, Surrey, BC V3W 0X1
Fax: 613-952-8045, 800-665-6878, org@cpc-cpp.gc.ca
Communications Branch, HSBC Place, 520 King St., 5th Fl., PO Box 5100, Fredericton, NB E3B 6G3
506-457-2356, Fax: 506-444-4697, Health.Sante@gnb.ca
Corporate Services Division, Marysville Place, PO Box 6000, Fredericton, NB E3B 5H1
506-453-3742, Fax: 506-444-4400, Reception.Marysville@gnb.ca
Correctional Service Canada, 340 Laurier Ave. West, Ottawa, ON K1A 0P9
613-992-5891, Fax: 613-943-1630
Health Services Information & Information Technology Cluster, 56 Wellesley St. West, 10th Fl., Toronto, ON M5S 2S3
416-314-4243, Fax: 416-314-0289
Health Workforce Division, Telus Plaza NT, 10025 Jasper Ave., 10th Fl., Edmonton, AB T5J 1S6
Housing, Seniors & Corporate Support, Jones Bldg., 11 Kent St., 2nd Fl., PO Box 2000, Charlottetown, PE C1A 7N8
Fax: 902-894-0242
Human Resources & Skills Development Canada, 140 Promenade du Portage, Gatineau, QC K1A 0J9
Immigration & Refugee Board of Canada, Canada Bldg, 344 Slater St., 12th Fl., Ottawa, ON K1A 0K1
613-995-6486, Fax: 613-943-1550, contact@irb-cisr.gc.ca
Legal Services Division, Bowker Building, 9833 - 109 St., 2nd Fl., Edmonton, AB T5K 2E8
780-422-0500
MERX, PO Box 11684 Centre-ville,Montreal, QC H3C 6H4
Fax: 888-235-5800, merx@merx.com
Military Police Complaints Commission, 270 Albert St., 10th Fl., Ottawa, ON K1P 5G8
613-947-5625, Fax: 613-947-5713, 800-632-0566, commission@mpcc-cppm.gc.ca
National Capital Commission, #202, 40 Elgin St., Ottawa, ON K1P 1C7
613-239-5000, Fax: 613-239-5063, 800-465-1867, info@ncc-ccn.ca; contracts-contrats@ncc-ccn.ca (Contracting)
National Defence Canada, Major-General George R. Pearkes Bldg., 101 Colonel By Dr., Ottawa, ON K1A 0K2
613-995-2534, Fax: 613-992-4739, 800-856-8488
National Parole Board, 410 Laurier Ave. West, Ottawa, ON K1A 0R1
613-954-7474, Fax: 613-995-4380, 800-874-2652, info@npb-cnlc.gc.ca
National Search & Rescue Secretariat, #400, 275 Slater St., Ottawa, ON K1A 0K2
613-992-0054, Fax: 613-996-3746, 800-727-9414, inquiry@nss.gc.ca
Public Service Commission, West Tower, 300 Laurier Ave. West, Ottawa, ON K1A 0M7
613-992-9562, Fax: 613-992-9352, infocom@psc-cfp.gc.ca
Public Service Commission, 2350 Albert St., Regina, SK S4P 4A6
306-787-7853, 866-319-5999, inquiry@psc.gov.sk.ca
Public Service Staffing Tribunal, 240 Sparks St., 6th Fl., Ottawa, ON K1A 0A5
613-949-6516, Fax: 613-949-6551, 866-637-4491, info@psst-tdfp.gc.ca
Public Works & Government Services Canada, Place du Portage, Phase III, 11, rue Laurier, Ottawa, ON K1A 0S5
questions@tpsgc-pwgsc.gc.ca
Royal Canadian Mounted Police, 1200 Vanier Pkwy., Ottawa, ON K1A 0R2
613-993-7267, Fax: 613-993-0260
Royal Canadian Mounted Police External Review Committee, PO Box 1159 B, Ottawa, ON K1P 5R2
613-998-2134, Fax: 613-990-8969, org@erc-cee.gc.ca
Security Intelligence Review Committee, Jackson Bldg., 122 Bank St., 4th Fl., PO Box 2430 D,Ottawa, ON K1P 5W5
613-990-8441, Fax: 613-990-5230, ellardm@sirc-csars.gc.ca
Veterans Affairs Canada, 161 Grafton St., PO Box 7700, Charlottetown, PE C1A 8M9
902-566-8888, 866-522-2111, information@vac-acc.gc.ca
Veterans Review & Appeal Board, Daniel J. MacDonald Bldg., 161 Grafton St., PO Box 9900, Charlottetown, PE C1A 8V7
902-566-8751, Fax: 902-566-7850, 800-450-8006, vrab_tacra@vac-acc.gc.ca
Alberta
Alberta Capital Finance Authority, Canadian Western Bank Place, #2450, 10303 Jasper Ave., Edmonton, AB T5J 3N6
780-427-9711, Fax: 780-422-2175, webacfa@gov.ab.ca
Alberta Health Services, Corporate Office, North Tower, Seventh Street Plaza, 10030 - 107th St. NW, 14th Fl., Edmonton, AB T5J 3E4
780-342-2000, Fax: 780-342-2060, 888-342-2471, ahsb.admin@albertahealthservices.ca
Alberta Pensions Services Corporation, 5103 Windermere Blvd. SW, Edmonton, AB T6W 0S9
780-427-2782, 800-661-8198, memberservices@apsc.ca; employerservices@apsc.ca; pay@apsc.ca
Energy Resources Conservation Board, #1000, 250 - 5 Ave. SW, Calgary, AB T2P 0R4
403-297-8311, Fax: 403-297-7336, 855-297-8311, inquiries@ercb.ca; infoservices@ercb.ca; ADR@ercb.ca
Alberta Infrastructure, Infrastructure Building, 6950 - 113 St., Edmonton, AB T6H 5V7
780-415-0507, Fax: 780-427-2187, -310-0000, Infra.Contact.Us.m@gov.ab.ca
Labour Relations Board, Labour Building, 10808 - 99 Ave., 5th Fl., Edmonton, AB T5K 0G5
780-422-5926, Fax: 780-422-0970, 800-463-2572, alrbinfo@lab.gov.ab.ca
Alberta Municipal Affairs, Communications Branch, Commerce Place, 10155 - 102 St., 18th Fl., Edmonton, AB T5J 4L4
780-427-2732, Fax: 780-422-1419, comments@gov.ab.ca
Municipal Government Board, Commerce Place, 10155 - 102 St., 15th Fl., Edmonton, AB T5J 4L4
780-427-4864, Fax: 780-427-0986, -310-0000, mgbmail@gov.ab.ca
Public Security Division, John E. Brownlee Building, 10365 - 97 St., 10th Fl., Edmonton, AB T5J 3W7
Alberta Tourism, Parks, & Recreation, Communications Branch, Commerce Place, 10155 - 102 St., 6th Fl., Edmonton, AB T5J 4L6
780-644-5589, TPR.Communications@gov.ab.ca
British Columbia
British Columbia Assessment Authority, #400, 3450 Uptown Blvd., Victoria, BC V8Z 0B9
250-595-6211, Fax: 250-595-6222, info@bcassessment.ca
British Columbia Ministry of Children & Family Development, PO Box 9770 Prov Govt,Victoria, BC V8W 9S5
250-387-7027, Fax: 250-356-3007, 877-387-7027, MCF.CorrespondenceManagement@gov.bc.ca
British Columbia Public Service Agency, #4, 810 Blanshard St., PO Box 9404 Prov Govt,Victoria, BC V8W 9V1
250-387-0518, Fax: 250-356-7074
British Columbia Transit, 520 Gorge Rd. East, Victoria, BC V8W 2P3
250-385-2551, Fax: 250-995-5639
British Columbia Ferry Services Inc., #500, 1321 Blanshard St., Victoria, BC V8W 0B7
250-381-1401, 888-223-3779
Local Government, PO Box 9490 Prov Govt,Victoria, BC V8W 9N7
250-356-6575, Fax: 250-387-7973
Office of the Representative for Children & Youth, #201, 546 Yates St., Victoria, BC V8W 1K8
250-356-6710, Fax: 250-356-0837, 800-476-3933, rcy@rcybc.ca
British Columbia Provincial Emergency Program, Block A, #200, 2261 Keating Cross Rd., Saanichton, BC V8M 2A5
250-952-4913, Fax: 250-952-4888, 888-257-4777
Manitoba
Advisory Council on Workplace Safety & Health, #200, 401 York Ave., Winnipeg, MB R3C 0P8
204-945-3446, Fax: 204-945-4556
Office of the Auditor General, #500, 330 Portage Ave., Winnipeg, MB R3C 0C4
204-945-3790, Fax: 204-945-2169, oag.contact@oag.mb.ca
Automobile Injury Compensation Appeal Commission, #301, 428 Portage Ave.., Winnipeg, MB R3C 0E2
204-945-4155, Fax: 204-948-2402, autoinjury@gov.mb.ca
Civil Service Commission Board, #935, 155 Carlton St., Winnipeg, MB R3C 3H8
204-945-1435, Fax: 204-945-1486
Manitoba Civil Service Commission, #935, 155 Carlton St., Winnipeg, MB R3C 3H8
204-945-2332, Fax: 204-945-1486, 800-282-8069, cschrp@gov.mb.ca
Credit Union Deposit Guarantee Corporation, #390, 200 Graham Ave., Winnipeg, MB R3C 4L5
204-942-8480, Fax: 204-947-1723, 800-697-4447, mail@cudgc.com
Manitoba Culture, Heritage & Tourism, Legislative Building, #118, 450 Broadway Ave., Winnipeg, MB R3C 0V8
204-945-3729, Fax: 204-945-5223, mincht@leg.gov.mb.ca
Emergency Measures Organization, 405 Broadway Ave., 15th Floor, Winnipeg, MB R3C 3L6
204-945-4772, Fax: 204-945-4929, 888-267-8298, emo@gov.mb.ca
Manitoba Family Services & Labour, #219, 114 Garry St., Winnipeg, MB R3C 4V6
204-945-3242, Fax: 204-945-2156, minfam@leg.gov.mb.ca

Manitoba Health, #100, 300 Carlton St., Winnipeg, MB R3B 3M9
204-786-7191, minhlt@leg.gov.mb.ca
Manitoba Healthy Living, Seniors & Consumer Affairs, #822, 155 Carlton St., Winnipeg, MB R3C 3H8
204-945-6565, Fax: 204-948-2514, 800-665-6565, seniors@gov.mb.ca
Manitoba Human Rights Commission, 175 Hargrave St., 7th Fl., Winnipeg, MB R3C 3R8
204-945-3007, Fax: 204-945-1292, 888-884-8681, hrc@gov.mb.ca
Manitoba Hydro, 360 Portage Ave., PO Box 815 Main,Winnipeg, MB R3C 2P4
204-474-3311, publicaffairs@hydro.mb.ca
Manitoba Immigration & Multiculturalism, Legislative Building, 317, 450 Broadway Ave., Winnipeg, MB R3C 0V8
204-945-4079, Fax: 204-945-8312, minlab@leg.gov.mb.ca
Manitoba Infrastructure & Transportation, Legislative Building, #203, 450 Broadway Ave., Winnipeg, MB R3C 0V8
204-945-3723, Fax: 204-945-7610
Manitoba Public Insurance, #B100, 234 Donald St., PO Box 6300, Winnipeg, MB R3C 4A4
204-985-7000, Fax: 204-985-3525, 800-665-2410
Manitoba Justice, Legislative Building, #104, 405 Broadway Ave., Winnipeg, MB R3C 3L6
204-945-3728, Fax: 204-945-2517, minjus@gov.mb.ca
Local Government Development Division, 59 Elizabeth Dr., PO Box 33, Thompson, MB R8N 1X4
204-677-6794, Fax: 204-677-6525
Manitoba Bureau of Statistics, #824, 155 Carlton St., Winnipeg, MB R3C 3H9
204-945-2406, Fax: 204-945-0695
Manitoba Film Classification Board, #216, 301 Weston St., Winnipeg, MB R3E 3H4
204-945-8962, Fax: 204-945-0890, 866-612-2399, mfcb@gov.mb.ca
Manitoba Housing & Renewal Corporation, 280 Broadway, Winnipeg, MB R3C 0R8
204-945-4895, Fax: 204-945-5710
Manitoba Housing Authority - Public Housing, #2100, 185 Smith St., Winnipeg, MB R3C 3G4
204-945-4663, Fax: 204-948-2013, 800-661-4663
Manitoba Labour Board, A.A. Heaps Bldg., #402, 258 Portage Ave., Winnipeg, MB R3C 0B6
204-945-3783, Fax: 204-945-1296, mlb@gov.mb.ca
Manitoba Land Value Appraisal Commission, 800 Portage Ave., Winnipeg, MB R3G 0N4
204-945-2941, Fax: 204-948-2235
Manitoba Minimum Wage Board, 614 - 401 York Ave., Winnipeg, MB R3C 0P8
204-945-4889, Fax: 204-948-2085, mw@gov.mb.ca
News Media Services, Legislative Bldg., #29, 450 Broadway Ave., Winnipeg, MB R3C 0V8
204-945-3746, Fax: 204-945-3988, nmservices@leg.gov.mb.ca
Office of the Fire Commissioner, #508, 401 York Ave., Winnipeg, MB R3C 0P8
204-945-3322, Fax: 204-948-2089, 800-282-8069, firecomm@gov.mb.ca
Provincial-Municipal Support Services, #508, 800 Portage Ave., Winnipeg, MB R3G 0N4
Public Health & Primary Health Care, 300 Carlton St., 2nd Floor, Winnipeg, MB R3B 3M9
Public Utilities Board, #400, 330 Portage Ave., Winnipeg, MB R3C 0C4
204-945-2638, Fax: 204-945-2643, 866-854-3698, publicutilities@gov.mb.ca
Manitoba Telecom Services Inc., 333 Main St., PO Box 6666, Winnipeg, MB R3C 3V6
204-941-4111, Fax: 204-772-6391
Manitoba Workers' Compensation Board, 333 Broadway Ave., Winnipeg, MB R3C 4W3
204-954-4321, Fax: 204-954-4999, 800-362-3340, wcb@wcb.mb.ca

New Brunswick

Premier's Council on the Status of Disabled Persons, Kings Place, #648, 440 King St., Fredericton, NB E3B 5H8
506-444-3000, Fax: 506-444-3001, 800-442-4412, pcsdp@gnb.ca
New Brunswick Human Rights Commission, PO Box 6000, Fredericton, NB E3B 5H1
506-453-2301, Fax: 506-453-2653, 888-471-2233, hrc.cdp@gnb.ca
Justice Services Division, Centennial Building, PO Box 6000, Fredericton, NB E3B 5H1
506-453-2458, Fax: 506-453-3651, general.comments@gnb.ca
New Brunswick Department of Health, PO Box 5100, Fredericton, NB E3B 5G8
506-457-4800, Fax: 506-453-5243, dh-ms@dh-ms.ca
New Brunswick Department of Post-Secondary Education, Training, & Labour, Chestnut Complex, PO Box 6000, Fredericton, NB E3B 5H1
506-453-2597, Fax: 506-453-3618, dpetlinfo@gnb.ca
New Brunswick Department of Social Development, Sartain MacDonald Bldg., 551 King St., PO Box 6000, Fredericton, NB E3B 5H1
506-453-2001, Fax: 506-453-7478, sd-ds@gnb.ca
Office of the Ombudsman, 767 Brunswick St., PO Box 6000, Fredericton, NB E3B 5H1
506-453-2789, Fax: 506-453-5599, 800-465-1100, nbombud@gnb.ca

Newfoundland & Labrador

C.A. Pippy Park Commission, Mount Scio House, 15 Mount Scio Rd., St. John's, NL A1B 3T2
709-737-3655, Fax: 709-737-3303, info@pippypark.com
Eastern Waste Management Commission, #200, 120 Lemarchant Rd., St. John's, NL A1C 2H2
709-579-7960, Fax: 709-579-5392, info@easternwaste.ca
Income & Employment Support Appeal Board, Confederation Bldg., PO Box 8700, St. John's, NL A1B 4J6
709-729-2479, Fax: 709-729-5139
Newfoundland & Labrador Department of Advanced Education & Skills, Confederation Building, West Block, 3rd Fl., PO Box 8700, St. John's, NL A1B 4J6
709-729-2480, aesweb@gov.nl.ca
Newfoundland & Labrador Department of Municipal Affairs, West Block, Main Fl., Confederation Bldg., PO Box 8700, St. John's, NL A1B 4J6
709-729-3046, Fax: 709-729-0943, mainfo@gov.nl.ca
Newfoundland & Labrador Department of Service NL, PO Box 8700, St. John's, NL A1B 4J6
709-729-4834, gsinfo@gov.nl.ca
Newfoundland & Labrador Department of Transportation & Works, Confederation Bldg., West Block, 6th Fl., PO Box 8700, St. John's, NL A1B 4J6
709-729-3679, Fax: 709-729-4285, twminister@gov.nl.ca
Newfoundland & Labrador Legal Aid Commission, #300, 251 Empire Ave., PO Box 399 C, St. John's, NL A1C 5J9
709-753-7863, Fax: 709-753-6226, 800-563-9911, nlac@legalaid.nl.ca
Newfoundland & Labrador Liquor Corporation, 90 Kenmount Rd., PO Box 8750 A, St. John's, NL A1B 3V1
709-724-1100, Fax: 709-754-0321, info@nfliquor.com
Newfoundland & Labrador Public Service Commission, 2 Canada Dr., 3rd Fl., PO Box 8700, St. John's, NL A1B 4J6
709-729-5810, Fax: 709-729-6234
Royal Newfoundland Constabulary Public Complaints Commission, Bally Rou Place, #E-160, 280 Torbay Rd., St. John's, NL A1A 3W8
709-729-0950, Fax: 709-729-1302, rnccomplaintscommission@gov.nl.ca

Northwest Territories

Department of Health & Social Services, Centre Square Tower, PO Box 1320, Yellowknife, NT X1A 2L9
Fax: 867-873-0266
Department of Municipal & Community Affairs, PO Box 1320, Yellowknife, NT X1A 2L9
867-873-7118, Fax: 867-873-0309
Department of Public Works & Services, PO Box 1320, Yellowknife, NT X1A 2L9
Northwest Territories Housing Corporation, Scotia Centre, 5102 50th Ave., PO Box 2100, Yellowknife, NT X1A 2P6
867-873-7853, Fax: 867-873-9426
Northwest Territories Power Corporation, 4 Capital Dr., Hay River, NT X0E 1G2
867-874-5200, Fax: 867-874-5251, info@ntpc.com
Victims Assistance Committee, c/o Community Justice Division, PO Box 1320, Yellowknife, NT X1A 2L9
867-920-6911, Fax: 867-873-0199
Northwest Territories Water Board, 125 Mackenzie Rd., PO Box 2531, Yellowknife, NT X0E 0T0
867-678-2942, Fax: 867-678-2943, info@nwtwb.com

Nova Scotia

Department of Community Services, Nelson Place, 5675 Spring Garden Rd., 8th Fl., PO Box 696, Halifax, NS B3J 2T7
902-424-4304, Fax: 902-428-0618
Nova Scotia Emergency Management Office, PO Box 2581, Halifax, NS B3J 3N5
902-424-5620, Fax: 902-424-5376, 866-424-5620, emo@gov.ns.ca
Department of Health & Wellness, Joseph Howe Bldg., 1690 Hollis St., 4th Fl., PO Box 488, Halifax, NS B3J 2R8
902-424-5818, Fax: 902-424-0730, 800-387-6665, DoHweb@gov.ns.ca
Nova Scotia Disabled Persons Commission, Dartmouth Professional Center, #104, 277 Pleasant St., Dartmouth, NS B2Y 4B7
902-424-8280, Fax: 902-424-0592, 800-565-8280
Nova Scotia Legal Aid Commission, #102, 137 Chain Lake Dr., Halifax, NS B3S 1B3
902-420-6573, Fax: 902-420-3471, nsla.exec@ns.sympatico.ca
Nova Scotia Police Commission, #300, 1601 Lower Water St., PO Box 1573, Halifax, NS B3J 2Y3
902-424-3246, Fax: 902-424-3919, uarb.polcom@gov.ns.ca
Department of Transportation & Infrastructure Renewal, Johnston Bldg., 1672 Granville St., 2nd Fl., PO Box 186, Halifax, NS B3J 2N2
902-424-2297, Fax: 902-424-0532, tpwpaff@gov.ns.ca
Workers' Advisers Program, #502, 5670 Spring Garden Rd., PO Box 1063, Halifax, NS B3J 2X1
902-424-5050, Fax: 902-424-0530, 800-774-4712

Nunavut

Department of Community & Government Services, W.G. Brown Bldg., 4th Fl., PO Box 1000 700,Iqaluit, NU X0A 0H0
867-975-5400, Fax: 867-975-5305
Department of Finance, Bldg. 1079, 1st Fl., PO Box 1000 330,Iqaluit, NU X0A 0H0
867-975-5800, Fax: 867-975-5805
Department of Health & Social Services, PO Box 1000 1000,Iqaluit, NU X0A 0H0
867-975-5700, Fax: 867-975-5705
Nunavut Emergency Management, PO Box 1000 700,Iqaluit, NU X0A 0H0
867-975-5403, Fax: 867-979-4221, 800-693-1666

Ontario

Advertising Review Board, Macdonald Block, #M2-56, 900 Bay St., 2nd Fl., Toronto, ON M7A 1N3
416-327-2183, Fax: 416-327-2179
Ontario Ministry of the Attorney General, McMurtry-Scott Bldg., 720 Bay St., 11th Fl., Toronto, ON M5G 2K1
416-326-2220, Fax: 416-326-4007, 800-518-7901
Ontario Ministry of Community & Social Services, Hepburn Block, 80 Grosvenor St., 6th Fl., Toronto, ON M7A 1E9
416-325-5666, Fax: 416-325-5172, 888-789-4199
Ontario Ministry of Community Safety & Correctional Services, George Drew Bldg., 25 Grosvenor St., 18th Fl., Toronto, ON M7A 1Y6
416-326-5000, Fax: 416-326-0498, 866-517-0571, mcscs.feedback@ontario.ca
Deposit Insurance Corporation of Ontario, #700, 4711 Yonge St., Toronto, ON M2N 6K8
416-325-9444, Fax: 416-325-9722, 800-268-6653
Fire Safety Commission, Place Nouveau Bldg., 5775 Yonge St., 7th Fl., Toronto, ON M2M 4J1
416-325-3100, Fax: 416-314-1217
Human Rights Tribunal of Ontario, 655 Bay St., 14th Fl., Toronto, ON M7A 2A3
416-326-1312, Fax: 416-326-2027, 866-598-0322, hrto.tdpo@ontario.ca
Hydro One Inc., North Tower, 483 Bay St., Toronto, ON M5G 2P5
416-345-5000, 877-955-1155, customercommunications@HydroOne.com
Independent Electricity System Operator, PO Box 4474 A,Toronto, ON M5W 4E5
905-403-6900, Fax: 905-403-6921, 888-448-7777, customer.relations@ieso.ca
Ontario Ministry of Municipal Affairs & Housing, College Park, 777 Bay St., 17th Fl., Toronto, ON M5G 2E5
416-585-7041, Fax: 416-585-6470, 866-220-2290, mininfo@ontario.ca
Office of the Employer Advisor, #704, 151 Bloor St. West., Toronto, ON M5S 1S4
416-327-0020, Fax: 416-327-0726, 800-387-0774
Office of the Worker Advisor, #1300, 123 Edward St., Toronto, ON M5G 1E2
416-325-8570, Fax: 416-325-4830, 800-435-8980
Ontario Pension Board, Sun Life Bldg., #2200, 200 King St. West, Toronto, ON M5H 3X6
416-364-8558, Fax: 416-364-7578, 800-668-6203, office.services@opb.on.ca
Ontario Power Generation, 700 University Ave., Toronto, ON M5G 1X6
416-592-2555, 877-592-2555, webmaster@opg.com
Social Benefits Tribunal, 1075 Bay St., 7th Fl., Toronto, ON M5S 2B1
416-326-0978, Fax: 416-325-5135, 800-753-3895
Southern Ontario Library Service, #902, 111 Peter St., Toronto, ON M5V 2H1
416-961-1669, Fax: 416-961-5122, 800-387-5765
Ontario Ministry of Transportation, Ferguson Block, 77 Wellesley St. West, 3rd Fl., Toronto, ON M7A 1Z8
416-235-4686, Fax: 905-704-2001, 800-268-4686

Prince Edward Island

Island Waste Management Corporation, 110 Watts Ave., Charlottetown, PE C1E 2C1
902-894-0330, Fax: 902-894-0331, 888-280-8111, reception@iwmc.pe.ca; info@iwmc.pe.ca

Prince Edward Island Department of Community Services & Seniors, Jones Bldg., 11 Kent St., 2nd Fl., PO Box 2000, Charlottetown, PE C1A 7N8
902-620-3777, Fax: 902-368-4740, 866-594-3777
Prince Edward Island Department of Health & Wellness, 105 Rochford St. North, 4th Fl., PO Box 2000, Charlottetown, PE C1A 7N8
902-368-6414, Fax: 902-368-4121
SkillsPEI, Atlantic Technology Centre, #212, 90 University Ave., Charlottetown, PE C1A 4K9
902-368-4260, Fax: 902-368-6340, 877-491-4766

Quebec

Ministère des Affaires municipales, des Régions et de l'Occupation du territoire, Aile Chaveau, 10, rue Pierre-Olivier-Chauveau, 3e étage, Québec, QC G1R 4J3
418-691-2019, Fax: 418-643-7385, communications@mamrot.gouv.qc.ca
Bureau des projets Centres hospitaliers universitaires de Montréal, CHUM, CUSM et CHU Sainte-Justine, #10.049, 2021, rue Union, Montréal, QC H3A 2S9
514-864-9883, Fax: 514-873-7362, info.construction3chu@msss.gouv.qc.ca
Commissariat des incendies, 455, rue Dupont, Québec, QC G1K 6N2
418-529-5706, Fax: 418-529-9922, cdelage@notarius.net
Commission administrative des régimes de retraite et d'assurances (Québec), 475, rue Saint-Amable, Québec, QC G1R 5X3
418-643-4881, Fax: 418-644-3839, 800-463-5533
Commission de la fonction publique (Québec), 800, Place d'Youville, 7e étage, Québec, QC G1R 3P4
418-643-1425, Fax: 418-643-7264, 800-432-0432, cfp@cfp.gouv.qc.ca
Commission municipale du Québec, Mezzanine, aile Chauveau, 10, rue Pierre-Olivier-Chauveau, Québec, QC G1R 4J3
418-691-2014, Fax: 418-644-4676, 866-353-6767, cmq@mamr.gouv.qc.ca
Conseil des services essentiels du Québec, #9.100, 500, boul René-Lévesque ouest, 9e étage, CP 38, Montréal, QC H2Z 1W7
514-873-7246, Fax: 514-873-3839, 800-337-7246, info@cses.gouv.qc.ca
Ministère de l'Emploi et de la Solidarité sociale, 425, rue St-Amable, 4e étage, Québec, QC G1R 4Z1
418-643-4721, 888-643-4721
Hydro-Québec, 75, boul René-Lévesque ouest, Montréal, QC H2Z 1A4
514-289-2211,
Office des personnes handicapées du Québec, 309, rue Brock, Drummondville, QC J2B 1C5
Fax: 819-475-8753, 800-567-1465, michael.magner@ophq.gouv.qc.ca
Palais des congrès de Montréal, 159, rue Saint-Antoine ouest, 9é étage, Montréal, QC H2Z 1H2
514-871-8122, Fax: 514-871-9389, 800-268-8122, info@congresmtl.com
Régie de l'assurance maladie du Québec, 1125, Grande Allée ouest, Québec, QC G1S 1E7
418-646-4636
Régie du logement du Québec, Pyramide Ouest, #2095, 5199, rue Sherbrooke est, Montréal, QC H1T 3X1
514-873-2245, Fax: 514-864-8077, 800-683-2245
Ministère de la Santé et des Services sociaux, Direction des communications, 1075, ch Sainte-Foy, 16e étage, Québec, QC G1S 2M1
418-643-9395, Fax: 418-643-4768, regisseur.web@msss.gouv.qc.ca
Société d'habitation du Québec, Aile St-Amable, 1054, rue Louis-Alexandre-Taschereau, 3e étage, Québec, QC G1R 5E7
418-643-4035, Fax: 418-643-2533, 800-463-4315
Société de l'assurance automobile du Québec, 333, boul Jean-Lesage, CP 19600 Terminus, Québec, QC G1K 8J6
418-643-7620, Fax: 418-644-0339, 800-361-7620, courrier@saaq.gouv.qc.ca
Ministère de la Sécurité publique, Tour des Laurentides, 2525, boul Laurier, 5e étage, Québec, QC G1V 2L2
418-643-2112, Fax: 418-646-6168, 866-644-6826
Urgences-santé Québec, 3232, rue Bélanger, Montréal, QC H1Y 3H5
514-723-5600, info@urgences-sante.qc.ca
Vérificateur général du Québec, 750, boulevard Charest est, 3e étage, Québec, QC G1K 9J6
418-691-5900, Fax: 418-644-4460, verificateur.general@vgq.gouv.qc.ca
École nationale des pompiers du Québec, #3.08, 2800, boul Saint-Martin ouest, Laval, QC H7T 2S9
450-680-6800, Fax: 450-680-6818, 866-680-3677

Saskatchewan

Crown Investments Corporation of Saskatchewan, #400, 2400 College Ave., Regina, SK S4P 1C8
306-787-6851, Fax: 306-787-8125
Ombudsman Saskatchewan, #150, 2401 Saskatchewan Dr., Regina, SK S4P 4H8
306-787-6211, Fax: 306-787-9090, 800-667-7180, ombreg@ombudsman.sk.ca
Provincial Auditor Saskatchewan, #1500, 1920 Broad St., Regina, SK S4P 3V2
306-787-6398, Fax: 306-787-6383, info@auditor.sk.ca
Saskatchewan Assessment Management Agency, #200, 2201 - 11th Ave., Regina, SK S4P 0J8
306-924-8000, Fax: 306-924-8070, 800-667-7262, info.request@sama.sk.ca
Saskatchewan Government Insurance, 2260 - 11th Ave., Regina, SK S4P 0J9
306-751-1200, Fax: 306-787-7477, 800-667-8015, sgiinquiries@sgi.sk.ca
Saskatchewan Legal Aid Commission, #502, 201 - 21 St. East, Saskatoon, SK S7K 0B8
306-933-5300, Fax: 306-933-6764, 800-667-3764
Saskatchewan Power Corporation (SaskPower), 2025 Victoria Ave., Regina, SK S4P 0S1
306-566-3306, Fax: 800-757-6937, 888-757-6937
Saskatchewan Social Services, 1920 Broad St., Regina, SK S4P 3V6
306-787-3700, 866-221-5200, socialservicesinquiry@gov.sk.ca
Saskatchewan Water Corporation (SaskWater), #200, 111 Fairford St. East, Moose Jaw, SK S6H 1C8
Fax: 306-694-3207, 888-230-1111, comm@saskwater.com; customerservice@saskwater.com
SaskEnergy Incorporated, 1777 Victoria Ave., Regina, SK S4P 4K5
306-777-9225, 800-567-8899

Yukon Territory

Yukon Community Services, PO Box 2703, Whitehorse, YT Y1A 2C6
867-667-5811, Fax: 867-393-6295, 800-661-0408, inquiry@gov.yk.ca
Emergency Measures Organization, Combined Services Bldg., 2nd Fl., 60 Norseman Rd, Airport, Whitehorse, YT Y1A 2C6
867-667-5220, Fax: 867-393-6266, 800-661-0408, emo.yukon@gov.yk.ca
Yukon Health & Social Services, PO Box 2703, Whitehorse, YT Y1A 2C6
867-667-3673, Fax: 867-667-3096, hss@gov.yk.ca
Yukon Housing Corporation, 410H Jarvis St., PO Box 2703, Whitehorse, YT Y1A 2H5
867-667-5759, Fax: 867-667-3664, 800-661-0408, ykhouse@housing.yk.ca
Yukon Public Service Commission, Yukon Government Administration Building, #2071-2nd Ave., PO Box 2703, Whitehorse, YT Y1A 2C6
867-667-5653, Fax: 867-667-5755, 800-661-0408, PSCWebsite@gov.yk.ca
Yukon Utilities Board, #19, 1114 - 1st Ave., PO Box 31728, Whitehorse, YT Y1A 6L3
867-667-5058, Fax: 867-667-5059, yub@utilitiesboard.yk.ca

PUBLIC TRUSTEE

British Columbia

Public Guardian & Trustee of British Columbia, #700, 808 West Hastings St., Vancouver, BC V6C 3L3
604-660-4444, Fax: 604-660-0374, 800-663-7867, mail@trustee.bc.ca

Manitoba

Office of the Public Trustee, #500, 155 Carlton St., Winnipeg, MB R3C 5R9
204-945-2700, Fax: 204-948-2251, publictrustee@gov.mb.ca

Newfoundland & Labrador

Newfoundland & Labrador Department of Justice, Confederation Bldg., East Block, 4th Fl., PO Box 8700, St. John's, NL A1B 4J6
709-729-2869, Fax: 709-729-0469, justice@gov.nl.ca

Nova Scotia

Public Trustee Office, #405, 5670 Spring Garden Rd., PO Box 685, Halifax, NS B3J 2T3
902-424-7760, Fax: 902-424-0616, PublicTrusteeHCD@gov.ns.ca (Health Care Decisions Division)

Quebec

Curateur public du Québec, 600, boul René-Lévesque ouest, Montréal, QC H3B 4W9
514-873-4074, Fax: 514-873-5033, 800-363-9020

PUBLIC UTILITIES

Yukon Territory

Yukon Energy Corporation, 2 Miles Canyon Rd., PO Box 5920, Whitehorse, YT Y1A 6S7
867-393-5300, 866-926-3749, communications@yukonenergy.ca

Alberta

Energy Resources Conservation Board, #1000, 250 - 5 Ave. SW, Calgary, AB T2P 0R4
403-297-8311, Fax: 403-297-7336, 855-297-8311, inquiries@ercb.ca; infoservices@ercb.ca; ADR@ercb.ca

British Columbia

British Columbia Hydro, 6911 Southpoint Dr., Burnaby, BC V3N 4X8
604-224-9376, 800-224-9376
British Columbia Utilities Commission, 900 Howe St., 6th Fl., PO Box 250, Vancouver, BC V6Z 2N3
604-660-4700, Fax: 604-660-1102, 800-663-1385, commission.secretary@bcuc.com

Manitoba

Manitoba Hydro, 360 Portage Ave., PO Box 815 Main,Winnipeg, MB R3C 2P4
204-474-3311, publicaffairs@hydro.mb.ca
Public Utilities Board, #400, 330 Portage Ave., Winnipeg, MB R3C 0C4
204-945-2638, Fax: 204-945-2643, 866-854-3698, publicutilities@gov.mb.ca

Newfoundland & Labrador

Churchill Falls (Labrador) Corporation Limited, Hydro Place, 500 Columbus Dr., PO Box 12500, St. John's, NL A1B 4K7
709-737-1859, Fax: 709-737-1816
Newfoundland & Labrador Hydro, Hydro Place, Columbus Dr., PO Box 12400, St. John's, NL A1B 4K7
709-737-1400, Fax: 709-737-1800, hydro@nlh.nl.ca
Newfoundland & Labrador Board of Commissioners of Public Utilities, PO Box 21040, St. John's, NL A1A 5B2
709-726-8600, Fax: 709-726-9604, 866-782-0006, ito@pub.nf.ca

Northwest Territories

Northwest Territories Power Corporation, 4 Capital Dr., Hay River, NT X0E 1G2
867-874-5200, Fax: 867-874-5251, info@ntpc.com
Northwest Territories Water Board, 125 Mackenzie Rd., PO Box 2531, Yellowknife, NT X0E 0T0
867-678-2942, Fax: 867-678-2943, info@nwtwb.com

Nova Scotia

Nova Scotia Utility & Review Board, Summit Place, 1601 Lower Water St., 3rd Fl., PO Box 1692 M,Halifax, NS B3J 3S3
902-424-4448, Fax: 902-424-3919, uarb.board@gov.ns.ca

Ontario

Hydro One Inc., North Tower, 483 Bay St., Toronto, ON M5G 2P5
416-345-5000, 877-955-1155, customercommunications@HydroOne.com
Independent Electricity System Operator, PO Box 4474 A,Toronto, ON M5W 4E5
905-403-6900, Fax: 905-403-6921, 888-448-7777, customer.relations@ieso.ca
Ontario Power Generation, 700 University Ave., Toronto, ON M5G 1X6
416-592-2555, 877-592-2555, webmaster@opg.com

Prince Edward Island

Prince Edward Island Regulatory & Appeals Commission, National Bank Tower, #501, 134 Kent St., PO Box 577, Charlottetown, PE C1A 7L1
902-892-3501, Fax: 902-566-4076, 800-501-6268, info@irac.pe.ca

Quebec

Hydro-Québec, 75, boul René-Lévesque ouest, Montréal, QC H2Z 1A4
514-289-2211
Régie de l'énergie, Tour de la Bourse, #2.55, 800, Place Victoria, Montréal, QC H4Z 1A2
514-873-2452, Fax: 514-873-2070, 888-873-2452, secretariat@regie-energie.qc.ca

Saskatchewan

Saskatchewan Power Corporation (SaskPower), 2025 Victoria Ave., Regina, SK S4P 0S1
306-566-3306, Fax: 800-757-6937, 888-757-6937
Saskatchewan Water Corporation (SaskWater), #200, 111 Fairford St. East, Moose Jaw, SK S6H 1C8
Fax: 306-694-3207, 888-230-1111, comm@saskwater.com; customerservice@saskwater.com
SaskEnergy Incorporated, 1777 Victoria Ave., Regina, SK S4P 4K5
306-777-9225, 800-567-8899

Yukon Territory

Yukon Utilities Board, #19, 1114 - 1st Ave., PO Box 31728, Whitehorse, YT Y1A 6L3
867-667-5058, Fax: 867-667-5059, yub@utilitiesboard.yk.ca

PUBLIC WORKS

New Brunswick

Corporate Services Division, Marysville Place, PO Box 6000, Fredericton, NB E3B 5H1
506-453-3742, Fax: 506-444-4400, Reception.Marysville@gnb.ca

Public Works & Government Services Canada, Place du Portage, Phase III, 11, rue Laurier, Ottawa, ON K1A 0S5
questions@tpsgc-pwgsc.gc.ca

Alberta

Alberta Infrastructure, Infrastructure Building, 6950 - 113 St., Edmonton, AB T6H 5V7
780-415-0507, Fax: 780-427-2187, -310-0000, Infra.Contact.Us.m@gov.ab.ca

British Columbia

British Columbia Ministry of Citizens' Services & Open Government, PO Box 9594 Prov Govt,Victoria, BC V8W 9E2
250-952-7623, Fax: 250-952-7628, 800-663-7867, EnquiryBC@gov.bc.ca

Manitoba

Manitoba Infrastructure & Transportation, Legislative Building, #203, 450 Broadway Ave., Winnipeg, MB R3C 0V8
204-945-3723, Fax: 204-945-7610

Newfoundland & Labrador

Newfoundland & Labrador Department of Transportation & Works, Confederation Bldg., West Block, 6th Fl., PO Box 8700, St. John's, NL A1B 4J6
709-729-3679, Fax: 709-729-4285, twminister@gov.nl.ca

Northwest Territories

Department of Public Works & Services, PO Box 1320, Yellowknife, NT X1A 2L9

Nova Scotia

Department of Transportation & Infrastructure Renewal, Johnston Bldg., 1672 Granville St., 2nd Fl., PO Box 186, Halifax, NS B3J 2N2
902-424-2297, Fax: 902-424-0532, tpwpaff@gov.ns.ca

Nunavut

Department of Community & Government Services, W.G. Brown Bldg., 4th Fl., PO Box 1000 700,Iqaluit, NU X0A 0H0
867-975-5400, Fax: 867-975-5305

Prince Edward Island

Prince Edward Island Department of Transportation & Infrastructure Renewal, Jones Bldg., 11 Kent St., 3rd Fl., PO Box 2000, Charlottetown, PE C1A 7N8
902-368-5100, Fax: 902-368-5395

Yukon Territory

Yukon Highways & Public Works, PO Box 2703, Whitehorse, YT Y1A 2C6
867-393-7193, Fax: 867-393-6218, 800-661-0408, hpw-info@gov.yk.ca

PUBLICATIONS

Public Works & Government Services Canada, Place du Portage, Phase III, 11, rue Laurier, Ottawa, ON K1A 0S5
questions@tpsgc-pwgsc.gc.ca

Manitoba

Statutory Publications, #20, 200 Vaughan St., Winnipeg, MB R3C 1T5
204-945-3101, Fax: 204-945-7172, 800-321-1203, statpub@gov.mb.ca

New Brunswick

Justice Services Division, Centennial Building, PO Box 6000, Fredericton, NB E3B 5H1
506-453-2458, Fax: 506-453-3651, general.comments@gnb.ca

Nova Scotia

Communications Nova Scotia, 1723 Hollis St., 3rd Fl., PO Box 608, Halifax, NS B3J 2R7
902-424-7690, Fax: 902-424-0515

Department of Service Nova Scotia & Municipal Relations, 1505 Barrington St., PO Box 216, Halifax, NS B3J 3K5
902-424-5200, Fax: 902-424-0581, 800-670-4357, askus@gov.ns.ca

Nunavut

Nunavut Legislative Assembly, 926 Federal Rd., PO Box 1200, Iqaluit, NU X0A 0H0
867-975-5000, Fax: 867-975-5190, 877-334-7266, leginfo@assembly.nu.ca

Quebec

Ministère de la Culture, des Communications & de la Condition féminine, 225, Grande Allée est, Québec, QC G1R 5G5
888-380-8882

Yukon Territory

Yukon Highways & Public Works, PO Box 2703, Whitehorse, YT Y1A 2C6
867-393-7193, Fax: 867-393-6218, 800-661-0408, hpw-info@gov.yk.ca

PURCHASING

Newfoundland & Labrador

Government Purchasing Agency, 30 Strawberry Marsh Rd., St. John's, NL A1B 4R4
709-729-3348, Fax: 709-729-5817, tenders@gov.nl.ca

MERX, PO Box 11684 Centre-ville,Montreal, QC H3C 6H4
Fax: 888-235-5800, merx@merx.com

Alberta

Alberta Infrastructure, Infrastructure Building, 6950 - 113 St., Edmonton, AB T6H 5V7
780-415-0507, Fax: 780-427-2187, -310-0000, Infra.Contact.Us.m@gov.ab.ca

British Columbia

British Columbia Ministry of Citizens' Services & Open Government, PO Box 9594 Prov Govt,Victoria, BC V8W 9E2
250-952-7623, Fax: 250-952-7628, 800-663-7867, EnquiryBC@gov.bc.ca

Newfoundland & Labrador

Newfoundland & Labrador Department of Service NL, PO Box 8700, St. John's, NL A1B 4J6
709-729-4834, gsinfo@gov.nl.ca

Northwest Territories

Department of Public Works & Services, PO Box 1320, Yellowknife, NT X1A 2L9

Nunavut

Department of Community & Government Services, W.G. Brown Bldg., 4th Fl., PO Box 1000 700,Iqaluit, NU X0A 0H0
867-975-5400, Fax: 867-975-5305

Prince Edward Island

Prince Edward Island Department of Transportation & Infrastructure Renewal, Jones Bldg., 11 Kent St., 3rd Fl., PO Box 2000, Charlottetown, PE C1A 7N8
902-368-5100, Fax: 902-368-5395

RAIL TRANSPORTATION

See Also: Transportation

Transportation Safety Board of Canada, 200 Promenade du Portage, 4th Fl., Ottawa, ON K1A 1K8
819-994-3741, Fax: 819-997-2239, 800-387-3557

VIA Rail Canada Inc., #500, 3, Place Ville-Marie, Montréal, QC H3B 2C9
514-871-6000, Fax: 514-871-6104, 888-842-7245

Manitoba

Manitoba Infrastructure & Transportation, Legislative Building, #203, 450 Broadway Ave., Winnipeg, MB R3C 0V8
204-945-3723, Fax: 204-945-7610

New Brunswick

New Brunswick Department of Transportation & Infrastructure, Kings Place, PO Box 6000, Fredericton, NB E3B 5H1
506-453-3939, Fax: 506-453-2900, Transportation.Web@gnb.ca

Newfoundland & Labrador

Newfoundland & Labrador Department of Transportation & Works, Confederation Bldg., West Block, 6th Fl., PO Box 8700, St. John's, NL A1B 4J6
709-729-3679, Fax: 709-729-4285, twminister@gov.nl.ca

Nova Scotia

Department of Transportation & Infrastructure Renewal, Johnston Bldg., 1672 Granville St., 2nd Fl., PO Box 186, Halifax, NS B3J 2N2
902-424-2297, Fax: 902-424-0532, tpwpaff@gov.ns.ca

Ontario

Metrolinx, #600, 20 Bay St., Toronto, ON M5J 2W3
416-869-3200, Fax: 416-869-3525, 888-438-6646

Quebec

Société du port ferroviaire Baie-Comeau-Hauterive, 18, rte Maritime, Baie-Comeau, QC G4Z 2L6
418-296-6785, Fax: 418-296-2377, societeduport@globetrotter.net

Ministère des Transports, 700, boul René-Lévesque est, 28e étage, Québec, QC G1R 5H1
418-643-6980, Fax: 418-643-2033, 888-355-0511, communications@mtq.gouv.qc.ca

Saskatchewan

Saskatchewan Highways & Infrastructure, Victoria Tower, 1855 Victoria Ave., Regina, SK S4P 3T2
306-787-4800, communications@highways.gov.sk.ca

REAL ESTATE

See Also: Land Titles

Canada Mortgage & Housing Corporation, 700 Montreal Rd., Ottawa, ON K1A 0P7
613-748-2000, Fax: 613-748-2098, 800-668-2642, chic@cmhc-schl.gc.ca

Alberta

Strategic Planning & Financial Services, Commerce Place, 10155 - 102 St., 13th Fl., Edmonton, AB T5J 4G8
780-422-8545

British Columbia

Real Estate Council of British Columbia, #900, 750 West Pender St., Vancouver, BC V6C 2T8
604-683-9664, Fax: 604-683-9017, 877-683-9664, info@recbc.ca

Nova Scotia

Department of Service Nova Scotia & Municipal Relations, 1505 Barrington St., PO Box 216, Halifax, NS B3J 3K5
902-424-5200, Fax: 902-424-0581, 800-670-4357, askus@gov.ns.ca

Nunavut

Legal Registries, Brown Bldg., 1st Fl., PO Box 1000 570,Iqaluit, NU X0A 0H0
Fax: 867-975-6594

Ontario

Ontario Realty Corporation, #2000, 1 Dundas St. West, Toronto, ON M5G 2L5
416-327-3937, Fax: 416-327-1906, 877-863-9672, feedback@ontariorealty.ca

REAL ESTATE

Ontario

Ontario Realty Corporation, #2000, 1 Dundas St. West, Toronto, ON M5G 2L5
416-327-3937, Fax: 416-327-1906, 877-863-9672, feedback@ontariorealty.ca

RECREATION

See Also: Tourism & Tourist Information

Canada Place Corporation, 504 - 999 Canada Place, Vancouver, BC V6C 3E1
604-775-7200, Fax: 604-775-6251, admin@canadaplace.ca

Canadian Heritage, 15 Eddy St., Gatineau, QC K1A 0M5
819-997-0055, 866-811-0055, info@pch.gc.ca

Canadian Tourism Commission, #1400, 1055 Dunsmuir St., PO Box 49230, Vancouver, BC V7X 1L2
604-638-8300

National Battlefields Commission, 390, av de Bernières, Québec, QC G1R 2L7
418-648-3506, Fax: 418-648-3638, information@ccbn-nbc.gc.ca

Parks, PO Box 2703 V-4, Whitehorse, YT Y1A 2C6
867-667-5648, Fax: 867-393-6223, 800-661-0408, yukon.parks@gov.yk.ca

Parks Canada, 25 Eddy St., Gatineau, QC K1A 0M5
613-860-1251, 888-773-8888, information@pc.gc.ca

Wascana Centre Authority, 2900 Wascana Dr., PO Box 7111, Regina, SK S4P 3S7
306-522-3661, Fax: 306-565-2742, wca@wascana.ca

Alberta

Alberta Sport, Recreation, Parks, & Wildlife Foundation, Standard Life Centre, #903, 10405 Jasper Ave., 9th Fl., Edmonton, AB T5J 4R7
780-415-1167, Fax: 780-415-0308, -310-0000

British Columbia

British Columbia Lottery Corporation, 74 West Seymour St., Kamloops, BC V2C 1E2
250-828-5500, Fax: 250-828-5631, 866-815-0222

British Columbia Ministry of Social Development, PO Box 9058 Prov Govt,Victoria, BC V8W 9E1

Office of the Superintendent of Motor Vehicles, PO Box 9254 Prov Govt,Victoria, BC V8W 9J2
250-387-7747, Fax: 250-387-4891, OSMV.Mailbox@gov.bc.ca

Manitoba

Manitoba Entrepreneurship, Training & Trade, #1000, 259 Portage Ave, Winnipeg, MB R3B 3P4
204-945-2475, Fax: 204-945-3977, minctt@leg.gov.mb.ca

Manitoba Lotteries Corporation, 830 Empress St., Winnipeg, MB R3G 3H3
204-957-2500, Fax: 204-957-3991, 800-265-2912, communications@casinosofwinnipeg.com

Manitoba Horse Racing Commission, c/o Boards, Commissions & Legislation Branch, #812, 401 York Ave., Winnipeg, MB R3C 0P8
204-945-4495, Fax: 204-948-2844, gordon.mackenzie@gov.mb.ca

Tourism Secretariat, 155 Carlton St., 7th Fl., Winnipeg, MB R3C 3H8
800-665-0040

New Brunswick

Corporate Services Division, Centennial Building, PO Box 6000, Fredericton, NB E3B 5H1
506-453-3707, Fax: 506-453-5428

New Brunswick Lotteries & Gaming Corporation, Centennial Bldg., 670 King St., PO Box 6000, Fredericton, NB E3B 5H1
506-444-3468, Fax: 506-444-5818

Newfoundland & Labrador
C.A. Pippy Park Commission, Mount Scio House, 15 Mount Scio Rd., St. John's, NL A1B 3T2
709-737-3655, Fax: 709-737-3303, info@pippypark.com
Newfoundland & Labrador Department of Tourism, Culture, & Recreation, Confederation Bldg., West Block, 2nd Fl., PO Box 8700, St. John's, NL A1B 4J6
709-729-0862, Fax: 709-729-0870, tcrinfo@gov.nl.ca
Ontario
Alcohol & Gaming Commission of Ontario, 90 Sheppard Ave. East, Toronto, ON M2N 0A4
416-326-8700, Fax: 416-326-5555, 800-522-2876
Ontario Ministry of Economic Development & Innovation, Hearst Block, 900 Bay St., 8th Fl., Toronto, ON M7A 2E1
416-325-6666, Fax: 416-325-6688, 866-668-4249, info@edt.gov.on.ca
Metro Toronto Convention Centre Corporation, 255 Front St. West, Toronto, ON M5V 2W6
416-585-8120, Fax: 416-585-8198, info@mtccc.com; sales@mtccc.com
Niagara Parks Commission, Oak Hall Administration Bldg., 7400 Portage Rd. South, PO Box 150, Niagara Falls, ON L2E 6T2
905-356-2241, Fax: 905-354-6041, 877-642-7275
Ontario Lottery & Gaming Corporation, Roberta Bondar Pl., #800, 70 Foster Dr., Sault Ste Marie, ON P6A 6V2
705-946-6464, Fax: 416-224-7000, 800-387-0098
Ontario Place Corporation, 955 Lake Shore Blvd. West, Toronto, ON M6K 3B9
416-314-9900, Fax: 416-314-9992
Ottawa Convention Centre, 55 Colonel By Dr., Ottawa, ON K1N 9J2
613-563-1984, Fax: 613-563-7646
St. Lawrence Parks Commission, RR#1, Morrisburg, ON K0C 1X0
613-543-3704, Fax: 613-543-2847, 800-437-2233
Ontario Ministry of Tourism & Culture, Hearst Block, 900 Bay St., 9th Fl., Toronto, ON M7A 2E1
416-326-9326, Fax: 416-314-7854, 800-668-2746
Prince Edward Island
Maritime Provinces Harness Racing Commission, 5 Gerald McCarville Dr., PO Box 128, Kensington, PE C0B 1M0
902-836-5500, Fax: 902-836-5320
Prince Edward Island Department of Community Services & Seniors, Jones Bldg., 11 Kent St., 2nd Fl., PO Box 2000, Charlottetown, PE C1A 7N8
902-620-3777, Fax: 902-368-4740, 866-594-3777
Prince Edward Island Department of Innovation & Advanced Learning, Shaw Bldg., 105 Rochford St., 5th Fl., PO Box 2000, Charlottetown, PE C1A 7N8
902-368-4240, Fax: 902-368-4242
Prince Edward Island Department of Tourism & Culture, PO Box 2000, Charlottetown, PE C1A 7N8
902-368-5540, Fax: 902-368-5277, tpswitch@gov.pe.ca
Quebec
Comité conjoint de chasse, de pêche et de piégeage, #C220, 383 rue Saint-Jacques, Montréal, QC H2Y 1N9
514-284-2151, Fax: 514-284-0039, infohftcc@cccpp-hftcc.com
Régie des alcools, des courses et des jeux, 560, boul Charest est, Québec, QC G1K 3J3
418-643-7667, Fax: 418-643-5971, 800-363-0320
Société des établissements en plein air du Québec, Place de la Cité, Tour Cominar, #250, 2640, boul Laurier, 2e étage, Québec, QC G1V 5C2
418-890-6527, Fax: 418-528-6025, 800-665-6527, inforeservation@sepaq.com
Saskatchewan
Saskatchewan Liquor & Gaming Authority, 2500 Victoria Ave., PO Box 5054, Regina, SK S4P 3M3
306-787-4213, inquiry@slga.gov.sk.ca
Yukon Territory
Yukon Tourism & Culture, 100 Hanson St., Whitehorse, YT Y1A 2C6
867-667-5036, Fax: 867-667-3546
Yukon Lottery Commission, 312 Wood St., Whitehorse, YT Y1A 2E6
867-633-7890, Fax: 867-668-7561, lotteriesyukon@gov.yk.ca

1470
See Also: 1470
See: 1470
Saskatchewan
Sport, Recreation, & Stewardship, 1919 Saskatchewan Dr., 9th Fl., Regina, SK S4P 4H2
306-787-7451, Fax: 306-787-0069
New Brunswick
New Brunswick Department of Culture, Tourism, & Healthy Living, Centennial Building, PO Box 6000, Fredericton, NB E3B 5H1
506-444-5205, Fax: 506-457-4984, taponlinedirectory@gnb.ca

RECYCLING
Alberta
Alberta Recycling Management Authority, Scotia Tower 1, #1310, 10060 Jasper Ave., PO Box 189, Edmonton, AB T5J 2J1
780-990-1111, Fax: 780-990-1122, 888-999-8762, info@albertarecycling.ca
Newfoundland & Labrador
Multi-Materials Stewardship Board, PO Box 8131 A, St. John's, NL A1B 3M9
709-753-0948, Fax: 709-753-0974, 800-901-6672, inquiries@mmsb.nl.ca

RESEARCH
Canada Foundation for Innovation, #450, 230 Queen St., Ottawa, ON K1p 5E4
613-947-6496, Fax: 613-943-0923, info@innovation.ca

RESEARCH & DEVELOPMENT
Bayfield Institute, 867 Lakeshore Rd., PO Box 5050, Burlington, ON L7R 4A6
905-336-6240,
Bedford Institute of Oceanography, 1 Challenger Dr., PO Box 1006, Dartmouth, NS B2Y 4A2
902-426-3492, Fax: 902-426-8484
Biotechnology Research Institute, 6100, av Royalmount, Montréal, QC H4P 2R2
514-496-6100, Fax: 514-496-1928, bri-info@cnrc-nrc.gc.ca
Canada Centre for Remote Sensing - Geomatics Canada, 588 Booth St., Ottawa, ON K1A 0Y7
613-995-0947, Fax: 613-947-1382
Canada Foundation for Innovation, #450, 230 Queen St., Ottawa, ON K1p 5E4
613-947-6496, Fax: 613-943-0923, info@innovation.ca
Canadian Hydraulics Centre, 1200 Montreal Rd., Ottawa, ON K1A 0R6
613-993-9381, Fax: 613-952-7679, info.chc@nrc-cnrc.gc.ca
Canadian Hydrographic Service, 615 Booth St., Ottawa, ON K1A 0E6
613-998-4931, Fax: 613-998-1217, chsinfo@dfo-mpo.gc.ca
Canadian Ice Service, 373 Sussex Dr., Block E, 3rd Fl., Ottawa, ON K1A 0H3
613-996-4489, 800-767-2885, cis-scg.cient@ec.gc.ca
Canadian Space Agency, John H. Chapman Space Centre, 6767, rte de l'Aéroport, Saint-Hubert, QC J3Y 8Y9
450-926-4800, Fax: 450-926-4352, promo@asc-csa.gc.ca
CANMET Energy Technology Centre-Varennes, 1615, boul Lionel-Boulet, CP 4800, Varennes, QC J3X 1S6
450-652-4621, Fax: 450-652-0999, 800-322-8122, canmetenergy.nrcan.gc.ca
Centre for Surface Transportation Technology, 2320 Lester Rd., Ottawa, ON K1V 1S2
613-998-9639, Fax: 613-957-0831, inquiries.cstt@nrc-cnrc.gc.ca
Chalk River Laboratories, NRC Canadian Neutron Beam Centre, Building 459, Station 18, Chalk River, ON K0J 1J0
613-584-8293, 800-364-6989
Fisheries Resource Conservation Council, PO Box 2001 D, Ottawa, ON K1P 5W3
613-998-0433, Fax: 613-998-1146, info@frcc-ccrh.ca
Freshwater Institute, 501 University Cres., Winnipeg, MB R3T 2N6
204-983-5000, Fax: 204-983-6285
Herzberg Institute of Astrophysics, 5071 West Saanich Rd., Victoria, BC V9E 2E7
250-363-0001, Fax: 250-363-0045, hia-www@nrc-cnrc.gc.ca
Industrial Materials Institute, 75, boul de Mortagne, Boucherville, QC J4B 6Y4
450-641-5000, Fax: 450-641-5101, Imi-Info@cnrc-nrc.gc.ca
Institut Maurice-Lamontagne, 850, rte de le Mer, CP 1000, Mont-Joli, QC G5H 3Z4
418-775-0555, Fax: 418-775-0730
Institute for Aerospace Research, 1200 Montreal Rd., Ottawa, ON K1A 0R6
613-990-0765, Fax: 613-952-7214
Institute for Biological Sciences, Bldg. M-54, 1200 Montreal Rd., Ottawa, ON K1A 0R6
613-993-5812, Fax: 613-957-7867
Institute for Chemical Process & Environmental Technology, Bldg. M-12, 1200 Montreal Rd., Ottawa, ON K1A 0R6
613-993-4041, Fax: 613-957-8231
Institute for Marine Biosciences, 1411 Oxford St., Halifax, NS B3H 3Z1
902-426-8332, Fax: 902-426-9413, communications.imb@nrc-cnrc.gc.ca
Institute for National Measurement Standards, Bldg. M-36, 1500 Montreal Rd., Ottawa, ON K1A 0R6
613-998-7018, Fax: 613-954-1473, alexandra.shaw@nrc-cnrc.gc.ca
Institute for Ocean Technology, Kerwin Pl. & Arctic Ave., PO Box 12093, St. John's, NL A1B 3T5
709-772-4939, Fax: 709-772-2462, Noel.Murphy@nrc-cnrc.gc.ca
Institute for Research in Construction, Bldg. M-24, 1500 Montreal Rd., Ottawa, ON K1A 0R6
613-993-2607, Fax: 613-952-7673, Irc.Client-Services@nrc-cnrc.gc.ca
Institute of Ocean Sciences, 9860 West Saanich Rd., PO Box 6000, Sidney, BC V8L 4B2
250-363-6517, Fax: 250-363-6390
London - Centre for Automotive Materials & Manufacturing, 800 Collip Circle, London, ON N6G 4X8
519-430-7166, Fax: 519-430-7064, John.Lyons@nrc-cnrc.gc.ca
National Institute of Nanotechnology, Bldg. NINT, University of Alberta, 11421 Saskatchewan Dr., Edmonton, AB T6G 2M9
780-641-1600, Fax: 780-641-1601, nintinfo@nrc.gc.ca
National Research Council Canada, Bldg. M-58, 1200 Montreal Rd., Ottawa, ON K1A 0R6
613-993-9101, Fax: 613-952-7928, 877-672-2672, info@nrc-cnrc.gc.ca
Natural Sciences & Engineering Research Council of Canada, Constitution Square, Tower II, 350 Albert St., Ottawa, ON K1A 1H5
613-995-4273, Fax: 613-943-1624, marie-josee.duval@nserc-crsng.gc.ca
Office of Energy Research & Development, 580 Booth St., 14th Fl., Ottawa, ON K1A 0E4
613-947-1421, Fax: 613-995-6146
Pacific Biological Station, 3190 Hammond Bay Rd., Nanaimo, BC V9T 6N7
250-756-7000, Fax: 250-756-7053
Plant Biotechnology Institute, 110 Gymnasium Pl., Saskatoon, SK S7N 0W9
306-975-5248, Fax: 306-975-4839, pbi-info@nrc-cnrc.gc.ca
Polar Continental Shelf Program, #487, 615 Booth St., Ottawa, ON K1A 0E4
613-947-1650, Fax: 613-947-1611, pcsp@nrcan-rncan.gc.ca
Research Branch, Tower 5, 1341 Baseline Rd., Ottawa, ON K1A 0C5
613-759-1000, Fax: 613-773-1866
Safe Environments Programme, Environmental Health Centre, Bldg. 8, 120 Parkdale Ave., Ottawa, ON K1A 0K9
613-954-0291, Fax: 613-952-2206
St. Andrews Biological Station, 531 Brandy Cove Rd., St Andrews, NB E5B 2L9
506-529-8854, Fax: 506-529-5862, XMARSABS@mar.dfo-mpo.gc.ca
Transportation Development Centre, Tour Ouest, Complexe Guy-Favreau, 800, boul René-Lévesque ouest, 6e étage, Montréal, QC H3B 1X9
514-283-0000, Fax: 514-283-7158, tdccdt@tc.gc.ca
Alberta
Alberta Innovates - Energy & Environmental Solutions, AMEC Place, #2540, 801 - 6th Ave. SW, Calgary, AB T2P 3W2
403-297-7089, ees@albertainnovates.ca
British Columbia
Powertech Labs Inc., 12388 - 88 Ave., Surrey, BC V8W 7R7
604-590-7500, Fax: 604-590-6611
New Brunswick
New Brunswick Research & Productivity Council, 921 College Hill Rd., Fredericton, NB E3B 6Z9
506-452-1212, Fax: 506-452-1395, info@rpc.ca
Northwest Territories
Aurora Research Institute, 191 MacKenzie Rd., PO Box 1450, Inuvik, NT X0E 0T0
867-777-3298, Fax: 867-777-4264, webmaster@nwtresearch.com
Ontario
Science & Information Resources Division, Roberta Bondar Pl., #400, 70 Foster Dr., Sault Ste Marie, ON P6A 6V5
705-755-2000, Fax: 705-755-2802, 800-667-1940
Prince Edward Island
Agricultural Insurance Corporation, 29 Indigo Cres., PO Box 1600, Charlottetown, PE C1A 7N3
902-368-4842, Fax: 902-368-6677
BIO FOOD TECH, 101 Belvedere Ave., PO Box 2000, Charlottetown, PE C1A 7N8
902-368-5548, Fax: 902-368-5549, 877-368-5548, biofoodtech@biofoodtech.ca
Quebec
Centre de recherche industrielle du Québec, 333, rue Franquet, Québec, QC G1P 4C7
418-659-1550, Fax: 418-652-2251, 800-667-2386, infocriq@criq.qc.ca
Fonds de la recherche en santé du Québec, #800, 500, rue Sherbrooke ouest, Montréal, QC H3A 3C6
514-873-2114, Fax: 514-873-8768

Fonds québécois de la recherche sur la nature et les technologies, #450, 140, Grande Allée est, Québec, QC G1R 5M8
418-643-8560, Fax: 418-643-1451, info@fqrnt.gouv.qc.ca
Innovatech Québec, #410, 888, rue St-Jean, Québec, QC G1R 5H6
418-528-9770, Fax: 418-528-9783, 866-605-1676

Saskatchewan
Saskatchewan Power Corporation (SaskPower), 2025 Victoria Ave., Regina, SK S4P 0S1
306-566-3306, Fax: 800-757-6937, 888-757-6937
Saskatchewan Research Council, #125, 15 Innovation Blvd., Saskatoon, SK S7N 2X8
306-933-5400, Fax: 306-933-7446, info@src.sk.ca

ROUND TABLES

National Round Table on the Environment & Economy, #200, 344 Slater St., Ottawa, ON K1R 7Y3
613-992-7189, Fax: 613-992-7385, info@nrtee-trnee.ca

Manitoba
Manitoba Round Table for Sustainable Development, #160, 123 Main St., Winnipeg, MB R3C 1A5
204-945-1869, Fax: 204-948-2357, mrtsd@gov.mb.ca

SALES TAX

British Columbia
Employment & Labour Market Services Division, PO Box 9762 Prov Govt,Victoria, BC V8W 1A4
250-356-0050, Fax: 250-953-3928
Financial Sector Regulation & Policy, Terrace Building, 9515 - 107 St., 4th Fl., Edmonton, AB T5K 2C3
Secretariat to Commission on the Reform of Ontario's Public Services, Frost Bldg. South, 7 Queen's Park Cres., 1st Fl., Toronto, ON M7A 1YA
416-326-9847, Fax: 416-212-7767

Manitoba
Taxation Division, #101, 401 York Ave., Winnipeg, MB R3C 0P8
204-945-6444, Fax: 204-948-2360

New Brunswick
Revenue & Taxation, Centennial Bldg., #671, 670 King St., PO Box 3000, Fredericton, NB E3B 5G5
506-444-2826, Fax: 506-444-4920

Northwest Territories
Department of Finance, Arthur Laing Building, 5th Fl., 5003 - 49th St., PO Box 1320, Yellowknife, NT X1A 2L9
867-873-7117, Fax: 867-873-0414

Nova Scotia
Provincial Tax Commission, Maritime Centre, 1505 Barrington St., 9th Fl., PO Box 2205, Halifax, NS B3J 2V4
902-424-6300, Fax: 902-424-7434, 800-565-2336

Nunavut
Department of Finance, Bldg. 1079, 1st Fl., PO Box 1000 330,Iqaluit, NU X0A 0H0
867-975-5800, Fax: 867-975-5805

Quebec
Centre de perception fiscale et des biens non réclamés, 3800, rue de Marly, Secteur 6-4-3, Québec, QC G1X 4A5

SCHOOL BOARDS

See: Education

Prince Edward Island
Eastern School District, PO Box 8600, Charlottetown, PE C1A 8V7
902-368-6990, Fax: 902-368-6960
French Language School Board, 1596, rte 124, Abram-Village, PE C0B 2E0
902-854-2975, Fax: 902-854-2981, cslf@edu.pe.ca
Western School Board of Prince Edward Island, Summerside Office, 272 MacEwen Dr., Summerside, PE C1N 2P7
902-888-8400, Fax: 902-888-8449

SCIENCE & NATURE

Aboriginal Affairs & Northern Development Canada, 10 Wellington St., North Tower, Gatineau, QC K1A 0H4
819-997-0380, Fax: 866-817-3977, 800-567-9604, infopubs@aadnc-aandc.gc.ca
Agriculture & Agri-Food Canada, 1341 Baseline Rd., Ottawa, ON K1A 0C5
613-773-1000, Fax: 613-773-2772, 866-345-7972, info@agr.gc.ca
Beverly & Qamanirjuaq Caribou Management Board, Secretariat, PO Box 629, Stonewall, MB R0C 2Z0
204-467-2438, caribounews@arctic-caribou.com
Canada Centre for Remote Sensing - Geomatics Canada, 588 Booth St., Ottawa, ON K1A 0Y7
613-995-0947, Fax: 613-947-1382
Canadian Institutes of Health Research, 160 Elgin St., 9th Fl., Ottawa, ON K1A 0W9
613-941-2672, Fax: 613-954-1800, 888-603-4178, info@cihr-irsc.gc.ca
Canadian Nuclear Safety Commission, 280 Slater St., PO Box 1046 B,Ottawa, ON K1P 5S9
613-995-5894, Fax: 613-995-5086, 800-668-5284
Canadian Polar Commission, Constitution Square, #1710, 360 Albert St., Ottawa, ON K1R 7X7
613-943-8605, Fax: 613-943-8607, 888-765-2701, mail@polarcom.gc.ca
Canadian Space Agency, John H. Chapman Space Centre, 6767, rte de l'Aéroport, Saint-Hubert, QC J3Y 8Y9
450-926-4800, Fax: 450-926-4352, promo@asc-csa.gc.ca
Centre for Surface Transportation Technology, 2320 Lester Rd., Ottawa, ON K1V 1S2
613-998-9639, Fax: 613-957-0831, inquiries.cstt@nrc-cnrc.gc.ca
Commission for Environmental Cooperation, Secretariat, #200, 393, rue St-Jacques ouest, Montréal, QC H2Y 1N9
514-350-4300, Fax: 514-350-4314, info@cec.org
Committee on the Status of Endangered Wildlife in Canada, c/o Canadian Wildlife Service, 351 St. Joseph Blvd, 4th Fl., Gatineau, QC K1A 0H3
819-953-3215, Fax: 819-994-3684, cosewic/cosepac@ec.gc.ca
Ecosystems & Fisheries Management, 200 Kent St., Ottawa, ON K1A 0E6
Electronic Commerce Branch, 300 Slater St., Ottawa, ON K1A 0C8
613-954-5031, Fax: 613-954-2340, 800-328-6189
Environment Canada, 10 Wellington St., Gatineau, QC K1A 0H3
819-997-2800, Fax: 819-994-1412, 800-668-6767, enviroinfo@ec.gc.ca
Environmental Sciences & Standards Division, 135 St. Clair Ave. West, 14th Fl., Toronto, ON M4V 1P5
416-314-6357, Fax: 416-314-6358
Fisheries & Oceans Canada, 200 Kent St., Ottawa, ON K1A 0E6
613-993-0999, Fax: 613-990-1866, info@dfo-mpo.gc.ca
Fisheries Resource Conservation Council, PO Box 2001 D, Ottawa, ON K1P 5W3
613-998-0433, Fax: 613-998-1146, info@frcc-ccrh.ca
Geological Survey of Canada, 601 Booth St., Ottawa, ON K1A 0E8
613-996-3919, Fax: 613-943-8742, esic@nrcan.gc.ca
Hazardous Materials Information Review Commission, 427 Laurier Ave. West, 7th Fl., Ottawa, ON K1A 1M3
613-993-4331, Fax: 613-993-4686, hmirc-ccrmd@hc-sc.gc.ca
Indian Oil & Gas Canada, #100, 9911 Chiila Blvd., Tsuu T'ina (Sarcee), AB T2W 6H6
403-292-5625, Fax: 403-292-5618, ContactIOGC@inac-ainc.gc.ca
Institute for Aerospace Research, 1200 Montreal Rd., Ottawa, ON K1A 0R6
613-990-0765, Fax: 613-952-7214
Institute for Information Technology, Bldg. M-50, 1200 Montreal Rd., Ottawa, ON K1A 0R6
613-991-3373, Fax: 613-952-0074, 877-672-2672
International Development Research Centre, 150 Kent St., PO Box 8500, Ottawa, ON K1G 3H9
613-236-6163, Fax: 613-238-7230, info@idrc.ca
Mackenzie Valley Environmental Impact Review Board, 200 Scotia Centre, #5102, 50th Ave., PO Box 938, Yellowknife, NT X1A 2N7
867-766-7050, Fax: 867-766-7074, 866-912-3472
National Energy Board, 444 - 7 Ave. SW, Calgary, AB T2P 0X8
403-292-4800, Fax: 403-292-5503, 800-899-1265, info@neb-one.gc.ca
National Research Council Canada, Bldg. M-58, 1200 Montreal Rd., Ottawa, ON K1A 0R6
613-993-9101, Fax: 613-952-7928, 877-672-2672, info@nrc-cnrc.ca
National Round Table on the Environment & Economy, #200, 344 Slater St., Ottawa, ON K1R 7Y3
613-992-7189, Fax: 613-992-7385, info@nrtee-trnee.ca
Natural Resources Canada, 580 Booth St., Ottawa, ON K1A 0E4
613-995-0947, Fax: 613-992-7211
Natural Sciences & Engineering Research Council of Canada, Constitution Square, Tower II, 350 Albert St., Ottawa, ON K1A 1H5
613-995-4273, Fax: 613-943-1624, marie-josee.duval@nserc-crsng.gc.ca
North American Bird Conservation Initiative, Canadian Wildlife Service, 351, boul St-Joseph, 3e étage, Gatineau, QC K1A 0H3
819-994-0512, Fax: 819-994-4445, nabci@ec.gc.ca
North American Waterfowl Management Plan, NAWCC (Canada) Secretariat, Place Vincent Massey, 351 St. Joseph Blvd., 7th Fl., Gatineau, QC K1A 0H3
819-934-6034, Fax: 819-934-6017, nawmp@ec.gc.ca
Nunavut Impact Review Board, PO Box 1360, Cambridge Bay, NU X0B 0C0
867-983-4600, Fax: 867-983-2594, 866-233-3033, info@nirb.ca
Nunavut Water Board, PO Box 119, Gjoa Haven, NU X0B 1J0
867-360-6338, Fax: 867-360-6369
Parks, PO Box 2703 V-4, Whitehorse, YT Y1A 2C6
867-667-5648, Fax: 867-393-6223, 800-661-0408, yukon.parks@gov.yk.ca
Pest Management Regulatory Agency, 2720 Riverside Dr., Ottawa, ON K1A 0K9
613-736-3401, Fax: 613-736-3798
Polar Continental Shelf Program, #487, 615 Booth St., Ottawa, ON K1A 0E4
613-947-1650, Fax: 613-947-1611, pcsp@nrcan-rncan.gc.ca
Porcupine Caribou Management Board, PO Box 31723, Whitehorse, YT Y1A 6L3
867-633-4780, Fax: 867-393-3904, pcmb@taiga.net
Program Policy, 200 Kent St., Ottawa, ON K1A 0E6
Provincial Services Division, #6540, 99 Wellesley St. West, Toronto, ON M7A 1W3
416-326-9504
Renewable Resources, Hugh John Flemming Forestry Centre, Suite 310, Fl 3rd, PO Box 6000, Fredericton, NB E3B 5H1
506-453-2684, Fax: 506-453-2684, dnrweb@gnb.ca
Social Sciences & Humanities Research Council of Canada, Constitution Sq., 350 Albert St., PO Box 1610 B,Ottawa, ON K1P 6G4
613-992-0691, Fax: 613-992-1787, info@sshrc.ca

Alberta
Access Advisory Council, Sterling Place, 9940 - 106 St., 4th Fl., Edmonton, AB
780-644-3183
Alberta Agriculture & Rural Development, JG O'Donoghue Bldg., #100A, 7000 - 113th St., Edmonton, AB T6H 5T6
780-427-2727, -310-3276, duke@gov.ab.ca
Alberta Environmental Appeals Board, Peace Hills Trust Tower, #306, 10011 - 109 St., Edmonton, AB T5J 3S8
780-427-6207, Fax: 780-427-4693
Alberta Innovates - Energy & Environmental Solutions, AMEC Place, #2540, 801 - 6th Ave. SW, Calgary, AB T2P 3W2
403-297-7089, ees@albertainnovates.ca
Alberta Innovates - Health Solutions, #1500, 10104 - 103 Ave., Edmonton, AB T5J 4A7
780-423-5727, Fax: 780-429-3509, 877-423-5727, health@albertainnovates.ca
Alberta Livestock & Meat Agency, Ellwood Office Park South, #101, 1003 Ellwood Rd. SW, Edmonton, AB T6X 0B3
780-638-1699, Fax: 780-638-6495, info@almaltd.ca
Alberta Recycling Management Authority, Scotia Tower 1, #1310, 10060 Jasper Ave., PO Box 189, Edmonton, AB T5J 2J1
780-990-1111, Fax: 780-990-1122, 888-999-8762, info@albertarecycling.ca
Alberta Research & Innvoation Authority, Phipps-McKinnon Bldg., #500, 101A Ave., Edmonton, AB T5J 3G2
780-427-1488, Fax: 780-427-0979, aria@albertainnovates.ca
Alberta Sport, Recreation, Parks, & Wildlife Foundation, Standard Life Centre, #903, 10405 Jasper Ave., 9th Fl., Edmonton, AB T5J 4R7
780-415-1167, Fax: 780-415-0308, -310-0000
Alberta Used Oil Management Association, Empire Building, #1008, 10080 Jasper Ave., Edmonton, AB T5J 1V9
780-414-1510, Fax: 780-414-1519, 866-414-1510, reception@usedoilrecycling.ca
Beverage Container Management Board, #750, 10707 - 100 Ave., Edmonton, AB T5J 3M1
780-424-3193, Fax: 780-428-4620, 888-424-7671
Alberta Energy, North Petroleum Plaza, 9945 - 108 St., Edmonton, AB T5K 2G6
780-427-8050, Fax: 780-422-0698, -310-0000, Library.Energy@gov.ab.ca
Alberta Environment & Sustainable Resource Development, Oxbridge Place, 9820 - 106 St., Main Fl., Edmonton, AB T5K 2J6
780-427-2700, Fax: 780-422-4086, -310-0000, env.infocent@gov.ab.ca; srd.infocent@gov.ab.ca
Irrigation Council, Provincial Bldg., 200 - 5 Ave. South, 3rd Fl., Lethbridge, AB T1J 4L1
403-381-5176, Fax: 403-382-4406
Land Compensation Board, 1229 - 91 St. SW, Edmonton, AB T6X 1E9
srb.lcb@gov.ab.ca
Natural Resources Conservation Board, Sterling Place, 9940 - 106 St., Edmonton, AB T5K 2N2
780-422-1977, Fax: 780-427-0607, 866-383-6722, info@nrcb.gov.ab.ca
Special Areas Board, Special Areas Board Administration, 212 - 2nd Ave. West, PO Box 820, Hanna, AB T0J 1P0
403-854-5600, Fax: 403-854-5527, specarea@telus.net

British Columbia

Agricultural Land Commission, #133, 4940 Canada Way, Burnaby, BC V5G 4K6
604-660-7000, Fax: 604-660-7033, ALCBurnaby@Victoria1.gov.bc.ca

British Columbia Farm Industry Review Board, 780 Blanshard St., PO Box 9129 Prov Govt, Victoria, BC V8W 9B5
250-356-8945, Fax: 250-356-5131, firb@gov.bc.ca

British Columbia Ministry of Agriculture, PO Box 9120 Prov Govt,Victoria, BC V8W 9E2
250-387-5121

British Columbia Ministry of Energy, Mines, & Natural Gas (& Responsible for Housing), PO Box 9053 Prov Govt,Victoria, BC V8W 9E2

British Columbia Ministry of Environment, PO Box 9339 Prov Govt,Victoria, BC V8W 9M1
250-387-1161, Fax: 250-387-5669, envmail@gov.bc.ca

British Columbia Ministry of Forests, Lands & Natural Resource Operations, PO Box 9352 Prov Govt,Victoria, BC V8W 9M1
250-387-4809, 877-855-3222, FLNRO.MediaRequests@gov.bc.ca

Emergency Management BC, PO Box 9223 Prov Govt,Victoria, BC V8W 9J1
250-953-4002, Fax: 250-953-4081, BC.CorSer@gov.bc.ca (Coroner); OFC@gov.bc.ca (Fire Commissioner)

Environmental Appeal Board, 747 Fort St., 4th Fl., PO Box 9425 Prov Govt, Victoria, BC V8W 3E9
250-387-3464, Fax: 250-356-9923, eabinfo@gov.bc.ca

Environmental Protection Division, PO Box 9339, Victoria, BC V8W 9M1
250-387-1288, Fax: 250-387-5669

Environmental Stewardship Division, PO Box 9339 Prov Govt,Victoria, BC V8W 9M1
250-356-0121, Fax: 250-387-5669

Forest Appeals Commission, 747 Fort St., 4th Fl., PO Box 9425 Prov Govt, Victoria, BC V8W 9V1
250-387-3464, Fax: 250-356-9923, facinfo@gov.bc.ca

Forest Practices Board, 1675 Douglas St., 3rd Fl., PO Box 9905 Prov Govt, Victoria, BC V8W 9R1
250-213-4700, Fax: 250-213-4725, 800-994-5899, fpboard@gov.bc.ca

Forestry Innovation Investment Ltd., #1200, 1130 West Pender St., Vancouver, BC V6E 4A4
604-685-7507, Fax: 604-685-5373, info@bcfii.ca

Islands Trust, #200, 1627 Fort St., Victoria, BC V8R 1H8
250-405-5151, Fax: 250-405-5155, information@islandstrust.bc.ca

Oil & Gas Commission, #100, 10003 - 110 Ave., Fort St John, BC V1J 6M7
250-794-5200, Fax: 250-794-5375

Timber Export Advisory Committee, PO Box 9514 Prov Govt, Victoria, BC V8W 9C2
250-387-8916, Fax: 250-387-5050

Manitoba

Manitoba Aboriginal & Northern Affairs, Legislative Bldg, 344-450 Broadway, Winnipeg, MB R3C 0V8
204-945-3719, Fax: 204-945-8374, anaweb@gov.mb.ca

Aboriginal Affairs Secretariat, #200, 500 Portage Ave., Winnipeg, MB R3C 3X1
204-945-2510, Fax: 204-945-3689

Agricultural Societies, 1129 Queens Ave., Brandon, MB R7A 1L9
204-726-6195, Fax: 204-726-6260

Manitoba Agriculture, Food & Rural Initiatives, Legislative Bldg., 165-450 Broadway, Winnipeg, MB R3C 0V8
204-945-3722, Fax: 204-945-3470, minagr@leg.gov.mb.ca

Clean Environment Commission, #305, 155 Carlton St., Winnipeg, MB R3C 3H8
204-945-0594, Fax: 204-945-0090

Manitoba Conservation & Water Stewardship, 200 Saulteaux Cres., Winnipeg, MB R3J 3W3
800-214-6497, mws@gov.mb.ca

Ecological Reserves Advisory Committee, c/o Manitoba Conservation, Parks & Natural Areas Branch, 200 Saulteaux Cres., Winnipeg, MB R3J 3W3
204-945-4148, Fax: 204-945-0012, hhernandez@gov.mb.ca

Endangered Species Advisory Committee, 200 Saulteaux Cres., PO Box 24, Winnipeg, MB R3J 3W3
204-945-7465, Fax: 204-945-3077

Farm Lands Ownership Board, #812, Norquay Bldg., 401 York Ave., Winnipeg, MB R3C 0P8
204-945-3149, Fax: 204-945-1489, 800-282-8069, robert.mckenzie@gov.mb.ca

Farm Machinery Board, Norquay Bldg., #812, 401 York Ave., Winnipeg, MB R3C 0P8
204-945-3856, Fax: 204-948-2844, randy.ozunko@gov.mb.ca

Manitoba Hydro, 360 Portage Ave., PO Box 815 Main,Winnipeg, MB R3C 2P4
204-474-3311, publicaffairs@hydro.mb.ca

Local Government Development Division, 59 Elizabeth Dr., PO Box 33, Thompson, MB R8N 1X4
204-677-6794, Fax: 204-677-6525

Manitoba Habitat Heritage Corporation, #200, 1555 St. James St., Winnipeg, MB R3H 1B5
204-784-4350, Fax: 204-784-7359, mhhc@mhhc.mb.ca

New Brunswick

New Brunswick Department of Agriculture, Aquaculture & Fisheries, Agricultural Research Station (Experimental Farm), PO Box 6000, Fredericton, NB E3B 5H1
506-453-2666, Fax: 506-453-7170, DAAF-MAAP@gnb.ca

New Brunswick Department of Environment & Local Government, Marysville Place, PO Box 6000, Fredericton, NB E3B 5H1
506-453-2690, Fax: 506-457-4994, elg/egl-info@gnb.ca

New Brunswick Department of Natural Resources, Hugh John Flemming Forestry Centre, PO Box 6000, Fredericton, NB E3B 5H1
506-453-3826, Fax: 506-444-4367, dnrweb@gnb.ca

New Brunswick Farm Products Commission, c/o Department of Agriculture, Aquaculture & Fisheries, PO Box 6000, Fredericton, NB E3B 5H1
506-453-3647, Fax: 506-444-5969

Northern Development Division, Harbourview Place, #400, 275 Main St., Bathurst, NB E2A 1A9
506-547-2227, Fax: 506-547-2269

New Brunswick Research & Productivity Council, 921 College Hill Rd., Fredericton, NB E3B 6Z9
506-452-1212, Fax: 506-452-1395, info@rpc.ca

Newfoundland & Labrador

C.A. Pippy Park Commission, Mount Scio House, 15 Mount Scio Rd., St. John's, NL A1B 3T2
709-737-3655, Fax: 709-737-3303, info@pippypark.com

Newfoundland & Labrador Department of Environment & Conservation, Confederation Bldg., West Block, 4th Fl., PO Box 8700, St. John's, NL A1B 4J6
709-729-2664, Fax: 709-729-6639, 800-563-6181, info@gov.nl.ca

Newfoundland & Labrador Department of Fisheries & Aquaculture, Petten Bldg., 30 Strawberry Marsh Rd., PO Box 8700, St. John's, NL A1B 4J6
709-729-3723, Fax: 709-729-6082, fisheries@gov.nl.ca

Newfoundland & Labrador Department of Natural Resources, Natural Resources Bldg., 50 Elizabeth Ave., 7th Fl., PO Box 8700, St. John's, NL A1B 4J6
709-729-2920, Fax: 709-729-0059

Professional Fish Harvesters Certification Board, 368 Hamilton Ave., PO Box 8541, St. John's, NL A1B 3P2
709-722-8170, Fax: 709-722-8201, pfh@pfhcb.com

Northwest Territories

Aurora Research Institute, 191 MacKenzie Rd., PO Box 1450, Inuvik, NT X0E 0T0
867-777-3298, Fax: 867-777-4264, webmaster@nwtresearch.com

Department of Environment & Natural Resources, PO Box 1320, Yellowknife, NT X1A 2L9

Nova Scotia

Department of Agriculture, 1741 Brunswick St., 3rd Fl., PO Box 2223, Halifax, NS B3J 3C4
902-424-4560, Fax: 902-424-4671

Crown Land Information Management Centre, Founders Square, #501, 1701 Hollis St., PO Box 698, Halifax, NS B3J 2T9
902-424-3171

Geomatics Centre, 160 Willow St., Amherst, NS B4H 3W5
902-667-7231, Fax: 902-667-6008, 800-798-0706, geoinfo@gov.ns.ca

Department of Natural Resources, Founder's Square, 1701 Hollis St., 3rd Fl., PO Box 698, Halifax, NS B3J 2T9
902-424-5935, Fax: 902-424-0594, 800-565-2224

Nova Scotia Farm Loan Board, PO Box 550, Truro, NS B2N 5E3
902-893-6506, Fax: 902-895-7693, flb@gov.ns.ca

Nunavut

Department of Environment, PO Box 1000 1300,Iqaluit, NU X0A 0H0
867-975-7700, Fax: 867-975-7742, environment@gov.nu.ca

Ontario

Advisory Council on Drinking Water Quality & Testing Standards, 40 St. Clair Ave. West, 3rd Fl., Toronto, ON M4V 1M2
416-212-7779, Fax: 416-212-7595

Ontario Ministry of Agriculture, Food & Rural Affairs, Ontario Government Bldg., 1 Stone Rd. West, Guelph, ON N1G 4Y2
519-826-3100, 888-466-2372

Algonquin Forestry Authority - Huntsville, 222 Main St. West, Huntsville, ON P1H 1Y1
705-789-9647, Fax: 705-789-3353, info@algonquinforestry.on.ca

Algonquin Forestry Authority - Pembroke, Victoria Centre, 84 Isabella St., 2nd Fl., Pembroke, ON K8A 5S5
613-735-0173, Fax: 613-735-4192, info@algonquinforestry.on.ca

Animal Care Review Board, 77 Grenville St., 8th Fl., Toronto, ON M5S 1B3
416-314-3509, Fax: 416-314-3518

Association of Ontario Land Surveyors, 1043 McNicoll Ave., Toronto, ON M1W 3W6
416-491-9020, Fax: 416-491-2576

Cancer Care Ontario, 620 University Ave., 15th Fl., Toronto, ON M5G 2L7
416-971-9800, Fax: 416-971-6888

Conservation Review Board, 400 University Ave. 4th Fl., Toronto, ON M7A 2R9
416-314-7137, Fax: 416-314-7175, conservation.review.board@ontario.ca

Ontario Ministry of Environment, 135 St. Clair Ave. West, Toronto, ON M4V 1P5
416-325-4000, Fax: 416-325-3159, 800-565-4923

Environmental Commissioner of Ontario, #605, 1075 Bay St., Toronto, ON M5S 2B1
416-325-3377, Fax: 416-325-3370, 800-701-6454, commissioner@eco.on.ca

Environmental Review Tribunal, #1500, 655 Bay St., Toronto, ON M5G 1E5
416-212-6349, Fax: 416-314-4506, 866-448-2248, erttribunalsecretary@ontario.ca

Lake of the Woods Control Board, c/o Executive Engineer, Ottawa, ON K1A 0H3
Fax: 819-953-4666, 800-661-5922, secretariat@lwcb.ca

Livestock Medicines Advisory Committee, 1 Stone Rd. West, 3rd Fl. Northeast, Guelph, ON N1G 4Y2
519-826-4110, Fax: 519-826-3254

Mines & Minerals Division, Willet Green Miller Centre, 933 Ramsey Lake Rd., Sudbury, ON P3E 6B5
705-670-5755, Fax: 705-670-5818, 888-415-9845

Ontario Ministry of Natural Resources, Whitney Block, #6630, 99 Wellesley St. West, 6th Fl., Toronto, ON M7A 1W3
800-667-1940

Niagara Parks Commission, Oak Hall Administration Bldg., 7400 Portage Rd. South, PO Box 150, Niagara Falls, ON L2E 6T2
905-356-2241, Fax: 905-354-6041, 877-642-7275

Ontario Ministry of Northern Development & Mines, 159 Cedar St., Sudbury, ON P3E 6A5
Fax: 416-327-0651, 888-415-9845

Ontario Clean Water Agency, 1 Yonge St., 17th Fl., Toronto, ON M5E 1E5
416-314-5600, Fax: 416-314-8300, 800-667-6292

Ontario Fish & Wildlife Heritage Commission, Robinson Pl., 300 Water St., PO Box 7000, Peterborough, ON K9J 8M5
705-755-1905, Fax: 705-755-1900

Ontario Geographic Names Board, Robinson Place, 300 Water St., 2nd Fl., PO Box 7000, Peterborough, ON K9J 8M5
705-755-2134

Ontario Moose & Bear Allocation Advisory Committee, PO Box 964, Sioux Lookout, ON P8T 1B3
807-737-2615, Fax: 807-737-4173

Ontario Science Centre, 770 Don Mills Rd., Toronto, ON M3C 1T3
416-696-1000, Fax: 416-696-3124

Pesticides Advisory Committee, 135 St. Clair Ave. West, 15th Fl., Toronto, ON M4V 1P5
416-314-9230, Fax: 416-314-9237

Rabies Advisory Committee, Trent University Science Complex, PO Box 4840, Peterborough, ON K9J 8N8
705-755-2270

Royal Botanical Gardens, 680 Plains Rd. West, Burlington, ON L7T 4H4
905-527-1158, Fax: 905-577-0375, 800-694-4769

Science & Information Resources Division, Roberta Bondar Pl., #400, 70 Foster Dr., Sault Ste Marie, ON P6A 6V5
705-755-2000, Fax: 705-755-2802, 800-667-1940

Science North, 100 Ramsey Lake Rd., Sudbury, ON P3E 5S9
705-522-3701, Fax: 705-522-4954

Shibogama Interim Planning Board, PO Box 105, Wunnumin, ON P0V 2Z0
807-442-2559, Fax: 807-442-2627

St. Lawrence Parks Commission, RR#1, Morrisburg, ON K0C 1X0
613-543-3704, Fax: 613-543-2847, 800-437-2233

Windigo Interim Planning Board, PO Box 299, Sioux Lookout, ON P8T 1A3
807-737-1585, Fax: 807-737-3133

Prince Edward Island

Agricultural Insurance Corporation, 29 Indigo Cres., PO Box 1600, Charlottetown, PE C1A 7N3
902-368-4842, Fax: 902-368-6677

Grain Elevators Corporation, 7 Gerald McCarville Dr., PO Box 250, Kensington, PE C0B 1M0
902-836-8935, Fax: 902-836-8926

Prince Edward Island Department of Agriculture & Forestry, Jones Bldg., 11 Kent St., PO Box 2000, Charlottetown, PE C1A 7N8
902-368-4880, Fax: 902-368-4857

Prince Edward Island Energy Corporation, Jones Bldg., 11 Kent St., 4th Fl., PO Box 2000, Charlottetown, PE C1A 7N8

Quebec

Ministère de l'Agriculture, des Pêcheries et de l'Alimentation, 200, ch Sainte-Foy, Québec, QC G1R 4X6
418-380-2110, 888-222-6272

Bureau d'audiences publiques sur l'environnement, Édifice Lomer-Gouin, #2.10, 575, rue Saint-Amable, Québec, QC G1R 6A6
418-643-7447, Fax: 418-643-9474, 800-463-4732, communication@bape.gouv.qc.ca

Comité consultatif de l'environnement Kativik, CP 930, Kuujjuaq, QC J0M 1C0
819-964-2961, Fax: 819-964-0694

Fondation de la faune du Québec, Place Iberville II, #420, 1175, av Lavigerie, Québec, QC G1V 4P1
418-644-7926, Fax: 418-643-7655, 877-639-0742, ffq@fondationdelafaune.qc.ca

Fonds québécois de la recherche sur la nature et les technologies, #450, 140, Grande Allée est, Québec, QC G1R 5M8
418-643-8560, Fax: 418-643-1451, info@fqrnt.gouv.qc.ca

Ottawa River Regulation Planning Board, 351 St Joseph Blvd., Hull, QC J8Y 3Z5
613-994-7079, 800-778-1246, secretariat@ottawariver.ca

Ministère des Ressources naturelles, 880, ch Sainte-Foy, Québec, QC G1S 4X4
418-627-8600, Fax: 418-644-6513, 866-248-6936, services.clientele@mrnf.gouv.qc.ca

Régie de l'énergie, Tour de la Bourse, #2.55, 800, Place Victoria, Montréal, QC H4Z 1A2
514-873-2452, Fax: 514-873-2070, 888-873-2452, secretariat@regie-energie.qc.ca

Société de développement de la Baie James, 110, boul Matagami, CP 970, Matagami, QC J0Y 2A0
819-739-4717, Fax: 819-739-4329, mat@sdbj.gouv.qc.ca

Saskatchewan

Agri-Food Council, #302, 3085 Albert St., Regina, SK S4S 0B1
306-787-5978, Fax: 306-787-5134, corey.ruud@gov.sk.ca

Agricultural Implements Board, #202, 3085 Albert St., Regina, SK S4S 0B1
306-787-4693, Fax: 306-787-1315

Enterprise Saskatchewan, #200, 3085 Albert St., Regina, SK S4S 0B1
306-787-4484, Fax: 306-798-0629, invest@gov.sk.ca

Farm Stress Unit, #125, 3085 Albert St., Regina, SK S4S 0B1
306-787-5196, Fax: 306-798-3042, 800-667-4442

Health Quality Council, 241, 111 Research Dr., Saskatoon, SK S7N 3R2
306-668-8810, Fax: 306-668-8820, info@hqc.sk.ca

Prairie Agricultural Machinery Institute, Hwy 5 West, PO Box 1150, Humboldt, SK S0K 2A0
306-682-2555, Fax: 306-682-5080, 800-567-7264, humboldt@pami.ca

Saskatchewan Agriculture, Walter Scott Bldg., 3085 Albert St., Regina, SK S4S 0B1
866-457-2377, aginfo@gov.sk.ca

Saskatchewan Conservation Data Centre, 3211 Albert St., Regina, SK S4S 5W6
306-787-9038, Fax: 306-787-9544

Saskatchewan Crop Insurance Corporation, 484 Prince William Dr., PO Box 3000, Melville, SK S0A 2P0
306-728-7200, Fax: 306-728-7202, 888-935-0000, customer.service@scic.gov.sk.ca

Saskatchewan Environment, 3211 Albert St., 2nd Fl., Regina, SK S4S 5W6
306-787-2584, Fax: 306-787-9544, 800-567-4224, Centre.Inquiry@gov.sk.ca

Saskatchewan Lands Appeal Board, #202, 3085 Albert St., Regina, SK S4S 0B1
306-787-4693, Fax: 306-787-1315, Donald.Brooks@gov.sk.ca

Saskatchewan Research Council, #125, 15 Innovation Blvd., Saskatoon, SK S7N 2X8
306-933-5400, Fax: 306-933-7446, info@src.sk.ca

Surface Rights Board of Arbitration, 113 - 2nd Ave. East, PO Box 1597, Kindersley, SK S0L 1S0
306-463-5447, Fax: 306-463-5449, surfacerightsboard@gov.sk.ca

Yukon Territory

Alsek Renewable Resource Council, PO Box 2077, Haines Junction, YT Y0B 1L0
867-634-2524, Fax: 867-634-2527

Carmacks Renewable Resource Council, PO Box 122, Carmacks, YT Y0B 1C0
867-863-6838, Fax: 867-863-6429, carmacksrrc@northwestel.net

Dawson District Renewable Resource Council, PO Box 1380, Dawson City, YT Y0B 1G0
867-993-6976, Fax: 867-993-6093, dawsonrrc@northwestel.net

Yukon Development Corporation, #2 Miles Canyon Rd., PO Box 5920, Whitehorse, YT Y1A 6S7
867-393-5337, Fax: 867-393-5401

Yukon Environment, PO Box 2703, Whitehorse, YT Y1A 2C6
867-667-5652, Fax: 867-393-7197, environment.yukon@gov.yk.ca

Mayo District Renewable Resources Council, PO Box 249, Mayo, YT Y0B 1M0
867-996-2942, Fax: 867-996-2948, mayorrc@yknet.yk.ca

North Yukon Renewable Resources Council, PO Box 80, Old Crow, YT Y0B 1N0
867-966-3034, Fax: 867-966-3036, vgrrc@yknet.yk.ca

Selkirk Renewable Resources Council, PO Box 32, Pelly Crossing, YT Y0B 1P0
867-537-3937, Fax: 867-537-3939, selkirkrrc@yknet.yk.ca

Teslin Renewable Resource Council, PO Box 186, Teslin, YT Y0A 1B0
867-390-2323, Fax: 867-390-2919, teslinrrc@northwestel.net

Yukon Fish & Wildlife Management Board, 106 Main St., 2nd Fl., Whitehorse, YT Y1A 5P7
867-667-3754, Fax: 867-393-6947, officemanager@yfwmb.ca

Yukon Land Use Planning Council, #201, 307 Jarvis St., Whitehorse, YT Y1A 2H3
867-667-7397, Fax: 867-667-4624, ylupc@planyukon.ca

SCIENCE & TECHNOLOGY

See Also: Business Development

Bedford Institute of Oceanography, 1 Challenger Dr., PO Box 1006, Dartmouth, NS B2Y 4A2
902-426-3492, Fax: 902-426-8484

Biotechnology Research Institute, 6100, av Royalmount, Montréal, QC H4P 2R2
514-496-6100, Fax: 514-496-1928, bri-info@cnrc-nrc.gc.ca

Canada Centre for Remote Sensing - Geomatics Canada, 588 Booth St., Ottawa, ON K1A 0Y7
613-995-0947, Fax: 613-947-1382

Canada Foundation for Innovation, #450, 230 Queen St., Ottawa, ON K1p 5E4
613-947-6496, Fax: 613-943-0923, info@innovation.ca

Canada Science & Technology Museum Corporation, PO Box 9724 T,Ottawa, ON K1G 5A3
613-991-6090, Fax: 613-990-3636, info@technomuses.ca

Canadian Food Inspection Agency, 1400 Merivale Rd., Ottawa, ON K1A 0Y9
613-225-2342, Fax: 613-228-6601, 800-442-2342

Canadian Hydraulics Centre, 1200 Montreal Rd., Ottawa, ON K1A 0R6
613-993-9381, Fax: 613-952-7679, info.chc@nrc-cnrc.gc.ca

Canadian Institutes of Health Research, 160 Elgin St., 9th Fl., Ottawa, ON K1A 0W9
613-941-2672, Fax: 613-954-1800, 888-603-4178, info@cihr-irsc.gc.ca

Canadian Space Agency, John H. Chapman Space Centre, 6767, rte de l'Aéroport, Saint-Hubert, QC J3Y 8Y9
450-926-4800, Fax: 450-926-4352, promo@asc-csa.gc.ca

CANMET Energy Technology Centre-Devon, 1 Oil Patch Dr., #A202, PO Box 1280, Devon, AB T9G 1A8
780-987-8614, Fax: 780-987-8690, hamza@nrcan.gc.ca

Chalk River Laboratories, NRC Canadian Neutron Beam Centre, Building 459, Station 18, Chalk River, ON K0J 1J0
613-584-8293, 800-364-6989

Environmental Sciences & Standards Division, 135 St. Clair Ave. West, 14th Fl., Toronto, ON M4V 1P5
416-314-6357, Fax: 416-314-6358

Freshwater Institute, 501 University Cres., Winnipeg, MB R3T 2N6
204-983-5000, Fax: 204-983-6285

Herzberg Institute of Astrophysics, 5071 West Saanich Rd., Victoria, BC V9E 2E7
250-363-0001, Fax: 250-363-0045, hia-www@nrc-cnrc.gc.ca

Industrial Materials Institute, 75, boul de Mortagne, Boucherville, QC J4B 6Y4
450-641-5000, Fax: 450-641-5101, Imi-Info@cnrc-nrc.gc.ca

Institut Maurice-Lamontagne, 850, rte de le Mer, CP 1000, Mont-Joli, QC G5H 3Z4
418-775-0555, Fax: 418-775-0730

Institute for Biological Sciences, Bldg. M-54, 1200 Montreal Rd., Ottawa, ON K1A 0R6
613-993-5812, Fax: 613-957-7867

Institute for Chemical Process & Environmental Technology, Bldg. M-12, 1200 Montreal Rd., Ottawa, ON K1A 0R6
613-993-4041, Fax: 613-957-8231

Institute for Marine Biosciences, 1411 Oxford St., Halifax, NS B3H 3Z1
902-426-8332, Fax: 902-426-9413, communications.imb@nrc-cnrc.gc.ca

Institute for National Measurement Standards, Bldg. M-36, 1500 Montreal Rd., Ottawa, ON K1A 0R6
613-998-7018, Fax: 613-954-1473, alexandra.shaw@nrc-cnrc.gc.ca

Institute for Ocean Technology, Kerwin Pl. & Arctic Ave., PO Box 12093, St. John's, NL A1B 3T5
709-772-4939, Fax: 709-772-2462, Noel.Murphy@nrc-cnrc.gc.ca

Institute for Research in Construction, Bldg. M-24, 1500 Montreal Rd., Ottawa, ON K1A 0R6
613-993-2607, Fax: 613-952-7673, Irc.Client-Services@nrc-cnrc.gc.ca

Institute of Ocean Sciences, 9860 West Saanich Rd., PO Box 6000, Sidney, BC V8L 4B2
250-363-6517, Fax: 250-363-6390

International Development Research Centre, 150 Kent St., PO Box 8500, Ottawa, ON K1G 3H9
613-236-6163, Fax: 613-238-7230, info@idrc.ca

National Research Council Canada, Bldg. M-58, 1200 Montreal Rd., Ottawa, ON K1A 0R6
613-993-9101, Fax: 613-952-7928, 877-672-2672, info@nrc-cnrc.ca

Natural Sciences & Engineering Research Council of Canada, Constitution Square, Tower II, 350 Albert St., Ottawa, ON K1A 1H5
613-995-4273, Fax: 613-943-1624, marie-josee.duval@nserc-crsng.gc.ca

Office of Energy Research & Development, 580 Booth St., 14th Fl., Ottawa, ON K1A 0E4
613-947-1421, Fax: 613-995-6146

Pacific Biological Station, 3190 Hammond Bay Rd., Nanaimo, BC V9T 6N7
250-756-7000, Fax: 250-756-7053,

Plant Biotechnology Institute, 110 Gymnasium Pl., Saskatoon, SK S7N 0W9
306-975-5248, Fax: 306-975-4839, pbi-info@nrc-cnrc.gc.ca

Polar Continental Shelf Program, #487, 615 Booth St., Ottawa, ON K1A 0E4
613-947-1650, Fax: 613-947-1611, pcsp@nrcan-rncan.gc.ca

Program Policy, 200 Kent St., Ottawa, ON K1A 0E6

Safe Environments Programme, Environmental Health Centre, Bldg. 8, 120 Parkdale Ave., Ottawa, ON K1A 0K9
613-954-0291, Fax: 613-952-2206

Soil, Plant & Feed Laboratory, Brookfield Rd., PO Box 8700, St. John's, NL A1B 4J6
709-729-6738, Fax: 709-729-6734

Spectrum, Information Technologies & Telecommunications, Journal Tower North, 300 Slater St., 20th Fl., Ottawa, ON K1A 0C8
613-998-0368, Fax: 613-952-1203

St. Andrews Biological Station, 531 Brandy Cove Rd., St Andrews, NB E5B 2L9
506-529-8854, Fax: 506-529-5862, XMARSABS@mar.dfo-mpo.gc.ca

Transportation Development Centre, Tour Ouest, Complexe Guy-Favreau, 800, boul René-Lévesque ouest, 6e étage, Montréal, QC H3B 1X9
514-283-0000, Fax: 514-283-7158, tdccdt@tc.gc.ca

Alberta

Alberta Innovates - Energy & Environmental Solutions, AMEC Place, #2540, 801 - 6th Ave. SW, Calgary, AB T2P 3W2
403-297-7089, ees@albertainnovates.ca

British Columbia

Leading Edge Endowment Fund Board, 1188 West Georgia St., 9th Fl., Vancouver, BC V6E 4A2
604-438-3220, contact@leefbc.ca

Powertech Labs Inc., 12388 - 88 Ave., Surrey, BC V8W 7R7
604-590-7500, Fax: 604-590-6611

Manitoba

Industrial Technology Centre, #200, 78 Innovation Dr., Winnipeg, MB R3T 6C2

Manitoba Education, Research & Learning Information Networks, #100 - 135 Innovation Dr., University of Manitoba, Winnipeg, MB R3T 6A8
204-474-7800, Fax: 204-474-7830, 800-430-6404

New Brunswick

Northern Development Division, Harbourview Place, #400, 275 Main St., Bathurst, NB E2A 1A9
506-547-2227, Fax: 506-547-2269

Partnerships & Innovation Division, Marysville Place, PO Box 6000, Fredericton, NB E3B 5H1
506-453-2862, Fax: 506-453-2265, elg/egl-info@gnb.ca

New Brunswick Research & Productivity Council, 921 College Hill Rd., Fredericton, NB E3B 6Z9
506-452-1212, Fax: 506-452-1395, info@rpc.ca

Northwest Territories

Aurora Research Institute, 191 MacKenzie Rd., PO Box 1450, Inuvik, NT X0E 0T0
867-777-3298, Fax: 867-777-4264, webmaster@nwtresearch.com

Nova Scotia

InNOVACorp, #1400, 1801 Hollis St., Halifax, NS B3J 3N4
902-424-8670, Fax: 902-424-4679, 800-565-7051, communications@innovacorp.ca

Ontario
Ontario Science Centre, 770 Don Mills Rd., Toronto, ON M3C 1T3
416-696-1000, Fax: 416-696-3124
Science North, 100 Ramsey Lake Rd., Sudbury, ON P3E 5S9
705-522-3701, Fax: 705-522-4954
Prince Edward Island
Prince Edward Island Department of Environment, Labour & Justice, Shaw Bldg. South, 95 Rochford St., 4th Fl., PO Box 2000, Charlottetown, PE C1A 7N8
902-620-3774, Fax: 902-368-4242, rrryder@gov.pe.ca
Quebec
Centre de recherche industrielle du Québec, 333, rue Franquet, Québec, QC G1P 4C7
418-659-1550, Fax: 418-652-2251, 800-667-2386, infocriq@criq.qc.ca
Fonds québécois de la recherche sur la nature et les technologies, #450, 140, Grande Allée est, Québec, QC G1R 5M8
418-643-8560, Fax: 418-643-1451, info@fqrnt.gouv.qc.ca
Saskatchewan
Saskatchewan Research Council, #125, 15 Innovation Blvd., Saskatoon, SK S7N 2X8
306-933-5400, Fax: 306-933-7446, info@src.sk.ca
Yukon Territory
Yukon Energy, Mines & Resources, PO Box 2703, Whitehorse, YT Y1A 2C6
867-667-3130, Fax: 867-456-3965, 800-661-0408, emr@gov.yk.ca

SECURITIES ADMINISTRATION
See Also: Finance
Newfoundland & Labrador
Consumer & Commercial Affairs Branch, PO Box 8700, St. John's, NL A1B 4J6
709-729-2570, Fax: 709-729-4151, gsinfo@gov.nl.ca
New Brunswick Securities Commission, #300, 85 Charloote St., Saint John, NB E2L 2J2
506-658-3060, Fax: 506-658-3059, 866-933-2222, information@nbsc-cvmnb.ca
Alberta
Alberta Securities Commission, #600, 250 - 5th St. SW, Calgary, AB T2P 0R4
403-297-6454, Fax: 403-297-6156, 877-355-0585, inquiries@asc.ca; media@asc.ca; complaints@asc.ca
British Columbia
British Columbia Securities Commission, Pacific Centre, 701 West Georgia St., 12th Fl., PO Box 10142, Vancouver, BC V7Y 1L2
604-899-6500, Fax: 604-899-6506, 800-373-6393, inquiries@bcsc.bc.ca
Manitoba
Manitoba Securities Commission, #500, 400 St. Mary Ave., Winnipeg, MB R3C 4K5
204-945-2548, Fax: 204-945-0330, 800-655-5244, securities@gov.mb.ca
Northwest Territories
Department of Justice, Courthouse, 4903 - 49th St., 6th Fl., PO Box 1320, Yellowknife, NT X1A 2L9
867-920-6197
Ontario
Ontario Securities Commission, #1903, 20 Queen St. West, PO Box 55, Toronto, ON M5H 3S8
416-597-0681, Fax: 416-593-8241
Saskatchewan
Saskatchewan Financial Services Commission, #601, 1919 Saskatchewan Dr., Regina, SK S4P 4H2
306-787-5645, Fax: 306-787-5899

SENIOR CITIZENS SERVICES
National Seniors Council, Place Vanier, Tower B, 355 North River Rd. 14th Fl., PO Box 4, Ottawa, ON K1A 0K9
Fax: 613-946-8871, 800-622-6232, nsc-cna@hrsdc-rhdcc.gc.ca
Office of the Commissioner of Review Tribunals, PO Box 8250 T, Ottawa, ON K1G 5S5
613-954-1313, Fax: 613-946-1588, 800-363-0076, info@ocrt-bctr.gc.ca
Alberta
Seniors Advisory Council for Alberta, Standard Life Centre, #600, 10405 Jasper Ave., 6th Fl., Edmonton, AB T5J 4R7
780-422-2321, Fax: 780-422-8762, -310-0000, saca@gov.ab.ca
Alberta Seniors, Communications, Standard Life Centre, 10405 Jasper Ave., 3rd Fl., Edmonton, AB T5J 4R7
780-415-9950, Fax: 780-644-1227, 866-477-8589, seniors.communications@gov.ab.ca
Manitoba
Manitoba Healthy Living, Seniors & Consumer Affairs, #822, 155 Carlton St., Winnipeg, MB R3C 3H8
204-945-6565, Fax: 204-948-2514, 800-665-6565, seniors@gov.mb.ca
New Brunswick
Program Design & Quality Management, Sartain MacDonald Bldg., #4007, 551 King St., PO Box 6000, Fredericton, NB E3B 5H1
506-453-2181, Fax: 506-453-3829
Nova Scotia
Seniors' Secretariat, Dennis Bldg., 1740 Granville St., 4th Fl., PO Box 2065, Halifax, NS B3J 2Z1
902-424-0065, Fax: 902-424-0561, 800-670-0065, seniors@gov.ns.ca
Nunavut
Department of Culture, Language, Elders & Youth, PO Box 1000 800,Iqaluit, NU X0A 0H0
867-975-5500, Fax: 867-975-5504, 866-934-2035
Ontario
Office of the Chief Information Officer, Mowat Block, 900 Bay St. 3rd FL, Toronto, ON M7A 1L2
416-325-4598
Quebec
Ministère de la Famille, 425, rue Saint-Amable, 1er étage, Québec, QC G1R 4Z1
877-216-6202
Ministère de la Santé et des Services sociaux, Direction des communications, 1075, ch Sainte-Foy, 16e étage, Québec, QC G1S 2M1
418-643-9395, Fax: 418-643-4768, regisseur.web@msss.gouv.qc.ca
Yukon Territory
Yukon Health & Social Services, PO Box 2703, Whitehorse, YT Y1A 2C6
867-667-3673, Fax: 867-667-3096, hss@gov.yk.ca

SEXUALLY TRANSMITTED DISEASE CONTROL
See Also: AIDS
Prince Edward Island
Prince Edward Island Department of Health & Wellness, 105 Rochford St. North, 4th Fl., PO Box 2000, Charlottetown, PE C1A 7N8
902-368-6414, Fax: 902-368-4121

SOCIAL AFFAIRS
Ontario
Ontario Trillium Foundation, 800 Bay St., 5th Fl., Toronto, ON M5S 3A9
416-963-4927, Fax: 416-963-8781, 800-263-2887, trillium@trilliumfoundation.org

SOCIAL SERVICES
See Also: Community Services
Alberta
Alberta Seniors, Communications, Standard Life Centre, 10405 Jasper Ave., 3rd Fl., Edmonton, AB T5J 4R7
780-415-9950, Fax: 780-644-1227, 866-477-8589, seniors.communications@gov.ab.ca
British Columbia
British Columbia College of Social Workers, #302, 1765 West 8th Ave., Vancouver, BC V6J 5C6
604-737-4916, Fax: 604-737-6809, info@bccsw.ca
British Columbia Ministry of Community, Sport, & Cultural Development, PO Box 9490 Prov Govt,Victoria, BC V8W 9N7
Manitoba
Social Services Appeal Board, 175 Hargrave St., 7th Fl., Winnipeg, MB R3C 3R8
204-945-3003, Fax: 204-945-1736, 800-282-8069
New Brunswick
New Brunswick Department of Social Development, Sartain MacDonald Bldg., 551 King St., PO Box 6000, Fredericton, NB E3B 5H1
506-453-2001, Fax: 506-453-7478, sd-ds@gnb.ca
Newfoundland & Labrador
Newfoundland & Labrador Department of Advanced Education & Skills, Confederation Building, West Block, 3rd Fl., PO Box 8700, St. John's, NL A1B 4J6
709-729-2480, aesweb@gov.nl.ca
Northwest Territories
Department of Health & Social Services, Centre Square Tower, PO Box 1320, Yellowknife, NT X1A 2L9
Fax: 867-873-0266
Nunavut
Department of Health & Social Services, PO Box 1000 1000,Iqaluit, NU X0A 0H0
867-975-5700, Fax: 867-975-5705
Ontario
Operations Division, Hepburn Block, 80 Grosvenor St., 6th Fl., Toronto, ON M7A 1E9
416-325-5581, Fax: 416-325-5432
Quebec
Ministère de la Santé et des Services sociaux, Direction des communications, 1075, ch Sainte-Foy, 16e étage, Québec, QC G1S 2M1
418-643-9395, Fax: 418-643-4768, regisseur.web@msss.gouv.qc.ca
Saskatchewan
Saskatchewan Social Services, 1920 Broad St., Regina, SK S4P 3V6
306-787-3700, 866-221-5200, socialservicesinquiry@gov.sk.ca

SOIL RESOURCES
Nova Scotia
Resource Stewardship Division, PO Box 550, Truro, NS B2N 5E3
Soil, Plant & Feed Laboratory, Brookfield Rd., PO Box 8700, St. John's, NL A1B 4J6
709-729-6738, Fax: 709-729-6734
Soils & Crops Research & Development Centre, 2560, boul Hochelaga, Québec, QC G1V 2J3
418-657-7980, Fax: 418-648-2402
Quebec
Commission de protection du territoire agricole du Québec, 200, ch Ste-Foy, 2e étage, Québec, QC G1R 4X6
418-643-3314, Fax: 418-643-2261, 800-667-5294, info@cptaq.gouv.qc.ca

SOLICITORS GENERAL
Manitoba
Manitoba Justice, Legislative Building, #104, 405 Broadway Ave., Winnipeg, MB R3C 3L6
204-945-3728, Fax: 204-945-2517, minjus@gov.mb.ca
Newfoundland & Labrador
Newfoundland & Labrador Department of Justice, Confederation Bldg., East Block, 4th Fl., PO Box 8700, St. John's, NL A1B 4J6
709-729-2869, Fax: 709-729-0469, justice@gov.nl.ca
Nova Scotia
Department of Justice, 5151 Terminal Rd., 4th Fl., PO Box 7, Halifax, NS B3J 2L6
902-424-4030, Fax: 902-424-0510, justweb@gov.ns.ca
Ontario
Ontario Ministry of Community Safety & Correctional Services, George Drew Bldg., 25 Grosvenor St., 18th Fl., Toronto, ON M7A 1Y6
416-326-5000, Fax: 416-326-0498, 866-517-0571, mcscs.feedback@ontario.ca
Quebec
Ministère de la Sécurité publique, Tour des Laurentides, 2525, boul Laurier, 5e étage, Québec, QC G1V 2L2
418-643-2112, Fax: 418-646-6168, 866-644-6826
Yukon Territory
Yukon Justice, Andrew Philipsen Law Centre, 2134 Second Ave., PO Box 2703, Whitehorse, YT Y1A 2C6
867-667-3033, Fax: 867-393-5790, jus.msb@gov.yk.ca

SPACE & ASTRONOMY
Canada Science & Technology Museum Corporation, PO Box 9724 T,Ottawa, ON K1G 5A3
613-991-6090, Fax: 613-990-3636, info@technomuses.ca
Canadian Space Agency, John H. Chapman Space Centre, 6767, rte de l'Aéroport, Saint-Hubert, QC J3Y 8Y9
450-926-4800, Fax: 450-926-4352, promo@asc-csa.gc.ca
Herzberg Institute of Astrophysics, 5071 West Saanich Rd., Victoria, BC V9E 2E7
250-363-0001, Fax: 250-363-0045, hia-www@nrc-cnrc.gc.ca
Institute for Aerospace Research, 1200 Montreal Rd., Ottawa, ON K1A 0R6
613-990-0765, Fax: 613-952-7214

SPORTS
See: Recreation
Prince Edward Island
Prince Edward Island Athletic Association, #101, 250 Water St., Summerside, PE C1N 1B6
902-438-4846, Fax: 902-438-4884
Saskatchewan Parks, Culture, & Sport, 1919 Saskatchewan Dr., 4th Fl., Regina, SK S4P 4H2
306-787-5729, Fax: 306-798-0033, 800-205-7070, info@tpcs.gov.sk.ca
Sport, Recreation, & Stewardship, 1919 Saskatchewan Dr., 9th Fl., Regina, SK S4P 4H2
306-787-7451, Fax: 306-787-0069

New Brunswick
New Brunswick Department of Culture, Tourism, & Healthy Living, Centennial Building, PO Box 6000, Fredericton, NB E3B 5H1
506-444-5205, Fax: 506-457-4984, taponlinedirectory@gnb.ca

STANDARDS

Institute for National Measurement Standards, Bldg. M-36, 1500 Montreal Rd., Ottawa, ON K1A 0R6
613-998-7018, Fax: 613-954-1473, alexandra.shaw@nrc-cnrc.gc.ca
Standards Council of Canada, #200, 270 Albert St., Ottawa, ON K1P 6N7
613-238-3222, Fax: 613-569-7808, info@scc.ca

STATISTICS

See Also: Vital Statistics
Statistics Canada, R.H. Coats Bldg., Tunney's Pasture, 150 Tunney's Pasture Driveway, Ottawa, ON K1A 0T6
613-951-8116, Fax: 877-287-4369, 800-263-1136, infostats@statcan.ca

Manitoba
Manitoba Bureau of Statistics, #824, 155 Carlton St., Winnipeg, MB R3C 3H9
204-945-2406, Fax: 204-945-0695

Nunavut
Department of Executive & Intergovernmental Affairs, 1084 Aeroplex bldg., PO Box 1000 200,Iqaluit, NU X0A 0H0
867-975-6000, Fax: 867-975-6099

Prince Edward Island
Prince Edward Island Department of Health & Wellness, 105 Rochford St. North, 4th Fl., PO Box 2000, Charlottetown, PE C1A 7N8
902-368-6414, Fax: 902-368-4121

STATISTICS (ENVIRONMENTAL)

Statistics Canada, R.H. Coats Bldg., Tunney's Pasture, 150 Tunney's Pasture Driveway, Ottawa, ON K1A 0T6
613-951-8116, Fax: 877-287-4369, 800-263-1136, infostats@statcan.ca

STUDENT AID

Yukon Territory
Advanced Education, PO Box 2703, Whitehorse, YT Y1A 2C6
867-667-5131, Fax: 867-667-8555, contact.education@gov.yk.ca

Nunavut
Department of Education, Sivummut Bldg., 2nd Fl., PO Box 1000 910,Iqaluit, NU X0A 0H0
867-975-5600, Fax: 867-975-5605

Quebec
Administration et aide financière aux études, 1035, rue De La Chevrotière, Québec, QC G1R 5A5
418-643-3750, 877-643-3750

Saskatchewan
Saskatchewan Education, 2220 College Ave., Regina, SK S4P 4V9
Iinquiry@gov.sk.ca

SUSTAINABLE DEVELOPMENT

Commissioner of the Environment & Sustainable Development, 240 Sparks St., Ottawa, ON K1A 0G6
613-995-3708, Fax: 613-957-0474, petitions@oag-bvg.gc.ca

Manitoba
Manitoba Round Table for Sustainable Development, #160, 123 Main St., Winnipeg, MB R3C 1A5
204-945-1869, Fax: 204-948-2357, mrtsd@gov.mb.ca

Quebec
Ministère du Développement durable, de l'Environnement, de la Faune, et des Parcs, Édifice Marie-Guyart, 675, boul René-Lévesque est, 29e étage, Québec, QC G1R 5V7
418-521-3830, Fax: 418-646-5974, 800-561-1616, info@mddep.gouv.qc.ca

TAXATION

See Also: Sales Tax
Canada Revenue Agency, 875 Heron Rd., Ottawa, ON K1A 0L5
800-267-6999
Financial Sector Regulation & Policy, Terrace Building, 9515 - 107 St., 4th Fl., Edmonton, AB T5K 2C3
First Nations Tax Commission, #321, 345 Yellowhead Hwy, Kamloops, BC V2H 1H1
250-828-9857, Fax: 250-828-9858, mailkamloops@fntc.ca
Secretariat to Commission on the Reform of Ontario's Public Services, Frost Bldg. South, 7 Queen's Park Cres., 1st Fl., Toronto, ON M7A 1YA
416-326-9847, Fax: 416-212-7767

Manitoba
Taxation Division, #101, 401 York Ave., Winnipeg, MB R3C 0P8
204-945-6444, Fax: 204-948-2360

New Brunswick
Revenue & Taxation, Centennial Bldg., #671, 670 King St., PO Box 3000, Fredericton, NB E3B 5G5
506-444-2826, Fax: 506-444-4920

Nova Scotia
Provincial Tax Commission, Maritime Centre, 1505 Barrington St., 9th Fl., PO Box 2205, Halifax, NS B3J 2V4
902-424-6300, Fax: 902-424-7434, 800-565-2336

Quebec
Centre de perception fiscale et des biens non réclamés, 3800, rue de Marly, Secteur 6-4-3, Québec, QC G1X 4A5

Saskatchewan
Board of Revenue Commissioners, #480, 2151 Scarth St., Regina, SK S4P 2H8
306-787-6221, Fax: 306-787-1610

TELECOMMUNICATIONS

See Also: Broadcasting
Canadian Broadcasting Corporation, 181 Queen St., PO Box 3220 C,Ottawa, ON K1Y 1E4
613-288-6033, liaison@radio-canada.ca
Canadian Radio-Television & Telecommunications Commission, Central Building, 1, Promenade du Portage, Les Terrasses de la Chaudière, Gatineau, QC J8X 4B1
819-997-0313, Fax: 819-994-0218, 877-249-2782
Communications Research Centre Canada, 3701 Carling Ave., PO Box 11490 H, Ottawa, ON K2H 8S2
613-991-3313, Fax: 613-998-5355, info@crc.gc.ca
Spectrum, Information Technologies & Telecommunications, Journal Tower North, 300 Slater St., 20th Fl., Ottawa, ON K1A 0C8
613-998-0368, Fax: 613-952-1203

Manitoba
Manitoba Telecom Services Inc., 333 Main St., PO Box 6666, Winnipeg, MB R3C 3V6
204-941-4111, Fax: 204-772-6391

Prince Edward Island
Prince Edward Island Department of Innovation & Advanced Learning, Shaw Bldg., 105 Rochford St., 5th Fl., PO Box 2000, Charlottetown, PE C1A 7N8
902-368-4240, Fax: 902-368-4242

Quebec
Ministère de la Culture, des Communications & de la Condition féminine, 225, Grande Allée est, Québec, QC G1R 5G5
888-380-8882
Société de télédiffusion du Québec (Télé-Québec), 1000, rue Fullum, Montréal, QC H2K 3L7
514-521-2424, Fax: 514-873-2601, 800-361-4362, info@telequebec.tv

Saskatchewan
Saskatchewan Telecommunications (SaskTel), 2121 Saskatchewan Dr., 7th Fl., Regina, SK S4P 4C3
306-777-3737, 800-727-5835, corporate.comments@sasktel.sk.ca

TOURISM & TOURIST INFORMATION

Canadian Tourism Commission, #1400, 1055 Dunsmuir St., PO Box 49230, Vancouver, BC V7X 1L2
604-638-8300
Canadian Tourism Commission, Four Bentall Centre, #1400, 1055 Dunsmuir St., PO Box 49230, Vancouver, BC V7X 1L2
604-638-8300
Charlottetown Civic Centre Management Inc., 46 Kensington Rd., Charlottetown, PE C1A 5H7
902-629-6600, Fax: 902-629-6650
Parks Canada, 25 Eddy St., Gatineau, QC K1A 0M5
613-860-1251, 888-773-8888, information@pc.gc.ca
Tourism Initiatives, 1919 Saskatchewan Dr., 2nd Fl., Regina, SK S4P 4H2
306-787-8985, Fax: 306-798-3177
Tourism Policy & Development Division, Hearst Block, 900 Bay St., 10th Fl., Toronto, ON M7A 2E1
416-326-9326, Fax: 416-325-6985
Tourism Saskatchewan, #189, 1621 Albert St., Regina, SK S4P 2S5
877-237-2273

Manitoba
Tourism Secretariat, 155 Carlton St., 7th Fl., Winnipeg, MB R3C 3H8
800-665-0040

New Brunswick
New Brunswick Department of Culture, Tourism, & Healthy Living, Centennial Building, PO Box 6000, Fredericton, NB E3B 5H1
506-444-5205, Fax: 506-457-4984, taponlinedirectory@gnb.ca

Newfoundland & Labrador
Newfoundland & Labrador Department of Tourism, Culture, & Recreation, Confederation Bldg., West Block, 2nd Fl., PO Box 8700, St. John's, NL A1B 4J6
709-729-0862, Fax: 709-729-0870, tcrinfo@gov.nl.ca

Northwest Territories
Department of Industry, Tourism & Investment, PO Box 1320, Yellowknife, NT X1A 2L9
Fax: 867-873-0306, info@iti.ca

Ontario
Ontario Ministry of Tourism & Culture, Hearst Block, 900 Bay St., 9th Fl., Toronto, ON M7A 2E1
416-326-9326, Fax: 416-314-7854, 800-668-2746

Prince Edward Island
Prince Edward Island Department of Tourism & Culture, PO Box 2000, Charlottetown, PE C1A 7N8
902-368-5540, Fax: 902-368-5277, tpswitch@gov.pe.ca

Quebec
Société des établissements en plein air du Québec, Place de la Cité, Tour Cominar, #250, 2640, boul Laurier, 2e étage, Québec, QC G1V 5C2
418-890-6527, Fax: 418-528-6025, 800-665-6527, inforeservation@sepaq.com
Ministère du Tourisme, #400, 900, boul René-Lévesque est, Québec, QC G1R 2B5
418-643-5959, Fax: 418-646-8723, 800-482-2433

Yukon Territory
Yukon Tourism & Culture, 100 Hanson St., Whitehorse, YT Y1A 2C6
867-667-5036, Fax: 867-667-3546,

TRADE

See Also: Business Development; Imports
Business Development Bank of Canada, #400, 5, Place Ville-Marie, Montréal, QC H3B 5E7
514-283-5904, Fax: 514-283-5626, 877-232-2269
Canadian Commercial Corporation, 50 O'Connor St., 11th Fl., Ottawa, ON K1A 0S6
613-996-0034, Fax: 613-995-2121, 800-748-8191
Canadian International Trade Tribunal, Standard Life Centre, 333 Laurier Ave. West, 15 Floor, Ottawa, ON K1A 0G7
613-990-2452, Fax: 613-990-2439, secretary@citt-tcce.gc.ca
Canadian Wheat Board, 423 Main St., PO Box 816 Main,Winnipeg, MB R3C 2P5
204-983-0239, Fax: 204-983-3841, 800-275-4292, questions@cwb.ca; farmerservice@cwb.ca
Commission for Environmental Cooperation, Secretariat, #200, 393, rue St-Jacques ouest, Montréal, QC H2Y 1N9
514-350-4300, Fax: 514-350-4314, info@cec.org
Export Development Canada, 151 Slater St., Ottawa, ON K1A 1K3
613-598-2500, Fax: 613-598-3811, 800-267-8510
Market & Industry Services Branch, Tower 5, 1341 Baseline Rd., Ottawa, ON K1A 0C5
613-759-1000, Fax: 613-773-1711
North American Free Trade Agreement (NAFTA) Secretariat, Canadian Section, #705, 90 Sparks St., Ottawa, ON K1P 5B4
613-992-9388, Fax: 613-992-9392, webmaster@nafta-alena.gc.ca
Northstar Trade Finance Inc., #833, 595 Burrard St., PO Box 49058, Vancouver, BC V7X 1C4
604-664-5828, Fax: 604-664-5838, 800-663-9288, vancouver@northstar.ca
The World Bank Group, 1818 H St. NW, Washington, DC
202-473-1000, Fax: 202-477-6391

Alberta
Intergovernmental Relations, Commerce Place, 10155 - 102 St., 12th Fl., Edmonton, AB T5J 4G8
780-427-6543, Fax: 780-427-0939

British Columbia
British Columbia Ministry of Social Development, PO Box 9058 Prov Govt,Victoria, BC V8W 9E1
Labour Market & Immigration Division, PO Box 9213, Vancouver, BC V8W 9J1
250-953-3585, Fax: 250-356-0033

Manitoba
Manitoba Entrepreneurship, Training & Trade, #1000, 259 Portage Ave, Winnipeg, MB R3B 3P4
204-945-2475, Fax: 204-945-3977, minctt@leg.gov.mb.ca

New Brunswick
New Brunswick Department of Economic Development, Centennial Building, PO Box 6000, Fredericton, NB E3B 5H1
506-453-3707, Fax: 506-453-3993, 800-665-1800, tradenb@gnb.ca

Nova Scotia
Department of Economic & Rural Development & Tourism, Centennial Building, #600, 1660 Hollis St., PO Box 2311, Halifax, NS B3J 1V7
902-424-0377, Fax: 902-424-0500, comm@gov.ns.ca

Prince Edward Island

Prince Edward Island Department of Innovation & Advanced Learning, Shaw Bldg., 105 Rochford St., 5th Fl., PO Box 2000, Charlottetown, PE C1A 7N8
902-368-4240, Fax: 902-368-4242

Quebec

Ministère du Développement économique, de l'Innovation et de l'Exportation, 710, place D'Youville, 3e étage, Québec, QC G1R 4Y4
418-691-5950, Fax: 418-644-0118, 866-680-1884

Ministère des Relations internationales, Édifice Hector-Fabre, 525, boul Réne-Lévesque est, Québec, QC G1R 5R9
418-649-2300, Fax: 418-649-2656

Yukon Territory

Yukon Economic Development, PO Box 2703, Whitehorse, YT Y1A 2C6
867-393-7191, Fax: 867-393-6412, 800-661-0408, ecdev@gov.yk.ca

TRADE - MEXICAN

Embassy of Mexico in Canada, #1000, 45 O'Connor St., Ottawa, ON K1P 1A4
613-233-8988, Fax: 613-235-9123, info@embamexcan.com

NAFTA Office of Mexico in Canada, #1030, 45 O'Connor St., Ottawa, ON K1P 1A4
613-235-7782, Fax: 613-235-1129, info@nafta-mexico.org

North American Development Bank, #300, 203 St. Mary's, San Antonio, TX
210-231-8000, Fax: 210-231-6232

TRADE - UNITED STATES

American National Standards Institute, 25 West 43rd St., New York, NY
212-642-4900, Fax: 212-398-0023

Environmental Protection Agency: Office of Acquisition Management, 1200 Pennsylvania Ave. NW, Washington, DC
202-564-4310, oam-web@epa.gov

General Services Administration, 1800 F St. NW, Washington, DC
202-501-0112, 877-495-4849, vendor.support@gsa.gov

Government Printing Office, 732 North Capitol St., Washington, DC
202-512-0526, Fax: 202-512-1782, gpoaccess@gpo.gov

National Electronic Procurement Assistance Center, #304, 55 Maple Ave., Rockville Center, NY
516-255-0500, Fax: 516-255-0509, 800-932-7761, online@cbdweb.com

National Technical Information Service, c/o Department of Commerce, 5285 Port Royal Rd., Springfield, VA
703-605-6000, Fax: 703-321-8547, info@ntis.gov

North American Development Bank, #300, 203 St. Mary's, San Antonio, TX
210-231-8000, Fax: 210-231-6232

United States Embassy in Canada, 490 Sussex Dr., Ottawa, ON K1N 1G8
613-238-5335, Fax: 613-688-3082, ottawareference@state.gov

US Commercial Service in Canada, c/o Department of Commerce, 14th & Constitution Ave. NW, Washington, DC
202-482-5777, Fax: 202-482-5013

TRADE-MARKS

See: Patents & Copyright

Prince Edward Island

Anne of Green Gables Licensing Authority Inc., 94 Euston, PO Box 910, Charlottetown, PE C1A 7L9
902-569-7787, Fax: 902-368-6301, kobaker@gov.pe.ca; aggla@bellnet.ca

TRAINING, ENVIRONMENTAL

Alberta

Community, Learner & Industry Connections Division, Phipps-McKinnon Bldg., 10020 - 101A Ave., 5th Fl., Edmonton, AB T5J 3G2

TRANSPORTATION

Atlantic Pilotage Authority, Cogswell Tower, #910, 2000 Barrington St., Halifax, NS B3J 3K1
902-426-2550, Fax: 902-426-4004, 877-272-3477, dispatch@atlanticpilotage.com

Canadian Air Transport Security Authority, 99 Bank St., 13th Fl., Ottawa, ON K1P 6B9
Fax: 613-990-1295, 888-294-2202

Canadian Coast Guard, Centennial Towers, #6S018, 200 Kent St., Ottawa, ON K1A 0E6
613-993-0999, Fax: 613-990-1866, info@dfo-mpo.gc.ca

Canadian Transportation Agency, Les Terrasses de la Chaudière, 15, rue Eddy, Gatineau, QC J8X 4B3
Fax: 819-997-6727, 888-222-2592, info@otc-cta.gc.ca

Centre for Surface Transportation Technology, 2320 Lester Rd., Ottawa, ON K1V 1S2
613-998-9639, Fax: 613-957-0831, inquiries.cstt@nrc-cnrc.gc.ca

Federal Bridge Corporation Limited, #1210, 55 Metcalfe St., Ottawa, ON K1P 6L5
613-993-6880, Fax: 613-993-6945, info@federalbridge.ca

Great Lakes Pilotage Authority, 202 Pitt St., 2nd fl., PO Box 95, Cornwall, ON K6H 5R9
613-933-2991, Fax: 613-932-3793, administration@glpa-apgl.com

Institute for Aerospace Research, 1200 Montreal Rd., Ottawa, ON K1A 0R6
613-990-0765, Fax: 613-952-7214

Laurentian Pilotage Authority, Head Office, #1501, 555, boul René-Lévesque ouest, Montréal, QC H2Z 1B1
514-283-6320, Fax: 514-496-2409, administration@apl.gc.ca; pilote-mtl@apl.gc.ca (Dispatch Center)

Marine Atlantic Inc., Corporate Office, Baine Johnston Centre, #302, 10 Fort William Pl., St. John's, NL A1C 1K4
800-897-2797, customer_relations@marine-atlantic.ca; marketing@marine-atlantic.ca

Old Port of Montréal Corporation Inc., 333, rue de la Commune ouest, Montréal, QC H2Y 2E2
514-283-5256, 800-971-7678

Pacific Pilotage Authority Canada, #1000, 1130 Pender St. West, Vancouver, BC V6E 4A4
604-666-6771, Fax: 604-666-1647, info@ppa.gc.ca

Parc Downsview Park Inc., #1, 35 Carl Hall Rd., Toronto, ON M3K 2B6
416-952-2222, Fax: 416-952-2225, info@downsviewpark.ca

Policy & Corporate Services Division, Twin Atria Building, 4999 - 98 Ave., 3rd Fl., Edmonton, AB T6B 2X3

St. Lawrence Seaway Management Corporation, 202 Pitt St., Cornwall, ON K6J 3P7
613-932-5170, Fax: 613-932-7286, marketing@seaway.ca

Transport Canada, Place de Ville, 330 Sparks St., Tower C, Ottawa, ON K1A 0N5
613-990-2309, Fax: 613-954-4731, 866-995-9737

Transportation & Civil Engineering Division, Twin Atria Building, 4999 - 98 Ave., 2nd Fl., Edmonton, AB T6B 2X3
780-422-2184, Fax: 780-415-1268

Transportation Appeal Tribunal of Canada, #1201, 333 Laurier Ave. West, 12th Fl., Ottawa, ON K1A 0N5
613-990-6906, Fax: 613-990-9153, info@tatc.gc.ca

Transportation Development Centre, Tour Ouest, Complexe Guy-Favreau, 800, boul René-Lévesque ouest, 6e étage, Montréal, QC H3B 1X9
514-283-0000, Fax: 514-283-7158, tdccdt@tc.gc.ca

Transportation Safety Board of Canada, 200 Promenade du Portage, 4th Fl., Ottawa, ON K1A 1K8
819-994-3741, Fax: 819-997-2239, 800-387-3557

Transportation Safety Services Division, Twin Atria Building, 4999 - 98 Ave., Main Fl., Edmonton, AB T6B 2X3
780-427-8901, Fax: 780-415-0782, 800-666-5036

Vehicle Management Agency, Vehicle Management Center, PO Box 6000, Fredericton, NB E3B 5H1
506-453-3939, Fax: 506-453-3628, Transportation.Web@gnb.ca

VIA Rail Canada Inc., #500, 3, Place Ville-Marie, Montréal, QC H3B 2C9
514-871-6000, Fax: 514-871-6104, 888-842-7245

Alberta

Alberta Automobile Insurance Rate Board, Canadian Western Bank Place, #2440, 10303 Jasper Ave., Edmonton, AB T5J 3N6
780-427-5428, Fax: 780-638-4254, -310-0000, airb@gov.ab.ca

Alberta Infrastructure, Infrastructure Building, 6950 - 113 St., Edmonton, AB T6H 5V7
780-415-0507, Fax: 780-427-2187, -310-0000, Infra.Contact.Us.m@gov.ab.ca

Transportation Safety Board, North Office, Twin Atria Building, 4999 - 98 Ave., Main Fl., Edmonton, AB T6B 2X3
780-427-7178, Fax: 780-422-9739, -310-0000

British Columbia

British Columbia Ferry Commission, PO Box 35119 Hillside, Victoria, BC V8T 5G2
250-590-2770, info@bcferrycommission.com

British Columbia Ministry of Transportation & Infrastructure, PO Box 9850 Prov Govt,Victoria, BC V8W 9T5
250-387-3198, Fax: 250-356-7706

British Columbia Transit, 520 Gorge Rd. East, Victoria, BC V8W 2P3
250-385-2551, Fax: 250-995-5639

British Columbia Ferry Services Inc., #500, 1321 Blanshard St., Victoria, BC V8W 0B7
250-381-1401, 888-223-3779

Passenger Transportation Board, #202, 940 Blanshard St., PO Box 9850 Prov Govt, Victoria, BC V8W 9T5
250-953-3777, Fax: 250-953-3788, ptboard@gov.bc.ca

Transportation Policy & Programs Department, PO Box 9850 Prov Govt,Victoria, BC V8W 9T5
250-387-5062, Fax: 250-387-6431

Manitoba

Highway Traffic Board/Motor Transport Board, #200, 301 Weston St., Winnipeg, MB R3E 3H4
204-945-8912, Fax: 204-783-6529

Manitoba Infrastructure & Transportation, Legislative Building, #203, 450 Broadway Ave., Winnipeg, MB R3C 0V8
204-945-3723, Fax: 204-945-7610

License Suspension Appeal Board/Medical Review Committee, #200, 301 Weston St., Winnipeg, MB R3E 3H4
204-945-7350, Fax: 204-948-2682

Taxicab Board, #200, 301 Weston St., Winnipeg, MB R3E 3H4
Fax: 204-948-2315

New Brunswick

New Brunswick Department of Transportation & Infrastructure, Kings Place, PO Box 6000, Fredericton, NB E3B 5H1
506-453-3939, Fax: 506-453-2900, Transportation.Web@gnb.ca

Newfoundland & Labrador

Newfoundland & Labrador Department of Transportation & Works, Confederation Bldg., West Block, 6th Fl., PO Box 8700, St. John's, NL A1B 4J6
709-729-3679, Fax: 709-729-4285, twminister@gov.nl.ca

Northwest Territories

Department of Transportation, Lahm Ridge Bldg., 4501 50 Ave., PO Box 1320, Yellowknife, NT X1A 2L9
867-920-3460, Fax: 867-873-0363

Highways & Marine, 4510 - 50 Ave., 2nd fl., PO Box 1320, Yellowknife, NT X1A 2L9
867-920-8771, Fax: 867-873-0288

Nova Scotia

Department of Transportation & Infrastructure Renewal, Johnston Bldg., 1672 Granville St., 2nd Fl., PO Box 186, Halifax, NS B3J 2N2
902-424-2297, Fax: 902-424-0532, tpwpaff@gov.ns.ca

Nunavut

Department of Community & Government Services, W.G. Brown Bldg., 4th Fl., PO Box 1000 700,Iqaluit, NU X0A 0H0
867-975-5400, Fax: 867-975-5305

Department of Economic Development & Transportation, Bldg. 1104 A, Inuksugait Plaza, PO Box 1000 1500,Iqaluit, NU X0A 0H0
867-975-7800, Fax: 867-975-7870, 888-975-5999, edt@gov.nu.ca

Ontario

Licence Appeal Tribunal, 20 Dundas St. West, 5th Fl., Toronto, ON M5G 2C2
416-314-4260, Fax: 416-314-4270, 800-255-2214

Metrolinx, #600, 20 Bay St., Toronto, ON M5J 2W3
416-869-3200, Fax: 416-869-3525, 888-438-6646

Ontario Highway Transport Board, 151 Bloor St. West, 10th Fl., Toronto, ON M5S 2T5
416-326-6732, Fax: 416-326-6738, ohtb@mto.gov.on.ca

Owen Sound Transportation Company Ltd., 717875, Hwy. 6, Owen Sound, ON N4K 5N7
519-376-8740, 800-265-3163

Road User Safety Division, Bldg A, #191, 1201 Wilson Ave., Downsview, ON M3M 1J8
416-235-2999, Fax: 416-235-4153

Ontario Ministry of Transportation, Ferguson Block, 77 Wellesley St. West, 3rd Fl., Toronto, ON M7A 1Z8
416-235-4686, Fax: 905-704-2001, 800-268-4686

Prince Edward Island

Prince Edward Island Department of Transportation & Infrastructure Renewal, Jones Bldg., 11 Kent St., 3rd Fl., PO Box 2000, Charlottetown, PE C1A 7N8
902-368-5100, Fax: 902-368-5395

Quebec

Abitibi-Témiscamingue, 80, av Québec, Rouyn-Noranda, QC J9X 6R1
819-763-3271, Fax: 819-763-3493, dat@mtq.gouv.qc.ca

Bas-Saint-Laurent—Gaspésie—Îles-de-la-Madeleine, #101, 92, 2e rue ouest, Rimouski, QC G5L 8E6
418-727-3674, Fax: 418-727-3673, dtbgi@mtq.gouv.qc.ca

Capitale-Nationale, 475, boul de l'Atrium, 2e étage, Québec, QC G1H 7H9
418-643-1911, Fax: 418-646-0003, dcnat@mtq.gouv.qc.ca

Chaudière-Appalaches, 1156, boul de la Rive-Sud, Saint-Romuald, QC G6W 5M6
418-839-5581, Fax: 418-834-7338, dtca@mtq.gouv.qc.ca

Commission des transports du Québec, 200, ch Sainte-Foy, 7e étage, Québec, QC G1R 5V5
Fax: 418-644-8034, 888-461-2433

Côte-Nord, #110, 625, boul Laflèche, Baie-Comeau, QC G5C 1C5
418-295-4765, Fax: 418-295-4766, cotenord@mtq.gouv.qc.ca

Est-de-la-Montérégie, 201, place Charles-Lemoyne, 5e étage, Longueuil, QC J4K 2T5
450-677-3413, Fax: 450-442-1317, dtem@mtq.gouv.qc.ca
Estrie, #2.02, 200, rue Belvédère nord, Sherbrooke, QC J1H 4A9
819-820-3280, Fax: 819-820-3118, dte@mtq.gouv.qc.ca
Laurentides-Lanaudière, 222, rue Saint-Georges, 2e étage, Saint-Jérôme, QC J7Z 4Z9
450-569-3057, Fax: 450-569-3072, dll@mtq.gouv.qc.ca
Laval-Mille-îles, 1725, boul Le Corbusier, Laval, QC H7S 2K7
450-680-6330, Fax: 450-973-4959, dtlmi@mtq.gouv.qc.ca
Mauricie—Centre-du-Québec, 100, rue Laviolette, 4e étage, Trois-Rivières, QC G9A 5S9
819-371-6896, Fax: 819-371-6136, dmcq@mtq.gouv.qc.ca
Ouest-de-la-Montérégie, #200, 180, boul d'Anjou, Châteauguay, QC J6K 1C4
450-698-3400, Fax: 450-698-3452, dtom@mtq.gouv.qc.ca
Outaouais, #5.110, 170, rue de l'Hôtel-de-Ville, Gatineau, QC J8X 4C2
819-772-3849, Fax: 819-772-3338, dto@mtq.gouv.qc.ca
Saguenay—Lac-Saint-Jean—Chibougamau, 3950, boul Harvey, Jonquière, QC G7X 8L6
418-695-7916, Fax: 418-695-7926, dt.slsjc@mtq.gouv.qc.ca
Société de l'assurance automobile du Québec, 333, boul Jean-Lesage, CP 19600 Terminus, Québec, QC G1K 8J6
418-643-7620, Fax: 418-644-0339, 800-361-7620, courrier@saaq.gouv.qc.ca
Société des traversiers du Québec, 250, rue Saint-Paul, Québec, QC G1K 9K9
418-643-2019, Fax: 418-643-7308, stq@traversiers.gouv.qc.ca
Société du port ferroviaire Baie-Comeau-Hauterive, 18, rte Maritime, Baie-Comeau, QC G4Z 2L6
418-296-6785, Fax: 418-296-2377, societeduport@globetrotter.net
Ministère des Transports, 700, boul René-Lévesque est, 28e étage, Québec, QC G1R 5H1
418-643-6980, Fax: 418-643-2033, 888-355-0511, communications@mtq.gouv.qc.ca
île-de-Montréal, 500, boul René-Lévesque ouest, 12e étage, CP 5, Montréal, QC H2Z 1W7
514-873-7781, Fax: 514-864-3867, dtim@mtq.gouv.qc.ca

Saskatchewan
Saskatchewan Highway Traffic Board, 1550 Saskatchewan Dr., Regina, SK S4P 0E4
306-775-6674, contactus@highwaytrafficboard.sk.ca
Saskatchewan Highways & Infrastructure, Victoria Tower, 1855 Victoria Ave., Regina, SK S4P 3T2
306-787-4800, communications@highways.gov.sk.ca

Yukon Territory
Yukon Community Services, PO Box 2703, Whitehorse, YT Y1A 2C6
867-667-5811, Fax: 867-393-6295, 800-661-0408, inquiry@gov.yk.ca
Driver Control Board, 2130 Second Ave., 3rd Fl., PO Box 2703, Whitehorse, YT Y1A 2C6
867-667-5111, Fax: 867-667-3609, dcb@gov.yk.ca
Yukon Highways & Public Works, PO Box 2703, Whitehorse, YT Y1A 2C6
867-393-7193, Fax: 867-393-6218, 800-661-0408, hpw-info@gov.yk.ca

TRANSPORTATION OF DANGEROUS GOODS

Nova Scotia
Department of Transportation & Infrastructure Renewal, Johnston Bldg., 1672 Granville St., 2nd Fl., PO Box 186, Halifax, NS B3J 2N2
902-424-2297, Fax: 902-424-0532, tpwpaff@gov.ns.ca

Ontario
Road User Safety Division, Bldg A, #191, 1201 Wilson Ave., Downsview, ON M3M 1J8
416-235-2999, Fax: 416-235-4153

Prince Edward Island
Prince Edward Island Department of Transportation & Infrastructure Renewal, Jones Bldg., 11 Kent St., 3rd Fl., PO Box 2000, Charlottetown, PE C1A 7N8
902-368-5100, Fax: 902-368-5395

Saskatchewan
Saskatchewan Highways & Infrastructure, Victoria Tower, 1855 Victoria Ave., Regina, SK S4P 3T2
306-787-4800, communications@highways.gov.sk.ca

TRAPPING & FUR INDUSTRY

Ontario
Ontario Moose & Bear Allocation Advisory Committee, PO Box 964, Sioux Lookout, ON P8T 1B3
807-737-2615, Fax: 807-737-4173

Quebec
Comité conjoint de chasse, de pêche et de piégeage, #C220, 383 rue Saint-Jacques, Montréal, QC H2Y 1N9
514-284-2151, Fax: 514-284-0039, infohftcc@cccpp-hftcc.com

Saskatchewan
Saskatchewan Environment, 3211 Albert St., 2nd Fl., Regina, SK S4S 5W6
306-787-2584, Fax: 306-787-9544, 800-567-4224, Centre.Inquiry@gov.sk.ca

TREASURY SERVICES

See Also: Finance

Ontario
Office of the Budget & Treasury Board, Frost Bldg. South, 95 Grosvenor St., 4th Fl., Toronto, ON M7A 1Z1
416-325-7620, Fax: 416-212-7767
Treasury Board of Canada, 140 O'Connor St., Ottawa, ON K1A 0R5
613-957-2400, Fax: 613-941-4000, 877-636-0656

British Columbia
Provincial Treasury, PO Box 9414 Prov Govt,Victoria, BC V8V 9V1
250-387-4541, Fax: 250-356-3041

New Brunswick
Treasury, Centennial Bldg., #376, 670 King St., PO Box 6000, Fredericton, NB E3B 5H1
506-453-3952, Fax: 506-453-2053

Nova Scotia
Nova Scotia Treasury & Policy Board, 1700 Granville St., 5th Fl., PO Box 1617, Halifax, NS B3J 2Y3
902-424-8910, Fax: 902-424-7638, TBenquiries@gov.ns.ca

Nunavut
Department of Finance, Bldg. 1079, 1st Fl., PO Box 1000 330,Iqaluit, NU X0A 0H0
867-975-5800, Fax: 867-975-5805

Quebec
Secrétariat du Conseil du trésor, 875, Grande Allée est, 5e étage, secteur 500, Québec, QC G1R 5R8
418-643-1529, Fax: 418-643-9226, 866-552-5158, communication@sct.gouv.qc.ca

URBAN RENEWAL & DESIGN

See Also: Municipal Affairs

Alberta
Local Government Services Division, Commerce Place, 10155 - 102 St., 17th Fl., Edmonton, AB T5J 4L4

Newfoundland & Labrador
Newfoundland & Labrador Housing Corporation, Sir Brian Dunfield Bldg., 2 Canada Dr., PO Box 220, St. John's, NL A1C 5J2
709-724-3000, Fax: 709-724-3250

Northwest Territories
Department of Municipal & Community Affairs, PO Box 1320, Yellowknife, NT X1A 2L9
867-873-7118, Fax: 867-873-0309

Ontario
Ontario Ministry of Municipal Affairs & Housing, College Park, 777 Bay St., 17th Fl., Toronto, ON M5G 2E5
416-585-7041, Fax: 416-585-6470, 866-220-2290, mininfo@ontario.ca

Prince Edward Island
SkillsPEI, Atlantic Technology Centre, #212, 90 University Ave., Charlottetown, PE C1A 4K9
902-368-4260, Fax: 902-368-6340, 877-491-4766

Quebec
Société d'habitation du Québec, Aile St-Amable, 1054, rue Louis-Alexandre-Taschereau, 3e étage, Québec, QC G1R 5E7
418-643-4035, Fax: 418-643-2533, 800-463-4315

VETERANS AFFAIRS

Ste-Anne's Hospital, 305 boul des Anciens-Combattants, Sainte-Anne-de-Bellevue, QC H9X 1Y9
514-457-3440, 800-361-9287, steanne@vac-acc.gc.ca
Veterans Affairs Canada, 161 Grafton St., PO Box 7700, Charlottetown, PE C1A 8M9
902-566-8888, 866-522-2111, information@vac-acc.gc.ca

VICE-REGAL REPRESENTATIVES

Governor General & Commander-in-Chief of Canada, Rideau Hall, 1 Sussex Dr., Ottawa, ON K1A 0A1
613-993-8200, Fax: 613-998-8760, 800-465-6890, info@gg.ca

Alberta
Office of the Lieutenant Governor, Office of the Lieutenant Governor of AB, Legislature Bldg., 10800 - 97 Ave., 3rd Fl., Edmonton, AB T5K 2B6
780-427-7243, Fax: 780-422-5134, ltgov@gov.ab.ca

British Columbia
Office of the Lieutenant Governor, Government House, 1401 Rockland Ave., Victoria, BC V8S 1V9
250-387-2080, Fax: 250-387-2078, ghinfo@gov.bc.ca

Manitoba
Office of the Lieutenant Governor, Legislative Building, #235, 450 Broadway Ave., Winnipeg, MB R3C 0V8
204-945-2753, Fax: 204-945-4329, ltgov@leg.gov.mb.ca

New Brunswick
Office of the Lieutenant-Governor, Government House, 51 Woodstock Rd., PO Box 6000, Fredericton, NB E3B 5H1
506-453-2505, Fax: 506-444-5280, LTgov@gnb.ca

Newfoundland & Labrador
Office of the Lieutenant Governor, Government House, Military Rd., PO Box 5517, St. John's, NL A1C 5W4
709-729-4494, Fax: 709-729-2234, governmenthouse@gov.nl.ca

Northwest Territories
Office of the Commissioner, #803 Northwest Tower, PO Box 1320, Yellowknife, NT X1A 2L9
867-873-7400, Fax: 867-873-0223, 888-270-3318, commissioner@gov.nt.ca

Nova Scotia
Office of the Lieutenant Governor, Government House, 1451 Barrington St., Halifax, NS B3J 1Z2
902-424-7001, Fax: 902-424-0537, lgoffice@gov.ns.ca

Nunavut
Office of the Commissioner, PO Box 2379, Iqaluit, NU X0A 0H0
867-975-5120, Fax: 867-975-5123, nunavutcommissioner@gov.nu.ca

Ontario
Office of the Lieutenant Governor, Room 131, Legislative Bldg., Queen's Park, Toronto, ON M7A 1A1
416-325-7780, Fax: 416-325-7787, ltgov@gov.on.ca

Prince Edward Island
Office of the Lieutenant Governor, Government House, PO Box 846, Charlottetown, PE C1A 7L9
902-368-5480, Fax: 902-368-5481

Quebec
Cabinet du Lieutenant-gouverneur, Édifice André-Laurendeau, 1050, rue des Parlementaires R.C., Québec, QC G1A 1A1
418-643-5385, Fax: 418-644-4677, 866-791-0766

Saskatchewan
Office of the Lieutenant Governor, Government House, 4607 Dewdney Ave., Regina, SK S4T 1B7
306-787-4070, Fax: 306-787-7716, lgo@ltgov.sk.ca

Yukon Territory
Office of the Commissioner, Closeleigh Manor, 1098 First Ave., Whitehorse, YT Y1A 0C1
867-667-5121, Fax: 867-393-6201, commissioner@gov.yk.ca

VIOLENCE

See Also: policing Services

New Brunswick
New Brunswick Department of Social Development, Sartain MacDonald Bldg., 551 King St., PO Box 6000, Fredericton, NB E3B 5H1
506-453-2001, Fax: 506-453-7478, sd-ds@gnb.ca

Nova Scotia
Department of Community Services, Nelson Place, 5675 Spring Garden Rd., 8th Fl., PO Box 696, Halifax, NS B3J 2T7
902-424-4304, Fax: 902-428-0618

VITAL STATISTICS

Vital Statistics, 254 Portage Ave., Winnipeg, MB R3C 0B8
204-945-3701, Fax: 204-948-3128, 800-282-8063, vitalstats@gov.mb.ca

Northwest Territories
Vital Statistics, Bag #9, Inuvik, NT X0E 0T0
867-777-7400, Fax: 867-777-3197, 800-661-0830, hsa@gov.nt.ca

Nova Scotia
Vital Statistics, Joseph Howe Bldg., 1690 Hollis St., Ground Floor, PO Box 157, Halifax, NS B3J 2M9
902-424-4071, Fax: 902-424-0678, 800-898-7668, vstat@gov.ns.ca

Prince Edward Island
Prince Edward Island Department of Health & Wellness, 105 Rochford St. North, 4th Fl., PO Box 2000, Charlottetown, PE C1A 7N8
902-368-6414, Fax: 902-368-4121

Quebec
Directeur de l'état civil, 2535, boul Laurier, Québec, QC G1V 5C5
418-643-3900, Fax: 418-646-3255, 800-567-3900, etatcivil@gouv.qc.ca

WASTE & GARBAGE

Low-Level Radioactive Waste Management Office, #200, 1900 City Park Dr., Ottawa, ON K1J 1A3
613-998-9442, Fax: 613-952-0760, 800-377-5995, info@llrwmo.org

Newfoundland & Labrador

Newfoundland & Labrador Department of Municipal Affairs, West Block, Main Fl., Confederation Bldg., PO Box 8700, St. John's, NL A1B 4J6
709-729-3046, Fax: 709-729-0943, mainfo@gov.nl.ca

Newfoundland & Labrador Department of Service NL, PO Box 8700, St. John's, NL A1B 4J6
709-729-4834, gsinfo@gov.nl.ca

Ontario

Ontario Ministry of Environment, 135 St. Clair Ave. West, Toronto, ON M4V 1P5
416-325-4000, Fax: 416-325-3159, 800-565-4923

Quebec

Bureau d'audiences publiques sur l'environnement, Édifice Lomer-Gouin, #2.10, 575, rue Saint-Amable, Québec, QC G1R 6A6
418-643-7447, Fax: 418-643-9474, 800-463-4732, communication@bape.gouv.qc.ca

Société québécoise de récupération et de recyclage, #200, 420, boul Charest est, Québec, QC G1K 8M4
418-643-0394, Fax: 418-643-6507, 866-523-8290, info@recyc-quebec.gouv.qc.ca

WASTE MANAGEMENT

See Also: Dangerous Goods & Hazardous Materials

Ontario

Integrated Environmental Policy Division, 77 Wellesley St. West, 11th Fl., Toronto, ON M7A 2T5
416-314-6338, Fax: 416-314-6346

Alberta

Alberta Recycling Management Authority, Scotia Tower 1, #1310, 10060 Jasper Ave., PO Box 189, Edmonton, AB T5J 2J1
780-990-1111, Fax: 780-990-1122, 888-999-8762, info@albertarecycling.ca

Alberta Used Oil Management Association, Empire Building, #1008, 10080 Jasper Ave., Edmonton, AB T5J 1V9
780-414-1510, Fax: 780-414-1519, 866-414-1510, reception@usedoilrecycling.ca

Beverage Container Management Board, #750, 10707 - 100 Ave., Edmonton, AB T5J 3M1
780-424-3193, Fax: 780-428-4620, 888-424-7671

Alberta Environment & Sustainable Resource Development, Oxbridge Place, 9820 - 106 St., Main Fl., Edmonton, AB T5K 2J6
780-427-2700, Fax: 780-422-4086, -310-0000, env.infocent@gov.ab.ca; srd.infocent@gov.ab.ca

Newfoundland & Labrador

Multi-Materials Stewardship Board, PO Box 8131 A, St. John's, NL A1B 3M9
709-753-0948, Fax: 709-753-0974, 800-901-6672, inquiries@mmsb.nl.ca

Northwest Territories

Department of Municipal & Community Affairs, PO Box 1320, Yellowknife, NT X1A 2L9
867-873-7118, Fax: 867-873-0309

Prince Edward Island

Island Waste Management Corporation, 110 Watts Ave., Charlottetown, PE C1E 2C1
902-894-0330, Fax: 902-894-0331, 888-280-8111, reception@iwmc.pe.ca; info@iwmc.pe.ca

Quebec

Société québécoise de récupération et de recyclage, #200, 420, boul Charest est, Québec, QC G1K 8M4
418-643-0394, Fax: 418-643-6507, 866-523-8290, info@recyc-quebec.gouv.qc.ca

Saskatchewan

Saskatchewan Environment, 3211 Albert St., 2nd Fl., Regina, SK S4S 5W6
306-787-2584, Fax: 306-787-9544, 800-567-4224, Centre.Inquiry@gov.sk.ca

Yukon Territory

Yukon Environment, PO Box 2703, Whitehorse, YT Y1A 2C6
867-667-5652, Fax: 867-393-7197, environment.yukon@gov.yk.ca

WATER & WASTEWATER

Bedford Institute of Oceanography, 1 Challenger Dr., PO Box 1006, Dartmouth, NS B2Y 4A2
902-426-3492, Fax: 902-426-8484

Canadian Hydraulics Centre, 1200 Montreal Rd., Ottawa, ON K1A 0R6
613-993-9381, Fax: 613-952-7679, info.chc@nrc-cnrc.gc.ca

Canadian Hydrographic Service, 615 Booth St., Ottawa, ON K1A 0E6
613-998-4931, Fax: 613-998-1217, chsinfo@dfo-mpo.gc.ca

Environment Canada, 10 Wellington St., Gatineau, QC K1A 0H3
819-997-2800, Fax: 819-994-1412, 800-668-6767, enviroinfo@ec.gc.ca

Fisheries & Oceans Canada, 200 Kent St., Ottawa, ON K1A 0E6
613-993-0999, Fax: 613-990-1866, info@dfo-mpo.gc.ca

Freshwater Institute, 501 University Cres., Winnipeg, MB R3T 2N6
204-983-5000, Fax: 204-983-6285

Institut Maurice-Lamontagne, 850, rte de le Mer, CP 1000, Mont-Joli, QC G5H 3Z4
418-775-0555, Fax: 418-775-0730

Institute for Marine Biosciences, 1411 Oxford St., Halifax, NS B3H 3Z1
902-426-8332, Fax: 902-426-9413, communications.imb@nrc-cnrc.gc.ca

Institute for Ocean Technology, Kerwin Pl. & Arctic Ave., PO Box 12093, St. John's, NL A1B 3T5
709-772-4939, Fax: 709-772-2462, Noel.Murphy@nrc-cnrc.gc.ca

Institute of Ocean Sciences, 9860 West Saanich Rd., PO Box 6000, Sidney, BC V8L 4B2
250-363-6517, Fax: 250-363-6390

Nunavut Water Board, PO Box 119, Gjoa Haven, NU X0B 1J0
867-360-6338, Fax: 867-360-6369

Alberta

Alberta Environment & Sustainable Resource Development, Oxbridge Place, 9820 - 106 St., Main Fl., Edmonton, AB T5K 2J6
780-427-2700, Fax: 780-422-4086, -310-0000, env.infocent@gov.ab.ca; srd.infocent@gov.ab.ca

Irrigation Council, Provincial Bldg., 200 - 5 Ave. South, 3rd Fl., Lethbridge, AB T1J 4L1
403-381-5176, Fax: 403-382-4406

British Columbia

British Columbia Ministry of Environment, PO Box 9339 Prov Govt,Victoria, BC V8W 9M1
250-387-1161, Fax: 250-387-5669, envmail@gov.bc.ca

British Columbia Utilities Commission, 900 Howe St., 6th Fl., PO Box 250, Vancouver, BC V6Z 2N3
604-660-4700, Fax: 604-660-1102, 800-663-1385, commission.secretary@bcuc.com

Manitoba

Manitoba Conservation & Water Stewardship, 200 Saulteaux Cres., Winnipeg, MB R3J 3W3
800-214-6497, mws@gov.mb.ca

Manitoba Water Services Board, PO Box 22080, Brandon, MB R7A 6Y9
204-726-6076, Fax: 204-726-6290

New Brunswick

New Brunswick Department of Environment & Local Government, Marysville Place, PO Box 6000, Fredericton, NB E3B 5H1
506-453-2690, Fax: 506-457-4994, elg/egl-info@gnb.ca

New Brunswick Department of Natural Resources, Hugh John Flemming Forestry Centre, PO Box 6000, Fredericton, NB E3B 5H1
506-453-3826, Fax: 506-444-4367, dnrweb@gnb.ca

Newfoundland & Labrador

Newfoundland & Labrador Department of Environment & Conservation, Confederation Bldg., West Block, 4th Fl., PO Box 8700, St. John's, NL A1B 4J6
709-729-2664, Fax: 709-729-6639, 800-563-6181, info@gov.nl.ca

Newfoundland & Labrador Board of Commissioners of Public Utilities, PO Box 21040, St. John's, NL A1A 5B2
709-726-8600, Fax: 709-726-9604, 866-782-0006, ito@pub.nf.ca

Northwest Territories

Department of Environment & Natural Resources, PO Box 1320, Yellowknife, NT X1A 2L9

Northwest Territories Water Board, 125 Mackenzie Rd., PO Box 2531, Yellowknife, NT X0E 0T0
867-678-2942, Fax: 867-678-2943, info@nwtwb.com

Nova Scotia

Department of Natural Resources, Founder's Square, 1701 Hollis St., 3rd Fl., PO Box 698, Halifax, NS B3J 2T9
902-424-5935, Fax: 902-424-0594, 800-565-2224

Nova Scotia Utility & Review Board, Summit Place, 1601 Lower Water St., 3rd Fl., PO Box 1692 M,Halifax, NS B3J 3S3
902-424-4448, Fax: 902-424-3919, uarb.board@gov.ns.ca

Waterfront Development Corporation Ltd., 1751 Lower Water St., 2nd Fl., Halifax, NS B3J 1S5
902-422-6591, Fax: 902-422-7582, info@wdcl.ca

Ontario

Ontario Ministry of Environment, 135 St. Clair Ave. West, Toronto, ON M4V 1P5
416-325-4000, Fax: 416-325-3159, 800-565-4923

Lake of the Woods Control Board, c/o Executive Engineer, Ottawa, ON K1A 0H3
Fax: 819-953-4666, 800-661-5922, secretariat@lwcb.ca

Ontario Ministry of Natural Resources, Whitney Block, #6630, 99 Wellesley St. West, 6th Fl., Toronto, ON M7A 1W3
800-667-1940

Ontario Clean Water Agency, 1 Yonge St., 17th Fl., Toronto, ON M5E 1E5
416-314-5600, Fax: 416-314-8300, 800-667-6292

Walkerton Clean Water Centre, 20 Ontario Rd., PO Box 160, Walkerton, ON N0G 2V0
519-881-2003, Fax: 519-881-4947, 866-515-0550, inquiry@wcwc.ca

Prince Edward Island

Prince Edward Island Department of Environment, Labour & Justice, Shaw Bldg. South, 95 Rochford St., 4th Fl., PO Box 2000, Charlottetown, PE C1A 7N8
902-620-3774, Fax: 902-368-4242, rrryder@gov.pe.ca

Prince Edward Island Department of Tourism & Culture, PO Box 2000, Charlottetown, PE C1A 7N8
902-368-5540, Fax: 902-368-5277, tpswitch@gov.pe.ca

Quebec

Ministère du Développement durable, de l'Environnement, de la Faune, et des Parcs, Édifice Marie-Guyart, 675, boul René-Lévesque est, 29e étage, Québec, QC G1R 5V7
418-521-3830, Fax: 418-646-5974, 800-561-1616, info@mddep.gouv.qc.ca

Saskatchewan

Saskatchewan Environment, 3211 Albert St., 2nd Fl., Regina, SK S4S 5W6
306-787-2584, Fax: 306-787-9544, 800-567-4224, Centre.Inquiry@gov.sk.ca

Saskatchewan Water Corporation (SaskWater), #200, 111 Fairford St. East, Moose Jaw, SK S6H 1C8
Fax: 306-694-3207, 888-230-1111, comm@saskwater.com; customerservice@saskwater.com

Saskatchewan Watershed Authority, 111 Fairford St. East, Moose Jaw, SK S6H 7X9
306-694-3900, Fax: 306-694-3944, comm@swa.ca

Yukon Territory

Yukon Environment, PO Box 2703, Whitehorse, YT Y1A 2C6
867-667-5652, Fax: 867-393-7197, environment.yukon@gov.yk.ca

WATER RESOURCES

See Also: Oceanography

Northwest Territories

Asset Management Division, Stuart M. Hodgson Bldg., 5009 - 49th St., 3rd Fl., Yellowknife, NT X1A 2L9

Drinking Water Management Division, 135 St. Clair Ave. West, Toronto, ON M4V 1P5
416-314-4475, Fax: 416-314-6935

Energy & Minerals Division, Jones Bldg., 4th Fl., Charlottetown, PE C1A 7N8
902-894-0288, Fax: 902-894-0290

Environmental Protection & Audit Division, 3211 Albert St., 5th Fl., Regina, SK S4S 5W6
306-787-2947

Environmental Stewardship Branch, 351 boul St-Joseph, Gatineau, QC K1A 0H3
819-997-1575, Fax: 819-953-9452

Freshwater Institute, 501 University Cres., Winnipeg, MB R3T 2N6
204-983-5000, Fax: 204-983-6285

Integrated Environmental Policy Division, 77 Wellesley St. West, 11th Fl., Toronto, ON M7A 2T5
416-314-6338, Fax: 416-314-6346

International Joint Commission, 234 Laurier Ave. West, 22nd Fl., Ottawa, ON K1P 6K6
613-947-1420, Fax: 613-993-5583, beckhoffb@ottawa.ijc.org

Monitoring & Science Division, Petroleum Plaza ST, 9915 - 108 St., 10th Fl., Edmonton, AB T5K 2G8

National Water Research Institute, 867 Lakeshore Rd., PO Box 5050, Burlington, ON L7R 4A6
905-336-4625, Fax: 905-336-6444, nwriscience.liaison@ec.gc.ca

Nunavut Water Board, PO Box 119, Gjoa Haven, NU X0B 1J0
867-360-6338, Fax: 867-360-6369

Water Science & Technology, 867 Lakeshore Rd., PO Box 5050, Burlington, ON L7R 4A6
905-336-4625, Fax: 905-336-6444

Alberta

Alberta Environment & Sustainable Resource Development, Oxbridge Place, 9820 - 106 St., Main Fl., Edmonton, AB T5K 2J6
780-427-2700, Fax: 780-422-4086, -310-0000, env.infocent@gov.ab.ca; srd.infocent@gov.ab.ca

British Columbia

Environmental Protection Division, PO Box 9339, Victoria, BC V8W 9M1
250-387-1288, Fax: 250-387-5669

Water Stewardship Division, PO Box 9339 Prov Govt,Victoria, BC V8W 9M1
Fax: 250-387-6003
Manitoba
Manitoba Water Services Board, PO Box 22080, Brandon, MB R7A 6Y9
204-726-6076, Fax: 204-726-6290
New Brunswick
Community Planning & Environmental Protection Division, Marysville Place, PO Box 6000, Fredericton, NB E3B 5H1
506-444-5119, Fax: 506-457-7333, elg/egl-info@gnb.ca
New Brunswick Department of Environment & Local Government, Marysville Place, PO Box 6000, Fredericton, NB E3B 5H1
506-453-2690, Fax: 506-457-4994, elg/egl-info@gnb.ca
Partnerships & Innovation Division, Marysville Place, PO Box 6000, Fredericton, NB E3B 5H1
506-453-2862, Fax: 506-453-2265, elg/egl-info@gnb.ca
Northwest Territories
Northwest Territories Water Board, 125 Mackenzie Rd., PO Box 2531, Yellowknife, NT X0E 0T0
867-678-2942, Fax: 867-678-2943, info@nwtwb.com
Nova Scotia
Department of Agriculture, 1741 Brunswick St., 3rd Fl., PO Box 2223, Halifax, NS B3J 3C4
902-424-4560, Fax: 902-424-4671
Nunavut
Department of Health & Social Services, PO Box 1000 1000,Iqaluit, NU X0A 0H0
867-975-5700, Fax: 867-975-5705
Ontario
Advisory Council on Drinking Water Quality & Testing Standards, 40 St. Clair Ave. West, 3rd Fl., Toronto, ON M4V 1M2
416-212-7779, Fax: 416-212-7595
Ontario Clean Water Agency, 1 Yonge St., 17th Fl., Toronto, ON M5E 1E5
416-314-5600, Fax: 416-314-8300, 800-667-6292
Walkerton Clean Water Centre, 20 Ontario Rd., PO Box 160, Walkerton, ON N0G 2V0
519-881-2003, Fax: 519-881-4947, 866-515-0550, inquiry@wcwc.ca
Quebec
Ministère du Développement durable, de l'Environnement, de la Faune, et des Parcs, Édifice Marie-Guyart, 675, boul René-Lévesque est, 29e étage, Québec, QC G1R 5V7
418-521-3830, Fax: 418-646-5974, 800-561-1616, info@mddep.gouv.qc.ca
Saskatchewan
Saskatchewan Environment, 3211 Albert St., 2nd Fl., Regina, SK S4S 5W6
306-787-2584, Fax: 306-787-9544, 800-567-4224, Centre.Inquiry@gov.sk.ca
Saskatchewan Water Corporation (SaskWater), #200, 111 Fairford St. East, Moose Jaw, SK S6H 1C8
Fax: 306-694-3207, 888-230-1111, comm@saskwater.com; customerservice@saskwater.com
Saskatchewan Watershed Authority, 111 Fairford St. East, Moose Jaw, SK S6H 7X9
306-694-3900, Fax: 306-694-3944, comm@swa.ca
Yukon Territory
Yukon Environment, PO Box 2703, Whitehorse, YT Y1A 2C6
867-667-5652, Fax: 867-393-7197, environment.yukon@gov.yk.ca

WEIGHTS & MEASURES

Standards Council of Canada, #200, 270 Albert St., Ottawa, ON K1P 6N7
613-238-3222, Fax: 613-569-7808, info@scc.ca

WILDLIFE RESOURCES

Canadian Wildlife Service, 351, boul St-Joseph, Gatineau, QC K1A 0H3
819-997-1301, Fax: 819-953-7177
Committee on the Status of Endangered Wildlife in Canada, c/o Canadian Wildlife Service, 351 St. Joseph Blvd, 4th Fl., Gatineau, QC K1A 0H3
819-953-3215, Fax: 819-994-3684, cosewic/cosepac@ec.gc.ca
Fish & Wildlife Division, Petroleum Plaza ST, 9915 - 108 St., 11th Fl., Edmonton, AB T5K 2G8
North American Bird Conservation Initiative, Canadian Wildlife Service, 351, boul St-Joseph, 3e étage, Gatineau, QC K1A 0H3
819-994-0512, Fax: 819-994-4445, nabci@ec.gc.ca
North American Waterfowl Management Plan, NAWCC (Canada) Secretariat, Place Vincent Massey, 351 St. Joseph Blvd., 7th Fl., Gatineau, QC K1A 0H3
819-934-6034, Fax: 819-934-6017, nawmp@ec.gc.ca
Alberta
Alberta Sport, Recreation, Parks, & Wildlife Foundation, Standard Life Centre, #903, 10405 Jasper Ave., 9th Fl., Edmonton, AB T5J 4R7
780-415-1167, Fax: 780-415-0308, -310-0000
British Columbia
Environmental Stewardship Division, PO Box 9339 Prov Govt,Victoria, BC V8W 9M1
250-356-0121, Fax: 250-387-5669
Manitoba
Endangered Species Advisory Committee, 200 Saulteaux Cres., PO Box 24, Winnipeg, MB R3J 3W3
204-945-7465, Fax: 204-945-3077
Newfoundland & Labrador
Forestry Services, Fortis Bldg., PO Box 2006, Corner Brook, NL A2H 6J8
709-637-2284, Fax: 709-634-4378
Nunavut
Department of Environment, PO Box 1000 1300,Iqaluit, NU X0A 0H0
867-975-7700, Fax: 867-975-7742, environment@gov.nu.ca
Ontario
Ontario Ministry of Environment, 135 St. Clair Ave. West, Toronto, ON M4V 1P5
416-325-4000, Fax: 416-325-3159, 800-565-4923
Ontario Fish & Wildlife Heritage Commission, Robinson Pl., 300 Water St., PO Box 7000, Peterborough, ON K9J 8M5
705-755-1905, Fax: 705-755-1900
Quebec
Fondation de la faune du Québec, Place Iberville II, #420, 1175, av Lavigerie, Québec, QC G1V 4P1
418-644-7926, Fax: 418-643-7655, 877-639-0742, ffq@fondationdelafaune.qc.ca
Ministère des Ressources naturelles, 880, ch Sainte-Foy, Québec, QC G1S 4X4
418-627-8600, Fax: 418-644-6513, 866-248-6936, services.clientele@mrnf.gouv.qc.ca

WOMEN'S ISSUES

See Also: Pay Equity
Status of Women Canada, 123 Slater St., 10th Fl., Ottawa, ON K1P 1H9
613-995-7835, Fax: 613-947-0761, 866-902-2719, infonational@swc-cfc.gc.ca
Alberta
Alberta Tourism, Parks, & Recreation, Communications Branch, Commerce Place, 10155 - 102 St., 6th Fl., Edmonton, AB T5J 4L6
780-644-5589, TPR.Communications@gov.ab.ca
Manitoba
Manitoba Women's Advisory Council, #301, 155 Carlton St., Winnipeg, MB R3C 3H8
204-945-6281, Fax: 204-945-6511, 800-282-8069, 001women@gov.mb.ca
Status of Women, #409, 401 York Ave., Winnipeg, MB R3C 0P8
204-945-6281, Fax: 204-945-6511, 800-263-0234, msw@gov.mb.ca
New Brunswick
New Brunswick Department of Social Development, Sartain MacDonald Bldg., 551 King St., PO Box 6000, Fredericton, NB E3B 5H1
506-453-2001, Fax: 506-453-7478, sd-ds@gnb.ca
New Brunswick Advisory Council on the Status of Women, 236 King St., Fredericton, NB E3B 1E2
506-444-4101, Fax: 506-444-4318, 800-332-3087, acswcccf@gnb.ca
Newfoundland & Labrador
Provincial Advisory Council on the Status of Women, #103, 15 Hallett Cres., St. John's, NL A1B 4C4
709-753-7270, Fax: 709-753-2606, 877-753-7270, info@pacsw.ca
Nova Scotia
Nova Scotia Advisory Council on the Status of Women, 1700 Granville St., PO Box 943, Halifax, NS B3J 2V9
902-424-7660, women@gov.ns.ca
Nunavut
Department of Culture, Language, Elders & Youth, PO Box 1000 800,Iqaluit, NU X0A 0H0
867-975-5500, Fax: 867-975-5504, 866-934-2035,
Ontario
Ontario Women's Directorate, 777 Bay St., 6th Fl., Toronto, ON M7A 2J4
416-314-0300, Fax: 416-314-0247, 866-510-5902, owd@ontario.ca
Quebec
Ministère de la Famille, 425, rue Saint-Amable, 1er étage, Québec, QC G1R 4Z1
877-216-6202
Yukon Territory
Yukon Women's Directorate, #1, 404 Hason St., Whitehorse, YT Y1A 1Y8
867-667-3030, Fax: 867-393-6270

WORKERS' COMPENSATION

Merchant Seamen Compensation Board, Secretary, Merchant Seamen Compensation Board, Phase II, Place du Portage, 10th Fl., Ottawa, ON K1A 0J2
819-953-8001, Fax: 819-994-5368
Alberta
Appeals Commission for Alberta Workers' Compensation, Energy Square Building, #901, 10109 - 106th St., Edmonton, AB T5J 3L7
780-412-8700, Fax: 780-412-8701, webmaster1@appealscommission.ab.ca
British Columbia
Workers' Compensation Appeal Tribunal, #150, 4600 Jacombs Rd., Richmond, BC V6V 3B1
604-664-7800, Fax: 604-664-7898, 800-663-2782
Workers' Compensation Board of British Columbia, PO Box 5350 Terminal,Vancouver, BC V6B 5L5
604-276-3100, Fax: 604-276-3247, 888-621-7233
Manitoba
Manitoba Workers' Compensation Board, 333 Broadway Ave., Winnipeg, MB R3C 4W3
204-954-4321, Fax: 204-954-4999, 800-362-3340, wcb@wcb.mb.ca
New Brunswick
Workplace Health, Safety & Compensation Commission of New Brunswick, 1 Portland St., PO Box 160, Saint John, NB E2L 3X9
506-632-2200, 800-222-9775, communications@ws-ts.nb.ca
Newfoundland & Labrador
Newfoundland & Labrador Workplace Health, Safety & Compensation Commission, 146 - 148 Forest Rd., PO Box 9000, St. John's, NL A1A 3B8
709-778-1000, Fax: 709-738-1714, 800-563-9000, general.inquiries@whscc.nl.ca
Northwest Territories
Northwest Territories & Nunavut Workers' Safety & Compensation Commission, Centre Square Tower, 5022 - 49th St., 5th Fl., PO Box 8888, Yellowknife, NT X1A 2R3
867-920-3888, Fax: 867-873-4596, 800-661-0792
Nova Scotia
Workers' Compensation Board of Nova Scotia, 5668 South St., PO Box 1150, Halifax, NS B3J 2Y2
902-491-8999, Fax: 902-491-8002, 800-870-3331, info@wcb.gov.ns.ca
Ontario
Workplace Safety & Insurance Board, 200 Front St. West, Ground Fl., Toronto, ON M5V 3J1
416-344-1000, Fax: 416-344-4684, 800-387-0750
Prince Edward Island
Prince Edward Island Workers Compensation Board, 14 Weymouth St., PO Box 757, Charlottetown, PE C1A 7L7
902-368-5680, Fax: 902-368-5696, 800-237-5049
Quebec
Commission des lésions professionnelles, #700, 900, Place d'Youville, Québec, QC G1R 3P7
418-644-7777, Fax: 418-644-6443, 800-463-1591
Commission de la santé et de la sécurité du travail du Québec, 524, rue Bourdages, CP 1200 Terminus postal,Québec, QC G1K 7E2
418-266-4850, Fax: 418-266-4669, 866-302-2778
Saskatchewan
Saskatchewan Workers' Compensation Board, #200, 1881 Scarth St., Regina, SK S4P 4L1
306-787-4370, Fax: 306-787-4311, 800-667-7590, internet_clientsvc@wcbsask.com
Yukon Territory
Yukon Workers' Compensation Health & Safety Board, 401 Strickland St., Whitehorse, YT Y1A 5N8
867-667-5645, Fax: 867-393-6279, 800-661-0443, worksafe@gov.yk.ca

YOUNG OFFENDERS

Justice Canada, East Memorial Bldg., 284 Wellington St., Ottawa, ON K1A 0H8
613-957-4222, Fax: 613-954-0811, webadmin@justice.gc.ca
Alberta
Alberta Justice & Solicitor General, Communications, Bowker Building, 9833 - 109 St., 3rd Fl., Edmonton, AB T5K 2E8
780-427-2745, 800-310-0000
British Columbia
British Columbia Ministry of Justice, PO Box 9044 Prov Govt,Victoria, BC V8W 9E2

Office of the Representative for Children & Youth, #201, 546 Yates St., Victoria, BC V8W 1K8
250-356-6710, Fax: 250-356-0837, 800-476-3933, rcy@rcybc.ca

Northwest Territories

Department of Justice, Courthouse, 4903 - 49th St., 6th Fl., PO Box 1320, Yellowknife, NT X1A 2L9
867-920-6197

Nova Scotia

Department of Justice, 5151 Terminal Rd., 4th Fl., PO Box 7, Halifax, NS B3J 2L6
902-424-4030, Fax: 902-424-0510, justweb@gov.ns.ca

Nunavut

Young Offenders, 1548 Federal Rd., PO Box 1439, Iqaluit, NU X0A 0H0
867-979-4452, Fax: 867-979-5506

Ontario

Ontario Ministry of the Attorney General, McMurtry-Scott Bldg., 720 Bay St., 11th Fl., Toronto, ON M5G 2K1
416-326-2220, Fax: 416-326-4007, 800-518-7901

YOUTH SERVICES

Alberta

Office of the Child & Youth Advocate, Peace Hills Trust Tower, #805, 10011 - 109 St., Edmonton, AB T5J 3S8
780-422-6056, Fax: 780-644-8833, 800-661-3446

British Columbia

Provincial Services, PO Box 9717 Prov Govt,Victoria, BC V8W 9S1
250-387-0978, Fax: 250-356-2079

New Brunswick

New Brunswick Advisory Council on Youth, Frederick Square, #130, 77 Westmorland St., PO Box 6000, Fredericton, NB E3B 5H1
506-453-3271, Fax: 506-444-4413, 888-830-5588, nbacy-ccjnb@gnb.ca

Nunavut

Department of Culture, Language, Elders & Youth, PO Box 1000 800,Iqaluit, NU X0A 0H0
867-975-5500, Fax: 867-975-5504, 866-934-2035

Ontario

Ontario Ministry of Children & Youth Services, 56 Wellesley St. West, 14th Fl., Toronto, ON M5S 2G3
Fax: 416-325-5191, 866-821-7770

Quebec

Ministère de la Santé et des Services sociaux, Direction des communications, 1075, ch Sainte-Foy, 16e étage, Québec, QC G1S 2M1
418-643-9395, Fax: 418-643-4768, regisseur.web@msss.gouv.qc.ca

ZONING

Alberta

Local Government Services Division, Commerce Place, 10155 - 102 St., 17th Fl., Edmonton, AB T5J 4L4

British Columbia

British Columbia Ministry of Community, Sport, & Cultural Development, PO Box 9490 Prov Govt,Victoria, BC V8W 9N7

Manitoba

Manitoba Municipal Board, #1144, 363 Broadway, Winnipeg, MB R3C 3N9
204-945-2941, Fax: 204-948-2235

Quebec

Commission municipale du Québec, Mezzanine, aile Chauveau, 10, rue Pierre-Olivier-Chauveau, Québec, QC G1R 4J3
418-691-2014, Fax: 418-644-4676, 866-353-6767, cmq@mamr.gouv.qc.ca

Government of Canada

c/o Canada Enquiry Centre, Service Canada, Ottawa, ON K1A 0J9

Tel: 613-941-1827
Toll-Free: 800-622-6232
canadasite@canada.gc.ca
www.canada.gc.ca
TTY: 800-926-9105

All political authority in Canada is divided between the federal & provincial governments, according to the provisions of the Constitution Act, 1867. Local municipalities are a concern of the provinces, & derive their authority from Acts of provincial legislation. The Parliament of Canada consists of Her Majesty Queen Elizabeth II (represented in Canada by the Governor General, His Excellency the Right Honourable David Johnston), an Upper House called the Senate, & an elected House of Commons.

Governor General & Commander-in-Chief of Canada / Gouverneur général et Commandant en chef du Canada

Rideau Hall, 1 Sussex Dr., Ottawa, ON K1A 0A1

Tel: 613-993-8200
Fax: 613-998-8760
Toll-Free: 800-465-6890
info@gg.ca
www.gg.ca

Canada is a constitutional monarchy. Under the terms of its Constitution, Her Majesty Queen Elizabeth II is the Head of State. The duties of the Head of State in Canada are undertaken by the Governor General as the Crown's representative. He is also Commander-in-Chief of the Canadian Forces, Chancellor & Principal Companion of the Order of Canada, Chancellor & Commander of the Order of Military Merit, & Head of the Canadian Heraldic Authority. The Office of the Governor General encompasses a number of responsibilities, both constitutional & traditional in nature. The Governor General of Canada exercises powers & responsibilities belonging to the Sovereign, with the advice of members of the Privy Council. He is involved in the promotion of Canadian sovereignty at home & represents Canada abroad. Canadian values, diversity, inclusion, culture, & heritage are promoted by the Governor General. National honours, decorations, & awards to recognize people who have demonstrated excellence, valour, bravery, or exceptional dedication to service are presented by the Governor General.

Governor General, Rt. Hon. David Johnston, C.C.
Tel: 613-993-8200
Fax: 613-993-1967

Secretary to the Governor General, Stephen Wallace
Tel: 613-993-0259
Fax: 613-993-1967

Director General, Corporate Services, Fady Abdul-Nour
Tel: 613-991-9091
Fax: 613-998-8762

Superintendent, Associated Services - Security, Sylvian Côté
Tel: 613-993-9332
Fax: 613-993-8641

The Chancellery of Honours / Chancellerie
1 Sussex Dr., Ottawa, ON K1A 0A1

Tel: 613-998-8732
Fax: 613-991-1681

Deputy Secretary & Deputy Herald Chancellor, Office of the Secretary to the Governor General, The Chancellery of Honours, Emmanuelle Sajous
Tel: 613-998-8731
Fax: 613-991-1681

Director, Honours, Office of the Secretary to the Governor General, Honours Directorate, Gabrielle Lappa
Tel: 613-991-0894
Fax: 613-991-1681

Chief Herald of Canada & Director, Office of the Secretary to the Governor General, The Canadian Heraldic Authority, Claire Boudreau
Tel: 613-991-2227
Fax: 613-990-5818

Deputy Chief Herald of Canada & Assistant Director, Office of the Secretary to the Governor General, Bruce Patterson
Tel: 613-991-2229
Fax: 613-990-5818

Policy, Program & Protocol Branch / Politique, programme et protocole
1 Sussex Dr., Ottawa, ON K1A 0A1

Deputy Secretary, Patricia Jaton
Tel: 613-990-9006
Fax: 613-993-4728

Chief, Visitor Services & Exhibits, Dominique Bergeron
Tel: 613-993-0311
Fax: 613-993-1656

Director, Security & Logistics, Sylvie Beaudry
Tel: 613-993-0439
Fax: 613-993-4728

Acting Director, Public Affairs, Annabelle Cloutier
Tel: 613-993-8158
Fax: 613-998-1664

Director, Events & Visitor Services, Christine MacIntyre
Tel: 613-993-1901
Fax: 613-991-5113

Director, Policy, Planning, & Correspondence, Duncan Mousseau
Tel: 613-993-1934
Fax: 613-993-1552

Director, Household Services, Philippe Wettel
Tel: 613-990-7629
Fax: 613-998-5579

Privy Council Office (PCO) / Bureau du Conseil privé (BCP)

#1000, 85 Sparks St., Ottawa, ON K1A 0A3

Tel: 613-957-5153
Fax: 613-997-5043
info@pco-bcp.gc.ca
www.pco-bcp.gc.ca
TTY: 613-957-5741
Other Communication: Media Phone: 613-957-5420

The Privy Council Office provides non-partisan advice & information from across the Public Service to the Prime Minister, the Cabinet, & its decision-making structures. The key roles of the Privy Council are as follows: advising the Prime Minister & supporting the Cabinet; managing the Cabinet's decision-making system & facilitating its efficient & effective functioning on a daily basis; & providing public service leadership, including the management of the appointments process for Crown corporations & agencies, & senior positions in federal departments. The Privy Council is led by the Clerk of the Privy Council. A member of the Privy Council is awarded the title, "Honourable", for life. The Governor General, the Prime Minister, & the Chief Justice of Canada are accorded the title, "The Right Honourable", for life.

Acts Administered:
Canadian Transportation Accident Investigation & Safety Board Act
Migratory Birds Convention Act, 1994 (in respect of any matter related to the Northern Pipeline as referred to in the Northern Pipeline Act)
Oaths of Allegiance Act
Representation Act, 1985
Royal Assent Act

President, Queen's Privy Council for Canada; Minister, Intergovernmental Affairs, Hon. Peter Penashue
Tel: 613-943-1838
Fax: 613-992-3700
peter.penashue@parl.gc.ca

Leader of the Government in the House of Commons (PCO Minister), Hon. Peter Van Loan
Tel: 613-996-7752
Fax: 613-992-8351
peter.vanloan@parl.gc.ca; info@pco-bcp.gc.ca
Other Communications: Department Phone: 613-957-5153

Leader of the Government in the Senate (PCO Minister), Hon. Marjory LeBreton
Tel: 613-943-0756
Toll-free: 800-267-7362
Fax: 613-943-1493
lebrem@sen.parl.gc.ca; Marjory.LeBreton@pco-bcp.gc.ca

Minister of State (Democratic Reform) (PCO Minister), Hon. Tim Uppal
Tel: 613-995-5609
Fax: 613-943-6976
tim.uppal@parl.gc.ca

Minister of State; Chief Government Whip (PCO Minister), Hon. Gordon O'Connor, B.A., B.Sc.
Tel: 613-992-1119
Fax: 613-992-1043
gordon.oconnor@parl.gc.ca

Clerk of the Privy Council & Secretary to the Cabinet, Wayne Wouters
Tel: 613-957-5400
Fax: 613-957-5729
info@clerk.gc.ca

National Security Advisor to the Prime Minister, Stephen Rigby
Tel: 613-957-5056
Fax: 613-957-5277

Special Advisor, Human Smuggling & Illegal Migration, Ward Elcock
Tel: 613-952-6732
Fax: 613-952-6794

Deputy Minister, Afghanistan Task Force, Greta Bossenmaier
Tel: 613-952-4900
Fax: 613-952-4924

Deputy Minister, Intergovernmental Affairs & Associate Secretary to the Cabinet, Janice Charette
Tel: 613-957-5466
Fax: 613-957-5089

Deputy Secretary to the Cabinet, Foreign & Defence Policy Advisor to the Prime Minister, Christine Hogan
Tel: 613-957-5476
Fax: 613-957-5365

Deputy Secretary to the Cabinet, Senior Personnel & Public Service Renewal, Patricia Hassard
Tel: 613-957-5360
Fax: 613-957-5006

Deputy Secretary to the Cabinet, Operations, Michael Martin
Tel: 613-957-5417
Fax: 613-957-5637

Deputy Secretary to the Cabinet, Plans & Consultation, William Pentney
Tel: 613-957-5462
Fax: 613-957-5487

Deputy Secretary to the Cabinet, Legislation & House Planning, & Machinery of Government, Counsel to the Clerk of the Privy Council, Yvan Roy
Tel: 613-957-5792
Fax: 613-952-4955

Executive Director, Administrative Services Review, Wilma Vreeswijk
Tel: 613-996-6538
Fax: 613-995-3506

Privy Council Members & Date When Sworn In
Hon. Paul Theodore Hellyer, Apr. 26, 1957
H.R.H. Prince Phillip, The Duke of Edinburg, Oct. 14, 1957
Rt. Hon. Martial Asselin, Mar. 18, 1963
Hon. Allan Joseph MacEachen, Apr. 22, 1963
Hon. Yvon Dupuis, Feb. 3, 1964
Rt. Hon. John Napier Turner, Dec. 18, 1965
Rt. Hon. Joseph Jacques Jean Chrétien, Apr. 4, 1967
Hon. Alexander Bradshaw Campbell, Jul. 5, 1967
Hon. Donald Stovel Macdonald, Apr. 20, 1968
Hon. Jean-Eudes Dubé, Jul. 6, 1968
Hon. Otto Emil Lang, Jul. 6, 1968
Rt. Hon. Herbert Eser Gray, Oct. 20, 1969
Hon. Robert D. George Stanbury, Oct. 20, 1969
Hon. Alastair William Gillespie, Aug. 12, 1971
Hon. Patrick Morgan Mahoney, Jan. 28, 1972
Hon. Eugene Francis Whelan, Nov. 27, 1972
Hon. William Warren Allmand, Nov. 27, 1972
Hon. James Hugh Faulkner, Nov. 27, 1972
Hon. André Ouellet, Nov. 27, 1972
Hon. Marc Lalonde, Nov. 27, 1972
Hon. J. Judd Buchanan, Aug. 8, 1974
Hon. Pierre Juneau, Aug. 29, 1975
Hon. Marcel Lessard, Sep. 26, 1975
Hon. Leonard Stephen Marchand, Sep. 15, 1976
Hon. Monique Bégin, Sep. 15, 1976
Hon. Jean-Jacques Blais, Sep. 15, 1976
Hon. Francis Fox, Sep. 15, 1976
Hon. Anthony Chisholm Abbott, Sep. 15, 1976
Hon. Iona Campagnolo, Sep. 15, 1976
Hon. Norman A. Cafik, Sep. 16, 1977
Hon. J. Gilles Lamontagne, Jan. 19, 1978
Hon. John M. Reid, Nov. 24, 1978
Hon. Pierre De Bané, Nov. 24, 1978
Rt. Hon. Charles Joseph Clark, Jun. 4, 1979
Hon. Flora Isabel MacDonald, Jun. 4, 1979
Hon. James Aloysius McGrath, Jun. 4, 1979
Hon. John Carnell Crosbie, Jun. 4, 1979
Hon. David Samuel Horne MacDonald, Jun. 4, 1979
Hon. Lincoln MacCauley Alexander, Jun. 4, 1979
Rt. Hon. Donald Frank Mazankowski, Jun. 4, 1979
Hon. Elmer MacIntosh MacKay, Jun. 4, 1979
Hon. Arthur Jacob Epp, Jun. 4, 1979
Hon. John Allen Fraser, Jun. 4, 1979
Hon. William H. Jarvis, Jun. 4, 1979
Hon. Sinclair McKnight Stevens, Jun. 4, 1979

Hon. John Wise, Jun. 4, 1979
Hon. Ronald George Atkey, Jun. 4, 1979
Hon. David Edward Crombie, Jun. 4, 1979
Hon. Henry Perrin Beatty, Jun. 4, 1979
Hon. J. Robert Howie, Jun. 4, 1979
Hon. Michael Holcombe Wilson, Jun. 4, 1979
Hon. Gerald Augustine Regan, Mar. 3, 1980
Hon. Robert Phillip Kaplan, Mar. 3, 1980
Hon. James Sydney Clark Fleming, Mar. 3, 1980
Hon. William H. Rompkey, Mar. 3, 1980
Hon. Pierre Bussières, Mar. 3, 1980
Hon. Charles Lapointe, Mar. 3, 1980
Hon. Edward C. Lumley, Mar. 3, 1980
Hon. Yvon Pinard, Mar. 3, 1980
Hon. Donald James Johnston, Mar. 3, 1980
Hon. Lloyd Axworthy, Mar. 3, 1980
Hon. Paul James Cosgrove, Mar. 3, 1980
Hon. Judith A. Erola, Mar. 3, 1980
Hon. Jacob Austin, Sep. 22, 1981
Hon. Serge Joyal, Sep. 22, 1981
Hon. Robert Gordon Robertson, Mar. 2, 1982
Hon. John Edward Broadbent, Apr. 17, 1982
Hon. William Grenville Davis, Apr. 17, 1982
Hon. William Richards Bennett, Apr. 17, 1982
Hon. John MacLennan Buchanan, Apr. 17, 1982
Hon. Alfred Brian Peckford, Apr. 17, 1982
Hon. James Matthew Lee, Apr. 17, 1982
Hon. Howard Russell Pawley, Apr. 17, 1982
Hon. David Michael Collenette, Aug. 12, 1983
Hon. Céline Hervieux-Payette, Aug. 12, 1983
Hon. Roger Simmons, Aug. 12, 1983
Hon. David Paul Smith, Aug. 12, 1983
Hon. Roy MacLaren, Aug. 17, 1983
Hon. Peter Michael Pitfield, Apr. 19, 1984
Rt. Hon. Martin Brian Mulroney, May 7, 1984
Rt. Hon. Edward Richard Schreyer, Jun. 3, 1984
Hon. Herb Breau, Jun. 30, 1984
Hon. Joseph Roger Rémi Bujold, Jun. 30, 1984
Hon. Jean-C. Lapierre, Jun. 30, 1984
Hon. Ralph Ferguson, Jun. 30, 1984
Hon. Robert Carman Coates, Sep. 17, 1984
Hon. Jack Burnett Murta, Sep. 17, 1984
Hon. Harvie Andre, Sep. 17, 1984
Hon. Otto John Jelinek, Sep. 17, 1984
Hon. Thomas Edward Siddon, Sep. 17, 1984
Hon. Charles James Mayer, Sep. 17, 1984
Hon. William Hunter McKnight, Sep. 17, 1984
Hon. Rev. Walter Franklin McLean, Sep. 17, 1984
Hon. Thomas Michael McMillan, Sep. 17, 1984
Hon. Patricia Carney, Sep. 17, 1984
Hon. André Bissonnette, Sep. 17, 1984
Hon. Suzanne Blais-Grenier, Sep. 17, 1984
Hon. Benoît Bouchard, Sep. 17, 1984
Hon. Andrée Champagne, Sep. 17, 1984
Hon. Michel Côté, Sep. 17, 1984
Hon. James Francis Kelleher, Sep. 17, 1984
Hon. Marcel Masse, Sep. 17, 1984
Hon. Barbara Jean McDougall, Sep. 17, 1984
Hon. Monique Vézina, Sep. 17, 1984
Hon. Saul Mark Cherniack, Nov. 30, 1984
Hon. Paule Gauthier, Nov. 30, 1984
Hon. Stewart Donald McInnes, Aug. 20, 1985
Hon. Frank Oberle, Nov. 20, 1985
Hon. Gordon F. Joseph Osbaldeston, Feb. 13, 1986
Hon. Lowell Murray, Jun. 30, 1986
Hon. Paul Wyatt Dick, Jun. 30, 1986
Hon. Pierre H. Cadieux, Jun. 30, 1986
Hon. Jean J. Charest, Jun. 30, 1986
Hon. Thomas Hockin, Jun. 30, 1986
Hon. Monique Landry, Jun. 30, 1986
Hon. Bernard Valcourt, Jun. 30, 1986
Hon. Gerry Weiner, Jun. 30, 1986
Hon. John William Bosley, Jun. 30, 1987
Hon. Douglas Grinslade Lewis, Aug. 27, 1987
Hon. Pierre Blais, Aug. 27, 1987
Hon. Lucien Bouchard, Mar. 31, 1988
Hon. Gerry St. Germain, Mar. 31, 1988
Hon. John Horton McDermid, Sep. 15, 1988
Hon. Shirley Martin, Sep. 15, 1988
Hon. Mary Collins, Jan. 30, 1989
Hon. Alan Redway, Jan. 30, 1989
Hon. William Charles Winegard, Jan. 30, 1989
Rt. Hon. A. Kim Campbell, Jan. 30, 1989
Hon. Gilles Loiselle, Jan. 30, 1989
Hon. Marcel Danis, Feb. 23, 1990
Hon. Audrey McLaughlin, Jan. 10, 1991
Hon. Pauline Browes, Apr. 21, 1991
Hon. J.J. Michel Robert, Dec. 5, 1991
Hon. Marcel Prud'homme, Jul. 1, 1992
Hon. Lorne Edmund Nystrom, Jul. 1, 1992
Hon. David Alexander Colville, Jul. 1, 1992
Hon. Paul Desmarais, Jul. 1, 1992
Hon. John Charles Polanyi, Jul. 1, 1992
Hon. Maurice F. Strong, Jul. 1, 1992
Hon. Antonine Maillet, Jul. 1, 1992
Hon. Richard Cashin, Jul. 1, 1992
Hon. Paul M. Tellier, Jul. 1, 1992
Hon. David Robert Peterson, Jul. 1, 1992
Hon. Conrad M. Black, Jul. 1, 1992
Hon. Charles Rosner Bronfman, Oct. 21, 1992
Hon. Pierre H. Vincent, Jan. 4, 1993
Hon. James Stewart Edwards, Jun. 25, 1993
Hon. Robert Douglas Nicholson, Jun. 25, 1993
Hon. Barbara Jane Sparrow, Jun. 25, 1993
Hon. Peter L. McCreath, Jun. 25, 1993
Hon. Ian Angus Ross Reid, Jun. 25, 1993
Hon. Larry Schneider, Jun. 25, 1993
Hon. Garth Turner, Jun. 25, 1993
Hon. David Anderson, Nov. 4, 1993
Hon. Ralph Edward Goodale, Nov. 4, 1993
Hon. David Charles Dingwall, Nov. 4, 1993
Hon. Ron Irwin, Nov. 4, 1993
Hon. Brian Tobin, Nov. 4, 1993
Hon. Joyce Fairbairn, Nov. 4, 1993
Hon. Sheila Maureen Copps, Nov. 4, 1993
Hon. Sergio Marchi, Nov. 4, 1993
Hon. John Manley, Nov. 4, 1993
Hon. Diane Marleau, Nov. 4, 1993
Rt. Hon. Paul Martin, Nov. 4, 1993
Hon. Douglas Young, Nov. 4, 1993
Hon. Michel Dupuy, Nov. 4, 1993
Hon. Arthur C. Eggleton, Nov. 4, 1993
Hon. Marcel Massé, Nov. 4, 1993
Hon. Anne McLellan, Nov. 4, 1993
Hon. Allan Rock, Nov. 4, 1993
Hon. Fernand Robichaud, Nov. 4, 1993
Hon. Ethel Blondin-Andrew, Nov. 4, 1993
Hon. Lawrence MacAulay, Nov. 4, 1993
Hon. Christine Stewart, Nov. 4, 1993
Hon. Raymond Chan, Nov. 4, 1993
Hon. Jon Gerrard, Nov. 4, 1993
Hon. Douglas Peters, Nov. 4, 1993
Hon. Alfonso Gagliano, Sep. 15, 1994
Hon. Lucienne Robillard, Feb. 22, 1995
Hon. Fred J. Mifflin, Jan. 25, 1996
Hon. Jane Stewart, Jan. 25, 1996
Hon. Stéphane Dion, Jan. 25, 1996
Hon. Pierre Pettigrew, Jan. 25, 1996
Hon. Martin Cauchon, Jan. 25, 1996
Hon. Hedy Fry, Jan. 25, 1996
Hon. James Andrew Grant, Sep. 30, 1996
Hon. Don Boudria, Oct. 4, 1996
Hon. Bernard Alasdair Graham, Jun. 11, 1997
Hon. Lyle Vanclief, Jun. 11, 1997
Hon. Herb Dhaliwal, Jun. 11, 1997
Hon. David Kilgour, Jun. 11, 1997
Hon. James Scott Peterson, Jun. 11, 1997
Hon. Andy Scott, Jun. 11, 1997
Hon. Andrew Mitchell, Jun. 11, 1997
Hon. Gilbert Normand, Jun. 18, 1997
Hon. Bob Rae, Apr. 30, 1998
Hon. Claudette Bradshaw, Nov. 23, 1998
Hon. Jocelyne Bourgon, Dec. 14, 1998
Hon. Raymond A. Speaker, Jun. 9, 1999
Hon. Frank Joseph McKenna, Jun. 9, 1999
Hon. George Baker, Aug. 3, 1999
Hon. Maria Minna, Aug. 3, 1999
Hon. Elinor Caplan, Aug. 3, 1999
Hon. Denis Coderre, Aug. 3, 1999
Hon. Robert Daniel Nault, Aug. 3, 1999
Hon. J. Bernard Boudreau, Oct. 4, 1999
Rt. Hon. Beverley M. McLachlin, Jan. 12, 2000
Hon. Sharon Carstairs, Jan. 9, 2001
Hon. Robert G. Thibault, Jan. 9, 2001
Hon. Rey Pagtakhan, Jan. 9, 2001
Hon. Gary Albert Filmon, Oct. 4, 2001
Hon. Susan Whelan, Jan. 15, 2002
Hon. Maurizio Bevilacqua, Jan. 15, 2002
Hon. Paul DeVillers, Jan. 15, 2002
Hon. Gar Knutson, Jan. 15, 2002
Hon. Denis Paradis, Jan. 15, 2002
Hon. Claude Drouin, Jan. 15, 2002
Hon. John McCallum, Jan. 15, 2002
Hon. Stephen Owen, Jan. 15, 2002
Hon. William Graham, Jan. 16, 2002
Hon. Gerry Byrne, Jan. 16, 2002
Hon. Jean Augustine, May 26, 2002
Hon. Arnold Wayne Easter, Oct. 22, 2002
Hon. Baljit Singh Chadha, Feb. 20, 2003
Hon. Steven W. Mahoney, Apr. 11, 2003
Hon. Roy J. Romanow, Nov. 13, 2003
Hon. Stan Kazmierczak Keyes, Dec. 12, 2003
Hon. Robert Speller, Dec. 12, 2003
Hon. Giuseppe (Joseph) Volpe, Dec. 12, 2003
Hon. Geoff Regan, Dec. 12, 2003
Hon. Tony Valeri, Dec. 12, 2003
Hon. David Pratt, Dec. 12, 2003
Hon. Jacques Saada, Dec. 12, 2003
Hon. Irwin Cotler, Dec. 12, 2003
Hon. Judy Sgro, Dec. 12, 2003
Hon. Hélène Chalifour Scherrer, Dec. 12, 2003
Hon. Ruben John Efford, Dec. 12, 2003
Hon. Liza Frulla, Dec. 12, 2003
Hon. Joseph Robert Comuzzi, Dec. 12, 2003
Hon. Albina Guarnieri, Dec. 12, 2003
Hon. Joseph McGuire, Dec. 12, 2003
Hon. Mauril Bélanger, Dec. 12, 2003
Hon. Carolyn Bennett, Dec. 12, 2003
Hon. M. Aileen Carroll, Dec. 12, 2003
Hon. André Harvey, Dec. 12, 2003
Hon. Susan Barnes, Dec. 12, 2003
Hon. David Price, Dec. 12, 2003
Hon. Jim Karygiannis, Dec. 12, 2003
Hon. Shawn Murphy, Dec. 12, 2003
Hon. Joseph Louis Jordan, Dec. 12, 2003
Hon. Roger Gallaway, Dec. 12, 2003
Hon. Paul Bonwick, Dec. 12, 2003
Hon. Eleni Bakopanos, Dec. 12, 2003
Hon. Georges Farrah, Dec. 12, 2003
Hon. Mark Eyking, Dec. 12, 2003
Hon. Dan McTeague, Dec. 12, 2003
Hon. Walt Lastewka, Dec. 12, 2003
Hon. Brenda Kay Chamberlain, Dec. 12, 2003
Hon. Larry Bagnell, Dec. 12, 2003
Hon. John Harvard, Dec. 12, 2003
Hon. Gurbax Singh Malhi, Dec. 12, 2003
Hon. Yvon Charbonneau, Dec. 12, 2003
Hon. Joseph Frank Fontana, Dec. 12, 2003
Hon. Jerry Pickard, Dec. 12, 2003
Hon. John McKay, Dec. 12, 2003
Hon. Scott Brison, Dec. 12, 2003
Hon. John Ferguson Godfrey, Dec. 12, 2003
Hon. Andrew Telegdi, Jan. 30, 2004
Hon. Rev. William Alexander Blaikie, Feb. 19, 2004
Hon. Grant Hill, Feb. 19, 2004
Right Hon. Stephen Joseph Harper, May 4, 2004
Hon. Joseph Marin Jacques Olivier, May 5, 2004
Hon. Ujjal Dosanjh, Jul. 20, 2004
Hon. Ken Dryden, Jul. 20, 2004
Hon. David Emerson, Jul. 20, 2004
Hon. Tony Ianno, Jul. 20, 2004
Hon. Peter Adams, Jul. 20, 2004
Hon. Sarmite Bulte, Jul. 20, 2004
Hon. Roy Cullen, Jul. 20, 2004
Hon. Marlene Jennings, Jul. 20, 2004
Hon. Dominic LeBlanc, Jul. 20, 2004
Hon. Judi Longfield, Jul. 20, 2004
Hon. Paul Macklin, Jul. 20, 2004
Hon. Keith P. Martin, Jul. 20, 2004
Hon. Karen Redman, Jul. 20, 2004
Hon. Raymond Simard, Jul. 20, 2004
Hon. Patricia Ann Torsney, Jul. 20, 2004
Hon. Bryon Wilfert, Jul. 20, 2004
Hon. Belinda Stronach, May 17, 2005
Hon. Aldéa Landry, Q.C., Jun. 24, 2005
Rt. Hon. Adrienne Clarkson, Oct. 3, 2005
Hon. Navdeep Bains, Oct. 7, 2005
Hon. Anita Neville, Oct. 7, 2005
Hon. Charles Hubbard, Oct. 7, 2005
Hon. Jean-Pierre Blackburn, Feb. 6, 2006
Hon. Greg Thompson, Feb. 6, 2006
Hon. Marjory LeBreton, Feb. 6, 2006
Hon. Monte Solberg, Feb. 6, 2006
Hon. Charles (Chuck) Strahl, Feb. 6, 2006
Hon. Gary Lunn, Feb. 6, 2006
Hon. Peter Gordon MacKay, Feb. 6, 2006
Hon. Loyola Hearn, Feb. 6, 2006
Hon. Stockwell Burt Day, Feb. 6, 2006
Hon. Carol Skelton, Feb. 6, 2006
Hon. Vic Toews, Feb. 6, 2006
Hon. Rona Ambrose, Feb. 6, 2006
Hon. Michael D. Chong, Feb. 6, 2006
Hon. Diane Finley, Feb. 6, 2006
Hon. Gordon O'Connor, Feb. 6, 2006
Hon. Beverley J. (Bev) Oda, Feb. 6, 2006
Hon. John Baird, Feb. 6, 2006
Hon. Maxime Bernier, Feb. 6, 2006
Hon. Lawrence Cannon, Feb. 6, 2006
Hon. Tony Clement, Feb. 6, 2006
Hon. James Michael (Jim) Flaherty, Feb. 6, 2006
Hon. Josée Verner, Feb. 6, 2006
Hon. Jim Prentice, Feb. 6, 2006
Hon. Michael Fortier, Feb. 6, 2006
Hon. John Reynolds, Feb. 6, 2006
Hon. Jay D. Hill, Feb. 16, 2006
Hon. Peter Van Loan, Nov. 27, 2006
Hon. Jason Kenney, Jan. 4, 2007
Hon. Gerry Ritz, Jan. 4, 2007
Hon. Helena Guergis, Jan. 4, 2007
Hon. Christian Paradis, Jan. 4, 2007
Hon. Daniel Philip Hays, Jan. 22, 2007
Hon. James Abbott, Oct. 15, 2007

Hon. Diane Ablonczy, Aug. 14, 2007
Hon. James Moore, Jun. 25, 2008
Hon. Denis Losier, Sep. 3, 2008
Hon. Arthur Thomas Porter, Sep. 3, 2008
Hon. Leona Aglukkaq, Oct. 30, 2008
Hon. Keith Ashfield, Oct. 30, 2008
Hon. Steven John Fletcher, Oct. 30, 2008
Hon. Gary Goodyear, Oct. 30, 2008
Hon. Peter Kent, Oct. 30, 2008
Hon. Denis Lebel, Oct. 30, 2008
Hon. Rob Merrifield, Oct. 30, 2008
Hon. Lisa Raitt, Oct. 30, 2008
Hon. Gail Shea, Oct. 30, 2008
Hon. Lynn Yelich, Oct. 30, 2008
Hon. Leonard Joseph Gustafson, Jan. 8, 2009
Hon. Frances Lankin, Jan. 22, 2009
Hon. Kevin Lynch, May 11, 2009
Hon. Rob Moore, Jan. 19, 2010
Hon. Michael Grant Ignatieff, May 7, 2010
Hon. Philippe Couillard, Jun. 21, 2010
Hon. John Duncan, Aug. 6, 2010
Hon. Rick Casson, Oct. 1, 2010
Hon. Laurie Hawn, Oct. 1, 2010
Hon. Julian Fantino, Jan. 4, 2011
Hon. Ted Menzies, Jan. 4, 2011
Hon. Steven Blaney, May 18, 2011
Hon. Edward Fast, May 18, 2011
Hon. Bal Gosal, May 18, 2011
Hon. Joe Oliver, May 18, 2011
Hon. Peter Penashue, May 18, 2011
Hon. Tim Uppal, May 18, 2011
Hon. Alice Wong, May 18, 2011
Hon. Peter Andrew Stewart Milliken, May 8, 2012
Hon. Ronald Cannan, Sept 13, 2012
Hon. Mike Lake, Sept 13, 2012
Hon. Thomas J. Mulcair, Sept 14, 2012

Associated Agencies, Boards & Commissions:
• Office of Intergovernmental Affairs / Affaires intergouvernementales

Senate of Canada / Sénat du Canada

Ottawa, QC K1A 0A4
Toll-Free: 866-599-4999
www.sen.parl.gc.ca

Senators are appointed by the Governor General, upon the recommendation of the Prime Minister of Canada. Senators hold their positions only until they attain the age of 75 years.
To be eligible for appointment, a senatorial candidate must be a Canadian citizen, & be at least 30 years of age. The person must own $4,000 of equity in land in his or her province or territory, & have a personal net worth of at least $4,000. A senator must also be a resident of the province or territory for which he or she is appointed.
The main tasks of the Senate are as follows: to examine bills; to approve, reject, or amend legislation; to investigate policy matters & to present recommendations; & to examine the government's spending proposals. No bill may become law unless it is passed by the Senate.
The main thrust of the Senate's work is carried out in committees, where bills are interpreted & reviewed clause by clause, & evidence is heard from groups & individuals who may be affected by the particular bill under review. Senators' committees, or study groups, investigate key issues, such as poverty, terrorism, literacy, children's rights, Aboriginal peoples, constitutional affairs, & foreign affairs. The Senate reports produced from these legislations have p roved to be valuable, & have often led to changes in government policy or legislation.
The Senate, as originally constituted at Confederation, consisted of 72 members. Through the addition of new provinces & territories, & the general growth of Canada, the Senate now has 105 regular members. By provinces & territories, representation in the Senate of Canada is as follows (September 2012):
Alberta 6;
British Columbia 6;
Manitoba 6;
New Brunswick 10;
Newfoundland & Labrador 6;
Northwest Territories 1;
Nova Scotia 10;
Nunavut 1;
Ontario 23;
Prince Edward Island 4;
Québec 24;
Saskatchewan 6;
Yukon 1;
Total 105.
By party affiliation, representation is as follows (September 2012):
Conservative 62;
Liberal 39;
Progressive Conservative 1;
Independent 2;
Vacant 1;
Total 105.

Political Officers

Speaker of the Senate, Hon. Noël Kinsella, Conservative Party
Tel: 613-992-4416
Toll-free: 800-267-7362
Fax: 613-992-9772
kinsen@sen.parl.gc.ca
www.sen.parl.gc.ca/nkinsella

Speaker pro tempore, Hon. Donald H. Oliver, Conservative Party
Tel: 613-943-1445
Toll-free: 800-267-7362
Fax: 613-943-1502
olived@sen.parl.gc.ca
www.senatordonaldoliver.ca

Leader of the Government in the Senate, Hon. Marjory LeBreton, Conservative Party
Tel: 613-943-0756
Toll-free: 800-267-7362
Fax: 613-943-1493
lebrem@sen.parl.gc.ca

Leader of the Opposition in the Senate, Hon. James S. Cowan, Liberal
Tel: 613-995-4268
Toll-free: 800-267-7362
Fax: 613-995-4287
cowanj@sen.parl.gc.ca

Deputy Leader of the Government in the Senate, Hon. Claude Carignan, Conservative Party
Tel: 613-992-0240
Toll-free: 800-267-7362
Fax: 613-992-0246
carigc@sen.parl.gc.ca
www.claudecarignan.ca

Deputy Leader of the Opposition in the Senate, Hon. Claudette Tardif, Liberal
Tel: 613-947-3589
Toll-free: 800-267-7362
Fax: 613-947-3609
tardic@sen.parl.gc.ca

Government Whip, Hon. Elizabeth (Beth) Marshall, Conservative Party
Tel: 613-992-3756
Toll-free: 800-267-7362
Fax: 613-943-1883
marshe@sen.parl.gc.ca

Opposition Whip, Hon. Jim Munson, Liberal
Tel: 613-947-2504
Toll-free: 800-267-7362
Fax: 613-947-2506
munsoj@sen.parl.gc.ca
jimmunson.sencanada.ca

Senators, with appointment year & political affiliation

Hon. Raynell Andreychuk, 1993, Conservative Party
Tel: 613-947-2239
Toll-free: 800-267-7362
Fax: 613-947-2241
andrer@sen.parl.gc.ca

Hon. Salma Ataullahjan, 2010, Conservative Party
Tel: 613-947-5906
Toll-free: 800-267-7362
Fax: 613-947-5908
atauls@sen.parl.gc.ca
senatorsalma.sencanada.ca

Hon. George S. Baker, 2002, Liberal
Tel: 613-947-2517
Toll-free: 800-267-7362
Fax: 613-947-1525
bakerg@sen.parl.gc.ca

Hon. Diane Bellemare, 2012, Conservative Party
Tel: 613-996-7293
Toll-free: 800-267-7362
Fax: 613-996-7365

Hon. Pierre-Hugues Boisvenu, 2010, Conservative Party
Tel: 613-943-4030
Toll-free: 800-267-7362
Fax: 613-943-4029
boisvp@sen.parl.gc.ca
www.boisvenu.ca

Hon. David Braley, 2010, Conservative Party
Tel: 613-943-0040
Toll-free: 800-267-7362
Fax: 613-943-0083
braled@sen.parl.gc.ca

Hon. Patrick Brazeau, 2008, Conservative Party
Tel: 613-947-4231
Toll-free: 800-267-7362
Fax: 613-947-4228
brazep@sen.parl.gc.ca
www.patrickbrazeau.ca

Hon. Bert Brown, 2007, Conservative Party
Tel: 613-944-3434
Toll-free: 800-267-7362
Fax: 613-944-3438
brownb@sen.parl.gc.ca

Hon. JoAnne L. Buth, 2012, Conservative Party
Tel: 613-996-7146
Toll-free: 800-267-7362
Fax: 613-996-7143
buthjo@sen.parl.gc.ca

Hon. Catherine S. Callbeck, 1997, Liberal
Tel: 613-943-0686
Toll-free: 800-267-7362
Fax: 613-943-0693
callbc@sen.parl.gc.ca
sen.parl.gc.ca/ccallbeck

Hon. Larry W. Campbell, 2005, Liberal
Tel: 613-995-4050
Toll-free: 800-267-7362
Fax: 613-995-4056
campbel@sen.parl.gc.ca
www.larrycampbell.ca

Hon. Claude Carignan, 2009, Conservative Party
Tel: 613-992-0240
Toll-free: 800-267-7362
Fax: 613-992-0246
carigc@sen.parl.gc.ca
www.claudecarignan.ca

Hon. Andrée Champagne, 2005, Conservative Party
Tel: 613-995-3999
Toll-free: 800-267-7362
Fax: 613-995-4034
champa@sen.parl.gc.ca

Hon. Maria Chaput, 2002, Liberal
Tel: 613-943-2435
Toll-free: 800-267-7362
Fax: 613-943-2482
chapum@sen.parl.gc.ca
www.mariachaput.ca

Hon. Marie-P. Charette-Poulin, 1995, Liberal
Tel: 613-947-8005
Toll-free: 800-267-7362
Fax: 613-947-8007
poulim@sen.parl.gc.ca

Hon. Ethel M. Cochrane, 1986, Conservative Party
Tel: 613-992-1577
Toll-free: 800-267-7362
Fax: 613-995-6691
cochre@sen.parl.gc.ca
sen.parl.gc.ca/ecochrane

Hon. Gerald J. Comeau, 1990, Conservative Party
Tel: 613-943-1448
Toll-free: 800-267-7362
Fax: 613-943-1556
comeag@sen.parl.gc.ca

Hon. Anne C. Cools, 1984, Independent
Tel: 613-992-2808
Toll-free: 800-267-7362
Fax: 613-992-8513
coolsa@sen.parl.gc.ca
senatorcools.sencanada.ca

Hon. Jane Marie Cordy, 2000, Liberal
Tel: 613-995-8409
Toll-free: 800-267-7362
Fax: 613-995-8432
cordyj@sen.parl.gc.ca
sen.parl.gc.ca/jcordy

Hon. James S. Cowan, 2005, Liberal
Tel: 613-995-4268
Toll-free: 800-267-7362
Fax: 613-995-4287
cowanj@sen.parl.gc.ca

Hon. Jean-Guy Dagenais, 2012, Conservative Party
Tel: 613-996-7644
Toll-free: 800-267-7362
Fax: 613-996-7649
dagenj@sen.parl.gc.ca
senateurdagenais.ca

LGen Hon. Roméo Dallaire, O.C., C.M.M., G.O.C, M.S.C., C.D., (Retired), 2005, Liberal
Tel: 613-995-4191
Toll-free: 800-267-7362
Fax: 613-995-4219
dallar@sen.parl.gc.ca
romeodallaire.sencanada.ca; www.romeodallaire.com

Hon. Dennis Dawson, 2005, Liberal
Tel: 613-995-3978
Toll-free: 800-267-7362
Fax: 613-995-3998
dawsod@sen.parl.gc.ca

Hon. Joseph A. Day, 2001, Liberal
Tel: 613-992-0833
Toll-free: 800-267-7362
Fax: 613-992-1175
dayja@sen.parl.gc.ca
jday.sencanada.ca

Hon. Pierre De Bané, 1984, Liberal
Tel: 613-992-8289
Toll-free: 800-267-7362
Fax: 613-995-6709
debanp@sen.parl.gc.ca
Hon. Jacques Demers, 2009, Conservative Party
Tel: 613-992-0151
Toll-free: 800-267-7362
Fax: 613-992-0128
tessil@sen.parl.gc.ca
Hon. Percy E. Downe, 2003, Liberal
Tel: 613-943-8107
Toll-free: 800-267-7362
Fax: 613-943-8109
pdowne@sen.parl.gc.ca
sen.parl.gc.ca/pdowne
Hon. Norman E. Doyle, 2012, Conservative Party
Tel: 613-996-7483
Toll-free: 800-267-7362
Fax: 613-996-7466
doylen@sen.parl.gc.ca
Hon. Michael Duffy, 2009, Conservative Party
Tel: 613-947-4163
Toll-free: 800-267-7362
Fax: 613-947-4157
mikeduffy@sen.parl.gc.ca
www.mikeduffy.ca
Hon. Lillian Eva Dyck, 2005, Liberal
Tel: 613-995-4318
Toll-free: 800-267-7362
Fax: 613-995-4331
dyckli@sen.parl.gc.ca
sen.parl.gc.ca/ldyck
Hon. Nicole Eaton, 2009, Conservative Party
Tel: 613-947-4047
Toll-free: 800-267-7362
Fax: 613-947-4044
eatonn@sen.parl.gc.ca
nicoleeaton.sencanada.ca
Hon. Art Eggleton, 2005, Liberal
Tel: 613-995-4230
Toll-free: 800-267-7362
Fax: 613-995-4237
egglea@sen.parl.gc.ca
www.senatorarteggleton.ca
Hon. Tobias C. Enverga Jr., 2012, Conservative Party
Tel: 613-996-7293
Toll-free: 800-267-7362
Fax: 613-996-7365
Hon. Joyce Fairbairn, 1984, Liberal
Tel: 613-996-4382
Toll-free: 800-267-7362
Fax: 613-995-3223
fairbj@sen.parl.gc.ca
Hon. Doug Finley, 2009, Conservative Party
Tel: 613-992-0172
Toll-free: 800-267-7362
Fax: 613-992-0169
finled@sen.parl.gc.ca
Hon. Suzanne Fortin-Duplessis, 2009, Conservative Party
Tel: 613-947-4036
Toll-free: 800-267-7362
Fax: 613-947-4004
fortis@sen.parl.gc.ca
www.fortin-duplessis.ca
Hon. Joan Fraser, 1998, Liberal
Tel: 613-943-9556
Toll-free: 800-267-7362
Fax: 613-943-9558
frasej@sen.parl.gc.ca
sen.parl.gc.ca/jfraser
Hon. Linda Frum, 2009, Conservative Party
Tel: 613-992-0310
Toll-free: 800-267-7362
Fax: 613-992-0316
fruml@sen.parl.gc.ca
www.lindafrum.ca
Hon. George Furey, 1999, Liberal
Tel: 613-943-7805
Toll-free: 800-267-7362
Fax: 613-943-7807
fureyg@sen.parl.gc.ca
sen.parl.gc.ca/gfurey
Hon. Irving R. Gerstein, 2009, Conservative Party
Tel: 613-947-4041
Toll-free: 800-267-7362
Fax: 613-947-4039
Hon. Stephen Greene, 2009, Conservative Party
Tel: 613-947-4210
Toll-free: 800-267-7362
Fax: 613-947-4224
greens@sen.parl.gc.ca
Hon. Mac Harb, 2003, Liberal
Tel: 613-996-2379
Toll-free: 800-267-7362
Fax: 613-996-2318
harbm@sen.parl.gc.ca
www.macharb.ca
Hon. Céline Hervieux-Payette, 1995, Liberal
Tel: 613-947-8008
Toll-free: 800-267-7362
Fax: 613-947-8010
hervic@sen.parl.gc.ca
www.eurekablogue.ca
Hon. Leo Housakos, 2009, Conservative Party
Tel: 613-947-4237
Toll-free: 800-267-7362
Fax: 613-947-4239
lacomd@sen.parl.gc.ca
Hon. Elizabeth Hubley, 2001, Liberal
Tel: 613-992-1177
Toll-free: 800-267-7362
Fax: 613-992-1516
hublee@sen.parl.gc.ca
sen.parl.gc.ca/ehubley
Hon. Mobina S.B. Jaffer, 2001, Liberal
Tel: 613-992-0189
Toll-free: 800-267-7362
Fax: 613-992-0673
jaffem@sen.parl.gc.ca
sen.parl.gc.ca/mjaffer
Hon. Janis G. Johnson, 1990, Conservative Party
Tel: 613-943-1430
Toll-free: 800-267-7362
Fax: 613-992-5029
johnsj@sen.parl.gc.ca
jjohnson.sencanada.ca
Hon. Serge Joyal, 1997, Liberal
Tel: 613-943-0434
Toll-free: 800-267-7362
Fax: 613-943-0441
joyals@sen.parl.gc.ca
sen.parl.gc.ca/sjoyal
Hon. Colin Kenny, 1984, Liberal
Tel: 613-996-2877
Toll-free: 800-267-7362
Fax: 613-996-3737
kennyco@sen.parl.gc.ca
www.colinkenny.ca
Hon. Noël A. Kinsella, 1990, Conservative Party
Tel: 613-992-4416
Toll-free: 800-267-7362
Fax: 613-992-9772
kinsen@sen.parl.gc.ca
sen.parl.gc.ca/nkinsella
Hon. Daniel Lang, 2009, Conservative Party
Tel: 613-947-4050
Toll-free: 800-267-7362
Fax: 613-947-4049
langd@sen.parl.gc.ca
www.danlang.ca
Hon. Marjory LeBreton, 1993, Conservative Party
Tel: 613-943-0756
Toll-free: 800-267-7362
Fax: 613-943-1493
lebrem@sen.parl.gc.ca
Hon. Sandra M. Lovelace Nicholas, 2005, Liberal
Tel: 613-943-3635
Toll-free: 800-267-7362
Fax: 613-943-3637
smithc@sen.parl.gc.ca
Hon. Michael L. MacDonald, 2009, Conservative Party
Tel: 613-995-1866
Toll-free: 800-267-7362
Fax: 613-995-1853
www.capebretonsenator.ca
Hon. Frank W. Mahovlich, 1998, Liberal
Tel: 613-943-2065
Toll-free: 800-267-7362
Fax: 613-943-2067
mahovf@sen.parl.gc.ca
Hon. Ghislain Maltais, 2012, Conservative Party
Tel: 613-996-7377
Toll-free: 800-267-7362
Fax: 613-996-7260
maltag@sen.parl.gc.ca
Hon. Fabian Manning, 2011, Conservative Party
Tel: 613-947-4203
Toll-free: 800-267-7362
Fax: 613-947-4170
mannif@sen.parl.gc.ca
Hon. Elizabeth (Beth) Marshall, 2010, Conservative Party
Tel: 613-943-4011
Toll-free: 800-267-7362
Fax: 613-943-4013
marshe@sen.parl.gc.ca
Hon. Yonah Martin, 2009, Conservative Party
Tel: 613-947-4078
Toll-free: 800-267-7362
Fax: 613-947-4082
martin@sen.parl.gc.ca
yonahmartin.sencanada.ca
Hon. Paul J. Massicotte, 2003, Liberal
Tel: 613-943-8110
Toll-free: 800-267-7362
Fax: 613-943-8129
massip@sen.parl.gc.ca
sen.parl.gc.ca/pmassicotte
Hon. Elaine McCoy, 2005, Progressive Conservative
Tel: 613-995-4293
Toll-free: 800-267-7362
Fax: 613-995-4304
mccoye@sen.parl.gc.ca
www.albertasenator.ca
Hon. Thomas Johnson McInnis, 2012, Conservative Party
Tel: 613-996-7293
Toll-free: 800-267-7362
Fax: 613-996-7365
Hon. Paul E. McIntyre, 2012, Conservative Party
Tel: 613-996-7293
Toll-free: 800-267-7362
Fax: 613-996-7365
Hon. Terry M. Mercer, 2003, Liberal
Tel: 613-996-2657
Toll-free: 800-267-7362
Fax: 613-947-2345
mercet@sen.parl.gc.ca
Hon. Pana Merchant, 2002, Liberal
Tel: 613-944-7777
Toll-free: 800-267-7362
Fax: 613-944-7778
merchp@sen.parl.gc.ca
Hon. Don Meredith, 2010, Conservative Party
Tel: 613-996-8572
Toll-free: 800-267-7362
Fax: 613-996-8570
meredd@sen.parl.gc.ca
donmeredith.sencanada.ca
Hon. Grant Mitchell, 2005, Liberal
Tel: 613-995-4254
Toll-free: 800-267-7362
Fax: 613-995-4265
mitchg@sen.parl.gc.ca
senatorgrantmitchell.ca
Hon. Percy Mockler, 2009, Conservative Party
Tel: 613-947-4225
Toll-free: 800-267-7362
Fax: 613-947-4227
mocklp@sen.parl.gc.ca
Hon. Wilfred P. Moore, 1996, Liberal
Tel: 613-947-1921
Toll-free: 800-267-7362
Fax: 613-943-1995
moorew@sen.parl.gc.ca
Hon. Jim Munson, 2003, Liberal
Tel: 613-947-2504
Toll-free: 800-267-7362
Fax: 613-947-2506
munsoj@sen.parl.gc.ca
jimmunson.sencanada.ca
Hon. Richard Neufeld, 2009, Conservative Party
Tel: 613-947-4055
Toll-free: 800-267-7362
Fax: 613-947-4065
neufer@sen.parl.gc.ca
senatorrichardneufeld.com
Hon. Thanh Hai Ngo, 2012, Conservative Party
Tel: 613-996-7293
Toll-free: 800-267-7362
Fax: 613-996-7365
Hon. Pierre Claude Nolin, 1993, Conservative Party
Tel: 613-943-1451
Toll-free: 800-267-7362
Fax: 613-943-1792
nolinp@sen.parl.gc.ca
Hon. Kelvin Kenneth Ogilvie, 2009, Conservative Party
Tel: 613-992-0331
Toll-free: 800-267-7362
Fax: 613-992-0334
ogilvk@sen.parl.gc.ca
Hon. Donald H. Oliver, 2009, Conservative Party
Tel: 613-943-1445
Toll-free: 800-267-7362
Fax: 613-943-1502
olived@sen.parl.gc.ca
www.senatordonaldoliver.ca
Hon. Dennis Glen Patterson, 2009, Conservative Party
Tel: 613-992-0480
Toll-free: 800-267-7362
Fax: 613-992-0495
patted@sen.parl.gc.ca
dpatterson.sencanada.ca

Hon. Robert W. Peterson, 2005, Liberal
Tel: 613-995-4220
Toll-free: 800-267-7362
Fax: 613-995-4229
russem@sen.parl.gc.ca
Hon. Donald Neil Plett, 2009, Conservative Party
Tel: 613-992-0180
Toll-free: 800-267-7362
Fax: 613-992-0186
plettd@sen.parl.gc.ca
www.donplett.ca
Hon. Rose-May Poirier, 2010, Conservative Party
Tel: 613-943-4027
Toll-free: 800-267-7362
Fax: 613-943-4026
poirir@sen.parl.gc.ca
Hon. Nancy Greene Raine, 2009, Conservative Party
Tel: 613-947-4052
Toll-free: 800-267-7362
Fax: 613-947-4054
rainen@sen.parl.gc.ca
sen.parl.gc.ca/nraine
Hon. Pierrette Ringuette, 2002, Liberal
Tel: 613-943-2248
Toll-free: 800-267-7362
Fax: 613-943-2245
ringup@sen.parl.gc.ca
sen.parl.gc.ca/pringuette
Hon. Michel Rivard, 2009, Conservative Party
Tel: 613-947-4107
Toll-free: 800-267-7362
Fax: 613-947-4110
rivarm@sen.parl.gc.ca
Hon. Jean-Claude Rivest, 1993, Independent
Tel: 613-947-2236
Toll-free: 800-267-7362
Fax: 613-947-2238
jcrivest@sen.parl.gc.ca
Hon. Fernand Robichaud, 1997, Liberal
Tel: 613-943-0675
Toll-free: 800-267-7362
Fax: 613-943-0677
Hon. Bob Runciman, 2010, Conservative Party
Tel: 613-943-4020
Toll-free: 800-267-7362
Fax: 613-943-4022
runcib@sen.parl.gc.ca
www.bobrunciman.com
Hon. Nancy Ruth, 2005, Conservative Party
Tel: 613-995-4174
Toll-free: 800-267-7362
Fax: 613-995-4188
mcgeed@sen.parl.gc.ca
www.nancyruth.ca
Hon. Gerry St. Germain, 1993, Conservative Party
Tel: 613-947-2242
Toll-free: 800-267-7362
Fax: 613-947-2244
stgerg@sen.parl.gc.ca
sen.parl.gc.ca/gstgermain
Hon. Hugh Segal, 2005, Conservative Party
Tel: 613-995-4059
Toll-free: 800-267-7362
Fax: 613-995-5259
kfl@sen.parl.gc.ca
www.hughsegal.ca
Hon. Judith Seidman, 2009, Conservative Party
Tel: 613-992-0110
Toll-free: 800-267-7362
Fax: 613-992-0118
seidmj@sen.parl.gc.ca
Hon. Dr. Asha Seth, 2012, Conservative Party
Tel: 613-996-7162
Toll-free: 800-267-7362
Fax: 613-996-7235
setha@sen.parl.gc.ca
Hon. Nick G. Sibbeston, 1999, Liberal
Tel: 613-943-7790
Toll-free: 800-267-7362
Fax: 613-943-7792
sibnic@sen.parl.gc.ca
sen.parl.gc.ca/nsibbeston
Hon. David P. Smith, Q.C., 2002, Liberal
Tel: 613-944-4079
Toll-free: 800-267-7362
Fax: 613-944-4083
smithd@sen.parl.gc.ca
Hon. Larry W. Smith, 2011, Conservative Party
Tel: 613-996-8555
Toll-free: 800-267-7362
Fax: 613-996-8565
Hon. Carolyn Stewart Olsen, 2009, Conservative Party
Tel: 613-992-0121
Toll-free: 800-267-7362
Fax: 613-992-0124
stewac@sen.parl.gc.ca
Hon. Terry Stratton, 1993, Conservative Party
Tel: 613-947-2224
Toll-free: 800-267-7362
Fax: 613-943-1563
stratt@sen.parl.gc.ca
www.terrystratton.ca
Hon. Claudette Tardif, 2005, Liberal
Tel: 613-947-3589
Toll-free: 800-267-7362
Fax: 613-947-3609
tardic@sen.parl.gc.ca
sen.parl.gc.ca/ctardif
Hon. David Tkachuk, 1993, Conservative Party
Tel: 613-947-3196
Toll-free: 800-267-7362
Fax: 613-947-3198
tkachd@sen.parl.gc.ca
senatortkachuk.com
Hon. Betty E. Unger, 2012, Conservative Party
Tel: 613-996-7420
Toll-free: 800-267-7362
Fax: 613-996-7407
ungerbe@sen.parl.gc.ca
Hon. Josée Verner, 2011, Conservative Party
Tel: 613-996-6999
Toll-free: 800-267-7362
Fax: 613-996-7004
vernej@sen.parl.gc.ca
Hon. John D. Wallace, 2009, Conservative Party
Tel: 613-947-4240
Toll-free: 800-267-7362
Fax: 613-947-4252
wallaj@sen.parl.gc.ca
Hon. Pamela Wallin, 2009, Conservative Party
Tel: 613-947-4097
Toll-free: 800-267-7362
Fax: 613-947-4091
wallinp@sen.parl.gc.ca
www.pamelawallin.com
Hon. Charlie Watt, 1984, Liberal
Tel: 613-992-2981
Toll-free: 800-267-7362
Fax: 613-990-5453
wattc@sen.parl.gc.ca
Hon. Vernon White, 2012, Conservative Party
Tel: 613-996-7602
Toll-free: 800-267-7362
Fax: 613-996-7654
whitev@sen.parl.gc.ca
sen.parl.gc.ca/vwhite
Hon. Rod A.A. Zimmer, 2005, Liberal
Tel: 613-995-4043
Toll-free: 800-267-7362
Fax: 613-995-4046
zimmer@sen.parl.gc.ca
rodaazimmer.sencanada.ca

Clerk of the Senate & Clerk of the Parliaments
Parliament Hill, Centre Block, #185-S, Ottawa, ON K1A 0A4
Clerk of the Senate & Clerk of the Parliaments, Gary W. O'Brien
Tel: 613-992-2493
Usher of the Black Rod, Kevin MacLeod
Tel: 613-992-8483
Director, Information Services Directorate, Hélène Bouchard
Tel: 613-993-5299
Fax: 613-992-7963
Director, Legislative Systems & Broadcasting Division, Diane Boucher
Tel: 613-992-1222
Director, Human Resources Directorate, Linda Dodd
Tel: 613-996-1096
Director, Audit & Planning, Jill Anne Joseph
Tel: 613-944-4070
Fax: 613-943-4610
Director, Finance & Procurement Directorate, Nicole Proulx
Tel: 613-943-0197
Fax: 613-943-4610
Acting Manager, Media Relations & Communications, Karen Schwinghamer
Tel: 613-995-3232

Parliamentary Precinct Services
Chambers Bldg., 40 Elgin St., 13th Fl., Ottawa, ON K1A 0A4
Director General, Gilles Duguay
Tel: 613-992-4787

House of Commons, Canada / Chambre des communes

House of Commons, Centre Block, Parliament Buildings, 111 Wellington St., Ottawa, ON K1A 0A6
Tel: 613-992-4793
Toll-Free: 866-599-4999
info@parl.gc.ca
www.parl.gc.ca
TTY: 613-995-2266
Information Service, Parliament of Canada
Ottawa, ON K1A 0A9

The House of Commons is the major law-making unit in Canada. The 308 members of the House represent each constituency, or riding, across Canada.

Members are elected in general elections, held at least once every five years. During general elections, one candidate per riding is elected, based on the largest number of votes, even if his or her vote is less than half the total. When a member resigns or dies between general elections, a by-election is held. The party that wins the largest number of seats in the general election usually forms the government. The party with the second largest number of votes becomes the Official Opposition. A minority government is created when one particular party holds no clear majority of seats in the House. In this case, the government is usually led by the party with the most seats in Parliament, providing it can sustain the support from other minor parties that enable it to pass legislation.

Any bills within federal jurisdiction must be passed by a majority of House members to become law. Members usually vote on proposed legislation according to party affiliation. They may vote against their party. They may also leave their elected party to sit as an independent within the House.

The Speaker of the House of Commons is a Member of Parliament, who is selected by fellow Members of Parliament through a secret ballot process. The Speaker's roles are to ensure that all procedures & rules are followed in the House, & to oversee administration in the House.

Officers & Officials of the House of Commons
Speaker of the House, Hon. Andrew Scheer, Conservative Party
Tel: 613-992-5042
Fax: 613-995-4253
andrew.scheer@parl.gc.ca; info@andrewscheer.ca
www.parl.gc.ca/About/House/Speaker/index-E.html
Other Communications: Speaker's Office: 613-992-5042; Fax: 613-995-4253
Social Media: twitter.com/andrewscheer, www.facebook.com/AndrewScheerMP
The HonourableAndrew Scheer, The Speaker's Office, House of Commons
111 Wellington St.
Ottawa, ON K1A 0A6
Deputy Speaker; Chair, Committees of theWhole, Joe Comartin, New Democratic Party
Tel: 613-947-3445
Fax: 613-947-3448
joe.comartin@parl.gc.ca
Social Media: twitter.com/joecomartin, www.facebook.com/joecomartin
Deputy Chair, Committees of the Whole, Barry Devolin, B.A., M.A., Conservative Party
Tel: 613-992-2474
Fax: 613-996-9656
barry.devolin@parl.gc.ca
Social Media: twitter.com/BarryDevolin_MP, www.facebook.com/barry.devolin
Assistant Deputy Chair, Committees of the Whole, Bruce Stanton, Conservative Party
Tel: 613-992-6582
Fax: 613-996-3128
bruce.stanton@parl.gc.ca
Social Media: twitter.com/bruce_stanton, www.facebook.com/pages/Bruce-Stanton/6236822310, www.linkedin.com/pub/bruce-stanton/28/19/95
Leader of the Government in the House of Commons; Conservative Party House Leader, Hon. Peter Van Loan, P.C., B.A., LL.B., M.A.,M.Sc.Pl., Conservative Party
Tel: 613-996-7752
Fax: 613-992-8351
peter.vanloan@parl.gc.ca
Note: Web Site: www.houseleader.gc.ca/index.asp?lang=eng&page=Team-equipe&doc=bio/bio-eng.htm
House Leader, Official Opposition, Nathan Cullen, New Democratic Party
Tel: 613-943-7881
Fax: 613-995-9696
nathan.cullen@parl.gc.ca; info@nathancullen.ca
www.nathancullen.com
Social Media: twitter.com/nathancullen, www.facebook.com/nathan.cullen1, www.linkedin.com/pub/nathan-cullen/21/24a/a36
House Leader, Liberal Party, Marc Garneau, C.C., C.D., B.Sc., Ph.D., F.C.A.S.I., Liberal

Tel: 613-995-2727
Fax: 613-995-8632
marc.garneau@parl.gc.ca
Social Media: twitter.com/MarcGarneau, www.facebook.com/pages/Marc-Garneau/21128206560

Acting House Leader, Bloc Québécois, Louis Plamondon, B.A.Ped., B.A.An, BQ
Tel: 613-995-9241
Toll-free: 866-693-2041
Fax: 613-995-6784
louis.plamondon@parl.gc.ca
www.louisplamondon.com
Social Media: www.facebook.com/LouisPlamondonBQ, www.linkedin.com/pub/louis-plamondon/36/b11/771

Chief Government Whip; Whip, Conservative Party of Canada, Hon. Gordon O'Connor, P.C., B.A., B.Sc., Conservative Party
Tel: 613-992-1119
Fax: 613-992-1043
gordon.oconnor@parl.gc.ca
www.gordonoconnor.ca
Social Media: www.facebook.com/pages/Gordon-OConnor/228442573837062?sk=info

Chief Opposition Whip, Nycole Turmel, New Democratic Party
Tel: 613-992-7550
Fax: 613-992-7599
Nycole.Turmel@parl.gc.ca
Social Media: twitter.com/nycole_turmel, www.facebook.com/Turmel.Nycole

Whip, Liberal Party, Judy Foote, B.A., B.Ed, Liberal
Tel: 613-995-7774
Fax: 613-992-5324
Judy.Foote@parl.gc.ca
Social Media: twitter.com/JudyFoote, www.facebook.com/pages/Judy-Foote/36948418784

Caucus Chair, Conservative Party, Guy Lauzon, Conservative Party
Tel: 613-992-2521
Fax: 613-996-2119
guy.lauzon@parl.gc.ca; info@guylauzon.ca
www.guylauzon.ca

Caucus Chair, New Democratic Party, Peter Julian, B.A., New Democratic Party
Tel: 613-995-7224
Fax: 613-947-9500
peter.julian@parl.gc.ca; peter.julian.c1@parl.gc.ca
www.peterjulian.ndp.ca
Social Media: twitter.com/MPJulian, www.facebook.com/MPPeterJulian

Caucus Chair, Liberal Party, Francis Scarpaleggia, B.A., M.A., M.B.A., Liberal
Tel: 613-995-8281
Fax: 613-995-0528
francis.scarpaleggia@parl.gc.ca
Social Media: twitter.com/scarpaleggiamp, www.facebook.com/Fscarpaleggia

Responsible, Conservative Party Research Office, Right Hon. Stephen Joseph Harper, P.C., B.A., M.A., Conservative Party
Tel: 613-992-4211
Fax: 613-941-6900
stephen.harper@parl.gc.ca; pm@pm.gc.ca
www.pm.gc.ca
Social Media: twitter.com/pmharper

Responsible, New Democratic Party Research Office, Thomas J. Mulcair, B.C.L. (Civil Law). LL.B (Common Law), New Democratic Party
Tel: 613-995-7691
Fax: 613-995-0114
thomas.mulcair@parl.gc.ca
www.thomasmulcair.ndp.ca; www.ndp.ca/thomasmulcair
Social Media: twitter.com/ThomasMulcair, www.facebook.com/ThomasMulcair

Responsible, Liberal Party Research Office, Hon. Ralph Goodale, P.C., B.A., LL.B., Liberal
Tel: 613-996-4743
Fax: 613-996-9790
ralph.goodale@parl.gc.ca; goodale@sasktel.net
www.ralphgoodale.liberal.ca
Social Media: twitter.com/RalphGoodale, www.facebook.com/ralphgoodale

Clerk, House of Commons, Audrey Elizabeth O'Brien
Tel: 613-992-2986
Fax: 613-995-6668

Deputy Clerk, House of Commons, Marc Bosc
Tel: 613-992-3156
Fax: 613-995-1449

Sergeant-at-Arms, Kevin M. Vickers
Tel: 613-992-2637
Fax: 613-995-4901
Office of the Sergeant-at-Arms, House of Commons
111 Wellington St.
Ottawa, ON K1A 0A6

Finance Services

Chief Financial Officer, Mark Watters
Tel: 613-996-0485
Fax: 613-995-4970

Chief Acquisitions Officer, Khalil Ibrahim
Tel: 613-996-2214
Fax: 613-992-3037

Head, Corporate Services, Murray Hodgins
Tel: 613-996-6065
Fax: 613-995-3072

Manager, Accounting, Nathalie Charpentier
Tel: 613-947-0946
Fax: 613-995-3072

Manager, Materiel Management & Warehousing, Stéphanie Charron
Tel: 613-947-2485
Fax: 613-943-8353

Manager, Financial Planning, Céline Laflamme
Tel: 613-995-1508
Fax: 613-947-3571

Manager, Standards & Performance Management, Dominique Lalonde
Tel: 613-947-6756
Fax: 613-992-3037

Manager, Corporate Policy Services, James MacKay
Tel: 613-992-1678
Fax: 613-947-3571

Manager, Contracting Services, Ghislaine Parent
Tel: 613-943-0838
Fax: 613-992-3037

Manager, Policy Services for Members, Jane Princi
Tel: 613-995-1618
Fax: 613-947-3571

Human Resources, Corporate Planning, & Communications Services

Chief Human Resources Officer, Kathryn Butler Malette
Tel: 613-992-0100
Fax: 613-947-0001

Director, Human Resources Strategies & Development, Marie-Andrée Bourgouin
Tel: 613-947-1175
Fax: 613-992-2599

Head, Corporate Communications, Léonie Bouvier
Tel: 613-992-9216
Fax: 613-995-3052

Head, Payroll Services & Benefits, Michel Fortin
Tel: 613-996-8768

Head, Corporate Planning, Kevin Whitehouse
Tel: 613-947-6776
Fax: 613-996-1698

Manager, Health, Safety & Environment, Sandra Benoît
Tel: 613-992-1379
Fax: 613-943-0848

Manager, Learning & Growth, Louise Chevrier
Tel: 613-943-4516
Fax: 613-992-2599

Manager, Staffing, Classification & Compensation, Pierre Côté
Tel: 613-995-6075
Fax: 613-995-1470

Manager, Administration, Planning, IM, & HR Systems, Sylvie Farrell
Tel: 613-992-2737
Fax: 613-947-0001

Manager, Labour Relations & Compensation, Chantal Paquette
Tel: 613-943-1500
Fax: 613-943-9772

Senior Communications Officer, Valérie Gervais
Tel: 613-944-6475
Fax: 613-995-3052

Senior Administrative Assistant, Employee Relations & Human Resources Services, Alda Da Silva
Tel: 613-995-3878
Fax: 613-943-9772

Information Services

Tel: 613-995-9631
Fax: 613-947-3547

Chief Information Officer, Louis Bard
Tel: 613-995-8884
Fax: 613-947-3547

Chief, Application Architecture & Development, Soufiane Ben Moussa
Tel: 613-943-1465
Fax: 613-943-1810

Chief, Publishing Service, Kim Buzzetti
Tel: 613-947-4911
Fax: 613-996-9496

Chief, Information Management, Leslie Hamel
Tel: 613-944-5227
Fax: 613-944-4118

Chief, Telecommunications, Sophie Hart
Tel: 613-947-6550
Fax: 613-995-4774

Chief, Finance, Administration, & Planning, Stéphane Jacques
Tel: 613-996-4994
Fax: 613-943-7890

Chief, Application Maintenance & Support Operations, Roger Roy
Tel: 613-996-4494
Fax: 613-943-1810

Chief, Reporting Services, Bruce Young
Tel: 613-995-1542
Fax: 613-991-1851

Director, IT Operations, Stéphan Aubé
Tel: 613-992-7449
Fax: 613-947-6292

Director, Printing Services, Benoit Giroux
Tel: 613-992-7398
Fax: 613-996-1589

Director, Parliamentary Publications, Michel Roy
Tel: 613-992-2420
Fax: 613-996-9496

Acting Deputy Director, IT Operations, Réal Charlebois
Tel: 613-947-0145
Fax: 613-947-6292

Manager, IT Project Management Office, Jean Forgues
Tel: 613-947-2397
Fax: 613-996-1414

Manager, Resources Applications, Michelle Guay-Leblanc
Tel: 613-992-3944
Fax: 613-943-1713

Acting Manager, IT Security, Christopher Karson
Tel: 613-947-7960
Fax: 613-947-6292

Manager, Television & Radio Services, Jean Leduc
Tel: 613-992-8102

Manager, Information Services Procurement Services, Christine Lemieux
Tel: 613-943-5727
Fax: 613-943-7890

Acting Manager, Event Support, François Patenaude
Tel: 613-995-1973
Fax: 613-992-4897

Television Producer, Multimedia Services, Alain Bourque
Tel: 613-992-1266
Fax: 613-995-3053

Television Producer, Multimedia Services, Pierre Ménard
Tel: 613-947-3405

Law Clerk & Parliamentary Counsel

Chief, Administrative Services, Suzanne Dupuis
Tel: 613-947-1997
Fax: 613-947-5556

Deputy Law Clerk & Parliamentary Counsel, Richard Denis
Tel: 613-943-2601
Fax: 613-947-5556

Office of the Clerk & Secretariat

Clerk of the House of Commons, Audrey O'Brien
Tel: 613-992-2986
Fax: 613-995-6668

Director, Audit & Review, Marie Nadeau
Tel: 613-996-2106
Fax: 613-943-2710

Director, Audit & Review, Jennifer Wall
Tel: 613-944-4080
Fax: 613-943-2710

Manager, Office of the Clerk, Suzanne Verville
Tel: 613-992-2986
Fax: 613-995-6668

Coordinator, Member's Orientation & Election Readiness Secretariat, Lyne Crêtes
Tel: 613-992-8282
Fax: 613-995-6668

Senior Administrative Coordinator, Anne-Marie Wszol
Tel: 613-996-1796
Fax: 613-995-6668

Senior Auditor, Michèle Serano
Tel: 613-995-1749
Fax: 613-943-2710

Risks & Controls Officer, Céline Gauthier
Tel: 613-943-9768
Fax: 613-943-2710

Parliamentary Precinct Services

Tel: 613-995-7521
Fax: 613-995-4901

Sergeant-at-Arms of the House of Commons, Kevin Vickers
Tel: 613-992-2637
Fax: 613-995-4901

Deputy Sergeant-at-Arms & Director General, John Janusz
Tel: 613-995-7020
Fax: 613-947-0692

Sergeant, Scanner Operations, Robert Couture
Tel: 613-996-9362
Fax: 613-947-9681

Sergeant, Chamber Security & Ceremonial Unit, Gérard Dignard
Tel: 613-992-7081
Fax: 613-947-3115
Executive Director to the Sergeant-At-Arms, Josée Knight
Tel: 613-943-0473
Fax: 613-995-4901
Director General, Parliamentary Accommodation, Michel Séguin
Tel: 613-996-7077
Fax: 613-995-7888
Chief, Parking Operations, Denis Deschambault
Tel: 613-947-5667
Fax: 613-947-0653
Chief, Postal, Distribution, Messenger, & Transportation Services, Robert Frenette
Tel: 613-996-1021
Fax: 613-996-0221
Chief, Press Gallery, Terry Guillon
Tel: 613-992-4511
Fax: 613-995-5795
Chief, Finance, Administration, & Planning, Brenda Hayter
Tel: 613-995-4704
Fax: 613-995-7888

Procedural Services
Deputy Clerk, Marc Bosc
Tel: 613-992-3156
Fax: 613-995-1449
Principal Clerk, Information Management, Colette Labrecque-Riel
Tel: 613-944-5652
Fax: 613-992-9427
Principal Clerk, Committees & Legislative Services Directorate, Jeffrey LeBlanc
Tel: 613-943-9484
Fax: 613-947-0309
Principal Clerk, Committees & Legislative Services Directorate, Ian McDonald
Tel: 613-995-0516
Fax: 613-947-0309
Principal Clerk, Journals Branch, Pierre Rodrigue
Tel: 613-996-1086
Fax: 613-947-5582
Clerk Assistant, House Proceedings, Beverley Isles
Tel: 613-943-6703
Fax: 613-995-2997
Manager, Resource Planning & Administration, Committees & Legislative Services Directorate, Jeannette Goneau
Tel: 613-995-9200
Fax: 613-947-0309
Manager, Administration & Finance, Office of the Clerk Assistant, Lynda Tremblay
Tel: 613-996-6599
Fax: 613-995-2997
Program Administrator, Parliamentary Internship Program, JoAnne Cartwright
Tel: 613-943-1228
Fax: 613-995-5357
Administration Officer, Canadian Study of Parliament Group, Table Research Branch, Dany Lamarque
Tel: 613-995-4033
Fax: 613-943-9949
Coordinator, Page Program, Lisa Chartier-Derouin
Tel: 613-947-3568
Fax: 613-947-2029

Committees of the House of Commons / Comités de la chambre des communes
Committees Directorate, House of Commons, 131 Queen St., 6th Fl., Ottawa, ON K1A 0A6
Tel: 613-992-3150
Fax: 613-947-3089
cmteweb@parl.gc.ca
www.parl.gc.ca/committeebusiness
A committee consists of parliamentarians from the House of Commons, the Senate, or both. Committee members are selected for study & consideration of matters, including bills. Items for consideration by committess are referred by the House of Commons or the Senate.
Types of committees include the following: Committees of the Whole; Joint Committees; Legislative Committees; Liaison Committee; Standing Committees; & Special Committees.
The following are the House of Commons Committees:
Aboriginal Affairs & Northern Development;
Access to Information, Privacy, & Ethics;
Agriculture & Agri-Food;
Bill C-11;
Bill C-18;
Canadian Heritage;
Citizenship & Immigration;
Environment & Sustainable Development;
Finance;
Fisheries & Oceans;
Foreign Affairs & International Development;
Government Operations & Estimates;
Health;
Human Resources, Skills & Social Development, & the Status of Persons with Disabilities;
Industry, Science, & Technology;
International Trade;
Justice & Human Rights;
Liaison;
National Defence;
Natural Resources;
Official Languages;
Proedure & House Affairs;
Public Accounts;
Public Safety & National Security;
Status of Women;
Transport, Infrastructure, & Communities; &
Veterans Affair s.
Principal Clerk, Committees Directorate & Legislative Services, Jeffrey LeBlanc
Tel: 613-943-9484
Fax: 613-947-0309
Principal Clerk, Committees Directorate & Legislative Services, Ian McDonald
Tel: 613-995-0516
Fax: 613-947-0309
Clerk, Aboriginal Affairs & Northern Development Committee, James M. Latminer
Tel: 613-996-1173
Fax: 613-992-9069
aano@parl.gc.ca
Clerk, Access to Information, Privacy, & Ethics Committee, Chad Mariage
Tel: 613-992-1240
Fax: 613-992-9069
ethi@parl.gc.ca
Clerk, Agriculture & Agri-Food Committee, David-Andrés Novoa
Tel: 613-947-6732
Fax: 613-943-0307
agri@parl.gc.ca
Clerk, Canadian Heritage Committee, Christine Holke David
Tel: 613-947-6729
Fax: 613-996-1626
chpc@parl.gc.ca
Clerk, Citizenship & Immigration Committee, Julie Lalande Prud'homme
Tel: 613-995-8525
Fax: 613-996-1962
cimm@parl.gc.ca
Clerk, Environment & Sustainable Development Committee, Marie-France Renaud
Tel: 613-992-5023
Fax: 613-996-1626
envi@parl.gc.ca
Clerk, Finance Committee, Jean-François Lafleur
Tel: 613-992-9753
Fax: 613-996-1626
fina@parl.gc.ca
Clerk, Fisheries & Oceans Committee, Georges Etoka
Tel: 613-996-3105
Fax: 613-996-1626
fopo@parl.gc.ca
Clerk, Foreign Affairs & International Development Committee, Miriam Burke
Tel: 613-996-1540
Fax: 613-992-7974
faae@parl.gc.ca
Clerk, Government Operations & Estimates Committee, Marc-Olivier Girard
Tel: 613-995-9469
Fax: 613-992-9069
oggo@parl.gc.ca
Clerk, Health Committee, Julie Pelletier
Tel: 613-995-4108
Fax: 613-992-7974
hesa@parl.gc.ca
Clerk, Human Resources, Skills, & Social Development & the Status of Persons with Disabilities Committee, Isabelle Dumas
Tel: 613-995-2622
Fax: 613-947-4177
huma@parl.gc.ca
Clerk, Industry, Science, & Technology Committee, Jean Michel Roy
Tel: 613-947-1971
Fax: 613-996-1626
indu@parl.gc.ca
Clerk, International Trade Committee, Paul Cardegna
Tel: 613-944-4364
Fax: 613-992-7974
ciit@parl.gc.ca
Clerk, Justice & Human Rights Committee, Jean-François Pagé
Tel: 613-996-1553
Fax: 613-992-1962
just@parl.gc.ca
Clerk, Liaison Committee, André Gagnon
Tel: 613-947-5623
Fax: 613-947-0309
liai@parl.gc.ca
Clerk, National Defence Committee, Leif-Erik Aune
Tel: 613-995-9461
Fax: 613-947-9670
nddn@parl.gc.ca
Clerk, Natural Resources Committee, Rémi Bourgault
Tel: 613-995-0047
Fax: 613-996-1626
rnnr@parl.gc.ca
Clerk, Official Languages Committee, Simon Larouche
Tel: 613-947-8891
Fax: 613-996-1962
lang@parl.gc.ca
Clerk, Procedure & House Affairs Committee, Michelle Tittley
Tel: 613-996-0506
Fax: 613-996-1626
proc@parl.gc.ca
Clerk, Public Accounts Committee, Joann Garbig
Tel: 613-996-1664
Fax: 613-996-1626
pacp@parl.gc.ca
Clerk, Public Safety & National Security Committee, Andrew Bartholomew Chaplin
Tel: 613-944-5635
Fax: 613-992-7974
secu@parl.gc.ca
Clerk, Status of Women Committee, Marlene Sandoval
Tel: 613-995-6119
Fax: 613-992-7974
fewo@parl.gc.ca
Clerk, Transport, Infrastructure, & Communities Committee, Alexandre Roger
Tel: 613-996-4663
Fax: 613-996-1626
tran@parl.gc.ca
Clerk, Veterans Affairs Committee, Cynara Corbin
Tel: 613-944-9354
Fax: 613-996-6616
acva@parl.gc.ca

Office of the Prime Minister, Conservative Party of Canada / Conservative Research Bureau

Langevin Block, 80 Wellington St., Ottawa, ON K1A 0A2
Tel: 613-992-4211
Fax: 613-995-0101
pm@pm.gc.ca
www.pm.gc.ca
TTY: 613-957-5741
The Prime Minister is the Head of Government in Canada & usually the leader of the party in power in the House of Commons.
The Prime Minister recommends the appointment of the Governor General to the monarchy, & is responsible for selecting a team of ministers, who are then appointed by the Governor General to the Queen's Privy Council. In addition, he or she also controls the appointment of senators, judges, & parliamentary secretaries. It is customary that the Prime Minister is also appointed to the Imperial Privy Council & is thus titled, "The Right Honourable". The Prime Minister has the right to dissolve parliament & can therefore control the timing of general elections.
The Prime Minister's Office is a central agency that features the executive staff of the Prime Minister, such as partisan political advisors & administrators, who provide support to the Prime Minister exclusively.

Prime Minister; Responsible, Conservative Party Research Office, Right Hon. Stephen Joseph Harper, P.C., B.A., M.A.
Tel: 613-992-4211
Fax: 613-941-6900
stephen.harper@parl.gc.ca; pm@pm.gc.ca
Social Media: twitter.com/pmharper

Leader of the Government in the House of Commons; Conservative Party House Leader, Hon. Peter Van Loan, P.C., B.A., LL.B., M.A., M.Sc.Pl.
Tel: 613-996-7752
Fax: 613-992-8351
peter.vanloan@parl.gc.ca

Caucus Chair, Conservative Party, Guy Lauzon
Tel: 613-992-2521
Fax: 613-996-2119
guy.lauzon@parl.gc.ca; info@guylauzon.ca
www.guylauzon.ca

Chief Government Whip, Hon. Gordon O'Connor, P.C., B.A., B.Sc.
Tel: 613-992-1119
Fax: 613-992-1043
gordon.oconnor@parl.gc.ca

www.gordonoconnor.ca
Social Media:
www.facebook.com/pages/Gordon-OConnor/228442573837062?sk=info

Deputy Government Whip, Harold Albrecht, D.D.S.
Tel: 613-992-4633
Fax: 613-992-9933
harold.albrecht@parl.gc.ca
www.haroldalbrechtmp.ca
Social Media:
www.facebook.com/pages/Gordon-OConnor/228442573837062?sk=info

Chief of Staff, Nigel Wright
Tel: 613-992-4211

Parliamentary Secretary to the Prime Minister, Dean Del Mastro, B. Comm. (Hons.)
Tel: 613-992-4211
Fax: 613-996-9800
dean.delmastro@parl.gc.ca
www.deandelmastro.ca
Social Media: www.twitter.com/mpdeandelmastro, www.facebook.com/deandelmastro
Office of the Parliamentary Secretary
80 Wellington St.
Ottawa, ON K1A 0A3

Principal Secretary, Raymond Novak
Tel: 613-992-4211

Executive Director, Conservative Research Bureau, Martin Bélanger
Tel: 613-996-5084
Fax: 613-943-8727
131 Queen St.
Ottawa, ON K1A 0A6

Director, Tour & Scheduling, Deborah Campbell
Tel: 613-952-4959

Director, Policy, Rachel Curran
Tel: 613-952-4211

Director, Caucus Services & Operations, Jonathan Ingraham
Tel: 613-996-5084
Fax: 613-943-8727

Director, Communications, Andrew MacDougall
Tel: 613-957-5555

Director, Planning, Alykhan Velshi
Tel: 613-992-4211

Director, Strategic Communications, Mike White
Tel: 613-957-5555

Director, Issues Management, Chris Woodcock
Tel: 613-960-4019

Senior Advisor, André Bachand
Tel: 613-948-6683

Office of the Leader, Official Opposition, New Democratic Party / New Democratic Party Research Bureau

111 Wellington St., Ottawa, ON K1A 0A6
Tel: 613-995-7224
Fax: 613-995-4565
www.npd.ca

Thomas Mulcair was elected leader of the Official Opposition & Leader of the New Democratic Party of Canada on March 24, 2011. Mulcair's election followed the August 2011 death of Jack Layton, Former Leader of the Official Opposition & Leader of the New Democratic Party. From July 28, 2011 to March 23, 2012, Nycole Turmel was the interim leader.

Leader, Official Opposition; Party Leader, New Democratic Party of Canada; Responsible, New Democratic Party Research Office, Thomas J. Mulcair, B.C.L. (Civil Law). LL.B (Common Law)
Tel: 613-995-7691
Fax: 613-995-0114
thomas.mulcair@parl.gc.ca
Social Media: twitter.com/ThomasMulcair, www.facebook.com/ThomasMulcair

Deputy Leader, New Democratic Party of Canada, David Christopherson
Tel: 613-995-1757
Fax: 613-992-8356
david.christopherson@parl.gc.ca; hamilton@davidchristopherson.ca
www.davidchristopherson.ndp.ca
Social Media: www.facebook.com/DavidChristophersonNDP

Deputy Leader, New Democratic Party of Canada, Libby Davies
Tel: 613-992-6030
Fax: 613-995-7412
libby.davies@parl.gc.ca
www.libbydavies.ca
Social Media: twitter.com/LibbyDavies, www.facebook.com/pages/Libby-Davies/7154945923?ref=nf

Deputy Leader, New Democratic Party of Canada, Megan Leslie, B.A. (Hons), LL.B.
Tel: 613-995-7614
Fax: 613-992-8569
megan.leslie@parl.gc.ca
www.meganleslie.ndp.ca
Social Media: twitter.com/meganleslieMP, www.facebook.com/MeganLeslieMP, www.linkedin.com/pub/megan-leslie/1a/369/886

House Leader, Official Opposition, Nathan Cullen
Tel: 613-943-7881
Fax: 613-995-9696
nathan.cullen@parl.gc.ca; info@nathancullen.ca
www.nathancullen.com
Social Media: twitter.com/nathancullen, www.facebook.com/nathan.cullen1, www.linkedin.com/pub/nathan-cullen/21/24a/a36

Deputy House Leader, Official Opposition, Sadia Groguhé
Tel: 613-947-3445
Fax: 613-954-0707
sadia.groguhe@parl.gc.ca
www.sadiagroguhe.ndp.ca
Social Media: www.facebook.com/Groguhe

Caucus Chair, New Democratic Party of Canada, Peter Julian, B.A.
Tel: 613-995-7224
Fax: 613-947-9500
peter.julian@parl.gc.ca; peter.julian.c1@parl.gc.ca
www.peterjulian.ndp.ca
Social Media: twitter.com/MPJulian, www.facebook.com/MPPeterJulian

Chief Opposition Whip, Nycole Turmel
Tel: 613-992-0336
Fax: 613-992-1160
nycole.turmel@parl.gc.ca
Social Media: twitter.com/nycole_turmel, www.facebook.com/Turmel.Nycole

Deputy Opposition Whip, Philip Toone
Tel: 613-995-9389
Fax: 613-992-6194
philip.toone@parl.gc.ca
Social Media:
www.facebook.com/pages/Philip-Toone/243294132367236

President, New Democratic Party of Canada, Rebecca Blaikie

National Director, New Democratic Party of Canada, Nathan Rotman

Chief of Staff, Leader of the Opposition, Anne McGrath
Tel: 613-992-2888
Fax: 613-995-6426

Chief of Staff, Chief Opposition Whip, Rob Sutherland
Tel: 613-992-9942
Fax: 613-992-1160

Office of the Leader, Liberal Party of Canada / Liberal Research Bureau

Centre Block, 111 Wellington St., Ottawa, ON K1A 0A6
Tel: 613-996-6740
Fax: 613-996-2551
info@liberal.ca
www.liberal.ca

The former leader of the Liberal Party of Canada, Michael Ignatieff announced his resignation on May 3, 2011, following the general election. Later that month, Bob Rae was appointed as the Interim Leader of the Liberal Party of Canada by the National Board of Directors in consultation with the caucus. The next leader of the party will be chosen on April 14, 2013.

Interim Party Leader, Liberal Party of Canada, Hon. Robert "Bob" Keith Rae, P.C., O.C., O.Ont., Q.C., B.A., B.Ph., LL.B.
Tel: 613-996-6740
Fax: 613-996-2551
bob.rae@parl.gc.ca; info@bobrae.ca
Social Media: twitter.com/bobraemp, www.facebook.com/pages/Bob-Rae/8034824801

House Leader, Liberal Party, Marc Garneau, C.C., C.D., B.Sc., Ph.D.,F.C.A.S.I.
Tel: 613-995-2727
Fax: 613-995-8632
marc.garneau@parl.gc.ca
Social Media: twitter.com/MarcGarneau, www.facebook.com/pages/Marc-Garneau/21128206560

Deputy House Leader, Liberal Party, Kevin Lamoureux
Tel: 613-996-6417
kevin.lamoureux@parl.gc.ca
Social Media: www.facebook.com/gokevin.ca

Caucus Chair, Liberal Party, Francis Scarpaleggia, B.A., M.A., M.B.A.
Tel: 613-995-8281
Fax: 613-995-0528
francis.scarpaleggia@parl.gc.ca
Social Media: twitter.com/scarpaleggiamp, www.facebook.com/Fscarpaleggia

Whip, Liberal Caucus, Judy Foote, B.A., B.Ed
Tel: 613-995-7774
Fax: 613-992-1065
Judy.Foote@parl.gc.ca
Social Media: twitter.com/JudyFoote, www.facebook.com/pages/Judy-Foote/36948418784

Deputy Whip, Liberal Party, Massimo Pacetti, B.Comm., F.C.G.A.
Tel: 613-995-9414
massimo.pacetti@parl.gc.ca
Social Media:
www.facebook.com/pages/Massimo-Pacetti/22800125080, www.linkedin.com/pub/massimo-pacetti/29/264/535

Responsible, Liberal Party Research Party, Hon. Ralph Goodale, P.C., B.A., LL.B.
Tel: 613-996-4743
Fax: 613-996-9790
ralph.goodale@parl.gc.ca;goodale@sasktel.net
www.ralphgoodale.liberal.ca
Social Media: twitter.com/RalphGoodale, www.facebook.com/ralphgoodale

Chief of Staff, Liberal Research Bureau, Peter Donolo
Tel: 613-996-6740
Fax: 613-947-0310
massimo.pacetti@parl.gc.ca

Chief Operating Officer, Liberal Research Bureau, Patricia Sorbara
Tel: 613-995-0741
Fax: 613-996-2551

Director, Policy; Director, Liberal Research Bureau, Brian Bohunicky
Tel: 613-947-6727
Fax: 613-996-2551

Director, Policy; Director, Liberal Research Bureau, Michael McNair
Tel: 613-996-9614
Fax: 613-996-2551

Press Secretary, Liberal Research Bureau, Michel Liboiron
Tel: 613-996-6535
Fax: 613-996-2551

Press Secretary, Liberal Research Bureau, Michael O'Shaughnessy
Tel: 613-943-4952
Fax: 613-996-2551

Office of the Leader, Bloc Québécois / Bureau du chef, Bloc Québécois

Centre Block, Ottawa, ON K1A 0A6
Tél: 613-992-6779
Téléc: 613-954-2121
www.blocquebecois.org

Following the May 2011 general election, Gilles Duceppe resigned as leader of the Bloc Québécois party. On December 11, 2011, Daniel Paillé became the Leader & President of the Bloc Québécois.

Party Leader & President, Bloc Québécois, Daniel Paillé,

B.A.A., M.Sc.
Tel: 514-526-3000
Fax: 514-526-2868
dpaille@bloc.org

Acting House Leader, Bloc Québécois, Louis Plamondon, B.A.Ped., B.A.An
Tel: 613-995-9241
Fax: 613-995-6784
louis.plamondon@parl.gc.ca
www.louisplamondon.com
Social Media: www.facebook.com/LouisPlamondonBQ, www.linkedin.com/pub/louis-plamondon/36/b11/771

Treasurer, Onil Arcand

Office of the Leader, Green Party of Canada

Confederation Building,, #518, 244 Wellington St., Ottawa, ON K1A 0A6

Tel: 613-996-1119
Fax: 613-996-0850
Toll-Free: 866-868-3447
leader@greenparty.ca; info@greenparty.ca
www.greenparty.ca
Other Communication: Media Requests, Phone: 613-562-4916, ext. 239

Elizabeth May was elected the Leader of the Green Party of Canada in 2006. In the May 2011 election, May became the first Green Party candidate to be elected to the House of Commons.

Leader, Green Party of Canada, Elizabeth May, O.C., LL.B.
Tel: 613-996-1119
Fax: 613-996-0850
elizabeth.may@parl.gc.ca
Social Media: twitter.com/elizabethmay, www.facebook.com/ElizabethMayGreenLeader, www.linkedin.com/pub/elizabeth-may/3/a91/69

The Canadian Ministry / The Cabinet

Information Service, Parliament of Canada, Ottawa, ON K1A 0A9

Tel: 613-992-4793
Toll-Free: 866-599-4999
info@parl.gc.ca
www.parl.gc.ca
TTY: 613-995-2266

The Canadian Ministry, or Cabinet, is the most significant of all federal government committees or councils. Cabinet members are selected & led by the Prime Minister. They must also be or become members of the Queen's Privy Council.
Cabinet ministers determine specific policies & are responsible for them in the House of Commons. The Cabinet is responsible for initiating all public bills in the House of Commons, & in some instances can create regulations that have the strength of law, termed decisions of the Governor-in-Council.
Cabinet meetings are usually closed to the public, allowing members to discuss their opinions on particular policy in secret. Once decided, members usually support all policy uniformly. If a minister is unable to support the Ministry, he or she is obligated to resign. Ministers are responsible to Parliament for their actions & the actions of their department.
The mailing address for all Cabinet members on Parliament Hill in Ottawa is as follows: House of Commons, Parliament Buildings, Ottawa, Ontario, K1A 0A6.
Members of the The Canadian Ministry are presented in order of precedence:

Members of The Canadian Ministry (Cabinet)

Prime Minister, Right Hon. Stephen Joseph Harper, P.C., B.A., M.A.
Constituency: Calgary Southwest, Alberta
Tel: 613-992-4211
Fax: 613-941-6900
pm@pm.gc.ca; stephen.harper@parl.gc.ca
Other Communications: PM's Office, Phone: 613-992-4211; Fax: 613-995-0101
Social Media: twitter.com/pmharper, www.facebook.com/group.php?gid=338690276206
Note: Web Sites: www.pm.gc.ca (Prime Minister of Canada);www.conservative.ca/leader/stephen_harper (Party Web Site)
Right Honourable Stephen Joseph Harper, Prime Minister, Office of the Prime Minister, Langevin Block
80 Wellington St.
Ottawa, ON K1A 0A2

Minister, Justice; Attorney General of Canada, Hon. Robert Douglas Nicholson, P.C., Q.C., B.A., LL.B.
Constituency: Niagara Falls, Ontario
Tel: 613-995-1547
Fax: 613-992-7910
rob.nicholson@parl.gc.ca
Other Communications: Justice, Phone: 613-992-4621; Fax:613-990-7255
TTY: 613-992-4556
Note: Web Sites: www.canada.justice.gc.ca/eng/mag-mpg/index.html(Department of Justice Canada); www.robnicholson.ca (Personal Web Site)
The Honourable Robert Douglas Nicholson, Minister of Justice & Attorney General of Canada
284 Wellington St.
Ottawa, ON K1A 0H8

Leader of the Goverment in the Senate, Hon. Marjory LeBreton, P.C.
Tel: 613-943-0756
Toll-free: 800-267-7362
Fax: 613-943-1493
Marjory.LeBreton@pco-bcp.gc.ca; lebrem@sen.parl.gc.ca
Note: Web Site: www.pco-bcp.gc.ca/lgs/default.asp?Language=E&Page=home
The Honourable MarjoryLeBreton, Leader of the Government in the Senate, Parliament Hill
#275S, Centre Block
Ottawa, ON K1A 0A4

Minister, National Defence, Hon. Peter Gordon MacKay
Constituency: Central Nova, Nova Scotia
Tel: 613-992-6022
Fax: 613-992-2337
dnd_mdn@forces.gc.ca; peter.mackay@parl.gc.ca
Other Communications: DND, Phone: 613-996-3100; Fax: 613-995-8189
TTY: 800-467-9877
Social Media: twitter.com/MacKayCPC
Note: Web Sites: www.forces.gc.ca/site/minister-ministre/index-eng.asp?WT.svl=ministerLef(Department of National Defence & the Canadian Forces); www.petermackay.ca (Personal Web Site)
Minister's Office, Major-General George R. Pearkes Building, National Defence Headquarters
101 Colonel By Dr.
Ottawa, ON K1A 0K2

Minister, Public Safety, Hon. Vic Toews, P.C., B.A., LL.B.
Constituency: Provencher, Manitoba
Tel: 613-992-3128
Toll-free: 800-830-3118
Fax: 613-995-1049
vic.toews@parl.gc.ca; communications@ps.gc.ca
Other Communications: Public Safety Canada, Phone: 613-991-2924
TTY: 866-865-5667
Note: Web Sites: www.publicsafety.gc.ca/abt/wwa/min-eng.aspx (Public SafetyCanada); www.victoews.com (Personal Web Site)
The Honourable Vic Toews, Minister of Public Safety, Minister's Office, Public Safety Canada
269 Laurier Ave. West
Ottawa, ON K1A 0P8

Minister, Public Works & Government Services; Minister for Status of Women, Hon. Rona Ambrose, P.C., B.A., M.A.
Constituency: Edmonton — Spruce Grove, Alberta
Tel: 613-996-9778
Toll-free: 866-902-2719
Fax: 613-996-0785
Rona.Ambrose@tpsgc-pwgsc.gc.ca;minister-ministre@swc-cfc.gc.ca
Other Communications: Status of Women: 819-956-4000; Fax: 613-995-1761
TTY: 613-996-1322
Social Media: twitter.com/MP_RonaAmbrose, www.linkedin.com/pub/rona-ambrose/16/bb0/668
Note: Web Sites: www.tpsgc-pwgsc.gc.ca/apropos-about/mnstr-eng.html (Public Works & Government Services Canada); www.swc-cfc.gc.ca/abu-ans/min/index-eng.html (Status of Women Canada); www.ronaambrose.com (PersonalWeb Site)
Office of the Minister of Public Works & Government Services Canada, Phase III, Place du Portage
#18A1, 11, rue Laurier
Gatineau, QC K1A0S5

Minister, Human Resources & Skills Development, Hon. Diane Finley, P.C., B.A., M.B.A.
Constituency: Haldimand — Norfolk, Ontario
Tel: 613-996-4974
Toll-free: 800-622-6232
Fax: 613-996-9749
diane.finley@hrsdc-rhdcc.gc.ca; diane.finley@parl.gc.ca
Other Communications: HR & Skills Dev.:819-994-2482; Fax: 819-994-0448
TTY: 800-926-9105
Note: Web Site:www.hrsdc.gc.ca/eng/corporate/ministers/index.shtml (Human Resources & Skills Development Canada); www.dianefinley.ca (Personal Web Site)
The Honourable Diane Finley, Office of the Minister, Human Resources & Skills Development
140, promenade du Portage
Gatineau, QC K1A OJ9

Minister, Foreign Affairs, Hon. John Baird, P.C., B.A.(Hons.)
Constituency: Ottawa West — Nepean, Ontario
Tel: 613-996-0984
Toll-free: 800-267-8376
Fax: 613-996-9880
john.baird@parl.gc.ca
Other Communications: Foreign Affairs, Phone: 613-995-1851
TTY: 613-944-9136
Social Media: twitter.com/JohnBairdOWN
Note: Web Sites: www.international.gc.ca/ministers-ministres/John_Baird.aspx?lang=eng&view=d (ForeignAffairs & International Trade Canada); www.johnbaird.com (Personal Web Site)
The HonourableJohn Baird, Minister, Foreign Affairs, Office of the Minister of Foreign Affairs
125 Sussex Dr.
Ottawa, ON K1A 0G2

Minister, Federal Economic Development Initiative for Northern Ontario; President, Treasury Board, Hon. Tony Clement, P.C., B.A., LL.B.
Constituency: Parry Sound — Muskoka, Ontario
Tel: 613-944-7740
Toll-free: 877-333-6673
Fax: 613-992-5092
tony.clement@parl.gc.ca
Other Communications: FedNor, Fax: 613-941-4553
Social Media: twitter.com/TonyclementCPC
Note: Web Sites:www.ic.gc.ca/eic/site/ic1.nsf/eng/06510.html (FedNor, Industry Canada); www.tonyclement.ca (Personal Web Site)
Minister for FedNor (Federal Economic Development Initiative for Northern Ontario), C.D. Howe Bldg.
235 Queen St.
Ottawa, ON K1A 0H5

Minister, Finance, Hon. James "Jim" Michael Flaherty, P.C., B.A., LL.B.
Constituency: Whitby — Oshawa, Ontario
Tel: 613-992-6344
Fax: 613-992-8320
jim.flaherty@parl.gc.ca
Other Communications: Finance Communications, Phone: 613-992-1573
TTY: 613-995-1455
Social Media: twitter.com/JimFlaherty, www.facebook.com/pages/Jim-Flaherty/49500135386
Note: Web Sites: www.fin.gc.ca/comment/minfin-eng.asp (Department of Finance Canada); www.jimflaherty.com(Personal Web Site)
TheHonourable James Flaherty, Minister of Finance, Department of Finance Canada
140 O'Connor St.
Ottawa, ON K1A 0G5

Leader, Government in the House of Commons, Hon. Peter Van Loan, P.C., B.A., LL.B., M.A., M.Sc.Pl.
Constituency: York — Simcoe, Ontario
Tel: 613-996-7752
Fax: 613-992-8351
peter.vanloan@parl.gc.ca
Other Communications: Office of Leader of Government in HoC:613-995-7226
Note: Web Sites:www.houseleader.gc.ca/index.asp?lang=eng&page=Team-equipe&doc=bio/bio-eng.htm (Leader of the Government in the House of Commons); www.petervanloan.com (Personal Web Site)
The Honourable Peter Van Loan, Office of the Leader of the Government in the House of Commons
111 Wellington St.
Ottawa, ON K1A 0A3

Minister, Citizenship, Immigration, & Multiculturalism, Hon. Jason Kenney, P.C.
Constituency: Calgary Southeast, Alberta
Tel: 613-992-2235
Fax: 613-992-1920
Minister@cic.gc.ca; jason.kenney@parl.gc.ca
Other Communications: Citizenship & Immigration, Phone:613-954-1064
Social Media: twitter.com/kenneyjason, www.facebook.com/pages/Jason-Kenney/29829307640
Note: Web Sites: www.cic.gc.ca/english/department/minister/index.asp (Citizenship &Immigration Canada); www.jasonkenney.com (Personal Web Site)
The Honourable Jason Kenney, P.C., M.P., Citizenship & Immigration Canada
365 Laurier Ave. West
Ottawa, ON K1A 1L1

Minister, Agriculture & Agri-Food; Minister, Canadian Wheat Board, Hon. Gerry Ritz, P.C.
Constituency: Battlefords — Lloydminster, Saskatchewan
Tel: 613-995-7080

Fax: 613-996-8472
gerry.ritz@parl.gc.ca
Other Communications: Agriculture & Agri-Food Canada, Fax:613-773-1081
Note: Web Sites:
www4.agr.gc.ca/AAFC-AAC/display-afficher.do?id=1203439690684&lang=eng(Agriculture & Agri-Food Canada); www.gerryritzmp.com (Personal Web Site)
The Honourable Gerry Ritz, Agriculture & Agri-Food Canada
1341 Baseline Rd.
Ottawa, ON K1A 0C5

Minister, Industry; Minister of State, Agriculture, Hon. Christian Paradis, P.C.
Constituency: Mégantic — L'Érable, Québec
Tel: 613-995-1377
Fax: 613-943-1562
minister.industry@ic.gc.ca; ParadC@parl.gc.ca
Other Communications: Agriculture & Agri-Food Canada, Fax:613-773-1081
Social Media: twitter.com/christianparad
Note: Web Sites:
www.ic.gc.ca/eic/site/ic1.nsf/eng/h_00279.html(Industry Canada);
www4.agr.gc.ca/AAFC-AAC/display-afficher.do?id=1262962138890&lang=eng (Agriculture & Agri-Food Canada); www.christianparadis.com (Personal Web Site)
The Hon. Christian Paradis, Minister, Industry & Minister of State (Agriculture), C.D. Howe Building
235 Queen St.
Ottawa, ON K1A 0H5

Minister, Canadian Heritage & Official Languages, Hon. James Moore, P.C., B.A.
Constituency: Port Moody — Westwood — Port Coquitlam, British Columbia
Tel: 613-992-9650
Toll-free: 866-811-0055
Fax: 613-992-9868
james.moore@pch.gc.ca; james.moore@parl.gc.ca
Other Communications: Canadian Heritage: 819-997-7788; Fax:819-994-1267
TTY: 888-997-3123
Social Media: twitter.com/JamesMoore_org, www.facebook.com/jamesmoore.org
Note: Web Sites:www.pch.gc.ca/pc-ch/minstr/moore/index-eng.cfm (Canadian Heritage); www.jamesmoore.org (Personal Web Site)
The Honourable James Moore, Minister of Canadian Heritage & Official Languages
15, rue Eddy
Gatineau, QC K1A 0M5

Minister, Transport, Infrastructure, & Communities; Minister, Economic Development Agency of Canada for the Regions of Québec, Hon. Denis Lebel, P.C.
Constituency: Roberval — Lac-Saint-Jean, Québec
Tél: 613-996-6236
Ligne sans frais: 866-995-9737
Téléc: 613-996-6252
denis.lebel@parl.gc.ca
Autre numéros: Economic Development: 514-283-6412; Fax: 514-496-5096
TTY: 888-675-6863
Les réseaux sociaux:
www.facebook.com/pages/Denis-Lebel/137888079554744
Note: Web Sites: www.tc.gc.ca/eng/minister-menu.htm (Transport Canada);
www.dec-ced.gc.ca/eng/minister/index.html (Canada Economic Development for Québec Regions); www.denislebel.com (Personal Web Site)
The Honourable Denis Lebel, Minister's Office, Canada Economic Development, Dominion Square Building
#900, 1255, rue Peel
Montréal, QC H3B2T9

Minister, Health; Minister, Canadian Northern Economic Development Agency, Hon. Leona Aglukkaq, P.C.
Constituency: Nunavut
Tel: 613-992-2848
Toll-free: 800-567-9604
Fax: 613-996-9764
Minister_Ministre@hc-sc.gc.ca; leona.aglukkaq@parl.gc.ca
Other Communications: Northern Economic Dev. Agency, Fax: 1-866-817-3977
TTY: 866-553-0554
Social Media: twitter.com/leonaaglukkaq
Note: Web Sites:www.hc-sc.gc.ca/ahc-asc/minist/index-eng.php (Health Canada); www.north.gc.ca/minstr-eng.asp (Canadian Northern Economic Development Agency);
www.leonaaglukkaq.ca/EN/5215/ (Personal Web Site)
The Honourable Leona Aglukkaq, P.C., M.P., Health Canada, Brooke Claxton Building, Tunney's Pasture
70 Colombine Driveway
PO Box 0906C
Ottawa, ON K1A 0K9

Minister, Fisheries & Oceans; Minister, Atlantic Gateway, Hon. Keith Ashfield, P.C.
Constituency: Fredericton, New Brunswick
Tel: 613-992-1067
Fax: 613-996-9955
Min@dfo-mpo.gc.ca; keith.ashfield@parl.gc.ca
Other Communications: Fisheries & Oceans, Phone:613-992-3474
TTY: 800-465-7735
Social Media: twitter.com/KeithAshfield11
Note: Web Sites:
www.dfo-mpo.gc.ca/minister-ministre/bio-eng.htm (Fisheries & OceansCanada); www.atlanticgateway.gc.ca (Canada's Atlantic Gateway); www.keithashfield.ca (Personal Web Site)
The Honourable Keith Ashfield, Minister's Office, Fisheries & Oceans Canada
200 Kent St.
Ottawa, ON K1A 0E6

Minister, Environment, Hon. Peter Kent, P.C.
Constituency: Thornhill, Ontario
Tel: 613-992-0253
Fax: 613-992-0887
Minister@ec.gc.ca; peter.kent@parl.gc.ca
Other Communications: Environment, Phone: 819-997-1441; Fax: 819-953-0279
Social Media: twitter.com/ec_minister; www.twitter.com/mpPeterKent, www.facebook.com/apps/application.php?id=135514873168072
Note: Web Sites: www.peterkent.ca (Personal Web Site); www.ec.gc.ca/default.asp?lang=En&n=B6832638-1 (EnvironmentCanada); Twitter (French): www.twitter.com/ministre_ec
The Honourable PeterKent, Minister, Environment, Les Terrasses de la Chaudière
10, rue Wellington, 28e étage
Gatineau, QC K1A 0H3

Minister, Labour, Hon. Lisa Raitt, P.C., B.Sc., M.Sc., LL.B.
Constituency: Halton, Ontario
Tel: 613-996-7046
Fax: 613-992-0851
lisa.raitt@hrsdc-rhdcc.gc.ca; lisa.raitt@parl.gc.ca
Other Communications: Labour, Phone: 819-953-5646; Fax: 819-994-5168
Social Media: twitter.com/lraitt, www.facebook.com/lisaraitt
Note: Web Sites:
www.hrsdc.gc.ca/eng/corporate/labour/minister/index.shtml (Labour, HumanResources & Skills Development Canada); www.lisaraittmp.ca (Personal Web Site)
The Honourable Lisa Raitt, Minister of Labour, Human Resources & Skills Development Canada
165, rue Hôtel-de-Ville
Gatineua, QC K1A 0J2

Minister, National Revenue, Hon. Gail Shea, P.C.
Constituency: Egmont, Prince Edward Island
Tel: 613-992-9223
Fax: 613-992-1974
gail.shea@parl.gc.ca; sheag1B@parl.gc.ca
Other Communications: Cda Revenue Agency: 613-995-2960; Fax: 613-952-6608
TTY: 800-665-0354
Social Media: twitter.com/CPCGailShea
Note: Web Sites:
www.cra-arc.gc.ca/gncy/mnstr/menu-eng.html (Canada Revenue Agency); www.gailshea.ca (Personal Web Site)
TheHonourable Gail Shea, Minister of National Revenue
555 MacKenzie Ave., 7th Fl.
Ottawa, ON K1A 0L5

Minister, Aboriginal Affairs & Northern Development, Hon. John Duncan, P.C., B.Sc.F.
Constituency: Vancouver Island North, British Columbia
Tel: 613-992-2503
Toll-free: 800-567-9604
Fax: 613-996-3306
john.duncan@parl.gc.ca
Other Communications: Aboriginal Affairs: 819-997-0002; Fax: 819-953-4941
TTY: 866-553-0554
Note: Web Sites:
www.ainc-inac.gc.ca/ai/min/index-eng.asp(Aboriginal Affairs & Northern Development Canada); www.johnduncanmp.com (Personal Web Site)
The Honourable John Duncan, Minister, Aboriginal Affairs & Northern Development Canada
10 Wellington St.
Gatineau, QC K1A 0H4

Minister, International Cooperation, Hon. Julian Fantino, P.C., C.O.M., O. Ont.
Constituency: Vaughan, Ontario
Tel: 613-996-4971
Toll-free: 800-230-6349
Fax: 613-996-4973
julian.fantino@parl.gc.ca
www.julianfantino.ca
Other Communications: CIDA, Phone: 819-953-6238; Fax:819-953-8525
TTY: 800-331-5018
Social Media: twitter.com/julianfantino, www.facebook.com/pages/Julian-Fantino/166075460072162
Note: Web Sites:www.acdi-cida.gc.ca/acdi-cida/acdi-cida.nsf/eng/NIC-5494720-J79 (Canadian International Development Agency); www.international.gc.ca/ministers-ministres/index.aspx?view=d (Foreign Affairs & International Trade)
The Honourable Julian Fantino, Minister, International Cooperation, Minister's Office
House of Commons
Ottawa, ON K1A 0A6

Minister, Veteran Affairs, Hon. Steven Blaney, P.C., M.B.A.
Constituency: Lévis — Bellechasse, Québec
Tél: 613-992-7434
Ligne sans frais: 866-522-2122
Téléc: 613-995-6856
steven.blaney@parl.gc.ca; blanes1@parl.gc.ca
Autre numéros: Veteran Affairs: 613-996-4649; Fax: 613-996-0287
Les réseaux sociaux: twitter.com/steven_blaney, www.facebook.com/people/Steven-Blaney/557166646
Note: Web Sites:
www.veterans.gc.ca/eng/sub.cfm?source=department/blaney-corner (Veteran Affairs Canada);www.stevenblaney.ca (Personal Web Site)
The Honourable Steven Blaney, Veterans Affairs Canada
66 Slater St., 14th Fl.
Ottawa, ON K1A 0P4

Minister, International Trade; Minister, Asia-Pacific Gateway, Hon. Edward Fast, P.C., LL.B.
Constituency: Abbotsford, British Columbia
Tel: 613-995-0183
Fax: 613-996-9795
ed.fast@parl.gc.ca; faste@parl.gc.ca; ed@edfast.ca
Other Communications: InternationalTrade: 613-992-7332; Fax: 613-996-8924
Note: Web Sites:www.international.gc.ca/commerce/edward_fast.aspx?lang=eng (Foreign Affairs & International Trade Canada); www.edfast.ca (Personal Web Site)
Office of the Minister for International Trade, Foreign Affairs & International Trade Canada
125 Sussex Dr.
Ottawa, ON K1A 0G2

Minister, Natural Resources, Hon. Joe Oliver, P.C., B.A., BCL, MBA
Constituency: Eglinton — Lawrence, Ontario
Tel: 613-992-6361
Fax: 613-992-9791
Minister.Ministre@NRCan-RNCan.gc.ca; joe.oliver@parl.gc.ca
Other Communications: Natural Resources: 613-996-2007; Fax:613-996-4516
Social Media: twitter.com/joeoliver1, www.facebook.com/profile.php?id=707035179, www.linkedin.com/pub/joseph-oliver/4/267/73b
Note: Web Sites:
www.nrcan.gc.ca/com/deptmini/minmin/minmin-biobio-eng.php (NaturalResources Canada); www.joeoliver.ca (Personal Web Site)
The Honourable Joe Oliver, Minister's Office, Natural Resources Canada
#C7-1, 580 Booth St., 21st Fl.
Ottawa, ON K1A 0E4

Minister, Intergovernmental Affairs; President, Queen's Privy Council for Canada, Hon. Peter Penashue, P.C.
Constituency: Labrador, Newfoundland & Labrador
Tel: 613-996-4630
Fax: 613-996-7132
peter.penashue@parl.gc.ca
Other Communications: Intergovernmental Affairs,Phone: 613-943-1838
Social Media: twitter.com/PeterPenashue, www.facebook.com/peterpenashue
Note: Web Site:
www.pco-bcp.gc.ca/aia/index.asp?lang=eng&page=min(Intergovernmental Affairs)
Minister of Intergovernmental Affairs & President of the Queen's Privy Council for Canada
#800, 66 Slater St.
Ottawa, ON K1A 0A3

Minister of State, Atlantic Canada Opportunities Agency; Minister of State, La Francophonie;, Associate Minister, National Defence, Hon. Bernard Valcourt, P.C., Q.C., B.A., LL.B., DHC
Constituency: Madawaska — Restigouche, New Brunswick
Tel: 613-995-0581
Toll-free: 800-561-7862
Fax: 613-996-9736
bernard.valcourt@parl.gc.ca; bvalcourt2011@hotmail.com
Other Communications: ACOA, Phone: 613-941-7241; Fax:

613-996-9736
TTY: 877-456-6500
Social Media: twitter.com/b_valcourt, www.facebook.com/pages/Bernard-Valcourt/214030968613999
Note: Web Sites: www.acoa-apeca.gc.ca/English/WhoWeAre/OurPeople/Pages/Minister.aspx?ProgramID= (ACOA); www.bernardvalcourt.ca (Personal);www.forces.gc.ca/site/minister-ministre/am-ma/gal/index-eng.asp (National Defence)
The Hon. Bernard Valcourt, Office of the Minister of State, Atlantic Canada OpportunitiesAgency
#800, 60, Queen St.
Ottawa, ON K1P 5Y7

Minister of State, Hon. Gordon O'Connor, P.C., B.A., B.Sc.
Constituency: Carleton — Mississippi Mills, Ontario
Tel: 613-992-1119
Fax: 613-992-1043
gordon.oconnor@parl.gc.ca
Other Communications: Minister of State, Phone: 613-995-2291
Social Media: www.facebook.com/pages/Gordon-OConnor/228442573837062?sk=info
Note: Web Site: www.gordonoconnor.ca (Personal Web Site)
The Honourable Gordon O'Connor,Minister of State, Centre Block
#215S, 111 Wellington St.
Ottawa, ON K1A 0A3

Minister of State, Small Business & Tourism, Hon. Maxime Bernier, P.C., B.Comm., LL.B.
Constituency: Beauce, Québec
Tél: 613-992-8053
Téléc: 613-995-0687
mossbt.industry@ic.gc.ca; maxime.bernier@parl.gc.ca
Autre numéros: Small Business:613-943-6183; Fax: 613-990-4056
Note: Web Sites: www.ic.gc.ca/eic/site/ic1.nsf/eng/00097.html (IndustryCanada); www.maximebernier.com (Personal Web Site)
The Honourable Maxime Bernier, Minister of State, Small Business & Tourism, C.D. Howe Building
235 Queen St.
Ottawa, ON K1A 0H5

Minister of State, Foreign Affairs (Americas & Consular Affairs), Hon. Diane Ablonczy, P.C., B.Ed., LL.B.
Constituency: Calgary — Nose Hill, Alberta
Tel: 613-996-2756
Toll-free: 800-267-8376
Fax: 613-992-2537
diane.ablonczy@parl.gc.ca; Calgary@ablonczy.com
Other Communications: ForeignAffairs, Phone: 613-944-2300
TTY: 613-944-9136
Social Media: twitter.com/dianeablonczymp
Note: Web Sites:www.international.gc.ca/ministers-ministres/Diane_Ablonczy.aspx?lang=eng&view=d (Foreign Affairs & International Trade Canada); www.dianeablonczy.com (Personal Web Site)
The Honourable Diane Ablonczy, Minister of State, Foreign Affairs (Americas & Consular Affairs)
125 Sussex Dr.
Ottawa, ON K1A 0G2

Minister of State, Western Economic Diversification, Hon. Lynne Yelich, P.C.
Constituency: Blackstrap, Saskatchewan
Tel: 613-995-5653
Fax: 613-995-0126
Lynne.Yelich@parl.gc.ca
Other Communications: Western Diversification, Phone: 613-952-2768
TTY: 877-303-3388
Social Media: twitter.com/Lynne_Yelich, www.facebook.com/pages/Lynne-Yelich/64666054978
Note: Web Sites: www.wd.gc.ca/eng/43.asp (Western Economic DiversificationCanada); www.lynneyelich.com (Personal Web Site)
TheHonourable Lynne Yelich, Minister of State for Western Economic Diversification, Gillin Building
#500, 141 Laurier Ave. West
Ottawa, ON K1P 5J3

Minister of State, Transport, Hon. Steven John Fletcher, P.C., B.Sc., M.B.A.
Constituency: Charleswood — St. James — Assiniboia, Manitoba
Tel: 613-995-5609
Fax: 613-992-3199
steven.fletcher@parl.gc.ca
Other Communications: Transport, Phone: 613-991-0700; Fax: 613-995-0327
Social Media: twitter.com/stevenjfletcher, www.facebook.com/StevenFletcherMP
Note: Web Sites: www.tc.gc.ca/eng/minister-state.htm (Transport Canada); www.stevenfletcher.com (PersonalWeb Site)
TheHonourable Steven John Fletcher, Minister of State, Transport
330 Sparks St.
Ottawa, ON K1A 0N5

Minister of State, Science & Technology; Minister of State, Federal Economic Development Agency for Southern Ontario, Hon. Dr. Gary Goodyear, P.C., D.C., F.C.C.S.S.
Constituency: Cambridge, Ontario
Tel: 613-996-1307
Fax: 613-996-8340
mosst.industry@ic.gc.ca; gary.goodyear@parl.gc.ca
Other Communications: Industry, Phone: 613-947-2956; Fax: 613-943-7598
Note: Web Sites: www.ic.gc.ca/eic/site/ic1.nsf/eng/02933.html (Industry Canada); www.garygoodyear.com (Personal Web Site)
Minister of State (Science & Tech.) (Federal Economic Development Agency for S. ON), CD Howe Bldg.
235 Queen St.
Ottawa, ON K1A0H5

Minister of State, Finance, Hon. Ted Menzies, P.C.
Constituency: Macleod, Alberta
Tel: 613-995-8471
Fax: 613-996-9770
ted.menzies@fin.gc.ca; ted.menzies@parl.gc.ca
Other Communications: Finance, Phone: 613-996-7861; Fax: 613-995-5176
Social Media: twitter.com/TedMenzies
Note: Web Sites: www.fin.gc.ca/comment/state-etat-eng.asp (Department of Finance Canada); www.tedmenzies.ca (Personal Web Site)
The HonourableTed Menzies, Minister of State, Finance, Finance Canada
140 O'Connor St.
Ottawa, ON K1A 0G5

Minister of State, Democratic Reform, Hon. Tim Uppal, P.C.
Constituency: Edmonton — Sherwood Park, Alberta
Tel: 613-995-3611
Fax: 613-995-3612
tim.uppal@parl.gc.ca
Other Communications: Democratic Reform: 613-992-3689; Fax: 613-947-8077
Social Media: twitter.com/TimUppal_MP, www.facebook.com/profile.php?id=560835735
Note: Web Sites: www.timuppal.ca (Personal Web Site); www.democraticreform.gc.ca/index.asp?lang=eng&page=min (Democratic Reform)
The Honourable Tim Uppal,Minister of State, Democratic Reform, Privy Council Office
66 Slater St., 8th Fl.
Ottawa, ON K1A 0A6

Minister of State, Seniors, Hon. Alice Wong, P.C., Ph.D.
Constituency: Richmond, British Columbia
Tel: 613-995-2021
Toll-free: 800-622-6232
Fax: 613-995-2174
alice.wong@parl.gc.ca; alice.wong.c1@parl.gc.ca
Other Communications: Seniors Canada, Fax: 613-957-1602
TTY: 800-926-9105
Social Media: twitter.com/AliceWongCanada, www.facebook.com/profile.php?id=100002648510727
Note: Web Sites:www.hrsdc.gc.ca/eng/corporate/ministers/index.shtml (Human Resources & Skills Development Canada); www.seniors.gc.ca/h.4m.2@.jsp (Seniors Canada); www.alicewong.ca (Personal Web Site)
The Hon. Alice Wong, Minister of State Office (Seniors), Human Resources & Skills Development Canada
140, promenade du Portage
Gatineau, QC K1A 0J9

Minister of State, Sport, Hon. Bal Gosal, P.C.
Constituency: Bramalea — Gore — Malton, Ontario
Tel: 613-992-9105
Fax: 613-947-0443
bal.gosal@pch.gc.ca; bal.gosal@parl.gc.ca
Other Communications: Sport, Phone: 819-934-1122; Fax: 819-953-8055
Social Media: twitter.com/MinStateSport, www.facebook.com/pages/Bal-Gosal/155006724554020
Note: Web Sites: www.pch.gc.ca/pc-ch/minstr/gosal/biograph-eng.cfm (Canadian Heritage); www.electbalgosal.ca (Personal Web Site)
The Honourable Bal Gosal,Minister of State, Sport, Canadian Heritage
25, rue Eddy
Gatineau, QC K1A 0M5

Forty-first Parliament - Canada

House of Commons, Parliament Buildings, Ottawa, AB K1A 0A6
www.parl.gc.ca

Members of the House of Commons are elected by the people. The Speaker is elected by the House.
Last General Election: May 2, 2011.
Political Party Leaders (August 2012):
Conservative Party of Canada - The Right Hon. Stephen Joseph Harper;
New Democratic Party - Thomas J. Mulcair;
Liberal Party of Canada - The Hon. Robert "Bob" Keith Rae (Interim Leader);
Bloc Québécois - Daniel Paillé;
Green Party of Canada - Elizabeth May.
Representation in the House of Commons by province is as follows (August 2012):
Alberta - Conservative Party of Canada 25, New Democratic Party 1, Independent 1, Vacant 1, Total 28;
British Columbia - Conservative Party of Canada 21, New Democratic Party 11, Liberal Party of Canada 2, Green Party of Canada 1, Vacant 1, Total 36;
Manitoba - Conservative Party of Canada 11, New Democratic Party 2, Liberal Party of Canada 1, Total 14;
New Brunswick - Conservative Party of Canada 8, New Democratic Party 1, Liberal Party of Canada 1, Total 10;
Newfoundland & Labrador - Conservative Party of Canada 1, New Democratic Party 2, Liberal Party of Canada 4, Total 7;
Northwest Territories - New Democratic Party 1, Total 1;
Nova Scotia - Conservative Party of Canada 4, New Democratic Party 3, Liberal Party of C anada 4, Total 11;
Nunavut - Conservative Party of Canada 1, Total 1
Ontario - Conservative Party of Canada 72, New Democratic Party 21, Liberal Party of Canada 11, Independent 1, Vacant 1, Total 106;
Prince Edward Island - Conservative Party of Canada 1, Liberal Party of Canada 3, Total 4;
Québec - Conservative Party of Canada 5, New Democratic Party 58, Liberal Party of Canada 8, Bloc Québécois 4, Total 75;
Saskatchewan - Conservative Party of Canada 13, Liberal Party of Canada 1, Total 14;
Yukon - Conservative Party of Canada 1, Total 1.
Representation in the House of Commons by party affiliation is as follows (August 2012):
Conservative Party of Canada 163;
New Democratic Party 100;
Liberal Party of Canada 35;
Bloc Québécois 4;
Green Party of Canada 1;
Independent 2;
Vacant 3;
Total 308.
Indemnities, Salaries, & Allowances (2011):
The basic sessional indemnity for each member of the House of Commons is $157,731. In addition to the indemnity, members who occupy certain positions in the House of Commons receive additional remuneration.
Prime Minister: $157,731, plus a car allowance of $2,112;
Minister $75,516, plus a car allowance of $2,122;
Minister of State: $56,637;
Secretary of State: $56,637;
Parliamentary Secretary: $15,834;
Speaker of the House of Commons: $75,516, plus a car allowance of $1,061, & a rent allowance of $3,000;
Deputy Speaker of the House of Commons: $39,179, plus a rent allowance of $1,500;
Leader of the Opposition in the House of Commons: $75,516, plus a car allowance of $2,122;
Leaders of Other Parties: $53,694;
Opposition House Leader: $39,179;
House Leader of Other Parties: $15,834;
Deputy House Leaders of Government & Official Opposition: $15,834;
Deputy House Leaders of Other Parties: $5,684;
Chief Government Whip: $28,420;
Chief Opposition Whip: $28,420;
Whip of Other Parties: $11,165;
Chief Government Whip's Assistant: $11,165;
Deputy Whip of the Official Opposition: $11,165;
Deputy Whip of Other Parties: $5,684;
Caucus Chair of the Government & the Official Opposition: $11,165;
Caucus Chair of Other Parties: $5,684;
Deputy Chair, Committees of the Whole: $15,834;
Assistant Deputy Chair, Committees of the Whole: $15,834;
Chair of Standing & Standing Joint Committee (excluding the Liaison Committee & the Standing Joint Committee on the Library of Parliament): $11,165
Vice-Chair of Standing & Standing Joint Committee (excluding the Liaison Committee & the Standing Joint Committee on the Library of Parliament): $5,684.
Mail may be sent postage-free to any Member of Parliament at the following address: House of Commons, Parliament Buildings, Ottawa, Ontario, K1A 0A6.
The following is a list of Members of Parliament, as of July 2012, with their constituency, number of electors on lists for the 2011 election, party affiliation, & contact information:

Members with Party Affiliation, Riding, & Contact Information

Minister of State, Foreign Affairs (Americas & Consular Affairs), Hon. Diane Ablonczy, P.C., B.Ed., LL.B.
Constituency: Calgary — Nose Hill, Alberta *No. of Constituents:* 101,910, Conservative Party
Tel: 613-996-2756
Fax: 613-992-2537
diane.ablonczy@parl.gc.ca;Calgary@ablonczy.com
Other Communications: Constituency Phone: 403-282-7980; Fax: 613-992-2537
Social Media: twitter.com/dianeablonczymp
Note: Web Sites: www.dianeablonczy.com (Personal Web Site);www.international.gc.ca/ministers-ministres/Diane_Ablonczy.aspx?lang=eng&view=d (Foreign Affairs & International Trade Canada)
Constituency Office
1107 - 17th Ave. NW
Calgary, AB T2M 0P7

Parliamentary Secretary to Minister, Veteran Affairs, Eve Adams, B.A.
Constituency: Mississauga — Brampton South, Ontario *No. of Constituents:* 94,531, Conservative Party
Tel: 613-995-7784
Fax: 613-996-9817
eve.adams@parl.gc.ca
www.voteadams.ca
Other Communications: Constituency Phone: 905-625-1201; Fax:905-625-1485
Social Media: twitter.com/MPEveAdams, www.facebook.com/eve.adams.mp, www.linkedin.com/in/eveadamsmississauga
Constituency Office
#7, 4870 Tomken Rd.
Mississauga, ON L4W 1J8

Mark Adler
Constituency: York Centre, Ontario *No. of Constituents:* 71,753, Conservative Party
Tel: 613-941-6339
Fax: 613-941-2421
mark.adler@parl.gc.ca
www.markadler.ca
Other Communications: Constituency Phone: 416-638-3700; Fax: 416-638-1407
Social Media: twitter.com/MarkAdlerMP
Constituency Office
#210, 638A Sheppard Ave.West
Toronto, ON M3H 2S1

Minister, Health; Minister, Canadian Northern Economic Development Agency, Hon. Leona Aglukkaq, P.C.
Constituency: Nunavut *No. of Constituents:* 17,349, Conservative Party
Tel: 613-992-2848
Toll-free: 866-267-7701
Fax: 613-996-9764
leona.aglukkaq@parl.gc.ca;Minister_Ministre@hc-sc.gc.ca
Other Communications: Constituency Phone: 867-979-4193; Fax: 867-979-4196
Social Media: twitter.com/leonaaglukkaq
Note: Web Sites: www.leonaaglukkaq.ca/EN/5215/ (Personal Web Site);www.hc-sc.gc.ca/ahc-asc/minist/index-eng.php (Health Canada); www.north.gc.ca/minstr-eng.asp (Canadian Northern Economic Development Agency)
Constituency Office, Building 208
PO Box 1930
Iqaluit, NU X0A 0H0

Dan Albas
Constituency: Okanagan — Coquihalla, British Columbia *No. of Constituents:* 86,195, Conservative Party
Tel: 613-995-1702
Fax: 613-995-1154
dan.albas@parl.gc.ca
www.danalbas.com
Other Communications: Constituency Phone: 250-770-4480; Fax: 250-770-4484
Social Media: twitter.com/DanAlbas, www.linkedin.com/in/danalbas
Constituency Office
#202, 301 Main St.
Penticton, BC V2A 5B7

Deputy Government Whip, Harold Albrecht, D.D.S.
Constituency: Kitchener — Conestoga, Ontario *No. of Constituents:* 88,766, Conservative Party
Tel: 613-992-4633
Fax: 613-992-9932
harold.albrecht@parl.gc.ca
www.haroldalbrechtmp.ca
Other Communications: Constituency Phone: 519-578-3777; Fax: 519-578-0138
Constituency Office
#2A, 153 Country Hill Dr.
Kitchener, ON N2E 2G7

Parliamentary Secretary to the Minister, National Defence, Chris Alexander
Constituency: Ajax — Pickering, Ontario *No. of Constituents:* 93,565, Conservative Party
Tel: 613-995-8042
Fax: 613-996-1289
chris.alexander@parl.gc.ca
www.chrisalexander.ca
Other Communications: Constituency Phone: 905-426-6808;Fax: 905-426-9564
Social Media: twitter.com/calxandr
Constituency Office
#101E, 100 Westney Rd. South
Ajax, ON L1S 7H3

Malcolm Allen
Constituency: Welland, Ontario *No. of Constituents:* 85,007, New Democratic Party
Tel: 613-995-0988
Fax: 613-995-5245
malcolm.allen@parl.gc.ca; malcolm.allen.c1@parl.gc.ca
www.malcolmallen.ca
Other Communications: Constituency Phone: 905-788-2204; Fax: 905-788-0071
Social Media: twitter.com/Malcolm_AllenMP, www.facebook.com/malcolmallenmp
ConstituencyOffice
#102, 60 King St.
Welland, ON L3B 6A4

Mike Allen, B.Admin., M.B.A.(Hons.)
Constituency: Tobique — Mactaquac, New Brunswick *No. of Constituents:* 53,073, Conservative Party
Tel: 613-947-4431
Toll-free: 800-671-6160
Fax: 613-947-4434
mike.allen@parl.gc.ca
www.mikeallen.ca
Other Communications: Constituency Phone: 506-473-6632; Fax: 506-473-3926
Social Media: twitter.com/mpmikea, www.facebook.com/mike.allen.mp, www.linkedin.com/pub/mike-allen/27/53a/232
ConstituencyOffice
#105, 218 Broadway Blvd.
Grand Falls, NB E3Z 2J9

Chair, Foreign Affairs & International Development Committee; Chair, Liaison Committee, Dean Allison, B.A.
Constituency: Niagara West — Glanbrook, Ontario *No. of Constituents:* 89,763, Conservative Party
Tel: 613-995-2772
Toll-free: 877-563-7900
Fax: 613-992-2727
Allison.D@parl.gc.ca;info@deanallison.ca
www.deanallison.ca
Other Communications: Constituency Phone: 905-563-7900; Fax: 905-563-7500
Social Media: twitter.com/DeanAllisonMP, www.facebook.com/pages/Dean-Allison/25765199451
Constituency Office
4994 King St.
Beamsville, ON L0R 1B0

Stella Ambler, BSc. (Hons.)
Constituency: Mississauga South, Ontario *No. of Constituents:* 78,551, Conservative Party
Tel: 613-992-4848
Fax: 613-996-3267
stella.ambler@parl.gc.ca; Stella@StellaAmbler.com
www.stellaambler.com
Other Communications: Constituency Phone: 905-486-1706
Social Media: www.facebook.com/pages/Stella-Ambler/135858743139392
Constituency Office
#5,Hurontario St.
Mississauga, ON L5G 3H2

Minister, Public Works & Government Services Canada; Minister, Status of Women, Hon. Rona Ambrose, P.C., B.A., M.A.
Constituency: Edmonton — Spruce Grove, Alberta *No. of Constituents:* 105,599, Conservative Party
Tel: 613-996-9778
Fax: 613-996-0785
rona.ambrose@parl.gc.ca;ambror1a@parl.gc.ca
Other Communications: Constituency Phone: 780-495-7705; Fax: 780-495-7741
Social Media: twitter.com/MP_RonaAmbrose, www.linkedin.com/pub/rona-ambrose/16/bb0/668
Note: Web Sites: www.ronaambrose.com (Personal Web Site);www.tpsgc-pwgsc.gc.ca/apropos-about/mnstr-eng.html (Public Works & Government Services Canada); www.swc-cfc.gc.ca/abu-ans/min/index-eng.html (Status of Women Canada)
Constituency Office
6801 - 170th St.
Edmonton, AB T5T 4W4

Rob Anders, B.A.
Constituency: Calgary West, Alberta *No. of Constituents:* 103,812, Conservative Party
Tel: 613-992-3066
Fax: 613-992-3256
rob.anders@parl.gc.ca; robanders@telus.net
www.robanders.com
Other Communications: Constituency Phone: 403-292-6666; Fax: 403-292-6670
Social Media: www.linkedin.com/pub/rob-anders/28/173/8b6
Constituency Office
11Spruce Centre SW
Calgary, AB T3C 3B3

Parliamentary Secretary to the Minister, Natural Resources & for the Canadian Wheat Board, David Anderson, B.A., M.Div
Constituency: Cypress Hills — Grasslands,Saskatchewan *No. of Constituents:* 44,539, Conservative Party
Tel: 613-992-0657
Fax: 613-992-5508
david.anderson@parl.gc.ca; david.anderson1@sasktel.net
www.davidanderson.ca
Other Communications: Constituency Phone: 306-778-4480; Fax: 306-778-6981
Social Media: twitter.com/DavidAndersonSK
Constituency Office, Chinook Building
#2, 240 Central Ave. North
Swift Current, SK S9H 0L2

Scott Andrews, B.A.
Constituency: Avalon, Newfoundland & Labrador *No. of Constituents:* 64,424, Liberal
Tel: 613-992-4133
Toll-free: 866-883-3424
Fax: 613-992-7277
scott.andrews@parl.gc.ca
www.scottandrews.ca
Other Communications: Constituency Phone: 709-834-3424; Fax: 709-834-3628
Social Media: twitter.com/ScottAndrewsMP, www.facebook.com/pages/Scott-Andrews/26946316089
Constituency Office
944-956Conception Bay Hwy.
PO Box 17171 Kelligrews Sta.
Conception Bay South, NL A1X 3H1

Charlie Angus
Constituency: Timmins — James Bay, Ontario *No. of Constituents:* 60,095, New Democratic Party
Tel: 613-992-2919
Fax: 613-995-0747
charlie.angus@parl.gc.ca; Angus.C@parl.gc.ca
www.charlieangus.ndp.ca
Other Communications: Constituency Phone: 705-567-2747; Fax: 705-567-5232
Social Media: twitter.com/CharlieAngusMP, www.facebook.com/profile.php?id=568261214&sk=info
Constituency Office
#201, 30 Second St.
PO Box 276
Kirkland Lake, ON P2N 3H7

Scott Armstrong, B.A., M.A., Ph.D.
Constituency: Cumberland — Colchester — Musquodoboit Valley, Nova Scotia *No. of Constituents:* 69,188, Conservative Party
Tel: 613-992-3366
Fax: 613-992-7220
scott.armstrong@parl.gc; armsts@parl.gc.ca; armsts2@parl.gc.ca
www.scottarmstrongmp.ca
Other Communications: Constituency Phone: 902-893-2455; Fax:902-893-1959
Social Media: twitter.com/SArmstrongCCMV, www.facebook.com/people/Scott-Armstrong/523045844, www.linkedin.com/pub/scott-armstrong/37/b0/1b4
Constituency Office
#101, 18 Willow St.
Truro, NS B2N 4Z4

Minister, Fisheries & Oceans, Hon. Keith Ashfield, P.C.
Constituency: Fredericton, New Brunswick *No. of Constituents:* 69,732, Conservative Party
Tel: 613-992-1067
Fax: 613-996-9955
keith.ashfield@parl.gc.ca
Other Communications: Constituency Phone: 506-452-4110; Fax: 506-452-4076
Social Media: twitter.com/KeithAshfield11
Note: Web Sites: www.keithashfield.ca (Personal Web Site); www.dfo-mpo.gc.ca/minister-ministre/bio-eng.htm (Fisheries & Oceans Canada)
Constituency Office
23 Alison Blvd.
Fredericton, NB E3C 2N5

Niki Ashton, B.A., M.A.
Constituency: Churchill, Manitoba *No. of Constituents:* 46,068, New Democratic Party
Tel: 613-992-3018
Toll-free: 866-785-0522
Fax: 613-996-5817
niki.ashton@parl.gc.ca

www.nikiashton.ndp.ca
Other Communications: Constituency Toll-Free Phone: 1-866-669-7770
Social Media: www.facebook.com/niki.ashton
Constituency Office
#307, 83Churchill Dr.
Thompson, MB R8N 0L4

Jay Aspin
Constituency: Nipissing — Timiskaming, Ontario *No. of Constituents:* 70,754, Conservative Party
Tel: 613-995-6255
Toll-free: 800-461-1394
Fax: 613-996-7993
jay.aspin@parl.gc.ca
www.jayaspin.ca
Other Communications: Constituency Phone: 705-647-6262; Fax: 705-647-6299
Social Media: twitter.com/JayAspin
Constituency Office
112 Whitewood Ave.West
New Liskeard, ON P0J 1P0

Alex Atamanenko, B.A., M.A.
Constituency: British Columbia Southern Interior, British Columbia *No. of Constituents:* 75,751, New Democratic Party
Tel: 613-996-8036
Toll-free: 800-667-2393
Fax: 613-943-0922
alex.atamanenko@parl.gc.ca; atamaa1@parl.gc.ca
www.alexndp.ca
Other Communications: Constituency Phone: 250-365-2792; Fax:250-365-2793
Social Media: www.facebook.com/pages/Alex-Atamanenko-MP/180017678676108
Constituency Officer
337 Columbia Ave.
Castlegar, BC V1N 1G6

Robert Aubin
Constituency: Trois-Rivières, Québec *No. of Constituents:* 79 520, New Democratic Party
Tél: 613-992-2349
Téléc: 613-995-9498
robert.aubin@parl.gc.ca
www.robertaubin.ndp.ca
Autre numéros: Constituency Phone: 819-371-5901; Fax: 819-371-5912
Constituency Office
214, rue Bonaventure
Trois-Rivières, QC G9A 2B1

Paulina Ayala
Constituency: Honoré-Mercier, Québec *No. of Constituents:* 81 736, New Democratic Party
Tel: 613-995-0580
Fax: 613-992-1710
Paulina.Ayala@parl.gc.ca
www.paulinaayala.ndp.ca
Other Communications: Constituency Phone: 514-353-5044; Fax: 514-353-3050
Constituency Office
7077, rue Beaubienest
Montréal, QC H1M 2Y2

Minister, Foreign Affairs, Hon. John Baird, P.C., B.A.(Hons.)
Constituency: Ottawa West — Nepean, Ontario *No. of Constituents:* 82,874, Conservative Party
Tel: 613-996-0984
Fax: 613-996-9880
john.baird@parl.gc.ca; bairdj1@parl.gc.ca
Other Communications: Constituency Phone: 613-990-7720;Fax: 613-993-6501
Social Media: twitter.com/JohnBairdOWN
Note: Web Sites: www.johnbaird.com (Personal Web Site);www.international.gc.ca/ministers-ministres/John_Baird.aspx?lang=eng&view=d (Foreign Affairs & International Trade Canada)
Constituency Office
#418, 2249 Carling Ave.
Ottawa, ON K2B 7E9

Joyce Bateman
Constituency: Winnipeg South Centre, Manitoba *No. of Constituents:* 58,075, Conservative Party
Tel: 613-992-9475
Fax: 613-992-9586
joyce.bateman@parl.gc.ca
www.joycebateman.ca
Other Communications: Constituency Phone: 204-983-1355; Fax: 204-984-3979
Constituency Office
#102, 611 CorydonAve.
Winnipeg, MB R3L 0P3

Hon. Mauril Bélanger, P.C., B.A.
Constituency: Ottawa — Vanier, Ontario *No. of Constituents:* 79,309, Liberal
Tel: 613-992-4766
Fax: 613-992-6448
mauril.bélanger@parl.gc.ca; BelanM1@parl.gc.ca
www.mauril.ca
Other Communications: Constituency Phone: 613-947-7961; Fax: 613-947-7963
Constituency Office
#504, 168 Charlotte St.
Ottawa, ON K1N 8K6

André Bellavance, B.A.
Constituency: Richmond — Arthabaska, Québec *No. of Constituents:* 82 637, BQ
Tél: 613-995-1554
Ligne sans frais: 877-751-1375
Téléc: 613-995-2026
andré.bellavance@parl.gc.ca; bellaa1@parl.gc.ca
www.andrebellavance.qc.ca
Autre numéros: Constituency Phone: 819-751-1375; Fax: 819-751-5517
Constituency Office
32, rue Notre-Dame est
Victoriaville, QC G6P 3Z5

Hon. Dr. Carolyn Bennett, P.C., M.D.
Constituency: St. Paul's, Ontario *No. of Constituents:* 83,367, Liberal
Tel: 613-995-9666
Fax: 613-947-4622
carolyn.bennett@parl.gc.ca
www.carolynbennett.liberal.ca
Other Communications: Constituency Phone: 416-952-3990; Fax: 416-952-3995
Social Media: twitter.com/Carolyn_Bennett, www.facebook.com/carolyn.bennett.stpauls, www.linkedin.com/pub/carolyn-bennett/13/a3/811
Constituency Office
#103, 1650 Yonge St.
Toronto, ON M4T 2A2

Chair, Natural Resources Committee, Leon Earl Benoit
Constituency: Vegreville — Wainwright, Alberta *No. of Constituents:* 83,790, Conservative Party
Tel: 613-992-4171
Toll-free: 800-463-1194
Fax: 613-996-9011
leon.benoit@parl.gc.ca; benoil1@parl.gc.ca
www.leonbenoit.ca
Other Communications: Constituency Phone: 780-763-6130; Fax:780-763-6132
Social Media: www.linkedin.com/pub/leon-benoit/17/b6a/a9a
Constituency Office, Professional Building
5004 - 49th St.
PO Box 300
Mannville, AB T0B 2W0

Tyrone Benskin
Constituency: Jeanne-Le Ber, Québec *No. of Constituents:* 89 365, New Democratic Party
Tel: 613-995-6403
Fax: 613-995-6404
tyrone.benskin@parl.gc.ca
www.tyronebenskin.ndp.ca
Other Communications: Constituency Phone: 514-496-4885; Fax: 514-496-8097
Social Media: www.facebook.com/pages/Tyrone-Benskin/105638686181284
Constituency Office
2403, rue duCentre
Montréal, QC H3K 1J9

Minister of State, Small Business & Tourism, Hon. Maxime Bernier, P.C., B.Comm., LL.B.
Constituency: Beauce, Québec *No. of Constituents:* 84 941, Conservative Party
Tél: 613-992-8053
Ligne sans frais: 888-470-2171
Téléc: 613-995-0687
maxime.bernier@parl.gc.ca; bernim1a@parl.gc.ca
Autre numéros: Constituency Phone: 418-227-2171; Fax: 418-227-3093
Note: Web Sites: www.maximebernier.com (Personal Web Site);www.ic.gc.ca/eic/site/ic1.nsf/eng/00097.html (Industry Canada)
Constituency Office
#430, 11535, 1re av
Saint-Georges, QC G5Y 7H5

Dennis Fraser Bevington, B.A.
Constituency: Western Arctic, Northwest Territories *No. of Constituents:* 29,020, New Democratic Party
Tel: 613-992-4587
Toll-free: 800-661-0802
Fax: 613-992-1586
dennis.bevington@parl.gc.ca
www.dennisbevington.ca
Other Communications: Constituency Phone: 867-873-6995; Fax: 867-920-4233
Social Media: twitter.com/nwtdennis, www.facebook.com/pages/Dennis-Bevington/28453715670
ConstituencyOffice
4908 - 49th St.
PO Box 1986
Yellowknife, NW X1A 2P5

Chair, National Defence Committee, James Bezan
Constituency: Selkirk — Interlake, Manitoba *No. of Constituents:* 66,370, Conservative Party
Tel: 613-992-2032
Toll-free: 888-247-9606
Fax: 613-992-6224
james.bezan@parl.gc.ca; office@jamesbezan.com
www.jamesbezan.com
Other Communications: Constituency Phone: 204-785-6151; Fax:204-785-6153
Social Media: twitter.com/jamesbezan, www.facebook.com/jamesbezan
Constituency Office
374 Main St.
Selkirk, MB R1A 1T7

Denis Blanchette
Constituency: Louis-Hébert, Québec *No. of Constituents:* 82 760, New Democratic Party
Tél: 613-995-4995
Téléc: 613-996-8292
denis.blanchette@parl.gc.ca
www.denisblanchette.npd.ca
Autre numéros: Constituency Phone: 418-648-3244
Les réseaux sociaux: twitter.com/DenisBlanchette, www.facebook.com/pages/Denis-Blanchette/13256142620
Constituency Office
#380, 360, ch Ste-Foy
Québec, QC G1V4H2

Lysane Blanchette-Lamothe
Constituency: Pierrefonds — Dollard, Québec *No. of Constituents:* 81,767, New Democratic Party
Tél: 613-992-2689
Téléc: 613-996-8478
lysane.blanchette-Lamothe@parl.gc
www.lysaneblanchettelamothe.ndp.ca
Autre numéros: Constituency Phone: 514-624-5725
Les réseaux sociaux: www.facebook.com/LysanePierrefondsDollard
Constituency Office
#303, 3883, boulSaint-Jean
Dollard-des-Ormeaux, QC H9G 3B9

Minister, Veteran Affairs, Hon. Steven Blaney, P.C., M.B.A.
Constituency: Lévis — Bellechasse, Québec *No. of Constituents:* 90 515, Conservative Party
Tél: 613-992-7434
Ligne sans frais: 877-630-0500
Téléc: 613-995-6856
steven.blaney@parl.gc.ca; blanes1@parl.gc.ca
Autre numéros: Constituency Phone: 418-830-0500;Fax: 418-830-0504
Les réseaux sociaux: twitter.com/steven_blaney, www.facebook.com/people/Steven-Blaney/557166646
Note: Web Sites: www.stevenblaney.ca (Personal Web Site);www.veterans.gc.ca/eng/sub.cfm?source=department/blaney-corner (Veteran Affairs Canada)
Constituency Office
#101, 115, rte du Président-Kennedy
Lévis, QC G6V 6C8

Kelly Block
Constituency: Saskatoon — Rosetown — Biggar, Saskatchewan *No. of Constituents:* 49,947, Conservative Party
Tel: 613-995-1551
Toll-free: 888-590-6555
Fax: 613-943-2010
kelly.block@parl.gc.ca
www.kellyblock.ca
Other Communications: Constituency Phone: 306-975-6555; Fax: 306-975-5786
Social Media: twitter.com/KellyBlockcpc, www.facebook.com/group.php?gid=75570595197
Constituency Office
904E - 22nd St.West
Saskatoon, SK S7M 0S1

Françoise Boivin, B.A., LL.L.
Constituency: Gatineau, Québec *No. of Constituents:* 89 537, New Democratic Party
Tél: 613-992-4351
Téléc: 613-992-1037
françoise.boivin@parl.gc.ca
www.francoiseboivin.com
Autre numéros: Constituency Phone: 819-561-5555; Fax: 819-561-0005
Les réseaux sociaux: twitter.com/FBoivinNPD, www.facebook.com/francoiseboivingatineau
Constituency Office
#104,160, boul de l'Hôpital
Gatineau, QC J8T 8J1

Charmaine Borg
Constituency: Terrebonne — Blainville, Québec *No. of Constituents:* 88 734, New Democratic Party

Tél: 613-947-4788
Téléc: 613-947-4879
charmaine.borg@parl.gc.ca
www.charmaineborg.ndp.ca
Autre numéros: Constituency Phone: 450-965-9417; Fax: 450-965-7742
Les réseaux sociaux: twitter.com/mpcharmaineborg
Constituency Office
3859, montéeGagnon
Terrebonne, QC J6Y 1K8

Ray Boughen, B.Sc., B.Ed., M.Sc.
Constituency: Palliser, Saskatchewan *No. of Constituents:* 50,175, Conservative Party
Tel: 613-992-9115
Fax: 613-992-0131
ray.boughen@parl.gc.ca; ray.boughen.c1@parl.gc.ca
www.rayboughen.ca
Other Communications: Constituency Phone: 306-691-3577; Fax: 306-691-3579
Constituency Office
#3, 54 Stadacona St. West
Moose Jaw, SK S6H 1Z1

Alexandre Boulerice
Constituency: Rosemont — La Petite-Patrie, Québec *No. of Constituents:* 81,961, New Democratic Party
Tél: 613-992-0423
Téléc: 613-992-0878
alexandre.boulerice@parl.gc.ca
www.alexandreboulerice.ndp.ca
Autre numéros: Constituency Phone: 514-729-5342; Fax: 514-729-5875
Les réseaux sociaux: twitter.com/alexboulerice, www.facebook.com/pages/Alexandre-Boulerice-NPD/26089638685
Constituency Office
#208, 1453,rue Beaubien est
Montréal, QC H2G 3C6

Marjolaine Boutin-Sweet
Constituency: Hochelaga, Québec *No. of Constituents:* 80 515, New Democratic Party
Tél: 613-947-4576
Téléc: 613-947-4579
marjolaine.boutin-sweet@parl.gc.ca
www.marjolaineboutinsweet.ndp.ca
Autre numéros: Constituency Phone: 514-283-2655; Fax: 514-283-6485
Les réseaux sociaux: twitter.com/marjboutinsweet, www.facebook.com/marjolaineboutinsweet
Constituency Office
#224, 2030, boul Pie-IX
Montréal, QC H1V 2C8

Tarik Brahmi
Constituency: Saint-Jean, Québec *No. of Constituents:* 85 777, New Democratic Party
Tél: 613-992-5296
Téléc: 613-992-9849
tarik.brahmi@parl.gc.ca
www.tarikbrahmi.ndp.ca
Autre numéros: Constituency Phone: 450-357-9100; Fax: 450-357-9109
Les réseaux sociaux: twitter.com/TarikBrahmi
Constituency Office
#117, 315, rueMacdonald
Saint-Jean-sur-Richelieu, QC J3B 8J3

Peter Braid, B.A.
Constituency: Kitchener — Waterloo, Ontario *No. of Constituents:* 95,966, Conservative Party
Tel: 613-996-5928
Fax: 613-992-6251
peter.braid@parl.gc.ca; peter.braid.c1@parl.gc.ca
www.peterbraid.ca
Other Communications: Constituency Phone: 519-746-1573; Fax: 519-746-6436
Social Media: twitter.com/peterbraid, www.facebook.com/PeterBraid?ref=ts, www.linkedin.com/pub/peter-braid/5/311/b1b
ConstituencyOffice
22 King St. South
Waterloo, ON N2J 1N8

Garry W. Breitkreuz
Constituency: Yorkton — Melville, Saskatchewan *No. of Constituents:* 50,797, Conservative Party
Tel: 613-992-4394
Toll-free: 800-667-6606
Fax: 613-992-8676
garry.breitkreuz@parl.gc.ca; garry.breitkreuz.c1@parl.gc.ca
www.garrybreitkreuz.com
Other Communications: Constituency Phone: 306-782-3309; Fax: 306-786-7207
Constituency Office
19 - 1st Ave. North
Yorkton, SK S3N 1J3

Hon. Scott Brison, P.C., B.Comm.
Constituency: Kings — Hants, Nova Scotia *No. of Constituents:* 65,355, Liberal
Tel: 613-995-8231
Fax: 613-996-9349
Brison.S@parl.gc.ca; kings.hants@ns.sympatico.ca
www.brison.ca
Other Communications: Constituency Phone: 902-542-4010; Fax: 902-542-4184
Social Media: twitter.com/scottbrison, www.linkedin.com/pub/scott-brison/9/a43/1a6
Constituency Office
#12, 360 Main St.
Wolfville, NS B4P 1C4

Ruth Ellen Brosseau
Constituency: Berthier — Maskinongé, Québec *No. of Constituents:* 90 838, New Democratic Party
Tel: 613-992-5681
Fax: 613-992-7276
RuthEllen.Brosseau@parl.gc.ca; RuthEllen.Brosseau.c1@parl.gc.ca
www.ruthellenbrosseau.ndp.ca
Other Communications: Constituency Phone: 819-228-1210; Fax:819-228-1181
Social Media: twitter.com/RE_Brosseau
Constituency Office
343, av Saint-Laurent
Louiseville, QC J5V 1K2

Gordon Brown, B.A. (Hons)
Constituency: Leeds — Grenville, Ontario *No. of Constituents:* 76,802, Conservative Party
Tel: 613-992-8756
Toll-free: 866-498-3096
Fax: 613-996-9171
gord.brown@parl.gc.ca; gord@gordbrownmp.ca
www.gordbrown.com
Other Communications: Constituency Phone: 613-498-3096; Fax: 613-498-3100
Constituency Office
27 King St. East
Brockville, ON K6V 1A7

Parliamentary Secretary to the Minister, International Cooperation, Lois Brown
Constituency: Newmarket — Aurora, Ontario *No. of Constituents:* 92,731, Conservative Party
Tel: 613-992-9310
Fax: 613-992-9407
lois.brown@parl.gc.ca
www.loisbrown.ca
Other Communications: Constituency Phone: 905-953-7515;Fax: 905-953-7527
Social Media: twitter.com/MPLoisBrown
Constituency Office
#206, 16600 Bayview Ave.
Newmarket, ON L3X 1Z9

Patrick W. Brown, LL.B.
Constituency: Barrie, Ontario *No. of Constituents:* 94,939, Conservative Party
Tel: 613-992-3394
Fax: 613-996-7923
patrick.brown@parl.gc.ca; barrie@servingbarrie.com
www.servingbarrie.com
Other Communications: Constituency Phone: 705-726-5959; Fax: 705-726-3340
Social Media: twitter.com/brownbarrie
Constituency Office
#302, 299 Lakeshore Dr.
Barrie, ON L4N 7Y9

Rod Bruinooge, B.A.
Constituency: Winnipeg South, Manitoba *No. of Constituents:* 64,144, Conservative Party
Tel: 613-995-7517
Fax: 613-943-1466
rod.bruinooge@parl.gc.ca; Rod@bruinooge.com
www.bruinooge.ca
Other Communications: Constituency Phone: 204-984-6787; Fax: 204-984-6792
Social Media: twitter.com/rodbruinooge, www.facebook.com/people/Rodney-Bruinooge/874415143
Constituency Office
#27, 2855 Pembina Hwy.
Winnipeg, MB R3T 2H5

Brad Butt
Constituency: Mississauga — Streetsville, Ontario *No. of Constituents:* 87,480, Conservative Party
Tel: 613-943-1766
Fax: 613-943-1768
Brad.Butt@parl.gc.ca
www.bradbutt.ca
Other Communications: Constituency Phone: 905-812-1811; Fax: 905-812-8464
Social Media: twitter.com/buttbrad
Constituency Office
#104, 154 Queen St. South
Mississauga, ON L5M 2P4

Hon. Gerry Byrne, P.C., B.Sc.
Constituency: Humber — St. Barbe — Baie Verte, Newfoundland & Labrador *No. of Constituents:* 59,109, Liberal
Tel: 613-996-5511
Toll-free: 800-563-9934
Fax: 613-996-9632
gerry.byrne@parl.gc.ca; info@gerrybyrne.ca
www.gerrybyrne.liberal.ca
Other Communications: Constituency Phone: 709-637-4540; 709-637-4537
Social Media: twitter.com/Gerry_Byrne
Constituency Office
14 Main St., 2nd Fl.
PO Box 1095
Corner Brook, NL A2H 6T2

Parliamentary Secretary to the Minister, Canadian Heritage, Paul Calandra
Constituency: Oak Ridges — Markham, Ontario *No. of Constituents:* 153,972, Conservative Party
Tel: 613-992-3640
Fax: 613-992-3642
paul.calandra@parl.gc.ca
www.paulcalandra.com
Other Communications: Constituency Phone: 905-640-1125; Fax:905-640-1182
Social Media: twitter.com/paulCalandra, www.facebook.com/pages/Paul-Calandra/97706410091, www.linkedin.com/pub/paul-calandra/25/149/697
Constituency Office
6060 Main St.
Stouffville, ON L4A 1B8

Chair, Bill C-18 Committee, Blaine Calkins, B.Sc.
Constituency: Wetaskiwin, Alberta *No. of Constituents:* 80,262, Conservative Party
Tel: 613-995-8886
Toll-free: 800-665-0865
Fax: 613-996-9860
blaine.calkins@parl.gc.ca; calkib1@parl.gc.ca
www.blainecalkinsmp.ca
Other Communications: Constituency Phone: 403-783-5530; Fax:403-783-5532
Social Media: twitter.com/blainecalkinsmp, www.facebook.com/pages/Blaine-Calkins/208129505866377
Constituency Office
#6A, 4612 - 50th St.
Ponoka, AB T4J 1S7

Ronald Cannan
Constituency: Kelowna — Lake Country, British Columbia *No. of Constituents:* 100,884, Conservative Party
Tel: 613-992-7006
Fax: 613-992-7636
ron.cannan@parl.gc.ca; ron@cannan.ca
www.cannan.ca
Other Communications: Constituency Phone: 250-470-5075; Fax: 250-470-5077
Social Media: twitter.com/RonCannan, www.linkedin.com/pub/ron-cannan/18/227/242
Constituency Office
#114, 1835Gordon Dr.
Kelowna, BC V1Y 3H4

John Carmichael, B.A.
Constituency: Don Valley West, Ontario *No. of Constituents:* 82,107, Conservative Party
Tel: 613-992-2855
Fax: 613-995-1635
john.carmichael@parl.gc.ca
www.johncarmichael.ca
Other Communications: Constituency Phone: 416-467-7275
Social Media: twitter.com/JohnBCarmichael, www.facebook.com/votecarmichael, www.linkedin.com/pub/john-carmichael/2/11b/b41
Constituency Office
#704, 18 Wynford Dr.
Toronto, ON M3C 3S2 Canada

Guy Caron, B.A., M.A.
Constituency: Rimouski-Neigette — Témiscouata — Les Basques, Québec *No. of Constituents:* 68 625, New Democratic Party
Tél: 613-992-5302
Téléc: 613-996-8298
guy.caron@parl.gc.ca
www.guycaron.ndp.ca
Autre numéros: Constituency Phone: 418-725-2562; Fax: 418-725-3993
Les réseaux sociaux: twitter.com/GuyCaronNPD
Constituency Office
#109, 140, rue SaintGermain
Rimouski, QC G5L 4B5

Parliamentary Secretary to the Minister, Health, Dr. Colin Carrie, B.Sc. (Hons.), D.C.
Constituency: Oshawa, Ontario *No. of Constituents:* 89,635, Conservative Party
Tel: 613-996-4756

Fax: 613-992-1357
colin.carrie@parl.gc.ca; colin@colincarriemp.ca
www.colincarriemp.ca
Other Communications: Constituency Phone: 905-440-4868; Fax: 905-440-4872
Social Media: twitter.com/ColinCarrie, www.facebook.com/people/Colin-Carrie/100001599242478
Constituency Office
#2B, 57 Simcoe St. South
Oshawa, ON L1H 4G4

Sean Casey, Q.C., B.B.A., LL.B.
Constituency: Charlottetown, Prince Edward Island *No. of Constituents:* 26,760, Liberal
Tel: 613-996-4714
Fax: 613-995-7685
sean.casey@parl.gc.ca
www.seancasey.ca
Other Communications: Constituency Phone: 902-566-7770; Fax: 902-566-7780
Social Media: twitter.com/SeanCaseyMP, www.facebook.com/pages/Sean-Casey/162651190466584, www.linkedin.com/pub/sean-casey/36/17/608
Constituency Office
#201, 75Fitzroy St.
Charlottetown, PE C1A 1R6

Andrew Cash
Constituency: Davenport, Ontario *No. of Constituents:* 66,731, New Democratic Party
Tel: 613-992-2576
Fax: 613- 99-5820
andrew.cash@parl.gc.ca; cash@cashfortoronto.ca
www.cashfortoronto.ca
Other Communications: Constituency Phone: 416-654-8048; Fax: 416-654-5083
Social Media: twitter.com/Cash4TO, www.facebook.com/cashfortoronto
Constituency Office
1162College St.
Toronto, ON M6H 1B6

Chris Charlton, B.A., M.A.
Constituency: Hamilton Mountain, Ontario *No. of Constituents:* 89,312, New Democratic Party
Tel: 613-995-9389
Toll-free: 866-878-5191
Fax: 613-992-7802
chris.charlton@parl.gc.ca; chris.charlton.c1@parl.gc.ca
www.chrischarlton.ca
Other Communications: Constituency Phone: 905-574-3331; Fax: 905-574-4980
Social Media: twitter.com/ChrisCharltonMP, www.facebook.com/pages/Chris-Charlton/25222718654, www.linkedin.com/pub/chris-charlton/8/8aa/4b9
Constituency Office
#232, 845 Upper James St., 2nd Fl.
Hamilton, ON L9C 3A3

Sylvain Chicoine
Constituency: Châteauguay — Saint-Constant, Québec *No. of Constituents:* 88 908, New Democratic Party
Tél: 613-996-7265
Téléc: 613-996-9287
sylvain.chicoine@parl.gc.ca
www.sylvainchicoine.ndp.ca
Autre numéros: Constituency Phone: 450-691-7044; Fax: 450-691-3114
Les réseaux sociaux: twitter.com/sylvainchicoine, www.facebook.com/group.php?gid=120841667990877
Constituency Office
253, bould'Anjou
Châteauguay, QC J6J 2R4

Robert Chisholm, B.A., M.A.
Constituency: Dartmouth — Cole Harbour, Nova Scotia *No. of Constituents:* 70,756, New Democratic Party
Tel: 613-995-9378
Fax: 613-995-9379
robert.chisholm@parl.gc.ca
www.robertchisholm.ndp.ca
Other Communications: Constituency Phone: 902-462-6453; Fax: 902-462-6493
Social Media: twitter.com/RobertNDP, www.facebook.com/RobertNDP
Constituency Office
#204, 530Portland St.
Dartmouth, NS B2Y 4V6

Corneliu Chisu, B.Eng., M.Eng.
Constituency: Pickering — Scarborough East, Ontario *No. of Constituents:* 78,501, Conservative Party
Tel: 613-995-8082
Fax: 613-993-6587
corneliu.chisu@parl.gc.ca
www.electchisu.ca
Other Communications: Constituency Phone: 416-287-0110; Fax: 416-287-6160
Social Media: twitter.com/cchisu, www.facebook.com/group.php?gid=229465150409635
Constituency Office
#4, 300Kingston Rd.
Pickering, ON L1V 1A2

Chair, Official Languages Committee, Hon. Michael D. Chong, P.C.
Constituency: Wellington — Halton Hills, Ontario *No. of Constituents:* 83,499, Conservative Party
Tel: 613-992-4179
Toll-free: 866-878-5556
Fax: 613-996-4907
michael.chong@parl.gc.ca
www.michaelchong.ca
Other Communications: Constituency Phone: 905-702-2597; Fax:905-702-2564
Social Media: www.linkedin.com/pub/michael-chong/15/632/353
Constituency Office
#205, 16 Mountainview Rd. South
Georgetown, ON L7G 4K1

François Choquette
Constituency: Drummond, Québec *No. of Constituents:* 77,280, New Democratic Party
Tél: 613-947-4550
Téléc: 613-947-4551
francois.choquette@parl.gc.ca
www.francoischoquette.ndp.ca
Autre numéros: Constituency Phone: 819-477-3611; Fax: 819-477-7116
Constituency Office
119B, rue desForges
Drummondville, QC J2B 6K1

Olivia Chow, B.A. (Hons.)
Constituency: Trinity — Spadina, Ontario *No. of Constituents:* 101,020, New Democratic Party
Tel: 613-992-2352
Fax: 613-992-6301
olivia.chow@parl.gc.ca
www.oliviachow.ca
Other Communications: Constituency Phone: 416-533-2710; Fax: 416-533-2236
Social Media: twitter.com/oliviachow, www.facebook.com/pages/Olivia-Chow/15535160141, www.linkedin.com/pub/olivia-riding-1-chow/6/845/202
Constituency Office
144 AugustaAve.
Toronto, ON M5T 2L5

Deputy Leader, New Democratic Party of Canada; Chair, Public Accounts Committee, David Christopherson
Constituency: Hamilton Centre, Ontario *No. of Constituents:* 78,562, New Democratic Party
Tel: 613-995-1757
Fax: 613-992-8356
david.christopherson@parl.gc.ca;hamilton@davidchristophers on.ca
www.davidchristopherson.ndp.ca
Other Communications: Constituency Phone: 905-526-0770; Fax: 905-526-9943
Social Media: www.facebook.com/DavidChristophersonNDP
Constituency Office
22 Tisdale St. South
Hamilton, ON L8N 2V9

Rob Clarke
Constituency: Desnethé — Missinippi — Churchill River, Saskatchewan *No. of Constituents:* 43,739, Conservative Party
Tel: 613-995-8321
Toll-free: 866-400-2334
Fax: 613-995-7697
rob.clarke@parl.gc.ca; rob.clarke.c1@parl.gc.ca
www.robclarkemp.ca
Other Communications: Constituency Phone: 306-425-2643; Fax: 306-425-2677
Social Media: twitter.com/rob_clarke_mp, www.facebook.com/pages/Rob-Clarke/123498939689
ConstituencyOffice
711 La Ronge Ave.
PO Box 612
La Ronge, SK S0J 1L0

Ryan Cleary
Constituency: St. John's South — Mount Pearl, Newfoundland & Labrador *No. of Constituents:* 67,025, New Democratic Party
Tel: 613-992-0927
Fax: 613-995-7858
ryan.cleary@parl.gc.ca
www.ryancleary.ndp.ca
Other Communications: Constituency Phone: 709-772-4608
Social Media: twitter.com/ClearyNDP, www.facebook.com/pages/Ryan-Cleary/218945144787655
Constituency Office
9 Commonwealth Ave.
Mount Pearl, NL A1N1W3

Minister, Federal Economic Development Initiative for Northern Ontario; President, Treasury Board, Hon. Tony Clement, P.C., B.A., LL.B.
Constituency: Parry Sound — Muskoka, Ontario *No. of Constituents:* 71,477, Conservative Party
Tel: 613-944-7740
Fax: 613-992-5092
tony.clement@parl.gc.ca; Clemet1@parl.gc.ca; Clemet2@parl.gc.ca
Other Communications: Constituency Phone: 705-789-4640; Fax: 705-789-8857
Social Media: twitter.com/TonyclementCPC
Note: Web Sites:www.ic.gc.ca/eic/site/ic1.nsf/eng/06510.html (FedNor, Industry Canada); www.tonyclement.ca (Personal Web Site)
Constituency Office
44A King William St.
Huntsville, ON P1H 1G3

Hon. Denis Coderre
Constituency: Bourassa, Québec *No. of Constituents:* 70 207, Liberal
Tél: 613-995-6108
Téléc: 613-995-9755
denis.coderre@parl.gc.ca; coderd1@parl.gc.ca
www.deniscoderre.liberal.ca
Autre numéros: Constituency Phone: 514-323-1212; Fax: 514-323-2875
Les réseaux sociaux: twitter.com/DenisCoderre, www.linkedin.com/pub/denis-coderre/12/451/97a
ConstituencyOffice
4975 Charleroi St.
Montréal, QC H1G 2Z2

Deputy Speaker; Chair, Committees of the Whole, Joe Comartin, LL.B.
Constituency: Windsor — Tecumseh, Ontario *No. of Constituents:* 84,458, New Democratic Party
Tel: 613-947-3445
Fax: 613-947-3448
joe.comartin@parl.gc.ca
www.joecomartin.ca
Other Communications: Constituency Phone: 519-988-1826; Fax:519-988-0152
Social Media: twitter.com/joecomartin, www.facebook.com/joecomartin
Constituency Office
1304B Lauzon Rd.
Windsor, ON N8S 3N1

Raymond Côté, B.A.
Constituency: Beauport — Limoilou, Québec *No. of Constituents:* 84 859, New Democratic Party
Tél: 613-992-4406
Téléc: 613-992-4544
raymond.cote@parl.gc.ca
www.raymondcote.ndp.ca
Autre numéros: Constituency Phone: 418-663-2113; Fax: 418-663-2988
Les réseaux sociaux: twitter.com/RCoteBL2011
Constituency Office
#101, 2000, avSanfaçon
Québec, QC G1E 3R7

Hon. Irwin Cotler, P.C., O.C., B.A., B.C.L., LL.M., LL.D., Ph.D.
Constituency: Mount Royal, Québec *No. of Constituents:* 68 556, Liberal
Tel: 613-995-0121
Fax: 613-992-6762
irwin.cotler@parl.gc.ca
www.irwincotler.liberal.ca
Other Communications: Constituency Phone: 514-283-0171; Fax:514-283-2407
Constituency Office
#316, 4770 Kent Ave.
Montréal, QC H3W 1H2

Jean Crowder, B.A.
Constituency: Nanaimo — Cowichan, British Columbia *No. of Constituents:* 99,872, New Democratic Party
Tel: 613-943-2180
Toll-free: 866-609-9998
Fax: 613-993-5577
jean.crowder@parl.gc.ca
www.jeancrowder.ca
Other Communications: Constituency Phone: 250-746-4896; Fax: 250-746-2354
Social Media: twitter.com/JeanCrowder, www.facebook.com/jeancrowder
Constituency Office
#101, 126Ingram St.
Duncan, BC V9L 1P1

House Leader, Official Opposition, Nathan Cullen, B.A.
Constituency: Skeena — Bulkley Valley, British Columbia *No. of Constituents:* 61,043, New Democratic Party
Tel: 613-993-6654
Fax: 613-993-9007
nathan.cullen@parl.gc.ca; info@nathancullen.ca
www.nathancullen.com
Other Communications: Constituency Phone: 250-877-4140;Fax: 250-877-4141

Social Media: twitter.com/nathancullen,
www.facebook.com/nathan.cullen1,
www.linkedin.com/pub/nathan-cullen/21/24a/a36
Note: Other constituency offices are located at #104, 4710 Lazelle Ave., Terrace, BC V8G 1T2 (250-615-5339) &818 Third Ave. West, Prince Rupert, BC V8J 1M6 (250-622-2413).
Constituency Office
1283 Main St., 2nd Fl.
PO Box 4914
Smithers, BC V0J 2N0

Rodger Cuzner, B.A.
Constituency: Cape Breton — Canso, Nova Scotia *No. of Constituents:* 57,331, Liberal
Tel: 613-992-6756
Toll-free: 866-282-0699
Fax: 613-992-4053
rodger.cuzner@parl.gc.ca; cuzner1@parl.gc.ca
www.rodgercuzner.liberal.ca
Other Communications: Constituency Phone: 902-842-9763; Fax: 902-842-9025
Social Media: twitter.com/RodgerCuzner,
www.facebook.com/rodger.cuzner
Constituency Office, Chedabucto Centre
78 Commercial St.
PO Box 2107
Dominion, NS B1G 1B4

Joe Daniel, B.Sc., M.Eng.
Constituency: Don Valley East, Ontario *No. of Constituents:* 69,690, Conservative Party
Tel: 613-995-4988
Fax: 613-995-1686
joe.daniel@parl.gc.ca; joedanieldve@gmail.com
www.joedaniel.ca
Other Communications: Constituency Phone: 647-624-6678; 647-624-6678
Social Media:
www.facebook.com/pages/Joe-Daniel/162888397199
ConstituencyOffice
#01, 1440 Don Mills Rd.
Toronto, ON M3B 3N6

Patricia Davidson
Constituency: Sarnia — Lambton, Ontario *No. of Constituents:* 79,688, Conservative Party
Tel: 613-957-2649
Fax: 613-957-2655
patricia.davidson@parl.gc.ca; davidp1@parl.gc.ca
www.patriciadavidson.ca
Other Communications: Constituency Phone: 519-383-6600; Fax: 519-383-0609
ConstituencyOffice
#2, 1000 Finch Dr.
Sarnia, ON N7S 6G5

Don Davies
Constituency: Vancouver Kingsway, British Columbia *No. of Constituents:* 82,619, New Democratic Party
Tel: 613-943-0267
Fax: 613-943-0219
don.davies@parl.gc.ca
www.dondavies.ndp.ca
Other Communications: Constituency Phone: 604-775-6263; Fax: 604-775-6284
Social Media: twitter.com/dondavies,
www.facebook.com/DonDaviesNDP,
www.linkedin.com/pub/don-davies/30/3ab/934
Constituency Office
2951 KingswayAve.
Vancouver, BC V5R 5J4

Deputy Leader, New Democratic Party of Canada, Libby Davies
Constituency: Vancouver East, British Columbia *No. of Constituents:* 81,801, New Democratic Party
Tel: 613-992-6030
Fax: 613-995-7412
libby.davies@parl.gc.ca
www.libbydavies.ca
Other Communications: Constituency Phone: 604-775-5800; Fax:604-775-5811
Social Media: twitter.com/LibbyDavies,
www.facebook.com/pages/Libby-Davies/7154945923?ref=nf
Constituency Office
2412 Main St.
Vancouver, BC V5T 3E2

Anne-Marie Day
Constituency: Charlesbourg — Haute-Saint-Charles, Québec *No. of Constituents:* 82,345, New Democratic Party
Tél: 613-995-8857
Téléc: 613-995-1625
anne-marie.day@parl.gc.ca
www.annemarieday.ndp.ca
Autre numéros: Constituency Phone: 418-624-0022; Fax: 418-624-1095
Les réseaux sociaux: twitter.com/AnneMarieDay,
www.facebook.com/pages/Anne-Marie-Day-NPD/191889404181173
Constituency Office
#204, 8400, boulHenri-Bourassa
Québec, QC G1G 4E2

Parliamentary Secretary to the Minister, Foreign Affairs, Bob Dechert
Constituency: Mississauga — Erindale, Ontario *No. of Constituents:* 105,430, Conservative Party
Tel: 613-995-7321
Fax: 613-992-6708
bob.dechert@parl.gc.ca; bob.dechert.c1@parl.gc.ca
www.bobdechertmp.ca
Other Communications: ConstituencyPhone: 905-897-1952; Fax: 905-897-6117
Constituency Office
#108, 1300 Central Pkwy. West
Mississauga, ON L5C 4G8

Parliamentary Secretary to the Prime Minister & to the Minister, Intergovernmental Affairs, Dean Del Mastro, B. Comm. (Hons.)
Constituency: Peterborough, Ontario *No. of Constituents:* 91,709, Conservative Party
Tel: 613-995-6411
Fax: 613-996-9800
dean.delmastro@parl.gc.ca; delmad1@parl.gc.ca
www.deandelmastro.ca
Other Communications: Constituency Phone: 705-745-2108; Fax: 705-741-4123
Social Media: twitter.com/mpdeandelmastro,
www.facebook.com/deandelmastro
Constituency Office
1875 Lansdowne St. West
PO Box 21030
Peterborough, ON K9J 8M7

Deputy Chair, Committees of the Whole, Barry Devolin, B.A., M.A.
Constituency: Haliburton — Kawartha Lakes — Brock, Ontario *No. of Constituents:* 93,250, Conservative Party
Tel: 613-992-2474
Toll-free: 866-688-9881
Fax: 613-996-9656
barry.devolin@parl.gc.ca
www.barrydevolin.ca
Other Communications: Constituency Phone: 705-324-2400; Fax:705-324-0880
Social Media: twitter.com/BarryDevolin_MP,
www.facebook.com/barry.devolin
Constituency Office
#1, 68 McLaughlin Rd.
Lindsay, ON K9V 6B5

Paul Dewar, B.A., B.Ed.
Constituency: Ottawa Centre, Ontario *No. of Constituents:* 90,008, New Democratic Party
Tel: 613-996-5322
Fax: 613-996-5323
paul.dewar@parl.gc.ca; pauldewar@ndp.ca
www.pauldewar.ca
Other Communications: Constituency Phone: 613-946-8682; Fax: 613-946-8680
Social Media: twitter.com/PaulDewar,
www.facebook.com/pages/Paul-Dewar/21201054432
Constituency Office
#304, 1306 Wellington St.
Ottawa, ON K1Y 3B2

Hon. Stéphane Dion, P.C., B.A., M.A., Ph.D.
Constituency: Saint-Laurent — Cartierville, Québec *No. of Constituents:* 78,870, Liberal
Tél: 613-996-5789
Téléc: 613-996-6562
stephane.dion@parl.gc.ca; dions1@parl.gc.ca
www.stephanedion.liberal.ca
Autre numéros: Constituency Phone: 514-335-6655; Fax:514-335-2712
Les réseaux sociaux:
www.facebook.com/pages/Stephane-Dion/7874631159
Constituency Office
#440, 750, boul Marcel Laurin
Saint-Laurent, QC H4M 2M4

Pierre Dionne Labelle
Constituency: Rivière-du-Nord, Québec *No. of Constituents:* 90 638, New Democratic Party
Tél: 613-992-3257
Téléc: 613-992-2156
Pierre.DionneLabelle@parl.gc.ca
www.pierredionnelabelle.ndp.ca
Autre numéros: Constituency Phone: 450-565-0061; Fax: 450-565-0118
Constituency Office
#101,227, rue St-Georges
St-Jérôme, QC J7Z 5A1

Fin Donnelly
Constituency: New Westminster — Coquitlam, British Columbia *No. of Constituents:* 84,337, New Democratic Party
Tel: 613-947-4455
Fax: 613-947-4458
fin.donnelly@parl.gc.ca; Donnelly.F@parl.gc.ca
www.findonnelly.ca
Other Communications: Constituency Phone: 604-664-9229; Fax: 604-664-9231
Social Media: twitter.com/FinDonnelly,
www.facebook.com/pages/Fin-Donnelly/107434010722,
www.linkedin.com/pub/fin-donnelly/4/968/919
Constituency Office
1116 Austin Ave.
Coquitlam, BC V3K 3P5

Rosane Doré Lefebvre, B.A.
Constituency: Alfred-Pellan, Québec *No. of Constituents:* 84 630, New Democratic Party
Tél: 613-992-0611
Téléc: 613-992-8556
rosane.dorelefebvre@parl.gc.ca
www.rosanedorelefebvre.ndp.ca
Autre numéros: Constituency Phone: 450-661-4117; Fax: 450-661-5623
Les réseaux sociaux: twitter.com/RosaneDL,
www.facebook.com/rosane.npd
Constituency Office
#304,3131, boul de la Concorde
Laval, QC H7E 4W4

Earl Dreeshen
Constituency: Red Deer, Alberta *No. of Constituents:* 93,723, Conservative Party
Tel: 613-995-0590
Fax: 613-995-6831
earl.dreeshen@parl.gc.ca; Dreese1@parl.gc.ca
www.earldreeshen.ca
Other Communications: Constituency Phone: 403-347-7426; Fax: 403-347-7423
Social Media: twitter.com/earl_dreeshen
Constituency Office
#100A, 4315 - 55th Ave.
Red Deer, AB T4N 4N7

Matthew Dubé
Constituency: Chambly — Borduas, Québec *No. of Constituents:* 99 210, New Democratic Party
Tél: 613-992-6035
Téléc: 613-995-6223
matthew.dube@parl.gc.ca
www.matthewdube.ndp.ca
Autre numéros: Constituency Phone: 450-441-7802; Fax: 450-441-3674
Les réseaux sociaux: twitter.com/MattDube,
www.facebook.com/matthewdube.chamblyborduas
Constituency Office
1, rue Robert
Saint-Basile-Le-Grand, QC J3N 1L7

Minister, Aboriginal Affairs & Northern Development, Hon. John Duncan, P.C., B.Sc.F.
Constituency: Vancouver Island North, British Columbia *No. of Constituents:* 90,374, Conservative Party
Tel: 613-992-2503
Toll-free: 800-667-8404
Fax: 613-996-3306
john.duncan@parl.gc.ca
Other Communications: Constituency Phone:250-338-9381; Fax: 250-338-9361
Note: Web Sites: www.johnduncanmp.com (Personal Web Site);www.ainc-inac.gc.ca/ai/min/index-eng.asp (Aboriginal Affairs & Northern Development Canada)
Constituency Office
#104, 576 England Ave.
Courtenay, BC V9N 2N3

Kirsty Duncan, B.A., PhD
Constituency: Etobicoke North, Ontario *No. of Constituents:* 63,014, Liberal
Tel: 613-995-4702
Fax: 613-995-8359
kirsty.duncan@parl.gc.ca
www.kirstyduncan.liberal.ca
Other Communications: Constituency Phone: 416-747-6003; Fax: 416-747-8295
Social Media: twitter.com/KirstyDuncanMP,
www.facebook.com/pages/Kirsty-Duncan/12293731397
Constituency Office
815 AlbionRd.
Toronto, ON M9V 1A3

Linda Francis Duncan, B.A., LL.B., LL.M.
Constituency: Edmonton — Strathcona, Alberta *No. of Constituents:* 73,444, New Democratic Party
Tel: 613-995-7325
Fax: 613-995-5342
linda.duncan@parl.gc.ca; duncal1@parl.gc.ca
www.lindaduncan.ndp.ca;www.edmontonstrathcona.ca/linda.html
Other Communications: Constituency Phone: 780-495-8404; Fax:780-495-8403
Social Media: twitter.com/LindaDuncanMP,
www.facebook.com/pages/Linda-Duncan/31779288732
Constituency Office

10049 - 81st Ave.
Edmonton, AB T6E 1W7

Pierre-Luc Dusseault
Constituency: Sherbrooke, Québec *No. of Constituents:* 82 918, New Democratic Party
Tél: 613-943-7896
Téléc: 613-943-7902
pierre-luc.dusseault@parl.gc.ca
www.pierrelucdusseault.ndp.ca
Autre numéros: Constituency Phone: 819-564-4200; Fax: 819-564-3745
Les réseaux sociaux: twitter.com/PLDusseault, www.facebook.com/PLDusseault
Constituency Office
#130, 100,rue Belvédère sud
Sherbrooke, QC J1H 4B5

Parliamentary Secretary to the Minister, Citizenship & Immigration, Richard Dykstra, B.A.
Constituency: St. Catharines, Ontario *No. of Constituents:* 83,475, Conservative Party
Tel: 613-992-3352
Fax: 613-947-4402
rick.dykstra@parl.gc.ca; info@rickdykstra.ca
www.rickdykstra.ca
Other Communications: Constituency Phone: 905-934-6767; Fax: 905-934-1577
Social Media: twitter.com/RickDykstra, www.facebook.com/RickDykstraMP
Constituency Office
61 Geneva St.
St. Catharines, ON L2R 4M2

Hon. Arnold Wayne Easter, P.C., Dipl.T., LL.D.(Hon.)
Constituency: Malpeque, Prince Edward Island *No. of Constituents:* 26,918, Liberal
Tel: 613-992-2406
Fax: 613-995-7408
wayne.easter@parl.gc.ca; eastew1@parl.gc.ca
www.wayneeaster.com
Other Communications: Constituency Phone: 902-964-2428; Fax:902-964-3242
Social Media: twitter.com/WayneEaster
Constituency Office
PO Box 70
Hunter River, PE C0A 1N0

Hon. Mark Eyking, P.C.
Constituency: Sydney — Victoria, Nova Scotia *No. of Constituents:* 60,719, Liberal
Tel: 613-995-6459
Fax: 613-995-2963
mark.eyking@parl.gc.ca
www.markeyking.liberal.ca
Other Communications: Constituency Phone: 902-567-6275; Fax: 902-564-2479
Constituency Office, Cabot House
#109,500 Kings Rd.
Sydney, NS B1S 1B2

Minister, International Cooperation, Hon. Julian Fantino, P.C., C.O.M., O. Ont.
Constituency: Vaughan, Ontario *No. of Constituents:* 125,059, Conservative Party
Tel: 613-996-4971
Fax: 613-996-4973
julian.fantino@parl.gc.ca; fantij@parl.gc.ca
Other Communications: ConstituencyPhone: 905-303-5000; Fax: 905-303-5002
Social Media: twitter.com/JulianFantino
Note: Web Sites: www.julianfantino.ca (Personal Web Site); www.acdi-cida.gc.ca/acdi-cida/acdi-cida.nsf/eng/NIC-5494720-J79(Canadian International Development Agency)
Constituency Office
#115, 9401 Jane St.
Maple, ON L6A 4H7

Minister, International Trade; Minister, Asia-Pacific Gateway, Hon. Edward Fast, P.C., LL.B.
Constituency: Abbotsford, British Columbia *No. of Constituents:* 85,143, Conservative Party
Tel: 613-995-0183
Fax: 613-996-9795
ed.fast@parl.gc.ca; faste@parl.gc.ca;ed@edfast.ca
Other Communications: Constituency Phone: 604-557-7888; Fax: 604-557-9918
Note: Web Sites: www.edfast.ca (Personal Web Site);www.international.gc.ca/commerce/edward_fast.aspx?lang=eng (Foreign Affairs & International Trade Canada)
Constituency Office
#205, 2825 Clearbrook Rd.
Abbotsford, BC V2T 6S3

Parliamentary Secretary to the Minister of Justice, Kerry-Lynne Findlay, Q.C., B.A., LL.B.
Constituency: Delta — Richmond East, British Columbia *No. of Constituents:* 80,821, Conservative Party
Tel: 613-992-2957
Fax: 613-992-3589
kerry-lynne.findlay@parl.gc.ca
www.kerrylynnefindlay.ca
Other Communications: ConstituencyPhone: 604-940-8040; Fax: 604-940-8041
Social Media: twitter.com/KLDF2011
Constituency Office
#202, 5000 Bridge St.
Delta, BC V4K 2K4

Minister, Human Resources & Skills Development, Hon. Diane Finley, P.C., B.A., M.B.A.
Constituency: Haldimand — Norfolk, Ontario *No. of Constituents:* 80,640, Conservative Party
Tel: 613-996-4974
Fax: 613-996-9749
diane.finley@parl.gc.ca;diane.finley@hrsdc-rhdcc.gc.ca
Other Communications: Constituency Phone: 519-426-3400; Fax: 519-426-0003
Note: Web Sites: www.dianefinley.ca (Personal Web Site);www.hrsdc.gc.ca/eng/corporate/ministers/index.shtml (Human Resources & Skills Development Canada)
Constituency Office
76 Kent St. South
Simcoe, ON N3Y 2Y1

Minister, Finance, Hon. James Michael (Jim) Flaherty, P.C., B.A., LL.B.
Constituency: Whitby — Oshawa, Ontario *No. of Constituents:* 103,125, Conservative Party
Tel: 613-992-6344
Fax: 613-992-8320
jim.flaherty@parl.gc.ca; jim@jimflahertymp.ca
Other Communications: Constituency Phone:905-665-8182; Fax: 905-665-8124
Social Media: twitter.com/JimFlaherty, www.facebook.com/pages/Jim-Flaherty/49500135386
Note: Web Sites: www.jimflaherty.com (Personal Web Site); www.fin.gc.ca/comment/minfin-eng.asp (Department ofFinance Canada)
Constituency Office
#204, 701 Rossland Rd. East
Whitby, ON L1N 8Y9

Minister of State, Transport, Hon. Steven John Fletcher, P.C., B.Sc., M.B.A.
Constituency: Charleswood — St. James — Assiniboia, Manitoba *No. of Constituents:* 62,609, Conservative Party
Tel: 613-995-5609
Fax: 613-992-3199
steven.fletcher@parl.gc.ca
Other Communications: Constituency Phone: 204-984-6432;Fax: 204-984-6451
Social Media: twitter.com/stevenjfletcher, www.facebook.com/StevenFletcherMP
Note: Web Sites: www.stevenfletcher.com (Personal Web Site); www.tc.gc.ca/eng/minister-state.htm (TransportCanada)
Constituency Office
3111A Portage Ave.
Winnipeg, MB R3K 0W4

Whip, Liberal Caucus, Judy Foote, B.A., B.Ed
Constituency: Random — Burin — St. George's, Newfoundland & Labrador *No. of Constituents:* 57,556, Liberal
Tel: 613-992-8655
Fax: 613-992-5324
Judy.Foote@parl.gc.ca
www.judyfoote.liberal.ca
Other Communications: Constituency Phone: 709-832-1383; Fax: 709-832-1380
Social Media: twitter.com/JudyFoote, www.facebook.com/pages/Judy-Foote/36948418784
ConstituencyOffice
3 Church St.
PO Box 370
Grand Bank, NL A0E 1W0

Jean-François Fortin, B.A.
Constituency: Haute-Gaspésie — La Mitis — Matane — Matapédia, Québec *No. of Constituents:* 59 397, Bloc Québécois
Tél: 613-995-1013
Téléc: 613-995-5184
jean-francois.fortin@parl.gc.ca
www.jffortin.info
Autre numéros: Constituency Phone: 418-562-0343; Fax: 418-562-7655
Les réseaux sociaux: twitter.com/fortjf, www.facebook.com/JFFortin.Bloc
Constituency Office
290,av St-Jérome
Matane, QC G4W 3A9

Mylène Freeman, B.A.
Constituency: Argenteuil — Papineau — Mirabel, Quebec *No. of Constituents:* 96 723, New Democratic Party
Tel: 613-992-0902
Fax: 613-992-2935
mylene.freeman@parl.gc.ca
www.mylenefreeman.ndp.ca
Other Communications: Constituency Phone: 450-562-0737; Fax: 450-562-2527
Social Media: twitter.com/MyleneFreeman, www.linkedin.com/in/mylenefreeman
Note: Mylène Freeman also has a constituency office in Saint-André-Avellin, Québec (149 Main St., J0V 1W0). The phone number in Saint-André-Avellin is 819-983-1577.
Constituency Office
499B, ruePrincipale
Lachute, QC J8H 1Y4

Hon. Hedy Fry, P.C., M.D., L.R.C.P.S.I., L.M.
Constituency: Vancouver Centre, British Columbia *No. of Constituents:* 102,201, Liberal
Tel: 613-992-3213
Fax: 613-995-0056
hedy.fry@parl.gc.ca
www.hedyfry.com
Other Communications: Constituency Phone: 604-666-0135; Fax: 604-666-0114
Social Media: twitter.com/hedyfry, www.facebook.com/pages/Dr-Hedy-Fry/6172639058
ConstituencyOffice
#106, 1030 Denman St.
Vancouver, BC V6G 2M6

Royal Galipeau
Constituency: Ottawa — Orléans, Ontario *No. of Constituents:* 89,802, Conservative Party
Tél: 613-995-1800
Téléc: 613-995-6298
royal.galipeau@parl.gc.ca; galipr1@parl.gc.ca
www.royalgalipeau.ca
Autre numéros: Constituency Phone: 613-995-1800; Fax: 613-590-1201
Les réseaux sociaux: twitter.com/GalipeauOrleans, www.facebook.com/royal.galipeau
Constituency Office
255 Centrum Blvd.
Orléans, ON K1E 3W3

Cheryl Gallant
Constituency: Renfrew — Nipissing — Pembroke, Ontario *No. of Constituents:* 78,307, Conservative Party
Tel: 613-992-7712
Toll-free: 866-295-7165
Fax: 613-995-2561
cheryl.gallant@parl.gc.ca; gallac1@parl.gc.ca
www.cherylgallant.com
Other Communications: Constituency Phone: 613-732-4404; Fax: 613-732-4697
Social Media: twitter.com/cherylgallant, www.facebook.com/CherylGallant, www.linkedin.com/pub/cheryl-gallant/36/336/366
Constituency Office
84 Isabella St., 2nd Fl.
Pembroke, ON K8A 5S5

House Leader, Liberal Party, Marc Garneau, C.C., C.D., B.Sc., Ph.D., F.C.A.S.I.
Constituency: Westmount — Ville-Marie, Québec *No. of Constituents:* 77,656, Liberal
Tel: 613-996-7267
Fax: 613-995-8632
marc.garneau@parl.gc.ca
www.marcgarneau.liberal.ca
Other Communications: Constituency Phone: 514-283-2013;Fax: 514-283-9790
Social Media: twitter.com/MarcGarneau, www.facebook.com/pages/Marc-Garneau/21128206560
Constituency Office
#340, 4060, rue Ste-Catherine ouest
Montréal, QC H3Z 2Z3

Randall Garrison
Constituency: Esquimalt — Juan de Fuca, British Columbia *No. of Constituents:* 98,477, New Democratic Party
Tel: 613-996-2625
Fax: 613-996-9779
randall.garrison@parl.gc.ca
www.randallgarrison.ca
Other Communications: Constituency Phone: 250-405-6550
Social Media: twitter.com/r_garrison, www.linkedin.com/pub/randall-garrison/15/922/193
Constituency Office
#2A, 100 AldersmithPl.
Victoria, BC V9A 7M8

Réjean Genest
Constituency: Shefford, Québec *No. of Constituents:* 84 666, New Democratic Party
Tél: 613-992-5279
Téléc: 613-992-7871
rejean.genest@parl.gc.ca
www.rejeangenest.ndp.ca
Autre numéros: Constituency Phone: 450-378-3221; Fax: 450-378-3380
Constituency Office
#101, 26 DufferinSt.
Granby, QC J2G 4W5

Jonathan Genest-Jourdain
Constituency: Manicouagan, Québec *No. of Constituents:* 65 648, New Democratic Party
Tél: 613-992-2363
Téléc: 613-996-7954
jonathan.genest-jourdain@parl.gc.ca
www.jonathangenestjourdain.ndp.ca
Autre numéros: Constituency Phone: 418-538-1632; Fax: 418-538-1736
Constituency Office
1158, rue Boreale, #B
Havre-St-Pierre, QC G0G 1P0

Alain Giguére
Constituency: Marc-Aurèle-Fortin, Québec *No. of Constituents:* 87 923, New Democratic Party
Tél: 613-992-2617
Téléc: 613-992-6069
alain.giguere@parl.gc.ca
www.alaingiguere.ndp.ca
Autre numéros: Constituency Phone: 450-965-0548; Fax: 450-965-3221
Constituency Office
#305, 83, rueTurgeon
Ste-Thérèse, QC J7E 3H7

Parm Gill
Constituency: Brampton — Springdale, Ontario *No. of Constituents:* 89,017, Conservative Party
Tel: 613-995-4843
Fax: 613-995-7003
parm.gill@parl.gc.ca
www.parmgillmp.ca
Other Communications: Constituency Phone: 905-840-0505; Fax: 905-840-1778
Social Media: twitter.com/ParmGill, www.facebook.com/profile.php?id=539745780&ref=ts
Constituency Office
#3000 - 180 Sandalwood Pkwy.East
Brampton, ON L6Z 1Y4

Parliamentary Secretary to the Minister, Finance, Shelly Glover
Constituency: Saint Boniface, Manitoba *No. of Constituents:* 65,604, Conservative Party
Tel: 613-995-0579
Fax: 613-996-7571
shelly.glover@parl.gc.ca
www.shellyglover.ca
Other Communications: Constituency Phone: 204-983-3183; Fax:204-983-4274
Social Media: www.facebook.com/MPShellyGlover
Constituency Office
#4, 213 St. Mary's Rd.
Winnipeg, MB R2H 1J2

Yvon Godin
Constituency: Acadie — Bathurst, New Brunswick *No. of Constituents:* 66,298, New Democratic Party
Tél: 613-992-2165
Téléc: 613-992-4558
yvon.godin@parl.gc.ca
www.yvongodin.ndp.ca
Autre numéros: Constituency Phone: 506-548-7511; Fax: 506-548-7418
Les réseaux sociaux: www.facebook.com/pages/Yvon-Godin/78947535300
Constituency Office
#311, 216 MainSt.
Bathurst, NB E2A 1A8

Parliamentary Secretary to the Minister, Justice, Robert Goguen, Q.C., B.B.A, LL.B.
Constituency: Moncton — Riverview — Dieppe, New Brunswick *No. of Constituents:* 75,298, Conservative Party
Tel: 613-992-8072
Fax: 613-992-8083
robert.goguen@parl.gc.ca
www.robertgoguen.ca
Other Communications: Constituency Phone:506-382-7175
Social Media: twitter.com/robertrgoguen, www.facebook.com/VoteGoguen
Constituency Office
34 King St.
Moncton, NB E1C 4M2

Peter Goldring
Constituency: Edmonton East, Alberta *No. of Constituents:* 92,507, Independent Con
Tel: 613-992-3821
Fax: 613-992-6898
peter.goldring@parl.gc.ca; goldrp1@parl.gc.ca
www.petergoldring.com
Other Communications: Constituency Phone: 780-495-3261; Fax: 780-495-5142
Note: Peter Goldring left the caucus of the Conservative Party of Canada in 2011. He has been recognized as an Independent Conservative since December 5,2011.
Constituency Office
9111 - 118th Ave. NW
Edmonton, AB T5B 0T9

Responsible, Liberal Party Research Office, Hon. Ralph Goodale, P.C., B.A., LL.B.
Constituency: Wascana, Saskatchewan *No. of Constituents:* 57,815, Liberal
Tel: 613-996-4743
Fax: 613-996-9790
ralph.goodale@parl.gc.ca; goodale@sasktel.net
www.ralphgoodale.liberal.ca
Other Communications: ConstituencyPhone: 306-585-2202; Fax: 306-585-2280
Social Media: twitter.com/RalphGoodale, www.facebook.com/ralphgoodale
Constituency Office
310 University Park Dr.
Regina, SK S4V 0Y8

Minister of State, Science & Technology & Federal Economic Development Agency for Southern Ontario, Hon. Dr. Gary Goodyear, P.C., D.C., F.C.C.S.S.
Constituency: Cambridge, Ontario *No. of Constituents:* 94,591, Conservative Party
Tel: 613-996-1307
Fax: 613-996-8340
gary.goodyear@parl.gc.ca; info@garygoodyear.com
Other Communications: Constituency Phone: 519-624-7440; Fax: 519-624-3517
Note: Web Sites: www.garygoodyear.com(Personal Web Site); www.ic.gc.ca/eic/site/ic1.nsf/eng/02933.html (Industry Canada)
Constituency Office
#3, 1425 Bishop St. North
Cambridge, ON N1R 6J9

Minister of State, Sport, Hon. Bal Gosal, P.C.
Constituency: Bramalea — Gore — Malton, Ontario *No. of Constituents:* 108,751, Conservative Party
Tel: 613-992-9105
Fax: 613-947-0443
bal.gosal@parl.gc.ca; bal.gosal@pch.gc.ca
Other Communications: Constituency Phone: 905-790-9211; Fax:905-790-9507
Social Media: twitter.com/MinStateSport, www.facebook.com/pages/Bal-Gosal/155006724554020
Note: Web Sites: www.electbalgosal.ca (Personal Web Site); www.pch.gc.ca/pc-ch/minstr/gosal/biograph-eng.cfm (CanadianHeritage)
Constituency Office
#44, 8500 Torbram Rd.
Brampton, ON L6T 5C6

Parliamentary Secretary to the Minister, Public Works & Government Services, for Official Languages, & for the Economic Development Agency for the Regions ofQuéebec, Jacques Gourde
Constituency: Lotbinière —Chutes-de-la-Chaudière, Québec *No. of Constituents:* 82 725, Conservative Party
Tél: 613-992-2639
Téléc: 613-992-1018
jacques.gourde@parl.gc.ca
Autre numéros: Constituency Phone: 418-836-0970; Fax: 418-836-6177
Les réseaux sociaux: twitter.com/JacquesGourde, www.facebook. com/jacques.gourde
Note: Web Sites: www.jacquesgourde.ca; www.tpsgc-pwgsc.gc.ca/apropos-about/scrtr-eng.html
Constituency Office
910, rte. Lagueux
Saint-Étienne-de-Lauzon, QC G6J 1B7

Claude Gravelle
Constituency: Nickel Belt, Ontario *No. of Constituents:* 72,280, New Democratic Party
Tel: 613-995-9107
Toll-free: 800-267-4829
Fax: 613-995-9109
claude.gravelle@parl.gc.ca
www.claudegravelle.ndp.ca
Other Communications: Constituency Phone: 705-897-2222; Fax: 705-897-2223
Social Media: www.facebook.com/pages/Claude-Gravelle/35478778040
Constituency Office
#203,2945 Hwy. 69 North
Val Caron, ON P3N 1N3

Nina Grewal, B.A.
Constituency: Fleetwood — Port Kells, British Columbia *No. of Constituents:* 95,797, Conservative Party
Tel: 613-996-2205
Fax: 613-995-7139
nina.grewal@parl.gc.ca; grewan1@parl.gc.ca
www.ninagrewal.ca
Other Communications: Constituency Phone: 604-501-5900; Fax: 604-501-5901
Social Media: twitter.com/MPNinaGrewal, www.facebook.com/NinaGrewalMP
Constituency Office
#201, 15957 - 84th Ave.
Surrey, BC V4N 0W7

Deputy House Leader, Official Opposition, Sadia Groguhé
Constituency: Saint-Lambert, Québec *No. of Constituents:* 73 523, New Democratic Party
Tél: 613-998-5961
Téléc: 613-954-0707
sadia.groguhe@parl.gc.ca
www.sadiagroguhe.ndp.ca
Autre numéros: Constituency Phone: 450-646-2423; Fax: 450-646-3018
Les réseaux sociaux: www.facebook.com/Groguhe
Constituency Office
1150, boul Desaulniers
Longueuil, QC J4K 1K7

Prime Minister; Responsible, Conservative Party Research Office, Right Hon. Stephen Joseph Harper, P.C., B.A., M.A.
Constituency: Calgary Southwest, Alberta *No. of Constituents:* 95,026, Conservative Party
Tel: 613-992-4211
Fax: 613-941-6900
stephen.harper@parl.gc.ca; pm@pm.gc.ca
Other Communications: Constituency Phone: 403-253-7990; Fax: 403-253-8203
Social Media: twitter.com/pmharper, www.facebook.com/pmharper
Note: Web Sites: www.pm.gc.ca (Prime Minister ofCanada); www.conservative.ca/leader/stephen_harper (Party Web Site)
Constituency Office
#203A, 1600 - 90th Ave. SW
Calgary, AB T2V 5A8

Dan Harris
Constituency: Scarborough Southwest, Ontario *No. of Constituents:* 69,389, New Democratic Party
Tel: 613-995-0284
Fax: 613-996-6309
dan.harris@parl.gc.ca
www.danharris.ndp.ca
Other Communications: Constituency Phone: 416-261-8613; Fax: 416-261-5268
Social Media: twitter.com/danharrisndp, www.facebook.com/pages/Dan-Harris/141741619229068
Constituency Office
1674 KingstonRd.
Toronto, ON M1N 1S5

Jack Harris, Q.C., B.A., LL.B., LL.M.
Constituency: St. John's East, Newfoundland & Labrador *No. of Constituents:* 76,424, New Democratic Party
Tel: 613-996-7269
Fax: 613-992-2178
jack.harris@parl.gc.ca
www.jackharris.ndp.ca
Other Communications: Constituency Phone: 709-772-7171; Fax: 709-772-7175
Social Media: twitter.com/JackHarrisNDP, www.facebook.com/pages/Jack-Harris/38470344017
Constituency Office
342Freshwater Rd.
St. John's, NL A1B 1C2

Richard M. Harris
Constituency: Cariboo — Prince George, British Columbia *No. of Constituents:* 76,216, Conservative Party
Tel: 613-995-6704
Toll-free: 800-668-4282
Fax: 613-996-9850
richard.harris@parl.gc.ca; harrir1@parl.gc.ca
www.dickharris.ca
Other Communications: Constituency Phone: 250-564-7771; Fax: 250-564-6224
Constituency Office
#206, 575 Quebec St.
Prince George, BC V2L 1W6

Sana Hassainia
Constituency: Verchères — Les Patriotes, Québec *No. of Constituents:* 80 472, New Democratic Party
Tél: 613-996-2998
Téléc: 613-995-1062
sana.hassainia@parl.gc.ca
www.sanahassainia.ndp.ca
Autre numéros: Constituency Phone: 450-652-4442; Fax: 450-652-4447
Les réseaux sociaux: twitter.com/sanouchka, www.linkedin.com/pub/sana-hassainia/21/690/915
Constituency Office
#118-119, 2071, rteMarie-Victorin
Varennes, QC J8X 1R3

Member, Treasury Board Sub-Committee on the Strategic & Operating Review, Hon. Laurie Hawn, P.C.
Constituency: Edmonton Centre, Alberta *No. of Constituents:* 86,408, Conservative Party
Tel: 613-992-4524
Fax: 613-943-0044
laurie.hawn@parl.gc.ca;Laurie.Hawn.C1@parl.gc.ca
www.lauriehawnmp.ca
Other Communications: Constituency Phone: 780-442-1888; Fax: 780-442-1891

Social Media: www.facebook.com/mplauriehawn, www.linkedin.com/pub/laurie-hawn/29/573/203
Constituency Office
11156 - 142nd St.
Edmonton, AB T5M 4G5

Bryan Hayes
Constituency: Sault Ste. Marie, Ontario *No. of Constituents:* 69,259, Conservative Party
Tel: 613-992-9723
Fax: 613-992-1954
bryan.hayes@parl.gc.ca
www.bryanhayes.ca
Other Communications: Constituency Phone: 705-941-2900; Fax: 705-941-2903
Social Media: www.facebook.com/group.php?gid=177199632299222
Constituency Office
#100, 369 Queen St. East
Sault Ste. Marie, ON P6A 1Z4

Russ Hiebert, B.A., M.B.A., LL.B.
Constituency: South Surrey — White Rock — Cloverdale, British Columbia *No. of Constituents:* 91,485, Conservative Party
Tel: 613-947-4497
Fax: 613-947-4500
russ.hiebert@parl.gc.ca; info@russhiebert.ca
www.russhiebert.ca
Other Communications: Constituency Phone: 604-542-9495; Fax: 604-542-9496
Social Media: twitter.com/HiebertRuss, www.facebook.com/russhiebert
Constituency Office
#106A, 2429 152nd St.
Surrey, BC V4P 1N4

Jim Hillyer
Constituency: Lethbridge, Alberta *No. of Constituents:* 90,036, Conservative Party
Tel: 613-996-0633
Fax: 613-995-5752
jim.hillyer@parl.gc.ca; hillyer@jimhillyer.com
www.jimhillyer.com
Other Communications: Constituency Phone: 403-320-0070; Fax: 403-380-4026
Constituency Office
255- 8th St. South
Lethbridge, AB T1J 4Y1

Randy Hoback
Constituency: Prince Albert, Saskatchewan *No. of Constituents:* 51,656, Conservative Party
Tel: 613-995-3295
Fax: 613-995-6819
randy.hoback@parl.gc.ca; hobacr1@parl.gc.ca; hobacr2@parl.gc.ca
www.randyhobackmp.ca
Other Communications: Constituency Phone: 306-953-8622; Fax: 306-953-8625
Social Media: twitter.com/RandyHobackMP, www.facebook.com/randyhobackmp
Constituency Office
137 - 15 St. East
Prince Albert, SK S6V 1G1

Parliamentary Secretary to the Minister, Public Safety, Candice Hoeppner
Constituency: Portage — Lisgar,Manitoba *No. of Constituents:* 59.799, Conservative Party
Tel: 613-995-9511
Toll-free: 866-856-2090
Fax: 613-947-0313
candice.hoeppner@parl.gc.ca; candice.hoeppner.c1a@parl.gc.ca
www.candicehoeppner.com
Other Communications: Constituency Phone: 204-822-7440; Fax: 204-822-7445
Social Media: twitter.com/CHoeppnerMP, www.facebook.com/pages/Candice-Hoeppner/144290685591209
Constituency Office
886 Thornhill St., #E
Morden, MB R6M 2E1

Ed Holder, B.A.
Constituency: London West *No. of Constituents:* 93,915, Conservative Party
Tel: 613-996-6674
Fax: 613-996-6772
ed.holder@parl.gc.ca
www.edholder.ca
Other Communications: Constituency Phone: 519-473-5955; Fax: 519-473-7333
Social Media: twitter.com/EdHolder_MP, www.facebook.com/group.php?gid=111702495519652, www.linkedin.com/pub/ed-holder/23/b96/92b
Constituency Office
#200, 390 Commissioners Rd.West
London, ON N6J 1Y3

Ted Hsu, B.Sc., Ph.D.
Constituency: Kingston & the Islands, Ontario *No. of Constituents:* 96,049, Liberal
Tel: 613-996-1955
Fax: 613-996-1958
ted.hsu@parl.gc.ca
www.tedhsu.ca
Other Communications: Constituency Phone: 613-542-3243; Fax: 613-542-5461
Social Media: twitter.com/tedhsu, www.facebook.com/tedhsu75, www.linkedin.com/in/tedhsu
Constituency Office
#14, 303 Bagot St.
Kingston, ON K7K 5W7

Carol Hughes
Constituency: Algoma — Manitoulin — Kapuskasing, Ontario *No. of Constituents:* 58,857, New Democratic Party
Tel: 613-996-5376
Toll-free: 800-463-3335
Fax: 613-995-6661
carol.hughes@parl.gc.ca
www.carolhughes.ndp.ca
Other Communications: Constituency Phone: 705-848-8080; Fax: 705-848-1818
Social Media: twitter.com/CarolHughesMP, www.facebook.com/pages/Carol-Hughes/38326584416
Constituency Office
20 PrinceEdward Walk
Elliot Lake, ON P5A 1Z7

Bruce Hyer, M.Sc.F.
Constituency: Thunder Bay — Superior North, Ontario *No. of Constituents:* 61,546, Independent
Tel: 613-996-4792
Toll-free: 888-266-8004
Fax: 613-996-9785
bruce.hyer@parl.gc.ca
www.brucehyer.ca
Other Communications: Constituency Phone: 807-345-1818; Fax: 807-345-4752
Social Media: twitter.com/brucehyer, www.facebook.com/brucehyer
Note: Bruce Hyer left the New Democratic Party in 2012. Since April 23, 2012, he has been an Independent Member of Parliament.
Constituency Office
69 NorthCourt St.
Thunder Bay, ON P7A 4T7

Pierre Jacob
Constituency: Brome — Missisquoi, Québec *No. of Constituents:* 80 371, New Democratic Party
Tél: 613-947-8185
Téléc: 613-947-8188
pierre.jacob@parl.gc.ca
www.pierrejacob.ndp.ca
Autre numéros: Constituency Phone: 450-266-6062; Fax: 450-266-6064
Les réseaux sociaux: twitter.com/@PJacobNPD, www.facebook.com/PierreJacobNPD
Constituency Office
#207, 505, rue South
Cowansville, QC J2K 2X9

Roxanne James
Constituency: Scarborough Centre, Ontario *No. of Constituents:* 70,274, Conservative Party
Tel: 613-992-6823
Fax: 613-943-1045
roxanne.james@parl.gc.ca
www.roxannejames.ca
Other Communications: Constituency Phone: 416-752-2358; Fax: 416-752-4624
Social Media: www.facebook.com/MP.RoxanneJames
Constituency Office
#211, 1450 MidlandAve.
Toronto, ON M1P 4Z8

Brian Jean, B.Sc., M.B.A., LL.B.
Constituency: Fort McMurray — Athabasca, Alberta *No. of Constituents:* 76,298, Conservative Party
Tel: 613-992-1154
Toll-free: 877-532-6272
Fax: 613-992-4603
brian.jean@parl.gc.ca; brian.jean.c1@parl.gc.ca
www.brianjean.ca
Other Communications: Constituency Phone: 780-743-2201; Fax: 780-743-2287
Social Media: twitter.com/BrianJean_MP
Constituency Office
#102, 9912 Franklin Ave.
Fort McMurray, AL T9H 2K5

Caucus Chair, New Democratic Party of Canada, Peter Julian, B.A.
Constituency: Burnaby — New Westminster, British Columbia *No. of Constituents:* 84,271, New Democratic Party
Tel: 613-992-4214
Fax: 613-947-9500
peter.julian@parl.gc.ca; peter.julian.c1@parl.gc.ca
www.peterjulian.ndp.ca
Other Communications: Constituency Phone:604-775-5707; Fax: 604-775-5743
Social Media: twitter.com/MPJulian, www.facebook.com/MPPeterJulian
Constituency Office
7615 - 6th St.
Burnaby, BC V3N 3M6

Parliamentary Secretary to the Minister, Fisheries & Oceans & for the Asia-Pacific Gateway, Randy Kamp, B.A.
Constituency: Pitt Meadows — Maple Ridge — Mission, British Columbia *No. of Constituents:* 89,613, Conservative Party
Tel: 613-947-4613
Toll-free: 888-255-8140
Fax: 613-947-4615
randy.kamp@parl.gc.ca;randy@randykamp.com
Other Communications: Constituency Phone: 604-466-2761; Fax: 604-466-7593
Social Media: twitter.com/RandyKamp_com
Note: Web Sites: www.randykamp.com;www.dfo-mpo.gc.ca/minister-ministre/bio-kamp-eng.htm
Constituency Office
22720 Lougheed Hwy.
Maple Ridge, BC V2X 2V6

Hon. Jim Karygiannis, P.C., B.A.Sc, F.B.A.
Constituency: Scarborough — Agincourt, Ontario *No. of Constituents:* 73,205, Liberal
Tel: 613-992-4501
Fax: 613-995-1612
jim.karygiannis@parl.gc.ca; jim@karygiannismp.com
www.karygiannismp.com
Other Communications: Constituency Phone: 416-321-5454; Fax:416-321-5456
Social Media: twitter.com/jimkarygiannis
Constituency Office
#206, 3850 Finch Ave. East
Toronto, ON M1T 3T6

Parliamentary Secretary to the Minister, International Trade, for the Atlantic Canada Opportunities Agency & for the AtlanticGateway, Gerald Keddy, B.A.
Constituency: SouthShore — St. Margaret's, Nova Scotia *No. of Constituents:* 67,296, Conservative Party
Tel: 613-996-0877
Toll-free: 888-816-4446
Fax: 613-996-0878
gerald.keddy@parl.gc.ca; keddyg@ns.sympatico.ca
Other Communications: Constituency Phone: 902-527-5655; Fax: 902-527-5656
Social Media: twitter.com/GeraldKeddy, www.linkedin.com/pub/gerald-keddy/27/540/9b3
Note: Web Sites: www.geraldkeddymp.ca; www.international.gc.ca/commerce/Gerald_Keddy.aspx
Constituency Office
#201, 129 Aberdeen Rd.
Bridgewater, NS B4V 2S7

Matthew Kellway
Constituency: Beaches — East York, Ontario *No. of Constituents:* 73,302, New Democratic Party
Tel: 613-992-2115
Fax: 613-996-7942
matthew.kellway@parl.gc.ca
www.matthewkellway.ndp.ca
Other Communications: Constituency Phone: 416-467-0860; Fax: 416-467-0905
Social Media: twitter.com/MatthewKellway, www.facebook.com/matthewkellway, www.linkedin.com/pub/matthew-kellway/19/976/763
Constituency Office
155 Main St.
Toronto, ON M4E 2V9

Minister, Citizenship, Immigration, & Multiculturalism, Hon. Jason Kenney, P.C.
Constituency: Calgary Southeast, Alberta *No. of Constituents:* 106,439, Conservative Party
Tel: 613-992-2235
Fax: 613-992-1920
jason.kenney@parl.gc.ca; calgary@jasonkenney.com
Other Communications: Constituency Phone: 403-225-3480; Fax: 403-225-3504
Social Media: twitter.com/kenneyjason, www.facebook.com/pages/Jason-Kenney/29829307640
Note: Web Sites: www.jasonkenney.com (Personal Web Site);www.cic.gc.ca/english/department/minister/index.asp
Constituency Office
1168 - 137 Ave. SE
Calgary, AB T2J 6T6

Minister, Environment, Hon. Peter Kent, P.C.
Constituency: Thornhill, Ontario *No. of Constituents:* 99,867, Conservative Party
Tel: 613-992-0253
Fax: 613-992-0887

peter.kent@parl.gc.ca; Minister@ec.gc.ca
Other Communications: Constituency Phone: 905-886-9911; Fax:905-886-5267
Social Media: twitter.com/mpPeterKent; twitter.com/ec_minister, www.facebook.com/apps/application.php?id=135514873168072
Note: Web Sites: www.peterkent.ca (Personal Web Site); www.ec.gc.ca/default.asp?lang=En&n=B6832638-1 (Environment Canada); Twitter (French):www.twitter.com/ministre_ec
Constituency Office
7600 Yonge St.
Thornhill, ON L4J 1V9

Chair, Veterans Affairs Committee, Greg Kerr, B.A., B.Ed.
Constituency: West Nova, Nova Scotia *No. of Constituents:* 67,938, Conservative Party
Tel: 613-995-5711
Toll-free: 866-280-5302
Fax: 613-996-9857
greg.kerr@parl.gc.ca
www.gregkerrmp.ca
Other Communications: Constituency Phone: 902-742-6808; Fax: 902-742-6815
Social Media: twitter.com/MPGregKerr, www.facebook.com/MPGregKerr
Constituency Office
233 Water St.
Yarmouth, NS B5A 1M1

Chair, Human Resources, Skills, & Social Development & the Status of Persons with Disabilities Committee, Ed Komarnicki
Constituency: Souris — Moose Mountain,Saskatchewan *No. of Constituents:* 47,061, Conservative Party
Tel: 613-992-7685
Toll-free: 866-249-4697
Fax: 613-995-8908
ed.komarnicki@parl.gc.ca; komare1@parl.gc.ca; komare2@parl.gc.ca
www.edkom.ca
Other Communications: Constituency Phone: 306-842-9000; Fax: 306-842-3854
Constituency Office
#2, 405 Souris Ave.
Weyburn, SK S4H 0C9

Daryl Kramp
Constituency: Prince Edward — Hastings, Ontario *No. of Constituents:* 89,208, Conservative Party
Tel: 613-992-5321
Fax: 613-996-8652
daryl.kramp@parl.gc.ca; daryl.kramp.c1@parl.gc.ca
www.darylkramp.ca
Other Communications: Constituency Phone: 613-969-3800; Fax: 613-969-3803
Social Media: twitter.com/darylkramp
Constituency Office
1Millennium Pkwy.
Belleville, ON K8N 4Z5

Parliamentary Secretary to the Minister, Industry, Mike Lake, B.Comm.
Constituency: Edmonton — Mill Woods — Beaumont, Alberta *No. of Constituents:* 86,529, Conservative Party
Tel: 613-995-8695
Toll-free: 866-670-0966
Fax: 613-995-6465
mike.lake@parl.gc.ca; LakeM@parl.gc.ca
www.mikelake.ca
Other Communications: Constituency Phone:780-495-2149; Fax: 780-495-2147
Social Media: twitter.com/MikeLakeMP, www.facebook.com/MikeLakeMP
Constituency Office
9225 - 28 Ave. NW
Edmonton, AB T6N 1N1

Deputy House Leader, Liberal Party, Kevin Lamoureux
Constituency: Winnipeg North, Manitoba *No. of Constituents:* 51,894, Liberal
Tel: 613-996-6417
Fax: 613-996-9713
kevin.lamoureux@parl.gc.ca
www.kevinlamoureux.liberal.ca
Other Communications: Constituency Phone: 204-984-1767; Fax: 204-984-1766
Social Media: www.facebook.com/gokevin.ca
Constituency Office
#6, 998 Keewatin Blvd.
Winnipeg, MB R2R 2V1

François Lapointe
Constituency: Montmagny — L'Islet — Kamouraska — Rivière-du-Loup, Québec *No. of Constituents:* 78 969, New Democratic Party
Tél: 613-995-0265
Téléc: 613-943-1229
francois.lapointe@parl.gc.ca
www.francoislapointe.ndp.ca
Autre numéros: Constituency Phone: 418-248-1211; Fax: 418-248-1244
Les réseaux sociaux: twitter.com/F_Lapointe
Constituency Office
114, av de laGare
Montmagny, QC G5V 2T3

Jean-François Larose
Constituency: Repentigny, Québec *No. of Constituents:* 94 047, New Democratic Party
Tél: 613-992-5257
Téléc: 613-996-4338
jean-francois.larose@parl.gc.ca
www.jeanfrancoislarose.ndp.ca
Autre numéros: Constituency Phone: 450-581-3896; Fax: 450-581-9958
Les réseaux sociaux: twitter.com/LaroseJF, www.facebook.com/pages/Jean-Francois-Larose/239453629399576
Constituency Office
#201, 184,rue Notre-Dame
Repentigny, QC J6A 2P9

Alexandrine Latendresse
Constituency: Louis-Saint-Laurent, Québec *No. of Constituents:* 86 945, New Democratic Party
Tel: 613-996-4151
Fax: 613-954-2269
alexandrine.latendresse@parl.gc.ca
www.alexandrinelatendresse.ndp.ca
Other Communications: Constituency Phone: 418-626-5522; Fax: 418-626-5646
Constituency Office
#220, 6655, boul Pierre Bertrand
Québec, QC G2K 1M1

Caucus Chair, Conservative Party, Guy Lauzon
Constituency: Stormont — Dundas — South Glengarry, Ontario *No. of Constituents:* 76,915, Conservative Party
Tel: 613-992-2521
Toll-free: 888-805-2515
Fax: 613-996-2119
guy.lauzon@parl.gc.ca; info@guylauzon.ca
www.guylauzon.ca
Other Communications: Constituency Phone: 613-937-3331; Fax:613-937-3251
Constituency Office
621 Pitt St.
Cornwall, ON K6J 3R8

Hélène Laverdière
Constituency: Laurier — Sainte-Marie, Québec *No. of Constituents:* 79 772, New Democratic Party
Tél: 613-992-6779
Téléc: 613-995-8461
helene.laverdiere@parl.gc.ca
www.helenelaverdiere.ndp.ca
Autre numéros: Constituency Phone: 514-522-1339; Fax: 514-522-9899
Les réseaux sociaux: www.facebook.com/Helene.Laverdiere.deputee
Constituency Office
#507, 1001, boulde Maisonneuve est
Montréal, QC H2L 4P9

Minister, Transport, Infrastructure, & Communities; Minister, Economic Development Agency of Canada for the Regions of Québec, Hon. Denis Lebel, P.C.
Constituency: Roberval — Lac-Saint-Jean, Québec *No. of Constituents:* 63 645, Conservative Party
Tél: 613-996-6236
Ligne sans frais: 800-667-2768
Téléc: 613-996-6252
denis.lebel@parl.gc.ca; mintc@tc.gc.ca
Autre numéros: Constituency Phone: 418-275-2768; Fax: 418-275-6535
Les réseaux sociaux: www.facebook.com/pages/Denis-Lebel/137888079554744
Note: Web Sites:www.denislebel.com (Personal Web Site); www.tc.gc.ca/eng/minister-menu.htm (Transport Canada); www.dec-ced.gc.ca/eng/minister/index.html (Canada Economic Development for Québec Regions)
Constituency Office
#102, 797, boul Saint-Joseph
Roberval, QC G8H 2L4

Hon. Dominic LeBlanc, P.C., B.A., LL.B., LL.M.
Constituency: Beauséjour, New Brunswick *No. of Constituents:* 63,267, Liberal
Tel: 613-992-1020
Toll-free: 800-432-0311
Fax: 613-992-3053
dominic.leblanc@parl.gc.ca
www.dominicleblanc.ca
Other Communications: Constituency Phone: 506-533-5700; Fax:506-533-5888
Social Media: www.facebook.com/pages/Dominic-LeBlanc/19671249720
Constituency Office
#1, 328 Main St.
Shediac, NB E4P 2E3

Hélène LeBlanc
Constituency: LaSalle — Émard, Québec *No. of Constituents:* 74 755, New Democratic Party
Tél: 613-943-6636
Téléc: 613-943-6637
helene.leblanc@parl.gc.ca
www.heleneleblanc.ndp.ca
Autre numéros: Constituency Phone: 514-363-0954; Fax: 514-367-5533
Les réseaux sociaux: twitter.com/HeleneLeBlanc, www.facebook.com/group.php?gid=196692170380605
Constituency Office
#307, 7475, boulNewman
Lasalle, QC H8N 1X3

Ryan Leef
Constituency: Yukon *No. of Constituents:* 24,341, Conservative Party
Tel: 613-995-9368
Fax: 613-995-0945
ryan.leef@parl.gc.ca
www.voteryanleef.ca
Other Communications: Constituency Phone: 867-668-6565; Fax: 867-668-6570
Social Media: www.facebook.com/group.php?gid=192960574077986
Constituency Office
#204, 204 BlackSt.
Whitehorse, YT Y1A 2M9

Parliamentary Secretary to the Minister, Human Resources & Skills Development & to the Minister, Labour, Dr. Kellie Leitch, O.Ont., M.D., M.B.A., F.R.C.S.(C)
Constituency: Simcoe — Grey, Ontario *No. of Constituents:* 99,354, Conservative Party
Tel: 613-992-4224
Fax: 613-992-2164
kellie.leitch@parl.gc.ca
www.kellieleitch.ca
Other Communications: Constituency Phone: 705-435-1809; Fax: 705-435-6448
Social Media: www.facebook.com/KellieLeitch#!/profile.php?id=731715176, www.linkedin.com/pub/dr-k-kellie-leitch/17/584/96
Note: Kellie Leitch also has a constituency office inCollingwood, Ontario (501 Hume St.). The phone number of the Collingwood office is 705-445-5557.
Constituency Office
23 Paris St.
Alliston, ON L9R 1J3

Parliamentary Secretary to the Minister, Agriculture, Pierre Lemieux, B.Eng., M.Sc.
Constituency: Glengarry — Prescott — Russell, Ontario *No. of Constituents:* 85,413, Conservative Party
Tel: 613-992-0490
Toll-free: 800-990-0490
Fax: 613-996-9123
pierre.lemieux@parl.gc.ca
www.pierrelemieux.ca
Other Communications: Constituency Phone:613-632-4162; Fax: 613-632-5668
Constituency Office
136 Main St. East
Hawkesbury, ON K6A 1A3

Deputy Leader, New Democratic Party of Canada, Megan Leslie, B.A. (Hons), LL.B.
Constituency: Halifax, Nova Scotia *No. of Constituents:* 73,357, New Democratic Party
Tel: 613-995-7614
Fax: 613-992-8569
megan.leslie@parl.gc.ca
www.meganleslie.ndp.ca
Other Communications: Constituency Phone: 902-426-8691;Fax: 902-426-8693
Social Media: twitter.com/meganleslieMP, www.facebook.com/MeganLeslieMP, www.linkedin.com/pub/megan-leslie/1a/369/886
Constituency Office
#1, 2207 Gottingin St.
Halifax, NS B3K 3B5

Parliamentary Secretary for Multiculturalism, Chungsen Leung, B.A., M.Sc.
Constituency: Willowdale, Ontario *No. of Constituents:* 93,584, Conservative Party
Tel: 613-992-4964
Fax: 613-992-1158
chungsen.leung@parl.gc.ca; info@chungsenleung.ca
www.chungsenleung.ca
Other Communications: ConstituencyPhone: 416-223 2858; Fax: 416-223 9715
Social Media: twitter.com/csleungmp, www.facebook.com/Chungsen.CS.Leung, www.linkedin.com/in/csleung
Constituency Office

#200, 250 Sheppard Ave. East
Toronto, ON M2N 6M9
Laurin Liu
Constituency: Rivière-des-Mille-Iles, Québec *No. of Constituents:* 79 689, New Democratic Party
Tel: 613-992-7330
Fax: 613-992-2602
laurin.liu@parl.gc.ca
www.laurinliu.ndp.ca
Other Communications: Constituency Phone: 450-473-4864; Fax: 450-473-9043
Social Media: twitter.com/laurinliu, www.facebook.com/group.php?gid=229547190392110
Constituency Office
172, rue Saint-Louis
Saint-Eustache, QC J7R 1Y3
Wladyslaw Lizon
Constituency: Mississauga East — Cooksville, Ontario *No. of Constituents:* 85,018, Conservative Party
Tel: 613-996-0420
Fax: 613-996-0279
wladyslaw.lizon@parl.gc.ca
www.wladyslawlizon.ca
Other Communications: Constituency Phone: 905-566-0009; Fax: 905-566-0017
Social Media: www.facebook.com/VoteLizon
Constituency Office
#303, 918 Dundas St.East
Mississauga, ON L4Y 2H9
Ben Lobb, B.Sc. Admin.
Constituency: Huron — Bruce, Ontario *No. of Constituents:* 78,695, Conservative Party
Tel: 613-992-8234
Fax: 613-995-6350
ben.lobb@parl.gc.ca
www.benlobb.com
Other Communications: Constituency Phone: 519-524-6560; Fax: 519-612-1141
Constituency Office
30 Victoria St.North
Goderich, ON N7A 2R6
Parliamentary Secretary to the Leader of the Government in the House of Commons, Tom Lukiwski
Constituency: Regina — Lumsden — Lake Centre, Saskatchewan *No. of Constituents:* 51,380, Conservative Party
Tel: 613-992-4573
Toll-free: 888-790-4747
Fax: 613-996-6885
tom.lukiwski@parl.gc.ca
www.tomlukiwski.com
Other Communications: Constituency Phone:306-790-4747; Fax: 613-996-6885
Social Media: twitter.com/TomLukiwski, www.facebook.com/TomLukiwski
Constituency Office
965 McIntosh St.
PO Box 31009
Regina, SK S4R 8R6
Dr. James Lunney, B.Sc., D.C.
Constituency: Nanaimo — Alberni, British Columbia *No. of Constituents:* 98,657, Conservative Party
Tel: 613-992-5243
Toll-free: 866-390-7550
Fax: 613-992-9112
james.lunney@parl.gc.ca
www.jameslunneymp.ca
Other Communications: Constituency Phone: 250-390-7550; Fax: 250-390-7551
Social Media: twitter.com/jameslunneymp
ConstituencyOffice
#6, 6894 Island Hwy. North
Nanaimo, BC V9V 1P6
Hon. Lawrence MacAulay, P.C.
Constituency: Cardigan, Prince Edward Island *No. of Constituents:* 27,581, Liberal
Tel: 613-995-9325
Fax: 613-995-2754
lawrence.macaulay@parl.gc.ca
www.lawrencemacaulay11.com
Other Communications: Constituency Phone: 902-838-4139; Fax: 902-838-3790
Social Media: www.facebook.com/lawrence.macaulay
Constituency Office
551 MainSt.
PO Box 1150
Montague, PE C0A 1R0
Minister, National Defence, Hon. Peter Gordon MacKay
Constituency: Central Nova, Nova Scotia *No. of Constituents:* 57,963, Conservative Party
Tel: 613-992-6022
Fax: 613-992-2337
peter.mackay@parl.gc.ca
Other Communications: Constituency Phone: 902-752-0226; Fax: 902-752-0284
Social Media: twitter.com/MacKayCPC
Note: Web Sites: www.petermackay.ca (Personal Web Site); www.forces.gc.ca/site/minister-ministre/index-eng.asp?WT.sv l=ministerLeft ((Department ofNational Defence & the Canadian Forces)
Constituency Office
980 East River Rd.
New Glasgow, NS B2H 3S8
Chair Justice & Human Rights Committee, Dave MacKenzie
Constituency: Oxford, Ontario *No. of Constituents:* 77,035, Conservative Party
Tel: 613-995-4432
Fax: 613-995-4433
dave.mackenzie@parl.gc.ca
www.davemackenzie.ca
Other Communications: Constituency Phone: 519-421-7214; Fax: 519-421-9704
Constituency Office
#4, 208 Huron St.
Woodstock, ON N4S 7A1
Hoang Mai
Constituency: Brossard — La Prairie, Québec *No. of Constituents:* 96 795, New Democratic Party
Tél: 613-995-9301
Téléc: 613-992-7273
hoang.mai@parl.gc.ca
www.hoangmai.ndp.ca
Autre numéros: Constituency Phone: 450-466-6872; Fax: 450-466-9822
Les réseaux sociaux: twitter.com/hoangmai_npd, www.linkedin.com/pub/hoang-mai/10/635/232
Constituency Office
#8A, 8080, boul Taschereau
Brossard, QC J4X 1C2
Wayne Marston
Constituency: Hamilton East — Stoney Creek, Ontario *No. of Constituents:* 85,710, New Democratic Party
Tel: 613-992-6535
Fax: 613-992-7764
wayne.marston@parl.gc.ca
www.waynemarston.ca
Other Communications: Constituency Phone: 905-662-4763; Fax: 905-662-2285
Social Media: twitter.com/WMarstonNDP, www.facebook.com/wayne.marston
Constituency Office
#2, 40 Centennial Pkwy.North
Hamilton, ON L8E 1H6
Chair, Government Operations & Estimates Committee, Pat Martin
Constituency: Winnipeg Centre, Manitoba *No. of Constituents:* 54,364, New Democratic Party
Tel: 613-992-5308
Fax: 613-992-2890
pat.martin@parl.gc.ca
www.patmartin.ca
Other Communications: Constituency Phone: 204-984-1675; Fax:204-984-1676
Social Media: twitter.com/PatMartinMP, www.facebook.com/pages/Pat-Martin/6587713095
Constituency Office
892 Sargent Ave.
Winnipeg, MB R3E 0C7
Brian Masse, B.A. (Hons.)
Constituency: Windsor West, Ontario *No. of Constituents:* 81,984, New Democratic Party
Tel: 613-996-1541
Fax: 613-992-5397
brian.masse@parl.gc.ca
www.brianmasse.ca
Other Communications: Constituency Phone: 519-255-1631; Fax: 519-255-7913
Social Media: twitter.com/BrianMasseMP, www.facebook.com/brianmassemp
Constituency Office
#2, 1398Ouellette Ave.
Windsor, ON N8X 1J8
Irene Mathyssen, B.A.(Hons), B.Ed.
Constituency: London — Fanshawe, Ontario *No. of Constituents:* 75,138, New Democratic Party
Tel: 613-995-2901
Fax: 613-943-8717
irene.mathyssen@parl.gc.ca
www.irenemathyssen.ca
Other Communications: Constituency Phone: 519-685-4745; Fax: 519-685-1462
Social Media: twitter.com/irenemathyssen, www.facebook.com/pages/Irene-Mathyssen/7711496179
Constituency Office
1700D Dundas St.
London, ON N5W 3C9
Leader, Green Party of Canada, Elizabeth May, O.C., LL.B.
Constituency: Saanich — Gulf Islands, British Columbia *No. of Constituents:* 93,380, Green Party of Canada
Tel: 613-996-1119
Fax: 613-996-0850
elizabeth.may@parl.gc.ca
www.elizabethmay.ca
Other Communications: Constituency Phone: 250-657-2000; Fax: 250-657-2004
Social Media: twitter.com/elizabethmay, www.facebook.com/ElizabethMayGreenLeader, www.linkedin.com/pub/elizabeth-may/3/a91/69
Constituency Office
#1, 9711 Fourth St.
Sidney, BC V8L 2Y8
Colin Mayes
Constituency: Okanagan — Shuswap, British Columbia *No. of Constituents:* 91,762, Conservative Party
Tel: 613-995-9095
Toll-free: 800-665-5040
Fax: 613-992-3195
colin.mayes@parl.gc.ca
www.colinmayes.ca
Other Communications: Constituency Phone: 250-260-5020; Fax: 250-260-5025
Constituency Office
3105 - 29thSt.
Vernon, BC V1T 5A8
Hon. John McCallum, P.C., B.A., Ph.D.
Constituency: Markham — Unionville, Ontario *No. of Constituents:* 92,638, Liberal
Tel: 613-996-3374
Fax: 613-992-3921
john.mccallum@parl.gc.ca
www.johnmccallum.liberal.ca
Other Communications: Constituency Phone: 905-479-8100; Fax: 905-479-3440
Social Media: twitter.com/JohnMcCallumMP, www.facebook.com/McCallumj1, www.linkedin.com/pub/john-mccallum/24/78a/217
Constituency Office
#21-22, 7750 Birchmount Rd.
Markham, ON L3R 0B4
Phil McColeman
Constituency: Brant, Ontario *No. of Constituents:* 95,508, Conservative Party
Tel: 613-992-3118
Fax: 613-992-6382
phil.mccoleman@parl.gc.ca
www.philmccolemanmp.ca
Other Communications: Constituency Phone: 519-754-4300; Fax: 519-751-8177
Social Media: twitter.com/Phil4Brant, www.facebook.com/profile.php?id=544956732
Constituency Office
#212, 505 Park Rd.North
Brantford, ON N3R 7K8
David McGuinty, B.A., LL.B, LL.M.
Constituency: Ottawa South, Ontario *No. of Constituents:* 87,399, Liberal
Tel: 613-992-3269
Fax: 613-995-1534
david.mcguinty@parl.gc.ca
www.davidmcguinty.liberal.ca
Other Communications: Constituency Phone: 613-990-8640; Fax: 613-990-2592
Social Media: twitter.com/DavidMcGuinty, www.facebook.com/davidmcguinty
Constituency Office
#205,2141 Thurston Dr.
Ottawa, ON K1G 6C9
Hon. John McKay, P.C., B.A., LL.B.
Constituency: Scarborough — Guildwood, Ontario *No. of Constituents:* 67,728, Liberal
Tel: 613-992-1447
Fax: 613-992-8968
john.mckay@parl.gc.ca
www.johnmckaymp.on.ca
Other Communications: Constituency Phone: 416-283-1226; Fax: 416-283-7935
Constituency Office
#10, 3785Kingston Rd.
Toronto, ON M1J 3H4
Parliamentary Secretary to the Minister, National Revenue, Cathy McLeod
Constituency: Kamloops — Thompson — Cariboo, British Columbia *No. of Constituents:* 90,855, Conservative Party
Tel: 613-995-6931
Toll-free: 877-619-3332
Fax: 613-995-9897
cathy.mcleod@parl.gc.ca
www.cathymcleod.com
Other Communications: Constituency Phone: 250-851-4991; Fax:250-851-4994
Social Media: twitter.com/Cathy_McLeod, www.facebook.com/cathymcleodMP

Constituency Office
979 Victoria St.
Kamloops, BC V2C 2C1
Costas Menegakis
Constituency: Richmond Hill, Ontario *No. of Constituents:* 90 924, Conservative Party
Tel: 613-992-3802
Fax: 613-996-1954
costas.menegakis@parl.gc.ca;
costas.menegakis.c1@parl.gc.ca
www.costasmenegakis.ca
Other Communications: Constituency Phone: 905-770-4440; Fax: 905-770-2221
Social Media:
www.facebook.com/pages/Costas-Menegakis/121337297944082
Constituency Office
#400, 9555 Yonge St.
Richmond Hill, ON L4C 9M5
Minister of State, Finance, Hon. Ted Menzies, P.C.
Constituency: Macleod, Alberta *No. of Constituents:* 85,720, Conservative Party
Tel: 613-995-8471
Toll-free: 866-636-9437
Fax: 613-996-9770
ted.menzies@parl.gc.ca; ted.menzies@fin.gc.ca
Other Communications: Constituency Phone: 403-625-5532; Fax:403-625-5592
Social Media: twitter.com/TedMenzies
Note: Web Sites: www.tedmenzies.ca (Personal Web Sites); www.fin.gc.ca/comment/state-etat-eng.asp (Department of Finance Canada
Constituency Office
4925 - 1st St. West
PO Box 40
Claresholm, AB T0L 0T0
Hon. Rob Merrifield, P.C.
Constituency: Yellowhead, Alberta *No. of Constituents:* 75,410, Conservative Party
Tel: 613-992-1653
Toll-free: 800-268-7117
Fax: 613-992-3459
rob.merrifield@parl.gc.ca
www.merrifieldmp.com
Other Communications: Constituency Phone: 780-723-6068; Fax: 780-723-5060
Constituency Office
119 - 50th St.
PO Box 7887 Main Sta.
Edson, AB T7E 1V9
Élaine Michaud, B.A.
Constituency: Portneuf — Jacques-Cartier, Quebec *No. of Constituents:* 81,093, New Democratic Party
Tél: 613-992-2798
Téléc: 613-995-1637
elaine.michaud@parl.gc.ca
www.elainemichaud.ndp.ca
Autre numéros: Constituency Phone: 418-873-5010; Fax: 418-873-5031
Les réseaux sociaux:
www.facebook.com/group.php?gid=219072564786090
Constituency Office
86, rue duCollège, #F
Pont-Rouge, QC G3H 3A8
Transport, Infrastructure, & Communities Committee, Larry Miller
Constituency: Bruce — Grey — Owen Sound, Ontario *No. of Constituents:* 79,977, Conservative Party
Tel: 613-996-5191
Fax: 613-952-0979
larry.miller@parl.gc.ca
www.larrymiller.ca
Other Communications: Constituency Phone: 519-371-1059; Fax:519-371-1752
Constituency Office
1131 - 2nd Ave. East
Owen Sound, ON N4K 2J1
Christine Moore
Constituency: Abitibi—Témiscamingue, Quebec *No. of Constituents:* 82,079, New Democratic Party
Tel: 613-996-3250
Toll-free: 800-567-6433
Fax: 613-992-3672
christine.moore@parl.gc.ca; christine.moore.c1@parl.gc.ca
www.christinemoore.ndp.ca
Other Communications: Constituency Phone: 819-762-3733; Fax: 819-762-8732
Social Media:
www.facebook.com/group.php?gid=146347468767378
Constituency Office
#15RC, 33A Gamble St. West
Rouyn-Noranda, QC J9X 2R3
Minister, Canadian Heritage & Official Languages, Hon. James Moore, P.C., B.A.
Constituency: Port Moody — Westwood — Port Coquitlam, British Columbia *No. of Constituents:* 86,190, Conservative Party
Tel: 613-992-9650
Fax: 613-992-9868
james.moore@parl.gc.ca; james.moore@pch.gc.ca
Other Communications: ConstituencyPhone: 604-937-5650; Fax: 604-937-5601
Social Media: twitter.com/JamesMoore_org, www.facebook.com/jamesmoore.org
Note: Web Sites: www.jamesmoore.org (Personal Web Site);www.pch.gc.ca/pc-ch/minstr/moore/index-eng.cfm (Canadian Heritage)
Constituency Office
2603 St. John's St.
Port Moody, BC V3H 2B5
Chair, Canadian Heritage Committee, Hon. Rob Moore, P.C., B.B.A., LL.B.
Constituency: Fundy Royal, New Brunswick *No. of Constituents:* 56,795, Conservative Party
Tel: 613-996-2332
Toll-free: 866-433-4677
Fax: 613-995-4286
rob.moore@parl.gc.ca
www.robmooremp.com
Other Communications: Constituency Phone: 506-832-4200; Fax:506-832-4235
Social Media: twitter.com/RobMoore_CPC
Constituency Office
#104, 599 Main St.
Hampton, NB E5N 6C2
Status of Women Committee, Dany Morin
Constituency: Chicoutimi — Le Fjord, Québec *No. of Constituents:* 79 369, New Democratic Party
Tél: 613-992-7207
Ligne sans frais: 866-599-4999
Téléc: 613-992-0431
dany.morin@parl.gc.ca
www.danymorin.ndp.ca
Autre numéros: Constituency Phone: 418-698-5648; Fax: 418-698-5611
Les réseaux sociaux: twitter.com/drdanymorin
Constituency Office
#240, rue Racine est
Chicoutimi, QC G7H 1R1
Isabelle Morin
Constituency: Notre-Dame-de-Grâce — Lachine, Québec *No. of Constituents:* 77,977, New Democratic Party
Tél: 613-995-2251
Téléc: 613-996-1481
isabelle.morin@parl.gc.ca
www.isabellemorin.ndp.ca
Autre numéros: Constituency Phone: 514-654-0841
Les réseaux sociaux: twitter.com/IsabelleMorinMP, www.facebook.com/IsabelleMorinMP
Constituency Office
#104, 735 rue Notre Dame
Lachine, QC H8S2B5
Marc-André Morin
Constituency: Laurentides — Labelle, Québec *No. of Constituents:* 92 025, New Democratic Party
Tél: 613-992-2289
Téléc: 613-992-9864
marc-andre.morin@parl.gc.ca
www.marcandremorin.ndp.ca
Autre numéros: Constituency Phone: 819-326-5098; Fax: 819-326-8262
Constituency Office
45, rueSt-Antoine
Sainte-Agathe-des-Monts, QC J8C 2C4
Marie-Claude Morin
Constituency: Saint-Hyacinthe — Bagot, Québec *No. of Constituents:* 79 289, New Democratic Party
Tel: 613-996-4585
Fax: 613-992-1815
marie-claude.morin@parl.gc.ca
www.marieclaudemorin.ndp.ca
Other Communications: Constituency Phone: 450-771-0505; Fax: 450-771-0767
Social Media:
www.facebook.com/profile.php?id=100000609131071
Constituency Office
1920, rueCascades ouest
St-Hyacinthe, QC J2S 3J5
Maria Mourani, B.A., M.A.
Constituency: Ahuntsic, Québec *No. of Constituents:* 73 254, BQ
Tél: 613-992-0983
Téléc: 613-992-1932
maria.mourani@parl.gc.ca
www.mariamourani.org
Autre numéros: Constituency Phone: 514-383-3709; Fax: 514-383-3589
Les réseaux sociaux:
www.facebook.com/group.php?gid=2314743183
Constituency Office
#100, 9880,rue Clark
Montréal, QC H3L 2R3
Leader of the Official Opposition; Party Leader, New Democratic Party of Canada; Responsible, New Democratic Party Research Office, Hon. Thomas J. Mulcair, B.C.L. (CivilLaw). LL.B (Common Law)
Constituency: Outremont, Québec *No. of Constituents:* 65 573, New Democratic Party
Tél: 613-995-7691
Téléc: 613-995-0114
thomas.mulcair@parl.gc.ca
www.thomasmulcair.ndp.ca; www.ndp.ca/thomasmulcair
Autre numéros: Constituency Phone: 514-736-2727; Fax: 514-736-2726
Les réseaux sociaux: twitter.com/ThomasMulcair, www.facebook.com/ThomasMulcair
Constituency Office
#310, 3333, ch Queen-Mary
Montréal, QC H3V 1A2
Joyce Murray
Constituency: Vancouver Quadra, British Columbia *No. of Constituents:* 87,224, Liberal
Tel: 613-992-2430
Fax: 613-995-0770
joyce.murray@parl.gc.ca
www.joycemurray.liberal.ca
Other Communications: Constituency Phone: 604-664-9220; Fax: 604-664-9221
Social Media: twitter.com/joycemurray, www.facebook.com/mpjoycemurray, www.linkedin.com/pub/joyce-murray/31/144/b64
Constituency Office
#206, 2112 BroadwayWest
Vancouver, BC V6K 2C8
Pierre Nantel
Constituency: Longueuil — Pierre-Boucher, Québec *No. of Constituents:* 78 791, New Democratic Party
Tél: 613-992-8514
Téléc: 613-992-2744
pierre.nantel@parl.gc.ca
www.pierrenantel.ndp.ca
Autre numéros: Constituency Phone: 450-928-4288; Fax: 450-928-4293
Les réseaux sociaux: twitter.com/pierrenantel, www.facebook.com/pierrenantel
Constituency Office
#200, 192, rueSaint-Jean
Longueuil, QC J4H 2X5
Peggy Nash, B.A. (Hons.)
Constituency: Parkdale — High Park, Ontario *No. of Constituents:* 74 463, New Democratic Party
Tel: 613-992-2936
Fax: 613-995-1629
peggy.nash@parl.gc.ca
www.peggynash.ndp.ca
Other Communications: Constituency Phone: 416-769-5072; Fax: 416-769-8343
Social Media: twitter.com/peggynash_, www.facebook.com/pages/Peggy-Nash/120766445468
Constituency Office
1596 Bloor St.West
Toronto, ON M6P 1A7
Jamie Nicholls, B.A., M.A.
Constituency: Vaudreuil — Soulanges, Quebec *No. of Constituents:* 104 325, New Democratic Party
Tel: 613-957-3744
Fax: 613-952-0874
jamie.nicholls@parl.gc.ca
www.jamienicholls.ndp.ca
Other Communications: Constituency Phone: 450-510-2305; Fax: 450-510-2383
Social Media: twitter.com/JPNichollsNPD, www.facebook.com/pages/Jamie-Nicholls/158685237528810, www.linkedin.com/pub/jamie-nicholls/11/76/452
Constituency Office
#210, 1965,ch Sainte-Angélique
Saint-Lazare, QC J7T 0E2
Attorney General of Canada; Minister, Justice, Hon. Robert Douglas Nicholson, P.C., Q.C., B.A., LL.B.
Constituency: Niagara Falls, Ontario *No. of Constituents:* 96,176, Conservative Party
Tel: 613-995-1547
Fax: 613-992-7910
rob.nicholson@parl.gc.ca
Other Communications: ConstituencyPhone: 905-353-9590; Fax: 905-353-9588
Note: Web Sites: www.robnicholson.ca (Personal Web Site); www.canada.justice.gc.ca/eng/mag-mpg/index.html(Department of Justice Canada)
Constituency Office
#11, 2895 St. Paul Ave.
Niagara Falls, ON L2J 2L3

Rick Norlock
Constituency: Northumberland — Quinte West, Ontario *No. of Constituents:* 96,154, Conservative Party
Tel: 613-992-8585
Fax: 613-995-7536
rick.norlock@parl.gc.ca; rick@ricknorlock.ca
www.ricknorlock.ca
Other Communications: Constituency Phone: 905-372-8757; Fax: 905-372-1500
Social Media: twitter.com/RickNorlock, www.facebook.com/group.php?gid=27428322342
Constituency Office
#2,277 Division St.
PO Box 290
Cobourg, ON K9A 3R2

José Nunez-Melo, B. Gest.
Constituency: Laval, Québec *No. of Constituents:* 85 204, New Democratic Party
Téléc: 613-996-1195
jose.nunez-melo@parl.gc.ca
www.josenunezmelo.ndp.ca
Autre numéros: Constituency Phone: 450-686-2562; Fax: 450-686-0450
Les réseaux sociaux: www.facebook.com/profile.php?id=1585725906
Constituency Office
2281, boul LeCorbusier
Laval, QC H7S 1Z4

Parliamentary Secretary to the Minister, Foreign Affairs, Deepak Obhrai
Constituency: Calgary East, Alberta *No. of Constituents:* 75 850, Conservative Party
Tel: 613-947-4566
Fax: 613-947-4569
deepak.obhrai@parl.gc.ca; deepak@deepakobhrai.com
Other Communications: ConstituencyPhone: 403-207-3030; Fax: 403-207-3035
Social Media: twitter.com/deepakobhrai, www.facebook.com/profile.php?id=1058993450
Note: Web Sites: www.deepakobhrai.com;www.international.gc.ca/ministers-ministres/deepak_obhrai.aspx?view=d
Constituency Office, Radisson Centre
#225, 525 - 28th St. SE
Calgary, AB T2A 6W9

Minister of State; Chief Government Whip; Whip, Conservative Party of Canada, Hon. Gordon O'Connor, P.C., B.A., B.Sc.
Constituency: Carleton — Mississippi Mills, Ontario *No. of Constituents:* 107,407, Conservative Party
Tel: 613-992-1119
Fax: 613-992-1043
gordon.oconnor@parl.gc.ca
www.gordonoconnor.ca
Other Communications: Constituency Phone: 613-592-3469; Fax: 613-592-4756
Social Media: www.facebook.com/pages/Gordon-OConnor/228442573837062?sk=info
Constituency Office
#101, 240 Michael Cowpland Dr.
Kanata, ON K2M 1P6

Minister, Natural Resources, Hon. Joe Oliver, P.C., B.A., BCL, MBA
Constituency: Eglinton — Lawrence, Ontario *No. of Constituents:* 73,522, Conservative Party
Tel: 613-992-6361
Fax: 613-992-9791
joe.oliver@parl.gc.ca; Minister.Ministre@NRCan-RNCan.gc.ca
Other Communications: ConstituencyPhone: 416-781-5583; Fax: 416-781-5586
Social Media: twitter.com/joeoliver1, www.facebook.com/FansofJoeOliver, www.linkedin.com/pub/joseph-oliver/4/267/73b
Note: Web Sites: www.joeoliver.ca (Personal Web Site);www.nrcan.gc.ca/com/deptmini/minmin/minmin-biobio-eng.php (Natural Resources Canada)
Constituency Office
511 Lawrence Ave. West
Toronto, ON M6A 1A3

Tilly O'Neill-Gordon
Constituency: Miramichi *No. of Constituents:* 43,547, Conservative Party
Tel: 613-992-5335
Fax: 613-996-8418
tilly.oneillgordon@parl.gc.ca
www.tillygordon.ca
Other Communications: Constituency Phone: 506-778-8448; Fax: 506-778-8150
Social Media: www.facebook.com/profile.php?id=1048071578
Constituency Office
4 RenaudSt.
Miramichi, NB E1V 6T1

Ted Opitz
Constituency: Etobicoke Centre, Ontario *No. of Constituents:* 81,765, Conservative Party
Tel: 613-947-5000
Fax: 613-947-4276
ted.opitz@parl.gc.ca
www.tedopitz.ca
Other Communications: Constituency Phone: 416-249-7322; Fax: 416-249-6117
Social Media: twitter.com/TedOpitz, www.facebook.com/profile.php?id=720902831&sk=info, www.linkedin.com/pub/ted-opitz/13/a61/84b
Constituency Office
#2, 577 Burnhamthorpe Rd.
Toronto, ON M9C 2Y3

Deputy Whip, Liberal Party, Massimo Pacetti, B.Comm., F.C.G.A.
Constituency: Saint-Léonard — Saint-Michel, Québec *No. of Constituents:* 71 999, Liberal
Tel: 613-995-9414
Fax: 613-992-8523
massimo.pacetti@parl.gc.ca
www.massimopacetti.liberal.ca
Other Communications: Constituency Phone: 514-256-4548; Fax:416-256-8828
Social Media: www.facebook.com/pages/Massimo-Pacetti/22800125080, www.linkedin.com/pub/massimo-pacetti/29/264/535
Constituency Office
#102, 5450, rue Jarry est
Saint-Léonard, QC H1P 1T9

Annick Papillon, B.A.
Constituency: Québec, Quebec *No. of Constituents:* 80 608, New Democratic Party
Tél: 613-992-8865
Téléc: 613-995-2805
annick.papillon@parl.gc.ca
www.annickpapillon.ndp.ca
Autre numéros: Constituency Phone: 418-523-6666; Fax: 418-523-6672
Constituency Office
275, boulCharest est
Québec, QC G1K 3G8

Minister, Industry; Minister of State, Agriculture, Hon. Christian Paradis, P.C.
Constituency: Mégantic — L'Érable, Québec *No. of Constituents:* 70 238, Conservative Party
Tél: 613-995-1377
Téléc: 613-943-1562
christian.paradis@parl.gc.ca; paradc1@parl.gc.ca
Autre numéros: Constituency Phone: 418-338-2903; Fax: 418-338-3631
Les réseaux sociaux: twitter.com/christianparad
Note: Web Sites: www.christianparadis.com;www.ic.gc.ca/eic/site/ic1.nsf/eng/h_00279.html; www4.agr.gc.ca/AAFC-AAC/display-afficher.do?id=1262962138890&lang=eng
Constituency Office
#1, 1313, boul Frontenac ouest
Thetford Mines, QC G6G 6K8

Claude Patry
Constituency: Jonquière — Alma, Quebec *No. of Constituents:* 81 098, New Democratic Party
Tél: 613-995-8425
Téléc: 613-947-2748
claude.patry@parl.gc.ca
www.claudepatry.ndp.ca
Autre numéros: Constituency Phone: 418-695-7554; Fax: 418-695-4467
Constituency Office
#204, 3885, boulHarvey
Jonquière, QC G7X 9B1

LaVar Payne
Constituency: Medicine Hat, Alberta *No. of Constituents:* 82,599, Conservative Party
Tel: 613-992-4516
Fax: 613-992-6181
lavar.payne@parl.gc.ca; paynel1@parl.gc.ca; paynel2@parl.gc.ca
www.lavarpayne.ca
Other Communications: Constituency Phone: 403-528-4698; Fax: 403-528-4365
Social Media: twitter.com/LaVarMP, www.facebook.com/profile.php?id=733796432, www.linkedin.com/pub/lavar-payne/16/318/767
Constituency Office
#112, 1310 Kingsway Ave. SE
Medicine Hat, AB T1A 2Y4

Ève Péclet
Constituency: La Pointe-de-l'Île, Québec *No. of Constituents:* 80 201, New Democratic Party
Tél: 613-995-6327
Téléc: 613-996-5173
eve.peclet@parl.gc.ca
www.evepeclet.ndp.ca
Autre numéros: Constituency Phone: 514-645-0101; Fax: 514-645-0032
Les réseaux sociaux: twitter.com/evepeclet, www.facebook.com/eve.pecletnpd
Constituency Office
#100, 12500, boulIndustriel
Montréal, QC H1B 5P5

Minister, Intergovernmental Affairs; President, Queen's Privy Council for Canada, Hon. Peter Penashue, P.C.
Constituency: Labrador, Newfoundland & Labrador *No. of Constituents:* 20,305, Conservative Party
Tel: 613-996-4630
Fax: 613-996-7132
peter.penashue@parl.gc.ca
Other Communications: Constituency Phone: 709-927-5210; Fax: 709-927-5830
Social Media: twitter.com/PeterPenashue, www.facebook.com/peterpenashue
Note: Web Site: www.pco-bcp.gc.ca/aia/index.asp?lang=eng&page=min (IntergovernmentalAffairs)
Constituency Office
53 Main Hwy.
PO Box 242
L'Anse au Loup, NL A0K 3L0

Manon Perreault
Constituency: Montcalm, Québec *No. of Constituents:* 107 677, New Democratic Party
Tél: 613-992-0164
Téléc: 613-992-5341
manon.perreault@parl.gc.ca
www.manonperreault.ndp.ca
Autre numéros: Constituency Phone: 450-474-1044; Fax: 450-474-1585
Les réseaux sociaux: twitter.com/MPerreaultNPD
Constituency Office
1095, montéeMasson
Mascouche, QC J7K 2M1

François Pilon
Constituency: Laval — Les Iles, Québec *No. of Constituents:* 92 755, New Democratic Party
Tél: 613-992-2659
Téléc: 613-992-9469
francois.pilon@parl.gc.ca
www.francoispilon.ndp.ca
Autre numéros: Constituency Phone: 450-689-5124; Fax: 450-689-5092
Les réseaux sociaux: twitter.com/francoispilon
Constituency Office
4201, boul Ste.Rose
Laval, QC H7R 4V5

Acting House Leader, Bloc Québécois, Louis Plamondon, B.A.Ped., B.A.An
Constituency: Bas-Richelieu — Nicolet — Bécancour, Quebec *No. of Constituents:* 77 290, BQ
Tél: 613-995-9241
Ligne sans frais: 866-693-2041
Téléc: 613-995-6784
louis.plamondon@parl.gc.ca
www.louisplamondon.com
Autre numéros: Constituency Phone: 450-742-0479; Fax:450-742-1976
Les réseaux sociaux: www.facebook.com/LouisPlamondonBQ, www.linkedin.com/pub/louis-plamondon/36/b11/771
Note: Another constituency office is located at 702, rue de Monseigneur-Panet, Nicolet, Québec, J3T1C6. The phone number in Nicolet is 819-293-2041.
Constituency Office
307 Marie-Victorin Rd.
Sorel-Tracy, QC J3R 1K6

Parliamentary Secretary to the Minister, Transport, Infrastructure & Communities, & for the Federal Economic Development Agency for SouthernOntario, Pierre Poilievre
Constituency: Nepean — Carleton,Ontario *No. of Constituents:* 112,535, Conservative Party
Tel: 613-992-2772
Fax: 613-992-1209
pierre.poilievre@parl.gc.ca
www.pierremp.ca
Other Communications: Constituency Phone: 613-990-4300; Fax: 613-990-4333
Social Media: www.facebook.com/pierre.poilievre
Constituency Office
250B Greenbank Rd., 2nd Level
Nepean, ON K2H 8X4

Procedure & House Affairs Committee, Joe Preston
Constituency: Elgin — Middlesex — London, Ontario *No. of Constituents:* 81,661, Conservative Party
Tel: 613-990-7769
Fax: 613-996-0194
joe.preston@parl.gc.ca; joe@joeprestonmp.ca

www.joeprestonmp.ca
Other Communications: Constituency Phone: 519-637-2255; Fax:519-637-3358
Social Media: twitter.com/Joe_Preston, www.facebook.com/Burgerguy, www.linkedin.com/pub/joe-preston/12/1a4/5a
Constituency Office
#2, 24 First Ave.
St. Thomas, ON N5R 4M5

Anne Minh-Thu Quach, B.A.
Constituency: Beauharnois — Salaberry, Québec *No. of Constituents:* 89 454, New Democratic Party
Tél: 613-995-2540
Téléc: 613-941-3300
anneminh-thu.quach@parl.gc.ca; anneminh-thu.quach.A1@parl.gc.ca
www.anneminhthuquach.ndp.ca
Autre numéros: Constituency Phone: 450-371-0644; Fax:450-371-3330
Les réseaux sociaux: twitter.com/AnneMTQuach, www.facebook.com/group.php?gid=248314418518470
Constituency Office
#230, 30 av du Centenaire
Salaberry-de-Valleyfield, QC J6S 5X4

Interim Party Leader, Liberal Party of Canada, Hon. Robert "Bob" Keith Rae, P.C., O.C., O.Ont., Q.C., B.A., B.Ph., LL.B.
Constituency: Toronto Centre, Ontario *No. of Constituents:* 88,810, Liberal
Tel: 613-992-5234
Fax: 613-996-9607
bob.rae@parl.gc.ca;info@bobrae.ca
www.bobrae.ca
Other Communications: Constituency Phone: 416-954-2222; Fax: 416-954-9649
Social Media: twitter.com/bobraemp, www.facebook.com/pages/Bob-Rae/8034824801
Constituency Office
514 Parliament St.
Toronto, ON M4X 1P4

John Rafferty, B.A., B.E.
Constituency: Thunder Bay — Rainy River, Ontario *No. of Constituents:* 62,765, New Democratic Party
Tel: 613-992-3061
Toll-free: 800-667-6186
Fax: 613-995-3515
Rae.B@parl.gc.ca
www.johnrafferty.ndp.ca
Other Communications: Constituency Phone: 416-954-2222; Fax: 416-954-9649
Social Media: twitter.com/JohnRaffertyMP, www.facebook.com/pages/John-Rafferty/19098359045
Constituency Office
409 GeorgeSt.
Thunder Bay, ON P7E 5Y9

Minister, Labour, Hon. Lisa Raitt, P.C., B.Sc., M.Sc., LL.B.
Constituency: Halton, Ontario *No. of Constituents:* 131,924, Conservative Party
Tel: 613-996-7046
Fax: 613-992-0851
lisa.raitt@parl.gc.ca; lisa.raitt@hrsdc-rhdcc.gc.ca
Other Communications: Constituency Phone:905-693-0166; Fax: 905-693-0704
Social Media: twitter.com/lraitt, www.facebook.com/lisaraitt
Note: Web Sites: www.lisaraittmp.ca (Personal Web Site); www.hrsdc.gc.ca/eng/corporate/labour/minister/index.shtml (Labour, HumanResources & Skills Development Canada)
Constituency Office
86 Main St. East
Milton, ON L9T 1N3

Chair, Finance Committee, James Rajotte, B.A.
Constituency: Edmonton — Leduc, Alberta *No. of Constituents:* 101,532, Conservative Party
Tel: 613-992-3594
Fax: 613-992-3616
james.rajotte@parl.gc.ca
www.jamesrajottemp.ca
Other Communications: Constituency Phone: 780-495-4351; Fax: 780-495-4485
Social Media: twitter.com/JamesRajotte, www.facebook.com/group.php?gid=134492869959367, www.linkedin.com/pub/james-rajotte/31/695/a57
ConstituencyOffice
#204, 596 Riverbend Sq.
Edmonton, AB T6R 2E3

Brent Rathgeber, Q.C., B.A., LL.B.
Constituency: Edmonton — St. Albert, Alberta *No. of Constituents:* 97,504, Conservative Party
Tel: 613-996-4722
Fax: 613-995-8880
brent.rathgeber@parl.gc.ca; brent.rathgeber.c1@parl.gc.ca
www.brentrathgeber.ca
Other Communications: Constituency Phone: 780-459-0809; Fax:780-460-1246
Social Media: twitter.com/brentrathgeber, www.facebook.com/profile.php?id=531147984
Constituency Office
#220, 20 Perron St.
St. Albert, AB T8N 1E4

Mathieu Ravignat, M.A. (Political Science)
Constituency: Pontiac, Québec *No. of Constituents:* 82 670, New Democratic Party
Tél: 613-992-5516
Téléc: 613-992-6802
mathieu.ravignat@parl.gc.ca; mathieu.ravignat.c1@parl.gc.ca
www.mathieuravignat.ndp.ca
Autre numéros: Constituency Phone: 819-281-2626;Fax: 819-281-2755
Les réseaux sociaux: twitter.com/MathieuRavignat, www.facebook.com/mathieu.ravignat
Constituency Office
127, rue Joseph
Gatineau, QC J8L 1G1

Francine Raynault
Constituency: Joliette, Québec *No. of Constituents:* 91 695, New Democratic Party
Tél: 613-996-6910
Téléc: 613-995-2818
francine.raynault@parl.gc.ca
www.francineraynault.ndp.ca
Autre numéros: Constituency Phone: 450-752-1940; Fax: 450-752-1719
Les réseaux sociaux: www.facebook.com/profile.php?id=100002301630440
Constituency Office
436, rueSaint-Viateur
Joliette, QC J6E 3B2

Hon. Geoff Regan, P.C., B.A., LL.B.
Constituency: Halifax West, Nova Scotia *No. of Constituents:* 72 862, Liberal
Tel: 613-996-3085
Fax: 613-996-6988
geoff.regan@parl.gc.ca; geoff@geoffregan.ca
www.geoffregan.ca
Other Communications: Constituency, Phone: 902-426-2217; Fax: 902-426-8339
Social Media: twitter.com/geoffregan, www.facebook.com/pages/Geoff-Regan/19891033712
Constituency Office
#222, 1496 Bedford Hwy.
Bedford, NS B4E 1E5

Scott Reid, B.A., M.A.
Constituency: Lanark - Frontenac - Lennox - Addington, Ontario *No. of Constituents:* 91,463, Conservative Party
Tel: 613-947-2277
Toll-free: 866-277-1577
Fax: 613-947-2278
scott.reid@parl.gc.ca
www.scottreid.ca
Other Communications: Constituency Phone: 613-257-8130; Fax: 613-257-4371
Social Media: www.facebook.com/profile.php?id=650980283&sk=info
Constituency Office
224Bridge St.
Carleton Place, ON K7C 3G9

Parliamentary Secretary to the Minister, Environment, Michelle Rempel
Constituency: Calgary Centre-North, Alberta *No. of Constituents:* 84,609, Conservative Party
Tel: 613-992-4275
Fax: 613-947-9475
michelle.rempel@parl.gc.ca
www.michellerempel.ca
Other Communications: Constituency Phone: 403-216-7777; Fax:403-230-4368
Social Media: twitter.com/MichelleRempel; twitter.com/MPRempelOffice, www.facebook.com/group.php?gid=126806667378661
Constituency Office
#105, 1318 Centre St. NE
Calgary, AB T2E 2R7

Blake Richards
Constituency: Wild Rose, Alberta *No. of Constituents:* 95,631, Conservative Party
Tel: 613-996-5152
Toll-free: 800-667-0410
Fax: 613-947-4601
blake.richards@parl.gc.ca; blake@blakerichards.ca
www.blakerichards.ca
Other Communications: Constituency Phone: 403-948-5103; Fax: 403-948-0879
Social Media: twitter.com/BlakeRichardsMP, www.facebook.com/vote.blake
Constituency Office
#16, 620 - 1st Ave. NW
Airdrie, AB T4B 2R3

Parliamentary Secretary to the Minister, Aboriginal Affairs & Northern Development, the Canadian Northern Economic Development Agency, & for the Federal EconomicDevelopment Initiative for Northern Ontario, Greg Rickford, MBA
Constituency: Kenora, Ontario *No. of Constituents:* 42,036, Conservative Party
Tel: 613-996-1161
Toll-free: 866-710-0008
Fax: 613-996-1759
greg.rickford@parl.gc.ca
www.gregrickford.ca
Other Communications: Constituency Phone: 807-468-2170; Fax: 807-468-4896
Constituency Office
#19, 308 Second St. South
Kenora, ON P9N 1G4

Minister, Agriculture & Agri-Food; Minister for the Canadian Wheat Board, Hon. Gerry Ritz, P.C.
Constituency: Battlefords — Lloydminster, Saskatchewan *No. of Constituents:* 50,655, Conservative Party
Tel: 613-995-7080
Fax: 613-996-8472
gerry.ritz@parl.gc.ca
Other Communications: Constituency Phone:306-445-2004; Fax: 306-445-0207
Note: Web Sites: www.gerryritzmp.com (Personal Web Site);www4.agr.gc.ca/AAFC-AAC/display-afficher.do?id=1203439690684&lang=eng
Constituency Office
1322 - 100th St.
North Battleford, SK S9A 0V8

Jean Rousseau, B.Sc.
Constituency: Compton — Stanstead, Québec *No. of Constituents:* 80 470, New Democratic Party
Tél: 613-995-2024
Téléc: 613-992-1696
jean.rousseau@parl.gc.ca
www.jeanrousseau.ndp.ca
Autre numéros: Constituency Phone: 819-347-2598; Fax: 819-347-3583
Constituency Office
5142, boulBourque
Sherbrooke, QC J1N 2K7

Romeo Saganash
Constituency: Abitibi — Baie-James — Nunavik — Eeyou, Quebec *No. of Constituents:* 59 325, New Democratic Party
Tel: 613-992-3030
Fax: 613-996-0828
romeo.saganash@parl.gc.ca
www.romeosaganash.ndp.ca
Other Communications: Constituency Phone: 819-824-2942; Fax: 819-824-2958
Social Media: twitter.com/RomeoSaganash, www.facebook.com/RomeoSaganash
Constituency Office
#204, 888 - 3e av
Val-d'Or, QC J9P 5E6

Jasbir Sandhu, B.A., M.B.A.
Constituency: Surrey North, British Columbia *No. of Constituents:* 72,145, New Democratic Party
Tel: 613-992-2922
Fax: 613-992-0252
jasbir.sandhu@parl.gc.ca
www.jasbirsandhu.ndp.ca
Other Communications: Constituency Phone:
Social Media: twitter.com/jasbirsandhu, www.facebook.com/sandhuj
Constituency Office
#107, 13979 - 104th Ave.
Surrey, BC V3P1X1

Parliamentary Secretary to the President, Treasury Board & for Western Economic Diversification, Andrew Saxton, B.A.
Constituency: North Vancouver, BritishColumbia *No. of Constituents:* 89,416, Conservative Party
Tel: 613-995-1225
Fax: 613-992-7319
andrew.saxton@parl.gc.ca
www.andrewsaxton.ca
Other Communications: Constituency Phone: 604-775-6333; Fax: 604-775-6332
Social Media: twitter.com/AndrewSaxton1, www.facebook.com/andrewsaxtonjr, www.linkedin.com/pub/andrew-saxton-jr/0/6b5/5a4
Constituency Office
102 West 3rd St.
North Vancouver, BC V7M 1E8

Caucus Chair, Liberal Party, Francis Scarpaleggia, B.A., M.A., M.B.A.
Constituency: Lac-Saint-Louis, Québec *No. of Constituents:* 82 542, Liberal
Tel: 613-995-8281
Fax: 613-995-0528
francis.scarpaleggia@parl.gc.ca

www.scarpaleggia.ca
Other Communications: Constituency Phone: 514-695-6661;Fax: 514-695-3708
Social Media: twitter.com/scarpaleggiamp, www.facebook.com/Fscarpaleggia
Constituency Office, East Tower
#635, 1, av Holiday
Pointe-Claire, QC H9R 5N3

Speaker of the House of Commons, Hon. Andrew Scheer
Constituency: Regina — Qu'Appelle, Saskatchewan *No. of Constituents:* 49,386, Conservative Party
Tel: 613-992-4593
Fax: 613-996-3120
andrew.scheer@parl.gc.ca; info@andrewscheer.ca
www.andrewmp.ca
Other Communications: Constituency Phone: 306-790-4727; Fax:306-790-4728
Social Media: twitter.com/andrewscheer, www.facebook.com/AndrewScheerMP
Constituency Office
984A Albert St.
Regina, SK S4R 2P7

Gary Schellenberger
Constituency: Perth — Wellington, Ontario *No. of Constituents:* 73 391, Conservative Party
Tel: 613-992-6124
Toll-free: 866-303-1400
Fax: 613-998-7902
gary.schellenberger@parl.gc.ca
www.schellenberger.ca
Other Communications: Constituency Phone: 519-273-1400; Fax: 519-273-9045
Social Media: twitter.com/GSchellenberger, www.facebook.com/gschellenberger
ConstituencyOffice
544 Huron St.
Stratford, ON N5A 5T9

Craig Scott
Constituency: Toronto — Danforth, Ontario *No. of Constituents:* 74,409, New Democratic Party
Tel: 613-992-9381
Fax: 613-992-9389
craig.scott@parl.gc.ca
www.craigscott.ndp.ca
Other Communications: Constituency Phone: 416-405-8914; Fax: 416-405-8919
Social Media: twitter.com/@craigscottNDP, www.facebook.com/CraigScottNDP
Note: Craig Scott was elected in a by-election on March 19, 2012, following the death of Jack Layton on August 22, 2011.
Constituency Office
#304, 741 Broadview Ave.
Toronto, ON M4K 3Y3

Kyle Seeback, B.A., LL.B.
Constituency: Brampton West, Ontario *No. of Constituents:* 117,926, Conservative Party
Tel: 613-995-5381
Fax: 613-995-6796
kyle.seeback@parl.gc.ca
www.kyleseeback.com
Other Communications: Constituency Phone: 905-846-0076; Fax: 905-846-3901
Social Media: twitter.com/KyleSeeback
Constituency Office
#29, 160 MainSt. South
Brampton, ON L6W 2E1

Djaouida Sellah
Constituency: Saint-Bruno — Saint-Hubert, Québec *No. of Constituents:* 82 381, New Democratic Party
Tél: 613-996-2416
Téléc: 613-995-6973
djaouida.sellah@parl.gc.ca
www.djaouidasellah.ndp.ca
Autre numéros: Constituency Phone: 450-926-5980; Fax: 450-926-5985
Les réseaux sociaux: twitter.com/DSellahNPD, www.facebook.com/pages/Djaouida-Sellah/19867495684826 7
Constituency Office
#110, 5440, ch deChambly
Saint-Hubert, QC J3Y 3P1

Hon. Judy Sgro, P.C.
Constituency: York West, Ontario *No. of Constituents:* 58,090, Liberal
Tel: 613-992-7774
Fax: 613-947-8319
judy.sgro@parl.gc.ca
www.judysgro.com
Other Communications: Constituency Phone: 416-744-1882; Fax: 416-952-1696
Social Media: twitter.com/JudySgro, www.facebook.com/pages/Judy-Sgro/29642650496, www.linkedin.com/in/judysgro
Constituency Office
#25, 2201 Finch Ave.West
Toronto, ON M9M 2Y9

Minister, National Revenue, Hon. Gail Shea, P.C.
Constituency: Egmont, Prince Edward Island *No. of Constituents:* 27,197, Conservative Party
Tel: 613-992-9223
Fax: 613-992-1974
gail.shea@parl.gc.ca; sheag1B@parl.gc.ca
Other Communications: Constituency Phone: 902-432-6899; Fax:902-432-6853
Social Media: twitter.com/CPCGailShea
Note: Web Sites: www.gailshea.ca (Personal Web Site); www.cra-arc.gc.ca/gncy/mnstr/menu-eng.html (Canada Revenue Agency)
Constituency Office
250 Water St., #F
Summerside, PE C1N 1B3

Bev Shipley
Constituency: Lambton — Kent — Middlesex, Ontario *No. of Constituents:* 79,754, Conservative Party
Tel: 613-947-4581
Toll-free: 800-586-4614
Fax: 613-947-4584
bev.shipley@parl.gc.ca
www.bevshipley.ca
Other Communications: Constituency Phone: 519-245-6561; Fax: 519-245-6736
Social Media: twitter.com/VoteBevShipley, www.facebook.com/profile.php?id=674005042
Constituency Office
380 Albert St.
PO Box 141
Strathroy, ON N7G 3J1

Devinder Shory
Constituency: Calgary Northeast, Alberta *No. of Constituents:* 87,307, Conservative Party
Tel: 613-947-4487
Fax: 613-947-4490
devinder.shory@parl.gc.ca
www.devindershory.ca
Other Communications: Constituency Phone: 403-291-0018; Fax: 403-291-9516
Social Media: twitter.com/NortheastShory, www.facebook.com/mpshory
Constituency Office
#140, 2635 - 37th Ave.NE
Calgary, AB T1Y 5Z6

Scott Simms, B.Comm.
Constituency: Bonavista — Gander — Grand Falls — Windsor, Newfoundland & Labrador *No. of Constituents:* 69,936, Liberal
Tel: 613-996-3935
Toll-free: 888-489-1901
Fax: 613-996-7622
scott.simms@parl.gc.ca
www.scottsimms.com
Other Communications: Constituency Phone: 709-256-3130; Fax: 709-256-3169
Social Media: twitter.com/Scott_Simms, www.facebook.com/MPScottSimms
Constituency Office
61Elizabeth Dr.
Gander, NL A1V 1G4

Jinny Jogindera Sims, B.Ed.
Constituency: Newton — North Delta, British Columbia *No. of Constituents:* 75,535, New Democratic Party
Tel: 613-992-0666
Fax: 613-992-1965
jinny.sims@parl.gc.ca
www.jinnysims.ndp.ca
Other Communications: Constituency Phone: 604-598-2200; Fax: 604-598-2212
Social Media: www.facebook.com/jinnysims
Constituency Office
#113, 8532 -120th St.
Surrey, BC V3W 3N5

Rathika Sitsabaiesan
Constituency: Scarborough — Rouge River, Ontario *No. of Constituents:* 85,183, New Democratic Party
Tel: 613-996-9681
Fax: 613-996-6643
rathika.sitsabaiesan@parl.gc.ca
www.rathika.ca
Other Communications: Constituency Phone: 416-298-4224, Fax: 416-298-6035
Social Media: twitter.com/rathikas, www.facebook.com/rathikaspage
Constituency Office
#104, 8130Sheppard Ave. East
Toronto, ON M1B 3W3

Chair, Health Committee, Joy Smith, B.Ed., M.Ed.(Hons.)
Constituency: Kildonan — St. Paul, Manitoba *No. of Constituents:* 63,866, Conservative Party
Tel: 613-992-7148
Fax: 613-996-9125
joy.smith@parl.gc.ca; joy@joysmith.ca
www.joysmith.ca
Other Communications: Constituency Phone: 204-984-6322; Fax:204-984-6415
Constituency Office, McIvor Mall
#13C, 1795 Henderson Hwy.
Winnipeg, MB R2G 1P3

Robert Sopuck, B.Sc., M.Sc.
Constituency: Dauphin — Swan River — Marquette, Manitoba *No. of Constituents:* 53,701, Conservative Party
Tel: 613-992-3176
Fax: 613-992-0930
robert.sopuck@parl.gc.ca; info@robertsopuck.ca
www.robertsopuck.ca
Other Communications: Constituency Phone: 204-622-4659; Fax: 204-622-4654
Social Media: www.facebook.com/pages/Robert-Sopuck/126578207395867
Constituency Office, Dauphin Marketplace Mall
#4C, 1450 Main St. South
Dauphin, MB R0J 1N0

Chair, Public Safety & National Security Committee, Kevin Sorenson
Constituency: Crowfoot, Alberta *No. of Constituents:* 88,881, Conservative Party
Tel: 780-608-4600
Toll-free: 800-665-4358
Fax: 613-947-4611
kevin.sorenson@parl.gc.ca
www.kevinsorenson.ca
Other Communications: Constituency Phone: 780-608-4600; Fax:780-608-4603
Constituency Office
4945 - 50th St.
Camrose, AB T4V 1P9

Assistant Deputy Chair, Committees of the Whole, Bruce Stanton
Constituency: Simcoe North, Ontario *No. of Constituents:* 90,779, Conservative Party
Tel: 613-992-6582
Toll-free: 800-265-6228
Fax: 613-996-3128
bruce.stanton@parl.gc.ca
www.brucestanton.ca
Other Communications: Constituency Phone: 705-327-0513; Fax:705-327-8310
Social Media: twitter.com/bruce_stanton, www.facebook.com/pages/Bruce-Stanton/6236822310, www.linkedin.com/pub/bruce-stanton/28/19/95
Constituency Office
#2A, 575 West St. South
Orillia, ON L3V 7N6

Lise St-Denis, B.A., M.A., M.Ed.
Constituency: Saint-Maurice — Champlain, Québec *No. of Constituents:* 80,534, Liberal
Tél: 613-995-4895
Téléc: 613-996-6883
lise.st-denis@parl.gc.ca; Lise.St-Denis.C1@parl.gc.ca
Autre numéros: Constituency Phone: 819-538-5291; Fax:819-538-7624
Note: Lise St-Denis left the New Democratic Party to join the Liberal Party on January 10, 2012.
Constituency Office
632, 6e av
Grand-Mère, QC G9T 2H5

Kennedy Stewart, B.A., M.A., Ph.D.
Constituency: Burnaby — Douglas, British Columbia *No. of Constituents:* 84,911, New Democratic Party
Tel: 613-996-5597
Fax: 613-992-5501
kennedy.stewart@parl.gc.ca
www.kennedystewart.ca
Other Communications: Constituency Phone: 604-291-8863; Fax: 604-666-0727
Social Media: twitter.com/kennedystewart, www.facebook.com/kennedy.stewart, www.linkedin.com/pub/kennedy-stewart/14/817/540
Constituency Office
4658 Hastings St.
Burnaby, BC V5C 2K5

Peter Stoffer
Constituency: Sackville — Eastern Shore, Nova Scotia *No. of Constituents:* 70,329, New Democratic Party
Tel: 613-995-5822
Toll-free: 888-701-5557
Fax: 613-996-9655
peter.stoffer@parl.gc.ca
www.peterstoffer.ndp.ca
Other Communications: Constituency Phone: 902-861-2311; Fax: 902-861-4620
Constituency Office
2900 Hwy.2
Fall River, NS B2T 1W4

Brian Storseth
Constituency: Westlock — St. Paul, Alberta *No. of Constituents:* 76,291, Conservative Party
Tel: 613-996-1783
Toll-free: 800-667-8450
Fax: 613-995-1415
brian.storseth@parl.gc.ca; brian@brianstorseth.ca
www.brianstorseth.ca
Other Communications: Constituency Phone: 780-349-8333; Fax: 780-349-8340
Social Media: twitter.com/BrianStorseth, www.facebook.com/Brian.Storseth.MP
Constituency Office
10623 - 100th Ave., #B
Westlock, ON T7P 2J4

Mark Strahl
Constituency: Chilliwack — Fraser Canyon, British Columbia *No. of Constituents:* 84,930, Conservative Party
Tel: 613-992-2940
Toll-free: 800-667-2808
Fax: 613-944-9376
mark.strahl@parl.gc.ca
www.markstrahl.com
Other Communications: Constituency Phone: 604-847-9711; Fax: 604-847-9744
Social Media: twitter.com/markstrahl, www.facebook.com/pages/Mark-Strahl/223322794358475
Constituency Office
#102, 7388Vedder Rd.
Chilliwack, BC V2R 4E4

Mike Sullivan
Constituency: York South — Weston, Ontario *No. of Constituents:* 68,361, New Democratic Party
Tel: 613-995-0777
Fax: 613-992-2949
mike.sullivan@parl.gc.ca
www.mikesullivan.ca
Other Communications: Constituency Phone: 416-656-2526
Social Media: twitter.com/mdsullivan, www.facebook.com/group.php?gid=161602783896439
Constituency Office
36 South Station St.
Toronto, ON M9N2B3

Chair, Industry, Science, & Technology Committee, David Sweet
Constituency: Ancaster — Dundas — Flamborough — Westdale, Ontario *No. of Constituents:* 86,382, Conservative Party
Tel: 613-996-4984
Fax: 613-996-4986
David.Sweet@parl.gc.ca; David.Sweet.c1@parl.gc.ca
www.davidsweet.ca/cms
Other Communications: Constituency Phone:905-627-9169; Fax: 905-627-3803
Social Media: twitter.com/DavidSweetMP, www.facebook.com/pages/David-Sweet/14043761823
Constituency Office
#3, 59 Kirby Ave.
Dundas, ON L9H 6P3

Chair, Bill C-11 Committee, Glenn Thibeault
Constituency: Sudbury, Ontario *No. of Constituents:* 72,019, New Democratic Party
Tel: 613-996-8962
Fax: 613-995-2569
glenn.thibeault@parl.gc.ca
www.glennthibeault.ndp.ca
Other Communications: Constituency Phone: 705-673-7107; Fax: 705-673-0944
Social Media: twitter.com/GlennThibeault, www.facebook.com/glennthibeaultmp
ConstituencyOffice, Rainbow Centre
#103A, 40 Elm St.
Sudbury, ON P3C 1S8

Chair, Citizenship & Immigration Committee, David Allan Tilson, Q.C., B.A.. LL.B.
Constituency: Dufferin — Caledon, Ontario *No. of Constituents:* 81,155, Conservative Party
Tel: 613-995-7813
Fax: 613-992-9789
david.tilson@parl.gc.ca; david.tilson.c1@parl.gc.ca
www.davidtilson.ca
Other Communications: Constituency Phone: 519-941-1832; Fax: 519-941-8660
Social Media: twitter.com/davidtilson
Constituency Office
#2, 229 Broadway
Orangeville, ON L9W 1K4

Lawrence Toet
Constituency: Elmwood — Transcona, Manitoba *No. of Constituents:* 59,154, Conservative Party
Tel: 613-995-6339
Fax: 613-995-6688
lawrence.toet@parl.gc.ca; lawrence@lawrencetoet.ca
www.lawrencetoet.ca
Other Communications: Constituency Phone: 204-984-2499; Fax: 204-984-2502
Social Media: www.facebook.com/pages/Lawrence-Toet/254206521258405
ConstituencyOffice
127 Regent Ave. West
Winnipeg, MB R2C 5G2

Minister, Public Safety, Hon. Vic Toews, P.C., B.A., LL.B.
Constituency: Provencher, Manitoba *No. of Constituents:* 64,104, Conservative Party
Tel: 613-992-3128
Fax: 613-995-1049
vic.toews@parl.gc.ca
Other Communications: Constituency Phone: 204-326-9889; Fax: 204-346-9874
Note: Web Sites: www.victoews.com (Personal Web Site); www.publicsafety.gc.ca/abt/wwa/min-eng.aspx (Public Safety Canada)
Constituency Office
#8, 227 Main St.
Steinbach, MB R5G 1Y7

Deputy Opposition Whip, Philip Toone
Constituency: Gaspésie — Iles-de-la-Madeleine, Québec *No. of Constituents:* 69,429, New Democratic Party
Tel: 613-992-6188
Toll-free: 866-368-1855
Fax: 613-992-6194
philip.toone@parl.gc.ca
www.philiptoone.ndp.ca
Other Communications: Constituency Phone: 418-368-1855; Fax: 418-368-1925
Social Media: www.facebook.com/pages/Philip-Toone/243294132367236
Note: Constituency offices are also located at #208, 735, rue Principal, Cap-aux-Meules, Québec G4T 1G8 (418-986-5552) & 642B, boul Perron,Carleton-sur-Mer, Québec G0C 1J0 (418-364-1401).
Constituency Office
3-1, rue Carter
Gaspé, QC G4X 1T5

Jonathan Tremblay
Constituency: Montmorency — Charlevoix — Haute-Côte-Nord, Québec *No. of Constituents:* 76,661, New Democratic Party
Tél: 613-995-9732
Ligne sans frais: 866-660-6776
Téléc: 613-996-2656
jonathan.tremblay@parl.gc.ca
www.jonathantremblay.gc.ca
Autre numéros: Constituency Phone: 418-660-6776; Fax: 418-660-6777
Les réseaux sociaux: twitter.com/Jonathan_tremb
Constituency Office
4611, boul Sainte-Anne
Québec, QC G1C 2J3

Brad Trost, B.A., B.Sc.
Constituency: Saskatoon — Humboldt, Saskatchewan *No. of Constituents:* 57,055, Conservative Party
Tel: 613-992-8052
Fax: 613-996-9899
brad.trost@parl.gc.ca
www.bradtrost.ca
Other Communications: Constituency Phone: 306-975-6133; Fax: 306-975-6670
Social Media: twitter.com/BradTrostCPC, www.facebook.com/pages/Brad-Trost-MP/183289298385094
Constituency Office
505B Nelson Rd.
Saskatoon, SK S7S 1P4

Bernard Trottier, B.Sc.Eng., MBA
Constituency: Etobicoke — Lakeshore, Ontario *No. of Constituents:* 87,188, Conservative Party
Tel: 613-995-9364
Fax: 613-992-5880
bernard.trottier@parl.gc.ca
www.bernardtrottiermp.ca
Other Communications: Constituency Phone: 416-251-5510; Fax: 416-251-2845
Social Media: twitter.com/btrottier, www.facebook.com/pages/Bernard-Trottier/128026606262?ref=ts, www.linkedin.com/pub/bernard-trottier/3/b47/836
Constituency Office
#200, 700 Kipling Ave.
Toronto, ON M8Z 5G3

Justin Trudeau, B.A., B.Ed.
Constituency: Papineau, Québec *No. of Constituents:* 70,973, Liberal
Tél: 613-995-8872
Téléc: 613-995-9926
justin.trudeau@parl.gc.ca
www.justin.ca
Autre numéros: Constituency Phone: 514-277-6020; Fax: 514-277-3454
Les réseaux sociaux: twitter.com/justinpjtrudeau, www.facebook.com/pages/Justin-Trudeau/21751825648
Constituency Office
#302, 529,rue Jarry est
Montréal, QC H2P 1V4

Parliamentary Secretary for Status of Women, Susan Truppe
Constituency: London North Centre, Ontario *No. of Constituents:* 88,478, Conservative Party
Tel: 613-992-0805
Fax: 613-992-9613
susan.truppe@parl.gc.ca; susan.truppe.c1@parl.gc.ca
www.susantruppe.ca
Other Communications: Constituency Phone:519-663-9777; Fax: 519-663-2238
Social Media: twitter.com/susantruppe, www.facebook.com/group.php?gid=222527324455927, www.linkedin.com/pub/susan-truppe/1b/3a5/a30
Constituency Office
546 King St.
London, ON N6B 1T5

Chief Opposition Whip, Nycole Turmel
Constituency: Hull — Aylmer, Quebec *No. of Constituents:* 91,958, New Democratic Party
Tél: 613-992-7550
Téléc: 613-992-7599
nycole.turmel@parl.gc.ca
www.nycoleturmel.ndp.ca
Autre numéros: Constituency Phone: 819-994-8844; Fax: 819-994-8557
Les réseaux sociaux: twitter.com/nycole_turmel, www.facebook.com/Turmel.Nycole
Constituency Office
200, boul St. Joseph
Gatineau, QC J8Y 3W9

Chair, Agriculture & Agri-Food Committee, Mervin C. Tweed
Constituency: Brandon — Souris, Manitoba *No. of Constituents:* 61,289, Conservative Party
Tel: 613-995-9372
Toll-free: 866-558-0555
Fax: 613-992-1265
merv.tweed@parl.gc.ca; merv.tweed.c1@parl.gc.ca
www.mervtweed.com
Other Communications: Constituency Phone:204-726-7600; Fax: 204-726-7699
Constituency Office, Redwood Plaza
#8, 223 - 18th St. North
Brandon, MB R7A 2V8

Minister of State, Democratic Reform, Hon. Tim Uppal, P.C.
Constituency: Edmonton — Sherwood Park, Alberta *No. of Constituents:* 94,602, Conservative Party
Tel: 613-995-3611
Fax: 613-995-3612
tim.uppal@parl.gc.ca
Other Communications: Constituency Phone: 780-467-4944; Fax: 780-449-1471
Social Media: twitter.com/TimUppal_MP, www.facebook.com/profile.php?id=560835735
Note: Web Sites: www.timuppal.ca (Personal Web Site); www.democraticreform.gc.ca/index.asp?lang=eng&page=min (Democratic Reform)
Constituency Office
141 Seneca Rd.
Sherwood Park, AB T8A 4G6

Minister of State, Atlantic Canada Opportunities Agency; Minister of State, La Francophonie; Associate Minister, National Defence, Hon. Bernard Valcourt, P.C., Q.C.,B.A., LL.B., DHC
Constituency: Madawaska — Restigouche,New Brunswick *No. of Constituents:* 50,966, Conservative Party
Tél: 613-995-0581
Téléc: 613-996-9736
bernard.valcourt@parl.gc.ca; bvalcourt2011@hotmail.com
Autre numéros: Constituency Phone: 506-739-4600; Fax: 506-739-4607
Les réseaux sociaux: twitter.com/b_valcourt, www.facebook.com/pages/Bernard-Valcourt/214030968613999
Note: Web Sites: www.bernardvalcourt.ca (Personal Web Site); www.acoa-apeca.gc.ca/English/WhoWeAre/OurPeople/Pages/Minister.aspx?ProgramID= (Atlantic Canada Opportunities Agency)
Constituency Office
14 Costigan St.
Edmundston, NB E3V 1W9

Frank Valeriote
Constituency: Guelph, Ontario *No. of Constituents:* 91,316, Liberal
Tel: 613-996-4758
Fax: 613-996-9922
frank.valeriote@parl.gc.ca
www.frankvaleriote.ca
Other Communications: Constituency Phone: 519-837-8276; Fax: 519-837-8443
Social Media: twitter.com/FrankValeriote, www.facebook.com/FrankValeriote

Constituency Office
40 Cork St. East
Guelph, ON N1H 2W8
Dave Van Kesteren
Constituency: Chatham-Kent — Essex, Ontario *No. of Constituents:* 74,231, Conservative Party
Tel: 613-992-2612
Fax: 613-992-1852
dave.vankesteren@parl.gc.ca
www.davevankesteren.ca
Other Communications: Constituency Phone: 519-358-7555; Fax: 519-358-1428
Social Media: www.facebook.com/davevankesteren
Constituency Office
8 King St.West
Chatham, ON N7M 1C6
Leader of the Government in the House of Commons; Conservative Party House Leader, Hon. Peter Van Loan, P.C., B.A., LL.B., M.A., M.Sc.Pl.
Constituency: York — Simcoe, Ontario *No. of Constituents:* 91,662, Conservative Party
Tel: 613-996-7752
Toll-free: 877-738-3748
Fax: 613-992-8351
peter.vanloan@parl.gc.ca
Other Communications: Constituency Phone: 905-898-1600; Fax: 905-898-4600
Note: Web Sites: www.petervanloan.com(Personal Web Site); www.houseleader.gc.ca/index.asp?lang=eng&page=Team-equipe&doc=bio/bio-eng.htm (Leader of the Government in the House of Commons)
Constituency Office, Grist Mill Plaza
#10, 45 Grist Mill Rd.
Holland Landing, ON L9N 1M7
Maurice Vellacott, B.R.E., M.Div., D.Min.
Constituency: Saskatoon — Wanuskewin, Saskatchewan *No. of Constituents:* 57,654, Conservative Party
Tel: 613-992-1899
Toll-free: 888-844-8886
Fax: 613-992-3085
maurice.vellacott@parl.gc.ca
www.mauricevellacott.ca
Other Communications: Constituency Phone: 306-975-4725; Fax: 306-975-4728
Constituency Office
#3, 844 - 51st St. East
Saskatoon, SK S7K 5C7
Mike Wallace, B.A.
Constituency: Burlington, Ontario *No. of Constituents:* 91,716, Conservative Party
Tel: 613-995-0881
Fax: 613-995-1091
mike.wallace@parl.gc.ca; mike.wallace.c1@parl.gc.ca
www.mikewallacemp.ca
Other Communications: Constituency Phone: 905-639-5757; Fax: 905-639-6031
Social Media: twitter.com/MikeWallaceMP, www.linkedin.com/pub/mike-wallace/1b/843/9b1
ConstituencyOffice, Burlington Mall
#209, 777 Guelph Line
Burlington, ON L7R 3N2
Chair, Environment & Sustainable Development Committee, Mark Warawa
Constituency: Langley, British Columbia *No. of Constituents:* 90,225, Conservative Party
Tel: 613-992-1157
Fax: 613-943-1823
mark.warawa@parl.gc.ca
www.markwarawa.com
Other Communications: Constituency Phone: 604-534-5955; Fax:604-534-5970
Social Media: twitter.com/MPmarkwarawa, www.facebook.com/markwarawa
Constituency Office
#104, 4769 - 222nd St.
Langley, BC V2Z 3C1
Chair, Aboriginal Affairs & Northern Development Committee, Chris Warkentin
Constituency: Peace River, Alberta *No. of Constituents:* 98,135, Conservative Party
Tel: 613-992-5685
Toll-free: 800-667-0456
Fax: 613-947-4782
chris.warkentin@parl.gc.ca; chris.warkentin.c1@parl.gc.ca
www.chriswarkentin.ca
Other Communications: Constituency Phone: 780-538-1677; Fax: 780-538-9257
Social Media: twitter.com/chriswarkentin, www.facebook.com/chriswarkentin
Constituency Office
#201, 10625 West Side Dr.
Grande Prairie, AB T8V 8E6
Jeff Watson
Constituency: Essex, Ontario *No. of Constituents:* 90,421, Conservative Party
Tel: 613-992-1812
Toll-free: 866-776-5333
Fax: 613-995-0033
jeff.watson@parl.gc.ca
www.jeffwatsonmp.ca
Other Communications: Constituency Phone: 519-776-4700; Fax: 519-776-1383
Social Media: www.facebook.com/JeffWatsonEssex
Constituency Office
186 Talbot St.South
Essex, ON N8M 1B6
Chair, Fisheries & Oceans Committee, John Weston
Constituency: West Vancouver — Sunshine Coast — Sea to Sky Country, British Columbia *No. of Constituents:* 99,642, Conservative Party
Tel: 613-947-4617
Toll-free: 800-665-6004
Fax: 613-947-4620
john.weston@parl.gc.ca
www.johnweston.ca
Other Communications: Constituency Phone: 604-981-1790; Fax:604-981-1794
Social Media: twitter.com/JohnWestonMP, www.facebook.com/JohnWestonMP
Constituency Office
#21, 285 - 17th St.
West Vancouver, BC V7V 3S6
Rodney Weston
Constituency: Saint John, New Brunswick *No. of Constituents:* 64,264, Conservative Party
Tel: 613-947-2700
Fax: 613-947-4574
rodney.weston@parl.gc.ca
www.rodneyweston.ca
Other Communications: Constituency Phone: 506-657-2500; Fax: 506-657-2504
Social Media: twitter.com/rodneywestonsj
Constituency Office
90 King St.
SaintJohn, NB E2L 1G4
David Wilks
Constituency: Kootenay — Columbia, British Columbia *No. of Constituents:* 67,663, Conservative Party
Tel: 613-995-7246
Fax: 613-996-9923
david.wilks@parl.gc.ca; david.wilks.c1@parl.gc.ca
www.david-wilks.ca
Other Communications: Constituency Phone: 250-417-2250; Fax: 250-417-2253
Social Media: twitter.com/DavidJohnWilks, www.facebook.com/david.wilks
Constituency Office
100B Cranbrook St. North
Cranbrook, BC V1C 3P9
John Williamson, B.A., MSc.
Constituency: New Brunswick Southwest, New Brunswick *No. of Constituents:* 49,578, Conservative Party
Tel: 613-995-5550
Toll-free: 888-350-4734
Fax: 613-995-5226
john.williamson@parl.gc.ca; john.williamson.c1@parl.gc.ca
www.votejohnwilliamson.ca
Other Communications: Constituency Phone: 506-466-3928; Fax: 506-466-2813
Social Media: www.facebook.com/pages/John-Williamson/172576949462450
Constituency Office
120 Milltown Blvd.
St. Stephen, NB E3L 1G6
Minister of State, Seniors, Hon. Alice Wong, P.C., Ph.D.
Constituency: Richmond, British Columbia *No. of Constituents:* 85,643, Conservative Party
Tel: 613-995-2021
Toll-free: 877-775-5790
Fax: 613-995-2174
alice.wong@parl.gc.ca; alice.wong.c1@parl.gc.ca
Other Communications: Constituency Phone: 604-775-5790;Fax: 604-775-6291
Social Media: twitter.com/AliceWongCanada, www.facebook.com/profile.php?id=100002648510727
Note: Web Sites: www.alicewong.ca (Personal Web Site); www.hrsdc.gc.ca/eng/corporate/ministers/index.shtml (HumanResources & Skills Development Canada); www.seniors.gc.ca/h.4m.2@.jsp (Seniors Canada)
Constituency Office
#360, 5951 No. 3 Rd.
Richmond, BC V6X 2E3
Stephen Woodworth, LL.B.
Constituency: Kitchener Centre, Ontario *No. of Constituents:* 80,480, Conservative Party
Tel: 613-995-8913
Fax: 613-996-7329
stephen.woodworth@parl.gc.ca
www.stephenwoodworth.ca
Other Communications: Constituency Phone: 519-741-2001; Fax: 519-579-2404
Social Media: twitter.com/WoodworthMP, www.facebook.com/WoodworthKitchenerCentre, www.linkedin.com/pub/stephen-woodworth/2b/84b/38
Constituency Office
#12, 300Victoira St. North
Kitchener, ON N2H 6R9
Minister of State, Western Economic Diversification, Hon. Lynne Yelich, P.C.
Constituency: Blackstrap, Saskatchewan *No. of Constituents:* 61,955, Conservative Party
Tel: 613-995-5653
Fax: 613-995-0126
Lynne.Yelich@parl.gc.ca
Other Communications: Constituency Phone: 306-975-6472; Fax:306-975-6492
Social Media: twitter.com/Lynne_Yelich, www.facebook.com/pages/Lynne-Yelich/64666054978
Note: Web Sites: www.lynneyelich.com (Personal Web Site); www.wd.gc.ca/eng/43.asp (Western Economic DiversificationCanada)
Constituency Office, Market Mall
#71, 2325 Preston Ave.
Saskatoon, SK S7J 2G2
Terence H. Young, B.A.
Constituency: Oakville, Ontario *No. of Constituents:* 85,920, Conservative Party
Tel: 613-995-4014
Fax: 613-992-0520
terence.young@parl.gc.ca
www.terenceyoung.com
Other Communications: Constituency Phone: 905-338-2008
Social Media: twitter.com/TerenceYoungMP, www.facebook.com/TerenceYoungMP
Constituency Office
#104, 165 Cross Ave.
Oakville, ON L6J 0A9
Wai Young, B.A.
Constituency: Vancouver South, British Columbia *No. of Constituents:* 82,509, Conservative Party
Tel: 613-995-7052
Fax: 613-995-2962
Wai.Young@parl.gc.ca; info@waiyoung.ca
www.waiyoung.ca
Other Communications: Constituency Phone: 604-775-5323; Fax: 604-775-5420
Social Media: twitter.com/WaiYoungMP, www.facebook.com/WaiYoungVancouverSouth, www.linkedin.com/pub/wai-young/2/4a7/a9a
Constituency Office
6406Victoria Dr.
Vancouver, BC V5P 3X7
Bob Zimmer, B.A.
Constituency: Prince George — Peace River, British Columbia *No. of Constituents:* 72,580, Conservative Party
Tel: 613-947-4524
Fax: 613-613-9474
Bob.Zimmer@parl.gc.ca
www.bobzimmer.ca
Other Communications: Constituency Phone: 250-561-7982; Fax: 250-561-7983
Social Media: twitter.com/ZimmerBob, www.facebook.com/group.php?gid=165836856816065, www.linkedin.com/pub/bob-zimmer/26/a21/ba6
Constituency Office
9916 - 100th Ave.
FortSt. John, BC V1J 1Y5
Vacant
Constituency: Calgary Centre, Alberta *No. of Constituents:* 89,536
Note: Lee Richardson, forner Conservative Member of Parliament for the Alberta riding of Calgary Cente, resigned onJune 6, 2012, to serve Alberta's Premier, Alison Redford as her Principal Secretary.
Vacant
Constituency: Durham, Ontario *No. of Constituents:* 92,470
Note: Bev Oda, former Conservative Member of Parliament for the Ontario riding of Durham, resigned on July 31,2012.
Vacant
Constituency: Victoria, British Columbia *No. of Constituents:* 89,750
Note: Denise Savoie, B.A., M.A., M.Ed., announced her retirement from politics on August 23, 2012. The NewDemocratic Member of Parliament also served as the Deputy Speaker & the Chair of the Committees of the Whole.

Federal Government Departments & Agencies / Agences et departements du gouvernement fédéral

Editor's Note: The entries listed below are entered alphabetically, using applied titles as registered by the Federal Identity

Program. Cross references are used to help you to locate the entry quickly. The two departments that incorporate Department of as part of their applied titles (Department of Finance Canada; Department of Justice Canada) are nevertheless listed alphabetically under Finance & Justice.

Aboriginal Affairs & Northern Development Canada (AANDC) / Affaires autochtones et Développement du Nord Canada (AADNC)

10 Wellington St., North Tower, Gatineau, QC K1A 0H4
Tel: 819-997-0380
Fax: 866-817-3977
Toll-Free: 800-567-9604
infopubs@aadnc-aandc.gc.ca
www.aadnc-aandc.gc.ca
TTY: 866-553-0554

AANDC supports First Nations, Inuit & Métis people in their effort to develop healthy, sustainable communities & achieve their economic & social aspirations. This mandate is derived largely from the Department of Indian & Northern Development Act, the Indian Act, territorial acts & legal obligations arising from section 91(24) of the Constitution Act, 1867. The department administers over 50 statutes.

Acts Administered:
(An Act for the) Settlement of Certain Questions Between the Governments of Canada & Ontario Respecting the Indian Reserve Lands Act
(An Act to confirm an) Agreement between the Governments of Canada & the province of New Brunswick respecting the Indian Reserves
(An Act to confirm an) Agreement between the Governments of Canada & the province of Nova Scotia respecting the Indian Reserves
Alberta Natural Resources Act
Arctic Waters Pollution Prevention Act (jointly with Transport Canada & Natural Resources)
British Columbia Indian Cut-off Lands Settlement Act
British Columbia Indian Lands Settlement Act
British Columbia Treaty Commission Act
Canada - Yukon Oil & Gas Accord Implementation Act
Canada Lands Surveys Act (jointly Natural Resources)
Canada Mining Regulations
Canada Oil & Gas Drilling & Production Regulations
Canada Oil & Gas Land Regulations
Canada Oil & Gas Operations Act (jointly with Natural Resources)
Canada Petroleum Resources Act (jointly with Natural Resources)
Canadian Polar Commission Act
Caughnawaga Indian Reserve Act
Claim Settlements (Alberta & Saskatchewan) Implementation Act
Condominium Ordinance Validation Act
Cree-Naskapi (of Québec) Act
Crown Waiver Orders
Department of Indian & Northern Affairs Development Act
Dominion Water Power Act
Fort Nelson Indian Reserve Minerals Revenue Sharing Act
Government Employees Land Acquisition Orders
Grassy Narrows & Islington Indian Band Mercury Pollution Claims Settlement Act
Gwich'in Land Claim Settlement Act
Indian (Soldier Settlement) Act
Indian Act
Indian Lands Agreement (1986) Act
Indian Oil & Gas Act
Indian Reserve Waste Disposal Regulations
James Bay & Northern Quebec Native Claims Settlement Act
Kanesatake Interim Land Base Governance Act
Kelowna Accord Implementation Act
Labrador Inuit Land Claims Agreement Act
Land Titles Repeal Act
Maanulth First Nations Final Agreement Act
Mackenzie Valley Resource Management Act
Manitoba Claim Settlements Implementation Act
Manitoba Natural Resources Act
Manitoba Supplementary Provisions Act
Natural Resources Transfer (School Lands) Amendments, Alberta, Manitoba & Saskatchewan
Nelson House First Nation Flooded Land Act
Nisga'a Final Agreement Act
Northern Canada Power Commission (Share Issuance & Sale Authorization) Act
Northern Canada Power Commission Yukon Assets Disposal Authorization Act
Northwest Territories Act
Northwest Territories Mining Districts Order & Nunavut Mining District
Northwest Territories Waters Act
Nunavik Inuit Land Claims Agreement Act
Nunavut Act
Nunavut Land Claims Agreement Act
Nunavut Waters & Nunavut Surface Rights Tribunal Act, 2002
Oil & Gas Land Orders
Orders Authorizing Acquisition of Interest in Certain Lands
Orders Respecting Withdrawal from Disposal of Certain Lands
Pictou Landing Indian Band Agreement Act
Polar Bear Pass Withdrawal Order
Railway Belt & Peace River Block Act
Railway Belt Act
Railway Belt Water Act
Reservations to Crown Waiver Orders
Sahtu Dene & Metis Land Claim Settlement Act
Saskatchewan Natural Resources Act
Saskatchewan Treaty Land Entitlement Act
Sechelt Indian Band Self-Government Act
Songhees Indian Reserve Act
Specific Claims Tribunal Act
Split Lake Cree First Nation Flooded Land Act
St. Peter's Reserve Act
St. Regis Islands Act
Territorial Coal Regulations
Territorial Dredging Regulations
Territorial Land Titles Offices Regulations
Territorial Land Use Regulations
Territorial Lands Act
Territorial Lands Act Exclusion Orders
Territorial Lands Regulations
Territorial Quarrying Regulations
Tlicho Land Claims & Self-Government Act
Tsawwassen First Nation Final Agreement Act
Westbank First Nation Self-Government Act
Western Arctic (Inuvialuit) Claims Settlement Act
Withdrawal of Certain Lands from Disposal Orders
Withdrawals of Disposal Orders
York Factory First Nation Flooded Land Act
Yukon Act
Yukon Environmental & Socio-Economic Assessment Act, 2003
Yukon First Nations Land Claims Settlement Act
Yukon First Nations Self-Government Act
Yukon Surface Rights Board Act

Minister, Indian Affairs & Northern Development; Minister of the Canadian Northern Economic Development Agency, Federal Interlocutor for Métis & Non-Status Indians, Hon. John Duncan, B.Sc.F.
Tel: 613-992-2503
Fax: 613-996-3306
Duncan.J@parl.gc.ca; Minister@ainc-inac.gc.ca
Other Communications: Indian Affairs & Northern Development: 819-997-0002

Parliamentary Secretary to the Minister of Aboriginal Affairs & Northern Development, Rod Bruinooge
Tel: 613-995-7517
Fax: 613-943-4666

Deputy Minister, Michael Wernick
Tel: 819-997-0133
Fax: 819-953-2251

Associate Deputy Minister, Colleen Swords
Tel: 819-934-0583
Fax: 819-953-2251

Director General, Communications, Dianne Clarke
Tel: 819-994-7526
Fax: 819-953-9465

Director General, Office of the Federal Interlocutor, Allan MacDonald
Tel: 613-992-8186
Fax: 613-947-7580

Senior General Counsel, Legal Services, Andrew Saranchuk
Tel: 819-994-4141
Fax: 819-953-7693

Director, Policy, Kym Purchase
Tel: 819-997-0002
Fax: 819-953-4941

Associated Agencies, Boards & Commissions:

• Beverly & Qamanirjuaq Caribou Management Board
Secretariat
PO Box 629
Stonewall, MB R0C 2Z0
Tel: 204-467-2438
caribounews@arctic-caribou.com
www.arctic-caribou.com
Group of hunters, biologists & wildlife managers working together to conserve Canada's vast Beverly & Qamanirjuaq caribou herds for the welfare of traditional caribou-using communities in northern Manitoba, Saskatchewan, Northwest Territories & Nunavut.

• First Nations Tax Commission (FNTC) / Commission de la fiscalité des premières nations (CFPN)
#321, 345 Yellowhead Hwy
Kamloops, BC V2H 1H1
Tel: 250-828-9857
Fax: 250-828-9858
mailkamloops@fntc.ca
www.fntc.ca
Other Communication: National Capital Region Email: mail@fntc.ca
The FNTC operates in the larger context of First Nation issues which goes beyond property tax. The FNTC is concerned with reducing the barriers to economic development on First Nation lands, increasing investor certainty, and enabling First Nations to be part of their regional economies. The FNTC is working to fill the institutional vacuum that has prevented First Nations from participating in the market economy and creating a national regulatory framework for First Nation tax systems that meets or beats the standards of provinces.

• Indian Oil & Gas Canada (IOGC) / Pétrole et gaz des Indiens du Canada
#100, 9911 Chiila Blvd.
Tsuu T'ina (Sarcee), AB T2W 6H6
Tel: 403-292-5625
Fax: 403-292-5618
ContactIOGC@inac-ainc.gc.ca
www.pgic-iogc.gc.ca
Indian Oil and Gas Canada (IOGC) is an organization committed to managing and regulating oil and gas resources on First Nation reserve lands. It is a special operating agency within Aboriginal Affairs & Northern Development Canada.

• Mackenzie Valley Environmental Impact Review Board
200 Scotia Centre
#5102, 50th Ave.
PO Box 938
Yellowknife, NT X1A 2N7
Tel: 867-766-7050
Fax: 867-766-7074
Toll-free: 866-912-3472
www.reviewboard.ca
In 1998, the Mackenzie Valley Environmental Impact Review Board was established under the Mackenzie Valley Resources Management Act. The co-management Review Board is made up of members nominated by First Nations & federal & territorial governments. Board members represent the interests of all residents of the Mackenzie Valley.

• Nunavut Impact Review Board
PO Box 1360
Cambridge Bay, NU X0B 0C0
Tel: 867-983-4600
Fax: 867-983-2594
Toll-free: 866-233-3033
info@nirb.ca
www.nirb.ca
An institution of the government established under the Nunavut Land Claims Agreement to conduct environmental & socio-economic assessments. The NIRB process involves participation by members of the community, Inuit organizations, the Government of Nunavut & the Government of Canada through the entire environmental assessment. Under the Canadian Environmental Assessment Act, the federal departments with specific responsibilities for the project must ensure that the requirements of the Act are met throughout the assessment process. This open process facilitates sound environmental stewardship & promotes economic & sustainable development.

• Nunavut Planning Commission
PO Box 2101
Cambridge Bay, NU X0B 0C0
Tel: 867-983-4625
Fax: 867-983-4626
www.nunavut.ca
Responsible for land use planning & environmental reporting & management in Nunavut.

• Nunavut Water Board
PO Box 119
Gjoa Haven, NU X0B 1J0
Tel: 867-360-6338
Fax: 867-360-6369
www.nunavutwaterboard.org
Responsible for the regulation, use & management of water in the Nunavut Settlement Area.

• Porcupine Caribou Management Board
PO Box 31723
Whitehorse, YT Y1A 6L3
Tel: 867-633-4780
Fax: 867-393-3904
pcmb@taiga.net
taiga.net/pcmb
Works to manage the Porcupine Caribou herd, one of the largest herds of migratory caribou in North America, & to protect & maintain its habitat.

Chief Financial Officer Sector / Secteur du dirigeant principal des finances
Tel: 819-953-1201
Fax: 819-953-4094

Chief Financial Officer, Susan MacGowan
Tel: 819-956-8188
Fax: 819-956-8193
Chief Information Officer, Information Management Branch, Tim Eryou
Tel: 819-994-3334
Fax: 819-956-8739
Director General, Planning & Resource Management, Pamela D'Eon
Tel: 819-994-6649
Fax: 819-953-8475
Director General, Corporate Accounting & Materiel Management, Andrew Francis
Tel: 819-994-6649
Fax: 819-953-8475
Director, Corporate Accounting & Reporting Directorate, Eva Jacobs
Tel: 819-934-0564
Fax: 819-953-3915

Education & Social Development Programs & Partnerships / Secteur des programmes et des partenariats en matière d'éducation et de dévelopment social
Fax: 819-953-4094

Assistant Deputy Minister, Françoise Ducros
Tel: 819-997-0020
Fax: 819-953-4094
Director General, Education Branch, Kathleen Keenan
Tel: 613-995-9392
Fax: 613-995-9393
Director General, Social Policy & Programs Branch, Sheilagh Murphy
Tel: 613-947-6508
Fax: 613-947-9242
Manager, Resources Planning & Management Directorate, Syndie Régimbal
Tel: 819-994-4406
Fax: 819-953-7627

Lands & Economic Development / Terres et Développement économique
Fax: 819-953-0248

Manages land-related statutory duties under the Indian Act & duties related to transferring land management services to First Nations. The Environment Directorate maintains an Inventory of Contaminated Sites on reserve land & coordinates remediation planning; responsible for the design & implementation of the Indian & Inuit Affairs Program Environmental Stewardship Strategy Action Plan; development of First Nations capacity, tools & enabling legislation in order that First Nations undertake their own environmental protection initiatives; supports First Nation, Métis & Inuit communities in efforts to promote environmental stewardship in a manner that is consistent with the principles of sustainable development.
Assistant Deputy Minister, Sara Filbee
Tel: 819-997-0114
Fax: 819-953-0248
Director General, Community Opportunities Branch, Andrew Beynon
Tel: 819-953-0517
Fax: 819-953-0649
Director General, Lands & Environmental Management, Margaret Buist
Tel: 819-997-8883
Fax: 819-953-3201
Director General, Policy & Coordination, Allan Clarke
Tel: 819-953-3004
Fax: 819-997-7054
Director General, Aboriginal Entrepreneurship Branch, Nicole Ladouceur
Tel: 819-953-0622
Fax: 819-997-7223

Northern Affairs / Affaires du Nord
Tel: 819-994-0044
Fax: 819-953-6121

Supports northern political & economic development through the management of federal interests; promotes sustainable development of the North's natural resources & northern communities. Works toward the devolution of all province-like responsibilities to northern governments of NWT, Nunavut & the Yukon. Develops & coordinates policies & programs related to northern environment & conservation, like the federal Northern Affairs Program Sustainable Development Strategy, the cleanup of northern hazardous waste sites, climate change & interdepartmental liaison with key policy departments like Environment Canada. Northern Contaminants Program is managed by AANDC in partnership with the federal departments of Health, Environment & Fisheries & Oceans, the territorial governments, Aboriginal organizations & university researchers, & its aim is to work toward reducing & eliminating, where possible, contaminants in traditionally harvested foods. The Northern Information Network is designed to link users to information about the Yukon, the Northwest Territories & Nunavut for more effective decision-making in areas such as resource management & economic development. NIN supports various research initiatives about the North, including project impact assessme nts, sustainable development strategies, wildlife management planning, land use planning & emergency preparedness. NIN has a directory of geo-referenced databases, provides a forum for discussion & has information & research documents pertaining to the North.
Assistant Deputy Minister, Janet King
Tel: 819-953-3760
Fax: 819-953-6121
Director General, Northern Oil & Gas Branch, Mimi Fortier
Tel: 819-953-9393
Fax: 819-934-6375
Director General, Natural Resources & Environment Branch, Paula Isaak
Tel: 819-997-9381
Fax: 819-953-8766
Acting Director General, Northern Policy & Science Integration Branch, John Kozij
Tel: 819-997-9449
Fax: 819-997-0552
Director General, Devolution & Territorial Relations, Stephen Van Dine
Tel: 819-997-0223
Fax: 819-953-9323
Executive Director, IPY 2012 Conference Secretariat, Julie Boyer
Tel: 613-995-6575
Fax: 613-995-7038
Director, Strategic Management Directorate, Trevor Thibault
Tel: 819-934-9886
Fax: 819-934-9888

Policy & Strategic Direction / Politique et direction stratégique
Fax: 819-953-5082

Senior Assistant Deputy Minister, Jean-François Tremblay
Tel: 819-994-7555
Fax: 819-953-5082
Director General, Strategic Planning & Analysis Branch, Claudine Gagnon
Tel: 819-994-7213
Fax: 819-953-0239
Director General, Strategic Policy & Research Branch, Nicole Kennedy
Tel: 819-953-3088
Fax: 819-994-7860
Director General, External Relations & Gender Issues Branch, Line Paré
Tel: 819-997-8212
Fax: 819-934-7192
Director General, Litigation Management & Resolution Branch, Daniel Ricard
Tel: 819-953-4968
Fax: 819-997-1679
Director General, Policy Services Branch, Jill Wherrett
Tel: 819-997-8359
Fax: 819-953-3320
Policy Analyst, Federal Relations & Issues Management, Nicholas Charney
Tel: 819-994-2658
Fax: 819-953-4366

Regional Operations / Opérations régionales
Fax: 819-953-9406

Senior Assistant Deputy Minister, Ron Hallman
Tel: 819-953-5577
Fax: 819-953-9406
Director General, Governance Branch, Brenda Kustra
Tel: 819-997-8154
Fax: 819-997-9541
Director General, Community Infrastructure Branch, Gail Mitchell
Tel: 819-953-4636
Fax: 819-997-3107

Resolution & Individual Affairs / Résolution et affaires individuelles
Fax: 613-996-2811

Assistant Deputy Minister, Élisabeth Châtillon
Tel: 613-996-2845
Fax: 613-996-2811
Director General, Kathryn Bruce
Tel: 613-947-6537
Fax: 613-996-2808
Director General, Settlement Agreement Operations, Marielle Doyon
Tel: 613-996-2890
Fax: 613-996-3053
Director General, Individual Affairs Branch, Ray Hatfield
Tel: 819-953-2605
Fax: 819-953-3371
Director General, Settlement Agreement Policy & Partnerships, Aideen Nabigon
Tel: 613-947-5209
Fax: 613-996-2456
Executive Director, Secure Certificate of Indian Status, Claudia Ferland
Tel: 819-934-7852
Fax: 819-953-9395
General Counsel & Director, Aboriginal Children's Issues, Caroline Clark
Tel: 613-996-0140
Fax: 613-996-1810
Manager, Business Integration & Modernization, Francine Duval
Tel: 800-567-9604
Fax: 819-953-9395

Treaties & Aboriginal Government / Traités et gouvernement autochtone
Fax: 819-953-3246

Senior Assistant Deputy Minister, Patrick Borbey
Tel: 819-953-3180
Fax: 819-953-3246
Director General, Policy Development & Coordination Branch, Perry Billingsley
Tel: 819-953-4315
Fax: 819-953-3855
Director General, Negotiations - West, Anita Boscariol
Tel: 604-775-7144
Fax: 604-775-7149
Director General, Specific Claims Branch, Anik Dupont
Tel: 819-994-2323
Fax: 819-994-4123
Director General, Implementation Branch, Stephen Gagnon
Tel: 819-994-3434
Fax: 819-953-6430
Director General, Negotiations - Central, Joëlle Montminy
Tel: 819-953-4365
Fax: 819-956-7011
Director General, Negotiations - East, Michael Nadler
Tel: 819-994-7521
Fax: 819-953-6768
Director General, Financial Management & Strategic Services, Tony Richard
Tel: 819-997-9757
Fax: 819-994-0273
Vancouver
Comprehensive Claims Branch, #600, 1138 Melville St., Vancouver, BC V6E 4S3
Tel: 604-775-7114
Fax: 604-775-7149

Regional Offices
Alberta
Canada Place, #620, 9700 Jasper Ave., Edmonton, AB T5J 4G2
Tel: 780-495-2773
Fax: 780-495-4354
Regional Director General, George Arcand Jr.
Tel: 780-495-2835
Fax: 780-495-4354
Atlantic
40 Havelock St., PO Box 160, Amherst, NS B4H 3Z3
Tel: 902-661-6201
Fax: 902-661-6237
Regional Director General, Ian Gray
Tel: 902-661-6262
Fax: 902-661-6237
British Columbia
#600, 1138 Melville St., Vancouver, BC V6E 4S3
Tel: 604-775-5100
Fax: 604-775-7149
Toll-Free: 866-553-0554
Regional Director General, Eric Magnuson
Tel: 604-666-5201
Fax: 604-775-7149
Manitoba
#200, 365 Hargrave St., Winnipeg, MB R3B 3A3
Tel: 204-983-2474
Fax: 866-817-3977
Toll-Free: 800-567-9604
Regional Director General, Anna Fontaine
Tel: 204-983-2474
Fax: 204-983-2936
Northwest Territories
#4914, 50th St., PO Box 1500, Yellowknife, NT X1A 2R3
Tel: 867-669-2500
Fax: 867-669-2709
Regional Director General, Trish Merrithew-Mercredi
Tel: 867-669-2501
Fax: 867-669-2703
Nunavut
PO Box 2200, Iqaluit, NU X0A 0H0
Tel: 867-975-4500
Fax: 867-975-4560
nuinfo@ainc-inac.gc.ca

Regional Director General, Robin Aitken
Tel: 867-975-4501
Fax: 867-975-4560
Director, Contaminated Sites, Natalie Plato
Tel: 867-975-4730
Ontario
25 St. Clair Ave. East, 8th Fl., Toronto, ON M4T 1M2
Tel: 416-973-6234
Fax: 416-954-6201
Toll-Free: 800-567-9604
TTY: 866-553-0554
Regional Director General, Joanne Wilkinson
Tel: 416-973-6201
Fax: 416-954-4326
Québec
#400, 320, rue St-Joseph est, Québec, QC G1K 9J2
Tél: 418-648-3270
Téléc: 866-817-3977
Ligne sans frais: 800-567-9604
TTY: 866-553-0554
Regional Director General, Pierre Nepton
Tel: 418-648-3270
Fax: 418-648-2266
Saskatchewan
#200, 1 First Nations Way, Regina, SK S4S 7K5
Tel: 306-780-5945
Fax: 306-780-5733
Other Communication: Other: 306-780-5392
Regional Director General, Riel Bellegarde
Tel: 306-780-6486
Fax: 306-780-7305
Yukon
#415C, 300 Main St., Whitehorse, YT Y1A 2B5
Tel: 867-667-3888
Fax: 867-667-3801
Toll-Free: 800-661-0451
ytinfo@inac-ainc.gc.ca
Regional Director General, Kerry Newkirk
Tel: 867-667-3300
Fax: 867-667-3801
Director, Environment, Michelle Edwards
Tel: 867-393-7934
Fax: 867-667-3861
Director, Governance, Dionne Savill
Tel: 867-667-3398
Fax: 867-667-3801

Agriculture & Agri-Food Canada / Agriculture et Agro-alimentaire Canada

1341 Baseline Rd., Ottawa, ON K1A 0C5
Tel: 613-773-1000
Fax: 613-773-2772
Toll-Free: 866-345-7972
info@agr.gc.ca
www.agr.ca
TTY: 613-773-2600
Other Communication: AgriInvest & AgriStability, Toll-Free Phone: 1-866-367-8506; Developing Innovative Agri-Products: 1-866-857-2287; Community Development Program: 1-877-295-7160

Agriculture & Agri-Food Canada is responsible for all matters related to agriculture. Examples of services provided by Agriculture & Agri-Food Canada include the following: research, development, & technology; policies & programs; the inspection & regulation of animals & plant-life forms; the coordination of rural development; the support of agricultural productivity & trade; the stabilization of farm incomes; & the provision of information. The goals of Agriculture & Agri-Food Canada are as follows: to achieve security of the food system; to ensure health of the environment; & to provide innovation for growth.
Agriculture & Agri-Food Canada reports to Parliament & Canadians through the Minister of Agriculture & Agri-Food & the Minister for the Canadian Wheat Board.

Acts Administered:
Agricultural Marketing Programs Act
Agricultural Products Marketing Act
Animal Pedigree Act
Canada Grain Act
Canadian Agricultural Loans Act
Canadian Dairy Commission Act
Canadian Wheat Board Act
Department of Agriculture & Agri-Food Act
Experimental Farm Stations Act
Farm Credit Canada Act
Farm Debt Mediation Act
Farm Income Protection Act
Farm Products Agencies Act
Prairie Farm Rehabilitation Act

Minister, Agriculture & Agri-Food; Minister, Canadian Wheat Board, Hon. Gerry Ritz
Tel: 613-773-1059
Fax: 613-773-1060
Ritz.G@parl.gc.ca

Parliamentary Secretary to the Minister, David Anderson
Tel: 613-773-1059
Fax: 613-992-5508
david.anderson@agr.gc.ca

Parliamentary Secretary to the Minister of Agriculture, Pierre Lemieux
Tel: 613-773-1059
Fax: 613-996-9123
lemieuxp@agr.gc.ca

Chief of Staff, Aaron Gairdner
Tel: 613-773-1059
Fax: 613-773-1060
aaron.gairdner@agr.gc.ca

Director, Issues Management, Steven Barrett
Tel: 613-773-1059
Fax: 613-773-1081
steven.barrett@agr.gc.ca

Director, Communications, Meagan Murdoch
Tel: 613-773-1059
Fax: 613-773-1060
meagan.murdoch@agr.gc.ca

Director, Policy, Mindy Pearce
Tel: 613-773-1059
Fax: 613-773-1081
mindy.pearce@agr.gc.ca

Regional Affairs Director, Andrea Smotra
Tel: 306-780-8236
Fax: 306-780-7292
andrea.smotra@agr.gc.ca

Director of Operations to the Ministry of State, Margaux Stastny
Tel: 613-773-1063
Fax: 613-773-1081
margaux.stastny@agr.gc.ca

Senior Policy Advisor, Jim Scott
Tel: 613-773-1059
Fax: 613-773-1060
jim.scott@agr.gc.ca

Policy Advisor, Karla House
Tel: 613-773-1059
Fax: 613-773-1060
karla.house@agr.gc.ca

Policy Advisor, Matthew J McBain
Tel: 613-773-1059
Fax: 613-773-1060
matthewj.mcbain@agr.gc.ca

Policy Advisor, Tyler McCann
Tel: 613-773-1059
Fax: 613-773-1081
tyler.mccann@agr.gc.ca

Policy Advisor, Dustin Pike
Tel: 613-773-1059
Fax: 613-773-1060
dustin.pike@agr.gc.ca

Regional Communications Advisor, Danielle Maier
Tel: 306-780-8236
Fax: 306-780-7292
danielle.maier@agr.gc.ca

Associated Agencies, Boards & Commissions:

• Canadian Dairy Commission (CDC) / Commission canadienne du lait
Central Experimental Farm, NCC Driveway, Bldg. 55
960 Carling Ave.
Ottawa, ON K1A 0Z2
Tel: 613-792-2000
Fax: 613-792-2009
TTY: 613-792-2082
cdc-ccl@cdc-ccl.gc.ca; carole.cyr@cdc-ccl.gc.ca
www.cdc.ca
Other Communication: Special Milk Class Permits, Phone: 613-792-2057; Dairy Imports & Exports, Phone: 613-792-2010

• Canadian Food Inspection Agency (CFIA) / Agence canadienne d'inspection des aliments
1400 Merivale Rd.
Ottawa, ON K1A 0Y9
Tel: 613-225-2342
Fax: 613-228-6601
Toll-free: 800-442-2342
TTY: 800-465-7735
www.inspection.gc.ca
Other Communication: Atlantic Area, Phone: 506-851-7400; Ontario Area: 519-837-9400; Québec Area: 514-283-8888; Western Area: 403-292-4301

• Canadian Grain Commission (CGC) / Commission canadienne des grains
#600, 303 Main St.
Winnipeg, MB R3C 3G8
Tel: 204-983-2770
Fax: 204-983-2751
Toll-free: 800-853-6705
TTY: 866-317-4289
contact@grainscanada.gc.ca
www.grainscanada.gc.ca
Other Communication: Grain Sanitation & Infestation Control Industry Services, Fax: 204-984-7550; Licensing & Security Unit, Fax: 204-983-4654; Statistics Unit, Phone: 204-983-2739

• Canadian International Grains Institute / Institut international du Canada pour le grain

• Canadian Wheat Board (CWB) / Commission canadienne du blé
423 Main St.
PO Box 816 Main
Winnipeg, MB R3C 2P5
Tel: 204-983-0239
Fax: 204-983-3841
Toll-free: 800-275-4292
questions@cwb.ca; farmerservice@cwb.ca
www.cwb.ca
Other Communication: Media relations, Phone: 204-983-3101; Government relations, Phone: 204-984-8167

• Canadian Pari-Mutuel Agency (CPMA)
Toll-free: 800-268-8835
cpmawebacpm@agr.gc.ca
www4.agr.gc.ca/AAFC-AAC/display-afficher.do?id=1204043533186&lang
Other Communication: Toll-Free Phone, French: 1-800-326-3344; Equine Drug Control Program, Phone: 613-949-0745

• Farm Credit Canada (FCC) / Financement agricole Canada
1800 Hamilton St.
PO Box 4320
Regina, SK S4P 4L3
Tel: 306-780-8100
Fax: 306-780-8919
Toll-free: 888-332-3301
TTY: 306-780-6974
csc@fcc-fac.ca
www.fcc-fac.ca
Other Communication: Careers, E-mail: hr-rh@fcc-fac.ca; Media & Publications: Communications@fcc-fac.ca; Legal Services: legal_services@fcc-fac.ca; FCC Learning: fcclearning@fcc-fac.ca

• Farm Products Council of Canada (FPCC)
Canada Bldg.
344 Slater St., 10th Fl.
Ottawa, ON K1R 7Y3
Tel: 613-995-6752
Fax: 613-995-2097
TTY: 613-943-3707
fpcc-cpac@agr.gc.ca
www.fpcc-cpac.gc.ca

Agri-Environment Services Branch (AESB)

Tower 4, 1341 Baseline Rd., Ottawa, ON K1A 0C5
Tel: 613-759-1000
Fax: 613-773-1211
www4.agr.gc.ca/AAFC-AAC/display-afficher.do?id=1187362338955&lang
Other Communication: Agroforestry Development Centre, Phone: 1-866-766-2284, Fax: 306-695-2568; Canada-Manitoba Crop Diversification Centre, Phone: 204-834-6000, Fax: 204-834-3777

The Agri-Environment Services Branch integrates the following components: Prairie Farm Rehabilitation Administration; National Land & Water Information Service; & Agri-Environmental Policy Bureau. The mission of the branch is to deliver innovative environmental solutions to the agriculture & agri-food sector.
Applied Technology Development Centres of the Agri-Environment Services Branch include the following: Agroforestry Development Centre (formerly known as the Prairie Farm Rehabilitation Administration); Canada-Saskatchewan Irrigation Diversification Centre; & the Canada-Manitoba Crop Diversification Centre.
Assistant Deputy Minister, Jamshed Merchant
Tel: 613-773-1200

Fax: 613-773-1211
jamshed.merchant@agr.gc.ca
Director General, Agri-Environmental Knowledge, Innovation, & Technology Directorate, Dr. Richard Butts
Tel: 506-452-4802
Fax: 506-474-7533
richard.butts@agr.gc.ca
850 Lincoln Rd.
PO Box 20280
Fredericton, NB E3B 4Z7
Acting Director General, Agri-Environmental Adaptation & Practice Change Directorate, Alan Parkinson
Tel: 306-780-5081
Fax: 306-780-6533
alan.parkinson@agr.gc.ca
FCC Tower
#408, 1800 Hamilton St.
Regina, SK S4P 4L2
Director General, Agri-Environmental Policy & Strategic Priorities Directorate, Greg Strain
Tel: 613-773-1207
Fax: 613-773-1222
greg.strain@agr.gc.ca
Tower 4
#208, 1341 Baseline Rd.
Ottawa, ON K1A 0C5

Communications & Consultations Branch
Tower 7, 1341 Baseline Rd., Ottawa, ON K1A 0C7
Tel: 613-759-1000
Fax: 613-773-2772

Assistant Deputy Minister, Jodi Redmond
Tel: 613-773-2922
Fax: 613-773-2772
jodi.redmond@agr.gc.ca
Director General, Communications Services, Jane Taylor
Tel: 613-773-2840
Fax: 613-773-2772
jane.taylor@agr.gc.ca
Director, E-Communications, Joan Anderson
Tel: 613-773-2601
Fax: 613-773-2398
joan.anderson@agr.gc.ca
Director, Strategic & Ministerial Communications, Steven Jurgutis
Tel: 613-773-2760
Fax: 613-773-2772
steven.jurgutis@agr.gc.ca
Director, Regions, Outreach & Events, Darell M. Pack
Tel: 613-773-2755
Fax: 613-773-2772
darell.pack@agr.gc.ca
Director, Translation & Revision Services, Caroline Rahal
Tel: 613-773-0986
Fax: 613-773-2397
caroline.rahal@agr.gc.ca

Corporate Management
Tower 4, 1341 Baseline Rd., Ottawa, ON K1A 0C5
Tel: 613-759-1000
Fax: 613-773-0911

Assistant Deputy Minister, Pierre Corriveau
Tel: 613-773-1330
Fax: 613-773-1233
pierre.corriveau@agr.gc.ca
Director General, Asset Management & Capital Planning, Lynden Hillier
Tel: 613-773-0923
Fax: 613-773-0966
lynden.hillier@agr.gc.ca
Director General, Finance & Resource Management Services, Bev Levere
Tel: 613-773-1332
Fax: 613-773-0777
bev.levere@agr.gc.ca
Acting Director General, Strategic Management, Debbie Winker
Tel: 613-773-1344
Fax: 613-773-0911
debbie.winker@agr.gc.ca
Acting Executive Director, Canadian Pari-Mutuel Agency, Steve Suttie
Tel: 613-949-0726
Fax: 613-949-0750
steve.suttie@agr.gc.ca

Deputy Minister's Office / Bureau du sous-ministre
Tower 7, 1341 Baseline Rd., Ottawa, ON K1A 0C5
Tel: 613-759-1011
Fax: 613-759-1040

The Deputy Minister's Office oversees the following organizations: Corporate Secretariat; Food Safety Review Secretariat; & Portfolio Coordination Secretariat.
Deputy Minister, Agriculture & Agri-Food Canada, John Knubley
Tel: 613-773-1101
Fax: 613-773-1040
john.knubley@agr.gc.ca
Associate Deputy Minister, Agriculture & Agri-Food Canada, Claude Carrière
Tel: 613-773-1011
Fax: 613-773-1061
claude.carriere@agr.gc.ca
Executive Director, Portfolio Coordination Secretariat, Todd F. Hunter
Tel: 613-773-1062
Fax: 613-773-1051
todd.hunter@agr.gc.ca
Executive Director, Food Safety Review Secretariat, Anna Romano
Tel: 613-773-2128
Fax: 613-773-2939
anna.romano@agr.gc.ca
Manager, Parliamentary Relations Office, Kristen Bassett
Tel: 613-773-1019
Fax: 613-773-1051
kristen.bassett@agr.gc.ca
Manager, Finance & Administration, Corporate Secretariat, Jeanne Johnson
Tel: 613-773-1057
Fax: 613-773-1061
jeanne.johnson@agr.gc.ca

Farm Financial Programs Branch / Direction générale des programmes de financement agricoles
Tower 7, 1341 Baseline Rd., Ottawa, ON K1A 0C5
Tel: 613-759-1000
Fax: 613-773-2121

The Farm Financial Programs Branch of Agriculture & Agri-Food Canada oversees the following organizations: Agriculture Transformation Programs Directorate; Business Risk Management Program Development; Centre of Program Excellence (COPE); Farm Income Programs Directorate; Finance & Renewal Programs Directorate; & Service Policy & Transformation Directorate.
Assistant Deputy Minister, Farm Financial Programs Branch, Rita Moritz
Tel: 613-773-2815
Fax: 613-773-2121
rita.moritz@agr.gc.ca
Acting Director General, Finance & Renewal Programs Directorate, Sean Malone
Tel: 613-773-2005
Fax: 613-773-2099
sean.malone@agr.gc.ca
Director General, Centre of Program Excellence (COPE), Ray Edwards
Tel: 613-773-0612
Fax: 613-773-1911
ray.edwards@agr.gc.ca
Director General, Business Risk Management Program Development, Danny Foster
Tel: 613-773-2100
Fax: 613-773-2198
danny.foster@agr.gc.ca
Acting Director General, Farm Income Programs Directorate, Patti Miller
Tel: 204-984-5645
Fax: 204-983-7557
patti.miller@agr.gc.ca
Director General, Agriculture Transformation Programs Directorate, Linda Parsons
Tel: 613-773-1900
Fax: 613-773-1911
linda.parsons@agr.gc.ca
Executive Director, Grants & Contributions Delivery Project, Johanne Y. Langevin
Tel: 613-773-2006
Fax: 613-773-2121
johanne.langevin@agr.gc.ca

Human Resources Branch / Direction générale des ressources humaines
Tower 1, 560 Rochester St., Ottawa, ON K1A 0C5
Tel: 613-759-1000
Fax: 613-759-7105

Assistant Deputy Minister, Human Resources Branch, Johanne Bélisle
Tel: 613-759-1196
Fax: 613-759-7105
johanne.belisle@agr.gc.ca
Acting Director General, Planning, Policy & Workplace Programs, Scott Aughey
Tel: 613-759-6527
scott.aughey@agr.gc.ca
Director General, Planning, Policy, & Workplace Programs, Catherine Conrad
Tel: 613-715-5056
Fax: 613-715-5150
catherine.conrad@agr.gc.ca
Director General, Workplace Relations, Caroline Dunn
Tel: 613-715-5260
Fax: 613-759-6143
caroline.dunn@agr.gc.ca
Acting Director General, Client Services, Maureen Meaney
Tel: 613-759-6231
Fax: 613-715-5244
maureen.meaney@agr.gc.ca
Senior Director, Learning, Development, & Official Languages, Laurie Hunter
Tel: 613-759-7434
Fax: 613-792-3426
laurie.hunter@agr.gc.ca
Acting Senior Director, Staffing & Recruitment, Strategic Resources, Brian McCarthy
Tel: 613-759-6683
Fax: 613-759-7767
brian.mccarthy@agr.gc.ca
Senior Director, Organizational Effectiveness & Compensation, Client Services, Michael Morin
Tel: 613-694-2578
Fax: 613-759-7471
michael.morin@agr.gc.ca

Information Systems Branch / Direction générale des systèmes d'information
Tower 4, 1341 Baseline Rd., Ottawa, ON K1A 0C5
Tel: 613-759-1000
Fax: 613-773-0676

The Information Systems Branch of Agriculture & Agri-Food Canada is reponsible for the following organizations: Applications Development Directorate; Information Management Services; IT Operations; & the Strategic Management Directorate.
Chief Information Officer, Peter Bruce
Tel: 613-773-1395
Fax: 613-773-0676
peter.bruce@agr.gc.ca
Director General, IT Operations, Gail Eagen
Tel: 613-773-0400
Fax: 613-773-0444
gail.eagen@agr.gc.ca
Director General, Applications Development Directorate, Angus Howieson
Tel: 613-759-7735
Fax: 613-759-6045
angus.howieson@agr.gc.ca
Director General, Information Management Services, Jeff Lamirande
Tel: 613-773-0304
Fax: 613-773-0666
jeff.lamirande@agr.gc.ca
Acting Director General, Strategic Management Directorate, Rama Rai
Tel: 613-773-0615
Fax: 613-773-0666
rama.rai@agr.gc.ca
Chief, Integrated Telecom Services, Systems Management, Pierre Cayen
Tel: 613-773-0537
Fax: 613-773-0500
pierre.cayen@agr.gc.ca
Director, Canadian Agriculture Library, Danielle Jacques
Tel: 613-773-1448
Fax: 613-773-1499
danielle.jacques@agr.gc.ca
Director, Programs & Corporate Applications, Cameron MacDonald
Tel: 613-759-6940
Fax: 613-694-2353
cameron.macdonald@agr.gc.ca

Legal Services / Services juridiques
Tower 7, 1341 Baseline Rd., Ottawa, ON K1A 0C5
Tel: 613-759-1000
Fax: 613-773-2929

General Counsel & Executive Director, Louise Sénéchal
Tel: 613-773-2901
Fax: 613-773-2929
louise.senechal@agr.gc.ca
Business Manager, Aysha Johnson
Tel: 613-773-2915
Fax: 613-773-2929
aysha.johnson@agr.gc.ca
Information Specialist, Aurora Bravar
Tel: 613-773-2920
Fax: 613-773-2929
aurora.bravara@agr.gc.ca
Senior Counsel, Duane Schippers
Tel: 613-773-2913
Fax: 613-773-2929
duane.schippers@agr.gc.ca
Senior Counsel, Theresa Siok
Tel: 613-773-2914

Fax: 613-773-2929
theresa.siok@agr.gc.ca

Market & Industry Services Branch (MISB) / Direction générale des services à l'industrie et aux marchés
Tower 5, 1341 Baseline Rd., Ottawa, ON K1A 0C5
Tel: 613-759-1000
Fax: 613-773-1711
Other Communication: Government of Canada Export Services Information, Toll-Free Phone: 1-888-576-4444
The Market & Industry Services Branch of Agriculture & Agri-Food Canada oversees the following organizations: Bilateral Relations & Technical Trade Policy Directorate; Food Value Chain Bureau; International Markets Bureau; Market Access Secretariat; Negotiations & Multilateral Trade Policy Directorate; & the Operations Directorate. The Operations Directorate operates regional offices throughout Canada, which provide access to market & trade programs & services. Marketing & trade officers offer the following information: statistics by country & product; market access advice; investment opportunities; regulatory issues; export counselling; & news about promotional events.
Assistant Deputy Minister, Steve Tierney
Tel: 613-773-1790
Fax: 613-773-1755
steve.tierney@agr.gc.ca
Director General, Multilateral Relations, Policy & Engagement Directorate, Blair Coomber
Tel: 613-773-1600
Fax: 613-773-1616
blair.coomber@agr.gc.ca
Director General & Chief Agriculture Negotiator, Trade Agreements & Negotiations, Gilles Gauthier
Tel: 613-773-0985
Fax: 613-773-1755
gilles.gauthier@agr.gc.ca
Director General, Market Access Secretariat, Fred Gorrell
Tel: 613-773-1512
Fax: 613-773-0199
fred.gorrell@agr.gc.ca
Director General, Operations Directorate, Dr. Jaspinder Komal
Tel: 613-773-1501
Fax: 613-773-1500
jaspinder.komal@agr.gc.ca
Director General, Sector Development & Analysis Directorate, Susie Miller
Tel: 613-773-1750
Fax: 613-773-0300
susie.miller@agr.gc.ca
Director General, International Markets Bureau, Paul Murphy
Tel: 613-773-1517
Fax: 613-773-1500
paul.murphy@agr.gc.ca

Market & Industry Services Branch Regional Offices
Market & Industry Services Branch Regional Offices
Alberta & Territories Regional Office
#720, 9700 Jasper Ave., Edmonton, AB T5J 4G5
Tel: 780-495-4141
Fax: 780-495-3324
Regional Director, Rodney Dlugos
Tel: 780-495-5525
Fax: 780-495-3324
rodney.dlugos@agr.gc.ca
Deputy Director, Janet Dorey
Tel: 780-495-5526
Fax: 780-495-3324
janet.dorey@agr.gc.ca
Atlantic Regional Office
#405, 1791 Barrington St., PO Box 248, Halifax, NS B3J 2N7
Tel: 902-426-3198
Fax: 902-426-3439
The Atlantic Regional Office in Halifax, Nova Scotia, is the headquarters for the following operations: New Brunswick Operations (Phone: 506-452-3706, Fax: 506-452-3509); Newfoundland & Labrador Operations (Phone: 709-772-4063, Fax: 709-772-4803); Nova Scotia Operations (Phone: 902-896-0332, Fax: 902-896-0100); & Prince Edward Island Operations (Phone: 902-566-7300, Fax: 902-566-7316).
Regional Director, Janet Steele
Tel: 902-426-7171
Fax: 902-426-3439
janet.steele@agr.gc.ca
Deputy Director, Prince Edward Island Operations, Heath Coles
Tel: 902-566-7305
Fax: 902-566-7316
heath.coles@agr.gc.ca
Deputy Director, Newfoundland & Labrador Operations, Brian Goldsworthy
Tel: 709-772-4055
Fax: 709-772-4803
brian.goldsworthy@agr.gc.ca
Acting Deputy Director, New Brunswick Operations, Dino Kubik
Tel: 506-452-3753
Fax: 506-452-3509
dino.kubik@agr.gc.ca
Deputy Director, Nova Scotia Operations, Shelley Manning
Tel: 902-896-0098
Fax: 902-896-0100
shelley.manning@agr.gc.ca
British Columbia Regional Office
#420, 4321 Stillcreek Dr., Burnaby, BC V5C 6S7
Tel: 604-666-6344
Fax: 604-666-7235
Regional Director, John Berry
Tel: 604-666-6344
Fax: 604-666-7235
john.berry@agr.gc.ca
Deputy Director, Michelle Soucie
Tel: 604-666-3054
Fax: 604-666-7235
michelle.soucie@agr.gc.ca
Manitoba Regional Office
303 Main St., Winnipeg, MB R3C 3G7
Tel: 204-983-3032
Fax: 204-983-4583
Acting Regional Director, Bob Nawolsky
Tel: 204-983-3891
Fax: 204-983-4583
bob.nawolsky@agr.gc.ca
Acting Deputy Director, Ron Wonneck
Tel: 204-983-4596
Fax: 204-983-4583
ron.wonneck@agr.gc.ca
Ontario Regional Office
174 Stone Rd. West, Guelph, ON N1G 4S9
Tel: 519-837-9400
Fax: 519-837-9782
Acting Regional Director, Marg Bancroft
Tel: 519-837-5821
Fax: 519-837-9782
marg.bancroft@agr.gc.ca
Deputy Director, Karl Michelazzi
Tel: 519-780-8097
Fax: 519-837-9782
karl.michelazzi@agr.gc.ca
Deputy Director, Bill Robinson
Tel: 519-837-5822
Fax: 519-837-9782
bill.robinson@agr.gc.ca
Québec Regional Office
2001, rue Université, 7e étage, Montréal, QC H3A 3N2
Tel: 514-283-8888
Fax: 514-496-3966
Regional Director, Sandra Gagné
Tel: 514-315-6170
Fax: 514-496-3966
sandra.gagne@agr.gc.ca
Regional Deputy Director, Scott Patterson
Tel: 514-315-6171
Fax: 514-496-3966
scott.patterson2@agr.gc.ca
Saskatchewan Regional Office
1800 Hamilton St., Regina, SK S4P 4K7
Tel: 306-780-5545
Fax: 306-780-7360
Regional Director, Dean L. Vey
Tel: 306-780-7065
Fax: 306-780-7360
dean.vey@agr.gc.ca
Deputy Director, Wendy Collinge
Tel: 306-780-5452
Fax: 306-780-7360
wendy.collinge@agr.gc.ca
Deputy Director, Markets & Trade, Gavin M. Conacher
Tel: 306-780-5216
Fax: 306-780-7360
gavin.conacher@agr.gc.ca

Regional Coordination & Correspondence
Tel: 613-759-7558
Fax: 613-773-1500
Deputy Director, Regional Coordination & Correspondence, Josy Parrotta-Marck
Tel: 613-773-1876
Fax: 613-773-1500
josy.parrotta-marck@agr.gc.ca
Senior Commerce Officer, Nathalie Bradbury
Tel: 613-773-0843
Fax: 613-773-1500
nathalie.bradbury@agr.gc.ca

Office of Audit & Evaluation
Tower 4, 1341 Baseline Rd., Ottawa, ON K1A 0C5
Tel: 613-759-1000
Fax: 613-773-0660
Agriculture & Agri-Food Canada's Office of Audit & Evaluation is responsible for the following services: evaluation; governance & review; & internal audit & assurance.
Chief Audit & Evaluation Executive, Graham Barr
Tel: 613-773-0650
Fax: 613-773-0660
graham.barr@agr.gc.ca
Director, Governance & Review Services, Jennifer Moher
Tel: 613-773-1773
Fax: 613-773-0660
jennifer.moher@agr.gc.ca
Director, Evaluation Services, Sally Scott
Tel: 613-773-0655
Fax: 613-773-0660
sally.scott@agr.gc.ca
Director, Internal Audit, Lyne Castonguay
Tel: 613-773-0669
Fax: 613-773-0660
lyne.castonguay@agr.gc.ca

Canada-Saskatchewan Irrigation Diversification Centre
901 McKenzie St. South, PO Box 700, Outlook, SK S0L 2N0
Tel: 306-867-5400
Fax: 306-867-9656
csidc@agr.gc.ca

Manitoba
#200, 303 Main St., Winnipeg, MB R3C 3G7
Tel: 204-984-3695
Fax: 204-983-2178

Manitoba Crop Diversification Centre
PO Box 309, Carberry, MB R0K 0H0
Tel: 204-834-6005
Fax: 204-834-3777

Northern Alberta & BC
Canada Place, #945, 9700 Jasper Ave. NW, Edmonton, AB T5J 4C3
Tel: 780-495-3307
Fax: 780-495-4504

Northern Saskatchewan
#1101, 11 Innovation Blvd., Saskatoon, SK S7N 3H5
Tel: 306-975-4693
Fax: 306-975-4594

Agroforestry Development Centre
PO Box 940, Indian Head, SK S0G 2K0
Tel: 306-695-2284
Fax: 306-695-2568

Southern Alberta
Harry Hays Bldg., #600, 138 - 4 Ave. SE, Calgary, AB T2G 4Z2
Tel: 403-292-5638
Fax: 403-292-5659

Southern Saskatchewan
#603, 1800 Hamilton St., Regina, SK S4P 4L2
Tel: 306-780-5150
Fax: 306-780-6778

Research Branch / Direction générale de la recherche
Tower 5, 1341 Baseline Rd., Ottawa, ON K1A 0C5
Tel: 613-759-1000
Fax: 613-773-1866
Agriculture & Agri-Food Canada's Research Branch consists of the following organizations: Innovation Directorate; International Scientific Cooperation Bureau; Land Resources; Science Centres Directorate, Science Partnerships Directorate; & Science Policy & Planning. Scientists from Agriculture & Agri-Food Canada work on projects to benefit the agricultural & agri-food sector at research centres located across Canada.
Acting Assistant Deputy Minister, Jody Aylard
Tel: 613-773-1860
Fax: 613-773-1866
jody.aylard@agr.gc.ca
Director General, Science Policy & Planning, Dr. Christiane Deslauriers, PhD
Tel: 613-773-1870
Fax: 613-773-1877
christiane.deslauriers@agr.gc.ca
Director General, Science Partnerships Directorate, Dr. Stephen D. Morgan Jones, PhD
Tel: 403-317-2200
Fax: 403-317-2197
steve.morganjones@agr.gc.ca
Director General, Science Centres Directorate, Dr. Gilles Saindon, PhD
Tel: 613-773-1843
Fax: 613-773-1844
gilles.saindon@agr.gc.ca
Director, Multilateral Science Relations, International Scientific Cooperation Bureau, Brad Fraleigh
Tel: 613-773-1838
Fax: 613-773-1822
brad.fraleigh@agr.gc.ca
Chief Scientist, International Scientific Cooperation Bureau, Dr. Yvon Martel, PhD
Tel: 613-773-1830

Fax: 613-773-1833
yvon.martel@agr.gc.ca
Chief Officer for Scientific Relations, China, International Scientific Cooperation Bureau, Jianqiang (Joe) Zhou, PhD
Tel: 613-759-1744
Fax: 613-773-1833
joe.zhou@agr.gc.ca

Research Centres

Atlantic Food & Horticulture Research Centre
32 Main St., Kentville, NS B4N 1J5
Tel: 902-679-5333
Fax: 902-679-2311
Acting Science Director, Crop Production Systems, Dr. Mark Hodges, PhD
Tel: 902-679-5544
Fax: 902-679-5784
mark.hodges@agr.gc.ca
Manager, Farm, Innovation & Renewal, David L. Bowlby
Tel: 902-679-5589
Fax: 902-670-0004
david.bowlby@agr.gc.ca

Brandon Research Centre
RR#3, PO Box 1000A, Brandon, MB R7A 5Y3
Tel: 204-726-7650
Fax: 204-728-3858
Manager, Research, Dr. Fernando Selles, PhD
Tel: 204-578-3539
Fax: 204-578-3528
fernando.selles@agr.gc.ca
Manager, Farm, Clay Jackson
Tel: 204-578-3610
Fax: 204-578-3522
clayton.jackson@agr.gc.ca

Cereal Research Centre
195 Dafoe Rd., Winnipeg, MB R3T 2M9
Tel: 204-983-5533
Fax: 204-983-4604
Manager, Research, Dr. David Wall
Tel: 204-983-0099
Fax: 204-984-6333
david.wall@agr.gc.ca
Science Director, Water & Soil Resources, Dr. Johanne B. Boisvert, PhD
Tel: 204-983-0466
Fax: 204-983-4604
johanne.boisvert@agr.gc.ca

Crops & Livestock Research Centre
440 University Ave., Charlottetown, PE C1A 4N6
Tel: 902-566-6800
Fax: 902-566-6821
The Crops & Livestock Research Centre (CLRC) in Charlottetown, Prince Edward Island is one of Agriculture and Agri-Food Canada's network of 19 research centres. The Centre's mandate is to develop scientific knowledge & new technologies in agriculture with the prime focus on Prince Edward Island & Atlantic Canada.
Manager, Research, Dr. Maria Rodriguez
Tel: 902-566-6817
Fax: 902-566-6821
maria.rodriguez@agr.gc.ca
Manager, Research Operations, Roddy C. Pratt
Tel: 902-672-6426
Fax: 902-566-6821
roddy.pratt@agr.gc.ca

Dairy & Swine Research & Development Centre
2000, rue College, CP 90 Lennoxville, Sherbrooke, QC J1M 1Z3
Tél: 819-565-9171
Téléc: 819-564-5507
The Dairy & Swine Research & Development Centre oversees the operations of the Beef Research Farm in Kapuskasing, Ontario, as well as the Office of Intellectual Property & Commercialization in Sherbrooke, Québec.
Manager, Research, Dr. Alain Giguère
Tel: 819-565-9174 ext: 103
Fax: 819-564-5407
alain.giguere@agr.gc.ca
Science Director, Livestock Production Systems, Dr. Jacques Surprenant, PhD, MPA
Tel: 819-565-9174 ext: 101
Fax: 819-564-4974
jacques.surprenant@agr.gc.ca
Head Herdsman, Kapuskasing Beef Research Farm, Maurice Portelance
Tel: 705-335-6148
Fax: 705-337-6000
maurice.portelance@agr.gc.ca

Eastern Cereal & Oilseed Research Centre
960 Carling Ave., Ottawa, ON K1A 0C6
Tel: 613-759-1858
Fax: 613-759-1970
Manager, Research, Dr. Marc Savard
Tel: 613-759-1683
Fax: 613-759-1970
marc.savard@agr.gc.ca
Manager, Research Support, Ron Wheeler
Tel: 613-759-1544
Fax: 613-952-6438
ron.wheeler@agr.gc.ca
Science Director, Food & Health, Dr. Michèle Marcotte, PhD, Eng
Tel: 613-759-1525
Fax: 613-759-1970
michele.marcotte@agr.gc.ca

Food Research & Development Centre
3600, boul Casavant ouest, Saint-Hyacinthe, QC J2S 8E3
Tel: 450-773-1105
Fax: 450-773-8461
Manager, Research, Dr. Christian J. Toupin, PhD
Tel: 450-768-3331
Fax: 450-773-2888
christian.toupin@agr.gc.ca
Science Director, Food Production, Safety, & Quality, Gabriel Piette
Tel: 450-768-3304
Fax: 450-773-2888
gabriel.piette@agr.gc.ca

Greenhouse & Processing Crops Research Centre
2585 Country Rd. 20, Harrow, ON N0R 1G0
Tel: 519-738-2251
Fax: 519-738-2929
Manager, Research, Ranjana Sharma
Tel: 519-738-1208
Fax: 519-738-2929
ranjana.sharma@agr.gc.ca
Manager, Integrated Services, Adrian Lancop
Tel: 519-738-1210
Fax: 519-738-2929
adrian.lancop@agr.gc.ca
Science Director, Integrated Pest Management, Environmental Health, Dr. Gary Whitfield
Tel: 519-738-1218
Fax: 519-738-3756
gary.whitfield@agr.gc.ca

Guelph Food Research Centre
93 Stone Rd. West, Guelph, ON N1G 5C9
Tel: 519-829-2400
Fax: 519-829-2600
Manager, Research, Dr. Punidadas Piyasena
Tel: 519-780-8063
Fax: 519-829-2602
puni.piyasena@agr.gc.ca
Science Director, Gabriel Piette
Tel: 450-768-3304
Fax: 450-773-2888
gabriel.pietter@agr.gc.ca

Horticulture Research & Development Centre
430, boul Gouin, Saint-Jean-sur-Richelieu, QC J3B 3E6
Tel: 450-346-4494
Fax: 450-346-7740
Manager, Research, Roger Chagnon
Tel: 450-515-2001
Fax: 450-346-7908
roger.chagnon@agr.gc.ca
Science Director, Jacques Suprenant
Tel: 819-565-9174 ext: 101
Fax: 450-346-7908
jacques.suprenant@agr.gc.ca
Manager, Greenhouse, Guy Boulet
Tel: 450-515-2016
Fax: 450-346-7740
guy.boulet@agr.gc.ca

Lacombe Research Centre
6000 C & E Trail, Lacombe, AB T4L 1W1
Tel: 403-782-8100
Fax: 403-782-6120
The Lacombe Research Centre is responsible for the operations of research farms in Beaverlodge & Fort Vermilion in Alberta.
Manager, Research, Rick Lawrence
Tel: 403-782-8110
Fax: 403-782-4308
rick.lawrence@agr.gc.ca
Science Director, Paul McCaughey
Tel: 306-956-7211
Fax: 306-956-7248
paul.mccaughey@agr.gc.ca
Manager, Farm, Ken B. Grimson
Tel: 403-782-8139
Fax: 403-782-8186
ken.grimson@agr.gc.ca
Foreman, Fort Vermilion Research Farm, Joe Unruh
Tel: 780-927-3253
Fax: 780-927-3330
joe.unruh@agr.gc.ca

Lethbridge Research Centre
5403 - 1st Ave. South, PO Box 3000, Lethbridge, AB T1J 4B1
Tel: 403-327-4561
Fax: 403-382-3156
The Lethbridge Research Centre oversees the operations of the Onefour Research Substation, the Stavely Research Substation, & the Vauxhall Research Substation in Alberta.
Manager, Research, Dr. Brian Freeze, PhD
Tel: 403-317-3445
Fax: 403-317-2211
brian.freeze@agr.gc.ca
Manager, Facility, Donavan T. Casson
Tel: 403-317-2233
Fax: 403-317-3491
donavan.casson@agr.gc.ca
Manager, Feed Mill, Dave Dancoisne
Tel: 403-317-3383
Fax: 403-382-3156
dave.dancoisne@agr.gc.ca
Manager, Stavely Research Substation Site, Albert J. Middleton
Tel: 403-549-2152
Fax: 403-549-3744
albert.middleton@agr.gc.ca
Manager, Vauxhall Research Substation Site, Jim Sukeroff
Tel: 403-654-2255
Fax: 403-654-4243
jim.sukeroff@agr.gc.ca
Manager, Onefour Research Substation Site, Ian Walker
Tel: 403-868-2364
Fax: 403-868-2489
ian.walker@agr.gc.ca
Science Director, Crop Genetic Enhancement, Dr. Jeff Stewart
Tel: 403-317-2208
Fax: 403-317-2197
jeff.stewart@agr.gc.ca

Pacific Agri-Food Research Centre (PARC)
4200 Hwy. 97, PO Box 5000, Summerland, BC V0H 1Z0
Tel: 250-494-7711
Fax: 250-494-0755
The Pacific Agri-Food Research Centre oversees the following organizations: the Agassiz Site, the Kamloops Range Research Unit, & the Summerland Site.
Research Manager, Summerland Site, Kenna MacKenzie
Tel: 250-494-6358
Fax: 250-494-6415
kenna.mackenzie@agr.gc.ca
Research Manager, Agassiz Site, Sankaran KrishnaRaj
Tel: 604-796-1709
Fax: 604-796-0359
sankaran.krishnaraj@agr.gc.ca
Facility Manager, Kamloops Range Research Unit, Larry Maio
Tel: 250-554-5227
Fax: 250-554-5229
larry.maio@agr.gc.ca
Integrated Services Manager, Summerland Site, Bruce Jensen
Tel: 250-494-6357
Fax: 250-494-0755
bruce.jensen@agr.gc.ca
Field Services Manager, Summerland Site, Mark Neufield
Tel: 250-494-6427
Fax: 250-494-0755
mark.neufield@agr.gc.ca
Grounds & Greenhouse Manager, Summerland Site, David Weir
Tel: 250-494-6387
Fax: 250-494-0755
david.weir@agr.gc.ca

Potato Research Centre
850 Lincoln Rd., PO Box 20280, Fredericton, NB E3B 4Z7
Tel: 506-452-3260
Fax: 506-452-3316
The Potato Research Centre is also responsible for the Senator Hervé J. Michaud Research Farm, located in Bouctouche, New Brunswick.
Manager, Research, Edward Hurley
Tel: 506-452-4845
Fax: 506-452-3212
edward.hurley@agr.gc.ca
Manager, Facilities, Sean Brown
Tel: 506-452-4839
Fax: 506-452-3316
sean.brown@agr.gc.ca
Manager, Integrated Services, Senator Hervé J Michaud Research Farm, Louise Boucher
Tel: 506-743-1140
Fax: 506-743-8316
louise.boucher@agr.gc.ca

Manager, Farm, Larry McMillan
Tel: 506-452-4838
Fax: 506-452-3316
larry.mcmillan@agr.gc.ca

Saskatoon Research Centre
107 Science Pl., Saskatoon, SK S7N 0X2
Tel: 306-956-7200
Fax: 306-956-7247
Manager, Research, Dr. Felicitas Katepa-Mupondwa
Tel: 306-956-2489
Fax: 306-956-7248
felicitas.katepa-mupondwa@agr.gc.ca
Science Director, Bioproducts Platforms & Genomics, Dr. Paul McCaughey
Tel: 306-956-7211
Fax: 306-956-7248
paul.mccaughey@agr.gc.ca

Semiarid Prairie Agricultural Research Centre
PO Box 1030, Swift Current, SK S9H 3X2
Tel: 306-778-7200
Fax: 306-778-3188
The Semiarid Prairie Agricultural Research Centre is responsible for the operations of research farms in Indian Head & Regina, Saskatchewan.
Manager, Research, Bruce McArthur
Tel: 306-778-7270
Fax: 306-778-3186
bruce.mcarthur@agr.gc.ca
Manager, Integrated Services, Debbie Biese
Tel: 306-778-7223
Fax: 306-778-3188
debbie.biese@agr.gc.ca
Manager, Regina Research Farm, Myron Knelsen
Tel: 306-780-7426
Fax: 306-780-5501
myron.knelsen@agr.gc.ca
General Supervisor, Indian Head Research Farm, Danny Petty
Tel: 306-695-4200
Fax: 306-695-3445
danny.petty@agr.gc.ca

Soils & Crops Research & Development Centre
2560, boul Hochelaga, Québec, QC G1V 2J3
Tel: 418-657-7980
Fax: 418-648-2402
The Soils & Crops Research & Development Centre is also responsible for a research farm in Normandin, Québec.
Manager, Research, Genevieve Levasseur
Tel: 418-210-5002
Fax: 418-648-7231
genevieve.levasseur@agr.gc.ca
Science Director, Claudel Lemieux
Tel: 418-210-5003
Fax: 418-648-7231
claudel.lemieux@agr.gc.ca
Manager, Integrated Services, Normandin Research Farm, Mario Fortin
Tel: 418-274-5881
Fax: 418-274-3386
mario.fortin@agr.gc.ca
Chief, Greenhouse, Normand Charest
Tel: 418-210-5014
Fax: 418-648-2402
normand.charest@agr.gc.ca

Southern Crop Protection & Food Research Centre
1391 Sandford St., London, ON N5V 4T3
Tel: 519-457-1470
Fax: 519-457-3997
The Southern Crop Protection & Food Research Centre oversees the operations of research farms in Delhi & Vineland, Ontario, as well as an Office of Intellectual Property & Commercialization in London, Ontario.
Manager, Research, Southern Crop Protection & Food Research Centre, Dr. Karl Volkmar
Tel: 519-457-1470
Fax: 519-457-3503
karl.volkmar@agr.gc.ca
Manager, Research, Vineland Research Farm, Antonet Svircev
Tel: 604-796-1709
Fax: 604-796-0359
antonet.svircev@agr.gc.ca
Manager, Facility, Joe Pratt
Tel: 519-457-1470
Fax: 519-457-3997
joe.pratt@agr.gc.ca
Supervisor, Farm Services, Delhi Research Farm, Albert Asztalos
Tel: 519-582-1950
Fax: 519-582-4223
albert.asztalos@agr.gc.ca

Rural & Co-operatives Secretariat / Le Secrétariat aux affaires rurales et aux coopératives
Tower 7, 1341 Baseline Rd., Ottawa, ON K1A 0C5
Tel: 613-759-1000
Fax: 613-773-2727
Executive Director, Michaela Huard
Tel: 613-773-2916
Fax: 613-773-2727
michaela.huard@agr.gc.ca
Associate Executive Director, Christine Burton
Tel: 613-773-2955
Fax: 613-773-2727
christine.burton@agr.gc.ca
Director, Partnerships & Programs, Louise Boudreau
Tel: 613-773-2988
Fax: 613-773-2198
louise.boudreau@agr.gc.ca
Manager, Program Development & Implementation, Partnerships & Programs, Lawrence Euteneier
Tel: 613-773-2943
Fax: 613-773-2198
lawrence.euteneier@agr.gc.ca
Manager, Financial Services, Theresa Hedquist
Tel: 613-773-2947
Fax: 613-773-2727
theresa.hedquist@agr.gc.ca
Manager, Co-op Policy & Research Unit, Co-operative Policy & Research, Anne Marie McInnis
Tel: 613-773-2971
Fax: 613-773-2199
anne-marie.mcinnis@agr.gc.ca
Manager, Partnerships & Programs, Alain Roy
Tel: 613-773-2925
Fax: 613-773-2198
alain.roy@agr.gc.ca
Officer, Rural Communications, Lauraine Watson
Tel: 204-983-8376
Fax: 204-983-8357
lauraine.watson@agr.gc.ca

Strategic Policy Branch / Direction générale des politiques stratégiques
Tower 7, 1341 Baseline Rd., Ottawa, ON K1A 0C5
Tel: 613-759-1000
Fax: 613-773-2111
The Strategic Policy Branch of Agriculture & Agri-Food Canada includes the following organizations: Policy Development & Analysis Directorate; Policy, Planning, & Integration Directorate; & the Research & Analysis Directorate.
Assistant Deputy Minister, Greg Meredith
Tel: 613-773-2930
Fax: 613-773-2121
greg.meredith@agr.gc.ca
Director General, Policy Development & Analysis Directorate, Paul Martin
Tel: 613-773-2700
Fax: 613-773-2111
paul.martin@agr.gc.ca
Director General, Research & Analysis Directorate, Andrew Goldstein
Tel: 613-773-0259
Fax: 613-773-2444
andrew.goldstein@agr.gc.ca
Manager, Branch Planning & Resource Management, Taryn Barone
Tel: 613-773-2301
Fax: 613-773-2333
taryn.barone@agr.gc.ca
Senior Policy Advisor, Lisa Foss
Tel: 613-773-1563
Fax: 613-773-2121
lisa.foss@agr.gc.ca
Executive Assistant to the ADM, Louise Galipeau
Tel: 613-773-2145
Fax: 613-773-2121
louise.galipeau@agr.gc.ca

Atlantic Canada Opportunities Agency (ACOA) / Agence de promotion économique du Canada atlantique (APECA)

Blue Cross Centre, 644 Main St., 3rd Fl., PO Box 6051, Moncton, NB E1C 9J8
Tel: 506-851-2271
Fax: 506-851-7403
Toll-Free: 800-561-7862
information@acoa-apeca.gc.ca
www.acoa-apeca.gc.ca
TTY: 877-456-6500
Other Communication: Secure fax: 506-875-1301; Access to information / privacy: 506-851-6202
The role of the Atlantic Canada Opportunities Agency is the development of opportunities for economic growth in Atlantic Canada. The agency achieves its mission in the following ways: assisting businesses to become more innovative, productive, & competitive; promoting the strengths of Atlantic Canada; & helping communities to develop more diversified local economies.

Minister of State (Atlantic Canada Opportunities Agency), Hon. Bernard Valcourt
Tel: 613-941-7241
Fax: 613-952-6393
bvalcourt2011@hotmail.com

President, Paul J. LeBlanc
Tel: 506-851-6128
Fax: 506-851-7403

Senior Vice-President, David Slade
Tel: 506-851-6141

Vice-President, Finance & Corporate Services, Denise Frenette
Tel: 506-851-6438

Director General, Human Resources, Kent Estabrooks
Tel: 506-851-3070

Director General, Communications, Susan Wisking
Tel: 506-851-7731
Fax: 613-952-6393
Other Communications: Alternate tel: 613-960-9010

Director, Regional Operations, Peter Hogan
Tel: 902-426-1288

Director, Energy, Environment Policy, & Coordination, Daniel McCarthy
Tel: 613-952-8216

Regional Offices
New Brunswick Regional Office
570 Queen St., 3rd Fl., PO Box 578, Fredericton, NB E3B 5A6
Tel: 506-452-3184
Fax: 506-452-3285
Toll-Free: 800-561-4030
TTY: 877-456-6500
The New Brunswick Regional Office oversees operations at the following offices: Campbellton (Phone: 506-789-4735); Edmundston (Phone: 506-735-4236); Fundy Region (Phone: 506-636-4485); Miramichi (506-778-1909); Northeast (Phone: 506-548-7420); Northwest (Phone: 506-473-5556); Southeast (Phone: 506-851-6432); Southwest (506-452-3135); & Tracadie-Sheila (506-395-1025).
Vice-President, New Brunswick, Janet Gagnon
Tel: 506-452-3342
Executive Director, New Brunswick Federal Council, Raymond Gallant
Tel: 506-452-4986
Director, Business Programs, André Charron
Tel: 506-452-2413
Director, Communications, Patricia Field
Tel: 506-452-4287
Director, Financial Management Services, David Hubbard
Tel: 506-452-2423
Director, Policy, Advocacy, & Coordination, Gail Moser
Tel: 506-452-3155
Newfoundland & Labrador Regional Office
John Cabot Building, 10 Barter's Hill, 11th Fl., PO Box 1060 C, St. John's, NL A1C 5M5
Tel: 709-772-2751
Fax: 709-772-2712
Toll-Free: 800-668-1010
TTY: 877-456-6500
The Newfoundland & Labrador Regional Office oversees the following offices throughout the province: Clarenville (Phone: 709-466-5980); Corner Brook (Phone: 709-637-4477); Gander (Phone: 709-651-4457); Grand Bank (Phone: 709-832-2517); Grand Falls-Windsor (Phone: 709-489-6600); & Labrador (709-896-2648).
Vice-President, Newfoundland & Labrador, Paul Mills
Tel: 709-772-4150
Director General, Policy, Advocacy, & Coordination, David Collins
Tel: 709-772-2334
Executive Director, Federal / Regional Council, Mark Butler
Tel: 709-772-2781
Director, Communications, Julie Afonso
Tel: 709-772-2984
Director, Community Development, John Kennedy
Tel: 709-772-2741
Director, Financial Management Services, Francis Mackey
Tel: 709-772-6286
Director, Enterprise Development, Kenneth Martin
Tel: 709-772-0212

Nova Scotia Regional Office
#600, 1801 Hollis St., PO Box 2284 C, Halifax, NS B3J 3C8
Tel: 902-426-6743
Fax: 902-426-2054
Toll-Free: 800-565-1228
TTY: 877-456-6500

The Nova Scotia Regional Office of the Atlantic Canada Opportunities Agency oversees the following offices throughout Nova Scotia: Antigonish (Phone: 902-867-6075); Bridgewater (Phone: 902-541-5543); Church Point Office (Phone: 902-260-3590); Kentville (902-679-5356); Pictou (Phone: 902-755-3746); Truro (902-895-2743), & Yarmouth (Phone: 902-742-0809).

Vice-President, Nova Scotia (acting), Peter Hogan
Tel: 902-426-1288
Director General, Regional Operations, Peter Hogan
Tel: 902-426-1288
Director, Finance & Management Services, Nancy Ives
Tel: 902-426-5968
Director, Intergovernmental Affairs & Coordination, Lisa Muton
Tel: 902-426-4820
Director, Communications, Alexander Smith
Tel: 902-426-9417
Fax: 902-426-5843

Prince Edward Island Regional Office
Royal Bank Building, 100 Sydney St., 3rd Floor, PO Box 40, Charlottetown, PE C1A 7K2
Tel: 902-566-7492
Fax: 902-566-7098
Toll-Free: 800-871-2596
TTY: 877-456-6500

The Prince Edward Island Regional Office oversees the Summerside District Office (Phone: 902-888-4145).

Vice-President, Prince Edward Island & Tourism, Patrick Dorsey
Tel: 902-368-0760
Director General, Enterprise Development & Policy, Wayne Hooper
Tel: 902-626-2877
Fax: 902-566-7098
Director General, Atlantic Tourism, Robert McCloskey
Tel: 902-626-2479
Fax: 902-566-7098
Executive Director, Prince Edward Island Federal Council, Catherine MacInnis
Tel: 902-368-0889
Fax: 902-566-7489
Director, Corporate Programs & Services, Lynne Beairsto
Tel: 902-566-7499
Director, Infrastructure Programs, Pat MacAulay
Tel: 902-626-2794
Director, Communicatons, Cindy Roy
Tel: 902-566-7569
Fax: 902-566-7098
Director, Trade & Business Programs, Douglas Smith
Tel: 902-368-0890

Ottawa Office
60 Queen Street, 4th Fl., PO Box 1667 B, Ottawa, ON K1P 5R5
Tel: 613-954-2422
Fax: 613-954-0429

Affiliated Crown Corporation
Enterprise Cape Breton Corporation (ECBC) / Société d'expansion du Cap-Breton
Silicon Island, 70 Crescent St., PO Box 1750, Sydney, NS B1P 6T7
Tel: 902-564-3600
Fax: 902-564-3825
Toll-Free: 800-705-3926
information@ecbc-secb.gc.ca
www.ecbc-secb.gc.ca

As the principal federal organization for economic development on Cape Breton Island, ECBC focuses on the major issues affecting the economy of the area. In partnership with all levels of government, the private sector, & other community stakeholders, ECBC promotes & assists the financing & development of communities and industry with a view to creating sustainable wealth on Cape Breton Island. In addition to its own programs, ECBC is responsible for the delivery of ACOA's programs on Cape Breton Island.

Chair, Paul J. LeBlanc
Tel: 506-851-6128
Fax: 506-851-7403
Chief Executive Officer, John Lynn
Tel: 902-564-3508
Fax: 902-564-2760

Atlantic Pilotage Authority (APA) / Administration de pilotage de l'Atlantique

Cogswell Tower, #910, 2000 Barrington St., Halifax, NS B3J 3K1
Tel: 902-426-2550
Fax: 902-426-4004
Toll-Free: 877-272-3477
dispatch@atlanticpilotage.com
www.atlanticpilotage.com
Other Communication: Toll-Free Fax: 1-877-745-3477; Fax to Email Direct: 1-866-774-2477

The Federal Crown Corporation is responsible for the safe & efficient operation, maintenance, & administration of marine pilotage service to Atlantic Canada.

Chief Executive Officer, R.A. Anthony McGuinness
Tel: 902-426-2553

Chief Financial Officer, Peter L. MacArthur
Tel: 902-426-8657

Director, Operations, Patrick Gates
Tel: 902-426-6389

Atomic Energy of Canada Limited (AECL) / Énergie atomique du Canada Ltée (EACL)

Head Office, Chalk River Laboratories, Chalk River, ON K0J 1J0
Tel: 613-584-3311
Toll-Free: 866-513-2325
librarycr@aecl.ca (library requests)
www.aecl.ca
Other Communication: Media Enquiries, Toll-Free Phone: 1-866-886-2325

Atomic Energy of Canada develops peaceful applications from nuclear technology. Services include research, design, engineering, waste management, & decommissioning.
The following offices & laboratories are part of Atomic Energy of Canada: Whiteshell Laboratories in Pinawa, Manitoba (204-753-2311); Low-Level Radioactive Waste Management in Ottawa, Ontario (613-998-9442); AECL Ottawa (613-237-3270); Port Hope Office & Laboratory in Port Hope, Ontario (905-885-9488); Port Hope Area Initiative (905-885-0291); & Centre for Nuclear Energy Research at the University of New Brunswick in Fredericton (506-453-5111).

President & Chief Executive Officer, Dr. Robert Walker

Senior Vice-President, Strategic Contracting, Allan A. Hawryluk

Senior Vice-President & General Manager, Jon Lundy

Chief Financial Officer & Vice-President, Steve Halpenny

Chief Nuclear Officer & Vice-President, Operations, Randy Lesco

Vice-President, General Counsel, & Corporate Secretary, Richard Fujarczuk

Vice-President, Research & Development, William Kupferschmidt

Vice-President, Decommissioning & Waste Management, Joan Miller

Low-Level Radioactive Waste Management Office (LLRWMO) / Bureau de gestion des déchets radioactifs de faible activité
#200, 1900 City Park Dr., Ottawa, ON K1J 1A3
Tel: 613-998-9442
Fax: 613-952-0760
Toll-Free: 800-377-5995
info@llrwmo.org
www.llrwmo.org

Carries out the responsibilities of the federal government for low-level radioactive waste (LLRW) management in Canada.

Auditor General of Canada / Vérificateur général du Canada

240 Sparks St., Ottawa, ON K1A 0G6
Tel: 613-995-3708
Fax: 613-957-0474
Toll-Free: 888-761-5953
communications@oag-bvg.gc.ca; infomedia@oag-bvg.gc.ca
www.oag-bvg.gc.ca
TTY: 613-954-8042
Other Communication: Media Relations, Phone: 613-952-0213, ext. 6292; Publications, Toll-Free Phone: 1-888-761-5953; Work Opportunities, E-mail: emplo@oag-bvg.gc.ca

The Office of the Auditor General of Canada was established in 1878. Today, the head office in Ottawa & regional offices in Halifax, Montréal, Edmonton, & Vancouver employ approximately 650 employees. The Office of the Auditor General of Canada provides objective, fact-based information required by Parliament to hold the federal government accountable for its stewardship of public funds. An Officer of Parliament, the Auditor General of Canada is responsible for auditing the following organizations: federal government departments; federal government agencies; most Crown corporations; many federal organizations; the government of the Yukon; the government of the Northwest Territories; & the government of Nunavut. The Auditor General, Michael Ferguson, reports publicly to the House of Commons about matters he believes should be brought to the attention of the House of Commons. The report can include chapters on audits & studies, sustainable development strategies, & environmental petitions.

Auditor General, Michael Ferguson

Chief Information Officer & Assistant Auditor General, Ira Greenblatt
Tel: 613-952-0213 ext: 434

Assistant Auditor General, IC, Aboriginal Issues, HRMA, Nunavut, Industry, & NRC, Ronnie Campbell
Tel: 613-952-0213 ext: 291

Assistant Auditor General, Crown Corporations Group, Nancy Cheng
Tel: 613-952-0213 ext: 626
Fax: 613-941-8284

Assistant Auditor General, Yukon & the Northwest Territories, Andrew Lennox
Tel: 613-952-0213 ext: 230

Assistant Auditor General, CBSA, CIDA, CSIS, CIC, CSC, IRB, Justice, Public Safety, & RCMP, Wendy Loschiuk
Tel: 613-952-0213 ext: 439

Assistant Auditor General, CDIC, CMHC, OP, FI, EDC, FCC, IDRC, & PSPIB, Clyde MacLellan
Tel: 613-952-0213 ext: 522

Assistant Auditor General, Health Canada, SC, CFIA, AAFC, & Fisheries & Oceans, Neil Maxwell
Tel: 613-952-0213 ext: 636

Assistant Auditor General, CRA, AA, FS, Separate Opinions, Income Tax, GST, & Performance Reporting, Marian McMahon
Tel: 613-952-0213 ext: 221

Assistant Auditor General, HRSDC, Small Entities, Crown Corporations, & Other Entities, Sylvain Ricard
Tel: 613-952-0213 ext: 535

Assistant Auditor General, Canadian Heritage Arts & Culture, Museums, NAC, CBC, TC, CATSA, VIA Rail, NCC, NRTEE, & ILO, John Rossetti
Tel: 613-952-0213 ext: 534

Assistant Auditor General, Corporate Services, Lyn Sachs
Tel: 613-952-0213 ext: 434

Principal, National Defence, Veteran Affairs Canada, Foreign Affairs, & International Trade Canada, Jerome Berthelette
Tel: 613-952-0213 ext: 450

Principal, Practice Review & Internal Audit, & Strategic Planning, Julie Charron
Tel: 613-952-0213 ext: 543

Principal, Forensic Audit Section, Linda Drainville
Tel: 613-952-0213 ext: 638

Principal, Parliamentary Liaison & International Relations, Jocelyne Therrien
Tel: 613-952-0213 ext: 435

Principal, Communications, Susan Wheeler
Tel: 613-952-0213 ext: 655

Commissioner, Environment & Sustainable Development, Scott Vaughan
Tel: 613-952-0213 ext: 640
Principal, Sustainable Development Strategies, Audits, & Studies, Andrew Ferguson
Tel: 613-952-0213 ext: 630
Principal, Sustainable Development Strategies, Audits, & Studies, James McKenzie
Tel: 613-952-0213 ext: 635

Principal, Sustainable Development Strategies, Audits, & Studies, Kimberly Leach
Tel: 613-952-0213 ext: 624
Principal, Sustainable Development Strategies, Audits, & Studies, Bruce Sloan
Tel: 613-952-0213 ext: 230

Regional Offices
Regional Offices
Edmonton
Manulife Place, #2460, 10180 - 101st St., Edmonton, AB T5J 3S4
Tel: 780-495-2028
Fax: 780-495-2031
Principal, Guy LeGras
Tel: 780-495-2029
Director, David Irving
Tel: 780-495-6338
Halifax/Dartmouth
Centennial Building, #414, 1660 Hollis St., Halifax, NS B3J 1V7
Tel: 902-426-7721
Fax: 902-426-8591
Principal, Heather McManaman
Tel: 902-426-7728
Director, Glenn Doucette
Tel: 902-426-2097
Director, Paul Kelly
Tel: 902-426-6512
Montréal
#545, 1255, rue Peel, Montréal, QC H3B 2T9
Tél: 514-283-6086
Téléc: 514-283-1715
Principal, René Béliveau
Tel: 514-283-8324
Director, Jean-Pierre Morin
Tel: 514-283-8136
Director, Tina Swiderski
Tel: 514-283-7793
Vancouver
#210, 351 Abbott St., Vancouver, BC V6B 0G6
Tel: 604-666-3596
Fax: 604-666-6162
Principal, Eric Hellsten
Tel: 604-666-7600

Bank of Canada / Banque du Canada

234 Wellington St., Ottawa, ON K1A 0G9
Tel: 613-782-7902
Fax: 613-782-7713
Toll-Free: 800-303-1282
info@bankofcanada.ca; communications@bankofcanada.ca (Media)
www.bankofcanada.ca
TTY: 888-418-1461
Other Communication: Access to information & privacy issues, E-mail: ATIP-AIPRP@bankofcanada.ca; Publications, E-mail: publications@bankofcanada.ca
Founded in 1934, the Bank of Canada was orignially a privately owned corporation. It became a Crown corporation, belonging to the federal government, in 1938. As Canada's central bank, the role of the Bank of Canada is the promotion of the economic & financial welfare of the nation. The following are the main responsibilities of the Bank of Canada: Canada's financial system; monetary policy; funds management; & bank notes. The Governor & Senior Deputy of the Bank of Canada are appointed by the Bank's Board of Directors, with the approval of the Cabinet. Regional offices of the Bank of Canada are located in the following cities: Halifax (Phone: 902-420-4600); Montréal (Phone: 514-496-4800); Toronto (Phone: 416-542-1251); Calgary (Phone: 403-215-6700); Vancouver (Phone: 604-643-6227); & New York (Phone: 212-596-1673).

Governor, Mark J. Carney

Senior Deputy Governor, Tiff Macklem

Deputy Governor, Jean Boivin

Deputy Governor, Agathe Côté

Deputy Governor, Timothy Lane

Deputy Governor, John Murray

Special Adviser to the Governor, Timothy Hodgson

General Counsel & Corporate Secretary, Executive & Legal Services, W. John Jussup

Chief, Information Technology Services, Sylvian Chalut

Chief, International Economic Analysis, Donald Coletti

Chief, Currency, Gerry T. Gaetz

Chief, Financial Markets, Donna Howard

Chief, Canadian Economic Analysis, Sharon Kozicki

Chief, Corporate Services, Colleen Leighton

Chief, Funds Management & Banking, Ron Morrow

Chief Internal Auditor, Carmen Prévost Vierula

Chief, Communications, Jill Vardy

Chief, Financial Services; Chief Accountant, Sheila Vokey

Chief, Financial Stability, Mark Zelmer

Chief Librarian, Information Resource Centre, Beverly Graham
Tel: 613-782-8466
Fax: 613-782-7387
ref1@bankofcanada.ca

Director, Data & Statistics Office, Arthur Berger

Archivist, Jane Boyko
Tel: 613-782-8673
Fax: 613-782-7387
archives@bankofcanada.ca

Business Development Bank of Canada (BDC) / Banque de développement du Canada (BDC)

#400, 5, Place Ville-Marie, Montréal, QC H3B 5E7
Tel: 514-283-5904
Fax: 514-283-5626
Toll-Free: 877-232-2269
www.bdc.ca
Other Communication: Toll-Free Fax 1-877-329-9232; Corporate Financing (Québec & Atlantic Regions), Fax: 514-283-8410
The Business Development Bank of Canada is a financial institution which is wholly owned by the Government of Canada. It was created by an Act of Parliament in 1944. The Bank is governed by an independent Board of Directors, & reports to the Minister of Industry. The mission of the Business Development Bank of Canada is to assist in the establishment & development of Canadian businesses in all industries. The Bank focuses its efforts on small & medium-sized enterprises. The following services are carried out by the Business Development Bank of Canada: consulting services; flexible financing, such as long term business financing & subordinate financing; & venture capital. Branches of the Business Development Bank of Canada are located throughout Canada. Smaller communities are served by satellite branches, consultants & travelling account managers.

Chair, John A. MacNaughton

President & Chief Executive Officer, Jean-René Halde

Executive Vice-President & Chief Financial Officer, Paul Buron

Executive Vice-President, Financing & Consulting, Edmée Métivier

Senior Vice President, Financing & Consulting, Québec, Patrice Bernard

Senior Vice President, Human Resources, Mary Karamanos

Senior Vice President, Financing & Consulting, Ontario, Peter Lawler

Senior Vice President, Strategy & Corporate Development, Jérôme Nycz

Senior Vice President, Legal Affairs; Corporate Secretary, Louise Paradis

Senior Vice President, Financing & Consulting, Atlantic, Terry Quinn

Senior Vice President, Credit Risk Management, André St-Pierre

National Vice President, Subordinate Financing, Roger Giraldeau

National Vice President, Subordinate Financing, Eastern Quebec, Montréal, North-Shore, & South-Shore, Danielle Landry

Vice President, Corporate Relations, Michel Bergeron

Vice President, Venture Capital, Charles Cazabon

Vice President, Securitization, Paula Cruickshank

Vice President, Information & Communication Technologies, Glen R. Egan

Vice President, Energy, Environment, Electronic, & Materials, Robert Inglese

Vice President, Consulting, Bruce McConnell

Vice President, Fund Investments, Frank Pho

Alberta Branches
Alberta Branches
Calgary Area Branch
Barclay Centre, #110, 444 - 7 Ave. SW, Calgary, AB T2P 0X8
Tel: 403-292-5600
Fax: 403-292-6616
Other Communication: Subordinate Financing (Prairies & Northwest Territories), Phone: 403-292-5000, Fax: 403-292-5862

Calgary North Branch
#100, 1935 - 32 Ave. NE, Calgary, AB T2E 7C8
Tel: 403-292-5333
Fax: 403-292-6651

Calgary South Branch
#200, 6700 MacLeod Trail SE, Calgary, AB T2H 0L3
Tel: 403-292-8882
Fax: 403-292-4345

Edmonton Branch
#200, 10665 Jasper Ave., Edmonton, AB T5J 3S9
Tel: 780-495-2277
Fax: 780-495-6616

Edmonton South Branch
#201, 4628 Calgary Trail NW, Edmonton, AB T6H 6A1
Tel: 780-495-7200
Fax: 780-495-7198

Edmonton West Branch
236 Mayfield Common, Edmonton, AB T5P 4B3
Tel: 780-442-7312
Fax: 780-495-3102

Grande Prairie Branch
#203, 10625 West Side Dr., Grande Prairie, AB T8V 8E6
Tel: 780-532-8875
Fax: 780-539-5130

Lethbridge Branch
520 - 5th Ave. South, Lethbridge, AB T1J 0T8
Tel: 403-382-3000
Fax: 403-382-3162

Medicine Hat Branch
#101, 2248 - 13th Ave. SE, Medicine Hat, AB T1A 8G6
Tel: 403-527-2601
Fax: 403-528-6899

Office by appointment.
Red Deer Branch
#107, 4815 - 50th Ave., Red Deer, AB T4N 4A5
Tel: 403-340-4203
Fax: 403-340-4243

British Columbia Branches
Cranbrook Branch
205B Cranbrook St. North, Cranbrook, BC V1C 3R1
Tel: 250-417-2200
Fax: 250-417-2213

Fort St. John Branch
#7, 10230 - 100th St., Fort St. John, BC V1J 3Y9
Tel: 250-787-0622
Fax: 250-787-9423

Kamloops Branch
205 Victoria St., Kamloops, BC V2C 2A1
Tel: 250-851-4900
Fax: 250-851-4925

Kelowna Branch
313 Bernard Ave., Kelowna, BC V1Y 6N6
Tel: 250-470-4802
Fax: 250-470-4832

Langley Branch
#101B, 6424 - 200th St., Langley, BC V2Y 2T3
Tel: 604-532-5150
Fax: 604-532-5166

Nanaimo Branch
#500, 6581 Aulds Rd., Nanaimo, BC V9T 6J6
Tel: 250-390-5757
Fax: 250-390-5753

Nelson Branch
#1, 619B Front St., Nelson, BC V1L 4B6
Tel: 250-352-3837
Fax: 250-352-3809

North Vancouver Branch
#3, 221 West Esplanade, North Vancouver, BC V7M 3J3
Tel: 604-666-7703
Fax: 604-666-1957

Prince George Branch
#150, 177 Victoria St., Prince George, BC V2L 5R8
Tel: 250-561-5323
Fax: 250-561-5512

South Vancouver Branch
#101, 5811 Cooney Rd., Richmond, BC V6X 3M1
Tel: 604-666-7850
Fax: 604-666-1068

Surrey Branch
#160, 10362 King George Blvd., Surrey, BC V3T 2W5
Tel: 604-586-2400
Fax: 604-586-2430

Terrace Branch
3233 Emerson St., Terrace, BC V8G 5L2
Tel: 250-615-5300
Fax: 250-615-5320

Tri-Cities Branch
#370, 2755 Lougheed Highway, Port Coquitlam, BC V3B 5Y9
Tel: 604-927-1400
Fax: 604-927-1415

Vancouver Branch
One Bentall Centre, #2100, 505 Burrard St., PO Box 6, Vancouver, BC V7X 1M6
Tel: 604-666-7850
Fax: 604-666-1068
Other Communication: Subordinate Financing (British Columbia & Yukon), Phone: 604-666-7875, Fax: 604-666-8482; Corporate Financing (Western Canada), Phone: 604-666-1068

British Columbia Branches
Vernon Branch
#302, 3105 - 33rd St., Vernon, BC V1T 9P7
Tel: 250-260-5061
Fax: 250-260-5011

Victoria Branch
990 Fort St., Victoria, BC V8V 3K2
Tel: 250-363-0161
Fax: 250-363-8029

Manitoba Branches
Manitoba Branches
Brandon Branch
#10, 940 Princess Ave., Brandon, MB R7A 0P6
Tel: 204-726-7570
Fax: 204-726-7555

Manitoba Branches
Winnipeg Branch
#1100, 155 Carlton St., Winnipeg, MB R3C 3H8
Tel: 204-983-7900
Fax: 204-983-0870

Manitoba Branches
Winnipeg West Branch
#200, 1655 Kenaston Blvd., Winnipeg, MB R3P 2M4
Tel: 204-983-6530
Fax: 204-983-6531

New Brunswick Branches
Bathurst Branch
#205, 275 Main St., Bathurst, NB E2A 1A9
Tel: 506-548-7360
Fax: 506-548-7381

Edmundston Branch
#407, 121, rue de l'Église, Edmundston, NB E3V 1J9
Tél: 506-739-8311
Téléc: 506-735-0019

Office by appointment.
Fredericton Branch
#504, 570 Queen St., PO Box 754, Fredericton, NB E3B 5B4
Tel: 506-452-3030
Fax: 506-452-2416

Moncton Branch
766 Main St., Moncton, NB E1C 1E6
Tel: 506-851-6120
Fax: 506-851-6033

Saint John Branch
53 King St., Saint John, NB E2L 1G5
Tel: 506-636-4751
Fax: 506-636-3892

Newfoundland & Labrador Branches
Corner Brook Branch
4 Herald Ave., 1st Fl., Corner Brook, NL A2H 4B4
Tel: 709-637-4515
Fax: 709-637-4522

Grand Falls-Windsor Branch
42 High St., PO Box 744, Grand Falls-Windsor, NL A2A 2M4
Tel: 709-489-2181
Fax: 709-489-6569

St. John's Branch
215 Water St., PO Box 520, St. John's, NL A1C 5K4
Tel: 709-722-5505
Fax: 709-772-2516

Northwest Territories & Nunavut Branches
Yellowknife & Nunavut Branch
4912 - 49th St., Yellowknife, NT X1A 1P3
Tel: 867-873-3565
Fax: 867-873-3501

Nova Scotia Branches
Halifax Branch
#1400, 2000 Barrington St., Halifax, NS B3J 2Z7
Tel: 902-426-7850
Fax: 902-426-6783

Vice-President & Area Manager, Craig Levangie
Tel: 902-426-7865
craig.levangie@bdc.ca

Sydney Branch
#117, 275 Charlotte St., Sydney, NS B1P 1C6
Tel: 902-564-7700
Fax: 902-564-3975

Truro Branch
622 Prince St., PO Box 1378, Truro, NS B2N 5N2
Tel: 902-895-6377
Fax: 902-893-7957

Yarmouth Branch
103 Water St., PO Box 98, Yarmouth, NS B5A 4B1
Tel: 902-742-7119
Fax: 902-742-8180

Ontario Branches
Barrie Branch
#301, 151 Ferris Lane, PO Box 876, Barrie, ON L4M 4Y6
Tel: 705-725-2533
Fax: 705-739-0467

Belleville Branch
284B Wallbridge-Loyalist Rd., Belleville, ON K8N 5B3
Tel: 613-969-4009
Fax: 613-969-4018

Office by appointment.
Brampton Branch
#100, 24 Queen St. East, Brampton, ON L6V 1A3
Tel: 905-450-9845
Fax: 905-450-7514

Brantford Branch
#10, 330 West St., Brantford, ON N3R 7V5
Tel: 519-751-3005
Fax: 519-751-3006

Office by appointment.
Burlington / Halton Branch
#401, 4145 North Service Rd., Burlington, ON L7L 6A3
Tel: 905-315-9230
Fax: 905-315-9243

Chatham Branch
62 Keil Dr. South, Chatham, ON N7M 3G8
Tel: 519-380-8886
Fax: 519-380-8850

Office by appointment.
Durham (Whitby) Branch
400 Dundas St. West, Whitby, ON L1N 2M7
Tel: 905-666-6694
Fax: 905-666-1059

Etobicoke Branch
#1001, 1243 Islington Ave., Toronto, ON M8X 1Y9
Tel: 416-954-2604
Fax: 416-954-2631
Other Communication: Subordinate Financing (Greater Toronto Area), Phone: 416-952-6291, Fax: 416-954-2630

Guelph Branch
#100, 120 Research Lane, Guelph, ON N1G 0B5
Tel: 519-826-2663
Fax: 519-826-2662

Hamilton Branch
#1900, 25 Main St. West, Hamilton, ON L8P 1H1
Tel: 905-572-2954
Fax: 905-572-4282

Kenora Branch
227 - 2nd St. South, Kenora, ON P9N 1G1
Tel: 807-467-3535
Fax: 807-467-3533

Kingston Branch
#201, 1000 Gardiners Rd., Kingston, ON K7P 3C4
Tel: 613-389-0999
Fax: 613-389-2543

Kitchener-Waterloo Branch
#110, 50 Queen St. North, Kitchener, ON N2H 6P4
Tel: 519-571-6676
Fax: 519-571-6685

London Branch
380 Wellington St., London, ON N6A 5B5
Tel: 519-645-4229
Fax: 519-645-5450
Other Communication: Subordinate Financing (Southwestern Ontario), Phone: 519-675-3114, Fax: 519-645-5989

Markham Branch
3130 Hwy. 7 East, Markham, ON L3R 5A1
Tel: 905-305-6867
Fax: 905-305-1969

Mississauga Branch
#100, 4310 Sherwoodtowne Blvd., Mississauga, ON L4Z 4C4
Tel: 905-566-6417
Fax: 905-566-6425

North Bay Branch
222 McIntyre St. West, North Bay, ON P1B 2Y8
Tel: 705-495-5700
Fax: 705-495-5707

North York Branch
#502, Islington Ave. West, North York, ON M3J 3H7
Tel: 416-736-3420
Fax: 416-736-3425

Ottawa Branch
55 Metcalfe St., Ground Fl., Ottawa, ON K1P 6L5
Tel: 613-995-0234
Fax: 613-995-9045
Other Communication: Subordinate Financing (Ottawa & Atlantic Regions), Phone: 613-995-4084, Fax: 613-943-9866

Ottawa West Branch
#100, 700 Silver Seven Rd., Kanata, ON K2V 1C3
Tel: 613-592-2968
Fax: 613-592-5053

Owen Sound Branch
173 - 8th St. East, Owen Sound, ON N4K 5N3
Tel: 519-371-5666
Fax: 519-371-1707

Office by appointment.
Peterborough Branch
340 George St. North, 4th Fl., PO Box 1419, Peterborough, ON K9J 7H6
Tel: 705-750-4800
Fax: 705-750-4808

Sarnia Branch
1086 Modeland Rd., Sarnia, ON N7S 6L2
Tel: 519-383-1848
Fax: 519-383-1849

Office by appointment.
Sault Ste Marie Branch
153 Great Northern Rd., Sault Ste Marie, ON P6B 4Y9
Tel: 705-941-3030
Fax: 705-941-3040

Scarborough Branch
#112, 305 Milner Ave., Toronto, ON M1B 3V4
Tel: 416-954-0709
Fax: 416-954-0716

St Catharines Branch
#100, 39 Queen St., PO Box 1193, St Catharines, ON L2R 7A7
Tel: 905-988-2874
Fax: 905-988-2890

Stratford Branch
516 Huron St., Stratford, ON N5A 5T7
Tel: 519-271-5650
Fax: 519-271-8472

Sudbury Branch
#10, 233 Brady St., Sudbury, ON P3B 4H5
Tel: 705-670-6482
Fax: 705-670-6387

Thunder Bay Branch
#102, 1136 Alloy Dr., Thunder Bay, ON P7B 6M9
Tel: 807-346-1780
Fax: 807-346-1790

Timmins Branch
#202, 85 Pine St. South, Timmins, ON P4N 2K1
Tel: 705-267-1246
Fax: 705-268-5437

Office by appointment.
Toronto Branch
#1200, 121 King St. West, Toronto, ON M5H 3T9
Tel: 416-973-0341
Fax: 416-954-5009
The King Street West branch offers corporate financing for the Greater Toronto Area.

Vaughan Branch
#600, 3901 Hwy. 7 West, Vaughan, ON L4L 8L5
Tel: 905-264-2100
Fax: 905-264-2122

Windsor Branch
#200, 2485 Ouellette Ave., Windsor, ON N8X 1L5
Tel: 519-257-6808
Fax: 519-257-6811

Prince Edward Island Branches
Charlottetown Branch
#230, 119 Kent St., PO Box 488, Charlottetown, PE C1A 7L1
Tel: 902-566-7454
Fax: 902-566-7459

Québec Branches
Boucherville Branch
1570 Ampère St, Boucherville, QC J4B 7L4
Tél: 450-928-4120
Téléc: 450-928-4127

Brossard Branch
#200, 4255, boul Lapinière, Brossard, QC J4Z 0C7
Tel: 450-926-7220
Fax: 450-926-7221

Chaudière - Appalaches (Saint-Romuald) Regional Branch
#100, 1175, boul de la Rive sud, Saint-Romuald, QC G6W 5M6
Tel: 418-834-5144
Fax: 418-834-1855

Des Moulins - Lanaudière (Terrebonne) Regional Branch
2785, boul des Plateaux, Terrebonne, QC J6X 4J9
Tél: 450-964-8778
Téléc: 450-964-8773

Drummondville Branch
1010, boul René-Lévesque, Drummondville, QC J2C 5W4
Tél: 819-478-4951
Téléc: 819-478-5864

Gatineau Branch
#104, 259, boul St-Joseph, Gatineau, QC J8Y 6T1
Tél: 819-997-4434
Téléc: 819-997-4435

Granby Branch
#302, 155, rue St-Jacques, Granby, QC J2G 9A7
Tél: 450-372-5202
Téléc: 450-372-2423

Laval Branch
#100, 2525, Daniel-Johnson, Laval, QC H7T 1S9
Tél: 450-973-3727
Téléc: 450-973-6860

Montréal Branch
#12525, 5, Place Ville-Marie, Montréal, QC H3B 2G2
Tél: 514-496-7966
Téléc: 514-496-7974
Autre numéros: Subordinate Financing (Montréal), Phone: 514-496-0626, Fax: 514-496-1020; Subordinate Financing (North-Shore & South-Shore), Phone: 514-283-8265, Fax: 514-496-1020

Pointe-Claire Branch
#110, 755, boul St-Jean, Pointe-Claire, QC H9R 5M9
Tel: 514-697-8014
Fax: 514-697-3160

Québec Branch
1134, Grande-Allée ouest, Québec, QC G1S 1E5
Tél: 418-648-3972
Téléc: 418-648-5525
Autre numéros: Subordinate Financing (Eastern Quebec), Phone: 418-648-5517, Fax: 418-649-6301

Québec North West Branch
#310, 1165, boul Lebourgneuf, Québec, QC G2K 2C9
Tel: 418-648-4740
Fax: 418-648-4745

Rimouski Branch
391, boul Jessop, Rimouski, QC G5L 1M9
Tél: 418-722-3300
Téléc: 418-722-3362

Rouyn-Noranda Branch
#301, 139, boul Québec, Rouyn-Noranda, QC J9X 6M8
Tél: 819-764-6701
Téléc: 819-764-5472

Saint-Jérôme Branch
#102, 55, rue Castonguay, Saint-Jérôme, QC J7Y 2H9
Tél: 450-432-7111
Téléc: 450-432-8366

Saint-Laurent Branch
#160, 3100, boul de la Côte-Vertu, Saint-Laurent, QC H4R 2J8
Tél: 514-496-7500
Téléc: 514-496-7510

Montreal East Branch
6347, rue Jean-Talon est, Saint-Léonard, QC H1S 3E7
Tél: 514-251-2818
Téléc: 514-251-2758

Sherbrooke Branch
2532, rue King ouest, Sherbrooke, QC J1J 2E8
Tél: 819-564-5700
Téléc: 819-564-4276

Thérèse-de-Blainville (Boisbriand) Regional Branch
3000, rue Cours le Corbusier, Boisbriand, QC J7G 3E8
Tél: 450-420-4900
Téléc: 450-420-4904

Trois-Rivières Branch
#150, 1500, rue Royale, Trois-Rivières, QC G9A 6E6
Tél: 819-371-5215
Téléc: 819-371-5220

Saguenay / Lac St-Jean Branch
#210, 325 des Saguenéens St, Chicoutimi, QC G7H 6K9
Tél: 418-698-5599
Téléc: 418-698-5678

Vaudreuil-Soulanges
450 Aimé-Vincent Street, Vaudreuil-Dorion, QC J7V 5V5
Tél: 450-455-9370
Téléc: 450-455-8126
Office by appointment.

Saskatchewan Branches
Prince Albert Branch
#1, 1499 - 10th Ave. E, Prince Albert, SK S6V 7S6
Tel: 306-953-8599
Fax: 306-953-1343
Office by appointment.

Regina
#320, 2220 - 12th Ave., Regina, SK S4P 0M8
Tel: 306-780-6478
Fax: 306-780-7516

Saskatoon
135 - 21st St. East, Main Fl., Saskatoon, SK S7K 0B4
Tel: 306-975-4822
Fax: 306-975-5955

Yukon Branches
Whitehorse
#202, 204 Lambert St., Whitehorse, YT Y1A 1Z4
Tel: 867-633-7510
Fax: 867-667-4058

Canada Border Services Agency (CBSA) / Agence des services frontaliers du Canada (ASFC)

Headquarters, 191 Laurier Ave. West, Ottawa, ON K1A 0L8
Toll-Free: 800-461-9999
Contact@cbsa.gc.ca; communications@ps.gc.ca (Public Safety)
www.cbsa-asfc.gc.ca
TTY: 866-335-3237
Other Communication: Border Information Service, Service in French, Toll-Free Phone: 1-800-959-2036; Public Safety Canada, Phone: 613-944-4875, Toll-Free: 1-800-830-3118

Established in 2003, as a response to the need for increased border services, the Canada Border Services Agency ensures the security & prosperity of Canada. The agency is responsible for managing the access of people & goods to & from Canada. To carry out its mission, Canada Border Services Agency administers more than ninety pieces of legislation. Some of the agencies duties include the following: managing over 100 border crossings; offering services at points throughout Canada & internationally; operating detention centres across the nation; conducting marine operations at the ports of Prince Rupert, Vancouver, Montréal, & Halifax; managing postal services at major mail centres in Montréal, Toronto, & Vancouver; & forming part of more than twenty Integrated Border Enforcement Teams across Canada.

Acts Administered:
Access to Information Act
Act to Establish the Canada Border Services Agency
Aeronautics Act
Agriculture & Agri-Food Administrative Monetary Penalties Act
Anti-Personnel Mines Convention Implementation Act (through EIPA)
Blue Water Bridge Authority Act
Bretton Woods & Related Agreements Act
Canada Agricultural Products Act
Canada Customs & Revenue Agency Act
Canada Grain Act
Canada Post Corporation Act
Canada Shipping Act
Canada-Chile Free Trade Agreement Implementation Act
Canada-Costa Rica Free Trade Agreement Implementation Act
Canada-Israel Free Trade Agreement Implementation Act
Canada-United States Free Trade Agreement Implementation Act
Canadian Dairy Commission Act
Canadian Environmental Protection Act, 1999
Canadian Food Inspection Agency Act
Canadian International Trade Tribunal Act
Canadian Wheat Board Act
Carriage by Air Act
Chemical Weapons Convention Implementation Act (through EIPA)
Citizenship Act
Civil International Space Station Agreement Implementation Act
Coastal Fisheries Protection Act
Coasting Trade Act
Consumer Packaging & Labelling Act
Controlled Drug & Substances Act
Convention on International Trade in Endangered Species of Wild Fauna & Flora
Copyright Act
Criminal Code
Cultural Property Export & Import Act
Customs & Excise Offshore Application Act
Customs Act
Customs Tariff Act
Defence Production Act
Department of Health Act
Department of Industry Act
Energy Administration Act
Energy Efficiency Act
Excise Act
Excise Act, 2001
Excise Tax Act
Explosives Act
Export & Import Permits Act
Export & Import of Rough Diamonds Act
Export Act
Federal-Provincial Fiscal Arrangements Act
Feeds Act
Fertilizers Act
Financial Administration Act
Firearms Act
Fish Inspection Act
Fisheries Act
Foods & Drugs Act
Foreign Missions & International Organizations Act
Freshwater Fish Marketing Act
Hazardous Products Act
Health of Animals Act
Immigration & Refugee Protection Act
Importation of Intoxicating Liquors Act
Integrated Circuit Topography Act
International Boundary Commission Act
Manganese-based Fuel Additives Act
Meat Inspection Act
Motor Vehicle Fuel Consumption Standards Act (not in force)
Motor Vehicle Safety Act
National Energy Board Act
Navigable Waters Protection Act
North American Free Trade Agreement Implementation Act
Nuclear Energy Act
Nuclear Safety & Control Act
Pest Control Products Act
Pilotage Act
Plant Breeders' Rights Act
Plant Protection Act
Precious Metals Marking Act
Preclearance Act
Privacy Act
Privileges & Immunities (North Atlantic Organization Act)
Proceeds of Crime (Money Laundering) & Terrorist Financing Act
Quarantine Act
Quebec Harbour, Port Warden Act
Radiation Emitting Devices Act
Radiocommunication Act
Seeds Act
Special Economic Measures Act
Special Import Measures Act
Statistics Act
Telecommunications Act
Textile Labelling Act
Trade-Marks Act
Transportation of Dangerous Goods Act, 1992
United Nations Act
United States Wreckers Act
Visiting Forces Act
Wild Animals & Plant Protection & Regulation of International & Interprovincial Trade Act

Minister, Public Safety, Hon. Vic Toews
Tel: 613-992-3128
Fax: 613-995-1049
Toews.V@parl.gc.ca

President, Luc Portelance
Tel: 613-952-3200
Fax: 613-948-3177

Executive Vice-President, Malcolm Brown
Tel: 613-952-3200
Fax: 613-952-1851

Associate Vice-President, Martin Bolduc
Tel: 613-952-5269
Fax: 613-948-7130

Regional Director General, Niagara Region, Rick Comerford
Tel: 905-994-6000
Fax: 905-994-6010
Other Communications: Executive Assistant, Phone: 905-994-6002

Regional Director General, Windsor - St. Clair Region, Pete Diponio
Tel: 519-967-4010

Regional Director General, Atlantic Region, Diane Giffin-Boudreau
Tel: 902-426-2914
Other Communications: Administrative Assistant, Phone: 902-426-2914

Regional Director General, Pacific Region, Roslyn MacVicar
Tel: 604-666-0760
Other Communications: Executive Assistant, Phone: 604-666-3305

Regional Director General, Northern Ontario Region, Denis R. Vinette
Tel: 613-991-0566
Other Communications: Executive Assistant, Phone: 613-991-0565

Regional Director General, Greater Toronto Area Region, Goran Vragrovic
Tel: 905-803-5595

Director, Prairie Region, Edmonton District, Bill Axten
Tel: 780-890-8040

Director, Atlantic Region, Southern New Brunswick & Prince Edward Island District, Don Collins
Tel: 506-636-4506
Other Communications: Administrative Assistant, Phone: 506-426-4501

Director, Atlantic Region, Northwestern New Brunswick District, John Dolimount
Tel: 506-324-8663
Other Communications: Administrative Assistant, Phone: 506-324-8660

Director, Prairie Region, Calgary District, Paul Dumouchel
Tel: 403-292-5690
Fax: 403-292-4840

Director, Pacific Region, Metro Vancouver District, John Dyck
Tel: 604-775-6790
Fax: 604-775-6792

Director, Atlantic Region, Newfoundland & Labrador Districtt, John Fagan
Tel: 709-772-2719
Other Communications: Administrative Assistant, Phone: 709-772-4335

Director, Northern Ontario Region, Northwest District, Gary Flanagan
Tel: 705-941-3052
Fax: 705-941-3060

Director, Pacific Region, Vancouver Airport District, Sari Hellsten
Tel: 604-666-1800
Fax: 604-666-1812
Other Communications: Executive Assistant, Phone: 604-666-9337

Director, Prairie Region, Southern Alberta District, Kevin Hewson
Tel: 403-344-2061

Director, Québec Region, Montérégie District, Claire Jacques
Tel: 450-246-2272

Director, Prairie Region, Southern Manitoba District, Darlene Klips
Tel: 204-373-2352
Fax: 204-373-2007

Director, Pacific Region, Okanagan & Kootenay District, Glyn Lee
Tel: 250-770-4512
Fax: 250-482-5983

Director, Atlantic Region, Nova Scotia District, Andrew LeFrank
Tel: 902-426-1784

Director, Prairie Region, Winnipeg & Northwest Territories District, Barry Lutz
Tel: 204-983-3770
Fax: 204-984-3106

Director, Northern Ontario Region, St. Lawrence District, Darko Nikolic
Tel: 613-382-8495
Fax: 613-382-4366

Director, Pacific Region, West Coast & Yukon District, Ivan Peterson
Tel: 250-363-3365
Fax: 250-363-8261

Director, Québec Region, St-Lawrence District, Danielle Petitclerc
Tel: 514-350-6100
Fax: 514-283-8591
Other Communications: Executive Assistant, Phone: 514-350-6100

Director, Québec Region, Airports District, Pierre Provost
Tel: 514-633-7702

Director, Pacific Region, Pacific Highway District, Kim Scoville
Tel: 778-538-3602
Fax: 604-541-5968
Other Communications: Executive Assistant, Phone: 778-545-5559

Director, Prairie Region, Saskatchewan District, Mike Shoobert
Tel: 306-780-7356
Fax: 306-780-8222

Director, Northern Ontario Region, Ottawa District, Debbie Zion
Tel: 613-991-1214
Fax: 613-991-1407

Comptrollership Branch
219 Laurier Ave. West, 9th Fl., Ottawa, ON K1A 0L8
Canada Border Services Agency's Comptrollership Branch consists of the following divisions & directorates: Agency Comptroller Directorate; Deputy Chief Financial Officer & Resource Management Directorate; Infrastructure & Environmental Operations Directorate; Infrastructure & Environmental Operations Directorate; Security & Professional Standards Directorate; Vice-President's Office
Vice-President, Sylvain St-Laurent
Tel: 613-948-8604
Fax: 613-948-8825
Director General; Deputy Chief Financial Officer, Simon Bonk
Tel: 613-941-6388
427 Laurier Ave. West, 6th Fl.
Ottawa, ON K1A 0L8
Director General, Infrastructure & Environmental Operations Directorate, David Champagne
Tel: 613-948-9717
410 Laurier Ave. West, 9th Fl.
Ottawa, ON K1A 0L8
Director General, Agency Comptroller Directorate, Terry Perkins
Tel: 613-946-9337
219 Laurier Ave. West, 10th Fl.
Ottawa, ON K1A 0L8
Senior Director, Strategic Financial Planning & Oversight Division, Marc Monette
Tel: 613-948-8606

Human Resources Branch
99 Metcalfe St., 3rd Fl., Ottawa, ON K1A 0L8
The Human Resources Branch consists of the following offices & directorates: Client Services Directorate; Corporate Human Resources Programs Directorate; Executive Group Services, Leadership & Talent Management Directorate; Labour Relations & Compensation Directorate; Strategic Branch Integration & Renewal Directorate; Training & Learning Directorate; Vice-President's Office; Workplace Development, Ethics & Employee Support Division
Vice-President, Human Resources Branch, Camille Therriault-Power
Tel: 613-948-3180
Fax: 613-952-1783
Director General, Labour Relations & Compensation Directorate, Patti Bordeleau
Tel: 613-948-9861
Director General, Client Services Directorate, Beverley Boyd
Tel: 613-948-1164
Director General, Training & Learning Directorate, Michael Gardiner
Tel: 613-946-4280
Director General, Executive Group Services, Leadership & Talent Management Directorate, France Guèvremont
Tel: 613-948-9828
Director General, Corporate Human Resources Programs Directorate, Scott Taymun
Tel: 613-957-3511
Director General, Strategic Branch Integration & Renewal Directorate, Lilia Trombetti
Tel: 613-954-7504

Information, Science & Technology Branch
191 Laurier Ave. West, 7th Fl., Ottawa, ON K1A 0L8
The Canada Border Services Agency Information, Science, & Technology Branch includes the following offices and directorates: Enterprise Architecture & Information Management Directorate; Infrastructure Services Directorate; Planning & Portfolio Management Directorate; Science & Engineering Directorate; Solutions Directorate; Vice-President's Office.
Vice-President, Information, Science, & Technology Branch, Deirdre Kerr-Perrott
Tel: 613-946-4884
Fax: 613-941-6557
Director General, Infrastructure Services Directorate, Anne Craig
Tel: 613-952-1920
#701, 2323 Riverside Dr., 7th Fl.
Ottawa, ON K1A 0L8
Director General, Solutions Directorate, Pierre Ferland
Tel: 613-960-8789
79 Bentley Ave.
Ottawa, ON K2E 6T7
Director General, Science & Engineering Directorate, Diane Keller
Tel: 613-954-2200
79 Bentley Ave.
Ottawa, ON K2E 6T7
Director General, Enterprise Architecture & Information Management Directorate, Gino Lechasseur
Tel: 613-960-8516
250 Tremblay Rd.
Ottawa, ON K1A 0L8
Director General, Planning & Portfolio Management Directorate, Brent McRoberts
Tel: 613-954-7056
Fax: 613-960-8777
150 Isabella St., 7th Fl.
Ottawa, ON K1A 0L8

Operations Branch
191 Laurier Ave. West, 18th Fl., Ottawa, ON K1A 0L8
The Operations Branch of the Canada Border Services Agency is responsible for the following offices & directorates: Border Operations Centre & Major Events Directorate; Border Operations Directorate; International Operations Directorate; Vice-President's Office.
Vice-President, Operations Branch, Pierre Sabourin
Tel: 613-948-4445
Fax: 613-948-7130
Associate Vice-President, Martin Bolduc
Tel: 613-952-5269
Fax: 613-948-7130
Director General, Border Operations Centre & Major Events Directorate, Megan Imrie
Tel: 613-952-2728
Fax: 613-941-9866
Director, Border Operations Directorate, Glenda Lavergne
Tel: 613-954-6990
Fax: 613-957-9723
Director, Operational Performance & Readiness Directorate, Arming Task Force, Arianne Reza
Tel: 613-948-1846
Fax: 613-952-0777

Programs Branch
191 Laurier Ave. West, 15th Fl., Ottawa, ON K1A 0L8
The Programs Branch of the Canadian Border Services Agency is responsible for the following offices & directorates: Anti-Dumping & Countervailing Directorate; Border Programs Directorate; Business Systems Support Directorate; eManifest & Major Projects Directorate; International & Partnerships Directorate; Office of the Vice President & Associate Vice President; Planning & Performance Management Directorate; Post-Border Programs Directorate; Pre-Border Programs Directorate; Risk Assessment Programs Directorate; Trade Programs & CBSA Assessment Revenue Management Directorate
Vice-President, Programs Branch, Cathy Munroe
Tel: 613-954-7220
Other Communications: Executive Assistant, Phone: 613-954-7287
Associate Vice-President, David Vigneault
Tel: 613-952-2531

150 Isabella St., 11th Fl.
Ottawa, ON K1A 0L8
Director General, Planning & Performance Management Directorate, Tim Coughlin
Tel: 613-946-3183
Fax: 613-952-2468
1686 Woodward Dr., 1st Fl.
Ottawa, ON K1A 0L8
Director General, Trade Programs & CBSA Assessment Revenue Management Directorate, Mike Feniak
Tel: 613-948-1838
150 Isabella St., 4th Fl.
Ottawa, ON K1A 0L8
Director General, Anti-Dumping & Countervailing Directorate, Daniel Giasson
Tel: 613-954-1642
191 Laurier Ave. West, 15th Fl.
Ottawa, ON K1L 0L8
Director General, International & Partnerships Directorate, Chris Henderson
Tel: 613-957-6623
150 Isabella St., 11th Fl.
Ottawa, ON K1A 0L8
Director General, Business Systems Support Directorate, Rachelle May
Tel: 613-954-1909
150 Isabella St., 11th Fl.
Ottawa, ON K1A 0L8
Director General, eManifest & Major Projects Directorate, Bruna Rados
Tel: 613-954-2157
150 Isabella St., 11th Fl.
Ottawa, ON K1A 0L8
Director General, Border Programs Directorate, Maureen Tracy
Tel: 613-954-6431
150 Isabella St., 11th Fl.
Ottawa, ON K1A 0L8

Canada Business Network / Réseau Entreprises Canada

235 Queen St., Ottawa, ON K1A 0H5
Toll-Free: 888-576-4444
www.canadabusiness.ca
TTY: 800-457-8466

Canada Business provides a wide range of information on government services, programs & regulations to Canadian business people. The base framework is an organized network of centres across Canada, one in each province & territory. The network of Canada Business is expanding to include regional access partners in many other communities across Canada. The centres offer various products & services aimed at helping clients obtain quick, accurate & comprehensive business information. Each centre exists as a result of cooperative arrangements between federal & provincial governments, & the private sector in some cases. Administration & management of the CBSC varies depending on location between the following federal agencies: Western Economic Diversification (WD), Industry Canada, the Canada Economic Development for Quebec Regions (CEDQR) & the Atlantic Canada Opportunities Agency (ACOA). The Federal Business Information System (BIS) is a collection of information on business-related programs, services & selected regulations which are accessible through the CBSC & on the CBSC web site (www.cbsc.org). The Federal BIS acts as a single window for individuals or businesses to access relevant information from all federal departments

Senior Project Manager, Canada Business Network Operations, Laura Collier
Tel: 613-952-5888
Fax: 613-954-5463

Project Manager, Canada Business Network Operations, Louise Cardinal
Tel: 613-946-1613
Fax: 613-954-5463

Regional Offices
The Business Link Business Service Centre
#100, 10237 - 104 St. NW, Edmonton, AB T5J 1B1
Tel: 780-422-7722
Fax: 780-422-0055
Toll-Free: 800-272-9675
TTY: 800-457-8466
Other Communication: Library Phone: 780-422-7780
Small Business BC
82 - 601 West Cordova St., Vancouver, BC V6B 1G1
Tel: 604-775-5525
Fax: 604-775-5520
Toll-Free: 800-667-2272
askus@smallbusinessbc.ca
www.smallbusinessbc.ca
TTY: 800-457-8466
Canada/Manitoba Business Service Centre
#250, 240 Graham Ave., PO Box 2609, Winnipeg, MB R3C 0J7
Tel: 204-984-2272
Fax: 204-983-3852
Toll-Free: 800-665-2019
TTY: 800-457-8466
Canada/New Brunswick Business Service Centre
Barker House, #102, 570 Queen St., Fredericton, NB E3B 6Z6
Tel: 506-444-6140
Fax: 506-444-6172
Toll-Free: 888-576-4444
TTY: 800-457-8466
Canada/Newfoundland & Labrador Business Service Centre
90 O'Leary Ave., PO Box 8687 A, St. John's, NL A1B 3T1
Tel: 709-772-6022
Fax: 709-772-6090
Toll-Free: 800-668-1010
TTY: 800-457-8466
Canada/NWT Business Service Centre
#701, 5201 - 50 Ave., Yellowknife, NT X1A 3S9
Tel: 876-873-7958
Fax: 876-873-7960
Toll-Free: 800-661-0599
TTY: 800-457-8466
Canada/Nova Scotia Business Service Centre (CNSBSC)
1575 Brunswick St., Halifax, NS B3J 2G1
Tel: 902-426-8604
Toll-Free: 888-576-4444
TTY: 800-457-8466
Canada/Nunavut Business Service Centre
Inuksugait Plaza, PO Box 1000 1198, Iqaluit, NU X0A 0H0
Tel: 867-975-7860
Fax: 867-975-7885
Toll-Free: 877-499-5199
TTY: 800-457-8466
Other Communication: Rankin Inlet, Phone: 867-645-8450, Fax: 867-645-8455; Cambridge Bay, Phone: 867-983-2095, Fax: 967-983-2075
Canada/Ontario Business Service Centre (COBSC)
151 Yonge St., 3rd Fl., Toronto, ON M5C 2W7
Toll-Free: 888-745-8888
www.cbo-eco.ca/en/locations.cfm
TTY: 800-457-8466
Canada/Prince Edward Island Business Service Centre (CPEIBSC)
100 Sydney St., 3rd Fl., PO Box 40, Charlottetown, PE C1A 7K2
Tel: 902-368-0771
Toll-Free: 888-576-4444
TTY: 800-457-8466
Canada/Saskatchewan Business Service Centre (CSBSC)
#2, 345 3rd Ave. South, Saskatoon, SK S7K 1M6
Tel: 306-956-2323
Fax: 306-956-2328
Toll-Free: 800-667-4374
TTY: 800-457-8466
Canada/Yukon Business Service Centre
#101, 307 Jarvis St., Whitehorse, YT Y1A 2H3
Tel: 867-667-2000
Fax: 867-667-2001
Toll-Free: 800-661-0543
TTY: 800-457-8466
Info entrepreneurs
#W204, 380, rue St-Antoine ouest, local 6000, Montréal, QC H2Y 3X7
Tél: 514-496-4636
Téléc: 514-496-5934
Ligne sans frais: 888-576-4444
infoentrepreneurs.org
TTY: 800-457-8466
Autre numéros: Toll Free Fax: 1-888-417-0442

Canada Council for the Arts / Conseil des Arts du Canada

350 Albert St., PO Box 1047, Ottawa, ON K1P 5V8
Tel: 613-566-4414
Fax: 613-566-4390
Toll-Free: 800-263-5588
www.canadacouncil.ca

The Canada Council for the Arts is a national arm's-length agency created by an Act of Parliament in 1957. According to the Canada Council Act, the role of the Council is to foster & promote the study & enjoyment of, & the production of works in the arts. To fulfill this mandate, the Council offers a broad range of grants & services to professional Canadian artists & arts organizations in dance, interdisciplinary work & performance art, media arts, music, interdisciplinary work, theatre, visual arts, & writing & publishing. The Council awards more than 100 prizes every year. It administers the Killam Program of scholarly awards, the Governor General's Literary Awards & the Governor General's Awards in Visual & Media Arts. The Canadian Commission for UNESCO & the Public Lending Right Commission operate under its aegis.

Director & Chief Executive Officer, Robert Sirman
Tel: 613-566-4414 ext: 420

Chair, Joseph L. Rotman
Tel: 613-566-4414 ext: 420
Other Communications: Toll-Free: 1-800-263-5588

Vice-Chair, Simon Brault
Tel: 613-566-4414 ext: 420
Other Communications: Toll-Free: 1-800-263-5588

Manager, Public Relations Team, Marketing Communications, Grace Thrasher
Tel: 613-566-4414 ext: 514

Canada Deposit Insurance Corporation (CDIC) / Société d'assurance-dépôts du Canada (SADC)

50 O'Connor St., 17th Floor, PO Box 2340 D, Ottawa, ON K1P 5W5
Fax: 613-996-6095
Toll-Free: 800-461-2342
info@cdic.ca; info@sadc.ca
www.cdic.ca; www.sadc.ca
Other Communication: Toll Free: 1-800-461-7232 (French)

CDIC, a Crown corporation established in 1967, ensures eligible deposits in member institutions (banks, trust companies, loan companies & cooperative credit associations) in case a member becomes insolvent. Funding is provided by its member institutions through premiums paid on insured deposits. Reports to government through the Minister of Finance. CDIC responsibilities include: providing deposit insurance in case of member failure; contributing to the stability of the Canadian financial system.

Chair, Bryan P. Davies
Tel: 416-973-3082

President & Chief Executive Officer, Michèle Bourque
Tel: 613-947-9332

Senior Vice-President, Insurance & Risk Assessment, Jeffery A. Johnson

Vice-President, Corporate Affairs; General Counsel & Corporate Secretary, M. Claudia Morrow

Vice-President, Finance & Administration; Chief Financial Officer, Thomas J. Vice

Canada Economic Development for Québec Regions / Développement économique Canada pour les régions du Québec

Édifice Dominion Square, #900, 1255, rue Peel, Montréal, QC H3B 2T9
Tel: 514-283-6412
Fax: 514-283-3302
Toll-Free: 866-385-6412
www.dec-ced.gc.ca
Secondary Address: 165, rue Hôtel de Ville
Place du Portage, Phase IIPO Box 1110 B Sta.
Gatineau, QC J8X 3X5 Canada
Fax: 819-997-3340

Defines federal objectives relating to development opportunities & delivers business assistance programs for small- & medium-sized businesses in Qu,bec for innovation, entrepreneurial & market development purposes. Supports a series of programs for appropriate environmental initiatives in various regions of Québec. The agency fosters alliances among the various environmental industry stakeholders including small- & medium-sized enterprises & industrial associations. Goals include a strengthening of existing & new partnerships, & an improvement of access to government programs. The agency also provides a significant amount of support for research & development in areas of environmental technology, demonstration, marketing & transfer projects. Supports initiatives that contribute to making Montréal an industrial centre of excellence in the environment. Aids small- & medium-sized firms in gaining access to federal procurement process, & encourages training & education focusing on business management. Helps business develop export markets through cooperative efforts with Industry Canada & Foreign Affairs & International Trade Canada

Minister Responsible, Hon. Christian Paradis
Tel: 613-995-1377
Fax: 613-943-1562
Paradis.C@parl.gc.ca

Minister of State, Economic Development Agency of Canada for the Regions of Québec, Hon. Denis Lebel

Tel: 613-996-6236
Fax: 613-996-6252
Lebel.D@parl.gc.ca; denis.lebel@dec-ced.gc.ca
Other Communications: Economic Development Agency (QC):514-496-1282

President, Suzanne Vinet
Tel: 514-283-4843
Fax: 514-283-7778

Chief of Staff, Yan Plante
Tel: 819-997-3319
Fax: 819-997-4469

Communications
Director General, Jean-Pierre Thibault
Tel: 514-283-8817
Fax: 514-283-7951

Legal Services
Executive Director, Christine Calvé
Tel: 514-283-2997
Fax: 514-283-1549

Operations / Opérations
Vice-President, Thao Pham
Tel: 514-283-3510
Fax: 514-283-4547
Director, Infrastructure, Lucie Perreault
Tel: 514-283-1333
Fax: 514-283-4131

Business Development & North Business Office
Director, Sophie Legendre
Tel: 514-283-8866
Fax: 514-283-3637

Infrastructure Directorate
Director, Lucie Perreault
Tel: 514-283-1333
Fax: 514-283-4131

Regional Coherence
Director General, Jacques Langelier
Tel: 514-283-3628
Fax: 514-283-7491

Policy & Planning / Politiques et planification
Vice-President, Rita Tremblay
Tel: 514-283-1294
Fax: 514-283-5940
Director General, Policy, Research & Programs Branch, Jean Pierre Lavoie
Tel: 514-283-2664
Fax: 514-283-8429
Director, Special Projects, Keltoum Bouhabel
Tel: 514-496-1299
Fax: 514-284-8429
Chief, Coordination & Administrative Services, Simon Labrecque
Tel: 514-283-2664
Fax: 514-283-8429
Abitibi-Témiscamingue
906, 5e av, Val-d'Or, QC J9P 1B9
Tel: 819-825-5260
Fax: 819-825-3245
Toll-Free: 800-567-6451
Regional Director, Sandra Lafleur
Tel: 819-825-5260
Fax: 819-825-3245
Bas St-Laurent
Édifice Trust général du Canada, #310, 2, rue Saint-Germain Est, Rimouski, QC G5L 8T7
Tel: 418-722-3282
Fax: 418-722-3285
Toll-Free: 800-463-9073
Regional Director, Pierre Roberge
Tel: 418-722-3255
Fax: 418-722-3285
Centre-du-Québec
#105, 1100 boul René-Lévesque, Drummondville, QC J2C 5W4
Tel: 819-478-4664
Fax: 819-478-4666
Toll-Free: 800-567-1418
Regional Director, Georges Arseneau
Tel: 819-478-4664
Fax: 819-478-4666
Côte-Nord
#202B, 701, boul Laure, PO Box 698, Sept-Iles, QC G4R 4K9
Tel: 418-968-3426
Fax: 418-968-0806
Toll-Free: 800-463-1707
Regional Director, Thomas Szalay
Tel: 418-968-3426
Fax: 418-968-0806
Estrie
Place Andrew Paton, #100, 202, rue Wellington nord, Sherbrooke, QC J1H 5C6
Tel: 819-564-5904
Fax: 819-564-5912
Toll-Free: 800-567-6084
Regional Director, Mariette Larochelle
Tel: 819-564-5904
Fax: 819-564-5912
Gaspésie—Iles-de-la-Madeleine
Place Jacques-Cartier, 120, rue de la Reine, 3e étage, Gaspé, QC G4X 2S1
Tel: 418-368-5870
Fax: 418-368-6256
Toll-Free: 866-368-0044
Regional Director, France Simard
Tel: 418-368-5879
Fax: 418-368-6256
Ile-de-Montréal
Édifice Dominion Square, #900, 1255, rue Peel, Montréal, QC H3B 2T9
Tel: 514-283-2500
Fax: 514-496-8310
Toll-Free: 800-322-4636
Regional Director, Marie-José Reid
Tel: 514-283-8153
Fax: 514-469-8310
Laval - Laurentides - Lanaudière
#410, 2990, av Pierre-Péladeau, Laval, QC H7T 3B3
Tel: 450-973-6844
Fax: 450-973-6851
Toll-Free: 800-430-6844
Regional Director, Carole Hart
Tel: 450-973-6845
Fax: 450-973-6851
Mauricie
Immeuble Bourg du Fleuve, #413, 25, rue des Forges, Trois-Rivières, QC G9A 2G4
Tel: 819-371-5182
Fax: 819-371-5186
Toll-Free: 800-567-8637
Regional Director, Pierre Lacoursière
Tel: 819-371-5182
Fax: 819-371-5186
Montérégie
Place Agropur, #400, 101, boul Roland-Therrien, Longueuil, QC J4H 4B9
Tel: 450-928-4088
Fax: 450-928-4097
Toll-Free: 800-284-0335
Regional Director, Charles Lambert
Tel: 450-928-4088
Fax: 450-928-4097
Nord-du-Québec
Édifice Dominion Square, #900, 1255 rue Peel, Montréal, QC H3B 2T9
Tel: 514-283-8131
Fax: 514-283-3637
Toll-Free: 800-561-0633
Regional Director, Sophie Legendre
Tel: 514-283-8866
Fax: 514-283-3637
Outaouais
#202, 259 boul Saint-Joseph, Gatineau, QC J8Y 6T1
Tel: 819-994-7442
Fax: 819-994-7846
Toll-Free: 800-561-4353
Regional Director, Marc Boily
Tel: 819-994-7442
Fax: 819-994-7846
Other Communications: Administrative Assistant, Phone: 819-944-7442
Québec - Chaudière - Appalaches
Place Iberville IV, #030, 2954, boul Laurier, Québec, QC G1V 4T2
Tel: 418-648-4826
Fax: 418-648-7291
Toll-Free: 800-463-5204
Regional Director, Christian Audet
Tel: 418-648-4451
Fax: 418-648-7291
Saguenay - Lac-Saint-Jean
#203, 100, rue Saint-Joseph sud, Alma, QC G8B 7A6
Tel: 418-668-3084
Fax: 418-668-7584
Toll-Free: 800-463-9808
Regional Director, Donald Hudon
Tel: 418-668-3084
Fax: 418-688-7584

Canada Industrial Relations Board (CIRB) / Conseil canadien des relations industrielles (CCRI)

240 Sparks St., 4th Fl. West, Ottawa, ON K1A 0X8
Fax: 613-941-4461
Toll-Free: 800-575-9696
info@cirb-ccri.gc.ca
www.cirb-ccri.gc.ca
TTY: 800-855-0511

The Board is an independent, administrative, quasi-judicial tribunal which administers Part I & certain provisions of Part II of the Canada Labour Code. Its responsibilities include the granting or revoking of collective bargaining rights, the mediation & adjudication of unfair labour practice complaints, the determination of unlawful strikes & lockouts & other matters.

Chair, Elizabeth MacPherson
Tel: 613-947-5366
Fax: 613-947-3894

Vice-Chairperson, Graham Clarke
Tel: 613-992-3979
Fax: 613-947-5407

Vice-Chairperson, Louise Fecteau
Tel: 613-992-3979
Fax: 514-283-3590

Vice-Chairperson, Judith F. MacPherson
Tel: 613-992-3979
Fax: 613-947-5407

Vice-Chairperson, William G. McMurray
Tel: 613-992-3979
Fax: 613-947-5407

Vice-Chairperson, Claude Roy
Tel: 613-992-3979
Fax: 514-283-3590
Other Communications: Executive Assistant, Phone: 613-944-6204

Research & Information Services Clerk, Marie-France Grenier
Tel: 613-947-5391
Fax: 613-947-5407

Communications
Director, Case Management Services, Justine Abel
Tel: 613-947-5432
Fax: 613-995-9493
Communications Officer, Joanne Maisonneuve
Tel: 613-992-4001
Fax: 613-947-5407
Communications Officer, Natalie Ouellette
Tel: 613-947-5386
Information Officer, Joanne Leclair
Tel: 613-947-5392
Fax: 613-947-5407

Legal Services
General Counsel & Director of Legal Services, David Demirkan
Tel: 613-944-5809
Fax: 613-947-5460
Senior Counsel, Marie-Claude Grignon
Tel: 514-283-3571
Fax: 514-283-3590
Senior Counsel, Susan Nicholas
Tel: 613-947-5456
Fax: 613-947-5460

Canada Lands Company Ltd. (CLCL) / Société immobilière du Canada limitée (SICL)

#1200, 1 University Ave., Toronto, ON M5J 2P1
Tel: 416-952-6111
Fax: 416-952-6115
Toll-Free: 888-252-5263
www.clcl.ca

CLCL is a Crown corporation with a mandate to enhance the quality of life of the communities in which it conducts business, to generate best value for the taxpayer through the orderly disposal of strategic real estate properties no longer required by the federal government, as well as the management of certain other select properties. The agency reports to government through the Minister of Transport, Infrastructure & Communities.

Chair, Grant B. Walsh
gwalsh@walshdeltagroup.com

President & Chief Executive Officer, Mark B. Laroche

Old Port of Montréal Corporation Inc. / Société du Vieux port de Montréal
333, rue de la Commune ouest, Montréal, QC H2Y 2E2
Tél: 514-283-5256
Ligne sans frais: 800-971-7678
www.oldportcorporation.com/home.html

Parc Downsview Park Inc.
#1, 35 Carl Hall Rd., Toronto, ON M3K 2B6
Tel: 416-952-2222
Fax: 416-952-2225
info@downsviewpark.ca
www.downsviewpark.ca
Chair, David Soknacki

Canada Mortgage & Housing Corporation (CMHC) / Société canadienne d'hypothèques et de logement (SCHL)

700 Montreal Rd., Ottawa, ON K1A 0P7
Tel: 613-748-2000
Fax: 613-748-2098
Toll-Free: 800-668-2642
chic@cmhc-schl.gc.ca
www.cmhc.ca; www.schl.ca
TTY: 613-748-2447
Other Communication: Canadian Housing Information Centre: 613-748-2367

CMHC works closely with a network of professional associations, groups & institutions concerned with regional planning & the residential sector. It prepares various research projects for the examination of relationships between urban areas, housing & sustainable development issues. Involved in numerous technical research projects addressing interrelationships between housing, energy & resource use. Through its research & information transfer function, CMHC will undertake initiatives such as identifying approaches & solutions that lead to more sustainable & healthy communities, examining barriers to potential development of brownfield sites. CMHC will focus on ways to reduce residential energy consumption in multiple-unit housing, educate consumers on energy-saving changes to homes. The Net Zero Healthy Healthy Housing Initiative combines passive solar, energy-efficient design, construction & appliances, integrated with renewable energy systems, to achieve net zero energy consumption on an annual basis, significantly reducing environmental impacts & GHG emissions. Twenty demonstration projects across Canada are underway.

Acts Administered:
CMHC Act
National Housing Act (NHA)

Minister Responsible, Minister of Human Resources & Skills Development, Hon. Diane Finley

Chair, Dino Chiesa

President & Chief Executive Officer; Board Member, Karen Kinsley
Tel: 613-748-2186

Vice-President, Corporate Services & Chief Financial Officer, Marc Joyal
Tel: 613-748-2958

Vice-President, Assisted Housing, Sharon Matthews
Tel: 613-748-2251

Vice-President, Insurance Underwriting, Servicing & Policy, Mark McInnis
Tel: 613-748-2134

Vice-President, Insurance Product & Business Development, Pierre Serré
Tel: 613-748-2818

Vice-President, Policy & Planning, Douglas A. Stewart
Tel: 613-748-2553

Vice-President, Human Resources, Gail Tolley
Tel: 613-748-2082

Executive Director, CMHC International, André Asselin
Tel: 613-748-2347

Executive Director, Communications, Peter De Barros
Tel: 613-748-2143

Executive Director, Corporate Marketing, Charles Chenard
Tel: 613-748-2505

Director, Risk Management, David Dmytryk
Tel: 613-748-2409

Director, Audit & Evaluation Services, Serge Gaudet
Tel: 613-748-4099

Atlantic Region
Barrington Tower, 9th Fl., 1894 Barrington St., Halifax, NS B3J 2A8
Tel: 902-426-3530
Fax: 902-426-9991
TTY: 800-309-3388
General Manager, Christina Haddad
Tel: 416-218-3321
Principal, Marketing, Info & Communications, Emily Poitras-Benedict
Tel: 902-426-8127 ext: 582

British Columbia
#200, 1111 West Georgia St., Vancouver, BC V6E 4S4
Tel: 604-731-5733
Fax: 604-737-4139
TTY: 800-309-3388
General Manager, Charles MacArthur
Tel: 604-737-4150
Manager, Business Development & Marketing, Marcia Freeman
Tel: 604-666-2529
Senior Consultant, Communications & Marketing, Tracy Wells
Tel: 604-737-4162

Ontario
#300, 100 Sheppard Ave. East, Toronto, ON M2N 6Z1
Tel: 416-221-2642
Fax: 416-218-3310
Toll-Free: 866-389-1742
TTY: 900-309-3388
General Manager, Peter Friedmann
Tel: 416-218-3300
Senior Consultant, Communications & Marketing, Michele McMaster
Tel: 416-218-3452

Prairie & Territories Region
#200, 1000 - 7 Ave. SW, Calgary, AB T2P 5L5
Tel: 403-515-3000
Fax: 403-515-2930
Toll-Free: 877-499-7245
TTY: 800-309-3388
General Manager, Gordon McHugh
Tel: 403-515-3001
Senior Consultant, Communications & Marketing, Kimberlee Jones
Tel: 403-515-3048

Québec
1100, boul René-Levesque ouest, 1er étage, Montréal, QC H3B 5J7
Tél: 514-283-2222
Ligne sans frais: 888-772-0772
TTY: 800-309-3388
General Manager, Sylvie Crispo
Tel: 514-283-3023
Director, Communications & Marketing, Lise Hamilton
Tel: 514-283-3151

Canada Pension Plan Investment Board / Office d'investissement du Régime de pensions du Canada

#2600, 1 Queen St. East, PO Box 101, Toronto, ON M5C 2W5
Tel: 416-868-4075
Fax: 416-868-8689
Toll-Free: 866-557-9510
csr@cppib.ca
www.cppib.ca
TTY: 416-868-6035

The CPP Investment Board is a Crown corporation created as part of 1997 reforms designed to ensure the soundness & sustainability of the CPP. The Board operates under similar investment rules as other pension plans in Canada, which require the prudent management of pension plan assets in the interests of plan contributors & beneficiaries.

Chair, Board of Directors, Robert Astley

President & Chief Executive Officer, David Denison

Executive Vice-President, Investments, Mark Wiseman

Senior Vice-President, Private Investments, André Bourbonnais

Senior Vice-President/General Counsel & Corporate Secretary, John H. Butler

Senior Vice-President, Real Estate Investments, Graeme Eadie

Vice-President, Head of Quantitative Research, Sterling Gunn

Senior Vice-President, Communications & Stakeholder Relations, Michel Leduc

Senior Vice-President, Human Resources, Saylor Millitz-Lee

Senior Vice-President, Chief Investment Strategist, Donald M. Raymond

Senior Vice-President & Chief Operating Officer, Benita M. Warmbold

Senior Vice-President, Public Market Investments, Eric M. Wetlaufer

Senior Vice-President & Chief Financial Officer, Nicholas Zelenczuk

Canada Place Corporation / Corporation Place du Canada

504 - 999 Canada Place, Vancouver, BC V6C 3E1
Tel: 604-775-7200
Fax: 604-775-6251
admin@canadaplace.ca
www.canadaplace.ca
Other Communication: Media, Filming & Public Relations, Phone: 604-775-6245, Fax: 604-775-6215, Email: media@canadaplace.ca

The Corporation is the landlord & in charge of property management at Canada Place in Vancouver, which includes a cruise ship facility, a trade & convention centre, a hotel, an IMAX theatre, & a parking structure

Chair, Robin Wilson

President & Chief Executive Officer, Michael J. Shardlow

Chief Operating Officer, Andrew Mann

Director, Communications & Public Affairs, Robyn McVicker

Director, Facilities, Andy O'Neill

Canada Post Corporation / Société canadienne des postes

Corporate Secretariat, 2701 Riverside Dr., Ottawa, ON K1A 0B1
Toll-Free: 866-607-6301
www.canadapost.ca; www.postescanada.ca
TTY: 800-267-2797
Other Communication: Postal Security, Phone: 1-800-267-1177

Federal commercial Crown corporation responsible for Canada's postal system. Reports to government through the Minister of Transport, Infrastructure & Communities. For postal rates, codes, abbreviations & other general information; see Postal Information in the main Index.

President & Chief Executive Officer, Deepak Chopra

Chief Financial Officer, Wayne Cheeseman

Chief Operating Officer, Jacques Côté

Senior Vice-President, Direct Marketing, Advertising & Publishing Business, Laurene Cihosky

Senior Vice-President, Postal Transformation, Cal Hart

Senior Vice-President, Operations, Douglas Jones

Senior Vice-President, Human Resources, André Joron

Senior Vice-President, Sales, Peter V. Melanson

Senior Vice-President/Chief Customer Officer, Louis O'Brien

Senior Vice-President, Parcels, Marvin Rosenzweig

Senior Vice-President, Transaction Mail, Mary Traversy

Senior Vice-President, Chief Information Technology Officer, André Turgeon

Senior Vice-President, Strategy, Philip Ventura

Vice-President/General Counsel, Corporate Secretary & Compliance, Bonnie Boretsky

Vice-President, Real Estate, Murray Dea

Vice-President, Customer Service, Stephen Edmondson

Vice-President, Engineering & Postal Transformation, John Farnand

Vice-President, Pension Fund/Chief Investment Officer, Douglas Greaves

Vice-President, Finance & Comptroller, Barbara MacKenzie

Vice-President, Government Relations & Policy, Susan Margles

Vice-President, General Business Sales, Serge Pitre

Vice-President, Communications & Public Affairs, Jo-Anne Polak

Vice-President, Mail Processing & Network, Brian Wilson

ePost / Postel
#1300, 393 University Ave., Toronto, ON M5G 2P7
Toll-Free: 877-376-1212
service@to.epost.ca

Office of the Ombudsman / Bureau de l'ombudsman
PO Box 90026, Ottawa, ON K1V 1J8
Fax: 800-204-4193
Toll-Free: 800-204-4198
www.ombudsman.postescanadapost.ca
Ombudsman, Nicole Goodfellow

Canada Post Communications Offices

Atlantic Division
6175 Almon St., Halifax, NS B3K 5N2
Tel: 902-494-4711

Huron Division
951 Highbury Ave., London, ON N5Y 1B0
Tel: 519-457-5362
Fax: 519-457-5346
President, Robert MacLeod
Coordinator, Tyler Campbell
Tel: 506-453-8420
Tyler.Campbell@inbcanada.ca

Pacific Division
PO Box 2110 STN Terminal, Vancouver, BC V6B 4Z3
Tel: 604-662-1592
Fax: 604-662-1710

Prairie Division
#1300, 10020 - 101A Ave., Edmonton, AB T5J 4J4
Tel: 780-944-3137
Fax: 780-944-3140
Secondary Address: #409, 266 Graham Ave. Winnipeg Office:
Winnipeg, MB R3C 0K0 Canada
Fax: 204-987-5110

Québec Division
#503, 300, rue St-Paul, Québec, QC G1K 3W0
Tel: 418-694-3161
Fax: 418-694-6993
Secondary Address: #1506, 555, rue McArthur Montréal Office:
Saint-Lauren, QC H4T 1T4 Canada
Fax: 514-345-4307

Greater Toronto Area & Regions
4567 Dixie Rd., Mississauga, ON L4W 1S2
Tel: 905-214-9595
Fax: 905-214-9244

Canada Revenue Agency (CRA) / Agence du revenu du Canada

875 Heron Rd., Ottawa, ON K1A 0L5
Toll-Free: 800-267-6999
www.cra-arc.gc.ca
TTY: 800-665-0354
Other Communication: Individual Income Tax Enquiries: 1-800-959-8281; Telerefund: 1-800-959-1956; Business & Self-Employed Individuals: 1-800-959-5525; GST/HST Credit: 1-800-959-1953

The Canada Revenue Agency administers tax laws for the Canadian federal government & for most provincial & territorial governments. The Agency is also responsible for various social & economic benefit & incentive programs, which are delivered through the tax system.

Acts Administered:
Canada Pension Plan Act, Part I
Customs & Excise Offshore Application Act
Customs Act
Customs Tariff Act
Department of National Revenue Act
Excise Act
Excise Tax Act
Special Import Measures Act
Unemployment Insurance Act, Part III & VII

Minister, National Revenue; Minister, Fisheries & Oceans, Hon. Gail Shea
Tel: 613-995-2960
Fax: 613-952-6608
Shea.G@parl.gc.ca

Commissioner & Chief Executive Officer, Linda Lizotte-MacPherson
Tel: 613-957-3688

Appeals Branch / Direction générale des appels
Assistant Commissioner, Anne-Marie Lévesque
Tel: 613-960-2388
Fax: 613-952-5965
Director General, Taxpayer Relief & Service Complaints, Lynn Atkinson
Tel: 613-960-2232
Fax: 613-952-5825
Director General, Tax & Charities Appeals, John Crowley
Tel: 613-960-2307
Fax: 613-941-8088
Director General, Program Management & Analysis, Sylvain St-Denis
Tel: 613-960-2374
Fax: 613-952-4281
Director, CPP/EI Appeals, Natalie Stibernik
Tel: 613-960-2205

Assessment & Benefit Services Branch / Direction générale des services de cotisation et de prestations
Assistant Commissioner, Arlene E. White
Tel: 613-954-6614
Fax: 613-954-4434
Deputy Assistant Commissioner, Dave J. Bennett
Tel: 613-941-5007
Fax: 613-954-4434
Director General, Individual Returns, Nathalie Dumais
Tel: 613-957-7497
Fax: 613-941-2090
Director General, Business Returns, Ted Gallivan
Tel: 613-954-7979
Director General, Benefit Programs, Cynthia Leblanc
Tel: 613-957-9338
Fax: 613-946-6719
Director General, Horizontal Integration & Management Services, Sue Wormington
Tel: 613-954-5755
Fax: 613-957-3365

Compliance Programs Branch / Programmes d'observation de la législation
Fax: 613-952-6772
Assistant Commissioner, Terrance I. McAuley
Tel: 613-957-3709
Fax: 613-952-6772
Deputy Assistant Commissioner, Richard Montroy
Tel: 613-957-3585
Fax: 613-952-6772
Director General, International & Large Business, Lucie Bergevin
Tel: 613-952-7472
Fax: 613-941-9673
Director General, Audit Professional Services, Susan Betts
Tel: 613-948-4744
Fax: 613-946-0044
Director General, Scientific Research & Experimental Development, Hélène Dompierre
Tel: 613-946-3447
Fax: 613-952-8071
Director General, Small & Medium Enterprises, Jim Gauvreau
Tel: 613-941-6756
Director General, Business Transformation & Corporate Management Directorate, Martin Leigh
Tel: 613-941-5126
Fax: 613-960-0328
Other Communications: Alternate Telephone: 613-791-6880
Director General, Compliance Strategy, Claude St-Pierre
Tel: 613-957-3648
Fax: 613-946-5931
Director General, Enforcement & Disclosures, Luc Vadnais
Tel: 613-957-7780
Fax: 613-941-9606

Corporate Audit & Evaluation Branch / Direction générale de la vérification et de l'évaluation de l'entreprise
Chief Audit Executive & Director General, Program Evaluation, Patricia A. MacDonald
Tel: 613-957-7522
Fax: 613-952-0512
Director, Internal Audit, Corporate Function, Annie Boudreau
Tel: 613-957-7552
Fax: 613-941-3657
Director, Professional Practice & Corporate Services, Maura Butko
Tel: 613-954-7840
Fax: 613-948-2314
Director, Internal Audit, Tax Operations, Gita Ghatt
Tel: 613-941-5664
Director, Program Evaluation, Myles Kennedy
Tel: 613-954-7881

Enterprise Risk Management Branch / Direction générale de la gestion des risques de l'entreprise
Assistant Commissioner & Chief Risk Officer, Brian Philbin
Tel: 613-960-5536
Fax: 613-960-5557
Director, Enterprise Risk Management, Valérie Bournival
Tel: 613-960-5534
Fax: 613-960-5557
Special Advisor to the Asst. Commissioner & CRO, Johanne Raby
Tel: 613-960-5535
Fax: 613-960-5557

Finance & Administration Branch / Direction générale des finances et de l'administration
Assistant Commissioner & Chief Financial Officer, Filipe Dinis
Tel: 613-946-1763
Fax: 613-948-5776
Director General, Security & Internal Affairs, Thérèse Awada
Tel: 613-948-2449
Fax: 613-952-2019
Director General, Financial Administration, Michel Bernard
Tel: 613-957-7343
Fax: 613-952-3087
Director General, Resource Management, Judy Cosby
Tel: 613-947-3262
Fax: 613-941-2264
Director General, Real Property & Service Integration, Bill Doering
Tel: 613-954-8330
Director General, Administration, Dennis Quinn
Tel: 613-947-3262
Fax: 613-941-2264
Acting Director General, Strategic Management & Program Support, Michael K. Walker
Tel: 613-957-7502
Fax: 613-957-7613

Human Resources Branch / Direction générale des ressources humaines
Fax: 613-957-2306
Assistant Commissioner, Cheryl Fraser
Tel: 613-954-8200
Fax: 613-952-8557
Deputy Assistant Commissioner, Dan Danagher
Tel: 613-946-4527
Fax: 613-952-8557
Director General, Strategic Business Integration, Claude Bourget
Tel: 613-954-8166
Director General, Training & Learning, Karen Butcher
Tel: 613-954-7573
Fax: 613-941-9411
Director General, Training & Learning, Judith Farley
Tel: 613-954-7573
Fax: 613-941-9411
Director General, Human Resources Operations, Claire Lavoie
Tel: 613-957-2319
Fax: 613-954-7214
Director General, Employment Programs, Anuradha Marisetti
Tel: 613-954-1623
Fax: 613-954-4194
Director General, Executive Personnel, Monique Potvin
Tel: 613-957-7623
Fax: 613-941-5132
Director General, Workplace Relations & Compensation, Claude P. Tremblay
Tel: 613-954-8150
Project Officer, Migration to the End-State PQPs Project, Violaine Chartrand
Tel: 613-957-7621

Information Technology Branch / Direction générale de l'informatique
Fax: 613-957-9058
Assistant Commissioner & Chief Information Officer, Peter Poulin
Tel: 613-954-8983
Fax: 613-957-9058
Deputy Assistant Commissioner, Keith Barrass
Tel: 613-948-2780
Director General, Technology Services, Annette Butikofer
Tel: 613-948-0814
Fax: 613-948-0487

Director General, Branch Business Management, Denis Lafrenière
Tel: 613-946-9473
Fax: 613-946-4992
Director General, Operations Services, Lorne Leech
Tel: 613-948-0976
Director General, Data & Assurance Services, Randall Rennie
Tel: 613-948-0396
Director, Distributed Services, Richard St-Jean
Tel: 613-946-4741
Fax: 613-946-4992

Legal Services Branch / Direction générale des services juridiques
Fax: 613-954-6282
Senior General Counsel, Charles McNab
Tel: 613-957-2358
Senior General Counsel, Jean-Marc Raymond
Tel: 613-954-5881

Legislative Policy & Regulatory Affairs / Politiques législatives et affaires réglementaires
Assistant Commissioner, Brian McCauley
Tel: 613-957-3708
Fax: 613-957-2067
Director General, Income Tax Rulings, Wayne Adams
Tel: 613-957-2132
Fax: 613-957-2088
Director General, Excise & GST/HST Rulings, Pierre Bertrand
Tel: 613-948-4398
Fax: 613-941-4451
Director General, Charities, Cathy Hawara
Tel: 613-954-0931
Fax: 613-954-2586
Director General, Registered Plans, Danielle Laflèche
Tel: 613-954-0933
Fax: 613-952-1343
Director General, Legislative Policy, Mickey Sarazin
Tel: 613-957-2061
Fax: 613-954-0896
Director, Planning & Management Services Division, Sherry Sharpe
Tel: 613-957-2375
Fax: 613-952-8674
Director, Reorganizations & Resources Division, Mark Symes
Tel: 613-957-8978
Fax: 613-957-2088
Special Advisor to the Assistant Commissioner, Terry de March
Tel: 613-941-1647
Fax: 613-954-2586

Public Affairs Branch / Direction générale des affaires publiques
Assistant Commissioner, Sandra Lavigne
Tel: 613-957-3508
Fax: 613-954-7955
Director General, Ministerial Services & Operations, Louise Dorval
Tel: 613-957-8438
Fax: 613-941-0914
Director General, Communications, Michel Hébert
Tel: 613-948-4847
Director, Policies & Standards, Geneviève Binet
Tel: 613-957-3265
Fax: 613-954-6441
Director, Access to Information & Privacy, Marie-Claude Juneau
Tel: 613-960-5378
Fax: 613-941-9395
Director, Branch Services, Patrick Mineault
Tel: 613-941-6865
Fax: 613-952-7939
Director, Electronic & Print Media, Christiane Séguin
Tel: 613-960-5523

Strategy & Integration Branch / Direction generale de la strategie et de l'integration
Assistant Commissioner, Catherine Bennett
Tel: 613-952-3660
Fax: 613-941-3438
Director General, Corporate Tax Administration for Ontario Directorate, Marilyn Gaudet
Tel: 613-960-5687
Fax: 613-960-5700
Director General, Client Relations, Mireille Éthier
Tel: 613-941-9964
Fax: 613-941-0181
Director General, Planning & Management Services Division, Rob Schumacher
Tel: 613-941-0798
Fax: 613-946-3312
Director General, Corporate Planning, Governance & Measurement, Normand Théberge
Tel: 613-954-6082
Fax: 613-952-0061
Director General, Statistics & Information Management, Patricia Whitridge
Tel: 613-957-8706
Fax: 613-952-6715
Director, Strategic Policy, Maxine Ifill
Tel: 613-941-6216
Fax: 613-946-8914
Director, Provincial Sales Tax Administration Reform Directorate, Cary O'Brien
Tel: 613-948-5319
Fax: 613-960-5700

Taxpayer Services & Debt Management Branch / Services aux contribuables et gestion des créances
Deputy Assistant Commissioner, Danielle Morin
Tel: 613-941-9801
Fax: 613-952-6395
Director General, Debt Management Research & Analytics, Richard Denis
Tel: 613-957-1863
Fax: 613-948-3162
Other Communications: Alternative Telephone: 613-859-8175

Director General, Taxpaper Services, Marj Ogden
Tel: 613-957-9362
Fax: 613-941-5100
Other Communications: Executive Assistant, Phone: 613-957-7849
Director General, Accounts Receivable Directorate, Michael Snaauw
Tel: 613-954-1532

Tax Services Offices
Toll-Free: 800-959-8281
TTY: 800-665-0354
Other Communication: For Business or Self-Employed, Toll-Free: 1-800-959-5525

Atlantic Region
Bathurst
201 George St., PO Box 8888, Bathurst, NB E2A 4L8
Fax: 506-548-7176
Charlottetown
161 St. Peters Rd., PO Box 8500, Charlottetown, PE C1A 8L3
Fax: 902-566-7197
Nova Scotia
1557 Hollis St., PO Box 638, Halifax, NS B3J 2T5
Fax: 902-426-7170
Moncton
50 King St., PO Box 1070, Moncton, NB E1C 8P2
Fax: 506-851-7018
Newfoundland & Labrador
Sir Humphrey Gilbert Building, 165 Duckworth St., PO Box 12075, St. John's, NL A1B 4R5
Fax: 709-754-5928
Saint John
126 Prince William St., Saint John, NB E2L 4H9
Fax: 506-636-5200

Northern Ontario Region
Barrie
81 Mulcaster St., Barrie, ON L4M 6T7
Fax: 705-721-0056
Belleville
11 Station St., Belleville, ON K8N 2S3
Fax: 613-969-7845
Kingston
31 Hyperion Ct., PO Box 2600, Kingston, ON K7L 5P3
Fax: 613-545-3272
Ottawa & Nunavut
333 Laurier Ave. West, Ottawa, ON K1A 0L9
Fax: 613-238-7125
Ottawa Technology Centre
875 Heron Rd., Ottawa, ON K1A 1A2
Fax: 613-739-1147
Peterborough
185 King St. West, Peterborough, ON K9J 8M3
Fax: 705-876-6422
Sudbury
1050 Notre Dame Ave., Sudbury, ON P3A 5C1
Fax: 705-671-3994
Thunder Bay
130 South Syndicate Ave., Thunder Bay, ON P7E 1C7
Fax: 807-622-8512

Pacific Region
Burnaby-Fraser
9737 King George Blvd., PO Box 9070 Main, Surrey, BC V3T 5W6
Fax: 604-587-2010
Northern BC & Yukon
280 Victoria St., Prince George, BC V2L 4X3
Fax: 250-561-7869
Southern Interior
277 Winnipeg St., Penticton, BC V2A 1N6
Fax: 250-492-8346
Vancouver
1166 West Pender St., Vancouver, BC V6E 3H8
Fax: 604-689-7536
Vancouver Island
1415 Vancouver St., Victoria, BC V8V 3W4
Fax: 250-363-8188

Prairie Region
Edmonton & NWT
#10, 9700 Jasper Ave., Edmonton, AB T5J 4C8
Fax: 780-495-3533
Lethbridge
#200, 419 - 7 St. South, Lethbridge, AB T1J 4A9
Fax: 403-382-4765
Red Deer
4996 - 49 Ave., Red Deer, AB T4N 6X2
Fax: 403-341-7053
Regina
#260, 1783 Hamilton St., Regina, SK S4P 2B6
Fax: 306-757-1412
Saskatoon
340 - 3rd Ave. North, Saskatoon, SK S7K 0A8
Fax: 306-652-3211
Calgary
220 - 4 Ave. SE, Calgary, AB T2G 0L1
Fax: 403-264-5843
Winnipeg
325 Broadway, Winnipeg, MB R3C 4T4
Fax: 204-984-5164
Brandon
1039 Princess Ave., Winnipeg, MB R7A 4J5
Fax: 204-726-7868

Southern Ontario Region
Hamilton
55 Bay St., PO Box 2220, Hamilton, ON L8N 3E1
Fax: 905-546-1615
Kitchener-Waterloo
166 Frederick St., Kitchener, ON N2G 4N1
Fax: 519-579-4532
London
451 Talbot St., London, ON N6A 5E5
Fax: 519-645-4029
St Catharines
32 Church St., PO Box 3038, St Catharines, ON L2R 3B9
Fax: 905-688-5996
Toronto Centre
1 Front St. West, Toronto, ON M5J 2X6
Fax: 416-360-8908
Toronto East
#427, 200 Town Centre Ct., Toronto, ON M1P 4Y3
Fax: 416-973-5126
Toronto North
5001 Yonge St., Toronto, ON M2N 6R9
Fax: 416-512-2558
Toronto West
5800 Hurontario St., Mississauga, ON L5R 4B4
Fax: 905-566-6182
Windsor
185 Ouellette Ave., Windsor, ON N9A 5S8
Fax: 519-257-6558

Québec Region
Chicoutimi
100, rue Lafontaine, Chicoutimi, QC G7H 6X2
Téléc: 418-698-6387
Laval
3400, av Jean-Béraud, Laval, QC H7T 2Z2
Téléc: 514-956-7071
Montérégie-Rive-Sud
3250, boul Lapinière, Brossard, QC J4Z 3T8
Téléc: 450-926-7100
Montréal
305, boul René-Lévesque ouest, Montréal, QC H2Z 1A6
Téléc: 514-496-1309
Outaouais
1100, boul Maloney ouest, Gatineau, ON K1A 1L4
Fax: 819-994-1103
Québec
165, rue de la Pointe-aux-Lièvres sud, Québec, QC G1K 7L3
Téléc: 418-649-6478
Rimouski
#101, 180, av de la Cathédrale, Rimouski, QC G5L 5H9
Téléc: 418-722-3027
Rouyn-Noranda
44, av du Lac, Rouyn-Noranda, QC J9X 6Z9
Téléc: 819-797-8366
Sherbrooke
50, Place de la Cité, CP 1300, Sherbrooke, QC J1H 5L8
Téléc: 819-821-8582
Trois-Rivières
#111, 25, rue des Forges, Trois-Rivières, QC G9A 2G4
Téléc: 819-371-2744

Canada School of Public Service (CCMD) / École de la fonction publique du Canada (EEPC)

373 Sussex Dr., Ottawa, ON K1N 6Z2
Tel: 819-953-5400
Fax: 819-953-7953
Toll-Free: 866-703-9598
info@csps-efpc.gc.ca
www.csps-efpc.gc.ca
TTY: 819-934-6194
Other Communication: Toll-Free Fax: 1-866-944-0454

Learning provider for the Public Service of Canada. The School brings together three well-established federal public service learning organizations: the Canadian Centre for Management Development, & from the Public Service Commission, Training & Development Canada & Language Training Canada. Contributes to building & maintaining a modern, high-quality, professional public service that is at the leading-edge of knowledge in modern public administration & public sector management. Through up-to-date adult learning techniques, it provides public servants across the country with access to the common learning opportunities they require to effectively serve Canada & Canadians

Acts Administered:
Canadian Centre for Management Development Act

Deputy Minister & President, Guy McKenzie
Tel: 613-992-8165
Fax: 613-943-1038
guy.mckenzie@csps-efpc.gc.ca

President Emeritus, Jocelyne Bourgon
Tel: 613-943-4311
Fax: 613-947-3130

Vice-President, Strategic Directions, Program Development & Marketing, Michele Brenning
Tel: 613-943-0321
Fax: 613-947-3706
Other Communications: Executive Assistant, Phone: 613-943-4296

Vice-President & Chief Financial Officer, Corporate Management & Registration Services, Chantale Cousineau-Mahoney
Tel: 613-947-1098
Fax: 613-995-5652
Other Communications: Executive Assistant, Phone: 613-947-4357

Vice-President, Penny Gotzaman
Tel: 613-995-4035
Fax: 613-943-7873

Acting Vice-President, Program Operations, Jayne Huntley
Tel: 613-943-0250
Fax: 613-992-3663

Director General, Functional Communities, Authority Delegation & Orientation, Élise Boisjoly
Tel: 819-934-7692
Fax: 819-953-2392
Other Communications: Executive Assistant, Phone: 819-994-5734

Director General, Physical Infrastructure & Administration, Alain Dorion
Tel: 613-943-8917
Fax: 613-995-0331

Director General, Strategic Directions, Innovation & Program Development, Jean-François Fleury
Tel: 613-992-8346
Fax: 613-943-4312

Director General, Language Training, Patricia Jaton
Tel: 819-994-5641
Fax: 819-953-7298

Director General, Registration Services & ILMS, Steven McLaughlin
Tel: 819-934-8279
Fax: 819-934-8300
Other Communications: Executive Assistant, Phone: 819-934-8258

Director General, Marketing, Communications & Engagement, Marie-Claude Petit
Tel: 613-943-4304
Fax: 613-943-5651

Director General, Leadership & Professional Development, Sandra Webber
Tel: 613-996-5489
Fax: 613-947-0490
Other Communications: Executive Assistant, Phone: 613-996-0295

Canadian Artists & Producers Professional Relations Tribunal / Tribunal canadien des relations professionnelles artistes-producteurs

C.D. Howe Bldg., 240 Sparks St., 1st Fl., West Tower, Ottawa, ON K1A 1A1
Tel: 613-996-4052
Fax: 613-947-4125
Toll-Free: 800-263-ARTS
info@capprt-tcrpap.gc.ca
www.capprt-tcrpap.gc.ca

The Tribunal administers legislation providing a framework for professional relations between self-employed artists & the producers in the federal jurisdiction who use their services.

Acts Administered:
The Status of the Artist Act

Executive Director & General Counsel, Diane Chartrand
Tel: 613-947-4263
Fax: 613-947-4125
chartrand.diane@capprt-tcrpap.gc.ca

Administrative & Financial Officer, Sylvie Besner
Tel: 613-947-4264
Fax: 613-947-4125
besner.sylvie@capprt-tcrpap.gc.ca
TTY: 800-267-6511

Administration & Communication Officer, Manon Allaire
Tel: 613-947-9607
Fax: 613-947-4125
allaire.manon@capprt-tcrpap.gc.ca
TTY: 800-267-6511

Director, Planning, Research & Communication, Brian K. Stewart
Tel: 613-996-4053
Fax: 613-947-4125
stewart.brianK@capprt-tcrpap.gc.ca
TTY: 800-267-6511

Manager, Corporate Services, Karen Berndt
Tel: 613-996-4054
Fax: 613-947-4125
TTY: 800-267-6511

Registrar & Legal Counsel, Steve Joanisse
Tel: 613-947-8413
Fax: 613-947-4125
joanisse.steve@capprt-tcrpap.gc.ca
TTY: 800-267-6511

Canadian Broadcasting Corporation (CBC) / Société Radio-Canada (SRC)

181 Queen St., PO Box 3220 C, Ottawa, ON K1Y 1E4
Tel: 613-288-6033
liaison@radio-canada.ca
www.cbc.radio-canada.ca
Other Communication: Toll Free: 1-866-306-4636

The Canadian Broadcasting Corporation (CBC) is a Crown corporation governed by the 1991 Broadcasting Act & subject to regulations of the Canadian Radio-television & Telecommunications Commission (CRTC). The CBC operates four national radio networks, CBC Radio One & CBC Radio Two in English, & La Radio de Radio-Canada & Espace musique in French, featuring information & general interest programs as well as classical music & cultural programs; two self-supporting specialty cable television services, CBC Newsworld in English & Le Réseau de l'information (RDI) in French which feature news & information programs 24 hours a day, seven days a week; & radio & television services for Canada's North in English, French & eight aboriginal languages. CBC also provides, on behalf of the Government of Canada, an international shortwave radio service, Radio Canada International, which broadcasts in seven languages.

Chair, Board of Directors, Timothy W. Casgrain

President & Chief Executive Officer, Hubert T. Lacroix

Executive Vice-President, French Services, Louis Lalonde

Executive Vice-President, English Services, Kirstine Stewart

Senior Vice-President, Corporate Secretary & Business Partnerships, Michel Tremblay

Vice President, Real Estate, Legal Services & General Counsel, Maryse Bertrand

Vice President, People & Culture, Roula Zaarour

Vice-President, Brand, Communications & Corporate Affairs, Real Estate Division, William B. Chambers

Vice-President & Chief Regulatory Officer, Steven Guiton

Vice-President & Chief Financial Officer, Suzanne Morris

CBC Ombudsman
Ombudsman, CBC, English Services, Kirk LaPointe
Tel: 416-205-2825
Fax: 416-205-2978
ombudsman@cbc.ca
PO Box 500 A Sta.
Toronto, ON M5W 1E6 Canada
Ombudsman, Radio-Canada, French Services, Julie Miville-Dechêne
Tél: 514-597-4757
Ligne sans frais: 877-846-4737
Téléc: 514-597-5253
ombudsman@radio-canada.ca
PO Box 6000
Montreal, QC H3C 3A8

Radio Canada International
1400, boul René-Lévesque est, CP 6000, Montréal, QC H2L 2M2
Tél: 514-597-7500
info@rcinet.ca
www.rcinet.ca

Radio Canada International produces daily and weekly programs in English, French, Spanish, Russian, Mandarin, Arabic & Portuguese. A wide variety of programs produced by CBC/Radio-Canada are also available. RCI also produces weekly and monthly short features & interviews for broadcast on numerous partner stations in English, French, Spanish, Russian and Mandarin. Radio Canada International is a member of several international organizations, such as NABA (North American Broadcasters Association), CBA (Commonwealth Broadcasting Association), CBU (Caribbean Broadcasting Union), ABU (Asia-Pacific Broadcasting Union) & DRM (Digital Radio Mondiale). RCI is an associate member of the UER (European Broadcasting Union).

CBC/Radio-Canada - English Services
250 Front St. W., PO Box 500 A, Toronto, ON M5W 1E6
Toll-Free: 866-306-4636
www.cbc.ca/contact/
TTY: 866-220-6045

CBC/Radio-Canada - French Services
1400, boul René-Lévesque est, CP 6000, Montréal, QC H3C 3A8
Tél: 514-597-6000
Ligne sans frais: 866-306-4636
auditoire@radio-canada.ca
www.radio-canada.ca/

Alberta (English & French)
10062 - 102nd Ave., PO Box 555, Edmonton, AB T5J 2P4
Tel: 780-468-7500
www.cbc.ca/edmonton/contact/

British Columbia (English & French)
PO Box 4600, Vancouver, BC V6B 4A2
Tel: 604-662-6000
Toll-Free: 866-306-4636
www.cbc.ca/bc/contact/

CBC North
PO Box 160, Yellowknife, NT X1A 2N2
Tel: 867-920-5400
www.cbc.ca/north/contact/

Manitoba (English & French)
541 Portage Ave., Winnipeg, MB R3B 2G1
Tel: 204-788-3222
www.cbc.ca/manitoba/contact/
TTY: 866-220-6045

Maritimes (English)
PO Box 3000, Halifax, NS B3J 3E9
Tel: 902-420-8311
www.cbc.ca/ns/contact/

Atlantic Provinces (French Services) / Radio-Canada Acadie
250, av Université, Moncton, NB E1C 8N8
Tel: 506-853-6666
www.cbc.ca/nb/contact

Newfoundland (English)
PO Box 12010 A, St. John's, NL A1B 3T8
Tel: 709-576-5000
www.cbc.ca/nl/contact/

Canadian Broadcasting Centre
250 Front St. W., PO Box 500 A, Toronto, ON M5W 1E6
Tel: 416-205-3311
www.cbc.ca/toronto/contact/

Ottawa Production Centre
181 Queen St., PO Box 3220 C, Ottawa, ON K1Y 1E4
Tel: 613-288-6000
www.cbc.ca/ottawa/contact/
Québec (English) / Maison de Radio-Canada
1400, boul René-Lévesque est, CP 6000, Montréal, QC H3C 3A8
Tél: 514-597-6000
www.cbc.ca/montreal/contact/
Québec (French) / Société Radio-Canada
880, rue Saint-Jean, CP 18800, Québec, QC G1K 9L4
Ligne sans frais: 800-267-1341
Saskatchewan (English & French)
2440 Broad St., Regina, SK S4P 4A1
Tel: 306-347-9540
www.cbc.ca/sask/contact/
Prince Edward Island (English & French)
430 University Ave., PO Box 2230, Charlottetown, PE C1A 8B9
Tel: 902-629-6400
Toll-Free: 866-306-4636
www.cbc.ca/pei/contact/

Canadian Centre for Occupational Health & Safety (CCOHS) / Centre canadien d'hygiène et de sécurité au travail (CCHST)

135 Hunter St. East, Hamilton, ON L8N 1M5
Tel: 905-572-2981
Fax: 905-572-2206
Toll-Free: 800-668-4284
www.ccohs.ca
Provides occupational health & safety & environmental information in the form of publications, responses to inquiries & a computerized information service available in various formats. Topics include: environmental acts & regulations; occupational & environmental health data; toxic effects of chemical substances; transport of dangerous goods; chemical evaluation; hazardous substances; & domestic substances listed under the Canadian Environmental Protection Act; biological hazards; ergonomics

President & Chief Executive Officer, S. Len Hong
Tel: 905-572-2981 ext: 443

Vice-President, Dr. Patabendi K. Abeytunga
Tel: 905-572-2981 ext: 453

Controller, Bonnie Easterbrook
Tel: 905-572-2981 ext: 440

Manager, Computer Systems & Services, David Brophy
Tel: 905-572-2981 ext: 449

Manager, General Health & Safety Services, Norma Gibson-MacDonald
Tel: 905-572-2981 ext: 452

Manager, Communications, Eleanor Westwood
Tel: 905-572-2981 ext: 440

Canadian Centre on Substance Abuse (CCSA) / Centre canadien de lutte contre l'alcoolisme et les toxicomanies (CCLAT)

#500, 75 Albert St., Ottawa, ON K1P 5E7
Tel: 613-235-4048
Fax: 613-235-8101
info@ccsa.ca
www.ccsa.ca
Other Communication: Publications, Email: publications@ccsa.ca
CCSA is a non-profit organization working to minimize the harm associated with the use of alcohol, tobacco, & other drugs.
Acts Administered:
CCSA Act

Interim Chair, Beverly Clarke

Chief Executive Officer, Michel Perron
Tel: 613-235-4048 ext: 232

Deputy Chief Executive Officer, Rita Notarandrea
Tel: 613-235-4048 ext: 239

Director, Research & Knowledge Exchange, Cheryl Arratoon
Tel: 613-235-4048 ext: 266

Director, Partnerships & Priorities, Rhowena Nebre Martin
Tel: 613-235-4048 ext: 287

Director, Human Resources, Sherry Read
Tel: 613-235-4048 ext: 254

Director, Finance, Anne Richer
Tel: 613-235-4048 ext: 231

Canadian Commercial Corporation (CCC) / Corporation commerciale canadienne

50 O'Connor St., 11th Fl., Ottawa, ON K1A 0S6
Tel: 613-996-0034
Fax: 613-995-2121
Toll-Free: 800-748-8191
www.ccc.ca
A Crown Corporation mandated to facilitate international trade, particularly in government markets. CCC specializes in international procurement markets for Canadian companies & provides services to help them win, negotiate & manage export contracts. As prime contractor, CCC offers a government-to-government agreement that simplifies customer access to Canadian technology & expertise. CCC contracts have a government guarantee for performance.

Chair, Robert C. Kay

President & Chief Executive Officer, Marc Whittingham
Tel: 613-996-0042
Fax: 613-992-2134
Other Communications: Alternative Telephone: 613-996-0043

Vice-President, Business Development & Sales, Pierre Alarie
Tel: 613-943-0953
Fax: 613-995-2121

Vice-President, Strategy & Organizational Development, Mariette Fyfe-Fortin
Tel: 613-943-4360
Fax: 613-995-2121

Vice-President, Contract Management & Procurement, Jacques Greffe
Tel: 613-996-0161
Fax: 613-995-2121

Vice-President/Legal General Counsel & Corporate Secretary, Legal Services, Tamara Parschin-Rybkin, Q.C.
Tel: 613-992-4419
Fax: 613-947-3903

Vice-President/Chief Financial Officer, Risk & Finance, Martin Zablocki
Tel: 613-992-9638
Fax: 613-995-2121

Canadian Dairy Commission (CDC) / Commission canadienne du lait (CCL)

Central Experimental Farm, NCC Driveway, Bldg. 55, 960 Carling Ave., Ottawa, ON K1A 0Z2
Tel: 613-792-2000
Fax: 613-792-2009
cdc-ccl@cdc-ccl.gc.ca
www.cdc.ca
TTY: 613-792-2082
Other Communication: Special Milk Class Permits, Phone: 613-792-2057; Dairy Imports & Exports, Phone: 613-792-2010
The federal Crown corporation serves the interests of all dairy stakeholders, including producers, processors, further processors, exporters, consumers & governments. The following are the key objectives of the CDC: providing efficient milk & cream producers with the opportunity to obtain a fair return for their labour & investment; & ensuring an adequate supply of high quality dairy products for consumers.

Chair, Randy Williamson

Chief Executive Officer, John Core
Tel: 613-792-2060
Fax: 613-792-2064
jcore@agr.gc.ca

Commissioner, Gilles Martin

Senior Director, Policy & Corporate Affairs, Gilles Froment
Tel: 613-792-2030
Fax: 613-792-2009
gfroment@agr.gc.ca

Senior Director, Finance & Operations, Gaëtan Paquette
Tel: 613-792-2070
Fax: 613-792-2009
gpaquette@agr.gc.ca

Director, Audit, Robert Hansis
Tel: 613-792-2050
Fax: 613-792-2009
rhansis@agr.gc.ca

Canadian Environmental Assessment Agency (CEAA) / Agence canadienne d'évaluation environnementale (ACEE)

Place Bell Canada, 160 Elgin St., 22nd Fl., Ottawa, ON K1A 0H3
Tel: 613-957-0700
Fax: 613-957-0862
Toll-Free: 866-582-1884
info@ceaa-acee.gc.ca
www.ceaa-acee.gc.ca
The Canadian Environmental Assessment Agency (CEAA) was established to administer the Canadian Environmental Assessment Act (the Act). The environmental assessment process identifies the environmental effects of proposed projects & measures to address those effects, in support of sustainable development. CEAA promotes environmental assessment as a tool to protect & sustain a healthy environment in harmony with a growing economy. The CEAA advocates high-quality environmental assessments by assisting federal departments & agencies with training & guidance & by investing in the research & development of best practices. CEAA provides administrative support to mediators & review panels & ensures that the public has opportunities to participate effectively in the environmental assessment process. Public participation strengthens the quality & credibility of environmental assessments by providing local & traditional knowledge, & insight into possible environmental effects. A publicly accessible master index of environmental assessments carried out by federal departments is available in the Canadian Environmental Assessment Registry (projects beginning before November 2003 are available in the Federal Environmental Assessment Index) located on the CEAA we b site. In addition, CEAA's participant funding program provides limited funds to ensure that interested individuals & groups have the opportunity to participate in mediations & panel reviews.
Accountable to the Minister of the Environment

President, Elaine Feldman
Tel: 613-948-2671
Fax: 613-948-2208
elaine.feldman@ceaa-acee.gc.ca

Vice-President, Policy Development, Helen Cutts
Tel: 613-948-2662
Fax: 613-957-0897
helen.cutts@ceaa-acee.gc.ca

Vice-President, Operations, Yves Leboeuf
Tel: 613-948-2665
Fax: 613-957-0935
yves.leboeuf@ceaa-acee.gc.ca

Executive Director, Project Reviews, Steve Burgess
Tel: 613-948-2663
Fax: 613-957-0941
steve.burgess@ceaa-acee.gc.ca

Director General, Corporate Services, Richard Gagné
Tel: 613-957-0467
Fax: 613-957-0946
richard.gagne@ceaa-acee.gc.ca

Director, Operational Support, Andrée Chevrier
Tel: 613-957-0641
Fax: 613-948-1354
andree.chevrier@ceaa-acee.gc.ca

Director, Communications, Charlene Gaudet
Tel: 613-957-0712
Fax: 613-957-0946
charlene.gaudet@ceaa-acee.gc.ca

Director, Legislative & Regulatory Affairs, John McCauley
Tel: 613-948-1785
Fax: 613-957-0897
john.mccauley@ceaa-acee.gc.ca

Director, Finance & Administration, Daniel Nadeau
Tel: 613-948-2677
Fax: 613-957-0862
daniel.nadeau@ceaa-acee.gc.ca

Director, Human Resources, Brigitte Schryer
Tel: 613-954-2201
Fax: 613-957-0858
brigitte.schryer@ceaa-acee.gc.ca

Senior Policy Analyst, Legislative & Regulatory Affairs, Natalie Deschamps
Tel: 613-957-0366

Fax: 613-857-0366
natalie.deschamps@ceaa-acee.gc.ca

General Counsel & Executive Director, Legal Services, Irene V. Gendron
Tel: 613-957-0735
Fax: 613-957-0942

Alberta & Northwest Territories
61 Airport Rd. NW, Edmonton, AB T5G 0W6
Tel: 780-495-2037
Fax: 780-495-2876

Ontario
#907, 55 St. Clair Ave. East, Toronto, ON M4T 1M2
Tel: 416-952-1576
Fax: 416-952-1573

Pacific & Yukon
#410, 701 Georgia St. West, Vancouver, BC V7Y 1K8
Tel: 604-666-2431
Fax: 604-666-6990

Prairie Region
#101, 167 Lobard Ave., Winnipeg, MB R3B OT6
Tel: 204-983-5127
Fax: 204-983-7174

Québec
1141, rte de l'Église, 2e étage, CP 9514 Ste-Foy, Québec, QC G1V 4B8
Tél: 418-649-6444
Téléc: 418-649-6443

Canadian Food Inspection Agency (CFIA) / Agence canadienne d'inspection des aliments (ACIA)

1400 Merivale Rd., Ottawa, ON K1A 0Y9
Tel: 613-225-2342
Fax: 613-228-6601
Toll-Free: 800-442-2342
www.inspection.gc.ca
TTY: 800-465-7735
Other Communication: Atlantic Area, Phone: 506-851-7400; Ontario Area: 519-837-9400; Québec Area: 514-283-8888; Western Area: 403-292-4301

The agency is responsible for all inspection services related to food safety, economic fraud, trade-related requirements, & animal & plant health programs.

Acts Administered:
Acts Administered in Part by the Canadian Food Inspection Agency
Agriculture & Agri-Food Administration Monetary Penalties Act
Canada Agricultural Products Act
Canadian Food Inspection Agency Act
Consumer Packaging & Labelling Act
Feeds Act
Fertilizers Act
Fish Inspection Act
Food & Drugs Act
Health of Animals Act
Meat Inspection Act
Plant Breeders' Rights Act
Plant Protection Act
Seeds Act

President, George Da Pont
Tel: 613-773-6000
Fax: 613-773-6060
George.DaPont@inspection.gc.ca

Executive Vice-President, Office of the President, Mary Komarynsky
Tel: 613-773-6500
Fax: 613-773-6060
Mary.Komarynsky@inspection.gc.ca

Vice-President, Operations, Stephen Baker
Tel: 613-773-5700
Fax: 613-773-5671
Stephen.Baker@inspection.gc.ca

Vice-President, Human Resources, Gérard Étienne
Tel: 613-773-5725
Fax: 613-773-5795
Gerard.Etienne@inspection.gc.ca

Vice-President, Policy & Programs, Neil Bouwer
Tel: 613-773-5734
Fax: 613-773-5791
Neil.Bouwer@inspection.gc.ca

Vice-President, Science, Vacant
Tel: 613-773-5722
Fax: 613-773-5797

Vice-President, Corporate Management, Peter Everson
Tel: 613-773-5759
Fax: 613-773-5792
Peter.Everson@inspection.gc.ca

Vice-President, Inspection Modernization, Cameron Prince
Tel: 613-773-7030
Fax: 613-773-5671
Cameron.Prince@inspection.gc.ca

Acting Vice-President, Information Management & Information Technology, Peter Bruce
Tel: 613-773-1395
Fax: 613-773-0676
Peter.Bruce@inspection.gc.ca

Vice-President, Public Affairs Branch, George W. Shaw
Tel: 613-773-5776
Fax: 613-773-5559
George.Shaw@inspection.gc.ca

Vice-President, Business Transformation, Bill Teeter
Tel: 613-221-3125
Fax: 613-221-3158
Bill.Teeter@inspection.gc.ca

Assoc. Vice-President, Integration & Management Services, Jim Butcher
Tel: 613-773-6298
Fax: 613-773-5791
Jim.Butcher@inspection.gc.ca

Executive Director, Strategic Communication, Laurel Herwig
Tel: 613-773-5501
Fax: 613-773-5618
Laurel.Herwig@inspection.gc.ca

Executive Director, Corporate Secretariat, Veronica McGuire
Tel: 613-773-5751
Fax: 613-773-5791
Veronica.McGuire@inspection.gc.ca

Executive Director, Audit, Evaluation & Risk Oversight, Brian Smithon
Tel: 613-773-5349
Fax: 613-773-5696
Brian.Smith@inspection.gc.ca

Director, Executive Support & Coordination, Aline Dimitri
Tel: 613-773-5542
Fax: 613-773-5606
Aline.Dimitri@inspection.gc.ca

Director, Corporate Planning & Reporting, Everett Ethier
Tel: 613-221-7571
Fax: 613-221-5270
Everett.Ethier@inspection.gc.ca

Canadian Forces Grievance Board / Comité des griefs des Forces canadiennes

60 Queen St., 10th Fl., Ottawa, ON K1P 5Y7
Tel: 613-996-8529
Fax: 613-996-6491
Toll-Free: 877-276-4193
www.cfgb-cgfc.gc.ca
TTY: 877-986-1666
Other Communication: Secure Fax: 613-995-8129

An administrative tribunal with quasi-judicial powers, independent from the Department of National Defence (DND) & the Canadian Forces (CF). The Board was created on March 1, 2000, in accordance with legislation enacted in December 1998 that contained amendments to the National Defence Act. The Board conducts objective & transparent reviews of grievances with due respect to fairness & equity for each individual member of the CF, regardless of rank or position. It plays a unique role within the military grievance review process because it ensures that the rights of CF personnel are considered fairly & impartially in the best interests of both parties concerned, thus balancing the rights of the grievor against the legal & operational requirements of the CF.

Acts Administered:
National Defence Act, ch. N-5, sec. 29
Queen's Regulation & Orders for the Canadian Forces, Ch. 7

Chair, Bruno Hamel
Tel: 613-996-6453
Fax: 613-995-8129
Other Communications: Executive Assistant, Phone: 613-996-8621

Vice-Chair, James Price
Tel: 613-996-8628
Fax: 613-996-6491

Executive Director, Corporate Services, Anne Sinclair
Tel: 613-996-7027
Fax: 613-996-6491
Other Communications: Executive Assistant, Phone: 613-995-7992

Director, Operations/General Counsel, Caroline Maynard
Tel: 613-995-5552
Fax: 613-996-6491
Other Communications: Executive Assistant, Phone: 613-995-5127

Senior Legal Counsel, Legal Services, Ann Boivin
Tel: 613-995-5599
Fax: 613-996-6491

Registrar, Andrée-Anne Paquette
Tel: 613-995-5126
Fax: 613-996-6491

Canadian Grain Commission (CGC) / Commission canadienne des grains (CCG)

#600, 303 Main St., Winnipeg, MB R3C 3G8
Tel: 204-983-2770
Fax: 204-983-2751
Toll-Free: 800-853-6705
contact@grainscanada.gc.ca
www.grainscanada.gc.ca
TTY: 866-317-4289
Other Communication: Grain Sanitation & Infestation Control Industry Services, Fax: 204-984-7550; Licensing & Security Unit, Fax: 204-983-4654; Statistics Unit, Phone: 204-983-2739

The CGC is Canada's official grain quality assurance agency. The CGC offers a wide range of programs & services. It regulates grain handling in Canada & establishes & maintains quality standards for Canadian grains. Responsibilities are as follows: officially inspecting & grading grain; weighing grain at terminal & transfer elevators; licensing grain elevators & dealers; conducting & publishing statistical & economic studies; & performing basic & applied research on Canadian grain.

Acts Administered:
Canada Grain Act

Chief Commissioner, Elwin Mermanson
Tel: 204-983-2735
Fax: 204-983-2751

Commissioner, Murdoch MacKay
Tel: 204-983-2732
Fax: 204-983-2751

Assistant Chief Commissioner, Jim Smolik
Tel: 204-983-2730
Fax: 204-983-2751

Chief Financial Officer, Cheryl Blahey
Tel: 204-984-7042
Fax: 204-984-7213

Chief Informatics Officer, Karl Daher
Tel: 204-984-6948
Fax: 204-983-0248

Chief Operating Officer, Gordon Miles
Tel: 204-983-2731
Fax: 204-983-2751

Director, Grain Research Laboratory, Peter Burnett
Tel: 204-983-2764

Director, Corporate Services, Sandy HayGlass
Tel: 204-983-2752
Fax: 204-983-0248

Director, Industry Services, Jim Stuart
Tel: 204-983-1549
Fax: 204-983-7550

Coordinator, Communications, Louise Worster
Tel: 204-983-2748

Canadian Heritage / Patrimoine canadien

15 Eddy St., Gatineau, QC K1A 0M5
Tel: 819-997-0055
Toll-Free: 866-811-0055
info@pch.gc.ca
www.pch.gc.ca
TTY: 888-997-3123

Canadian Heritage works to achieve a more cohesive & creative nation. Goals of the department are for Canadians to express & share their cultural experiences with others in their own country & globally & for Canadians to live in an inclusive society with

intercultural understanding & citizen participation.
Responsibilities are carried out by the following sectors: Citizenship & Heritage; Cultural Affairs; Sport, Major Events & Regions; & Strategic Policy, Planning & Corporate Affairs.
Acts Administered:
An Act to Incorporate the Jules & Paul-Émile Léger Foundation
Broadcasting Act
Canada Council for the Arts Act
Canadian Charter of Rights & Freedoms
Canadian Radio-television & Telecommunications Commission
Copyright Act
Cultural Property Export & Import Act
Department of Canadian Heritage Act
Fitness & Amateur Sport Act
Foreign Publishers Advertising Services Act
Holidays Act
Income Tax Act
Investment Canada Act
Laurier House Act
Library & Archives of Canada Act
Lieutenant Governors Superannuation Act
Museums Act
National Anthem Act
National Arts Centre Act
National Battlefields at Québec Act
National Film Act
National Horse of Canada Act
National Sports of Canada Act
National Symbol of Canada Act
Official Languages Act
Parliamentary Employment & Staff Relations Act
Physical Activity & Sport Act
Public Servants Disclosure Protection Act
Public Service Employment Act
Public Service Labour Relations Act
Salaries Act
Sir John A. Macdonald Day & the Sir Wilfred Laurier Day Act
Status of the Artist Act
Telefilm Canada Act
Trademarks Act

Minister, Canadian Heritage & Official Languages, Hon. James Moore
Tel: 819-997-7788
Fax: 819-994-1267
james.moore@pch.gc.ca

Minister of State (Status of Women), Hon. Rona Ambrose
Tel: 819-956-4000
Fax: 613-995-1761
minister-ministre@swc-cfc.gc.ca

Minister of State (Sport), Hon. Bal Gosal
Tel: 819-934-1122
Fax: 819-953-8055
bal.gosal@pch.gc.ca

Deputy Minister, Daniel Jean
Tel: 819-994-1132
Fax: 819-997-0979
daniel.jean@pch.gc.ca

Director, Communications, James Maunder
Tel: 819-997-7788
Fax: 819-994-1267
james.maunder@pch.gc.ca

Liaison & Agenda Officer, Associate Deputy Minister's Office, Joanne Courchesne
Tel: 819-997-1356
Fax: 819-997-2978
joanne.courchesne@pch.gc.ca

Associated Agencies, Boards & Commissions:
• Canada Council for the Arts / Conseil des Arts du Canada
350 Albert St.
PO Box 1047
Ottawa, ON K1P 5V8
Tel: 613-566-4414
Fax: 613-566-4390
Toll-free: 800-263-5588
www.canadacouncil.ca
• Canada Science & Technology Museum Corporation / Musée des sciences et de la technologie du Canada
• Canadian Broadcasting Corporation (CBC) / Société Radio-Canada (SRC)
See: Entry Name Index for detailed listing.
• Canadian Museum of Civilization (CMC) / Musée canadien des civilisations
• Canadian Museum of Nature (CMN) / Musée canadien de la nature (MCN)
See: Entry Name Index for detailed listing.
• Canadian Museum of Civilization (CMC) / Musée canadien des civilisations
• Canadian Museum of Nature (CMN) / Musée canadien de la nature (MCN)
See: Entry Name Index for detailed listing.
• Canadian Radio-television & Telecommunications Commission (CRTC) / Conseil de la radiodiffusion et des télécommunications canadiennes
• Library & Archives Canada
• National Arts Centre (NAC) / Centre national des Arts (CNA)
See: Entry Name Index for detailed listing.
• National Battlefields Commission / Commission des champs de bataille nationaux
• National Film Board of Canada / Office national du film du Canada
• National Gallery of Canada / Musée des Beaux-Arts du Canada
• National Gallery of Canada / Musée des beaux-arts du Canada
• Public Service Commission of Canada / Commission de la fonction publique du Canada
• Status of Women Canada / Condition féminine Canada
• Telefilm Canada / Téléfilm Canada

Citizenship & Heritage Sector / Citoyenneté et patrimoine
Assistant Deputy Minister, Tom Scrimger
Tel: 819-997-2832
Fax: 819-994-5032
tom.scrimger@pch.gc.ca
Director General, Canadian Heritage Information Network (CHIN), Gabrielle Blais
Tel: 819-997-0091
Fax: 819-994-9555
Gabrielle.Blais@pch.gc.ca
Director General, Canadian Conservation Institute & Chief Operating Officer, Jeanne E. Inch
Tel: 613-998-3721
Fax: 613-952-1431
jeanne.inch@pch.gc.ca
Director General, Strategic Management & Human Rights, Martha LaBarge
Tel: 819-997-1588
Fax: 819-997-0329
Martha.Labarge@pch.gc.ca
Director General, Citizen Participation, Michel Lemay
Tel: 819-953-5999
Fax: 819-953-3515
Michel.Lemay@pch.gc.ca
Director General, Official Languages Support Programs, Hubert Lussier
Tel: 819-994-0943
Fax: 819-953-9353
Hubert.Lussier@pch.gc.ca
Director General, Aboriginal Affairs, Patricia Neri
Tel: 819-994-6035
Fax: 819-934-6704
patricia.neri@pch.gc.ca
Director, Heritage Group, Pierre Derome
Tel: 819-956-5555
Fax: 819-934-3201
pierre.derome@pch.gc.ca
Director, Policy & Research, Yvan M. Déry
Tel: 819-994-2224
Fax: 819-994-3697
yvan.dery@pch.gc.ca
Atlantic
#106, 1045 Main St., Moncton, NB E1C 1H1
Tel: 506-851-7066
Fax: 506-851-7079
Toll-Free: 866-811-0055
pch-atlan@pch.gc.ca
TTY: 888-997-3123
Regional Executive Director, Paul Landry
Tel: 506-851-7069
Fax: 506-851-7079
Paul.Landry@pch.gc.ca
Ontario
#400, 150 John St., Toronto, ON M5V 3T6
Tel: 416-954-0395
Fax: 416-954-2909
Toll-Free: 866-811-0055
pch-ontario@pch.gc.ca
TTY: 888-997-3123
Executive Director, Marie Moliner
Tel: 416-954-0396
Fax: 416-954-2909
marie.moliner@pch.gc.ca
Prairies & Northern Region
#510, 240 Graham Ave., PO Box 2160, Winnipeg, MB R3C 3R5
Tel: 204-983-3601
Fax: 204-984-6996
Toll-Free: 866-811-0055
pnr-rpn@pch.gc.ca
TTY: 888-997-3123
Regional Executive Director, Louis Chagnon
Tel: 204-983-0261
Fax: 204-984-2303
Louis.Chagnon@pch.gc.ca
Québec
Complexe Guy-Favreau, Tour Ouest, 200, boul René-Lévesque ouest, 6e étage, Montréal, QC H2Z 1X4
Tel: 514-283-5191
Toll-Free: 866-811-0055
pch-qc@pch.gc.ca
TTY: 888-997-3123
Regional Executive Director, Marc Lemay
Tel: 514-283-5797
Fax: 514-283-8762
Marc.Lemay@pch.gc.ca
Western
#400, 300 West Georgia St., Vancouver, BC V6B 6C6
Tel: 604-666-0176
Fax: 604-666-3508
Toll-Free: 866-811-0055
wr-ro@pch.gc.ca
TTY: 888-997-3123
Other Communication: LAN Fax: 604-666-8801
Regional Executive Director, Patrick Tobin
Tel: 604-666-2060
Fax: 604-666-6040
Patrick.Tobin@pch.gc.ca

Canadian Human Rights Commission / Commission canadienne des droits de la personne

344 Slater St., 8th Fl., Ottawa, ON K1A 1E1
Tel: 613-995-1151
Fax: 613-996-9661
Toll-Free: 888-214-1090
www.chrc-ccdp.ca
TTY: 888-643-3304

The Commission administers the Canadian Human Rights Act which applies to federal government departments & agencies, & businesses under federal jurisdiction. The Commission accepts complaints of discrimination based on race, national or ethnic origin, colour, religion, age, sex, marital & family status, pardoned offence, disability & sexual orientation. It also administers the Employment Equity Act to remove barriers for four designated groups: women, Aboriginal peoples, persons with disabilities & members of visible minorities. Collect calls accepted throughout Canada.

Chief Commissioner, Jennifer Lynch, QC
Tel: 613-943-9144

Deputy Chief Commissioner, David Langtry
Tel: 613-943-9148

Secretary General, Karen Mosher
Tel: 613-943-9134

Director General, Knowledge Center, Linda Dabros
Tel: 613-943-9153

Director General, Dispute Resolution Branch, Ian Fine
Tel: 613-943-9090

Director General, Discrimination Prevention Branch, Myriam Montrat
Tel: 613-943-9155

Director General, Corporate Management Branch, Heather Throop
Tel: 613-943-9033
Fax: 613-941-6808

Director, Outreach & Communications Branch, David Gollob
Tel: 613-943-9138

Western Region
Canada Place, #1645, 9700 Jasper Ave., PO Box 21, Edmonton, AB T5J 4C3
Tel: 780-495-4040
Fax: 780-495-4044
Toll-Free: 888-214-1090
TTY: 780-495-4108
Other Communication: Toll-Free TYY: 1-888-643-3304
Regional Manager, Hilda Andresen
Tel: 780-495-5936
Fax: 780-495-4044
Eastern Region
#903, 425, boul de Maisonneuve ouest, Montréal, QC H3A 3G5
Tel: 514-283-5218
Fax: 514-283-5084
Toll-Free: 888-214-1090
TTY: 514-283-1869
Other Communication: Toll-Free TTY: 1-888-643-3304
Regional Manager, Michel Bibeau
Tel: 514-496-2932
Fax: 514-283-5084
National Aboriginal Initiative
#750, 175 Hargrave St., Winnipeg, MA RC3 3R8
Tel: 204-983-2189
Fax: 204-983-6132
Toll-Free: 866-772-4880
TTY: 866-772-4840
Director, Sherri Helgason
Tel: 204-983-4648

Canadian Human Rights Tribunal (CHRT) / Tribunal canadien des droits de la personne (TCDP)

160 Elgin St., 11th Fl., Ottawa, ON K1A 1J4
Tel: 613-995-1707
Fax: 613-995-3484
registrar@chrt-tcdp.gc.ca
www.chrt-tcdp.gc.ca
TTY: 613-947-1070

Quasi-judicial body that adjudicates complaints of discrimination referred to it by the Canadian Human Rights Commission & determines whether the activities violate the Canadian Human Rights Act.
Acts Administered:
Canadian Human Rights Act
Employment Equity Act

Chair, Shirish P. Chotalia
Tel: 613-995-1707
Fax: 613-995-3484

Vice-Chair, Susheel Gupta
Tel: 613-995-1707
Fax: 613-995-3484

Executive Directory & Registrar, Frederick Gloade
Tel: 613-947-1028
Fax: 613-995-3484
Frederick.Gloade@chrt-tcdp.gc.ca

Director, Registry Operations, Michelle Costello
Tel: 613-947-1122
Fax: 613-947-3484
michelle.costello@chrt-tcdp.gc.ca

Director, Financial Services, Doreen Dyet
Tel: 613-947-1169
Fax: 613-995-3484

Director, Administrative Services, Bernard Fournier
Tel: 613-947-1038
Fax: 613-995-3484
bernard.fournier@chrt-tcdp.gc.ca

Director, Information Technology Services, Julie Sibbald
Tel: 613-947-1185
julie.sibbald@chrt-tcdp.gc.ca

Canadian Institutes of Health Research (CIHR) / Instituts de recherche en santé du Canada (IRSC)

160 Elgin St., 9th Fl., Ottawa, ON K1A 0W9
Tel: 613-941-2672
Fax: 613-954-1800
Toll-Free: 888-603-4178
info@cihr-irsc.gc.ca
www.cihr-irsc.gc.ca

Promotes health research excellence in Canada through training & funding programs in basic, clinical, health systems & services, & population health research. Research is carried out in universities, in the health sciences faculties, affiliated hospitals & institutions & other faculties where research projects are highly relevant to human health. University-Industry programs create the opportunity for collaboration between Canadian companies & researchers conducting research in Canadian universities or affiliated institutions. Also manages the health-related Networks of Centres of Excellence.

President, Alain Beaudet
Tel: 613-954-1808

Executive Vice-President, Christine Fitzgerald
Tel: 613-957-6134

Vice-President, Knowledge Translation & Public Outreach, Ian Graham
Tel: 613-948-2318

Executive Director, Secretariat on Research Ethics, Susan Zimmerman
Tel: 613-947-7148

Director, PAN - Institute Affairs & Initiatives, Terry Campbell
Tel: 613-960-6211

Director, Ethics Office, Geneviève Dubois-Flynn
Tel: 613-954-1801

Director, Human Resources, Diane Massicotte
Tel: 613-957-8762

Director, Evaluations, Internal Audit & Risk Management, Martin Rubenstein
Tel: 613-941-3557

Director, Communications & Marketing, Karen Spierkel
Tel: 613-954-1812

Canadian Intergovernmental Conference Secretariat (CICS) / Secrétariat des conférences intergouvernementales canadiennes

222 Queen St., 10th Fl., PO Box 488 A, Ottawa, ON K1N 8V5
Tel: 613-995-2341
Fax: 613-996-6091
info@scics.gc.ca
www.scics.gc.ca

CICS is a conference support body which provides the administrative services required for the planning & the conduct of federal-provincial-territorial & provincial-territorial conferences at the First Ministers, ministers & deputy ministers level. The agency is at the disposal of individual federal, provincial & territorial government departments which may be called upon to organize & chair such meetings.

Secretary, André M. McArdle

Director, Corporate Services, Anik Lapointe

Director, Information Services, Bernard Latulippe

Director, Conference Services, Louise Seaward-Gagnon
Louise.Seaward-Gagnon@scics.gc.ca

Canadian International Development Agency (CIDA) / Agence canadienne de développement international (ACDI)

200, Promenade du Portage, Gatineau, QC K1A 0G4
Tel: 819-997-5456
Fax: 819-953-6088
Toll-Free: 800-230-6349
info@acdi-cida.gc.ca
www.acdi-cida.gc.ca
TTY: 819-953-5023
Other Communication: Toll-Free TTY: 1-800-331-5018

Major agency responsible for delivering most of Canada's foreign aid. CIDA is committed to supporting sustainable development in developing countries to meet the needs of current & future generations. The mission statement demands that criteria of sustainability be integrated into each project undertaken by the Agency in order to improve the economic, social, cultural, ecological & political condition of the world's developing nations. Many of the projects CIDA supports are aimed directly at the environment. Projects include reforestation & watershed rehabilitation, small scale fishing development (to increase output & food), water projects (to improve health), increased food production, improved rural quality, & supply & generation of electricity. Various other projects help nations develop the legal & administrative framework needed to promote environmentally sustainable development.

Minister, International Cooperation, Hon. Julian Fantino
Tel: 819-953-6238
Fax: 819-953-8525

Parliamentary Secretary to the Minister of International Cooperation, Hon. Lois Brown
Tel: 613-992-9310
Fax: 613-992-9407

Chief of Staff, Neil Desai
Tel: 819-953-6238

Senior Vice-President, Geographic Programs Branch, Hau Sing Tse
Tel: 819-997-1665

Acting Vice-President, Afghanistan & Pakistan Task Force, Francoise Ducros
Tel: 819-997-1408

Vice-President, Multilateral & Global Programs Branch, Diane Jacovella
Tel: 819-997-7537
Fax: 819-953-5348

Vice-President, Pan Geographic Programs, Nadia Kostiuk
Tel: 819-997-1643

Vice-President, Strategic Policy & Performance Branch, Vincent Rigby
Tel: 819-997-6133
Fax: 819-997-9049

Acting Chief Information Officer, Jacques Mailloux
Tel: 819-994-3855

Acting Director General, Communications Branch, Bernard Etzinger
Tel: 819-953-9574

Acting Director General, Human Resources Branch, Sheila Tenasco-Banerjee
Tel: 819-934-4682

Director General, Multilateral Development Institutions Directorate, Paul Samson
Tel: 819-994-3967

Director General, Strategic Planning & Operations Directorate, Naresh Singh
Tel: 819-956-8266

Administrative Officer, Claudine Taillefer
Tel: 819-997-6912

Canadian International Trade Tribunal / Tribunal canadien du commerce extérieur

Standard Life Centre, 333 Laurier Ave. West, 15 Floor, Ottawa, ON K1A 0G7
Tel: 613-990-2452
Fax: 613-990-2439
secretary@citt-tcce.gc.ca
www.citt-tcce.gc.ca

The Tribunal is an independent, quasi-judicial body, which carries out both judicial & advisory functions relating to trade remedies for the North American Free Trade Agreement. In this capacity, the Tribunal succeeds the Procurement Review Board of Canada. Reports to government through the Minister of Finance.
Acts Administered:
Canadian International Trade Tribunal Act
Customs Act
Excise Tax Act
Special Import Measures Act

Acting Chair, Serge Fréchette
Tel: 613-990-2432
Fax: 613-990-9881
Other Communications: Executive Assistant, Phone: 613-990-9881

Vice-Chair, Diane Vincent
Tel: 613-990-1476
Fax: 613-990-9881

Secretary, Dominique Laporte
Tel: 613-993-3595
Fax: 613-998-1322
Other Communications: Executive Assistant, Phone: 613-949-2309

Director General, Research, Rose Ritcey
Tel: 613-990-8718
Fax: 613-990-2431
Other Communications: Executive Assistant, Phone: 613-990-8145

General Counsel, Reagan Walker

Tel: 613-991-9247
Fax: 613-990-7132
Other Communications: Executive Assistant, Phone: 613-993-4372

Canadian Judicial Council / Conseil canadien de la magistrature

150 Metcalfe St., 15th Fl., Ottawa, ON K1A 0W8
Tel: 613-288-1566
Fax: 613-288-1575
info@cjc-ccm.gc.ca
www.cjc-ccm.gc.ca/

The members of the Council include the Chief Justice of Canada (who acts as Chair), the Chief Justices & Associate Chief Justices of each Superior Court or Branch or Division thereof, the senior judges of the Supreme Court of the Yukon Territory, the Supreme Court of the Northwest Territories & the Nunavut Court of Justice, the Chief Judge & Associate Chief Judge of the Tax Court of Canada, & the Chief Justice of the Court Martial Court of Canada.

Executive Director & Senior General Counsel, Norman Sabourin

Senior Administrative Officer, Odette Dagenais

General Counsel, Julie Durette

Director, Committees Management, Caroline Collard

Director, Communications & Strategic Issues, Johanna Laporte

Canadian Museum of Civilization Corporation (CMCC) / Musée canadien des civilisations

100 Laurier St., Gatineau, QC K1A 0M8
Tel: 819-776-7000
Toll-Free: 800-555-5621
www.civilization.ca
TTY: 819-776-7003

The Museum of Civilization Corporation was established by the Museums Act. The Crown corporation manages the Canadian Museum of Civilization & the Canadian War Museum in its efforts to promote increased awareness & understanding of Canadian history, culture, & identity.

President & Chief Executive Officer, Mark O'Neill
Tel: 819-776-7116

Chief Financial Officer, Linda Hurdle
Tel: 819-776-8363
Fax: 819-776-8535

Chief Operating Officer, David Loye
Tel: 819-776-8258
Fax: 819-776-7156

Chief Information Officer, Bruce Watkinson
Tel: 819-776-8403

Vice-President, Exhibitions & Programs, Jean-Marc Blais
Tel: 819-776-8302
Fax: 819-776-8301

Vice-President, Human Resources, Elizabeth S. Goger
Tel: 819-776-8268

Vice-President, Public Affairs & Publishing, Chantal Schryer
Tel: 819-776-8499
Fax: 819-776-7187

Executive Director, Development, Robert Ryan
Tel: 819-776-8468

Director, Library, Archives, & Documentation Services, Nicolas Gauvin
Tel: 819-776-7179
Fax: 819-776-8491

Director, Public Research & Evaluation, Karen Graham
Tel: 819-776-7123

Director, Collections Management & Planning, Bill Moore
Tel: 819-776-8319

Director, Visitor Services, Heather Paszkowski
Tel: 819-776-8288

Director General, Canadian War Museum; Vice-President, Canadian Museum of Civilization Corporation, James Whitham
Tel: 819-776-8646

Director, Collections Management, Planning, & Programs, Tony Glen
Tel: 819-776-8619

Director, Research, Exhibition, & Interpretation, Dean Oliver
Tel: 819-776-8654

Librarian, Lara Andrews
Tel: 819-776-8680

Head, Military History Research Centre, Jane Naisbitt
Tel: 819-776-8674

Canadian Museum of Nature (CMN) / Musée Canadien de la Nature (MCN)

PO Box 3443 D, Ottawa, ON K1P 6P4
Tel: 613-566-4700
Fax: 613-364-4021
Toll-Free: 800-263-4433
www.nature.ca
TTY: 613-566-4770
Other Communication: Toll-Free TTY: 1-866-600-8801

A diverse natural history collection encompassing some 10 million specimens, & thousands of species. Provides access to specimens & data for research & access to knowledge on biodiversity, biosystematics & the environment. Carries out research on management & care of collections & employs a staff of researchers working on national & international projects. Through public programs, CMN communicates knowledge & promotes understanding of science & nature to diverseaudiences. It includes permanent, special & travelling exhibits, curriculum-based & interpretive programs, & print, electronic, audiovisual & multimedia publications.

Canadian Nuclear Safety Commission (CNSC) / Commission canadienne de sûreté nucléaire (CCSN)

280 Slater St., PO Box 1046 B, Ottawa, ON K1P 5S9
Tel: 613-995-5894
Fax: 613-995-5086
Toll-Free: 800-668-5284
www.nuclearsafety.gc.ca

Federal agency which regulates activities involving nuclear energy & prescribed substances in the interests of health & safety for workers & the public. Areas covered under the AECB's licensing process include the nuclear fuel cycle (from mining to waste disposal), heavy water plants, research reactors & accelerators, & radioisotopes. Operations ensure that the use of nuclear energy in Canada does not pose undue risk to health, safety, security & the environment. The Research & Support Program (RSP) augments & extends the AECB's regulatory program beyond the capability of in-house resources. It produces pertinent & independent information that will assist the Board & its staff in making sound, timely & credible decisions on regulating nuclear facilities & materials. The nine sectors of the program include: safety of nuclear facilities; radioactive waste management; health physics; physical security; development of regulatory processes; & social services

President, Michael Binder
Tel: 613-992-8828
Fax: 613-995-5086

Executive Vice-President/Chief Regulatory Operations Officer, Ramzi Jammal
Tel: 613-947-8899
Fax: 613-995-5086
Other Communications: Executive Assistant, Phone: 613-947-8896

Vice-President/CSB & Chief Financial Officer, Corporate Services Branch, Michel Cavallin
Tel: 613-995-0104
Fax: 613-995-5086
Other Communications: Executive Assistant, Phone: 613-992-4543

Vice-President, Technical Support Branch, Terry Jamieson
Tel: 613-947-8931
Fax: 613-995-5086
Other Communications: Executive Assistant, Phone: 613-996-0260

Vice-President, Regulatory Affairs, Gordon White
Tel: 613-943-7662
Fax: 613-995-5086
Other Communications: Executive Assistant, Phone: 613-996-9505

Director General, Security & Safeguards, Raoul R. Awad
Tel: 613-992-2943
Fax: 613-995-5086

Director General, Strategic Planning, Jason K. Cameron
Tel: 613-947-3773
Fax: 613-995-5086

Director General, Finance & Administration, Stéphane Cyr
Tel: 613-995-8273
Fax: 613-995-5086

Director General, Regulatory Policy, Mark Dallaire
Tel: 613-947-3728
Fax: 613-995-5086

Director General, Nuclear Cycle & Facilities Regulation, Peter H. Elder
Tel: 613-943-8948
Fax: 613-995-5086

Director General, Assessment & Analysis, Gerry Frappier
Tel: 613-995-2031
Fax: 613-995-5086

Director General, Safety Management, Kathleen Heppell-Masys
Tel: 613-991-3220
Fax: 613-995-5086

Director General, Regulatory Improvement & Major Projects Management, Barclay Howden
Tel: 613-943-0179
Fax: 613-995-5086

Director General, Nuclear Substance Regulation, André Régimbald
Tel: 613-993-7699
Fax: 613-995-5086

Director General, Information Management & Technology, Hugh Robertson
Tel: 613-949-9498
Fax: 613-995-5086

Director General, Power Reactor Regulation, Greg Rzentkowski
Tel: 613-995-2655
Fax: 613-995-5086

Director General, Environmental & Radiation Protection & Assessment, Patsy Thompson
Tel: 613-947-3352
Fax: 613-995-5086

Canadian Polar Commission (CPC) / Commission canadienne des affaires polaires (CCAP)

Constitution Square, #1710, 360 Albert St., Ottawa, ON K1R 7X7
Tel: 613-943-8605
Fax: 613-943-8607
Toll-Free: 888-765-2701
mail@polarcom.gc.ca
www.polarcom.gc.ca

Mandated to enhance the public's awareness of polar regions & to foster both international & domestic liaison & cooperation in circumpolar research & technology development. One of the Commission's main objectives in the short term is focus on climate change & energy. Maintains the Canadian Polar Information System (CPIS) which, in addition to polar data & information, includes services such as the Polar Science Forum, Researcher's Directory, Researcher's Toolbox, & links to International Partners. In September 2005, the federal government announced it will provide $150 million in new funding over six years for International Polar Year 2007-2008, an international research program.

Chair, Bernard Funston

Executive Director, Steven Bigras
Tel: 613-943-8606
steven.bigras@polarcom.gc.ca

Manager, Information, John Bennett
Tel: 613-943-0716
Fax: 613-943-8607
john.bennett@polarcom.gc.ca

Senior Science Advisor, Jean-Marie Beaulieu
Tel: 613-947-9108
Fax: 613-943-8607
jean-marie.beaulieu@polarcom.gc.ca

Executive Secretary, Sandy Bianchini
Tel: 613-943-8605

Financial Analyst, Tom Egan

Tel: 613-943-0718
Fax: 613-943-8607

Polar Research Analyst, Laurie Buckland
laurie.buckland@polarcom.gc.ca

Canadian Race Relations Foundation (CRRF) / Fondation canadienne des relations raciales (TCRR)

#701, 4576 Yonge St., Toronto, ON M2N 6N4
Tel: 416-952-3500
Fax: 416-952-3326
Toll-Free: 888-240-4936
www.crr.ca
Other Communication: Toll-Free Fax: 1-888-399-0333
Crown corporation operating at arms length from the federal government from which it receives no funding. The Foundation is committed to building a national framework for the fight against racism in Canadian society.
Acts Administered:
Canadian Race Relations Foundation Act

Executive Director, Ayman Al-Yassini
Tel: 416-952-3500
Fax: 416-952-3326

Director, Finance & Administration, Arsalan Tavassoli
Tel: 416-952-5063
Fax: 416-952-3326

Canadian Radio-Television & Telecommunications Commission (CRTC) / Conseil de la radiodiffusion et des télécommunications Canadiennes

Central Building, 1, Promenade du Portage, Les Terrasses de la Chaudière, Gatineau, QC J8X 4B1
Tel: 819-997-0313
Fax: 819-994-0218
Toll-Free: 877-249-2782
www.crtc.gc.ca
TTY: 819-994-0423
Other Communication: Toll-Free TTY: 1-877-909-2782
Mailing Address: CRTC
Ottawa, ON K1A 0N2 Canada
The CRTC is vested with the authority to regulate & supervise all aspects of the Canadian broadcasting system, as well as to regulate telecommunications common carriers & service providers that fall under federal jurisdiction. Reports to Parliament through the Minister of Canadian Heritage.
Acts Administered:
Bell Canada Act
Broadcasting Act
Canadian Radio-television & Telecommunications Commission Act
Telecommunications Act

Chair, Konrad W. von Finckenstein
Tel: 819-997-3430
Fax: 819-953-1555

Vice-Chair, Telecommunications, Leonard Katz
Tel: 819-997-4644
Fax: 819-997-4923

Vice-Chair, Broadcasting, Tom Pentefountas
Tel: 819-997-8766
Fax: 819-997-4923

Commissioner, Michel Morin
Tel: 819-953-4375
Other Communications: Executive Assistant, Phone: 819-997-3917

Commissioner, Marc Patrone
Tel: 819-953-9958
Other Communications: Executive Assistant, Phone: 819-997-4126

Commissioner, Alberta/Northwest Territories Regions, Peter Menzies
Tel: 819-953-5241
Fax: 819-994-0218

Commissioner, Atlantic/Nunavut Regions, Elizabeth A. Duncan
Tel: 819-997-4764
Fax: 819-997-4923
Other Communications: Executive Assistant, Phone: 819-997-3917

Commissioner, British Columbia/Yukon Regions, Stephen B. Simpson
Tel: 819-953-6026
Other Communications: Executive Assistant, Phone: 819-997-3917

Commissioner, Manitoba/Saskatchewan Regions, Candice J. Molnar
Tel: 306-780-3423

Commissioner, Ontario Region, Rita Cugini
Tel: 819-997-2431
Fax: 819-994-0218

Commissioner, Québec Region, Suzanne Lamarre
Tel: 819-934-6347
Fax: 819-997-3917

Executive Director, Policy Development & Research, Namir Anani
Tel: 819-997-4534
Fax: 819-994-0218

Executive Director, Broadcasting, Scott Hutton
Tel: 819-997-4573
Fax: 819-994-0218

Executive Director, Telecommunications, John Traversy
Tel: 819-953-5889
Fax: 819-997-4550

Acting Director General, Strategic Communications & Parliamentary Affairs, Sally Southey
Tel: 819-997-9372
Fax: 819-997-4245

Director General, Finance & Administrative Service, Jim Stefanik
Tel: 819-997-0108
Fax: 819-953-5107

Secretary General, Corporate & Operations, Robert A. Morin
Tel: 819-994-0233
Fax: 819-994-0218

Senior General Counsel, John Keogh
Tel: 819-953-3990
Fax: 819-953-0589

Alberta
#403, 100 4th Ave. SW., Calgary, AB T2P 3N2
Tel: 403-292-6660
Fax: 403-292-6686
Administrative Officer, Margot Anderson

British Columbia
#290, 858 Beatty St., Vancouver, BC V6B 1C1
Tel: 604-666-2111
Fax: 604-666-8322
Administrative Officer, Jo-Anne Platt
Tel: 604-666-2111

Manitoba
#1810, 275 Portage Ave., Winnipeg, MB R3B 2B3
Tel: 204-983-6306
Fax: 204-983-6317
Acting Director, Western & Northern Region, Cheryl Grossi
Tel: 204-983-6599
Fax: 204-983-6317
TTY: 877-249-2782
Administrative Officer, Judy Henry
Tel: 204-983-6306

Nova Scotia
Metropolitan Place, #1410, 99 Wyse Rd., Dartmouth, NS B3A 4S5
Tel: 902-426-7997
Fax: 902-426-2721
Manager, Eastern & Atlantic Regions, Donna Shewfelt
Tel: 902-426-7268
Fax: 902-426-2721
Administrative Officer, Diane Mallet
Tel: 902-426-7997

Ontario
#624, 55 St. Clair Ave. East, Toronto, ON M4T 1M2
Tel: 416-954-6271
Administrative Officer, Andrea Mullin
Tel: 416-954-6271

Québec
#504, 205, av Viger ouest, Montréal, QC H2Z 1G2
Tel: 514-283-6607
Administrative Officer, Monique Cyr
Tel: 514-496-4077

Saskatchewan
Cornwall Professional Bldg., #620, 2220 12th Ave., Regina, SK S4P 0M8
Tel: 306-780-3422
Administrative Officer, Janet LaBar
Tel: 306-780-3422

Canadian Security Intelligence Service (CSIS) / Service canadien du renseignement de sécurité

PO Box 9732 T, Ottawa, ON K1G 4G4
Tel: 613-993-9620
Fax: 613-231-0612
www.csis.gc.ca
TTY: 613-991-9228
Acts Administered:
Anti-terrorism Act
Canadian Security Intelligence Service Act
Charities Registration (Security Information) Act
Citizenship Act
Employment Equity Act
Immigration & Refugee Protection Act
Proceeds of Crime (Money Laundering) & Terrorist Financing Act
Public Safety Act
Security of Information Act

Director, Richard B. Fadden
Tel: 613-842-1200

Deputy Director, Charles Bisson
Tel: 613-231-0986

Chief Financial Officer, Laura Danagher
Tel: 613-842-1191

Chief Information Officer, Susan Brown
Tel: 613-842-1531

Canadian Space Agency (CSA) / Agence spatiale canadienne (ASC)

John H. Chapman Space Centre, 6767, rte de l'Aéroport, Saint-Hubert, QC J3Y 8Y9
Tel: 450-926-4800
Fax: 450-926-4352
promo@asc-csa.gc.ca
www.asc-csa.gc.ca
Other Communication: Client Services, Phone: 450-926-4351
Established in 1989, & responsible for coordinating all civil, space-related policies & programs on behalf of the Government of Canada. Scientific research & industrial development in earth observation, space science & exploration, satellite communications, & space awareness & learning. RADARSAT International (RSI) develops products & services demanded by world markets. RADARSAT-1, the first Canadian commercial Earth Observation (EO) satellite, is uniquely capable of responding to disasters around the world. The system can support the operational mapping & monitoring of natural disasters in four critical ways: prevention, preparedness, emergency response & recovery. Moreover, the development of the high performance RADARSAT-2 to be launched in 2007, will further enhance Canada's competitive position. RADARSAT-2 will offer improved quality of data images to meet the growing world demand of Earth observation information. The SCISAT satellite is used in ozone depletion research.
Acts Administered:
Canadian Space Agency Act

Minister, Industry; Minister Responsible, Canadian Space Agency, Hon. Christian Paradis
Tel: 613-995-9001
Fax: 613-992-0302
Minister.Industry@ic.gc.ca

President & Chief Astronaut, Steven MacLean
Tel: 450-926-4301
Fax: 450-926-4315

Vice-President, Chummer Farina
Tel: 613-998-5284
Fax: 613-990-4994

Chief Financial Officer, Marie-Claude Guerard
Tel: 450-926-4407
Fax: 450-926-4424

Chief Information Officer, Charles Ouellette
Tel: 450-926-4851

Chief, Management & Liaison Services, Agathe Jérôme
Tel: 613-991-3250
Fax: 613-990-4994

Chief, Human Resources Officer, Yves Saulnier
Tel: 450-926-4815
Fax: 450-926-5194

Chief of the Astronauts, Jean-Marc Comtois
Tel: 450-926-4755

Director General, Space Science, David Kendall

Tel: 450-926-4770
Fax: 450-926-4766

Director General, Space Exploration, Gilles Leclerc
Tel: 450-926-4606
Fax: 450-926-4323

Director General, Corporate Services, Benoît Marcotte
Tel: 450-926-4667
Fax: 450-926-4612

Canadian Tourism Commission (CTC) / Commission canadienne du tourisme (CCT)

Four Bentall Centre, #1400, 1055 Dunsmuir St., PO Box 49230, Vancouver, BC V7X 1L2
Tel: 604-638-8300
www.canadatourism.com

A Crown corporation owned entirely by the Canadian government, the Commission seeks to promote a thriving tourism industry in Canada, & encourage relationships between the private sector & the governments of Canada at all levels.

Chair, Steve Allan

President & Chief Executive Officer, Michele McKenzie

Senior Vice-President, Marketing Strategy & Communications, Greg Klassen

Senior Vice-President, Corporate Affairs/Corporate Secretary, Chantal Péan

Vice-President, Finance/Chief Financial Officer, Lena Bullock

Vice-President, International, Charles McKee

Vice-President, Strategy & Corporate Communications, Paul Nursey

Canadian Transportation Agency (CTA) / Office des transports du Canada (OTC)

Les Terrasses de la Chaudière, 15, rue Eddy, Gatineau, QC J8X 4B3
Fax: 819-997-6727
Toll-Free: 888-222-2592
info@otc-cta.gc.ca
www.cta-otc.gc.ca
TTY: 800-669-5575

Responsible for the economic regulation of transportation in Canada. The agency requires that all applications for new railway lines, modifications to existing railway lines, disputed railway crossings at grade, grade separation, utility crossings & private crossings be accompanied by an environment impact assessment

Acts Administered:
Canada Marine Act
Canada Transportation Act
Coasting Trade Act
Pilotage Act
Railway Safety Act

Chair & Chief Executive Officer, Geoffrey C. Hare
Tel: 819-997-9233
Fax: 819-953-9979
geoffrey.hare@otc-cta.gc.ca

Vice-Chair, John Scott
Tel: 819-953-8915
Fax: 819-953-9979
john.scott@otc-cta.gc.ca

Director General, Industry Regulation & Determinations Branch, Ghislain Blanchard
Tel: 819-953-4657
Fax: 819-994-8807
ghislain.blanchard@otc-cta.gc.ca

Director General, Dispute Resolution Branch, Nina Frid
Tel: 819-953-5074
Fax: 819-953-5562
nina.frid@otc-cta.gc.ca

Director General, Corporate Management Branch, Arun Thangaraj
Tel: 819-997-6764
Fax: 819-953-9842

Senior Director, Regulatory Approvals & Compliance Directorate, Carole Girard
Tel: 819-997-8761
Fax: 819-953-5562
carole.girard@otc-cta.gc.ca

Director, Communications Directorate, Jacqueline Bannister
Tel: 819-953-7666
Fax: 819-953-8353
jacqueline.bannister@otc-cta.gc.ca

Director, Rail, Air & Marine Disputes Directorate, Joseph Dion
Tel: 819-953-0327
Fax: 819-953-8353
joseph.dion@otc-cta.gc.ca

Senior Counsel, Legal Services, Claude Jacques
Tel: 819-997-9323
Fax: 819-953-9269
claude.jacques@otc-cta.gc.ca

Atlantic
#109, 1045 Main St., Moncton, NB E1C 1H1
Tel: 506-851-6950
Fax: 506-851-2518
sap-amp@otc-cta.gc.ca

Central
#702, 269 Main St., PO Box 27007 Winnipeg Square, Winnipeg, MB R3C 4T3
Tel: 204-984-6092
Fax: 204-984-6093
sap-amp@otc-cta.gc.ca

Ontario
#300, 4900 Yonge St., Toronto, ON M2N 6A5
Tel: 416-952-7895
Fax: 416-952-7897
sap-amp@otc-cta.gc.ca

Pacific
#560, 800 Burrard St., Vancouver, BC V6Z 2V8
Tel: 604-666-0620
Fax: 604-666-1267
sap-amp@otc-cta.gc.ca

Enforcement Officer, Wayne Wooldridge

Québec
#510, 101, boul Roland-Therrien, Longueuil, QC J4H 4B9
Tel: 450-928-4173
Fax: 450-928-4174
sap-amp@otc-cta.gc.ca

Enforcement Officer, Richard Laliberté

Western
#1100, 9700 Jasper Ave. NW, Edmonton, AB T5J 4C3
Tel: 780-495-6618
Fax: 780-495-5639
sap-amp@otc-cta.gc.ca

Enforcement Officer, Linda Brooklyn

Canadian Wheat Board (CWB) / Commission canadienne du blé

423 Main St., PO Box 816 Main, Winnipeg, MB R3C 2P5
Tel: 204-983-0239
Fax: 204-983-3841
Toll-Free: 800-275-4292
questions@cwb.ca; farmerservice@cwb.ca
www.cwb.ca
Other Communication: Media relations, Phone: 204-983-3101; Government relations, Phone: 204-984-8167

The market agency serves farmers in Western Canada who grow wheat, durum wheat, & barley. The Canadian Wheat Board's main function is to market these grains in Canada & abroad.

Acts Administered:
Canadian Wheat Board Act

Minister, Agriculture & Agri-Food; Minister, Canadian Wheat Board, Hon. Gerry Ritz
Tel: 613-995-7080
Fax: 613-996-8472

President & Chief Executive Officer, Ian White

Chair, Allen Oberg
Tel: 780-582-2171
Fax: 780-582-4127
allen_oberg@cwb.ca

Chief Financial Officer, Brita Chell

Chief Information Officer, Information & Technology, Graham Paul

Chief Operating Officer, Ward Weisensel

Vice-President, Farmer Relations & Public Affairs, Dave Burrows

Vice-President, People & Organizational Services, Diane Wiesenthal

Ottawa
21 Florence St., Ottawa, ON K2P 0W6
Tel: 613-236-3633
Fax: 613-236-5749

China
Tower B, Beijing COFCO Plaza, #708, 8 Jianguomen Nei St., Beijing, 100005 China
Other Communication: 011-86-10-6526-3908; Fax: 011-86-10-6526-3907

Japan
Tomoecho Annex 2, 4 Fl., 3-8-27 Toranomon, Minato-ku, Tokyo, 105-0001 Japan
Other Communication: 011-81-3-5425-1055; Fax: 011-81-3-5425-0036

Citizenship & Immigration Canada / Citoyenneté et Immigration Canada

Jean Edmonds, South Tower, 365 Laurier Ave. West, Ottawa, ON K1A 1L1
Tel: 613-954-9019
Fax: 613-954-2221
Toll-Free: 888-242-2100
www.cic.gc.ca
TTY: 888-576-8502

The Department of Citizenship & Immigration administers Canada's citizenship & immigration policies, procedures & service. The department is responsible for the following: examining immigrants, visitors & people claiming refugee status at land borders, seaports & airports; processing applications for permanent residence, extensions of visitor status requests & sponsorships for relatives & refugees overseas; admitting students, temporary workers & qualified business immigrants; investigating & removing people who are in Canada illegally; working with & helping fund a network of settlement agencies & services to help immigrants adapt to & participate in day-to-day Canadian life; promoting the acceptance of immigrants by Canadians; cooperating with various levels of government on enforcement, program development & the delivery of services; accepting applications & verifying the eligibility & documentation of applicants; granting citizenship & administration of the Oath of numerous community facilities across Canada; confirming Canadian citizenship status &; issuing proofs of citizenship to Canadians. The Immigration & Refugee Board reports to Parliament through the minister.

Acts Administered:
Canadian Heritage Languages Institute Act
Canadian Multiculturalism Act
Canadian Race Relations Foundation Act
Citizenship Act
Department of Citizenship & Immigration Act
Immigration & Refugee Protection Act

Minister, Citizenship, Immigration, & Multiculturalism, Hon. Jason Kenney
Tel: 613-992-2235
Fax: 613-992-1920
jason.kenney@parl.gc.ca; Minister@cic.gc.ca

Parliamentary Secretary Assistant, Andrea Khanjin
Tel: 613-954-1064
Fax: 613-957-2688

Special Assistant for Multiculturalism, Felix Wong
Tel: 613-954-1064

Deputy Minister, Neil Yeates
Tel: 613-954-3501

Director, Audit, Jacques Marquis
Tel: 613-946-5651
Fax: 613-952-6556

Canada Immigration Centres & Citizenship Offices / Centres d'immigration et de citoyenneté

Immigration visa offices are located in most Canadian Embassies & Consulates abroad. Immigration centres are located at most ports of entry in Canada, & citizenship & immigration offices in major cities throughout the country. For specific addresses & other information contact 1-888-242-2100.

Office of the Assistant Deputy Attorney General / Bureau du Sous-procureur général adjoint

Assistant Deputy Attorney General, Micheline Van-Erum
Tel: 613-957-4811
Fax: 613-941-1221

Senior Counsel, Legal Services, Deborah Horowitz
Tel: 613-946-9980
Fax: 613-941-1221

General Counsel, Legal Services, Deen Olsen
Tel: 613-946-9992
Fax: 613-941-1221

Office of the Assistant Deputy Minister, Operations / Bureau de la sous-ministre adjointe, Opérations
Assistant Deputy Minister, Claudette Deschênes
Tel: 613-954-5335
Fax: 613-957-8887

Office of the Assistant Deputy Minister, Corporate Services / Bureau de la sous-ministre adjointe, Services ministériels
Assistant Deputy Minister, Manon Brassard
Tel: 613-957-3338
Fax: 613-954-7360
Chief Technology Officer, Wade Daley
Tel: 613-941-0015
Fax: 613-954-6209
Chief Information Officer/Director General, David Adamson
Tel: 613-954-2700
Fax: 613-954-6209
Director General, Administration, Security & Accommodation, Bob Lanouette
Tel: 613-954-4223
Fax: 613-954-3754
Director General, Human Resources, Diane Mikaelsson
Tel: 613-941-7788
Fax: 613-957-3882
Director General, Global Case Management System, Soyoung Park
Tel: 613-946-3901
Fax: 613-946-0581
Director General, Corporate Affairs, Dr. Raman Srivastava
Tel: 613-941-7018
Fax: 613-957-5946

Office of the Assistant Deputy Minister, Chief Financial Officer / Bureau de la sous-ministre adjointe, administrateur principal des finances
Assistant Deputy Minister/Chief Financial Officer, Mark G. Watters
Tel: 613-954-4443
Fax: 613-946-6048

Office of the Assistant Deputy Minister, Strategic & Program Policy / Cabinet du sous-ministre adjoint, Politiques stratégiques et de programmes
Assistant Deputy Minister, Les Linklater
Tel: 613-954-7353
Fax: 613-946-6048
Director General, Refugees, Sarita Bhatla
Tel: 613-957-5874
Fax: 613-957-5869
Director General, Admissibility, Alain Desruisseaux
Tel: 613-954-6132
Fax: 613-952-9187
Director General, International & Intergovernmental Relations, Brian Grant
Tel: 613-957-5878
Fax: 613-957-5913
Director General, Strategic Policy, Sandra Harder
Tel: 613-957-5948
Fax: 613-954-5896
Director General, Research & Evaluation, Ümit Kiziltan
Tel: 613-954-6526
Fax: 613-957-5936
Director General, Information Sharing Project Branch, Stéphane Larue
Tel: 613-948-2473
Director General, Immigration, David Manicom
Tel: 613-941-8989
Fax: 613-941-9323
Director General, Foreign Credentials Referral Office, Corinne Prince St-Amand
Tel: 613-941-2769
Fax: 613-941-5314
Director General, Integration, Deborah Tunis
Tel: 613-957-3257
Fax: 613-954-9144
Director, Policy & Knowledge Development, Mondher BenHassine
Tel: 613-991-2241
Fax: 613-991-2485
Executive Head, Metropolis Project, Julie Boyer
Tel: 613-957-5966
Fax: 613-957-5968
Executive Head, Metropolis Project, Howard Duncan
Tel: 613-957-5916
Fax: 613-957-5968
Director General, Deborah Tunis
Tel: 613-957-3257
Fax: 613-954-9144
Director, Horizontal Policy Development & Coordination, Angela Connidis
Tel: 613-946-0572
Fax: 613-954-9144
Director, Integrated Business Services, François Des Rosiers
Tel: 613-957-6527
Fax: 613-952-7416

Office of the Conflict of Interest & Ethics Commissioner / Commissariat aux conflits d'intérêts et à l'éthique

Commissioner's Office, 66 Slater St., 22nd Fl., Ottawa, ON K1A 0A6
Tel: 613-995-0721
Fax: 613-995-7308
ciec-ccie@parl.gc.ca
www.ciec-ccie.gc.ca

The Conflict of Interest & Ethics Commissioner is an independent Officer of Parliament. Responsibilities include assisting elected & appointed officials to avoid conflicts between their private interests & public duties.
Acts Administered:
Conflict of Interest Act
Conflict of Interest Code for Members of the House of Commons

Conflict of Interest & Ethics Commissioner, Mary E. Dawson
Tel: 613-995-0721
Fax: 613-995-7308

Executive Advisor, Robert LeBlond
Tel: 613-995-5764
Fax: 613-995-7308

Assistant Commissioner, Advisory & Compliance, Lyne Robinson-Dalpé
Tel: 613-996-6020
Fax: 613-995-7308

Director, Corporate Management, Denise Benoit
Tel: 613-996-6025
Fax: 613-995-7308

Director, Reports & Investigations, Eppo Maertens
Tel: 613-943-3763
Fax: 613-995-7308

Director, Policy, Research, & Communications, Sherry Perreault
Tel: 613-996-4880
Fax: 613-995-7308

General Counsel, Legal Services, Nancy Bélanger
Tel: 613-996-6028
Fax: 613-995-7308
Director General, Sarita Bhatla
Tel: 613-957-5874
Fax: 613-957-5869
Acting Director, Asylum Policy & Programs, Jennifer Irish
Tel: 613-941-8331
Fax: 613-941-6413
Director, Refugee Program Support, Josée Brennan
Tel: 613-952-2119
Fax: 613-941-2960
Director, Resettlement, Debra Pressé
Tel: 613-957-5833
Fax: 613-957-5836
Senior Policy Analyst, Horizontal Policy & International Protection Development, Jessie Thomson
Tel: 613-960-7628
Fax: 613-957-5869

Copyright Board of Canada / Commission du droit d'auteur du Canada

#800, 56 Sparks St., Ottawa, ON K1A 0C9
Tel: 613-952-8621
Fax: 613-952-8630
secretariat@cb-cda.gc.ca
www.cb-cda.gc.ca

The Board is an economic regulatory body empowered to establish, either mandatorily or at the request of an interested party, the royalties to be paid for the use of copyrighted works, when the administration of such copyright is entrusted to a collective-administration society. The Board also has the right to supervise agreements between users & licensing bodies & issues licences when the copyright owner cannot be located.

Chair, William J. Vancise
Tel: 613-952-8621

Vice-Chair & Chief Executive Officer, Claude Majeau
Tel: 613-952-8621

Acting Secretary General, Gilles McDougall
Tel: 613-952-8624
gilles.mcdougall@cb-cda.gc.ca

General Counsel, Mario Bouchard
Tel: 613-954-6470
mario.bouchard@cb-cda.gc.ca

Director, Research & Analysis, Vacant
Tel: 613-946-4457

Office of the Correctional Investigator / L'Enquêteur correctionnel Canada

PO Box 3421 D, Ottawa, ON K1P 6L4
Fax: 613-990-9091
Toll-Free: 877-885-8848
org@oci-bec.gc.ca
www.oci-bec.gc.ca

Investigates complaints from inmates in Canadian institutions. Reports on problems inmates have that fall within the responsibility of the Department of Public Safety & Emergency Preparedness & meet certain conditions.
Acts Administered:
Corrections and Conditional Release Act (Part III)

Correctional Investigator, Howard Sapers
Tel: 613-990-2689

Executive Director, Dr. Ivan Zinger
Tel: 613-990-2690

Director of Investigations, Marie-France Kingsley
Tel: 613-998-6960

Director of Investigations, Paul McKenzie
Tel: 613-990-2691

Director, Policy & Research, David Hooey
Tel: 613-990-2693

Director, Corporate Services & Planning, Manuel Marques
Tel: 613-990-2692

Correctional Service Canada (CSC) / Service correctionnel Canada

340 Laurier Ave. West, Ottawa, ON K1A 0P9
Tel: 613-992-5891
Fax: 613-943-1630
www.csc-scc.gc.ca

An agency within Public Safety & Emergency Preparedness Canada responsible for the administration of sentences with respect to convicted offenders sentenced to two or more years as decided by the federal courts, & certain provincial inmates who have been transferred to a federal institution. CSC is also responsible for the supervision of inmates who have been granted conditional release by the authority of the National Parole Board.
Acts Administered:
Corrections & Conditional Release Act
Criminal Code
Extradition Act
Old Age Security Act
Prisons & Reformatories Act
Transfer of Offenders Act

Chief Executive Officer, CORCAN, John Sargent
Tel: 613-996-4530
Fax: 613-947-8875

Commissioner, Don Head
Tel: 613-995-5781
Fax: 613-943-1630

Deputy Commissioner, Women, Jennifer Oades
Tel: 613-992-6067
Fax: 613-992-4692

Assistant Commissioner, Corporate Services, Liette Dumas-Sluyter
Tel: 613-996-4242
Fax: 613-992-8443

Assistant Commissioner, Human Resource Management, Fraser Macaulay
Tel: 613-995-8899
Fax: 613-992-9208

Assistant Commissioner, Health Services, Leslie MacLean
Tel: 613-995-8023
Fax: 613-995-6277

Assistant Commissioner, Policy & Research, Ian McCowan
Tel: 613-996-2180
Fax: 613-995-3603

Executive Director & General Counsel, Legal Services, Carole Johnson

Tel: 613-992-9009
Fax: 613-995-9971

Assistant Commissioner, Correctional Operations & Programs, Chris Price
Tel: 613-943-0499
Fax: 613-996-6174

Assistant Commissioner, Communications & Engagements, Elizabeth Van Allen
Tel: 613-995-6867
Fax: 613-947-0091

Atlantic
1045 Main St., 2nd Fl., Moncton, NB E1C 1H1
Tel: 506-851-6313
Fax: 506-851-6316

Deputy Commissioner, Thérèse Leblanc
Tel: 506-851-6377
Fax: 506-851-2418

Ontario
440 King St. West, PO Box 1174, Kingston, ON K7L 4Y8
Tel: 613-536-4527
Fax: 613-545-8684

Assistant Commissioner, Lori MacDonald
Tel: 613-545-8131
Fax: 613-545-8684

Pacific
32560 Simon Ave., 2nd Fl., PO Box 4500, Abbotsford, BC V2T 5L7
Tel: 604-870-2500
Fax: 604-870-2430

Deputy Commissioner, Anne Kelly
Tel: 604-870-2501
Fax: 604-870-2430

Prairies
2313 Hanselman Pl., PO Box 9223, Saskatoon, SK S7K 6A9
Tel: 306-975-4850
Fax: 306-975-4435

Regional Director, Darcy Emann
Tel: 306-975-5026

Québec
3, pl Laval, 2e étage, Laval, QC H7N 1A2
Tel: 450-967-3333
Fax: 450-967-3326

Regional Director, Youssef Mani
Tel: 450-664-6640 ext: 391
Fax: 450-664-6641

Northern/Interior Area
#203, 1635 Abbott St., Kelowna, BC V1Y 1A9
Tel: 250-470-5166
Fax: 250-470-5173

Central Ontario
#215, 180 Dundas St. West, Toronto, ON M5G 1Z8
Tel: 416-973-2393
Fax: 416-973-1779

East & West Québec
#202, 212, boul. Curé-Labelle, Sainte-Thérèse, QC J7E 2X7
Tel: 450-435-3932
Fax: 450-420-7600

Acting District Director, Lise Bouthillier

Northeast Ontario
191 Gilmour St., Ottawa, ON K2P 0N8
Tel: 613-996-7011
Fax: 613-954-1687

Fraser Valley
#100, 32544 George Ferguson Way, Abbotsford, BC V2T 4Y1
Tel: 604-870-2730
Fax: 604-870-2731

Hamilton & Niagara
55 Bay St. North, 2nd Fl., Hamilton, ON L8R 3P7
Tel: 905-572-2695
Fax: 905-572-2072

Manitoba/Sask/Northwestern Ontario
#102, 123 Main St., Winnipeg, MB R3C 1A3
Tel: 204-983-4306
Fax: 204-983-5869

Montréal-Métropolitan
#917, Tour Ouest, 200, boul René-Lévesque ouest, Montréal, QC H2Z 1X4
Tél: 514-283-1776
Téléc: 514-283-1783

New Brunswick & PEI
1 Factory Lane, 1st Fl., Moncton, NB E1C 9M3
Tel: 506-851-3038
Fax: 506-851-2057

Newfoundland & Labrador
531 Charter Ave., St. John's, NL A1A 1P7
Tel: 709-772-5359
Fax: 709-772-6415

Northern Alberta, NWT
9530 - 101 Ave., 2nd Fl., Edmonton, AB T5H 0B3
Tel: 780-495-4900
Fax: 780-495-4975

Ottawa
191 Gilmour St., Ottawa, ON K2P 0N8
Tel: 613-996-7011
Fax: 613-954-1687

Nova Scotia
#102, 2131 Gottingen St., Halifax, NS B3K 5Z7
Tel: 902-426-3408
Fax: 902-426-6579

Nunavut
1043 Woodhouse St., Iqaluit, NU X0A 0H0
Tel: 867-979-8892
Fax: 867-979-7441

Saskatchewan
#603, 230 - 22 St. East, Saskatoon, SK S7K 0E9
Tel: 306-975-4070
Fax: 306-975-4532

Southern Alberta
#140, 1925 - 18 Ave. NE, Calgary, AB T2E 7T8
Tel: 403-292-5522
Fax: 403-292-5510

Vancouver Area
#401, 877 Expo Blvd., Vancouver, BC V6B 1K9
Tel: 604-666-8004
Fax: 604-666-2000

Vancouver Island
#200, 256 Wallace St., Nanaimo, BC V9R 5B3
Tel: 250-754-0264
Fax: 250-754-0266

District Director, Dave Keating

Western Ontario
#117, 255 Woodlawn Rd. West, Guelph, ON N1H 8J1
Tel: 519-826-2139
Fax: 519-826-2143

Defence Construction Canada (DCC) / Construction de Défense Canada (CDC)

Constitution Square, 350 Albert St., 19th Fl., Ottawa, ON K1A 0K3
Tel: 613-998-9548
Fax: 613-998-1061
Toll-Free: 800-514-3555
info@dcc-cdc.gc.ca
www.dcc-cdc.gc.ca

Federal government crown corporation responsible for the contracting & supervising of major military construction & maintenance projects required by National Defence. Services include construction, project management, environmental services & operational support services. DCC provides environmental science & environmental engineering services to help fulfill the Department of National Defence's sustainable development strategy, including: environmental impact & site assessment; environmental site remediation; environmental support for project & program management; sustainable development strategy support services; policy, compliance & advisory services; site decommissioning services; facility deconstruction & demolition; firing range decommissioning; waste management auditing & planning; waste reduction planning; landfill inventories & investigations; hazardous waste management; UST removals; training & education; ISO 14000 environmental management systems; environmental CIS applications; environmental checklists for property transactions & decommissioning; environmental monitoring & compliance auditing; designated substances inventories; environmental disclosures reporting; treatment & disposal facilities conceptual designs; environmental contrac ting & contract management; energy conservation. Projects include: the DEW (Distant Early Warning) Line cleanup, a dismantling of the DEW sites, scheduled for completion in 2012, & a major environmental project in the Canadian Arctic; green demolition at CFB Comox; biodiesel pilot program at 4 Wing Cold Lake, launched in 2005

President & Chief Executive Officer, James S. Paul
Tel: 613-998-9541
Fax: 613-998-1218

Senior Vice-President, Operations, Ron de Vries, P.Eng
Tel: 613-998-9543
Fax: 613-998-1218

Vice-President, Operations, Steve Irwin, P.Eng
Tel: 613-949-7721
Fax: 613-998-1218

Vice-President, Operations, Randy McGee, P.Eng., GSC
Tel: 613-949-0052
Fax: 613-998-1218

Vice-President, Corporate Services & CFO, Angelo Ottoni, C.A.
Tel: 613-998-1001

Director, Atlantic Region, Business Operations - Atlantic Region, Ross Welsman, P.Eng., PMP
Tel: 902-426-5640
Fax: 902-426-9655
#202, 1597 Bedford Hwy.
Bedford, NS B4A 1E7

Manager, Operations Coordination, Business Operations - Atlantic Region, George Theoharopoulos
Tel: 902-426-4040
Fax: 902-426-9655

Director, Ontario Region, Environmental Services - Ontario, John Graham, P.Eng., PMP
Tel: 613-384-1256 ext: 230
Fax: 613-384-7747
Howard Maitland Building
#205, 780 Midpark Dr.
Kingston, ON K7M 7P6

Manager, Environmental Services - Ontario, Dennis Katic
Tel: 613-384-1256 ext: 227
Fax: 613-384-7747

Director, Quebec Region, Environmental Services - Québec, Marc Lanteigne, P.Eng.
Tel: 514-496-2729
Fax: 514-283-8347
Village olympique Pyramide Ouest
#2700, 5199, rue Sherbrooke est
Montréal, QC H1T 3X2

Manager, Environmental Services - Québec, Alain Dufresne
Tel: 514-283-8165
Fax: 514-283-8347

Director, Western Region, Environmental Services - Western Region, Stephen G. Karpyshin, P.Eng.
Tel: 780-495-2555
Fax: 780-495-5959
#210, 13220 St. Albert Trail
Edmonton, AB T5L 4W1

Manager, Environmental Services - Western Region, Sabrina Rock
Tel: 780-495-3979
Fax: 780-495-5959

Director, Contract Services, Contract Services, Melinda Nycholat, P.Eng., PMP
Tel: 613-991-9313
Fax: 613-998-9547
Constitution Square
350 Albert St., 17th Fl.
Ottawa, ON K1A 0K3

Executive Administrative Assistant, Claire Péladeau
Tel: 613-991-3475
Fax: 613-998-1218

Defence Research & Development Canada / Recherche et développement pour la défense Canada

305 Rideau St., Ottawa, ON K1A 0K2
Tel: 613-992-7237
info@drdc-rddc.gc.ca
www.drdc-rddc.gc.ca
TTY: 800-467-9877

Provides research & development both nationally & internationally by providing the Canadian Forces with relevant & timely technologies, while at the same time offering attractive collaborative opportunities to other government departments, the private sector, academia & international allies.

Chief Executive Officer, Dr. Marc Fortin
Tel: 613-996-2020

Director General, Science & Technology Operations, Richard Williams
Tel: 613-992-5776

Director General, Corporate Services, Colin McEwan
Tel: 613-992-6105

Director General, Research & Development Programs, Maria Rey
Tel: 613-998-2303
Fax: 613-993-6095

Elections Canada / Élections Canada

The Jackson Bldg., 257 Slater St., Ottawa, ON K1A 0M6
Tel: 613-993-2975
Fax: 613-954-8584
Toll-Free: 800-463-6868
www.elections.ca
TTY: 800-361-8935

The Chief Electoral Officer of Canada is responsible for the conduct of federal elections & referendums in Canada & for ensuring that all provisions of the Canada Elections Act are complied with & enforced. Major activities include the maintenance of the National Register of Electors, the production of lists of electors, the training of returning officers, the revisions of polling division boundaries & the acquisition of election materials & supplies. Elections Canada is also responsible for the compilation & publishing of statutory & statistical reports, & the provision of advice & assistance to Parliament, as required. The agency also implements public education & information programs. As well, its mandate includes the registration of political parties & third parties engaged in election advertising, & the certification of statutory payments to be made to auditors, political parties, & candidates under the election expenses provisions of the Act. Following each decennial census, the Chief Electoral Officer must calculate the number of electoral districts to be assigned to each province according to rules contained in s. 51 of the Constitution Act, prepare population distribution maps for use by the ten electoral boundaires commission s (one per province) that are directly responsible for readjusting federal electroal boundaries & publish their reports.

Chief Electoral Officer, Marc Mayrand
Tel: 613-993-5755
Fax: 613-993-5380

Chief of Staff, Office of the CEO, Vivian Cousineau
Tel: 613-993-3748
Fax: 613-993-5380

Deputy Chief Information Officer, Pierre LaFrance
Tel: 613-993-4121
Fax: 613-990-3662

Commissioner, Canada Elections, William H. Corbett
Tel: 613-998-4051
Fax: 613-990-4877

General Counsel, Canada Elections, Johanne Gauthier
Tel: 613-998-4051
Fax: 613-990-4877

Acting Chief Financial Officer, Finance, Internal Audit & Administration, Brian Berry
Tel: 613-998-8440
Fax: 613-993-8517

Deputy Chief Electoral Officer, Electoral Events, Rennie Molnar
Tel: 613-949-3125
Fax: 613-954-2874
Other Communications: Administrative Assistant, Gargi Bose: 613-990-3440

Acting Director, Outreach, Communications & Research, Marc Lamontagne
Tel: 613-990-2979
Fax: 613-954-8584

Director/General Counsel, Electoral Affairs, Michèle René de Cotret
Tel: 613-990-7239
Fax: 613-993-5880

Chief Information Officer, Stéphane Cousineau
Tel: 613-991-2401

Deputy Chief Electoral Officer, Policy, Planning & Public Affairs, Belaineh Deguefé
Tel: 613-991-4640

Deputy Chief Electoral Officer, Political Financing, François Bernier
Tel: 613-998-0670
Fax: 613-990-7241
Other Communications: Executive Assistant, Lyne Michaud: 613-990-7241

Chief Human Resources Officer, Human Resources, Pierrette Lacroix
Tel: 613-998-5262
Fax: 613-998-7561

Senior General Counsel/Senior Director, Stéphane Perrault
Tel: 613-990-6846
Fax: 613-993-5880

Environment Canada (EC) / Environnement Canada

10 Wellington St., Gatineau, QC K1A 0H3
Tel: 819-997-2800
Fax: 819-994-1412
Toll-Free: 800-668-6767
enviroinfo@ec.gc.ca
www.ec.gc.ca
TTY: 819-994-0736
Other Communication: Environmental Emergencies (24-hour): 819-997-3742; TTY: 819-994-0736

Fosters a national capacity for sustainable development in cooperation with other governments, departments of government & the private sector that will result in a safe & healthy environment & a sound & prosperous economy by: undertaking & promoting programs to augment understanding of the environment; supporting environmentally responsible public & private decision-making; warning Canadians of risks to & from the environment; engaging Canadians as partners in measurably beneficial action to conserve, protect & restore the integrity of Canada's environment for the benefit of present & future generations.

Acts Administered:
Acts Administered in Part by Environment Canada
Acts in which Environment Canada Provides Assistance
Administration, Management & Control of Certain Public Lands
Agricultural & Rural Development Act (Agriculture & Agri-Foods)
Air Pollution Regulations
Alberta Equivalency Order
Alternative Fuels Act & Regulations (Treasury Board)
Antarctic Environmental Protection Act
Arctic Shipping Pollution Prevention Regulations
Arctic Waters Pollution Prevention Act
Arctic Waters Pollution Prevention Regulations
Asbestos Mines & Mills Release Regulations
Atomic Energy Control Act
Auditor General Act (Treasury Board)
Benzene in Gasoline Regulations
Canada Agricultural Products Act
Canada Emission Reduction Incentives Agency Act
Canada Marine Act (Transport Canada)
Canada Oil & Gas Certificate of Fitness Regulations
Canada Oil & Gas Drilling Regulations
Canada Oil & Gas Geophysical Operations Regulations
Canada Oil & Gas Operations Act (Indian & Northern Affairs/Natural Resources)
Canada Oil & Gas Operations Regulations
Canada Oil & Gas Production & Conservation Regulations
Canada Petroleum Resources Act (Indian Affairs & Northern Development/Natural Resouces)
Canada Port Authority Environmental Assessment Regulations
Canada Shipping Act
Canada Water Act
Canada Wildlife Act
Canada-Chile Free Trade Agreement Implementation Act (International Trade)
Canada-Newfoundland Atlantic Accord Implementation Act
Canada-Nova Scotia Offshore Petroleum Resources Accord Implementation Act
Canadian Environment Week Act
Canadian Environmental Assessment Act
Canadian Environmental Protection Act
Canadian Transportation Accident Investigation & Safety Board Act (Privy Council)
Chlor-Alkali, Mercury Release Regulations
Chlor-alkali Mercury Liquid Effluent Regulations
Chlorobiphenyls Regulations
Clean Air Act
Comprehensive Study List Regulation
Contaminated Fuel Regulations
Controlled Products Regulations
Dangerous Chemicals & Noxious Liquid Substances Regulations
Department of the Environment Act
Disposal at Sea Regulations
Electricity Regulations
Emergency Preparedness Act (National Defence)
Energy Supplies Emergency Act (National Research)
Environment Canada Related Acts & Regulations
Environmental Emergency Regulations
Environmental Studies Research Fund Regions Regulations
Exclusion List Regulation
Export & Import of Hazardous Wastes Regulations
Export Control List of Notification Regulations
Export of Substances under the Rotterdam Convention Regulations
Federal Authorities Regulations
Federal Halocarbon Regulations
Federal Mobile PCB Treatment & Destruction Regulations
Federal Registration of Storage Tank Systems for Petroleum Products & Allied Petroleum Products on Federal Lands or Aboriginal Lands Regulations
Fisheries Act (Fisheries & Oceans)
Food & Drugs Act (Agriculture & Agri-Foods/Health Canada)
Fuels Information Regulations, No. 1
Garbage Pollution Prevention Regulations
Gasoline & Gasoline Blend Dispensing Flow Rate Regulations
Gasoline Regulations
Great Lakes Sewage Pollution Prevention Regulations
Greenhouse Gas Technology Investment Fund Act
Hazardous Products Act (Health Canada)
Inclusion List Regulation
International Boundary Waters Treaty Act (Foreign Affairs)
International River Improvements Act
Interprovincial Movement of Hazardous Waste Regulations
James Bay & Northern Québec Native Claims Settlement Act
Kemano Completion Project Guidelines Order
Lac Seul Conservation Act
Lake of the Woods Control Board Act
Law List Regulation
List of Hazardous Waste Authorities
List of Toxic Substances Authorities
Mackenzie Valley Resource Management Act (Indian & Northern Affairs)
Manganese-Based Fuel Additives Act
Masked Name Regulations
Meat & Poultry Products Plant Liquid Effluent Regulations
Metal Mining Effluent Regulations
Migratory Bird Regulations
Migratory Bird Sanctuary Regulations
Migratory Birds Convention Act
Motor Vehicle Safety Act (Transport)
National Energy Board Act (Natural Resources/Transport Canada)
National Round Table on the Environment & the Economy Act (Prime Minister)
National Wildlife Week Act
New Substances Fees Regulations
New Substances Notification Regulations
Newfoundland Offshore Area Oil & Gas Operations Regulations
Newfoundland Offshore Area Petroleum Geophysical Operations Regulations
Newfoundland Offshore Area Petroleum Production & Conservation Regulations
Newfoundland Offshore Certificate of Fitness Regulations
Newfoundland Offshore Petroleum Drilling Regulations
Newfoundland Offshore Petroleum Installations Regulations
Non-Pleasure Craft Sewage Pollution Prevention Regulations
North American Free Trade Agreement Implementation Act
Northern Pipeline Act (Natural Resources)
Northern Pipeline Socio-Economic & Environmental Terms & Conditions (Northern BC, Southern BC, AB, SK & Swift River Portion in BC)
Nova Scotia Offshore Petroleum Drilling Regulations
Nuclear Energy Act (Natural Resources)
Oceans Act (Fisheries & Oceans)
Off-Road Small Spark-Ignition Engine Emission Regulations
Oil & Gas Regulations
Oil Pollution Prevention Regulations
On-Road Vehicle & Engine Emission Regulations
Onshore Pipeline Regulations
Ozone Depleting Substances Regulations
PCB Waste Export Regulations
Persistence & Bioaccumulation Regulations
Pest Control Products Act & Regulations (Health Canada)
Petroleum Refinery Liquid Effluent Regulations
Phosphorus Concentration Regulations
Pleasure Craft Sewage Pollution Prevention Regulations
Pollutant Discharge Reporting Regulations
Pollutant Substances Regulations
Port Alberni Pulp & Paper Effluent Regulations
Potato Processing Plant Liquid Effluent Regulations
Prohibition of Certain Toxic Substances
Projects Outside Canada Environmental Assessment Regulations
Pulp & Paper Effluent Regulations
Pulp & Paper Mill Defoamer & Wood Chip Regulations
Pulp & Paper Mill Effluent Chlorinated Dioxins & Furans Regulations
Regulations respecting Applications for Permits for Disposal at Sea
Resources & Technical Surveys Act (Natural Resources/Fisheries & Oceans)
Rules for Procedures for Boards of Review
Rules of Practice & Procedure
Secondary Lead Smelter Release Regulations
Ship-Source Oil Pollution Fund Regulations
Solvent Degreasing Regulations
Species at Risk Act, 2002
Storage of PCB Material Regulations
Sulphur in Diesel Fuel Regulations
Sulphur in Gasoline Regulations
Tetrachloroethylene (Use in Dry Cleaning & Reporting Requirements) Regulations
Transport Packaging of Radioactive Materials Regulations
Transportation Safety Board Regulations

Transportation of Dangerous Goods Act & Regulations (Transport Canada)
Tributyltetradeclyphosphonium Chloride Regulations
Uranium & Thorium Mining Regulations
Vinyl Chloride Release Regulations
Weather Modification Information Act
Wild Animal & Plant Protection & Regulation of International & Interprovincial Trade Act
Wildlife Area Regulations

Minister, Environment, Hon. Peter Kent
Tel: 819-997-1441
Fax: 819-953-0279
minister@ec.gc.ca

Deputy Minister, Bob Hamilton
Tel: 819-997-4203
Fax: 819-953-6897

Associate Deputy Minister, Andrea Lyon
Tel: 819-997-4203
Fax: 819-953-6897

Executive Assistant Deputy Minister, Debra Tompkins-Caron
Tel: 819-994-5020

Director General, Audit & Evaluation, Robert D'Aoust
Tel: 819-953-5471
Fax: 819-953-2459

Director General, Communications Branch, David Henley
Tel: 819-997-6820
Fax: 819-953-1599

Director General, Corporate Secretariat, Pierre Bernier
Tel: 819-953-2743
Fax: 819-953-0749

Director, Parliamentary Affairs, Lori Dawe
Tel: 819-997-1441

Associated Agencies, Boards & Commissions:

• Committee on the Status of Endangered Wildlife in Canada (COSEWIC) / Comité sur la situation des espèces en péril au Canada
c/o Canadian Wildlife Service
351 St. Joseph Blvd, 4th Fl.
Gatineau, QC K1A 0H3
Tel: 819-953-3215
Fax: 819-994-3684
cosewic/cosepac@ec.gc.ca
www.cosewic.gc.ca
Other Communication: Species at Risk Act Public Registry: www.sararegistry.gc.ca
Committee of experts that assesses & designates which wild species are in some danger of disappearing from Canada. COSEWIC determines the national status of wild Canadian species, subspecies & separate populations suspected of being at risk. COSEWIC bases its decisions on the best up-to-date scientific information & Aboriginal traditional knowledge available. All native mammals, birds, reptiles, amphibians, fish, mollusks, lepidopterans (butterflies & moths), vascular plants, mosses & lichens are included in its current mandate. In its 2010 Annual report, COSEWIC's assessment results indicate there are 602 species in the risk category (extirpated, endangered, threatened or of special concern) & 13 species found to be extinct.

• North American Waterfowl Management Plan (NAWMP) / Le plan nord-américain de gestion de la sauvagine
NAWCC (Canada) Secretariat, Place Vincent Massey
351 St. Joseph Blvd., 7th Fl.
Gatineau, QC K1A 0H3
Tel: 819-934-6034
Fax: 819-934-6017
nawmp@ec.gc.ca
www.nawmp.ca
The North American Waterfowl Management Plan is an international action plan to conserve migratory birds throughout the continent. The Plan's goal is to return waterfowl populations to their 1970's levels by conserving wetland & upland habitat. Canada & the United States signed the Plan in 1986 in reaction to critically low numbers of waterfowl. Mexico joined in 1994 making it a truly continental effort. The Plan is a partnership of federal, provincial/state & municipal governments, non-governmental organizations, private companies & many individuals, all working towards achieving better wetland habitat for the benefit of migratory birds, other wetland-associated species & people. The Plan's unique combination of biology, landscape conservation & partnerships comprise its exemplary conservation legacy. Plan projects are international in scope, but implemented at regional levels. These projects contribute to the protection of habitat & wildlife species across the North American landscape.

• North American Bird Conservation Initiative (NABCI)
Canadian Wildlife Service
351, boul St-Joseph, 3e étage
Gatineau, QC K1A 0H3
Tel: 819-994-0512
Fax: 819-994-4445
nabci@ec.gc.ca
www.nabci.net
The NABCI is a coordinated effort among Canada, the United States & Mexico to maintain the diversity & abundance of all North American birds. National coordination of this effort in Canada occurs through the NABCI Canada Council, chaired by the Asst. Deputy Minister of Environment Canada's Environmental Conservation Service. Council members include representatives from provincial governments, non-government organizations, four bird plans (waterfowl, landbirds, shorebirds, waterbirds), & habitat joint ventures. In Canada, the joint venture conservation projects has three habitat joint ventures (Pacific Coast, Prairie Habitat, Eastern Habitat) & three species (Arctic Goose, Black Duck, Sea Duck.)

Enforcement Branch / Direction générale de l'application de la loi
351 boul St-Joseph, Gatineau, QC K1A 0H3
Tel: 819-997-2019
Fax: 819-997-0086
The Branch is built around the principle of ensuring that companies & individuals comply with the pollution prevention & conservation goals of environmental & wildlife protection acts & regulations. Enforcement is delivered through the work of in-the-field enforcement officers across Canada working through the Environmental Enforcement Directorate & The Wildlife Enforcement Directorate. Their work is carried out in cooperation with other federal, provincial & territorial governments & with international organizations involved in enforcement such as the United States Fish & Wildlife Service, the United States Environmental Protection Agency & Interpol.

Environmental Stewardship Branch / Direction générale de l'intendance environnementale
351 boul St-Joseph, Gatineau, QC K1A 0H3
Tel: 819-997-1575
Fax: 819-953-9452
Assessment & management of risk associated with domestic & international sources of pollution. The range of activity is broad, assessment of substances & practices that pose a risk to the environment, development & implementation of environmental protection measures including pollution prevention, regulations, permits & technology advancement & ensuring compliance with federal pollution & wildlife laws. These activities lead to improvements in environmental quality which helps to support the health of Canadians & their economic security.
Assistant Deputy Minister, Coleen Volk
Tel: 819-953-1711
Fax: 819-953-9452
Associate Assistant Deputy Minister, Mike Beale
Tel: 819-956-9500
Director General, Chemicals Sector, Margaret Kenny
Tel: 819-934-4960
Fax: 819-953-3213
Director General, Energy & Transportation, Steve McCauley
Tel: 819-997-1298
Fax: 819-953-9547
Director General, Public & Resources Sectors, Randall Meades
Tel: 819-934-4205
Director General, Strategic Priorities, Louise Métivier
Tel: 819-994-5022
Fax: 819-953-7941
Director General, Environmental Protection Operations, Sue Milburn-Hopwood
Tel: 819-934-5666
Fax: 819-934-6531

Finance Branch / Direction générale des finances
Tel: 819-953-7026
Fax: 819-953-4064
Acting Assistant Deputy Minister, Carol Najm
Tel: 819-953-4736
Acting Director General, Corporate Management, Karen Turcotte
Tel: 819-953-5842
Acting Director General, Finance Directorate, Randy Larkin
Tel: 819-953-9569
Fax: 819-953-2459
Acting Director General, Integrated Enterprise Services, Cheryl Bertrand
Tel: 819-953-8911
Fax: 819-953-4064

International Affairs / Direction générale des affaires internationales
Tel: 819-997-4882
Fax: 819-953-5981
Assistant Deputy Minister, Dan McDougall
Tel: 819-934-6020
Fax: 819-953-9412
Director General, Americas, Dean Knudson
Tel: 819-994-1670
Fax: 819-997-0199
Director General, Climate Change International, Stephen de Boer
Tel: 819-953-6830
Fax: 819-953-9333
Director General, Multilateral & Bilateral Affairs, France Jacovella
Tel: 819-956-5263
Fax: 819-994-6227
Director, Partnerships Division, Darren Goetze
Tel: 819-953-9525
Fax: 819-953-9333

Legal Services / Services juridiques
Tel: 819-953-3680
Fax: 819-953-9110

Meteorological Service of Canada (MSC) / Le service météorologique du Canada
Tel: 819-997-2696
Fax: 819-994-8841
The Meteorological Service of Canada monitors water quantities, provides information & conducts research on climate, atmospheric science, air quality, ice & other environmental issues.
Assistant Deputy Minister, David Grimes
Tel: 613-943-5585
Fax: 613-943-5737
Director General, Business Policy, Danielle Lacasse
Tel: 613-943-5532
Fax: 613-995-0389
Director General, Weather & Environmental Monitoring, Jim Abraham
Tel: 416-739-4965
Fax: 416-739-4261
Director General, Weather & Environmental Monitoring, Michel Jean
Tel: 514-421-4601
Fax: 514-421-7250
Director General, Weather & Environmental Prediction & Services, Diane E. Campbell
Tel: 613-947-9200
Fax: 613-943-6440

Science & Technology Branch / Direction générale des sciences et de la technologie
Tel: 819-994-4751
Fax: 819-997-1541
Assistant Deputy Minister, Karen L. Dodds
Tel: 819-934-6851
Director General, Wildlife & Landscape Science, Kevin J. Cash, PhD
Tel: 613-998-0329
Fax: 613-998-0458
Director General, Science & Technology Strategies, Dr. Javier A. Gracia-Garza
Tel: 819-953-3090
Fax: 819-953-9029
Director General, Atmospheric Science & Technology, Charles A. Lin
Tel: 416-739-4995
Fax: 416-739-4265
Acting Director General, Science & Risk Assessment, David Morin
Tel: 819-953-3091
Fax: 819-953-7155
Director General, Water Science & Technology, Dan Wicklum, PhD
Tel: 819-994-4533

Strategic Policy / Direction générale de la politique stratégique
Tel: 819-953-4818
Fax: 819-953-5981
Assistant Deputy Minister, Michael Keenan
Tel: 819-953-4818
Fax: 819-953-5981
Director General, Sustainability Directorate, Jan Dyer
Tel: 819-934-6028
Fax: 819-994-8864
Director General, Strategic Policy Directorate, Lawrence Hanson
Tel: 819-934-4149
Fax: 819-953-4679
Acting Director General, Intergovernmental & Stakeholder Relations Directorate, Nancy Roberts
Tel: 819-953-3353
Fax: 819-994-6787
Director General, Economic Analysis Directorate, Tony Young
Tel: 819-953-7624
Fax: 819-953-5916

Environment Canada Regional Offices
Atlantic
Queen Sq., 45 Alderney Dr., Dartmouth, NS B2Y 2N6
Tel: 902-426-7231
Fax: 902-426-6348
15th.reception@ec.gc.ca
atlantic-web1.ns.ec.gc.ca/index_e.html
TTY: 819-994-0736
Acting Regional Director General, Jackie Olsen
Tel: 902-426-0628
Fax: 902-426-6348
Pacific & Yukon
201, 401 Burrard St., Vancouver, BC V6C 3S5
Tel: 604-664-9145
Fax: 604-664-9190
greenlane.pyr@ec.gc.ca
www.pyr.ec.gc.ca
Regional Director General, Paul Kluckner
Tel: 604-664-9145
Fax: 604-664-9190
Contact, Pacific Environment Centre Office, Marlene Elliot
Tel: 604-666-5958
Other Communications: Office Phone: 604-666-8425
Ontario
4905 Dufferin St., Toronto, ON M3H 5T4
Tel: 416-739-4826
Fax: 416-739-4776
enviroinfo.ontario@ec.gc.ca
www.on.ec.gc.ca
Acting Regional Director General, Michael Goffin
Tel: 416-739-4666
Fax: 416-739-4691
Prairie & Northern
Twin Atria Bldg., #200, 4999 - 98 Ave., Edmonton, AB T6B 2X3
Tel: 780-951-8869
Fax: 780-495-3086
Acting Regional Director General, Mike Norton
Tel: 780-951-8869
Fax: 780-495-2758
Québec
1141, rte de l'Église, 6e étage, CP 10100, Québec, QC G1V 4H5
Tél: 418-648-4077
Téléc: 418-648-4613
Ligne sans frais: 800-463-4311
quebec.lavoieverte@ec.gc.ca
Regional Director General, Philippe Morel
Tel: 418-648-4077
Fax: 418-649-6213

National Guidelines & Standards Office (NGSO)
Environment Canada, 200 boul. Sacré-Coeur, Gatineau, QC K1A 0H3
Tel: 819-953-1550
ceqg-rcqe@ec.gc.ca
ceqg-rcqe.ccme.ca
The National Guidelines & Standards Office (NGSO) provides nationally approved, science-based measures of environmental quality including guidelines, standards, & objectives. The primary focus of the group is developing national guidelines for water, sediment & soil quality, & aquatic tissue residues. Guidelines are recommended numerical or narrative limits for a variety of substances & environmental quality characteristics (such as dissolved oxygen or pH), which, if exceeded, may impair the health of Canadian ecosystems. Guidelines are mandated federally under the Canadian Environmental Protection Act (CEPA) & nationally under various federal-provincial agreements (Canadian Council of Ministers of the Environment, Great Lakes Water Quality Agreement). In addition, the NGSO leads & supports various ecosystem management initiatives (with a focus on consultative, community-based, right-to-know approaches) cooperatively with the CCME, Environment Canada Regions & other federal departments. The NGSO's thrust is to develop & promote effective implementation of science-based guidelines, objectives & indicators to achieve ecosystem health & sustainable development.
Manager, Pat Falletta

St. Lawrence Centre (SLC) / Centre Saint-Laurent
#105 McGill St., 7th Fl., Montréal, QC H2Y 2E7
quebec.csl@ec.gc.ca
www.qc.ec.gc.ca/csl/
SLC is the only federal research & development centre devoted entirely to the river ecosystem. SLC experts study the ecosystems of the St. Lawrence River & conduct research programs with the aim of better understanding how these ecosystems function & maintaining knowledge of the St. Lawrence River up to date. SLC is divided into four sections Environmental Chemistry, Environmental Biology, State of the St. Lawrence Environment & Information Management.

Black Duck
Environment Canada, Canadian Wildlife Service, 335 River Rd., Ottawa, ON K1A 0H3
Tel: 613-949-8254
www.blackduckjv.org
Coordinator, Brigitte Collins
brigitte.collins@ec.gc.ca
Coordinator, Tasha Sargent
tasha_sargent@pcjv.org

Commission for Environmental Cooperation (CEC) / Commission coopération environnementale

Secretariat, #200, 393, rue St-Jacques ouest, Montréal, QC H2Y 1N9
Tel: 514-350-4300
Fax: 514-350-4314
info@cec.org
www.cec.org
The Commission for Environmental Cooperation (CEC) is an international organization created by Canada, Mexico & the United States under the North American Agreement on Environmental Cooperation (NAAEC). The CEC was established to address regional environmental concerns, help prevent potential trade & environmental conflicts & to promote the effective enforcement of environmental law. The Agreement complements the environmental provisions of the North American Free Trade Agreement (NAFTA).

Executive Director, Evan Lloyd
Tel: 514-350-4303
melhadj@cec.org

Legal Officer, Submission on Enforcement Matters Unit, Paolo Solano
Tel: 514-350-4321
psolano@cec.org

Legal Officer, Submission on Enforcement Matters Unit, Paolo Solano
Tel: 514-350-4321
psolano@cec.org

Program Manager, Air Quality & PRTR, Orlando Cabrera-Rivera
Tel: 514-350-4323
ocabrera@cec.org

Program Manager, Chemicals Management, Ned T. Brooks
Tel: 514-350-4372
nbrooks@cec.org

Program Manager, Environmental Information, Karen Richardson
Tel: 514-350-4326
krichardson@cec.org

Program Manager, Environmental Law, Marco Antonio Heredia Fragoso
Tel: 514-350-4302
maheredia@cec.org

Council Secretary, Nathalie Daoust
Tel: 514-350-4310
ndaoust@cec.org

Environmental Protection Review Canada / Révision de la protection de l'environnement Canada

240 Sparks St., 1st Fl. West, Ottawa, ON K1A 1A1
Tel: 613-995-7599
Fax: 613-992-4918
eprc-rpec@eprc-rpec.gc.ca
www.eprc-rpec.gc.ca
Environmental Protection Review Canada is a group of expert adjudicators, entirely separate from Environment Canada, that conducts reviews of Environmental Protection Compliance Orders (EPCOs). Under the Canadian Environmental Protection Act, 1999 (CEPA, 1999), enforcement officers have the power to issue EPCOs to prevent a violation, to stop an on-going violation or to require that violations be corrected. Any person who has been issued an EPCO may ask for an independent review conducted by a Review Officer. Review Officers have the authority to confirm or cancel an EPCO. They may also amend, suspend, add or delete a term or condition of the Order. The decisions of Review Officers may be appealed to the Federal Court, Trial Division.

Chief Review Officer, Allan Pope
Tel: 613-997-4060
Fax: 613-992-4918

Review Officer, Louis LaPierre, Ph.D.
Tel: 506-863-2056
Fax: 506-863-2000
lapierl@umoncton.ca

Export Development Canada (EDC) / Exportation et développement Canada (SEE)

151 Slater St., Ottawa, ON K1A 1K3
Tel: 613-598-2500
Fax: 613-598-3811
Toll-Free: 800-267-8510
www.edc.ca
TTY: 866-574-0451
A financial services corporation assisting Canadian business to succeed in foreign markets. EDC provides a wide range of financial solutions to exporters across Canada & their customers around the world. The corporation's risk management services include: export-credit insurance protecting exporters against losses due to non-payment relating to commercial & political risks; & flexible medium- or long-term financing & guarantees. As a financially self-sustaining Crown corporation, EDC operates on commercial principles, charging fees & premiums for its products & interest on its loans. EDC is governed by a board of directors composed of representatives from both the private & public sectors, & reports to Parliament through the minister for international trade. An Environmental Review Directive is used to assess the environmental impacts of projects EDC is asked to support. EDC pursues an international multilateral consensus on environmental review practices so that all exporters are subject to the same rules. EDC has adopted & implemented the OECD Recommendation on Common Approaches on Environment & Officially Supported Export Credits. EDC has signed the UNEP Statement of Financial Institutions. Through the EnviroExport initiative, EDC helps Canadia n environmental exporters succeed internationally through financing products. Where EDC is considering providing financing support, political risk insurance or equity to the sponsor of a Category A project under the Environmental Review Directive, EDC will seek consent to inform the public on its website that it is considering support to such a project.

President & Chief Executive Officer, Stephen S. Poloz

Senior Vice-President, Business Development, Benoit Daignault

Senior Vice-President, Human Resources & Corporate Services, Susanne Laperle

Senior Vice-President, Business Solutions & Technology, Sherry L. Noble

Senior Vice-President, Financing Products Group, Rajesh Sharma

Senior Vice-President, Insurance, Pierre Gignac

Senior Vice-President, Legal Services & Secretary, Jim McArdle

Senior Vice-President/CFO, Finance, Ken Kember

Media Contact, Phil Taylor
Tel: 613-598-2904
ptaylor@edc.ca

EDC Regional Offices
Calgary
#2403, 308-4th Ave. SW, Calgary, AB T2P 0H7
Tel: 403-817-6700
Fax: 403-817-6701
Edmonton
#1150, 10810 - 101 St., Edmonton, AB T5J 3S4
Tel: 780-702-5233
Fax: 780-702-5235
Halifax
Tower 2, #1605, 1969 Upper Water St., Halifax, NS B3J 3R7
Tel: 902-442-5205
Fax: 902-442-5204
London
#1512, 148 Fullarton St., London, ON N6A 5P3
Tel: 519-963-5400
Fax: 519-963-5407
Moncton
#400, 735 Main St., Moncton, NB E1C 1E5
Tel: 506-851-6066
Fax: 506-851-6406
Montréal
Tour de la Bourse, #4520, 800, Victoria Square, CP 124, Montréal, QC H4Z 1C3
Tél: 514-908-9200
Téléc: 514-878-9891

Québec
D-3, #600, 2875, boul Laurier, Québec, QC G1V 2M2
Tel: 418-577-7408
Fax: 418-577-7419

St. John's
90 O'Leary Ave., St. John's, NL A1B 2C7
Tel: 709-772-8808
Fax: 709-772-8693

Toronto
#3120, 155 Wellington St. West, Toronto, ON M5V 3L3
Tel: 416-349-6515
Fax: 416-349-6516

Vancouver
Bentall Four, #400, 1055 Dunsmuir St., PO Box 49086, Vancouver, BC V7X 1G4
Tel: 604-638-6950
Fax: 604-638-6955

Winnipeg
Commodity Exchange Tower, #2075, 360 Main St., Winnipeg, MB R3C 3Z3
Tel: 204-975-5090
Fax: 204-975-5094

Farm Credit Canada / Financement agricole Canada

1800 Hamilton St., PO Box 4320, Regina, SK S4P 4L3
Tel: 306-780-8100
Fax: 306-780-8919
Toll-Free: 888-332-3301
csc@fcc-fac.ca
www.fcc-fac.com
TTY: 306-780-6974

Federal Crown corporation reporting to Parliament through the Minister of Agriculture & Agri-Food. Under the Farm Credit Canada Act FCC offers financing to primary producers & agribusiness through 100 offices in rural communities across Canada.

President & Chief Executive Officer, Greg Stewart, P.Ag.

Executive Vice-President & Chief Financial Officer, Moyez Somani, CMA, MBA, FCMA

Executive Vice-President & Chief Operating Officer, Operations, Rémi Lemoine, MBA, FCI

Senior Vice-President, Marketing, Lyndon Carlson, P.Ag.

Senior Vice-President, Strategy, Knowledge & Reputation, Kellie Garrett, ABC, MA

Senior Vice-President, Human Resources, Greg Honey

Senior Vice-President, Portfolio & Credit Risk, Michael Hoffort, P.Ag.

Office of the Commissioner for Federal Judicial Affairs / Commissariat à la magistrature fédérale Canada

99 Metcalfe St., 8th Fl., Ottawa, ON K1A 1E3
Tel: 613-995-5140
Fax: 613-995-5615
Toll-Free: 877-583-4266
www.fja-cmf.gc.ca

Established in 1978, the Office of the Commissioner for Federal Judicial Affairs is responsible for the administration of Part I of the Judges Act. Federally appointed judges are provided with administrative services independent of the Department of Justice. Approximately 1,100 active judges & 800 retired judges are served by the Commissioners' Office.
The Office is also engaged in the following duties: management of the Judicial Appointments Secretariat & the Federal Courts Reports Section; coordination of initiatives related to the judiciary's role in international cooperation; preparation of a budget; administration of a judical intranet & a virtual library; & the provision of language training to judges.

Commissioner for Federal Judicial Affairs Canada, William A. Brooks
Tel: 613-947-1793
Fax: 613-995-5192

Deputy Commissioner, Marc A. Giroux
Tel: 613-995-7438
Fax: 613-995-5615

Chief, Administrative Services, Anne Barnabé
Tel: 613-995-2310
Fax: 613-995-5615

Executive Director, Judicial Appointments; Senior Legal Counsel, Véronique Joly
Tel: 613-992-9400
Fax: 613-941-0607

Executive Editor, Federal Courts Reports, François Boivin
Tel: 613-947-8491
Fax: 613-995-5615

Director, Information Systems Services, Normand Bernier
Tel: 613-996-5536
Fax: 613-995-5615

Director, Compensation, Pension, Benefits, & Human Resources, Nikki Clemenhagen
Tel: 613-947-9899
Fax: 613-995-5615

Director, Finance & Administration, Wayne Osborne
Tel: 613-992-8185
Fax: 613-995-5615

Director, Judges' Language Training, Hardyal Sewdat
Tel: 613-992-2909
Fax: 613-995-5615

Director, International Programs, Oleg Shakov
Tel: 613-992-2990
Fax: 613-995-5615

Finance Canada / Finances Canada

L'esplanade Laurier, 140 O'Connor St., Ottawa, ON K1A 0G5
Tel: 613-992-1573
Fax: 613-943-0938
finpub@fin.gc.ca
www.fin.gc.ca
TTY: 613-995-1455
Other Communication: Library Services: 613-995-5877

The Department of Finance Canada is responsible for providing the federal government with analysis & advice on financial & economic issues. It also monitors & researches the performance of the Canadian economy's major factors (output, growth, employment, income, price stability, monetary policy, & long-term change). Interacting with various other federal departments & agencies, the Department encourages coordination in all federal initiatives with an impact on the economy. Emphasis is placed on consulting with the public regarding policy directions & options.

Acts Administered:
Air Canada Public Participation Act
Air Travellers Security Charge Act
An Act Respecting Payments to a Trust Established to Provide Provinces & Territories with Funding for Community Development
An Act Respecting the Provision of Funding for Diagnostic & Medical Equipment
Bank for International Settlements (Immunity) Act
Bank of British Columbia Business Continuation Act
Bank of Canada Act
Beechwood Power Project Act
Bills of Exchange Act
Borrowing Authority Act
Bretton Woods & Related Agreements Act
Budget Implementation Acts & Acts Implementing Measures Announced in Economic Statements
Canada Deposit Insurance Corporation Act
Canada Employment Insurance Financing Board Act
Canada Health Care, Early Childhood Development & Other Social Services Funding Act
Canada Pension Plan Act
Canada Pension Plan Investment Board Act
Canada-Newfoundland Atlantic Accord Implementation Act
Canada-Nova Scotia Offshore Petroleum Resources Accord Implementation Act
Canada-US Free Trade Agreement Implementation Act
Canadian Commercial Bank Financial Assistance Act
Canadian International Trade Tribunal Act
Canadian Payments Act
Canadian Securities Regulation Regime Transition Office Act
Co-operative Credit Associations Act
Crown Corporations Dissolution or Transfer Authorization Act
Currency Act
Customs & Excise Offshore Application Act
Customs Tariff Act
Depository Bills & Notes Act
Diplomatic Service (Special) Superannuation Act
Economic Development Agency of Canada for Regions of Quebec Act
Eldorado Nuclear Limited Reorganization & Divestiture Act
Energy Costs Assistance Measures Act
European Bank for Reconstruction & Development Agreement Act
Excise Tax Act, 2001
Export Credits Insurance, Parts I & II
Federal-Provincial Fiscal Arrangements Act
Federal-Provincial Fiscal Revisions Act
Financial Administration Act
Financial Consumer Agency of Canada Act
Financial Institutions & Deposit Insurance System Amendment Act
Financial Institutions Depositors Compensation Act
First Nations Goods & Services Tax Act
First Nations Sales Tax Act
Garnishment, Attachment, & Pension Diversion Act
Halifax Relief Commission Pension Continuation Act
Income Tax Act
Income Tax Conventions Interpretation Act
Insurance Companies Act
Interest Act
Newfoundland Additional Finance Assistance Act
Nordion & Theatronics Divestiture Authorization Act
Nova Scotia & Newfoundland & Labrador Additional Fiscal Equalization Offset
Office of the Superintendent of Financial Institutions Act
Oil Export Tax Act
Payment Card Networks Act
Payment Clearing & Settlement Act
Pension Benefits Standards Act
Petro-Canada Public Participation Act
Prince Edward Island Subsidy Act
Proceeds of Crime (Money Laundering) & Terrorist Financing Act
Provincial Subsidies Act
Special Import Measures Act
Spending Control Act
Supplementary Fiscal Equalization Payments Act, 1982-87
Tax Convention Acts
Tax-Back Guarantee Act
Teleglobe Canada Reorganization & Divestiture Act
Telesat Canada Reorganization & Divestiture Act
Trust & Loan Companies Act

Minister, Finance, Hon. James Michael (Jim) Flaherty, B.A., LL.B.
Tel: 613-992-6344
Fax: 513-992-8320
FlaheJ@parl.gc.ca; jflaherty@fin.gc.ca

Minister of State (Finance), Ted Menzies
Tel: 613-996-7861
Fax: 613-995-5176
ted.menzies@fin.gc.ca

Deputy Minister, Michael Horgan
Tel: 613-992-4925
Fax: 613-952-9569

Associate Deputy Minister & G-7 Deputy for Canada, Paul Rochon
Tel: 613-943-2314
Fax: 613-952-9569

Associate Deputy Minister, Louise Levonian
Tel: 613-996-1963
Fax: 613-952-9569

Assistant Deputy Minister, Denis Gauthier
Tel: 613-992-1527
Fax: 613-992-0387

Associated Agencies, Boards & Commissions:
• **Auditor General of Canada / Vérificateur Général du Canada**
• **Bank of Canada / Banque du Canada**
• **Canada Deposit Insurance Corporation / Société d'assurance-dépôts du Canada**
• **Canada Savings Bonds (CSB) / Obligations d'épargne du Canada (OEC)**
#900, 110 Yonge St.
Toronto, ON M5C 1T4
Tel: 416-952-1252
Fax: 416-952-1270
Toll-free: 800-575-5151
csb@csb.gc.ca
www.csb.gc.ca
• **Canada Revenue Agency / Agence du revenu du Canada**
• **Financial Consumer Agency of Canada / Agence de la consommation en matière financière du Canada**
• **Financial Transactions & Reports Analysis Centre of Canada (FINTRAC) / Centre d'analyse des opérations et déclarations financières du Canada (CANAFE)**
234 Laurier Ave. West, 24th Fl.
Ottawa, ON K1P 1H7
Fax: 613-943-7931
Toll-free: 866-346-8722
guidelines-lignesdirectrices@fintrac-canafe.gc.ca
www.fintrac.gc.ca
Created in 2000, FINTRAC is Canada's financial intelligence unit, a specialized agency created to collect, analyze & disclose financial information & intelligence on suspected money laundering & terrorist activities financing.

• **Office of the Superintendent of Financial Institutions / Bureau du surintendant des institutions financières Canada**

Consultations & Communications Branch / Direction des consultations et des communications
East Tower, 140 O'Connor St., 19th Fl., Ottawa, ON K1A 0G5
Tel: 613-992-1573
finpub@fin.gc.ca
TTY: 613-995-1455
Secondary Address: #135P, 300 Laurier Ave. West
Distribution Centre, West Tower
Ottawa, ON
Fax: 613-996-0518
services-distribution@fin.gc.ca
Assistant Deputy Minister, Jean-Michel Catta
Tel: 613-992-1369
Fax: 613-943-0938
Director, Public Affairs & Operations, David Gamble
Tel: 613-992-7763

Corporate Services Branch / Direction des services ministériels
Provides joint services for the federal Treasury Board Secretariat & Finance Canada.
Acting Assistant Deputy Minister, Sherry Harrison
Tel: 613-995-1408
Fax: 613-995-1408
Executive Director/Chief Information Officer, Information Management & Technology, Robert Aubé
Tel: 613-996-0313
Fax: 613-943-2077
Executive Director, Human Resources Division, Edward Poznanski
Tel: 613-992-1105
Fax: 613-943-2807

Economic & Fiscal Policy Branch / Direction de la politique économique et fiscale
Assistant Deputy Minister, Benoit Robidoux
Tel: 613-992-6930
Fax: 613-992-5773
General Director, Jim Haley
Tel: 613-992-0321
Fax: 613-992-5773

Economic Development & Corporate Finance / Développement économique et finances intégrées
Assistant Deputy Minister, Denis Gauthier
Tel: 613-992-1527
Fax: 613-992-0387
General Director, Richard Botham
Tel: 613-992-1011
Fax: 613-995-0387

Federal-Provincial Relations & Social Policy Branch / Direction des relations fédérales-provinciales et de la politique sociale
Assistant Deputy Minister, Chris Forbes
Tel: 613-996-0735
Fax: 613-992-7754
General Director, Chantal Maheu
Tel: 613-992-3998
Fax: 613-992-7754

Financial Sector Policy Branch / Direction de la politique du secteur financier
Assistant Deputy Minister, Jeremy Rudin
Tel: 613-992-4679
Fax: 613-952-1596
General Director, Diane Lafleur
Tel: 613-992-5885
Fax: 613-943-8436
Senior Chief, Securities Regulation & Intergovernmental Issues, Roger Charland
Tel: 613-992-7056
Fax: 613-947-5467
Director, Financial Sector, Leah Anderson
Tel: 613-992-6516
Fax: 613-943-8436
Director, Financial Markets Division, Wayne Foster
Tel: 613-947-2353
Fax: 613-943-2039
Director, Securities Policy, David M. Murchison
Tel: 613-947-8614
Fax: 613-947-5467
Director, Financial Institutions, Jane Pearse
Tel: 613-992-1631
Fax: 613-943-1334

International Trade & Finance / Finances et échanges internationaux
Assistant Deputy Minister, Rob Stewart
Tel: 613-992-6985
Fax: 613-992-7347
General Director, Jean-François Perrault
Tel: 613-996-8927
Fax: 613-992-7347
Senior Chief, International Finance & Development, Lise Carrière
Tel: 613-992-2984
Fax: 613-943-0279

Law Branch / Direction juridique
Assistant Deputy Minister, Sandra Hassan
Tel: 613-996-4667
Fax: 613-995-7223

Tax Policy Branch / Direction de la politique de l'impôt
Assistant Deputy Minister, Nancy Horsman
Tel: 613-992-1630
Fax: 613-996-1630
General Director, Tax Policy, Brian Ernewein
Tel: 613-992-3045
Fax: 613-996-0660
Director, Personal Income Tax, Sean Keenan
Tel: 613-992-6729
Fax: 613-943-5597
Director, Tax Legislation, Gerald Lalonde
Tel: 613-992-0405
Fax: 613-992-4450
Director, Intergovernmental Tax Policy, Evaluation & Research, Kei Moray
Tel: 613-947-3341
Fax: 613-947-1677
Director, Sales Tax Division, Lise Potvin
Tel: 613-992-6298
Fax: 613-995-8970
Director, Business Income Tax Division, Geoff Trueman
Tel: 613-992-1008
Fax: 613-943-2486
Director, Personal Income Tax, Baxter Williams
Tel: 613-992-2555
Fax: 613-996-0660

Financial Consumer Agency of Canada (FCAC) / Agence de la consommation en matière financière du Canada (ACFC)

427 Laurier Ave. West, 6th Fl., Ottawa, ON K1R 1B9
Fax: 613-941-1436
info@fcac-acfc.gc.ca
www.fcac-acfc.gc.ca
TTY: 866-914-6097
Other Communication: Toll-Free: 1-866-461-FCAC (3222) for services in English; 1-866-461-ACFC (2232) for services in French; www.twitter.com/fcacan
Created by Parliament in 2001, the Financial Consumer Agency of Canada (FCAC) exists to protect Canada's financial consumers; to make them aware of their rights & responsibilities; & to inform Canadians about the financial products & services available to them. The FCAC ensures that the nearly 500 federally regulated financial institutions respect the consumer provisions in the laws that govern them & monitors the voluntary codes of conduct financial institutions have adopted. As well as informing people about their rights as financial consumers, the FCAC provides information & tools to help consumers shop around for the best financial product/service for their situation. As of July 2010, the FCAC oversees payment card network operators & their commerical practices.
Acts Administered:
Bank Act
Co-operative Credit Associations Act
Financial Consumer Agency of Canada Act
Green Shield Canada Act
Insurance Companies Act
Payment Card Network Act
Trust & Loan Companies Act

Commissioner, Ursula Menke
Tel: 613-941-4300

Deputy Commissioner, Lucie Tedesco
Tel: 613-941-4335

Senior Counsel, Legal Services, Joseph de Pencier
Tel: 613-941-1425

Director, Marketing & Communications, André-Marc Allain
Tel: 613-941-4770

Director, Corporate & Administrative Services, Martin Pachéco
Tel: 613-941-4239

Director, Financial Literacy & Consumer Education, Jane Rooney
Tel: 613-941-1528

Director, Compliance & Enforcement Research, John Rossi
Tel: 613-941-3929

Office of the Superintendent of Financial Institutions (OSFI) / Bureau du surintendant des institutions financières Canada

Kent Square, 255 Albert St., Ottawa, ON K1A 0H2
Tel: 613-990-7788
Fax: 613-990-5591
Toll-Free: 800-385-8647
information@osfi-bsif.gc.ca
www.osfi-bsif.gc.ca
TTY: 613-943-3980
Responsible for regulating & supervising financial institutions & pension plans under federal jurisdiction. Included under federal jurisdiction are: banks, some insurance companies, trust companies, loan companies, cooperative credit associations, & fraternal benefit societies. OSFI monitors & examines these institutions & pension plans for solvency, liquidity, & compliance with legislation, regulations & Office guidelines. Provides actuarial services & advice to the Government of Canada. Reports to government through the Minister of Finance.

Superintendent, Julie Dickson
Tel: 613-990-3667
Fax: 613-993-6782
julie.dickson@osfi-bsif.gc.ca

Director, Security Services, Raymond Bullard
Tel: 613-990-7781
Fax: 613-990-0081
raymond.bullard@osfi-bsif.gc.ca

Communications Officer, Léonie Roux
Tel: 613-949-8942
Fax: 613-660-5591
leonie.roux@osfi-bsif.gc.ca

Audit & Consulting Services / Services de vérification et de consultation
Fax: 416-954-3169
Capital Consultant, Robert J. Hanna
Tel: 613-990-7278
Fax: 613-993-6525
bob.hanna@osfi-bsif.gc.ca

Corporate Services Sector / Secteur des services intégrés
Fax: 613-949-3968
Other Communication: Alt. Fax: 613-993-6782
Assistant Superintendent, Gary Walker
Tel: 613-990-8761
Fax: 613-990-6328
gary.walker@osfi-bsif.gc.ca
Managing Director, Finance & Corporate Planning, Michele Bridges
Tel: 613-991-4607
Fax: 613-990-6328
michele.briddges@osfi-bsif.gc.ca
Director, Communications & Consultations, Margaret Pearcy
Tel: 613-993-0577
Fax: 613-990-5591
margaret.pearcy@osfi-bsif.gc.ca

Office of the Chief Actuary / Bureau de l'actuaire en chef
Fax: 613-990-9900
Chief Actuary, Jean-Claude Ménard
Tel: 613-990-7577
Fax: 613-990-9900
jean-claude.menard@osfi-bsif.gc.c

Regulation Sector / Secteur de la réglementation
Fax: 613-993-6525
Assistant Superintendent, Mark White
Tel: 416-973-1655
Fax: 416-973-1655
mark.white@osfi-bsif.gc.ca
Senior Director, Actuarial, Stuart Wason
Tel: 416-973-2056
Fax: 416-952-0664
stuart.wason@osfi-bsif.gc.ca
Senior Director, Capital Division, Gilbert Ménard
Tel: 613-990-8081
Fax: 613-991-6822
gilbert.menard@osfi-bsif.gc.ca
Senior Director, AML & Compliance, Nicolas Burbridge
Tel: 416-973-6117
Fax: 416-954-3169
nicolas.burbridge@osfi-bsif.gc.ca
Senior Director, Legislation & Approvals, Patricia (Patty) A. Evanoff
Tel: 613-990-9004
Fax: 613-998-6716
patty.evanoff@osfi-bsif.gc.ca
Managing Director, International Advisory Group, Arvind Baghel
Tel: 416-973-6758

Fax: 416-952-1662
arvind.baghel@osfi-bsif.gc.ca
Senior Director, Accounting Policy, Karen F. Stothers
Tel: 416-973-0744
Fax: 416-952-1662
karen.stothers@osfi-bsif.gc.ca
Director, Research, Gerald Goldstein
Tel: 613-990-8911
Fax: 613-991-6822
gerald.goldstein@osfi-bsif.gc.ca
General Counsel, Legal Services, Alain Prévost
Tel: 613-990-7787
Fax: 613-952-5031
alain.prevost@csfi-bsif.gc.ca

Supervision Sector / Secteur de la surveillance
Other Communication: Toronto Fax: 416-973-1168; Ottawa Fax: 613-993-6782
Assistant Superintendent, Ted F. Price
Tel: 416-973-4385
Fax: 416-973-1168
ted.price@osfi-bsif.gc.ca
Senior Director, Financial Institutions Group, Karen Badgerow-Croteau
Tel: 416-952-3909
Fax: 416-954-5015
karen.badgerow-croteau@osfi-bsif.gc.ca
Senior Director, Regulatory & Supervisory Practices Division, Bruce J. Rutherford
Tel: 416-973-4378
Fax: 416-973-8994
bruce.rutherford@osfi-bsif.gc.ca
Managing Director, Operational Risk & Capital Assessment Services, Abhilash D. Bhachech
Tel: 416-973-6654
Fax: 416-952-1663
abhilash.bhachech@osfi-bsif.gc.ca
Senior Director, Property & Casualty Insurance Group, Penny M. Lee
Tel: 416-952-0557
Fax: 416-954-6478
penny.lee@osfi-bsif.gc.ca
Managing Director, Strategic Initiatives, Pamela H. Hopkins
Tel: 416-973-6657
Fax: 416-973-1168
pamela.hopkins@osfi-bsif.gc.ca
Director, Supervision, Maria Moutafis
Tel: 416-973-3699
Fax: 416-973-8994
maria.moutafis@osfi-bsif.gc.ca
Managing Director, Capital Markets/Risk Assessment, Douglas Sannuto
Tel: 416-973-1671
Fax: 416-954-3170
douglas.sannuto@osfi-bsif.gc.ca

Fisheries & Oceans Canada (DFO) / Pêches et Océans Canada (MPO)

200 Kent St., Ottawa, ON K1A 0E6
Tel: 613-993-0999
Fax: 613-990-1866
info@dfo-mpo.gc.ca
www.dfo-mpo.gc.ca
TTY: 800-465-7735

The Department of Fisheries & Oceans (DFO), on behalf of the Government of Canada, is responsible for policies & programs in support of Canada's economic, ecological & scientific interests in the oceans & freshwater fish habitat; for the conservation & sustainable utilization of Canada's fisheries resources in marine & inland waters; & for safe, effective & environmentally sound marine services responsive to the needs of Canadians in a global economy. The Department's mandate is extremely broad & covers management & protection of the marine & fisheries resources inside the 200-mile exclusive economic zone; management & protection of freshwater fisheries resources; marine safety along the world's longest coastline; facilitation of marine transportation; protection of the marine environment; support to other federal government institutions & objectives, as the government's civilian marine service; & research to support government priorities such as climate change & biodiversity. Because of its broad mandate, DFO does not operate alone. Federal & provincial governments share jurisdiction in a number of areas related to the Department's mandate. A $28-million investment over two years for the first phase of the Oceans Action Plan was announced in Feb ruary, 2005. The Plan is designed to develop ocean resources while protecting marine ecosystems, through sustainable development, integrated management plans, & marine protected areas.

Acts Administered:
Aboriginal Communal Fishing Licences Regulations
Alberta Fishery Regulations, 1998
Alice Arm Tailings Deposit Regulations
Atlantic Fisheries Restructuring Act
Atlantic Fishery Regulations
Basic Head Marine Protected Area Regulations
British Columbia Gravel Removal Order
British Columbia Logging Order
British Columbia Sport Fishing Regulations
Canada Shipping Act
Coastal Fisheries Protection Act
Confederation Bridge Area Provincial (PEI) Laws Application Regulations
Department of Fisheries & Oceans Act
Eastport Marine Protected Area Regulations
Endeavour Hydrothermal Vents Marine Protected Areas Regulations
Fish Health Protection Regulations
Fish Toxicant Regulations
Fisheries & Oceans Canada Orders
Fisheries Act
Fisheries Development Act
Fisheries Improvement Loans Act
Fishery (General) Regulations
Fishing & Recreational Harbours Act
Fishing Zones of Canada (Zone 6) Order
Fishing Zones of Canada (Zones 1, 2 & 3) Order
Fishing Zones of Canada (Zones 4 & 5) Order
Foreign Vessel Fishing Regulations
Freshwater Fish Marketing Act
Gilbert Bay Marine Protected Area Regulations
Great Lakes Fisheries Convention Act
Gully Marine Protected Area Regulations
Management of Contaminated Fisheries Regulations
Manitoba Fishery Regulations
Marine Mammal Regulations
Maritime Provinces Fishery Regulations
Navigable Waters Protection Act
Newfoundland & Labrador Fishery Regulations
Northwest Territories Fishery Regulations
Oceans Act
Ontario Fishery Regulations
Pacific Fishery Management Area Regulations
Pacific Fishery Regulations
Pleasure Craft Sewage Pollution Prevention Regulations
Potato Processing Plant Liquid Effluent Regulations
Provincial Regulations
Pulp & Paper Effluent Regulations
Quebec Fishery Regulations
Saskatchewan Fishery Regulations
Species at Risk Act
Territorial Sea Geographical Coordinated Order
Territorial Sea Geographical Coordinates (Area 7) Order
Yukon Territory Fishery Regulations

Minister, Fisheries & Oceans, Hon. Keith Ashfield
Tel: 613-992-3474
Fax: 613-992-1974
Min@dfo-mpo.gc.ca
Other Communications: Fisheries & Oceans, Phone: 613-992-3474

Deputy Minister, Claire Dansereau
Tel: 613-993-2200
Fax: 613-993-2194

Parliamentary Secretary to the Minister of Fisheries & Oceans, Randy Kamp
Tel: 613-992-3474
Fax: 613-947-4615
Kamp.R@parl.gc.ca

Director General, Communications, Louise Girouard
Tel: 613-990-0219
Fax: 613-993-8277

Executive Director & Senior General Counsel, Legal Services Unit, Lynn Lovett
Tel: 613-993-0966

Chief of Staff to the Deputy Minister, Blair Hodgson
Tel: 613-993-9226
Fax: 613-993-2194
blair.hodgson@dfo-mpo.gc.ca

Associated Agencies, Boards & Commissions:
• Fisheries Resource Conservation Council (FRCC) / Le Conseil pour la conservation des ressources halieutiques (CCRH)
PO Box 2001 D
Ottawa, ON K1P 5W3
Tel: 613-998-0433
Fax: 613-998-1146
info@frcc-ccrh.ca
www.frcc.ca
Created in 1993 to form a partnership between scientific & academic expertise, & all sectors of the fishing industry. Council members make public recommendations to the Minister of Fisheries & Oceans on conservation measures for the Atlantic fishery.
• Freshwater Fish Marketing Corporation / Office de commercialisation du poisson d'eau douce

Canadian Coast Guard (CCG) / Garde côtière canadienne
Centennial Towers, #6S018, 200 Kent St., Ottawa, ON K1A 0E6
Tel: 613-993-0999
Fax: 613-990-1866
info@dfo-mpo.gc.ca
www.ccg-gcc.gc.ca
TTY: 613-941-6517
The Canadian Coast Guard provides the following maritime programs & services: search & rescue; marine communications & traffic services, including radio communications & radio navigational aids services; marine navigation services, a program which establishes & maintains navigational aids to assist vessels in safe navigation; enrvironmental response program, which works to minimize impacts of marine pollution incidents & to provide humanitarian aid in disasters; aids to navigation, such as the Differential Global Positioning System (DGPS) & Notices to Mariners (NOTMAR); icebreaking services; & client relations & international affairs.
Commissioner, Marc Grégoire
Tel: 613-998-1571
Fax: 613-990-2780
Assistant Commissioner, Newfoundland & Labrador Region, John Butler
Tel: 709-772-5150
Fax: 709-772-4194
Assistant Commissioner, Quebec Region, Marc Demonceaux
Tel: 418-648-4535
Fax: 418-649-6066
Assistant Commissioner, Mario Pelletier
Tel: 613-991-6108
Fax: 613-993-5333
Assistant Commissioner, Canadian Coast Guard, Vija Poruks
Tel: 604-775-8810
Assistant Commissioner, Maritimes Region, Gary Sidock
Tel: 902-425-3907
Fax: 613-993-3421
Assistant Commissioner, Central & Arctic Region, Vacant
Tel: 519-383-1800
Fax: 519-383-1998
Assistant Commissioner, Pacific Region, Vacant
Deputy Commissioner, Vessel Procurement, Michel G. Vermette
Tel: 613-994-9220
Fax: 613-949-6816
Special Advisor to the Commissioner, David G. Faulkner
Tel: 613-993-1628
Fax: 613-993-5333
Director General, Operations, Wade Spurrell
Tel: 613-990-9172
Fax: 613-995-4700

Ecosystems & Fisheries Management / Gestion des écosystèmes et des pêches
200 Kent St., Ottawa, ON K1A 0E6
Responsible for the management & development of all federal fisheries & habitat in Canada. The division conserves, protects, develops & enhances fishery resources & habitats, encompassing the Atlantic & Pacific sectors, adjacent provinces, & the 200-mile offshore zone. Also manages Canadian parts of trans-boundary rivers.
Senior Assistant Deputy Minister, David Balfour
Tel: 613-990-9864
Associate Assistant Deputy Minister, Mitch Bloom
Tel: 613-993-1798
Director General, Ecosystem Management, Sharon Ashley
Tel: 613-990-0007
Acting Director General, Integrated Business Management, Jaime Caceres
Tel: 613-990-7556
Director General, Small Craft Harbours, Micheline Leduc
Tel: 613-990-8989
Director General, Aboriginal Programs & Governance, David Millette
Tel: 613-990-7201
Director General, Conservation & Protection, Paul Steele
Tel: 613-998-9537
Director General, Conservation & Protection, Trevor Swerdfager
Tel: 613-949-4919
Executive Director, Aquaculture Operations Management Directorate, Steve Burgess
Tel: 613-993-1884

Ecosystems & Oceans Science / Océans et science
200 Kent St., Ottawa, ON K1A 0E6
Services include: oceans sciences (ocean's physical properties, behaviour of organic & inorganic materials & their impact on fish & ecosystems, pollutants); regulation, enforcement & management of fisheries resources & habitat that are exploited for aboriginal, commercial & recreational purposes. The Marine Protected Areas Policy & the National Framework for Establishing & Managing Marine Protected Areas represents DFO's approach to establishing & maintaining MPOs in Canada.

Assistant Deputy Minister, Siddika Mithani
Tel: 613-993-5123
Director General, Ecosystem Science, David Gillis
Tel: 613-990-0271
Director General, Strategic & Regulatory Science, Wayne Moore
Tel: 613-990-0001
Fax: 613-990-0313
Director General, Canadian Hydrographic Service, Savithri Narayanan
Tel: 613-995-4413

Human Resources & Corporate Services / Services généraux
200 Kent St., Ottawa, ON K1A 0E6
Acting Assistant Deputy Minister, Richard Nadeau
Tel: 613-993-8726
Fax: 613-993-3246
Chief Information Officer & Director General, Information Management & Technology Services, Filippo Gagliardi
Tel: 613-993-2051
Director General, Real Property, Safety & Security, Daniel Leclair
Tel: 613-993-9291
Director General, Human Resources, Bhagwant Sandhu
Tel: 613-990-0013
Director, Human Resources, Marie LeBlanc
Tel: 506-851-6973
Fax: 506-851-2605
Director, Finance & Assets Management, Robert C. Richard
Tel: 506-851-2029
Fax: 506-851-2599

Program Policy / Politiques relatives aux programmes
200 Kent St., Ottawa, ON K1A 0E6
Services provided by the science sector include the following: research & data gathering; provision of information & advice in the fields of fisheries sciences (fish, invertebrates, marine mammals & plants, & ecosystems), oceans sciences (ocean's physical properties, behaviour of organic & inorganic materials & their impact on fish & ecosystems, pollutants), & hydrography (bathymetric, tide & current systems); & regulation, enforcement & management of fisheries resources & habitat that are exploited for aboriginal, commercial & recreational purposes. The sector assesses major stocks of exploited species of anadromous & marine fish, invertebrates, mammals & plants in Canada's Atlantic, Pacific, Arctic & marine waters, as well as freshwater fish in the Yukon & Northwest Territories. Research is conducted in the following areas: the biology & population of fish stocks, in order to provide scientific information & advice to fishery managers; the effects of changes in the ocean environment on the recruitment & distribution of fish populations; & studies to improve the productivity of aquaculture.
Assistant Deputy Minister, Kevin Stringer
Tel: 613-993-0850
Director General, Aquaculture Management, Guy Beaupré
Tel: 613-991-4315
Director General, Fisheries & Aboriginal Policy, Nadia Bouffard
Tel: 613-998-3111
Director General, Ecosystem Programs Policy, Christine Loth
Tel: 613-998-9088
Fax: 613-998-8158

Strategic Policy / Politiques
200 Kent St., Ottawa, ON K1A 0E6
Provides leadership in recommending, developing & monitoring policy frameworks that advance DFO's initiatives, support DFO programs, & are responsive to the changing needs of DFO clients. Provides strategic advice on departmental programs, develops long-term planning priorities for the department & coordinates cross-sectoral activities in support of government goals & departmental objectives.
Senior Assistant Deputy Minister, France Pégeot
Tel: 613-993-1808
Director General, Science & Policy Integration, Pardeep Ahluwalia
Tel: 613-990-0417
Fax: 613-998-8158
Director General, Economic Analysis & Statistics, Robert Elliott
Tel: 613-993-8597
Director General, Strategic Policy & Priorities, Dilhari Fernando
Tel: 613-990-0287
Director General, Legislative & Intergovernmental Affairs, Jeff MacDonald
Tel: 613-991-6651
Fax: 613-990-2811
Director General, Executive Secretariat, Michael Olsen
Tel: 613-998-5012
Fax: 613-949-9022
Director General, International Affairs, Michael Pearson
Tel: 613-993-1908
Acting Executive Advisor to the Senior ADM, Tanya Dagenais
Tel: 613-993-0823
Fax: 613-993-6958

Central & Arctic
#703, 201 Front St., Sarnia, ON N7T 8B1
Tel: 519-383-1810
Fax: 519-464-5128
Acting Regional Director General, David Burden
Tel: 519-383-1810
Fax: 519-464-5128
Gulf
PO Box 5030, Moncton, NB E1C 9B6
Tel: 506-851-7747
Fax: 506-851-2435
Regional Director General, Serge Theriault
Tel: 506-851-7750
Fax: 506-851-2224
Maritimes
176 Portland St., Halifax, NS B2Y 4T3
Tel: 902-426-2581
Fax: 902-426-2479
Regional Director General, Faith Scattolon
Tel: 902-426-2581
Newfoundland & Labrador
PO Box 5667 Whitehills, St. John's, NL A1C 5X1
Tel: 709-772-4423
Fax: 709-772-4880
Regional Director General, James Baird
Tel: 709-772-4417
Fax: 709-772-6306
Pacific
#200, 401 Burrard St., Vancouver, BC V6C 3S4
Tel: 604-666-0384
Fax: 604-666-8956
Regional Director General, Paul Sprout
Tel: 604-666-6098
Fax: 604-666-8756
Québec
104, rue Dalhousie, Québec, QC G1K 7Y7
Tél: 418-648-7747
Téléc: 418-648-4758
Associate Regional Director General, Johanne Benoit-Guillot
Tel: 418-648-7863
Fax: 418-648-4758

Bayfield Institute
867 Lakeshore Rd., PO Box 5050, Burlington, ON L7R 4A6
Tel: 905-336-6240
Comprises fisheries research, habitat management, hydrographic surveys & chart production & ships support. Together with the Freshwater Institute in Winnipeg, it provides the federal Fisheries & Oceans science programs for the Central & Arctic Region. Multiple partnerships with a variety of external stakeholders allow the Institute to be recognized internationally as a site of leading research in freshwater science.
District Manager, Ron DesJardine
Tel: 705-750-4017

Bedford Institute of Oceanography (BIO) / L'institut océanographique de Bedford
1 Challenger Dr., PO Box 1006, Dartmouth, NS B2Y 4A2
Tel: 902-426-3492
Fax: 902-426-8484
www.bio.gc.ca
Administered by Fisheries & Oceans, Bedford Institute of Oceanography (BIO) is Canada's largest centre for ocean research. Scientists, engineers & technicians primarily from Fisheries & Oceans, & Natural Resources Canada, (smaller components are from National Defense & Environment Canada) perform targeted research & provide advice on Atlantic marine environments. Programs include: fisheries research, ocean sciences & management, habitat ecology, marine chemistry, Canadian Hydrographic Service (producing navigation charts for the Atlantic & Arctic areas), marine environmental regional & resources geoscience, & seabird research & management. BIO based staff also conduct joint projects, such as sea floor mapping & exploration, & provide scientific response to marine environmental emergencies. Also located at Bedford is the Canadian Shark Research Laboratory & the Otolith Research Laboratory.
Regional Science Director, Dr. Michael Sinclair
sinclairm@mar.dfo-mpo.gc.ca

Freshwater Institute / Institut des eaux douces
501 University Cres., Winnipeg, MB R3T 2N6
Tel: 204-983-5000
Fax: 204-983-6285
Main areas of research are: fish habitats; limnology emphasizing mechanisms & processes of biological production & decomposition in lakes; studies related to energy development use, acidification, radionuclide & heavy metal pollution. Arctic research emphasizes commercially important fish & marine mammals & associated ecosystems, & the effects of hydroelectric developments & toxic chemical pollution on aquatic ecosystems. The Institute supports a major field camp at the Experimental Lakes Area. Activities include freshwater & arctic science, science oceans initiative, fish habitat management, fisheries management, small craft harbours, corporate services, communications & regional senior management. The federal fish inspection program, recently transferred to the new Canadian Food Inspection Agency (CFIA), continues to operate out of the FWI.
Administrative Assistant, Judy Fredette
Tel: 204-983-5118

Gulf Fisheries Centre / Centre de poissonerie du gulfe
343, av Université, 5th Fl., Moncton, NB E1C 9B6
Tél: 506-851-3886
Téléc: 506-851-7732
Regional Director General, Serge Thériault
Tel: 506-851-7750
Fax: 506-851-2224

Institut Maurice-Lamontagne / Maurice Lamontagne Institute
850, rte de le Mer, CP 1000, Mont-Joli, QC G5H 3Z4
Tél: 418-775-0555
Téléc: 418-775-0730
www.qc.dfo.ca/iml/en/intro.htm
Provides extensive research on: fisheries, fish habitat, oceanography, hydrography; development of marine renewable resources in the fields of fisheries, ocean industry development, commercial shipping & recreational boating. Main area of focus centres on the Gulf of St. Lawrence & estuary, Saguenay Fjord, Canadian Arctic, & the James, Hudson & Ungava Bays. Also performs the following research: environmental chemistry research on the distribution, transport & fate of contaminants in sediments, water & the food chain; ecotoxicology research & field assessments for biomarkers, fish pathology & embryotoxicity; molecular toxicology research for biomarkers, fish reproduction & steroid hormones; bioremediation study on the microbial degradation of petroleum oil hydrocarbons & microbial bioassays. Projects include the temporal & spatial monitoring of organic & inorganic contaminants in fish, shellfish & sediments of the St. Lawrence gulf & estuary. Also studying the effects of pulp & paper effluents & mercury & municipal effluents on the reproduction of fish.
Regional Director, Regional Science Branch, Ariane Plourde

Centre for Aquaculture & Environmental Research
4160 Marine Dr., West Vancouver, BC V7V 1N6
Tel: 604-666-7453
Fax: 604-666-3497
The Center for Aquaculture & Environmental Research (CAER) is a specialized centre for aquaculture & coastal research co-founded by Fisheries & Oceans Canada & the University of British Columbia.
Regional Director, Science Branch, Laura Richards
Tel: 250-729-8369
Fax: 250-756-7053

Institute of Ocean Sciences (IOS) / Institut des sciences de la mer (ISM)
9860 West Saanich Rd., PO Box 6000, Sidney, BC V8L 4B2
Tel: 250-363-6517
Fax: 250-363-6390
Science divisions at IOS include: Canadian Hydrographic Service, Marine Environment & Habitat Science, Ocean Science & Productivity. Other departments & organizations at the IOS facility include: GSC Pacific - Sidney Pacific Geoscience Centre, Canadian Wildlife Service, Canadian Coast Guard, North Pacific Marine Science Organization (PICES).
Director, Denis D'Amours
Tel: 250-363-6347

Pacific Biological Station (PBS) / La station de biologie du Pacifique
3190 Hammond Bay Rd., Nanaimo, BC V9T 6N7
Tel: 250-756-7000
Fax: 250-756-7053
Research at PBS responds to stock assessment, aquaculture, marine environment & habitat science, & ocean science & productivity priorities.
Regional Director, Science Branch, Laura Richards
Tel: 250-729-8369

St. Andrews Biological Station / La Station biologique de St. Andrews
531 Brandy Cove Rd., St Andrews, NB E5B 2L9
Tel: 506-529-8854
Fax: 506-529-5862
XMARSABS@mar.dfo-mpo.gc.ca
www.mar.dfo-mpo.gc.ca/sabs
Chemical & ecological studies on the interaction between oceanography & fisheries/aquaculture & the aquatic environment. Stock assessments & associated research on commercially important groundfish, pelagic finfish, invertebrate species in the Bay of Fundy & other areas of Atlantic Canada. Research in support of the existing salmon aquaculture industry & research on other species with potential for aquaculture in Atlantic Canada. Major environmental research projects include: risk assessment of organic chemicals to fisheries; biochemical indicators of health of aquatic animals; aquatic toxicity of marine phytotoxins; molluscan toxins, techniques & improvements; phytotoxin research; aquaculture ecology research;

effectiveness of acid rain control programs; effects of aquaculture in the coastal environment.
Section Head, Lara Cooper
Tel: 506-529-5951
Fax: 902-529-5862

Ecosystem Research Division (ERD) / Division de la recherche écosystémique (DRE)
www2.mar.dfo-mpo.gc.ca/science/ocean/sci/sci-e.html
Manager, Ecosystem Research, Glenn Harrison
Tel: 902-426-3879
glenn.harrison@dfo-mpo.gc.ca

Ocean Sciences
www2.mar.dfo-mpo.gc.ca/science/ocean/osd/osd-e.html
Manager, Ocean Sciences, Michel Mitchell
Tel: 902-426-8366
michel.mitchell@dfo-mpo.gc.ca

Integrated Science Data Management (ISDM) / Gestion des données scientifiques intégrées (GDSI)
Tel: 613-990-0265
Fax: 613-993-4658
service@meds-sdmm.dfo-mpo.gc.ca
www.meds-sdmm.dfo-mpo.gc.ca/isdm-gdsi/index-eng.html
Manages & archives ocean data collected by DFO or acquired through national or international programmes conducted in ocean areas adjacent to Canada; disseminates data, data products & services to the marine community. MEDS is a member of the International Oceanographic Data & Information Exchange, whose mission is to enhance marine research, exploitation & development by facilitating the exchange of oceanographic information between participating member countries.
Senior Technical & Policy Advisor, J. Robert Keeley
keeley@meds-sdmm.dfo-mpo.gc.ca

Foreign Affairs & International Trade Canada (FAIT) / Affaires étrangères et Commerce international Canada (AECT)

125 Sussex Dr., Ottawa, ON K1A 0G2
Tel: 613-944-4000
Fax: 613-996-9709
Toll-Free: 800-267-8376
enqserv@international.gc.ca
www.international.gc.ca
TTY: 613-944-4000
Other Communication: Media Relations: 613-995-1874

FAIT works to ensure that its policies, programmes & operations reflect sustainable development criteria & to make a difference in sustainable development terms in the international arena. The Department defines its intent in a 3-year SD strategy which is tabled in Parliament. Annual progress reports are also tabled in Parliament. The current strategy, Agenda 2006, covers the 2004-2006 period. FAIT strives to defend & advance Canada's international interests in environmental protection & sustainable development in bilateral, multilateral & regional fora including issues relating to climate change, trade & environment, sustainable forest management, hazardous & toxic substances, desertification, human settlements, biological diversity, biosafety, genetic resources for food & agriculture, air & marine pollution, whaling, & non-Canada-USA freshwater. To achieve progress in this area of responsibility, FAIT's Environmental & Sustainable Development Bureau works with the major international environmental & sustainable development organizations. It also recommends & oversees funding where appropriate. Domestically, the Bureau works toward agreement & productive partnerships with other government departments, agencies & non-governmental environmental, no nuclear energy, developmental & business organizations. It prepares & monitors implementation of the Department's Sustainable Development Strategy & provides advice & assistance in the areas of environmental assessment & the greening of departmental operations both in Canada & at the 157 missions abroad. FAIT established an environmental management system (EMS), based on the International Organization for Standardization's (ISO) 14000 series, in a commitment to incorporate best environmental management practices into its operations. A database of international environmental treaties to which Canada is a party may be searched at www.treaty-accord.gc.ca

Acts Administered:
Asia-Pacific Foundation of Canada Act
Bretton Woods Agreements Act
Canadian Commercial Corporation Act
Canadian Institute for International Peace & Security Act
Comprehensive Nuclear Test-Ban Treaty Implementation Act
Cultural Property Export & Import Act
Department of Foreign Affairs & International Trade Act
Diplomatic & Consular Privileges & Immunities Act
Export & Import Permits Act
Export Development Act
Food & Agriculture Organization of the United Nations Act
Forgiveness of Certain Official Development Assistance Debts Act
Fort-Falls Bridge Authority Act
Geneva Conventions Act
High Commissioner of the United Kingdom Act
International Boundary Waters Treaty Act
International Development (Financial Institutions) Continuing Assistance Act
International Development Research Centre Act
Meat Import Act
North American Free Trade Agreement Implementation Act
Northern Pipeline Act
Privileges & Immunities (International Organizations) Act
Privileges & Immunities (North Atlantic Treaty Organization) Act
Prohibition of International Air Services Act
Rainy Lake Watershed Emergency Control Act
Roosevelt-Campobello International Park Commission Act
Skagit River Valley Treaty Implementation Act
State Immunity Act
United Nations Act

Minister, Foreign Affairs, Hon. John Baird
Tel: 613-995-1851

Minister, International Trade, Hon. Edward Fast
Tel: 613-992-7332

Minister of State of Foreign Affairs, Diane Ablonczy
Tel: 613-994-2300

Associated Agencies, Boards & Commissions:
• Canadian International Development Agency / Agence canadienne de développement international
• International Joint Commission (Canadian Section) / Commission mixte internationale

Deputy Minister of Foreign Affairs / Sous-ministre des Affaires étrangères
Deputy Minister, Morris Rosenberg
Tel: 613-944-4491
Associate Deputy Minister, Gerald Cossette
Tel: 613-994-2771
Parliamentary Secretary to the Minister of Foreign Affairs, Deepak Obhrai
Tel: 613-947-4566
Fax: 613-947-4569
Chief Audit Executive, Yves Vaillancourt
Tel: 613-943-4743
Fax: 613-947-9374
Director General, Office of Transformation, Rick Savone
Tel: 613-944-0206

Office of Protocol / Bureau du Protocole
125 Sussex Dr., Ottawa, ON K1A 0G2
Tel: 613-996-8683
Fax: 613-943-1075
Chief of Protocol, Margaret Huber
Tel: 613-992-2344
Deputy Chief of Protocol & Director, Diplomatic Corps Services, Isabelle Martin
Tel: 613-995-5185
Fax: 613-943-1075

Communications Bureau / Direction générale des communications
125 Sussex Dr., Ottawa, ON K1A 0G2
Tel: 613-944-0404
Fax: 613-944-0811
Director General, Communications Bureau, Debora Brown
Tel: 613-944-2482
Director, Foreign Policy & Corporate Communications, Latifa Belmahdi
Tel: 613-996-2107
Fax: 613-995-0667
Director, E-Communications, Communications Products & Services, Yan Michaud
Tel: 613-992-7005
Fax: 613-992-2432
Director, Media Relations Office, Ulric Shannon
Tel: 613-992-0956

Global Issues / Enjeux mondiaux
Assistant Deputy Minister, Keith Christie
Tel: 613-944-2273
Fax: 613-944-1315
Director General, International Organizations, Human Rights & Democracy Bureau, David J. Angell
Tel: 613-944-0928
Fax: 613-944-0722
Director General, Energy, Climate & Circumpolar Affairs Bureau, Sheila Riordon
Tel: 613-944-0886
Director General, Economic Policy Bureau, Renatta Siemens
Tel: 613-992-7825

International Security Branch & Political Director / Sécurité international et directeur politique
Assistant Deputy Minister, Kerry Buck
Tel: 613-944-4228
Fax: 613-944-1180
Director General, International Security Bureau, Donald Sinclair
Tel: 613-992-3402
Director, International Crime & Terrorism, Michael Walma
Tel: 613-996-1430
Fax: 613-944-4827

Strategic Policy & Planning
125 Sussex Dr., Ottawa, ON K1A 0G2
Tel: 613-944-2696
Fax: 613-944-0285
Assistant Deputy Minister, Carmen Sylvain
Tel: 613-944-3022
Director General, Strategic Planning & Reporting Bureau, Patricia Fuller
Tel: 613-944-4150
Fax: 613-992-8732
Director General, Policy Planning Bureau, Arif Lalani
Tel: 613-944-3179
Fax: 613-944-3189

Deputy Minister of International Trade / Sous-ministre du Commerce international
Tel: 613-944-5000
Fax: 613-944-8493
Deputy Minister of International Trade, Louis Lévesque
Tel: 613-944-5000
Fax: 613-944-8493
Director, Arun Alexander
Tel: 613-944-0358
Deputy Director & Executive Assistant, Shalini Anand
Tel: 613-944-0357

Assistant Deputy Minister, Asia & Chief Trade Commissioner / Sous-ministre adjoint, Asie et Délégué commercial en chef
Tel: 613-944-2697
Fax: 613-944-3473
Assistant Deputy Minister (Asia), Peter McGovern
Tel: 613-944-2695
Fax: 613-944-2697
Director General, Geographic Strategy & Services Bureau, Roxanne Dubé
Tel: 613-995-7759
Director General, South, Southeast Asia & Oceania, Kenneth Macartney
Tel: 613-992-6129
Fax: 613-996-5897
Director General, Office of the Chief Trade Commissioner, Louis Marcotte
Tel: 613-996-0550
Fax: 613-944-3473

International Business Development, Investment & Innovation / Développement du commerce international, investissement et innovation
Tel: 613-944-3178
Acting Assistant Deputy Minister, Grant Manuge
Tel: 613-944-0504
Fax: 613-944-3062
Chief Economist, André Downs
Tel: 613-992-7776
Director General, International Trade Strategy & Portfolio Bureau, Michael Fine
Tel: 613-992-7979
Director General, Global Business Opportunities, Peter MacArthur
Tel: 613-996-1745
Director General, Trade Commissioner Service - Operations, Judith St George
Tel: 613-944-1678
Director General, Invest in Canada, Danielle Thibault
Tel: 613-996-2213
Fax: 613-944-3312
Director General, Canada Bureau, Randle Wilson
Tel: 613-992-8785
Atlantic
Senior Trade Commissioner, Regional Office - Moncton, Sarah Dionne
Tel: 506-851-4965
Fax: 506-851-6429
Ontario
Senior Trade Commissioner & Director, Regional Office - Toronto, Jim Feir
Tel: 416-954-6326
Fax: 416-973-8161
Pacific
Senior Trade Commissioner & Regional Director, Regional Office - Vancouver, Anna Biolik
Tel: 604-666-888
Prairie & Northern
Senior Trade Commissioner, Regional Office - Calgary, Patricia L. Elliott
Tel: 403-292-6409
Québec
Senior Trade Commissioner & Director, Regional Office - Montréal, Michel Charland

Tel: 514-283-3531
Fax: 514-283-8974

Trade Policy & Negotiations Branch / Secteur de la politique et des négociations commerciales
Tel: 613-996-5677
Fax: 613-996-1667

Assistant Deputy Minister, Ian Burney
Tel: 613-992-0293
Chief Trade Negotiator (Canada-India), Don Stephenson
Tel: 613-944-6900
Chief Trade Negotiator (Canada-European Union), Steve Verheul
Tel: 613-944-5880
Fax: 613-947-7483
Director General, North America Trade Policy Bureau, Laurent Cardinal
Tel: 613-944-0462
Fax: 613-944-0231
Director General, Trade Negotiations Bureau, Kirsten Hillman
Tel: 613-944-2002
Director General, Trade Negotiations Bureau, Anne McCaskill
Tel: 613-992-3386
Fax: 613-944-0757
Director General & Chief Air Negotiator, Intellectual Property & Services Trade Policy Bureau, Robert Ready
Tel: 613-944-1116
Fax: 613-944-0023

Passport Canada
Le 70 Crémazie, 70 Crémazie St., Gatineau, QC K1A 0G3
Fax: 819-953-5856
Toll-Free: 800-567-6868
www.pptc.gc.ca
Other Communication: TTY: 1-866-255-7655

CEO, Christine Desloges
Tel: 819-994-3530
Fax: 819-994-7150
Information Officer, Denis Bertrand
Tel: 819-953-1087
Information Officer, Patrice Brière
Tel: 819-956-4981
Information Officer, Claire Delisle
Tel: 819-934-3263
Information Officer, Anne Dubeau
Tel: 819-934-9991
Information Officer, Mouland Nait-Yahia
Tel: 819-934-6985
Information Officer, Trina Picard
Tel: 819-934-6981
Information Officer, Jennifer Proulx
Tel: 819-934-6354

Brampton
#401, 40 Gillingham Dr., Brampton, ON
Calgary
Harry Hays Bldg., #150, 220 - 4th Ave. SE, Calgary, AB
Calgary South
14331 Macleod Trail SW, Calgary, AB
Edmonton
Canada Place Building, #126, 9700 Jasper Ave., Edmonton, AB
Fredericton
Frederick Square, #430, 77 Westmorland St., Fredericton, NB
Gatineau
Place du Centre, Commercial Level 2, 200 Promenade du Portage, Gatineau, QC
Halifax
Maritime Centre, #1508, 1505 Barrington St., Halifax, NS
Hamilton
Standard Life Bldg., #330, 120 King St. West, Hamilton, ON
Kelowna
#110, 1835 Gordon Dr., Kelowna, BC
Kitchener
40 Weber St. East, Kitchener, ON
Laval
#500, 3, place Laval, Laval, QC
London
#201, 400 York St., 2nd Fl., London, ON
Mississauga
Central Parkway Mall, #116, 377 Burnhamthorpe Rd. East, 2nd Fl., Mississauga, ON
Montréal
Complexe Guy Favreau, Tour Ouest, #103, 200, boul René-Lévesque ouest, Montréal, QC
North York
Joseph Shepard Bldg., #380, 4900 Yonge St., North York, ON
Ottawa
Level C, East Tower, C.D. Howe Bldg., 240 Sparks St., Ottawa, ON
Pointe Claire
Fairview Pointe-Claire Shopping Center, 6815, rte Transcanadienne, Pointe-Claire, QC
Québec
Tour Cominar, Place de la Cité, #200, 2640, boul Laurier, 2e étage, Québec, QC
Regina
#500, 1870 Albert St., Regina, SK
Richmond
#310, 5611 Cooney Rd., Richmond, BC
Saguenay
Immeuble St-Michel, #408, 3885, boul Harvey, Saguenay, QC
St. Catharines
Landmark Bldg., #600, 43 Church St., St Catharines, ON
St. John's
TD Place, #802, 140 Water St., St. John's, NL
Saint-Laurent
#100, 2089 boul Marcel-Laurin, Saint-Laurent, QC
Saskatoon
Federal Bldg., #405, 101 - 22 St. East, Saskatoon, SK
Scarborough
#210, 200 Town Centre Crt., Scarborough, ON
Surrey
10153 King George Blvd., Surrey, BC
Thunder Bay
979 Alloy Dr., 2nd Fl., Thunder Bay, ON
Toronto
#300, 74 Victoria St., Toronto, ON
Vancouver
Sinclair Centre, #200, 757 West Hastings St., Vancouver, BC
Victoria - Bay Centre
1150 Douglas St., 4th Fl., Victoria, BC
Whitby
Whitby Mall, 1615 Dundas St. East, Whitby, ON
Windsor
CIBC Building, #503, 100 Ouellette Ave., Windsor, ON
Winnipeg
#400, 433 Main St., Winnipeg, MB

Canada Post Receiving Agents
Acton
53 Bower St., Acton, ON L7J 1E0
Tel: 519-853-0410
Ancaster
27 Legend Court, Ancaster, ON L9K 1J0
Toll-Free: 866-607-6301
Anjou
7200 rue Joseph-Renaud, Anjou, QC H1K 3W0
Toll-Free: 866-607-6310
Aurora
20 Wellington St. East, Aurora, ON L4G 1H0
Toll-Free: 866-607-6301
Barrie
150 Collier St., Barrie, ON L4M 1G0
Toll-Free: 866-607-6301
Belleville
Station Main, 21 College St. West, #D, Belleville, ON K8N 3B0
Tel: 613-968-3599
Boucherville
131 rue Jacques-Ménard, Boucherville, QC J4B 5B0
Tel: 450-655-5782
Bracebridge
98 Manitoba St., Bracebridge, ON P1L 1A0
Tel: 705-645-9955
Bradford
50 Barrie St., PO Box L3Z 1A0, Bradford, ON
Tel: 905-775-3002
Brantford
58 Dalhousie St., Brantford, ON N3T 2J0
Toll-Free: 866-607-6301
Brossard
10 Place du Commerce, Brossard, QC J4W 4T0
Toll-Free: 866-607-6301
Cap Rouge
#122, 1100 de la Chaudiere Blvd., Cap-Rouge, QC G1Y 1C0
Tel: 418-651-4194
Charlottetown
135 Kent St., Charlottetown, PE C1A 1M0
Tel: 902-628-4400
Chatham
120 Wellington St. West, Chatham, ON N7M 4V0
Tel: 519-352-1310
Georgetown
112 Guelph St., Georgetown, ON L7G 3Z0
Tel: 905-877-1917
Guelph
88 Wyndham St. North, Guelph, ON N1H 4E0
Tel: 519-822-3537
Kanata
145 Roland Michener Dr., Kanata, ON K2T 1G0
Tel: 905-607-6301
Kelowna
Banks Centre Retail Post Office, 2453 Hwy. 97 North, Kelowna, BC V1X 4J0
Toll-Free: 866-607-6301
Kingston
120 Clarence St., Kingston, ON K7L 1X0
Tel: 613-530-2260
Kirkland
16997 Aut. Transcanadienne, Kirkland, QC H9H 5J0
Toll-Free: 866-607-6301
Lasalle
7565 Newman Blvd., Lasalle, QC H8N 2X0
Toll-Free: 866-607-6301
Lévis
4870 de la Rive-Sud boul, Lévis, QC G6V 3P0
Toll-Free: 866-607-6301
Markham
21 Main St. North, Markham, ON L3P 1X0
Toll-Free: 866-607-6301
Midland
525 Dominion Ave., Midland, ON L4R 1P0
Tel: 705-526-5571
Moncton
281 St. George St., Moncton, NB E1C 1H0
Tel: 506-857-7258
North Bay
101 Worthington Ave., North Bay, ON P1B 1H0
Toll-Free: 866-607-6301
Oakville
193 Church St., Oakville, ON L6J 1N0
Toll-Free: 866-607-6301
Orangeville
216 Broadway Ave., Orangeville, ON L9W 1L0
Tel: 519-941-1160
Orillia
25 Peter St. North, Orillia, ON L3V 4Y0
Tel: 705-327-2918
Ottawa
1424 Sanford Fleming Ave., Ottawa, ON K1G 1C0
Toll-Free: 866-607-6301
Ottawa - Riverside Dr.
2701 Riverside Dr., Ottawa, ON K1A 0B1
Tel: 613-734-4338
Owen Sound
901 3rd Ave. East, Owen Sound, ON N4K 2K0
Tel: 519-371-5028
Peterborough
150 King St., Peterborough, ON K9J 2R0
Tel: 705-743-7705
Pickering
1740 Kingston Rd., Pickering, ON L1V 1C0
Toll-Free: 866-607-6301
Pointe-Claire
15 Donegani Ave., Pointe-Claire, QC H9R 2V0
Toll-Free: 866-607-6301
Prince George
1323 - 5th Ave., Prince George, BC V2L 3L0
Toll-Free: 866-607-6301
Québec - Galleries de la Capitale
#119, 5401, boul Des Galleries, Québec, QC G2K 1A0
Toll-Free: 866-607-6301
Québec - Haute-Ville
5, rue Dufort, Québec, QC G1R 2J0
Toll-Free: 866-607-6301
Québec
Succ. Québec Centre, 710 rue Bouvier, #145, Québec, QC G2J 1C0
Toll-Free: 866-607-6301
Rimouski
136 St-Germain St. West, Rimouski, QC G5L 4B0
Tel: 418-725-7378
Saint Bruno
50 de la Rabastalière St. West, Saint Bruno, QC J3V 1Y0
Tel: 450-441-1583
Saint John
125 Rothesay Ave., Saint John, NB E2L 2B0
Toll-Free: 866-607-6301
Sarnia
105 Christina St. South, Sarnia, ON N7T 2M0
Tel: 519-344-1644
Sault-Sainte-Marie
451 Queen St. East, Sault Ste Marie, ON P6A 1Z0
Toll-Free: 866-607-6301
Sherbrooke
50 Place de la Cité, Sherbrooke, QC H1H 4G0
Tel: 819-823-9449
Stratford
75 Waterloo St. South, Stratford, ON N5A 4A0
Toll-Free: 866-607-6301
Sudbury - Lasalle Blvd.
1776 Lasalle Blvd., Sudbury, ON P3A 2A0
Toll-Free: 866-607-6301
Sudbury - Lisgar St.
1 Lisgar St., Sudbury, ON P3E 3L0
Toll-Free: 866-607-6301
Summerside
57 Central St., Summerside, PE C1N 3K0
Tel: 902-436-5852

Sydney
269 Charlotte St., Sydney, NS B1P 1T0
Toll-Free: 866-607-6301
Toronto
2384 Yonge St., Toronto, ON M4P 2E0
Toll-Free: 866-607-6301
Trois-Rivières
1285 Notre Dame St., Trois-Rivières, QC G9A 4X0
Tel: 819-691-4215
Uxbridge
67 Brock St. West, Uxbridge, ON L9P 1A0
Tel: 905-852-7231
Woodstock
433 Norwich Ave., Woodstock, ON N4S 3W0
Toll-Free: 866-607-6301
Yarmouth
15 Willow St., Yarmouth, NS B5A 1T0
Tel: 902-742-4221
Abbotsford
32525 Simon Ave., Abbotsford, BC
TTY: 800-926-9105
Ajax
274 Mackenzie Ave., Ajax, ON
TTY: 800-926-9105
Amherst
#202, 26-28 Prince Arthur St., Amherst, NS
TTY: 800-926-9105
Asbestos
#204, 309 Chase St., Asbestos, QC
TTY: 800-926-9105
Baie Comeau
#204, Laflèche Blvd. ouest, 2e étage, Baie-Comeau, QC
TTY: 800-926-9105
Barrie
48 Owen St., Barrie, ON
TTY: 800-926-9105
Bedford
1597 Bedford Hwy., 2nd Fl., Bedford, NS
TTY: 800-926-9105
Bracebridge
Federal Building, 98 Manitoba St., 2nd Fl., Bracebridge, ON
TTY: 800-926-9105
Brandon
#100, 1039 Princess Ave., Brandon, MB
Bridgewater
77 Dufferin St., Bridgewater, NS
TTY: 800-926-9105
Brockville
The Fuller Building, 14 Courthouse Ave., Brockville', ON
TTY: 800-926-9105
Brooks
#608, 2 St. West, Brooks, AB
TTY: 800-926-9105
Brossard
2501 Lapinere Blvd., Brossard, QC
TTY: 800-926-9105
Burnaby
#100, 3480 Gilmore Way, Burnaby, BC
TTY: 800-926-9105
Calgary (East)
Marlborough Mall, #1502, 515 Marlborough Way NE, Calgary, AB
TTY: 800-926-9105
Calgary (North)
One Executive Place, 1816 Crowchild Trail NW, Calgary, AB
TTY: 800-926-9105
Calgary (South)
Fisher Park Place II, #100, 6712 Fisher St. SE, Calgary, AB
TTY: 800-926-9105
Campbellton
157 Water St., Campbellton, NB
TTY: 800-926-9105
Cambridge Bay
PO Box 2010, Cambridge Bay, NU
Campbellton
157 Water St., Campbellton, NB
Canmore
Canmore Gateway Shops, #113, 802 Bow Valley Trail, Building C, Canmore, AB
TTY: 800-926-9105
Charlottetown
Jean Canfield Government of Canada Building, 191 University Ave., Charlottetown, PE
TTY: 800-926-9105
Chibougamau
623, 3e rue, Chibougamau, QC
TTY: 800-926-9105
Chicoutimi
100 Lafontaine Ave., Chicoutimi, QC
TTY: 800-926-9105
Chilliwack
45860 Cheam Ave., Chilliwack, BC
TTY: 800-926-9105

Coaticook
#300, 14 Adams St., Coaticook, QC
TTY: 800-926-9105
Collingwood
44 Hurontario St., Collingwood, ON
TTY: 800-926-9105
Coquitlam
#100, 2963 Glen Drive, Coquitlam, BC
TTY: 800-926-9105
Corner Brook
1 Regent Sq., Corner Brook, NL
Cornwall
#100, 111 Water St. East, Cornwall, ON
TTY: 800-926-9105
Courtenay
130-19th St., Courtenay, BC
TTY: 800-926-9105
Cowansville
224 South St., 2nd Fl., Cowansville, QC
TTY: 800-926-9105
Cranbrook
1113 Baker St., Cranbrook, BC
TTY: 800-926-9105
Drummondville
1525 Saint-Joseph Blvd., Drummondville, QC
TTY: 800-926-9105
Edmonton Meadowlark
Meadowlark Shopping Centre, #120, 15710 87th Ave. NW, Edmonton, AB
Edmonton Millbourne
148 Millbourne Market Mall, 38 Ave. & Millwoods Rd., Edmonton, AB
Edmonton North
Northgate Centre, #2000, 9499 137th Ave. NW, Edmonton, AB
TTY: 800-926-9105
Edmundston
Federal Building, 22 Emmerson St., Edmundston, NB
TTY: 800-926-9105
Edson
4905 4th Ave., Edson, AB
TTY: 800-926-9105
Elliot Lake
Algo Centre, 151 Ontario Ave., Upper Mall, Elliot Lake, ON
TTY: 800-926-9105
Espanola
#200, 721 Centre St., Espanola, ON
TTY: 800-926-9105
Estevan
1314 3rd St., Estevan, SK
TTY: 800-926-9105
Flin Flon
111 Main St., Flin Flon, MB
Fort Frances
301 Scott St., Fort Frances, ON
TTY: 800-926-9105
Fort McMurray
Provincial Bldg., Main Fl., 9915 Franklin Ave., Fort McMurray, AB
Fort Simpson
9606 - 100 St., Fort Simpson, NT
Fort Smith
136 McDougal Rd., Fort Smith, NT
Gander
1 Markham Pl., Gander, NL
Gaspé
Frederica-Giroux Building, 98 de la Reine St., Gaspé, QC
TTY: 800-926-9105
Georgetown
232 Guelph St., Georgetown, ON
TTY: 800-926-9105
Glace Bay
Senator's Place, #100, 633 Main St., Glace Bay, NS
TTY: 800-926-9105
Grand Falls (Grand-Sault)
#100, 441 Madawaska Rd., Grand Falls (Grand-Sault), NB
TTY: 800-926-9105
Grand Prairie
Town Centre Mall, #100, 9845 99th Ave., Grand Prairie, AB
TTY: 800-926-9105
Happy Valley
23 Broomfield St., Jau Valley-Goose Bay, NL
Hawkesbury
134 Main St. East, Hawkesbury, ON
TTY: 800-926-9105
Hay River
#204, 41 Capital Dr., Hay River, NT
Inuvik
170 McKenzie Rd., Inuvik, NT
Iqaluit
#300, Iqaluit House, Iqaluit, NU
Kamloops
317 Seymour St., Kamloops, BC
TTY: 800-926-9105

Kapuskasing
8 Queen St., Kapuskasing, ON
TTY: 800-926-9105
Kelowna
471 Queensway Ave., Kelowna, BC
TTY: 800-926-9105
Kentville
Federal Building, 495 Main St., 2nd Fl., Kentville, NS
TTY: 800-926-9105
Kenora
308 Second St., Kenora, ON
TTY: 800-926-9105
Labrador City
500 Vanier Ave., Labrador City, NL
Langley
#202, 8747 204th St., Langley, BC
TTY: 800-926-9105
Lasalle
7655 Newman Blvd., Lasalle, QC
TTY: 800-926-9105
La Tuque
290, rue St-Joseph, La Tuque, QC
TTY: 800-926-9105
Lethbridge
Crowsnest Trail Plaza, #101, 920 2A Ave. North, Lethbridge, AB
Lloydminster
5016 48th St., Lloydminster, AB
TTY: 800-926-9105
Longueuil
#100, 1195 Du Tremblay Rd., Longueuil, QC
TTY: 800-926-9105
Magog
100A, 1700 Sherbrooke St., Magog, QC
TTY: 800-926-9105
Maple Ridge
22325 Lougheed Hwy., Maple Ridge, BC
TTY: 800-926-9105
Marystown
#130, 140 Ville Marie Dr., Marystown, NL
Medicine Hat
78 8th St. NW, Medicine Hat, AB
Melfort
104 McKendry Plaza, Melfort, SK
TTY: 800-926-9105
Miramichi
150 Pleasant St., Miramichi, NB
TTY: 800-926-9105
Moncton
Heritage Court, #310, 95 Foundry St., Moncton, NB
TTY: 800-926-9105
Montague
541 Main St., Montague, PE
TTY: 800-926-9105
Montréal
5455 Chauvreau St., Montréal, QC
TTY: 800-926-9105
Moose Jaw
Victoria Place, #501, 111 Fairford St. E., Moose Jaw, SK
TTY: 800-926-9105
Morden
158 Stephen St., Morden, MB
Nanaimo
#201, 60 Front St., Nanaimo, BC
TTY: 800-926-9105
Nelson
Kutenai Building, 333 Victoria St., Nelson, BC
TTY: 800-926-9105
New Liskeard
290 Armstrong St. North, New Liskeard, ON
TTY: 800-926-9105
Newmarket
1-18183 Yonge St., East Gwillimbury, Newmarket, ON
TTY: 800-926-9105
New Westminster
#201, 620 Royal Ave., New Westminster, BC
TTY: 800-926-9105
North Vancouver
#100, 221 West Esplanade, North Vancouver, BC
TTY: 800-926-9105
North Battleford
9800 Territorial Dr., North Battleford, SK
TTY: 800-926-9105
Notre-Dame-de-Lourdes
51 Rodgers St., Notre Dame de Lourdes, MB
Oakville
#B5, 117 Cross Ave., Oakville, ON
TTY: 800-926-9105
Orangeville
#102, 210 Broadway Ave., Orangeville, ON
TTY: 800-926-9105
Oshawa
Midtown Mall, #C6, 200 John St. West, Oshawa, ON
TTY: 800-926-9105

Ottawa (East)
2339 Ogilvie Rd., Ottawa, ON
TTY: 800-926-9105

Ottawa (West)
Lincoln Heights Galleria, 2525 Carling Ave., Ottawa, ON
TTY: 800-926-9105

Owen Sound
Heritage Place Shopping Centre, 1350 16th St. East, Owen Sound, ON
TTY: 800-926-9105

Parry Sound
74 James St., Parry Sound, ON
TTY: 800-926-9105

The Pas
Government of Canada Building, 305 4th St. West, The Pas, MB

Pembroke
141 Lake St., Pembroke, ON
TTY: 800-926-9105

Penticton
#101, 386 Ellis St., Penticton, BC
TTY: 800-926-9105

Peterborough
#101, 185 King St., Peterborough, ON
TTY: 800-926-9105

Placentia
Dalfens Mall, 61 Blockhouse Rd., Placentia, NL

Powell River
7061 Duncan St., Powell River, BC
TTY: 800-926-9105

Prince George
1363-4th Ave., Prince George, BC
TTY: 800-926-9105

Rankin Inlet
PO Box 97, Rankin Inlet, NU

Red Deer
First Red Deer Place, 4911 51st St., 2nd Fl., Red Deer, AB
TTY: 800-926-9105

Regina
1783 Hamilton St., Regina, SK
TTY: 800-926-9105

Repentigny
#54, 155 Notre-Dame St., Repentigny, QC
TTY: 800-926-9105

Richmond Hill
35 Beresford Dr., Richmond Hill, ON
TTY: 800-926-9105

Rouyn-Noranda
Réal Caouette Building, #300, 151 du Lac Avenue, Rouyn-Noranda, QC
TTY: 800-926-9105

Saint-Hyacinthe
Galerie St-Hyacinthe Shopping Mall, #2550, 3225 Cusson Ave., 2nd Fl., Saint-Hyacinthe, QC
TTY: 800-926-9105

Saint John
1 Agar Place, Saint John, NB
TTY: 800-926-9105

Saint-Quentin
193 Canada St., Saint-Quentin, NB
TTY: 800-926-9105

Salmon Arm
191 Shuswap St. NW, Salmon Arm, BC
TTY: 800-926-9105

Sault-Sainte-Marie
Sault-Sainte-Marie, ON
TTY: 800-926-9105

St. Anthony
Viking Mall, 1 Goose Cove Rd., St. Anthony, NL

St. Stephen
Canada Post Building, 93 Milltown Blvd., St. Stephen, NB
TTY: 800-926-9105

Sept-Iles
701 Laure Blvd., 3rd Fl., Sept-Iles, QC
TTY: 800-926-9105

Sherbrooke
124 Wellington St. North, Sherbrooke, QC
TTY: 800-926-9105

Souris
IGA Mall, 173 Main St., 2nd Fl., Souris, PE
TTY: 800-926-9105

Steinbach
321 Main St., Steinbach, MB
TTY: 800-926-9105

Summerside
Government of Canada Building, 294 Church St., Summerside, PE
TTY: 800-926-9105

Terrace
4630 Lazelle Ave., Terrace, BC

Thetford Mines
#500, 250 Frontenac Blvd. West, Thetford Mines, QC
TTY: 800-926-9105

Thompson
#118, 3 Station Rd., Thompson, MB

Timmins
120 Cedar St. South, Timmins, ON
TTY: 800-926-9105

Toronto (Centre)
Arthur Meighen, 25 St. Clair Ave. East, Toronto, ON
TTY: 800-926-9105

Toronto (Lakeside)
Dufferin Mall, #0001, 900 Dufferin St., Toronto, ON
TTY: 800-926-9105

Toronto (Lawrence Square)
Lawrence Square Mall, #103-105, 700 Lawrence Ave. West, Toronto, ON
TTY: 800-926-9105

Trois-Rivières
Le Bourg du Fleuve, 55 Des Forges St., Trois-Rivières, QC
TTY: 800-926-9105

Val d'Or
400 Central Ave., Val-d'Or, QC
TTY: 800-926-9105

Valleyfield
#100, 73 Maden St., Valleyfield, QC
TTY: 800-926-9105

Vancouver
Harry Stevens Building, 125 10th Ave. East, Vancouver, BC
TTY: 800-926-9105

Verdun
4110 Wellington St., 2nd Fl., Montréal, QC
TTY: 800-926-9105

Victoria
595 Pandora Ave., Victoria, BC
TTY: 800-926-9105

Whitehorse
#125, 300 Main St., Whitehorse, YT
TTY: 800-926-9105

Woodstock
Canada Post Building, 680 Main St. East, Woodstock, NB
TTY: 800-926-9105

Yellowknife
5101 - 50th Ave., Yellowknife, NT
TTY: 800-926-9105

Yorkton
214 Smith St. East, Yorkton, SK

Canadian Trade Commissioner Service / Service des délégués commerciaux du Canada
c/o Foreign Affairs & International Trade, 125 Sussex Dr., Ottawa, ON K1A 0G2
Tel: 613-944-9991
Fax: 613-996-9709
Toll-Free: 888-306-9991
enqserv@international.gc.ca
www.tradecommissioner.gc.ca

The Virtual Trade Commissioner (VTC) is a federal service that provides Canadian businesses with export assistance to increase overseas sales. VTC provides access to free services of the Canadian Trade Commissioner Service, with over 500 trade officers in 140 cities worldwide, information & services available through a personalized webpage & access to international business leads from the International Business Opportunities Centre.

Spokesperson, Caitlin Workman
Tel: 613-996-2000
Fax: 613-996-9276
cmr@international.gc.ca
Director, Marcel Lebleu
Tel: 613-996-3024

Bancomext
#2712, 66 Wellington St. West, PO Box 32, Toronto, ON M5K 1A1
Tel: 416-867-9292
Fax: 416-867-9325
cc-toronto@bancomext.gob.mx
www.bancomext.com

Main business development bank in Mexico which promotes international competitiveness within Mexican companies, & develops Mexico's foreign trade. It also encourages the inflow of foreign investment & the establishment of cooperative investments with companies & agencies from other countries.

Montréal
1540, 1501 McGill College, Montréal, QC H3A 3M8
Tel: 514-287-0899
Fax: 514-287-1844
montreal@bancomext.gob.mx

Vancouver
#1365, 200 Granville St., Vancouver, BC V6C 1S4
Tel: 604-682-3648
Fax: 604-682-1355
bancomext@trademexbc.com

Canada Trade Missions / Missions commerciales du Canada
Tel: 613-996-6117
trade.missions@international.gc.ca
www.tradecommissioner.gc.ca

Website contains links to trade missions in order to expand a business into foreign markets.

Canadian Chamber of Commerce in Mexico / Chambre de commerce du Canada au Mexique
Blvd. M. µvila Camacho No.1 Piso 8, Col. Polanco, México, D.F., 11560
www.canchammx.com
Other Communication: Ph: (52 55) 5580 3690
General Manager, Natalie Buylla
nbulla@canchammx.com

Embassy of Mexico in Canada / Ambassade du Mexique au Canada
#1000, 45 O'Connor St., Ottawa, ON K1P 1A4
Tel: 613-233-8988
Fax: 613-235-9123
info@embamexcan.com
embamex.sre.gob.mx/canada

Ambassador, Francisco J. Barrio Terrazas
Minister, Special Projects, Carlos Enrique L¢pez-Araiza Gebis
clopezaraiza@embamexcan.com

North American Development Bank
#300, 203 St. Mary's, San Antonio, TX 78205 USA
Tel: 210-231-8000
Fax: 210-231-6232
www.nadbank.org

NADB is a bilaterally funded, international organization, funded & governed by the United States & Mexico for the purpose of financing environmental infrastructure projects along their joint border.

Managing Director, Ger¢nimo Gutiérrez Fernández

Secretariat of Environment & Natural Resources (SEMARNAT)
Col. Jardines en la Monta¤a, Tlalpan, 4209 Blvd. Adolfo Ruiz Cortines, México, D.F., 14210 Mexico
web@semernat.gob.mx
www.semarnat.gob.mx/
Other Communication: Ph: (52 54) 90 09 00

Government agency whose main purpose is to develop environmental protection policy.

C. Secretario, Juan Rafael Elvira Quesada

Freshwater Fish Marketing Corporation / Office de commercialisation du poisson d'eau douce

1199 Plessis Rd., Winnipeg, MB R2C 3L4
Tel: 204-983-6601
Fax: 204-983-6497
sandi.cain@freshwaterfish.com
www.freshwaterfish.com

The Corporation is a buyer, processor & marketer of freshwater fish, harvested from over 400 lakes in Manitoba, Saskatchewan, Alberta, the Northwest Territories & Northwestern Ontario. Reports to the government through the Minister of Fisheries & Oceans.

President & Chief Executive Officer, John Wood

Chief Financial Officer, Stan Lazar

Great Lakes Pilotage Authority / Administration de pilotage des Grands Lacs

202 Pitt St., 2nd fl., PO Box 95, Cornwall, ON K6H 5R9
Tel: 613-933-2991
Fax: 613-932-3793
administration@glpa-apgl.com
www.glpa-apgl.com

The Authority provides pilotage services in the waters of the St. Lawrence River commencing at the northern entrance of St. Lambert Lock, the Great Lakes area & the Port of Churchill, Manitoba. Reports to government through the Minister of Transport.

Chief Executive Officer, Robert Lemire, C.A.
rlemire@glpa-apgl.com

Secretary-Treasurer, Réjean Ménard
rmenard@glpa-apgl.com

Administrative Assistant, Nancy McAteer
nmcateer@glpa-apgl.com

Head Office & Cornwall Dispatch
202 Pitt St., 2nd Fl., Cornwall, ON K6H 5R79
Tel: 613-933-2991
Fax: 613-932-3793

Thorold Office
Lock 7, Welland Canal, Thorold, ON
Tel: 905-688-3399
Fax: 905-688-5599

Health Canada / Santé Canada

Tunney's Pasture, Ottawa, ON K1A 0K9
Tel: 613-957-2991
Fax: 613-941-5366
Toll-Free: 866-225-0709
info@hc-sc.gc.ca
www.hc-sc.gc.ca
Other Communication: Office of the Access to Information: 613-954-8744

In partnership with provincial & territorial governments, Health Canada (HC) develops health policy, enforces health regulations, promotes disease prevention, & enhances healthy living for all Canadians. HC ensures that health services are available & accessible to First Nations & Inuit communities. It works closely with other federal departments, agencies & health stakeholders to reduce health & safety risks to Canadians. Through its Health Intelligence Network, HC works with other levels of government & the health care system in the surveillance, prevention, control & research of disease outbreaks across Canada & around the world. It also monitors health & safety risks related to the sale & use of drugs, food, chemicals, pesticides, medical devices & certain consumer products. HC negotiates agreements regarding hazardous materials in the workplace, performs medical assessments for pilots & air traffic controllers, & conducts environmental health assessments.

Acts Administered:
Appeal Board Procedures Regulations
Assisted Human Reproduction Act
Canada Health Act
Canada Medical Act
Canadian Centre on Substance Abuse Act
Canadian Institutes of Health Research Act
Consumer Chemicals & Containers Regulations
Controlled Drug Substances Act
Controlled Products Regulations
Department of Health Act
Financial Administration Act
Fitness & Amateur Sport Act
Food & Drugs Act (Agriculture & Agri-Food Canada)
Hazardous Material Information Review Regulations
Hazardous Materials Information Review Act (Human Resources & Skills Development)
Hazardous Products Act
Hazardous Products Regulations (Cellulose Insulation, Charcoal, Crocidolite Asbestos, Liquid Coating Materials, etc.)
Ingredient Disclosure List
Medical Research Council Act
Patent Act
Pest Control Products Act, 2002
Pesticide Residue Compensation Act
Quarantine Act
Queen Elizabeth II Canadian Research Fund Act
Radiation Emitting Devices Act
Tobacco Act

Minister, Health, Hon. Leona Aglukkaq
Tel: 613-957-0200
Fax: 613-952-1154
aglukkaq.l@parl.gc.ca; minister_ministre@hc-sc.gc.ca

Director, Policy, Leah Canning
Tel: 613-957-0200

Director, Parliamentary Affairs, Andrea Paine
Tel: 613-957-0200

Director, Communications, Tim Vail
Tel: 613-957-0200
Fax: 613-952-1154

Director, Operations & CanNor, Rossana Whissell
Tel: 613-957-0200

Chief of Staff, Scott Tessier
Tel: 613-957-0200

Associated Agencies, Boards & Commissions:

• Canadian Institutes of Health Research / Instituts de recherche en santé du Canada

• Hazardous Materials Information Review Commission (HMIRC) / Conseil de contrôle des renseignements relatifs aux matières dangereuses
427 Laurier Ave. West, 7th Fl.
Ottawa, ON K1A 1M3
Tel: 613-993-4331
Fax: 613-993-4686
hmirc-ccrmd@hc-sc.gc.ca
www.hmirc-ccrmd.gc.ca
The HMIRC is an administrative agency charged with carrying out a multi-faceted mandate under the authority of the Hazardous Materials Information Review Act, & provincial & territorial occupational health & safety acts. The mandate includes: formally registering claims for trade-secret exemptions & issuing registry numbers; adjudicating & issuing decisions on the validity of claims for exemption using prescribed regulatory criteria; making decisions on the compliance of material safety data sheets (MSDSs) & labels within the Workplace Hazardous Materials Information System (WHMIS) requirements; & convening independent, tripartite boards to hear appeals from claimants or affected parties on decisions & orders issued by HMIRC. Clients consist of a number of WHMIS stakeholders: suppliers & employers in the chemical industry who wish to protect their trade secrets from being disclosed on MSDSs or labels; employers who rely on supplier MSDS information to prepare their own workplace MSDSs & training programs; & labour organizations representing all workers who are exposed to these products.

• Pest Management Regulatory Agency (PMRA) / Agence de réglementation de la lutte antiparasitaire (ARLA)
2720 Riverside Dr.
Ottawa, ON K1A 0K9
Tel: 613-736-3401
Fax: 613-736-3798
www.hc-sc.gc.ca/cps-spc/pest/index-eng.php
Other Communication: Pesticides Information: 1-800-267-6315
The PMRA determines if proposed pesticides can be used safely when label directions are followed & will be effective for their intended use. If there is reasonable certainty from scientific evaluation that no harm to human health, future generations or the environment will result from exposure to or use of a pesticide, its registration for use in Canada will be approved. Once the pesticides are on the market, the PMRA monitors their use through a series of education, compliance & enforcement programs. Pesticides are also reviewed every fifteen years or sooner as new information is discovered & as science evolves. Companies are also required to report any incident they receive about their products, just as the public is encouraged to report any incidents to these companies or through the Incident Reporting Program. The PMRA administers the Pest Control Products Act on behalf of the Minister of Health.

• Public Health Agency of Canada / Agence de santé publique du Canada
130 Colonnade Rd.
Ottawa, ON K1A 0K9
www.phac-aspc.gc.ca
Other Communication: Alberta/NWT: 780-495-2754; Atlantic: 902-426-2700; BC/Yukon: 604-666-2729; Manitoba/Saskatchewan: 204-789-2000; Ontario/Nunavut: 416-973-0003; Quebec: 514-283-2858
Promotes & protects the health & safety of all Canadians. Its activities focus on preventing chronic diseases, including cancer & heart disease, preventing injuries, & responding to public health emergencies & infectious disease outbreaks.

Audit & Accountability Bureau (AAB) / Bureau de la vérification et de la responsabilisation (BVR)

Tel: 613-946-0361
Fax: 613-941-7319
aab-bvr@hc-sc.gc.ca
TTY: 800-267-1245

The AAB provides independent & objective advice & assurance to the Deputy Minister, on the effectiveness of risk management, controls & governance processes.

Chief Audit Executive, Guy Chevalier
Tel: 613-954-2215
Fax: 613-957-8910
guy.chevalier@hc-sc.gc.ca

Executive Coordinator, Christina Gauthier
Tel: 613-957-6820
Fax: 613-957-8910
christina.gauthier@hc-sc.gc.ca

Chief Financial Officer Branch (CFOB) / Direction générale du contrôleur ministériel (DGCM)

Tel: 613-957-3889
Fax: 613-952-9660
DPED_DEPM@hc-sc.gc.ca
Other Communication: Management Accountability Division: mcs-sfcm@hc-sc.gc.ca

The CFOB is the departmental focal point of accountability to ensure rigorous stewardship of resources & managing for results. The CFO provides the Minister, Deputy Minister, Associate Deputy Minister & the Departmental Executive with strategic advice on efficiency of expenditures & value-for-money, as well as anticipating & promoting future trends. The CFO reports directly to the Deputy Minister & is a key member of Health Canada's Senior Management Board. The CFO is also the lead executive with Central Agencies for overall financial management, with a functional reporting relationship to the Comptroller General of Canada.

Chief Financial Officer, Jamie Tibbetts
Tel: 613-952-3985
Fax: 613-952-7580
jamie.tibbetts@hc-sc.gc.ca

Executive Assistant to the ADM, Kateri Beauregard
Tel: 613-952-3984
Fax: 613-952-7580
kateri.beauregard@hc-sc.gc.ca

Coordinator, Correspondence, Cabinet Affairs & Parliament Relations, Jean Burns
Tel: 613-952-1299
Fax: 613-952-7580
jean.burns@hc-sc.gc.ca

Manager, Correspondence, Cabinet Affairs & Parliament Relations, Roxanne Fraser
Tel: 613-946-6363
Fax: 613-952-7580
roxanne.fraser@hc-sc.gc.ca

Senior Advisor, Cheryl Larabie
Tel: 613-952-3986
Fax: 613-952-7580
cheryl.larabie@hc-sc.gc.ca

Special Advisor, Gregory Wright
Tel: 613-952-3987
gregory.wright@hc-sc.gc.ca

Corporate Services Branch (CSB) / Direction générale aux services de gestion

The CSB provides corporate support & services across the Department in the following areas: human resources management; official languages; real property & facilities management; occupational health, safety emergency & security management; information technology & information management; executive correspondence; & access to information & privacy requests/issues.

Assistant Deputy Minister, Kin Choi
Tel: 613-946-3209
Fax: 613-946-3236
kin.choi@hc-sc.gc.ca

Acting Director General, Planning, Integration & Management Services, Brenda Baxter
Tel: 613-946-8132
Fax: 613-957-1587
brenda.baxter@hc-sc.gc.ca

Director General, Human Resources, Gerard Etienne
Tel: 613-957-3236
Fax: 613-941-1814
gerard.etienne@hc-sc.gc.ca

Director General, Facilities & Security Directorate, Gary Lacey
Tel: 613-692-6190
Fax: 613-946-0807
gary.lacey@hc-sc.gc.ca

Executive Director, Solutions Centre, Christiana Cavazzoni
Tel: 613-595-1371
Fax: 613-595-1822
christiana.cavazzoni@hc-sc.gc.ca

Director, Policy, Planning & Information, Sandi Wright
Tel: 613-946-3208
Fax: 613-946-0807
sandi.wright@hc-sc.gc.ca

Team Lead, Solutions Centre, Andrew Nice
Tel: 613-668-2790
andrew.nice@hc-sc.gc.ca

Senior Business Analyst, Information Services Business Management, Steve Morphy
Tel: 613-595-1657
Fax: 613-595-1657
steve.morphy@hc-sc.gc.ca

Project Officer, Planning, Integration & Management Services, Suzane-Renee Collette
Tel: 613-957-7818
suzane-renee.collette@hc-sc.gc.ca

Project Officer, Information Services Business Management, Manon Allard
Tel: 613-451-2038
Fax: 613-595-0726
manon.allard@hc-sc.gc.ca

Advisor, Human Resources, Leonce Philoctete
Tel: 613-946-3756
Fax: 613-946-3804
leonce.philoctete@hc-sc.gc.ca

Deputy Minister's Office / Bureau de la Sous-Ministre

Deputy Minister, Glenda Yeates
Tel: 613-957-0212
Fax: 613-952-8422
glenda.yeates@hc-sc.gc.ca

Associate Deputy Minister, Associate Deputy Minister's Office, Anne-Marie Robinson
Tel: 613-954-5904
Fax: 613-952-8422
anne-marie.robinson@hc-sc.gc.ca

Director General, Associate Deputy Minister's Office, Sony Perron
Tel: 613-941-2567
sony.perron@hc-sc.gc.ca

Director, Operations, Danielle Dubois
Tel: 613-948-6420
danielle.dubois@hc-sc.gc.ca
Director, Associate Deputy Minister's Office, Robert Ianiro
Tel: 613-941-2526
robert.ianiro@hc-sc.gc.ca

First Nations & Inuit Health Branch (FNIHB) / Direction générale de la santé des Premières nations et des Inuits (DGSPNI)
Assists First Nations & Inuit communities & people to address health inequalities & diseases threats through health surveillance & population health interventions. Ensures the availability of, or access to, health services for First Nations & Inuit people. Devolves control & management of community-based health services to First Nations & Inuit communities & organizations. The Environmental Health Division addresses conditions in the environment that could affect the health of community members, such as drinking water quality, mould, food safety, facilities inspections, transportation of dangerous goods. The Environmental Research Division conducts, coordinates & funds contaminants-related research, coordinates the replacement or upgrading of diesel-fuel tanks & remediation of fuel oil-contaminated sites, lab services for testing of PCBs & mercury, drinking water-related research & testing.
Assistant Deputy Minister, Michel Roy
Tel: 613-957-7701
Fax: 613-957-1118
michel.roy@hc-sc.gc.ca
Chief Dental Officer, Office of the Chief Dental Officer, Peter Cooney
Tel: 613-941-4748
Fax: 613-957-3687
peter.cooney@hc-sc.gc.ca
Senior Director General, Debbie L. Reid
Tel: 613-952-3135
Fax: 613-957-1118
debbie.l.reid@hc-sc.gc.ca
Acting Director General, Non-Insured Health Benefits, Scott Doidge
Tel: 613-954-8825
Fax: 613-954-5265
scott.doidge@hc-sc.gc.ca
Director General, Business Planning & Management Directorate, Stephane Hardy
Tel: 613-946-8853
Fax: 613-948-4307
stephane.hardy@hc-sc.gc.ca
Director General, Community Programs, Kathy Langlois
Tel: 613-952-9616
Fax: 613-941-3170
kathy.langlois@hc-sc.gc.ca
Director General, Strategic Policy, Planning & Analysis, Valerie Gideon
Tel: 613-957-3402
valerie.gideon@hc-sc.gc.ca
Acting Executive Director, Office of Nursing Services, Dorothy Laplante
Tel: 613-946-0442
Fax: 613-957-9986
dorothy.laplante@hc-sc.gc.ca
Executive Director, Office of Community Medicine, Dr. RoseMarie Ramsingh
Tel: 613-941-5358
Fax: 613-952-6407
rosemarie.ramsingh@hc-sc.gc.ca
Acting Director, Policy & Operations, Lori Brooks
Tel: 613-941-4400
lori.brooks@hc-sc.gc.ca
Director, Environmental Public Health, Primary Health Care & Public Health, Ivy Chan
Tel: 613-948-7773
Fax: 613-952-8639
ivy.chan@hc-sc.gc.ca
Director, Environmental Health Research, Primary Health Care & Public Health, Roy Kwiatkowski
Tel: 613-952-2828
Fax: 613-954-0692
roy.kwiatkowski@hc-sc.gc.ca
Director, Strategic Relations, Strategic Policy, Planning & Analysis, Paul McKinstry
Tel: 204-983-0989
Fax: 204-983-0079
paul.mckinstry@hc-sc.gc.ca
Director, Primary Health Care & Public Health, Shelagh Jane Woods
Tel: 613-941-1956
Fax: 613-941-8904
shelagh.jane.woods@hc-sc.gc.ca

Health Canada Regulations / Section de la réglementation
Fax: 613-954-4627
General Counsel & Director, Claude Lesage
Tel: 613-952-9645
Fax: 613-954-4627
claude.lesage@hc-sc.gc.ca
Senior Counsel, Wendy Gordon
Tel: 613-954-4761
Fax: 613-954-4627
wendy.gordon@hc-sc.gc.ca

Health Products & Food Branch (HPFB) / Direction générale des produits de santé et des aliments (DGPSA)
HPFB's mandate is to take an integrated approach to the management of risks & benefits related to health products & food by minimizing health factors to Canadians while maximizing the safety provided by the regulatory system for health products & food; & to promote conditions that enable Canadians to make healthy choices & provide information so that they can make informed decisions about their health. The Environmental Impact Initiative develops strategy & policy in response to the Canadian Environmental Protection Act requirement that all new substances for use in Canada must be assessed for direct & indirect impact on human health & the environment.
Assistant Deputy Minister, Paul Glover
Tel: 613-957-1804
Fax: 613-957-3954
paul_glover@hc-sc.gc.ca
Associate Assistant Deputy Minister, Catherine MacLeod
Tel: 613-957-6817
Fax: 613-957-3954
catherine_macleod@hc-sc.gc.ca
Director General, Veterinary Drugs Directorate, Daniel Chaput
Tel: 613-954-1873
Fax: 613-954-5694
daniel.chaput@hc-sc.gc.ca
Director General, Office of Consumer & Public Involvement, Lucie Desforges
Tel: 613-948-8431
lucie.desforges@hc-sc.gc.ca
Director General, Food Directorate, Dr. Samuel Godefroy
Tel: 613-957-1821
Fax: 613-954-4674
samuel.godefroy@hc-sc.gc.ca
Director General, Biologics & Genetic Therapies Directorate, Elwyn Griffiths
Tel: 613-957-8065
Fax: 613-957-1679
elwyn.griffiths@hc-sc.gc.ca
Director General, Office of Nutrition Policy & Promotion, Dr. Hasan Hutchinson
Tel: 613-957-8330
Fax: 613-946-8073
hasan.hutchinson@hc-sc.gc.ca
Director General, Natural Health Products, Scott Sawler
Tel: 613-952-2558
Fax: 613-948-6810
scott.sawler@hc-sc.gc.ca
Director General, Therapeutic Products Directorate, Dr. Supriya Sharma
Tel: 613-957-6466
Fax: 613-952-7756
supriya.sharma@hc-sc.gc.ca
Director General, Marketed Health Products Directorate, Dr. Chris Turner
Tel: 613-941-8889
Fax: 613-952-7738
chris.turner@hc-sc.gc.ca
Director General, Policy, Planning & International Affairs Directorate, Kendal Weber
Tel: 613-952-8149
Fax: 613-954-9981
kendal.weber@hc-sc.gc.ca

Healthy Environments & Consumer Safety (HECSB) / Direction générale, santé environnementale et sécurité des consommateurs (DGSESC)
The HECSB mission is to help Canadians to maintain & improve their health by promoting healthy & safe living, working & recreational environments & by reducing the harm caused by tobacco, alcohol, controlled substances, environmental contaminants, & unsafe consumer & industrial products.
Assistant Deputy Minister, Hilary Geller
Tel: 613-946-6701
Fax: 613-946-6666
hilary.geller@hc-sc.gc.ca
Director General, Consumer Product Safety, Athana Mentzelopoulos
Tel: 613-960-4725
Fax: 613-946-1100
athana.mentzelopoulos@hc-sc.gc.ca
Director General, Environmental & Radiation Health Sciences, Beth Pieterson
Tel: 613-954-3859
beth.pieterson@hc-sc.gc.ca
Director General, Controlled Substances & Tobacco, Cathy A. Sabiston
Tel: 613-941-1977
Fax: 613-946-6460
cathy.a.sabiston@hc-sc.gc.ca
Director, Planning & Administrative Services, Policy, Planning & Integration, Wendy Kiernan
Tel: 613-941-3137
Fax: 613-941-8632
wendy.kiernan@hc-sc.gc.ca
Director, Planning & Administrative Services, Safe Environments, Karen Lloyd
Tel: 613-954-0291
Fax: 613-952-2206
karen.lloyd@hc-sc.gc.ca
Director, Office of Controlled Substances, Johanne Beaulieu
Tel: 613-952-2177
Fax: 613-946-4224
johanne.beaulieu@hc-sc.gc.ca

Legal Services / Services juridiques
www.hc-sc.gc.ca/ahc-asc/branch-dirgen/ls-sj/index-eng.php
Senior General Counsel; Head, Legal Services, Irit Weiser
Tel: 613-957-3766
Fax: 613-954-9485
irit.weiser@hc-sc.gc.ca
Director, Planning & Operations, Steven Blake
Tel: 613-941-5343
steven.blake@hc-sc.gc.ca

Pest Management Regulatory Agency (PMRA) / Agence de réglementation de la lutte antiparasitaire (ARLA)
The PMRA is responsible for pesticide regulation in Canada. Created in 1995, this branch of Health Canada consolidates the resources & responsibilities for pest management regulation. Pesticides are stringently regulated in Canada to ensure they pose minimal risk to human health & the environment. Health Canada also promotes & verifies compliance with the Act & enforces situations of non compliance warranting action.
Executive Director, Richard Aucoin
Tel: 613-736-3701
Fax: 613-736-3707
richard.aucoin@hc-sc.gc.ca
Director General, Health Evaluation, Dr. Peter Chan, PhD
Tel: 613-736-3510
Fax: 613-736-3909
peter.chan@hc-sc.gc.ca
Director General, Re-evaluation Management, Margherita Conti
Tel: 613-736-3485
Fax: 613-736-9840
margherita.conti@hc-sc.gc.ca
Director General, Policy, Communications & Regulatory Affairs, Trish MacQuarrie
Tel: 613-736-3660
Fax: 613-736-3659
trish.macquarrie@hc-sc.gc.ca
Director General, Environmental Assessment, Mary Mitchell
Tel: 613-736-3715
mary.mitchell@hc-sc.gc.ca
Director General, Compliance, Lab Services & Regional Operations, Dr. Martin Tomkin
Tel: 613-736-3484
Fax: 613-736-3540
martin.tomkin@hc-sc.gc.ca
Director General, Value & Sustainability Assessment, John Worgan
Tel: 613-736-3780
Fax: 613-736-3770
john.worgan@hc-sc.gc.ca
Director, Strategic Planning, Financial & Business Operations, Anne Lapierre
Tel: 613-736-3411
anne.lapierre@hc-sc.gc.ca

Public Affairs, Consultation & Communications (PACCB) / Direction générale des affaires publiques, de la consultation et des communications (DGAPCC)
The PACCB integrates national & regional perspectives into all of its policies & strategies, communications & consultation functions. The Branch plays a key role in delivering Health Canada's commitment to transparency. Through PACCB, Health Canada will continue to improve communications & the flow of information to & from stakeholders, clients, partners, media & the Canadian public.
Assistant Deputy Minister, Anne Lamar
Tel: 613-960-2176
Fax: 613-960-2183
anne.lamar@hc-sc.gc.ca
Director General, Marketing & Communications Services, Jane Hazel
Tel: 613-957-0215
Fax: 613-948-8092
jane.hazel@hc-sc.gc.ca
Director General, Strategic Communications, Charles Mojsej
Tel: 613-948-8916
Fax: 613-957-1729
charles.mojsej@hc-sc.gc.ca

Director General, Consultations, Planning & Coordination, Aruna Sadana
Tel: 613-960-6043
Fax: 613-960-6063
aruna.sadana@hc-sc.gc.ca

Regions & Programs Branch / Direction générale des régions et des programmes
Assistant Deputy Minister, Michel C. Doré
Tel: 613-941-8081
Fax: 613-948-0082
michel.c.dore@hc-sc.gc.ca
Acting Senior Director General, Programs, Debbie Beresford-Green
Tel: 613-952-3579
Fax: 613-941-7360
debbie.beresford-green@hc-sc.gc.ca
Director General, Emergency Preparedness & Occupational Health, Anthony Sangster
Tel: 613-957-7669
Fax: 613-954-5822
anthony.sangster@hc-sc.gc.ca
Director General, Branch Management Services, Nicholas Trudel
Tel: 613-954-0681
Fax: 613-941-7360
nicholas.trudel@hc-sc.gc.ca
Director, Colleen Ryan
Tel: 613-952-2074
Fax: 613-941-7360
colleen.ryan@hc-sc.gc.ca
Alberta
9700 Jasper Ave., Edmonton, AB T5J 4C3
Tel: 780-495-6815
Fax: 780-495-5551
Regional Director General, Arthur J. Murphy
Tel: 780-495-6737
arthur.j.murphy@hc-sc.gc.ca
Associate Regional Director General, Ward Chickoski
Tel: 780-495-3857
Fax: 780-495-5551
ward.chickoski@hc-sc.gc.ca
Atlantic
#1525, 1505 Barrington St., Halifax, NS B3J 3Y6
Tel: 902-426-2038
Fax: 902-426-3768
Regional Director General, Simon d'Entremont
Tel: 902-426-4097
Fax: 902-426-6659
simon.dentremont@hc-sc.gc.ca
Associate Regional Director General, Cheryl Flemming
Tel: 902-426-2622
Fax: 902-426-6659
cheryl.flemming@hc-sc.gc.ca
British Columbia
Winch Bldg., #410, 757 West Hastings St., Vancouver, BC V6C 1A1
Tel: 604-666-2083
Fax: 604-666-2258
Regional Director General, Catherine Lappe
Tel: 604-775-7003
catherine.lappe@hc-sc.gc.ca
Associate Regional Director General, Bruce Cuddihey
Tel: 604-666-0511
Fax: 604-775-8716
bruce.cuddihey@hc-sc.gc.ca
Manitoba Region
#450, 391 York Ave., Winnipeg, MB R3C 4W1
Tel: 204-983-2508
Fax: 204-983-3972
Regional Director General, Laurette Burch
Tel: 204-984-4363
Fax: 204-983-5325
laurette.burch@hc-sc.gc.ca
Northern Region
#1400, 60 Queen St., PO Box 3914A, Ottawa, ON K1A 0K9
Tel: 613-946-8081
Fax: 613-948-2428
Other Communication: General inquiries: 866-509-1769
Regional Director General, Cathy Praamsma
Tel: 613-946-8104
Fax: 613-948-2428
cathy.praamsma@hc-sc.gc.ca
Ontario
180 Queen St. West, Toronto, ON M5V 3L7
Tel: 416-973-4389
Fax: 416-973-1423
Toll-Free: 866-999-7612
Acting Regional Director General, Lucy Butts
Tel: 416-954-3592
Fax: 416-954-3599
lucy.butts@hc-sc.gc.ca
Québec
Guy-Favreau Complexe, Tour Est, 200, boul René-Lévesque ouest, 2e étage, Montréal, QC H2Z 1X4
Tél: 450-646-1353
Téléc: 514-283-6739
Ligne sans frais: 800-561-3350
Regional Director General, Marie-France Bérard
Tel: 514-283-2856
Fax: 514-283-0910
marie-france.berard@hc-sc.gc.ca
Saskatchewan
2045 Broad St., Regina, SK S4P 3T7
Regional Director General, Alexander Campbell
Tel: 306-780-3115
alexander.campbell@hc-sc.gc.ca

Strategic Policy Branch (SPB) / Direction générale de la politique stratégique (DGPS)
The SPB plays a lead role in health policy, communications & consultations. The SPB's objective is to promote national coordination & development of a strong, shared knowledge base to address health & health care priorities for all Canadians. They also aim to facilitate successful health system adaptation to changes in technology, society, industry & the environment, such that Canadians will continue to be protected from health risks, have access to quality health care, & gain positive health benefits from information & innovation.
Assistant Deputy Minister, Abby Hoffman
Tel: 613-946-1791
Fax: 613-954-0336
abby.hoffman@hc-sc.gc.ca
Associate Assistant Deputy Minister, Michelle Kovacevic
Tel: 613-954-2645
michelle.kovacevic@hc-sc.gc.ca
Acting Director General, Health Care Policy, Gavin Brown
Tel: 613-957-8994
Fax: 613-648-4663
gavin.brown@hc-sc.gc.ca
Director General, Science Policy, Dr. Pierre Charest
Tel: 613-941-3003
Fax: 613-941-3007
pierre.charest@hc-sc.gc.ca
Director General, International Affairs, Bersabel Ephrem
Tel: 613-941-3335
Fax: 613-952-7417
bersabel.ephrem@hc-sc.gc.ca
Director General, Legislative & Regulatory Policy, Regi Mathew
Tel: 613-960-7353
regi.mathew@hc-sc.gc.ca
Director General, Applied Research & Analysis, Sylvain Paradis
Tel: 613-946-8030
sylvain.paradis@hc-sc.gc.ca
Executive Director, Office of Nursing Policy, Sandra MacDonald-Rencz
Tel: 613-941-4314
Fax: 613-946-3166
sandra.macdonald-rencz@hc-sc.gc.ca
Acting Executive Director, Office of Pharmaceuticals Management Strategies, Jean Pruneau
Tel: 613-941-8218
Fax: 613-941-5258
jean.pruneau@hc-sc.gc.ca
Director, Canada Health Act Division, Gigi Mandy
Tel: 613-954-8685
Fax: 613-952-8542
gigi.mandy@hc-sc.gc.ca
Acting Director, Federal/Provincial Relations, Noel Kivimaki
Tel: 613-946-8860
Fax: 613-954-3580
noel.kivimaki@hc-sc.gc.ca
Director, Policy Coordination & Planning, Phyllis Colvin
Tel: 613-957-3085
phyllis.colvin@hc-sc.gc.ca

Hazardous Materials Information Review Commission (HMIRC)

427 Laurier Ave. West, Ottawa, ON K1A 1M3
www.hmirc-ccrmd.gc.ca
The Hazardous Materials Information Review Commission works with the Ministry of Health to help safeguard the workers and trade secrets of Canada's chemical industry.

Human Resources & Skills Development Canada (HRSDC) / Ressources humaines et Développement des compétences Canada (RHDCC)

140 Promenade du Portage, Gatineau, QC K1A 0J9
www.hrsdc.gc.ca
Other Communication: Media enquiries: 819-994-5559
HRSDC works to build a competitive country & to support Canadians in making choices to live productively. The following are key responsibilities of the federal department: developing policies to assist Canadaians to use their talents, skills & resources to participate in learning, work, & their community; creating programs to support initiative to help citizens in life transitions; improving outcomes for people through services offered by Service Canada & other partners; & establishing a healthy work environment.
Acts Administered:
Aviation Occupational Safety & Health Regulations
Canada Labour Code
Canada Occupational Health & Safety Regulations
Canada Pension Plan
Canada Student Financial Assistance Act
Canada Student Loans Act
Canadian Centre for Occupational Health & Safety Act
Coal Mines (CBDC) Occupational Safety & Health Regulations
Coal Mining Safety Commission Regulations
Corporations & Labour Unions Returns Act
Department of Human Resources Development Act
Employment Equity Act
Employment Insurance Act
Fair Wages & Hours of Labour Act
Family Orders & Agreements Enforcement Assistance Act
Federal-Provincial Fiscal Arrangements Act
Government Annuities Act
Government Employees Compensation Act
Labour Adjustment Benefits Act
Marine Occupational Safety & Health Regulations
Merchant Seamen Compensation Act
Non-smokers' Health Act (Transport Canada)
Oil & Gas Occupational Safety & Health Regulations
Old Age Security Act
On Board Trains Occupational Safety & Health Regulations
Status of the Artist Act
Unemployment Assistance Act
Vocational Rehabilitation of Disabled Persons Act
Wages Liability Act

Minister, Human Resources & Skills Development, Hon. Diane Finley, B.A., M.B.A.
Tel: 819-994-2482
Fax: 819-994-0448
diane.finley@hrsdc-rhdcc.gc.ca

Minister, Labour, Hon. Lisa Raitt
Tel: 819-953-5646
Fax: 819-994-5168
lisa.raitt@hrsdc-rhdcc.gc.ca

Minister of State (Seniors), Hon. Alice Wong
Tel: 613-995-2021
Fax: 819-995-2174

Parliamentary Secretary to the Minister of Human Resources & Skills Development Canada & to the Minister of Labour, Dr. Kellie Leitch
Tel: 613-992-4224
Fax: 613-992-2164

Deputy Minister, Labour, Hélène Gosselin
Tel: 819-934-3320
Fax: 819-934-7066
helene.gosselin@labour-travail.gc.ca

Deputy Minister, Human Resources & Skills Development Canada, Ian Shugart
Tel: 819-994-4514
Fax: 819-953-5603
ian.shugart@hrsdc-rhdcc.gc.ca

Chief Audit Executive, Vincent DaLuz
Tel: 819-953-0821
Fax: 819-953-0831
vincent.daluz@hrsdc-rhdcc.gc.ca

Associated Agencies, Boards & Commissions:
• **Canada Employment Insurance Commission (CEIC) / Commission de l'assurance-emploi du Canada (CAEC)**
140, Promenade du Portage, Phase IV
Gatineau, QC K1A 0J9
Toll-free: 800-206-7218
www.ei-ae.gc.ca
Manages the Employment Insurance Program.
• **Canada Industrial Relations Board / Conseil canadien des relations industrielles**
• **Canadian Centre for Occupational Health & Safety / Centre canadien d'hygiène et de sécurité au travail**
• **Canadian Council of Directors of Apprenticeship / Conseil canadien des directeurs de l'apprentissage**
140 Promenade du Portage, 5th Fl, Phase IV
Gatineau, QC K1A 0J9
Tel: 819-953-7443
Fax: 819-994-0202
redseal-sceaurouge@hrsdc-rhdcc.gc.ca
www.red-seal.ca
A national body responsible for the certification of skilled workers, in the regulated trade, under the Interprovincial Standards (Red Seal) Program. This program is designed to

facilitate the mobility of workers employed in the apprenticeable occupations in Canada through the establishment of common standards for certification. The apprenticeship program is generally administered by provincial & territorial departments responsible for education, labour & training (under the direction of the provincial & territorial Director of Apprenticeship) with authority delegated from the legislation in each province & territory. Through the program, apprentices who have completed their training & certified journeymen are able to obtain a Red Seal endorsement on their Certificate of Qualification by successfully completing an Interprovincial Standards Examination. The program encourages standardization of provincial & territorial apprenticeship training & certification programs. The Red Seal allows qualified trade persons to practice the trade in any province or territory in Canada where the trade is designated without having to write further examinations.

• Merchant Seamen Compensation Board / Commission d'indemnisation des marins marchands du Canada
Secretary, Merchant Seamen Compensation Board
Phase II, Place du Portage, 10th Fl.
Ottawa, ON K1A 0J2
Tel: 819-953-8001
Fax: 819-994-5368
The Merchant Seamen Compensation Board consists of three members who are appointed by the Governor in Council pursuant to the Merchant Seamen Compensation Act . The Board reports to the federal Minister of Labour who has the overall responsibility for the Act. The Board hears & decides claims arising under the Act. The Act provides benefits to merchant seamen who are injured or disabled as a result of their work. Employers are liable to pay benefits awarded & the administrative expenses of the Board. They must maintain insurance against the risk of claims & report all accidents to the Board.

• Office of the Commissioner of Review Tribunals / Bureau du Commissaire des tribunaux de revision
PO Box 8250 T
Ottawa, ON K1G 5S5
Tel: 613-954-1313
Fax: 613-946-1588
Toll-free: 800-363-0076
info@ocrt-bctr.gc.ca
www.ocrt-bctr.gc.ca
Review Tribunals were created to provide a body independent from government to make determinations about eligibility for persons claiming CPP & OAS benefits that had previously been denied.

• Pension Appeals Board / Commission d'appel des pensions
PO Box 8567 T
Ottawa, ON K1G 3H9
Tel: 613-995-0612
Fax: 613-995-6834
Toll-free: 888-640-8001
info@pab-cap.gc.ca
www.pab-cap.gc.ca
The Pension Appeals Board is the final opportunity for appeal under the Canada Pension Plan. Responsible for the hearing of appeals which arise from the decisions of the Review Tribunals of the Office of the Commissioner.

Chief Financial Officer's Office / Bureau de l'agent principal des finances
Chief Financial Officer, Alfred Tsang
Tel: 819-994-5898
Fax: 613-997-0699
alfred.tsang@hrsdc-rhdcc.gc.ca
Senior Director General, Investment, Asset & Procurement, Jane Cochran
Tel: 819-934-1749
Fax: 819-994-1114
jane.cochran@hrsdc-rhdcc.gc.ca
Senior Director General, Financial Management Advisory Services, Alain R. Gélinas
Tel: 819-953-8266
Fax: 819-953-0177
alain.r.gelinas@hrsdc-rhdcc.gc.ca
Director General, Corporate Accounting & Reporting, Patrick Amyot
Tel: 819-953-0033
Fax: 819-997-6149
patrick.amyot@hrsdc-rhdcc.gc.ca
Director General, Financial Policy, Internal Control & Business Services, Eddy G. Reitberger
Tel: 819-934-8434
Fax: 819-953-0177
eddy.reitberger@hrsdc-rhdcc.gc.ca
Acting Director General, Contracting & Procurement, Lisa Reynolds
Tel: 819-934-1749
Fax: 819-994-4463
lisa.reynolds@hrsdc-rhdcc.gc.ca
Director General, Quebec Finance & Administration Services Director, Marie E. Steward
Tel: 514-982-2384 ext: 200
Fax: 514-283-2882
marie.steward@hrsdc-rhdcc.gc.ca
Director General, Corporate Resource Management, Claude P. Tremblay
Tel: 819-997-6510
Fax: 819-956-9730
claude.tremblay@hrsdc-rhdcc.gc.ca
Senior Director, Enabling Services, Sara Lantz
Tel: 819-953-2241
sara.lantz@hrsdc-rhdcc.gc.ca

Human Resources Services Branch / Direction générale des services des ressources humaines
Human Resources Services provides human resource services & technical expertise to HRSDC including succession planning, career development, orientation & training; compensation & benefits; classification & staffing; organizational renewal design & development; labour relations; occupational health & safety; & employment equity & official languages.
Assistant Deputy Minister, Gina Rallis
Tel: 819-997-5564
Fax: 819-934-6620
gina.rallis@hrsdc-rhdcc.gc.ca
Director General, Operations Service Centre, Marilyn Dingwall
Tel: 819-994-4015
Fax: 819-953-1271
marilyn.dingwall@hrsdc-rhdcc.gc.ca
Director General, Transformation & Change Leadership Office, Anne Duguay
Tel: 819-953-1273
Fax: 819-994-7930
anne.duguay@hrsdc-rhdcc.gc.ca
Acting Director General, Executive Services, Linda Fréchette
Tel: 819-953-1265
Fax: 819-953-1271
linda.frechette@hrsdc-rhdcc.gc.ca
Director General, Transformation & Change Leadership Office, Jacqueline Hilton
Tel: 613-990-4661
jacqueline.hilton@hrsdc-rhdcc.gc.ca
Director General, Management Services Branch, Sylvian Patenaude
Tel: 819-956-7189
Fax: 819-954-6097
sylvain.patenaude@hrsdc-rhdcc.gc.ca

Innovation, Information & Technology Branch / Direction générale d'innovation, information et technologie
Innovation, Information & Technology provides information & technology services to HRSDC including business applications that support & streamline work processes, access data, & process millions of benefit-related transactions to address Canadians' needs. It is also responsible for the provision & management of telephony & data networks, applications & data stores, & new processes & technologies.
Chief Information Officer, Charles Nixon
Tel: 819-997-1620
Fax: 819-953-2407
charles.nixon@hrsdc-rhdcc.gc.ca
Chief Technology Officer, Senior Director General, Patrice Rondeau
Tel: 819-934-3289
Fax: 819-956-2010
patrice.rondeau@hrsdc-rhdcc.gc.ca
Chief Solutions Officer, Guylaine Montplaisir
Tel: 819-997-5413
Fax: 819-997-8880
guylaine.montplaisir@hrsdc-rhdcc.gc.ca
Director General, Chief, Strategy Architecture, Lorne Sundby
Tel: 780-495-2358
Fax: 780-495-4250
lorne.sundby@hrsdc-rhdcc.gc.ca
Director, Business Management Services, Gaétan Ouellette
Tel: 819-994-7850
Fax: 819-994-9706
gaetan.ouellette@hrsdc-rhdcc.gc.ca
Acting Director, Chief Solutions Office, Kathleen Webster
Tel: 819-953-0254
Fax: 819-997-8888
kathleen.c.webster@hrsdc-rhdcc.gc.ca

Income Security & Social Development Branch / Direction générale de la sécurité du revenu et du développement social
Income Security & Social Development is the focal point for social policy & programs designed to ensure that children, families, seniors, people with disabilities, the homeless & those at risk of homelessness, communities & others who are facing social challenges have the support, knowledge, & information they need to maintain their well-being & facilitate their participation in society.
Senior Assistant Deputy Minister, Income Security & Social Development Branch, Jacques Paquette
Tel: 613-957-3111
Fax: 613-957-1185
jacques.paquette@hrsdc-rhdcc.gc.ca
Director General, Seniors & Pensions Policy Secretariat, Dominique La Salle
Tel: 613-957-1626
Fax: 613-946-8871
dominique.lasalle@hrsdc-rhdcc.gc.ca
Director General, Homelessness Partnering Secretariat, Barbara Lawless
Tel: 819-997-5464
Fax: 819-994-4211
barbara.lawless@hrsdc-rhdcc.gc.ca
Director General, Strategic Integration, Planning & Accountability, Ouassim Meguellati
Tel: 613-954-0885
Fax: 613-952-4655
ouassim.meguellati@hrsdc-rhdcc.gc.ca
Director General, Office for Disability Issues, Nancy Milroy-Swainson
Tel: 819-994-1941
Fax: 819-994-8634
nancy.milroyswainson@hrsdc-rhdcc.gc.ca
Director General, Canada Pension Plan Directorate, Mary Pichette
Tel: 613-946-3005
Fax: 613-954-2578
mary.pichette@hrsdc-rhdcc.gc.ca
Director General, Community Development & Partnerships Directorate, John Walker
Tel: 613-941-1180
Fax: 613-946-3024
john.walker@hrsdc-rhdcc.gc.ca

Labour Program / Programme du travail
The Labour Program promotes safe, healthy, cooperative & productive workplaces. They develop, administer & enforce workplace legislation & regulations, such as the Canada Labour Code, which covers industrial relations, health & safety & employment standards, & the Employment Equity Act, which promotes workplace equality by removing the barriers faced by women, Aboriginal peoples, persons with disabilities & visible minorities while on the job. These laws cover federally regulated workers & employers.
Deputy Minister, Hélène Gosselin
Tel: 819-934-3320
Fax: 819-934-7066
helene.gosselin@labour-travail.gc.ca
Assistant Deputy Minister, Compliance, Operations & Program Development, Bayla Kolk
Tel: 819-956-9646
Fax: 819-997-9957
bayla.kolk@labour-travail.gc.ca
Assistant Deputy Minister, Policy, Dispute Resolution & International Affairs, Marie-Geneviève Mounier
Tel: 819-997-1493
Fax: 819-953-5685
mg.mounier@labour-travail.gc.ca
Director General, Federal Mediation & Conciliation Service, Guy Baron
Tel: 819-994-1118
Fax: 819-997-1693
guy.baron@labour-travail.gc.ca
Director General, Program Development & Guidance Directorate, Caroline Cyr
Tel: 819-934-3331
Fax: 819-953-8883
caroline.cyr@labour-travail.gc.ca
Director General, Strategic Policy, Analysis & Workplace, Anthony J. Giles
Tel: 819-997-4621
Fax: 819-994-0165
anthony.giles@labour-travail.gc.ca
Director General, Regional Operations & Compliance Directorate, Danica Shimbashi
Tel: 819-997-0252
Fax: 613-956-7521
danica.shimbashi@labour-travail.gc.ca
Director General, International & Intergovernmental Labour Affairs, Debra Young
Tel: 819-953-7405
Fax: 819-953-0227
debra.young@labour-travail.gc.ca
Senior Director, Occupational Health & Safety & Fire Protection Services, Louis-Philippe Delage
Tel: 819-953-7768
Fax: 819-953-4830
louisphilippe.delage@hrsdc-rhdcc.gc.ca
Senior Director, Strategic Policy & Legislative Reform, Lenore Duff
Tel: 819-953-0241
Fax: 819-997-3667
lenore.duff@labour-travail.gc.ca
Senior Director, Labour Standards & Workplace Equity, Jan Michaels
Tel: 819-934-5745

Fax: 819-997-3701
jan.michaels@labour-travail.gc.ca
Executive Director & Senior Counsel, Occupational Health & Safety Tribunal Canada, Marie-Claude Turgeon
Tel: 613-957-4105
Fax: 613-954-6404
marieclaude.turgeon@ohstc-tsstc.gc.ca

Learning Branch / Apprentissage
The Learning branch helps Canadians attend college, university & trade schools by providing advice, loans, assistance, grants to students, by encouraging individuals & organizations to save for a child's post-secondary education, & by assisting children from low-income families through grants. It is responsible for programs & services related to learning, including student financial assistance, savings incentives for post-secondary education, & literacy.
Assistant Deputy Minister, Kathryn McDade
Tel: 819-953-3712
Fax: 819-953-7427
kathryn.mcdade@hrsdc-rhdcc.gc.ca
Director General, Canada Education Savings Program, David Swol
Tel: 819-953-1530
Fax: 819-953-6500
david.swol@hrsdc-rhdcc.gc.ca
Director General, Program Policy Planning, Danièle Besner
Tel: 819-953-1966
Fax: 819-994-1868
daniele.besner@hrsdc-rhdcc.gc.ca
Director, Canada Student Loans Directorate, Del Carrothers
Tel: 819-997-3333
Fax: 819-997-4660
del.carrothers@hrsdc-rhdcc.gc.ca

Legal Services / Services juridiques
Legal Services provides legal services to support the core operations & key initiatives of HRSDC. The services provided include: legal advice on program statutes & policies administered by the Department, policy advice for developing policy & legislative or regulatory proposals, & representing the Department before boards, tribunals & courts.
Senior Counsel & Group Head, Carol MacLean
Tel: 819-997-2440
Fax: 819-997-7547
carol.mclean@hrsdc-rhdcc.gc.ca
Deputy Head & General Counsel, Stephen Sharzer
Tel: 819-953-8302
Fax: 819-953-7317
stephen.sharzer@hrsdc-rhdcc.gc.ca
Director, Anne Mongeon
Tel: 819-997-7383
Fax: 819-997-7547
anne.mongeon@hrsdc-rhdcc.gc.ca

Program Operations / Opérations des programmes
Program Operations handles the operation & coordination of the Grant & Contributions programs across the Department.
Assistant Deputy Minister, Program Operations Branch, Joanne Lamothe
Tel: 819-934-7067
Fax: 819-934-7614
joanne.lamothe@hrsdc-rhdcc.gc.ca
Director General, Labour Market & Social Development Program Operations, Nancy Gardiner
Tel: 819-953-4662
Fax: 819-953-9354
nancy.gardiner@hrsdc-rhdcc.gc.ca
Director General, Program Operations Management & Accountability, Kenneth Kerr
Tel: 819-997-1551
Fax: 819-994-7580
kenneth.kerr@hrsdc-rhdcc.gc.ca
Director General, Aboriginal Program Operations, Marie-France Lamarche
Tel: 819-997-7583
Fax: 819-934-6339
mariefrance.lamarche@hrsdc-rhdcc.gc.ca

Public Affairs & Stakeholder Relations / Affaires publiques et Relations avec les intervenants
Public Affairs & Stakeholder Relations informs Canadians about HRSDC's mandate, policies & programs. It also supports departmental activities in engaging & communicating with stakeholders & citizens.
Assistant Deputy Minister, Peter Larose
Tel: 819-934-5760
Fax: 819-934-5751
peter.larose@hrsdc-rhdcc.gc.ca
Director General, Program Communications, Public Affairs & Stakeholder Relations, Barry Frewer
Tel: 819-994-1361
Fax: 819-934-5751
barry.frewer@hrsdc-rhdcc.gc.ca
Director General, Strategic Communications & Stakeholders Relations, Benoit Trottier
Tel: 819-953-1308
Fax: 819-953-3981
benoit.trottier@hrsdc-rhdcc.gc.ca
Senior Director, Strategic Planning & Management Services, Anne Schroder
Tel: 819-997-2192
Fax: 819-934-5751
anne.schroder@hrsdc-rhdcc.gc.ca
Director, Ministerial Communications Services, Brian Laghi
Tel: 819-934-5582
Fax: 819-994-6609
brian.laghi@hrsdc-rhdcc.gc.ca

Service Canada
140, Promenade du Portage, Gatineau, QC K1A 0J9
Toll-Free: 800-622-6232
www.servicecanada.gc.ca
TTY: 800-926-9105
Service Canada was created in 2005 to improve the delivery of government programs & services to Canadians, by making access to them faster, easier, & more convenient. Service Canada offers single-window access to a wide range of Government of Canada programs & services for citizens through more than 600 points of service located across the country, call centres, & the Internet.
Senior Assistant Deputy Minister, Carolina Giliberti
Tel: 819-934-1504
Fax: 819-934-1505
carolina.giliberti@servicecanada.gc.ca
Head, Service Delivery, Robin Flaherty
Tel: 613-990-9105
Fax: 613-941-1827
robin.flaherty@servicecanada.gc.ca
Director General, Citizen Service Strategy, Zahra Pourjafar-Ziaei
Tel: 613-957-6727
Fax: 613-957-4400
zahra.pourjafarziaei@servicecanada.gc.ca
Director General, Business Transformation, Mary O'Neill
Tel: 819-956-7659
Fax: 819-997-9194
mary.oneill@servicecanada.gc.ca
Director, Web Strategies & Product Management, Minh Doan
Tel: 613-957-6220
Fax: 613-957-6767
minh.doan@servicecanada.gc.ca

Service Canada Centres
Toll-Free: 800-622-6232
Other Communication: CPP/OAS: 800-277-9914; Record of Employment: 800-367-5693; Telephone Info Service: 800-206-7218; Telephone Reporting Service: 800-531-7555
Brooks
Cassils Plaza, 608 - 2 St. West, Brooks, AB T1R 1A8
Calgary Centre
#270, 220 - 4 Ave. SE, Calgary, AB T2G 4X3
Calgary East
#1502, 515 Marlborough Way NE, Calgary, AB T2A 7E7
Calgary North
One Executive Place, 1816 Crowchild Trail NW, PO Box 65037 North Hill, Calgary, AB T2N 4T6
Calgary South
Fisher Park Place II, #100, 6712 Fisher St. SE, Calgary, AB T2H 1X3
Camrose
Federal Bldg., 4901 - 50 Ave., Camrose, AB T4V 0S2
Canmore
Bldg. C, #113, 802 Bow Valley Trail, Canmore, AB T1W 1N6
Edmonton Canada Place
Canada Place, 9700 Jasper Ave., Main Fl., Edmonton, AB T5J 4C1
Edmonton Meadowlark
#120, 15710 - 87 Ave. NW, Edmonton, AB T5R 5W9
Edmonton Millbourne
148 Millbourne Market Mall, 38 Ave. & Millwoods Rd., Edmonton, AB T6K 3L6
Edmonton North
#2000, 9499 - 137 Ave. NW, Edmonton, AB T5E 5R8
Tel: 780-495-3904
Toll-Free: 800-622-6232
Edson
4905 - 4 Ave., Edson, AB T7E
Fort McMurray
Provincial Bldg., 9915 Franklin Ave., Main Fl., Fort McMurray, AB T9H 2K4
Grande Prairie
Towne Centre Mall, #100, 9845 - 99 Ave., Grande Prairie, AB T8V 0R3
Lethbridge
Crowsnest Trail Plaza, 101, 920 - 2A Ave. North, Lethbridge, AB T1H 0E3
Lloydminster
5016 - 48 St., Lloydminster, AB T9V 0H8
Medicine Hat
Northside Centre, 78 - 8 St. NW, Medicine Hat, AB T1A 6P1
Red Deer
First Red Deer Place, 4911 - 51 St., 2nd Fl., Lethbridge, AB T4N 6A4
Slave Lake
Sawridge Plaza, 100 Main St. South, Slave Lake, AB T0G 2A3
St Paul
5126 - 50 Ave., St Paul, AB T0A 3A0
Abbotsford
100, 32525 Simon Ave., Abbotsford, BC V2T 6T6
Burnaby
#100, 3480 Gilmore Way, Burnaby, BC V5G 4Y1
Campbell River
#101, 950 Alder St., Campbell River, BC V9W 2P8
Chilliwack
9345 Main St., Chilliwack, BC V2P 4M3
Comox Valley
130 - 19 St., Courtenay, BC V9N 8S1
Coquitlam
#100, 2963 Glen Dr., Coquitlam, BC V3B 2P7
Cowichan
211 Jubilee St., Duncan, BC V9L 1W8
Cranbrook
1113 Baker St., Cranbrook, BC V1C 1A7
Dawson Creek
#103, 1508 - 102 Ave., Dawson Creek, BC V1G 2E2
Kamloops
317 Seymour St., 1st Fl., Kamloops, BC V2C 2E8
Kelowna
#106, 471 Queensway Ave., Kelowna, BC V1Y 6S5
Langley
#102, 8747 - 204 St., Langley, BC V1M 2Y5
Nanaimo
#201, 60 Front St., Nanaimo, BC V9R 5H7
Nelson
Kutenai Bldg., 333 Victoria St., Main Fl., Nelson, BC V1L 4K3
New Westminster
#201, 620 Royal Ave., New Westminster, BC V3M 1J2
North Shore
#100, 221 West Esplanade, North Vancouver, BC V7M 3N7
Penticton
#100, 386 Ellis St., Penticton, BC V2A 8C9
Port Alberni
4805 Mar St., #A, Port Alberni, BC V9Y 8J5
Powell River
7061 Duncan St., #A, Powell River, BC V8A 1W1
Prince George
1363 - 4 Ave., Prince George, BC V2L 3J6
Prince Rupert
#100, 215 - 3 St., Prince Rupert, BC V8J 3J9
Quesnel
283 Reid St. East, Quesnel, BC V2J 2A8
Richmond
#350, 5611 Cooney Rd., Richmond, BC V6X 3K5
Ridge Meadows
22325 Lougheed Hwy., Maple Ridge, BC V2X 8T1
Salmon Arm
191 Shuswap St. NW, 1st Fl., Salmon Arm, BC
Sinclair Centre
#415, 757 Hastings St. West, Vancouver, BC V6B 1N9
Smithers
1020 Murray St., Smithers, BC V0J 2N3
Squamish
1440 Winnipeg St., Squamish, BC V8B 0J2
Surrey North
13889 - 104 Ave., Surrey, BC V3T 1W7
Surrey
7404 King George Hwy., Surrey, BC V3W 0L4
Terrace
4630 Lazelle Ave., Terrace, BC V8G 1S6
Trail
#101, 1101 Dewdney Ave., Trail, BC V1R 4A5
Vancouver East
1420 Kingsway, Vancouver, BC V5N 2R5
Vancouver
125 - 10 Ave. East, Vancouver, BC V5T 1Z3
Vanderhoof
189 Stewart St. East, Vanderhoof, BC
Vernon
3202 - 31 St., Vernon, BC V1T 5J1
Victoria
595 Pandora Ave., Victoria, BC V8W 1N6
Williams Lake
79 - 4 Ave. South, Williams Lake, BC V2G 1H2
Aboriginal Single Window
Aboriginal Centre, #100, 181 Higgins Ave., Winnipeg, MB R3B 3G1
Brandon
Government of Canada Building, 1039 Princess Ave., Brandon, MB R7A 6E2
Churchill
1 Mantayo Seepee Meskanow, Churchill, MB

Dauphin
135 - 2 Ave. NE, Dauphin, MB R7N 0Z6
Flin Flon
Government of Canada Bldg., 111 Main St., Flin Flon, MB R8A 1J9
Morden
Government of Canada Bldg., 158 Stephen St., Morden, MB R6M 1T3
Notre-Dame-des-Lourdes
51 Rodgers St., Notre Dame de Lourdes, QC R0G 1M0
Portage la Prairie
Government of Canada Bldg., 1016 Saskatchewan Ave. East, Portage la Prairie, MB R1N 3V2
Saint-Pierre-Jolys
427 Sabourin St., Saint-Pierre-Jolys, MB R0A 1V0
Selkirk
Government of Canada Bldg., 237 Manitoba Ave., Main Fl., Selkirk, MB R1A 2M8
Steinbach
Steinbach, 321 Main St., Main Fl., Steinbach, MB R5G 1Z2
Swan River
#1, 355 Kelsey Trail, Swan River, MB R0L 1Z0
The Pas
Government of Canada Bldg., 305 - 4 St. West, The Pas, MB
Thompson
North Centre Mall, #118, 3 Station Rd., Thompson, MB R8N 0N3
Winnipeg Centre
Stanley Knowles Bldg., 391 York Ave., Winnipeg, MB R3C 1T9
Winnipeg La Verendrye
#100, 614 des Meurons St., Winnipeg, MB R2H 2R1
Winnipeg North-East
Kildonan Village Mall, 1122 Henderson Hwy., Winnipeg, MB R2G 1L1
Winnipeg South-West
Westwood Centre, 3338 Portage Ave., Winnipeg, MB R3K 0Z1
Winnipeg St. Vital
1001 St. Mary's Rd., Winnipeg, MB R2M 3S4
Bathurst
Nicolas Denys Bldg., 120 Harbourview Blvd., 1st Fl., Bathurst, NB E2A 1R6
Campbellton
Campbellton City Center Mall, #111, 157 Water St., Campbellton, NB E3N 3L3
Caraquet
Bellevue Place, 20E St. Pierre Blvd. West, Caraquet, NB E1W 1B6
Dalhousie
Darlington Mall, 110 Plaza Blvd., Dalhousie, NB E8C 2A3
Edmundston
Federal Bldg., 22 Emmerson St., Edmundston, NB E3V 1R7
Fredericton
Federal Bldg., 633 Queen St., Fredericton, NB E3B 5G4
Grande Falls
#100, 441 Madawaska Rd., Grand Falls, NB E3Y 1A3
Miramichi
Roach Bldg., 150 Pleasant St., Miramichi, NB E1V 1Y1
Moncton
Heritage Court, #310, 95 Foundry St., Moncton, NB E1C 8R5
Richibucto
Cartier Place, 25 Cartier Blvd., Richibucto, NB E4W 3W7
Sackville
East Main Plaza, 170 Main St., Sackville, NB E4L 4S2
Saint John
1 Agar Place, 1st Fl., Saint John, NB E2L 5G4
Saint Quentin
193 Canada St., Saint-Quentin, NB E8A 1G9
Shediac
Centre-Ville Mall, 342 Main St., Shediac, NB E4P 2E7
Shippagan
196A J.D. Gauthier Blvd., 1st Fl., Shippagan, NB E8S 1P3
Shippagan
Post Office Bldg., 93 Milltown Blvd., St. Stephen, NB E3L 3E2
Sussex
Mapleton Place, 10 Gateway St., Sussex, NB E4E 3E5
Tracadie-Sheila
Le Rond Point Shopping Center, #17, 3409 Principale St., Tracadie-Sheila, NB E1X 1A4
Woodstock
Post Office Bldg., 680 Main St., Woodstock, NB E7M 5Z7
Clarenville
Park Place, 50 Manitoba Dr., Clarenville, NL A5A 1K5
Corner Brook
Joseph R. Smallwood Bldg., 1 Regent Sq., Corner Brook, NL A2H 491
Gander
McCurdy Complex, 1 Markham Place, 3rd Fl., Gander, NL A1V 1W7
Grand Falls-Windsor
Bailey Bldg., #100, 4A Bayley St., Grand Falls, NL A2A 2Y3

Happy Valley
23 Broomfield St., Happy Valley-Goose Bay, NL A0P 1E0
Harbour Grace
Babb Bldg., 33-35 Harvey St., Harbour Grace, NL A0A 2M0
Labrador City
Labrador Mall, 500 Vanier Ave., Labrador City, NL A2V 2W7
Marystown
Jerrett Bldg., #130, 140 Ville Marie Dr., Marystown, NL A0E 1L0
Placentia
Dalfens Mall, 61 Blockhouse Rd., Placentia, NL A0B 2Y0
Port Aux Basques
#4, 10 High St., Channel-Port aux Basques, NL A0M 1C0
Rocky Harbour
Budgeon Bldg., 118 Pond Rd., Rocky Harbour, NL A0K 4N0
Springdale
Wells Bldg., 130 Main St., Springdale, NL A0J 1T0
St. Anthony
Viking Mall, 1 Goose Cove Rd., St. Anthony, NL A0K 4S0
St. John's
Bldg. 223, Pleasantville, 223 Churchill Ave., St. John's, NL A1B 3P3
Stephenville
133 Carolina Ave., Stephenville, NL A2N 2S5
Fort Simpson
Federal Bldg., 9606 - 100 St., Fort Simpson, NT X0E 0N0
Tel: 867-695-2238
Fax: 867-695-2229

Fort Smith
Federal Bldg., 149 McDougal Rd., Fort Smith, NT X0E 0P0
Tel: 867-872-2747

Hay River
#204, 41 Capital Dr., Hay River, NT X0E 1G2
Tel: 867-874-6739
Fax: 867-874-6100

Inuvik
85 Kingmingya Rd., Inuvik, NT X0E 0T0
Tel: 867-777-2122
Fax: 867-777-4369

Yellowknife
Greenstone Bldg., 5101 - 50 Ave., Main Fl., Yellowknife, NT X1A 3Z4
Tel: 867-766-8300
Fax: 867-873-3621

Amherst
#202, 26-28 Prince Arthur St., Amherst, NS B4H 1V6
Fax: 902-661-6637

Antigonish
Federal Bldg., 325 Main St., 2nd Fl., Antigonish, NS B2G 2C3
Fax: 902-863-7053

Bedford
Royal Bank Bldg., 1597 Bedford Hwy., 2nd Fl., Bedford, NS B4A 1E8
Fax: 902-426-5552

Bridgewater
Dawson B. Dauphinee Bldg., 77 Dufferin St., Bridgewater, NS B4V 2G1
Fax: 902-527-5624

Dartmouth
Royal Bank Bldg., 46 Portland St., 5th Fl., Dartmouth, NS B2Y 1H2
Fax: 902-426-7301

Digby
Maud Lewis Provincial Bldg., 84 Warwick St., Digby, NS B0V 1A0
Fax: 902-245-6226

Glace Bay
Senator's Place, #201, 633 Main St., Glace Bay, NS B1A 6J3
Fax: 902-842-2655

Guysborough
Chedabucto Centre, 9996 Hwy. 16, Guysborough, NS B0H 1N0
Fax: 902-533-2891

Halifax
Mumford Towers, Tower II, 7001 Mumford Rd., Halifax, NS B3L 4T8
Fax: 902-426-7690

Inverness
15926 Central Ave., Inverness, NS B0E 1X0
Fax: 902-258-3036

Kentville
Federal Bldg., 495 Main St., 2nd Fl., Kentville, NS B4N 3W5
Fax: 902-679-5786

New Glasgow
340 East River Rd., New Glasgow, NS B2H 3P7
Fax: 902-755-7869

North Sydney
105 King St., Main Fl., North Sydney, NS B2A 3S1
Fax: 902-794-5724

Port Hawkesbury
Shediac Shopping Centre, #8, 811 Reeves St., Port Hawkesbury, NS B9A 2S4
Fax: 902-625-4137

Shelburne
Loyalist Plaza, 218 Water St., Shelburne, NS B0T 1W0
Fax: 902-875-3505

Sydney
Commerce Tower, 15 Dorchester St., 1st Fl., Sydney, NS B1P 5Y9
Fax: 902-564-7104

Truro
#8, 60 Lorne St., Truro, NS B2N 3K3
Fax: 902-893-0075

Windsor
80 Water St., Windsor, NS B0P 1L0
Fax: 902-798-5816

Yarmouth
Canada Post Office Bldg., 13 Willow St., 2nd Fl., Yarmouth, NS B5A 1T8
Fax: 902-742-0815

Ajax
#200, 274 Mackenzie Ave., Ajax, ON L1S 1P7
Arnprior
Heritage Square, #1 & 2, 75 Elgin St. West, Arnprior, ON K7S 3T9
Bancroft
Fairway Plaza, 5 Fairway Blvd., Bancroft, ON K0L 1C0
Barrie
48 Owen St., 1st Fl., Barrie, ON L4M 1G6
Belleville
Business Bldg., 1 North Front St., 2nd Fl., Belleville, ON K8P 3A7
Bracebridge
Federal Bldg., 98 Manitoba St., 2nd Fl., Bracebridge, ON P1L 1S1
Brampton
18 Corporation Dr., Brampton, ON L6S 6B2
Brantford
58 Dalhousie St., 2nd Fl., Brantford, ON N3T 2J2
Brockville
Thomas Fuller Bldg., 14 Court House Ave., 1st Fl., Brockville, ON K6V 3X3
Burlington
Burlington Resource Centre, 440 Elizaebth St., Burlington, ON L7R 2M1
Cambridge
350 Conestoga Blvd., #C2, Cambridge, ON N1R 7L7
Carleton Place
46 Lansdowne Ave., Carleton Place, ON K7C 3S9
Chatham-Kent
Federal Bldg., 120 Wellington St. West, Chatham, ON N7M 4V9
Cobourg
Fleming Bldg., #103, 1005 Elgin St. West, Cobourg, ON K9A 5J4
Collingwood
44 Huronontario St., Collingwood, ON L9Y 2L6
Cornwall
#100, 111 Water St. East, Cornwall, ON K6H 6S2
Dryden
41C Duke St., Dryden, ON P8N 1E6
Elliot Lake
Algo Centre, Upper Mall, 151 Ontario Ave., Elliot Lake, ON P5A 2T2
Espanola
#2, 721 Centre St., Espanola, ON P5E 1H7
Fort Frances
301 Scott St., Fort Frances, ON P9A 1H1
Gananoque
5 Charles St. South, Gananoque, ON K7G 1V9
Georgetown
232 Guelph St., 1st Fl., Georgetown, ON L7G 4B1
Geraldton
208 Beamish Ave. West, Geraldton, ON P0T 1M0
Goderich
52 East St., Goderich, ON N7A 1N3
Guelph
259 Woodlawn Rd. West, Suite C, Guelph, ON N1H 8J1
Hamilton - East
2255 Barton St. East, Hamilton, ON L8H 7T4
Hamilton - Main
1550 Upper James St., 1st Fl., Hamilton, ON L9B 1K3
Hawkesbury
134 Main St. East, Hawkesbury, ON K6A 1A3
Kapuskasing
8 Queen St., Kapuskasing, ON P5N 1G7
Kenora
Kenora Market Square, #201, 308 2 St. South, Kenora, ON P9N 1G3
Kingston
299 Concession St., Kingston, ON K7L 5H5
Kirkland Lake
10 Government Rd. East, Kirkland Lake, ON P2N 1A2
Kitchener
409 Weber St. West, Kitchener, ON N2H 4B1

Leamington
Leamington Mall, 215 Talbot St. East, Leamington, ON N8H 3X5
Lindsay
65 Kent St. West, Lindsay, ON K9V 2Y3
Listowel
210 Main St. East, Listowel, ON N4W 2B7
London
Dominion Public Bldg., 457 Richmond St., London, ON N6A 3E3
Malton
#5, 6877 Goreway Dr., Malton, ON L4V 1L9
Marathon
#105, 52 Peninsula Rd., Marathon, ON P0T 2E0
Markham
#14, 5051 Hwy. 7 East, Markham, ON L3T 7T1
Midland
Huronia Mall, 9225 Hwy. 93, Midland, ON L4R 4K4
Milton
Trafalgar Square, 310 Main St. East, Milton, ON L9T 1P4
Mississauga - East
2525 Dixie Rd., Mississauga, ON L4Y 2A1
Mississauga - West
3085A Glen Erin Dr., Mississauga, ON L5L 1J3
Napanee
Murphy's Plaza, 2 Dairy Ave., Napanee, ON K7R 3T1
New Liskeard
280 Armstrong St. North, New Liskeard, ON P0J 1P0
Newmarket
#1, 18183 Yonge St. East, East Gwillimbury, ON L3Y 4V8
Niagara Falls
Customs Bldg., 5853 Peer St., Niagara Falls, ON L2G 1X4
North Bay
Canada Place, #102, 107 Shirreff Ave., North Bay, ON P1B 7K8
Oakville
117 Cross Ave., #5B, Oakville, ON L6J 2W7
Orangeville
#102, 210 Broadway, Orangeville, ON L9W 5G4
Orillia
#101, 50 Andrew St. South, Orillia, ON L3V 7T5
Oshawa
Midtown Mall, 200 John St. West, Unit C6, Oshawa, ON L1J 2B4
Ottawa - Centre
L'Esplanade Laurier, 300 Laurier Ave. West, 2nd Fl., Ottawa, ON K2P 1W5
Ottawa - East
Beacon Hill Shopping Centre, 2339 Ogilvie Rd., Ottawa, ON K1A 0J6
Ottawa Government
110 Laurier Ave. West, Ottawa, ON K1P 1J1
Ottawa - West
Lincoln Fields Galleria, 2525 Carling Ave., 1st Fl., Ottawa, ON K2B 7Z2
Owen Sound
Heritage Place Shopping Centre, 1350 - 16 St. East, Owen Sound, ON N4K 6N7
Parry Sound
74 James St., 2nd Fl., Parry Sound, ON P2A 1T8
Pembroke
141 Lake St., Pembroke, ON K8A 5L8
Perth
The Factory, 40 Sunset Blvd., Perth, ON K7H 2Y4
Peterborough
Jackson Square, #101, 185 King St., Peterborough, ON K9J 2R8
Picton
229 Main St., Picton, ON K0K 2T0
Prescott
292 Centre St., Prescott, ON K0E 1T0
Tel: 613-925-2808
Fax: 613-925-3846
ontario.inquiry@hrsdc-rhdcc.gc.ca
Renfrew
350 Raglan St. South, Renfrew, ON K7V 1R6
Richmond Hill
35 Beresford Dr., Richmond Hill, ON L4B 4M3
Sarnia
529 Exmouth St., Sarnia, ON N7T 7S5
Sault Ste Marie
22 Bay St., 1st Fl., Sault Ste Marie, ON P6A 5S2
Simcoe
5 Queensway East, Simcoe, ON N3Y 5K2
Smiths Falls
#115, 91 Cornelia St. West, Smiths Falls, ON K7A 5L3
St Catherines
Henley Square Plaza, 395 Ontario St., Unit E & F, St Catharines, ON L2N 7N6
St Thomas
#34, 1010 Talbot St., St Thomas, ON N5P 4N2
Stratford
#2, 61 Lorne Ave., Ground Fl., Stratford, ON N5A 6S4

Sturgeon Falls
#2, 186 Main St., Sturgeon Falls, ON P2B 1N9
Sudbury
Federal Bldg., 19 Lisgar St., Main Fl., Sudbury, ON P3E 6L1
Thunder Bay
975 Alloy Dr., Thunder Bay, ON P7B 6N5
Tillsonburg
96 Tillson Ave., Tillsonburg, ON N4G 3A1
Timmins
120 Cedar St. South, 1st Fl., Timmins, ON P4N 1G2
Toronto - Centre
Arthur Meighen Bldg., 25 St. Clair Ave. East, 1st Fl., Toronto, ON M4T 3A4
Toronto - City Hall
City Hall, 100 Queen St. West, 1st Fl., Toronto, ON M5H 2N2
Toronto - Dufferin Mall
Dufferin Mall, #0001, 900 Dufferin St., Toronto, ON M6H 4B1
Toronto - Etobicoke
5343 Dundas St. West, Toronto, ON M9B 6K6
Toronto - Gerrard Square
Gerrard Square Mall, 1000 Gerrard St. East, #DD10/11, 2nd Fl., Toronto, ON M4M 1Z3
Toronto - Lawrence Square
Lawrence Square Mall, #103-105, 700 Lawrence Ave. West, Toronto, ON M6B 4L4
Toronto - Malvern
Malvern Town Centre Mall, 31 Tapscott Rd., Toronto, ON M1B 3G7
Toronto - North
3737 Chesswood Dr., Toronto, ON M3J 2P6
Toronto - Scarborough
Canada Centre, 200 Town Centre Ct., 1st Fl., Toronto, ON M1P 4X9
Toronto - Willowdale
Joseph Shepard Bldg., 4900 Yonge St., 1st Fl., Toronto, ON M2N 6B1
Trenton
50 Dundas St. West, Trenton, ON K8V 6R5
Walkerton
200 McNab St., Walkerton, ON N0G 2V0
Wallaceburg
Municipal Service Centre, 786 Dufferin Ave., 2nd Fl., Wallaceburg, ON N8A 2V3
Welland
250 Thorold Rd. West, Welland, ON L3C 3W3
Tel: 905-988-2700
Fax: 905-735-7036
Windsor
#103, 400 City Hall Sq. East, Windsor, ON N9A 7K6
Woodstock
#101, 959 Dundas St., Woodstock, ON N4S 1H2
Charlottetown
Jean Canfield Goverment of Canada Bldg., 191 University Ave., Charlottetown, PE C1A 2A1
Fax: 902-368-0178
Montague
491 Main St., Montague, PE C0A 1R0
Fax: 902-838-3439
O'Leary
371 Main St., O'Leary, PE C0B 1V0
Fax: 902-859-1286
Souris
Save Easy Mall, 173 Main St., 2nd Fl., Souris, PE C0A 2B0
Fax: 902-687-3722
Summerside
Government of Canada Bldg., 294 Church St., Summerside, PE C1N 3H8
Fax: 902-432-6808
Alma
Jacques-Gagnon Complex, #105, 100, rue St-Joseph sud, Alma, QC G8B 6S9
Amos
101 - 1re av est, Amos, QC J9T 1H4
Fax: 819-732-7997
Asbestos
#204, 309, rue Chassé, Asbestos, QC J1T 2B3
Fax: 819-879-2501
Baie-Comeau
Centre commercial Laflèche, #204, 625, boul Laflèche ouest, Baie-Comeau, QC G5C 1C5
Fax: 418-295-1313
Beauport (Québec)
Centre commercial Les Promenades Beauport, #265, 3333, rue du Carrefour, 2e étage, Québec, QC G1C 7E1
Fax: 418-681-4810
Bécancour
#200, 1580, boul Port-Royal, 1e étage, Bécancour, QC G9H 1X6
Fax: 819-233-4398
Brossard
2501, boul Lapinière, Brossard, QC J4Z 3P1
Fax: 450-445-5760

Buckingham (Gatineau)
101, rue MacLaren est, 2e étage, Gatineau, QC J8L 2X1
Fax: 819-953-0267
Campbell's Bay
2, rue John, Campbell's Bay, QC J0X 1K0
Fax: 819-648-5102
Cap-aux-Meules
#200, 380, chemin Principal, Cap-aux-Meules, QC G4T 1J7
Fax: 418-986-2764
Causapscal
8, rue St-Jacques nord, Causapscal, QC G0J 1J0
Fax: 418-756-6002
Chandler
#201, 75 boul René-Lévesque est, Chandler, QC G0C 1K0
Fax: 418-689-4900
Chibougamau
623 - 3e Rue, Chibougamau, QC G8P 3A2
Fax: 418-748-6730
Chicoutimi
98, rue Racine est, Chicoutimi, QC G7H 1R7
Chisasibi
Complexe administratif, Chisasibi, QC
Tel: 819-855-2675
Fax: 819-855-2109
Châteauguay
#101, 245, boul St-Jean Baptiste, Châteauguay, QC J6K 3C3
Fax: 450-691-4247
Coaticook
#300, 14, rue Adams, Coaticook, QC J1A 2B4
Fax: 819-849-4196
Cowansville
224, rue du Sud, 2e étage, Cowansville, QC J2K 1M7
Fax: 450-263-8838
Côte-des-Neiges (Montréal)
Carré Décarie, #3015, 6900, boul Décarie, 3e étage, Cote-St-Luc, QC H3X 2K5
Fax: 514-496-1335
Dolbeau
1500, rue des Érables, Dolbeau-Mistassini, QC G8L 1C4
Donnacona
#110, 100, rte 138, Donnacona, QC G3M 1C1
Fax: 418-681-4810
Drummondville
Édifice Surprenant, 1525, boul St-Joseph, Drummondville, QC J2C 2E9
Fax: 819-478-8137
Forestville
Centre Forestville, #800, 25, rte 138 est, Forestville, QC G0T 1E0
Fax: 418-587-4956
Gaspé
Édifice Frédérica-Giroux, 98, rue de la Reine, 1e étage, Gaspé, QC G4X 1E5
Fax: 418-368-2785
Gatineau
#150, 85, rue Bellehumeur, Gatineau, QC J8T 8B7
Fax: 819-561-2726
Granby
#201, 35, rue Dufferin, Granby, QC J2G 4W6
Fax: 450-378-5719
Hull-Aylmer (Gatineau)
920, boul St-Joseph, Gatineau, QC J8Z 1S9
Fax: 819-953-0267
Joliette
Comlexe Joliette, #100, 46, rue Gauthier sud, Joliette, QC J6E 4J4
Fax: 450-756-2579
Jonquière
#102, 3750, boul du Royaume, Ville de Saguenay, QC G7X 0A4
La Malbaie
541, rue St-Étienne, La Malbaie, QC G5A 1J3
Fax: 418-681-4810
La Pocatière
Les Cours Painchaud, #103, 708, 4e av, La Pocatière, QC G0R 1Z0
Fax: 418-856-3688
La Sarre
Centre commercial Carrefour La Sarre, #30, 255 - 3e rue est, La Sarre, QC J9Z 3N7
Fax: 819-333-3612
La Tuque
Centre commercial Carrefour La Tuque, 290, rue St-Joseph, La Tuque, QC G9X 1L1
Fax: 819-523-6028
Lac Mégantic
#201, 5200, rue Frontenac, 2e étage, Lac-Mégantic, QC G6B 2E7
Fax: 819-583-0944
Lasalle (Montréal)
7655, boul Newman, Lasalle, QC H8N 1X7
Fax: 514-363-9059

Laval
1041, boul des Laurentides, Laval, QC H7G 2W2
Fax: 450-682-3856
Lévis
Place Lévis, #175, 50 rte du Président-Kennedy, Lévis, QC G6V 6C7
Fax: 418-834-2551
Longueuil
#100, 1195, ch Du Tremblay, Longueuil, QC J4N 1A2
Fax: 450-448-7506
Louisville
507, rue Marcel, Louisville, QC J5V 1T7
Fax: 819-228-3848
Magog
1700, rue Sherbrooke, #100A, Magog, QC J1X 5B6
Fax: 819-843-5427
Maniwaki
Galeries Maniwaki, #220, 100, rue Principale sud, Maniwaki, QC J9E 1Z9
Fax: 819-449-7087
Matane
Les Galeries du Vieux Port, #220, 750, av du Phare ouest, Matane, QC G4W 1V4
Fax: 418-562-9200
Mercier (Montréal)
5455 rue Chauveau, 1e étage, Montréal, QC H1N 1G8
Fax: 514-355-8914
Mont-Laurier
431, rue de la Madone, 1e étage, Mont-Laurier, QC J9L 1S2
Fax: 819-623-7113
Montmagny
37, av Sainte-Brigitte sud, Montmagny, QC G5V 2Y3
Fax: 418-834-2551
Montréal (Centre-ville)
Complexe Guy-Favreau, #034, 200, boul René-Lévesque ouest, Montréal, QC H2Z 1X4
Fax: 514-496-5951
New Richmond
Carrefour Baie-des-Chaleurs, 122, boul Perron ouest, 2e étage, New Richmond, QC G0C 2B0
Fax: 418-392-4346
Nunavik
5207, ch de l'Aéroport, Kuujjuaq, QC J0M 1C0
Tel: 866-351-6278
Fax: 866-534-5860
Pointe-Claire (Montréal)
#100, 181, boul Hymus, Pointe-Claire, QC H9R 1E9
Fax: 514-496-1335
Pointe-aux-Trembles (Montréal)
13313, rue Sherbrooke est, Montréal, QC H1A 1C2
Fax: 514-642-7640
Québec (Centre-ville)
330, rue de la Gare-du-Palais, Québec, QC G1K 7R1
Téléc: 418-681-4810
Repentigny
Place Repentigny, #54, 155, rue Notre-Dame, Repentigny, QC J6A 7G5
Fax: 450-585-2180
Rimouski
Édifice Boisé Langevin, #201, 287, rue Pierre-Saindon, Rimouski, QC G5L 9A7
Fax: 418-722-3369
Rivière-du-Loup
298, boul Armand-Thériault, 2e étage, Rivière-du-Loup, QC G5R 4Y4
Fax: 418-862-1923
Roberval
Plaza Roberval, #202, 755, boul Saint-Joseph, Roberval, QC G8H 2L5
Rouyn-Noranda
Édifice Réal-Caouette, #300, 151, av du Lac, Rouyn-Noranda, QC J9X 6Z4
Fax: 819-762-4605
Saint-Eustache
250, boul Arthur-Sauvé, Saint-Eustache, QC J7R 2H9
Fax: 450-473-9020
Saint-Georges
11400 - 1re av est, 2e étage, Saint-Georges, QC G5Y 6R1
Fax: 418-335-3715
Saint-Hyacinthe
Galeries St-Hyacinthe, #2500, 3225, av Cusson, 2e étage, Saint-Hyacinthe, QC J2S 0H7
Fax: 450-773-8276
Saint-Jean-sur-Richelieu
#106, 320, boul du Séminaire nord, Saint-Jean-sur-Richelieu, QC J3B 5L1
Fax: 450-348-5303
Saint-Jérôme
#100, 339, boul Jean-Paul-Hogue, Saint-Jérôme, QC J7Z 7A5
Fax: 866-613-5613
Saint-Léonard (Montréal)
#500, 6020, rue Jean-Talon est, Saint-Léonard, QC H1S 3B1
Fax: 514-355-8914
Sainte-Agathe-des-Monts
118, rue Principale est, 2e étage, Sainte-Agathe-des-Monts, QC J8C 1L1
Fax: 819-326-6205
Sainte-Anne-des-Monts
230, 1ére av ouest, Sainte-Anne-des-Monts, QC G4V 1E2
Fax: 418-763-7414
Sainte-Foy (Québec)
Édifice Saint-Mathieu, #200, 3175, ch des Quatre-Bourgeois, 2e étage, Québec, QC G1X 2Z7
Fax: 418-681-4810
Sainte-Thérèse
#110, 100, boul Ducharme, Sainte-Thérèse, QC J7E 1X2
Fax: 450-430-5885
Senneterre
761 - 10e av, Senneterre, QC J0Y 2M0
Fax: 819-737-8872
Sept-Îles
701, boul Laure, 3e étage, Sept-Îles, QC G4R 1X8
Fax: 418-962-8301
Shawinigan
444 - 5e rue, Shawinigan, QC G9N 1E6
Fax: 819-536-7063
Sherbrooke
124, rue Wellington nord, Sherbrooke, QC J1H 5X8
Fax: 819-564-5769
Sorel-Tracy
101, rue Augusta, Sorel, QC J3P 1A7
Fax: 450-743-8338
Terrebonne
835, montée Masson, Terrebonne, QC J6W 2P4
Fax: 450-471-2417
Thetford Mines
#500, 350, boul Frontenac ouest, Thetford Mines, QC G6G 6K2
Fax: 418-335-3715
Trois-Rivières
Édifice Bourg du Fleuve, 55, rue des Forges, Trois-Rivières, QC G9A 2G6
Fax: 819-379-3085
Val-d'Or
400, av Centrale, Val-d'Or, QC J9P 1P4
Fax: 819-825-0726
Valleyfield
#100, 73, rue Maden, Salaberry-de-Valleyfield, QC J6S 3V4
Fax: 450-373-2356
Vaudreuil-Dorion
2555, rue Dutrisac, Vaudreuil-Dorion, QC J7V 7E6
Fax: 450-424-0506
Verdun
4110, rue Wellington, 2e étage, Montréal, QC H4G 2P4
Fax: 514-496-6986
Victoriaville
84, boul Labbé sud, Victoriaville, QC G6P 0E4
Fax: 819-758-7809
Ville-Marie
18, rue Notre-Dame-de-Lourdes, Ville-Marie, QC J9V 1X7
Fax: 819-629-3496
Villeray (Montréal)
#300, 1415, rue Jarry est, 3e étage, Montréal, QC H2E 3B4
Tel: 514-723-7273
Fax: 514-723-6249

Estevan
1314 - 3 St., Estevan, SK S4A 1E9
La Ronge
1016 La Ronge Ave., La Ronge, SK S0J 1L0
Melfort
McKendry Plaza, 104 McKendry Ave. West, Melfort, SK S0E 1A0
Moose Jaw
Victoria Place, #501, 111 Fairford St. East, Moose Jaw, SK S6H 0B8
North Battleford
Territorial Place, #15, 9800 Territorial Dr., North Battleford, SK S9A 3N6
Prince Albert
1288 Central Ave., Prince Albert, SK S6V 3B3
Regina
Alvin Hamilton Bldg., 1783 Hamilton St., Regina, SK S4P 4B4
Saskatoon
Federal Bldg., 101 - 22 St. East, Saskatoon, SK S7K 0E1
Swift Current
Chinook Bldg., 250 Central Ave. North, Swift Current, SK S9H 0L2
Weyburn
City Centre Mall, 110 Souris Ave., Main Fl., Weyburn, SK S4H 2Z8
Yorkton
Imperial Plaza, 214 Smith St. East, Yorkton, SK S3N 3S6
Whitehorse
Elijah Smith Bldg., #125, 300 Main St., Whitehorse, YT Y1A 2B5

Skills & Employment / Direction générale des compétences et de l'emploi

Skills & Employment provides programs & initiatives that promote skills development, labour market participation & inclusiveness, as well as ensuring labour market efficiency. Specifically, these programs seek to address the employment & skills needs of those facing employment barriers, & contribute to life long learning & building a skilled inclusive labour force. Other programs that support an efficient labour market include the labour market integration of recent immigrants, the entry of temporary foreign workers, the mobility of workers across Canada & the dissemination of labour market information. This branch is also responsible for programs that provide temporary income support to eligible unemployed workers.

Senior Assistant Deputy Minister, Frank Vermaeten
Tel: 819-997-9236
Fax: 819-934-4040
frank.vermaeten@hrsdc-rhdcc.gc.ca
Associate Assistant Deputy Minister, Louis Beauséjour
Tel: 819-997-9427
Fax: 819-934-4040
louis.beausejour@hrsdc-rhdcc.gc.ca
Director General, Active Employment Measures, John Atherton
Tel: 819-994-4553
Fax: 819-934-7107
john.atherton@hrsdc-rhdcc.gc.ca
Acting Director General, Federal/Provincial/Territorial Partnerships, Michel C. Caron
Tel: 819-997-5136
Fax: 819-934-7818
michel.caron@hrsdc-rhdcc.gc.ca
Acting Director General, Program Policy, Planning & Coordination, Alexis Conrad
Tel: 819-997-0037
Fax: 819-934-5333
alexis.conrad@hrsdc-rhdcc.gc.ca
Director General, Workplace Partnerships, Silvano Tocchi, 20110720
Tel: 819-953-0243
Fax: 819-997-6777
silvano.tocchi@hrsdc-rhdcc.gc.ca
Director General, Temporary Foreign Workers, Andrew Kenyon
Tel: 819-994-1021
Fax: 819-997-5979
andrew.kenyon@hrsdc-rhdcc.gc.ca
Director General, Employment Insurance Policy, Mireille Laroche
Tel: 819-997-8622
Fax: 819-934-6631
mireille.laroche@hrsdc-rhdcc.gc.ca
Director General, Labour Market Integration, Jean-François LaRue
Tel: 819-997-9217
Fax: 819-934-6630
jeanfrancois.larue@hrsdc-rhdcc.gc.ca
Director General, Office of Literacy & Essential Skills, Silvano Tocchi
Tel: 819-953-6967
Fax: 819-997-6777
silvano.tocchi@hrsdc-rhdcc.gc.ca
Director, Aboriginal Affairs, Alfred M. Linklater
Tel: 819-934-6640
Fax: 819-994-3297
alfred.linklater@hrsdc-rhdcc.gc.ca

Strategic Policy & Research / Direction générale de la politique stratégique et de la recherche

Strategic Policy & Research leads on integrating human resources & social development issues in strategic policy, evaluation, & knowledge & research dissemination. It also leads on emerging & long-term policy development, corporate planning, & central agency, intergovernmental & international relations.

Senior Assistant Deputy Minister, David McGovern
Tel: 819-953-3729
Fax: 819-997-7329
david.mcgovern@hrsdc-rhdcc.gc.ca
Associate Assistant Deputy Minister, Allen Sutherland
Tel: 819-994-6013
Fax: 819-997-7329
allen.sutherland@hrsdc-rhdcc.gc.ca
Acting Director General, Strategy & Integration, David Bailey
Tel: 819-953-4416
Fax: 819-953-0519
david.bailey@hrsdc-rhdcc.gc.ca
Director General, Knowledge & Data Management, Christian Dea
Tel: 819-934-7655
Fax: 819-953-1947
christian.dea@hrsdc-rhdcc.gc.ca
Acting Director General, Policy Research Directorate, Jeff Frank
Tel: 819-953-6892
Fax: 819-953-8868
jeff.frank@hrsdc-rhdcc.gc.ca

Director General, Learning Policy Directorate, Mark Hopkins
Tel: 819-953-8005
Fax: 819-997-5433
mark.hopkins@hrsdc-rhdcc.gc.ca
Director General, Corporate Planning & Accountability, Bobby Matheson
Tel: 819-994-2098
Fax: 819-994-2374
bobby.matheson@hrsdc-rhdcc.gc.ca
Acting Director General, Social Policy, François Weldon
Tel: 819-994-3184
Fax: 819-953-9119
francois.weldon@hrsdc-rhdcc.gc.ca
Director General, Intergovernmental Relations, David Whillans
Tel: 819-994-4538
Fax: 819-953-4701
david.whillans@hrsdc-rhdcc.gc.ca
Director, Resource Management Directorate, Kata Kitaljevich
Tel: 819-953-2368
Fax: 819-953-4962
kata.kitaljevich@hrsdc-rhdcc.gc.ca

Immigration & Refugee Board of Canada (IRB) / Commission de l'immigration et du statut de réfugié du Canada (CISR)

Canada Bldg, 344 Slater St., 12th Fl., Ottawa, ON K1A 0K1
Tel: 613-995-6486
Fax: 613-943-1550
contact@irb-cisr.gc.ca
www.irb-cisr.gc.ca

The IRB is an independent administrative tribunal that reports to Parliament through the Minister of Citizenship & Immigration Canada (CIC). The Board's mission, on behalf of Canadians, is to make well-reasoned decisions on immigration & refugee matters efficiently, fairly, & in accordance with the law. As Canada's largest federal tribunal, the IRB consists of three divisions. The Refugee Protection Division decides claims for refugee protection made by persons in Canada. The Immigration Division conducts detention reviews & immigration inquiries for certain categories of people believed to be inadmissable, or removable from, Canada. The Immigration Appeal Division hears appeals of sponsorship applications refused by officials of Citizenship & Immigration Canada; appeals from certain removal orders made against permanent residents, refugees & other protected persons, & holders of permanent resident visas; appeals by permanent residents who have been found outside Canada not to have fulfilled their residency obligation; & appeals by CIC from decisions of the Immigration Division at admissability hearings.

Chair, Brian Goodman
Tel: 613-996-4752
Fax: 613-947-5338
brian.goodman@irb-cisr.gc.ca

Executive Director, Simon Coakeley
Tel: 613-947-1040
simon.coakeley@irb-cisr.gc.ca

Deputy Chairperson, Immigration Appeal Division, Shari Stein
Tel: 613-995-7289
shari.stein@irb-cisr.gc.ca

Deputy Chairperson, Refugee Protection Division, Ken Sandhu
Tel: 613-947-6711
ken.sandhu@irb-cisr.gc.ca

Director General, Corporate Planning & Services Branch, Serge Gascon
Tel: 613-947-6679
serge.gascon@irb-cisr.gc.ca

Director General, Human Resources & Professional Development Branch, Diane Lacelle
Tel: 613-995-0805
diane.lacelle@irb-cisr.gc.ca

Director General, Immigration Division, Susan Bibeau
Tel: 613-947-6922
susan.bibeau@irb-cisr.gc.ca

Deputy Director General, Operations Branch, Thomas Vulpe
Tel: 613-947-7184
thomas.vulpe@irb-cisr.gc.ca

Director General, Strategic Communication & Partnerships, Kevin White
Tel: 613-995-3513
kevin.white@irb-cisr.gc.ca

Senior General Counsel, Legal Services, Sylvia Cox-Duquette
Tel: 613-943-2310
Fax: 613-947-2607
sylvia.cox-duquette@irb-cisr.gc.ca

Director, Communications, Aarin Masson
Tel: 613-996-1329
aarin.masson@irb-cisr.gc.ca

Communications Officer, Christopher Slaney
Tel: 613-943-3940
christopher.slaney@irb-cisr.gc.ca

Industry Canada / Industrie Canada

C.D. Howe Building, 235 Queen St., Ottawa, ON K1A 0H5
Tel: 613-954-5031
Fax: 613-954-2340
Toll-Free: 800-328-6189
info@ic.gc.ca
www.ic.gc.ca
TTY: 866-694-8389

The mission of Industry Canada is to help make Canadians more productive & competitive in a global, knowledge-based economy. The department's policies, programs & services assist in the creation of an economy that provides more & better-paying jobs for Canadians; supports stronger business growth through sustained improvements in productivity; & gives consumers, businesses & investors confidence that the marketplace is fair, efficient & competitive. To reach its clients, Industry Canada collaborates extensively with partners at all levels of government & the private sector.

Acts Administered:
Agreement on Internal Trade Implementation Act
Agricultural & Rural Development Act
Atlantic Fisheries Restructuring Act
Bankruptcy & Insolvency Act
Bell Canada Act
Bills of Exchange Act
Boards of Trade Act
British Columbia Telephone Company Act
Budget Implementation Act, 1997
Business Development Bank of Canada Act
Canada Business Corporations Act
Canada Co-operative Associations Act
Canada Corporations Act
Canada Small Business Financing Act
Canadian Space Agency Act
Canadian Tourism Commission Act
Civil International Space Station Agreement Act
Companies' Creditors Arrangement Act
Competition Act
Competition Tribunal Act
Consumer Packaging & Labelling Act
Copyright Act
Corporations & Labour Unions Returns Act
Department of Industry Act
Electricity & Gas Inspection Act
Employment Support Act
Government Corporations Operations Act
Industrial & Regional Development Act
Industrial Design Act
Integrated Circuit Topography Act
Investment Canada Act
National Research Council Act
Natural Sciences & Engineering Research Council Act
Patent Act
Pension Fund Societies Act
Personal Information Protection & Electronic Dociuments Act
Precious Metals Marking Act
Public Documents Act
Public Officers Act
Public Servants Inventions Act
Radiocommunication Act
Regional Development Incentives Act
Seals Act
Small Business Loans Act
Social Sciences & Humanities Research Council Act
Special Areas Act
Standards Council of Canada Act
Statistics Act
Telecommunications Act
Teleglobe Canada Reorganization & Divestiture Act
Telesat Canada Reorganization & Divestiture Act
Textile Labelling Act
Timber Marking Act
Trade Unions Act
Trade-marks Act
Weights & Measures Act
Winding-up & Restructuring Act

Minister, Industry; Minister, State (Agriculture), Hon. Christian Paradis
Tel: 613-995-9001
minister.industry@ic.gc.ca

Minister, State (Small Business & Tourism), Hon. Maxime Bernier
Tel: 613-943-6183
Fax: 613-990-4056

Minister, State (Science & Technology), Hon. Gary Goodyear
Tel: 613-947-2956
Fax: 613-943-7598

Deputy Minister, Richard Dicerni
Tel: 613-992-4292
Fax: 613-954-3272
richard.dicerni@ic.gc.ca

Senior Associate Deputy Minister, Simon Kennedy
Tel: 613-943-7164
Fax: 613-954-2137

Associated Agencies, Boards & Commissions:

• Canadian Tourism Commission (CTC) / Commission canadienne du tourisme (CCT)
#1400, 1055 Dunsmuir St.
PO Box 49230
Vancouver, BC V7X 1L2
Tel: 604-638-8300
en-corporate.canada.travel
CTC is a unique partnership between tourism business & associations, provincial & territorial governments, & the Government of Canada. The CTC's Board of Directors is a decision-making body composed of 26 members with a wide variety of skills & knowledge, representing all regions of the country. The CTC's mission is to sustain a vibrant & profitable Canadian tourism industry.

• Communications Research Centre Canada (CRC) / Centre de recherches sur les communications
3701 Carling Ave.
PO Box 11490 H
Ottawa, ON K2H 8S2
Tel: 613-991-3313
Fax: 613-998-5355
info@crc.gc.ca
www.crc.gc.ca
Dedicated to advanced communications research & development for over 50 years. Key research areas include radio science, terrestrial wireless systems, satellite communications broadcasting & broadband network technologies. CRC has a long history of technology transfer. CRC operates an Innovation Centre, a technology incubator for small & medium-sized high-tech start-ups, which provides increased access to CRC's technologies, research expertise & unique laboratories & facilities.

• Competition Tribunal / Tribunal de la concurrence
Thomas D'Arcy McGee Bldg.
#600, 90 Sparks St.
Ottawa, ON K1P 5B4
Tel: 613-957-3172
Fax: 613-957-3170
tribunal@ct-tc.gc.ca
www.ct-tc.gc.ca
Hears & decides all applications made under Parts V11.1 & VIII of the Competition Act.

• Electronic Commerce Branch / Direction générale du commerce électronique
300 Slater St.
Ottawa, ON K1A 0C8
Tel: 613-954-5031
Fax: 613-954-2340
Toll-free: 800-328-6189
TTY: 866-694-8389
www.ic.gc.ca/eic/site/ecic-ceac.nsf/eng/h_gv00002.html
Coordinates the development & implementation of a national electronic commerce strategy. It is responsible for both domestic & international aspects of electronic commerce. The Canadian Electronic Commerce Strategy was announced in September 1998. The Strategy, which was developed in collaboration with provincial & territorial governments, industry & consumer groups, among others, establishes a framework, goals, timetable, & implementation plan for electronic commerce domestically. The Strategy involves coordinating strategic elements that fall within the federal government's responsibilities, including the policy development areas of encryption & privacy.

• Enterprise Cape Breton Corporation (ECBC) / Société d'expansion du Cap-Breton
Silicon Island
70 Crescent St.
Sydney, NS B1S 2Z7
Tel: 902-564-3600
Fax: 902-564-3825
Toll-free: 800-705-3926
information@ecbc-secb.gc.ca
www.ecbc-secb.gc.ca

Crown corporation established pursuant to Part II of the Government Organization Act, Atlantic Canada, 1987, with a jurisdictional mandate which includes all of Cape Breton Island & a portion of mainland Nova Scotia in & around the Town of Mulgrave. The Corporation is charged with the responsibility for promoting & assisting the financing & development of industry in the region, providing employment outside the coal-producing sector & broadening the base of the local economy.

• **Standards Council of Canada / Conseil canadien des normes**
#200, 270 Albert Street
Ottawa, ON K1P 6N7
Tel: 613-238-3222
Fax: 613-569-7808
info@scc.ca
www.scc.ca
The Standards Council of Canada (SCC) works to promote the development & use of national & international standards and reports to Parliament through the Minister of Industry. It consists of 15 members and a staff of 90.

Audit & Evaluation Branch (AEB) / Direction générale de la vérification et de l'évaluation (DGVE)
Tel: 613-943-7047
Fax: 613-995-8568
Director General, Audit & Evaluation, Susan Hart, CAE
Tel: 613-954-5084
Fax: 613-954-5070

Canadian Intellectual Property Office (CIPO) / Office de la propriété intellectuelle du Canada (OPIC)
Place du Portage I, #C-229, 50 Victoria Street, Gatineau, QC K1A 0C9
Tel: 866-997-1936
Fax: 819-953-7620
cipo.contact@ic.gc.ca
www.cipo.ic.gc.ca
TTY: 866-442-2476
Other Communication: International calls: 819-934-0544
Commissioner, Patents; Registrar, Trademarks; Chief Executive Officer, Sylvain Laporte
Tel: 819-997-1057
Fax: 819-997-1890

Communications & Marketing Branch (CMB) / Direction générale des communications et du marketing (DGCM)
Director General, Brian Spurling
Tel: 613-947-2597
Fax: 613-954-6436

Competition Bureau / Bureau de la concurrence
Place du Portage, Phase I, 50 Victoria Street, Ottawa, ON K1A 0C9
Tel: 819-997-4282
Fax: 819-997-0324
Toll-Free: 800-348-5358
www.competitionbureau.gc.ca
TTY: 800-642-3844
The Competition Bureau is the organization responsible for the enforcement of the Competition Act, the Consumer Packaging & Labelling Act except as it relates to food, the Precious Metals Marking Act & the Textile Labelling Act. The Competition Bureau ensures compliance by the business community with legislation administered by the Bureau, & oversees the development of policy & dissemination of information aimed at ensuring optimal compliance levels.
Commissioner of Competition, Melanie Aitken
Tel: 819-997-3304
Fax: 819-953-5013
Deputy Commissioner, Vicky Eatrides
Tel: 819-997-5222
Fax: 819-953-5013

Industry Sector / Secteur de l'industrie
Tel: 613-954-3395
Fax: 613-941-1134
Industry Sector (IS) assists Canadian industry & businesses compete, expand & create jobs in the knowledge-based economy. IS contributes to Industry Canada's strategic objectives, trade, investment, innovation, connectedness & marketplace. It facilitates delivery of industrial, related policy analyses & strategies to promote global competitiveness of Canadian industry. IS provides a broad range of services, information resources, sector policies & strategies to support business growth. IS provides Canadian businesses with timely information products, business tools, research, strategic analyses, data & information resources.
Assistant Deputy Minister, Marta Morgan
Tel: 613-954-3798
Fax: 613-941-1134
Associate Assistant Deputy Minister, Philip Jennings
Tel: 613-946-4448
Fax: 613-941-1134

Aerospace, Defence & Marine Branch / Aérospatiale, defense et la marine
Tel: 613-954-3786
Fax: 613-998-6703
Director General, Brian Gear
Tel: 613-941-8123
Fax: 613-998-6703
Senior Policy Advisor, Katie Durling
Tel: 613-960-9403
Fax: 613-998-6703

Automotive & Transportation Industries Branch / Direction générale des industries de l'automobile et des transports
Tel: 613-952-0441
Fax: 613-952-8088
Director General, Alison Tait
Tel: 613-954-2949
Fax: 613-941-2379

Life Science Industries Branch / Sciences de la vie
Tel: 613-946-3144
Fax: 613-946-3144
Director General, Leah Clark
Tel: 613-954-5258
Fax: 613-952-5822

Manufacturing & Resource Processing Industries Branch / Industries de la fabrication et de la transformation des ressources naturelles
Tel: 613-954-2892
Fax: 613-941-8048
strategis.gc.ca/rpib
Director General, Ailish Campbell
Tel: 613-954-2990
Fax: 613-954-3107
Director, Forestry & Energy Industries Directorate, Jyotsna Dalvi
Tel: 613-941-2274
Fax: 613-941-8048
Acting Director, Resource Manufacturing Industries Directorate, Patrick Hum
Tel: 613-954-2703
Fax: 613-954-3107
Director, Business Services to Manufacturing & Consumer Products, Patrick Hurens
Tel: 613-952-1710
Fax: 613-954-3107
Director, Environmental & Clean Energy Industries, Tim Karlsson
Tel: 613-955-2991
Fax: 613-941-8048

Regional Operations / Opérations régionales
Tel: 613-941-3095
Fax: 613-954-4883
Acting Assistant Deputy Minister, Mitch Davies
Tel: 613-954-3405
Fax: 613-954-4883
Senior Advisor to the Assistant Deputy Minister, Diane St-Gelais
Tel: 613-954-3407
Fax: 613-954-4883
Director General & Director, Regional Policy & Coordination Branch; National Access Program Directorate, Lisa Setlakwe
Tel: 613-952-0564
Fax: 613-946-2835

Small Business, Tourism & Marketplace Services / Services axés sur le marché, le tourisme et la petite entreprise
Tel: 613-995-9305
Fax: 613-941-1938
Assistant Deputy Minister, Marie-Josée Thivierge
Tel: 613-995-9605
Fax: 613-948-9088

Chief Informatics Office / Bureau principal de l'informatique
Tel: 613-954-3570
Fax: 613-941-1938
Chief Informatics Officer, Rick Rinholm
Tel: 613-954-3574
Fax: 613-941-1938

Corporations Canada
365 Laurier Avenue West, Ottawa, ON K1A 0C8
Tel: 613-941-4550
Fax: 613-941-0601
Director General, Corporations Canada, Marcie Girouard
Tel: 613-954-3576
Fax: 613-941-5783

Information Management Branch / Direction générale de la gestion de l'information
Tel: 613-954-3749
Fax: 613-990-4848
Director General, Nancy Graham
Tel: 613-952-6368
Fax: 613-990-4848

Investment Review & Strategic Planning Branch / Direction générale de l'examen des investissements et de la planification stratégique
Tel: 613-954-1887
Fax: 613-996-2515
investcan.ic.gc.ca
Director General, Jenifer Aitken
Tel: 613-946-9108
Fax: 613-996-2515

Measurement Canada / Mesures Canada
151 Tunney's Pasture Driveway, Ottawa, ON K1A 0C9
Tel: 613-952-0652
Fax: 613-957-1265
mc.ic.gc.ca
President, Alan Johnston
Tel: 613-952-0655
Fax: 613-957-1265
Vice-President, Engineering & Laboratory Services, Rene Magnan
Tel: 613-952-0610
Fax: 613-952-1754
Vice-President, Innovative Services Directorate, Sonia Roussy
Tel: 613-952-4285
Fax: 613-952-1736
Vice-President, Program Development Directorate, Gilles Vinet
Tel: 613-941-8918
Fax: 613-952-1736

Office of the Superintendent of Bankruptcy / Bureau du surintendant des faillites
155 Queen Street, Ottawa, ON K1A 0H5
Tel: 613-941-1000
Fax: 613-941-2862
osb-bsf.ic.gc.ca
Superintendent of Bankruptcy, Bill James
Tel: 613-941-2691
Fax: 613-946-9205
Deputy Superintendent, Patricia Alferez
Tel: 613-946-2157
Fax: 613-946-6367
Director General, Program Policy & Regulatory Affairs, Elisabeth Lang
Tel: 613-946-2166
Fax: 613-946-2168
Director General, Outreach Services, Ginette Trahan
Tel: 613-941-2854
Fax: 613-941-2862

Small Business / Direction générale de la petite entreprise
Tel: 613-954-5479
Fax: 613-946-1035
Director General, Éric Dagenais
Tel: 613-954-5489
Fax: 613-946-1035

Tourism Branch / Direction générale du tourisme
Director General, Billy Hewett
Tel: 613-960-8958
Fax: 613-952-0290
Senior Director, Horizontal Policy Integration, Ilona Rehberg
Tel: 613-946-1881
Fax: 613-952-0290

Spectrum, Information Technologies & Telecommunications / Spectre, technologies de l'information et télécommunications
Journal Tower North, 300 Slater St., 20th Fl., Ottawa, ON K1A 0C8
Tel: 613-998-0368
Fax: 613-952-1203
Contributes to the Industry Canada mandate by fostering the early development & use of information & communications technologies, infrastructures & services. The sector uses its policy & regulatory rule-making powers, & marketplace & industry sectoral development services to ensure Canada has a world-class telecommunications & information infrastructure; promote the international competitiveness of Canadian information technologies by all sectors of the Canadian economy; & ensure effective & efficient use of the radio frequency spectrum.
Senior Assistant Deputy Minister, Helen McDonald
Tel: 613-998-0368
Fax: 613-952-1203
Assistant Deputy Minister, Susan Bincoletto
Tel: 613-998-0368
Fax: 613-952-1203
Director General, Information & Communications Technologies Branch, Alain Beaudoin
Tel: 613-954-5598
Fax: 613-957-4076
Director General, Governance, Policy Coordination & Planning, Carol Bradley
Tel: 613-946-9077
Fax: 613-946-9084
Director General, Electronic Commerce Branch, Janet DiFrancesco

Tel: 613-990-2225
Fax: 613-941-1164
Director General, Engineering, Planning & Standards Branch, Marc Dupuis
Tel: 613-990-4820
Fax: 613-954-6091
Director General, Spectrum Management Operations Branch, Fiona Gilfillan
Tel: 613-990-4817
Fax: 613-993-4433

Office of the Information Commissioner of Canada / Commissariat à l'information du Canada

Place de Ville, Tower B, 112 Kent St., 7th Fl., Ottawa, ON K1A 1H3

Tel: 613-995-2410
Fax: 613-947-7294
Toll-Free: 800-267-0441
general@oic-ci.gc.ca
www.oic-ci.gc.ca
TTY: 613-947-0388

The Office of the Information Commissioner of Canada was established in 1983. It investigates complaints from people & organizations who believe they have been denied rights under the Access of Information Act, Canada's freedom of information legislation.
An independent ombudsperson appointed by Parliament, the Information Commissioner has strong investigative powers. The Information Commissioner mediates between government institutions & dissatisfied applicants, & may refer cases to the Federal Court for resolution.
Acts Administered:
Access to Information Act

Information Commissioner, Suzanne Legault
Tel: 613-995-9976
Fax: 613-995-1501
Social Media: www.facebook.com/OICCANADA

Assistant Information Commissioner, Complaints Resolution & Compliance, Andrea J. Neill
Tel: 613-995-2665
Fax: 613-947-7294

Interim Director General, Corporate Services Branch, Layla Michaud
Tel: 613-995-2864
Fax: 613-995-1501

General Counsel, Legal Services, Emily McCarthy
Tel: 613-947-1834
Fax: 613-947-5252

Infrastructure Canada

180 Kent St., Ottawa, ON K1P 0B6

Tel: 613-948-1148
Toll-Free: 877-250-7154
info@infc.gc.ca
www.infrastructure.gc.ca
TTY: 800-465-7735
Other Communication: Media Relations, Phone: 613-960-9251, E-mail: mediarelations.relationsmedias@infc.gc.ca

Infrastructure Canada is engaged in the following tasks to ensure modern public infrastructure for the benefit of Canadians: developing policies; establishing partnerships; fostering knowledge; making investments; & delivering programs.
To address local, regional, & national priorities, Infrastructure Canada works with municipalities, provinces & territories, other federal departments & agencies, as well as private companies & the non-profit sector to build & revitalize the infrastructure required by Canadians.

Minister, Transport, Infrastructure & Communities; Minister, Economic Development Agency of Canada for the Regions of Québec, Hon. Denis Lebel, P.C.
Tel: 613-991-0700
Fax: 613-995-0327
mintc@tc.gc.ca; denis.lebel@parl.gc.ca
Minister'sOffice, Tower C
330 Sparks St.
Ottawa, ON K1A 0N5

Associate Deputy Minister, Infrastructure, Marie Lemay
Tel: 613-948-8157
Fax: 613-948-2963
marie.lemay@infc.gc.ca

Parliamentary Secretary to the Minister, Transport, Infrastructure & Communities, & for the Federal Economic Development Agency for Southern Ontario, Pierre Poilievre
Tel: 513-992-2772
Fax: 613-992-1209
www.resultsforyou.ca
Social Media: www.facebook.com/pierre.poilievre
#680, La Promenade Buidling
111Wellington St.
Ottawa, ON K1A 0A6

Senior Counsel, Legal Services, Richard Ouellet
Tel: 613-990-5783
Fax: 613-990-5777
ouellet.richard@tc.gc.ca

Audit & Evaluation Branch

#1100, 180 Kent St., Ottawa, ON K1P 0B6

Independent audits are conducted to ensure proper processes of Infrastructure Canada. Evaluation programs are also carried out to assess the value of the department's programs & initiatives. The work of the Audit & Evaluation Branch supports decision making within Infrastructure Canada.
Chief Audit & Evaluation Executive, Raymond Kunze
Tel: 613-954-4879
Fax: 613-941-5050
raymond.kunze@infc.gc.ca
Director, Evaluation, Alison Taylor
Tel: 613-954-7750
Fax: 613-941-5050
alison.taylor@infc.gc.ca
Director, Audit, Inanc Yazar
Tel: 613-946-8751
Fax: 613-941-5050
inanc.yazar@infc.gc.ca
Manager, Professional Practices, Vilma Youmaran
Tel: 613-960-9665
Fax: 613-960-8902
vilma.youmaran@infc.gc.ca

Corporate Services Branch

#1100, 180 Kent St., Ottawa, ON K1P 0B6

The Corporate Services Branch supports corporate functions & provides information management & technology services. Specific duties include administration, human resources services, procurement, financial services, & maintenance of the Shared Information Management System for Infrastructure.
Assistant Deputy Minister; Chief Financial Officer, David Miller
Tel: 613-948-9161
Fax: 613-960-6348
david.miller@infc.gc.ca
Director General, Human Resources, Security, & Administration, Nancy Martel
Tel: 613-948-3773
Fax: 613-948-3772
nancy.martel@infc.gc.ca
Director, Operational Support & Web Services, IM / IT Directorate, Patrick Boulé
Tel: 613-960-5661
Fax: 613-960-9648
pat.boule@infc.gc.ca
Director, Application Services, IM / IT Directorate, André Bourdon
Tel: 613-948-9719
Fax: 613-960-9423
andre.bourdon@infc.gc.ca
Director, Finance & Administration, Cynthia Cantlie
Tel: 613-948-4424
Fax: 613-960-6348
cynthia.cantlie@infc.gc.ca
Director, Planning, Standards, & Project Delivery, IM / IT Directorate, Mohamad Hamzeh
Tel: 613-960-6396
Chief Risk Officer, Denis Bouvier
Tel: 613-946-7874
Fax: 613-960-6348
denis.bouvier@infc.gc.ca
Chief, Financial Planning & Analysis, Danielle Byrne
Tel: 613-941-7955
Fax: 613-960-6348
danielle.byrne@infc.gc.ca
Chief Information Officer, Jennifer Dawson
Tel: 613-946-0509
Fax: 613-960-9649
jennifer.dawson@infc.gc.ca
Chief, Corporate Resourcing, Julie Parker
Tel: 613-948-7239
Fax: 613-960-6348
julie.parker@infc.gc.ca

Policy & Communications Branch

#1100, 180 Kent St., Ottawa, ON K1P 0B6

The following responsibilities are handled by the Policy & Communications Branch: identifying infrastructure priorities; conducting research that contributes to policy development; assessing investments; providing correspondence services; & coordinating communications on infrastructure & sharing knowledge.
Assistant Deputy Minister, Policy & Communications, Taki Sarantakis
Tel: 613-946-5188
Fax: 613-960-9648
taki.sarantakis@infc.gc.ca
Director General, Policy & Planning, Samantha Tattersall
Tel: 613-948-7237
Fax: 613-948-9393
samantha.tattersall@infc.gc.ca
Director General, Communications, Peter Wallace
Tel: 613-948-2940
Fax: 613-948-2963
peter.wallace@infc.gc.ca
Director, Policy, Francis Bilodeau
Tel: 613-948-9160
Fax: 613-960-9648
francis.bilodeau@infc.gc.ca
Director, Special Projects, Louise Payette
Tel: 613-960-6807
Fax: 613-960-9289
louise.payette@infc.gc.ca
Director, Environmental Initiatives, Sonya Read
Tel: 613-960-9507
Fax: 613-960-9648
sonya.read@infc.gc.ca
Director, Reporting & Coordination, Tom Roberts
Tel: 613-946-9922
Fax: 613-960-9648
tom.roberts@infc.gc.ca
Director, Economic & Community Initiatives, Michael Rutherford
Tel: 613-952-3366
Fax: 613-960-6949
michael.rutherford@infc.gc.ca
Coordinator, Access to Information & Privacy, Veronique Vieira
Tel: 613-960-9622
Fax: 613-948-9393
veronique.vieira@infc.gc.ca

Program Operations Branch

#1100, 180 Kent St., Ottawa, ON K1P 0B6

The Program Operations Branch is responsible for the following activities: implementing programs; administering funding agreements; managing the federal Gas Tax transfer to Canadian municipalities to support environmentally sustainable infrastructure; & conducting environment assessments & program evaluations.
Assistant Deputy Minister, Program Operations, Natasha Rascanin
Tel: 613-948-8003
Fax: 613-960-9423
natasha.rascanin@infc.gc.ca
Director General, Program Integration, Claude Blanchette
Tel: 613-948-9392
Fax: 613-948-9394
claude.blanchette@infc.gc.ca
Director General, North, Atlantic, Ontario Program Operations, Deryck Trehearne
Tel: 613-960-6774
Fax: 613-960-9423
deryck.trehearne@infc.gc.ca
Director, West Region, Marie-Josée Lafleur
Tel: 613-948-1905
Fax: 613-948-2965
marie-josee.lafleur@infc.gc.ca
Director, Program Integration, Bogdan Makuc
Tel: 613-960-9247
Fax: 613-941-5050
bogdan.makuc@infc.gc.ca
Director, Québec Region, Isabel Romero
Tel: 613-960-6140
Fax: 613-960-9428
isabel.romero@infc.gc.ca
Director, North Program Operations, Paul Truant
Tel: 613-960-6802
Fax: 613-938-2965
paul.truant@infc.gc.ca

Office of Intergovernmental Affairs (IGA) / Affaires intergouvernementales

c/o Privy Council Office, #1000, 85 Slater St., Ottawa, ON K1A 0A3

Tel: 613-957-5153
Fax: 613-957-5043
info@pco-bcp.gc.ca
www.pco-bcp.gc.ca/aia
TTY: 613-957-5741

The federal government office is responsible for the management of federal-provincial-territorial relations.
The office supports & advises the Prime Minister & the Minister of Intergovernmental Affairs about issues related to federal-provincial-territorial relations, such as communications, policies, & parliamentary affairs. Fiscal federalism, the evolution of the federation, & Canadian unity are key areas for the IGA.

Minister, Intergovernmental Affairs; President, Queen's Privy Council for Canada, Hon. Peter Penashue, P.C.

Tel: 613-996-4630
Fax: 613-996-7132
peter.penashue@parl.gc.ca
Social Media: www.twitter.com/PeterPenashue, www.facebook.com/peterpenashue

Deputy Minister; Associate Secretary to the Cabinet, Janice Charette, B.Comm. (Hons.)
Tel: 613-957-5466

Parliamentary Secretary to the Prime Minister & to the Minister, Intergovernmental Affairs, Dean del Mastro, B. Comm. (Hons.)
Tel: 613-995-6411
Fax: 613-996-9800
dean.delmastro@parl.gc.ca; delmad1@parl.gc.ca
Social Media: www.twitter.com/mpdeandelmastro, www.facebook.com/deandelmastro

International Development Research Centre (IDRC) / Centre de recherches pour le développement international (CRDI)

150 Kent St., PO Box 8500, Ottawa, ON K1G 3H9
Tel: 613-236-6163
Fax: 613-238-7230
info@idrc.ca
www.idrc.ca

Helps scientists in developing countries identify long-term, practical solutions to pressing development problems. Support is given directly to scientists working in universities, private enterprise, government & non-profit-making organizations. Priority is given to research aimed at achieving equitable & sustainable development. One of the three program areas of focus is Environmental & Natural Resource Management. Initiatives in this area include a rural poverty & environment program initiative, an urban poverty & environment program, ecosystem approaches to human health, an international model forest network, biodiversity & regional water demand initiative.

Chair, Barbara McDougall
Tel: 613-236-6163 ext: 238
Fax: 613-565-8212
bmcdougall@idrc.ca

President, David M. Malone
Tel: 613-236-6163 ext: 259
Fax: 613-235-6391
dmalone@idrc.ca

Vice-President, Resources & Chief Financial Officer, Sylvain Dufour
Tel: 613-236-6163 ext: 218
Fax: 613-236-7293
sdufour@idrc.ca

Vice-President, Programs & Partnership Branch, Rohinton Medhora
Tel: 613-236-6163 ext: 231
Fax: 613-567-7748
rmedhora@idrc.ca

Director, Communications Division, Angela Prokopiak
Tel: 613-236-6163 ext: 259
Fax: 613-563-2476
aprokopiak@idrc.ca

Director, Environmental & Natural Resource Management, Jean Lebel
Tel: 613-236-6163 ext: 253
Fax: 613-567-7748
jlebel@idrc.ca

Eastern & Southern Africa
IDRC, Liasion House, 2nd Floor, State House Avenue, Nairobi, 62084 00200 Kenya
vngugi@idrc.ca
www.idrc.ca/esaro
Other Communication: Tel: 254-20-2713160; Fax: 254-20-2711063

Latin America & the Caribbean
Avenida Brasil 2655, Montevideo, 11300 Uruguay
lacroinf@idrc.ca
www.idrc.ca/lacro
Other Communication: Tel: 598-2-709-0042; Fax: 598-2-708-6776

Middle East & North Africa
8 Ahmed Nessim St., 8th fl., PO Box 14, Giza, Cairo
skamel@idrc.ca
www.idrc.ca/cairo
Other Communication: Tel: 20-2-336-7051; Fax: 20-2-336-7056

South Asia & China
IDRC, 208 Jor Bagh, New Delhi, 110 003 India
saro@idrc.ca
www.idrc.ca/saro
Other Communication: Tel: 91-11-2461-9411; Fax: 91-11-2462-2707

Southeast & East Asia
IDRC, Tanglin, #02-55 - 22 Cross St., Singapore, 048421 Singapore
asro@idrc.ca
www.idrc.ca/asro
Other Communication: Tel: 65-6438-7877; Fax: 65-6438-4844

West & Central Africa
CRDI, CD Annexe, BP 11007, Peytavin, Dakar
waro@idrc.ca
www.idrc.ca/waro
Other Communication: Tel: 221-33-864-0000; Fax: 221-33-825-3255

International Joint Commission (IJC) / Commission mixte internationale (CMI)

234 Laurier Ave. West, 22nd Fl., Ottawa, ON K1P 6K6
Tel: 613-947-1420
Fax: 613-993-5583
beckhoffb@ottawa.ijc.org
www.ijc.org
Other Communication: Great Lakes Water Quality Information: 519-257-6700

Established by the Boundary Waters Treaty of 1909 & is responsible for approving (by Order of Approval) certain works in boundary waters which affect levels & flows on both sides of the Canada-US border. The commission provides recommendations on matters along the common boundary which have been referred to the Commission by the governments. Also monitors & assesses the Great Lakes Water Quality Agreement (GLWQA) & is responsible for reviewing & commenting on Remedial Action Plans (RAPs) in coordination with eight US states & the province of Ontario.

Chair, Joseph Comuzzi

Commissioner, Lyall D. Knott

Commissioner, Pierre Trépanier

Great Lakes Regional Office
100 Ouellette Ave., 8th fl., Windsor, ON N9A 6T3
Tel: 519-257-6733
Fax: 519-257-6740
nevinj@windsor.ijc.org
Other Communication: Information: 519-257-6700

Director, Great Lakes Regional Office, Dr. Saad Y. Jasim
Tel: 519-257-6715
jasims@windsor.ijc.org

United States Section / Section des États-Unis
#615, 2000 L Street, Northwest, Washington, DC 20440 USA
Tel: 202-736-9024
Fax: 202-643-2007
bevacquaf@washington.ijc.org

Chair, Lana Pollack
Commissioner, Dereth Glance
Commissioner, Rich Moy
Public Information Officer, Frank Bevacqua
Tel: 202-736-9024
bevacquaf@washington.ijc.org

Justice Canada

East Memorial Bldg., 284 Wellington St., Ottawa, ON K1A 0H8
Tel: 613-957-4222
Fax: 613-954-0811
webadmin@justice.gc.ca
www.justice.gc.ca
TTY: 613-992-4556
Other Communication: Media Relations Phone: 613-957-4207; Access to Information and Privacy Phone: 613-952-8361

The Department ensures that the Canadian justice system is fair, accessible & efficient. Responsibilities are as follows: provision of policy & program advice & direction by the development of the legal content of bills, regulations, & guidelines; prosecution of federal offences throughout Canada; litigation of civil cases by or on behalf of the federal Crown; & provision of legal advice to federal law enforcement agencies & other government departments.

Acts Administered:
Access to Information Act (President of the Treasury Board)
Annulment of Marriages (Ontario) Act
Anti-Terroism Act
Bills of Lading Act (Minister of Transport)
Canada Evidence Act
Canada Prize Act
Canada-United Kingdom Civil & Commercial Judgments Convention Act
Canadian Bill of Rights
Canadian Human Rights Act
Commercial Arbitration Act
Contraventions Act
Controlled Drugs & Substance Act
Criminal Code (Solicitor General & Minister of Agriculture & Agri-Foods)
Crown Liability & Proceedings Act
Department of Justice Act
Divorce Act
Escheats Act
Extradition Act
Family Orders Agreements Enforcement Assistance Act
Federal Courts Act
Firearms Act
Foreign Enlistment Act
Foreign Extraterritorial Measures Act
Fugitive Offenders Act
Garnishment, Attachment Pension Diversion Act (Minister of National Defense, Minister of Finance & Minister of Public Works & Government Services)
Identification of Criminals Act
International Sale of Goods Contracts Convention Act
Interpretation Act
Judges Act
Law Commission of Canada Act
Marriage (Prohibited Degrees) Act
Minister of Justice shares responsibility to Parliament for the following Acts:
Mutual Legal Assistance in Criminal Matters Act
Official Languages Act
Postal Services Interruption Relief Act
Privacy Act (President of the Treasury Board)
Revised Statutes of Canada, 1985 Act
Security Offences Act
State Immunity Act
Statute Revision Act
Statutory Instruments Act
Supreme Court Act
Tax Court of Canada Act
United Nations Foreign Arbitral Awards Convention Act
Youth Criminal Justice Act

Minister, Justice; Attorney General of Canada, Hon. Robert Douglas Nicholson
Tel: 613-992-4621
Fax: 613-992-7910
Nicholson.R@parl.gc.ca

Parliamentary Secretary to the Minister of Justice, Anita McGuire
Tel: 613-995-4621
Fax: 613-990-7255
anita.mcguire@parl.gc.ca

Deputy Minister & Deputy Attorney General, Miles J. Kirvan
Tel: 613-957-4998

Associate Deputy Minister, Yves Côté
Tel: 613-941-4073
Fax: 613-941-4074

Chief Audit Executive, Steve Samuels
Tel: 613-991-8200
Fax: 613-998-4030

Federal Ombudsman for Victims of Crime, Sue O'Sullivan
Tel: 613-957-6554
Fax: 613-941-3498

Head, Integration, Barbara Ritzen
Tel: 780-495-4074
Fax: 780-495-5835
Other Communications: Alternate telephone: 613-960-3420

Executive Director & General Counsel, Canadian Heritage, Legal Services, Marc Tremblay
Tel: 819-997-2729
Fax: 819-997-2801

Aboriginal Affairs Portfolio / Portfeuille des affaires autochtones
Fax: 613-954-4737

Assistant Deputy Attorney General, Pamela McCurry
Tel: 613-946-6633
Fax: 613-954-4737

Deputy Assistant Deputy Attorney General, Michael Hudson
Tel: 604-775-5173
Fax: 604-775-5152
Other Communications: Alt. Phone: 613-946-1385

Senior General Counsel & Senior Advisor to the ADAG, Tom Saunders
Tel: 613-957-4969
Fax: 613-954-4737

Senior General Counsel & Senior Advisor to the ADAG, Ronald S. Stevenson
Tel: 613-946-6636
Fax: 613-954-4737
Acting Director General & Senior General Counsel, Aboriginal Law & Strategic Policy, Julie Jai
Tel: 613-946-3838
Head of Legal Services & Senior General Counsel, Aboriginal Affairs & Northern Development Canada, Andrew Saranchuk
Tel: 819-994-4141
Senior General Counsel, Resolution, Geoffrey Bickert
Tel: 613-946-3839
Fax: 613-946-6896
Senior Counsel, Aboriginal Consultation Secretariat, Marja J. Bulmer
Tel: 604-775-6513
Fax: 604-775-7922

Business & Regulatory Law Portfolio / Portefeuille du droit des affaires et du droit réglementaire
Fax: 613-946-9988
Assistant Deputy Minister, Pierre Legault
Tel: 613-947-4944
Fax: 613-946-9988
Deputy Assistant Deputy Minister, A. François Daigle
Tel: 613-957-4650
Fax: 613-946-9988

Central Agencies Portfolio / Groupes centraux
Fax: 613-995-7223
Assistant Deputy Minister & Counsel to the Deptartment of Finance, Sandra Hassan
Tel: 613-996-4667
Fax: 613-995-7223
Senior General Counsel, Public Service Commission, Gaston Arseneault
Tel: 613-995-0445
Fax: 613-995-0198
Senior General Counsel, Treasury Board, Michel LeFrançois
Tel: 613-952-3379
Fax: 613-954-5806
General Counsel, Finance - Tax Counsel Division, Sonia Beaulieu
Tel: 613-992-4827
Fax: 613-992-2571
General Counsel & Director, Finance - General Legal Services, Rambod Behboodi
Tel: 613-995-8724
Fax: 613-995-7223
General Counsel, Financial Transactions & Reports Analysis Centre of Canada, Paul Dabrule
Tel: 613-943-3396
Fax: 613-943-3393
General Counsel, Office of the Superintendent of Financial Institutions, Alain Prévost
Tel: 613-990-7787
Senior Counsel, Office of the ADM, Yvonne Milosevic
Tel: 613-943-0418
Fax: 613-995-7223

Chief Financial Officer Branch / Direction générale du dirigeant principal des finances
Chief Financial Officer, Daniel Schnob
Tel: 613-948-5117
Fax: 613-946-1389
Deputy Chief Financial Officer & Director, Micheline Saurette
Tel: 613-941-4095
Fax: 613-960-4871

Communications Branch
284 Wellington St., Ottawa, ON K1A 0H8
Fax: 613-941-2329
Director General, Suesan Saville
Tel: 613-957-9596
Fax: 613-941-2329
Information Officer, Valerie Laforce
Tel: 613-957-4223
Fax: 613-954-0811
Acting Director, Creative Services, Outreach & Electronic Communications Division, Jennifer Buffam
Tel: 613-957-4216
Fax: 613-948-2983
Director, Strategic Communications Division, John Dunn
Tel: 613-941-4021
Manager, Public & Media Relations, Christian Girouard
Tel: 613-941-7326
Fax: 613-954-0811

Corporate Secretariat / Secrétariat corporatif
Fax: 613-957-8382
Acting Senior Counsel & Director, Phaedra Glushek
Tel: 613-941-8826
Fax: 613-941-2279
Chief, Cabinet Affairs Unit, Jacinthe Lareau
Tel: 613-946-6929
Fax: 613-957-8382
Chief, Ministerial Liaison Unit, Jenny Greig
Tel: 613-946-6914
Fax: 613-941-2279
Chief & Legal Counsel, Parliamentary Affairs Unit, Yanike Legault
Tel: 613-952-8354
Fax: 613-957-8382
Chief, Writing & Editing Services, Ministerial Correspondence Unit, Aida Saghbini
Tel: 613-948-2205
Fax: 613-957-3559

Legislative Services Branch / Division des services législatifs
Chief Legislative Counsel, John Mark Keyes
Tel: 613-954-5786
Fax: 613-952-4080
Chief Legislative Editor, Legislative Revising & Editing Services, Ingrid Ludchen
Tel: 613-957-8497
Fax: 613-957-7866
Deputy Chief Legislative Counsel, Philippe Hallée
Tel: 613-941-4178
Fax: 613-941-1193

Litigation Branch / Direction du contentieux
Assistant Deputy Attorney General, Simon Fothergill
Tel: 613-957-4840
Fax: 613-941-1972
Director General & Senior General Counsel, International Assistance Group, Janet Henchey
Tel: 613-948-3003
Fax: 613-957-8412
Director General & Senior General Counsel, Civil Litigation Section, Alain Préfontaine
Tel: 613-946-3815
Fax: 613-954-1920
Director General & Senior General Counsel, Management of Class Actions & Mass Litigation Unit, Paul B. Vickery
Tel: 613-948-1483
Fax: 613-941-5879

Management Sector / Secteur de la gestion
Acting Assistant Deputy Minister, Joel A. Oliver
Tel: 613-941-7890
Fax: 613-957-6377
Corporate Counsel, Deborah MacNair
Tel: 613-952-1578
Fax: 613-946-2216
Chief Information Officer, Marj Akerley
Tel: 613-941-3444
Chief, Strategic Operations, Business Centre, Lise Jubinville
Tel: 613-946-8890
Fax: 613-952-2178
Director General, Strategic Planning & Performance Management, Nick Falcon
Tel: 613-946-3867
Fax: 613-941-3315
Director General & Senior General Counsel, Law Practice Management Directorate, Michel Francoeur
Tel: 613-952-5024
Fax: 613-946-3411
Director General, Human Resources & Professional Development Directorate, Joan Pratt
Tel: 613-941-1867
Fax: 613-954-3000
Acting Director General, Administration Directorate, Ivan Sicard
Tel: 613-957-6654
Fax: 613-941-0220
Senior Director, Portfolio Design & Development, Peter Mathieson
Tel: 613-952-3905
Fax: 613-941-3315
Director, Access to Information & Privacy Office, Francine Farley
Tel: 613-954-1207
Fax: 613-957-2303

Policy Sector / Secteur des politiques
Senior Assistant Deputy Minister, Donald K. Piragoff
Tel: 613-957-4730
Fax: 613-957-9949
Acting Director General & General Counsel, Youth Justice & Strategic Initiatives, David Dendooven
Tel: 613-954-3233
Fax: 613-954-3275
Acting Director General, International Legal Programs Section, Deborah Friedman
Tel: 613-952-6595
Fax: 613-948-8910
Director General & Senior General Counsel, Criminal Law Policy, Catherine Kane
Tel: 613-957-4690
Fax: 613-952-1110
Director General, Policy Integration & Coordination Section, Stan E. Lipinski
Tel: 613-941-2267
Fax: 613-957-4019
Director General, Programs Branch, Barbara Merriam
Tel: 613-957-4344
Fax: 613-954-4893
Senior Director, Policy Implementation Directorate, Elizabeth Hendy
Tel: 613-941-1085
Fax: 613-941-5446
Director & Senior Counsel, International Legal Programs, Aly N. Alibhai
Tel: 613-952-4032
Fax: 613-948-8910
Director & General Counsel, Security, Terrorism & Governance, Criminal Law Policy, Doug Breithaupt
Tel: 613-957-4743
Fax: 613-941-9310
Director, International Relations Group, Michelle Douglas
Tel: 613-957-4959
Fax: 613-948-8910
Director, Programs & Corporate Affairs, Youth & Strategic Initiatives Section, Hana Hruska
Tel: 613-957-3140
Fax: 613-954-3348
Director & General Counsel, Cabinet & Leg, Criminal Law Policy, Carole Morency
Tel: 613-941-4044
Fax: 613-941-9310
Director, Business Management, Senior Assistant Deputy Minister's Office, Paul Roy
Tel: 613-954-3890
Fax: 613-957-9949
Senior General Counsel, Family, Children & Youth Section, Elissa Lieff
Tel: 613-957-1200
Fax: 613-952-5740
Senior Counsel, Youth & Strategic Initiatives Section, Paula Kingston
Tel: 613-954-3187
Fax: 613-954-3275

Public Law Sector / Secteur du Droit public
Assistant Deputy Minister, Carolyn P. Kobernick
Tel: 613-957-4939
Fax: 613-957-1403
Director General, Trade Law Bureau, Matthew Kronby
Tel: 613-943-2803
Fax: 613-944-0027
Director General & Senior General Counsel, Human Rights Law Section, Jodie van Dieen
Tel: 613-952-4131
Fax: 613-952-4137
Director General & Senior General Counsel, Constitutional, Administrative & International Law Section, Laurie Wright
Tel: 613-941-2317
Fax: 613-941-1937
General Counsel & Director, Information Law & Privacy Section, Denis Kratchanov
Tel: 613-957-4624
Fax: 613-941-2002
General Counsel & Director, International Private Law Section, Kathryn Sabo
Tel: 613-957-4967
Fax: 613-957-3854
General Counsel & Director, Official Languages Law Section, Marie Tremblay
Tel: 613-941-4037
Fax: 613-952-0677
Senior General Counsel, Constitutional & Administrative Law Section, Ann Chaplin
Tel: 613-948-2992
Fax: 613-941-1937

Public Safety, Defence & Immigration Portfolio / Sécurité Publique, défense & immigration
Assistant Deputy Attorney General, Daniel Therrien
Tel: 613-952-4774
Fax: 613-957-7840
Executive Director & Senior General Counsel, Citizenship & Immigration Canada, Marie Bourry
Tel: 613-952-4763
Fax: 613-952-4770
Executive Director & Senior General Counsel, Public Safety Canada, Legal Services, Paul Shuttle
Tel: 613-991-9375
Director & General Counsel, Crimes Against Humanity & War Crimes, Terry Beitner
Tel: 613-954-2351
Fax: 613-952-7370

Tax Law Services Portfolio / Services du droit fiscal
Assistant Deputy Attorney General, Michelline van Erum
Tel: 613-957-4811
Fax: 613-941-1221

Senior General Counsel, Tax Law Services, Gordon Bourgard
Tel: 613-952-9810
Fax: 613-946-7449
Senior General Counsel, Canada Revenue Agency, Charles MacNab
Tel: 613-957-2358
Senior General Counsel, Canada Revenue Agency, Jean-Marc Raymond
Tel: 613-954-5881
Senior General Counsel, Tax Law Services Section, John Shipley
Tel: 613-957-4816
Fax: 613-941-2293

Laurentian Pilotage Authority (LPA) / Administration de pilotage des Laurentides (APL)

Head Office, #1501, 555, boul René-Lévesque ouest, Montréal, QC H2Z 1B1
Tél: 514-283-6320
Téléc: 514-496-2409
administration@apl.gc.ca; pilote-mtl@apl.gc.ca (Dispatch Center)
www.pilotagestlaurent.gc.ca
Autre numéros: Dispatch Center, Toll-Free Phone: 800-361-0747; Billing Department, Phone: 514-283-6320

In 1972, the Laurentian Pilotage Authority was created under the Pilotage Act.
The Crown corporation has the following objectives: to operate a pilotage service in Canadian waters in & around the province of Québec, except the waters of Cap d'Espoir & Chaleur Bay; to maintain a service in the interest of navigational safety; & to charge pilotage tariffs in order to finance operations.

Chief Executive Officer, Fulvio Fracassi

Director, Administrative Services, Claude Lambert
Tel: 514-283-6320 ext: 212

Director, Dispatch Services, Sylvia Masson
Tel: 514-283-6320 ext: 211

Director, Operations, Denys Pouliot
Tel: 514-283-6320 ext: 299

Officer, Human Resources, Nicole Sabourin
Tel: 514-283-6320 ext: 213

Secretary; Legal Advisor, Mario St-Pierre
Tel: 514-283-6320 ext: 209

Library & Archives Canada (LAC) / Bibliothèque et archives Canada

395 Wellington St., Ottawa, ON K1A 0N4
Tel: 613-996-5115
Fax: 613-995-6274
Toll-Free: 866-578-7777
www.bac-lac.gc.ca
TTY: 866-299-1699
Other Communication: Media Relations, Phone: 613-293-4298; Publication Orders: 819-994-4531; Interlibrary Loans: 613-996-7527; Theses Canada: 819-953-6221; Copyright Bureau: 613-992-2567

The mission of Library & Archives Canada is to collect & preserve the documentary heritage of Canada. Library & Archives Canada ensures that publications, archival records, photographs, sound & audio-visual materials, & electronic documents are accessible to all Canadians. The organization also works to facilitate cooperation among communities involved in the acquisition, preservation, & diffusion of knowledge. Library & Archives Canada provides services the the public, government, plus libraries, archives, & publishers.

Deputy Head, Librarian & Archivist of Canada; Chair, Heads of Federal Agencies, Daniel J. Caron
Tel: 819-934-5800
Fax: 819-934-5888
danielj.caron@lac-bac.gc.ca

Assistant Deputy Minister, Policy & Collaboration; Corporate Secretary, Hervé Déry
Tel: 819-994-6982
Fax: 819-934-4422
herve.dery@bac-lac.gc.ca

Chief Financial Officer; Senior Director General, Corporate Resouring, Mark C. Melanson
Tel: 819-934-4627
Fax: 819-934-4428
mark.melanson@bac-lac.gc.ca

Chief Operating Officer, Cecilia Muir
Tel: 819-934-5840
Fax: 819-934-4422
cecilia.muir@bac-lac.gc.ca

Senior Director General, Business Integration Office, Stuart Campbell
Tel: 613-293-7767
Fax: 819-934-4388
stuart.campbell@bac-lac.gc.ca

Director General, Strategic Planning & Infrastructure Management, Stéphan Déry
Tel: 819-934-5876
Fax: 819-934-5266
stephan.dery@bac-lac.gc.ca

Director General, Communications, Julie Hébert
Tel: 819-994-6766
Fax: 819-934-5839
JulieJ.Hebert@bac-lac.gc.ca

Director General, Open Data, Fabien Lengellé
Tel: 613-996-3405
Fax: 613-947-2706
fabien.lengelle@bac-lac.gc.ca

Director General, Appraisal & Acquisitions, Chantal Marin-Comeau
Tel: 819-934-5860
Fax: 819-934-7534
chantal.marin-comeau@bac-lac.gc.ca

Director General, Analogue Preservation, Robert McIntosh
Tel: 613-762-9354
Fax: 819-953-0070
robert.mcintosh@bac-lac.gc.ca

Director General, Stakeholder Relations, Fabio Onesi
Tel: 819-934-5858
Fax: 819-934-4422
fabio.onesi@bac-lac.gc.ca

Director General, Strategic Research & Policies, Lucie L. Séguin
Tel: 819-934-4310
Fax: 819-934-4388
luciel.seguin@bac-lac.gc.ca

Director General, Information Technology, Ronald Surette
Tel: 819-997-4111
Fax: 819-994-6835
ronald.surette@bac-lac.gc.ca

Director General, Business Architecture, Duc-Chi Tran
Tel: 613-222-0526
Fax: 819-953-0291
Duc-Chi.Tran@bac-lac.gc.ca

Library of Parliament / Bibliothèque du Parlement

Parliamentary Buildings, Ottawa, ON K1A 0A9
Tel: 613-992-4793
Toll-Free: 866-599-4999
info@parl.gc.ca
www.parl.gc.ca/About/Library/VirtualLibrary/index-e.asp
TTY: 613-995-2266
Other Communication: Visitor Information, Phone: 613-996-0896

The Library of Parliament provides services to parliamentarians & the public.
The Library of Parliament's Parliamentary Budget Officer offers analysis to Parliament about the country's finances & trends in the Canadian economy. Information is also available about proposed legislation, plus legislative summaries & research publications.
Services to the public include information about Parliament, classroom resources, & guided tours of the Parliament buildings.

Parliamentary Librarian, Sonia L'Heureux
Tel: 613-992-3122

Director General, Economic & Fiscal Analysis, Mostafa Askari
Tel: 613-992-8045

Director General, Information & Document Resource Service, Lynn Brodie
Tel: 613-996-8558
Fax: 613-947-9235

Director General, Learning & Access Services, Dianne Brydon
Tel: 613-996-0238

Director General, Parliamentary Information & Research Service, Jean-Denis Frechette
Tel: 613-995-1213

Director General, Expenditure & Revenue Analysis, Sahir Khan
Tel: 613-992-8044

Director General, Corporate Services, Lynn Potter
Tel: 613-992-6826

Senior Director, Industry, Infrastructure, & Resources, Lalita Acharya
Tel: 613-995-6494

Senior Director, Legal & Legislative Affairs, Kristen Douglas
Tel: 613-995-3476

Senior Director, Social Affairs, Yvan Gervais
Tel: 613-995-7383

Senior Director, Reference & Strategic Analysis, Joseph Jackson
Tel: 613-995-6363

Senior Director, International Affairs, Trade, & Finance, James Kalwarowsky
Tel: 613-995-2728

Director, Knowledge Management & Preservation, Sonia Bebbington
Tel: 613-996-3156

Director, Executive Services, Ted Buglas
Tel: 613-943-6375
Fax: 613-943-6383

Director, Information Technology Directorate, Ken Cameron
Tel: 613-944-7820

Director, Budget, Estimates, & Reporting, Jason Jacques
Tel: 613-995-3315

Director, Knowledge Organization & Discovery, Hélène Larouche
Tel: 613-995-0407

Director, Public Education Programs, Benoit Morin
Tel: 613-943-6401

Director, Collection Development, Chantal Poliquin
Tel: 613-996-1387

Director, Human Resources, Shirley Squires
Tel: 613-943-5929

Associate Director, Corporate Communications, Cynthia Cusinato
Tel: 613-992-8001
Fax: 613-943-6383

Parliamentary Budget Officer, Kevin Page
Tel: 613-992-8026

General Counsel, James Robertson
Tel: 613-995-9404

Marine Atlantic Inc. / Marine Atlantique

Corporate Office, Baine Johnston Centre, #302, 10 Fort William Pl., St. John's, NL A1C 1K4
Toll-Free: 800-897-2797
customer_relations@marine-atlantic.ca;
marketing@marine-atlantic.ca
www.marine-atlantic.ca

Marine Atlantic is a Crown corporation that strives to provide safe & environmentally responsible ferry service between the island of Newfoundland & the province of Nova Scotia.
Two routes are available. A year round service is provided between Port aux Basques, Newfoundland & Labrador & North Sydney, Nova Scotia. The second route is available between mid-June & late September between Argentia, Newfoundland & Labrador & North Sydney, Nova Scotia.

Chair, Robert Crosbie

President & Chief Executive Officer, Paul John Griffin

Chief Information Officer, Colin Tibbo

Vice-President, Customer Experience, Donald Barnes

Vice-President, Human Resources, Rhona Green

Vice-President, Finance, Shawn Leamon

Director, Passenger Services, Neil Paterson

Manager, Marketing, Vicki Rose

National Arts Centre (NAC) / Centre national des Arts (CNA)

53 Elgin St., PO Box 1534 B, Ottawa, ON K1P 5W1
Tel: 613-947-7000
Fax: 613-996-9578
Toll-Free: 866-850-2787
info@nac-cna.ca
www.nac-cna.ca
TTY: 613-947-7100

The National Arts Centre is a multidisciplinary, bilingual performing arts centre that was created by an Act of the Parliament of Canada & opened to the public in 1969. It is home to the National Arts Centre Orchestra. The National Arts Centre works to develop performing arts in the National Capital Region & to help the Canada Council develop performing arts throughout Canada.
The Centre raises approximately half of its revenues from ticket, food, & parking sales, & well as hall rental fees & fundraising through the National Arts Centre Foundation. Other revenues are derived from the federal government.

Chair, National Arts Centre Board of Trustees, Julia E. Foster
Tel: 613-947-7000 ext: 221
Fax: 613-996-9578

President & Chief Executive Officer, Peter Herrndorf
Tel: 613-947-7000 ext: 200
Fax: 613-238-4556

Chief Executive Officer, National Arts Centre Foundation, Jayne Watson
Tel: 613-947-7000 ext: 331
Fax: 613-947-8786

Chief Financial Officer, Daniel Senyk
Tel: 613-947-7000 ext: 585
Fax: 613-943-1399

Managing Director, NACO, Christopher Deacon
Tel: 613-947-7000 ext: 363
Fax: 613-943-1400

Managing Director, English Theatre, Nancy Webster
Tel: 613-947-7000 ext: 319
Fax: 613-943-1401

Director, Operations, Georges Bouchard
Tel: 613-947-7000 ext: 650
Fax: 613-947-4512

Director, Music Education & Community Engagement, Geneviève Cimon
Tel: 613-947-7000 ext: 374
Fax: 613-992-5225

Director, Human Resources, Debbie Collins
Tel: 613-947-7000 ext: 518
Fax: 613-943-1402

Director, Administrative Services & Information Technology, Doug Eide
Tel: 613-947-7000 ext: 403
Fax: 613-952-7682

Director, Production Operations, Paul Hennig
Tel: 613-947-7000 ext: 234
Fax: 613-943-8692

Director, Marketing, Diane Landry
Tel: 613-947-7000 ext: 328
Fax: 613-996-2828

Artistic Director, French Theatre, Wajdi Mouawad
Tel: 613-947-7000 ext: 311
Fax: 613-943-1401

Director, Communications & Public Affairs, Rosemary Thompson
Tel: 613-947-7000 ext: 260
Fax: 613-996-9578

Director, Patron Services, Fran Walker
Tel: 613-947-7000 ext: 275
Fax: 613-996-9578

National Battlefields Commission (NBC) / Commission des champs de bataille nationaux

390, av de Bernières, Québec, QC G1R 2L7
Tel: 418-648-3506
Fax: 418-648-3638
information@ccbn-nbc.gc.ca
www.ccbn-nbc.gc.ca
Other Communication: Communications, Phone: 418-649-6251; Customer Service: 418-649-6159; Archives: 418-648-2589; Finances: 418-648-4666; Activities: 418-648-4071

In 1908, an Act was passed to create the National Battlefields Commission. The purpose of the Commission is to acquire & preserve historical battlefields & to create national parks from these battlefields for the benefit of the public. The federal government agency, with its nine-member board of directors, operates under the portfolio of the Minister of Canadian Heritage.
The Commission has a sustainable development policy for the conservation of the Plains of Abraham park.

Secretary - Director General, André Beaudet
Tel: 418-648-3553
Fax: 418-648-3638

Director, Administration; Financial Services Agent, Paule Veilleux
Tel: 418-648-4666
Fax: 418-649-6345

Chief, Security Service, Jean St-Pierre
Tel: 418-648-4655
Fax: 418-649-6152

Officer, Customer Service, Marie Cantin
Tel: 418-649-6159
Fax: 418-648-3809

Officer, Cultural & Technical Services, Martin Duchesneau
Tel: 418-648-4687
Fax: 418-648-2263

Officer, Development & Marketing, Benoit Gilbert
Tel: 418-648-4796
Fax: 418-648-3809

Officer, Material Management, Philippe Lafrenière
Tel: 418-648-4599
Fax: 418-649-6345

Officer, Communications, Joanne Laurin
Tel: 418-649-6251
Fax: 418-648-3809

Historian; Archivist, Hélène Quimper
Tel: 418-648-2589
Fax: 418-648-3638

Forest Engineer; Supervisor, Major Events, Marc Pelletier
Tel: 418-648-7052
Fax: 418-649-6576

Consultant, Landscape & Envrionment, Marc Boilard
Tel: 418-648-4795
Fax: 418-648-3809

National Capital Commission (NCC) / Commission de la capitale nationale (CCN)

#202, 40 Elgin St., Ottawa, ON K1P 1C7
Tel: 613-239-5000
Fax: 613-239-5063
Toll-Free: 800-465-1867
info@ncc-ccn.ca; contracts-contrats@ncc-ccn.ca (Contracting)
www.canadascapital.gc.ca
TTY: 866-661-3530
Other Communication: Emergency Service, Phone: 613-239-5353; Gatineau Park Visitor Centre: 819-827-2020; Volunteer Centre: 613-239-5373; Skateway: 613-239-5234; Sponsorship: 613-239-5625

The National Capital Commission is a Crown corporation. It was established by Parliament in 1959 to act as a steward for federal buildings & lands in Canada's National Capital Region.
The Commission works to ensure that the region is a place of national significance & pride. It consists of the following corporate, advisory, & special committees: Executive; Audit; Governance; Advisory Committee on Planning, Design, & Realty; Advisory Committee on Communications, Marketing, & Programming; Advisory Committee on the Official Residences of Canada; & Canadiana Fund.
In accordance with the *National Capital Act*the Commission's board of directors is appointed by the Minister of Foreign Affairs, with the approval of the Governor-in-Council. The National Capital Commission is accountable to Parliament & reports through the Minister of Foreign Affairs.

Chair, Russell Andrew Mills

Chief Executive Officer, Jean-François Trépanier

Senior Vice-President, Public & Corporate Affairs Management, Diane Dupuis
Tel: 613-239-5363
Fax: 613-239-5007

Vice-President, Environment, Capital Lands, & Parks, Michelle Comeau
Tel: 613-239-5209
Fax: 613-239-5337

Vice-President, Finance & Procurement; Chief Financial Officer, Pierre Désautels
Tel: 613-239-5086
Fax: 613-239-5007

Vice-President, Capital Planning, François Lapointe
Tel: 613-239-5579
Fax: 613-239-5302

Vice-President, Real Estate Managemtn, Design, & Construction, Roland Morin
Tel: 613-239-5589
Fax: 613-239-5302

Vice-President, Human Resources, Manon Rochon
Tel: 613-239-5576
Fax: 613-239-5552

Director, Information Technologies & Geomatics Services, Martin Bernier
Tel: 613-239-5650
Fax: 613-239-5507

Director, Environmental Management & Protection, Steve Blight
Tel: 613-239-5583
Fax: 613-239-5336

Director, Digitial Communications Outreach & Youth Programs, Daniel Feeny
Tel: 613-239-5766
Fax: 613-239-5300

Director, Audit & Corporate Ethics; Chief Audit Executive, Jayne Hinchliff-Milne
Tel: 613-239-5629
Fax: 613-239-5695

Director, Marketing, Susan Kay
Tel: 613-239-5056
Fax: 613-239-5300

Director, Strategic Communications, Kathryn Keyes
Tel: 613-239-5636
Fax: 613-239-5758
kathryn.keyes@ncc-ccn.ca

Director, Official Residences, Art Marcotte
Tel: 613-993-2613
Fax: 613-993-8244

Director, Corporate Planning, Louise Mignault
Tel: 613-239-5734
Fax: 613-239-5039

Director, Public Affairs & Information Management, Sandra Pecek
Tel: 613-239-5155
Fax: 613-239-5274

Director, Design & Construction, Claude Robert
Tel: 613-239-5651
Fax: 613-239-5694

Director, Capital Celebrations & Program Operations, Guy Tanguay
Tel: 613-239-5245
Fax: 613-239-5013

Director, Capital Interpretation & Commemorations, Sylvie Tilden
Tel: 613-239-5242
Fax: 613-239-5333

General Counsel; Commission Secretary, Mark Dehler
Tel: 613-239-5102
Fax: 613-239-5404

National Defence Canada / Défense nationale

Major-General George R. Pearkes Bldg., 101 Colonel By Dr., Ottawa, ON K1A 0K2
Tel: 613-995-2534
Fax: 613-992-4739
Toll-Free: 800-856-8488
www.forces.gc.ca
TTY: 800-467-9877
Other Communication: Access to Information: 613-992-0996; Media Inquiries: 613-996-2353

The Minister of National Defence is responsible for the Department of National Defence (DND), the Canadian Forces (CF), & related organizations. Canadian Forces members protect Canada, defend North America, & contribute to international peace & security. The work of DND & CF includes the following: assisting civil authorities to protect national interests, to handle national emergencies & to maintain an adequate level of emergency preparedness throughout Canada; protecting Canadian approaches to the continent; promoting Arctic security; pursuing opportunities for Canada-U.S.A. defence co-operation; participating in multilateral operations through international organizations, such as the United Nations (UN) & the North Atlantic Treaty Organization (NATO); supporting humanitarian relief efforts; assisting in the restoration of conflict-devastated places; & participating in confidence-building measures, like arms-control programs.

Acts Administered:
Aeronautics Act, with respect to any matter relating to defence
Army Benevolent Act
Canadian Forces Superannuation Act
Defence Services Pension Continuation Act
Emergencies Act
Emergency Preparedness Act
Garnishment, Attachment & Pension Diversion Act, with respect to members & former members of the Canadian Forces
In addition, the DND administers, under the general direction of the Chief Electoral Officer, the Special Voting Rules (Schedule II to the Canada Elections Act) as they relate to Canadian Forces electors.
National Defence Act
Pension Benefits Division Act, with respect to members & former members of the Canadian Forces
Visiting Forces Act

Minister, National Defence, Hon. Peter Gordon MacKay
Tel: 613-992-6022
Fax: 613-992-2337
MacKay.P@parl.gc.ca; Mackay.P@forces.gc.ca

Parliamentary Secretary to the Minister of National Defence, Chris Alexander
Tel: 613-995-8042

Associate Minister, Hon. Bernard Valcourt
Tel: 613-996-3100

Deputy Minister, Robert Fonberg
Tel: 613-992-4258
Fax: 613-995-2028

Chief of Defence Staff, Gen. Walter Natynczyk
Tel: 613-992-7031
Fax: 613-992-3945
Note: In August 2012, Lt.-Gen. Thomas Lawson was announced as the next Chief of Defence Staff.

Vice-Chief of Defence Staff, V.-Adm. Bruce Donaldson
Tel: 613-992-6052
Fax: 613-992-3945
Other Communications: Secure Telephone: 613-995-0016

Associate Deputy Minister, National Defence, Matthew King
Tel: 613-992-0275
Fax: 613-945-7011

Chief, Review Services, Greg Jarvis
Tel: 613-992-7975
Fax: 613-992-0528

Chair, Defence Science Advisory Board, Wayne Williams
Tel: 613-992-4070
Fax: 613-996-9168

Legal Advisor, Oonagh Fitzgerald
Tel: 613-995-0828
Fax: 613-995-0943

Director, General Safety, Sylvie Chateauvert
Tel: 613-996-3551
Fax: 613-992-1512

Director, Civillian Employment Policies, Elaine Coldwell
Tel: 613-971-0525
Fax: 613-971-0300

Director, Diversity & Well-Being, Lorraine MacIver
Tel: 613-944-7002
Fax: 613-944-7055

Director, Military Personnel Research & Analysis, Susan Truscott
Tel: 613-992-6162
Fax: 613-995-5785

Director General, Policy Coordination, Nada Vrany
Tel: 613-995-8332
Fax: 613-995-2876

Director, Defence Force Planning, Col. Carl Wohlgemuth
Tel: 613-996-2776
Fax: 613-992-5484

Associated Agencies, Boards & Commissions:

• Communications Security Establishment / Centre de la sécurité des telecommunications
1500 Bronson Ave.
PO Box 9703 Terminal
Ottawa, ON K1A OK2
Tel: 613-991-7600
Fax: 613-991-8514
www.cse-cst.gc.ca
The Communications Security Establishment is Canada's national cryptologic agency, providing the Government of Canada with two key services: foreign signals intelligence in support of defence & foreign policy, & the protection of electronic information & communication.

• Office of the Communications Security Establishment Commissioner / Bureau du Commissaire du Centre de la sécurité des télécommunications
PO Box 1984 B
Ottawa, ON K1P 5R5
Tel: 613-992-3044
csec-ccst.gc.ca
The Commissioner reviews the activities of the Communications Security Establishment for compliance with the law; advises the Minister of National Defence & the Attorney General of Canada of any CSE activity not in compliance with the law; receives complaints about CSE activities; carries out specific duties under the public interest provisions of the Security of Information Act.

• Military Police Complaints Commission / Commission d'examen des plaintes concernant la police militaire
270 Albert St., 10th Fl.
Ottawa, ON K1P 5G8
Tel: 613-947-5625
Fax: 613-947-5713
Toll-free: 800-632-0566
commission@mpcc-cppm.gc.ca
Other Communication: Toll Free Fax: 1-877-947-5713
Quasi-judicial, independent civilian agency examines complaints arising from either the conduct of military police members in the exercise of policing duties or functions or from interference in or obstruction of their police investigations.

Commands / Commandes

Chief of the Air Staff, Air Command, L.Gen. Angus Watt
Tel: 613-995-9141
Fax: 613-995-8687
Other Communications: Secure Telephone: 613-996-5355
Chief of the Land Staff, Land Force Command, L.Gen. Andrew Leslie
Tel: 613-945-0442
Fax: 613-945-0445
Chief of Maritime Staff, Maritime Command, V.Adm. Dean McFadden
Tel: 613-945-0540
Fax: 613-945-7243
Commander, Canadian Operational Support Command, M.Gen. Daniel Benjamin
Commander, Canadian Expeditory Forces Command, L.Gen. Michel Gauthier
Commander, Canadian Special Forces Operations Command, Col. David Barr
Commander, Canadian Command, L.Gen. Walter Semianiw

Communications Security Establishment Canada / Centre de la sécurité des télécommunications Canada

Chief, John Adams
Tel: 613-991-7241
Fax: 613-991-8514
Chief of Staff to the CSEC Chief, Laurie Storsater
Tel: 613-991-7241
Fax: 613-991-8514
Deputy Chief, SIGINT, Shelly Bruce
Tel: 613-991-7240
Fax: 613-991-8514
Acting Deputy Chief & Chief Information Officer, Richard McDonald
Tel: 613-991-8880
Fax: 613-998-5811
Deputy Chief, IT Security, Toni Moffa
Tel: 613-991-7391
Fax: 613-991-8514
Director General, Audit, Evaluation & Ethics, Sue Greaves
Tel: 613-998-4954
Fax: 613-991-8514
Director General, Policy & Communications, Kathleen (Kathy) Thompson
Tel: 613-998-2595
Fax: 613-991-8514

Finance & Corporate Services / Finances et serices du ministère

Assistant Deputy Minister, Kevin Lindsey
Tel: 613-992-5669
Fax: 613-992-9693
Director General, Financial Management, Robert Bertrand
Tel: 613-992-6907
Director General, Financial Operations, Patricia Laviolette
Tel: 613-971-6506
Director General, Corporate & Shared Services, Larry Surtees
Tel: 613-996-6402
Fax: 613-992-8712

Human Resources - Civilian / Ressources humaines - Civils

Assistant Deputy Minister, Cynthia Binnington
Tel: 613-992-7447
Fax: 613-995-8938
Chief of Staff, Gail Johnson
Tel: 613-971-0248
Fax: 613-971-0236
Comptroller, LCol Marc Larochelle
Tel: 613-995-7238
Fax: 613-992-2648
Director General, Labour Relations & Compensation, Mandy Hanlon
Tel: 613-945-1278
Fax: 613-945-1190
Director General, Learning & Professional Development, Stephanie Poliquin
Tel: 819-997-2937
Fax: 819-994-1187
Director General, Civilian Human Resources Management Operations, Cheryl Read
Tel: 613-971-0524
Fax: 613-971-0103

Information Management / Gestion de l'information

Assistant Deputy Minister, John Turner
Tel: 613-995-2017
Fax: 613-995-2189
Chief of Staff, Guy Thibault
Tel: 613-992-5420
Fax: 613-995-2189
Director General, Information Management Technology, Len Bastien
Tel: 613-990-3625
Fax: 613-990-3773
Acting Director General, Information Management Project Delivery, Donald Messier
Tel: 613-992-9119
Fax: 613-944-8031
Director General, Enterprise Application Services, Michelle Tilley
Tel: 613-960-9915
Fax: 613-960-9920

Infrastructure & Environment / Infrastructure et environnement

Assistant Deputy Minister, Scott Stevenson
Tel: 613-945-7545
Fax: 613-995-6653
Chief of Staff, M.Gen. Daniel Benjamin
Tel: 613-995-7243
Fax: 613-996-9527
Chief Executive Officer, Canadian Forces Housing Agency, Dominique Francoeur
Tel: 613-998-5904
Fax: 613-991-1988
Director General, Real Property, Susan Chambers
Tel: 613-995-0923
Fax: 613-995-1031
Acting Director General, Nuclear Safety, Sandy Dewar
Tel: 613-992-8546
Fax: 613-992-5537
Director General, Environment, Rose Kattackal
Tel: 613-995-5586
Fax: 613-995-1031
Director General & Chief, Military Engineering, Col. Sylvain Sirois
Tel: 613-995-2415
Fax: 613-995-8261

Judge Advocate General's Office / Juge-avocat général
Tel: 613-992-5678
Fax: 613-992-1211
Judge Advocate General, B.Gen. Ken Watkin
Tel: 613-992-3019
Fax: 613-992-5678
Acting Deputy Judge Advocate General, Operations, Cdr. Geneviève Bernachez
Tel: 613-996-8998
Fax: 613-995-5737
Deputy Judge Advocate General, Military Justice & Administrative Law, Col. Blaise Cathcart
Tel: 613-996-4812
Fax: 613-995-3155
Deputy Judge Advocate General, Regional Services - Ottawa, Col. Dominic McAlea
Tel: 613-996-6456
Fax: 613-995-3155

Materiel / Matériels
Assistant Deputy Minister, Dan Ross
Tel: 613-992-6622
Fax: 613-945-0949
Chief of Staff, David Jacobson
Tel: 613-992-6794
Fax: 613-995-0028
Director General, Major Project Delivery (Air), André Fillion
Tel: 819-997-6306
Fax: 819-997-9699
Director, Major Project Services, Trish Cullen
Tel: 819-997-6134
Fax: 819-997-6072
Director, Major Project Delivery (Land & Sea), Ian Mack
Tel: 819-997-7429
Fax: 819-997-7310

Aerospace Equipment Program Management / Gestion du programme d'équipement aérospatial
Fax: 613-990-5236
Director General, William Kelly
Tel: 613-993-3354
Fax: 613-990-5236

International & Industry Programs / Programmes Internationaux et industriels
Fax: 613-995-0028
Director General, Wendy Gilmour
Tel: 613-992-3730
Fax: 613-995-0028

Land Equipment Program Management / Gestion du programme d'équipement terrestre
Fax: 819-994-3143
Director General, B.Gen. Alex Patch
Tel: 819-997-9474
Fax: 819-994-3143

Maritime Equipment Program Management / Gestion du programme d'équipement maritime
Fax: 819-997-7058
Director General, Cmdre. Richard Greenwood
Tel: 819-994-8718
Fax: 819-997-7058

Materiel Systems & Supply Chain / Systèmes de matériel et chaîne d'approvisionnement
Fax: 819-994-1627
Director General, Geneviève O'Sullivan
Tel: 819-994-9461
Fax: 819-994-1627

Procurement Services / Services d'acquisition
Fax: 613-992-7735
Acting Director General, Charles McColgan
Tel: 613-996-8935
Fax: 613-992-7735

Office of the Ombudsman / Bureau de l'ombudsman
Fax: 613-996-3280
Ombudsman, Pierre Daigle
Tel: 613-996-2089
Fax: 613-996-3280
Other Communications: Secure Fax: 613-996-9562
Director General, Operations, Nathalie Neault
Tel: 613-992-0780
Fax: 613-992-3167

Operational Research / Recherche opérationnelle
Director, Operational Research (Corporate, Air & Maritime), John Evans
Tel: 613-992-5026
Fax: 613-992-3342
Director, Operational Research (Joint & Land), Robert Dickinson
Tel: 613-992-6866
Fax: 613-992-3342
Director, Military Personnel Operational Research & Analysis, Kelly Farley
Tel: 613-996-1280
Fax: 613-995-2701
Director, DRDC CORA Director Corporate Services, Edward Pitula
Tel: 613-992-5209
Fax: 613-992-3342
Chief Scientist, DRDC CORA Director Corporate Services, Mr. Paul Comeau
Tel: 613-996-6502
Fax: 613-992-3342

Policy / Politiques
Assistant Deputy Minister, Jill Sinclair
Tel: 613-992-3458
Fax: 613-995-2876
Director General, International Security Policy, Michael Grant
Tel: 613-992-2769
Fax: 613-992-3990
Director General, Policy Planning, Michael Margolian
Tel: 613-992-0799
Fax: 613-995-0446
Director General, Policy Coordination, Nada Vrany
Tel: 613-995-8332
Fax: 613-995-2876

Public Affairs / Affaires publiques
Assistant Deputy Minister, Josée Touchette
Tel: 613-996-0562
Fax: 613-995-2610
Chief of Staff & Director, Col. Jacques Poitras
Tel: 613-995-1497
Fax: 613-995-2610
Director General, Marketing, Lisa Allaire
Tel: 819-997-1846
Fax: 819-997-1880
Director, Public Affairs Operations, Capt. (N) James David Scanlon
Tel: 613-995-0022
Fax: 613-995-2610

Science & Technology / Science et technologie
Assistant Deputy Minister, Dr. Robert Walker
Tel: 613-996-2020
Fax: 613-995-3402
Chief of Staff, René Larose
Tel: 613-996-7215
Fax: 613-995-3402
Director General, Defence Research & Development Canada - Centre for Security Science, Dr. Anthony Ashley
Tel: 613-944-8195
Fax: 613-995-0002
Director General, Research & Development Corporate Services, Colin McEwan
Tel: 613-992-6105
Fax: 613-996-0038
Director General, Defence Research & Development Canada - Centre for Operational Research & Analysis, Maria Rey
Tel: 613-992-5025
Fax: 613-992-3342
Director General, Science & Technology Operations, Rick Williams
Tel: 613-992-5776
Fax: 613-995-3402
Director, Science & Technology (Maritime), Keith Hendy
Tel: 613-992-7695
Fax: 613-996-7063
Director, Science & Technology (Human Performance), Kurtis Simpson
Tel: 613-947-7810
Fax: 613-990-1205
Director, Science & Technology (Land), Michel Szymaczak
Tel: 613-992-2608
Fax: 613-996-5177
Director, Science & Technology (Air), Joseph Templin
Tel: 613-992-4338
Fax: 613-996-5177
Director, Military Personnel Research & Analysis, Susan Truscott
Tel: 613-992-6162
Fax: 613-995-5785

Land Force Atlantic Area (Headquarters)
Halifax, NS
Tel: 902-427-7631

Land Force Central Area (Headquarters)
Toronto, ON
Tel: 416-633-6200
Commander, B. Gen. O.H. Lavoie, OMM, MSC, CD

Land Force Western Area (Headquarters)
Edmonton, AB
Tel: 780-973-4011
Commander, B.Gen J.C.G. Juneau

Maritime Forces Atlantic (Headquarters)
Halifax, NS
Tel: 902-427-6355
Commander, Rear Adm. Dave Gardam

Maritime Forces Pacific (Headquarters)
Victoria, BC
Tel: 250-363-2800
Commander, R.Adm. Bill Truelove

Secteur du Québec de la Force terrestre
Montréal, QC
Tel: 514-252-2777
Commander, B.Gen. Simon Hébert
BFC Bagotville
Alouette, QC G0C 1A0
CFB Borden
Borden, ON L0M 1C0
CFB Cold Lake
Cold Lake, AB T9M 2C6
CFB Comox
Lazo, BC V0R 2K0
CFB Edmonton
PO Box 10500, Edmonton, AB T5J 4J5
CFB Esquimalt
FMO, Victoria, BC V9A 7N2
CFB Gagetown
Oromocto, NB E2V 4J5
CFB Gander
PO Box 6000, Gander, NL A1V 1X1
CFB Goose Bay
Goose Airport, Happy Valley-Goose Bay, NL A0P 1S0
CFB Greenwood
Greenwood, NS B0P 1N0
CFB Halifax
Halifax, NS B3K 5X5
CFB Kingston
Vimy Post Office, Kingston, ON K7K 7B4
BFC Montréal
Richelain, QC J0J 1R0
CFB Moose Jaw
PO Box 5000, Moose Jaw, SK S6H 7Z8
CFB North Bay
Hornell Heights, ON P0H 1P0
CFB Petawawa
Petawawa, ON K8H 2X3
CFB ASU Shilo
Shilo, MB R0K 2A0
CFB Suffield
PO Box 6000, Medicine Hat, AB T1A 8K8
CFB Trenton
Astra, ON K0K 3W0
BFC Valcartier
Courcelette, QC G0A 4Z0
CFB Winnipeg
Westwin, MB R3J 3Y5
CFS Alert Unit of CFB Trenton
Belleville, ON K8N 5W6
CFS Leitrim
Ottawa, ON K1A 0K5
CFS Masset
PO Box 2000, Masset, BC V0T 1M0
CFS St. John's
PO Box 2028, St. John's, NL A1C 6B5

Canadian Forces College
Toronto, ON
Tel: 416-482-6800
Commandant, B.Gen. D.C. Hilton

Canadian Land Forces Command & Staff College
Kingston, ON
Tel: 613-451-5818
Commandant, Col. BWG McPherson

Royal Military College
Kingston, ON
Tel: 613-541-6000
Commandant, Commodore William S. Truelove
Calgary
#418, 100 - 4th Ave. SW, Calgary, AB T2P 3N2
Tel: 403-974-2822
Fax: 403-974-2829
ndpaocal@nucleus.com
Halifax
#209, 6080 Young Street, PO Box 99000 Forces, Halifax, NS B3K 5X5
Tel: 902-427-7452
Fax: 902-427-7455
ndpaoatlantic@ns.aliantzinc.ca
Québec
Tour Ouest, Guy-Favreau Complex, #911, 200, boul René-Lévesque, Montréal, QC H2Z 1X4
Tel: 514-283-5272
Fax: 514-283-5351
ndpao.mtl@videotron.ca

Toronto
4900 Yonge St., 6th Fl., Toronto, ON M2N 6B7
Tel: 416-635-4406
Fax: 416-635-2795
Toll-Free: 888-564-8625
NDPAO@bellnet.ca

Vancouver
#201, 1090 West Pender, Vancouver, BC V6E 2N7
Tel: 604-666-0199
Fax: 604-666-0156
pacificpa@forces.gc.ca

National Energy Board (NEB) / Office national de l'énergie (ONE)

444 - 7 Ave. SW, Calgary, AB T2P 0X8
Tel: 403-292-4800
Fax: 403-292-5503
Toll-Free: 800-899-1265
info@neb-one.gc.ca
www.neb-one.gc.ca
TTY: 800-632-1663
Other Communication: Toll-free fax: 877-288-8803

Federal regulatory tribunal whose powers include: authorizing oil, natural gas & electricity exploration; certifying interprovincial & international pipelines & designated power lines; & setting tolls & tariffs for oil & gas pipelines under federal jurisdiction. The NEB reviews Canadian supply of all major commodities, with emphasis on electricity, oil, natural gas, & oil & natural gas by-products. It also reviews the demand for Canadian energy in Canada & in export markets. In addition to its regulatory role, the NEB is responsible for advising the government on the development & use of energy resources. Its responsibilities include regulating exploration, development & production of oil & gas on frontier lands in a manner that promotes worker safety, environmental protection & resource conservation. The NEB is responsible for environmental matters relating to the construction & operation of facilities & programs within its jurisdiction. Its environmental activities are carried out in three phases: The first phase involves evaluating the potential environmental effects of proposed projects. In the second phase, the environment is protected through monitoring & enforcement of terms & conditions attached to project approval. The third phase include s ongoing monitoring of operations to ensure that cleanup, restoration & maintenance of sites & rights of way are conducted to acceptable standards. The Board also verifies that emergency response plans are in place & that it or the operator can respond immediately to any incidents

Acts Administered:
Canada Oil & Gas Operations Act
Canada Petroleum Resources Act
Canada Transportation Act
Canadian Environmental Assessment Act
Energy Administration Act
National Energy Board Act
Northern Pipeline Act

Chair & Chief Executive Officer, Gaétan Caron
Tel: 403-299-2724
Fax: 403-299-5503
gaetan.caron@neb-one.gc.ca

Farm Products Council of Canada (FPCC) / Conseil des produits agricoles du Canada (CPAC)

Building 59, Central Experimental Farm, 960 Carling Ave., Ottawa, ON K1A 0C6
Tel: 613-759-1555
Fax: 613-759-1566
fpcc-cpac@agr.gc.ca
www.fpcc-cpac.gc.ca
TTY: 613-759-1737

In 1972, the Natioanl Farm Products Council was established by Parliament. The National Farm Products Council became known as the Farm Products Council of Canada in 2009.
The mission of the council is as follows: to oversee the national supply management agencies for poultry & eggs & the national promotion research agencies; to liaise with provincial governments interested in the work of the national agencies; to review operations of the national agencies to ensure they act in accordance with the *Farm Products Agencies Act*; to investigate complaints in relation to national agency decisions & to hold public hearings if necessary; to administer the *Agricultural Products Marketing Act* & to encourage effective marketing of farm products; & to advise the Minister on matters related to the national agencies.
The Council consists of at least three members & up to seven. Members of the Council are appointed by Cabinet.

Acts Administered:
Agricultural Products Marketing Act, 1949
Farm Products Marketing Agencies Act, 1972
Farm Products Marketing Agencies Act, 1972

Chair, Laurent Pellerin

Vice-Chair, Brent Montgomery

National Film Board of Canada (NFB) / Office national du film du Canada

3155, rue Côte de Liesse, CP 1600 Centre-ville, Saint-Laurent, QC H4N 2N4
Tél: 514-283-9000
Téléc: 514-283-7564
Ligne sans frais: 800-267-7710
www.nfb.ca

The Board is mandated to initiate & promote the production & distribution of films in the national interest, with the primary object of interpreting Canada to Canadians & to other nations. Reports to government through the Minister of Canadian Heritage.

Government Film Commissioner & Chair, Tom Perlmutter
Tel: 514-283-9245

Director General, Accessibility & Digital Enterprises, Deborah Drisdell
Tel: 514-283-9246

Director General, Marketing & Communications, Nathalie Courville
Tel: 514-283-9246

Director General, English Program Branch, Cindy Witten
Tel: 514-283-9501

Director General, Finance, Operations & Technology, Luisa Frate
Tel: 514-283-9051

Director General, French Program Branch, Monique Simard
Tel: 514-283-9285

Director, Human Resources, Robert Paquette
Tel: 514-283-9108

Director, Technical Innovation & Resources, Joanne Carrière
Tel: 514-283-9258

Director, Administration, Luisa Frate
Tel: 514-283-9051

Edmonton
#100, 10815 - 104 Ave., Edmonton, AB T5J 4N6
Tel: 780-495-3013
Fax: 780-495-6412

Executive Producer, David Christensen
Tel: 780-495-3015

Halifax
#201 - 5475 Spring Garden Rd., Halifax, NS B3J 1G2
Tel: 902-426-6000
Fax: 902-426-8901

Executive Producer, Kent Martin
Tel: 902-426-7351

Moncton
#100, 95 Foundry St., Moncton, NB E1C 5H7
Fax: 506-851-2246
Toll-Free: 866-663-8331

Executive Producer, Jacques Turgeon
Tel: 506-851-6105

Montréal
1564, rue St-Denis, Montréal, QC H2X 3K2
Tel: 514-496-6887
Fax: 514-283-2816
cinerobotheque@nfb.ca

Québec
#368, 901 Cap Diamant, Québec, QC G1K 4K1
Tel: 418-649-6377
Fax: 418-649-6379

Toronto
150 John St., Toronto, ON M5V 3C3
Tel: 416-973-0904
Fax: 416-973-9640
ontarioinfo@nfb.ca

Toronto (French Program)
150 John St., Toronto, ON M5V 3C3
Tel: 416-973-5382
Fax: 416-973-2594

Vancouver
#250, 351 Abbott St., Vancouver, BC V6B 0G6
Tel: 604-666-3838
Fax: 604-666-1569

Executive Producer, Tracey Friesen
Tel: 604-666-3411

Winnipeg
#300, 136 Market Ave., Winnipeg, MB R3B 0P4
Tel: 204-983-3160
Fax: 204-983-0742

Executive Producer, Derek Mazur
Tel: 204-983-7985

France
5, rue de Constantine, Paris, 75007 France
paris@onf.ca
Other Communication: 33-1-44-18-35-40; Fax: 33-1-47-05-75-89

USA
#4820, 350 Fifth Ave., New York, NY 10118 USA
Tel: 212-629-8890
Fax: 212-629-8502

Head, North American Sales, Heather Wyer

National Gallery of Canada (NGC) / Musée des Beaux-Arts du Canada (MBAC)

380 Sussex Dr., PO Box 427 A, Ottawa, ON K1N 9N4
Tel: 613-990-1985
Fax: 613-993-4385
Toll-Free: 800-319-2787
info@gallery.ca; info@beaux-arts.ca
www.national.gallery.ca
TTY: 613-990-0777
Other Communication: Bookstore: 613-990-1970

The permanent collection of the National Gallery comprises paintings, sculpture, prints & drawings, photographs, film & video art from the Canadian, European, American & Asian schools. Special exhibitions as well as permanent installations of the gallery's collections are on display. The gallery also sends its exhibitions on tour across the country & participates in international exhibitions. Services provided to the public include lectures, talks, tours, films, workshops, concerts & a bookstore.

Chair, Michael J. Audain

Vice-Chair, Michael J. Tims

Director & Chief Executive Officer, Marc Mayer
Tel: 613-990-1927

Chief Curator & Deputy Director, David Franklin
Tel: 613-990-0497
dfrankli@gallery.ca

Deputy Director, Administration & Finance, David Baxter
Tel: 613-991-0040

Deputy Director, Exhibitions & Installations, Karen Colby-Stothart
Tel: 613-998-4917

Director, Corporate Secretariat & Ministerial Liaison, Matthew Symonds
Tel: 613-990-9232

Director, Human Resources Services, Michelle Miner
Tel: 613-993-2856

Curator, Canadian Art, Charles Hill
Tel: 613-990-0486
chill@gallery.ca

Curator, Contemporary Art, Josée Drouin-Brisebois
Tel: 613-990-7645

Curator, European & American Art, Dr. Graham Larkin
Tel: 613-990-8580

Curator, Indigenous Art, Greg Hill
Tel: 613-949-0327

Curator, Photographs Collection, Ann Thomas
Tel: 613-990-1961
athomas@gallery.ca

Associate Curator, Prints & Drawings, Sonia Couturier
Tel: 613-990-8981

Senior Media & Public Relations Officer, Josée (Britanie) Mallet
Tel: 613-990-6835

National Joint Council (NJC) / Conseil national mixte (CNM)

C.D. Howe Bldg., 240 Sparks St. West, 7th Fl., PO Box 1525 B, Ottawa, ON K1P 5V2
Tel: 613-990-1805
Fax: 613-990-7071
email.courrier@njc-cnm.gc.ca
www.njc-cnm.gc.ca

Provides a forum for consultation on labour issues between the Government of Canada & the bargaining agents for its employees.

General Secretary, Barry Fennessy
Tel: 613-990-1807
Barry.Fennessy@njc-cnm.gc.ca
c/o Human Resources Branch, Treasury Board
300 Laurier Ave. West, 4th fl.
Ottawa, ON K1A 0R5 Canada

Manager, NJC Operations, Nicole Paré
Tel: 613-990-1806
Fax: 613-990-7071
nicole.pare@njc-cnm.gc.ca

Committee Advisor, Jennifer Murphy
Tel: 613-990-1725
Fax: 613-990-7071
jennifer.murphy@njc-cnm.gc.ca

National Parole Board / Commission nationale des libérations conditionnelles

410 Laurier Ave. West, Ottawa, ON K1A 0R1
Tel: 613-954-7474
Fax: 613-995-4380
Toll-Free: 800-874-2652
info@npb-cnlc.gc.ca
www.npb-cnlc.gc.ca
Other Communication: Communications Inquiries Phone: 613-954-6549; Pardons - Requests for Application Kit Toll Free: 1-800-874-2652; Victims Information Line Toll Free: 1-866-789-4636

Part of the criminal justice system, the National Parole Board makes independent, conditional release & pardon decisions & clemency recommendations. The Board also works to facilitate integration of offenders as law-abiding citizens.

Acts Administered:
Corrections & Conditional Release Act
Criminal Code
Criminal Records Act

Chair, Harvey Cenaiko
Tel: 613-941-1154
Fax: 613-941-9426

Executive Vice-Chair, Marie-France Pelletier
Tel: 613-954-6120

Executive Director, Shelley Trevethan
Tel: 613-954-1153

Manager, Appeal Division, Denise Leblanc
Tel: 613-954-5940

Director, Communications, Caroline Douglas
Tel: 613-954-6547

Senior Counsel, Legal Services, Gertrude Lavigne
Tel: 613-954-7451

Atlantic
1045 Main St., 1st Fl., Moncton, NB E1C 1H1
Tel: 506-851-6345
Fax: 506-851-6926

Regional Director General, Brian Chase
Tel: 506-851-6492
Vice-Chairperson, Louis-Philippe McGraw
Tel: 506-851-6490

Ontario
516 O'Connor Dr., Kingston, ON K7P 1N3
Tel: 613-634-3857
Fax: 613-634-3861

Regional Director General, Denise Preston
Tel: 613-384-7621
Vice-Chairperson, Fred Tufnell

Pacific
1925 McCallum Road, 2nd Floor, Abbotsford, BC V2S 3N2
Tel: 604-870-2468
Fax: 604-870-2498

Regional Director General, Harold Massey
Vice-Chairperson, Kelly-Ann Speck
Tel: 604-870-2479

Prairies - Saskatoon
101 - 22 St. East, 6th Fl., Saskatoon, SK S7K 0E1
Tel: 306-975-4228
Fax: 306-975-5892

Regional Director General, Michelle Van De Bogart
Tel: 780-442-6770

Prairies - Edmonton
Scotia Place, Scotia 2, #401, 10060 Jasper Avenue, 4th Floor, Edmonton, AB T5J 3R8
Tel: 780-495-3404
Fax: 780-495-3475

Regional Director General, Michelle Van De Bogart

Québec
Complexe Guy-Favreau, Tour ouest, #1001, 200, boul René-Lévesque ouest, Montréal, QC H2Z 1X4
Tel: 514-283-4584
Fax: 514-283-5484

Regional Director, Jean-Marc Trudeau
Tel: 514-283-4584
Vice-Chairperson, Denis Couillard
Tel: 514-283-4584

National Research Council Canada (NRC) / Conseil national de recherches Canada (CNRC)

Bldg. M-58, 1200 Montreal Rd., Ottawa, ON K1A 0R6
Tel: 613-993-9101
Fax: 613-952-7928
Toll-Free: 877-672-2672
info@nrc-cnrc.ca
www.nrc-cnrc.ca
TTY: 613-952-9907
Other Communication: IRAP Information: 613-993-1790; CISTI Information: 613-993-1600

NRC is Canada's principal public science & technology agency. It performs, supports & promotes scientific & industrial research for economic & social benefits, research & development in the national interest. Contributions are made to the national science & technology infrastructure & the development of a highly skilled workforce is fostered. Activities focus on strengthening industrial partnerships to bolster competitiveness in key information & telecommunications technologies. The Canada Institute for Scientific & Technical Information (CISTI), a component of NRC, provides access to hundreds of national/international databases, more than 50,000 journals, millions of books, technical reports & conference proceedings. Provides: customized literature searches; current awareness services; access to scientific, technical & medical databases; & referrals to experts. CISTI has an integrated online catalog accessible via the Internet. It publishes 14 international research journals including "Environmental Reviews". The NRC Industrial Research Assistance Program (IRAP) is Canada's national technology transfer & diffusion network helping Canadian firms develop world-class technology they cannot generate on their own. Advisory services involve assisting firms to: define technical needs; identify technical opportunities; obtain technical information & assistance; solve process & production problems; access or acquire technology & expertise from Canadian or foreign firms; & access financial assistance where appropriate. Technical & financial assistance is provided for R&D projects & for adapting existing technologies, with emphasis on advancing unproven technologies to the point of performance testing

President, Dr. John R. McDougall
Tel: 613-993-2024
Fax: 613-957-8850

Vice-President, Research, Life Sciences, Dr. Roman Szumski
Tel: 613-993-9244
Fax: 613-954-2066

Vice-President, Research, Physical Sciences, Dr. Danial D. Wayner
Tel: 613-998-5404
Fax: 613-949-1314

Vice-President, Technology & Industry Support, Patricia Mortimer
Tel: 613-998-3664
Fax: 613-998-3839

Vice-President, Engineering, Dr. Ian Potter
Tel: 613-949-5955
Fax: 613-949-5987

Acting Vice-President, Corporate Management & CFO, Shane Brunas
Tel: 613-991-3773
Fax: 613-991-3774

Acting Secretary General, Robert G. James
Tel: 613-998-4579
Fax: 613-991-0398

Director General, Canada Institute for Scientific & Technical Information, Pam Bjornson
Tel: 613-993-2341
Fax: 613-952-9112

Director General, Industrial Research Assistance Program (IRAP), Dr. Tony Rahilly
Tel: 613-993-0695
Fax: 613-954-0501

Alberta & Northwest Territories
250 Karl Clark Rd., Edmonton, AB T6N 1E4
Tel: 780-495-6509
Fax: 780-495-6510

Director, Dr. Kashmir Gill
Tel: 780-495-2136
Fax: 780-495-6510
kashmir.gill@nrc-cnrc.gc.ca

Atlantic/Nunavut Region
1411 Oxford St., Halifax, NS B3H 3Z1
Tel: 902-426-3138
Fax: 902-426-1624

Executive Director, Bradley C. Goodyear
Tel: 902-426-1055
Fax: 902-426-1624

Pacific Region
#650 - 1185 West Georgia St., Vancouver, BC V6E 4E6
Tel: 604-221-3100
Fax: 604-221-3101

Executive Director, Christopher Ryan
Tel: 604-221-3163
Fax: 604-221-3101
christopher.ryan@nrc-cnrc.gc.ca

Newfoundland & Labrador
Kerwin Place & Arctic Ave., Memorial University, PO Box 12093, St. John's, NL A1B 3T5
Tel: 709-772-5228
Fax: 709-772-5067

New Brunswick
PO Box 5678 W, Fredericton, NB E3B 5G4
Tel: 506-452-3831
Fax: 506-452-3827
Toll-Free: 877-994-4727

Executive Director, David Healey

Ontario
#903 55 St. Clair Ave. E, Toronto, ON M4T 1M2
Tel: 416-973-4484
Fax: 416-973-4303

Acting Executive Director, Tomas Matulis
Tel: 519-880-9699
Fax: 519-880-1360

Québec
#P-101, 75, boul de Montagne, Boucherville, QC J4B 6Y4
Tel: 450-641-5300
Fax: 450-641-5301

Executive Director, Bogdan Ciobanu
Tel: 450-641-5305
Fax: 450-641-5301
bogdan.ciobanu@cnrc-nrc.gc.ca

Saskatchewan & Manitoba
435 Ellice Ave., Winnipeg, MB R3B 1X6
Tel: 204-983-0092
Fax: 204-983-8835

Director, Vivian Sullivan
Tel: 204-984-6477
Fax: 204-983-8835
vivian.sullivan@nrc-cnrc.gc.ca

Biotechnology Research Institute (BRI) / Institut de recherche en biotechnologie (IRB)

6100, av Royalmount, Montréal, QC H4P 2R2
Tel: 514-496-6100
Fax: 514-496-1928
bri-info@cnrc-nrc.gc.ca
www.nrc-cnrc.gc.ca/eng/ibp/bri.html

Prevention & pollution control, including technology & process development, identification & behaviour of pollutants, monitoirng & ecotoxicological risk evaluation; green technologies & sustainable development. BRI scientists have unique expertise in the biotreatment of contaminated soils, groundwater, sediments, air, & industrial wastewater. The Sector works closely with industry on the R&D of innovative environmental technologies. BRI is also a founding member of the Montreal Centre of Excellence in Brownfields Rehabilitation (MCEBR), a joint initiative between government & industry to carry out research, development, & demonstration projects associated with soil decontamination & site rehabilitation.

Director General, Dr. Michel Desrochers
Tel: 514-496-6101
Fax: 514-496-6388

Herzberg Institute of Astrophysics (HIA) / Institut Herzberg d'astrophysique (IHA)

5071 West Saanich Rd., Victoria, BC V9E 2E7
Tel: 250-363-0001
Fax: 250-363-0045
hia-www@nrc-cnrc.gc.ca
www.nrc-cnrc.gc.ca/eng/ibp/hia.html

Operation & maintenance of astronomical observatories as national facilities available to all interested scientists. Conducts research programs in the fields of astronomy, space science & studies solar activity measurements of trace elements in the atmosphere.

Director General, Dr. Greg Fahlman
Tel: 250-363-0040

Fax: 250-363-8483
Gregory.Fahlman@nrc-cnrc.gc.ca
Director, Dominion Astrophysical Observatory, James E. Hesser
Tel: 250-363-0007
Fax: 250-363-6970
James.Hesser@nrc-cnrc.gc.ca
Director, Dominion Radio Astrophysical Observatory, Dr. Sean Dougherty
Tel: 250-497-2359
Fax: 250-497-2355
sean.dougherty@nrc-cnrc.gc.ca
Director Operations, Central Services, Susanna Gibson
Tel: 250-363-0567
Fax: 250-363-0063
susanna.gibson@nrc-cnrc.gc.ca

Industrial Materials Institute (IMI) / Institut des matériaux industriels
75, boul de Mortagne, Boucherville, QC J4B 6Y4
Tel: 450-641-5000
Fax: 450-641-5101
Imi-Info@cnrc-nrc.gc.ca
www.nrc-cnrc.gc.ca/imi-imi
Materials processing technologies for the metal, polymer, aerospace & automotive sectors; virtual fabrication; advanced instrumentation & materials; envionmental technologies.
Director General, Dr. Blaise Champagne, Eng., Ph.D.
Tel: 450-641-5050
Fax: 450-641-5101
Blaise.Champagne@cnrc-nrc.gc.ca
Acting Director, Aluminium Technology Centre, Bernard Arsenault
Tel: 418-545-5546
Fax: 418-545-5543
Bernard.Arsenault@cnrc-nrc.gc.ca
Director, Modelling & Diagnostics, Jean F. Bussière
Tel: 450-641-5252
Fax: 450-641-5106
Jean.Bussiere@cnrc-nrc.gc.ca
Director, London - Center for Automotive Materials & Manufacturing (CAMM), Sylvain Pelletier
Tel: 450-641-5239
Fax: 450-641-5105
Sylvain.Pelletier@imi.cnrc-nrc.gc.ca

Institute for Aerospace Research (NRC) / Institut de recherche aérospatiale (IAR)
1200 Montreal Rd., Ottawa, ON K1A 0R6
Tel: 613-990-0765
Fax: 613-952-7214
www.nrc-cnrc.gc.ca/iar-ira
Development & use of national aeronautical facilities; advanced design & manufacture; transportation & safety; aerospace & the environment; international programs & strategic intelligence.
Director General, Jerzy P. Komorowski
Tel: 613-993-0141
jerzy.komorowski@nrc-cnrc.gc.ca
Director, Aerodynamics Laboratory, Dr. Steven J. Zan
Tel: 613-993-2423
Fax: 613-957-4309
Director, Aerospace Manufacturing Technology Centre, Pierre Dicaire
Tel: 514-283-9139
Fax: 514-283-9484
Director, Flight Research Laboratory, Stewart W. Baillie
Tel: 613-998-3071
Fax: 613-952-1704
Director, Gas Turbine Laboratory, Dr. Ibrahim A. Yimer
Tel: 613-991-1139
Director, Operations, Andrew B. Sullivan
Tel: 613-993-9447
Director, Structures, Materials & Performance Laboratory, Dr. Prakash Patnaik
Tel: 613-991-6915
Fax: 613-990-7444
Communications Officer, Sheila Noble
Tel: 613-991-5738
sheila.noble@nrc-cnrc.gc.ca

Institute for Biodiagnostics / Institut du biodiagnostic
435 Ellice Ave., Winnipeg, MB R3B 1Y6
Tel: 204-983-7692
Fax: 204-984-7217
Neela.Mitra@nrc-cnrc.gc.ca
www.nrc-cnrc.gc.ca/ibd-ibd
Director General, Dr. Ian Smith
Tel: 204-983-7526
Fax: 204-984-6978
Ian.Smith@nrc-cnrc.gc.ca
Director, Business & Corporate Services, Paul Wiebe
Tel: 204-984-6223
Fax: 204-983-3154
Paul.Wiebe@nrc-cnrc.gc.ca
Director, Research, Roxanne Deslauriers
Tel: 204-984-5146
Fax: 204-984-6978
Roxanne.Deslauriers@nrc-cnrc.gc.ca
Communications Officer, Valerie McPherson
Tel: 204-984-4890
Fax: 204-983-3154
Valerie.McPherson@nrc-cnrc.gc.ca

Institute for Biological Sciences (IBS) / Institut des sciences biologiques
Bldg. M-54, 1200 Montreal Rd., Ottawa, ON K1A 0R6
Tel: 613-993-5812
Fax: 613-957-7867
www.nrc-cnrc.gc.ca/ibs-isb
Research in molecular genetics, immunochemistry, microbiology, biochemistry, neurobiology including cell signaling, transduction, in vivo & in vitro models for therapeutics evaluation.
Director General, Dr. James Richards
Tel: 613-993-7506
Fax: 613-957-7867
James.Richards@nrc-cnrc.gc.ca
Director, Business Development & Research Services, Scott Ferguson
Tel: 613-990-5948
Fax: 613-952-5136
Scott.Ferguson@nrc-cnrc.gc.ca
Director, Immunobiology Program, Jean-Robert Brisson
Tel: 613-990-3244
Fax: 613-941-1327
Jean-Robert.Brisson@nrc-cnrc.gc.ca

Institute for Chemical Process & Environmental Technology (ICPET) / Institut de technologie des procédés chimiques et de l'environnement
Bldg. M-12, 1200 Montreal Rd., Ottawa, ON K1A 0R6
Tel: 613-993-4041
Fax: 613-957-8231
www.nrc-cnrc.gc.ca/icpet-itpce
Focuses expertise in the areas of process & materials chemistry, process technology & related environmental technology. Supports environmentally responsible manufacturing in the fuel cell, oil sands & bioproducts sectors. Aids manufacturing & industrial clients in optimizing their process operations & reducing the impact of their operations on the environment. Promotes business opportunities in collaborative research, technology licensing & fee-for-service arrangements.
Director General, Dr. Janusz Lusztyk
Janusz.Lusztyk@nrc-cnrc.gc.ca
Director, Commercialization, Kanu Sikka
Tel: 613-990-4624
Fax: 613-991-2384
Kanu.Sikka@nrc-cnrc.gc.ca
Director, Research, Kevin A. Jonasson
Tel: 613-993-6570
Fax: 613-991-2384
kevin.jonasson@nrc-cnrc.gc.ca

Institute for Fuel Cell Innovation (IFCI) / Institut d'innovation en piles à combustible
4250 Wesbrook Mall, Vancouver, BC V6T 1W5
Tel: 604-221-3000
Fax: 604-221-3001
info.ifci-iipac@nrc-cnrc.gc.ca
www.nrc-cnrc.gc.ca/ifci-iipc
Strategic research aimed at advancing fuel cell science & technology & facilitating the commercialization of hydrogen & fuel cell systems.
Director General, Maja Veljkovic
Tel: 604-221-3024
Fax: 604-221-3002
Maja.Veljkovic@nrc-cnrc.gc.ca
Director, Operations, David Semczyszyn
Tel: 604-221-3013
David.Semczyszyn@nrc-cnrc.gc.ca
Director, Science & Technology, Dr. Dave Ghosh
Tel: 604-221-3040
Dave.Ghosh@nrc-cnrc.gc.ca

Institute for Information Technology (IIT) / Institut de technologie de l'information
Bldg. M-50, 1200 Montreal Rd., Ottawa, ON K1A 0R6
Tel: 613-991-3373
Fax: 613-952-0074
Toll-Free: 877-672-2672
www.nrc-cnrc.gc.ca/eng/ibp/iit.html
Acting Director General, Andrew Reddick
Tel: 506-444-0555
Fax: 506-444-6187
andrew.reddick@nrc-cnrc.gc.ca
Acting Director, Research Programs, NCR, Charles-Antoine Gauthier
Tel: 613-993-8551
Fax: 613-952-7998
Charles-Antoine.Gauthier@nrc-cnrc.gc.ca

Institute for Marine Biosciences (IMB) / Institut des biosciences marines (IBM)
1411 Oxford St., Halifax, NS B3H 3Z1
Tel: 902-426-8332
Fax: 902-426-9413
communications.imb@nrc-cnrc.gc.ca
www.nrc-cnrc.gc.ca/imb-ibm
Aquatic animal health & nutrition; natural toxins; mass spectrometry & proteomics; cell & molecular biology.
Director General, Dr. Joan C. Kean-Howie
Tel: 902-426-8278
Fax: 902-426-8514
Joan.Kean-Howie@nrc-cnrc.gc.ca
Director, Corporate & Business Relations, Denise LeBlanc MacDonald
Tel: 902-426-2496
Denise.LeBlancMacDonald@nrc-cnrc.gc.ca
Director, Research, Aleksander Patrzykat
Tel: 902-426-4080
Aleksander.Patrzykat@nrc-cnrc.gc.ca

Institute for Microstructural Sciences (IMS) / Institut des sciences des microstructures
Bldg. M-50, 1200 Montreal Rd., Ottawa, ON K1A 0R6
Tel: 613-949-9660
Fax: 613-957-8734
ims.info@nrc-cnrc.gc.ca
www.nrc-cnrc.gc.ca/eng/ibp/ims.html
Director General, Marie D'Iorio
Tel: 613-993-4597
Fax: 613-957-8734
Director, Applications Technologies, Sylvain Charbonneau
Tel: 613-998-9414
Sylvain.Charbonneau@nrc-cnrc.gc.ca
Director, Materials Technologies, Thomas E. Jackman
Tel: 613-993-6711
Thomas.Jackman@nrc-cnrc.gc.ca
Director, Research Support Operations, Cheryl Lambert
Tel: 613-991-4650
Cheryl.Lambert@nrc-cnrc.gc.ca

Institute for National Measurement Standards / Institut des étalons nationaux de mesure
Bldg. M-36, 1500 Montreal Rd., Ottawa, ON K1A 0R6
Tel: 613-998-7018
Fax: 613-954-1473
alexandra.shaw@nrc-cnrc.gc.ca
www.nrc-cnrc.gc.ca/inms-ienm
Canada's national metrology institute (NMI), charged with the responsibility to investigate & determine standards & methods of measurement.
Director General, Dr. James W. McLaren
Tel: 613-993-7319
Fax: 613-952-5113
James.McLaren@nrc-cnrc.gc.ca

Institute for Nutrisciences & Health / Institut des sciences nutritionelles et de la santé
550 University Ave., Charlottetown, PE C1A 4P3
Tel: 902-566-7000
Fax: 902-569-4289
inh@nrc-cnrc.gc.ca
www.nrc-cnrc.gc.ca/inh-isns
Director General, Research, Dr. Joan C. Kean-Howie
Tel: 902-426-8278
Fax: 902-426-8514

Institute for Ocean Technology (IOT) / Institut des technologies océaniques (ITO)
Kerwin Pl. & Arctic Ave., PO Box 12093, St. John's, NL A1B 3T5
Tel: 709-772-4939
Fax: 709-772-2462
Noel.Murphy@nrc-cnrc.gc.ca
www.nrc-cnrc.gc.ca/iot-ito
Ocean technology research in the areas of offshore engineering, marine vessel design, underwater vehicles, propulsion, electronic navigation, ice-vessel & ice structure interaction. Provides assistance to Canadian ocean technology companies & Canadian government departments. Research services performed in the following areas: tanker offloading & stationkeeping, offshore platform efficiency, navigation safety, all aspects of ocean technology. The Ocean Technology Enterprise Centre assists in the growth & development of new ventures in ocean technology. The centre helps new & established enterprises to develop their concepts & technologies in a supportive environment, with access to IOT facilities & expertise.
Director General, Dr. F. Mary Williams
Tel: 709-772-2469
Fax: 709-772-3101
f.williams@nrc-cnrc.gc.ca
Director, Facilities, Carl J. Harris
Tel: 709-772-2326
Fax: 709-772-2462
Carl.Harris@nrc-cnrc.gc.ca

Director, Research, Dr. Bruce Parsons
Tel: 709-772-2326
Fax: 709-772-2462
bruce.parsons@nrc-cnrc.gc.ca
Communications Coordinator, Derek J. Yetman
Tel: 709-772-6001
Fax: 709-772-2462
Derek.Yetman@nrc-cnrc.gc.ca

Institute for Research in Construction (IRC) / Institut de recherche en construction
Bldg. M-24, 1500 Montreal Rd., Ottawa, ON K1A 0R6
Tel: 613-993-2607
Fax: 613-952-7673
Irc.Client-Services@nrc-cnrc.gc.ca
www.nrc-cnrc.gc.ca/irc-irc
Research areas include building envelope & structure, indoor environment, urban infrastructure, fire research, sustainable built environment & climate change. A special initiative is the National Guide to Sustainable Municipal Infrastructure, in partnership with the Federation of Canadian Municipalities, Infrastructure Canada & the Canadian Public Works Association, a collection of best practices for core infrastructure.
Director General, Morad R. Atif
Tel: 613-993-2443
Fax: 613-941-0822
Morad.Atif@nrc-cnrc.gc.ca

London - Centre for Automotive Materials & Manufacturing (CAMM) / Centre des matériaux et fabrication pour l'automobile
800 Collip Circle, London, ON N6G 4X8
Tel: 519-430-7166
Fax: 519-430-7064
John.Lyons@nrc-cnrc.gc.ca
www.nrc-cnrc.gc.ca/eng/facilities/imi/camm.html
The Centre for Automotive Materials & Manufacturing serves as the national headquarters for the National Research Council's automotive-related capabilities and facilities across Canada. Their purpose is to lead in the development of scalable, sustainable manufacturing technologies for green vehicles. CAMM research is focused on laser materials processing, electrolytic, physical & chemical vapor deposition technologies & composites in manufacturing.
Director, Dr. Sylvain Pelletier
Tel: 450-641-5239
Fax: 450-641-5105
Sylvain.Pelletier@imi.cnrc-nrc.gc.ca

National Institute of Nanotechnology / Institut national de nanotechnologie
Bldg. NINT, University of Alberta, 11421 Saskatchewan Dr., Edmonton, AB T6G 2M9
Tel: 780-641-1600
Fax: 780-641-1601
nintinfo@nrc.gc.ca
www.nrc-cnrc.gc.ca/eng/ibp/nint.html
Multi-disciplined research in physics, chemistry, engineering, biology, informatics, pharmacy & medicine, with applications in medicine & biotechnology, energy & environment, computing & telecommunications.
Acting Director General, Dr. Marie D'Iorio
Tel: 780-641-1610
Fax: 780-641-1601
Director, Business Development & External Relations, Richard Brommeland
Tel: 780-641-1620
Richard.Brommeland@nrc-cnrc.gc.ca
Director, Research Programs, Dr. Christopher J. Haugen
Tel: 780-641-1615
Chris.Haugen@nrc-cnrc.gc.ca
Research Officer, Nano Ethical, Environmental, Economic, Legal & Societal Issues (NEEELS), Michael D. Lounsbury
Tel: 780-492-1684
Fax: 780-492-3325
ml37@ualberta.ca

Plant Biotechnology Institute (PBI) / Institut de biotechnologie des plantes (IBP)
110 Gymnasium Pl., Saskatoon, SK S7N 0W9
Tel: 306-975-5248
Fax: 306-975-4839
pbi-info@nrc-cnrc.gc.ca
www.nrc-cnrc.gc.ca/pbi-ibp
Canada's national laboratory for advanced research in new exploitable methods for genetic alteration of plants & for biochemical control of plant development in agriculture. Engineering projects include cell & molecular biology of higher plants. Technical services include: DNA synthesis & sequencing, bio-nuclear magnetic resonance spectroscopy, mass spectroscopy, advanced training services, & expert consultancy.
Director General, Jerome Konecsni
Tel: 306-975-5575
Fax: 306-975-4191
Jerome.Konecsni@nrc-cnrc.gc.ca
Director, Business & Corporate Services, Jeffrey P. Parker
Tel: 306-975-5568
Fax: 306-975-4839
Jeff.Parker@nrc-cnrc.gc.ca
Director, Research, Suzanne R. Abrams
Tel: 306-975-5569
Fax: 306-975-4191
Sue.Abrams@nrc-cnrc.gc.ca

Steacie Institute for Molecular Sciences / Institut Steacie des sciences moléculaires
100 Sussex Dr., Ottawa, ON K1A 0R6
Tel: 613-993-1212
Fax: 613-954-5242
Huguette.Morin-Dumais@nrc-cnrc.gc.ca
www.nrc-cnrc.gc.ca/sims-issm
NRC-SIMS conducts cutting-edge interdisciplinary research in selected areas of molecular sciences that have the potential to stimulate entirely new or emerging sectors of the Canadian economy. Strategic molecular sciences research fields for NRC-SIMS include: nanoscience, chemical biology, diagnostics, laser science, molecular interfaces, advanced materials, & their related technologies.
Acting Director General, Dr. James B. Webb
Tel: 613-990-0915
James.Webb@nrc-cnrc.gc.ca

Canadian Hydraulics Centre (CHC) / Centre canadien d'hydraulique (CCH)
1200 Montreal Rd., Ottawa, ON K1A 0R6
Tel: 613-993-9381
Fax: 613-952-7679
info.chc@nrc-cnrc.gc.ca
www.nrc-cnrc.gc.ca/chc-chc
One of North America's largest hydraulic engineering laboratories, with expertise & experience in physical & numerical modeling, analysis & field studies to solve a wide range of hydraulic engineering problems. Specializations include: coastal engineering; marine structures; cold regions; environmental hydraulics; laboratory technologies; numerical models. Environmental hydraulics services include: coastal ecosystem management; river & watershed management; flood management & dam break; chemical & oil spill migration; water quality & pollutant transport; sediment transport, including shoreline erosion & dredged spoil disposal; aquaculture management; environmental information & simulation systems.
Acting General Manager, Eric Magel
Tel: 613-993-2417
Fax: 613-952-7679
Group Leader, Coastal Engineering, Andrew M. Cornett
Tel: 613-993-6690
Andrew.Cornett@nrc-cnrc.gc.ca

Centre for Surface Transportation Technology (CSTT) / Centre de technologie des transports de surface (CTTS)
2320 Lester Rd., Ottawa, ON K1V 1S2
Tel: 613-998-9639
Fax: 613-957-0831
inquiries.cstt@nrc-cnrc.gc.ca
www.nrc-cnrc.gc.ca/cstt-ctts
Road & rail vehicle performance technology, studies & rail tribology; climatic engineering.
Director General, Paul Treboutat
Tel: 613-998-9635
Paul.Treboutat@nrc-cnrc.gc.ca
Director, Rail Division, Harold M. Kohn
Tel: 613-991-5522
Harold.Kohn@nrc-cnrc.gc.ca
Director, Road Vehicles & Military Systems Division, Michael S. Halasz
Tel: 613-998-8015
Michael.Halasz@nrc-cnrc.gc.ca

National Round Table on the Environment & Economy (NRTEE) / Table ronde nationale sur l'environnement et l'économie (TRNEE)

#200, 344 Slater St., Ottawa, ON K1R 7Y3
Tel: 613-992-7189
Fax: 613-992-7385
info@nrtee-trnee.ca
www.nrtee-trnee.ca
The National Round Table on the Environment & the Economy is an independent agency of the federal government committed to providing decision makers & opinion leaders with reliable information & objective views on the current state of the debate on the environment & the economy. Working with stakeholders across Canada, the NRTEE carries out its mandate by identifying key issues with both environmental & economic implications, fully exploring these implications, & suggesting action designed to balance economic prosperity with environmental preservation. A multistakeholder approach, combined with impartiality & neutrality, are the hallmarks of the NRTEE's activities. By creating an atmosphere in which all points of view can be expressed freely & debated openly, the NRTEE has established a process whereby stakeholders themselves define the environment/economy interface within issues, determine areas of consensus & identify the reasons for disagreement in other areas. The NRTEE's programs focus on the following areas: energy & climate change; capital markets & sustainability; climate change adaptation

Acting President & Chief Executive Officer, Jim McLaughlin
Tel: 613-947-4507
jim.mclachlan@nrtee-trnee.gc.ca

Director, Policy & Research, René Drolet
Tel: 613-996-4501
rene.drolet@nrtee-trnee.gc.ca

Director, Communications & Public Affairs, Marie-Josée Lapointe
Tel: 613-943-2054
mariejosee.lapointe@nrtee-trnee.gc.ca

Manager, Human Resources & Administrative Services, Hélène Sutton
Tel: 613-992-7181

Manager, Finance & Contracts, Duane Wilson
Tel: 613-947-4421
duane.wilson@nrtee-trnee.gc.ca

Office & Facility Coordinator, Corporate Services, Kim Laforge
Tel: 613-947-4419
kim.laforge@nrtee-trnee.gc.ca

National Search & Rescue Secretariat / Secrétariat national de recherches et sauvetage

#400, 275 Slater St., Ottawa, ON K1A 0K2
Tel: 613-992-0054
Fax: 613-996-3746
Toll-Free: 800-727-9414
inquiry@nss.gc.ca
www.nss.gc.ca
Provides a central managerial role in the overall coordination of search & rescue. It addresses program & policy issues related to the National Search & Rescue Program, & advises the Lead Minister for search & rescue.

Executive Director, Géraldine Underdown
Tel: 613-992-0054
Fax: 613-996-3746

Communications Officer, Kim Fauteux
Tel: 613-992-3472
Fax: 613-996-3746

National Seniors Council (NSC) / Conseil national des aînés (CNA)

Place Vanier, Tower B, 355 North River Rd. 14th Fl., PO Box 4, Ottawa, ON K1A 0K9
Fax: 613-946-8871
Toll-Free: 800-622-6232
nsc-cna@hrsdc-rhdcc.gc.ca
www.seniorscouncil.gc.ca
TTY: 800-926-9105
The Council, formerly known as the National Advisory Council on Aging, advises the Minister of Health on issues related to the aging of the Canadian population & the quality of life of seniors. It reviews the needs & problems of seniors & recommends remedial action, liaises with other groups interested in aging, encourages public discussion & publishes & disseminates information on aging.

Chair, Jean-Guy Souliere

Natural Resources Canada (NRCan) / Ressources naturelles Canada (RNCan)

580 Booth St., Ottawa, ON K1A 0E4
Tel: 613-995-0947
Fax: 613-992-7211
www.nrcan-rncan.gc.ca/com/
TTY: 613-996-4397
Other Communication: Emergency Operations Centre: 613-995-5555, 613-943-0000
Advances development of Canada's economy by contributing to the development & use of Canada's mineral & energy resources in a manner consistent with federal environmental & social objectives; advances knowledge of the Canadian landmass through scientific & science-related activities.
Acts Administered:
Acts Administered in Part by Natural Resources Canada
Administration of Acts with respect to Changes in Provincial Boundaries

Alberta Act
Alberta/BC Boundary Act, 1974
Alberta/NWT Boundary Act, 1958
Arctic Shipping Pollution Prevention Regulations
Arctic Waters Experimental Pollution Regulations
Arctic Waters Pollution Prevention Act
Arctic Waters Pollution Prevention Act (Transport Canada/Indian & Northern Affairs)
Arctic Waters Pollution Prevention Regulations
BC-Yukon-NWT Boundary Act, 1967
British Columbia 1857, 1866
Canada Foundation for Sustainable Development Technology Act
Canada Lands Survey Act (Indian & Northern Affairs)
Canada Lands Surveys Examination Regulation
Canada Oil & Gas Certificate of Fitness Regulations
Canada Oil & Gas Diving Regulations
Canada Oil & Gas Drilling Regulations
Canada Oil & Gas Geophysical Operations Regulations
Canada Oil & Gas Installations Regulations
Canada Oil & Gas Operations Act (Indian Affairs & Northern Development)
Canada Oil & Gas Operations Regulations
Canada Oil & Gas Production & Conservation Regulations
Canada Petroleum Resources Act
Canada Petroleum Resources Act (Indian & Northern Affairs)
Canada-Newfoundland Atlantic Accord Implementation Act
Canada-Newfoundland Oil & Gas Spills & Debris Liability Regulations
Canada-Newfoundland Oil & Gas Spills & Debris Liability Regulations
Canada-Nova Scotia Offshore Petroleum Resources Accord Implementation Act
Canada-Nova Scotia Oil & Gas Spills & Debris Liability Regulations
Canadian Nuclear Safety Commission Rules of Procedure
Canadian Ownership & Control Determination Act
Cape Breton Development Corporation Act
Class I Nuclear Facilities Regulations
Class II Nuclear Facilities & Prescribed Equipment Regulations
Co-operative Energy Act
Department of Natural Resources Act
Energy Administration Act
Energy Efficiency Act
Energy Monitoring Act
Energy Supplies Emergency Act
Environmental Studies Research Fund Regions Regulations
Explosives Act
Forestry Act
Frontier Lands Petroleum Royalty Regulations
Frontier Lands Registration Regulations
General Nuclear Safety & Control Regulations
Gros Morne Forestry Timber Regulations
Hibernia Development Project Act
International Boundary Commission Act
Keewatin Act
Lancaster Sound Designated Area Regulations
Land Survey Tariff Regulations
Lands Surveyors Act
Lands Surveys Act
Manitoba Boundaries Extension Act, 1912
Manitoba-NWT Boundary Act, 1966
Manitoba/Saskatchewan Boundary Act, 1966
Motor Vehicle Fuel Consumption Standards Act
National Energy Board Act
National Energy Board Act (Transport Canada)
National Energy Board Coast Recovery Regulations
National Energy Board Electricity Regulations
National Energy Board Export & Import Reporting Regulations
National Energy Board Pipeline Crossing Regulations, I & II
National Energy Board Processing Plant Regulations
National Energy Board Rules of Practice & Procedure
National Energy Board Substituted Service Regulations
New Brunswick, 1851
Newfoundland & Labrador Offshore Area Line Regulations
Newfoundland Offshore Area Oil & Gas Operations Regulations
Newfoundland Offshore Area Oil & Gas Operations Regulations
Newfoundland Offshore Area Petroleum Diving Regulations
Newfoundland Offshore Area Petroleum Diving Regulations
Newfoundland Offshore Area Petroleum Geophysical Operations Regulations
Newfoundland Offshore Area Petroleum Geophysical Operations Regulations
Newfoundland Offshore Area Petroleum Production & Conservation Regulations
Newfoundland Offshore Area Petroleum Production & Conservation Regulations
Newfoundland Offshore Area Registration Regulations
Newfoundland Offshore Area Registration Regulations
Newfoundland Offshore Certificate of Fitness Regulations
Newfoundland Offshore Petroleum Drilling Regulations
Newfoundland Offshore Petroleum Drilling Regulations
Newfoundland Offshore Petroleum Installations Regulations
Newfoundland Offshore Petroleum Installations Regulations
Newfoundland Offshore Petroleum Resource Revenue Fund Regulations
Newfoundland, 1949
Northern Pipeline Act
Northwest Territories, 1905
Nova Scotia Offshore Area Certificate of Fitness Regulations
Nova Scotia Offshore Area Petroleum Diving Regulations
Nova Scotia Offshore Area Petroleum Drilling Regulations
Nova Scotia Offshore Area Petroleum Geophysical Operations Regulations
Nova Scotia Offshore Area Petroleum Installations Regulations
Nova Scotia Offshore Area Petroleum Production & Conservation Regulations
Nova Scotia Offshore Area Production & Conservation Regulations
Nova Scotia Resources (Ventures) Limited Drilling Assistance Regulations
Nova Scotia Resources (Ventures) Ltd. Drilling Assistance Regulations
Nova Scotia, 1851
Nuclear Energy Control Act
Nuclear Fuel Waste Act, 2002
Nuclear Liability Act
Nuclear Non-Proliferation Import & Export Control Regulations
Nuclear Safety & Control Act
Nuclear Security Regulations
Nuclear Substances & Radiation Devices Regulations
Nunavut, 1993
Oil & Gas Spills & Debris Liability Regulations
Oil Substitution & Conservation Act
Onshore Pipeline Regulations
Ontario Boundaries Extension Act, 1912
Ontario, 1889
Ontario-Manitoba Boundary Act
Order Exempting the United States Coast Guard Icebreaker \Healy\" from the Application of the Arctic Shipping Pollution Prevention Regulations"
Orders Prohibiting the Issuance of Interests at Lapierre House Historic Site (Yukon) & Rampart House (Yukon)
Packaging & Transport of Nuclear Substances Regulations
Pipeline Arbitration Committee Procedure Rules
Power Line Crossing Regulations
Prince Edward Island, 1873
Québec Boundaries Extension Act, 1912
Radiation Protection Regulations
Report on the State of Canada's Forests Regulations
Resources & Technical Surveys Act (Fisheries & Oceans/Environment)
Saskatchewan, 1905
Saskatchewan/NWT Boundary Act, 1966
Shipping Safety Control Zones Order
Timber Regulations
Uranium Mines & Mills Regulations
Uranium Mines (Ontario) Occupational Health & Safety Regulations
Uranium Mines (Ontario) Occupational Health & Safety Regulations
Yukon, 1898

Minister, Natural Resources, Hon. Joe Oliver
Tel: 613-996-2007
Fax: 613-996-4516
Minister.Ministre@NRCan-RNCan.gc.ca

Director of Parliamentary Affairs, Johnues Penner
Tel: 613-996-2007
Fax: 613-943-0662
john.penner@NRCan-RNCan.gc.ca

Deputy Minister, Serge Dupont
Tel: 613-992-3280
Fax: 613-992-3828
Serge.Dupont@NRCan-RNCan.gc.ca

Associate Deputy Minister, Karen Ellis
Tel: 613-996-9753
Fax: 613-992-3828
Karen.Ellis@NRCan-RNCan.gc.ca

Assistant Deputy Minister, Johanne Mongeon
Tel: 613-992-3457
Fax: 613-992-3828
Johanne.Mongeon@NRCan-RNCan.gc.ca

Chief Scientist, Geoff Munro
Tel: 613-947-1435
Fax: 613-944-4747
geoff.Munro@NRCan-RNCan.gc.ca

Chief Audit Executive, Joe Freamo
Tel: 613-996-4940
Fax: 613-992-8799
Joe.Freamo@NRCan-RNCan.gc.ca

Director General, Corporate Renewal Office, Sylvie Letellier
Tel: 613-947-7403
Fax: 613-992-8922
Sylvie.Letellier@NRCan-RNCan.gc.ca

Director General, External Relations, Mark Pearson
Tel: 613-996-6055
Fax: 613-996-0478
Mark.Pearson@NRCan-RNCan.gc.ca

Associated Agencies, Boards & Commissions:
• National Energy Board

Canadian Forest Service (CFS) / Service canadien des forêts
Tél: 613-995-0947
Téléc: 613-947-1208
CFS-SCF@NRCan-RNCan.gc.ca
cfs.nrcan.gc.ca
TTY: 613-996-4397

Promotes the sustainable development of Canada's forests & competitiveness of the Canadian forest sector for the well-being of present & future generations of Canadians. It focuses on forest science & technology, & related national policy coordination. The CFS maintains five research centres across the country that share responsibility for research in the areas of biodiversity; biotechnology; climate change; ecology & ecosytems; entomology; forest conditions, monitoring & reporting; forest fires; forest & landscape management; pathology; silviculture & regeneration; & socioeconomics.
Assistant Deputy Minister, Tom Rosser
Tel: 613-947-7400
Fax: 613-947-7395
Tom.Rosser@NRCan-RNCan.gc.ca
Atlantic Forestry Centre / Centre de foresterie de l'Atlantique
1350 Regent St. South, PO Box 4000, Fredericton, NB E3B 5P7
Tel: 506-452-3500
Fax: 506-452-3525
cfs.nrcan.gc.ca/regions/afc
Responsible for the overall Canadian Forest Service operations & programs in the Atlantic region. Liaises & negotiates with provincial government, industry officials, & other sector-related senior management on behalf of the CFS in the region.
Acting Regional Director General, Derek MacFarlane
Tel: 506-452-3508
Derek.MacFarlane@NRCan-RNCan.gc.ca
Director, Forest Production & Protection, Derek MacFarlane
Tel: 506-452-3680
Derek.MacFarlane@NRCan-RNCan.gc.ca
Director, Science, Bruce Pendrel
Tel: 506-452-3505
Bruce.Pendrel@NRCan-RNCan.gc.ca
Canadian Wood Fibre Centre (CWFC) / Centre canadien sur la fibre de bois (CCFB)
580 Booth Street, 8th Floor, Ottawa, ON K1A 0E4
Tel: 613-947-9001
Fax: 613-947-8863
cfs.nrcan.gc.ca/subsite/cwfc
The Canadian Wood Fibre Centre (CWFC) brings together forest sector researchers to develop solutions for the Canadian forest sector's wood fibre related industries in an environmentally responsible manner. Its mission is to create innovative knowledge to expand the economic opportunities for the forest sector to benefit from Canadian wood fibre.
Executive Director, George Alexande Bruemmer
Tel: 613-947-7331
Fax: 613-947-8863
GeorgeAlexande.Bruemmer@NRCan-RNCan.gc.ca
Great Lakes Forestry Centre / Centre de foresterie des Grands Lacs
1219 Queen St. East, PO Box 490, Sault Ste Marie, ON P6A 2E5
Tel: 705-949-9461
Fax: 705-541-5700
cfs.nrcan.gc.ca/regions/glfc
Responsibilities include: forest research & regional forestry activities in Ontario; provides the primary federal focus for forestry in Ontario; emphasis on boreal mixed wood forest management & environmental impacts of pollutants & forestry practices; efforts also directed at the reduction of losses from insects, disease & fire; ecosystem dynamics & classification; nutrient problems & impacts from forestry practices; acid rain impacts (carbon dioxide/nitrogen oxide interactions).
Director General, Theodore Van Lunen
Tel: 705-541-5555
Theodore.VanLunen@NRCan-RNCan.gc.ca

Laurentian Forestry Centre / Centre de foresterie des Laurentides
1055, rue du PEPS, CP 10380 Sainte-Foy, Québec, QC G1V 4C7
Tél: 418-648-3335
Téléc: 418-648-5849
lucie.labrecque@RNCan-NRCan-gc.ca
scf.rncan.gc.ca/regions/cfl
Responsibilities include: increasing scientific & technical knowledge in the area of forest biology which includes biodiversity, tree biotechnology & advanced genetics, pest management methods, & in the area of forest ecosystem which cover forest ecosystem processes, effects of forestry practices, landscape management & climate change.
Director General, Jacinthe Leclerc
Tel: 418-648-3957
Jacinthe.Leclerc@RNCan-NRCan.gc.ca
Director, Forest Biology Program, Lise Caron
Tel: 418-648-7616
Fax: 418-649-6956
Lise.Caron@RNCan-NRCan.gc.ca
Research Director, Forest Ecosystems, Vincent Roy
Tel: 418-648-3770
Fax: 418-649-6956
Vincent.Roy@RNCan-NRCan.gc.ca
Director, Planning & Development, Normand Laflamme
Tel: 418-648-2528
Fax: 418-648-2529
Normand.Laflamme@RNCan-NRCan.gc.ca
Northern Forestry Centre / Centre de foresterie du Nord
5320 - 122 St., Edmonton, AB T6H 3S5
Tel: 780-435-7210
Fax: 780-435-7359
cfs.nrcan.gc.ca/regions/nofc
Responsibilities include: socio-economics & forest sociology; fire ecology, environment, & advanced fire management & prediction systems; climate change & forest interactions; carbon budget modeling; forest health, insect, & disease monitoring & management systems; remote sensing applications & landscape level classification systems; ecosystems productivity; biodiversity. Regional coordination of national programs relating to Model Forests & First Nation Forestry. Responsible for the direction of forestry programs in the provinces of Alberta, Saskatchewan, Manitoba & the NWT, including R&D, & four federal-provincial partnership agreements in forestry.
Director General, Timothy Sheldan
Tel: 780-435-7202
Fax: 780-435-7396
Timothy.Sheldan@RNCan-NRCan.gc.ca
Pacific Forestry Centre / Centre de foresterie du Pacifique
506 West Burnside Rd., Victoria, BC V8Z 1M5
Tel: 250-363-0600
Fax: 250-363-0775
cfs.nrcan.gc.ca/regions/pfc
Responsibilities include: forest management of federal lands; first nations programs; first nations land claims resource analysis; economic analysis of the regional forest sector (value-added, labour costs, & industrial sustainability); national strategic planning for the forestry practices & landscape management networks; science & technology programs in both forest biology (ecosystems processes, climate change, pest management, & tree biotechnology). Advises the CFS ADM on all forestry matters relating to the Pacific & Yukon region. The Mountain Pine Beetle Action Plan 2005-2010 set out strategies for confronting the infestation.
Director General, Kami Ramcharan
Tel: 250-363-0608
Fax: 250-363-6088
Kami.Ramcharan@RNCan-NRCan.gc.ca

Corporate Management & Services Sector / Secteur de la gestion et des services intégrés
Tel: 613-995-4243
Fax: 613-922-8922
Assistant Deputy Minister & Chief Financial Officer, Bill Merklinger
Tel: 613-995-4252
Fax: 613-992-8922
Bill.Merklinger@RNCan-NRCan.gc.ca
Director General, Dr. David Boerner
Tel: 613-995-4314
Fax: 613-996-6575
David.Boerner@RNCan-NRCan.gc.ca
Director General, Human Resources & Security Management Branch, Kiran Hanspal
Tel: 613-996-4008
Fax: 613-995-0025
kiran.hanspal@RNCan-NRCan.gc.ca
Director General & Chief Information Officer, Information Management Branch, Michel Lessard
Tel: 613-943-0469
Fax: 613-996-2953
Michel.Lessard@RNCan-NRCan.gc.ca
Director General, Corporate Renewal Officer, Sylvie Letellier
Tel: 613-947-7403
Fax: 613-992-8922
Sylvie.Letellier@NRCan-RNCan.gc.ca
Director General, Financial Management Branch, Thérèse Roy
Tel: 613-943-8763
Fax: 613-996-2151
Therese.Roy@NRCan-RNCan.gc.ca
Director, Security, Safety & Emergency Management, Guy Morin
Tel: 613-943-0594
Fax: 613-943-0336
guy.morin@NRCan-RNCan.gc.ca

Earth Sciences Sector / Secteur des sciences de la Terre
ess.nrcan.gc.ca/index_e.php
Provides Canadians with timely & reliable geomatics & geoscience knowledge, products & services of the highest standards & in the most cost-effective manner possible. The Earth Sciences Sector is a predominantly science- & technology-based sector & includes the Geological Survey of Canada, Geomatics Canada, & the Polar Continental Shelf Project. These groups are major contributors to the comprehensive geoscience knowledge base of Canada & provide surveying, mapping, remote sensing, & digital information services describing the Canadian landmass.
Assistant Deputy Minister, Brian Gray
Tel: 613-992-9983
Fax: 613-995-1509
brian.gray@NRCan-RNCan.gc.ca

Canada Centre for Remote Sensing - Geomatics Canada / Centre canadien de télédétection - Géomatique Canada
Director General, Douglas Bancroft
Tel: 613-947-1358
Fax: 613-947-1382
Douglas.Bancroft@NRCan-RNCan.gc.ca

Coordination & Strategic Issues Branch / Direction de la coordination et des enjeux stratégiques
Director General, Marian Campbell Jarvis
Tel: 613-992-5032
Marian.CampbellJarvis@NRCan-RNCan.gc.ca

Geological Survey of Canada (GSC) / Commission géologique du Canada
601 Booth St., Ottawa, ON K1A 0E8
Tel: 613-996-3919
Fax: 613-943-8742
esic@nrcan.gc.ca
gsc.nrcan.gc.ca
Other Communication: Bookstore: 613-995-4342
Geoscientific information & research, geoscience surveys, sustainable development of Canada's resources, environmental protection, technology innovation.
Director General, Central & Northern Canada Branch, Daniel Lebel
Tel: 613-992-1400
Fax: 613-996-6575
Daniel.Lebel@NRCan-RNCan.gc.ca
Chief Geologist, Canada Nunavut Geoscience Office, David Mate
Tel: 867-975-4412
Fax: 867-979-0708
David.Mate@NRCan-RNCan.gc.ca
Program Officer, Atlantic & Western Branch, Dan Richardson
Tel: 613-996-9151
Fax: 613-996-6575
dan.richardson@NRCan-RNCan.gc.ca

Mapping Information Branch / Direction de l'information cartographique
Director General, Prashant Shukle
Tel: 613-947-0467
Fax: 613-994-6749
Prashant.Shukle@NRCan-RNCan.gc.ca

Energy Sector / Secteur de la politique énergétique
Tel: 613-996-7432
Fax: 613-992-1405
www.nrcan-rncan.gc.ca/eneene/polpol/index-eng.php
Develops & promotes economic, regulatory & voluntary approaches to encourage sustainable development of energy resources to meet domestic needs & export markets. Advises the government on federal energy policies, strategies, emergency plans & activities; promotes efficient energy use.
Assistant Deputy Minister, Mark Corey
Tel: 613-947-2751
Mark.Corey@NRCan-RNCan.gc.ca

Innovation & Energy Technology Sector / Secteur de l'innovation et de la technologie énergétique
Assistant Deputy Minister & Chief Scientist, Geoff Munro
Tel: 613-947-1435
Fax: 613-944-4747
Geoff.Munro@NRCan-RNCan.gc.ca
Director General, Strategic Science-Technology Branch, Martin Aubé
Tel: 613-996-8109
Fax: 613-947-1016
Martin.Aube@NRCan-RNCan.gc.ca
Acting Director General, Operations, Philippe Dauphin
Tel: 613-943-4195
Fax: 613-995-7868
Philippe.Dauphin@NRCan-RNCan.gc.ca
Director General, Devon Research Centre, Dr. Hassan Hamza
Tel: 780-987-8617
Fax: 780-987-8690
Hassan.Hamza@NRCan-RNCan.gc.ca
Director General, Varennes Research Centre, Gilles Jean
Tel: 450-652-6639
Fax: 450-652-5994
Gilles.Jean@RNCan-NRCan.gc.ca
Director General, Ottawa Research Centre, John Marrone
Tel: 613-996-8201
Fax: 613-947-2318
John.Marrone@NRCan-RNCan.gc.ca

Minerals & Metals Sector (MMS) / Secteur des minéraux et des métaux
Tel: 613-947-6580
info-mms@nrcan-rncan.gc.ca
www.nrcan-rncan.gc.ca/mms-smm
TTY: 613-996-4397
MMS is the federal government's primary source of scientific & technological knowledge, & policy advice, on Canada's mineral & metal resources & on explosives regulation & technology. In addition to housing three scientific research institutions, MMS has the government lead in promoting sustainable development & responsible use of Canada's mineral & metal resources. The Sector is a leader in the generation & dissemination of knowledge on the Canadian minerals & metals industry, & collaborates with & provides research services to governmental, institutional & industrial clients for the development of new technology with economic, environmental & social benefits to Canadians.
Assistant Deputy Minister, Anil Arora
Tel: 613-992-2490
Fax: 613-996-7425
Anil.Arora@NRCan-RNCan.gc.ca
Chief, Exploration, Industry Economics & Taxation Division, Louis Arseneau
Tel: 613-995-0959
Fax: 613-943-8453
Louis.Arseneau@NRCan-RNCan.gc.ca
Chief, Health & Safety, CANMET Mining & Mineral Sciences Laboratories, Katrina Nicholson
Tel: 613-996-0826
Fax: 613-943-0575
Katrina.Nicholson@NRCan-RNCan.gc.ca
Chief, Program Policy & Administration Division, Explosives Safety & Security Branch, Joseph Prokipcak
Tel: 613-941-9034
Fax: 613-948-5195
Joseph.Prokipcak@NRCan-RNCan.gc.ca
Inspector of Explosives, Explosives Safety & Security Branch, Mike Farbod
Tel: 613-996-6877
Fax: 613-947-1200
Mike.Farbod@NRCan-RNCan.gc.ca
Director General, Minerals, Metals & Materials Policy Branch, Ginny Flood
Tel: 613-996-5309
Fax: 613-952-7501
Ginny.Flood@NRCan-RNCan.gc.ca
Director General, CANMET Materials Technology Laboratory, Dr. Jennifer Jackman
Tel: 613-995-8248
Fax: 613-992-8735
Jennifer.Jackman@NRCan-RNCan.gc.ca
Director General, Explosives Safety & Security Branch, Patrick O'Neill
Tel: 613-948-5181
Fax: 613-948-5195
Director General, Minerals, Metals & Materials Knowledge Branch, Christiane Villemure
Tel: 613-996-5525
Fax: 613-943-8453
Christiane.Villemure@NRCan-RNCan.gc.ca
Director & Chief Inspector, Explosives Regulatory Division, Christopher Watson
Tel: 613-948-5170
Fax: 613-948-5195
Christopher.Watson@NRCan-RNCan.gc.ca
Director General, Joy Senack
Tel: 613-995-2821
Fax: 613-996-5943
Joy.Senack@NRCan-RNCan.gc.ca
Director, Analysis & Modelling Division, Hertsel Labib
Tel: 613-995-8762
Fax: 613-996-8123
hertsel.labib@nrcan-rncan.gc.ca
Director, Economic & Fiscal Analysis Division, Phyllis Odenbach-Sutton
Tel: 613-996-2663

Fax: 613-996-7837
phyllis.odenbach-sutton@nrcan-rncan.gc.ca
Director, International Environment Policy Division, David Henry
Tel: 613-996-6474
Fax: 613-947-6799
david.henry@nrcan-rncan.gc.ca
Director, Strategic Policy Division, Sheryl Groeneweg
Tel: 613-996-5473
Fax: 613-996-5943
Sheryl.Groeneweg@NRCan-RNCan.gc.ca
Director, International Energy Division, Kristi Varangu
Tel: 613-996-8904
Fax: 613-995-5576
kristi.varangu@nrcan-rncan.gc.ca

Natural Sciences & Engineering Research Council of Canada (NSERC) / Conseil des recherches en sciences naturelles et en génie du Canada (CRSNG)

Constitution Square, Tower II, 350 Albert St., Ottawa, ON K1A 1H5
Tel: 613-995-4273
Fax: 613-943-1624
marie-josee.duval@nserc-crsng.gc.ca
www.nserc.gc.ca

Science & Engineering Research Canada (NSERC) is a federal agency whose role is to make investments in people, discovery & innovation for the benefit of all Canadians. With an annual budget of more than $860 million, it supports more than 20,000 university students & postdoctoral fellows in their advanced studies. NSERC promotes discovery by funding more than 10,000 university professors every year & helps make innovation happen by encouraging more than 500 Canadian companies to participate & invest in university research projects.

President, Dr. Suzanne Fortier
Tel: 613-995-5840
suzanne.fortier@nserc-crsng.gc.ca

Vice-President, Research Grants & Scholarships Directorate, Isabelle Blain
Tel: 613-995-5833
isabelle.blain@nserc-crsng.gc.ca

Vice-President, Research Partnerships Programs Directorate, Janet Walden
Tel: 616-139-9215
Fax: 613-947-6371
janet.walden@nserc-crsng.gc.ca

Director, Communications Division, Jacqueline Couture
Tel: 613-995-5993
Jacqueline.Couture@nserc-crsng.gc.ca

Vice-President, Common Administrative Services Directorate, Jaime Pitfield
Tel: 613-995-3914
Fax: 613-991-0969
Jaime.Pitfield@nserc-crsng.gc.ca

Vice-President, Common Administrative Services, Michel Cavallin

Director, Finance & Awards Administration Division, Dominique Osterrath
Tel: 613-996-8269
dominique.osterrath@nserc-crsng.gc.ca

North American Free Trade Agreement (NAFTA) Secretariat / Secrétariat de l'ALÉNA

Canadian Section, #705, 90 Sparks St., Ottawa, ON K1P 5B4
Tel: 613-992-9388
Fax: 613-992-9392
webmaster@nafta-alena.gc.ca
www.nafta-alena.gc.ca

The NAFTA Secretariat, comprised of a Canadian Section, a United States Section & a Mexican Section, is responsible for the administration of the dispute settlement provisions of the North American Free Trade Agreement. The Canadian Section also carries responsibility for similar provisions under the Canada-Chile, Canada-Israel & Canada-Costa Rica free trade agreements.

Canadian Secretary, Marie-Josée, Langlois
Tel: 613-992-9380
marie.josee.langlois@nafta-alena.gc.ca

Registrar/Acting Deputy Secretary, Feleke Bogale
Tel: 613-992-9384
Fax: 613-992-9392
feleke.bogale@nafta-alena.gc.ca

Records & Information Management Officer, Marie-France Meunier
Tel: 613-992-2303
Fax: 613-992-9392
mariefrance.meunier@nafta-alena.gc.ca

Northern Pipeline Agency Canada (NPAC) / Administration du pipe-line du Nord Canada (APNC)

580 Booth St., Ottawa, ON K1A 0E4
Tel: 613-992-9612
Fax: 613-995-1913

Established to carry out federal responsibilities in relation to the planning & construction of the Canadian portion of the Alaska Natural Gas Transportation System.

Commissioner, Serge Dupont
Tel: 613-992-3280
Fax: 613-992-3828

Assistant Commissioner & Comptroller, Christopher Cuddy
Tel: 613-995-4297
Fax: 613-996-5354

Administrator, Carole Matte
Tel: 613-992-1150
Fax: 613-996-5354

Office of the Commissioner of Official Languages / Commissariat aux langues officielles

344 Slater St., 3rd fl., Ottawa, ON K1A 0T8
Tel: 613-996-6368
Fax: 613-993-5082
Toll-Free: 877-996-6368
www.ocol-clo.gc.ca
TTY: 800-880-1990

Responsible for ensuring the equality of English & French in Parliament, within the Government of Canada, the federal administration, & the institutions subject to the Official Languages Act; the preservation & development of official language communities in Canada; & the equality of English & French in Canadian society.
Acts Administered:
Official Languages Act

Commissioner of Official Languages, Graham Fraser
Tel: 613-995-7488
Fax: 613-943-2255

Director, Audits, Nycole Lafond
Tel: 613-943-1159
Fax: 613-943-0451

Director, Finance & Procurement, Colette M. Lagacé
Tel: 613-995-0412
Fax: 613-993-5082

Director, Human Resources, Mario Séguin
Tel: 613-943-0390
Fax: 613-944-5477

Director, Information Management & Technology, JoHanne Verrier
Tel: 613-943-0220
Fax: 613-947-4751

Director, Investigations, Carole Beauvais
Tel: 613-943-1161
Fax: 613-943-0451

Director & General Counsel, Legal Affairs, Johane Tremblay
Tel: 613-995-9069
Fax: 613-996-9671

Director, Operational Integration Initiative, Corita Harty
Tel: 613-992-9874
Fax: 613-995-1161

Director, Policy & Research, Johanne Lapointe
Tel: 613-943-0429
Fax: 613-995-1161

Director, Strategic Communications & Production, Robin Cantin
Tel: 613-995-9356
Fax: 613-995-1161

Director, Strategic Performance Measurement, Pierre Coulombe
Tel: 613-995-0815
Fax: 613-943-0451

Pacific Pilotage Authority Canada / Administration de pilotage du Pacifique Canada

#1000, 1130 Pender St. West, Vancouver, BC V6E 4A4
Tel: 604-666-6771
Fax: 604-666-1647
info@ppa.gc.ca
www.ppa.gc.ca
Other Communication: Vancouver Dispatch: 604-666-6776, Fax: 604-666-6093; Victoria Dispatch: 250-363-3878, Fax: 250-363-3293

Operates pilotage services in Canadian waters in & around British Columbia. Reports to government through the Minister of Transportation.

President & Chief Executive Officer, Capt. Kevin Obermeyer

Chair, David K. Gardiner

Director, Finance, Bruce Chadwick

Director, Operations, Capt. Brian Young

Parks Canada / Parcs Canada

25 Eddy St., Gatineau, QC K1A 0M5
Tel: 613-860-1251
Toll-Free: 888-773-8888
information@pc.gc.ca
www.pc.gc.ca
TTY: 866-787-6221

Responsible for the protection, management, operation & maintenance of national parks, historic sites, canals & other significant examples of Canada's natural & cultural heritage, for the benefit, understanding & enjoyment of Canadians. Administers one of the largest park systems in the world. Working towards establishing parks in each of 39 distinct natural regions. In addition to the national parks, national historic sites & national marine conservation areas, Parks Canada coordinates other heritage programs, including federal heritage buildings, heritage railway stations, grave sites of Canadian Prime Ministers, heritage rivers, archaeology programs, international programs.

Minister of Environment; Minister Responsible, Hon. Peter Kent
Tel: 613-992-0253
Fax: 613-992-0887
kentp@parl.gc.ca

Chief Executive Officer, Alan Latourelle
Tel: 819-997-9525
Fax: 819-953-9745

Chief Audit & Evaluation Executive, Office of Internal Audit & Evaluation, Brian Evans
Tel: 819-997-9928
Fax: 819-997-5285
Other Communications: Alt. Phone: 613-889-1675

Ombudsman, Luc Martin
Tel: 819-934-7000
Fax: 819-210-3645

Director General, National Parks, Ron Hallman
Tel: 819-994-2657
Fax: 819-994-5140

Director General, National Historic Sites, Larry S. Ostola
Tel: 819-994-1808
Fax: 819-934-1526

Communications Advisor, Joanne Huppé
Tel: 819-953-8699
Fax: 819-953-5523
Other Communications: Alt. Phone: 613-799-6269

Associated Agencies, Boards & Commissions:
• Historic Sites & Monuments Board of Canada / Commission des lieux et monuments historiques du Canada
Terrasses de la Chaudière
25 Eddy St.
Gatineau, QC K1A 0M5
Fax: 819-934-1115
Toll-free: 855-283-8730
hsmbc-clmhc@pc.gc.ca
www.pc.gc.ca/clmhc-hsmbc/
A seventeen-member advisory board which reports to the Minister of Environment & recommends whether persons, places or events are of national historic &/or architectural significance, & therefore warrant commemoration. The board also makes recommendations concerning the designation of heritage railway stations.

Canal Offices
Carillon
230, rue du Barrage, Saint-André-d'Argenteuil, QC J0V 1X0
Tel: 450-537-3534
Fax: 450-658-2428
parkscanada-que@pc.gc.ca
www.pc.gc.ca/canalcarillon

Chambly
1899, boul Périgny, Chambly, QC J3L 4C3
Tel: 450-658-6525
Fax: 450-658-2428
parkscanada-que@pc.gc.ca
www.pc.gc.ca/canalchambly
Other Communication: Lock #9 (Saint-Jean), Phone: 450-348-3392

Lachine
200, boul René-Lévesque ouest, tour Ouest, 6e étage, Montréal, QC H2Z 1X4
Tel: 514-283-6054
Fax: 514-496-1263
parcscanada-que@pc.gc.ca
www.pc.gc.ca/canallachine

Rideau
34 Beckwith St. South, Smiths Falls, ON K7A 2A8
Tel: 613-283-5170
Fax: 613-283-0677
RideauCanal-info@pc.gc.ca
www.pc.gc.ca/eng/lhn-nhs/on/rideau/index.aspx

Sainte-Anne-de-Bellevue
170, rue Sainte-Anne, Sainte-Anne, QC H9X 1N1
Tel: 514-457-5546
Fax: 450-658-2428
parkscanada-que@pc.gc.ca
www.pc.gc.ca/canalsteanne

Saint-Ours
2930, ch des Patriotes, Saint-Ours, QC J0G 1P0
Tél: 450-785-2212
Téléc: 450-658-2428
www.pc.gc.ca/canalstours

St. Peters
PO Box 8, St Peters, NS B0E 3B0
Tel: 902-733-2280
Fax: 902-733-2362
information@pc.gc.ca
www.pc.gc.ca/stpeterscanal

Sault Ste Marie
1 Canal Dr., Sault Ste Marie, ON P6A 6W4
Tel: 705-941-6262
Fax: 705-941-6206
info-saultcanal@pc.gc.ca
www.pc.gc.ca/eng/lhn-nhs/on/ssmarie/index.aspx

Trent-Severn Waterway
PO Box 567, Peterborough, ON K9J 6Z6
Tel: 705-750-4900
Fax: 705-742-9644
Toll-Free: 888-773-7777
Ont.Trentsevern@pc.gc.ca
www.pc.gc.ca/trentsevern
TTY: 705-750-4949

Atlantic National Parks/National Historic Sites

Alexander Graham Bell Historic Site of Canada
PO Box 159, Baddeck, NS B0E 1B0
Tel: 902-295-2069
Fax: 902-295-3496
information@pc.gc.ca
www.pc.gc.ca/eng/lhn-nhs/ns/grahambell/index.aspx

Ardgowan National Historic Site of Canada
2 Palmer's Lane, Charlottetown, PE C1A 5V8
Tel: 902-566-7050
Fax: 902-566-7226
www.pc.gc.ca/eng/lhn-nhs/pe/ardgowan/index.aspx

Bank Fishery National Heritage Exhibit
PO Box 9080 A, Halifax, NS B3K 5M7
Tel: 902-426-5080
Fax: 902-426-4228
information@pc.gc.ca
www.pc.gc.ca/lhn-nhs/ns/bank/index.aspx

Boishébert & Beaubears Shipbuilding National Historic Sites of Canada
186, route 117, Kouchibouguac National Park, NB E4X 2P1
Tel: 506-876-2443
Fax: 506-876-4802
kouch.info@pc.gc.ca
www.pc.gc.ca/lhn-nhs/nb/boishebert/index.aspx
TTY: 506-876-4205

Canso Islands National Historic Site of Canada
PO Box 159, Baddeck, NS B0E 1B0
Tel: 902-295-2069
Fax: 902-295-3496
information@pc.gc.ca
www.pc.gc.ca/lhn-nhs/ns/canso/index.aspx

Cape Breton Highlands National Park of Canada
Ingonish Beach, NS B0C 1L0
Tel: 902-224-2306
Fax: 902-285-2866
information@pc.gc.ca
www.pc.gc.ca/pn-np/ns/cbreton/index.aspx

Cape Spear National Historic Site of Canada
PO Box 1268, St. John's, NL A1C 5M9
Tel: 709-772-5367
Fax: 709-772-6302
cape.spear@pc.gc.ca
www.pc.gc.ca/lhn-nhs/nl/spear/index.aspx

Carleton Martello Tower National Historic Site of Canada
454 Whipple St., Saint John, NB E2M 2R3
Tel: 506-636-4011
Fax: 506-636-4574
info.martello@pc.gc.ca
www.pc.gc.ca/lhn-nhs/nb/carleton/index.aspx
TTY: 506-887-6015

Castle Hill National Historic Site of Canada
PO Box 10, Jerseyside, Placentia Bay, NL A0B 2G0
Tel: 709-227-2401
Fax: 709-227-2452
castle.hill@pc.gc.ca
www.pc.gc.ca/lhn-nhs/nl/castlehill/index.aspx
Other Communication: Off-season: 709-772-5367, Fax: 709-772-6302

Fort Amherst/Port-La-Joye National Historic Site of Canada
2 Palmers Lane, Charlottetown, PE C1A 5V8
Tel: 902-566-7626
Fax: 902-566-8295
www.pc.gc.ca/lhn-nhs/pe/amherst/index.aspx
Other Communication: July 1-August 31 Phone: 902-675-2220

Fort Anne National Historic Site of Canada
PO Box 9, Annapolis Royal, NS B0S 1A0
Tel: 902-532-2397
Fax: 902-532-2232
information@pc.gc.ca
www.pc.gc.ca/lhn-nhs/ns/fortanne/index.aspx
Other Communication: Off-season: 902-532-2321

Fort Beauséjour National Historic Site of Canada
111 Fort Beauséjour Rd., Aulac, NB E4L 2W5
Tel: 506-364-5080
Fax: 506-536-4399
fort.beausejour@pc.gc.ca
www.pc.gc.ca/lhn-nhs/nb/beausejour/index.aspx

Fort Edward National Historic Site of Canada
PO Box 9, Annapolis Royal, NS B0S 1A0
Tel: 902-532-2321
Fax: 902-532-2232
www.pc.gc.ca/lhn-nhs/ns/edward/index.aspx
Other Communication: July & August: 902-798-4706

Fort McNab National Historic Site of Canada
PO Box 9080 A, Halifax, NS B3K 5M7
Tel: 902-426-5080
Fax: 902-426-4228
halifax.citadel@pc.gc.ca
www.pc.gc.ca/lhn-nhs/ns/mcnab/index.aspx

Fortress of Louisbourg National Historic Site
259 Park Service Rd., Louisbourg, NS B1C 2L2
Tel: 902-733-2280
Fax: 902-733-2362
information@pc.gc.ca
www.pc.gc.ca/lhn-nhs/ns/louisbourg/index.aspx
TTY: 902-733-3607

Fundy National Park of Canada
PO Box 1001, Alma, NB E4H 1B4
Tel: 506-887-6000
Fax: 506-887-6008
fundy.info@pc.gc.ca
www.pc.gc.ca/pn-np/nb/fundy/index.aspx
TTY: 506-887-6015

Grand Pré National Historic Site of Canada
PO Box 150, Grand Pré, NS B0P 1M0
Tel: 902-542-3631
Fax: 902-542-1691
Toll-Free: 866-542-3631
grandpre.info@pc.gc.ca; contact@grand-pre.com
www.pc.gc.ca/lhn-nhs/ns/grandpre/index.aspx; www.grand-pre.com
TTY: 902-532-7472

Georges Island National Historic Site of Canada
PO Box 9080 A, Halifax, NS B3K 5M7
Tel: 902-426-5080
Fax: 902-426-4228
georges.island@pc.gc.ca
www.pc.gc.ca/lhn-nhs/ns/georges/index.aspx

Green Gables Heritage Place
2 Palmer's Lane, Charlottetown, PE C1A 5V6
Tel: 902-963-7874
greengables.info@pc.gc.ca
www.pc.gc.ca/lhn-nhs/pe/greengables/index.aspx

Gros Morne National Park of Canada
PO Box 130, Rocky Harbour, NL A0K 4N0
Tel: 709-458-2417
Fax: 709-458-2059
grosmorne.info@pc.gc.ca
www.pc.gc.ca/pn-np/nl/grosmorne/index.aspx
TTY: 709-772-4564

Halifax Citadel National Historic Site of Canada
PO Box 9080 A, Halifax, NS B3K 5M7
Tel: 902-426-5080
Fax: 902-426-4228
halifax.citadel@pc.gc.ca
www.pc.gc.ca/lhn-nhs/ns/halifax/index.aspx

Hawthorne Cottage National Historic Site of Canada
PO Box 5542, St. John's, NL A1C 5W4
Tel: 709-753-9262
Fax: 709-753-0879
info@historicsites.ca
www.pc.gc.ca/lhn-nhs/nl/hawthorne/index.aspx
Other Communication: Off-season: 709-528-4004

Kejimkujik National Park of Canada
PO Box 236, Maitland Bridge, NS B0T 1B0
Tel: 902-682-2772
Fax: 902-682-3367
kejimkujik.info@pc.gc.ca
www.pc.gc.ca/pn-np/ns/kejimkujik/index_e.asp

Kouchibouguac National Park of Canada
186, Route 117, Kouchibouguac National Park, NB E4X 2P1
Tel: 506-876-2443
Fax: 506-876-4802
kouch.info@pc.gc.ca
www.pc.gc.ca/pn-np/nb/kouchibouguac/index.aspx
TTY: 506-876-4205

L'Anse aux Meadows National Historic Site of Canada
PO Box 70, St-Lunaire-Griquet, NL A0K 2X0
Tel: 709-458-2417
Fax: 709-623-2028
viking.lam@pc.gc.ca
www.pc.gc.ca/lhn-nhs/nl/meadows/index.aspx

Marconi National Historic Site of Canada
PO Box 159, Baddeck, NS B0E 1B0
Tel: 902-295-2069
Fax: 902-295-3496
information@pc.gc.ca
www.pc.gc.ca/lhn-nhs/ns/marconi/index.aspx

Monument Lefebvre National Historic Site of Canada
480 rue Centrale, Memramcook, NB E4K 3S6
Tel: 506-758-9808
Fax: 506-758-9813
monument@nbnet.nb.ca
www.pc.gc.ca/lhn-nhs/nb/lefebvre/index.aspx

Port-au-Choix National Historic Site of Canada
PO Box 140, Port au Choix, NL A0K 4C0
Tel: 709-458-2417
Fax: 709-861-3827
pac-historic-site@pc.gc.ca
www.pc.gc.ca/lhn-nhs/nl/portauchoix/index.aspx
Other Communication: Seasonal: 709-861-3522

Port Royal National Historic Site of Canada
PO Box 9, Annapolis Royal, NS B0S 1A0
Tel: 902-532-2898
Fax: 902-532-2232
information@pc.gc.ca
www.pc.gc.ca/lhn-nhs/ns/portroyal/index.aspx
Other Communication: Off-season: 902-532-2232

Prince Edward Island National Park of Canada
2 Palmers Lane, Charlottetown, PE C1A 5V8
Tel: 902-672-6350
Fax: 902-672-6370
pnipe.peinp@pc.gc.ca
www.pc.gc.ca/pn-np/pe/pei-ipe/index.aspx
TTY: 902-566-7061

Prince of Wales Tower National Historic Site
PO Box 9080 A, Halifax, NS B3K 5M7
Tel: 902-426-5080
Fax: 902-426-4228
halifax.citadel@pc.gc.ca
www.pc.gc.ca/lhn-nhs/ns/prince/index.aspx

Province House National Historic Site of Canada
2 Palmer's Lane, Charlottetown, PE C1A 5V8
Tel: 902-566-7626
Fax: 902-566-8295
information@pc.gc.ca
www.pc.gc.ca/lhn-nhs/pe/provincehouse/index.aspx

Red Bay National Historic Site of Canada
PO Box 103, Red Bay, NL A0K 4K0
Tel: 709-920-2142
Fax: 709-458-2144
redbay.info@pc.gc.ca
www.pc.gc.ca/lhn-nhs/nl/redbay/index.aspx
Other Communication: Summer: 709-920-2051; Alt. Phone: 709-458-2417

Ryan Premises National Historic Site
PO Box 1451, Bonavista, NL A0C 1B0
Tel: 709-468-1600
Fax: 709-468-1604
ryan.premises@pc.gc.ca
www.pc.gc.ca/lhn-nhs/nl/ryan/index.aspx

St. Andrews Blockhouse National Historic Site of Canada
454 Whipple St., Saint John, NB E2M 2R3
Tel: 506-636-4011
Fax: 506-636-4574
fundy.info@pc.gc.ca
www.pc.gc.ca/lhn-nhs/nb/standrews/index.aspx
TTY: 506-887-6015
Other Communication: Summer: 506-529-4270

St. Peters Canada National Historic Site of Canada
PO Box 8, St Peters, NS B0E 3B0
Tel: 902-733-2280
Fax: 902-733-2362
information@pc.gc.ca
www.pc.gc.ca/lhn-nhs/ns/stpeters/index.aspx

Signal Hill National Historic Site of Canada
PO Box 1268, St. John's, NL A1C 5M9
Tel: 709-772-5367
Fax: 709-772-6302
signal.hill@pc.gc.ca
www.pc.gc.ca/lhn-nhs/nl/signalhill/index.aspx

Terra Nova National Park of Canada
General Delivery, Glovertown, NL A0G 2L0
Tel: 709-533-2801
Fax: 709-533-2706
info.tnnp@pc.gc.ca
www.pc.gc.ca/pn-np/nl/terranova/index.aspx

York Redoubt National Historic Site of Canada
PO Box 9080 A, Halifax, NS B3K 5M7
Tel: 902-426-5080
Fax: 902-426-4228
halifax.citadel@pc.gc.ca
www.pc.gc.ca/lhn-nhs/ns/york/index.aspx

Ontario National Parks/National Historic Sites

Battle of the Windmill National Historic Site of Canada
370 Vankoughnet St., PO Box 479, Prescott, ON K0E 1T0
Tel: 613-925-2896
Fax: 613-925-1536
ont.wellington@pc.gc.ca
www.pc.gc.ca/lhn-nhs/on/windmill/index.aspx

Bellevue House National Historic Site of Canada
35 Centre St., Kingston, ON K7L 4E5
Tel: 613-545-8666
Fax: 613-545-8721
bellevue.house@pc.gc.ca
www.pc.gc.ca/lhn-nhs/on/bellevue/index.aspx
TTY: 613-545-8668

Bethune Memorial House National Historic Site of Canada
235 John St. North, Gravenhurst, ON P1P 1G4
Tel: 705-687-4261
Fax: 705-687-4935
ont-bethune@pc.gc.ca
www.pc.gc.ca/lhn-nhs/on/bethune/index.aspx

Bois Blanc Island Lighthouse National Historic Site of Canada
c/o Fort Malden N.H.S., 100 Laird Ave., PO Box 38, Amherstburg, ON N9V 2Z2
Tel: 519-736-5416
Fax: 519-736-6603
ont.fort-malden@pc.gc.ca
www.pc.gc.ca/lhn-nhs/on/boisblanc/index.aspx

Bruce Peninsula National Park
PO Box 189, Tobermory, ON N0H 2R0
Tel: 519-596-2233
Fax: 519-596-2298
bruce-fathomfive@pc.gc.ca
www.pc.gc.ca/pn-np/on/bruce/index.aspx

Butler's Barracks c/o Fort George National Historic Site
25 Eddy St., Gatineau, QB K1A 0M5
Tel: 905-468-6614
Fax: 905-468-4638
ont-niagara@pc.gc.ca
www.pc.gc.ca/lhn-nhs/on/fortgeorge/index.aspx

Fort George National Historic Site of Canada
25 Eddy St., Gatineau, QB K1A 0M5
Tel: 905-468-6614
Fax: 905-468-4638
ont-niagara@pc.gc.ca
www.pc.gc.ca/lhn-nhs/on/fortgeorge/index.aspx

Fathom Five National Marine Park of Canada
PO Box 189, Tobermory, ON N0H 2R0
Tel: 519-596-2233
Fax: 519-596-2298
bruce-fathomfive@pc.gc.ca
www.pc.gc.ca/eng/amnc-nmca/on/fathomfive/index.aspx

Fort Malden National Historic Site
100 Laird Ave., PO Box 38, Amherstburg, ON N9V 2Z2
Tel: 519-736-5416
Fax: 519-736-6603
ont.fort-malden@pc.gc.ca
www.pc.gc.ca/eng/lhn-nhs/on/malden/index.aspx

Fort Mississauga National Historic Site of Canada
26 Queen St., PO Box 787, Niagara on the Lake, ON L0S 1J0
Tel: 905-468-6614
Fax: 905-468-4638
www.friendsoffortgeorge.ca

Fort St. Joseph National Historic Site of Canada
PO Box 220, Richards Landing, ON P0R 1J0
Tel: 705-246-2664
Fax: 705-246-1796
fortstjoseph-info@pc.gc.ca
www.pc.gc.ca/lhn-nhs/on/stjoseph.aspx

Fort Wellington National Historic Site of Canada
PO Box 479, Prescott, ON K0E 1T0
Tel: 613-925-2896
Fax: 613-925-1536
ont-wellington@pc.gc.ca
www.pc.gc.ca/lhn-nhs/on/wellington.aspx
TTY: 613-925-2896

Georgian Bay Islands National Park of Canada
901 Wye Valley Rd., PO Box 9, Midland, ON L4R 4K6
Tel: 705-526-9804
Fax: 705-526-5939
info.gbi@pc.gc.ca
www.pc.gc.ca/eng/pn-np/on/georg/index.aspx

Inverarden House National Historic Site of Canada
370 Vankoughnet St., PO Box 479, Prescott, ON K0E 1T0
Tel: 613-925-2896
Fax: 613-925-1536
ont-wellington@pc.gc.ca
www.pc.gc.ca/lhn-nhs/on/inverarden/index.aspx

Kingston Martello Towers
35 Centre St., Kingston, ON K7L 4E5
Tel: 613-545-8666
Fax: 613-545-8721
www.pc.gc.ca/lhn-nhs/on/bellevue/index.aspx
TTY: 613-545-8668

Laurier House National Historic Site of Canada
335 Laurier Ave. East, Ottawa, ON K1A 6R4
Tel: 613-992-8142
Fax: 613-947-4851
laurier-house@pc.gc.ca
www.pc.gc.ca/lhn-nhs/on/laurier.aspx

Point Clark Lighthouse National Historic Site of Canada
c/o Woodside National Historic Site, 528 Wellington St. North, Kitchener, ON N2H 5L5
Tel: 519-571-5684
Fax: 519-571-5286
ont-woodside@pc.gc.ca
www.pc.gc.ca/lhn-nhs/on/clark.aspx

Point Pelee National Park of Canada
407 Monarch Lane, RR#1, Leamington, ON N8H 3V4
Tel: 519-322-2365
Fax: 519-322-1277
pelee.info@pc.gc.ca
www.pc.gc.ca/fra/pn-np/on/pelee.aspx

Pukaskwa National Park of Canada
PO Box 212, Heron Bay, ON P0T 1R0
Tel: 807-229-0801
Fax: 807-229-2097
ont-pukaskwa@pc.gc.ca
www.pc.gc.ca/pn-np/on/pukaskwa.aspx

Queenston Heights & Brock's Monument
26 Queen St., PO Box 787, Niagara on the Lake, ON L0S 1J0
Tel: 905-468-4257
Fax: 905-468-4638
ont-niagara@pc.gc.ca
www.pc.gc.ca/lhn-nhs/on/queenston/index.aspx

St. Lawrence Islands National Park of Canada
2 County Rd. 5, RR#3, Mallorytown Landing, ON K0E 1R0
Tel: 613-923-5261
Fax: 613-923-1021
ont-sli@pc.gc.ca
www.pc.gc.ca/pn-np/on/lawren/index.aspx

Sir John Johnson National Historic Site of Canada
c/o Fort Wellington National Historic Site, 370 Vanhoughnet St., PO Box 479, Prescott, ON K0E 1T0
Tel: 613-925-2896
Fax: 613-925-1536
ont.wellington@pc.gc.ca; sirjohnjohnson@sympatico.ca
www.pc.gc.ca/lhn-nhs/on/johnjohnson/index.aspx

Woodside National Historic Site of Canada
528 Wellington St. North, Kitchener, ON N2H 5L5
Tel: 519-571-5684
Fax: 519-571-5686
ont-woodside@pc.gc.ca
www.pc.gc.ca/lhn-nhs/on/woodside/index.aspx

Quebec National Parks/National Historic Sites

Artillery Park National Historic Site of Canada
2, rue d'Auteuil, CP 10 B, Québec, QC G1K 7A1
Tél: 418-648-7016
Téléc: 418-648-2506
parkscanada-que@pc.gc.ca
www.pc.gc.ca/lhn-nhs/qc/artiller.aspx

Battle of the Châteauguay National Historic Site of Canada
2371, ch de la Rivière Châteauguay nord, CP 250, Howick, QC J0S 1G0
Tél: 450-829-2003
Téléc: 450-829-3325
parkscanada-que@pc.gc.ca
www.pc.gc.ca/lhn-nhs/qc/chateauguay/index.aspx

Battle of the Restigouche National Historic Site of Canada
Route 132, CP 359, Pointe-à-la-Croix, QC G0C 1L0
Tél: 418-788-5676
Téléc: 418-788-5895
parkscanada-que@pc.gc.ca
www.pc.gc.ca/lhn-nhs/qc/ristigouche.aspx

Carillon Barracks National Historic Site of Canada
1899, boul. Périgny, Chambly, QC J3L 4C3
Tel: 450-658-0681
Fax: 450-658-2428
parkscanada-que@pc.gc.ca
www.pc.gc.ca/lhn-nhs/qc/carillon/index.aspx

Cartier-Brébeuf National Historic Site of Canada
175, rue de l'Espinay, CP 10 B, Québec, QC G1K 7A1
Tél: 418-648-4038
Téléc: 418-948-9181
parkscanada-que@pc.gc.ca
www.pc.gc.ca/lhn-nhs/qc/cartierbrebeuf.aspx

Coteau-du-Lac National Historic Site of Canada
308 A, ch du Fleuve, Coteau-du-Lac, QC J0P 1B0
Tél: 450-763-5631
Téléc: 450-763-1654
parkscanada-que@pc.gc.ca
www.pc.gc.ca/lhn-nhs/qc/coteaudulac.aspx

Forges du Saint-Maurice National Historic Site of Canada
10000, boul des Forges, Trois-Rivières, QC G9C 1B1
Tel: 819-378-5116
Fax: 819-378-0887
parkscanada-que@pc.gc.ca
www.pc.gc.ca/lhn-nhs/qc/saintmaurice.aspx

Forillon National Park of Canada
122, boul Gaspé, Gaspé, QC G4X 1A9
Tél: 418-368-5505
Téléc: 418-368-6837
parkscanada-que@pc.gc.ca
www.pc.gc.ca/pn-np/qc/forillon.aspx

Fort Chambly National Historic Site of Canada
2, rue de Richelieu, Chambly, QC J3L 2B9
Tel: 450-658-1585
Fax: 450-658-7216
parkscanada-que@pc.gc.ca
www.pc.gc.ca/lhn-nhs/qc/fortchambly/index.aspx

Fort Lennox National Historic Site of Canada
1 - 61e av, St-Paul-de-l'Ile-aux-Noix, QC J0J 1G0
Tél: 450-291-5700
Téléc: 450-291-4389
parkscanada-que@pc.gc.ca
www.pc.gc.ca/lhn-nhs/qc/lennox.aspx

Fort Témiscamingue National Historic Site of Canada
830, ch du Vieux-Fort, Duhamel ouest, QC J9V 1N7
Tél: 819-629-3222
Téléc: 819-629-2977
fort.temiscaminque@pc.gc.ca
www.pc.gc.ca/fra/lhn-nhs/qc/temiscamingue.aspx

Fortifications of Québec National Historic Site of Canada
2, rue d'Auteuil, PO Box 10 B, Québec, QC G1K 7A1
Tel: 418-648-7016
Fax: 418-648-2506
www.pc.gc.ca/lhn-nhs/qc/fortifications/index.aspx

Grosse Ile & the Irish Memorial National Historic Site of Canada
2 rue D'Auteuil, CP 10 B, Québec, QC G1K 7A1
Tél: 418-234-8841
Téléc: 866-790-8991
parkscanada-que@pc.gc.ca
www.pc.gc.ca/lhn-nhs/qc/grosseile/index.aspx

La Mauricie National Park of Canada
702, 5e rue, CP 160 Bureau-Chef, Shawinigan, QC G9N 6T9
Tél: 819-538-3232
Téléc: 819-536-3661
parkscanada-que@pc.gc.ca
www.pc.gc.ca/fra/pn-np/qc/mauricie.aspx

Lévis Forts National Historic Site of Canada
41, ch du Gouvernement, CP 10 B, Québec, QC G1K 7A1
Tél: 418-835-5182
Téléc: 418-948-9119
parkscanada-que@pc.gc.ca
www.pc.gc.ca/lhn-nhs/qc/levis/index.aspx

Louis S. St-Laurent National Historic Site of Canada
6790, rte Louis-St-Laurent, Compton, QC J0B 1L0
Tel: 819-835-5448
Fax: 819-835-9101
parkscanada-que@pc.gc.ca
www.pc.gc.ca/fra/lhn-nhs/qc/stlaurent.aspx

Manoir Papineau National Historic Site of Canada
500, rue Notre-Dame, Montebello, QC J0V 1L0
Tél: 819-423-6965
Téléc: 819-423-6455
parkscanada-que@pc.gc.ca
www.pc.gc.ca/fra/lhn-nhs/qc/manoirpapineau/index.aspx

Mingan Archipelago National Park Reserve of Canada
1340, rue de la Digue, CP 1180, Havre-Saint-Pierre, QC G0G 1P0
Tél: 418-538-3331
Téléc: 418-538-3595
parkscanada-que@pc.gc.ca
www.pc.gc.ca/pn-np/qc/mingan.aspx
Autre numéros: Information and/or Reservation: 418-538-3285; 418-949-2126

Pointe-au-Père Lighthouse National Historic Site of Canada
1034, rue du Phare, Pointe-au-Père, QC G5M 1L8
Tel: 418-724-6214
Fax: 418-721-0815
parkscanada-que@pc.gc.ca
www.pc.gc.ca/lhn-nhs/qc/pointaupere/index.aspx

Saguenay St. Lawrence Marine Park of Canada
182, rte de l'Église, CP 220, Tadoussac, QC G0T 2A0
Tél: 418-235-4703
Téléc: 418-235-4686
parkscanada-que@pc.gc.ca
www.pc.gc.ca/amnc-nmca/qc/saguenay/default.aspx

Sir George-Étienne Cartier National Historic Site of Canada
458, rue Notre-Dame est, Montréal, QC H2Y 1C8
Tel: 514-283-2282
Fax: 514-283-5560
cartier.maison@pc.gc.ca
www.pc.gc.ca/lhn-nhs/qc/etiennecartier.aspx

Sir Wilfrid Laurier National Historic Site of Canada
#945, 12e av, St-Lin-Laurentides, QC J5M 2W4
Tél: 450-439-3702
Téléc: 450-439-5721
parkscanada-que@pc.gc.ca
www.pc.gc.ca/fra/lhn-nhs/qc/wilfridlaurier.aspx

The Fur Trade at Lachine National Historic Site of Canada
1255, boul Saint-Joseph, Lachine, QC H8S 2M2
Tel: 514-637-7433
Fax: 514-637-5325
parkscanada-que@pc.gc.ca
www.pc.gc.ca/lhn-nhs/qc/lachine/index.aspx
Other Communication: Winter, Phone: 514-283-6054; Fax: 514-496-1263

Western & Northern Canada National Parks/National Historic Sites

Aulavik National Park of Canada
PO Box 29, Sachs Harbour, NT X0E 0Z0
Tel: 867-690-3904
Fax: 867-690-4808
inuvik.info@pc.gc.ca
pc.gc.ca/pn-np/nt/aulavik/index_e.asp

Auyuittuq National Park of Canada
PO Box 353, Pangnirtung, NU X0A 0R0
Tel: 867-473-2500
Fax: 867-473-8612
nunavut.info@pc.gc.ca
www.pc.gc.ca/pn-np/nu/auyuittuq/index_e.asp

Banff National Park of Canada
PO Box 900, Banff, AB T1L 1K2
Tel: 403-762-1550
Fax: 403-762-1551
banff.vrc@pc.gc.ca
www.pc.gc.ca/pn-np/ab/banff/index_e.asp

Banff Park Museum National Historic Site of Canada
PO Box 900, Banff, AB T1L 1K2
Tel: 403-762-1558
Fax: 403-762-1565
banff.vrc@pch.gc.ca
www.pc.gc.ca/lhn-nhs/ab/banff/index_E.asp

Bar U Ranch National Historic Site of Canada
PO Box 168, Longview, AB T0L 1H0
Tel: 403-395-2212
Fax: 403-395-2331
BarU.Info@pc.gc.ca
www.pc.gc.ca/lhn-nhs/ab/baru/index_e.asp

Batoche National Historic Site of Canada
RR#1 Box 1040, Wakaw, SK S0K 4P0
Tel: 306-423-6227
Fax: 306-423-5400
batoche@pc.gc.ca
www.pc.gc.ca/eng/lhn-nhs/sk/batoche/index.aspx
TTY: 306-423-5540

Cave & Basin National Historic Site of Canada
PO Box 900, Banff, AB T1L 1K2
Tel: 403-762-1566
Fax: 403-762-1565
banff.vrc@pc.gc.ca
www.pc.gc.ca/lhn-nhs/ab/caveandbasin/index_e.asp

Chilkoot Trail National Historic Site of Canada
#205, 300 Main St., Whitehorse, YT Y1A 2B5
Tel: 867-667-3910
Fax: 867-393-6701
Toll-Free: 800-661-0486
whitehorse.info@pc.gc.ca
www.pc.gc.ca/lhn-nhs/yt/chilkoot/index_e.asp

Dawson Historical Complex National Historic Site of Canada

PO Box 390, Dawson City, YT Y0B 1G0
Tel: 867-993-7200
Fax: 867-993-7203
dawson.info@pc.gc.ca
www.pc.gc.ca/lhn-nhs/yt/dawson/index_E.asp

Dredge No. 4 National Historic Site of Canada
PO Box 390, Dawson City, YT Y0B 1G0
Tel: 867-993-7200
Fax: 867-993-7203
dawson.info@pc.gc.ca
www.pc.gc.ca/lhn-nhs/yt/klondike.aspx

Elk Island National Park of Canada
RR#1, Site 4, Fort Saskatchewan, AB T8L 2N7
Tel: 780-992-5790
Fax: 780-992-2951
elk.island@pc.gc.ca
www.pc.gc.ca/pn-np/ab/elkisland/index_e.asp
Other Communication: Administration: 780-992-2950

Fisgard Lighthouse National Historic Site of Canada
603 Fort Rodd Hill Rd., Victoria, BC V9C 2W8
Tel: 250-478-5849
Fax: 250-478-2816
fort.rodd@pc.gc.ca
www.pc.gc.ca/lhn-nhs/bc/fisgard/index_e.asp

Fort Battleford National Historic Site of Canada
PO Box 70, Battleford, SK S0M 0E0
Tel: 306-937-2621
Fax: 306-937-3370
battleford-info@pc.gc.ca
www.pc.gc.ca/lhn-nhs/sk/battleford/index_e.asp
TTY: 306-937-3199

Fort Langley National Historic Site of Canada
23433 Mavis Ave., PO Box 129, Fort Langley, BC V1M 2R5
Tel: 604-513-4777
Fax: 604-513-4798
fort.langley@pc.gc.ca
www.pc.gc.ca/lhn-nhs/bc/langley/index_e.asp

Fort Rodd Hill National Historic Site of Canada
603 Fort Rodd Hill Rd., Victoria, BC V9C 2W8
Tel: 250-478-5849
Fax: 250-478-2816
fort.rodd@pc.gc.ca
www.pc.gc.ca/lhn-nhs/bc/fortroddhill/index_e.asp

Fort St. James National Historic Site of Canada
PO Box 1148, Fort St James, BC V0J 1P0
Tel: 250-996-7191
Fax: 250-996-8566
stjames@pc.gc.ca
www.pc.gc.ca/lhn-nhs/bc/stjames/index_e.asp

Fort Walsh National Historic Site of Canada
PO Box 278, Maple Creek, SK S0N 1N0
Tel: 306-662-3590
Fax: 306-662-2711
fort.walsh@pc.gc.ca
www.pc.gc.ca/lhn-nhs/sk/walsh/index_e.asp
TTY: 306-662-3124
Other Communication: Administration: 306-662-2645

Gitwangak Battle Hill National Historic Site of Canada
PO Box 37, Queen Charlotte, BC V0T 1S0
Tel: 250-559-8818
Fax: 250-559-8366
gwaii.haanas@pc.gc.ca
www.pc.gc.ca/lhn-nhs/bc/kitwanga/index_E.asp
TTY: 250-559-8139

Glacier National Park of Canada
PO Box 350, Revelstoke, BC V0E 2S0
Tel: 250-837-7500
Fax: 250-837-7536
revglacier.reception@pc.gc.ca
www.pc.gc.ca/pn-np/bc/glacier/index_e.asp

Grasslands National Park of Canada
PO Box 150, Val Marie, SK S0N 2T0
Fax: 306-298-2042
Toll-Free: 877-345-2257
grasslands.info@pc.gc.ca
www.pc.gc.ca/pn-np/sk/grasslands/index_e.asp

Gulf Islands National Park Reserve of Canada
2220 Harbour Rd., Sidney, BC V8L 2P6
Tel: 250-654-4000
Fax: 250-654-4014
Toll-Free: 866-944-1744
gulf.islands@pc.gc.ca
www.pc.gc.ca/pn-np/bc/gulf/index_E.asp

Gulf of Georgia Cannery National Historic Site of Canada
12138 Fourth Ave., Richmond, BC V7E 3J1
Tel: 604-664-9009
Fax: 604-664-9008
gog.info@pc.gc.ca
www.pc.gc.ca/lhn-nhs/bc/georgia/index_e.asp

Gwaii Haanas National Park Reserve & Haida Heritage Site of Canada
60 Second Beach Rd., PO Box 37, Queen Charlotte, BC V0T 1S0
Tel: 250-559-8818
Fax: 250-559-8366
Toll-Free: 877-559-8818
gwaii.haanas@pc.gc.ca
www.pc.gc.ca/pn-np/bc/gwaiihaanas/index_e.asp

Ivvavik National Park of Canada
PO Box 1840, Inuvik, NT X0E 0T0
Tel: 867-777-8800
Fax: 867-777-8820
inuvik.info@pc.gc.ca
www.pc.gc.ca/pn-np/yt/ivvavik/index_e.asp

Jasper National Park of Canada
PO Box 10, Jasper, AB T0E 1E0
Tel: 780-852-6176
Fax: 780-852-6152
pnj.jnp@pc.gc.ca
www.pc.gc.ca/pn-np/ab/jasper/index_e.asp

Kluane National Park & Reserve of Canada
PO Box 5495, Haines Junction, YT Y0B 1L0
Tel: 867-634-7250
Fax: 867-634-7208
kluane.info@pc.gc.ca
www.pc.gc.ca/pn-np/yt/kluane/index_e.asp

Kootenay National Park of Canada
PO Box 220, Radium Hot Springs, BC V0A 1M0
Tel: 250-347-9505
Fax: 250-347-9980
kootenay.info@pc.gc.ca
www.pc.gc.ca/pn-np/bc/kootenay/index_e.asp

Lower Fort Garry National Historic Site of Canada
5925 Highway 9, St. Andrews, MB R1A 4A8
Tel: 204-785-6050
Fax: 204-482-5887
lfg.info@pc.gc.ca
www.pc.gc.ca/lhn-nhs/mb/fortgarry/index_e.asp

Motherwell Homestead National Historic Site of Canada
PO Box 70, Abernethy, SK S0A 0A0
Tel: 306-333-2116
Fax: 306-333-2210
Motherwell.Homestead@pc.gc.ca
www.pc.gc.ca/lhn-nhs/sk/motherwell/index_e.asp

Mount Revelstoke National Park of Canada
PO Box 350, Revelstoke, BC V0E 2S0
Tel: 250-837-7500
Fax: 250-837-7536
revglacier.reception@pc.gc.ca
www.pc.gc.ca/pn-np/bc/revelstoke/index_e.asp
TTY: 866-787-6221

Nahanni National Park Reserve of Canada
10002 - 100 Street, PO Box 348, Fort Simpson, NT X0E 0N0
Tel: 867-695-7750
Fax: 867-695-2446
nahanni.info@pc.gc.ca
www.pc.gc.ca/pn-np/nt/nahanni/index_e.asp

Pacific Rim National Park Reserve of Canada
2185 Ocean Terrace Rd., PO Box 280, Ucluelet, BC V0R 3A0
Tel: 250-726-3500
Fax: 250-726-3520
pacrim.info@pc.gc.ca
www.pc.gc.ca/pn-np/bc/pacificrim/index_e.asp

Prince Albert National Park of Canada
PO Box 100, Waskesiu Lake, SK S0J 2Y0
Tel: 306-663-4522
panp.info@pc.gc.ca
www.pc.gc.ca/pn-np/sk/princealbert/index_e.asp

Prince of Wales Fort National Historic Site of Canada
PO Box 127, Churchill, MB R0B 0E0
Tel: 204-675-8863
Fax: 204-675-2026
mannorth.nhs@pc.gc.ca
www.pc.gc.ca/lhn-nhs/mb/prince/index_e.asp

Quttinirpaaq National Park of Canada
PO Box 278, Iqaluit, NU X0A 0H0
Tel: 867-975-4673
Fax: 867-975-4674
nunavut.info@pc.gc.ca
www.pc.gc.ca/pn-np/nu/quttinirpaaq/index_e.asp

Riding Mountain National Park of Canada
Wasagaming, MB R0J 2H0
Tel: 204-848-7275
Fax: 204-848-2596
rmnp.info@pc.gc.ca
www.pc.gc.ca/pn-np/mb/riding/index_e.asp

Riel House National Historic Site of Canada
330 River Rd. (St. Vidal), PO Box 73, Winnipeg, MB R2N 3X9
Tel: 204-257-1783
Fax: 204-983-2221
riel.info@pc.gc.ca
www.pc.gc.ca/lhn-nhs/mb/riel/index_E.asp
TTY: 866-787-6221
Other Communication: Winter: 204-983-6757

Rocky Mountain House National Historic Site of Canada
Site 127, Comp 6, RR#4, Rocky Mountain House, AB T4T 2A4
Tel: 403-845-2412
Fax: 403-845-5320
rocky.info@pc.gc.ca
www.pc.gc.ca/lhn-nhs/ab/rockymountain/index_E.asp

Sirmilik National Park of Canada
PO Box 300, Pond Inlet, NU X0A 0S0
Tel: 867-899-8092
Fax: 867-899-8104
sirmilik.info@pc.gc.ca
www.pc.gc.ca/pn-np/nu/sirmilik/index_E.asp

SS Keno National Historic Site of Canada
PO Box 390, Dawson City, YT Y0B 1G0
Tel: 867-993-7200
Fax: 867-993-7203
dawson.info@pc.gc.ca
www.pc.gc.ca/lhn-nhs/yt/sskeno/index_e.asp

SS Klondike National Historic Site of Canada
#205, 300 Main St., Whitehorse, YT Y1A 2B5
Fax: 867-393-6701
Toll-Free: 800-661-0486
whitehorse.info@pc.gc.ca
www.pc.gc.ca/lhn-nhs/yt/ssklondike/index_E.asp
Other Communication: Summer: 867-667-4511

St. Andrews Rectory National Historic Site of Canada
374, chemin River, St. Andrews, MB R1A 2Y1
Tel: 204-785-6050
Fax: 204-482-5887
lfg.info@pc.gc.ca
www.pc.gc.ca/lhn-nhs/mb/standrews/contact_e.asp

The Forks National Historic Site of Canada
401-25 Forks Market Rd., Winnipeg, MB R3C 4S8
Tel: 204-983-6757
Fax: 204-983-2221
forks.fourche@pc.gc.ca
www.pc.gc.ca/lhn-nhs/mb/forks/index_e.asp

Tuktut Nogait National Park of Canada
PO Box 91, Paulatuk, NT X0E 1N0
Tel: 867-580-3233
Fax: 867-580-3234
inuvik.info@pc.gc.ca
www.pc.gc.ca/pn-np/nt/tuktutnogait/index_e.asp

Ukkusiksalik National Park of Canada
PO Box 220, Repulse Bay, NU X0C 0H0
Tel: 867-462-4500
Fax: 867-462-4095
ukkusiksalik.info@pc.gc.ca
www.pc.gc.ca/pn-np/nu/ukkusiksalik/index_E.asp

Vuntut National Park of Canada
PO Box 19, Old Crow, YT Y0B 1N0
Tel: 867-667-3910
Fax: 867-393-6701
vuntut.info@pc.gc.ca
www.pc.gc.ca/pn-np/yt/vuntut/index_E.asp

Wapusk National Park of Canada
Churchill Office, PO Box 127, Churchill, MB R0B 0E0
Tel: 204-675-8863
Fax: 204-675-2026
wapusk.np@pc.gc.ca
www.pc.gc.ca/pn-np/mb/wapusk/index_e.asp

Waterton Lakes National Park of Canada
PO Box 200, Waterton Park, AB T0K 2M0
Tel: 403-859-5133
Fax: 403-859-5152
waterton.info@pc.gc.ca
www.pc.gc.ca/pn-np/ab/waterton/index_E.asp

Wood Buffalo National Park of Canada
PO Box 750, Fort Smith, NT X0E 0P0
Tel: 867-872-7900
Fax: 867-872-3910
wbnp.info@pc.gc.ca
www.pc.gc.ca/pn-np/nt/woodbuffalo/index_e.asp
TTY: 867-872-7961
Other Communication: 24 Hour Hotline: 867-872-7962

Yoho National Park of Canada
PO Box 99, Field, BC V0A 1G0
Tel: 250-343-6783
Fax: 250-343-6012
yoho.info@pc.gc.ca
www.pc.gc.ca/pn-np/bc/yoho/index_E.asp

York Factory National Historic Site of Canada
PO Box 127, Churchill, MB R0B 0E0
Tel: 204-675-8863
Fax: 204-675-2026
Toll-Free: 888-773-8888
mannorth.nhs@pc.gc.ca
www.pc.gc.ca/lhn-nhs/mb/yorkfactory/index_E.asp
TTY: 866-787-6221

Patented Medicine Prices Review Board / Conseil d'examen du prix des médicaments brevetés

Standard Life Centre, #1400, 333 Laurier Ave. West, PO Box L40, Ottawa, ON K1P 1C1
Tel: 613-954-8299
Fax: 613-952-7626
Toll-Free: 877-861-2350
pmprb@pmprb-cepmb.gc.ca
www.pmprb-cepmb.gc.ca
TTY: 613-957-4373

The Patented Medicine Prices Review Board (PMPRB) is an independent quasi-judicial body established by Parliament in 1987 under the Patent Act (Act). The PMPRB is responsible for regulating the prices that patentees charge, the "factory-gate" price, for prescription & non-prescription patented drugs sold in Canada, to wholesalers, hospitals or pharmacies, for human and veterinary use to ensure that they are not excessive. The PMPRB regulates the price of each patented drug product, including each strength of each dosage form of each patented medicine sold in Canada.

Chair, Mary Catherine Lindberg
Tel: 613-952-3300

Vice-Chair, Mitchell Levine
Tel: 613-960-4570
Fax: 613-952-7626

Executive Director, Michelle Boudreau
Tel: 613-957-3656
Fax: 613-952-7626
Other Communications: Executive Assistant, Phone: 613-952-7617

Director, Board Secretariat & Communications, Sylvie Dupont
Tel: 613-954-8299
Fax: 613-952-7626

Director, Corporate Services, Marian Eagen
Tel: 613-952-3304
Fax: 613-952-7626

Director, Policy & Economic Analysis Branch, Gregory Gillespie
Tel: 613-952-3305
Fax: 613-952-7626

Acting Director, Policy & Economic Analysis Branch, Karen Reynolds
Tel: 613-941-0023
Fax: 613-952-7626

Director, Regulatory Affairs & Outreach, Ginette Tognet
Tel: 613-954-8297
Fax: 613-952-7626

Privacy Commissioner of Canada / Commissariat à la protection de la vie privée du Canada

Tower B, Place de Ville, 112 Kent St., 3rd Fl., Ottawa, ON K1A 1H3
Tel: 613-947-1698
Fax: 613-947-6850
Toll-Free: 800-282-1376
www.privcom.gc.ca
TTY: 613-992-9190

The Privacy Commissioner of Canada is an Officer of Parliament mandated to protect & promote privacy rights. She works independently from Government, reporting directly to the House of Commons & the Senate. The Privacy Commissioner oversees two federal privacy laws: the Privacy Act, which covers the federal government, & the new Personal Information Protection & Electronic Documents (PIPEDA) Act, which covers the collection use & disclosure of personal information in the course of commercial activities, except in provinces which have not, by then, enacted legislation that is deemed to be substantially similar to the federal law. The Privacy Commissioner's powers include: investigating complaints & conducting audits under both federal privacy laws; publishing information about personal information handling practices in the public & private sectors; conducting research into privacy issues; & promoting awareness & understanding of privacy issues in Canada.

Privacy Commissioner, Jennifer Stoddart
Tel: 613-947-6000
Fax: 613-947-6850
Other Communications: Executive Assistant, Phone: 613-947-6000

Assistant Privacy Commissioner, Chantal Bernier
Tel: 613-995-6402
Fax: 613-995-1139
Other Communications: Executive Assistant, Phone: 613-995-6402

Public Safety Canada / Sécurité publique Canada

269 Laurier Ave. West, Ottawa, ON K1A 0P8
Tel: 613-944-4875
Fax: 613-954-5186
Toll-Free: 800-830-3118
communications@ps.gc.ca
www.publicsafety.gc.ca; www.securitepublique.gc.ca
TTY: 866-865-5667
Other Communication: National Crime Prevention Centre Toll Free: 1-877-302-6272; E-mail: prevention@ps.gc.ca; National Office for Victims Toll-Free: 866-525-0554; Media: 613-991-0657

Public Safety Canada works to keep Canadians safe in cases of natural disasters, crime, & terrorism. Policies are developed, & programs & services are delivered in the following areas: emergency management, including information about emergency preparedness; national security, which features the administration of the Government Operations Centre to monitor potential threats to the national interest; law enforcement, including the contribution of funds for policing services in First Nations & Inuit communities; federal corrections effectiveness, efficiency & accountability, with the development of federal policy & legislation; & crime prevention, such as work with other governments, businesses, & volunteer groups to support projects to reduce offences.

Acts Administered:
Canadian Security Intelligence Act
Corrections & Conditional Release Act
Criminal Records Act
Customs Act
DNA Identification Act
Department of the Solicitor General Act
Emergency Preparedness Act
Firearms Act
Prisons & Reformatories Act
Royal Canadian Mounted Police Act
Royal Canadian Mounted Police Pension Continuation Act
Transfer of Offenders Act
Witness Protection Program Act

Minister, Public Safety, Hon. Vic Toews
Tel: 613-992-3128
Fax: 613-995-1049
Toews.V@parl.gc.ca
Other Communications: Public Safety & Emergency Preparedness: 613-991-2924

Deputy Minister, William V. Baker
Tel: 613-991-2895

Parliamentary Secretary to the Minister of Public Safety, Dave MacKenzie
Tel: 613-991-2924

Chief of Staff, Minister's Office, Andrew House
Tel: 613-991-2924

Assistant Inspector General, Canadian Security Intelligence Service (CSIS), Ian Blackie
Tel: 613-993-7431

Deputy Executive Director & Senior Counsel, Legal Services, Caroline Fobes
Tel: 613-949-9724

Senior Counsel & Strategic Policy Advisor, Mary-Anne Kirvan
Tel: 613-954-1067

Associated Agencies, Boards & Commissions:

• Canada Firearms Program (CAFC) / Centre des armes à feu Canada
Ottawa, ON K1A 0R2
Fax: 613-825-0297
Toll-free: 800-731-4000
cfp-pcaf@rcmp-grc.gc.ca
www.rcmp.gc.ca/cfp
The Canada Firearms Centre oversees the administration of the Firearms Act and the Canadian Firearms Program (CFP).

• Canadian Security Intelligence Service (CSIS) / Service canadien du renseignement de sécurité (SCRS)
See: Entry Name Index for detailed listing.

• Commission for Public Complaints Against the Royal Canadian Mounted Police / Commission des plaintes du public contre la Gendarmerie royale du Canada
National Intake Office
PO Box 88689
Surrey, BC V3W 0X1
Fax: 613-952-8045
Toll-free: 800-665-6878
TTY: 866-432-5837
org@cpc-cpp.gc.ca
www.cpc-cpp.gc.ca
The Commission is responsible for the receipt of complaints from the public about the conduct of members of the RCMP. It is also responsible for the review of complaints when complainants are not satisfied with the disposition of their complaints by the RCMP. The Commission can inquire into complaints by means of public hearings & the chair of the Commission can investigate complaints. Annually, the chair reports to Parliament through the Minister of Public Safety & Emergency Preparedness Canada.

• Correctional Service of Canada / Service correctionnel Canada

• National Parole Board

• Royal Canadian Mounted Police

• Royal Canadian Mounted Police External Review Committee / Comité externe d'examen de la Gendarmerie royale du Canada
PO Box 1159 B
Ottawa, ON K1P 5R2
Tel: 613-998-2134
Fax: 613-990-8969
org@erc-cee.gc.ca
www.erc-cee.gc.ca
The RCMP External Review Committee is an independent agency reporting to Parliament through the Minister of Public Safety Canada. It aims to independently and impartially promote fair and equitable labour relations within the RCMP, in accordance with applicable principles of law. To this end the Committee conducts an independent review of appeals in disciplinary and discharge and demotion matters, as well as certain categories of grievances that can be referred to it pursuant to s. 33 of the RCMP Act and s. 36 of the RCMP Regulations.

Communications Directorate / Direction générale des communications

Director General, Stéphanie Durand
Tel: 613-991-2799
Associate Director General, Jamie Tomlinson
Tel: 613-990-2642

Community Safety & Partnerships Branch / Sécurité de la population et des partenariats

340 Laurier Ave. West, Ottawa, ON K1A 0P8
The Community Safety & Partnerships Branch consist of the Aboriginal Policing Directorate, the Corrections & Criminal Justice Directorate, & the National Crime Prevention Centre.
Assistant Deputy Minister, Shawn Tupper
Tel: 613-993-4325

Aboriginal Policing Directorate / Direction générale de la police des autochtones

Director General, Mary Donaghy
Tel: 613-990-2666
Senior Director, Policy & Coordination, Annie LeBlanc
Tel: 613-991-4762
Senior Director, Operations, Claude Turgeon
Tel: 613-990-8434

Corrections & Criminal Justice Directorate / Direction générale des affaires correctionnelles et de la ustice pénale

Director General, Mary Campbell
Tel: 613-991-2952

National Crime Prevention Centre / Centre national de prévention du crime

Executive Director, Wayne Stryde
Tel: 613-957-9639
Regional Director, Northern Region, Kimberly Chemerika
Tel: 778-433-9701
Regional Director, Quebec Region, Kurtis Clifford
Tel: 514-283-7790
Fax: 514-283-2016
Regional Director, British Columbia Region, Sue Olsen
Tel: 604-666-5705
Regional Director, Atlantic Region, Karen Swan
Tel: 902-426-0012

Corporate Management Branch / Secteur de la gestion ministérielle

340 Laurier Ave. West, Ottawa, ON K1A 0P8
Assistant Deputy Minister, Elisabeth Nadeau
Tel: 613-990-2615
Chief Information Officer, Rosanna Di Paola
Tel: 613-944-4878
Comptroller, Hélène Filion
Tel: 613-998-0053
Director General, Corporate Services, René Bolduc
Tel: 613-990-6101
Director General, Human Resources, Denis Desharnais
Tel: 613-990-3496

Emergency Management & National Security Branch / Secteur de la gestion des urgences et de la sécurité nationale

340 Laurier Ave. West, Ottawa, ON K1A 0P8
The Emergency Management & National Security Branch consists of the following directorates & secretariat: Coordination Directorate; Emergency Management Policy Directorate; National Security Policy Directorate; Operations Directorate; Preparedness & Recovery Directorate; & the Cyber Security Strategy Secretariat.
Assistant Deputy Minister, Lynda Clairmont
Tel: 613-990-4976
Assistant Deputy Minister, Gina Wilson
Tel: 613-990-2743
Associate Assistant Deputy Minister, Daniel Lavoie
Tel: 613-990-2743
Director General, Science & Technology Policy, Ashley Anthony
Tel: 613-991-3376
Director General, Emergency Management Policy, Serge C. Beaudoin
Tel: 613-991-2944
Director General, National Security Policy, John Davies
Tel: 613-991-1970
Director General, Regional Operations Directorate, Jamie Deacon
Tel: 613-991-1699
Director General, National Cyber Security, Robert Dick
Tel: 613-990-2661
Director General, Preparedness & Recovery, Robert Lesser
Tel: 613-944-4853
Director General, National Security Operations, Michael MacDonald
Tel: 613-993-4595
Director General, Operations, Continuity of Government, Preparedness & Recovery, Richard Moreau
Tel: 613-990-7016
Director General, Critical Infrastructure & Strategic Coordination, Suki Wong
Tel: 613-991-3583
Associate Director General, Operations, Craig Oldham
Tel: 613-991-7728
Senior Director, Public Service Renewal, Kevin Phillips
Tel: 613-947-6492
Executive Director, Canadian Emergency Management College, Gary Donovan
Tel: 613-949-5000
Senior Analyst, National Cyber Security, Tom Campbell
Tel: 613-990-3577

Law Enforcement & Policing Branch / Secteur de la Police, et de l'application de la loi

340 Laurier Ave. West, Ottawa, ON K1A 0P8
The Policing, Law Enforcement & Interoperability Branch includes the following directorates: Law Enforcement & Border Strategies; Policing Policy; & Public Safety Interoperability.
Assistant Deputy Minister, Richard Wex
Tel: 613-990-2703
Director General, Law Enforcement & Border Strategies Directorate, Trevor Bhupsingh
Tel: 613-991-4281
Director General, Office of the Assistant Deputy Minister, Law Enforcement & Policing, Richard Clair
Tel: 613-990-3969
Director General, Police Services Agreements, Marty Muldoon
Tel: 613-949-3097
Director General, Policing Policy Directorate, Mark Potter
Tel: 613-991-1632

Strategic Policy Branch / Secteur de politiques stratégiques

340 Laurier Ave. West, Ottawa, ON K1A 0P8
Assistant Deputy Minister, Paul MacKinnon
Tel: 613-949-6435

Director General, Intergovernmental Affairs & Citizen Engagement Directorate, Patrick Boucher
Tel: 613-949-6553
Director General, Evaluation, Denis Gorman
Tel: 613-990-2646
Director General, Cabinet, Parliamentary & Executive Services, Randall Koops
Tel: 613-949-0477
Director General, Border Policy & International Affairs, Barbara Motzney
Tel: 613-949-7260
Director General, Strategic Policy, Planning & Research, Robert Mundie
Tel: 613-991-2824

Public Service Commission (PSC) / Commission de la fonction publique (CFP)

West Tower, 300 Laurier Ave. West, Ottawa, ON K1A 0M7
Tel: 613-992-9562
Fax: 613-992-9352
infocom@psc-cfp.gc.ca
www.psc-cfp.gc.ca
TTY: 800-532-9397

An independent agency that reports directly to Parliament. For administrative purposes, the Minister of Canadian Heritage speaks on its behalf in the House of Commons, but has no jurisdiction over it. The commission is also responsible for safeguarding the values of a professional Public Service: competence, non-partisanship & representatives.
Acts Administered:
Canadian Charter of Rights & Freedoms
Canadian Human Rights Act
Employment Equity Act
Official Languages Act
Public Service Employment Act
Public Service Modernization Act

President, Maria Barrados
Tel: 613-992-2788
Fax: 613-996-4337

Commissioner, Manon Vennat
Tel: 613-943-8709

Senior Vice-President, Policy, Hélène Laurendeau
Tel: 613-995-6135
Fax: 613-995-0221

Vice-President, Investigations, Denis Bilodeau
Tel: 613-992-5418
Fax: 613-995-6985

Vice-President, Corporate Management Branch, Richard Charlebois
Tel: 613-992-2425
Fax: 613-992-7519

Vice-President, Audit, Evaluation & Studies, Elizabeth Murphy-Walsh
Tel: 613-947-0219
Fax: 613-995-6044

Vice-President, Staffing & Assessment Services, Gerry Thom
Tel: 613-992-0894
Fax: 613-992-9905

Director General, Corporate Management Practices & Evaluation, Marvin Bedward
Tel: 613-992-1225
Fax: 613-995-3795

Director General; Chief Information Officer, Information Technology Services, Hachem Ben Essalah
Tel: 613-992-1981
Fax: 613-992-5948

Director General, Human Resources Management, Judith Flynn-Bédard
Tel: 613-992-1225
Fax: 613-995-3795

Director General, Communications & Parliamentary Affairs, Andrew McGillivary
Tel: 613-992-5428
Fax: 613-943-7723

Director General, Finance & Administration, Rafid Warsalee
Tel: 613-992-0847
Fax: 613-947-9747

Alberta & NWT
Canada Place, #830, 9700 Jasper Ave., Edmonton, AB T5J 4G3
Tel: 780-495-6134
Fax: 780-495-3145
TTY: 780-495-3130

Atlantic
Maritime Centre, 1505 Barrington St., 17th Fl., Halifax, NS B3J 3Y6
Fax: 888-457-5333
Toll-Free: 800-645-5605
TTY: 902-426-6246
Other Communication: Information: 1-877-998-7979

BC & Yukon
#210, 757 West Hastings St., Vancouver, BC V6C 3M2
Fax: 866-280-6356
Toll-Free: 800-645-5605
TTY: 604-666-6868

Central & Southern Ontario
Dominion Public Bldg., 1 Front St. West, 6th Fl., Toronto, ON M5J 2X5
Tel: 416-973-3131
Fax: 888-515-4447
TTY: 416-973-2269

Central Prairies & Nunavut
320 Donald St., 1st Fl., Winnipeg, MB R3B 2H3
Tel: 204-983-2486
Fax: 204-983-8188
TTY: 204-983-6066

National Capital & Eastern Ontario
66 Slater St., 4th Fl., Ottawa, ON K1A 0M7
Fax: 613-996-8048
Toll-Free: 800-645-5605
TTY: 613-996-1205

Québec
Complexe Guy-Favreau, Tour Est, 200, boul René-Lévesque ouest, 8e étage, Montréal, QC H2Z 1X4
Fax: 866-667-4936
Toll-Free: 800-645-5605
TTY: 514-283-2467

Director General, Hervé Déry
Tel: 613-992-5354
Fax: 613-995-0221
Director, Strategic Policy, Policy Research & Library, Margaret Hill
Tel: 613-947-2578
Fax: 613-992-9610
Director General, Equity & Diversity, Paula Green
Tel: 613-943-8262
Fax: 613-992-9977
Director General, Policy Development, Jennifer Miles
Tel: 613-947-0716
Fax: 613-943-2481
Director General, Political Activities, Kathy Nakamura
Tel: 613-995-1125
Fax: 613-995-7699

Public Service Staffing Tribunal (PSSRB) / Tribunal de la dotation de la fonction publique

240 Sparks St., 6th Fl., Ottawa, ON K1A 0A5
Tel: 613-949-6516
Fax: 613-949-6551
Toll-Free: 866-637-4491
info@psst-tdfp.gc.ca
www.psst-tdfp.gc.ca
TTY: 866-389-6901

Established under the Public Service Employment Act, the Tribunal deals with complaints related to internal appointments & lay offs in the federal public service. The Tribunal conducts hearings & provides mediation services in order to resolve complaints.
Acts Administered:
Public Service Employment Act

Chair & Chief Executive Officer, Guy Giguère
Tel: 613-949-5435
Fax: 613-949-5514

Vice-Chair, John Mooney
Tel: 613-949-5510
Fax: 613-949-5514

Executive Director & General Counsel, Josée Dubois
Tel: 613-949-5511
Fax: 613-949-5514

Director, Human Resources & Corporate Services, Julie Brunet
Tel: 613-949-9753
Fax: 613-949-5514

Director, Planning, Communications & Information Management, Brian Boudreau
Tel: 613-949-5513
Fax: 613-949-6551

Director, Registry, Operations & Policy, Christine Landry
Tel: 613-949-6518
Fax: 613-949-6551
christine.landry@psst-tdfp.gc.ca

Director, Dispute Resolution, Serge Roy
Tel: 613-949-6518
Fax: 613-949-6551
serge.roy@psst-tdfp.gc.ca

Public Works & Government Services Canada (PWGSC) / Travaux publics et services gouvernementaux

Place du Portage, Phase III, 11, rue Laurier, Ottawa, ON K1A 0S5
questions@tpsgc-pwgsc.gc.ca
www.tpsgc-pwgsc.gc.ca
TTY: 800-926-9105

Primary department responsible for purchasing goods & services for the Government of Canada. Purchases a variety of goods & services, construction, architectural, engineering & maintenance services & provides leasing services related to federal government works & facilities. Also maintains source lists of potential suppliers for some products. Ensures that the government's operational requirements are met in a cost-effective & timely manner, while taking into account the government's objectives including environmental considerations. As builders & caretakers of buildings, the department protects the environment by reducing solid waste, greening the construction & operation of buildings, conserving energy & water, improving fleet management, minimizing the effects of operations on climate change, & increasing environmental protection & conservation.
Acts Administered:
Anti-Personnel Mines Convention Implementation Act
Bridges Act
Canadian Arsenals Limited Divestiture Authorization Act
Defence Production Act
Dry Docks Subsidies Act
Expropriation Act
Federal District Commission to have acquired certain lands, An Act to Confirm the Authority of
Garnishment, Attachment & Pension Diversion Act
Government Property Traffic Act
Ottawa River, Act Respecting Certain Works
Pension Benefits Division Act
Public Works & Government Services Act
Seized Property Management Act
Statutes Act
Surplus Crown Assets Act
Translation Bureau Act

Minister, Public Works & Government Services; Minister for Status of Women, Receiver General for Canada, Hon. Rona Ambrose
Tel: 819-997-5421
Fax: 819-956-8382
Rona.Ambrose@tpsgc-pwgsc.gc.ca

Parliamentary Secretary, Jacques Gourde
Tel: 613-992-2639
Fax: 613-992-1018
Gourdj@parl.gc.ca

Deputy Minister & Deputy Receiver General for Canada, François Guimont
Tel: 819-956-1706
Fax: 819-956-8280
francois.guimont@tpsgc-pwgsc.gc.ca

Associate Deputy Minister, Andrew Treusch
Tel: 819-956-4472
Fax: 819-956-8280
Andrew.Treusch@tpsgc-pwgsc.gc.ca

Assistant Deputy Minister, Human Resources, Diane Lorenzato
Tel: 819-956-7548
Fax: 819-934-2523
diane.lorenzato@tpsgc-pwgsc.gc.ca

Assistant Deputy Minister, Departmental Oversight, Barbara Glover
Tel: 819-997-1094
Fax: 819-956-9949
barbara.glover@tpsgc-pwgsc.gc.ca

Chief of Staff, Office of the Minister, Michele Austin
Tel: 819-997-5421

Fax: 819-956-8920
michele.austin@tpsgc-pwgsc.gc.ca

Chief of Staff, Deputy Minister's Office, Anik Trépanier
Tel: 819-956-1710
Fax: 819-956-8280
anik.trepanier@tpsgc-pwgsc.gc.ca

Chief Executive Officer, Translation Bureau, Donna Achimov
Tel: 819-997-8825
Fax: 819-997-9227
donna.achimov@tpsgc-pwgsc.gc.ca
Other Communications: Alternate Phone: 613-240-2552

Acting Senior General Counsel & Executive Director, Legal Services Branch, Micheline Langlois
Tel: 819-956-0993
Fax: 819-953-3974
micheline.langlois@tpsgc-pwgsc.gc.ca

Associated Agencies, Boards & Commissions:
- **Canadian Wheat Board / Commission canadienne du blé**
- **Defence Construction Canada / Construction de Défense Canada**

Accounting, Banking & Compensation Branch / Direction générale de la comptabilité, gestion bancaire et rémunération

Responsible for managing the operations of the federal treasury, including issuing Receiver General payments for major government programs as well as maintaining the Accounts of Canada & producing the Government's financial statements. Responsible for providing government-wide accounting & reporting services. Directs the management & delivery of the administration of the public service pension & group insurance plans & maintains accounts for the various pension funds. Focuses in the financial management & control framework for the Department.

Assistant Deputy Minister, Accounting, Banking & Compensation, Renée Jolicoeur
Tel: 819-934-0497
Fax: 819-934-0932
renee.jolicoeur@tpsgc-pwgsc.gc.ca
Director General, Central Accounting & Reporting, Kim Croucher
Tel: 819-956-2875
Fax: 819-956-8400
kim.croucher@tpsgc-pwgsc.gc.ca
Director General, Pension Modernization & Centralization, Lucie Lanctôt
Tel: 613-948-6218
lucie.lanctot@tpsgc-pwgsc.gc.ca
Director General, Compensation, Carrie Roussin
Tel: 819-956-0481
Fax: 819-956-3000
carrie.roussin@tpsgc-pwgsc.gc.ca

Acquisitions Branch / Direction générale des approvisionnements

Provides departments & agencies with expert assistance at each stage of the supply cycle & offers tools that simplify & accelerate the acquisition of goods & services. It ensures that the government exercises due diligence & maintains the integrity of the procurement process. It is a primary service provider offering client departments a broad base of procurement solutions aimed at securing best value for their procurement dollar.

Assistant Deputy Minister, Tom Ring
Tel: 819-956-1711
Fax: 819-953-1058
tom.ring@tpsgc-pwgsc.gc.ca
Director General, Washington Sector, Martine Belanger
Tel: 202-682-7609
Fax: 202-682-7613
martine.belanger@pwgsc-tpsgc.gc.ca
Director General, Commercial Acquisitions & Supply Management Sector, Claire Caloren
Tel: 819-956-6098
Fax: 819-956-4491
claire.caloren@tpsgc-pwgsc.gc.ca
Acting Director General, Business Management Sector, Susan Daly
Tel: 819-956-8166
Fax: 819-956-8303
susan.daly@tpsgc-pwgsc.gc.ca
Director General, Services & Specialized Acquisitions Management Sector, Vicki L. Ghadban
Tel: 819-956-1649
Fax: 819-956-4944
vicki.ghadban@tpsgc-pwgsc.gc.ca
Director General, Marine Sector, Scott Leslie
Tel: 613-943-3338
Fax: 613-944-7870
scott.leslie@tpsgc-pwgsc.gc.ca
Director General, Services & Technology Acquisition Management Sector, Normand Masse
Tel: 819-956-3937
Fax: 819-956-2675
normand.masse@tpsgc-pwgsc.gc.ca
Director General, Office of Small & Medium Enterprises, Shereen Benzvy Miller
Tel: 819-956-8416
Fax: 819-956-6859
shereen.miller@tpsgc-pwgsc.gc.ca
Acting Director General, Defence & Major Projects Sector, Johanne Provencher
Tel: 819-956-0010
Fax: 819-956-9110
johanne.provencher@tpsgc-pwgsc.gc.ca
Director General, Policy, Risk, Integrity & Strategic Management Sector, Alain Vauclair
Tel: 819-956-0299
Fax: 819-956-0355
alain.vauclair@tpsgc-pwgsc.gc.ca

Communications Branch / Direction générale des communications

Director General, Kathleen Kieley
Tel: 819-956-2304
Fax: 819-956-9062

Corporate Services & Strategic Policy Branch / Direction générale des services ministériels et des politiques stratégiques

Assistant Deputy Minister, Caroline Weber
Tel: 819-956-4056
Fax: 819-956-5145
caroline.weber@tpsgc-pwgsc.gc.ca
Director General, Strategic Governance & Intergovernmental Affairs Unit, Kata Kitaljevich
Tel: 819-956-0809
Fax: 819-956-5145
kata.kitaljevich@tpsgc-pwgsc.gc.ca
Other Communications: Secure Fax: 819-956-4522
Director General, Strategic Policy & Planning, Jonathan Higdon
Tel: 819-956-0893
Fax: 819-956-5145
jonathan.higdon@tpsgc-pwgsc.gc.ca
Director General, Corporate Services, Penny Levesque
Tel: 819-956-3121
penny.levesque@tpsgc-pwgsc.gc.ca
Acting Director General, Executive Secretariat, John Longair
Tel: 819-956-5132
Fax: 819-956-9538
john.longair@tpsgc-pwgsc.gc.ca
Acting Director General, Office of Greening Government Operations, Micheline E. Paquette
Tel: 819-956-3334
Fax: 819-956-1130
micheline.e.paquette@tpsgc-pwgsc.gc.ca

Departmental Oversight Branch / Direction générale de la surveillance

Assistant Deputy Minister, Barbara Glover
Tel: 819-997-1094
Fax: 819-956-9949
barbara.glover@tpsgc-pwgsc.gc.ca
Chief Audit & Evaluation Executive, Linda Anglin
Tel: 819-956-2971
Fax: 819-956-9721
linda.anglin@tpsgc-pwgsc.gc.ca
Director General, Industrial Security Sector, Jennifer E. Stewart
Tel: 613-948-1777
Fax: 613-948-4144
jennifer.stewart@pwgsc-tpsgc.gc.ca

Audit Services Canada / Services de vérification Canada
Tower B, Place de Ville, 112 Kent St., Ottawa, ON K1A 0S5
Tel: 613-996-0188

Chief Executive Officer, André Auger
Tel: 613-996-2279
Fax: 613-947-2436
andre.auger@tpsgc-pwgsc.gc.ca
Acting Director, NCR Operations, Daren Penteluke
Tel: 613-992-6947
Fax: 613-947-2436
daren.penteluke@tpsgc-pwgsc.gc.ca
Acting Regional Director, Ontario, Jerry Jeremiah
Tel: 416-973-4196
Fax: 416-954-1729
jerry.jeremiah@pwgsc-tpsgc.gc.ca
Regional Director, Pacific & Western, Badrudin Moosa
Tel: 604-666-8228
Fax: 604-666-7330
Badrudin.Moosa@pwgsc-tpsgc.gc.ca
Acting Regional Director, Atlantic, Montague J. Onyett
Tel: 902-426-0521
Fax: 902-426-5419
montague.onyett@pwgsc-tpsgc.gc.ca

Finance Branch / Direction générale des finances
Fax: 819-956-5060

Chief Financial Officer, Alex Lakroni
Tel: 819-956-7226
Fax: 819-956-5060
alex.lakroni@tpsgc-pwgsc.gc.ca
Director General, SIGMA, Jacques Cormier
Tel: 819-934-9967
Fax: 819-934-4535
jacques.cormier@tpsgc-pwgsc.gc.ca
Director General, Financial Operations, André G. Léger
Tel: 819-956-1258
Fax: 819-956-1090
andre.g.leger@tpsgc-pwgsc.gc.ca
Director General, Financial Management, Sue Morgan
Tel: 819-934-0949
Fax: 819-953-9595
sue.morgan@tpsgc-pwgsc.gc.ca
Director General, Budget & Investment Management, Maria Pagliarello
Tel: 819-956-8504
Fax: 819-956-0162
maria.pagliarello@tpsgc-pwgsc.gc.ca

Human Resources Branch / Direction générale des ressources humaines
Fax: 819-956-7724

Assistant Deputy Minister, Diane Lorenzato
Tel: 819-956-7548
Fax: 819-934-2523
diane.lorenzato@tpsgc-pwgsc.gc.ca
Director General, Labour Relations, OHSD & Compensation Sector, André V. Latreille
Tel: 819-956-7378
Fax: 819-956-5547
andre.v.latreille@tpsgc-pwgsc.gc.ca
Director General, Corporate Human Resources Policies, Programs & Systems, Louis Seguin
Tel: 819-956-9716
Fax: 819-956-9955
louis.seguin@tpsgc-pwgsc.gc.ca
Director General, Human Resources Operations, Line Vallières
Tel: 819-956-8365
Fax: 819-956-4760
line.vallieres@tpsgc-pwgsc.gc.ca

Information Technology Services Branch / Services d'infotechnologie

Provides common telecommunications & informatics services to government departments, agencies & organizations, to facilitate universal access to information throughout the federal government. Focussing on network & computer services, telecommunications, & application development, ITS is a key player in government-wide initiatives such as the Secure Channel, IM/IT community renewal, & Government-On-Line (GoL).

Chief Information Officer, John Rath-Wilson
Tel: 819-956-2632
Fax: 819-956-5189
john.rath-wilson@tpsgc-pwgsc.gc.ca
Director General, Strategic Planning & Enterprise Architecture, François Audet
Tel: 819-956-4745
Fax: 819-956-4261
francois.audet@tpsgc-pwgsc.gc.ca
Director General, Application Management & IT Operational Services, Douglas Gauen
Tel: 819-956-2354
Fax: 819-956-2960
doug.gauen@tpsgc-pwgsc.gc.ca
Director General, Client Engagement, Paul Hession
Tel: 819-956-0226
paul.hession@tpsgc-pwgsc.gc.ca
Director General, Project Delivery Office, Claude Lareau
Tel: 819-956-8283
Fax: 819-956-6476
claude.lareau@tpsgc-pwgsc.gc.ca
Director General, Information Technology Services Branch, Christianne Poirier
Tel: 819-956-7054
christianne.poirier@tpsgc-pwgsc.gc.ca
Senior Director, Strategic Planning & Program Management, James Brooks
Tel: 819-956-9495
Fax: 819-956-4986
james.brooks@tpsgc-pwgsc.gc.ca
Senior Director & Information Security Officer, Office of the Chief Technology Officer, Brigitte Hébert
Tel: 819-956-7054
brigitte.hebert@tpsgc-pwgsc.gc.ca
Senior Director, Portfolio Management - A, Robert Laframboise
Tel: 819-956-7909
Fax: 819-956-2758
robert.laframboise@tpsgc-pwgsc.gc.ca
Senior Director, Application Engineering Services, John MacKenzie
Tel: 819-956-2372

Fax: 819-956-2418
john.mackenzie@tpsgc-pwgsc.gc.ca
Senior Director, Enterprise Revenue & Client Planning, Marc J. Thivierge
Tel: 819-956-4600
Fax: 819-956-4627
marc.j.thivierge@tpsgc-pwgsc.gc.ca
Senior Director, IT Services Plans & Performance Management, Michelle Tite-Soldaat
Tel: 819-956-8448
Fax: 819-956-5306
michelle.tite-soldaat@tpsgc-pwgsc.gc.ca
Executive Director, Service Transitions & Major Projects, Charles Duffett
Tel: 819-956-3162
charles.duffett@tpsgc-pwgsc.gc.ca
Director, Business Planning & Management Services, Paul Butler
Tel: 819-934-5125
Fax: 819-956-4986
paul.butler@tpsgc-pwgsc.gc.ca
Director, Service Management, Strategy & Optimization, Jim King
Tel: 613-748-2365
jim.king@tpsgc-pwgsc.gc.ca

Integrated Services Branch / Direction generale des services intégrés
Acting Assistant Deputy Minister, Sarah Paquet
Tel: 613-992-0679
sarah.paquet@tpsgc-pwgsc.gc.ca
Acting Director General, Shared Services Integration Sector, Stéphane J. Guèvremont
Tel: 613-992-3248
Fax: 613-944-4958
stephane.guevremont@tpsgc-pwgsc.gc.ca
Acting Director General, Business Planning & Management Services, Jacqeline Jodoin
Tel: 613-943-8425
Fax: 613-992-5980
jacqeline.jodoin@tpsgc-pwgsc.gc.ca
Director General, Service Integration Sector, Daniel Leclair
Tel: 819-956-9368
Fax: 819-956-9538
daniel.leclair@tpsgc-pwgsc.gc.ca
Acting Director General, Government Consulting Services, Danl Loewen
Tel: 613-995-1918
Fax: 613-944-4958
danl.loewen@tpsgc-pwgsc.gc.ca
Director General, Government Information Services Sector, Marc Saint-Pierre
Tel: 613-992-9218
Fax: 613-947-6949
marc.saint-pierre@tpsgc-pwgsc.gc.ca

MERX
PO Box 11684 Centre-ville, Montreal, QC H3C 6H4
Fax: 888-235-5800
merx@merx.com
www.merx.com
Other Communication: Suppliers Support: 1-800-964-MERX (6379); Buyers Support: 1-888-738-3005 (Ottawa: 613-737-3796)

The federal government's Government Electronic Tendering Service (GETS) contracts MERX to advertise government procurement opportunities online. Architectural & engineering consulting services, or services related to real property above $84,000 are advertised on MERX; below $84,000, they are handled through SELECT. Construction opportunities above $100,000 are advertised through MERX; below are handled through SELECT. MERX is used for printing services valued at $10,000 or above, & most goods & services valued at $25,000 or above. Below this level PWGSC uses a variety of bid solicitation methods: T-buys (purchasing by telephone when the product or service is required quickly & can easily be identified over the phone); RFQ (Request for Quotation); an Invitation to Tender (ITT) is used for straightforward requirements above $25,000 & where the lowest price will determine the awarding of the contract; RFP (Request for Proposal) for more complex requirements above $25,000; RFSO (Request for Standing Offer); RFSA (Request for Supply Arrangement); Sole-sourcing, subject to trade agreements & government contracting regulations. For products, individual departments have authority to buy up to $5,000 directly from suppliers; above $5,000, the department must go to PWGSC. Departments have authority to purchase nearly all their services; for program delivery services, departments may buy directly from suppliers up to $400,000 competitively or up to $100,000 without competition; they may also buy competitively up to $2 million when they advertise their requirements through MERX. Subscribers to MERX have access to an opportunity matching service, may view historical opportunities, review contract awards & international opportunities

Office of the Procurement Ombudsman / Bureau de l'ombudsman de l'approvisionnement
Constitution Square Bldg., #1150, 340 Albert St., 11th Fl., PO Box 151, Ottawa, ON K1R 7Y6

Parliamentary Precinct Branch / Direction générale de la cité parlementaire
Assistant Deputy Minister, Pierre-Marc Mongeau
Tel: 819-775-7325
Fax: 819-775-7496
pierre-marc.mongeau@tpsgc-pwgsc.gc.ca
Director General, Planning & Operations, Joanne Monette
Tel: 819-775-7150
Fax: 819-775-7496
joanne.monette@tpsgc-pwgsc.gc.ca
Director General, Major Crown Projects, Robert A. Wright
Tel: 819-775-7170
Fax: 819-775-7369
robert.a.wright@tpsgc-pwgsc.gc.ca
Director, Sylvian Lepage
Tel: 613-996-3883
sylvain.lepage@tpsgc-pwgsc.gc.ca
Director, Business Planning & Management Services, Robert Porter
Tel: 819-775-7310
Fax: 819-775-5725
robert.porter@tpsgc-pwgsc.gc.ca

Real Property Branch / Biens immobiliers
Fax: 613-736-2789

Manages office space & other general-purpose property; acts as custodian for $7.6 billion of real property holdings; administers 2,000 lease contracts; provides working space for 241,000 public servants in 1,810 locations across Canada; provides professional & technical services to government departments & agencies. Government buildings are 34 per cent more energy efficient & 24 per cent more greenhouse gas efficient than in 1990. Green Leases address key environmental standards such as proper management of wastewater, indoor air quality, recycling, energy efficient lighting fixtures, greenhouse gas reduction. Works with other departments on the remediation of contaminated sites & is the federal lead in the cleanup of the Sydney Tar Ponds in Nova Scotia.
Assistant Deputy Minister, John McBain
Tel: 819-956-3189
Fax: 819-956-7130
john.mcbain@tpsgc-pwgsc.gc.ca
Director General, Accommodation, Portfolio Management & Real Estate Services, Anne Auger
Tel: 819-956-6304
Fax: 819-956-4347
anne.auger@tpsgc-pwgsc.gc.ca
Director General, AFD Sector, Mark Campbell
Tel: 819-775-7217
Fax: 819-775-7279
mark.campbell@tpsgc-pwgsc.gc.ca
Director General, Special Initiatives Sector, Ralph Collins
Tel: 613-947-9335
Fax: 613-947-9300
ralph.collins@tpsgc-pwgsc.gc.ca
Director General, Professional & Technical Service Management, Anna Cullinan
Tel: 819-956-2039
Anna.Cullinan@tpsgc-pwgsc.gc.ca
Director General, National Capital Area Operations Sector, Rick DeBenetti
Tel: 819-956-2469
Fax: 819-956-2720
rick.debenetti@tpsgc-pwgsc.gc.ca
Director General, CRA Portfolio, Bill Doering
Tel: 613-954-8330
Fax: 613-949-1284
bill.doering@tpsgc-pwgsc.gc.ca
Acting Director General, Client Consultancy & Real Property Solutions, Peter Marella
Tel: 613-960-6713
Fax: 613-960-6399
peter.marella@tpsgc-pwgsc.gc.ca
Director General, Strategic Planning, Administration & Renewal Sector, Diane Orange
Tel: 819-956-6443
Fax: 819-956-7154
Diane.Orange@tpsgc-pwgsc.gc.ca
Acting Director General, NCA Portfolio Management, Claude Séguin
Tel: 819-956-6363
Fax: 819-956-0603
claude.seguin@tpsgc-pwgsc.gc.ca
Director General, Program Management Sector, Stephen Twiss
Tel: 819-956-6452
Fax: 819-934-0980
stephen.twiss@tpsgc-pwgsc.gc.ca
Acting Director General, Engineering Assets Strategy, Jacques A. Vachon
Tel: 819-956-6422

Fax: 819-934-1415
jean.vezina@tpsgc-pwgsc.gc.ca
Other Communications: Alternate Phone: 604-666-5191
Director General, Major Crown Projects, Jean Vézina
Tel: 819-956-4935
Fax: 819-956-7384
jean.vezina@tpsgc-pwgsc.gc.ca

Translation Bureau / Bureau de traduction
Richelieu Bldg., 975 St-Joseph Blvd., 5th Fl., Gatineau, QC K1A 0S5
Tel: 819-934-0496
Fax: 819-997-9227

Chief Executive Officer, Donna Achimov
Tel: 819-997-8825
Fax: 819-997-9227
donna.achimov@tpsgc-pwgsc.gc.ca
Other Communications: Alternate Phone: 613-240-2552
Vice-President, Professional Services, Donald Barabé
Tel: 819-994-1391
Fax: 819-934-0770
donald.barabe@tpsgc-pwgsc.gc.ca
Vice-President, Corporate Services, Gisèle Côté
Tel: 819-994-5221
gisele.cote@tpsgc-pwgsc.gc.ca
Vice-President, Client Services, Anne Nicholls
Tel: 819-997-6339
Fax: 819-997-8917
anne.nicholls@tpsgc-pwgsc.gc.ca
Director, Terminology Standardization, Gabriel Huard
Tel: 819-997-6843
Fax: 819-953-8443
gabriel.huard@tpsgc-pwgsc.gc.ca
Director, Interpretation & Parliamentary Translation, Alain Wood
Tel: 613-992-0294
Fax: 613-996-8794
wooda@parl.gc.ca
Acting Director General, Richard Robesco
Tel: 819-956-1649
Fax: 819-956-4944
richard.robesco@tpsgc-pwgsc.gc.ca
Senior Director, Major Projects Services, Rami Acouri
Tel: 819-934-0960
Fax: 819-956-4944
rami.acouri@tpsgc-pwgsc.gc.ca
Director, Space Program Directorate, François Gougeon
Tel: 450-926-4528
Fax: 450-926-4574
francois.gougeon@tpsgc-pwgsc.gc.ca
Senior Director, Shared Travel Services, Michael Corbett
Tel: 613-946-9915
Fax: 613-952-0434
michael.corbett@tpsgc-pwgsc.gc.ca
Director, Traffic Management Directorate, Jacques Amyot
Tel: 613-956-7301
Fax: 613-956-4944
jacques.amyot@tpsgc-pwgsc.gc.ca

Royal Canadian Mint / Monnaie royale canadienne

320 Sussex Dr., Ottawa, ON K1A 0G8
Tel: 613-993-3500
Fax: 613-993-4092
Toll-Free: 800-267-1871
www.rcmint.ca
TTY: 613-949-7731

The RCM has two plants located in Ottawa & Winnipeg. Foreign & domestic circulating coinage is manufactured in Winnipeg. The Ottawa facility is responsible for the production of foreign & domestic numismatic products, precious metals & the refining of gold. Reports to government through Public Works & Government Services.

Vice-Chairman of the Board of Directors, James B. Love

President & Chief Executive Officer, Ian E. Bennett
Tel: 613-993-1716

Vice-President, General Counsel & Corporate Secretary, Corporate & Legal Affairs, Marguerite F. Nadeau
Tel: 613-993-1732

Vice-President & Chief Financial Officer, Finance & Administration, J. Marc Brûlé
Tel: 613-993-5384

Royal Canadian Mounted Police (RCMP) / Gendarmerie royale du Canada (GRC)

1200 Vanier Pkwy., Ottawa, ON K1A 0R2
Tel: 613-993-7267
Fax: 613-993-0260
www.rcmp-grc.gc.ca

In 1873 the North West Mounted Police was constituted to provide Police protection in the unsettled portions of the North

West. In 1904 the title Royal was given to the Force. In 1920 The Dominion Police was amalgamated with this Force & the name changed to Royal Canadian Mounted Police. The headquarters was moved from Regina to Ottawa & the Force may be called upon to perform duties in any portion of the Dominion. In 1928 the RCMP absorbed the Saskatchewan Provincial Police & in 1932 the Provincial Police Forces of Alberta, Manitoba, New Brunswick, Nova Scotia & PEI were absorbed in like manner.

Acts Administered:
Canadian Peacekeeping Service Medal Act
Controlled Drugs & Substances Act
Criminal Code
Criminal Records Act
DNA Identification Act
Employment Equity Act
Excise Act
Export & Import Permits Act
Firearms Act
Foreign Missions & International Organizations Act
National Defence Act
Royal Canadian Mounted Police Act
Royal Canadian Mounted Police Pension Continuation Act
Royal Canadian Mounted Police Superannuation Act
Security Offences Act
Witness Protection Program Act

Commissioner, Bob Paulson

Director General, National Headquarters, Claude Bisson
Tel: 613-993-3627
Fax: 613-998-9444
Other Communications: Alternate Telephone: 613-794-5050

Deputy Commissioner, Atlantic Region, Steve Graham
Tel: 902-496-5042

Deputy Commissioner, Contract & Aboriginal Policing, Doug Lang

Deputy Commissioner, North Western Region, Gerry B. Braun
Tel: 306-780-6816

Deputy Commissioner, Pacific Region, Gary Bass
Tel: 604-264-2003

Deputy Commissioner, National Police Service, Joseph Buckle
Tel: 613-993-1736

Deputy Commissioner, Operations & Integration, Tim Killam
Tel: 613-993-3724

Deputy Commissioner, Special Advisor, Bill Sweeney
Tel: 613-949-4760
Fax: 613-993-1941

Deputy Commissioner, Federal Policing, Raf Souccar
Tel: 613-993-0403

Deputy Commissioner, Chief Human Resources Officer, Allen Nause
Tel: 613-843-4634
Fax: 613-825-4790

Chief Financial & Administrative Officer, Corporate Management & Comptrollership, Alain P. Séguin
Tel: 613-993-3193
Fax: 613-993-3770

Director General, National Communication Services, Supt. Tim Cogan
Tel: 613-991-9164
Fax: 613-993-0953

Director General, Internal Audit, Denise Nesrallah
Tel: 613-843-5453

Executive Director, Public Affairs, Sheila Bird
Tel: 613-993-3113
Fax: 613-993-3936
sheila.bird@rcmp-grc.gc.ca

Director, Professional Practice & Administration, Ian Christie
Tel: 613-843-5495

Director, Access to Information & Privacy Branch, Supt. Yves Marineau
Tel: 613-993-5162
Fax: 613-993-5080

Director, Executive Services & Ministerial Liaison, Kathryn McElhone
Tel: 613-843-4611
Fax: 613-825-1949

Director, Staff Relations Representative Program Office, Greg Nixon
Tel: 613-843-5616

Director, Adjudications, Supt. John Reid
Tel: 613-991-0753

RCMP Divisions & Commanding Officers

A Division
155 McArthur Ave., Ottawa, ON K1A 0R4
Tel: 613-993-8860
Fax: 613-993-5870
Acting Commanding Officer, A/Commr. Allen Nause
Tel: 613-993-8860
Fax: 613-993-5870

B Division
PO Box 9700 B, St. John's, NL A1A 3T5
Tel: 709-772-5465
Commanding Officer, Assistant Commissioner, A/Commr. Bill Smith

C Division
4225, boul Dorchester ouest, Westmount, QC H3Z 1V5
Tél: 514-939-8300
Téléc: 514-283-2169
Ligne sans frais: 800-771-5401
Commanding Officer, A/Commr. François Deschênes

D Division
1091 Portage Ave., PO Box 5650, Winnipeg, MB R3C 3K2
Tel: 204-983-5420
Commanding Officer, Bill Robinson

E Division
657 West 37 St., Vancouver, BC V5Z 1K6
Tel: 604-264-3111
Fax: 604-264-3196
Commanding Officer, A/Commr. Peter Hourihan

F Division
6101 Dewdney Ave. West, PO Box 2500, Regina, SK S4P 3K7
Tel: 306-780-5477
Fax: 306-780-5410
Commanding Officer, Russ Mirasty

G Division
Henry Larsen Bldg., 5010 - 49th Ave., PO Box 5010, Yellowknife, NT X1A 2R3
Tel: 867-669-5100
Commanding Officer, Chief Superintendent, Tom Middleton

H Division
3139 Oxford St., PO Box 2286, Halifax, NS B3J 3E1
Tel: 902-426-3940
Fax: 902-426-2481
Commanding Officer, DL Bishop
Tel: 902-426-3940

J Division
1445 Regent St., PO Box 3900, Fredericton, NB E3B 4Z8
Tel: 506-452-3400
Commanding Officer, Wayne Lang

K Division
11140 - 109 St., Edmonton, AB T5G 2T4
Tel: 780-945-5444
Fax: 780-945-5601
Commanding Officer, R.R. (Rod) Knecht

L Division
450 University Ave., PO Box 1360, Charlottetown, PE C1A 7N1
Tel: 902-566-7112
Fax: 902-566-7235
Commanding Officer, Tracy Hardy

M Division
4100 - 4th Ave., Whitehorse, YT Y1A 1H5
Tel: 867-667-5551
Fax: 867-393-6791
Commanding Officer, Peter Clark

O Division
130 Dufferin Ave., 5th Fl., PO Box 3240 B, London, ON N6A 4K3
Tel: 519-640-7267
Fax: 519-640-7255
TTY: 519-640-7495
Commanding Officer, Norm Mazerolle

V Division
PO Box 500 B, Iqaluit, NU X0A 0H0
Tel: 867-975-4409
Commanding Officer, C/Supt. Steve McVarnock

Canadian Police College / École de police canadienne
PO Box 8900, Ottawa, ON K1G 3J2
Tel: 613-993-9500
Fax: 613-990-9738
cpc-ccp@rcmp-grc.gc.ca
www.cpc.gc.ca
Director General & Chief Superintendent, Cal Corley
Tel: 613-998-0883

RCMP Training Academy / Académie d'entrainement
6101 Dewdney Ave., Regina, SK S4P 3J7
Tel: 306-780-5002
Fax: 306-780-7940
Officer in Charge, Centralized Training, Robert Castonguay

St. Lawrence Seaway Management Corporation (SLSMC) / Corporation de Gestion de la Voie Maritime du Saint-Laurent (CGVMSL)

202 Pitt St., Cornwall, ON K6J 3P7
Tel: 613-932-5170
Fax: 613-932-7286
marketing@seaway.ca
www.greatlakes-seaway.com
Other Communication: billing@seaway.ca (Statistics & Research)

A not-for-profit corporation responsible for the safe & efficient movement of marine traffic through Canadian Seaway facilities. It shares operations with its American counterpart, the Saint Lawrence Seaway Development Corporation, in operating & maintaining 15 locks between Montréal & Lake Erie.

President & Chief Executive Officer, Terence F. Bowles

Maisonneuve
151, rue Ecluse, Saint-Lambert, QC J4R 2V6
Vice-President, A. Juster

Niagara
508 Glendale Ave., St Catharines, ON L2R 6V8
Vice-President, M. Drolet

Security Intelligence Review Committee (SIRC) / Comité de Surveillance des activités de renseignement de sécurité (CSARS)

Jackson Bldg., 122 Bank St., 4th Fl., PO Box 2430 D, Ottawa, ON K1P 5W5
Tel: 613-990-8441
Fax: 613-990-5230
ellardm@sirc-csars.gc.ca
www.sirc-csars.gc.ca

Has as its mandate, under the Canadian Security Intelligence Service Act, to carry out the independent & external review of the Canadian Security Intelligence Service (CSIS) & to investigate complaints about CSIS activities. It is also required to investigate complaints from individuals who have had their employment prospects affected by the denial of a security clearance, & complaints referred to it by the Human Rights Commission. It is required to investigate reports made to it by the Minister of Citizenship & Immigration, & the Solicitor General of Canada, which relate to national security or to an individual's involvement in organized crime. The Committee is required to report annually to Parliament through the Minister of Public Safety & Emergency Preparedness on these matters.

Acts Administered:
Canadian Security Intelligence Service Act

Chair, Hon. Arthur Porter
Tel: 613-991-9111
Fax: 613-990-5230

Executive Director, Susan Pollak
Tel: 613-991-9111
Fax: 613-990-5230

Deputy Executive Director, Lori Biesenthal
Tel: 613-991-9112
Fax: 613-990-5230

Social Sciences & Humanities Research Council of Canada (SSHRC) / Conseil de recherches en sciences humaines du Canada (CRSH)

Constitution Sq., 350 Albert St., PO Box 1610 B, Ottawa, ON K1P 6G4
Tel: 613-992-0691
Fax: 613-992-1787
info@sshrc.ca
www.sshrc-crsh.gc.ca

The key national research agency investing in the knowledge & skills Canada needs to build the quality of its social, cultural &

economic life. SSHRC supports university-based research & training in the human sciences. It funds basic, applied & collaborative research, student training, research partnerships, knowledge transfer & the communication of research findings in all disciplines of the social sciences & humanities. Grants & fellowships are awarded through national competitions adjudicated by eminent researchers & scholars.

President, Chad Gaffield
Tel: 613-995-5488
Chad.Gaffield@sshrc-crsh.gc.ca

Executive Vice-President, Carmen Charette
Tel: 613-947-3275
carmen.charette@sshrc-crsh.gc.ca

Vice-President, Research Capacity Directorate, Brent Herbert-Copley
Tel: 613-995-5457
Brent.Herbert-Copley@sshrc-crsh.gc.ca

Vice-President, Common Administrative Services, Jaime Pitfield
Tel: 613-995-3914
Fax: 613-991-0969
Jaime.Pitfield@sshrc-crsh.gc.ca

Vice-President, Partnerships, Research Directorate, Gisèle Yasmeen
Tel: 613-947-6938
gisele.yasmeen@sshrc-crsh.gc.ca

Specific Claims Tribunal Canada (SCT) / Tribunal des revendications particulières Canada (TRP)

#400, 427 Laurier Ave. West, PO Box 31, Ottawa, ON K1R 7Y2
Tel: 613-947-0751
Fax: 613-943-0586
info@sct-trp.ca
www.sct-trp.ca

Created in 2008 as part of the federal government's Justice at Last policy. The Tribunal is an independent group of six federal judges who can make binding rulings on monetary damage claims filed by First Nations groups against the Crown.

Chairperson, Hon. Harry Slade

Justice, Hon. Patrick Smith

Justice, Hon. Johanne Mainville

Standards Council of Canada (SCC) / Conseil canadien des normes (CCN)

#200, 270 Albert St., Ottawa, ON K1P 6N7
Tel: 613-238-3222
Fax: 613-569-7808
info@scc.ca
www.scc.ca

Federal Crown corporation with the mandate to promote efficient & effective standardization. The organization reports to Parliament through the Minister of Industry & oversees Canada's National Standards System. The National Standards System comprises organizations & individuals involved in voluntary standards development, promotion & implementation. In addition, more than 400 organizations have been accredited by the Standards Council, including environmental management systems (EMS) registration organizations that perform registrations to ISO 14000 series standards. The Council offers accreditation to registration bodies for specialized environmental management systems in industry-specific areas, including sustainable forestry management (CAN/CSZ809-02). Manages the Program for the Accreditation of Laboratories - Canada (PALCAN) which seeks to identify & accredit competent testing laboratories. Initial assessment is made & regular follow-up audits are performed; accredited organizations are included in the Standards Council directory of accredited testing organizations. Users of testing services can eliminate or reduce their need to establish the competence of a prospective lab. In cooperation with the Canadian Association of Environmental Analy tical Laboratories (CAEAL), SCC operates an accreditation program for environmental analytical laboratories. SCC's website provides free access to a wide variety of standards information, including searchable databases containing information on Canadian, foreign & international standards, regulations & SCC-accredited organizations. More speacialized information is available through SCC's information & Research Service. Other accreditation programs include ones for registrars of ISO 14000 environmental management systems; environmental auditor certifiers & auditor training course providers.

Chair, Hugh Krentz
Tel: 613-238-3222
Fax: 613-569-7808

Executive Director, John Walter
Tel: 613-238-3222 ext: 400
Fax: 613-569-7808
jwalter@scc.ca

Manager, Communications, Pilar Castro
Tel: 613-238-3222 ext: 405
Fax: 613-569-7808
pcastro@scc.ca

Statistics Canada / Statistique Canada

R.H. Coats Bldg., Tunney's Pasture, 150 Tunney's Pasture Driveway, Ottawa, ON K1A 0T6
Tel: 613-951-8116
Fax: 877-287-4369
Toll-Free: 800-263-1136
infostats@statcan.ca
www.statcan.ca
TTY: 800-363-7629

Agency of the federal government, headed by the Chief Statistician of Canada which reports to Parliament through the Minister of Industry. As Canada's central statistical agency, it has a mandate to collect, compile, analyse, abstract & publish statistical information relating to the commercial, industrial, financial, social, economic & general activities & condition of the people of Canada; coordinates activities with its federal & provincial partners in the national statistical system to avoid duplication of effort & to ensure the consistency & usefulness of statistics. The agency profiles & measures both social & economic changes in Canada. It presents a comprehensive picture of the national economy through statistics on manufacturing, agriculture, retail sales, services, prices, productivity changes, trade, transportation, employment & unemployment, & aggregate measures such as gross domestic product. It also presents a comprehensive picture of social conditions through statistics on demography, health, areas.

Acts Administered:
Corporations Returns Act
Statistics Act

Chief Statistician of Canada, Wayne Smith
Tel: 613-951-9757
Fax: 613-951-3880
Wayne.Smith@statcan.gc.ca

Calgary
Discovery Place, #201, 3553-31 St. NW, Edmonton, AB T2L 2K7
Tel: 780-495-3027
Fax: 780-495-5318

Edmonton
Park Square, 10001 Bellamy Hill, Edmonton, AB T5J 3B6
Tel: 780-495-3027
Fax: 780-495-5318

Halifax
1770 Market St., 3rd Fl., Halifax, NS B3J 3M3

Montréal
Tour Est, Complexe Guy-Favreau, 200, boul René-Lévesque ouest, 4e étage, Montréal, QC H2Z 1X4

Ottawa
R.H. Coats Bldg., Lobby, Holland Ave., Ottawa, ON K1A 0T6

Regina
Avord Tower, 2001 Victoria Ave., 9th Fl., Regina, SK S4P 0R7

Toronto
Arthur Meighen Bldg., 25 St. Clair Ave. East, 10th Fl., Toronto, ON M4T 1M4

Vancouver
Library Square Tower, #600, 300 West Georgia St., Vancouver, BC V6B 6C7

Winnipeg
Via Rail Bldg., #200, 123 Main St., Winnipeg, MB R3C 4V9

Status of Women Canada (SWC) / Condition féminine Canada

123 Slater St., 10th Fl., Ottawa, ON K1P 1H9
Tel: 613-995-7835
Fax: 613-947-0761
Toll-Free: 866-902-2719
infonational@swc-cfc.gc.ca
www.swc-cfc.gc.ca
TTY: 613-996-1322

The federal government agency promotes gender equality, & the participation of women in the economic, social, cultural, & political life in Canada. Status of Women Canada focuses its work in the following areas: improvement of women's economic autonomy & well-being; elimination of systemic violence against women & children; & the advancement of women's human rights. To achieve results, SWC works with & supports research organizations, equality-seeking organizations, the non-governmental, voluntary & private sectors, & international organizations.

Minister, Public Works & Government Services; Minister for Status of Women, Hon. Rona Ambrose
Tel: 613-956-4000
Fax: 613-995-1761
minister-ministre@swc-cfc.gc.ca

Parliamentary Secretary for Status of Women, Susan Truppe
Tel: 613-992-0805
Fax: 613-992-9613

Coordinator/Head of Agency, Suzanne Clement
Tel: 613-995-7838
Fax: 613-943-0449
suzanne.clement@swc-cfc.gc.ca

Director General, Policy, Sébastien Goupil
Tel: 613-995-4761
Fax: 613-947-0530
sebastien.goupil@swc-cfc.gc.ca

Director, Women's Program, Linda Savoie
Tel: 613-947-0355
Fax: 613-947-0761
linda.savoie@swc-cfc.gc.ca

Director General, Communications & Strategic Planning Directorate, Nanci-Jean Waugh
Tel: 613-995-7839
Fax: 613-943-2386
nanci-jean.waugh@swc-cfc.gc.ca

Telefilm Canada / Téléfilm Canada

#500, 360, rue Saint-Jacques, Montréal, QC H2Y 1P5
Tél: 514-283-6363
Téléc: 514-283-2365
Ligne sans frais: 800-567-0890
info@telefilm.gc.ca
www.telefilm.gc.ca

Telefilm Canada is a Crown corporation reporting to Parliament through the Department of Canadian Heritage. Headquartered in Montréal, Telefilm provides services to the Canadian audiovisual industry by means of four regional offices located in Vancouver, Toronto, Montréal and Halifax. Dedicated to the development and promotion of the Canadian audiovisual industry.

Chair, Michel Roy

Executive Director, Carolle Brabant

Director, Communications, Denise Arab

Director, Business Affairs & Certification, Dave Forget

Director, National & International Business Development, Sheila de La Varende

Director, Public & Government Affairs, Jean-Claude Mahé

Director, Legal Services & Access to Information; Corporate Secretary, Stéphane Odesse

Director, Administration & Corporate Services, Denis Pion

Director, Projects Financing, Michel Pradier

Atlantic Region
1717 Barrington St., 4th Fl., Halifax, NS B3J 2A4
Tel: 902-426-8425
Fax: 902-426-4445
Toll-Free: 800-565-1773
hal@telefilm.gc.ca

Ontario & Nunavut
#100, 474 Bathurst St., Toronto, ON M5T 2S6
Tel: 416-973-6436
Fax: 416-973-8606

Western Region
#410, 609 Granville St., Vancouver, BC V7Y 1G5
Tel: 604-666-1566
Fax: 604-666-7754

Transport Canada (TC) / Transports Canada

Place de Ville, 330 Sparks St., Tower C, Ottawa, ON K1A 0N5
Tel: 613-990-2309
Fax: 613-954-4731
Toll-Free: 866-995-9737
www.tc.gc.ca
TTY: 888-675-6863

Using EMS 14000 standards, Transport Canada incorporates environmental considerations in all decision-making to fulfill the department's sustainable development strategy. Working with airports & airlines to minimize environmental effects of de-icing fluids; working with Environment Canada & industry to more effectively manage road salt; participating with ICAO's Committee on Aviation Environmental Protection (CAEP) concerning aircraft emissions, noise & land use planning. Ongoing contaminated sites management program. The Moving on Sustainable Transportation (MOST) Program supports projects that educate, raise awareness & provide tools to understand, promote & encourage sustainable transportation, such as neighbourhood transit passes, idle-free workplaces, school walking routes. Development of strategies to reduce greenhouse gas emissions from freight transportation; information on fuel consumption. Urban Transportation Showcase Program aims to reduce greenhouse gas emissions through showcasing demonstrations in communities across Canada
(www.tc.gc.ca/eng/programs/environment-utsp-menu-964.htm)

Acts Administered:

Aeronautics Act
Air Canada Public Participation Act
Airport Transfer (Miscellaneous Matters) Act
Arctic Waters Pollution Prevention Act (Indian & Northern Affairs)
Bills of Landing Act
Blue Water Bridge Authority Act
Bridges Act
Buffalo & Fort Erie Public Bridge Company Act
CN Commercialization Act
Canada Marine Act
Canada Post Corporation Act
Canada Shipping Act, 2001 (Fisheries & Oceans)
Canada Strategic Infrastructure Fund Act
Canada Transportation Act
Canadian Air Transport Security Authority Act
Canadian National Montréal Terminals Act
Carriage by Air Act
Civil Air Navigation Services Commercialization Act
Coasting Trade Act
Department of Transport Act
Government Property Traffic Act
Harbour Commissions Act
International Bridges & Tunnels Act
International Interests in Mobile Equipment (aircraft equipment) Act
Marine Insurance Act
Marine Liability Act
Marine Transportation Security Act
Montréal Port Wardens Act
Motor Vehicle Fuel Consumption Standards Act
Motor Vehicle Safety Act
Motor Vehicle Transport Act
National Energy Board Act
Navigable Waters Projection Act
Northern Transportation Company Ltd. Disposal Authorization Act
Northumberland Strait Crossing Act
Pilotage Act
Pre-clearance Act
Québec Habor, Port Wardens Act
Railway Relocation & Crossing Act
Railway Safety Act
Safe Containers Convention Act
Transportation Appeal Tribunal of Canada Act
Transportation of Dangerous Goods Act, 1992
United States Wreckers Act

Minister, Transport, Infrastructure, & Communities, Hon. Denis Lebel
Tel: 613-991-0700
Fax: 613-995-0327
mintc@tc.gc.ca

Deputy Minister, Yaprak Baltacioglu
Tel: 613-990-4507
Fax: 613-991-0851
yaprak.baltacioglu@tc.gc.ca

Associate Deputy Minister, Anita Biguzs
Tel: 613-949-2960
Fax: 613-991-0851
anita.biguzs@tc.gc.ca

Parliamentary Secretary to the Minister of Transport, Infrastructure, & Communities, Pierre Poilievre
Tel: 613-992-2772
Fax: 613-992-1209
pierre.poilievre@parl.gc.ca

Chief, Audit & Evaluation Executive, Laura Ruzzier
Tel: 613-990-5462
Fax: 613-990-6455
laura.ruzzier@tc.gc.ca

Integrity Officer, Transport Canada Office of Integrity, Ted Cherrett
Tel: 613-998-9654
ted.cherrett@tc.gc.ca

Director General, Corporate Secretariat, Natalie Bossé
Tel: 613-998-8058
Fax: 613-993-5146
natalie.bosse@tc.gc.ca

Director General, Communications & Marketing, Dan Dugas
Tel: 613-990-6138
Fax: 613-991-6719
dan.dugas@tc.gc.ca

Acting Executive Director to the Deputy Minister, Doreen Gagnon
Tel: 613-990-9002
Fax: 613-990-1878
doreen.gagnon@tc.gc.ca

Executive Director, Legal Services, Henry K. Schultz
Tel: 613-990-5768
Fax: 613-990-5777
henry.schultz@tc.gc.ca

Associated Agencies, Boards & Commissions:

• Atlantic Pilotage Authority Canada / Administration de pilotage de l'Atlantique Canada
• Canada Lands Company / Société Immobilière du Canada
• Canada Mortgage & Housing Corporation / Société canadienne d'hypothèques et de logement
• Canada Post Corporation / Société canadienne des postes

• Canadian Air Transport Security Authority (CATSA) / Administration canadienne de la sûreté du transport aérien (ACSTA)
99 Bank St., 13th Fl.
Ottawa, ON K1P 6B9
Fax: 613-990-1295
Toll-free: 888-294-2202
TTY: 613-949-5534
www.catsa-acsta.gc.ca
CATSA secures critical elements of the air transportation system - from passenger screening to baggage screening - & encourages Canadians to Pack Smart for the benefit of all air travellers.
• Canadian Transportation Agency / Office des transports du Canada
• Federal Bridge Corporation Limited (FBCL) / Société des ponts fédéraux Limitée
#1210, 55 Metcalfe St.
Ottawa, ON K1P 6L5
Tel: 613-993-6880
Fax: 613-993-6945
info@federalbridge.ca
www.federalbridge.ca
The FBCL was incorporated in 1998 to assume the non-navigational management responsibilities of the St. Lawrence Seaway Authority, including the Jacques Cartier & Champlain Bridges Incorporated, & in a joint venture with its U.S. partner, the Seaway International Bridge Corporation, Ltd. At the same time, the FBCL assumed responsibility for the management of the Canadian portion of the Thousand Islands International Bridge. In 2000, the FBCL acquired the Canadian half of the Sault Ste. Marie International Bridge.
• Great Lakes Pilotage Authority / Administration de pilotage des Grands Lacs
• Laurentian Pilotage Authority / Administration de pilotage des Laurentides Canada
• Marine Atlantic Inc. / Marine Atlantique
• Pacific Pilotage Authority / Administration de Pilotage du Pacifique Canada
• Royal Canadian Mint / Monnaie royale canadienne
• Transportation Appeal Tribunal of Canada / Anciennement le Tribunal de l'aviation civile
#1201, 333 Laurier Ave. West, 12th Fl.
Ottawa, ON K1A 0N5
Tel: 613-990-6906
Fax: 613-990-9153
info@tatc.gc.ca
www.tatc.gc.ca
The Tribunal provides an independent review process for anyone who has been given notice of an administrative or enforcement action taken by the Minister of Transport, railway safety inspectors or the Canadian Transportation Agency under various federal transportation Acts.
• Transportation Safety Board of Canada / Bureau de la sécurité des transports du Canada
• VIA Rail Canada Inc.

Communications & Marketing Group / Groupe Communications et marketing
Tel: 613-993-0055
Fax: 613-991-6719

Director General, Dan Dugas
Tel: 613-990-6138
Fax: 613-991-6719
dan.dugas@tc.gc.ca
Executive Director, Marian Hubley
Tel: 613-993-7649
Fax: 613-995-0351
marian.hubley@tc.gc.ca
Director, Web Creative & Internal Communications, Catherine Betz
Tel: 613-990-6721
catherine.betz@tc.gc.ca
Director, Client Services, Operations, Robert Greenslade
Tel: 613-990-6140
robert.greenslade@tc.gc.ca
Director, Strategic Initiatives & Marketing, Joan Pollock
Tel: 613-990-2366
Fax: 613-957-4260
joan.pollock@tc.gc.ca

Corporate Services / Services généraux
Corporate Services is part of the Department's administration business line & is responsible for providing services & functional expertise in the areas of finance & administration, technology & information management, human resources & access to information, Crown corporation portfolio coordination, internal audit & evaluation services.
Director General, Crown Corporation Governance, April Nakatsu
Tel: 613-991-2998
Fax: 613-991-4277
april.nakatsu@tc.gc.ca
Executive Director, Corporate Planning & Reporting, Marie-Christine Haubert
Tel: 613-998-9293
Fax: 613-991-0426
marie-christine.haubert@tc.gc.ca

Finance & Administration / Finances et administration
Director General, Deloranda Munro
Tel: 613-993-4307
Fax: 613-991-4410
deloranda.munro@tc.gc.ca
Senior Director, Financial Management, Claude Corbin
Tel: 613-990-3800
Fax: 613-998-1337
claude.corbin@tc.gc.ca

Human Resources Directorate / Direction générale des ressources humaines
Director General, Linda Brouillette
Tel: 613-991-6317
linda.brouillette@tc.gc.ca
Chief, Diversity & Official Languages, Corporate HR Policy & Programs, Francine Charbonneau
Tel: 613-990-5690
Fax: 613-998-4614
francine.charbonneau@tc.gc.ca
Chief, Resources, Projects & Issues Management Branch, Patrice Faria
Tel: 613-993-7900
Fax: 613-998-4614
patrice.faria@tc.gc.ca
Chief, Values, Ethics & Wellness, Eric Saint-Onge
Tel: 613-949-1976
Fax: 613-998-1345
eric.saint-onge@tc.gc.ca
Senior Director, Human Resources Client Services, George Thwaites
Tel: 613-993-8976
Fax: 613-990-1880
george.thwaites@tc.gc.ca
Senior Director, Corporate, HR Policy, Programs, Planning & Systems, Robert Sincennes
Tel: 613-991-6485
Fax: 613-990-1880
robert.sincennes@tc.gc.ca

Technology & Information Management Services Directorate / Direction générale des services de gestion de la technologie et de l'information
Director General, Chris Molinski
Tel: 613-998-6465
chris.molinski@tc.gc.ca
Director, Application Services, Tracey Boicey
Tel: 613-998-0739
Fax: 613-954-4493
tracey.boicey@tc.gc.ca
Director, IM/IT Architecture & Planning, Joël Comeau
Tel: 613-993-8040

Fax: 613-954-5858
joel.comeau@tc.gc.ca
Director, Computer Operations & Network Services, Rick Huard
Tel: 613-990-5380
rick.huard@tc.gc.ca
Director, Information Management, Diane Lavigne
Tel: 613-991-2867
Fax: 613-990-2469
diane.lavigne@tc.gc.ca
Director, IT/IM Security & Infrastructure Planning, Richard Ruta
Tel: 613-993-7066
Fax: 613-954-5858
richard.ruta@tc.gc.ca

Policy Group / Groupe de politiques
Responsible for setting policies relating to rail, marine, highways & borders, motor carrier, air, airports & accessible transportation, as well as setting departmental strategic policy & coordinating intergovernmental relations; assessing the performance of the overall transportation systems & its components, & developing supporting databases, forecasts & economic analysis; administering the management agreement with the St. Lawrence Seaway Management Corporation; & supporting rail passenger services through payments to VIA Rail & three regional railways, & ferry services through payments to Marine Atlantic & to provincial & private operators & border infrastructure improvements.
Assistant Deputy Minister, Kristine Burr
Tel: 613-998-1880
Fax: 613-991-1440
kristine.burr@tc.gc.ca
Executive Director, Policy Initiatives, Marc Rioux
Tel: 613-993-1718
Fax: 613-991-6445
marc.rioux@tc.gc.ca
Director, Business Planning & Group Services, Malick Sidibé
Tel: 613-949-0245
Fax: 613-998-3987
malick.sidibe@tc.gc.ca
Human Resources Special Project Officer, Bruce Vo
Tel: 613-949-7272
Fax: 613-949-9415
bruce.vo@tc.gc.ca
Senior Policy Advisor, Félix Meunier
Tel: 613-998-1877
Fax: 613-991-6445

Air Policy / Politique du transport aérien
Fax: 613-991-6445
Director General, Brigita Gravitis-Beck
Tel: 613-993-0054
brigita.gravitis-beck@tc.gc.ca
Chief, Policy Analysis, Donald Park
Tel: 613-991-9082
donald.park@tc.gc.ca
Canada's Permanent Representative to the International Civil Aviation Organization, Mark Allen
Tel: 613-991-6405
mark.allen@tc.gc.ca

Economic Analysis / Analyse économiques
Fax: 613-957-3280
Director General, Richard Thivierge
Tel: 613-998-1881
Fax: 613-957-3280
richard.thivierge@tc.gc.ca

Environmental Policy / Politiques environnementales
Director General, Pierre Marin
Tel: 613-949-2677
Fax: 613-949-9415
pierre.marin@tc.gc.ca

International & Intergovernmental Relations / Relations internationales et intergouvernementales
Director General, Arlene Turner
Tel: 613-991-6500
arlene.turner@tc.gc.ca
Chief, International & Intergovernmental Policy Coordination & Special Projects, Jennifer Little
Tel: 613-991-6505
jennifer.little@tc.gc.ca

Marine Policy / Politique maritime
Fax: 613-998-1845
Director General, Tim Meisner
Tel: 613-991-3536
Fax: 613-998-1845
tim.meisner@tc.gc.ca
Chief, International Marine Policy, Doug O'Keefe
Tel: 613-991-6526
doug.okeefe@tc.gc.ca
Executive Director, International Marine Policy & Liability, Jerry Rysanek
Tel: 613-998-0708
Fax: 613-998-1845
jerry.rysanek@tc.gc.ca

Strategic Policy / Politiques stratégiques
Tel: 613-949-9596
Fax: 613-990-1719
Director General, Sandra LaFortune
Tel: 613-998-0402
Fax: 613-990-1719
sandra.lafortune@tc.gc.ca
Executive Director, Continental Gateway & System Analysis, Jacques Rochon
Tel: 613-991-2967
jacques.rochon@tc.gc.ca

Surface Transportation Policy / Politiques de transport terrestre
Fax: 613-998-2686
Director General, Annette Gibbons
Tel: 613-998-2689
Fax: 613-998-2686
annette.gibbons@tc.gc.ca
Executive Director, Windsor Gateway Project Team, Sean O'Dell
Tel: 613-991-4702
Fax: 613-998-2686
sean.odell@tc.gc.ca

Transportation Technology & Innovation / Technologie des transports ed de l'innovation
Director General, Marc Fortin
Tel: 613-998-8242
Fax: 613-998-3987
marc.fortin@tc.gc.ca
Chief, Advanced Technology, Transportation Development Centre, Howard Posluns
Tel: 613-993-6254
Fax: 613-991-5928
howard.posluns@tc.gc.ca

Programs Group / Groupe des programmes
www.tc.gc.ca/eng/programs-menu.htm
Responsible for the transfer of ports, harbours & airports to communities & other interests; the oversight & lease management of divested facilities; the operation of facilities not yet divested; & real property management. Responsible for environmental programs & policies, including environmental management system, sustainable development strategies, environmental assessment & national environmental issues in transportation, such as climate change.
Director, Strategic Planning & Integration, Aline M. M. MacDougall
Tel: 613-949-4157
Fax: 613-990-1427
aline.macdougall@tc.gc.ca

Airport & Port Programs / Programmes aeroportuaires et portuaires
Tel: 613-993-4466
Fax: 613-990-8889
Acting Director General, Marc Brazeau
Tel: 613-990-1340
Fax: 613-990-8889
marc.brazeau@tc.gc.ca
Senior Director, Authorities Management & Real Property, Richard Barbeau
Tel: 613-949-5721
Fax: 613-990-8889
richard.barbeau@tc.gc.ca

Environmental Affairs / Affaires environnementales
Fax: 613-957-4260
Director General, Catherine Higgens
Tel: 613-991-5995
Fax: 613-993-8674
catherine.higgens@tc.gc.ca
Chief, Energy & Advanced Vehicle Program, Nicole Galvin
Tel: 613-990-4321
nicole.galvin@tc.gc.ca
Senior Director, Environmental Management, Alec Simpson
Tel: 613-990-0512
alec.simpson@tc.gc.ca

Surface Infrasturcture Programs / Programmes des infrastructures
Fax: 613-990-9639
Director General, Jane Weldon
Tel: 613-998-8137
Fax: 613-990-9639
jane.weldon@tc.gc.ca
Senior Director, Highways & Borders, Jim Lothrop
Tel: 613-998-1902
jim.lothrop@tc.gc.ca

Safety & Security Group / Groupe de sécurité et sûreté
The ADM, Safety & Security, directs the development of transportation safety & security legislation, regulations & national standards; is responsible for the uniform implementation of monitoring, testing, inspection, research & development, & subsidy programs in the aviation, marine, rail & road modes of transport; oversees the delivery of aircraft services to government & other transportation bodies; & is responsible for development & enforcement of regulations & standards under federal jurisdiction, to protect public safety in the transportation of dangerous goods, & to prevent unlawful interference in the aviation, marine & railways modes of transport, as well as ensuring that the department is prepared to respond to transportation & transportation-related emergencies.
Assistant Deputy Minister, Gerard A. McDonald
Tel: 613-990-3838
Fax: 613-990-2947
gerard.mcdonald@tc.gc.ca
Associate Assistant Deputy Minister, Laureen E. Kinney
Tel: 613-949-2394
Fax: 613-990-2947
laureen.kinney@tc.gc.ca
Chief, Ministerial Liaison & Strategic Issues Management, Christine Martel
Tel: 613-993-8803
Fax: 613-990-3994
christine.martel@tc.gc.ca
Chief, Corporate Services, Joseé L. Sabourin
Tel: 613-990-5492
Fax: 613-990-3894
josee.sabourin@tc.gc.ca
Executive Director, National Organization Transition Implementation Project, Dena Palamedes
Tel: 613-991-6006
Fax: 613-949-7779
dena.palamedes@tc.gc.ca
Director, Executive Services Secretariat, Lynn Gauthier
Tel: 613-990-3890
lynn.gauthier@tc.gc.ca

Aircraft Services / Services des aéronefs
Tel: 613-998-7991
Fax: 613-991-0365
Director General, Michel Gaudreau
Tel: 613-998-3316
Fax: 613-991-0365
michel.gaudreau@tc.gc.ca
Chief, Strategic Planning, Financial & Administrative Services, Lorraine Stairs
Tel: 613-998-8655
lorraine.stairs@tc.gc.ca
Chief, Flight Operations Training, Turbo-jet, Simon Pinsonneault
Tel: 613-949-5841
simon.pinsonneault@tc.gc.ca
Chief, Facilities Environmental & Site Safety, Sandra L. Phillips-McRae
Tel: 613-949-0559
Fax: 613-998-8235
sandra.phillips-mcrae@tc.gc.ca

Aviation Security Directorate / Direction générale de la sûreté aérienne
Director General, Erin O'Gorman
Tel: 613-990-3651
Fax: 613-990-5046
erin.ogorman@tc.gc.ca

Civil Aviation / Aviation civile
Tel: 613-990-1322
Fax: 613-957-4208
Director General, Martin J. Eley
Tel: 613-990-1322
martin.eley@tc.gc.ca
Acting Chief, Program Management, Standards, Brigitte Ouellet
Tel: 613-990-3716
Fax: 613-998-7416
brigitte.ouellet@tc.gc.ca

Marine Safety / Sécurité maritime
www.tc.gc.ca/marine/menu.htm
Responsible for the administration of national & international laws designed to ensure the safe operation, navigation, design & maintenance of ships, protection of life & property, & prevention of ship-source pollution. Transport Canada has assumed responsibility for environmental response from Fisheries & Oceans Canada. Strictly enforces pollution prevention regulations through the inspection of ships for compliance with pollution prevention regulations & through investigation of pollution incidents.
Director General, Donald Roussel
Tel: 613-998-0610
Fax: 613-954-1032
donald.roussel@tc.gc.ca
Chief, Marine Safety Application Management, Program & Technical Training Services, Lousie D. Gagné
Tel: 613-998-8310
louise.gagne@tc.gc.ca
Executive Director, Regulatory Services & Quality Assurance, Sylvian Lachance
Tel: 613-998-0600
Fax: 613-954-1032
sylvain.lachance@tc.gc.ca

Marine Security / Sûreté maritime
Director General, Fulvio Fracassi
Tel: 613-991-4173
Fax: 613-993-1714
fulvio.fracassi@tc.gc.ca

Rail Safety / Sécurité ferroviaire
www.tc.gc.ca/rail/menu.htm
Administers the Railway Safety Act & associated regulations; provides funding for improvements to railway grade crossings; administers Part II of the Canada Labour Code, relating to the safety & health of employees; & ensures, for specific railway works, that environmental impacts are assessed in compliance with the Canadian Environmental Assessment Act.
Director General, Luc Bourdon
Tel: 613-998-2984
Fax: 613-990-2924
Chief Engineer, Rail Safety Operations, Engineering, Daniel Lafonatine
Tel: 613-990-4515
daniel.lafontaine@tc.gc.ca

Road Safety & Motor Vehicle Registration / Direction de la sécurité routière et de la réglementation automobile
Tel: 613-998-8616
Toll-Free: 800-333-0371
www.tc.gc.ca/road/menu.htm
Administers the Motor Vehicle Safety Act by developing vehicle & motor vehicle equipment safety standards, emission standards & testing procedures; responds to public enquiries & complaints of alleged vehicle safety defects, emission defects & fuel consumption deficiencies; &, in conjunction with Natural Resources Canada, provides fuel consumption information through vehicle labels & the Fuel Consumption Guide. Also administers the Motor Vehicle Transport Act, which governs the safety fitness of extra-provincial trucks & buses. The enforcement of this act is largely delegated to the provinces.
Director General, Kash Ram
Tel: 613-993-6735
Acting Chief, Resources & Strategic Planning, Nicole MacIsaac
Tel: 613-991-3109
Fax: 613-998-4831
nicole.macisaac@tc.gc.ca

Security Program Support / Soutien au programme de sûreté
Responsible for the development & enforcement of regulations & standards to prevent unlawful interference with air, rail & marine transportation; management of departmental security.
Director General, Emilia Warriner
Tel: 613-990-2208
Fax: 613-949-6637
emilia.warriner@tc.gc.ca
Chief, Security Education & Training Programs, Security Expertise Programs, Ginette Charlebois
Tel: 613-991-3095
Fax: 613-998-8238
ginette.charlebois@tc.gc.ca
Chief, Intelligence Security Screening Programs, Lise Ranger
Tel: 613-998-9773
Fax: 613-991-3205
lise.ranger@tc.gc.ca

Strategies & Integration / Strategies et intégration
Director General, Melanie Tod
Tel: 613-949-0864
Fax: 613-990-5058
melanie.tod@tc.gc.ca
Acting Chief, Administrative Services, Program Support, Nadine Vincent
Tel: 613-991-3022
Fax: 613-990-5058
nadine.vincent@tc.gc.ca
Director General, Dominique Blanchard
Tel: 613-949-7778
Fax: 613-990-2015
dominique.blanchard@tc.gc.ca

Transportation of Dangerous Goods / Transport des marchandises dangereuses
Regulatory development, information & guidance on dangerous goods transport for the public, industry & government. Represents Canada on international organizations responsible for establishing uniform international requirements, such as the United Nations Committee of Experts on the Transport of Dangerous Goods, Association of American Railroads (AAR) Tankcar Committee & International Civil Aviation Organization (ICAO) Dangerous Goods Panel. Branches are responsible for regulatory affairs, research, evaluation, compliance & response, review of remedial measures, development of training programs.

Director General, Marie-France Dagenais
Tel: 613-990-1147
Fax: 613-990-2917
marie-france.dagenais@tc.gc.ca

Atlantic
Heritage Court, 95 Foundry St., 6th Fl., Moncton, NB E1C 5H7
Tel: 506-851-7131
Fax: 506-851-2563

Ontario
#300, 4900 Yonge St., Toronto, ON M2N 6A5
Tel: 416-952-0215
Fax: 416-952-0196

Pacific
#620, 800 Burrard St., Vancouver, BC V6Z 2J8
Tel: 604-666-5575
Fax: 604-666-4839

Prairie & Northern
344 Edmonton St., 1st Fl., Winnipeg, MB R3C 0P6
Tel: 204-983-4341
Fax: 204-984-2069

Québec
700, Leigh Capréol, 2e étage, Dorval, QC H4Y 1G7
Tel: 514-633-3580
Fax: 514-633-3585

Transportation Safety Board of Canada / Bureau de la sécurité des transports du Canada

200 Promenade du Portage, 4th Fl., Ottawa, ON K1A 1K8
Tel: 819-994-3741
Fax: 819-997-2239
Toll-Free: 800-387-3557
www.tsb.gc.ca
TTY: 819-953-7287
The Board is an independent agency reporting to Parliament through the President of the Queen's Privy Council. The formal name for the Board is the Canadian Transportation Accident Investigation & Safety Board. Its sole aim is the advancement of transportation safety in the marine, rail, pipeline & air modes of transport. The TSB conducts independent investigations into selected transportation occurences in order to make findings as to their causes & contributing factors; identifies safety deficiences, & makes recommendations designed to prevent further occurences. Because the Board is independent, its transportation accident investigations are completely separate from the regulatory agencies responsible for transportation. In making findings & recommendations it is not the function of the Board to assign fault or determine civil liability.
Acts Administered:
Access to Information Act
Canadian Transportation Accident Investigation & Safety Board Act
Privacy Act

Chair, Wendy A. Tadros
Tel: 819-994-8000
Fax: 819-994-9759
Wendy.Tadros@tsb.gc.ca
Other Communications: Executive Assistant, Phone: 819-994-8002

Chief Operating Officer, Jean L. Laporte
Tel: 819-994-8004
Fax: 819-994-9759
Jean.Laporte@bst-tsb.gc.ca

Director, Investigations, Air, Mark Clitsome
Tel: 819-994-3813
Fax: 819-953-9586

Director, Investigations, Rail/Pipeline, Kirby Jang
Tel: 819-953-6470
Fax: 819-953-7876
Kirby.jang@bst-tsb.gc.ca
Other Communications: Administrative Assistant, Phone: 819-953-1646

Director, Investigations, Marine, Marc-André Poisson
Tel: 819-953-1398
Marc-Andre.Poisson@bst-tsb.gc.ca

Manager, Communications Products & Services, Publishing & Linquistic Services, Jacynthe Dubé
Tel: 819-934-1762
Fax: 819-953-1733
Jacynthe.Dube@bst-tsb.gc.ca

Acting Manager, Publishing & Linguistic Services, Chantal Laflamme
Tel: 819-994-8032
Fax: 819-953-1733
chantal.laflamme@bst-tsb.gc.ca

Treasury Board of Canada / Conseil du Trésor du Canada

140 O'Connor St., Ottawa, ON K1A 0R5
Tel: 613-957-2400
Fax: 613-941-4000
Toll-Free: 877-636-0656
www.tbs-sct.gc.ca
TTY: 613-957-9090
The Treasury Board is a Cabinet Committee of government headed by the President of the Treasury Board. The committee constituting the Treasury Board includes, in addition to the President, the Minister of Finance & four other ministers appointed by the Governor-in-Council. The main role of the Treasury Board is the management of the government's financial, personnel & administrative responsibilities. The Treasury Board derives its authority primarily from the Financial Administration Act & is supported by the Treasury Board Secretariat.
Acts Administered:
Alternative Fuels Act
Federal Real Property & Federal Immovables Act

Minister, FedNor; President, Treasury Board, Hon. Tony Clement
Tel: 613-944-7740
Fax: 613-992-5092

Parliamentary Secretary to the President of the Treasury Board, Andrew Saxton
Tel: 613-995-1225
Fax: 613-992-7319
Saxton.A@parl.gc.ca

Secretary, Michelle d'Auray
Tel: 613-952-1777
Fax: 613-952-6596

Associate Secretary, Alister Smith
Tel: 613-941-1843
Fax: 613-952-6596

Assistant Secretary, Regulatory Cooperation Council Secretariat, Robert Carberry
Tel: 613-946-9335
Fax: 613-960-1975

Assistant Secretary, Red Tape Reduction Commission Secretariat, Roger Scott-Douglas
Tel: 613-960-3277
Fax: 613-992-4881

Director, Policy, President's Office, Neil Brodie
Tel: 613-957-2666

Director, Communications, President's Office, Jennifer Gearey
Tel: 613-957-2666
Fax: 613-990-2806

Director, Evaluation, Internal Audit & Evaluation Bureau, Ramona Helm
Tel: 613-992-4835
Fax: 613-992-3331

Director, Parliament Affairs & Issues Management, President's Office, David Pierce
Tel: 613-957-2666

Senior General Counsel, Treasury Board Secretariat Legal Services, Michel LeFrançois
Tel: 613-952-3379
Fax: 613-954-5806

Associated Agencies, Boards & Commissions:
• Public Sector Pension Investment Board / Office d'investissement des régimes de pensions du secteur public
#200, 440 Laurier Ave. West
Ottawa, ON K1R 7X6
Tel: 613-782-3095
Fax: 613-782-6864
info@investpsp.ca
www.investpsp.ca
Crown corporation established by Parliament by the Public Sector Pension Investment Board Act (September 1999). The mandate of PSP Investments is to manage employer & employee contributions made after April 1, 2000 to the federal Public Service, the Canadian Forces & the Royal Canadian Mounted Police pension funds.

• Canada Public Service Agency (CPSA) / Agence de la fonction publique du Canada (AFPC)
122 Bank St.
Ottawa, ON K1A 0R5
Created in 2003 to put in place a new human resources management regime in the public service of Canada. Formerly the Public Service Human Resources Management Agency of Canada (PSHRMAC).
• Public Service Labour Relations Board / Commission des relations de travail dans la fonction publique
CD Howe Building
240 Sparks St., 6th Fl.
PO Box 1525 B
Ottawa, ON K1P 5V2
Tel: 613-990-1800
Fax: 613-990-1849
Toll-free: 866-931-3454
mail.courrier@pslrb-crtfp.gc.ca
www.pslrb-crtfp.gc.ca
Independent, quasi-judicial statutory tribunal responsible for administering the collective bargaining & grievance adjudication systems in the federal Public & Parliamentary Service. Also provides mediation & conflict resolution services, compensation analysis & research services.

Chief Information Officer Branch / Direction du dirigeant principal de l'information
Chief Information Officer, Corinne Charette
Tel: 613-957-7070
Fax: 613-952-8536
Deputy Chief Information Officer, Pierre Boucher
Tel: 613-957-8990
Fax: 613-952-8536

Corporate Services Sector / Secteur des services ministériels
Assistant Secretary, Christine Walker
Tel: 613-992-0554
Fax: 613-943-8683
Chief of Staff, Jodi C. Tognarelli
Tel: 613-947-3662
Fax: 613-947-4461

Economic Sector / Secteur des programmes économiques
Assistant Secretary, Gavin Liddy
Tel: 613-957-0556
Fax: 613-957-0557

Expenditure Management Sector / Secteur de la gestion des dépenses
Assistant Secretary, Bill Matthews
Tel: 613-946-3061
Fax: 613-946-3718
Deputy Assistant Secretary, David Enns
Tel: 613-960-0778
Fax: 613-946-3718

Government Operations Sector / Secteur des opérations gouvernementales
Assistant Secretary, Jean-Pierre Blais
Tel: 613-946-4199
Fax: 613-957-0160

Human Resources Division / Division des ressources humaines
Executive Director, Mary McLaren
Tel: 613-948-4713
Fax: 613-957-8289
Chief, HR Services, Mélanie Beck
Tel: 613-947-4988
Fax: 613-948-1144

International Affairs, Security & Justice / Secteur des affaires internationales, de la sécurité et de la justice
Assistant Secretary, John Ossowski
Tel: 613-957-0531
Fax: 613-957-0525

Office of the Comptroller General / Bureau du contrôleur général
Comptroller General of Canada, James Ralston
Tel: 613-957-7820
Fax: 613-952-0354
Assistant Comptroller General, Internal Audit, Brian Aiken
Tel: 613-957-3851
Fax: 613-952-3698
Assistant Comptroller General, Financial Management & Analysis, Gonzague Guéranger
Tel: 613-957-9659
Fax: 613-952-9613
Assistant Comptroller General, Acquired Services & Assets, Marc O'Sullivan
Tel: 613-957-0299
Fax: 613-957-0557

Office of the Chief Human Resources Officer / Bureau du dirigeant principal des ressources humaines
Chief Human Resources Officer, Daphne Meredith
Tel: 613-952-1225
Fax: 613-952-1177
Chief of Staff, Mario Baril
Tel: 613-960-6915
Fax: 613-952-1177
Assistant Deputy Minister, Compensation & Labour Relations Sector, Marc-Arthur Hyppolite
Tel: 613-952-3000
Fax: 613-952-8100
Assistant Deputy Minister, Executive Policies & Talent Management Sector, Yazmine Laroche
Tel: 613-992-9160
Fax: 613-996-2228
Assistant Deputy Minister, Governance, Planning & Policy Sector, Ross MacLeod
Tel: 613-952-1173
Fax: 613-941-9450

Priorities & Planning / Priorités et planification
Assistant Secretary, Frank Des Rosiers
Tel: 613-954-0048
Fax: 613-946-3716

Regulatory Affairs / Affaires réglementaires
Assistant Secretary, Michael Presley
Tel: 613-943-5069
Fax: 613-995-2873

Social & Cultural Sector / Secteur des programmes sociaux et culturels
Assistant Secretary, Leslie MacLean
Tel: 613-957-2609
Fax: 613-941-5096

Strategic Communications & Ministerial Affairs / Communications stratégiques et affaires ministérielles
Assistant Secretary, Monique Lebel-Ducharme
Tel: 613-957-2422
Fax: 613-952-3658

Veterans Affairs Canada / Anciens combattants Canada

161 Grafton St., PO Box 7700, Charlottetown, PE C1A 8M9
Tel: 902-566-8888
Toll-Free: 866-522-2111
information@vac-acc.gc.ca
www.vac-acc.gc.ca
Other Communication: Toll-Free French: 1-866-522-2022
Secondary Address: Ottawa: 66 Slater St.
Ottawa, ON K1A 0P4 Canada
Provides pensions for disability or death, economic support in the form of allowances, and health care benefits and services to veterans and members of the Canadian Armed Forces, members and ex-members of the RCMP, and their dependents.
Acts Administered:
Aeronautics Act, section 9
Canadian Forces Members & Veterans Re-establishment & Compensation Act
Children of Deceased Veterans Education Assistance Act
Civilian War-related Benefits Act
Department of Veterans Affairs Act
Halifax Relief Commission Pension Continuation Act
Indian Soldier Settlement Act
Pension Act
Related Acts
Returned Soldiers' Insurance Act
Royal Canadian Mounted Police Pension Continuation Act (in Part)
Royal Canadian Mounted Police Superannuation Act (in Part)
Soldier Settlement Act
Special Operators War Service Benefits Act
Supervisors War Service Benefits Act
Veterans Benefit Act
Veterans Insurance Act
Veterans Review & Appeal Board Act
Veterans' Land Act
War Services Grants Act
War Veterans Allowance Act
Women's Royal Naval Services & the South African Military Nursing Service (Benefits) Act

Minister, Veterans Affairs, Hon. Steven Blaney
Tel: 613-992-7434
Fax: 613-995-6856
steven.blaney@parl.gc.ca

Parliamentary Secretary to the Minister of Veterans Affairs, Eve Adams
Tel: 613-995-7784
Fax: 613-996-9817
Eve.Adams@parl.gc.ca

Associate Deputy Minister, Mary Chaput
Tel: 902-370-4784
Fax: 902-370-4818

Chief of Staff, Frédérik Boisvert
Tel: 613-996-4649
Fax: 613-996-0287

Director, Policy, Andrew Bernardo
Tel: 613-996-4649
Fax: 613-954-1054

Director, Parliamentary Affairs, Erin McClelland
Tel: 613-996-4649
Fax: 613-954-1054

Director, Communications, Codie Taylor
Tel: 613-996-4649
Fax: 613-996-0287

Senior Counsel, Legal Services Unit, Neil Robinson
Tel: 902-566-8992
Fax: 902-566-8793

Associated Agencies, Boards & Commissions:
• Veterans Review & Appeal Board / Tribunal des anciens combattants (révision et appel)
Daniel J. MacDonald Bldg.
161 Grafton St.
PO Box 9900
Charlottetown, PE C1A 8V7
Tel: 902-566-8751
Fax: 902-566-7850
Toll-free: 800-450-8006
vrab_tacra@vac-acc.gc.ca
www.vrab-tacra.gc.ca
Other Communication: Ligne sans frais: 1-877-368-0859
The Board is an independent Board with full and exclusive jurisdiction to hear appeals from the decisions of the Minister of Veterans Affairs. The Board may affirm, vary or reverse the Minister's decisions, or refer decisions back to the Minister for reconsideration. The Board is completely independent from the Department of Veterans Affairs.
Deputy Minister, Suzanne Tining
Tel: 902-566-8666
Fax: 902-566-7868
Associate Deputy Minister, Mary Chaput
Tel: 902-370-4784
Fax: 902-370-4818
Director General, Transformation, Associate Deputy Minister's Office, David M. Robinson
Tel: 902-566-8302
Fax: 902-370-4818

Audit & Evaluation Division / Direction générale de la vérification et de l'évaluation
Director General, Don Love
Tel: 902-566-8018
Fax: 902-566-8343

Bureau of Pensions Advocates, Head Office / Bureau de services juridiques des pensions
Executive Director & Chief Pensions Advocate, Brian McKenna
Tel: 902-566-8916
Fax: 902-566-7804
Other Communications: Alt Phone: 604-666-3627
Director, Legal Operations, Mark Belliveau
Tel: 902-566-8021
Fax: 902-566-7804
Director, Strategic Planning & Management Support Directorate, Sue Lemaistre
Tel: 902-566-6923
Fax: 902-368-0450

Corporate Services / Coordination des politiques
Assistant Deputy Minister, Heather Parry
Tel: 902-566-8047
Fax: 902-566-8521
Director General, Corporate Planning Division, Murielle Belliveau
Tel: 902-368-0510
Fax: 902-368-0437
Director General, Finance Division, André Joannette
Tel: 902-566-8320
Fax: 902-368-0411
Director General, Information Technology & Information Management Division, John Walker
Tel: 902-566-8236
Fax: 902-566-8351
Director, Information Management Services Directorate, Anne Murtha
Tel: 902-566-7060
Fax: 902-368-0496

Federal Healthcare Partnership Secretariat / Secrétariat de partenariat fédéral pour les soins de santé
Chief Information Officer, LCol James Kirkland
Tel: 613-947-3808
Fax: 613-992-8747
Director, Research, Analysis & Negotiations, Pierre de Montigny
Tel: 613-947-4014
Fax: 613-992-8747

Human Resources Division / Direction générale des ressources humaines
Director General, Anthony Saez
Tel: 902-566-8408
Fax: 902-566-8425
Senior Director, HR Services Directorate, Donna MacDonald
Tel: 902-566-8373
Fax: 902-566-8425
Director, Strategic Business Initiatives, Strategic Business Initiatives & HR Systems, Judy Gallant-MacIsaac
Tel: 902-370-4475
Fax: 902-566-8425
Director, Corporate Labour Relations, Workplace Management Directorate, Pierre Lapointe
Tel: 902-566-8375
Fax: 902-370-4768
Director, Workplace Management Directorate, Louise Wallis
Tel: 902-368-0957
Fax: 902-566-8534
Regional Director, Human Resources Charlottetown Division, Cheryl Gotell
Tel: 902-370-4725
Fax: 902-566-7924

Policy, Communications & Commemoration / Politiques, communications et commémoration
Assistant Deputy Minister, James Gilbert
Tel: 902-566-8100
Fax: 902-566-8780
Director General, Policy & Research Division, Bernard Butler
Tel: 902-566-7438
Fax: 902-370-4727
Director General, Canada Remembers Division, Derek Sullivan
Tel: 902-566-8026
Fax: 902-566-7056
Director General, Communications Division, Peter Yendall
Tel: 613-996-0484
Fax: 613-996-9969
Other Communications: Executive Assistant, Phone: 613-996-2340

Service Delivery Branch / Prestation des services
Assistant Deputy Minister, Keith Hillier
Tel: 902-626-2723
Fax: 902-566-8172
Director General, Service Delivery & Program Management Division, Sonia Gogoh
Tel: 902-368-0646
Fax: 902-566-8073
Director General, Centralized Operations Division, Nancy McRae
Tel: 902-566-8644
Fax: 902-566-8337
Director General, Business Re-engineering, Andrée Métivier
Tel: 902-995-8114

Ste-Anne's Hospital / Hôpital Sainte-Anne
305 boul des Anciens-Combattants, Sainte-Anne-de-Bellevue, QC H9X 1Y9
Tel: 514-457-3440
Toll-Free: 800-361-9287
steanne@vac-acc.gc.ca
The Hospital provides Veterans with long-term or respite care in addition to offering support services, through its day centre, to clients who still reside in the community and to Veterans and other clients who require mental health services or short-term hospitalization, through the National Centre for Operational Stress Injuries (NCOSI).
Executive Director, Rachel Corneille-Gravel
Tel: 514-457-8400
Fax: 514-457-5741

Veterans Ombudsman (Charlottetown) / Ombudsman des vétérans (Charlottetown)
134 Kent St., PO Box 7700, Charlottetown, PE C1A 8M9
Fax: 888-566-7582
Toll-Free: 877-330-4343
Director, Early Intervention, Michel Guay
Tel: 902-626-2663
Fax: 902-566-7582
Acting Director, Corporate Services & Liaison, Wilma Hanscome
Tel: 902-626-2913
Fax: 902-566-7582
Senior Projects Officer, Paulette McNally
Tel: 902-566-8577
Fax: 902-626-2950

Veterans Ombudsman (Ottawa) / Ombudsman des vétérans (Ottawa)
PO Box 18 B, Ottawa, ON K1P 6C3
Fax: 888-566-7582
Toll-Free: 877-330-4343
Veterans Ombudsman, Guy Parent
Tel: 613-944-2940
Fax: 613-944-2939
Other Communications: Executive Assistant, Phone: 613-943-3076
Director General, Operations, Gary Walbourne
Tel: 613-944-2943
Fax: 613-944-2939
Other Communications: Executive Assistant, Phone: 613-943-3028
Director, Research & Investigation, Pierre Guénette
Tel: 613-943-3027
Fax: 613-944-2939
Director, Communications Operations, Lynda Leblanc
Tel: 613-944-2941
Fax: 613-944-2939
Legal Advisor, Diane Guilmet-Harris
Tel: 613-944-2942
Fax: 613-944-2939
Atlantic Region
40 Alderney Dr., 3rd Fl., Dartmouth, NS B2Y 2N5
Tel: 902-426-0629
Fax: 902-426-7447
Toll-Free: 866-522-2122
Other Communication: Toll-Free French: 866-522-2022
Director General, Krista Locke
Tel: 902-426-6305
Fax: 902-426-0555
Ontario Region
Bag Service 4000, 145 Government Rd. West, Kirkland Lake, ON P2N 2E8
Tel: 705-567-9571
Fax: 705-567-7565
Toll-Free: 866-522-2122
Other Communication: Toll-Free French: 866-522-2022
Regional Director General, Dan Fenety
Tel: 705-568-4132
Québec Region
Place Bonaventure, #6505, 800, rue de la Gauchetière Ouest, Montréal, QC H5A 1L8
Tél: 514-496-6412
Téléc: 514-283-2102
Ligne sans frais: 866-522-2122
Autre numéros: Toll-Free French: 866-522-2022
Regional Director General, Charlotte Bastien
Tel: 514-496-6412
Fax: 514-496-7303
Western Region (Vancouver)
#900, 605 Robson St., PO Box 5600, Vancouver, BC V6B 5G4
Tel: 604-666-2675
Fax: 604-666-8839
Toll-Free: 866-522-2122
Other Communication: Toll-Free French: 866-522-2022
Regional Director General, Gisèle Toupin
Tel: 604-666-2675
Fax: 604-666-8839
Western Region (Winnipeg)
#610, 234 Donald St., PO Box 6050, Winnipeg, MB R3C 4G5
Tel: 204-983-5316
Fax: 204-983-6286
Regional Director General, Gisèle Toupin
Tel: 204-983-5316
Fax: 204-983-6286

VIA Rail Canada Inc.

#500, 3, Place Ville-Marie, Montréal, QC H3B 2C9
Tél: 514-871-6000
Téléc: 514-871-6104
Ligne sans frais: 888-842-7245
www.viarail.ca
TTY: 800-268-9503
Established in 1977, VIA Rail Canada is a Crown corporation that manages the national passenger rail network. The corporation serves 450 communities throughout Canada. VIA works to offer safe, efficient, & environmentally responsible public transportation.
Environmental intiatives include a reduction in emissions & a reduce, re-use & recycle program. Under the capital investment plan, older locomotives & passenger cars are being rebuilt. The corporation also offers a Green Procurement Guide to promote the use of environmentally responsible products in all its activities.

Chair, Paul G. Smith

President & Chief Executive Officer, Marc Laliberté

Chief Information Officer, Yves Bourbonnais

Chief Human Resources Officer, Laurent F. Caron

Chief Marketing & Sales Officer, Steve Del Bosco

Chief Legal & Corporate Affairs Officer; Corporate Secretary, Yves Desjardins-Siciliano

Chief Customer Experience & Operating Officer, Denis Pinsonneault

Chief Financial & Administrative Officer, Robert St-Jean

Senior Director, Safety, Security, & Risk Management, Jean Tierney

Western Economic Diversification Canada (WD) / Diversification de l'économie de l'Ouest Canada (DEO)

Canada Place, #1500, 9700 Jasper Ave. NW, Edmonton, AB T5J 4H7
Tel: 780-495-4164
Fax: 780-495-4557
Toll-Free: 888-338-9378
www.wd-deo.gc.ca
TTY: 877-303-3388
Responsible for promoting economic growth & diversification in the West. By investing in innovation, fostering entrepreneurship & using partnerships to enhance community sustainability, WD is helping to create a more prosperous future for western Canadians.Invests in R&D & commercialization in environmental technologies as a focus area for innovation strategies.

Minister of State (Western Economic Diversification), Hon. Lynne Yelich
Tel: 613-952-2768
Fax: 613-952-1155
lynne.yelich@parl.gc.ca

Deputy Minister, Daniel Watson
Tel: 780-495-5772
Fax: 780-495-6222
Other Communications: Ottawa: 613-952-9382

Chief of Staff, Office of the Minister, Stacey Gairdner
Tel: 613-952-2768
Fax: 613-957-1155

Director General, Planning & Programs, Nadean Langlois
Tel: 780-495-4973
Fax: 780-495-6876

Director General, Audit, Evaluation & Disclosure, Donald MacDonald
Tel: 780-495-8437
Fax: 780-495-6223

Director General, Finance & Management Accountability, Cathy Matthews
Tel: 780-495-6336
Fax: 780-495-4434

Executive Director, Alberta Federal Council, Marcel Préville
Tel: 780-495-5413

Executive Director, Finance & Corporate Management, Jim Saunderson
Tel: 780-495-4301
Fax: 780-495-7618
Other Communications: Administrative Assistant, Phone: 780-495-5791

Headquarters / Administration centrale
Tel: 780-495-4164
Fax: 780-495-5808
Director General, Planning & Programs, Nadean Langlois
Tel: 780-495-4873
Fax: 780-495-6876
Director General, Audit, Evaluation & Disclosure, Donald MacDonald
Tel: 780-495-8437
Fax: 780-495-6223
Director General, Finance & Management Accountability, Cathy Matthews
Tel: 780-495-6336
Fax: 780-495-4434
Executive Director, Policy Planning & Performance Measurement, Brant Popp
Tel: 780-495-6549
Fax: 780-495-6876
Executive Director, Finance & Corporate Management, Jim Saunderson

Tel: 780-495-4301
Fax: 780-495-7618
Alberta (Edmonton)
Canada Place, #1500, 9700 Jasper Ave. Northwest, Edmonton, AB T5J 4H7
Tel: 780-495-4164
Fax: 780-495-4557
Toll-Free: 888-338-9378
TTY: 877-303-3388
Assistant Deputy Minister, Doug Maley
Tel: 780-495-4168
Fax: 780-495-6222
Other Communications: Executive Assistant, Phone: 780-495-4960
Director General, Operations, David Woynorowski
Tel: 780-495-4970
Fax: 780-495-4557
Director, Policy, Planning & External Relations, Neil Kirkpatrick
Tel: 780-495-6796
Fax: 780-495-4557
British Columbia (Vancouver)
Price Waterhouse Bldg., #700, 333 Seymour St., Vancouver, BC V6B 5G9
Tel: 604-666-6256
Fax: 604-666-2353
Toll-Free: 888-338-9378
TTY: 877-303-3388
Assistant Deputy Minister, Gerry Salembier
Tel: 604-666-6366
Fax: 604-666-1510
Director General, Naina Sloan
Tel: 604-666-7011
Fax: 604-666-2353
Director, Innovation & Competitiveness, Tammy Schulz
Tel: 604-666-1889
Fax: 604-666-2353
Director, Policy, Planning & Performance Integration, Martin Sutherland
Tel: 604-666-4766
Fax: 604-666-2353
Calgary
#300, 639 - 5 Ave. SW, Calgary, AB T2P 0M9
Tel: 403-292-5458
Fax: 403-292-5487
Toll-Free: 888-338-9378
TTY: 877-303-3388
Acting Director, Neil Kirkpatrick
Tel: 403-292-4426
Fax: 403-292-5487
Manitoba (Winnipeg)
The Cargill Bldg., #620, 240 Graham Ave., Winnipeg, MB R3C 0J7
Tel: 204-983-4472
Fax: 204-983-3852
Toll-Free: 888-338-9378
TTY: 877-303-3388
Assistant Deputy Minister, Marilyn Kapitany
Tel: 204-983-5715
Fax: 204-983-0966
Other Communications: Executive Assistant, Phone: 204-983-4467
Executive Director, Manitoba Federal Council Secretariat, Cynthia Foreman
Tel: 204-984-6815
Fax: 204-984-0105
Director General, Operations, Derryl Millar
Tel: 204-983-4531
Fax: 204-983-1280
Director, Economic Recovery Branch, France Guimond
Tel: 204-984-2438
Fax: 204-983-1280
Director, Policy, Planning & External Relations, Tim Hibbard
Tel: 204-983-0689
Fax: 204-984-0360
Associate Director, Infrastructure Secretariat, Ivan Didiuk
Tel: 204-945-5557
Fax: 204-948-2035
Ottawa Liaison Office
#500, 141 Laurier Ave. West, Ottawa, ON K1P 5J3
Tel: 613-952-2768
Fax: 613-952-9384
TTY: 877-303-3388
Assistant Deputy Minister, James Meddings
Tel: 613-952-7096
Fax: 613-954-1044
Director, Strategic Policy & Advocacy, Francesco Del Bianco
Tel: 613-954-9640
Fax: 613-952-3434
Director, Consultation, Marketing & Communications, Peter G. Wallace
Tel: 613-952-7101
Fax: 613-952-6775

Saskatchewan (Saskatoon)
S.J. Cohen Bldg., #601, 119 - 4 Ave. South, PO Box 2025, Saskatoon, SK S7K 3S7
Tel: 306-975-4373
Fax: 306-975-5484
Toll-Free: 888-338-9378
TTY: 877-303-3388
Assistant Deputy Minister, Sharon Lee Smith
Tel: 306-975-5858
Fax: 306-975-5484
Executive Director, Saskatchewan Federal Council, Rhonda Laing
Tel: 306-975-5944
Fax: 306-975-5484
Director General, Operations, Doug Zolinsky
Tel: 306-975-6988
Fax: 306-975-5484

Government of Alberta

Seat of Government: PO Box 1333, Edmonton, AB T5J 2N2
Tel: 780-427-2711
Fax: 780-422-2852
Toll-Free: -310-0000
www.alberta.ca
TTY: 800-232-7215
Other Communication: TTY: 427-9999 (in Edmonton)
Alberta was proclaimed as a province on September 1, 1905. The province has an elected Legislative Assembly, consisting of 83 members. The Premier & the Cabinet exercise executive power. The representative of the Crown is the Lieutenant Governor, who is appointed by the Governor General. The population as of the census of 2011 was 3,645,257.

Office of the Lieutenant Governor

Office of the Lieutenant Governor of AB, Legislature Bldg., 10800 - 97 Ave., 3rd Fl., Edmonton, AB T5K 2B6
Tel: 780-427-7243
Fax: 780-422-5134
ltgov@gov.ab.ca
www.lieutenantgovernor.ab.ca
The representative of the Crown in Alberta is the Lieutenant Governor, who is appointed by the Governor General, with the advice of the Prime Minister of Canada.

Lieutenant Governor, Hon. Donald S. Ethell, OC, OMM, AOE, MSC, CD, LLD
Tel: 780-427-7243
Note: The Queen's representative in Alberta is a retired Colonel.

Private Secretary to the Lieutenant Governor, Barb Walline
Tel: 780-427-7243
Fax: 780-422-5134
barb.walline@gov.ab.ca

Communications Officer, Janet Resta
Tel: 780-427-9222
Fax: 780-422-5134
janet.resta@gov.ab.ca

Office of the Premier

Office of the Premier, Legislature Building, #307, 10800 - 97 Ave., Edmonton, AB T5K 2B6
Tel: 780-427-2251
Fax: 780-427-1349
Toll-Free: -310-0000
www.premier.alberta.ca
The head of government in Alberta is the Premier. The Premier of the province is the leader of the political party that has the most seats in the Legislative Assembly. The Premier is head of the Executive Council, which works to put government policy into practice.
On October 1, 2011, Alison Redford was elected leader of Alberta's Progressive Conservative Party. She was sworn-in as the fourteenth premier of the province on October 7, 2011.
The Office of the Premier is led by the Chief of Staff. The following services are provided by the Office of the Premier: the provision of support to the Premier; issues management; the provision of strategic advice; correspondence; & scheduling.

Premier; President, Executive Council; Chair, Agenda & Priorities Committee, Hon. Alison Redford, QC
Tel: 780-427-2251
Fax: 780-427-1349
premier@gov.ab.ca
307 Legislature Bldg.
10800 - 97 Ave.
Edmonton, AB T5K2B6

Chief of Staff, Farouk Adatia
Tel: 780-427-2251
Fax: 780-427-1349
farouk.adatia@gov.ab.ca

Principal Secretary, Lee Richardson
Tel: 780-427-2251
Fax: 780-427-1349
lee.richardson@gov.ab.ca

Director, Legislative & House Procedures, Sherry Kozak
Tel: 780-427-2251
Fax: 780-427-1349
sherry.kozak@gov.ab.ca

Executive Director, Southern Alberta Office, Hunter Wight
Tel: 403-297-6464
Fax: 403-297-4276
hunter.wight@gov.ab.ca
Social Media: ca.linkedin.com/pub/hunter-wight/8/281/821
McDougall Centre
455 - 6th St. SW
Calgary, AB T2P 4A2

Director, Communications, Jay O'Neill
Tel: 780-427-2251
Fax: 780-422-3669
jay.o'neill@gov.ab.ca

Executive Scheduler, Lindsay Hoffman
Tel: 780-427-2251
Fax: 780-427-1349
lindsay.hoffman@gov.ab.ca

Director, Strategic Communications, Stefan Baranski
Tel: 780-427-2251
Fax: 780-427-1349
stefan.baranski@gov.ab.ca

Director, Operations, Darren Cunningham
Tel: 780-427-2251
Fax: 780-427-1349
darren.cunningham@gov.ab.ca

Assistant Director of Operations, Matthew Macdonald
Tel: 780-427-2251
Fax: 780-427-1349
matthew.macdonald@gov.ab.ca

Special Assistant to the Premier, John Hampson
Tel: 780-427-2251
Fax: 780-427-1349
john.hampson@gov.ab.ca

Manager, Correspondence, Liz Coupland
Tel: 780-415-1439
Fax: 780-422-3843
liz.coupland@gov.ab.ca

Press Secretary to Premier & Deputy Premier, Kim Misik
Tel: 780-427-2251
Fax: 780-422-3669
kim.misik@gov.ab.ca

Manager, Issues, Tracy Balash
Tel: 780-427-2251
Fax: 780-422-3669
tracy.balash@gov.ab.ca

Executive Council

Legislature Building, 10800 - 97 Ave., Edmonton, AB T5K 2B6
Tel: 780-427-2711
Toll-Free: -310-0000
The Executive Council consists of the Premier & cabinet ministers. Cabinet ministers are selected by the Premier from elected members of the Premier's party.
The Cabinet carries out the following functions: approving Orders in Council; ratifying policy matters; & acting as the final authority on issues related to the operation of the government.
The following is a list of members of the Executive Council, presented in order of precedence:

Premier; President, Executive Council; Chair, Agenda & Priorities Committee, Hon. Alison Redford, QC
Constituency: Calgary-Elbow
Tel: 780-427-2251
Fax: 780-427-1349
premier@gov.ab.ca
www.alisonredford.ca; alberta.ca/premier.cfm
Social Media: twitter.com/Premier_Redford, www.facebook.com/PremierRedford
Legislature Building
#307, 10800 - 97 Ave.
Edmonton, AB T5K 2B6

Deputy Premier; Chair, Operations Policy Committee; Liaison to the Canadian Forces, Hon. Thomas Lukaszuk
Constituency: Edmonton-CastleDowns
Tel: 780-427-5777
Fax: 780-422-8733
Social Media: twitter.com/lukaszukmla, www.facebook.com/108139349208353
Legislature Building
#408, 10800 - 97 Ave. NW
Edmonton, AB T5K 2B6

Minister, Finance; President, Treasury Board, Hon. Doug Horner
Constituency: Spruce Grove-St. Albert
Tel: 780-415-4855
Fax: 780-415-4853
sprucegrove.stalbert@assembly.ab.ca
horner.votepc.ca
Social Media: twitter.com/DougHornerMLA, www.facebook.com/DougHornerForAlberta, www.linkedin.com/pub/doug-horner/30/310/206
Legislature Building
#423, 10800 - 97 Ave.
Edmonton, AB T5K 2B6

Minister, Human Services; Government House Leader, Hon. David Hancock, QC
Constituency: Edmonton-Whitemud
Tel: 780-643-6210
Fax: 780-643-6214
hancock.votepc.ca
Social Media: twitter.com/davehancockmla, www.facebook.com/dave.hancock.376, www.linkedin.com/pub/dave-hancock/16/207/959
Legislature Building
#224, 10800 - 97 Ave.
Edmonton, AB T5K 2B6

Minister, International & Intergovernmental Relations, Hon. Cal Dallas
Constituency: Red Deer-South
Tel: 780-643-6225
Fax: 780-643-6228
dallas.votepc.ca
Social Media: twitter.com/CalDallas, www.facebook.com/caldallasmla, ca.linkedin.com/pub/cal-dallas/39/557/281
Legislature Building
#320, 10800 - 97 Ave.
Edmonton, AB T5K 2B6

Minister, Environment & Sustainable Resource Development, Hon. Diana McQueen
Constituency: Drayton Valley-Devon
Tel: 780-427-2391
Fax: 780-422-6259
www.mcqueen.mypcmla.ca
Social Media: twitter.com/ministermcqueen, www.facebook.com/dianamcqueenmla, ca.linkedin.com/pub/diana-mcqueen/17/24/b62
Legislature Building
#204, 10800 - 97 Ave.
Edmonton, AB T5K 2B6

Minister, Health, Hon. Fred Horne
Constituency: Edmonton-Rutherford
Tel: 780-427-3665
Fax: 780-415-0961
www.fredhorne.ca
Social Media: twitter.com/fredhornemla, www.facebook.com/FredHorne
Legislature Building
#208, 10800 - 97 Ave.
Edmonton, AB T5K 2B6

Minister, Energy, Hon. Ken Hughes
Constituency: Calgary-West
Tel: 780-427-3740
Fax: 780-422-0195
hughes.mypcmla.ca
Social Media: twitter.com/kenhughes4mla, www.facebook.com/KenHughes4MLA, www.linkedin.com/pub/ken-hughes/4/8a9/aab/sv
Legislature Building
#404, 10800 - 97 Ave.
Edmonton, AB T5K 2B6

Minister, Education, Hon. Jeff Johnson
Constituency: Athabasca-Sturgeon-Redwater
Tel: 780-427-5010
Fax: 780-427-5018
Social Media: www.facebook.com/JeffJohnsonPC
Legislature Building
#424, 10800 - 97 Ave.
Edmonton, AB T5K 2B6

Minister, Agriculture & Rural Development, Hon. Verlyn Olson, QC
Constituency: Wetaskiwin-Camrose
Tel: 780-427-2137
Fax: 780-422-6035
olson.votepc.ca
Social Media: www.facebook.com/verlynolsonmla
Legislature Building
#228, 10800 - 97 Ave.
Edmonton, AB T5K 2B6

Minister, Justice & Solicitor General; Deputy House Leader, Hon. Jonathan Denis, QC
Constituency: Calgary-Acadia
Tel: 780-427-2339
Fax: 780-422-6621
calgary.acadia@assembly.ab.ca
www.jonathandenis.com
Social Media: twitter.com/ministerjono, www.facebook.com/jonathandenismla
Legislature Building
#403, 10800 - 97 Ave.
Edmonton, AB T5K2B6

Minister, Municipal Affairs, Hon. Doug Griffiths
Constituency: Battle River-Wainwright
Tel: 780-427-3744
Fax: 780-422-9550
griffiths.votepc.ca
Social Media: twitter.com/GriffMLA, www.facebook.com/griffiths.mla, www.linkedin.com/in/mlagriff13ways
Legislature Building
#104, 10800 - 97 Ave.
Edmonton, AB T5K 2B6

Minister, Aboriginal Relations; Deputy House Leader, Hon. Robin Campbell
Constituency: West Yellowhead
Tel: 780-422-4144
Fax: 780-644-8389
campbell.mypcmla.ca
Social Media: www.facebook.com/robin.campbell.3990
Legislature Building
#323, 10800 - 97 Ave.
Edmonton, AB T5K 2B6

Minister, Culture, Hon. Heather Klimchuk
Constituency: Edmonton-Glenora
Tel: 780-422-3559
Fax: 780-427-7729
klimchuk.votepc.ca
Social Media: twitter.com/heatherklimchuk, www.facebook.com/Heather.Klimchuk
Legislature Building
#107, 10800 - 97 Ave.
Edmonton, AB T5K2B6

Minister, Service Alberta, Hon. Manmeet S. Bhullar
Constituency: Calgary-Greenway
Tel: 780-422-6880
Fax: 780-422-2496
Social Media: twitter.com/manmeetsbhullar
Legislature Building
#131, 10800 - 97 Ave.
Edmonton, AB T5K 2B6

Minister, Infrastructure, Hon. Wayne Drysdale
Constituency: Grande Prairie-Wapiti
Tel: 780-427-5041
Fax: 780-422-2002
drysdale.votepc.ca
Social Media: twitter.com/mla_w_drysdale, www.facebook.com/waynedrysdalemla, www.linkedin.com/pub/wayne-drysdale/1a/159/473
Legislature Building
#324, 10800 - 97 Ave.
Edmonton, AB T5K 2B6

Minister, Enterprise & Advanced Education, Hon. Stephen Khan
Constituency: St. Albert
Tel: 780-427-2025
Fax: 780-427-5582
khan.votepc.ca
Social Media: twitter.com/StephenKhanMLA, www.facebook.com/StephenKhanPC
Legislature Building
#402, 10800 - 97 Ave.
Edmonton, AB T5K 2B6

Minister, Transportation; Deputy House Leader, Hon. Ric McIver
Constituency: Calgary-Hays
Tel: 780-427-2080
Fax: 780-422-2722
ricmciver.ca
Social Media: twitter.com/ricmciver, www.facebook.com/RicMcIver, www.linkedin.com/pub/ric-mciver/10/498/34a
Legislature Building
#425, 10800 - 97 Ave.
Edmonton, AB T5K 2B6

Minister, Tourism, Parks, & Recreation, Hon. Christine Cusanelli
Constituency: Calgary-Currie
Tel: 780-427-4928
Fax: 780-427-0188
cusanelli.votepc.ca
Social Media: twitter.com/cc4currie, www.facebook.com/ccinyyc
Legislature Building
#229, 10800 - 97 Ave.
Edmonton, AB T5K 2B6

Corporate Human Resources (CHR)
Peace Hills Trust Tower, 10011 - 109 St., 7th Fl., Edmonton, AB T5J 3S8
Toll-Free: -310-0000
www.chr.alberta.ca

Corporate Human Resources offers advice to the Alberta provincial government about human resource administration. The following are some of the tasks performed by Corporate Human Resources: providing a corporate executive search program; coordinating job postings; delivering information about benefits, workplace health, labour relations, & other issues; advancing employee engagement; & offering learning opportunities to provincial government employees.

Public Service Commissioner, Dwight Dibben
Tel: 780-408-8450
Fax: 780-422-5428

Executive Director, Human Resources, CHR, Liz Kennedy
Tel: 780-408-8443
Fax: 780-644-4599
liz.kennedy@gov.ab.ca

Executive Director, Labour Relations, & Workplace Health, Lenore Neudorf
Tel: 780-408-8430
Fax: 780-427-5131
lenore.neudorf@gov.ab.ca

Executive Director, Compensation, Job Evaluation, & Benefits, Debra Smith
Tel: 780-408-8477
Fax: 780-422-3034
debra.smith@gov.ab.ca

Director, Corporate Recruitment & HR Community Development, Ray Chow
Tel: 780-644-1783
Fax: 780-644-1698
raymond.chow@gov.ab.ca

Director, Management Development, Ken Freier
Tel: 780-408-8415
Fax: 780-422-0835
ken.freier@gov.ab.ca

Director, Physical Sector, Tim Hajar
Tel: 780-408-8371
Fax: 780-415-9438
tim.hajar@gov.ab.ca

Director, Staffing Programs, Carole Kereliuk
Tel: 780-408-8410
Fax: 780-644-1698
carole.kereliuk@gov.ab.ca

Director, Organizational Learning, Chantal MacLean
Tel: 780-427-1438
Fax: 780-422-0835
chantal.maclean@gov.ab.ca

Director, Executive Search, Trish Mills
Tel: 780-408-8372
Fax: 780-422-0468
trish.mills@gov.ab.ca

Director, Employee Engagement, Jody Nisbet
Tel: 780-408-8463
Fax: 780-422-0835
jody.nisbet@gov.ab.ca

Director, Leadership Development, Torri Parkin
Tel: 780-408-8442
Fax: 780-422-0835
torri.parkin@gov.ab.ca

Director, Health Practices, Tim Royer
Tel: 780-408-8428
Fax: 780-415-9438
tim.royer@gov.ab.ca

Director, Information Technology Services, Roger Harris
Tel: 780-408-8496

Fax: 780-644-1698
roger.harris@gov.ab.ca
Assistant Deputy Minister, Organizational Transformation, Heather Caltagirone
Tel: 780-408-8462
Fax: 780-422-0835
heather.caltagirone@gov.ab.ca
Assistant Deputy Minister, Organizational Transformation, Connie Harrison
Tel: 780-427-5801
Fax: 780-422-0835
connie.harrison@gov.ab.ca
Assistant Commissioner, Attraction & Technology & Human Resource Community Development, Lori Cooper
Tel: 780-644-7520
Fax: 780-644-1698
lori.cooper@gov.ab.ca
Public Affairs Officer, Communications, Cara Smith
Tel: 780-644-5602
Fax: 780-427-6596
cara.smith@gov.ab.ca

Deputy Minister's Office
Executive Branch, Legislature Building, #305, 10800 - 97th Ave., Edmonton, AB T5K 2B6
The Executive Council Office is led by the Deputy Minister of the Executive Council.
Deputy Minister, Executive Council, Peter Watson
Tel: 780-422-4910
Fax: 780-422-1882
peter.watson@gov.ab.ca
Assistant Deputy Minister, Social Policy, Bruce McDonald
Tel: 780-644-5286
Fax: 780-427-0305
bruce.mcdonald@gov.ab.ca
Deputy Chief, Policy Coordination, Grant D. Sprague, Q.C.
Tel: 780-415-2388
Fax: 780-427-0305
grant.sprague@gov.ab.ca
Assistant Deputy Minister, Strategic Planning & Coordination, Bryce Stewart
Tel: 780-422-5353
bryce.stewart@gov.ab.ca
Assistant Deputy Minister, Economic Policy, Wendy Boje
Tel: 780-422-7050
Fax: 780-427-0305
wendy.boje@gov.ab.ca
Assistant Deputy Minister, Natural Resources & Environment Policy, John Donner
Tel: 780-638-4141
Fax: 780-427-0305
john.donner@gov.ab.ca

Protocol
Executive Branch, Legislature Annex, 9718 - 107 St., 11th Fl., Edmonton, AB T5K 1E4
Tel: 780-422-1542
Fax: 780-422-0786
Chief, Protocol, Betty Anne Spinks
Tel: 780-422-2236
Fax: 780-422-0786
bettyanne.spinks@gov.ab.ca
Deputy Chief, Protocol, Norm Davies
Tel: 780-422-1845
Fax: 780-422-0786
norm.davies@gov.ab.ca
Manager, Government House, Gino Gadowsky
Tel: 780-427-2281
Fax: 780-422-6508
gino.gadowsky@gov.ab.ca
Executive Branch
12845 - 102 Ave.
Edmonton, AB T5N 0M6
Coordinator, Government House, Christine Taylor
Tel: 780-427-2281
Fax: 780-422-6508
christine.taylor@gov.ab.ca
Executive Branch
12845 - 102 Ave.
Edmonton, AB T5N 0M6

Public Affairs Bureau
Park Plaza, 10611 - 98 Ave., Edmonton, AB T5K 2P7
Tel: 780-427-2754
Fax: 780-422-4168
Managing Director, Public Affairs Bureau, Lee Funke
Tel: 780-644-5655
Fax: 780-427-1010
lee.funke@gov.ab.ca
Executive Director, Corporate Services, Elaine Dougan
Tel: 780-422-4097
Fax: 780-422-4168
elaine.dougan@gov.ab.ca
Executive Director, Strategic Communications, Kathy Lazowski
Tel: 780-644-4623
Fax: 780-427-1010
kathy.lazowski@gov.ab.ca
Executive Director, Corporate Communications, Terry Willock
Tel: 780-422-2787
Fax: 780-415-9485
terry.willock@gov.ab.ca
Manager, Marketing Services, Shelley Gangl
Tel: 780-427-9356
Fax: 780-422-4650
shelley.gangl@gov.ab.ca
Senior Manager, Communications, Joanne Rosnau
Tel: 780-644-8106
Fax: 780-427-1010
joanne.rosnau@gov.ab.ca

Regulatory Review Secretariat
Legislature Annex, 9718 - 107 St, 11th Fl., Edmonton, AB T5K 1E4
Tel: 780-422-1736
regulatoryreview@gov.ab.ca
alberta.ca/regulatoryreviewsecretariat.cfm
The Regulatory Review Secretariat undertakes the following activities: ensuring that regulations in Alberta are up-to-date & meet Government priorities; analyzing new regulations or changes to existing regulations; improving regulations through communication with the public & businesses; evaluating Alberta's regulatory system; working with governments across Canada to improve regulations in Alberta & in other provinces
Executive Director, Regulatory Review Secretariat, George Samoil
Tel: 780-422-1736
Fax: 780-415-4860
george.samoil@gov.ab.ca
Manager, Regulatory Review, Meenakshi Joshi
Tel: 780-422-9341
Fax: 780-415-4860
meenakshi.joshi@gov.ab.ca
Manager, Regulatory Review Strategic Support, Keren Perla
Tel: 780-422-3498
Fax: 780-415-4860
keren.perla@gov.ab.ca

Cabinet Policy Committees
The following are Alberta's cabinet policy committees: Community Development; Education; Energy; Finance; & Public Health & Safety.
Chair, Community Development Cabinet Policy Committee, Hector Goudreau
Tel: 780-643-6452
Fax: 780-643-6456
Social Media:
www.facebook.com/pages/Hector-Goudreau/195236593554
Executive Branch, Legislature Building
#127, 10800 - 97 Ave.
Edmonton, AB T5K 2B6
Chair, Education Cabinet Policy Committee, Genia Leskiw
Tel: 780-415-0995
Fax: 780-643-6449
Social Media: www.facebook.com/genia.leskiw1?ref
Executive Branch, Legislature Building
#131, 10800 - 97 Ave.
Edmonton, AB T5K 2B6
Chair, Energy Cabinet Policy Committee, Doug Elniski
Tel: 780-427-0858
Fax: 780-643-6456
Social Media: www.twitter.com/dougelniski
Executive Branch, Legislature Building
#128, 10800 - 97 Ave.
Edmonton, AB T5K 2B6
Chair, Finance Cabinet Policy Committee, Dave Quest
Tel: 780-643-6458
Fax: 780-643-6449
Social Media: www.twitter.com/davequestMLA, www.facebook.com/DaveQuestMLA
Executive Branch, Legislature Building
#131, 10800 - 97 Ave.
Edmonton, AB T5K 2B6
Chair, Public Health & Safety Cabinet Policy Committee, George Rogers
Tel: 780-422-2229
Fax: 780-427-4974
leduc.beaumont@assembly.ab.ca
Social Media: www.twitter.com/rogersofleduc, www.facebook.com/George-Rogers/215811019107
Executive Branch, Legislature Building
#130, 10800 - 97 Ave.
Edmonton, AB T5K 2B6

Legislative Assembly of Alberta

Legislature Annex, 9718 - 107 St., Edmonton, AB T5K 1E4
Tel: 780-427-2826
Fax: 780-427-1623
laocommunications@assembly.ab.ca
www.assembly.ab.ca
Other Communication: Reference information: library.requests@assembly.ab.ca; Visitor Services Office: visitorinfo@assembly.ab.ca
The Legislative Assembly of Alberta is elected by voters. It consists of government members & opposition members.
The Legislative Assembly Office carries out the following main responsibilities: supporting the Speaker of the Legislative Assembly; supporting members; recording proceedings & maintaining records of the Legislative Assembly; educating the public; & providing services to external clients.
The Legislative Assembly Office is organized by services such as the following: management & communication services; house & committee services; legal services; human resource services; financial management & administrative services; visitor, ceremonial, & security services; library services; public information & reporting services; & information technology services.

Clerk, Dr. David McNeil
Tel: 780-427-2478
Fax: 780-427-5688
david.mcneil@assembly.ab.ca
Note: The Clerk acts as the Chief Executive Officer of the Legislative Assembly Office. In the Chamber, the Clerk advises the Speakerabout procedure. He also calls out the daily order of business.

Sergeant-at-Arms; Director, Visitor, Ceremonial & Security Services, Brian Hodgson
Tel: 780-427-6048
Fax: 780-415-5829
brian.hodgson@assembly.ab.ca
Note: The following duties are performed: management of visitors' servicesfor the Legislative Assembly; provision of security services; & the execution of ceremonial functions for the Legislative Assembly.

Senior Financial Officer; Director, Financial Management & Administrative Services, Scott Ellis
Tel: 780-427-1566
Fax: 780-415-1714
scott.ellis@assembly.ab.ca
Note: Financial Management & Administrative Services isresponsible for financial processing, reporting, & control.

Director, Human Resources, Information Technology & Broadcast Services, Cheryl Scarlett
Tel: 780-427-1368
Fax: 780-427-6436
cheryl.scarlett@assembly.ab.ca
Note: Customized human resource management services are provided tosupport the operation of the Legislative Assembly of Alberta.

Legislature Librarian, Valerie Footz
Tel: 780-427-0202
Fax: 780-427-6016
val.footz@assembly.ab.ca
Note: The Legislature Library provides services to Members of the Legislative Assembly of Alberta, Members' staff, LegislativeAssembly Office staff, & the general public.

Managing Editor, Hansard, Liz Sim
Tel: 780-427-1875
Fax: 780-427-1623
liz.sim@assembly.ab.ca
Note: Hansard is the official report of the debates of a Legislature or a Parliament & its committees. It is named after theHansard family, the printers who published the first official record of the British parliamentary debates in the 19th century.

Auditor General, Merwan Saher
Tel: 780-422-6195
Fax: 780-422-9555
Note: Web Site: www.oag.ab.ca
Office of the Auditor General
9925 - 109th St., 8th Fl.
Edmonton, AB T5K 2J8

Chief Electoral Officer, Brian O. Fjeldheim
Tel: 780-427-1035
Fax: 780-422-2900
brian.fjeldheim@elections.ab.ca
Note: Web Site: www.elections.ab.ca
Office of the Chief Electoral Officer, Queen's Printer Building

11510 Kingway Ave., 1st Fl.
Edmonton, AB T5G2Y5

Ethics Commissioner, Neil R. Wilkinson
Tel: 780-422-2273
Fax: 780-422-2261
generalinfo@ethicscommissioner.ab.ca
Note: Web Site:www.ethicscommissioner.ab.ca
Office of the Ethics Commissioner
9925 - 109th St., 12th Fl.
Edmonton, AB T5K 2J8

Information & Privacy Commissioner, Jill Clayton
Tel: 780-422-6860
Fax: 780-422-5682
jclayton@oipc.ab.ca
Note: Web Site:www.oipc.ab.ca
Office of the Information & Privacy Commissioner
9925 - 109th St., 4th Fl.
Edmonton, AB T5K 2J8

Director, Corporate Services, Suzanne Richford
Tel: 780-415-2510
Fax: 780-427-2759
suzanne.richford@ombudsman.ab.ca
Note: WebSite: www.ombudsman.ab.ca
Office of the Ombudsman. Canadian Western Bank Building
10303 Jasper Ave., 28th Fl.
Edmonton, AB T5J 5C3

Ombudsman, Peter Hourihan
Tel: 780-427-2756
Fax: 780-427-2759
Note: Web Site: www.ombudsman.ab.ca
Office of the Ombudsman. Canadian Western Bank Building
10303 Jasper Ave., 28th Fl.
Edmonton, AB T5J 5C3

Office of the Child & Youth Advocate
Peace Hills Trust Tower, #805, 10011 - 109 St., Edmonton, AB T5J 3S8
Tel: 780-422-6056
Fax: 780-644-8833
Toll-Free: 800-661-3446
www.alberta.ca/advocate
Other Communication: Southern Alberta Advocacy Services, Phone: 403-297-8435, Fax: 403-297-4456
Secondary Address: 301 - 14 St. NW
Southern Alberta Advocacy Services, Professional Bldg.
Calgary, AB T2N 2A1
As of April 1, 2012, the Child & Youth Advocate is an independent officer reporting to the Legislature under the newly created Child & Youth Advocate Act.
Acts Administered:
Child & Youth Advocate Act
Child, Youth & Family Enhancement Act
Protection of Sexually Exploited Children Act
Child & Youth Advocate (Alberta), Del Graff
Tel: 780-644-8281
Fax: 780-644-8833
del.graff@gov.ab.ca
Executive Director, Child & Youth Advocacy, Jackie Stewart
Tel: 780-422-6056
Manager, Legal Representation for Children & Youth Service, Terri Davies
Tel: 780-415-8936
Fax: 780-644-7227
terri.davies@gov.ab.ca
Director, Strategic Support, Bonnie Russell
Tel: 780-422-2966
Fax: 780-644-8833
bonnie.russell@gov.ab.ca
Director, Systemic Advocacy & Outreach, Randy Baker
Tel: 780-422-2632
Fax: 780-638-3718
randy.baker@gov.ab.ca

Office of the Speaker
Legislative Branch, Legislature Building, 10800 - 97th Ave., Edmonton, AB T5K 2B6
The Speaker of the Alberta Legislative Assembly maintains orderly debate in the Chamber. He cannot engage in debate in the Assembly. As head of the Legislative Assembly Office, the Speaker also plays a role in the maintenance of records of the Assembly & the provision of services to members.
Speaker, Hon. Gene Zwozdesky
Tel: 780-427-2464
Fax: 780-422-9553
gene.zwozdesky@assembly.ab.ca
Executive Assistant, Bev Alenius
Tel: 780-427-2464
Fax: 780-422-9553
bev.alenius@assembly.ab.ca

Government Members' Caucus Office
Legislative Branch, Legislature Building, #132, 10800 - 97th Ave., Edmonton, AB T5K 2B6
Tel: 780-427-1800
support@mypcmla.ca
www.mypcmla.ca
Alberta's Progressive Conservatives hold the most seats in the Legislature & are the governing party in Alberta. Government Caucus is led by a whip, who sets agendas & chairs meetings.
Whip; Member, Legislative Assembly, Steve Young
Tel: 780-427-1879
Fax: 780-415-0968
Director, Caucus, Douglas Mills
Tel: 780-427-1198
Fax: 780-415-0968
douglas.mills@assembly.ab.ca
Director, Research & Communications, Eldon McIlwain
Tel: 780-427-8219
Fax: 780-422-5266
eldon.mcilwain@assembly.ab.ca

Wildrose Alliance Party of Alberta Office
Legislature Annex, #502A, 9718 - 107 St., Edmonton, AB T5K 1E4
Tel: 780-415-0975
Fax: 780-638-3506
www.wildrose.ca
The Wildrose Alliance Party of Alberta, led by Danielle Smith, occupies four seats in the Legislative Assembly.
Leader, Alberta Wildrose Alliance Official Opposition, Danielle Smith
Tel: 403-769-0999
Toll-free: 888-262-1888
Fax: 866-620-4791
rob.anderson@assembly.ab.ca
Social Media: www.twitter.com/ElectDanielle, www.facebook.com/ElectDanielle, www.linkedin.com/in/electdanielle
Wildrose Alliance Party
#408, 919 Centre St. NW
Calgary, AB T2E 2P6
Director, Communications, Brock Harrison
Tel: 780-643-4032
Fax: 780-638-3506
brock.harrison@assembly.ab.ca
Director, Legislative Affairs, Shannon Stubbs
Tel: 780-415-8799
Fax: 780-638-3506
shannon.stubbs@assembly.ab.ca
Director, Policy & Research, Bill Bewick
Tel: 780-638-2897
Fax: 780-638-3506
bill.bewick@assembly.ab.ca

Liberal Caucus Office
Legislature Annex, 9718 - 107 St., 2nd Fl., Edmonton, AB T5K 1E4
Tel: 780-427-2292
Fax: 780-427-3697
liberal.correspondence@assembly.ab.ca
www.albertaliberalcaucus.com
Led by party leader, Dr. Raj Sherman, the Liberal Party occupies nine seats in the Legislative Assembly.
Leader, Liberal Party of Alberta, Dr. Raj Sherman
Tel: 780-415-0976
Fax: 780-638-4313
Social Media: www.twitter.com/RajShermanMLA, www.facebook.com/rajshermanmla
Note: Web Site: www.electraj.ca
Chief of Staff, Jonathan Huckabay
Tel: 780-447-2292
Fax: 780-427-3697
jonathan.huckabay@assembly.ab.ca
Director, Southern Alberta Liberal Caucus Office, Vacant
Tel: 403-233-8250
Fax: 403-233-8269
Southern Alberta Liberal Caucus Office
#103, 602 - 11 Ave. SW, 3rd Fl.
Calgary, AB T2R 1J8
Senior Research Analyst / Communications Consultant, Denis Lapointe
Tel: 780-427-2292
Fax: 780-427-3697
denis.lapointe@assembly.ab.ca

New Democratic Party Caucus Office
#501, 9718 - 107 St., Edmonton, AB T5K 1E4
Tel: 780-415-1800
Fax: 780-415-0701
nd@assembly.ab.ca
www.ndpopposition.ab.ca
The New Democratic Party has two seats in the Legislative Assembly.
Leader, New Democratic Party Opposition, Brian Mason
Constituency: Edmonton-Highlands-Norwood
Tel: 780-415-1800
Fax: 780-415-0701
brian.mason@assembly.ab.ca
Social Media: www.twitter.com/bmasonNDP, www.facebook.com/Brian-Mason/26993021019
Note: Web Site: www.brianmason.ca
Chief, Staff, Adrienne King
Tel: 780-644-4556
Fax: 780-415-0701
Adrienne.king@assembly.ab.ca
Director, Research, Doug Bailie
Tel: 780-415-2266
doug.bailie@assembly.ab.ca
Officer, Administration, John Ashton
Tel: 780-415-1800
Fax: 780-415-0701
john.ashton@assembly.ab.ca
Officer, Outreach, Pascal Ryffel
Tel: 780-415-1801
Fax: 780-415-0701
pascal.ryffel@assembly.ab.ca

Alberta Party Office
Legislative Branch, Legislature Annex, #401, 9718 - 107 St., PO Box 1045 Main, Edmonton, AB T5K 1E4
Toll-Free: 877-683-3126
info@albertaparty.ca
www.albertaparty.ca
The Alberta Party has one member in the Legislative Assembly.
Leader, Alberta Party, Glenn Taylor
glenn@albertaparty.ca
Member, Legislative Assembly, Dave Taylor
Tel: 780-427-2298
Fax: 780-638-3958
Research Assistant, Evan Galbraith
Tel: 780-638-3956
Fax: 780-638-3958
evan.galbraith@assembly.ab.ca
Office Assistant, Jacquie Lycka
Tel: 780-427-2298
Fax: 780-638-3958
jacquie.lycka@assembly.ab.ca

Committees of the Legislative Assembly of Alberta
Legislative Branch, Legislature Annex, #801, 9718 - 107 St., Edmonton, AB T5K 1E4
committees@assembly.ab.ca
Committees of the Legislative Assembly of Alberta include select special committees, special standing committees, policy field committees, & standing committees.
Current select special committees include the Select Special Information & Privacy Commissioner Search Committee & the Select Special Ombudsman Search Committee.
There is one special standing committee, the Special Standing Committee on Members' Services.
Policy field committees include the following: Standing Committee on Community Services; Standing Committee on Health; Satnding Committee on Public Safety & Services; Standing Committee on Resources & Environment; & the Standing Committee on the Economy.
Current standing committees are as follows: Standing Committee on Legislative Offices; Standing Committee on Private Bills; Standing Committee on Privileges & Elections, Standing Orders & Printing; Standing Committee on Public Accounts; & the Standing Committee on the Alberta Heritage Savings Trust Fund.
Chair, Select Special Information & Privacy Commissioner Search Committee, Leonard Mitzel
Constituency: Cypress-Medicine Hat, Progressive Conservative
Tel: 780-415-9590
Fax: 780-422-0351
Chair, Select Special Ombudsman Search Committee, Leonard Mitzel
Constituency: Cypress-Medicine Hat, Progressive Conservative
Tel: 780-415-9590
Fax: 780-422-0351
Chair, Special Standing Committee on Members' Services, Hon. Ken Kowalski
Constituency: Barrhead-Morinville-Westlock, Progressive Conservative
Tel: 780-427-2464
Fax: 780-422-9553
ken.kowalski@assembly.ab.ca
Social Media: www.facebook.com/ken.kowalski
Chair, Standing Committee on the Alberta Heritage Savings Trust Fund, Janis Tarchuk
Constituency: Banff-Cochrane, Progressive Conservative
Tel: 780-415-0993
Fax: 780-427-1835
Chair, Standing Committee on the Economy, Naresh Bhardwaj
Constituency: Edmonton-Ellerslie, Progressive Conservative
Tel: 780-644-3845
Fax: 780-422-1671

Chair, Standing Committee on Health, Barry McFarland
Constituency: Little Bow, Progressive Conservative
Tel: 780-427-0879
Fax: 780-422-0351
Chair, Standing Committee on Legislative Offices, Leonard Mitzel
Constituency: Cypress-Medicine Hat, Progressive Conservative
Tel: 780-415-9590
Fax: 780-422-0351
Chair, Standing Committee on Private Bills, Dr. Neil Brown, Q.C.
Constituency: Calgary-Nose Hill, Progressive Conservative
Tel: 780-415-8368
Fax: 780-427-1234
Chair, Standing Committee on Privileges & Elections, Standing Orders & Printing, Raymond Prins
Constituency: Lacombe-Ponoka, Progressive Conservative
Tel: 780-422-3353
Fax: 780-422-0351
Chair, Standing Committee on Public Accounts, Hugh MacDonald
Constituency: Edmonton-Gold Bar
Tel: 780-427-2292
Fax: 780-427-3697
hugh.macdonald@assembly.ab.ca
Chair, Standing Committee on Public Safety & Services, Wayne Drysdale
Constituency: Grande Prairie-Wapiti, Progressive Conservative
Tel: 780-415-0107
Fax: 780-422-1671
Chair, Standing Committee on Resources & Environment, Raymond Prins
Constituency: Lacombe-Ponoka, Progressive Conservative
Tel: 780-422-3353
Fax: 780-422-0351

Twenty-eighth Legislature - Alberta

Legislature Bldg., 10800 - 97 Ave., Edmonton, AB T5K 2B6
Tel: 780-427-2826
laocommunications@assembly.ab.ca
www.assembly.ab.ca
Other Communication: Reference Information, E-mail: library.requests@assembly.ab.ca

Last General Election, April 23, 2012.
Party Leaders:
Progressive Conservative Party: Hon. Alison Redford, Premier;
Liberal Party: Dr. Raj Sherman;
Wildrose Alliance Party: Danielle Smith;
New Democratic Party: Brian Mason.
Party Standings:
Progressive Conservative Party 61;
Wildrose Alliance Party 17;
Alberta Liberal 5;
New Democratic Party 4;
Total 87.
Indemnities, Salaries, & Allowances:
MLA indemnity $52,092, plus $26,046 MLA tax free allowance.
In addition to this are the following indemnities & allowances:
Premier $81,312;
Speaker $63,912;
Ministers with portfolio $63,912;
Ministers without portfolio $28,392;
Leader of the Official Opposition $63,912;
Deputy Speaker & Chair, Committees $31,968;
Deputy Chair of Committees $15,984;
Leader of a recognized opposition parties $28,392.
The following are special members' allowances:
Official Opposition House Leader: $13,596;
Third Party House Leader (recognized opposition party): $10,872;
Chief Government Whip: $10,872;
Assistant Government Whip: $8,136;
Chief Opposition Whip: $8,136;
Assistant Opposition Whip: $6,792;
Third Party Whip: $6,792.
The following is a list of members, with their constituency, the number of electors in the ele ectoral division, the party affiliation, & contact information:

Members, Legislative Assembly of Alberta

Member, Legislative Assembly, Mike Allen
Constituency: Fort McMurray-Wood Buffalo *No. of Constituents:* 19,796, Progressive Conservative
Tel: 780-427-1800
Fax: 780-415-0968
fortmcmurray.woodbuffalo@assembly.ab.ca
www.pickmike.ca
Other Communications: Constituency Phone: 780-790-6014; Fax: 780-791-3683
Social Media: twitter.com/Mike_Allen47, www.facebook.com/pages/Mike-Allen-Campaign/183446135092911
Constituency Office
#102, 9925 Biggs Ave.
Fort McMurray, AB T9H 1S2
Member, Legislative Assembly, Moe Amery
Constituency: Calgary-East *No. of Constituents:* 28,318, Progressive Conservative
Tel: 780-427-1800
Fax: 780-415-0968
calgary.east@assembly.ab.ca; MoeAmery@gmail.com
www.moeamery.ca
Other Communications: Constituency Phone: 403-216-5450; Fax: 403-216-5452
Social Media: www.facebook.com/people/Moe-Amery/783777229
ConstituencyOffice
#550, 2710 - 17th Ave. SE
Calgary, AB T2A 0P6
Member, Legislative Assembly, Rob Anderson
Constituency: Airdrie *No. of Constituents:* 28,928, Wildrose Alliance Party of Alberta
Tel: 780-638-3505
Toll-free: 888-948-8741
Fax: 780-638-3506
airdrie@assembly.ab.ca
www.robanderson.ca
Other Communications: Constituency Phone: 403-948-8741; Fax: 403-948-8744
Social Media: twitter.com/randersonmla, www.facebook.com/pages/Rob-Anderson/199265040654
Constituency Office
209Bowers St.
Airdrie, AB T4B 0R6
Member, Legislative Assembly, Joe Anglin
Constituency: Rimbey-Rocky Mountain House-Sundre *No. of Constituents:* 25,598, Wildrose Alliance Party of Alberta
Tel: 780-638-3505
Fax: 780-638-3506
rimbey.rockymountainhouse.sundre@assembly.ab.ca
www.joeanglin.ca
Other Communications: Constituency Phone: 403-638-5025; Fax: 403-638-5026
Social Media: twitter.com/JoeAnglin2, www.facebook.com/group.php?gid=190805771034042
ConstituencyOffice
101 Main Ave. SE
PO Box 1626
Sundre, AB T0M 1X0
Member, Legislative Assembly, Drew Barnes
Constituency: Cypress-Medicine Hat *No. of Constituents:* 25,247, Wildrose Alliance Party of Alberta
Tel: 780-638-3505
Toll-free: 866-339-2191
Fax: 780-638-3506
cypress.medicinehat@assembly.ab.ca
www.barnesforwildrose.ca
Other Communications: Constituency Phone: 403-528-2191; Fax: 403-528-2278
Social Media: twitter.com/drew_barnes, www.facebook.com/barneswildrose
ConstituencyOffice, Trans Canada Place
#5, 1299 Trans Canada Way
Medicine Hat, AB T1B 1H9
Member, Legislative Assembly, Naresh Bhardwaj
Constituency: Edmonton-Ellerslie *No. of Constituents:* 24,945, Progressive Conservative
Tel: 780-427-1800
Fax: 780-415-0968
edmonton.ellerslie@assembly.ab.ca
www.bhardwaj.votepc.ca
Other Communications: Constituency Phone: 780-414-2000; Fax: 780-414-6383
Social Media: twitter.com/NareshBhardwaj, www.facebook.com/profile.php?id=646264668
Constituency Office
5732- 19A Ave.
Edmonton, AB T6L 1L8
Member, Legislative Assembly, Hon. Manmeet S. Bhullar
Constituency: Calgary-Greenway *No. of Constituents:* 24,816, Progressive Conservative
Tel: 780-427-1800
Fax: 780-415-0968
calgary.greenway@assembly.ab.ca
Other Communications: Constituency Phone: 403-248-4487; Fax: 403-273-2898
Social Media: twitter.com/manmeetsbhullar, www.facebook.com/manmeetbhullarmla
ConstituencyOffice
#1017, 2220 - 68 St. NE
Calgary, AB T1Y 6Y7
Member, Legislative Assembly, Gary Bikman
Constituency: Cardston-Taber-Warner *No. of Constituents:* 23,606, Wildrose Alliance Party of Alberta
Tel: 780-638-3505
Toll-free: 888-600-6080
Fax: 780-638-3506
cardston.taberwarner@assembly.ab.ca
www.whygary.ca; www.wildrose.ca/mlas/gary-bikman
Other Communications: Cardston Phone: 403-653-5100; Taber: 403-223-0001
Social Media: twitter.com/garybikman, www.facebook.com/garybikman, ca.linkedin.com/pub/gary-bikman/14/67b/9a1
ConstituencyOffice
24 - 3rd Ave. West
PO Box 1539
Cardston, AB T0K 0K0
Member, Legislative Assembly, Deron Bilous
Constituency: Edmonton-Beverly-Clareview *No. of Constituents:* 28,620, New Democratic Party
Tel: 780-415-1800
Fax: 780-415-0701
edmonton.beverlyclareview@assembly.ab.ca
www.albertandp.ca/deron
Other Communications: Constituency Phone: 780-476-6467; Fax: 780-476-6473
Social Media: twitter.com/DeronBilous, www.facebook.com/electderonbilous
ConstituencyOffice
552 Hermitage Mall
Edmonton, AB T5A 4N2
Member, Legislative Assembly, Laurie Blakeman
Constituency: Edmonton-Centre *No. of Constituents:* 23,995, Liberal
Tel: 780-427-2292
Fax: 780-427-3697
edmonton.centre@assembly.ab.ca
www.laurieblakeman.com
Other Communications: Constituency Phone: 780-414-0743; Fax: 780-414-0772
Social Media: twitter.com/laurieblakeman, www.facebook.com/laurieblakeman
Constituency Office
#3,9908 - 109 St.
Edmonton, AB T5K 1H5
Member, Legislative Assembly, Dr. Neil Brown, Q.C.
Constituency: Calgary-Mackay-Nose Hill *No. of Constituents:* 27,966, Progressive Conservative
Tel: 780-427-1800
Fax: 780-415-0968
calgary.mackay.nosehill@assembly.ab.ca
www.neilbrown.ca
Other Communications: Constituency Phone: 403-215-7710; Fax: 403-216-5410
Social Media: twitter.com/@rneilbrown, www.facebook.com/DrNeilBrown
ConstituencyOffice
#16, 5440 - 4th St. NW
Calgary, AB T2K 1A8
Member, Legislative Assembly, Pearl Calahasen
Constituency: Lesser Slave Lake *No. of Constituents:* 17,001, Progressive Conservative
Tel: 780-427-1800
Toll-free: 866-625-0648
Fax: 780-415-0968
lesser.slavelake@assembly.ab.ca
Other Communications: Constituency Phone: 780-523-3171; Fax: 780-523-5150
Social Media: www.facebook.com/pearlcalahasen
ConstituencyOffice
5001 - 49 St.
PO Box 598
High Prairie, AB T0G 1E0
Member, Legislative Assembly, Robin Campbell
Constituency: West Yellowhead *No. of Constituents:* 19,115, Progressive Conservative
Tel: 780-427-1800
Toll-free: 800-661-6517
Fax: 780-415-0968
west.yellowhead@assembly.ab.ca
Other Communications: Constituency Phone: 780-865-9796; Fax: 780-865-9760
Social Media: www.facebook.com/RobinCampbellAB
ConstituencyOffice
#6, 554 Carmichael Lane
Hinton, AB T7V 1S8
Member, Legislative Assembly, Wayne Cao
Constituency: Calgary-Fort *No. of Constituents:* 24,755, Progressive Conservative
Tel: 780-427-1800
Fax: 780-415-0968
calgary.fort@assembly.ab.ca
www.waynecao.ca
Other Communications: Constituency Phone: 403-216-5454; Fax: 403-216-5455
Social Media: www.facebook.com/caoboys
Constituency Office
2784 GlenmoreTrail SE
Calgary, AB T2C 2E6

Member, Legislative Assembly, Ron Casey
Constituency: Banff-Cochrane *No. of Constituents:* 26,362, Progressive Conservative
Tel: 780-427-1800
Toll-free: 866-760-8281
Fax: 780-415-0968
banff.cochrane@assembly.ab.ca; ron@roncasey.com
www.casey.votepc.ca
Other Communications: Constituency Phone: 403-760-8281; Fax: 403-760-5009
Social Media: twitter.com/casey_ron
Constituency Office
229 Bear St., 4th Fl.
PO Box 790
Banff, AB T1L 1A8

Member, Legislative Assembly, Christine Cusanelli
Constituency: Calgary-Currie *No. of Constituents:* 26,906, Progressive Conservative
Tel: 780-427-1800
Fax: 780-415-0968
calgary.currie@assembly.ab.ca
Other Communications: Constituency Phone: 403-246-4794; Fax: 403-686-1543
Social Media: twitter.com/cc4currie, www.facebook.com/ccinyyc
Constituency Office
2108B - 33 Ave. SW
Calgary, AB T2T 1Z6

Member, Legislative Assembly, Hon. Cal Dallas
Constituency: Red Deer-South *No. of Constituents:* 31,049, Progressive Conservative
Tel: 780-427-1800
Fax: 780-415-0968
reddeer.south@assembly.ab.ca
www.dallas.votepc.ca
Other Communications: Constituency Phone: 403-340-3565; Fax: 403-346-9260
Social Media: twitter.com/CalDallas, www.facebook.com/caldallasmla, ca.linkedin.com/pub/cal-dallas/39/557/281
Constituency Office
#503, 4901- 48 St.
Red Deer, AB T4N 6M4

Member, Legislative Assembly, Alana DeLong
Constituency: Calgary-Bow *No. of Constituents:* 24,390, Progressive Conservative
Tel: 780-427-1800
Fax: 780-415-0968
calgary.bow@assembly.ab.ca
www.delong.votepc.ca
Other Communications: Constituency Phone: 403-216-5400; Fax: 403-216-5402
Social Media: twitter.com/alanadelong, www.facebook.com/alana.delong, ca.linkedin.com/pub/alana-delong/27/226/373
Constituency Office
6307 BownessRd. NW
Calgary, AB T3B 0E4

Member, Legislative Assembly, Hon. Jonathan Denis, Q.C.
Constituency: Calgary-Acadia *No. of Constituents:* 25,293, Progressive Conservative
Tel: 780-427-1800
Fax: 780-415-0968
calgary.acadia@assembly.ab.ca
www.denismla.ca
Other Communications: Constituency Phone: 403-640-1363; Fax: 403-640-2970
Social Media: twitter.com/MinisterJono, www.facebook.com/jonathandenismla, ca.linkedin.com/pub/jonathan-denis/4/7ab/746
Constituency Office
#10, 8318 Fairmount Dr. SE
Calgary, AB T2H 0Y8

Member, Legislative Assembly, Ian Donovan
Constituency: Little Bow *No. of Constituents:* 22,225, Wildrose Alliance Party of Alberta
Tel: 780-638-3505
Toll-free: 800-563-0917
Fax: 780-638-3506
little.bow@assembly.ab.ca
www.iandonovan.net; www.wildrose.ca/mlas/ian-donovan
Other Communications: Constituency Phone: 403-643-2077; Fax: 403-643-2024
Social Media: www.facebook.com/group.php?gid=178095635541802
Constituency Office
111Carman St.
Carmangay, AB T0L 0N0

Member, Legislative Assembly, David Dorward
Constituency: Edmonton-Gold Bar *No. of Constituents:* 30,349, Progressive Conservative
Tel: 780-427-1800
Fax: 780-415-0968
edmonton.goldbar@assembly.ab.ca
www.votedorward.ca
Other Communications: Constituency Phone: 780-414-1015; Fax: 780-414-1017
Social Media: twitter.com/VoteDorward, www.facebook.com/votedorward, ca.linkedin.com/pub/david-dorward/6/121/501
Constituency Office
#102,7024 - 101 Ave. NW
Edmonton, AB T6A 0H7

Member, Legislative Assembly, Wayne Drysdale
Constituency: Grande Prairie-Wapiti *No. of Constituents:* 27,374, Progressive Conservative
Tel: 780-427-1800
Fax: 780-415-0968
grandeprairie.wapiti@assembly.ab.ca
drysdale.votepc.ca
Other Communications: Constituency Phone: 780-538-1800; Fax: 780-538-1802
Social Media: twitter.com/mla_w_drysdale, www.facebook.com/waynedrysdalemla, ca.linkedin.com/pub/wayne-drysdale/1a/159/473
Constituency Office,Junction Point Village
#101, 9814 - 97 St.
Grande Prairie, AB T8V 8H5

Member, Legislative Assembly, David Eggen
Constituency: Edmonton-Calder *No. of Constituents:* 27,274, New Democratic Party
Tel: 780-415-1800
Fax: 780-415-0701
edmonton.calder@assembly.ab.ca; davideggen@albertandp.ca
www.albertandp.ca/davideggen
Other Communications: Constituency Phone: 780-451-2345; Fax: 780-451-2344
Social Media: twitter.com/davideggenAB, www.facebook.com/ElectDavidEggen
Constituency Office, Circle Square
#316, 11808 St. Albert Trail
Edmonton, AB T5L 4G4

Member, Legislative Assembly, Kyle Fawcett
Constituency: Calgary-Klein *No. of Constituents:* 27,637, Progressive Conservative
Tel: 780-427-1800
Fax: 780-415-0968
calgary.klein@assembly.ab.ca
www.kylefawcett.ca
Other Communications: Constituency Phone: 403-216-5430; Fax: 403-216-5432
Social Media: twitter.com/kyleMLA, www.facebook.com/pages/Kyle-Fawcett/201067916433, ca.linkedin.com/pub/kyle-fawcett/22/20b/7b0
Constituency Office
#9, 2400Centre St. NE
Calgary, AB T2E 2T9

Member, Legislative Assembly, Jacquie Fenske
Constituency: Fort Saskatchewan-Vegreville *No. of Constituents:* 28,029, Progressive Conservative
Tel: 780-427-1800
Fax: 780-415-0968
fortsaskatchewan.vegreville@assembly.ab.ca
www.fenske.votepc.ca
Other Communications: Ft. Sk, Phone: 780-992-6560; Vegreville: 780-632-6840
Social Media: twitter.com/jacquiefenske, www.facebook.com/pages/Jacquie-Fenske/317593138268237, ca.linkedin.com/pub/jacquie-fenske/14/4b7/8a3
ConstituencyOffice
9925B - 104 St.
Fort Saskatchewan, AB T8L 2E7

Member, Legislative Assembly, Heather Forsyth
Constituency: Calgary-Fish Creek, Wildrose Alliance Party of Alberta
Tel: 780-415-0058
Fax: 780-638-3506
calgary.fishcreek@assembly.ab.ca
www.heatherforsyth.com
Other Communications: Constituency Phone: 403-278-4444; Fax: 403-278-7875
Social Media: twitter.com/HeatherMLA, www.facebook.com/profile.php?id=1420582509, ca.linkedin.com/pub/heather-forsyth/27/589/158
Constituency Office
#7,1215 Lake Sylvan Dr. SE
Calgary, AB T2J 3Z5

Member, Legislative Assembly, Rodney Fox
Constituency: Lacombe-Ponoka *No. of Constituents:* 24,071, Wildrose Alliance Party of Alberta
Tel: 780-638-3505
Toll-free: 800-565-6432
Fax: 780-638-3506
lacombe.ponoka@assembly.ab.ca
www.wildrose.ca/mlas/rod-fox
Other Communications: Constituency Phone: 403-782-7725; Fax: 403-782-3307
Social Media: www.facebook.com/RodFoxWildrose, ca.linkedin.com/pub/rodney-fox/30/40/655
Constituency Office
#101, 4892 - 46 St.
Lacombe, AB T4L 2B4

Member, Legislative Assembly, Rick Fraser
Constituency: Calgary-South East *No. of Constituents:* 28,046, Progressive Conservative
Tel: 780-427-1800
Fax: 780-415-0968
calgary.southeast@assembly.ab.ca
www.rfraser.votepc.ca
Social Media: twitter.com/Fraser4MLA, www.facebook.com/RickFraserYYCSE, ca.linkedin.com/pub/rick-fraser/30/192/55

Member, Legislative Assembly, Yvonne Fritz
Constituency: Calgary-Cross *No. of Constituents:* 26,330, Progressive Conservative
Tel: 780-427-1800
Fax: 780-415-0968
calgary.cross@assembly.ab.ca
www.fritz.votepc.ca
Other Communications: Constituency Phone: 403-280-4022; Fax: 403-280-3877
Social Media: www.facebook.com/YvonneFritzYYC.Cross, ca.linkedin.com/pub/yvonne-fritz/46/108/999
Constituency Office
#15, 6208Rundlehorn Dr. NE
Calgary, AB T1Y 2X1

Member, Legislative Assembly, Hector Goudreau
Constituency: Dunvegan-Central Peace-Notley *No. of Constituents:* 13,950, Progressive Conservative
Tel: 780-427-1800
Toll-free: 866-835-4988
Fax: 780-415-0968
dunvegan.centralpeace.notley@assembly.ab.ca
Other Communications: Phone, Falher: 780-837-3846; Fairview: 780-835-7211
Constituency Office
035 - 1st Av. SW
PO Box 1054
Falher, AB T0H 1M0

Member, Legislative Assembly, Hon. Doug Griffiths
Constituency: Battle River-Wainwright *No. of Constituents:* 24,255, Progressive Conservative
Tel: 780-427-1800
Fax: 780-415-0968
battleriver.wainwright@assembly.ab.ca; info@betteralberta.ca
www.douggriffiths.ca
Other Communications: Constituency Phone: 780-842-6177; Fax:780-842-3171
Social Media: twitter.com/Griff4MLA, www.facebook.com/Griffs4ABsFuture, ca.linkedin.com/in/mlagriff13ways
Constituency Office
#201, 1006 - 4 Ave.
Wainwright, AB T9W 2R3

Member, Legislative Assembly, Jason Hale
Constituency: Strathmore-Brooks *No. of Constituents:* 25,850, Wildrose Alliance Party of Alberta
Tel: 780-638-3505
Fax: 780-638-3506
strathmore.brooks@assembly.ab.ca
www.jasonhale.ca
Other Communications: Constituency Phone: 403-362-6973; Fax: 403-362-5923
Social Media: twitter.com/JasonHaleWRP, www.facebook.com/jasonhale.2011, ca.linkedin.com/pub/jason-hale/41/334/715
Constituency Office
403 - 2ndAve. West
PO Box 873
Brooks, AB T1R 1B7

Member, Legislative Assembly, Hon. David Hancock, QC
Constituency: Edmonton-Whitemud *No. of Constituents:* 31,898, Progressive Conservative
Tel: 780-427-1800
Fax: 780-415-0968
edmonton.whitemud@assembly.ab.ca; dave.hancock@gov.ab.ca
www.davehancock.ca
Other Communications: Constituency Phone: 780-413-5970; Fax:780-413-5971
Social Media: twitter.com/DaveHancockMLA, www.facebook.com/people/Dave-Hancock/532170905, ca.linkedin.com/pub/dave-hancock/16/207/959
Constituency Office
#203, 596 Riverbend Sq.
Edmonton, AB T6R 2E3

Member, Legislative Assembly, Kent Hehr
Constituency: Calgary-Buffalo *No. of Constituents:* 22,638, Liberal
Tel: 780-427-2292

Fax: 780-427-3697
calgary.buffalo@assembly.ab.ca; info@kenthehr.com
www.kenthehr.comcom
Other Communications: Constituency Phone: 403-244-7737; Fax: 403-541-9106
Social Media: twitter.com/kenthehr, www.facebook.com/kent.hehr, ca.linkedin.com/pub/kent-hehr/8/329/538
ConstituencyOffice
#130, 1177 - 11 Ave. SW
Calgary, AB T2R 1K9

Member, Legislative Assembly, Hon. Fred Horne
Constituency: Edmonton-Rutherford *No. of Constituents:* 25,392, Progressive Conservative
Tel: 780-427-1800
Fax: 780-415-0968
edmonton.rutherford@assembly.ab.ca
www.horne.votepc.ca
Other Communications: Constituency Phone: 780-414-1311; Fax: 780-414-1314
Social Media: twitter.com/FredHorneMLA, www.facebook.com/FredHorne
Constituency Office
308Saddleback Rd.
Edmonton, AB T6J 4R7

Member, Legislative Assembly, Hon. Doug Horner
Constituency: Spruce Grove-St. Albert *No. of Constituents:* 32,548, Progressive Conservative
Tel: 780-427-1800
Fax: 780-415-0968
sprucegrove.stalbert@assembly.ab.ca
Other Communications: Constituency Phone: 780-962-6606; Fax: 780-962-1568
Social Media: twitter.com/DougHornerMLA, www.facebook.com/DougHornerForAlberta, www.linkedin.com/pub/doug-horner/30/310/206
Constituency Office
#50, 210 McLeod Ave.
Spruce Grove, AB T7X 2K5

Member, Legislative Assembly, Ken Hughes
Constituency: Calgary-West *No. of Constituents:* 26,125, Progressive Conservative
Tel: 780-427-1800
Fax: 780-415-0968
calgary.west@assembly.ab.ca
www.hughes.votepc.ca
Other Communications: Constituency Phone: 780-216-5439; Fax: 780-216-5441
Social Media: twitter.com/#!/KenHughes4MLA, www.facebook.com/KenHughes4MLA, ca.linkedin.com/pub/ken-hughes/4/8a9/aab
Constituency Office
#230, 30Springborough Blvd. SW
Calgary, AB T3H 0N9

Member, Legislative Assembly, Mary Anne Jablonski
Constituency: Red Deer-North *No. of Constituents:* 27,705, Progressive Conservative
Tel: 780-427-1800
Fax: 780-415-0968
reddeer.north@assembly.ab.ca
Other Communications: Constituency Phone: 403-342-2263; Fax: 403-340-3185
Social Media: twitter.com/majablonski, www.facebook.com/profile.php?id=1017282631
Constituency Office
#200,4814 Ross St.
Red Deer, AB T4N 1X4

Member, Legislative Assembly, Sandra Jansen
Constituency: Calgary-North West *No. of Constituents:* 28,638, Progressive Conservative
Tel: 403-427-1800
Fax: 403-415-0968
calgary.northwest@assembly.ab.ca
www.jansen.votepc.ca
Other Communications: Constituency Phone: 403-216-5444; Fax: 403-216-5442
Social Media: twitter.com/SANDRA4PCNW, www.facebook.com/SandraJansenYYCNW, ca.linkedin.com/pub/sandra-jansen/25/148/288
Constituency Office
#29,735 Ranchlands Blvd. NW
Calgary, AB T3G 3A9

Member, Legislative Assembly, Matt Jeneroux
Constituency: Edmonton-South West *No. of Constituents:* 26,469, Progressive Conservative
Tel: 403-427-1800
Fax: 403-415-0968
edmonton.southwest@assembly.ab.ca; info@mattjeneroux.ca
www.mattjeneroux.ca
Social Media: twitter.com/jeneroux, www.facebook.com/mattjeneroux, ca.linkedin.com/pub/matt-jeneroux/13/787/49a

Member, Legislative Assembly, Hon. Jeff Johnson
Constituency: Athabasca-Sturgeon-Redwater *No. of Constituents:* 23,415, Progressive Conservative
Tel: 780-427-1800
Fax: 780-415-0968
athabasca.sturgeon.redwater@assembly.ab.ca
Other Communications: Constituency Phone: 780-675-3232; Fax: 780-675-2396
Social Media: www.facebook.com/JeffJohnsonPC
ConstituencyOffice
4807 - 50 St.
Athabasca, AB T9S 1C8

Member, Legislative Assembly, Linda Johnson
Constituency: Calgary-Glenmore *No. of Constituents:* 32,940, Progressive Conservative
Tel: 780-427-1800
Fax: 780-415-0968
calgary.glenmore@assembly.ab.ca
www.ljohnson.votepc.ca
Other Communications: Constituency Phone: 403-216-5421; Fax: 403-216-5423
Social Media: twitter.com/pclindaj, www.facebook.com/LindaJ4Glenmore, ca.linkedin.com/pub/linda-johnson/5/a28/34a
Constituency Office
#210A,1600 - 90th Ave. SW
Calgary, AB T2V 5A8

Member, Legislative Assembly, Darshan Kang
Constituency: Calgary-McCall *No. of Constituents:* 21,750, Liberal
Tel: 780-427-2292
Fax: 780-427-3697
calgary.mccall@assembly.ab.ca
www.constituency.dkang.ca
Other Communications: Constituency Phone: 403-216-5424; Fax: 403-216-5426
Social Media: twitter.com/darshankang, www.facebook.com/yycKang
Constituency Office
#12, 2110 -41 Ave. NE
Calgary, AB T2E 8Z7

Member, Legislative Assembly, Donna Kennedy-Glans
Constituency: Calgary-Varsity *No. of Constituents:* 27,466, Progressive Conservative
Tel: 780-427-1800
Fax: 780-415-0968
calgary.varsity@assembly.ab.ca
www.donnapc.ca
Other Communications: Constituency Phone: 403-216-5436; Fax: 403-216-5438
Social Media: twitter.com/dkennedyglans, www.facebook.com/donnakennedyglans, ca.linkedin.com/pub/donna-kennedy-glans/11/778/b34
Constituency Office
#108, 4616 Valiant Dr. NW
Calgary, AB T3A 0X9

Member, Legislative Assembly, Steve Khan
Constituency: St. Albert *No. of Constituents:* 31,065, Progressive Conservative
Tel: 780-427-1800
Fax: 780-415-0968
st.albert@assembly.ab.ca; stephenkhanpc@gmail.com
www.khan.votepc.ca
Other Communications: Constituency Phone: 403-459-9113; Fax: 403-460-9815
Social Media: twitter.com/stephenkhanpc, www.facebook.com/StephenKhanPC
ConstituencyOffice
14 Perron St.
St. Albert, AB T8N 1E4

Member, Legislative Assembly, Hon. Heather Klimchuk
Constituency: Edmonton-Glenora *No. of Constituents:* 26,626, Progressive Conservative
Tel: 780-427-1800
Fax: 780-415-0968
edmonton.glenora@assembly.ab.ca
www.klimchuk.votepc.ca
Other Communications: Constituency Phone: 780-455-7979; Fax: 780-455-2197
Social Media: twitter.com/HeatherKlimchuk, www.facebook.com/Heather.Klimchuk
Constituency Office
10649 - 124 St.
Edmonton, AB T5N 1S5

Member, Legislative Assembly, Maureen Kubinec
Constituency: Barrhead-Morinville-Westlock *No. of Constituents:* 25,351, Progressive Conservative
Tel: 780-427-1800
Fax: 780-415-0968
barrhead.morinville.westlock@assembly.ab.ca
www.kubinec.votepc.ca
Other Communications: Constituency Phone: 780-674-3225; Fax: 780-674-6183
Social Media: www.facebook.com/MaureenKubinecBMW
ConstituencyOffice
5110 - 50 Ave.
Barrhead, AB T7N 1L1

Member, Legislative Assembly, Ken Lemke
Constituency: Stony Plain *No. of Constituents:* 27,243, Progressive Conservative
Tel: 780-427-1800
Fax: 780-415-0968
stony.plain@assembly.ab.ca
www.lemke.votepc.ca
Other Communications: Constituency Phone: 780-963-1444; Fax: 780-963-1730
Social Media: twitter.com/KenLemkeMLA, www.facebook.com/KenLemkePC, ca.linkedin.com/in/kenlemke
Constituency Office
#103, 5101 - 48thSt.
Stony Plain, AB T7Z 1L8

Member, Legislative Assembly, Genia Leskiw
Constituency: Bonnyville-Cold Lake *No. of Constituents:* 20,329, Progressive Conservative
Tel: 780-427-1800
Fax: 780-415-0968
bonnyville.coldlake@assembly.ab.ca
www.genialeskiw.ca
Other Communications: Constituency Phone: 780-826-5658; Fax: 780-826-2165
Social Media: www.facebook.com/genia.leskiw1
Constituency Office
#2,4428 - 50 Ave.
PO Box 5160
Bonnyville, AB T9N 2G4

Member, Legislative Assembly, Jason Luan
Constituency: Calgary-Hawkwood *No. of Constituents:* 32,150, Progressive Conservative
Tel: 780-427-1800
Fax: 780-415-0968
calgary.hawkwood@assembly.ab.ca
www.jasonluan.ca
Other Communications: Constituency Phone: 403-216-5439;403-216-5441
Social Media: twitter.com/Jason_Luan_, www.facebook.com/people/Jason-Luan/100000106974054, ca.linkedin.com/pub/jason-luan/48/68b/332

Member, Legislative Assembly, Hon. Thomas Lukaszuk
Constituency: Edmonton-Castle Downs *No. of Constituents:* 29,226, Progressive Conservative
Tel: 780-427-1800
Fax: 780-415-0968
edmonton.castledowns@assembly.ab.ca
www.thomasmla.com
Other Communications: Constituency Phone: 780-414-0705; Fax: 780-414-0707
Social Media: twitter.com/lukaszukmla, www.facebook.com/thomaslukaszuk
ConstituencyOffice
12120 - 161 Ave.
Edmonton, AB T5X 5M8

Member, Legislative Assembly, Brian Mason
Constituency: Edmonton-Highlands-Norwood *No. of Constituents:* 37,045, New Democratic Party
Tel: 780-415-1800
Fax: 780-415-0701
edmonton.highlandsnorwood@assembly.ab.ca
www.albertandp.ca/brianmason
Other Communications: Constituency Phone: 780-414-0682; Fax: 780-414-0684
Social Media: twitter.com/bmasonNDP, www.facebook.com/brianmasonleader
Constituency Office
6519 - 112 Ave.
Edmonton, AB T5W 0P1

Member, Legislative Assembly, Bruce McAllister
Constituency: Chestermere-Rocky View *No. of Constituents:* 29,542, Wildrose Alliance Party of Alberta
Tel: 403-638-3505
Toll-free: 866-843-4314
Fax: 403-638-3506
chestermere.rockyview@assembly.ab.ca
www.brucemcallister.ca; www.wildrose.ca/mlas/bruce-mcalliste
Other Communications: Constituency Phone: 403-216-2221; Fax: 403-216-2225
Social Media: twitter.com/McAllisterBruce, www.facebook.com/BruceMcAllisterWildrose?sk=wall, ca.linkedin.com/pub/bruce-mcallister/44/a54/666
Constituency Office
#6, 160 Maclaurin Dr.
Calgary, AB T3Z 3S4

Member, Legislative Assembly, Everett McDonald
Constituency: Grande Prairie-Smoky *No. of Constituents:* 26,123, Progressive Conservative
Tel: 403-427-1800
Fax: 403-415-0968

grandeprairie.smoky@assembly.ab.ca
www.mcdonald.votepc.ca; www.electmcdonald.com
Other Communications: Constituency Phone: 780-513-1233; Fax: 780-513-1247
Social Media: twitter.com/electmcdonald, www.facebook.com/electmcdonald
Constituency Office
#105, 9804 - 100 Ave.
Grande Prairie, AB T8V 0T8

Member, Legislative Assembly, Ric McIver
Constituency: Calgary-Hays *No. of Constituents:* 26,750, Progressive Conservative
Tel: 403-427-1800
Fax: 403-415-0968
calgary.hays@assembly.ab.ca
www.ricmciver.ca
Other Communications: Constituency Phone: 403-215-4380; Fax: 403-215-4383
Social Media: twitter.com/RicMcIver; info@ricmciver.ca, www.facebook.com/RicMcIver, ca.linkedin.com/pub/ric-mciver/10/498/34a
Constituency Office
#255, 11488 -24th St. SE
Calgary, AB T2Z 4C9

Member, Legislative Assembly, Hon. Diana McQueen
Constituency: Drayton Valley-Devon *No. of Constituents:* 23,051, Progressive Conservative
Tel: 780-427-1800
Toll-free: 800-542-7307
Fax: 780-415-0968
draytonvalley.devon@assembly.ab.ca
www.mcqueen.votepc.ca
Other Communications: Constituency Phone: 780-542-3355; Fax: 780-542-3331
Social Media: twitter.com/mcqueenmla, www.facebook.com/dianamcqueenmla, ca.linkedin.com/pub/diana-mcqueen/17/24/b62
Constituency Office
5136B - 52 Ave.
Drayton Valley, AB T7A 1S5

Member, Legislative Assembly, Rachel Notley
Constituency: Edmonton-Strathcona *No. of Constituents:* 24,171, New Democratic Party
Tel: 780-415-1800
Fax: 780-415-0701
edmonton.strathcona@assembly.ab.ca
Other Communications: Constituency Phone: 780-414-0702; Fax: 780-414-0703
Social Media: twitter.com/RachelNotley, www.facebook.com/rachelnotley
Note: Web Site: www.ndpopposition.ab.ca/rachelnotley
Constituency Office,Strathcona Professional Centre
10328 - 81 Ave. NW, Main Fl.
Edmonton, AB T6E 1X2

Member, Legislative Assembly, Hon. Frank Oberle
Constituency: Peace River *No. of Constituents:* 18,280, Progressive Conservative
Tel: 780-427-1800
Fax: 780-415-0968
peace.river@assembly.ab.ca
Other Communications: Constituency Phone: 780-624-5400; Fax: 780-624-5464
Note: Web Site: oberle.mypcmla.ca
Constituency Office
9907 - 101Ave.
PO Box 6299
Peace River, AB T8S 1S2

Member, Legislative Assembly, Cathy Olesen
Constituency: Sherwood Park *No. of Constituents:* 29,081, Progressive Conservative
Tel: 780-427-1800
Fax: 780-415-0968
sherwood.park@assembly.ab.ca
Other Communications: Constituency Phone: 780-417-4747; Fax: 780-417-4748
Note: Web Site: olesen.votepc.ca
Constituency Office
#116B, 937Fir St.
Sherwood Park, AB T8A 4N6

Member, Legislative Assembly, Hon. Verlyn Olson, QC
Constituency: Wetaskiwin-Camrose *No. of Constituents:* 25,844, Progressive Conservative
Tel: 780-427-1800
Fax: 780-415-0968
wetaskiwin.camrose@assembly.ab.ca
Other Communications: Constituency Phone: 780-672-0000; Fax: 780-672-6945
Social Media: www.facebook.com/verlynolsonmla
Note: Web Sites: olson.votepc.ca (Personal Web Site); www.justice.alberta.ca (Justice & Attorney General)
Constituency Office
4870 - 51 St.
Camrose, AB T4V 1A1

Member, Legislative Assembly, Bridget A. Pastoor
Constituency: Lethbridge-East *No. of Constituents:* 30,256, Progressive Conservative
Tel: 780-427-1800
Fax: 780-427-0968
lethbridge.east@assembly.ab.ca
Other Communications: Constituency Phone: 403-320-1011; Fax: 403-328-6613
Note: Web Site: www.albertaliberal.com/team.php?MLA=16084
Constituency Office
2816- 5 Ave. North
Lethbridge, AB T1H 0P1

Member, Legislative Assembly, Blake Pedersen
Constituency: Medicine Hat *No. of Constituents:* 27,820, Wildrose Alliance Party of Alberta
Tel: 780-638-3505
Toll-free: 800-565-6432
Fax: 780-638-3506
medicine.hat@assembly.ab.ca
Other Communications: Constituency Phone: 403-782-7725; Fax: 403-782-3307
Social Media: twitter.com/teamwildrose, www.facebook.com/100003355571499
Note: Web Site: www.blakepedersen.ca
ConstituencyOffice
620 - 3rd St. SE
Medicine Hat, AB T1A 0H5

Member, Legislative Assembly, Sohail Quadri
Constituency: Edmonton-Mill Woods *No. of Constituents:* 24,316, Progressive Conservative
Tel: 780-427-1800
Fax: 780-415-0968
edmonton.millwoods@assembly.ab.ca
Other Communications: Constituency Phone: 780-414-1000; Fax: 780-414-1278
Note: Web Site: www.sohailquadri.com
Constituency Office
#218,4128A - 97 St. NW
Edmonton, AB T6E 5Y6

Member, Legislative Assembly, Dave Quest
Constituency: Strathcona-Sherwood Park *No. of Constituents:* 30,173, Progressive Conservative
Tel: 780-643-6458
Fax: 780-643-6449
strathcona.sherwoodpark@assembly.ab.ca
Other Communications: Constituency Phone: 416-416-2492; Fax: 780-416-7093
Note: Web Site: www.davequest.ca
Constituency Office
#168, 2301 Premier Way
Sherwood Park, AB T8H 2K8

Member, Legislative Assembly, Hon. Alison Redford, QC
Constituency: Calgary-Elbow *No. of Constituents:* 30,338, Progressive Conservative
Tel: 780-427-1800
Fax: 780-415-0968
calgary.elbow@assembly.ab.ca
Other Communications: Constituency Phone: 403-252-0346; Fax: 403-252-0520
Note: Web Site: www.alisonredford.ca
Constituency Office
#6,22 Richard Way SW
Calgary, AB T3E 7M9

Member, Legislative Assembly, Dave Rodney
Constituency: Calgary-Lougheed *No. of Constituents:* 28,727, Progressive Conservative
Tel: 780-427-1800
Fax: 780-415-0968
calgary.lougheed@assembly.ab.ca
Other Communications: Constituency Phone: 403-238-1212; Fax: 403-251-5453
Note: Web Site: rodney.votepc.ca
Constituency Office
#311A,2525 Woodview Dr. SW
Calgary, AB T2W 4N4

Member, Legislative Assembly, George Rogers
Constituency: Leduc-Beaumont *No. of Constituents:* 28,815, Progressive Conservative
Tel: 780-427-1800
Fax: 780-415-0968
leduc.beaumont@assembly.ab.ca
Other Communications: Constituency Phone: 780-986-4652; Fax: 780-986-5228
Social Media: www.twitter.com/rogersofleduc
Note: Web Site: rogers.mypcmla.ca
Constituency Office
#54, 5203- 50 St.
Leduc, AB T9E 6Z5

Member, Legislative Assembly, Bruce Rowe
Constituency: Olds-Didsbury-Three Hills *No. of Constituents:* 26,626, Wildrose Alliance Party of Alberta
Tel: 780-638-3505
Fax: 780-638-3506
oldsdidsbury.threehills@assembly.ab.ca
Other Communications: Constituency Phone: 780-986-4652; Fax: 780-986-5228
Social Media: twitter.com/teambrucerowe
Note: Web Site: www.brucerowe.ca
Constituency Office
#3,4530 - 49 Ave.
Olds, AB T4H 1A4

Member, Legislative Assembly, Peter Sandhu
Constituency: Edmonton-Manning *No. of Constituents:* 26,987, Progressive Conservative
Tel: 780-427-1800
Fax: 780-415-0968
edmonton.manning@assembly.ab.ca
Other Communications: Constituency Phone: 780-414-0714; Fax: 780-414-0716
Social Media: twitter.com/PeterSandhuMLA, www.facebook.com/petersandhumla
Note: Web Site: sandhu.mypcmla.ca
Constituency Office
5523 -137 Ave.
Edmonton, AB T5A 3L4

Member, Legislative Assembly, Janice Sarich
Constituency: Edmonton-Decore *No. of Constituents:* 27,648, Progressive Conservative
Tel: 780-427-1800
Fax: 780-415-0968
edmonton.decore@assembly.ab.ca
Other Communications: Constituency Phone: 780-414-1328; Fax: 780-414-1328
Social Media: www.facebook.com/janicesarich
Note: Web Site: sarich.mypcmla.ca
Constituency Office
#5, 9228- 144th Ave.
Edmonton, AB T5E 6A3

Member, Legislative Assembly, Shayne Saskiw
Constituency: Lac La Biche-St. Paul-Two Hills *No. of Constituents:* 19,463, Wildrose Alliance Party of Alberta
Tel: 780-427-1800
Fax: 780-415-0968
laclabiche.stpaul.twohills@assembly.ab.ca
Other Communications: Constituency Phone: 780-645-6999; Fax: 780-645-5787
Social Media: twitter.com/ShayneSaskiw, www.facebook.com/100107776715015
Note: Web Site: www.saskiw.ca
ConstituencyOffice
4434 - 50th Ave.
St. Pail, AB T0A 3A2

Member, Legislative Assembly, Don Scott
Constituency: Fort McMurray-Conklin *No. of Constituents:* 13,272, Progressive Conservative
Tel: 780-427-1800
Fax: 780-415-0968
fortmcmurray.conklin@assembly.ab.ca
Social Media: twitter.com/DonaldKScott, www.facebook.com/DonScottforMLA
Note: Web Site: scott.votepc.ca
Constituency Office

Member, Legislative Assembly, Dr. Raj Sherman
Constituency: Edmonton-Meadowlark *No. of Constituents:* 25,665, Liberal
Tel: 780-427-2292
Fax: 780-427-3697
edmonton.meadowlark@assembly.ab.ca
Other Communications: Constituency Phone: 780-414-0711; Fax: 780-414-0713
Social Media: www.twitter.com/RajShermanMLA, www.facebook.com/rajshermanmla
Note: Web Site: www.electraj.ca
Constituency Office
#220, 8944 - 182 St.
Edmonton, AB T5T 2E3

Member, Legislative Assembly, Danielle Smith
Constituency: Highwood *No. of Constituents:* 29,758, Wildrose Alliance Party of Alberta
Tel: 780-638-3505
Fax: 780-638-3506
highwood@assembly.ab.ca
Other Communications: Constituency Phone: 403-652-7100; Fax: 403-652-7757
Social Media: twitter.com/electdanielle, www.facebook.com/ElectDanielle
Note: Web Site: www.daniellesmith.ca
Constituency Office
103 - 3rd Ave.West
PO Box 5243
High River, AB T1V 1M4

Member, Legislative Assembly, Richard Starke
Constituency: Vermilion-Lloydminster *No. of Constituents:* 22,548, Progressive Conservative
Tel: 780-427-1800
Toll-free: 800-567-7644

Fax: 780-415-0968
vermilion.lloydminster@assembly.ab.ca
Other Communications: Constituency Phone: 780-853-4202; Fax: 780-853-5770
Social Media: twitter.com/RichardStarke, www.facebook.com/133911663391787
Note: Web Site: starke.votepc.ca
Constituency Office
5036 - 49th Ave.
Vermilion, AB T9X 1B7

Member, Legislative Assembly, Mr. Pat Stier
Constituency: Livingstone-Macleod *No. of Constituents:* 26,862, Wildrose Alliance Party of Alberta
Tel: 780-638-3505
Toll-free: 800-565-0962
Fax: 780-638-3506
livingstone.macleod@assembly.ab.ca
Other Communications: Constituency Phone: 403-553-2400; Fax: 403-553-2133
Social Media: www.facebook.com/Riverhawc
Note: Web Site: www.wildrose.ca/mlas/pat-stier
ConstituencyOffice
2115 - 2nd Ave.
PO Box 69
Fort Macleod, AB T0L 0Z0

Member, Legislative Assembly, Rick Strankman
Constituency: Drumheller-Stettler *No. of Constituents:* 23,320, Wildrose Alliance Party of Alberta
Tel: 780-638-3505
Fax: 780-638-3506
drumheller.stettler@assembly.ab.ca
Other Communications: Constituency Phone: 403-742-4284; Fax: 780-742-4295
Social Media: www.facebook.com/rickstrankman
Note: Web Site: www.wildrose.ca/mlas/rick-strankman
Constituency Office
4820- 50th St.
PO Box 2022
Stettler, AB T0C 2L2

Member, Legislative Assembly, Dr. David Swann
Constituency: Calgary-Mountain View *No. of Constituents:* 26,198, Liberal
Tel: 780-427-2292
Fax: 780-427-3697
calgary.mountainview@assembly.ab.ca
Other Communications: Constituency Phone: 403-216-5445; Fax: 403-216-5447
Social Media: twitter.com/davidswann, www.facebook.com/DrDavidSwann
Note: Web Site: www.davidswann.ca
Constituency Office
#102, 723 - 14 St. NW
Calgary, AB T2N 2A4

Member, Legislative Assembly, Kerry Towle
Constituency: Innisfail-Sylvan Lake *No. of Constituents:* 25,857, Wildrose Alliance Party of Alberta
Tel: 780-638-3505
Toll-free: 888-655-2535
Fax: 780-638-3506
innisfail.sylvanlake@assembly.ab.ca
Other Communications: Constituency Phone: 403-227-1500; Fax: 403-227-5350
Social Media: twitter.com/KerryTowle, www.facebook.com/138721419537532
Note: Web Site: kerrytowle.com
ConstituencyOffice
#18, 4804 - 42nd Ave.
Innisfail, AB T4G 1T4

Member, Legislative Assembly, Hon. George VanderBurg
Constituency: Whitecourt-Ste. Anne *No. of Constituents:* 22,910, Progressive Conservative
Tel: 780-427-1800
Toll-free: 800-786-7136
Fax: 780-415-0968
whitecourt.steanne@assembly.ab.ca
Other Communications: Constituency Phone: 780-786-1997; Fax: 780-786-1995
Note: Web Site: vanderburg.mypcmla.ca
Constituency Office
4811 Crockett St.
PO Box 3618
Mayerthorpe, AB T0E 1N0

Member, Legislative Assembly, Hon. Greg Weadick
Constituency: Lethbridge-West *No. of Constituents:* 26,681, Progressive Conservative
Tel: 780-427-1800
Fax: 780-415-0968
lethbridge.west@assembly.ab.ca
Other Communications: Constituency Phone: 403-329-4644; Fax: 403-329-4289
Note: Web Sites: weadick.mypcmla.ca (Personal Web Site); www.advancededucation.gov.ab.ca/ministry/about/minister.aspx (Advanced Education & Technology)
Constituency Office
404 -8 St. South
Lethbridge, AB T1J 2J7

Member, Legislative Assembly, Len Webber
Constituency: Calgary-Foothills *No. of Constituents:* 28,360, Progressive Conservative
Tel: 780-427-1800
Fax: 780-415-0968
calgary.foothills@assembly.ab.ca
Other Communications: Constituency Phone: 403-288-4453; Fax: 403-247-9863
Social Media: www.facebook.com/lenwebbermla
Note: Web Site: webber.mypcmla.ca
Constituency Office
#217, 45Edenwold Dr. NW
Calgary, AB T3A 3S8

Member, Legislative Assembly, Jeff Wilson
Constituency: Calgary-Shaw *No. of Constituents:* 28,785, Wildrose Alliance Party of Alberta
Tel: 780-638-3505
Fax: 780-638-3506
calgary.shaw@assembly.ab.ca
Other Communications: Constituency Phone: 403-256-8969; Fax: 403-256-8970
Social Media: twitter.com/JeffWilson_WRP, www.facebook.com/295069673889189
Note: Web Site: www.calgaryshaw.org
Constituency Office
#328, 22Midlake Blvd. SE
Calgary, AB T2X 2X7

Member, Legislative Assembly, Hon. Teresa Woo-Paw
Constituency: Calgary-Northern Hills *No. of Constituents:* 31,056, Progressive Conservative
Tel: 780-427-1800
Fax: 780-415-0968
calgary.northernhills@assembly.ab.ca
Other Communications: Constituency Phone: 403-274-1931; Fax: 403-275-8421
Social Media: www.facebook.com/teresawoopawmla
Note: Web Sites: woo-paw.mypcmla.ca
ConstituencyOffice
#103, 200 Country Hills Landing NW
Calgary, AB T3K 5P3

Member, Legislative Assembly, David H. Xiao
Constituency: Edmonton-McClung *No. of Constituents:* 25,706, Progressive Conservative
Tel: 780-427-1800
Fax: 780-415-0968
edmonton.mcclung@assembly.ab.ca
Other Communications: Constituency Phone: 780-408-1860; Fax: 780-408-1864
Note: Web Site: xiao.mypcmla.ca
Constituency Office
#301,6650 - 177 St.
Edmonton, AB T5T 4J5

Member, Legislative Assembly, Steve Young
Constituency: Edmonton-Riverview *No. of Constituents:* 26,706, Progressive Conservative
Tel: 780-427-1800
Fax: 780-415-0968
edmonton.riverview@assembly.ab.ca
Other Communications: Constituency Phone: 780-414-0719; Fax: 780-414-0721
Note: Web Site: young.votepc.ca
Constituency Office
9202B -149 St.
Edmonton, AB T5R 1C3

Member, Legislative Assembly, Gene Zwozdesky
Constituency: Edmonton-Mill Creek *No. of Constituents:* 23,412, Progressive Conservative
Tel: 780-427-1800
Fax: 780-415-0968
edmonton.millcreek@assembly.ab.ca
Other Communications: Constituency Phone: 780-466-3737; Fax: 780-468-3359
Note: Web Site: zwozdesky.mypcmla.ca
Constituency Office
8207Argyll Rd.
Edmonton, AB T6C 4B2

Alberta Government Departments & Agencies

Alberta Aboriginal Relations

Commerce Place, 10155 - 102 St., 20th Fl., Edmonton, AB T5J 4G8
Aboriginal Relations works with Aboriginal communities & other partners to enhance social & economic opportunities for Alberta's Aboriginal people.
Acts Administered:
Métis Settlements Accord Implementation Act
Métis Settlements Act, 1990
Métis Settlements Land Protection Act, 1990

Minister, Aboriginal Relations, Robin Campbell
Tel: 780-422-4144
Fax: 780-644-8389
Social Media: www.facebook.com/robin.campbell.3990
Legislature Building
#323, 10800 - 97 Ave.
Edmonton, AB T5K 2B6

Deputy Minister, Bill Werry
Tel: 780-643-9081
Fax: 780-422-2745
bill.werry@gov.ab.ca

Acting Director, Communications, David Dear
Tel: 780-427-4210
Fax: 780-415-9548
david.dear@gov.ab.ca

Director, Business Integration & Strategy, Dale Unrau
Tel: 780-638-4331
Fax: 780-422-2745
dale.unrau@gov.ab.ca

Writer/Editor, Ministerial Correspondence Unit, Joanna Verhelst
Tel: 780-427-4627
Fax: 780-422-2745
joanna.verhelst@gov.ab.ca

Associated Agencies, Boards & Commissions:
• Métis Settlements Appeal Tribunal (MSAT)
14605 - 134 Ave. NW
Edmonton, AB T5L 4S9
Tel: 780-422-1541
Fax: 780-422-0019
Toll-free: 800-661-8864
• Métis Settlements Ombudsman Office
#203, 10525 - 170 St.
Edmonton, AB T5P 4W2
Tel: 780-427-9828
Fax: 780-427-9962
Toll-free: 866-427-6813

Consultation & Land Claims
Commerce Place, 10155 - 102 St., 20th Fl., Edmonton, AB T5J 4G8
Tel: 780-427-0417
Fax: 780-427-0401

Assistant Deputy Minister, Stan Rutwind, Q.C.
Tel: 780-643-1731
Fax: 780-427-0401
stan.rutwind@gov.ab.ca

Executive Director, Aboriginal Consultation, Cole Pederson
Tel: 780-427-8441
Fax: 780-427-0401
cole.pederson@gov.ab.ca

Director, Land Claims, Steven Andres
Tel: 780-427-6084
Fax: 780-427-0401
steven.andres@gov.ab.ca

Director, Aboriginal Consultation, Cory Enns
Tel: 780-644-1055
Fax: 780-427-0401
cory.enns@gov.ab.ca

Senior Manager, Consultation Policy & Regional Land Issues, Ashley Bodnar
Tel: 780-644-1036
Fax: 780-427-0401
ashley.bodnar@gov.ab.ca

Manager, Negotiation Support, Land Claims, Kathryn Coxson
Tel: 780-644-1003
Fax: 780-427-0401
kathryn.coxson@gov.ab.ca

First Nations & Metis Relations
Commerce Place, 10155 - 102 St., 19th Fl., Edmonton, AB T5J 4G8

Assistant Deputy Minister, Donavon Young
Tel: 780-422-5925
Fax: 780-427-4019
donavon.young@gov.ab.ca

Executive Director, Policy & Planning, Henry Cameron
Tel: 780-427-2008
Fax: 780-427-0401
cameron.henry@gov.ab.ca

Executive Director, Métis Relations, Thomas Droege
Tel: 780-427-9431
Fax: 780-427-4019
thomas.droege@gov.ab.ca

Executive Director, First Nations Relations, Cynthia Dunnigan
Tel: 780-415-6141
Fax: 780-427-1760
cynthia.dunnigan@gov.ab.ca

Director, First Nations Development Fund, Peter Croseen
Tel: 780-415-6142
Fax: 780-427-0401
peter.crossen@gov.ab.ca

Director, Aboriginal Economic Partnerships, Lanny Der
Tel: 780-644-1057
Fax: 780-427-1760
lanny.der@gov.ab.ca
Director, Métis Relations, Linda Lewis
Tel: 780-644-1004
Fax: 780-427-4019
linda.lewis@gov.ab.ca
Director, First Nations & Urban Initiatives, Kristina Midbo
Tel: 780-427-9394
Fax: 780-427-1760
kristina.midbo@gov.ab.ca
Director, Aboriginal Community Initiatives, Bronwyn Shoush
Tel: 780-427-3060
Fax: 780-427-4019
bronwyn.shoush@gov.ab.ca
Director, Planning & Research, Ellen Tian
Tel: 780-422-4061
Fax: 780-427-1760
ellen.tian@gov.ab.ca
Registrar, Métis Settlements Land Registry, Lisa Chartrand
Tel: 780-415-0168
Fax: 780-427-3656
lisa.chartrand@gov.ab.ca

Alberta Agriculture & Rural Development

JG O'Donoghue Bldg., #100A, 7000 - 113th St., Edmonton, AB T6H 5T6
Tel: 780-427-2727
Toll-Free: -310-3276
duke@gov.ab.ca
www.agric.gov.ab.ca

Alberta's Agriculture & Rural Development is engaged in the following key activities: facilitating sustainable industry growth, enhancing rural sustainability, & strengthening business risk management.

Acts Administered:
Agricultural Operations Practices Act
Agricultural Pests Act
Agricultural Service Board Act
Agricultural Societies Act
Agriculture Financial Services Act
Agriculture Satutes Repeal Act, 2008
Alberta Wheat & Barley Test Market Act
Animal Health Act
Animal Keepers Act
Animal Protection Act
Bee Act
Crop Liens Priorities Act
Crop Payments Act
Dairy Industry Act
Farm Implement Act
Farm Implement Dealerships Act
Feeder Associations Guarantee Act
Fuel Tax Act
Fur Farms Act
Gas Distribution Act
Government Accountability Act
Government Organization Act
Heating Oil & Propane Rebate Act
Horned Cattle Purchases Repeal Act
Irrigation Districts Act
Line Fence Act
Livestock & Livestock Products Act
Livestock Identification & Commerce Act
Livestock Industry Diversification Act
Marketing of Agricultural Products Act
Meat Inspection Act
Rural Electrification Loan Act
Rural Electrification Long-term Financing Act
Rural Utilities Act
Soil Conservation Act
Stray Animals Act
Vegetable Sales (Alberta) Repeal Act
Weed Control Act
Wheat Board Money Trust Act
Women's Institute Act

Minister, Agriculture & Rural Development, Hon. Verlyn Olson, QC
Constituency: Wetaskiwin-Camrose
Tel: 780-427-2137
Fax: 780-422-6035
olson.votepc.ca
Social Media: www.facebook.com/verlynolsonmla
Legislature Building
#228, 10800 - 97 Ave.
Edmonton, AB T5K2B6

Deputy Minister, John Knapp
Tel: 780-427-2145
Fax: 780-415-6002
john.knapp@gov.ab.ca
JG O'Donoghue Building
7000 - 113 St., 3rd Fl.
Edmonton, AB T6H 5T6

Executive Director, Human Resource Services & Facilities Management Services, Heather K.M. Behman
Tel: 780-427-2430
Fax: 780-427-3398
heather.behman@gov.ab.ca
JG O'Donoghue Building
7000 - 113 St., 3rd Fl.
Edmonton, AB T6H5T6

Acting Director, Communications Branch, David Hennig
Tel: 780-422-1177
Fax: 780-638-4477
david.hennig@gov.ab.ca

Executive Director/Senior Financial Officer, Financial & Business Planning Services Division, Anne Halldorson
Tel: 780-427-3216
Fax: 780-422-6529
anne.halldorson@gov.ab.ca

Associated Agencies, Boards & Commissions:

• Agricultural Products Marketing Council
JG O'Donoghue Bldg.
7000 - 113 St., 3rd Fl.
Edmonton, AB T6H 5T6
Tel: 780-427-2164
Fax: 780-422-9690
The Alberta Agricultural Products Marketing Council supports legislation & regulations & offers policy advice to the Minister of Agriculture & Rural Development & industry organizations.

• Alberta Grains Council (AGC)
JG O'Donoghue Bldg.
7000 - 113 St., 3rd Fl.
Edmonton, AB T6H 5T6
Tel: 780-427-7329
Fax: 780-422-9690
www1.agric.gov.ab.ca/$department/deptdocs.nsf/all/agc2620
The Alberta Grains Council makes recommendations to the Minister of Agriculture & Rural Affairs about issues in the grain industry.

• Alberta Livestock & Meat Agency (ALMA)
Ellwood Office Park South
#101, 1003 Ellwood Rd. SW
Edmonton, AB T6X 0B3
Tel: 780-638-1699
Fax: 780-638-6495
info@almaltd.ca
www.alma.alberta.ca
The provincial government agency was established to advance the Alberta Livestock & Meat Strategy. The goal of the Alberta Livestock & Meat Agency is to develop a profitable & competitive Alberta livestock & meat industry, by offering information & investment opportunities to the industry & the Government of Alberta.

• Irrigation Council
Provincial Bldg.
200 - 5 Ave. South, 3rd Fl.
Lethbridge, AB T1J 4L1
Tel: 403-381-5176
Fax: 403-382-4406
www1.agric.gov.ab.ca/$department/deptdocs.nsf/all/irc9432
The Irrigation Council was established under Section 50 of the Irrigation Districts Act. The provincial agency reports to the Minister of Agriculture & Rural Development.

• Office of the Farmers' Advocate
JG O'Donoghue Bldg.
7000 - 113 St.
Edmonton, AB T6H 5T6
Tel: 780-644-5365
Toll-free: -310-3276
www1.agric.gov.ab.ca/$department/deptdocs.nsf/all/ofa2621
The Farmers' Advocate Office offers rural consumer protection, rural opportunities, & fair process for rural Albertans. The Office supports programs to settle disputes or offer appeals privately.

Food Safety & Technology Sector
3rd fl. JG O'Donoghue Bldg., 7000 - 113 St., Edmonton, AB T6H 5T6
Tel: 780-427-6159
Assistant Deputy Minister, Jamie Curran
Tel: 780-422-6166
Fax: 780-422-6317
jamie.curran@gov.ab.ca

Food Safety & Animal Health Division
Agriculture & Rural Development, OS Longman Bldg., 6909 - 116 St., Edmonton, AB T6H 4P2
Tel: 780-427-6159
Executive Director, Food Safety & Animal Health Division, Greg Orriss
Tel: 780-427-6159
Fax: 780-427-1437
greg.orriss@gov.ab.ca

Office of the Chief Provincial Veterinarian
OS Longman Bldg., 6909 - 116 St., Edmonton, T6H 4P2
Tel: 780-427-3448
Fax: 780-415-0810
Chief Provincial Veterinarian, Dr. Gerald Hauer
Tel: 780-415-9503
Fax: 780-415-0810
gerald.hauer@gov.ab.ca
Program Veterinarian, Dr. Hernan Ortegon
Tel: 780-644-2148
Fax: 780-427-1437
hernan.ortegon@gov.ab.ca
Branch Head & Deputy Chief, Animal Health Branch, Dr. Chris Morley
Tel: 780-427-6406
Fax: 780-427-1437
chris.morley@gov.ab.ca
Unit Leader, Livestock Welfare, Michelle Follensbee
Tel: 780-644-3072
Fax: 780-415-0810
michelle.follensbee@gov.ab.ca

Information Management Division
JG O'Donoghue Bldg, 7000 - 113 St., 1st Fl., Edmonton, AB T6H 5T6
Tel: 780-427-2727
Fax: 780-427-2861
Director, Information Management, Gerard Vaillancourt
Tel: 780-422-6796
Fax: 780-427-2861
gerard.vaillancourt@gov.ab.ca
Division Administrator, Information Management, Rita Splawinski
Tel: 780-422-3375
Fax: 780-427-2861
rita.splawinski@gov.ab.ca

Information Technology Division
JG O'Donoghue Bldg., 7000 - 113 St., 2nd Fl., Edmonton, AB T6H 5T6
Executive Director, Information Technology, Rob Pungor
Tel: 780-422-6660
Fax: 780-422-4004
rob.pungor@gov.ab.ca
Manager, Business Services, Dean Pratt
Tel: 780-422-2142
Fax: 780-422-4004
dean.pratt@gov.ab.ca
Manager, Infrastructure, Chris Wright
Tel: 780-415-2361
Fax: 780-422-4004
chris.wright@gov.ab.ca

Regulatory Services Division
JG O'Donoghue Bldg., 7000 - 113 St., 3rd Fl., Edmonton, AB T6H 5T6
Tel: 780-422-7197
Fax: 780-422-4513
Executive Director, Regulatory Services Division, Cliff Munroe
Tel: 780-422-7249
Fax: 780-422-4513
cliff.munroe@gov.ab.ca
Branch Head, Meat Inspection Branch, Jake Kotowich
Tel: 780-644-2371
Fax: 780-422-4513
jake.kotowich@gov.ab.ca
Branch Head, Inspection & Investigation Branch, Lyle Marianchuk
Tel: 403-340-5320
Fax: 403-340-5870
yle.marianchuk@gov.ab.ca

Rural Utilities Division
JG O'Donoghue Bldg., 7000 - 113 St., 2nd Fl., Edmonton, AB T6H 5T6
Tel: 780-427-0125
Fax: 780-422-1613
Executive Director, Rural Utilities, Terry Holmes
Tel: 780-427-0134
Fax: 780-422-1613
terry.holmes@gov.ab.ca
Branch Head, Rural Electric & Information Systems Branch, Tom Kee
Tel: 780-427-0944
Fax: 780-422-1613
tom.kee@gov.ab.ca
Branch Head, Safety & Technical Services Branch, Bruce Partington
Tel: 780-427-0111
Fax: 780-422-1613
bruce.partington@gov.ab.ca

Industry & Market Development Sector
JG O'Donoghue Bldg., 7000 - 113 St., Edmonton, AB T6H 5T6
Assistant Deputy Minister, Jo-Ann Hall
Tel: 780-427-2439

Fax: 780-422-6317
jo-ann.hall@gov.ab.ca

Research & Innovation Division
JG O'Donoghue Bldg., 7000 - 113 St., 3rd Fl., Edmonton, AB T6H 5T6
Tel: 780-679-5172
Fax: 780-679-5175

Director, Research & Innovation, Connie Phillips
Tel: 780-644-8124
Fax: 780-427-1057
connie.phillips@gov.ab.ca

Branch Head, Livestock Research Branch, Wesley Johnson
Tel: 780-415-0828
Fax: 780-427-1057
wesley.johnson@gov.ab.ca

Branch Head, Bio-Industrial Opportunities Branch, Hong Qi
Tel: 780-644-8128
Fax: 780-638-3586
hong.qi@gov.ab.ca

Senior Manager, Pest Surveillance Branch, Paul Laflamme
Tel: 780-422-4911
Fax: 780-427-1057
paul.laflamme@gov.ab.ca

Branch Head, Food & Bio-Industrial Crops Branch, James Jones
Tel: 780-422-5028
Fax: 780-422-5028
james.jones@gov.ab.ca

Branch Head, Feed Crops Branch, Mark MacNaughton
Tel: 780-782-8033
Fax: 780-782-5514
mark.macnaughton@gov.ab.ca

Food Processing Division
Development Centre, 6309 - 45 St., Leduc, AB T9E 7C5
Tel: 780-986-4793
Fax: 780-986-5138

Executive Director, Food Processing Division, Ken Gossen
Tel: 780-980-4860
Fax: 780-986-5138
ken.gossen@gov.ab.ca

Senior Programs Manager, Programs Branch, Karen Erin
Tel: 780-980-4864
Fax: 780-986-5138
karen.erin@gov.ab.ca

Senior Operations Manager, Operations Branch, Robert Gibson
Tel: 780-980-4866
Fax: 780-980-4250
robert.gibson@gov.ab.ca

Rural Extension & Industry Development Division
Provincial Building, 4709 - 44 Ave., Stony Plain, AB T7Z 1N4
Tel: 780-968-3557
Fax: 780-963-4709

Executive Director, Rural Extension & Industry Development Division, Vacant
Tel: 780-968-3512
Fax: 780-963-4709

Branch Head, Crop Business Development Branch, James Calpas
Tel: 403-340-5329
Fax: 403-340-4896
james.calpas@gov.ab.ca

Branch Head, Agriculture Grant Programs Branch, Murray Greer
Tel: 780-980-4722
Fax: 780-980-4237
murray.greer@gov.ab.ca

Branch Head, Alberta Ag-Info Centre, Ross Hutchison
Tel: 403-742-7542
Fax: 403-742-7527
ross.hutchison@gov.ab.ca

Branch Head, Local / Domestic Market Expansion Branch, Shauna Johnston
Tel: 780-968-3553
Fax: 780-968-3554
shauna.johnston@gov.ab.ca

Branch Head, Livestock & Farm Business Branch, Carlyon Rod
Tel: 780-349-4466
Fax: 780-349-5240
rod.carlyon@gov.ab.ca

Branch Head, Ag-Industry Extension Branch, Barb Shackel-Hardman
Tel: 780-968-3550
Fax: 780-968-3554
barb.shackel.hardman@gov.ab.ca

Branch Head, 4-H Branch, Marguerite Stark
Tel: 403-948-8510
Fax: 780-948-2069
marguerite.stark@gov.ab.ca

Branch Head, Processing Industry Business Development Branch, Lynn Stegman
Tel: 403-340-7010
Fax: 403-340-4896
lynn.stegman@gov.ab.ca

Traceability Division
JG O'Donoghue Bldg., 7000 - 113 St., 3rd Fl., Edmonton, T6H 5T6
Tel: 780-643-1572
Fax: 780-422-3655

Executive Director, Traceability Division, John Brown
Tel: 780-427-2799
Fax: 780-422-3655
john.brown@gov.ab.ca

Coordinator, Traceability Education, Kelly Gordon
Tel: 780-638-3148
Fax: 780-422-3655
kelly.gordon@gov.ab.ca

Policy & Environment Sector
JG O'Donoghue Bldg., 7000 - 113 St., 3rd Fl., Edmonton, AB T6H 5T6

Assistant Deputy Minister, Colin Jeffares
Tel: 780-427-1957
Fax: 780-422-6317
colin.jeffares@gov.ab.ca

Economics & Competitiveness Division
JG O'Donoghue Bldg., 7000 - 113 St., 3rd Fl., Edmonton, AB T6H 5T6
Tel: 780-422-3771
Fax: 780-427-5220

Acting Executive Director, Economics & Competitiveness Division, Don Brown
Tel: 780-644-5634
Fax: 780-427-5220
don.brown@gov.ab.ca

Branch Head, Competitiveness & Market Analysis Branch, Darren Chase
Tel: 780-422-4056
Fax: 780-427-5220
darren.chase@gov.ab.ca

Branch Head, Statistics & Data Development Branch, Reynold Jaipaul
Tel: 780-427-5376
Fax: 780-427-5220
reynold.jaipaul@gov.ab.ca

Acting Branch Head, Economics Branch, Diane McCann-Hiltz
Tel: 780-422-6081
Fax: 780-427-5220
diane.mccann-hiltz@gov.ab.ca

Environmental Stewardship Division
JG O'Donoghue Bldg., 7000 - 113 St., 3rd Fl., Edmonton, AB T6H 5T6

Executive Director, Environmental Stewardship Division, Brenda Brindle
Tel: 780-427-0674
Fax: 780-422-9745
brenda.brindle@gov.ab.ca

Branch Head, Technology & Innovation Branch, Rick Atkins
Tel: 780-427-9801
Fax: 780-422-9745
rick.atkins@gov.ab.ca

Branch Head, Agri-Environmental Management Branch, Sandi Jones
Tel: 403-556-4278
Fax: 403-556-7545
sandi.jones@gov.ab.ca

Irrigation & Farm Water Division
Agriculture Centre, #100, 5401 - 1 Ave. South, Lethbridge, AB T1J 4V6

Executive Director, Irrigation & Farm Water Division, Brent Paterson
Tel: 403-381-5143
Fax: 403-381-5903
brent.paterson@gov.ab.ca

Branch Head, Irrigation Secretariat, Roger Hohm
Tel: 403-381-5176
Fax: 403-382-4406
roger.hohm@gov.ab.ca

Branch Head, Rural Water Program, Marshall Eliason
Tel: 780-427-4615
Fax: 780-422-9745
marshall.eliason@gov.ab.ca

Policy, Strategy, & Intergovernmental Affairs Division
JG O'Donoghue Bldg., 7000 - 113 St., 2nd Fl., Edmonton, AB T6H 5T6
Tel: 780-422-9167
Fax: 780-427-5921

Director, Strategy & Intergovernmental Affairs Division, Andre Tremblay
Tel: 780-415-9755
Fax: 780-427-5921
andre.tremblay@gov.ab.ca

Manager, International Relations & Marketing Branch, Annalisa Baer
Tel: 780-427-4148
Fax: 780-427-5921
annalisa.baer@gov.ab.ca

Branch Head, Policy Coordination & Research Branch, Dr. Shiferaw Adilu
Tel: 780-422-7196
Fax: 780-427-5921
shiferaw.adilu@gov.ab.ca

Branch Head, Strategy & Program Delivery Branch, Linda Hawk
Tel: 780-427-4463
Fax: 780-427-5921
linda.hawk@gov.ab.ca

Branch Head, Domestic & International Trade Policy Branch, Peter Kuperis
Tel: 780-415-8608
Fax: 780-427-5921
peter.kuperis@gov.ab.ca

Branch Head, Growing Forward Coordination & Program Policy Branch, Wendy McCormick
Tel: 403-340-5306
Fax: 403-340-4896
wendy.mccormick@gov.ab.ca

Rural Development Division
JG O'Donoghue Bldg., 7000 - 113 St., Edmonton, AB T6H 5T6
Tel: 780-427-2409
Fax: 780-427-4227

Executive Director, Rural Development, Ron Popek
Tel: 780-422-1858
Fax: 780-427-4227
ron.popek@gov.ab.ca

Senior Manager, Rural Initiatives & Research Unit, Robert Hornbrook
Tel: 780-427-4218
Fax: 780-427-4227
robert.hornbrook@gov.ab.ca

Agri-Environmental Management Branch
Provincial Bldg., 5030 - 50 St., 2nd Fl., Olds, AB T4H 1S1
Tel: 780-422-3771
Fax: 780-427-5220

Branch Head, Agri-Environmental Management Branch, Sandi Jones
Tel: 403-556-4278
Fax: 403-556-7545
sandi.jones@gov.ab.ca

Section Head, AOPA/CFO Extension Section, Brian Koberstein
Tel: 780-674-8255
Fax: 780-674-8309
brian.koberstein@gov.ab.ca

Section Lead, Land Use Section, Len Kryzanowski
Tel: 780-422-1252
Fax: 780-422-9745
len.kryzanowski@gov.ab.ca

Acting Section Lead, Nutrient Management Section, Tanya Moskal-Hebert
Tel: 780-427-2933
Fax: 780-422-9745
tanya.moskal-hebert@gov.ab.ca

Financial & Business Planning Services Division
JG O'Donoghue Bldg., 7000 - 113 St., 2nd Fl., Edmonton, AB T6H 5T6
Tel: 780-427-2151
Fax: 780-422-6529

Senior Writer & Supervisor, Correspondence Unit, Jared Schapansky
Tel: 780-644-1206
Fax: 780-422-6529
jared.schapansky@gov.ab.ca

Human Resource Services & Facilities Management Services
JG O'Donoghue Bldg., 7000 -113 St., Edmonton, AB T6H 5T6
Tel: 780-427-2111
Fax: 780-427-3398
resumes@agric.gov.ab.ca

Executive Director, Human Resources Services and Facilities Management Services, Heather K.M. Behman
Tel: 780-427-2430
Fax: 780-427-3398
heather.behman@gov.ab.ca

Director, Human Resource Consulting Services, Helene Vegh
Tel: 780-427-2967
Fax: 780-427-3398
helene.vegh@gov.ab.ca

Coordinator, Facilities Management Unit, Rose Alwood
Tel: 780-422-4915
Fax: 780-427-4227
rose.alwood@gov.ab.ca

Alberta Office of the Auditor General

9925 - 109 St., 8th Fl., Edmonton, AB T5K 2J8
Tel: 780-427-4222
Fax: 780-422-9555
info@oag.ab.ca
www.oag.ab.ca
The Auditor General of Alberta is the independent auditor of all Government of Alberta ministries, departments, regulated funds, & agencies. Audits identify areas where improvement is required for the use of public resources & provide recommendations to improve practices.

Auditor General, Merwan Saher, CA
Tel: 780-422-6195
Fax: 780-422-9555

Senior Financial Officer, Jeff Olson, CMA, MBA
Tel: 780-422-6517
Fax: 780-427-5080
jolson@oag.ab.ca

General Counsel, Kerry Langford, LLB
Tel: 780-422-6359
Fax: 780-422-9555
klangford@oag.ab.ca

Director, Human Resources, Jacquie M. Pylypiuk, CA, CHRP
Tel: 780-422-6370
Fax: 780-427-5080
jpylypiuk@oag.ab.ca

Manager, Communications, Lori Trudgeon
Tel: 780-422-6655
Fax: 780-422-9555
ltrudgeon@oag.ab.ca

Alberta Culture

Communications Branch, Standard Life Centre, 10405 Jasper Ave., 7th Fl., Edmonton, AB T5J 4R7
Tel: 780-427-6530
Toll-Free: 800-232-7215
ccs.communications@gov.ab.ca
www.culture.alberta.ca
TTY: 780-427-9999
Formerly known as Culture & Community Services, & before that Culture & Community Spirit, until name changes in 2011 & 2012 under Premier Redford, Alberta's Culture continues to support arts & cultural industries throughout Alberta. Financial assistance is provided to the non-profit sector, film, the arts, & heritage.
The following agencies, boards, & commissions report directly to the Minister: Alberta Foundation for the Arts, Alberta Historical Resources Foundation, Government House Foundation, & the Historic Resources Fund.
Acts Administered:
Alberta Foundation for the Arts Act
Alberta Human Rights Act
Emblems of Alberta Act
Film & Video Classification Act
First Nations Sacred Ceremonial Objects Repatriation Act
Foreign Cultural Property Immunity Act
Government House Act
Government Organization Act
Historical Resources Act
Holocaust Memorial Day & Genocide Remembrance Act
Queen Elizabeth II Golden Jubilee Recognition Act
Recreation Development Act

Minister, Culture, Hon. Heather Klimchuk
Tel: 780-422-3559
Fax: 780-427-7729
Social Media: twitter.com/heatherklimchuk, www.facebook.com/Heather.Klimchuk
Legislature Bldg.
#107, 10800 - 97 Ave.
Edmonton, AB T5K 2B6

Deputy Minister, Culture, Barry Day
Tel: 780-427-2921
Fax: 780-427-5362
barry.day@gov.ab.ca

Chief Information Officer, Culture & Community Services, Lorie Baddock
Tel: 780-427-7828
Fax: 780-427-0255
lorie.baddock@gov.ab.ca

Executive Director/Senior Financial Officer, Financial Services, Pam Arnston
Tel: 780-427-0120
Fax: 780-427-0255
pam.arnston@gov.ab.ca

Executive Director, Policy, Planning, & Legislative Services, Susan Cribbs
Tel: 780-422-1290
Fax: 780-427-0255
susan.cribbs@gov.ab.ca

Executive Director, Human Resources, Diane Dunn
Tel: 780-422-5779
Fax: 780-422-3142
diane.dunn@gov.ab.ca

Executive Director, Francophone Secretariat, Denis Tardif
Tel: 780-415-3232
Fax: 780-422-7533
denis.tardif@gov.ab.ca
Other Communications: Main Secretariat Number: 780-415-3348

Director, Legal & Legislative Services, Barbara Adamson
Tel: 780-644-7741
Fax: 780-427-0255
barbara.adamson@gov.ab.ca

Director, Planning & Performance Measurement, Brad Babiak
Tel: 780-644-3272
Fax: 780-427-0255
brad.babiak@gov.ab.ca

Director, Communications, John Tuckwell
Tel: 780-427-2395
Fax: 780-427-1496
john.tuckwell@gov.ab.ca

Acting Director, Policy Coordination & Program Evaluation, David Middagh
Tel: 780-427-0617
Fax: 780-427-0255
david.middagh@gov.ab.ca

Acting Director, Financial Planning, Jeanette Stead
Tel: 780-644-8101
Fax: 780-427-0255
jeanette.stead@gov.ab.ca

Director, Financial Reporting & Operations, Carmen Vidaurri
Tel: 780-644-5511
Fax: 780-427-0255
carmen.vidaurri@gov.ab.ca

Associated Agencies, Boards & Commissions:
• **Alberta Foundation for the Arts (AFA)**
10708 - 105 Ave.
Edmonton, AB T5H 0A1
Tel: 780-427-9968
Toll-free: -310-0000
www.affta.ab.ca
The Foundation supports the development of arts throughout Alberta. It works to maintain & expand the AFA art collection for Albertans.
• **Alberta Historical Resources Foundation (AHRF)**
Old St. Stephen's College
8820 - 112 St.
Edmonton, AB T6G 2P8
Tel: 780-431-2300
Fax: 780-427-5598
www.culture.alberta.ca/ahrf
Established through the Historical Resources Act, The Alberta Historical Resource Foundation raises awareness of Alberta's heritage.
• **Government House Foundation**
12845 - 102 Ave. NW
Edmonton, AB T5N 0M6
Tel: 780-427-2281
Fax: 780-422-6508
governmenthouseinfo@gov.ab.ca
Established in 1976, the Government House Foundation consist of a board of up to 12 directors. The Lieutenant Governor appoints the directors who are responsible to the Minister of Culture & Community Spirit.
The board of directors is engaged in the following activities: advising the Minister of Culture & Community Services about the preservation of Government House, raising public awareness of the architectural development of Government House, & soliciting property for display in Government House.
• **Historic Resources Fund**
c/o Culture & Community Spirit, Old St. Stephen's College
8820 - 112 St.
Edmonton, AB T6G 2P8
Tel: 780-431-2300
Fax: 780-427-5598
Under the authority of the Historical Resources Act, the Historic Resource Fund carries out its purpose to protect, enhance, display, & promote the historic resources of Alberta. It funds programs that are designated by the Lieutenant Governor.

Culture, Community, & Voluntary Services Division
Standard Life Centre, 9th Fl., 10405 Jasper Ave., 9th Fl., Edmonton, AB T5J 4R7
Assistant Deputy Minister, Shannon Marchand
Tel: 780-422-0194
Fax: 780-422-2891
shannon.marchand@gov.ab.ca
Alberta Film Commissioner, Alberta Film, Jeff Brinton
Tel: 780-422-8581
Fax: 780-422-8582
jeff.brinton@gov.ab.ca
Other Communications: Alberta Film, Toll-Free Phone: 1-888-813-1738
Alberta Film, Whitemud Crossing
#140, 4211 - 106 St.
Edmonton, AB T6J6L7
Executive Director, Arts Branch, Jeffrey Anderson
Tel: 780-415-0283
Fax: 780-422-9132
jeffrey.anderson@gov.ab.ca
Executive Director, Community Engagement & Inclusion Branch, Carol Moerth
Tel: 780-415-4874
Fax: 780-427-4155
carol.moerth@gov.ab.ca
Director, Program Development & Special Initiatives, Pat Blakney
Tel: 780-422-1724
Fax: 427-427-4155
pat.blakney@gov.ab.ca
Director, Alberta Nonprofit / Voluntary Sector Initiative (ANVSI), Bruce Milne
Tel: 780-415-0856
Fax: 427-427-4155
bruce.milne@gov.ab.ca
Director, Policy, Planning and Strategic Initiatives, John Pryde
Tel: 780-381-5234
Fax: 427-329-8816
john.pryde@gov.ab.ca
Director, Lottery Funding Programs, Carl Royan
Tel: 780-422-9525
Fax: 427-422-8739
carl.royan@gov.ab.ca

Heritage Division
Old St. Stephen's College, 8820 - 112 St., Edmonton, AB T6G 2P8
Assistant Deputy Minister, David Link
Tel: 780-431-2313
Fax: 780-427-5598
david.link@gov.ab.ca
Executive Director & Provincial Archivist, Provincial Archives of Alberta, Leslie Latta-Guthrie
Tel: 780-427-0058
Fax: 780-427-4646
leslie.latta-guthrie@gov.ab.ca
Other Communications: Provincial Archives of Alberta, Phone: 780-427-1750
ProvincialArchives of Alberta
8555 Roper Rd.
Edmonton, AB T6E 5W1
Executive Director, Royal Tyrrell Museum of Palaeontology, Andy Neuman
Tel: 403-820-6201
Fax: 403-823-7131
andrew.neuman@gov.ab.ca
PO Box 7500
Drumheller, AB T0J 0Y0
Executive Director, Royal Alberta Museum, Chris Robinson
Tel: 780-453-9168
Fax: 780-454-6629
chris.robinson@gov.ab.ca
12845 - 102 Ave.
Edmonton, AB T5N 0M6
Executive Director, Historic Sites & Museums, Catherine Whalley
Tel: 780-431-2306
Fax: 780-427-5598
catherine.whalley@gov.ab.ca
Director, Policy & Program Coordination, Marilyn Kimura
Tel: 780-431-2314
Fax: 780-427-5598
marilyn.kimura@gov.ab.ca

Alberta Education

Commerce Place, 10155 - 102 St., 7th Fl., Edmonton, AB T5J 4L5
Tel: 780-427-7219
Fax: 780-427-0591
Toll-Free: -310-0000
www.education.alberta.ca
Other Communication: Media Inquiries, Phone: 780-422-4495
From Early Childhood Services (ECS) to Grade 12, Alberta Education supports students, parents, teachers & administrators. The Ministry is engaged in the following activities: developing & evaluating curriculum; setting standards; assessing outcomes; supporting the education of special needs, Aboriginal, & francophone students; developing & certifying teachers; funding & supporting school boards; overseeing educational policies & regulations; & managing the Alberta Initiative for School Improvement (AISI).
Acts Administered:
Alberta School Boards Association Act
Financial Administration Act
Freedom of Information & Protection of Privacy Act
Government Accountability Act
Government Organization Act
Northland School Division Act
Remembrance Day Act
School Act & Regulations
Teachers' Pension Plans Act & Regulations
Teaching Profession Act & Regulations

Minister, Education, Hon. Thomas Lukaszuk
Tel: 780-427-5010
Fax: 780-427-5018
Social Media: www.twitter.com/lukaszukml, www.facebook.com/Thomas-A-Lukaszuk/662272836

Deputy Minister, Keray Henke
Tel: 780-427-3659
Fax: 780-427-7733
keray.henke@gov.ab.ca

Director, Communications, Kathy Telfer
Tel: 780-427-5423
Fax: 780-427-0591
kathy.telfer@gov.ab.ca

Parliamentary Assistant, Janice Sarich
Tel: 780-415-9462
Fax: 780-415-0951
keray.henke@gov.ab.ca

Associated Agencies, Boards & Commissions:
• Council on Alberta Teaching Standards (COATS)
10044 - 108 St.
Edmonton, AB T5J 5E6
Tel: 780-427-2045
Fax: 780-422-4199
www.teachingquality.ab.ca
Established by a Ministerial Order in 1985, the Council on Alberta Teaching Standards offers recommendations related to teaching to the Minister. Advice is provided on matters such as teacher certification, teacher preparation, & practice review.

Education Program Standards & Assessment Division
Commerce Place, 10155 - 102 St., 7th Fl., Edmonton, AB T5J 4L5
Assistant Deputy Minister, Ellen Hambrook
Tel: 780-427-7484
Fax: 780-422-1400
ellen.hambrook@gov.ab.ca
Executive Director, French & International Education Services Sector, Paul Lamoureux
Tel: 780-422-7793
Fax: 780-422-1947
paul.lamoureux@gov.ab.ca
10044 - 108 St., 9th Fl.
Edmonton, AB T5J 5E6
Acting Executive Director, Planning & Standards, Joan Engel
Tel: 780-422-0629
Fax: 780-422-3745
joan.engel@gov.ab.ca
10044 - 108 St., 8th Fl.
Edmonton, AB T5J 5E6
Executive Director, Learner Assessment Sector, Neil Fenske
Tel: 780-427-0010
Fax: 780-422-4200
neil.fenske@gov.ab.ca
10044 - 108 St., 6th Fl.
Edmonton, AB T5J 5E6
Communications Coordinator, Programs of Study & Resources, Wendy Narang
Tel: 780-422-5631
Fax: 780-422-3745
wendy.narang@gov.ab.ca
10044 - 108 St., 8th Fl.
Edmonton, AB T5J 5E6

Learning Supports & Information Management Division
Commerce Place, 10155 - 102 St., 7th Fl., Edmonton, AB T5J 4L5
Assistant Deputy Minister, Dean Lindquist
Tel: 780-427-2051
Fax: 780-415-8938
dean.lindquist@gov.ab.ca
Executive Director, Learning & Program Resources Sector, Rick Baker
Tel: 780-427-5277
Fax: 780-422-0130
rick.baker@gov.ab.ca
Executive Director, Capital Planning Sector, Laura Cameron
Tel: 780-427-0289
Fax: 780-644-2284
laura.cameron@gov.ab.ca
Executive Director, FNMI & Field Services Sector, Rick Hayes
Tel: 780-427-5378
Fax: 780-422-9682
rick.hayes@gov.ab.ca
Executive Director, Information & Technology Management Sector, Aziza Jivraj
Tel: 780-427-3880
Fax: 780-422-0880
aziza.jivraj@gov.ab.ca
Executive Director, Program Delivery Sector, Lorraine Stewart
Tel: 780-422-6554
Fax: 780-643-1188
lorraine.stewart@gov.ab.ca
Director, School Technology Sector, Bette Gray
Tel: 780-427-1509
Fax: 780-415-1091
bette.gray@gov.ab.ca

People & Research Division
Commerce Place, 10155 - 102 St., Edmonton, AB T5J 4L5
Acting Assistant Deputy Minister, Gene Williams
Tel: 780-644-3578
Fax: 780-638-3272
gene.williams@gov.ab.ca
Director, Teacher Relations Branch, Doug Aitkenhead
Tel: 780-643-1277
Fax: 780-638-4197
doug.aitkenhead@gov.ab.ca
Director & Team Lead, Strategic Planning, Workplace Planning & Development Branch, Mark Bevan
Tel: 780-644-3579
Fax: 780-644-3591
mark.bevan@gov.ab.ca
Executive Director, Human Resources Branch, Bernadette Welham
Tel: 780-644-7503
Fax: 780-422-5362
bernadette.welham@gov.ab.ca
Director, School Research & Improvement Branch, Dr. Dianna Millard
Tel: 780-427-7882
Fax: 780-415-2481
dianna.millard@gov.ab.ca
Director & Registrar, Professional Standards Branch, Marc Prefontaine
Tel: 780-427-2045
Fax: 780-422-4199
marc.prefontaine@gov.ab.ca

Strategic Services Division
Commerce Place, 10155 - 102 St., 7th Fl., Edmonton, AB T5J 4L5
Assistant Deputy Minister, Michael Walter
Tel: 780-427-3663
Fax: 780-422-0408
michael.walter@gov.ab.ca
Executive Director, Policy & Planning, Don Napier
Tel: 780-427-9998
Fax: 780-422-5126
don.napier@gov.ab.ca
Executive Director, Strategic Financial Services Sector, Brad J. Smith
Tel: 780-422-0920
Fax: 780-422-6996
bsmith@gov.ab.ca
Director, Strategic Business Services Sector, Hank Koning
Tel: 780-422-3279
Fax: 780-415-6546
hank.koning@gov.ab.ca

Alberta Office of the Chief Electoral Officer / Elections Alberta (OOCEO)

11510 Kingsway Ave., 1st Fl., Edmonton, AB T5G 2Y5
Tel: 780-427-7191
Fax: 780-422-2900
info@electionsalberta.ab.ca
www.electionsalberta.ab.ca
The Office of the Chief Electoral Officer is engaged in the following activities: administering impartial, open, & fair elections; offering necessary information to political participants & voters; providing a high standard of customer service; training election officials; & adopting best practices & new technologies.
Acts Administered:
Election Act
Election Finances & Contributions Disclosure Act
Senatorial Selection Act

Chief Electoral Officer, O. Brian Fjeldheim
Tel: 780-427-1035
Fax: 780-422-2900
brian.fjeldheim@elections.ab.ca

Deputy Chief Electoral Officer, Lori McKee-Jeske
Tel: 780-427-6860
Fax: 780-422-2900
lori.mckeejeske@elections.ab.ca

Director, Information Technology & Geomatics, Keila Johnston
Tel: 780-643-1105
Fax: 780-422-2900
keila.johnston@elections.ab.ca

Director, Election Finances, CJ Rhamey
Tel: 780-427-1036
Fax: 780-422-2900
cj.rhamey@elections.ab.ca

Director, Election Operations & Communications, Drew Westwater
Tel: 780-427-1038
Fax: 780-422-2900
drew.westwater@elections.ab.ca

Alberta Energy

North Petroleum Plaza, 9945 - 108 St., Edmonton, AB T5K 2G6
Tel: 780-427-8050
Fax: 780-422-0698
Toll-Free: -310-0000
Library.Energy@gov.ab.ca
www.energy.gov.ab.ca
TTY: 780-427-9999
Other Communication: Calgary, Phone: 403-297-8955; TTY Toll-Free: 1-800-232-7215; Library Services, Phone: 780-415-0351
Alberta Energy is responsible for the development of Alberta's non-renewable resources & renewable energy. Non-renewable resources include natural gas, conventional oil & oil sands, coal, & minerals. Renewable resources include wind, solar, geothermal, & hydro.
Other responsibilities of Alberta Energy are as follows: establishing & administering fiscal & royalty systems; granting the right to explore & develop resources; promoting energy conservation; & encouraging investment to create economic prosperity.
Acts Administered:
Alberta Corporate Tax Act
Alberta Utilities Commission Act
Ammonite Shell Regulations
CO2 Projects Royalty Credit Regulation
Coal Conservation Act
Coal Sales Act
Electric Utilities Act
Energy Resources Conservation Act
Exploration Regulation
Flare Gas Generation Regulation
Freehold Mineral Rights Tax Act
Gas Processing Efficiency Assistance Regulation
Gas Resources Preservation Act
Gas Utilities Act
Hydro & Electric Energy Act
Independent Power & Small Power Regulation
Innovative Energy Technologies Regulation
Metallic & Industrial Minerals Exploration Regulation
Metallic & Industrial Minerals Regulation
Mineral Rights Compensation Regulation
Mines & Minerals Act
Natural Gas Marketing Act
Natural Gas Price Protection Act
Oil & Gas Conservation Act
Oil Sands Conservation Act
Oil Sands Tenure Regulation

Petroleum Marketing Act
Pipeline Act
Public Utilities Act
Security Management Regulation
Small Power Research & Development Act
Turner Valley Unit Operations Act
Water, Gas & Electric Companies Act

Minister, Energy, Hon. Ken Hughes
Tel: 780-427-3740
Fax: 780-422-0195
minister.energy@gov.ab.ca
Legislature Building
10800 - 97th Ave.
Edmonton, AB T5K 2B6

Deputy Minister, Energy, Jim Ellis
Tel: 780-415-8434
Fax: 780-427-7737
jim.ellis@gov.ab.ca
Petroleum Plaza NT
9945 - 108 St.
Edmonton, AB T5K 2G5

Executive Director, Human Resources, Dave Prince
Tel: 780-427-6294
Fax: 780-422-4299
dave.prince@gov.ab.ca
Petroleum Plaza NT
9945 - 108 St.
Edmonton, AB T5K 2G5

Director, Communications, Janice Schroeder
Tel: 780-422-3667
Fax: 780-422-0698
janice.schroeder@gov.ab.ca
Petroleum Plaza NT
9945 - 108 St.
Edmonton, AB T5K 2G5

Manager, Planning & Communications, Matthew Good
Tel: 780-638-3812
Fax: 780-427-7737
matthew.good@gov.ab.ca

Associated Agencies, Boards & Commissions:
• Alberta Utilities Commission (AUC)
Fifth Avenue Place
425 - 1st St. SW, 4th Fl.
Calgary, AB T2P 3L8
Tel: 403-592-8845
Fax: 403-592-4406
Toll-free: -310-0000
info@auc.ab.ca; utilitiesconcerns@auc.ab.ca
www.auc.ab.ca
Other Communication: Edmonton Office, Phone: 780-427-4901; Edmonton Office, Fax: 780-427-6970
The Alberta Utilities Commission was established by the Government of Alberta as a quasi-judicial independent agency. It is responsible for regulating the utilities sector & the electricity & natural gas markets in Alberta to ensure that the delivery of utility service is responsible, fair, & in the public interest.
• Energy Resources Conservation Board (ERCB)
#1000, 250 - 5 Ave. SW
Calgary, AB T2P 0R4
Tel: 403-297-8311
Fax: 403-297-7336
Toll-free: 855-297-8311
inquiries@ercb.ca; infoservices@ercb.ca; ADR@ercb.ca
www.ercb.ca
Other Communication: Appropriate Dispute Resolution Program, Phone: 403-297-6252; ERCB Applications Help Line, Phone: 403-297-4369; E-mail: Directive56.Help@ercb.ca
As an independent, quasi-judicial agency of the Government of Alberta, the Energy Resources Conservation Board is responsible for regulating the safe & responsible development of energy resources in Alberta. The province's energy resources include coal, natural gas, oil, & oil sands.

Clean Energy Division
Centre West Building, 10035 - 108 St., Edmonton, AB T5J 3E1
Assistant Deputy Minister, Clean Energy Division, John Donner
Tel: 780-638-4141
Fax: 780-638-4134
john.donner@gov.ab.ca
Director, Business Planning & Performance, Sandra Stemmer
Tel: 780-643-1438
Fax: 780-422-0800
sandra.stemmer@gov.ab.ca

Electricity, Alternative Energy, & Carbon Capture & Storage Division
Petroleum Plaza NT, 9945 - 108 St., 6th Fl., Edmonton, AB T5K 2G6
Assistant Deputy Minister, Sandra Locke
Tel: 780-644-7126
Fax: 780-427-7737
sandra.locke@gov.ab.ca
Executive Director, Carbon Capture & Storage Development / Energy Efficiency & Conservation Branch, Mikera Fernandez
Tel: 780-415-6414
Fax: 780-422-0229
mike.fernandez@gov.ab.ca
Executive Director, Infrastructure & Alternative Energy Branch, Ian McKay
Tel: 780-422-8726
Fax: 780-427-8065
ian.mckay@gov.ab.ca
Executive Director, Electricity Markets Branch, Kathryn Wood
Tel: 780-644-1232
Fax: 780-427-8065
kathryn.wood@gov.ab.ca

Oil Sands Strategy & Operations
Petroleum Plaza NT, 9945 - 108 St., 6th Fl., Edmonton, AB T5K 2G6
Chief Assistant Deputy Minister of Oil Sands Division, Jennifer Steber
Tel: 780-427-6370
Fax: 780-427-7737
jennifer.steber@gov.ab.ca
Executive Director, Oil Sands Strategy, Anne Denman
Tel: 780-422-9212
Fax: 780-427-8065
anne.denman@gov.ab.ca
Branch Head, External Relations & Advocacy, Lyn Bilida
Tel: 780-415-6187
Fax: 780-644-3234
lyn.bilida@gov.ab.ca
Branch Head, Operations, Steve Tkalcic
Tel: 780-422-9121
Fax: 780-422-0692
steve.tkalcic@gov.ab.ca
Branch Head, Business Design & Evaluation, Larry Ziegenhagel
Tel: 780-427-6384
Fax: 780-422-0692
larry.ziegenhagel@gov.ab.ca

Oil Sands Sustainable Development Secretariat
Oxbridge Place, 9820 - 106 St., 3rd Fl., Edmonton, AB T5K 2J6
Tel: 780-644-1473
The Oil Sands Sustainable Development Secretariat works with governments & stakeholders to provide an integrated policy approach & to share information about Alberta's oil sands regions. The Secretariat also considers the economic, environmental, & social impacts of the oil sands, by leading the implementation of a strategy entitled, Responsible Actions: A Plan for Alberta's Oil Sands.
Executive Director, Sandra Klashinsky
Tel: 780-427-7242
Fax: 780-427-2852
sandra.klashinsky@gov.ab.ca
Director, Community & Regional Planning, Gary Haynes
Tel: 780-644-4542
Fax: 780-427-2852
gary.haynes@gov.ab.ca
Director, Strategic Policy & Planning, Mel Miller
Tel: 780-643-1936
Fax: 780-427-2852
mel.miller@gov.ab.ca
Senior Manager & Project Coordinator, Karen Henderson
Tel: 780-415-8629
Fax: 780-427-2852
karen.henderson@gov.ab.ca

Regulatory Enhancement Project Implementation
Petroleum Plaza NT, 9945 - 108 St., 10th Fl., Edmonton, AB T5K 2G6
Assistant Deputy Minister, John Buie
Tel: 780-427-2159
Fax: 780-644-1784
john.buie@gov.ab.ca
Executive Advisor, Robert Burwood
Tel: 780-427-4300
Fax: 780-644-1784
robert.burwood@gov.ab.ca
Executive Advisor, Charleen Schmidt
Tel: 780-427-2368
Fax: 780-644-1784
charleen.schmidt@gov.ab.ca

Resource Development Policy Division
Petroleum Plaza NT, 9945 - 108 St., Edmonton, AB T5K 2G6
Assistant Deputy Minister, Resource Development Policy Division, Martin Chamberlain
Tel: 780-422-1045
Fax: 780-427-7737
martin.chamberlain@gov.ab.ca
Executive Director, Resource Development, Sharla Rauschning
Tel: 780-427-6230
Fax: 780-644-3604
sharla.rauschning@gov.ab.ca
Branch Head, Environment & Resource Services, Audrey Murray
Tel: 780-427-6383
Fax: 780-422-3044
audrey.murray@gov.ab.ca
Associate Branch Head, Economics & Markets, Matthew Foss
Tel: 780-422-5059
Fax: 780-422-9677
matthew.foss@gov.ab.ca
Director, Energy Markets & Forecasting, Paul Tsounis
Tel: 780-643-1292
Fax: 780-427-6504
paul.tsounis@gov.ab.ca
Branch Administrator, Aboriginal Relations / Single Aboriginal Affairs Branch, Tiffany Bailey
Tel: 780-427-5110
Fax: 780-644-1271
tiffany.bailey@gov.ab.ca

Revenue & Operations Division
Petroleum Plaza NT, 9945 - 108 St., 10th Fl., Edmonton, AB T5K 2G6
Assistant Deputy Minister, Revenue & Operations Division, Rhonda Wehrhahn
Tel: 780-422-9430
Fax: 780-422-1123
rhonda.wehrhahn@gov.ab.ca
Branch Head, Tenure, Brenda Allbright
Tel: 780-422-9393
Fax: 780-422-1123
brenda.allbright@gov.ab.ca
Branch Head, Petroleum Registry of Alberta (Edmonton / Calgary), Wally Goeres
Tel: 780-415-2079
Fax: 780-422-0229
wally.goeres@gov.ab.ca
Branch Head, Compliance & Assurance, Larry McGuinness
Tel: 403-297-6742
Fax: 403-297-5199
larry.mcguinness@gov.ab.ca
Branch Head, Royalty Operations, Salim Merali
Tel: 780-422-9124
Fax: 780-427-0865
salim.merali@gov.ab.ca
Branch Head, Petroleum Marketing & Valuation, & Site Services, Gale Robins
Tel: 403-297-5460
gale.robins@gov.ab.ca
Branch Head, Coal & Mineral Development, Gary V. White
Tel: 780-415-0349
Fax: 780-422-5447
gary.v.white@gov.ab.ca

Strategic Initiatives Division
Petroleum Plaza NT, 9945 - 108 St., 10th Fl., Edmonton, AB T5K 2G6
Assistant Deputy Minister, Mike Ekelund
Tel: 780-422-0813
Fax: 780-427-7737
mike.ekelund@gov.ab.ca
Director, Strategic Initiatives, Menzie McEachern
Tel: 780-638-4045
Fax: 780-427-7737
menzie.mceachern@gov.ab.ca

Strategic Services Division
Petroleum Plaza NT, 9945 - 108 St., 10th Fl., Edmonton, AB T5K 2G6
Director, Business Planning & Reporting, Sandra Stemmer
Tel: 780-643-1438
Fax: 780-422-0800
sandra.stemmer@gov.ab.ca
Branch Head, Finance & Business Services, Douglas Borland
Tel: 780-427-6223
Fax: 780-422-4281
douglas.borland@gov.ab.ca
Branch Head, FOIP & Records Management Branch, Marlene Bruyere
Tel: 780-644-3778
Fax: 780-644-3786
marlene.bruyere@gov.ab.ca
Branch Head, Information Management & Technology Services, Carol Anne Pasutto
Tel: 780-415-2083
Fax: 780-427-5696
carolanne.pasutto@gov.ab.ca

Alberta Enterprise & Advanced Education

Legislature Bldg., #324, 10800 - 97 Ave., Edmonton, AB T5K 2B6

Tel: 780-422-5400
Toll-Free: -310-0000
eae.alberta.ca

The key responsibilities of Enterprise & Advanced Education include post-secondary matters, apprenticeship & industry training, adult learning, research & innovation, economic development, immigration & labour attraction, & labour force development.

The following are some specific activities: funding public post-secondary institutions in Alberta; developing program standards with industry; counselling apprentices & employers; certifying apprentices & occupational trainees; providing student financial assistance; funding education providers; funding apprentices; working with various industry sectors, government councils, businesses, communities, & alliances to grow Alberta's economy; funding the Alberta Innovates programs; Facilitating technology commercialization & development; providing assistance to new immigrants; addressing & providing solutions for labour force issues

Acts Administered:
Access to the Future Act
Advanced Education & Technology Grants Regulation
Alberta Enterprise Corporation Act
Alberta Public Agencies Governance Act
Alberta Research & Innovation Act
Apprenticeship & Industry Training Act
Financial Administration Act
Freedom of Information & Protection of Privacy Act
Post-secondary Learning Act (PSLA)
Private Vocational Training Act
Student Support Legislation (various)

Minister, Enterprise & Advanced Education, Hon. Stephen Khan
Tel: 780-427-2025
Fax: 780-427-5582
Social Media: twitter.com/StephenKhanMLA, www.facebook.com/StephenKhanPC
Legislature Building
#402, 10800 - 97 Ave.
Edmonton, AB T5K2B6

Deputy Minister, David Morhart
Tel: 780-415-4744
Fax: 780-422-1801
david.morhart@gov.ab.ca

Executive Director & Senior Financial Officer, Corporate Services, Darrell Dancause
Tel: 780-427-1897
Fax: 780-415-9823
darrell.dancause@gov.ab.ca

Executive Director, Human Resources, Dianna Wilk
Tel: 780-422-5324
Fax: 780-427-3316
dianna.wilk@gov.ab.ca

Director, Legislative & Governance Services, Susan Bacock
Tel: 780-415-8985
Fax: 780-415-6546
susan.bocock@gov.ab.ca

Director, Communications, Michael Shields
Tel: 780-422-1562
Fax: 780-427-0821
michael.shields@gov.ab.ca

Director, Corporate Planning & Reporting, Magdalena DesLauriers
Tel: 780-415-4866
Fax: 780-422-3014
magdalena.deslauriers@gov.ab.ca

Director, Financial & Administrative Operations, Benedict Dy
Tel: 780-422-3070
Fax: 780-415-9823
benedict.dy@gov.ab.ca

Director, Financial Planning, McKnight Cindy
Tel: 780-415-6681
Fax: 780-415-9823
cindy.mcknight@gov.ab.ca

Director, Business Integration, Richard Wosnack
Tel: 780-427-6976
Fax: 780-422-7376
richard.wosnack@gov.ab.ca

Manager, Ministerial Correspondence Unit, Pauline Nealon
Tel: 780-422-9631
Fax: 780-422-1801
pauline.nealon@gov.ab.ca

Associated Agencies, Boards & Commissions:

• Access Advisory Council
Sterling Place
9940 - 106 St., 4th Fl.
Edmonton, AB
Tel: 780-644-3183
The council is appointed by the Minister of Advanced Education & Technology. The role of the council is to offer advice regarding the Access to the Future Fund.

• Alberta Apprenticeship & Industry Training Board
Commerce Place
10155 - 102nd St., 10th Fl.
Edmonton, AB T5J 4L5
Tel: 780-427-8765
Fax: 780-422-7376
Toll-free: -310-0000
TTY: 780-427-9999
www.tradesecrets.gov.ab.ca
Other Communication: TTY Toll-Free: 1-800-232-7215
Board members are appointed by the Lieutenant Governor in Council, upon recommendation of the Minister of Advanced Education & Technology. The mission of the board is to maintain high quality training & certification standards in the apprenticeship & industry training system. The board offers recommendations to the Minister about the needs of the labour market in Alberta & the training & certification of persons in designated trades & occupations.

• Alberta Council on Admissions & Transfer (ACAT)
Commerce Place
10155 - 102 St., 11th Fl.
Edmonton, AB T5J 4L5
Tel: 780-422-9021
Fax: 780-422-3688
Toll-free: -310-0000
TTY: 780-427-9999
acat@gov.ab.ca
www.acat.gov.ab.ca
Other Communication: TTY Toll-Free: 1-800-232-7215
The independent body advocates for learners by working to ensure transferability of educational courses & programs to benefit students. The role of the council is to develop policies & procedures to facilitate transfer agreements among post-secondary institutions.

• Alberta Economic Development Authority (AEDA)
McDougall Centre
455 - 6th St. SW
Calgary, AB T2P 4E8
Tel: 403-297-3022
Fax: 403-297-6435
Toll-free: -310-0000
www.aeda.alberta.ca
Working in partnership with the provincial government, the Alberta Economic Development Authority offers recommendations on key economic issues. The Alberta Economic Development Authority consists of business, municipal, & academic leader from throughout Alberta.

• Alberta Enterprise Corporation Board
Alberta Enterprise Corporation
#1100, 10830 Jasper Ave.
Edmonton, AB T5J 2B3
Tel: 780-392-3901
The Alberta Enterprise Corporation Board was established in 2008 through the Alberta Enterprise Corporation Act. The Alberta Enterprise Fund is the corporation's fund that targets technology venture capital funds.

• Alberta Innovates - Bio Solutions (AI Bio)
Phipps McKinnon Bldg.
10020 - 101A Ave.
Edmonton, AB T5J 3G2
Tel: 780-427-1956
Fax: 780-427-3252
Toll-free: 877-828-0444
bio@albertainnovates.ca
www.albertainnovates.ca/bio
Other Communication: General inquiries related to research & innovation organizations throughout Alberta, Phone: 877-828-0444
Alberta Innovates Bio Solutions was established in 2010 under the Alberta Research & Innovation Act. It is part of the Alberta Innovates system, which reports to the Minister of Alberta Advanced Education & Technology. Investments are made in research & innovation to benefit Alberta's forestry, agriculture, & food sectors.

• Alberta Innovates - Energy & Environmental Solutions
AMEC Place
#2540, 801 - 6th Ave. SW
Calgary, AB T2P 3W2
Tel: 403-297-7089
ees@albertainnovates.ca
www.albertainnovates.ca/energy/introduction
The Alberta energy & environmental research organization works to develop innovative methods for the conversion of natural resources into environmentally responsible, market-ready energy.

• Alberta Innovates - Health Solutions (AIHS)
#1500, 10104 - 103 Ave.
Edmonton, AB T5J 4A7
Tel: 780-423-5727
Fax: 780-429-3509
Toll-free: 877-423-5727
health@albertainnovates.ca
www.ahfmr.ab.ca
Alberta Innovates - Health Solutions supports research & innovation for the improvement of Albertans' health & well-being. The organization also works to create health related social & economic benefits.

• Alberta Innovates - Technology Futures
250 Karl Clark Rd.
Edmonton, AB T6N 1E4
Tel: 780-450-5111
Fax: 780-450-5333
referral@albertainnovates.ca
www.albertatechfutures.ca
As part of the research & innovation system in Alberta, the organization works to build healthy, sustainable businesses. Technology Futures offers technical services, program funding, as well as regionally accessible commercialization support.

• Alberta Research & Innvoation Authority (ARIA)
Phipps-McKinnon Bldg.
#500, 101A Ave.
Edmonton, AB T5J 3G2
Tel: 780-427-1488
Fax: 780-427-0979
aria@albertainnovates.ca
www.albertainnovates.ca/research/introduction
The advisory body offers recommendations to the Government of Alberta about research, emerging technologies, & policy direction.

• Campus Alberta Quality Council (CAQC)
Commerce Place
10155 - 102 St., 11th Fl.
Edmonton, AB T5J 4L5
Tel: 780-427-8921
Fax: 780-427-4185
caqc@gov.ab.ca
www.caqc.gov.ab.ca
The arms-length quality assurance agency makes recommendations to the Minister of Advanced Education & Technology on applications from post-secondary institutions that want to offer new degree programs. All degree programs, except for degrees in divinity, offered by resident institutions & non-resident institutions in Alberta must be approved by the Minister.

• Northern Alberta Development Council (NADC)
Peace River Office, Provincial Building
#206, 9621 - 96 Ave.
PO Box 900-14
Peace River, AB T8S 1T4
Tel: 780-624-6274
Fax: 780-624-6184
Toll-free: -310-0000
nadc.council@gov.ab.ca
www.nadc.ca
Other Communication: Bursary Information, E-mail: nadc.bursary@gov.ab.ca
The Northern Alberta Development Council focuses on the advancement of the northern economy. The Council is engaged in projects involving tourism, transportation, educational initiatives, value-added agriculture, & inter-jurisdictional projects.

• Student Financial Assistance Appeal Committee
Students Finance
PO Box 28000 Main
Edmonton, AB T5J 4R4
Tel: 780-427-3722
Toll-free: 800-222-6485
The committees in Edmonton & Calgary hear appeals from students who were not provided the entire amount of financial assistance requested, or who had their application for assistance refused. The committees make a recommendation to the Minister, who make a decision on the appeal.

• Students Finance Board

Established in 1953, the Students Finance Board advises the Minister of Advanced Education & Technology about student financial assistance, including scholarships.

Advanced Technology Industries Division
Phipps-McKinnon Bldg., 10020 - 101A Ave., 5th Fl., Edmonton, AB T5J 3G2
Branches & sections in this division include the following: Emerging Technology Industries; Information & Technology Management; Innovation Client Services; & Technology Industry Development.
Assistant Deputy Minister, Mel Wong
Tel: 780-427-2084
Fax: 780-427-5924
mel.wong@gov.ab.ca
Executive Director & Chief Information Officer, Information & Technology Management Section, Leslie Sim-Kaiser
Tel: 780-415-0813
Fax: 780-422-0880
leslie.sim-kaiser@gov.ab.ca
Commerce Place
10155 - 102 St., 9thFl.
Edmonton, AB T5J 4L5
Executive Director, Technology Industry Development Section, Robert Lai
Tel: 780-427-7722
Fax: 780-427-5924
robert.lai@gov.ab.ca
Director, Emerging Technology Industries Branch, Mathew Anil
Tel: 780-415-8751
Fax: 780-427-5924
mathew.anil@gov.ab.ca
Branch Head, Emerging Technology Industries Branch, Ryan Leskiw
Tel: 780-644-2587
Fax: 780-427-5924
ryan.leskiw@gov.ab.ca
Branch Head, Innovation Client Services Branch, Alex Umnikov
Tel: 780-427-6620
Fax: 780-427-5924
alex.umnikov@gov.ab.ca

Community, Learner & Industry Connections Division
Phipps-McKinnon Bldg., 10020 - 101A Ave., 5th Fl., Edmonton, AB T5J 3G2
Units of the Community Learner & Industry Connections Division include Apprenticeship & Industry Training & Learner Assistance.
Assistant Deputy Minister, Darlene Bouwsema
Tel: 780-422-1185
Fax: 780-422-2420
darlene.bouwsema@gov.ab.ca
Executive Director, Policy & Standards, Mark Douglas
Tel: 780-643-1466
Fax: 780-422-7376
mark.douglas@gov.ab.ca
Other Communications: General Apprentice Inquiries, Phone: 780-427-8517
Executive Director, Learner Assistance, Schubert Kwan
Tel: 780-422-4498
Fax: 780-422-4517
schubert.kwan@gov.ab.ca
Other Communications: Learner Assistance, Main Phone: 780-422-0555
Sterling Place
9940 - 106 St., 9th Fl.
Edmonton, AB T5K2V1
Director, Program, Policy & Systens Support, Trudy Dupre
Tel: 780-422-1208
Fax: 780-422-4517
trudy.dupre@gov.ab.ca
Sterling Place
9940 - 106 St., 9th Fl.
Edmonton, AB T5K 2V1
Director, Financial Operations & Control Services, John Koehn
Tel: 780-422-5109
Fax: 780-422-4517
john.koehn@gov.ab.ca
Sterling Place
9940 - 106 St., 9th Fl.
Edmonton, AB T5K 1V1
Director, Learner Funding, Launa Lebeau
Tel: 780-427-9820
Fax: 780-422-4516
launa.lebeau@gov.ab.ca
Sterling Place
9940 - 106 St., 7th Fl.
Edmonton, AB T5K 1V1

Enterprise Division
Phipps-McKinnon Bldg., 10020 - 101A Ave., 6th Fl., Edmonton, AB T5J 3G2
Units of the Enterprise Division include Regional Development, the Alberta Economic Development Authority, Industry Development, Economic Development Policy & Analysis, & the Northern Alberta Development Council.
Assistant Deputy Minister, Justin Riemer
Tel: 780-427-6302
Fax: 780-422-0626
justin.riemer@gov.ab.ca
Executive Director, Industry Development, Kirsty Piquette
Tel: 780-427-6987
Fax: 780-422-2091
kirsty.piquette@gov.ab.ca
Executive Director, Economic Development Policy & Analysis, Duane Pyear
Tel: 780-427-0850
Fax: 780-422-0061
duane.pyear@gov.ab.ca
Executive Director, Regional Development, Diane Simsovic
Tel: 780-427-6656
Fax: 780-422-5804
diane.simsovic@gov.ab.ca
Senior Director, North Region & Regional Development Best Practices, George Brosseau
Tel: 780-427-0802
Fax: 780-422-5804
george.brosseau@gov.ab.ca
Senior Director, Productivity Alberta, Lori Schmidt
Tel: 780-422-0545
Fax: 780-422-2091
lori.schmidt@gov.ab.ca
Senior Director, South Region, Elvira Smid
Tel: 403-529-3733
Fax: 403-529-3140
elvira.smid@gov.ab.ca
Director, Metro Regions & Small Business Support, Karen Wronko
Tel: 780-422-8420
Fax: 780-422-5804
karen.wronko@gov.ab.ca
Team Lead, Energy & Value Added Development (EVAD), Jerry MacPherson
Tel: 780-427-6591
Fax: 780-422-2091
jerry.macpherson@gov.ab.ca

Immigration Division
Labour Building, 10808 - 99 Ave., 9th Fl., Edmonton, AB T5K 0G5
The main units of the Immigration Division are: Immigration Policy & Programs, Labour Force Development, & Strategic Marketing & Labour Attraction.
Assistant Deputy Minister, Maryann Everett
Tel: 780-422-9493
Fax: 780-422-2889
maryann.everett@gov.ab.ca
Executive Director, Strategic Marketing & Labour Attraction, Danielle Comeau
Tel: 780-427-0528
Fax: 780-644-3329
danielle.comeau@gov.ab.ca
Executive Director, Immigration Policy & Programs, Percy Cummins
Tel: 780-415-8945
Fax: 780-643-0905
percy.cummins@gov.ab.ca
Director, Economic Immigration, Gosia Cichy-Weclaw
Tel: 780-644-2948
Fax: 780-644-3329
gosia.cichy-weclaw@gov.ab.ca
Director, Foreign Qualifications Recognition/International Qualifications Assessment Services, Gail Sarkany-Coles
Tel: 780-643-6782
Fax: 780-422-9734
gail.sarkany-coles@gov.ab.ca
Managing Director, Alberta Immigrant Nominee Program, Brad Trefan
Tel: 780-427-6496
Fax: 780-427-6560
brad.trefan@gov.ab.ca
Director, Immigration Policy & Planning, Peter Weclaw
Tel: 780-415-8830
peter.weclaw@gov.ab.ca

Post Secondary & Community Education Division
Commerce Place, 10155 - 102 St., 7th Fl., Edmonton, AB T5J 4L5
Campus Alberta Partnerships, Post-secondary Investments & Outcomes, & Strategic Directions make up the Post-secondary & Community Education Division.
Assistant Deputy Minister, Connie Harrison
Tel: 780-427-5607
Fax: 780-427-9430
connie.harrison@gov.ab.ca
Executive Director, Campus Alberta Partnerships, Dan Rizzoli
Tel: 780-415-2966
Fax: 780-427-0423
dan.rizzoli@gov.ab.ca
Executive Director, Strategic Directions, Kurt Schreiner
Tel: 780-427-9635
kurt.schreiner@gov.ab.ca
Executive Director, Post-secondary Investments & Outcomes, Gerry Waisman
Tel: 780-427-9667
Fax: 780-427-4185
gerry.waisman@gov.ab.ca

Research & Innovation Division
Phipps-McKinnon Bldg., 10020 - 101A Ave., 5th Fl., Edmonton, AB T5J 3G2
The Research & Innovation Division consists of Cross Ministry Initiatives, Innovation Planning & Accountability, Alberta Research & Innovation Authority, Innovation Policy, & Alberta Innovates.
Executive Director, Innovation Planning & Accountability, Lisa Bowes
Tel: 780-422-3117
Fax: 780-427-1430
lisa.bowes@gov.ab.ca
Executive Director, Cross Ministry Initiatives, Daphne Cheel
Tel: 780-422-0054
Fax: 780-427-3252
daphne.cheel@gov.ab.ca
Director, Innovation Policy, Sandra Duxbury
Tel: 780-427-4498
Fax: 780-427-5924
sandra.duxbury@gov.ab.ca

Alberta Environment & Sustainable Resource Development

Oxbridge Place, 9820 - 106 St., Main Fl., Edmonton, AB T5K 2J6
Tel: 780-427-2700
Fax: 780-422-4086
Toll-Free: -310-0000
env.infocent@gov.ab.ca; srd.infocent@gov.ab.ca
environment.alberta.ca
TTY: 780-427-9999
Other Communication: 24-hour Environment Hotline (to report an environmental emergency or file a complaint): 1-800-222-6514; Media Enquiries, Phone: 780-427-6267; TTY: 1-800-232-7215
Alberta Environment & Sustainable Resource Development, created in 2012 by Premier Redford, works as a partner to protect & enhance the natural environment of Alberta.
The Minister of Environment & Sustainable Resource Development is repsonsible for the Environmental Appeals Board, & oversees the following agencies & boards: Alberta Recycling Management Authority, Alberta Used Oil Management Association, & the Beverage Container Management Board.
Acts Administered:
Boundary Surveys Act
Climate Change & Emissions Management Act
Environmental Protection & Enhancement Act
Expropriation Act (sections 25 to 28 & 72)
Fisheries (Alberta) Act
Forest & Prairie Protection Act
Forest Reserves Act
Forests Act
Government Organization Act (sections 4(2)(f) & (g) of Schedule 5, in common with the Minister of Environment & the Minister of Infrastructure)
Mines & Minerals Act (aections 108(g), (h), & (j), in common with the Minister of Energy)
Natural Resources Conservation Board Act (in common with the Minister of Environment)
Public Lands Act
Surface Rights Act
Surveys Act
Water Act
Wildlife Act

Minister, Environment & Sustainable Resource Development, Hon. Diana McQueen
Tel: 780-427-2391
Fax: 780-422-6259
Social Media: twitter.com/ministermcqueen, www.facebook.com/dianamcqueenmla, ca.linkedin.com/pub/diana-mcqueen/17/24/b62
Legislature Building
#204, 10800 - 97 Ave.
Edmonton, AB T5K 2B6

Deputy Minister, Environment & Sustainable Resource Development, Dana Woodworth
Tel: 780-427-1799
Fax: 780-415-9669
dana.woodworth@gov.ab.ca
Petroleum Plaza ST
9915 - 108 St., 10th Fl.
Edmonton, AB T5K 2G8

Director, Communications, Andy Weiler
Tel: 780-427-8122

Fax: 780-427-1874
andy.weiler@gov.ab.ca

Associated Agencies, Boards & Commissions:

• Alberta Environmental Appeals Board
Peace Hills Trust Tower
#306, 10011 - 109 St.
Edmonton, AB T5J 3S8
Tel: 780-427-6207
Fax: 780-427-4693
www.eab.gov.ab.ca
The Environmental Appeals Board strives to offer fair, impartial, & efficient resolutions to matters in order to advance the protection & enhancement of the environment in Alberta.

• Alberta Recycling Management Authority (ARMA)
Scotia Tower 1
#1310, 10060 Jasper Ave.
PO Box 189
Edmonton, AB T5J 2J1
Tel: 780-990-1111
Fax: 780-990-1122
Toll-free: 888-999-8762
info@albertarecycling.ca
www.albertarecycling.ca
Other Communication: Toll-Free Fax: 1-866-990-1122; Electronics Recycling: electronics@albertarecycling.ca; Tire Recycling: tires@albertarecycling.ca; Paint: paint@albertarecycling.ca
Reporting to the Minister of Environment, the not-for-profit association manages tire, paint, & electronics recycling programs throughout Alberta.

• Alberta Used Oil Management Association (AUOMA)
Empire Building
#1008, 10080 Jasper Ave.
Edmonton, AB T5J 1V9
Tel: 780-414-1510
Fax: 780-414-1519
Toll-free: 866-414-1510
reception@usedoilrecycling.ca
www.usedoilrecycling.com/en/ab
Other Communication: Info Line (for information about the nearest Alberta Eco Centre / Collection Facility): 1-888-922-2298

The not-for-profit association encourages Albertans to return used oil, filters, & containers to collection facilities so they can be disposed of properly. The program is funded by an Environmental Handling Charge, & a Return Incentive is paid to private sector collectors.

• Beverage Container Management Board (BCMB)
#750, 10707 - 100 Ave.
Edmonton, AB T5J 3M1
Tel: 780-424-3193
Fax: 780-428-4620
Toll-free: 888-424-7671
www.bcmb.ab.ca
The Beverage Container Management Board is an alliance of the Alberta Government, municipalities, beverage manufacturers, environmental organizations, & the public. It was established in 1997 as a management board, under the Beverage Container Recycling Regulation pursuant to Section 175 of the Environmental Protection & Enhancement Act.
The Beverage Container Management Board oversees the collection & recycling of beverage containers throughout Alberta. Its policy parameters are established by the Minister of Environment. Funding is through a levy based on the returns of beverage containers.

• Disabled Hunter Review Committee
c/o Fish & Wildlife Div,, Sustainable Resource Development
9915 - 108 St., 11th Fl.
Edmonton, AB T5K 2G8
Toll-free: -310-0000
The Disabled Hunter Review Committee is engaged in hearing appeals & reviewing applications by persons who received a negative decision when attempting to obtain a licences or permit for hunting. Depending upon the number of applications, the Committee holds hearings annually.

• Environmental Response Centre
Twin Atria Bldg.
4999 - 98 Ave., 1st Fl.
Edmonton, AB T6B 2X3
Tel: 780-427-2700
Other Communication: Environment Hotline (for reporting an environmental emergency or filing a complaint): 1-800-222-6514
Complaints about contraventions of the Environmental Protection & Enhancement Act are investigated.

• Land Compensation Board (LCB)
1229 - 91 St. SW
Edmonton, AB T6X 1E9
srb.lcb@gov.ab.ca
www.landcompensation.gov.ab.ca
The Land Compensation Board listens to disputes & delivers a decision, within it legislated mandate, about the compensation for landowners or tenants when land is taken by an authority for public works projects. Applications to the Board can be made through forms found in the Expropriation Act Rules of Procedure & Practice.

• Natural Resources Conservation Board (NRCB)
Sterling Place
9940 - 106 St.
Edmonton, AB T5K 2N2
Tel: 780-422-1977
Fax: 780-427-0607
Toll-free: 866-383-6722
info@nrcb.gov.ab.ca
www.nrcb.gov.ab.ca
Established in 1991 by the Government of Alberta, the Natural Resources Conservation Board carries out its responsibilities under the Natural Resources Conservation Board Act. The quasi-judicial agency, which is accountable to the Minister of Sustainable Resource Development, reviews non-energy natural resource projects. The Board considers environmental, economic, & social effects in deciding if a project is in the public interest.
In accordance with the Agricultural Operation Practices Act, the Natural Resources Conservation Board also has regulatory authority for confined feeding operations in Alberta. Its work in this area includes administering policies, fulfilling applications, & conducting board reviews.

• Surface Rights Board (SRB)
1229 - 91 St. SW
Edmonton, AB T6X 1E9
Tel: 780-427-2444
Fax: 780-427-5798
Toll-free: -310-0000
srb.lcb@gov.ab.ca
www.surfacerights.gov.ab.ca
The Surface Rights Board holds hearings on disputes related to energt activities & land access. The hearing usually involves a panel of three members of the Surface Rights Board. Members of the Board are appointed by an Order in Counsel, according to the Surface Rights Act. Affected parties may also participate in the hearings, which are open to the public.
The Board delivers decisions, within its legislated mandate, about compensation to landowners, surrounding issues such as oil & gas & power line activity. In determining compensation, the Board considers factors such as the value of the land, loss of use, inconvenience, nuisance, & noise, & adverse effects on remaining land.

• Wildfire Costs Assessment Committee
c/o Office of the Farmer's Advocate, JG O'Donoghue Building
7000 - 113 St., 3rd Fl.
Edmonton, AB T6H 5T6
The Wildfire Costs Assessment Committee is administered by the Farmers' Advocate Office. When a party is deemed responsible for starting a wildfire, the Committee evaluates that party's ability to pay the cost of fighting the fire.

• Wildlife Predator & Shot Livestock Compensation Committee
c/o Fish & Wildlife Div., Sustainable Resource Development
9920 - 108 St., 3rd Fl.
Edmonton, AB T5K 2M4
The reimbursement paid to a livestock producer, when an animal has been injured by a wildlife predator, or shot, is determined by the Predator & Shot Livestock Compensation Committee of Alberta. Compensation provided to the livestock owner is based upon a schedule for losses or injury to specified livestock.

Clean Energy Division
Centre West Building, 10035 - 108 St., 8th Fl., Edmonton, AB T5J 3E1

Assistant Deputy Minister, John Donner
Tel: 780-638-4141
Fax: 780-638-4134
john.donner@gov.ab.ca

Acting Executive Director, Policy Management Office, Heather von Hauff
Tel: 780-638-4139
Fax: 780-638-4134
heather.vonhauff@gov.ab.ca

Senior Operations Manager, Chris Hunt
Tel: 780-644-1259
Fax: 780-638-4134
chris.hunt@gov.ab.ca

Corporate Services Division
Petroleum Plaza ST, 9915 - 108 St., 10th Fl, Edmonton, AB T5K 2G8
Tel: 780-643-0890
Fax: 780-644-8469

Assistant Deputy Minister, Tom Davis
Tel: 780-644-3205
Fax: 780-427-0923
tom.davis@gov.ab.ca

Chief Information Officer, Office of the CIO & Information Management & Technology Branch, Roger Burns
Tel: 780-644-5065
roger.burns@gov.ab.ca
Oxbridge Place
9820 - 106 St.
Edmonton, AB T5K 2J6

Chief Information Officer, Resource Information Management Branch, Sustainable Resource Development, James Greengrass
Tel: 780-422-5719
Fax: 780-422-0712
james.greengrass@gov.ab.ca
Oxbridge Place
9820 - 106 St.
Edmonton, AB T5K2J6

Executive Director & Senior Financial Officer, Finance & Administration Branch, Mike Dalrymple
Tel: 780-427-9148
Fax: 780-427-0923
mike.dalrymple@gov.ab.ca

Executive Director & Senior Financial Officer, Finance & Administration Branch, Greg Kliparchuk
Tel: 780-638-3199
Fax: 780-427-2512
greg.kliparchuk@gov.ab.ca

Executive Director, Corporate Busines Support Branch, Scott Milligan
Tel: 780-422-0672
Fax: 780-644-4682
scott.milligan@gov.ab.ca

Director, Planning & Policy Coordination, Fiona Salkie
Tel: 780-422-0561
Fax: 780-644-4682
fiona.salkie@gov.ab.ca

Director, Information Communication Technology, Joe Vance
Tel: 780-644-8619
Fax: 780-427-7434
joe.vance@gov.ab.ca

Fish & Wildlife Division
Petroleum Plaza ST, 9915 - 108 St., 11th Fl., Edmonton, AB T5K 2G8

Assistant Deputy Minister, Rick Blackwood
Tel: 780-427-1139
Fax: 780-427-8884
rick.blackwood@gov.ab.ca

Executive Director, Wildlife Management, Ron Bjorge
Tel: 780-427-9503
Fax: 780-422-9557
ron.bjorge@gov.ab.ca

Director, Fisheries Management Branch, Travis Ripley
Tel: 780-427-7763
Fax: 780-422-9559
travis.ripley@gov.ab.ca

Forestry Division
Petroleum Plaza ST, 9915 - 108 St. 11th Fl., Edmonton, AB T5K 2G8

Assistant Deputy Minister, Bruce Mayer
Tel: 780-427-3542
Fax: 780-422-6068
bruce.mayer@gov.ab.ca

Executive Director, Wildfire Management Branch, Hugh Boyd
Tel: 780-442-7781
Fax: 780-415-1509
hugh.boyd@gov.ab.ca

Executive Director, Forest Management Branch, Darren Tapp
Tel: 780-427-5324
Fax: 780-427-0085
darren.tapp@gov.ab.ca

Executive Director, Forest Industry Development Branch, Dan Wilkinson
Tel: 780-427-6372
Fax: 780-644-5728
dan.wilkinson@gov.ab.ca

Director, Wildfire Operations Section, John Brewer
Tel: 780-427-7925
Fax: 780-422-7230
john.brewer@gov.ab.ca

Director, Wildfire Prevention Section, Herman Stegehuis
Tel: 780-415-9969
Fax: 780-427-0292

Land Use Secretariat
Centre West Building, 10035 - 108 St., Edmonton, AB T5J 3E1
Tel: 780-644-7972
Fax: 780-644-1034
luf@gov.ab.ca
www.landuse.alberta.ca

The Land Use Secretariat is a leader in the implementation of Alberta's Land-use Framework. The Secretariat assists regional advisory councils in offering advice to government about developing regional plans.

Executive Director, Regional Planning, Crystal Damer
Tel: 780-644-5014
Fax: 780-644-1034
crystal.damer@gov.ab.ca

Commissioner, Stewardship, Morris Seiferling
Tel: 780-644-7978
Fax: 780-644-1034
morris.seiferling@gov.ab.ca
Coordinator, Budget & Projects, Ursula Hung
Tel: 780-427-9195
Fax: 780-644-1034
ursula.hung@gov.ab.ca
Manager, Communications & Web, Tim Kulak
Tel: 780-415-9547
Fax: 780-644-1034
tim.kulak@gov.ab.ca

Lands Division
Petroleum Plaza ST, 9915 - 108 St., 11th Fl., Edmonton, AB T5K 2G8
Tel: 780-415-1396
Fax: 780-422-6068
Assistant Deputy Minister, Glenn Selland
Tel: 780-427-7061
Fax: 780-422-6068
glenn.selland@gov.ab.ca
Executive Director, Land Management Branch, Jeff Reynolds
Tel: 780-644-1752
Fax: 780-427-1185
jeff.reynolds@gov.ab.ca
Acting Executive Director, Rangeland Management Branch, Dan Smith
Tel: 780-427-3595
Fax: 780-422-0454
dan.smith@gov.ab.ca
Director, Land Dispositions Branch, Val Hoover
Tel: 780-427-3464
Fax: 780-422-2545
val.hoover@gov.ab.ca
Director, Project Management Branch, Todd Letwin
Tel: 780-427-4768
Fax: 780-644-1142
todd.letwin@gov.ab.ca

Monitoring & Science Division
Petroleum Plaza ST, 9915 - 108 St., 10th Fl., Edmonton, AB T5K 2G8
Assistant Deputy Minister, Bob Barraclough
Tel: 780-427-0029
Fax: 780-422-4192
bob.barraclough@gov.ab.ca
Acting Director, Data Monitoring & Validation Branch, Tom Dickson
Tel: 780-415-9367
Fax: 780-422-8606
tom.dickson@gov.ab.ca
Administrative Coordinator, Jannette Wombold
Tel: 780-427-8315
Fax: 780-427-6334
jannette.wombold@gov.ab.ca

Operations Division
Petroleum Plaza ST, 9915 - 108 St., Edmonton, AB T5K 2G8
Tel: 780-427-1335
Fax: 780-427-1335
Assistant Deputy Minister, Rick Brown
Tel: 780-427-1335
Fax: 780-422-5141
rick.brown@gov.ab.ca
Director, Water Management Operations, David Ardell
Tel: 780-297-5892
Fax: 780-297-6389
dave.ardell@gov.ab.ca
Director, Regional Integration Branch, Colin Blair
Tel: 780-427-8536
Fax: 780-422-4086
colin.blair@gov.ab.ca
Director, Environmental Support & Emergency Response Team, Greg Carter
Tel: 780-415-0989
Fax: 780-427-2278
greg.carter@gov.ab.ca
Acting Team Leader, Environmental Assessment, Environmental Impact Assessmnet Group, Corinne Kristensen
Tel: 780-427-9116
Fax: 780-427-9102
corinne.kristensen@gov.ab.ca

Policy Division
Petroleum Plaza ST, 9915 - 108 St., Edmonton, AB T5K 2G8
Tel: 780-415-8183
Fax: 780-415-6492
Assistant Deputy Minister, Shannon Flint
Tel: 780-422-8463
Fax: 780-427-0923
shannon.flint@gov.ab.ca
Acting Director, Policy & Legislation Innovation Branch, Janet McLean
Tel: 780-427-9888
Fax: 780-422-4192
janet.mclean@gov.ab.ca
Director, Clean Energy Policy Branch, Roger Ramcharita
Tel: 780-644-5290
Fax: 780-415-1718
roger.ramcharita@gov.ab.ca
Director, Water Policy Branch, Andy Ridge
Tel: 780-638-4198
Fax: 780-442-4192
andy.ridge@gov.ab.ca
Acting Director, Climate Change Secretariat, Bob Savage
Tel: 780-644-4918
Fax: 780-415-1718
robert.savage@gov.ab.ca
Office Coordinator, Air, Land, & Waste Policy Branch, Lynn Lockhart
Tel: 780-427-8249
Fax: 780-422-4192
lynn.lockhart@gov.ab.ca

Strategy Division
Petroleum Plaza ST, 9915 - 108 St., 10th Fl., Edmonton, AB T5K 2G8
Assistant Deputy Minister, Bev Yee
Tel: 780-427-6247
Fax: 780-427-1014
bev.yee@gov.ab.ca
Executive Director, SREM Aboriginal Affairs Branch (SAAB), Norman Calliou
Tel: 780-422-7898
Fax: 780-421-0028
norman.calliou@gov.ab.ca
Director, Strategy Development & Foresight, Stephanie Clarke
Tel: 780-422-1874
Fax: 780-644-7571
stephanie.clarke@gov.ab.ca
Director, Transboundary Secretariat, Robert Harrison
Tel: 780-427-9288
Fax: 780-638-3187
robert.harrison@gov.ab.ca
Acting Director, Systems Management, Christine Lazaruk
Tel: 780-422-9100
Fax: 780-422-5120
christine.lazaruk@gov.ab.ca

Alberta Office of the Ethics Commissioner

#1250, 9925 - 109 St. NW, Edmonton, AB T5K 2J8
Tel: 780-422-2273
Fax: 780-422-2261
generalinfo@ethicscommissioner.ab.ca
www.ethicscommissioner.ab.ca
Established in 1992, the Office of the Ethics Commissioner for the Province of Alberta is engaged in the promotion of public confidence in the ethics of each Member of the Legislative Assembly.
Acts Administered:
Alberta Conflicts of Interest Act

Alberta Ethics Commissioner, Neil R. Wilkinson
Tel: 780-422-2273
Fax: 780-422-2261
generalinfo@ethicscommissioner.ab.ca

Chief Administrative Officer, Office of the Ethics Commissioner, Glen Resler
Tel: 780-422-4974
Fax: 780-422-2261
gresler@ethicscommissioner.ab.ca

Registrar, Lobbyists Act, & General Counsel, Brad Odsen, QC
Tel: 780-644-3879
Fax: 780-422-2261
bodsen@ethicscommissioner.ab.ca

Alberta Health

PO Box 1360 Main, Edmonton, AB T5J 2N3
Tel: 780-427-7164
Fax: 780-427-1171
Toll-Free: -310-0000
www.health.alberta.ca; www.seniors.gov.ab.ca
TTY: 800-232-7215
Other Communication: Seniors Phone: 780-644-9992; Fax: 780-422-5954; Toll-Free: 1-877-644-9992
Formerly Alberta Health & Wellness, Alberta Health is involved in the following activities: establishing legislation, policy, & standards; supporting the health system; allocating resources; & administering provincial programs. As of 2012, Alberta Health also incorporates elements of the former Alberta Seniors.
Acts Administered:
ABC Benefits Corporation Act
Alberta Cancer Prevention Legacy Act
Alberta Evidence Act
Alberta Health Act
Alberta Health Care Insurance Act
Alberta Housing Act (jointly with other Ministries)
Charitable Donation of Food Act
Dependent Adults Act
Emergency Health Services Act
Emergency Medical Aid Act
Government Organization Act
Health Care Protection Act
Health Disciplines Act
Health Facilities Review Committee Act
Health Governance Transition Act
Health Information Act
Health Insurance Premiums Act
Health Professions Act
Hospitals Act
Human Tissue & Organ Donation Act
M.S.I. Foundation Act
Mandatory Testing & Disclosure Act
Mental Health Act
Nursing Homes Act
Opticians Act
Personal Directives Act
Pharmacy & Drug Act
Physical Therapy Profession Act
Podiatry Act
Prevention of Youth Tobacco Use Act
Protection for Persons in Care Act
Protection of Children Abusing Drugs Act
Provincial Health Authorities of Alberta Act
Public Health Act
Regional Health Authorities Act
Seniors Advisory Council for Alberta Act
Seniors Benefit Act
Supportive Living Accommodation Licensing Act
Tobacco Reduction Act

Minister, Health, Hon. Fred Horne
Tel: 780-427-3665
Fax: 780-415-0961
health.minister@gov.ab.ca
Social Media: twitter.com/fredhornemla, www.facebook.com/FredHorne
Legislature Building
#208, 10800 - 97 Ave.
Edmonton, AB T5K 2B6

Associate Minister, Wellness, Hon. Dave Rodney
Tel: 780-415-0482
Fax: 780-415-2255
Legislature Building
#418, 10800 - 97 Ave.
Edmonton, AB T5K 2B6

Associate Minister, Seniors, Hon. George VanderBurg
Tel: 780-415-9550
Fax: 780-415-9411
Legislature Building
#227, 10800 - 97 Ave.
Edmonton, AB T5K 2B6

Deputy Minister, Health, Marcia Nelson
Tel: 780-422-0747
Fax: 780-427-1016
marcia.nelson@gov.ab.ca
Telus Plaza NT
10025 Jasper Ave., 22nd Fl.
Edmonton, AB T5J 1S6

Mental Health Patient Advocate, Fay Orr
Tel: 780-422-1812
Fax: 780-422-0695
fay.orr@gov.ab.ca
Centre West Building
10025 - 108 St., 12th Fl.
Edmonton, AB T5J 3E1

Executive Director, Human Resources, F.W. (Rick) Brick
Tel: 780-427-1060
Fax: 780-422-1700
rick.brick@gov.ab.ca

Director, Communications, Carol Chawrun
Tel: 780-427-5344
Fax: 780-427-1171
carol.chawrun@gov.ab.ca

Manager, Organizational Effectiveness, Lynsey Nault
Tel: 780-644-6825
Fax: 780-422-1700
lynsey.nault@gov.ab.ca

Manager, Executive Correspondence Unit, Monica Ulmer
Tel: 780-638-4562

Fax: 780-427-1851
monica.ulmer@gov.ab.ca

Associated Agencies, Boards & Commissions:
• Alberta Health Services (AHS)
Corporate Office, North Tower, Seventh Street Plaza
10030 - 107th St. NW, 14th Fl.
Edmonton, AB T5J 3E4
Tel: 780-342-2000
Fax: 780-342-2060
Toll-free: 888-342-2471
ahsb.admin@albertahealthservices.ca
www.albertahealthservices.ca
Other Communication: Board Office, Phone: 866-943-1120; Fax: 403-943-1124
Alberta Health Services was established in 2008, and became operational in 2009. The provincial health authority plans & delivers health services throughout Alberta.
• Health Quality Council of Alberta (HQCA)
#210, 811 - 14 St. NW
Calgary, AB T2N 2A4
Tel: 403-297-8162
Fax: 403-297-8258
info@hqca.ca
www.hqca.ca
Other Communication: Edmonton Office, Phone: 780-429-3008, Fax: 780-429-0985
The Health Quality Council of Alberta is legislated under the Regional Health Authorities Act. The Council's responsibilities are set forth in the Health Quality Council of Alberta Regulation. The independent organization strives to improve the health service quality, patient safety, & performance of the health system in Alberta.
• Office of the Chief Medical Officer of Health (OCMOH)
Telus Plaza NT
10025 Jasper Ave., 24th Fl.
Edmonton, AB T5J 1S6
Tel: 780-427-5263
The Office of the Chief Medical Officer of Health offers guidelines to Alberta Health Services about public health policy. The Office also provides information to the public about communicable diseases & public health programs.
The Chief Medical Officer of Health works under the authority of the Public Health Act to promote & protect the health of the people of Alberta.
• Seniors Advisory Council for Alberta
Standard Life Centre
#600, 10405 Jasper Ave., 6th Fl.
Edmonton, AB T5J 4R7
Tel: 780-422-2321
Fax: 780-422-8762
Toll-free: -310-0000
saca@gov.ab.ca
www.seniors.alberta.ca/services_resources/advisory_council
The Seniors Advisory Council for Alberta consults with senior citizens & seniors' organizations in communities throughout Alberta. The Council then informs the Government of Alberta, through the Minister of Seniors & Community Supports, about the issues that affect Alberta's seniors.
The Seniors Advisory Council for Alberta is also engaged in planning the Seniors' Week celebration each years, supporting workshops for frontline workers & seniors, & participating in research projects.

Alberta Aids to Daily Living (AADL)
Milner Building, 10040 - 104 St., 10th Fl., Edmonton, AB T5J 0Z2
Tel: 780-427-0731
Fax: 780-422-0968
www.seniors.gov.ab.ca/aadl
The AADL provides financial assistance to Albertans with long-term disabilities, chronic or terminal illnesses, who live at home, in lodges, or in group homes.
Acting Director, Barb Martini
Tel: 780-422-6985
Fax: 780-422-0968
barb.martini@gov.ab.ca
Manager, Medical & Surgical Benefits, Lauran Chittim
Tel: 780-422-4846
Fax: 780-422-0968
lauran.chittim@gov.ab.ca
Manager, Prosthetics & Orthotics, Seating & Footwear Benefits, Cathy Johnson
Tel: 780-422-6319
Fax: 780-422-0968
cathy.johnson@gov.ab.ca
Program Manager, Mobility & Large Equipment Benefits, Sheron Parmar
Tel: 780-422-8025
Fax: 780-422-0968
sheron.parmar@gov.ab.ca
Manager, AADL Business Unit, Erin Stevens
Tel: 780-422-7684
Fax: 780-422-0968
erin.stevens@gov.ab.ca
Manager, Hearing & Communication Benefits, Patti-Jo Sullivan
Tel: 780-422-6567
Fax: 780-422-0968
patti-jo.sullivan@gov.ab.ca
Respiratory Therapy Consultant, Respiratory Benefits, Mariana Chan
Tel: 780-422-4864
Fax: 780-422-0968
mariana.chan@gov.ab.ca

Family & Population Health Division
Telus Plaza NT, 10025 Jasper Ave., 24th Fl., Edmonton, AB T5J 1S6
Assistant Deputy Minister, Margaret King
Tel: 780-415-2783
Fax: 780-422-3671
margaret.king@gov.ab.ca
Executive Director, Health Protection, Dawn Friesen
Tel: 780-415-2818
Fax: 780-427-1470
dawn.friesen@gov.ab.ca
Executive Director, Wellness Branch, Neil MacDonald
Tel: 780-415-2759
Fax: 780-422-5474
neil.macdonald@gov.ab.ca
Executive Director, Surveillance & Assessment, Kathy Ness
Tel: 780-422-2561
Fax: 780-427-1470
kathy.ness@gov.ab.ca

Financial & Corporate Services Division
Telus Plaza NT, 10025 Jasper Ave., 19th Fl., Edmonton, AB T5J 1S6
Assistant Deputy Minister, David Breakwell
Tel: 780-415-1599
Fax: 780-422-3672
david.breakwell@gov.ab.ca
Executive Director, Corporate Services, Stephen Arthur
Tel: 780-415-0201
Fax: 780-427-1643
stephen.arthur@gov.ab.ca
Executive Director, Health Facilities Planning, Wayne Campbell
Tel: 780-638-3546
Fax: 780-422-3672
wayne.campbell@gov.ab.ca
Acting Executive Director, Corporate Services, Scott McIntyre
Tel: 780-427-6011
Fax: 780-427-7432
scott.mcintyre@gov.ab.ca
Executive Director, Financial Planning Branch, Charlene Wong
Tel: 780-427-7100
Fax: 780-422-3672
charlene.wong@gov.ab.ca
Legislative Counsel, Denise C. Gagnon
Tel: 780-415-0230
Fax: 780-422-2512
denise.gagnon@gov.ab.ca

Health Benefits & Compliance Division
Telus Plaza NT, 10025 Jasper Ave., 18th Fl., Edmonton, AB T5J 1S6
Executive Director, Pharmaceutical Funding & Guidance, Steve Long
Tel: 780-427-8019
Fax: 780-422-3646
steve.long@gov.ab.ca
Executive Director, Health Insurance Programs Branch, Donna Manuel
Tel: 780-644-3149
Fax: 780-644-1445
donna.manuel@gov.ab.ca
Executive Director, Monitoring & Investigations Branch, Lorraine McKay
Tel: 780-415-1424
Fax: 780-643-1527
lorraine.mckay@gov.ab.ca
Executive Director, Standards Licensing & Compliance Branch, Marjory Sutherland
Tel: 780-422-8219
Fax: 780-644-5499
marjory.sutherland@gov.ab.ca

Health Information Technology & Systems Division
Telus Plaza NT, 10025 Jasper Ave., 21st Fl., Edmonton, AB T5J 1S6
Assistant Deputy Minister & Chief Information Officer, Health Information Technology & Systems Division, Mark Brisson
Tel: 780-427-1572
Fax: 780-422-5176
mark.brisson@gov.ab.ca
Executive Director, EHR Delivery Services, Susan Anderson
Tel: 780-415-2492
Fax: 780-415-2289
susan.anderson@gov.ab.ca
Executive Director, Information Systems Delivery Branch, Chris Kearney
Tel: 780-415-2704
Fax: 780-415-2289
chris.kearney@gov.ab.ca
Executive Director, Information Management Branch, Sue Kessler
Tel: 780-415-2788
Fax: 780-422-6663
sue.kessler@gov.ab.ca
Executive Director, Information Technology & Operations, Blaine Steward
Tel: 780-415-1562
Fax: 780-644-3091
blaine.steward@gov.ab.ca

Health Workforce Division
Telus Plaza NT, 10025 Jasper Ave., 10th Fl., Edmonton, AB T5J 1S6
Assistant Deputy Minister, Glenn Monteith
Tel: 780-415-2745
Fax: 780-415-8455
glenn.monteith@gov.ab.ca
Acting Executive Director, Workforce Policy & Planning Branch & Senior Manager, Research & Planning, Bernard Anderson
Tel: 780-415-2749
Fax: 780-415-1094
bernard.anderson@gov.ab.ca
Executive Director, Labour Relations Branch, Deb Kaweski
Tel: 780-415-0212
Fax: 780-415-1094
deb.kaweski@gov.ab.ca
Acting Executive Director, Innovative Compensation & Director, Academic Medicine, Sharon McCaughan
Tel: 780-427-8067
Fax: 780-422-5208
sharon.mccaughan@gov.ab.ca

Primary Health Care Division
Telus Plaza NT, 10025 Jasper Ave., 18th Fl., Edmonton, AB T5J 1S6
Assistant Deputy Minister, Susan A. Williams
Tel: 780-644-3086
Fax: 780-415-0570
susan.williams@gov.ab.ca
Executive Director, Acute/EMS Services Branch, Line Porfon
Tel: 780-415-2762
Fax: 780-422-1515
line.porfon@gov.ab.ca
Executive Director, Addictions & Mental Health, Silvia Vajushi
Tel: 780-422-1344
Fax: 780-422-6663
silvia.vajushi@gov.ab.ca
Executive Director, Clinical Advisory & Research Branch, & Acting Senior Provincial Clinical Advisor, Joan Berezanski
Tel: 780-422-9325
Fax: 780-422-4482
joan.berezanski@gov.ab.ca

Seniors Services & Continuing Care Division
Standard Life Centre, 10405 Jasper Ave., 6th Fl., Edmonton, AB T5J 4R7
Assistant Deputy Minister, Chi Loo
Tel: 780-422-3179
Fax: 780-422-5954
chi.loo@gov.ab.ca
Executive Director, Continuing Care Branch, Tyler James
Tel: 780-422-9678
Fax: 780-422-1515
tyler.james@gov.ab.ca
Executive Director, Seniors Financial Assistance Branch, John Cabral
Tel: 780-422-7270
Fax: 780-422-5954
john.cabral@gov.ab.ca
Director, Seniors Supplementary Supports Branch, Kindy Joseph
Tel: 780-644-8613
Fax: 780-422-5954
kindy.joseph@gov.ab.ca
Director, Seniors Policy & Community Partner Branch, Sarah Carr
Tel: 780-644-2975
Fax: 780-422-5954
sarah.carr@gov.ab.ca

Strategic Services Division
Telus Plaza NT, 10025 Jasper Ave., 22nd Fl., Edmonton, AB T5J 1S6
Assistant Deputy Minister, Linda Mattern
Tel: 780-422-2720
Fax: 780-643-9421
linda.mattern@gov.ab.ca
Executive Director, Deputy Minister Supports Branch, Shannon Haggarty
Tel: 780-415-0953
Fax: 780-643-9421
shannon.haggarty@gov.ab.ca

Executive Director, Information & Analysis, Dee-Jay King
Tel: 780-427-8596
Fax: 780-427-1577
dee-jay.king@gov.ab.ca
Acting Executive Director, Planning, Measuring & Reporting Branch, John Quince
Tel: 780-415-1505
Fax: 780-422-2880
john.quince@gov.ab.ca
Director, Strategic Policy Branch, Hilary Lynas
Tel: 780-643-0978
Fax: 780-422-1515
hilary.lynas@gov.ab.ca

Alberta Human Services

Office of the Minister, Legislature Building, #224, 10800 - 97 Ave., Edmonton, AB T5K 2B6
Tel: 780-644-5135
Toll-Free: 866-644-5135
www.humanservices.alberta.ca
Other Communication: Alberta Supports Contact Centre, Toll-Free Phone: 1-877-644-9992; Family Violence Info Line: 310-1818; Bullying Help Line: 1-888-456-2323
The Ministry of Human Services was created in 2011, under Premier Redford. The ministry is responsible for programs & services in the following areas: children & youth; employment & immigration; homelessness support; & Alberta Supports.
Children & youth services include the following: adoption, child care & early childhood development, child intervention, family support for children with disabilities, & the prevention of family violence & bullying.
Employment & immigration services oversee Alberta Works, employment standards, labour market information, labour relations, occupational health & safety, & immigration.
Homelessness support is involved in the administration of Alberta's Plan to End Homelessness, the Alberta Secretariat for Action on Homelessness, the Gunn Centre, & emergency shelters.
Alberta Supports includes the Alberta Supports Contact Centre.
As of 2012, Human Services is also responsible for programs relating to seniors & persons with disabilities.
Acts Administered:
Administrative Procedures Act
Adult Interdependent Relationships Act
Agrologists Act
Architects Act
Assured Income for the Severely Handicapped Act
Blind Persons' Rights Act
Child Care Licensing Act
Child, Youth, Family Enhancement Act
Consulting Engineers of Alberta Act
Dower Act
Drug-endangered Children Act
Energy Resources Conservation Act
Engineering, Geological & Geophysical Professions Act
Expropriation Act
Family & Community Support Services Act
Family Law Act
Family Support for Children with Disabilities Act
Financial Administration Act
Income & Employment Supports Act
Interjurisdictional Support Orders Act
Interpretation Act
Land Agents Licensing Act
Land Surveyors Act
Land Titles Act
Maintenance Enforcement Act
Métis Settlements Act
Métis Settlements Land Protection Act
Occupational Health & Safety Act
Persons with Developmental Disabilities Community Governance Act
Premier's Council on the Status of Persons with Disabilities Act
Professional & Occupational Associations Registration Act
Protection Against Family Violence Act
Protection of Sexually Exploited Children Act
Regulated Accounting Profession Act
Regulated Forestry Profession Act
Service Dogs Act
Social Care Facilities Licensing Act
Social Care Facilities Review Committee Act
Surface Rights Act
Surveys Act
Veterinary Profession Act

Minister, Human Services; Government House Leader, Hon. David Hancock, QC
Tel: 780-643-6210
Fax: 780-643-6214
Social Media: twitter.com/davehancockmla, www.facebook.com/dave.hancock.376, www.linkedin.com/pub/dave-hancock/16/207/959
Legislature Building
#224, 10800 - 97 Ave.
Edmonton, AB T5K 2B6

Associate Minister, Services for Persons with Disabilities, Hon. Frank Oberle
Tel: 780-415-8700
Fax: 780-415-8738

Deputy Minister, Human Services, Steve MacDonald
Tel: 780-427-6448
Fax: 780-422-9044
steve.macdonald@gov.ab.ca

Executive Director, Alberta's Promise Secretariat, Ruth Copot
Tel: 780-403-2599
Fax: 780-297-6664
ruth.copot@gov.ab.ca

Executive Director, Human Resources, Rick Nisbet
Tel: 780-427-7274
Fax: 780-427-3937
rick.nisbet@gov.ab.ca

Executive Director, Organizational Renewal, Dawn White
Tel: 780-415-8964
Fax: 780-415-2003
dawn.white@gov.ab.ca

Director, Communications, Kathy Telfer
Tel: 780-415-6490
Fax: 780-422-3071
kathy.telfer@gov.ab.ca

Associated Agencies, Boards & Commissions:
• Appeals Commission for Alberta Workers' Compensation
Energy Square Building
#901, 10109 - 106th St.
Edmonton, AB T5J 3L7
Tel: 780-412-8700
Fax: 780-412-8701
webmaster1@appealscommission.ab.ca
www.appealscommission.ab.ca
Other Communication: Phone, Calgary: 403-508-8800
The Appeals Commission for Alberta Workers' Compensation strives to offer an independent, fair, & timely appeals process. The Commission works to operate consistently with legislation & policy.
• Calgary Citizens Appeal Panel
Human Services, AMEC Pl.
801 - 6 Ave. SW
Calgary, AB T2P 3W2
Tel: 403-297-5636
• Edmonton Citizens Appeal Panel
Centre West Building
100335 - 108th St.
Edmonton, AB T5J 3E1
Tel: 780-427-2709
Fax: 780-422-1088
• Labour Relations Board (ALRB)
Labour Building
10808 - 99 Ave., 5th Fl.
Edmonton, AB T5K 0G5
Tel: 780-422-5926
Fax: 780-422-0970
Toll-free: 800-463-2572
alrbinfo@lab.gov.ab.ca
www.alrb.gov.ab.ca
The independent & impartial tribunal is involved in the application & interpretation of labour lawa in Alberta. The Alberta Labour Relations Board administers the Labour Relations Code to handle disputes between trade unions & employers.
• Lethbridge Citizens Appeal Panel
Human Services, Administration Building
#408, 909 - 3 Ave. North
Lethbridge, AB T1H 0H5
• Occupational Health & Safety Council (OHSC)
Labour Building
10808 - 99 Ave., 9th Fl.
Edmonton, AB T5K 0G5
Tel: 780-415-8690
Toll-free: 866-415-8690
Under the Occupational Health & Safety Act, the Occupational Health & Safety Council advises the Minister about matters related to the health & safety of Alberta's workers. Nine members serve on the Council, including the chair & representatives from employers, employees, & the public.
• Persons with Developmental Disabilities Community Boards
c/o PDD Program Branch, Peace Hills Trust Tower
10011 - 109 St., 4th Fl.
Edmonton, AB T5J 3S8
Tel: 780-427-1177
Fax: 780-427-1220
Toll-free: 800-310-0000
PDDinfo@gov.ab.ca
www.seniors.alberta.ca/pdd
Six Persons with Developmental Disabilities Community Boards were established by the Persons with Developmental Disabilities Community Governance Act. The boards deliver supports to adults with developmental disabilities. The following services are funded by the program: community living supports for persons in their home environment; employment supports to educate & train individuals; community access supports; & specialized community supports.
• Premier's Council on the Status of Persons with Disabilities
HSBC Building
10055 - 106 St., 11th Fl.
Edmonton, AB T5J 1G3
Tel: 780-422-1095
Toll-free: 800-272-8841
pcspd@gov.ab.ca
www.seniors.alberta.ca/PremiersCouncil
Established in 1988, the mandate for the Premier's Council on the Status of Persons with Disabilities is outlined in the Premier's Council on the Status of Persons with Disabilities Act. The Premier's Council consists of up to fifteen volunteer members who communicate the concerns of Alberta's disability community to the provincial government.
• Red Deer Citizens Appeal Panel
Human Services, Provincial Building
4920 - 51 St.
Red Deer, AB T4N 6K8
• Social Care Facilities Review Committee
Sterling Place
9940 - 106 St., 3rd Fl.
Edmonton, AB T5K 2N2
Other Communication: Complaint Line: 780-427-3010
• Workers' Compensation Board (WCB)
9912 - 107 St.
Edmonton, AB T5J 2S5
Tel: 780-498-3999
Fax: 780-427-5863
Toll-free: 866-922-9221
TTY: 780-498-7895
www.wcb.ab.ca
Other Communication: Calgary, Phone: 403-517-6000; Toll-Free Phone, outside Alberta: 1-800-661-9608; Claims, Toll-Free Fax: 1-800-661-1993
The independent organization manages workers' compensation insurance, based on legislation. The Alberta Workers' Compensation Board compensates injured workers for costs such as lost income & health care.

Aboriginal Policy & Community Engagement Division
Sterling Place, 9940 - 106 St., 10th Fl., Edmonton, AB T5K 2N2
Assistant Deputy Minister, Catherine Twinn
Tel: 780-643-1157
Fax: 780-422-5415
catherine.twinn@gov.ab.ca
Director, Partnerships, Analysis, Initiatives & Research (PAIR), Mary Berube
Tel: 780-422-4781
Fax: 780-422-0562
mary.berube@gov.ab.ca
Director, Community, Capacity & Planning (CCP), Bree Claude
Tel: 780-638-4115
Fax: 780-644-2646
bree.claude@gov.ab.ca
Director, Aboriginal Relations, Arlene Thunder
Tel: 780-422-1690
Fax: 780-422-0562
arlene.thunder@gov.ab.ca

Child & Family Services Delivery Division
Sterling Place, 9940 - 106 St., 12th Fl., Edmonton, AB T5K 2N2
Services for Alberta's families & children are delivered from ten Child & Family Services Authorities located in regions throughout the province.
Assistant Deputy Minister, Bonnie Johnston
Tel: 403-408-8478
Fax: 403-422-6642
bonnie.johnston@gov.ab.ca
Director, Collaborative Policy & Analysis, Stephen Gauk
Tel: 403-422-7960
Fax: 403-415-5841
stephen.gauk@gov.ab.ca
Director, Governance Services, Mary Jane Graham
Tel: 403-422-5873

Fax: 403-644-6880
maryjane.graham@gov.ab.ca
Region #1, Southwest Alberta, Chief Executive Officer, Lonnie Slezina
Tel: 403-381-5570
Fax: 403-381-5791
lonnie.slezina@gov.ab.ca
Other Communications: Region #1 Main Phone: 403-381-5543
Note: Web Site: www.southwestalbertacfsa.gov.ab.ca
Children & Youth Services, Southwest Alberta Region #1, PalliserCentre
#107, 3305 - 18th Ave. North
Lethbridge, AB T1H 5S1
Region #2, Southeast Alberta, Chief Executive Officer, Bryan Heninger
Tel: 403-529-3756
Fax: 403-528-5244
bryan.heninger@gov.ab.ca
Other Communications: Region #2 Main Phone: 403-529-3753
Children & Youth Services, Southeast Alberta Region #2,Provincial Building
346 - 3rd St. SE, 1st Fl.
Medicine Hat, AB T1A 0G7
Region #4, Central Alberta, Chief Executive Officer, David Tunney
Tel: 403-341-8655
Fax: 403-755-6184
david.tunney@gov.ab.ca
Other Communications: Region #4 Main Phone: 403-341-8642
Note: Web Site: www.centralalbertacfsa.gov.ab.ca
Children & Youth Services, Central Alberta Region #4, Bishop's Place
4826 Ross St., 3rd Fl.
Red Deer, AB T4N 1X4
Region #5, East Central Alberta, Chief Executive Officer, Brian Holden
Tel: 780-662-7055
Fax: 780-662-3854
brian.holden@gov.ab.ca
Other Communications: Region #5 Main Phone: 780-385-7160
Note: Web Site: www.eastcentralalbertacfsa.gov.ab.ca
Children & Youth Services, East Central Alberta Region #5
4811 -49th Ave.
Killam, AB T0B 2L0
Region #6, Edmonton & Area, Chief Executive Officer, Carole Anne Patenaude
Tel: 780-415-2291
Fax: 780-422-6864
caroleanne.patenaude@gov.ab.ca
Other Communications: Region #6 Main Phone: 780-427-2250
Note: Web Site: www.edmontonandareacfsa.gov.ab.ca
Children & Youth Services, Edmonton & Area Region #6,Oxbridge Place
9820 - 106th St., 7th Fl.
Edmonton, AB T5K 2J6
Region #7, North Central Alberta, Chief Executive Officer, Dr. David Rideout
Tel: 780-305-2435
Fax: 780-305-2444
david.rideout@gov.ab.ca
Other Communications: Region #7 Main Phone: 780-305-2440
Children & Youth Services, North Central Alberta Region #7,Administrative Building
5143 - 50th St.
Barrhead, AB T7N 1A6
Region #8, Northwest Alberta, Chief Executive Officer, Rick Flette
Tel: 780-538-5248
Fax: 780-538-5137
rick.flette@gov.ab.ca
Other Communications: Region #8 Main Phone: 780-538-5122
Children & Youth Services, Northwest Alberta Region #8, Place South
#214, 10130 - 99th Ave., 4th Fl.
Grande Prairie, AB T8V 2V4
Region #9, Northeast Alberta, Chief Executive Officer, Ron Benson
Tel: 780-743-7462
Fax: 780-743-7474
ron.benson@gov.ab.ca
Children & Youth Services, Northeast Alberta Region #9, Provincial Building
9915 Franklin Ave., 4thFl.
Fort McMurray, AB T9H 2K4
Region #10, Métis Settlement, Chief Executive Officer, Lillian Parenteau
Tel: 780-415-6170
Fax: 780-415-0177
lillian.parenteau@gov.ab.ca
Other Communications: Region #10 Main Phone: 780-427-1033
Children & Youth Services, Métis Settlement Region #10,Centurion Plaza
#210, 10335 - 172 St.
Edmonton, AB T5S 1K9

Child Intervention Program Quality & Supports Division
Sterling Pl., 9940 - 106 St., 10th Fl., Edmonton, AB T5K 2N2
Tel: 780-422-0305
Fax: 780-422-5415

Assistant Deputy Minister, Mark Hattori
Tel: 780-415-1548
Fax: 780-422-5415
mark.hattori@gov.ab.ca
Director, Field Operations Support, Fred Anderson
Tel: 780-644-6990
Fax: 780-422-5415
fred.anderson@gov.ab.ca
Director, Program Information, Evaluation, & Performance, Maureen Mooney
Tel: 780-422-5674
Fax: 780-422-5415
maureen.mooney@gov.ab.ca
Senior Manager, Post Adoption Registry, Maureen Landry
Tel: 780-422-3389
Fax: 780-427-2048
maureen.landry@gov.ab.ca
Senior Manager, Adoption Services, Anne Scully
Tel: 780-644-3099
Fax: 780-427-2048
anne.scully@gov.ab.ca

Community Disability Services Division
Standard Life Centre, 10405 Jasper Ave., 3rd Fl., Edmonton, AB T5J 4R7
Assistant Deputy Minister, Brenda Lee Doyle
Tel: 780-427-2593
Fax: 780-427-1689
brendalee.doyle@gov.ab.ca
Acting Executive Director, Persons with Developmental Disabilities Program, Jim Menzies
Tel: 780-427-1216
Fax: 780-427-1220
jim.menzies@gov.ab.ca
Director, Family Support for Children with Disabilities (FSCD) Branch, Laura Alcock
Tel: 780-427-5869
Fax: 780-415-0651
laura.alcock@gov.ab.ca
Acting Director, Office of the Public Guardian, Shirley Peleshytyk
Tel: 780-422-2029
Fax: 780-422-6051
shirley.peleshytyk@gov.ab.ca
Other Communications: Main Number: 780-422-1868
Director, Program Development & Innovation, Tim Weinkauf
Tel: 780-427-1206
Fax: 780-427-1220
tim.weinkauf@gov.ab.ca
Public Trustee, Cindy Bentz
Tel: 780-422-3141
Fax: 780-422-9136
cindy.bentz@gov.ab.ca
Public Guardian - Calgary, Mohinder Bajwa
Tel: 403-297-3393
Fax: 403-297-3427
mohinder.bajwa@gov.ab.ca
Public Guardian - Central Region, Betty Lou Bowles
Tel: 403-340-5502
Fax: 403-340-7131
bettylou.bowles@gov.ab.ca
Public Guardian - South, Connie MacDonald
Tel: 403-381-5653
Fax: 403-381-5774
connie.macdonald@gov.ab.ca
Acting Public Guardian - North, Teresa Overgaard
Tel: 780-645-6296
Fax: 780-645-6260
teresa.overgaard@gov.ab.ca
Assistant Public Guardian - Edmonton, Debbie Urquhart
Tel: 780-422-7824
Fax: 780-422-9138
debbie.urquhart@gov.ab.ca

Community Strategies & Workforce Supports Division
Sterling Place, 9940 - 106 St., 10th Fl., Edmonton, AB T5K 2N2
Tel: 780-427-6428
Fax: 780-422-9045

Assistant Deputy Minister, Karen Ferguson
Tel: 780-427-6428
Fax: 780-422-9045
karen.ferguson@gov.ab.ca
Executive Director, Alberta Works Programs, David Schneider
Tel: 780-415-9106
Fax: 780-422-0032
david.schneider@gov.ab.ca
Executive Director, Business Innovations, Brian Payne
Tel: 780-427-6678
Fax: 780-422-6768
brian.payne@gov.ab.ca
Director, Community Partnerships, Ken Dropko
Tel: 780-644-2485
Fax: 780-644-2671
ken.dropko@gov.ab.ca
Director, Child Care, Lynn Jerchel
Tel: 780-422-4538
Fax: 780-427-1258
lynn.jerchel@gov.ab.ca
Director, Forum of Labour Market Ministers (FLMM) Secretariat, Heather Collier
Tel: 780-427-3975
Fax: 780-427-0354
heather.collier@gov.ab.ca
Senior Manager, Early Childhood Development Initiatives, Deborah Hopkins
Tel: 780-644-4492
Fax: 780-427-1258
deborah.hopkins@gov.ab.ca
Senior Manager, Fetal Alcohol Spectrum Disorder Initiatives / Children's Mental Health, Denise Milne
Tel: 780-415-0523
Fax: 780-644-2671
denise.milne@gov.ab.ca
Senior Manager, Child Development Services, Jennifer Weber
Tel: 780-644-2506
Fax: 780-427-1258
jennifer.weber@gov.ab.ca
Senior Manager, Centrally Delivered Child Care Services, Linda Yurdiga
Tel: 780-427-7599
Fax: 780-427-1258
linda.yurdiga@gov.ab.ca

Corporate Services Division
Standard Life Centre, 10405 Jasper Ave., 2nd Fl., Edmonton, AB T5J 4R7
Tel: 780-638-3560
Assistant Deputy Minister & Senior Financial Officer, Carol Ann Kushlyk
Tel: 780-422-8550
Fax: 780-644-2524
carolann.kushlyk@gov.ab.ca
Chief Information Officer, Vicki Ozaruk
Tel: 780-427-8398
Fax: 780-427-4310
vicki.ozaruk@gov.ab.ca
Executive Director & Senior Financial Officer, Shelley Engstrom
Tel: 780-427-0034
Fax: 780-422-2861
shelley.engstrom@gov.ab.ca
Executive Director & Chief Information Officer, Kevin Molcak
Tel: 780-644-1125
Fax: 780-427-9376
kevin.molcak@gov.ab.ca
Director, Appeals Secretariat, Kevin Young
Tel: 780-422-9079
Fax: 780-422-1088
kevin.young@gov.ab.ca

Disability Policy & Supports Division
Milner Building, 10040 - 104 St., 12th Fl., Edmonton, AB T5J 0Z2
Tel: 780-427-1245
Fax: 780-427-5148
Other Communication: Assured Income for the Severely Handicapped (AISH) Info Line: 1-866-477-8589
Assistant Deputy Minister, Donna Ludvigsen
Tel: 780-644-4555
Fax: 780-427-5148
donna.ludvigsen@gov.ab.ca
Executive Director, Assured Income for the Severely Handicapped (AISH) Delivery Services, Dale Beesley
Tel: 780-644-4731
Fax: 780-644-3299
dale.beesley@gov.ab.ca
Executive Director, Policy, Innovation & Partnerships, Sherri Wilson
Tel: 780-644-9910
Fax: 780-644-2315
sherri.wilson@gov.ab.ca
Director, Assured Income for the Severely Handicapped (AISH) Program & Disability Policy, Gisela Kwok
Tel: 780-422-0714
Fax: 780-644-2315
gisela.kwok@gov.ab.ca
Senior Manager, Finance & Contracting Services, Jackie Lee
Tel: 780-644-5179

Fax: 780-427-9145
jackie.lee@gov.ab.ca
Senior Manager, Fetal Alcohol Spectrum Disorder Initiatives/Children's Mental Health, Denise Milne
Tel: 780-415-0523
Fax: 780-415-0651
denise.milne@gov.ab.ca
Manager, Issues Management & Corporate Support, Susan West
Tel: 780-427-2065
Fax: 780-427-5148
susan.west@gov.ab.ca

Employment Services Delivery Division
Labour Building, 10808 - 99 Ave., 10th Fl., Edmonton, AB T5K 0G5
Tel: 780-415-2946
Fax: 780-427-7548
Assistant Deputy Minister, Ken Shewchuk
Tel: 780-415-2583
Fax: 780-427-7548
ken.shewchuk@gov.ab.ca
Executive Director, Centrally Delivered Services, Chuck Conroy
Tel: 780-644-1911
Fax: 780-415-1667
chuck.conroy@gov.ab.ca
Regional Director, Central Region, Clay Buchanan
Tel: 403-340-7001
Fax: 403-340-7057
Provincial Building
4920 - 51 St., 5th Fl.
Red Deer, AB T4N 6K8
Regional Director, Edmonton Region, Elvin Collins
Tel: 780-422-6993
Fax: 780-422-5125
elvin.collins@gov.ab.ca
South Tower, Seventh Street Plaza
10030 - 107 St., 8th Fl.
Edmonton, AB T5J 4X7
Regional Director, Northeast Region, Bev Parker
Tel: 780-623-5133
Fax: 780-623-5355
bev.parker@gov.ab.ca
Lakeview Building
15 Nipewan Rd.
Lac La Biches, AB T0A 2C0
Regional Director, Northwest Region, Nancy Schneider
Tel: 780-324-3239
Fax: 780-324-3235
nancy.schneider@gov.ab.ca
Provincial Building
10320 - 99th St.
Grande Prairie, AB T8V 6J4
Regional Director, South Region, Noelle Becker
Tel: 403-345-7979
Fax: 403-345-4915
noelle.becker@gov.ab.ca
2105 - 20th Ave.
Coaldale, AB T1M 1M2

Family Violence Prevention & Homeless Supports Division
Capital Boulevard, #44, 10044 - 108 St., 3rd Fl., Edmonton, AB T5J 5E6
Tel: 780-643-6648
Fax: 780-644-5796
Assistant Deputy Minister, Susan Taylor
Tel: 780-415-8907
Fax: 780-644-5796
susan.taylor@gov.ab.ca
Executive Director, Alberta Secretariat for Action on Homelessness, Stephen Manley
Tel: 403-297-7461
Fax: 403-297-6138
stephen.manley@gov.ab.ca
Acting Executive Director, Family Violence Prevention, Paulette Rodziewicz
Tel: 403-643-6651
Fax: 403-427-2039
paulette.rodziewicz@gov.ab.ca
Director, Gunn Centre, Lynn Bell
Tel: 780-967-2221
Fax: 780-967-3494
lynn.bell@gov.ab.ca
Director, Cross Ministry Initiatives Branch, Barry Bezuko
Tel: 780-643-0757
Fax: 780-415-9345
barry.bezuko@gov.ab.ca
Director, Youth Homelessness, Darren Joslin
Tel: 780-422-5680
Fax: 780-644-5796
darren.joslin@gov.ab.ca

Service Delivery Transformation Initiative
Standard Life Centre, 10405 Jasper Ave., 4th Fl., Edmonton, AB T5J 4R7

Strategic Services Division
Labour Building, 10808 - 99 Ave., 10th Fl., Edmonton, AB T5K 0G5
Tel: 780-427-4093
Fax: 780-422-8462
Assistant Deputy Minister, Lana Lougheed
Tel: 780-643-0766
Fax: 780-427-5971
lana.lougheed@gov.ab.ca
Executive Director, Data Development & Evaluation, Yvonne McFadzen
Tel: 780-427-9644
Fax: 780-422-5070
yvonne.mcfadzen@gov.ab.ca
Executive Director, Social Policy Framework Project Team, Lora Pillipow
Tel: 780-422-2816
Fax: 780-644-5240
lora.pillipow@gov.ab.ca
Director, Strategic Planning, & Reporting Branch, Tessa Ford
Tel: 780-644-5066
Fax: 780-427-1689
tessa.ford@gov.ab.ca
Director, Career & Workplace Resources, Geoff Perry
Tel: 780-422-5312
Fax: 780-422-5319
geoff.perry@gov.ab.ca
Director, Intergovernmental Relations, John Vellacott
Tel: 780-422-5996
Fax: 780-422-0274
john.vellacott@gov.ab.ca
Director, Legal Services - Sterling Place, Susan Wismer
Tel: 780-427-7207
Fax: 780-422-0912
susan.wismer@gov.ab.ca

Workplace Standards Division
Labour Building, 10808 - 99 Ave., 9th Fl., Edmonton, AB T5K 0G5
Tel: 780-644-1500
Fax: 780-422-0014
Other Communication: Employment Standards Inquiries, Toll-Free Phone: 1-877-427-3731
The Division includes occupational health & saftety & employment standards program delivery.
Assistant Deputy Minister, Andrew Sharman
Tel: 780-643-1391
Fax: 780-422-0014
andrew.sharman@gov.ab.ca
Executive Director, Occupational Health & Safety Delivery, Brent McEwan
Tel: 780-415-0603
Fax: 780-644-1508
brent.mcewan@gov.ab.ca
Executive Director, Occupational Health & Safety Policy & Program Development, Ross Nairne
Tel: 780-644-8672
Fax: 780-422-0014
ross.nairne@gov.ab.ca
Executive Director, Employment Standards Program Delivery, Eric Reitsma
Tel: 780-422-5932
Fax: 780-644-5424
eric.reitsma@gov.ab.ca
Executive Director, Workplace Policy, Legislation & Program Development, Tim Thompson
Tel: 780-415-0527
Fax: 780-422-0014
tim.thompson@gov.ab.ca
Director, Parnerships in Injury Reduction, Rob Feagan
Tel: 780-415-0608
Fax: 780-427-5698
rob.feagan@gov.ab.ca
Director, Mediation Services (Labour Mediation), Bertha Greenstein
Tel: 780-415-0530
Fax: 780-427-6327
bertha.greenstein@gov.ab.ca
Manager/Registrar of Appeals & Employment Standards, Verna Carlson
Tel: 780-644-4517
Fax: 780-644-7173
verna.carlson@gov.ab.ca

Alberta Office of the Information & Privacy Commissioner

Office of the Information & Privacy Commissioner (Edmonton), #410, 9925 - 109 St., 4th Fl., Edmonton, AB T5K 2J8
Tel: 780-422-6860
Fax: 780-422-5682
Toll-Free: 888-878-4044
generalinfo@oipc.ab.ca
www.oipc.ab.ca
Other Communication: Calgary Office, Phone: 403-297-2728, Fax: 403-297-2711

The Information & Privacy Commissioner has offices in Calgary & Edmonton. In Calgary, issues related to the Personal Information Protection Act are addressed. The Edmonton office handles issues under the Freedom of Information & Protection of Privacy Act & the Health Information Act.

Information & Privacy Commissioner, Frank Work
Tel: 780-422-6860
Fax: 780-422-5682
fwork@oipc.ab.ca

Assistant Commissioner, Freedom of Information & Protection of Privacy Act Team (FOIP), Marilyn Mun
Tel: 780-422-7617
Fax: 780-422-5682
mmun@oipc.ab.ca

Director, Legal Services, Sharon Ashmore
Tel: 780-422-6860
Fax: 780-422-5682
sashmore@oipc.ab.ca

Director, Human Resources & Finance, Donna Check
Tel: 780-422-9037
Fax: 780-644-6997
dcheck@oipc.ab.ca

Director, Adjudication Team, Christina Gauk
Tel: 780-422-6860
Fax: 780-422-5682
cgauk@oipc.ab.ca

Director, Health Information Act Team, Brian Hamilton
Tel: 780-415-6676
Fax: 780-422-5682
bhamilton@oipc.ab.ca

Director, Personal Information Protection Act Team (PIPA) - Calgary Office, Diane McLeod-McKay
Tel: 403-297-6452
Fax: 403-297-2711
dmcleod-mckay@oipc.ab.ca
AMEC Place
801 - 6 Ave. SW, 24th fl.
Calgary, AB T2P 3W2

Director, Communications, Wayne Wood
Tel: 780-644-4015
Fax: 780-422-5682
wwood@oipc.ab.ca
AMEC Place
801 - 6 Ave. SW, 24th Fl.
Calgary, AB T2P 3W2

Alberta Infrastructure

Infrastructure Building, 6950 - 113 St., Edmonton, AB T6H 5V7
Tel: 780-415-0507
Fax: 780-427-2187
Toll-Free: -310-0000
Infra.Contact.Us.m@gov.ab.ca
www.infrastructure.alberta.ca

The Ministry supports the provision of well designed, high quality public infrastructure for the people of Aberta.

Acts Administered:
Builders' Lien Act
Government Organization Act (section 3 of schedule 1; section 4(2) (f) & (g) & 9 of schedule 5; sections 4 to 8 of schedule 5; sections 1, 4, 5, 6-10, & 11-13 of schedule 11)
Hospitals Act (sections 28(1)(a), 42, & 43(h) to (j))
Land Assembly Project Area Act
Mental Health Act (section 53(1)(c))
Nursing Homes Act (sections 6, 11, 23(g) & (j), & 24(l))
Post-secondary Learning Act (sections 66(2) & (3), 67, 72(3) & (4), 73, 80, 99(1)(a) & (2) to (6))
Public Works Act
School Act (part 7, sections 195-206 & section 274)
Water, Gas & Electric Companies Act (section 4)

Deputy Minister, Ray Gilmour
Tel: 780-427-3835

Fax: 780-422-6565
ray.gilmour@gov.ab.ca

Executive Director, Human Resources Branch, Dana Thompson
Tel: 780-422-4623
Fax: 780-422-5138
dana.thompson@gov.ab.ca

Director, Human Resources Consulting Services, Linda Flynn
Tel: 780-427-7371
Fax: 780-422-5138
linda.flynn@gov.ab.ca

Director, Communications, Sharon Lopatka
Tel: 780-644-8596
Fax: 780-427-2187
sharon.lopatka@gov.ab.ca

Capital Projects Division
Infrastructure Building, 6950 - 113 St., 2nd Fl., Edmonton, AB T6H 5V7
Tel: 780-427-3700

Assistant Deputy Minister, Diane Dagleish
Tel: 780-422-7436
Fax: 780-422-7599
diane.dalgleish@gov.ab.ca
Executive Director, Health Facilities Branch, Brian Fedor
Tel: 780-422-0616
Fax: 780-638-4158
brian.fedor@gov.ab.ca
Executive Director, Technical Services Branch, Tom O'Neill
Tel: 780-422-7447
Fax: 780-422-7479
Executive Director, Project Delivery Branch, Kent Phillips
Tel: 780-422-0770
Fax: 780-422-9749
kent.phillips@gov.ab.ca
Executive Director, Learning Facilities & Alternative Procurement Branch, Guy A. Smith
Tel: 780-422-7459
Fax: 780-427-5816
guy.smith@gov.ab.ca
Executive Director, Project Services Branch, Brian Soutar
Tel: 780-422-7461
Fax: 780-422-9594
brian.soutar@gov.ab.ca
Director, Divisional Coordination Branch, Lara McClelland
Tel: 780-638-4365
Fax: 780-422-7599
lara.mcclelland@gov.ab.ca

Policy & Corporate Services Division
Twin Atria Building, 4999 - 98 Ave., 3rd Fl., Edmonton, AB T6B 2X3

Assistant Deputy Minister, Alan Humphries
Tel: 780-415-1386
Fax: 780-422-1070
alan.humphries@gov.ab.ca
Executive Director, Strategic Policy Branch, Dr. Ross Danyluk
Tel: 780-644-2663
Fax: 780-422-1070
ross.danyluk@gov.ab.ca
Executive Director & Chief Information Officer, Information Management Branch, Ken Bainey
Tel: 780-644-5114
Fax: 780-644-7028
ken.bainey@gov.ab.ca
Executive Director & Senior Financial Officer, Finance Branch, Winnie Yiu-Young
Tel: 780-427-1440
Fax: 780-643-0803
winnie.yiu-young@gov.ab.ca
Director, Strategic & Business Planning, Darcy Kolodnicki
Tel: 780-427-8427
Fax: 780-644-1100
darcy.kolodnicki@gov.ab.ca
Director, Legislative Planning & FOIP, Mark Minenko
Tel: 780-422-8223
Fax: 780-638-3497
mark.minenko@gov.ab.ca

Properties Division
Infrastructure Building, 6950 - 113 St., 3rd Fl., Edmonton, AB T6H 5V7
Tel: 780-427-3881
Fax: 780-422-1389

Assistant Deputy Minister, John Enns
Tel: 780-427-3875
Fax: 780-422-1389
john.enns@gov.ab.ca
Executive Director, Reality Services Branch, Dave Bentley
Tel: 780-422-7489
Fax: 780-415-1641
dave.bentley@gov.ab.ca
Executive Director, Property Development Branch, Rod Dushnicky
Tel: 780-422-3597
Fax: 780-422-5832
rod.dushnicky@gov.ab.ca
Executive Director, Property Management Branch - North Region, Ken Grey
Tel: 780-427-9225
Fax: 780-422-0284
ken.grey@gov.ab.ca
Executive Director, Property Management Branch - South Region, George Tribe
Tel: 780-427-2710
Fax: 780-422-0284
george.tribe@gov.ab.ca
Director, Divisional Coordination Branch, Scott Beeby
Tel: 780-422-9591
Fax: 780-427-6905
scott.beeby@gov.ab.ca

Alberta International & Intergovernmental Relations

Commerce Place, 10155 - 102 St., 12th Fl., Edmonton, AB T5J 4G8
Tel: 780-422-1510
Toll-Free: -310-0000
www.international.alberta.ca

In 2012, under Premier Alison Redford, the new Ministry of International & Intergovernmental Relations was created. International & Intergovernmental Relations coordinates Alberta's regional, national, & global relationships. The ministry also strives to facilitate trade & to attract investment. Another responsibility of the ministry is the management of Alberta's international offices. The following international offices work to promote trade & to attract investment & other interests such as culture & education: Alberta China Office; Alberta Germany Office; Alberta Hong Kong Office; Alberta Japan Office; Alberta Korea Office; Alberta Mexico Office; Alberta Shanghai Office; Alberta Taiwan Office; Alberta United Kingdom Office; & Alberta Washington, D.C. Office.

Acts Administered:
Constitution of Alberta Amendment Act, 1990
Constitutional Referendum Act
Government Organization Act
International Trade & Investment Agreements Implementation Act
Senatorial Selection Act

Minister, International & Intergovernmental Relations, Hon. Cal Dallas
Tel: 780-643-6225
Fax: 780-643-6228
Social Media: twitter.com/CalDallas, www.facebook.com/caldallasmla, ca.linkedin.com/pub/cal-dallas/39/557/281
Legislature Building
#320, 10800 - 97 Ave.
Edmonton, AB T5K2B6

Associate Minister, International & Intergovernmental Affairs, Hon. Teresa Woo-Paw
Tel: 780-415-2363
Fax: 780-422-0471
calgary.northernhills@assembly.ab.ca
Legislature Building
#130, 10800 - 97 Ave.
Edmonton, AB T5K2B6

Deputy Minister, Roxanna Benoit
Tel: 780-415-0900
Fax: 780-415-6144
roxanna.benoit@gov.ab.ca

Director, Communications, David Sands
Tel: 780-422-2524
Fax: 780-422-2635
david.sands@gov.ab.ca

Senior Manager, Ministerial Issues & Correspondence, Allison Murphy
Tel: 780-422-7296
Fax: 780-422-2635
allison.murphy@gov.ab.ca

Alberta's Representative to Asia, Gary Mar
Tel: 780-427-6079
Fax: 780-427-0699
gary.mar@gov.ab.ca

Corporate Services
Commerce Place, 10155 - 102 St., 12th Fl., Edmonton, AB T5J 4G8
Tel: 780-427-6543
Fax: 780-427-0939

Assistant Deputy Minister, Lorne Harvey
Tel: 780-422-2429
Fax: 780-427-0939
lorne.harvey@gov.ab.ca
Executive Director, Human Resource Services, Pat Connolly
Tel: 780-422-1341
Fax: 780-427-1272
pat.connolly@gov.ab.ca
Executive Director, Finance & Administration, Howard Wong
Tel: 780-427-0793
Fax: 780-427-0939
howard.wong@gov.ab.ca
Director, FOIP, Gerry Kushlyk
Tel: 780-427-9658
Fax: 780-644-4939
gerry.kushlyk@gov.ab.ca
Director, IMIT, Carol Lawrence
Tel: 780-427-0269
Fax: 780-427-4625
carol.lawrence@gov.ab.ca
Director, Corporate Planning, Carol Mayers
Tel: 780-644-1160
Fax: 780-644-4939
carol.mayers@gov.ab.ca
Director, Financial Planning & Administration, Sharon Miskiw
Tel: 780-415-1941
Fax: 780-427-0939
sharon.miskiw@gov.ab.ca
Manager, Corporate Administration, Helen Stiles
Tel: 780-422-0980
Fax: 427-093-9625
helen.stiles@gov.ab.ca

Intergovernmental Relations
Commerce Place, 10155 - 102 St., 12th Fl., Edmonton, AB T5J 4G8
Tel: 780-427-6543
Fax: 780-427-0939

Assistant Deputy Minister, Garry Pocock
Tel: 780-422-0453
Fax: 780-427-0939
garry.pocock@gov.ab.ca
Executive Director, Trade Policy - International, Daryl Hanak
Tel: 780-422-1339
Fax: 780-427-0699
daryl.hanak@gov.ab.ca
Acting Executive Director, Immigration Policy, Don Kwas
Tel: 780-422-0487
Fax: 780-427-0939
don.kwas@gov.ab.ca
Executive Director, Trade Policy - Domestic, Shawn Robbins
Tel: 780-422-1129
Fax: 780-427-0699
shawn.robbins@gov.ab.ca
Executive Director, Federal / Provincial Relations, Bruce Tait
Tel: 780-422-1127
Fax: 780-427-0939
bruce.tait@gov.ab.ca
Executive Director, Social & Economic Policy, Gordon Vincent
Tel: 780-415-6548
Fax: 780-427-0939
gordon.vincent@gov.ab.ca
Director, Federalism, Constitutional Federal / Provincial Relations, Heather Edwards
Tel: 780-644-1223
Fax: 780-427-0939
heather.edwards@gov.ab.ca
Director, Economics & Resources, Randy Fischer
Tel: 780-422-0959
Fax: 780-427-0939
randy.fischer@gov.ab.ca
Director, Canadian Intergovernmental Policy, Clean Energy & Natural Resources / Social Policy, Carla White
Tel: 780-422-0937
Fax: 780-427-0939
carla.white@gov.ab.ca

International Relations
Commerce Place, 10155 - 102 St., 4th Fl., Edmonton, AB T5J 4L6
Tel: 780-427-6543
Fax: 780-427-0699

Assistant Deputy Minister, Jason Krips
Tel: 780-422-5276
Fax: 780-427-0392
jason.krips@gov.ab.ca
Executive Director, Europe, US & International Offices, Chris Heseltine
Tel: 403-297-6377
Fax: 403-297-6168

chris.heseltine@gov.ab.ca
Standard Life Building
639 - 5 Ave. SW, 3rd Fl.
Calgary, AB T2P 0M9
Executive Director, Southern Hemisphere, Greg Jardine
Tel: 780-427-6368
Fax: 780-422-9127
greg.jardine@gov.ab.ca
Executive Director, North Asia & Business Planning, Yvette Ng
Tel: 780-422-2305
Fax: 780-427-0699
yvette.ng@gov.ab.ca
Executive Director, Advocacy, US Relations, & Mission Planning, Marvin Schneider
Tel: 780-422-2332
Fax: 780-422-5486
marvin.schneider@gov.ab.ca
Senior Director, Trade Investment, Middle East / North Africa, Norm Morrison
Tel: 780-427-6421
Fax: 780-422-9127
norm.morrison@gov.ab.ca
Senior Director, Southeast Asia & Oceania, Rahul Sharma
Tel: 780-427-6354
Fax: 780-422-9127
rahul.sharma@gov.ab.ca

International Relations - Alberta International Offices

Alberta has ten international offices. The manadate for each office is to meet the province's priorities in the region.
Alberta China Office Managing Director, Josephine Choi
josephine.choi@international.gc.ca
Other Communications: Phone: 011-86-10-5139-4272; Fax: 011-86-10-5139-4465
c/o Canadian Embassy
19 Dongzhimenwai Dajie, ChaoyangDistrict
Beijing, 100600 China
Alberta Germany Office Commercial & Administrative Assistant, Ilka Jung
ilka.jung@international.gc.ca
Other Communications: Phone: 011-49-89-2199-5741; Fax: 011-49-89-2199-5745
Alberta Germany Office, Canadian Consulate
Tal 29
Munich, 80331 Germany
Alberta Hong Kong Office Trade Director, Christopher Liu
chris.liu@alberta.org.hk
Other Communications: Phone: 011-852-2528-4729; Fax: 011-852-2529-8115
Tower Two, Admiralty Centre
#1004, 18 Harcourt Rd.
Hong Kong, China
Alberta Japan Office Manager (Acting), Norihiro Saito
norihiro.saito@altanet.or.jp
Other Communications: Phone: 011-81-3-3475-1174; Fax: 011-81-3-3470-3939
Place Canada, 3rd Fl.
3-37 Akasaka 7 - chomeMinato-ku
Tokyo, 107-0052 Japan
Alberta Korea Office Commercial Director, Won-il Chung
wonil.chung@international.gc.ca
Other Communications: Phone: 011-82-2-3783-6142; Fax: 011-82-2-3783-6147
c/o Embassy of Canada
21 Jeongdong-gil (Jeong-dong),Jung-gu
Seoul, 110-1202 South Korea
Alberta Mexico Office Managing Director, Tim Hazlett
Tel: 780-427-6679
Fax: 780-422-2091
tim.hazlett@gov.ab.ca
Alberta Taiwan Office Representative, Li-an Chen
lian.chen@international.gc.ca
Other Communications: Phone: 011-886-2-8789-2006; Fax: 011-886-2-8789-1878
Canadian Trade Office
6F, No. 1, Song Zhi Rd., ZinYi District
Taipei City, 11047 Taiwan
Alberta United Kingdom Office Managing Director, Jeffrey Sundquist
jeffrey.sundquist@international.gc.ca
Other Communications: Phone: 011-44-20-7258-6472; Fax: 011-44-20-7258-6309
Canadian High Commission, MacDonald House
1 GrosvenorSq.
London, W1K 4AB UK
Alberta Washington DC Office Director, Alberta - USA Relations, Tristan Sanregret
Tel: 202-448-6474
Fax: 202-448-6477
tristan.sanregret@gov.ab.ca
Canadian Embassy
501 Pennsylvania Ave. NW
Washington, DC 20001 USA

Alberta Justice & Solicitor General

Communications, Bowker Building, 9833 - 109 St., 3rd Fl., Edmonton, AB T5K 2E8
Tel: 780-427-2745
Toll-Free: 800-310-0000
www.justice.alberta.ca

In 2012, Premier Alison Redford announced the creation of the Ministry of Justice & Solicitor General, through the merger of Alberta Solicitor General & Public Security with Alberta Justice. The mission of Alberta Justice & Solicitor General is to provide a fiar & safe province. Its core businesses are as follows: promoting safe communities for the people of Alberta; facilitating access to justice; & providing legal & strategic services to government.

Acts Administered:
Administration of Estates Act
Administrative Procedures & Jurisdiction Act
Adult Interdependent Relationships Act
Age of Majority Act
Alberta Evidence Act (except section 9)
Alberta Human Rights Act
Alberta Personal Property Bill of Rights
Arbitration Act
Body Armour Control Act
Civil Enforcement Act
Class Proceedings Act
Commissioners for Oaths Act
Conflicts of Interest Act
Contributory Negligence Act
Corrections Act
Court of Appeal Act
Court of Queen's Bench Act
Criminal Notoriety Act
Dangerous Dogs Act
Daylight Saving Time Act
Defamation Act
Devolution of Real Property Act
Election Act
Election Finances & Contributions Disclosure Act
Electoral Boundaries Commission Act
Electoral Divisions Act
Expropriation Act (except sections 25 to 28 & 72)
Extra-provincial Enforcement of Custody Orders Act
Factors Act
Family Law Act
Fatal Accidents Act
Fatality Inquiries Act
Fisheries (Alberta) Act
Fraudulent Preferences Act
Frustrated Contracts Act
Government Organization Act, Schedule 3.1, 9, & 15
Guarantees Acknowledgment Act
Gunshot & Stab Wound Mandatory Disclosure Act
Innkeepers Act
Interjurisdictional Support Orders Act
International Child Abduction Act
International Commercial Arbitration Act
International Conventions Implementation Act
Interpretation Act
Interprovincial Subpoena Act
Judgment Interest Act
Judicature Act
Jury Act
Justice of the Peace Act
Landlord's Rights on Bankruptcy Act
Languages Act / Loi Linguistique
Legal Profession Act
Limitations Act
Lobbyists Act
Maintenance Enforcement Act
Married Women's Act
Masters & Servants Act
Maternal Tort Liability Act
Matrimonial Property Act
Missing Persons Act
Motor Vehicle Accident Claims Act (except sections 2 & 3)
Notaries Public Act
Notice to the Attorney General Act
Oaths of Office Act
Occupiers' Liability Act
Ombudsman Act
Peace Officer Act
Perpetuities Act
Personal Property Security Act (Part 5 only)
Petty Trespass Act
Police Act
Powers of Attorney Act
Proceedings Against the Crown Act
Property Rights Advocate Act
Provincial Court Act
Provincial Offences Procedure Act
Public Inquiries Act
Queen's Counsel Act
Reciprocal Enforcement of Judgments Act
Recording of Evidence Act
Regulations Act
Revised Statutes 1980 Act
Road Building Machinery Equipment Act
Safer Communities & Neighbourhoods Act
Sale of Goods Act
Security Services & Investigators Act
Statute Revision Act
Survival of Actions Act
Tort-Feasors Act
Trespass to Premises Act
Trustee Act
Unconscionable Transactions Act
Victims Restitution & Compensation Payment Act
Victims of Crime Act
Warehouse Receipts Act
Wildlife Act (Section 1.1 only)
Wills & Succession Act
Witness Security Act
Youth Justice Act

Minister, Justice; Solicitor General, Hon. Jonathan Denis
Tel: 780-427-2339
Fax: 780-422-6621
calgary.acadia@assembly.ab.ca
Legislature Building
#403, 10800 - 97 Ave.
Edmonton, AB T5K 2B6

Deputy Minister, Justice; Deputy Attorney General, Ray Bodnarek, QC
Tel: 780-427-5032
Fax: 780-422-9639
ray.bodnarek@gov.ab.ca

Deputy Minister, Public Security; Deputy Solicitor General, Jay Ramotar
Tel: 780-427-3814
Fax: 780-427-0727
jay.ramotar@gov.ab.ca
John E. Brownlee Building
10365 - 97 St., 9th Fl
Edmonton, AB T5J 3W7

Executive Director, Human Resources, Lynn Cook
Tel: 780-427-0441
Fax: 780-422-5575
lynn.cook@gov.ab.ca

Director, Issues Management, Sarah Dafoe
Tel: 780-427-5032
Fax: 780-422-9639
sarah.dafoe@gov.ab.ca

Director, Organizational Development & Effectiveness, Andrea Hayes
Tel: 780-644-2355
Fax: 780-422-1330
andrea.hayes@gov.ab.ca

Director, Communications, Dan Laville
Tel: 780-427-6154
Fax: 780-422-7363
dan.laville@gov.ab.ca

Senior Manager, Employee & Labour Relations, Glenna Quinn
Tel: 780-644-1393
Fax: 780-422-1330
glenna.quinn@gov.ab.ca

Senior Manager, Consulting Services, James Zomerman
Tel: 780-427-1140
Fax: 780-422-1330
james.zomerman@gov.ab.ca

Associated Agencies, Boards & Commissions:
• Alberta Human Rights Commission
Northern Regional Office, Standard Life Centre
#800, 10405 Jasper Ave.
Edmonton, AB T5J 4R7
Tel: 780-427-7661
Fax: 403-297-6567
Toll-free: 800-232-7215
TTY: 780-427-1597
humanrights@gov.ab.ca;
educationcommunityservices@gov.ab.ca
www.albertahumanrights.ab.ca
Other Communication: Education & Community Services, Phone: 403-297-8407
The Alberta Human Rights Act established the Alberta Human Rights Commission. In accordance with the Alberta Human Rights Act, the Commission works to foster equality & to reduce discrimination.

The address of the Alberta Human Rights Commission's Southern Regional Office is as follows: Duff Building, 525 - 11th Ave. SW., 3rd Fl., Calgary, AB T2R 0C9. The confidential inquiry line for the Southern Regional Office is 403-297-6571. TTY service is also available for persons who are deaf or hard of hearing. The TTY number in Calgary is 403-297-5639. The fax number for the Southern Regional Office is 403-297-6567.

• **Alberta Review Board**
Oxford Tower
10235 - 101 St., 11th Fl.
Edmonton, AB T5J 3E9
Tel: 780-422-5994
Fax: 780-427-1762
The Alberta Review Board is composed of nine members who are appointed by the Lieutenant Governor in Council.
The Board is responsible for making or reviewing dispositions about any accused person for whom one of the following verdicts is rendered: "unfit to stand trial" or "not criminally responsible because of mental disorder". The Alberta Review Board also determines whether a person is subject to a detention order, a conditional discharge, or an absolute discharge.

• **Criminal Injuries Review Board (CIRB)**
#1502, 10025 - 102A Ave.
Edmonton, AB T5J 2Z2
Tel: 780-427-7330
Fax: 780-427-7347
cirb@gov.ab.ca
Established in 1997, the Criminal Injuries Review Board operates as an autonomous body, in accordance with the Victims of Crime Act. Members of the Board are appointed by the Lieutenant Governor in Council, as recommended by the Minister. They review the decisions of the Director of Victims of Crime Financial Benefits Program, or his or her designate.

• **Fatality Review Board**
4070 Bowness Rd. NW
Calgary, AB T3B 3R7
Tel: 403-297-8123
Fax: 403-297-3429
The Lieutenant Governor in Council appoints the members of the Fatality Review Board. The board consists of the chief medical examiner, a physician, a lawyer, & a layperson.
The Fatality Review Board reviews deaths investigated by the Office of the Chief Medical Examiner & makes recommendations to the Minister of Justice & Solicitor General about whether or not a public fatality inquiry should take place in order to prevent similar deaths in the future.

• **Law Enforcement Review Board (LERB)**
City Centre Place
#1502, 10025 - 102A Ave.
Edmonton, AB T5J 2Z2
Tel: 780-422-9376
Fax: 780-422-4782
lerb@gov.ab.ca
Established under Alberta's Police Act, the Law Enforcement Review Board conducts its business as an independent, quasi-judicial organization. Members of the Board are appointed by the Lieutenant Governor in Council as recommended by the Minister. They are charged with the responsibility of reviewing public complaints about the conduct of police officers & appeals by police officers.

Corporate Services Division (Justice)
Bowker Building, 9833 - 109 St., 2nd Fl., Edmonton, AB T5K 2E8
The Corporate Services Division consists of the following services: business, finance, information, JIMS program support, & planning & reporting.
Assistant Deputy Minister, Bruce M. Perry
Tel: 780-427-3301
Fax: 780-422-9639
bruce.m.perry@gov.ab.ca
Executive Director, JIMS Program Support Office, Stephen Bull
Tel: 780-644-8414
Fax: 780-644-8424
stephen.bull@gov.ab.ca
Sun Life Place
10123 -99 St., 3rd Fl.
Edmonton, AB T5J 3H1
Executive Director, Information Services; Chief Information Officer, Barry Chatwin
Tel: 780-415-6067
Fax: 780-427-6002
barry.chatwin@gov.ab.ca
Executive Director, Financial Services; Senior Financial Officer, Shawkat Sabur
Tel: 780-427-4997
Fax: 780-422-1648
shawkat.sabur@gov.ab.ca
Director, Planning & Reporting Services, Mark Ham
Tel: 780-422-2640
Fax: 780-422-2829
mark.ham@gov.ab.ca
Assistant, Director Business Services, Janet Brzezicki
Tel: 780-427-6465
Fax: 780-415-2575
janet.brzezicki@gov.ab.ca

Corporate Services Division (Solicitor General)
John E. Brownlee Building, 10365 - 97 St., 9th Fl., Edmonton, AB T5J 3W7
The division consists of the following branches: financial & business services; information technology; & planning & policy.
Assistant Deputy Minister, Jim Bauer
Tel: 780-422-1033
Fax: 780-644-2537
jim.bauer@gov.ab.ca
Chief Information Officer; Executive Director, Information Technology Branch, Ayaaz Janmohamed
Tel: 780-644-3171
Fax: 780-415-2887
ayaaz.janmohamed@gov.ab.ca
#154, Millbourne Market Mall
Edmonton, AB T6K 3L6
Executive Director, Planning & Policy Branch, Rae-Ann Lajeunesse
Tel: 780-644-3010
Fax: 780-644-2763
rae-ann.lajeunesse@gov.ab.ca
Executive Director, Financial & Business Services Branch, Michael Michalski
Tel: 780-427-7516
Fax: 780-427-2789
michael.michalski@gov.ab.ca
Director, Alberta Solicitor General & Public Security Staff College, Curtis Clarke
Tel: 780-644-1778
Fax: 780-422-2854
curtis.clarke@gov.ab.ca
Alberta Solicitor General & Public Security Staff College
1568 HectorRd.
Edmonton, AB T6R 2H2

Correctional Services Division
John E. Brownlee Building, 10365 - 97 St., 10th Fl., Edmonton, AB T5J 3W7
Tel: 780-427-3440
The following branches make up the Correctional Services Division: adult centre operations; community corrections & release program; strategic services; & young offenders.
The division also oversees the New Edmonton Remand Centre, as well as the correctional services intelligence unit & the security standards, audits, & investigations unit.
Assistant Deputy Minister, Bruce V. Anderson
Tel: 780-427-3440
Fax: 780-427-5905
bruce.v.anderson@gov.ab.ca
Executive Director, Young Offender Branch, Judith Barlow
Tel: 780-422-5019
Fax: 780-422-0732
judith.barlow@gov.ab.ca
Executive Director, Strategic Services Branch, Jim Cook
Tel: 780-427-4568
Fax: 780-427-1903
jim.cook@gov.ab.ca
Executive Director, Community Corrections & Release Program Branch, Brent Doney
Tel: 780-422-5757
Fax: 780-422-3098
brent.doney@gov.ab.ca
Executive Director, Adult Centre Operations Branch, Terry Garnett
Tel: 780-427-4703
Fax: 780-427-1904
terry.garnett@gov.ab.ca
Executive Director, New Edmonton Remand Centre, Mike Tholenaer
Tel: 780-638-5298
mike.tholenaer@gov.ab.ca
New Edmonton Remand Centre
18415 - 127 St.
Edmonton, AB T6V 1B1
Director, Security Standards, Audits, & Investigations Unit, Gord Barinecutt
Tel: 780-638-5109
Fax: 780-422-0732
gord.barinecutt@gov.ab.ca
Deputy Director, Adult Centre Operations Branch, Leonard Goueffic
Tel: 780-427-3669
Fax: 780-427-1904
leonard.goueffic@gov.ab.ca
Deputy Director Inspector, Security Standards, Audits, & Investigations Unit, Michael Kinnee
Tel: 780-427-3152
Fax: 780-422-0732
New Edmonton Remand Centre
18415 - 127 St.
Edmonton, AB T6V 1B1
Deputy Director, Strategic Services Branch, Fiona Lavoy
Tel: 780-644-2092
Fax: 780-427-1903
fiona.lavoy@gov.ab.ca
Deputy Director, New Edmonton Remand Centre, Cathy Scott
Tel: 780-638-5299
cathy.scott@gov.ab.ca
New Edmonton Remand Centre
18415 - 127 St.
Edmonton, AB T6V 1B1
Administrative Assistant, Correctional Services Intelligence Unit, Carrie Grieves
Tel: 780-644-2788
Fax: 780-422-0732
carrie.grieves@gov.ab.ca

Court Services Division
Bowker Building, 9833 - 109 St., 5th Fl., Edmonton, AB T5K 2E8
Tel: 780-427-4992
Fax: 780-422-6613
The Court Services Division oversees the Court of Appeal, the Court of Queen's Bench, the Provincial Court, Law Information Centres, & Alberta Law Libraries.
Assistant Deputy Minister, Lynn Varty
Tel: 780-644-8105
Fax: 780-422-6613
lynn.varty@gov.ab.ca
Registrar, Court of Appeal, Sue Stushnoff
Tel: 780-422-7710
Fax: 780-422-7710
sue.stushnoff@gov.ab.ca
Law Courts Building South
1A Sir Winston Churchill Sq., 5th Fl.
Edmonton, AB T5J 0R2
Executive Director, Calgary Court Operations, Sharon Lepetich
Tel: 403-297-2313
Fax: 403-297-7152
sharon.lepetich@gov.ab.ca
Calgary Courts Centre
601 - 5th St, SW
Calgary, AB T2P 5P7
Executive Director, Edmonton Court Operations, Lorna Ross
Tel: 780-422-2426
Fax: 780-422-9585
lorna.ross@gov.ab.ca
Law Courts Building South
1A Sir Winston Churchill Sq., Mezzanine Fl.
Edmonton, AB T5J 0R2
Executive Director, Regional Court Operations, Ed Towers
Tel: 780-986-6903
Fax: 780-986-2429
ed.towers@gov.ab.ca
Court House
4612 - 50th St.
Leduc, AB T9E 6L1
Executive Director, Strategic Initiatives, Court Services Division Head Office, Barb Turner, Q.C.
Tel: 780-427-4995
Fax: 780-422-6613
barb.turner@gov.ab.ca
Director, Judicial Administration, Court of Queen's Bench, Bonita Dueck
Tel: 403-297-4661
Fax: 403-297-8625
bonita.dueck@gov.ab.ca
Calgary Courts Centre
601 - 5th St. SW
Calgary, AB T2P 5P7
Director, Court Technology Services, Faye Morrison
Tel: 780-427-3430
Fax: 780-422-2962
faye.morrison@gov.ab.ca
Law Courts Annex
1A Sir Winston Churchill Sq., 4th Fl.
Sherwood Park, AB T5J 0R2
Director, Alberta Law Libraries, Sonia Poulin
Tel: 780-422-1011
Fax: 780-427-0397
sonia.poulin@gov.ab.ca
Law Courts Building North
1A Sir Winston Churchill Sq., 5th Fl.
Edmonton, AB T5J 0R2
Senior Manager, Provincial Court, Basem Hage
Tel: 403-297-3681
Fax: 403-592-4896
basem.hage@gov.ab.ca
Calgary Courts Centre
601 - 5th St. SW
Calgary, AB T2P 5P7
Senior Manager, Provincial Court, Edmonton, Brenda Haynes
Tel: 780-427-7869
Fax: 780-422-9736
brenda.haynes@gov.ab.ca
Law Courts Building North

1A Sir Winston Churchill Sq., Main Fl.
Edmonton, AB T5J 0R2
Regional Manager, Regional Family Justice Services & the Provincial Court Civil Claims Mediation Program, Yogesh Gupta
Tel: 780-980-4202
Fax: 780-980-3552
yogesh.gupta@gov.ab.ca
Court House
4612 - 50th St.
Leduc, AB T9E6L1
District Manager, South Regional Court Operations, Clara Finan
Tel: 403-381-5453
Fax: 403-381-5762
clara.finan@gov.ab.ca
Court House
320 - 4 St., 1st Fl.
Lethbridge, AB T1J 1Z8
District Manager, Central Regional Court Operations, Ursula Owre
Tel: 780-980-3550
Fax: 780-980-3551
ursula.owre@gov.ab.ca
Court House
4612 - 50 St.
Leduc, AB T9E 6L1
District Manager, North Regional Court Operations, Wendy Smith
Tel: 780-538-5360
Fax: 780-538-5454
wendy.smith@gov.ab.ca
Court House
10260 - 99 St.
Grande Prairie, AB T8V 2H4
Business Manager, Regional Family Justice Services, Joan Thember
Tel: 780-980-7579
Fax: 780-980-3552
joan.thember@gov.ab.ca
Court House
4612 - 50th St.
Leduc, AB T9E 6L1
Project Manager, Calgary Court Operations, Charles Hanna
Tel: 403-297-3866
Fax: 403-297-7152
charles.hanna@gov.ab.ca
Calgary Courts Centre
601 - 5th St. SW
Calgary, AB T2P 5P7
Project Manager, Regional Court Operations, Wendy Komarnisky
Tel: 780-992-6832
Fax: 780-992-6831
wendy.komarnisky@gov.ab.ca
Court House
10504 - 100 Ave.
Fort Saskatchewan, AB T8L 3S9
Project Manager, Edmonton Court Operations, Tracey Switzer
Tel: 780-422-5210
Fax: 780-422-9585
tracey.switzer@gov.ab.ca
Law Courts Building
1A Sir Winston Churchill Sq., Mezz. Fl.
Edmonton, AB T5J 0R2
Manager, Transcript Management, Carol Clark
Tel: 403-297-7386
Fax: 403-297-7034
carol.clark@gov.ab.ca
Calgary Courts Centre
601 - 5th St. SW
Calgary, AB T2P 5P7
Manager, Provincial Court (Traffic & Civil), Linda Hawryluk
Tel: 403-427-5913
Fax: 780-427-5791
linda.hawryluk@gov.ab.ca
Law Courts Building North
1A Sir Winston Churchill Sq., Main Fl.
Edmonton, AB T5J 0R2
Manager, Provincial Court (Family & Youth), Lisa Lindquist
Tel: 403-297-3926
Fax: 403-297-3461
lisa.lindquist@gov.ab.ca
Calgary Courts Centre
601 - 5th St. SW
Calgary, AB T2P 5P7

Criminal Justice Division
Bowker Building, 9833 - 109 St., 2nd Fl., Edmonton, AB T5K 2E8

Assistant Deputy Minister, Gregory Lepp, Q.C.
Tel: 780-427-5046
Fax: 780-422-9639
greg.lepp@gov.ab.ca
Executive Director, Special Prosecutions (Edmonton), Sheila Brown, Q.C.
Tel: 780-422-0640
Fax: 780-422-1217
sheila.brown@gov.ab.ca
John E. Brownlee Building
10365 - 97 St., 5th Fl.
Edmonton, AB T5J 3W7
Executive Director, Strategic & Business Services, Peter Teasdale, Q.C.
Tel: 780-427-5050
Fax: 780-988-7639
peter.teasdale@gov.ab.ca
Executive Director, Appeals, Education, & Prosecution Policy Branch, Eric Tolppanen, Q.C.
Tel: 403-297-6005
Fax: 403-297-3453
eric.tolppanen@gov.ab.ca
Centrium Place
#300, 332 - 6th Ave. SW
Calgary, AB T2P 0B2
Assistant Executive Director, Specialized Prosecutions (Calgary), Brian Holtby, Q.C.
Tel: 403-297-8477
Fax: 403-355-4518
brian.holtby@gov.ab.ca
Centrium Place
#300, 332 - 6th Ave. SW
Calgary, AB T2P 0B2
Chief Crown Prosecutor, Edmonton, Steven Bilodeau, Q.C.
Tel: 780-422-1111
Fax: 780-422-9756
steven.bilodeau@gov.ab.ca
Chief Crown Prosecutor, Fort McMurray, Bina Border
Tel: 780-743-7285
Fax: 780-791-6387
bina.border@gov.ab.ca
Chief Crown Prosecutor, Wetaskiwin, Rodney Clark
Tel: 780-361-1206
Fax: 780-361-1468
rodney.clark@gov.ab.ca
Chief Crown Prosecutor, Lethbridge, Robert Coleman, Q.C.
Tel: 403-381-5211
Fax: 403-381-5760
robert.coleman@gov.ab.ca
Chief Crown Prosecutor, Grande Prairie, Steven Hinkley
Tel: 780-538-5338
Fax: 780-538-5500
steven.hinkley@gov.ab.ca
Chief Crown Prosecutor, Hinton, Robert Marr
Tel: 780-865-8285
Fax: 780-865-8328
robert.marr@gov.ab.ca
Chief Crown Prosecutor, Fort Saskatchewan, Jeffrey Morrison
Tel: 780-998-1269
Fax: 780-998-9599
jeffrey.morrison@gov.ab.ca
Chief Crown Prosecutor, Red Deer, Anders Quist
Tel: 403-340-5190
Fax: 403-340-7193
anders.quist@gov.ab.ca
Chief Crown Prosecutor, Calgary, Lloyd Robertson, Q.C.
Tel: 403-297-8444
Fax: 403-297-4311
lloyd.robertson@gov.ab.ca
Chief Crown Prosecutor, Medicine Hat, Ramona Robins
Tel: 403-488-4556
Fax: 403-529-3121
ramona.robins@gov.ab.ca
Chief Crown Prosecutor, St. Paul, Jeff Rudiak
Tel: 780-645-6381
Fax: 780-645-6363
jeff.rudiak@gov.ab.ca
Chief Crown Prosecutor, Peace River, David Stilwell
Tel: 780-624-6270
Fax: 780-624-6312
david.stilwell@gov.ab.ca
Project Lead, Court Case Management - JIMS Quick Wins, Tim Owens
Tel: 780-644-2932
Fax: 780-422-9747
tim.owens@gov.ab.ca
Sun Life Place
10123 - 99 St., 4th Fl.
Edmonton, AB T5J 3H1

Justice Services Division
Bowker Building, 9833 - 109 St., 2nd Fl., Edmonton, AB T5K 2E8

The Justice Services Division oversees claims & recoveries, the maintenance enforcement program, & the Medical Examiner's Office.

Executive Director, Maintenance Enforcement Program, Esther de Vos
Tel: 780-401-7500
Fax: 780-401-7575
esther.devos@gov.ab.ca
John E. Brownlee Building
10365 - 97 St., 7th Fl.
Edmonton, AB T5J 3W7
Executive Director, Claims & Recoveries, Tracy Wyrstiuk
Tel: 780-422-2610
Fax: 780-415-2200
tracy.wyrstiuk@gov.ab.ca
Sun Life Building
10123 - 99 St.
Edmonton, AB T5J 3H1
Chief Medical Examiner, Anny Sauvageau, MD
Tel: 780-427-4987
Fax: 780-422-1265
anny.sauvageau@gov.ab.ca
7007 - 116 St.
Edmonton, AB T6H 5R8
Chief Toxicologist, Graham Jones
Tel: 780-427-4987
Fax: 780-422-1265
graham.jones@gov.ab.ca
7007 - 116 St.
Edmonton, AB T6H 5R8
Director, Policy & Strategic & Legislative Issues, Donan Carrier
Tel: 780-643-6305
Fax: 780-422-9639
donan.carrier@gov.ab.ca
Director, Policy & Strategic Issues, Legal Aid, Suzanne Harbottle
Tel: 780-643-6738
Fax: 780-422-9639
suzanne.harbottle@gov.ab.ca

Legal Services Division
Bowker Building, 9833 - 109 St., 2nd Fl., Edmonton, AB T5K 2E8
Tel: 780-422-0500

The following branches are part of the Legal Services Division: divisional planning & management; government client services; & legal policy & ministerial services.

Assistant Deputy Minister, Denise Perret
Tel: 780-427-0912
Fax: 780-422-9639
denise.perret@gov.ab.ca
Executive Director, Corporate Legal Services, R. Neil Dunne, Q.C.
Tel: 780-422-8787
Fax: 780-425-0307
r.neil.dunne@gov.ab.ca
Executive Director, Departmental Legal Services Delivery, Government Client Services Branch, Barbara Mason
Tel: 780-427-9618
Fax: 780-425-0310
barb.mason@gov.ab.ca
Executive Director, Legal Services Coordination, Government Client Services Branch, Lorne Merryweather, Q.C.
Tel: 780-422-9501
Fax: 780-427-1230
lorne.merryweather@gov.ab.ca
Executive Director, Constitutional Law, Nolan Steed, Q.C.
Tel: 780-422-9653
Fax: 780-425-0307
nolan.steed@gov.ab.ca
Executive Director, Departmental Legal Services Delivery, Government Client Services Branch, Rita Sumka
Tel: 780-422-3715
Fax: 780-427-5914
rita.sumka@gov.ab.ca
Chief Legislative Counsel, Legislative Counsel Office, Peter Pagano, Q.C.
Tel: 780-427-0303
Fax: 780-422-7366
peter.pagano@gov.ab.ca
Director, Litigation, Edmonton, Susan Bercov
Tel: 780-422-9200
Fax: 780-427-1230
ken.caron@gov.ab.ca
Co-Director, Central Services, Edmonton, Mary-Kay Brook
Tel: 780-422-7720
Fax: 780-425-0310
mary-kay.brook@gov.ab.ca
Director, Divisional Planning & Management Branch, Ken Caron
Tel: 780-422-8855
Fax: 780-425-0307
ken.caron@gov.ab.ca
Co-Director, Central Services, Edmonton, Jennifer Head
Tel: 780-422-9180
Fax: 780-425-0310
jennifer.head@gov.ab.ca
Director, Aboriginal Law, Edmonton, Donald Kruk
Tel: 780-422-4850
Fax: 780-643-0852
donald.kruk@gov.ab.ca
Director, Legislative Reform, Averie McNary
Tel: 780-422-8838
Fax: 780-425-0307
averie.mcnary@gov.ab.ca

Director, Environmental Law, Darin Stepaniuk
Tel: 780-427-6121
Fax: 780-427-4343
darin.stepaniuk@gov.ab.ca
Branch Head, Energy Law, Bruce Laycock
Tel: 780-422-8085
Fax: 780-427-1871
bruce.laycock@gov.ab.ca
Counsel, Health Law, George Christidis
Tel: 780-415-2822
Fax: 780-422-2512
george.christidis@gov.ab.ca

Public Security Division
John E. Brownlee Building, 10365 - 97 St., 10th Fl., Edmonton, AB T5J 3W7
The following branches are part of the Public Security Division: commercial vehicle enforcement; fish & wildlife enforcement; law enforcement & oversight; parks enforcement; policy & program development; & sheriffs & security operations. The division is also responsible for the Alberta Serious Incident Response Team.
Assistant Deputy Minister, Bill Meade
Tel: 780-427-7952
Fax: 780-427-1194
bill.meade@gov.ab.ca
Chief Transport Officer, Commercial Vehicle Enforcement Branch, Steve Callahan
Tel: 403-340-5225
Fax: 403-340-5074
steve.callahan@gov.ab.ca
Provincial Building
4920 - 51 St., 4th Fl.
Red Deer, AB T4N 6K8
Executive Director, Sheriffs & Security Operations Branch, Vince Caleffi
Tel: 780-422-3500
Fax: 780-422-3365
vince.caleffi@gov.ab.ca
City Centre Place
10025 - 102A Ave.
Edmonton, AB T5J 2Z2
Executive Director, Policy & Program Development Branch, Kathy Collins
Tel: 780-427-7051
Fax: 780-422-4213
kathy.collins@gov.ab.ca
Executive Director, Fish & Wildlife Enforcement Branch, Deryl Empson
Tel: 780-422-0044
Fax: 780-422-9560
deryl.empson@gov.ab.ca
Great West Life Building
9920 - 108 St., 3rd Fl.
Edmonton, AB T5K 2M4
Executive Director, Law Enforcement & Oversight Branch, Gloria Ohrt
Tel: 780-427-6887
Fax: 780-427-5916
gloria.ohrt@gov.ab.ca
Executive Director, Alberta Serious Incident Response Team (ASIRT), Clif Purvis
Tel: 780-644-1487
Fax: 780-644-1497
clif.purvis@gov.ab.ca
Petroleum Plaza
9915 - 108 St., 14th Fl.
Edmonton, AB T5K 2G8
Director, Law Enforcement Standards & Audits, Matthew Barker
Tel: 780-427-6896
Fax: 780-427-5916
matthew.barker@gov.ab.ca
Director, Conservation Officer Programs, John Findlay
Tel: 780-427-8522
Fax: 780-427-1194
john.findlay@gov.ab.ca
Director, First Nations Policing, Ron Hepperle
Tel: 780-427-4774
Fax: 780-427-5916
ron.hepperle@gov.ab.ca
Director, Court Security & Prisoner Transport, Chris Kluthe
Tel: 780-427-2098
Fax: 780-422-3365
chris.kluthe@gov.ab.ca
City Centre Place
10025 - 102A Ave., 7th Fl.
Edmonton, AB T5J 2Z2
Director, Protection Services, Neil LeMay
Tel: 780-415-2216
Fax: 780-422-3365
neil.lemay@gov.ab.ca
City Centre Place
10025 - 102A Ave., 7th Fl.
Edmonton, AB T5J 2Z2
Director, Public Complaints, Contract Policing & Policing Oversight, Wendy Moshuk
Tel: 780-644-6935
Fax: 780-427-5916
wendy.moshuk@gov.ab.ca
Director, Victim Services, Julie Peacock
Tel: 780-427-6792
Fax: 780-422-4213
julie.peacock@gov.ab.ca

Safe Communities & Strategic Policy Division
University of Lethbridge Tower, #800, 10707 - 100 Ave., Edmonton, AB T5J 3M1
Tel: 780-644-5595
Fax: 780-644-5609
Assistant Deputy Minister, Kurt Sandstrom, Q.C.
Tel: 780-422-4160
Fax: 780-422-9639
kurt.sandstrom@gov.ab.ca
Bowker Building
9833 - 109 St., 2nd Fl.
Edmonton, AB T5K 2E8
Executive Director, Strategic Policy, Jeanette Fedorak
Tel: 780-422-9760
Fax: 780-644-5609
jeanette.fedorak@gov.ab.ca
Director, Stakeholder Relations & Communications, Jennifer Berglind
Tel: 780-644-5737
Fax: 780-644-5609
jennifer.berglind@gov.ab.ca
Director, Alberta Gang Reduction Strategy, Darren Caul
Tel: 780-643-1347
Fax: 780-644-5609
darren.caul@gov.ab.ca
Director, Legislative Initiatives, Kelly Hillier
Tel: 780-638-3744
Fax: 780-644-5609
kelly.hillier@gov.ab.ca
Director, Safe Communities, Gerald Lamoureux
Tel: 780-644-5626
Fax: 780-638-2870
gerald.lamoureux@gov.ab.ca
Co-Manager, Safe Communities Innovation Fund, Doug Darwish
Tel: 780-643-1346
Fax: 780-638-2870
doug.darwish@gov.ab.ca
Co-Manager, Safe Communities Innovation Fund, Bev Sochatsky
Tel: 780-643-1345
Fax: 780-638-2870
bev.sochatsky@gov.ab.ca

Alberta Municipal Affairs

Communications Branch, Commerce Place, 10155 - 102 St., 18th Fl., Edmonton, AB T5J 4L4
Tel: 780-427-2732
Fax: 780-422-1419
comments@gov.ab.ca
www.municipalaffairs.alberta.ca
In 2011, under Premier Redford, the Ministry of Municipal Affairs took on the responsibilities of the former Ministry of Housing & Urban Affairs.
Alberta's Ministry of Municipal Affairs is engaged in the following activities: assisting Alberta's municipalities in the provision of well-managed, accountable local government; managing municipal & library system boards; administering a safety system for the construction & maintenance of equipment & buildings; ensuring safe, affordable, & sustainable housing for Albertans; & assisting urban communities.
Acts Administered:
Alberta Housing Act
City of Lloydminster Act
Emergency Management Act
Government Organization Act
Libraries Act
Local Authorities Election Act
Municipal Government Act
Parks Towns Act
Public Highways Development Act
Safety Codes Act
Social Care Facilities Licensing Act
Special Areas Act

Minister, Municipal Affairs, Hon. Doug Griffiths
Tel: 780-427-3744
Fax: 780-422-9550
Social Media: www.twitter.com/griffmla, www.facebook.com/Griffs4ABsFuture?sk=app_53267368995
Legislature Building
#104, 10800 - 97 Ave.
Edmonton, AB T5K 2B6

Associate Minister, Hon. Greg Weadick
Tel: 780-422-5627
Fax: 780-422-8983

Deputy Minister, Paul Whittaker
Tel: 780-427-4826
Fax: 780-422-9561
paul.whittaker@gov.ab.ca

Chief of Staff, Tim Morrison
Tel: 780-427-3744
Fax: 780-422-9550
tim.morrison@gov.ab.ca

Coordinator, Scheduling, Camille Hauck
Tel: 780-427-3744
Fax: 780-422-9550
camille.hauck@gov.ab.ca

Executive Director, Human Resource Services, Sandra Kraatz
Tel: 780-422-8681
Fax: 780-422-0214
sandra.kraatz@gov.ab.ca
HSBC Building
10055 - 106 St., 5th Fl.
Edmonton, AB T5J 1G3

Director, Communications, Cameron Traynor
Tel: 780-415-4758
Fax: 780-422-1419
cameron.traynor@gov.ab.ca

Director & Solicitor, Legal Services, Bill Nugent, Q.C.
Tel: 780-422-8795
Fax: 780-427-0996
bill.nugent@gov.ab.ca
Commerce Place
10155 - 102 St., 18th Fl.
Edmonton, AB T5J 4L4

Manager, Executive Correspondence, Chuck Costello
Tel: 780-422-9338
Fax: 780-422-1419
chuck.costello@gov.ab.ca

Associated Agencies, Boards & Commissions:
• Alberta Emergency Management Agency (AEMA)
c/o Alberta Municipal Affairs, Communications Branch
10155 - 102 St., 18th Fl.
Edmonton, AB T5J 4L4
Tel: 780-422-9000
Fax: 780-644-1044
Toll-free: -310-0000
aema@gov.ab.ca
www.aema.alberta.ca
Other Communication: Alberta Emergency Management Agency Response Readiness Centre, Phone: 1-866-618-2362
The Alberta Emergency Management Agency coordinates organizations, such as government, municipalities, & first responders, which are involved in the prevention, preparedness, & response to emergencies.
• Capital Region Board
Bell Tower
#1405, 10104 - 103 Ave.
Edmonton, AB T5J 0H8
Tel: 780-638-6000
Fax: 780-638-6009
www.capitalregionboard.ab.ca
The Government of Alberta established the Capital Region Board in 2008. The Board consists of members from twenty-four participating municipalities. They serve on the following committees: land use; transit; Geographic Information Services; housing; & governance.
The following are the municipalities of the Capital Region Board: Town of Beaumont; Town of Bon Accord; Town of Bruderheim; Town of Calmar; Town of Devon; City of Edmonton; City of Fort Saskatchewan; Town of Gibbons; Lamont County; Town of Lamont; City of Leduc; Leduc County; Town of Legal; Town of Morinville; Parkland County; Town of Redwater; City of St. Albert; City of Spruce Grove; Town of Stony Plain; Strathcona County; Sturgeon County; Village of Thorsby; Village of Wabamun; & the Village of Warburg.
• Gunn Centre
PO Box 130
Gunn, AB T0E 1A0
Tel: 780-967-2221
Fax: 780-967-3494
Since 1941, the Gunn Centre has offered services to disadvantaged men. The Centre provides temporary accommodation & support services to help men reestablish their lives.

• Municipal Government Board (MGB)
Commerce Place
10155 - 102 St., 15th Fl.
Edmonton, AB T5J 4L4
Tel: 780-427-4864
Fax: 780-427-0986
Toll-free: -310-0000
mgbmail@gov.ab.ca
www.municipalaffairs.alberta.ca
Operating as an independent & impartial body, the Municipal Government Board decides upon certain appeals & disputes from the Municipal Government Act. Examples of issues dealt with by the Municipal Government Board are as follows: disputes between municipalities; annexation matters; linear property assessment complaints; & appeals about equalized assessment & subdivisions.

• Safety Codes Council (SCC)
#1000, 10665 Jasper Ave. NW
Edmonton, AB T5J 3S9
Tel: 780-413-0099
Fax: 780-424-5134
Toll-free: 888-413-0099
sccinfo@safetycodes.ab.ca
www.safetycodes.ab.ca
Other Communication: Toll-Free Fax: 1-888-424-5134
The Safety Codes Council is a corporation that supports the Ministry of Municipal Affairs' administration of the Safety Codes Act. The Council has the following business units: Accreditation & Appeals; Administration; Certification & Policy; Electronic Business Solutions; & Training.

• Special Areas Board
Special Areas Board Administration
212 - 2nd Ave. West
PO Box 820
Hanna, AB T0J 1P0
Tel: 403-854-5600
Fax: 403-854-5527
specarea@telus.net
www.specialareas.ab.ca
Other Communication: Hanna, Phone: 403-854-5625; Oyen, Phone: 403-664-3618, Fax: 403-664-3320; Consort, Phone: 403-577-3523, Fax: 403-577-2446; Youngstown, Phone: 403-779-3733
The Special Areas Board is responsible for the management of public land in Alberta's three Special Areas. The Board also provides municipal services to eastern Alberta's dryland region. The following are examples of programs & services offered by the Special Areas Board: protective & emergency services; construction & maintenance of local roads; provision of water services; management of public land; operation & maintenance of Special Areas recreational parks & community pastures; conservation programming; agricultural development; & economic development programs.

Corporate Strategic Services Division
Commerce Place, 10155 - 102 St., 18th Fl., Edmonton, AB T5J 4L4
Assistant Deputy Minister, Anthony Lemphers
Tel: 780-415-9099
Fax: 780-422-4923
anthony.lemphers@gov.ab.ca
Executive Director & Senior Financial Officer, Financial Services, Dan Balderston
Tel: 780-644-8098
Fax: 780-422-5840
dan.balderston@gov.ab.ca
Executive Director, Corporate Planning & Policy, Indira Breitkreuz
Tel: 780-422-7317
Fax: 780-422-4923
indira.breitkreuz@gov.ab.ca
Director, Information Technology, Heather Cox
Tel: 780-427-6097
Fax: 780-422-0776
heather.cox@gov.ab.ca
Director, Public Library Services, Diana Davidson
Tel: 780-415-0284
Fax: 780-415-8594
diana.davidson@gov.ab.ca
Director, Information Management, Legislative & Administrative Services, Wilma Sisk
Tel: 780-422-8834
Fax: 780-643-1090
wilma.sisk@gov.ab.ca

Housing & Urban Affairs
44 Capital Boulevard, 10044 - 108 St. 3rd Fl., Edmonton, AB T5J 5E6
Tel: 780-422-0122
Coordinator, Correspondence Management Unit, Dianne Singh
Tel: 780-422-8422
Fax: 780-644-5796
dianne.singh@gov.ab.ca
Program Advisor, Kelly Santarossa
Tel: 780-422-8240
Fax: 780-644-5796
kelly.santarossa@gov.ab.ca
#301, 7015 Macleod Trail South
Calgary, AB T2H 2K6
ARTS Administrator, Sherry Wynnyk
Tel: 780-644-5284
Fax: 780-644-5796
sherry.wynnyk@gov.ab.ca

Housing Development & Operations
44 Capital Boulevard, 10044 - 108 St. 3rd Fl., Edmonton, AB T5J 5E6
Tel: 780-643-1020
Fax: 780-422-8462
Other Communication: Rural & Native Mortgage Portfolio, Phone: 780-427-6897
Assistant Deputy Minister, Mike Leathwood
Tel: 780-638-3383
Fax: 780-422-8462
mike.leathwood@gov.ab.ca
Executive Director, Housing Development, Don Squire
Tel: 780-427-5786
Fax: 780-422-5124
don.squire@gov.ab.ca
Manager, Program Delivery, Walter Tauber
Tel: 780-427-8137
Fax: 780-422-5124
walter.tauber@gov.ab.ca
Director, Financial Monitoring & Contract Administration, Philip Henke
Tel: 780-422-8157
Fax: 780-422-5124
philip.henke@gov.ab.ca
Director, Financial Support, Peggy Kornega
Tel: 780-422-8255
Fax: 780-427-0418
peggy.kornega@gov.ab.ca
Administrator, Rent Supplement Program, Karen Butkowski
Tel: 780-422-8202
Fax: 780-422-8551
karen.butkowski@gov.ab.ca
Manager, North Operations, Bill Draper
Tel: 780-427-5785
Fax: 780-422-8551
bill.draper@gov.ab.ca
Manager, South Operations, David Staines
Tel: 780-297-5773
Fax: 780-297-6138
david.staines@gov.ab.ca
Manager, Special Operations, Lana Braidot
Tel: 780-415-1237
Fax: 780-415-9345
lana.braidot@gov.ab.ca

Local Government Services Division
Commerce Place, 10155 - 102 St., 17th Fl., Edmonton, AB T5J 4L4
Assistant Deputy Minister, Michael Merritt
Tel: 780-427-9660
Fax: 780-427-0453
michael.merritt@gov.ab.ca
Executive Director, Municipal Services Branch, Gary Sandberg
Tel: 780-422-8034
Fax: 780-420-1016
gary.sandberg@gov.ab.ca
Executive Director, Assessment Services Branch, Steve White
Tel: 780-422-1377
Fax: 780-422-3110
steve.white@gov.ab.ca
Director, Strategic Planning & Program Integration, James Acheson
Tel: 780-422-8908
Fax: 780-427-0453
james.acheson@gov.ab.ca
Director, Education Tax & Assessment Advisory, Lynda Downey
Tel: 780-422-8313
Fax: 780-422-3110
lynda.downey@gov.ab.ca
Director, Legislative Projects, Erin Foster-O'Riordan
Tel: 780-644-5684
Fax: 780-644-4941
safety.services@gov.ab.ca
Director, Assessment Audit, Brian Ferguson
Tel: 780-422-8396
Fax: 780-422-3110
brian.ferguson@gov.ab.ca
Director, Capacity Building, Colin Doupe
Tel: 780-427-9290
Fax: 780-420-1016
colin.doupe@gov.ab.ca
Director, Municipal Collaboration, Theresa Ostrum
Tel: 780-422-8053
Fax: 780-420-1016
theresa.ostrum@gov.ab.ca
Director, Linear Property Assessment, Chris Risling
Tel: 780-422-8414
Fax: 780-422-3110
chris.risling@gov.ab.ca
Executive Director, Grants & Education Property Tax Branch, Janice Romanyshyn
Tel: 780-415-0833
Fax: 780-422-9133
janice.romanyshyn@gov.ab.ca
Director, Planning & Policy Advisory, Bill Symonds
Tel: 780-422-8355
Fax: 780-422-8624
bill.symonds@gov.ab.ca
Director, Regulated Assessment Policy, Sheila Young
Tel: 780-422-8078
Fax: 780-644-4941
sheila.young@gov.ab.ca
Executive Director, Major Legislative Projects & Strategic Planning, Brandy Cox
Tel: 780-415-9786
Fax: 780-644-6941
brandy.cox@gov.ab.ca

Public Safety Division
Commerce Place, 10155 - 102 St., 16th Fl., Edmonton, AB T5J 4L4
Assistant Deputy Minister, Ivan Moore
Tel: 780-638-3245
Fax: 780-427-2538
ivan.moore@gov.ab.ca
Executive Director, Safety Services Branch, Chris Tye
Tel: 780-644-5691
Fax: 780-427-8686
safety.services@gov.ab.ca
Director, Legislation & Strategic Projects, Joan Armstrong
Tel: 780-427-2279
Fax: 780-427-2538
joan.armstrong@gov.ab.ca
Director, Risk Management & Finance, Diane McLean
Tel: 780-427-6133
Fax: 780-427-2538
diane.mclean@gov.ab.ca
Director, Safety Assurance Services, Alex Morrison
Tel: 780-644-1010
Fax: 403-297-4174
safety.services@gov.ab.ca
Director, Codes & Standards, James Orr
Tel: 780-644-1010
Fax: 780-427-8686
safety.services@gov.ab.ca
Director, Field Technical Services, Randy Paulson
Tel: 780-644-1010
Fax: 780-427-8686
safety.services@gov.ab.ca
Manager, Operational Support Services, Don Rebus
Tel: 780-644-1010
Fax: 780-427-8686
safety.services@gov.ab.ca
Project Coordinator, Tank Site Remediation Program, Stephen Hoare
Tel: 780-415-8665
Fax: 780-415-8664
stephen.hoare@gov.ab.ca

Strategic Services
44 Capital Boulevard, 10044 - 108 St. 3rd Fl., Edmonton, AB T5J 5E6
Tel: 780-638-3736
Assistant Deputy Minister, Bruce McDonald
Tel: 780-422-3188
Fax: 780-422-5124
bruce.mcdonald@gov.ab.ca
Chief Information Officer & Executive Director, Information Management & Technology, Dean Lussier
Tel: 780-427-1751
Fax: 780-427-0418
dean.lussier@gov.ab.ca
Executive Director & Senior Financial Officer, Finance & Administrative Services, Robert Lee
Tel: 780-643-1324
Fax: 780-427-0418
robert.lee@gov.ab.ca
Director, Strategic Planning & Legislative Program Services, Cynthia Evans
Tel: 780-422-8306
Fax: 780-422-5124
cynthia.evans@gov.ab.ca
Director, Strategic Policy & Urban Affairs, Patti Giberson
Tel: 780-644-2609
Fax: 780-422-5124
patti.giberson@gov.ab.ca
Director, Financial Services, Trevor Mireau
Tel: 780-643-1655
Fax: 780-427-0418
trevor.mireau@gov.ab.ca

Director, Financial Planning, Christine Oness
Tel: 780-427-2925
Fax: 780-427-0418
christine.oness@gov.ab.ca
Senior Manager, Federal - Provincial Relations, Kildy Yuen
Tel: 780-422-8133
Fax: 780-422-5124
kildy.yuen@gov.ab.ca
Advisor, Privacy & Information, Holly Simpson
Tel: 780-638-2979
Fax: 780-427-0418
holly.simpson@gov.ab.ca

Alberta Office of the Ombudsman

Canadian Western Bank Building, #2800, 10303 Jasper Ave. NW, 28th Fl., Edmonton, AB T5J 5C3

Tel: 780-427-2756
Fax: 780-427-2759
Toll-Free: 888-455-2756
info@ombudsman.ab.ca
www.ombudsman.ab.ca
Secondary Address: #2560, 801 - 6 Ave. SW
Calgary Regional Office
Calgary, AB T2P 3W2
Fax: 403-297-5121

As an Officer of the Legislative Assembly of Alberta, the Alberta Ombudsman reports directly to the Legislative Assembly. The Ombudsman carries out his role under the authority of Alberta's Ombudsman Act.
The Alberta Ombudsman operates independently from the Alberta government to investigate & respond to written complaints about unfair treatment from Alberta government authorities, designated professional organizations. The Ombudsman also handles the patient concerns resolution process of Alberta Health Services.

Ombudsman, Peter Hourihan

Director, Corporate Services, Suzanne Richford
Tel: 780-415-2510
Fax: 780-427-2759

Team Leader & Senior Investigator, Ombudsman Alberta, Edmonton Office, Diann Bowes
Tel: 780-427-2756
Fax: 780-427-2759

Team Leader & Senior Investigator, Ombudsman Alberta, Calgary Office, Joanne Roper
Tel: 403-297-6185
Fax: 403-297-5121

Alberta Public Affairs Bureau (PAB)

Park Plaza, 10611 - 98 Ave., 6th Fl., Edmonton, AB T5K 2P7

Tel: 780-427-2754
Fax: 780-422-4168
Toll-Free: -310-0000
www.publicaffairs.alberta.ca

Communications are provided by the Public Affairs Bureau to support Alberta's government ministries. The Public Affairs Bureau provides information about government policies & programs to Albertans. The Bureau is also responsible for coordinating communications during public emergencies.

Managing Director, Lee Funke
Tel: 780-644-5655
Fax: 780-427-1010
lee.funke@gov.ab.ca

Senior Manager, Communications, Joanne Rosnau
Tel: 780-644-8106
Fax: 780-427-1010
joanne.rosnau@gov.ab.ca

Officer, Public Affairs, Chelsey Chapman
Tel: 780-644-5300
Fax: 780-427-1010
chelsey.chapman@gov.ab.ca

Alberta Seniors

Communications, Standard Life Centre, 10405 Jasper Ave., 3rd Fl., Edmonton, AB T5J 4R7

Tel: 780-415-9950
Fax: 780-644-1227
Toll-Free: 866-477-8589
seniors.communications@gov.ab.ca
www.seniors.alberta.ca

The main responsibility of Alberta's Ministry of Seniors is the development & delivery of programs & services to Albertans. The Ministry is divided into the following divisions: Community Support Programs & Strategic Planning; Seniors Services; & Disability Supports.
The Community Support Programs & Strategic Planning Division oversees the following programs & services: the provision of direct guardianship services for dependent adults; the administration of the Protection for Persons in Care Act; monitoring the quality of services for the Persons with Developmental Disabilities program; monitoring accommodation standards for long-term care & supportive living facilities; & administration of the Seniors Lodge, Senior Self-Contained, & Unique Homes programs.
The Senior Services Division oversees programs such as the Alberta Seniors Benefit, the Special Needs Assistance for Seniors program, dental & optical programs, & the Education Property Tax Assistance program. The Division also provides information through the Seniors Information Line, Seniors Information Services Offices, & publications such as the annual "Senior Programs & Services Information Guide".
The Disability Supports Division administers the Alberta Aids to Daily Living program, as well as the Assured Income for the Severely Handicapped program. Community supports are also provided to persons with special needs, through programs such as the Fetal Alcohol Spectrum Disorder initiative & the Alberta Brain Injury initiative.

Minister, Seniors, Hon. George VanderBurg
Tel: 780-415-9550
Fax: 780-415-9411
Social Media:
www.facebook.com/George-VanderBurg/195871217330
Legislature Building
#227, 10800 - 97 Ave.
Edmonton, AB T5K 2B6

Deputy Minister, Robert Bhatia
Tel: 780-415-1357
Fax: 780-415-1686
robert.bhatia@gov.ab.ca

Executive Director, Human Resource Services, Dawn White
Tel: 780-415-8964
Fax: 780-415-2003
dawn.white@gov.ab.ca

Director, Communications, Michael Shields
Tel: 780-644-1108
Fax: 780-644-1227
michael.shields@gov.ab.ca

Senior Manager, Human Resource Programs & Strategies, Cheryl Beck
Tel: 780-644-1818
Fax: 780-415-2003
cheryl.beck@gov.ab.ca

Senior Manager, Consulting Services, Alana Chwaklinski
Tel: 780-643-1076
Fax: 780-415-2003
alana.chwaklinski@gov.ab.ca

Parliamentary Assistant, Alana DeLong
Tel: 780-415-9459
Fax: 780-427-1835

Administrator, Ministerial Correspondence, Claire Puyaoan
Tel: 780-644-1236
Fax: 780-415-1686
claire.puyaoan@gov.ab.ca

Senior Consultant, Occupational Health & Safety, Derrick Richards
Tel: 403-340-5740
Fax: 403-340-7140
derrick.richards@gov.ab.ca

Community Support Programs & Strategic Planning Division

Standard Life Centre, 10405 Jasper Ave., 3rd Fl., Edmonton, T5J 4R7

Tel: 780-415-2466
Fax: 780-427-1689

Assistant Deputy Minister, Brenda Lee Doyle
Tel: 780-427-2593
Fax: 780-427-1689
brendalee.doyle@gov.ab.ca
Executive Director, Persons with Developmental Disabilities Program, Jim Menzies
Tel: 780-427-1216
Fax: 780-427-1220
jim.menzies@gov.ab.ca
Peace Hills Trust Tower
10011 - 109 St., 4th Fl.
Edmonton, AB T5J3S8
Director, Protection for Persons in Care, Edith Baraniecki
Tel: 780-427-0552
Fax: 780-415-8611
edith.baraniecki@gov.ab.ca
Executive Co-Lead, Persons with Developmental Disabilities Implementation Team, Ruth Hofer
Tel: 780-427-7200
Fax: 780-427-1220
ruth.hofer@gov.ab.ca
Manager, Strategic Support & Issues Management, Lois Flynn
Tel: 780-415-9498
Fax: 780-427-1689
lois.flynn@gov.ab.ca
Public Guardian Representative, Office of the Public Guardian, Lincoln Mar
Tel: 780-638-3501
Fax: 780-422-6051
lincoln.mar@gov.ab.ca

Disability Supports Division

Milner Building, 10040 - 104 St., 12th Fl., Edmonton, AB T5J 0Z2

Assistant Deputy Minister, Donna Ludvigsen
Tel: 780-427-1245
Fax: 780-427-5148
donna.ludvigsen@gov.ab.ca
Executive Director, Delivery Services, Dale Beesley
Tel: 780-644-4731
Fax: 780-644-3299
dale.beesley@gov.ab.ca
Executive Director, Policy, Innovation, & Partnerships, Sherri Wilson
Tel: 780-644-9910
Fax: 780-644-2315
sherri.wilson@gov.ab.ca
Director, Health Related Supports, Marianne Baird
Tel: 780-422-6985
Fax: 780-422-0968
marianne.baird@gov.ab.ca
Manager, Financial Services, Jackie Lee
Tel: 780-644-5179
Fax: 780-644-3299
jackie.lee@gov.ab.ca
Manager, Divisional Coordination & Issues Management Unit, Rosa Spadavecchia
Tel: 780-427-2065
Fax: 780-427-5148
rosa.spadavecchia@gov.ab.ca

Seniors Services Division

Standard Life Centre, 10405 Jasper Ave., 6th Fl., Edmonton, AB T5J 4R7

Assistant Deputy Minister, Chi Loo
Tel: 780-422-3179
Fax: 780-644-7602
chi.loo@gov.ab.ca
Director, Seniors Financial Assistance Branch, John Cabral
Tel: 780-422-7270
Fax: 780-644-1602
john.cabral@gov.ab.ca
Director, Seniors Policy & Planning, Sarah Carr
Tel: 780-644-2975
Fax: 780-644-7602
sarah.carr@gov.ab.ca
Director, Client & Information Services Branch, Denine Ritchie
Tel: 780-415-0845
Fax: 780-422-8762
denine.ritchie@gov.ab.ca

Strategic Services Division

Standard Life Centre, 10405 Jasper Ave., 2nd Fl., Edmonton, AB T5J 4R7

Assistant Deputy Minister & Senior Financial Officer, Carol Ann Kushlyk
Tel: 780-422-8550
Fax: 780-644-2524
carolann.kushlyk@gov.ab.ca
Executive Director & CIO, Corporate Services Branch, Kevin Molcak
Tel: 780-644-1125
Fax: 780-427-9376
kevin.molcak@gov.ab.ca
Executive Director, Supportive Living & Long Term Care Branch, Marjory Sutherland
Tel: 780-422-8219
Fax: 780-644-5499
marjory.sutherland@gov.ab.ca
Director, Financial Planning & Reporting, Financial Planning Branch, Bill Cruikshank
Tel: 780-644-1858
Fax: 780-644-2524
bill.cruikshank@gov.ab.ca
Director, Financial Services & Accountability Branch, Mahmud Dhala
Tel: 780-427-2190
Fax: 780-644-2524
mahmud.dhala@gov.ab.ca

Senior Manager, Corporate Planning, Policy, & Research Branch, Glen Hughes
Tel: 780-427-1985
Fax: 780-427-1689
glen.hughes@gov.ab.ca

Service Alberta

Government of Alberta, PO Box 1333, Edmonton, AB T5J 2N2
Tel: 780-427-4088
Toll-Free: -310-0000
service.alberta@gov.ab.ca
www.servicealberta.ca
Other Communication: Consumer Information, E-mail: cs@gov.ab.ca; Corporate Registry, E-mail: cr@gov.ab.ca; Land Titles, E-mail: lto@gov.ab.ca; Landlords & Tenants, E-mail: rta@gov.ab.ca

The Ministry of Service Alberta offers information, services, & products to Albertans. The following are examples of the ministry's services: delivery of shared services to ministries, such as printing documents & technical support; management of the government's vehicle fleet; administration of the Freedom of Information & Protection of Privacy legislation; provision of licensing & registry services; & enforcement of high standards of consumer protection.

Acts Administered:
Agricultural & Recreational Land Ownership Act
Builders' Lien Act
Business Corporations Act
Cemeteries Act
Cemetery Companies Act
Change of Name Act
Charitable Fundraising Act
Companies Act
Condominium Property Act
Cooperatives Act
Debtors' Assistance Act
Dower Act
Electronic Transactions Act
Fair Trading Act
Franchises Act
Freedom of Information & Protection of Privacy Act
Funeral Services Act
Garage Keepers' Lien Act
Government Organization Act
Land Titles Act
Law of Property Act
Marriage Act
Mobile Home Sites Tenancies Act
Motor Vehicle Accident Claims Act
Partnership Act
Personal Information Protection Act
Personal Property Security Act
Possessory Liens Act
Queen's Printer Act
Real Estate Act
Religious Societies' Land Act
Residential Tenancies Act
Societies Act
Surveys Act
Traffic Safety Act
Vital Statistics Act
Warehousemen's Lien Act
Woodmen's Lien Act

Minister, Service Alberta, Hon. Manmeet S. Bhullar
Tel: 780-422-6880
Fax: 780-422-2496
Social Media: www.twitter.com/manmeetsbhullar, www.facebook.com/manmeetbhullarmla
Legislature Building
#103, 10800 - 97 Ave.
Edmonton, AB T5K2B6

Associate Minister of Accountability, Transparency & Transformation, Hon. Don Scott
Tel: 780-415-1356
Fax: 780-415-1711

Deputy Minister, Doug Lynkowski
Tel: 780-427-1990
Fax: 780-427-4999
doug.lynkowski@gov.ab.ca
Telus Plaza South
10020 - 100 St., 29th Fl.
Edmonton, AB T5J 0N3

Chief of Staff, Emir Mehinagic
Tel: 780-422-6880
Fax: 780-422-2496
emir.mehinagic@gov.ab.ca

Executive Director, Human Resource Services, Gerry Jacubo
Tel: 780-427-8352
Fax: 780-427-4999
gerry.jacubo@gov.ab.ca

Director, Communications, Gerald Kastendieck
Tel: 780-427-6699
Fax: 780-415-9816
gerald.kastendieck@gov.ab.ca

Manager, Ministry Advisory Services, Diane Carter
Tel: 780-644-4524
Fax: 780-422-0956
diane.carter@gov.ab.ca

Associated Agencies, Boards & Commissions:

• Alberta Funeral Services Regulatory Board (AFSRB)
11810 Kingsway Ave.
Edmonton, AB T5G 0X5
Tel: 780-452-6130
Fax: 780-452-6085
Toll-free: 800-563-4652
office@afsrb.ab.ca; complaints@afsrb.ab.ca; education@afsrb.ab.ca
www.afsrb.ab.ca
In 1992, the Alberta Funeral Services Regulatory Board was established under the Licensing of Trades & Businesses Act & the Funeral Services Business Licensing Regulation. The Board provides the following services: establishing educational standards; licensing pre-need salespeople, funeral directors, embalmers, funeral businesses, & crematories; monitoring performance standards; & investigating consumer complaints.

• Alberta Motor Vehicle Industry Council (AMVIC)
#303, 9945 - 50 St.
Edmonton, AB T6A 0L4
Tel: 780-466-1140
Fax: 780-462-0633
www.amvic.org
Other Communication: Investigations, Toll-Free Phone: 1-877-279-8200; Licensing, Toll-Free Phone: 1-877-979-8100
The Alberta Motor Vehicle Industry Council is responsible for the administration & enforcement of automotive industry regulations, under Alberta's Fair Trading Act.

• Money Mentors
Quikcard Centre
#175, 17010 - 102rd Ave.
Edmonton, AB T5S 1K7
Fax: 780-423-2791
Toll-free: 888-294-0076
info@moneymentors.ca
www.moneymentors.ca
Formerly known as Credit Counselling Services of Alberta, Money Mentors is a not-for-profit credit counselling & money coaching organization. It serves Albertans by educating them about personal money management & offering alternatives for those who encounter financial difficulties.

• Real Estate Council of Alberta (RECA)
#350, 4954 Richard Rd. SW
Calgary, AB T3E 6L1
Tel: 403-228-2954
Fax: 403-228-3065
Toll-free: 888-425-2754
info@reca.ca
www.reca.ca
Operating under the Real Estate Act of Alberta, the Real Estate Council of Alberta is responsible for the regulation of professionals in the real estate, real estate appraisal, & mortgage broker industries. The Council is made up of the following committees: Audit, Finance, Governance, Hearings, & the Education Ad Hoc Committee.

Business Services

Telus Plaza South, 10020 - 100 St., 29th Fl., Edmonton, AB T5J 0N3
Toll-Free: -310-0000
Other Communication: Consumer Contact Centre, Phone: 1-877-427-4088

Assistant Deputy Minister, Bruce McDonald
Tel: 780-415-2272
Fax: 780-422-0956
bruce.mcdonald@gov.ab.ca

Executive Director, Procurement Services, Bill Moulton
Tel: 780-427-4120
Fax: 780-422-9672
bill.moulton@gov.ab.ca

Executive Director, Client Services Operations, Liane Stangenberg
Tel: 780-644-2316
Fax: 780-415-6091
liane.stangenberg@gov.ab.ca

Director, Business Operations, Derek Thomson
Tel: 780-643-1464
Fax: 780-415-2722
derek.thomson@gov.ab.ca

Consumer Services

Telus Plaza South, 10020 - 100 St., 29th Fl., Edmonton, AB T5J 0N3
Toll-Free: -310-0000
Other Communication: Consumer Contact Centre, Phone: 1-877-427-4088

Consumer Services administers & enforces consumer protection legislation, in support of a fair & effective marketplace for Albertans. The Office of the Utilities Consumer Advocate is also the responsibility of Consumer Services. It ensures that consumers have the information & protection required for the electricity & natural gas markets in Alberta.

Acting Assistant Deputy Minister, Steve Burford
Tel: 780-644-4527
Fax: 780-644-1015
steve.burford@gov.ab.ca

Assistant Deputy Minister, Shared Network Services, Brian Fischer
Tel: 780-427-2214
Fax: 780-644-1015
brian.fischer@gov.ab.ca

Executive Director, Shared Network Services, Dennis Mudryk
Tel: 780-427-6005
Fax: 780-638-5947
dennis.mudryk@gov.ab.ca

Executive Director, Consumer Services Programs, Rob Phillips
Tel: 780-422-8177
Fax: 780-427-3033
rob.phillips@gov.ab.ca

Director, Information Technology, Kim Smadis
Tel: 780-415-6010
Fax: 780-427-2959
kim.smadis@gov.ab.ca

Manager, Regulatory Operations, Office of the Utilities Consumer Advocate, Barry Shymanski
Tel: 780-644-5477
Fax: 780-644-5129
barry.shymanski@gov.ab.ca
TD Tower
10088 - 102 Ave., 17th Fl.
Edmonton, AB T5J 2Z1

Enterprise Services

Telus Plaza South, 10020 - 100 St., 29th Fl., Edmonton, AB T5J 0N3

Enterprise Services oversees information & communication technology infrastructure services to government departments, plus some agencies, boards, & commissions. The Alberta government's Chief Information Officer Council also receives secretariat support from Enterprise Services.

Assistant Deputy Minister, Kate Rozmahel
Tel: 780-644-4529
Fax: 780-422-0956
kate.rozmahel@gov.ab.ca

Executive Director, ICT Service Delivery & Support, Ron Boehm
Tel: 780-644-2536
Fax: 780-422-0956
ron.boehm@gov.ab.ca

Director, Office of the Corporate Chief Information Officer, Steve French
Tel: 780-427-1466
steve.french@gov.ab.ca

Executive Director, Corporate Architecture & Planning, Rob Godin
Tel: 780-644-4541
Fax: 780-427-0238
rob.godin@gov.ab.ca

Executive Director, Enterprise Technology Infrastructure Services, Dale Huhtala
Tel: 780-427-2295
dale.huhtala@gov.ab.ca

Executive Director, Strategic Infrastructure Projects, Andrew Mak
Tel: 780-644-2014
andrew.mak@gov.ab.ca

Information Services

Telus Plaza South, 10020 - 100 St., 29th Fl., Edmonton, AB T5J 0N3

Assistant Deputy Minister, Cathryn Landreth
Tel: 780-427-0057
Fax: 780-422-0956
cathryn.landreth@gov.ab.ca

Executive Director, Service Delivery, Ray Keroack
Tel: 780-427-0254
Fax: 780-422-8287
ray.keroack@gov.ab.ca

Executive Director, Records & Information Management Branch, Laurel Frank
Tel: 780-422-0267
Fax: 780-422-0818
laurel.frank@gov.ab.ca

Director, Audit & Investigation Branch, Brian Breakey
Tel: 780-422-8008

Fax: 780-644-3536
brian.breakey@gov.ab.ca
Director, Policy & Governance, Cheryl Naundorf
Tel: 780-427-6369
Fax: 780-427-1120
cheryl.naundorf@gov.ab.ca
Director, FOIP & Legislative Services, Di Nugent
Tel: 780-422-7840
Fax: 780-427-1120
di.nugent@gov.ab.ca
Manager, Library Services, Linda R. Scott
Tel: 780-415-8344
Fax: 780-427-8287
linda.r.scott@gov.ab.ca

Registry Services
Telus Plaza South, 10020 - 100 St., 29th Fl., Edmonton, AB T5J 0N3
Registries Services is responsible for ensuring that Albertans have access to registry information & services for motor vehicles, personal property, vital statistics, licensing, & businesses & non-profit groups. Land title services are provided under the Torrens Land Registration System. The Special Investigations Unit of Registries Services offers court certificates, facial recognition analysis, & support to the Ministries of Infrastructure & Transportation.
Assistant Deputy Minister, Janet Skinner
Tel: 780-427-4095
Fax: 780-644-1015
janet.skinner@gov.ab.ca
Executive Director, Motor Vehicles & Agent Support, Doug Morrison
Tel: 780-415-2847
Fax: 780-644-1040
doug.morrison@gov.ab.ca
Executive Director, Land Titles, Vital Statistics, & Corporate Registry, Les Speakman
Tel: 780-427-0108
Fax: 780-422-3105
les.speakman@gov.ab.ca

Strategic Planning & Financial Services
Commerce Place, 10155 - 102 St., 13th Fl., Edmonton, AB T5J 4G8
Tel: 780-422-8545
Executive Director & Senior Financial Officer, Strategic Planning & Financial Services, Althea Hutchinson
Tel: 780-415-8975
Fax: 780-427-0307
althea.hutchinson@gov.ab.ca
Director, Planning & Performance Measurement, Chrenan Borradaile
Tel: 780-427-0282
Fax: 780-427-0307
chrenan.borradaile@gov.ab.ca
Director, Financial Reporting & Policy, Rene Mella
Tel: 780-427-1882
Fax: 780-427-0307
rene.mella@gov.ab.ca
Manager, Shared Services Administration & Special Projects, Gerry Boily
Tel: 780-427-6622
Fax: 780-427-0307
gerry.boily@gov.ab.ca
Manager, Financial Planning & Analysis, Jennifer Gleave
Tel: 780-422-8167
Fax: 780-427-0307
jennifer.gleave@gov.ab.ca

Alberta Tourism, Parks, & Recreation

Communications Branch, Commerce Place, 10155 - 102 St., 6th Fl., Edmonton, AB T5J 4L6
Tel: 780-644-5589
TPR.Communications@gov.ab.ca
www.tpr.alberta.ca
TTY: 780-427-9999
Other Communication: TTY Toll-Free: 1-800-232-7215
Alberta's Ministry of Tourism, Parks, & Recreation was established in 2008.
The Ministry works to develop the tourism industry in Alberta by facilitating the profitability & sustainability of both existing & new tourism operations, positioning land for tourism, creating a positive policy environment, assisting with regulatory processes, & promoting tourism investment.
The Ministry of Tourism, Parks, & Recreation is also responsible for Alberta's network of parks & protected areas. These areas offer Albertans & tourists opportunities to appreciate the province's natural heritage & to participate in educational & recreational activities.
Promoting recreation & sports for healthy living & athletic excellence is another goal of the Ministry of Tourism, Parks, & Recreation. The government ministry works with recreation & sport associations & provides funding for recreation facilities across the province to achieve this goal.

Acts Administered:
Alberta Sport, Recreation, Parks, & Wildlife Foundation Act
Government Organization Act
Provincial Parks Act
Provincial Parks Amendment Act
Recreation Development Act
Travel Alberta Act
Wilderness Areas, Ecological Reserves, Natural Areas, & Heritage Rangelands Act
Willmore Wilderness Park Act

Minister, Tourism, Parks, & Recreation, Hon. Christine Cusanelli
Tel: 780-427-4928
Fax: 780-427-0188
Legislature Building
#229, 10800 - 97 Ave.
Edmonton, AB T5K 2B6

Deputy Minister, Brad Pickering
Tel: 780-644-5139
Fax: 780-644-5145
brad.pickering@gov.ab.ca

Acting Director, Communications, Katrina Bluetchen
Tel: 780-427-8761
Fax: 780-644-5586
katrina.bluetchen@gov.ab.ca

Director, Issues Management, Paul Leeder
Tel: 780-415-1098
Fax: 780-644-5145
paul.leeder@gov.ab.ca

Coordinator, Correspondence, Rubena Hassan
Tel: 780-644-5139
Fax: 780-644-5145
rubena.hassan@gov.ab.ca

Associated Agencies, Boards & Commissions:
• Alberta Sport, Recreation, Parks, & Wildlife Foundation (ASRPWF)
Standard Life Centre
#903, 10405 Jasper Ave., 9th Fl.
Edmonton, AB T5J 4R7
Tel: 780-415-1167
Fax: 780-415-0308
Toll-free: -310-0000
www.cd.gov.ab.ca/asrpwf
Supported by the Alberta Lottery Fund, the Alberta Sport, Recreation, Parks, & Wildlife Foundation reports to the Minister of Alberta Tourism, Parks, & Recreation. The Foundation's objectives are provided in the Alberta, Sport, Recreation, Parks, & Wildlife Foundation Act.
The Alberta Sport, Recreation, Parks, & Wildlife Foundation develops partnerships with sport, recreation, active living, & parks & wildlife programs, in order to encourage & enhance athletic excellence, active lifestyles, & the conservation of natural areas. The Foundation funds a variety of organizations throughout Alberta, such as Alberta Active Living agencies, the Percy Page Centre, sport & recreation associations, & sport development centres.
• Travel Alberta
2500
Edmonton, AB T5J 2Z4
Tel: 780-427-4321
Toll-free: 800-252-3782
travelinfo@TravelAlberta.com
www.travelalberta.com
Travel Alberta is a marketing organization that is engaged in the following activities: promotion of Alberta as a tourist destination; administration of the Tourism Information System; management of the Travel Alberta Contact / Distribution Centre; & the operation of a network of Visitor Information Centres.

Parks Division
Oxbridge Place, 9820 - 106 St., 2nd Fl., Edmonton, AB T5K 2J6
Tel: 780-427-3582
Fax: 780-427-5980
Toll-Free: 866-427-3582
Assistant Deputy Minister, Graham Statt
Tel: 780-644-4948
Fax: 780-427-5980
graham.statt@gov.ab.ca
Executive Director, Program Coordination, Parks & Protected Areas Program, Steve Donelon
Tel: 403-678-5500
Fax: 403-678-5505
steve.donelon@gov.ab.ca
Director, Policy & Strategic Support, Brian Kelly
Tel: 780-427-9382
Fax: 780-427-5980
brian.kelly@gov.ab.ca
Director, Land Management, Archie Landals
Tel: 780-427-9470
Fax: 780-427-5980
archie.landals@gov.ab.ca
Director, Parks Finance Section, Dale Schinkel
Tel: 780-427-8224
Fax: 780-427-5980
dale.schinkel@gov.ab.ca
Director, Operations, Learning, & Stewardship, Mark Storie
Tel: 780-427-9383
Fax: 780-427-5980
mark.storie@gov.ab.ca

Recreation & Sport Development Division
Standard Life Centre, 10405 Jasper Ave., 9th Fl., Edmonton, AB T5J 4R7
Assistant Deputy Minister, Tim Moorhouse
Tel: 780-422-3305
Fax: 780-415-0308
tim.moorhouse@gov.ab.ca
Executive Director, Sport Excellence Branch, Lloyd Bentz
Tel: 780-415-0263
Fax: 780-415-0308
lloyd.bentz@gov.ab.ca
Director, Marketing & Provincial Sport Branch, Dennis Allen
Tel: 403-297-2729
Fax: 403-297-6669
dennis.allen@gov.ab.ca
Director, Physical Activity Branch, Roger Kramers
Tel: 780-415-0272
Fax: 780-427-5140
roger.kramers@gov.ab.ca
Director, Outdoor Development Branch, Bernie MacDonald
Tel: 780-415-0268
Fax: 780-427-5140
bernie.macdonald@gov.ab.ca
Director, High Performance Sport Branch, Scott Fraser
Tel: 780-422-8310
Fax: 780-427-5140
scott.c.fraser@gov.ab.ca

Special Projects Division
Commerce Place, 10155 - 102 St., 6th Fl., Edmonton, AB T5J 4L6
Assistant Deputy Minister, Bob Scott
Tel: 780-415-0892
Fax: 780-427-0778
bob.scott@gov.ab.ca

Strategic Corporate Services Division
Commerce Place, 10155 - 102 St., Edmonton, AB T5J 4L6
Tel: 780-415-0257
Chief Information Officer & Executive Director, Information Management & Technology Services, Mark Diner
Tel: 780-427-1075
Fax: 780-644-1286
mark.diner@gov.ab.ca
Executive Director & Senior Financial Officer, Financial Services Branch, Cameron Steenveld
Tel: 780-644-2714
Fax: 780-644-5586
cameron.steenveld@gov.ab.ca

Tourism Division
Commerce Place, 10155 - 102 St., 6th Fl., Edmonton, AB T5J 4L6
Tel: 780-427-3164
Assistant Deputy Minister, Reegan McCullough
Tel: 780-643-1997
Fax: 780-427-6454
reegan.mccullough@gov.ab.ca
Director, Tourism Services Branch, Elizabeth Kuhnel
Tel: 780-427-6743
Fax: 780-415-0896
elizabeth.kuhnel@gov.ab.ca
Director, Tourism Business Development, Ressearch, & Investment Branch, Moe Rehemtulla
Tel: 780-427-6689
Fax: 780-427-6454
moe.rehemtulla@gov.ab.ca
Manager, Contact Centre & Tourism Information System, Robin Luini
Tel: 780-427-4965
Fax: 780-415-0896
robin.luini@gov.ab.ca
Manager, Visitor Information Centres & Support Services, Noel Ma
Tel: 780-427-6512
Fax: 780-415-0896
noel.ma@gov.ab.ca
Manager, Tourism Research, Sid Nieuwenhuis
Tel: 780-422-1058
Fax: 780-422-1759
sid.nieuwenhuis@gov.ab.ca

Alberta Transportation

Twin Atria Building, 4999 - 98 Jasper Ave., 2nd Fl., Edmonton, AB T6B 2X3
Tel: 780-427-2731
Toll-Free: -310-0000
Trans.Contact.Us.m@gov.ab.ca
www.transportation.alberta.ca

Alberta's Ministry of Transportation consists of the Department of Transportation & the Transportation Safety Board. The Ministry strives to provide a safe & sustainable transportation system & water management infrastructure throughout the province.
Key activities of the Department are as follows: leading the planning, construction & preservation of highways across Alberta; offering information & education about transportation safety services & enforcement programs; designing, building, & maintaining the water management infrastructure in the province; managing grant programs to assist municipalities; & representing Alberta at all levels of government to ensure regulatory harmonization.

Acts Administered:
Dangerous Goods Transportation & Handling Act
Government Organization Act (jointly with other ministries)
Highways Development & Protection Act
Provincial Parks Act (jointly with other ministries)
Railway (Alberta) Act
Regional Airports Authorities Act
Traffic Safety Act
Water Act (jointly with other ministries)
Water, Gas, & Electric Companies Act (jointly with other ministries)

Associated Agencies, Boards & Commissions:
• Transportation Safety Board
North Office, Twin Atria Building
4999 - 98 Ave., Main Fl.
Edmonton, AB T6B 2X3
Tel: 780-427-7178
Fax: 780-422-9739
Toll-free: -310-0000
www.atsb.alberta.ca
The Alberta Transportation Safety Board reports to the Minister of Transportation, through the Chair. The Board's members are chosen through a public recruitment process.
The Board hears appeals about licence suspensions & vehicle seizures. Its decisions are made in accordance with the Traffic Safety Act & the Railway (Alberta) Act.

Policy & Corporate Services Division
Twin Atria Building, 4999 - 98 Ave., 3rd Fl., Edmonton, AB T6B 2X3
The Policy & Corporate Services Division provides the following services: strategic policy, legislative planning, FOIP, finance, & information management.
Executive Director, Strategic Policy Branch, Arthur Arruda
Tel: 780-415-8730
Fax: 780-422-1070
arthur.arruda@gov.ab.ca
Executive Director & Senior Financial Officer, Finance Branch, Winnie Yiu-Young
Tel: 780-427-1440
Fax: 780-415-1219
winnie.yiu-young@gov.ab.ca
Director, Transportation Development & Coordination, Jeff Paruk
Tel: 780-415-2562
Fax: 780-422-1070
jeff.paruk@gov.ab.ca
Project Manager, Records & Information Management Initiative, Dennis Mitchell
Tel: 780-427-3900
Fax: 780-427-6905
dennis.mitchell@gov.ab.ca

Transportation & Civil Engineering Division
Twin Atria Building, 4999 - 98 Ave., 2nd Fl., Edmonton, AB T6B 2X3
Tel: 780-422-2184
Fax: 780-415-1268
The Transportation & Civil Engineering Division carries out the following functions: planning & delivering highway construction & rehabilitation projects & special projects throughout the province; managing highway maintenance activities; constructing & upgrading management facilities; & managing grant programs, such as the Canada-Alberta Municipal Rural Infrastructure Fund.

Assistant Deputy Minister, Bruno Zutautas
Tel: 780-422-2184
Fax: 780-415-1268
bruno.zutautas@gov.ab.ca
Executive Director, Planning Branch, Jim Der
Tel: 780-415-1300
Fax: 780-422-2027
jim.der@gov.ab.ca
Executive Director, Technical Standards Branch, Moh Lali
Tel: 780-415-1083
Fax: 780-422-2027
moh.lali@gov.ab.ca
Executive Director, Major Capital Projects Branch, Tom Loo
Tel: 780-415-4876
Fax: 780-415-0475
tom.loo@gov.ab.ca
Executive Director, Program Management Branch, Ranjit Tharmalingam
Tel: 780-422-7672
Fax: 780-427-0783
ranjit.tharmalingam@gov.ab.ca
Executive Director, Divisional Services, Gordon Zack
Tel: 780-427-4548
Fax: 780-415-1268
gordon.zack@gov.ab.ca
Director & Chair, Strategic Planning, Louise Nelson
Tel: 780-427-2595
Fax: 780-422-1070
louise.nelson@gov.ab.ca

Transportation Safety Services Division
Twin Atria Building, 4999 - 98 Ave., Main Fl., Edmonton, AB T6B 2X3
Tel: 780-427-8901
Fax: 780-415-0782
Toll-Free: 800-666-5036
The Transportation Safety Services Division is responsible for the following services: monitoring the motor carrier industry & provincial railways; driver licensing & driver's licence enforcement; driver, vehicle, & road safety programs; impaired driving intervention programs; & dangerous goods control.
Assistant Deputy Minister, Shaun Hammond
Tel: 780-415-1146
Fax: 780-415-0782
shaun.hammond@gov.ab.ca
Chief Transport Officer, Commercial Vehicle Enforcement Branch, Steve Callahan
Tel: 403-340-5225
Fax: 403-340-5074
steve.callahan@gov.ab.ca
Executive Director, Office of Traffic Safety, Jeanette Espie
Tel: 780-427-6588
Fax: 780-422-3682
jeanette.espie@gov.ab.ca
Executive Director, Driver Programs, Mitch Fuhr
Tel: 780-644-4576
Fax: 780-427-0833
mitch.fuhr@gov.ab.ca
Director, Transport Engineering, Kim Durdle
Tel: 403-340-5189
Fax: 403-340-5092
kim.durdle@gov.ab.ca
Director, Dangerous Goods, Vehicle, & Rail Safety Branch, Terry Wallace
Tel: 780-427-7508
Fax: 780-422-9193
terry.wallace@gov.ab.ca

Alberta Treasury Board & Finance

Oxbridge Place, 9820 - 106 St., 5th Fl., Edmonton, AB T5K 2J6
Tel: 780-415-4519
Toll-Free: -310-000
www.finance.alberta.ca

Alberta's Treasury Board manages government spending by carrying out the following responsibilities: leading the provincial government's capital planning process; providing advice & analysis on costs & capital spending; identifying alternatives for financing capital projects; & ensuring accounting standards & financial reporting. The ministry also oversees economic development & corporate human resources.
Alberta Finance offers financial, economic, & fiscal policy advice to government. The Ministry also provides tax & regulatory administration to support strong government finances & to ensure that Alberta has a productive & competitive economy.
The two ministries were combined in 2012 by Premier Redford.

Acts Administered:
Alberta Capital Finance Authority Act
Alberta Competitiveness Act
Alberta Corporate Tax Act
Alberta Economic Development Authority Act
Alberta Heritage Savings Trust Fund Act
Alberta Income Tax Act
Alberta Investment Management Corporation (AIMCo) Act
Alberta Personal Income Tax Act
Alberta Stock Exchange Restructuring Act
Alberta Taxpayer Protection Act
Alberta Treasury Branches Act
Appropriation Act
Civil Service Garnishee Act
Credit Union Act
Electric Utilities Act
Employment Pension Plans Act
Farm Credit Stability Act
Financial Administration Act
Financial Consumers Act
Financial Sector Statutes Amendment Act, 2003
Fiscal Responsibility Act
Fuel Tax Act
Government Accountability Act
Government Fees & Charges Review Act
Government Organization Act
Hospitals Act
Income Trusts Liability Act
Insurance Act
Loan & Trust Corporations Act
Members of the Legislative Assembly Pension Plan Act
Municipal Debentures Act
Northern Alberta Development Council Act
Office of Statistics & Information Act
Pension Fund Act
Public Sector Pension Plans Act
Public Service Act
Securities Act
Securities Transfer Act
Teachers' Pension Plans Act
Tobacco Tax Act
Tourism Levy Act
Unclaimed Personal Property & Vested Property Act

President, Treasury Board; Minister, Finance, Hon. Doug Horner
Tel: 780-415-4855
Fax: 780-415-4853
sprucegrove.stalbert@assembly.ab.ca
Social Media: www.twitter.com/hornerforab, www.facebook.com/DougHornerForAlberta, www.linkedin.com/pub/doug-horner/30/310/206
Legislature Building
#423, 10800 - 97 Ave.
Edmonton, AB T5K 2B6

Associate Minister, Hon. Kyle Fawcett
Tel: 780-643-9094
Fax: 780-643-9099
Social Media: www.twitter.com/kyleMLA, www.facebook.com/pages/Kyle-Fawcett/201067916433

Deputy Minister, Annette Trimbee
Tel: 780-415-4515
Fax: 780-427-6596
annette.trimbee@gov.ab.ca

Executive Director, Human Resource Services, Rodney Yaremchuk
Tel: 780-415-9109
Fax: 780-422-0421
rodney.yaremchuk@gov.ab.ca

Director, Communications, Robyn Cochrane
Tel: 780-415-1541
Fax: 780-427-1147
robyn.cochrane@gov.ab.ca

Director, Information Technology Services, Caleb Kwok
Tel: 780-427-8812
Fax: 780-422-2164
caleb.kwok@gov.ab.ca

Manager, Finance & Administration, Reema Puri
Tel: 780-643-0613
reema.puri@gov.ab.ca

Associated Agencies, Boards & Commissions:
• Alberta Automobile Insurance Rate Board
Canadian Western Bank Place
#2440, 10303 Jasper Ave.
Edmonton, AB T5J 3N6
Tel: 780-427-5428
Fax: 780-638-4254
Toll-free: -310-0000
airb@gov.ab.ca
www.airb.alberta.ca
The Automobile Insurance Rate Board is engaged in the following activities: setting premiums for basic coverage; monitoring premiums for optional coverage; & reviewing & approving rating programs for new insurers.
• Alberta Capital Finance Authority (ACFA)
Canadian Western Bank Place
#2450, 10303 Jasper Ave.
Edmonton, AB T5J 3N6
Tel: 780-427-9711
Fax: 780-422-2175
webacfa@gov.ab.ca
www.acfa.gov.ab.ca
Other Communication: Rate Information Line: 780-422-2632
Established in 1956, the Alberta Capital Finance Authority is a non-profit corporation that acts under the authority of the Alberta

Capital Finance Authority Act (Alberta). Flexible funding for capital projects is provided by the provincial authority to Alberta's municipalities, school boards, & other local entities, at interest rates based on the cost of its borrowings.

• Alberta Investment Management Corporation (AIMCo)
1100 - 10830 Jasper Ave.
Edmonton, AB T5J 2B3
Tel: 780-392-3600
inquiries@aimco.alberta.ca
www.aimco.alberta.ca
Other Communication: Toronto Office, Phone: 416-304-1160; Media Inquiries, Phone: 403-538-5645
Established as a Crown corporation in 2008, the Alberta Investment Management Corporation provides investment management services for a group of Alberta public sector funds.

• Alberta Pensions Services Corporation (APS)
5103 Windermere Blvd. SW
Edmonton, AB T6W 0S9
Tel: 780-427-2782
Toll-free: 800-661-8198
memberservices@apsc.ca; employerservices@apsc.ca; pay@apsc.ca
www.apsc.ca
Alberta Pensions Services Corporation was incorporated in 1995, under the Business Corporations Act of Alberta. The Crown Corporation administers seven statutory pension plans & two supplementary retirement plans.

• Alberta Securities Commission (ASC)
#600, 250 - 5th St. SW
Calgary, AB T2P 0R4
Tel: 403-297-6454
Fax: 403-297-6156
Toll-free: 877-355-0585
inquiries@asc.ca; media@asc.ca; complaints@asc.ca
www.albertasecurities.com
Other Communication: Commission Proceedings, E-mail: registrar@asc.ca; Investor Education, E-mail: checkfirst@asc.ca; Records & File Requests, E-mail: records.requests@asc.ca
The Alberta Securities Commission is a regulatory agency that is responsible for the administration of the Alberta Securities Act. The capital market in Alberta is regulated by the Alberta Securities Commission to protect investors.
The Alberta Securities Commission also works as a member of the Canadian Securities Administrators to coordinate & improve the regulation of Canada's capital markets.

• Alberta Teachers' Retirement Fund (ATRF)
Barnett House
11010 - 142 St. NW
Edmonton, AB T5N 2R1
Tel: 780-451-4166
Fax: 780-452-3547
Toll-free: 800-661-9582
info@atrf.com; member@atrf.com; pensioner@atrf.com
www.atrf.com
Other Communication: Employer Inquiries, E-mail: helpdesk@atrf.com
Established under the Teachers' Pension Plans Act, the Alberta Teachers' Retirement Fund has administered a pension plan for teachers employed in Alberta's school jurisdictions & charter schools since 1939.
The independent corporation also administers the Private School Teachers' Pension Plan for teachers at Alberta's private schools that have joined the plan.

• ATB Financial
9888 Jasper Ave.
Edmonton, AB T5J 1P1
Tel: 403-245-8110
Toll-free: 800-332-8383
www.atb.com
Other Communication: Privacy, Phone: 1-866-858-4175; Online Banking, Phone: 1-866-282-4932; Lost or stolen ATB Financail products, Phone: 1-800-224-3979
Established in 1938, ATB Financial has been a provincial Crown corporation since 1997. As the largest Alberta-based financial institution, ATB Financial serves people across Alberta through 165 branches, 131 agencies, & a Customer Contact Centre.

• Credit Union Deposit Guarantee Corporation (CUDGC)
#2000, 10104 - 103 St.
Edmonton, AB T5J 0H8
Tel: 780-428-6680
Fax: 780-428-7571
Toll-free: 800-661-0351
mail@cudgc.ab.ca
www.cudgc.ab.ca
Established untder the Alberta Credit Union Act, the Credit Union Deposit Guarantee Corporation is a provincial corporation. The Corporation is administered by a Board of Directors, who are appointed by the Lieutenant Governor in Council of Alberta. The Credit Union Deposit Guarantee Corporation guarantees deposits held with Alberta's credit unions & works to ensure that credit unions employ sound business practices.

• Locked-in Account Advisory Committee (LAAC)
Financial Hardship Unlocking
PO Box 982
Edmonton, AB T5J 2L8
Tel: 780-427-8322
fhu@gov.ab.ca; employment.pensions@gov.ab.ca
The Locked-in Account Advisory Committee was created under the Government Organization Act. The advisory agency is accountable to the Minister of Finance & Enterprise.
The Committee provides guidance regarding applicants to the Superintendent of Pensions who request acccess to locked-in accounts.

Corporate Internal Audit Services
Oxbridge Place, 9820 - 106th St., 4th Fl., Edmonton, AB T5K 2J6
Tel: 780-644-7185
Corporate Internal Audit Services works with Alberta's government ministries to identify areas for improvement. Following the performance of internal audits, recommendations are provided to better operations & fiscal management.

Chief Internal Auditor, Dan Stadlwieser
Tel: 780-644-4736
Fax: 780-644-4761
dan.stadlwieser@gov.ab.ca

Executive Director, Internal Audit Operations, Kathleen Gora
Tel: 780-644-5271
Fax: 780-644-4761
kathleen.gora@gov.ab.ca

Director, Enterprise Audits, Enterprise Audits & Professional Practice, Nimal Chellappah
Tel: 780-422-0065
Fax: 780-644-4761
nimal.chellappah@gov.ab.ca

Director, Professional Practice, Enterprise Audits & Professional Practice, Jonn Robertson
Tel: 780-644-3438
Fax: 780-644-4761
jonn.robertson@gov.ab.ca

Budget & Fiscal Planning
Terrace Building, 9515 - 107 St., 4th Fl., Edmonton, AB T5K 2C3

Assistant Deputy Minister, Stephen LeClair
Tel: 780-427-8417
Fax: 780-427-1296
stephen.leclair@gov.ab.ca

Chief Economist & Executive Director, Economics, Demography, & Public Finance, Katherine White
Tel: 780-643-0980
Fax: 780-426-3951
katherine.white@gov.ab.ca

Executive Director, Tax Policy, Nancy Cuelenaere
Tel: 780-427-8893
Fax: 780-426-4564
nancy.cuelenaere@gov.ab.ca

Executive Director, Budget Planning & Integration, James Forrest
Tel: 780-427-8752
Fax: 780-426-4564
james.forrest@gov.ab.ca

Director, Office of Statistics & Information (OSI), Joanne Sasges
Tel: 780-427-9648
Fax: 780-422-5070
joanne.sasges@gov.ab.ca

Financial Sector Regulation & Policy (FSRP)
Terrace Building, 9515 - 107 St., 4th Fl., Edmonton, AB T5K 2C3

Asst. Deputy Minister, Financial Sector Regulation & Policy & Superintendent, Financial Institutions, Insurance, & Pensions, Mark Prefontaine
Tel: 780-427-9722
Fax: 780-427-1636
mark.prefontaine@gov.ab.ca

Executive Director, Pension Policy, Ellen Nygaard
Tel: 780-415-0513
Fax: 780-644-7771
ellen.nygaard@gov.ab.ca

Director, Public Sector Pension Policy, Lorna Mathews
Tel: 780-427-8896
Fax: 780-644-7771
lorna.mathews@gov.ab.ca

Administrator, Financial Hardship Unlocking Program, James Skitsko
Tel: 780-415-9225
Fax: 780-644-7279
james.skitsko@gov.ab.ca

Office of the Controller
Oxbridge Place, 9820 - 106 St., 4th Fl., Edmonton, AB T5K 2J6
The Office of the Controller handles the following responsibilities: overseeing financial management & control policies; ensuring government accounting standards; reporting financial information; & planning.

Acting Controller/Executive Director, Financial Accounting & Standards, Gisele Simard
Tel: 780-415-9253
Fax: 780-422-2164
gisele.simard@gov.ab.ca

Executive Director, Business Process Reengineering Office, Nilam Jetha
Tel: 780-643-0772
Fax: 780-422-2164
nilam.jetha@gov.ab.ca

Acting Executive Director, Performance Planning & Reporting, Scott Kashuba
Tel: 780-644-7133
Fax: 780-422-2164
scott.kashuba@gov.ab.ca

Executive Director, Agency Governance Secretariat, Anita Lunden
Tel: 780-643-1465
Fax: 780-422-2164
anita.lunden@gov.ab.ca

Spending Management & Planning
Oxbridge Place, 9820 - 106 St., 5th Fl., Edmonton, AB T5K 2J6
The Spending Management & Planning division works with Alberta Finance to monitor the fiscal activities of Alberta's ministries. The division offers recommendations about the budgeting, spending proposals, & spending of the provincial ministries.

Assistant Deputy Minister, Aaron Neumeyer
Tel: 780-644-8078
Fax: 780-644-3907
aaron.neumeyer@gov.ab.ca

Executive Director, SMP 2, Darren Hedley
Tel: 780-415-4733
Fax: 780-644-3907
darren.hedley@gov.ab.ca

Executive Director, SMP 3, Greg Findlay
Tel: 780-415-9258
Fax: 780-644-3907
greg.findlay@gov.ab.ca

Executive Director, SMP 4, Dale Fulford
Tel: 780-427-8736
Fax: 780-644-3907
dale.fulford@gov.ab.ca

Director, Coordination & Integration, Wallace Currie
Tel: 780-427-8702
Fax: 780-644-3907
wallace.currie@gov.ab.ca

Strategic & Business Services
Terrace Building, 9515 - 107 St., 4th Fl., Edmonton, AB T5K 2C3
Tel: 780-427-3052

Assistant Deputy Minister, Darwin Bozek
Tel: 780-415-9718
Fax: 780-427-1296
darwin.bozek@gov.ab.ca

Executive Director, Financial Services, Richard Isaak
Tel: 780-415-9149
Fax: 780-422-2163
richard.isaak@gov.ab.ca

Director, Corporate Technology Services, Neil Bracegirdle
Tel: 780-415-9166
Fax: 780-415-6416
neil.bracegirdle@gov.ab.ca

Director, Administrative & Information Services, Roger Mariner
Tel: 780-415-9180
Fax: 780-422-7235
roger.mariner@gov.ab.ca

Director, Corporate Planning Services, Dave Olson
Tel: 780-644-2614
Fax: 780-638-3128
dave.olson@gov.ab.ca

Strategic Capital Planning
Oxbridge Place, 9820 - 106 St., 5th Fl., Edmonton, AB T5K 2J6
The Strategic Capital Planning division is responsible for the development & management of the Capital Plan. Advice & analysis are provided about planning & capital spending. Strategic Capital Planning also has responsibility for the Air Transportation Service. The Service serves government departments, boards, & agencies by providing air travel services.

Assistant Deputy Minister, Neill McQuay
Tel: 780-415-1076
Fax: 780-440-8719
neill.mcquay@gov.ab.ca

Executive Director, Capital Planning & Spending, Tim Cartmell
Tel: 780-427-8898
Fax: 780-644-3906
tim.cartmell@gov.ab.ca

Executive Director, Alternative Capital Financing, Faye McCann
Tel: 780-644-8774

Fax: 780-644-3906
faye.mccann@gov.ab.ca
Director, Air Transportation Service, Rob Madden
Tel: 780-427-7341
Fax: 780-422-1232
rob.madden@gov.ab.ca

Tax & Revenue Administration
Sir Frederick W. Haultain Building, 9811 - 109 St., 2nd Fl., Edmonton, AB T5K 2L5
Tel: 780-427-3044

Assistant Deputy Minister, Ian Ayton
Tel: 780-427-9403
Fax: 780-422-0899
ian.ayton@gov.ab.ca
Executive Director, Audit, Melissa Banks
Tel: 780-644-4212
Fax: 780-422-2090
melissa.banks@gov.ab.ca
Executive Director, Revenue Operations, Kent Heine
Tel: 780-644-4257
Fax: 780-644-4921
kent.heine@gov.ab.ca
Executive Director, Tax Services, Angelina Leung
Tel: 780-644-4064
Fax: 780-427-5074
angelina.leung@gov.ab.ca
Acting Executive Director, Business Technology Management, Patrick Marshall
Tel: 780-644-4164
Fax: 780-644-5016
patrick.marshall@gov.ab.ca
Director, Strategic & Client Services, Irene Chan
Tel: 780-644-4171
Fax: 780-422-0899
irene.chan@gov.ab.ca

Treasury & Risk Management
Terrace Building, 9515 - 107 St., 3rd Fl., Edmonton, AB T5K 2C3
Assistant Deputy Minister, Treasury & Risk Management, Rod Matheson
Tel: 780-415-0752
Fax: 780-427-2435
rod.matheson@gov.ab.ca
Executive Director, Risk Management & Insurance, Mark Day
Tel: 780-644-4045
Fax: 780-422-5271
mark.day@gov.ab.ca
Executive Director, Capital Markets, Lowell Epp
Tel: 780-422-4052
Fax: 780-427-2435
lowell.epp@gov.ab.ca
Executive Director, Financial Institutions Policy, James Flett
Tel: 780-415-9233
Fax: 780-644-7759
james.flett@gov.ab.ca
Director, Banking & Cash Forecasting, David Hinman
Tel: 780-415-9184
Fax: 780-427-0780
david.hinman@gov.ab.ca
Director, Capital Markets Policy, Marsha Manolescu
Tel: 780-415-9243
Fax: 780-644-7759
marsha.manolescu@gov.ab.ca

Government of British Columbia

Seat of Government: Parliament Bldgs., Victoria, BC V8V 1X4
Tel: 250-387-6121
Toll-Free: 800-663-7867
www.gov.bc.ca
TTY: 800-661-8773
Other Communication: Vancouver, Phone: 604-660-2421; Vancouver, TDD: 604-775-0303; Outside BC, Phone: 604-660-2421

The Province of British Columbia entered Confederation on July 20, 1871. According to the 2011 Census, the population of the province is 4,400,057. British Columbia's land area is 922,509.29 square kilometres.

Office of the Lieutenant Governor

Government House, 1401 Rockland Ave., Victoria, BC V8S 1V9
Tel: 250-387-2080
Fax: 250-387-2078
ghinfo@gov.bc.ca
www.ltgov.bc.ca

Lieutenant Governor, British Columbia, Hon. Steven L. Point, OBC

Private Secretary to the Lieutenant Governor & Executive Director, Government House, Herb A. LeRoy
Tel: 250-387-2083
Fax: 250-387-2078

Director, Operations & Management Services, Jerymy Brownridge
Tel: 250-387-2087

Office of the Premier

West Annex, Parliament Bldgs., PO Box 9041 Prov Govt, Victoria, BC V8W 9E1
Tel: 250-387-1715
Fax: 250-387-0087
premier@gov.bc.ca
www.gov.bc.ca/premier
Other Communication: Premier's Vancouver Office, Phone: 604-775-1600, Fax: 604-775-1688

Christy Clark won the leadership of the Liberal party in February 2011, following the resignation of former premier, Gordon Campbell. She was sworn in as the 35th Premier of British Columbia on March 14, 2011.

Premier, Hon. Christy Clark

Chief of Staff, Dan Doyle

Deputy Chief of Staff, Operations, Kim Haakstad

Parliamentary Secretary to the Premier, Doug Horne
Tel: 250-953-4611
Fax: 250-387-9100

Press Secretary, Michael Morton

Managing Director, Correspondence, Antoinette De Wit
Tel: 250-387-3570
Fax: 250-356-1385
Antoinette.DeWit@gov.bc.ca

Director, Communications, Sara MacIntyre

Director, Outreach, Pamela Martin
Tel: 604-775-1600
Fax: 604-775-1688

Director, Issues Management, Shane Mills

Executive Scheduling Coordinator, Tamara Davidson
Tel: 250-356-2089
Fax: 250-356-5972

Deputy Minister's Office
PO Box 9041 Prov Govt, Victoria, BC V8W 9E1
Tel: 250-387-2226
Fax: 250-356-7258

Deputy Minister to the Premier; Cabinet Secretary; Head of the Public Service, John Dyble
Tel: 250-356-2209
Fax: 250-356-7258
Deputy Minister, Corporate Priorities & Planning, Neil Sweeney
Tel: 250-387-5830
Fax: 250-356-7258
Director, Executive Operations, Michelle Leamy
Tel: 250-387-5894
Fax: 250-356-7258
Michelle.Leamy@gov.bc.ca
Director, Corporate Priorities & Performance Management, Sandy Wharf
Tel: 250-387-3563
Fax: 250-356-7258
Sandy.Wharf@gov.bc.ca
Executive Administrative Coordinator, Alisha Olson
Tel: 250-356-2605
Fax: 250-356-7258
Alisha.Olson@gov.bc.ca

Intergovernmental Relations Secretariat (IGRS)
PO Box 9333 Prov Govt, Victoria, BC V8W 9N3
Tel: 250-387-0752
Fax: 250-387-1920
igrs@gov.bc.ca; protocol@gov.bc.ca
www.igrs.gov.bc.ca

The Intergovernmental Relations Secretariat consists of the following sections: Intergovernmental & International Relations; Office of Protocol; & the Francophone Affairs Program.
The mission of Intergovernmental & International Relations is to ensure that the province's relations with provincial & territorial governments, the federal government, the United States, the Asia-Pacific region, & other international governments advance British Columbia's interests. Advice is given to the Premier & cabinet ministers.
The Office of Protocol offers leadership in government protocol, ceremonial, & diplomatic events. Examples of these activities include the installation of cabinet members & the opening of the legislature.
Information about the provincial government's services & publications available in French is found by using the following link: www2.gov.bc.ca/gov/bienvenue/index.page.

Associate Deputy Minister, Intergovernmental Relations Secretariat, Pierrette Maranda
Tel: 250-387-0752
Fax: 250-387-1920
Pierrette.Maranda@gov.bc.ca
Executive Director, Federalism & Canadian Intergovernmental Policy, Paul Craven
Tel: 250-356-2272
Fax: 250-387-1920
Paul.Craven@gov.bc.ca
Executive Director, USA Relations & Partnerships, Bryant Fairley
Tel: 250-387-1134
Fax: 250-387-1920
Bryant.Fairley@gov.bc.ca
Executive Director, Economic Policy & Asia Pacific Relations; Advisor to the Deputy Minister's Office, Donald Haney
Tel: 250-387-5628
Fax: 250-387-1920
Donald.Haney@gov.bc.ca
Executive Director & Chief of Protocol, Marc-André Ouellette
Tel: 250-387-4304
Fax: 250-356-2814
Sukumar.Periwal@gov.bc.ca
PO Box 9422 Prov Govt Sta.
Victoria, BC V8W 9N3
Executive Director, Strategic Policy & Planning, Sukumar Periwal
Tel: 250-387-0761
Fax: 250-387-1920
Sukumar.Periwal@gov.bc.ca
Manager, Intergovernmental Events, Helen Carr
Tel: 250-356-2891
Fax: 250-356-2814
Claudia.Fabbri@gov.bc.ca
Manager, International Relations, Claudia Fabbri
Tel: 250-387-1174
Fax: 250-387-1920
Claudia.Fabbri@gov.bc.ca
Manager, Honours, Karen Felker
Tel: 250-356-1139
Fax: 250-356-2814
Manager, International Visits, Karen Geiger
Tel: 250-356-9414
Fax: 250-356-2814
Karen.Geiger@gov.bc.ca
Manager, Diplomatic & Consular Services, Manjit Khaira
Tel: 250-356-9459
Fax: 250-356-2814
Manager, Intergovernmental Events, Lucy Lobmeier
Tel: 250-356-6177
Fax: 250-356-2814
Manager, Federal - Provincial Agreement on Official Languages, Veronique Mercier
Tel: 250-387-4791
Fax: 250-387-1920
Veronique.Mercier@gov.bc.ca
Manager, Intergovernmental Relations, Judi Sigudson
Tel: 250-387-3463
Fax: 250-387-1920

Executive Council of the Government of British Columbia

Cabinet Operations, 617 Government St., 1st Fl., PO Box 9487 Prov Govt, Victoria, BC V8W 9W6
www.gov.bc.ca/premier/cabinet_ministers

British Columbia Premier Christy Clark announced a new cabinet on September 5, 2012. The cabinet shuffle followed announcements by some former cabinet ministers that they will not seek re-election in the provincial election in May 2013.

Cabinet Ministers
Premier; President, Executive Council, Hon. Christy Clark
Tel: 250-387-1715
Fax: 250-387-0087
premier@gov.bc.ca; christy@christyclark.ca
www.christyclark.ca
PO Box 9041 Prov Govt Sta.
Victoria, BC V8W 9E1
Deputy Premier; Minister, Energy, Mines, & Natural Gas; Minister Responsible, Housing, Hon. Rich Coleman
Tel: 250-387-5896
Fax: 250-356-2965
EMH.Minister@gov.bc.ca
www.gov.bc.ca/ener
Social Media: twitter.com/colemancountry
PO Box 9060 Prov Govt Sta.
Victoria, BC V8W 9E2
Minister, Finance; Government House Leader, Hon. Michael de Jong, Q.C.
Tel: 250-387-3751

Fax: 250-387-5594
FIN.Minister@gov.bc.ca
www.gov.bc.ca/fin
Social Media: twitter.com/mike_de_jong
PO Box 9048 Prov Govt Sta.
Victoria, BC V8W 9E2

Minister, Aboriginal Relations & Reconciliation, Hon. Ida Chong
Tel: 250-953-4844
Fax: 250-953-4856
ABR.Minister@gov.bc.ca
www.gov.bc.ca/arr
Social Media: twitter.com/Ida_Chong, www.facebook.com/idachongmla
PO Box 9051 Prov Govt Sta.
Victoria, BC V8W 9E2

Minister, Advanced Education, Innovation, & Technology; Minister Responsible, Multiculturalism, Hon. John Yap
Tel: 250-356-0179
Fax: 250-952-0260
AVED.Minister@gov.bc.ca
www.gov.bc.ca/aved
Social Media: twitter.com/John_Yap
PO Box 9080 Prov Govt Sta.
Victoria, BC V8W9E2

Minister, Agriculture, Hon. Norm Letnick
Tel: 250-387-1023
Fax: 250-387-1522
AGR.Minister@gov.bc.ca
www.gov.bc.ca/agri
Social Media: twitter.com/normletnick
PO Box 9043 Prov Govt Sta.
Victoria, BC V8W 9E2

Minister, Children & Family Development, Hon. Stephanie Cadieux
Tel: 250-387-9699
Fax: 250-387-9722
MCF.Minister@gov.bc.ca
www.gov.bc.ca/mcf
Social Media: twitter.com/mlacadieux
PO Box 9057 Prov Govt Sta.
Victoria, BC V8W 9E2

Minister, Citizens' Services & Open Government, Hon. Ben Stewart
Tel: 250-952-7623
Fax: 250-952-7628
www.gov.bc.ca/citz
PO Box 9056 Prov Govt Sta.
Victoria, BC V8W 9E2

Minister, Community, Sport, & Cultural Development, Hon. Bill Bennett
Tel: 250-387-2283
Fax: 250-387-4312
CSCD.minister@gov.bc.ca
www.gov.bc.ca/cscd
Social Media: twitter.com/KootenayBill
PO Box 9056 Prov Govt Sta.
Victoria, BC V8W 9E2

Minister, Education, Hon. Don McRae
Tel: 250-387-1977
Fax: 250-387-3200
Minister.Educ@gov.bc.ca
www.gov.bc.ca/bced
Social Media: twitter.com/DonMcRaeMLA, www.facebook.com/donmcrae
PO Box 9045 Prov Govt Sta.
Victoria, BC V8W 9E2

Minister, Environment; Deputy House Leader, Hon. Terry Lake
Tel: 250-387-1187
Fax: 250-387-1356
ENV.Minister@gov.bc.ca
www.gov.bc.ca/env
Social Media: twitter.com/terrylakeMLA
#247, Parliament Buildings
PO Box 9047 Prov Govt Sta.
Victoria, BC V8W9E2

Minister, Forests, Lands, & Natural Resource Operations, Hon. Steve Thomson
Tel: 250-356-6211
Fax: 250-387-1040
FLNR.Minister@gov.bc.ca
www.gov.bc.ca/for
PO Box 9049 Prov Govt Sta.
Victoria, BC V8W 9E2

Minister, Health, Hon. Dr. Margaret MacDiarmid
Tel: 250-953-3547
Fax: 250-356-9587
hlth.minister@gov.bc.ca
www.gov.bc.ca/health
Social Media: twitter.com/@DrMacDiarmid, www.facebook.com/margaretmacdiarmid
PO Box 9050 Prov Govt Sta.
Victoria, BC V8W9E2

Minister, Jobs, Tourism, & Skills Training; Minister Responsible, Labour, Hon. Patrick Bell
Tel: 250-356-2771
Fax: 250-356-3000
JTI.Minister@gov.bc.ca
www.gov.bc.ca/jti
Social Media: twitter.com/patbellbc
PO Box 9067 Prov Govt Sta.
Victoria, BC V8W 9E9

Minister, Justice; Attorney General, Hon. Shirley Bond
Tel: 250-387-1866
Fax: 250-387-6411
JAG.Minister@gov.bc.ca
www.gov.bc.ca/justice
Social Media: twitter.com/shirleybond, www.facebook.com/shirley.bond
PO Box 9044 Prov Govt Sta.
Victoria, BC V8W9E2

Minister, Social Development, Hon. Dr. Moira Stilwell
Tel: 250-356-7750
Fax: 250-356-7292
SD.Minister@gov.bc.ca
www.gov.bc.ca/hsd
Social Media: twitter.com/DrMoiraStilwell
PO Box 9058 Prov Govt Sta.
Victoria, BC V8W 9E1

Minister, Transportation & Infrastructure, Hon. Mary Polak
Tel: 250-387-1978
Fax: 250-356-2290
Minister.Transportation@gov.bc.ca
www.gov.bc.ca/tran
Social Media: twitter.com/MaryPolakMLA, www.facebook.com/MLAPolak
PO Box 9055 Prov Govt Sta.
Victoria, BC V8W 9E2

Minister of State for Seniors, Hon. Ralph Sultan
Tel: 250-356-0912
Fax: 250-356-0931

Minister of State for Small Business, Hon. Naomi Yamamoto
Tel: 250-356-0179
Fax: 250-952-0260
Social Media: twitter.com/naomiyamamoto, www.facebook.com/naomi.yamamoto.mla

Cabinet Operations
617 Government St., 1st Fl., PO Box 9487 Prov Govt, Victoria, BC V8W 9W6
Fax: 250-387-7392

Cabinet Secretary; Deputy Minister to the Premier; Head of the Public Service, John Dyble
Tel: 250-356-2209
Fax: 250-356-7258

Deputy Cabinet Secretary, Elizabeth MacMillan
Tel: 250-387-6020
Fax: 250-387-7392

Manager, Cabinet Operations, Debbie Tsukayama
Tel: 250-387-0869
Fax: 250-387-7392
Debbie.Tsukayama@gov.bc.ca

Coordinator, Cabinet Documents, Joyce Gillespie
Tel: 250-387-5509
Fax: 250-387-7392
Joyce.Gillespie@gov.bc.ca

Coordinator, OIC, Gillian Henuset
Tel: 250-387-5503
Fax: 250-387-7392
Gillian.Henuset@gov.bc.ca

Coordinator, Document Processing, Sheila A. Johnstone
Tel: 250-387-5553
Fax: 250-387-7392
Sheila.Johnstone@gov.bc.ca

BC Legislative Assembly & Independent Offices

Clerk's Office, #221, Parliament Bldgs., Victoria, BC V8V 1X4
Tel: 250-387-3785
Fax: 250-387-0942
ClerkHouse@leg.bc.ca
www.leg.bc.ca

Clerk, E. George MacMinn, Q.C.
Tel: 250-387-3785
Fax: 250-387-0942

Speaker, Legislative Assembly, Hon. Bill Barisoff
Tel: 250-387-3952
Fax: 250-387-2813
#207, Parliament Bldgs.
Victoria, BC V8V 1X4

Deputy Speaker, Legislative Assembly, Linda Reid
Tel: 250-953-4887
Fax: 250-356-0596
#207, Parliament Bldgs.
Victoria, BC V8V 1X4

Sergeant-at-Arms, Gary Lenz
Tel: 250-356-6966

Legislative Comptroller, Dan Arbic
Tel: 250-356-8588
Fax: 250-356-7517
Comptroller@leg.bc.ca
Parliament Bldgs.
612 Government St.
Victoria, BC V8V 1X4

Acting Director, Hansard Production, Rob Sutherland
Tel: 250-387-0944
Fax: 250-356-5681
Hansard.Services@leg.bc.ca
Parliament Bldgs.
612 Government St.
Victoria, BC V8V 1X4

Director, Legislative Library Administration Office, Peter Gourlay
Tel: 250-387-6508
Fax: 250-356-1373
Other Communications: URL: www.llbc.leg.bc.ca
#214, Parliament Bldgs.
Victoria, BC V8V 1X4

Auditor General, John Doyle
Tel: 250-419-6100
Fax: 250-387-1230
Other Communications: URL: www.bcauditor.com
8 Bastion Sq., 2nd Fl.
PO Box 9036 Prov Govt Sta.
Victoria, BC V8W 9A2

Conflict of Interest Commissioner, Paul D.K. Fraser
Tel: 250-356-9283
Fax: 250-356-6580
conflictofinterest@coibc.ca
Other Communications: URL: www.coibc.ca

Information & Privacy Commissioner, Elizabeth Denham
Tel: 250-387-5629
Fax: 250-387-1696
info@oipc.bc.ca
Other Communications: URL: www.oipc.bc.ca

Merit Commissioner, Fiona Spencer
Tel: 250-953-4208
Fax: 250-953-4160
merit@meritcomm.bc.ca
Other Communications: www.meritcomm.bc.ca

Police Complaint Commissioner, Stan T. Lowe
Tel: 250-356-7458
Fax: 250-356-6503
info@opcc.bc.ca

Ombudsperson, Kim Carter
Tel: 250-356-1559
Fax: 250-387-0198
info@opcc.bc.ca

Acting Chief Electoral Officer, Elections British Columbia, Craig James
Tel: 250-387-5305
Fax: 250-387-3578
ElectionsBC@elections.bc.ca

Representative for Children & Youth, Mary Ellen Turpel-Lafond
Tel: 250-356-6710
Fax: 250-356-0837
rcy@rcybc.ca

Government Caucus Office (Liberal)
East Annex, Parliament Buildings, Victoria, BC V8V 1X4
Tel: 250-356-6171
Fax: 250-356-6176
www.governmentcaucus.bc.ca

Premier; Leader, Liberal Party of British Columbia, Hon. Christy Clark, Liberal
Tel: 250-387-1715
Fax: 250-387-0087
premier@gov.bc.ca

Government House Leader; Minister, Finance, Hon. Michael de Jong, Q.C., Liberal
Tel: 250-387-3751
Fax: 250-387-5594
Michael.DeJong@gov.bc.ca
Social Media: twitter.com/mike_de_jong

Deputy House Leader; Minister, Environment, Hon. Terry Lake
Tel: 250-387-1187

Fax: 250-387-1356
Social Media: twitter.com/terrylakeMLA
Government Whip, Eric Foster
Tel: 250-356-9574
Fax: 250-356-0596
Deputy Government Whip, Pat Pimm
Tel: 250-952-6784
Fax: 250-387-9100
Executive Director, Government Caucus, Primrose Carson
Tel: 250-387-2950
Fax: 250-387-9066
Director, Communications, Ben James
Tel: 250-208-7052
Fax: 250-387-7957
Director, Research, Blair Phelps
Tel: 250-387-8943
Fax: 250-356-0329
Director, Operations, Christie Pruden
Tel: 250-356-6134
Fax: 250-387-9066
Manager, Outreach, Melissa Nowakowski
Tel: 250-387-1774
Fax: 250-387-9066

Office of the Opposition (New Democrat)
#201, Parliament Bldgs., Victoria, BC V8V 1X4
Tel: 250-387-3655
Fax: 250-387-4680
ndp@leg.bc.ca

Leader, Adrian Dix
Tel: 250-387-3655
Fax: 250-387-4680
Adrian.Dix.MLA@leg.bc.ca
Executive Director, Mary O'Donoghue
Tel: 250-387-3655
Fax: 250-387-4680
Director, Research, AnneMarie Delorey
Tel: 250-387-3655
Fax: 250-387-4680

Legislative Committees
#224, Parliament Bldgs., Victoria, BC V8V 1X4
Tel: 250-356-2933
Fax: 250-356-8172
ClerkComm@leg.bc.ca

At the beginning of each session, Select Standing Committees are established by the Legislative Assembly in British Columbia. The following nine Select Standing Committees have been established: Aboriginal Affairs; Children & Youth; Crown Corporations; Education; Finance & Government Services; Health; Legislative Initiatives; Parliamentary Reform, Ethical Conduct, Standing Orders, & Private Bills; & Public Accounts.
Clerk Assistant & Acting Clerk of Committees, Kate Ryan-Lloyd
Tel: 250-356-2895
Fax: 250-356-8172

Thirty-ninth Legislature - British Columbia

Parliament Buildings, Victoria, BC V8V 1X4
Tel: 250-387-3785
Fax: 250-387-0942
ClerkHouse@leg.bc.ca
www.leg.bc.ca

Last General Election: May 12, 2009.
Next General Election: May 14, 2013.
Party Standings (September 2012):
Liberal 46;
New Democratic Party 36;
Independent 3;
Total 85.
Salaries, Indemnities, & Allowances: (2009):
Annual Basic Compensation per Member $101,859.00.
Additional Salaries:
Premier $91,673.10;
Leader of the Official Opposition $50,929.50;
Leader of a recognized political party other than the government or the Official Opposition $25,464.75;
Member, Executive Council with portfolio $50,929.50;
Member, Executive Council without portfolio $35,650.65;
Speaker $50,929.50;
Deputy Speaker $35,650.65;
Assistant Deputy Speaker $35,650.65;
Government Whip $20,371.80;
Deputy Government Whip $15,278.85;
Official Opposition Whip $20,371.80;
Official Opposition Deputy Whip $15,278.85
Party Whip of a recognized political party other than the government or the Official Opposition $10,185.90;
House Leader $20,371.80;
House Leader of a recognized political party other than the government or the Official Opposition $10,185.90;
Deputy Chair, Committee of the Whole $20,371.80;
Parliamentary Secretary $15,278.85.
The following is a list of each Member of the Legislative Assembly of British Columbia, the c onstituency, the total number of registered voters for the 2009 provicial general election, party affiliation, & contact information:

Members of the Legislative Assembly of British Columbia

Member, Legislative Assembly, Hon. George Abbott
Constituency: Shuswap *No. of Constituents:* 40,773, Liberal
Tel: 250-387-1977
Toll-free: 877-771-7557
Fax: 250-387-3200
george.abbott.mla@leg.bc.ca
Other Communications: Constituency Phone: 250-833-7414, Fax:250-833-7422
#310, Parliament Buildings
Victoria, BC V8V 1X4
Member, Legislative Assembly, Robin Austin
Constituency: Skeena *No. of Constituents:* 21,066, New Democratic Party
Tel: 250-387-3655
Fax: 250-387-4680
robin.austin.mla@leg.bc.ca
Other Communications: Terrace Constituency Phone: 250-638-7906
#201, ParliamentBuildings
Victoria, BC V8V 1X4
Member, Legislative Assembly, Harry Bains
Constituency: Surrey-Newton *No. of Constituents:* 30,628, New Democratic Party
Tel: 250-387-3655
Fax: 250-387-4680
harry.bains.mla@leg.bc.ca
Other Communications: Constituency Phone: 604-597-8248, Fax: 604-597-8882
#201, ParliamentBuildings
Victoria, BC V8V 1X4
Member, Legislative Assembly, Hon. Bill Barisoff
Constituency: Penticton *No. of Constituents:* 42,109, Liberal
Tel: 250-387-3952
Toll-free: 866-387-3952
Fax: 250-387-2813
bill.barisoff.mla@leg.bc.ca
Other Communications: Constituency Phone: 250-487-4400, Fax:250-487-4405
#207, Parliament Buildings
Victoria, BC V8V 1X4
Member, Legislative Assembly, Donna Barnett
Constituency: Cariboo-Chilcotin *No. of Constituents:* 20,890, Liberal
Tel: 250-387-3820
Fax: 250-387-9066
donna.barnett.mla@leg.bc.ca
Other Communications: 100 Mile House Constituency Phone: 250-395-3916
East Annex,Parliament Buildings
Victoria, BC V8V 1X4
Member, Legislative Assembly; Minister, Jobs, Tourism, & Skills Training; Minister Responsible, Labour, Hon. Patrick Bell
Constituency: Prince George-Mackenzie *No. of Constituents:* 32,913, Liberal
Tel: 250-356-2771
Fax: 250-356-3000
pat.bell.mla@leg.bc.ca; JTI.Minister@gov.bc.ca
www.patbellmla.bc.ca
Other Communications: Prince George Constituency Phone: 250-612-4194
Social Media: twitter.com/patbellbc
#138, Parliament Buildings
Victoria, BC V8V 1X4
Member, Legislative Assembly; Minister, Community, Sport, & Cultural Development, Hon. Bill Bennett
Constituency: Kootenay East *No. of Constituents:* 29,463, Liberal
Tel: 250-387-2283
Toll-free: 866-417-6022
Fax: 250-387-4312
CSCD.minister@gov.bc.ca
Other Communications: Constituency Phone:250-417-6022, Fax: 250-417-6026
Social Media: twitter.com/KootenayBill
East Annex, Parliament Buildings
Victoria, BC V8V 1X4
Member, Legislative Assembly, Dawn Black
Constituency: New Westminster *No. of Constituents:* 42,765, New Democratic Party
Tel: 250-387-3655
Fax: 250-387-4680
dawn.black.mla@leg.bc.ca
Other Communications: Constituency Phone: 604-775-2101, Fax: 604-775-2121
#201, ParliamentBuildings
Victoria, BC V8V 1X4
Member, Legislative Assembly, Hon. Harry Bloy
Constituency: Burnaby-Lougheed *No. of Constituents:* 35,705, Liberal
Tel: 250-356-7750
Fax: 250-356-7292
harry.bloy.mla@leg.bc.ca
Other Communications: Constituency Phone: 604-664-0847, Fax: 604-664-0815
#124, ParliamentBuildings
Victoria, BC V8V 1X4
Member, Legislative Assembly; Minister, Justice; Attorney General, Hon. Shirley Bond
Constituency: Prince George-Valemount *No. of Constituents:* 34,727, Liberal
Tel: 250-387-1866
Fax: 250-387-6411
shirley.bond.mla@leg.bc.ca; JAG.Minister@gov.bc.ca
www.shirleybondmla.bc.ca
Other Communications: Constituency Phone: 250-612-4181, Fax: 250 612-4188
Social Media: twitter.com/shirleybond, www.facebook.com/shirley.bond
#232, Parliament Buildings
Victoria, BC V8V 1X4
Member, Legislative Assembly, Jagrup Brar
Constituency: Surrey-Fleetwood *No. of Constituents:* 33,039, New Democratic Party
Tel: 250-387-3655
Fax: 250-387-4680
jagrup.brar.mla@leg.bc.ca
Other Communications: Constituency Phone: 604-501-8227, Fax: 604-501-8233
#201, ParliamentBuildings
Victoria, BC V8V 1X4
Member, Legislative Assembly; Minister, Children & Family Development, Hon. Stephanie Cadieux
Constituency: Surrey-Panorama *No. of Constituents:* 38,685, Liberal
Tel: 250-387-9699
Fax: 250-387-9722
stephanie.cadieux.mla@leg.bc.ca
www.stephaniecadieuxmla.bc.ca
Other Communications: ConstituencyPhone: 604-574-5662, Fax: 604-574-5691
#236, Parliament Buildings
Victoria, BC V8V 1X4
Member, Legislative Assembly, Ron Cantelon
Constituency: Parksville-Qualicum *No. of Constituents:* 40,805, Liberal
Tel: 250-387-2203
Fax: 250-387-9066
ron.cantelon.mla@leg.bc.ca
Other Communications: Constituency Phone: 250-951-6018, Fax: 250-951-6020
East Annex,Parliament Buildings
Victoria, BC V8V 1X4
Member, Legislative Assembly, Spencer Chandra Herbert
Constituency: Vancouver-West End *No. of Constituents:* 35,370, New Democratic Party
Tel: 250-387-3655
Fax: 250-387-4680
s.chandraherbert.mla@leg.bc.ca
Other Communications: Constituency Phone: 604-660-7307, Fax: 604-660-7300
#201, Parliament Buildings
Victoria, BC V8V 1X4
Member, Legislative Assembly; Minister, Aboriginal Relations & Reconciliation, Hon. Ida Chong
Constituency: Oak Bay-Gordon Head *No. of Constituents:* 38,415, Liberal
Tel: 250-953-4844
Fax: 250-953-4856
ida.chong.mla@leg.bc.ca; ABR.Minister@gov.bc.ca
Other Communications: Gordon Head Constituency Phone: 250-472-8528
Social Media: twitter.com/Ida_Chong, www.facebook.com/idachongmla
#323, Parliament Buildings
Victoria, BC V8V 1X4
Member, Legislative Assembly, Raj Chouhan
Constituency: Burnaby-Edmonds *No. of Constituents:* 34,288, New Democratic Party
Tel: 250-387-3655
Fax: 250-387-4680
raj.chouhan.mla@leg.bc.ca
Other Communications: Constituency Phone: 604-660-7301, Fax: 250-387-4680
#201, ParliamentBuildings
Victoria, BC V8V 1X4
Member, Legislative Assembly; Premier; President, Executive Council, Hon. Christy Clark
Constituency: Vancouver-Point Grey *No. of Constituents:* 41,181, Liberal
Tel: 250-387-1715
Fax: 250-387-0087
premier@gov.bc.ca; christy@christyclark.ca
www.christyclark.ca
Other Communications: ConstituencyPhone: 604-775-1003, Fax: 604 775-1026

Note: Christy Clark became the 35th Premier of British Columbia on March 14, 2011. She was elected in a by-election on May 12,2011.
West Annex, Parliament Buildings
Victoria, BC V8V 1X4

Member, Legislative Assembly, Murray Coell
Constituency: Saanich North & the Islands *No. of Constituents:* 43,989, Liberal
Tel: 250-387-8381
Toll-free: 866-655-5711
Fax: 250-387-9066
murray.coell.mla@leg.bc.ca
Other Communications: Constituency Phone: 250-655-5711, Fax: 250-655-5710
EastAnnex, Parliament Buildings
Victoria, BC V8V 1X4

Member, Legislative Assembly; Minister, Energy, Mines, & Natural Gas; Minister Responsible, Housing, Hon. Rich Coleman
Constituency: Fort Langley-Aldergrove *No. of Constituents:* 43,243, Liberal
Tel: 250-387-5896
Fax: 250-356-2965
rich.coleman.mla@leg.bc.ca; EMH.Minister@gov.bc.ca
Other Communications: Constituency Phone: 604-882-3151, Fax: 604-882-3154
Social Media: twitter.com/colemancountry
#128, Parliament Buildings
Victoria, BC V8V 1X4

Member, Legislative Assembly, Katrine Conroy
Constituency: Kootenay West *No. of Constituents:* 30,934, New Democratic Party
Tel: 250-387-3655
Toll-free: 888-755-0556
Fax: 250-387-4680
katrine.conroy.mla@leg.bc.ca
Other Communications: Constituency Phone: 250-304-2783, Fax: 250-304-2655
#201, Parliament Buildings
Victoria, BC V8V 1X4

Member, Legislative Assembly, Gary Earl Coons
Constituency: North Coast *No. of Constituents:* 15,681, New Democratic Party
Tel: 250-387-3655
Toll-free: 866-624-7734
Fax: 250-387-4680
gary.coons.mla@leg.bc.ca
Other Communications: Constituency Phone: 250-624-7734, Fax: 250-624-7737
#201,Parliament Buildings
Victoria, BC V8V 1X4

Member, Legislative Assembly, Kathy Corrigan
Constituency: Burnaby-Deer Lake *No. of Constituents:* 34,488, New Democratic Party
Tel: 250-387-3655
Fax: 250-387-4680
kathy.corrigan.mla@leg.bc.ca
Other Communications: Constituency Phone: 604-775-2414, Fax: 604-775-2550
#201,Parliament Buildings
Victoria, BC V8V 1X4

Member, Legislative Assembly, Marc Dalton
Constituency: Maple Ridge-Mission *No. of Constituents:* 35,200, Liberal
Tel: 250-953-4769
Toll-free: 877-899-3215
Fax: 250-387-9100
marc.dalton.mla@leg.bc.ca
Other Communications: Maple Ridge Constituency Phone: 604-476-4530
East Annex,Parliament Buildings
Victoria, BC V8V 1X4

Member, Legislative Assembly; Minister, Finance; Government House Leader, Hon. Michael de Jong, QC
Constituency: Abbotsford West *No. of Constituents:* 30,822, Liberal
Tel: 250-953-3547
Fax: 250-356-9587
mike.dejong.mla@leg.bc.ca;FIN.Minister@gov.bc.ca
Other Communications: Constituency Phone: 604-870-5486, Fax: 604-870-5444
Social Media: twitter.com/mike_de_jong
#337, Parliament Buildings
Victoria, BC V8V 1X4

Member, Legislative Assembly, Adrian Dix
Constituency: Vancouver-Kingsway *No. of Constituents:* 56,715, New Democratic Party
Tel: 250-387-3655
Fax: 250-387-4680
adrian.dix.mla@leg.bc.ca
Other Communications: Constituency Phone: 604-660-0314, Fax: 604-660-1131
#201, ParliamentBuildings
Victoria, BC V8V 1X4

Member, Legislative Assembly, Doug Donaldson
Constituency: Stikine *No. of Constituents:* 13,131, New Democratic Party
Tel: 250-387-3655
Fax: 250-387-4680
doug.donaldson.mla@leg.bc.ca
Other Communications: Hazelton Constituency Phone: 250-842-6338
#201, ParliamentBuildings
Victoria, BC V8V 1X4

Member, Legislative Assembly, Mable Elmore
Constituency: Vancouver-Kensington *No. of Constituents:* 36,057, New Democratic Party
Tel: 250-387-3655
Fax: 250-387-4680
mable.elmore.mla@leg.bc.ca
Other Communications: Constituency Phone: 604-775-1033, Fax: 604-775-1330
#201, ParliamentBuildings
Victoria, BC V8V 1X4

Member, Legislative Assembly, Hon. Kevin Falcon
Constituency: Surrey-Cloverdale *No. of Constituents:* 40,268, Liberal
Tel: 250-387-3751
Fax: 250-387-5594
kevin.falcon.mla@leg.bc.ca
Other Communications: Constituency Phone: 604-576-3792, Fax: 604-576-3797
#153,Parliament Buildings
Victoria, BC V8V 1X4

Member, Legislative Assembly, Mike Farnworth
Constituency: Port Coquitlam *No. of Constituents:* 37,009, New Democratic Party
Tel: 250-387-3655
Fax: 250-387-4680
mike.farnworth.mla@leg.bc.ca
Other Communications: Constituency Phone: 604-927-2088, Fax: 604-927-2090
#201,Parliament Buildings
Victoria, BC V8V 1X4

Member, Legislative Assembly, Rob Fleming
Constituency: Victoria-Swan Lake *No. of Constituents:* 38,359, New Democratic Party
Tel: 250-387-3655
Fax: 250-387-4680
rob.fleming.mla@leg.bc.ca
Other Communications: Constituency Phone: 250-360-2023, Fax: 250-360-2027
#201, ParliamentBuildings
Victoria, BC V8V 1X4

Member, Legislative Assembly, Eric Foster
Constituency: Vernon-Monashee *No. of Constituents:* 45,410, Liberal
Tel: 250-356-9574
Fax: 250-356-0596
eric.foster.mla@leg.bc.ca
Other Communications: Constituency Phone: 250-503-3600, Fax: 250-503-3603
East Annex,Parliament Buildings
Victoria, BC V8V 1X4

Member, Legislative Assembly, Scott Fraser
Constituency: Alberni-Pacific Rim *No. of Constituents:* 30,818, New Democratic Party
Tel: 250-387-3655
Toll-free: 866-870-4190
Fax: 250-387-4680
scott.fraser.mla@leg.bc.ca
Other Communications: Port Alberni Constituency Phone: 250-720-4515
#201,Parliament Buildings
Victoria, BC V8V 1X4

Member, Legislative Assembly, Guy Gentner
Constituency: Delta North *No. of Constituents:* 34,851, New Democratic Party
Tel: 250-387-3655
Fax: 250-387-4680
guy.gentner.mla@leg.bc.ca
Other Communications: Constituency Phone: 604-597-1488, Fax: 604-597-1466
#201, ParliamentBuildings
Victoria, BC V8V 1X4

Member, Legislative Assembly, Sue Hammell
Constituency: Surrey-Green Timbers *No. of Constituents:* 29,799, New Democratic Party
Tel: 250-387-3655
Fax: 250-387-4680
sue.hammell.mla@leg.bc.ca
Other Communications: Constituency Phone: 604-590-5868, Fax: 604-590-5873
#201, ParliamentBuildings
Victoria, BC V8V 1X4

Member, Legislative Assembly, Hon. Colin Hansen
Constituency: Vancouver-Quilchena *No. of Constituents:* 39,067, Liberal
Tel: 250-952-7270
Fax: 250-387-9100
colin.hansen.mla@leg.bc.ca
Other Communications: Constituency Phone: 604-664-0748, Fax: 604-664-0750
East Annex,Parliament Buildings
Victoria, BC V8V 1X4

Member, Legislative Assembly, Randy Hawes
Constituency: Abbotsford-Mission *No. of Constituents:* 34,412, Liberal
Tel: 250-952-7275
Toll-free: 866-370-6203
Fax: 250-387-9100
randy.hawes.mla@leg.bc.ca
Other Communications: Mission Constituency Phone: 604-820-6203
East Annex,Parliament Buildings
Victoria, BC V8V 1X4

Member, Legislative Assembly, Dave S. Hayer
Constituency: Surrey-Tynehead *No. of Constituents:* 34,037, Liberal
Tel: 250-387-8076
Fax: 250-387-9100
dave.hayer.mla@leg.bc.ca
Other Communications: Constituency Phone: 604-586-3747, Fax: 604-584-4741
East Annex,Parliament Buildings
Victoria, BC V8V 1X4

Member, Legislative Assembly, Kash Heed
Constituency: Vancouver-Fraserview *No. of Constituents:* 38,262, Liberal
Tel: 250-356-0963
Fax: 250-387-9066
kash.heed.mla@leg.bc.ca
Other Communications: Constituency Phone: 604-775-2246, Fax: 604-775-2422
East Annex, ParliamentBuildings
Victoria, BC V8V 1X4

Member, Legislative Assembly, Hon. Gordon Hogg
Constituency: Surrey-White Rock *No. of Constituents:* 39,598, Liberal
Tel: 250-952-7638
Fax: 250-387-9066
gordon.hogg.mla@leg.bc.ca
Other Communications: Constituency Phone: 604-542-3930, Fax: 604-542-3933
East Annex,Parliament Buildings
Victoria, BC V8V 1X4

Member, Legislative Assembly, John Horgan
Constituency: Juan de Fuca *No. of Constituents:* 33,812, New Democratic Party
Tel: 250-387-3655
Fax: 250-387-4680
john.horgan.mla@leg.bc.ca
Other Communications: Constituency Phone: 250-391-2801, Fax: 250-391-2804
#201, ParliamentBuildings
Victoria, BC V8V 1X4

Member, Legislative Assembly, Douglas Horne
Constituency: Coquitlam-Burke Mountain *No. of Constituents:* 31,397, Liberal
Tel: 250-953-4611
Toll-free: 800-691-9158
Fax: 250-387-9100
douglas.horne.mla@leg.bc.ca
Other Communications: Constituency Phone: 604-949-1424, Fax: 604-949-1481
EastAnnex, Parliament Buildings
Victoria, BC V8V 1X4

Member, Legislative Assembly, Rob Howard
Constituency: Richmond Centre *No. of Constituents:* 42,007, Liberal
Tel: 250-952-7616
Fax: 250-387-9100
rob.howard.mla@leg.bc.ca
Other Communications: Constituency Phone: 604-775-0754
East Annex, Parliament Buildings
Victoria, BC V8V 1X4

Member, Legislative Assembly, Vicki Huntington
Constituency: Delta South *No. of Constituents:* 34,331, Independent
Tel: 250-952-7594
Fax: 250-952-7598
vicki.huntington.mla@leg.bc.ca
Other Communications: Constituency Phone: 604-940-7924
#145, ParliamentBuildings
Victoria, BC V8V 1X4

Member, Legislative Assembly, Carole James
Constituency: Victoria-Beacon Hill *No. of Constituents:* 42,615, New Democratic Party
Tel: 250-387-3655
Fax: 250-387-4680
carole.james.mla@leg.bc.ca
Other Communications: Constituency Phone: 250-952-4211,

Fax: 250-952-4586
#201, ParliamentBuildings
Victoria, BC V8V 1X4
Member, Legislative Assembly, Maurine Karagianis
Constituency: Esquimalt-Royal Roads *No. of Constituents:* 37,546, New Democratic Party
Tel: 250-387-3655
Fax: 250-387-4680
maurine.karagianis.mla@leg.bc.ca
Other Communications: Constituency Phone: 250-479-8326, Fax: 259-479-5003
#201,Parliament Buildings
Victoria, BC V8V 1X4
Member, Legislative Assembly, Leonard Krog
Constituency: Nanaimo *No. of Constituents:* 39,273, New Democratic Party
Tel: 250-387-3655
Fax: 250-387-4680
leonard.krog.mla@leg.bc.ca
Other Communications: Constituency Phone: 250-714-0630, Fax: 250-714-0859
#201, ParliamentBuildings
Victoria, BC V8V 1X4
Member, Legislative Assembly, Hon. Kevin Krueger
Constituency: Kamloops-South Thompson *No. of Constituents:* 40,645, Liberal
Tel: 250-952-7269
Fax: 250-952-7263
kevin.krueger.mla@leg.bc.ca
Other Communications: Constituency Phone: 250-314-6031, Fax: 250-314-6040
East Annex,Parliament Buildings
Victoria, BC V8V 1X4
Member, Legislative Assembly, Jenny Wai Ching Kwan
Constituency: Vancouver-Mount Pleasant *No. of Constituents:* 38,267, New Democratic Party
Tel: 250-387-3655
Fax: 250-387-4680
jenny.kwan.mla@leg.bc.ca
Other Communications: Constituency Phone: 604-775-0790, Fax: 604-775-0881
#201,Parliament Buildings
Victoria, BC V8V 1X4
Member, Legislative Assembly; Minister, Environment; Deputy House Leader, Hon. Terry Lake
Constituency: Kamloops-North Thompson *No. of Constituents:* 38,245, Liberal
Tel: 250-387-1187
Fax: 250-387-1356
terry.lake.mla@leg.bc.ca; ENV.Minister@gov.bc.ca
Other Communications: Constituency Phone: 250-554-5413, Fax: 250-554-5417
Social Media: twitter.com/terrylakeMLA
#112, Parliament Buildings
Victoria, BC V8V 1X4
Member, Legislative Assembly, Harry Lali
Constituency: Fraser-Nicola *No. of Constituents:* 21,663, New Democratic Party
Tel: 250-387-3655
Toll-free: 877-378-4802
Fax: 250-384-4680
harry.lali.mla@leg.bc.ca
Other Communications: Constituency Phone: 250-378-4802, Fax: 250-378-4852
#201,Parliament Buildings
Victoria, BC V8V 1X4
Member, Legislative Assembly, Richard T. Lee
Constituency: Burnaby North *No. of Constituents:* 38,404, Liberal
Tel: 250-356-3052
Fax: 250-387-9100
richard.lee.mla@leg.bc.ca
Other Communications: Constituency Phone: 604 775-0778, Fax: 604-775-0833
East Annex,Parliament Buildings
Victoria, BC V8V 1X4
Member, Legislative Assembly, Hon. Blair Lekstrom
Constituency: Peace River South *No. of Constituents:* 17,397, Liberal
Tel: 250-387-1978
Toll-free: 877-784-1330
Fax: 250-356-2290
blair.lekstrom.mla@leg.bc.ca
Other Communications: Constituency Phone: 250-784-1330, Fax:250-784-1333
#342, Parliament Buildings
Victoria, BC V8V 1X4
Member, Legislative Assembly, John Les
Constituency: Chilliwack *No. of Constituents:* 36,138, Liberal
Tel: 250-356-6171
Toll-free: 866-424-8350
Fax: 250-387-3698
john.les.mla@leg.bc.ca
Other Communications: Constituency Phone: 604-702-5214
East Annex, ParliamentBuildings
Victoria, BC V8V 1X4
Member, Legislative Assembly; Minister, Agriculture, Hon. Norm Letnick
Constituency: Kelowna-Lake Country *No. of Constituents:* 41,947, Liberal
Tel: 250-387-1023
Toll-free: 866-765-8516
Fax: 250-387-1552
norm.letnick.mla@leg.bc.ca; AGR.Minister@gov.bc.ca
Other Communications: Constituency Phone:205-765-8516, Fax: 250-765-7283
Social Media: twitter.com/normletnick
East Annex, Parliament Buildings
Victoria, BC V8V 1X4
Member, Legislative Assembly; Minister, Health, Hon. Dr. Margaret MacDiarmid
Constituency: Vancouver-Fairview *No. of Constituents:* 41,748, Liberal
Tel: 250-953-3547
Fax: 250-356-9587
margaret.macdiarmid.mla@leg.bc.ca; hlth.minister@gov.bc.ca
Other Communications: Constituency Phone: 604-660-7061, Fax: 604-660-7065
Social Media: twitter.com/@DrMacDiarmid, www.facebook.com/margaretmacdiarmid
#346, Parliament Buildings
Victoria, BC V8V 1X4
Member, Legislative Assembly, Norm Macdonald
Constituency: Columbia River-Revelstoke *No. of Constituents:* 24,071, New Democratic Party
Tel: 250-387-3655
Toll-free: 866-870-4188
Fax: 250-387-4680
norm.macdonald.mla@leg.bc.ca
Other Communications: Constituency Phone: 250-344-4816, Fax: 250-344-4815
#201, Parliament Buildings
Victoria, BC V8V 1X4
Member, Legislative Assembly, Joan McIntyre
Constituency: West Vancouver-Sea to Sky *No. of Constituents:* 34,911, Liberal
Tel: 250-953-4613
Fax: 250-387-9100
joan.mcintyre.mla@leg.bc.ca
Other Communications: Constituency Phone: 604-981-0045, Fax: 604-981-0060
East Annex,Parliament Buildings
Victoria, BC V8V 1X4
Member, Legislative Assembly, Hon. Mary McNeil
Constituency: Vancouver-False Creek *No. of Constituents:* 34,211, Liberal
Tel: 250-387-9699
Fax: 250-387-9722
mary.mcneil.mla@leg.bc.ca
Other Communications: Constituency Phone: 604-775-2601, Fax: 604-775-2607
#306, ParliamentBuildings
Victoria, BC V8V 1X4
Member, Legislative Assembly; Minister, Education, Hon. Don McRae
Constituency: Comox Valley *No. of Constituents:* 48,367, Liberal
Tel: 250-387-1977
Fax: 250-387-3200
don.mcrae.mla@leg.bc.ca; Minister.Educ@gov.bc.ca
Other Communications: Constituency Phone:250-703-2422, Fax: 250-703-2425
Social Media: twitter.com/DonMcRaeMLA, www.facebook.com/donmcrae
#301, Parliament Buildings
Victoria, BC V8V 1X4
Member, Legislative Assembly, Michelle Mungall
Constituency: Nelson-Creston *No. of Constituents:* 27,565, New Democratic Party
Tel: 250-387-3655
Toll-free: 877-388-4498
Fax: 250-387-4680
wally.oppal.mla@leg.bc.ca
Other Communications: Constituency Phone: 250-354-5944, Fax: 250-354-5937
#201, Parliament Buildings
Victoria, BC V8V 1X4
Member, Legislative Assembly, Gwen O'Mahony
Constituency: Chilliwack-Hope *No. of Constituents:* 32,709, New Democratic Party
Tel: 250-387-3655
Fax: 250-387-4680
gwen.o'mahony.mla@leg.bc.ca
Other Communications: Constituency Phone: 604-702-9633, Fax: 604-702-9623
Social Media: twitter.com/gwenomahony, www.facebook.com/gwenomahony
Note: Gwen O'Mahony was elected in a by-election on April 19, 2012.
#201, ParliamentBuildings
Victoria, BC V8V 1X4
Member, Legislative Assembly, Pat Pimm
Constituency: Peace River North *No. of Constituents:* 23,253, Liberal
Tel: 250-952-6784
Toll-free: 877-332-0101
Fax: 250-387-9100
pat.pimm.mla@leg.bc.ca
Other Communications: Constituency Phone: 250-263-0101, Fax: 250-263-0104
East Annex,Parliament Buildings
Victoria, BC V8V 1X4
Member, Legislative Assembly; Minister, Transportation & Infrastructure, Hon. Mary Polak
Constituency: Langley *No. of Constituents:* 42,918, Liberal
Tel: 250-387-1978
Fax: 250-356-2290
mary.polak.mla@leg.bc.ca;Minister.Transportation@gov.bc.ca
www.marypolakmla.bc.ca
Other Communications: Constituency Phone: 604-514-8206, Fax: 604-514-0195
Social Media: twitter.com/MaryPolakMLA, www.facebook.com/MLAPolak
#325, Parliament Buildings
Victoria, BC V8V 1X4
Member, Legislative Assembly, Lana Popham
Constituency: Saanich South *No. of Constituents:* 37,612, New Democratic Party
Tel: 250-387-3655
Fax: 250-387-4680
lana.popham.mla@leg.bc.ca
Other Communications: Constituency Phone: 250-479-4154, Fax: 250-479-4176
#201, ParliamentBuildings
Victoria, BC V8V 1X4
Member, Legislative Assembly, Bruce Ralston
Constituency: Surrey-Whalley *No. of Constituents:* 33,557, New Democratic Party
Tel: 250-387-3655
Fax: 250-387-4680
bruce.ralston.mla@leg.bc.ca
www.bruceralstonmla.ca
Other Communications: Constituency Phone: 604-586-2740, Fax: 604-586-2800
Social Media: twitter.com/BruceRalston
#201, ParliamentBuildings
Victoria, BC V8V 1X4
Member, Legislative Assembly, Linda Reid
Constituency: Richmond East *No. of Constituents:* 41,331, Liberal
Tel: 250-953-4887
Fax: 250-356-0596
linda.reid.mla@leg.bc.ca
Other Communications: Constituency Phone: 604-775-0891, Fax: 604-775-0999
East Annex, ParliamentBuildings
Victoria, BC V8V 1X4
Member, Legislative Assembly, Bill Routley
Constituency: Cowichan Valley *No. of Constituents:* 41,612, New Democratic Party
Tel: 250-387-3655
Toll-free: 877-715-0127
Fax: 250-387-4680
bill.routley.mla@leg.bc.ca
Other Communications: Constituency Phone: 250-715-0127, Fax: 250-715-0139
#201,Parliament Buildings
Victoria, BC V8V 1X4
Member, Legislative Assembly, Doug Routley
Constituency: Nanaimo-North Cowichan *No. of Constituents:* 38,832, New Democratic Party
Tel: 250-387-3655
Fax: 250-387-4680
douglas.routley.mla@leg.bc.ca
Other Communications: Ladysmith Constituency Phone: 250-245-9375
#201, ParliamentBuildings
Victoria, BC V8V 1X4
Member, Legislative Assembly, John Rustad
Constituency: Nechako Lakes *No. of Constituents:* 16,318, Liberal
Tel: 250-953-4892
Toll-free: 877-964-5650
Fax: 250-387-9066
john.rustad.mla@leg.bc.ca
Other Communications: Vanderhoof Constituency Phone: 250-567-6820
East Annex,Parliament Buildings
Victoria, BC V8V 1X4

Member, Legislative Assembly, Michael Sather
Constituency: Maple Ridge-Pitt Meadows *No. of Constituents:* 36,716, New Democratic Party
Tel: 250-387-3655
Fax: 250-387-4680
michael.sather.mla@leg.bc.ca
Other Communications: Constituency Phone: 604-476-9823, Fax: 604-476-9820
#201,Parliament Buildings
Victoria, BC V8V 1X4

Member, Legislative Assembly, Nicholas Simons
Constituency: Powell River-Sunshine Coast *No. of Constituents:* 36,304, New Democratic Party
Tel: 250-387-3655
Toll-free: 866-373-0792
Fax: 250-387-4680
nicholas.simons.mla@leg.bc.ca
www.nicholassimons.ca
Other Communications: Powell River Constituency Office Phone:604-485-1249
Social Media: twitter.com/NicholasSimons
#201, Parliament Buildings
Victoria, BC V8V 1X4

Member, Legislative Assembly, Bob Simpson
Constituency: Cariboo North *No. of Constituents:* 23,631, Independent
Tel: 250-387-8347
Toll-free: 866-991-0296
Fax: 250-387-8338
bob.simpson.mla@leg.bc.ca
Other Communications: Quesnel Constituency Phone: 250-991-0296
#027, ParliamentBuildings
Victoria, BC V8V 1X4

Member, Legislative Assembly, Shane Simpson
Constituency: Vancouver-Hastings *No. of Constituents:* 39,006, New Democratic Party
Tel: 250-387-3655
Fax: 250-387-4680
shane.simpson.mla@leg.bc.ca
Other Communications: Constituency Phone: 604-775-2277, Fax: 604-775-2352
#201, ParliamentBuildings
Victoria, BC V8V 1X4

Member, Legislative Assembly, John Slater
Constituency: Boundary-Similkameen *No. of Constituents:* 28,822, Liberal
Tel: 250-953-4869
Toll-free: 877-652-4304
Fax: 250-387-9100
john.slater.mla@leg.bc.ca
Other Communications: Constituency Phone: 250-495-2042, Fax: 250-495-2077
EastAnnex, Parliament Buildings
Victoria, BC V8V 1X4

Member, Legislative Assembly; Minister, Citizens' Services & Open Government, Ben Stewart
Constituency: Westside-Kelowna *No. of Constituents:* 41,155, Liberal
Tel: 250-952-7623
Fax: 250-952-7628
ben.stewart.mla@leg.bc.ca
www.benstewartmla.bc.ca
Other Communications: Constituency Phone:250-768-8426, Fax: 250-768-8436
East Annex, Parliament Buildings
Victoria, BC V8V 1X4

Member, Legislative Assembly; Minister, Social Development, Hon. Dr. Moira Stilwell
Constituency: Vancouver-Langara *No. of Constituents:* 38,142, Liberal
Tel: 250-356-7750
Fax: 250-356-7292
moira.stilwell.mla@leg.bc.ca; SD.Minister@gov.bc.ca
Other Communications: Constituency Phone: 604-660-8380, Fax: 604-660-8383
Social Media: twitter.com/DrMoiraStilwell
East Annex, Parliament Buildings
Victoria, BC V8V 1X4

Member, Legislative Assembly; Minister of State for Seniors, Hon. Ralph Sultan
Constituency: West Vancouver-Capilano *No. of Constituents:* 39,288, Liberal
Tel: 250-356-0912
Fax: 250-356-0931
ralph.sultan.mla@leg.bc.ca
www.ralphsultanmla.ca
Other Communications: Constituency Phone: 604-981-0050,Fax: 604-981-0055
East Annex, Parliament Buildings
Victoria, BC V8V 1X4

Member, Legislative Assembly; Minister, Forests, Lands, & Natural Resource Operations, Hon. Steve Thomson
Constituency: Kelowna-Mission *No. of Constituents:* 42,344, Liberal
Tel: 250-387-6240
Fax: 250-387-1040
steve.thomson.mla@leg.bc.ca;FLNR.Minister@gov.bc.ca
Other Communications: Constituency Phone: 250-712-3620, Fax: 250-712-3626
#248, Parliament Buildings
Victoria, BC V8V 1X4

Member, Legislative Assembly, Diane Thorne
Constituency: Coquitlam-Maillardville *No. of Constituents:* 37,342, New Democratic Party
Tel: 250-387-3655
Fax: 250-387-4680
diane.thorne.mla@leg.bc.ca
Other Communications: Constituency Phone: 604-933-2001, Fax: 604-933-2022
#201, ParliamentBuildings
Victoria, BC V8V 1X4

Member, Legislative Assembly, Jane Thornthwaite
Constituency: North Vancouver-Seymour *No. of Constituents:* 37,071, Liberal
Tel: 250-387-2796
Fax: 250-387-9100
jane.thornthwaite.mla@leg.bc.ca
Other Communications: Constituency Phone: 604-983-9852, Fax: 604-983-9978
EastAnnex, Parliament Buildings
Victoria, BC V8V 1X4

Member, Legislative Assembly, Joe Trasolini
Constituency: Porty Moody-Coquitlam *No. of Constituents:* 33,487, New Democratic Party
Tel: 250-387-3655
Fax: 250-387-4680
joe.trasolini.mla@leg.bc.ca
www.joetrasolini.ca
Other Communications: Constituency Phone: 604-931-5477, Fax: 604-931-8328
Social Media: twitter.com/JoeTrasolini, www.facebook.com/pages/Joe-Trasolini/143050492467234
Note: Joe Trasolini was elected in a by-election on April 19, 2012.
#201, ParliamentBuildings
Victoria, BC V8V 1X4

Member, Legislative Assembly, Claire Trevena
Constituency: North Island *No. of Constituents:* 40,040, New Democratic Party
Tel: 250-387-3655
Toll-free: 866-387-5100
Fax: 250-387-4680
claire.trevena.mla@leg.bc.ca
Other Communications: Campbell River Constituency Phone: 250-287-5100
#201,Parliament Buildings
Victoria, BC V8V 1X4

Member, Legislative Assembly, John van Dongen
Constituency: Abbotsford South *No. of Constituents:* 33,979, Liberal
Tel: 250-387-8950
Fax: 250-952-7263
john.vandongen.mla@leg.bc.ca
Other Communications: Constituency Phone: 604-870-5945, Fax: 604-870-5950
East Annex,Parliament Buildings
Victoria, BC V8V 1X4

Member, Legislative Assembly; Minister of State for Small Business, Hon. Naomi Yamamoto
Constituency: North Vancouver-Lonsdale *No. of Constituents:* 38,088, Liberal
Tel: 250-356-0179
Fax: 250-952-0260
naomi.yamamoto.mla@leg.bc.ca
www.naomiyamamotomla.bc.ca
Other Communications: Constituency Phone:604-981-0033, Fax: 604-981-0044
Social Media: twitter.com/naomiyamamoto, www.facebook.com/naomi.yamamoto.mla
#133, Parliament Buildings
Victoria, BC V8V 1X4

Member, Legislative Assembly; Minister, Advanced Education, Innovation, & Technology; Minister Responsible, Multiculturalism, Hon. John Yap
Constituency: Richmond-Steveston *No. of Constituents:* 42,336, Liberal
Tel: 250-356-1631
Fax: 250-952-7263
john.yap.mla@leg.bc.ca; AVED.Minister@gov.bc.ca
www.johnyapmla.bc.ca
Other Communications: Constituency Phone: 604-241-8452, Fax: 604-241-8493
Social Media: twitter.com/John_Yap
#124, Parliament Buildings
Victoria, BC V8V 1X4

British Columbia Government Departments & Agencies

British Columbia Ministry of Aboriginal Relations & Reconciliation

2957 Jutland Rd., PO Box 9100 Prov Govt, Victoria, BC V8W 9B1
Tel: 250-387-6121
Toll-Free: 800-663-7867
abrinfo@gov.bc.ca
www.gov.bc.ca/arr
Other Communication: Vancouver Phone: 604-660-2421; Information, Toll-Free Line: 1-800-880-1022

The Ministry of Aboriginal Relations & Reconciliation works to achieve the following goals: reconciliation with Aboriginal peoples; negotiation of lasting agreements; strengthening relationships with the Métis Nation; development of partnerships with Aboriginal people, organizations, & communities; support of capacity building in Aboriginal communities; provision of advice on policy related to Aboriginal people; & revitalization of Aboriginal language & culture.

Minister, Aboriginal Relations & Reconciliation, Hon. Ida Chong
Tel: 250-953-4844
Fax: 250-953-4856
ABR.Minister@gov.bc.ca
Social Media: twitter.com/Ida_Chong, www.facebook.com/idachongmla
PO Box 9051 Prov Govt Sta.
Victoria, BC V8W 9E2

Deputy Minister, Aboriginal Relations & Reconciliation, Steve Munro
Tel: 250-356-1394
Fax: 250-387-6073
PO Box 9100 Prov Govt Sta.
Victoria, BC V8W 9B1

Correspondence Manager, Jeanette Sidhu-Scherer
Tel: 250-953-3530
Fax: 250-387-6073
Jeanette.SidhuScherer@gov.bc.ca
PO Box 9100 Prov Govt Sta.
Victoria, BC V8W 9B1

Associated Agencies, Boards & Commissions:

• British Columbia Treaty Commission (BCTC)
#700, 1111 Melville St.
Vancouver, BC V6E 3V6
Tel: 604-482-9200
Fax: 604-482-9222
Toll-free: 800-665-8330
info@bctreaty.net
www.bctreaty.net
The independent & neutral body facilitates treaty negotiations among the governments of Canada, British Columbia, & First Nations in BC.

• Native Economic Development Advisory Board
c/o Director, Economic Initiatives
PO Box 9100 Prov Govt
Victoria, BC V8W 9B1
Tel: 250-387-2536
Fax: 250-356-9467
www.gov.bc.ca/arr/economic/fcf/nedab.html
Supporting sustainable Aboriginal economic development throughout British Columbia is the role of the Native Economic Development Advisory Board.

Fiscal Negotiations Team

Chief Negotiator, Rob Draeseke
Tel: 250-356-8768
Fax: 250-356-5213
Rob.Draeseke@gov.bc.ca

Fiscal Negotiator, Heidi Reinebeck
Tel: 250-356-5484
Fax: 250-387-5213
Heidi.Reinebeck@gov.bc.ca
Other Communications: Cell Phone: 250-896-5390

Director, Cost-sharing & Financial Mandates, Elisabeth Ellis
Tel: 250-356-9070
Fax: 250-356-6073
Elisabeth.Ellis@gov.bc.ca
Other Communications: Cell Phone: 250-886-6192

Director, Fiscal Arrangements & Climate Change, Michael Matsubuchi
Tel: 250-387-6387
Fax: 250-356-5312
Michael.Matsubuchi@gov.bc.ca
Other Communications: Cell Phone: 250-744-7454

Acting Director, Cost-sharing & Financial, Bademа Karabegovic
Tel: 250-953-3506
Fax: 250-387-6073
Badema.Karabegovic@gov.bc.ca

Negotiations & Regional Operations Division
Assistant Deputy Minister, Charles Porter
Tel: 250-953-3541
Fax: 250-387-6073
Divisional Coordinator, Shawna Hill
Tel: 250-953-3542
Fax: 250-387-6073
Shawna.Hill@gov.bc.ca
Chief Negotiator, Beedle Team, Tom Ethier
Tel: 250-387-0024
Fax: 250-387-0887
Tom.Ethier@gov.bc.ca
Other Communications: Alternate Phone: 250-361-7372
Chief Negotiator, Lofthouse Team, Heinz Dyck
Tel: 250-356-6599
Fax: 250-356-6159
Heinz.Dyck@gov.bc.ca
Chief Negotiator, Lofthouse Team, Mark Lofthouse
Tel: 250-356-8769
Fax: 250-387-0887
Mark.Lofthouse@gov.bc.ca
Other Communications: Cell Phone: 250-480-8899
Executive Director, Negotiations & Regional Operations, Trish Balcaen
Tel: 250-953-3954
Trish.Balcaen@gov.bc.ca

Partnerships & Community Renewal Division
Assistant Deputy Minister, Arlene Paton
Tel: 250-356-8750
Fax: 250-387-6073
Arlene.Paton@gov.bc.ca
Divisional Coordinator, Janice Rashbrook
Tel: 250-356-0213
Fax: 250-387-6073
Janice.Rashbrook@gov.bc.ca
Chief Negotiator, Negotiations & Community Renewal Branch, Roger Graham
Tel: 250-356-6599
Fax: 250-356-0366
Roger.Graham@gov.bc.ca
Other Communications: Cell Phone: 250-812-8244
Executive Director, Intergovernmental & Community Relations, Ken Armour
Tel: 250-387-2161
Fax: 250-356-9467
Ken.Armour@gov.bc.ca
Executive Director, Implementation & Legislation, Lloyd Roberts
Tel: 250-952-4482
Fax: 250-952-4485
Lloyd.Roberts@gov.bc.ca
Other Communications: Cell Phone: 250-380-8568

Strategic Initiatives Division
Assistant Deputy Minister, Julian C. Paine
Tel: 250-387-6838
Fax: 250-387-6073
Other Communications: Cell Phone: 250-387-6838
Chief Negotiator, Glenn Ricketts
Tel: 250-953-4004
Fax: 250-356-0366
Glenn.Ricketts@gov.bc.ca
Other Communications: Cell Phone: 250-889-1695
Executive Director, Cross Government Initiatives, Lynn Beak
Tel: 250-356-7214
Fax: 250-356-0366
Lynn.Beak@gov.bc.ca
Other Communications: Cell Phone: 250-920-6286
Executive Director, Strategic Policy & Planning Branch, Jaclynn Hunter
Tel: 250-356-5267
Fax: 250-356-0366
Jaclynn.Hunter@gov.bc.ca
Executive Director, Special Projects, Giovanni Puggioni
Tel: 250-952-0530
Fax: 250-356-0366
Giovanni.Puggioni@gov.bc.ca

British Columbia Ministry of Advanced Education, Innovation, & Technology (& Responsible for Multiculturalism)

PO Box 9059 Prov Govt, Victoria, BC V8W 9E2
Tel: 250-952-6508
Fax: 250-356-6942
www.gov.bc.ca/aved

The Ministry of Advanced Education, Innovation & Technology is responsible for the following: universities; colleges; post-secondary policy & accountability; post secondary financing; student financial assistance; research, innovation, & technology; & multiculturalism.

Acts Administered:
Accountants (Certified General) Act
Accountants (Chartered) Act
Accountants (Management) Act
Applied Science Technologists & Technicians Act
Architects (Landscape) Act
Architects Act
College & Institute Act
Degree Authorization Act
Engineers & Geoscientists Act
Music Teachers (Registered) Act
Private Career Training Institutions Act
Public Education Flexibility & Choice Act
Public Education Labour Relations Act
Royal Roads University Act
Thompson Rivers University Act
University Act
University Foundations Act

Minister, Advanced Education, Innovation, & Technology; Minister Responsible, Multiculturalism, Hon. John Yap
Tel: 250-356-0179
Fax: 250-952-0260
AVED.Minister@gov.bc.ca
Social Media: twitter.com/John_Yap
PO Box 9080 Prov Govt Sta.
Victoria, BC V8W 9E2

Deputy Minister, Advanced Education, Innovation, & Technology, Cheryl Wenezenki-Yolland
Tel: 250-356-5173
Fax: 250-356-5468
AVED.DeputyMinister@gov.bc.ca
PO Box 9884 Prov Govt Sta.
Victoria, BC V8W 9T6

Manager, Executive Operations & Strategic Support, Jennifer Meadows
Tel: 250-952-6842
Fax: 250-356-5468

Manager, Operations & Ministerial Correspondence & Research Unit, Judy Shaw
Tel: 250-356-6284
Fax: 250-356-5468

Parliamentary Secretary for Innovation & Technology to the Minister of Advanced Education, Innovation, & Technology, Ron Cantelon
Tel: 250-387-2203
Fax: 250-387-9066

Associated Agencies, Boards & Commissions:

• **British Columbia Innovation Council (BCIC)**
1188 West Georgia St., 9th Fl.
Vancouver, BC V6E 4A2
Tel: 604-683-2724
Fax: 604-683-6567
Toll-free: 800-665-7222
info@bcic.ca
www.bcic.ca
The British Columbia Innovation Council strives to advance innovation & commercialization by focusing on the following strategies: developing, recruiting & retaining science & technology professionals; fostering innovation & entrepreneurship; & bringing innovation to commercial success by establishing partnerships.

• **Degree Quality Assessment Board**
Degree Quality Assessment Board Secretariat
PO Box 9177 Prov Govt
Victoria, BC V8W 9H8
Tel: 250-387-5163
DQABsecretariat@gov.bc.ca
www.aved.gov.bc.ca/degree-authorization/board/welcome.htm
The Degree Quality Assessment Board reviews applications from British Columbia public post-secondary institutions, & private & out-of-province public post-secondary institutions. Applications concern new degree programs & exempt status, & the use of the word "university". Recommendations are then made to the Minister of Advanced Education & Labour Market Development.

• **Multicultural Advisory Council of BC**
Multiculturalism & Inclusive Communities Office
605 Robson St., 5th Fl.
Vancouver, BC V6B 5J3
Tel: 604-660-2203
Fax: 604-775-0670
www.embracebc.ca/embracebc/multiculturalism
Members of the Multicultural Advisory Council advise the minister responsible for multiculturalism about issues related to multiculturalism & anti-racism. The Multiculturalism Act of British Columbia guides the council.

• **Premier's Technology Council**
Tel: 604-775-2122
Fax: 604-775-2129
premiers.technologycouncil@gov.bc.ca
www.gov.bc.ca/premier/technology_council
The 23 member Premier's Technology Council advises the Premier on all technology related issues that affect British Columbia & its residents.

• **Private Career Training Institutions Agency**
#300, 5172 Kingsway
Burnaby, BC V5H 2E8
Tel: 604-660-4400
Fax: 604-660-3312
Toll-free: 800-661-7441
info@pctia.bc.ca
www.pctia.bc.ca
The Private Career Training Institutions Agency is the regulatory agency for private training institutions in British Columbia. The Agency works in accordance with the Private Career Training Institutions Act, Regulations & Bylaws.

Students, Institutions & Programs Division
PO Box 9191 Prov Govt, Victoria, BC V8W 9E6
Fax: 250-356-5468
Acting Assistant Deputy Minister, Mark Gillis
Tel: 250-952-0698
Fax: 250-356-5468
Mark.Gillis@gov.bc.ca
Executive Director, Research Universities & Health Programs Branch, Susan B. Brown
Tel: 250-387-6193
Fax: 250-356-8851
AVED.ResearchUniversities&HlthProgBr@gov.bc.ca
PO Box 9162 Prov Govt Sta.
Victoria, BC V8W 9H8
Executive Director, Teaching Universities, Institutes & Aboriginal Programs Branch, Deborah Hull
Tel: 250-356-8382
Fax: 250-356-5962
MSUUAPB@gov.bc.ca
Executive Director, Governance & Quality Assurance Branch, Tony Loughran
Tel: 250-356-7254
Executive Director, Colleges & Skills Development Branch, Dawn Minty
Tel: 250-387-8871
Fax: 250-952-6110
RESD.Agencies&QualityAssuranceBr@gov.bc.ca
PO Box 9894 Prov Govt Sta.
Victoria, BC V8W 9T6
Executive Director, StudentAid BC, Victoria Thibeau
Tel: 250-387-3605
Fax: 250-356-5468
Victoria.Thibeau@gov.bc.ca

Decision Support & Accountability Division
PO Box 9324 Prov Govt, Victoria, BC V8W 9N3
Tel: 250-952-0606
Fax: 250-356-5468
Assistant Deputy Minister, Corporate Services, Brian Hansen
Chief Information Officer, Technology & Business Solutions Branch, Suzanne Manahan
Tel: 250-952-0729
Fax: 250-952-0739
Executive Director, Open Government, Allan Pollock
Tel: 250-356-7210
Allan.Pollock@gov.bc.ca
PO Box 9149 Prov Govt Sta.
Victoria, BC V8W 9H1
Executive Director, Policy Planning & Intergovernmental Relations, Jacqui Stewart
Tel: 250-387-5029
Fax: 250-387-1377
AVED.PolicyPlanning&IntergovRelationsBr@gov.bc.ca
Executive Director, Post Secondary Funding & Corporate Finance Branch, Joseph Thompson
Tel: 250-387-8820
Fax: 250-356-7922
Joe.Thompson@gov.bc.ca
PO Box 9147 Prov Govt Sta.
Victoria, BC V8W 9H1
Executive Director, Talent Strategies Branch, Lori Wiedeman
Tel: 250-356-1777
Fax: 250-356-5468
Lori.Wiedeman@gov.bc.ca
PO Box 9324 Prov Govt Sta.
Victoria, BC V8W 9N3
Director, Research & Analysis, Patty Beatty-Guenter
Tel: 250-387-1105
Fax: 250-952-0606
AVED.PolicyPlanning&IntergovRelationsBr@gov.bc.ca
Director, Projects & Planning, Kursti Calder
Tel: 250-387-8874
Fax: 250-952-0606
AVED.PolicyPlanning&IntergovRelationsBr@gov.bc.ca
Director, Corporate Policy, Kate Cotie
Tel: 250-387-6197
Fax: 250-952-0606
AVED.PolicyPlanning&IntergovRelationsBr@gov.bc.ca

Director, Post Secondary Finance, Colin Fowler
Tel: 250-387-6142
Fax: 250-952-6103
Colin.Fowler@gov.bc.ca
Director, Financial Operations, Jennifer Ingram-Kum
Tel: 250-356-1409
Fax: 250-387-6360
Jennifer.IngramKum@gov.bc.ca
Director, Capital Unit, Catherine Nickerson
Tel: 250-356-7896
Fax: 250-356-7922
Catherine.Nickerson@gov.bc.ca
Director, Corporate Policy, Vincent Portal
Tel: 250-356-6356
Fax: 250-952-0606
AVED.PolicyPlanning&IntergovRelationsBr@gov.bc.ca
Director, Corporate Finance, Donna Porter
Tel: 250-356-6819
Fax: 250-387-6360
Donna.Porter@gov.bc.ca
Director, Workforce Planning & Analysis, Kathy Philps
Tel: 250-387-5600
Fax: 250-356-5468
Kathy.Philps@gov.bc.ca

British Columbia Ministry of Agriculture

PO Box 9120 Prov Govt, Victoria, BC V8W 9E2
Tel: 250-387-5121
www.gov.bc.ca/agri
Other Communication: Agriculture Communications Office, Phone: 250-387-1693

The mission of the Ministry of Agriculture is to stabilize & expand agrifoods production & incomes, to safeguard animal, plant, & human health, & to encourage environmental stewardship. Responsibilities include agriculture, acquacultures & food industry development, fish processing, meat processing policy, food safety & quality, & crop insurance.

Acts Administered:
Agri-Food Choice & Quality Act
Agricultural Land Commission Act
Agricultural Produce Grading Act
Agrologists Act
Animal Disease Control Act
Bee Act
Farm Income Insurance Act
Farm Practices Protection (Right to Farm) Act
Farmers & Womens Institutes Act
Farming & Fishing Industries Development Act
Fish Inspection Act
Fisheries Act (except Part 3 as it relates to the licensing of aquaculture)
Food Products Standards Act
Fur Farm Act
Game Farm Act
Insurance for Crops Act
Livestock Act
Livestock Identification Act
Livestock Lien Act
Local Government Act (ss. 916-919)
Milk Industry Act (s. 12 as it relates to tank milk receiver licences, & the remainder of the Act)
Ministry of Agriculture & Food Act
Ministry of Forestry & Range Act (s. 4 (d) (ii) & (e) as that provision relates to the portfolio of the Minister of Agriculture)
Natural Products Marketing (BC) Act
Plant Protection Act
Prevention of Cruelty to Animals Act
Range Act (ss. 39-41, 42 & 43; ss. 1 (2) & (3), 44, 45, 76, 79 & 80 as those provisions relate to the portfolio of the Minister of Agriculture)
Seed Potato Act
Special Accounts Appropriation & Control Act (s. 9.2)
Veterinarians Act
Veterinary Drugs Act

Minister, Agriculture, Hon. Norm Letnick
Tel: 250-387-1023
Fax: 250-387-1522
AGR.Minister@gov.bc.ca
Social Media: twitter.com/normletnick
PO Box 9043 Prov Govt Sta.
Victoria, BC V8W 9E2

Deputy Minister, Agriculture, Wes Shoemaker
Tel: 250-356-1800
Fax: 250-356-8392
PO Box 9120 Prov Govt Sta.
Victoria, BC V8W 9B4

Manager, Executive Operations, Sandra Roe
Tel: 250-356-5126
Fax: 250-356-8392
Sandra.Roe@gov.bc.ca

Operations, Project, & Administrative Coordinator, Correspondence Unit, Naomi Boulay
Tel: 250-356-1804
Fax: 250-356-8392
Naomi.Boulay@gov.bc.ca

Associated Agencies, Boards & Commissions:

• Agricultural Land Commission (ALC)
#133, 4940 Canada Way
Burnaby, BC V5G 4K6
Tel: 604-660-7000
Fax: 604-660-7033
ALCBurnaby@Victoria1.gov.bc.ca
www.alc.gov.bc.ca
The independent Crown agency strives to preserve agricultural land in British Columbia. The Provincial Agricultural Land Commission also works to encourage & enable farm businesses throughout the province. The Commission's chief responsibility is the administration of the Agricultural Land Commission Act.

• British Columbia Broiler Hatching Egg Commission (BCBHEC)
#180, 32160 South Fraser Way
Abbotsford, BC V2T 1W5
Tel: 604-850-1854
Fax: 604-850-1683
info@bcbhec.com
www.bcbhec.com
The British Columbia Broiler Hatching Egg Commission was formed in 1988 under the British Columbia Natural Products Marketing Act, & seeks to promote a better understanding of the broiler hatching egg industry.

• British Columbia Chicken Marketing Board (BCCMB)
#101, 32450 Simon Ave.
Abbotsford, BC V2T 4J2
Tel: 604-859-2868
Fax: 604-859-2811
info@bcchicken.ca
www.bcchicken.ca
The purpose of the BC Chicken Marketing Board is to monitor & regulate the production of chicken in British Columbia. The Board works closely with hatcheries, growers, truckers & processors, & carries out field inspections, to accomplish this.

• British Columbia Cranberry Marketing Commission (BCCMC)
c/o #71, 4001 Old Clayburn Rd.
Abbotsford, BC V3S 1C5
Tel: 604-302-1046
cranberries@telus.net
www.bccranberries.com
Since 1968 the BCCMC has administered the British Columbia Cranberry Marketing Scheme, established under the Natural Products Marketing (BC) Act. The Commission reports to the British Columbia Farm Industry Review Board.

• British Columbia Egg Marketing Board (BCEMB)
#250, 32160 South Fraser Way
Abbotsford, BC V2T 1W5
Tel: 604-556-3348
Fax: 604-556-3410
bcemb@bcegg.com
www.bcegg.com
The BCEMB was established in 1967 in order to better regulate the price of eggs.

• British Columbia Farm Industry Review Board (BCFIRB)
780 Blanshard St.
PO Box 9129 Prov Govt
Victoria, BC V8W 9B5
Tel: 250-356-8945
Fax: 250-356-5131
firb@gov.bc.ca
www.firb.gov.bc.ca
The British Columbia Farm Industry Review Board is a statutory appeal body. It is engaged in the general supervision of marketing boards & commodity boards which operate in the agricultural & aquaculture sectors.

• British Columbia Hog Marketing Commission (BCHMC)
PO Box 8000-280
Abbotsford, BC V2S 6H1
Tel: 604-897-9252
Fax: 604-677-6058
dianned@bcpork.ca
www.bcpork.ca
The Commission seeks to promote BC-grown pork through the use of its logo on all BC pork products.

• British Columbia Milk Marketing Board (BCMMB)
#200, 32160 South Fraser Way
Abbotsford, BC V2T 1W5
Tel: 604-556-3444
Fax: 604-556-7717
info@milk-bc.com
bcmilkmarketing.worldsecuresystems.com/
The Board is reponsible for promoting, controlling & regulating the production, transportation, packing, storing & marketing of all BC milk products.

• British Columbia Turkey Marketing Board (BCTMB)
#106, 19329 Enterprise Way
Surrey, BC V3S 6J8
Tel: 604-534-5644
Fax: 604-534-3651
info@bcturkey.com
www.bcturkey.com
Established in 1966, the Board oversees the licensing of turkey farmers and processors; prices for live turkeys; maintaining of a quota system; & promoting turkey products, under the authority of the Natural Products Marketing (BC) Act.

• British Columbia Vegetable Marketing Commission (BCVMC)
#207, 15252 32nd Ave.
Surrey, BC V3S 0R7
Tel: 604-542-9734
Fax: 603-542-9753
info@bcveg.com
The Commission is responsible for promoting controlled marketing for BC vegetable producers, under the authority of the Natural Products Marketing (BC) Act.

Agriculture Science & Policy

PO Box 9120 Prov Govt, Victoria, BC V8W 9B4
Tel: 250-356-1816
Fax: 250-356-7279

Director, Innovation & Governance Branch, Sean Darling
Tel: 250-356-5338
Fax: 250-356-5367
Sean.Darling@gov.bc.ca
Director/Chief Veterinary Officer, Plant & Animal Health Branch, Abbotsford, Paul Kitching
Tel: 604-556-3038
Fax: 604-556-3010
Paul.Kitching@gov.bc.ca
Director, Policy & Industry Competitiveness, Grant Thompson
Tel: 250-356-8299
Fax: 250-387-0357
Grant.Thompson@gov.bc.ca
Assistant Director, Policy & Industry Competitiveness, Gavin Last
Tel: 250-356-7640
Fax: 250-387-0357
Gavin.Last@gov.bc.ca

Animal Health Center

Tel: 604-556-3003
Fax: 604-556-3010

Avian Pathologist, Dr. Victoria Bowes
Tel: 604-556-3041
Victoria.Bowes@gov.bc.ca
Veterinary Pathologist, Dr. Ann Britton
Tel: 604-556-3039
Ann.P.Britton@gov.bc.ca
Fish Pathologist, Dr. Gary Marty
Tel: 604-556-3123
Gary.Marty@gov.bc.ca
Veterinary Pathologist, Dr. Stephen Raverty
Tel: 604-556-3026
Stephen.Raverty@gov.bc.ca
Veterinary Virologist, Dr. John Robinson
Tel: 604-556-3036
John.H.Robinson@gov.bc.ca
Microbiologist/Supervisor, Dr. Sean Byrne
Tel: 604-556-3025
Sean.Byrne@gov.bc.ca
Poultry Health Veterinarian, Dr. William Cox
Tel: 604-556-3150
William.Cox@gov.bc.ca

Strategic Industry Partnerships Division

PO Box 9120 Prov Govt, Victoria, BC V8W 9B4
Tel: 250-356-1122
Fax: 250-356-7279

Assistant Deputy Minister, Grant Parnell
Tel: 250-356-1802
Grant.Parnell@gov.bc.ca
Director, Head Office, Gary Falk
Tel: 250-861-7232
Fax: 250-861-7490
Gary.Falk@gov.bc.ca
Director, Sustainable Agriculture Management, Land Program Services, Ken Nickel
Tel: 604-556-3103
Fax: 604-556-3030
Ken.Nickel@gov.bc.ca
780 Blanshard St.
PO Box 9308 Prov Govt Sta.
Victoria, BC V8W 9N1
Director, Food Protection Branch, Jim Russell
Tel: 250-897-7561
Fax: 250-334-1410
Jim.Russell@gov.bc.ca
Assistant Director, Sustainable Agriculture Management, Leslie S. MacDonald

Tel: 604-556-3074
Fax: 604-556-3030
Leslie.MacDonald@gov.bc.ca
Agrologist, Head Office, Phil Croteau
Tel: 250-861-7419
Fax: 250-861-7490
Phil.Croteau@gov.bc.ca

Office of the Auditor General

PO Box 9036 Prov Govt, Victoria, BC V8W 9A2
Tel: 250-419-6100
Fax: 250-387-1230
www.bcauditor.com

The chief responsibility of the Office of the Auditor General is auditing most of the British Columbia provincial government, with its ministries, Crown corporations, & other organizations.

Auditor General, John Doyle, MAcc, CA

Executive Director, Michael Macdonell, MBA, CA
Tel: 250-419-6109
mmacdonell@bcauditor.com

Financial Audit
Assistant Auditor General, Bill Gilhooly, BEcon, CA
Tel: 250-419-6102
bgilhooly@bcauditor.com
Assistant Auditor General, Russ Jones, MBA, CA
Tel: 250-419-6103
rjones@bcauditor.com
Executive Director, Peter Bourne, CA, CIA
Tel: 250-419-6141
pbourne@bcauditor.com
Other Communications: Alternate Phone: 250-387-5600
Executive Director, Lisa Moore, CA
Tel: 250-419-6188
lmoore@bcauditor.com
Executive Director, Jason Reid, BComm, CA
Tel: 250-419-6204
jreid@bcauditor.com
Director, Ada Chiang
Tel: 250-419-6144
achiang@bcauditor.com
Director, Bob Faulkner
Tel: 250-419-6152
bfaulkner@bcauditor.com
Director, IT Audit, Pam Hamilton
Tel: 250-419-6164
phamilton@bcauditor.com
Director, David K. Lau
Tel: 250-419-6118
dlau@bcauditor.com

Performance Audit
Assistant Auditor General, Governance, Accountability & Education, Malcolm Gaston, CMA, CPFA
Tel: 250-419-6105
mgaston@bcauditor.com
Assistant Auditor General, Sustainability & Environment, Morris Sydor, MBA, CA
Tel: 250-419-6106
msydor@bcauditor.com
Director, Tara Anderson
Tel: 250-419-6134
tanderson@bcauditor.com
Director, Sheila Dodds
Tel: 250-419-6149
sdodds@bcauditor.com
Director, Mike McStravick
Tel: 250-419-6185
mmcstravick@bcauditor.com
Director, Paul Nyquist
Tel: 250-419-6194
pnyquist@bcauditor.com

Standards & Quality
Assistant Auditor General, Professsional Practices & Quality Assurance, Beverly Romeo-Beehler
Tel: 250-419-6107
barombee@bcauditor.com
Executive Director, Professsional Practices & Quality Assurance, Brian Jones
Tel: 250-419-6171
bjones@bcauditor.com
Director, Finance & Human Capital, Marc LeFebvre
Tel: 250-419-6120
mlefebvre@bcauditor.com

British Columbia Centre for Disease Control (BCCDC)

655 West 12th Ave., Vancouver, BC V5Z 4R4
Tel: 604-707-2400
Fax: 604-707-2401
admininfo@bccdc.ca
www.bccdc.ca

The BCCDC is both a provincial & national leader in public health as it detects, treats, & prevents diseases in its patients. Not only does it offer direct services for people with diseases & health concerns, but it also provides analytical & policy support to health authorities at all levels of government.

British Columbia Ministry of Children & Family Development (MCFD)

PO Box 9770 Prov Govt, Victoria, BC V8W 9S5
Tel: 250-387-7027
Fax: 250-356-3007
Toll-Free: 877-387-7027
MCF.CorrespondenceManagement@gov.bc.ca
www.gov.bc.ca/mcf
TTY: 800-667-4770
Other Communication: Helpline for Children: 310-1234; Emergencies outside office hours: 604-660-4927 (Vancouver); 604-660-8180 (Lower Mainland); 1-800-663-9122 (remainder of province)

The Ministry of Children & Family Development works to support healthy child development, to maximize the potential of children & youth, & to achieve meaningful outcomes for children, youth, & families. A client-centered approach is used to deliver services. The following services are available to families throughout British Columbia: adoption servies; early childhood development & child care services; child safety, family support, & children in care services; services for children & youth with special needs; mental health services for children & youth; & youth justice services.

Acts Administered:
Adoption Act
Child Care BC Act
Child Care Subsidy Act
Child, Family, & Community Service Act
Community Care & Assisted Living Act (ss. 8 & 34 (2) (h) & (h.1) & (6))
Community Services Interim Authorities Act
Employment & Assistance Act (except ss. 17 (3) & (4), 18-20, 21 (1), 22 (1)-(3), (4) (b), (5) & (6), 23 (1) (a) (ii) & (iii) & (b) (ii) & (iii), 23 (2), 24 (1), (2) (a) & (3)-(7) & 29)
Health & Social Services Delivery Improvement Act (Part 3)
Human Resource Facility Act (except s. 1.1 (b), (c) & (d))
Social Workers Act
Youth Justice Act (except Part 1 & s. 44 (2) (a) & (b))

Minister, Children & Family Development, Hon. Stephanie Cadieux
Tel: 250-387-9699
Fax: 250-387-9722
MCF.Minister@gov.bc.ca; stephanie.cadieux.mla@leg.bc.ca
Social Media: twitter.com/mlacadieux
PO Box 9057 Prov Govt Sta.
Victoria, BC V8W 9E2

Deputy Minister, Children & Family Development, Stephen Brown
Tel: 250-387-2000
Fax: 250-356-2920
mcf.deputyministersoffice@gov.bc.ca
PO Box 9721 Prov Govt Sta.
Victoria, BC V8W 9S2

Assistant Deputy Minister; Provincial Director, Child Welfare, Doug Hughes
Tel: 250-953-3835
Fax: 250-387-7756
PO Box 9767 Prov Govt Sta.
Victoria, BC V8W 9S5

Advocate for Service Quality, Jane Holland
Tel: 604-775-1238
Fax: 604-660-1505

Director, Executive Operations, Debbie Godfrey
Tel: 250-387-3717
Fax: 250-356-2920

Associated Agencies, Boards & Commissions:
• British Columbia College of Social Workers (BCCSW)
#302, 1765 West 8th Ave.
Vancouver, BC V6J 5C6
Tel: 604-737-4916
Fax: 604-737-6809
info@bccsw.ca
www.bccollegeofsocialworkers.ca

The regulatory body for the practice of social work in British Columbia is the Board of Registration for Social Workers in BC. The Board's responsibility is establishing & supporting high standards for Registered Social Workers in the province.

Aboriginal Policy & Service Support Team
PO Box 9721 Prov Govt, Victoria, BC V8W 9S2
Tel: 250-387-5275
Fax: 250-356-6534
Assistant Deputy Minister, Debra Foxcroft
Tel: 250-387-3810
Fax: 250-356-6534
Director/Project Director, Aboriginal Policy & Legislation/Jordan's Principle Implementation Team, Dena Carroll
Tel: 250-356-5581
Fax: 250-387-1732
Other Communications: Team Phone: 250-356-9791, Fax: 250-387-1732
PO Box 9774 Prov Govt Sta.
Victoria, BC V8W9S5
Acting First Nations Director, Aboriginal Services, Ray Bronson
Tel: 250-387-0726
Fax: 250-387-1732
PO Box 977 Prov Govt Sta.
Victoria, BC V8W 9S5
Director, Operations, Aboriginal Services, Rob Parenteau
Tel: 250-387-7073
Fax: 250-387-1732
PO Box 977 Prov Govt Sta.
Victoria, BC V8W 9S5
Executive Coordinator, Lisa Marshman
Tel: 250-953-3450
Fax: 250-387-1732
PO Box 977 Prov Govt Sta.
Victoria, BC V8W 9S5

Integrated Quality Assurance
PO Box 9721 Prov Govt, Victoria, BC V8W 9S2
Tel: 250-356-9808
Fax: 250-356-6534
Assistant Deputy Minister, Sandra Griffin
Senior Director, Practice Support, Karen Blackman
Tel: 250-387-7416
Fax: 250-387-8000
PO Box 9766 Prov Govt Sta.
Victoria, BC V8W 9S1
Senior Director, Practice Support, Joan Easton
Tel: 250-387-7814
Fax: 250-387-7618
PO Box 9766 Prov Govt Sta.
Victoria, BC V8W 9S1
Director, Advocacy, Kathy Berggren-Clive
Tel: 604-775-2165
Fax: 604-660-4007
865 Hornby St., 9th Fl.
Vancouver, BC V6Z 9S2
Provincial Director, Adoptions, Anne Clayton
Tel: 250-387-2281
Fax: 250-387-7914
PO Box 9766 Prov Govt Sta.
Victoria, BC V8W 9S1

Office of the Chief Operating Officer
PO Box 9721 Prov Govt, Victoria, BC V8W 9S2
Tel: 250-387-3006
Fax: 250-356-6534
Assistant Deputy Minister, Integrated Policy & Legislation, Randi Mjolsness
Tel: 250-387-7090
Fax: 250-356-2481
Chief Operating Officer, Derek Sturko
Tel: 250-387-3006
Fax: 250-356-6534
Chief Information Officer, Information Management & Technology, Martin P. Wright
Tel: 250-356-0463
Fax: 250-387-7421
Craig.Wilkinson@gov.bc.ca
Executive Financial Officer, Financial Services, Craig Wilkinson
Tel: 250-356-2954
Fax: 250-356-2899
Craig.Wilkinson@gov.bc.ca
Executive Director, Strategic Policy & Operations, Integrated Policy & Legislation, Jennifer Erickson
Tel: 250-387-7418
Executive Director, Accountability, Tessa Graham
Tel: 250-953-3446
Fax: 250-356-6534
Executive Director, Legislation & Litigation, Integrated Policy & Legislation, Michael Turanski
Tel: 250-387-6434
Fax: 250-356-8182
Keva.Glynn@gov.bc.ca
Senior Director, Early Years Policy, Integrated Policy & Legislation, Keva Glynn

Tel: 250-387-9714
Fax: 250-356-0399
Keva.Glynn@gov.bc.ca
Senior Director, Children & Youth with Special Needs Provincial Operations, Integrated Policy & Legislation, Arif Lalani
Tel: 250-387-7762
Fax: 250-356-0399
Senior Director, Child, Youth & Family Policy, Integrated Policy & Legislation, Sandy Wiens
Tel: 250-387-1551
Fax: 250-356-0399
Director, Child Welfare Policy, Integrated Policy & Legislation, Mona Herring
Tel: 250-356-2777
Fax: 250-356-2995
Director, Child & Youth Mental Health Policy, Integrated Policy & Legislation, Deborah Saari
Tel: 250-356-5201
Fax: 250-356-0580
Director, Children & Youth with Special Needs, Integrated Policy & Legislation, Aleksandra Stevanovic
Tel: 250-387-1828
Fax: 250-356-0399
Director, CYSN Services Transfer & Cross-Ministry Youth Transitions Framework, Integrated Policy & Legislation, Frank Van Zandwijk
Tel: 250-356-2857
Fax: 250-953-4234
Director, Legislation, Leah Bailey
Tel: 250-387-0372
Fax: 250-356-8182
Director, Infrastructure & Administrative Services, Information Management & Technology Branch, Dwayne Quesnel
Tel: 250-387-7697
Fax: 250-387-2481
Director, Information Management & Governance, Information Management & Technology Branch, Ken Reimer
Tel: 250-356-2831
Fax: 250-387-7726
Director, Client Services & Projects, Information Management & Technology Branch, Steve Wilson
Tel: 250-356-9043
Fax: 250-387-7726

Provincial Services
PO Box 9717 Prov Govt, Victoria, BC V8W 9S1
Tel: 250-387-0978
Fax: 250-356-2079

Senior Executive Director, Alan Markwart
Executive Director, Youth Custody Services, Barry Lynden
Tel: 604-356-1970
Fax: 604-356-2079
PO Box 9719 Prov Govt Sta.
Victoria, BC V8W 9S5
Assistant Executive Director, Youth Custody Service, Rick Faoro
Tel: 778-452-2065
Fax: 778-452-2076
Director, Case Management, Victoria Youth Custody Service, Jeff Haas
Tel: 250-708-2218
Fax: 250-704-0283
Jeff.Haas@gov.bc.ca
Director, Victoria Youth Custody Service, Phil Hawley
Tel: 250-708-2206
Fax: 250-704-0283
Jeff.Haas@gov.bc.ca
Acting Director, Operations, Victoria Youth Custody Service, Mike Macphee
Tel: 250-708-2225
Fax: 250-704-0283
Mike.MacPhee@gov.bc.ca
Director, Programs, Victoria Youth Custody Service, Blade Tickner
Tel: 250-708-2219
Fax: 250-704-0283
Blade.Tickner@gov.bc.ca
Director, Operations, Prince George Youth Custody Service, Jim Arnold
Tel: 250-649-3852
Fax: 250-649-3878
Director, Victoria Youth Custody Service, Kim Fogtmann
Tel: 250-562-5393
Fax: 250-649-3878
Director, Programs, Prince George Youth Custody Service, Shawn Young
Tel: 250-562-5393
Fax: 250-565-6930
Director, Staffing Support Services, Burnaby Youth Custody Service, Doug Charmichael
Fax: 604-660-5994
Director, Operations, Burnaby Youth Custody Service, Andrew Cronkhite
Tel: 604-419-1618
Fax: 604-660-5994
Director, Case Management, Burnaby Youth Custody Service, Anita McDonnell
Tel: 604-419-1613
Fax: 604-660-5994
Director, Youth Justice Policy & Program Support, Chris Zatylny
Tel: 250-387-1335
Fax: 250-356-2079
Provincial Director, Youth Forensic Psychiatric Services, Andre Picard
Tel: 778-452-2202
Fax: 778-452-2201
Provincial Clinical Director, Youth Forensic Psychiatric Services, Dr. Kulwant Riar
Tel: 778-452-2205
Fax: 778-452-2201
Director, Maples Adolescent Treatment Centre, Ken Moore
Tel: 604-660-5811
Fax: 604-660-5814
3405 Willingdon Ave.
Burnaby, BC V5G 3H4

Strategic Human Resource & Sectoral Relations
PO Box 9757 Prov Govt, Victoria, BC V8W 9S3
Tel: 250-356-6883
Fax: 250-952-6880
Executive Director, Patrick Doyle
Tel: 250-356-7103
Director, Strategic Human Resources Projects & Recruitment, Cheryl Howarth
Tel: 250-387-7659
Acting Director, Human Resources Services, Tim Osborne
Tel: 250-387-2466
Director, Sectoral Relations, Brian Scofield
Tel: 250-953-3833
Acting Director, Learning & Development, Annemarie Travers
Tel: 250-387-7665

Regional Offices
Fraser & Vancouver Coastal Regions
Tel: 604-660-2433
Fax: 604-660-1090
Assistant Deputy Minister, Beverly Dicks
Fax: 604-660-4005
Regional Executive Director, Fraser Regional Office, Barbara Walsh
Tel: 604-586-4121
Fax: 604-596-4151
Regional Executive Director, Vancouver Coastal Regional Office, Dennis Padmore
Tel: 604-660-2433
Fax: 604-660-1090
Executive Director, Practice, Fraser Regional Office, Bruce McNeill
Tel: 604-586-4123
Fax: 604-586-4153
Director, Support to Operations, Fraser Regional Office, Donna Mathiasen
Tel: 604-586-4109
Fax: 604-596-4151
Director, Practice, Fraser Regional Office, Amarjit Sahota
Tel: 604-586-2628
Fax: 604-586-4153
Director, Aboriginal Service Change, Fraser Regional Office, Virge Silveira
Tel: 604-586-4132
Fax: 604-586-4153
Director, Quality Assurance Practice, Fraser Regional Office, Susan Waldron
Tel: 604-586-4100
Fax: 604-586-4153
Acting Director, Operations, Vancouver Coastal Regional Office, Holden Chu
Tel: 604-660-2141
Fax: 604-660-5346
Meena.Sanghera@gov.bc.ca
Director, Financial Management & Administration, Vancouver Coastal Regional Office, Philip Dong
Tel: 604-660-2433
Fax: 604-660-1090
Director, Practice, Vancouver Coastal Regional Office, Sheila Robinson
Tel: 604-660-5673
Fax: 604-660-5072
Meena.Sanghera@gov.bc.ca
Interior Region
PO Box 9767 Prov Govt, Victoria, BC V8W 9S5
Fax: 250-387-7756
Regional Executive Director, Nancy McComb
Tel: 250-354-6465
Fax: 250-354-6530
Director, Support to Practice, Karen Wallace
Tel: 250-953-3835
Executive Coordinator, Faye McClinton
Tel: 250-387-1068

North Region
Tel: 250-565-4367
Fax: 250-565-4427
Assistant Deputy Minister, Peter Cunningham
Acting Regional Executive Director, Shirley Reimer
Executive Director, Practice/Director, Child Welfare, Robert Watts
Tel: 250-565-4312
Director, Corporate Services, Sue Risby
Tel: 250-565-4315
Deputy Director, Child Welfare, Joanne White
Tel: 250-992-4158
Vancouver Island
PO Box 9767 Prov Govt, Victoria, BC V8W 9S5
Tel: 250-387-7744
Fax: 250-387-7756
Assistant Deputy Minister, Chuck Eamer
Regional Executive Director, Mark Armitage
Tel: 250-390-5458
Fax: 250-390-5477
Executive Director, Child Care Programs & Services Branch, Lenora Angel
Tel: 250-952-6089
Fax: 250-953-3327
Lenora.Angel@gov.bc.ca
Director, Child Care Subsidy Service Centre - Operations, Doug Bell
Toll-free: 888-338-6622
Fax: 250-387-0699
Director, Child Care Programs & Services, Andrew Morgan
Tel: 250-356-5391
Director, Operations/Office Manager, Regional Finance & Administration, Susan Rivers
Tel: 250-390-6018
Fax: 250-952-4282
Director, Program Support, Daniel Sobhana
Tel: 250-952-0893
Director, Child Welfare, Director CF & Community Services, Thomas Weber
Tel: 250-334-5820
Fax: 250-334-5844
Assistant Director, Child Care Subsidy Service Centre - Operations, Tim Anderson
Toll-free: 888-338-6622
Fax: 250-387-0699

British Columbia Ministry of Citizens' Services & Open Government

PO Box 9594 Prov Govt, Victoria, BC V8W 9E2
Tel: 250-952-7623
Fax: 250-952-7628
Toll-Free: 800-663-7867
EnquiryBC@gov.bc.ca
www.gov.bc.ca/citz
Other Communication: Victoria, Phone: 250-387-6121; Vancouver, Phone: 604-660-2421

The Ministry of Citizens' Services & Open Government oversees the following: Board Resourcing & Development Office; BC OnLine; BC Stats; Enquiry BC; government communications & public engagement; business & personal property registries; information & privacy policy; Queen's Printer; corporate accounting services; procurement & supply services; & telecommunications infrastructure.

Acts Administered:
BC Online Act
Business Corporations Act (as it relates to the establishment & operation of the Corporate Registry)
Business Number Act
Cooperative Association Act (as it relates to the establishment & operation of the Corporate Registry)
Credit Union Incorporation Act (as it relates to the establishment and operation of the Corporate Registry)
Document Disposal Act
Electronic Transactions Act
Emergency Intervention Disclosure Act
Family Day Act
Financial Institutions Act (as it relates to the establishment & operation of the Corporate Registry)
Fire Department Act
Freedom of Information & Protection of Privacy Act
Government Buildings Act
Insurance (Captive Company) Act (as it relates to the establishment & operation of the Corporate Registry)
Knowledge Network Corporation Act
Legislative Assembly Management Committee Act
Legislative Assembly Privilege Act
Legislative Library Act
Legislative Procedure Review Act
Manufactured Home Act (as it relates to the establishment & operation of the Manufactured Home Registry)
Members' Remuneration & Pensions Act
Ministry of Provincial Secretary & Government Services Act

Miscellaneous Registrations Act, 1992 (as it relates to the establishment or operation of the Personal Property Registry)
Mutual Fire Insurance Companies Act (as it relates to the establishment & operation of the Corporate Registry)
Partnership Act (as it relates to the establishment & operation of the Corporate Registry)
Pension Fund Societies Act (as it relates to the establishment and operation of the Corporate Registry)
Personal Information Protection Act
Personal Property Security Act (as it relates to the establishment & operation of the Personal Property Registry)
Procurement Services Act
Public Agency Accommodation Act
Queen's Printer Act
Repairers Lien Act (as it relates to the establishment & operation of the Personal Property Registry)
Society Act (as it relates to the establishment & operation of the Corporate Registry)
Statistics Act

Minister, Citizens' Services & Open Government, Hon. Ben Stewart
Tel: 250-952-7623
Fax: 250-952-7628
PO Box 9056 Prov Govt Sta.
Victoria, BC V8W 9E2

Deputy Minister, Citizens' Services & Open Government, Kim Henderson
Tel: 250-387-8852
Fax: 250-387-8561
PO Box 9440 Prov Govt Sta.
Victoria, BC V8W 9V3

Deputy Minister, Government Communications & Public Engagement, Athana Mentzelopoulos
Tel: 250-356-7398
Fax: 250-356-2872
Athana.Mentzelopoulos@gov.bc.ca
PO Box 9409 Prov Govt Sta.
Victoria, BC V8W 9V1

Manager, Communications, David Haslam
Tel: 250-387-0172
David.Haslam@gov.bc.ca

Coordinator, Administration, Yvette Marquis
Tel: 250-952-7623
Fax: 250-952-7628

Associated Agencies, Boards & Commissions:
• Knowledge Network Corporation
4355 Mathissi Pl.
Burnaby, BC V5G 4S8
Tel: 604-431-3222
Fax: 604-431-3387
Toll-free: 877-456-6988
info@knowledge.ca; hr@knowledge.ca (employment information)
www.knowledge.ca
Other Communication: Press, E-mail: press@knowledge.ca
The Knowledge Network Corporation is a provincial Crown agency, operating under British Columbia's Ministry of Citizens' Services & Open Government. The corporation is British Columbia's public broadcaster, which is licensed by the Canadian Radio-television & Telecommunications Commission. Arts & culture & children's programs are featured through television & the Internet.
The network is commercial-free. Funds for the provision of educational broadcasting services are received the British Columbia provincial government, public supporters, & Knowledge Partners.

BC OnLine
Operations Centre, #400A, 4000 Seymour Pl., Victoria, BC V8X 5J8
Tel: 250-953-8250
Fax: 250-953-8222
Toll-Free: 800-663-6102
bconline@apicanada.com; bcolhelp@apicanada.com (support issues)
www.bconline.gov.bc.ca
Other Communication: Help Desk, Phone: 250-953-8200
BC OnLine serves government, legal, & business professionals by providing access to provincial government computer systems through the Internet. Examples of e-government services include Court Services Online, Land Title & Survey Authority Electronic Services, Personal Property Registry, Corporate Registry, Gas & Electrical Permits, & the Wills Registry.
Director, Operations, Allan Crawshaw
Tel: 250-953-8277
Fax: 250-953-8222
Allan.Crawshaw@apicanada.com
Chief Financial Officer, Harvey Coomber
Tel: 250-953-8276
Fax: 250-953-8222
Manager, Contract Administration, Bob Dearborn
Tel: 250-953-8266
Fax: 250-953-8222
Bob.Dearborn@apicanada.com
Coordinator, Client Support Services, Valeska Campbell
Tel: 250-953-8200
Fax: 250-953-8222
Valeska.Campbell@apicanada.com

BC Registry Services
PO Box 9431 Prov Govt, Victoria, BC V8W 9V3
Tel: 250-356-8661
Fax: 250-356-9422
www.bcregistryservices.gov.bc.ca
Other Communication: Corporations Unit, Phone: 250-356-8626; Societies & Cooperatives: 250-356-8609; OneStop Business Registry: 250-356-8689; Personal Property Registry: 250-952-7976
BC Registry Services support commerce by overseeing the Corporate Registry, the Personal Property Registry, the Manufactured Home Registry, & the OneStop Business Registry.

Manager, Registries Programs (Trade Agreements), Janice Gignac
Tel: 250-952-6025
Fax: 250-356-8923
Janice.Gignac@gov.bc.ca
Financial Analyst, Cassey Zhou
Tel: 250-356-8665
Fax: 250-356-9422
Cassey.Zhou@gov.bc.ca

BC Stats
553 Superior St., PO Box 9410 Prov Govt, Victoria, BC V8W 9V1
Tel: 250-387-0327
Fax: 250-387-0380
BC.Stats@gov.bc.ca
www.bcstats.gov.bc.ca
Operating under the direction of the Britisih Columbia Statistics Act, R.S.B.C. 1996, C. 439, BC Stats is the central statistical agency of the Province of British Columbia. The organization serves government & voluntary clients through the dissemination of general statistical information.
BC Stats carries out its activities through the following sections: Data Services; Business Statistics; Economic Statistics; Labour & Social Statistics; Demographic Analysis, & Public Sector Research & Evaluation.
Executive Director & Provincial Statistician, Angelo Cocco
Tel: 250-356-2119
Fax: 250-387-0380
Director, Data Services, Paul Gosh
Tel: 250-387-9221
Fax: 250-387-0380
Paul.Gosh@gov.bc.ca
Director, Public Sector Research & Evaluation, Martin Monkman
Tel: 250-356-0025
Fax: 250-387-0380
Martin.Monkman@gov.bc.ca
Director, Labour & Social Statistics, Cathy Stock
Tel: 250-953-3703
Fax: 250-387-0380
Cathy.Stock@gov.bc.ca
Director, Demographic Analysis, Jackie Storen
Tel: 250-216-2291
Fax: 250-387-0380
Jackie.Storen@gov.bc.ca
Manager, Finance & Administration, Michael Griffin
Tel: 250-387-6744
Fax: 250-387-0380
Michael.Griffin@gov.bc.ca
Manager, Economic Statistics, Lillian Hallin
Tel: 250-387-0366
Fax: 250-387-0380
Lillian.Hallin@gov.bc.ca
Manager, Business Operations, Margaret Johnson
Tel: 250-387-9062
Fax: 250-387-0380
Margaret.Johnson@gov.bc.ca
Manager, Trade & Business Statistics, Dan Schrier
Tel: 250-387-0376
Fax: 250-387-0380
Dan.Schrier@gov.bc.ca

Board Resourcing & Development Office
Tel: 604-660-1170
Fax: 604-775-0158
abc@gov.bc.ca
www.gov.bc.ca/brdo
The Board Resourcing & Development Office has the following responsibilities: forming guidelines for appointments to agencies; ensuring an open & consistent appointment process; & confirming that appointees to agencies receive orientation & continuing professional development.
Managing Director, Ann Wicks
Tel: 604-775-1668
Fax: 604-775-0158
Ann.Wicks@gov.bc.ca
Legislative Analyst, Monica Jang
Tel: 604-775-2072
Fax: 604-775-0158
Monica.Jang@gov.bc.ca
Senior Analyst, Larkin MacKenzie-Ast
Tel: 604-775-2084
Fax: 604-775-0158
Larkin.MacKenzieAst@gov.bc.ca

Office of the Chief Information Officer (OCIO)
PO Box 9412 Prov Govt, Victoria, BC V8W 9V1
Tel: 250-387-0401
Fax: 250-387-5693
Toll-Free: 800-663-7867
ciowebcommunications@gov.bc.ca; CPIAadmin@gov.bc.ca (privacy help)
www.cio.gov.bc.ca
Other Communication: To report an information incident, such as a privacy breach, phone: 1-866-660-0811, option 3; BC Privacy Helpline, Phone: 250-356-1851, Fax: 250-953-0455
The Office of the Chief Information Officer guides & promotes the management of government information as an asset to business.
Examples of responsibilities include records management, legislation that governs the protection of privacy & personal information, freedom of information requests, & governance for corporate IM/IT policy, such as technology architecture & standards, data access, & information security.
Branches of the Office of the Chief Information Officer are as follows: Architecture & Standards; Community & External Initiatives; Corporate Operations & Finance; Knowledge & Information Services; Information Security; & Strategic Initiatives.
Associate Deputy Minister & Government Chief Information Officer for the Province of British Columbia, Dave Nikolejsin
Tel: 250-387-8509
Fax: 250-387-1940
Dave.Nikolejsin@gov.bc.ca
Assistant Deputy Minister, Strategic Partnerships, CJ Ritchie
Tel: 250-356-1789
Fax: 250-387-1940
CJ.Ritchie@gov.bc.ca
Executive Director, Architecture & Standards, Ian Bailey
Tel: 250-387-8053
Fax: 250-952-6250
Ian.Bailey@gov.bc.ca
Executive Director, Provincial IDIM Program, Kevena Bamford
Tel: 250-360-7336
Fax: 250-387-5693
Kevena.Bamford@gov.bc.ca
Executive Director, Strategic Initiatives, Gary Cooney
Tel: 250-387-5975
Fax: 250-953-3555
Gary.Cooney@gov.bc.ca
Executive Director, Knowledge & Information Services, Charmaine Lowe
Tel: 250-356-2507
Fax: 250-356-1182
charmaine.lowe@gov.bc.ca
Executive Director, Finance, Matt Mannix
Tel: 250-356-8321
Fax: 250-387-1940
Matt.Mannix@gov.bc.ca
Executive Director, Cross Government IM/IT Initiatives, Peter Watkins
Tel: 250-387-2184
Fax: 250-387-5693
Peter.Watkins@gov.bc.ca

Communications & Media Relations Division
PO Box 9409 Prov Govt, Victoria, BC V8W 9V1
Tel: 250-387-3534
Assistant Deputy Minister, Communications & Media Relations, Kelly Gleeson
Tel: 250-356-8608
Fax: 250-356-2872
Kelly.Gleeson@gov.bc.ca
Director, Communications, Matt Gordon
Tel: 250-356-6482
Fax: 250-356-2872
Matt.Gordon@gov.bc.ca
Manager, Multicultural Communications, Pavan Bajwa
Tel: 250-387-5033
Fax: 250-387-6070
Pavan.Bajwa@gov.bc.ca
Manager, Media Relations, Karen Murry
Tel: 250-387-0779

Fax: 250-387-6070
Karen.Murry@gov.bc.ca
Manager, Media Monitoring Services, Scott Ryckman
Tel: 250-356-5735
Fax: 250-356-5901
Scott.Ryckman@gov.bc.ca

Corporate Services Division
PO Box 9409 Prov Govt, Victoria, BC V8W 9V1
Tel: 250-387-1449
Fax: 250-387-6687

The Corporate Services Division oversees facilities & administration, financial services, human resources, records management, & systems architecture.
Executive Director, Operations & Human Resources, Denise Champion
Tel: 250-953-4685
Fax: 250-387-3534
Denise.Champion@gov.bc.ca
Director, Systems Solutions & Architecture, Stephen Bamford
Tel: 250-217-6137
Fax: 250-387-6687
Stephen.Bamford@gov.bc.ca
Manager, Human Resources, Michelle Rowsell
Tel: 250-387-8067
Fax: 250-387-3534
Michelle.Rowsell@gov.bc.ca
Officer, Records Services, Bruce Foster
Tel: 250-812-2122
Fax: 250-387-6687
Bruce.Foster@gov.bc.ca
Officer, Administrative Services, Susan Smith
Tel: 250-387-1449
Fax: 250-387-6687
Susan.Smith@gov.bc.ca
Officer, Financial Services, Dawn Stewart
Tel: 250-356-8595
Fax: 250-387-6687
Dawn.Stewart@gov.bc.ca

Enquiry BC
PO Box 9594 Prov Govt, Victoria, BC V8W 9K4
Tel: 250-387-6121
Toll-Free: 800-663-7867
EnquiryBC@gov.bc.ca
TTY: 800-661-8773
Other Communication: Vancouver, Phone: 604-660-2421

Inquiries are handled about services provided by provincial governmen ministries, Crown corporations, & public agencies.
Program Manager, Catherine Wollner
Tel: 250-387-4845
Fax: 250-387-5633
Program Analyst, Craig Smith
Tel: 250-356-1487
Fax: 250-387-5633
Craig.Smith@gov.bc.ca

Queen's Printer
PO Box 9452 Prov Govt, Victoria, BC V8W 9V7
Tel: 250-387-3309
Fax: 250-356-6036
Toll-Free: 800-663-6105
QPGazette@gov.bc.ca (BC Gazette); QPLegalEzeQgov.bc,ca
www.qp.gov.bc.ca

British Columbia's Queen's Printer provides printing & specialized scanning services, plus multimedia duplication to the province's government ministries & the public sector.
Senior Director, Queen's Printer / BC Mail Plus, Don Swagar
Tel: 250-387-6691
Fax: 250-356-7380
Don.Swagar@gov.bc.ca
Director, Queen's Printer, Sherry Brown
Tel: 250-356-6876
Fax: 250-387-0388
Sherry.Brown@gov.bc.ca
Manager, Crown Publications, Wendy Pope
Tel: 250-356-5392
Fax: 250-387-1120
Wendy.Pope@gov.bc.ca

Service BC
PO Box 9804 Prov Govt, Victoria, BC V8W 9W1
Tel: 250-387-6121
Fax: 250-387-5633
Toll-Free: 800-663-7867
www.servicebc.gov.bc.ca
TTY: 800-661-8773
Other Communication: Vancouver & outside B.C., Phone: 604-660-2421; Southeast Service BC Centre, Phone: 250-354-6109; Vancouver Island / South Coast Service BC Centre: 250-356-7302

Service BC provides frontline government services & information to businesses, residents, & visitors in British Columbia. Areas of service include education, training, employment & labour standards, doing business in the province, licensing & registration, taxation, health services, legal services, family support services, property, transportation, tourism, recreation, & publications. Service is available by phone, online, or in person at Service BC Centres throughout the province.
Assistant Deputy Minister, Service BC, Bette-Jo Hughes
Tel: 250-387-9170
Fax: 250-387-5633
Executive Director, Regional Operations, Ron Hinshaw
Tel: 250-356-2031
Fax: 250-387-5633
Ron.Hinshaw@gov.bc.ca
Director, Financial Operations, Tavish Annis
Tel: 250-387-0390
Fax: 250-387-5633
Tavish.Annis@gov.bc.ca
Director, Operations & Client Services, Brad Boquist
Tel: 250-356-2039
Fax: 250-387-5633
Brad.Boquist@gov.bc.ca
Project Director, John Hammond
Tel: 250-356-1356
Fax: 250-387-5633
John.Hammond@gov.bc.ca
Regional Director, Interior Northeast Service BC Centre, Deborah Lipscombe
Tel: 250-828-4545
Fax: 250-828-4542
Deborah.Lipscombe@gov.bc.ca
Regional Director, Northwest Service BC Centre, Perry Slump
Tel: 250-565-4488
Fax: 250-565-6638
Perry.Slump@gov.bc.ca
Manager, Clients & Special Projects, Kathy Ham-Rowbottom
Tel: 250-356-1444
Fax: 250-387-5633
Kathleen.HamRowbottom@gov.bc.ca
Executive Coordinator, Keri Merrick
Tel: 250-387-9170
Fax: 250-387-5633
Keri.Merrick@gov.bc.ca

Strategic Planning & Public Engagement Division
PO Box 9409 Prov Govt, Victoria, BC V8W 9V1
Tel: 250-356-2872

Assistant Deputy Minister, Strategic Planning & Public Engagement, John Paul Fraser
Tel: 250-356-8527
Fax: 250-356-2872
JohnPaul.Fraser@gov.bc.ca
Executive Director, Marketing & Communications Support Service, Mary Dila
Tel: 250-356-7823
Fax: 250-387-6070
Mary.Dila@gov.bc.ca
Executive Director, Citizen Engagement, Tanya Twynstra
Tel: 250-507-2163
Fax: 250-387-0718
Tanya.Twynstra@gov.bc.ca
Corporate Director, Public Engagement, Susan Ibbott
Tel: 250-356-7363
Fax: 250-387-6070
Susan.Ibbott@gov.bc.ca
Manager, Writing & Editorial Services, Jon Chant
Tel: 250-387-7194
Fax: 250-387-6687
Jon.Chant@gov.bc.ca
Manager, Engagement Programming, Jamieson Dunlop
Tel: 250-307-0291
Fax: 250-387-0718
Jamieson.Dunlop@gov.bc.ca
Manager, Social Media & Digital Services, Brooke Finnigan
Tel: 250-387-6693
Fax: 250-387-6070
Brooke.Finnigan@gov.bc.ca
Manager, Graphic Design Services, Andrew Pratt
Tel: 250-356-8120
Fax: 250-387-6070
Andrew.Pratt@gov.bc.ca
Manager, Advertising & Marketing Services, Adrienne Watt
Tel: 250-387-1374
Fax: 250-387-1435
Adrienne.Watt@gov.bc.ca

Columbia Power Corporation (CPC)

#200, 445 - 13th Ave., Castlegar, BC V1N 1G1
Tel: 250-304-6060
Fax: 250-304-6083
cpc.info@columbiapower.org
www.columbiapower.org

Columbia Power Corporation was established under the Company Act in 1994. A Crown corporation, it is wholly owned & controlled by the Province of British Columbia. On a joint venture basis with the Columbia Basin Trust, Columbia Power Corporation undertakes power project investments as the agent of the Province of British Columbia. Some power projects include the following: Arrow Lakes Generating Station, Brilliant Expansion Project, & Waneta Expansion Project.

Chair, Lee Doney

Vice-Chair, Tim Stanley

President/Chief Executive Officer, Jane Bird

Chief Technical Officer, Victor Jmaeff

Vice-President, Capital Projects, Giulio Ambrosone

Vice-President, Human Resources & Corporate Services, Debbie Martin

Corporate Secretary, Don Rose

British Columbia Ministry of Community, Sport, & Cultural Development

PO Box 9490 Prov Govt, Victoria, BC V8W 9N7
www.gov.bc.ca/cscd
Other Communication: Media Inquiries, Phone: 250-953-3677, Fax: 250-356-1070

Enabling local governments & citizens of British Columbia to build well-governed communities with opportunities to participate in the arts & sports is the goal of the Ministry of Community, Sport, & Cultural Development.
The following are examples of the ministry's responsibilities: providing policies & programs so that local governments can govern effectively; offering advice & funding for community economic growth; ensuring a fair & flexible property assessment system; & supporting the provincial sport system, cultural organizations, & artists.
Acts Administered:
Arts Council Act
Assessment Act
Assessment Authority Act
Athletic Commissioner Act
Auditor General for Local Government Act
British Columbia Enterprise Corporation (except as it relates to the B.C. Pavilion Corporation)
Capital Commission Act
Community Charter Act
Gaming Control Act (Part 6)
Land Title Act (s. 219 (1), (2), (3) (a) & (b), (4)-(9.2), (10), (11) (a), (12) & (14), as that provision relates to the portfolio of the Minister of Community, Sport, & Cultural Development)
Local Government Act (except ss. 692, 693 & 916-919)
Local Government Grants Act
Local Services Act
Manufactured Home Tax Act
Ministry of Municipal Affairs Act
Municipal Aid Act
Municipal Finance Authority Act
Municipalities Enabling & Validating Act
Municipalities Enabling & Validating Act (No. 2)
Municipalities Enabling & Validating Act (No. 3)
Municipalities Enabling & Validating Act (No. 4)
Museum Act
Recreational Facility Act
Resort Associations Act
Resort Municipality of Whistler Act
Sechelt Indian Government District Enabling Act (s. 4)
Special Accounts Appropriation & Control Act (ss. 8 & 9)
Tourist Accommodation (Assessment Relief) Act
University Endowment Land Act (except ss. 2 (1) (a) & (d) & 3 (b))
Vancouver Charter Act

Minister, Community, Sport, & Cultural Development, Hon. Bill Bennett
Tel: 250-387-2283
Fax: 250-387-4312
CSCD.minister@gov.bc.ca
Social Media: twitter.com/KootenayBill
PO Box 9056 Prov Govt Sta.
Victoria, BC V8W 9E2

Deputy Minister, Community, Sport, & Cultural Development, Don Fast
Tel: 250-387-4104
Fax: 250-387-7973
Don.Fast@gov.bc.ca

Administrative Coordinator, Connie Roberts
Tel: 250-387-2283
Fax: 250-387-4312

Executive Coordinator, Lee Valentine
Tel: 250-387-4104
Fax: 250-387-7973
Lee.Valentine@gov.bc.ca

Parliamentary Secretary for Rural Communities to the Minister, Community, Sport, & Cultural Development, Donna Barnett
Tel: 250-387-3820
Fax: 250-387-9066

Associated Agencies, Boards & Commissions:

• British Columbia Assessment Authority (BCAA)
#400, 3450 Uptown Blvd.
Victoria, BC V8Z 0B9
Tel: 250-595-6211
Fax: 250-595-6222
info@bcassessment.ca
www.bcassessment.bc.ca
The British Columbia Assessment Authority is an independent, provincial Crown corporation. Governed by a Board of Directors, the role of BC Assessment is the production of annual property assessments for each property owner in British Columbia. Area offices are located across the province.

• British Columbia Games Society
#200, 990 Fort St.
Victoria, BC V8V 3K2
Tel: 250-387-1375
Fax: 250-387-4489
info@bcgames.org
www.bcgames.org
The BC Games Society is incorporated under the Societies Act. With responsibility to British Columbia's Minister of Healthy Living & Sport, the Crown Agency works with its partners to provide event management leadership. The Society strives to create development opportunities for athletes, coaches, & officials, sport organizations, & host communities.

• Board of Examiners
Tel: 250-387-4085
Fax: 250-387-7972
www.cscd.gov.bc.ca/lgd/gov_structure/board_examiners/index.htm

• Islands Trust
#200, 1627 Fort St.
Victoria, BC V8R 1H8
Tel: 250-405-5151
Fax: 250-405-5155
information@islandstrust.bc.ca
www.islandstrust.bc.ca
Other Communication: Northern Office: 250-247-2063; Salt Spring Office: 250-537-9144
The Islands Trust area covers the following islands & waters between the British Columbia mainland & southern Vancouver Island: Bowen, Denman, Gabriola, Galiano, Gambier, Hornby, Lasqueti, Mayne, North Pender, Salt Spring, Saturna, South Pender, & Thetis. The Trust is a federation of independent local governments. The federation plans land use & regulates development to preserve & protect the area and its environment.

• Property Assessment Appeal Board (PAAB)
#10, 10551 Shellbridge Way
Richmond, BC V6X 2W9
Tel: 604-775-1740
Fax: 604-775-1742
Toll-free: 888-775-1740
office@paab.bc.ca
www.assessmentappeal.bc.ca
Other Communication: Toll-Free Fax: 1-888-775-1742
The Board assists with assessment appeals for all types of properties, dealing with issues such as market value, classification, and qualification for tax exemption.

Arts, Culture & Sport
PO Box 9490 Prov Govt, Victoria, BC V8W 9N7
Tel: 250-356-6914
Fax: 250-387-7973

Assistant Deputy Minister, David Galbraith
Tel: 250-356-7139
Fax: 250-387-7973
David.Galbraith@gov.bc.ca

Executive Director, Arts & Culture Branch, Andrea Henning
Tel: 250-356-6614
Fax: 250-387-4099
Andrea.Henning@gov.bc.ca

Executive Director, Sport Branch, Margo Ross
Tel: 250-356-7168
Fax: 250-356-2842
Margo.Ross@gov.bc.ca

Executive Director, BC Arts Council, Gillian Wood
Tel: 250-356-1725
Fax: 250-387-4099
Gillian.Wood@gov.bc.ca

Director, Business Development, Liz Lilly
Tel: 250-356-7096
Fax: 250-387-4099
Liz.Lilly@gov.bc.ca

Acting Director, Sport Branch, Sharon White
Tel: 250-387-5651
Fax: 250-356-2842
Sharon.D.White@gov.bc.ca

Director, Sport Branch, Doug Wrean
Tel: 250-356-0364
Fax: 250-356-2842
Doug.Wrean@gov.bc.ca

Senior Financial Officer, Robert Easton
Tel: 250-356-9416
Fax: 250-387-7973
Robert.Easton@gov.bc.ca

BC Film Commissioner, Susan Croome
Tel: 604-660-3235
Fax: 604-660-4790
susanc@bcfilmcommission.com

Local Government
PO Box 9490 Prov Govt, Victoria, BC V8W 9N7
Tel: 250-356-6575
Fax: 250-387-7973
www.cd.gov.bc.ca/lgd

Working with a great range of partners, the Local Government Department develops communities that can manage change & offer affordable services to residents of British Columbia. The Department's programs include the following: developing local government legislation; facilitating partnerships with local governments & First Nations; fostering positive inter-governmental relations to facilitate community & regional planning; offering financial support; & providing information & advice.

Assistant Deputy Minister/Inspector of Municipalities, Mike Furey
Tel: 250-356-6575
Fax: 250-387-7973

Executive Director, Local Government Infrastructure & Finance, Glen Brown
Tel: 250-387-4067
Fax: 250-356-1873
Glen.T.Brown@gov.bc.ca
800 Johnson St., 4th Fl.
PO Box 9838 Prov Govt Sta.
Victoria, BC V8W 9T1

Executive Director, Intergovernmental Relations & Planning, Lois-Leah Goodwin
Tel: 250-356-1128
Fax: 250-387-6212
LoisLeah.Goodwin@gov.bc.ca
800 Johnson St., 6th Fl.
PO Box 9841 Prov Govt Sta.
Victoria, BC V8W 9T2

Executive Director, Local Government Policy & Research, Nicola Marotz
Tel: 250-356-6257
Fax: 250-387-6212
Nicola.Marotz@gov.bc.ca
800 Johnson St., 6th Fl.
PO Box 9847 Prov Govt Sta.
Victoria, BC V8W 9T2

Executive Director, Governance & Structure, Gary Paget
Tel: 250-953-4129
Fax: 250-387-7972
Gary.Paget@gov.bc.ca
800 Johnson St., 4th Fl.
PO Box 9839 Prov Govt Sta.
Victoria, BC V8W 9T1

Director, Structure, Governance & Structure, Marijke Edmondson
Tel: 250-387-4058
Fax: 250-387-7972
Marijke.Edmondson@gov.bc.ca
800 Johnson St., 4th Fl.
PO Box 9839 Prov Govt Sta.
Victoria, BC V8W 9T1

Director, Advisory Services, Governance & Structure, Don Sutherland
Tel: 250-387-4025
Fax: 250-387-7972
Don.Sutherland@gov.bc.ca
800 Johnson St., 4th Fl.
PO Box 9839 Prov Govt Sta.
Victoria, BC V8W 9T1

Director, Regional Initiatives, Governance & Structure, Derek Trimmer
Tel: 250-356-9621
Fax: 250-387-7972
Derek.Trimmer@gov.bc.ca
800 Johnson St., 4th Fl.
PO Box 9839 Prov Govt Sta.
Victoria, BC V8W 9T1

Director, Commuity Relations, Governance & Structure, Cathy Watson
Tel: 250-387-4057
Fax: 250-387-7972
Cathy.Watson@gov.bc.ca
800 Johnson St., 4th Fl.
PO Box 9839 Prov Govt Sta.
Victoria, BC V8W 9T1

Director, Intergovernmental Relations, Intergovernmental Relations & Planning Division, Rejan Farley
Tel: 250-387-4046
Fax: 250-387-6212
Rejan.Farley@gov.bc.ca
800 Johnson St., 4th Fl.
PO Box 9839 Prov Govt Sta.
Victoria, BC V8W9T1

Director, Planning Programs, Intergovernmental Relations & Planning Division, Meggin Messenger
Tel: 250-387-4045
Fax: 250-387-6212
Meggin.Messenger@gov.bc.ca
800 Johnson St., 4th Fl.
PO Box 9839 Prov Govt Sta.
Victoria, BC V8W9T1

Director, Infrastructure, Local Government Infrastructure & Finance, Liam Edwards
Tel: 250-356-0218
Fax: 250-356-1873
Liam.Edwards@gov.bc.ca
800 Johnson St., 4th Fl.
PO Box 9839 Prov Govt Sta.
Victoria, BC V8W 9T1

Director, Local Government Finance, Local Government Infrastructure & Finance, Talitha Soldera
Tel: 250-387-4063
Fax: 250-356-1873
Talitha.Soldera@gov.bc.ca
800 Johnson St., 4th Fl.
PO Box 9839 Prov Govt Sta.
Victoria, BC V8W9T1

Director, Legislation, Local Government Policy & Research, Meagan Gergley
Tel: 250-387-4052
Fax: 250-387-6212
Meagan.Gergley@gov.bc.ca
800 Johnson St., 4th Fl.
PO Box 9839 Prov Govt Sta.
Victoria, BC V8W 9T1

Management Services
PO Box 9842 Prov Govt, Victoria, BC V8W 9T2
Tel: 250-387-8705
Fax: 250-387-7973

Assistant Deputy Minister, Shauna Brouwer
Tel: 250-387-9180
Fax: 250-387-7973
Shauna.Brouwer@gov.bc.ca

Executive Director/Chief Information Officer, Information Systems, Debbie Fritz
Tel: 250-356-0803
Fax: 250-387-1590
Debbie.Fritz@gov.bc.ca
800 Johnson St., 3rd Fl.
PO Box 9802 Prov Govt Sta.
Victoria, BC V8W 9W1

Executive Director, Strategic Human Resources & Corporate Policy & Planning, Kim Russell
Fax: 250-387-1407
800 Johnson St., 2nd Fl.
PO Box 9806 Prov Govt Sta.
Victoria, BC V8W 9W1

Director/Chief Financial Officer, Finance & Administrative Services, Jim MacAulay
Tel: 250-387-9179
Fax: 250-387-1590
Jim.MacAulay@gov.bc.ca
800 Johnson St., 3rd Fl.
PO Box 9843 Prov Govt Sta.
Victoria, BC V8W 9T2

Director, Policy & Planning, Strategic Human Resources & Corporate Policy & Planning, Shannon Mullen
Tel: 250-953-4334
Fax: 250-387-1407
Shannon.Mullen@gov.bc.ca
800 Johnson St., 3rd Fl.
PO Box 9843 Prov Govt Sta.
Victoria, BC V8W9T2

Office of the Conflict of Interest Commissioner

#101, 431 Menzies St., Victoria, BC V8V 1X4
Tel: 250-356-0750
Fax: 250-356-6580
conflictofinterest@coibc.ca
www.gov.bc.ca/oci

The Conflict of Interest Commissioner is an independent Officer of the Legislative Assembly. The following roles are carried out by the Commissioner: advising Members of the Legislative Assembly; meeting with Members of the Legislative Assembly for review of disclosure of Members' interests, & obligations imposed by the Members' Conflict of Interest Act; & undertaking investigations into alleged contraventions of the Act or the Constitution Act, section 25.

Acts Administered:
Members' Conflict of Interest Act

Commissioner, Paul D. K. Fraser, Q.C.
Tel: 250-356-9283

Executive Coordinator, Daphene Thompson

British Columbia Ministry of Education

PO Box 9161 Prov Govt, Victoria, BC V8W 9H3
Toll-Free: 888-879-1166
EDUC.Correspondence@gov.bc.ca
www.gov.bc.ca/bced
Other Communication: Nedia Inquiries, Phone: 250-356-5963; Fax: 250-356-5945

The Ministry of Education works with stakeholders in all stages of the education system, from early learning programs & kindergarten to grade 12 to life-long literacy. Early learning programs include the ministry initiative, StrongStart. Life-long literacy initiatives include programs at community learning centres & public libraries.

Acts Administered:
Education Improvement Act
First Nations Education Act
Independent School Act
Library Act
School Act (except as it relates to the collection of public money, as defined in section 1 of the Financial Administration Act, other than a fine, or the administration of deposits & securities payable
Special Accounts Appropriation & Control Act (s. 9.4)
Teachers Act

Minister, Education, Hon. Don McRae
Tel: 250-387-1977
Fax: 250-387-3200
Minister.Educ@gov.bc.ca
Social Media: twitter.com/DonMcRaeMLA, www.facebook.com/donmcrae
PO Box 9045 Prov Govt Sta.
Victoria, BC V8W 9E2

Deputy Minister, Education, James Gorman
Tel: 250-356-1234
Fax: 250-356-6007
dm.education@gov.bc.ca
PO Box 9179 Prov Govt Sta.
Victoria, BC V8W 9H8

Parliamentary Secretary for Independent School to the Minister of Education, Marc Dalton
Tel: 250-953-4769
Fax: 250-387-9100

Parliamentary Secretary for Student Support & Parent Engagement to the Minister of Education, Jane Thornthwaite
Tel: 250-387-2796
Fax: 250-387-9100

Executive Administrative Coordinator, Heather Langton
Tel: 250-387-2026
Fax: 250-356-6007
Heather.Langton@gov.bc.ca
PO Box 9179 Prov Govt Sta.
Victoria, BC V8W 9H8

Associated Agencies, Boards & Commissions:

• **British Columbia College of Teachers**
#400, 2025 West Broadway
Vancouver, BC V6J 1Z6
Tel: 604-731-8170
Fax: 604-731-9142
Toll-free: 800-555-3684
www.bcct.ca
The College was created in 1987 by the Teaching Profession Act to impose standards of quality & education on its members. Its duties include: assessing applicants for admission into the College; issuing certificates of qualification; reviewing certificate holders; & administering disciplinary action when necessary.

• **British Columbia Council on Admissions & Transfer**
#709, 555 Seymour St.
Vancouver, BC V6B 3H6
Tel: 604-412-7700
Fax: 604-683-0576
info@bccat.ca
www.bccat.ca

Achievement Division
PO Box 9187 Prov Govt, Victoria, BC V8W 9H3
Tel: 250-356-2332
Fax: 250-356-0407

Superintendent, Achievement, Rick Davis
Tel: 250-558-8722
Fax: 250-356-0407
EDUC.Achievement@gov.bc.ca
Project Director, Sector Leadership Development, Cathy Elliott
Tel: 604-649-0035
Fax: 604-356-0407
EDUC.Achievement@gov.bc.ca

Business, Technology & Online Services Division
PO Box 9132 Prov Govt, Victoria, BC V8W 9B5
Tel: 250-356-6068
Fax: 250-387-0044
EDUC.ADMO.Knowledge.Management@gov.bc.ca

Assistant Deputy Minister, Renate Butterfield
Tel: 250-356-6068
EDUC.ADMO.Knowledge.Management@gov.bc.ca
Director, Open School BC, Eleanor Liddy
Tel: 250-508-1119
Fax: 250-356-6036
Eleanor.Liddy@gov.bc.ca
Director, Common Business Initiatives, Andrew Macauley
Tel: 250-415-2736
Fax: 250-356-9460
Andrew.Macauley@gov.bc.ca
Director, Student Certification Branch, Brenda Neufeld
Tel: 250-216-7168
Fax: 250-356-9460
educ.dmsc@gov.bc.ca
Other Communications: Cell Phone: 250-216-7168
Manager, Transcripts & Examinations, Emille Hillier
Tel: 250-356-7270
Fax: 250-356-0271
Emilie.Hillier@gov.bc.ca
Director, ITMB Business Management, Information & Technology Management Branch, Margaret Parkinson
Tel: 250-516-0591
Fax: 250-356-1520
EDUC.InformationManagement@gov.bc.ca
Director, ITMB Strategic Initiatives, Information & Technology Management Branch, Hwee Boon Teo
Tel: 250-217-9756
Fax: 250-356-8267
EDUC.InformationManagement@gov.bc.ca

Governance, Legislation & Regulation
PO Box 9146 Prov Govt, Victoria, BC V8W 9H1
Tel: 250-356-1404
Fax: 250-953-4908
EDUC.GovernanceDepartment@gov.bc.ca

Responsibilities include legislation for & governance of the public school system, homeschooling, independent schools, & offshore schools.

Assistant Deputy Minister, Claire Avison
Tel: 250-356-6760
Fax: 250-953-4908
EDUC.GovernanceDepartment@gov.bc.ca
Executive Director & Inspector, Independent Schools, International Education, Ed Vanderboom
Tel: 250-387-3711
Fax: 250-953-4908
EDUC.IndependentSchoolsOffice@gov.bc.ca
Other Communications: URL: www.bced.gov.bc.ca/independentschools
Inspector, Independent Schools, Theo Vandeweg
Tel: 250-387-3711
Fax: 250-953-4908
EDUC.IndependentSchoolsOffice@gov.bc.ca
Other Communications: URL: www.bced.gov.bc.ca/independentschools
Acting Deputy Inspector, Nick Poeschek
Tel: 250-356-1265
EDUC.IndependentSchoolsOffice@gov.bc.ca
Director, Governance & Legislation, Dave Duerksen
Tel: 250-356-1404
Fax: 250-953-4908
EDUC.GovernanceDepartment@gov.bc.ca
Other Communications: URL: www.bced.gov.bc.ca/legislation

Director, Cross Sector and Strategic Initiatives, Heather Beaton
Tel: 250-356-7680
EDUC.GovernanceDepartment@gov.bc.ca
Director, Governance and Legislation, Mary Shaw
Tel: 250-217-8199
EDUC.GovernanceDepartment@gov.bc.ca
Senior Legislative Analyst, Governance and Legislation, Karen Loughran
Tel: 250-896-1701
EDUC.GovernanceDepartment@gov.bc.ca

Learning Division
PO Box 9887 Prov Govt, Victoria, BC V8W 9T6
Tel: 250-387-2046
Fax: 250-356-6007

Superintendent of Learning, Rod Allen
Tel: 250-213-3000
Fax: 250-356-6007
Roderick.Allen@gov.bc.ca

Liason Division
Tel: 604-660-1415
Fax: 604-660-2124
www.bced.gov.bc.ca/departments/liaison

Open Government & Community Partnership Division
PO Box 9161 Prov Govt, Victoria, BC V8W 9H3
Tel: 250-387-6399
Fax: 250-356-6007
EDUCADMO@Victoria1.gov.bc.ca
www.bced.gov.bc.ca/departments/partnerships_plan/

Assistant Deputy Minister, Paige MacFarlane
Tel: 250-387-6399
EDUCADMO@Victoria1.gov.bc.ca
Director, Open Government & Community Partnerships Division, Beverley Shaw
Tel: 250-415-1662
Bev.Shaw@gov.bc.ca
Director, Citizen Engagement, Eve Gaudet
Tel: 250-415-3966
Fax: 250-387-0044
Eve.Gaudet@gov.bc.ca
Director, Accountability & Public Assurance, Caroline Ponsford
Tel: 250-216-6347
Fax: 250-356-0891
IGR.Education@gov.bc.ca
Director, Libraries & Literacy, Jacqueline van Dyk
Tel: 604-356-1791
Fax: 604-953-3225
Jacqueline.vanDyk@gov.bc.ca

Resource Management Division
PO Box 9151 Prov Govt, Victoria, BC V8W 9H1
Tel: 250-356-2588
Fax: 250-356-8332
www.bced.gov.bc.ca/departments/resource_man/

Assistant Deputy Minister, Keith F. Miller
Tel: 250-356-2588
Fax: 250-387-1451
Director, School District Financial Reporting, Ian Aaron
Tel: 250-387-0893
Fax: 250-387-1451
Director, Funding & Compliance, Dave Duerksen
Tel: 250-217-1574
Executive Director, Chief Financial Officer, Financial Services Branch, Brian Fraser
Tel: 250-387-6282
Fax: 250-387-9695
Financial.Services@gov.bc.ca
Director, Capital Management, Doug Stewart
Tel: 250-217-8656
Fax: 250-953-4985

Elections British Columbia

PO Box 9275 Prov Govt, Victoria, BC V8W 9J6
Tel: 250-387-5305
Fax: 250-387-3578
Toll-Free: 800-661-8683
electionsbc@elections.bc.ca
www.elections.bc.ca
TTY: 888-456-5448
Other Communication: Toll-free Fax: 1-866-466-0665

Elections British Columbia is a non-partisan, independent Office of the Legislature. Its responsibility is the administration of the electoral process in the province, including provincial general elections, by-elections, provincial referendums, & recall & initiative petitions & votes.

Acting Chief Electoral Officer, Craig James
Tel: 250-387-5305

Assistant Chief Electoral Officer, Electoral Operations, Anton Boegman
Tel: 250-387-5305
Anton.Boegman@elections.bc.ca

Assistant Chief Electoral Officer, Funding & Disclosure, M. Nola Western
Tel: 250-387-4141
Nola.Western@elections.bc.ca

Director, Information Technology, Bob Jasperse
Tel: 250-387-4139
Bob.Jasperse@elections.bc.ca

Director, Voter Registration & Boundaries, Peter Gzowski
Tel: 250-387-7258
Peter.Gzowski@elections.bc.ca

British Columbia Ministry of Energy, Mines, & Natural Gas (& Responsible for Housing)

PO Box 9053 Prov Govt, Victoria, BC V8W 9E2
www.gov.bc.ca/ener

In September 2012, changes were made to the Ministry of Energy & Mines to reinforce natural gas, which is an economic development priority of the provincial government.

The development of sustainable & competitive energy & mineral resource sectors in British Columbia is the focus of the Ministry of Energy, Mines, & Natural Gas. To develop legislation & guidelines, the ministry consults with other ministries & levels of government, as well as communities, First Nations, the public, energy & mining companies, & environmental organizations.

Acts Administered:
Assistance to Shelter Act
BC Hydro Public Power Legacy & Heritage Contract Act
Building Officials' Association Act
Clean Energy Act (except Part 6 & s. 38; s. 36 (2))
Coal Act
Coalbed Gas Act
Commercial Tenancy Act
Energy Efficiency Act
Gaming Control Act
Gas Utility Act
Geothermal Resources Act
Greenhouse Gas Reduction (Renewable & Low Carbon Fuel Requirements) Act
Homeowner Protection Act (except ss. 2 (2) & 10.1 & Part 9; (b) ss. 10, 32 & 36)
Hydro & Power Authority Act
Hydro Power Measures Act
Liquor Control & Licencing Act
Liquor Distribution Act
Local Government Act (ss. 692 & 693)
Manufactured Home Park Tenancy Act
Mineral Land Tax Act (except as it relates to (a) the collection of public money, as defined in section 1 of the Financial Administration Act, other than a fine, or (b) the administration of deposits & securities payable)
Mineral Tax Act (except as it relates to (a) the collection of public money, as defined in section 1 of the Financial Administration Act, other than a fine, or (b) the administration of deposits and securities payable)
Mineral Tenure Act
Mines Act
Mining Right of Way Act
Ministry of Energy & Mines Act
Ministry of Lands, Parks, & Housing Act (ss. 5 (c), 8.1 & 10)
Natural Gas Price Act
Oil & Gas Activities Act (except Division 2 of Part 2)
Petroleum & Natural Gas (Vancouver Island Railway Lands) Act
Petroleum & Natural Gas Act (except (a) ss 74-77; (b) except as it relates to (i) the collection of public money, as defined in section 1 of the Financial Administration Act, other than a fine, or (ii) the administration ofdeposits & securities payable)
Power for Jobs Development Act
Rent Distress Act
Residential Tenancy Act
Safety Authority Act
Safety Standards Act
Shelter Aid for Elderly Renters Act
Special Accounts Appropriation & Control Act (s. 9.3, s. 9.5)
Strata Property Act
Vancouver Island Natural Gas Pipeline Act

Minister; Energy, Mines, & Natural Gas; Minister Responsible for Housing; Deputy Premier, Hon. Rich Coleman
Tel: 250-387-5896
Fax: 250-356-2965
EMH.Minister@gov.bc.ca
Social Media: twitter.com/colemancountry
PO Box 9060 Prov Govt Sta.
Victoria, BC V8W 9E2

Deputy Minister, Energy, Mines, & Natural Gas, Steve Carr
Tel: 250-952-0504
Fax: 250-952-0269
Steve.Carr@gov.bc.ca
PO Box 9319 Prov Govt Sta.
Victoria, BC V8W 9N3

Director, Cabinet & Legislative Initiatives & Executive Operations, Rhonda De Champlain
Tel: 250-952-0253
Fax: 250-952-0269
Rhonda.DeChamplain@gov.bc.ca
PO Box 9319 Prov Govt Sta.
Victoria, BC V8W 9N3

Parliamentary Secretary for the Northeast to the Minister of Energy, Mines, & Natural Gas, Pat Pimm
Tel: 250-952-6784
Fax: 250-387-9100

Officer, Public Affairs, Jake Jacobs
Tel: 250-952-0628
Fax: 250-952-0627
Jake.Jacobs@gov.bc.ca

Associated Agencies, Boards & Commissions:

• British Columbia Lottery Corporation
74 West Seymour St.
Kamloops, BC V2C 1E2
Tel: 250-828-5500
Fax: 250-828-5631
Toll-free: 866-815-0222
www.bclc.com
Other Communication: Vancouver Phone: 604-215-0649

• Building Code Appeal Board (BCAB)
c/o Building & Safety Standards Branch
PO Box 9844 Prov Govt
Victoria, BC V8W 1A4
Tel: 250-387-3133
Fax: 250-387-8164
Building.Safety@gov.bc.ca
www.housing.gov.bc.ca/bcab

• Homeowner Protection Office (HPO)
c/o BC Housing
#650, 4789 Kingway
Burnaby, BC V5H 0A3
Tel: 604-646-7050
Fax: 604-646-7051
Toll-free: 800-407-7757
hpo@hpo.bc.ca
www.hpo.bc.ca
The Homeowner Protection Office seeks to protect buyers of new homes, to regulate the quality of residential construction, and to support residential construction research and education in British Columbia.

• Oil & Gas Commission (OGC)
#100, 10003 - 110 Ave.
Fort St John, BC V1J 6M7
Tel: 250-794-5200
Fax: 250-794-5375
www.bcogc.ca
Other Communication: Incident Reporting: 1-800-663-3456; Victoria: 250-419-4400; Dawson Creek: 250-795-2140
The Oil & Gas Commission was enacted under the Oil & Gas Commission Act, The Commission regulates British Columbia's oil & gas activities & pipelines.

Electricity & Alternative Energy
PO Box 9314 Prov Govt, Victoria, BC V8W 9N1
Tel: 250-387-2814
Fax: 250-952-0258

Assistant Deputy Minister, Les MacLaren
Tel: 250-952-0204
Fax: 250-952-0926
Les.MacLaren@gov.bc.ca

Executive Director, ICE Fund, Dan Green
Tel: 250-952-0279
Fax: 250-952-0351
Dan.Green@gov.bc.ca

Acting Executive Director, Electricity Transmission & Inter-jurisdictional Branch, Derek Griffin
Tel: 250-952-0265
Fax: 250-952-0258

Executive Director, Alternative Energy/Renewable Energy Development Branch, Paul Wieringa
Tel: 250-952-0651
Fax: 250-952-0657

Director, Electricity Transmission & Inter-jurisdictional Branch, Scott Barillaro
Tel: 250-952-0267
Fax: 250-952-0258
Scott.Barillaro@gov.bc.ca

Director, Electricity Generation & Regulation Branch, Sue Bonnyman
Tel: 250-953-3365
Fax: 250-952-0258
Sue.Bonnyman@gov.bc.ca

Director, Renewable Energy Development Branch, Janice Larson
Tel: 250-952-0706
Fax: 250-952-0258
Janice.Larson@gov.bc.ca

Director, Energy Efficiency Branch, Andrew Pape-Salmon
Tel: 250-952-0819
Fax: 250-952-0258
Andrew.PapeSalmon@gov.bc.ca

Director, ICE Fund, Liz Wouters
Tel: 250-387-2883
Fax: 250-952-0351
Liz.Wouters@gov.bc.ca

Gaming Policy & Enforcement
PO Box 9311 Prov Govt, Victoria, BC V8W 9N1
Tel: 250-387-1301
Fax: 250-387-1818
www.hsd.gov.bc.ca/gaming

Assistant Deputy Minister, Douglas S. Scott
Tel: 250-953-4482
Fax: 250-387-1818
Douglas.S.Scott@gov.bc.ca

Executive Director, Policy, Responsible Gambling & Business Services Division, Sue Birge
Tel: 250-387-3211
Fax: 250-356-1910
Sue.Birge@gov.bc.ca

Executive Director, Licensing & Grants, Ursula Cowland
Tel: 250-356-2975
Fax: 250-356-8149
Ursula.Cowland@gov.bc.ca

Executive Director, Racing, Samuel Hawkins
Tel: 604-660-7405
Fax: 604-660-7414
Samuel.Hawkins@gov.bc.ca

Executive Director, Internal Compliance & Risk Management, Bill McCrea
Tel: 250-356-1109
Fax: 250-387-1818
Bill.McCrea@gov.bc.ca

Executive Director, Registration & Certification Division, Rick Saville
Tel: 250-356-0981
Fax: 250-952-5225
Rick.Saville@gov.bc.ca

Executive Director, Audit & Compliance Division, Terri Van Sleuwen
Tel: 604-660-0274
Fax: 604-660-0267
Terri.VanSleuwen@gov.bc.ca

Executive Director, Investigations & Regional Operations Division, Larry Vander Graaf
Tel: 604-660-0276
Fax: 604-660-0267
Larry.VanderGraaf@gov.bc.ca

Director, Personnel Registration, Garth Baillie
Tel: 250-356-0983
Fax: 250-952-5225
Garth.Baillie@gov.bc.ca

Director, Casino Investigations, Derek Dickson
Tel: 604-660-0299
Fax: 604-660-2030
Derek.Dickson@gov.bc.ca

Director, Licensing, Kathy Elder
Tel: 250-356-6479
Fax: 250-356-8149
Kathy.Elder@gov.bc.ca

Director, Charitable Gaming Audit, Anna Fitzgerald
Tel: 604-660-0269
Fax: 604-660-0267
Anna.Fitzgerald@gov.bc.ca

Director, Forensic Investigations, Al Giesbrecht
Tel: 250-356-5550
Fax: 250-356-0782
Al.Giesbrecht@gov.bc.ca

Director, Responsible Gambling Strategy, David Horricks
Tel: 250-953-3078
Fax: 250-356-1910
David.Horricks@gov.bc.ca

Director, Grants, Ron C. Johnson
Tel: 250-356-2967
Fax: 250-356-8149
Ron.Johnson@gov.bc.ca

Director, Commercial Gaming Audit (Lottery), Karen Kraan
Tel: 604-775-1103
Fax: 604-660-0267
Karen.Kraan@gov.bc.ca

Director, Certification & Game Integrity, Steve Lefler
Tel: 250-356-6166
Fax: 250-356-0782
Stephen.Lefler@gov.bc.ca

Director, Lotteries Registration, Len Meilleur
Tel: 250-356-6320
Fax: 250-356-0782
Len.Meilleur@gov.bc.ca

Director, Corporate Registration, Ron Merchant
Tel: 250-356-0989
Fax: 250-356-5225
Ron.Merchant@gov.bc.ca

Director, Lottery Investigations, William Mulcahy
Tel: 604-660-0278
Fax: 604-660-0267
William.Mulcahy@gov.bc.ca

Director, Commercial Gaming Audit (Casino/Bingo), David Pyatt
Tel: 604-775-1198
Fax: 604-660-0267
David.Pyatt@gov.bc.ca

Director, Business Services, Susan Quesnel
Tel: 250-356-9150
Fax: 250-356-1910
Susan.Quesnel@gov.bc.ca
Director, Race Operations, Doug Scott
Tel: 604-328-1671
Fax: 604-660-7414
Douglas.F.Scott@gov.bc.ca

Liquor Control & Licensing Branch
PO Box 9292 Prov Govt, Victoria, BC V8W 9J8
Tel: 250-952-5787
Fax: 250-952-7066
www.pssg.gov.bc.ca/lclb

Assistant Deputy Minister/General Manager, Karen Ayers
Tel: 250-952-5791
Fax: 259-852-7066
Karen.Ayers@gov.bc.ca
Registrar, Elizabeth Barker
Tel: 250-952-5793
Fax: 250-952-7066
Elizabeth.Barker@gov.bc.ca
Deputy General Manager, Licensing, Cheryl Caldwell
Tel: 250-952-7046
Fax: 250-952-7060
Cheryl.Caldwell@gov.bc.ca
Deputy General Manager, Compliance & Enforcement Division, Bruce Edmundson
Tel: 250-952-7037
Fax: 250-952-7059
Bruce.Edmundson@gov.bc.ca
Director, Policy, Planning & Communications, Barry Bieller
Tel: 250-952-5755
Fax: 250-952-7066
Barry.Bieller@gov.bc.ca
Director, Management Services, Jan Evans
Tel: 250-952-7031
Fax: 250-952-7066
Jan.L.Evans@gov.bc.ca

Liquor Distribution Branch
3200 East Broadway, Vancouver, BC V5M 1Z6
Tel: 604-252-3000
Fax: 604-252-3026

General Manager, Jay Chambers
Tel: 604-252-3021
Fax: 603-252-3026
Jay.Chambers@bcldb.com
Chief Financial Officer, Roger Bissoondatt
Tel: 604-252-3151
Fax: 604-252-3175
Roger.Bissoondatt@bcldb.com
Executive Director, Information Services, Don Farley
Tel: 604-252-3264
Fax: 604-252-3283
Don.Farley@bcldb.com
Executive Director, Human Resources, Michael Procopio
Tel: 604-252-3243
Fax: 604-252-3200
Michael.Procopio@bcldb.com
Executive Director, Retail Services, Kelly Wilson
Tel: 604-252-3103
Fax: 604-252-3127
Kelly.Wilson@bcldb.com
Director, Store Operations, Gary Branham
Tel: 604-252-3109
Fax: 604-252-3127
Gary.Branham@bcldb.com
Director, Recruitment & Compensation, Terry Dobrozdravich
Tel: 604-252-2977
Fax: 604-252-3274
Terry.Dobrozdravich@bcldb.com
Acting Director, Employee Relations & Occupational Health & Safety, Rita Ferrara
Tel: 604-252-2948
Fax: 604-252-3274
Rita.Ferrara@bcldb.com
Director, Regulatory Division, Mark Fukuhara
Tel: 604-252-3226
Fax: 604-252-3350
Mark.Fukuhara@bcldb.com
Director, Corporate Policy, Gord Hall
Tel: 604-252-3035
Fax: 604-252-3026
Gord.Hall@bcldb.com
Acting Director, Information Technology Architecture & Planning, Rob James
Tel: 604-252-3073
Rob.James@bcldb.com
Acting Director, Technical Services, Peter Kho
Tel: 604-252-3046
Peter.Kho@bcldb.com
Director, Financial Planning & Reporting, Elaine Low
Tel: 604-252-3158
Elaine.Low@bcldb.com

Director, Wholesale Business, Donna Mohn
Tel: 604-252-3098
Fax: 604-252-3106
Donna.Mohn@bcldb.com
Director, Corporate Security/Emergency Management, Donna Morse
Tel: 604-252-3051
Fax: 604-252-3450
Donna.Morse@bcldb.com
Acting Director, Corporate Projects, Amin Nanji
Tel: 604-252-3408
Amin.Nanji@bcldb.com
Director, Marketing, Paulette Parry
Tel: 604-252-3238
Fax: 604-252-3127
Paulette.Parry@bcldb.com
Director, Internal Audit, Patrick Seeley
Tel: 604-252-3222
Patrick.Seeley@bcldb.com
Director, Finance Administration, Al Shariff
Tel: 604-252-3354
Al.Shariff@bcldb.com
Acting Director, Application Services, Martin Straith
Tel: 604-252-2901
Martin.Straith@bcldb.com
Director, Revenue Division, Norman Thompson
Tel: 604-252-2998
Norman.Thompson@bcldb.com
Director, Real Estate, Bob Tougas
Tel: 604-252-3133
Fax: 604-252-3141
Bob.Tougas@bcldb.com
Director, Distribution, Don Wilcox
Tel: 604-252-3129
Fax: 604-252-3390
Don.Wilcox@bcldb.com

Mines & Mineral Resources
PO Box 9319 Prov Govt, Victoria, BC V8W 9N3
Acting Assistant Deputy Minister, Anne Currie
Tel: 250-952-0470
Fax: 250-952-0491
Anne.Currie@gov.bc.ca
Chief Inspector, Mines, Al Hoffman
Tel: 250-952-0494
Fax: 250-952-0491
Al.Hoffman@gov.bc.ca
Chief Geologist & Director, British Columbia Geological Survey, Dave Lefebvre
Tel: 250-952-0374
Fax: 250-952-0381
Dave.Lefebure@gov.bc.ca
Deputy Chief Gold Commissioner & Director, Mineral Titles (Vancouver), Ed Collazzi
Tel: 604-660-2814
Fax: 604-660-2653
Ed.Collazzi@gov.bc.ca
Acting Director, Mineral Development Office, Kirk Hancock
Tel: 250-952-0433
Fax: 604-775-0313
Kirk.Hancock@gov.bc.ca
Other Communications: Alternate Phone: 604-660-3332
Director, Resource Information Section, Larry Jones
Tel: 250-952-0386
Fax: 250-952-0381
Larry.Jones@gov.bc.ca
Director, Cordilleran Geoscience, Stephen Rowins
Tel: 250-952-0454
Fax: 250-952-0381
Stephen.Rowins@gov.bc.ca
Director, Mining Operations (Kamloops), Joe Seguin
Tel: 250-828-4448
Fax: 250-828-4154
Joe.Seguin@gov.bc.ca
Regional Director, Mining Operations (Victoria), Ed Taje
Tel: 250-952-0732
Fax: 250-952-0491
Eddy.Taje@gov.bc.ca

Office of Housing & Construction Standards
PO Box 9319 Prov Govt, Victoria, BC V8W 9N3
Fax: 250-952-0269

Assistant Deputy Minister, Jeff Vasey
Tel: 250-387-2001
Fax: 250-387-8164
Jeff.Vasey@gov.bc.ca
Acting Executive Director, Building & Safety Standards Branch, Trudy Rotgans
Tel: 250-387-3754
Fax: 250-387-8164
Trudy.Rotgans@gov.bc.ca
Executive Director, Housing Policy Branch, Gregory Steves
Tel: 250-387-3087
Fax: 250-356-8182
Gregory.Steves@gov.bc.ca

Director, Crown Agency Liaison, Simon Clews
Tel: 250-387-1018
Fax: 250-356-8182
Simon.Clews@gov.bc.ca

Oil & Gas
PO Box 9323 Prov Govt, Victoria, BC V8W 9N3
Fax: 250-952-0926

Assistant Deputy Minister, Graeme McLaren
Tel: 250-952-0115
Fax: 250-952-0926
Graeme.McLaren@gov.bc.ca
Executive Director, GeoScience & Natural Gas Development Branch, Richard Bader
Tel: 250-356-1307
Fax: 250-953-3770
Richard.Bader@gov.bc.ca
Executive Director, Major Initiatives, Linda Beltrano
Tel: 250-356-1183
Fax: 250-952-0255
Executive Director, Royalty Policy Branch, Ines Piccinino
Tel: 250-356-9825
Fax: 250-952-0271
Ines.Piccinino@gov.bc.ca
Director, O&G Business Practices, Olga Klimko
Tel: 250-953-3766
Fax: 250-952-0255
Olga.Klimko@gov.bc.ca
Director, Royalty & Policy, Aaron Nelson
Tel: 250-953-3740
Fax: 250-953-3770
Aaron.Nelson@gov.bc.ca
Director, Infrastructure & Development Section, Stephen Pal
Tel: 250-953-3738
Fax: 250-953-3770
Stephen.Pal@gov.bc.ca
Acting Director, Major Initiatives Branch, Michelle Schwabe
Tel: 250-387-1585
Fax: 250-953-3770
Michelle.Schwabe@gov.bc.ca
Director, Economic Development, Ingrid Strauss
Tel: 250-952-0185
Fax: 250-952-0255
Ingrid.Strauss@gov.bc.ca

Titles & Corporate Relations
PO Box 9315 Prov Govt, Victoria, BC V8W 9N1
Fax: 250-356-5092

Acting Assistant Deputy Minister, Laurel Nash
Tel: 250-356-9569
Fax: 250-356-5092
Laurel.Nash@gov.bc.ca
Executive Director, Corporate Policy, Planning & Legislation, Karen Koncohrada
Tel: 250-952-0274
Fax: 250-952-0637
Karen.Koncohrada@gov.bc.ca
Acting Executive Director/Director, Titles Branch/Resource Development, May Mah-Paulson
Tel: 250-952-0335
Fax: 250-952-0291
May.Mah-Paulson@gov.bc.ca
Acting Director, Policy & Planning, Kelly Finck
Tel: 250-952-0709
Fax: 250-952-0331
Kelly.Finck@gov.bc.ca
Director, Division Operation & Revenue Systems Branch, Debbie Fischer
Tel: 250-952-0336
Fax: 250-952-0331
Debbie.Fischer@gov.bc.ca
Acting Director, Corporate Policy & Legislation, Barbara Thomson
Tel: 250-952-0533
Fax: 250-952-0637
Barbara.Thomson@gov.bc.ca
Acting Director, Resource Development/Policy & Planning, Garth Thoroughgood
Tel: 250-952-6382
Fax: 250-952-0331
Garth.Thoroughgood@gov.bc.ca

British Columbia Ministry of Environment

PO Box 9339 Prov Govt, Victoria, BC V8W 9M1
Tel: 250-387-1161
Fax: 250-387-5669
envmail@gov.bc.ca
www.gov.bc.ca/env
Other Communication: Environmental Emergencies: 1-800-663-3456; Report All Poachers & Polluters (RAPP): 1-877-952-7277; Media Enquiries, Phone: 250-387-9973

The following responsibilities are handled by the Ministry of the Environment: establishment of standards; administration of legislation; promotion of stewardship & sustainability, through environmental protection; development of partnerships, by engaging stakeholders, First Nations, & citizens in policy & program development; & conservation, maintenance, & enhancement of ecosystems & native species.

Acts Administered:
College of Applied Biology Act
Ecological Reserve Act
Environmental Assessment Act
Environmental Management Act (except (a) s. 5 (f), as that provision relates to the portfolio of the Minister of Forests, Lands, & Natural Resource Operations; (b) Divisions 1 & 3 of Part 8)
Greenhouse Gas Reduction (Cap & Trade) Act
Greenhouse Gas Reduction (Vehicle Emissions Standards) Act
Greenhouse Gas Reduction Targets Act
Integrated Pest Management Act
Land Title Act (s. 219 (1), (2), (3) (a) & (b), (4)-(9.2), (10), (11) (a), (12) & (14), as that provision relates to the portfolio of the Minister of Environment)
Ministry of Environment Act (except s. 4 (2) (d); ss. 4 (2) (b), (e), (f) & (g) & 6.1 as those provisions relate to the portfolio of the Minister of Forests, Lands, & Natural Resource Operations)
Ministry of Lands, Parks, & Housing Act (ss. 5 (b), 6 & 9, as those provisions relate to the portfolio of the Minister of Environment)
Park Act
Protected Areas of British Columbia Act
Special Accounts Appropriation & Control (s. 9.6)
Sustainable Environment Fund Act
Wildlife Act (s. 3 (b), as that provision relates to the portfolio of the Minister of Environment; ss. 6 & 108 (2) (a))

Minister, Environment; Deputy House Leader, Hon. Terry Lake
Tel: 250-387-1187
Fax: 250-387-1356
ENV.minister@gov.bc.ca
Social Media: twitter.com/terrylakeMLA
PO Box 9047 Prov Govt Sta.
Victoria, BC V8W 9E2

Deputy Minister, Environment, Cairine MacDonald
Tel: 250-387-5429

Associated Agencies, Boards & Commissions:
• British Columbia Environmental Assessment Office

Climate Action Secretariat
PO Box 9486 Prov Govt, Victoria, BC V8W 9W6
Fax: 250-356-7286
climateactionsecretariat@gov.bc.ca
www.env.gov.bc.ca/cas//index.html

Head, James Mack
Tel: 250-387-9456
Fax: 250-356-7286
Chief Negotiator/Executive Director, Business Development, Tim Lesiuk
Tel: 250-387-9216
Fax: 250-356-7286
Other Communications: Cell Phone: 250-216-5893
Executive Director, Climate Policy, Lee Thiessen
Tel: 250-356-7917
Fax: 250-356-7286
Director, Carbon Neutral Government & Outreach, Colleen Sparks
Tel: 250-356-1810
Fax: 250-356-7286
Colleen.Sparks@gov.bc.ca
Lead Negotiator/Director, Business Development, Jessica Verhagen
Tel: 604-660-0788
Fax: 250-356-7286
Jessica.Verhagen@gov.bc.ca

Compliance Division - Enforcement Program / Conservation Officer Service
PO Box 9376 Prov Govt, Victoria, BC V8W 9M1
Tel: 250-356-9234
Fax: 250-356-9197
conservation.officer.service@gov.bc.ca
www.env.gov.bc.ca/cos/
Other Communication: Wildlife conflict: 1-877-952-7277

Chief Conservation Officer, Enforcement Program/Conservation Officer Service, Ed Illi
Tel: 250-356-9100
Fax: 250-356-9197
Ed.Illi@gov.bc.ca
Executive Director, Enforcement Program/Conservation Officer Service, Tom D. Clark
Tel: 250-356-9443
Fax: 250-953-3414
Tom.D.Clark@gov.bc.ca
Other Communications: Cell Phone: 250-893-0990
Chief Superintendent, Program Governance, Lance Sundquist
Tel: 250-751-3119
Fax: 250-751-7383
Lance.Sundquist@gov.bc.ca
Other Communications: Alternate Phone: 250-356-9121
Chief Superintendent, Program Governance, Barry Farynuk
Tel: 250-354-6336
Fax: 250-354-6277
Barry.Farynuk@gov.bc.ca

Environmental Protection Division
PO Box 9339, Victoria, BC V8W 9M1
Tel: 250-387-1288
Fax: 250-387-5669
www.env.gov.bc.ca/epd/

Assistant Deputy Minister, Jim Standen
Tel: 250-387-1288
Fax: 250-387-5669
Jim.Standen@gov.bc.ca
Director, Environmental Management, Jim Hofweber
Tel: 250-387-9971
Fax: 250-387-8897
Jim.Hofweber@gov.bc.ca
Director, Air Protection Branch, Glen Okrainetz
Tel: 250-953-3417
Fax: 250-952-1713
Glen.Okrainetz@gov.bc.ca
Director, Environmental Standards Branch, David Ranson
Tel: 250-387-9933
Fax: 250-356-7197
David.Ranson@gov.bc.ca
Deputy Director, Regional Operations, Christa Zacharias-Homer
Tel: 250-356-8174
Fax: 250-356-5496
Christa.ZachariasHomer@gov.bc.ca
Regional Manager, Thompson Regional Office, Rick Adams
Tel: 250-371-6299
Fax: 250-828-4000
Rick.P.Adams@gov.bc.ca
1259 Dalhousie Dr.
Kamloops, BC V2C 5Z5
Regional Manager, Vancouver Island Regional Office, Randy Alexander
Tel: 250-751-3176
Fax: 250-751-3103
Randy.Alexander@gov.bc.ca
2080A Labieux Rd.
Nanaimo, BC V9T 6J9
Regional Manager, Lower Mainland Regional Office, Jonn Braman
Tel: 604-582-5284
Fax: 604-584-9751
10470 - 152nd St., 2nd Fl.
Surrey, BC V3R 0Y3
Regional Manager, Omineca Regional Office, Dean Cherkas
Tel: 250-565-6443
Fax: 250-565-6629
Dean.Cherkas@gov.bc.ca
1011 - 4th Ave., 3rd Fl.
Prince George, BC V2L 3H9
Regional Manager, Kootenay & Okanagan Regional Office, Robyn Roome
Tel: 250-354-6362
Fax: 250-354-6332
Robyn.Roome@gov.bc.ca
#401, 333 Victoria St.
Nelson, BC V1L 4K3
Regional Manager, Skeena Regional Office, Ian Sharpe
Tel: 250-847-7251
Fax: 250-847-7591
Ian.Sharpe@gov.bc.ca
3726 Alfred Ave.
PO Box 5000
Smithers, BC V0J 2N0
Section Head, Cariboo Regional Office, Douglas Hill
Tel: 250-398-4542
Fax: 250-398-4214
#400, 640 Borland St.
Williams Lake, BC V2G 4T1

Environmental Stewardship Division
PO Box 9339 Prov Govt, Victoria, BC V8W 9M1
Tel: 250-356-0121
Fax: 250-387-5669

Director, Regional Operations, Brian J. Clark
Tel: 250-356-0874
Fax: 250-356-9299
Brian.J.Clark@gov.bc.ca
Manager, First Nations Relations, Bryan Williams
Tel: 250-751-3155
Fax: 250-751-3208
Manager, Strategic Initiatives, Chris Tunnoch
Tel: 604-942-2224
Fax: 604-924-2244
Chris.Tunnoch@gov.bc.ca
Regional Manager, Vancouver Island Regional Office, Don Cadden
Tel: 250-751-3211
Fax: 250-751-3208
Don.Cadden@gov.bc.ca
Regional Manager, Thompson Regional Office, Jeff Leahy
Tel: 250-371-6304
Fax: 250-828-4000
Jeff.Leahy@gov.bc.ca
Acting Regional Manager, Omineca Regional Office, Ted Zimmerman
Tel: 250-614-9904
Fax: 250-565-6940
Ted.Zimmerman@gov.bc.ca
Section Head, Skeena Regional Office, Larry Boudreau
Tel: 250-847-7655
Fax: 250-847-7728
Larry.Boudreau@gov.bc.ca
Section Head, Kootenay Regional Office, Glenn Campbell
Tel: 250-489-8595
Fax: 250-489-8506
Glenn.Campbell@gov.bc.ca
Section Head, Cariboo Regional Office, Murray Carruthers
Tel: 250-398-4924
Fax: 250-398-4214
Murray.Carruthers@gov.bc.ca
Section Head, Lower Mainland Regional Office, Vicki Haberl
Tel: 604-898-3678
Fax: 604-898-4171
Vicki.Haberl@gov.bc.ca
Section Head, Okanagan Regional Office, Dave Richmond
Tel: 250-490-8259
Fax: 250-490-2231
Dave.Richmond@gov.bc.ca

Environmental Sustainability & Strategic Policy Division
PO Box 9335 Prov Govt, Victoria, BC V8W 9M1
Tel: 250-387-9666
Fax: 250-387-8894

Assistant Deputy Minister, Mark Zacharias
Tel: 250-356-0121
Fax: 250-387-5669
Executive Director, Strategic Policy Branch, Anthony J. Danks
Tel: 250-387-8483
Fax: 250-387-8894
Anthony.Danks@gov.bc.ca
Director, Ecosystems Branch, Kaaren Lewis
Tel: 250-387-9731
Fax: 250-356-5104
Kaaren.Lewis@gov.bc.ca
Director, Knowledge Management Branch, Fern Schultz
Tel: 250-387-6722
Fax: 250-356-1202
Fern.Schultz@gov.bc.ca
Director, Water Protection & Sustainability Branch, Lynn Kriwoken
Tel: 250-387-9446
Fax: 250-356-1202
Lynn.Kriwoken@gov.bc.ca

Parks & Protected Areas Division
PO Box 9339 Prov Govt, Victoria, BC V8W 9M9
Fax: 250-953-3414

Assistant Deputy Minister, Lori Halls
Tel: 250-387-9997
Fax: 250-953-3414
Director, Parks Planning & Management Branch, Brian Bawtinheimer
Tel: 250-387-4355
Fax: 250-387-5757
Brian.Bawtinheimer@gov.bc.ca
Director, Visitor Services Branch, Christine Houghton
Tel: 250-356-9241
Fax: 250-387-5757
Christine.Houghton@gov.bc.ca

Water Stewardship Division
PO Box 9339 Prov Govt, Victoria, BC V8W 9M1
Fax: 250-387-6003

Regional Manager, Vancouver Island Regional Office, Larry Barr
Tel: 250-751-7105
Fax: 250-751-7079
Larry.Barr@gov.bc.ca
2080A Labieux Rd.
Nanaimo, BC V9T 6J9
Regional Manager, Lower Mainland Regional Office, Julia Berardinucci
Tel: 604-582-5353
Fax: 604-582-5235
Julia.Berardinucci@gov.bc.ca
10470 - 152nd St., 2nd Fl.
Surrey, BC V3R 0Y3
Regional Manager, Omineca, Peace, & Skeena Regional Offices, Norm Bilodeau
Tel: 250-565-6424
Fax: 250-565-6629
Normand.Bilodeau@gov.bc.ca

4051 - 18th Ave.
Prince George, BC V2N 1B3

British Columbia Ministry of Justice

PO Box 9044 Prov Govt, Victoria, BC V8W 9E2
www.gov.bc.ca/justice

The Ministry of Justice works to ensure safety for the people of British Columbia by seeing that public affairs are administered according to the law & by leading law reform.
The following are examples of general responsibilities of the ministry: legal services to government; consumer services; crime prevention programs; emergency social services; provincial emergency management; criminal justice; legal aid; court administration; police & correctional services; victim assistance; & the protection order registry.

Acts Administered:
Administrative Tribunals Act
Administrative Tribunals Appointment & Administration Act
Adult Guardianship Act
Age of Majority Act
Apology Act
Armoured Vehicle & After-Market Compartment Control
Attorney General Act
Body Armour Control Act
British Columbia Neurotrauma Fund Contribution
Builders Lien Act
Business Practices & Consumer Protection Act
Business Practices & Consumer Protection Authority Act
Charitable Purposes Preservation Act
Civil Forfeiture Act
Civil Resolution Tribunal Act
Civil Rights Protection Act
Class Proceedings Act
Coastal Ferry Act
Commercial Arbitration
Commercial Transport Act (except s. 3; ss. 1, 4, 5, 8, 9, 11, & 12 as those provisions relate to highway infrastructure & weigh scales; & ss. 1, 4, 5, 8, 9, 11, 12, & 14 as those provisions relate to affairs of CommercialVehicle Safety & Enforcement)
Conflict of Laws Rules for Trusts Act
Constitution Act (except ss. 25-27)
Constitutional Amendment Approval Act
Constitutional Question Act
Coroners Act
Correction Act
County Boundary Act
Court Agent Act
Court Jurisdiction & Proceedings Transfer Act
Court Order Enforcement Act
Court Order Interest Act
Court Rules Act
Court of Appeal Act
Cremation, Interment & Funeral Services Act
Crime Victim Assistance Act
Criminal Asset Management Act
Criminal Injury Compensation Act
Criminal Records Review Act
Crown Counsel Act
Crown Franchise Act
Crown Proceeding Act
Debtor Assistance Act
Disciplinary Authority Protection Act
Election Act
Electoral Boundaries Commission Act
Electoral Districts Act
Electoral Reform Referendum 2009 Act
Emergency Communications Corporations Act
Emergency Program Act
Enforcement of Canadian Judgments & Decrees Act
Environmental Management Act (Divisions 1 & 3 of Part 8)
Escheat Act
Estate Administration Act
Estates of Missing Persons Act
Evidence Act
Expropriation Act
Family Compensation Act
Family Law Act
Family Maintenance Enforcement Act
Family Relations Act
Federal Courts Jurisdiction Act
Financial Disclosure Act
Fire Services Act (except s. 47 (2) (g) & (h))
Firearm Act
Fireworks Act
Flood Relief Act
Food Donor Encouragement Act
Foreign Arbitral Awards Act
Foreign Money Claims Act
Forest & Range Practices Act (s. 166, as that provision relates to the portfolio of the Minister of Justice)
Forest Practices Code of British Columbia (Part 9)
Fraudulent Conveyance Act
Fraudulent Preference Act
Frustrated Contract Act
Good Samaritan Act
Guide Animal Act
Gunshot & Stab Wound Disclosure
Holocaust Memorial Day Act
Human Rights Code Act
Infants Act
Insurance Corporation Act (Part 2)
Interjurisdictional Support Orders Act
International Commercial Arbitration Act
International Sale of Goods Act
International Trusts Act
Interpretation Act
Judicial Compensation Act
Judicial Review Procedure Act
Jury Act
Justice Administration Act
Law & Equity Act
Law Reform Commission Act
Legal Profession Act
Legal Services Society Act
Libel & Slander Act
Limitation Act
Lobbyists Registration Act
Local Government Bylaw Notice Enforcement Act
Members' Conflict of Interest Act
Metal Dealers & Recyclers Act
Ministry of Consumer & Corporate Affairs Act
Ministry of Provincial Secretary & Government Services Act
Motion Picture Act
Motor Dealer Act
Motor Vehicle Act (with some exceptions related to highway infrastructure & weigh scales & to affairs of Commercial Vehicle Safety & Enforcement)
Negligence Act
Notaries Act
Occupiers Liability Act
Offence Act
Oil & Gas Activities Act
Ombudsperson Act
Parental Responsibility Act
Partition of Property Act
Patients Property Act
Perpetuity Act
Police Act
Power of Appointment Act
Power of Attorney Act
Privacy Act
Probate Recognition Act
Property Law Act
Provincial Court Act
Public Guardian & Trustee Act
Public Inquiry Act
Queen's Counsel Act
Recall & Initiative Act
Referendum Act
Representation Agreement Act
Representative for Children & Youth Act
Safe Streets Act
Sale of Goods Act
Security Services Act
Settlement of International Investment Disputes Act
Sex Offender Registry Act
Sheriff Act
Small Claims Act
Special Accounts Appropriation & Control Act (ss. 7 & 10 (2) (a) & (b))
Statute Revision Act
Subpoena (Interprovincial) Act
Supreme Court Act
Survivorship & Presumption of Death Act
Trespass Act
Trust & Settlement Variation Act
Trustee (Church Property) Act
Trustee Act
Utilities Commission Act
Victims of Crime Act
Wills Act (except Part 2)
Wills Variation Act
Wills, Estates & Succession Act
Youth Justice Act

Minister, Justice; Attorney General, Hon. Shirley Bond
Tel: 250-387-1866
Fax: 250-387-6411
JAG.Minister@gov.bc.ca
Social Media: twitter.com/shirleybond, www.facebook.com/shirley.bond

Deputy Minister, Justice, Richard Fyfe, QC
Tel: 250-356-0149
Fax: 250-387-6224
PO Box 9290 Prov Govt Sta.
Victoria, BC V8W 9J7

Deputy Minister, Justice, Lori Wanamaker
Tel: 250-356-0149
Fax: 250-387-6224
PO Box 9290 Prov Govt Sta.
Victoria, BC V8W 9J7

Assistant Deputy Minister, Justice Services, Jay Chalke, QC
Tel: 250-356-6582
Victoria, BC V8W 9J7

Assistant Deputy Minister, Management Services, Tara Faganello
Tel: 250-387-5258
Tara.Faganello@gov.bc.ca
Victoria, BC V8W 9J7

Assistant Deputy Minister, Kevin Jardine
Tel: 250-356-1526
Victoria, BC V8W 9J7

Executive Director, Business Intelligence & Performance Management, Allan Castle
Tel: 250-356-0111
Fax: 250-387-6224

Executive Advisor, Corporate Communications & Change Management, Barbara Greeniaus
Tel: 250-356-0169
Fax: 250-387-6224
Barbara.Greeniaus@gov.bc.ca

Director, Investigation & Standards, Sydney Swift
Tel: 250-387-5948
Fax: 250-356-9875

Manager, Strategic Coordination, Darrion Campbell
Tel: 250-356-5203
Fax: 250-953-4072
Darrion.Campbell@gov.bc.ca

Associated Agencies, Boards & Commissions:

• British Columbia Ferry Commission
PO Box 35119 Hillside
Victoria, BC V8T 5G2
Tel: 250-590-2770
info@bcferrycommission.com
www.bcferrycommission.com
The British Columbia Ferry Commission was established under the Coastal Ferry Act. The fares & service levels of the province's ferry operator, British Columbia Ferry Services Inc., are regulated by the Commission.

• British Columbia Human Rights Tribunal
#1170, 605 Robson St.
Vancouver, BC V6B 5J3
Tel: 604-775-2000
Fax: 604-775-2020
Toll-free: 888-440-8844
TTY: 604-775-2021
BCHumanRightsTribunal@gov.bc.ca
www.bchrt.bc.ca
The independent, quasi-judicial body was established by the British Columbia Human Rights Code. The British Columbia Human Rights Tribunal is engaged in accepting, screening, mediating, & adjudicating human rights complaints.

• British Columbia Law Institute (BCLI)
University of British Columbia
1822 East Mall
Vancouver, BC V6T 1Z1
Tel: 604-822-0142
Fax: 604-822-0144
bcli@bcli.org
www.bcli.org
The Institute was created in 1997 under the Provincial Society Act, & is tasked with promoting clarity in modern law; improvement in the administration of justice; & scholarly legal research.

• British Columbia Office of the Police Complaint Commissioner
#501, 947 Fort St.
PO Box 9895 Prov Govt
Victoria, BC V8W 9T8
Tel: 250-356-7458
Fax: 250-356-6503
Toll-free: 877-999-8707
info@opcc.bc.ca
www.opcc.bc.ca

• British Columbia Pension Corporation
2995 Jutland Rd.
PO Box 9460
Victoria, BC V8W 9V8
Tel: 250-387-1002
Fax: 250-953-0429
Toll-free: 800-663-8823
PensionCorp@pensionsbc.ca;
Retired.Members@pensionsbc.ca
www.pensionsbc.ca
Other Communication: College Pension Plan: 250-953-4324; Municipal Pension Plan: 250-953-3000; Public Service Pension Plan: 250-953-3033; Teachers' Pension Plan: 250-953-3022

• British Columbia Review Board
#1020, 510 Burrard St.
Vancouver, BC V6C 3A8
Tel: 604-660-8789
Fax: 604-660-8809
Toll-free: 877-305-2277
www.bcrb.bc.ca
The British Columbia Review Board was created in accordance with the Criminal Code of Canada. The Board is an independent tribunal, with responsibility for holding hearings to establish & review dispositions. The dispositions involve persons who have been charged with criminal offenses & received verdicts of not criminally responsible on account of mental disorder, or unfit to stand trial on account of mental disorder.

• Coroners Service of British Columbia
Metrotower II
#800, 4720 Kingsway
Burnaby, BC V5H 4N2
Tel: 604-660-7745
Fax: 604-660-7766
BC.CorSer@gov.bc.ca
www.pssg.gov.bc.ca/coroners

• Criminal Injury Compensation Program (Workers' Compensation Board) / CICP
PO Box 5350
Vancouver, BC V6B 5L5
Tel: 604-244-6400
Fax: 604-244-6480

• Elections British Columbia

• Environmental Appeal Board (EAB)
747 Fort St., 4th Fl.
PO Box 9425 Prov Govt
Victoria, BC V8W 3E9
Tel: 250-387-3464
Fax: 250-356-9923
eabinfo@gov.bc.ca
www.eab.gov.bc.ca

• Forest Appeals Commission (FAC)
747 Fort St., 4th Fl.
PO Box 9425 Prov Govt
Victoria, BC V8W 9V1
Tel: 250-387-3464
Fax: 250-356-9923
facinfo@gov.bc.ca
www.fac.gov.bc.ca

• Judicial Council of British Columbia
Pacific Centre
#602, 700 West Georgia St.
PO Box 10287
Vancouver, BC V7Y 1E8
Tel: 604-660-2864
Fax: 604-660-1108
info@provincialcourt.bc.ca
www.provincialcourt.bc.ca/judicialcouncil
As designated by the Provincial Court Act, the Judicial Council of British Columbia consists of nine members. The process of the Judicial Council is governed by a Procedure Bylaw. The overall goal of the Council is the improvement of the quality of judicial service in the province.

• Justice Education Society (JES)
#260, 800 Hornby St.
Vancouver, BC V6Z 2C3
Tel: 604-660-9870
Fax: 604-775-3476
info@justiceeducation.ca
www.justiceeducation.ca
Formerly the Law Courts Education Society, renamed in 2009, the Justice Education Society seeks to promote the understanding of, and access to, Canada's justice system for all groups of people, but especially youth, Aboriginals, ethnic & immigrant communities, deaf people, those with learning disabilities, & other groups as required.

• Legal Services Society (LSS)
#400, 510 Burrard St.
Vancouver, BC V6C 3A8
Tel: 604-601-6000
www.lss.bc.ca
Other Communication: Call Centre: 1-866-577-2525; 604-408-2172 (Greater Vancouver); Media inquiries: 604-601-6004
The Legal Services Society was established by the Legal Services Society Act. The non-profit Society provides legal information, advice, & representation services to assist British Columbians in the resolution of their legal issues. Regional centres & local agents' offices are located throughout the province.

• Office of the Representative for Children & Youth (RCY)
#201, 546 Yates St.
Victoria, BC V8W 1K8
Tel: 250-356-6710
Fax: 250-356-0837
Toll-free: 800-476-3933
rcy@rcybc.ca
www.rcybc.ca
Other Communication: Northern Office - Prince George: 250-561-4626; Lower Mainland Office - Burnaby: 604-775-3213
Acting in accordance with British Columbia's Representative for Children and Youth Act, the Representative for Children & Youth is responsible for advocacy, monitoring, & investigation.

• Public Guardian & Trustee of British Columbia (PGT)
#700, 808 West Hastings St.
Vancouver, BC V6C 3L3
Tel: 604-660-4444
Fax: 604-660-0374
Toll-free: 800-663-7867
mail@trustee.bc.ca
www.trustee.bc.ca
Other Communication: Communications & Media Relations: 604-660-4474; Child & Youth Svs.: 604-775-3480; Estate & Personal Trust Svs.: 604-660-4444
The Public Guardian & Trustee of British Columbia was established under the Public Guardian and Trustee Act. The corporation offers the following programs: Child & Youth Services; Services to Adults; & Estate & Personal Trust Services.

Corrections Branch
PO Box 9278 Prov Govt, Victoria, BC V8W 9J7
Tel: 250-387-5059
Fax: 250-387-5698
www.pssg.gov.bc.ca/corrections
Other Communication: Adult Custody Phone: 250-387-5098; Community Corrections & Corporate Programs Phone: 250-356-7930
The Corrections Branch consists of the Adult Custody Division & the Community Corrections & Corporate Programs Division. The Adult Custody Division operates correctional centres for persons awaiting trial or serving a provincial custody sentence. The Community Corrections & Corporate Programs Division operates over fifty community corrections offices throughout British Columbia.

Assistant Deputy Minister, Corrections, Brent Merchant
Tel: 250-387-5363
Fax: 250-387-5698

Provincial Director, Adult Custody Division, Pete Coulson
Tel: 250-387-5959
Fax: 250-952-6883
Peter.Coulson@gov.bc.ca

Provincial Director, Community Corrections & Corporate Programs Division, Michelia Cameron
Tel: 250-387-5930
Fax: 250-952-6883
Micheila.Cameron@gov.bc.ca

Deputy Provincial Director, Community Corrections & Corporate Programs Headquarters, Elenore Clark
Tel: 250-387-5936
Fax: 250-387-5039
Elenore.Clark@gov.bc.ca

Acting Deputy Provincial Director, Operations, Debbie Hawboldt
Tel: 250-356-5868
Fax: 250-952-6883
Debbie.Hawboldt@gov.bc.ca

Deputy Provincial Director, Capital Projects, Tedd Howard
Tel: 250-514-8851
Fax: 250-952-6883
Tedd.Howard@gov.bc.ca

Deputy Provincial Director, Community Corrections & Corporate Programs Headquarters, Bill Small
Tel: 250-387-6040
Fax: 250-387-5039
Bill.Small@gov.bc.ca

Court Services Branch
PO Box 9249 Prov Govt, Victoria, BC V8W 9J2
Tel: 250-356-1550
Fax: 250-356-8152

Executive Director, Corporate Support, Brenda Miller
Tel: 250-356-1525
Fax: 250-387-4743

Acting Director, Court Reform, Business Transformation & Corporate Planning, Kashmiro Cheema
Tel: 250-356-1826
Fax: 250-356-8152
Kashmiro.Cheema@gov.bc.ca
#202, 668 Carnarvon St.
New Westminster, BC V3M 5Y6

Executive Director, Business Transformation & Corporate Planning, Trish Shwart
Tel: 250-356-6428
Fax: 250-356-8152
Trish.Shwart@gov.bc.ca

Director, Service Transformation, Business Transformation & Corporate Planning, Alanna Valentine
Tel: 250-356-9534
Fax: 250-356-8152
Alanna.Valentine@gov.bc.ca
#202, 668 Carnarvon St.
New Westminster, BC V3M5Y6

Director, Financial Management & Administration, Ted Stevens
Tel: 250-356-9469
Fax: 250-356-8152
Ted.Stevens@gov.bc.ca
#202, 668 Carnarvon St.
New Westminster, BC V3M 5Y6

Director, Strategic Information & Business Applications, Dan Chiddell
Tel: 250-356-1565
Fax: 250-356-8152
Dan.Chiddell@gov.bc.ca
#202, 668 Carnarvon St.
New Westminster, BC V3M 5Y6

Criminal Justice Branch
1001 Douglas St., 9th Fl., PO Box 9276 Prov Govt, Victoria, BC V8W 9J7
Tel: 250-387-3840
Fax: 250-387-0090
www.ag.gov.bc.ca/prosecution-service/

Assistant Deputy Attorney General, Robert W.G. Gillen, Q.C.
Tel: 250-387-3840
Fax: 250-387-0090

Emergency Management BC
PO Box 9223 Prov Govt, Victoria, BC V8W 9J1
Tel: 250-953-4002
Fax: 250-953-4081
BC.CorSer@gov.bc.ca (Coroner); OFC@gov.bc.ca (Fire Commissioner)
www.pssg.gov.bc.ca/coroners; www.pssg.gov.bc.ca/firecom
Other Communication: Office of the Chief Coroner: 604-660-7745; Office of the Fire Commissioner Phone: 250-356-9000, Toll Free: 1-888-988-9488; Provincial Emergency Program: 250-952-4913
Emergency Management BC oversees the Coroners Service of British Columbia, the Office of the Fire Commissioner, & the Provincial Emergency Program (www.pep.bc.ca).
B.C. Coroners Service investigates all unexpected, unnatural, unexplained, & unattended deaths in the province.
Improvements to public safety & recommendations to prevent similar deaths are made by the Coroners Service.
The Office of the Fire Commissioner administers & enforces fire safety legislation, trains local assistants to the fire commissioner, certifies fire fighters, provides public fire safety education, advises local governments, responds to major fires, & investigates fires.
The Provincial Emergency Program provides training & support to local governments.

Fire & Emergency Management Commissioner, Becky Denlinger
Tel: 250-953-4083
Fax: 250-387-4872
Becky.Denlinger@gov.bc.ca

Executive Officer, Cameron Lewis
Tel: 250-953-4036
Fax: 250-953-4081
Cameron.Lewis@gov.bc.ca

Executive Director, Corporate Services, David Curtis
Tel: 250-953-4034
Fax: 250-953-4081
David.Curtis@gov.bc.ca

Director, Flood Protection Program, Carol Loski
Tel: 250-953-4003
Fax: 250-953-4081

BC Coroners Service
Metrotower II, #800, 4720 Kingsway, Burnaby, BC V5H 4N2
Tel: 604-660-7745
Fax: 604-660-7766
BC.CorSer@gov.bc.ca
www.pssg.gov.bc.ca/coroners/

Chief Coroner, Lisa Lapointe
Tel: 604-660-7745
Fax: 604-660-7766

Deputy Chief Coroner, Norm Leibel
Tel: 604-660-7745
Fax: 604-660-7766
Norm.Leibel@gov.bc.ca

Executive Director, Kellie Kilpatrick
Tel: 604-660-2556
Fax: 604-660-2640
Kellie.Kilpatrick@gov.bc.ca

Executive Director, Medical Services, Dr. Karla Pederson
Tel: 604-660-7745
Fax: 604-660-7766
Director, Legal Services & Inquests, Rodrick MacKenzie
Tel: 604-660-7745
Fax: 604-660-7766
Rodrick.MacKenzie@gov.bc.ca

Provincial Emergency Program
PO Box 9201 Prov Govt, Victoria, BC V8W 9J1
Tel: 250-952-4913
Fax: 250-952-4888
Toll-Free: 800-663-3456
www.pep.bc.ca

Executive Director, Emergency Coordination, Chris Duffy
Tel: 250-952-4544
Fax: 250-952-4888
Chris.Duffy@gov.bc.ca
Executive Director, Strategic Planning, Policy & Legislation, Cam Filmer
Tel: 250-952-4881
Fax: 250-952-4888
Cam.Filmer@gov.bc.ca
Director, Integrated Public Safety Unit, Heather Lyle
Tel: 604-586-4358
Fax: 604-586-4334
Heather.Lyle@gov.bc.ca
Director, Integrated Planning, Aja Norgaard
Tel: 250-952-4854
Fax: 250-952-4888
Aja.Norgaard@gov.bc.ca
Senior Regional Manager/Assistant Director, Northwest & Vancouver Island Regions, Ralph Mohrmann
Tel: 250-952-4895
Fax: 250-952-4888
Ralph.Mohrmann@gov.bc.ca
Other Communications: Vancouver Fax: 250-952-4304

Finance & Administration Division
PO Box 9256 Prov Govt, Victoria, BC V8W 9J4
Tel: 250-387-5505
Fax: 250-356-8739

Chief Financial Officer, David Hoadley
Tel: 250-356-5393
Fax: 250-356-8739
David.Hoadley@gov.bc.ca
Director, Financial Planning & Analysis, Paul Cumberland
Tel: 250-356-5499
Fax: 250-356-8739
Paul.Cumberland@gov.bc.ca
Director, Special Projects, Financial Planning & Analysis Division, Rod Seginson
Tel: 250-356-7068
Fax: 250-356-8739
Rod.Seginson@gov.bc.ca
Director, Accounting, Budgeting & Reporting, William Skrlac
Tel: 250-356-7077
Fax: 250-356-9185
William.Skrlac@gov.bc.ca

Information Technology Services Division
PO Box 9262 Prov Govt, Victoria, BC V8W 9J4
Tel: 250-356-8972
Fax: 250-356-8739

Acting Executive Director/Chief Information Officer, Frank D'Argis
Tel: 250-387-5258
Fax: 250-356-8739
Chief Technology Officer, Operations, Evan Schlaak
Tel: 250-356-6061
Fax: 250-356-7699
Evan.Schlaak@gov.bc.ca
Chief Enterprise Architect, Stuart F. Cayzer
Tel: 250-387-1111
Fax: 250-356-7699
Stuart.Cayzer@gov.bc.ca
Acting Director, Enterprise Architecture, Chris Mah
Tel: 250-952-0591
Fax: 250-356-7699
Chris.Mah@gov.bc.ca
Director, Client Services, IM/IT Client Services, Larry Bjelde
Tel: 250-356-9285
Fax: 250-356-7699
Larry.Bjelde@gov.bc.ca
Director, Technical Support Services, Ross Harris
Tel: 250-415-3197
Fax: 250-356-7699
Ross.Harris@gov.bc.ca
Director, Application & Infrastructure Services, Carol Barnsley
Tel: 250-356-1164
Fax: 250-356-7699
Carol.Barnsley@gov.bc.ca

Justice Service Branch
PO Box 9222 Prov Govt, Victoria, BC V8W 9J1

Provincial Executive Director, Family Justice Services, Irene Robertson
Tel: 250-387-5903
Fax: 250-356-1279
Executive Director, Maintenance Enforcement & Locate Services, Christopher Beresford
Tel: 604-660-2528
Fax: 604-660-1346
Chris.Beresford@gov.bc.ca
Executive Director, Civil Policy & Legislation Office, Nancy Carter
Tel: 250-356-6182
Fax: 250-387-4525
Nancy.Carter@gov.bc.ca
Executive Director, Criminal Justice & Legal Access Policy Division, James Deitch
Tel: 250-387-2109
Fax: 250-356-6552
Executive Director, Administrative Justice, Dianne Flood
Tel: 250-387-0116
Fax: 250-387-0079
Executive Director, Dispute Resolution Office, David Merner
Tel: 250-514-5507
Fax: 250-387-1189
David.Merner@gov.bc.ca
Director, Integrated Criminal Justice, Criminal Justice & Legal Access Policy Division, Allan Castle
Tel: 250-356-6518
Fax: 250-356-6552
Allan.Castle@gov.bc.ca
Director, Criminal Justice Transformation Projects, Criminal Justice & Legal Access Policy Division, Judy Klima
Tel: 250-387-0801
Fax: 250-356-6552
Judy.Klima@gov.bc.ca
Director, FPT Criminal Justice, Criminal Justice & Legal Access Policy Division, Jacquelyn Nelson
Tel: 250-387-5004
Fax: 250-356-6552
Jacquelyn.Nelson@gov.bc.ca
Deputy Director, Maintenance Enforcement & Locate Services, Ringo Dosanjh
Tel: 604-660-3746
Fax: 604-660-3728
Ringo.Dosanjh@gov.bc.ca
Director, Strategic Projects, Dispute Resolution Office, Kate Kimberley
Tel: 250-356-6180
Fax: 250-387-1189

Legal Services Branch
PO Box 9280 Prov Govt, Victoria, BC V8W 9J7

Assistant Deputy Attorney General, Richard Fyfe, Q.C.
Tel: 250-356-9260
Fax: 250-356-5111
Richard.Fyfe@gov.bc.ca
Acting Chief Legislative Counsel, Kenneth Downing, Q.C.
Fax: 250-356-5758
Ken.Downing@gov.bc.ca
Acting Director, Library & Research Services, Craig Huggins
Tel: 250-356-8490
Fax: 250-387-5758
Craig.Huggins@gov.bc.ca
Director, Strategic & Business Initiatives, Patricia J. Kimmitt-Huxley
Tel: 250-952-7540
Fax: 250-952-7555
Patricia.KimmittHuxley@gov.bc.ca
Director, Business Operations, Aaron Plater
Tel: 250-952-7550
Fax: 250-952-7555
Aaron.Plater@gov.bc.ca
Director, Finance & Human Resources, Kyle Pollner
Tel: 250-952-7554
Fax: 250-952-7555
Kyle.Pollner@gov.bc.ca
Supervising Counsel, Barristers Division - Aboriginal Litigation, Elizabeth Argall
Tel: 250-356-5365
Fax: 250-387-0343
Elizabeth.Argall@gov.bc.ca
Supervising Counsel, Barristers Division - Civil Litigation, Gordon Houston
Tel: 250-356-6175
Fax: 250-953-4348
Gordon.Houston@gov.bc.ca
Supervising Counsel, Barristers Division - Constitutional & Administrative Law, Craig Jones
Tel: 250-387-3129
Fax: 250-356-9154
Craig.Jones@gov.bc.ca
Other Communications: Alternate Phone: 604-660-5476
Acting Supervising Solicitor, Solicitors Division - Resource, Environmental & Land Law, Christopher Jones
Tel: 250-356-0464
Fax: 250-387-6597
Christopher.H.Jones@gov.bc.ca
Supervising Solicitor, Solicitors Division - Finance, Commercial & Transportation, Lauren Knoblauch
Tel: 250-356-5744
Fax: 250-387-1010
Lauren.Knoblauch@gov.bc.ca
Supervising Solicitor, Solicitors Division - Justice, Education Law Group, Jean Morgan
Tel: 250-356-8465
Fax: 250-356-9254
Jean.Morgan@gov.bc.ca
Supervising Solicitor, Solicitors Division - Aboriginal Law Group, Geoff Moyse
Tel: 250-356-8937
Fax: 250-356-8939
Geoff.Moyse@gov.bc.ca
Supervising Solicitor, Solicitors Division - Revenue, Taxation, Jeff Pottinger
Tel: 250-356-8845
Fax: 250-387-0700
Jeff.Pottinger@gov.bc.ca
Supervising Solicitor, Solicitors Division - Health & Social Services, Fiona St. Clair
Tel: 250-356-8444
Fax: 250-356-8992
Fiona.StClair@gov.bc.ca

Office of the Superintendent of Motor Vehicles (OSMV)
PO Box 9254 Prov Govt, Victoria, BC V8W 9J2
Tel: 250-387-7747
Fax: 250-387-4891
OSMV.Mailbox@gov.bc.ca
www.pssg.gov.bc.ca/osmv

The Office of the Superintendent of Motor Vehicles is responsible for regulating drivers in British Columbia. The following services are provided: establishment & maintenance of standards for driving behaviour & medical fitness; provision of an independent method of appeal of certain Insurance Corporation of British Columbia decisions; scheduling & hearing evidence related to proposals by the Insurance Corporation of British Columbia concerning licences, driving training schools, & AirCare Certified repair facilities; & reviewing driving prohibitions & vehicle impoundments imposed by police.

Superintendent, Motor Vehicles, Steve Martin
Tel: 250-387-5692
Fax: 250-356-5577
Director, Hearings & Fair Practices, Stephanie Melvin
Tel: 250-953-3818
Fax: 250-356-5577
Stephanie.Melvin@gov.bc.ca
Director, Management Services, Deidre Moran
Tel: 250-356-9482
Fax: 250-356-5568
Director, Policy & Research, Dana Tadla
Tel: 250-356-0097
Fax: 250-356-5568

British Columbia Environmental Assessment Office

836 Yates St., 1st Fl., PO Box 9426 Prov Govt, Victoria, BC V8W 9V1
Tel: 250-356-7479
Fax: 250-356-6448
eaoinfo@gov.bc.ca
www.eao.gov.bc.ca

Operating independently, the Environmental Assessment Office (EAO) coordinates the assessment of proposed projects in British Columbia. The Office acts under the requirements of the Environmental Assessment Act. Working with the public, government agencies, & First Nations, the Environmental Assessment Office ensures that projects are developed in a sustainable manner.

Acting Executive Director, John Mazure
Tel: 250-356-7475
Fax: 250-356-7477
John.Mazure@gov.bc.ca

Acting Executive Project Assessment Director, Kathy Eichenberger
Tel: 250-387-2307
Fax: 250-387-2208
Kathy.Eichenberger@gov.bc.ca

Director, Strategy & Quality Assurance, Michelle Carr
Tel: 250-387-6748
Fax: 250-356-6448
Michelle.Carr@gov.bc.ca

Director, Business Operations, Terri Starkes
Tel: 250-356-5770
Fax: 250-356-7477
Terri.Starkes@gov.bc.ca

Project Assessment Director, Coal & Aggregates Mining Projects, Karen L. Christie
Tel: 250-387-9675
Fax: 250-356-6448
Karen.L.Christie@gov.bc.ca

Project Assessment Director, Food Processing & Waste Management Projects, Chris Hamilton
Tel: 250-387-1032
Fax: 250-387-2208
Chris.Hamilton@gov.bc.ca

Project Assessment Director, Power & Industrial Projects, Brian Murphy
Tel: 250-387-2402
Fax: 250-387-2208
Brian.Murphy@gov.bc.ca

Project Assessment Director, Metal Mining & Transportation Projects, Shelley Murphy
Tel: 250-387-1447
Shelley.Murphy@gov.bc.ca

Project Assessment Director, Destination Resorts & Oil & Gas Projects, Archie Riddell
Tel: 250-952-6507
Fax: 250-387-2208
David.Riddell@gov.bc.ca

British Columbia Ferry Services Inc.

#500, 1321 Blanshard St., Victoria, BC V8W 0B7
Tel: 250-381-1401
Toll-Free: 888-223-3779
www.bcferries.com
Other Communication: Outside North America Phone: 250-386-3431
BC Ferries operates as the primary provider of coastal ferry service in British Columbia. The fleet covers 25 routes.
Acts Administered:
Coastal Ferry Act

Chair, Donald P. Hayes

President/Chief Executive Officer, David L. Hahn

Executive Vice-President & Chief Financial Officer, Rob Clarke

Executive Vice-President & Chief Operating Officer, Mike Corrigan

Executive Vice-President, Human Resources & Corporate Development, Glen N. Schwartz

British Columbia Ministry of Finance

PO Box 9417 Prov Govt, Victoria, BC V8W 9V1
Toll-Free: 877-388-4440
CTBTaxQuestions@gov.bc.ca (tax inquiries)
www.gov.bc.ca/fin
Other Communication: Media Inquiries, Phone: 250-356-9872, Fax: 250-356-2822
The Ministry of Finance establishes, implements, & reviews the government's financial management, fiscal, economic, & taxation policies. Responsibilities are as follows: economic planning, budgeting, & reporting; policy development for the financial, corporate, & real estate sectors; overseeing financial & administrative governance for the public service; banking & risk management services for government; tax & non-tax administration; loan administration & collection; administering a governance framework for Crown agencies; & regulating the financial services & real estate sectors.
Acts Administered:
Auditor General Act
BC Railway Act
Balanced Budget & Ministerial Accountability Act
Bonding Act
Budget Transparency & Accountability Act
Business Corporations Act
Business Number Act
Capital Financing Authority Repeal & Debt Restructuring Act
Community Services Labour Relations Act
Constitution Act, ss. 25-27
Cooperative Association Act
Credit Union Incorporation Act
Creditor Assistance Act
Financial Administration Act
Financial Information Act
Financial Institutions Act
Industrial Development Act
Insurance (Captive Company) Act
Insurance (Marine) Act
Insurance Act
International Financial Business Act
Manufactured Home Act
Ministerial Accountability Bases (2004, 2004-2005) Acts
Ministry of Consumer & Corporate Affairs Act, ss. 3-4
Ministry of Intergovernmental Relations Act, s. 3
Miscellaneous Registrations Act, 1992
Mortgage Brokers Act
Mutual Fire Insurance Companies Act
Pacific North Coast Native Cooperative Act
Partnership Act
Pension Agreement Act
Pension Benefits Standards Act
Pension Fund Societies Act
Personal Property Security Act
Ports Property Tax Act
Probate Fee Act
Public Education Support Staff Collective Bargaining Assistance Act
Public Works Agreement Act
Real Estate Development Marketing Act
Real Estate Services Act
Repairers Lien Act
Securities (Forged Transfer) Act
Society Act
Strata Property Act
Tugboat Worker's Lien Act
Unclaimed Property Act
Warehouse Lien Act
Warehouse Receipt Act
Woodworker Lien Act

Minister, Finance; Government House Leader, Hon. Michael de Jong, Q.C.
Tel: 250-387-3751
Fax: 250-387-5594
FIN.Minister@gov.bc.ca; Michael.DeJong@gov.bc.ca
Social Media: twitter.com/mike_de_jong
PO Box 9048 Prov Govt Sta.
Victoria, BC V8W 9E2

Deputy Minister, Finance, Peter Milburn
Tel: 250-387-3184
Fax: 250-387-1655

Assistant Deputy Minister, Strategic Initiatives, Doug Foster
Tel: 250-387-9022
Fax: 250-387-1655
Doug.Foster@gov.bc.ca

Associate Deputy Minister, Sheila Taylor
Tel: 250-387-8499
Fax: 250-387-1655

Manager, Executive Operations, Shelley MacLean
Tel: 250-356-6696
Fax: 250-387-1655

Associated Agencies, Boards & Commissions:
• **Auditor Certification Board**
PO Box 9431 Prov Govt
Victoria, BC V8W 9V3
Tel: 250-356-8658
Fax: 250-356-9422
Kelly.Fitzsimonds@gov.bc.ca
The Auditor Certification Board is authorized under the Business Corporations Act. The Board receives applications from individuals who apply to becertified as auditors. Persons with the necessary qualifications are then certified.
• **British Columbia Securities Commission**
Pacific Centre
701 West Georgia St., 12th Fl.
PO Box 10142
Vancouver, BC V7Y 1L2
Tel: 604-899-6500
Fax: 604-899-6506
Toll-free: 800-373-6393
inquiries@bcsc.bc.ca
www.bcsc.bc.ca
The British Columbia Securities Commission is an independent provincial government agency. Through administration of the Securities Act, the Commission regulates securities trading in British Columbia.
• **Crown Agencies Resource Office (CARO)**
PO Box 9469 Prov Govt
Victoria, BC V8V 9V8
Tel: 250-387-8770
Fax: 250-387-9061
CAS@gov.bc.ca
www.gov.bc.ca/caro
Implementation of the governance framework for British Columbia's Crown agencies is the role of the Crown Agencies Secretariat. The Secretariat advises Ministries & Crown agencies on the requirements of the Crown Agency Accountability System. It also maintains the Crown Agency Registry.
• **Financial Institutions Commission (FICOM)**
#1200, 13450 - 102 Ave.
Surrey, BC V3T 5X3
Tel: 604-953-5300
Fax: 604-953-5301
Toll-free: 866-206-3030
FICOM@ficombc.ca; HR@ficombc.ca
www.fic.gov.bc.ca
Other Communication: Complaints & inquiries: 604-953-5200
The Financial Institutions Commission is a regulatory agency of British Columbia's Ministry of Finance. The Commission's responsibility is the administration of statutes that regulate the financial services, pension, & real estate sectors in the province.
• **Insurance Council of British Columbia**
#300, 1040 West Georgia St.
PO Box 7
Vancouver, BC V6E 4H1
Tel: 604-688-0321
Fax: 604-662-7767
Toll-free: 877-688-0321
www.insurancecouncilofbc.com
The Insurance Council of British Columbia reports to the province's Minister of Finance. The Council has the following responsibilities: Licensing insurance agents, salespersons, & adjusters; Regulating insurance licensees; & Investigating & disciplining licensees.
• **Public Sector Employers' Council Secretariat (PSEC)**
#210, 880 Douglas St.
PO Box 9400 Prov Govt
Victoria, BC V8V 9V1
Tel: 250-387-0842
Fax: 250-387-6258
www.aved.gov.bc.ca/psec
The coordination of the management of labour relations policies & practices in the public sector is the principal responsibility of the Public Sector Employers' Council. The Council consists of the following members: eight Ministers or Deputy Ministers; Commissioner of the BC Public Service Agency; & representatives from six public sector employers' associations. The Public Sector Employers' Council Secretariat carries out the work of the Council.
• **Real Estate Council of British Columbia**
#900, 750 West Pender St.
Vancouver, BC V6C 2T8
Tel: 604-683-9664
Fax: 604-683-9017
Toll-free: 877-683-9664
info@recbc.ca
www.recbc.ca
The Real Estate Council of British Columbia is a regulatory agency with the following responsibilities under the requirements of the Real Estate Services Act: Licensing individuals & brokerages involved in real estate sales, rental & strata property management; Enforcing licensing qualifications & licensee conduct; & Investigating complaints against licensees & imposing discipline.

Corporate & Ministry Support Services
PO Box 9415 Prov Govt, Victoria, BC V8W 9V1
Assistant Deputy Minister, Deborah Fayad
Tel: 250-387-8139
Fax: 250-387-8586
Deborah.Fayad@gov.bc.ca
Other Communications: Cell Phone: 250-589-2480
Chief Information Officer & Executive Director, Information Management, Michael Carpenter
Tel: 250-387-3485
Fax: 250-356-1494
Michael.Carpenter@gov.bc.ca
PO Box 9424 Prov Govt Sta.
Victoria, BC V8W 9V1
Executive Director, Strategic Human Resources, Elaine Jones
Tel: 250-387-2984
Fax: 250-356-7326
Elaine.F.Jones@gov.bc.ca
PO Box 9420 Prov Govt Sta.
Victoria, BC V8W 9V1
Executive Director & Chief Financial Officer, Financial Services & Administration, Steve Klak
Tel: 250-356-1387
Fax: 250-356-7326
Steve.Klak@gov.bc.ca
Executive Director, Performance Management & Corporate Priorities Branch, Donna Selbee
Tel: 250-387-4733
Fax: 250-356-7326
Donna.Selbee@gov.bc.ca
Director, Facilities Management, Shelly Akam
Tel: 250-387-8125
Fax: 250-387-8586
Shelly.Akam@gov.bc.ca
Other Communications: Cell Phone: 250-588-3614

Director, Divisional Operations Branch, Heather L. Clark
Tel: 250-356-9606
Fax: 250-387-8586
Heather.L.Clark@gov.bc.ca
Other Communications: Cell Phone: 250-216-4149
Director, Strategic Human Resources Branch, Bert Elliott
Tel: 250-387-9504
Fax: 250-356-7326
Bert.Elliott@gov.bc.ca
Director, Operational Support, Tim Furmek
Tel: 250-387-8962
Fax: 250-356-1494
Tim.Furmek@gov.bc.ca
Director, Business & Client Services, Mike Holt
Tel: 250-953-3950
Fax: 250-356-1494
Mike.Holt@gov.bc.ca
Director, Financial Services, Kanwaljeet Kuckreja
Tel: 250-387-3867
Fax: 250-356-7326
Kanwaljeet.Kuckreja@gov.bc.ca
Director, Financial Management & Reporting, Martha Okot Thomas
Tel: 250-356-0403
Martha.Thomas@gov.bc.ca
Director, Financial Planning, Philip Twyford
Tel: 250-387-9530
Fax: 250-356-7326
Philip.Twyford@gov.bc.ca

Deputy Secretary to Treasury Board
PO Box 9469 Prov Govt, Victoria, BC V8W 9V8
Assistant Deputy Minister/Deputy Secretary to Treasury Board, Sabine Feulgen
Tel: 250-356-5427
Fax: 250-387-9054
Sabine.Feulgen@gov.bc.ca
Executive Director, SUCH Ministries, Gord Enemark
Tel: 250-356-5032
Fax: 250-387-9054
Gord.Enemark@gov.bc.ca
Executive Director, Estimates & Reporting, Don Epp
Tel: 250-387-9008
Fax: 250-387-0300
Don.Epp@gov.bc.ca
Executive Director, Performance Budgeting Office, David Fairbotham
Tel: 250-387-8773
Fax: 250-387-9061
David.Fairbotham@gov.bc.ca
Executive Director, Social Policy, Kerri Harrison
Tel: 250-387-9041
Fax: 250-387-9054
Kerri.Harrison@gov.bc.ca
Executive Director, Fiscal Planning, Dave Riley
Tel: 250-387-9030
Fax: 250-387-0300
Dave.Riley@gov.bc.ca
Executive Director, Economic Development Policy, Marie Ty
Tel: 250-952-6200
Fax: 250-387-9054
Marie.Ty@gov.bc.ca
Director, Performance Budgeting Office, Rebecca John
Tel: 250-387-9034
Fax: 250-387-9054
Rebecca.John@gov.bc.ca
Manager, TB Operations, Jennifer Mitchell
Tel: 250-387-9070
Fax: 250-356-7624
Jennifer.Michell@gov.bc.ca

Economics & Policy Division
Fax: 250-952-0137
Assistant Deputy Minister, Heather Wood
Tel: 250-356-9911
Fax: 250-952-0137
Acting Executive Director, Financial & Corporate Sector Policy Branch, Marcus Gill
Tel: 250-387-9090
Fax: 250-387-9093
Marcus.Gill@gov.bc.ca
Executive Director & Chief Economist, Economic Forecasting & Policy Analysis, Llew Hamdi
Tel: 250-387-0368
Fax: 250-387-0300
Llew.Hamdi@gov.bc.ca
Executive Director, Intergovernmental Fiscal Relations, Rory Molnar
Tel: 250-387-4174
Fax: 250-387-9061
Rory.Molnar@gov.bc.ca
Executive Director, Tax Policy Branch, Glen Armstrong
Tel: 250-387-9011
Fax: 250-387-9061
Rory.Molnar@gov.bc.ca
Director, Intergovernmental Fiscal Relations, Patrick Ewing
Tel: 250-952-0936
Fax: 250-387-9093
Patrick.Ewing@gov.bc.ca
Director, Financial & Corporate Sector Policy Branch, Mary Kimpton
Tel: 250-387-9077
Fax: 250-387-9093
Mary.Kimpton@gov.bc.ca
Director, Intergovernmental Fiscal Relations, Russell Mellett
Tel: 604-775-0703
Fax: 250-387-9061
Russell.Mellett@gov.bc.ca
Director, Intergovernmental Fiscal Relations, Grant Smith
Tel: 250-387-1510
Fax: 250-387-9061
Grant.H.Smith@gov.bc.ca
Director, Intergovernmental Fiscal Relations, Brad Underwood
Tel: 250-356-0513
Fax: 250-387-9061
Brad.Underwood@gov.bc.ca

Office of the Comptroller General
PO Box 9413 Prov Govt, Victoria, BC V8W 9V1
Tel: 250-356-2001
Comptroller.General@gov.bc.ca
www.fin.gov.bc.ca/ocg.htm
Other Communication: Legal Encumbrance Inquiries, Phone: 250-387-3364

The Office of the Comptroller General oversees the quality & integrity of the government's financial management & control systems. The Office consists of the following branches: Activity Based Management; Corporate Compliance & Controls Monitoring Branch & Corporate Operations; Financial Management Branch; Financial Reporting & Advisory Services; Internal Audit & Advisory Services; & Procurement Governance Office.

Comptroller General, Stuart Newton
Tel: 250-387-6692
Fax: 250-356-2001
Stuart.Newton@gov.bc.ca
Executive Director, Financial Reporting & Advisory Services, Carl Fischer
Tel: 250-356-9272
Fax: 250-356-8388
Carl.Fischer@gov.bc.ca
Executive Director, Corporate Compliance & Controls Monitoring, Greg Gudgeon
Tel: 250-356-7434
Fax: 250-356-0560
greg.gudgeon@gov.bc.ca
Executive Director, Financial Management, Steve Rossander
Tel: 250-387-0279
Fax: 250-356-6164
Steve.Rossander@gov.bc.ca
Director, Investigation & Forensic Unit, Dan Peck
Tel: 250-387-8542
Fax: 250-356-2001
Dan.Peck@gov.bc.ca
Director, Procurement & Financial Management Governance, David Pilling
Tel: 250-387-8189
Fax: 250-356-6164
David.Pilling@gov.bc.ca
Director, Corporate Operations, Ron Tannhauser
Tel: 250-387-8551
Fax: 250-356-6164
Ron.Tannhauser@gov.bc.ca

Provincial Treasury
PO Box 9414 Prov Govt, Victoria, BC V8V 9V1
Tel: 250-387-4541
Fax: 250-356-3041
www.fin.gov.bc.ca/pt.htm

The Provincial Treasury consists of the following branches: Banking / Cash Management; Corporate Operations; Corporate & Project Finance; Debt Management; Information Systems; Risk Management; & BC Registry Services.

Assistant Deputy Minister, Jim Hopkins
Tel: 250-387-5729
Fax: 250-356-3041
Jim.Hopkins@gov.bc.ca
Chief Security Officer, Risk Mitigation & Government Security, Shaun Fynes
Tel: 250-387-0522
Fax: 250-356-6222
Shaun.Fynes@gov.bc.ca
Executive Director, Risk Management, Phil Grewar
Tel: 250-387-0521
Fax: 250-356-6222
Phil.Grewar@gov.bc.ca
Executive Director, Debt Management, Darshi Klear
Tel: 250-387-8815
Fax: 250-387-3024
Director, Information Systems, Tom Caldwell
Tel: 250-356-5473
Fax: 250-387-6577
Tom.Caldwell@gov.bc.ca
Director, Client Services - Core Government & Crowns, Glen Frederick
Tel: 250-356-8915
Fax: 250-356-6222
Glen.Frederick@gov.bc.ca
Director, Client Services - Education, Andrew Green
Tel: 250-952-0785
Fax: 250-356-6222
Andrew.Green@gov.bc.ca
Director, Underwriting & Analysis, Laura Hughs
Tel: 250-387-0519
Fax: 250-356-6222
Laura.Hughes@gov.bc.ca
Director, Client Services - Health Care, Linda Irvine
Tel: 250-952-0849
Fax: 250-953-3050
Linda.Irvine@gov.bc.ca
Director, Banking/Cash Management, Nicholas Krischanowsky
Tel: 250-387-7105
Nick.Krischanowsky@gov.bc.ca
Director, Claims & Litigation Management, Kim Oldham
Tel: 250-952-0837
Fax: 250-356-0661
Kim.Oldham@gov.bc.ca
Director, Corporate & Project Finance, Matthew O'Rae
Tel: 250-356-9370
Fax: 250-387-3024
Manager, Corporate Operations, Ida Stephenson
Tel: 250-387-7124
Fax: 250-387-6577
Ida.Stephenson@gov.bc.ca

Revenue Programs Division
Fax: 250-387-3000
Assistant Deputy Minister, Elan Symes
Tel: 250-387-0665
Elan.Symes@gov.bc.ca
Executive Director, Consumer Taxation Programs Branch, Jordan Goss
Tel: 250-387-0611
Executive Director, Income Taxation Branch, Paula Harper
Tel: 250-387-3968
Fax: 250-356-9243
Executive Director, Property Taxation Branch, Tara Richards
Tel: 250-387-0532
Fax: 250-387-2210
Tara.Richards@gov.bc.ca
Acting Executive Director, Mineral, Oil & Gas Revenue Branch, Andrew Ritonja
Tel: 250-356-0670
Fax: 250-952-0191
Andrew.Ritonja@gov.bc.ca
Director, Real Property Taxation, Art Chambers
Tel: 250-356-9565
Fax: 250-387-2210
Art.Chambers@gov.bc.ca
Director, Audit & Compliance, Hilary Harley
Tel: 250-387-0602
Fax: 250-953-3094
Hilary.Harley@gov.bc.ca
Director, Property Tax Services & Tax Deferment, Lori Kirk
Tel: 250-387-5469
Fax: 250-386-5347
Lori.Kirk@gov.bc.ca
Director, Investigations Unit, Carson Kong
Tel: 604-586-4172
Fax: 604-586-4172
Carson.Kong@gov.bc.ca
Director, Income Tax Advisory & Intergovernmental Relations, Jeffery Krasnick
Tel: 250-953-3091
Fax: 250-356-9243
Jeffrey.Krasnick@gov.bc.ca
Director, Income Tax Programs, Steve Pleva
Tel: 250-387-1201
Fax: 250-356-9243
Steve.Pleva@gov.bc.ca
Audit Director, Audit (Victoria), Carol O'Brien
Tel: 250-387-9667
Fax: 250-356-0434
Carol.OBrien@gov.bc.ca

Revenue Services
Fax: 250-952-0113
Assistant Deputy Minister, Janet Baltes
Tel: 250-387-1158
Fax: 250-952-0113
Janet.Baltes@gov.bc.ca
Executive Director, Revenue Solutions Branch, Pat Parkinson
Tel: 250-356-9670

Fax: 250-356-1709
Pat.Parkinson@gov.bc.ca
Executive Director, Tax Appeals & Administrative Services Branch, Wayne Sparanese
Tel: 250-387-0662
Wayne.Sparanese@gov.bc.ca
Acting Director, Integrated Services, Gina Curran
Tel: 250-387-1199
Fax: 250-356-1706
Gina.Curran@gov.bc.ca
Director, Compliance & Customer Care, Gregg Danderfer
Tel: 250-356-2522
Fax: 250-356-1706
Gregg.Danderfer@gov.bc.ca
Director, Student Loans Management Team, Steven Emery
Tel: 250-387-1182
Fax: 250-356-1706
Steven.Emery@gov.bc.ca
Director, Performance & Reporting, Darrell Eng
Tel: 250-356-2517
Fax: 250-356-1706
Darrell.Eng@gov.bc.ca
Director, Receivables Management Office, Dennis Forbes
Tel: 250-356-8031
Fax: 250-356-5604
Dennis.Forbes@gov.bc.ca
Director, Appeals, Kinsburh Healey
Tel: 250-387-5881
Fax: 250-387-5883
Kinsburh.Healey@gov.bc.ca
Acting Director, Appeals, Renny Lubberts
Tel: 250-356-2758
Fax: 250-387-5883
Renny.Lubberts@gov.bc.ca
Director, ASD Contracts, David Sherwood
Tel: 250-387-3864
Fax: 250-356-1706
David.Sherwood@gov.bc.ca
Other Communications: Cell Phone: 250-888-6480
Director, Client Portfolio, Elaine Smith
Tel: 250-356-1564
Fax: 250-356-1706
Elaine.Smith@gov.bc.ca
Director, Appeals, Hilary Vance
Tel: 250-952-0708
Fax: 250-387-5883
Hilary.Vance@gov.bc.ca
Manager, Corporate Operations, Leona Frenette
Tel: 250-387-4175
Fax: 250-952-0113
Leona.Frenette@gov.bc.ca

British Columbia Ministry of Forests, Lands & Natural Resource Operations

PO Box 9352 Prov Govt, Victoria, BC V8W 9M1
Tel: 250-387-4809
Toll-Free: 877-855-3222
FLNRO.MediaRequests@gov.bc.ca
www.gov.bc.ca/for
TTY: 800-661-8773
Other Communication: Media Phone: 250-356-5261

The Ministry of Forests, Lands & Natural Resource Operations establishes policies for access to & use of British Columbia's forests, land, & natural resources. Services provided enable stewardship & sustainable management of the province's resources. Responsibilities of the ministry include Aboriginal consultation; Crown land administration policy; resource roads & bridges policy; forest, range, & grazing stewardship policy; pest & disease management policy; water use planning; timber supply & sales; fish, wildlife, & habitat management; licensing for hunting, trapping, & angling; recreation sites & trails; & wildfire management.

Acts Administered:
Boundary Act
Creston Valley Wildlife Act
Dike Maintenance Act
Drainage, Ditch & Dike Act
Environment & Land Use Act
Environmental Management Act (s. 5 (f), as that section relates to the portfolio of the Minister of Forests, Lands, & Natural Resource Operations)
Fish Protection Act
Fisheries Act (Part 3, as it relates to the licensing of aquaculture)

Flathead Watershed Area Conservation Act
Forest & Range Practices Act (except the collection of public money, as defined in the Financial Administration Act, other than a fine, or the administration of deposits & securities payable; & s. 166, as that relates tothe Justice portfolio)
Forest Act (except the collection of public money, as defined in section 1 of the Financial Administration Act, other than a fine, or the administration of deposits & securities payable)
Forest Practices Code of British Columbia Act (except the collection of public money, as defined in section 1 of the Financial Administration Act, other than a fine, or the administration of deposits & securities payable; &Part 9)
Forest Stand Management Fund Act (except the collection of public money, as defined in section 1 of the Financial Administration Act, other than a fine, or the administration of deposits & securities payable)
Foresters Act
Forestry Revitalization Act
Forestry Service Providers Protection Act
Greenbelt Act
Heritage Conservation Act
Hunting & Fishing Heritage Act
Industrial Operation Compensation Act
Land (Spouse Protection) Act
Land Act
Land Survey Act
Land Surveyors Act
Land Title & Survey Authority Act
Land Title Act (except s. 77.2; s. 219 (1), (2), (3) (a) & (b), (4) - (9.2), (10), (11) (a), (12) & (14) as that provision relates to the portfolio of the Minister of Community, Sport, & Cultural Dev. or to the portfolio ofthe Minister of Environment)
Land Title Inquiry Act
Land Transfer Form Act
Libby Dam Reservoir Act
Ministry of Environment Act (s. 4 (2) (d); ss. 4 (2) (b), (e), (f) & (g) & 6.1 as those provisions relate to the portfolio of the Minister of Forests, Lands & Natural Resource Operations)
Ministry of Forests & Range Act (except the collection of public money, as defined in the Financial Administration Act, other than a fine, or the administration of deposits & securities payable; & s. 4 (d) (ii) & (e) asthat relates to Agriculture)
Ministry of Lands, Parks, & Housing (except ss. 5 (c), 8.1 & 10; & ss. 5 (b), 6 & 9 as those provisions relate to the portfolio of the Minister of Environment)
Motor Vehicle (All Terrain) Act
Muskwa-Kechika Management Area Act
Natural Resource Compliance Act
Private Managed Forest Land Act
Protected Areas Forests Compensation Act
Railway Act (s. 33)
Range Act (except collection of public money, defined in the Financial Administration Act, other than a fine or the administration of deposits & securities payable; ss. 39, 41, 42 (1) & 43; (c) ss. 1 (2) & (3), 44, 45, 76,79 & 80 related to Agriculture)
Resort Timber Administration Act
Skagit Environmental Enhancement Act
Special Accounts Appropriation & Control (s. 5)
Tugboat Worker Lien Act
University Endowment Land Act (ss. 2 (1) (a) & (d) & 3 (b))
Water Act
Water Protection Act
Water Utility Act
Weed Control Act
Wildfire Act (except as it relates to the collection of public money, as defined in section 1 of the Financial Administration Act, other than a fine, or the administration of deposits & securities payable)
Wildlife Act (except s. 3 (b) as that provision relates to the portfolio of the Minister of Environment; & ss. 6 & 108 (2) (a))
Woodworker Lien Act
Zero Net Deforestation Act

Minister, Forests, Lands, & Natural Resource Operations, Hon. Steve Thomson
Tel: 250-356-6211
Fax: 250-387-1040
FLNR.Minister@gov.bc.ca
PO Box 9049 Prov Govt Sta.
Victoria, BC V8W 9E2

Deputy Minister, Doug Konkin
Tel: 250-952-6500
Fax: 250-387-3291
1520 Blanshard St., 3rd Fl.
PO Box 9525 Prov Govt Sta.
Victoria, BC V8W 9C3

Parliamentary Secretary for Forestry to the Minister of Forests, Lands, & Natural Resource Operations, John Rustad
Tel: 250-953-4892
Fax: 250-387-9066

Associated Agencies, Boards & Commissions:
• Assayers Certification Board of Examiners (ACBE)
PO Box 9333 Prov Govt
Victoria, BC V8W 9N3
Tel: 250-952-0396
The Board of Examiners administers the Assayers Certification Program, invigilate the examinations, grade papers, and recommend candidates for qualification to the Responsible Minister. The Board operates under the Ministry of Energy & Mines Act.
• Forest Practices Board (FPB)
1675 Douglas St., 3rd Fl.
PO Box 9905 Prov Govt
Victoria, BC V8W 9R1
Tel: 250-213-4700
Fax: 250-213-4725
Toll-free: 800-994-5899
fpboard@gov.bc.ca
www.fpb.gov.bc.ca
Other Communication: Toll-Free Fax: 1-877-708-4607
British Columbia's Forest Practices Board is responsible for reporting to the government & public about compliance with the Forest & Range Practices Act. The Board engages in the following activities: Investigation of public complaints; Undertaking special investigations; Auditing forest practices of government, government enforcement of the Forest & Range Practices Act, & licence holders on public lands; Participation in appeals; & Provision of reports & recommendations.
• Muskwa-Kechika Advisory Board (M-KAB)
coordinator@muskwa-kechika.com
www.muskwa-kechika.com
The Board oversees the preservation of the Muskwa-Kechika Management Area, & ensures that activities carried out within the area meet the standards set by the Muskwa-Kechika Management Plan.
• Timber Export Advisory Committee
PO Box 9514 Prov Govt
Victoria, BC V8W 9C2
Tel: 250-387-8916
Fax: 250-387-5050

Corporate Initiatives

PO Box 9352 Prov Govt, Victoria, BC V8W 9M1
Acting Executive Director, Christine Gelowitz
Tel: 250-387-8885
Fax: 250-356-5797
Christine.Gelowitz@gov.bc.ca
Acting Director, Strategic Initiatives, Gail P. Brewer
Tel: 250-356-5299
Fax: 250-953-3481
Director, Legislation, Richard Grieve
Tel: 250-387-8606
Fax: 250-356-7903
Richard.Grieve@gov.bc.ca
Acting Director, Natural Resource Authorization, Brian Westgate
Tel: 250-953-4205
Brian.Westgate@gov.bc.ca
Senior Manager, Strategic Planning & Policy, Melissa Friesen
Tel: 250-356-7278
Fax: 250-953-3603
Melissa.Friesen@gov.bc.ca

Integrated Resource Operations Division

PO Box 9352 Prov Govt, Victoria, BC V8W 9M1
Tel: 250-356-1874
Fax: 250-387-2335
Assistant Deputy Minister, Gary Townsend
Tel: 250-356-1874
Fax: 250-387-2335
Executive Director, Field Operations, Jim Maxwell
Tel: 250-387-1236
Fax: 250-953-3687
Jim.Maxwell@gov.bc.ca
Executive Director, GeoBC & Compliance & Enforcement, Francesca Wheler
Tel: 250-387-3745
Director, Range, Invasive Plants & Ecosystem Restoration, David Borth
Tel: 250-371-3827
Fax: 250-828-4987
David.Borth@gov.bc.ca
Other Communications: Alternate Phone: 250-371-3836
441 Columbia St.
Kamloops, BC V2C 2T3
Acting Director, Compliance & Enforcement, Kevin Edquist
Tel: 250-387-8372
Fax: 250-387-2569
Kevin.Edquist@gov.bc.ca
Director, Recreation Sites & Trails BC, Bill Marshall
Tel: 250-953-3678
Bill.Marshall@gov.bc.ca
Director, Wildfire Management Headquarters, Brian Simpson
Tel: 250-356-1068
Fax: 250-387-5685
Brian.Simpson@gov.bc.ca
Manager, Regional Service Delivery, GeoBC, Janet Adams
Tel: 250-387-9338
Fax: 250-356-5797
Janet.Adams@gov.bc.ca

Major Projects, First Nations & Community Opportunities Division
PO Box 9352 Prov Govt, Victoria, BC V8W 9M1
Fax: 250-387-2335

Assistant Deputy Minister, Peter Walters
Tel: 250-356-7723
Fax: 250-387-2335
Executive Director, Major Projects Branch, Jennifer C. Davis
Tel: 250-387-0738
Fax: 250-387-2335
Jennifer.C.Davis@gov.bc.ca
Executive Director, Resort Development, Norman Lee
Tel: 250-952-0478
Fax: 250-356-2842
Norman.K.Lee@gov.bc.ca
Director, Archeology Branch, Justine Batten
Tel: 250-953-3355
Fax: 250-953-3340
Justine.Batten@gov.bc.ca
Director, Crown Land Opportunities & Restoration, Ron Bronstein
Tel: 250-387-1544
Fax: 250-356-6791
Ron.Bronstein@gov.bc.ca
Director, Heritage Branch, Jennifer Iredale
Tel: 250-356-1431
Fax: 250-356-2842
Jennifer.Iredale@gov.bc.ca
Director, First Nation Relations Branche, Darrell A. Robb
Tel: 250-387-6719
Fax: 250-356-6076
Darrell.Robb@gov.bc.ca

Coast
2100 Labieux Rd., Nanaimo, BC V9T 6E9
Tel: 250-751-7001
Fax: 250-751-7190
Forests.CoastRegionOffice@gov.bc.ca
www.for.gov.bc.ca/rco

Assistant Deputy Minister, Jody Shimkus
Tel: 250-387-9773
Fax: 250-356-2150
Jody.Shimkus@gov.bc.ca
Regional Executive Director, Coast, Brian J. Clark
Tel: 250-356-0874
Fax: 250-356-9299
Brian.J.Clark@gov.bc.ca
Regional Executive Director, West Coast, Sharon Hadway
Tel: 250-751-7161
Fax: 250-751-7196
Sharon.Hadway@gov.bc.ca
Regional Executive Director, South Coast, Heather MacKnight
Tel: 604-586-2892
Fax: 604-586-4434
Heather.MacKnight@gov.bc.ca
Director, Resource Management (West Coast), Larry Barr
Tel: 250-751-7105
Fax: 250-741-5686
Larry.Barr@gov.bc.ca
Director, Pricing/Tenures/Mines, Denis Collins
Tel: 250-751-7121
Fax: 250-751-7196
Denis.Collins@gov.bc.ca
Director, Authorizations, Myles Mana
Tel: 250-751-7308
Fax: 250-751-7081
Myles.Mana@gov.bc.ca
Director, Resource Management (South Coast), Jennifer McGuire
Tel: 604-582-5370
Fax: 604-930-7119
Jennifer.Mcguire@gov.bc.ca
Manager, Business Innovation & Information, Angus Carnie
Tel: 250-387-3874
Fax: 250-387-5757
Angus.Carnie@gov.bc.ca
Manager, Permit & Authorization Service Bureau, Yvonne Foxall
Tel: 250-387-3787
Fax: 250-387-1814
Yvonne.Foxall@gov.bc.ca
Manager, Wildlife Management, Ian Hatter
Tel: 250-387-9792
Fax: 250-387-0239
Ian.Hatter@gov.bc.ca
Manager, Private Land & Wildlife, Jeff Morgan
Tel: 250-371-6347
Fax: 250-828-4000
Manager, Fish & Wildlife Recovery, Chris Ritchie
Tel: 250-614-9910
Fax: 250-565-6940
Chris.Ritchie@gov.bc.ca
Manager, Fisheries Management, Andrew Wilson
Tel: 250-387-9788
Fax: 250-387-0239
Andrew.Wilson@gov.bc.ca
Manager, Habitat Management, Andy Witt
Tel: 250-356-2353
Fax: 250-356-5104
Andy.Witt@gov.bc.ca

North Area
1011 - 4 Ave., 5th Fl., Prince George, BC V2L 3H9
Tel: 250-565-6100
www.for.gov.bc.ca/rni

Assistant Deputy Minister, Kevin Kriese
Tel: 250-952-0596
Executive Director, Nick Crisp
Tel: 250-356-7275
Fax: 250-356-5450
Nick.Crisp@gov.bc.ca
Executive Director, Site C, Norm Marcy
Tel: 250-387-1780
Norman.Marcy@gov.bc.ca
Executive Director, Butch Morningstar
Tel: 250-387-0844
Fax: 250-952-0491
Butch.Morningstar@gov.bc.ca
Other Communications: Cell Phone: 250-847-0856
Regional Executive Director, Northeast, Dale Morgan
Tel: 250-784-1200
Dale.Morgan@gov.bc.ca
Regional Executive Director, Skeena, Eamon O'Donoghue
Tel: 250-847-7495
Fax: 250-847-7347
Eamon.ODonoghue@gov.bc.ca
Regional Executive Director, Omineca, Bill Warner
Tel: 250-565-6102
Fax: 250-565-6671
Bill.Warner@gov.bc.ca
Director, Authorizations (Prince George), Joyce Beaudry
Tel: 250-565-4131
Fax: 250-565-6671
Joyce.Beaudry@gov.bc.ca
Director, Resource Management (Omenica), Normand Bilodeau
Tel: 250-565-6424
Director, Major Projects (Northeast), Todd Bondaroff
Tel: 250-784-1245
Fax: 250-787-3219
Todd.Bondaroff@gov.bc.ca
Director, Pricing & Tenures (Omineca), Heather Cullen
Tel: 250-565-6102
Fax: 250-565-6671
Heather.Cullen@gov.bc.ca
Director, Resource Management (Skeena), Loren Kelly
Tel: 250-847-7653
Fax: 250-847-7603
Loren.Kelly@gov.bc.ca
Director, Authorizations (Skeena), Bobby Love
Tel: 250-847-7517
Fax: 250-847-7347
Bobby.Love@gov.bc.ca
Director, Resource Authorizations (Northeast), Karrilyn Vince
Tel: 250-787-3534
Fax: 250-787-3219
Karrilyn.Vince@gov.bc.ca
District Manager, Resource Operations (Vanderhoof/Fort St. James), Lynda Currie
Tel: 250-996-5241
Fax: 250-996-5290
Lynda.Currie@gov.bc.ca
District Manager, Resource Operations (Mackenzie), Dave Francis
Tel: 250-997-2203
Fax: 250-997-2203
Dave.Francis@gov.bc.ca
District Manager, Resource Operations (Dawson Creek), Robert Kopecky
Tel: 250-784-1205
Fax: 250-784-1203
District Manager, Resource Operations (Fort Nelson), Steve Lindsey
Tel: 250-774-5520
Fax: 250-774-3704
Steve.Lindsey@gov.bc.ca
District Manager, Resource Operations (Prince George), Greg Rawling
Tel: 250-614-7400
Fax: 250-614-7435
Greg.Rawling@gov.bc.ca
District Manager, Kalum, Barry Dobbin
Tel: 250-638-5100
Fax: 250-638-5176
Barry.Dobbin@gov.bc.ca
District Manager, Skeena Stikine, Jane Lloyd-Smith
Tel: 250-847-6305
Fax: 250-847-6353
Jane.LloydSmith@gov.bc.ca
District Manager, Nadina, Josh Pressey
Tel: 250-692-2224
Fax: 250-692-7461
Josh.Pressey@gov.bc.ca

South
441 Columbia St., Kamloops, BC V2C 2T3
Tel: 250-828-4131
Fax: 250-828-4154
www.for.gov.bc.ca/rsi

Acting Assistant Deputy Minister, Rick Manwaring
Tel: 250-828-4292
Acting Executive Director, Madeline Maley
Tel: 250-828-4114
Other Communications: Alternate Phone: 250-371-3747
Regional Executive Director, Thompson Okanagan, Kevin Dickenson
Tel: 250-828-4445
Fax: 250-828-4442
Kevin.Dickenson@gov.bc.ca
Regional Executive Director, Cariboo, Gerry MacDougall
Gerry.MacDougall@gov.bc.ca
Regional Executive Director, Kootenay Boundary, Tony Wideski
Tel: 250-426-1741
Fax: 250-426-1767
Tony.Wideski@gov.bc.ca
Director, Resource Management (Kootenay), Tom G. Bell
Tel: 250-354-6345
Fax: 250-354-6332
Tom.Bell@gov.bc.ca
Director, Resource Authorizations (Kamloops), Peter Lishman
Tel: 250-828-4239
Fax: 250-828-4442
Peter.Lishman@gov.bc.ca
Director, Resource Management (Kamloops), Dan Peterson
Tel: 250-828-4124
Fax: 250-828-4154
Dan.Peterson@gov.bc.ca
Director, Pricing & Tenures (Kamloops), Jim Schafthuizen
Tel: 250-828-4625
Fax: 250-828-4154
Jim.Schafthuizen@gov.bc.ca
Director, Resource Management (Cariboo), Rodger Stewart
Tel: 250-398-4549
Fax: 250-398-4214
Rodger.Stewart@gov.bc.ca
Other Communications: Cell Phone: 250-305-8536
Director, Resource Operations (Cariboo), Ken Vanderburgh
Tel: 250-398-4225
Fax: 250-398-4836
Ken.Vanderburgh@gov.bc.ca
District Manager, Natural Resource Operations (100 Mile House), Patrick Byrne
Tel: 250-395-7804
Fax: 250-395-7810
Pat.Byrne@gov.bc.ca
District Manager, Natural Resource Operations (Quensel), Steve Dodge
Tel: 250-992-4465
Fax: 250-992-4403
Steve.Dodge@gov.bc.ca
Acting District Manager, Natural Resource Operations (Kamloops), Jennifer Fraser
Tel: 250-371-6503
Jennifer.Fraser@gov.bc.ca
District Manager, Natural Resource Operations (Kamloops), Dave Hails
Tel: 250-558-1729
Fax: 250-549-5485
Dave.Hails@gov.bc.ca
District Manager, Natural Resource Operations (Cascades), Charles van Hemmen
Tel: 250-378-8402
Fax: 250-378-8481
Charles.vanHemmen@gov.bc.ca
Other Communications: Cell Phone: 250-315-3773
District Manager, Natural Resource Operations (Central Cariboo/Chilcotin), Mike Pedersen
Tel: 250-398-4355
Fax: 250-398-4790
Mike.Pedersen@gov.bc.ca
Other Communications: Alternate Phone: 250-398-4345

Resource Stewardship Division
PO Box 9525 Prov Govt, Victoria, BC V8W 9C3
Tel: 250-387-1296
Fax: 250-953-3687

Chief Forester, Jim Snetsinger
Tel: 250-387-1296
Fax: 250-953-3687
Jim.Snetsinger@gov.bc.ca
Acting Deputy Chief Forester, Susanna Laaksonen-Craig
Tel: 250-387-1296
Fax: 250-953-3687
Susanna.LaaksonenCraig@gov.bc.ca
Chief Financial Officer, Water Allocation & Safety, Ron Simmons
Tel: 250-387-6308

Fax: 250-953-5124
Ron.Simmons@gov.bc.ca
Director, Tree Improvement Branch, Brian Barber
Tel: 250-356-0888
Fax: 250-356-8124
Brian.Barber@gov.bc.ca
Other Communications: URL: www.for.gov.bc.ca/hti/
Director & Comptroller, Water Rights, Water Management, Glen Davidson, P.Eng
Tel: 250-387-6949
Fax: 250-356-0605
Glen.Davidson@gov.bc.ca
Director, Resource Management Objectives, Allan Lidstone
Tel: 250-387-8372
Fax: 250-387-2410
Allan.Lidstone@gov.bc.ca
Director, Forest Analysis & Inventory Branch, Albert Nussbaum
Tel: 250-356-5958
Fax: 250-953-3838
Forests.ForestAnalysisBranchOffice@gov.bc.ca
Director, Resource Practices Branch, Jim D. Sutherland
Tel: 250-398-4527
Fax: 250-387-2136
Jim.D.Sutherland@gov.bc.ca
Other Communications: Alternate Phone: 250-387-0088
Director, Regional Operations, Water Stewardship, Brian Symonds
Tel: 250-490-8255
Fax: 250-490-2231
Brian.Symonds@gov.bc.ca
Director, Operations, Keith Thomas
Tel: 250-952-0193
Fax: 250-953-3687
Keith.Thomas@gov.bc.ca
Assistant Deputy Minister, Dave Peterson
Tel: 250-387-1057
Fax: 250-356-6791
Executive Director, Tenures, Duncan Williams
Tel: 250-387-1810
Fax: 250-356-2150
Duncan.Williams@gov.bc.ca
Director, Compensation & Business Analysis Branch, Peter Jacobsen
Tel: 250-387-8643
Fax: 250-356-7903
Peter.Jacobsen@gov.bc.ca
Other Communications: Cell Phone: 250-415-6638
Director, Forest Tenures Branch, Doug Stewart
Tel: 250-387-8729
Fax: 250-387-6445
Doug.B.Stewart@gov.bc.ca
Director, Land Tenures Branch, Ward Trotter
Tel: 250-356-2166
Fax: 250-356-6791
Ward.Trotter@gov.bc.ca
Branch Coordinator, Competitiveness & Innovation Branch, Judith Elkins
Tel: 250-356-7880
Fax: 250-356-7903
Judith.Elkins@gov.bc.ca

Timber Operations & Pricing Division
PO Box 9525 Prov Govt, Victoria, BC V8W 9C3
Fax: 250-953-3687
Assistant Deputy Minister, Tom Jensen
Tel: 250-387-3656
Fax: 250-953-3687
Tom.Jensen@gov.bc.ca
Chief Engineer, Brian Chow
Tel: 250-953-4370
Fax: 250-953-3687
Brian.Chow@gov.bc.ca
Executive Director, Field Operations, Mike Falkiner
Tel: 250-387-8309
Fax: 250-953-3687
Mike.Falkiner@gov.bc.ca
Executive Director, Timber Operations & Pricing, Diane Medves
Tel: 250-356-9287
Fax: 250-953-3687
Diane.Medves@gov.bc.ca
Other Communications: Alternate Phone: 250-751-7196
Director, Resource Worker Safety, Tom Jackson
Tel: 250-956-5105
Fax: 250-956-5045
Tom.Jackson@gov.bc.ca
Director, Timber Pricing Branch, Murray Stech
Tel: 250-356-9807
Fax: 250-387-5670
Murray.Stech@gov.bc.ca
Director, Engineering Branch, Peter Wyatt
Tel: 250-387-1295
Fax: 250-953-3687
Peter.Wyatt@gov.bc.ca

Corporate Services for the Natural Resouces Sector

Finance, Client Services, Facilities, Infrastructure & Strategic Services
PO Box 9339 Prov Govt, Victoria, BC V8W 9M1
Tel: 250-387-9878
Fax: 250-953-3414
Assistant Deputy Minister/Executive Financial Officer, Agriculture & Environment, Denise Bragg
Tel: 250-387-9878
Fax: 250-953-3414
Denise.Bragg@gov.bc.ca
Chief Financial Officer, Aboriginal Relations & Reconciliation/Energy & Mines, Ranbir Parmar
Tel: 250-387-1421
Fax: 250-387-1574
Ranbir.Parmar@gov.bc.ca
Chief Financial Officer, Agriculture & Environment, Anne Minnings
Tel: 250-356-9220
Fax: 250-356-9239
Anne.Minnings@gov.bc.ca
Chief Financial Officer/Executive Director, Forests, Lands & Natural Resource Operations, Terry Gelinas
Tel: 250-952-0174
Fax: 250-952-0161
Terry.Gelinas@gov.bc.ca
Executive Director, Client Services Branch, Trish Dohan
Tel: 250-356-9221
Fax: 250-356-9239
Trish.Dohan@gov.bc.ca
Executive Director, Strategic & Operational Services Branch, Jeanne Sedun
Tel: 250-387-7564
Jeanne.Sedun@gov.bc.ca
Director, Financial Planning & Reporting (Aboriginal Relations/Energy & Mines), Mary Myers
Tel: 250-356-6624
Fax: 250-387-8818
Mary.Myers@gov.bc.ca
Director, Financial Policy & Compliance (Aboriginal Relations/Energy & Mines), Diane Ross
Tel: 250-387-8800
Fax: 250-387-8864
Diane.Ross@gov.bc.ca
Director, Financial Planning & Reporting (Agriculture/Environment), Michael Lord
Tel: 250-356-6132
Fax: 250-356-1769
Michael.Lord@gov.bc.ca
Director, Financial Operations (Agriculture/Environment), Sandra Winter
Tel: 250-356-9227
Fax: 250-356-9239
Sandra.Winter@gov.bc.ca
Acting Director, Revenue (Forests), Cathy Gauthier
Tel: 250-387-1589
Fax: 250-356-9239
Director, Financial Planning, Systems & Reporting (Forests), Barb Searle
Tel: 250-387-1575
Michael.Lord@gov.bc.ca
Director, Fleet & Assets, Kevin Doran
Tel: 250-387-3442
Fax: 250-387-1574
Kevin.Doran@gov.bc.ca
Director, Infrasturcture, Policy & Records, Diane St. Hilair
Tel: 250-952-4944
Diane.StHilair@gov.bc.ca
Director, Corporate Security, Tina St. Hilaire
Tel: 250-356-7641
Tina.St.Hilaire@gov.bc.ca

Information Management/Information Technology
PO Box 9352 Prov Govt, Victoria, BC V8W 9M1
Tel: 250-953-4745
Fax: 250-953-3603
Assistant Deputy Minister/Executive Financial Officer (Forests), Craig Sutherland
Tel: 250-953-4745
Fax: 250-356-5797
Craig.Sutherland@gov.bc.ca
Chief Information Officer/Executive Director, Information Management Branch, Doug Say
Tel: 250-356-5216
Fax: 250-356-9836
Doug.Say@gov.bc.ca
Director, Business Service Desk, Mike Kelley
Tel: 250-953-4201
Fax: 250-356-5797
Mike.Kelley@gov.bc.ca
Director, Business Applications, Bonnie Laine Farrell
Tel: 250-356-2890
Fax: 250-387-5132
Bonnie.LaineFarrell@gov.bc.ca
Director, Client Business Solutions, Denise Rossander
Tel: 250-356-7695
Fax: 250-356-9836
Denise.Rossander@gov.bc.ca
Other Communications: Cell Phone: 250-213-5206
Director, Information Security, Fary Eriksson
Tel: 250-387-1373
Fax: 250-953-3752
Fary.Eriksson@gov.bc.ca
Director, Infrastructure Management, Terry Gunning
Tel: 250-387-9975
Fax: 250-356-9836
Terry.Gunning@gov.bc.ca
Director, Middle Tier & Database Administration, Colleen Coccola
Tel: 250-356-0603
Fax: 250-356-9836
Colleen.Coccola@gov.bc.ca
Director, Technology & Communication Services, Dave Rejminiak
Tel: 250-387-6358
Fax: 250-387-5132
Dave.Rejminiak@gov.bc.ca

People & Workplace Strategies
PO Box 9339 Prov Govt, Victoria, BC V8W 9M1
Tel: 250-356-8794
Fax: 250-953-3414
Assistant Deputy Minister/Executive Financial Officer (Agriculture & Energy & Mines), Neilane Mayhew
Tel: 250-356-8794
Fax: 250-953-3414
Executive Director, Mike R. Hykaway
Tel: 250-952-6626
Fax: 250-387-9086
Mike.Hykaway@gov.bc.ca
Director, Ingrid Fee
Tel: 250-952-4930
Fax: 250-952-4925
Ingrid.Fee@gov.bc.ca
Director, Sonja Martins
Tel: 250-387-9299
Fax: 250-387-3522
Sonja.Martins@gov.bc.ca

British Columbia Ministry of Health

1515 Blanshard St., Victoria, BC V8W 3C8
Toll-Free: 800-663-7100
hlth.health@gov.bc.ca
www.gov.bc.ca/health
Other Communication: Senior Health Care Support Line: 1-877-952-3181; Media Inquiries, Phone: 250-952-1887, Fax: 250-952-1883

The Ministry of Health is responsible for ensuring quality, timely, & cost effective health services for all citizens of British Columbia. To guide & enhance British Columbia's health services, the ministry works with health authorities, agencies, care providers, & other groups.

Acts Administered:
Access to Abortion Services Act
Anatomy Act
Community Care & Assisted Living Act (except ss. 8 & 34 (2) (h) & (h.1) & (6))
Continuing Care Act
Drinking Water Protection Act
E-Health Act (Personal Health Information Access & Protection of Privacy)
Emergency & Health Services Act
Food Safety Act
Forensic Psychiatry Act
Health & Social Services Delivery Improvement Act (except Part 3)
Health Act
Health Authorities Act
Health Care (Consent) & Care Facility (Admission) Act
Health Care Costs Recovery Act
Health Professions Act
Health Sector Partnerships Agreement Act
Health Special Account Act
Hospital Act
Hospital District Act
Hospital Insurance Act
Human Resource Facility Act (s. 1.1(d))
Human Tissue Gift Act
Marriage Act
Medicare Protection Act (except ss. 5 (1) (b), 7 (5), 8 (4), 8.1, 8.2 & 32)
Mental Health Act
Milk Industry Act (s. 12, except as that provision relates to tank milk receiver licences)
Ministry of Health Act
Name Act
Patient Care Quality Review Board Act
Pharmaceutical Services Act

Pharmacy Operations & Drug Scheduling Act
Public Health Act
Tobacco Control Act
Tobacco Damages & Health Care Costs Recovery Act
Wills Act (Part 2)

Minister, Health, Hon. Dr. Margaret MacDiarmid
Tel: 250-953-3547
Fax: 250-356-9587
hlth.minister@gov.bc.ca
Social Media: twitter.com/@DrMacDiarmid, www.facebook.com/margaretmacdiarmid
PO Box 9050 Prov Govt Sta.
Victoria, BC V8W 9E2

Deputy Minister, Health, Graham Whitmarsh
Tel: 250-952-1590
Fax: 250-952-1909
hlth.dmoffice@gov.bc.ca

Director, Executive Operations, Grace Foran
Tel: 250-952-1410
Fax: 250-952-1909
hlth.dmoffice@gov.bc.ca

Associated Agencies, Boards & Commissions:

• British Columbia Ambulance Service (BCAS)
PO Box 9600 Prov Govt
Victoria, BC V8W 9P1
Tel: 250-953-3298
Fax: 250-953-3119
www.bcas.ca/
The BCAS operates under the Emergency Health Services Commission, legislated by the Emergency & Health Services Act.

• Emergency & Health Services Commission (EHSC)
2261 Keating Cross Rd.
Saanichton, BC V8M 2A5
Tel: 250-953-3298
Fax: 250-953-3119
www.health.gov.bc.ca/ehsc/
Governed by the Emergency & Health Services Act, the EHCS allows British Columbia residents & health care professionals to access pre-hospital emergency services, as well as non-emergency health & information services (HealthLink BC).

• Hospital Appeal Board (HAB)
747 Fort St., 4th Fl.
PO Box 9425 Prov Govt
Victoria, BC V8W 9V1
Tel: 250-387-3464
Fax: 250-356-9923
Toll-free: 800-663-7867
hab@gov.bc.ca
www.hab.gov.bc.ca
The Hospital Appeal Board of British Columbia is an independent, quasi-judicial administrative appeal tribunal, which was created by the Hospital Act. The Board provides an appeal process for medical practitioners. The role of the Board is to review hospital board of management decisions concerning hospital privileges. Board members are appointed by British Columbia's Minister of Health.

• Medical Services Commission (MSC)
1515 Blanshard St., 3rd Fl.
Victoria, BC V8W 3C8
Tel: 250-952-3073
Fax: 250-952-3131
www.health.gov.bc.ca/msp/legislation/msc.html
The Medical Services Commission is a statutory body made up of nine members. In accordance with the Medicare Protection Act & Regulations, the Commission acts on behalf of the Government of British Columbia to manage the Medical Services Plan. The Commission works to ensure British Columbia residents have access to medical care, & to manage the provision & payment of medical services.

• Mental Health Review Board (MHRB)
Dogwood Building
2601 Lougheed Hwy.
Coquitlam, BC V3C 4J2
Tel: 604-524-7220
Fax: 604-524-7216

Office of the Chief Administrative Officer
Tel: 250-952-1164
Fax: 250-952-1909

Chief Administrative Officer, John Bethel
Tel: 250-952-2404
Fax: 250-952-1390
Acting Executive Director, Labour Relations Unit, Ted Patterson
Tel: 250-952-1026
Fax: 250-952-1034
Ted.Patterson@gov.bc.ca
Director, Regulatory Services, Emergency Medical Assistants Licensing Board, Julie Brown
Tel: 250-952-2613
Fax: 250-952-1222
emalb@victoria1.gov.bc.ca
Director/Registrar, Emergency Medical Assistants Licensing Board, Judy Thompson
Tel: 250-952-1203
Fax: 250-952-1222
emalb@victoria1.gov.bc.ca
Manager, Corporate Services & Program Operations Standards, Anne Stearn
Tel: 250-952-2636
Fax: 250-952-1909
Executive Director, Medical Services Branch, Stephanie Power
Tel: 250-952-2671
stephanie_power@gov.bc.ca
Executive Director, Primary Healthcare and Specialists Services, Nichola Manning
Tel: 250-952-2961
nichola_manning@gov.bc.ca

Medical Services & Health Human Resources Division
Tel: 250-952-3465
Fax: 250-952-3131

Assistant Deputy Minister, Sheila Taylor
Tel: 250-952-3465
Fax: 250-952-3131
Sheila.Taylor@gov.bc.ca
Executive Director, Laboratory, Diagnostic & Blood Services Branch, Jane Crickmore
Tel: 250-952-1323
Fax: 250-952-3133
Jane.Crickmore@gov.bc.ca
Executive Director, Physician Human Resource Management, Rod Frechette
Tel: 250-952-3146
Fax: 250-952-3486
Rod.Frechette@gov.bc.ca
Executive Director, Medical Servcies Branch, Nichola Manning
Tel: 250-952-1204
Fax: 250-952-3133
Executive Director, Health Human Resources Planning (Physicians), Libby Posgate
Tel: 250-952-1107
Fax: 250-952-2125
Libby.Posgate@gov.bc.ca
Executive Director, Health Human Resources Planning (Nursing & Allied), Sharon Stewart
Tel: 250-952-3656
Fax: 250-952-2125
Sharon.Stewart@gov.bc.ca
Executive Director, Primary Health Care, Valerie Tregillus
Tel: 250-952-2961
Fax: 250-952-1417
Valerie.Tregillus@gov.bc.ca

Health Sector Information Management/Information Technology
Tel: 250-952-2563
Fax: 250-952-1827

Assistant Deputy Minister, Linsday Kislock
Tel: 250-952-2160
Fax: 250-952-2109
Executive Director, Business Management Office, Carolyn Bell
Tel: 250-952-6202
Fax: 250-952-6084
Executive Director, Corporate Management & Operations, Darcy Goodwin
Tel: 250-952-1432
Fax: 250-952-1186
Darcy.Goodwin@gov.bc.ca
Executive Director, eHealth Privacy, Security & Legislation, Deb McGinnis
Tel: 250-952-2663
Fax: 250-952-3492
Executive Director, Public Health Systems, Kelly Moran
Tel: 250-356-2434
Fax: 250-356-2530
Kelly.Moran@gov.bc.ca
Chief Data Steward/Executive Director, Strategic Policy, Information Management & Data Stewardship, Chris Norman
Tel: 250-952-1822
Fax: 250-952-2202
Chris.Norman@gov.bc.ca
Executive Director, Integrated Health Information Technology Branch, Paul Shrimpton
Tel: 250-356-2401
Fax: 250-356-2530

Pharmaceutical Services
Tel: 250-952-1464
Fax: 250-952-1584

Assistant Deputy Minister, Bob Nakagawa
Tel: 250-952-1464
Fax: 250-952-1584
Acting Executive Director, Business Management & Supplier Relations, Dennis Chan
Tel: 604-660-5422
Fax: 604-660-2108
Executive Director, Drug Intelligence, Eric Lun
Tel: 250-952-2272
Fax: 250-952-2216
Executive Director, Drug Use Optimization, Suzanne Taylor
Tel: 604-660-1217
Fax: 604-660-2108
Suzanne.Taylor@gov.bc.ca
Executive Director, Policy, Outcomes Evaluation & Research, Darlene Therrien
Tel: 250-952-1149
Fax: 250-952-1391
Darlene.Therrien@gov.bc.ca

Office of the Chief Operating Officer
Fax: 250-952-1909

Chief Operating Officer, Michael MacDougall
Tel: 250-952-1764
Fax: 250-952-1909
Michael.MacDougall@gov.bc.ca
Executive Director, Intergovernmental Relations, Mariana Diacu
Tel: 250-952-1304
Fax: 250-952-2516
Executive Director, Organizational Development & Engagement, Dale Samsonoff
Tel: 250-952-1175
Fax: 250-952-2125
Acting Executive Director, Emergency Management Unit, Chris Smith
Tel: 250-952-1456
Fax: 250-952-2467
Executive Project Director, Nikki Sieben
Tel: 250-952-1170
Fax: 250-952-1909
Acting Director, Planning & Programs, Kirsten Brown
Tel: 250-952-3214
Fax: 250-952-2467
Director, Operational Readiness, Dave Burgess
Tel: 604-418-1634
Fax: 604-586-4334
Director, Intergovernmental Relations, Gayle Downey
Tel: 250-952-1645
Fax: 250-952-2516
Director, Strategic Initiatives, Sandra Maxson
Tel: 250-952-1685
Fax: 250-952-1909

Planning & Innovation Division
Fax: 250-952-1909

Assistant Deputy Minister, Elaine McKnight
Tel: 250-952-2563
Fax: 250-952-1827
Elaine.McKnight@gov.bc.ca
Executive Director, Management Information Branch, Nick Grant
Tel: 250-952-1116
Fax: 250-952-2002
Nick.Grant@gov.bc.ca
Executive Director, Legislation & Professional Regulation, Christine Massey
Tel: 250-952-2281
Fax: 250-952-2205
HLTH.LPRAdmin@gov.bc.ca
Acting Executive Director, Financial Analysis Branch, Ted Patterson
Tel: 250-952-1435
Fax: 250-952-2605
Glynis.Soper@gov.bc.ca
Executive Director, Modeling & Analysis Branch, Ian Rongve
Tel: 250-952-1343
Fax: 250-952-3676
Ian.Rongve@gov.bc.ca
Executive Director, Strategic Management Planning, Anne Sandbu
Tel: 250-952-1438
Fax: 250-952-2605
Anne.Sandbu@gov.bc.ca
Executive Director, Business Intelligence Branch, Glynis Soper
Tel: 250-952-2406
Fax: 250-952-2605
Glynis.Soper@gov.bc.ca
Executive Director, Research, Knowledge Translation & Library Services Branch, Elisabeth Wagner
Tel: 250-952-2282
Fax: 250-952-2516

Population & Public Health
Tel: 250-952-1731
Fax: 250-952-1021

Acting Assistant Deputy Minister, Laurie Woodland
Acting Executive Director, Seniors' Healthy Living Secretariat, Silas Brownsey
Tel: 250-356-1474
Fax: 250-387-1407
Silas.Brownsey@gov.bc.ca

Acting Executive Director, Healthy Women, Children & Youth Secretariat, Joan Geber
Tel: 250-952-3678
Fax: 250-952-1570
Executive Director, Business Operations & Surveillance, Tom Gregory
Tel: 250-952-1467
Fax: 250-952-1713
Acting Executive Director, Chronic Disease/Injury Prevention & Built Environment, Matt Herman
Tel: 250-952-2847
Fax: 250-952-1570
Acting Executive Director, Health Protection, Tim Lambert
Tel: 250-952-1987
Fax: 250-952-1713
Executive Director, Aboriginal Healthy Living, Shannon McDonald
Tel: 250-952-2811
Fax: 250-952-1570
Acting Executive Director, Communicable Disease Prevention, Harm Reduction & Mental Health Promotion, Warren O'Briain
Tel: 250-952-2481
Fax: 250-952-1570
Acting Executive Director, Health Promotion Supports & Engagement, Kate Fagan Taylor
Tel: 250-356-9814
Fax: 250-387-8720
Kate.Fagan.Taylor@gov.bc.ca

Financial & Corporate Services
Tel: 250-952-2067
Fax: 250-952-1573
Assistant Deputy Minister, Manjit Sidhu
Tel: 250-952-2066
Fax: 250-952-1573
Chief Financial Officer/Executive Director, Finance & Decision Support, Hilary Woodward
Tel: 250-952-2016
Fax: 250-952-2089
Executive Director, Capital Services, Kevin Brewster
Tel: 250-952-1102
Fax: 250-952-2873
Executive Director, Regional Grants - Decision Support, Gordon Cross
Tel: 250-952-1120
Fax: 250-952-1420
Director, Health Authority Funding, Rhonda Beveridge
Tel: 250-952-1054
Fax: 250-952-1420
Director, Health Authority Funding, Blair Boland
Tel: 250-952-2250
Fax: 250-952-1420
Director, Accounting Operations Branch, Ted Boomer
Tel: 250-952-2053
Fax: 250-952-2090
Director, Decision Support - MSD, Betty-Anne Brazier
Tel: 250-952-2048
Fax: 250-952-0989
Director, Health Authority Funding, Harry Hitchman
Tel: 250-952-3673
Fax: 250-952-1420
Director, Finance, Decision Support - Pharmaceutical Services, Vitali Kozubenko
Tel: 250-952-1953
Fax: 250-952-2089
Director, Capital Services, Shelley Moen
Tel: 250-952-1518
Fax: 250-952-2873
Shelley.Moen@gov.bc.ca
Director, Financial Verification, Maria Perri
Tel: 250-952-1011
Fax: 250-952-1573
Director, Capital Services, Cathy Sleeva
Tel: 250-952-1510
Fax: 250-952-2873
Cathy.Sleeva@gov.bc.ca
Director, Decision Support - Health Sector Information Management/Information Technology, Glen Stusek
Tel: 250-952-2100
Fax: 250-952-0989
Acting Director, Audit & Investigations Branch, Marie Thelisma
Tel: 250-952-1665
Fax: 250-952-2089
Director, Capital Services, Scarlette Verjinschi
Tel: 250-952-1494
Fax: 250-952-2873
Cathy.Sleeva@gov.bc.ca
Director, Capital Finance, Bonnie Wong
Tel: 250-952-1646
Fax: 250-952-0989
Director, Finance & Funding, Mark Taylor
Tel: 250-952-1177
Fax: 250-952-1420

Health Authorities Division
Tel: 250-952-1049
Fax: 250-952-1052
Assistant Deputy Minister, Heather Davidson
Assisted Living Registrar, Susan Adams
Tel: 604-714-3378
Fax: 604-733-5996
info@alregistrar.bc.ca

Clinical Care & Patient Safety
Tel: 250-952-1975
Fax: 250-952-1014
Executive Director, Brenda Canitz
Tel: 250-952-2738
Fax: 250-952-1014
Director, Patient Safety, Brian G. Sagar
Tel: 250-952-2753
Fax: 250-952-1014
Director, Clinical Innovation, Marc Woons
Tel: 250-952-1950
Fax: 250-952-1014
Manager, Heather Davidson
Tel: 250-952-3540
Fax: 250-952-1014

Health Authority Relations & Corporate Services
Tel: 250-952-1382
Fax: 250-952-1689
For a certificate of a registration or record: $25 per copy. For each search for one registration or record for each three-year period or fraction thereof over which the search is conducted: $25.
Executive Director, Teri Collins
Tel: 250-952-2871
Fax: 250-952-1052
Director, Planning & Divisional Support, Kim Grantham
Tel: 250-952-2175
Fax: 250-952-1052
Director, Health Authority Relations, Valerie Stevens
Tel: 250-952-1990
Fax: 250-952-1689

Home, Community & Integrated Care
Tel: 250-952-3594
Fax: 250-952-1282
Executive Director, Leigh Ann Seller
Tel: 250-952-1274
Fax: 250-952-1282
Director, Community Care Licensing, Sue Bedford
Tel: 250-952-1442
Fax: 250-952-1713
Director, Service Redesign & Caregiving & Health-care Facilities, Katie Hill
Tel: 250-952-1564
Fax: 250-952-1282
Director, Program Monitoring, Ramani Kumar
Tel: 250-952-2011
Fax: 250-952-1282
Manager, Service Redesign Policy & Planning, Karen Archibald
Tel: 250-952-2784
Fax: 250-952-1282
Manager, Program Monitoring, Shana Hall
Tel: 250-952-1159
Fax: 250-952-1282
Manager, Residential Services, Brenda Higham
Tel: 250-952-1188
Fax: 250-952-1282
Manager, End-of-Life Care & Special Populations, Pauline James
Tel: 250-952-1536
Fax: 250-952-1282

Hospital & Provincial Services Branch
Tel: 250-952-1178
Fax: 250-952-1052
Executive Director, Effie Henry
Tel: 250-952-1514
Fax: 250-952-1282
Director, Priority Projects-Surgical Services, Minjeet (Margi) Bhalla
Tel: 250-952-1040
Fax: 250-952-1282
Director, Acute Program, Tricia Braidwood-Looney
Tel: 250-952-1012
Fax: 250-952-1282
Director, Diagnostic Imaging & Piority Projects, Kirk Eaton
Tel: 250-952-1599
Fax: 250-952-1052
Director, Performance Accountability, Provincial Health Services Authority, Alex Scheiber
Tel: 250-952-3595
Fax: 250-952-1282
Director, Program Monitoring Hospital Service, Nancy South
Tel: 250-952-3593
Fax: 250-952-1282

Mental Health & Substance Abuse
Tel: 250-952-1608
Fax: 250-952-1689
Executive Director, Ann Marr
Tel: 250-952-3519
Fax: 250-952-1689
Director, Program Monitoring, Ross Hayward
Tel: 250-952-3638
Fax: 250-952-1689
Director, Mental Health, Gerrit van der Leer
Tel: 250-952-1610
Fax: 250-952-1689
Director, Mental Health & Substance Abuse, Anita Snell
Tel: 250-952-1270
Fax: 250-952-1689

HealthLink BC
PO Box 9600 Prov Govt, Victoria, BC V8W 9P1
Tel: 604-215-8110
Fax: 250-952-6509
healthlinkbc@healthlinkbc.ca
www.HealthLinkBC.ca
Other Communication: HealthLink BC hotline: 8-1-1; TTY: 7-1-1
HealthLink BC allows residents of British Columbia to access health care information by phone or online, and incorporates the following previously existing services: BC HealthGuide, BC HealthFiles, BC NurseLine & Pharmacist service, & Dial-a-Dietitian.
Executive Lead, Bob Bell
Tel: 250-356-0685
Fax: 250-952-6509
Other Communications: Alternate Phone: 250-356-0767
Executive Director, Clinical Practice & Integrated Knowledge Management, Alyse Capron
Tel: 604-215-5191
Executive Director, Information Management, Simon Hall
Tel: 250-356-3015
Fax: 250-952-6509
Simon.Hall@gov.bc.ca
Executive Director, Navigation Services, Michele Lane
Tel: 604-215-5156
Fax: 604-215-8105
Executive Director, Business Development, Mark MacKinnon
Tel: 250-952-6293
Fax: 250-952-6509
Executive Director, Operations, Marie Root
Tel: 604-215-5118
Fax: 250-952-6509
Executive Director, Planning & Business Support, Dave Van Swieten
Tel: 250-952-6294
Fax: 250-952-6509
Director, Change Management & Business Transformation, Lake Apted
Tel: 250-952-6144
Fax: 250-952-6509
Director, Clinical Infomatics/Decision Support, Lee Ashbourne
Tel: 250-953-4299
Fax: 250-952-6509
Director, Business Development, Kevin Brown
Tel: 250-952-6281
Fax: 250-952-6509
Director, Business Development, Collette Christney
Tel: 250-356-0339
Fax: 250-952-6509
Director, Marketing & Communications Services, Kate Jobling
Tel: 250-953-3234
Director, Dietitian Services, Barbara Leslie
Tel: 604-215-5138
Director, Business Development, Janice Linton
Tel: 250-952-6280
Fax: 250-952-6509
Director, Information Technology & Telecom Ops & Architecture, John Martin
Tel: 604-215-5128
Director, Quality Management & Professional Management, Peter Quick
Tel: 604-215-5197
Director, Nursing Services, Kim Schmidt
Tel: 604-215-5103
Director, Project Management Office, Irina Sladecek
Tel: 250-356-0225
Fax: 250-952-6509
Manager, Directory Services, Adriana Poveda
Tel: 604-215-7171
Fax: 250-953-0481
chard.support@gov.bc.ca

British Columbia Hydro

6911 Southpoint Dr., Burnaby, BC V3N 4X8
Tel: 604-224-9376
Toll-Free: 800-224-9376
www.bchydro.com
Secondary Address: 333 Dunsmuir St.
Corporate Address
Vancouver, BC V6B 5R3

The Clean Energy Act consolidated BC Hydro & the BC Transmission Corporation in 2010. BC Hydro is a crown corporation that reports to the British Columbia Ministry of Energy, Mines, & Natural Gas. The mission of the corporation is the delivery of energy, in an envrionmentally & socially responsible manner, to meet the province's demand for electricity. Thirty-one hydroelectric facilities & three thermal generating plants are operated by BC Hydro.

President & Chief Executive Officer, Charles Reid

Chief Human Resources Officer & Senior Vice-President, Debbie Nagle

Chief Financial Officer & Executive Vice-President, Cheryl Yaremko

Executive Vice-President, Generation, Chris O'Riley

Executive Vice-President, Transmission & Distribution, Greg Reimer

Executive Vice-President, Site C Clean Energy Project, Susan Yurkovich

Senior Vice-President, Corporate Services & General Counsel, Ray Aldeguer

Associated Agencies, Boards & Commissions:

• Powerex Corp.
#1400, 666 Burrard St.
Vancouver, BC V6C 2X8
Tel: 604-891-5000
Fax: 604-891-6060
Toll-free: 800-220-4907
Brian.Moghadam@powerex.com
www.powerex.com
A wholly-owned subsidiary of BC Hydro, Powerex Corp. markets wholesale energy products & services to utilities, power pools, industrials, & power marketers in North America, particularly western Canada, the western United States.

• Powertech Labs Inc.
12388 - 88 Ave.
Surrey, BC V8W 7R7
Tel: 604-590-7500
Fax: 604-590-6611
www.powertechlabs.com
A wholly owned subsidiary of BC Hydro, Powertech Labs offers environmental, mechanical, electrical, metallurgical, civil, chemical, gas technologies, & structural engineering to deal with technical problems with power equipment & systems.

Office of the Information & Privacy Commissioner for British Columbia (OIPC)

947 Fort St., 4th Fl., PO Box 9038 Prov Govt, Victoria, BC V8W 9A4
Tel: 250-387-5629
Fax: 250-387-1696
Toll-Free: 800-663-7867
info@oipc.bc.ca
www.oipc.bc.ca
Other Communication: Vancouver Phone: 604-660-2421

Operating independently from the government, the Office of the Information & Privacy Commissioner is responsible for monitoring & enforcing the following acts in British Columbia: Freedom of Information & Protection of Privacy Act; & Personal Information Protection Act.

Commissioner, Elizabeth Denham

Assistant Commissioner, Investigation & Mediation, Catherine Tully

Assistant Commissioner, Policy & Adjudication, LeRoy Brower

Communications & Research officer, Maria Dupuis
Tel: 250-387-5629
Fax: 250-387-1696
info@oipc.bc.ca

Senior Investigator, Jim Burrows

Senior Investigator, Patrick Egan

Registrar of Inquiries, Cindy Hamilton

Insurance Corporation of British Columbia (ICBC)

151 West Esplanade, North Vancouver, BC V7M 3H9
Tel: 604-661-2800
Toll-Free: 800-663-3051
www.icbc.com
Other Communication: New Claims, Lower Mainland Phone: 604-520-8222; Elsewhere in BC, Toll Free: 1-800-910-4222; TIPS Lower Mainland, Phone: 604-661-6844; TIPS BC Line: 1-800-661-6844

A provincial Crown corporation, The Insurance Corporation of British Columbia was established in 1973. The main responsibilities of the Insurance Corporation of British Columbia are as follows: Provision of universal auto insurance to motorists in British Columbia; Registration & licensing of vehicles; & Driver licensing.

Chair, Nancy McKinstry

President/Chief Executive Officer, Jon Schubert

Chief Financial Officer, Geri Prior

Chief Information Officer, Ward Chapin

Senior Vice-President, Insurance, Mark Blucher

Senior Vice-President, Claims, Craig Horton

Senior Vice-President, Corporate Affairs, Donnie Wing

Vice-President, Business Transformation, Sheila Eddin

Vice-President, Driver Licensing, Fred Hess

Vice-President, Human Resources & Corporate Law, Len Posyniak

Vice-President, Strategic Marketing, Jeff Schulz

British Columbia Ministry of Jobs, Tourism, & Skills Training (& Responsible for Labour)

PO Box 9071 Prov Govt, Victoria, BC V8W 9E2
EnquiryBC@gov.bc.ca; GCPE.JTI.Media.Requests@gov.bc.ca
www.gov.bc.ca/jti
Other Communication: Media Relations, Phone: 250-356-8177

In September 2012, the Ministry of Jobs, Tourism, & Innovation was reorganized to become the Ministry of Jobs, Tourism, & Skills Training. The minister of the ministry is also responsible for labour. The change was made to ensure citizens of British Columbia are equipped with useful skills to preserve a strong economy.

General responsibilities of the ministry are as follows: WorkBC; export market development; trade initiatives; the Canada-BC Business Service Centre; the Community Business Loans Program; labour relations; employment standards; regional economic & rural development; Rural BC Secretariat; tourism strategies; Aboriginal tourism; industry training; & occupational health & safety.

Acts Administered:
BC-Alcan Northern Development Fund Act
British Columbia Enterprise Corporation Act (as it relates to the B.C. Pavilion Corporation)
British Columbia Innovation Council Act
Columbia Basin Trust Act
Employee Investment Act
Hotel Guest Registration Act
Hotel Keepers Act
Industrial Development Act
Industry Training Authority Act
Labour Mobility Act
Ministry of International Business & Immigration Act
Miscellaneous Statutes Amendment Act (No. 3), 2010 (s. 40)
Multiculturalism Act
New West Partnership Trade Agreement Implementation Act
North Island-Coast Development Initiative Trust
Northern Development Initiative Trust Act
Small Business Venture Capital Act
Southern Interior Development Initiative Trust Act
Tourism Act
Trade, Investment, & Labour Mobility Agreement Implementation Act
Vancouver Tourism Levy Enabling Act
Wood First Act

Minister, Jobs, Tourism, & Skills Training; Minister Responsible, Labour, Hon. Patrick Bell
Tel: 250-356-2771
Fax: 250-356-3000
JTI.Minister@gov.bc.ca
Social Media: twitter.com/patbellbc
PO Box 9067 Prov Govt Sta.
Victoria, BC V8W 9E9

Deputy Minister, Jobs, Tourism, & Skills Training, Dave Byng
Tel: 250-952-0103
Fax: 250-356-1195
Dave.Byng@gov.bc.ca
PO Box 9846 Prov Govt Sta.
Victoria, BC V8W 9T2

Manager, Correspondence, Darla Cooper
Tel: 250-387-4648
Darla.Cooper@gov.bc.ca

Manager, Small Business Roundtable Secretariat, Sean Murry
Tel: 250-387-9083
Fax: 250-952-0113

Parliamentary Secretary for Asia Pacific to the Minister of Jobs, Tourism, & Skills Training, Richard T. Lee
Tel: 250-356-3052
Fax: 250-387-9100
Richard.Lee.MLA@leg.bc.ca

Director, Executive Operations, Maureen Yelovatz
Tel: 250-952-0104
Fax: 250-356-1195

Associated Agencies, Boards & Commissions:

• British Columbia Labour Relations Board
Oceanic Plaza
#600, 1066 West Hastings St.
Vancouver, BC V6E 3X1
Tel: 604-660-1300
Fax: 604-660-1892
information@lrb.bc.ca
www.lrb.bc.ca
The British Columbia Labour Relations Board is an independent, administrative tribunal. The Board is responsible for mediating & adjudicating employment & labour relations matters related to unionized workplaces.

• Employment Standards Tribunal
Oceanic Plaza
#650, 1066 West Hastings St.
Vancouver, BC V6E 3X1
Tel: 604-775-3512
Fax: 604-775-3372
registrar.est@bcest.bc.ca
www.bcest.bc.ca
Established under the Employment Standards Act, the Employment Standards Tribunal operates as an administrative tribunal. The responsibility of the Tribunal is to provide an independent appeal of Determinations made by the Director of Employment Standards.

• Forestry Innovation Investment Ltd. (FII)
#1200, 1130 West Pender St.
Vancouver, BC V6E 4A4
Tel: 604-685-7507
Fax: 604-685-5373
info@bcfii.ca
www.bcfii.ca
British Columbia's Forestry Innovation Investment strives to support a prosperous & environmentally sustainable forest economy in the province. The role of the organization includes the following activities: Promotion of British Columbia's forest practices & wood products to international markets; Working in partnership with the forestry sector, the Government of British Columbia, & the Government of Canada; & Assisting the forestry sector with issues such as Mountain Pine Beetle outbreak.

• Industry Training Authority (ITA)
#1223, 13351 Commerce Pkwy.
Richmond, BC V6V 2X7
Tel: 604-214-8700
Fax: 604-214-8701
Toll-free: 866-660-6011
info@itabc.ca; customerservice@itabc.ca
www.itabc.ca
Other Communication: Customer Service: 778-328-8700
British Columbia's Industry Training Authority is a provincial government agency which oversees the province's training & apprenticeship system. The ITA works with industry, employers, training providers, trainees, & apprentices.

• Leading Edge Endowment Fund Board (LEEF)
1188 West Georgia St., 9th Fl.
Vancouver, BC V6E 4A2
Tel: 604-438-3220
contact@leefbc.ca
www.leefbc.ca
To encourage social & economic development in British Columbia, the provincial government established the Leading Edge Endowment Fund in 2002. The Fund establishes Leadership Research Chairs at the province's public,

post-secondary institutions, & Regional Innovation Chairs through colleges, university-colleges, & institutes.

• Northern Development Initiative Trust
#301, 1268 Fifth Ave.
Prince George, BC V2L 3L2
Tel: 250-561-2525
Fax: 250-561-2563
info@northerndevelopment.bc.ca
northerndevelopment.bc.ca
The Northern Trust consists of a Board of Directors which makes funding decisions for programs of the Trust. According to provincial legislation, investments can be made in the following areas: agriculture, economic development, energy, forestry, mining, Olympic opportunities; pine beetle recovery, small business, tourism, & transportation.

• Southern Interior Development Initiative Trust
#204, 3131 29th St.
Vernon, BC V1T 5A8
Tel: 250-545-6829
Fax: 250-545-6896
admin@sidit-bc.ca
www.sidit-bc.ca
The government of British Columbia enacted legislation in 2006 to establish the Southern Interior Development Initiative Trust. The mission of the Trust is to grow & diversify the economy of the Southern Interior of British Columbia through investments in economic development projects that will benefit the area.

• Workers' Compensation Appeal Tribunal (WCAT)
#150, 4600 Jacombs Rd.
Richmond, BC V6V 3B1
Tel: 604-664-7800
Fax: 604-664-7898
Toll-free: 800-663-2782
www.wcat.bc.ca
The Workers' Compensation Appeal Tribunal of British Columbia is an independent appeal tribunal, which was established by the Workers Compensation Amendment Act (No. 2), 2002. The Tribunal decides appeals from workers & employers from decisions of the Workers' Compensation Board (WorkSafeBC).

Competitiveness & Innovation
PO Box 9327 Prov Govt, Victoria, BC V8W 9N3
Fax: 250-952-0137

Acting Assistant Deputy Minister, Jane Burnes
Tel: 250-889-1054
Fax: 250-952-0137
Jane.Burnes@gov.bc.ca

Executive Director, Small Business Branch, Simone Decosse
Tel: 250-387-0661
Simone.Decosse@gov.bc.ca

Acting Executive Director, Research & Innovation, Melanie Friesen
Tel: 250-356-1894
Fax: 250-387-3725
Melanie.Friesen@gov.bc.ca

Director, Economic Analysis, Dr. Linda ChaseWilde
Tel: 250-952-0338
Fax: 250-952-0675
Linda.ChaseWilde@gov.bc.ca

Director, Knowledge Transfer & Commercialization, Tim Ewanchuk
Tel: 250-356-1593
Fax: 250-387-3725
Tim.Ewanchuk@gov.bc.ca

Director, Division Operations, Jennifer Meadows
Tel: 250-952-0710
Fax: 250-952-0137
Jennifer.Meadows@gov.bc.ca

Director, Small Business Programs, Darryl Soper
Tel: 250-356-7532
Fax: 250-952-0113
Darryl.L.Soper@gov.bc.ca

Director, Research & Knowledge Development, Claudia Trudeau
Tel: 250-387-6157
Fax: 250-387-3725
Claudia.Trudeau@gov.bc.ca

Manager, Land Use Initiatives, Alison Coyne
Tel: 250-356-0807
Fax: 250-952-0137
Alison.Coyne@gov.bc.ca

Investment Capital Branch
PO Box 9800 Prov Govt, Victoria, BC V8W 9V1
Fax: 250-952-0371

Vice-President/Executive Director, Investments/Venture Capital Programs, Todd Tessler
Tel: 250-952-0612
Fax: 250-952-0371
Todd.Tessier@gov.bc.ca

Senior Portfolio Manager, Venture Capital Programs, Melanie Achtemichuk
Tel: 604-660-6812
Fax: 604-660-6812
Melanie.Achtemichuk@gov.bc.ca

Senior Portfolio Manager, Venture Capital Programs, Matthew Brown
Tel: 250-952-0631
Fax: 250-952-0371
Matthew.J.Brown@gov.bc.ca

Senior Portfolio Manager, International Business Activities, Lina Duong-Aihara
Tel: 250-952-0420
Fax: 250-952-0371
Lina.Duong-Aihara@gov.bc.ca

Senior Portfolio Manager, Venture Capital Programs, Ian Wong
Tel: 250-952-6396
Fax: 250-952-0371
Ian.Wong@gov.bc.ca

Straightforward BC
PO Box 9822 Prov Govt, Victoria, BC V8W 9N3
Fax: 250-952-0113

Executive Director, Simone Decosse
Tel: 250-387-0661
Fax: 250-952-0113

Acting Director, Strategic Planning & Partnership, Jennifer Gorman
Tel: 250-387-8469
Fax: 250-952-0113

Director, Regulatory Reform, Heather Holley
Tel: 250-387-8469
Fax: 250-952-0113
Heather.Holley@gov.bc.ca

Senior Advisor, Regulatory Reform, Melanie Iwanow
Tel: 250-952-0157
Fax: 250-952-0113
Melanie.Iwanow@gov.bc.ca

Senior Advisor, Regulatory Reform, Carmen Ross
Tel: 250-356-8098
Fax: 250-952-0113
Carmen.Ross@gov.bc.ca

Economic Development Division

Assistant Deputy Minister, Sandra Carroll
Tel: 250-952-0601
Sandra.Carroll@gov.bc.ca

Chief Strategy Officer, Wood First & Wood Inovation & Design Centre, Joan Elangovan
Tel: 250-952-6529
Fax: 250-356-1195
Joan.Elangovan@gov.bc.ca

Executive Director, Economic Development, Steve Anderson
Tel: 250-952-0644
Fax: 250-952-0351
Steve.Anderson@gov.bc.ca

Executive Director, Pine Beetle Epidemic Response Branch, Gord Borgstrom
Tel: 250-371-3741
Fax: 250-371-3735
Gordon.Borgstrom@gov.bc.ca

Executive Director, RuralBC Secretariat Strategic Initiatives Branch, Greg Goodwin
Tel: 250-953-3008
Fax: 250-387-7972
Greg.Goodwin@gov.bc.ca

Executive Director, Economic Initiatives Branch, Dean Sekyer
Tel: 250-952-0409
Fax: 250-952-0646
Dean.Sekyer@gov.bc.ca

Executive Director, Community Development Trust, Tracey Thompson
Tel: 250-387-3130
Fax: 250-387-4425
Tracey.Thompson@gov.bc.ca

Director, Pine Beetle Epidemic Response Branch (Fort St. James), Jim Burck
Tel: 250-996-5200
Fax: 250-387-1590
Jim.Burck@gov.bc.ca

Director, Pine Beetle Epidemic Response Branch (Williams Lake), Hugh Flinton
Tel: 250-398-4224
Fax: 250-371-3735
Hugh.Flinton@gov.bc.ca

Director, Economic Initiatives, Chris Gilmore
Tel: 250-952-0139
Fax: 250-952-0351
Christopher.Gilmore@gov.bc.ca

Director, Pine Beetle Epidemic Response Branch (Kamloops), Marc Imus
Tel: 250-371-3937
Fax: 250-371-3735
Marc.Imus@gov.bc.ca

Director, Strategic Policy & Corporate Planning, Debra Larusson
Tel: 250-952-0225
Fax: 250-889-3114
Debra.Larusson@gov.bc.ca

Director, Industrial Initiatives, Gary Schick
Tel: 250-952-0643
Fax: 250-952-0646
Gary.Schick@gov.bc.ca

Director, Business Analysis, Sylvia Selig
Tel: 250-387-7555
Fax: 250-952-0351
Sylvia.Selig@gov.bc.ca

International Trade & Investment Attraction Division
Tel: 604-775-2100
Fax: 604-660-6835

Assistant Deputy Minister, Shom Sen
Tel: 604-775-0005
Fax: 604-660-6832
Shom.Sen@gov.bc.ca

Executive Director, International Partnerships & Programs, Chris Carter
Tel: 604-660-5896
Fax: 604-660-6835
Chris.Carter@gov.bc.ca

Executive Director/Practice Lead, International Relations & Business Development/Global Industry Practices, Marcus Ewert-Jones
Tel: 604-775-2145
Fax: 604-775-2197
Marcus.Johns@gov.bc.ca

Acting Executive Director, Investor Services, Michael Track
Tel: 604-775-2202
Fax: 604-775-2197
Michael.Track@gov.bc.ca

Executive Director, Trade Initiatives, Don D. White
Tel: 250-952-0708
Don.D.White@gov.bc.ca

Director, Internal Trade, Gail Greenwood
Tel: 250-387-7575
Fax: 250-952-0137
Gail.Greenwood@gov.bc.ca

Director, BC Business Services & Olympic Legacy, Brian Krieger
Tel: 604-660-0220
Fax: 604-775-2197
Brian.Krieger@gov.bc.ca

Director, Special Projects, Christine Little
Tel: 250-953-3479
Christine.Little@gov.bc.ca

Director, International Operations & Logistics, Gregory Matisz
Tel: 605-660-5899
Fax: 604-660-2520
Gregory.Matisz@gov.bc.ca

Director, Trade Policy, Robert Musgrave
Tel: 250-952-0711
Fax: 250-952-0716
Robert.Musgrave@gov.bc.ca

Director, International Trade, Janel Quiring
Tel: 250-356-5867
Fax: 250-952-0351
Janel.Quiring@gov.bc.ca

Director, International Marketing Secretariat, Nancy Taylor
Tel: 250-953-3397
Fax: 250-952-0716
Nancy.Taylor@gov.bc.ca

Director, Special Projects, Gloria Yang-Mason
Tel: 604-660-5895
Fax: 604-660-6935
Gloria.Yang-Mason@gov.bc.ca

Labour Market & Immigration Division
PO Box 9213, Vancouver, BC V8W 9J1
Tel: 250-953-3585
Fax: 250-356-0033

Assistant Deputy Minister, Shannon Baskerville
Shannon.Baskerville@gov.bc.ca

Acting Executive Director, Policy & Stakeholder Relations Branch, Sohee Ahn
Tel: 250-952-6567
Fax: 250-387-0878
Sohee.Ahn@gov.bc.ca

Executive Director, Economic Immigration Programs Branch, Ian Mellor
Tel: 604-775-2183
Fax: 604-660-4092
Ian.Mellor@gov.bc.ca

Executive Director, Labour Market Programs Branch, Melanie J. Stewart
Tel: 250-387-3661
Fax: 250-387-4788
Melanie.J.Stewart@gov.bc.ca

Executive Director, Immigrant Integration Branch, Deb Zehr
Tel: 250-356-1125
Fax: 250-356-0033
Deb.Zehr@gov.bc.ca

Director, Senior Relations, Dudley Alison
Tel: 604-775-0694
Fax: 604-775-0670
Alison.Dudley@gov.bc.ca

Director, Immigration Policy, Francois Bertrand
Tel: 604-660-3463

Fax: 604-660-4092
Francois.Bertrand@gov.bc.ca
Director, Client Engagement, Asha Bhat
Tel: 250-387-3679
Fax: 250-356-0033
Asha.Bhat@gov.bc.ca
Director, Strategic Occupations, Michael Chew
Tel: 604-775-2215
Fax: 604-660-4092
Michael.Chew@gov.bc.ca
Director, Labour Market Policy & Intergovernmental Relations, Suzanne Ferguson
Tel: 250-387-7587
Fax: 250-387-4788
Suzanne.Ferguson@gov.bc.ca
Director, Skills For Growth, Keith Godin
Tel: 250-387-5631
Fax: 250-387-4789
Keith.Godin@gov.bc.ca
Director, Partnerships & Productivity Unit, Nicola Lemmer
Tel: 250-952-7584
Fax: 250-387-4788
Nicola.Lemmer@gov.bc.ca
Director, Program Management & Evaluation, Ben Pollard
Tel: 604-775-0293
Fax: 604-775-0670
Ben.Pollard@gov.bc.ca
Director, Settlement Policy Unit, Catherine Poole
Tel: 250-953-3292
Fax: 250-356-0033
Catherine.Poole@gov.bc.ca
Director, Business Immigration, S.P. Poon
Tel: 604-775-2216
Fax: 604-660-4092
SP.Poon@gov.bc.ca
Director, Labour Market Agreement, Deb Rhymer
Tel: 250-952-0642
Fax: 250-387-4789
Deborah.Rhymer@gov.bc.ca
Director, Labour Market Information Services, Brenda Scott
Tel: 250-387-3517
Fax: 250-387-4788
Brenda.Scott@gov.bc.ca
Director, Program & Regional Operations, Lucy Swib
Tel: 604-775-0458
Fax: 604-775-0670
Lucy.Swib@gov.bc.ca
Director, Industry Training Programs, Bev Verboven
Tel: 250-356-9827
Fax: 250-387-4789
Bev.Verboven@gov.bc.ca
Director, Labour Market & Immigration Forecasting Unit, Kerry Young
Tel: 250-387-5790
Fax: 250-387-4788
Kerry.Young@gov.bc.ca

Tourism Division
510 Burrard St., 12th Fl., Vancouver, BC V6C 3A8
Fax: 604-660-3383
Assistant Deputy Minister, Grant Mackay
Tel: 604-660-6319
Fax: 604-660-3383
Grant.Mackay@gov.bc.ca
Director, Tourism Strategy, Policy & Research, Heather Brazier
Tel: 250-952-6024
Fax: 250-356-8246
Heather.Brazier@gov.bc.ca
Director, Partnership Marketing, Peter Harrison
Tel: 250-387-8578
Fax: 250-356-8246
Peter.Harrison@gov.bc.ca
Other Communications: URL: www.HelloBC.com
Director, Marketing (Overseas), Reg Krake
Tel: 604-660-3769
Fax: 604-660-3383
Director, Industry Relations, Ray LeBlond
Tel: 604-660-3233
Fax: 604-660-3383
Ray.LeBlond@gov.bc.ca
Director, Sector Development & City Destinations, Richard Lewis
Tel: 604-660-3701
Fax: 604-660-3383
Richard.Lewis@gov.bc.ca
Director, Marketing Communications, Kathleen Lorentsen
Tel: 604-660-4257
Fax: 604-660-3383
Kathleen.Lorentsen@gov.bc.ca
Director, Tourism Product Management, Margaret McCormick
Tel: 604-660-4705
Fax: 604-660-3688
Margaret.McCormick@gov.bc.ca
Director, Marketing (North America), Carol Nelson
Tel: 604-660-3755
Fax: 604-660-3383
Carol.Nelson@gov.bc.ca
Director, Visitor Services, Ninette Ollgaard
Tel: 250-356-0453
Fax: 250-356-8246
Ninette.Ollgaard@gov.bc.ca
Director, Research, Planning & Evaluation, Richard Porges
Tel: 250-356-9936
Fax: 250-356-8246
Richard.Porges@gov.bc.ca
Operations Manager, British Columbia Magazine, Lesley Christian
Tel: 604-660-3703
Leslie.Christian@gov.bc.ca

Management Services Division
PO Box 9842 Prov Govt, Victoria, BC V8W 9T2
Tel: 250-387-8705
Fax: 250-387-7973
Assistant Deputy Minister, Shauna Brouwer
Tel: 250-387-9180
Fax: 250-387-7973
Shauna.Brouwer@gov.bc.ca
Chief Information Officer/Executive Director, Debbie Fritz
Tel: 250-356-0803
Fax: 250-387-1590
Debbie.Fritz@gov.bc.ca
Executive Director, Strategic Human Resources & Corporate Policy & Planning, Kim Russell
Tel: 250-387-8976
Fax: 250-387-8772
Kim.Russell@gov.bc.ca
Chief Financial Officer/Director, Finance & Administrative Services, Murray Jacobs
Tel: 250-356-6950
Fax: 250-387-7973
Murray.Jacobs@gov.bc.ca
Director, Corporate Policy & Planning, Shannon Mullen
Tel: 250-953-4334
Fax: 250-387-1407
Shannon.Mullen@gov.bc.ca

Office of the Ombudsperson

947 Fort St., 2nd Fl., PO Box 9039 Prov Govt, Victoria, BC V8W 9A5
Tel: 250-387-5855
Fax: 250-387-0198
Toll-Free: 800-567-3247
systems@bcombudsperson.ca (Information technology inquiries)
www.ombudsman.bc.ca

Complaints about the services of public agencies are submitted to the Office of the Ombudsperson. The responsibility of the Office of the Ombudsperson is to investigate impartially these inquiries about the practices of public agencies within its jurisdiction. The Office determines if public agencies acted fairly in accordance with relevant legislation & policies.

Ombudsperson, Kim Carter
Tel: 250-356-1559

Executive Director, Corporate Services, Shelley Forrester
Tel: 250-356-7761

Executive Director, Investigations, Linda Carlson
Tel: 250-387-0189

Executive Director, Intake & Systemic Investigations, Bruce Ronayne
Tel: 250-387-0196

British Columbia Pavilion Corporation (PavCo)

#850, 999 West Hastings St., PO Box 16, Vancouver, BC V6C 2W2
Tel: 604-482-2200
Fax: 604-681-9017
info@bcpavco.com
www.bcpavco.com

The BC Pavilion Corporation is a provincial crown corporation of British Columbia's Ministry of Energy, Mines, & Natural Gas. The corporation's divisions include Corporate Services, BC Place, & the Vancouver Convention Centre.

Chair, David R. Podmore

President & Chief Executive Officer, Dana Hayden

Chief Financial Officer & Corporate Secretary, John Harding

BC Place
777 Pacific Blvd., Vancouver, BC V6B 4Y8
Tel: 604-669-2300
Fax: 604-661-3412
stadium@bcpavco.com
www.bcplace.com
General Manager, Howard Crosley
Director, Construction, Brian Griffin
Director, Business Development, Graham Ramsay
Director, Operations Division, Harvey Repp

Vancouver Convention Centre
1055 Canada Pl., Vancouver, BC V6C 0C3
Tel: 604-689-8232
Fax: 604-647-7232
info@vancouverconventioncentre.com
www.vancouverconventioncentre.com
General Manager, Ken Cretney
Vice-President, Sales & Marketing, Claire Smith
Vice-President, Operations, Catherine Wong

British Columbia Provincial Emergency Program (PEP)

Block A, #200, 2261 Keating Cross Rd., Saanichton, BC V8M 2A5
Tel: 250-952-4913
Fax: 250-952-4888
Toll-Free: 888-257-4777
www.pep.bc.ca
Other Communication: Emergency Coordination Centre: 1-800-663-3456; Recovery & Funding Programs Phone: 250-952-5505

The Provincial Emergency Program (PEP) is a division of the Ministry of Public Safety & Solicitor General, Emergency Management BC. PEP works with local governments to provide the following training & support services for emergencies: awareness & education to lessen the effects of emergencies; promotion of preparedness for disasters, through planning & exercises; coordination & assistance in response to emergencies; & development & implementation of recovery measures.

Executive Director, Strategic Planning, Policy & Legislation, Cam Filmer
Tel: 250-952-4881
Cam.Filmer@gov.bc.ca
Block A
#200, 2261 Keating Cross Rd.
Saanichton, BC V8M 2A5

Executive Director, Strategic Planning, Policy & Legislation, Cam Filmer
Tel: 250-952-4881
Cam.Filmer@gov.bc.ca
Block A
#200, 2261 Keating Cross Rd.
Saanichton, BC V8M 2A5

Executive Director, Emergency Coordination, Chris Duffy
Tel: 250-952-4544
Chris.Duffy@gov.bc.ca
Block A
#200, 2261 Keating Cross Rd.
Saanichton, BC V8M 2A5

Director, Integrated Planning, Aja Norgaard
Tel: 250-952-4854
Aja.Norgaard@gov.bc.ca
Block A
#200, 2261 Keating Cross Rd.
Saanichton, BC V8M 2A5

Senior Regional Manager/Assistant Director, Operations, Ralph Mohrmann
Tel: 250-952-4895
Ralph.Mohrmann@gov.bc.ca
Block A
#200, 2261 Keating Cross Rd.
Saanichton, BC V8M 2A5

Office of the Fire Commissioner
PO Box 9201 Prov Govt, Victoria, BC V8W 9J1
Tel: 250-952-4913
Fax: 250-952-4888
Toll-Free: 888-988-9488
OFC@gov.bc.ca
www.pssg.gov.bc.ca/firecom/index.htm
Deputy Fire Commissioner, Community Support, Dave Ferguson
Tel: 250-952-4919
Fax: 250-952-4888
Dave.Ferguson@gov.bc.ca
Assistant Fire Commissioner, Investigations, Rob Owens
Tel: 250-952-4913

Fax: 250-952-4888
Rob.Owens@gov.bc.ca

British Columbia Public Service Agency

#4, 810 Blanshard St., PO Box 9404 Prov Govt, Victoria, BC V8W 9V1
Tel: 250-387-0518
Fax: 250-356-7074
www.bcpublicserviceagency.gov.bc.ca/

The provision of human resource management services is the responsibility of the British Columbia Service Agency. The services are provided to persons & organizations working in the provinces's public sector.

Head, British Columbia Public Service Agency, Lynda Tarras
Tel: 250-387-2166
Fax: 250-356-7074
Lynda.Tarras@gov.bc.ca

Assistant Deputy Minister, Talent Management, Deborah Bowman
Tel: 250-387-0428
Fax: 250-356-7074
Deborah.Bowman@gov.bc.ca

Assistant Deputy Minister, Employee Relations, Doug Caul
Tel: 250-356-7448
Fax: 250-356-7074
Doug.Caul@gov.bc.ca

Assistant Deputy Minister, Client Services, Laurie Duncan
Tel: 250-356-6830
Fax: 250-356-7074
Laurie.Duncan@gov.bc.ca

Executive Director, Executive Account Management, Lorne DeLarge
Tel: 250-356-0708
Fax: 250-356-7074
Lorne.DeLarge@gov.bc.ca

Executive Director, Business Performance Division, Marguerite Vickery
Tel: 250-356-5431
Fax: 250-356-7074
Marguerite.Vickery@gov.bc.ca

British Columbia Ministry of Social Development

PO Box 9058 Prov Govt, Victoria, BC V8W 9E1
www.gov.bc.ca/hsd

The main responsibilities of the Ministry of Social Development include supporting community living services that assist persons with developmental disabilities; providing employment programs & services to unemployed & underemploye persons; & delivering income assistance to persons in need.

Acts Administered:
Community Living Authority Act
Employment & Assistance Act (ss 17 (3) & (4), 18-20, 21 (1), 22 (1)-(3), (4) (b), (5) & (6), 23 (1) (a) (ii) & (iii) & (b) (ii) & (iii), 23 (2), 24 (1), (2) (a) & (3)-(7) & 29; & provisions except those that relate to thechild in the home of a relative)
Employment & Assistance for Persons with Disabilities Act
Human Resource Facility Act

Minister, Social Development, Hon. Dr. Moira Stilwell
Tel: 250-356-7750
Fax: 250-356-7292
SD.Minister@gov.bc.ca
Social Media: twitter.com/DrMoiraStilwell
PO Box 9058 Prov Govt Sta.
Victoria, BC V8W 9E1

Deputy Minister, Social Development, Mark Sieben
Tel: 250-387-2325
Fax: 250-356-7801
PO Box 9934 Prov Govt Sta.
Victoria, BC V8W 9R2

Manager, Executive Operations, Karen MacMillan
Tel: 250-387-2807
Fax: 250-387-5775

Manager, Executive Correspondence Services, Sheena Marshall
Tel: 250-387-7660
Fax: 250-387-4264

Manager, Communications, Joanne Whittier
Tel: 250-356-1670
Fax: 250-356-7801

Parliamentary Secretary for Non-Profit Partnerships to the Minister of Social Development, Gordon Hogg

Associated Agencies, Boards & Commissions:
• Employment & Assistance Appeal Tribunal
PO Box 9994 Prov Govt
Victoria, BC V8W 9R7
Tel: 250-356-6374
Fax: 250-356-9687
Toll-free: 866-557-0035
eaat@gov.bc.ca
www.gov.bc.ca/eaat/

Employment & Labour Market Services Division
PO Box 9762 Prov Govt, Victoria, BC V8W 1A4
Tel: 250-356-0050
Fax: 250-953-3928

Assistant Deputy Minister, Allison Bond
Tel: 250-953-3924
Fax: 250-953-3928
Executive Director, Employment Program Management & Development, Sergei Bouslov
Tel: 250-356-8128
Fax: 250-387-2069
Executive Director, Service Delivery, Tami Currie
Tel: 250-387-9625
Fax: 250-356-2734
Tami.Currie@gov.bc.ca
Director, Multiculturalism Unit, Meharoona Ghani
Tel: 604-660-5140
Fax: 604-775-0670
Director, Employment & Labour Market Programming, Anne A. Hill
Tel: 250-387-2098
Fax: 250-387-2069
Anne.A.Hill@gov.bc.ca
Director, Stakeholder Relationships, Rachel Holmes
Tel: 250-953-3917
Fax: 250-953-3928
Rachel.Holmes@gov.bc.ca
Acting Director, Planning & Reporting, Tiffany Ma
Tel: 250-953-4514
Fax: 250-953-3928
Tiffany.Ma@gov.bc.ca
Director, Disabilities & Specialized Employment, Sandy Rodgers
Tel: 604-775-2065
Fax: 604-775-2075
Sandy.Rodgers@gov.bc.ca
Executive Project Director, ICM Branch, Dexter Ratcliff
Tel: 250-216-8721
Project Director, Social Integration, Bernard Achampong
Tel: 250-953-4538
Fax: 250-953-3928
Bernard.Achampong@gov.bc.ca
Project Director, Business Transformation, Linda Bradford
Tel: 250-953-3917
Fax: 250-387-2089
Linda.Bradford@gov.bc.ca

Integrated Case Management
PO Box 9436 Prov Govt, Victoria, BC V8W 9W3
Tel: 250-356-6633

Assistant Deputy Minister, Jill Kot
Tel: 250-356-6633
Fax: 250-356-1053
Executive Director, Kathleen Asher
Tel: 250-356-2688
Fax: 250-356-1053
Executive Director, Robert O'Neill
Tel: 250-356-9253
Fax: 250-356-5405
Executive Director, Wayne Powell
Tel: 250-387-2223
Fax: 250-387-9737
Director, Vendor Management, Brad Boquist
Tel: 250-387-1568
Director, Solution Alignment, Marcin Zaranski
Tel: 250-387-5129

Management Services Division
PO Box 9940 Prov Govt, Victoria, BC V8W 9R2
Tel: 250-387-3159
Fax: 250-387-2418

Assistant Deputy Minister/Executive Financial Officer, Wes Boyd
Tel: 250-387-3159
Fax: 250-387-2418
Wes.Boyd@gov.bc.ca
Executive Director/Chief Financial Officer, Financial & Administrative Services Branch, Len Dawes
Tel: 250-356-7047
Fax: 250-356-5994
Len.Dawes@gov.bc.ca
Executive Director/Chief Information Officer, Information Management Branch, Jeff Gauthier
Tel: 250-387-3112
Fax: 250-387-6439
Jeff.Gauthier@gov.bc.ca
Executive Director, Engagement & Workforce Development, David Glockzin
Tel: 250-387-7667
Fax: 250-387-4264
David.Glockzin@gov.bc.ca
Acting Director, Business Services, Shelley Burnham
Tel: 250-356-8988
Fax: 250-356-1612
Shelley.Burnham@gov.bc.ca
Director, Financial Accounting & Reporting, Rob Byers
Tel: 250-387-2132
Fax: 250-356-1051
Rob.Byers@gov.bc.ca
Director, Infrastructure Services, Claudia Lang
Tel: 250-356-5103
Fax: 250-387-6439
Claudia.Lang@gov.bc.ca
Director, Facilities & Workplace Solutions, Joyce Metcalfe
Tel: 250-217-4971
Fax: 250-356-5994
Joyce.Metcalfe@gov.bc.ca
Director, Budget Management & Assurance, Cindy Petrowski
Tel: 250-387-1623
Fax: 250-356-5994
Cindy.Petrowski@gov.bc.ca
Director, Application Services, Jay Prill
Tel: 250-356-7661
Fax: 250-387-6439
Jay.Prill@gov.bc.ca
Director, Corporate Planning & Performance, Kashi Tanaka
Tel: 250-387-9075

Policy & Research Division
PO Box 9936 Prov Govt, Victoria, BC V8W 9R2
Tel: 250-356-5065
Fax: 250-387-5775

Assistant Deputy Minister, Molly Harrington
Tel: 250-356-5065
Fax: 250-387-2418
Executive Director, Employment & Income Assistance Branch, Robert Bruce
Tel: 250-387-1486
Fax: 250-387-8164
Robert.Bruce@gov.bc.ca
Executive Director, Employment & Income Assistance Branch, Mark Medgyesi
Tel: 250-953-3923
Fax: 250-387-8164
Mark.Medgyesi@gov.bc.ca
Executive Director, Disability Services Branch, Harb Sihota
Tel: 250-356-0923
Fax: 250-387-8164
Harb.Sihota@gov.bc.ca
Executive Director, Ministry of Social Development-Ministry of Children & Family Development Legislation & Litigation Branch, Michael Turnaski
Tel: 250-387-6434
Fax: 250-356-8182
Michael.Turanski@gov.bc.ca
Other Communications: Cell Phone:250-588-9677
Executive Director, Provincial Services, Debi Upton
Tel: 250-356-8506
Fax: 250-387-8261
Director, Legislation, Leah M. Bailey
Tel: 250-387-0372
Fax: 250-356-8182
Leah.Bailey@gov.bc.ca
Director, Employment & Income Assistance Branch, Alison Bath
Tel: 250-356-5002
Fax: 250-387-8164
Alison.Bath@gov.bc.ca
Director, Health Assistance Branch, Paul Beardmore
Tel: 250-356-1746
Fax: 250-356-7290
Paul.Beardmore@gov.bc.ca
Director, Disability Services Branch, Ian Brethour
Tel: 250-387-3764
Fax: 250-387-8164
Director, Disability Services Branch, Odette Dantzer
Tel: 250-356-2249
Fax: 250-387-8164
Director, Evaluation, Performance Management & Intergovernmental Relations, Linda DeBenedictis
Tel: 250-387-4622
Fax: 250-387-8164
Linda.DeBenedictis@gov.bc.ca

Regional Services Division
PO Box 9934 Prov Govt, Victoria, BC V8W 9R2
Tel: 250-387-6905
Fax: 250-387-2418

Assistant Deputy Minister, Sharon Moysey
Tel: 250-387-6905
Fax: 250-387-2418
Executive Director, Fraser Regional Office, Patricia Boyle
Tel: 604-586-2959
Fax: 604-586-2681
Off300@gov.bc.ca
Executive Director, Regional Operations, Janice Nakamura
Tel: 250-356-2220
Fax: 250-952-6450
Executive Director, Prevention & Loss Management Services, Kim Saastad
Tel: 250-356-8200
Fax: 250-356-1615
Executive Director, Vancouver Coastal Regional Office, Nancy Shewchuk
Tel: 604-660-3224
Fax: 604-660-2503
Executive Director, Interior Regional Office, Bruce Smith
Tel: 888-939-9278
Fax: 250-828-4614
Bruce.Smith@gov.bc.ca
Other Communications: Alternate Phone: 250-828-4600
Director, Policy Interpretation & Stakeholder Relations Liaison Branch, Judy D'Gal
Tel: 250-387-9271
Fax: 250-952-6450
Director, Project Management & Implementation Branch, Raymond Fieltsch
Tel: 250-387-3865
Fax: 250-952-6450
Raymond.Fieltsch@gov.bc.ca

Prevention & Loss Management Services
PO Box 9930 Prov Govt, Victoria, BC V8W 9R2
Tel: 250-356-8200
Fax: 250-356-1615

British Columbia Ministry of Transportation & Infrastructure

PO Box 9850 Prov Govt, Victoria, BC V8W 9T5
Tel: 250-387-3198
Fax: 250-356-7706
www.gov.bc.ca/tran
Other Communication: Media Enquiries, Phone: 250-387-7787, Fax: 250-356-2950

The mission of the Ministry of Transportation & Infrastructure is to plan tranportation networks, to establish policies, to provide transportation services & infrastructure, & to administer acts & regulations related to transportation & infrastructure.
Specific responsibilities include the following: working with partners to fund cost-effective public transit, ferry services, & cycling networks; managing funding for public infrastructure; maintaining highways; setting commercial vehicle operating standards & overseeing vehicle safety inspections; & licensing commercial passenger transporation.

Acts Administered:
British Columbia Rail Benefits (First Nations) Trust Act
British Columbia Railway Act
British Columbia Transit Act
Coastal Ferry Act (except Part 4 & ss. 70, 72 & 73)
Commercial Transport Act (s. 3; ss. 1, 4, 5, 8, 9, 11, & 12, as those provisions relate to highway infrastructure & weigh scales; & ss. 1, 4, 5, 8, 9, 11, 12, & 14, as those provisions relate to Commercial Vehicle Safety &Enforcement)
Industrial Roads Act
Land Title Act (s. 77.2)
Motor Vehicle Act (ss. 116.1, 118.94-118.992, 119-125.1, 126-135.1, 136-148.1, 149-169.1, 170-182, 185-209, 212-212.2, 213, 214, 216-218, 219, 223, 237, 239-240; ss. 1, 75-76, 78, 83, 83.1, 183 & 210; ss. 1, 66, 73, 75-76,78, 82-83, 210, 211, 220, 238)
Passenger Transportation Act
Public Works Agreement Act
Railway Act (except s. 33)
Railway Safety Act
Significant Projects Streamlining Act
South Coast British Columbia Transportation Authority Act (except Part 7.1)
Transport of Dangerous Goods Act
Transportation Act
Transportation Investment Act

Minister, Transportation & Infrastructure, Hon. Mary Polak
Tel: 250-387-1978
Fax: 250-356-2290
Minister.Transportation@gov.bc.ca
Social Media: twitter.com/MaryPolakMLA, www.facebook.com/MLAPolak
PO Box 9055 Prov Govt Sta.
Victoria, BC V8W 9E2

Deputy Minister, Grant Main
Tel: 250-387-3280
Fax: 250-387-6431
Grant.Main@gov.bc.ca
PO Box 9850 Prov Govt Sta.
Victoria, BC V8W 9T5

Manager, Executive Operations, Vanessa Ginger
Tel: 250-387-3077
Fax: 250-387-6431
Vanessa.Ginger@gov.bc.ca

Information Officer, Katerina Anastasiadis
Tel: 250-660-5887
Fax: 250-660-6833

Coordinator, Documents, Elizabeth Nicholls
Tel: 250-356-1937
Fax: 250-387-6431
Elizabeth.Nicholls@gov.bc.ca

Associated Agencies, Boards & Commissions:
- **British Columbia Ferry Services Inc.**
- **British Columbia Railway Company**

#600, 221 West Esplanade
North Vancouver, BC V7M 3J3
Tel: 604-678-4735
Fax: 604-678-4736
westerhouts@bcrco.com
www.bcrco.com
- **British Columbia Transit**

520 Gorge Rd. East
Victoria, BC V8W 2P3
Tel: 250-385-2551
Fax: 250-995-5639
www.bctransit.com
Other Communication: Community transit information: transitinfo@bctransit.com; Media: pr@bctransit.com
A provincial crown agency, BC Transit coordinates the delivery of public transportation in British Columbia, outside the Greater Vancouver Regional District. The corporation's specific role, in accordance with the BC Transit Act, is the planning, acquisition, construction, operation, & maintenance of public passenger transportation systems & rail systems.
- **Passenger Transportation Board**

#202, 940 Blanshard St.
PO Box 9850 Prov Govt
Victoria, BC V8W 9T5
Tel: 250-953-3777
Fax: 250-953-3788
ptboard@gov.bc.ca
www.ptboard.bc.ca
The Passenger Transportation Board carries out its responsibilities in accordance with the Passenger Transportation Act. The independent tribunal makes decisions regarding the operation of passenger directed vehicles and inter-city buses in British Columbia.

Finance & Management Services Department
PO Box 9850, Victoria, BC V8W 9T5
Tel: 250-387-3100
Fax: 250-387-6431
Assistant Deputy Minister, Finance & Management Services, Nancy Bain
Tel: 250-387-3100
Fax: 250-387-6431
Nancy.Bain@gov.bc.ca
Chief Financial Officer, Financial Management, Dave Stewart
Tel: 250-387-7505
Fax: 250-356-7706
Dave.Stewart@gov.bc.ca
Other Communications: Cell Phone: 250-818-5806
Executive Director, Crown Agencies, Carol Bishop
Tel: 250-387-1936
Fax: 250-356-7706
Carol.Bishop@gov.bc.ca
Other Communications: Cell Phone: 250-888-1251
Executive Director/Chief Information Officer, Information Management Branch, Debbie Fritz
Tel: 250-387-3580
Fax: 250-356-7184
Debbie.Fritz@gov.bc.ca
Director, Reporting & Analysis, Gail Silvestrini
Tel: 250-387-3104
Fax: 250-387-7645
Gail.Silvestrini@gov.bc.ca
Director, Finance (British Columbia Transportation Finance Authority), Gary So
Tel: 250-387-7873
Fax: 250-387-7645
Gary.So@gov.bc.ca

Highways Department
PO Box 9850, Victoria, BC V8W 9T5
Tel: 250-387-3260
Fax: 250-387-6431
Assistant Deputy Minister, Mike Proudfoot
Tel: 250-387-3260
Fax: 250-387-6431
Dave.Duncan@gov.bc.ca
Chief Engineer, Dirk Nyland
Tel: 250-387-2310
Fax: 250-387-7735
Dirk.Nyland@gov.bc.ca
Other Communications: Cell Phone: 250-812-6645
Executive Director, Highway Operations, Shanna Mason
Tel: 250-387-0159
Fax: 250-387-6431
Shanna.Mason@gov.bc.ca
Other Communications: Cell Phone: 250-889-3707
Director, Provincial Field Services, Keith Callander
Tel: 250-828-4151
Fax: 250-828-4277
Keith.Callander@gov.bc.ca
Other Communications: Cell Phone: 604-880-2336
Director, Construction & Maintenance, Rodney Chapman
Tel: 250-387-7626
Fax: 250-356-8143
Rodney.Chapman@gov.bc.ca
Other Communications: Cell Phone: 250-213-7499
Director, Rehabilitation & Maintenance, Reg Fredrickson
Tel: 250-387-7627
Fax: 250-356-7276
Reg.Fredrickson@gov.bc.ca
Other Communications: Cell Phone: 250-480-9729
Director, Social Media Branch, Russel Lolacher
Tel: 250-356-9682
Fax: 250-356-8767
Russel.Lolacher@gov.bc.ca
Other Communications: Cell Phone: 778-679-2482
Director, Commercial Vehicle Safety & Enforcement Branch, Brian Murray
Tel: 250-953-4024
Fax: 250-952-0578
Brian.Murray@gov.bc.ca
Other Communications: Cell Phone: 778-888-8436
Director, Business Management Branch, Sandra Toth Nacey
Tel: 250-356-9768
Fax: 250-256-8767
Sandra.TothNacey@gov.bc.ca
Other Communications: Cell Phone: 778-679-2483
Director, Engineering Systems, Al Szczawinski
Tel: 250-387-7777
Fax: 250-387-8081
Al.Szczawinski@gov.bc.ca

Partnerships Department
PO Box 9850 Prov Govt, Victoria, BC V8W 9T5
Tel: 250-356-1403
Fax: 250-387-6431
Acting Assistant Deputy Minister, Kirsten Pedersen
Kirsten.Pedersen@gov.bc.ca
Director, Properties & Land Management Branch, Svein Haugen
Tel: 250-356-7904
Fax: 250-356-6970
Svein.Haugen@gov.bc.ca
Director, Transit Branch, Jim Hester
Tel: 250-387-6024
Fax: 250-387-5012
Jim.Hester@gov.bc.ca
Director, Real Esate, Richard Myhill Jones
Tel: 604-678-4703
Fax: 604-678-4702
Richard.MyhillJones@gov.bc.ca
Director, Procurement & Operations, Bruce McAllister
Tel: 250-356-7108
Fax: 250-356-6970
Bruce.McAllister@gov.bc.ca
Director, Partnership & Project Development, Bob Steele
Tel: 250-356-2051
Fax: 250-356-2112
Bob.Steele@gov.bc.ca

Transportation Policy & Programs Department
PO Box 9850 Prov Govt, Victoria, BC V8W 9T5
Tel: 250-387-5062
Fax: 250-387-6431
Assistant Deputy Minister, Jacquie Dawes
Tel: 250-387-5062
Fax: 250-387-6431
Jacquie.Dawes@gov.bc.ca
Registrar/Director, Passenger Transportation Branch, Dawn Major
Tel: 604-453-4278
Dawn.Major@gov.bc.ca
Other Communications: Cell Phone: 604-992-9140
Acting Director, Transportation Policy Branch, Greg Gilks
Tel: 250-387-0882
Fax: 250-356-0897
Greg.Gilks@gov.bc.ca

Infrasturcture Department
PO Box 9850 Prov Govt, Victoria, BC V8W 9T5
Tel: 250-387-6742
Fax: 250-387-6431

Assistant Deputy Minister, Kevin Richter
Tel: 250-387-6742
Fax: 250-387-6431
Kevin.Richter@gov.bc.ca
Executive Director, Planning & Programming Branch, David Marr
Tel: 250-356-2100
Fax: 250-356-0897
David.Marr@gov.bc.ca
Acting Executive Project Director, Evergreen Line Project, Jon Buckle
Tel: 604-927-4452
Fax: 604-927-4453
Jon.Buckle@gov.bc.ca
Director, Marine Branch, Krik Handrahan
Tel: 250-952-0678
Fax: 250-356-0897
Kirk.Handrahan@gov.bc.ca
Director, Infrastructure Development, Renee Mounteney
Tel: 250-953-3689
Fax: 250-356-0897
Renee.Mounteney@gov.bc.ca
Other Communications: Cell Phone: 250-208-8876

British Columbia Utilities Commission

900 Howe St., 6th Fl., PO Box 250, Vancouver, BC V6Z 2N3
Tel: 604-660-4700
Fax: 604-660-1102
Toll-Free: 800-663-1385
commission.secretary@bcuc.com
www.bcuc.com

The British Columbia Utilities Commission is an independent regulatory agency of the Provincial Government of British Columbia. The Commission's regulates the province's natural gas & electricity utilities. Other activities of the Utilities Commission include the regulation of universal compulsory automobile insurance & intra-provincial pipelines.
Acts Administered:
Utilities Commission Act

Chair/Chief Executive Officer, Len Kelsey
Tel: 604-660-4757
len.kelsey@bcuc.com

Commission Secretary, Erica Hamilton
Tel: 604-660-4727
Erica.Hamilton@bcuc.com

Acting Commission Secretary, Alanna Gillis
Tel: 604-660-4727
alanna.gillis@bcuc.com

Director, Strategic Services, Doug Chong
Tel: 604-660-4737
doug.chong@bcuc.com

Director, Rates & Finance, Philip W. Nakoneshny
Tel: 604-660-4736
philip.nakoneshny@bcuc.com

Director, Emerging Technologies & Innovation, Mark Thomas
Tel: 604-660-4726
mark.thomas@bcuc.com

Director, Engineering & Energy Markets, Brian Williston
Tel: 604-660-4773
brian.williston@bcuc.com

British Columbia Vital Statistics Agency

PO Box 9657 Prov Govt, Victoria, BC V8W 9P3
Tel: 250-952-2681
Fax: 250-952-9097
VSOFFCEO@gov.bc.ca
www.vs.gov.bc.ca

The Vital Statistics Agency operates under the Ministry of Health, and offers the following services: Birth registration; marriage certificates; death certificates; wills; name changes; and geneaology.

Chief Executive Officer, Jack Shewchuk
Tel: 250-952-9039
Fax: 250-952-9097
Jack.Shewchuk@gov.bc.ca

Director, Bruce Klette
Tel: 250-952-9040
Fax: 250-952-9097
Bruce.Klette@gov.bc.ca

Workers' Compensation Board of British Columbia

PO Box 5350 Terminal, Vancouver, BC V6B 5L5
Tel: 604-276-3100
Fax: 604-276-3247
Toll-Free: 888-621-7233
www.worksafebc.com

Other Communication: Head Office Physical Address: 6951 Westminster Hwy., Richmond, BC; Claims: 604-231-8888, Fax: 604-233-9777; Employer services/Assessments: 604-244-6181
The Workers' Compensation Board of British Columbia, or WorkSafeBC, assists workers & employers in British Columbia by promoting health & safety in workplaces. WorkSafeBC's key responsiblities are as follows: consultation with & education of employers & workers; monitoring compliance with the Occupational Health & Safety Regulation; & provision of return-to-work compensation, rehabilitation, health care benefits, & other services for parties affected by work-related injuries or diseases.

Chair, George Morfitt

President/Chief Executive Officer, David Anderson

Chief Financial Officer/Senior Vice-President, Finance Division, Steve Barnett

Senior Vice-President, Corporate Affairs, Roberta Ellis

Senior Vice-President, Operations, Diana Miles

Vice-President, Human Resources & Facilities, Pamela Cohen

Vice-President, Claims Services, Ian Munroe

Vice-President, Prevention Services, Betty Pirs

Vice-President, Industry Services & Sustainability, Donna Wilson

General Counsel & Secretary, Ed Bates

Government of Manitoba

Seat of Government: Legislative Building, Rm. 237, Winnipeg, MB R3C 0V8
Tel: 204-945-3636
Fax: 204-948-2507
clerkla@leg.gov.mb.ca
www.gov.mb.ca

The Province of Manitoba entered Confederation July 15, 1870. It has an area of 647,797 km2, & the StatsCan census population in 2011 was 1,208,268.

Office of the Lieutenant Governor

Legislative Building, #235, 450 Broadway Ave., Winnipeg, MB R3C 0V8
Tel: 204-945-2753
Fax: 204-945-4329
ltgov@leg.gov.mb.ca
www.lg.gov.mb.ca

Lieutenant Governor, Hon. Philip S. Lee, C.M., O.M.

Chief of Staff/ Private Secretary, Phyllis Fraser
Tel: 204-945-2752
phyllis.fraser@leg.gov.mb.ca

Scheduling Coordinator, Elaine Embury
Tel: 204-945-2753
elaine.embury@leg.gov.mb.ca

Government House Event Coordinator, Lisa Vermette
Tel: 204-945-2753
lisa.vermette@leg.gov.mb.ca

Office of the Premier

Legislative Building, #204, 450 Broadway Ave., Winnipeg, MB R3C 0V8
Tel: 204-945-3714
Fax: 204-949-1484
premier@leg.gov.mb.ca
www.gov.mb.ca

Premier, Hon. Greg Selinger
Tel: 204-945-3714
Fax: 204-949-1484

Deputy Premier, Hon. Rosann Wowchuk
Tel: 204-945-3952
Fax: 204-945-6057

Clerk of the Executive Council & Cabinet Secretary, Paul Vogt
Tel: 204-945-5640
Fax: 204-945-8390

Chief of Staff, Michael Balagus
Tel: 204-945-8753

Administrative Officer, Sonia Stubler
Tel: 204-945-1494

Press Secretary to Cabinet, Rachel Morgan
Tel: 204-945-1494

Executive Council

Legislative Building, 450 Broadway Ave., Winnipeg, MB R3C 0V8
The following is a list of Cabinet Ministers of the Government of Manitoba in order of precedence:

Premier; President, Executive Council; Minister, Federal-Provincial Relations; Minister Responsible. Francophone Affairs, Hon. Gregory Selinger
Tel: 204-945-3714
Fax: 204-949-1484
premier@leg.gov.mb.ca
Legislative Building
#204,450 Broadway
Winnipeg, MB R3C 0V8

Minister, Infrastructure & Transportation; Minister Responsible, Emergency Measures; Minister charged with the administration of The Manitoba Lotteries Corporation Act, Hon. Steve Ashton
Tel: 204-945-3723
Fax: 204-945-7610
minmit@leg.gov.mb.ca
Legislative Building
#203, 450 Broadway
Winnipeg, MB R3C 0V8

Minister, Innovation, Energy, & Mines; Minister charged with the administration of The Gaming Control Act, & the administration of The Manitoba Hydro Act, Hon. David Chomiak
Tel: 204-945-5356
Fax: 204-948-2692
miniem@leg.gov.mb.ca
Legislative Building
#343, 450 Broadway
Winnipeg, MB R3C 0V8

Minister, Conservation & Water Stewardship, Hon. Gord Mackintosh
Tel: 204-945-3730
Fax: 204-945-3586
minconws@leg.gov.mb.ca
Legislative Building
#330, 450 Broadway
Winnipeg, MB R3C 0V8

Deputy Premier; Minister, Aboriginal & Northern Affairs; Minister Responsible, Sport, Aboriginal Education, & the MB Floodway & East Side Road Authority Act; Minister charged with the administration of The Communities EconomicDevelopment Fund Act, Hon. Eric Robinson
Tel: 204-945-3719
Fax: 204-945-8374
minna@leg.gov.mb.ca
Legislative Building
#344, 450 Broadway
Winnipeg, MB R3C 0V8

Minister, Local Government, Hon. Ron Lemieux
Tel: 204-945-3788
Fax: 204-945-1383
minlg@leg.gov.mb.ca
Legislative Building
#103, 450 Broadway
Winnipeg, MB R3C 0V8

Minister, Finance; Minister Responsible, Civil Service; Minister charged with the administration of The Crown Corporations Public Review & AccountabilityAct, Hon. Stan Struthers
Tel: 204-945-3952
Fax: 204-945-6057
minfin@leg.gov.mb.ca
Legislative Building
#103, 450 Broadway
Winnipeg, MB R3C 0V8

Minister, Education, Hon. Nancy Allan
Tel: 204-945-3720
Fax: 204-945-1291

minedu@leg.gov.mb.ca
Legislative Building
#168, 450 Broadway
Winnipeg, MB R3C 0V8

Minister, Healthy Living, Seniors, & Consumer Affairs; Minister charged with the administration of The Liquor Control Act, Hon. Jim Rondeau
Tel: 204-945-1373
Fax: 204-945-2703
Minhliv@leg.gov.mb.ca
Legislative Building
#310, 450Broadway
Winnipeg, MB R3C 0V8

Minister, Entrepreneurship, Training & Trade, Hon. Peter Bjornson
Tel: 204-945-0067
Fax: 204-945-4882
minett@leg.gov.mb.ca
Legislative Building
#333, 450 Broadway
Winnipeg, MB R3C 0V8

Minister, Immigration & Multiculturalism, Hon. Christine Melnick
Tel: 204-945-1133
Fax: 204-948-2684
minwsd@leg.gov.mb.ca
Legislative Building
#314, 450 Broadway
Winnipeg, MB R3C 0V8

Minister, Health, Hon. Theresa Oswald
Tel: 204-945-3731
Fax: 204-945-0441
minhlt@leg.gov.mb.ca
Legislative Building
#302, 450 Broadway
Winnipeg, MB R3C 0V8

Minister, Housing & Community Development, Hon. Kerri Irvin-Ross
Tel: 204-945-6190
Fax: 204-945-1491
minhcd@leg.gov.mb.ca
Legislative Building
#358, 450 Broadway
Winnipeg, MB R3C 0V8

Minister, Justice; Attorney General; Minister Responsible, Constitutional Affairs; Minister, charged with the administration of The Manitoba Public Insurance Act; Keeper of the Great Seal of the Province ofManitoba, Hon. Andrew Swan
Tel: 204-945-3728
Fax: 204-945-2517
minjus@leg.gov.mb.ca
Legislative Building
#104, 450 Broadway
Winnipeg, MB R3C 0V8

Minister, Family Services & Labour; Minister Responsible for the Status of Women; Minister, charged with the administration of The Workers Compensation Act; Government House Leader, Hon. Jennifer Howard
Tel: 204-945-4173
Fax: 204-945-5149
minfsl@leg.gov.mb.ca
Legislative Building
#357, 450 Broadway
Winnipeg, MB R3C 0V8

Minister, Culture, Heritage, & Tourism, Hon. Flor Marcelino
Tel: 204-945-3729
Fax: 204-945-5223
mincht@leg.gov.mb.ca
Legislative Building
#118, 450 Broadway
Winnipeg, MB R3C 0V8

Minister, Advanced Education & Literacy, Hon. Erin Selby
Tel: 204-945-0825
Fax: 204-948-2216
minaed@leg.gov.mb.ca
Legislative Building
#162, 450 Broadway
Winnipeg, MB R3C 0V8

Minister, Childrem & Youth Opportunities; Minister Responsible for Healthy Child Manitoba, Hon. Kevin Chief
Tel: 204-945-1133
Fax: 204-948-2519
mincyo@leg.gov.mb.ca
Legislative Building
#314, 450 Broadway
Winnipeg, MB R3C0V8

Minister, Agriculture, Food, & Rural Initiatives, Hon. Ron Kostyshyn
Tel: 204-945-3722
Fax: 204-945-3470
minagr@leg.gov.mb.ca
Legislative Building
#165, 450 Broadway
Winnipeg, MB R3C 0V8

Cabinet Office
Legislative Assistant to the Premier, Bidhu Jha
Tel: 204-945-6021
bjha@leg.gov.mb.ca
Legislative Assistant, Agriculture, Food & Rural Initiatives, Thomas Nevakshonoff
Tel: 204-945-4966
tnevakshonoff@leg.gov.mb.ca
Legislative Assistant, Brandon & Western Manitoba, Drew Caldwell
Legislative Assistant, Culture, Heritage, Tourism & Sport, Flor Marcelino
Legislative Assistant, Family Services & Housing, Doug Martindale
Tel: 204-945-2645
dmartindale@leg.gov.mb.ca
Legislative Assistant, Labour & Immigration, Justice, Marilyn Brick

Cabinet Committees
Community & Economic Development Committee; Treasury Board Committee; Priorities & Planning Committee

Manitoba Legislative Assembly

c/o Clerk's Office, Legislative Bldg., #237, 450 Broadway, Winnipeg, MB R3C 0V8
Tel: 204-945-3636
Fax: 204-948-2507
clerkla@leg.gov.mb.ca
www.gov.mb.ca/legislature

Clerk of the Legislative Assembly, Patricia Chaychuk
Tel: 204-945-3636
clerk@leg.gov.mb.ca

Speaker of the House, Hon. Daryl Reid
Tel: 204-945-3706
speaker@leg.gov.mb.ca

Ombudsman, Irene Hamilton
Tel: 204-982-9130
Toll-free: 800-665-0531
Fax: 204-942-7803
ombudsma@ombudsman.mb.ca

Commissioner, Conflict of Interest, Ron Perozzo
Tel: 204-948-1018
Fax: 204-945-4585

Children's Advocate, Ms. Billie Schibler
Tel: 204-988-7440
Toll-free: 800-263-7146
Fax: 204-988-7472
bschibler@childrensadvocate.mb.ca

Manager, Investigation, Access & Privacy, Nancy Love
Tel: 204-982-9130
nancy.love@gov.mb.ca

Auditor General, Carol Bellringer
Tel: 204-945-3790
carol.bellringer@gov.mb.ca

ADM/Chief Financial Officer, Mala Sachdeva
Tel: 204-945-2540
mala.sachdeva@gov.mb.ca

Journals Clerk, Claude Michaud
Tel: 204-945-6331

Government Caucus Office (New Democratic Party)
Legislative Bldg., #234, 450 Broadway Ave., Winnipeg, MB R3C 0V8
Tel: 204-945-3710
Fax: 204-948-2005
www.ndpcaucus.mb.ca

Premier & Leader, Hon. Greg Selinger
Tel: 204-945-3714
Fax: 204-949-1484
premier@leg.gov.mb.ca
Deputy Premier, Hon. Rosann Wowchuk
Tel: 204-945-3722
Fax: 204-945-3470
Government House Leader, Hon. David Walter Chomiak
Tel: 204-945-3728
Fax: 204-945-2517

Progressive Conservative Caucus Office
Legislative Building, #227, 450 Broadway Ave., Winnipeg, MB R3C 0V8
Tel: 204-945-3709
Fax: 204-945-1284
Toll-Free: 800-282-8069
pccaucus@leg.gov.mb.ca
www.manpc.mb.ca

Leader of the Opposition, Hugh McFadyen
Tel: 204-945-3593
Fax: 204-945-1299
hugh.mcfadyen@leg.gov.mb.ca
Communications Officer, Liz Peters
Tel: 204-945-5519
Fax: 204-945-5921
liz.peters@leg.gov.mb.ca

Office of the Liberal Party of Canada in Manitoba
635 Broadway Ave., Winnipeg, MB R3C 0X1
Tel: 204-988-9380
Fax: 204-284-1492
manager@manitobaliberals.ca
mlp.manitobaliberals.ca

Leader, Hon. Jon Gerrard
Tel: 204-945-5194
Fax: 204-948-3220
jon.gerrard@leg.gov.mb.ca

Legislative Committees
Legislative Building, #249, 450 Broadway Ave., Winnipeg, MB R3C 0V8
Fax: 204-945-0038

Contact, Committee Clerks, Rick Yarish
Tel: 204-945-4729
rick.yarish@leg.gov.mb.ca

Fortieth Legislature - Manitoba

Legislative Building, 450 Broadway Ave., Winnipeg, MB R3C 0V8
Tel: 204-945-3636
Fax: 204-948-2507
clerkla@leg.gov.mb.ca
www.gov.mb.ca/legislature

Last General Election: Oct. 4, 2011.
Next General Election: Oct. 6, 2015.
Party Standings (July 2012): New Democratic Party 37;
Progressive Conservative Party 19;
Liberal 1;
Total - 57.
MLA Pay (effective Mar. 26, 2011):
MLA basic annual salary $85,564;
Additional Annual Salaries:
Premier $55,944;
Cabinet Ministers $36,745;
Cabinet Ministers without portfolio $32,570;
Speaker $45,931;
Deputy Speaker $9,047;
Leader of the Official Opposition $45,931;
Deputy Chairperson of the Committee of the Whole $6,462;
Government House Leader $9,047;
Government Whip $6,462;
Official Opposition House Leader $6,462;
Official Opposition Whip $5,171;
Leader of Other Recognized Parties $40,713;
Other Opposition House Leader $5,171;
Other Opposition Whip $3,880;
Caucus Chair $5,570;
Permanent Chairperson, Standing or Special Committees $166.00 per meeting to an annual maximum of $3,880.
All members of the Legislative Assembly of Manitoba may be reached at the following address: 450 Broadway, Winnipeg, MB R3C 0V8.
The following is a list of Mmembers of the Legislative Assembly of Manitoba, with their constituency, number of registered voters in the constituency, party affiliation, & contact information:
Members of the Legislative Assembly of Manitoba
Minister, Education, Hon. Nancy Allan
Constituency: St. Vital *No. of Constituents:* 13,918, New Democratic Party
Tel: 204-945-3720
Fax: 204-945-1291
minedu@leg.gov.mb.ca
www.nancyallan.ca
Other Communications: Constituency Phone: 204-237-8771; Fax: 204-231-0499
Social Media: www.facebook.com/nancyforstvital
Constituency Office

51D St. Anne'sRd.
Winnipeg, MB R2M 2Y4
James Allum
Constituency: Fort Garry-Riverview *No. of Constituents:* 14,307, New Democratic Party
Tel: 204-945-3710
james.allum@leg.gov.mb.ca
Other Communications: Constituency Phone: 204-475-2270; Fax: 204-475-2293
Social Media: www.facebook.com/group.php?gid=149263358470609
Constituency Office
#9, 222 Osborne St. South
Winnipeg, MB R3L1Z3
Rob Altemeyer
Constituency: Wolseley *No. of Constituents:* 12,624, New Democratic Party
Tel: 204-945-3710
Fax: 204-948-2005
rob.altemeyer@leg.gov.mb.ca
Other Communications: Constituency Phone: 204-775-8575; Fax: 204-779-0326
Social Media: www.facebook.com/RobAltemeyerMLA
Constituency Office
#202, 222 Furby St.
Winnipeg, MB R3C 2A7
Minister, Infrastructure & Transportation; Minister Responsible, Emergency Measures; Minister charged with the administration of The Manitoba Lotteries Corporation Act, Hon. Steve Ashton
Constituency: Thompson *No. of Constituents:* 10,328, New Democratic Party
Tel: 204-945-3723
Fax: 204-945-7610
minmit@leg.gov.mb.ca; ashton@mts.net
www.steveashton.ca
Other Communications: Constituency Phone: 204-778-8601; Fax: 866-279-8651
Constituency Office
3 Station Rd., 2nd Fl.
Thompson, MB R8N 0N3
Minister, Entrepreneurship, Training, & Trade, Hon. Peter Bjornson
Constituency: Gimli *No. of Constituents:* 14,769, New Democratic Party
Tel: 204-945-0067
Fax: 204-945-4882
minett@leg.gov.mb.ca
Other Communications: Constituency Phone: 204-642-4977; Fax: 204-642-8991
Constituency Office
#105, 94 First Ave.
Gimli, MB R3C 0V8
Sharon Blady
Constituency: Kirkfield Park *No. of Constituents:* 15,329, New Democratic Party
Tel: 204-945-0932
Fax: 204-948-2005
sharon.blady@leg.gov.mb.ca
Other Communications: Constituency Phone: 204-832-2318; Fax: 204-837-1023
Constituency Office
3059 Portage Ave., #B
Winnipeg, MB R3K OW4
Erna Braun
Constituency: Rossmere *No. of Constituents:* 15,921, New Democratic Party
Tel: 204-945-3710
Fax: 204-948-2005
erna.braun@leg.gov.mb.ca
Other Communications: Constituency Phone: 204-667-7244; Fax: 204-668-8473
Constituency Office
#3, 935 McLeod Ave.
Winnipeg, MB R2GOY4
Stuart Briese
Constituency: Agassiz *No. of Constituents:* 13,509, Progressive Conservative
Tel: 204-945-4698
Fax: 204-945-5921
stuart.briese@leg.gov.mb.ca
Other Communications: Constituency Phone: 204-476-3736; Fax: 204-476-3462
Constituency Office
PO Box 1482
Neepawa, MB R0J 1H0
Drew Caldwell
Constituency: Brandon East *No. of Constituents:* 13,305, New Democratic Party
Tel: 204-945-3710
Fax: 204-948-2005
drew.caldwell@leg.gov.mb.ca
Other Communications: Constituency Phone: 204-727-8734; Fax: 204-725-1795
Constituency Office
119 - 10th St.
Brandon, MB R7A4E7
Minister, Children & Youth Opportunities; Minister Responsible for Healthy Child Manitoba, Hon. Kevin Chief
Constituency: Point Douglas *No. of Constituents:* 11,858, New Democratic Party
Tel: 204-945-1133
Fax: 204-948-2519
mincyo@leg.gov.mb.ca
Other Communications: Constituency Phone:204-421-9126; Fax: 204-421-9127
Constituency Office
788 Selkirk Ave.
Winnipeg, MB R2W 2N6
Minister, Innovation, Energy, & Mines; Minister charged with the administration of The Gaming Control Act, & the administration of The Manitoba Hydro Act, Hon. David Chomiak
Constituency: Kildonan *No. of Constituents:* 14,775, New Democratic Party
Tel: 204-945-5356
Fax: 204-945-2692
miniem@leg.gov.mb.ca
Other Communications: Constituency Phone: 204-334-5060; Fax: 204-334-4878
Constituency Office
640 Leila Ave.
Winnipeg, MB R2V 3N7
Deanne Crothers
Constituency: St. James *No. of Constituents:* 14,403, New Democratic Party
Tel: 204-945-3710
Fax: 204-948-2005
deanne.crothers@leg.gov.mb.ca
Other Communications: Constituency Phone: 204-415-0883; Fax: 204-415-0747
Constituency Office
2003 PortageAve.
Winnipeg, MB R3J 0K3
Cliff Cullen
Constituency: Spruce Woods *No. of Constituents:* 13,940, Progressive Conservative
Tel: 204-945-5083
Fax: 204-945-5921
cliff.cullen@leg.gov.mb.ca
Other Communications: Constituency Phone: 204-827-3956; Fax: 204-827-3957
Constituency Office
101 BroadwaySt.
PO Box 129
Glenboro, MB R0K 0X0
Greg Dewar
Constituency: Selkirk *No. of Constituents:* 14,053, New Democratic Party
Tel: 204-945-3710
Fax: 204-948-2005
greg.dewar@leg.gov.mb.ca
Other Communications: Constituency Phone: 204-482-7066; Fax: 204-482-4745
Constituency Office
218C Manitoba Ave.
Selkirk, MB R1A0Y5
Myrna Driedger
Constituency: Charleswood *No. of Constituents:* 14,249, Progressive Conservative
Tel: 204-945-3280
Fax: 204-948-2092
myrna.driedger@leg.gov.mb.ca
Other Communications: Constituency Phone: 204-885-0594; Fax: 204-885-5525
Constituency Office
5120B RoblinBlvd.
Winnipeg, MB R3R 0G9
Ralph Eichler
Constituency: Lakeside *No. of Constituents:* 13,451, Progressive Conservative
Tel: 204-945-0541
Fax: 204-948-2092
ralph.eichler@leg.gov.mb.ca
Other Communications: Constituency Phone: 204-467-9482; Fax: 204-467-7580
Constituency Office
323 MainSt.
PO Box 1845
Stonewall, MB ROC 2Z0
Wayne Ewasko
Constituency: Lac du Bonnet *No. of Constituents:* 13,844, Progressive Conservative
Tel: 204-945-8989
Fax: 204-945-6613
wayne.ewasko@leg.gov.mb.ca
Other Communications: Constituency Phone: 204-945-8989; Fax: 204-268-3976
Constituency Office
638 ParkAve.
PO Box 1299
Beausejour, MB R0E 0C0
Cameron Friesen
Constituency: Morden-Winkler *No. of Constituents:* 14,195, Progressive Conservative
Tel: 204-945-4469
Fax: 204-948-2092
cameron.friesen@leg.gov.mb.ca
Other Communications: Constituency Phone: 204-822-1088; Fax: 204-822-1086
Constituency Office
108A - 8th St.
Morden, MB R6M 1Y7
Dave Gaudreau
Constituency: St. Norbert *No. of Constituents:* 13,736, New Democratic Party
Tel: 204-945-3710
Fax: 204-948-2005
dave.gaudreau@leg.gov.mb.ca
Other Communications: Constituency Phone: 204-261-1794; Fax: 204-261-6707
Constituency Office
3489 PembinaHwy.
Winnipeg, MB R3V 1A4
Hon. Jon Gerrard
Constituency: RiverHeights *No. of Constituents:* 14,325, Liberal
Tel: 204-945-5194
Fax: 204-948-3220
jon.gerrard@leg.gov.mb.ca
MLA Office. Legislative Building
#167, 450 Broadway
Winnipeg, MB R3C 0V8
Kelvin Goertzen
Constituency: Steinbach *No. of Constituents:* 12,934, Progressive Conservative
Tel: 204-945-0231
Fax: 204-948-2092
kelvin.goertzen@leg.gov.mb.ca
Other Communications: Constituency Phone: 204-326-5763; Fax: 204-346-9913
Constituency Office
227 MainSt.
Steinbach, MB R5G 1Y7
Cliff Graydon
Constituency: Emerson *No. of Constituents:* 12,453, Progressive Conservative
Tel: 204-945-5639
Fax: 204-942-6613
cliff.graydon@leg.gov.mb.ca
Other Communications: Constituency Phone: 204-324-9901; Fax: 204-324-9902
Constituency Office
67 St. NE
PO Box 2099
Altona, MB R0G0B0
Reg Helwer
Constituency: Brandon West *No. of Constituents:* 14,607, Progressive Conservative
Tel: 204-945-8165
Fax: 204-942-6613
reg.helwer@leg.gov.mb.ca
Other Communications: Constituency Phone: 204-728-2410; Fax: 204-726-4740
Constituency Office
2 - 18th St.
Brandon, MB R7A 5A3
Minister, Family Services & Labour; Minister Responsible for the Status of Women; Minister, charged with the administration of The Workers Compensation Act; Government HouseLeader, Hon. Jennifer Howard
Constituency: Fort Rouge *No. of Constituents:* 14,429, New Democratic Party
Tel: 204-945-4173
Fax: 204-945-5149
minfsl@leg.gov.mb.ca
Other Communications: Constituency Phone: 204-946-0272; Fax: 204-946-0550
Constituency Office
#9, 222 Osborne St. South
Winnipeg, MB R3L 1Z3
Minister, Housing & Community Development, Hon. Kerri Irvin-Ross
Constituency: Fort Richmond *No. of Constituents:* 12,040, New Democratic Party
Tel: 204-945-6190
Fax: 204-945-1491
minhcd@leg.gov.mb.ca
Other Communications: Constituency Phone: 204-475-9433; Fax: 204-475-9438
Constituency Office

1060 Pembina Hwy.
Winnipeg, MB R3T 1Z8
Bidhu Jha
Constituency: Radisson *No. of Constituents:* 14,899, New Democratic Party
Tel: 204-945-3710
Fax: 204-948-2005
bidhu.jha@leg.gov.mb.ca
Other Communications: Constituency Phone: 204-222-0074; Fax: 204-222-2840
Constituency Office
549 Regent Ave. West
Winnipeg, MB R2C1R9
Minister, Agriculture, Food, & Rural Initiatives, Hon. Ron Kostyshyn
Constituency: Swan River *No. of Constituents:* 12,853, New Democratic Party
Tel: 204-945-3722
Fax: 204-945-3470
minagr@leg.gov.mb.ca
Other Communications: Constituency Phone: 204-734-4900; Fax: 204-734-2302
Constituency Office
#102, 6th Ave. North
Swan River, MB R0L 1Z0
Minister, Local Government, Hon. Ron Lemieux
Constituency: Dawson Trail *No. of Constituents:* 14,118, New Democratic Party
Tel: 204-945-3788
Fax: 204-945-1383
minlg@leg.gov.mb.ca
Other Communications: Constituency Phone: 204-878-4644; Fax: 204-878-4649
Constituency Office
#101, 1309Dawson Rd.
Lorette, MB R0A 0Y0
Minister, Conservation & Water Stewardship, Hon. Gord Mackintosh
Constituency: St. Johns *No. of Constituents:* 13,119, New Democratic Party
Tel: 204-945-3730
Fax: 204-945-3586
minconws@leg.gov.mb.ca
Other Communications: Constituency Phone: 204-945-3730; Fax: 204-586-3736
Constituency Office
1763 Main St.
Winnipeg, MB R2V 1Z8
Larry Maguire
Constituency: Arthur-Virden *No. of Constituents:* 14,613, Progressive Conservative
Tel: 204-945-4975
Fax: 204-945-5921
larry.maguire@leg.gov.mb.ca
Other Communications: Constituency Phone: 204-748-6443; Fax: 204-748-6492
Constituency Office
PO Box 459
Virden, MB R0M2C0
Jim Maloway
Constituency: Elmwood *No. of Constituents:* 13,578, New Democratic Party
Tel: 204-945-3710
Fax: 204-948-2005
jim.maloway@leg.gov.mb.ca
MLA Office, Legislative Building
#234, 450 Broadway
Winnipeg, MB R3C0V8
Minister, Culture, Heritage, & Tourism, Hon. Flor Marcelino
Constituency: Logan *No. of Constituents:* 10,698, New Democratic Party
Tel: 204-945-3729
Fax: 204-945-5229
mincht@leg.gov.mb.ca
Other Communications: Constituency Phone: 204-788-0800; Fax: 204-788-4444
ConstituencyOffice
849 Notre Dame Ave.
Winnipeg, MB R3E OM4
Ted Marcelino
Constituency: Tyndall Park *No. of Constituents:* 11,201, New Democratic Party
Tel: 204-945-3710
Fax: 204-948-2005
ted.marcelino@leg.gov.mb.ca
Other Communications: Constituency Phone: 204-945-3710; Fax: 204-948-2005
Constituency Office
#24, 360 KeewatinSt.
Winnipeg, MB R2X 2Y3
Leader of the Official Opposition, Hugh McFadyen
Constituency: Fort Whyte *No. of Constituents:* 14,542, Progressive Conservative
Tel: 204-945-3593
Fax: 204-945-1299
hugh.mcfadyen@leg.gov.mb.ca
Other Communications: Constituency Phone: 204-488-3560; Fax: 204-488-3561
ConstituencyOffice
#152, 99 Scurfield Blvd.
Winnipeg, MB R3Y 1Y1
Minister, Immigration & Multiculturalism, Hon. Christine Melnick
Constituency: Riel *No. of Constituents:* 15,257, New Democratic Party
Tel: 204-945-4079
Fax: 204-945-8312
minimm@leg.gov.mb.ca
Other Communications: Constituency Phone: 204-253-5162; Fax: 204-253-0222
Constituency Office
#4, 1549 St. Mary's Rd.
Winnipeg, MB R2M 5G9
Bonnie Mitchelson
Constituency: River East *No. of Constituents:* 15,332, Progressive Conservative
Tel: 204-945-0008
Fax: 204-948-2092
bonnie.mitchelson@leg.gov.mb.ca
Other Communications: Constituency Phone: 204-334-7866; Fax: 204-338-7697
Constituency Office
#13E, 1795 HendersonHwy.
Winnipeg, MB R2G 1P3
Thomas Nevakshonoff
Constituency: Interlake *No. of Constituents:* 12,586, New Democratic Party
Tel: 204-945-3710
Fax: 204-948-2005
tom.nevakshonoff@leg.gov.mb.ca
Other Communications: Constituency Phone: 204-664-2000; Fax: 204-948-2005
Constituency Office
PO Box 44
Poplarfield, MB R0C2N0
Minister, Health, Hon. Theresa Oswald
Constituency: Seine River, New Democratic Party
Tel: 204-945-3731
Fax: 204-945-0441
minhlt@leg.gov.mb.ca
Other Communications: Constituency Phone: 204-255-7840; Fax: 204-504-6678
Constituency Office
1631 St. Mary'sRd., #H
Winnipeg, MB R2N 1Z4
Blaine Pedersen
Constituency: Midland *No. of Constituents:* 14,467, Progressive Conservative
Tel: 204-945-7909
Fax: 204-942-6613
blaine.pedersen@leg.gov.mb.ca
Other Communications: Constituency Phone: 204-745-2203; Fax: 204-745-2205
Constituency Office
148 MainSt.
PO Box 1944
Carman, MB R0G OJO
Clarence Petterson
Constituency: Flin Flon *No. of Constituents:* 9,409, New Democratic Party
Tel: 204-945-3710
Fax: 204-948-2005
clarence.pettersen@leg.gov.mb.ca
Other Communications: Constituency Phone: 204-687-3367; Fax: 204-687-3398
Constituency Office
24 Main St.
PO Box 331
FlinFlon, MB R8A 1N1
Speaker, Hon. Daryl Reid
Constituency: Transcona *No. of Constituents:* 15,120, New Democratic Party
Tel: 204-945-3706
Fax: 204-945-1443
Speaker@leg.gov.mb.ca
Other Communications: Constituency Phone: 204-222-0040; Fax: 204-222-2840
Constituency Office
#1, 549 Regent Ave. West
Winnipeg, MB R2C 1R9
Deputy Premier; Minister, Aboriginal & Northern Affairs; Minister Responsible, Sport, Aboriginal Education, & the MB Floodway & East Side Road Authority Act; Minister charged withthe administration of The Communities Economic Development Fund Act, Hon. Eric Robinson
Constituency: Kewatinook *No. of Constituents:* 10,081, New Democratic Party
Tel: 204-943-2274
Fax: 204-957-7010
minna@leg.gov.mb.ca
Other Communications: Constituency Phone: 204-943-2274; Fax: 204-957-7010
Constituency Office, Legislative Building
#22, 450Broadway
Winnipeg, MB R3C OV8
Minister, Healthy Living, Seniors, & Consumer Affairs; Minister charged with the administration of The Liquor Control Act, Hon. Jim Rondeau
Constituency: Assiniboia *No. of Constituents:* 14,170, New Democratic Party
Tel: 204-945-1373
Fax: 204-948-2703
minhliv@leg.gov.mb.ca
Other Communications: Constituency Phone: 204-888-7722; Fax: 204-889-0300
Constituency Office
839A Cavalier Dr.
Winnipeg, MB R2Y 1C6
Leanne Rowat
Constituency: Riding Mountain *No. of Constituents:* 14,165, Progressive Conservative
Tel: 204-945-0258
Fax: 204-945-5921
leanne.rowat@leg.gov.mb.ca
Other Communications: Constituency Phone: 204-867-2297; Fax: 204-867-3641
Constituency Office
114 Main St.
PO Box 1074
Minnedosa, MB R0J 1E0
Mohinder Saran
Constituency: The Maples *No. of Constituents:* 13,772, New Democratic Party
Tel: 204-945-3710
Fax: 204-948-2005
mohinder.saran@leg.gov.mb.ca
Other Communications: Constituency Phone: 204-632-7933; Fax: 204-697-2031
Constituency Office
80 MandalayDr.
Winnipeg, MB R2P 1V8
Ron Schuler
Constituency: St. Paul *No. of Constituents:* 16,075, Progressive Conservative
Tel: 204-945-4321
Fax: 204-942-6613
ron.schuler@leg.gov.mb.ca
Other Communications: Constituency Phone: 204-444-4371; Fax: 204-444-4372
Constituency Office
#3, 777 Cedar Pl.
PO Box 150
Oakbank, MB R0E 1J0
Minister, Advanced Education & Literacy, Hon. Erin Selby
Constituency: Southdale *No. of Constituents:* 15,574, New Democratic Party
Tel: 204-945-0825
Fax: 204-948-2216
minaed@leg.gov.mb.ca
Other Communications: Constituency Phone: 204-253-3918; Fax: 204-253-3946
ConstituencyOffice
#310, 119 Vermillion Rd.
Winnipeg, MB R2J 4A9
Premier; President, Executive Council; Minister, Federal-Provincial Relations; Minister Responsible. Francophone Affairs, Hon. Gregory Selinger
Constituency: St. Boniface *No. of Constituents:* 14,496, New Democratic Party
Tel: 204-945-3417
Fax: 204-949-1484
premier@leg.gov.mb.ca
Other Communications: Constituency Phone: 204-237-9247; Fax: 204-237-9488
Constituency Office
123 Enfield Cres.
Winnipeg, MB R2H 1A8
Hon. Dennis Smook
Constituency: La Verendrye *No. of Constituents:* 13,119, Progressive Conservative
Tel: 204-945-4339
Fax: 204-942-6613
dennis.smook@leg.gov.mb.ca
Other Communications: Constituency Phone: 204-424-5406; Fax: 204-424-5458
Constituency Office
217B Fournier St.
LaBroquerie, MB R0A 0W0
Heather Stefanson
Constituency: Tuxedo *No. of Constituents:* 14,778, Progressive Conservative
Tel: 204-945-0827
Fax: 204-945-5921

heather.stefanson@leg.gov.mb.ca
Other Communications: Constituency Phone: 204-487-0013; Fax: 204-487-0078
Constituency Office
1840 Grant Ave.
Winnipeg, MB R3N 0N4

Minister, Finance; Minister Responsible, Civil Service; Minister charged with the administration of The Crown Corporations Public Review & Accountability Act, Hon. Stan Struthers
Constituency: Dauphin *No. of Constituents:* 13,181, New Democratic Party
Tel: 204-945-3952
Fax: 204-945-6057
minfin@leg.gov.mb.ca
Other Communications: Constituency Phone: 204-622-7630; Fax: 204-622-7633
Constituency Office
21B - 3rd Ave. NE
Dauphin, MB R7N OY5

Minister, Justice; Attorney General; Minister Responsible, Constitutional Affairs; Minister, charged with the administration of The Manitoba Public Insurance Act; Keeper of theGreat Seal of the Province of Manitoba, Hon. Andrew Swan
Constituency: Minto *No. of Constituents:* 11,796, New Democratic Party
Tel: 204-945-3728
Fax: 204-945-2517
minjus@leg.gov.mb.ca
Other Communications: Constituency Phone: 204-783-9860; Fax: 204-772-6129
Constituency Office
892 Sargent Ave.
Winnipeg, MB R3E 0C7

Mavis Taillieu
Constituency: Morris *No. of Constituents:* 15,228, Progressive Conservative
Tel: 204-945-3525
Toll-free: 866-989-6633
Fax: 204-942-6613
mavis.taillieu@leg.gov.mb.ca
Other Communications: Constituency Phone: 204-832-6633; Fax: 204-832-6833
Constituency Office
5423A PortageAve.
Headingley, MB R4H 1E5

Frank Whitehead
Constituency: The Pas *No. of Constituents:* 13,459, New Democratic Party
Tel: 204-945-3710
Fax: 204-948-2005
frank.whitehead@leg.gov.mb.ca
Other Communications: Constituency Phone: 204-623-3358; Fax: 204-623-6955
Constituency Office
234A Fisher Ave.
The Pas, MB R9A 1R7

Matt Wiebe
Constituency: Concordia *No. of Constituents:* 12,834, New Democratic Party
Tel: 204-945-3710
Fax: 204-948-2005
matt.wiebe@leg.gov.mb.ca
Other Communications: Constituency Phone: 204-654-1857; Fax: 204-663-1943
Constituency Office
#106, 1111 Munroe Ave.
Winnipeg, MB R2K 3Z5

Melanie Wight
Constituency: Burrows *No. of Constituents:* 11,025, New Democratic Party
Tel: 204-945-3710
Fax: 204-948-2005
melanie.wight@leg.gov.mb.ca
Other Communications: Constituency Phone: 204-421-9414; Fax: 204-421-9415
Constituency Office
685 McPhillipsSt.
Winnipeg, MB R2X 2H6

Ian Wishart
Constituency: Portage la Prairie *No. of Constituents:* 13,521, Progressive Conservative
Tel: 204-945-8088
Fax: 204-942-6613
ian.wishart@leg.gov.mb.ca
Other Communications: Constituency Phone: 204-857-9267; Fax: 204-857-9841
Constituency Office
306 Saskatchewan Ave. East
Portagela Prairie, MB R1N 0K8

Associated Agencies, Boards & Commissions:

• Progressive Conservative Party
Legislative Bldg
#227, 450 Broadway
Winnipeg, MB R3C 0V8
Tel: 204-945-3709
Fax: 204-945-1284
Toll-free: 800-282-8069
pccaucus@leg.gov.mb.ca
www.manpc.mb.ca

• New Democratic Party
Legislative Bldg
#234, 450 Broadway
Winnipeg, MB R3C 0V8
Tel: 204-945-3710
Fax: 204-948-2005
www.ndpcaucus.mb.ca/newCaucus

• Liberal Party
Legislative Bldg
#169, 450 Broadway
Winnipeg, MB R3C 0V8
Tel: 204-945-5194
Fax: 204-948-3220
jgerrard@leg.gov.mb.ca

Manitoba Government Departments & Agencies

Manitoba Aboriginal & Northern Affairs

Legislative Bldg, 344-450 Broadway, Winnipeg, MB R3C OV8

Tel: 204-945-3719
Fax: 204-945-8374
anaweb@gov.mb.ca
www.gov.mb.ca/ana/

The goals of Manitoba's Aboriginal & Northern Affairs are as follows: to improve the quality of life & opportunities for Aboriginal & Northern people; to facilitate better services, opportunities & results for Manitoba's Aboriginal & northern people; to support the mental, emotional, physical & spiritual health of northern communities & Aboriginal people; to resolve outstanding provincial obligations to Aboriginal/northern communities; to foster self-determination, accountability & sustainable growth; & to strengthen the participation of Aboriginal & northern people in Manitoba's economy.

Acts Administered:
Manitoba Floodway and East Side Road Authority Act
Northern Affairs Act
Planning Act

Minister, Hon. Eric Robinson
Tel: 204-945-3719
Fax: 204-954-8374
minna@leg.gov.mb.ca

Deputy Minister, Harvey Bostrom
Tel: 204-945-0565
Fax: 204-945-1256
dmna@leg.gov.mb.ca

Director, Finance & Administrative Services, Justin Nedd
Tel: 204-677-6609
Fax: 204-677-6753

Executive Director, Local Government Development Division, Freda Albert
Tel: 204-677-6795

Director, Policy & Strategic Initiatives, Eleanor Brokington
Tel: 204-945-0572

Director, Agreements Management, Dave Hicks
Tel: 204-945-2506

Associated Agencies, Boards & Commissions:
• Communities Economic Development Fund
#100, 23 Station Rd.
Thompson, MB R8N 0N6
Tel: 204-778-4138
Fax: 204-778-4313
Toll-free: 800-561-4315
www.cedf.mb.ca

Aboriginal Affairs Secretariat
#200, 500 Portage Ave., Winnipeg, MB R3C 3X1
Tel: 204-945-2510
Fax: 204-945-3689

Executive Director, Joe Morriseau
Tel: 204-945-3689
Fax: 204-945-3689
jmorrissea@gov.mb.ca

Agreements Management
#200, 500 Portage Ave., Winnipeg, MB R3C 3X1
Tel: 204-945-8337
Fax: 204-945-3689

Director, David Hicks
Tel: 204-945-2506
Fax: 204-945-3689
dhicks@gov.mb.ca

Local Government Development Division
59 Elizabeth Dr., PO Box 33, Thompson, MB R8N 1X4
Tel: 204-677-6794
Fax: 204-677-6525

The Local Government Development Division provides support to 50 northern & remote communities, including public works, environmental services, & infrastructure development. It promotes cooperative, community-driven sustainable development.

Executive Director, Freda Albert
Tel: 204-677-6795
falbert@gov.mb.ca
Director, Program Planning & Development, Jeff Gordon
Tel: 204-945-1713
jgordon@gov.mb.ca

Dauphin
Provincial Bldg., 27 Second Ave. SW, PO Box 15, Dauphin, MB R7N 3E5
Tel: 204-622-2110
Fax: 204-622-2305

Regional Director, Karen Barker
kbarker@gov.mb.ca

Thompson
59 Elizabeth Dr., PO Box 27, Thompson, MB R8N 1X4
Tel: 204-677-6786
Fax: 204-677-6525

Regional Director, Jean Merasty
jmerasty@gov.mb.ca

Manitoba Advanced Education & Literacy

Legislative Building, #162, 450 Broadway Ave., Winnipeg, MB R3C 0V8

Tel: 204-945-0825
Fax: 204-948-2216
minaed@leg.gov.mb.ca
www.edu.gov.mb.ca

Acts Administered:
Adult Learning Centres Act
Adult Literacy Act
Advanced Education Administration Act
Brandon University Act
Colleges Act
Council on Post-Secondary Education Act
Degree Granting Act
Private Vocational Institutions Act
Student Aid Act
University College of the North Act
University of Manitoba Act
University of Winnipeg Act

Minister, Hon. Erin Selby
Tel: 204-945-0825
Fax: 204-948-2216
minaed@leg.gov.mb.ca

Deputy Minister, Heather Reichert
Tel: 204-945-1648
Fax: 204-945-8330
dmedu@leg.gov.mb.ca

Director, Human Resources, Robert Berube
Tel: 204-945-6892

Manager, Pay & Benefits, Peggy Fontaine
Tel: 204-945-6890

Director, Financial and Administrative Sevices, Claude Fortier
Tel: 204-945-1117

Associated Agencies, Boards & Commissions:
• Council on Post-Secondary Education
#608, 330 Portage Ave.
Winnipeg, MB R3C 0C4
Tel: 204-945-1833
Fax: 204-945-1841
info@copse.mb.ca
www.copse.mb.ca

Council on Post-Secondary Education
#608, 330 Portage Ave., Winnipeg, MB R3C 0C4
Tel: 204-945-1833
Fax: 204-945-1841
info@copse.mb.ca
www.copse.mb.ca

Deputy Minister, Adult Learning and Literacy, Lynette Plett
Tel: 204-945-4399
Fax: 204-948-1008
Manager, Policy Development & Analysis, Dan Smith
Tel: 204-945-4720

Chief Financial Officer, Carlos Matias
Tel: 204-945-1839
Director, Institutional Relations, Josh Watt
Tel: 204-945-8597
#401, 1181 Portage Ave.
Winnipeg, MB R3G 0N4

College Expansion Initiative Branch
#401, 1181 Portage Ave., Winnipeg, MB R3G 0T3
Tel: 204-945-5150
Fax: 204-948-2676
www.copse.mb.ca/en/cei/
Manager, College Relations, COPSE, Ray Karasevich
ray.karasevich@gov.mb.ca

Aboriginal Education Directorate
Director, Helen Robinson-Settee
Tel: 204-945-4763
Program Manager & Evaluation Consultant, Dino Altieri
Tel: 204-945-6181

Manitoba Agriculture, Food & Rural Initiatives

Legislative Bldg., 165-450 Broadway, Winnipeg, MB R3C 0V8
Tel: 204-945-3722
Fax: 204-945-3470
minagr@leg.gov.mb.ca
www.gov.mb.ca/agriculture/

Acts Administered:
Agricultural Producers' Organization Funding Act
Agricultural Societies Act
Agrologists Act
Animal Care Act
Animal Diseases Act
Animal Liability Act
Cattle Producers Association Act
Coarse Grain Marketing Control Act
Community development Bonds Act
Crown Lands Act, (in part) Sections 6, 7, 10, 12(1), 14, 16, 17, 18, 21, 23, 24 to 28 both inclusive
Dairy Act
Department of Agriculture, Food and Rural Initiatives Act
Family Farm Protection Act
Farm Income Assurance Plans Act
Farm Lands Ownership Act
Farm Machinery & Equipment Act
Farm Practices Protection Act
Food Safety Act
Fruit & Vegetable Sales Act
Horse Racing Commission Act
Income Tax Act
Land Rehabilitation Act
Livestock & Livestock Products Act
Livestock Industry Diversification Act
Manitoba Agricultural Services Corporation Act
Milk Prices Review Act
Natural Products Marketing Act
Noxious Weeds Act
Organic Agricultural Products Act
Pesticides & Fertilizers Control Act
Plant Pests and Diseases Act
Property Tax and Insulation Assistance Act
Seed & Fodder Relief Act
Veterinary Medical Act
Veterinary Science Scholarship Fund Act
Veterinary Services Act
Wildlife Act, (in part) Section 89(e)
Women's Institute Act

Minister, Hon. Stan Struthers
Tel: 204-945-3722
Fax: 204-945-3470
minagr@leg.gov.mb.ca

Deputy Minister, Barry Todd
Tel: 204-945-3734
Fax: 204-948-2095
dmagr@leg.gov.mb.ca

Executive Director, Strategic Planning, Maurice Bouvier
Tel: 204-792-5406

Chief Veterinary Officer, Food Safety Knowledge Centre, Wayne Lees
Tel: 204-945-7685

Director, Crops Knowledge Centre, Mike Kagan
Tel: 204-745-5653

Director, Land Use Planning Knowledge Centre, Robert Fleming
Tel: 204-867-6551

Associated Agencies, Boards & Commissions:

• Agricultural Societies
1129 Queens Ave.
Brandon, MB R7A 1L9
Tel: 204-726-6195
Fax: 204-726-6260
Promotes improvement in agriculture & development of Manitoba agricultural products. Provide organizational assistance to rural & urban people.

• Farm Lands Ownership Board
#812, Norquay Bldg.
401 York Ave.
Winnipeg, MB R3C 0P8
Tel: 204-945-3149
Fax: 204-945-1489
Toll-free: 800-282-8069
robert.mckenzie@gov.mb.ca
www.web2gov.mb.ca/agriculture/programs/

• Farm Machinery Board
Norquay Bldg.
#812, 401 York Ave.
Winnipeg, MB R3C 0P8
Tel: 204-945-3856
Fax: 204-948-2844
randy.ozunko@gov.mb.ca
www.web2.gov.mb.ca/agriculture/programs/

• Farm Practices Protection Board
c/o Boards, Commissions & Legislation Branch
#812, 401 York Ave.
Winnipeg, MB R3C 0P8
Tel: 204-945-0630
Fax: 204-948-2844
www.web2.gov.mb.ca/agriculture/programs/

• Farm Products Marketing Council
c/o Boards, Commissions & Legislation Branch
#812, 401 York Ave.
Winnipeg, MB R3C 0P8
Tel: 204-945-4495
Fax: 204-948-2844
gordon.mackenzie@gov.mb.ca
www.web2.gov.mb.ca/agriculture/programs/

• Food Development Centre
810 Phillips St.
PO Box 1240
Portage la Prairie, MB R1N 3J9
Tel: 204-239-3150
Fax: 204-239-3180
Toll-free: 800-870-1044
www.gov.mb.ca/agriculture/fdc
The Food Development Centre (FDC) is a Special Operating Agency of Manitoba Agriculture, Food and Rural Initiatives (MAFRI). Its mandate is to assist the agri-food industry in the development and commercialization of conventional and functional foods and natural health products.

• Manitoba Agricultural Services Corporation (MASC)
#100, 1525 First St. South
Brandon, MB R7A 7A1
Tel: 204-726-6850
Fax: 204-726-6849
mailbox@masc.mb.ca
www.masc.mb.ca
Formerly the Manitoba Agricultural Credit Corporation & the Manitoba Crop Insurance Corporation. Manitoba Agricultural Services Corporation (MASC) fully supports the province's producers and rural communities, through innovative and targeted risk management and financial programs. MASC is represented across Manitoba by 19 insurance offices and 16 lending offices, with corporate offices located in Portage la Prairie and Brandon.

• Manitoba Farm Mediation Board
c/o Boards, Commissions & Legislation Branch
#812, 401 York Ave.
Winnipeg, MB R3C 0P8
Tel: 204-945-0357
Fax: 204-945-1489
robert.mckenzie@gov.mb.ca
www.web2.gov.mb.ca/agriculture/programs/
Mediates options to legal action by creditors when farmers cannot meet their obligations.

• Manitoba Horse Racing Commission
c/o Boards, Commissions & Legislation Branch
#812, 401 York Ave.
Winnipeg, MB R3C 0P8
Tel: 204-945-4495
Fax: 204-948-2844
gordon.mackenzie@gov.mb.ca
www.web2.gov.mb.ca/agriculture/programs/
Governs, directs, controls, & regulates horse racing & the operation of all race tracks in Manitoba.

• Manitoba Milk Prices Review Commission
c/o Boards, Commissions & Legislation Branch
#812, 401 York Ave.
Winnipeg, MB R3C 0P8
Tel: 204-945-3854
Fax: 204-948-2844
randy.ozunko@gov.mb.ca
www.web2.gov.mb.ca/agriculture/programs/

Agri-Food & Rural Development Division
Asst. Deputy Minister, Gerald Huebner
Tel: 204-945-3735
Executive Director, Strategic Planning Directorate, Mona Cornock
Tel: 204-726-7192
Director, Food Commercialization & Marketing Knowledge Centre, Randy Stoyko
Tel: 204-795-2437
Director, GO Teams, Gerald Huebner
Tel: 204-797-4522
Fax: 204-886-3657
Central Plains
Morris Ave., PO Box 532, Gladstone, MB R0J 0T0
Tel: 204-871-4219
GO Team Leader, Dennis Beernaert
Eastman
20 First St. South, PO Box 50, Beausejour, MB R0E 0C0
Tel: 204-268-6099
Fax: 204-268-6060
GO Team Manager, Shaunda Rossington
North Interlake
317 River Rd., PO Box 2000, Arborg, MB R0C 0A0
Fax: 204-376-3311
GO Team Manager, Bob Penner
Tel: 204-641-4910
North Parkland
27 Second Ave. SW, Dauphin, MB R7N 3E5
Fax: 204-734-5271
GO Team Manager, Debra Watson
Pembina
279 Carlton St., PO Box 189, Somerset, MB R0G 2L0
GO Team Leader, Shane Dobson
Red River
67 - 2 St. NE, PO Box 969, Altona, MB R0G 0B0
Fax: 204-324-2803
GO Team Leader, Jacquie Cherewayko
South Interlake
77 Main St., PO Box 70, Teulon, MB R0C 3B0
Fax: 204-886-3657
GO Team Manager, Wray Whitmore
South Parkland
221 Elm St., Hwy 21 N, PO Box 50, Hamiota, MB R0M 0T0
GO Team Manager, Gwenda Skayman
Southwest
247 Wellington St., PO Box 850, Virden, MB R0M 2C0
Fax: 204-748-4775
GO Team Manager, John Corbey
Tel: 204-851-2442
Valleys North
120 - 6th Ave. North, PO Box 370, Swan River, MB R0L 1Z0
Fax: 204-734-5271
GO Team Manager, Allen Muggaberg

Agri-Industry Development & Innovation Division
Asst. Deputy Minister, Allan Preston
Tel: 204-945-3736
Acting Director, Agri-Environment, Leloni Scott
Tel: 204-745-5658
Director, Agri-Food Innovation & Adaptation, Daryl Domitruk
Tel: 204-745-0214
Director, Crops, Mike Kagan
Tel: 204-745-5653
Director, Food Safety & Chief Veterinary Office, Dr. John Taylor
Tel: 204-945-7690
Fax: 204-945-4327
Acting Director, Land Use Planning & Manager, Agricultural Crown Lands, Robert Fleming
Tel: 204-867-6551

Office of the Auditor General

#500, 330 Portage Ave., Winnipeg, MB R3C 0C4
Tel: 204-945-3790
Fax: 204-945-2169
oag.contact@oag.mb.ca
www.oag.mb.ca
Established under The Auditor General Act, the Office of the Auditor General is an independent office of the Legislative Assembly. Through audit of management practices & accountability reports, the Office contributes to effective governance & public trust.

Auditor General, Carol Bellringer, FCA, MBA
cbellringer@aog.mb.ca

Deputy Auditor General, Mala Sachdeva, CA
Tel: 204-945-2686

Executive Director, Strategic Initiatives, Norman Ricard, CA
Tel: 204-945-2782

Executive Director, Quality Assurance & Professional Practice, Greg MacBeth, CA
Tel: 204-945-6883

Director, Special Audits, Jack Buckwold, BA, B. Comm.
Tel: 204-945-1620

Manitoba Children & Youth Opportunities

Legislative Bldg., #314, 450 Broadway, Winnipeg, MB R3C 0V8
Tel: 204-945-1133
Fax: 204-948-2519
www.gov.mb.ca/cyo/index.html

Minister & Chair, Healthy Child Committee of Cabinet, Kevin Chief
mincyo@leg.gov.mb.ca

Deputy Minister, Jan Sanderson
Tel: 204-945-6707

Executive Director, Crime Prevention Unit, Todd Clarke
Tel: 204-945-6884

Director, MB4Youth, & Recreation & Regional Services, Annette Willborn
Tel: 204-945-0371

Healthy Child Manitoba Office
Chief Executive Officer, Jan Sanderson
Tel: 204-945-6707
Executive Director, Programs & Administration, Susan Tessler
Tel: 204-945-1275
Director, Policy Development, Research & Evaluation, Leanne Boyd
Tel: 204-945-5447
Director, Parenting Initiatives, Steven Feldgaier
Tel: 204-945-3084

Manitoba Civil Service Commission

#935, 155 Carlton St., Winnipeg, MB R3C 3H8
Tel: 204-945-2332
Fax: 204-945-1486
Toll-Free: 800-282-8069
cschrp@gov.mb.ca
www.gov.mb.ca/csc/

Acts Administered:
Employment Standards Code
Freedom of Information & Protection of Privacy Act
Labour Relations Act
Manitoba Act
Personal Health Information Act
The Civil Service Act

Minister responsible, Hon. Gregory F. Selinger
Tel: 204-945-3952
Fax: 204-945-6057
minfin@leg.gov.mb.ca

Deputy Minister & Commissioner, Debra Woodgate

Associated Agencies, Boards & Commissions:
• **Civil Service Commission Board**
#935, 155 Carlton St.
Winnipeg, MB R3C 3H8
Tel: 204-945-1435
Fax: 204-945-1486

Manitoba Conservation & Water Stewardship

200 Saulteaux Cres., Winnipeg, MB R3J 3W3
Toll-Free: 800-214-6497
mws@gov.mb.ca
www.gov.mb.ca/conservation; www.gov.mb.ca/waterstewardship
Manitoba Conservation protects, conserves, manages & sustains development of forest, fisheries, wildlife, water, energy & Crown & Park land resources. It also protects environmental integrity, & ensures a high level of environmental quality.
The department is the lead agency for providing outdoor recreational opportunities for Manitobans & visitors.
It is a contributor to the economic development & well-being of the province, through resource-based harvesting operations, & in cooperation with other departments responsible for agriculture & tourism. Protecting people & property from floods, wildfires, & adverse effects of other natural occurrences, are also major roles.
The department administers legislation & regulations protecting the environment & public health, participates in approval, licensing & appeals for industrial development activities, administers waste reduction & pollution prevention activities, & monitors environmental quality.
Acts Administered:
Burning of Crop Residue & Non-Crop Herbage Regulation
Campgrounds Regulation
Classes of Development Regulation
Climate Change and Emissions Reductions Act
Conservation Agreement Forms Regulation
Conservation Agreements Act
Conservation Districts Act
Contaminated Sites Remediation Act
Crown Lands Act
Dangerous Goods Handling & Transportation Act
Dangerous Goods Handling & Transportation Fees Regulation
Dangerous Goods Handling & Transportation Regulation
Designation of Wild Animals Regulation
Designation of Wildlife Lands Regulation
Disposal of Whey Regulation
Drinking Water Safety Act, 2004
Dyking Authority Act
East Side Traditional Lands Planning and Special Protected Areas Act
Ecological Reserves Act
Ecological Reserves Designation Regulation
Eligible Conservation Agencies Regulation
Endangered Species Act
Environment Act
Environment Act Fees Regulation
Environmental Accident Reporting Regulation
Environmental Assessment Hearing Costs Recovery Regulation
Fisheries Act
Fishermen's Assistance & Polluter's Liability Act
Floodway Authority Act
Forest Act
Generator Registration & Carrier Licensing Regulation
Ground Water & Water Well Act
Ground Water & Water Well Act
High Level Radioactive Waste Act
Incinerators Regulation
Inco Ltd. & Hudson Bay Mining & Smelting Co., Ltd. Smelting Complex Regulation
International Peace Garden Act
Joint Environmental Assessment Regulation
Lake of the Woods Control Board Act
Litter Regulation
Livestock Manure & Mortalities Management Regulation
Manifest Regulation
Manitoba Hazardous Waste Management Corporation Act
Manitoba Natural Resources Transfer Act
Manitoba Natural Resources Transfer Act
Manitoba Natural Resources Transfer Act, Amendment Act
Manitoba Natural Resources Transfer Act, Amendment Act, 1963
Multi-Material Stewardship (Interim Measures) Regulation
Natural Resources Agreement Act
Onsite Wastewater Management Systems Regulation
Ozone Depleting Substances Act
PCB Storage Site Regulation
Participant Assistance Regulation
Peat Smoke Control Regulation
Pesticides Regulation
Plant Pests & Diseases Act
Polar Bear Protection Act, 2003
Protection of Water Resources Regulation
Provincial Parks Act
Public Health Act
Public Health Act
Resource Tourism Operators Act
Rockwood Sensitive Area Regulation
Sanitary Areas Regulation
Special Waste (Shredder Residue) Regulation
Storage & Handling of Petroleum Products & Allied Products Regulation
Surveys Act (Part II)
Sustainable Development Act
Threatened, Endangered & Extirpated Species Regulation
Tire Stewardship Regulation
Used Oil, Oil Filters & Containers Stewardship Regulation
Waste Disposal Grounds Regulation
Waste Reduction & Prevention Act
Wastewater Management Systems Regulations
Water & Wastewater Facility Operators Regulation
Water Commission Act
Water Power Act
Water Resources Administration Act
Water Resources Conservation & Protection Act
Water Resources Conservation Act
Water Rights Act
Water Rights Act
Water Supplies Regulation
Water Supply Commissions Act
Water Works, Sewage & Sewage Disposal Regulations
Well Drilling Regulation
Wild Rice Act
Wildlife Act

Minister, Hon. Gord Mackintosh
Tel: 204-945-3730
Fax: 204-945-3586
minconws@leg.gov.mb.ca

Deputy Minister, Fred Meier
Tel: 204-945-3785
Fax: 204-948-2403
dmcon@leg.gov.mb.ca

Executive Director, Corporate Crown Lands Policy, Marlene Zyluk
Tel: 204-945-7370

Associated Agencies, Boards & Commissions:
• **Clean Environment Commission**
#305, 155 Carlton St.
Winnipeg, MB R3C 3H8
Tel: 204-945-0594
Fax: 204-945-0090
www.cecmanitoba.ca/
Arm's-length provincial agency that holds public hearings on the subject of the regulation of a broad range of private industry, municipal or provincial government operations. Investigates environmental matters or considers proposed abatement projects with public hearings. Reports to the Minister with advice & recommendations & acts as a mediator between two or more parties to an environmental dispute.
• **Ecological Reserves Advisory Committee**
c/o Manitoba Conservation, Parks & Natural Areas Branch
200 Saulteaux Cres.
Winnipeg, MB R3J 3W3
Tel: 204-945-4148
Fax: 204-945-0012
hhernandez@gov.mb.ca
• **Endangered Species Advisory Committee**
200 Saulteaux Cres.
PO Box 24
Winnipeg, MB R3J 3W3
Tel: 204-945-7465
Fax: 204-945-3077
• **Lake of the Woods Control Board**
c/o Executive Engineer
Ottawa, ON K1A 0H3
Fax: 819-953-4666
Toll-free: 800-661-5922
secretariat@lwcb.ca
www.lwcb.ca
• **Manitoba Conservation Districts Commission**
Secretariat c/o Planning & Coordination Branch
123 Main St.
PO Box 20000
Neepawa, MB R0J 1H0
Tel: 204-476-7033
Fax: 204-476-7539
whildebran@gov.mb.ca
The Conservation Districts Program has been delivering a comprehensive, sustainable approach to water & soil management for over 25 years. Conservation Districts are established under the authority of The Conservation District Act. There are 16 Conservation Districts covering approximately 60% of Agro-Manitoba. Individual district boundaries may vary depending on the needs of the people. Districts are usually based on the drainage basin or watershed of the major river in the area.

Administration & Finance Division
Assistant Deputy Minister, Bruce Gray
Tel: 204-945-3840
Director, Comptrollership, Grants & Contract Review, Rodney Dieleman
Tel: 204-945-4187
Director, Financial Services, Giselle Martel
Tel: 204-945-8266
Director, Business Transformation & Technology, Maria Villarba
Tel: 204-945-2929

Climate Change & Environmental Protection
Assistant Deputy Minister, Dan McInnis
Tel: 204-296-4199
Director, Environmental Assessment & Licensing, Tracey Braun
Tel: 204-945-7071
Director, Climate Change, Neil Cunningham
Tel: 204-945-8793
Director, Environmental Programs & Strategies, Mike Gilbertson
Tel: 204-471-9338
Director, Don Labossiere
Tel: 204-945-7005

Conservation Programs Division
Manages Manitoba's natural resources, parks, lands, forests, fish, wildlife, & the environment. Implements the principles of sustainable development.
Assistant Deputy Minister, Serge Scrafield
Tel: 204-945-7008
Chief Operating Officer, Green Manitoba, Christina McDonald
Tel: 204-945-1819
123 Main St. West
PO Box 20000
Neepawa, MB R0J 1H0
Director, Forestry, John Dojack
Tel: 204-945-7998
Director, GeoManitoba, Greg Carlson
Tel: 204-945-7952
123 Main St. West
PO Box 20000
Neepawa, MB R0J 1H0
Director, Wildlife & Ecosystem Protection, James Duncan
Tel: 204-945-7465

Corporate Policy Division
Executive Director, Jocelyn Baker
Tel: 204-945-6658
Director, Aboriginal Relations, Ron Missyabit
Tel: 204-945-7088
Director, Sustainable Resource & Policy Management, Charlotte Price
Tel: 204-945-6944

Ecological Services Division
Assistant Deputy Minister, Dwight Williamson
Tel: 204-945-7030
Director, Water Science & Management Branch, Nicole Armstrong
Tel: 204-945-3991
Director, Planning & Coordination, Rhonda McDougal
Tel: 204-945-8271
Director/Manager, Office of Drinking Water, Kim Philip
Tel: 204-945-7010
Senior Information Management Specialist, Fisheries Branch, Robert Moszynski
Tel: 204-945-2916

Manitoba Round Table for Sustainable Development (MRTSD)
#160, 123 Main St., Winnipeg, MB R3C 1A5
Tel: 204-945-1869
Fax: 204-948-2357
mrtsd@gov.mb.ca
www.gov.mb.ca/conservation/susresmb/mrtsd
The Manitoba Round Table for Sustainable Development is an advisory body to the provincial government. It provides advice & support to decision makers toward making responsible resource, land use, environment, social, & economic development decisions for the province.
Chair, Hon. Stan Struthers

Regional Operations Division
Operates six regional offices in rural Manitoba & co-ordinated from Headquarters operations in Winnipeg. The Division co-ordinates the delivery of programs & services at the community level
Asst. Deputy Minister, Bruce Bremner
Tel: 204-945-4842
Central (Gimli)
75 - 7th Ave., PO Box 6000, Gimli, MB R0C 1B0
Tel: 204-642-6070
Fax: 204-642-6108
Regional Director, Rob Nedotiafko
Tel: 204-642-6096
Central (Winnipeg)
#160, 123 Main St., Winnipeg, MB R3C 1A5
Tel: 204-945-7100
Fax: 204-948-2338
Eastern
Provincial Hwy. #502, CP 4000, Lac du Bonnet, MB R0E 1A0
Tél: 204-345-1431
Téléc: 204-345-1440
Chief of Park Operations, Don Hallett
Tel: 204-345-1480
Northeastern
59 Elizabeth Dr., PO Box 28, Thompson, MB R8N 1X4
Tel: 204-677-6648
Fax: 204-677-6359
Regional Director, Pierce Roberts
Tel: 204-677-6893
Northwestern
3rd St. & Ross Ave., PO Box 2550, The Pas, MB R9A 1M4
Tel: 204-627-8215
Fax: 204-623-5733
Regional Director, Wayde Roberts
Tel: 204-627-8399
Western
1129 Queens Ave., PO Box 13, Brandon, MB R7A 1L9
Tel: 204-726-6441
Fax: 204-726-6301
Regional Director, Luke Peloquin
Tel: 204-726-6299

Manitoba Culture, Heritage & Tourism

Legislative Building, #118, 450 Broadway Ave., Winnipeg, MB R3C 0V8
Tel: 204-945-3729
Fax: 204-945-5223
mincht@leg.gov.mb.ca
www.gov.mb.ca/chc
Committed to the development & implementation of programs & services which promote & enhance the well-being, identity & creativity of Manitobans & which contribute to Manitoba's continued economic growth & steadily rising quality of life. Working with its partners in the community & with government, the Department raises the national & international profile of the talents & abilities of our people, encourages healthy active living, promotes pride of place, creates jobs & attracts & maintains investment in our province
Acts Administered:
Amusements Act (except Part II)
Arts Council Act
Coat of Arms, Emblems & The Manitoba Tartan Act
Foreign Cultural Objects Immunity from Seizure Act
Freedom of Information & Protection of Privacy Act
Heritage Manitoba Act
Heritage Resources Act
Income Tax Act
Le Centre Culturel Franco-Manitobain Act
Legislative Library Act
Legislative Library Act
Manitoba Museum Act
Public Libraries Act
Public Printing Act
Travel Manitoba Act

Minister, Hon. Florfina Marcelino
Tel: 204-945-3729
Fax: 204-945-5223
mincht@leg.gov.mb.ca

Deputy Minister, Cindy Stevens
Tel: 204-945-4136
Fax: 204-948-3102

Associated Agencies, Boards & Commissions:
• Le Centre Culturel franco-manitobain/Franco-Manitoban Cultural Centre
340, boul Provencher
St Boniface, MB R2H 0G7
Tel: 204-233-8972
Fax: 204-233-3324
ccfm@ccfm.mb.ca
www.ccfm.mb.ca
• Heritage Grants Advisory Council
213 Notre Dame Ave., 3rd Fl.
Winnipeg, MB R3B 1N3
Tel: 204-945-2213
Fax: 204-948-2086
• Manitoba Arts Council
#525, 93 Lombard Ave.
Winnipeg, MB R3B 3B1
Tel: 204-945-2237
Fax: 204-945-5925
Toll-free: 866-994-2787
info@artscouncil.mb.ca
www.artscouncil.mb.ca
An arms-length agency of the provincial government dedicated to artistic excellence. It offers a broad-based granting program for professional artists & arts organizations. It promotes, preserves, supports & advocates for the arts as essential to the quality of life of all the people of Manitoba.
• Manitoba Centennial Centre Corporation
555 Main St.
Winnipeg, MB R3B 1C3
Tel: 204-956-1360
Fax: 204-944-1390
• Manitoba Film Classification Board
#216, 301 Weston St.
Winnipeg, MB R3E 3H4
Tel: 204-945-8962
Fax: 204-945-0890
Toll-free: 866-612-2399
mfcb@gov.mb.ca
www.gov.mb.ca/filmclassification
• Manitoba Heritage Council
213 Notre Dame Ave., Main Fl.
Winnipeg, MB R3B 1N3
Tel: 204-945-2118
Fax: 204-948-2384
hrb@gov.mb.ca
Protects, interprets & promotes the heritage resources of the province; offers advice & recommendations on places & events which should be protected by the department; protection of significant buildings & sites.
• Manitoba Museum / Musée du Manitoba
190 Rupert Ave.
Winnipeg, MB R3B 0N2
Tel: 204-956-2830
Fax: 204-942-3679
info@manitobamuseum.mb.ca
www.manitobamuseum.mb.ca
Other Communication: Info Line:|204/943-3139
• Manitoba Film & Sound Recording Development Corporation
#410, 93 Lombard Ave.
Winnipeg, MB R3B 3B1
Tel: 204-947-2040
Fax: 204-956-5261
carole@mbfilmsound.mb.ca
www.mbfilmsound.mb.ca
Pomotes the province's film & sound recording artists & industries.

Administration & Finance Division
Fax: 204-945-5760
Executive Director, David Paton
Tel: 204-945-2233
Acting IT Director, Information Systems, Lori Constant
Tel: 204-945-4356
Director, Financial Services, Jennifer Hibbert
Tel: 204-945-3946

Communications Services Manitoba
155 Carlton St., 10th Fl., Winnipeg, MB R3C 3H8
Tel: 204-945-3765
Fax: 204-948-2147
Acting Assistant Deputy Minister, Debbie MacKenzie
Tel: 204-945-4271
Fax: 204-948-2219
Acting Director, Public Affairs, Angela Jamieson
Tel: 204-945-4971
Fax: 204-948-2147
Director, Creative Services, Cam McCullough
Tel: 204-945-8830
Fax: 204-948-2147
Director, Advertising & Program Promotion, Michelle Wallace
Tel: 204-945-5164
Fax: 204-948-2147
Manager, Internet Services, Carol Bartmanovich
Tel: 204-945-0870
Manager, Production & Media Procurement, Heather A. Coleman
Tel: 204-945-7121
Fax: 204-945-1366
Supervisor, Statutory Publications, Keith Holness
Tel: 204-945-3101
Fax: 204-945-7172
statpub@gov.mb.ca
200 Vaughan St.
Winnipeg, MB R3C 1T5
Director, Stu Fawcett
Tel: 204-945-3746
News Editor, Tobi Brown
Tel: 204-945-1014

Culture & Heritage Programs Division
Assistant Deputy Minister, Veronica Dyck
Tel: 204-945-4078
Fax: 204-948-2739
Director, Historic Resources, Donna Dul
Tel: 204-945-4389
Fax: 204-948-2384
Acting Director, Public Library Services, Trevor Surgenor
Tel: 204-726-6864
Fax: 204-726-6868
#200, 1595 - 1 St.
Brandon, MB R7A 7A1
Administrative Officer, Arts Branch, Donna Monkman
Tel: 204-945-4577

Provincial Services Division
#100, 200 Vaughan St., Winnipeg, MB R3C 1T5
Acting Executive Director, Melanie Cwikla
Tel: 204-945-3096
Legislative Librarian, Tannis Gretzinger
Tel: 204-945-4245
Archivist of Manitoba, Scott Goodine
Tel: 204-945-6140

Director, Information & Privacy Policy Secretariat, Michael Baudic
Tel: 204-945-2523
Office Manager, Translation Services, Diane Schipper
Tel: 204-945-0525

Tourism Secretariat
155 Carlton St., 7th Fl., Winnipeg, MB R3C 3H8
Toll-Free: 800-665-0040
www.travelmanitoba.com
Executive Director, Tourism Manitoba, Terry Welsh
Tel: 204-945-2449

Manitoba Development Corporation (MDC)

#555, 155 Carlton St., Winnipeg, MB R3C 3H8
Tel: 204-945-7626
Fax: 204-945-1193

Minister Responsible, Hon. Peter Bjornson
Tel: 204-945-0067
Fax: 204-945-4882
minett@leg.gov.mb.ca

Chair, Hugh Eliasson

Manitoba Education

#168, Legislative Bldg., 450 Broadway, Winnipeg, MB R3C 0V8
Tel: 204-945-3720
Fax: 204-945-1291
minedu@leg.gov.mb.ca
www.edu.gov.mb.ca

Acts Administered:
Blind & Deaf Persons' Maintenance & Education Act
Education Administration Act
Property Tax and Insualtion Assistance Act (Part III.2)
Public Schools Act
Public Schools Finance Board Act
Teachers' Pension Act
Teachers' Society Act

Minister, Hon. Nancy Allan
Tel: 204-945-3720
Fax: 204-945-1291
minedu@leg.gov.mb.ca

Deputy Minister, Gerald Farthing
Tel: 204-945-1648
Fax: 204-945-8330
dmedu@leg.gov.mb.ca

Executive Director, Public Schools Finance, Rick Dedi
Tel: 204-945-5534

Director, Schools' Finance Branch, Lynne Mavins
Tel: 204-945-4061

Associated Agencies, Boards & Commissions:
• **Public Schools Finance Board**
#506, 1181 Portage Ave.
Winnipeg, MB R3G 0T3
Tel: 204-945-6628
Fax: 204-948-2001
• **Teachers' Retirement Allowances Fund Board**
#330 Johnston Terminal
35 Forks Market Rd.
Winnipeg, MB R3C 4S8
Tel: 204-949-0048
Fax: 204-944-0361

Division du Bureau de l'éducation française / French Language Education Office
#509, 1181 av Portage, Winnipeg, MB R3C 0T3
Tél: 204-945-6916
Téléc: 204-945-1625
Sous-ministre adjoint, Jean-Vianney Auclair
Tél: 204-945-6928
Téléc: 204-948-2994
Directeur, Programmes de langues officielles et services administratifs, Kassy Assie
Tél: 204-945-6029
Téléc: 204-945-1625
Directrice, La production de Bibliothèque et Matériaux, Lynette Chartier
Tél: 204-945-1342
Directrice, Services de soutien en éducation, Florence Girouard
Tél: 204-945-8797
Directeur, Developpement et implantation des programmes, Gilbert Michaud
Tél: 204-945-6022

Education Administration Services / Services Administratifs de l'Éducation
#507, 1181 av Portage, Winnipeg, MB R3C 0T3
Tél: 204-945-6897
Téléc: 204-945-2154
Director, David Yeo
Tel: 204-945-8664
Program Director, Professional Certification & Student Records, Allan Tataryn
Tel: 204-773-2998
Senior Field Officer, Pupil Transportation, Chris Hagen
Tel: 204-945-6898

School Programs Division
#5, 1567 Dublin Ave, Winnipeg, MB R3E 3J5
Tel: 204-945-7934
Fax: 204-945-8303
Assistant Deputy Minister, Aileen Najduch
Tel: 204-945-7935
Chief Operating Officer, Manitoba Text Book Bureau, Brenda McKinny
Tel: 204-483-5035
Director, Instruction, Curriculum & Assessment, Daryl Gervais
Tel: 204-945-0294
Director, Program & Student Services, Joanna Blais
Tel: 204-945-7911
Fax: 204-945-7914
Coordinator, Development, Carole Bilyk
Tel: 204-945-1773
Coordinator, Assessment, Ken Clark
Tel: 204-945-3666
Coordinator, Early Childhood Education, Wenda Dickens
Tel: 204-945-1095
Coordinator, Media Production Services, Ani Granson
Tel: 204-945-5266
Coordinator, Distance Learning, Susan Lee
Tel: 204-325-1717
Financial Coordinator, Yvonne Pennings
Tel: 204-945-3546
Coordinator, Deaf & Hard of Hearing Services, Karen Priestley
Tel: 204-945-2051
Coordinator, Financial & Administration Unit, Joanne Prins
Tel: 204-945-7821
Coordinator, Learning Support & Technology, Cheryl Prokopanko
Tel: 204-945-6435
Coordinator, Instructional Resources, John Tooth
Tel: 204-945-7833

Shared Services
510 Selkirk Ave., Winnipeg, MB R2W 2M7
Director, Aboriginal Education Directorate, Helen Robinson-Settee
Tel: 204-945-4763
Fax: 204-948-2010
Acting Director, Systems & Technology Services, Shirley McLellan
Tel: 204-945-5421
Executive Financal Officer, Claude Fortier
Tel: 204-945-1117
Fax: 204-948-2851
Translator/French Language Coordinator, Translation Services, Rene Tondji-Simen
Tel: 204-945-6889

Elections Manitoba

#120, 200 Vaughan St., Winnipeg, MB R3C 1T5
Tel: 204-945-3225
Fax: 204-945-6011
Toll-Free: 866-628-6837
election@elections.mb.ca
www.electionsmanitoba.ca
Independent from government, Elections Manitoba conducts fair elections. It ensures that political financing laws are followed, & increases public awareness of the electoral process

Chief Electoral Officer, Richard D. Balasko
Tel: 204-945-3225

Deputy Chief Electoral Officer, Scott Gordon
Tel: 204-945-7156

Manager, Elections Finances, Shipra Verma, CA
Tel: 204-945-1283

Analyst, Financial Compliance, Maggie Anderson
Tel: 416-945-7559

Officer, Communications & Community Relations, Amanda Jeninga
Tel: 204-945-3804

Manitoba Entrepreneurship, Training & Trade

#1000, 259 Portage Ave, Winnipeg, MB R3B 3P4
Tel: 204-945-2475
Fax: 204-945-3977
minctt@leg.gov.mb.ca
www.gov.mb.ca/ctt
The mission of Manitoba's Entrepreneurship, Training & Trade is to support the growth of business in the province, to meet provincial labour demands, to increase training opportunities, & to expand global trade relations.

Acts Administered:
Biofuels Act
Crocus Investment Fund
Design Institute Act
Development Corporations Act
Drilling & Production Regulation
Economic Innovation & Technology Council Act
Electronic Commerce & Information Act (except part 5)
Energy Act
Gas Allocation Act
Gas Pipe Line Act
Greater Winnipeg Gas Distribution Act (S.M. 1988-89, C.40)
Income Tax Act (S. 7.5 & 7.10)
Labour-Sponsored Venture Capital Corporations Act
Manitoba Health Research Council Act
Mines & Minerals Act
Mining & Metallurgy Compensation Act
Oil & Gas Act
Oil & Gas Production Tax Act
Statistics Act
Surface Rights Act
Sustainable Development Act

Minister, Hon. Peter Bjornson
Tel: 204-945-0067
Fax: 204-945-4882
minett@leg.gov.mb.ca

Deputy Minister, Hugh Eliasson
Tel: 204-945-4076
Fax: 204-945-1561
dmett@leg.gov.mb.ca

Executive Director, Manitoba Trade & Investment, Don Callis
Tel: 204-945-8695

Executive Director, Financial & Administration Services, Craig Halwachs
Tel: 204-945-3675
chalwachs@gov.mb.ca

Director, Policy, Planning & Coordination, Alan Barber
Tel: 204-945-8714
abarber@gov.mb.ca

Associated Agencies, Boards & Commissions:
• **Apprenticeship & Certification Board**
#1010, 401 York Ave.
Winnipeg, MB R3C 0P8
Tel: 204-945-3337
Fax: 204-948-2346
Toll-free: 877-978-7233
The Board is an advisory body which makes recommendations regarding the designation and regulation of trades and which approves apprenticeship training standards.
• **Convention Centre Corporation Board of Directors**
375 York Ave.
Winnipeg, MB R3C 3J3
Tel: 204-956-1720
Fax: 204-943-0310
Toll-free: 800-565-7776
audra@wcc.mb.ca
The Board manages and administers the affairs of the corporation.
• **Manitoba Development Corporation (MDC)**
#1040, 259 Portage Ave.
Winnipeg, MB R3B 3P4
Tel: 204-945-0141
Fax: 204-945-1193
The Board provides financial services and manages financial instruments on behalf of the Province of Manitoba to assist with economic development initiatives.
• **Manitoba Opportunity Fund (MOF)**
#600, 259 Portage Ave.
Winnipeg, MB R3B 2A9
Tel: 204-945-1872
MOF holds and invests the Provincial allocation of immigrants investments made through the Federal Department of Citizenship and Immigration Canada's Immigrant Investor Program.

• Manitoba Trade & Investment Corporation (MTIC)
#1100, 259 Portage Ave.
Winnipeg, MB R3B 3P4
Tel: 204-945-2466
Fax: 204-957-1793
MTIC is an administrative mechanism that supports the economic priorities of Building the Manitoba economy through increased exports and industry investments.
• Manitoba Taking Charge! Inc
276 Colony St.
Winnipeg, MB R3C 1W3
Tel: 204-945-1100
Taking Charge! Inc. is a non-profit organization under the leadership & direction of a Board of Directors that also oversees the employment programming & Taking Care, the licensed day care.

Community & Economic Development Committee of Cabinet Secretariat
#648, 155 Carlton St., Winnipeg, MB R3C 3H8
Tel: 204-945-8221
Fax: 204-945-8229

Director, Anna Rothney
Tel: 204-945-3036
Administrative Officer, Colleen Davies
Tel: 204-945-4346
codavies@gov.mb.ca

Business Services Division
To encourage & facilitate entrepreneurial & employment opportunities within the Province through the establishment of new businesses or the expansion/retention of existing Manitoba businesses. The Branch promotes increased access to capital for industry by serving as a principal source of financial advice & assistance for businesses to expand or locate in Manitoba. The Branch develops & administers a number of third party delivered pools of risk capital
Senior Executive Director, Financial Services, Jim Kilgour
Tel: 204-945-7626
Director, Small Business Development, Tony Romeo
Tel: 204-945-2019
Senior Manager, Competitiveness Initiatives, Paul Pierlot
Tel: 204-945-5633
Senior Manager, Industry Consulting & Marketing Support, David Sprange
Tel: 204-945-7938
Librarian, Small Business Development, Peggy Neal
Tel: 204-984-0779

Labour Market Skills & Employment Income Assistance
Senior Executive Coordinator, Kimberley Puhach
Tel: 204-945-5034
Executive Director, Employment & Income Assistance Programs, Dave Fisher
Tel: 204-945-8730
Acting Executive Director, Industry Workforce Development, Lynn Houghton
Tel: 204-945-0122
Acting Executive Director, Apprenticeship Manitoba, Jacueline Ratte Kohut
Tel: 204-945-3337

Manitoba Bureau of Statistics
#824, 155 Carlton St., Winnipeg, MB R3C 3H9
Tel: 204-945-2406
Fax: 204-945-0695
Chief Statistician, Wilf Falk
Tel: 204-945-2988
wfalk@mbs.gov.mb.ca

Premier's Economic Advisory Council
#648, 155 Carlton St., Winnipeg, MB R3C 3N8
Tel: 204-945-6133
Fax: 204-945-8229

Executive Coordinator, Alissa Brandt
Tel: 204-945-5297

Manitoba Family Services & Labour

#219, 114 Garry St., Winnipeg, MB R3C 4V6
Tel: 204-945-3242
Fax: 204-945-2156
minfam@leg.gov.mb.ca
www.gov.mb.ca/fs
Supports citizens in need to achieve fuller participation in society & greater self-suffiency & independence. Helps keep children, families & communities safe & secure & promotes healthy citizen development & well-being. Mission is accomplished through: provision of financial support; provision of services & supports that assist individuals improve their attachment to the labour market; provision of supports & services for adults & children with disabilities; provision of child protection & related services; assistance to people facing family violence or family disruption; provision of services & supports to promote the healthy development & well-being of children & families; assistance to Manitobans to access safe, appropriate & affordable housing; fostering community capacity & engaging the broader community to participate in & contribute to decision-making; & respectful & appropriate delivery of programs & services
Acts Administered:
Adoption Act
Child & Family Services Act
Child & Family Services Authorities Act
Community Child Day Care Standards Act
Elderly & Infirm Person's Housing Act
Elderly & Infirm Persons' Housing Act
Employment & Income Assistance Act
Intercountry Adoption (Hague Convention) Act
Parents' Maintenance Act (s. 10)
Social Services Administration Act
Social Services Appeal Board Act
Vulnerable Persons Living with a Mental Disability Act

Minister, Hon. Jennifer Howard
Tel: 204-945-4173
Fax: 204-945-5149
minfsl@leg.gov.mb.ca

Deputy Minister, Jeff Parr
Tel: 204-945-6700
Fax: 204-948-1896
dmfsl@leg.gov.mb.ca

Assistant Deputy Minister, Cross-Department Coordination Initiatives, Marcia Thomson
Tel: 204-945-4895

Acting Executive Director, Policy & Planning, Lissa Donner
Tel: 204-945-3231

Associated Agencies, Boards & Commissions:
• Disabilities Issues Office
#630, 240 Graham Ave.
Winnipeg, MB R3C 0J7
Tel: 204-945-7613
Fax: 204-948-2896
TTY: 204-948-2901
dio@gov.mb.ca
• Manitoba Housing Authority - Public Housing
#2100, 185 Smith St.
Winnipeg, MB R3C 3G4
Tel: 204-945-4663
Fax: 204-948-2013
Toll-free: 800-661-4663
www.gov.mb.ca/fs/housing/mha.html
• Manitoba Housing & Renewal Corporation
280 Broadway
Winnipeg, MB R3C 0R8
Tel: 204-945-4895
Fax: 204-945-5710
www.gov.mb.ca/fs/org/eih/mhrc.html
• Social Services Appeal Board
175 Hargrave St., 7th Fl.
Winnipeg, MB R3C 3R8
Tel: 204-945-3003
Fax: 204-945-1736
Toll-free: 800-282-8069
TTY: 204-948-2037
www.gov.mb.ca/fs/ssab/index.html

Child & Family Services
Assistant Deputy Minister, Carolyn Loeppky
Tel: 240-945-3257
Acting Assistant Deputy Minister, Sid Rogers
Tel: 240-945-3257
Acting Executive Director, Child Protection, Brian Ridd
Tel: 240-945-4575
Acting Executive Director, Strategic Initiatives & Program Support, Ben Van Haute
Tel: 240-945-8300
Director, Operations, All Nations Coordinated Response Network (ANCR), Terry Driedger
Tel: 240-944-4142
Director, Family Violence Prevention, Paulette Fortier
Tel: 240-945-1709

Community Service Delivery
Assistant Deputy Minister, Peter Dubienski
Tel: 204-945-2204
Executive Director, Rural & Northern Services, Debbie Besant
Tel: 204-945-4998
Executive Director, Winnipeg Services, Michelle Dubik
Tel: 204-945-2685
Executive Director, Child & Family Services of Central MB, Kathleen Wightman
Tel: 204-857-8751
Executive Director, Service Delivery Support, Tom Sidebottom
Tel: 204-945-1268
Director, Provincial Services, Kathy Brooks
Tel: 204-945-6854

Disability Programs & Early Learning & Child Care
Assistant Deputy Minister, Charlene Paquin
Tel: 204-945-6374
Vulnerable Persons' Commissioner, JoAnne Reinsch
Tel: 204-945-0564
Acting Executive Director, Disability Programs, Carol Antkowiak
Tel: 204-945-3848
Director, Manitoba Early Learning & Child Care, Margaret Ferniuk
Tel: 204-945-2668
Director, Policy & Program Development, Catherine Gates
Tel: 204-945-0028
Director, Quality Assurance & Program Support, Darren Macdonald
Tel: 204-945-5660

Labour Programs
Executive Assistant to the ADM of Labour Programs, Michelle Tabaka
Tel: 204-945-8216
Fire Investigator, Office of the Fire Commissioner, Bill Harrow
Tel: 204-986-2742

Status of Women
#409, 401 York Ave., Winnipeg, MB R3C 0P8
Tel: 204-945-6281
Fax: 204-945-6511
Toll-Free: 800-263-0234
msw@gov.mb.ca
www.gov.mb.ca/msw
Senior Policy Analyst, Crystal Gartside
Tel: 204-945-5969

Manitoba Finance

#109, Legislative Bldg., Winnipeg, MB R3C 0V8
Tel: 204-945-3754
Fax: 204-945-8316
minfin@leg.gov.mb.ca
www.gov.mb.ca/finance/

Established in 1969 under authority of the Financial Administration Act. Responsible for central accounting, payroll & financial reporting services for the government, consumer & corporate affairs & central financial control of cost-shared agreements. The ministry manages government borrowing programs & is responsible for federal-provincial relations.
Acts Administered:
Bedding, Upholstered & Stuffed Articles Regulation
Business Names Registration Act
Business Practices Act
Cemeteries Act
Change of Name Act
Charities Endorsement Act
Commodity Futures Act
Condominium Act
Consumer Protection Act
Cooperatives Act
Corporation Capital Tax Act
Corporations Act
Credit Unions & Caisses Populaires Act
Electronic Commerce & Information Act
Embalmers & Funeral Directors Act
Energy Rate Stabilization Act
Financial Administration Act
Fire Insurance Reserve Fund Act
Fiscal Stabilization Fund Act
Gasoline Tax Act
Health & Post Secondary Education Tax Levy Act
Hospital Capital Financing Authority Act
Housing & Renewal Corporation Act
Hudson's Bay Company Land Register Act
Income Tax Act
Insurance Act
Insurance Corporations Tax Act
Landlord & Tenant Act
Life Leases Act
Manitoba Evidence Act (Part II & III)
Manitoba Investment Pool Authority Act
Manitoba Investment Pool Authority Act
Marriage Act
Mining Claim Tax Act
Mining Tax Act
Mortgage Act (Part III)
Mortgage Dealers Act
Motive Fuel Tax Act
Pari-Mutuel Levy Act
Partnership Act
Personal Investigations Act
Personal Property Security Act
Prearranged Funeral Services Act
Professional Home Economists Act
Property Tax & Insulation Assistance Act
Provincial-Municipal Tax Sharing Act
Public Health Act
Public Officers Act

Public Utilities Board Act
Real Estate Brokers Act
Real Property Act
Registry Act
Religious Societies' Lands Act
Residential Tenancies Act
Retail Sales Tax Act
Revenue Act
Securities Act
Special Survey Act
Succession Duty Act
Suitors' Moneys Act
Surveys Act (Part I)
The title to Certain Lands Act (R.S.M. 1990, c.259).
Tobacco Tax Act
Trade Practises Inquiry Act
Vital Statistics Act

Minister, Hon. Stan Struthers
Tel: 204-945-3722
Fax: 204-945-3470
minfin@leg.gov.mb.ca

Deputy Minister, Hugh, Eliasson
Tel: 204-945-5343
dmfin@leg.gov.mb.ca

Secretary, Treasury Board Secretariat, Tannis Mindell
Tel: 204-945-1100

Assoc. Secretary, Treasury Board, David Woodbury
Tel: 204-945-1524

Executive Director, Francophone Affairs Secretariat, Guy Jourdain
Tel: 204-945-4915

Peformance Management Coordinator, Administrative Policy, Sally Correia
Tel: 204-945-1084

Associated Agencies, Boards & Commissions:

• Automobile Injury Compensation Appeal Commission
#301, 428 Portage Ave..
Winnipeg, MB R3C 0E2
Tel: 204-945-4155
Fax: 204-948-2402
autoinjury@gov.mb.ca
www.gov.mb.ca/cca/autom

• Claimant Adviser Office
#200, 330 Portage Ave.
Winnipeg, MB R3C 0C4
Tel: 204-945-7413
Fax: 204-948-3157

• Credit Union Deposit Guarantee Corporation
#390, 200 Graham Ave.
Winnipeg, MB R3C 4L5
Tel: 204-942-8480
Fax: 204-947-1723
Toll-free: 800-697-4447
mail@cudgc.com
www.cudgc.com

• Crown Corporations Council / Conseil des corporations de la Couronne
#1130, 444 St. Mary Ave.
Winnipeg, MB R3C 3T1
Tel: 204-949-5270
Fax: 204-949-5283
crowncc@mts.net
www.crowncc.mb.ca

• Manitoba Securities Commission
#500, 400 St. Mary Ave.
Winnipeg, MB R3C 4K5
Tel: 204-945-2548
Fax: 204-945-0330
Toll-free: 800-655-5244
securities@gov.mb.ca
www.msc.gov.mb.ca
The Manitoba Securities Commission is an independent agency of the Government of Manitoba that protects investors and promotes fair and efficient capital markets throughout the province.

• Public Utilities Board
#400, 330 Portage Ave.
Winnipeg, MB R3C 0C4
Tel: 204-945-2638
Fax: 204-945-2643
Toll-free: 866-854-3698
publicutilities@gov.mb.ca
www.pub.gov.mb.ca
Regulate the rates charged by Manitoba Hydro (electrical utility), Manitoba Public Insurance (auto insurance), some gas or propane utilities (Centra Gas, Stittco, Swan Valley Gas Corp.) and all water and sewer utilities outside Winnipeg.

• Residential Tenancies Commission
#1650, 155 Carlton St.
Winnipeg, MB R3C 3H8
Tel: 204-945-2028
Fax: 204-945-5453
Toll-free: 800-782-8403
rtc@gov.mb.ca
www.gov.mb.ca/finance/cca/residtc
Landlords and tenants may appeal orders and decisions issued by the Residential Tenancies Branch. The commission hears these appeals. Appeals are heard by a panel of three consisting of one landlord and one tenant representative and either the chief commissioner or a deputy commissioner as the neutral chairperson.

Administration & Finance Division
Executive Financial Officer, Erroll Kavanagh
Tel: 204-945-4319
Director, Amalgamated Human Resources, Melanie Schade
Tel: 204-945-3001
Director, Insurance & Risk Management, John Rislahti
Tel: 204-945-2482

Manitoba Gaming Control Commission

#800, 215 Garry St., Winnipeg, MB R3C 3P3
Tel: 204-945-9400
Fax: 204-945-9450
Toll-Free: 800-782-0363
information@mgcc.mb.ca
www.mgcc.mb.ca

Established in 1969 under authority of the Financial Administration Act. Responsible for central accounting, payroll & financial reporting services for the government, consumer & corporate affairs & central financial control of cost-shared agreements. The ministry manages government borrowing programs & is responsible for federal-provincial relations.

Minister, Hon. David Chomiak
Tel: 204-945-9400

Chairperson, Darlene Dziewit

Vice-Chairperson, Lucille Cenerini

Commissioner, Barbara Bruce

Commissioner, Brenda Johnston

Commissioner, Dennis Meeches

Commissioner, Joe Stadnyk

Comptroller Division
#715, 401 York Ave., Winnipeg, MB R3C 0P8
Tel: 204-945-4920
Fax: 204-945-2394
Provides central accounting, payroll & financial reporting services, & central financial control of cost-shared agreements for the government. The division develops government-wide financial systems, policies & procedures, & provides policy advice for financial & management systems. The division coordinates, develops & maintains departmental data processing systems, & provides direction to the government on the effective use of information systems technology
Provincial Comptroller, Betty-Anne Pratt
Tel: 204-945-4919
Director, Internal Audit & Consulting Services, Jane Holatko
Tel: 204-945-8110
Director, Disbursements & Accounting, Terry Patrick
Tel: 204-945-1343
Director, Information Technology Management, Michael Antonio
Tel: 204-232-3560

Consumer & Corporate Affairs Division
Asst. Deputy Minister, Alexandra Morton, Q.C.
Tel: 204-945-3742
Fax: 204-945-4009
Director, Research & Planning, Ian Anderson
Tel: 204-945-7892
Director, Consumers' Bureau, Nancy Anderson
Tel: 204-945-4062
Acting Director, Residential Tenancies Branch, Laura Gowerluk
Tel: 204-945-0377
Fax: 204-945-6273
Director, Claimant Advisor Office, Bob Sample
Tel: 204-945-8171

Federal-Provincial Relations & Research Division
#910, 386 Broadway, Winnipeg, MB R3C 3R6
Tel: 204-945-3757
Fax: 204-945-5051
Provides research & analytical support for national/provincial fiscal & economic matters & inter-governmental financial relations. Also administers fiscal arrangements & tax collection agreements with the federal government & tax credit programs with federal & municipal governments
Asst. Deputy Minister, Heather Wood
Tel: 204-945-4120
Fax: 204-945-5051
Director, Economic & Fiscal Analysis, Jim Hrichishen
Tel: 204-945-1468
Acting Director, Intergovernmental Finance, René Perreault
Tel: 204-945-1478
Director, Taxation Analysis Branch, Stephen Watson
Tel: 204-945-1473

Taxation Division
#101, 401 York Ave., Winnipeg, MB R3C 0P8
Tel: 204-945-6444
Fax: 204-948-2360

Treasury Division
Created as a separate entity in 1976, to address the need for placing greater emphasis on the management of substantial amounts of money, debt & investments. Currency & interest rate risk management programs have been developed due to the increase in volumes & dollar values. The division assists with the arrangement of financing for municipalities, schools & hospitals
Asst. Deputy Minister, Gary Gibson
Tel: 204-945-1184
Director, Capital Markets, Deborah Deen
Tel: 204-945-6637
Director, Treasury & Banking Operations, Scott Wiebe
Tel: 204-945-6677

Companies Office
#1010, 405 Broadway, Winnipeg, MB R3C 3L6
Tel: 204-945-2500
Fax: 204-945-1459
companies@gov.mb.ca
companiesoffice.gov.mb.ca
Chief Operating Officer, Myron Pawlowsky
Tel: 204-945-4206

Financial Institutions Regulation Branch
#1115, 405 Broadway, Winnipeg, MB R3C 3L6
Tel: 204-945-2542
Fax: 204-948-2268
Superintendent, Financial Institutions, Jim Scalena
Tel: 204-945-3911
Deputy Superintendent, Lofgren Ken
Tel: 204-945-6111
Deputy Superintendent, Insurance, Scott Moore
Tel: 204-945-1150

Property Registry
Acting Director, Grant Kernested
Tel: 204-945-1946

Vital Statistics
254 Portage Ave., Winnipeg, MB R3C 0B8
Tel: 204-945-3701
Fax: 204-948-3128
Toll-Free: 800-282-8063
vitalstats@gov.mb.ca
www.gov.mb.ca/cca/vital
Other Communication: Fax Certificate Requests: 204-948-3128
Provincial agency responsible for the issuance of birth, death, change of name & marriage certificates. Written or faxed requests must be submitted.

Manitoba Health

#100, 300 Carlton St., Winnipeg, MB R3B 3M9
Tel: 204-786-7191
minhlt@leg.gov.mb.ca
www.gov.mb.ca/health/index.html

Responsible for the overall quality of the health system in the province, for maintaining the health system, & for ensuring that the health needs of Manitobans are met. Services are provided through regional delivery systems, hospitals & other health care facilities. The Department also makes insured benefits claims payments for residents of Manitoba related to the cost of medical, hospital, personal care, pharmacare & other health services. To lead the way to quality health care, built with creativity, compassion, confidence, trust & respect; empower Manitobans through knowledge, choices & access to the best possible health resources; & build partnerships & alliances for healthy & supportive communities. To foster innovation in the health care system. This is accomplished through: developing mechanisms to assess & monitor quality of care, utilization & cost effectiveness; fostering behaviours & environments which promote health; & promoting responsiveness & flexibility of delivery systems, & alternative & less expensive services.

Acts Administered:
Anatomy Act
Atmospheric Pollution Regulation
Cancer Care Manitoba Act
Chiropractic Act
Collection & Disposal of Wastes Regulation
Dental Association Act
Dental Health Services Act

Dental Health Workers Act
Denturists Act
Department of Health Act
District Health & Social Services Act
Elderly & Infirm Persons' Housing Act (with respect to elderly persons housing units as defined in the Act)
Emergency Medical Response and Stretcher Transportation Act
Fumigation & Pest Control Regulation
Health Services Act
Health Services Insurance Act
Hearing Aid Act
Hospitals Act
Human Tissue Act
Licensed Practical Nurses Act
Manitoba Medical Association Dues Act
Medical Act
Medical Laboratory Technologists Act
Mental Health Act (except parts 9 & 10 & clauses 125 (1)(i) & (j)
Midwifery Act
Naturopathic Act
Occupational Therapists Act
Opticians Act
Optometry Act
Personal Health Information Act
Pharmaceutical Act
Physiotherapists Act
Podiatrists Act
Prescription Drugs Cost Assistance Act
Private Hospitals Act
Protection for Persons in Care Act
Protection of Water Sources Regulation
Psychologists Registration Act
Public Health Act
Regional Health Authorities Act
Registered Dieticians Act
Registered Nurses Act
Registered Psychiatric Nurses Act
Registered Respiratory Therapists Act
Sanitation Regulation
Sanitorium Board of Manitoba Act
Tobacco Damages and Health Care Cost Recovery Act (not yet proclaimed)
Water Supplies Regulation
Water Works, Sewerage & Sewage Disposal Regulation
X-Ray Safety Regulation

Minister, Hon. Theresa Oswald
Tel: 204-945-3731
Fax: 204-945-0441
minhlt@leg.gov.mb.ca

Deputy Minister, Milton Sussman
Tel: 204-945-3771
Fax: 204-945-4564
dmhlt@leg.gov.mb.ca

Chief Medical Officer of Health, Dr. Joel Kettner
Tel: 204-788-6766
Fax: 204-948-2204

Provincial Director, Patient Access, Dr. Luis Oppenheimer

Administrative Secretary, Betty Rubin
Tel: 204-786-7191
Fax: 204-774-1325
brubin@gov.mb.ca

Associated Agencies, Boards & Commissions:
• Appeal Panel for Home Care
#4012, 300 Carlton St.
Winnipeg, MB R3B 3M9
Tel: 204-788-6788
Fax: 204-948-2024
Toll-free: 800-491-4993
appeals@gov.mb.ca

Associated Agencies, Boards & Commissions:
• Manitoba Drug Standards & Therapeutics Committee
#1014, 300 Carlton St.
Winnipeg, MB R3B 3M9
Tel: 204-786-7317
Fax: 204-942-2030
• Manitoba Health Appeal Board
#4011, 300 Carlton St.
Winnipeg, MB R3B 3M9
Tel: 204-788-6704
Fax: 204-948-2024
Toll-free: 866-744-3257
Quasi-judicial body responsible for making decisions on appeals under The Health Services Insurance Act, The Ambulance Services Act & The Mental Health Act.

• Addictions Foundation of Manitoba (AFM) / Fondation manitobaine de lutte contre les dépendances
1031 Portage Ave.
Winnipeg, MB R3G 0R8
Tel: 204-944-6200
Fax: 204-786-7768
library@afm.mb.ca
www.afm.mb.ca
• Manitoba Seniors & Healthy Aging Secretariat

Finance
Chief Financial Officer & Asst. Deputy Minister, Karen Herd
Tel: 204-788-2525
Fax: 204-775-3412

Health Workforce
Assistant Deputy Minister, Bethy Beaupre
Tel: 204-786-6674
Executive Assistant, Karen Hanks
Tel: 204-788-2500

Provincial Policy & Programs
Fax: 204-775-3712
Asst. Deputy Minister, Milton Sussman
Tel: 204-945-3771
Central File Clerk, Provincial Drug Programs, Arsenia Amigo
Tel: 204-788-2530
Director, Corporate Services, Jeff Gunter
Tel: 204-788-6749
Manager, Protection for Persons in Care, Chris Campbell
Tel: 204-786-7264
Acting Director, Information Systems - Technical Services & Operations, Ken Browne
Tel: 204-788-2521
Coordinator, French Language Services, Richard Loiselle
Tel: 204-788-6698
Fax: 204-772-2943
Director, Drug Management Policy, Jeff Onyskiw
Tel: 204-788-6436
Director, Provincial Blood Programs, Carol Renner
Tel: 204-786-7395

Public Health & Primary Health Care
300 Carlton St., 2nd Floor, Winnipeg, MB R3B 3M9
Mission is to encourage the prevention of illness & injury, coordinate access to health care, & strengthen existing primary health care services with new initiatives
Assistant Deputy Minister, Terry Goertzen
Tel: 204-788-6656
Director, Health System Innovations, Kristin Anderson
Tel: 204-788-6746
Executive Director, Primary Health Care Branch, Barbara Wasilewski
Tel: 204-786-7176

Regional Policy & Programs
Assistant Deputy Minister, Jean Cox
Tel: 204-786-7301
Project Manager for the ADM/Regional Programs & Services, Thelma Findlay
Tel: 204-786-6692

Associated Agencies, Boards & Commissions:
• Assiniboine Regional Health Authority
192 - 1st Ave.
PO Box 579
Souris, MB R0K 2C0
Tel: 204-483-5000
Fax: 204-483-5005
Toll-free: 888-682-2253
assineboinerha@arha.ca
www.assiniboine-rha.ca

Associated Agencies, Boards & Commissions:
• Brendon Regional Health Authority
150 - 7th St.
Brandon, MB R7A 7M2
Tel: 204-578-2300
Fax: 204-578-2820
www.brandonrha.mb.ca
• Burntwood Regional Health Authority
867 Thompson Dr. South
Thompson, MB R8N 1Z4
Tel: 204-677-5353
Fax: 204-677-5366
www.brha.mb.ca
• Central Regional Health Authority
180 Centennaire Dr.
Southport, MB R0H 1N0
Tel: 204-428-2720
Fax: 204-428-2779
Toll-free: 800-742-6509
www.rha-central.mb.ca

• Churchill Regional Health Authority
Churchill Health Centre
Churchill, MB R0H 0E0
Tel: 204-675-8318
Fax: 204-675-2243
www.churchillrha.com
• Interlake Regional Health Authority
589 - 3rd Ave. South
Stonewall, MB R0C 2Z0
Tel: 204-467-4742
Fax: 204-467-4750
Toll-free: 888-488-2299
www.irha.mb.ca
• Nor-Man Regional Health Authority
84 Church St.
PO Box 130
Flin Flon, MB R8A 1M7
Tel: 204-687-1300
Fax: 204-687-6405
www.norman-rha.mb.ca
• North Eastman Regional Health Authority
24 Aberdeen Ave.
PO Box 339
Pinawa, MB R0E 1L0
Tel: 204-753-3101
Fax: 204-753-2015
Toll-free: 800-753-2012
www.neha.mb.ca
• Parkland Regional Health Authority
625 Third St. SW
Dauphin, MB R7N 1R7
Tel: 204-638-2118
Fax: 204-622-6232
Toll-free: 800-259-7541
www.prha.mb.ca
• South Eastman Regional Health Authority
PO Box 470
La Broquerie, MB R0A 0W0
Tel: 204-424-5880
Fax: 204-424-5888
Toll-free: 866-716-5633
www.sehealth.mb.ca
• Winnipeg Regional Health Authority
650 Main St.
Winnipeg, MB R3B 1E2
Tel: 204-926-7000
Fax: 204-926-7007
www.wrha.mb.ca

Manitoba Healthy Child Office

#219, 114 Garry St., Winnipeg, MB R3C 1G1
Tel: 204-945-2266
Toll-Free: 888-848-0140
healthychild@gov.mb.ca
Office provides leadership & encourages actions that address health concerns & reduces the need for medical care for children

Acts Administered:
Manitoba Prenatal Benefit Regulation
The Addictions Foundation Act
The Non-Smokers Health Protection Act

Minister, Hon. Kerri Irvin-Ross
Tel: 204-945-1373
Fax: 204-948-2703

Chief Executive Officer, Healthy Child Manitoba, Jan Sanderson
Tel: 204-945-6707
Fax: 204-948-2585

Director, Programs, Susan Tessler
Tel: 204-945-1275

Manitoba Healthy Living, Seniors & Consumer Affairs

#822, 155 Carlton St., Winnipeg, MB R3C 3H8
Tel: 204-945-6565
Fax: 204-948-2514
Toll-Free: 800-665-6565
seniors@gov.mb.ca
www.gov.mb.ca/shas

Deputy Minister, Cindy Stevens
Tel: 204-945-4136

Associated Agencies, Boards & Commissions:
• Manitoba Council on Aging
#822, 155 Carlton St.
Winnipeg, MB R3C 3H8
Tel: 204-945-6565
Fax: 204-948-2514
Toll-free: 800-665-6565

Administration & Finance
#822, 155 Carlton St., Winnipeg, MB R3C 3H8
Tel: 204-945-6565
Fax: 204-948-2514
Toll-Free: 800-665-6565
seniors@gov.mb.ca
www.gov.mb.ca/shas

Consumer & Corporate Affairs
#822, 155 Carlton St., Winnipeg, MB R3C 3H8
Tel: 204-945-6565
Fax: 204-948-2514
Toll-Free: 800-665-6565
seniors@gov.mb.ca
www.gov.mb.ca/shas

Healthy Living & Populations
#822, 155 Carlton St., Winnipeg, MB R3C 3H8
Tel: 204-945-6565
Fax: 204-948-2514
Toll-Free: 800-665-6565
seniors@gov.mb.ca
www.gov.mb.ca/shas

The Property Registry
#822, 155 Carlton St., Winnipeg, MB R3C 3H8
Tel: 204-945-6565
Fax: 204-948-2514
Toll-Free: 800-665-6565
seniors@gov.mb.ca
www.gov.mb.ca/shas

Director of Finance, Grant Kernested
Tel: 204-945-1946
Director of Information Technology, Cecilia Antonio
Tel: 204-945-2244

Manitoba Housing & Community Development

175 Hargrave St., 7th Fl., Winnipeg, MB R3C 3R8
Tel: 204-945-3007
Fax: 204-945-1292
Toll-Free: 888-884-8681
hrc@gov.mb.ca
www.gov.mb.ca/hrc/
TTY: 204-945-3442

Deputy Minister, Joy Cramer
Tel: 204-945-5600

Chief Executive Officer, Manitoba Housing, Darrell Jones
Tel: 204-945-7647

Minister, Minister's Office, Kerri Irvin-Ross
Tel: 204-945-6190

Manitoba Human Rights Commission

175 Hargrave St., 7th Fl., Winnipeg, MB R3C 3R8
Tel: 204-945-3007
Fax: 204-945-1292
Toll-Free: 888-884-8681
hrc@gov.mb.ca
www.gov.mb.ca/hrc/
TTY: 204-945-3442

Executive Director, Dianna Scarth
Tel: 204-945-3020

Manitoba Hydro

360 Portage Ave., PO Box 815 Main, Winnipeg, MB R3C 2P4
Tel: 204-474-3311
publicaffairs@hydro.mb.ca
www.hydro.mb.ca

Manitoba Hydro (MH) is a major energy utility. One of the largest electricity & natural gas utilities in Canada, it serves 521,600 electric customers throughout Manitoba & 261,150 gas customers in various communities throughout southern Manitoba. Virtually all electricity generated by the provincial Crown Corporation is from self-renewing water power. MH is the major distributor of natural gas in the province. Developing & implementing an environmental management system consistent with ISO standards. Actively pursuing a vairety or projects & programs aimed at reducing GHG & vehicle emissions, recycling, conserving energy, digging out contaminated soils, partnering with NGOs

Minister responsible, Hon. Dave Chomiak
Tel: 204-945-5356
Fax: 204-948-2692
miniem@leg.gov.mb.ca

President/CEO, Bob B. Brennan
Tel: 204-474-3600

Chair, Victor H. Schroeder, Q.C.

Vice-President, Customer Service & Marketing, Gerry W. Rose

Vice-President, Finance & Administration & CFO, Vince A. Warden

Vice-President, Power Supply, Ken R. Adams

Vice-President, Transmission & Distribution, Al M. Snyder

General Counsel & Corporate Secretary, Ken M. Tennenhouse

Manitoba Immigration & Multiculturalism

Legislative Building, 317, 450 Broadway Ave., Winnipeg, MB R3C 0V8
Tel: 204-945-4079
Fax: 204-945-8312
minlab@leg.gov.mb.ca
www.gov.mb.ca/labour

Acts Administered:
Amusements Act (Part II)
Architects & Engineers Scope of Practice Dispute Settlement Act
Architects Act
Buildings & Mobile Homes Act
Construction Industry Safety Regulation
Construction Industry Wages Act
Department of Labour & Immigration Act
Electricians' Licence Act
Elevator Act
Employment Services Act
Employment Standards Code
Engineering & Geoscientific Professions Act
Fair Registration Practices in Regulated Professions Act
Fibrosis & Silicosis Regulation
Firefighters & Paramedics Arbitration Act
Fires Prevention & Emergency Response Act
Forestry, Logging & Log Hauling Regulation
Gas & Oil Burner Act
Hearing Conservation & Noise Control Regulation
Holocaust Memorial Day Act
Labour Relations Act
Manitoba Ethnocultural Advisory & Advocacy Council Act
Manitoba Immigration Council Act
Manitoba Multiculturalism Act
Manitoba Women's Advisory Council Act
Minimum Wage & Working Conditions Regulation
Operation of Mines Regulation
Pay Equity Act
Pension Benefits Act
Power Engineers Act
Remembrance Day Act
Retail Business Holiday Closing Act
Sanitary & Hygienic Welfare Regulation
Steam & Pressure Plants Act
Worker Recruitment and Protection Act
Workplace Hazardous Materials Information System Regulation
Workplace Health Hazard Regulation
Workplace Safety & Health Act
Workplace Safety & Health Committee Regulation
Workplace Safety Regulation

Minister, Christine Melnick
Tel: 204-945-4079
Fax: 204-945-8312
minimm@leg.gov.mb.ca

Deputy Minister, Hugh Eliasson
Tel: 204-945-4076

Director, Multiculturalism Secretariat, Benjamin Amoyaw
Tel: 204-945-6290

Program Officer, Multiculturalism Secretariat, Simi Jerez
Tel: 204-945-6245

Associated Agencies, Boards & Commissions:
- **Advisory Council on Workplace Safety & Health**
#200, 401 York Ave.
Winnipeg, MB R3C 0P8
Tel: 204-945-3446
Fax: 204-945-4556
www.gov.mb.ca/labour/safety/council.html
The Advisory Council on Workplace Safety & Health was established in 1977 under the authority of the Workplace Safety & Health Act. The council reports directly to the Minister of Labour & Immigration. The council advises & makes recommendations to the Minister of Labour & Immigration concerning general workplace safety & health issues, protection of workers in specific situations & appointment of consultants & advisors.
- **Board of Electrical Examiners**
#500, 401 York Ave
Winnipeg, MB R3C 0P8
Tel: 204-945-3507
terry.rieger@gov.mb.ca
- **Gas Advisory Board**
terry.reiger@gov.mb.ca
- **Manitoba Ethnocultural Advisory & Advocacy Council**
215 Notre Dame Ave. 4th Fl.
Winnipeg, MB R3B 1N3
Tel: 204-945-2339
Fax: 204-948-2323
Toll-free: 800-665-8332
meaac@gov.mb.ca
www.gov.mb.ca/labour/immigrate/multiculturalism/5.html
- **Manitoba Labour Board**
A.A. Heaps Bldg.
#402, 258 Portage Ave.
Winnipeg, MB R3C 0B6
Tel: 204-945-3783
Fax: 204-945-1296
mlb@gov.mb.ca
www.gov.mb.ca/labour/labbrd
- **Manitoba Minimum Wage Board**
614 - 401 York Ave.
Winnipeg, MB R3C 0P8
Tel: 204-945-4889
Fax: 204-948-2085
mw@gov.mb.ca
www.gov.mb.ca/labour/labmgt/resbr/wages/minwagbd.html
- **Manitoba Women's Advisory Council**
#301, 155 Carlton St.
Winnipeg, MB R3C 3H8
Tel: 204-945-6281
Fax: 204-945-6511
Toll-free: 800-282-8069
001women@gov.mb.ca
- **Multiculturalism Secretariat**
213 Notre Dame Ave., 4th Fl.
Winnipeg, MB R3B 1N3
Tel: 204-945-1156
Fax: 204-948-2323
- **Office of the Fire Commissioner**
#508, 401 York Ave.
Winnipeg, MB R3C 0P8
Tel: 204-945-3322
Fax: 204-948-2089
Toll-free: 800-282-8069
firecomm@gov.mb.ca
www.firecomm.gov.mb.ca/
- **Pension Commission of Manitoba**
#1004, 401 York Ave.
Winnipeg, MB R3C 0P8
Tel: 204-945-2740
Fax: 204-948-2375
pensions@gov.mb.ca
www.gov.mb.ca/labour/pension/index.html

Manitoba Infrastructure & Transportation

Legislative Building, #203, 450 Broadway Ave., Winnipeg, MB R3C 0V8
Tel: 204-945-3723
Fax: 204-945-7610
www.gov.mb.ca/mit/

Acts Administered:
CentrePort Canada Act
Crown Lands Act
Drivers & Vehicles Act
Government Air Services Act
Government House Act
Government Purchases Act
Highway Traffic Act
Highways & Transportation Act
Highways & Transportation Construction Contracts Disbursement Act
Highways Protection Act
Land Acquisition Act
Manitoba Floodway Authority Act
Manitoba Water Services Board Act
Off-Road Vehicles Act
Provincial Parks Act
Provincial Railways Act
Public Works Act
Taxicab Act
Trans-Canada Highway Act
Water Resources Administration Act
Wild Rice Act

Minister, Hon. Steve Ashton
Tel: 204-945-3723
Fax: 204-945-7610
mininfratran@leg.gov.mb.ca

Associate Deputy Minister, Paul Rochon
Tel: 204-945-3887
215 Garry St., 17th Fl.
Winnipeg, MB R3C 3Z1

Assistant Deputy Minister, Engineering & Operations Division, Lance Vigfusson
Tel: 204-945-3733
215 Garry St., 17th Fl.
Winnipeg, MB R3C 3Z1

Associated Agencies, Boards & Commissions:
• Lake Winnipeg Stewardship Board
PO Box 305
Gimli, MB R0C 1B0
Tel: 204-642-4899
www.lakewinnipeg.org
Established in 2003 to assist the government of Manitoba to achieve the main commitments in the Lake Winnipeg Action Plan of reducing phosphorus & nitrogen in the lake to pre-1970 levels. The Lake Winnipeg Stewardship Board's Interim Report (Jan. 2005), contained 32 sets of recommendations & was followed by public discussions.
• Highway Traffic Board/Motor Transport Board
#200, 301 Weston St.
Winnipeg, MB R3E 3H4
Tel: 204-945-8912
Fax: 204-783-6529
• Manitoba Floodway Authority (MFA)
#200, 155 Carlton St.
Winnipeg, MB R3C 3H8
Tel: 204-945-4900
Fax: 204-948-2462
Toll-free: 866-356-6355
floodway@gov.mb.ca
Separate, independent, publicly accountable provincial agency that will manage the expansion & maintenance of the Red River Floodway on behalf of Manitobans.
• Manitoba Habitat Heritage Corporation
#200, 1555 St. James St.
Winnipeg, MB R3H 1B5
Tel: 204-784-4350
Fax: 204-784-7359
mhhc@mhhc.mb.ca
www.mhhc.mb.ca
• License Suspension Appeal Board/Medical Review Committee
#200, 301 Weston St.
Winnipeg, MB R3E 3H4
Tel: 204-945-7350
Fax: 204-948-2682
• Manitoba Water Services Board
PO Box 22080
Brandon, MB R7A 6Y9
Tel: 204-726-6076
Fax: 204-726-6290
www.gov.mb.ca/waterstewardship/mwsb/
Assists rural residents outside Winnipeg in developing safe & sustainable water &/or sewerage facilities.
• Manitoba Land Value Appraisal Commission
800 Portage Ave.
Winnipeg, MB R3G 0N4
Tel: 204-945-2941
Fax: 204-948-2235
• Taxicab Board
#200, 301 Weston St.
Winnipeg, MB R3E 3H4
Fax: 204-948-2315

Accommodation Services Division
1700 Portage Ave., Winnipeg, MB R3J 0E1
Asst. Deputy Minister, Chris Hauch
Tel: 204-945-7535
Fax: 204-945-2546
Acting Director, Corporate Services, Accommodation Policy & Planning, Don Armstrong
Tel: 204-945-2009
Director, Project Services, Pat Landry
Tel: 204-945-6615
Director, Operations, Susanne Parent
Tel: 204-945-7528
Director, Leasing, Accommodation Management & Parking, Andrea Clarke
Tel: 204-945-7588
Supervisor, Accounting Service, Divisional Support Services, Heather Wilson
Tel: 204-945-7550

Emergency Measures Organization (EMO)
405 Broadway Ave., 15th Floor, Winnipeg, MB R3C 3L6
Tel: 204-945-4772
Fax: 204-945-4929
Toll-Free: 888-267-8298
emo@gov.mb.ca
www.manitobaemo.ca
Coordinates emergency response, municipal emergency planning & training, & disaster recovery programs
Executive Director, Chuck Sanderson
Tel: 204-945-5228
Fax: 204-945-4929

Supply & Services Division
270 Osborne St. North, Winnipeg, MB R3C 1V7
Asst. Deputy Minister, Tracey Danowski
Tel: 204-945-6340
Fax: 204-948-2509
COO, Fleet Vehicles Agency, Al Franchuk
Tel: 204-945-0275
626 Henry Ave.
Winnipeg, MB R3A 1P7
Director, Procurement Services, David Ash
Tel: 204-945-6380
Fax: 204-945-1455
270 Osborne St. North, 2nd Fl.
Winnipeg, MB R3C 1V7
COO, Materials Distribution Agency, David Bishop
Tel: 204-945-6043
Fax: 204-948-3273
#7, 1715 St. James St.
Winnipeg, MB R3H 1H3

Transportation
Legislative Bldg., #209, 450 Broadway, Winnipeg, MB R3C 0V8
Deputy Minister, Andrew Horosko
Tel: 204-945-3768
Fax: 204-945-4766

Construction & Maintenance Branch
#1610, 215 Garry St., Winnipeg, MB R3C 3Z1
Fax: 204-945-3841
Other Communication: Highway Condition Information: 204-945-3705, 1-877-627-6237
Executive Director, Ron Weatherburn
Tel: 204-945-3775
Director, Mechanical Equipment Services, Mike Knight
Tel: 204-945-8567
Fax: 204-948-3274

Administrative Services Division
215 Garry St., 17th Fl., Winnipeg, MB R3C 3Z1
Fax: 204-945-5115
Asst. Deputy Minister, Ian Hasanally
Tel: 204-945-2964
Acting Director, Financial Services, Todd Callin
Tel: 204-945-3883
Director, Information Technology Services, Dan Buhler
Tel: 204-945-4512
215 Garry St., 12th Fl.
Winnipeg, MB R3C 3Z1
Acting Director, Occupation Safety, Health Risk Management, Tim Lucko
Tel: 204-945-4102
#600, 155 Carlton St.
Winnipeg, MB R3C 3H8

Engineering & Operations Division
215 Garry St., 16th Fl., Winnipeg, MB R3C 3Z1
Fax: 204-945-3841
Asst. Deputy Minister, Lance Vigfusson
Tel: 204-945-3733
Director, Northern Airports & Marine, Mary Bartman
Tel: 204-945-3421
Executive Director, Construction & Maintenance, Ron Weatherburn
Tel: 204-945-3775
Executive Director, Highway Regional Opertaions, Don McKibbin
Tel: 204-726-6809
Director, Water Control & Structures, Ron Richardson
Tel: 204-945-6494
Executive Director, Highway Engineering, Walter T. Burdz
Tel: 204-945-3772

Manitoba Floodway & East Side Road Authority

Motor Carrier Division
Assistant Deputy Minister, John Spacek
Tel: 204-945-1025
Executive Director, Darren Christle
Tel: 204-945-7693
Director, Safety Programs, Bruce McCormick
Tel: 204-945-6651
Director, Motor Carrier Permits & Development, Sheila Champagne
Tel: 204-945-8909

Director, Strategic Initiatives Branch, Lawrence Mercer
Tel: 204-945-1894

Safety & Supply Services Division
Assistant Deputy Minister, Tracey Danowski
Tel: 204-945-6340
Director, Procurement Services, David Ash
Tel: 204-945-6380
Acting Chief Operating Officer, Crown Lands and Property Agency, Tracey Danowski
Tel: 204-239-3561
Chief Operating Officer, Vehicle and Equipment Management Agency, Al Franchuk
Tel: 204-945-0275

Transportation Policy Division
215 Garry St., 15th Fl., Winnipeg, MB R3C 3Z1
Fax: 204-945-5539
Asst. Deputy Minister, John Spacek
Tel: 204-945-1025
Director, Legislative & Regulatory Services Branch, Lucille McLaughlin
Tel: 204-945-7996
Director, Transportation Policy & Service Development, Richard Danis
Tel: 204-945-0800
Acting Director, Transportation Systems Planning & Development, David Duncan
Tel: 204-945-3646

Manitoba Innovation, Energy & Mines

Tel: 204-945-3744
Toll-Free: 866-626-4862
mgi@gov.mb.ca

Acts Administered:
Gaming Control Act
Manitoba Hydro Act

Minister, Dave Chomiak
Tel: 204-945-5356

Special Advisor to the Minister, Manitoba Hydro, Carolina Stecher
Tel: 204-945-3365

Associated Agencies, Boards & Commissions:
• Industrial Technology Centre
#200, 78 Innovation Dr.
Winnipeg, MB R3T 6C2
www.itc.mb.ca
• Mining Board
#360, 1395 Ellice Ave.
Winnipeg, MB R3G 3P2
Tel: 204-489-0018
Arbitration of disputes between surface rights holders & mineral rights holders with respect to accessing of minerals other than oil & gas.
• Surface Rights Board
#360, 1395 Ellice Ave.
Winnipeg, MB R3G 3P2
Tel: 204-945-0731
Fax: 204-948-2578
Toll-free: 800-282-8069
bmiskimmin@gov.mb.ca
Arbitrates disputes relating to right of entry or compensation for surface rights used by holders of oil & gas rights.
• Manitoba Education, Research & Learning Information Networks (MERLIN)
#100 - 135 Innovation Dr., University of Manitoba
Winnipeg, MB R3T 6A8
Tel: 204-474-7800
Fax: 204-474-7830
Toll-free: 800-430-6404
www.merlin.mb.ca
• Manitoba Health Research Council
#P216, 770 Bannatyne Ave.
Winnipeg, MB R3E 0W3
Tel: 204-775-1096
Fax: 204-786-5401
info@mhrc.mb.ca
mhrc.mb.ca

Administration & Finance
Executive Director, Financial & Administrative Services (Shared), Craig Halwachs
Tel: 905-945-3675
Director Finance & Accountability, Peter Moreira
Tel: 204-945-7281
Supervisor of Accounting Services, Shirley Dimaala-Martin
Tel: 204-945-2176

Business Transformation & Technology
Asst. Deputy Minister, Gisela Rempel
Tel: 204-945-2692
Executive Director, ICT Management Services, Marion Gislason
Tel: 204-945-7629

Executive Director, ICT Strategic Services & Innovation, Ken K. Lamoureux
Tel: 204-945-7385

Legislative Building Information Systems
Acting Office Manager, Legislative Building Information Systems, Corazon Magnayon
Tel: 204-945-6219
Manager, Application Development, Bryan Lam
Tel: 204-945-0121
Manager, LBIS, Technical Services, Robert Bazzocchi
Tel: 204-945-0544
Senior Technical Specialist, Technical Services, Harry Van Ry
Tel: 204-945-0766
Chief Operating Officer, Greg Baylis
Tel: 204-474-7800

Mineral Resources Division
343 Legislative Bldg., 450 Broadway, Winnipeg, MB R3C 0V8
Fax: 204-948-2692
Assistant Deputy Minister, John Fox
Tel: 204-945-4317
Director, Manitoba Geological Survey, Ric Syme
Tel: 204-945-6556
Coordinator, Aboriginal Consultation, Minerals Policy & Business Development, Garry Courchene
Tel: 204-945-6563
Coordinator, Minerals Convention, Minerals Policy & Business Developments, Shirley Holgate
Tel: 204-945-2691
Director, Mines Branch, Ernie Armitt
Tel: 204-945-6505
Director, Petroleum Branch, Keith Lowdon
Tel: 204-945-6574

Science, Innovation & Business Development
343 Legislative Bldg., 450 Broadway, Winnipeg, MB R3C 0V8
Fax: 204-948-2692
Business Development Associate, Tim McIsaac
Tel: 204-945-0287
Director, Broadband Initiatives, Maurice Montreuil
Tel: 204-474-7098
Acting Director, Business Development, Knowledge Enterprises, Cindy Hodges
Tel: 204-945-6657
Senior Executive Director, Life Sciences, Douglas McCartney
Tel: 204-945-6298

Manitoba Local Government

#301, 450 Broadway Ave., Winnipeg, MB R3C 0V8
Fax: 204-945-1383
mnia@leg.gov.mb.ca
www.gov.mb.ca/ia/

The mission is to improve the economic, social & environmental wellbeing of Manitoba communities & citizens. The Department serves individuals, local governments, community organizations & businesses; & establishes a legislative, financial, planning & policy framework that supports democratic, accountable, effective & financially efficient local government, & the sustainable development of our communities. Programs are aimed at meeting particular needs for training, on-going advice, technical analysis & funding related to community revitalization & development, infrastructure development, land management, business support & local governance. The Department functions as an advocate of community needs, a catalyst & co-ordinator of action, promotes & participates in partnerships with private sector & non-government organizations & intergovernmental alliances.

Acts Administered:
An Act respecting Debts Owing by Municipalities to School Districts
Capital Region Partnership Act
Cemeteries Act
City of Winnipeg Charter
Emergency 911 Public Safety Answering Point Act
Emergency Measures Act
Local Government Districts Act
Manitoba Trade & Investment Corporation Act
Municipal Act
Municipal Affairs Administration Act
Municipal Assessment Act
Municipal Board Act
Municipal Councils & School Boards Elections Act
Municipal Revenue (Grants & Taxation) (Part 2)
Official Time Act
Planning Act (in part)
Prearranged Funeral Services Act
Regional Waste Management Authorities Act
Soldiers' Taxation Relief Act
Unconditional Grants Act

Minister, Hon. Ron Lemieux
Tel: 204-945-3788
Fax: 204-945-1383
minlg@leg.gov.mb.ca

Deputy Minister, Intergovernmental Affairs, Linda McFadyen
Tel: 204-945-4309
Fax: 204-945-5255
dmlg@leg.gov.mb.ca

Manager, Accounting Services, Financial & Administrative Services, Gary Sawchuk
Tel: 204-945-2201

Associated Agencies, Boards & Commissions:
• Manitoba Liquor Control Commission
1555 Buffalo Pl.
PO Box 1023
Winnipeg, MB R3C 2X1
Tel: 204-284-2501
Fax: 204-475-7666
info@mlcc.mb.ca
www.mlcc.mb.ca
• Manitoba Municipal Board
#1144, 363 Broadway
Winnipeg, MB R3C 3N9
Tel: 204-945-2941
Fax: 204-948-2235

Canada-Manitoba Infrastructure Secretariat
Tel: 204-945-4074
Fax: 204-945-2035
Toll-Free: 800-268-4883
infra@gov.mb.ca
Executive Director, Karlene Debance
Tel: 204-945-4431
Director, Infrastructure Programs, Barb Harrison
Tel: 204-945-7624
Director, Economic Development Programs, Tara Pratt
Tel: 204-945-8666

Community Planning & Development
Assistant Deputy Minister, Ramona Mattix
Tel: 204-945-6117
Director, Community & Regional Planning, David Neufeld
Tel: 204-945-2192
Fax: 204-945-5059
Director, Planning Policy & Programs, Jon Gunn
Tel: 204-945-3864

Provincial-Municipal Support Services
#508, 800 Portage Ave., Winnipeg, MB R3G 0N4
Assistant Deputy Minister, Laurie Davidson
Tel: 204-945-2565
Fax: 204-948-2107
Provincial Municipal Assessor, Assessment Branch, Mark Boreskie
Tel: 204-945-2604
Fax: 204-945-1994
assessment@gov.mb.ca
Other Communications: Web Site: www.gov.mb.ca/assessment
Director, Information Systems, Debbie Champagne
Tel: 204-945-2602
Fax: 204-945-1994
Director, Municipal Finance & Advisory Services, Matt Dryburgh
Tel: 204-945-1944
Fax: 204-948-2780

Urban Strategic Initiatives
#607, 800 Portage Ave., Winnipeg, MB R3G 0N4
Fax: 204-948-3512
Asst. Deputy Minister, Vacant
Director, Programs & Policy, Jon Gunn
Tel: 204-945-3864
Director, Winnipeg Partnership Agreement, Vacant
Tel: 204-984-1806
Fax: 204-983-3844
Coordinator, Neighbourhoods Alive!, Bob Dilay
Tel: 204-945-3379
Fax: 204-945-5059

Manitoba Justice

Legislative Building, #104, 405 Broadway Ave., Winnipeg, MB R3C 3L6
Tel: 204-945-3728
Fax: 204-945-2517
minjus@gov.mb.ca
www.gov.mb.ca/justice/index.html

Promotes a safe, just & peaceful society supported by a justice system that is fair, effective, trusted & understood by: providing a fair & effective prosecution service; managing offenders in an environment that promotes public safety & rehabilitation; providing mechanisms for timely & peaceful resolution of civil & criminal matters; providing legal advice & services to government; providing programs which assist in protecting & enforcing individual & collective rights; providing support & assistance to victims of crime; & promoting effective policing & crime prevention initiatives

Acts Administered:
Canada-United Kingdom Judgements Enforcement Act
Child Custody Enforcement Act
Constitutional Questions Act
Correctional Services Act
Court Security Act
Court of Appeal Act
Court of Queens' Bench Act
Crime Prevention Foundation Act
Crown Attorneys Act
Department of Justice Act
Discriminatory Business Practices Act
Domestic Violence & Stalking Prevention, Protection & Compensation Act
Enforcement of Judgements Conventions Act
Escheats Act
Executive Government Organization Act (subsection 12(2), only, as Keeper of the Great Seal)
Expropriation Act
Fatality Inquiries Act
Fortified Buildings Act
Helen Betty Osborne Memorial Foundation Act
Human Rights Code
Inter-jurisdictional Support Orders Act
International Commercial Arbitration Act
International Sale of Goods Act
Interprovincial Subpoena Act
Intoxicated Persons Detention Act
Jury Act
Law Enforcement Review Act
Law Fees & Probate Charge Act
Law Reform Commission Act
Legal Aid Services Society of Manitoba Act
Mental Health Act Part 10 & clauses 125(1)(i) & (j)
Minors Intoxicating Substances Control Act
Privacy Act
Private Investigators & Security Guards Act
Proceedings Against the Crown Act
Provincial Police Act
Public Trustee Act
Reciprocal Enforcement of Judgement Act
Regulations Act
Safer Communities & Neighbourhood Act
Sheriffs Act
Summary Convictions Act
Transboundary Pollution Reciprocal Access Act
Uniform Law Conference Commissioners Act
Vacant Property Act
Victims' Bill of Rights

Minister & Attorney General, Hon. Andrew Swan
Tel: 204-945-3728
Fax: 204-945-2517
minjus@leg.gov.mb.ca

Deputy Minister & Deputy Attorney General, Jeffrey Schnoor, Q.C.
Tel: 204-945-3739
dmjus@leg.gov.mb.ca

Executive Director, Administration & Finance, Patrick J Sinnott
Tel: 204-945-2880

Associated Agencies, Boards & Commissions:
• Compensation for Victims of Crime
1410 - 405 Broadway
Winnipeg, MB R3C 3L6
Tel: 204-945-0899
Fax: 204-948-3071
Toll-free: 800-262-9344
www.gov.mb.ca/justice/victims/index.html
The Compensation for Victims of Crime Program provides compensation for personal injury or death resulting from certain crimes occurring within Manitoba.
• Law Enforcement Review Agency (LERA)
#420, 155 Carlton St.
Winnipeg, MB R3C 3H8
Tel: 204-945-8667
Fax: 204-948-1014
Toll-free: 800-282-8069
lera@gov.mb.ca
www.gov.mb.ca/justice/lera
The mission of the Law Enforcement Review Agency (LERA) is to deliver a judicious, timely, impartial, client-oriented service to the public and to the police services and police officers within its jurisdiction.

• Law Reform Commission
#432, 405 Broadway
Winnipeg, MB R3C 3L6
Tel: 204-945-2896
Fax: 204-948-2184
lawreform@gov.mb.ca
www.gov.mb.ca/justice/mlrc
The Manitoba Law Reform Commission is an independent agency of the Government of Manitoba established by The Law Reform Commission Act, C.C.S.M. c. L95. The Commission's duties are to inquire into and consider any matter relating to law in Manitoba with a view to making recommendations for the improvement, modernization and reform of law.

• Legal Aid Manitoba
402 - 294 Portage Ave.
Winnipeg, MB R3C 0B9
Tel: 204-985-8500
Fax: 204-944-8582
Toll-free: 800-261-2960
info@legalaid.mb.ca
www.legalaid.mb.ca
Legal Aid Manitoba works to ensure people with low incomes have the protections guaranteed in Canada by the The Charter of Rights and Freedoms, enacted as part of The Constitution Act in 1982.

• Manitoba Gaming Control Commission
#800, 215 Garry St.
Winnipeg, MB R3C 3P3
Tel: 204-954-9400
Fax: 204-954-9450
Toll-free: 800-782-0363
information@mgcc.mb.ca
www.mgcc.mb.ca
Other Communication: Toll Free Fax: 1-866-999-6688
To regulate and control gaming activity in Manitoba by protecting the public interest, being proactive and responsive to Manitoba's evolving gaming environment and working in consultation with our clients, stakeholders and partners to establish fair, balanced and responsible gaming practices.

• Manitoba Human Rights Commission

• Office of the Chief Medical Examiner
#210, 1 Wesley Ave.
Winnipeg, MB R3C 4C6
Tel: 204-945-2088
Fax: 204-945-2442
Toll-free: 800-282-9069
www.gov.mb.ca/justice/about/chief.html
The Chief Medical Examiner's Office investigates deaths where the cause is not readily known or when the death is a result of violence.

• Office of the Public Trustee
#500, 155 Carlton St.
Winnipeg, MB R3C 5R9
Tel: 204-945-2700
Fax: 204-948-2251
publictrustee@gov.mb.ca
www.gov.mb.ca/publictrustee/index.html
The Public Trustee of Manitoba is a provincial government Special Operating Agency that manages and protects the affairs of Manitobans who are unable to do so themselves and have no one else willing or able to act. This includes mentally incompetent and vulnerable adults, deceased estates, and children.

• Manitoba Review Board
408 York Ave., 2nd Fl.
Winnipeg, MB R3C 0P9
Tel: 204-945-4438
Fax: 204-945-5751

Civil Legal Services
Acting Director, Civil Legal Services, Lynn Romeo
Tel: 204-945-2846
Director, Constitutional Law, Heather Leonoff
Tel: 204-945-0679
Director, Family Law, Joan A. MacPhail, Q.C.
Tel: 204-945-0268
Fax: 204-948-2004

Corrections Division
#810, 405 Broadway Ave., Winnipeg, MB R3C 3L6
Tel: 204-945-7291
Asst. Deputy Minister, Greg Graceffo
Tel: 204-945-7291
Fax: 204-945-5537
Executive Director, Adult Custody, Reg Forester
Tel: 204-945-7283
Fax: 204-945-5537
Acting Executive Director, Youth Correctional Services, Carolyn Brock
Tel: 204-945-6063
Fax: 204-948-2166
Acting Director, Adult Probation Services, Bob Dojack
Tel: 204-945-4639
Fax: 204-948-2166

Courts Division
405 Broadway, 2nd Fl., Winnipeg, MB R3C 3L6
Asst. Deputy Minister, Jeff Schnoor
Tel: 204-945-3027
Acting Executive Director, Judicial Services, Lavonne Ross
Tel: 204-945-0413
Executive Director, Regional Courts, Vacant
Tel: 204-726-6561
Executive Director, Winnipeg Courts & Acting Director, Court Services, Debra Baker
Tel: 204-945-5883
Other Communications: Court Services: 204/945-1579

Criminal Justice Division
Asst. Deputy Minister, Mike Horn
Tel: 204-945-2887
Director, Aboriginal & Community Law Enforcement, Al Brolly
Tel: 204-945-5556
Director, Victim Services, Vacant
Tel: 204-945-4589

Legislative Counsel Division
#410, 405 Broadway Ave., Winnipeg, MB R3C 3L6
Tel: 204-945-5758
Legislative Counsel & Asst. Deputy Minister, Valerie Perry
Tel: 204-945-1727
Director, Legal Translation, Michel Nantel
Tel: 204-945-4597

Prosecutions Division
#510, 405 Broadway Ave., Winnipeg, MB R3C 3L6
Tel: 204-945-2852
Asst. Deputy Attorney General, Vacant
Tel: 204-945-2873
Director, Regional Prosecutions & Legal Education, Brian Kaplan
Tel: 204-945-2860
Director, Specialized Prosecutions & Appeals, Don Slough
Tel: 204-945-2868
Director, Winnipeg Prosecutions, Jacqueline St.Hill
Tel: 204-945-3228
Director, Policy Development & Analysis, Jeff Schnoor
Tel: 204-945-2900
Director, Business Operations, Carol Abbott
Tel: 204-945-3417

•

Manitoba Liquor Control Commission

1555 Buffalo Place, PO Box 1023, Winnipeg, MB R3C 2X1
Tel: 204-284-2501
contact@mlcc.mb.ca
www.mlcc.mb.ca

Minister, Hon. Greg Selinger
Tel: 204-284-2501

Chair, Carmen Neufeld

Vice-Chair, Fran Frederickson

President & CEO, Ken Hildahl

Commissioner, Ed Azure

Commissioner, Janine Ballingall Scotten

Commissioner, Les Crisostomo

Commissioner, Garry Hammerback

Commissioner, Eugene Kostyra

Commissioner, Maria Moore

Commissioner, Aidan O'Brien

Commissioner, Myrna A. Phillips

Manitoba Lotteries Corporation

830 Empress St., Winnipeg, MB R3G 3H3
Tel: 204-957-2500
Fax: 204-957-3991
Toll-Free: 800-265-2912
communications@casinosofwinnipeg.com
www.mlc.mb.ca

President/CEO, Winston Hodgins

Communications Coordinator, Lindsay Sprange
Tel: 204-957-3930

Manitoba Government Inquiry
Tel: 204-945-3744
Fax: 204-945-4261
Toll-Free: 866-626-4862
mgi@gov.mb.ca
TTY: 204-945-4796
Answers queries regarding Manitoba's provincial government departments & agencies.
Supervisor, Aggie Hasselfield
Tel: 204-945-2424
ahasselfield@gov.mb.ca

Statutory Publications
#20, 200 Vaughan St., Winnipeg, MB R3C 1T5
Tel: 204-945-3101
Fax: 204-945-7172
Toll-Free: 800-321-1203
statpub@gov.mb.ca
www.gov.mb.ca/chc/statpub/
Sale & distribution of Manitoba statutes, regulations & a wide variety of other government publications & forms
Supervisor, Keith Holness
Tel: 204-945-3101
Fax: 204-945-7172
kholness@gov.mb.ca

Manitoba Office of the Ombudsman

750 - 500 Portage Ave., Winnipeg, MB R3C 3X1
Tel: 204-982-9130
Fax: 204-942-7803
Toll-Free: 800-665-0531
ombudsma@ombudsman.mb.ca
www.ombudsman.mb.ca
The Ombudsman, an independent & non-partisan Officer of the Legislative Assembly, investigates complaints from persons who feel they have been unfairly dealt with by government departments or agencies

Manitoba Ombudsman, Irene Hamilton

Manitoba Public Insurance

#B100, 234 Donald St., PO Box 6300, Winnipeg, MB R3C 4A4
Tel: 204-985-7000
Fax: 204-985-3525
Toll-Free: 800-665-2410
www.mpi.mb.ca
TTY: 204-985-8832
Administers Manitoba's Public Automobile Insurance Program & sells extension auto coverage on a competitive basis.

Minister responsible, Hon. Andrew Swan
Tel: 204-945-3728
Fax: 204-945-2517
minjus@leg.gov.mb.ca

President/CEO, Marilyn McLaren

Vice-President, Claims Operations & Safety Operations, Ted Hlynsky

Vice-President, Community & Corporate Relations, MaryAnn Kempe

Vice-President, Finance & CFO, Don Palmer

Vice-President, Service Operations, Christine Martin

Vice-President, Strategy & Innovation & Chief Information Officer, Dan Guimond

General Counsel & Corporate Secretary, Kathy Kalinowsky

Manitoba Telecom Services Inc. (MTS)

333 Main St., PO Box 6666, Winnipeg, MB R3C 3V6
Tel: 204-941-4111
Fax: 204-772-6391
www.mts.mb.ca/

Chair, Thomas E. Stefanson

CEO, Pierre Blouin

President, Enterprise Solutions, John A. MacDonald

President, Consumer Markets, Kelvin Shepherd, P.Eng.

CFO, Wayne S. Demkey, CA

Manitoba Treasury Board Secretariat

#200, 386 Broadway, Winnipeg, MB R3C 3R6
Tel: 204-945-4150
Fax: 204-948-4878
The Treasury Board Secretariat provides financial and analytical support and advice to the Minister of Finance and Treasury Board.

Minister responsible, Hon. Rosann Wowchuk
Tel: 204-945-3952
Fax: 204-945-6057
minfin@leg.gov.mb.ca

Secretary to the Treasury Board, Tannis Mindell
Tel: 204-945-1100

Asst. Deputy Minister, Labour Relations, Richard (Rick) Stevenson
Tel: 204-945-2136

Asst. Deputy Minister, Fiscal Management & Capital Planning, Barb Dryden
Tel: 204-945-1096

Manitoba Workers' Compensation Board

333 Broadway Ave., Winnipeg, MB R3C 4W3
Tel: 204-954-4321
Fax: 204-954-4999
Toll-Free: 800-362-3340
wcb@wcb.mb.ca
www.wcb.mb.ca

President/CEO, Doug Sexsmith

CFO, Harold Dueck

Vice President, Prevention, Assessments & Customer Service, Alice Sayant

Vice President, Rehabilitation & Compensation Services, Dave Scott

General Counsel & Corporate Secretary, Lori Ferguson Sain

Associate Vice President, Human Resources & Administration, Rob Campbell

Director, Communications/SAFE Work, Warren Preece

Government of New Brunswick

Seat of Government: PO Box 6000, Fredericton, NB E3B 5H1
www.gnb.ca
The Province of New Brunswick entered Confederation July 1, 1867. It has an area of 71,355.12 km2. The Statistics Canada census population in 2011 was 751,171.

Office of the Lieutenant-Governor

Government House, 51 Woodstock Rd., PO Box 6000, Fredericton, NB E3B 5H1
Tel: 506-453-2505
Fax: 506-444-5280
LTgov@gnb.ca
www.gnb.ca/lg
The Lieutenant-Governor represents The Queen of Canada, Her Majesty Queen Elizabeth II in New Brunswick. The Lieutenant-Governor is appointed by the Governor General-in-Council on the recommendation of the Prime Minister of Canada.
The following are some responsibilities of the Lieutenant-Governor: opening, proroguing, & dissolving the Legislative Assembly of New Brunswick; swearing in the Premier & cabinet ministers; delivering the Speech from the Throne; giving royal assents to bills passed by the legislature; presenting awards; lending patronage to non-for-profit organizations; & participating in dedications & investitures.

Lieutenant-Governor of New Brunswick / Lieutenant-gouverneur du Nouveau-Brunswick, Hon. Graydon Nicholas
graydon.nicholas@gnb.ca

Principal Secretary, Tim Richardson
tim.richardson@gnb.ca

Office of the Premier / Cabinet du Premier ministre

Centennial Bldg., 670 King St., PO Box 6000, Fredericton, NB E3B 5H1
Tel: 506-453-2144
Fax: 506-453-7407
premier@gnb.ca
www.gnb.ca/premier

Premier; President, Executive Council; Minister, Intergovernmental Affairs; Minister Responsible, Premier's Council on the Status of Disabled Persons; Minister Responsible, Aboriginal Affairs Secretariat, Citizens' Engagement, Hon. David Alward
david.alward@gnb.ca; Premier@gnb.ca

Chief of Staff, Nancy McKay
nancy.mckay@gnb.ca

Correspondence Manager, Correspondence, Linda Landry-Guimond
Tel: 506-453-2144
Fax: 506-453-7407
linda.laundry-guimond@gnb.ca

Press Secretary, Communications, Jesse Robichaud
jesse.robichaud@gnb.ca

Executive Council

Centennial Building, PO Box 6000, Fredericton, NB E3B 5H1
Tel: 506-444-4417
Fax: 506-453-2266
Executivecouncilofflce@gnb.ca
www2.gnb.ca/content/gnb/en/departments/executive_council.ht ml
The following members of The Cabinet of the Government of New Brunswick are listed in the order their departments appear in the Executive Council Act:

Premier; President, Executive Council; Minister Responsible, Intergovernmental Affairs, Aboriginal Affairs Secretariat, Premier's Council on the Status of Disabled Persons, Citizens' Engagement, Office of Government Review;Chair, Policy & Priorities Committee, Hon. David Alward
Tel: 506-453-2144
Fax: 506-453-7407
premier@gnb.ca; premierministre@gnb.ca; david.alward@gnb.ca
Office of the Premier, Centennial Building
670 King St.
PO Box 6000
Fredericton, NB E3B5H1

Minister, Justice; Attorney General; Minister Responsible, Women's Issues, Hon. Marie-Claude Blais, Q.C.
Tel: 506-453-3132
Fax: 506-453-3651
marie-claude.blais@gnb.ca
Centennial Building
670 King St.
PO Box 6000
Fredericton, NB E3B5H1

Minister, Public Safety; Solicitor General, Hon. Robert B. Trevors
Tel: 506-453-7414
Fax: 506-453-3870
robert.trevors@gnb.ca; robert.trevors.mla@bellaliant.com
Argyle Place
364 Argyle St.
PO Box 6000
Fredericton, NB E3B5H1

Minister, Finance; Minister, Office of Human Resources; Minister Responsible, New Brunswick Liquor Corporation, New Brunswick Investment Management Corporation, & New Brunswick Lotteries & Gaming Corporation; Chair, Board ofManagement, Hon. Blaine Higgs
Tel: 506-444-2627
Fax: 506-457-4989
Blaine.Higgs@gnb.ca
Centennial Building
670 King St.
PO Box 6000
Fredericton, NB E3B 5H1

Minister, Transportation & Infrastructure; Minister Responsible, Supply & Services, Hon. Claude Williams
Tel: 506-457-7345
Fax: 506-453-7987
Claude.Williams@gnb.ca
Kings Place
440 King St.
PO Box 6000
Fredericton, NB E3B5H1

Minister, Natural Resources, Hon. Bruce Northrup
Tel: 506-453-2510
Fax: 506-444-5839
bruce.northrup@gnb.ca
Hugh John Flemming Forestry Centre
1350 Regent St.
PO Box 6000
Fredericton, NB E3B 5H1

Minister, Agriculture, Aquaculture, & Fisheries, Hon. Michael Olscamp
Tel: 506-453-2662
Fax: 506-453-3402
Mike.Olscamp@gnb.ca
Agricultural Research Station (Experimental Farm)
850 Lincoln Rd.
PO Box 6000
Fredericton, NB E3B5H1

Minister, Health, Hon. Madeleine Dubé
Tel: 506-457-4800
Fax: 506-453-5442
Madeleine.Dubé@gnb.ca
HSBC Place
520 King St.
PO Box 5100
Fredericton, NB E3B 5G8

Minister, Culture, Tourism, & Healthy Living, Hon. Trevor Holder
Tel: 506-453-3009
Fax: 506-457-4984
trevor.holder@gnb.ca
Centennial Building
670 King St.
PO Box 6000
Fredericton, E3

Minister, Social Development; Minister Responsible for Seniors, Housing, & Community Non-Profit Organizations, Hon. Sue Stultz
Tel: 506-453-2001
Fax: 506-453-2164
sue.stultz@gnb.ca
Sartain MacDonald Building
551 King St.
PO Box 6000
Fredericton, NB E3B 5H1

Minister, Post-Secondary Education, Training, & Labour, Hon. Martine Coulombe
Tel: 506-453-2342
Fax: 506-453-3038
martine.coulombe@gnb.ca
Chestnut Complex
470 York St.
PO Box 6000
Fredericton, NB E3B 5H1

Minister, Education Early Childhood Development, Hon. Jody Carr
Tel: 506-453-2523
Fax: 506-457-4810
jody.carr@gnb.ca
Place 2000
250 King St.
PO Box 6000
Fredericton, NB E3B 5H1

Minister, Environment & Local Government; Minister Responsible for the Energy Efficiency & Conservation Agency of NB, Hon. Bruce Fitch
Tel: 506-444-5136
Fax: 506-453-3377
Bruce.Fitch@gnb.ca
Marysville Place
20 McGloin St.
PO Box 6000
Fredericton, NB E3B 5H1

Minister, Economic Development; Minster Responsible for la Francophonie; Deputy Premier; Government House Leader, Hon. Paul Robichaud
Tel: 506-453-5898
Fax: 506-453-6389
paul.robichaud@gnb.ca
Centennial Building
670 KingSt.

PO Box 6000
Fredericton, NB E3B 5H1

Minister, Government Services; Acting Minister, Energy; Minister Responsible, New Brunswick Internal Services Agency, Service New Brunswick, Hon. Craig Leonard
Tel: 506-453-2240
Fax: 506-453-5329
Craig.Leonard@gnb.ca;EECA/AECE.Customer.Service@gnb.ca
Andal Building
225 King St.
PO Box 6000
Saint John, NB E3B 5H1

Executive Council Office

Centennial Building, #273, 670 King St., PO Box 6000, Fredericton, NB E3B 5H1
Tel: 506-444-4417
Fax: 506-453-2266
www.gnb.ca/0012/index-e.asp

The Executive Council Office is responsible for the provision of secretariat & administrative services to the following: the Executive Council; ministers with policy coordination responsibilities; & the Policy & Priorities Committee.

Premier; President, Executive Council; Minister Responsible, Intergovernmental Affairs, Aboriginal Affairs Secretariat, Premier's Council on the Status of Disabled Persons, Citizens' Engagement, Office of Government Review;Chair, Policy & Priorities Committee, Hon. David Alward
Tel: 506-453-2144
Fax: 506-453-7407
premier@gnb.ca; premierministre@gnb.ca;
david.alward@gnb.ca

Deputy Minister; Clerk of the Executive Council; Secretary to Cabinet, Byron James
Tel: 506-444-4417
Fax: 506-453-2266
Byron.James@gnb.ca

Deputy Minister, Responsible for Strategic Initiatives, Dallas McCready
Tel: 506-453-2144
Fax: 506-453-7407
dallas.mccready@gnb.ca

Assistant Deputy Minister, Patricia MacKenzie
Tel: 506-453-2314
Fax: 506-453-2266
patricia.mackenzie@gnb.ca

Secretary to the Policy & Priorities Committee of Cabinet, Greg Lutes
Tel: 506-462-5003
Fax: 506-453-2266
greg.lutes@gnb.ca

Aboriginal Affairs Secretariat / Secrétariat des affaires autochtones
Kings Place, #237, 440 King St., PO Box 6000, Fredericton, NB E3B 5H8
Tel: 506-462-5177
Fax: 506-444-5142
aboriginalaffairssecretariat@gnb.ca
www.gnb.ca/aboriginal

The Aboriginal Affairs Secretariat strives to enhance the Government of New Brunswick's relationship with Mi'kmaq & Maliseet (or Wolastoqiyik) communities & Aboriginal organizations. The Secretariat acts as a gateway for contact between First Nations & the province. It works with all provincial departments to address issues such as health, housing, education, family & community services, economic development, & natural resource management.

Premier; President, Executive Council; Minister Responsible, Intergovernmental Affairs, Aboriginal Affairs Secretariat, Premier's Council on the Status of Disabled Persons, Citizens' Engagement, Office of Government Review;Chair, Policy & Priorities Committee, Hon. David Alward
Tel: 506-453-2144
Fax: 506-453-7407
premier@gnb.ca; premierministre@gnb.ca;
david.alward@gnb.ca
Director, Susanne Derrah
Susi.Derrah@gnb.ca
Director, John Smith
Tel: 506-444-4665
Fax: 506-444-5142
John.Smith6@gnb.ca
Officer, Jason Peters
jason.peters@gnb.ca
Legislature & Program Officer, Lisa Rivett
lisa.rivett@gnb.ca

Intergovernmental Affairs Division
Centennial Bldg., #274, 670 King St., PO Box 6000, Fredericton, NB E3B 5H1
Tel: 506-457-7275
Fax: 506-453-2995
iga@gnb.ca

The Intergovernmental Affairs Division manages relations with other governments, communities, & organizations.
Acts Administered:
Maritime Economic Cooperation Act
Order of New Brunswick Act

Premier; President, Executive Council; Minister Responsible, Intergovernmental Affairs, Aboriginal Affairs Secretariat, Premier's Council on the Status of Disabled Persons, Citizens' Engagement, Office of Government Review;Chair, Policy & Priorities Committee, Hon. David Alward
Tel: 506-453-2144
Fax: 506-453-7407
premier@gnb.ca; premierministre@gnb.ca;
david.alward@gnb.ca

North American Relations Division / Division des relations nord-américaines
Centennial Building, #274, 670 King St., PO Box 6000, Fredericton, NB E3B 5H1
Tel: 506-444-6775
Fax: 506-453-2995
iga@gnb.ca

The North American Relations Division has the following mission: to protect New Brunswick's interests in the Canadian federation & with the United States; to pursue increased federal investment in New Brunswick; to promote regional cooperation to achieve the province's social & economic priorities; & to increase the benefits for New Brunswick as a member of the Council of Maritime Premiers, the Council of Atlantic Premiers, & the Conference of New England Governors and Eastern Canadian Premiers.

Assistant Deputy Minister, Jocelyne Mills
Tel: 506-457-7275
Fax: 506-457-6507
jocelyne.mills@gnb.ca
Director, Phyllis Mockler-Caissie
Tel: 506-444-2481
Fax: 506-453-2995
Phyllis.Mockler-Caissie@gnb.ca

Women's Issues Branch
Sartain MacDonald Bldg., PO Box 6000, Fredericton, NB E3B 5H1
Tel: 506-453-8126
Fax: 506-453-7977
WIB-DQF@gnb.ca
www.gnb.ca/0012/Womens-Issues/index-e.asp

Women's Issues, a branch of the Executive Council Office, consists of the following units: Violence Prevention Initiatives; Wage Gap Reduction Initiatives; & Policy Assessment & Advice. The branch provides support on women's issues to the Minister Responsible for Women's Issues & to departments of the provincial government.

Assistant Deputy Minister, Norma Dubé
Tel: 506-453-2975
Fax: 506-453-7977
Norma.Dube@gnb.ca
Director, Wage Gap Reduction Initiatives, Nicole McCarty
Tel: 506-453-8126
Fax: 506-453-7977
Nicole.McCarty@gnb.ca
Director, Violence Prevention Initiatives, Martine Stewart
Tel: 506-453-8126
Fax: 506-453-7977
Martine.Stewart@gnb.ca
Coordinator, Policy, Sonja Perley
Tel: 506-462-5023
Fax: 506-453-7977
sonja.perley@gnb.ca

Legislative Assembly of New Brunswick / Assemblée législative

Centre Block, Legislative Building, 706 Queen St., PO Box 6000, Fredericton, NB E3B 5H1
Tel: 506-453-2506
Fax: 506-453-7154
wwwleg@gnb.ca
www.gnb.ca/legis/index-e.asp

The Office of the Legislative Assembly is responsible for the following services: assisting Members of the Legislative Assembly, their staff, & the public; recording the proceedings of the Legislative Assembly; maintaining the records of the Legislative Assembly; & providing information services on behalf of the Legislative Assembly.

Speaker of the Legislative Assembly, Hon. Dale Graham
Tel: 506-453-2907
Fax: 506-453-7154
dale.graham@gnb.ca

Deputy Speaker, Claude Landry
Tel: 506-453-7494
Fax: 506-453-3461
claude.landry@gnb.ca

Deputy Speaker, Carl Urquhart
Tel: 506-453-7494
Fax: 506-453-3461
carl.urquhart@gnb.ca

Clerk of the Legislative Assembly, Loredana Catalli Sonier
Tel: 506-453-2506
Fax: 506-453-7154
l.catalli.sonier@gnb.ca

Director, Finance & Human Resources, Peter Wolters
Tel: 506-453-2506
Fax: 506-444-3331
peter.wolters@gnb.ca

Sergeant-at-Arms, Daniel Bussières
Tel: 506-453-2527
Fax: 506-453-7154
dan.bussieres@gnb.ca

Commissioner, Office of the Conflict of Interest, Hon. Patrick A.A. Ryan, Q.C.
Tel: 506-457-7890
Toll-free: 877-333-9831
Fax: 506-444-5224
coi@gnb.ca
Edgecombe House
736 King St.
Fredericton, NB E3B 1G2

Official Reporter, Hansard Office, Linda Fahey
Tel: 506-453-2531
Fax: 506-453-3199
linda.fahey@gnb.ca
West Block
96 Saint John St.
PO Box 6000
Fredericton, NB E3B 5H1

Legislative Librarian, Kenda Clark-Gorey
Tel: 506-453-8346
Fax: 506-444-5889
kenda.clark.gorey@gnb.ca

Manager, Debates Translation, Aurella Losier-Vienneau
Tel: 506-453-6270
Fax: 506-453-3126
aurella.losier.vienneau@gnb.ca
Edgecombe House
736 King St.
Fredericton, NB E3B 1G2

Officer, Special Projects, Valmond LeBlanc
Tel: 506-472-0214
Fax: 506-472-4724
vall2@rogers.com
Edgecombe House
736 King St.
Fredericton, NB E3B 1G2

Government Members Office (Progressive Conservative Party)
West Block, Departmental Building, 96 Saint John St., PO Box 6000, Fredericton, NB E3B 5H1
Tel: 506-453-7494
Fax: 506-453-3461
pcmemb@gnb.ca

Leader of the Government (Premier); President, Executive Council; Minister Responsible, Intergovernmental Affairs, Aboriginal Affairs Secretariat, Premier's Council on the Status of Disabled Persons, Citizens' Engagement,Office of Government Review, Hon. David Nathan Alward
Tel: 506-453-2144
Fax: 506-453-7407
premier@gnb.ca; premierministre@gnb.ca;
david.alward@gnb.ca
Office of the Premier, Centennial Building
670 King St.
PO Box 6000
Fredericton, NB E3B 5H1
Government House Leader; Deputy Premier; Minister, Economic Development; Minister Responsible for la Francophonie, Hon. Paul Robichaud
paul.robichaud@gnb.ca
Deputy Government House Leader, Wes McLean
wes.mclean@gnb.ca

Director, Research, Carole Caron
carole.caron2@gnb.ca
Director, Communications (Government Members), Heidi Cyr
heidi.cyr@gnb.ca
Director, Translation & Communications, Melanie Sivret
melanie.sivret@gnb.ca
Manager, Office Administration (Government Members), Kathy Legere
kathy.legere@gnb.ca

Office of the Official Opposition (Liberal Party) / Bureau de l'opposition officielle
East Block, Old Education Building, 710 Queen St., PO Box 6000, Fredericton, NB E3B 5H1
Tel: 506-453-2548
Fax: 506-453-3956
Leader, Official Opposition, Victor Éric Boudreau
victor.boudreau@gnb.ca
Chief of Staff, Greg Byrne
greg.byrne@gnb.ca
Director, Research & Communications, Carl Davies
carl.davies@gnb.ca
Press Secretary, Hillary Casey
hillary.casey@gnb.ca
Office Manager, Administrative Services, Linda Haché
lindahache@gnb.ca

Standing Committees of the Legislative Assembly of New Brunswick
The following are the Standing Committees of the Legislative Assembly of New Brunswick: Crown Corporations; Estimates; Health Care; Law Amendments; Legislative Administration; Legislative Officers; Private Bills; Privileges; Procedure; & Public Accounts.
Chair, Standing Committee on Crown Corporations, Jack Carr, Progressive Conservative
jack.carr@gnb.ca
Chair, Standing Committee on Estimates, Dorothy Shephard, Progressive Conservative
dorothy.shephard@gnb.ca
Chair, Standing Committee on Health Care, Hon. Madeleine Dubé, Progressive Conservative
madeleine.dube@gnb.ca
Chair, Standing Committee on Law Amendments, Hon. Marie-Claude Blais, Q.C., Progressive Conservative
marie-claude.blais@gnb.ca
Chair, Legislative Administration Committee, Hon. Dale Graham, Progressive Conservative
dale.graham@gnb.ca
Contact, Standing Committee on Legislative Officers, Greg Davis, Progressive Conservative
greg.davis@gnb.ca
Chair, Standing Committee on Private Bills, Carl Killen, Progressive Conservative
carl.killen@gnb.ca
Chair, Standing Committee on Privileges, Bev Harrison, Progressive Conservative
bev.harrison@gnb.ca
Chair, Standing Committee on Procedure, Carl Urquhart, Progressive Conservative
carl.urquhart@gnb.ca; MLA@CarlUrquhart.com
Chair, Public Accounts, Rick Doucet, Liberal
rick.doucet@gnb.ca

Select Committees of the Legislative Assembly of New Brunswick
The following are the Select Committees of the Legislative Assembly of New Brunswick: Point Lepreau; Revision of the Official Languages Act; & Legislative Reform.
Chair, Select Committee on Point Lepreau, Kirk MacDonald, Progressive Conservative
kirk.macdonald@gnb.ca
Chair, Select Committee on the Revision of the Official Languages Act, Hon. Marie-Claude Blais, Q.C., Progressive Conservative
marie-claude.blais@gnb.ca
Contact, Select Committee on Legislative Reform, Wes McLean, Progressive Conservative
wes.mclean@gnb.ca

Fifty-seventh Legislative Assembly - New Brunswick

Centre Block, Legislative Building, 706 Queen St., PO Box 6000, Fredericton, NB E3B 5H1
Tel: 506-453-2506
Fax: 506-453-7154
wwwleg@gnb.ca
www.gnb.ca/legis/index-e.asp
Last General Election, September 27, 2010.
Next General Election: September 22, 2014.
Party Standings (July 2012):
Progressive Conservatives 42;
Liberal 13;
Total 55.
Members' Salaries, Indemnities, & Allowances (2010):
Members' annual indemnity $85,000.
Additional Members' Salaries, Indemnities, & Allowances:
Premier $79,000;
Cabinet Ministers $52,614;
Leader of the Opposition $55,300;
Leader of a Registered Political Party: $19,750;
Speaker $52,614;
Deputy Speaker $26,307;
Government Whip $26,307;
Official Opposition Whip $19,730;
Government House Leader $26,307;
Opposition House Leader $19,730.
Members of the Legislative Assembly may be reached at the following address: Members of the Legislative Assembly, Province of New Brunswick, PO Box 6000, Fredericton, NB E3B 5H1.
The following is a list of Members of the Legislative Assembly with their riding, the number of electors from the official list for the 2010 election, party affiliation, & contact information:

Members of the Legislative Assembly of New Brunswick
Hon. Hédard Albert
Constituency: Caraquet, ElectoralDistrict 6 *No. of Constituents:* 8,833, Liberal
Tel: 506-726-2929
Fax: 506-726-2966
hedard.albert@gnb.ca
Constituency Office
#25, 7 St. Pierre Blvd. West
Caraquet, NB E1W 1B8
Premier; President, Executive Council; Minister Responsible, Intergovernmental Affairs, Aboriginal Affairs Secretariat, Premier's Council on the Status of Disabled Persons,Citizens' Engagement, Office of Government Review; Chair, Policy & Priorities Committee, Hon. David Nathan Alward
Constituency: Woodstock, Electoral District 49 *No. of Constituents:* 9,749, Progressive Conservative
Tel: 506-453-2144
Fax: 506-453-7407
david.alward@gnb.ca; premier@gnb.ca; premierministre@gnb.ca
www2.gnb.ca/content/gnb/en/departments/premier.html
Other Communications: Constituency Phone: 506-325-4990; Fax:506-325-4991
Constituency Office
107 Connell St.
PO Box 6746
Woodstock, NB E7M 1K7
Hon. Donald Arseneault
Constituency: Dalhousie-RestigoucheEast, Electoral District 2 *No. of Constituents:* 9,770, Liberal
Tel: 506-685-5252
Fax: 506-685-5255
donald.arseneault@gnb.ca
Social Media: twitter.com/donarseneault, ca.linkedin.com/pub/donald-arseneault/3b/b71/732
Constituency Office
#2, 389 Adelaide St.
Dalhousie, NB E8C 1B5
John Willis Betts
Constituency: Moncton-Crescent, ElectoralDistrict 24 *No. of Constituents:* 12,919, Progressive Conservative
Tel: 506-869-6579
Fax: 506-869-6614
johnw.betts@gnb.ca
Constituency Office
1351 Mountain Rd.
Moncton, NB E1C 2T9
Minister, Justice; Attorney General; Minister Responsible, Women's Issues, Hon. Marie-Claude Blais, Q.C.
Constituency: Moncton North, Electoral District 23 *No. of Constituents:* 9,249, Progressive Conservative
Tel: 506-453-3132
Fax: 506-453-3651
marie-claude.blais@gnb.ca
www.gnb.ca/0062/index-e.asp (Justice & Attorney General)
Other Communications: ConstituencyPhone: 506-869-7050; Fax: 506-869-7096
Constituency Office
587 Mountain Rd.
Moncton, NB E1C 2N9
Yvon Bonenfant
Constituency: Madawaska-les-Lacs, ElectoralDistrict 55 *No. of Constituents:* 8,743, Progressive Conservative
Tel: 506-737-4420
Fax: 506-737-4436
yvon.bonenfant@gnb.ca
Constituency Office
193 Principale St.
Saint-Jacques, NB E7B 1W7
Leader, Official Opposition, Victor Éric Boudreau
Constituency: Shediac-Cap-Pelé, Electoral District 17 *No. of Constituents:* 11,258, Liberal
Tel: 506-453-2548
Fax: 506-453-3956
victor.boudreau@gnb.ca
Other Communications: Constituency Phone: 506-533-3450; Fax: 506-533-345
ConstituencyOffice
328 Main St., #H
Shediac, NB E4P 2E3
Jack Carr
Constituency: New Maryland-Sunbury West,Electoral District 46 *No. of Constituents:* 8,606, Progressive Conservative
Tel: 506-368-2938
Fax: 506-368-2939
jack.carr@gnb.ca
Social Media: twitter.com/jackcarr_mla, ca.linkedin.com/pub/jack-carr/47/871/407
Constituency Office
#1, 189A Sunbury Dr.
Fredericton Junction, NB E5L 1R5
Minister, Education & Early Childhood Development, Hon. Jody Carr
Constituency: Oromocto, Electoral District 40 *No. of Constituents:* 7,590, Progressive Conservative
Tel: 506-453-2523
Fax: 506-457-4810
jody.carr@gnb.ca
Other Communications: Constituency Phone: 506-357-4141; Fax: 506-357-4147
Constituency Office
281 Restigouche Rd.
PO Box 20022
Oromocto, NB E2V 2R6
Christopher Michael Collins
Constituency: Moncton East,Electoral District 21 *No. of Constituents:* 10,382, Liberal
Tel: 506-856-2595
Fax: 506-856-2596
chris.collins@gnb.ca
Social Media: ca.linkedin.com/pub/chris-collins/18/859/118
Constituency Office
137 McLaughlin Dr.
Moncton, NB E1A 4P4
Minister, Post-Secondary Education, Training, & Labour, Hon. Martine Coulombe
Constituency: Restigouche-la-Vallée, Electoral District 53 *No. of Constituents:* 9,172, Progressive Conservative
Tel: 506-453-2342
Fax: 506-453-3038
martine.coulombe@gnb.ca
www.gnb.ca/redirect/0105/index.htm (Post-Secondary Ed.)
Other Communications: Constituency Phone: 506-235-6111; Fax:506-235-6133
Constituency Office
168B Canada St.
Saint-Quentin, NB E8A 1G7
Greg Davis
Constituency: Campbellton-Restigouche Centre, ElectoralDistrict 1 *No. of Constituents:* 9,473, Progressive Conservative
Tel: 506-759-4118
Fax: 506-453-3461
greg.davis@gnb.ca
Constituency Office
19 Aberdeen St.
Campbellton, NB E3N 2J6
Rick Doucet
Constituency: Charlotte-The Isles, ElectoralDistrict 38 *No. of Constituents:* 8,478, Liberal
Tel: 506-755-4200
Fax: 506-755-4207
rick.doucet@gnb.ca
Social Media: ca.linkedin.com/pub/hon-rick-doucet/30/19a/171
Constituency Office
28 Mt. Pleasant St.
St George, NB E5C 3K4
Minister, Health, Hon. Madeleine Dubé
Constituency: Edmundston-Saint-Basile, Electoral District 54 *No. of Constituents:* 10,458, Progressive Conservative
Tel: 506-457-4800
Fax: 506-453-5442
madeleine.dube@gnb.ca
www.gnb.ca/0051/index-e.asp (Health)
Other Communications: Constituency Phone: 506-735-2528; Fax: 506-735-2583
Constituency Office
59 del'Église St.
Edmundston, NB E3V 1J6
Minister, Environment & Local Government; Minister Responsible for the Energy Efficiency & Conservation Agency of NB, Hon. Bruce Fitch
Constituency: Riverview, Electoral District 26 *No. of Constituents:* 10,457, Progressive Conservative
Tel: 506-444-5136
Fax: 506-453-3377
bruce.fitch@gnb.ca

www.bfitch.ca
Other Communications: Constituency Phone: 506-869-6117; Fax: 506-869-6114
Social Media: twitter.com/brucefitchmla
Constituency Office
#18A, 567 Coverdale Rd.
Riverview, NB E1B 3K7

Hugh John (Ted) Flemming III
Constituency: Rothesay, Electoral District32 *No. of Constituents:* 8,713, Progressive Conservative
Tel: 506-848-5440
Fax: 506-848-5442
hugh.flemming@gnb.ca
Note: Hugh John (Ted) Flemming won a by-elction on June 25, 2012. Former energy minister, Margaret-Ann Blaney resigned to become president of Efficiency New Brunswick.
Constituency Office
70 Hampton Rd.
Rothesay, NB

Bill Fraser
Constituency: Miramichi-Bay du Vin, ElectoralDistrict 11 *No. of Constituents:* 8,619, Liberal
Tel: 506-228-2003
Fax: 506-624-5517
bill.fraser@gnb.ca
Social Media: twitter.com/billfrasermla
Constituency Office
125 Wellington St.
Miramichi, NB E1N 1L3

Speaker of the Legislative Assembly, Hon. Dale Graham
Constituency: Carleton, Electoral District 50 *No. of Constituents:* 8,780, Progressive Conservative
Tel: 506-453-2907
Fax: 506-453-7154
dale.graham@gnb.ca
Other Communications: Constituency Phone: 506-276-4016; Fax: 506-276-4020
ConstituencyOffice
787 Central St.
PO Box 631
Centreville, NB E7K 3H5

Hon. Shawn M. Graham
Constituency: Kent, Electoral District15 *No. of Constituents:* 8,310, Liberal
Tel: 506-523-7980
Fax: 506-523-7982
Shawn.Graham2@gnb.ca
Constituency Office
#3, 79 Main St
Rexton, NB E4W 1Z9

Roland Haché
Constituency: Nigadoo-Chaleur, ElectoralDistrict 3 *No. of Constituents:* 9,700, Liberal
Tel: 506-542-2424
Fax: 506-542-2425
roland.hache@gnb.ca
Social Media: ca.linkedin.com/pub/roland-hache-roland-hache/3b/342/9aa
Constituency Office
691 Principale St.
Petit-Rocher, NB E8J 1G1

Bev Harrison
Constituency: Hampton-Kings, Electoral District29 *No. of Constituents:* 10,431, Progressive Conservative
Tel: 506-832-6464
Fax: 506-832-6466
bev.harrison@gnb.ca
Constituency Office
#4, 46 Keirstead Ave.
Hampton, NB E5N 5A4

Minister, Finance; Minister, Office of Human Resources; Minister Responsible, New Brunswick Liquor Corporation, New Brunswick Investment Management Corporation, & NewBrunswick Lotteries & Gaming Corporation; Chair, Board of Management, Hon. Blaine Higgs
Constituency: Quispamsis, Electoral District 30 *No. of Constituents:* 11,079, Progressive Conservative
Tel: 506-444-2627
Fax: 506-457-4989
blaine.higgs@gnb.ca
www.blainehiggs.com
Other Communications: Constituency Phone: 506-848-5422; Fax: 506-848-5429
Social Media: www.facebook.com/group.php?gid=133631310011919
Constituency Office
25 William Ct.
Quispamsis, NB E2E4B1

Minister, Culture, Tourism, & Healthy Living, Hon. Trevor Holder
Constituency: Saint John Portland, Electoral District 35 *No. of Constituents:* 9,079, Progressive Conservative
Tel: 506-453-3009
Fax: 506-457-4984
trevor.holder@gnb.ca
Other Communications: Constituency Phone: 506-657-2335; Fax: 506-657-2335
Constituency Office
#3, 229 Churchill Blvd.
Saint John, NB E2K 3E2

Brian Kenny
Constituency: Bathurst, Electoral District 4 *No. of Constituents:* 9,085, Liberal
Tel: 506-549-5355
Fax: 506-549-5261
brian.kenny@gnb.ca
Social Media: ca.linkedin.com/pub/brian-kenny/23/825/433
Constituency Office
111 Main St.
Bathurst, NB E2A 1A6

Carl Killen
Constituency: Saint John Harbour, Electoral District34 *No. of Constituents:* 8,331, Progressive Conservative
Tel: 506-642-9774
Fax: 506-642-9794
carl.killen@gnb.ca
Social Media: twitter.com/carlkillen, www.facebook.com/pages/Carl-Killen/109855392374217, ca.linkedin.com/pub/carl-killen/19/b57/290
Constituency Office
72 Germain St.
Saint John, NB E2L 2E7

Deputy Speaker, Claude Landry
Constituency: Tracadie-Sheila, Electoral District 9 *No. of Constituents:* 9,097, Progressive Conservative
Tel: 506-453-7494
Fax: 506-453-3461
claude.landry@gnb.ca
Other Communications: Constituency Phone: 506-395-9162; Fax: 506-393-7794
Constituency Office
422 Arseneau St.
Tracadie-Sheila, NB E1X 1B3

Denis Landry
Constituency: Centre-Péninsule —Saint-Saveur, Electoral District 8 *No. of Constituents:* 8,995, Liberal
Tel: 506-764-2530
Fax: 506-764-2535
denis.landry2@gnb.ca
Constituency Office
1344-3 des Fondateurs St.
Paquetville, NB E8R 1A4

Bernard LeBlanc
Constituency: Memramcook-Lakeville-Dieppe,Electoral District 19 *No. of Constituents:* 9,423, Liberal
Tel: 506-758-4088
Fax: 506-758-4089
bernard.leblanc@gnb.ca
Constituency Office
488 Centrale St.
Memramcook, NB E4K 3S6

Bertrand LeBlanc
Constituency: Rogersville-Kouchibouguac, Electoral District 14 *No. of Constituents:* 8,735, Liberal
Tel: 506-876-3592
Fax: 506-876-3590
bertrand.leblanc@gnb.ca
Constituency Office
83B Beauséjour St.
Saint-Louis-de-Kent, NB E4X 1A6

Minister, Government Services; Acting Minister, Energy; Minister Responsible, New Brunswick Internal Services Agency, Service New Brunswick, Hon. Craig Leonard
Constituency: Fredericton-Lincoln, Electoral District44 *No. of Constituents:* 9,912, Progressive Conservative
Tel: 506-453-2240
Fax: 506-453-5329
craig.leonard@gnb.ca; EECA/AECE.Customer.Service@gnb.ca
Other Communications: Constituency Phone: 506-453-5723; Fax: 506-453-6057
Social Media: twitter.com/craig_leonard
Constituency Office
#4, 618 Queen St., 3rd Fl.
Fredericton, NB E3B 1C2

Troy Lifford
Constituency: Fredericton-Nashwaaksis, Electoral District 42 *No. of Constituents:* 10,727, Progressive Conservative
Tel: 506-449-3902
Fax: 506-449-0433
troy.lifford@gnb.ca
Social Media: twitter.com/troylifford
Constituency Office, Brookside Mall
#36A, 435 Brookside Dr.
Fredericton, NB E3A 8V4

Pam Lynch
Constituency: Fredericton-Fort Nashwaak, ElectoralDistrict 43 *No. of Constituents:* 11,009, Progressive Conservative
Tel: 506-444-3322
Fax: 506-444-3384
pam.lynch@gnb.ca
www.pamlynch.ca
Constituency Office
121 Gibson St.
Fredericton, NB E3A 4E1

Brian MacDonald
Constituency: Fredericton-Silverwood, Electoral District 45 *No. of Constituents:* 11,124, Progressive Conservative
Tel: 506-453-8461
Fax: 506-453-6057
brian.t.macdonald@gnb.ca
www.brian-macdonald.com
Social Media: twitter.com/bmacdonald_pc, www.facebook.com/Brian.T.Macdonald
Constituency Office
#4, 618 Queen St., 3rd Fl.
Fredericton, NB E3B 1C2

Kirk MacDonald
Constituency: York North,Electoral District 48 *No. of Constituents:* 9,950, Progressive Conservative
Tel: 506-363-4949
Fax: 506-363-4998
kirk.macdonald@gnb.ca
Constituency Office, Keswick Landing Mall
#7, 9 Yerxa Lane
Keswick, NB E6L 1N7

Curtis Malloch
Constituency: Charlotte-Campobello,Electoral District 39 *No. of Constituents:* 8,640, Progressive Conservative
Tel: 506-466-7688
Fax: 506-466-2191
curtis.malloch@gnb.ca
www.curtismalloch.com
Constituency Office
#101, 123 Milltown Blvd.
St Stephen, NB E3L 1G5

Deputy Government House Leader, Wes McLean
Constituency: Victoria-Tobique, Electoral District 51 *No. of Constituents:* 7,446, Progressive Conservative
Tel: 506-453-7494
Fax: 506-453-3461
wes.mclean@gnb.ca
Other Communications: Constituency Phone: 506-273-2460; Fax: 506-453-3461
Constituency Office
1153 WestRiverside Dr.
Perth-Andover, NB E7H 5G5

Roger Melanson
Constituency: DieppeCentre-Lewisville, Electoral District 20 *No. of Constituents:* 14,028, Liberal
Tel: 506-869-7000
Toll-free: 800-561-4041
Fax: 506-869-7007
roger.l.melanson@gnb.ca
www.rogermelanson.ca
Social Media: twitter.com/RogerMelanson, www.facebook.com/votevotezroger
Constituency Office
260 Champlain St.
Dieppe, NB E1A 1P3

Minister, Natural Resources, Hon. Bruce Northrup
Constituency: Kings East, Electoral District 28 *No. of Constituents:* 9,581, Progressive Conservative
Tel: 506-453-2510
Fax: 506-444-5839
bruce.northrup@gnb.ca
Other Communications: Constituency Phone: 506-432-2686; Fax: 506-432-2647
ConstituencyOffice
PO Box 3339
Sussex, NB E4E 3P9

Minister, Agriculture, Aquaculture, & Fisheries, Hon. Michael Olscamp
Constituency: Tantramar, Electoral District 18 *No. of Constituents:* 6,893, Progressive Conservative
Tel: 506-453-2662
Fax: 506-453-3402
mike.olscamp@gnb.ca
Other Communications: Constituency Phone: 506-364-4774; Fax: 506-364-4775
Constituency Office
43 Main St.
PO Box 6059
Sackville, NB E4L 1G6

Jim Parrott
Constituency: Fundy-River Valley, Electoral District 37 *No. of Constituents:* 8,935, Progressive Conservative
Tel: 506-757-2088
Fax: 506-757-1009
jim.parrott@gnb.ca; jimparrottmla@bellaliant.com
Constituency Office
#2, 192 River Valley Dr.
Grand Bay-Westfield, NB E5K1A4

Ryan Riordon
Constituency: Nepisiguit, Electoral District 5 *No. of Constituents:* 8,132, Progressive Conservative
Tel: 506-547-2355
Fax: 506-547-2353
ryan.riordon@gnb.ca
Social Media:
www.facebook.com/group.php?gid=135907896450302
Constituency Office
845 Riordon Ave.
Bathurst, NB E2A 4W7

Deputy Premier; Minister, Economic Development; Minister Responsible for la Francophonie; Government House Leader, Hon. Paul Robichaud
Constituency: Lamèque-Shippagan-Miscou, Electoral District 7 *No. of Constituents:* 8,742, Progressive Conservative
Tel: 506-453-7494
Fax: 506-453-3461
paul.robichaud@gnb.ca
Other Communications: Constituency Phone: 506-336-3388; Fax: 506-336-3387
Constituency Office
233 J.D. Gauthier Blvd.
Shippagan, NB E8S 1N2

Serge Robichaud
Constituency: Miramichi Bay-Neguac, ElectoralDistrict 10 *No. of Constituents:* 8,516, Progressive Conservative
Tel: 506-776-4005
Fax: 506-776-4006
serge.j.robichaud@gnb.ca
Constituency Office
1124 Principale St.
Neguac, NB E9G 1P1

Glenn Savoie
Constituency: SaintJohn-Fundy, Electoral District 31 *No. of Constituents:* 9,464, Progressive Conservative
Tel: 506-658-6333
Fax: 506-658-5982
glensavoie@gnb.ca; glensavoie@bellaliant.com
Constituency Office
2075 Loch Lomond Rd.
Saint John, NB E2N 1A1

Dorothy Shephard
Constituency: Saint John Lancaster,Electoral District 36 *No. of Constituents:* 9,919, Progressive Conservative
Tel: 506-643-2900
Fax: 506-658-9885
dorothy.shephard@gnb.ca
Constituency Office
649 Manawagonish Rd.
Saint John, NB E2M 3W4

Danny Soucy
Constituency: Grand Falls-Drummond-Saint-André,Electoral District 52 *No. of Constituents:* 8,463, Progressive Conservative
Tel: 506-473-7740
Fax: 506-473-7745
danny.soucy@gnb.ca
Constituency Office
285 Broadway Blvd.
Grand Falls, NB E3Z 2K1

Wayne Steeves
Constituency: Albert, Electoral District27 *No. of Constituents:* 9,187, Progressive Conservative
Tel: 506-856-3006
Fax: 506-856-3000
wayne.steeves@gnb.ca
Constituency Office
1029 Rte. 114
Lower Coverdale, NB E1J 1A1

Jake Stewart
Constituency: Southwest-Miramichi, Electoral District13 *No. of Constituents:* 8,264, Progressive Conservative
Tel: 506-843-7729
Fax: 506-843-7726
jake.stewart@gnb.ca
Social Media:
www.facebook.com/pages/Jake-Stewart/110545285660161
Constituency Office
137 Main St.
Blackville, NB E9B 1B9

Minister, Social Development; Minister Responsible for Seniors, Housing, & Community Non-Profit Organizations, Hon. Sue Stultz
Constituency: Moncton West, Electoral District 22 *No. of Constituents:* 9,718, Progressive Conservative
Tel: 506-453-2001
Fax: 506-453-2164
sue.stultz@gnb.ca
Other Communications: Constituency Phone: 506-869-6164; Fax: 506-869-6553
Constituency Office
#120, 272 St. George St.
Moncton, NB E1C 1W6

Glen Tait
Constituency: Saint John East,Electoral District 33 *No. of Constituents:* 10,060, Progressive Conservative
Tel: 506-643-3200
Fax: 506-643-3201
glen.tait@gnb.ca
Constituency Office, Building C
#15, 535 Westmorland Rd.
Saint John, NB E2J 3T3

Minister, Public Safety; Solicitor General, Hon. Robert B. Trevors
Constituency: Miramichi Centre, Electoral District 12 *No. of Constituents:* 8,632, Progressive Conservative
Tel: 506-453-7414
Fax: 506-453-3870
robert.trevors@gnb.ca; robert.trevors.mla@bellaliant.com
Other Communications: Constituency Phone:506-462-4214; Fax: 506-624-2151
Constituency Office
237 Pleasant St.
Miramichi, NB E1V 1Y6

Deputy Speaker, Carl Urquhart
Constituency: York, Electoral District 47 *No. of Constituents:* 8,462, Progressive Conservative
Tel: 506-453-7494
Fax: 506-453-3461
carl.urquhart@gnb.ca; MLA@CarlUrquhart.com
www.carlurquhart.com
Constituency Office
#1, 1757 Hanwell Rd.
Hanwell, NB E3C2B9

Ross Wetmore
Constituency: Grand Lake-Gagetown, ElectoralDistrict 41 *No. of Constituents:* 8,950, Progressive Conservative
Tel: 506-488-3577
Toll-free: 877-632-2083
Fax: 506-488-3511
ross.wetmore@gnb.ca
Constituency Office
56 Front St.
Gagetown, NB E5M 1A1

Minister, Transportation & Infrastructure; Minister Responsible, Supply & Services, Hon. Claude Williams
Constituency: Kent South, Electoral District 16 *No. of Constituents:* 10,202, Progressive Conservative
Tel: 506-457-7345
Fax: 506-453-7984
claude.williams@gnb.ca
Other Communications: ConstituencyPhone: 506-525-4025; Fax: 506-525-4034
Constituency Office
24-1, av de l'Église
Saint-Antoine, NB E4V 1M3

Sherry Wilson
Constituency: Petitcodiac, Electoral District25 *No. of Constituents:* 10,456, Progressive Conservative
Tel: 506-372-3301
Fax: 506-372-3304
sherry.wilson@gnb.ca
Constituency Office
3118 Main St.
Salisbury, NB E4J 2L6

New Brunswick Government Departments & Agencies / Ministères et organismes du gouvernement du Nouveau-Brunswick

New Brunswick Department of Agriculture, Aquaculture & Fisheries / Agriculture, Aquaculture et Pêches

Agricultural Research Station (Experimental Farm), PO Box 6000, Fredericton, NB E3B 5H1
Tel: 506-453-2666
Fax: 506-453-7170
DAAF-MAAP@gnb.ca
www.gnb.ca/aquaculture

Acts Administered:
Agricultural Associations Act
Agricultural Commodity Price Stabilization Act
Agricultural Development Act
Agricultural Insurance Act
Agricultural Land Protection & Development Act
Agricultural Operation Practices Act
Agricultural Producers Registration and Farm Organizations Funding
Apiary Inspection Act
Aquaculture Act
Diseases of Animals Act
Farm Credit Corporation Assistance Act
Farm Improvement Assistance Loans Act
Farm Income Assurance Act
Farm Machinery Loans Act
Fish & Wildlife Act (in part)
Fisheries and Aquaculture Development Act
Inshore Fisheries Representation Act
Livestock Incentives Act
Livestock Operations Act
Marshland Reclamation Act
Mining Act
Natural Products Act
New Brunswick Grain Act
Plant Health Act
Potato Disease Eradication Act
Poultry Health Protection Act
Real Property Tax Act
Seafood Processing Act
Sheep Protection Act
Women's Institute & Institut féminin Act

Minister, Agriculture, Aquaculture, & Fisheries, Hon. Michael Olscamp
Tel: 506-453-2662
Fax: 506-453-3402
Mike.Olscamp@gnb.ca

Deputy Minister, Robert Rioux
Tel: 506-453-2450
Robert.Rioux@gnb.ca

Director, Communications, Gisèle Regimbal
Tel: 506-444-4218
Fax: 506-444-5022
Gisele.Regimbal@gnb.ca

Director, Policy & Planning, Shirley Stuible
Tel: 506-453-3451
Fax: 506-453-5210
shirley.stuible@gnb.ca

Associated Agencies, Boards & Commissions:

• New Brunswick Agricultural Insurance Commission / Commission de L'assurance Agricole du Nouveau-Brunswick
c/o Department of Agriculture, Aquaculture & Fisheries
PO Box 6000
Fredericton, NB E3B 5H1
Tel: 506-453-2185
Fax: 506-453-7406
daa-maa@gnb.ca
Agricultural Insurance Commission is responsible for administering the delivery to producers of an agricultural insurance plan to provide insurance protection against losses of production. This plan is funded through producer premiums and through contributions from the Province of New Brunswick and the Government of Canada.

• New Brunswick Farm Products Commission / Commission des produits de ferme du Nouveau-Brunswick
c/o Department of Agriculture, Aquaculture & Fisheries
PO Box 6000
Fredericton, NB E3B 5H1
Tel: 506-453-3647
Fax: 506-444-5969
Products Act. ment/administrative support to the Commission in the monitoring of commodity boards under the provisions of the Natural Products Act.

Agriculture & Bio-Economy Division / Agriculture et Bioéconomie
DAAF-MAAP@gnb.ca
www.gnb.ca/agriculture
To encourage the development of a prosperous, globally competitive & sustainable agriculture & agri-food business using the latest technologies to produce & market innovative & safe food as well as other bio-products.

Asst. Deputy Minister, Kevin McKendy
Tel: 506-453-2366
Fax: 506-444-5022
kevin.mckendy@gnb.ca

Executive Director, Livestock Development, Michael Maloney
Tel: 506-453-2457
michael.maloney@gnb.ca

Director, Crop Development, Kevin McCully
Tel: 506-453-3481
kevin.mccully@gnb.ca

Director, Agricultural Financial Programs, Cathy Larochelle
Tel: 506-444-2728
cathy.larochelle@gnb.ca

Director, Land & Environment, Sandi McGeachy
Tel: 506-453-2109
sandi.mcgeachy@gnb.ca

Director, Regional Agri-Business Development, Gerry Chevrier
Tel: 506-453-2172
gerald.chevrier@gnb.ca

Manager, Veterinary Laboratory & Pathology Services, James Goltz
Tel: 506-453-5488
jim.goltz@gnb.ca

Manager, Food Safety & Quality, Clinton McLean
Tel: 506-453-6735
clint.mclean@gnb.ca
Bathurst
Bathurst Agriculture Building, 1425 King Ave., Bathurst, NB E2A 1S7
Tel: 506-547-2088
Fax: 506-547-2064
DAAF-MAAP@gnb.ca
Regional Manager, Jean Marc Clavette
Bon Accord
Bon Accord Elite Seed Potato Centre, 790 Kincardine Rd., Bon Accord, NB E7H 2K8
Tel: 506-273-4741
Fax: 506-273-4742
DAAF-MAAP@gnb.ca
Regional Manager, Pelkey Shaun
Edmundston
36 Court St., Edmundston, NB E3V 1S3
Tel: 506-735-2060
Fax: 506-735-2754
DAAF-MAAP@gnb.ca
Regional Manager, Charles Mallet
Grand Falls
PO Box 5001, Grand Falls, NB E3Z 1G1
Tel: 506-473-7755
Fax: 506-473-6641
DAAF-MAAP@gnb.ca
Specialist, Jacques Lavoie
Miramichi
Chatham Town Centre, 1780 Water St., Miramichi, NB E1N 1B6
Tel: 506-778-6030
Fax: 506-778-6679
DAAF-MAAP@gnb.ca
Regional Manager, Scott McFarlane
Moncton
PO Box 5001, Moncton, NB E1C 8R3
Tel: 506-856-2277
Fax: 506-856-2092
DAAF-MAAP@gnb.ca
Regional Manager, Claude Robichaud
Saint-Quentin
366 Canada St., #A, Saint-Quentin, NB E8A 1H8
Tel: 506-235-6050
Fax: 506-235-6055
DAA-MAA@gnb.ca
Regional Manager, André Clavet
Tracadie-Sheila
Place Tracadie, 3518-1 Principale St., Tracadie-Sheila, NB E1X 1C9
Tel: 506-394-4128
Fax: 506-394-4128
DAA-MAA@gnb.ca
Coordinator, Denis Prince
Wicklow
Potato Development Centre, 39 Barker Lane, Wicklow, NB E7L 3S4
Tel: 506-392-5100
Fax: 506-392-5089
Toll-Free: 888-622-4742
DAA-MAA@gnb.ca
Regional Manager, Brian Duplessis

Fisheries Division / Pêches
DAAF-MAAP@gnb.ca
www.gnb.ca/agriculture
Asst. Deputy Minister, Perron Sadie
Tel: 506-457-6964
Fax: 506-444-5022
sadie.perron@gnb.ca
Executive Director, Fisheries Management & Operations, Yvon Chiasson
Tel: 506-453-8432
Fax: 506-462-5929
yvon.chiasson@gnb.ca
Director, Business Development, Louis Arsenault
Tel: 506-743-7222
louis.arsenault@gnb.ca
Director, Licensing & Technical Services, Ghislain Chiasson
Tel: 506-453-2252
ghislain.chiasson@gnb.ca
Bouctouche
26 Acadie St., Bouctouche, NB E4S 2T2
Tel: 506-743-7222
Fax: 506-743-7229
DAAF-MAAP@gnb.ca
Regional Director, Louis Arsenault
Caraquet
22 St-Pierre Blvd. East, Caraquet, NB E1W 1B6
Tel: 506-726-2400
Fax: 506-726-2419
MDP-DOF@gnb.ca
Regional Director, Mario Gaudet
Shippagan
104 Aquarium St., Shippagan, NB E8S 1H9
Tel: 506-336-3751
Fax: 506-336-3057
DAA-MAA@gnb.ca
Regional Director, Christian Noris

Office of the Auditor General / Bureau du Vérificateur général

HSBC Place, 520 King St., 6th Fl., Fredericton, NB E3B 6G3
Tel: 506-453-2243
Fax: 506-453-3067
www.gnb.ca/OAG-BVG/Index.htm
The role of the Office of the Auditor General is the promotion of accountability. On behalf of the Legislative Assembly, the Office of the Auditor General audits the accounts of the province & certain Crown agencies. Objective information is provided to the citizens of New Brunswick through the Legislative Assembly.

Auditor General, Kim MacPherson, C.A.
Tel: 506-453-2465
Kim.MacPherson@gnb.ca

Deputy Auditor General, Kenneth Robinson, C.A.
Tel: 506-453-6751
ken.robinson@gnb.ca

Director, Value-for-money Audit, Brent White, C.A.
Tel: 506-453-6752
brent.white@gnb.ca

Director, Financial Audit, Paul Jewett, C.A.
Tel: 506-453-6754
paul.jewett@gnb.ca

Office of the Comptroller / Bureau du Contrôleur

Centennial Bldg., 670 King St., Fredericton, NB E3B 1G1
Tel: 506-453-2565
Fax: 506-453-2917
wwwooc@gnb.ca
www.gnb.ca/0087/index-e.asp
The Office of the Comptroller provides leadership in accounting & internal auditing services to clients & encourages the effective management of the resources of the province.

Comptroller, Janet Gallagher
Tel: 506-453-2565
janet.gallagher@gnb.ca

Director, Accounting Services, Karen Cunningham
Tel: 506-453-8975
karen.cunningham@gnb.ca

Director, Audit & Consulting Services, Stephen Thompson, C.M.A.
Tel: 506-444-4560
steve.t.thompson@gnb.ca

New Brunswick Department of Culture, Tourism, & Healthy Living

Centennial Building, PO Box 6000, Fredericton, NB E3B 5H1
Tel: 506-444-5205
Fax: 506-457-4984
taponlinedirectory@gnb.ca
www2.gnb.ca/content/gnb/en/departments/cthl.html
The Department of Culture, Tourism, & Healthy Living is engaged in facilitating community cultural development throughout New Brunswick, maximizing the profile of the province's tourism industry, & improving population health.
Acts Administered:
Arts Development Trust Fund (except administration of fund)
Assessment (s.15.3) (Concurrent jurisdiction with the Minister responsible for Service New Brunswick)
Heritage Conservation
Municipalities (subsection 188(3))
Off-Road Vehicle (sections 7.2(1), 7.2(3), 7.2(5), 7.3, & 7.5(1))
Parks
Sport Development Trust Fund (except administration of fund)
Tourism Development Act, 2008
Youth Assistance (section 11)

Minister, Culture, Tourism, & Healthy Living, Hon. Trevor Holder
Tel: 506-453-3009
Fax: 506-457-4984
trevor.holder@gnb.ca

Deputy Minister, Carolyn Mackay
Tel: 506-453-3261
carolyn.mackay@gnb.ca

Director, Strategic Planning & Policy, Shannon Ferris
Tel: 506-462-5053
shannon.ferris@gnb.ca

Director, Communications, Jane Matthews-Clark
Tel: 506-444-4454
jane.matthews-clark@gnb.ca

Associated Agencies, Boards & Commissions:
• **New Brunswick Arts Board / Conseil des arts Nouveau-Brunswick**
61 Carleton St.
Fredericton, NB E3B 3T2
Tel: 506-444-4444
Fax: 506-444-5543
Toll-free: 866-460-2787
www.artsnb.ca
The New Brunswick Arts Board promotes the creation of art. The arts funding agency also administers funding programs for professional artists throughout New Brunswick.

Corporate Services
Centennial Building, 6th Fl., PO Box 6000, Fredericton, NB E3B 5H1
Tel: 506-453-3115
Fax: 506-444-5760
taponlinedirectory@gnb.ca
Corporate services includes financial planning, monitoring, & consulting, plus human resource services to enhance individual & organizational effectiveness, & information technology services.
Director, Financial Services, Jo-Anne Lang
Tel: 506-444-5813
jo-anne.lang@gnb.ca
Director, Human Resource Services, Barbara Lapointe
Tel: 506-453-2198
barbara.legacy@gnb.ca
Director, Information Technology Services, Doug Waugh
Tel: 506-457-7324
doug.waugh@gnb.ca

Culture & Healthy Living
Place 2000, PO Box 6000, Fredericton, NB E3B 5H1
Tel: 506-453-2909
Fax: 506-453-6668
WCScommunication@gnb.ca
Cultural responsiblities include development of the arts, heritage, cultural industries, & the New Brunswick Museum.
The province of New Brunswick also invests in improving health & wellness in homes, schools, workplaces, & communities.
Assistant Deputy Minister, Culture & Healthy Living, Ronald Durelle
Tel: 506-453-3989
Ron.durelle@gnb.ca
Chief Executive Officer, New Brunswick Museum, Jane Fullerton
Tel: 506-643-2346
jane.fullerton@nbm-mnb.ca
Director, Wellness, Michelle Bourgoin
Tel: 506-453-5526
michelle.bourgoin@gnb.ca
Director, Arts Devlopment, Nathalie Dubois
Tel: 506-453-2729
nathalie.dubois@gnb.ca
Director, Sport & Recreation, Roger Duval
Tel: 506-457-4950
roger.duval@gnb.ca
Director, Heritage, William Hicks
Tel: 506-444-5320
bill.hicks@gnb.ca

Marketing, Development & Operations
Centennial Building, 670 King St., 6th Fl., Fredericton, NB E3B 1G1
Tel: 506-444-6752
Fax: 506-453-2854
taponlinedirectory@gnb.ca
Activities include industry & media relations, as well as visit engagement through tourism communication & visitor information centres.
Assistant Deputy Minister, Kelly Cain
Tel: 506-444-4118
kelly.cain@gnb.ca
Director, Sales, Partnerships, & Business Development, Cindy Creamer Rouse
Tel: 506-444-4097
cindy.creamer-rouse@gnb.ca
Director, Product Development, Bruno Laplante
Tel: 506-444-3788
bruno.laplante@gnb.ca
Director, Marketing, Kim Matthews
Tel: 506-453-4284
kim.matthews@gnb.ca
Director, Content Development, Susan Morell
Tel: 506-453-5896
susan.morell@gnb.ca

Tourism Operations
Centennial Building, 6th Fl., PO Box 6000, Fredericton, NB E3B 5H1
Tel: 506-444-6752
Fax: 506-453-2854
taponlinedirectory@gnb.ca

Tourism Operations oversees the following provincial parks & historical sites: De la République, Sugarloaf, Mactaquac, New River Beach, Herring Cove, Parlee Beach, Murray Beach, The Ancorage, Mount Carleton, Hopewell Rocks, Village Historique Acadien, Kings Landing, & Miscou.

Director, Tourism Operations, Alain Basque
Tel: 506-453-2170
alain.basque@gnb.ca
Assistant Director, Tourism Operations, Martin MacMullin
Tel: 506-444-5339
martin.macmullin@gnb.ca
Executive Director, Kings Landing Historical Site, Kevin Cormier
Tel: 506-363-4957
kevin.cormier@gnb.ca
Director, Village Historique Acadien, Gabriel Lebreton
Tel: 506-726-2600
gabriel.lebreton@gnb.ca
Director, Mactaquac Provincial Park, Neill Sandwith
Tel: 506-363-4905
neill.sandwith@gnb.ca
Manager, Herring Cove Provincial Park, Dorinda Anthony
Tel: 506-752-7010
Dorinda.Anthony@gnb.ca
Manager, Mount Carleton Provincial Park, Louis Comeau
Tel: 506-235-0793
Louis.Comeau@gnb.ca
Manager, Hopewell Rocks, Guy Daigle
Tel: 506-734-3538
guy.daigle2@gnb.ca
Manager, Sugarloaf Provincial Park, Greg Dion
Tel: 506-789-2366
greg.dion@gnb.ca
Manager, New River Beach Provincial Park & The Anchorage Provincial Park, Lenora Lomax
Tel: 506-755-4042
lenora.lomax@gnb.ca
Manager, New River Beach Provincial Park, Lenora Lomax
Tel: 506-755-4042
lenora.lomax@gnb.ca
Manager, Parlee Beach Provincial Park, Marcel Richard
Tel: 506-533-3363
marcel.richard2@gnb.ca
Manager, De la République Provincial Park, Jocelyne St. Onge
Tel: 506-735-2702
jocelyne.st-onge@gnb.ca
Supervisor, Murray Beach Provincial Park, M. Banks
Tel: 506-538-2628
murraybeach@gnb.ca

Premier's Council on the Status of Disabled Persons / Conseil du Premier ministre sur la condition des personnes handicapées

Kings Place, #648, 440 King St., Fredericton, NB E3B 5H8
Tel: 506-444-3000
Fax: 506-444-3001
Toll-Free: 800-442-4412
pcsdp@gnb.ca
www.gnb.ca/0048

The role of the Premier's Council on the Status of Disabled Persons is to provide advice to the provincial government of New Brunswick & the public about issues of interest & concern that affect the status of persons with disabilities.

Premier; President, Executive Council; Minister, Intergovernmental Affairs; Minister Responsible, Premier's Council on the Status of Disabled Persons; Minister Responsible, Citizens'Engagement, Hon. David Alward
Tel: 506-453-2144
Fax: 506-453-7407
david.alward@gnb.ca
Centennial Bldg.
670 King St.
Fredericton, NB E3B 5H1

Chairperson, Michelle Horncastle
Tel: 506-444-3000
Fax: 506-444-3001
pcsdp@gnb.ca
TTY: 506-444-3000

Executive Director, Christyne Allain
Tel: 506-444-3004
Fax: 506-444-3001
pcsdp@gnb.ca

New Brunswick Department of Economic Development

Centennial Building, PO Box 6000, Fredericton, NB E3B 5H1
Tel: 506-453-3707
Fax: 506-453-3993
Toll-Free: 800-665-1800
tradenb@gnb.ca
www2.gnb.ca/content/gnb/en/departments/economic_development.html

The mission of the New Brunswick Department of Economic Development is to retain & expand business, & to develop business clusters that focus on biosciences, industrial fabrication, aerospace & defence, & value-added food & value-added wood. The department achieves its goals through the following divisions: Business Development, Communications, Corporate Services, & Financial Programs & Policy & Planning.

Acts Administered:
Economic Development
Invest New Brunswick
Regional Development Corporation
Research & Productivity Council
Youth Assistance

Minister, Economic Development; Minster Responsible for la Francophonie; Deputy Premier; Government House Leader, Hon. Paul Robichaud
Tel: 506-453-5898
Fax: 506-453-6389
paul.robichaud@gnb.ca
Centennial Bldg.
670 King St.
PO Box 6000
Fredericton, NB E3B 5H1

Deputy Minister, Bill Levesque
Tel: 506-453-5897
bill.levesque@gnb.ca

Associated Agencies, Boards & Commissions:
- **Invest NB**
HSBC Place
PO Box 6000
Fredericton, NB E3B 5H1
- **New Brunswick Industrial Development Board**
Centennial Building
PO Box 6000
Fredericton, NB E3B 5H1
Tel: 506-453-4200
Fax: 506-457-7282

Business Development Division
Centennial Building, PO Box 6000, Fredericton, NB E3B 5H1
Tel: 506-453-3412
Fax: 506-453-3783
tradenb@gnb.ca
www.newbrunswick.ca

The Business Development Division assists businesses in New Brunswick to become more innovative & competitive.

Assistant Deputy Minister, Eric Beaulieu
Tel: 506-453-3412
eric.beaulieu@gnb.ca
Executive Director, Export Development, Joel Richardson
Tel: 506-453-3412
joel.richardson@gnb.ca
Director, Export Development, Michel Albert
Tel: 506-444-5053
michel.albert@gnb.ca
Manager, Knowledge Industries & Innovation, Jonathan Downey
Tel: 506-444-6758
Jon.downey@gnb.ca
Project Executive, Industry Services, Gilles Johnson
Tel: 506-444-2025
gilles.johnson@gnb.ca

Communications Division
Centennial Bldg., PO Box 6000, Fredericton, NB E3B 5H1
Tel: 506-453-8607
Fax: 506-453-3993
www.newbrunswick.ca

The Communications Division promotes the department's efforts to retain businesses & to create key economic clusters.

Director, Communications, Bruce MacFarlane
Tel: 506-453-8607
bruce.macfarlane@gnb.ca
Officer, Communications, Marie-Berthe Losier
marie-berthe.losier@gnb.ca

Corporate Services Division
Centennial Building, PO Box 6000, Fredericton, NB E3B 5H1
Tel: 506-453-3707
Fax: 506-453-5428
www.newbrunswick.ca

The Corporate Services Division assists the department through records management, financial administration, & information technology management.

Director, Information Technology, Doug Waugh
Tel: 506-457-7324
doug.waugh@gnb.ca
Manager, Financial Administration, Jean-Bernard Guignard
Tel: 506-453-3707
jean-bernard.guignard@gnb.ca
Supervisor, Records Management, Daphne MacKay
Tel: 506-453-8162
daphne.mackay2@gnb.ca

Financial Programs & Policy & Planning Division
Centennial Bldg., PO Box 6000, Fredericton, NB E3B 5H1
Tel: 506-453-2875
Fax: 506-444-4128
www.newbrunswick.ca

The Financial Programs & Policy & Planning Division offers financial assistance & capital investment to existing & new entrepreneurs. The goal is to increase sustainable employment throughout New Brunswick.

Assistant Deputy Minister, Financial Programs & Policy & Planning, Eric Beaulieu
Tel: 506-462-5277
eric.beaulieu@gnb.ca
Executive Director, Policy & Planning, Shannon Sanford
Tel: 506-444-5854
shannon.sanford@gnb.ca
Executive Director, Business Financial Support, Daniel Seems
Tel: 506-453-6291
dan.seems@gnb.ca
Director, Financial Programs, Bernie Fontaine
Tel: 506-444-5852
bernie.fontaine@gnb.ca
Manager, Monitoring & Program Delivery, Joe Richard
Tel: 506-453-3231
joe.richard@gnb.ca

Northern Development Division
Harbourview Place, #400, 275 Main St., Bathurst, NB E2A 1A9
Tel: 506-547-2227
Fax: 506-547-2269
www.newbrunswick.ca

The Northern Development Division is engaged in the administration of financial programs.

Assistant Deputy Minister, Northern Development, Roger Robichaud
Tel: 506-547-2227
roger.robichaud@gnb.ca
Director, Northern Development, Rick Lloyd
Tel: 506-547-2227
rick.lloyd@gnb.ca
Director, Northern Development, Denis Roy
Tel: 506-547-2227
denis.roy2@gnb.ca
Financial Officer, Financial Programs, Sylvain Savoie
Tel: 506-547-2227
sylvain.savoie@gnb.ca

New Brunswick Department of Education & Early Childhood Development / Éducation

Place 2000, PO Box 6000, Fredericton, NB E3B 5H1
Tel: 506-453-3678
Fax: 506-453-3325
edcommunication@gnb.ca
www.gnb.ca/education

The Department of Education & Early Childhood Development consists of an Early Learning & Child Care Sector, an Anglophone Sector, & a Francophone Sector.
The Early Learning & Child Care Sector oversees the following programs & services: Prenatal Benefit Program; the Postnatal Benefit Program; the Infant Parent Attachment Program; Excellence in Parenting; the Pay Equity Program for Child Care Staff; early intervention standards; child day care; Early Childhood Development Centers; the Early Childhood Strategy; the Early Learning & Child Care Trust Fund; the curriculum for early learning & child care; & services for preschool children with autism.
The English Educational Services Division is responsible for curriculum development, student services, e-learning, & student evaluation & assessment.
The Francophone Educational Services Division oversees curriculum development & implementation, special education, psychology, guidance counselling, professional development, & assessment & evaluation.

Acts Administered:
Early Learning & Childcare Act
Education Act

Minister, Education & Early Childhood Development, Hon. Jody Carr

Tel: 506-453-2523
jody.carr@gnb.ca

Deputy Minister / Sous-ministre, Roger Doucet
Tel: 506-453-2409
roger.doucet@gnb.ca

Deputy Minister, Wendy McLeod MacKnight
Tel: 506-453-2529
wendy.mcleodmacknight@gnb.ca

Director, Communications, Christina Winsor
Tel: 506-444-2455
christina.winsor@gnb.ca

Accountability & Quality Assurance
Huttle Building, PO Box 6000, Fredericton, NB E3B 5H1
Tel: 506-453-8679
Fax: 506-457-4810
teachercertification@gnb.ca
www.gnb.ca/education

Executive Director, Accountability & Quality Assurance, Deidre Green, CA
Tel: 506-453-8679
deidre.green@gnb.ca
Manager, Mark Comeau
Tel: 506-453-8619
mark.comeau@gnb.ca

Corporate Services
Place 2000, PO Box 6000, Fredericton, NB E3B 5H1
Tel: 506-453-2085
Fax: 506-457-4810
edcommunication@gnb.ca
www.gnb.ca/education

Assistant Deputy Minister, Michel Thériault
Tel: 506-453-2085
michel.theriault@gnb.ca
Director, Corporate Relations, Manon Arsenault
Tel: 506-453-6433
manon.arsenault@gnb.ca
Director, Human Resources, Valmond Guimond
Tel: 506-444-4914
Valmond.Guimond@gnb.ca
Director, Information Systens, Louise Ouellette
Tel: 506-453-7158
Louise.Ouellette@gnb.ca
Director, Educational Facilities & Pupil Transportation, Ron White
Tel: 506-453-2242
ron.white@gnb.ca
Senior Financial Officer, Mylène Chiasson
Tel: 506-453-4231
mylene.chiasson@gnb.ca

Early Childhood Development
Place 2000, PO Box 6000, Fredericton, NB E3B 5H1
Tel: 506-453-2950
Fax: 506-453-2082
edcommunication@gnb.ca
www.gnb.ca/education

Executive Director, Nicole Gervais
Tel: 506-453-2950
nicole.gervais@gnb.ca
Director, Early Learning & Child Care, Diane Lutes
Tel: 506-869-6878
diane.lutes@gnb.ca

Educational Services (Anglophone)
Place 2000, PO Box 6000, Fredericton, NB E3B 5H1
Tel: 506-453-3326
Fax: 506-457-4810
edcommunication@gnb.ca
www.gnb.ca/education

Assistant Deputy Minister, Zoë Watson
Tel: 506-453-3326
zoe.watson@gnb.ca
Director, Professional Learning Services, Inga Boehler
Tel: 506-453-3696
inga.boehler@gnb.ca
Director, Student Services, Brian Kelly
Tel: 506-453-2816
inga.boehler@gnb.ca
Director, Assessment & Evaluation, Sandra Mazerall
Tel: 506-453-2744
sandra.mazerall@gnb.ca
Director, Strategic Partnerships, Dawn Weatherbie
Tel: 506-453-2771
dawn.weatherbie@gnb.ca
Director, Curriculum Development & Implementation K-12, Darlene Whitehouse-Sheehan
Tel: 506-453-2155
darlene.whitehouse-sheehan@gnb.ca
Registrar, Teacher Certification, Yves King
Tel: 506-453-2785
Yves.king@gnb.ca

Policy & Planning
Place 2000, PO Box 6000, Fredericton, NB E3B 5H1
Tel: 506-453-3090
Fax: 506-453-3111
edcommunication@gnb.ca
www.gnb.ca/education

Executive Director, Policy & Planning, Lise Bellefleur
Tel: 506-453-8299
lise.bellefleur@gnb.ca
Director, Corporate Data Management & Analysis, Monica LeBlanc
Tel: 506-453-6124
monica.leblanc@gnb.ca
Director, Policy & Legislative Affairs, Catherine Stewart
Tel: 506-453-8832
catherine.stewart@gnb.ca
Senior Policy Analyst, Vincent French
Tel: 506-453-3090
vincent.french@gnb.ca

Secteur des services éducatifs francophones
Place 2000, PO Box 6000, Fredericton, NB E3B 9M9
Tel: 506-453-2086
Fax: 506-457-4810

Director, Services intégrées, Bob Eckstein
Tel: 506-444-2618
bob.eckstein@gnb.ca
Director, Initiatives, relations stratégiques et éducation internationale, Luc Handfield
Tel: 506-453-8882
luc.handfield@gnb.ca
Director, Mesure et évaluation, Robert Laurie
Tel: 506-453-2157
robert.laurie@gnb.ca
Director, Programmes d'études et de l'apprentissage, Marcel Lavoie
Tel: 506-453-2743
Marcel.lavoie@gnb.ca
Director, École communautaire, du leadership et de la technologie, Alain Poitras
Tel: 506-444-2575
alain.poitras@gnb.ca
Director, Services aux élèves, Gina St-Laurent
Tel: 506-453-5876
gina.st-laurent@gnb.ca

Special Project Team
Place 2000, 250 King St., 4th Fl., Fredericton, NB E3B 5H1
Tel: 506-444-2906
Fax: 506-444-5523
edcommunication@gnb.ca
www.gnb.ca/education

Project Executive, Amanda Harpelle
Tel: 506-453-6723
amanda.harpelle@gnb.ca
Project Executive, Claude Marquis
Tel: 506-453-8884
claude.marquis@gnb.ca

Office of the Chief Electoral Officer / Bureau de la directrice générale des élections

PO Box 6000, Fredericton, NB E3B 5H1
Tel: 506-453-2218
Fax: 506-457-4926
Toll-Free: 800-308-2922
www.gnb.ca/elections

Chief Electoral Officer, Michael Quinn
Tel: 506-453-2218
michael.quinn@electionsnb.ca

Director, Operations, Craig Astle
Tel: 506-453-2218
Fax: 506-457-4926
craig.astle@electionsnb.ca

Manager, Voter Information Systems, Ronald Armitage
Tel: 506-453-2218
Fax: 506-457-4926
ron.armitage@electionsnb.ca

Manager, Policy & Development, Peggy Scott
Tel: 506-453-2218
Fax: 506-457-4926
peggy.scott@electionsnb.ca

Supervisor, Finance & Human Resources, Theresa Comeau
Tel: 506-453-2218
Fax: 506-453-6121
theresa.comeau@electionsnb.ca

New Brunswick Department of Energy

Brunswick Square, #100M, 1 Germain St., Saint John, NB E2L 4V1
Tel: 506-658-3180
Fax: 506-643-2919
DOEweb@gnb.ca
www.gnb.ca/energy

The New Brunswick Department of Energy is responsible for the following: ensuring a reliable, secure, & cost effective energy supply; promoting economic efficiency in energy systems; encouraging economic development opportunities; protecting & improving the environment; & ensuring an effective regulatory regime.

Acts Administered:
Electricity
Energy Efficiency
Energy Efficiency & Conservation Agency of New Brunswick Act
Gas Distribution, 1999
Petroleum Products Pricing
Pipeline

Minister, Government Services; Acting Minister, Energy; Minister Responsible, New Brunswick Internal Services Agency, Service New Brunswick, Hon. Craig Leonard
Tel: 506-453-2240
Fax: 506-453-5329
Craig.Leonard@gnb.ca;EECA/AECE.Customer.Service@gnb.ca

Deputy Minster, Phil Lepage
Tel: 506-453-2501
phil.lepage@gnb.ca

Assistant Deputy Minster, Neil Jacobsen
Tel: 506-658-3132
neil.jacobsen@gnb.ca

Director, Communications, Tyler Campbell
Tel: 506-453-8420
tyler.campbell@gnb.ca

Alternative Energy & Energy Efficiency Division
Brunswick Square, #M100, 1 Germain St., Saint John, NB E2L 4V1
Tel: 506-658-3180
Fax: 506-658-3191
DOEweb@gnb.ca
www.gnb.ca/energy

The division focuses upon energy management initiatives to improve the use & diversity of energy resources. The work of the Alternative Energy & Energy Efficiency Division benefits the environment & the economy.
Director, Alternative Energy & Energy Efficiency Division, Bill Breckenridge
Tel: 506-658-3180
bill.breckenridge@gnb.ca
Policy Advisor, David Duplisea
Tel: 506-658-3180
David.Duplisea@gnb.ca
Policy Advisor, Keith Melvin
Tel: 506-658-3180
Keith.melvin@gnb.ca

Electricity & Nuclear Energy Division
Brunswick Square, #100M, 1 Germain St., Saint John, NB E2L 4V1
Tel: 506-658-3180
Fax: 506-658-3191
DOEweb@gnb.ca

The Electricity & Nuclear Energy works to improve the security of energy supply throughout the province.
Director, Electricity & Nuclear Energy, Stephen Waycott
Tel: 506-658-3126
stephen.waycott@gnb.ca
Policy Advisor, Heather Quinn
Tel: 506-658-3180
Heather.Quinn@gnb.ca
Policy Advisor, David Sollows
Tel: 506-658-3180
david.sollows@gnb.ca

Hydrocarbon Energy Legislative & Regulatory Affairs Division
Brunswick Square, #100M, 1 Germain St., Saint John, NB E2L 4V1
Tel: 506-658-3180
Fax: 506-658-3191
Doeweb@gnb.ca

Through ongoing infrastructure growth & regulatory reform, the Department of Energy works to develop & improve energy sources.
Director, Hydrocarbon Energy Legislative & Regulatory Affairs Division, Patrick Ervin
Tel: 506-658-3180
patrick.ervin@gnb.ca

Policy Advisor, Mary Ann Mann
Tel: 506-658-3180
maryann.mann@gnb.ca
Policy Advisor, Sacha Patino
Tel: 506-658-3180
sacha.patino@gnb.ca

New Brunswick Department of Environment & Local Government

Marysville Place, PO Box 6000, Fredericton, NB E3B 5H1
Tel: 506-453-2690
Fax: 506-457-4994
elg/egl-info@gnb.ca
www2.gnb.ca/content/gnb/en/departments/elg.html
Other Communication: Toll-free phone to report pesicide, oil, chemical spills, & other environmental emergencies: 1-800-565-1633

The Departmemt of Environment & Local Government is responsible for environmental stewardship, Efficiency NB, & consultation with municipal governments & Local Service Districts concerning governance issues.

Acts Administered:
Agricultural Land Protection & Development (subsection 10(2) & section 11)
Assessment & Planning Appeal Board
Beverage Containers
Business Improvement Areas
Cemetery Companies (paragraph 5(1)(c))
Clean Air
Clean Environment
Clean Water
Community Planning
Control of Municipalities
Days of Rest
Edmundston Act, 1998
Environmental Trust Fund (except administration of fund)
Evidence (sections 88, 89 & 90)
Gas Distribution Act, 1999 (subsection 18(2), paragraph 32(1)(a), & subsection 39(1))
Highway (sections 58 to 62.1)
Metric Conversion
Mining (subsection 68(2))
Municipal Assistance
Municipal Capital Borrowing
Municipal Debentures
Municipal Thoroughfare Easements
Municipalities (other than subsection 19(8), 125(1), & 188(3))
New Brunswick Municipal Finance Corporation (section 14 & subsection 16(4))
Pesticides Control
Police (paragraph 17.05(2)(b), subsections 17.06(3), & (4), paragraph 17.2(3)(b), & subsections 17.4(3), & (4))
Real Property Tax (section 4 & subsection 5(10))
Service New Brunswick (paragraph 15.1(3)(b))
Society for the Prevention of Cruelty to Animals
Taxation of the LNG Terminal, An Act to Comply with the Request of The City of Saint John
Topsoil Preservation
Unsightly Premises

Minister, Environment & Local Government; Minister Responsible for the Energy Efficiency & Conservation Agency of NB, Hon. Bruce Fitch
Tel: 506-453-2807
Bruce.Fitch@gnb.ca

Deputy Minister, Environment & Local Government; President, Efficiency NB, Denis Caron
Tel: 506-453-3256
denis.caron@gnb.ca

Contact, Public Affairs, Marie-Claude Wedge
Tel: 506-453-3700
Fax: 506-453-3843
Marie-Claude.Wedge@gnb.ca

Associated Agencies, Boards & Commissions:

• Assessment & Plannning Appeal Board
City Centre
PO Box 6000
Fredericton, NB E3B 5H1
Tel: 506-453-2126
Fax: 506-444-4881
lg/gl-info@gnb.ca
The Assessment & Planning Appeal Board hears property assessment appeals, appeals of land use & planning decisions, & appeals of local heritage review board decisions. The board consists of eleven regional panels from across New Brunswick.

• Royal District Planning Commission (RDPC)
#1, 49 Winter St.
Sussex, NB E4E 2W8
Tel: 506-432-7530
Fax: 506-432-7539
Toll-free: 888-245-9155
info@royaldpc.com
www.royaldpc.com
Established by a Ministerial Order under the Community Planning Act of the Province of New Brunswick, the Royal District Planning Commission is composed of board members who are appointed by the Minister of Environment & Local Government & municipal partners. It provides land use planning services to the municipalities & unincorporated areas.
The Commission oversees a staff that manages the daily work of the Commission, such as approving subdivision plans & developments; issuing building permits; inspecting new developments & buildings; administering & enforcing subdivision, building, & zoning by-laws; & providing planning advice to the Minister of Environment & Local Government, municipalities, & rural community committees.

Community Planning & Environmental Protection Division

Marysville Place, PO Box 6000, Fredericton, NB E3B 5H1
Tel: 506-444-5119
Fax: 506-457-7333
elg/egl-info@gnb.ca
The division is concerned with the state of the environment, sustainable development, impact evaluation & management, standard setting, & enforcement.
Executive Director, State of the Environment, David Schellenberg
Tel: 506-457-4844
dave.schellenberg@gnb.ca
Director, Standards Setting, Program Operations, & Enforcement, Mike Cormier
Tel: 506-444-3635
Mike.Cormier@gnb.ca
Director, Analytical Services, Peter McLaughlin
Tel: 506-453-2477
Peter.McLaughlin@gnb.ca
Director, Performance Excellence Process & Continuous Improvement, Colleen Mullin
Tel: 506-444-5119
Colleen.Mullin@gnb.ca
Director, Environmental Evaluation & Reporting, Darryl Pupek
Tel: 506-457-4844
Darryl.Pupek@gnb.ca
Director, Sustainable Development, Planning, & Impact Evaluation, Paul Vanderlaan
Tel: 506-444-4599
paul.vanderlaan@gnb.ca
Bathurst Regional Office
PO Box 5001, Bathurst, NB E2A 3Z9
Tel: 506-547-2092
Fax: 506-547-7655
elg/egl-info@gnb.ca
Regional Director, Paul Fournier
Tel: 506-547-2092
Paul.Fournier@gnb.ca
Engineer, Gaétan Landry
Tel: 506-547-2092
Gaetan.Landry@gnb.ca
Fredericton Regional Office
Priestman Centre, PO Box 6000, Fredericton, NB E3B 5H1
Tel: 506-444-5149
Fax: 506-453-2893
elg/egl-info@gnb.ca
Director, Serge Gagnon
Tel: 506-444-5149
Serge.Gagnon@gnb.ca
Engineer, Jennifer Bishop
Tel: 506-444-5149
jennifer.bishop@gnb.ca
Grand Falls Regional Office
PO Box 5001, Grand Falls, NB E3Z 1G1
Tel: 506-473-7744
Fax: 506-475-2510
elg/egl-info@gnb.ca
Regional Director, Richard Keeley
Tel: 506-473-7744
Richard.Keeley@gnb.ca
Engineer, Roger Bélanger
Tel: 506-473-7744
Roger.Belanger@gnb.ca
Miramichi Regional Office
Industrial Park, 316 Dalton Ave., Miramichi, NB E1V 3N9
Tel: 506-778-6032
Fax: 506-778-6796
elg/egl-info@gnb.ca
Regional Director, Denis Daigle
Tel: 506-778-6032
Denis.Daigle@gnb.ca
Moncton Regional Office
PO Box 5001, Moncton, NB E1C 8R3
Tel: 506-856-2374
Fax: 506-856-2370
elg/egl-info@gnb.ca
Regional Director, Laurie Collette
Tel: 506-856-2374
Laurie.Collette@gnb.ca
Saint John Regional Office
PO Box 5001, Saint John, NB E2L 4Y9
Tel: 506-658-2558
Fax: 506-658-3046
elg/egl-info@gnb.ca
Director, Patrick Stull
Tel: 506-658-2558
patrick.stull@gnb.ca
Engineer, Barry Leger
Tel: 506-658-2558
Barry.Leger@gnb.ca
Biologist, Aaron Bennett
Tel: 506-658-2558
Aaron.Bennett@gnb.ca

Corporate Services, Community Funding & Technical Services Division

Marysville Place, PO Box 6000, Fredericton, NB E3B 5H1
Tel: 506-453-2020
Fax: 506-457-7800
lg/gl-info@gnb.ca
The division oversees human resources & administrative services, information & technology management, corporate finance, & community funding.
Assistant Deputy Minister, Corporate Services, Community Funding, & Technical Services Division, Alan Roy
Tel: 506-453-6285
alan.roy@gnb.ca
Director, Community Funding & Technical Services, André Chenard
Tel: 506-457-4947
Andre.Chenard@gnb.ca
Director, Information & Technology Management, Laurie Robichaud
Tel: 506-453-2020
Laurie.Robichaud@gnb.ca
Director, Corporate Finance, Yvonne Samson
Tel: 506-453-2020
Yvonne.Samson@gnb.ca
Director, Human Resources & Administration, Mary Ellen Somerville
Tel: 506-453-2020
MaryEllen.Somerville@gnb.ca

Local Government Division

Marysville Place, PO Box 6000, Fredericton, NB E3B 5H1
Tel: 506-453-2690
Fax: 506-457-4994
lg/gl-info@gnb.ca
The Local Government Division provides liaison services, financial support, & assistance with municipal functions. Examples of activities include overseeing the restructuring of municipalities & rural communities, & assisting Business Improvement Areas to improve downtown cores.
Assistant Deputy Minister, Local Government, Stephen Battah
Tel: 506-444-4423
stephen.battah@gnb.ca
Executive Director, Local & Regional Governance, Rob Kelly
Tel: 506-453-2154
Rob.Kelly@gnb.ca
Director, Local & Regional Governance, Susan Atkinson
Tel: 506-453-2154
susan.atkinson@gnb.ca
Director, Public Affairs, Ryan Donaghy
Tel: 506-444-4693
Ryan.Donaghy@gnb.ca
Director, Community Finances, Alexandra Ferris
Tel: 506-453-2154
Ali.Ferris@gnb.ca
Director, Special Projects, Sandra Jessop-Roach
Tel: 506-453-2154
Sandra.Roach@gnb.ca
Director, Capacity Building & Local Services, Peter Kavanagh
Tel: 506-444-4423
peter.kavanagh@gnb.ca
Director, Local Governance Policy, Christy Shaw
Tel: 506-453-3700
Christy.Shaw@gnb.ca

Partnerships & Innovation Division

Marysville Place, PO Box 6000, Fredericton, NB E3B 5H1
Tel: 506-453-2862
Fax: 506-453-2265
elg/egl-info@gnb.ca
The Partnerships & Innovation Division manages the Climate Change Secretariat & the Green Economy Project.
The Climate Change Secretariat is concerned with greenhouse

gas emission reductions & adaptations. The secretariat also manages engagement with federal, provincial, territorial, & international jurisdictions on climate change issues. Public awareness & education programs are also produced.
The Green Economy Project focuses upon sustainable development & achieving a green economy.
Executive Director, Climate Change Secretariat & Green Economy Project, Darwin Curtis
Tel: 506-457-4844
Darwin.Curtis@gnb.ca
Coordinator, Adaptation, Robert Hughes
Tel: 506-457-4844
Robert.Hughes@gnb.ca
Community Planner, Paul Jordan
Tel: 506-457-4844
paul.jordan@gnb.ca

Policy & Strategic Initiatives Division
Marysville Place, PO Box 6000, Fredericton, NB E3B 5H1
Tel: 506-453-3700
Fax: 506-453-7128
elg/egl-info@gnb.ca
The division is responsible for ensuring that policies & strategic planning intitiatives are developed & implemented to support the Department of Environment & Local Government.
Executive Director, Policy & Strategic Initiatives Division, Elizabeth Hayward
Tel: 506-453-8788
bebo.hayward@gnb.ca
Director, Stakeholder Education & Engagement, Michelle Daigle
Tel: 506-453-3700
Michelle.Daigle@gnb.ca
Director, Strategic Planning & Policy Development, Kim Hughes
Tel: 506-453-3700
kim.hughes@gnb.ca
Director, Environmental Policy, Katherine Lefeuvre
Tel: 506-453-3700
katherine.lefeuvre@gnb.ca
Director, Legislative Renewal & Legal Affairs, Denyse Smart
Tel: 506-453-3700
Denyse.Smart@gnb.ca
Director, Inter-governmental Affairs, Stephanie Whalen
Tel: 506-453-3700
Stephanie.Whalen@gnb.ca

New Brunswick Department of Finance / Finances

670 King St., PO Box 6000, Fredericton, NB E3B 5H1
Tel: 506-453-2451
Fax: 506-457-4989
wwwfin@gnb.ca
www.gnb.ca/0024/index-e.asp
The Department of Finance manages the public finances of New Brunswick.
Acts Administered:
Appropriation Act
Arts Development Trust Fund
Auditor General Act (subsections 4(3) & 16(1) & Section 17
Beaverbrook Art Gallery Act (Section 9)
Beaverbrook Auditorium Act (Section 7)
Crown Construction Contracts Act
Environmental Trust Fund (administration of fund)
Expenditure Management Act, 1991
Expenditure Management Act, 1992
Fees Act
Financial Administration Act (expect provisions assigned to the Office of the Comptroller or to the Board of Management)
Financial Administration Act (responsibilities pursuant to subsection 2(1))
Financial Administration Act (responsibilties pursuant to subsection 2(2) & Section 6
Financial Corporation Capital Tax Act
Fiscal Responsibility and Balanced Budget Act
Fiscal Stabilization Fund
Fishermen's Disaster Fund Act (functions vested in Provincial Secretary-Treasurer)
Fredericton-Moncton Highway Financing Act
Gaming Control Act (part 2)
Gasoline & Motive Fuel Tax Act
Harmonized Sales Tax Act
Health Care Funding Guarantee Act
Income Tax Act
Loan Act
Maritime Provinces Harness Racing Commission Act
Member's Pension Act
Members Superannuation Act
Metallic Minerals Act
Mining Act
Municipal Assistance Act (except Section 5, 9 & 10)
Municipalities Act (subsection 19(8) & paragraphs 87.1(b) & (2)(b)
New Brunswick Income Tax Act
New Brunswick Investment Management Corporation Act
New Brunswick Liquor Corporation Act
New Brunswick Municipal Finance Corporation Act
Northumberland Strait Crossing Act
Oil and Natural Gas Act
Ombudsman Act (pension provision, subsection 2(4))
Pari-Mutuel Tax Act
Petrolium Act (part13, except S.88)
Provincial Court Act (pension provisions)
Provincial Court Judges' Pension Act
Provincial Loans Act
Public Service Labour Relations Act (61)
Public Service Superannuation Act
Quarrible Substances Act
Real Property Tax Act (except Sections 4 & subsection 5 (10))
Real Property Transfer Tax Act
Retirement Plan Benificiaries Act
Revenue Administration Act
Small Business Investment Tax Credit Act
Social Services & Education Tax Act
Special Appropriations Act
Special Retirement Program Act
Sport Development Trust Fund Act (administration of fund)
Statistics Act
Statutes under the Jurisdiction of the Minister of Finance & Administered by a Board, Commission or Corporation
Statutes under the Jurisdiction of the Minister of Finance & Administered by the Office of the Comptroller
Statutes under the Jurisdiction of the Minister of Finance in the Minister's Capacity as Chairman of the Board of Management
Taxpayers Protection Act
Teachers' Pension Act
Tobacco Tax Act
Tuition Tax Cash Back Credit Act

Minister, Finance; Minister, Office of Human Resources; Minister Responsible, New Brunswick Liquor Corporation, New Brunswick Investment Management Corporation, & New Brunswick Lotteries & Gaming Corporation; Chair, Board ofManagement, Hon. Blaine Higgs
Tel: 506-444-2627
Fax: 506-457-4989
Blaine.Higgs@gnb.ca

Deputy Minister, Michael Ferguson, C.A.
Tel: 506-453-2534
Fax: 506-457-4989
mike.ferguson@gnb.ca

Chief Operating Officer, Minister's Office, Jane Washburn
Tel: 506-452-6500
Fax: 506-453-4225
jane.washburn@gnb.ca

Policy Advisor, Minister's Office, Graham Little
Tel: 506-453-2144
Fax: 506-457-4989
graham.little@gnb.ca

Executive Secretary, Minister's Office, Pauline Taylor
Tel: 506-444-2627
Fax: 506-457-4989
pauline.taylor@gnb.ca

Executive Assistant, Minister's Office, Bill Oliver
Tel: 506-444-2627
Fax: 506-457-4989
bill.oliver@gnb.ca

Executive Secretary, Deputy Head's Office, Jocelyne MacFarlane
Tel: 506-453-2354
Fax: 506-457-4989
jocelyne.macfarlane@gnb.ca

Associated Agencies, Boards & Commissions:
• New Brunswick Investment Management Corporation (NBIMC) / Société de gestion des placements du Nouveau-Brunswick
York Tower
#581, 440 King St.
Fredericton, NB E3B 5H8
Tel: 506-444-5800
Fax: 506-444-5025
comments@nbimc.com
www.nbimc.com
The New Brunswick Investment Management Corporation assists in the development of the financial services industry & capital markets in the province of New Brunswick.

• New Brunswick Lotteries & Gaming Corporation
Centennial Bldg.
670 King St.
PO Box 6000
Fredericton, NB E3B 5H1
Tel: 506-444-3468
Fax: 506-444-5818
www.gnb.ca/0162/gaming/nblgc_welcome-e.asp
The name of the Lotteries Commission of New Brunswick, which was established as a Crown corporation under the Lotteries Act, was changed to the New Brunswick Lotteries & Gaming Corporation.

Budget & Financial Management / Gestion financière et budgétaire
Centennial Bldg., #250, 670 King St., PO Box 6000, Fredericton, NB E3B 5H1
Tel: 506-453-2808
Fax: 506-444-4499
The Budget & Financial Management Division has the following responsibilities: implementation of multi-year expenditure plans; development & monitoring of budgets; & offering options for the government to consider.
Senior Financial Analyst, Bernice Cook
Tel: 506-453-2808
Fax: 506-444-4499
bernice.cook@gnb.ca
Director, Board of Management, Kelly Barr
Tel: 506-453-2808
kelly.barr@gnb.ca
Assistant Secretary, Board of Management, Keith MacNevin
Tel: 506-453-2808
Keith.MacNevin@gnb.ca

Communications Services / Service des communications
Centennial Bldg., #373, 670 King St., PO Box 6000, Fredericton, NB E3B 5H1
Tel: 506-453-2451
Fax: 506-457-4989
wwwfin@gnb.ca
www.gnb.ca/finance
The Budget & Financial Management Division has the following responsibilities: Implementation of multi-year expenditure plans; Development & monitoring of budgets; & Offering options for the government to consider.
Director, Brendan Langille
Tel: 506-453-2565
Fax: 506-457-4989
brendan.langille@gnb.ca

Finance & Administration / Finances et administration
Centennial Bldg., #375, 670 King St., PO Box 6000, Fredericton, NB E3B 5H1
Tel: 506-453-2451
Fax: 506-444-4724
This division uses a shared services model to provide a blend of corporate services to about 600 clients who work for 10 departments and 22 agencies, boards and commissions. The corporate services include financial services, information technology services and human resources services.
Assistant Deputy Minister, Jane Garbutt
Tel: 506-444-5686
Fax: 506-457-4989
jane.garbutt@gnb.ca
Assistant Director, Shauna Woodside
Tel: 506-453-2286
Fax: 506-462-5056
shauna.woodside@gnb.ca

Financial Services / Services financiers
Tel: 506-453-2286
Fax: 506-444-5056
This division uses a shared services model to provide a blend of corporate services to about 600 clients who work for 10 departments and 22 agencies, boards and commissions. The corporate services include financial services, information technology services and human resources services.

Human Resources Services / Services des ressources humaines
Tel: 506-453-2451
Fax: 506-444-4724
This division uses a shared services model to provide a blend of corporate services to about 600 clients who work for 10 departments and 22 agencies, boards and commissions. The corporate services include financial services, information technology services and human resources services.
Director, Peter Trask
Tel: 506-444-5099
Fax: 506-444-4724
peter.trask@gnb.ca
Assistant Director, Terry Charters
Tel: 506-453-6905
Fax: 506-444-4724
terry.charters@gnb.ca

Information Management & Technology / Gestion de l'information et de la technologie
Tel: 506-453-2096
Fax: 506-444-3471
This division uses a shared services model to provide a blend of corporate services to about 600 clients who work for 10 departments and 22 agencies, boards and commissions. The corporate services include financial services, information technology services and human resources services.
Director, Pam Gagnon
Tel: 506-453-3310
Fax: 506-444-3471
pam.gagnon@gnb.ca
Senior Programmer/Analyst, Vasco Gabriel Bonilla Perris
Tel: 506-444-4568
Fax: 506-444-3471
vascogabriel.bonillaperris@gnb.ca
Project Manager, Colleen Benson
Tel: 506-453-6090
Fax: 506-444-3471
colleen.benson@gnb.ca

Policy & Planning / Politiques et de la planification
Tel: 506-453-2451
Fax: 506-444-4724
This division uses a shared services model to provide a blend of corporate services to about 600 clients who work for 10 departments and 22 agencies, boards and commissions. The corporate services include financial services, information technology services and human resources services.
Director, Ann Deveau
Tel: 506-444-4498
Fax: 506-444-4724
ann.deveau@gnb.ca
Legislative Coordinator, Carole Beaulieu
Tel: 506-453-8010
Fax: 506-444-4724
carole.beaulieu@gnb.ca

Fiscal Policy / Politiques fiscales
Centennial Bldg., #245, 670 King St., PO Box 6000, Fredericton, NB E3B 5H1
Tel: 506-453-2096
Fax: 506-453-2281
The Fiscal Policy Division provides the following services: Advice & analysis in the areas of fiscal & budget policy, federal-provincial fiscal relations, & the economy; Statistical services for the government; & Forecasting & monitoring of government revenues & the economy.
Assistant Deputy Minister, Fiscal Policy, Peter Kieley
Tel: 506-453-6921
Fax: 506-453-2281
Peter.Kieley@gnb.ca

Fiscal Policy & Economics / Direction des politiques fiscales et de l'économie
Tel: 506-453-2096
Fax: 506-453-2281
The Fiscal Policy Division provides the following services: Advice & analysis in the areas of fiscal & budget policy, federal-provincial fiscal relations, & the economy; Statistical services for the government; & Forecasting & monitoring of government revenues & the economy.
Director, George Richardson
Tel: 506-453-6917
Fax: 506-453-2281
george.richardson@gnb.ca
Senior Economist, Terry Loughead
Tel: 506-453-3646
Fax: 506-453-2281
terry.loughead@gnb.ca
Senior Economist, Todd Selby
Tel: 506-444-5399
Fax: 506-453-2281
todd.selby@gnb.ca

Federal-Provincial Fiscal & Statistical Relations / Direction des relations fédérales-provinciales, finances et statistiques
Tel: 506-453-2096
Fax: 506-453-2281
The Fiscal Policy Division provides the following services: Advice & analysis in the areas of fiscal & budget policy, federal-provincial fiscal relations, & the economy; Statistical services for the government; & Forecasting & monitoring of government revenues & the economy.
Senior Economist, Kathy Wyrwas
Tel: 506-453-6966
Fax: 506-453-2281
kathy.wyrwas@gnb.ca

Revenue & Taxation / Revenu et Impôt
Centennial Bldg., #671, 670 King St., PO Box 3000, Fredericton, NB E3B 5G5
Tel: 506-444-2826
Fax: 506-444-4920
Provision of effective, efficient and fair administration of assigned revenue acts. In addition, provides policy and administration support to the Lotteries Commission.
Assistant Deputy Minister, James Turgeon
Tel: 506-444-2826
James.Turgeon@gnb.ca
Provincial Tax Commissioner, Richard McCullough
Tel: 506-444-2826
Rick.McCullough@gnb.ca

Treasury / Trésorerie
Centennial Bldg., #376, 670 King St., PO Box 6000, Fredericton, NB E3B 5H1
Tel: 506-453-3952
Fax: 506-453-2053
The Treasury Division is responsible for financing the Province's cash requirements, cash management, administration of outstanding debt, investment management and administration of pension, sinking and special purpose trust funds, financial policy analysis and advice and Crown corporation and municipal financing.
Assistant Deputy Minister, Leonard Lee-White
Leonard.lee-white@gnb.ca

New Brunswick Department of Government Services

Marysville Place, 20 McGloin St., Fredericton, NB E3A 5T8
Tel: 506-453-6100
Fax: 506-462-5049
www2.gnb.ca/content/gnb/en/departments/government_services.html

New Brunswick's Department of Government Services is responsible for Service New Brunswick, the New Brunswick Internal Services Agency, services associated with procurement, printing, translation, & records management, plus marketing, graphic design, & web & event management.
Acts Administered:
Air Space
Archives
Assessment
Boundaries Confirmation
Business Corporations
Change of Name
Common Business Identifier
Companies
Condominium Property
Corporations
Foreign Resident Corporations
Land Titles
Limited Partnership
Marriage
New Brunswick Internal Services Agency
Partnership
Partnerships & Business Names Registration
Personal Property Security
Public Purchasing
Registry
Residential Property Tax Relief
Residential Tenancies
Right to Information & Protection of Privacy
Service New Brunswick
Special Corporate Continuance
Standard Forms of Conveyance
Surveys
Vital Statistics
Winding-up

Minister, Government Services; Acting Minister, Energy; Minister Responsible, New Brunswick Internal Services Agency, Service New Brunswick, Hon. Craig Leonard
Tel: 506-453-2240
Fax: 506-453-5329
Craig.Leonard@gnb.ca;EECA/AECE.Customer.Service@gnb.ca

Deputy Minister, Government Services; President, Service New Brunswick; President, New Brunswick Internal Services Agency, Sylvie Levesque-Finn
Tel: 506-444-2897
Sylvie.Levesque-Finn@gnb.ca

Director, Communications, Brent Staeben
Tel: 506-453-6100
brent.staeben2@gnb.ca

Officer, Communications, Donna Leggatt
Tel: 506-453-3742
Donna.Leggatt@gnb.ca

Corporate Marketing Division
Marysville Place, 20 McGloin St., Fredericton, NB E3A 5T8
Tel: 506-453-6100
Fax: 506-462-5049
The Corporate Marketing Division oversees marketing & design services, web services, & operations, such as event planning.
Executive Director, Corporate Marketing, Tim Porter
Tel: 506-453-6191
tim.porter@gnb.ca
Director, Web Services, Bonnie Buckingham Landry
Tel: 506-453-2240
bonnie.buckingham-landry@gnb.ca
Director, Marketing & Design Services, Rob MacLeod
Tel: 506-453-2425
rob.macleod@gnb.ca
Manager, Marketing & Design Services, Susan McCloskey
Tel: 506-453-2916
susan.mccloskey@gnb.ca
Manager, Operations, Bruce Melanson
Tel: 506-444-3515
bruce.melanson@gnb.ca

Corporate Services Division
Marysville Place, PO Box 6000, Fredericton, NB E3B 5H1
Tel: 506-453-3742
Fax: 506-444-4400
Reception.Marysville@gnb.ca
The following services are provided by the Corporate Services Division: finance & administration, technology support, human resources, & policy & planning.
Acting Executive Director, Corporate Services Division & Director, Human Resources, Ray Butler
Tel: 506-453-3742
ray.butler@gnb.ca
Director, Finance & Administration, Lise Chiasson
Tel: 506-453-3742
lise.chiasson@gnb.ca
Director, Technology Support, Christine Colborne
Tel: 506-453-3742
Director, Policy & Planning, Joanne Fletcher
Tel: 506-453-3742
joanne.fletcher@gnb.ca

Strategic Procurement Division
Marysville Place, PO Box 6000, Fredericton, NB E3B 5H1
Tel: 506-453-2245
Fax: 506-444-4400
Reception.Marysville@gnb.ca
A great variety of services are provided by the Strategic Procurement Division. The division serves government departments & agencies as well as the general public. Responsibilities include translation & interpretation, procurement processes for goods & services, & archival & reference services.
Director, Strategic Procurement Division, Dylan Chester
Tel: 506-453-2245
dylan.chester@inbcanada.ca
Director, Provincial Archives, Marion Beyea
Tel: 506-453-2122
Marion.Beyea@gnb.ca
Director, Publications & Distribution, Gilles Boudreau
Tel: 506-453-2545
gilles.boudreau@gnb.ca
Director, Translation Bureau, Jo-Ann Leblanc
Tel: 506-453-2920
jo-annm.leblanc@gnb.ca
Director, Procurement, Janice York
Tel: 506-453-8880
janice.york@gnb.ca

New Brunswick Department of Health / Santé

PO Box 5100, Fredericton, NB E3B 5G8
Tel: 506-457-4800
Fax: 506-453-5243
dh-ms@dh-ms.ca
www.gnb.ca/0051/index-e.asp
The mission of New Brunswick's Department of Health is to work with New Brunswickers in achieving well-being, by promoting self-sufficiency & personal responsibility, & providing approved services as required.
The development & delivery of health programs & services to New Brunswick residents is supported by a range of internal department functions, such as administration, planning & evaluation, & program support. The department provides the continuum of services to prevent illness & disability. Education & awareness raising initiatives promote the health & well-being of New Brunswickers of all ages, so that they can achieve their best potential, while enjoying an independent & healthy lifestyle for as long as possible.
Acts Administered:
Ambulance Services Act
Anatomy Act
Automated Defibrillator Act
Cemetery Companies Act
Clean Air (Paragraph 8(2a) & Subsection 4)
Clean Water Act (in part)
Health Services Act
Hospital Act(except section 21)

Hospital Services Act
Human Tissues Gift Act
Insurance Act
Liquor Control Act
Medical Consent of Minors Act
Medical Services Payment Act
Mental Health Act
Mental Health Services Act
Motor Vehicle Act (in part)
Municipalities Act
Personal Health Information Privacy and Access Act
Pesticides Control Act (in part)
Prescription Drug Payment Act
Public Health
Regional Health Authorities Act
Smoke-Free Places Act, 2004
Tobacco Damages and Health Care Costs Recovery
Tobacco Sales Act

Minister, Health, Hon. Madeleine Dubé
Tel: 506-457-4800
Fax: 506-453-5442
Madeleine.Dubé@gnb.ca

Deputy Minister, Donald Ferguson
Tel: 506-475-4800
don.j.ferguson@gnb.ca

Executive Secretary, Deputy Head's Office, Hélène Moffatt
Tel: 506-475-4800
helene.moffatt@gnb.ca

Administrative Support, Kathy Densmore
Tel: 506-453-2536
Fax: 506-444-4697
kathy.densmore@gnb.ca

Associated Agencies, Boards & Commissions:

• Psychiatric Patient Advocate Services Review Board
c/o Dept. of Health, Psychiatric Patient Advocate Services
#505, 860 Main St.
Moncton, NB E1C 1G2
Tel: 506-869-6818
Fax: 506-869-6101
Toll-free: 888-350-4133
A senior lawyer, a psychiatrist (or a physician, if a psychiatrist is unavailable), & a lay person serve on the Psychiatric Patient Advocate Services Review Board, as required under section 30(2) of the Mental Health Act.
The Review Board is engaged in the following activities: granting certificates of detention; delivering an order to administer a treatment; reviewing a treatment; reviewing the status of an involuntary patient; reviewing a patient's competence to give consent; reviewing the patient's access to information regarding his treatment; reviewing a transfer to another jurisdiction; & reviewing the ability of an involuntary patient to manage his estate

• Psychiatric Patient Advocate Services Tribunal
c/o Dept. of Health, Psychiatric Patient Advocate Services
#505, 860 Main St.
Moncton, NB E1C 1G2
Tel: 506-869-6818
Fax: 506-869-6101
Toll-free: 888-350-4133
The Psychiatric Patient Advocate Services Tribunal is made up of a lawyer & two members of the public. The tribunal authorizes involuntary admission according to the Mental Health Act. It also authorize the treatment of involuntary patients.

Addiction, Mental Health, Primary Health Care & Extra Mural Services Division / Services de traitement des dépendances, de santé mentale, de soins de santé primaires et extra-muraux
HSBC Place, 520 King St., 5th Fl., PO Box 5100, Fredericton, NB E3B 5G8
Tel: 506-457-4800
Fax: 506-453-5243
Health.Sante@gnb.ca
www.gnb.ca/0051/index-e.asp
Asst. Deputy Minister, Kenneth Ross
Tel: 506-457-4800
ken.ross@gnb.ca
Executive Director, Addiction & Mental Health Services, Barbara Whitenect
Tel: 506-444-4442
Barbara.Whitenect@gnb.ca
Director, Adult Services, Sylvie Martin
Tel: 506-444-5241
sylvie.martin@gnb.ca
Director, Child & Youth Services, Yvette Doiron
Tel: 506-444-4442
yvette.doiron-brun@gnb.ca
Director, Primary Health Care, Bronwyn Davies
Tel: 506-453-7926
bronwyn.davies@gnb.ca
Director, Extra-Mural Program, Jean Bustard
Tel: 506-453-4303
jean.bustard@gnb.ca

Communications Branch / Communications
HSBC Place, 520 King St., 5th Fl., PO Box 5100, Fredericton, NB E3B 6G3
Tel: 506-457-2356
Fax: 506-444-4697
Health.Sante@gnb.ca
www.gnb.ca/0051/index-e.asp
Public Health services are delivered through the province's seven health regions, under the management of Regional Directors. A Chief Medical Officer of Health & a Deputy Chief Medical Officer of Health oversee the development of policy & regulations, & provide medical operational support to the regional Medical Officers of Health. Public Health Services support healthy growth & development, foster healthy lifestyles, control communicable diseases, & protect the public from adverse health consequences of exposure to chemical, physical & biological agents.
Director, Tracy Burkhardt
Tel: 506-453-2536
tracy.burkhardt@gnb.ca
Media Relations Coordinator, Danielle Phillips
Tel: 506-453-2536
danielle.phillips@gnb.ca

Corporate Services / Services ministériels
HSBC Place, 520 King St., 5th Fl., PO Box 5100, Fredericton, NB E3B 6G3
Tel: 506-457-2775
Fax: 506-453-5243
Health.Sante@gnb.ca
www.gnb.ca/0051/index-e.asp
Public Health services are delivered through the province's seven health regions, under the management of Regional Directors. A Chief Medical Officer of Health & a Deputy Chief Medical Officer of Health oversee the development of policy & regulations, & provide medical operational support to the regional Medical Officers of Health. Public Health Services support healthy growth & development, foster healthy lifestyles, control communicable diseases, & protect the public from adverse health consequences of exposure to chemical, physical & biological agents.

Human Resources Branch / Ressources humaines
HSBC Place, 520 King St., 4th Fl., PO Box 5100, Fredericton, NB E3B 6G3
Tel: 506-453-2843
Fax: 506-453-2843
Health.Sante@gnb.ca
www.gnb.ca/0051/index-e.asp
Public Health services are delivered through the province's seven health regions, under the management of Regional Directors. A Chief Medical Officer of Health & a Deputy Chief Medical Officer of Health oversee the development of policy & regulations, & provide medical operational support to the regional Medical Officers of Health. Public Health Services support healthy growth & development, foster healthy lifestyles, control communicable diseases, & protect the public from adverse health consequences of exposure to chemical, physical & biological agents.
Director, Joanne Stone
Tel: 506-444-2521
joanne.stone@gnb.ca

Institutional Services Division / Services en établissements
HSBC Place, 520 King St., 5th Fl., PO Box 5100, Fredericton, NB E3B 6G3
Tel: 506-457-4800
Fax: 506-453-5243
Health.Sante@gnb.ca
www.gnb.ca/0051/index-e.asp
Public Health services are delivered through the province's seven health regions, under the management of Regional Directors. A Chief Medical Officer of Health & a Deputy Chief Medical Officer of Health oversee the development of policy & regulations, & provide medical operational support to the regional Medical Officers of Health. Public Health Services support healthy growth & development, foster healthy lifestyles, control communicable diseases, & protect the public from adverse health consequences of exposure to chemical, physical & biological agents.
Acting Assistant Deputy Minister, Lyne St-Pierre-Ellis
Tel: 506-457-4800
lyne.st-pierre-ellis@gnb.ca

New Brunswick Cancer Network / Réseau - Cancer Nouveau-Brunswick
HSBC Place, 520 King St., 2nd Fl., PO Box 5100, Fredericton, NB E3B 6G3
Tel: 506-457-5521
Fax: 506-453-5522
Health.Sante@gnb.ca
www.gnb.ca/0051/index-e.asp
Public Health services are delivered through the province's seven health regions, under the management of Regional Directors. A Chief Medical Officer of Health & a Deputy Chief Medical Officer of Health oversee the development of policy & regulations, & provide medical operational support to the regional Medical Officers of Health. Public Health Services support healthy growth & development, foster healthy lifestyles, control communicable diseases, & protect the public from adverse health consequences of exposure to chemical, physical & biological agents.

Office of the Associate Deputy Minister of Health - Francophone Services Division / Bureau de la sous-ministre déléguée du ministère de la santé - Services aux francophones
HSBC Place, 520 King St., 5th Fl., PO Box 5100, Fredericton, NB E3B 6G3
Tel: 506-453-2582
Fax: 506-453-5523
Health.Sante@gnb.ca
www.gnb.ca/0051/index-e.asp
Public Health services are delivered through the province's seven health regions, under the management of Regional Directors. A Chief Medical Officer of Health & a Deputy Chief Medical Officer of Health oversee the development of policy & regulations, & provide medical operational support to the regional Medical Officers of Health. Public Health Services support healthy growth & development, foster healthy lifestyles, control communicable diseases, & protect the public from adverse health consequences of exposure to chemical, physical & biological agents.
Associate Deputy Minister, Lyne St-Pierre-Ellis
Tel: 506-453-2582
lyne.st-pierre-ellis@gnb.ca

Office of the Chief Medical Officer of Health Division / Bureau du Médecin-hygiéniste en chef du ministère de la santé - Services aux francophones
HSBC Place, 520 King St., 5th Fl., PO Box 5100, Fredericton, NB E3B 6G3
Tel: 506-444-2112
Fax: 506-453-5243
Health.Sante@gnb.ca
www.gnb.ca/0051/index-e.asp
Public Health services are delivered through the province's seven health regions, under the management of Regional Directors. A Chief Medical Officer of Health & a Deputy Chief Medical Officer of Health oversee the development of policy & regulations, & provide medical operational support to the regional Medical Officers of Health. Public Health Services support healthy growth & development, foster healthy lifestyles, control communicable diseases, & protect the public from adverse health consequences of exposure to chemical, physical & biological agents.
Executive Director, Scott Maclean
Tel: 506-453-2427
scott.maclean@gnb.ca
Manager, Patrick Guest
Tel: 506-444-2112
pat.guest@gnb.ca

Planning, Pharmaceutical Services & Privacy Division / Planification, services pharmaceutiques et protection de la vie privée
HSBC Place, 520 King St., 5th Fl., PO Box 5100, Fredericton, NB E3B 6G3
Tel: 506-457-4800
Fax: 506-453-5523
Health.Sante@gnb.ca
www.gnb.ca/0051/index-e.asp
Public Health services are delivered through the province's seven health regions, under the management of Regional Directors. A Chief Medical Officer of Health & a Deputy Chief Medical Officer of Health oversee the development of policy & regulations, & provide medical operational support to the regional Medical Officers of Health. Public Health Services support healthy growth & development, foster healthy lifestyles, control communicable diseases, & protect the public from adverse health consequences of exposure to chemical, physical & biological agents.
Assistant Deputy Minister, Kelli Simmonds
Tel: 506-457-4800
kelli.simmonds@gnb.ca

Office of Human Resources / Bureaux des ressources humaines

Centennial Bldg, #345, 670 King St., PO Box 6000, Fredericton, NB E3B 5H1
Tel: 506-453-2264
Fax: 506-453-7195
www.gnb.ca/0163/index-e.asp
The Office of Human Resources has responsibility for the policies which govern the following human resources issues: recruitment; compensation; & staff development for the provision of quality public services.

Acts Administered:
Civil Services Act (staffing responsibilities)
Public Interest Disclosure Act

Minister, Finance; Minister, Office of Human Resources; Minister Responsible, New Brunswick Liquor Corporation, New Brunswick Investment Management Corporation, & New Brunswick Lotteries & Gaming Corporation; Chair, Board ofManagement, Hon. Blaine Higgs
Tel: 506-444-2627
Fax: 506-457-4989
blaine.higgs@gnb.ca

Deputy Minister, Brian Durelle
Tel: 506-453-3036
Fax: 506-453-7195
Brian.Durelle@gnb.ca

Communications
Centennial Bldg., #344, 670 King St., PO Box 6000, Fredericton, NB E3B 5H1
Tel: 506-453-2264
Fax: 506-453-4225
Director, Brendon Langille
Tel: 506-444-4594
brendan.langille@gnb.ca

Employee Relations Services
Centennial Bldg., #360, 670 King St., PO Box 6000, Fredericton, NB E3B 5H1
Tel: 506-453-2115
Fax: 506-444-5786
Assistant Deputy Minister, Dorine P. Pirie
Tel: 506-457-6739
Dorine.Pirie@gnb.ca
Director, Compensation, Classification & Corporate Research, Lori Anne Mccracken
Tel: 506-457-7216
LoriAnne.Mccracken@gnb.ca
Director, Labor Relations, Frédéric Finn
Tel: 506-453-8006
Frederic.Finn@gnb.ca

Human Resource Strategy & Programs
Centennial Bldg., #344, 670 King St., PO Box 6000, Fredericton, NB E3B 5H1
Tel: 506-453-2264
Fax: 506-453-2124
Acting Director, HR Strategy & Development Branch, Jennifer Wilkins
Tel: 506-453-2141
Fax: 506-453-2124
Jennifer.Wilkins@gnb.ca
Director, HR Programs & Official Languages, Janique Robichaud-Savoie
Tel: 506-453-6088
Janique.Robichaud@gnb.ca

Pensions & Employee Benefits
York Tower, Kings Place, #680, 440 King St., PO Box 6000, Fredericton, NB E3B 5H8
Tel: 506-453-2296
Fax: 506-457-7388
Toll-Free: 800-561-4012
www.gnb.ca/0163/pension/pension-e.asp
Assistant Deputy Minister, Pensions & Employee Benefits, Gaudet Mark
Tel: 506-453-2296
Fax: 506-457-7388
Mark.Gaudet@gnb.ca
Director, Human Resources, Troy Mann
Tel: 506-453-2296
Fax: 506-457-7388
Troy.Mann@gnb.ca
Manager, Benefit Services, Kim Fraser
Tel: 506-453-2296
Fax: 506-457-7388
kim.fraser@gnb.ca
Manager, Committee Support & Development, Carolyn Roberts
Tel: 506-453-2296
Fax: 506-457-7388
carolyn.roberts@gnb.ca
Manager, Finance & Administration, Marilyn Mcconnell
Tel: 506-453-2296
marilyn.mcconnell@gnb.ca
Manager, Applications & System Management, Michael Mclaughlin
Tel: 506-453-2296
Michael.Mclaughlin@gnb.ca
Manager, Data Services, Raymond David
Tel: 506-453-2296
raymond.david@gnb.ca

New Brunswick Human Rights Commission / Commission des droits de la personne

PO Box 6000, Fredericton, NB E3B 5H1
Tel: 506-453-2301
Fax: 506-453-2653
Toll-Free: 888-471-2233
hrc.cdp@gnb.ca
TTY: 506-453-2911

The Human Rights Commission is a provincial government agency. It promotes equality & investigates & tries to settle complaints of discrimination & harassment. The Commission also works to prevent discrimination by promoting human rights & offering educational opportunities to employers, service providers, & the general public.

Chairperson, Randy Dickinson
Tel: 506-453-2301
hrc.cdp@gnb.ca

Director, Jill Peters
Tel: 506-453-2301
jill.peters@gnb.ca

Legal Counsel, Sarina Mckinnon
Tel: 506-453-2301
sarina.mckinnon@gnb.ca

Lawyer, Chantal Gauthier
Tel: 506-453-2301
chantal.gauthier@gnb.ca

New Brunswick Department of Justice & Attorney General

Centennial Building, PO Box 6000, Fredericton, NB E3B 5H1
Tel: 506-462-5100
Fax: 506-453-3651
justice.comments@gnb.ca
www.gnb.ca/0062/index-e.asp

The Department of Justice & Attorney General promotes the impartial administration of justice & ensures protection of the public interest.

Acts Administered:
Absconding Debtors
Age of Majority
Arbitration
Arrest & Examinations
Assignments & Preferences
Attorney General, An Act Respecting the Role of the Attorney General
Auctioneers Licence
Canadian Judgments
Charter Compliance Acts
Civil Forfeiture
Class Proceedings
Co-operative Associations
Collection Agencies
Commissioners for Taking Affidavits
Conflict of Laws Rules for Trusts
Consumer Product Warranty & Liability
Contributory Negligence
Cost of Credit Disclosure
Court Security
Credit Unions
Creditors Relief
Criminal Prosecution Expenses
Crown Debts
Defamation
Demise of the Crown
Devolution of Estates
Direct Sellers
Easements
Electronic Transactions
Entry Warrants
Escheats & Forfeitures
Evidence
Executors & Trustees
Expropriation
Factors & Agents
Family Services (Part VII)
Fatal Accidents
Federal Courts Jurisdiction
Foreign Judgments
Franchises
Frustrated Contracts
Garnishee
Gift Cards
Great Seal
Guardianship of Children
Infirm Persons
Innkeepers
Inquiries
Insurance
Interjurisdictional Support Orders
International Child Abduction
International Commercial Arbitration
International Sale of Goods
International Trusts
International Wills
Interpretation
Interprovincial Subpoena
Judges Disqualification Removal
Judicature
Jury
Landlord & Tenant
Law Reform
Legal Aid
Liens on Goods & Chattels
Limitation of Actions
Loan & Trust Companies
Management of Seized & Forfeited Property
Marital Property
Mechanics' Lien
Memorials & Executions
Notaries Public
Nova Scotia Grants
Nursing Homes Pension Plans
Pension Benefits
Postal Services Interruption
Pre-arranged Funeral Services
Premium Tax
Presumption of Death
Probate Court
Proceedings Against the Crown
Property
Protection of Persons Acting Under Statute
Provincial Court
Provincial Offences Procedure
Provincial Offences Procedure for Young Persons
Provision for Dependants
Public Records
Queen's Counsel & Precedence
Queen's Printer
Quieting of Titles
Real Estate Agents
Reciprocal Enforcement of Judgments
Reciprocal Recognition & Enforcement of Judgments in Civil & Commercial Matters
Recording of Evidence
Regulations
Removal of Archaic Terminology from the Acts of New Brunswick
Sale of Goods
Sale of Lands Publication
Securities Transfer
Sheriffs
Special Insurance Companies
Statute Law Amendment
Statute Revision
Statute of Frauds
Storer's Lien
Succession Law Amendment
Support Enforcement
Survival of Actions
Survivorship
Tortfeasors
Trespass
Trustees
Unconscionable Transactions Relief
Wage Earners Protection
Warehouse Receipts
Wills
Woods Workers' Lien

Minister, Justice; Attorney General; Minister Responsible, Women's Issues, Hon. Marie-Claude Blais, Q.C.
Tel: 506-453-3132
Fax: 506-453-3651
marie-claude.blais@gnb.ca

Deputy Minister; Deputy Attorney General, Judith Keating
Tel: 506-453-2208
judith.keating@gnb.ca

Director, Communications, Dave MacLean
Tel: 506-462-5100
Dave.MacLean@gnb.ca

Senior Policy Advisor, Cynthia Davis
Tel: 506-462-5100
Cynthia.Davis@gnb.ca

Associated Agencies, Boards & Commissions:

• New Brunswick Legal Aid Services Commission
#501, 500 Beaverbrook Ct.
Fredericton, NB E3B 5X4
Tel: 506-444-2776
Fax: 506-444-2290
info@legalaid.nb.ca
www.legalaid.nb.ca
Local legal aid offices are located in the following places:
Baththurst (506-546-5010);
Campbellton (506-753-6453);
Edmundston (506-735-4213);
Fredericton (506-444-2777);
Miramichi (506-622-1061);
Moncton (506-853-7300);
Saint John (506-633-6030);
Tracadie-Sheila (506-395-1507);
Woodstock (506-328-8127.

• New Brunswick Securities Commission / Commission des valeurs mobilières du Nouveau-Brunswick
#300, 85 Charloote St.
Saint John, NB E2L 2J2
Tel: 506-658-3060
Fax: 506-658-3059
Toll-free: 866-933-2222
information@nbsc-cvmnb.ca
www.nbsc-cvmnb.ca
The New Brunswick Securities Commission adminsters the province's Securities Statute. Staff of the commission are responsible for the following services: review of prospectuses; registration of companies & persons operating in the province's securities industry; consideration of exemption applications; & enforcement of securities laws.

Administrative Services Division
Centennial Building, PO Box 6000, Fredericton, NB E3B 5H1
Tel: 506-453-2719
Fax: 506-453-8718
general.comments@gnb.ca
The Administrative Services Division supports the operations of the Department of Justice & Attorney General by providing the following services: expropriation advisory services; human resources; information management & technology; financial services; & facilities management.
Director, Human Resources Services, Julie Comeau
Tel: 506-444-2191
Julie.M.Comeau@gnb.ca
Director, Financial Services, Gayle Howard
Tel: 506-444-4015
gayle.howard@gnb.ca
Director, Information Management & Technology, Lachlan MacQuarrie-McLeod
Tel: 506-444-5855
lachlan.macquarrie-mcleod@gnb.ca

Court Services Division
Centennial Building, PO Box 6000, Fredericton, NB E3B 5H1
Tel: 506-453-2933
Fax: 506-453-3651
general.comments@gnb.ca
The Court Services Division ensures uniform access for all citizens to criminal & civil courts.
Court services are located in the following regions:
Bathurst / Campbellton / Tracadie (506-547-2150);
Edmundston / Grand Falls (506-735-2029);
Fredericton / Oromocto / Woodstock (506-453-2015);
Miramichi (506-627-4023);
Moncton / Richibucto (506-856-2305);
Saint John / Hampton / St. Stephen (506-658-2400).
Assistant Deputy Minister, Court Services Division, Marilyn Born
Tel: 506-453-2933
marilyn.born@gnb.ca
Director, Program Support Services, Anne McKay
Tel: 506-453-8498
Anne.Mckay@gnb.ca
Registrar, Registrar Services, Michael Bray
Tel: 506-453-2803
Michael.Bray@gnb.ca
Regional Director, Saint John / Hampton / St. Stephen Court Services, Thomas Bishop
Tel: 506-658-2400
tom.bishop@gnb.ca
Regional Director, Bathurst / Campbellton / Tracadie Court Services, Grégoire Boudreau
Tel: 506-547-2150
gregoire.boudreau@gnb.ca
Regional Director, Miramichi Clerk's Office, Matthew Cripps
Tel: 506-627-4023
matthew.cripps@gnb.ca
Regional Director, Fredericton / Oromocto / Woodstock Court Services, Andrea Hull
Tel: 506-453-2015
Andrea.Hull@gnb.ca
Regional Director, Moncton / Richibucto Court Services, David Léger
Tel: 506-856-2305
David.Leger@gnb.ca
Clerk, Edmundston Clerk's Regional Office, Jean-Francois Cyr
Tel: 506-735-2029
jean-francois.cyr@gnb.ca

Justice Services Division
Centennial Building, PO Box 6000, Fredericton, NB E3B 5H1
Tel: 506-453-2458
Fax: 506-453-3651
general.comments@gnb.ca
The Justice Services Division works to ensure the protection & uniform treatment of all citizens.
Under the Public Prosecutions Branch, family & youth justice crown services are located in the following places:
Bathurst (506-547-2160);
Campbellton (506-789-2308);
Edmundston (506-735-2027);
Fredericton (506-453-2819);
Miramichi (506-627-4015);
Moncton (506-869-6211);
Saint John (506-658-2580).
Also operating under the Public Prosecutions Branch are the following offices that offer crown prosecutor services:
Bathurst (506-547-2160);
Campbellton (506-789-2308);
Caraquet (506-726-2794);
Edmundston (506-735-2027);
Fredericton (506-453-2819);
Grand Falls (506-473-7702);
Miramichi (506-627-4015);
Moncton (506-856-2310);
Oromocto / Burton (506-357-4033);
Richibucto (506-523-7990);
Saint John (506-658-2580);
St. Stephen (506-466-7397);
Tracadie-Sheila (506-394-3727);
Woodstock (506-325-4416).
Sheriff services are available at the following locations:
Bathurst (506-547-2163);
Campbellton (506-789-2100);
Edmundston (506-735-2032);
Fredericton (506-453-2801);
Miramichi (506-627-4026);
Moncton (506-856-2315);
Saint John (506-658-2569);
Woodstock (506-325-4426).
Assistant Deputy Minister, Justice Services Division, Suzanne Bonnell-Burley
Tel: 506-453-2458
suzanne.bonnell-burley@gnb.ca
Assistant Deputy Attorney General, Public Prosecutions, Luc Labonté
Tel: 506-453-2784
Executive Director, Public Prosecutions, Pierre Castonguay
Tel: 506-453-2784
Executive Director, Litigation Group, Nancy Forbes
Tel: 506-453-2222
nancy.forbes@gnb.ca
Director, Legislative Drafting (Anglophone) & Registrar of Regulations, Susan Burns
Tel: 506-453-2569
Susan.Burns@gnb.ca
Director, Employment & Administrative Law Group, Andrea Folster
Tel: 506-453-2222
andrea.folster@gnb.ca
Director, Corporate & Property Law Group, John Logan
Tel: 506-453-2222
john.logan@gnb.ca
Director, Credit Unions, Co-operatives & Trust Companies, & Examinations, Pierre LeBlanc
Tel: 506-453-2315
pierre.leblanc@gnb.ca
Director, Legislative Drafting (Francophone), Joanne Léger-Daigle
Tel: 506-453-2855
joanne.leger-daigle@gnb.ca
Director, Legislative Affairs, Elizabeth Strange
Tel: 506-453-2855
Elizabeth.Strange@gnb.ca
Superintendent, Office of the Superintendent of Pensions, Angela Mazerolle Stephens
Tel: 506-453-2055
angela.mazerollestephens@gnb.ca
Superintendent, Insurance, Deborah McQuade
Tel: 506-453-2512
deborah.mcquade@gnb.ca
Chief Sheriff, Sheriff Services, Marilyn Born
Tel: 506-462-5100
marilyn.born@gnb.ca

Public Legal Education & Information Service of New Brunswick (PLEIS-NB)
PO Box 6000, Fredericton, NB E3B 5H1
Tel: 506-453-5369
Fax: 506-462-5193
pleisnb@web.ca
www.legal-info-legale.nb.ca
The mission of the Public Legal Education & Information Service is to assist the public by developing bilingual educational projects & services about the law. The service promotes access to the legal system & improves citizens' abilities to handle legal issues.
Executive Director, Deborah Doherty, Ph.D.
Project Coordinator, Emily Bell, LL.B.
Officer, Family Law Information, Chantal Lajoie, LL.B.

New Brunswick Liquor Corporation (Alcool NB Liquor) / Société des alcools du Nouveau-Brunswick

170 Wilsey Rd., PO Box 20787, Fredericton, NB E3B 5B8
Tel: 506-452-6826
Fax: 506-462-2024
info@anbl.com
www.nbliquor.com
Other Communication: Public Affairs Phone: 506-452-6453
The Crown corporation manufactures, buys, imports, & sells liquor of every kind.

Minister, Finance; Minister, Office of Human Resources; Minister Responsible, New Brunswick Liquor Corporation, New Brunswick Investment Management Corporation, & New Brunswick Lotteries & Gaming Corporation; Chair, Board ofManagement, Hon. Blaine Higgs
Tel: 506-444-2627
Fax: 506-457-4989
Blaine.Higgs@gnb.ca

Chairperson, Ron Lindala
Tel: 506-452-6826
ron.lindala@anbl.com

President/CEO, Daniel Allain
Tel: 506-452-6522
daniel.allain@anbl.com

Senior Vice-President, Richard A. Smith
Tel: 506-452-6826
rick.smith@anbl.com

Vice-President/CFO, Chris Evans
Tel: 506-452-6460
chris.evans@anbl.com

Vice-President, Supply Chain/ Products & Marketing, Mike O'Brien
Tel: 506-452-6505
mike.o'brien@anbl.com

Vice-President, Customer Service & Retail Operations, Brad Cameron
Tel: 506-452-6511
brad.cameron@anbl.com

New Brunswick Department of Natural Resources / Ressources naturelles

Hugh John Flemming Forestry Centre, PO Box 6000, Fredericton, NB E3B 5H1
Tel: 506-453-3826
Fax: 506-444-4367
dnrweb@gnb.ca
www.gnb.ca/naturalresources
The Department of Natural Resources manages all natural resources within the province including fish & wildlife, timber, minerals, Crown lands, & water resources. It is also responsible for the development, protection, allocation, & utilization of resources in a way that is considered economically, environmentally, & socially acceptable.
Acts Administered:
Act Respecting Angling Lease Number 7
Acts administered by an Associated Agency, Board, Commission or Corporation
Bituminous Shale Act
Conservation Easements Act
Crown Grant Restrictions Act
Crown Lands & Forests Act
Endangered Species Act
Fish & Wildlife Act
Forest Fires Act
Forest Products Act
Grants Act

Kouchibouguac National Park, An Act to Implement Recommendation 16 of the Report of the Special Inquiry on
Leasing Regulation
Maritime Forestry Complex Coporation Act
Mining Act (in part)
National Parks Act
Natural Products Act (in part)
Off-Road Vehicle Act
Oil & Natural Gas Act
Ownership of Minerals Act
Parks Act
Petroleum Act (except most of Part 13)
Protected Natural Areas Act, 2003
Quarriable Substances Act
Roosevelt Campobello International Park Act
Scalers Act
St. Croix International Waterway Commission Act
Territorial Divisions Act
Transportation of Primary Forest Products Act
Underground Storage Act

Minister, Natural Resources, Hon. Bruce Northrup
Tel: 506-453-2510
Fax: 506-444-5839
bruce.nortrup@gnb.ca

Deputy Minister, Phil Lepage
Tel: 506-453-2501
Fax: 506-453-2930
Phil.Lepage@gnb.ca

Director, Communications, Steven Benteau
Tel: 506-453-2614
Fax: 506-457-4881
Steve.Benteau@gnb.ca

Executive Secretary, Ginette Delfrate
Tel: 506-453-2501
Fax: 506-457-4881
Ginette.Delfrate@gnb.ca

Associated Agencies, Boards & Commissions:
• **New Brunswick Wildlife Council**
c/o New Brunswick Wildlife Trust Fund
PO Box 30030
Fredericton, NB E3B 0H8
Tel: 506-453-6655
Fax: 506-462-5054
wildcoun@nbnet.nb.ca
www.nbwtf.ca/council-membership.asp
The New Brunswick Wildlife Council manages the New Brunswick Wildlife Trust Fund. The Fund was created by the Department of Natural Resources Minister in 1997. Under the Fish & Wildlife Act (O.C. 2002-49), the New Brunswick Wildlife Trust Fund evaluates project applications & advises the Department of Natural Resources Minister. The New Brunswick Wildlife Council is composed of seventeen members who represent environmental, naturalist, Aboriginal, hunting, angling, & trapping groups.

Corporate Services Division / Services Généraux Division
Hugh John Flemming Forestry Centre, 3rd Fl, PO Box 6000, Fredericton, NB E3B 5H1
Tel: 506-453-2178
Fax: 506-453-2930
Assistant Deputy Minister, Corporate Services, Janet Higgins
Tel: 506-453-2501
Fax: 506-453-2930
Janet.Higgins@gnb.ca
Director, Policy and Strategic Initiatives, Lesley Chenier-Aussant
Tel: 506-444-4688
lesley.chenier-aussant@gnb.ca
Director, Human Resource Services, Kathleen Good Waite
Tel: 506-453-2197
Kathleen.GoodWaite@gnb.ca
Director, Financial Services, Jean-Guy Leblanc
Tel: 506-453-3826
JeanGuy.LeBlanc@gnb.ca
Assistant Director, Employee Relations, Barb Macintosh
Tel: 506-453-3863
Barb.Macintosh@gnb.ca
Director, Information Services and Systems, Doris Wu
Tel: 506-457-4922
Doris.Wu@gnb.ca

Lands, Minerals & Petroleum Division / Terres, Minéraux et Pétrole Division
Hugh John Flemming Forestry Centre, PO Box 6000, Fredericton, NB E3B 5H1
Tel: 506-453-2684
Fax: 506-453-2930
dnrweb@gnb.ca
www.gnb.ca/0078/minerals/index-e.asp
Asst. Deputy Minister, Samuel McEwan
Tel: 506-453-2684
Sam.McEwan@gnb.ca
Director, Crown Lands, Peter Macnutt
Tel: 506-453-6656
Peter.MacNutt@gnb.ca
Director, Geological Surveys Branch, Leslie Fyffe
Tel: 506-444-5005
Les.Fyffe@gnb.ca
Acting Director, Minerals & Petroleum Development, Endresen Keith
Tel: 506-444-2683
keith.endresen@gnb.ca

Renewable Resources / Ressources renouvelables
Hugh John Flemming Forestry Centre, Suite 310, Fl 3rd, PO Box 6000, Fredericton, NB E3B 5H1
Tel: 506-453-2684
Fax: 506-453-2684
dnrweb@gnb.ca
www.gnb.ca/naturalresources
Asst. Deputy Minister, Paul Orser
Tel: 506-453-2684
Paul.Orser@gnb.ca
Director, Fish & Wildlife, Michael Sullivan
Tel: 506-453-7114
Mike.Sullivan@gnb.ca
Director, Forest Management, Thomas MacFarlane
Tel: 506-453-6673
Tom.MacFarlane@gnb.ca
Executive Director, Regional Operations & Support Services, Julius Tarjan
Tel: 506-453-2684
Julius.Tarjan@gnb.ca

Office of the Ombudsman / Bureau de l'ombudsman

767 Brunswick St., PO Box 6000, Fredericton, NB E3B 5H1
Tel: 506-453-2789
Fax: 506-453-5599
Toll-Free: 800-465-1100
nbombud@gnb.ca
www.gnb.ca/ombudsman

Ombudsman, François Levert
Tel: 506-453-2789
Fax: 506-453-5599
Francois.Levert@gnb.ca

Executive Director, Steve Gilliland
Tel: 506-453-2789
Fax: 506-453-5599
Steve.Gilliland@gnb.ca

Executive Secretary, Julie Dickison
Tel: 506-453-2789
Fax: 506-453-5599
Julie.Dickison@gnb.ca

New Brunswick Police Commission (NBPC) / Commission de police du Nouveau-Brunswick

Fredericton City Centre, #202, 435 King St., Fredericton, NB E3B 1E5
Tel: 506-453-2069
Fax: 506-457-3542
nbpc@gnb.ca
www.gnb.ca/0075/index-e.asp
The New Brunswick Police Commission is engaged in the following activities: investigating & determining complaints alleging misconduct by municipal & regional police officers; investigating any matter relating to any aspect of policing in any area of the province; determining the adequacy of municipal, regional, & RCMP police forces within the province.

Chair, Peter Seheult
Tel: 506-453-2069
Fax: 506-457-3542

Vice-Chair, Donald R. Butler
Tel: 506-453-2069
Fax: 506-457-3542

Executive Director, Pierre Beaudoin
Tel: 506-453-2069
Fax: 506-457-3542
Pierre.Beaudoin@gnb.ca

New Brunswick Department of Post-Secondary Education, Training, & Labour

Chestnut Complex, PO Box 6000, Fredericton, NB E3B 5H1
Tel: 506-453-2597
Fax: 506-453-3618
dpetlinfo@gnb.ca
www.gnb.ca/post-secondary
New Brunswick's Department of Post-Secondary Education, Training, & Labour consists of the following divisions: Adult Learning & Employment; Communications; Corporate Services; Labour & Planning; Population Growth; & Post-Secondary Education.
Acts Administered:
Adult Education & Training Act
Apprenticeship & Occupational Certification Act (except sections 10 and 11.5)
Degree Granting Act
Employment Development Act
Employment Standards Act
Fisheries Bargaining Act (sections 32, 33(3), 33(4), 50 to 55, 57 to 62, 63(2), 70 to 73, 80, 87, 92(5), 94, 103(1), 106(1), 106(3), 109, 110 to 112, 113(3), 113(4), 113(5), 113(8), 114(1), 114(2) and 117)
Higher Education Foundation Act
Human Rights Act
Industrial Relations Act
Labour Market Research Act
Maritime Provinces Higher Education Commission Act
New Brunswick Community Colleges Act
New Brunswick Public Libraries Act
Post Secondary Student Financial Assistance
Private Occupational Training Act
Silicosis Compensation Act

Minister, Hon. Martine Coulombe
Tel: 506-453-2342
martine.coloumbe@gnb.ca

Deputy Minister, Marc Léger
Tel: 506-453-2343
Marc.Leger@gnb.ca

Adult Learning & Employment Division
Chestnut Complex, PO Box 6000, Fredericton, NB E3B 5H1
Tel: 506-453-8202
Fax: 506-453-3038
dpetlinfo@gnb.ca
Adult Learning & Employment Division is composed of the following branches: Aprenticeship & Occupational Certification; Community Adult Learning Services; Employment Development; & the New Brunswick Library Service.
Assistant Deputy Minister, Adult Learning & Employment, Lily Fraser
Tel: 506-444-3479
lily.fraser@gnb.ca
Executive Director, New Brunswick Public Library Service, Sylvie Nadeau
Tel: 506-453-7141
sylvie.nadeau@gnb.ca
Director, Employment Programs & Services, Hélène Bouchard
Tel: 506-453-2814
helene.bouchard@gnb.ca
Director, Employment Development, Diane Hawkins
Tel: 506-453-8707
diane.hawkins@gnb.ca
Director, Community Adult Learning Services, Guy Lamarche
Tel: 506-444-4331
guy.lamarche@gnb.ca
Director, Employment Development Program Design & Support, Cindy Lanteigne
Tel: 506-444-5867
cindy.lanteigne@gnb.ca
Director, Apprenticeship & Occupational Certification, Daniel Mills
Tel: 506-444-3657
daniel.Mills@gnb.ca
Public Services Development Librarian, New Brunswick Public Library Service, Leah Brisco
Tel: 506-457-6713
leah.brisco@gnb.ca
Research & Planning Librarian, New Brunswick Public Library Service, Teresa Johnson
Tel: 506-453-3429
Teresa.Johnson@gnb.ca

Communications Division
Chestnut Complex, PO Box 6000, Fredericton, NB E3B 5H1
Tel: 506-444-3465
Fax: 506-444-4314
dpetlinfo@gnb.ca
The Communications Division offers services to every branch & group within the Department of Post-Secondary Education, Training, & Labour. Employees in the division follow the directives of the Cabinet Policy on Communications.
Director, Communications, Marie-Josee Groulx
Tel: 506-444-3465
marie-josee.groulx@gnb.ca

Corporate Services Division
Chestnut Complex, PO Box 6000, Fredericton, NB E3B 5H1
Tel: 506-453-3038
dpetlinfo@gnb.ca

Branches within the Corporate Services Division include the following: Corporate Information Management & Administrative Services; Financial Services: Information Technology Services; Facilities Management; Human Resource Services; Departmental Coordination; & Internal Audit & Portfolio Debt Management.
Executive Director, Corporate Services, Lyne Paquet
Tel: 506-453-2587
lyne.paquet@gnb.ca
Director, Information Technology Services, Suzanne Bourgeois
Tel: 506-453-2588
suzanne.bourgeois@gnb.ca
Director, Financial Services, Georges Breau
Tel: 506-444-5225
george.breau@gnb.ca
Director, Departmental Coordination, Linda Clayton
Tel: 506-453-8132
linda.clayton@gnb.ca
Director, Human Resource Services, Michael Murray
Tel: 506-453-8209
michael.murray@gnb.ca
Manager, Facilities Management, Michel Cormier
Tel: 506-453-8244
Michel.Cormier@gnb.ca
Supervisor, Administrative Services, Mavis Banks-Carr
Tel: 506-444-6750
mavis.banks-carr@gnb.ca
Librarian, Corporate Information Management, Mary Comeau
Tel: 506-453-8247
mary.comeau@gnb.ca
Auditor & Consultant, Internal Audit & Portfolio Debt Management, Erica Brown
Tel: 506-444-2157
Erica.Brown@gnb.ca

Labour & Planning Division
Chestnut Complex, PO Box 6000, Fredericton, NB E3B 5H1
Tel: 506-453-8202
Fax: 506-453-3038
dpetlinfo@gnb.ca
The Labour & Planning Division consists of the following branches: Employers' Advocate; Employment Standards; Industrial Relations; Labour Market Analysis; Policy & Planning; & Workers' Advocate.
Assistant Deputy Minister, Gérin Girouard
Tel: 506-453-8202
gerin.girouard@gnb.ca
Director, Policy & Planning, Dianne Nason
Tel: 506-444-2071
dianne.nason@gnb.ca
Director, Industrial Relations & Employment Standards, Paula Ultican
Tel: 506-453-2261
paula.ultican@gnb.ca
Manager, Labour Market Analysis, Hope Brewer
Tel: 506-457-7891
Hope.Brewer@gnb.ca
Manager, Workers' Advocate, Guy Dagenais
Tel: 506-453-2149
guy.dagenais@gnb.ca
Manager, Employers' Advocate, Richard Fitzgerald
Tel: 506-457-3510
richard.fitzgerald@gnb.ca

Population Growth Division
Kings Place, PO Box 6000, Fredericton, E3B 5H1
Tel: 506-457-7640
Fax: 506-453-3899
pgs-scd@gnb.ca
Issues such as immigration, attraction & repatriation, settlement & multiculturalism, & retention are handled by the Population Growth Division.
Assistant Deputy Minister, Charles Ayles
Tel: 506-444-5663
charles.ayles@gnb.ca
Director, Settlement & Multiculturalism, Ashraf Ghanem
Tel: 506-457-7644
ashraf.ghanem@gnb.ca
Director, Repatriation & Attraction, Ryan Jacobson
Tel: 506-457-7646
ryan.jacobson@gnb.ca
Manager, Immigration, Tammy Caseley
Tel: 506-444-5072
tammy.caseley@gnb.ca
Manager, Immigration, George Itoafa
Tel: 506-444-5055
george.itoafa@gnb.ca
Manager, Federal / Provincial / Territorial Relations & Research, Stephanie Eardley
Tel: 506-457-7642
Stephanie.Eardley@gnb.ca

Post-Secondary Education Division
Beaverbrook Building, PO Box 6000, Fredericton, NB E3B 5H1
The Post-Secondary Division is made up of the College Support Service Branch, the University Relations Branch, the Private Occupational Training Branch, & Student Financial Services. The division also oversees the New Brunswick College of Craft & Design.
Assistant Deputy Minister, Yves Pelletier
Tel: 506-457-4891
yves.pelletier@gnb.ca
Executive Director, College Support Service, Daniel Fraser
Tel: 506-453-8230
daniel.fraser@gnb.ca
Director, College Admissions Service, Doris Adams
Tel: 506-789-2016
doris.adams@gnb.ca
Director, Student Financial Services, Michael Barnett
Tel: 506-453-3790
michael.barnett@gnb.ca
Director, New Brunswick College of Craft & Design, Donna Boudreau
Tel: 506-444-2435
donna.boudreau@gnb.ca
Director, University Relations, René Beaulieu
Tel: 506-462-5135
rene.boudreau@gnb.ca
Dean, New Brunswick College of Craft & Design, Keith McAlpine
Tel: 506-444-4056
keith.mcalpine@gnb.ca
Registrar, New Brunswick College of Craft & Design, Nancy Beaulieu
Tel: 506-453-6491
nancy.beaulieu@gnb.ca
Manager, Post-Secondary Education, Margie Layden-Oreto
Tel: 506-462-5127
margie.layden-oreto@gnb.ca
Manager, Financial Assistance Delivery, Gisèle Parkinson
Tel: 506-453-2025
gisele.parkinson@gnb.ca

New Brunswick Department of Public Safety / Sécurité publique

364 Argyle St., PO Box 6000, Fredericton, NB E3B 5H1
Tel: 506-453-3992
Fax: 506-453-3870
DPS-MSP.Information@gnb.ca
www.gnb.ca/0276/index-e.asp
The Department of Public Safety provides leadership in the areas of public order & community safety.
It provides fair, accessible, community-focused, & coordinated public safety programs & services. The department also ensures effective inspection & enforcement of designated public safety programs & services. Acting in partnership with communities, the department works to prevent crime, assist victims, & create opportunities for offenders to change.
The Public Safety Department coordinates & cooperates with the federal government in the administration of correctional services & law enforcement in New Brunswick.
Acts Administered:
Boiler & Pressure Vessel Act
Coroners Act
Corrections Act
Cross Border Policing Act
Custody & Detention of Young Persons Act
Electrical Installation & Inspection Act
Elevators & Lifts Act
Emergency 911 Act
Emergency Measures Act
Film & Video Act
Fire Prevention Act
Gaming Control (except Part 2)
Industrial Relations (subsection 1(8.11))
Intoxicated Persons Detention Act
Liquor Control Act
Motor Vehicle Act
New Brunswick Building Code Act
Plumbing Installation & Inspection Act
Police Act (Parts I, I1 & IV)
Private Investigators & Security Services Act
Restricted Beverage Act
Salvage Dealers Licensing Act
Transportation of Dangerous Goods Act
Victim Services Act

Minister, Public Safety; Solicitor General, Hon. Robert B. Trevors
Tel: 506-453-7414
Fax: 506-453-3870
robert.trevors@gnb.ca; robert.trevors.mla@bellaliant.com

Deputy Minister, Dale Wilson
Tel: 506-453-7412
Dale.Wilson@gnb.ca

Director, Communications & Public Awareness, Deborah Nobes
Tel: 506-444-3323
Deborah.Nobes@gnb.ca

Director, Financial Services, Deborah Carpenter
Tel: 506-453-5446
Fax: 506-444-4743
Deborah.Carpenter@gnb.ca

Director, Human Resources, Andrew Currie
Tel: 506-453-3903
Fax: 506-453-7481
andrew.currie@gnb.ca

Director, Information Technology, Virender Ambwani
Tel: 506-444-4433
Fax: 506-453-3321
vic.ambwani@gnb.ca

Executive Director, Jerome Connors
Tel: 506-453-5975
Jerome.Connors@gnb.ca

Safety Services / Direction des services de sécurité
Provides leadership in the areas of law enforcement & community safety in order to preserve & enhance the quality of life in New Brunswick.
Asst. Deputy Minister, Michael Cameau
Tel: 506-453-7142
Fax: 506-453-3870
michael.cameau@gnb.ca
Executive Director, Michael Johnston
Tel: 506-453-7472
Mike.Johnston@gnb.ca
Director, Agency Services, Denis Deveau
Tel: 506-453-2336
Denis.Deveau@gnb.ca
Director, Gaming Control, Brian Fillmore
Tel: 506-453-3992
Director, Licensing & Registration, Darlene Harnish
Tel: 506-453-7472
Darlene.Harnish@gnb.ca
Director, Gaming Control, Chris O'Connell
Tel: 506-453-4332
Chris.O'Connell@gnb.ca
Deputy Registrar, Drivers & Vehicles, Susan Mccracken
Tel: 506-453-2410
Inspector, Technical Inspections Services, Michel LaBlanc
Tel: 506-453-2336
Inspector, Motor Vehicle Inspection Program, Guy Imbeault
Tel: 506-547-5403
Guy.Imbeault@gnb.ca
Chief Fire Inspector, Fire Inspection Program, Kenneth Harris
Tel: 506-453-8292
Ken.Harris@gnb.ca
Inspector, Motor Vehicle Inspection Program, Greg Bonnar
Tel: 506-444-4814
Chief Inspector, Plumbing Inspection Program, William Fallow
Tel: 506-453-2336
william.fallow@gnb.ca
Chief Coroner, Coroner Services, Gregory J. Forestell
Tel: 506-453-3604
Greg.Forestell@gnb.ca

Regional Development Corporation (RDC) / Société d'aménagement régional (SAR)

RDC Bldg., 836 Churchill Row, PO Box 428, Fredericton, NB E3B 5R4
Tel: 506-453-2277
Fax: 506-453-7988
www2.gnb.ca/content/gnb/en/departments/regional_development.html
The Regional Development Corporation is a Crown corporation which carries out its mandate in accordance with the Regional Development Corporation Act. The following are responsibilities of the Corporation: administration & management of development agreements between the Province of New Brunswick & the federal government; assistance in the establishment & development of enterprises & institutions; assistance to municipalities in the planning & development of projects to benefit the public; assistance in the development of tourism & recreational facilities; planning, coordinating, & guiding regional development; & performing duties assigned by the Lieutenant-Governor-in-Council.

Minister Responsible, Hon. Paul Robichaud
Tel: 506-453-5898
Fax: 506-453-6389
paul.robichaud@gnb.ca

President, Denis Caron
Tel: 506-453-8542
denis.caron@gnb.ca

Acting Vice-President, Financial Services, Ann Marie Wood-Seems
Tel: 506-453-8526
annmarie.wood-seems@gnb.ca

Vice-President, Development & Special Initiatives, Serge Doucet
Tel: 506-457-4912
serge.doucet@gnb.ca

Corporate Secretary, Bruce Macfarlane
Tel: 506-444-4606
bruce.macfarlane@gnb.ca

New Brunswick Research & Productivity Council (RPC) / Conseil de la recherche et de la productivité du Nouveau-Brunswick (RPC)

921 College Hill Rd., Fredericton, NB E3B 6Z9
Tel: 506-452-1212
Fax: 506-452-1395
info@rpc.ca
www.rpc.ca

The New Brunswick Research & Productivity Council's vision is to excel in technological innovation, enabling its partners in business & industry to create wealth & high quality employment opportunities in New Brunswick.
The council works to steadily improve its capacity to develop & apply new technology, in partnership with firms in the private sector. It provides an expanding range of high quality technical services to clients in the global marketplace.
The Research & Productivity Council is registered to the ISO 9001:2000 International Standard.

Executive Director, Eric Cook, P.Eng.
Tel: 506-452-0585
eric.cook@rpc.ca

Chief Financial Officer, Stephen A. Fox
Tel: 506-452-1380
stephen.fox@rpc.ca

Head, Physical Metallurgy, John Aikens
Tel: 506-460-5766
john.aikens@rpc.ca

Head, Food, Fisheries & Aquaculture, Dr. Rachael Ritchie
Tel: 506-452-1365
rachael.ritchie@rpc.ca

Head, Inorganic Analytical Services, Ross Kean
Tel: 506-452-1399
ross.kean@rpc.ca

Head, Mechanical Systems & Diagnostics, John Aikens
Tel: 506-460-5766
john.aikens@rpc.ca

Manager, Organic Analytical Services, Bruce Phillips
Tel: 506-452-1369
bruce.phillips@rpc.ca

Manager, High Res Section, Dr. John Macaulay
Tel: 506-452-1369
john.macaulay@rpc.ca

Manager, Process Technology, Ross Gilders
Tel: 506-460-5672
ross.gilders@rpc.ca

Manager, Air Quality Services, Thelma Green
Tel: 506-452-0586
thelma.green@rpc.ca

Coordinator, Susi Chamberlain
Tel: 506-452-1244
susi.chamberlain@rpc.ca

Executive Assistant, Linda Horsman
Tel: 506-452-1363
Fax: 506-452-1386
linda.horsman@rpc.ca

Senior & Healthy Aging Secretariat

Sartain MacDonald Bldg., 4th Fl., PO Box 6000, Fredericton, NB E3B 5H1
Tel: 506-453-2001
Fax: 506-453-2164
seniors@gnb.ca
www.gnb.ca/seniors

The Senior & Healthy Aging Secretariat has the following responsibilities: promoting the healthy aging & wellness of seniors; supporting the Minister Responsible for Seniors; overseeing initiatives under the Renewed Long Term Care Strategy; coordinating strategies that increase support for informal caregivers; producing & disseminating information for seniors; coordinating the Senior Goodwill Ambassador Program; & working with organizations related to seniors.

Minister, Social Development; Minister Responsible for Seniors, Housing, & Community Non-Profit Organizations, Hon. Sue Stultz
Tel: 506-453-2001
Fax: 506-453-2164
sue.stultz@gnb.ca

Deputy Minister, Edith Doucet
Tel: 506-453-2590
Fax: 506-453-2164
Edith.Doucet@gnb.ca

Director, Senior & Healthy Aging Secretariat, André Lepine
Tel: 506-457-6856
Fax: 506-453-2869
Andre.Lepine@gnb.ca

Manager, Communications, Judy Cole
Tel: 506-444-3522
Fax: 506-453-2164
judy.cole@gnb.ca

Advisor, Janice Clarke
Tel: 506-444-4076
Fax: 506-453-2869
janice.clarke@gnb.ca

New Brunswick Advisory Council on the Status of Women / Conseil consultatif sur la condition de la femme au Nouveau-Brunswick

236 King St., Fredericton, NB E3B 1E2
Tel: 506-444-4101
Fax: 506-444-4318
Toll-Free: 800-332-3087
acswcccf@gnb.ca
www.acswcccf.nb.ca

Chair, Elsie Hambrook
acswcccf@gnb.ca

Executive Director, Rosella Melanson
rosella.melanson@gnb.ca

New Brunswick Department of Social Development / Développement social

Sartain MacDonald Bldg., 551 King St., PO Box 6000, Fredericton, NB E3B 5H1
Tel: 506-453-2001
Fax: 506-453-7478
sd-ds@gnb.ca
www.gnb.ca/socialdevelopment

The Department of Social Development oversees services to the following citizens of New Brunswick: seniors & persons with disabilities who need long-term care & nursing home services; children who require assistance to prepare for school; abused & neglected children & adults; families in need of affordable day care; & persons in need of affordable housing & social assistance.
Acts Administered:
Charitable Donation of Food Act
Economic and Social Inclusion Act
Education Act (section 19)
Employment Standards Act (subsection 44.02(6))
Essential Services in Nursing Homes
Family Income Security Act
Family Services Act (except Part VII)
Hospital Act (section 21)
Intercountry Adoption Act
Nursing Homes Act
Reciprocal Enforcement of Maintenance Orders Act (section 10)
Vocational Rehabilitation of Disabled Persons Act

Minister, Social Development; Minister Responsible for Seniors, Housing, & Community Non-Profit Organizations, Hon. Sue Schultz
Tel: 506-453-2001
Fax: 506-453-2164
sue.stultz@gnb.ca

Deputy Minister, Edith Doucet
Tel: 506-453-2590
Fax: 506-453-2164
Edith.Doucet@gnb.ca

Director, Communications, Jason Humphrey
Tel: 506-444-2416
Fax: 506-453-6555
jason.humphrey@gnb.ca

Director, Human Resources Services, Manon Daigle
Tel: 506-444-6715
Fax: 250-453-6555
manon.daigle@gnb.ca

Planning & Corporate Services / Planification et services corporatif

Sartain MacDonald Bldg., 551 King St., 4th Fl., PO Box 6000, Fredericton, NB E3B 5H1
Tel: 506-453-2181
Fax: 506-453-3829

Assistant Deputy Minister, Jack Brown
Tel: 506-453-2181
Fax: 506-453-3829
Jack.Brown@gnb.ca
Director, Finance & Administration, Paulette Boudreau-Clark
Tel: 506-457-6735
Fax: 506-453-2128
paulette.boudreau-clark@gnb.ca
Director, Information Technology Services, Carol LaChapelle
Tel: 506-453-2033
Fax: 506-453-2841
carol.lachapelle@gnb.ca
Director, Policy, Legislation & Intergovernmental Relations, Bill MacKenzie
Tel: 506-457-4803
Fax: 506-462-5150
Bill.MacKenzie@gnb.ca
Acting Director, Integrated Planning, Reporting & Accountabilities, Janet P. Thomas
Tel: 506-444-3380
Fax: 506-462-5150
Janet.Thomas@gnb.ca

Program Delivery / Délivrance des programmes

Sartain MacDonald Bldg., 551 King St., 4th Fl., PO Box 6000, Fredericton, NB E3B 5H1
Tel: 506-453-2379
Fax: 506-453-2164

Assistant Deputy Minister, Social Development, Hon. Geraldine Poirier-Baiani
Tel: 506-453-2379
Fax: 506-453-2164
geraldine.poirier-baiani@gnb.ca
Minister Responsible, Community Non-Profit Organizations, Hon. Sue Stultz
Tel: 506-453-2001
Fax: 506-444-2978
info.nonprofitsector@gnb.ca
Director, Operational Support, Charles Boulay
Tel: 506-444-4828
Fax: 506-453-2152
Charles.Boulay@gnb.ca

Program Design & Quality Management / Division de la conception des programmes et de gestion de la qualité

Sartain MacDonald Bldg., #4007, 551 King St., PO Box 6000, Fredericton, NB E3B 5H1
Tel: 506-453-2181
Fax: 506-453-3829

Assistant Deputy Minister, Lisa Doucette
Tel: 506-453-2181
Fax: 506-453-2164
Lisa.Doucette@gnb.ca
Acting Director, Adults with Disabilities & Senior Services & Nursing Homes Services, André Lepine
Tel: 416-457-6856
Fax: 506-453-2869
andre.lepine@gnb.ca
Director, Child & Youth Services, Claude Savoie
Tel: 506-453-3622
claude.savoie@gnb.ca
Director, Community & Individual Development, Amélie Deschenês
Tel: 506-453-7450
Amélie.Deschênes@gnb.ca
Manager, Nursing Homes Services, Rose-Marie St-Pierre
Tel: 506-453-2376
RoseMarie.St-Pierre@gnb.ca
Manager, Community & Human Resources Development, John Otteson
Tel: 506-444-2333
John.Otteson@gnb.ca
Manager, Long Term Care & Disability Support, Joan Mccarthy
Tel: 506-462-5155
Joan.Mccarthy@gnb.ca
Manager, Clinical Auditing & Child Welfare Training, Wendy Chisholm-Spragg
Tel: 506-457-6797
Wendy.Chisholm-Spragg@gnb.ca

New Brunswick Department of Transportation & Infrastructure

Kings Place, PO Box 6000, Fredericton, NB E3B 5H1
Tel: 506-453-3939
Fax: 506-453-2900
Transportation.Web@gnb.ca
www.gnb.ca/0113/index-e.asp

The mission of the Department of Transportation & Infrastructure is the maintenance of a safe transportation system & infrastructure within the province of New Brunswick's jurisdiction. The department also monitors & advises on transportation & infrastructure issues of federal jurisdiction.

Acts Administered:
Gas Distribution, 1999 (subsections 18(2) & 39(1))
Highway (except sections 58 to 62.1)
Motor Carrier Act (except licensing of motor carriers)
Public Landings
Public Works
Shortline Railways
Telephone Companies (Chief Highway Engineer under subsection 5(3))

Minister, Transportation & Infrastructure; Minister Responsible, Supply & Services, Hon. Claude Williams
Tel: 506-457-7345
Fax: 506-453-7987
claude.williams@gnb.ca

Deputy Minister, Jean-Marc Dupuis
Tel: 506-453-2549
jean-marc.dupuis@gnb.ca

Director, Communications, Judy Cole
Tel: 506-453-5634
judy.cole@gnb.ca

Associated Agencies, Boards & Commissions:
• Vehicle Management Agency
Vehicle Management Center
PO Box 6000
Fredericton, NB E3B 5H1
Tel: 506-453-3939
Fax: 506-453-3628
Transportation.Web@gnb.ca
The Vehicle Management Agency provides vehicle maintenance & fleet management services to the Government of New Brunswick.

Buildings Division

Marysville Place, PO Box 6000, Fredericton, NB E3B 5H1
Tel: 506-453-3742
Fax: 506-444-4400
Reception.Marysville@gnb.ca

The Building Division oversees the construction & maintenance of New Brunswick's provincial government buildings & leased premises. The division is also responsible for the acquisition & sale of government property.

Assistant Deputy Minister, Buildings Division, Robert Martin
Tel: 506-453-2228
bob.martin@gnb.ca
Executive Director, Design & Construction, Bob Daigle
Tel: 506-453-6118
Bob.Daigle@gnb.ca
Executive Director, Special Projects Development, Scott Gibson
Tel: 506-325-4520
Scott.Gibson@gnb.ca
Director, Planning & Project Development, Pam Barteaux
Tel: 506-453-2362
Pam.Barteaux@gnb.ca
Director, Design Services, Joel Bragdon
Tel: 506-444-5519
Joel.Bragdon@gnb.ca
Director, Property Management, Leah Essensa
Tel: 506-453-2221
Leah.Essensa@gnb.ca

Corporate Services & Fleet Management Division

Kings Place, PO Box 6000, Fredericton, NB E3B 5H1
Tel: 506-453-3939
Fax: 506-453-7987
Transportation.Web@gnb.ca

The following services are provided by the Corporate Services & Fleet Management Division: administration; financial services; human resources; information technology services; & fleet management for the Government of New Brunswick.

Assistant Deputy Minister, Corporate Services & Fleet Management, Kim Daley
Tel: 506-453-3939
kim.daley@gnb.ca
Director, Human Resources, Myrna Belyea-Tracy
Tel: 506-444-5531
Myrna.Belyea-Taccy@gnb.ca
Director, Information Management & Technology, Colleen Boldon
Tel: 506-453-4498
colleen.boldon@gnb.ca
Director, Financial & Administrative Services, Charlotte Valley
Tel: 506-453-3389
Charlotte.Valley@gnb.ca

Engineering Services Division

Kings Place, PO Box 6000, Fredericton, NB E3B 5H1
Tel: 506-453-3939
Fax: 506-453-7987
Transportation.Web@gnb.ca

Responsibilities of the Engineering Services Division are as follows: offering technical expertise; supporting the design of highway & bridge projects; & coordinating technical transportation research.

Assistant Deputy Minister, Dale Forster
Tel: 506-453-3939
dale.forster@gnb.ca
Executive Director, Operations, David Cogswell
Tel: 506-453-3939
david.cogswell@gnb.ca
Executive Director, Engineering Services, Carol MacQuarrie
Tel: 506-453-3939
carol.macquarrie@gnb.ca
Director, Maintenance & Traffic, Kevin Maclean
Tel: 506-444-2134
kevin.maclean@gnb.ca

Facilities Management Division

Marysville Place, PO Box 6000, Fredericton, NB E3B 5H1
Tel: 506-453-3742
Fax: 506-444-4400
Reception.Marysville@gnb.ca

Responsibilities of the Facilities Management Division include the following: negotiating & administering leases; operating provincially-owned buildings; inspecting buildings; & offering technical support services to government departments, hospitals, & schools.

Executive Director, Facilities Management, Gary Lynch
Tel: 506-444-4527
gary.lynch@gnb.ca
Manager, Facilities Management Technical Services, Peter Davis
Tel: 506-444-4541
peter.davis@gnb.ca
Manager, Financial Administration & Space Management, Kimberly Lebritton
Tel: 506-444-4538
Kim.Lebritton@gnb.ca

Policy, Strategic Development, & Intergovernmental Relations Division

Kings Place, PO Box 6000, Fredericton, NB E3B 5H1
Tel: 506-453-3939
Fax: 506-453-5859
Transportation.Web@gnb.ca

Transportation plans & policies are developed in consultation with provincial & federal governments, the transporation industry, & stakeholders.

Assistant Deputy Minister, Policy, Strategic Development, & Intergovernmental Relations Division, Margaret Grant-McGivney
Tel: 506-453-3939
margaret.grant-mcgivney@gnb.ca
Director, Transportation Policy, Kelly Rodgers-Sturgeon
Tel: 506-444-4356
kelly.rodgers-sturgeon@gnb.ca
Senior Policy Advisor, Strategic Development, John Weatherhead
Tel: 506-444-3185
john.weatherhead@gnb.ca

Workplace Health, Safety & Compensation Commission of New Brunswick (WHSCC) / La commission de la santé, de la sécurité et de l'indemnisation des accidents au travail du Nouveau-Brunswick

1 Portland St., PO Box 160, Saint John, NB E2L 3X9
Tel: 506-632-2200
Toll-Free: 800-222-9775
communications@ws-ts.nb.ca
www.whscc.nb.ca

The Workplace Health, Safety & Compensation Commission (WHSCC) of New Brunswick is a crown corporation charged with overseeing the implementation & application of the New Brunswick Occupational Health & Safety Act, the Workers' Compensation Act of New Brunswick, & the Workplace Health, Safety & Compensation Commission Act of New Brunswick on behalf of the workers & employers of this province. The Commission administers no-fault workplace accident & disability insurance & comprehensive accident prevention health & safety initiatives for employers & their workers, funded solely through premiums paid by employers.

Acts Administered:
Firefighters' Compensation Act
Occupational Health & Safety Act
Workers' Compensation Act
Workplace Health, Safety & Compensation Commission Act

Chair, Sharon Tucker

President/CEO, Peter Murphy

Chair, Appeals Tribunal, Ronald Gaffney

Member Representing Workers, Danny King

Member Representing Workers, Maureen Wallace

Member Representing Workers, Michéle Caron

Member Representing Employers, David Ellis

Member Representing Employers, Marty Martell

New Brunswick Advisory Council on Youth (NBACY) / Conseil consultatif de la jeunesse du Nouveau-Brunswick (CCJNB)

Frederick Square, #130, 77 Westmorland St., PO Box 6000, Fredericton, NB E3B 5H1
Tel: 506-453-3271
Fax: 506-444-4413
Toll-Free: 888-830-5588
nbacy-ccjnb@gnb.ca
www.gnb.ca

The Lieutenant Governor in Council appoints thirteen young people from all regions of New Brunswick, & from both official language groups, to a two-year term on the New Brunswick Advisory Council on Youth. Representative of youth, the Council on Youth voices the concerns, interests, needs, & perspectives of persons between fifteen & twenty-four years of age. The provincial body presents its recommendations to government.

Chair, Kara Hachey
Kara.Hachey@gnb.ca

Executive Director, Ivan Corbett
Ivan.Corbett@gnb.ca

Director, Communications, Brendan Languille
Tel: 506-444-5070

Government of Newfoundland & Labrador

Seat of Government: Confederation Bldg., St. John's, NL A1B 4J6
info@gov.nl.ca
www.gov.nl.ca

The Province of Newfoundland & Labrador entered Confederation March 31, 1949. It has an area of 370,494.89 km2, & the StatsCan census population in 2011 was 514,536.

Office of the Lieutenant Governor

Government House, Military Rd., PO Box 5517, St. John's, NL A1C 5W4
Tel: 709-729-4494
Fax: 709-729-2234
governmenthouse@gov.nl.ca
www.govhouse.nl.ca

Lieutenant Governor, The Hon. John C. Crosbie
Tel: 709-729-4494
Fax: 709-729-2234

Private Secretary, Gary Cake
Tel: 709-729-4494
Fax: 709-729-2234
gcake@gov.nl.ca

Office of the Premier

East Block, Confederation Bldg., PO Box 8700, St. John's, NL A1B 4J6
Tel: 709-729-3570
Fax: 709-729-5875
premier@gov.nl.ca
www.premier.gov.nl.ca

Kathy Dunderdale was sworn in as Newfoundland & Labrador's tenth Premier on December 3, 2010. She is the first female Premier of the province. In the general election of October 11, 2011, Premier Dunderdale was re-elected.

Premier, Hon. Kathy Dunderdale
kathydunderdale@gov.nl.ca

Chief of Staff, Brian Taylor

Director, Communications, Glenda Power

Director, Operations, Derrick Rideout

Press Secretary, Millyck Brown

Executive Council

c/o Communications Branch, East Block, Confederation Building, 10th Fl., St. John's, NL A1B 4J6
info@gov.nl.ca
www.exec.gov.nl.ca/exec
The mailing address for all Ministers of the Government of Newfoundland & Labrador is as follows: Confederation Building, PO Box 8700, St. John's NL A1B 4J6.
The following is a list of Cabinet Ministers by their department:

Minister, Advanced Educaton & Skills; Minister Responsible for the Status of Persons with Disabilities & for YouthEngagement, Hon. Joan Burke
Tel: 709-729-3580
Toll-free: 866-838-5620
Fax: 709-729-6996
joanburke@gov.nl.ca
www.aes.gov.nl.ca/department/minister.html

Minister, Child, Youth, & Family Services; Minister Responsible for the Status of Women, Hon. Charlene Johnson
Tel: 709-729-0173
Toll-free: 800-809-0106
Fax: 709-729-1049
charlenejohnson@gov.nl.ca
www.gov.nl.ca/cyfs/department/minister.html

Minister, Education, Hon. Clyde Jackman
Tel: 709-729-5040
Toll-free: 800-423-3301
Fax: 709-729-0414
clydejackman@gov.nl.ca
www.ed.gov.nl.ca/edu

Minister, Environment & Conservation; Minister Responsible for the Labour Relations Agency, the Multi Materials Stewardship Board, & the Office of Climate Change, Energy Efficiency, & Emissions Trading, Hon. Terry French
Tel: 709-729-5907
Fax: 709-729-5819
Terryfrench@gov.nl.ca
www.env.gov.nl.ca/env/department/minister.html

Minister, Finance; President, Treasury Board; Minister Responsible for the Public Service Secretariat, Public Service Commission, & the Newfoundland & Labrador Liquor Corporation, Hon. Thomas W. Marshall, Q.C.
Tel: 709-729-2858
Fax: 709-729-2232
tommarshall@gov.nl.ca
www.fin.gov.nl.ca/fin
Social Media: twitter.com/tommarshall_he

Minister, Fisheries & Aquaculture; Deputy Government House Leader, Hon. Darin T. King, Ph.D
Tel: 709-729-0340
Fax: 709-729-0414
darinking@gov.nl.ca
www.fishaq.gov.nl.ca

Minister, Health & Community Services; Minister Responsible for Aging & Senior, & Francophone Affairs, Hon. Susan Sullivan
Tel: 709-709-4893
Toll-free: 888-610-4440
Fax: 709-489-5480
SusanSullivan@gov.nl.ca
www.health.gov.nl.ca/health
Social Media: ca.linkedin.com/pub/susan-sullivan/43/339/687

Minister, Intergovernmental & Aboriginal Affairs; Minister Responsible for Labrador Affairs & Voluntary & Non-Profit Sector, Hon. Nick McGrath
Tel: 709-729-1066
Fax: 709-729-1425
nickmcgrath@gov.nl.ca
www.exec.gov.nl.ca/exec/igas

Minister, Innovation, Business, & Rural Development; Minister Responsible, Rural Secretariat, & the Research & DevelopmentCorporation, Hon. Keith Hutchings
Tel: 709-729-1390
Toll-free: 800-634-5504
Fax: 709-729-2463
keithhutchings@gov.nl.ca
www.ibrd.gov.nl.ca

Minister, Justice; Attorney General, Hon. Felix Collins
Tel: 709-729-2869
Toll-free: 877-898-0898
Fax: 709-729-0469
felixcollins@gov.nl.ca
www.justice.gov.nl.ca/just/department/minister.html
Social Media: ca.linkedin.com/pub/felix-collins/2b/2b7/543

Minister, Municipal Affairs; Minister Responsible for Fire & Emergency Services - NL, & Registrar General, Hon. Kevin O'Brien
Tel: 709-729-3046
Toll-free: 800-813-6850
Fax: 709-729-0943
kevinobrien@gov.nl.ca
www.ma.gov.nl.ca/ma
Social Media: ca.linkedin.com/pub/kevin-o-brien/43/b6/b45

Minister, Natural Resources; Minister Responsible for the Foresetry & Agrifoods Agency; Government House Leader, Hon. Jerome Kennedy, Q.C.
Tel: 709-729-2920
Toll-free: 877-998-9933
Fax: 709-729-0059
JeromeKennedy@gov.nl.ca
www.nr.gov.nl.ca/nr

Minister, Service Newfoundland & Labrador; Minister Responsible for the Government Purchasing Agency, Office of the CIO, Workplace Health, Safety, & Compensation Committee, Hon. Paul Davis
Tel: 709-729-6670
Fax: 709-729-6244
padavis@gov.nl.ca

Minister, Tourism, Culture, & Recreation, Hon. Derrick Dalley
Tel: 709-729-7895
Toll-free: 888-783-9990
Fax: 709-729-3306
derrickdalley@gov.nl.ca
www.tcr.gov.nl.ca/tcr
Social Media: ca.linkedin.com/pub/derrick-dalley/43/6bb/430

Minister, Transportation & Works; Minister Responsible for the Newfoundland & Labrador Housing Corporation, Hon. Tom Hedderson
Tel: 709-729-3679
Toll-free: 877-787-0707
Fax: 709-729-4285
thedderson@gov.nl.ca
www.tw.gov.nl.ca/department/minister.html
Social Media: twitter.com/tomhedderson

Cabinet Secretariat

Fax: 709-729-5218
Clerk, Executive Council & Secretary to the Cabinet, Robert Thompson
Tel: 709-729-2853
Fax: 709-729-5218
rthompson@gov.nl.ca
Deputy Clerk, Executive Council & Associate Secretary to the Cabinet, Julia Mullaley
Tel: 709-729-2844
Fax: 709-729-5218
Assistant Secretary, Economic Policy, Dennis Hogan
Tel: 709-729-2845
Fax: 709-729-5218
Assistant Secretary, Social Policy, Colleen Janes
Tel: 709-729-2850
Fax: 709-729-5218
cjanes@gov.nl.ca
Executive Director, Planning & Co-ordination, Paula Burt
Tel: 709-729-4340
Fax: 709-729-5218
paulaburt@gov.nl.ca

Office of the Chief Information Officer (OCIO)

40 Higgins Line, PO Box 8700, St. John's, NL A1B 4J6
Tel: 709-729-4000
Fax: 709-729-6767
ocio@gov.nl.ca
The OCIO provides a professional Information Technology & Information Management capability aligned to support the business of government & the citizens of Newfoundland & Labrador.
Minister Responsible, Hon. Paul Davis
Tel: 709-729-6670
Fax: 709-729-1503
padavis@gov.nl.ca
Chief Information Officer, Ellen MacDonald
Tel: 709-729-2617
Fax: 709-729-1464
Executive Director, Application Services, Craig Slaney
Tel: 709-729-5694
craigslaney@gov.nl.ca
Executive Director, Corporate Operations & Client Services, Jean Tilley
Tel: 709-729-4110
Fax: 709-729-6767
jeantilley@gov.nl.ca
Executive Director, Information Management, Shelley Smith
Tel: 709-729-6260
ssmith@gov.nl.ca
Executive Director, Operations, Randy Mouland
Tel: 709-729-5227
randymouland@gov.nl.ca
Executive Director, Solution Delivery, Colin Tibbo
Tel: 709-729-3617
colint@gov.nl.ca

Office of Climate Change, Energy Efficiency & Emissions Trading

PO Box 8700, St. John's, NL A1B 4J6
Tel: 709-729-1210
Fax: 709-729-1119
climatechange@gov.nl.ca
www.exec.gov.nl.ca/exec/cceeet/
Has lead responsibility within Government for strategy & policy development on climate change, energy efficiency & emissions trading. CCEEET is a central agency located within Executive Council.
Minister Responsible, Hon. Terry French
Tel: 709-729-2577
Fax: 709-729-0112
terryfrench@gov.nl.ca
Assistant Deputy Minister, Jackie Janes
Tel: 709-729-7971
Fax: 709-729-1119
jackiejanes@gov.nl.ca
Director, Evidence, Gerald Crane
Tel: 709-729-0379
Fax: 709-729-1119
geraldcrane@gov.nl.ca
Director, Government Relations, Patrick Griffin
Tel: 709-729-7955
patgriffin@gov.nl.ca

Intergovernmental & Aboriginal Affairs Secretariat

Confederation Bldg., East Block, 7th Fl., PO Box 8700, St. John's, NL A1B 4J6
Tel: 709-729-3164
Fax: 709-729-5038
iga@gov.nl.ca
www.exec.gov.nl.ca/exec/igas/index.html
Acts Administered:
Intergovernmental Affairs Act
Minister, Hon. Nick McGrath
Tel: 709-729-3400
Deputy Minister, Sean Dutton
Tel: 709-729-2134
sdutton@gov.nl.ca
Assistant Deputy Minister, Tracy English
Tel: 709-729-3164
Fax: 709-729-5038
tenglish@gov.nl.ca
Communications Specialist, Lesley Clarke
Tel: 709-729-6026
lesleyclarke@gov.nl.ca
Acting Director, Social & Economic Policy, Cameron Bodnar
Tel: 709-729-1341
Fax: 709-729-5038
cameronbodnar@gov.nl.ca
Acting Director, Resource & Fiscal Policy, John Cowan
Tel: 709-729-6267
Fax: 709-729-1330
jcowan@gov.nl.ca

Labrador Affairs Office (LAO)

21 Broomfield St., PO Box 3014, Happy Valley - Goose Bay, NL A0P 1E0
laa@gov.nl.ca
Assistant Deputy Minister, Ron Bowles
Tel: 709-896-4449
Fax: 709-896-4748
rabowles@gov.nl.ca
Director, Michelle Watkins
Tel: 709-896-1780
Fax: 709-896-0045
michellewatkins@gov.nl.ca

Public Service Secretariat

Confederation Bldg., Main Fl., East Block, PO Box 8700, St. John's, NL A1B 4J6
Tel: 709-729-6479
Fax: 709-729-2156

Minister Responsible, Hon. Tom Marshall, Q.C.
Tel: 709-729-3775
Fax: 709-729-2232
tommarshall@gov.nl.ca
Deputy Minister, Brenda Caul
Tel: 709-729-2633
Fax: 709-729-1746
bcaul@gov.nl.ca
Director, Communications - Finance, Mark King
Tel: 709-729-6830
Fax: 709-729-2232
markking@gov.nl.ca

Rural Secretariat
PO Box 8700, St. John's, NL A1B 4J6
Tel: 709-729-7380
Fax: 709-729-1673
ruralinfo@gov.nl.ca
www.exec.gov.nl.ca/rural

The Rural Secretariat is a unique & innovative provincial government entity that strives to advance the sustainability of rural Newfoundland & Labrador communities & regions. It does this by supporting the development of citizen-based policy advice, engaging citizens in the future of their province, & supporting collaboration between & among rural stakeholders including governments.

Minister Responsible, Hon. Keith Hutchings
Tel: 709-729-4728
Fax: 709-729-0654
keithhutchings@gov.nl.ca
Asst. Deputy Minister, Dr. Bruce Gilbert
Tel: 709-729-1611
brucegilbert@gov.nl.ca

Voluntary & Non-Profit Sector
PO Box 8700, St. John's, NL A1B 4J6
volunteers@gov.nl.ca

Deputy Minister, Ross Reid
Tel: 709-729-2824
Fax: 709-729-2226
rossreid@gov.nl.ca
Director, Policy & Strategic Planning, Dana Spurrell
Tel: 709-729-2249
Fax: 709-729-2226
danaspurrell@gov.nl.ca

Women's Policy Office
Minister Responsible, Hon. Susan Sullivan
Tel: 709-729-5040
Fax: 709-729-0414
ssullivan@gov.nl.ca
Asst. Deputy Minister, Heather MacLellan
Tel: 709-729-5098
Fax: 709-729-2331
hmaclellan@gov.nl.ca

House of Assembly

c/o Clerk's Office, Confederation Bldg., PO Box 8700, St. John's, NL A1B 4J6
Tel: 709-729-3405
Fax: 709-729-4820
www.gov.nl.ca/hoa
Other Communication: Legislative Library: 709-729-3604

Speaker, Hon. Roger Fitzgerald
Tel: 709-729-3404
Fax: 709-729-4820
rfitzgerald@gov.nl.ca

Citizens' Representative, Barry Fleming
Tel: 709-729-7647
Fax: 709-729-7696
citrep@gov.nl.ca

Sergeant-at-Arms, Elizabeth Gallagher
Tel: 709-729-3630
egallagher@gov.nl.ca

Director, Information Management (Legislative Library), Kimberley Hammond
Tel: 709-729-5646
Fax: 709-729-0234
Kimberleyhammond@gov.nl.ca

Information & Privacy Commissioner, Ed Ring
Tel: 709-729-6309
Toll-free: 877-729-6309
Fax: 709-729-6500
commissioner@oipc.nl.ca

Child & Youth Advocate, Carol A. Chafe
Tel: 709-753-3888
Toll-free: 877-753-3888
Fax: 709-753-3988
office@ocya.nl.ca

Government Caucus Office (Progressive Conservative Party)
PO Box 8700, St. John's, NL A1B 4J6
Premier; Leader, Progressive Conservative Party, Kathy Dunderdale
Tel: 709-729-3570
Fax: 709-729-5875
Government House Leader, Jerome Kennedy
Tel: 709-729-2920
Toll-free: 877-998-9933
Fax: 709-729-0059
Caucus Whip, Progressive Conservative Party, Tony Cornect
Tel: 709-643-0813
Fax: 709-643-0814
tonycornect@gov.nl.ca
Caucus Chair, Progressive Conservative Party, Clayton Forsey
Tel: 709-258-2519
Toll-free: 888-554-7799
Fax: 709-258-2518
claytonforsey@gov.nl.ca
Deputy Government House Leader, Darin T. King, Ph.D.
Tel: 709-729-3705
Toll-free: 877-997-9933
Fax: 709-729-0360
darinking@gov.nl.ca
Parliamentary Assistant to the Premier, Vaughn Granter
Tel: 709-729-3093
Fax: 709-729-5774
vaughngranter@gov.nl.ca

Office of the Official Opposition (Liberal)
East Block, 5th Fl., PO Box 8700, St. John's, NL A1B 4J6
Tel: 709-729-5202
Toll-Free: 800-813-9157
www.liberaloppositionnl.com

Interim Leader, Liberal Pary of Newfoundland & Labrador; Leader, Official Opposition;, Opposition Critic for Child, Youth, & Family Services, Finance, Health & Community Services, & Tourism, Culture, &Recreation, Dwight Ball
Tel: 709-729-3391
Toll-free: 877-635-0132
Fax: 709-729-5202
dwightball@gov.nl.ca
Opposition House Leader; Critic, Intergovernmental Affairs, Labrador Affairs, Natural Resources, Status of Women, Voluntary & Non-ProfitSector, Yvonne Jones
Tel: 709-729-6925
Toll-free: 800-286-9118
Fax: 709-729-5202
yvonnejones@gov.nl.ca
Caucus Whip; Critic, Municipal Affairs & Transportation & Works, Eddie Joyce
Tel: 709-634-7883
Fax: 709-634-7885
ejoyce@gov.nl.ca
Caucus Chair; Critic, Aboriginal Affairs, Environment & Conservation, & Service Newfoundland & Labrador, Randy Edmunds
Tel: 709-923-2471
Toll-free: 877-923-2471
Fax: 709-923-2473
randyedmunds@gov.nl.ca
Chair, Public Accounts Committee; Critic, Fisheries & Aquaculture, & Innovation, Business & Rural Development, Jim Bennett
Tel: 709-729-6356
Toll-free: 800-898-6751
jimbennett@gov.nl.ca
Deputy Opposition House Leader; Critic, Advanced Education & Skills, Education, Child, Youth, & Family Services, &Justice, Andrew Parsons
Tel: 709-695-3585
Toll-free: 800-518-9479
Fax: 709-695-5800
andrewparsons@gov.nl.ca
Director, Research, Joy Buckle
Tel: 709-729-6948
joybuckle@gov.nl.ca
Director, Communications, Peter Miles
Tel: 709-729-6151
petermiles@gov.nl.ca

Caucus Office of the Third Party (New Democratic Party)
Confederation Building, PO Box 8700, St. John's, NL A1B 4J6
Tel: 709-729-0270
Fax: 709-576-1443
Toll-Free: 855-729-0270
ndpinfo@gov.nl.ca
www.nlndpcaucus.ca

In the 2011 general election, five members of the New Democratic Party were elected to the House of Assembly. This is the largest Newfoundland & Labrador New Democratic Party Caucus in history.

Leader, New Democratic Party; Critic, Finance, Treasury Board, Health & Community Services, Natural Resources, Intergovernmental & Aboriginal Affairs, Labrador Affairs, Voluntary & Non-Profit Sector, NL Liquor Corporation, &Francophone Affairs, Lorriane Michael
Tel: 709-729-0270
Fax: 709-576-1443
lorrainemichael@gov.nl.ca
Social Media: twitter.com/lorrainemichael, www.facebook.com/LorraineMichaelNDP
Caucus Whip, New Democratic Party; Critic, Municipal Affairs, Environment & Conservation, & Transportation & Works, George Murphy
Tel: 709-729-3651
Fax: 709-576-1443
georgemurphy@gov.nl.ca
Caucus Chair, New Democratic Party, Gerry Rogers
Tel: 709-729-2638
Fax: 709-576-1443
gerryrogers@gov.nl.ca
Director, Communications, Jean Graham
Tel: 709-729-2137
Fax: 709-693-9172
jeangraham@gov.nl.ca

Forty-seventh House of Assembly - Newfoundland & Labrador

Confederation Building, PO Box 8700, St. John's, NL A1B 4J6
Tel: 709-729-3405
ClerkHOA@gov.nl.ca
www.assembly.nl.ca
Other Communication: Speaker's Office, Phone: 709-729-3404; Legislative Library, Phone: 709-729-3604; Tours, Phone: 709-729-3670

Last General Election, October 11, 2011. Next General Election: 2015.
Party Standings (September 2012):
Progressive Conservative 36;
Liberal 6;
New Democratic Party (NDP) 5;
Independent 1;
Total 48.
Authorized Salaries & Committee Allowance for Members of the House of Assembly (December 2009): Member, Base Salary $95,357.
In addition to this base salary are the following salaries for office holders:
Speaker $54,072;
Leader of the Opposition $54,072;
Deputy Speaker & Chair of Committees $27,033;
Opposition House Leader $27,033;
Leader of a Third Party $18,918;
Deputy Opposition House Leader $18,457;
Deputy Chair of Committees $13,517;
Chair, Public Accounts Committee $13,517;
Party Whip $13,517;
Caucus Chair $13,517.
All members of the House of Assembly may be reached by including the member's name, the member's district, plus the following address: Confederation Building, PO Box 8700, St. John's NL, A1B 4J6.
The following is an alphabetical list of the members of the House of Assembly, with their electoral district, the total number of registered electors in their district for the 2011 election, plus the members' contact information:

Members of the House of Assembly
Interim Leader, Liberal Pary of Newfoundland & Labrador; Leader, Official Opposition, Dwight Ball
Constituency: Humber Valley *No. of Constituents:* 8,026, Liberal
Tel: 709-635-0132
Toll-free: 877-635-0132
Fax: 709-635-0133
dwightball@gov.nl.ca; dwight.ball@nf.sympatico.ca
www.dwightball.ca
District Office
13A North Main St.
Deer Lake, NL A8A 1W7
Jim Bennett
Constituency: St. Barbe *No. of Constituents:* 7,062, Liberal
Tel: 709-729-6356
Toll-free: 800-898-6751
jimbennett@gov.nl.ca; jim@jimbennett.ca
www.jimbennett.ca
Other Communications: District Phone: 709-458-3257; Fax: 709-458-3259
District Office
16 West Link Rd.
Rocky Harbour, NL A0K4N0
David Brazil
Constituency: Conception Bay East — Bell Island *No. of Constituents:* 11,225, Progressive Conservative

Tel: 709-729-0334
Fax: 709-729-1503
davidbrazil@gov.nl.ca; info@davidbrazilforpc.ca
www.davidbrazilforpc.ca
Government Members' Office, East Block, Confederation Building, 5th Fl.
PO Box 8700
St. John's, NL A1B4J6

Minister, Advanced Educaton & Skills; Minister Responsible for the Status of Persons with Disabilities & for Youth Engagement, Hon. Joan Burke
Constituency: St. George's-Stephenville East *No. of Constituents:* 7,959, Progressive Conservative
Tel: 709-729-3580
Toll-free: 866-838-5620
Fax: 709-729-6996
Joanburke@gov.nl.ca
www.aes.gov.nl.ca/department/minister.html
Other Communications: District Phone: 709-643-8663; Fax: 709-643-8677
District Office, Harmon Building
58 Oregon Dr., 2nd Fl.
Stephenville, NL A2N 2Y1

Minister, Justice; Attorney General, Hon. Felix Collins
Constituency: Placentia — St. Mary's *No. of Constituents:* 7,383, Progressive Conservative
Tel: 709-729-2869
Toll-free: 877-898-0898
Fax: 709-729-0469
felixcollins@gov.nl.ca
www.justice.gov.nl.ca/just/department/minister.html
Other Communications: District Phone: 709-729-6926
Social Media: ca.linkedin.com/pub/felix-collins/2b/2b7/543
Department of Jusice, East Block,Confederation Building, 4th Fl.
PO Box 8700
St. John's, NL A1B 4J6

Parliamentary Secretary to the Minister of Health & Community Services, Sandy Collins
Constituency: Terra Nova *No. of Constituents:* 8,390, Progressive Conservative
Tel: 709-467-1018
Toll-free: 800-670-2850
Fax: 709-467-1010
sandycollins@gov.nl.ca
District Office
PO Box 100
Musgravetown, NL A0C1Z0

Caucus Whip, Progressive Conservative Party, Tony Cornect
Constituency: Port auPort *No. of Constituents:* 8,449, Progressive Conservative
Tel: 709-643-0813
Fax: 709-643-0814
tonycornect@gov.nl.ca
District Office
143 Main St.
Stephenville, NL A2N 1J5

Eli Cross
Constituency: Bonavista North *No. of Constituents:* 6,935, Progressive Conservative
Tel: 709-729-0032
Toll-free: 866-929-0032
Fax: 709-729-1503
elicross@gov.nl.ca
East Block, Confederation Building, 5th Fl.
PO Box 8700
St. John's, NL A1B 4J6

Dan Crummell
Constituency: St. John'sWest *No. of Constituents:* 7,774, Progressive Conservative
Tel: 709-729-5869
Fax: 709-729-5774
dancrummell@gov.nl.ca
Social Media: twitter.com/dancrummell
Government Members' Office, East Block, Confederation Building, 5th Fl.
PO Box 8700
St. John's, NL A1B 4J6

Minister, Tourism, Culture, & Recreation, Hon. Derrick Dalley
Constituency: The Isles of Notre Dame *No. of Constituents:* 7,004, Progressive Conservative
Tel: 709-729-7895
Toll-free: 888-783-9990
Fax: 709-729-3306
derrickdalley@gov.nl.ca
Other Communications: District Phone: 709-884-1226; Fax: 709-884-1227
Social Media: ca.linkedin.com/pub/derrick-dalley/43/6bb/430
District Office
PO Box 430
Twillingate, NL A0G 4M0

Minister, Service Newfoundland & Labrador; Minister Responsible for the Government Purchasing Agency, Office of the CIO, Workplace Health, Safety, & Compensation Committee, Hon. Paul Davis
Constituency: Topsail *No. of Constituents:* 11,345, Progressive Conservative
Tel: 709-729-6670
Fax: 709-729-6244
padavis@gov.nl.ca
Government Members' Office, East Block, Confederation Building, 5th Fl.
PO Box 8700
St. John's, NL A1B 4J6

John Dinn
Constituency: Kilbride *No. of Constituents:* 10,416, Progressive Conservative
Tel: 709-729-3758
Fax: 709-729-1082
johndinn@gov.nl.ca
Social Media: ca.linkedin.com/pub/john-dinn/22/147/2
Government Members' Office, Confederation Building
PO Box 8700
St. John's, NL A1B 4J6

Premier, Hon. Kathy Dunderdale
Constituency: Virginia Waters *No. of Constituents:* 10,168, Progressive Conservative
Tel: 709-729-3570
Fax: 709-729-5875
kathydunderdale@gov.nl.ca; premier@gov.nl.ca
www.premier.gov.nl.ca (Office of the Premier)
East Block, Confederation Building
Elizabeth Ave.
PO Box 8700
St. John's, NL A1B 4J6

Randy Edmunds
Constituency: Torngat Mountains *No. of Constituents:* 2,139, Liberal
Tel: 709-923-2471
Toll-free: 877-923-2471
Fax: 709-923-2473
randyedmunds@gov.nl.ca
Social Media: twitter.com/EdmundsMHA

Clayton Forsey
Constituency: Exploits *No. of Constituents:* 7,723, Progressive Conservative
Tel: 709-258-2519
Toll-free: 888-554-7799
Fax: 709-258-2518
claytonforsey@gov.nl.ca
District Office
6 Dominic St.
PO Box 340
Bishop's Falls, NL A0H 1C0

Minister, Environment & Conservation; Minister Responsible for the Labour Relations Agency, the Multi Materials Stewardship Board, & the Office of Climate Change, Energy Efficiency, & EmissionsTrading, Hon. Terry French
Constituency: Conception Bay South *No. of Constituents:* 10,239, Progressive Conservative
Tel: 709-729-5907
Fax: 709-729-5819
Terryfrench@gov.nl.ca
www.env.gov.nl.ca/env/department/minister.html
West Block, Confederation Building
PO Box 8700
St. John's, NL A1B 4J6

Vaughn Granter
Constituency: Humber West *No. of Constituents:* 8,368, Progressive Conservative
Tel: 709-729-3093
Fax: 709-729-5774
vaughngranter@gov.nl.ca
Other Communications: District Phone: 709-637-4056; Fax: 709-637-4058
Social Media: twitter.com/granterhw, www.facebook.com/vaughngranter
District Office
Sir Richard Squires Building, 10th Fl.
PO Box 2006
Corner Brook, NL A2H 6J8

Minister, Transportation & Works; Minister Responsible for the Newfoundland & Labrador Housing Corporation, Hon. Tom Hedderson
Constituency: Harbour Main *No. of Constituents:* 9,098, Progressive Conservative
Tel: 709-729-3679
Toll-free: 877-787-0707
Fax: 709-729-4285
thedderson@gov.nl.ca
www.tw.gov.nl.ca/department/minister.html
Other Communications: District Phone:709-229-0160; Fax: 709-229-0169
Social Media: twitter.com/tomhedderson
District Office
402 Conception Bay Hwy.
PO Box 129
Holyrood, NL A0A 2R0

Ray Hunter
Constituency: Grand Falls-Windsor — Green Bay South *No. of Constituents:* 7,082, Progressive Conservative
Tel: 709-729-6932
Toll-free: 877-585-0505
Fax: 709-729-1503
rhunter@gov.nl.ca
Confederation Building
PO Box 8700
St. John's, NL A1B 4J6

Minister, Innovation, Business, & Rural Development; Minister Responsible, Rural Secretariat, & the Research & Development Corporation, Hon. Keith Hutchings
Constituency: Ferryland *No. of Constituents:* 8,693, Progressive Conservative
Tel: 709-729-1390
Toll-free: 800-634-5504
Fax: 709-729-2463
keithhutchings@gov.nl.ca
www.ibrd.gov.nl.ca
Innovation, Business, & Rural Development, Confederation Building
PO Box 8700
St. John's, NL A1B 4J6

Minister, Education, Hon. Clyde Jackman
Constituency: Burin — Placentia West *No. of Constituents:* 7,591, Progressive Conservative
Tel: 709-729-5040
Toll-free: 800-423-3301
Fax: 709-729-0414
clydejackman@gov.nl.ca
www.ed.gov.nl.ca/edu
Other Communications: District Phone: 709-891-5607
West Block, Confederation Building, 3rd Fl.
PO Box 8700
St.John's, NL A1B 4J6

Minister, Child, Youth, & Family Services; Minister Responsible for the Status of Women, Hon. Charlene Johnson
Constituency: Trinity — Bay De Verde *No. of Constituents:* 6,947, Progressive Conservative
Tel: 709-729-0173
Toll-free: 800-809-0106
Fax: 709-729-1049
charlenejohnson@gov.nl.ca
www.gov.nl.ca/cyfs/department/minister.html
Other Communications: District Phone: 709-729-2543
Main Office
95 Elizabeth Ave.
PO Box 8700
St. John's, NL A1B 4J6

Opposition House Leader, Yvonne Jones
Constituency: Cartwright — L'Anse au Clair *No. of Constituents:* 3,142, Liberal
Tel: 709-729-6925
Toll-free: 800-286-9118
Fax: 709-729-5202
yvonnejones@gov.nl.ca
Other Communications: District Phone: 709-729-6925, Fax: 709-729-5202
Opposition Office, East Block, ConfederationBuilding, 3rd Fl.
PO Box 8700
St. John's, NL A1B 4J6

Eddie Joyce
Constituency: Bay of Islands *No. of Constituents:* 7,725, Liberal
Tel: 709-634-7883
Fax: 709-634-7885
ejoyce@gov.nl.ca
www.eddiejoyce.com
District Office, Fortis Tower
#203, 4 Herald Ave., 2nd Fl.
PO Box 2006
Corner Brook, NL A2H 6J8

Minister, Natural Resources; Minister Responsible for the Foresetry & Agrifoods Agency; Government House Leader, Hon. Jerome Kennedy, Q.C.
Constituency: Carbonear — Harbour Grace *No. of Constituents:* 9,272, Progressive Conservative
Tel: 709-729-2920
Toll-free: 877-998-9933
Fax: 709-729-0059
jeromekennedy@gov.nl.ca
www.nr.gov.nl.ca/nr
Other Communications: District Phone: 709-576-8051
District Office
27 Goff Ave.
Carbonear, NL A1Y 1A6

Deputy Chair of Committees, Steve Kent
Constituency: Mount Pearl North *No. of Constituents:* 9,865, Progressive Conservative
Tel: 709-729-1526
Fax: 709-364-1639
stevekent@gov.nl.ca
www.stevekent.ca

Social Media: twitter.com/stephenkent, www.facebook.com/stevekentpc, ca.linkedin.com/in/stephenpkent
House of Assembly Office, West Block, Confederation Building, 5th Fl.
PO Box 8700
St. John's, NL A1B 4J6

Minister, Fisheries & Aquaculture; Deputy Government House Leader, Hon. Darin T. King, Ph.D
Constituency: Grand Bank *No. of Constituents:* 6,921, Progressive Conservative
Tel: 709-729-3705
Toll-free: 877-997-9933
Fax: 709-729-0360
darinking@gov.nl.ca
www.darinking.ca; www.fishaq.gov.nl.ca
Other Communications: District Phone: 709-832-2531; Fax: 709-832-2534
District Office
26 Water St.
PO Box 400
Grand Bank, NL A0E 1W0

Dale Kirby
Constituency: St. John's North *No. of Constituents:* 9,048, NDP
Tel: 709-729-6921
Fax: 709-576-1443
dalekirby@gov.nl.ca
www.dalekirby.com
Main Office, East Block, Confederation Building
PO Box 8700
St. John's, NL A1B 4J6

Paul Lane
Constituency: Mount Pearl South *No. of Constituents:* 8,154, Progressive Conservative
Tel: 709-729-2231
Fax: 709-729-1503
paullane@gov.nl.ca
www.paullanenl.ca
Social Media: twitter.com/paullanenl, www.facebook.com/PaulLaneNL
Main Office, East Block, Confederation Building, 5th Fl.
PO Box 8700
St. John's, NL A1B 4J6

Glenn Little
Constituency: Bonavista South *No. of Constituents:* 6,823, Progressive Conservative
Tel: 709-468-2132
Toll-free: 800-600-4875
Fax: 709-468-2134
glenlittle@gov.nl.ca
Other Communications: District Assistant, Phone: 709-468-2132
District Office
134 Confederation Dr.
Bonavista, NL A0C 1B0

Glenn Littlejohn
Constituency: Port DeGrave *No. of Constituents:* 9,002, Progressive Conservative
Tel: 709-786-1372
Fax: 709-786-1380
glittlejohn@gov.nl.ca
www.votelittlejohn.ca
Social Media: twitter.com/GlennLittlejohn
District Office, Bay Roberts Dental Clinic Building
400 Conception Bay Hwy.
PO Box 960
Bay Roberts, NL A0A 1G0

Minister, Finance; President, Treasury Board; Minister Responsible for the Public Service Secretariat, Public Service Commission, & the Newfoundland & Labrador Liquor Corporation, Hon. Thomas W. Marshall, Q.C.
Constituency: HumberEast *No. of Constituents:* 8,780, Progressive Conservative
Tel: 709-729-2858
Fax: 709-729-2232
tommarshall@gov.nl.ca
www.fin.gov.nl.ca/fin
Other Communications: District Phone: 709-637-2061; Fax: 709-637-4133
Social Media: twitter.com/tommarshall_he
District Office
Sir Richard Squires Building, 4th Fl.
PO Box 2006
Corner Brook, NL A2H 6J8

Minister, Intergovernmental & Aboriginal Affairs; Minister Responsible for Labrador Affairs & Voluntary & Non-ProfitSector, Hon. Nick McGrath
Constituency: Labrador West *No. of Constituents:* 6,702, Progressive Conservative
Tel: 709-729-1066
Fax: 709-729-1425
nickmcgrath@gov.nl.ca
www.exec.gov.nl.ca/exec/igas
Confederation Building
PO Box 8700
St. John's, NL A1B 4J6

Leader of the Third Party, Lorraine Michael
Constituency: Signal Hill— Quidi Vidi *No. of Constituents:* 8,366, NDP
Tel: 709-729-0270
Fax: 709-576-1443
lorrainemichael@gov.nl.ca
Social Media: twitter.com/lorrainemichael, www.facebook.com/LorraineMichaelNDP
East Block, Confederation Building, 3rd Fl.
PO Box 8700
St. John's, NL A1B 4J6

Christopher Mitchelmore
Constituency: The Straits — White Bay North *No. of Constituents:* 6,847, NDP
Tel: 709-454-2633
Toll-free: 888-729-6091
Fax: 709-454-2652
cmitchelmore@gov.nl.ca
Other Communications: District Assistant, Phone: 709-454-2646
District Office, Public Building
270 West St.
PO Box 620
St.Anthony, NL A0K 4S0

George Murphy
Constituency: St. John's East *No. of Constituents:* 8,322, NDP
Tel: 709-729-3651
Fax: 709-576-1443
georgemurphy@gov.nl.ca
Other Communications: District Assistant, Phone: 709-729-3651
Main Office, East Block, Confederation Building, 3rd Fl. North
PO Box 8700
St. John's, NL A1B 4J6

Minister, Municipal Affairs; Minister Responsible for Fire & Emergency Services - NL, & Registrar General, Hon. Kevin O'Brien
Constituency: Gander *No. of Constituents:* 9,284, Progressive Conservative
Tel: 709-729-3046
Toll-free: 800-813-6850
Fax: 709-729-0943
kevinobrien@gov.nl.ca
www.ma.gov.nl.ca/ma
Other Communications: District Phone:709-256-3729; Fax: 709-256-1410
Social Media: ca.linkedin.com/pub/kevin-o-brien/43/b6/b45
District Office
PO Box 2222
Gander, NL A1V 2N9

Tom Osborne
Constituency: St. John's South *No. of Constituents:* 8,076, Independent
Tel: 709-729-4882
tosborne@gov.nl.ca
Note: On September 13, 2012, TomOsborne announced that he will sit as an Independent Member.
Main Office, East Block, Confederation Building, 3rd Fl.
St. John's, NL A1B 4J6

Deputy Opposition House Leader, Andrew Parsons
Constituency: Burgeo — La Poile *No. of Constituents:* 7,576, Liberal
Tel: 709-695-3585
Toll-free: 800-518-9479
Fax: 709-695-5800
andrewparsons@gov.nl.ca
Other Communications: District Assistant, Phone: 709-695-3585
District Office
52 Main St.
PO Box 2263
Channel-Port aux Basques, NL A0M 1C0

Kevin Parsons
Constituency: Cape St. Francis *No. of Constituents:* 10,676, Progressive Conservative
Tel: 709-729-6979
Fax: 709-729-5774
kevinparsons@gov.nl.ca
Other Communications: District Assistant, E-mail: Barbaracaddigan@gov.nl.ca
Social Media: twitter.com/kevinparsonspc, ca.linkedin.com/pub/kevin-parsons/43/100/280
Main Office, East Block, Confederation Building
PO Box 8700
St. John's, NL A1B 4J6

Calvin Peach
Constituency: Bellevue *No. of Constituents:* 7,649, Progressive Conservative
Tel: 709-729-1546
Toll-free: 888-458-4440
Fax: 709-729-1503
calvinpeach@gov.nl.ca
Main Office, East Block, Confederation Building
PO Box 8700
St. John's, NL A1B 4J6

Tracy Perry
Constituency: Fortune Bay-Cape La Hune *No. of Constituents:* 6,091, Progressive Conservative
Tel: 709-538-3112
Toll-free: 888-538-3112
Fax: 709-538-3079
traceyperry@gov.nl.ca
District Office
101 Main St.
PO Box 429
St. Alban's, NL A0H 2E0

Kevin Pollard
Constituency: Baie Verte-Springdale *No. of Constituents:* 8,107, Progressive Conservative
Tel: 709-729-0371
Toll-free: 800-598-1806
Fax: 709-727-1503
kevinpollard@gov.nl.ca
Other Communications: District Phone: 709-532-2243; Fax: 709-532-2239
District Office, BVPEDA Building
319 Hwy. #410
PO Box 128
BaieVerte, NL A0K 1B0

Gerry Rogers
Constituency: St. John's Centre *No. of Constituents:* 7,940, NDP
Tel: 709-729-2638
Fax: 709-576-1443
gerryrogers@gov.nl.ca
Main Office, East Block, Confederation Building, 3rd Fl.
PO Box 8700
St. John's, NL A1B 4J6

Keith Russell
Constituency: Lake Melville *No. of Constituents:* 6,710, Progressive Conservative
Tel: 709-896-7975
Fax: 709-896-7977
keithrussell@gov.nl.ca
District Office
21 Broomfield St.
PO Box 2532 B Sta.
Happy Valley-Goose Bay, NL A0P 1E0

Minister, Health & Community Services; Minister Responsible for Aging & Senior, & Francophone Affairs, Hon. Susan Sullivan
Constituency: Grand Falls-Windsor — Buchans *No. of Constituents:* 7,549, Progressive Conservative
Tel: 709-489-3409
Toll-free: 888-610-4440
Fax: 709-489-5480
susansullivan@gov.nl.ca
www.health.gov.nl.ca/health
Social Media: ca.linkedin.com/pub/susan-sullivan/43/339/687
MainOffice, Health & Community Services, West Block, Confederation Building
PO Box 8700
St. John's, NL A1B 4J6

Deputy Speaker of the House of Assembly; Chair of Committees, Wade Verge
Constituency: Lewisporte *No. of Constituents:* 7,759, Progressive Conservative
Tel: 709-729-3399
Toll-free: 877-585-0515
Fax: 709-729-1082
wadeverge@gov.nl.ca
Other Communications: District Phone: 709-535-2131; Fax: 709-535-2138
DistrictOffice
PO Box 248
Lewisporte, A0G 3A0

Speaker of the House of Assembly, Ross Wiseman
Constituency: Trinity North *No. of Constituents:* 8,419, Progressive Conservative
Tel: 709-729-3404
Toll-free: 800-514-9073
Fax: 709-729-4820
rosswiseman@gov.nl.ca
Other Communications: District Phone: 709-466-4165; Fax: 709-466-4178
District Office
#208, 86 ManitobaDr.
Clarenville, NL A5A 1K7

Newfoundland & Labrador Government Departments & Agencies

Newfoundland & Labrador Department of Advanced Education & Skills

Confederation Building, West Block, 3rd Fl., PO Box 8700, St. John's, NL A1B 4J6

Tel: 709-729-2480
aesweb@gov.nl.ca
www.aes.gov.nl.ca
Other Communication: Communications, Phone: 709-729-0753; Employment Supports & Services, Toll-Free: 1-800-563-6600

To meet the needs of a growing economy, Newfoundland & Labrador's Department of Advanced Education & Skills works to ensure that the province has highly educated graduates & skilled workers.

The department focuses upon the following tasks: assisting youth in the development of leadership skills; helping employers by providing access to needed workers; assisting people to find employment; improving the inclusion of persons with disabilities in society; supporting communities to attract & welcome immigrants; supporting persons during disasters; providing financial support for people with little or no income; & reducing poverty.

Income & financial services are available at the following locations: Avalon Region (1-877-729-7888); Central Region (1-888-632-4555); Labrador Region (1-888-773-9311); & Western Region (1-866-417-4753)

Acts Administered:
Apprenticeship & Certification Act
College Act
Degree Granting Act
Emergency Services Act
Income & Employment Support Act & Regulations
Memorial University Act
Memorial University Foundation Act
Memorial University Pensions Act
Private Training Institutions Act & Regulations
Student Financial Assistance Act
Support Orders Enforcement Act

Minister, Advanced Educaton & Skills; Minister Responsible for the Status of Persons with Disabilities & for YouthEngagement, Hon. Joan Burke
Tel: 709-729-3580
Toll-free: 866-838-5620
Fax: 709-729-6996
Joanburke@gov.nl.ca

Deputy Minister, Advanced Education & Skills, Rose Baxter
Tel: 709-729-3582
Fax: 709-729-6996
brose@gov.nl.ca

Assistant Deputy Minister, responsible for Labour Market Recruitment, Bill Duggan
Tel: 709-729-1334
bduggan@gov.nl.ca

Assistant Deputy Minister, Regional Operations, Roxie Wheaton
Tel: 709-729-2320
roxiewheaton@gov.nl.ca

Associated Agencies, Boards & Commissions:

• Income & Employment Support Appeal Board
Confederation Bldg.
PO Box 8700
St. John's, NL A1B 4J6
Tel: 709-729-2479
Fax: 709-729-5139

• Labour Relations Board
Beothuck Bldg.
20 Crosbie Pl., 5th Fl.
PO Box 8700
St. John's, NL A1B 4J6
Tel: 709-729-2707
Fax: 709-729-5738
lrb@gov.nl.ca
www.hrle.gov.nl.ca/lrb

• Standing Fish Price Setting Panel
Beothuck Bldg.
20 Crosbie Pl., 3rd Fl.
PO Box 8700
St. John's, NL A1B 4J6
Tel: 709-729-2711
Fax: 709-729-5905

Advanced Studies Branch
c/o Department of Advanced Education & Skills, PO Box 8700, St. John's, NL A1B 4J6

The Advanced Studies Branch consists of the following divisions: Apprenticeship & Trade Certification; Student Financial Services; Student Loan Corporation of Newfoundland & Labrador; Adult Learning & Literacy; Skills Development; & Institutional Services.

The following are some services provided by the branch: providing student financial assistance; regulating private training institutions; administering Red Seal examinations; developing curriculum for adult basic education, & apprenticeship training; registering apprentices; & analyzing post-secondary data.

Assistant Deputy Minister, Advanced Studies, Bruce Belbin
Tel: 709-729-3026
Fax: 709-729-2828
BruceBelbin@gov.nl.ca

Corporate Services Branch
c/o Department of Advanced Education & Skills, PO Box 8700, St. John's, NL A1B 4J6

The Corporate Services Branch handles policy planning & evaluation, human resources, information technology services, & financial operations for the provincial office & regions.

Assistant Deputy Minister, Corporate Services, Dave Lewis
Tel: 709-729-3594
davidlewis@gov.nl.ca

Manager, Finance & General Operations, Angela Piercey
Tel: 709-729-6918
angelapiercey@gov.nl.ca

Manager, Research & Evaluation, Jon Waterhouse
Tel: 709-729-4904
Fax: 709-729-5560
jonwaterhouse@gov.nl.ca

Income, Employment, & Youth Services Branch
c/o Department of Advanced Education & Skills, PO Box 8700, St. John's, NL A1B 4J6

Tel: 709-729-5151
Other Communication: Poverty Reduction Strategy, E-mail: povertyreduction@gov.nl.ca

The Income, Employment, & Youth Services Branch consists of the following divisions: Career, Employment, & Youth Services; Income Support; & Poverty Reduction. Services provided by the branch include the Support During Disasters Program & the Support Application Social Worker Program.

Assistant Deputy Minister, Income, Employment, & Youth Services, Marilyn Field
Tel: 709-729-5151
marilynfield@gov.nl.ca

Director, Income Support, Donna O'Brien
Tel: 709-729-2665
Fax: 709-729-5139
donnaobrien@gov.nl.ca

Specialist, Program & Policy Development, Poverty Reduction Strategy, Amanda Hannaford
Tel: 709-729-1382
amandahannaford@gov.nl.ca

Labour Market Development & Client Services Branch
c/o Department of Advanced Education & Skills, PO Box 8700, St. John's, NL A1B 4J6

Other Communication: Labour Market & Career Information: Toll-Free Hotline: 1-800-563-6600, Web Site: www.lmiworks.nl.ca

Services of the branch include the following: distributing labour market information across the province; providing income support plus career & youth services programs; supporting the development of labour market policies & initiatives; & developing services for communities to support displaced fish plant workers.

Senior Director, Labour Market Services, Pamela Toope
Tel: 709-729-6516
pamtoope@gov.nl.ca

Director, Workforce Adjustment, Dominic Gerard
Tel: 709-729-5190
Fax: 709-729-1129
GerardDominic@gov.nl.ca

Director, Labour Market Development, Walt Mavin
Tel: 709-729-0939
waltmavin@gov.nl.ca

Senior Manager, Client Services, Daphne Bavis
Tel: 709-729-1042
Fax: 709-729-5712

Senior Manager, Labour Market Partnerships, Sean Hanrahan
Tel: 709-729-1045
Fax: 709-729-5712

Manager, Labour Market Research & Analysis, Stephen Dale
Tel: 709-729-5670
Fax: 709-729-1129
StephenDale@gov.nl.ca

Manager, Employer Services, LoreLei Roberts-Loder
Tel: 709-729-1324
Fax: 709-729-5712
LRobertsLoder@gov.nl.ca

Manager, Try the Trades, Mike Rose
Tel: 709-729-6553
Fax: 709-729-5712
MikeRose@gov.nl.ca

Manager, Youth Retention & Attraction Strategy, Rhonda Tulk-Lane
Tel: 709-729-0426
Fax: 709-729-1129
RhondaTulk-Lane@gov.nl.ca

Office of Immigration & Multiculturalism (OIM)
c/o Department of Advanced Education & Skills, PO Box 8700, St. John's, NL A1B 4J6

Tel: 709-729-6607
Fax: 709-729-7381
Toll-Free: 888-632-4555
immigration@gov.nl.ca
www.nlimmigration.ca
TTY: 877-292-4205
Other Communication: Provincial Nominee Program, E-mail: pnp@gov.nl.ca

The Office of Immigration & Multiculturalism is engaged in the implementation of the Provincial Immigration Strategy, which involves attracting & retaining immigrants to Newfoundland & Labrador.

Executive Director, Office of Immigration & Multiculturalism, Nellie Burke
Tel: 709-729-6967
Fax: 709-729-7381
nellieburke@gov.nl.ca

Director, Joshi Smita
Tel: 709-729-7140
Fax: 709-729-7381
smitajoshi@gov.nl.ca

Specialist, Provincial Nominee Program, Julia Greenwood-Meyers
Tel: 709-729-0129
Fax: 709-729-7381
juliameyers@gov.nl.ca

Specialist, Policy & Program Development, Kamrul Islam
Tel: 709-729-1332
Fax: 709-729-7381
kamrulislam@gov.nl.ca

Specialist, Senior Provincial Nominee Program, MaryAnn Scanlon
Tel: 709-729-7730
Fax: 709-729-7381
MaryAnnScanlon@gov.nl.ca

Specialist, Immigration, Portal, & Multiculturalism, Jamie Valvasori
Tel: 709-729-7200
Fax: 709-729-7381
JamieValvasori@gov.nl.ca

Office of the Auditor General

PO Box 8700, St. John's, NL A1B 4J6

Tel: 709-729-2695
Fax: 709-729-5970
oagmail@oag.nl.ca
www.ag.gov.nl.ca

The Auditor General's fundamental role is to bring an independent audit and reporting process to bear upon the manner in which Government and its various entities discharge their responsibilities, report on their planned programs and their use of public resources.

Newfoundland & Labrador Department of Child, Youth & Family Services

PO Box 8700, St. John's, NL A1B 4J6

Tel: 709-729-0760
www.gov.nl.ca/cyfs
Other Communication: Adoption Services Phone: 709-752-4406; Youth Corrections Program: 709-729-2794

Acts Administered:
Adoption Act
Child Care Services Act
Children & Youth Care & Protection Act
Young Persons Offences Act
Youth Criminal Justice Act

Minister, Hon. Charlene Johnson
Tel: 709-729-0173
charlenejohnson@gov.nl.ca

Deputy Minister, Sheree MacDonald
Tel: 709-729-0583
smacdonald@gov.nl.ca

Assistant Deputy Minister, Policy & Program, Lori Ann Companion
Tel: 709-729-0088
loriannecompanion@gov.nl.ca

Assistant Deputy Minister, Corporate Services, Genevieve Dooling
Tel: 709-729-0656
gdooling@gov.nl.ca

Assistant Deputy Minister, Services Delivery & Regional Operations, Genevieve Dooling
Tel: 709-729-0656
gdooling@gov.nl.ca

Director, Communications, Michelle Hunt
Tel: 709-729-5148
michellehunt@gov.nl.ca

Newfoundland & Labrador Department of Education

West Block, Confederation Bldg., 100 Prince Philip Dr., 3rd Fl., PO Box 8700, St. John's, NL A1B 4J6
Tel: 709-729-5097
Fax: 709-729-5896
education@gov.nl.ca
www.ed.gov.nl.ca

Responsible for the K-12 & post-secondary school system, literacy & library services; comprises four executive branches: Primary, Elementary & Secondary Education, Corporate Services Branch; Post-Secondary Branch; International Education & Planning Branch; Literacy School Services; reporting to the department through their various boards are the Provincial Information & Library Resources Board, the Literacy Development Council, 4 geographical school boards & a Francophone school board. In October 2011, a separate Department called Advanced Education & Skills was created by Premier Kathy Dunderdale.

Acts Administered:
Apprenticeship & Certification Act
College Act
Degree Granting Act
Memorial University Act
Memorial University Foundation Act
Memorial University Pensions Act
Private Training Institutions Act
Public Libraries Act
School Boards' Association Act
Schools Act, 1997
Student Financial Assistance Act
Teacher Training Act
Teachers' Association Act

Minister, Hon. Clyde Jackman
Tel: 709-729-5040
Toll-free: 866-838-5620
Fax: 709-729-0414
clydejackman@gov.nl.ca

Acting Assistant Deputy Minister, Infrastructure, Ingrid E. Clarke
Tel: 709-729-2496

Assistant Deputy Minister, Corporate Services, Ramona Cole
Tel: 709-729-3025
ramonacole@gov.nl.ca

Assistant Deputy Minister, Primary, Elementary & Secondary Education, Janet Vivian-Walsh
Tel: 709-729-5720
janetvivianwalsh@gov.nl.ca

Director, Communications, Heather May
Tel: 709-729-0048
heathermay@gov.nl.ca

Associated Agencies, Boards & Commissions:
• Provincial Information & Library Resources Board
48 St. George's Ave
Stephenville, NL A2H 1K9
Tel: 709-643-0900
Fax: 709-643-0925
www.nlpl.ca
To establish & operate those public libraries in the province that it considers necessary & provide support to ensure that library materials, information & programs are available to meet the needs of the public.

Advanced Studies Branch
Assistant Deputy Minister, Bruce Belbin
Tel: 709-729-3026
brucebelbin@gov.nl.ca
Director, Adult Learning & Literacy, Candice Ennis-Williams
Tel: 709-729-1738
candiceennis-williams@gov.nl.ca
Director, Institutional & Industrial Education, Cliff Mercer
Tel: 709-729-2350
cliffordmercer@gov.nl.ca
Director, Student Loan Corporation of Newfoundland & Labrador, Julie Moore
Tel: 709-729-6465
juliemoore@gov.nl.ca
Director, Student Financial Services, David Pike
Tel: 709-729-3576
davidpike@gov.nl.ca

Corporate Services Branch
Assistant Deputy Minister, Ramona Cole
Tel: 709-729-3025
rcole@gov.nl.ca
Acting Assistant Deputy Minister, Infrastructure, Ingrid Clarke
Tel: 709-729-3025
ingridclarke@gov.nl.ca
Director, Information Management & Special Projects, Brian Evans
Tel: 709-729-1841
brianevans@gov.nl.ca
Director, Financial Services, Don Stapleton
Tel: 709-729-0837
Fax: 709-729-1330
donjstapleton@gov.nl.ca
Director, Policy, Planning & Accountability, Renee Williams
Tel: 709-729-7425
reneewilliams@gov.nl.ca

Primary, Elementary & Secondary Education
Assistant Deputy Minister, Janet Vivian-Walsh
Tel: 709-729-5720
Fax: 709-729-0987
janetvivianwalsh@gov.nl.ca
Director, Program Development, Bradley Clarke
Tel: 709-729-3004
bradclarke@gov.nl.ca
Director, Student Support Services, Dan Goodyear
Tel: 709-729-3023
dangoodyear@gov.nl.ca
Director, School Services, Bob Gardiner
Tel: 709-729-3034
obgardiner@gov.nl.ca
Director, Early Childhood Learning, Paula Hennessey
Tel: 709-729-5128
paulahennessey@gov.nl.ca
Director, Centre for Distance Learning & Innovation, Jim Tuff
Tel: 709-729-7614
Toll-free: 866-836-3559
jimtuff@gov.nl.ca
Director, Evaluation & Research Division, Ron Smith
Tel: 709-729-3000
ronsmith@gov.nl.ca

Office of the Chief Electoral Officer

39 Hallett Cr., St. John's, NL A1B 4C4
Tel: 709-729-0712
Fax: 709-729-0679
Toll-Free: 877-729-7987
enl@gov.nl.ca
www.gov.nl.ca/elections

Chief Electoral Officer, Victor Powers
Tel: 702-729-6068
vpowers@gov.nl.ca

Assistant Chief Electoral Officer & Director, Election Finance, Bruce Chaulk
Tel: 709-729-4116
brucechaulk@gov.nl.ca

Director, Elections Operations & Special Ballot Administrator, Isabel Collins
Tel: 709-729-0713
icollins@gov.nl.ca

Newfoundland & Labrador Department of Environment & Conservation

Confederation Bldg., West Block, 4th Fl., PO Box 8700, St. John's, NL A1B 4J6
Tel: 709-729-2664
Fax: 709-729-6639
Toll-Free: 800-563-6181
info@gov.nl.ca
www.env.gov.nl.ca

To protect, conserve & enhance the Province's environment through the management of water resources, the environmental assessment of undertakings & the control & management of substances & activities that may pollute the environment. The Department is actively working towards reducing the number of landfill sites & implementing the Provincial Waste Management Strategy.The strategy will divert 50 percent of materials from landfill sites, phase out municipal solid waste incinerators by 2008 & prohibit such facilities from being built in the future.

Acts Administered:
Air Pollution Control Regulations, 2004
Dangerous Goods Transportation Act
Endangered Species Act
Environmental Assesment Act, 2000
Environmental Assessment Regulations, 2003
Environmental Control Water & Sewage Regulations
Environmental Protection Act
Gasoline Volatility Control Regulations, 2003
Geographical Names Board Act
Halocarbon Regulations
Heating Oil Storage Tank System Regulations
Land Surveyors Act
Lands Act
National Park Lands Act
Notices of Protected Water Supplies, Watershed Areas, Wellhead Protected Water Supplies
Ozone Depleting Substances Regulations, 2003
Pesticides Control Regulations, 2003
Provincial Parks Act
Species Status Advisory Committee Regulations
Storage & Handling of Gasoline & Associated Products Regulations, 2003
Storage of PCB Waste Regulations, 2003
Used Oil Control Regulations
Waste Management Regulations, 2003
Waste Material Disposal Areas Regulations
Water Power Rental Regulations, 2003
Water Resources Act
Well Drilling Regulations, 2003
Wild Life Act
Wild Life Park Order
Wild Life Park Regulations
Wild Life Regulations
Wild Life Reserve Regulations
Wilderness & Ecological Reserves Act

Minister, Hon. Terry French
Tel: 709-729-2577
Fax: 709-729-0112
terryfrench@gov.nl.ca

Minister, Hon. Terry French
Tel: 709-729-2577
Fax: 709-729-0112
terryfrench@gov.nl.ca

Deputy Minister, Bill Parrott
Tel: 709-729-2572
Fax: 709-729-0112
wparrott@gov.nl.ca

Director, Communications, Melony O'Neil
Tel: 709-729-2575
Fax: 709-729-1930
moneill@gov.nl.ca

Director, Policy & Planning, John Drover
Tel: 709-729-1090
Fax: 709-729-5818
jdrover@gov.nl.ca

Associated Agencies, Boards & Commissions:
• Multi-Materials Stewardship Board (MMSB)
PO Box 8131 A
St. John's, NL A1B 3M9
Tel: 709-753-0948
Fax: 709-753-0974
Toll-free: 800-901-6672
inquiries@mmsb.nl.ca
www.mmsb.nf.ca

Environment Branch
Other Communication: Spill Reporting (24 hours): 709-772-2083; Environmental Assessment: 1-800-563-6181
Assistant Deputy Minister, Martin Goebel
Tel: 709-729-2559
Fax: 709-729-7413
mgoebel@gov.nl.ca
Director, Environmental Assessment Division, Bas Cleary
Tel: 709-729-0673
Fax: 709-729-5518
clearyb@gov.nl.ca
Director, Policy & Planning, John Drover, P. Eng
Tel: 709-729-1090
Fax: 709-729-5818
jdrover@gov.nl.ca
Director, Water Resources, Hassen Khan
Tel: 709-729-2535
Fax: 709-729-0320
hkhan@gov.nl.ca
Director, Pollution Prevention, Derrick Maddocks
Tel: 709-729-5782
Fax: 709-729-6969
dmaddocks@gov.nl.ca
Manager, Environmental Science & Monitoring, Peter Haring
Tel: 709-729-4147
Fax: 709-729-6969
pharing@gov.nl.ca
Manager, Petroleum Storage & Management, John Dutton
Tel: 709-729-2561

Fax: 709-729-6969
jdutton@gov.nl.ca
Acting Manager, Industrial Compliance, Dexter Pittman
Tel: 709-729-6771
Fax: 709-729-6969
dpittman@gov.nl.ca
Manager, Industrial Projects, Dan Michielsen
Tel: 709-729-6697
Fax: 709-729-6969
michielsend@gov.nl.ca
Manager, Pesticide Control, Karen Linfield
Tel: 709-729-3395
Fax: 709-729-6969
karenlinfield@gov.nl.ca
Manager, Waste Management, Craig Bugden
Tel: 709-729-0483
Fax: 709-729-6969
cbugden@gov.nl.ca

Lands Branch
Director, Surveys & Mapping Division, Allan Chafe
Tel: 709-729-0602
achafe@gov.nl.ca
Director, Lands Management Division, Reginald Garland
Tel: 709-729-3844
rgarland@gov.nl.ca
Director, Crown Lands Administration Division, Peter Howe
Tel: 709-729-3174
phowe@gov.nl.ca

Natural Heritage
Assistant Deputy Minister, Ross Firth
Tel: 709-637-2135
Fax: 709-637-2180
rossfirth@gov.nl.ca
Director, Wildlife Division, John Blake
Tel: 709-637-2008
Fax: 709-637-2180
johnblake@gov.nl.ca
Director, Parks & Natural Areas, Sian French
Tel: 709-637-4520
Fax: 709-635-4541
sianfrench@gov.nl.ca

Sustainable Development & Strategic Science Branch
Executive Director, Policy & Legislation, Shane P. Mahoney
Tel: 709-729-2542
Fax: 709-729-7677
shanemahoney@gov.nl.ca
Director, Science, Monitoring & Data Synthesis, Rob Otto
Tel: 709-637-6200 ext: 639
Fax: 709-639-7591
rotto@gov.nl.ca

Newfoundland & Labrador Department of Finance

Confederation Bldg., PO Box 8700, St. John's, NL A1B 4J6
Tel: 709-729-6165
Fax: 709-729-2070
finance@gov.nl.ca
www.fin.gov.nl.ca

Acts Administered:
Crown Guarantee & Loan Act
Crown Royalties Act
Department of Finance Act
Financial Administration Act
Government Money Purchase Pension Plan Act
Government-Corner Brook Pump & Paper Limited Agreements Act
Income Tax Act
Industrial Development Corporation Act
Labour-Sponsored Venture Capital Tax Credit Act
Liquor Corporation Act
Loan & Guarantee Act, 1957
Loan Act
Local Authority Guarantee Act, 2005
Lotteries Act
Medication Association Agreement Act
Members of the House of Assembly Retiring Allowances Act
Municipal Financing Corporation Act
Offshore Area Corporate Income Tax Act
Pension Contributions Reduction Act
Pensions Funding Act
Portability of Pensions Act
Provincial Court Judges' Pension Plan Act
Public Service Pensions Act, 1991
Revenue Administration Act
School Tax Authorities Winding Up Act
Service Charges Act
Statistics Agency Act
Stock Savings Tax Credit Act
Supply Act
Tax Agreement Act
Taxation of Utilities & Cable Television Companies Act
Teachers' Pensions Act
Tobacco Tax Act
Uniformed Services Pensions Act
Venture Capital Act
War Service Pensions Act

Minister & President, Treasury Board, Hon. Tom Marshall, Q.C.
Tel: 709-729-3775
Fax: 709-729-2232
financeminister@gov.nl.ca; tommarshall@gov.nl.ca

Deputy Minister, Terry Paddon
Tel: 709-729-2946
tpaddon@gov.nl.ca

Comptroller General, Finance, Ron Williams
Tel: 709-729-4866
rwilliams@gov.nl.ca

Director, Communications, Luke Joyce
Tel: 709-729-6830
Fax: 709-729-2232
lukejoyce@gov.nl.ca

Director, Policy, Planning, Accountability & Information Management, K. Gail Boland
Tel: 709-729-2950
Fax: 709-729-2070
gailboland@gov.nl.ca

Director, Policy Support, Norman Wally
Tel: 709-729-2907
Fax: 709-729-2070
wnorman@gov.nl.ca

Associated Agencies, Boards & Commissions:
• C.A. Pippy Park Commission
Mount Scio House
15 Mount Scio Rd.
St. John's, NL A1B 3T2
Tel: 709-737-3655
Fax: 709-737-3303
info@pippypark.com
www.pippypark.com
C.A. Pippy Park was established by an Act of the Newfoundland Legislature in 1968. The Act created the C.A. Pippy Park Commission, a semi-autonomous Crown Corporation under the laws of the Province of Newfoundland & Labrador. The Commission currently reports to the Minister of Finance.
• Newfoundland & Labrador Municipal Financing Corporation (NMFC)
Confederation Bldg.
PO Box 8700
St. John's, NL A1B 4J6
Tel: 709-729-6686
Fax: 709-729-2095
Newfoundland & Labrador Municipal Financing Corporation is a Crown Corporation established to consolidate the long-term borrowing programs of all municipalities in one central agency.
• Newfoundland & Labrador Liquor Corporation
90 Kenmount Rd.
PO Box 8750 A
St. John's, NL A1B 3V1
Tel: 709-724-1100
Fax: 709-754-0321
info@nfliquor.com
www.nfliquor.com
The Newfoundland Labrador Liquor Corporation (NLC) is a provincial crown corporation responsible for managing the importation, sale & distribution of beverage alcohol within the province.

Economics & Statistics
Assistant Deputy Minister, Alton Hollett
Tel: 709-729-3255
ahollett@gov.nl.ca
Director, Economic Research & Analysis, Rod Forsey
Tel: 709-729-0864
rforsey@gov.nl.ca
Director, Newfoundland & Labrador Statistics Agency, Robert Reid
Tel: 709-729-0158
Fax: 709-729-0393
robertr@gov.nl.ca

Financial Planning & Benefits Administration
Assistant Deputy Minister, Laurie Skinner
Tel: 709-729-4039
laurieskinner@gov.nl.ca
Director, Insurance, James Doody
Tel: 709-729-7471
jamesdoody@gov.nl.ca
Director, Budgeting, Glenn Grandy
Tel: 709-729-1054
Fax: 709-729-2156
glenngrandy@gov.nl.ca
Director, Pensions Administration, Maureen McCarthy
Tel: 709-729-5983
Fax: 709-729-6790
mccarthym@gov.nl.ca

Office of the Comptroller General
Comptroller General, Ronald Williams, C.A.
Tel: 709-729-5926
Fax: 709-729-7627
rwilliams@gov.nl.ca
Director, Government Accounting, Ann Marie Miller, C.M.A.
Tel: 709-729-2341
Fax: 709-729-7627
millera@gov.nl.ca
Director, Professional Services & Internal Audit, David Hill
Tel: 709-729-0702
Fax: 709-729-7144
davehill@gov.nl.ca
Director, Financial Systems Control, David Drover
Tel: 709-729-6530
Fax: 709-729-2098
droverd@gov.nl.ca
Director, Corporate Services, Denise Hanrahan
Tel: 709-729-1414
Fax: 709-729-0670
hanrahand@gov.nl.ca
Director, Compensation and Benefits, Byron Mercer
Tel: 709-729-6368
Fax: 709-729-6395
byronmercer@gov.nl.ca

Taxation & Fiscal Policy Branch
Assistant Deputy Minister, Bob Constantine
Tel: 709-729-2944
rconstantine@gov.nl.ca
Director, Fiscal Policy, Chris Butt
Tel: 709-729-6714
cbutt@gov.nl.ca
Director, Tax Policy, Jay Griffin
Tel: 709-729-6847
jgriffin@gov.nl.ca
Director, Project Analysis, Brian Hurley
Tel: 709-729-3664
bhurley@gov.nl.ca
Director, Debt Management, Paul Myrden
Tel: 709-729-6848
Director, Tax Administration, Cathy M. Whalen
Tel: 709-729-6307
Fax: 709-729-2277
cathywhalen@gov.nl.ca

Newfoundland & Labrador Department of Fisheries & Aquaculture

Petten Bldg., 30 Strawberry Marsh Rd., PO Box 8700, St. John's, NL A1B 4J6
Tel: 709-729-3723
Fax: 709-729-6082
fisheries@gov.nl.ca
www.fishaq.gov.nl.ca
Other Communication: Aquaculture Phone: 709-292-4100; Fax: 709-292-4113; Email: aquaculture@gov.nl.ca
Contributes to economic & community growth in the province by encouraging sustainable growth & development of the harvesting, processing, & distribution sectors; includes providing support for the marketing of fish & aquaculture products produced in Newfoundland & Labrador for domestic & export markets. Responsible for: setting & enforcing standards for the processing & sale of fish products in the province; licensing fish processing establishments; undertaking developmental initiatives in the harvesting, processing, & marketing sectors of the fishing industry; developing, promoting & licensing of aquaculture facilities; developing & maintaining strategic fisheries infrastructure; articulating policies & providing advice for the management & development of fisheries & aquaculture; providing statistical information.
Acts Administered:
Aquaculture Act
Fish Inspection Act
Fish Processing Licensing Board Act
Fisheries Act
Fishing Industry Collective Bargaining Act
Professional Fish Harvesters Act

Minister, Hon. Darin King
Tel: 709-729-3705
Fax: 709-729-0360
DarinKingMHA@gov.nl.ca

Deputy Minister, Alastair O'Rielly
Tel: 709-729-3707
Fax: 790-729-4219
aorielly@gov.nl.ca

Director, Communications, Jason Card

Tel: 709-729-3733
jasoncard@gov.nl.ca

Manager, Finance & Budgeting, Barry Aylward
Tel: 709-729-4764
Fax: 709-729-2092
baylward@gov.nl.ca

Associated Agencies, Boards & Commissions:
• Fish Processing Licensing Board
c/o Fish Processing Licensing Board Secretariat
30 Strawberry Marsh Rd.
St. John's, NL A1B 4J6
fplbsecretariat@gov.nl.ca
• Professional Fish Harvesters Certification Board (PFHCB)
368 Hamilton Ave.
PO Box 8541
St. John's, NL A1B 3P2
Tel: 709-722-8170
Fax: 709-722-8201
pfh@pfhcb.com
www.pfhcb.com

Aquaculture Branch
Fax: 709-729-0360
The Branch is responsible for licensing & aquaculture development.
Assistant Deputy Minister, Brian Meaney
Tel: 709-729-3710
Fax: 709-729-1882
bmeaney@gov.nl.ca
Director & Provincial Aquaculture Veterinarian, Dr. Daryl Whelan
Tel: 709-729-6872
Fax: 709-729-1882
darylswhelan@gov.nl.ca

Fisheries Branch
Fax: 709-729-6082
Assistant Deputy Minister, Shawn Robinson
Tel: 709-729-3723
Fax: 709-729-6082
Director, Licensing & Quality Assurance, Ian Burford
Tel: 709-729-3736
Fax: 709-729-5995
iburford@gov.nl.ca
Director, Innovation & Development, Mark Rumboldt
Tel: 709-729-3749
Fax: 709-729-1884
mrumboldt@gov.nl.ca
Director, Compliance & Enforcement, Milly Meaney
Tel: 709-729-3717
Fax: 709-729-1881
mmeaney@gov.nl.ca

Marketing & Development Branch
This branch is responsible for promoting & supporting the diversification & development of the harvesting, processing, & marketing sectors of the seafood industry through public & private sector partnerships.
Executive Director, Marketing Development & Renewal, Mike Warren
Tel: 709-729-3708
Fax: 709-729-6082
mikewarren@gov.nl.ca
Director, Seafood Marketing & Support Services, Pat McDonald
Tel: 709-729-3390
Fax: 709-729-1884
pmcdonald@gov.nl.ca
Market Development Supervisor, Sean Barry
Tel: 709-729-0634
Fax: 709-729-1884
seanbarry@gov.nl.ca

Policy Development & Planning Branch
Provides policy & program planning services to the Department. Through the Sustainable Fisheries & Oceans Policy Division participates in oceans policy & governance issues, in addition to the resource assessment & management process of the federal Department of Fisheries & Oceans, including local, national, & international bodies responsible for fisheries conservation & management.
Assistant Deputy Minister, David Lewis
Tel: 709-729-3713
Fax: 709-729-0360
davidlewis@gov.nl.ca
Director, Sustainable Fisheries & Oceans Policy, Tom Dooley
Tel: 709-729-0335
Fax: 709-729-6082
Director, Fishing Industry Renewal & Adjustment, Paul Martin
Tel: 709-729-1073
Fax: 709-729-6082
pdmartin@gov.nl.ca
Director, Planning Services, Wandalee Wiseman
Tel: 709-729-3765
Fax: 709-729-6082
wandaleewiseman@gov.nl.ca

Avalon & Eastern
Tel: 709-832-2860
Fax: 709-832-1669
Regional Director, Rex Matthews
Tel: 709-832-2860
Fax: 709-832-1669
rmatthews@gov.nl.ca
Northern
Tel: 709-896-3412
Fax: 709-896-3483
Regional Director, Craig Taylor
Tel: 709-896-3412
Fax: 709-896-3483
craigtaylor@gov.nl.ca
Western/Central
Tel: 709-861-3537
Fax: 709-861-3556
Regional Director, Wilson Goosney
Tel: 709-861-3537
Fax: 709-637-2908

Newfoundland & Labrador Department of Health & Community Services (HCS)

West Block, Confederation Bldg., PO Box 8700, St. John's, NL A1B 4J6
Tel: 709-729-5021
Fax: 709-729-5824
healthinfo@gov.nl.ca
www.health.gov.nl.ca

Provides a leadership role in health & community service programs & policy development for the Province. This involves working in partnership with a number of key stakeholders including regional boards, community organizations, professional associations, post-secondary educational institutions, unions, consumer & other government departments.
Acts Administered:
Adoption Act
Adult Protection Act
Centre for Health Information Act
Child Care Services Act
Chiropractors Act, 2009
Communicable Diseases Act
Dental Act
Denturists Act
Dieticians Act
Dispensing Opticians Act
Emergency Medical Aid Act
Food & Drug Act
Health & Community Services Act
Health Care Association Act
Health Professions Act
Health Research Ethics Authority Act
Hearing Aid Practitioners
Hospital Insurance Agreement Act
Human Tissue Act
Licensed Practical Nurses Act
Massage Therapy Act
Medical Act, 2011
Medical Care Insurance Act, 1999
Mental Health Care & Treatment Act
Neglected Adults Welfare Act
Occupational Therapists Act
Optometry Act
Personal Health Information Act
Pharmaceutical Services Act
Pharmacy Act
Physiotherapy Act
Psychologists Act
Regional Health Authorities Act
Registered Nurses Act
Self-managed Home Support Services Act
Smoke-free Environment Act
Social Workers Act
Tobacco Control Act
Young Persons Offences Act
Youth Criminal Justice Act (Canada)

Minister, Hon. Susan Sullivan
Tel: 709-729-3124
Toll-free: 800-514-9073
Fax: 709-729-0121
SusanSullivan@gov.nl.ca

Deputy Minister, Bruce Cooper
Tel: 709-729-3125
Fax: 709-729-0121

Assistant Deputy Minister, Professional Services, Colleen Janes
Tel: 709-729-1716
Fax: 709-729-5218
cjanes@gov.nl.ca

Assistant Deputy Minister, Tracy King
Tel: 709-729-3103
Fax: 709-729-0121
tracyking@gov.nl.ca

Assistant Deputy Minister, Denise Tubrett
Tel: 709-729-0580
Fax: 709-729-0640
dtubrett@gov.nl.ca

Assistant Deputy Minister, Regional Health Operations, Tony Wakeham
Tel: 709-729-3127
tonywakeham@gov.nl.ca

Chief Nurse, Anita Ludlow
Tel: 709-729-2039
anitaludlow@gov.nl.ca

Director, Communications, Jennifer Tulk
Tel: 709-729-1377
Fax: 709-699-6524
jennifertulk@gov.nl.ca

Associated Agencies, Boards & Commissions:
• Newfoundland & Labrador Centre for Health Information
70 O'Leary Ave.
St. John's, NL A1B 2C7
Tel: 709-752-6000
Fax: 709-752-6011
• Newfoundland & Labrador Health Boards Associations
Beothuck Bldg.
20 Crosbie Pl., 2nd Fl.
St. John's, NL A1B 3Y8
Tel: 709-364-7701
Fax: 709-364-6460
www.nlhba.nl.ca

Corporate Services Branch
Director, Corporate Initiatives, Harry Hutchings
Tel: 709-729-0444
hhutchings@gov.nl.ca
Financial Manager, Financial Services, Pam Barnes
Tel: 709-729-5323
pbarnes@gov.nl.ca
Budgeting Manager, Financial Services, Linda Boland
Tel: 709-729-7956
Fax: 709-729-3151
lindaboland@gov.nl.ca
Senior Manager, Regional Health Authority - Audits, Sheree Snow
Tel: 709-729-4911
shereesnow@gov.nl.ca

Medical Services Division
Associate Deputy Minister, Dr. Cathi Bradbury
Tel: 709-729-1574
Fax: 709-729-0121
cathibradbury@gov.nl.ca
Provincial Director, Pathology and Laboratory Medicine, Beverly Carter
Tel: 709-729-7652
beverlycarter@gov.nl.ca
Director, Health Emergency Management, Dennis Davis
Tel: 709-729-3912
ddavis@gov.nl.ca
Program & Policy Development Specialist, Darlene Ricketts
Tel: 709-729-0719
Fax: 709-729-7778
darlenericketts@gov.nl.ca

Policy and Planning Branch
Acting Director, Policy and Program Evaluation Consultant, Linda Carter
Tel: 709-729-3117
Fax: 709-729-5824
lindacarter@gov.nl.ca
Director, Legislative and Regulatory Affairs, Reginald Coates
Tel: 709-729-3421
rcoates@gov.nl.ca
Director, Policy Development, Wanda Legge
Tel: 709-729-5249
wlegge@gov.nl.ca
Director, Office of Aging and Seniors, Suzanne Brake
Tel: 709-729-4957
suzannebrake@gov.nl.ca
Director & Chief Nurse, Office of the Chief Nurse, Anita Ludlow
Tel: 709-729-2039
anitaludlow@gov.nl.ca

Public Health & Wellness Branch
Chief Medical Officer of Health, Public Health Division, Dr. Faith Stratton
Tel: 709-729-3430

Director, Health Emergency Management, Dennis Davis
Tel: 709-729-3912
Director, Environmental Public Health, Darryl Johnson
Tel: 709-729-3422
Fax: 709-729-0730
djohnson@gov.nl.ca
Director, Health Promotion & Wellness, Eleanor Swanson
Tel: 709-729-5023
Director, Disease Control, Cathy O'Keefe
Tel: 709-729-5019
Fax: 709-729-5824
cokeefe@gov.nl.ca

Newfoundland & Labrador Housing Corporation (NLHC)

Sir Brian Dunfield Bldg., 2 Canada Dr., PO Box 220, St. John's, NL A1C 5J2
Tel: 709-724-3000
Fax: 709-724-3250
www.nlhc.nl.ca

Minister Responsible, Hon. Thomas J. Hedderson
Tel: 709-729-3679
Fax: 709-729-4285
thedderson@gov.nl.ca

Chair & Chief Executive Officer, Len Simms
Tel: 709-724-3054
lensimms@nlhc.nl.ca

Manager, Communications, Jenny Bowring
Tel: 709-724-3055
jmbowring@nlhc.nl.ca

Corporate Secretary, Janette Loveless
Tel: 709-724-3067
Fax: 709-724-3250
jmloveless@nlhc.nl.ca

Newfoundland & Labrador Human Rights Commission

PO Box 8700, St. John's, NL A1B 4J6
Tel: 709-729-2709
Fax: 709-729-0790
Toll-Free: 800-563-5808
humanrights@mail.gov.nl.ca
www.justice.gov.nl.ca/hrc

Vice Chair, Stephanie Newell, Q.C.

Newfoundland & Labrador Hydro

Hydro Place, Columbus Dr., PO Box 12400, St. John's, NL A1B 4K7
Tel: 709-737-1400
Fax: 709-737-1800
hydro@nlh.nl.ca
www.nlh.nl.ca

Crown corporation, owned by the Province of Newfoundland & Labrador. Hydro generates, transmits & distributes electrical power & energy to utility, residential & industrial customers throughout the province. Hydro is the parent company of the Hydro Group of Companies (Hydro Group), comprising Newfoundland & Labrador Hydro, Churchill Falls (Labrador) Corporation Limited (CF(L)Co), Lower Churchill Development Corporation Limited (LCDC), Gull Island Power Company Limited (GIPCo), & Twin Falls Power Corporation Limited (TwinCo). The Hydro Group's installed generating capacity is the fourth largest of all utility companies in Canada, consisting of ten hydroelectric plants, including the Churchill Falls hydraulic plant, which is the largest underground powerhouse in the world with a rated capacity of 5,428 megawatts (MW) of power, one oil-fired plant, four gas turbines & 26 diesel plants.

President & Chief Executive Officer, Ed Martin

Vice-President, Finance & Chief Financial Officer, Derrick Sturge

Vice-President, Human Resources & Organzational Effectiveness, Gerard McDonald

Vice-President, Regulated Operations, Jim Haynes

Churchill Falls (Labrador) Corporation Limited
Hydro Place, 500 Columbus Dr., PO Box 12500, St. John's, NL A1B 4K7
Tel: 709-737-1859
Fax: 709-737-1816
Churchill Falls (Labrador) Corporation operates a hydroelectric generating plant & transmission facilities.
President & Chief Executive Officer, Ed Martin
Vice-President, Finance & Chief Financial Officer, Derrick Sturge

Gull Island Power Co. Ltd.
President & Chief Executive Officer, Ed Martin
Vice-President, Regulated Operations, Jim Haynes
Vice-President, Finance & Chief Financial Officer, Derrick Sturge

Lower Churchill Development Corporation Ltd.
Member, Board of Directors, Jim Haynes
Vice-President, Finance & Chief Financial Officer, Derrick Sturge

Twin Falls Power Corporation
PO Box 12500, St. John's, NL A1B 3T5
Twin Falls Power Corporation has developed a hydroelectric generating plant on the Unknown River in Labrador. The plant has been inoperative since 1974.
President, James R. Haynes
Vice-President, Finance & Chief Financial Officer, Derrick Sturge

Newfoundland & Labrador Department of Innovation, Business, & Rural Development

Confederation Bldg., West Block, PO Box 8700, St. John's, NL A1B 4J6
Tel: 709-729-7000
Fax: 709-729-0654
intrd@gov.nl.ca
www.intrd.gov.nl.ca

The Department was created in 2004 to reflect the enhanced empasis placed on the innovation aspect of the provincial economic agenda. It is the lead agency for economic development in the province & in each of its regions.
Acts Administered:
Business Investment Corporation Act
Economic Diversification and Growth Enterprises Act
Research Council Act
Research and Development Council Act

Minister, Hon. Keith Hutchings
Tel: 709-729-4728
Fax: 709-729-0654
keithhutchings@gov.nl.ca

Deputy Minister, Brent Meade
Tel: 709-729-4731
Fax: 709-729-0654
bmeade@gov.nl.ca

Director, Communications, Scott Barfoot
Tel: 709-729-4570
Fax: 709-729-5124
scottbarfoot@gov.nl.ca

Director, Ireland Business Partnerships (IBP), Diane Hooper
Tel: 709-729-1684
Fax: 709-729-7234

Director, Policy & Strategic Planning, Sheila Fudge
Tel: 709-729-7019
Fax: 709-729-5124
sfudge@gov.nl.ca

Director, The Strategic Partnership, Derek Staubitzer
Tel: 709-729-7043
Fax: 709-729-7135
dstaubit@gov.nl.ca

Innovation
Assistant Deputy Minister, Jackie Collins
Tel: 709-729-7102
Fax: 709-729-7234
jackiecollins@gov.nl.ca
Director, Innovation, Research & Technology, Sharon Tiller
Tel: 709-729-7068
stiller@gov.nl.ca
Director, Information Management, Ruth Parsons
Tel: 709-729-1940
Fax: 709-729-5124
ruthparsons@gov.nl.ca

Regional Development
Assistant Deputy Minister, Rita Malone
Tel: 709-637-2977
Fax: 709-639-7713
rmalone@gov.nl.ca
Director, Regional Economic Development, John Wickham
Tel: 709-729-7260
Fax: 709-729-5124
jwickham@gov.nl.ca
Avalon
28 Pippy Place, St. John's, NL A1B 3X4
Fax: 709-729-7135
Acting Regional Director, Jim Antsey
Tel: 709-729-7124
Fax: 709-729-7135
jkantsey@gov.nl.ca
Central
McCurdy Complex, Markham Place, PO Box 2222, Gander, NL A1V 2N9
Fax: 709-256-1490
Regional Director, Percy Farwell
Tel: 709-256-1483
pfarwell@gov.nl.ca
Eastern
211B Memorial Drive, Clarenville, NL A5A 1R3
Fax: 709-466-1306
Acting Regional Director, Denis Sullivan
Tel: 709-466-4171
Fax: 709-466-1306
sullivan@gov.nl.ca
Labrador
2 Hillcrest Rd., PO Box 3014 B, Happy Valley-Goose Bay, NL A0P 1E0
Tel: 709-896-2400
Fax: 709-896-0234
Regional Director, Reg Kean
Tel: 709-896-0306
rkean@gov.nl.ca
Western
PO Box 2006, Corner Brook, NL A2H 6J8
Fax: 709-639-7713
Acting Regional Director, John Davis
Tel: 709-637-2981
jdavis@gov.nl.ca

Strategic Industries & Business Development Branch
Assistant Deputy Minister, Peter W. Au
Tel: 709-729-4711
Fax: 709-729-4858
peterau@gov.nl.ca
Director, Strategic Industries Development, Kirk Tilley
Tel: 709-729-7080
Fax: 709-729-5124
ktilley@gov.nl.ca
Acting Director, Business Analysis, Ken Thompson
Tel: 709-729-5622
Fax: 709-729-5124
kthompson@gov.nl.ca

Trade & Export Development Branch
Specializes in assisting provincial businesses develop an export plan to enter new markets, find export business partners & research national & international market opportunities.
Assistant Deputy Minister, Judith Hearn
Tel: 709-729-0882
Fax: 709-729-7234
judithhearn@gov.nl.ca
Director, Linda Spurrell
Tel: 709-729-7483
Fax: 709-729-5124
lspurrel@gov.nl.ca
Director, Strategic Partnership, Derek Staubitzer
Tel: 709-729-7043
Fax: 709-729-5124
derekstaubitzer@gov.nl.ca

Newfoundland & Labrador Department of Justice

Confederation Bldg., East Block, 4th Fl., PO Box 8700, St. John's, NL A1B 4J6
Tel: 709-729-2869
Fax: 709-729-0469
justice@gov.nl.ca
www.justice.gov.nl.ca

The Department of Justice ensures the impartial administration of justice & the protection of the public interest through the dual offices of the Attorney General & Minister of Justice.
Acts Administered:
Access to Information & Protection of Privacy Act
Adult Corrections Act
Advance Health Care Directives Act
Age of Majority Act
Agreement for Policing the Province Act
Apology Act
Apportionment Act
Arbitration Act
Bankers' Books Act
Blind Persons' Rights Act
Canada & United Kingdom Reciprocal Recognition & Enforcement of Judgments Act
Chattels Real Act
Children's Law Act (jointly with Government Services & Lands)
Commissioners for Oaths Act
Contributory Negligence Act
Correctional Services Act
Corrections & Conditional Release Act (Canada)
Court Security Act, 2010
Criminal Code
Defamation Act

Detention of Intoxicated Persons Act
Electoral Boundaries Act
Enduring Powers of Attorney Act
Enforcement of Canadian Judgments Act
Evidence Act
Exhumation Act
Family Law Act
Family Relief Act
Family Violence Protection Act
Fatal Accidents Act
Fatalities Investigations Act
Federal Courts Jurisdiction Act
Fraudulent Conveyances Act (jointly with Government Services & Lands)
Frustrated Contracts Act
Gunshot & Stab Wound Reporting Act
Human Rights Act, 2010
Interjurisdictional Support Orders Act
International Commercial Arbitration Act
International Interests in Mobile Aircraft Equipment Act
International Sale of Goods Act
International Trusts Act
Interpretation Act
Interprovincial Subpoena Act
Intestate Succession Act
Judgment Enforcement Act
Judgment Interest Act
Judicature Act
Jury Act, 1991
Justices & Public Authorities Protection Act
Justices Act
Law Society Act, 1999
Leaseholds in St. John's Act
Legal Aid Act
Limitations Act
Lobbyist Registration Act
Mentally Disabled Persons' Estates Act
Notaries Public Act
Oaths Act
Oaths of Office Act
Partnership Act
Petty Trespass Act
Presumption of Death Act
Prisons & Reformatories Act (Canada)
Prisons Act
Privacy Act
Proceedings Against the Crown Act
Proof of Death Members of Armed Forces Act
Provincial Court Act, 1991
Provincial Offences Act
Public Inquiries Act
Public Investigations Evidence Act
Public Trustee Act, 2009
Public Utilities Acquisition of Lands Act
Public Utilities Act
Queen's Counsel Act
Quieting of Titles Act
Reciprocal Enforcement of Judgments Act
Recording of Evidence Act
Revised Statutes, 1990 Act
Royal Newfoundland Constabulary Act, 1992
Safer Communities & Neighbourhoods Act
Settlement of International Investment Disputes Act
Sheriff's Act, 1991
Small Claims Act
Statutes & Subordinate Legislation Act
Statutes Act
Statutes Amendment Act, 1992
Support Orders Enforcement Act (jointly with Social Services)
Survival of Actions Act
Survivorship Act
Tobacco Health Care Costs Recovery Act
Victims of Crime Services Act
Wills Act
Youth Criminal Justice Act (Canada) & Young Persons Offences Act (jointly with Social Services)

Minister & Attorney General, Hon. Felix Collins
Tel: 709-729-2869
Fax: 709-729-0469
felixcollins@gov.nl.ca

Deputy Minister, Donald Burrage, Q.C.
Tel: 709-729-2872
Fax: 709-729-0469
donburrage@gov.nl.ca

Assistant Deputy Minister, Donna Ballard, Q.C.
Tel: 709-729-0288
Fax: 709-729-2129
dballard@gov.nl.ca

Executive Director, Human Rights Commission, Carey Majid
Tel: 709-729-2709
careymajid@gov.nl.ca

Director, Quality Management & Support Services, Dan Chafe
Tel: 709-729-1078
Fax: 709-729-5100

Director, Communications, Vanessa Colman-Sadd
Tel: 709-729-6985
Fax: 709-729-0469
vanessacolmansadd@gov.nl.ca

Director, Legal Information Services, Sean Dawe
Tel: 709-729-2861
Fax: 709-729-1370
seand@gov.nl.ca
Health Sciences Complex
300 Prince Philip Dr.
St. John's, NL A1B 3V6 Canada

Director, Policy & Strategic Planning, Jackie Lake-Kavanagh
Tel: 709-729-0543
Fax: 709-729-3949
jackiekavanagh@gov.nl.ca

Director, Fines Administration, Susan Roberts
Tel: 709-729-0250
Fax: 709-729-0595

Director, Court Services, Pamela Ryder-Lahey
Tel: 709-729-2081
Fax: 709-729-2161

Associated Agencies, Boards & Commissions:
• Human Rights Commission
• Newfoundland & Labrador Board of Commissioners of Public Utilities
• Newfoundland & Labrador Legal Aid Commission
#300, 251 Empire Ave.
PO Box 399 C
St. John's, NL A1C 5J9
Tel: 709-753-7863
Fax: 709-753-6226
Toll-free: 800-563-9911
nlac@legalaid.nl.ca
The Legal Aid Commission ensures that persons with limited financial means have access to legal counsel.
• Royal Newfoundland Constabulary Public Complaints Commission
Bally Rou Place
#E-160, 280 Torbay Rd.
St. John's, NL A1A 3W8
Tel: 709-729-0950
Fax: 709-729-1302
rncomplaintscommission@gov.nl.ca
www.justice.gov.nl.ca/rncpcc
The Royal Newfoundland Constabulary Public Complaints Commission is an independent review authority established under Statute to hear & investigate complaints against members of the Royal Newfoundland Constabulary &, when appropriate, to conduct public hearings in respect of particular complaints.

Courts & Legal Services
Assistant Deputy Minister, Donna Ballard
Tel: 709-729-0288
Fax: 709-729-2129
dballard@gov.nl.ca
Director, Legal Information Services, Sean Dawe
Tel: 709-729-2861
Fax: 709-729-1370
seand@gov.nl.ca

Public Prosecutions Division
Assistant Deputy Minister & Director, Pamela Goulding, Q.C.
Tel: 709-729-2868
Fax: 709-729-2129
pamelagoulding@gov.nl.ca
Assistant Director, Molloy Donovan
Tel: 709-729-1179
Fax: 709-729-2129
donovanmolloy@gov.nl.ca
Manager, Administrative Support, Lily Pittman
Tel: 709-729-0509
Fax: 709-729-0716
lilyp@gov.nl.ca

Public Safety & Enforcement
Assistant Deputy Minister, Paul Noble
Tel: 709-729-7357
Fax: 709-729-2129
pauln@gov.nl.ca
Superintendent, Prisons, Graham Rogerson
Tel: 709-729-2978
Fax: 709-729-4312
grahamrogerson@gov.nl.ca
Chief, Royal Newfoundland Constabulary, R.P. Johnston
Tel: 709-729-8155

Senior Legislative Counsel
Assistant Deputy Minister & Chief Legislative Counsel, Kimberly Hawley-George
Tel: 709-729-4766
Fax: 709-729-2129
kimhawle@gov.nl.ca

Strategic and Corporate Services
Assistant Deputy Minister, Heather Jacobs
Tel: 709-729-2880
Fax: 709-729-2129
heatherj@gov.nl.ca
Director, Strategic Human Resource Management, Wanda Penney
Tel: 709-729-4256
wandapenney@gov.nl.ca
Director, Policy and Strategic Planning, Jackie Lake Kavanagh
Tel: 709-729-0284
Fax: 709-729-3949
jackkiekavanagh@gov.nl.ca
Commissioner for the Lobbyist Registration Act, Finance and General Operations, LeeAnn Montgomery
Tel: 709-729-2918
leeannmontgomery@gov.nl.ca
Manager, Integrated Disability, Bonnie Abbott
Tel: 709-729-0274
Fax: 709-729-6344
bonnieabbott@gov.nl.ca

Newfoundland & Labrador Department of Municipal Affairs

West Block, Main Fl., Confederation Bldg., PO Box 8700, St. John's, NL A1B 4J6
Tel: 709-729-3046
Fax: 709-729-0943
mainfo@gov.nl.ca
www.ma.gov.nl.ca

Works with municipalities to ensure communities are properly managed & planned to ensure residents have a high standard of living in a clean, healthy & safe environment. The department is responsible for community-related activities such as the Office of the Fire Commissioner, the Emergency Measures Organization, Engineering & Land Use Planning.

Acts Administered:
Assessment Act, 2006
Avian Emblem Act
Building Standards Act
City of Corner Brook Act
City of Mount Pearl Act
City of St. John's Act
City of St. John's Municipal Taxation Act
Coat of Arms Act
Commemoration Day Act
Crown Corporations Local Taxation Act
Emergency Services Act
Evacuated Communities Act
Family Homes Expropriation Act
Fire Prevention Act, 1991
Fire Protection Services Act
Firefighters' Protection Act
Floral Emblem Act
Housing Act
Labrador Act
Mineral Emblem Act
Municipal Affairs Act
Municipal Authorities Amendment Act, 1991
Municipal Elections Act
Municipalities Act, 1999
Provincial Anthem Act
Provincial Flag Act
Remembrance Day Act
St. John's Centennial Foundation Act
St. John's Municipal Council Parks Act
Standard Time Act
Taxation of Utilities & Cable Television Companies Act
Urban & Rural Planning Act, 2000

Minister, Hon. Kevin O'Brien
Tel: 709-729-3046
Fax: 709-729-0943
kevinobrien@gov.nl.ca

Deputy Minister, Sandra Barnes
Tel: 709-729-3049
Fax: 709-729-0943
sbarnes@gov.nl.ca

Director, Communications, Ken Morrissey
Tel: 709-729-1983

Fax: 709-729-0943
kenmorrissey@gov.nl.ca

Associated Agencies, Boards & Commissions:

• Burin Peninsula Waste Management Corporation
PO Box 510
Burin Bay Arm, NL A0E 1G0
Tel: 709-891-1717
Fax: 709-891-1727
info@burinpenwaste.com
burinpenwaste.com

• Eastern Waste Management Commission
#200, 120 Lemarchant Rd.
St. John's, NL A1C 2H2
Tel: 709-579-7960
Fax: 709-579-5392
info@easternwaste.ca
easternwaste.ca

• Fire & Emergency Services
25 Hallett Cres.
PO Box 8700
St. John's, NL A1B 4J6
Tel: 709-729-1608
Fax: 709-729-2524
www.gov.nl.ca/fes/
Other Communication: Emergency Management: 709-729-3703 (Tel.), 709-729-3757 (Fax)

• Green Bay Waste Authority
PO Box 116
South Brook, NL A0J 1S0
Tel: 709-657-2233
Fax: 709-657-2133
Toll-free: 877-657-2233
info@greenbaywaste.com
greenbaywaste.com

• Northern Peninsula Regional Service Board
PO Box 130
St. Anthony, NL
Tel: 709-454-3110
Fax: 709-454-3818
nprsb@nf.aibn.com
norpenwaste.com

Assistant Deputy Minister, Rick Healey
Tel: 709-729-3016
Fax: 709-729-0943
rhealey@gov.nl.ca

Director, Financial & General Operations, Scott Jones
Tel: 709-729-5292
Fax: 709-729-5535
scottjones@gov.nl.ca

Director, Keith Mullett
Tel: 709-729-6766
Fax: 709-729-2019
kmullett@gov.nl.ca

Assistant Deputy Minister, Cluney Mercer
Tel: 709-729-3051
Fax: 709-729-0477
mercerc@gov.nl.ca

Director, Randy Dillon
Tel: 709-729-5328
rdillon@gov.nl.ca

Director, Waste Management, Cory Grandy
Tel: 709-729-7482
corygrandy@gov.nl.ca

Assistant Deputy Minister, Paul C. Smith
Tel: 709-729-3066
Fax: 709-729-4475
smithp@gov.nl.ca

Director, Local Governance, Chad M. Blundon
Tel: 709-729-5519
Fax: 709-729-4475
chadbludon@gov.nl.ca

Director, Eastern & Central Regional Office, Dan Noseworthy
Tel: 709-729-0259
Fax: 709-729-0477
dannoseworthy@gov.nl.ca

Director, Municipal Finance, Paul Tucker
Tel: 709-729-5381
Fax: 709-729-5535
ptucker@gov.nl.ca

Director, Regional Cooperation, Keith Warren
Tel: 709-729-5928
Fax: 709-729-0477
kwarren@gov.nl.ca

Manager, Western & Labrador Regional Office, Dan Hynes
Tel: 709-637-2332
Fax: 709-637-2548
dhynes@gov.nl.ca

Manager, Eastern Regional Office, Lori Evoy
Tel: 709-729-5020
Fax: 709-779-0477
lorievoy@gov.nl.ca

Manager, Labrador Regional Office, Bob MacAulay
Tel: 709-896-2941
Fax: 709-896-8847
bmacaulay@gov.nl.ca

Newfoundland & Labrador Department of Natural Resources

Natural Resources Bldg., 50 Elizabeth Ave., 7th Fl., PO Box 8700, St. John's, NL A1B 4J6
Tel: 709-729-2920
Fax: 709-729-0059
www.nr.gov.nl.ca

Responsible for the management of the province's mineral, energy, land, forest & wildlife resources in a manner that will ensure optimum benefits for the people of the province.

Acts Administered:
Abitibi-Consolidated Inc. & Abitibi Partner Exemption Order, 2002
Abitibi-Consolidated Rights & Assets Act
Agricultural Products Marketing Board Appeal Regulations
Agricultural Products Marketing Board Order
Agrologists Act
Animal Health & Protection Act
Animal Protection Act
Assessment of Over-Marketing Regulations, 2009
Berry Regulations
Canada-Newfoundland & Labrador Atlantic Accord Implementation Newfoundland & Labrador Act
Canada-Newfoundland & Labrador Oil & Gas Spills & Debris Liability Newfoundland & Labrador Regulations
Chicken Farmers of Newfoundland & Labrador Licensing Regulations
Chicken Farmers of Newfoundland & Labrador Marketing Board Regulations
Chicken Farmers of Newfoundland & Labrador Quota Regulations
Churchill Falls (Labrador) Corporation Limited (Lease) Act, 1961
Consolidated Chicken Farmers of Newfoundland & Labrador Order
Control of Nurseries & Dealers in Nursery Stock Regulations
Copper-in-Concentrate Exemption Order, 2009
Corner Brook Pulp & Paper Limited Exemption Order
Crop Insurance Act
Cutting of Timber Regulations
Description of Lands Open for Staking in respect of which the Mineral Claims Recorder shall Issue only Map Staked Licenses Order
Designation of Inspectors Order
Directed Sale of Timber Regulations
Dog Act
Donation of Food Act (jointly with Department of Health & Community Services)
Egg Grading & Inspection Regulations
Egg Regulations
Egg Scheme, 2000
Electrical Power Control Act, 1994
Endangered Species Act (jointly with Department of Environment and Conservation)
Energy Corporation Act
Energy Corporation of Newfoundland & Labrador Water Rights Act
Farm Practices Protection Act
Farm Products Corporation Act
Food & Drug Act
Forest Fire Offence & Penalty Regulation
Forest Fire Regulations
Forest Fires Liability & Compensation Regulations
Forest Land Management & Taxation Regulations
Forest Management Districts Proclamation
Forest Protection Act
Forestry Act
Granite Canal Hydroelectric Project Exemption Order
Health & Community Services Act (jointly with Department of Health & Community Services)
Heritage Animals Act
Hydro Corporation Act, 2007
Labrador Hydro Project Exemption Order
Labrador Inuit Land Claims Agreement Act
Livestock Act
Livestock Health Act
Livestock Health Regulations
Livestock Insurance Act
Livestock Owners Compensation Order
Livestock Regulations
Lower Churchill Development Act
Meat Inspection Act
Meat Inspection Regulations
Milk Regulations, 1998
Milk Scheme, 1998
Mill Regulations
Mineral Act
Mineral Act Baie Verte Area Exemption Regulations
Mineral Holdings Impost Act
Mineral Holdings Impost Regulations
Mineral Regulations
Mining Act
Mining Regulations
Miscellaneous Financial Provisions Act, 1975
Motorized Snow Vehicles & All-Terrain Vehicles Act (jointly with Government Services)
Motorized Snow Vehicles & All-Terrain Vehicles Regulations
Natural Products Marketing Act
Newfoundland & Labrador Chicken Marketing Scheme
Newfoundland & Labrador Hydro-Abitibi Consolidated Inc. Exemption Order
Newfoundland & Labrador Hydro-Abitibi Consolidated Inc. Stephensville Operations Exemption Order
Newfoundland & Labrador Hydro-Corner Brook Pulp & Paper Limited Exemption Order
Newfoundland & Labrador Power Commission (Water Power) Act
Newfoundland Pony Designation Order
Nickel-in-Concentrate Exemption Order, 2009
Offshore Area Oil & Gas Operations Regulations
Offshore Area Petroleum Diving Newfoundland & Labrador Regulations
Oil Royalty Regulations
Petroleum & Natural Gas Act
Petroleum Drilling Regulations
Petroleum Regulations
Plant Protection Act
Plant Quarantine Regulations
Plebiscite Regulations
Port au Port Peninsula Petroleum & Natural Gas Development Area Order
Poultry & Poultry Products Act
Quarry Leases Rental Order
Quarry Materials Act, 1998
Quarry Materials Regulations
Revenue Administration Act
Royalty Regulations, 2003
Seed Potato Regulations
Small Scale Operations Regulations
Timber Royalty Regulations
Timber Scaling Regulations
Undeveloped Minerals Areas Act
Undeveloped Minerals Areas Order
Vegetable Grading Act
Veterinary Medical Act, 2004
Voisey's Bay Nickel Company Limited Matte Plant Exemption Order
Voisey's Bay Nickel Company Limited Primary Production Order
Water Management Regulations
Wilderness & Ecological Reserves Act (jointly with Environment and Conservation)

Minister, Hon. Jerome P. Kennedy
Tel: 709-729-2920
Fax: 709-729-0059
JeromeKennedy@gov.nl.ca

Deputy Minister, Diana Dalton
Tel: 709-729-2766
Fax: 709-729-0059
dianadalton@gov.nl.ca

Assistant Deputy Minister, Keith Deering
Tel: 709-729-2488
Fax: 709-637-2461
keithdeering@gov.nl.ca

Chief Executive Officer, Len Moores
Tel: 709-637-2627
lmoores@gov.nl.ca

Executive Director, Labrador, Paul Carter
Tel: 709-944-7940
paulcarter@gov.nl.ca

Director, Communications, Heather Maclean
Tel: 709-729-5282
Fax: 709-729-0059
heathermaclean@gov.nl.ca

Director, Strategic Planning & Policy Coordination, Tanya Noseworthy
Tel: 709-729-1466
tanyanoseworthy@gov.nl.ca

Director, Information Manangement, Renée Pendergast
Tel: 709-729-1651
reneependergast@gov.nl.ca

Associated Agencies, Boards & Commissions:

• Canada - Newfoundland & Labrador Offshore Petroleum Board (C-NLOPB)
TD Place
140 Water St., 5th Fl.
St. John's, NL A1C 6H6
Tel: 709-778-1400
Fax: 709-778-1473
information@cnlopb.nl.ca
www.cnlopb.nl.ca
Other Communication: Core Storage & Research Centre, Phone: 709-778-1500, E-mail: csrc@cnlopb.nl.na
Established in 1985, the Canada - Newfoundland & Labrador Offshore Petroleum Board applies the provisions of the *Atlantic Accord* & the *Atlantic Accord Implementation Acts.*
The Board regulates the oil & gas industrr for the Newfoundland & Labrador Offshore Area. Operator activity is overseen for legislative & regulatory compliance in the areas of environmental protection, resource management, offshore safety, & industrial benefits.
The role of the Canada - Newfoundland & Labrador Offshore Petroleum Board facilitates the exploration for & development of hydrocarbon resources.

Agrifoods Development
Provincial Agriculture Bldg., Brookfield Rd., PO Box 8700, St. John's, NL A1B 4J6
Tel: 709-729-6588
Fax: 709-729-2674
To contribute to economic & rural development throughout the province by promoting the continued development, expansion & diversification of competitive & sustainable primary & value-added agrifood businesses.
Assistant Deputy Minister, Keith Deering
Tel: 709-729-3787
Fax: 709-729-0973
keithdeering@gov.nl.ca
Director, Production & Market Development, Otto Goulding
Tel: 709-637-2047
Fax: 709-637-2591
ottogoulding@gov.nl.ca
Director, Production & Marketing Division, Dave Jennings
Tel: 709-637-2046
davejennings@gov.nl.ca
Director, Agriculture Business Development Division, Cindy MacDonald
Tel: 709-637-2077
Director, Land Resource Stewardship, Carey Richard
Tel: 709-637-2081
Fax: 709-637-2586
rcarey@gov.nl.ca
Director, Animal Health Division & Chief Veterinary Officer, Dr. Hugh Whitney
Tel: 709-729-6879
Fax: 709-729-0055
hughwhitney@gov.nl.ca

Energy Branch
Associate Deputy Minister, Charles Bown
Tel: 709-729-2349
Fax: 709-729-2871
cbown@gov.nl.ca
Assistant Deputy Minister, Petroleum Development, Wes Foote
Tel: 709-729-2206
Fax: 709-729-2508
wesfoote@gov.nl.ca
Assistant Deputy Minister, Royalties & Benefits, Vanessa Newhook
Tel: 709-729-1644
Fax: 709-729-2871
vnewhook@gov.nl.ca
Director, Regulatory Affairs, Fred Allen
Tel: 709-729-2778
fredallen@gov.nl.ca
Director, Energy Economics, Wayne Andrews
Tel: 709-729-5899
wayneandrews@gov.nl.ca
Director, Electricity & Alternative Energy, Dave Bazeley
Tel: 709-729-6760
Fax: 709-729-2508
dbazeley@gov.nl.ca
Director, Petroleum Engineering, Keith Hynes
Tel: 709-729-7188
Fax: 709-729-2508
keithhynes@gov.nl.ca
Director, Royalties & Benefits, Craig Martin
Tel: 709-729-0463
Fax: 709-729-2508
cmartin@gov.nl.ca
Director, Energy Policy, Rob McGrath
Tel: 709-729-1421
robmcgrath@gov.nl.ca
Director, Petroleum Geoscience, David Middleton
Tel: 709-729-1821
davidmiddleton@gov.nl.ca
Director, Electricity & Alternative Energy, Walter Parsons
Tel: 709-729-6760
Fax: 709-729-2508
walterparsons@gov.nl.ca
Director, Energy Policy, Paul Scott
Tel: 709-729-1406
Fax: 709-729-3374
paulscott@gov.nl.ca
Director, Marketing & Promotion, Darrell Spurrell
Tel: 709-729-0579
Fax: 709-729-4011
darrellspurrell@gov.nl.ca
Director, Industrial Benefits, Bryon Sparkes
Tel: 709-729-3906
Fax: 709-729-4011
bsparkes@gov.nl.ca

Forestry & Agrifoods Agency

Forestry Branch (Newfoundland Forest Service) (NFS)
Fortis Bldg., PO Box 2006, Corner Brook, NL A2H 6J8
Tel: 709-637-2349
Fax: 709-637-2403
Assistant Deputy Minister, James Evans
Tel: 709-637-2339
Fax: 709-637-2461
Director, Forest Engineering & Industry Services, Eric Young
Tel: 709-637-2350
Fax: 709-637-2403
emyoung@gov.nl.ca
Director, Forest Ecosystem Management, Ivan Downton
Tel: 709-634-2284
idownton@gov.nl.ca
Director, Legislation & Compliance, Hubert Smith
Tel: 709-637-2041
Fax: 709-637-2083
hubertsmith@gov.nl.ca

Forestry Services
Fortis Bldg., PO Box 2006, Corner Brook, NL A2H 6J8
Tel: 709-637-2284
Fax: 709-634-4378
Manages & conserves the Province's ecosystems, under the principles of sustainable development, using an ecologically based management philosophy, & sound environmental practices. This is achieved through the implementation of forest management programs, such as silviculture, access road construction, forest fire suppression, insect control, management planning, tree nursery operations, inventory, dealing with wildlife in residential areas, collisions or similar situations, & public relations. In addition the Department is responsible for issuing permits under various legislation as well as the enforcement of forestry & wildlife regulations in such areas as hunting & timber harvesting.

Mines Branch
Promotes & facilitates the sustainable development of the province's mineral & energy resources through its resource assessment, management & development activities for the overall benefit of the citizens of Newfoundland & Labrador.
Assistant Deputy Minister, David Liverman
Tel: 709-729-2768
Fax: 709-729-2871
dliverman@gov.nl.ca
Director, Mineral Lands Division, Kenneth Andrews
Tel: 709-729-6425
Fax: 709-729-6782
kenandrews@gov.nl.ca
Acting Director, Mineral Development, Alex Smith
Tel: 709-729-6379
Fax: 709-729-3493
Director, Geological Survey Division, Lawrence Dickson
Tel: 709-729-2453
Fax: 709-729-4270
wldickson@gov.nl.ca

Policy & Planning Division
Promotes & facilitates the sustainable development of the province's mineral & energy resources through its resource assessment, management & development activities for the overall benefit of the citizens of Newfoundland & Labrador.

Strategic Resource Development Division
Tel: 709-729-0651
Fax: 709-729-0973
Director, Ed O'Reilly
Tel: 709-729-1643
edoreilly@gov.nl.ca
Eastern
PO Box 2222, Gander, NL A1V 5T4
Tel: 709-256-1450
Fax: 709-256-1459
Regional Ecosystem Director, David Fong
Tel: 709-256-1451
Labrador
PO Box 3014 B, Happy Valley-Goose Bay, NL A0P 1E0
Tel: 709-896-3405
Other Communication: Fax: 709-896-3747 (Forestry); 896-0188 (Wildlife)
Regional Ecosystem Director, Carroll Colin
Tel: 709-896-9377
Fax: 709-896-3747
colincarroll@gov.nl.ca
Western
Massey Drive Bldg., PO Box 2006, Corner Brook, NL A2H 6J8
Tel: 709-637-2409
Fax: 709-639-1377
Regional Ecosystem Director, Perry Benoit
Tel: 709-637-2692

Newfoundland & Labrador Public Service Commission

2 Canada Dr., 3rd Fl., PO Box 8700, St. John's, NL A1B 4J6
Tel: 709-729-5810
Fax: 709-729-6234
www.gov.nl.ca/psc

Acts Administered:
Public Service Commission Act

Minister Responsible, Hon. Tom Marshall, Q.C.
Tel: 709-729-3775
Fax: 709-729-2232
tommarshall@gov.nl.ca

Chair & Chief Executive Officer, Ed Walsh
Tel: 709-729-2650
Fax: 709-729-3178
ewalsh@gov.nl.ca

Commissioner, Ann Chafe
Tel: 709-729-2659
Fax: 709-729-3178
annchafe@gov.nl.ca

Human Resources
Assistant Deputy Minister, Chantelle McDonald Newhook
Tel: 709-729-3106
cnewhook@gov.nl.ca
Acting Director, Strategic Initiatives, Jeff Butt
Tel: 709-729-2223
jeffkbutt@gov.nl.ca
Director, Policy & Planning, Marie Wells
Tel: 709-729-7350
mwells@gov.nl.ca

Labour Relations
Assistant Deputy Minister, Geoff Williams
Tel: 709-729-3559
Fax: 709-729-1746
geoffwilliams@gov.nl.ca
Executive Director, Employee Relations, Brian Miller
Tel: 709-729-1585
Fax: 709-729-6842
brianmiller@gov.nl.ca
Director, Organizational Management & Design, Tony Cuomo
Tel: 709-729-3387
Fax: 709-729-2156
tcuomo@gov.nl.ca
Director, Classification & Compensation, Terry Kennedy
Tel: 709-729-7284
Fax: 709-729-7455
kennedyt@gov.nl.ca

Newfoundland & Labrador Board of Commissioners of Public Utilities

PO Box 21040, St. John's, NL A1A 5B2
Tel: 709-726-8600
Fax: 709-726-9604
Toll-Free: 866-782-0006
ito@pub.nf.ca
www.pub.nf.ca
Regulates electrical utilities in Newfoundland & Labrador.
Acts Administered:
Access to Information & Protection of Privacy Act
Automobile Insurance Act
Electric Power Control Act
Expropriation Act
Hydro Corporation Act
Insurance Companies Act
Motor Carrier Act
Petroleum Products Act
Public Utilities Acquisition of Lands Act
Public Utilities Act

Chair & CEO, Andy Wells
Tel: 709-726-1133
awells@pub.nl.ca

Vice-Chair, Darlene Whalen
Tel: 709-726-0955
dwhalen@pub.nl.ca

Director, Corporate Services & Board Secretary, G. Cheryl Blundon
Tel: 709-726-8600
Fax: 709-726-9604
cblundon@pub.nl.ca

Director, Regulatory & Advisory Services, Robert Byrne
Tel: 709-726-0742
rbyrne@pub.nl.ca

Newfoundland & Labrador Research & Development Corporation (RDC)

187 Kenmount Rd., PO Box 13067 A, St. John's, NL A1B 3V8
Tel: 709-758-0913
Fax: 709-758-0927
info@researchnl.com
www.researchnl.com

The RDC is a provincial Crown corporation established in 2008 to improve Newfoundland & Labrador's research & development capabilities.

Minister Responsible, Hon. Keith Hutchings
Tel: 709-729-4728
Fax: 709-729-0654
keithhutchings@gov.nl.ca

Chair, Jackie Sheppard

Chief Executive Officer, Glenn Janes

Director, Business Development, Steve Mercer
Tel: 709-758-0984
stevemercer@researchnl.com

Manager, Marketing & Communications, Jeff Green
Tel: 709-758-0973
jeffsgreen@researchnl.com

Executive Assistant, Brenda Baird
Tel: 709-758-0912
Fax: 709-758-0927
brendabaird@researchnl.com

Newfoundland & Labrador Department of Service NL

PO Box 8700, St. John's, NL A1B 4J6
Tel: 709-729-4834
gsinfo@gov.nl.ca
www.servicenl.gov.nl.ca

Service NL provides a great range of services to the people of Newfoundland & Labrador. Areas of attention include public health, public safety, environmental protection, vital statistics, motor vehicles, printing services, provincially regulated financial institutions, the operation of Government Service Centres, consumer & commercial affairs, & occupational health & safety. The department works in accordance with more than 150 pieces of legislation, regulations, standards, & codes of practice.
Service NL operates as a single access point for the public to common government services, such as licencing, permitting, & inspecting. The department handles the following responsibilities: issuing birth, marriage, & death certificates; testing & issuing driver licenses; issuing vehicle registrations; mediating landlord & tenant issues; registering companies, deeds, & lobbyists; investigating workplace incidents; issuing charitable gaming licences; & protecting the interests of consumers.
Service NL strives to provide services with a staff of more than 500 people at over 30 locations throughout Newfoundland & Labrador.

Acts Administered:
Accident & Sickness Insurance Act
Adoption Act
Architects Act
Automobile Insurance Act
Building Standards Act
Buildings Accessibility Act
Business Electronic Filing Act
Certified General Accountants Act
Certified Management Accountants Act
Change of Name Act
Chartered Accountants Act
Child Care Services Act
Child, Youth, & Family Services Act
Children's Law Act
Co-operatives Act
Collections Act
Communicable Diseases Act
Condominium Act, 2009
Consumer Protection & Business Practices Act
Conveyancing Act
Corporations Act
Credit Union Act
Dangerous Goods Transportation Act
Electronic Commerce Act
Embalmers & Funeral Directors Act
Engineers & Geoscientists Act
Environmental Protection Act
Fire Insurance Act
Fire Prevention Act
Fisheries Act
Food & Drug Act
Fraudulent Conveyances Act
Health & Community Services Act
Highway Traffic Act
Income Tax Savings Plans Act
Insurance Adjusters, Agents, & Brokers Act
Insurance Companies Act
Insurance Contracts Act
Life Insurance Act
Limited Partnership Act
Lobbyist Registration Act
Marriage Act
Meat Inspection Act
Mechanics' Lien Act
Mortgage Brokers Act
Motor Carrier Act
Motorized Snow Vehicles & All-Terrain Vehicles Act
Occupational Health & Safety Act
Partnership Act
Pension Benefits Act, 1997
Pension Plans Designation of Beneficiaries Act
Perpetuities & Accumulations Act
Personal Property Security Act
Prepaid Funeral Services Act
Printing Services Act
Private Investigations & Security Services Act
Public Accountancy Act
Public Safety Act
Radiation Health & Safety Act
Real Estate Trading Act
Registration of Deeds Act, 2009
Residential Tenancies Act
Sale of Goods Act
Securities Act
Smoke-Free Environment Act
Solemnization of Marriage Act
Tobacco Control Act
Trustee Act
Urban & Rural Planning Act, 2000
Warehouser Receipts Act
Warehouser's Lien Act
Water Resources Act
Wildlife Act
Workplace Health, Safety, & Compensation Act
Works, Services, & Transportation Act

Minister, Service Newfoundland & Labrador; Minister Responsible for the Government Purchasing Agency, Office of the CIO, Workplace Health, Safety, & Compensation Committee, Hon. Paul Davis
Tel: 709-729-6670
Fax: 709-729-6244
padavis@gov.nl.ca

Deputy Minister, David Norman
Tel: 709-729-4752
Fax: 709-729-4754
davidnorman@gov.nl.ca

Director, Strategic Human Resource Management, Barbara Brenton
Tel: 709-729-5102
Fax: 709-729-6661
BarbaraBrenton@gov.nl.ca

Director, Policy & Strategic Planning, Elizabeth Day
Tel: 709-729-6470
Fax: 709-729-4754
elizabethday@gov.nl.ca

Director, Communications, Hugh Donnan
Tel: 709-729-4860
Fax: 709-729-4754
hughdonnan@gov.nl.ca

Director, Information Management, Susanna Duke
Tel: 709-729-2544
Fax: 709-729-4754
susannaduke@gov.nl.ca

Associated Agencies, Boards & Commissions:

• Credit Union Deposit Guarantee Corporation
PO Box 340
Marystown, NL A0E 2M0
Tel: 709-279-0170
Fax: 709-279-0177
Toll-free: 877-279-0170
www.cudgcnl.com
The Credit Union Deposit Guarantee Corporation is a provincial Crown corporation. The corporation administers the Credit Union Act & Regulations. The Credit Union Deposit Guarantee Corporation is responsible for ensuring compliance with the Credit Union Act & Regulations by credit unions, & insuring deposits of credit union members & associate members in Newfoundland & Labrador.

• Government Purchasing Agency
30 Strawberry Marsh Rd.
St. John's, NL A1B 4R4
Tel: 709-729-3348
Fax: 709-729-5817
tenders@gov.nl.ca
The Government Purchasing Agency is the Government of Newfoundland & Labrador's central procurement unit. The agency manages the procurement process for goods & services for all government departments. It administers the the Agreement on Internal Trade & the Atlantic Procurement Agreement.

Consumer & Commercial Affairs Branch

PO Box 8700, St. John's, NL A1B 4J6
Tel: 709-729-2570
Fax: 709-729-4151
gsinfo@gov.nl.ca
Other Communication: Commercial Registrations: 709-729-3317

The Consumer & Commercial Affairs Branch of Service NL carries out its functions through the Commercial Registrations Division, the Financial Services Regulation Division, & the Consumer Affairs Division.
The Commercial Registrations Division is involved in administering the registries of deeds, personal property, condominiums, mechanics liens, co-operatives, limited partnerships, companies, & lobbyists.
In the area of financial services, responsibilities include the regulation of industries such as the following: insurance, securities, real estate, mortgage broker, & pension. The Financial Services Regulation Division also administers the Consumer Protection Fund for Prepaid Funerals.
The Consumer Affairs Division strives to safeguard the consumer interests of Newfoundlanders & Labradorians. In the area of consumer protection, the division operates under the authority of the following acts: Architects Act; Business Electronic Filing Act; Certified General Accountants Act; Certified Management Accountants Act; Chartered Accountants Act; Collections Act; Consumer Protection & Business Practices Act; Electronic Commerce Act; Embalmers & Funeral Directors Act; Engineers & Geoscientists Act; Public Accountancy Act; & Sale of Goods Act. Associate d regulations include the following: Collections Regulations; Embalmers & Funeral Directors Regulations; Engineers & Geoscientists Regulations; & Lottery Licensing Regulations. The Consumer Affairs Division also handles mediation of disputes between landlords & tenants.
Other services include regulation of the licencing of the following: charitable & non-profit oranganizations' lottery fundraising activities; corporations & individuals who provide private investigation & security services; direct sales contracts between business entities & consumers; & corporations & individuals who facilitate the collection of outstanding debts.

Assistant Deputy Minister, Consumer & Commercial Affairs, Julian McCarthy
Tel: 709-729-2570
Fax: 709-729-4151
jmccarth@gov.nl.ca

Director, Consumer Affairs, Gerry Burke
Tel: 709-729-2618
Fax: 709-729-6998
gburke@gov.nl.ca

Director, Financial Services Regulation, Douglas Connolly
Tel: 709-729-4909
Fax: 709-729-3205
connolly@gov.nl.ca

Director, Commercial Registrations, Dean Doyle
Tel: 709-729-4043
Fax: 709-729-0232
doyled@gov.nl.ca

Government Services Branch

PO Box 8700, St. John's, NL A1B 4J6
Other Communication: Engineering & Inspection Services, Phone: 709-729-2747

The Government Services Branch oversees the following: Government Service Centres; motor vehicle registration; the Office of the Queen's Printer; vital statistics; engineering & inspections; & program & support services. Government services staff handle matters related to vital statistics, public health & safety, environmental issues, accessibility, highway

safety, as well as the processing of permits, licences, approvals, & inspections.
Government Service Centres are located in the following places, presented in alphabetical order:
Clarenville (709-466-4060);
Corner Brook (709-637-2204);
Gander (709-256-1420);
Grand Bank (709-832-2326);
Grand Falls-Windsor (709-292-4206);
Harbour Grace (709-945-3107);
Happy Valley-Goose Bay (709-896-5428);
Labrador City (709-944-5282);
Lewisporte (709-535-0262);
Marystown (709-279-0837);
Port aux Basques (709-695-2835);
St. Anthony (709-454-8833);
St. John's (709-729-3699);
Stephenville (709-643-8650);
Springdale (709-673-4218).
Newfoundland & Labrador's motor vehicle registration services are available in the following places:
Clarenville (1-877-636-6867);
Corner Brook (1-877-636-6867);
Gander (1-877-636-6867);
Grand Falls-Windsor (1-877-636-686);
Happy Valley-Goose Ba y (1-877-636-6867);
Harbour Grace (1-877-636-6867);
Labrador City (1-877-636-6867);
Mount Pearl (1-877-636-6867).
Assistant Deputy Minister, Government Services, Donna Kelland
Tel: 709-729-3056
Fax: 709-729-4151
dkelland@gov.nl.ca
Director, Program & Support Services, Rick Curran
Tel: 709-729-4875
Director, Engineering & Inspections, Dennis Eastman
Tel: 709-729-2747
Fax: 709-729-2071
deastman@gov.nl.ca
Registrar, Vital Statistics, Ken Mullaly
Tel: 709-729-3311
Fax: 709-729-1402
kmullaly@gov.nl.ca
Queen's Printer, Office of the Queen's Printer, William E. Parsons
Tel: 709-729-3210
Fax: 709-729-1900
williamparsons@gov.nl.ca

Occupational Health & Safety Branch
PO Box 8700, St. John's, NL A1B 4J6
Other Communication: Safety Bulletins & Recalls, Toll-Free: 1-563-5471
The Occupational Health & Safety Branch of Service NL works to ensure the health & safety of employees in the workplace in Newfoundland & Labrador.
The branch oversees administration of the Occupational Health & Safety Act, the Radiation Health & Safety Act, & the Workplace Health, Safety, & Compensation Act. Related regulations include the following: Asebestos Abatement Regulations; the Asbestos Exposure Code Regulations; the Occupational Health & Safety Regulations; the Occupational Health & Safety First Aid Regulations; the Radiation Health & Safety Regulations; the Workplace Hazardous Materials Information System (WHMIS) Regulations; & the Workplace Health, Safety, & Compensation Regulations.
Responsibilities of the Occupational Health & Safety Branch are as follows: development of health & safety legislation; compliance inspections of provincially regulated workplaces; hygiene assessments in workplaces; inspection of radiation control measures in workplaces; investigation of workplace incidents; & enforcement of health & safety legislation.
Assistant Deputy Minister, Occupational Health & Safety, Kim Dunphy
Tel: 709-729-5548
Fax: 709-729-4151
kdunphy@gov.nl.ca

Provincial Advisory Council on the Status of Women

#103, 15 Hallett Cres., St. John's, NL A1B 4C4
Tel: 709-753-7270
Fax: 709-753-2606
Toll-Free: 877-753-7270
info@pacsw.ca
www.pacsw.com

Minister Responsible, Hon. Charlene Johnson
Tel: 709-729-0173
Fax: 709-729-1049
charlenejohnson@gov.nl.ca

President/CEO, Linda Ross
Tel: 709-753-7270
lindaross@pacsw.ca

Director, Communications, Danielle Finney
daniellefinney@pacsw.ca

Office Manager, Sandy Abbott
Tel: 709-753-7270
Fax: 709-753-2606
sandyabbot@pacsw.ca

Newfoundland & Labrador Department of Tourism, Culture, & Recreation

Confederation Bldg., West Block, 2nd Fl., PO Box 8700, St. John's, NL A1B 4J6
Tel: 709-729-0862
Fax: 709-729-0870
tcrinfo@gov.nl.ca
www.tcr.gov.nl.ca
Ensures the development of provincial vacation & business travel markets. The department conserves, preserves & protects natural & cultural resources & promotes the resources for economic benefit, sport & recreation in the province. It also protects, preserves & develops the historic resources of the province. Programs promote the development of travel & tourism & assist in transforming the province's natural & cultural attractions into opportunities for employment & revenue generation.
Acts Administered:
Arts Council Act
Books Preservation of Copies Act
Boxing Authority Act
Colonial Buildings Act
Cruiseship Authority Act
Grand Concourse Authority Act
Historic Resources Act
Inkeepers Act
Newspapers & Books Act
Rooms Act
Tourist Establishments Act

Minister, Hon. Derrick Dalley
Tel: 709-729-0659
Toll-free: 877-787-0707
Fax: 709-729-0662
DerrickDalley@gov.nl.ca

Deputy Minister, Rick Hayward
Tel: 709-729-3555
Fax: 709-729-0662

Director, Communications, Diana Quinton
Tel: 709-729-0928
Fax: 709-729-0662
DianaQuinton@gov.nl.ca

Director, Strategic Planning & Policy, Janet Miller-Pitt
Tel: 709-729-5623
Fax: 709-729-0870
jpitt@gov.nl.ca

Associated Agencies, Boards & Commissions:
• **Newfoundland & Labrador Arts Council**
1 Springdale St.
PO Box 98
St. John's, NL A1C 5H5
Tel: 709-726-2212
Fax: 709-726-0619
Toll-free: 866-726-2212
nlacmail@nlac.ca
www.nlac.ca
• **Newfoundland & Labrador Film Development Corporation**
12 King's Bridge Rd.
St. John's, NL A1C 3K3
Tel: 709-738-3456
Fax: 709-739-1680
Toll-free: 877-738-3456
info@nlfdc.ca
www.nlfdc.ca

Culture & Recreation
The department administers archeology permits, the Art Procurement Program, the Heritage Foundation of Newfoundland & Labrador, provides grants to artists, arts organizations, museums & archives through the Newfoundland & Labrador Arts Council, provides grants to assists the Newfoundland & Labrador Film Development Corporation & administers provincial historic sites.
Assistant Deputy Minister, Mark Jones
Tel: 709-729-3609
Fax: 709-729-0870
markjones@gov.nl.ca
Chief Executive Officer, The Rooms, Dean Brinton
Tel: 709-757-8012
Fax: 709-757-8017
Director, The Rooms Provincial Art Gallery, Anne Chafe
Tel: 709-757-8077
annechafe@therooms.ca
Director, Arts, Arts & Culture Centres Division, Eleanor Dawson
Tel: 709-729-7397
Fax: 709-729-0870
eleanordawson@gov.nl.ca
Director, The Rooms Regional Museums, Penny Houlden
Tel: 709-757-8022
Director, Finance & General Operations, Vicky Lewis
Tel: 709-757-8015
Director, Arts & Culture Centres, Doreen McCarthy
Tel: 709-729-3453
Fax: 709-729-5952
mccarthyd@artsandculturecentre.com
Archivist, Government Records, John Mowbray
Tel: 709-757-8035
Director, The Rooms Provincial Art Gallery, Sheila Perry
Tel: 709-757-8042
sheilaperry@therooms.ca
Provincial Archeologist, Martha Drake
Tel: 709-729-2462
Fax: 709-729-0870
mdrake@gov.nl.ca
Confederation Bldg.
PO Box 8700
St. John's, NL A1B 4J6
Director & Provincial Archivist, The Rooms Provincial Archives, Greg Walsh
Tel: 709-757-8032
Archivist, Still & Moving Images, Sandra Ronayne
Tel: 709-757-8087
Director, Culture, Recreation & Sport, Jim Tee
Tel: 709-729-5241
Fax: 709-729-5293
Archivist, Exhibitions, Craig Tucker
Tel: 709-757-8038
Archivist, Reference & Access, Melanie Tucker
Tel: 709-757-8062
Manager, St. John's Arts & Culture Centre, Aiden Flynn
Tel: 709-729-3453
Fax: 709-729-5952
aflynn@artsandculturecentre.com
Prince Philip Dr.
PO Box 1854
St. John's, NL AIC 5P9
Manager, Provincial Historic Sites, Gerry Osmond
Tel: 709-729-7212
Fax: 709-729-7989
gerryosmond@gov.nl.ca

Tourism
Assistant Deputy Minister, Mary Taylor-Ash
Tel: 709-729-2821
Fax: 709-729-5293
mtaylorash@gov.nl.ca
Director, Tourism Product Development, Juanita Keel-Ryan
Tel: 709-729-1708
Fax: 709-729-0474
jkeelryan@gov.nl.ca
Director, Tourism Marketing Division, Carmela Murphy
Tel: 709-729-2831
Fax: 709-729-0057
carmelamurphy@gov.nl.ca
Director, Tourism Research Division, Michaela Roebothan
Tel: 709-729-6024
Fax: 709-729-0870
michaelaroebothan@gov.nl.ca

Newfoundland & Labrador Department of Transportation & Works

Confederation Bldg., West Block, 6th Fl., PO Box 8700, St. John's, NL A1B 4J6
Tel: 709-729-3679
Fax: 709-729-4285
twminister@gov.nl.ca
www.tw.gov.nl.ca
To provide a safe, efficient & sustainable transportation system & to provide landlord services & support services such as leasing & mail services for all government departments. The department liaises with other agencies & the federal government to ensure the overall public works & transportation needs & interest of the province are fully provided & protected.
Acts Administered:
Expropriation Act
Highway Traffic Act
Local Road Boards Act
Motor Carrier Act
Rail Service Act
Transportation & Works Act

Minister, Hon. Thomas J. Hedderson
Tel: 709-729-3679
Toll-free: 866-996-5670
Fax: 709-729-4285
thedderson@gov.nl.ca

Deputy Minister, Jamie Chippett
Tel: 709-729-3676
Fax: 709-729-4285

Director, Communications, Jason Card
Tel: 709-729-3015
Fax: 709-729-4285
jasoncard@gov.nl.ca

Legal Advisor, David Jones
Tel: 709-729-1966
Fax: 709-729-6934
davidj@gov.nl.ca

Marine Transportation Services
Other Communication: Tel.: 709-729-6882 (St. John's), 709-735-6202 (Lewisporte); Fax: 709-729-3418 (St. John's), 709-535-6245 (Lewisporte)

Road & Air Transportation
Assistant Deputy Minister, Gary Goose
Tel: 709-729-3796
Fax: 709-729-0283
gosseg@gov.nl.ca
Director, Highway Design & Construction, Brandon MacDonald
Tel: 709-729-0648
Fax: 709-729-0283
Director, Maintenance & Support, Dean Osmond
Tel: 709-729-3636
Fax: 709-729-6934
Senior Engineer, Highway Design, Bill Skanes
Tel: 709-729-5962
Fax: 709-729-0283
Chief Operating Officer, Marine Services, Tom Prim
Tel: 709-429-3278
Fax: 709-729-6934

Strategic & Corporate Services
Tel: 709-729-3019
Fax: 709-729-4658
Assistant Deputy Minister, Weldon Moores
Tel: 709-729-6882
Fax: 709-729-3418
wmoores@gov.nl.ca
Director, Financial Operations, Kevin Antle
Tel: 709-729-5356
Fax: 709-729-0703
kantle@gov.nl.ca
Director, Policy, Planning & Evaluation, Lynn Bryant
Tel: 709-729-5344
Fax: 709-729-3418
lbryant@gov.nl.ca
Director, Human Resources, Cindy Hussey
Tel: 709-729-3292
cindyhussey@gov.nl.ca

Works Branch
Tel: 709-729-3019
Fax: 709-729-4658
Assistant Deputy Minister, Cory Grandy
Tel: 709-729-5672
Fax: 709-729-5934
corygrandy@gov.nl.ca
Director, Building Design & Construction, Paul Lahey
Tel: 709-729-3342
Fax: 709-729-0646
laheyp@gov.nl.ca
Director, Engineering Support Services, Keith Noel
Tel: 709-729-5786
Fax: 709-729-5934
noelka@gov.nl.ca
Director, Realty Services, Martin Balodis
Tel: 709-729-3690
Fax: 709-729-0984

Newfoundland & Labrador Workplace Health, Safety & Compensation Commission

146 - 148 Forest Rd., PO Box 9000, St. John's, NL A1A 3B8
Tel: 709-778-1000
Fax: 709-738-1714
Toll-Free: 800-563-9000
general.inquiries@whscc.nl.ca
www.whscc.nf.ca
Other Communication: Grand Falls toll-free: 800-563-3448; Corner Brook toll-free: 800-563-2772
Utilizing skilled, professional employees, in partnership with workplace parties, the commission facilitates safe & healthy workplaces by assisting employers & workers to prevent accidents, & manage workplace injuries/illnesses & return-to-work processes. Operating as the administrator of the workers' compensation insurance program, the commission provides a reasonable level of benefits to injured workers & their dependents based on reasonable assessment rates for employers, while maintaining or exceeding service level performance when compared to other jurisdictions in Canada.

Minister Responsible, Hon. Paul Davis
Tel: 709-729-6670
Fax: 709-729-1503
padavis@gov.nl.ca

Chair, Ralph Tucker

CEO, Leslie Galway

Government of the Northwest Territories

Seat of Government: PO Box 1320, Yellowknife, NT X1A 2L9
www.gov.nt.ca
The Northwest Territories was reconstituted September 1, 1905. It has an area of 1,140,834.90 km2, & the StatsCan census in 2011 showed the population was 41,462. On April 1, 1999, the Northwest Territories was divided into two new territories: Nunavut Territories and the as yet unnamed territory (known as the Northwest Territories). The Northwest Territories is governed by a fully elected Legislative Assembly of 19 members elected for a four-year term. Government is by consensus rather than party politics. The Legislature elects the Premier & a seven-member Executive Council, which is charged with the operation of government & the establishment of program & spending priorities. The Commissioner of the Northwest Territories is appointed by the Federal Government, & serves a role similar to that of a Lieutenant Governor in provincial jurisdictions.

Department of the Executive
PO Box 1320, Yellowknife, NT X1A 2L9
executive@gov.nt.ca
Minister, Hon. Bob McLeod
Tel: 867-669-2311
Fax: 867-873-0385
bob_mcleod@gov.nt.ca
Deputy Minister & Secretary to Cabinet, Penny Ballantyne
Tel: 867-873-7100
penny_ballantyne@gov.nt.ca
Assistant Deputy Minister & Deputy Secretary to Cabinet, Allan Cash
Tel: 867-873-7652
allan_cash@gov.nt.ca
Assistant Deputy Minister, Executive Operations, David Stewart
Tel: 867-920-6378
david_stewart@gov.nt.ca
Executive Director, Devolution, Martin Goldney
Tel: 867-873-7172
martin.goldney@gov.nt.ca
Director, Program Review Office, Michael Kalnay
Tel: 867-873-7778
michael_kalnay@gov.nt.ca
Legislation Coordinator, Legislation and House Planning, Kevin O'Keefe
Tel: 867-669-2239
kevin_o'keefe@gov.nt.ca
Special Advisor, Status of Women, Gail Cyr
Tel: 867-920-3106
gail_cyr@gov.nt.ca
Manager, Corporate Services, Lisa Turner
Tel: 867-920-3169
lisa_turner@gov.nt.ca

Cabinet Secretariat
Tel: 867-873-7817
Fax: 867-873-0279
Secretary to Cabinet, Dave Ramsden
Tel: 867-873-7100
dave_ramsden@gov.nt.ca
Deputy Secretary to Cabinet, Alan Cash
Tel: 867-873-7652
Fax: 867-873-0279
alan_cash@gov.nt.ca
Asst. Deputy Minister, Executive Operations, David Stewart
Tel: 867-873-7823
david_stewart@gov.nt.ca
Director, Corporate Services, Cathy Myres
Tel: 867-873-7148
cathy_myres@gov.nt.ca
Advisor, Status of Women, Gail Cyr
Tel: 867-920-3106
gail_cyr@gov.nt.ca
Chief of Protocol, Carmen Moore
Tel: 867-873-7167
carmen_moore@gov.nt.ca

Territorial Statistician, Bureau of Statistics, Angelo Cocco
Tel: 867-873-7147
angelo_cocco@gov.nt.ca

Office of the Commissioner

#803 Northwest Tower, PO Box 1320, Yellowknife, NT X1A 2L9
Tel: 867-873-7400
Fax: 867-873-0223
Toll-Free: 888-270-3318
commissioner@gov.nt.ca
www.commissioner.gov.nt.ca

Commissioner, Hon. George Tuccaro
Tel: 867-873-7400
Fax: 867-873-0223
george_tuccaro@gov.nt.ca

Deputy Commissioner, Margaret M Thom
margaret_thom@gov.nt.ca

Assistant to the Commissioner, Phila Fyten
Tel: 867-873-7332
phila_fyten@gov.nt.ca

Office of the Premier

Legislative Assembly Bldg., PO Box 1320, Yellowknife, NT X1A 2L9
Tel: 867-669-2311
Fax: 867-873-0385
premier@gov.nt.ca
www.premier.gov.nt.ca

Premier, Hon. Bob McLeod
Tel: 867-669-2311
Fax: 867-873-0385
bob_mcleod@gov.nt.ca

Press Secretary, Drew Williams
Tel: 867-669-2304
drew_williams@gov.nt.ca

Executive Assistant, Stephen Dunbar
Tel: 867-669-2307
stephen_dunbar@gov.nt.ca

Executive Council

PO Box 1320, Yellowknife, NT X1A 2L9
executive@gov.nt.ca
www.executive.gov.nt.ca
Other Communication: Protocol: executive_protocol@gov.nt.ca; Corporate Communications: executive_communications@gov.nt.ca; Corporate Services: executive_services@gov.nt.ca
Coordination & advisory functions are performed for the Government of the Northwest Territories.

Premier-elect, Hon. Bob McLeod
Tel: 867-669-2311
Fax: 867-873-0385
bob_mcleod@gov.nt.ca

Minister, Portfolio Undecided, Hon. Glen Abernethy
Tel: 867-669-2223
Fax: 867-873-0276
glen_abernethy@gov.nt.ca

Minister, Portfolio Undecided, Hon. Tom Beaulieu
Tel: 867-669-2223
Fax: 867-873-0276
tom_beaulieu@gov.nt.ca

Minister, Portfolio Undecided, Hon. Jackson Lafferty
Tel: 867-669-2399
Fax: 867-873-0274
jackson_lafferty@gov.nt.ca

Minister, Portfolio Undecided, Hon. Robert C. McLeod
Tel: 867-669-2223
Fax: 867-873-0276
robert_c_mcleod@gov.nt.ca

Minister, Portfolio Undecided, Hon. J. Michael Miltenberger
Tel: 867-669-2355
Fax: 867-873-0596
michael_miltenberger@gov.nt.ca
Note: The Honourable J. Michael Miltenberger is also the Minister Responsible for the NorthwestTerritories Housing Corporation.

Minister, Portfolio Undecided, Hon. David Ramsay
Tel: 867-669-2223

Fax: 867-873-0276
david_ramsay@gov.nt.ca

Intergovernmental Affairs - Ottawa
Tel: 613-234-6525
Fax: 613-234-9667
Contact, Rose McConville
rose_mcconville@gov.nt.ca

Legislation & House Planning
Legislative Coordinator, Kevin O'Keefe
Tel: 867-669-2239
Fax: 867-873-0139
kevin_o'keefe@gov.nt.ca

NWT Legislative Assembly

c/o Clerk's Office, PO Box 1320, Yellowknife, NT X1A 2L9
Tel: 867-669-2299
Fax: 867-920-4735
Toll-Free: 800-661-0784
www.assembly.gov.nt.ca

Clerk, Tim Mercer
Tel: 867-669-2299
tim_mercer@gov.nt.ca

Speaker-elect, Hon. Jackie Jacobson
Tel: 867-669-2200
Toll-free: 800-661-0784
jackie_jacobson@gov.nt.ca

Deputy Clerk, Doug Schauerte
Tel: 867-669-2277
doug_schauerte@gov.nt.ca

Director, Corporate Services, Darrin Ouellette
Tel: 867-669-2334
Fax: 867-920-4735
darrin_ouellette@gov.nt.ca

Director, Research Services, Colette Langlois
Tel: 867-669-2212
colette_langlois@gov.nt.ca

Legislative Librarian, Vera Raschke
Tel: 867-669-2203
Fax: 867-873-0207
vera_raschke@gov.nt.ca

Chief Electoral Officer, Elections NWT, David Brock
Tel: 867-920-6999
david_brock@gov.nt.ca

Elections NWT/Plebiscite Office
YK Centre East, #7, 4915-48th St., 3rd Fl., Yellowknife, NT X1A 3S4
Tel: 867-920-6999
Fax: 867-873-0366
Toll-Free: 800-661-0796
electionsnwt@gov.nt.ca
www.electionsnwt.com
Other Communication: Toll-Free Fax: 1-800-661-0872
Chief Electoral Officer, David M. Brock
Tel: 867-920-6999
david_brock@gov.nt.ca

Office of the Languages Commissioner
Laing Bldg., 5003 - 49 St., Yellowknife, NT X1A 2P4
Tel: 867-873-7034
Fax: 867-873-0357
Toll-Free: 800-661-0889
langcom@gov.nt.ca
www.nwtlanguagescommissioner.ca
Languages Commissioner, Sarah Jerome
Tel: 876-678-2200
Fax: 867-678-2201
sarah_jerome@gov.nt.ca
Information & Privacy Commissioner, Elaine Keenan-Bengts
Tel: 867-669-0976
Fax: 867-920-2511
atippcom@theedge.ca
Conflict of Interest Commissioner, Gerald Gerrand
Tel: 867-669-2298
Fax: 867-873-0276

Standing Committees of the Legislature
www.assembly.gov.nt.ca/_live/pages/wpPages/Committees.aspx

Priorities & Planning; Economic Development & Infrastructure; Rules & Procedures; Government Operations; Social Programs

Seventeenth Legislature - Northwest Territories

PO Box 1320, Yellowknife, NT X1A 2L9
Tel: 867-669-2200
Fax: 867-920-4735
Toll-Free: 800-661-0784

Last General Election: October 3, 2011.
Maximum Duration: Four years.
Salaries, Indemnities & Allowances (2011):
Members of the Legislative Assembly are entitled to a basic indemnity of $90,199. Members are entitled to a non-taxable annual expense allowance of $6,962 for a Minister or for Members living within commuting distance of the capital. Members, who are not Ministers, & who do not live within commuting distance of the capital, are entitled to an additional non-taxable non-accountable allowance of $6,962 for expenses incurred while inthe capital while on constituency business or business as a Member. Up to $29,500 annually is paid to Members for capital accommodation, when their residence is not within 80 km of Yellowknife, & when they are attending sittings of the Legislature, committee meetings & performing constituency duties in Yellowknife. Members are provided with a set operating budget to defray the expenses of working on behalf of their constituents. In addition are the following remunerations:
Premier $73,482;
Minister $51,709;
Speaker $42,053;
Deputy Speaker $6,804;
Deputy Chairperson of Committee of the Whole $4,083.
The address for all contacts is as follows: PO Box 1320, Yellowknife, NT, X1A 2L9. The following is a list of Members of the Legislative Assembly, with their constituency, the number of electors on the voting list for the the most recent election, plus contact information:
Members
Hon. Glen Abernethy
Constituency: Yellowknife - Great Slave *No. of Constituents:* 1,857
Tel: 867-669-2290
Fax: 867-873-0276
glen_abernethy@gov.nt.ca
Hon. Tom Beaulieu
Constituency: Tu Nedhe *No. of Constituents:* 526
Tel: 867-669-2287
Fax: 867-873-0276
tom_beaulieu@gov.nt.ca
Other Communications: Additional Phone: 867-444-8463
Wendy Bisaro
Constituency: Yellowknife - Frame Lake *No. of Constituents:* 1,996
Tel: 867-669-2274
Fax: 867-873-0276
wendy_bisaro@gov.nt.ca
Frederick Blake Jr.
Constituency: Mackenzie Delta *No. of Constituents:* 1,343
Tel: 867-669-2223
Fax: 867-873-0274
frederick_blake@gov.nt.ca
Constituency Office
PO Box 266
Fort McPherson, NT X0E 0J0
Robert Bouchard
Constituency: Hay River North *No. of Constituents:* 1,386
Tel: 867-669-2223
Fax: 867-873-0276
robert_bouchard@gov.nt.ca
Constituency Office
#202, 76 Capital Dr.
Hay River, NT X0E 1G2
Bob Bromley
Constituency: Yellowknife - Weledeh *No. of Constituents:* 2,088
Tel: 867-669-2272
Fax: 867-873-0276
bob_bromley@gov.nt.ca
Daryl Dolynny
Constituency: Yellowknife - Range Lake *No. of Constituents:* 1,998
Tel: 867-669-2223
Fax: 867-873-0270
daryl_dolynny@gov.nt.ca
Jane Groenewegen
Constituency: Hay RiverSouth *No. of Constituents:* 1,330
Tel: 867-874-6141
Fax: 867-874-6143
jane_groenewegen@gov.nt.ca
Other Communications: Yellowknife Phone: 867-669-2292; Fax: 867-873-0276
Constituency Office
#3, 66 Woodland Dr.
Hay River, NT X0E 1G1
Robert Hawkins
Constituency: Yellowknife Centre *No. of Constituents:* 2,134
Tel: 867-669-2265
Fax: 867-873-0276
robert_hawkins@gov.nt.ca
Hon. Jackie Jacobson
Constituency: Nunakput *No. of Constituents:* 913
Tel: 867-669-2276
Fax: 867-873-0276
jackie_jacobson@gov.nt.ca
Hon. Jackson Lafferty
Constituency: Monfwi *No. of Constituents:* 1,546
Tel: 867-669-2399
Fax: 867-873-0169
jackson_lafferty@gov.nt.ca
Hon. Bob McLeod
Constituency: Yellowknife South *No. of Constituents:* 1,529
Tel: 867-669-2388
Fax: 867-873-0169
bob_mcleod@gov.nt.ca
Hon. Robert C. McLeod
Constituency: Inuvik Twin Lakes *No. of Constituents:* 604
Tel: 867-669-2279
Fax: 867-873-0276
robert_mcleod@gov.nt.ca
Other Communications: Additional Phone: 867-678-0319
Kevin A. Menicoche
Constituency: Nahendeh *No. of Constituents:* 1,527
Tel: 867-695-3780
Fax: 867-695-3781
kevin_menicoche@gov.nt.ca
Other Communications: Yellowknife Phone: 867-669-2294; Fax: 867-873-0276
Constituency Office
PO Box 266
Fort Simpson, NT X0E 0N0
Hon. J. Michael Miltenberger
Constituency: Thebacha *No. of Constituents:* 1,569
Tel: 867-872-5511
Fax: 867-872-5642
michael_miltenberger@gov.nt.ca
Other Communications: Minister's Office: 867-669-2355; Fax: 867-873-0169
Constituency Office
102 Wilderness Dr.
Fort Smith, NT X0E 0P0
Alfred Moses
Constituency: Inuvik Boot Lake *No. of Constituents:* 608
Tel: 867-669-2223
Fax: 867-873-0276
alfred_moses@gov.nt.ca
Constituency Office
181 Mackenzie Rd.
PO Box 1998
Inuvik, NT X0E 0T0
Michael Nadli
Constituency: Deh Cho *No. of Constituents:* 931
Tel: 867-669-2223
Fax: 867-873-0276
michael_nadli@gov.nt.ca
Constituency Office
PO Box 149
Fort Providence, NT X0E 0L0
Hon. David Ramsay
Constituency: Kam Lake *No. of Constituents:* 1,777
Tel: 867-669-2296
Fax: 867-873-0276
david_ramsay@gov.nt.ca
Norman Yakeleya
Constituency: Sahtu *No. of Constituents:* 1,574
Tel: 867-669-2366
Fax: 867-873-0169
norman_yakeleya@gov.nt.ca

Northwest Territories Government Departments & Agencies

Department of Aboriginal Affairs & Intergovernmental Relations

4910 - 52nd St., PO Box 1320, Yellowknife, NT X1A 2L9
Tel: 867-873-7143
Fax: 867-873-0233
Toll-Free: 877-838-8194
nancy_gardiner@gov.nt.ca
www.daair.gov.nt.ca

The Department of Aboriginal Affairs & Intergovernmental Relations is charged with the following responsibilities: to negotiate, implement, & monitor land, resource & self-government agreements; to manage governmental relationships with Aboriginal, federal, provincial, & territorial governments, & with circumpolar countries; to provide advice on federal-provincial-territorial-Aboriginal relations; & to contribute to the political & constitutional development of the Northwest Territories.
Acts Administered:
National Aboriginal Day Act

Tlicho Community Government Act
Tlicho Community Services Agency Act
Tlicho Land Claims & Self-Government Agreement Act

Minister, Hon. Bob McLeod
Tel: 867-669-2311
Fax: 867-873-0385
bob_mcleod@gov.nt.ca

Acting Deputy Minister, Andy Bevan
Tel: 867-873-7143
Fax: 867-873-0233
andy_bevan@gov.nt.ca

Director, Implementation, Scott B. Alexander
Tel: 867-873-7149
Fax: 867-873-0540
scott_alexander@gov.nt.ca

Acting Director, Intergovernmental Relations, Jennifer Dallman-Sanders
Tel: 867-873-7112
Fax: 867-873-0233
jennifer_dallman-sanders@gov.nt.ca

Director, Policy, Planning & Communications, Richard Robertson
Tel: 867-920-3141
Fax: 867-873-0540
richard_robertson@gov.nt.ca

Director, Negotiations, Fred Talen
Tel: 867-873-7388
Fax: 867-873-0593
fred_talen@gov.nt.ca

Aurora Research Institute (ARI)

191 MacKenzie Rd., PO Box 1450, Inuvik, NT X0E 0T0
Tel: 867-777-3298
Fax: 867-777-4264
webmaster@nwtresearch.com
www.nwtresearch.com
Other Communication: Twitter: twitter.com/nwtresearch

A division of Aurora College that is dedicated to excellence, leadership & innovations in Northern education & research. Administers the research licencing provisions of the Northwest Territories Scientists Act & provides year round logistical assistance for researchers.

Director, Pippa Seccombe
Tel: 867-777-3298 ext: 235
pseccombe-hett@auroracollege.nt.ca

Northwest Territories Business Development & Investment Corporation (BDIC)

#701, 5201 - 50th Ave., Yellowknife, NT X1A 3S9
Tel: 867-920-6455
Fax: 867-765-0652
www.bdic.ca

The BDIC provides access to business financing, support, & development assistance to communities throughout the Northwest Territories. Their focus is the small and mid-sized business sector.

Chair, Darrell Beaulieu

Chief Executive Officer, Pawan Chugh
Tel: 867-920-3348

Director, Policy, Planning & Operations, Ron Chiasson
Tel: 867-920-3355

Director, Finance & Subsidiaries, Leonard Kwong
Tel: 867-920-3339

Department of Education, Culture & Employment (ECE)

PO Box 1320, Yellowknife, NT X1A 2L9
Tel: 867-669-2399
Fax: 867-873-0431
Toll-Free: 866-606-5627
www.ece.gov.nt.ca
Other Communication: Jobs North Phone: 867-873-7690; Fax: 867-873-0636; Email: jobsnorth@gov.nt.ca

The Ministry's responsibilities cover the following areas: Early Childhood; Kindergarten to Grade 12; Adult & Post-Secondary Education; Career Development & Employment; Apprenticeship & Occupational Certification; Culture, Heritage & Languages; Income Security; & Labour Services.

Acts Administered:
Apprenticeship, Trade & Occupations Certification Act
Archives Act
Aurora College Act
Child Day Care Act
Education Act
Employment Standards Act
Historical Resources Act
Occupational Training Agreements Act
Official Languages Act
Public Libraries Act
Scientists Act
Senior Citizens Benefits Act
Social Assistance Act
Student Financial Assistance Act

Minister, Hon. Jackson Lafferty
Tel: 867-669-2399
Fax: 867-873-0274
jackson_lafferty@gov.nt.ca

Deputy Minister, Gabriela Eggenhofer
Tel: 867-920-6240
Fax: 867-873-0338
gabriela_eggenhofer@gov.nt.ca

Associate Deputy Minister, Gloria Iatridis
Tel: 867-920-6240
Fax: 867-873-0338
gloria_iatridis@gov.nt.ca

Director, Official Languages, Albert Canadien
Tel: 867-920-6484
albert_canadien@gov.nt.ca

Director, Education Operations & Development, Joanne McGrath
Tel: 867-873-7673
joanne_mcgrath@gov.nt.ca

Manager, Public Affairs, Jacqueline McKinnon
Tel: 867-920-6222
jacqueline_mckinnon@gov.nt.ca

Registrar of Appeals, Appeals Office - ECE Programs & Services, Moses Hernandez
Tel: 867-920-6324
moses_hernandez@gov.nt.ca

Executive Director, Secretariat aux affaires francophones/Francophone affairs secreatariat, Benoit Boutin
Tel: 867-920-3107
benoit_boutin@gov.nt.ca

Director, Early Childhood & School Services, Angela James
Tel: 867-920-7176
angela_james@gov.nt.ca

Associated Agencies, Boards & Commissions:
• Northwest Territories Apprenticeship, Trade & Occupations Certification Board
PO Box 1320
Yellowknife, NT X1A 2L9
Tel: 867-873-7357
Fax: 867-873-0200
• NWT Arts Council
PO Box 1320 Main
Yellowknife, NT X1A 2L9
Tel: 867-920-6370
Fax: 867-873-0205
pwnhc.learnnet.nt.ca/artscouncil/

Advanced Education
Director, Advanced Education, Laurie Morton
Tel: 867-873-7552
Fax: 867-873-0200
laurie_morton@gov.nt.ca

Culture & Heritage
Director, Culture & Heritage, Barb Cameron
Tel: 867-873-7551
barb_cameron@gov.nt.ca

ECE Service Centres

Income Security Programs Division
Director, Lois Walbourne
Tel: 867-920-8921
lois_walbourne@gov.nt.ca

Strategic & Business Development
Director, Strategic & Business Services, Paul Devitt
Tel: 867-873-7739
paul_devitt@gov.nt.ca
Legislative Policy Advisor, Policy & Planning, Tricia Ralph
Tel: 867-873-7670
tricia_ralph@gov.nt.ca
Manager, Planning & Analysis, Marissa Martin
Tel: 867-920-3129
marissa_martin@gov.nt.ca

Department of Environment & Natural Resources (ENR)

PO Box 1320, Yellowknife, NT X1A 2L9
www.enr.gov.nt.ca

Operations cover a broad spectrum of activities directed at promoting a healthy environment that supports traditional lifestyles within a modern economy. The wise use & protection of natural resources are encouraged. The Department's activities are carried out through the following divisions: Environmental Protection, Forest Management, Policy, Legislation & Communications, Protected Areas Strategy, Informatics, & Wildlife.

Acts Administered:
Asphalt Paving Industry Emission Regulations
Beverage Container Regulations
Certification & Disposal of Wildlife Regulations
Critical Wildlife Areas Regulations
Environmental Protection Act
Environmental Rights Act
Forest Management Act
Forest Protection Act
Natural Resources Conservation Trust Act
Pesticide Act
Sale of Wildlife Regulations
Species At Risk NWT Act (Not in force)
Spill Contingency Planning & Reporting Regulations
Trapping Regulations
Used Oil & Waste Fuel Management Regulations
Waste Reduction & Recovery Act
Water Resources Agreement Act
Wildlife Act
Wildlife Export Regulations
Wildlife General Regulations
Wildlife Management Areas & Zones Regulations
Wildlife Preserves Regulations
Wildlife Sanctuaries Regulations

Minister, Hon. Michael Miltenberger
Tel: 867-669-2355
Fax: 867-873-0596
Michael_Miltenberger@gov.nt.ca

Deputy Minister, Ernie Campbell
Tel: 867-873-7401
ernie_campbell@gov.nt.ca

Assistant Deputy Minister, Operations, Jack Bird
Tel: 867-920-6389
jack_bird@gov.nt.ca

Assistant Deputy Minister, Corporate & Strategic Planning, Ray Case
Tel: 867-920-6389
ray_case@gov.nt.ca

Director, Environment, Lisa Dyer
Tel: 867-873-7654
Fax: 867-873-0221
lisa_dyer@gov.nt.ca

Director, Land & Water, Mary Tapsell
Tel: 867-920-8069
Fax: 867-873-4229
mary_tapsell@gov.nt.ca

Director, Policy and Strategic Planning, Field Support Unit, Evan Walz
Tel: 867-920-8046
evan_walz@gov.nt.ca

Deh Cho
Milton Bldg., 2nd Fl., PO Box 240, Fort Simpson, NT X0E 0N0
Tel: 867-695-7450
Fax: 867-695-2381
Regional Superintendent, Carl Lafferty
Tel: 867-695-7451
carl_lafferty@gov.nt.ca

Inuvik
Semmler Bldg., 2nd Fl., Bag Service #1, Inuvik, NT X0E 0T0
Fax: 867-678-6699
Regional Superintendent, Stephen Charlie
Tel: 867-678-6690
stephen_charlie@gov.nt.ca

North Slave
PO Box 2668, Yellowknife, NT X1A 2P9
Tel: 867-873-7184
Fax: 867-873-6230

Regional Superintendent, Fred Mandeville
Tel: 867-920-6114
fred_mandeville@gov.nt.ca
Sahtu
PO Box 130, Norman Wells, NT X0E 0V0
Tel: 867-587-3500
Fax: 867-587-3516
Acting Regional Superintendent, Jeff Walker
Tel: 867-587-3532
jeff_walker@gov.nt.ca
Fort Smith (South Slave)
Sweetgrass Bldg., PO Box 390, Fort Smith, NT X0E 0P0
Tel: 867-872-6400
Fax: 867-872-4250
Acting Regional Superintendent, Troy Vermillion
Tel: 867-872-6404
troy_vermillion@gov.nt.ca

Environment
Tel: 867-873-7654
Fax: 867-873-0221
To protect & enhance the environmental quality in the North. Departmental programs are designed to control the discharge of contaminants & reduce their impacts on the natural environment. This is a shared responsibility with federal, territorial, Aboriginal & municipal agencies, as well as every resident of the Northwest Territories. To promote energy conservation & the use of energy efficient technology in the Northwest Territories, identify & facilitate the development of alternative, local energy sources which strengthen community economies, & promote & facilitate energy planning.

Forest Management Division
PO Box 7, Fort Smith, NT X0E 0P0
Fax: 867-874-2077
forestmanagement.enr.gov.nt/
Provides the policy, planning & regulatory framework for the stewardship, protection & sustainable management of forest resources on 33 million hectares of land in the Northwest Territories, eight per cent of Canada's entire forested area. Working with First Nations governments, communities, other governments & non-governmental agencies on such a vast land mass presents unique & complex challenges for forest managers. The FMD coordinates & facilitates the implementation of forest management programs & services among the five administrative regions of ENR. The regional offices have the primary responsibility for delivery of programs. Regional staff implement forest resource & fire management programs for the Department. Regional personnel receive applications for approval to harvest, supervise harvesting activities, ensure compliance with standards, support community protection planning efforts & carry out fire management activities under the direction of the Forest Management Division. The Forest Management

Policy & Strategic Planning
Fax: 867-873-0114
Provides services in the area of policy, legislation, environmental assessment, land claims & self-government, resource management & public affairs & communications.

Wildlife
Fax: 867-874-2347
www.nwtwildlife.com/
Activities are directed towards maintaining productive populations of all native wildlife in their natural habitats, encouraging the wise use of wildlife populations within the limits of sustainable yield & encouraging the active participation of northern residents in the management of wildlife resources. In addition to assistance programs that are designed to support the hunting & trapping economy, the division provides support to organizations of resource users to allow them to become more involved in wildlife management.

Department of Finance

Arthur Laing Building, 5th Fl., 5003 - 49th St., PO Box 1320, Yellowknife, NT X1A 2L9
Tel: 867-873-7117
Fax: 867-873-0414
www.fin.gov.nt.ca
The government of the Northwest Territories has a budget of over $700,000,000 (including federal government transfers of over $500,000,000). The Department of Finance obtains the financial resources to carry on the functions of government & for intergovernmental fiscal negotiations & arrangements.
Acts Administered:
Appropriation Act
Borrowing Authorization Act
Central Trust Company Act
Certified General Accountants' Association Act
Financial Administration Act
Financial Agreement Act
Forgiveness of Debts Act
Income Tax Act
Income Tax Collection Agreement Questions Act
Institute of Chartered Accountants Act
Insurance Act
Liquor Act
Loan Authorization Act
Northern Employee Benefits Services Pension Plan Protection Act
Northwest Territories Energy Corporation Ltd. Loan Guarantee Act
Payroll Tax Act, 1993
Petroleum Products Tax Act
Property & Assessment Taxation Act (jointly with Department of Municipal & Community Affairs)
Public Utilities Income Tax Rebates Act
Retirement Plan Beneficiaries Act
Revolving Funds Act
Risk Capital Investment Tax Credit Act
Society of Management Accountants Act
Supplementary Appropriation Act
Tobacco Tax Act
Union of Northern Workers Act
Write-Off of Assets & Debts Act

Minister, Hon. J. Michael Miltenberger
Tel: 867-669-2355
Fax: 867-873-0596
Michael_Miltenberger@gov.nt.ca

Deputy Minister, Mike Aumond
Tel: 867-873-7117
Fax: 867-873-0414
mike_aumond@gov.nt.ca

Associated Agencies, Boards & Commissions:
• Northwest Territories Liquor Commission
#201, 31 Capital Dr.
Hay River, NT X0E 1G2
Tel: 867-874-2100
Fax: 867-874-2180
• Northwest Territories Liquor Licensing Board
#210, 31 Capital Dr.
Hay River, NT X0E 1G2
Tel: 867-874-2906
Fax: 867-874-6011
delilah_st-arneault@gov.nt.ca
• Northwest Territories Liquor Licensing & Enforcement
#210, 31 Capital Dr.
Hay River, NT X0E 1G2
Tel: 867-874-2906
Fax: 867-874-6011

Budget, Treasury & Debt Management
Tel: 867-873-7308
Fax: 867-873-0325
Treasury is responsible for managing the government's cash position; conducting banking, borrowing & investment activities; protecting the government's activities & assets from risk of loss by means of appropriate insurance coverage & risk management activities; & regulating insurance companies, agents, brokers & adjusters operating in the NWT.
Director, Treasury, Doug Doak
Tel: 867-920-3423
doug_doak@gov.nt.ca
Director, Management Board Secretariat, Olin Lovely
Tel: 867-920-6431

Fiscal Policy
Tel: 867-920-6436
Fax: 867-873-0128
Responsible for developing policies & providing research, analysis & recommendations on the fiscal policies of government. The Division also administers the Formula Financing Agreement with Canada & is responsible for intergovernmental fiscal relations.
Director, Kelly Bluck
Tel: 867-920-6436
kelly_bluck@gov.nt.ca

Financial Management Board Secretariat (FMBS)

c/o Secretary of the FMB / Comptroller General, 5003 - 49 St., PO Box 1320, Yellowknife, NT X1A 2L9
Coordinating & promoting the efficient use of the Government's financial & information resources are the chief responsibilities of the Financial Management Board Secretariat. The central agency, that supports the Minister of Finance, provides leadership in functions related to governmental business planning, information management, & program & service evaluation. The FMBS also supports sustainable resource development, self-government development, & the improvement of programs & services.

Minister Responsible, Hon. J. Michael Miltenberger
Tel: 867-669-2355
Fax: 867-873-0385
J_Michael_Miltenberger@gov.nt.ca

Comptroller General, Warren St Germaine
Tel: 867-920-6196
Fax: 867-873-0296
warren_stgermaine@gov.nt.ca

Manager, Budget Development, Chuck Gibson
Tel: 867-873-7883
chuck_gibson@gov.nt.ca

Deputy Secretary, Sandy Kalgutkar
Tel: 867-920-6196
sandy_kalgutkar@gov.nt.ca

Vital Statistics
Bag #9, Inuvik, NT X0E 0T0
Tel: 867-777-7400
Fax: 867-777-3197
Toll-Free: 800-661-0830
hsa@gov.nt.ca
Birth certificates: $10
Registrar General, Jenetta Day
Tel: 867-777-7422
jenetta_day@gov.nt.ca
Deh Cho
PO Box 246, Fort Simpson, NT X0E 0N0
Tel: 867-695-3815
Fax: 867-695-2920
Tlicho
Bag #5, Behchoko, NT X0E 0Y0
Tel: 867-392-3000
Fax: 867-392-3001
Fort Smith
PO Box 1080, Fort Smith, NT X0E 0P0
Tel: 867-872-6200
Fax: 867-872-6275
Hay River
3 Gaetz Dr., Hay River, NT X0E 0R8
Tel: 867-874-7100
Fax: 867-874-7118
Beaufort-Delta
Bag #2, 285 Mackenzie Rd., Inuvik, NT X0E 0T0
Tel: 867-777-8000
Fax: 867-777-8062
Sahtu
PO Box 340, Norman Wells, NT X0E 0V0
Tel: 867-587-3650
Fax: 867-587-3436
Stanton
PO Box 10, Yellowknife, NT X1A 2N1
Tel: 867-669-4224
Fax: 867-669-4128
www.srhb.org
Yellowknife
Jan Stirling Bldg., 4702 Franklin Ave., PO Box 608, Yellowknife, NT X1A 2N5
Tel: 867-873-7276
Fax: 867-920-7025
yhssa@gov.nt.ca
www.yhssa.org

Department of Health & Social Services

Centre Square Tower, PO Box 1320, Yellowknife, NT X1A 2L9
Fax: 867-873-0266
www.hlthss.gov.nt.ca
The Department of Health & Social Services is mandated to provide a broad range of health & social programs & services to the residents of the NWT. Seven regional Health & Social Services Authorities plan, manage & deliver a full spectrum of community & facility-based services for health care & social services. Community health programs include daily sick clinics, public health clinics, home care, school health programs & educational programs. Visiting physicians & specialists routinely visit the communities.
Acts Administered:
Aboriginal Custom Adoption Recognition Act
Adoption Act
Change of Name Act
Child & Family Services Act
Communicable Diseases Regulation
Dental Auxiliaries Act
Dental Mechanics Act
Dental Profession Act
Emergency Medical Aid Act
General Sanitation Regulations
Guardianship & Trusteeship Act (jointly with Deptartment of Justice)
Hospital Insurance & Health & Social Services Administration Act
Human Tissue Act
Intercountry Adoption (Hague Convention) Act
Licensed Practical Nurses Act
Marriage Act

Meat Inspection Regulations
Medical Care Act
Medical Profession Act
Mental Health Act
Midwifery Profession Act
Nursing Profession Act
Ophthalmic Medical Assistants Act
Optometry Act
Personal Directives Act
Pharmacy Act
Psychologists Act
Public Health Act
Public Sewerage Systems Regulation
Public Water Supply Regulations
Tobacco Control Act
Veterinary Profession Act
Vital Statistics Act

Minister, Hon. Tom Beaulieu
Tel: 867-669-2315
Tom_Beaulieu@gov.nt.ca

Deputy Minister, Debbie DeLancey
Tel: 867-920-6173
Fax: 867-873-0266
debbie_delancey@gov.nt.ca

Associate Deputy Minister, Dana Heide
Tel: 867-873-7737
Fax: 867-873-0266
dana_heide@gov.nt.ca

Assistant Deputy Minister, Corporate Services, Derek Elkin
Tel: 867-920-3356
derek_elkin@gov.nt.ca

Director, Policy, Legislation & Communications, Denise Canuel
Tel: 867-920-3283
Fax: 867-873-0204
denise_canuel@gov.nt.ca

Director, Corporate Planning, Reporting & Evaluation, Lisa Cardinal
Tel: 867-873-7908
Fax: 867-873-0484
lisa_cardinal@gov.nt.ca

Director, Health Services Administration, Nick Saturnino
Tel: 867-777-7400
Toll-free: 800-661-0830
Fax: 867-777-3197
nick_saturnino@gov.nt.ca

Director, Population Health, Laura Seddon
Tel: 867-920-3231
laura_seddon@gov.nt.ca

Deputy Chief Public Health Officer, Dr. Kami Kandola
Tel: 867-873-7721
Fax: 867-873-0442
kami_kandola@gov.nt.ca

Communications Officer, Dorothy Westerman
Tel: 867-920-3373
Fax: 867-873-0204
dorothy_westerman@gov.nt.ca

Chief Environmental Health Officer, Environmental Health, Duane Fleming
Tel: 867-873-2183
duane_fleming@gov.nt.ca

Territorial Epidemiologist, Disease Registries, Maria Santos
Tel: 867-920-3241
maria_santos@gov.nt.ca

Director, Infrastructure Planning, Perry Heath
Tel: 867-873-7703
perry_heath@gov.nt.ca

Northwest Territories Housing Corporation

Scotia Centre, 5102 50th Ave., PO Box 2100, Yellowknife, NT X1A 2P6

Tel: 867-873-7853
Fax: 867-873-9426
www.nwthc.gov.nt.ca
Other Communication: Official Languages Coordination Phone: 867-873-7899; Fax: 867-669-7901

The mandate of the Northwest Territories Housing Corporation is to ensure, where necessary, a sufficient supply of affordable, adequate & suitable housing to meet the needs of residents. To accomplish this mandate, the corporation works with citizens, communities, Local Housing Organizations, aboriginal organizations, the business community, non-government organizations, & other governments. Through Housing Choices, the following four programs are available: Providing Assistance for Territorial Homeownership (PATH); Contributing Assistance for Repairs and Enhancements (CARE); Homeowner Entry Level Program (HELP); & Solutions to Educate People (STEP).

Minister Responsible, Hon. Robert C. McLeod
Tel: 867-669-2366
Robert_C_McLeod@gov.nt.ca

President, Jeff Polakoff
Tel: 867-873-7853
Fax: 867-873-9426
jeff_polakoff@gov.nt.ca

Vice President, Finance & Infrastructure Services, Jeff Anderson
Tel: 867-873-7873
Fax: 867-920-8024
jeff_anderson@gov.nt.ca

Vice-President, Programs & District Operations, Franklin Carpenter
Tel: 867-873-7858
Fax: 867-669-7901
franklin_carpenter@gov.nt.ca

Director, Infrastructure Services, Scott Reid
Tel: 867-873-7875
Fax: 867-669-7010
scott_reid@gov.nt.ca

Department of Human Resources

PO Box 1320, Yellowknife, NT X1A 2L9

Tel: 867-920-3409
Fax: 867-873-0306
Toll-Free: 866-475-8162
www.hr.gov.nt.ca
Other Communication: Yellowknife Recruitment Office Phone: 867-920-8900; Fax: 867-873-0282; Email: jobsyk@gov.nt.ca; Current Employment Opportunites: www.hr.gov.nt.ca/employment

The Department services the people of the Northwest Territories & supports the development of employees in the northern public service. Services are provided through the following divisions: Management & Recruitment Services; Corporate Human Resource Services; Human Resource Strategy & Policy; & Employee Services.

Acts Administered:
Public Service Act
Teachers' Association Act

Minister, Hon. Glen Abernethy
Tel: 867-669-2388
Fax: 867-873-0306
Glen_Abernethy@gov.nt.ca

Deputy Minister, Sheila Bassi-Kellett
Tel: 867-873-7187
Fax: 867-873-0667
sheila_bassi-kellett@gov.nt.ca

Assistant Deputy Minister, Sharilyn Alexander
Tel: 867-873-7187
Fax: 867-873-0667
sharilyn_alexander@gov.nt.ca

Director, Corporate Human Resources, Laura Gareau
Tel: 867-873-7850
laura_gareau@gov.nt.ca

Director, Strategy & Policy, Michelle Beard
Tel: 867-873-7786
michelle_beard@gov.nt.ca

Director, Management & Recruitment Services, Caroline Larocque
Tel: 867-920-6910
caroline_larocque@gov.nt.ca

Director, Employee Services, Alison Welch
Tel: 867-873-7906
Fax: 867-873-0167
alison_welch@gov.nt.ca

Manager, Finance & Corporate Support, Hilda Balsillie
Tel: 867-920-8948
hilda_balsillie@gov.nt.ca

Department of Industry, Tourism & Investment (ITI)

PO Box 1320, Yellowknife, NT X1A 2L9

Fax: 867-873-0306
info@iti.ca
www.iti.gov.nt.ca

The Department of Industry, Tourism & Investment promotes & supports economic prosperity & community self-reliance in the Northwest Territories by providing programs & services. Programs & services are available through the following departmental divisions: Diamonds; Energy Planning; Industrial Initiatives; Informatics; Investment & Economic Analysis; Mackenzie Valley Pipeline Office; Minerals, Oil & Gas; Policy, Legislation & Communications; & Tourism & Parks.

Acts Administered:
Agricultural Products Marketing Act
Business Development & Investment Corporation Act
Co-operative Associations Act (jointly with Department of Justice)
Credit Union Act
Freshwater Fish Marketing Act
Herd & Fencing Act
Territorial Parks Act

Minister, Hon. David Ramsey
Tel: 867-669-2377
Fax: 867-873-0306
David_Ramsay@gov.nt.ca

Deputy Minister, Peter Vician
Tel: 867-920-8048
Fax: 867-873-0563
peter_vician@gov.nt.ca

Assistant Deputy Minister, Kelly Kaylo
Tel: 867-873-7115
kelly_kaylo@gov.nt.ca

Director, Minerals, Oil & Gas, Deborah Archibald
Tel: 867-920-3222
deborah_archibald@gov.nt.ca

Director, Planning Coordination, Mackenzie Valley Pipeline Office, Tim Coleman
Tel: 867-874-5405
tim_coleman@gov.nt.ca

Director, Shared Services, Finance & Administration, Nancy Magrum
Tel: 867-920-8649
Fax: 867-920-2756
nancy_magrum@gov.nt.ca

Director, Energy Planning, Dave Nightingale
Tel: 867-920-3274
dave_nightingale@gov.nt.ca

Director, Policy, Legislation & Communications, Sonya Saunders
Tel: 867-873-7005
Fax: 867-873-0645
sonya_saunders@gov.nt.ca

Director, Investment & Economic Analysis, John Colford
Tel: 867-873-7361
Fax: 867-873-0101
john_colford@gov.nt.ca

Director, Tourism & Parks, Richard Zieba
Tel: 867-873-7903
Fax: 867-873-0163
richard_zieba@gov.nt.ca

Chief Geologist, Northwest Territories Geoscience Office, Scott Cairns
Tel: 867-669-2479
scott_cairns@gov.nt.ca

Senior Contract Reporting Officer, The BIP Monitoring Office, Lori Gaukel
Tel: 867-873-7235
lori_gaukel@gov.nt.ca

Department of Justice

Courthouse, 4903 - 49th St., 6th Fl., PO Box 1320, Yellowknife, NT X1A 2L9

Tel: 867-920-6197
www.justice.gov.nt.ca
Other Communication: Access to Information and Protection of Privacy Phone: 867-920-6418

The following are some of the services offered by the Department of Justice: Aboriginal Rights Court Challenges Program; Access to Information & Protection of Privacy; Commissioner for Oaths/Notary Public; Coroner; Corporate

Registries; Land Titles Office; Legal Aid; Maintenance Enforcement; Mental Disorder Review Board; Personal Property Registry; Public Trustee; Rental Office; Securities Registry; Victim Services; Witness Expense Assistance Program; & Youth Justice.

Acts Administered:
Access to Information & Protection of Privacy Act (jointly with Legislative Assembly)
Adoption of the French Version of Statutes & Statutory Instruments Act
Age of Majority Act
Arbitration Act
Business Corporations Act
Children's Law Act
Choses In Action Act
Commercial Tenancies Act
Condominium Act
Conflict of Interest Act
Contributory Negligence Act
Coroners Act
Corrections Act
Court Security Act
Creditors Relief Act
Defamation Act
Department of Justice Act
Dependants Relief Act
Devolution of Real Property Act
Donation of Food Act
Engineering & Geoscience Professions Act
Evidence Act
Exemptions Act
Expropriation Act
Factors Act
Family Law Act
Fatal Accidents Act
Fine Option Act
Frustrated Contracts Act
Garage Keepers Lien Act
Hotel Keepers Act
Interjurisdictional Support Orders Act
International Child Abduction Act
International Commercial Arbitration Act
International Interests in Mobile Aircraft Equipment Act
International Sale of Goods Act
Interpretation Act
Interprovincial Subpoenas Act
Intestate Succession Act
Judicature Act
Jury Act
Justices of the Peace Act
Land Titles Act
Legal Profession Act
Legal Questions Act
Legal Services Act
Limitation of Actions Act
Maintenance Orders Enforcement Act
Married Women's Property Act
Mechanics Lien Act
Miners Lien Act
Partnership Act
Perpetuities Act
Personal Property Security Act
Powers of Attorney Act
Presumption of Death Act
Professional Corporations Act
Protection Against Family Violence Act
Public Inquiries Act
Public Printing Act
Public Service Garnishee Act
Public Trustee Act
Reciprocal Enforcement of Judgments (Canada-UK) Act
Reciprocal Enforcement of Judgments Act
Religious Societies Land Act
Residential Tenancies Act
Retirement Plan Beneficiaries Act (jointly with Department of Finance)
Royal Canadian Mounted Police Agreements Act
Sale of Goods Act
Securities Act
Securities Transfer Act
Seizures Act
Settlement of International Investment Disputes Act
Societies Act
Statute Revision Act
Statutory Instruments Act
Summary Conviction Procedures Act
Survivorship Act
Tenants in Common Act
Territorial Court Act
Trustee Act
Variation of Trusts Act
Victims of Crime Act
Warehouse Keepers Lien Act
Wills Act
Youth Justice Act

Minister, Hon. Glen Abernethy
Tel: 867-669-2388
Glen_Abernethy@gov.nt.ca

Deputy Minister, Sylvia Haener
Tel: 867-920-6197
Fax: 867-873-0307
sylvia_haener@gov.nt.ca

Assistant Deputy Minister & Attorney General, Mark Aitken
Tel: 867-920-6197
mark_aitken@gov.nt.ca

Assistant Deputy Minister & Solicitor General, Shirley Kemeys-Jones
shirley_kemeysjones@gov.nt.ca

Chief Coroner, Coroner's Office, Cathy Menard
Tel: 867-973-7448
Fax: 867-873-0426
cathy_menard@gov.nt.ca

Chief Information Officer, Norm Embleton
Tel: 867-920-6100
Fax: 867-873-0197
norm_embleton@gov.nt.ca

Public Trustee, Public Trustee's Office, Brian Asmundson
Tel: 867-873-7464
Toll-free: 866-535-0423
Fax: 867-873-0184
larry_pontus@gov.nt.ca

Executive Director, Legal Services Board, Charlene Doolittle
Tel: 867-873-7450
Fax: 867-873-5320
charlene_doolittle@gov.nt.ca

Acting Director, Legislation Division, Kelly McLaughlin
Tel: 867-920-8778
Fax: 867-873-0234
kelly_mclaughlin@gov.nt.ca

Director, Corrections Services, Greg Debogorski
Tel: 867-920-8922
Fax: 867-873-0299
greg_debogorski@gov.nt.ca

Director, Court Services, Anne Mould
Tel: 867-920-8852
Fax: 867-873-0307
anne_mould@gov.nt.ca

Director, Community Justice & Community Policing, Parker Kennedy
Tel: 867-873-7002
Fax: 867-873-0199
parker_kennedy@gov.nt.ca

Director, Legal Registries, Gary MacDougall
Tel: 867-873-7490
Fax: 867-873-0243
gary.macdougall@gov.nt.ca

Director, Finance, Kim Schofield
Tel: 867-873-7641
Fax: 867-873-0173
kim_schofield@gov.nt.ca

Director, Policy & Planning, Glen Rutland
Tel: 867-920-3225
Fax: 867-873-0659
glen_rutland@gov.nt.ca

Director, Legal Division, Brad Patzer
Tel: 867-920-3248
Fax: 867-873-0234
brad_patzer@gov.nt.ca

Registrar, Land Titles, Tom Hall
Tel: 867-920-8986
Fax: 867-873-0243
tom_hall@gov.nt.ca

Registrar, Corporate Registries, Donald MacDougall
Tel: 867-920-8984
Fax: 867-873-0243
donald_macdougall@gov.nt.ca

Administrator, Commissioner for Oaths / Notary Public, Cindy Pettes
Tel: 867-920-8985
Fax: 867-873-0243
cindy_pettes@gov.nt.ca

Associated Agencies, Boards & Commissions:
- **Judicial Council**
PO Box 550
Yellowknife, NT X1A 2N4
Tel: 867-873-7105
Fax: 867-873-0287
- **Legal Services Board of the Northwest Territories**
PO Box 1320
Yellowknife, NT X1A 2L9
Tel: 867-873-7450
Fax: 867-873-5320
- **Victims Assistance Committee**
c/o Community Justice Division
PO Box 1320
Yellowknife, NT X1A 2L9
Tel: 867-920-6911
Fax: 867-873-0199

Department of Municipal & Community Affairs

PO Box 1320, Yellowknife, NT X1A 2L9
Tel: 867-873-7118
Fax: 867-873-0309
www.maca.gov.nt.ca

Supports capable, accountable & self-directed community governments providing a safe, sustainable & healthy environment for community residents. Works with community governments & other partners in supporting community residents as they organize & manage democratic, responsible & accountable community governments. The Department assists municipalities with administrative services & infrastructure project management, provides expertise in engineering to communities & arranges for debentures on behalf of communities which are undertaking public works programs. Advisory services are supplied to community councils for the planning, development & administration of public lands within municipal boundaries. Technical expertise is provided for mapping, surveying & air photography & zoning by-law administration.

Acts Administered:
Area Development Act
Business Licence Act
Charter Communities Act
Cities, Towns & Villages Act
Civil Emergency Measures Act
Commissioner's Land Act
Community Employees Benefits Act
Consumer Protection Act
Curfew Act
Dog Act
Film Classification Act
Fire Prevention Act
Hamlets Act
Home Owner's Property Tax Rebate Act
Local Authorities Elections Act
Lotteries Act
Pawnbrokers & Second-Hand Dealers Act
Planning Act
Property Assessment & Taxation Act (jointly with Department of Finance)
Real Estate Agent's Licensing Act
Senior Citizens' & Disabled Persons' Property Tax Relief Act
Settlements Act
Tlicho Community Government Act
Western Canada Lotteries Act

Minister, Hon. Robert C. McLeod
Tel: 867-669-2366
Robert_C_McLeod@gov.nt.ca

Deputy Minister, Tom R. Williams
Tel: 867-873-7118
Fax: 867-873-0309
tom_williams@gov.nt.ca

Assistant Deputy Minister, Regional Operations, Eleanor Young
Tel: 867-873-7118
Fax: 867-873-0309
eleanor_young@gov.nt.ca

Director, Corporate Affairs, Gary Schauerte
Tel: 867-873-7512
gary_schauerte@gov.nt.ca

Director, Community Operations, Bill Buckle
Tel: 867-873-7571
bill_buckle@gov.nt.ca

Director, Sport, Recreation & Youth, Ian Legaree

Tel: 867-873-7245
Fax: 867-920-6467
ian_legaree@gov.nt.ca

Director, Public Safety, Kevin Brezinski
Tel: 867-873-7565
kevin_brezinski@gov.nt.ca

Manager, Emergency Measures, Wayne Norris
Tel: 867-873-7583
wayne_norris@gov.nt.ca

Fire Marshal, Stephen Moss
Tel: 867-873-7469
Fax: 867-873-0260
stephen_moss@gov.nt.ca

Records Coordinator, Corporate Affairs, Terry Kungl
Tel: 867-873-7474
terry_kungl@gov.nt.ca

Associated Agencies, Boards & Commissions:
• **Assessment Appeal Tribunal of the Northwest Territories**
#400, 5201 - 50th Ave.
PO Box 1320
Yellowknife, NT X1A 2L9
Tel: 867-873-7125
Fax: 867-873-0609
• **Territorial Board of Revision**
#400, 5201 - 50th Ave.
PO Box 1320
Yellowknife, NT X1A 2L9
Tel: 867-873-7125
Fax: 867-873-0609

Lands Administration

Tel: 867-873-7569
Fax: 867-920-6156

Responsible for the administration of Commissioner's lands in & around the communities of the Northwest Territories. Commissioner's lands make up about 2 percent of all land in the North. The Federal Government administers about 97 percent & municipal corporations administer the remaining 1 percent. Under the Lands Program, MACA is in the process of transferring certain lands from the Commissioner to municipalities. Land administration is being decentralized from MACA headquarters to regional offices or to the communities. As authority for land devolves, MACA will take on a training & advisory role, teaching & advising communities how to look after their own lands. The division supplies information & advice regarding land leases, surrenders, transfers, & mortgage registration for Commissioner's land & notifications.
Director, Emerald Murphy
Tel: 867-920-6284
emerald_murphy@gov.nt.ca
Manager, Lands Policy/Program Development, Michelle Chappell
Tel: 867-920-6318
michelle_chappell@gov.nt.ca

School of Community Government
#500, 5201 - 50th Ave., Yellowknife, NT X1A 3S9

Tel: 867-920-3159
Fax: 867-873-0584
Toll-Free: 877-531-9194

Director, Dan Schofield
Tel: 867-873-7755
Fax: 867-873-0584
dan_schofield@gov.nt.ca

Sport, Recreation & Youth

Tel: 867-873-7245
Fax: 867-920-6467

Director, Ian Legaree
Tel: 867-873-7245
ian_legaree@gov.nt.ca

Northwest Territories Power Corporation

4 Capital Dr., Hay River, NT X0E 1G2

Tel: 867-874-5200
Fax: 867-874-5251
info@ntpc.com
www.ntpc.com

Other Communication: Fort Simpson: 800-288-4784; Fort Smith: 800-661-0855; Inuvik: 800-661-0856; Yellowknife: 800-661-0854
Made up of 28 separate power systems, the NWT Power Corporation serves approximately 42,000 people in communities across the Northwest Territories. Facilities include hydro-electric, diesel & natural gas generation plants, transmission systems, & several isolated electrical distribution systems. The Corporation works to provide environmentally sound, safe, reliable, cost-effective energy & related services in the territories.

Minister Responsible, Hon. Floyd K. Roland
Tel: 867-669-2311
Fax: 867-873-0169
Floyd_K_Roland@gov.nt.ca

Chair, Brendan Bell

Acting President/Chief Executive Officer & Chief Operating Officer, Emanuel DaRosa

Chief Financial Officer, Judith Goucher

Public Utilities Board of the Northwest Territories (PUB)

#203, 62 Woodland Dr., PO Box 4211, Hay River, NT X0E 1G1

Tel: 867-874-3944
Fax: 867-874-3639
www.nwtpublicutilitiesboard.ca

The independent, quasi-judicial agency of the Government of the Northwest Territories is responsible for the regulation of public utilities in the territory. Its authority is from the Public Utilities Act. Issues are handled by an application & decision process.

Minister Responsible, Hon. Bob McLeod
Tel: 867-669-2388
Fax: 867-873-0431
Bob_McLeod@gov.nt.ca

Chair, Joe Acorn

Board Secretary, Louise-Ann Larocque
louise-ann_larocque@gov.nt.ca

Department of Public Works & Services

PO Box 1320, Yellowknife, NT X1A 2L9

www.pws.gov.nt.ca

Designs, constructs, maintains & operates territorial buildings; implements energy efficiency projects; provides essential petroleum products to the public where they are not available from the private sector; provides data systems & communication services to government departments.
Acts Administered:
Architects Act
Boilers & Pressure Vessels Act
Electrical Protection Act
Gas Protection Act
Purchasing Management Association Act

Minister, Hon. Glen Abernethy
Tel: 867-669-2388
glen_abernethy@gov.nt.ca

Deputy Minister, Paul Guy
Tel: 867-873-7114
Fax: 867-873-0226
paul_guy@gov.nt.ca

Director, Technical Support Section, Sukhi Cheema
Tel: 867-920-8088
sukhi_cheema@gov.nt.ca

Director, Technology Service Centre (TSC), Laurie Gault
Tel: 867-873-7836
Fax: 867-873-0135
laurie_gault@gov.nt.ca

Director, Corporate Services, Steve Lewis
Tel: 867-920-8672
Fax: 867-873-0212
steve_lewis@gov.nt.ca

Director, Facility Management Section, Brian Nagel
Tel: 867-920-6465
brian_nagel@gov.nt.ca

Executive Secretary, Marvia Rivet
Tel: 867-873-7114
Fax: 867-873-0226
marvia_rivet@gov.nt.ca

Asset Management Division
Stuart M. Hodgson Bldg., 5009 - 49th St., 3rd Fl., Yellowknife, NT X1A 2L9
Estimates the cost of building construction & renovation; consults in the plan of buildings so they meet program needs; reviews consultant designs of buildings & works; implements the Safe Drinking Water Initiatives.
Assistant Deputy Minister, Mike Burns
Tel: 867-920-6142
Fax: 867-873-0226
mike_burns@gov.nt.ca
Director, Facility Management Section, Brian Nagel
Tel: 867-920-6465
Fax: 867-873-0226
brian_nagel@gov.nt.ca
Manager, Gas/Boilers & Electrical, Ron McRae
Tel: 867-920-8801
ron_mcrae@gov.nt.ca

Petroleum Products Division
Stuart M. Hodgson, 5009 - 49th St., 1st Fl., Yellowknife, NT X1A 2L9

Tel: 867-920-3447
Fax: 867-873-0100

Provides essential petroleum products to the public where they are not available from the private sector.
Director, John Vandenburg
Tel: 867-920-3447
Fax: 867-873-0100
john_vandenberg@gov.nt.ca
Senior Operations Officer, Mike Squirrel
Tel: 867-695-7257
Fax: 867-695-3034
mike_squirrel@gov.nt.ca
Coordinator, Fuel Operations, Susan Eveleigh
Tel: 867-873-7796
Fax: 867-920-6297
susan_eveleigh@gov.nt.ca

Status of Women Council of the Northwest Territories

PO Box 1320, Yellowknife, NT X1A 2L9

Tel: 867-920-6177
Fax: 867-873-0285
Toll-Free: 888-234-4485
council@statusofwomen.nt.ca
www.statusofwomen.nt.ca

To work towards the equality of women through advice to the government; research; public education; advocacy on behalf of women; & workshops & other support for the development of women's groups, & other groups working on issues of concern to women.

Minister Responsible, Hon. Sandy Lee
Tel: 867-669-2344
Fax: 867-873-0481
Sandy_Lee@gov.nt.ca

President, Therese Dolly Simon

Vice-President, Su-Ellen Kolback

Executive Director, Lorraine Phaneuf
lorraine@statusofwomen.nt.ca

Department of Transportation

Lahm Ridge Bldg., 4501 50 Ave., PO Box 1320, Yellowknife, NT X1A 2L9

Tel: 867-920-3460
Fax: 867-873-0363
www.dot.gov.nt.ca

Acts Administered:
All-Terrain Vehicles Act
Deh Cho Bridge Act
Motor Vehicles Act
Public Airports Act
Public Highways Act
Transportation of Dangerous Goods Act, 1990
Transportation of Dangerous Goods Regulations

Minister, Hon. David Ramsay
Tel: 867-669-2377
Fax: 867-873-0388
David_Ramsay@gov.nt.ca

Deputy Minister, Russell Neudorf
Tel: 867-920-3460
Fax: 867-873-0363
russell_neudorf@gov.nt.ca

Assistant Deputy Minister, Daniel Auger
Tel: 867-920-3461
Fax: 867-873-0363
daniel_auger@gov.nt.ca

Director, Corporate Services, Jim Martin
Tel: 867-920-3459
Fax: 867-873-0283
jim_martin@gov.nt.ca

Director, Planning, Policy & Environment Division, Jayleen Robertson
Tel: 867-920-3366
Fax: 867-920-2565
jayleen_robertson@gov.nt.ca

Director, Mackenzie Valley Highway, Jim Stevens
Tel: 867-920-6247
jim_stevens@gov.nt.ca

Airports
YK Centre, 4922 - 28th St., 4th fl., PO Box 1320, Yellowknife, NT X1A 2L9
Tel: 867-873-7725
Fax: 867-873-0297

Director, Delia Chesworth
Tel: 867-873-7561
delia_chesworth@gov.nt.ca
Assistant Director, Airport Facilities, Mark Cronk
Tel: 867-873-7845
mark_cronk@gov.nt.ca
Assistant Director, Programs & Standards, Ben Webber
Tel: 867-873-7822
Fax: 867-873-0297
ben_webber@gov.nt.ca

Highways & Marine
4510 - 50 Ave., 2nd fl., PO Box 1320, Yellowknife, NT X1A 2L9
Tel: 867-920-8771
Fax: 867-873-0288

Director, Kevin McLeod
Tel: 867-873-7800
Fax: 867-873-0288
kevin_mcleod@gov.nt.ca
Head, Structures, Ann Kulmatycki
Tel: 867-920-8010
ann_lanteigne@gov.nt.ca

Road Licensing & Safety
4510 - 50 Ave., 1st fl., PO Box 1320, Yellowknife, NT X1A 2L9
Tel: 867-873-7972
Fax: 867-873-0120

Acting Director, Michael Conway
Tel: 867-920-3068
Fax: 867-873-0120
michael_conway@gov.nt.ca

Northwest Territories Water Board

125 Mackenzie Rd., PO Box 2531, Yellowknife, NT X0E 0T0
Tel: 867-678-2942
Fax: 867-678-2943
info@nwtwb.com
www.nwtwb.com

Responsible for the development, maintenance & conservation of water resources; administers licences for utilizing water or disposing of wastes into water under the Northwest Territories Waters Act; has federal/territorial jurisdiction.

Chair, Eddie T. Dillon

Executive Director, Mike Harlow
Tel: 867-678-8609
harlowm@nwtwb.com

Office & Finance Administrator, Freda Wilson
Tel: 867-678-2942
wilsonf@nwtwb.com

Northwest Territories & Nunavut Workers' Safety & Compensation Commission (WCB)

Centre Square Tower, 5022 - 49th St., 5th Fl., PO Box 8888, Yellowknife, NT X1A 2R3
Tel: 867-920-3888
Fax: 867-873-4596
Toll-Free: 800-661-0792
www.wscc.nt.ca
Other Communication: Toll Free Fax: 1-866-277-3677; Incident/Accident Line: 1-800-661-0792

The Workers' Safety & Compensation Commission is engaged in the following activities: ensuring compensation & pensions are awarded to injured workers or their dependents; assessing sufficiently & fairly to meet obligations; maintaining balance in providing benefits to injured workers, while keeping costs to employers as low as possible; & promoting safe workplaces through education & enforcement.
Acts Administered:
Asbestos Safety Regulations
Environmental Tobacco Smoke Worksite Regulations
Explosives Use Act
Mine Health & Safety Act
Mine Health & Safety Regulations
Safety Act
Summary Convictions Procedures Act
Work Site Hazardous Materials Information System Regulations
Workers' Compensation Act

Minister Responsible, Hon. Robert C. McLeod
Tel: 867-669-2366
Robert_C_McLeod@gov.nt.ca

President/Chief Executive Officer, Dave Grundy
Tel: 867-669-4442

Vice-President, Revenue & Financial Services, Gloria Badari
Tel: 867-920-3824

Vice-President, Prevention Services, Cara Benoit
Tel: 867-669-4407

Vice-President, Client & Central Services, Kim Collins Riffel
Tel: 867-920-3821

Vice-President, Nunavut Operations, Derek Dinham
Tel: 902-979-8507

Vice-President, Corporate Communications & Policy Services, Edith Johnston-Ryder
Tel: 867-669-4431

Chief Information Officer, Harmeet Jagpal
Tel: 867-669-4446

General Counsel, Amy Groothuis
Tel: 867-920-3813

Government of Nova Scotia

Seat of Government: Province House, 1726 Hollis St., Halifax, NS B3J 2T3
www.gov.ns.ca

The Province of Nova Scotia entered Confederation July 1, 1867. It has an area of 52,917,46 km2, & the StatsCan census population in 2011 was 921,727.

Office of the Lieutenant Governor

Government House, 1451 Barrington St., Halifax, NS B3J 1Z2
Tel: 902-424-7001
Fax: 902-424-0537
lgoffice@gov.ns.ca
www.lt.gov.ns.ca
Other Communication: Invitation to the Lieutenant Governor, E-mail: invite-lg@gov.ns.ca; Greeting requests from the Lieutenant Governor, Nova Scotia Protocol Office Phone: 902-424-4463

On April 12, 2012, Brigadier-General The Honourable J.J. Grant, CMM, ONS, CD (Ret'd) was installed as Her Majesty's representative in Nova Scotia.

Lieutenant Governor of Nova Scotia, Hon. John James Grant, CMM, ONS, CD (Ret'd)
Note: On February 16, 2012, the Right Honourable Stephen Harper announced the appointment of Brigadier-General Grant as thethirty-second Lieutenant Governor of Nova Scotia.

Executive Director, Government House; Private Secretary to the Lieutenant Governor, Dr. Christopher McCreery, MVO

Coordinator, In-house Events, Kelly Clelland

Office of the Premier

One Government Place, 1700 Granville St., 7th Fl., PO Box 726, Halifax, NS B3J 2T3
Tel: 902-424-6600
Fax: 902-424-7648
Toll-Free: 800-267-1993
premier@gov.ns.ca
www.premier.gov.ns.ca

Premier, Hon. Darrell Dexter
premier@gov.ns.ca

Deputy Premier, Frank Corbett
Tel: 902-862-9550
Fax: 902-862-9501
corbetf@gov.ns.ca

Chief of Staff, Dan O'Connor
oconnoda@gov.ns.ca

Director, Communications, Shawn Fuller
Tel: 902-240-7575
fullersz@gov.ns.ca

Director, Strategic Operations, Shawna Martin
martinsl@gov.ns.ca

Principal Secretary to the Premier, Matt Hebb
hebbmg@gov.ns.ca

Manager, Administration, Operations, Events Management, Military/ Protocol Liasion & Special Projects, Jo Anne Fisher
fisherjc@gov.ns.ca

Executive Council

One Government Place, 1700 Granville St., 5th Fl., PO Box 2125, Halifax, NS B3J 3B7
Tel: 902-424-5970
Fax: 902-424-0667
execounc@gov.ns.ca
www.gov.ns.ca/exec_council
TTY: 866-206-6844
Other Communication: 902-424-6611 (General Inquiries)

The ECO is non-departmental in function & purpose. It serves the Executive Council (Cabinet) & its committees, the exectuve teams of Treasury Board Office & the Office of Policy & Priorities, as well as departments, agencies, boards, & commissions. The office aims to ensure that the business of the Cabinet and its committees is conducted in a timely, efficient way & that proper collective information is provided. The ECO works to improve agenda management for the Cabinet its committees, by developing policies & procedures for more efficient & effective operations of the decision-making process.

Premier & President, Executive Council, Minister, Policy & Priorities; Minister, Intergovernmental Affairs; Minister, Aboriginal Affairs; Min. responsible for Military Relations, Hon. Darrell Dexter
Tel: 902-424-6600
Toll-free: 800-261-1933
Fax: 902-424-7648
premier@gov.ns.ca

Deputy Premier & Deputy President, Executive Council, Minister, Public Service Commission; Minister, Communications Nova Scotia; Minister, Information Management; Chair, Treasury Board, Hon. Frank Corbett
Tel: 902-424-5465
Fax: 902-424-0555
min_psc@gov.ns.ca

Minister, Fisheries & Aquaculture; Minister, Environment, Hon. Sterling Belliveau
Tel: 902-424-3736
Fax: 902-424-1599
min_env@gov.ns.ca; min_dfa@gov.ns.ca

Minister, Transportation & Infrastructure Renewal; Minister, Gaelic Affairs; Minister Responsible, Sydney Tar Ponds Agency, Sydney Steel Corporation Act, Insurance Act, & Nova Scotia Police Review Board; Member, Treasury BoardCommittee, Hon. Maurice Smith
Tel: 902-424-5875
Fax: 902-424-0171
tirmin@gov.ns.ca; gaelicinfo@gov.ns.ca

Minister, Education; Minister Responsible for Youth; Member of Treasury Board Committee, Hon. Ramona Jennex
Tel: 902-424-4236
Fax: 902-424-0680
educmin@gov.ns.ca

Attorney General & Minister, Justice; Provincial Secretary, Responsible for Human Rights Act, Regulations Act, Workers' Compensation Act (Part II), Retail Business Uniform Closing Day Act, & Elections, Hon. Ross Landry
Tel: 902-424-4044
Fax: 902-424-0510
justmin@gov.ns.ca

Minister, Labour & Advanced Education; Minister, Immigration; & Minister, Voluntary Sector, Responsible for the Advisory Council on the Status of Women Act, Apprenticeship & Trades Qualifications Act, Workers Compensation Act, Hon. Marilyn More
Tel: 902-424-6647
Fax: 902-424-0575
min_lae@gov.ns.ca

Minister, Economic & Rural Development & Tourism; Minister, African Nova Scotian Affairs, Minister Responsible for the Gateway Initiative, Nova Scotia Business Incorporated, & Innovation Corporation Act, Hon. Percy Paris
Tel: 902-424-5790
Fax: 902-424-0514
econmin@gov.ns.ca

Minister, Natural Resources; Minister, Energy, Hon. Charlie Parker
Tel: 902-424-4037
Fax: 902-424-0594
min_dnr@gov.ns.ca; energyminister@gov.ns.ca

Minister, Community Services; Minister, Seniors, Minister Responsible for the Disabled Persons' Commission Act; Chair of the Senior Citizens'Secretariat, Hon. Denise Peterson-Rafuse
Tel: 902-424-4304
Fax: 902-428-0618
petersdj@gov.ns.ca

Minister, Health & Wellness; Minister, Acadian Affairs, Hon. Dave Wilson
Tel: 902-424-3377
Fax: 902-424-0559
health.minister@gov.ns.ca; min-oaa@gov.ns.ca

Minister, Agriculture; Minister, Service Nova Scotia & Municipal Relations, Minister Responsible for the Residential Tenancies Act, Maritime Provinces Harness Racing Commission Act, & Gaming Control Act (Part II), Hon. John MacDonell
Tel: 902-424-4388
Fax: 902-424-0699
min_dag@gov.ns.ca
Note: Member of Treasury Board Committee

Minister, Finance; Minister Responsible for the Securities Act, Liquor Control Act, Credit Union Act, Utility & Review Board Act, Nova Scotia Liquor Corporation; Member of Treasury Board Committee, Hon. Maureen MacDonald
Tel: 902-424-5720
Fax: 902-424-0635
financeminister@gov.ns.ca

Minister, Communities, Culture, & Heritage; Minister Responsible for the Heritage Property Act & Gaming Control Act (Part I), Hon. Leonard Preyra
Tel: 902-424-4889
Fax: 902-424-4872
min_cch@gov.ns.ca

Legislative House of Assembly

c/o Clerk's Office, Province House, 1st Fl., PO Box 1617, Halifax, NS B3J 2Y3

Tel: 902-424-5978
Fax: 902-424-0632
www.gov.ns.ca/legi/house.htm
Other Communication: 902-424-0526 (Fax, Office of the Speaker)

Chief Clerk of the House, Neil R. Ferguson
Tel: 902-424-8941

Speaker, House of Assembly, Hon. Gordie Gosse
Tel: 902-424-5707
Fax: 902-424-0526
gordiegosse@ns.aliantzinc.ca; gossego@gov.ns.ca
www.gordiegosse.net
Other Communications: Administration Office, Phone: 902-424-4478
Speaker's Administration Office
1724 Granville St.
PO Box 1617
Halifax, NS B3J 1X5

Deputy Speaker, Leo Glavine
Tel: 902-424-8637
Fax: 902-424-0539
leoglavinemla@eastlink.ca
www.leoglavine.com

Deputy Speaker, Becky Kent
Tel: 902-424-4134
Fax: 902-424-0504
kentbj@gov.ns.ca
Social Media: ca.linkedin.com/pub/becky-kent/29/a38/20

Deputy Speaker, Alfie MacLeod
Tel: 902-424-2731
Fax: 902-424-7484
alfiemacleodmla@ns.aliantzinc.ca
Social Media: ca.linkedin.com/pub/becky-kent/29/a38/20

Sergeant-at-Arms, Kenneth Greenham, C.D.
Tel: 902-424-4603

Legislative Librarian, Margaret Murphy
Tel: 902-424-5932
Fax: 902-424-0220
leglib@gov.ns.ca
Legislative Library, Province House
1726, Hollis St.
PO Box 396
Halifax, NS B3J 2P8

Editor, Hansard, Robert Kinsman
Tel: 902-424-5706
Fax: 902-424-0593
publications@gov.ns.ca
Note:
www.nslegislature.ca/index.php/people/offices/hansard-reporting-services/

Chief Legislative Counsel, Gordon D. Hebb
Tel: 902-424-8941
Fax: 902-424-0547
legc.office@gov.ns.ca
Office of the Legislative Counsel, CIBC Building
#802, 1809 Barrington St.
PO Box 1116
Halifax, NS B3J 2X1

Assistant Clerk; Legislative Counsel, Annette M. Boucher, QC
Tel: 902-424-6187

Director, Administration, Deborah Lusby
Tel: 902-424-4479
Fax: 902-424-2404
lusbyda@gov.ns.ca

Director, Legislative TV, Jim MacInnes
Tel: 902-424-3875
Fax: 902-424-0604
macinnjt@gov.ns.ca

Government Caucus Office (New Democratic Party)

New Democratic Party Caucus Office, Centennial Building, #1006, 1660 Hollis St., Halifax, NS B3J 1V7

Tel: 902-424-4134
Fax: 902-423-9618
Toll-Free: 800-753-7696
ndpcaucus@gov.ns.ca
www.ndpcaucus.ns.ca; www.ns.ndp.ca

Premier; Leader, New Democratic Party of Nova Scotia; President, Executive Council; Minister, Intergovernmental Affairs; Minister, Policy & Priorities; Minister, Aboriginal Affairs; Minister Responsible, MilitaryRelations, Hon. Darrell Dexter
Tel: 902-424-6600
Fax: 902-424-7648
ddexter.mla@gmail.com; premier@gov.ns.ca
premier.gov.ns.ca
Social Media: twitter.com/PremierDexter

Chair, New Democratic Party Caucus, Vicki Conrad
Tel: 902-424-4134
Fax: 902-424-0504
vconrad@vickiconrad.ca

Deputy Premier; Government House Leader; Deputy President, Executive Council; Chair, Treasury Board, Minister, Public Service Commission; Minister, Communications Nova Scotia; Minister, InformationManagement, Hon. Frank Corbett
Tel: 902-424-5465
Fax: 902-424-0555
frankmla@ns.sympatico.ca; min_psc@gov.ns.ca

Deputy House Leader, New Democratic Party, Clarrie MacKinnon
Tel: 902-424-4134
Fax: 902-424-0504
clarriemla@ns.aliantzinc.ca
www.clarriemla.ca

Whip, Government Caucus, Mat Whynott
Tel: 902-424-4134
Fax: 902-424-0504
mat.mla@ns.sympatico.ca
www.mattwynott.ca
Social Media: twitter.com/matmla, www.facebook.com/matmla

President, New Democratic Party of Nova Scotia, David Wallbridge

Office of the Official Opposition (Liberal Party)

Nova Scotia Liberal Caucus Office, #1402, 5151 George St., PO Box 741, Halifax, NS B3J 2T3

Tel: 902-424-8637
Fax: 902-424-0539
Toll-Free: 877-778-1917
info@nsliberalcaucus.ca
www.nsliberalcaucus.ca

The Official Opposition of the Nova Scotia House of Assembly consists of thirteen Liberal MLAs.

Leader, Official Opposition, Nova Scotia House of Assembly; Leader, Nova Scotia Liberal Party, Hon. Stephen McNeil, ECNS
Tel: 902-424-8637
Fax: 902-424-0539
stephenmcneil@ns.aliantzinc.ca
www.liberal.ns.ca/nslp_9244.html
Social Media: twitter.com/StephenMcNeil, www.facebook.com/StephenMcNeilMLA

Chair, Liberal Caucus, Diana Whalen
Tel: 902-424-8637
Fax: 902-424-0539
whalendc@gov.ns.ca
www.dianawhalen.com
Social Media: twitter.com/dianawhalenMLA

House Leader, Official Opposition, Hon Michel P. Samson
Tel: 902-424-8637
Fax: 902-424-0539
michelsamson@ns.sympatico.ca
www.michelsamson.ca
Social Media: twitter.com/msamsonliberal, www.facebook.com/michel.samson.mla

Deputy House Leader, Liberal Party, Andrew Younger
Tel: 902-424-8637
Fax: 902-424-0539
info@andrewyounger.ca
www.andrewyounger.ca
Social Media: twitter.com/AndrewMLA

Whip, Liberal Caucus, Kelly Regan
Tel: 902-424-8637
Fax: 902-424-0539
kelly@kellyregan.ca
www.kellyregan.ca
Social Media: twitter.com/KellyReganNS, www.facebook.com/kelly.regan1?ref=ts

Chief of Staff, Kelly McVicar
mcvicaks@gov.ns.ca

Director, Communications, Kyley Harris
Tel: 902-223-2387
harriskz@gov.ns.ca

Director, Outreach (Metro), Kristan Hines
hineskl@gov.ns.ca

Director, Research, Tracey Preeper
preepetk@gov.ns.ca

Manager, Human Resources & Office, Shirley-Anne Williams
williasd@gov.ns.ca

Office of the Progressive Conservative Party

PC Caucus Office, Bank of Monteal Building, #601, 5151 George St., 6th Fl., Halifax, NS B3J 1M5

Tel: 902-424-2731
Fax: 902-424-7484
Toll-Free: 800-363-1998
www.pccaucus.ns.ca; www.pcparty.ns.ca
Other Communication: Media Inquiries, Phone: 902-499-9948

Leader, Progressive Conservative Party of Nova Scotia, Hon. Jamie Baillie
Tel: 902-424-2731
Fax: 902-424-7484
jamiebaillie@bellaliant.com
www.jamiebailliemla.ca
Social Media: twitter.com/JamieBaillie, www.facebook.com/jamie.baillie.988

Caucus Chair, Progressive Conservative Party, Keith Bain
Tel: 902-424-2731
Fax: 902-424-7484
keithbainmla@ns.sympatico.ca; keith@keithbainmla.ca
www.keithbainmla.ca

House Leader, Progressive Conservative Party, Hon. Christopher A. d'Entremont
Tel: 902-424-2731
Fax: 902-424-7484
info@chrisdentremont.com
www.chrisdentremont.com
Social Media: twitter.com/@ChrisMLA

Whip, Progressive Conservative Party, Allan MacMaster
Tel: 902-424-2731
Fax: 902-424-7484
mlamacmaster@bellaliant.com
www.allanmacmaster.ca

President, Nova Scotia Progressive Conservative Party, Janet Fryday Dorey

Press Secretary to the Progressive Conservative Leader, Angie Zinck
Tel: 902-225-1630
zinckal@gov.ns.ca

Standing Committees of the House

Committees Office, 1740 Granville St., 3rd Fl., PO Box 2630 M, Halifax, NS B3J 3N5

Tel: 902-424-4432
Fax: 902-424-0513
legcomm@gov.ns.ca
www.nslegislature.ca/index.php/committees/

Legislative committees are appointed by the Nova Scotia House of Assembly & are comprised of Members of the House. The committee system allows for detailed examination of matters in a

manner which would not be possible in the larger House & also allows members of the public to have direct input into the parliamentary process by making submissions & attending public hearings.
Clerk, Legislative Committees, Darlene Henry

Sixty-first Assembly - Nova Scotia

Province House, 1726 Hollis St., Halifax, NS B3J 2Y3
Tel: 902-424-4661
Fax: 902-424-0574

Last General Election, June 9, 2009.
Maximum Duration, 5 years.
Party Standings (September 2012):
New Democratic Party (NDP) 31;
Liberal (Lib.) 13;
Progressive Conservative (PC) 7;
Independent 1;
Total: 52.
MLA Remuneration (January 2012):
MLA Indemnity 87,485.20;
Additional Indemnity:
Premier 110,579.61;
Speaker 48,084.81;
Deputy Speaker 24,042.40;
Minister with portfolio 48,084.81;
Minister without portfolio 48,084.81;
Leader of the Opposition 48,084.81;
Leader of a Recognized Opposition Party 24,042.40.
The following list features members, with their constituency, the number of electors on the official list for the 2009 provincial general election, party affiliation, & contact information:

Members of the Legislative Assembly of Nova Scotia

Hon. Jamie Baillie
Constituency: Cumberland South *No. of Constituents:* 10,075, Progressive Conservative
Tel: 902-424-2731
Fax: 902-424-7484
jamiebaillie@bellaliant.com
www.jamiebailliemla.ca
Other Communications: Constituency Phone: 902-597-1998
Social Media: twitter.com/JamieBaillie, www.facebook.com/jamie.baillie.988
Note: The Honourable Jamie Baillie was elected to the Nova Scotia House of Assembly in a by-election that took place on October 25, 2010.
Constituency Office
6 McFarlane St.
Springhill, NS B0M 1X0

Keith Bain
Constituency: Victoria-The Lakes *No. of Constituents:* 9,328, Progressive Conservative
Tel: 902-424-2731
Fax: 902-424-7484
keithbainmla@ns.sympatico.ca; keith@keithbainmla.ca
www.keithbainmla.ca
Other Communications: Constituency Phone: 902-674-0089,Fax: 902-674-0191
Constituency Office
1551 Old Rte. 5
Big Bras d'Or, NS B1X 1B5

Hon. Sterling Belliveau
Constituency: Shelburne *No. of Constituents:* 11,661, New Democratic Party
Tel: 902-424-8953
Fax: 902-428-3145
mlashelburne@eastlink.ca; min_dfa@gov.ns.ca;min_env@gov.ns.ca
www.sterlingbelliveau.ca
Other Communications: Constituency Phone: 902-637-3200, Fax: 902-637-3530
Constituency Office
#9, 3640 Hwy. 3
PO Box 595
Barrington Passage, NS B0W 1G0

Pam Birdsall
Constituency: Lunenburg *No. of Constituents:* 13,703, New Democratic Party
Tel: 902-424-4134
Toll-free: 877-634-9110
Fax: 902-424-0504
pambirdsallmla@bellaliant.com
www.pambirdsall.ca
Other Communications: Constituency Phone: 902-634-9110, Fax: 902-634-8489
Social Media: www.facebook.com/pam.birdsall
Constituency Office
119 PelhamSt.
PO Box 1509
Lunenburg, NS B0J 2C0

Jim Boudreau
Constituency: Guysborough-Sheet Harbour *No. of Constituents:* 9,505, New Democratic Party
Tel: 902-424-4134
Toll-free: 888-465-7575
Fax: 902-424-0504
jimboudreaumla@bellaliant.com
www.jimboudreau.ca
Other Communications: Constituency Phone: 902-366-3033, Fax: 902-366-3858
Social Media: www.facebook.com/groups/10565684630
Constituency Office
1290 UnionSt.
PO Box 69
Canso, NS B0H 1H0

Gary Burrill
Constituency: Colchester-Musquodoboit Valley *No. of Constituents:* 13,422, New Democratic Party
Tel: 902-424-4134
Toll-free: 877-582-0277
Fax: 902-424-0504
garyburrill@ns.sympatico.ca
Other Communications: Constituency Phone: 902-639-2277; Fax: 902-639-9776
Constituency Office
20 Dunrovin Ave.
PO Box 129
Stewiacke, NS B0N 2J0

Hon. Karen Casey
Constituency: Colchester North *No. of Constituents:* 13,686, Liberal
Tel: 902-424-8637
Fax: 902-424-0539
karencasey@ns.aliantzinc.ca
www.karencasey.ca
Other Communications: Constituency Phone: 902-893-2180, Fax: 902-893-3064
Note: On January 10, 2011, The Honourable Karen Casey resigned from the PC Causcus & joined the Liberal Caucus.
Constituency Office
30 Duke St.
Truro, NS B2N 2A1

Zach Churchill
Constituency: Yarmouth *No. of Constituents:* 13,197, Liberal
Tel: 902-424-8637
Fax: 902-424-0539
churchzj@gov.ns.ca
www.zachchurchill.ca
Other Communications: Constituency Phone: 902-742-4444, Fax: 902-742-7391
Social Media: twitter.com/zachchurchill, www.facebook.com/pages/Zach-Churchill/130216460347628
Note: Zach Churchill was elected to the Nova Scotia House of Assembly in a by-election on June 22, 2010.
Constituency Office
#100, 396 Main St.
Yarmouth, NS B5A 1E9

Hon. Keith Colwell
Constituency: Preston *No. of Constituents:* 7,680, Liberal
Tel: 902-424-8637
Fax: 902-424-0539
colwelkw@gov.ns.ca
www.keithcolwell.ca
Other Communications: Constituency Phone: 902-433-1494, Fax: 902-435-1712
Social Media: twitter.com/keithcolwellmla, www.facebook.com/keithcolwellNS
Constituency Office
Box 1, Comp. 4, 2345 Hwy. 7
East Preston, NS B2Z 1G6

Vicki Conrad
Constituency: Queens *No. of Constituents:* 9,974, New Democratic Party
Tel: 902-424-4134
Toll-free: 888-354-5203
Fax: 902-424-0504
vconrad@vickiconrad.ca
www.vickiconrad.ca
Other Communications: Constituency Phone: 902-354-5203, Fax: 902-354-5247
Constituency Office
43 Carten St.
PO Box 430
Liverpool, NS B0T 1K0

Public Service Commission; Minister, Communications NovaScotia; Minister, Information Management, Hon. Frank Corbett
Constituency: Cape Breton Centre *No. of Constituents:* 12,317, New Democratic Party
Tel: 902-424-5465
Fax: 902-424-0555
frankmla@ns.sympatico.ca; min_psc@gov.ns.ca
Other Communications: Constituency Phone: 902-862-9550, Fax: 902-862-9501
Constituency Office
3397 Plummer Ave.
PO Box 1
New Waterford, NS B1H1Z1

Hon. Christopher A. d'Entremont
Constituency: Argyle *No. of Constituents:* 6,474, Progressive Conservative
Tel: 902-424-2731
Fax: 902-424-7484
info@chrisdentremont.com
www.chrisdentremont.com
Other Communications: Constituency Phone: 902-648-2020, Fax:902-648-2001
Social Media: twitter.com/@ChrisMLA
Constituency Office
PO Box 94
Tusket, NS B0W 3M0

Intergovernmental Affairs; Minister, Policy & Priorities; Minister, AboriginalAffairs; Minister Responsible, Military Relations, Hon. Darrell Dexter
Constituency: Cole Harbour *No. of Constituents:* 15,720, New Democratic Party
Tel: 902-424-6600
Fax: 902-424-7648
ddexter.mla@gmail.com; premier@gov.ns.ca
premier.gov.ns.ca
Other Communications: Constituency Phone: 902-462-5300, Fax: 902-462-5306
Social Media: twitter.com/PremierDexter
Constituency Office
971 Cole Harbour Rd.
Cole Harbour, NS B2V 1E8

Howard Epstein
Constituency: Halifax Chebucto *No. of Constituents:* 14,382, New Democratic Party
Tel: 902-424-4134
Fax: 902-424-0504
hepstein@ns.aliantzinc.ca; howard@howardepstein.ca
www.howardepstein.ca
Other Communications: Constituency Phone: 902-425-8521, Fax: 902-429-6082
Social Media: twitter.com/hepsteinmla
Constituency Office
#103, 6009 Quinpool Rd.
Halifax, NS B3K 5J6

Hon. Bill Estabrooks
Constituency: Timberlea-Prospect *No. of Constituents:* 15,984, New Democratic Party
Tel: 902-424-4134
Fax: 902-424-0504
billestabrooks@navnet.net
Other Communications: Constituency Phone: 902-876-2472, Fax: 902-876-2192
Constituency Office, BLT RecreationCentre
1492 St. Margaret's Bay Rd.
Lakeside, NS B3T 1B3

Hon. Wayne J. Gaudet
Constituency: Clare *No. of Constituents:* 6,905, Liberal
Tel: 902-424-8637
Fax: 902-424-0539
waynej@ns.aliantzinc.ca
Other Communications: Constituency Office: 902-769-3131, Fax: 902-769-2239
Constituency Office
RR#1
PO Box 106
Church Point, NS B0W 1M0

Leo Glavine
Constituency: Kings West *No. of Constituents:* 14,706, Liberal
Tel: 902-424-8637
Fax: 902-424-0539
leoglavinemla@eastlink.ca
www.leoglavine.com
Other Communications: Constituency Phone: 902-765-4083, Fax: 902-765-4176
Constituency Office, SouthgateCourt
780 Central Ave.
PO Box 1501
Greenwood, NS B0P 1N0

Hon. Gordie Gosse
Constituency: Cape Breton Nova *No. of Constituents:* 10,748, New Democratic Party
Tel: 902-424-5707
Fax: 902-424-0526
gordiegosse@ns.aliantzinc.ca; gossego@gov.ns.ca
www.gordiegosse.net
Other Communications: Constituency Phone: 902-564-9161, Fax:902-564-9975
Constituency Office
758 Victoria Rd.
Sydney, NS B1N 1J6

Hon. Ramona Jennex
Constituency: Kings South *No. of Constituents:* 17,062, New Democratic Party
Tel: 902-424-4236
Fax: 902-424-0680
ramonajennexmla@bellaliant.com; educmin@gov.ns.ca
www.ramonajennex.ca

Other Communications: Constituency Phone:902-681-3741, Fax: 902-681-6261
Social Media: www.facebook.com/pages/Ramona-Jennex/65006196043
Constituency Office
#2, 8985 Commercial St.
New Minas, NS B4N 3E3

Becky Kent
Constituency: Cole-Harbour-Eastern Passage *No. of Constituents:* 13,158, New Democratic Party
Tel: 902-424-4134
Fax: 902-424-0504
kentbj@gov.ns.ca
Other Communications: Constituency Phone: 902-465-3180, Fax: 902-465-3179
Social Media: ca.linkedin.com/pub/becky-kent/29/a38/20
Constituency Office
1490 Main Rd.
PO Box 152
Eastern Passage, NS B3G 1M4

Min. Responsible, Regulations Act; Min. Responsible,Part II, Workers' Comp Act; Min. Responsible, Retail Business Uniform Closing Day Act, Hon. Ross Landry
Constituency: Pictou Centre *No. of Constituents:* 12,929, New Democratic Party
Tel: 902-424-4044
Fax: 902-424-0510
pictoucentremla@rosslandry.ca; justmin@gov.ns.ca
www.rosslandry.ca
Other Communications: Constituency Phone: 902-752-7677, Fax: 902-752-7922
ConstituencyOffice
115 MacLean St.
New Glasgow, NS B2H 4M5

Hon. Manning MacDonald
Constituency: Cape Breton South *No. of Constituents:* 16,838, Liberal
Tel: 902-424-8637
Fax: 902-424-0539
manningm@ns.sympatico.ca
Other Communications: Constituency Phone: 902-539-6032, Fax: 902-539-6860
Constituency Office
253 Newlands Ave.
Sydney, NS B1S 1Y7

Nova Scotia Liquor Corporation; Min. Responsible, Securities Act;Min. Responsible, Utility & Review Board Act, Hon. Maureen MacDonald
Constituency: Halifax Needham *No. of Constituents:* 16,241, New Democratic Party
Tel: 902-424-5720
Fax: 902-424-0635
mmacdonald@navnet.net; financeminister@gov.ns.ca
www.maureenmacdonald.ca
Other Communications: Constituency Phone: 902-455-2926, Fax: 902-455-3929
Constituency Office
3115 Veith St.
Halifax, NS B3K3G9

Maritime Provinces Harness Racing Comm. Act; Min. Responsible, Part II, Gaming ControlAct; Min. Responsible, Residential Tenanancies Act, Hon. John MacDonell
Constituency: Hants East *No. of Constituents:* 18,019, New Democratic Party
Tel: 902-424-5550
Toll-free: 888-827-2212
Fax: 902-424-0581
john.macdonell@ns.sympatico.ca; min_dag@gov.ns.ca
Other Communications: Constituency Phone: 902-883-7308, Fax: 902-883-7627
Constituency Office
#5, 202 Hwy.2
PO Box 330
Enfield, NS B2T 1C8

Clarrie MacKinnon
Constituency: Pictou East *No. of Constituents:* 11,673, New Democratic Party
Tel: 902-424-4134
Fax: 902-424-0504
clarriemla@ns.aliantzinc.ca
www.clarriemla.ca
Other Communications: Constituency Phone: 902-396-1853, Fax:902-396-1803
Constituency Office
1905 Main St.
PO Box 914
Westville, NS B0K 2A0

Geoff MacLellan
Constituency: Glace Bay *No. of Constituents:* 12,993, Liberal
Tel: 902-424-8637
Fax: 902-424-0539
mla@geoffmaclellan.ca; info@geoffmaclellan.ca
www.geoffmaclellan.ca
Other Communications: Constituency Phone: 902-842-4390, Fax: 902-842-4389
Social Media: twitter.com/GeoffMacLellan, www.facebook.com/geoffmaclellanmla
Note: Geoff MacLellan was elected to the Nova Scotia House of Assembly in a by-election on June 22, 2010.
Constituency Office,Peoples Mall
219 Commercial St., #D
Glace Bay, NS B1A 3B9

Alfie MacLeod
Constituency: Cape Breton West *No. of Constituents:* 14,843, Progressive Conservative
Tel: 902-424-2731
Fax: 902-424-7484
alfiemacleodmla@ns.aliantzinc.ca
Other Communications: Constituency Phone: 902-564-8679, Fax: 902-564-1204
Constituency Office
1990Kings Rd.
Sydney, NS B1L 1C4

Allan MacMaster
Constituency: Inverness *No. of Constituents:* 14,453, Progressive Conservative
Tel: 902-424-2731
Toll-free: 888-968-7652
Fax: 902-424-7484
mlamacmaster@bellaliant.com
www.allanmacmaster.ca
Other Communications: Constituency Phone: 902-258-2216, Fax: 902-258-3231
Note: Alan MacMaster was elected to the Nova Scotia House of Assembly in a by-election in 2009.
Constituency Office
15759 Central Ave.
PO Box 238
Inverness, NS B0E 1N0

Hon. Stephen McNeil, ECNS
Constituency: Annapolis *No. of Constituents:* 14,429, Liberal
Tel: 902-424-8637
Toll-free: 800-317-8533
Fax: 902-424-0539
stephenmcneil@ns.aliantzinc.ca
www.liberal.ns.ca/nslp_9244.html
Other Communications: Constituency Phone: 902-825-2093, Fax: 902-825-6306
Social Media: twitter.com/StephenMcNeil, www.facebook.com/StephenMcNeilMLA
Constituency Office
142 Commercial St.
PO Box 1420
Middleton, NS B0S1P0

Advisory Council on the Status of Women Act; Min. Responsible,Apprenticeship & Trades Qualifications Act; Min. Responsible, Workers' Comp., Hon. Marilyn More
Constituency: Dartmouth South-Portland Valley *No. of Constituents:* 18,609, New Democratic Party
Tel: 902-424-7627
Fax: 902-428-3178
marilynmoremla@ns.aliantzinc.ca; min_lae@gov.ns.ca
www.marilynmore.ca
Other Communications: Constituency Phone: 902-463-6673, Fax: 902-463-4973
Constituency Office
135 Portland St.
PO Box 534
Dartmouth, NS B2Y 3Y8

Jim Morton
Constituency: Kings North *No. of Constituents:* 14,803, New Democratic Party
Tel: 902-424-4134
Fax: 902-424-0504
jimmorton@kingsnorthmla.ca
www.kingsnorthmla.ca
Other Communications: Constituency Phone: 902-678-6880, Fax: 902-678-6945
Constituency Office
401 MainSt.
PO Box 1577
Kentville, NS B4N 3W4

Eddie Orrell
Constituency: Cape Breton North *No. of Constituents:* 14,397, Progressive Conservative
Tel: 902-424-2731
Fax: 902-424-7484
eddieorrell@bellaliant.com
Other Communications: Constituency Phone: 902-794-9445, Fax: 902-794-1815
Social Media: twitter.com/eddieorrell, www.facebook.com/eddie.orrell.9
Note: Eddie Orrell was elected to the Nova Scotia House of Assembly in a by-election that took place on June 21, 2011.
Constituency Office
#5, 309 Commercial St.
North Sydney, NS B2A 1B9

Nova Scotia Business Incorporated; Minister Responsible,Innovation Corporation Act; Minister Responsible, Gateway Initiative, Hon. Percy Paris
Constituency: Waverley-Fall River — Beaverbank *No. of Constituents:* 15,741, New Democratic Party
Tel: 902-424-5790
Fax: 902-424-0514
percy@percyparis.ca; econmin@gov.ns.ca
www.percyparis.ca
Other Communications: Constituency Phone: 902-860-4004, Fax: 902-860-0197
Constituency Office
273 Windsor JunctionRd.
Windsor Junction, NS B2T 1G7

Hon. Charlie Parker
Constituency: Pictou West *No. of Constituents:* 10,996, New Democratic Party
Tel: 902-424-7793
Fax: 902-424-3265
charlieparkermla@ns.aliantzinc.ca; min_dnr@gov.ns.ca
Other Communications: Constituency Phone:902-485-4550, Fax: 902-485-7088
Constituency Office
49 Water St.
Pictou, NS B0K 1H0

Senior Citizens' Secretariat, Hon. DeniseP. Peterson-Rafuse
Constituency: Chester-St. Margaret's *No. of Constituents:* 15,409, New Democratic Party
Tel: 902-424-0065
Toll-free: 877-740-3378
Fax: 902-424-0561
denisepetersmla@bellaliant.com; DCSMIN@gov.ns.ca
www.denisepetersonrafusemla.ca
Other Communications: Constituency Phone: 902-857-3378, Fax: 902-857-3386
Social Media: twitter.com/deniseprafuse, www.facebook.com/DeniseMLA
Constituency Office
#213, 9977 St. Margaret's Bay Rd., RR#2
Hubbards, NS B0J 1T0

Chuck Porter
Constituency: Hants West *No. of Constituents:* 14,887, Progressive Conservative
Tel: 902-424-2731
Fax: 902-424-7484
chuck@chuckporter.ca; Cportermla@eastlink.ca
www.chuckporter.ca
Other Communications: Constituency Phone: 902-798-5779, Fax: 902-798-4093
Social Media: twitter.com/chuckportermla, www.facebook.com/chuck.porter.102
Constituency Office
58 GerrishSt.
PO Box 3873
Windsor, NS B0N 2T0

Sidney Prest
Constituency: Eastern Shore *No. of Constituents:* 12,078, New Democratic Party
Tel: 902-424-4134
Fax: 902-424-0504
sidprest.mla@ns.aliantzinc.ca
Other Communications: Constituency Phone: 902-889-2112, Fax: 902-889-3190
Constituency Office
#2, 7907 Hwy. 7
PO Box 6
Musquodoboit Harbour, NS B0J 2L0

Heritage PropertyAct, Hon. Leonard Preyra
Constituency: Halifax Citadel — SableIsland *No. of Constituents:* 15,240, New Democratic Party
Tel: 902-424-4889
Fax: 902-424-4872
preyra@eastlink.ca; min_cch@gov.ns.ca
www.preyra.ca
Other Communications: Constituency Phone: 902-444-3238, Fax: 902-444-3278
Constituency Office
989 Young Ave.
Halifax, NS B3H 2V9

Gary Ramey
Constituency: Lunenberg West *No. of Constituents:* 14,339, New Democratic Party
Tel: 902-424-4134
Fax: 902-424-0504
gary.ramey.mla@eastlink.ca
Other Communications: Constituency Phone: 902-530-8080, Fax: 902-530-8081
Social Media: ca.linkedin.com/pub/gary-ramey/47/489/594
Constituency Office
410 King St.
Bridgewater, NS B4V 1A9

Michèle Raymond
Constituency: Halifax Atlantic *No. of Constituents:* 16,705, New Democratic Party

Tel: 902-424-4134
Fax: 902-424-0504
mhraymondmla@eastlink.ca
www.mhraymond.ca
Other Communications: Constituency Phone: 902-477-4100, Fax: 902-477-4810
Constituency Office
47 Williams Lake Rd.
Halifax, NS B3P 1S9

Kelly Regan
Constituency: Bedford-Birch Cove *No. of Constituents:* 19,154, Liberal
Tel: 902-424-8637
Toll-free: 877-778-1917
Fax: 902-424-0539
kelly@kellyregan.ca
www.kellyregan.ca
Other Communications: Constituency Phone: 902-407-3777, Fax: 902-407-3779
Social Media: twitter.com/KellyReganNS, www.facebook.com/kelly.regan1?ref=ts
Constituency Office
#555, 1550 Bedford Hwy.
Bedford, NS B4A 1E6

Hon. Michel P. Samson
Constituency: Richmond *No. of Constituents:* 7,954, Liberal
Tel: 902-424-8637
Fax: 902-424-0539
michelsamson@ns.sympatico.ca
www.michelsamson.ca
Other Communications: Constituency Phone: 902-345-0778, Fax: 902-345-0779
Social Media: twitter.com/msamsonliberal, www.facebook.com/michel.samson.mla
Constituency Office, Richmond Industrial Mall
PO Box 57
Louisdale, NS B0E 1V0

Brian Skabar
Constituency: Cumberland North *No. of Constituents:* 14,452, New Democratic Party
Tel: 902-424-4134
Fax: 902-424-0504
office@brianskabarmla.ca
www.brianskabarmla.ca
Other Communications: Constituency Phone: 902-667-9812, Fax: 902-667-9811
Constituency Office
30 1/2 ChurchSt.
Amherst, NS B4H 3A8

NS Police Complaints Comm.; Min. Responsible, NSPolice Review Bd.; Min. Responsible, Sydney Steel Corp. Act; Min. Responsible, Tar Ponds, Hon. Maurice G. Smith
Constituency: Antigonish *No. of Constituents:* 15,005, New Democratic Party
Tel: 902-424-4298
Fax: 902-424-0171
mauricesmithmla@bellaliant.com; tirmin@gov.ns.ca
www.mauricesmithmla.ca
Other Communications: Constituency Phone: 902-863-0444, Fax: 902-424-0171
Note: Maurice Smith was elected to the Legislative Assembly in a by-election in 2009.
Constituency Office
#102, 275 Main St.
Antigonish, NS B2G 2C3

Hon. Graham G. Steele
Constituency: Halifax Fairview *No. of Constituents:* 14,508, New Democratic Party
Tel: 902-424-4134
Fax: 902-424-0504
graham@grahamsteele.ca
www.grahamsteele.ca
Other Communications: Constituency Phone: 902-453-5556, Fax: 902-453-4566
Constituency Office
#101, 7105 ChebuctoRd.
Halifax, NS B3L 4W8

Harold (Junior) Theriault
Constituency: Digby-Annapolis *No. of Constituents:* 9,883, Liberal
Tel: 902-424-8637
Fax: 902-424-0539
junior@ns.aliantzinc.ca
Other Communications: Constituency Phone: 902-245-2991, Fax: 902-245-6853
Social Media: www.facebook.com/haroldjunior.theriaultmla
Constituency Office
310 Hwy.303
PO Box 1038
Digby, NS B0V 1A0

Diana Whalen
Constituency: Halifax Clayton Park *No. of Constituents:* 19,976, Liberal
Tel: 902-424-8637
Fax: 902-424-0539
whalendc@gov.ns.ca
www.dianawhalen.com
Other Communications: Constituency Phone: 902-443-8318, Fax: 902-445-9287
Social Media: twitter.com/dianawhalenMLA
Constituency Office
#303, 287Lacewood Dr.
Halifax, NS B3M 3Y7

Mat Whynott
Constituency: Hammonds Plains - Upper Sackville *No. of Constituents:* 17,937, New Democratic Party
Tel: 902-424-4134
Fax: 902-424-0504
mat.mla@ns.sympatico.ca
www.mattwynott.ca
Other Communications: Constituency Phone: 902-864-5310, Fax: 902-864-8681
Social Media: twitter.com/matmla, www.facebook.com/matmla
Constituency Office
1651Sackville Dr.
Middle Sackville, NS B4E 3A9

Hon. David Wilson
Constituency: Sackville-Cobequid *No. of Constituents:* 14,882, New Democratic Party
Tel: 902-424-0497
Fax: 902-428-0124
dave@davidawilsonmla.ca; health.minister@gov.ns.ca
www.davidwilsonmla.ca
Other Communications: Constituency Phone:902-864-0396, Fax: 902-864-8409
Constituency Office
#105, 51 Cobequid Rd.
Lower Sackville, NS B4C 2N1

Andrew Younger
Constituency: Dartmouth East *No. of Constituents:* 15,240, Liberal
Tel: 902-424-8637
Fax: 902-424-0539
info@andrewyounger.ca
www.andrewyounger.ca
Other Communications: Constituency Phone: 902-406-4420, Fax: 902-406-4421
Social Media: twitter.com/AndrewMLA
ConstituencyOffice
#600, 73 Tacoma Dr.
Dartmouth, NS B2W 3Y6

Lenore Zann
Constituency: Truro-Bible Hill *No. of Constituents:* 15,647, New Democratic Party
Tel: 902-424-4134
Fax: 902-424-0504
lenorezannmla@bellaliant.com
www.lenorezannmla.ca
Other Communications: Constituency Phone: 902-897-9266, Fax: 902-897-1841
Social Media: twitter.com/lenorezann, www.facebook.com/LenoreZannMLA
Constituency Office
#212, 35 Commercial St.
Truro, NS B2N 3H9

Trevor Zinck
Constituency: Dartmouth North *No. of Constituents:* 14,728, Independent
Tel: 902-404-8414
tzinck@ns.aliantzinc.ca
Other Communications: Constituency Phone: 902-404-8413, Fax: 902-404-8415
Constituency Office
#3, 102 Albro Lake Rd.
Dartmouth, NS B3A3Y6

Nova Scotia Government Departments & Agencies

Office of Aboriginal Affairs

5251 Duke St., 5th Fl., PO Box 1617, Halifax, NS B3J 1P3
Tel: 902-424-7409
Fax: 902-424-0728
oaa@gov.ns.ca
www.gov.ns.ca/abor/

The Office undertakes activities that increase the level of pubic awareness of Aboriginal people and the issues they face. It also works collaboratively with Aboriginal communities and organizations and other levels of government to coordinate Aboriginal and tri-partite initiatives, develop strategies, and build and maintain a sustainable foundation for Aboriginal-Government relations.

Minister, Hon. Darrell Dexter
Tel: 902-424-7648
Toll-free: 800-267-1993
Fax: 902-424-7648
premier@gov.ns.ca

Deputy Minister, Judith Sullivan-Corney
Tel: 902-424-3219
Fax: 902-424-4166
corneyjm@gov.ns.ca

Director, Consultation, Jay Hartling
Tel: 902-424-4214
hartlij@gov.ns.ca

Director, Negotiations, Tom Soehl
Tel: 902-424-4224
Fax: 902-424-4225
soehlto@gov.ns.ca

Director, Policy, Ernest Walker
Tel: 902-424-4931
Fax: 902-424-4225

Office of Acadian Affairs

Dennis Building, 1740 Granville St., 7th Fl., PO Box 682, Halifax, NS B3J 2T7
Tel: 902-424-1267
Fax: 902-428-0124
Toll-Free: 866-382-5811
bonjour@gov.ns.ca
www.gov.ns.ca/acadian/e

The mission of the Office of Acadian Affairs is to offer advice & support to departments, offices, agencies, & Crown corporations so they can develop & adapt policies, programs, & services that reflect the needs of the Acadian & francophone community of Nova Scotia.

Minister, Hon. Dave Wilson
min-oaa@gov.ns.ca

Deputy Minister & Chief Executive Officer, Vaughne Madden
Tel: 902-424-3821
maddenve@gov.ns.ca

Office of African Nova Scotian Affairs (OANSA)

#604, 5670 Spring Garden Rd., PO Box 2691, Halifax, NS B3J 1H6
Tel: 902-424-5555
Fax: 902-424-7189
Toll-Free: 866-580-2672
ansa_newsletter@gov.ns.ca
www.gov.ns.ca/ansa

The mission of the Office of African Nova Scotian Affairs is to serve as a broker between community members & government, & to advocate for cross-cultural understanding.

Minister, Hon. Percy Paris

Cape Breton
Sydney Commerce Towers, #501, 15 Dorchester St., Sydney, NS B1P 5Y9
Tel: 902-563-3735
Fax: 902-563-2700

Department of Agriculture

1741 Brunswick St., 3rd Fl., PO Box 2223, Halifax, NS B3J 3C4
Tel: 902-424-4560
Fax: 902-424-4671
www.gov.ns.ca/nsafPO Box 550 Sta.
Truro, NS B2N 5E3 Canada

The Department of Agriculture has a legislated mandate to support & develop the agriculture & food industries, recognizing that these sectors are economic engines of Nova Scotia's rural communities. Fosters prosperous & sustainable agriculture & food industries through the delivery of quality public services for the betterment of rural communities in Nova Scotia.

Acts Administered:
Agriculture & Marketing Act
Agriculture & Rural Credit Act
Agriculture Marshland Conservation Act
Agrologists Act
Animal Cruelty Prevention Act
Animal Health & Protection Act
Animal Health & Protection Regulations
Animal Protection Act
Baby Chick Protection Act
Bee Industry Act
Cattle Pest Control Act
Crop & Livestock Insurance Act
Dairy Industry Act
Farm Practices Act
Farm Registration Act
Federations & Agriculture Act
Fences & Detention of Stray Livestock Act
Health Act (Food Safety, Inspection & Regulations)

Health Protection Act (Food Regulations & Milk Production, Transportation & Pasteurization Regulations only)
Imitation Dairy Products Act
Livestock Brands Act
Livestock Health Services Act
Livestock Health Services Regulations
Margarine Act
Maritime Provinces Harness Racing Commission Act
Marsh Land Use Regulations: Bishop-Beckwith, Dentiballis, Dugau/Ryerson, Grand Pré, Lower Truro, Masstown, Victoria Diamond Jubilee, Wellington
Meat Inspection Act
Natural Products Act
Non-Agricultural Use Land Exemption Regulations
Potato Industry Act
Provincial Berry Act
Sheep Protection Act
Veterinary Medical Act
Weed Control Act
Wildlife Act
Women's Institute of Nova Scotia Act

Minister, Hon. John MacDonnell
Tel: 902-424-4388
Fax: 902-424-0699
min_dag@gov.ns.ca

Deputy Minister, Paul LaFleche
Tel: 902-424-0300
Fax: 902-424-0698
laflecpt@gov.ns.ca

Acting Director, Policy & Planning, Mike Chisholm
Tel: 902-424-8860
chishomg@gov.ns.ca

Director, Communications, Celeste Sulliman
Tel: 902-424-0192
Fax: 902-424-3948
sullimcc@gov.ns.ca

Executive Secretary, Yvelle Poirier
Tel: 902-424-4388
ypoirier@gov.ns.ca

Associated Agencies, Boards & Commissions:

• Nova Scotia Crop & Livestock Insurance Commission
MacRae Library Building
137 College Rd.
PO Box 1092
Truro, NS B2N 5G9
Tel: 902-424-4560
Fax: 902-895-4622
nsclic@gov.ns.ca
www.gov.ns.ca/agri/ci
Under the Crop & Livestock Insurance Act, the Commission is responsible for administering the program under the direction, supervision, & control of the Minister of Agriculture.

• Nova Scotia Farm Loan Board
PO Box 550
Truro, NS B2N 5E3
Tel: 902-893-6506
Fax: 902-895-7693
flb@gov.ns.ca
www.gov.ns.ca/agri/farmlb/
Other Communication: Kentville location: Phone: 902-679-6009, Fax: 902-679-4997
The Nova Scotia Farm Loan Board operates as a Corporation of the Crown & supports the development of sustainable agriculture & agri-rural business in Nova Scotia through responsible lending.

• Nova Scotia Farm Practices Board
PO Box 550
Truro, NS B2N 5E3
Tel: 902-893-7314
www.gov.ns.ca/agri/legislaton/fpb.shtml
The Farm Practices Board provides a structure to hear complaints & decide on normal farm practices. The Board provides a mechanism for resolving issues between farmers & their neighbours regarding odour, noise, dust, vibration, light, smoke or other disturbance resulting from a farming activity.

• Nova Scotia Natural Products Marketing Council
179 College Rd.
PO Box 550
Truro, NS B2N 5E3
Tel: 902-893-6306
Fax: 902-893-7579
www.gov.ns.ca/agri/npmc/
The Council, an agency of the NS Government, is responsible for the administration of the Natural Products Act & the Dairy Industry Act. Ten marketing boards are established under the Natural Products Act & the Dairy Farmers of Nova Scotia is established under the Dairy Industry Act. These boards are producer elected & the Council delegates or regulates authority to them specific to their farm product. The Council is a regulatory & supervisory body, a major role of which is to balance industry interests with teh broader public interest.

Agriculture Services
www.gov.ns.ca/agri/department/divisions/agservices.shtml
The mission of Agriculture Services is to ensure a prosperous & sustainable agriculture industry through the development of rural people & resources for the benefit of all Nova Scotians.
Executive Director, Alan Grant
Tel: 902-893-6591

Resource Stewardship Division
PO Box 550, Truro, NS B2N 5E3
Encourages the best available management of agricultural resources to ensure sustainable & sound environmental farm practices. Environmental Management conducts research & technology adaptation initiatives that support a sustainable economic atmosphere for rural people. It also has a close working relationship with the Nova Scotia Federation of Agriculture & provides resources in support of the Environmental Farm Plan Program. Pest Management, Regulation & Environmental Coordination adapts & develops regulatory programs & related methods to prevent or minimize introduction & spread of designated diseases & pests of concern to agriculture; delivers enforcement of related regulations; conducts regular assessments to determine risk invasion of agricultural pests. Land Protection has the responsibilities to carry out maintenance work on system of tidal dykes in Nova Scotia. Staff of the Resource Stewardship Division also chair & provide administrative services to the Nova Scotia Soils Institute
Manager, Environmental Services, Marion MacAulay
Tel: 902-893-6518
macaulmt@gov.ns.ca
Manager, Regional Services, Arthur Pick
Tel: 902-893-6587
pickaa@gov.ns.ca
Engineer, Land Protection Services, Dave Browning
Tel: 902-893-6569
brownida@gov.ns.ca
Chief Inspector (Weed Control Act), Pest Management Regulation & Environmental Coordination, Joe Calder
Tel: 902-893-6549
calderjr@gov.ns.ca
Resource Management Specialist, Environmental Management, Lorne Crozier
Tel: 902-893-6548
crozielm@gov.ns.ca

Legislation & Compliance Services
www.gov.ns.ca/agri/department/divisions/legcom.shtml
Licenses meat processing, retail food outlets & restaurants, fur & game farms, oversees activities related to food & consumer safety, as well as on-farm quality evaluation. Responsible for monitoring & enforcing compliance with departmental regulations.
Executive Director, Leo Muise
Tel: 902-424-0337
muiselj@gov.ns.ca

Nova Scotia Agricultural College (NSAC)
PO Box 550, Truro, NS B2N 5E3
Tel: 902-893-6600
Toll-Free: 888-700-6722
webmaster@snac.ca
www.nsac.ca
Co-President, Bernie MacDonald
Tel: 902-893-6034
Fax: 902-893-4601
bmacdonald@nsac.ca
Co-President, Leslie MacLaren
Tel: 902-893-6030

Office of the Auditor General

#302, 1888 Brunswick St., Halifax, NS B3J 3J8
Tel: 902-424-5907
Fax: 902-424-4350
www.oag-ns.ca
The mission of the Auditor General is to make a significant contribution to enhanced accountability & performance in the provincial sector. The Auditor General serves the public interest as the House of Assembly's primary source of assurance on government performance.

Auditor General, Jacques R. Lapointe, B.A., C.A., C.I.A., C.G.A.P.
Tel: 902-424-4046
lapoinjr@gov.ns.ca

Deputy Auditor General, Alan D. Horgan, C.A.
Tel: 902-424-3945
horganad@gov.ns.ca

Asst. Auditor General, Evangeline Colman-Sadd, C.A.
Tel: 902-424-4347
colmansa@gov.ns.ca

Asst. Auditor General, Ann T. McDonald, C.A.
Tel: 902-424-4970
mcdonaat@gov.ns.ca

Asst. Auditor General, Terry M. Spicer, C.M.A.
Tel: 902-424-8565
spicert@gov.ns.ca

Communications Nova Scotia

1723 Hollis St., 3rd Fl., PO Box 608, Halifax, NS B3J 2R7
Tel: 902-424-7690
Fax: 902-424-0515
www.gov.ns.ca/cns/
Other Communication: Queen's Printer: 902-424-4481
Communications Nova Scotia strives to help Nova Scotians understand what their government is doing & why. They provide a complete range of professional communications services to provincial government departments, agencies, boards & commissions.

Minister, Hon. Frank Corbett
corbetfr@gov.ns.ca

Deputy Minister, Gregory P. Keefe
Tel: 902-424-8940
Fax: 902-428-3191
keefeg@gov.ns.ca

Associate Deputy Minister, Tracey Taweel
Tel: 902-424-3839
taweelt@gov.ns.ca

Director, Production, Diane Leblanc
Tel: 902-424-2077

Director, Communications, Tom Peck
Tel: 902-424-1593

Director, Communications, Catherine Shaw
Tel: 902-424-8787

Director, Communications, Celeste Sulliman
Tel: 902-424-7957

Director, Communications, Kristen Tynes MacEachern
Tel: 902-424-4038

Director, Communications, Webster Natalie Joy
Tel: 902-424-7280

Director, Communications, Valerie Bellafontaine
Tel: 902-424-7942

Director, Communications, Carla Burns
Tel: 902-424-2876

Director, Communications, Daniel Davis
Tel: 902-424-8978

Director, Communications, Michelle Robin Lucas
Tel: 902-424-3731

Director, Communications, Catherine MacIsaac
Tel: 902-424-6283

Director, Communications, Susan McKeage
Tel: 902-424-7942

Director, Communications, Ross McLaren
Tel: 902-424-4536

Director, Communications, Janet Lynn McNeil
Tel: 902-424-7420

Department of Communities, Culture & Heritage

World Trade & Convention Centre, 1800 Argyle St., 6th Fl., PO Box 456, Halifax, NS B3J 3N8
Tel: 902-424-4510
Fax: 902-424-0710
culture@gov.ns.ca
www.gov.ns.ca/tch
The Department of Communities, Culture & Heritage is responsible for contributing to the well-being & prosperity of Nova Scotia's diverse & creative communities through the promotion, development, preservation & celebration of culture, heritage, identity & languages, and by providing leadership, expertise, & innovation to stakeholders.

Acts Administered:
Art Council Act
Art Gallery of Nova Scotia Act
Cemeteries Protection Act
Cultural Foundation Act

Government Records Act
Heritage Property Act
Libraries Act
Multiculturalism Act
Nova Scotia Museum Act
Nova Scotia Tartan Act
Order of Nova Scotia Act
Peggy's Cove Commission Act
Public Archives Act
Schooner Bluenose Foundation Act
Sherbrooke Restoration Commission Act
Special Places Protection Act (Ecological Site Designations: Abraham Lake, Bornish Hill, Duncans Cove, Great Barren & Quinan Lakes, Indian Man Lake, MacFarlane Woods, Panuke Lake, Ponhook Lake, Quinns Meadow, RiverInhabitants, Roman Valley)
Tourist Accommodations Act

Minister, Hon. Leonard Preyra
Tel: 902-424-4889
Fax: 902-424-4872
min_cch@gov.ns.ca

Deputy Minister, Laura Lee Langley
Tel: 902-424-4938
Fax: 902-424-4872
langley@gov.ns.ca

Director, Lang Jongmans
Tel: 902-424-7121

Director, Communications, Michael Noonan
Tel: 902-424-1593
Fax: 902-424-4872
noonanmg@gov.ns.ca

Associated Agencies, Boards & Commissions:
• Nova Scotia Tourism Partnership Council
World Trade & Convention Centre
#603, 1800 Argyle St.
Halifax, NS B3J 3N8
Tel: 902-424-0048
Fax: 902-424-0723
www.gov.ns.ca/econ/tourism/nstpc/
The Council is an industry & government partnership that shares in planning & decision making for tourism marketing, research & product development in Nova Scotia.

NS Archives
6016 University Ave., Halifax, NS B3H 1W4
Tel: 902-424-6060
Fax: 902-424-0628
nsarm@gov.ns.ca
www.gov.ns.ca/nsarm/
Other Communication: www.facebook.com/novascotiaarchvies; www.twitter.com/NS_Archives
As a documentary heritage institution for the province, the NS Archives serves as the permanent repository for the archival records of the government of Nova Scotia; acquires & preserves provincially significant archival records from the private sector; delivers a range of professional, client-centred reference services; develops & maintains two websites; & provides strategic support & financial assistance to strengthen the provincial archival community.
Director, Public Services, Lois Yorke
Tel: 902-424-6068
yorkelk@gov.ns.ca
Director, Archives Management, Margaret Campbell
Tel: 902-424-6076
campbemj@gov.ns.ca

Culture Division
#601, 1800 Argyle St., PO Box 456, Halifax, NS B3J 2R5
Tel: 902-424-4510
Fax: 902-424-0710
culture@gov.ns.ca
www.gov.ns.ca/tch/culture_mandate.asp
Responsible for Nova Scotia museums which administer the Special Places Protection Act; preserves ecological sites in the province.
Interim Executive Director, Culture Division, Marcel Philip McKenough
Tel: 902-424-6393

Heritage Division
1747 Summer St., Halifax, NS B3H 3A6
Tel: 902-424-7344
Fax: 902-424-0560
Toll-Free: 800-632-1114
heritage@gov.ns.ca
www.gov.ns.ca/tch/heritage_mandate.asp
The mission of Heritage Division is to protect, enhance, & celebrate heritage for all Nova Scotians & for future generations.
Executive Director, Heritage Division, Bill Greenlaw
Tel: 902-424-4986
greenlbe@gov.ns.ca

Department of Community Services

Nelson Place, 5675 Spring Garden Rd., 8th Fl., PO Box 696, Halifax, NS B3J 2T7
Tel: 902-424-4304
Fax: 902-428-0618
www.gov.ns.ca/coms
The Department of Community Services is committed to a sustainable social service system that promotes the independence, self-reliance, & security of the people it serves.
Acts Administered:
Adoption Information Act
Children & Family Services Act
Day Care Act
Disabled Persons' Commission Act
Employment Support & Income Assistance Act
Homes for Special Care Act
Housing Act
Housing Development Corporation Act
Intercountry Adoption Act
North Queens Nursing Home Act
Protection for Persons in Care Act
Senior Citizens' Financial Aid Act
Senior Citizens' Secretariat Act
Senior Citizens' Social Services Act
Social Assistance Act

Minister, Hon. Denise Peterson-Rafuse
petersdj@gov.ns.ca

Deputy Minister, Robert Wood
Tel: 902-424-4325
Fax: 902-424-3287
woodrj@gov.ns.ca

Executive Director, Finance & Administration, George Hudson
Tel: 902-424-2750

Associated Agencies, Boards & Commissions:
• Nova Scotia Disabled Persons Commission (NSDPC)
Dartmouth Professional Center
#104, 277 Pleasant St.
Dartmouth, NS B2Y 4B7
Tel: 902-424-8280
Fax: 902-424-0592
Toll-free: 800-565-8280
www.gov.ns.ca/disa
The NSDPC gives people with disabilities a way to participate in the provincial government policy-making process. Its mission is to champion the social & economic inclusion of citizens with disabilities.

Affordable Housing & Repairs
www.gov.ns.ca/coms/housing/index.html
The provincial government offers a number of programs to help lower income households maintain, acquire or rent safe, adequate & ffordable housing.
Director, Housing, Neil MacDonald
Tel: 902-424-2409

Children, Youth & Families
Fax: 902-424-0708
Executive Director, George Savoury
Tel: 902-424-8256
Director, Services for Persons with Disabilities, Lorna McPherson
Tel: 902-424-3387
Director, Child Welfare, Victoria Wood
Tel: 902-424-5653

Employment Support & Income Assistance
Fax: 902-424-0721
The Employment Support & Income Assistance (ESIA) program helps by giving money for living costs, or providing other kinds of help, when individuals are unable to support themselves or their family.
Director, Income Assistance, Janet Rathbun
Tel: 902-424-6104
Director, Employment Support Services, Mike Townsend
Tel: 902-424-4329
Director, Employment Support Services, Neil MacDonald
Tel: 902-424-2409

Services for Persons with Disabilities
The SPD Program serves children, youth & adults with intellectual disabilities, long-term mental illness, & physical disabilities in a range of community-based, residential & vocational/day programs.
Director, Lorna McPherson
Tel: 902-424-3787
Eastern
#25, 360 Prince St., Sydney, NS B1P 5L1
Tel: 902-563-3302
Fax: 902-563-5693
Regional Administrator, Cyril Leblanc
Tel: 902-563-2125
Central
McDonald Bldg., 2131 Gottingen St., PO Box 2623, Halifax, NS B3J 3E4
Tel: 902-424-5074
Fax: 902-424-5115
Regional Administrator, Lynn Brogan
Tel: 902-424-2681
Northern
161 Terra Cotta Drive, New Glasgow, NS B2H 6B6
Tel: 902-755-7023
Fax: 902-752-5088
Regional Administrator, Catherine Berliner
Western
#202, 10 Webster St., Kentville, NS B4N 1H7
Tel: 902-679-6715
Fax: 902-679-6127
Regional Administrator, Phil Warren
Tel: 902-863-6716

Council of Atlantic Premiers (CAP)

Council Secretariat, #1006, 5161 George St., PO Box 2044, Halifax, NS B3J 2Z1
Tel: 902-424-7590
Fax: 902-424-8976
info@cap-cpma.ca
www.cap-cpma.ca
The Premiers of New Brunswick, Newfoundland & Labrador, Nova Scotia & Prince Edward Island constitute the Council. It was established by memorandum of understanding to: promote unity of purpose among their respective Governments; ensure maximum coordination of the activities of the Governments & their agencies; & establish a framework for joint action & undertakings. The Council meets up to four times annually to discuss matters of mutual interest or concern to the four Atlantic governments. A Secretariat acts as the focal point for coordinating the efforts of the four Governments in identifying potential benefits that could result from a regional approach to policy formulation & program development.

Secretary to Council, Don Osmond
Tel: 902-424-7600

Chief Financial Officer, Rod Casey
Tel: 902-424-5078

Associated Agencies, Boards & Commissions:
• Council of Atlantic Ministers of Education & Training
PO Box 2044
Halifax, NS B3J 2Z1
Tel: 902-424-5352
Fax: 902-424-8976
camet_camef@cap-cpma.ca
www.camet-camef.ca
• Maritime Provinces Higher Education Commission (MPHEC) / Commission de l'engseignement supérieur des Provinces Maritimes (CESPM)
#401, 82 Westmorland
Fredericton, PE E3B 5H1
Tel: 506-453-2844
Fax: 506-453-2106
mphec@mphec.ca
www.mphec.ca
As an Agency of the Council of Atlantic Premiers that provides advice to Ministers responsible for Post-Secondary Education in the Maritimes, the Commission assists institutions & governments in enhancing a post-secondary learning environment that reflects quality, accessibility, mobility, relevance, accountability, scholarship & research.
• Maritime Provinces Harness Racing Commission
5 Gerald McCarville Dr.
PO Box 128
Kensington, PE C0B 1M0
Tel: 902-836-5500
Fax: 902-836-5320
www.mphrc.ca
The Commission governs, regulates, & supervises harness racing in all of its forms relevant & related to pari-mutuel betting.

Department of Economic & Rural Development & Tourism

Centennial Building, #600, 1660 Hollis St., PO Box 2311, Halifax, NS B3J 1V7
Tel: 902-424-0377
Fax: 902-424-0500
comm@gov.ns.ca
www.gov.ns.ca/econ/

The office assists with knowledge management, trade policy, special projects, government relations regarding economic development issues, labour advice, regarding the work force of the future, information on the business climate & assistance on strategic infrastructure. It provides assistance with strategic management & rural development regarding the business climate, & services such as the Rural Development Branch, Rural Development Service Locations & Co-operatives Branch, dealing with trade policy negotiations & agreements.

Acts Administered:
Business Development Corporation Act
Cooperation Associations Act
Economic Renewal Agency Act
Industrial Development Act
Industrial Estates Limited Act
Industrial Loan Act
Industrial Property Act
Industry Closing Act
Innovation Corporation Act
Nova Scotia Business Incorporated Act
Nova Scotia Film Development Corporation Act
Regional Community Development Act
Research Foundation Corporation Act
Small Business Development Act
Sydney Steel Corporation Act
Tourist Accommodations Act
Trade Development Authority Act
Venture Corporation Act
Venture Corporation Act - Regulations
Voluntary Planning Act

Minister, Hon. Percy Paris
Tel: 902-424-5790
Fax: 902-424-0514
econmin@gov.ns.ca

Associate Deputy Minister, Christopher Daly

Executive Director, Tourism Division, John Somers
Tel: 902-424-4554
somersjh@gov.ns.ca

Director, Program Managment, Elizabeth D. Beck
Tel: 902-424-4641

Director, Robert Edwin Book
Tel: 902-424-7577

Director, Procurement, Rick Draper
Tel: 902-424-4557

Acting Director, Communications, Jennifer Gavin
Tel: 902-424-4998
Fax: 902-424-7008

Director, Economic Strategies & Initiatives, Bruce Hennebury
Tel: 902-424-5757
hennebub@gov.ns.ca

Director, Decision Support, Liliani Kumaranayake
Tel: 902-424-4641

Director, Development Initiatives, Marvyn C. Robar
Tel: 902-424-3973

Associated Agencies, Boards & Commissions:

• Canada - Nova Scotia Offshore Petroleum Board (CNSOPB)
TD Centre
1791 Barrington St., 18th Fl.
Halifax, NS B3J 3K9
Tel: 902-422-5588
Fax: 902-422-1799
postmaster@cnsopb.ns.ca
www.cnsopb.ns.ca
Created in 1990, the Canada - Nova Scotia Offshore Petroleum Board regulates petroleum activities in the Nova Scotia Offshore Area.
The following are some of the responsibilities of the Board: protecting the environment; overseeing the health & safety of offshore workers; managing the conservation of offshore petroleum resources; issuing licences for offshore exploration & development; collecting & distributing data; & complying with provisions of the *Accord Acts* that deal with employment & industrial benefits.

• InNOVACorp
#1400, 1801 Hollis St.
Halifax, NS B3J 3N4
Tel: 902-424-8670
Fax: 902-424-4679
Toll-free: 800-565-7051
communications@innovacorp.ca
www.innovacorp.ns.ca
Other Communication: www.twitter.com/innovacorp
A network of business resources for the early stage technology entrepreneur. Key services include research & development support, business advice, investment & partnership advice. Focuses on two main growth sectors: life sciences & information technology.

• Nova Scotia Business Inc. (NSBI)
World Trade & Convention Centre
#701, 1800 Argyle St.
PO Box 2374
Halifax, NS B3J 3N8
Tel: 902-424-6650
Fax: 902-424-5739
Toll-free: 800-260-6682
info@nsbi.ca
www.novascotiabusiness.com
Other Communication: www.twitter.com/nsbi; www.facebook.com/novscotiabusiness
NSBI is the first point of contact for local companies that want to grow in Nova Scotia, and for international companies that have heard about the province and want to know more.

• Film Nova Scotia
Collins Bank Bldg.
1869 Upper Water St., 3rd Fl.
Halifax, NS B3J 1S9
Tel: 902-424-7177
Fax: 902-424-0617
Toll-free: 888-360-2111
www.film.ns.ca
Created in 1990 under the Film Development Corporation Act, Film Nova Scotia is a Provincial Crown Corporation reporting to the Minister of Economic and Rural Development. A Board of Directors, appointed by the Governor in Council, directs the Corporation's activities.

• Trade Centre Limited
1800 Argyle St.
PO Box 955
Halifax, NS B3J 2V9
Tel: 902-421-8686
Fax: 902-422-2922
www.tradecentrelimited.com
Trade Centre Limited creates economic benefits by bringing people together in Halifax & Nova Scotia.

• Waterfront Development Corporation Ltd.
1751 Lower Water St., 2nd Fl.
Halifax, NS B3J 1S5
Tel: 902-422-6591
Fax: 902-422-7582
info@wdcl.ca
www.my-waterfront.ca/about-wdcl
Other Communication: www.facebook.com/pages/my-waterfront/139091936107397; www.twitter.com/my_waterfront
Coordinates the commercial & recreational development of the downtown waterfront of Halifax & Dartmouth.

Amherst
35 Church St., Amherst, NS B4H 4A1
Tel: 902-667-3233
Fax: 902-667-2270

Antigonish
#4, 149 Church St., Antigonish, NS B2G 2E2
Tel: 902-863-7539
Fax: 902-863-7477

Bridgewater
220 North St., Bridgewater, NS B4V 2V6
Tel: 902-530-3117
Fax: 902-543-1156

Halifax
Centennial Building, #600, 1660 Hollis St., PO Box 2311, Halifax, NS B3J 1V7
Tel: 902-424-4319
Fax: 902-424-1263
Toll-Free: 800-565-2009

Kentville
#103, 35 Webster St., Kentville, NS B4N 1H4
Tel: 902-679-6116
Fax: 902-679-6094

Sydney
#207, 275 Charlotte St., Sydney, NS B1P 1C6
Tel: 902-563-2070
Fax: 902-563-0500

Truro
#3-80 Walker St., Truro, NS B2N 4A7
Tel: 902-893-6212
Fax: 902-893-6108

Yarmouth
Pier One Complex, 103 Water St., Yarmouth, NS B5A 4P4
Tel: 902-742-8404
Fax: 902-742-0019

Department of Education

Trade Mart Bldg., #402-2021 Brunswick St., PO Box 578, Halifax, NS B3J 2S9
Tel: 902-424-5168
Fax: 902-424-0680
www.ednet.ns.ca
Other Communication: www.twitter.com/nseducation

The mission of the Department of Education is to provide excellence in education & training for personal fulfillment & for a productive, prosperous society.

Acts Administered:
Acadia University Act
Agriculture & Marketing Act, as it pertains to the Agreements of the Nova Scotia Agricultural College Regulations
Apprenticeship & Trades Qualifications Act
Atlantic Provinces Special Education Act
Atlantic School of Theology Act
Barbers Act
Community Colleges Act
Cosmetology Act
Dalhousie College & University Act
Dalhousie-Technical University Amalgamation Act
Degree Granting Act
Education Act
Education Assistance Act
Hospital Education Assistance Act
Libraries Act
Maritime Provinces Higher Education (Nova Scotia) Act
Mi'kmaq Education Act
Mount Saint Vincent University Act
Nova Scotia College of Art & Design Act
Nova Scotia School Boards Association Act
Nova Scotia Teachers College Foundation Act
Private Career Colleges Regulations Act
Registered Barbers Act
Saint Mary's University Act
School Loan Fund Act
Southwestern Nova Scotia Community College Act
St. Francis Xavier University Act
Student Aid Act
Teachers' Collective Bargaining Act
Teaching Profession Act
Universities Assistance Act
University College of Cape Breton Act
University Foundations Act
University Kings College Act
Université Saint-Anne Act
Youth Secretariat Act

Minister, Hon. Ramona Jennex
Tel: 902-424-4236
Fax: 902-424-0680
educmin@gov.ns.ca

Deputy Minister, Rosalind C. Penfound
Tel: 902-424-5643
repenfou@gov.ns.ca

Associated Agencies, Boards & Commissions:

• Nova Scotia Advisory Board on Colleges & Universities
2021 Brunswick St.
PO Box 2086 M
Halifax, NS B3J 3B7
Fax: 902-424-0651

Acadian & French Language Services

Tel: 902-424-3927
Fax: 902-424-3937
www.ednet.ns.ca/afls.shtml
Other Communication: www.dsalf.ednet.ns.ca

The Acadian & French Language Services Branch monitors & approves curriculum development for French first language education, collaborates with other branches of the department to ensure common services are available in French for first language schools, coordinates activities related to federal-provincial funding agreements for French minority language education and French language instruction, & coordinates & manages implementation of national official language programs in Nova Scotia.

Senior Executive Director, Acadian & French Language Programs, Gilles LeBlanc
Tel: 902-424-6097
leblangg@gov.ns.ca

Director, French Programs, Margelaine Holding
Tel: 902-424-6626

Corporate Policy

Tel: 902-424-5294
Fax: 902-424-0519
www.ednet.ns.ca/corporatepolicy.shtml
Other Communication: 902-424-4684 (Freedom of Information & Protection of Privacy Review Office)

Corporate Policy is responsible for providing assistance & support in policy, planning, legislation, research, coordination, & information & publishing services to all areas of the department.

It also coordinates departmental accountability processes including the departmental business plan & support to school board planning processes.
Officer, Freedom of Information & Protection of Privacy Review, Dulcie McCallum
Tel: 902-424-8277
mccalld@gov.ns.ca
Director, Policy & Planning, Shannon Delbridge
Tel: 902-424-5242
delbrisd@gov.ns.ca

Corporate Services
www.ednet.ns.ca/corporateservices.shtml
This branch comprises Financial Management, Education Funding & Accountability, Facilities Management, Information Technology Services, Statistics & Data Management, & Teacher Certification. It is responsible for the delivery of business & support services to the Department of Education, including financial management & controllership responsibilities, provision of facilities planning & capital projects, coordination of pupil transportation with boards, information technology, and province-wide delivery of data communications.
Chief Operating Officer, Frank Dunn
Tel: 902-423-7635
Fax: 902-424-1866
dunnfm@gov.ns.ca
Director, Financial Management, Ben McIntyre
Tel: 902-424-5698
Fax: 902-424-1866
mcintybr@gov.ns.ca
Director, Grants & Audits, Joe MacEachern
Tel: 902-424-3956
Fax: 902-424-1866
maceacj@gov.ns.ca
Director, Information Technology Services, John Fahie
Tel: 902-424-2823
Fax: 902-424-0874
fahiejw@gov.ns.ca

Public Schools
www.ednet.ns.ca/publicschools.shtml
The Public Schools Branch designs, develops, implements, & evaluates programs, courses, services, related policies & resources including student & teaching resources to support implementation, for the public school system, correspondence studies, & on-line learning.
Senior Executive Director, Alan Lowe
Tel: 902-424-5829
lowead@gov.ns.ca
Executive Director, English Program Services, Ann Blackwood
Tel: 902-424-5475
Director, Mi'Kmaq Liasion Office, Candy Palmater
Tel: 902-424-8625

Elections Nova Scotia

#6-7037 Mumford Rd., PO Box 2246, Halifax, NS B3J 2J1
Tel: 902-424-8584
Fax: 902-424-6622
Toll-Free: 800-565-1504
elections@gov.ns.ca
www.electionsnovascotia.ns.ca
TTY: 866-774-7074
Secondary Address: 6-7037 Mumford Rd.
Election Supply Centre
Halifax, NS B3T 2J1
Elections Nova Scotia is independent of any political affiliation, including the government in power. It ensures that every election, by-election, & liquor plebiscite is held in a fair & impartial manner (according to the Elections Act and other relevant laws) & that all political parties & candidates act within the rules.

Chief Electoral Officer, Christine McCulloch
mccullca@gov.ns.ca

Nova Scotia Emergency Management Office (EMO)

PO Box 2581, Halifax, NS B3J 3N5
Tel: 902-424-5620
Fax: 902-424-5376
Toll-Free: 866-424-5620
emo@gov.ns.ca
www.gov.ns.ca/emo
Coordinating agency of the Nova Scotia Government with the responsibility of assisting municipalities to plan & prepare for emergencies; responsible for the implementation of the province-wide 911 service. Coordinates emergency efforts of provincial & federal departments & agencies, as well as private health & social services, to provide assistance to disaster areas; sponsors the Ground Search & Rescue Program; maintains a professional planner at all offices. Coordinates all emergency preparedness training for municipal staff at the Emergency Preparedness College (Arnprior, ON) & through the Joint Emergency Preparedness Program (JEPP), which provides a federal government cost-sharing formula for emergency equipment for first-response agencies.
Acts Administered:
Emergency 911 Act
Emergency Management Act

Minister Responsible, Hon. Ross Landry
Tel: 902-424-4044
Fax: 902-424-0510
justmin@gov.ns.ca

Chief Executive Officer & Deputy Minister, Marian Tyson
tysonmf@gov.ns.ca

Director, Emergency Services, Michael Myette
Tel: 902-424-6206

Director, Emergency Services, Michelle Perry
Tel: 902-424-0284
perrymx@gov.ns.ca

Department of Energy

Bank of Montreal Bldg., #400, 5151 George St., PO Box 2664, Halifax, NS B3J 3P7
Tel: 902-424-4575
Fax: 902-424-0528
energyinfo@gov.ns.ca
www.gov.ns.ca/energy
To serve as the government's focal point in the development of the province's energy resources, as outlined in the Energy Strategy. Responsible for a wide range of initiatives in the following areas: energy transportation & utilization policy & analysis; resource assessment & royalties; climate change; business & technology; communications & public education.
Acts Administered:
Canada-Newfoundland Labrador Offshore Area Regulations
Canada-Nova Scotia Offshore Petroleum Resources Accord Implementation (Nova Scotia) Act
Electricity Act
Energy Resources Conservation Act
Energy-Efficient Appliances Act
Gas Distribution Act
Gas Plant Facility Regulations
Land Acquisition Regulations
Natural Gas Transmission Pipeline Assessment Regulations
Nova Scotia Offshore Area Certificate of Fitness Regulations
Nova Scotia Offshore Area Oil & Gas Spills & Debris Liability Regulations
Nova Scotia Offshore Area Petroleum Diving Regulations
Nova Scotia Offshore Area Petroleum Drilling Regulations
Nova Scotia Offshore Area Petroleum Geophysical Operations Regulations
Nova Scotia Offshore Area Petroleum Installations Regulations
Nova Scotia Offshore Petroleum Production & Conservation Regulations
Offshore Petroleum Royalty Act
Onshore Petroleum Drilling Regulations
Onshore Petroleum Geophysical Exploration Regulations
Onshore Petroleum Geophysical Exploration Regulations
Petroleum Resources Act
Petroleum Resources Removal Permit Act
Pipeline Act
Pipeline Benefits Plan Regulations
Pipeline Regulations
Sable Offshore Energy Project Regulations
Underground Hydrocarbons Storage Act

Minister, Hon. Charlie Parker
Tel: 902-424-7793
Fax: 902-424-3265
energyminister@gov.ns.ca

Deputy Minister, Murray Coolican
Tel: 902-424-4450
Fax: 902-424-3265
coolicm@gov.ns.ca

Executive Secretary to the Minister, Diane Bernard
Tel: 902-424-7793
Fax: 902-424-3265
bernardm@gov.ns.ca

Associated Agencies, Boards & Commissions:
• Utility & Review Board (UARB)
Summit Place
1601 Lower Water St., 3rd Fl.
PO Box 1692 M
Halifax, NS B3J 3S3
Tel: 902-424-4448
Fax: 902-424-3919
uarb.board@gov.ns.ca
www.nsuarb.ca
The Nova Scotia Utility & Review Board is an independent quasi-judicial body which has both regulatory adjudicative jurisdiction flowing from the Utility and Review Board Act.

Business & Technology
www.gov.ns.ca/energy/what-we-do.asp#business-technology
Director, Charles Bernard MacDonald
Tel: 902-424-2704

Communications & Public Education
www.gov.ns.ca/energy/what-we-do.asp#communications
Director, Communications, Nancy Watson
Tel: 902-424-1195
watsonnm@gov.ns.ca

Energy Fiscal Affairs
Tel: 902-424-6673
www.gov.ns.ca/energy/what-we-do.asp#energy-fiscal
Director, Energy Markets, Reginald Scott McCoombs
Tel: 902-424-7305
Director, Chris Spencer

Energy Markets
www.gov.ns.ca/energy/what-we-do.asp#energy-markets

Resource Assessment
www.gov.ns.ca/energy/what-we-do.asp#resource-assessment

Strategic Policy, Planning & Services
www.gov.ns.ca/energy/what-we-do.asp#spps

Department of Environment

5151 Terminal Rd., 5th Fl., PO Box 442, Halifax, NS B3J 2P8
Tel: 902-424-3600
Fax: 902-424-0503
Toll-Free: 877-936-8476
www.gov.ns.ca/nse
Major program responsibilities for Nova Scotia Environment are environmental & natural areas management, environmental monitoring & compliance, & climate change. Pollution prevention, the NS Youth Conservation Corps., solid waste reduction & recycling, & environmental trade & innovation are all part of the new Nova Scotia Environment.
Acts Administered:
Anti-idling Act
Court & Administrative Reform Act (Department of Justice)
Environment Act
Environmental Goals & Sustainable Prosperity Act
Health Protection Act
Non-essential Pesticides Control Act
Off-highway Vehicles Act
Special Places Protection Act
Wilderness Areas Protection Act

Minister, Hon. Sterling Belliveau
Tel: 902-424-3736
Fax: 902-424-1599
min_env@gov.ns.ca

Deputy Minister, Sara Jane Snook
Tel: 902-424-8150
Fax: 902-424-1599
snooksj@gov.ns.ca

Executive Secretary, Virginia Messervey
Tel: 902-424-3736
messerv@gov.ns.ca

Acting Director, Jason Hollett
Tel: 902-424-0784
holletjn@gov.ns.ca

Communications
www.gov.ns.ca/nse/dept/division.communications.asp
The Communications Division provides strategic communications planning & advice for the department. It is responsible for all external communications functions carried out for the department, including issues management, advertising, & media relations, & shares responsibility within the department for internal communications.
Director, Karen White
whitekl@gov.ns.ca

Environmental Monitoring & Compliance
Tel: 902-424-2547
Fax: 902-424-0569
Toll-Free: 877-936-8476
emc@gov.ns.ca
www.gov.ns.ca/nse/dept/division.emc.asp
The Environmental Monitoring Compliance Division is responsible for the majority of field operations relating to environmental protection.
Executive Director, Regional & District Offices, Darlene Fenton
Tel: 902-424-2547
Toll-free: 877-936-8476
Fax: 902-424-0569

Regional Offices

Central - HRM, East Hants, West Hants
Bedford Commons, #115, 30 Damascus Rd., Bedford, NS B4A 0C1
Tel: 902-424-7773
Fax: 902-424-0597

Eastern - Port Hawkesbury, Sydney
295 Charlotte St., Sydney, NS B1P 6H7
Tel: 902-563-2100
Fax: 902-563-2387

Regional Director, Roger Munroe
Tel: 902-563-2100
Fax: 902-563-2387

Eastern - Richmond Co., Southern Inverness, Mulgrave, Auld's Cove
#12, 218 MacSween St., Port Hawkesbury, NS B9A 2J9
Tel: 902-625-0791
Fax: 902-625-3722

District Manager, Terry MacPherson

Northern - Amherst, Antigosh, Truro, Pictou
#3, 36 Inglis Place, 2nd Fl., PO Box 824, Truro, NS B2N 5G6
Tel: 902-667-6205
Fax: 902-667-6214

Northern - Antigosh, Guysborough Counties
#205, 155 Main St., Antigosh, NS B2N 2B6
Tel: 902-667-6205
Fax: 902-667-6214

District Manager, Paul Keats

Northern - Colchester County
Tel: 902-667-6205
Fax: 902-667-6214

District Manager, Wayne Faulkner

Northern - Cumberland County
71 East Victoria St., Amherst, NS B4H 1X7
Tel: 902-667-6205
Fax: 902-667-6214

District Manager, Brad Skinner

Northern - Colchester County
20 Pumphouse Rd., RR3, New Glasgow, NS B2H 5C6
Tel: 902-396-4194
Fax: 902-396-4765

District Manager, Penny McLeod

Western - Bridgewater, Kentville, Yarmouth
136 Exhibition St., Kentville, NS B4N 4E5
Tel: 902-679-6088
Fax: 902-679-6186

Regional Director, Adrian Fuller
District Manager, Jennifer Lonergan

Western - Digby, Yarmouth & Shelburne Counties
13 First St., Yarmouth, NS B5A 1S9
Tel: 902-742-8985
Fax: 902-742-7796

Western - Lunenberg & Queens Counties
60 Logan Rd., Bridgewater, NS B4V 3J8
Tel: 902-543-4685
Fax: 902-527-5480

District Manager, Kristen Martell

Environment & Sustainable Prosperity Partnerships
www.gov.ns.ca/nse/dept/division.espp.asp
The Division aims to provide leadership & coordination of community engagement activities in Environment (and more broadly) is responsible for delivery of major environmental service contracts with the private sector.

Environmental Science & Program Management
www.gov.ns.ca/nse/dept/division.espm.asp
The Environmental Science & Program Management Division promotes sustainable management & protection of the environment through both regulatory & non-regulatory means, including developing & implementing plans, standards, guidelines, & policies for the management & protection of Nova Scotia's air, water & terrestrial resources including protected areas, & by providing regionally-based regulatory approval, inspection, monitoring & enforcement.
Director, Kimberly MacNeil
Tel: 902-424-2386

Policy & Corporate Services
www.gov.ns.ca/nse/dept/division.pcs.asp
Founded in 2009, this division combines former divisions (Competitiveness & Compliance, Environmental Assessment, Information & Business Services, & Policy).
Director, Scott Nicholson
nicholsw@gov.ns.ca
Environmental Analyst, Helen MacPhail
Tel: 902-424-0126
Librarian, Natalie MacPherson
Tel: 902-424-8474
macphend@gov.ns.ca

Department of Finance

Provincial Bldg., 1723 Hollis St., 7th Fl., PO Box 187, Halifax, NS B3J 2N3
Tel: 902-424-5554
Fax: 902-424-0635
FinanceWeb@gov.ns.ca
www.gov.ns.ca/fina
Other Communication: www.twitter.com/NSFinance

The Department of Finance's vision is to provide financial leadership that strengthens Nova Scotia; & their mission is to provide corporate financial services & manage the province's financial affairs & policies in the interests of Nova Scotians.

Acts Administered:
Corporation Capital Tax Act
Credit Union Act
Equity Tax Credit Act
Finance Act
Gaming Control Act - Part I
Halifax-Dartmouth Bridge Commission Act
Home Ownership Savings Plan (Nova Scotia) Act
Homeowners' Incentive Act
Income Tax Act
Insurance Act
Insurance Premiums Tax Act
Members' Retiring Allowances Act
NS Power Privatization Act
Public Sector Compensation Disclosure Act
Public Sector Unpaid Leave Act
Public Service Superannuation Act
Revenue Act
Sales Tax Act
Securities Act
Sydney Steel Corporation Sale Act
Tax Collection Agreement (1961) Act
Teachers' Pension Act
Trust & Loan Companies Act
Utility & Review Board Act

Minister, Hon. Maureen MacDonald
Tel: 902-424-5720
financeminister@gov.ns.ca

Deputy Minister, Margaret MacDonald
Tel: 902-424-5744
macdonmf@gov.ns.ca

Associate Deputy Minister, Bryon Rafuse
Tel: 902-424-4168
rafusebg@gov.ns.ca

Executive Secretary to the Deputy Minister, Barbara Alison MacIsaac
Tel: 902-424-5553
macisaab@gov.ns.ca

Associated Agencies, Boards & Commissions:

• Nova Scotia Pension Agency
Purdy's Landing
1949 Upper Water St.
PO Box 371
Halifax, NS B3J 3N3
Tel: 902-424-5070
Fax: 902-424-0662
Toll-free: 800-774-5070
pensionsinfo@gov.ns.ca
www.novascotiapension.ca

• Nova Scotia Utility & Review Board (NSUARB)
Summit Place
1601 Lower Water St., 3rd Fl.
Halifax, NS B3J 3P6
Tel: 902-424-4448
Fax: 902-424-3919
uarb.board@gov.ns.ca
www.nsuarb.ca
The Nova Scotia Utility & Review Board (NSUARB) is an independent quasi-judicial body which has both regulatory & adjudicative jurisdiction flowing from the Utility & Review Board Act. It reports to the Legislature through the Minister of Finance.

Capital Markets Administration
www.gov.ns.ca/finance/en/home/aboutfinance/divisions.aspx
The Capital Markets Administration division provides all post trade settlement & accounting functions for the Nova Scotia Pension Agency investment & the Province's debt portfolio activities.
Director, Vicki Dimick

Communications
www.gov.ns.ca/finance/en/home/aboutfinance/divisions.aspx
The Communications division promotes the Department of Finance's programs & policies to the public, primarily Nova Scotians.
Director, Michelle Lucas
Tel: 902-424-3731

Corporate Information Systems (CIS)
www.gov.ns.ca/finance/en/home/aboutfinance/divisions.aspx
CIS provides ongoing support for the SAP systems within provincial departments & agencies, school boards, regional housing authorities & six municipalities within Nova Scotia.
Director, Steve Feindel
Tel: 902-424-2939
feindesj@gov.ns.ca

Finance Corporate Services Unit (CSU)
The Finance CSU supplies support in all aspects of financial management to other government departments.
Director, Joyce McDonald
Tel: 902-424-7395
mcdonajm@gov.ns.ca

Financial Institutions
Tel: 902-424-6331
Fax: 902-424-1298
The Financial Institutions Division regulates the operations of credit unions, trust & loan companies & insurance companies, agents, brokers & adjusters in the Province. The Division also provides a complaint & enquiry service to the public relating to financial institutions & the insurance industry & collects & verifies the insurance premiums tax.
Director, Doug Murphy
Tel: 902-424-7552
murphydh@gov.ns.ca
Manager, Audit & Examination, William Ngu
Tel: 902-424-2787

Fiscal & Economic Policy Branch
www.gov.ns.ca/finance/en/home/aboutfinance/divisions.aspx
Executive Director, Michael DeCoste
Tel: 902-424-2421
Director, Economic & Statistics, Thomas Storring
Tel: 902-424-2410
storrith@gov.ns.ca
Director, Taxation & Fiscal Policy, Paul Davies
Tel: 902-424-4655
Fax: 902-424-0590
daviespb@gov.ns.ca

Government Accounting
www.gov.ns.ca/finance/en/home/aboutfinance/divisions.aspx
Director, Financial Accounting, Suzanne Wile
Tel: 902-424-7021
wilesm@gov.ns.ca

Information Management
www.gov.ns.ca/finance/en/home/aboutfinance/divisions.aspx
Promotes the coordinated & consistent management of records & information throughout their life cycle. IM supports informed decision making, access to information & protection of privacy, & due diligence through good record keeping.
Manager, Angela Smith
Tel: 902-424-7932
ajsmith@gov.ns.ca

Internal Audit Centre
www.gov.ns.ca/finance/en/home/aboutfinance/divisions.aspx
Internal Audit strives to improve the effectiveness of risk management, control, & governance processes. It examines & evaluates internal controls to determine if they're adequate & effective. Compliance issues are regularly addressed & operational reviews assess efficiency & performance.
Executive Director, Ted Doane
DOANEET@gov.ns.ca

Liability Management & Treasury Services
www.gov.ns.ca/finance/en/home/aboutfinance/divisions.aspx
Responsible for ensuring effective money management, maximizing return on investments & minimizing debt servicing costs within risk tolerances acceptable to government.
Executive Director, Peter Urbanc
Tel: 902-424-2435
urbancpv@gov.ns.ca

Middle Office Compliance & Reporting
www.gov.ns.ca/finance/en/home/aboutfinance/divisions.aspx
Ensures that the investment & debt management activities are compliant with legislature as well as Finance's objectives & policy limits by guaranteeing that best-in-class practices/policies/processes are in place to adequately control activities, such as monitoring & reporting ongoing investment & debt activities to management & Governance Committees.
Director, Vicki Dimick
dimickvc@gov.ns.ca

Payroll Services
www.gov.ns.ca/finance/en/home/aboutfinance/divisions.aspx
Provides payroll services for employees of the Province, the regional school boards, & selective crown corporations, agencies & boards, as well as for retirees of the province & teachers superannuation plans.
Director, Blair McNaughton
MCNAUGBN@gov.ns.ca

Policy & Planning
www.gov.ns.ca/finance/en/home/aboutfinance/divisions.aspx
Works in cooperation with the Treasury & Policy Board to develop corporate fiscal & economic policies, & supports coordinated information flows into & out of the department & intra & inter-departmental collaboration.
Executive Director, Diana Eisenhauer
eisendi@gov.ns.ca

Department of Fisheries & Aquaculture

1741 Brunswick St., 3rd Fl., PO Box 2223, Halifax, NS B3J 3C4
Tel: 902-424-4560
Fax: 902-424-4671
www.gov.ns.ca/fish

The Department of Fisheries & Aquaculture's mission is to foster prosperous and sustainable fisheries, aquaculture and food industries through the delivery of quality public services for the betterment of coastal communities and of all Nova Scotians.
Acts Administered:
Fisheries & Coastal Resources Act
Fisheries Organizations Support Act
Wildlife Act (Fishing Regulations only)

Minister, Hon. Sterling Belliveau
Tel: 902-637-3200
Fax: 902-637-3530
min_dfa@gov.ns.ca
Other Communications: 902-875-9090 (Shelburne office)

Deputy Minister & Chief Executive Officer, Paul LaFleche
Tel: 902-424-0300
laflecpt@gov.ns.ca

Associate Deputy Minister, Gregory Roach
Tel: 902-424-0348
Fax: 902-424-1766
roachg@gov.ns.ca

Director, Communications, Celeste Sulliman
Tel: 902-424-0192
sullimcc@gov.ns.ca

Associated Agencies, Boards & Commissions:
- **Fisheries & Aquaculture Loan Board**
1741 Brunswick St., 3rd Fl.
PO Box 2223
Halifax, NS B3J 3C4
Tel: 902-424-0318
Fax: 902-424-3502
www.gov.ns.ca/nsaf/loanboards/fishlb/

Marine Division
Manager, Innovations & Field Services, Bruce Osborne
Tel: 902-424-0352
osbornbd@gov.ns.ca

Aquaculture Division
Director, Marshall Giles
Tel: 902-424-3664
gilesm@gov.ns.ca

Inland Fisheries Division
Director, Donald MacLean
Tel: 902-485-7021
macleand@gov.ns.ca

Office of Gaelic Affairs (OGA)

Johnston Building, 1672 Granville St., 2nd Fl., PO Box 186, Halifax, NS B3J 2N2
Tel: 902-424-4298
Fax: 902-424-0171
Toll-Free: 888-842-3542
gaelicinfo@gov.ns.ca; fiosgaidhlig@gov.ns.ca
www.gov.ns.ca/oga

The OGA's mission is to renew the Gaelic language through its work with Nova Scotians across the province.

Minister, Hon. Maurice Smith

Antigonish
155 Main St., 2nd Fl., Antigonish, NS B2G 2B6
Tel: 902-863-7578
Fax: 902-863-7428

Halifax
World Trade & Convention Centre, #603, 1800 Argyle St., PO Box 456, Halifax, NS B3J 2V9
Tel: 902-424-4298
Fax: 902-424-0171

Mabou
11485 Hwy. 19, PO Box 261, Mabou, NS B0E 1X0
Tel: 902-945-2114
Fax: 902-945-2628

Department of Health & Wellness

Joseph Howe Bldg., 1690 Hollis St., 4th Fl., PO Box 488, Halifax, NS B3J 2R8
Tel: 902-424-5818
Fax: 902-424-0730
Toll-Free: 800-387-6665
DoHweb@gov.ns.ca
www.gov.ns.ca/health
TTY: 800-670-8888
Other Communication: TeleHealth Network: 1-800-889-5949

Mission: Working together to empower individuals, families, partners, and communities to promote, improve, and maintain the health of Nova Scotians through a proactive and sustainable health care system.
Acts Administered:
Chiropractic Act
Cobequid Multi-Service Centre Act
Dental Act
Dental Hygienists Act
Dental Technicians Act
Denturist Act
Department of Health Promotion & Protection Act
Disabled Persons Commissions Act
Dispensing Opticians Act
Drug Dependency Act
Fair Drug Pricing Act
Health Act
Health Authorities Act
Health Protection Act
Health Research Foundation Act
Health Services & Insurance Act
Homemakers' Services Act
Homes for Special Care Act
Hospitals Act
Involuntary Psychiatric Treatment Act
Licensed Practical Nurses Act
Mandatory Testing & Disclosure Act
Medical Act
Medical Laboratory Technology Act
Medical Professional Corporations Act
Medical Radiation Technologists Act
Midwifery Act
Municipal Hospitals Loan Act
Occupational Therapists Act
Optometry Act
Part I - Gaming Control Act
Pharmacy Act
Physiotherapy Act
Prescription Monitoring Act
Protection for Persons in Care Act
Psychologists Act
Registered Nurses Association Act
Registered Nurses' Act
Registered Therapists Act
Safer Needles in Healthcare Workplaces Act
Smoke-free Places Act
Social Assistance Act
Tanning Beds Act
Tobacco Access Act

Minister, Hon. Dave Wilson
Tel: 902-424-3377
Fax: 902-424-0559
health.minister@gov.ns.ca

Deputy Minister, Kevin McNamara
Tel: 902-424-7570
Fax: 902-424-4570
mcnamakd@gov.ns.ca

Associate Deputy Minister, Frances Martin
Tel: 902-424-2080
martinfr@gov.ns.ca

Chief Financial Officer, Linda Ruth Penny
Tel: 902-424-4840

Executive Director, Strategic Financial Operations, Abram James Almeda
Tel: 902-424-4476

Executive Director, Health System Workforce, Carmelle d'Entremont
Tel: 902-424-8686

Executive Director, Policy & Planning, Tracey Williams
Tel: 902-424-7931

Senior Director, Labour Relations, Richard Anderson
Tel: 902-424-7730

Senior Director, Janet Braunstein
Tel: 902-424-5187

Senior Director, Sport & Research, Farida Gabbani
Tel: 902-424-7554

Chief Medical Director, Carman Giacomantonio
Tel: 902-473-6177

Senior Director, Physical Activity, Sport & Recreation, Farida Gabbani
Tel: 902-424-7554
gabbanfg@gov.ns.ca

Senior Director, Legislative Policy, Dennis Holland
Tel: 902-424-3351

Director, Communications, Sherri Aikenhead
Tel: 902-424-5579
sherri.aikenhead@gov.ns.ca

Director, Policy & Planning, Tracey Barbrick
Tel: 902-424-7337

Director, Acute & Tertiary Care, Lewis Bedford
Tel: 902-424-5497

Director, Health Intergovernmental Affairs, Vijay Bhashyakarla
Tel: 902-424-2842

Director, Heather Jane Christian
Tel: 902-424-5869

Director, Carolyn Davison
Tel: 902-424-7218
davisocj@gov.ns.ca

Director, Technical Operations, Anthony Eden
Tel: 902-424-4429

Director, Health Services, Kevin Elliott
Tel: 902-424-6869

Director, Acute Care, Katherine Fraser
Tel: 902-424-4878

Director, Active & Healthy Living, Rick Gilbert
Tel: 902-424-2772
Fax: 902-424-0520
gilberrf@gov.ns.ca

Director, Fin. & Admin. Internal Support, Gary Glessing
Tel: 902-424-6138

Director, Primary Health Care, Lisa Ruth Grandy
Tel: 902-424-4617

Director, Long Term Care, Dean Hirtle
Tel: 902-424-1797

Director, Chronic Disease & Injury Prevention, Nancy Hoddinott
Tel: 902-424-5840

Director, Lindsay Marja Hugenholtz
Tel: 902-490-3200

Director, Health Economics, Michael Joyce
Tel: 902-427-6879

Director, Health Privacy Office, Maria Lasheras
Tel: 902-424-8214

Director, Insured Services, Harold McCarthy
Tel: 902-424-7538

Director, Karen McDuff
Tel: 902-424-2635

Director, Environmental Health, Gary O'Toole
Tel: 902-424-1262

Director, AIDS Commission, Michelle Proctor-Simms
Tel: 902-424-4741

Director, Standards & Policy, Susan Stevens
Tel: 902-424-6857

Director, Emergency Managment Centre, Russell Stuart
Tel: 902-424-0000

Associated Agencies, Boards & Commissions:

• Nova Scotia Advisory Commission on AIDS
Dennis Bldg.
1740 Granville St., 6th Fl.
Halifax, NS B3J 1X5
Tel: 902-424-5730
Fax: 902-424-4727
AIDS@gov.ns.ca
www.gov.ns.ca/aids/
• Seniors' Secretariat
Dennis Bldg.
1740 Granville St., 4th Fl.
PO Box 2065
Halifax, NS B3J 2Z1
Tel: 902-424-0065
Fax: 902-424-0561
Toll-free: 800-670-0065
seniors@gov.ns.ca
www.gov.ns.ca/seniors/

Office of the Chief Public Health Officer
PO Box 488, Halifax, NS B3J 2R8
The Office of the Chief Public Health Officer is responsible for the Department of Health's legislated responsibility to protect & promote the public's health in the following areas: communicable disease control, environmental health, emergency preparedness & response. In addition, staff in the Office of the Chief Public Health Officer, in collaboration with academic expertise at Dalhousie University, function as an expert resource in community health science & an epidemiological resource for the department, the health districts, & other relevant government & community groups.
Chief Public Health Officer/Chief Medical Officer of Health, Dr. Robert Strang
Tel: 902-424-2358
Fax: 902-424-4716

Nova Scotia Human Rights Commission

Joseph Howe Bldg., 1690 Hollis St., 6th Fl., Halifax, NS B3J 3C4
Tel: 902-424-4111
Fax: 902-424-0596
hrcinquiries@gov.ns.ca
www.humanrights.gov.ns.ca
TTY: 902-424-3139

Acts Administered:
Human Rights Act

Minister, Justice, Hon. Ross Landry
Tel: 902-424-4044
Fax: 902-424-0510
justmin@gov.ns.ca

Digby
84 Warwick St., PO Box 1029, Digby, NS B0V 1A0
Tel: 902-245-4791
Fax: 902-245-7103

Sydney
Provincial Bldg., 360 Prince St., Sydney, NS B1P 5L1
Tel: 902-563-2140
Fax: 902-563-5613

Office of Immigration

#110A, 1741 Brunswick St., PO Box 1535, Halifax, NS B3J 2Y3
Tel: 902-424-5230
Fax: 902-424-7936
immigration@gov.ns.ca
www.novascotiaimmigration.com

Minister, Hon. Marilyn More
Tel: 902-424-7627
Fax: 902-428-3178
min_immigration@gov.ns.ca

Deputy Minister, Hon. Judith Ferguson
Tel: 902-424-3603
fergusjf@gov.ns.ca

Director, Communications, Tom Peck
Tel: 902-423-3742
peckto@gov.ns.ca

Department of Intergovernmental Affairs

Duke Tower, 5251 Duke St., 5th Fl., PO Box 1617, Halifax, NS B3J 2Y3
Fax: 902-424-0728
iga@gov.ns.ca
www.gov.ns.ca/iga
Provides leadership in the development of corporate strategies for Nova Scotia's relations with governments & organizations.

Minister, Hon. Darrell Dexter
Tel: 902-424-6600
Toll-free: 800-267-1993
Fax: 902-424-7648
premier@gov.ns.ca

Deputy Minister, Judith Sullivan-Corney
Tel: 902-424-3219
corneyjm@gov.ns.ca

Associate Deputy Minister, Scott Logan
Tel: 902-424-2094
logansm@gov.ns.ca

Director, Regional Relations, Darryl C. Eisan
Tel: 902-424-4535
dceisan@gov.ns.ca

Director, Strategic Policy, Norma MacIsaac
Tel: 902-424-7662
macisanj@gov.ns.ca

Director, Economic Policy & Analysis, André Moore
Tel: 902-424-7728
mooreac@gov.ns.ca

Director, Environmental & Social Affairs, Albert Walzak
Tel: 902-424-7748
walzakag@gov.ns.ca

Department of Justice

5151 Terminal Rd., 4th Fl., PO Box 7, Halifax, NS B3J 2L6
Tel: 902-424-4030
Fax: 902-424-0510
justweb@gov.ns.ca
www.gov.ns.ca/just/

Acts Administered:
Age of Majority Act
Alimony Act
Alternative Penalty Act
Apportionment Act
Arbitration Act
Architects Act
Assignments & Preferences Act
Barristers & Solicitors Act
Beneficiaries Designation Act
Bills of Lading Act
Canada & the United Kingdom Reciprocal Recognition & Enforcement of Judgments Act
Canadian Forces Reservists Protection Act
Cape Breton Barristers' Society Act
Change of Name Act
Child Abduction Act
Collection Act
Communications & Information Act
Compensation for Victims of Crime Act
Constables Act
Constables' Protection Act
Constitutional Questions Act
Contributory Negligence Act
Controverted Elections Act
Conveyancing Act
Corporations Miscellaneous Provisions Act
Correctional Services Act
Corrections Act
Costs & Fees Act
Court & Administrative Reform
Court Houses & Lockup Houses Act
Court Officials Act
Court Security Act
Court for Divorce & Matrimonial Causes Act
Creditors' Relief Act
Defamation Act
Demise of the Crown Act
Descent of Property Act
Divorce Act
Domestic Violence Act
Elections Act
Enforcement of Canadian Judges & Decrees Act
Engineering Profession Act
Escheats Act
Estate Actions Act
Estreats Act
Evidence Act
Expropriation Act
Family Court Act
Family Maintenance Act
Family Orders Information Release Act
Fatal Injuries Act
Fatality Investigations Act
Federal/Provincial Power Act
Flea Markets Regulation Act
Floral Emblem Act
Forcible Entry & Detainer Act
Freedom of Information & Protection of Privacy Act
Guardianship Act
Gunshot Wounds Act
House of Assembly Act
Human Rights Act
Incompetent Persons Act
Indigent Debtors Act
Inebriates' Guardianship Act
Interest on Judgements Act
Interior Designers Act
Interjurisdictional Act
International Commercial Arbitration Act
Interpretation Act
Interprovincial Subpoena Act
Intestate Succession Act
Judicature Act
Judicial Disqualifications Removal Act
Juries Act
Justices of the Peace Act
Land Actions Venue Act
Law Reform Commission Act
Legal Aid Act
Liberty of the Subject Act
Lieutenant Governor & Great Seal Act
Limitation of Actions Act
Lobbyists' Registration Act
Maintenance & Custody Act
Maintenance Enforcement Act
Maintenance Orders Enforcement Act
Married Women's Deed Act
Married Women's Property Act
Matrimonial Property Act
Mechanics' Lien Act
Medal of Bravery Act
Members & Public Employees Disclosure Act
Municipal Conflict of Interest Act
Night Courts Act
Notaries & Commissioners Act
Nova Scotia Tartan Act
Occupiers Liability Act
Official Tree Act
Ombudsman Act
Overholding Tenants Act
Partition Act
Payment into Court Act
Personal Directives Act
Personal Information International Disclosure Protection Act
Pledging of Service Emblems Act
Police Act
Police Services Act
Powers of Attorney Act
Presumption of Death Act
Private Investigators & Private Guards Act
Probate Act
Proceedings Against the Crown Act
Protection of Property Act
Provincial Bird Act
Provincial Court Act
Provincial Dog Act
Public Inquiries Act
Public Prosecutions Act
Public Service Act
Public Subscriptions Act
Public Trustee Act
Quieting Titles Act
Real Property Act
Real Property Transfer Validation Act
Reciprocal Enforcement of Judgment Orders Act
Regulations Act
Religious & Charitable Corporations Property Act
Religious Congregations & Societies Act
Remembrance Day Act
Remission of Penalties Act
Residential Tenancies Act
Retail Business Uniform Closing Day Act
Safer Communities & Neighbours Act
Sale of Goods Act
Sale of Land under Execution Act
Salvage Yards Licensing Act
Securities Act
Small Claims Court Act
Solemnization of Marriage Act
Statute Revision Act
Summary Proceedings Act
Supreme & Exchequer Courts of Canada Act
Sureties Act
Survival of Actions Act
Survivorship Act
Taxing Masters Act
Tenancies & Distress for Rent Act
Testators' Family Maintenance Act
Ticket of Leave Act
Time Definition Act
Tortfeasors Act
Trustee Act
Unclaimed Articles Act
Uniform Law Act

Utility & Review Board Act
Variation of Trusts Act
Vendors & Purchasers Act
Victims' Rights & Services Act
Volunteer Services Act
Warehouse Receipts Act
Warehousemen's Lien Act
Wills Act
Woodmen's Lien Act
Workers' Compensation Act
Young Persons Summary Proceedings Act
Youth Criminal Justice Act
Youth Justice Act

Minister & Attorney General, Hon. Ross Landry
Tel: 902-424-4044
Fax: 902-424-0510
justmin@gov.ns.ca

Deputy Minister, Marian F. Tyson, Q.C.
Tel: 902-424-4223
tysonmf@gov.ns.ca

Director, Regional & Canada US Relations, Daryl Eisan

Director, Contracts, Edward Kirby
Tel: 902-424-3178

Director, Emergency Programs, Andrew Lathem
Tel: 000-424-5620

Director, Economic Policy & Analysis, Andre Moore

Director, Emergency Services, Michael Myette
Tel: 902-424-6206

Director, Information Technology, Charles Purcell
Tel: 902-424-6349

Director, Social & Environmental Affairs, Albert Walzak
Tel: 902-563-5648

Associated Agencies, Boards & Commissions:
• Human Rights Commission
Joseph Howe Building
1690 Hollis St., 6th Fl.
PO Box 2221
Halifax, NS B3J 3C4
Tel: 902-424-4111
Fax: 902-424-0596
Toll-free: 877-269-7699
TTY: 877-424-3139
hrcinquiries@gov.ns.ca
www.humanrights.gov.ns.ca/
• Nova Scotia Legal Aid Commission
#102, 137 Chain Lake Dr.
Halifax, NS B3S 1B3
Tel: 902-420-6573
Fax: 902-420-3471
nsla.exec@ns.sympatico.ca
www.nslegalaid.ca
• Office of the Chief Medical Examiner
Halifax Insurance Bldg.
#701, 5670 Spring Garden Rd.
Halifax, NS B3J 1H7
Tel: 902-424-2722
Fax: 902-424-0607
www.gov.ns.ca/just/CME.asp
• Nova Scotia Police Commission
#300, 1601 Lower Water St.
PO Box 1573
Halifax, NS B3J 2Y3
Tel: 902-424-3246
Fax: 902-424-3919
uarb.polcom@gov.ns.ca
www.gov.ns.ca/just/polcomm.htm
• Public Trustee Office
#405, 5670 Spring Garden Rd.
PO Box 685
Halifax, NS B3J 2T3
Tel: 902-424-7760
Fax: 902-424-0616
PublicTrusteeHCD@gov.ns.ca (Health Care Decisions Division)
www.gov.ns.ca/just/pto/
• Workers' Compensation Appeals Tribunal
#1002, 5670 Spring Garden Rd.
Halifax, NS B3J 1H6
Tel: 902-424-2250
Fax: 902-424-2321
Toll-free: 800-274-8281
www.gov.ns.ca/wcat/

Communications
Tel: 902-424-7640
Fax: 902-424-0692

Director, Donna Chislett
Tel: 902-424-3313
Fax: 902-424-0510
chisledp@gov.ns.ca
Director, Ross McLaren
Tel: 902-424-3313
Fax: 902-424-0510
MCLARENR@gov.ns.ca

Correctional Services
Tel: 902-424-7640
Fax: 902-424-0692

Executive Director, Corrections, Diana MacKinnon
Tel: 902-424-5661
Director, David Bungay
Tel: 902-563-2362
Director, David William Horner
Tel: 902-424-6437
Director, Sean Kelly
Tel: 902-424-5342

Court Services
Tel: 902-424-7640
Fax: 902-424-0692

Director, William Clancey
Tel: 902-424-6414
Director, Shauna Lee Wilson
Tel: 902-563-3545

Finance & Administration
Tel: 902-424-7640
Fax: 902-424-0692

Director, Finance, Lisa MacKinnon
Tel: 902-424-6530

Maintenance Enforcement Program
Tel: 902-424-7640
Fax: 902-424-0692

Director, Judith Crump
Tel: 902-424-3641

Policy & Information Management
Tel: 902-424-7640
Fax: 902-424-0692

Executive Director, Judith McPhee
Tel: 902-424-4632

Department of Labour & Advanced Education

5151 Terminal Rd., 6th Fl., PO Box 697, Halifax, NS B3J 2T8
Tel: 902-424-5301
Fax: 902-424-0575
www.gov.ns.ca/lwd

Focuses on labour issues, employment rights & responsibilities, adult learning, apprenticeship training & trade qualification, skill development, public & workplace safety, industry regulation, licensing & pensions.
Acts Administered:
Amusement Devices Safety Act
Apprenticeship & Trades Qualifications Act
Building Code Act
Court & Administrative Reform Act (Labour Relations Board Orders Regulations only)
Degree Granting Act
Electrical Installation & Inspection Act
Elevators & Lifts Act
Fire Safety Act
Labour Standards Code
Occupational Health & Safety Act
Pay Equity Act
Pension Benefits Act
Private Career Colleges Regulation Act
Registered Barbers Act
Retail Business Designated Day Closing Act
Retail Business Uniform Closing Day Act
Student Aid Act
Teachers' Collective Bargaining Act
Technical Safety Act
Theatres & Amusements Act
Trade Union Act
Universities Assistance Act
University Foundations Act
Voluntary Fire Services Act
Voluntary Protection Act
Voluntary Services Act
Workers' Compensation Act

Minister, Hon. Marilyn More
Tel: 902-424-6647
Fax: 902-424-0575
min_lae@gov.ns.ca

Deputy Minister, Judith Ferguson
Tel: 902-424-4148
fergusjf@gov.ns.ca

Associate Deputy Minister, Jeff Conrad
Tel: 902-424-6270
conradja@gov.ns.ca

Director, Communications, Karen Stone
Tel: 902-424-2107
Fax: 902-424-0644
stonekk@gov.ns.ca

Associated Agencies, Boards & Commissions:
• Nova Scotia Apprenticeship Board
2021 Brunswick St.
PO Box 578
Halifax, NS B3J 2S9
Tel: 902-424-0872
Fax: 902-424-0488
Toll-free: 800-494-5651
bedgoomm@gov.ns.ca
www.gov.ns.ca/lae/Apprenticeshipboard
Other Communication: 902-424-5651 (Registration & Renewals)
The Nova Scotia Apprenticeship Board is the voice of industry to the Minister of Labour & Advanced Education. The primary role of the board is to consult with industry on apprenticeship matters & to make recommendations to the Minister. In particular, the Board reviews current trade regulations & recommends proposed trades for designation & compulsory certification.
• Crane Operators Appeal Board
5151 Terminal Rd., 7th Fl.
PO Box 697
Halifax, NS B3J 2T8
Tel: 902-424-8595
Fax: 902-424-0217
fernanfs@gov.ns.ca
www.gov.ns.ca/lae/coab
The Crane Operators Appeal Board was created pursuant to the Crane Operators & Power Engineers Act, which came into force on September 1, 2001. It is an independent adjudicative tribunal charged with considering appeals filed under Part I of the Act.
• Elevators & Lifts Appeal Board
5151 Terminal Rd., 7th Fl.
PO Box 697
Halifax, NS B3J 2T8
Tel: 902-424-8595
Fax: 902-424-0217
www.gov.ns.ca/lae/elab
• Occupational Health & Safety Advisory Council
PO Box 697
Halifax, NS B3J 2T8
Tel: 902-424-2484
Fax: 902-424-5640
www.gov.ns.ca/lae/abct/ohsadvisory.asp
• Pay Equity Commission
5151 Terminal Rd., 6th Fl.
PO Box 697
Halifax, NS B3J 2T8
Tel: 902-424-2385
Fax: 902-424-0575
www.gov.ns.ca/lwd/payequity
The Pay Equity Commission is responsible for administrating the Pay Equity Act. In addition to monitoring the pay equity process, the Commission has the power to resolve disputes when employers and employees cannot agree, conducts research, maintains statistics, and advises the Minister of Labour on matters relating to pay equity.
• Power Engineers & Operators Appeal Committee
5151 Terminal Rd., 7th Fl.
PO Box 697
Halifax, NS B3J 2T8
Tel: 902-424-8595
Fax: 902-424-0217
www.gov.ns.ca/lae/peoac/
• Workers' Advisers Program
#502, 5670 Spring Garden Rd.
PO Box 1063
Halifax, NS B3J 2X1
Tel: 902-424-5050
Fax: 902-424-0530
Toll-free: 800-774-4712
www.gov.ns.ca/lwd/wap
The Workers' Advisers Program is a legal clinic that is funded by the provincial government offering services to injured workers. Our purpose is to provide legal assistance when an injured worker has been denied Workers' Compensation Board benefits.

Advanced Education
Brunswick Place, 2021 Brunswick St., 4th Fl., PO Box 578, Halifax, NS B3J 2S9
www.gov.ns.ca/lae/divisions/
Consists of Post-Secondary Disability Services, Private Career Colleges, Student Assistance, & Universities & Colleges.

Alcohol & Gaming
780 Windmill Rd., 2nd Fl., PO Box 545, Dartmouth, NS B2Y 3Y8
Fax: 902-424-6160
Toll-Free: 877-565-0556
www.gov.ns.ca/lae/divisions/
Consists of Post-Secondary Disability Services, Private Career Colleges, Student Assistance, & Universities & Colleges.

Labour Services Branch
www.gov.ns.ca/lae/divisions/
Consists of Conciliation & Labour Tribunals, Labour Standards, Pension Regulation, & Workers' Advisers Program.
Executive Director, Labour Services, Barbara Jones-Gordon
Tel: 902-424-2385
Director, Labour Services, William Grant
Tel: 902-424-3549
grantwa@gov.ns.ca
Director, Labour Standards, Lynn Hartley
Tel: 902-424-3345
hartleel@gov.ns.ca
Chief Worker Advisor, Workers' Advisers Program, Kenny LeBlanc
Tel: 902-424-0460
Director, Labour Standards, J. Anne Partridge
Tel: 902-424-2219

Policy, Planning & Professional Services Branch
www.gov.ns.ca/lae/policy/
Other Communication: www.gov.ns.ca/lae/ProfessionalServices.asp
Consists of Federal/Provincial Relations & Research, Policy & Planning, & Professional Services
Executive Director, Marjorie Davison
Tel: 902-424-5191
Director, Professional Services, Stewart Sampson
Tel: 902-424-8055

Safety Branch
www.gov.ns.ca/lae/publicsafety/
Other Communication: www.gov.ns.ca/lae/ohs/
Consists of Building, Fire & Technical Safety/Office of the Fire Marshall, & Occupational Health & Safety.
Executive Director, James LeBlanc
Tel: 902-424-8477
Regional Director, David Clark
Tel: 902-752-2641
Director & Fire Marshal, Harold James Pothier
Tel: 902-538-4112
Director, Technical Safety, David Wigmore
Tel: 902-424-5434

Skills & Learning Branch
www.gov.ns.ca/lae/divisions/
Consists of Adult Education, Apprenticeship Training, Employment Nova Scotia, & Skill Development.
Director, Apprenticeship, Joseph Rudderham
Tel: 902-424-3206

Volunteerism
www.gov.ns.ca/lae/volunteerism/

Nova Scotia Liquor Corporation

Bayers Lake Business Park, 93 Chain Lake Dr., Halifax, NS B3S 1A3
Tel: 902-450-6752
Toll-Free: 800-567-5874
www.mynslc.com
Other Communication: www.facebook.com/theNSLC?ref=td; www.twitter.com/theNSLC

Minister Responsible, Hon. Maureen MacDonald

Chair, Sherry Porter
Tel: 902-420-5243
sherry.porter@thenslc.com

President & Chief Executive Officer, Bret Mitchell
Tel: 902-450-5802
bret.mitchell@thenslc.com

Department of Natural Resources

Founder's Square, 1701 Hollis St., 3rd Fl., PO Box 698, Halifax, NS B3J 2T9
Tel: 902-424-5935
Fax: 902-424-0594
Toll-Free: 800-565-2224
www.gov.ns.ca/natr
Responsible for the administration & management of provincial Crown lands, development of mineral & energy resources, protection & sustainable development of forest resources & operation & maintenance of parks system, & promoting the conservation & sustainable use of wildlife populations, habitat & ecosystems.Initiatives include: a State of the Forest report; working with other departments on State of the Environment report; leading the development of a provincial climate change strategy; implementing recovery plans for endangered & threatened wildlife species; & developing strategic land use plans for Crown lands using an integrated resource management planning process.
Acts Administered:
Act to Confer Certain Powers Upon the Lieutenant Governor in Council & to amend the Mines Act
Angling Act
Beaches Act
Blueberry Association Act
Bowater Mersey Agreement Act
Christmas Tree Grading Regulations
Christmas Tree Levy Regulations
Conservation Easements Act
Dutch Elm Disease Regulations
Endangered Species Act
Expropriation Act
Forest Fire Protection Regulations
Forest Sustainability Regulations
Forests Act
General Wildlife Regulations
Gypsum Mining Income Tax Act
Halifax Power & Pulp Company Limited Agreement Act, 1962
Indian Lands Act
Land Holdings Disclosure Act
Land Surveyors Act
Mineral Resources Act
Mines Act
Nova Scotia Federation of Anglers & Hunters Act
Off Highway Vehicles Act
Primary Forest Products Marketing Act
Private Ways Act
Provincial Parks Act
Registration & Statistical Returns Regulations
Scalers Act
Scott Maritimes Limited Agreement (1965) Act
Special Places Protection Act (jointly with Tourism, Culture & Heritage)
Stora Forest Industries Agreement Act
Timber Loan Board Regulations
Trails Act
Treasure Trove Act
Wildlife Act
Wildlife Habitat & Watercourses Protection Regulations

Minister, Hon. Charlie Parker
Tel: 902-424-4037
Fax: 902-424-0594
min_dnr@gov.ns.ca

Deputy Minister, Rick Williams
Tel: 902-424-7751
Fax: 902-428-2137
williarm@gov.ns.ca

Director, Information Technology, Barbara Curry
Tel: 902-424-4142

Director, Communications, Dan Davis
Tel: 902-424-2354
Fax: 902-424-7735
davisds@gov.ns.ca

Director, Financial Services, Weldon Myers
Tel: 902-424-3288

Director, Human Resources, Leslie Shanahan
Tel: 902-424-8861
Fax: 902-424-8407

Associated Agencies, Boards & Commissions:
• Crown Land Information Management Centre
Founders Square
#501, 1701 Hollis St.
PO Box 698
Halifax, NS B3J 2T9
Tel: 902-424-3171
• NS Primary Forest Products Marketing Board
#804, 45 Alderney Dr.
Dartmouth, NS B2Y 2N6
Tel: 902-424-7598
Fax: 902-424-6965
www.gov.ns.ca/pfpmb/

Land Services Branch
www.gov.ns.ca/natr/thedepartment/landservices.asp
The Land Services Branch management oversees, coordinates & approves all activities within the Branch relating to the administration of Crown land. The Branch provides advice on legislative revisions & advises & drafts policies relating to the administration of Crown land.
Executive Director, Gretchen Pohlkamp
Tel: 902-424-4267
pohlkagg@gov.ns.ca
Director, Land Administration, Arlene D'Eon
Tel: 902-424-6335
Director, Land Services Renewal, Eli Elias
Tel: 902-424-1190
Director, Surveys, Bruce Albert MacQuarrie
Tel: 902-424-3144

Mineral Resources Branch
Fax: 902-424-7735
www.gov.ns.ca/natr/meb/
Implements policies & programs dealing with the exploration, development, management & efficient use of energy & mineral resources, promotes scientific studies of the geology of the province for use by government, industry & the public, provides a mineral rights tenure system to establish legal rights to minerals for exploration & development. Promotes concepts of environmental responsibility & sustainability.
Executive Director, Don James
Tel: 902-424-2523
Director, Mineral Management, Alan Davidson
Tel: 902-424-5618
Director, Geological Services, Rob Naylor
Tel: 902-424-8119

Policy, Planning & Support Services
Provides planning & policy coordination support to the Department, ensures that policies & plans developed in the Department are coordinated, supports the integrated management of natural resources. Also provides a range of administrative, planning, research, information management, information distribution, graphics, cartographic, communication, & occupational health & safety-related services.
Executive Director, Patricia Bernadette MacNeil
Tel: 902-424-4988
macneipb@gov.ns.ca

Regional Services Branch
Delivers departmental programs & services through a field office network, responsible for forest protection & planning, forest nurseries, research & development, enforcement, coordination of the hunter safety program, regional geological services, Crown land surveys, operation & maintenance of provincial parks, resource conservation, forest fire prevention & monitoring of forest insects & diseases.
Executive Director, Brian Stanley Gilbert
Tel: 902-424-3949
Director, Resource Management, Dan Eidt
Tel: 902-424-7594
Director, Enforcement Division, John Mombourquette
Tel: 902-424-5254
jamombou@gov.ns.ca
Director, Operations, William Smith
Tel: 902-424-4445
Director, Fleet Management, Ross Wickwire
Tel: 902-758-3438
Central
PO Box 68, Truro, NS B2N 5B8
Tel: 902-893-6350
Fax: 902-893-5613
Secondary Address: 664 Prince St.
Arlington Place
Truro, NS B2N 1G6
Regional Director, J. Allan Eddy
Tel: 902-893-5627
Eastern
300 Mountain Rd., Sydney, NS B1L 1A9
Tel: 902-563-3370
Fax: 902-567-2535
Other Communication: Alternate Phone: 902-563-3372
Regional Director, Donald Feldman
Tel: 902-533-3370
Western
PO Box 6000, Lunenberg, NS B0J 2C0
Tel: 902-634-7555
Fax: 902-634-7577
Secondary Address: 312 Green St.
Lunenburg, NS B0J 2C0
Regional Director, Gerald Joudrey
Tel: 902-543-0622
gtjoudre@gov.ns.ca

Renewable Resources
Executive Director, Julie Towers
Tel: 902-679-6139
Director, Forest Protection, Walter Fanning
Tel: 902-758-7236
Director, Forestry, Jonathan Kierstead
Tel: 902-893-5673
Director, Program Development, Peter MacQuarrie
Tel: 902-424-7708
gpmacqua@gov.ns.ca

Director, Wildlife, Robert Petrie
Tel: 902-679-4366

Office of the Ombudsman

#700, 5670 Spring Garden Rd., PO Box 2152, Halifax, NS B3J 3B7
Tel: 902-424-6780
Fax: 902-424-6675
Toll-Free: 800-670-1111
ombudsman@gov.ns.ca
www.gov.ns.ca/ombu

Ombudsman, Dwight Bishop

Office Manager, Lois Smith
Tel: 902-424-5401
Fax: 902-424-6675

Executive Director, Janet Anne McKinnon
Tel: 902-424-8898
Fax: 902-424-6675

Office of Policy & Priorities

1700 Granville St., 3rd Fl., 1 Government Place, Halifax, NS B3J 2Y3
Tel: 902-424-7751
Fax: 902-428-2137
PPenquiries@gov.ns.ca

On July 9, 2009, a new government committee was established to provide policy direction to government. It is responsible for all affairs & matters pertaining to identification, prioritization, & development of government policy issues, plans & strategies.

Minister, Hon. Darrell Dexter
premier@gov.ns.ca

Deputy Minister, Rick Williams, EdD
willarm@gov.ns.ca

Public Service Commission

1800 Argyle St., 5th Fl., PO Box 943, Halifax, NS B3J 2V9
Tel: 902-424-7660
www.gov.ns.ca/psc

Minister, Human Resources, Hon. Frank Corbett
Tel: 902-424-5465
min_psc@gov.ns.ca
Deputy Minister, Kelliann Dean
Tel: 902-424-6617
deankm@gov.ns.ca
Executive Director, Policy & Systems Performance, Gordon Adams
Tel: 902-424-5969
Executive Director, Employee Relations, Gordon MacLean
Tel: 902-424-7644
macleang@gov.ns.ca
Executive Director, Patti Pike
Executive Director, Client Service Delivery, Sharalyn Young
Tel: 902-424-0944
Director, Compensation & Benefits, John F. Campbell
Tel: 902-424-2824
Social Media:
www.linkedin.com/pub/john-campbell/26/691/881
Director, Evaluation & Accountability, Katherine Cox-Brown
Tel: 902-424-8383
coxbrokm@gov.ns.ca
Director, Communications, Sue McKeage
Tel: 902-424-7280
mckeagsm@gov.ns.ca
Director, Recruitment Services, Jocelyn Pletz
Tel: 902-722-1327
Social Media: www.linkedin.com/pub/jocelyn-pletz/7/4a5/9ab

Department of Seniors

1740 Granville St., PO Box 2065, Halifax, NS B3J 2Z1
Tel: 902-424-0065
Fax: 902-424-0561
Toll-Free: 800-670-0065
seniors@gov.ns.ca
www.gov.ns.ca/seniors

Committed to ensuring the inclusion, well-being, & independence of seniors in Nova Scotia by facilitating the development of policies on aging & programs for seniors across government & through the provision & coordination of strategic planning, support, services, programs & information.

Minister, Hon. Denise Peterson-Rafuse
petersdj@gov.ns.ca

Deputy Minister, Kelliann Dean
Tel: 902-424-6617
deankm@gov.ns.ca

Chief Executive Officer, Valerie White
Tel: 902-424-6322
whitevj@gov.ns.ca

Director, Programs, Wendy Aird
Tel: 902-424-4649

Director, Corporate Strategy & Policy, Faizal Nanji
Tel: 902-424-7921

Director, Communications, Natalie Webster
Tel: 902-424-7957

Nova Scotia Securities Commission

Joseph Howe Building, 1690 Hollis St., 2nd Fl., PO Box 458, Halifax, NS B3J 3J9
Tel: 902-424-7768
Fax: 902-424-4625
Toll-Free: 855-424-2499
www.gov.ns.ca/nssc/

Established to provide investors with protection in accordance with Nova Scotia's securities laws from practices & activities that tend to undermine investor confidence in the fairness & efficiency of capital markets.

Chairman, H. Leslie O'Brien, Q.C.
Tel: 902-424-7079
obrienhl@gov.ns.ca

Vice Chair, Sarah P. Bradley
Tel: 902-424-7768

Executive Director, Securities, J. William Slatterly
slattejw@gov.ns.ca

Director, Policy & Market Regulation, Shirley Lee
leesp@gov.ns.ca

Director, Corporate Finance, Kevin G. Redden
reddenkg@gov.ns.ca

Department of Service Nova Scotia & Municipal Relations

1505 Barrington St., PO Box 216, Halifax, NS B3J 3K5
Tel: 902-424-5200
Fax: 902-424-0581
Toll-Free: 800-670-4357
askus@gov.ns.ca
www.gov.ns.ca/snsmr
TTY: 877-404-0720
Other Communication: Nova Scotia Business Registry: 1-800-670-4357

Provides leadership in the achievement of effective local government, assessment services, business licensing & registration, vehicle registration & driver licensing, taxation & revenue collection, vital statistics & an integrated land information management system to meet the needs of local & provincial agencies & residents of Nova Scotia.

Acts Administered:
Assessment Act
Business Electronic Filing Act
Cemetery & Funeral Services Act
Change of Name Act
Chartered Accountants Act
Collection Agencies Act
Communications & Information Act
Companies Act
Condominium Act
Consumer Creditors' Conduct Act
Consumer Protection Act
Consumer Reporting Act
Consumer Services Act
Corporations Registration Act
Direct Sellers' Regulation Act
Embalmers & Funeral Directors Act
Land Registration Act
Limited Partnerships Act
Liquor Control Act
Lobbyists' Registration Act
Marketable Titles Act
Mortgage Brokers' & Lenders' Registration Act
Motor Vehicle Act
Municipal Conflict of Interest Act
Municipal Elections Act
Municipal Finance Corporation Act
Municipal Fiscal Year Act
Municipal Government Act
Municipal Government Act Resource Binder
Municipal Grants Act
Municipal Housing Corporations Act
Municipal Loan & Building Fund Act
Off-Highway Vehicles Act
Oil Refineries & L.N.G. Plants Municipal Taxation Act
Part II of the Gaming Control Act
Part IV of the Revenue Act for administrative purposes
Part X of the Bankruptcy & Insolvency Act
Partnership Act
Partnerships & Business Names Registration Act
Personal Property Security Act
Petroleum Products Pricing Act
Private Investment Holding Companies Act
Property Valuation Services Corporation Act
Public Accountants Act
Real Estate Trading Act
Registry Act
Rent Review Act
Rental Property Conversion Act
Residential Tenancies Act
Rural Fire District Act
Sales Tax Act
Societies Act
Solemnization of Marriage Act
Unconscionable Transactions Relief Act
Vital Statistics Act
Wind Turbine Facilities Municipal Taxation Act

Minister, Hon. John MacDonnell
Tel: 902-424-5550
Fax: 902-424-0581
snsmrmin@gov.ns.ca

Deputy Minister, Kevin Malloy
Tel: 902-424-4100
Fax: 902-424-0581
keefeg@gov.ns.ca

Executive Director, Strategic & Transition Planning, Cheryl Burgess
Tel: 902-424-5604
Fax: 902-424-0581

Executive Director, Human Resources Services & Client Support, Sharalyn Young
Tel: 902-424-0944
Fax: 902-424-0581

Director, Human Resources, Kimberley Aselstine
Tel: 902-424-3930
Fax: 902-424-0581

Director, Compensation & Benefits, John Campbell
Tel: 902-424-2824
Fax: 902-424-0581

Director, Audit & Evaluation, Katharine Cox-Brown
Tel: 902-424-8383
Fax: 902-424-0581

Director, Human Resources, Isabel Hache
Tel: 902-424-7840
Fax: 902-424-0581

Director, Human Resources, Catherine Francis Martin
Tel: 902-424-2751
Fax: 902-424-0581

Director, Communications, Penny McCormick
Tel: 902-424-6336
Fax: 902-424-0581

Director, Recruitment Services, Jocelyn Pletz
Tel: 902-722-1327
Fax: 902-424-0581

Director, Human Resources, Dale Rushton
Tel: 902-424-6498
Fax: 902-424-0581

Director, Human Resources, Leslie Shanahan
Tel: 902-424-8861
Fax: 902-424-0581

Director, Human Resources, Marica Mary Smythe
Tel: 902-424-3443
Fax: 902-424-0581

Director, Staff Relations, Cynthia Yazbek
Tel: 902-424-4588
Fax: 902-424-0581

Associated Agencies, Boards & Commissions:
• Nova Scotia Municipal Finance Corporation
Maritime Centre
1505 Barrington St., 10th Fl. South
PO Box 850 M
Halifax, NS B3J 2V2
Tel: 902-424-4590
Fax: 902-424-0525
www.gov.ns.ca/nsmfc

NSMFC issues pooled debentures that provide low-cost, long-term capital financing for municipal capital projects. The NSMFC issues in capital markets twice a year, generally in the spring & fall. On occasion the NSMFC will do a single issue, provided the size is large enough.

Access Nova Scotia
www.gov.ns.ca/snsmr/access/default.asp

Municipal Services Division
Fax: 902-424-0821
www.gov.ns.ca/snsmr/muns/http://www.gov.ns.ca/snsmr/muns/
Executive Director, Nathan Gorall
Tel: 902-424-2499
Acting Director, Advisory Services, Mark Peck
Tel: 902-424-7917
Director, Policy & Finance, Jeff Shute
Tel: 902-424-6161
Acting Director, Planning, Dave Smith
Tel: 902-424-7918
Director, Grants & Programs, Aileen Waller-Hebb
Tel: 902-424-7414
Director, Strategy & Sector Relations, Brant Wishart
Tel: 902-424-7418

Co-operatives Branch
#3, 80 Walker St., Truro, NS B2N 4A7
Tel: 902-893-6190
Fax: 902-893-6108
nscoop@gov.ns.ca
Other Communication: www.gov.ns.ca/snmr/access/business/registry-joint-stock-companies/co-operatives.asp
Inspector, Lynda C. H. Russell

Land Programs
PO Box 1523, Halifax, NS B3J 2Y3
Fax: 902-424-0639
Toll-Free: 866-518-4640
propertyonline@gov.ns.ca
Other Communication: www.gov.ns.ca/snsmr/access/land/land-services-information/land-registry.asp
Registrar General & Director, Norman Hill
Tel: 902-722-5079

Provincial Tax Commission
Maritime Centre, 1505 Barrington St., 9th Fl., PO Box 2205, Halifax, NS B3J 2V4
Tel: 902-424-6300
Fax: 902-424-7434
Toll-Free: 800-565-2336
www.gov.ns.ca/snsmr/taxcomm/

Registry of Deeds
PO Box 2205, Halifax, NS B3J 3C4
Fax: 902-424-5872
www.gov.ns.ca/snsmr/property/default.asp?mn=282.46.1064
Registrar, L. Nellie Anderson
Tel: 902-667-6540
Registrar, Shelley Archibald
Tel: 902-893-5869
Registrar, Elaine Marie Deion
Tel: 902-837-3500
Registrar, C. Darlene Dixon
Tel: 902-485-7176
Registrar, Elaine Howatt
Tel: 902-742-0776
Registrar, Marian MacPherson
Tel: 902-863-2677
Registrar, Joan Plunkett
Tel: 902-543-5095
Registrar, Mary Elizabeth Shaw
Tel: 902-226-2818
Registrar, Peggy Zwicker
Tel: 902-354-5715

Registry of Joint Stock Companies
Maritime Centre, 1505 Barrington St., 9th Fl., Halifax, NS B3J 3K5
Tel: 902-424-7770
Fax: 902-424-4633
Toll-Free: 800-225-8227
joint-stock@gov.ns.ca
www.gov.ns.ca/snsmr/rjsc
Registrar, Hayley Clarke
Tel: 902-424-7742
clarkehe@gov.ns.ca
Social Media: www.linkedin.com/in/hayleyclarke

Registry of Motor Vehicles
1505 Barrington St., 8th Fl. North, PO Box 1652, Halifax, NS B3J 2Z3
Tel: 902-424-7801
Fax: 902-424-0772
Toll-Free: 800-898-7668
www.gov.ns.ca/snsmr/rmv/
Registrar & Director, Paul Arsenault
Tel: 902-424-7801
Social Media: www.linkedin.com/pub/paul-arsenault/18/49b/259

Service Delivery
Maritime Centre, 1505 Barrington St., 9th Fl., Halifax, NS B3J 3K5
Tel: 902-424-2850
Fax: 902-424-0602
Executive Director, Service Delivery, Nancy MacLellan
Tel: 902-424-5181
Senior Project Executive, Natasha Clarke
Tel: 902-722-5042
Director, Regional Services, Barbara Brown
Tel: 902-869-3606
Director, E-Service, D. Darlene Joyce
Tel: 902-424-7523
Director, Property Registry, Donna MacRury
Tel: 902-563-2234

Vital Statistics
Joseph Howe Bldg., 1690 Hollis St., Ground Floor, PO Box 157, Halifax, NS B3J 2M9
Tel: 902-424-4071
Fax: 902-424-0678
Toll-Free: 800-898-7668
vstat@gov.ns.ca
www.gov.ns.ca/snsmr/access/vitalstats.asp
Deputy Registrar General, Michelle MacFarlane
Tel: 902-424-6274

Geomatics Centre
160 Willow St., Amherst, NS B4H 3W5
Tel: 902-667-7231
Fax: 902-667-6008
Toll-Free: 800-798-0706
geoinfo@gov.ns.ca
www.gov.ns.ca/snsmr/land/
Manager, Robert Neil Caldwell
Tel: 902-667-6287

Information Management Services
Executive Director, Robert Devet
Tel: 902-424-5022
Director, Project & Portfolio Management, Peter Arnburg
Tel: 902-424-6833
Social Media: www.linkedin.com/pub/peter-arnburg/4/8b4/298

Director, Geographic Information Services, Nancy Saunders
Tel: 902-424-4305
nsaunders@gov.ns.ca
Social Media: www.linkedin.com/pub/nancy-saunders/3a/136/bb2
Bridgewater
80 Logan Rd., Bridgewater, NS B4V 3J8
Antigonish
Antigosh Mall Annex, #3, 149 Church St., Antigonish, NS B2G 2E2
Toll-Free: 800-670-4357
Dartmouth
Super Store Mall, 650 Portland St., Dartmouth, NS B2W 6A3
Halifax
Bayers Lake Business Park, 300 Horseshoe Lake Drive, Halifax, NS B3S 0B7
Port Hawkesbury
Provincial Building, #22, 218 MacSween St., Port Hawkesbury, NS B9A 2J9
Kentville
5 Shylah Drive, Kentville, NS B4N 0H2
Sydney
Moxam Centre, 380 King's Rd., Sydney, NS B1S 1A8
Truro
#3, 80 Walker St., Truro, NS B2N 4A7
Yarmouth
Provincial Bldg., #127, 10 Starrs Rd., Yarmouth, NS B5A 2T1
Tel: 902-742-8565
Fax: 902-742-6244
info@yarmouth-town.com
www.yarmouth-town.com

Program Management & Corporate Services
Acting Executive Director, Cameron MacNeil
Tel: 902-424-4417

Nova Scotia Advisory Council on the Status of Women

1700 Granville St., PO Box 943, Halifax, NS B3J 2V9
Tel: 902-424-7660
women@gov.ns.ca
www.women.gov.ns.ca

The agency advocates for improved legislation, policies & programs for women, & provides research & policy advice to government on ways in which public policies & programs could better serve women.

Minister Responsible, Hon. Marilyn More
Tel: 902-424-8662
Fax: 902-424-0573

Executive Director, Stephanie MacInnis-Langley
Tel: 902-424-7548

Department of Transportation & Infrastructure Renewal

Johnston Bldg., 1672 Granville St., 2nd Fl., PO Box 186, Halifax, NS B3J 2N2
Tel: 902-424-2297
Fax: 902-424-0532
tpwpaff@gov.ns.ca
www.gov.ns.ca/tran
TTY: 888-432-3233

Provides a transportation network for the safe & efficient movement of people & goods; serves the building, property & accommodation needs of government departments & agencies; employs professional, dedicated people & offers a high level of customer service.

Acts Administered:
Dangerous Goods Transportation Act
Dangerous Goods Transportation Regulations
Ferries Act
Highway 104: Western Alignment Act
Motor Carrier Act
Motor Vehicle Act
Off-Highway Vehicles Act
Public Highways Act
Railways Act
Surplus Crown Property Disposal Act

Minister, Hon. Maurice Smith
Tel: 902-424-5875
Fax: 902-424-0171
tirmin@gov.ns.ca

Deputy Minister, David Darrow
Tel: 902-424-4036
Fax: 902-424-2014
ddarrow@gov.ns.ca

Executive Director, John Bernard O'Connor
Tel: 902-424-2756

Executive Director, Human Resources & Client Support, Sharalyn Young
Tel: 902-424-0944
Social Media: www.linkedin.com/pub/sharalyn-young/39/794/112

Director, Information Technology, George Cooper
Social Media: www.linkedin.com/pub/george-cooper/21/864/338

Director, Policy & Planning, Brian Michael Gallivan
Tel: 902-424-2907

Director, Engineering, Design & Construction, Tom Gouthro
Tel: 902-860-2999
Fax: 902-861-4828
gouthrto@gov.ns.ca

Director, Central district, Peter Hackett
Tel: 902-860-5600
Social Media: www.linkedin.com/pub/peter-hackett/29/71a/820

Director, Eastern district, Gerard Jessome
Tel: 902-563-2250
Social Media: www.linkedin.com/pub/gerard-jessome/17/438/542

Director, Public Affairs & Communications, Cathy MacIsaac
Tel: 902-424-8978
Fax: 902-424-0532
macisacl@gov.ns.ca

Director, Western district, Stephen MacIsaac
Tel: 902-543-4121
Social Media: www.linkedin.com/pub/steve-macisaac/32/456/416

Director, Northern district, Peter Emile Merritt
Tel: 902-424-5328

Associated Agencies, Boards & Commissions:

• **Sydney Tar Ponds Agency**
1 Inglis St.
PO Box 1028 A
Sydney, NS B1P 6J7
Tel: 902-567-1035
Fax: 902-567-1032
www.tarpondscleanup.ca

Highway Operations
www.gov.ns.ca/tran/highways
This division provides for provincial highway & bridge maintenance, as well as the operation of the Department's fleet management & a strategic planning section. District Services provides general services on primary & secondary roads & works with private sector contractors to provide the public with enhanced road systems.
Executive Director, Highway Engineering & Construction, Kevin Caines
Tel: 902-424-5687
Executive Director, Highway Maintenance & Operations, Charles Joseph MacDonald
Tel: 902-295-2700
Director, Highway / Engineering Services, Bernard Clancey
Tel: 902-424-4268

Public Works
www.gov.ns.ca/tran/works/
This division provides technical expertise & services required by the Department's highway, building & property divisions. The Highway Engineering Services section provides delivery of highway planning, geometric & structural design, traffic engineering, capital program maintenance & asset management business functions. The Engineering & Design section provides engineering, architectural, environmental & technical services & project management services for projects that are related to maintaining & constructing highway & building infrastructure. The Building Services & Operations section oversees the management, operation, maintenance & renovation of government buildings, infrastructure & properties, as well as the provision of trade & contract services in both leased & owned premises.
Executive Director, Strategiec Capital & Infrastructure Planning, Jane Fraser-Coutts
Tel: 902-424-8600
Director, Don Sutherland
Tel: 902-424-6038
Social Media: www.linkedin.com/pub/don-sutherland/21/610/696
Director, Building Services, Neil Whyte
Tel: 902-424-2883
Manager, Environmental Services, Chris Moir
Tel: 902-424-4725

Nova Scotia Treasury & Policy Board

1700 Granville St., 5th Fl., PO Box 1617, Halifax, NS B3J 2Y3
Tel: 902-424-8910
Fax: 902-424-7638
TBenquiries@gov.ns.ca
www.gov.ns.ca/tpb

On July 9, 2009, a new government committee was established to provide policy direction to the government. Treasury & Policy Board was separated into a Policy & Priorities Committee & a stand-alone Treasury Board.

President, Executive Council, Hon. Darrell E. Dexter
Tel: 902-424-6600
Fax: 902-424-7648
premier@gov.ns.ca

Deputy Minister, Treasury Board, Gregory P. Keefe
keefeg@gov.ns.ca

Chair, Treasury Board, Hon. Frank Corbett
Tel: 902-424-8910
Fax: 902-424-7638

Nova Scotia Utility & Review Board

Summit Place, 1601 Lower Water St., 3rd Fl., PO Box 1692 M, Halifax, NS B3J 3S3
Tel: 902-424-4448
Fax: 902-424-3919
uarb.board@gov.ns.ca
www.nsuarb.ca

The Board has a very broad mandate encompassing a number of Acts. Operations fall into two categories, regulatory & adjudicative. The regulatory category includes the regulation of public utilities, licensing of public passenger carriers, monitoring of automobile insurance rates, the approval of Halifax-Dartmouth bridge fares, & the regulation of natural gas distribution & pipelines. The Board conducts hearings relating to gaming control, liquor control & film classification. The adjudicative category includes appeals or applications relating to property assessments, expropriation compensation claims, planning & subdivisions, heritage properties, criminal injury compensation claims, municipal boundaries, municipal & school board electoral boundaries, as well as gasoline, diesel oil & tobacco taxes. The Board receives its authority from the Public Inquiries Act & the Utility & Review Board Act.
Acts Administered:
Assessment Act
Education Act
Electrical Installation & Inspection Act
Energy & Mineral Resources Conservation Act
Expropriation Act
Fire Safety Act
Gaming Control Act (Part II)
Gas Distribution Act
Halifax-Dartmouth Bridge Commission Act
Liquor Control Act
Motor Carrier Act (public passenger only)
Motor Vehicle Transport Act of Canada, 1987 (Federal)
Municipal Government Act
Nova Scotia Power Finance Corporation Act
Nova Scotia Power Privatization Act
Petroleum Products Pricing Act
Petroleum Resources Removal Permit Act
Pipeline Act
Public Utilities Act
Railways Act
Revenue Act
Theatres & Amusement Act
Underground Hydrocarbons Storage Act
Utility & Review Board Act
Victims' Rights & Services Act

Chair, Peter W. Gurnham, Q.C.
uarb.board@gov.ns.ca

Administrator, Paul G. Allen
Tel: 902-424-4448
uarb.paul@gov.ns.ca

Workers' Compensation Board of Nova Scotia

5668 South St., PO Box 1150, Halifax, NS B3J 2Y2
Tel: 902-491-8999
Fax: 902-491-8002
Toll-Free: 800-870-3331
info@wcb.gov.ns.ca
www.wcb.ns.ca

Coordinates the workers' compensation system to assist injured workers & their employers by providing timely medical & rehabilitative support to help injured workers return to work. Also, to provide appropriate compensation for work-related injuries & illnesses.

Chair, Elaine Sibson

CEO, Nancy MacCready-Williams
Tel: 902-491-8300

Deputy Chair, Chris Power

Government of Nunavut

Seat of Government: PO Box 1200, Iqaluit, NU X0A 0H0
Toll-Free: 888-252-9869
info@gov.nu.ca
www.gov.nu.ca

On April 1, 1999, Nunavut Territory was created as part of the Nunavut Land Claims Agreement signed in 1993. It has area of 1,932,254.97 km2, & the StatsCan census in 2011 showed the population was 31,906. Nunavut Territory is governed by a fully elected Legislative Assembly of 19 members elected for a five-year term. Government is by consensus rather than party politics. The Legislature elects the Premier & a seven-member Executive Council, which is charged with the operation of government & the establishment of program & spending priorities. Nunavut Territory acts under the same conditions as other territories in Canada. For an explanation of the difference between provinces & territories please see the Yukon Territory listing. The Commissioner of Nunavut Territory is appointed by the Federal Government, & serves a role similar to that of the Lieutenant Governor in provincial jurisdictions.

Office of the Commissioner

PO Box 2379, Iqaluit, NU X0A 0H0
Tel: 867-975-5120
Fax: 867-975-5123
nunavutcommissioner@gov.nu.ca
www.gov.nu.ca/commissioner

Commissioner, Hon. Edna Ekhivalak Elias

Asst. to the Commissioner, Marie Fortier
Tel: 867-975-5120
Fax: 867-975-5123
mfortier@gov.nu.ca

Office of the Premier

Legislative Assembly Bldg., 2nd Fl., PO Box 2410, Iqaluit, NU X0A 0H0
Tel: 867-975-5050
Fax: 867-975-5051
www.gov.nu.ca

Premier, Hon. Eva Aariak
Tel: 867-975-5050
Fax: 867-975-5051
premier@gov.nu.ca

Principal Secretary, Paul Crowley
Tel: 867-975-5050
Fax: 867-975-5051
jkunuk@gov.nu.ca
Social Media: www.linkedin.com/pub/paul-crowley/23/929/36b

Executive Assistant, Madeleine Allakariallak
mallakariallak@gov.nu.ca

Executive Council

Legislative Bldg., 2nd Fl., Box 2410, Iqaluit, NU X0A 0H0
Tel: 867-975-5090
Fax: 867-975-5095

Premier & Minister, Executive & Intergovernmental Affairs; Status of Women; Immigration; Aboriginal Affairs; Education, Hon. Eva Aariak
Tel: 867-975-5050
Fax: 867-975-5051
premier@gov.nu.ca

Deputy Premier & Minister, Economic Development & Transportation; Nunavut Business Credit Corporation; Nunavut Development Dorporation; Mines, Hon. Peter Taptuna
Tel: 867-975-5076
Fax: 867-975-5016

Minister, Health & Social Services & Minister; Nunavut Housing Corporation; Homelessness; Workers' Safety & Compensation Commission, Hon. Tagak Curley
Tel: 867-975-5005
Fax: 867-975-5095

Government House Leader & Minister, Community & Government Services; Energy; Qulliq Energy Corporation, Hon. Lorne Kusuqak
Tel: 867-975-5003
Fax: 867-975-5095

Minister, Finance; Justice; Public Agencies Council; Labour Standards Board; Liquor Licensing Board, Hon. Keith Peterson
Tel: 867-975-5007
Fax: 867-975-5095

Minister, Environment; Nunavut Arctic College, Hon. Daniel Shewchuk
Tel: 867-975-5001
Fax: 867-975-5044

Minister, Culture, Language, Elders & Youth; Languages; Utility Rates Review Council, Hon. James Arreak
Tel: 867-924-6423
Fax: 867-924-6429

Executive Secretary, Dorcas Nattaq-Hamioui
Tel: 867-975-5050
Fax: 867-975-5051
dnattaq-hamioui@gov.nu.ca

Nunavut Legislative Assembly

926 Federal Rd., PO Box 1200, Iqaluit, NU X0A 0H0
Tel: 867-975-5000
Fax: 867-975-5190
Toll-Free: 877-334-7266
leginfo@assembly.nu.ca
www.assembly.nu.ca

Clerk of the Assembly, John Quirke
Tel: 867-975-5100
jquirke@assembly.nu.ca

Speaker, Hon. Hunter Tootoo
Tel: 867-975-5023
Fax: 867-975-5095
htootoo@assembly.nu.ca

Deputy Clerk, Nancy Tupik
Tel: 867-975-5115
ntupik@assembly.nu.ca

Legislative Librarian, Yvonne Earle
Tel: 867-975-5134
yearle@assembly.nu.ca
PO Box 1200
Iqaluit, NU X0A 0H0 Canada

Third Legislature - Nunavut

PO Box 1200, Iqaluit, NU X0A 0H0
www.assembly.nu.ca

Last General Election: Oct. 27, 2008.
Maximum Duration, five years.
Salaries, Indemnities & Allowances (effective 2011):
MLAs $90,396 including $1,000 tax free allowance;
Premier $179,683 total;
Deputy Premier $167,094 total;
Ministers & Speaker $160,505 total;
Deputy Speaker $108,475 total.
A taxable Northern allowance ranging between $15,000 & $34,500 is paid to all Members & is dependent upon the community & residence of the Member.
The address for all members of the Legislative Assembly is as follows: Legislative Assembly of Nunavut, PO Box 1200, Iqaluit NU X0A OHO. The following is a list of members, their constituency, the number of persons on the official voters list for the most recent election, & contact information:

Hon. Eva Aariak
Constituency: Iqaluit East *No. of Constituents:* 958
Tel: 867-979-0410
Fax: 867-979-0415
eva.aariak@gov.nu.ca
Other Communications: Legislature Phone: 867-975-5050

Hon. James Arreak
Constituency: Uqqummiut (Clyde River, Qikiqtarjua) *No. of Constituents:* 637
Tel: 867-924-6423
Fax: 867-924-6429
jarreak@assembly.nu.ca
Other Communications: Legislature Phone: 867-975-5019

Moses Aupaluktuq
Constituency: Baker Lake *No. of Constituents:* 965
Tel: 867-793-4949
Fax: 867-793-4950
maupaluktuq@assembly.nu.ca
Other Communications: Legislature Phone: 867-975-5030

Hon. Tagak Curley
Constituency: Rankin Inlet North *No. of Constituents:* 535
Tel: 867-645-4900
Fax: 867-645-4981
tagak.curley@gov.nu.ca
Other Communications: Legislature Phone: 867-975-5026

Hon. Monica Ell
Constituency: Iqaluit West *No. of Constituents:* 808
Tel: 867-979-5807
Fax: 867-979-2226
Other Communications: Legislature Phone: 867-975-5027

Ron Elliot
Constituency: Quttiktuq *No. of Constituents:* 562
Tel: 867-439-8050
Fax: 867-439-8051
relliott@assembly.nu.ca
Other Communications: Legislature Phone: 867-975-5015

Joe Enook
Constituency: Tununiq *No. of Constituents:* 678
Tel: 867-899-8999
Fax: 867-899-8713
jenook@assembly.nu.ca
Other Communications: Legislature Phone: 867-975-5035

Hon. Lorne Kusugak
Constituency: Rankin Inlet South / Whale Cove *No. of Constituents:* 843
Tel: 867-645-4866
Fax: 867-645-4865
lorne.kusugak@gov.nu.ca
Other Communications: Legislature Phone: 867-975-5020

John Ningark
Constituency: Akulliq *No. of Constituents:* 672
Tel: 867-462-4363
Fax: 867-462-4364
jningark@assembly.nu.ca
Other Communications: Legislature Phone: 867-975-5014

Johnny Ningeongan
Constituency: Nanulik *No. of Constituents:* 533
Tel: 867-925-9890
Fax: 867-925-9891
jningeongan@assembly.nu.ca
Other Communications: Legislature Phone: 867-975-5021

Hezakiah Oshutapik
Constituency: Pangnirtung *No. of Constituents:* 647
Tel: 867-473-8220
Fax: 867-473-8227
Other Communications: Legislature Phone: 867-975-5047

Hon. Keith Peterson
Constituency: Cambridge Bay *No. of Constituents:* 660
Tel: 867-983-3777
Fax: 867-983-3778
keith.peterson@gov.nu.ca
Other Communications: Legislature Phone: 867-975-5028

Allan Rumbolt
Constituency: Hudson Bay *No. of Constituents:* 414
Tel: 867-266-8518
Fax: 867-266-8315
arumbolt@assembly.nu.ca
Other Communications: Legislature Phone: 867-975-5032

Hon. Fred Schell
Constituency: South Baffin (Cape Dorset, Kimmirut) *No. of Constituents:* 872
Tel: 867-897-8753
Fax: 867-897-8645
fschell@assembly.nu.ca
Other Communications: Legislature Phone: 867-975-5031

Hon. Daniel Shewchuk
Constituency: Arviat *No. of Constituents:* 972
Tel: 867-857-4485
Fax: 867-857-4486
daniel.shewchuk@gov.nu.ca
Other Communications: Legislature Phone: 867-975-5024

Louis Tapardjuk
Constituency: Amittuq *No. of Constituents:* 1,061
Tel: 867-934-4070
Fax: 867-934-4071
ltapardjuk@assembly.nu.ca
Other Communications: Legislature Phone: 867-975-5070

Hon. Peter Taptuna
Constituency: Kugluktuk *No. of Constituents:* 651
Tel: 867-982-4232
Fax: 867-982-5733
ptaptuna@gov.nu.ca
Other Communications: Legislature Phone: 867-975-5075

Hon. Hunter Tootoo
Constituency: Iqaluit Centre *No. of Constituents:* 826
Tel: 867-979-2210
Fax: 867-979-2211
htootoo@assembly.nu.ca
Other Communications: Legislature Phone: 867-975-5023

Jeannie Ugyuk
Constituency: Tununiq *No. of Constituents:* 672
Tel: 867-360-6337
Fax: 867-360-6819
jugyuk@assembly.nu.ca
Other Communications: Legislature Phone: 867-975-5048

Nunavut Territory Government Departments & Agencies

Department of Community & Government Services

W.G. Brown Bldg., 4th Fl., PO Box 1000 700, Iqaluit, NU X0A 0H0
Tel: 867-975-5400
Fax: 867-975-5305
Other Communication: 867-975-5306

To support the development, provision & maintenance of programs & services which affect the communities in all areas of municipal responsibility & transportation.

Acts Administered:
Area Development Act
Boilers & Pressure Vessels Act
Business Licenses Act
Cities, Towns & Villages Act
Commissioner's Airport Lands Regulations
Commissioner's Land Act
Commissioner's Land Regulations
Community Employees' Benefits Program Transfer Act
Conflict of Interest Act
Consumer Protection Act
Dog Act
Electrical Protection Act
Emergency Measures Act
Film Classification Act
Fire Prevention Act
Fire Prevention Regulations
Fireworks Regulations
Gas Protection Act
Hamlets Act
Home Owners Property Tax Rebate Act
Iqaluit By-Law Exemption Order
Local Authorities Elections Act
Lotteries Act
Pawnbrokers & Second-Hand Dealers Act
Planning Act
Propane Cylinder Storage
Property Assessment & Taxation Act
Real Estate Agents Licencing Act
Religious Societies Lands Act
Residential Tenancies Act
Resolute Bay Development Area Regulations
Senior Citizens & Disabled Persons Property Tax Relief Act
Settlements Act
Strathcona Sound Development Area Regulations
Technical Standards & Safety Act
Town of Iqaluit Continuation Order

Minister, Hon. Lorne Kusuqak
Tel: 867-975-5003
Fax: 867-975-5095

Deputy Minister (interim), Shawn Maley
Tel: 867-645-8101
Fax: 867-645-8141

Asst. Deputy Minister, Lorne Levy
Tel: 867-975-5306
Fax: 867-975-5305
smaley@gov.nu.ca

Executive Director, Municipal Training Organization (MTO), Matthew Ayres
Tel: 867-975-5346
mayres@gov.nu.ca

Executive Director, NCIAC, Catherine Foo
Tel: 867-975-5336
cfoo@gov.nu.ca

Director, Policy & Procedures, Lucy Magee
Tel: 867-975-5309
Fax: 867-975-5351
lmagee@gov.nu.ca

Director, Financial Services, Alma Power
Tel: 867-975-5333
apower@gov.nu.ca

Director, Protection Services, Ed Zebedee
Tel: 867-975-5319
Fax: 867-975-5453
ezebedee@gov.nu.ca

Director, Corporate Services and Human Resources, Carmen Levi
Tel: 867-975-5332
clevi@gov.nu.ca

Senior Manager, Operations and Networks, Jeff Bisson
Tel: 867-975-6474
jbisson@gov.nu.ca

Senior Manager, Research and Development, Bu Lam
Tel: 867-975-5462
blam@gov.nu.ca

Senior Manager, Informatics, Planning and Services (IPS), Dean Wells
Tel: 867-975-6439
dwells@gov.nu.ca

Senior Consumer Affairs Officer, Leah Aupaluktuq
Tel: 867-793-3303
Fax: 867-793-3321

Administrative Officer, Dorothy Kaludjak
Tel: 867-975-5306
Fax: 867-975-5305
dkaludjak@gov.nu.ca

Regional Offices
Regional Offices
Kitikmeot
PO Box 200, Cambridge Bay, NU X0B 0C0
Regional Director, Kevin Niptanatiak
Tel: 867-983-4138
Fax: 867-983-4026
Qikiqtaaluk
PO Box 330, Cape Dorset, NU X0A 0C0
Regional Director, Timoon Toonoo
Tel: 867-897-3607
ttoonoo@gov.nu.ca
Kivalliq
PO Box 490, Rankin Inlet, NU X0C 0G0
Regional Director, Ralph Ruediger
Tel: 867-645-8153
Fax: 867-645-8197

Department of Culture, Language, Elders & Youth (CLEY)

PO Box 1000 800, Iqaluit, NU X0A 0H0
Tel: 867-975-5500
Fax: 867-975-5504
Toll-Free: 866-934-2035
www.cley.gov.nu.ca

Responsible for the protection, preservation & promotion of Inuit languages. Cultural initiatives & departmental goals are reached in coordination with & in support of elder & youth groups. Acts in respect to issues concerning women & people with disabilities. The government is dedicated to preserving & promoting elements that make up the Inuit identity.

Acts Administered:
Archives Act
Historical Resources Act
Official Languages Act

Minister, Hon. James Arreak
Tel: 867-975-5019
Fax: 867-975-5114
jarreak@assembly.nu.ca

Deputy Minister, Simon Awa
Tel: 867-975-5501
simon.awa@gov.nu.ca

Asst. Deputy Minister, Naullaq Arnaquq
Tel: 867-975-5532
Fax: 867-975-5504
narnaquq@gov.nu.ca

Director, Elders & Youth, Joanna Quassa
Tel: 867-934-2032
jquassa@gov.nu.ca

Director, Culture & Heritage, Dr. Douglas Stenton
Tel: 867-975-5524
dstenton1@gov.nu.ca

Director, Corporate Services, Nikki Nweze
Tel: 867-975-5514
nnweze@gov.nu.ca

Director, Inuit Quajimajatuqangit, Shuvinai Mike
Tel: 867-975-5525
Fax: 867-975-5504
smike@gov.nu.ca

Director, Official Languages, Stephanie Clouter
Tel: 867-975-5507
scloutier1@gov.nu.ca

Director, Policy & Planning, Jodi Durdle
Tel: 867-975-5505
jdurdle@gov.nu.ca

Director, Sports & Recreation, Kyle Seeley
Tel: 867-793-3301
kseeley@gov.nu.ca

Director, Inuit Uqausinginnik Taiguusiliuqtiit, Eileen Kilabuk-Weber
Tel: 867-975-5527
ekilabuk-weber@gov.nu.ca

Director, Piqqusilirivvik, Jonathan Palluq
Tel: 867-899-7392
jpalluq@gov.nu.ca

Manager, Nunavut Public Library Services, Ron Knowling
Tel: 867-899-3353
rknowling@gov.nu.ca

Director, Stephane Cloutier
scloutier@gov.nu.ca
Director, Joanna Quassa
jquassa@gov.nu.ca
Director, Kyle Seeley
kseeley@gov.nu.ca
Director, Shuvinai Mike
smike@gov.nu.ca

Department of Economic Development & Transportation

Bldg. 1104 A, Inuksugait Plaza, PO Box 1000 1500, Iqaluit, NU X0A 0H0
Tel: 867-975-7800
Fax: 867-975-7870
Toll-Free: 888-975-5999
edt@gov.nu.ca
www.edt.gov.nu.ca

Acts Administered:
All-Terrain Vehicles Act
All-Terrain Vehicles Regulations
Carrier Fitness Regulations
Economic Development Agreements Act
Exemption of Motor Vehicles Act Regulations
Guide Exemption Regulations
Highway Designation & Classification Regulations
Highway Signs Regulations
Hours of Service Regulations
Large Vehicle Control Regulations
Motor Vehicle Equipment Regulations
Motor Vehicles Act
Nunavut Development Corporation
Outfitter Regulations
Public Highways Act
School Bus Regulations
Seasonal Highway Regulations
Special All-Terrain Vehicles Fees Regulations
Special All-Terrain Vehicles Helmet Regulations
Tourist Establishment Regulations
Transportation of Dangerous Goods Act
Transportation of Dangerous Goods Regulations
Travel & Tourism Act
Travel Development Area Regulations

Minister, Hon. Peter Taptuna
Tel: 867-975-5076
Fax: 867-975-5016

Deputy Minister, Robert Long
Tel: 867-975-7829
rlong@gov.nu.ca

Director, Transportation Policy & Planning, John Hawkins
Tel: 867-975-7826
jhawkins@gov.nu.ca

Director, Policy, Planning & Communications, Matthew Bowler
Tel: 867-975-7808
mbowler@gov.nu.ca

Director, Finance & Administration, Tanya Winmill
Tel: 867-975-7816
twinmill@gov.nu.ca

Manager, Communications, Matthew Illaszewicz
Tel: 867-975-7818
Fax: 867-975-7870

Associated Agencies, Boards & Commissions:
• Nunavut Business Credit Corporation
Parnaivak Bldg.
#100
PO Box 2548
Iqaluit, NU X0A 0H0
Tel: 867-975-7891
Fax: 867-975-7897
Toll-free: 800-758-0038
credit@nbcc.nu.ca
www.nbcc.nu.ca

Economic Development
Asst. Deputy Minister, Gordon MacKay
Tel: 867-975-7822
gmackay@gov.nu.ca
Director, Community Operations, Kitikmeot, Vacant
Director, Community Operations, Kivalliq, Laura MacKenzie
Tel: 867-645-8458
lmackenzie@gov.nu.ca
Director, Community Operations, Qikiqtaaluk, Rhoda Katsak
Tel: 867-899-7339
rkatsak@gov.nu.ca
Director, Minerals & Petroleum Resources, Eric Prosh
Tel: 867-975-7827
eprosh@gov.nu.ca
Director, Tourism & Cultural Industries, Vacant

Transportation
Asst. Deputy Minister, Methusalah Kunuk
Tel: 867-975-7832
Fax: 867-975-7880
mkunuk@gov.nu.ca
Director, Iqaluit International Airport, John Graham
Tel: 867-979-5224
jgraham@gov.nu.ca
Director, Motor Vehicles, Lorna Gee
Tel: 867-360-4614
lgee@gov.nu.ca
Director, Nunavut Airports, Shawn Maley
Tel: 867-645-8203
smaley@gov.nu.ca
Director, Transportation Policy & Planning, John Hawkins
Tel: 867-975-7826
jhawkins@gov.nu.ca

Kitikmeot
PO Box 316, Kugluktuk, NU X0B 0E0
Tel: 867-982-7453

Director, Vacant
Tel: 867-982-7459
Fax: 867-982-3204

Kivalliq
PO Box 2, Rankin Inlet, NU X0C 0G0
Tel: 867-645-8450

Director, Laura MacKenzie
Tel: 867-645-8458
Fax: 867-645-8455

Qikiqtaaluk
#1045, PO Box 389, Pond Inlet, NU X0A 0S0
Tel: 867-899-7338
Toll-Free: 888-899-7338

Director, Rhoda Katsak
Tel: 867-899-7339
Fax: 867-899-7348

Department of Education

Sivummut Bldg., 2nd Fl., PO Box 1000 910, Iqaluit, NU X0A 0H0
Tel: 867-975-5600
Fax: 867-975-5605
www.edu.gov.nu.ca

Acts Administered:
Apprenticeship, Trade & Occupation Certification Act
Child Care Act
Education Act
Federation of Nunavut Teachers Act
Library Act (CLEY)
Occupational Training Agreement Act
Official Languages Act (CLEY)
Public Colleges Act
Scientists & Education Act (CLEY)
Senior Citizens Benefits Act
Social Assistance Act
Student Financial Assistance Act

Minister, Hon. Eva Aariak
Tel: 867-975-5050
Fax: 867-975-5051

Deputy Minister, Kathy Okpik
Tel: 867-975-5601
Fax: 867-975-5635

Director, Corporate Services, Murray Horn
Tel: 867-975-5616
Fax: 867-975-5605
mhorn@gov.nu.ca

Director, Policy & Planning, Brad Chambers
Tel: 867-975-5606
bchambers@gov.nu.ca

Adult Learning, Career & Early Childhood Services
Fax: 867-857-3090
Asst. Deputy Minister, Irene Tanuyak
Tel: 867-975-5604
Fax: 867-975-5635
itanuyak@gov.nu.ca
Director, Income Support, Sandy Teiman
Tel: 867-975-5685
Fax: 867-975-5690
steiman@gov.nu.ca
Director, Adult Learning & Post-Secondary Services, Edward Duru
Tel: 867-857-3056
eduru@gov.nu.ca
Director, Career Development Services and Adult Special Project, David Lloyd
Tel: 867-975-5648
dlloyd@gov.nu.ca

Curriculum & School Services
Asst. Deputy Minister, Peter Geikie
Tel: 867-975-5604
Fax: 867-975-5635
Director, Curriculum Development, Cathy McGregor
Tel: 867-975-5641
Fax: 867-975-5635
cmcgregor@gov.nu.ca
Director, French, Leonie Aissaoui
Tel: 867-975-5627
laissaoui@gov.nu.ca

Early Childhood Services
Regional Director, Quikiqtani Region, John MacDonald
Tel: 867-473-2600
Fax: 867-473-2647
jmacdonald@gov.nu.ca
Regional Director, Kivalliq Region, Richard Mackenzie
Tel: 867-645-5040

Fax: 867-645-2148
rmackenzie@gov.nu.ca
Regional Director, Kitikmeot Region, Brenda Jancke
Tel: 867-983-4031
Fax: 867-983-4025
bjancke@gov.nu.ca

Regional Offices
Regional Offices
Tel: 867-983-7214
Fax: 867-983-2004
Cambridge Bay
Tel: 867-983-4031
Fax: 867-983-7309
Director, Career & Early Childhood, Brenda Jancke
Tel: 867-983-4030
Fax: 867-983-4191
bjancke@gov.nu.ca
Kivalliq
Tel: 867-645-5040
Fax: 867-645-2148

Nunavut Emergency Management

PO Box 1000 700, Iqaluit, NU X0A 0H0
Tel: 867-975-5403
Fax: 867-979-4221
Toll-Free: 800-693-1666
cgs.gov.nu.ca/en/nunavut-emergency-management
Other Communication: 867-979-6262

Manager, Emergency Services, Glen Higgins
Tel: 867-975-5403
Fax: 867-979-4221
ghiggins@gov.nu.ca

Deputy Fire Marshall, Robert Prima
Tel: 867-645-8127
rprima@gov.nu.ca

Department of Environment

PO Box 1000 1300, Iqaluit, NU X0A 0H0
Tel: 867-975-7700
Fax: 867-975-7742
environment@gov.nu.ca
Acts Administered:
Asphalt Paving Industry Emission Regulations
Big Game Hunting Regulations
Birds of Prey Regulations
Certification & Disposal of Wildlife Regulations
Community Parks Order
Critical Wildlife Areas Regulations
Dempster Highway Special Management Area Regulations
Environmental Protection Act
Environmental Rights Act
Establishing Freshwater Fish Marketing Corporation Regulations
Flood Damage Reduction Agreements Act
Forest Management Act
Forest Management Regulations
Forest Protection Act
Freshwater Fish Marketing Act
Herd & Fencing Act
Heritage Parks, Natural Environment Parks & Recreation Parks Regulations
Historic Parks Order
Natural Environment Recreation Park Order
Nuisance Bison Control Regulations
Outdoor Recreation Parks Order
Outfitter Regulations
Pesticides Act
Polar Bear Defence Kill Regulations
Sale of Wildlife Regulations
Small Game Hunting Regulations
Spill Contingency Planning & Reporting
Territorial Parks Act
Territorial Parks Regulations
Tourist Establishment Regulations
Trapping Regulations
Travel & Tourism Act
Travel Development Area Regulation
Used Oil & Waste Fuel Management
Waste Reduction & Recovery Act
Water Resources Agreements Act
Wayside Parks Order
Wildlife Act
Wildlife Business Regulations
Wildlife Export Regulations
Wildlife General Regulations
Wildlife Licenses & Permits Regulations
Wildlife Management Barren Ground Caribou Area Regulation
Wildlife Management Grizzly Bear Area Regulations
Wildlife Management Muskox Areas Regulations
Wildlife Management Outfitter Area Regulations
Wildlife Management Polar Bear Areas Regulations
Wildlife Management Units Regulations
Wildlife Management Wood Bison Area Regulations
Wildlife Management Zones Regulations
Wildlife Preserves Regulations
Wildlife Regions Regulations
Wildlife Sanctuaries Regulations

Minister, Hon. Daniel Shewchuk
Tel: 867-975-5001
Fax: 867-975-5044

Deputy Minister, David Akeeagok
Tel: 867-975-7705
dakeeagok@gov.nu.ca

Asst. Deputy Minister, Earle Baddaloo
Tel: 867-975-7705
Fax: 867-975-7740
ebaddaloo@gov.nu.ca

Director, Corporate Services, Camilius Egeni
Tel: 867-975-7708
Fax: 867-975-7740
cegeni@gov.nu.ca

Director, Policy, Planning & Legislation, Steve Pinksen
Tel: 867-975-7718
Fax: 867-975-7740
spinksen@gov.nu.ca

Director, Fisheries & Sealing, Wayne Lynch
Tel: 867-975-7750
Fax: 867-975-7742
cegeni@gov.nu.ca

Executive Secretary, Lena Hughes
Tel: 867-975-7705
Fax: 867-975-7740
lhughes@gov.nu.ca

Regional Offices
Regional Offices

Baffin
PO Box 569, Pond Inlet, NU X0A 0S0
Regional Wildlife Manager, Alex Millar
Tel: 867-899-8034
Fax: 867-889-8050
amillar@gov.nu.ca
Kitikmeot
PO Box 377, Kugluktuk, NU X0B 0E0
Kivalliq
PO Box 120, Arviat, NU X0C 0E0

Department of Executive & Intergovernmental Affairs

1084 Aeroplex bldg., PO Box 1000 200, Iqaluit, NU X0A 0H0
Tel: 867-975-6000
Fax: 867-975-6099
www.eia.gov.nu.ca
The department provides advice & administrative support to Cabinet & the government, works to ensure that the Nunavut Land Claims Agreement & Nunavut's relationships with other governments in Canada & the circumpolar world are used to support common goals. The department compiles & communicates information & evaluates government programs & data.The Intergovernmental Affairs Division is responsible for the management & development of government strategies, policies & initiatives relating to federal, provincial, territorial, circumpolar & aboriginal affairs. This office participates in preparations for Intergovernmental activities such as the Western & Annual Premiers Conferences, First Ministers meetings & the Social Union Framework Agreement, the Arctic Council, the Nunavut Implementation Panel & the Clyde River Protocol.
Acts Administered:
Nunavut Power Corporation Assets Transfer Confirmation Act
Public Utilities Act
Public Utilities Regulations

Minister, Hon. Eva Aariak
Tel: 867-975-5050
Fax: 867-975-5051

Deputy Minister of Executive, Daniel Vandermeulen
Tel: 867-975-6011
Fax: 867-975-6095
dvandermeuleneia@gov.nu.ca

Deputy Minister, Intergovernmental Affairs, Aluki Rojas
Tel: 867-975-6034
Fax: 867-975-6091
arojas@gov.nu.ca

Asst. Deputy Minister, Intergovernmental Affairs - Ottawa Liason, Robert Carson
Tel: 613-233-9890 ext: 235
Fax: 613-233-2543

Asst. Deputy Minister, Policy, Planning & Evaluation, Paul Suvega
Tel: 867-975-6009
Fax: 867-975-6089

Director, Aboriginal & Circumpolar Affairs, Letia Obed
Tel: 867-975-6036
Fax: 867-975-6091
lobed@gov.nu.ca

Director, Policy, Planning & Evaluation, Rachel Mark
Tel: 867-975-6029
Fax: 867-975-6029
rmark@gov.nu.ca

Director, Corporate Services, David Pealow
Tel: 867-975-6002
dpealow@gov.nu.ca

Director, Communications, Pam Coulter
Tel: 867-975-6049
pcoulter2@gov.nu.ca

Director, Statistics, Ron McMahon
Tel: 867-473-2693
Fax: 867-473-2626
rmcmahon@gov.nu.ca

Director, Devolution Division, Mark Thompson
Tel: 867-975-6070
mthompson1@gov.nu.ca

Manager, Access Information, Jessica Bell
Tel: 867-975-6044
jessica.bell@gov.nu.ca

Manager, Women's Secretariat, Tanya Campbell
Tel: 867-975-6018
tcampbell@gov.nu.ca

Commissioner, Commissioner's Office, Edna Elias
Tel: 867-975-5120
elias@gov.nu.ca

Senior Advisor, Energy Policy, Chris Down
Tel: 867-975-6043
cdown@gov.nu.ca

Department of Finance

Bldg. 1079, 1st Fl., PO Box 1000 330, Iqaluit, NU X0A 0H0
Tel: 867-975-5800
Fax: 867-975-5805
www.finance.gov.nu.ca
The Department of Finance is committed to provide direction and leadership to ensure fiscal responsibility and to create a secure base for Nunavut's economic growth, while promoting and maintaining public confidence in the prudence, propriety and integrity of government financial operations and respecting the principles of Inuit Qaujimajatuqangit (IQ).
Acts Administered:
Environmental Tobacco Smoke Work Site Reguations
Explosives Use Act
Mine Health & Safety Act
Safety Act
Technical Standards & Safety Act
Worker's Compensation Act

Minister, Hon. Keith Peterson
Tel: 867-975-5070

Deputy Minister, Health and Social Services, Peter Ma
Tel: 867-975-5803
Fax: 867-975-5805
pma@gov.nu.ca

Comptroller General, Jeff Chown
Tel: 867-975-5833
Fax: 867-975-5896
jchown@gov.nu.ca

Deputy Minister, Finance, Chris D'Arcy
Tel: 867-975-6865
Fax: 867-975-5805

Director, Finance, Kerry Angidlik
Tel: 867-645-8515
kangidlik@gov.nu.ca

Director, Corporate Services, Scott Mariott
Tel: 867-975-6803

Fax: 867-975-6868
smarriott@gov.nu.ca

Director, Accounting Policy & System Management, Vacant

Acting Director, Expenditure Management, Jeff Chown
Tel: 867-975-5835
Fax: 867-975-6825
jchown@gov.nu.ca

Acting Manager, Taxation, Daniel Young
Tel: 867-975-5812
Fax: 867-975-5845
dyoung1@gov.nu.ca

Director, Compensation & Benefits, Nasim Bhanji
Tel: 867-975-5847
Fax: 867-975-5863
nbhanji@gov.nu.ca

Acting Chief Internal Auditor, Grace Wilk
Tel: 867-975-6848
Fax: 867-975-6842
gwilk@gov.nu.ca

Associated Agencies, Boards & Commissions:
• Nunavut Liquor Licensing Board
Bag 002
Rankin Inlet, NU X0C 0G0
Fax: 867-645-3327

Regional Offices
Regional Offices
Tel: 867-983-4043
Fax: 867-983-4041

Kitikmeot
Director, Regional Financial Services, Sandra Peterson
Tel: 867-983-4042
speterson@gov.nu.ca
Kivalliq
Director, Regional Financial Services, Kerry Angidlik
Tel: 867-645-8515
Fax: 867-645-8511
kangidlik@gov.nu.ca
Qikiqtaaluk
Tel: 867-934-2056
Fax: 867-934-8677
Director, Regional Financial Services, Vacant

Department of Health & Social Services

PO Box 1000 1000, Iqaluit, NU X0A 0H0
Tel: 867-975-5700
Fax: 867-975-5705
www.hss.gov.nu.ca

The Environmental Health Specialist provides recommendations & direction, consultation, development of standards, monitoring, maintenance & evaluation of all environmental health programs within Nunavut. Reviews the Public Health Act & Regulations & environmental health standards & policies & makes recommendations for revisions. Guides the regional environmental health officers in development & implementation of programs & policies in prevention of diseases caused by environmental factors, including food, water, waste disposal, housing & the sanitation of public places, including schools, day cares & other institutional facilities. Guides the Regional Environmental Health Officers in water & food-borne related illness investigations & food recalls. Guides the regions in the monitoring of drinking water supplies. Assists with development of health education & promotional materials & activities related to environmental health.

Acts Administered:
Boards of Management Dissolution Act
Camp Sanitation Regulations
Communicable Diseases Regulations
Disease Registries Act
General Sanitation Exemption Regulations
General Sanitation Regulations
Meat Inspection Regulations
Public Health Act
Public Sewerage Systems Regulations
Public Water Supply Regulations
Reportable Diseases Order
Tobacco Control Act
Tourist Accomodation Health Regulations

Minister, Hon. Tagak Curley
Tel: 867-975-5005
Fax: 867-975-5095

Deputy Minister, Peter Ma
pma@gov.nu.ca

Chief Medical Officer of Health, Dr. Geraldine Osborne
Tel: 867-975-5774
gosborne@gov.nu.ca

Director, Finance, Ramanath Kamath
Tel: 867-975-5736
rkamath@gov.nu.ca

Asst. Deputy Minister, Operations, Monita O'Connor
Tel: 867-975-5704
mo'connor@gov.nu.ca

Executive Director, Corporate Services, Debora Voth
Tel: 867-975-5742
dvoth@gov.nu.ca

Executive Director, Population Health, Gogi Greeley
Tel: 867-975-5709
ggreeley@gov.nu.ca

Acting Director, Communications, Yasmine Pepa
Tel: 867-975-5714
Fax: 867-975-5705

Director, Health & Social Services, Virginia Turner
Tel: 867-473-2629
Fax: 867-473-2657
vturner@gov.nu.ca

Acting Director, Medical Affairs & Telehealth, Dr. William MacDonald
Tel: 867-979-7601
Fax: 876-979-7346
wmacdonald2@gov.nu.ca

Director, Health Information, Martin Joy
Tel: 867-975-5903
mjoy@gov.nu.ca

Director, Policy and Planning, Rian Van Bruggen
Tel: 867-975-5717
rvanbruggen@gov.nu.ca

Director / Manager, Child Welfare / Social Services, Norm Murray
Tel: 867-975-5750
nmurray@gov.nu.ca

Manager, Public Health, Kristine Hutchinson
Tel: 867-975-4805
khutchinson@gov.nu.ca

Manager, Health Protection, Janet Brewster
Tel: 867-975-5703
jbrewster@gov.nu.ca

Manager, Human Resources, Shawn Burke
Tel: 867-975-5749
sburke@gov.nu.ca

Home Care Coordinator, Tracy Palm
Tel: 867-266-8965
tpalm@gov.nu.ca

Nunavut Housing Corporation

PO Box 480, Arviat, NU X0C 0E0
Tel: 867-857-3000
Fax: 867-857-3040
www.nunavuthousing.ca

Minister Responsible, Hon. Tagak Curley
Tel: 867-975-5005
Fax: 867-975-5095

President, Alain Barriault
Tel: 867-975-7200 ext: 720
Fax: 867-979-4194
abarriault@gov.nu.ca

Vice-President, Jamie Flaherty
Tel: 867-975-7200 ext: 721
Fax: 867-979-4194
jflahertynhc@gov.nu.ca

Manager, Rental Programs, Don Moors
Tel: 867-857-3006
Fax: 867-857-3040
dmoors@gov.nu.ca

Executive Director, Corporate Services & CFO, Lori Kimball
Tel: 867-975-7200 ext: 720
Fax: 867-979-4194
dmoors@gov.nu.ca

Department of Human Resources

PO Box 1000 400, Iqaluit, NU X0A 1H0
Fax: 867-975-6216
Toll-Free: 888-668-9993
gnhr@gov.nu.ca

Minister, Hon. Fred Schell
Tel: 867-897-8753
Fax: 867-897-8645
fschell@assembly.nu.ca
Other Communications: Legislature Phone: 867-975-5031

Deputy Minister, Joe Adla Kunuk
Tel: 867-975-6213
Fax: 867-975-6216
jkunuk@gov.nu.ca

Assistant Deputy Minister, Richard Paton
Tel: 867-975-6204
rpaton1@gov.nu.ca

Executive Secretary, Lizzie Ryan
Tel: 867-975-6213
Fax: 867-975-6216
lryan1@gov.nu.ca

Acting Director, Corporate Services, David Kolot
Tel: 867-975-6203
Fax: 867-975-6266
dkolot@gov.nu.ca

Director, Employee Relations, Deborah Evans
Tel: 867-975-6257
Fax: 867-975-6241

Acting Director, Inuit Employee Planning, Steven Lonsdale
Tel: 867-975-6272
Fax: 867-975-6280
slonsdale@gov.nu.ca

Director, Job Evaluation & Organization Design, Diane Stenton
Tel: 867-975-6208
Fax: 867-975-6215

Director, Policy & Planning Division, David Kolot
Tel: 867-975-6203
Fax: 867-975-6216
dkolot@gov.nu.ca

Director, Recruitment and Staffing, Sheyla Kolola
Tel: 867-975-6223
skolola@gov.nu.ca

Director, Employee Relations and Job Evaluation, Crystal Tobin
Tel: 867-975-6211
ctobin@gov.nu.ca

Regional Offices
Regional Offices

Cambridge Bay
PO Box 2375, Cambridge Bay, NU X0B 0C0
Tel: 867-983-4058
Fax: 867-983-4061
Toll-Free: 866-667-6624
Director, Community Operations, Alice Lafrance
Tel: 867-983-4060
Fax: 867-983-4061
alafrance@gov.nu.ca
Qikigtaaluk
PO Box 233, Igloolik, NU X0A 0L0
Fax: 867-934-2027
Toll-Free: 800-682-9033

Rankin Inlet
PO Box 930, Rankin Inlet, NU X0C 0G0
Fax: 867-645-8097
Toll-Free: 800-933-3072
Director, Community Operations, Jacqueline Curley
Tel: 867-645-8064
Fax: 867-645-8097
jcurley@gov.nu.ca

Department of Justice

Sivummut, 1st Fl., PO Box 1000 500, Iqaluit, NU X0A 0H0
Tel: 867-975-6170
Fax: 867-975-6195
justice@gov.nu.ca
www.justice.gov.nu.ca

Acts Administered:
Engineers, Geologists & Geophysicists Act

Expropriation Act
Land Titles Act

Minister, Hon. Keith Peterson
Tel: 867-975-5007
Fax: 867-975-5095

Deputy Minister, Janet Slaughter
Tel: 867-975-6180
Fax: 867-975-6195
janet.slaughter@gov.nu.ca

Assistant Deputy Minister, Rebekah Williams
Tel: 867-975-6180
Fax: 867-975-6195
rwilliams@gov.nu.ca

Director, Legal & Constitutional Law, Norman Tarnow
Tel: 867-975-6332
Fax: 867-975-6151
ntarnow@gov.nu.ca

Director, Corporate Services, Edward Dingle
Tel: 867-975-6181
Fax: 867-975-6188
edingle@gov.nu.ca

Associated Agencies, Boards & Commissions:

• Baffin Correctional Centre
1550 Federal Rd.
PO Box 368
Iqaluit, NU X0A 0H0
Tel: 867-979-8100
Fax: 867-979-4646

• Office of the Chief Coroner
PO Box 1000 590
Iqaluit, NU X0A 0H0

• Legal Services Board of Nunavut
PO Box 125
Gjoa Haven, NU X0A 0H0
Fax: 867-360-6112

• Young Offenders
1548 Federal Rd.
PO Box 1439
Iqaluit, NU X0A 0H0
Tel: 867-979-4452
Fax: 867-979-5506

Community Justice

Director, Alan Hartley
Tel: 867-975-6176
Fax: 867-975-6160
ahartley@gov.nu.ca
Manager, Community Corrections, Vacant

Corporate Services

Tel: 867-975-6170
Fax: 867-975-6188
justice.corporate@gov.nu.ca

Corrections

Tel: 867-975-6500
Fax: 867-975-6515
justice.corrections@gov.nu.ca

Court Services
PO Box 297, Iqaluit, NU X0A 0H0

Other Communication: www.nunavutcourtofjustice.ca

Director, Lou Hall
Tel: 867-975-6131
Fax: 867-975-6511
lhall@gov.nu.ca
Sheriff, Chris Kennedy
Tel: 867-975-6119
Fax: 867-975-6168
ckennedy@gov.nu.ca

Legal & Constitutional Law

Tel: 867-975-6321
Fax: 867-975-6349

Director, Norman M. Tarnow
Tel: 867-975-6332
Fax: 867-975-6349
ntarnow@gov.nu.ca
Legal Counsel, Adrienne Silk
Tel: 867-975-6172
asilk@gov.nu.ca
Legal Counsel, Erin George
Tel: 867-975-6354
egeorge@gov.nu.ca
Public Trustee, Esmeralda Bautista
Tel: 867-975-6311
Fax: 867-975-6343
ebautista@gov.nu.ca

Legal Registries
Brown Bldg., 1st Fl., PO Box 1000 570, Iqaluit, NU X0A 0H0

Fax: 867-975-6594

Director, Louis Arki
Tel: 867-975-6587
larki@gov.nu.ca
Registrar, Land Titles, Vacant
Tel: 867-975-6590
Deputy Registrar, Securities & Corporate Registry, Tammy Heffernan
Tel: 867-975-6597
theffernan@gov.nu.ca

Legislation

Tel: 867-975-6330
Fax: 867-975-6189

Director & Registrar, Regulations, Susan Hardy
Tel: 867-975-6334
shardy@gov.nu.ca
Manager, Legal Translation - Inuktitut & Inuinnaqtun, Betty Brewster
Tel: 867-975-6164
bbrewster@gov.nu.ca
Manager, Legal Translation - French, Vacant
Tel: 867-975-6336

Policy & Planning

Fax: 867-975-6151

Acting Director, Stephanie Lachance
Tel: 867-645-8062
slachance@gov.nu.ca

Northwest Territories & Nunavut Workers' Safety & Compensation Commission (WCB)

For a detailed listing please see Northwest Territories.

Government of Ontario

Seat of Government: Queen's Park, Toronto, ON M7A 1A2

Tel: 416-326-1234
Toll-Free: 800-267-8097
www.gov.on.ca
TTY: 800-268-7095

The Province of Ontario entered Confederation July 1, 1867. It has an area of 907,573.82 km2, & the StatsCan census population in 2011 was 12,851,821.

Office of the Lieutenant Governor

Room 131, Legislative Bldg., Queen's Park, Toronto, ON M7A 1A1

Tel: 416-325-7780
Fax: 416-325-7787
ltgov@gov.on.ca
www.lt.gov.on.ca

Represents Her Majesty The Queen in Ontario. The Office coordinates, supports & promotes the activities of the Lieutenant Governor. In his constitutional role, the Lieutenant Governor swears-in the Executive Council, outlines the Government's plans in the Speech from the Throne, provides the Royal Assent needed for bills to become laws, approves orders-in-council & appointments recommended by Cabinet, & prorogues or dissolves each session of Parliament. In his community role, he represents the people of Ontario & acts as the Province's official host, welcoming world leaders & diplomats. He hosts or attends hundreds of community events throughout Ontario & presents honours & awards to outstanding Ontarians. His Honour has focused on three themes: reducing the stigma of mental illness, fighting racism, & supporting aboriginal youth. His Honour is also a champion for people living with disabilities.

Lieutenant Governor, Hon. David C. Onley, O.Ont.
Tel: 416-325-7780
Fax: 416-325-7787
ltgov@gov.on.ca

Chief of Staff, Nanda Casucci-Bryne
Tel: 416-325-7781
nanda.casuccibyrne@ontario.ca

Chief Aide-de-Camp, A.G. (Sandy) Cameron
Tel: 416-325-7780
ltgov@gov.on.ca

Chief Steward, Robert Adams
Tel: 416-325-7794
robert.adams@ontario.ca

Office of the Premier

Legislative Bldg., #281, 1 Queen's Park Cres. South, Toronto, ON M7A 1A1

Tel: 416-325-1941
Fax: 416-325-3745
www.premier.gov.on.ca
TTY: 800-387-5559

Premier, Hon. Dalton McGuinty
Tel: 416-325-1941
Fax: 416-325-3745
dmcguinty.mpp.co@liberal.ola.org

Parliamentary Assistant, David Orazietti
Tel: 705-949-6959
dorazietti.mpp.co@liberal.ola.org

Chief of Staff, Chris Morley
Tel: 416-325-2228
Fax: 416-325-9895

Press Secretary, Jane Almeida
Tel: 416-314-8975
Fax: 416-325-0803

Deputy Chief of Staff, Operations, Dave Gene
Tel: 416-325-2486
Fax: 416-325-6749

Executive Director, Policy & Research, Alex Johnston
Tel: 416-314-2598
Fax: 416-314-3853

Executive Director, Communications, Aaron Lazarus
Tel: 416-325-5972
Fax: 416-325-0803

Director & Executive Assistant, Tracey Sobers
Tel: 416-325-2228
Fax: 416-325-9895

Director, Caucus Relations, Rod MacDonald
Tel: 416-325-2491
Fax: 416-314-5189

Director, Issues Management & Legislative Affairs, Alicia Johnston
Tel: 416-325-8510
Fax: 416-325-0246

Special Assistant to the Chief of Staff, Wendy Wai
Tel: 416-325-1619
Fax: 416-325-9895

Executive Council

Whitney Block, Queen's Park, 99 Wellesley St. West, 6th Fl., Toronto, ON M7A 1A1

Tel: 416-325-5721
Fax: 416-314-1551

Premier & President, Council, Hon. Dalton McGuinty
Tel: 416-325-1941
Fax: 416-325-3745
premier@gov.on.ca; dmcguinty.mpp.co@liberal.ola.org
TTY: 416-325-7702
Social Media: www.twitter.com/Dalton_McGuinty, www.facebook.com/PremierMcGuinty
Queen's Park
#281, Main Legislative Bldg.
Toronto, ON M7A 1A1 Canada

Minister, Northern Development, Mines & Forestry; Chair of Cabinet, Hon. Rick Bartolucci
Tel: 416-327-0633
Fax: 416-327-0665
rbartolucci.mpp.co@liberal.ola.org
Social Media: www.twitter.com/rickbartolucci, www.facebook.com/rick.bartolucci
Ministry of Northern Development, Mines & Forestry
#5630, 99 Wellesley St.West, 5th Fl.
Toronto, ON M7A 1W3

Minister, Energy, Hon. Chris Bentley
Tel: 416-327-6758
Fax: 416-327-6754
cbentley.mpp.co@liberal.ola.org
Social Media: www.twitter.com/Chris_Bentley
Ministry of Energy & Infrastructure, Hearst Block
900 Bay St., 4th Fl.
Toronto, ON M7A2E1

Minister, Consumer Services, Hon. Margarett Best
Tel: 416-327-8300

Fax: 416-326-1947
mbest.mpp.co@liberal.ola.org
Social Media:
www.facebook.com/people/Margarett-Best/772159453,
www.linkedin.com/pub/christina-bisanz/2/7a4/599
Ministry of Consumer Services, Mowat Block
900 Bay St., 6th Fl.
Toronto, ON M7A 1L2

Minister, Environment, Hon. James J. Bradley
Tel: 416-314-6790
Fax: 416-314-6748
jbradley.mpp.co@liberal.ola.org
Social Media: www.facebook.com/votebradley
Ministry of the Environment, Ferguson Block
77 Wellesley St. West, 11th Fl.
Toronto, ON M7A 2T5

Minister, Education; Responsible for Women's Issues, Hon. Laurel Broten
Tel: 416-325-2600
Fax: 416-325-2608
lbroten.mpp.co@liberal.ola.org
Ministry of Education, Mowat Block
900 Bay St., 22nd Fl.
Toronto, ON M7A1L2

Minister, Tourism & Culture, Hon. Michael Chan
Tel: 416-326-9326
Fax: 416-314-7854
mchan.mpp.co@liberal.ola.org
Social Media:
www.facebook.com/group.php?gid=2401349051
Ministry Office, Hearst Block
900 Bay St., 9th Fl.
Toronto, ON M7A2E1

Minister, Infrastructure, Hon. Bob Chiarelli
Tel: 416-325-5270
Fax: 416-325-8860
bchiarelli.mpp.co@liberal.ola.org
Social Media: www.Bob_Chiarelli,
www.facebook.com/BobChiarelliMPP
Ministry of Infrastructure, Mowat Block
900 Bay St., 5th Fl.
Toronto, ON M7A 1C2

Minister, Transportation, Hon. Bob Chiarelli
Tel: 416-327-9200
Fax: 416-327-9188
bchiarelli.mpp.co@liberal.ola.org
Social Media: www.Bob_Chiarelli,
www.facebook.com/BobChiarelliMPP
Ministry of Transportation, Ferguson Block
77 Wellesley St. West, 3rd Fl.
Toronto, ON M7A1Z8

Minister, Economic Development & Innovation, Hon. Brad Duguid
Tel: 416-325-6900
Fax: 416-325-6918
bduguid.mpp.co@liberal.ola.org
Social Media: www.twitter.com/VoteBradDuguid,
www.facebook.com/VoteBradDuguid,
www.linkedin.com/pub/brad-duguid/3/b01/6a3
Ministry of Economic Development & Trade, Hearst Block
900 Bay St., 8th Fl.
Toronto, ON M7A 2E1

Minister, Finance; Deputy Premier; Chair, Management Board of the Cabinet, Hon. Dwight Duncan
Tel: 416-325-0400
Fax: 416-325-0374
dduncan.mpp.co@liberal.ola.org
Social Media: www.twitter.com/DwightDuncan,
www.facebook.com/dwight1?sk=wall,
www.linkedin.com/pub/dwight-duncan/31/774/8b1
Ministry of Finance, Frost Building South
7 Queen's Park Cres., 7th Fl.
Toronto, ON M7A 1Y7

Minister, Natural Resources, Hon. Michael Gravelle
Tel: 416-314-2301
Fax: 416-325-5316
mgravelle.mpp.co@liberal.ola.org
Ministry of Natural Resources, Whitney Block
#6630, 99 Wellesley St. West, 6th Fl.
Toronto, ON M7A1W3

Minister, Children & Youth Services, Hon. Eric Hoskins
Tel: 416-212-7432
Fax: 416-212-7431
ehoskins.mpp.co@liberal.ola.org
Social Media: www.twitter.com/DrEricHoskins,
www.facebook.com/drerichoskins
Ministry Office
56 Wellesley St. West, 14th Fl.
Toronto, ON M5S 2S3

Minister, Labour; Responsible for Seniors' Secretariat, Hon. Linda Jeffrey
Tel: 416-326-7600
Fax: 416-326-1449
ljeffrey.mpp.co@liberal.ola.org
Social Media: www.twitter.com/LindaJeffrey
Ministry of Labour
400 University Ave., 14th Fl.
Toronto, ON M7A 1T7

Minister, Health & Long-Term Care, Hon. Deborah Matthews
Tel: 416-327-4300
Fax: 416-327-3679
dmatthews.mpp.co@liberal.ola.org
Social Media: www.twitter.com/Deb_Matthews
Ministry of Health & Long-Term Care, Hepburn Block
80 Grosvenor St., 10th Fl.
Toronto, ON M7A 2C4

Minister, Agriculture, Food & Rural Affairs, Hon. Ted McMeekin
Tel: 416-326-3074
Fax: 416-326-3083
tmcmeekin.mpp.co@liberal.ola.org
Social Media: www.twitter.com/TedMcMeekin
Ministry of Agriculture, Food & Rural Affairs
77 Grenville St., 11th Fl.
Toronto, ON M5S 1B3

Minister, Community Safety & Correctional Services; Responsible for Francophone Affairs, Hon. Madeleine Meilleur
Tel: 416-325-0408
Fax: 416-325-6067
mmeilleur.mpp.co@liberal.ola.org
Social Media:
www.facebook.com/group.php?gid=5634816945&v=info
777 Bay St., 17th Fl.
Toronto, ON M5G 2E5

Minister, Community & Social Services; Government House Leader, Hon. John Milloy
Tel: 416-325-5225
Fax: 416-325-3347
jmilloy.mpp.co@liberal.ola.org
Social Media: www.twitter.com/John_Milloy
Ministry of Community & Social Services, Hepburn Block
80 Grosvenor St., 6th Fl.
Toronto, ON M7A 1E9

Minister, Training, Colleges & Universities, Hon. Glen Murray
Tel: 416-326-1600
Fax: 416-326-1656
gmurray.mpp.co@liberal.ola.org
Social Media: www.twitter.com/Glen4TC,
www.facebook.com/GlenMurrayMPP,
www.linkedin.com/in/glenmurraympp
Ministry of Training, Colleges & Universities, Mowat Block
900 Bay St., 3rd Fl.
Toronto, ON M7A1L2

Minister, Citizenship & Immigration, Hon. Charles Sousa
Tel: 416-325-6200
Fax: 416-325-6195
csousa.mpp.co@liberal.ola.org
Social Media: www.twitter.com/SousaCharles,
www.facebook.com/people/Charles-Sousa/541270855,
www.linkedin.com/in/charlessousa
Ministry of Citizenship & Immigration
400 University Ave., 6th Fl.
Toronto, ON M7A 2R9

Minister, Government Services, Hon. Harinder S. Takhar
Tel: 416-327-2333
Fax: 416-327-3790
htakhar.mpp.co@liberal.ola.org
Social Media: www.twitter.com/harindertakhar,
www.facebook.com/HarinderTakharMPP,
www.linkedin.com/pub/hon-harinder-takhar/34/a2a/58
Ministry of Government Services, Whitney Block
#4320, 99 Wellesley St. West
Toronto, ON M7A 1W3

Minister, Aboriginal Affairs, Hon. Kathleen Wynne
Tel: 416-325-5110
Fax: 416-314-2701
kwynne.mpp.co@liberal.ola.org
Social Media: www.twitter.com/Kathleen_Wynne,
www.facebook.com/kwynnempp,
www.linkedin.com/in/kathleenwynne
#400, 160 Bloor St. East
Toronto, ON M7A 2E6

Minister, Municipal Affairs & Housing, Hon. Kathleen Wynne
Tel: 416-585-7000
Fax: 416-585-6470
kwynne.mpp.co@liberal.ola.org
Social Media: www.twitter.com/Kathleen_Wynne,
www.facebook.com/kwynnempp,
www.linkedin.com/in/kathleenwynne
777 Bay St., 17th Fl.
Toronto, ON M5G 2E5

Cabinet Office

Whitney Block, 99 Wellesley St. West, 6th Fl., Toronto, ON M7A 1A1

Tel: 416-325-7635
Fax: 416-325-3004
TTY: 416-314-5721

Secretary of the Cabinet & Head of the Ontario Public Service, Peter Wallace
Tel: 416-325-7641
Fax: 416-314-8980
peter.wallace@ontario.ca

Deputy Minister, Communications & Associate Secretary of Cabinet, Lynn Betzner
Tel: 416-325-9698
Fax: 416-325-1979
lynn.betzner@ontario.ca

Deputy Minister, Intergovernmental Affairs; Francophone Affairs & Associate Secretary of the Cabinet, Paul Genest
Tel: 416-314-9710
Fax: 416-325-4787
paul.genest@ontario.ca

Deputy Minister, Policy & Delivery & Associate Secretary of Cabinet, Giles Gherson
Tel: 416-325-3759
Fax: 416-325-7631
giles.gherson@ontario.ca

Assistant Deputy Minister, Corporate Planning & Services, Linda Jackson
Tel: 416-314-0817
Fax: 416-325-2388
linda.jackson@ontario.ca

Associated Agencies, Boards & Commissions:
• Executive Development Committee
Queen's Park
Toronto, ON M5G 2K1
Tel: 416-325-1750

Ontario Legislative Assembly

c/o Clerk's Office, #104, Legislative Bldg., Queen's Park, Toronto, ON M7A 1A2

Tel: 416-325-7500
Fax: 416-325-7489
assemblyinternet@ontla.ola.org
www.ontla.on.ca
TTY: 416-325-9426

Other Communication: Hansard Email: hansard@ontla.ola.org
Acts Administered:
Election Act
Election Finances Act
Fewer Politicians Act, 1996
Freedom of Information & Protection of Privacy Act
Legislative Assembly Act
Legislative Assembly Retirement Allowances Act
Members' Integrity Act
Ombudsman Act

Speaker, Hon. Dave Levac
Tel: 416-325-6261
Fax: 416-325-6358
dlevac.mpp@liberal.ola.org

Deputy Speaker & Chair, Committee of the Whole House, Hon. Bas Balkissoon
Tel: 416-325-3804

Clerk, Deborah Deller
Tel: 416-325-7340
Fax: 416-325-7344
debbie_deller@ontla.ola.org

Executive Director, Administrative Services, Sylvia

Nemanic
Tel: 416-325-3568
Fax: 416-314-5995
sylvia_nemanic@ontla.ola.org
#2501, Whitney Block, Queen's Park
Toronto, ON M7A 1A2 Canada

Deputy Clerk & Executive Director, Legislative Services, Todd Decker
Tel: 416-325-3502
Fax: 416-325-5848
todd_decker@ontla.ola.org
#1302, Whitney Block, Queen's Park
99 Wellesley St. W
Toronto, ON M7A 1A2 Canada

Executive Director & Legislative Librarian, Information & Technology Services, Vicki Whitmell
Tel: 416-325-3939
Fax: 416-325-3909
vicki_whitmell@ontla.ola.org
Other Communications: Reference Inquiries: 416-325-3900
#1413, Whitney Block
Toronto, ON M7A1A9 Canada

Sergeant-at-Arms & Executive Director, Precinct Properties Division, Dennis M. Clark
Tel: 416-325-7446
Fax: 416-325-7154
dennis_clark@ontla.ola.org
#411, North Wing, Legislative Bldg., Queen
Toronto, ON M7A1A2 Canada

Executive Assistant to the Clerk, Zina Decker
Tel: 416-325-7343
Fax: 416-325-7344
zina_decker@ontla.ola.org

Government Members Services
#124, North Wing, Legislative Bldg., Queen's Park, 111 Wellesley St. West, Toronto, ON M7A 1A8
Tel: 416-325-7200
Fax: 416-325-3810

Government House Leader, Hon. John Milloy
Tel: 416-325-5225
Fax: 416-325-3347
jmilloy.mpp.co@liberal.ola.org
Office of the Government House Leader
#223, Main Legislative Bldg.
Toronto, ON M7A 1A4
Chief Government Whip, Jeff Leal
Tel: 416-325-0534
Chair, Management Board of the Cabinet, Hon. Dwight Duncan
Tel: 416-325-0400
Fax: 416-325-0374
dduncan.mpp.co@liberal.ola.org

Office of the Opposition (PC)
Legis. Bldg., North Wing, #381, Queen's Park, Toronto, ON M7A 1A8
Tel: 416-325-0445
Fax: 416-325-0491
www.ontariopc.com
TTY: 416-325-5771

Leader, Tim Hudak
Tel: 416-325-0445
Fax: 416-325-0491
Deputy Leader, Christine Elliott
Tel: 416-325-1331
Fax: 416-325-1423
Opposition House Leader, John Yakabuski
Tel: 416-325-2170
Fax: 416-325-2196
john.yakabuski@pc.ola.org
Deputy House Leader, Ted Arnott
Tel: 416-325-3880
Fax: 416-325-6649
Chief Opposition Whip, Norm Miller
Tel: 416-325-7736
Fax: 416-325-7739
norm.miller@pc.ola.org
Opposition Caucus Chair, Toby Barrett
Tel: 416-325-8404
Fax: 416-325-8408

New Democratic Party
Legislative Bldg., #113, Queen's Park, Toronto, ON M7A 1A5
Tel: 416-325-7116
Fax: 416-325-8222
www.ontariondp.com
TTY: 416-325-6564

Leader, Andrea Horwath
Tel: 416-325-8300
Fax: 416-325-8222

Standing Committees of the Legislative Assembly
Standing Committees of the Legislative Assembly

Estimates Committee
Clerk, Valerie Quioc Lim
Tel: 416-325-7352
valerie_quioc@ontla.ola.org

Finance & Economic Affairs Committee
Clerk, Valerie Quioc Lim
Tel: 416-325-7352
valerie_quioc@ontla.ola.org

General Government Committee
Clerk, Sylwia Przezdziecki
Tel: 416-325-3515
sylwia_przezdziecki@ontla.ola.org

Government Agencies
Clerk, Trevor Day
Tel: 416-325-3509
trevor_day@ontla.ola.org

Justice Policy Committee
Clerk, William Short
Tel: 416-325-3883
william_short@ontla.ola.org

Legislative Assembly Committee
Clerk, Trevor Day
Tel: 416-325-3509
trevor_day@ontla.ola.org

Public Accounts Committee
Clerk, William Short
Tel: 416-325-3883
william_short@ontla.ola.org

Regulations & Private Bills Committee
Clerk, Tamara Pomanski
Tel: 416-325-3506
tamara_pomanski@ontla.ola.org

Social Policy
Clerk, Katch Koch
Tel: 416-325-3526
katch_koch@ontla.ola.org

Fortieth Provincial Parliament - Ontario

Clerk's Office, #104, Legislative Building, Queen's Park, Toronto, ON M7A 1A2
Tel: 416-325-7500
Fax: 416-325-7489
tourbookings@ontla.ola.org
www.ontla.on.ca
TTY: 416-325-9426

Last General Election, October 6, 2011.
Maximum Duration, 5 years.
Party Standings (September 2012):
Liberal Party 53;
Progressive Conservative Party 36;
New Democratic Party 18;
Total Seats 107.
Salary Disclosure for 2011:
Premier $208,974;
Leader, Official Opposition $180,885.96;
Leader, Third Party $158,157.96;
Minister, Finance $165,851.03;
Speaker $152,913.96;
Chief Government Whip $137,879.04;
Chief Whip, Official Opposition $129,577.32;
Chief Whip, Third Party $129,722.63;
House Leader, Official Opposition $130,549.04;
House Leader, Third Party $134,732.04.
The following list features members, with their constituency, the number of names on the list of electors for the 2011 election, party affiliation, & contact information:

Members of Provincial Parliament

Laura Albanese
Constituency: York South-Weston *No. of Constituents:* 69,580, Liberal
Tel: 416-243-7984
Fax: 416-243-0327
lalbanese.mpp.co@liberal.ola.org
www.lauraalbanese.onmpp.ca/Contact.aspx
Other Communications: Queen's Park Phone: 416-325-1800; Fax: 416-325-1802
Social Media: www.twitter.com/Laura_Albanese, www.facebook.com/pages/Laura-Albanese-MPP/313504007063
Constituency Office
#102, 2301 Keele St.
Toronto, ON M6M3Z9
Teresa Armstrong
Constituency: London-Fanshawe *No. of Constituents:* 75,165, NDP
Tel: 519-451-0099
www.teresaarmstrong.ca/tag/ndp/
Social Media: www.twitter.com/Teresa_NDP
Constituency Office
London, ON
Ted Arnott
Constituency: Wellington-Halton Hills *No. of Constituents:* 82,926, Progressive Conservative
Tel: 519-787-5247
Toll-free: 800-265-2366
Fax: 519-787-5249
ted.arnottco@pc.ola.org; ted.arnott@pc.ola.org
www.tedarnottmpp.com
Other Communications: Queen's Park Phone: 416-325-3880; Fax: 416-325-6649
Social Media: www.facebook.com/ted.arnott.ont
Constituency Office
181 St. Andrew St. East, 2ndFl.
Fergus, ON N1M 1P9
Robert (Bob) Bailey
Constituency: Sarnia-Lambton *No. of Constituents:* 78,646, Progressive Conservative
Tel: 519-337-0051
Fax: 519-337-3246
bob.bailey@pc.ola.org; bob.baileyco@pc.ola.org
www.bobbaileympp.com
Other Communications: Queen's Park Phone: 416-325-1715; Fax: 416-325-1852
Social Media: www.twitter.com/BobBaileyPC
Constituency Office
836 Upper Canada Dr.
Sarnia, ON N7W 1A4
Bas Balkissoon
Constituency: Scarborough-Rouge River *No. of Constituents:* 85,338, Liberal
Tel: 416-325-3804
Fax: 416-212-4174
bbalkissoon.mpp.co@liberal.ola.org
www.basbalkissoon.onmpp.ca
Other Communications: Queen's Park Phone: 416-212-3066; Fax: 416-325-3862
Social Media: www.twitter.com/basbalkissoon, www.facebook.com/pages/Bas-Balkissoon/191306360704
Constituency Office
4559 Sheppard Ave. East, #B
Toronto, ON M1S 1V3
Hon. Rick Bartolucci
Constituency: Sudbury *No. of Constituents:* 65,130, Liberal
Tel: 705-675-1914
Fax: 705-675-1456
rbartolucci.mpp.co@liberal.ola.org
www.voterickbartolucci.com
Other Communications: Queen's Park Phone: 416-585-7000; Fax: 416-585-6470
Social Media: www.twitter.com/rickbartolucci, www.facebook.com/rick.bartolucci
Constituency Office
#302, 93 Cedar St.
Sudbury, ON P3C1A7
Hon. Christopher Bentley
Constituency: London West *No. of Constituents:* 93,852, Liberal
Tel: 519-657-3120
Toll-free: 800-518-7901
Fax: 519-657-0368
cbentley.mpp@liberal.ola.org;
cbentley.mpp.co@liberal.ola.org
www.chrisbentley.onmpp.ca
Other Communications: Queen's Park Phone: 416-326-2220; Fax: 416-326-4007
TTY: 416-326-4012
Social Media: www.twitter.com/Chris_Bentley
Constituency Office
#8,11 Base Line Rd. East
London, ON N6C 5Z8
Lorenzo Berardinetti
Constituency: Scarborough Southwest *No. of Constituents:* 69,553, Liberal
Tel: 416-261-9525
Fax: 416-261-0381
lberardinetti.mpp@liberal.ola.org
www.lorenzoberardinetti.onmpp.ca
Other Communications: Queen's Park Phone: 416-325-1008; Fax: 416-325-1219
Social Media: www.twitter.com/LBerardinetti, www.facebook.com/berardinetti
Constituency Office
#403B, 3090 Kingston Rd.
Scarborough, ON M1M1P2
Hon. Margarett Best
Constituency: Scarborough-Guildwood *No. of Constituents:* 67,408, Liberal
Tel: 416-281-2787
Fax: 416-281-2360
mbest.mpp.co@liberal.ola.org; mbest.mpp@liberal.ola.org

www.margarettbest.onmpp.ca
Other Communications: Queen's Park Phone: 416-326-8500; Fax: 416-326-8520
Social Media: www.facebook.com/people/Margarett-Best/772159453, www.linkedin.com/pub/christina-bisanz/2/7a4/599
Constituency Office
#109, 4117 Lawrence Ave. East
Toronto, ON M1E 2S2

Christina Bisanz
Constituency: Newmarket-Aurora *No. of Constituents:* 92,231, Liberal
Tel: 905-726-8122
www.christinabisanz.ca
Social Media: www.twitter.com/ChristinaBisanz, www.facebook.com/votebisanz
Constituency Office
#B, 11 Wellington St. East
Aurora, ON L4G 1H5

Gilles Bisson
Constituency: Timmins-JamesBay *No. of Constituents:* 49,723, New Democratic Party
Tel: 705-268-6400
Toll-free: 800-461-9878
Fax: 705-266-9125
gbisson@ndp.on.ca
www.gillesbisson.com
Other Communications: Queen's Park Phone: 416-325-7122; Fax: 416-325-7111
Social Media: www.twitter.com/bissongilles, www.facebook.com/pages/Gilles-Bisson/104067992963846, www.linkedin.com/pub/gilles-bisson/32/42b/363
Constituency Office
#202, 60 Wilson Ave
Timmins, ON P4N 2S7

Hon. James J. Bradley
Constituency: St Catharines *No. of Constituents:* 84,078, Liberal
Tel: 905-935-0018
Fax: 905-935-0191
jbradley.mpp.co@liberal.ola.org; jbradley.mpp@liberal.ola.org
Other Communications: Queen's Park Phone: 416-585-7000; Fax: 416-585-6470
Social Media: www.facebook.com/votebradley
Constituency Office
#2, 2 Secord Dr.
StCatharines, ON L2N 1K8

Hon. Laurel C. Broten
Constituency: Etobicoke-Lakeshore *No. of Constituents:* 87,390, Liberal
Tel: 416-259-2249
Fax: 416-259-3704
lbroten.mpp@liberal.ola.org; lbroten.mpp.co@liberal.ola.org
www.laurelbroten.onmpp.ca
Other Communications: Queen's Park Phone: 416-212-7432; Fax: 416-212-7431
Constituency Office
#100, 701 EvansAve.
Toronto, ON M8V 1A3

Sarah Campbell
Constituency: Kenora-Rainy River *No. of Constituents:* 48,369, New Democratic Party
Tel: 807-467-2415
Toll-free: 800-465-8501
Fax: 807-467-2641
www.sarah4nwo.ca
Other Communications: Queen's Park Phone: 416-325-2750; Fax: 416-325-1645
Social Media: www.twitter.com/Sarah4NWO, www.facebook.com/sarah4nwo
Constituency Office
300 McClellan Ave, East Room
Kenora, ON P9N 1A8

Donna H. Cansfield
Constituency: Etobicoke Centre *No. of Constituents:* 81,413, Liberal
Tel: 416-234-2800
Fax: 416-234-2276
dcansfield.mpp@liberal.ola.org; dcansfield.mpp.co@liberal.ola.org
www.donnacansfield.onmpp.ca
Other Communications: Queen's Park Phone: 416-585-7007; Fax: 416-585-4035
Social Media: www.twitter.com/DCansfield, www.facebook.com/DonnaCansfield, www.linkedin.com/pub/donna-cansfield/39/3a0/735
Constituency Office
#200, 4800 Dundas St.West
Toronto, ON M9A 1B1

Hon. Michael Chan
Constituency: Markham-Unionville *No. of Constituents:* 92,232, Liberal
Tel: 905-305-1935
Fax: 905-305-1938
mchan.mpp@liberal.ola.org; mchan.mpp.co@liberal.ola.org
www.michaelchan.onmpp.ca
Other Communications: Queen's Park Phone: 416-326-9326; Fax: 416-326-9338
Social Media: www.facebook.com/group.php?gid=2401349051
Constituency Office
#5, 450 Alden Rd.
Markham, ON L3R5H4

Hon. Bob Chiarelli
Constituency: OttawaWest-Nepean *No. of Constituents:* 82,187, Liberal
Tel: 613-721-8075
Fax: 613-721-5756
bchiarelli.mpp.co@liberal.ola.org
www.bobchiarelli.onmpp.ca
Other Communications: Queen's Park Phone: 416-325-8841; Fax: 416-325-8860
Social Media: www.Bob_Chiarelli, www.facebook.com/BobChiarelliMPP
Constituency Office
#201, 2249 Carling Ave.
Ottawa, ON K2B 7E9

Ted Chudleigh
Constituency: Halton *No. of Constituents:* 128,643, Progressive Conservative
Tel: 905-878-1729
Fax: 905-878-5144
ted.chudleigh@pc.ola.org
www.tedchudleigh.com
Other Communications: Queen's Park Phone: 416-325-5747; Fax: 416-325-5750
Social Media: www.twitter.com/TChudleigh2011
Constituency Office
#1, 172 Mill St.
Milton, ON L9T 1S2

Steve Clark
Constituency: Leeds-Grenville *No. of Constituents:* 75,797, Progressive Conservative
Tel: 613-342-9522
Toll-free: 800-267-4408
Fax: 613-342-2501
steve.clark@pc.ola.org
www.steveclarkmpp.com
Other Communications: Queen's Park Phone: 416-325-1522; Fax: 416-325-1493
Social Media: www.twitter.com/steveclarkelib, www.facebook.com/VoteSteveClarke
Constituency Office
#101, 100 Strowger Blvd.
Brockville, ON K6V 5J9

Mike Colle
Constituency: Eglinton-Lawrence *No. of Constituents:* 74,309, Liberal
Tel: 416-781-2395
Fax: 416-781-4116
mcolle.mpp@liberal.ola.org; mcolle.mpp.co@liberal.ola.org
www.mikecolle.com
Other Communications: Queen's Park Phone: 416-325-4091; Fax: 416-325-4136
Social Media: www.twitter.com/mikecolleMPP, www.linkedin.com/pub/mike-colle-mpp/15/55a/748
Constituency Office
2882 Dufferin St.
Toronto, ON M6B 3S6

Michael Coteau
Constituency: Don ValleyEast *No. of Constituents:* 69,851, Liberal
Tel: 416-494-6856
Fax: 416-494-9937
Other Communications: Queen's Park Phone: 416-325-3290; Fax: 416-325-3204
Social Media: www.twitter.com/coteau, www.facebook.com/michaelcoteau
Constituency Office
2062 Sheppard Ave. East
Toronto, ON M2J 5B3

Grant Crack
Constituency: Glengarry-Prescott-Russell *No. of Constituents:* 84,584, Liberal
Tel: 613-446-4010
Toll-free: 800-355-9666
Fax: 613-446-6605
www.grantcrack.ca
Other Communications: Queen's Park Phone: 416-325-7289; Fax: 416-325-2827
Social Media: www.twitter.com/GrantCrack
Constituency Office
345A Laurier St.
Rockland, ON K4K 1K4

Kim Craitor
Constituency: Niagara Falls *No. of Constituents:* 95,266, Liberal
Tel: 905-357-0681
Fax: 905-357-9456
kcraitor.mpp@liberal.ola.org; kcraitor.mpp.co@liberal.ola.org
www.kimcraitor.com
Other Communications: Queen's Park Phone: 416-325-3715; Fax: 416-212-7155
Social Media: www.facebook.com/people/Kim-Craitor-Mpp/100002625582257, www.linkedin.com/pub/kim-craitor/30/291/771
Constituency Office
#8, 3930 Montrose Rd.
NiagaraFalls, ON L2H 3C9

Dipika Damerla
Constituency: Mississauga East-Cooksville *No. of Constituents:* 84,330, Liberal
www.votedipika.com
Social Media: www.twitter.com/DipikaDamerla, www.facebook.com/DipikaDamerla.MEC?sk=wall&filter=2

Bob Delaney
Constituency: Mississauga-Streetsville *No. of Constituents:* 87,297, Liberal
Tel: 905-569-1643
Fax: 905-569-6416
bdelaney.mpp@liberal.ola.org; bdelaney.mpp.co@liberal.ola.org
www.bobdelaney.com
Other Communications: Queen's Park Phone: 416-325-0161; Fax: 416-325-0186
Social Media: www.facebook.com/BobDelaneyMPP, www.linkedin.com/in/bobdelaneympp
Constituency Office
Plaza IV, #22, 2000 Argentia Rd., 2ndFl.
Mississauga, ON L5N 1W1

Steven Del Duca
Constituency: Vaughan *No. of Constituents:* 121,154, Liberal
Tel: 905-851-4698
steven@votedelduca.ca
www.votedelduca.ca
Social Media: twitter.com/@stevendelduca, www.facebook.com/votedelduca
Note: On August 1, 2012, Greg Sorbara announced his departure as MPP for theriding of Vaughan. He will continue to be Co-Chair of the Liberal campaign. Steven Del Duca won the Sept. 6, 2012 by-election with 50 per cent of the popular vote.
Constituency Office
#19, 7887 Weston Rd.
Vaughan, ON L4L 1A6

Vic Dhillon
Constituency: Brampton West *No. of Constituents:* 115,431, Liberal
Tel: 905-796-8669
Fax: 905-796-8069
vdhillon.mpp@liberal.ola.org; vdhillon.mpp.co@liberal.ola.org
www.vicdhillon.onmpp.ca
Other Communications: Queen's Park Phone: 416-325-0241; Fax: 416-325-0272
Social Media: www.twitter.com/dhillonvic, www.facebook.com/dhillonvic
Constituency Office
#304, 37 George St.North
Brampton, ON L6X 1R5

Joe Dickson
Constituency: Ajax-Pickering *No. of Constituents:* 92,745, Liberal
Tel: 905-427-2060
Fax: 905-427-6976
jdickson.mpp@liberal.ola.org
www.joedickson.onmpp.ca
Other Communications: Queen's Park Phone: 416-325-1182; Fax:416-325-1191
Social Media: www.twitter.com/votejoedickson
Constituency Office
#201A, 50 Commercial Ave.
Ajax, ON L1S 2H5

Cheri DiNovo
Constituency: Parkdale-High Park *No. of Constituents:* 77,163, New Democratic Party
Tel: 416-763-5630
Fax: 416-763-5640
dinovoc-qp@ndp.on.ca; dinovoc-co@ndp.on.ca
www.cheridinovo.ca
Other Communications: Queen's Park phone: 416-325-0244; Fax: 416-325-0305
Social Media: www.twitter.com/cheridinovo, www.facebook.com/CheriDiNovoParkdaleHighPark, www.linkedin.com/pub/cheri-dinovo/12/715/157
Constituency Office
3136 Dundas St. West
Toronto, ON M6P 2A1

Hon. Brad Duguid
Constituency: Scarborough Centre *No. of Constituents:* 70,958, Liberal
Tel: 416-615-2183

Fax: 416-615-2011
bduguid.mpp@liberal.ola.org; bduguid.mpp.co@liberal.ola.org
www.bradduguid.ca
Other Communications: Queen's Park Phone: 416-327-6758; Fax: 416-327-6754
Social Media: www.twitter.com/VoteBradDuguid, www.facebook.com/VoteBradDuguid, www.linkedin.com/pub/brad-duguid/3/b01/6a3
Constituency Office
#204, 1450 MidlandAve.
Scarborough, ON M1P 4Z8

Hon. Dwight Duncan
Constituency: Windsor-Tecumseh *No. of Constituents:* 83,807, Liberal
Tel: 519-251-5199
Fax: 519-251-5299
dduncan.mpp@liberal.ola.org; dduncan.mpp.co@liberal.ola.org
www.dwightduncan.ca
Other Communications: Queen's Park Phone: 416-325-0400; Fax: 416-325-0374
Social Media: www.twitter.com/DwightDuncan, www.facebook.com/dwight1?sk=wall, www.linkedin.com/pub/dwight-duncan/31/774/8b1
Constituency Office
#211, 2825 LauzonParkway
Windsor, ON N8T 3H5

Garfield Dunlop
Constituency: Simcoe North *No. of Constituents:* 89,474, Progressive Conservative
Tel: 705-326-3246
Toll-free: 800-304-7341
Fax: 705-326-9579
garfield.dunlop@pc.ola.org; garfield.dunlopco@pc.ola.org
www.garfielddunlopmpp.com
Other Communications: Queen's Park Phone: 416-325-3855; Fax: 416-325-9035
Social Media: www.twitter.com/Garfield_Dunlop, www.facebook.com/pages/Garfield-Dunlop/119367071443387
Constituency Office
14 Coldwater Rd. West
PO Box 2320
Orillia, ON L3V 6S2

Christine Elliott
Constituency: Whitby-Oshawa *No. of Constituents:* 102,672, Progressive Conservative
Tel: 905-430-1141
Fax: 905-430-1840
christine.elliott@pc.ola.org
www.christineelliottmpp.com
Other Communications: Queen's Park Phone: 416-325-1331; Fax: 416-325-1423
Social Media: www.twitter.com/votechristine
Constituency Office
#101, 114 Dundas St. East
Whitby, ON L1N 2H7

Vic Fedeli
Constituency: Nipissing *No. of Constituents:* 59,481, Liberal
Tel: 705-474-8340
Fax: 705-474-9747
www.fedeli.com
Other Communications: Queen's Park Phone: 416-325-7754; Fax: 416-325-7755
Social Media: www.twitter.com/victorfedeli, www.facebook.com/pages/Vic-Fedeli/195238410500602?sk=wall, www.linkedin.com/in/victorfedeli
Constituency Office
165 Main St. East
North Bay, ON P1B 1A9

Catherine Fife
Constituency: Kitchener-Waterloo *No. of Constituents:* 98,268, New Democratic Party
Tel: 519-725-4888
catherinefife@on.ndp.ca
www.catherinefife.com
Social Media: twitter.com/CfifeKW, www.facebook.com/catherinefifeNDP
Note: Catherine Fife won Kitchener-Waterloo for the first time in NDP history, in a Sept. 2012by-election, after Elizabeth Witmer was nominated to be Chair of the Workplace Safety & Insurance Board (WSIB) by Premier Dalton McGuinty, in May 2012.
182 Weber St.
Waterloo, ON N2J 3H4

Kevin Daniel Flynn
Constituency: Oakville *No. of Constituents:* 85,971, Liberal
Tel: 905-827-5141
Fax: 905-827-3786
kflynn.mpp@liberal.ola.org; kflynn.mpp.co@liberal.ola.org
www.kevinflynn.onmpp.ca
Other Communications: Queen's Park Phone: 416-325-7215; Fax: 416-325-9295
Social Media: www.twitter.com/OakvilleMPP, www.linkedin.com/pub/kevin-flynn/1b/73a/9b1
Constituency Office
2330 Lakeshore Rd.West
Oakville, ON L6L 1H3

Cindy Forster
Constituency: Welland *No. of Constituents:* 85,141, New Democratic Party
Tel: 905-732-6884
Fax: 905-732-9782
Other Communications: Queen's Park Phone: 416-325-7106
Social Media: www.facebook.com/CindyForsterNDP
Constituency Office
#103, 60 King St.
Welland, ON L3B 6A4

France Gélinas
Constituency: Nickel Belt *No. of Constituents:* 62,276, New Democratic Party
Tel: 705-969-3621
Fax: 705-969-3538
fgelinas-co@ndp.on.ca; fgelinas-qp@ndp.on.ca
www.francegelinas.ca
Other Communications: Queen's Park Phone: 416-325-9203; Fax: 416-325-9185
Social Media: www.twitter.com/NickelBelt
Constituency Office
#15, 5085 Hwy. 69 North
Hanmer, ON P3P 1P7

Hon. John Gerretsen
Constituency: Kingston & the Islands *No. of Constituents:* 95,966, Liberal
Tel: 613-547-2385
Fax: 613-547-5001
jgerretsen.mpp@liberal.ola.org; jgerretsen.mpp.co@liberal.ola.org
www.johngerretsen.onmpp.ca
Other Communications: Queen's Park Phone: 416-327-8300; Fax: 416-326-1947
Constituency Office
#2, 303 BagotSt.
Kingston, ON K7K 5W7

Hon. Michael Gravelle
Constituency: Thunder Bay-Superior North *No. of Constituents:* 54,443, Liberal
Tel: 807-345-3647
Toll-free: 888-516-5555
Fax: 807-345-2922
mgravelle.mpp@liberal.ola.org
www.michaelgravelle.ca
Other Communications: Queen's Park Phone: 416-327-0633; Fax: 416-327-0665
Constituency Office
#101, 215 Van Norman St.
Thunder Bay, ON P7A4B6

Ernie Hardeman
Constituency: Oxford *No. of Constituents:* 76,804, Progressive Conservative
Tel: 519-537-5222
Toll-free: 800-265-4046
Fax: 519-537-3577
ernie.hardeman@pc.ola.org; ernie.hardemanco@pc.ola.org
www.erniehardemanmpp.com
Other Communications: Queen's Park Phone: 416-325-1239; Fax: 416-325-1259
Social Media: www.facebook.com/people/Ernie-Hardeman/505534292, www.linkedin.com/pub/ernie-hardeman/2b/18a/37a
Constituency Office
12 Perry St., 2nd Fl.
Woodstock, ON N4S 3C2

Michael Harris
Constituency: Kitchener-Conestoga *No. of Constituents:* 87,992, Progressive Conservative
Tel: 519-954-3276 ext: 867
Fax: 519-748-9876
info@michaelharrispc.ca
www.michaelharrispc.ca
Social Media: www.twitter.com/Michaelharrispc, www.facebook.com/group.php?gid=2418112067
Constituency Office
771 Wilson Ave.
Kitchener, ON N2C 1J1

Randy Hillier
Constituency: Lanark-Frontenac-Lennox& Addington *No. of Constituents:* 89,150, Progressive Conservative
Tel: 613-267-8293
Fax: 613-267-7398
randy.hillierco@pc.ola.org
www.randyhilliermpp.com
Other Communications: Queen's Park Phone: 416-325-2244; Fax: 416-325-2166
Social Media: www.twitter.com/randyhillier, www.facebook.com/pages/Randy-Hillier-MPP/178772728799738, www.linkedin.com/pub/randy-hillier/34/496/41b
Constituency Office
#1, 105 Dufferin St.
Perth, ON K7H 3A5

Andrea Horwath
Constituency: Hamilton Centre *No. of Constituents:* 79,524, New Democratic Party
Tel: 905-544-9644
Fax: 905-544-5152
ahorwath-qp@ndp.on.ca; ahorwath-co@ndp.on.ca
www.ontariondp.com
Other Communications: Queen's Park Phone: 416-325-2777; Fax: 416-325-2770
Social Media: www.twitter.com/andreahorwath, www.facebook.com/AndreaHorwathONDP
Constituency Office
200 - 20 Hughson St. South
Hamilton, ON L8N 2A1

Hon. Eric Hoskins
Constituency: St.Paul's *No. of Constituents:* 85,451, Liberal
Tel: 416-656-0943
Fax: 416-656-0875
ehoskins.mpp.co@liberal.ola.org
www.erichoskins.onmpp.ca
Other Communications: Queen's Park Phone: 416-325-6200; Fax: 416-325-6195
Social Media: www.twitter.com/DrEricHoskins, www.facebook.com/drerichoskins
Constituency Office
803 St. Clair Ave. West
Toronto, ON M6C 1B9

Tim Hudak
Constituency: NiagaraWest-Glanbrook *No. of Constituents:* 89,489, Progressive Conservative
Tel: 905-563-1755
Toll-free: 800-665-3697
Fax: 905-563-1317
tim.hudakco@pc.ola.org
www.timhudakmpp.com
Other Communications: Queen's Park Phone: 416-325-8454; Fax: 416-325-0998
Social Media: www.twitter.com/timhudak, www.facebook.com/timhudak, www.linkedin.com/in/timhudak
Constituency Office
#M1, 4961 King St. East
Beamsville, ON L0R 1B0

Rod Jackson
Constituency: Barrie *No. of Constituents:* 94,114, Progressive Conservative
Tel: 705-881-1519
www.rodjackson.ca
Social Media: www.twitter.com/RodneyJackson, www.facebook.com/pages/Elect-Rod-Jackson/168359439854698?sk=wall
Constituency Office
200 Fairview Dr.
Barrie, ON

Helena Jaczek
Constituency: OakRidges-Markham *No. of Constituents:* 151,959, Liberal
Tel: 905-294-4931
Toll-free: 866-531-9551
Fax: 905-294-0014
hjaczek.mpp@liberal.ola.org
www.helenajaczek.ca
Other Communications: Queen's Park Phone: 416-325-0737; Fax: 416-325-4112
Social Media: www.twitter.com/helenajaczek, www.facebook.com/helenajaczek, www.linkedin.com/pub/helena-jaczek/4/6a5/b77
Constituency Office
#201, 137 Main St. North
Markham, ON L3P 1Y2

Hon. Linda Jeffrey
Constituency: Brampton-Springdale *No. of Constituents:* 87,543, Liberal
Tel: 905-495-8030
Fax: 905-495-1041
ljeffrey.mpp@liberal.ola.org; ljeffrey.mpp.co@liberal.ola.org
www.lindajeffrey.onmpp.ca
Other Communications: Queen's Park Phone: 416-314-2301; Fax: 416-325-5316
Social Media: www.twitter.com/LindaJeffrey
Constituency Office
#13, 380 Bovaird Dr. East
Brampton, ON L6Z 2S7

Sylvia Jones
Constituency: Dufferin-Caledon *No. of Constituents:* 79,918, Progressive Conservative
Tel: 519-941-7751
Fax: 519-941-3246
sylvia.jones@pc.ola.org; sylvia.jonesco@pc.ola.org
www.sylviajonesmpp.ca
Other Communications: Queen's Park Phone: 416-325-1898; Fax: 416-325-1936

Social Media: www.twitter.com/SylviaJonesMPP, www.facebook.com/group.php?gid=336959233065
Constituency Office
244 Broadway Ave.
Orangeville, ON L9W 1K5

Monte Kwinter
Constituency: York Centre *No. of Constituents:* 71,531, Liberal
Tel: 416-630-0080
Fax: 416-630-8828
mkwinter.mpp@liberal.ola.org; mkwinter.mpp.co@liberal.ola.org
www.montekwinter.com
Other Communications: Queen's Park Phone: 416-325-0036; Fax: 416-325-0316
Social Media: www.twitter.com/MonteKwinter, www.facebook.com/ReElectMonteKwinter
Constituency Office
539 Wilson HeightsBlvd.
Toronto, ON M3H 2V7

Jeff Leal
Constituency: Peterborough *No. of Constituents:* 91,908, Liberal
Tel: 705-742-3777
Fax: 705-742-1822
jleal.mpp@liberal.ola.org; jleal.mpp.co@liberal.ola.org
www.jeffleal.ca
Other Communications: Queen's Park Phone: 416-325-0534; Fax: 416-325-0570
Social Media: www.twitter.com/reelectjeffleal
Constituency Office
236 King St.
Peterborough, ON K9J7L8

Rob Leone
Constituency: Cambridge *No. of Constituents:* 92,310, Progressive Conservative
Tel: 519-623-5852
Fax: 519-623-3250
www.robleone.ca
Other Communications: Queen's Park Phone: 416-325-8451; Fax: 416-325-8413
Social Media: www.twitter.com/robleone
Constituency Office
#2, 410 Hespeler Rd.
Cambridge, ON N1R 6J6

Hon. Dave Levac
Constituency: Brant *No. of Constituents:* 94,717, Liberal
Tel: 519-759-0361
Fax: 519-759-6439
dlevac.mpp@liberal.ola.org; dlevac.mpp.co@liberal.ola.org
www.davelevac.on.ca
Other Communications: Queen's Park Phone: 416-325-6261, Fax: 416-325-6358
Constituency Office
#101, 96 Nelson St.
Brantford, ON N3T2N1

Tracy MacCharles
Constituency: Pickering-Scarborough East *No. of Constituents:* 78,835, Liberal
Tel: 905-492-8683
www.votemaccharles.ca
Other Communications: Queen's Park Phone: 416-325-3581; Fax: 416-325-3453
Social Media: www.twitter.com/votemaccharles, www.facebook.com/votemaccharles
Constituency Office
#1, 300 Kingston Rd.
Pickering, ON L1V 6Z9

Jack MacLaren
Constituency: Carleton-MississippiMills *No. of Constituents:* 105,368, Progressive Conservative
Tel: 513-599-3000
Toll-free: 800-267-1020
Fax: 613-599-8183
www.jackmaclaren.com
Other Communications: Queen's Park Phone: 416-314-7900; Fax: 416-314-7966
Social Media: www.twitter.com/jackmaclaren, www.facebook.com/pages/Jack-MacLaren/181470968553829?sk=info
Constituency Office
#100, 240 Michael Cowpland Dr.
Katana, ON K2M 1P6

Lisa MacLeod
Constituency: Nepean-Carleton *No. of Constituents:* 110,662, Progressive Conservative
Tel: 613-823-2116
Fax: 613-823-8284
lisa.macleod@pc.ola.org
www.lisamacleod.com; www.lismacleod.ca
Other Communications: Queen's Park Phone: 416-325-6351; Fax: 416-325-6364
Social Media: www.facebook.com/LisaMacLeodMPP, www.linkedin.com/pub/lisa-macleod/13/675/163
Constituency Office
#10, 3500 Fallowfield Rd.
Nepean, ON K2J4A7

Amrit Mangat
Constituency: Mississauga-Brampton South *No. of Constituents:* 93,563, Liberal
Tel: 905-696-0367
Fax: 905-696-7545
amangat.mpp.co@liberal.ola.org
www.amritmangat.onmpp.ca
Other Communications: Queen's Park Phone: 416-325-1050; Fax: 416-325-1138
Social Media: www.twitter.com/amrit_mangat, www.facebook.com/pages/Amrit-Mangat/265148843495306?v=info
Constituency Office
#203, 7045 Edwards Blvd.
Mississauga, ON L5S 1X2

Michael Mantha
Constituency: Algoma-Manitoulin *No. of Constituents:* 52,919, New Democratic Party
Tel: 705-848-0431
mikemantha@ontariondp.ca
Social Media: www.facebook.com/MikeManthaONDP
Constituency Office
#151-5B Ontario St.
Elliot Lake, ON P5A 2T2

Rosario Marchese
Constituency: Trinity-Spadina *No. of Constituents:* 109,565, New Democratic Party
Tel: 416-603-9664
Fax: 416-603-1241
rmarchese-co@ndp.on.ca
www.rosariomarchese.ca
Other Communications: Queen's Park Phone: 416-325-9092; Fax: 416-325-4976
Social Media: www.twitter.com/RMarcheseMPP, www.facebook.com/RosarioMarcheseMPP
Constituency Office
854 Dundas St. West
Toronto, ON M6J 1V5

Hon. Deborah Matthews
Constituency: London North Centre *No. of Constituents:* 91,638, Liberal
Tel: 519-432-7339
Fax: 519-432-0613
dmatthews.mpp@liberal.ola.org; dmatthews.mpp.co@liberal.ola.org
www.debmatthews.ca
Other Communications: Queen's Park Phone: 416-327-4300; Fax: 416-327-3679
Social Media: www.twitter.com/Deb_Matthews
Constituency Office
242 Piccadilly St.
London, ON N6A 1S4

Bill Mauro
Constituency: ThunderBay-Atikokan *No. of Constituents:* 57,027, Liberal
Tel: 807-623-9237
Fax: 807-623-4983
bmauro.mpp.co@liberal.ola.org
www.billmauro.onmpp.ca
Other Communications: Queen's Park Phone: 416-327-6611; Fax: 416-327-6618
Social Media: www.twitter.com/billmaurompp, www.linkedin.com/pub/bill-mauro/1a/447/6a8
Constituency Office
240 South Syndicate Ave.
Thunder Bay, ON P7E 1C8

Jim McDonell
Constituency: Stormont-Dundas-South Glengarry *No. of Constituents:* 75,975, Progressive Conservative
Tel: 613-933-7447
jimmcdonellcampaign@gmail.com
www.mcdonell.ca
Constituency Office
#B, 900 Pitt St.
Cornwall, ON K6J 3S5

Hon. Dalton McGuinty
Constituency: OttawaSouth *No. of Constituents:* 87,766, Liberal
Tel: 613-736-9573
Fax: 613-736-7374
dmcguinty.mpp.co@liberal.ola.org
www.daltonmcguinty.onmpp.ca
Other Communications: Queen's Park Phone: 416-325-1941; Fax: 416-325-3745
Social Media: www.twitter.com/Dalton_McGuinty, www.facebook.com/PremierMcGuinty
Constituency Office
1795 Kilborn Ave.
Ottawa, ON K1H 6N1

Jane McKenna
Constituency: Burlington *No. of Constituents:* 90,964, Progressive Conservative
Tel: 905-639-7924
Fax: 905-639-3284
www.janemckenna.ca
Other Communications: Queen's Park Phone: 416-325-5362; Fax: 416-325-5357
Social Media: www.twitter.com/VoteJaneMcKenna
Constituency Office
#44, 760 Brant Street
Burlington, ON L7R 4B7

Hon. Ted McMeekin
Constituency: Ancaster-Dundas-Flamborough-Westdale *No. of Constituents:* 88,080, Liberal
Tel: 905-690-6552
Toll-free: 888-566-6614
Fax: 905-690-6562
tmcmeekin.mpp@liberal.ola.org; tmcmeekin.mpp.co@liberal.ola.org
Other Communications: Queen's Park Phone: 416-326-1600; Fax: 416-326-2807
Social Media: www.twitter.com/TedMcMeekin
Constituency Office
299 Dundas St. East
PO Box 1240
Waterdown, ON L0R 2H0

Monte McNaughton
Constituency: Lambton-Kent-Middlesex *No. of Constituents:* 78,683, Progressive Conservative
Tel: 519-205-8875
www.montemcnaughton.com
Social Media: www.twitter.com/MonteMcNaughton/
Constituency Office
81 Front St. West
PO Box 420
Strathroy, ON N0L 1M0

Phil McNeely
Constituency: Ottawa-Orléans *No. of Constituents:* 89,726, Liberal
Tel: 613-834-8679
Fax: 613-834-7647
pmcneely.mpp@liberal.ola.org; pmcneely.mpp.co@liberal.ola.org
www.philmcneely.onmpp.ca
Other Communications: Queen's Park Phone: 416-325-0505; Fax: 416-325-0532
Social Media: www.twitter.com/PhilMcNeelyMPP
Constituency Office
#6, 110 Bearbrook Rd.
Gloucester, ON K1B 5R2

Hon. Madeleine Meilleur
Constituency: Ottawa-Vanier *No. of Constituents:* 81,712, Liberal
Tel: 613-744-4484
Toll-free: 800-628-7507
Fax: 613-744-0889
mmeilleur.mpp.co@liberal.ola.org; ofa@ofa.gov.on.ca
www.madeleinemeilleur.onmpp.ca
Other Communications: Queen's Park Phone: 416-325-5225; Fax: 416-325-5191
Social Media: www.facebook.com/group.php?gid=5634816945&v=info
Constituency Office
237 Montreal Rd.
Vanier, ON K1L 6C7

Norm Miller
Constituency: ParrySound-Muskoka *No. of Constituents:* 69,651, Progressive Conservative
Tel: 705-746-4266
Toll-free: 888-701-1176
Fax: 705-746-1578
norm.millerco@pc.ola.org
www.normmillermpp.ca; www.normmillerpc.com
Other Communications: Queen's Park Phone: 416-325-1012; Fax: 416-325-1153
Social Media: www.twitter.com/normmillermpp
Constituency Office
17 James St.
Parry Sound, ON P2A 1T4

Paul Miller
Constituency: HamiltonEast-Stoney Creek *No. of Constituents:* 85,908, New Democratic Party
Tel: 905-545-0114
Fax: 905-545-9024
pmiller-co@ndp.on.ca; pmiller-qp@ndp.on.ca
www.paulmillermpp.ca
Other Communications: Queen's Park Phone: 416-325-0707; Fax: 416-325-0853
Constituency Office
289 Queenston Rd.
Hamilton, ON L8K 1H2

Rob Milligan
Constituency: Northumberland-Quinte West *No. of Constituents:* 93,720, Progressive Conservative
Tel: 905-372-5433

rrmilligan@hotmail.ca
www.robmilligan.ca
Social Media: www.twitter.com/RobMilligan,
www.facebook.com/pages/Rob-Milligan/210851462262701
Constituency Office
87 King St. West
Cobourg, ON

Hon. John Milloy
Constituency: Kitchener Centre *No. of Constituents:* 80,170, Liberal
Tel: 519-579-5460
Fax: 519-579-2121
jmilloy.mpp@liberal.ola.org; jmilloy.mpp.co@liberal.ola.org
www.johnmilloy.onmpp.ca; www.johnmilloy.ca
Other Communications: Queen's Park Phone: 416-326-1600; Fax: 416-326-1656
Social Media: www.twitter.com/John_Milloy
Constituency Office
#6C, 1770 King St.East
Kitchener, ON N2G 2P1

Reza Moridi
Constituency: Richmond Hill *No. of Constituents:* 91,010, Liberal
Tel: 905-884-8080
Fax: 905-884-1040
rmoridi.mpp@liberal.ola.org
www.rezamoridi.onmpp.ca
Other Communications: Queen's Park Phone: 416-326-5968; Fax: 416-326-5834
Social Media: www.twitter.com/rezamoridi,
www.facebook.com/rmoridi,
www.linkedin.com/pub/reza-moridi-mpp/6/673/bb4
Constituency Office
9891 Yonge St.
Richmond Hill, ON L4C 1V1

Julia Munro
Constituency: York-Simcoe *No. of Constituents:* 90,599, Progressive Conservative
Tel: 905-478-2572
Toll-free: 866-206-1373
Fax: 905-478-8470
julia.munro@pc.ola.org; julia.munroco@pc.ola.org
www.juliamunrompp.com
Other Communications: Queen's Park Phone: 416-325-3392; Fax: 416-325-3466
Social Media: www.twitter.com/juliamunropc,
www.facebook.com/juliamunropc
Constituency Office
18977 Leslie St.
PO Box 1129
Sharon, ON L0G1V0

Hon. Glen R. Murray
Constituency: TorontoCentre *No. of Constituents:* 95,466, Liberal
Tel: 416-972-7683
Fax: 416-972-7686
gmurray.mpp.co@liberal.ola.org
www.glenmurray.onmpp.ca
Other Communications: Queen's Park Phone: 416-325-5744; Fax: 416-325-5754
Social Media: www.twitter.com/Glen4TC,
www.facebook.com/GlenMurrayMPP,
www.linkedin.com/in/glenmurraympp
Constitutency Office
514 Parliament St.
Toronto, ON M4X 1P4

Taras Natyshak
Constituency: Essex *No. of Constituents:* 89,549, New Democratic Party
Tel: 519-776-4957
Toll-free: 866-660-1460
www.tarasnatyshakndp.ca
Social Media: www.twitter.com/Taras4EssexMPP,
www.facebook.com/TarasNatyshakMPP
Constituency Office
361 Talbot St. North
Essex, ON N8M 2E1

Yasir Naqvi
Constituency: Ottawa Centre *No. of Constituents:* 94,553, Liberal
Tel: 613-722-6414
Fax: 613-722-6703
ynaqvi.mpp@liberal.ola.org
www.yasirnaqvimpp.ca
Other Communications: Queen's Park Phone: 416-327-4394; Fax: 416-314-9369
Social Media: www.twitter.com/Yasir_Naqvi,
www.facebook.com/YasirNaqviMPP,
www.linkedin.com/in/yasirnaqvimpp
Constituency Office
#204, 411 Roosevelt Ave.
Ottawa, ON K2A 3X9

Rick Nicholls
Constituency: Chatham-Kent-Essex *No. of Constituents:* 73,727, Progressive Conservative
www.ricknicholls.com
Social Media: www.twitter.com/RickNicholls,
www.facebook.com/RickNichollsPCofCKEX?sk=wall,
www.linkedin.com/pub/rick-nicholls/10/280/b05
Constituency Office
657 Grand Ave. West
Chatham, ON N7L 1C5

David Orazietti
Constituency: Sault Ste. Marie *No. of Constituents:* 59,698, Liberal
Tel: 705-949-6959
Fax: 705-946-6269
dorazietti.mpp@liberal.ola.org;
dorazietti.mpp.co@liberal.ola.org
www.davidorazietti.onmpp.ca
Other Communications: Queen's Park Phone: 416-314-6467; Fax: 416-314-6470
Social Media: www.twitter.com/DavidOrazietti,
www.facebook.com/davidorazietti?v=info
Constituency Office
726 Queen St. East
Sault SteMarie, ON P6A 2A9

John O'Toole
Constituency: Durham *No. of Constituents:* 92,096, Progressive Conservative
Tel: 905-697-1501
Toll-free: 800-661-2433
Fax: 905-697-1506
john.otoole@pc.ola.org; john.otooleco@pc.ola.org
www.johnotoolempp.com
Other Communications: Queen's Park Phone: 416-325-6745; Fax: 416-325-6255
Constituency Office
75 King St. East
Bowmanville, ON L1C1N4

Jerry J. Ouellette
Constituency: Oshawa *No. of Constituents:* 89,767, Progressive Conservative
Tel: 905-723-2411
Fax: 905-723-1054
jerry.ouellette@pc.ola.org; jerry.ouelletteco@pc.ola.org
www.oshawampp.com; www.jerryouellette.ca
Other Communications: Queen's Park Phone: 416-325-2147; Fax: 416-325-2169
Social Media:
www.linkedin.com/pub/jerry-ouellette/27/12b/751
Constituency Office
170 Athol St. East
Oshawa, ON L1H1K1

Randy Pettapiece
Constituency: Perth-Wellington *No. of Constituents:* 71,629, Progressive Conservative
www.randypettapiece.com
Social Media: www.twitter.com/randypettapiece,
www.facebook.com/pages/Randy-Pettapiece/116053045144846
Constituency Office
165 Argyle Ave. North
Listowel, ON N5A 6S4

Teresa Piruzza
Constituency: Windsor West *No. of Constituents:* 82,773, Liberal
Tel: 519-977-7191
Fax: 519-977-7029
www.votepiruzza.ca
Other Communications: Queen's Park Phone: 416-325-6900; Fax: 416-325-6918
Social Media: www.twitter.com/VotePiruzza,
www.facebook.com/VotePiruzza?sk=wall&filter=2,
www.linkedin.com/pub/teresa-piruzza/21/461/486
Constituency Office
1368 Ouellette Ave., 1st Fl.
Windsor, ON N8X 1J9

Michael Prue
Constituency: Beaches-EastYork *No. of Constituents:* 74,450, New Democratic Party
Tel: 416-690-1032
Fax: 416-690-8420
mprue-qp@ndp.on.ca; mprue-co@ndp.on.ca
www.michaelprue.com
Other Communications: Queen's Park Phone: 416-325-1303; Fax: 416-325-1367
Constituency Office
1821 Danforth Ave.
Toronto, ON M4C 1J2

Shafiq Qaadri
Constituency: Etobicoke North *No. of Constituents:* 62,472, Liberal
Tel: 416-745-2859
Fax: 416-745-4601
sqaadri.mpp@liberal.ola.org; sqaadri.mpp.co@liberal.ola.org
www.shafiqqaadri.com
Other Communications: Queen's Park Phone: 416-325-6679; Fax: 416-325-6691
Social Media: www.linkedin.com/in/doctorqca
Constituency Office
823 Albion Rd.
Etobicoke, ON M9V1A3

Liz Sandals
Constituency: Guelph *No. of Constituents:* 93,308, Liberal
Tel: 519-836-4190
Fax: 519-836-4191
lsandals.mpp@liberal.ola.org;
lsandals.mpp.co@liberal.ola.org
www.lizsandals.onmpp.ca; www.lizsandals.ca
Other Communications: Queen's Park Phone: 416-327-1322; Fax: 416-325-3862
Constituency Office
173 Woolwich St.
Guelph, ON N1H 3V4

Jonah Schein
Constituency: Davenport *No. of Constituents:* 68,998, New Democratic Party
Tel: 416-531-7495
jonah@jonahschein.ca
www.electjonahschein.com
Social Media: www.twitter.com/jonahschein,
www.facebook.com/votejonahschein
Constituency Office
Toronto, ON

Laurie Scott
Constituency: Haliburton-Kawartha Lakes-Brock *No. of Constituents:* 89,830, Liberal
Tel: 705-880-5674
www.votelaurie.com
Social Media: www.twitter.com/LaurieScott_PC,
www.facebook.com/pages/Laurie-Scott/199126813450886?v=info
Constituency Office
Lindsay, ON K9V 2Y1

Mario Sergio
Constituency: YorkWest *No. of Constituents:* 58,255, Liberal
Tel: 416-743-7272
Fax: 416-743-3292
msergio.mpp@liberal.ola.org
www.mariosergio.com
Other Communications: Queen's Park Phone: 416-325-4925; Fax: 416-325-4926
Social Media: www.linkedin.com/pub/mario-sergio/18/b65/28
Constituency Office
#38, 2300 Finch Ave. West
Toronto, ON M9M 2Y3

Peter Shurman
Constituency: Thornhill *No. of Constituents:* 99,517, Progressive Conservative
Tel: 905-731-8462
Fax: 905-731-2984
peter.shurman@pc.ola.org; peter.shurmanco@pc.ola.org
www.petershurman.com
Other Communications: Queen's Park Phone: 416-325-1415; Fax: 416-325-3810
Social Media: www.twitter.com/shurmanator,
www.facebook.com/pages/Peter-Shurman/136034076479824
Constituency Office
#204, 7330 Yonge St.
Thornhill, ON L4J 7Y7

Jagmeet Singh
Constituency: Bramalea-Gore-Malton *No. of Constituents:* 07,820, Liberal
Tel: 905-456-7125
contact@jagmeetsingh.ca
www.jagmeetsingh.ca
Social Media: www.twitter.com/JagmeetSingh,
www.facebook.com/jagmeetndp?sk=pe
Constituency Office
#18, 470 Chrysler Dr.
Brampton, ON L6S 0C1

Todd Smith
Constituency: Prince Edward-Hastings *No. of Constituents:* 86,304, Progressive Conservative
www.electtoddsmith.ca
Social Media: www.twitter.com/toddsmithpc
Constituency Office
#13, 97 Main St.
Picton, ON K0K 2T0

Hon. Charles Sousa
Constituency: Mississauga South *No. of Constituents:* 78,746, Liberal
Tel: 905-274-8228
Fax: 905-274-8552
csousa.mpp@liberal.ola.org; csousa.mpp.co@liberal.ola.org
www.charlessousa.ca
Other Communications: Queen's Park Phone: 416-327-6611; Fax: 416-327-6618
Social Media: www.twitter.com/SousaCharles,
www.facebook.com/people/Charles-Sousa/541270855,
www.linkedin.com/in/charlessousa

Constituency Office
#1 & 2, 120 Lakeshore Road W.
Mississauga, ON L5H 1E8
Peter Tabuns
Constituency: Toronto-Danforth *No. of Constituents:* 75,815, New Democratic Party
Tel: 416-461-0223
Fax: 416-461-9542
tabunsp-qp@ndp.on.ca; tabunsp-co@ndp.on.ca
www.petertabuns.ca
Other Communications: Queen's Park Phone: 416-325-3250; Fax: 416-325-3252
Constituency Office
421 Donlands Ave.
Toronto, ON M4J 3S2
Hon. Harinder S. Takhar
Constituency: Mississauga-Erindale *No. of Constituents:* 104,254, Liberal
Tel: 905-828-8989
Fax: 905-828-8670
htakhar.mpp@liberal.ola.org; htakhar.mpp.co@liberal.ola.org
www.hstakhar.com
Other Communications: Queen's Park Phone: 416-327-2333; Fax: 416-327-3790
Social Media: www.twitter.com/harindertakhar, www.facebook.com/HarinderTakharMPP, www.linkedin.com/pub/hon-harinder-takhar/34/a2a/58
Constituency Office
#4, 2160 Dunwin Dr.
Mississauga, ON L5L 5M8
Monique Taylor
Constituency: Hamilton Mountain *No. of Constituents:* 90,355, New Democratic Party
Tel: 905-546-0606
moniquetaylor@ontariondp.ca
www.moniquetaylor.ca
Social Media: www.twitter.com/MoniqueONDP, www.facebook.com/group.php?gid=151616944893613
Constitutency Office
#6, 841 Upper Wentworth St.
PO Box L9A 4W5
Hamilton, ON
Lisa Thompson
Constituency: Huron-Bruce *No. of Constituents:* 75,853, Liberal
Tel: 519-482-5630
Toll-free: 800-668-9320
Fax: 519-482-3149
www.lisathompson4huronbruce.ca
Constituency Office
PO Box 1794
Clinton, ON N0M 1L0
John Vanthof
Constituency: Timiskaming-Cochrane *No. of Constituents:* 50,554, New Democratic Party
Tel: 705-647-3940
www. johnvanthof.ca
Social Media: www.facebook.com/JohnVanthof
Constituency Office
19 Armstrong St.
PO Box 1799
Bill Walker
Constituency: Bruce-Grey-Owen Sound *No. of Constituents:* 75,809, Progressive Conservative
Tel: 519-371-2421
Toll-free: 800-461-2664
Fax: 519-371-0953
www.billwalkerpc.com
Other Communications: Queen's Park Phone: 416-325-6242; Fax: 416-325-6248
Social Media: www.twitter.votebillwalker, www.facebook.com/pages/Bill-Walker/231771823522746?sk=photos
Constituency Office
1047 - 2nd Ave. East
Owen Sound, ON N4K 2H8
Jim Wilson
Constituency: Simcoe-Grey *No. of Constituents:* 97,272, Progressive Conservative
Tel: 705-446-1090
Toll-free: 800-268-7542
Fax: 705-446-3397
jim.wilson@pc.ola.org; jim.wilsonco@pc.ola.org
www.jimwilsonmpp.com
Other Communications: Queen's Park Phone: 416-325-2069; Fax: 416-325-2079
Social Media: www.twitter.com/jwilsonmpp
Constituency Office
50 Hume St.
Collingwood, ON L9Y 1V2
Soo Wong
Constituency: Scarborough-Agincourt *No. of Constituents:* 73,583, Liberal
Tel: 416-297-6568
Fax: 416-297-4962
www.votesoowong.com
Other Communications: Queen's Park Phone: 416-325-3628; Fax: 416-314-7421
Social Media: www.twitter.com/votesoo
Constituency Office
#204, 4002 Sheppard Ave. East
Toronto, ON M1S 4R5
Hon. Kathleen Wynne
Constituency: Don Valley West *No. of Constituents:* 82,533, Liberal
Tel: 416-425-6777
Fax: 416-425-0350
kwynne.mpp@liberal.ola.org; kwynne.mpp.co@liberal.ola.org
www.kathleenwynne.onmpp.ca
Other Communications: Queen's Park Phone: 416-327-9200; Fax: 416-327-9188
Social Media: www.twitter.com/Kathleen_Wynne, www.facebook.com/kwynnempp, www.linkedin.com/in/kathleenwynne
Constituency Office
#101, 795 Eglinton Ave. East
Toronto, ON M4G 4E4
John Yakabuski
Constituency: Renfrew-Nipissing-Pembroke *No. of Constituents:* 74,191, Progressive Conservative
Tel: 613-735-6627
Fax: 613-735-6692
john.yakabuski@pc.ola.org; john.yakabuskico@pc.ola.org1
www.johnyakabuski.com
Other Communications: Queen's Park Phone: 416-325-2170; Fax: 416-325-2196
Social Media: www.twitter.com/JYakabuskiMPP
Constituency Office
84 Isabella St.
Pembroke, ON K8A 5S5
Jeff Yurek
Constituency: Elgin-Middlesex-London *No. of Constituents:* 80,858, Progressive Conservative
Tel: 519-631-0280
votejeff@yurek.com
www.jeffyurek.ca
Social Media: www.twitter.com/jeffreyyurek
Constituency Office
829 Talbot St.
St. Thomas, ON N5P 1E4
David Zimmer
Constituency: Willowdale *No. of Constituents:* 95,694, Liberal
Tel: 416-733-7878
Fax: 416-733-7709
dzimmer.mpp@liberal.ola.org; dzimmer.mpp.co@liberal.ola.org
www.davidzimmer.ca
Other Communications: Queen's Park Phone: 416-327-4516; Fax: 416-325-4175
Social Media: www.facebook.com/group.php?gid=81031428325
Constituency Office
#3, 5801 Yonge St.
Toronto, ON M2M 3T9
Toby Barrett
Constituency: Haldimand-Norfolk *No. of Constituents:* 78,030, Progressive Conservative
Tel: 519-428-0446
Fax: 519-428-0835
toby.barrett@pc.ola.org
www.tobybarrett.com
Other Communications: Queen's Park Phone: 416-325-8404; Fax: 416-325-8408
Social Media: www.twitter.com/tobybarretmpp
Constituency Office
39 Norfolk St. North
Simcoe, ON N3Y 3N6

Ontario Government Departments & Agencies

Ontario Ministry of Aboriginal Affairs / Ministère des Affaires autochtones

160 Bloor St. East, 4th & 9th Fl., Toronto, ON M7A 2E6
Tel: 416-326-4740
Fax: 416-326-4017
www.aboriginalaffairs.gov.on.ca

The Ministry operates with the following units: Office of the Deputy Minister of Aboriginal Affairs; Office of the Assistant Deputy Minister of Aboriginal Affairs; Policy & Relationships Branch; Ipperwash Response Team; Negotiations Branch; Legal Services Branch; Communications Branch; & the Business Services Unit.

Acts Administered:
English & Wabigoon River Systems Mercury Contamination Settlement Agreement Act

Minister, Hon. Kathleen Wynne
Tel: 416-325-5110
Fax: 416-314-2701
kwynne.mpp.co@liberal.ola.org

Deputy Minister, Lori Sterling
Tel: 416-314-1141
Fax: 416-314-1165
lori.sterling@ontario.ca

Parliamentary Assistant, David Zimmer
Tel: 416-733-7878
dzimmer.mpp.co@liberal.ola.org

Director, Communications Services, Greg Coleman
Tel: 416-314-5383
greg.coleman@ontario.ca

Director, Legal Services, Grant Wedge
Tel: 416-326-2372
grant.wedge@ontario.ca

Aboriginal Relations & Ministry Partnership Division

Tel: 416-326-4740
Fax: 416-314-2102

Assistant Deputy Minister, Deborah Richardson
Tel: 416-325-0304
deborah.richardson@ontario.ca
Director, Social & Education, Hanita Tiefenbach
Tel: 416-325-7032
hanita.tiefenbach@ontario.ca
Director, Resource & Economic Development, Pam Wheaton
Tel: 416-326-4053
pam.wheaton@ontario.ca

Negotiations & Reconciliation

Tel: 416-326-4740
Fax: 416-326-2361

The branch carries out the following responsibilities: researching & conducting land claim negotiations; managing & coordinating negotiations; representing the province for federally-led governance negotiations; & implementing settlements.
Assistant Deputy Minister, Doug Carr
Tel: 416-326-4741
doug.carr@ontario.ca
Director, David Didluck
Tel: 416-326-2839
Fax: 416-326-4017
david.didluck@ontario.ca
Director, Community Initiatives - Brantford/Toronto, Bruce Leslie
Tel: 519-720-9350
bruce.leslie@ontario.ca

Office of the Chief Administrative Officer - Corporate Management Division

Whitney Block, #6540, 99 Wellesley St. W., Toronto, ON M7A 1W3
Fax: 416-314-6091

Chief Administrative Officer, David Lynch
Tel: 416-314-1939
david.lynch@ontario.ca
Director, Strategic Human Resources, Pat Freistatter
Tel: 705-755-3131
pat.freistatter@ontario.ca
Director, Corporate Management, Carlene Jackson
Tel: 416-212-1633
carlene.jackson@ontario.ca

Office of the Chief Information Officer, Land & Resources I&IT Cluster

Whitney Block, #6601, 99 Wellesley St. W., Toronto, ON M7A 1W3
Fax: 416-314-6091

Chief Information Officer, Robert Hollis
Tel: 416-314-1528
robert.hollis@ontario.ca
Acting Director, Organizational Performance, Judy Tomarin
Tel: 416-212-7560
judy.tomarin@ontario.ca
Acting Manager, Business & Financial Services, Glenn Wetherall
Tel: 519-826-4769
glenn.wetherall@ontario.ca

Strategic Policy & Planning

160 Bloor St. E., 4th Fl., Toronto, ON M7A 2E6
Tel: 416-326-4743
Fax: 416-326-4777

The branch is engaged in the following key activities: developing & coordinating government-wide Aboriginal policy; providing corporate planning & policy advice on Aboriginal matters; & developing & maintaining positive relationships with Aboriginal leaders.
Assistant Deputy Minister, Bryan Kozman
Tel: 416-212-2302
bryan.cozman@ontario.ca
Director, Jonathan Lebi
Tel: 416-314-1607
jonathan.lebi@ontario.ca

Ontario Ministry of Agriculture, Food & Rural Affairs (OMAFRA)

Ontario Government Bldg., 1 Stone Rd. West, Guelph, ON N1G 4Y2

Tel: 519-826-3100
Toll-Free: 888-466-2372
www.omafra.gov.on.ca
Secondary Address: 77 Grenville St., 11th Fl.
Toronto, ON M5S 1B3 Canada

The ministry works in partnership with an industry that employs over 640,000 people & contributes over $25 billion annually to the provincial economy. The ministry plays a key role in bringing a strong agricultural & rural perspective to provincial policies. The ministry works with other ministries to resolve local economic issues & assists rural communities in retaining & attracting business. Staff at the ministry's Guelph headquarters & across the province provide a wide range of agri-food & rural economic development programs & services to clients.

Acts Administered:
AgriCorp Act
Agricultural & Horticultural Organizations Act
Agricultural Employees Protection Act 2002
Agricultural Lands Regulations
Agricultural Research Institute of Ontario Act
Agricultural Tile Drainage Installation Act
Animal Health Act
Animals for Research Act
Beef Cattle Marketing Act
Bees Act
Commodity Board Members Act
Commodity Boards & Marketing Agencies Act
Crop Insurance Act (Ontario)
Drainage Act
Farm Implements Act
Farm Products Container Act
Farm Products Grades & Sales Act
Farm Products Marketing Act
Farm Products Payments Act
Farm Registration & Farm Organizations Funding Act
Farming & Food Production Protection Act
Food Safety & Quality Act, 2001
Grains Act
Livestock & Livestock Products Act
Livestock Community Sales Act
Livestock Identification Act
Livestock Medicines Act
Milk Act
Ministry of Agriculture, Food & Rural Affairs Act
Ministry of Energy Act (sections dealing with the Ontario Ethanol Growth Fund program)
Nutrient Management Act, 2002
Ontario Agriculture Week Act
Ontario Food Terminal Act
Plant Diseases Act
Pounds Act
Protection of Livestock & Poultry from Dogs Act
Tile Drainage Act
Veterinarians Act
Weed Control Act

Minister, Hon. Ted McMeekin
Tel: 416-326-3074
Fax: 416-326-3083
tmcmeekin.mpp.co@liberal.ola.org

Deputy Minister, John Burke
Tel: 416-326-3101

Parliamentary Assistant, Grant Crack
Tel: 613-446-4010
gcrack.mpp.co@liberal.ola.org

Director, Communications, Diane Gumbs
Tel: 416-326-5196
diane.gumbs@ontario.ca

Director, Legal Services, Michael Brady
Tel: 519-826-3378
Fax: 519-826-3385
michael.p.brady@ontario.ca

Associated Agencies, Boards & Commissions:

• AGRICORP
1 Stone Rd. West, 3rd Fl.
PO Box 3660 Central
Guelph, ON N1H 8M4
Fax: 519-826-4118
Toll-free: 888-247-4999
cac@agricorp.com
www.agricorp.com
Responsible for delivering government & non-government priority products & services that assist Ontario's agri-food industry in managing risks. Since its inception, AGRICORP has developed a reputation for innovation, excellent customer service & reliable, cost-effective delivery

• Agricultural Research Institute of Ontario (ARIO)
1 Stone Rd. West, 2nd Fl.
Guelph, ON N1G 4Y2
Tel: 519-826-4199
Fax: 519-826-4211
The role of ARIO is to enquire into programs of research with respect to agriculture, veterinary medicine & consumer studies, select & recommend areas of research for the betterment of agriculture, veterinary medicine & consumer studies, & stimulate interest in research as a means of developing a high degree of efficiency in the production & marketing of agricultural products in Ontario.

• Agriculture, Food & Rural Affairs Tribunal
1 Stone Rd. West, 2nd Fl.
Guelph, ON N1G 4Y2
Tel: 519-826-3433
Fax: 519-826-4232
appeals.tribunal@omafra.gov.on.ca

• College of Veterinarians of Ontario
2106 Gordon St.
Guelph, ON N1L 1G6
Tel: 519-824-5600
Fax: 519-824-6497
Toll-free: 800-424-2856
inquiries@cvo.org
www.cvo.org

• Board of Negotiation
1 Stone Rd. West
Guelph, ON N1G 4Y2

• Grain Financial Protection Board
1 Stone Rd. West, 1st Fl. Northeast
PO Box 3660 Central
Guelph, ON N1H 8M4
Tel: 519-826-3949
Fax: 519-826-3367

• Livestock Financial Protection Board
1 Stone Rd. West, 5th Fl. Northwest
Guelph, ON N1G 4Y2
Tel: 519-826-3886
Fax: 519-826-4375

• Livestock Medicines Advisory Committee
1 Stone Rd. West, 3rd Fl. Northeast
Guelph, ON N1G 4Y2
Tel: 519-826-4110
Fax: 519-826-3254

• Normal Farm Practices Protection Board
1 Stone Rd. West, 3rd Fl.
Guelph, ON N1G 4Y2
Fax: 519-826-3259
Toll-free: 877-424-1300

• Ontario Farm Products Marketing Commission
1 Stone Rd. West, 5th Fl. Southwest
Guelph, ON N1G 4Y2
Tel: 519-826-4220
Fax: 519-826-3400

• Ontario Food Terminal Board
165 The Queensway
Toronto, ON M8Y 1H8
Tel: 416-259-5479
Fax: 416-259-4303
www.oftb.com

• Rural Economic Development (RED) Panel
1 Stone Rd. West, 4th Fl.
Guelph, ON N1G 4Y2
Fax: 519-826-4336
Toll-free: 888-588-4111
red.omafra@ontario.ca
www.ontario.ca/rural

Economic Development Division

Tel: 519-826-4304
Fax: 519-826-4416

Regional Offices
Central Region
Elora Resource Centre, #10, 6484 Wellington Rd. 7, Elora, ON N0B 1S0
East Region, Kemptville District Office
59 Ministry Dr., PO Box 2004, Kemptville, ON K0G 1J0
North Region
Caldwell Twp. Hall Bldg., Hwy. 64, PO Box 521, Verner, ON P0H 2M0
Southwest Region
London Resource Centre, 667 Exeter Rd., London, ON N6E 1L3

Food Safety & Environment Division

Tel: 519-826-4304
Fax: 519-826-4416

Assistant Deputy Minister, Dr. Dave Hope
Tel: 519-826-4301
Fax: 519-826-4416
dave.hope@ontario.ca

Director, Animal Health & Welfare, Dr. Jim Richardson
Tel: 519-826-3577
Fax: 519-826-4375
jim.richardson@ontario.ca

Director, Food Inspection Branch, Gavin Downing
Tel: 519-826-4366
Fax: 519-826-4375
gavin.downing@ontario.ca

Acting Director, Food Safety Programs, Gwen McBride
Tel: 519-826-3112
Fax: 519-826-4466
gwen.mcbride@ontario.ca

Director, Environmental Management, Clarence Haverson
Tel: 519-826-4975
Fax: 519-826-6611
clarence.haverson@ontario.ca

Acting Director, Animal Health & Welfare/ Office of the Chief Veterinarian for Ontario, Jim Richardson
Tel: 519-826-3577
jim.richardson@ontario.ca

Office of the Chief Information Officer, Land & Resources I&IT Cluster

Chief Information Officer, Robert Hollis
Tel: 416-314-1528
robert.hollis@ontario.ca

Acting Director, Organizational Performance, Judy Tomarin
Tel: 416-212-7560
judy.tomarin@ontario.ca

Manager, Business & Financial Management, Glenn Wetherall
Tel: 519-826-4769
glenn.wetherall@ontario.ca

Head, Service Management, Uwe Helmer
Tel: 519-826-5160
uwe.helmer@ontario.ca

Head, Strategy Information & Program Management, Doug Green
Tel: 519-826-3236
doug.greeen@ontario.ca

Policy Division

Tel: 519-826-4020
Fax: 519-826-3492

Responsible for the ministry's policy processes, the administration & delivery of several farm business risk management programs & the management of the ministry's strategic partnership with AGRICORP.

Assistant Deputy Minister, Dave Antle
Tel: 519-826-4151
Fax: 519-826-3492
dave.antle@ontario.ca

Director, Farm Finance, Tracy Dallaire
Tel: 519-826-3244
Fax: 519-826-3170
tracy.dallaire@ontario.ca

Director, Economic Development Policy, Thom Hagerty
Tel: 519-826-3918
thom.hagerty@ontario.ca

Director, Food Safety & Environmental Policy Branch, Rena Hubers
Tel: 519-826-3241
Fax: 519-826-3492
rena.hubers@ontario.ca

Director, Strategic Policy, George McCaw
Tel: 519-826-4002
george.mccaw@ontario.ca

Research & Corporate Services Division

1 Stone Road W., 2nd Fl. Northwest, Guelph, ON N1G 4Y2

Tel: 519-826-4551
Fax: 519-826-3390

Assistant Deputy Minister, Karen D. Chan
Tel: 519-826-6599
Fax: 519-826-3390
karen.chan@ontario.ca

Director, Strategic Business Unit, Jim Felker
Tel: 519-826-3739
jim.felker@ontario.ca

Director, Business Planning & Financial Management, Phil Cooke
Tel: 519-826-3336
phil.cooke@ontario.ca

Director, Business Services Branch, Shelly Gibson
Tel: 519-826-4698
shelley.gibson@ontario.ca

Director, Research & Innovation, Dr. Michael Toombs
Tel: 519-826-4172
Fax: 519-826-4211
michael.toombs@ontario.ca

Director, Financial Management, Lee-Ann Walker
Tel: 519-826-3336
Fax: 519-826-4130
leeann.walker@ontario.ca

Manager, French Language Services, Louise Gagnon
Tel: 416-212-4274
louise.gagnon@ontario.ca
Director, Internal Audit Services, Nancy Lavoie
Tel: 905-704-2870
Fax: 705-755-1599
nancy.lavoie@ontario.ca

Ontario Ministry of the Attorney General

McMurtry-Scott Bldg., 720 Bay St., 11th Fl., Toronto, ON M5G 2K1

Tel: 416-326-2220
Fax: 416-326-4007
Toll-Free: 800-518-7901
www.attorneygeneral.jus.gov.on.ca
TTY: 416-326-4012

Justice services are delivered to Ontarians by the Ministry of the Attorney General. The Ministry is engaged in the following activities: supporting victims of crime; providing justice support services to vulnerable people in the province; ensuring the availability of effective & efficient criminal, civil & family courts, plus related justice services; prosecuting crime; & giving legal advice & services to government.

Acts Administered:
Absconding Debtors Act
Absentees Act
Accumulations Act
Administration of Justice Act
Age of Majority & Accountability Act
Alcohol & Gaming Regulation & Public Protection Act (Part I)
Aliens' Real Property Act
Apology Act
Arbitration Act
Architects Act
Assessment Review Board Act
Bail Act
Barristers Act
Blind Persons' Rights Act
Bulk Sales Act
Business Records Protection Act
Certified General Accountants Act
Certified Management Accountants Act
Charities Accounting Act
Chartered Accountants Act
Child & Family Services Act (sec. 162-174)
Children's Law Reform Act
Civil Remedies Act
Class Proceedings Act
Commercial Mediation Act
Commissioners for Taking Affidavits Act
Compensation for Victims of Crime Act
Construction Lien Act
Conveyancing & Law of Property Act
Costs of Distress Act
Courts of Justice Act
Crown Administration of Estates Act
Crown Agency Act
Crown Attorneys Act
Crown Witnesses Act
Declarations of Death Act
Disorderly Houses Act
Dog Owners' Liability Act
Donation of Food Act
Education Act (sec. 57)
Election Act
Election Finances Act
Electoral System Referendum Act
Electronic Commerce Act
Employers & Employees Act
Enforcement of Judgement Conventions Act
Environmental Review Tribunal Act
Escheats Act
Estates Act
Estates Administration Act
Evidence Act
Execution Act
Executive Council Act
Expropriations Act
Family Law Act
Fines & Forfeitures Act
Fraudulent Conveyances Act
Frustrated Contracts Act
Gaming Control Act
Good Samaritan Act
Habeas Corpus Act
Hospitals & Charitable Institutions Inquiries Act
Human Rights Code
Inter-Provincial Summonses Act
Interjurisdictional Support Orders
International Commercial Arbitration Act
International Interests in Mobile Equipment Act (Aircraft Equipment)
International Sale of Goods Act
Judicial Review Procedure Act
Juries Act
Justices of the Peace Act
Law Society Act
Legal Aid Services Act
Legislation Act
Legislative Assembly Act
Libel & Slander Act
Lieutenant Governor Act
Limitations Act
Liquor Licence Act
Members' Integrity Act
Mercantile Law Amendment Act
Ministry of the Attorney General Act
Mortgages Act
Negligence Act
Notaries Act
Occupiers' Liability Act
Ombudsman Act
Ontario Association of Former Parliamentarians Act
Ontario Heritage Act
Ontario Municipal Board Act
Ontario Works Act (Part IV)
Parental Responsibility Act
Partition Act
Pawnbrokers Act
Perpetuities Act
Police Services Act (s. 113)
Powers of Attorney Act
Proceedings Against the Crown Act
Professional Engineers Act
Prohibiting Profiting from Recounting Crimes Act
Property & Civil Rights Act
Provincial Offences Act
Public Accounting Act
Public Authorities' Protection Act
Public Guardian & Trustee Act
Public Officers Act
Real Property Limitations Act
Reciprocal Enforcement of Judgements (U.K.) Act
Reciprocal Enforcement of Judgements Act
Religious Freedom Act
Religious Organizations' Lands Act
Representation Act
Rescuing Children from Sexual Exploitation Act (Parts III & IV)
Residential Tenancies Act (in part)
Revised Statutes Confirmation & Corrections Act
Safe Streets Act
Sale of Goods Act
Settled Estates Act
Settlement of International Investment Disputes Act
Short Forms of Leases Act
Solicitors Act
Statute of Frauds
Statutory Powers Procedure Act
Substitute Decisions Act
Succession Law Reform Act
Ticket Speculation Act
Time Act
Tobacco Damages & Health Care Costs Recovery
Transboundary Pollution Reciprocal Access Act
Trespass to Property Act
Trustee Act
Unconscionable Transactions Relief Act
Variation of Trusts Act
Vendors & Purchasers Act
Victims Bill of Rights Act
Wages Act
Warehouse Receipts Act

Attorney General, Hon. John Gerretsen
Tel: 416-326-2220
Toll-free: 800-518-7901
Fax: 416-326-4007
jgerretsen.mpp.co@liberal.ola.org
TTY: 416-326-4012

Deputy Attorney General, Murray Segal
Tel: 416-326-2640
Fax: 416-326-4018
Murray.Segal@ontario.ca

Parliamentary Assistant, Lorenzo Berardinetti
Tel: 416-261-9525
lberardinetti.mpp.co@liberal.ola.org

Acting Director, Communications, Marianne Summers
Tel: 416-326-2604
Fax: 416-326-4007
marianne.summers@ontario.ca

Associated Agencies, Boards & Commissions:

• Alcohol & Gaming Commission of Ontario
90 Sheppard Ave. East
Toronto, ON M2N 0A4
Tel: 416-326-8700
Fax: 416-326-5555
Toll-free: 800-522-2876
www.agco.on.ca

• Assessment Review Board
Eaton Tower
#1500, 655 Bay St.
Toronto, ON M5G 1E5
Tel: 416-212-6349
Fax: 416-314-3717
Toll-free: 866-448-2248
TTY: 877-849-2066
assessment.review.board@ontario.ca
www.arb.gov.on.ca

• Chief Inquiry Officer - Expropriations Act
McMurtry-Scott Bldg.
720 Bay St., 8th Fl.
Toronto, ON M7A 2S9
Tel: 416-314-2226

• Criminal Injuries Compensation Board
439 University Ave., 4th Fl.
Toronto, ON M5G 1Y8
Tel: 416-326-2900
Fax: 416-326-2883
Toll-free: 800-372-7463
info.cicb@ontario.ca
www.cicb.gov.on.ca
Other Communication: Victim Support Line: 1-888-579-2888

• Human Rights Tribunal of Ontario
655 Bay St., 14th Fl.
Toronto, ON M7A 2A3
Tel: 416-326-1312
Fax: 416-326-2027
Toll-free: 866-598-0322
TTY: 416-326-2027
hrto.tdpo@ontario.ca
www.hrto.ca
Other Communication: Toll-Free TTY: 1-866-607-1240

• Judicial Appointments Advisory Committee
McMurtry-Scott Bldg.
720 Bay St., 3rd Fl.
Toronto, ON M7A 2S9
Tel: 416-326-4060
Fax: 416-212-7316

• Legal Aid Ontario
#404, 375 University Ave.
Toronto, ON M5G 2G1
Tel: 416-979-1446
Fax: 416-979-8669
Toll-free: 800-668-8258
TTY: 416-598-8867
info@lao.on.ca
www.legalaid.on.ca
Other Communication: Toll-Free TTY: 1-866-641-8867

• Office for Victims of Crime
700 Bay St., 3rd Fl.
Toronto, ON M5G 1Z6
Tel: 416-326-1682
Fax: 416-326-4497
Toll-free: 887-435-7661
TTY: 416-325-9341

• Office of the Independent Police Review Director
655 Bay St., 10th Fl.
Toronto, ON M7A 2T4
Tel: 416-246-7071
Fax: 416-327-8332
Toll-free: 877-411-4773
TTY: 877-414-4773
www.oiprd.on.ca
Other Communication: Toll-Free Fax: 877-415-4773

• Ontario Human Rights Commission

• Ontario Municipal Board & Board of Negotiation
655 Bay St., 15th Fl.
Toronto, ON M5G 1E5
Tel: 416-326-6800
Fax: 416-326-5370
Toll-free: 866-887-8820
www.omb.gov.on.ca

• Social Justice Tribunals Ontario
40 Dundas St. West
Toronto, ON M7A 0A9
Tel: 416-212-8000
Fax: 416-212-8024

Corporate Services Management Division
Assistant Deputy Attorney General & Chief Admin. Officer, Dante Pontone
Tel: 416-326-9844
dante.pontone@ontario.ca
Director, Business & Fiscal Planning, Maureen Buckley
Tel: 416-326-4020

Fax: 416-326-4019
maureen.buckley@ontario.ca
Director, Human Resources Branch, Barbara Ross
Tel: 416-326-3283
Fax: 416-326-2298
barbara.ross@ontario.ca
Director, Facilities Management, Judy Stamp
Tel: 416-326-4033
Fax: 416-326-4029
judy.stamp@ontario.ca
Director, Diversity & Inclusion Office, Tom Fagan
Tel: 416-314-3590
thomas.fagan@ontario.ca
Director, Ontario Internal Audit, Justice Audit Service, David Horie
Tel: 705-329-6747
david.horie@ontario.ca

Court Services Division
Asst. Deputy Attorney General, Lynne Wagner
Tel: 416-326-2609
Fax: 416-326-2652
lynne.wagner@ontario.ca
Head, Business Solutions, Chris Walpole
Tel: 416-326-4267
Fax: 416-212-4981
chris.walpole@ontario.ca
Director, Family Policy & Programs, Anne Marie Predko
Tel: 416-326-7867
annemarie.predko@ontario.ca
Acting Director, Corporate Planning, Sheila Bristo
Tel: 416-314-4608
Fax: 416-326-1011
sheila.bristo@ontario.ca
Director, Criminal/POA Policy & Programs Branch, Diana Hunt
Tel: 416-326-2531
Fax: 416-326-1869
diana.hunt@ontario.ca
Central East
#201, 1091 Gorham St., Newmarket, ON L3Y 8X7
Tel: 905-836-5621
Fax: 905-836-5620
Acting Director, Court Operations, Sarina Kashak
Tel: 905-836-5484
Fax: 905-836-5620
sarina.kashak@ontario.ca
Central West
#518B, 45 Main St. East, Hamilton, ON L8N 2B7
Tel: 905-645-5333
Fax: 905-645-5375
Director, Court Operations, Joanne Spriet
Tel: 905-645-5333
Fax: 905-645-5375
joanne.spriet@ontario.ca
East
#100 - 343 Preston St., Ottawa, ON K1S 1N4
Tel: 613-239-1551
Fax: 613-239-1273
Director, Court Operations, Viviane Carpentier
Tel: 613-239-1597
viviane.carpentier@ontario.ca
Northeast
501, 159 Cedar St., Sudbury, ON P3E 6A5
Tel: 705-564-7675
Fax: 705-564-7664
Director, Court Operations, Robert Gordon
Tel: 807-343-2701
robert.gordon@ontario.ca
Northwest
277 Camelot St., Thunder Bay, ON P7A 4B3
Tel: 807-343-2747
Fax: 807-345-6383
Director, Court Operations, Robert Gordon
Tel: 807-343-2701
Fax: 807-345-6383
robert.gordon@ontario.ca
Toronto
#1601, 700 Bay St., Toronto, ON M5G 1Z6
Tel: 416-326-4249
Fax: 416-326-2073
Regional Director, Lynn Norris
Tel: 416-326-4250
Fax: 416-326-2073
lynn.norris@ontario.ca
West
80 Dundas St., Unit D, London, ON N6A 6A4
Tel: 519-660-3090
Fax: 519-660-3098
Director, Court Operations, Paul Langlois
Tel: 519-660-3094
paul.langlois@ontario.ca

Courts of Justice
Osgoode Hall, 130 Queen St. W., Toronto, ON M5H 2N5
Tel: 416-327-5020
Other Communication: Fax: 416-327-6256 (Appeal Scheduling), 416-327-5032 (Intake Office)

Criminal Law Division
McMurty-Scott Bldg., 720 Bay St., 6th fl., Toronto, ON M5G 2K1
Tel: 416-326-4656
Fax: 416-326-2063
Director, Criminal Law Policy Branch, Mary Nethery
Tel: 416-325-8663
mary.nethery@ontario.ca
Deputy Director, Crown Law Office - Criminal, John Corelli
Tel: 416-326-2618
john.corelli@ontario.ca
Deputy Director, Crown Law Office - Criminal, Rosella Cornaviera
Tel: 416-326-4616
rosella.cornaviera@ontario.ca
Deputy Director, Crown Law Office - Criminal, David Finley
Tel: 416-326-4587
david.finley@ontario.ca
Deputy Director, Crown Law Office - Criminal, Howard Leibovich
Tel: 416-326-2002
howard.leibovich@ontario.ca
Deputy Director, Crown Law Office - Criminal, Susan Reid
Tel: 416-326-2682
susan.reid@ontario.ca
Director, Divisional Planning & Administration, Stephanie Crawford
Tel: 416-326-2099
Fax: 416-326-2423
stephanie.crawford@ontario.ca
Acting Director, Law & Technology, Alexander Smith
Tel: 416-212-1166
alexander.smith@ontario.ca
Senior Advisor to the ADAG, Lisa Gold
Tel: 416-325-8597
lisa.gold@ontario.ca

Justice Technology Services
#300, 21 College St., Toronto, ON M5G 2B3

Legal Services Division
McMurty-Scott Bldg., 720 Bay St., 6th fl., Toronto, ON M5G 2K1
Tel: 416-326-0891
Fax: 416-326-6996
Acting Assistant Deputy Attorney General, Malliha Wilson
Tel: 416-326-2505
Fax: 416-326-6996
malliha.wilson@ontario.ca
Director, Constitutional Law, Michel Y. Hélie
Tel: 416-326-4454
Fax: 416-326-4015
michel.helie@ontario.ca
Director, Crown Law Office-Civil, Craig Slater
Tel: 416-326-4100
Fax: 416-326-4181
craig.slater@ontario.ca
Director, Legal Services Program Support Branch, Paula Konstantinidis
Tel: 416-326-4173
Fax: 416-314-7926
paula.konstantinidis@ontario.ca

Civil Remedies for Illicit Activities
77 Wellesley St. West, PO Box 333, Toronto, ON M7A 1N3
Tel: 416-212-0556
Fax: 416-314-3714
Legal Director, Jeff Simser
Tel: 416-326-4188
Fax: 416-314-3714
jeff.simser@ontario.ca

Legislative Counsel
Whitney Block, #3600, 99 Wellesley St. West, Toronto, ON M7A 1A2
Tel: 416-326-2841
Fax: 416-326-2806
Chief Legislative Counsel, Mark Spakowski
Tel: 416-326-2740
mark.spakowski@ontario.ca
Associate Chief Legislative Counsel, Cornelia Schuh
Tel: 416-326-2741
cornelia.schuch@ontario.ca
Director, French Legislative Services, Gerard Hernando
Tel: 416-326-2793
gerard.hernando@ontario.ca

Policy & Adjudicative Tribunals Division
McMurtry-Scott Bldg, 720 Bay St, 11th Fl., Toronto, ON M7A 2S9
Tel: 416-326-2500
Fax: 416-326-2699
Asst. Deputy Attorney General, Mark Leach
Tel: 416-326-2711
mark.leach@ontario.ca
Director, Corporate Policy & Agency Relations Branch, Martha Otton
Tel: 416-326-4932
martha.otton@ontario.ca
393 University Ave., 14th Fl.
Toronto, ON M5G 1W9 Canada
Director, Justice Policy Development Branch, Andrea Storm
Tel: 416-326-2482
595 Bay St., 8th Fl.
Toronto, ON M5G 2M6 Canada
Director, Special Investigations Unit, Ian Scott
Tel: 416-622-0748
ian.scott@ontario.ca

Victims & Vulnerable Persons Division
18 King St. E, 7th Fl., Toronto, ON M5C 1C4
Tel: 416-325-3265
Fax: 416-212-1091
Asst. Deputy Minister, Irwin Glasberg
Tel: 416-326-0190
irwin.glasberg@ontario.ca
Director, Programs & Community Development, Linda D. Haldenby
Tel: 416-326-2428
Fax: 416-212-1091
linda.d.haldenby@ontario.ca
Director, Policy & Program Development, Patricia Bishop
Tel: 416-325-3695
Fax: 416-212-1091
patricia.bishop@ontario.ca

Office of the Auditor General

Atrium on Bay, #1530, 20 Dundas St. West, PO Box 105, Toronto, ON M5G 2C2
Tel: 416-327-2381
Fax: 416-327-9862
comments@auditor.on.ca
www.auditor.on.ca
TTY: 416-327-6123

Auditor General, Jim R. McCarter
Tel: 416-327-1326
jim.mccarter@auditor.on.ca

Deputy Auditor General, Gary Peall
Tel: 416-327-1658
gary.peall@auditor.on.ca

Director, Crown Agencies (2) Portfolio, Laura Bell
Tel: 416-327-2377
laura.bell@auditor.on.ca

Director, Community, Social Services & Revenue Portfolio, Walter Bordne
Tel: 416-327-1329
walter.bordne@auditor.on.ca

Director, Public Accounts, Finance, Environment & Natural Resources Portfolio, Gus Chagani
Tel: 416-327-2395
gus.chagani@auditor.on.ca

Director, Education & Training Portfolio, Gerard Fitzmaurice
Tel: 416-327-1371
gerard.fitzmaurice@auditor.on.ca

Director, Health & Long-term Care Providers Portfolio, Susan Klein
Tel: 416-327-1668
susan.klein@auditor.on.ca

Director, Justice & Regulatory Portfolio, Vince Mazzone
Tel: 416-327-1669
vince.mazzone@auditor.on.ca

Director, Crown Agencies (1) Portfolio, John McDowell
Tel: 416-327-1656
john.mcdowell@auditor.on.ca

Manager, Transportation, Infrastructure & Municipal Affairs Portfolio, Kim Cho
Tel: 416-327-3059
kim.cho@auditor.on.ca

Ontario Ministry of Children & Youth Services

56 Wellesley St. West, 14th Fl., Toronto, ON M5S 2G3
Fax: 416-325-5191
Toll-Free: 866-821-7770
www.children.gov.on.ca
TTY: 800-387-5559

Working collaboratively with community partners, as well as the Ministries of Education, Health & Long-Term Care, Community & Social Services, Citizenship & Immigration, Culture, & Tourism & Recreation to integrate a number of Ontario's children & youth programs & services. By bringing these programs under one roof, this government is making children a top priority to give them the best start in life, to prepare youth to become productive adults, & to make it easier for families to get the services they need at all stages of a child's development.

Acts Administered:
British Home Child Day Act
Child & Family Services Act
Day Nurseries Act
Health Protection and Promotion Act
Intercountry Adoption Act, 1998
Ministry of Community and Social Services Act
Ministry of Correctional Services Act
Ontario Child Benefit Equivalent Act
Poverty Reduction Act
Provincial Advocate for Children & Youth Act
Rescuing Children from Sexual Exploitation Act

Minister, Hon. Eric Hoskins
Tel: 416-212-7432
Fax: 416-212-7431
ehoskins.mpp.co@liberal.ola.org

Deputy Minister, Alexander Bezzina
Tel: 416-212-2280
alexander.bezzina@ontario.ca

Parliamentary Assistant, Tracy MacCharles
Tel: 905-509-0336
tmaccharles.mpp.co@liberal.ola.org

Chief Information Officer, Children, Youth & Social Services, Corbin Kerr
Tel: 416-326-4330
Fax: 416-325-0266
corbin.kerr@ontario.ca

Director, Communications & Marketing Branch, Jean-Claude Camus
Tel: 416-326-3512
Fax: 416-325-5191
jean-claude.camus@ontario.ca

Director, Legal Services Branch, Diane Zimnica
Tel: 416-314-5173
Fax: 416-327-0568
diane.zimnica@ontario.ca

Provincial Advocate, Office of The Provincial Advocate for Children & Youth, Irwin Elman
Tel: 416-325-5989
Fax: 416-325-5681
irwin.elman@provincialadvocate.on.ca
Other Communications: URL: www.provincialadvocate.on.ca

Business Planning & Corporate Services
Assistant Deputy Minister, Lorraine Graham-Watson
Tel: 416-325-5588
lorraine.graham-watson@ontario.ca
Director, Capital & Accommodation Services, Angela James
Tel: 416-325-4600
angela.james@ontario.ca
Director, Emergency Management Program, Linda MacQueen
Tel: 416-327-3950
linda.macqueen@ontario.ca
Director, Financial Planning & Business Management, Martin Thumm
Tel: 416-325-5139
martin.thumm@ontario.ca
Director, Human Resources, Frank Caccia
Tel: 416-327-4753
frank.caccia@ontario.ca
Director, Internal Audit Services, David W. Johnston
Tel: 416-585-6550
david.w.johnston@ontario.ca

Children, Youth & Social Services Cluster, I&IT
56 Wellesley St. W, 14th Fl., Toronto, ON M5S 2S3
Tel: 416-327-4865
Fax: 416-314-1862

Policy Development & Program Design
56 Wellesley St. W, 14th Fl., Toronto, ON M5S 2S3
Tel: 416-327-4865
Fax: 416-314-1862

Assistant Deputy Minister, Aryeh Gitterman
Tel: 416-212-1961
Fax: 416-314-1862
aryeh.gitterman@ontario.ca
Senior Adviser, Pamela Loring
Tel: 416-314-5857
Fax: 416-314-1862
pamela.loring@ontario.ca
Director, Specialized Services & Supports Branch, Susan Capling
Tel: 416-325-5331
Fax: 416-325-8330
susan.capling@ontario.ca
Director, Children & Youth at Risk, Marian Mlakar
Tel: 416-212-5205
Fax: 416-212-2021
marian.mlakar@ontario.ca
Director, Child Welfare Secretariat, Jennifer Morris
Tel: 416-325-3560
jennifer.morris@ontario.ca

Service Delivery Division
Assistant Deputy Minister, Nancy Matthews
Tel: 416-212-3141
nancy.matthews@ontario.ca
Director, Client Services, Greg Douglas
Tel: 416-327-2531
greg.douglas@ontario.ca
Director, Resource Management, Sally Johnson
Tel: 416-325-5510
sally.johnson@ontario.ca

Strategic Policy & Planning Division
56 Wellesley St., 14th Fl., Toronto, ON M5S 2S3
Tel: 416-327-9460
Fax: 416-314-1862

Assistant Deputy Minister, Darryl Sturtevant
Tel: 416-327-9481
Fax: 416-314-1862
darryl.sturtevant@ontario.ca
Director, Early Learning & Child Development Branch, Julie Mathien
Tel: 416-325-5874
Fax: 416-326-0478
Director, Research & Outcome Measurement, Anne Premi
Tel: 416-325-5944
Fax: 416-327-0570
anne.premi@ontario.ca
Director, Strategic Planning, Rachel Simeon
Tel: 416-314-1489
Fax: 416-326-3140
rachel.simeon@ontario.ca

Youth Justice Services
56 Wellesley St. W, 14th fl., Toronto, ON M5S 2S3
Tel: 416-314-3502
Fax: 416-327-0478

Assistant Deputy Minister, JoAnn Miller-Reid
Tel: 416-327-9910
joann.miller-reid@ontario.ca
Director, Operational Support, John Scarfo
Tel: 416-212-7609
Fax: 416-327-2418
john.scarfo@ontario.ca
Director, Planning & Program Development, Trish Moloughney
Tel: 416-212-7610
trish.moloughney@ontario.ca
Director, Information Management Unit, Cindy Cowper
Tel: 705-494-3117
cindy.cowper@ontario.ca

Toronto
477 Mount Pleasant Rd., 3rd Fl., Toronto, ON M7A 1G1
Tel: 416-325-0500
Fax: 416-325-0541
Toll-Free: 416-325-3600

Central East
#1, 17310 Yonge St., Newmarket, ON L3Y 7R8
Tel: 905-868-8900

Central West
#200, 6733 Mississauga Rd., Mississauga, ON L5N 6J5
Tel: 905-567-7177
Fax: 905-567-3215
Toll-Free: 877-832-2818

Eastern
347 Preston St., Ottawa, ON K1S 2T7
Tel: 613-234-1188
Fax: 613-787-5252
Toll-Free: 800-267-5111

Hamilton Niagara
Ellen Fairclough Bldg., 119 King St., Hamilton, ON L8P 4Y7
Tel: 905-521-7280
Fax: 905-546-8277
TTY: 905-546-8276

North East
621 Main St., North Bay, ON P1B 2V6
Tel: 705-474-3540
Fax: 705-474-5815
Toll-Free: 800-461-6977
TTY: 705-474-7665

Northern
#1002, 199 Larch St., Sudbury, ON P3E 5P9
Tel: 705-564-6699
Fax: 705-564-3099
Toll-Free: 800-265-1222

South East
11 Beechgrove Lane, Kingston, ON K7M 9A6
Tel: 613-545-0539
Fax: 613-536-7272
Toll-Free: 800-646-3209
TTY: 613-536-7304

South West
#203, 217 York St., PO Box 5217, London, ON N6A 5R1
Tel: 519-438-5111
Fax: 519-672-9510
Toll-Free: 800-265-4197
TTY: 519-663-5276

Ontario Ministry of Citizenship & Immigration

400 University Ave., 6th Fl., Toronto, ON M7A 2R9
Tel: 416-327-2422
Fax: 416-314-4965
Toll-Free: 800-267-7329
www.citizenship.gov.on.ca
TTY: 416-326-0148
Other Communication: Information URL: ontarioimmigration.ca

Acts Administered:
Fair Access to Regulated Professions Act
Holocaust Memorial Day Act
Holodomor Memorial Day Act
Ministry of Citizenship & Culture Act (in part)
Ontario Human Rights Code
Remembrance Day Observance Act
Vimy Ridge Day Act

Minister, Hon. Charles Sousa
Tel: 416-325-6200
Fax: 416-325-6195
csousa.mpp.co@liberal.ola.org
TTY: 888-335-6611

Deputy Minister, Chisanga Puta-Chekwe
Tel: 416-325-6220
chisanga.puta-chekwe@ontario.ca

Parliamentary Assistant, Teresa Piruzza
Tel: 519-977-7191
tpiruzza.mpp.ca@liberal.ola.org

Director, Communications, Deborah Swain
Tel: 416-314-7606
Fax: 416-314-4965
deborah.swain@ontario.ca

Assistant Director & Manager, Issues, Media Relations & Program Communications - Program Communications Unit, Mary Dowding-Paré
Tel: 416-314-7230
mary.dowding-pare@ontario.ca

Associated Agencies, Boards & Commissions:
• Office of the Fairness Commissioner
#1201, 595 Bay St.
Toronto, ON M7A 2B4
Tel: 416-325-9380
Fax: 416-326-6081
Toll-free: 877-727-5365
ofc@ontario.ca

Citizenship & Immigration Division
400 University Ave., 3rd Fl., Toronto, ON M7A 2R9
Tel: 416-314-7541
Fax: 416-314-7599

Assistant Deputy Minister, Marsha Barnes
Tel: 416-325-6278
marsha.barnes@ontario.ca
Director, Immigration Programs, Catherine Finlay
Tel: 416-212-4290
Fax: 416-314-7307
catherine.finlay@ontario.ca
Director, Immigration Policy, Alice Young
Tel: 416-326-8595
Fax: 416-314-7307
alice.young@ontario.ca

Office of the Chief Information Officer
Mowat Block, 900 Bay St. 3rd FL, Toronto, ON M7A 1L2
Tel: 416-325-4598

Assistant Deputy Minister, Soussan Tabari
Tel: 416-326-8216
tabari.soussan@ontario.ca
Director, Technology & Business Solutions, Sanaul Haque
Tel: 416-585-6746
sanaul.haque@ontario.ca

Project Planning Coordinator, Business and Financial Services, Dianna Robinson
Tel: 416-325-2287
dianna.robinson@ontario.ca

Ontario Internal Audit, Culture & Innovation Audit Service Team
College Park, 777 Bay St., 25th Fl., Toronto, ON M5G 2E5
Tel: 416-326-0800
Fax: 416-326-1712
Director, Charles Meehan
Tel: 416-325-5983
charles.meehan@ontario.ca

Regional & Corporate Services Division
400 University Ave., 2nd fl., Toronto, ON M7A 2R9
Tel: 416-314-7311
Fax: 416-314-7313
Assistant Deputy Minister & Chief Administration Officer, Robert Montgomery
Tel: 416-314-7311
Fax: 416-314-7313
robert.m.montgomery@ontario.ca
Chief Information Officer, French Language Services, Education & Community Services Cluster, Dominique Guillaumant
Tel: 416-326-9749
dominique.guillaumant@ontario.ca
Director, Human Resources, Cindy Lam
Tel: 416-212-2783
Fax: 416-325-6371
cindy.lam@ontario.ca
Director, Regional Services, Brian Lemiere
Tel: 416-314-6680
Fax: 416-314-6686
brian.lemire@ontario.ca
Director, Finance & Business Management Council, Heather Taylor
Tel: 416-325-6135
heather.taylor@ontario.ca
Bracebridge
15 Dominion St., Bracebridge, ON P1L 2E7
Tel: 705-646-0641
Fax: 705-646-0544
Hamilton
119 King St. West, 14th Fl., Hamilton, ON L8P 4Y7
Tel: 905-521-7459
Fax: 905-521-7398
Toll-Free: 877-998-9927
Regional Advisor, Lorraine Hogan
Tel: 905-521-7459
lorraine.hogan@ontario.ca
Huntsville
207 Main St. West, Huntsville, ON P1H 1Z9
Tel: 705-789-4448
Fax: 705-789-9533
Regional Advisor, Larry Curley
Tel: 705-789-4448
larry.curley@ontario.ca
Midhurst
2284 Nursery Rd., Midhurst, ON L0L 1X0
Fax: 705-739-6697
Toll-Free: 877-395-4105
Regional Advisor (Bilingual), Judy Adams
Tel: 705-739-6800
judy.adams@ontario.ca
Regional Advisor, Catherine Campbell
Tel: 705-737-3010
catherine.campbell@ontario.ca
Toronto
180 Dundas St. West, 5th Fl., Toronto, ON
Tel: 416-314-6044
Fax: 416-314-2024
Toll-Free: 877-395-4105
Regional Advisor, Freba Shahsamand
Tel: 416-314-1990
freba.shahsamand@ontario.ca
Regional Advisor, Roya Alaei
Tel: 416-212-6504
roya.alaei@ontario.ca
Regional Advisor, Carol Law
Tel: 416-325-6542
carol.law@ontario.ca
Dryden
Ontario Government Bldg., 479 Government Rd., PO Box 3000, Dryden, ON P8N 3B3
Fax: 807-223-8502
Toll-Free: 800-525-8785
Regional Advisor, Natasha Lovenuk Markham
Tel: 807-223-8682
natasha.lovenukmarkham@ontario.ca
Kenora
810 Robertson St., Kenora, ON P9N 4J4
Tel: 807-468-2540
Fax: 807-468-2788
Toll-Free: 800-465-1108
North Bay
447 McKeown Ave., North Bay, ON P1B 9S9
Tel: 705-494-4182
Fax: 705-494-4069
Toll-Free: 800-461-9563
Sault Ste. Marie
Roberta Bondar Place, #200, 70 Foster Dr., Sault Ste Marie, ON P6A 6V8
Tel: 705-945-5885
Fax: 705-945-5931
Toll-Free: 800-461-7284
Sioux Lookout
62 Queen St., PO Box 267, Sioux Lookout, ON P8T 1A3
Fax: 807-737-3419
Toll-Free: 800-529-6619
Sudbury
Ontario Government Bldg., #401, 199 Larch St., Sudbury, ON P3E 5P9
Tel: 705-564-3035
Fax: 705-564-3043
Toll-Free: 800-461-4004
Thunder Bay
#334, 435 James St. South, Thunder Bay, ON P7E 6S7
Tel: 807-475-1683
Fax: 807-475-1297
Toll-Free: 800-465-6861
Regional Advisor, Marlene Wright
Tel: 807-475-1658
marlene.wright@ontario.ca
Timmins
Ontario Government Complex, Hwy. 101 East, PO Box 3085, South Porcupine, ON P0N 1H0
Tel: 705-235-1550
Fax: 705-235-1553
Toll-Free: 800-305-4442
Kingston
Ontario Government Bldg., Beechgrove Complex, 51 Heakes Lane, Kingston, ON K7M 9B1
Tel: 613-531-5580
Fax: 613-531-5585
Toll-Free: 800-293-7543
Ottawa
347 Preston St., 4th Fl., Ottawa, ON K1S 3J4
Tel: 613-742-3360
Fax: 613-742-5300
Toll-Free: 800-267-9340
Manager, Valerie Andrews
Tel: 613-742-3366
valerie.andrews@ontario.ca
Peterborough
Robinson Pl., South Tower, 300 Water St., 2nd Fl., Peterborough, ON K9J 8M5
Tel: 705-755-2624
Fax: 705-755-2631
Toll-Free: 800-461-7629
Kitchener
#405, 30 Duke St. West, Kitchener, ON N2H 3W5
Tel: 519-578-3600
Fax: 519-578-1632
Toll-Free: 800-265-2189
Regional Advisor, Sonja Erstic
Tel: 519-571-6117
sonja.erstic@ontario.ca
London
659 Exeter Rd., 2nd Fl., London, ON N6A 1L3
Fax: 519-873-4061
Toll-Free: 800-265-4730
St Catharines
301 St Paul St., 9th Fl., St Catharines, ON L2R 7R4
Fax: 905-704-3955
Toll-Free: 800-263-2441
Walkerton
Bldg. 3, 220 Trillum Crt., Walkerton, ON N0G 2V0
Fax: 519-881-0525
Toll-Free: 800-265-5520
Windsor
221 Mill St., Windsor, ON N9C 2R1
Fax: 519-973-1414
Toll-Free: 800-265-1330

Ontario Ministry of Community & Social Services (MCSS)

Hepburn Block, 80 Grosvenor St., 6th Fl., Toronto, ON M7A 1E9
Tel: 416-325-5666
Fax: 416-325-5172
Toll-Free: 888-789-4199
www.mcss.gov.on.ca
TTY: 800-387-5559
Other Communication: Welfare Fraud Hotline:|1-800-394-7867
Acts Administered:
Accessibility for Ontarians with Disabilities Act
Child & Family Services Act
Deaf-Blind Awareness Month Act
District Social Services Administration Boards Act
Family Responsibility & Support Arrears Enforcement Act
Indian Welfare Services Act
Ministry of Community & Social Services Act
Ontarians with Disabilities Act
Ontario Disability Support Program Act, 1997
Ontario Works Act, 1997
Services & Supports to Promote the Social Inclusion of Persons with Developmental Disabilities Act
Social Work & Social Service Work Act, 1998
Soldiers' Aid Commission Act

Minister & Government House Leader, Hon. John Milloy
Tel: 416-325-5225
Fax: 416-325-3347
jmilloy.mpp.co@liberal.ola.org

Deputy Minister, Marguerite Rappolt
Tel: 416-325-5225
Fax: 416-325-5240
marguerite.rappolt@ontario.ca

Parliamentary Assistant, Bas Balkissoon
Tel: 416-297-5040
bbalkissoon.mpp.co@liberal.ola.org

Director, Communications & Marketing, Karin Dillabough
Tel: 416-325-5203
karin.dillabough@ontario.ca

Director, Legal Services, Diane Zimnica
Tel: 416-314-5173
diane.zimnica@ontario.ca

Associated Agencies, Boards & Commissions:
• Social Benefits Tribunal
1075 Bay St., 7th Fl.
Toronto, ON M5S 2B1
Tel: 416-326-0978
Fax: 416-325-5135
Toll-free: 800-753-3895
TTY: 416-325-3408
www.sbt.gov.on.ca
Other Communication: Toll-Free TTY: 1-800-268-7095

Accessibility Directorate of Ontario
#601, 777 Bay St., Toronto, ON M7A 2J4
Tel: 416-326-0207
Fax: 416-325-5615
Toll-Free: 866-515-2025
TTY: 800-268-7095
Asst. Deputy Minister, Ellen Waxman
Tel: 416-325-5247
Fax: 416-326-9725
Director, Outreach & Compliance, Alfred Spencer
Tel: 416-314-7289
Fax: 416-326-9725
alfred.spencer@ontario.ca
Director, Standards, Policy & Coordination, Brenda Lewis
Tel: 416-325-5586
Fax: 416-327-9725
brenda.lewis@ontario.ca

Business Planning & Corporate Services Division
Hepburn Block, 80 Grosvenor St., 6th Fl., Toronto, ON M7A 1E9
Tel: 416-325-5595
Fax: 416-325-5615
Assistant Deputy Minister, Lorraine Graham-Watson
Tel: 416-325-5588
Fax: 416-325-5615
lorraine.graham-watson@ontario.ca
Director, Human Resources, Frank Caccia
Tel: 416-327-4753
Fax: 416-325-0561
frank.caccia@ontario.ca
Director, Capital & Accommodation Services, Angela James
Tel: 416-325-4600
Fax: 416-325-5397
angela.james@ontario.ca
Director, Ontario Internal Audit, David W. Johnston
Tel: 416-585-6550
david.w.johnston@ontario.ca
Director, Financial Planning & Business Management Branch, Martin Thumm
Tel: 416-325-5139
martin.thumm@ontario.ca

Family Responsibility Office
1201 Wilson Ave., PO Box 220, Toronto, ON M3M 3A3
Fax: 416-240-2402
Assistant Deputy Minister, Bohodar Rubashewsky
Tel: 416-240-2477
bohar.rubashewsky@ontario.ca

Chief Information Officer, Children, Youth & Social Services Cluster, Corbin Kerr
Tel: 416-326-4330
Fax: 416-325-0266
corbin.kerr@ontario.ca

Operations Division
Hepburn Block, 80 Grosvenor St., 6th Fl., Toronto, ON M7A 1E9
Tel: 416-325-5581
Fax: 416-325-5432
Other Communication: Client Information & Support Services: 416-325-5766; 1-800-665-6129

Assistant Deputy Minister, David Zuccato
Tel: 416-325-5579
Fax: 416-325-5432
david.zuccato@ontario.ca
Director, Social Assistance & Municipal Operations, Maxine Daley
Tel: 416-212-1246
maxine.daley@ontario.ca
Director, Controllership & Accountability, Sandy Henderson
Tel: 416-325-4401
sandy.henderson@ontario.ca
Director, Developmental Services Implementation Project Office, Linda Henry
Tel: 416-438-5111 ext: 317
linda.henry@ontario.ca
Director, Services & Supports Branch, Nancy Lytle
Tel: 416-325-5446
nancy.lytle@ontario.ca

Regional Offices
Regional Offices
Central East
#1, 17310 Yonge St., Newmarket, ON L3Y 7R8
Tel: 905-868-8900
Fax: 905-895-4330
Toll-Free: 877-669-6658
TTY: 905-715-7759

Regional Director, Claudine Cousins
Tel: 905-952-1871
claudine.cousins@ontario.ca
Central West
#200, 6733 Mississauga Rd., Mississauga, ON L5N 6J5
Tel: 905-567-7177
Fax: 905-567-3215
Toll-Free: 877-832-2818
TTY: 905-567-3219
Other Communication: French Phone: 905-567-7177
Regional Director, Vince Tedesco
Tel: 905-567-7177 ext: 310
vince.tedesco@ontario.ca
Eastern
347 Preston St., 2nd & 3rd fl., Ottawa, ON K1S 3H8
Tel: 613-234-1188
Fax: 613-787-3990
Toll-Free: 800-267-5111

Regional Director, Suzanne Gagnon
Tel: 613-787-3962
suzanne.gagnon@ontario.ca
Hamilton Niagara
Ellen Fairclough bldg., 119 King St. West, 7th Fl., Hamilton, ON L8P 4Y7
Tel: 905-521-7280
Fax: 905-546-8277
TTY: 866-221-2229

Regional Director, Sandra Datars Bere
Tel: 905-521-7844
Northern
#1002, 199 Larch St., Sudbury, ON P3E 5P9
Tel: 705-564-6699
Fax: 705-564-3099
Toll-Free: 800-265-1222

Regional Director, June Kelloway-Tarrant
Tel: 807-223-2241
North East
621 Main St. West, North Bay, ON P1B 2V6
Tel: 705-474-3540
Fax: 705-474-5815
Toll-Free: 800-461-6977
TTY: 705-474-7665

Regional Director, Monique Legault
Tel: 705-474-3540 ext: 200
monique.legault@ontario.ca
South East
11 Beechgrove Lane, Kingston, ON K7M 9A6
Tel: 613-545-0539
Fax: 613-536-7272
Toll-Free: 800-646-3209
TTY: 613-536-7304

Executive Assistant/Project Manager, Mary-Anne Baun
Tel: 613-536-7262
mary-anne.baun@ontario.ca

South West
#203, 217 York St., PO Box 5217, London, ON N6A 5R1
Tel: 519-483-5111
Fax: 519-672-9510
Toll-Free: 800-265-4197
TTY: 519-663-5276

Regional Director, Peter Steckenreiter
Tel: 519-438-5111 ext: 313
Toronto
477 Mount Pleasant Rd., 3rd Fl., Toronto, ON M7A 1G1
Tel: 416-325-0500
Fax: 416-325-0541
TTY: 416-325-3600

Regional Director, Richard K. Jackson
Tel: 416-325-0536
Fax: 416-325-0541
richard.k.jackson@ontario.ca

Social Policy Development Division
Hepburn Block, 80 Grosvenor St, 6th fl., Toronto, ON M7A 1E9
Tel: 416-325-5421
Fax: 416-325-9408

Assistant Deputy Minister, David Carter-Whitney
Tel: 416-325-3592
Fax: 416-325-9408
david.carter-whitney@ontario.ca
Director, Policy Research & Analysis, Peter Amenta
Tel: 416-212-6274
Fax: 416-325-8764
peter.amenta@ontario.ca
Director, Planning & Strategic Policy, Erin Hannah
Tel: 416-325-5550
erin.hannah@ontario.ca
Director, Community & Developmental Services, Carol Latimer
Tel: 416-325-5359
Fax: 416-325-8865
carol.latimer@ontario.ca
Director, Ontario Disabilities Support Program, Patti Redmond
Tel: 416-314-1122
Fax: 416-326-1735
patti.redmond@ontario.ca
Acting Director, Ontario Works, Tanya Vrooman
Tel: 416-325-1107
tanya.vrooman@ontario.ca
Director, ODSP Modernization Team, Susan Waring
Tel: 416-326-3302
Fax: 416-325-8865
susan.waring@ontario.ca

Ontario Ministry of Community Safety & Correctional Services

George Drew Bldg., 25 Grosvenor St., 18th Fl., Toronto, ON M7A 1Y6
Tel: 416-326-5000
Fax: 416-326-0498
Toll-Free: 866-517-0571
mcscs.feedback@ontario.ca
www.mcscs.jus.gov.on.ca
TTY: 416-326-5511
Other Communication: TTY Toll Free: 1-866-517-0572

The Ministry ensures that communities across the province are protected by safe, effective & accountable law enforcement and public safety systems. General responsibilities of the ministry are as follows: correctional services; public safety & security; & policing services.

Acts Administered:
Ammunition Regulation Act, 1994
Anatomy Act
Christopher's Law (Sex Offender Registry), 2000
Coroners Act
Emergency Management & Civil Protection Act
Fire Protection & Prevention Act, 1997
Firefighters' Memorial Day Act
Imitation Firearms Regulation Act
Interprovincial Policing Act, 2009
Mandatory Blood Testing Act
Mandatory Gunshot Wounds Reporting Act
Ministry of Correctional Services Act
Ministry of the Solicitor General Act
Ontario Society for the Prevention of Cruelty to Animals Act
Police Services Act
Private Security & Investigative Services Act, 2005
Public Works Protection Act

Minister, Hon. Madeleine Meilleur
Tel: 416-325-0408
Fax: 416-325-6067
mmeilleur.mpp.co@liberal.ola.org

Parliamentary Assistant, Soo Wong
Tel: 416-297-6568
swong.mpp.co@liberal.ola.org

Deputy Minister, Community Safety, Ian Davidson
Tel: 416-326-5060
ian.davidson@ontario.ca

Deputy Minister, Correctional Services, Jay Hope
Tel: 416-327-9734
jay.hope@ontario.ca

Acting Director, Communications, Debbie Conrad
Tel: 416-326-5004
Fax: 416-326-3200
debbie.conrad@ontario.ca

Assistant Director, Strategic Communications, Stuart McGetrick
Tel: 416-326-5008
stuart.mcgetrick@ontario.ca

Commissioner, Community Safety, Dan Hefkey
Tel: 416-212-7656
dan.hefkey@ontario.ca

Commissioner, Ontario Provincial Police, Chris D. Lewis
Tel: 705-329-6199
chris.d.lewis@ontario.ca
Lincoln M. Alexander Bldg.
777 Memorial Ave., 3rd Fl.
Orillia, ON L3V 7V3

Chief Coroner for Ontario, Dr. Andrew McCallum
Tel: 416-314-4008
andrew.mccallum@ontario.ca

Deputy Chief Coroner, Dr. Bonita Marie Bengert
Tel: 416-314-6808
bonita.porter@ontario.ca

Chief Forensic Pathologist for Ontario, Dr. Michael Pollanen
Tel: 416-314-4040
michael.pollanen@ontario.ca
Coroners Bldg.
26 Grenville St.
Toronto, ON M7A 2G9

Chief, Emergency Management Ontario, Allison J. Stuart
Tel: 416-314-6186
allison.j.stuart2@ontario.ca
77 Wellesley St. W.
PO Box 222
Toronto, ON M7A 1N3

Fire Marshal of Ontario, Ted Wieclawek
Tel: 416-325-3101
ted.wieclawek@ontario.ca

Associated Agencies, Boards & Commissions:
• Animal Care Review Board
77 Grenville St., 8th Fl.
Toronto, ON M5S 1B3
Tel: 416-314-3509
Fax: 416-314-3518
• Death Investigation Oversight Council
George Drew Bldg.
25 Grosvenor St., 1st Fl.
Toronto, ON M7A 1Y6
Tel: 416-212-4041
dioc@ontario.ca
www.dioc.gov.on.ca
• Fire Safety Commission
Place Nouveau Bldg.
5775 Yonge St., 7th Fl.
Toronto, ON M2M 4J1
Tel: 416-325-3100
Fax: 416-314-1217
• Ontario Civilian Police Commission (OCPC)
250 Dundas St. West, 6th Fl.
Toronto, ON M7A 2T3
Tel: 416-314-3004
Fax: 416-314-0198
Toll-free: 888-515-5005
www.ocpc.ca
Other Communication: Complaints (GTA): 416-326-1189; Toll-Free Fax: 1-888-311-7555
• Ontario Parole Board
#1803, 415 Yonge St.
Toronto, ON M5B 2E7
Tel: 416-325-4480
Fax: 416-325-4485
Toll-free: 888-579-2888
www.operb.gov.on.ca

• Ontario Police Arbitration Commission
George Drew Bldg.
25 Grosvenor St., 1st Fl.
Toronto, ON M7A 1Y6
Tel: 416-314-3520
Fax: 416-314-3522
www.policearbitration.on.ca

Community Services
150 Dufferin Ave., London, ON N6A 5N6
Assistant Deputy Minister, Marg Welch
Tel: 519-661-1773
marg.welch@ontario.ca

Corporate Services
George Drew bldg., 25 Grosvenor St., 13th fl., Toronto, ON M7A 1Y6
Tel: 416-325-3445
Fax: 416-325-3465
Assistant Deputy Minister & Chief Administration Officer, Allan Gunn
Tel: 416-325-9208
Fax: 416-326-3149
allan.gunn@ontario.ca
Director, Human Resources, Jane Albright
Tel: 416-212-3555
Fax: 416-314-5559
jane.albright@ontario.ca
Director, Internal Audit, Justice Audit Services, David Horie
Tel: 705-329-6747
david.horie@ontario.ca
Acting Director, Facilities, Peter Kaftarian
Tel: 416-314-6683
Fax: 416-327-1470
peter.kaftarian@ontario.ca
Director, Business & Financial Planning, Shawn Lawson
Tel: 416-326-1016
Fax: 416-325-3465
shawn.lawson@ontario.ca

Correctional Services
Assistant Deputy Minister, Adult Community Corrections, Marg Welch
Tel: 519-661-1773
marg.welch@ontario.ca
Assistant Deputy Minister, Adult Institutional Services, Steven F. Small
Tel: 416-327-9992
Fax: 416-314-6669
steve.small@ontario.ca
Director, Management & Operational Support, Lynn Kenn
Tel: 416-327-9918
Fax: 416-314-5987
lynn.kenn@ontario.ca
Director, Strategic & Operational Initiatives, Wendy Love
Tel: 416-327-2329
Fax: 416-314-5987
wendy.love@ontario.ca

Regional Offices
Central Region
Other Communication: Community Services: phone 416-212-6714, fax 416-327-4468; Institutional Services: phone 905-279-6997, fax 905-279-6710
Regional Director, Institutional Services, Mike Conry
Tel: 905-279-6366
mike.conry@ontario.ca
Regional Director, Community Services, David Mitchell
Tel: 416-212-6708
david.mitchell@ontario.ca
Deputy Regional Director, Institutional Services, Rose Buhagiar
Tel: 416-325-8605
rose.buhagiar@ontario.ca
Deputy Regional Director, Institutional Services, Gary Calverley
Tel: 905-279-6375
gary.calverley@ontario.ca
Deputy Regional Director, Community Services, Allar Viinamae
Tel: 416-314-8379
allar.viinamae@ontario.ca
Acting Deputy Regional Director, Community Services, Winston Wong
Tel: 416-327-4448
winston.wong@ontario.ca

Institutional Services
George Drew Bldg., 17th Fl., Toronto, ON M7A 1Y6
Tel: 416-326-6950
Fax: 416-326-1104
Assistant Deputy Minister, Steven F. Small
Tel: 416-327-9992
steve.small@ontario.ca
Eastern Region
25 Heakes Lane, Kingston, ON K7M 9B1
Tel: 613-536-7350
Other Communication: Fax: 613-531-8496 (Community Services), 613-544-6460 (Institutional Services)
Regional Director, Community Services, Peter Lesperance
Tel: 613-536-7390
peter.lesperance@ontario.ca
Regional Director, Institutional Services, Marilyn Tomkinson
Tel: 613-536-7353
marilyn.tomkinson@ontario.ca
Deputy Regional Director, Institutional Services, Kevin T. Bell
Tel: 613-536-7358
kevin.t.bell@ontario.ca
Acting Deputy Regional Director, Community Services, Michael Lawless
Tel: 613-536-7366
michael.lawless@ontario.ca
Deputy Regional Director, Community Services, Lori Potter
Tel: 613-536-7360
lori.potter@ontario.ca
Northern Region
200 First Ave. W., 4th Fl., North Bay, ON P1B 3B9
Other Communication: Institutional Services: phone 705-494-3430, fax 705-494-3435; Community Services: phone 807-343-7521 (Thunder Bay), fax 705-494-3459
Regional Director, Institutional Services, Kathy Klinger
Tel: 807-468-2999
Regional Director, Community Services, Mary-Jo Knappett
Tel: 705-494-3645
maryjo.knappett@ontario.ca
Acting Deputy Regional Director, Institutional Services, John McFarlane
Tel: 705-494-3359
john.mcfarlane@ontario.ca
Deputy Regional Director, Community Services, Martin O'Grady
Tel: 705-739-6480 ext: 219
martin.ogrady@ontario.ca
Acting Deputy Regional Director, Institutional Services, Daryl Pitfield
Tel: 705-494-3725
daryl.pitfield@ontario.ca
Deputy Regional Director, Institutional Services, Dan Smith
Tel: 519-881-3442 ext: 201
daniel.smith@ontario.ca
Western Region
#704, 150 Dufferin Ave., London, N6A 5N6
Tel: 519-675-7757
Fax: 519-679-0699
Regional Director, Institutional Services, David Hatt
Tel: 519-661-1693
david.hatt@ontario.ca
Regional Director, Community Services, Emelie Milloy
Tel: 519-661-1694
emelie.milloy@ontario.ca
Acting Deputy Regional Director, Community Services, Michelle Amlin
Tel: 519-675-7080
michelle.amlin2@ontario.ca
Acting Deputy Regional Director, Institutional Services, Christina Danylchenko
Tel: 519-661-6178
christina.danylchenko@ontario.ca
Deputy Regional Director, Institutional Services, Barry McDonnell
Tel: 519-661-6661
barry.mcdonnell@ontario.ca
Acting Deputy Regional Director, Community Services, Barb Forbes
Tel: 519-661-1688
barb.forbes@ontario.ca

Justice Technology Services
#300, 21 College St, Toronto, ON M5G 2B3
Tel: 416-326-6950
Fax: 416-326-1104
Assistant Deputy Minister & Chief Information Officer, John DiMarco
Tel: 416-326-6954
Fax: 416-326-1104
john.dimarco@ontario.ca
Manager, I&IT Security, Gregory Wilson
Tel: 416-212-0602
gregory.wilson@ontario.ca
Head, Court Business Solutions Branch, Chris Walpole
Tel: 416-326-4267
chris.walpole@ontario.ca
Head, Technology Solutions, Sandy Mannering
Tel: 705-494-3226
sandy.mannering@ontario.ca

Legal Services
#501, 655 Bay St., Toronto, ON M7A 0A8
Director, Denise Dwyer
Tel: 416-326-4108
denise.dwyer@ontario.ca

Organizational Effectiveness
George Drew Bldg., 25 Grosvenor St., 17th Fl., Toronto, ON M7A 1Y6
Assistant Deputy Minister, Steve Small
Tel: 416-212-5025
steve.small@ontario.ca

Policy & Strategic Planning
George Drew Bldg., 25 Grosvenor St., 9th Fl., Toronto, ON M7A 1Y6
Assistant Deputy Minister, Karen Maxwell
Tel: 416-314-8789

Public Safety
George Drew Bldg., 25 Grosvenor St., 12th Fl., Toronto, ON M7A 2H3
Assistant Deputy Minister, Glenn Murray
Tel: 416-325-3454
Project Director, Rudy Gheysen
Tel: 519-873-4269
rudy.gheysen@ontario.ca
Project Director, Fay Patey
Tel: 416-314-3015
fay.patey@ontario.ca
Director, Forensic Sciences, Analytical Laboratory Council, Dr. Ray Prime
Tel: 416-314-3224
ray.prime@ontario.ca
Acting Director, Police Support Services, Dr. Stephen Waldie
Tel: 416-325-3132
stephen.waldie@ontario.ca

Ontario Ministry of Consumer Services

Mowat Block, 900 Bay St., 6th Fl., Toronto, ON M7A 1L2
Tel: 416-327-8300
Fax: 416-326-1947
Toll-Free: 866-665-0662
infomcs@ontario.ca
www.sse.gov.on.ca
TTY: 877-666-6545
Other Communication: Consumer Protection Branch Phone: 416-326-8800; Fax: 416-326-8665; TTY: 416-229-6086; Email: consumer@ontario.ca

The Ministry seeks to educate, protect & serve consumers in Ontario by maintaining a fair, safe & informed marketplace; providing modern information services; & regulating practices that serve the interests of Ontarians.

Acts Administered:
Apportionment Act
Arthur Wishart Act (Franchise Disclosure)
Assignments & Preferences Act
Athletics Control Act
Bailiffs Act
Business Corporations Act (in part)
Business Names Act (in part)
Business Regulation Reform Act (in part)
Cemeteries Act (Revised)
Collection Agencies Act
Collision Repair Standards Act
Condominium Act (in part)
Consumer Protection Act
Consumer Reporting Act
Corporations Act (in part)
Corporations Information Act (in part)
Debt Collectors Act
Discriminatory Business Practices Act
Electricity Act (in part)
Electronic Registration Act (in part)
Extra-Provincial Corporations Act (in part)
Factors Act
Film Classification Act
Funeral Directors & Establishments Act
Funeral, Burial & Cremation Services Act
Horse Riding Safety Act
Limited Partnerships Act
Ministry of Consumer & Business Services Act
Motor Vehicle Dealers Act, 2002
Not-for-Profit Corporations Act (in part)
Ontario New Home Warranties Plan Act
Paperback & Periodical Distributors Act
Partnerships Act
Payday Loans Act
Personal Property Security Act
Real Estate & Business Brokers Act
Repair & Storage Liens Act (in part)
Residential Complex Sales Representation Act
Retail Business Holidays Act
Safety & Consumer Statutes Administration Act
Securities Transfer Act
Technical Standards & Safety Act
Travel Industry Act
Vinters Quality Alliance Act
Wine Content & Labelling Act

Minister, Hon. Margarett Best
Tel: 416-327-8300

Fax: 416-326-1947
mbest.mpp.co@liberal.ola.org

Deputy Minister, George Ross
Tel: 416-327-8342
Fax: 416-314-7167
george.ross@ontario.ca

Parliamentary Assistant, Amrit Mangat
Tel: 905-696-0367
amangat.mpp.co@liberal.ola.org

Director, Legal Services, James Girling
Tel: 416-212-4273
james.girling@ontario.ca

Director, Communications, Cindy Greeniaus
Tel: 416-326-7208
Fax: 416-326-7445
cindy.greeniaus@ontario.ca

Director, Internal Audit, Culture & Innovation Audit Service, Charles Meehan
Tel: 416-325-5983
Fax: 416-326-1712
charles.meehan@ontario.ca

Associated Agencies, Boards & Commissions:
• Ontario Film Review Board
#101B, 4950 Yonge St.
Toronto, ON M1N 6K1
Tel: 416-314-2626
Fax: 416-314-3632
www.ofrb.gov.on.ca

Corporate Services Division
Hearst Block, 900 Bay St., 7th Fl., Toronto, ON M7A 2E1
Tel: 416-325-6486
Fax: 416-325-6392

Assistant Deputy Minister & Chief Administrative Officer, David Clifford
Tel: 416-325-6600
david.clifford@ontario.ca
Director, Business Planning & Finance, Robert Burns
Tel: 416-327-1137
Fax: 416-327-4236
robert.burns@ontario.ca
Director, Strategic Human Resources Business Unit, Dan Keating
Tel: 416-325-6598
Fax: 416-325-6715
dan.keating@ontario.ca
Director, Service Management & Facilities, Isolina Kuzminski
Tel: 416-325-9366
Fax: 416-325-1118
isolina.kuzminski@ontario.ca

Policy & Consumer Protection Services Division
College Park, 777 Bay St., 5th Fl., Toronto, ON M7A 2J3
Tel: 416-326-8578
Fax: 416-325-6192

Assistant Deputy Minister, Frank Denton
Tel: 416-326-2826
frank.denton@ontario.ca
Director, Consumer Policy & Liaison, David Brezer
Tel: 416-326-8868
david.brezer@ontario.ca
Director, Consumer Protection, Barbara Duckitt
Tel: 416-326-8598
barbara.duckitt@ontario.ca
Director, Public Safety, Nicole Stewart
Tel: 416-326-8877
nicole.stewart@ontario.ca

Ontario Ministry of Economic Development & Innovation

Hearst Block, 900 Bay St., 8th Fl., Toronto, ON M7A 2E1
Tel: 416-325-6666
Fax: 416-325-6688
Toll-Free: 866-668-4249
info@edt.gov.on.ca
www.mri.gov.on.ca
TTY: 416-325-4402

Promotes economic development & job creation in Ontario by creating a climate for business to prosper & eliminate red tape as well as stimulating trade. This Ministry markets the province as a desirable place to live, work, invest & raise a family. It works with its private sector partners to ensure that its core responsibilities of employment & business development, investment & trade continue to help Ontario businesses compete globally; contribute to a highly-skilled, well-educated workforce; & generate prosperity for all Ontarians. In Northern Ontario, the Ministry is represented by the Northern Development Division of the Ministry of Northern Development & Mines.

Acts Administered:
Development Corporations Act
Dissolution of Inactive Corporations Act
Idea Corporation Act
Ministry of Industry, Trade & Technology Act
Ontario Capital Growth Corporation Act
Research Foundation Act
Water Opportunities Act

Minister, Hon. Brad Duguid
Tel: 416-325-6900
Fax: 416-325-6918
bduguid.mpp.co@liberal.ola.org

Deputy Minister, Wendy Tilford
Tel: 416-325-6927
wendy.tilford@ontario.ca

Parliamentary Assistant, Monte Kwinter
Tel: 416-325-0036
mkwinter.mpp.co@liberal.ola.org

Director, Communications Branch, Clare Barnett
Tel: 416-325-8058
clare.barnett@ontario.ca

Acting Director, Legal Services Branch, Andrew Macdonald
Tel: 416-212-8392
andrew.macdonald@ontario.ca

Associated Agencies, Boards & Commissions:
• Ontario Capital Growth Corporation
#1701, 393 University Ave.
Toronto, ON M5G 1E6
Tel: 416-325-6874
Fax: 416-212-0794
Toll-free: 877-422-5818
www.ocgc.gov.on.ca
The OCGC was established by the Ontario Capital Growth Corporation Act, 2008. The Corporation's main focus is the management of the Government of Ontario's interests in the Ontario Venture Capital Fund LP and the Ontario Emerging Technologies Fund.

Corporate Services Division
Hearst Block, 900 Bay St., 7th fl., Toronto, ON M7A 2E1
Tel: 416-325-6486
Fax: 416-325-6392

Assistant Deputy Minister & Chief Executive Officer, David Clifford
Tel: 416-325-6600
david.clifford@ontario.ca
Director, Business Planning & Finance Branch, Robert Burns
Tel: 416-327-1137
robert.burns@ontario.ca
Director, Strategic Human Resources Business Unit, Dan Keating
Tel: 416-325-6598
dan.keating@ontario.ca
Director, Service Management & Facilities Branch, Isolina Kuzminski
Tel: 416-325-9366
isolina.kuzminski@ontario.ca

Research, Commercialization & Entrepreneurship Division
56 Wellesley St. West, 11th Fl., Toronto, ON M7A 2E7
Tel: 416-314-1163
Fax: 416-314-4344

Acting Assistant Deputy Minister, Bill Mantel
Tel: 416-327-2889
bill.mantel@ontario.ca
Director, Commercialization Branch, George Cadete
Tel: 416-314-0670
Fax: 416-314-0680
george.cadete@ontario.ca
Manager, Access to Capital & Business Development Secretariat, Maxx-Phillippe Hollott
Tel: 416-325-4899
Maxx-Phillippe.Hollott@ontario.ca
Director, Entrepreneurship Branch, Sam Boonstra
Tel: 416-314-3809
sam.boonstra@ontario.ca
Director, Research Branch, Allison Barr
Tel: 416-212-6990
allison.barr@ontario.ca

Trade & Marketing Division
Hearst Block, 900 Bay St., 5th fl., Toronto, ON M7A 2E1
Tel: 416-325-9802
Fax: 416-325-5617

Assistant Deputy Minister, Cameron Sinclair
Tel: 416-325-9801
cameron.sinclair@ontario.ca
Director, International Trade Branch, Hope Jaglowitz
Tel: 416-325-6515
hope.jaglowitz@ontario.ca
Director, International Representation & Strategies Branch, Guy Poirier
Tel: 416-325-6752
guy.poirier@ontario.ca
Acting Director, Marketing Branch, Margaret Steeves
Tel: 416-325-6690
margaret.steeves@ontario.ca
Acting Director, Access to Capital & Business Development Branch, Marie Larose
Tel: 416-327-4430
marie.larose@ontario.ca
Acting Director, Direct Marketing & Lead Generation Branch, Trisha Grant
Tel: 416-326-8886
trisha.grant@ontario.ca

Investment & Industry Division
Hearst Block, 900 Bay St., 5th fl., Toronto, ON M7A 2E1
Tel: 416-212-0864
Fax: 416-212-3658

Assistant Deputy Minister, Tony LaMantia
Tel: 416-325-6623
tony.lamantia@ontario.ca
Director, Business Advisory Services Branch, Brian Love
Tel: 416-325-6522
brian.love@ontario.ca
Director, Science, Technology & Services Branch, Richard Kikuta
Tel: 416-212-7469
richard.kikuta@ontario.ca
Manager, Business Immigration, Ramneet Aujla
Tel: 416-325-1462
ramneet.aujla@ontario.ca
Acting Director, Manufacturing Investment Branch, Trish Grant
Tel: 416-325-6758
trisha.grant@ontario.ca
Director, Regional Economic Development & Coordination Branch, Reed Barrett
Tel: 416-325-9897
reed.barrett@ontario.ca

Ontario—Open for Business
#700-375 University Ave., Toronto, ON M5G 2J5
Tel: 416-326-7206
Fax: 416-212-3288

Assistant Deputy Minister, Katherine Hewson
Tel: 416-212-3283
katherine.hewson@ontario.ca
Acting Director, Sunil Johal
Tel: 416-314-5525
sunil.johal@ontario.ca

Small & Medium Enterprise Division
56 Wellesley St. W., Toronto, ON M7A 2E7
Fax: 416-326-5154

Policy & Strategy Division
Hearst Block, 900 Bay St., 3rd Fl., Toronto, ON M7A 2E7
Tel: 416-212-6653
Fax: 416-326-6393

Assistant Deputy Minister, John Whitehead
Tel: 416-325-4655
john.whitehead@ontario.ca
Director, Trade Policy Branch, Katherine McGuire
Tel: 416-325-6930
katherine.mcguire@ontario.ca
Director, Strategic Policy Branch, Steve Romanyshyn
Tel: 416-325-8554
steve.romanyshyn@ontario.ca
Director, Science & Technology Branch, Elaine Leung
Tel: 416-314-5744
elaine.leung@ontario.ca
Director, SME Policy & Outreach Branch, Allison Rickaby
Tel: 416-212-1823
allison.rickaby@ontario.ca
Acting Director, Strategic Planning & Policy Branch, Ryan Lock
Tel: 416-326-6237
ryan.lock@ontario.ca

Ontario Ministry of Education

Mowat Block, 900 Bay St., 22nd. Fl., Toronto, ON M7A 1L2
Tel: 416-325-2929
Fax: 416-325-2934
Toll-Free: 800-387-5514
info@edu.gov.on.ca
www.edu.gov.on.ca
TTY: 500-263-2892

Acts Administered:
Day Nurseries Act
Early Childhood Educators Act
Education Act
Education Quality & Accountability Office Act, 1996
Fairness for Parents & Employees Act (Teachers' Withdrawal of Services), 1997
Ministry of Community & Social Services Act

Ontario College of Teachers Act, 1996
Ontario Educational Communications Authority Act
Ontario French-Language Educational Communications Authority Act
Ontario Institute for Studies in Education Repeal Act, 1996
Ontario School Trustees' Council Act
Ottawa-Carleton French-Language School Board Transferred Employees Act
Provincial Schools Negotiations Act
Sabrina's Law
School Trust Conveyances Act
Teachers' Pension Act
Teaching Profession Act

Minister, Hon. Laurel Broten
Tel: 613-325-2600
Fax: 416-325-2608
ldombrowsky.mpp.co@liberal.ola.org

Deputy Minister, Kevin Costante
Tel: 416-325-2600
kevin.costante@ontario.ca

Parliamentary Assistant, Bob Delaney
Tel: 905-569-1643
bdelaney.mpp.co@liberal.ola.org

Chief Information Officer, Soussan Tabari
Tel: 416-326-8216
Fax: 416-325-8371
soussan.tabari@ontario.ca

Director, Communications, Murray Leaning
Tel: 416-325-2742
Fax: 416-212-4158
murray.leaning@ontario.ca
Mowat Block
900 Bay St., 14th Fl.
Toronto, ON M7A 1L2 Canada

Associated Agencies, Boards & Commissions:

• Education Quality & Accountability Office (EQAO)
#1200, 2 Carlton St.
Toronto, ON M5B 2M9
Tel: 416-314-0146
Fax: 416-325-2956
Toll-free: 888-327-7377
www.eqao.com

• Languages of Instruction Commission of Ontario
Mowat Block
900 Bay St., 8th Fl.
Toronto, ON M7A 1L2
Tel: 416-314-3500
Fax: 416-325-2979

• Minister's Advisory Council on Special Education
900 Bay St., 18th Fl.
Toronto, ON M7A 1L2
Tel: 416-314-2333
Fax: 416-314-0637
Toll-free: 877-699-5431
macse@ontario.ca
www.edu.gov.on.ca/eng/general/abcs/acse/acse_eng.html

• Ontario Educational Communications Authority (TVO)
2180 Yonge St.
PO Box 200 Q
Toronto, ON M4T 2T1
Tel: 416-484-2600
Toll-free: 800-613-0513
www.tvo.org

• Provincial Schools Authority
255 Ontario St. South
Milton, ON L9T 2M5
Tel: 905-878-2851
TTY: 905-878-8405

Corporate Management & Services Division
Mowat Block, #342, 900 Bay St., Toronto, ON M7A 1L2
Tel: 416-325-2772
Fax: 416-325-2778

Chief Administrative Officer & Assistant Deputy Minister, David Fulford
Tel: 416-325-2773
david.fulford@ontario.ca

Director, Legal Services, John Calcott
Tel: 416-325-2399
Fax: 416-325-2410
john.calcott@ontario.ca

Director, Strategic Human Resources Branch, Sandra Diprospero
Tel: 416-325-4511
Fax: 416-327-9043
sandra.diprospero@ontario.ca

Director, Corporate Finance & Services Branch, Dasha Hubschmann
Tel: 416-325-1822
Fax: 416-325-1835
dasha.hubschmann@ontario.ca

Director, Internal Audit Services, Warren McCay
Tel: 416-212-4814
Fax: 416-325-1120
warren.mccay@ontario.ca

Early Learning Division
Mowat Block, 900 Bay St., 24th Fl., Toronto, ON M7A 1L2
Tel: 416-212-4714
Fax: 416-314-7836

Assistant Deputy Minister, Jim Grieve
Tel: 416-314-9393
jim.grieve@ontario.ca

Director, Early Learning & Child Care Policy & Program Branch, Rupert Gordon
Tel: 416-314-8241
rupert.gordon@ontario.ca

Director, Early Learning & Child Care Implementation Branch, Pam Musson
Tel: 416-314-8192
pam.musson@ontario.ca

Director, Child Care Quality Assurance & Licensing Branch, Jill Vienneau
Tel: 416-314-2190
jill.vienneau@ontario.ca

Elementary/Secondary Business & Finance Division
Mowat Block, 900 Bay St., 20th fl., Toronto, ON M7A 1L2
Tel: 416-325-6127
Fax: 416-325-9560

Assistant Deputy Minister, Gabriel Sékaly
Tel: 416-325-6127
Fax: 416-325-9560
gabriel.sekaly@ontario.ca

Director, Financial Analysis & Accountability Branch, Andrew Davis
Tel: 416-314-3711
Fax: 416-325-2007
andrew.davis@ontario.ca

Director, School Business Support Branch, Cheri Hayward
Tel: 416-327-7503
Fax: 416-212-3990
cheri.hayward@ontario.ca

Acting Director, Capital Policy Branch, Grant Osborn
Tel: 416-325-1705
Fax: 416-326-9959
grant.osborn@ontario.ca

Director, Education Finance Branch, Grant Osborne
grant.osborne@ontario.ca

Director, Capital Programs Branch, Nancy Whynot
Tel: 416-325-4030
Fax: 416-325-4024
nancy.whynot@ontario.ca

French Language, Aboriginal Learning & Research Division
Mowat Block, 900 Bay St., 22nd fl., Toronto, ON M7A 1L2
Tel: 416-325-2132
Fax: 416-327-1182

Assistant Deputy Minister, Raymond Theberge
Tel: 416-325-2132
Fax: 416-327-1182
raymond.theberge@ontario.ca

Director, Aboriginal Education Office, Alayne Bigwin
Tel: 416-325-8561
alayne.bigwin@ontario.ca

Director, Education Statistics & Analysis Branch, Taddesse Haile
Tel: 416-325-9122
taddesse.haile@ontario.ca

Acting Director, Education Research & Evaluation Strategy Branch, Doris McWhorter
Tel: 416-314-3819
doris.mcwhorter@ontario.ca

Director, French Language Education Policy & Programs, Ginette Plourde
Tel: 416-327-9072
Fax: 416-325-2156
ginette.plourde@ontario.ca

Director, Field Services, Kathy Verduyn
Tel: 416-325-2588
kathy.verduyn@ontario.ca

Instruction & Leadership Development Division
Mowat Block, 900 Bay St., 13th fl., Toronto, ON M7A 1L2
Tel: 416-314-3664
Fax: 416-325-7019

Assistant Deputy Minister, Barry Pervin
Tel: 416-325-2411
Fax: 416-325-7019
barry.pervin@ontario.ca

Director, Teaching Policy & Standards, Paul Anthony
Tel: 416-325-7744
Fax: 416-326-1113
paul.anthony@ontario.ca

Director, Learning Environment Branch, Marg Connor
Tel: 416-325-7645
Fax: 416-325-2664
marg.connor@ontario.ca

Director, Leadership Development Branch, Bruce Drewett
Tel: 416-325-1079
Fax: 416-325-7019
bruce.drewett@ontario.ca

Director, Inclusive Education Branch, Ruth Flynn
Tel: 416-326-7597
Fax: 416-325-7019
ruth.flynn@ontario.ca

Director, Labour Relations & Governance Branch, Margot Trevelyan
Tel: 416-325-2826
Fax: 416-325-7247
margot.trevelyan@ontario.ca

Learning & Curriculum Division
Mowat Block, 900 Bay st., 22nd fl., Toronto, ON M7A 1L2
Tel: 416-325-2135
Fax: 416-327-1182

Assistant Deputy Minister, Grant Clarke
Tel: 416-314-5788
Fax: 416-327-1182
grant.clarke@ontario.ca

Director, Curriculum & Assessment Policy Branch, Sue Durst
Tel: 416-325-2576
Fax: 416-325-2575
sue.durst@ontario.ca

Director, Special Education Policy & Programs Branch, Barry Finlay
Tel: 416-325-2889
Fax: 416-314-0637
barry.finlay@ontario.ca

Director, Provincial Schools Branch, Nancy Sanders
Tel: 905-878-2851 ext: 214
Fax: 905-878-1354
nancy.sanders@ontario.ca

Student Achievement Division
Mowat Block, 900 Bay St., 10th Fl., Toronto, ON M7A 1L2

Chief Student Achievement Officer of Ontario & Assistant Deputy Minister, Mary Jean Gallagher
Tel: 416-325-9964
maryjean.gallagher@ontario.ca

Senior Executive Officer, Literacy & Numeracy Secretariat, Roderick Benns
Tel: 416-325-9389
roderick.benns@ontario.ca

Director, Implementation and Training Unit, Rob J. Andrews
Tel: 416-326-9369
Rob.J.Andrews@ontario.ca

Director, Student Success/Learning to 18 Strategic Policy Branch, Richard Franz
Tel: 416-314-1410
richard.franz@ontario.ca

Elections Ontario

51 Rolark Dr., Toronto, ON M1R 3B1
Tel: 416-326-6300
Fax: 416-326-6200
Toll-Free: 888-668-8683
info@elections.on.ca
www.elections.on.ca
TTY: 866-479-1118
Other Communication: Election Finances 416-325-9401 or 866-566-9066; Fax: 416-325-9466

Acts Administered:
Election Act
Elections Finance Act

Chief Electoral Officer, Greg Essensa
Tel: 416-326-6383
Fax: 416-326-6201
greg.essensa@elections.on.ca

Deputy Chief Electoral Officer, Loren A. Wells
Tel: 416-326-6387
Fax: 416-326-6201
loren.wells@elections.on.ca

Chief Operating Officer, Michael Stockfish
Tel: 416-325-9450
Fax: 416-326-6201
michael.stockfish@elections.on.ca

Communications
Lalitha Flach
Tel: 416-326-5688
lalitha.flach@elections.on.ca

Corporate Services
Director, Lisa Forte
Tel: 416-326-4394
lisa.forte@elections.on.ca

Election Finances
Director, Jonathan Batty
Tel: 416-212-3367
jonathan.batty@elections.on.ca

Electoral Event Services
Director, Barbara McEwan
Tel: 416-326-1971
barbara.mcewan@elections.on.ca

Technology Services
Andrew Herd
Tel: 416-326-1972
andrew.herd@elections.on.ca

Ontario Ministry of Energy

Hearst Block, 900 Bay St., 4th Fl., Toronto, ON M7A 2E1
Tel: 416-327-6758
Fax: 416-325-8440
Toll-Free: 888-668-4636
write2us@ontario.ca
www.energy.gov.on.ca
TTY: 800-239-4224

The Ministry of Energy's responsibility is to ensure that Ontario's electricity system functions at the highest level of reliability & productivity. The electricity system lies at the heart of the economy & way of life & by ensuring the system remains reliable, efficient & secure, the ministry is making sure Ontario remains one of the best places in the world in which to live, work, invest & raise a family. The Ministry of Energy is also focused on promoting ingenuity & innovation in the energy sector. By encouraging the development of new ideas & technologies it is helping to make Ontario a world leader in the global energy market. Protecting the environment is also a top priority for the Ministry. Developing renewable sources of energy, cleaner forms of fuel, as well as fostering a conservation culture, are all cornerstones of the Ministry's vision for Ontario's electricity future.

Acts Administered:
Electricity Act
Energy Consumer Protection Act
Green Energy Act
Hydro One Inc. Directors & Officers Act, 2002
Ministry of Energy Act, 2011
Ontario Clean Energy Benefit Act
Ontario Energy Board Act
Power Corporation Act
Toronto District Heating Corporation Act

Minister, Hon. Chris Bentley
Tel: 416-327-6758
Fax: 416-327-6754
bduguid.mpp.co@liberal.ola.org

Deputy Minister, David Lindsay
Tel: 416-327-6734
david.lindsay@ontario.ca

Parliamentary Assistant, Reza Moridi
Tel: 905-884-8080
rmoridi.mpp.co@liberal.ola.org

Director, Legal Services Branch, Halyna Perun
Tel: 416-325-6681
Fax: 416-325-1781
halyna.perun2@ontario.ca

Director, Communications Branch, John Whytock
Tel: 416-327-6541
Fax: 416-326-3947
john.whytock@ontario.ca

Associated Agencies, Boards & Commissions:
- **Hydro One Inc.**
- **Independent Electricity System Operator**
- **Ontario Energy Board**
#2700, 2300 Yonge St.
Toronto, ON M4P 1E4
Tel: 416-481-1967
Fax: 416-440-7656
Toll-free: 888-632-6273
www.ontarioenergyboard.ca
- **Ontario Power Authority**
#1600, 120 Adelaide St. West
Toronto, ON M5H 1T1
Tel: 416-967-7474
Fax: 416-967-1947
Toll-free: 800-797-9604
info@powerauthority.on.ca
www.powerauthority.on.ca
- **Ontario Power Generation**

Corporate Development Division
880 Bay St., 5th Fl., Toronto, ON M7A 2C1
Tel: 416-327-7106
Fax: 416-314-3354

Provides a structure to identify strategic issues, to coordinate policy & program development; & to coordinate & integrate action by the Ministry & other governments.
Assistant Deputy Minister & Interim Chief Administrative Officer, John Whitehead
Tel: 416-325-6544
john.whitehead@ontario.ca
Director, Service Management Branch, Betty Morgan
Tel: 416-314-3309
Fax: 416-314-3354
betty.morgan@ontario.ca
Acting Director, Business & Resource Planning, Lourdes Valenton
Tel: 416-327-7227
Fax: 416-314-3354
lourdes.valenton@ontario.ca

Energy Supply, Transmission & Distribution Policy
880 Bay St., 3rd Fl., Toronto, ON M7A 2C1
Tel: 416-327-7353
Fax: 416-314-6224

Assistant Deputy Minister, Rick Jennings
Tel: 416-314-6190
Fax: 416-314-6224
rick.jennings@ontario.ca
Director, Energy Supply - Nuclear Branch, Cedric Jobe
Tel: 416-325-6545
Fax: 416-212-1117
cedric.jobe@ontario.ca
Director, Energy Supply & Competition, Garry McKeever
Tel: 416-325-8627
Fax: 416-325-7023
garry.mckeever@ontario.ca
Director, Transmission & Distribution Policy, Jonathan Norman
Tel: 416-326-1759
Fax: 416-325-7023
jonathan.norman@ontario.ca

Regulatory Affairs & Strategic Policy
Mowat Block, 900 Bay St., 5th Fl., Toronto, ON M7A 2E3
Tel: 416-325-6559
Fax: 416-325-7041

Provides strategic policy coordination & development for the ministry as well as policy analysis & advice related to energy conservation & efficiency, demand management, & conservation.

Assistant Deputy Minister, John Whitehead
Tel: 416-325-6559
Fax: 416-325-7041
john.whitehead@ontario.ca
Director, Planning & Agency Relations Branch, Alex Killoch
Tel: 416-326-5572
Fax: 416-325-7041
alex.killoch@ontario.ca
Director, Strategic Policy & Research Branch, Kaili Sermat-Harding
Tel: 416-327-5555
kaili.sermat-harding@ontario.ca

Renewables & Energy Efficiency
880 Bay St., 6th Fl., Toronto, ON M7A 2C1
Tel: 416-314-6216
Fax: 416-325-3438

The branch provides analysis, advice & policy development on issues relating to energy efficiency, demand management & conservation as well as administering the Energy Efficiency Act.

Ontario Ministry of Environment (MOE)

135 St. Clair Ave. West, Toronto, ON M4V 1P5
Tel: 416-325-4000
Fax: 416-325-3159
Toll-Free: 800-565-4923
www.ene.gov.on.ca
TTY: 800-515-2759
Other Communication: Pollution Hotline: 1-866-MOE-TIPS (1-866-663-8477); Spills or Emergencies: 1-800-268-6060; Public Information: 1-800-565-4923

The ministry is responsible for protecting clean & safe air, land & water to ensure healthy communities, ecological protection & sustainable development for present & future generations of Ontarians. Using stringent regulations, targeted enforcement & a variety of innovative programs & initiatives, the ministry continues to address environmental issues that have local, regional &/or global effects. The ministry has built a strong foundation of clear laws, stringent regulations, tough standards & rigorous permits & approvals. The ministry monitors pollution & restoration trends in an effort to determine the effectiveness of its activities & to assess risks to human health & the environment. This information is used to develop & implement environmental legislation, regulations, standards, policies, guidelines & programs to enhance environmental protection.

Acts Administered:
Adams Mine Lake Act, 2004
Additional Charges Regulation
Air Contaminants from Ferrous Foundries Regulation
Air Pollution - Local Quality Regulations
Airborne Contaminant Discharge Monitoring & Reporting Regulations
Ambient Air Quality Criteria Regulations
Blue Box Waste Regulations, 2002
Boilers Regulation
Capital Investment Plan Act
Certificates of Approval Exemptions Air Regulation
Certification of Drinking-Water System Operators & Water Quality Analysts
Classes of Contaminants Exemption Regulations
Classification & Exemption of Spills Regulations
Clean Water Act
Compliance & Enforcement
Consolidated Hearings Act
Containers Regulation
Deep Well Disposal Regulation
Definitions of "Deficiency" & "Municipal Drinking-Water System" Regulations
Definitions of Words & Expressions Used in the Act Regulations, 2003
Designation of Waste Regulation
Designations & Exemptions
Discharge of Sewage from Pleasure Boats Regulation
Disposable Containers for Milk Regulations
Disposable Paper Containers for Milk Regulations
Drinking-Water Systems Regulations, 2003
Drinking-Water Testing Services Regulations, 2003
Dry Cleaners Regulations
Effluent Monitoring & Effluent Limits Regulations
Electricity Projects Regulation
Emissions Trading Regulation
Environmental Assessment Act
Environmental Assessment General Regulations
Environmental Bill of Rights Act
Environmental Protection Act
Environmental Review Tribunal Act, 2000
Ethanol in Gasoline
Exemption Regulations
Gasoline Volatility Regulation
General Waste Management Regulation
Ground Source Heat Pumps Regulation
Halon Fire Extinguishing Equipment Regulation
Hot Mix Asphalt Facilities Regulation
Industrial, Commercial & Institutional Source Separation Programs Regulation
Industry Emissions - Nitrogen Oxides & Sulphur Dioxide
Lake Simcoe Protection Act
Lakeview Generating Station Regulations
Lambton Industry Meteorology Alert Regulation
Land Disposal Restrictions
Landfilling Sites Regulation
Licensing of Sewage Works Operators Regulations
Marinas Regulation
Ministry of the Environment Act
Mobil PCB Destruction Facilities Regulation
Motor Vehicles Regulation
Municipal Sewage & Water & Roads Class Environmental Assessment Project Regulation
Municipal Water & Sewage Transfer Act
Municipalities, Secured Creditors, Receivers, Trustees in Bankruptcy & Fiduciaries, Pt.XV.2 of the Act Regulations, 2002
Non-Residential & Non-Municipal Seasonal Residential Systems that do not Service Designated Facilities
Nutrient Management Act
Ontario Drinking-Water Quality Standards Regulations, 2003
Ontario Power Generation Regulations
Ontario Water Resources Act
Ozone Depleting Substances Regulation
Packaging Audits & Packaging Reduction Work Plans Regulation
Pesticides Act
Records of Site Condition, Pt.XV.1 of the Act Regulations, 2004
Recovery of Gasoline Vapour in Bulk Transfers Regulation
Recycling & Composting of Municipal Waste Regulation
Refillable Containers for Carbonated Soft Drink Regulation
Refrigerants Regulation
Reporting Requirements, Sulphur Levels in Gasoline Regulations
Safe Drinking Water Act, 2002
Schools, Private Schools & Day Nurseries Regulations, 2003
Secured Creditors, Receivers, Trustees in Bankruptcy Regulations, 2002
Sewage System Regulations & Exemptions
Sewage Works Subject to Approval under the Environmental Assessment Act Regulations
Solvents Regulation

Spills Regulation
Sterilants Regulation
Sulphur Content of Fuels Regulation
Sustainable Water & Sewage Systems Act, 2002
Toxins Reduction Act
Transitional Provisions Relating to the Repeal of Pt.VIII of the Environmental Protection Act Regulations
Used Oil Material Regulations, 2003
Used Tires Regulations, 2003
Waste Audits & Waste Reduction Workplans Regulation
Waste Disposal Sites & Waste Management Systems Subject to Approval under the Environmental Assessment Act Regulations
Waste Diversion Act, 2002
Waste Electrical & Electronic Equipment
Waste Management (PCBs) Regulation
Water Opportunities Act
Water Taking & Transfer Regulation
Wells Regulation

Minister, Hon. James J. Bradley
Tel: 416-314-6790
Fax: 416-314-6748
jbradley.mpp.co@liberal.ola.org

Deputy Minister, Gail Beggs
Tel: 416-314-6753
Fax: 416-314-6791

Parliamentary Assistant, Helena Jaczek
Tel: 905-294-4931
hjaczek.mpp.co@liberal.ola.org

Chief Information Officer, Robert Hollis
Tel: 416-314-1528
Fax: 705-755-1599
robert.hollis@ontario.ca

Acting Director, Communications Branch, Michelle Garrett
Tel: 416-314-6695
Fax: 416-314-6711
michelle.garrett@ontario.ca

Director, Legal Services Branch, Rand Roszell
Tel: 416-212-0853
Fax: 416-212-0863
rand.roszell@ontario.ca
Other Communications: Southwest Region Counsel Fax: 519-682-9539

Associated Agencies, Boards & Commissions:

• Office of Consolidated Hearings
#1500, 655 Bay St.
Toronto, ON M5G 1E5
Tel: 416-212-6349
Fax: 416-314-4506
Under the Consolidated Hearings Act, the Environmental Assessment Board holds public hearings in conjunction with the Ontario Municipal Board. This occurs when a proposal requires more than one tribunal hearing under more than one of the acts set out in the schedule to the Consolidated Hearings Act, 1981. The hearings registrar must receive written notice from the person proposing the undertaking, specifying the nature of the undertaking, required hearings & governing acts. The matter is then referred to the chairs of the two boards, who establish a joint board for the hearing. The board's decision can be varied or rescinded only by the Lieutenant-Governor-in-Council or, on a question of law, may be appealed to the Divisional Court.

• Advisory Council on Drinking Water Quality & Testing Standards
40 St. Clair Ave. West, 3rd Fl.
Toronto, ON M4V 1M2
Tel: 416-212-7779
Fax: 416-212-7595

• Environmental Review Tribunal
#1500, 655 Bay St.
Toronto, ON M5G 1E5
Tel: 416-212-6349
Fax: 416-314-4506
Toll-free: 866-448-2248
TTY: 800-855-1155
erttribunalsecretary@ontario.ca
www.ert.gov.on.ca
The Environmental Review Tribunal's primary role is adjudicating applications & appeals under various environmental & planning statutes. The Tribunal hears applications & appeals under the Environmental Assessment Act, the Environmental Protection Act, the Ontario Water Resources Act, & the Pesticides Act, & leave to appeal applications under the Environmental Bill of Rights, 1993. The Environmental Review Tribunal also functions as the Office of Consolidated Hearings to hear applications made under the Consolidated Hearings Act & as the Niagara Escarpment Hearing Office to hear development permit appeals & Niagara Escarpment Plan amendment applications under the Niagara Escarpment Planning & Development Act.

• Ontario Clean Water Agency (OCWA)
1 Yonge St., 17th Fl.
Toronto, ON M5E 1E5
Tel: 416-314-5600
Fax: 416-314-8300
Toll-free: 800-667-6292
www.ocwa.com
The Ontario Clean Water Agency (OCWA) was established as a Provincial Crown Agency in November 1993 & is committed to providing safe & reliable clean water services. The Agency is an established leader in the operation, maintenance & management of water & wastewater treatment facilities & their associated distribution & collection systems. OCWA operates hundreds of water & wastewater facilities, ranging in size from small wells & pumping stations to large-scale urban water & wastewater systems.

• Pesticides Advisory Committee
135 St. Clair Ave. West, 15th Fl.
Toronto, ON M4V 1P5
Tel: 416-314-9230
Fax: 416-314-9237
www.opac.gov.on.ca
This committee advises the Minister of the Environment on matters pertaining to pesticides. It annually reviews the Pesticides Act & regulations, & government publications respecting pesticides & control of pests. The committee also recommends classifications for all new pesticide products prior to their marketing & use in Ontario, & publishes an annual report, which is available upon request. For other ministry publications on pests & pest control & information on pesticide licensing, contact the Standards Development Branch, Pesticides Section.

• Walkerton Clean Water Centre
20 Ontario Rd.
PO Box 160
Walkerton, ON N0G 2V0
Tel: 519-881-2003
Fax: 519-881-4947
Toll-free: 866-515-0550
inquiry@wcwc.ca
www.wcwc.ca
The vision of the Walkerton Clean Water Centre is to create a world-class intitute dedicated to clean & secure drinking water for the people of Ontario. Established by Ontario Regulation 304/04 as a crown agency of the Ministry of the Environment in October 2004, & governed by a 12-member board of directors, the Centre's work will complement & support that of the Ministry with a focus on ensuring that training, education & information is available & accessible to owners, operators & operating authorities of Ontario's drinking water systems, particularly in rural & remote communities.

Corporate Management Division
135 St. Clair Ave. West, 14th Fl., Toronto, ON M4V 1P5
Tel: 416-314-6426
Fax: 416-314-6425

Assistant Deputy Minister & Chief Administrative Officer, Debra Sikora
Tel: 416-314-6424
debra.sikora@ontario.ca
Director, Business & Fiscal Planning, Rob W. Campbell
Tel: 416-314-7370
Fax: 416-314-7858
rob.w.campbell@ontario.ca
Director, Strategic Human Resources Branch, Jacques LeGris
Tel: 416-314-9305
Fax: 416-314-9313
jacques.legris@ontario.ca
Director, Information Management & Access Branch, Jim Lewis
Tel: 416-314-3856
Fax: 416-314-6872
jim.d.lewis@ontario.ca
Director, Legal Services Branch, Rand Roszell
Tel: 416-212-0853
Fax: 416-314-6579
rand.roszell@ontario.ca
Director, Transition Office, Becky Taylor
Tel: 416-314-5606
Fax: 416-325-7962
becky.taylor@ontario.ca
Manager, Environmental Bill of Rights Office, Jacqueline Gallacher
Tel: 416-314-9615
Fax: 416-314-6872
jacqueline.gallacher@ontario.ca

Drinking Water Management Division
135 St. Clair Ave. West, Toronto, ON M4V 1P5
Tel: 416-314-4475
Fax: 416-314-6935

The Drinking Water Management Division, led by the Chief Drinking Water Inspector, has lead responsibility for program & operational activities related to the protection & provision of safe drinking water in Ontario.

Assistant Deputy Minister & Chief Drinking Water Inspector, John Stager
Tel: 416-314-4463
john.stager@ontario.ca
Director, Safe Drinking Water Branch, Paul Neiweglowski
Tel: 416-314-1977
Fax: 416-212-7576
paul.nieweglowski@ontario.ca
Director, Drinking Water Programs Branch, Orna Salamon
Tel: 416-212-2355
Fax: 416-314-9477
orna.salamon@ontario.ca
Director, Source Protection Programs Branch, Ian R. Smith
Tel: 416-212-6459
Fax: 416-212-2757
ian.r.smith@ontario.ca

Environmental Programs Division
135 St. Clair Ave. West, 14th Fl., Toronto, ON M4V 1P5
Tel: 416-326-7203
Fax: 416-327-8777

Assistant Deputy Minister, George Rocoski
Tel: 416-314-9530
Fax: 416-327-8777
george.rocoski@ontario.ca
Director, Aboriginal Affairs Branch/Lake Simcoe Project, Mary Hennessy
Tel: 416-327-6953
Fax: 416-326-8114
mary.hennessy@ontario.ca
Director, Program Planning & Implementation Branch/Toxics Reduction Project, Kevin Perry
Tel: 416-327-9730
Fax: 416-325-8475
kevin.perry@ontario.ca
Director, Modernization of Approvals Project, Marcia Wallace
Tel: 416-327-9466
Fax: 416-325-7962
marcia.wallace@ontario.ca
Director, Environmental Innovations Branch, Douglas S. Wright
Tel: 416-325-8068
Fax: 416-314-7919
douglas.wright@ontario.ca

Environmental Sciences & Standards Division
135 St. Clair Ave. West, 14th Fl., Toronto, ON M4V 1P5
Tel: 416-314-6357
Fax: 416-314-6358

The Environmental Sciences & Standards Division (ESSD) provides the best available science & technology to support decisions about the natural environment, & implements those decisions by developing & managing programs & partnerships, setting scientifically credible standards, monitoring the environment & providing valuable analytical & scientific expertise. Programs such as Drive Clean, that improve the environment & increase public awareness, are central to the ministry's efforts to strengthen environmental protection.

Assistant Deputy Minister, Deb Stark
Tel: 416-314-6310
deb.stark@ontario.ca
Director, Drive Clean Office, Dale Henry
Tel: 416-327-5543
Fax: 416-314-4160
dale.henry@ontario.ca
Director, Standards Development, Steve Klose
Tel: 416-314-1501
Fax: 416-327-2936
steve.klose@ontario.ca
Director, Environmental Monitoring & Reporting Branch, John Mayes
Tel: 416-235-6160
Fax: 416-235-5770
john.mayes@ontario.ca
Director, Laboratory Services, Joseph Odumeru
Tel: 416-235-5747
Fax: 416-235-5744
joseph.odumeru@ontario.ca

Integrated Environmental Policy Division
77 Wellesley St. West, 11th Fl., Toronto, ON M7A 2T5
Tel: 416-314-6338
Fax: 416-314-6346

Integrated Environmental Planning Division is responsible for integrating the overall policy development & planning functions of the Ministry. This involves integrating & synthesizing all information, data & perspectives on the many aspects of the Ministry's mandate. The division consults extensively on developing policies, strategies & programs that support the Ministry's core business of conservation & environmental protection.

Assistant Deputy Minister, Paul Evans
Tel: 416-314-6352
Fax: 416-314-6346
paul.evans@ontario.ca

Director, Land & Water Policy, Sharon Bailey
Tel: 416-314-7020
Fax: 416-314-7200
sharon.bailey@ontario.ca
Director, Environmental Intergovernmental Affairs Branch, Brian Nixon
Tel: 416-212-1340
brian.nixon2@ontario.ca
Acting Director, Strategic Policy, Debbie Ramsay
Tel: 416-327-9743
Fax: 416-325-8181
debbie.ramsay@ontario.ca
Director, Air Policy & Climate Change, Adam Redish
Tel: 416-314-5148
Fax: 416-314-4128
adam.redish@ontario.ca
Director, Waste Management Policy, Greg Sones
Tel: 416-326-1825
Fax: 416-325-4233
greg.sones@ontario.ca
Director, Air Policy Instruments & Programs Design Branch, Jim Whitestone
Tel: 416-314-8562
jim.whitestone@ontario.ca

Operations Division
135 St. Clair Ave. West, 8th Fl., Toronto, ON M4V 1P5
Tel: 416-314-6378
Fax: 416-314-6396

The Operations Division is the operations & program delivery arm of the ministry. It is responsible for delivering programs to protect air quality, to protect surface & ground water quality & quantity, to ensure appropriate management of wastes, to ensure an adequate quality of drinking water & to control the use of pesticides. In addition, the division is responsible for administering the ministry's approvals & licensing programs as well as an investigative & enforcement program to ensure compliance with environmental laws. The division has a province-wide network of regional, district & area offices.
Assistant Deputy Minister, Kevin French
Tel: 416-314-6366
Fax: 416-314-6396
kevin.french@ontario.ca
Director, Sector Compliance, Andy Dominski
Tel: 416-314-4241
Fax: 416-314-4464
andy.dominski@ontario.ca
Director, Environmental Approvals Access & Service Integration, Doris Dumais
Tel: 416-314-8171
Fax: 416-314-8452
doris.dumais@ontario.ca
Elle Fairclough Bldg.
119 King St. West, 12th Fl.
Hamilton, ON L8P 4Y7 Canada
Director, Investigations & Enforcement Branch, Lisa Feldman
Tel: 416-326-3444
Fax: 416-326-5256
lisa.feldman@ontario.ca
5775 Yonge St., 8th Fl.
Toronto, ON M2M 4J1 Canada
Director, Environmental Approvals, Agatha Garcia-Wright
Tel: 416-314-7288
Fax: 416-314-8452
agatha.garciawright@ontario.ca
Elle Fairclough Bldg.
119 King St. West, 12th Fl.
Hamilton, ON L8P 4Y7 Canada
Director, Operations Integration, Jim O'Mara
Tel: 416-314-3994
james.omara@ontario.ca
Elle Fairclough Bldg.
119 King St. West, 12th Fl.
Hamilton, ON L8P 4Y7 Canada
Director, Central Regional Office, Dolly Goyette
Tel: 416-314-3920
Toll-free: 800-810-8048
Fax: 416-325-6345
dolly.goyette@ontario.ca
Elle Fairclough Bldg.
119 King St. West, 12th Fl.
Hamilton, ON L8P 4Y7 Canada
Director, Eastern Regional Office, Hollee Kew
Tel: 613-548-6901
Fax: 613-548-6911
hollee.kew@ontario.ca
133 Dalton Ave.
PO Box 820
Kingston, ON K7L 4X6 Canada
Director, Northern Regional Office, John P. Taylor
Tel: 807-475-1690
Fax: 807-475-1754
john.p.taylor@ontario.ca
#331, 435 James St. South
Thunder Bay, ON P7E 6S7 Canada
Director, Southwestern Regional Office, Franca Dignem
Tel: 519-873-5001
Toll-free: 800-265-7672
Fax: 519-873-5020
franca.dignem@ontario.ca
659 Exeter Rd., 2nd Fl.
London, ON N6E 1L3 Canada
Director, West Central Regional Office, Bill Bardswick
Tel: 905-521-7652
Toll-free: 800-668-4557
Fax: 905-521-7820
bill.bardswick@ontario.ca
Elle Fairclough Bldg.
119 King St. West, 12th Fl.
Hamilton, ON L8P 4Y7 Canada

Environmental Commissioner of Ontario (ECO)

#605, 1075 Bay St., Toronto, ON M5S 2B1
Tel: 416-325-3377
Fax: 416-325-3370
Toll-Free: 800-701-6454
commissioner@eco.on.ca
www.eco.on.ca

An independent officer of the Legislative Assembly of Ontario, the Environmental Commissioner of Ontario promotes the values, goals & purposes of the Environmental Bill of Rights (EBR) to improve the quality of Ontario's natural environment. The ECO monitors & reports on the application of the EBR, provides public education to facilitate Ontario residents' participation in the EBR & reviews government accountability for environmental decision-making.

Commissioner, Gord Miller

Director, Operations, Peter Lapp
Tel: 416-325-3369
peter.lapp@eco.on.ca

Ontario Ministry of Finance

Frost Bldg. South, 7 Queen's Park Cres., 7th Fl., Toronto, ON M7A 1Y7
Fax: 866-888-3850
Toll-Free: 866-668-8297
financecommunications.fin@ontario.ca
www.fin.gov.on.ca
TTY: 800-263-7776
Other Communication: Toll Free (French): 1-800-668-5821
Secondary Address: Oshawa Office: 33 King St. WestPO Box 627 Sta.
Oshawa, ON L1H 8H5 Canada

The Ministry of Finance recommends taxation, fiscal & economic policies. Other responsibilities include the management of provincial finances & the development & allocation of Ontario's budget.

Acts Administered:
Alcohol & Gaming Regulation & Public Protection Act
Assessment Act
Auditor General Act
Automobile Insurance Rate Stabilization Act, 2003
Canadian Public Accountability Board Act (Ontario)
Capital Investment Plan Act, 1993
Co-operative Corporations Act
Commercial Concentration Tax Act
Commodity Futures Act
Community Small Business Investment Funds Act
Compulsory Automobile Insurance Act
Corporations Tax Act
Credit Unions and Caisses Populaires Act, 1994
Crown Foundations Act, 1996
Education Act (in part)
Employer Health Tax Act
Estate Administration Tax Act
Estate Administration Tax Act, 1998
Financial Administration Act
Financial Services Commission of Ontario Act, 1997
Fiscal Transparency and Accountability Act, 2004
Fuel Tax Act
Gasoline Tax Act
Highway Traffic Act (only specific provisions)
Income Tax Act
Insurance Act
Interim Appropriation for 2011-2012 Act
Investing in Ontario Act
Land Transfer Tax Act
Liquor Control Act
Loan & Trust Corporations Act
MPPs Pension Act, 1996
Marine Insurance Act
Mining Tax Act
Ministry of Revenue Act
Mortgage Brokerages, Lenders & Administrators Act, 2006
Motor Vehicle Accident Claims Act
Municipal Property Assessment Corporation Act, 1997
Ontario Clean Energy Benefit Act
Ontario Guaranteed Annual Income Act
Ontario Home Ownership Savings Plan Act
Ontario Loan Act, 2005, S.O. 2005, c. 28, Sched. K
Ontario Loan Act, 2006, S.O. 2006, c. 9, Sched. J
Ontario Loan Act, 2007, S.O. 2007, c. 7, Sched. 29
Ontario Loan Act, 2008, S.O. 2008, c. 7, Sched. P
Ontario Loan Act, 2009 (No. 2), S.O. 2009, c. 34, Sched. O
Ontario Loan Act, 2009, S.O. 2009, c. 18, Sched. 21
Ontario Loan Act, 2010, S.O. 2010, c. 1, Schedule 22
Ontario Loan Act, 2011, S.O. 2011, c. 9, Schedule 33
Pension Benefits Act 1990
Prepaid Hospital & Medical Services Act
Province of Ontario Savings Office Act
Province of Ontario Savings Office Privatization Act, 2002
Provincial Land Tax Act, 2006
Public Sector Compensation Restraint to Protect Public Services Act
Public Sector Salary Disclosure Act, 1996
Race Tracks Tax Act
Racing Commission Act
Registered Insurance Brokers Act
Retail Sales Tax Act
Securities Act
SkyDome Act (Bus Parking), 2002
Small Business Development Corporations Act, 2009
Social Contract Act, 1993
Statistics Act
Succession Duty Act Supplementary Provisions Act, 1980
Succession Duty Legislation Repeal Act, 2009
Supplementary Interim Appropriation Act, 2011
Supply Act, 2011
Tax Incentive Zones Act (Pilot Projects), 2002
Tax Increment Financing Act, 2006
Taxation Act
Taxation Act, 2007
Taxpayer Protection Act, 1999
Tobacco Tax Act
Toronto Stock Exchange Act
Trust Beneficiaries' Liability Act
Unclaimed Intangible Property Act

Minister; Chair, Treasury Board; Chair, Management Board of Cabinet, Hon. Dwight Duncan
Tel: 416-325-0400
Fax: 416-325-0374
dduncan.mpp.co@liberal.ola.org

Deputy Minister & Secretary, Treasury Board, Steve Orsini
Tel: 416-325-1592
Fax: 416-325-1595
steve.orsini@ontario.ca

Parliamentary Assistant, Donna Cansfield
Tel: 416-325-0702
dcansfield.mpp.co@liberal.ola.org

Parliamentary Assistant, Yasir Naqvi
Tel: 613-722-6414
ynaqvi.mpp.co@liberal.ola.org

Director, Legal Services, James D. Sinclair
Tel: 416-325-1450
Fax: 416-325-1460
james.sinclair@ontario.ca

Director, Communications, Dianne Lone
Tel: 416-212-1440
Fax: 416-325-0339
dianne.lone@ontario.ca

Deputy Director, Legal Services Branch, Malle Hanslep
Tel: 416-325-1457
malle.hanslep@ontario.ca

Associated Agencies, Boards & Commissions:
• Deposit Insurance Corporation of Ontario
#700, 4711 Yonge St.
Toronto, ON M2N 6K8
Tel: 416-325-9444
Fax: 416-325-9722
Toll-free: 800-268-6653
www.dico.com
The Deposit Insurance Corporation of Ontario provides deposit insurance, to the extent provided under the Credit Unions and Caisses Populaires Act, on deposits of members of credit unions and caisses populaires.

• Financial Services Commission of Ontario (FSCO)
New York City Ctr.
5160 Yonge St., 17th Fl.
PO Box 85
Toronto, ON M2N 6L9
Tel: 416-250-7250
Fax: 416-590-7070
Toll-free: 800-668-0128
TTY: 800-387-0584
www.fsco.gov.on.ca
Regulates insurance, pensions plans, credit unions, caisses populaires, mortgage brokers, cooperative corporations & loan & trust companies in Ontario. FSCO provides regulatory services that protect financial services consumers & pension plan beneficiaries & support a healthy & competitive financial services industry.

• Liquor Control Board of Ontario (LCBO)
55 Lake Shore Blvd. East
Toronto, ON M5E 1A4
Tel: 416-365-5900
Fax: 416-864-2476
Toll-free: 800-668-5226
infoline@lcbo.com
www.lcbo.com
The Liquor Control Board of Ontario (LCBO) is a provincial Crown corporation in Ontario, Canada established in 1927 by Lieutenant Governor William Donald Ross, on the advice of his Premier, Howard Ferguson, to sell liquor, wine, and beer through a chain of retail stores.

• Ontario Electricity Financial Corporation (OEFC)
#1400, 1 Dundas St. West
Toronto, ON M7A 1Y7
Tel: 416-325-8000
Fax: 416-325-8005
www.oefc.on.ca

• Ontario Financing Authority (OFA)
#1400, 1 Dundas St. West
Toronto, ON M7A 1Y7
Tel: 416-325-8000
Fax: 416-325-8005
www.ofina.on.ca
The Ontario Financing Authority (OFA) is an agency of the Province of Ontario that manages the Province's debt and borrowing program. The OFA is governed by a Board of Directors that reports to the Minister of Finance.

• Ontario Lottery & Gaming Corporation (OLG)
Roberta Bondar Pl.
#800, 70 Foster Dr.
Sault Ste Marie, ON P6A 6V2
Tel: 705-946-6464
Fax: 416-224-7000
Toll-free: 800-387-0098
TTY: 800-563-5357
www.olg.ca
Created on April 1, 2000 under the Ontario Lottery and Gaming Corporation Act, 1999, the Ontario Lottery and Gaming Corporation (OLG) is a provincial agency operating and managing province-wide lotteries, casinos and slots facilities at horse racing tracks.

• Ontario Racing Commission (ORC)
#400, 10 Carlson Crt.
Toronto, ON M9W 6L2
Tel: 416-213-0520
Fax: 416-213-7827
inquiry@ontarioracingcommission.ca
www.ontarioracingcommission.ca

• Ontario Securities Commission (OSC) / Commission des valeurs mobilières de l'Ontario
#1903, 20 Queen St. West
PO Box 55
Toronto, ON M5H 3S8
Tel: 416-597-0681
Fax: 416-593-8241
www.osc.gov.on.ca
The mandate of the Ontario Securities Commission (OSC) is to protect investors while fostering capital formation and the efficiency and integrity of Ontario's and Canada's capital markets.

• Stadium Corporation of Ontario Ltd.
33 King St. West, 6th Fl.
Oshawa, ON L1H 8H5
Tel: 416-314-5158
Fax: 905-433-6688
The corporation continues to exist to comply with legal commitments by the Province of Ontario as part of the sale of SkyDome. The agency is currently commercially active as it addresses obligations to provide a permanent solution to SkyDome bus parking. The agency has real estate assets in the form of a bus parking facility.

Corporate & Quality Service Division
Michael Starr Bldg., 33 King St. West, 6th Fl., Toronto, ON L1H 8H5
Tel: 905-433-6844
Fax: 905-433-6688
Other Communication: Freedom of Information & Protection of Privacy: 416-325-8370, Toll Free: 1-800-263-7965, Ligne sans frais: 1-800-668-5821

Assistant Deputy Minister & Chief Administrative Officer, Helmut Zisser
Tel: 416-314-5158
helmut.zisser@ontario.ca
Director, Corporate Planning & Finance Branch, Linda Gibney
Tel: 905-433-5637
Fax: 905-433-5124
linda.gibney@ontario.ca
Director, Business Services Branch, Paula Reid
Tel: 905-440-4263
paula.reid@ontario.ca
Acting Director, Strategic Human Resources Services Branch, Allyson Thompson
Tel: 905-433-5482
allyson.thompson@ontario.ca

Office of Economic Policy
Frost Bldg. North, 95 Grosvenor St., 5th Fl., Toronto, ON M7A 1Z1
Tel: 416-325-0840
Fax: 416-325-9224

Assistant Deputy Minister & Chief Economist, Patrick Deutscher
Tel: 416-325-0850
Fax: 416-325-9224
pat.deutscher@ontario.ca
Director, Industrial & Financial Policy Branch, Alvaro del Castillo
Tel: 416-325-0928
Fax: 416-325-1187
alvaro.delcastillo@ontario.ca
Director, Labour & Demographic Analysis Branch, Ambaye Kidane
Tel: 416-325-0801
Fax: 416-325-0841
ambaye.kidane@ontario.ca
Acting Director, Economic & Revenue Forecasting & Analysis, David West
Tel: 416-325-0778
Fax: 416-325-0796
david.west@ontario.ca

Office of Taxation, Agencies & Pensions
Frost Bldg. South, 7 Queen's Park Cres., 7th Fl., Toronto, ON M7A 1Y7
Tel: 416-325-0400
Fax: 416-325-0290

Acting Assistant Deputy Minister, Pension, Income Security & Research Division, Steve Orsini
Tel: 416-325-1592
Fax: 416-327-0160
steve.orsini@ontario.ca
Assistant Deputy Minister, Revenue Agencies Oversight Division, Barry Goodwin
Tel: 416-325-2880
barry.goodwin@ontario.ca
Assistant Deputy Minister, Taxation Policy Division, Sriram Subrahmanyan
Tel: 416-327-7294
sriram.subrahmanyan@ontario.ca
Director, Alcohol & Fees Policy Branch, Barbara Hewett
Tel: 416-314-4288
barbara.hewett@ontario.ca
Acting Director, Gaming Policy Branch, Elizabeth Yeigh
Tel: 416-212-7401
elizabeth.yeigh@ontario.ca
Director, Corporate & Commodity Taxation Branch, Ann Langleben
Tel: 416-327-0222
ann.langleben@ontario.ca
Director, Pension Policy Branch, Bruce Macnaughton
Tel: 416-327-0140
bruce.macnaughton@ontario.ca
Director, Personal Tax Policy & Design Branch, Kostas Plainos
Tel: 416-327-0246
kostas.plainos@ontario.ca
Director, Strategic Quantitative Research Branch, Charles Whitfield
Tel: 416-327-0143
charles.whitfield@ontario.ca

Office of the Budget & Treasury Board
Frost Bldg. South, 95 Grosvenor St., 4th Fl., Toronto, ON M7A 1Z1
Tel: 416-325-7620
Fax: 416-212-7767

Associate Deputy Minister, Greg Orencsak
Tel: 416-325-4569
greg.orencsak@ontario.ca
Assistant Deputy Minister, BPS Supply Chain Secretariat, Peggy Mooney
Tel: 416-314-1869
peggy.mooney@ontario.ca
Other Communications: URL: www.fin.gov.on.ca/bpssupplychain
Assistant Deputy Minister & Acting Provincial Controller, Murray Lindo
Tel: 416-325-8017
Fax: 416-325-2029
murray.lindo@ontario.ca
Director, Health & Demand Forecasting Branch, Jay Coghill
Tel: 416-325-8244
jay.coghill@ontario.ca
Director, Education, Justice & Quantitative Management Branch, Maria Duran-Schneider
Tel: 416-212-9693
Fax: 416-327-9115
maria.duran-schneider@ontario.ca
Director, General Government, Planning & Resources Branch, Joshua Paul
Tel: 416-327-0206
joshua.paul@ontario.ca
Director, Social Policy & Fiscal Framework Branch, Tim Schuurman
Tel: 416-327-0173
tim.schuurman@ontario.ca

Ontario Internal Audit Division
777 Bay St., 25th Fl., Toronto, ON M5G 2E5
Chief Internal Auditor & Assistant Deputy Minister, Richard Kennedy
Tel: 416-327-9319
Fax: 416-327-9486
richard.kennedy@ontario.ca
Audit Director, Larry Yarmolinsky
Tel: 416-464-7488
Fax: 416-327-9486
larry.yarmolinsky@ontario.ca

Provincial-Local Finance Division
College Park, 777 Bay St., 10th Fl., Toronto, ON M5G 2C8
Tel: 416-327-0264
Fax: 416-325-7644

Acting Assistant Deputy Minister, Allan Doheny
Tel: 416-327-9592
allan.doheny@ontario.ca
Acting Director, Property Tax Analysis & Municipal Funding Policy, Chris Broughton
Tel: 416-314-3801
Fax: 416-314-3853
chris.broughton@ontario.ca
Director, Provincial Local Initiatives, Helen Harper
Tel: 416-314-2286
Fax: 416-314-3853
helen.harper@ontario.ca
Director, Property Tax Legislation & Assessment Policy, Diane Ross
Tel: 416-327-0266
Fax: 416-314-7670
diane.ross@ontario.ca

Secretariat to Commission on the Reform of Ontario's Public Services
Frost Bldg. South, 7 Queen's Park Cres., 1st Fl., Toronto, ON M7A 1YA
Tel: 416-326-9847
Fax: 416-212-7767

Assistant Deputy Minister & Executive Lead, Scott Thompson
Tel: 416-327-2060
d.scott.thompson@ontario.ca

Tax & Benefits Administration
Michael Starr Bldg., 33 King St. West, 6th Fl., Oshawa, ON L1H 8H5
Associate Deputy Minister, Mahmood Nanji
Tel: 905-433-2292
mahmood.nanji@ontario.ca
Other Communications: Alternate Phone: 416-326-9524
Assistant Deputy Minister, Compliance Programs Division, John Andersen
Tel: 905-837-5236
john.andersen@ontario.ca
Assistant Deputy Minister, Program Delivery Division, Terry Hewak
Tel: 905-433-5614
terry.hewak@ontario.ca
Assistant Deputy Minister, Strategic Partnerships & Program Policy Division, Bob Laramy
Tel: 905-433-6219
bob.laramy@ontario.ca
Chief Information Officer, Central Agencies Information & IT Cluster, Jim Hamilton
Tel: 905-433-6890
jim.hamilton@ontario.ca

Office of Francophone Affairs

#200, 777 Bay St., Toronto, ON M7A 0A2
Tel: 416-325-4949
Fax: 416-325-4980
Toll-Free: 800-268-7507
ofa@ontario.ca
www.ofa.gov.on.ca
TTY: 416-325-0017

A central agency that assists the Government of Ontario in its delivery of services in French, & in the development of policies & programs that meet the needs of the province's francophones.
Acts Administered:
French Language Services Act

Minister Responsible, Hon. Madeleine Meilleur
Tel: 416-744-4484
Fax: 416-325-4980
mmeilleur.mpp.co@liberal.ola.org

Deputy Minister, Paul Genest
Tel: 416-314-9710
Fax: 416-325-5240
paul.genest@ontario.ca

Parliamentary Assistant, Grant Crack
Tel: 613-446-4010
gcrack.mpp.co@liberal.ola.org

Assistant Deputy Minister, Daniel Cayen
Tel: 416-325-4936
daniel.cayen@ontario.ca

Acting Director, Policy & Ministry Services, Éric Mézin
Tel: 416-325-4943
eric.mezin@ontario.ca

Director, Strategic Communications Branch, Charles Jean Sucsan
Tel: 416-325-4968
charlesjean.sucsan@ontario.ca

Ontario Ministry of Government Services (MGS)

Whitney Block, #4320, 99 Wellesley St. West, 4th Fl., Toronto, ON M7A 1W3
Tel: 416-326-1234
Fax: 416-327-3790
Toll-Free: 800-268-1142
www.mgs.gov.on.ca
TTY: 416-326-8566
Other Communication: Consumer Protection, Phone: 416-326-8800; Toll Free: 1-800-889-9768

MGS is responsible for the delivery of government services, the government workforce, procurement & technology resources. The ministry is engaged in the following main activities: providing government information to individuals & businesses, including distribution through Publications Ontario; protecting consumers through information about frauds & scams & mediating complaints about businesses; & issuing birth, death & marriage certificates, & managing Land Registry Offices throughout the province.
Acts Administered:
Adjudicative Tribunals Accountability, Governance & Appointments Act
Archives & Recordkeeping Act
Boundaries Act
Broader Public Sector Accountability Act
Business Corporations Act
Business Names Act
Business Regulation Reform Act
Cabinet Ministers' & Opposition Leaders' Expenses Review & Accountability Act
Change of Name Act
Condominium Act, 2011
Corporations Act
Corporations Information Act
Electronic Land Registration Services Act
Electronic Registration Act
Extra-Provincial Corporations Act
Flag Act
Floral Emblem Act
Freedom of Information & Protection of Privacy Act
Government Advertising Act
Highway Traffic Act
Land Registration Reform Act
Land Titles Act
Licence Appeal Tribunal Act
Limited Partnerships Act
Lobbyists Registration Act
Marriage Act
Ministry of Government Services Act
Municipal Freedom of Information & Protection of Privacy Act
Not-for-Profit Corporations Act, 2010
Official Notices Publication Act
Ontario Provincial Police Collective Bargaining Act
Ontario Public Service Employees' Union Pension Act
Partnerships Act
Personal Property Security Act
Public Sector Expenses Review Act
Public Service Pension Act
Public Service of Ontario Act
Registry Act
Repair & Storage Liens Act
Residential Complex Sales Representation Act
Vital Statistics Act

Minister, Hon. Harinder S. Takhar
Tel: 416-327-2333
Fax: 416-327-3790
htakhar.mpp.co@liberal.ola.org

Deputy Minister, MGS, Associate Secretary of the Cabinet & Secretary of Mgmt Board of Cabinet, Ron McKerlie
Tel: 416-325-1607
Fax: 416-325-1612
ron.mckerlie@ontario.ca

Parliamentary Assistant, Shafiq Qaadri
Tel: 416-745-2859
sqaadri.mpp.co@liberal.ola.org

Assistant Deputy Minister, Labour Relations Secretariat, Tim Hadwen
Tel: 416-326-4195
Fax: 416-326-5265

Assistant Deputy Minister, Ontario Public Service Green Office, Neil Sentance
Tel: 416-327-3536
neil.sentance@ontario.ca

Chief Officer, Diversity & Accessibility, Shamira Madhany
Tel: 416-314-6989
shamira.madhany@ontario.ca

Director, Operations, Deborah E. Brown
Tel: 416-325-1609
Fax: 416-325-1612
deborah.e.brown@ontario.ca

Director, Legal Services, Sean Kearney
Tel: 416-327-6396
Fax: 416-326-6383
sean.kearney@ontario.ca

Acting Director, Communications, Sevaun Palvetzian
Tel: 416-325-1376
Fax: 416-327-2817
sevaun.palvetzian@ontario.ca

Associated Agencies, Boards & Commissions:
• Advertising Review Board
Macdonald Block
#M2-56, 900 Bay St., 2nd Fl.
Toronto, ON M7A 1N3
Tel: 416-327-2183
Fax: 416-327-2179
• Conflict of Interest Commissioner
#1802, 2 Bloor St. East
Toronto, ON M4W 3J6
Tel: 416-325-1571
Fax: 416-325-4330
• Licence Appeal Tribunal (LAT)
20 Dundas St. West, 5th Fl.
Toronto, ON M5G 2C2
Tel: 416-314-4260
Fax: 416-314-4270
Toll-free: 800-255-2214
www.lat.gov.on.ca
Other Communication: Toll Free Fax: 1-800-720-5292
The LAT hears appeals when a decision or order to suspend or a proposal is made to cancel or to refuse to grant or renew a registration, certificate or a licence, or when a claim for compensation has been denied.
• Ontario Pension Board
Sun Life Bldg.
#2200, 200 King St. West
Toronto, ON M5H 3X6
Tel: 416-364-8558
Fax: 416-364-7578
Toll-free: 800-668-6203
office.services@opb.on.ca
www.opb.on.ca
• OPSEU Pension Trust
#1200, 1 Adelaide St. East
Toronto, ON M5C 3A7
Tel: 416-681-6161
Fax: 416-681-6175
Toll-free: 800-637-0024
www.optrust.com
• Provincial Judges Pension Board
c/o Ontario Pension Board
#1100, 1 Adelaide St. East
Toronto, ON M5C 2X6
Tel: 416-327-8395
Fax: 416-366-0199
• Public Service Commission
Whitney Block
99 Wellesley St. West, 5th Fl.
Toronto, ON M7A 1W4
Tel: 416-325-1750

Corporate Services Division
College Park, 777 Bay St., 5th Fl., Toronto, ON M7A 2J3
Tel: 416-314-5187
Fax: 416-327-2866

Assistant Deputy Minister & Chief Administrative Officer, Karen Hughes
Tel: 416-325-3311
karen.hughes@ontario.ca
Director, Business Planning & Financial Management Branch, Lillian Duda
Tel: 416-212-3124
lillian.duda@ontario.ca
Director, Service Management & service Delivery Branch, Karl Cunningham
Tel: 416-326-8896
karl.cunningham@ontario.ca
Director, Enterprise Services Strategic Business Unit, Tracey McConnell
Tel: 416-327-3821
tracey.mcconnell@ontario.ca
Manager, French Language Services, Richard Martel
Tel: 416-327-3818
richard.martel@ontario.ca

Enterprise Services Cluster
Ferguson Block, 77 Wellesley St. West, 8th Fl., Toronto, ON M7A 1N3
Tel: 416-326-2700
Fax: 416-326-3347

Chief Information Officer, Enterprise Services Cluster, Ron Huxter
Tel: 416-327-1476
ron.huxter@ontario.ca
Head, Enterprise HR Systems Branch, John Deans
Tel: 416-327-9210
john.deans@ontario.ca
Head, Enterprise Financial Systems, Tricia Ireland
Tel: 416-326-9624
tricia.ireland@ontario.ca
Head, Information Technology Source, Fred Pitt
Tel: 416-327-5010
fred.pitt@ontario.ca
Head, Technology & Applied Architecture, John Van den Hoven
Tel: 416-326-9477
john.vandenhoven@ontario.ca
Head, Business & Application Modernization, Russ Whitehead
Tel: 416-327-3431
russ.whitehead@ontario.ca

Government Services
Macdonald Block, 900 Bay St, Ground Flr Rm M1-72, Toronto, ON M7A 1N3
Tel: 416-326-5366
Fax: 416-326-5265

Assistant Deputy Minister, Tim Hadwen
Tel: 416-326-4195
tim.hadwen@ontario.ca
Director, Labour Strategy, Michael Uhlmann
Tel: 416-326-3865
michael.uhlmann@ontario.ca
Manager, Research and Analysis, Peter Marques
Tel: 416-212-6082
peter.marques@ontario.ca

HR Ontario
Whitney Block, #5320, 99 Wellesley St. West, Toronto, ON M7A 1N3
Tel: 416-212-2057
Fax: 416-325-6317

Associate Deputy Minister, Angela Coke
Tel: 416-325-5065
angela.coke@ontario.ca
Assistant Deputy Minister, HR Management & Corporate Policy Division, Catherine D. Brown
Tel: 416-327-9223
catherine.brown@ontario.ca

Assistant Deputy Minister, Employee Relations Division, David Logan
Tel: 416-325-1476
david.logan@ontario.ca
Assistant Deputy Minister, HR Service Delivery Division, Debbie Moretta
Tel: 416-325-7612
debbie.moretta@ontario.ca
Assistant Deputy Minister, Centre for Leadership & Learning, Kerry Pond
Tel: 416-325-1777
kerry.pond@ontario.ca
Assistant Deputy Minister, Centre for Organizational Excellence, Leslie Slater
Tel: 416-325-1737
leslie.slater@ontario.ca
Director, Strategic Business Performance Branch, Lisa Sherin
Tel: 416-326-8774
lisa.sherin@ontario.ca

Information, Privacy & Archives Division
134 Ian Macdonald Blvd., Toronto, ON M7A 2C5
Tel: 416-327-1600
Fax: 416-327-1999
Toll-Free: 800-668-9933
www.archives.gov.on.ca
Acting Chief Privacy Officer & Archivist of Ontario, Angela Forest
Tel: 416-327-1602
Fax: 416-327-1992
angela.forest@ontario.ca
Director, Archives Management and Information Storage, Mary Anne Henderson
Tel: 416-327-1577
maryanne.henderson@ontario.ca
Director, Policy and Planning, Heather Clarke
Tel: 416-327-1467
heather.clarke@ontario.ca
Senior Manager, Finance & Administration and Information & Privacy, Pam Gould
Tel: 416-327-1562
pam.gould@ontario.ca

Office of the Corporate Chief Information Officer (OCCIO)
Ferguson Block, 77 Wellesley St. West, 5th Fl., Toronto, ON M7A 1N3
Tel: 416-327-3442
Fax: 416-327-3264
Corporate Chief Information & Information Technology Officer, David Nicholl
Tel: 416-327-9696
david.nicholl@ontario.ca
Corporate Chief, Infrastructure Technology Services, Marty Gallas
Tel: 416-326-7224
marty.gallas@ontario.ca
Corporate Chief Strategist, Samantha Liscio
Tel: 416-212-1624
Fax: 416-314-7710
samantha.liscio@ontario.ca
Acting Head, I&IT Strategy, Policy & Planning Branch, Linda Haldenby
Tel: 416-314-2060
linda.haldenby@ontario.ca
Head, Corporate Security, Peter Macaulay
Tel: 416-327-0413
Fax: 416-327-3262
peter.macaulay@ontario.ca

Ontario Shared Services
700 University Ave., 6th Fl., Toronto, ON M7A 2S4
Tel: 416-326-9300
Toll-Free: 866-979-9300
Associate Deputy Minister, Lois Bain
Tel: 416-212-7550
lois.bain@ontario.ca
Assistant Deputy Minister, Strategy & Enterprise Services, Glen Medeiros
Tel: 416-212-6569
Fax: 416-327-4246
Assistant Deputy Minister, Enterprise Financial Services, Roman Zydownyk
Tel: 416-212-3713
Fax: 416-212-3715
roman.zydownyk@ontario.ca
Assistant Deputy Minister, Pay & Benefits Services Division, Riet Verheggen
Tel: 416-212-6731
Fax: 416-325-1165
riet.verheggen@ontario.ca

Supply Chain Management
Tel: 413-212-0967
Fax: 416-327-3573
www.ontario.ca/supplychain
Develops & implements an integrated corporate procurement strategy to: leverage & optimize government procurement of goods & services; identify and implement procurement process improvements; enhance procurement controllership; provide strategic advice on large scale procurements; develop innovative policy frameworks to support service delivery through third party service providers.
Assistant Deputy Minister, Marian Macdonald
Tel: 416-327-7508
Fax: 416-327-3573
marian.macdonald@ontario.ca
Director, Procurement Policy & Planning Branch, Susan Hoyle-Howieson
Tel: 416-327-8765
Fax: 416-327-3573
susan.hoyle-howieson@ontario.ca
Director, Enterprise Procurement Branch, Wes Lapish
Tel: 416-327-3518
Fax: 416-327-3573
wes.lapish@ontario.ca
Director, Procurement Strategies & Enablement Branch, Ben Sopel
Tel: 416-325-7553
Fax: 416-327-3573
ben.sopel@ontario.ca

ServiceOntario
College Park, 777 Bay St., 15th fl., Toronto, ON M7A 2J3
Tel: 416-326-1234
Fax: 416-326-1313
Toll-Free: 800-267-8097
www.serviceontario.ca
TTY: 800-268-7095
Deputy Minister & Chief Executive Officer, Bob Stark
Tel: 416-326-7102
bob.stark@ontario.ca
Assistant Deputy Minister, Business Improvement, Bev Hawton
Tel: 416-326-6062
bev.hawton@ontario.ca
Assistant Deputy Minister, Business Development Division, Frank D'Onofrio
Tel: 416-314-3709
Fax: 416-326-0277
frank.d'onofrio@ontario.ca
Assistant Deputy Minister, Central Services Division, Sam Erry
Tel: 416-314-4877
sam.erry@ontario.ca
Assistant Deputy Minister, Customer Care Division, Helga Iliadis
Tel: 416-326-2784
helga.iliadis@ontario.ca
Assistant Deputy Minister, Service Delivery Strategy Division, Richard Steele
Tel: 416-325-8804
richard.steele@ontario.ca

Algoma
420 Queen St. East, Sault Ste Marie, ON P6A 1Z7
Tel: 705-253-8887
Fax: 705-253-9245

Brant
Court House, 80 Wellington St., Brantford, ON N3T 2L9
Tel: 519-752-8321
Fax: 519-752-0273

Bruce
203 Cayley St., PO Box 1690, Walkerton, ON N0G 2V0
Tel: 519-881-2259
Fax: 519-881-2322

Cochrane
143 - 4th Ave., PO Box 580, Cochrane, ON P0L 1C0
Tel: 705-272-5791
Fax: 705-272-2951
Toll-Free: 877-817-6636

Dufferin
#7, 41 Briadway Ave., Orangeville, ON L9W 1J7
Tel: 519-941-1481
Fax: 519-941-6444

Dundas
8 Fifth St., PO Box 645, Morrisburg, ON K0C 1X0
Tel: 613-543-2583
Fax: 613-543-4541

Durham
590 Rossland Rd. East, Whitby, ON L1N 9G5
Tel: 416-665-4007
Fax: 416-665-5247

Elgin
#36, 1010 Talbot St., St Thomas, ON N5P 4N2
Tel: 519-631-3015
Fax: 519-631-8182

Essex
#100, 949 McDougall St., Windsor, ON N9A 1L9
Tel: 519-971-9980
Fax: 519-971-9937

Frontenac
1 Court St., Kingston, ON K7L 2N4
Tel: 613-548-6767
Fax: 613-548-6766

Glengarry
63 Kenyon St. West, Alexandria, ON K0C 1A0
Tel: 613-525-1315
Fax: 613-525-0509

Grenville
499 Centre St., PO Box 1660, Prescott, ON K0E 1T0
Tel: 613-925-3177
Fax: 613-925-0302

Grey
East Court Plaza, #1-2, 1555 - 16th St. East, Owen Sound, ON N4K 5N3
Tel: 519-376-1637
Fax: 519-376-1639

Haldimand
10 Echo St. West, PO Box 310, Cayuga, ON N0A 1E0
Tel: 905-772-3531
Fax: 905-772-0105

Haliburton
12 Newcastle St., PO Box 270, Minden, ON K0M 2K0
Tel: 705-286-1391
Fax: 705-286-4324

Halton
2800 Highpoint Dr., 2nd Fl., Milton, ON L9T 6P4
Tel: 905-864-3500
Fax: 905-864-3549

Hastings
#109, 199 Front St., Belleville, ON K8N 5H5
Tel: 613-968-4597
Fax: 613-968-3606
Land Registrar, David Faires
Tel: 613-968-4597 ext: 210

Huron
38 North St., Goderich, ON N7A 2T4
Tel: 519-524-9562
Fax: 519-524-2482

Kenora
220 Main St. South, Kenora, ON P9N 1T2
Tel: 807-468-2794
Fax: 807-468-2796

Kent
40 William St. North, Chatham, ON N7M 4L2
Tel: 519-352-5520
Fax: 519-352-3222

Lambton
#102, 700 North Christina St., Sarnia, ON N7V 3C2
Tel: 519-337-2393
Fax: 519-337-8371

Lanark
2 Industrial Dr., PO Box 1180, Almonte, ON K0A 1A0
Tel: 613-256-1496
Fax: 613-256-0940

Leeds
7 King St. West, Brockville, ON K6V 3P7
Tel: 613-345-5751
Fax: 613-345-7390

Lennox
#2, 7 Snow Rd., Napanee, ON K7R 0A2
Tel: 613-354-3751
Fax: 613-354-1474

Manitoulin
Courthouse, 27 Phipps St., PO Box 619, Gore Bay, ON P0P 1H0
Tel: 705-282-2442
Fax: 705-282-2131

Middlesex
100 Dundas St., London, ON N6A 5B6
Tel: 519-675-7600
Fax: 519-675-7611

Muskoka
15 Dominion St. North, Bracebridge, ON P1L 2E7
Tel: 705-645-4415
Fax: 705-645-7826

Niagara North & South
59 Church St., St. Catharines, ON L2R 3C3
Tel: 905-684-6351
Fax: 905-684-5874

Nipissing
360 Plouffe St., North Bay, ON P1B 9L5
Tel: 705-474-2270
Fax: 705-495-8511

Norfolk
Court House, #201, 50 Frederick Hobson VC Dr., Simcoe, ON N3Y 4K8
Tel: 519-426-2216
Fax: 519-426-9627

Northumberland
Fleming Bldg., #105, 1005 Elgin St. West, Cobourg, ON K9A 5J4
Tel: 705-372-3813
Fax: 905-372-4758

Ottawa-Carleton
Court House, 161 Elgin St., 4th Fl., Ottawa, ON K2P 2K1
Tel: 613-239-1230
Fax: 613-239-1422

Oxford
75 Graham St., Woodstock, ON N4S 6J8
Tel: 519-537-6287
Fax: 519-537-3107

Parry Sound
28 Miller St., Parry Sound, ON P2A 1T1
Tel: 705-746-5816
Fax: 705-746-6517

Peel
7765 Hurontario St., 1st Fl., Brampton, ON L6W 4S8
Tel: 905-874-4008
Fax: 905-874-4012

Perth
5 Huron St., Stratford, ON N5A 5S4
Tel: 519-271-3343
Fax: 519-271-2550

Peterborough
Robinson Pl. North Tower, 300 Water St., 1st Fl., PO Box 7000, Peterborough, ON K9J 8M5
Tel: 705-755-1342
Fax: 705-755-1343

Prescott
499 Centre St., PO Box 1660, Prescott, ON K0E 1T0
Tel: 613-925-3177
Fax: 613-925-0302

Prince Edward
1 Pitt St., PO Box 1310, Picton, ON K0K 2T0
Tel: 613-476-3219
Fax: 613-476-7908

Rainy River
353 Church St., Fort Frances, ON P9A 1C9
Tel: 807-274-5451
Fax: 807-274-1704

Renfrew
400 Pembroke St. East, Pembroke, ON K8A 3K8
Tel: 613-732-8331
Fax: 613-732-0297

Russell
1122 Concession St., PO Box 10, Russell, ON K4R 1C8
Tel: 613-445-2138
Fax: 613-445-0614

Simcoe
Court House, 114 Worsley St., Barrie, ON L4M 1M1
Tel: 705-725-7232
Fax: 705-725-7246

Stormont
#2, 720 14th St. West, Cornwall, ON K6J 5T9
Tel: 613-932-4522
Fax: 613-932-4524

Sudbury
#300, 199 Larch St., Sudbury, ON P3E 5P9
Tel: 705-675-4300
Fax: 705-675-4148

Thunder Bay
189 Red River Rd., 2nd Fl., Thunder Bay, ON P7B 1A2
Tel: 807-343-7436
Fax: 807-343-7439

Timiskaming
375 Main St., PO Box 159, Haileybury, ON P0J 1K0
Tel: 705-672-3332
Fax: 705-672-3906

Toronto (Metropolitan Registry)
Atrium on Bay, #420, 20 Dundas St. West, PO Box 117, Toronto, ON M5G 2C2
Tel: 416-314-4430
Fax: 416-314-4453

Toronto (Metropolitan Land Titles)
#420, 20 Dundas St. West, PO Box 117, Toronto, ON M5G 2C2
Tel: 416-314-4430
Fax: 416-314-4453

Victoria
322 Kent St. West, Lindsay, ON K9V 4T7
Tel: 705-324-4912
Fax: 705-324-6290

Waterloo
30 Duke St. West, 2nd Fl., Kitchener, ON N2H 3W5
Tel: 519-571-6043
Fax: 519-571-6067

Wellington
1 Stone Rd. West, Guelph, ON N1G 4Y2
Tel: 519-826-3372
Fax: 519-826-3373

Land Registrar, Donna Trevors
Tel: 519-826-3372
Fax: 519-826-3373
donna.trevors@ontario.ca

Wentworth
119 King St. West, 4th Fl., Hamilton, ON L8P 4Y7
Tel: 905-521-7561
Fax: 905-521-7505

York Region
50 Bloomington Rd. West, Aurora, ON L4G 0L8
Tel: 905-713-7798
Fax: 905-713-7799

Ontario Ministry of Health & Long-Term Care

Hepburn Block, 80 Grosvenor St., 10th Fl, Toronto, ON M7A 2C4
Tel: 416-327-4327
Toll-Free: 800-268-1153
www.health.gov.on.ca
TTY: 800-387-5559

The ministry is responsible for administering the health care system & providing services to the Ontario public through such programs as health insurance, drug benefits, assistive devices, care for the mentally ill, long-term care, home care, community & public health, & health promotion & disease prevention. It also regulates hospitals & nursing homes, operates psychiatric hospitals & medical laboratories, & co-ordinates emergency health services.

Acts Administered:
Alcoholism & Drug Addiction Research Foundation Act
Ambulance Act
Audiology & Speech-Language Pathology Act
Brain Tumour Awareness Month Act, 2001
Broader Public Sector Accountability Act, 2010
Cancer Act
Chase McEachern Act (Heart Defibrillator Civil Liability), 2007
Chiropody Act, 2009
Chiropractic Act
Commitment to the Future of Medicare Act, 2004
Community Care Access Corporations Act
Community Recreation Centres Act
Dental Hygiene Act, 1991
Dental Technology Act, 1991
Dentistry Act, 1991
Denturism Act, 1991
Dietetics Act, 1991
Drug & Pharmacies Regulation Act
Drug Interchangeability & Dispensing Fee Act
Drugless Practitioners Act
Elderly Persons Centres Act
Excellent Care for All Act, 2010
Fluoridation Act
Healing Arts Radiation Protection Act
Health Care Consent Act
Health Facilities Special Orders Act
Health Insurance Act
Health Protection & Promotion Act
Home Care & Community Services Act, 1994
Homemakers & Nurses Services Act
Homeopathy Act, 2007
Homes for Special Care Act
Immunization of School Pupils Act
Independent Health Facilities Act
Katelyn Bedard Bone Marrow Awareness Month Act, 2010
Kinesiology Act
Laboratory & Specimen Collection Centres Licensing Act
Local Health System Integration Act, 2006
Long-Term Care Homes Act, 2007
Massage Therapy Act
Medical Laboratory Technology Act
Medical Radiation Technology Act
Medicine Act
Mental Health Act
Midwifery Act, 1991
Ministry of Community & Social Services Act (sections 11.1 & 12 re: long-term care programs & services only)
Ministry of Health & Long-Term Care Act
Ministry of Health & Long-Term Care Appeal & Review Boards Act
Narcotics Safety & Awareness Act
Natruopathy Act
Nursing Act
Occupational Therapy Act
Ontario Agency for Health Protection & Promotion Act, 2007
Ontario Drug Benefit Act
Ontario Medical Association Dues Act, 1991
Ontario Mental Health Foundation Act
Opticianry Act, 1991
Optometry Act, 1991
Patient Restraints Minimization Act
Personal Health Information Protection Act
Pharmacy Act, 1991
Physiotherapy Act, 1991
Private Hospitals Act
Psychology Act, 1991
Psychotherapy Act
Public Hospitals Act
Quality of Care Information Protection Act
Regulated Health Professions Act, 1991
Respiratory Therapy Act, 1991
Smoke-Free Ontario Act
Traditional Chinese Medicine Act
Trillium Gift of Life Network Act
University Health Network Act
University of Ottawa Heart Institute Act

Minister, Hon. Deborah Matthews
Tel: 416-327-4300
Fax: 416-327-2679
dmatthews.mpp.co@liberal.ola.org

Deputy Minister, Saäd Rafi
Tel: 416-327-4496
Fax: 416-326-1570
saad.rafi@ontario.ca

Parliamentary Assistant, Phil McNeely
Tel: 613-834-8679
pmcneely.mpp.co@liberal.ola.org

Parliamentary Assistant, Liz Sandals
Tel: 519-836-4190
lsandals.mpp.co@liberal.ola.org

Associate Deputy Minister, Transformation Secretariat, Helen Angus
Tel: 416-212-4030
helen.angus@ontario.ca

Associate Deputy Minister, David Hallett
Tel: 416-327-2605
david.hallett@ontario.ca

Executive Director, Communications, Kevin Finnerty
Tel: 416-327-4352
kevin.finnerty@ontario.ca

Director, Legal Services Branch, Janice B. Crawford
Tel: 416-327-8565
janice.b.crawford@ontario.ca

Associated Agencies, Boards & Commissions:

• **Cancer Care Ontario**
620 University Ave., 15th Fl.
Toronto, ON M5G 2L7
Tel: 416-971-9800
Fax: 416-971-6888
www.cancercare.on.ca

• **Consent & Capacity Board**
151 Bloor St. West, 10th Fl.
Toronto, ON M5S 2T5
Tel: 416-327-4142
Fax: 416-924-8873
Toll-free: 866-777-7391
TTY: 877-301-0889
www.ccboard.on.ca
Other Communication: Toll-Free Fax: 1-866-777-7273
Hears appeals relating to involuntary placement in a psychiatric facility, capacity to make personal care & financial decisions & access to personal records from a psychiatric facility.

• **eHealth Ontario**
College Park
#701, 777 Bay St.
Toronto, ON M5G 2C8
Tel: 416-586-6535
Fax: 416-586-4363
Toll-free: 888-411-7742
TTY: 855-645-3390
info@ehealthontario.on.ca
www.ehealthontario.on.ca

• **Health Boards Secretariat**
151 Bloor St. West, 9th Fl.
Toronto, ON M5S 2T5
Tel: 416-327-8512
Fax: 416-327-8524
Toll-free: 866-282-2179

• **Health Quality Ontario**
#702, 130 Bloor St. West
Toronto, ON M5S 1N5
Tel: 416-323-6868
www.ohqc.ca

• **Medical Eligibility Committee**
370 Select Dr.
PO Box 168
Kingston, ON K7M 8T4
Tel: 613-548-6405
Deals with the eligibility of insured services as well as other matters assigned to it by the act or the regulation or by the minister; makes recommendations to the general manager with respect to these decisions.

• **Ontario Mental Health Foundation**
441 Jarvis St., 2nd Fl.
Toronto, ON M4Y 2G8
Tel: 416-920-7721
Fax: 416-920-0026
grants@omhf.on.ca
www.omhf.on.ca

• Ontario Review Board
151 Bloor St. West, 10th Fl.
Toronto, ON M5S 2T5
Tel: 416-327-8866
Fax: 416-327-8867
www.orb.on.ca

• Public Health Ontario
#300, 480 University Ave.
Toronto, ON M5G 1V2
Tel: 647-260-7100
Fax: 647-260-7600
www.oahpp.ca

• Trillium Gift of Life Network
#900, 522 University Ave.
Toronto, ON M5G 1W7
Tel: 416-363-4001
Fax: 416-363-4002
Toll-free: 800-263-2833
www.giftoflife.on.ca

Chief Medical Officer of Health
Hepburn Block, 80 Grosvenor St., 11th Fl., Toronto, ON M7A 1R3
Tel: 416-212-3831
Fax: 416-325-8412

Chief Medical Officer of Health, Dr. Arlene King
Tel: 416-212-3831
Fax: 416-325-8412
arlene.king@ontario.ca
Associate Chief Medical Officer of Health, Protection & Prevention, Dr. David Williams
Tel: 416-326-0392
david.williams@ontario.ca
Associate Chief Medical Officer of Health, Transition, Dr. Robin Williams
Tel: 416-325-7672
dr.robin.williams@ontario.ca
Associate Chief Medical Officer, Health, Environmental Health, Vacant
Associate Chief Medical Officer, Health, Health Promotion, Chronic Diseases & Injury Prevention, Vacant
Executive Director, Public Health, Roselle Martino
Tel: 416-327-9555
Fax: 416-325-8412
roselle.martino@ontario.ca
Director, Public Health Policy & Programs, Nina Arron
Tel: 416-212-4873
nina.arron@ontario.ca
Director, Emergency Management, Gerilynne Carroll
Tel: 416-212-5229
gerilynne.carroll@ontario.ca
Director, Public Health Standards, Practice & Accountability, Sylvia Shedden
Tel: 416-327-7423
sylvia.shedden@ontario.ca
Director, Public Health Planning & Liaison, Elizabeth Walker
Tel: 416-212-6359
elizabeth.walker@ontario.ca

Corporate Services Division
Hepburn Block, 80 Grosvenor St., 11th Fl., Toronto, ON M7A 1R3
Tel: 416-327-4266
Fax: 416-314-5915

Assistant Deputy Minister & Chief Administrative Officer, Ruth Hawkins
Tel: 416-327-4387
Fax: 416-314-5915
ruth.hawkins@ontario.ca
Director, HR Ontario Strategic Business Unit, Lori Aselstine
Tel: 416-327-8747
Fax: 416-327-7580
lori.aselstine@ontario.ca
Director, Health Audit Service Team, Ken Flynn
Tel: 416-327-7786
Fax: 416-327-7809
ken.flynn@ontario.ca
Director, Supply Chain & Facilities Branch, Paul Latremouille
Tel: 416-327-0782
Fax: 416-327-7312
paul.latremouille@ontario.ca
Director, Corporate Management Branch, Michele Sanborn
Tel: 416-326-5725
Fax: 416-327-2714
michele.sanborn@ontario.ca
Director, Accounting Policy & Financial Reporting, Joy Stevenson
Tel: 416-327-7350
Fax: 416-327-7364
joy.stevenson@ontario.ca
Director, Financial Management Branch, Pier Faltico
Tel: 416-212-0723
Fax: 416-212-0683
pier.falotico@ontario.ca

Direct Services Division
56 Wellesley St. West, 2nd Fl., Toronto, ON M5S 2S3
Tel: 416-314-5915

Assistant Deputy Minister, Patricia Li
Tel: 416-327-4845
Fax: 416-314-5915
patricia.li@ontario.ca
Director, Emergency Health Services (Land & Air), Malcolm Bates
Tel: 416-327-7909
Fax: 416-327-7879
malcolm.bates@ontario.ca
Director, Psychiatric Patient Advocate Office, Vahe Kehyayan
Tel: 416-327-7007
Fax: 416-327-7008
vahe.kehyayan@ontario.ca
Director, Assistive Devices Program, Susan Picarello
Tel: 416-212-5906
Fax: 416-327-8192
susan.picarello@ontario.ca
Director, Registration & Claims Branch, Dianne Wylie
Tel: 613-548-6454
Fax: 416-548-6320
dianne.wylie@ontario.ca

Health Human Resources Strategy Division
Macdonald Block, #M2-61, 900 Bay St., 2nd Fl., Toronto, ON M7A 1R3
Tel: 416-212-6115
Fax: 416-314-3751

Acting Assistant Deputy Minister, Suzanne McGurn
Tel: 416-212-7688
Fax: 416-314-3751
suzanne.mcgurn@ontario.ca
Provincial Chief Nursing Officer, Debra Bournes
Tel: 416-212-4835
Fax: 416-327-1878
debra.bournes@ontario.ca
Director, Health Sector Labour Market Policy, John Amodeo
Tel: 416-212-0873
Fax: 416-325-9827
john.amodeo@ontario.ca
Director, Health Human Resources Policy, Jeff Goodyear
Tel: 416-327-7482
Fax: 416-327-9429
jeff.goodyear@ontario.ca
Director, Health Professionals Regulatory Policy & Programs Branch, Marilyn Wang
Tel: 416-327-8888
Fax: 416-327-8879
marilyn.wang@ontario.ca

Health Promotion Division
College Park, #1903, 777 Bay St., 19th Fl., Toronto, M7A 1S5

Assistant Deputy Minister, Kate Manson-Smith
Tel: 416-326-4790
kate.manson-smith@ontario.ca
Acting Director, Strategic Initiatives Branch, Olha Dobush
Tel: 416-212-7785
olha.dobush@ontario.ca
Director, Standards, Programs & Community Development, Laura Pisko
Tel: 416-327-7445
laura.pisko@ontario.ca
Acting Manager, Policy Development & Liaison, Strategic Policy, Partnership & Research Branch, Kelci Gershon
Tel: 416-326-4368
kelci.gershon@ontario.ca

Health Services Information & Information Technology Cluster
56 Wellesley St. West, 10th Fl., Toronto, ON M5S 2S3
Tel: 416-314-4243
Fax: 416-314-0289

Chief Information Officer, Lorelle Taylor
Tel: 416-314-1276
Fax: 416-314-0289
lorelle.taylor@ontario.ca
Director, Business & Financial Services Branch, Raj Sharda
Tel: 416-327-6962
Fax: 416-314-4182
raj.sharda@ontario.ca
Head, Business Consulting & Governance Branch, Joan Berry
Tel: 416-326-7133
Fax: 416-314-0289
joan.berry@ontario.ca
Head, Health Solutions Delivery, Kevan Malden
Tel: 613-548-6395
Fax: 613-548-6587
kevan.malden@ontario.ca
Director, Ontario Public Health Intregrated Solutions, Karen McKibbin
Tel: 416-326-7169
Karen.McKibbin@ontario.ca
Head, Technology Management & Solutions Integration, Shelley Woods
Tel: 613-548-6688
Fax: 416-327-4429
shelley.woods@ontario.ca
Head, I&IT Strategy & Architecture Branch, Evan Woodhead
Tel: 416-327-1002
evan.woodhead@ontario.ca

Health System Accountability & Performance Division
Hepburn Block, 80 Grosvenor St., 5th Fl., Toronto, ON M7A 1R3
Tel: 416-212-1859

Acting Assistant Deputy Minister, Rachel E. Kampus
Tel: 416-212-1134
rachel.e.kampus@ontario.ca
Provincial Lead, Critical Care & Trauma, Dr. Bernard Lawless
Tel: 416-340-4800 ext: 556
Fax: 416-212-1859
lawlessb@smh.toronto.on.ca
Director, Implementation Branch, Melissa Farrell
Tel: 416-327-7135
melissa.farrell@ontario.ca
Acting Director, Performance Improvement & Compliance Branch, Rachel E. Kampus
Tel: 416-212-2362
rachel.e.kampus@ontario.ca
Director, LHIN Liaison Branch, Kathryn McCulloch
Tel: 416-314-1864
kathryn.mcculloch@ontario.ca

Health System Information Management & Investment Division
1075 Bay St., 13th Fl., Toronto, ON M5S 2B1
Tel: 416-212-1852
Fax: 416-327-8835

Assistant Deputy Minister, Don Young
Tel: 416-327-8854
don.young@ontario.ca
Director, Health Capital Investment Branch, James Alberding
Tel: 416-314-0402
james.alberding@ontario.ca
Director, Health Analytics Branch, Sten Ardal
Tel: 416-327-6483
sten.ardal@ontario.ca
Director, Information Management Strategy & Policy Branch, Alison Blair
Tel: 416-212-4433
alison.blair@ontario.ca
Director, Special Projects, Aileen Chan
Tel: 416-325-2311
aileen.chan@ontario.ca
Director, E-Health Liaison Branch, Greg Hein
Tel: 416-325-9075
greg.hein@ontario.ca
Director, Health System Funding Policy, Christina Hoy
Tel: 416-326-5707
christina.hoy@ontario.ca
Director, Health Data Branch, Jeanette Munshaw
Tel: 416-212-9163
jeanette.munshaw@ontario.ca
Director, Knowledge Management Branch, Ann-Marie Strapp
Tel: 416-327-8453
ann-marie.strapp@ontario.ca

Health System Strategy & Policy Division
Hepburn Block, 80 Grosvenor St., 8th Fl., Toronto, ON M7A 1R3
Tel: 416-327-8295
Fax: 416-327-5109

Assistant Deputy Minister, Dr. Vasanthi Srinivasan
Tel: 416-327-7261
Fax: 416-327-5109
vasanthi.srinivasan@ontario.ca
Senior Medical Scientific & Health Technology Advisor, Dr. Leslie Levin
Tel: 416-314-0249
les.levin@ontario.ca
Director, Community & Population Health Branch, Sheree Davis
Tel: 416-327-8319
Fax: 416-314-8275
sheree.davis@ontario.ca
Acting Director, System Policy & Strategy Branch, Sylvia Moustacalis
Tel: 416-212-4366
sylvia.moustacalis@ontario.ca
Director, Policy Care Standards Branch, Susan Paetkau
Tel: 416-327-8533
susan.paetkau@ontario.ca
Acting Director, Planning, Research & Analysis Branch, Alison Paprica
Tel: 416-327-0951
Fax: 416-327-3200
alison.paprica@ontario.ca

Director, Policy Care Standards, Susan Paetkau
Tel: 416-327-8533
susan.paetkau@ontario.ca
Director, Strategic Alignment Branch, Richard Prial
Tel: 416-327-1535
Fax: 416-212-7144
richard.prial@ontario.ca
Manager, Intergovernmental Relations Unit, Louis Dimitracopoulos
Tel: 416-327-8850
louis.dimitracopoulos@ontario.ca

Negotiations & Accountability Management Division
Hepburn Block, 80 Grosvenor St., 5th Fl., Toronto, ON M7A 1R3
Tel: 416-212-7012
Fax: 416-327-5186

Assistant Deputy Minister, Susan Fitzpatrick
Tel: 416-212-7012
susan.fitzpatrick@ontario.ca
Director, Health Quality Branch, L. Miin Alikhan
Tel: 416-325-2658
miin.alikhan@ontario.ca
Acting Director, Negotiations, David Clarke
Tel: 613-212-4904
david.w.clarke@ontario.ca
Director, Primary Health Care, Mary Fleming
Tel: 613-650-5430
mary.fleming@ontario.ca
Director, Diagnostic Services & Planning Branch, Sandy Nuttall
Tel: 416-212-4576
sandy.nuttall@ontario.ca
Director, Provincial Programs Branch, Kathryn Pagonis
Tel: 416-326-3834
kathryn.pagonis@ontario.ca
Director, Health Services Branch, Pauline Ryan
Tel: 613-536-3031
pauline.ryan@ontario.ca

Ontario Public Drug Programs Division
Hepburn Block, 80 Grosvenor St., 9th Fl., Toronto, ON M7A 1R3
Tel: 416-212-4724
Fax: 416-327-5219

Assistant Deputy Minister & Executive Officer, Diane MacArthur
Tel: 416-327-0902
diane.mcarthur@ontario.ca
Director, Drug Program Services, Brent Fraser
Tel: 416-327-8315
brent.fraser@ontario.ca
Director, Exceptional Access Program Branch, Lana Sheinbaum
Tel: 416-327-8118
lana.sheinbaum@ontario.ca

Ontario Human Rights Commission

180 Dundas St. West, 7th Fl., Toronto, ON M7A 2R9
Tel: 416-326-9511
Fax: 416-314-4494
Toll-Free: 800-387-9080
www.ohrc.on.ca
TTY: 800-308-5561

Chief Commissioner, Barbara Hall
Tel: 416-314-4536

Chief Administrative Officer, Karen Pereira
Tel: 416-314-4480
Fax: 416-314-4494
karen.pereira@ohrc.on.ca

Executive Director, Nancy Austin
Tel: 416-326-0567
Fax: 416-325-2004
nancy.austin@ohrc.on.ca

Acting Director, Policy, Education, Monitoring & Outreach, Shaheen Azmi
Tel: 416-314-4532
Fax: 416-314-4533
shaheen.azmi@ohrc.on.ca

Hydro One Inc.

North Tower, 483 Bay St., Toronto, ON M5G 2P5
Tel: 416-345-5000
Toll-Free: 877-955-1155
customercommunications@HydroOne.com
www.HydroOne.com

President & Chief Executive Officer, Laura Formusa

Chief Financial Officer & Executive Vice-President, Corporate Support, Sandy Struthers

Chief Risk Officer & Senior Vice-President, John Fraser

Chief Investment & Pension Officer & Senior Vice-President, Robert Cultraro

Executive Vice-President, Operations, Peter Gregg

Executive Vice-President, Strategy, Carmine Marcello

Senior Vice-President, Customer Operations & President/Chief Executive Officer, Hydro One Remotes Inc., Myles D'Arcey

Senior Vice-President, Engineering & Project Delivery, Nairn McQueen

Senior Vice-President, Grid Operations, Wayne Smith

Vice-President, Health, Safety & Environment, John Macnamara

President & Chief Executive Officer, Hydro One Telecom Inc., Paul Marchant

President & Chief Executive Officer, Hydro One Brampton Inc., Remy Fernandes

General Counsel, Joe Agostino

Independent Electricity System Operator (IESO)

PO Box 4474 A, Toronto, ON M5W 4E5
Tel: 905-403-6900
Fax: 905-403-6921
Toll-Free: 888-448-7777
customer.relations@ieso.ca
www.ieso.ca

President & Chief Executive Officer, Paul Murphy
paul.murphy@ieso.ca

Vice-President, Resource Integration, Bruce Campbell
Tel: 416-506-2829
bruce.campbell@ieso.ca

Vice-President, Finance, Ted Leonard
ted.leonard@ieso.ca

Vice-President, Organizational Development, Bill Limbrick
bill.limbrick@ieso.ca

Vice-President, Operations, Kim Warren
kim.warren@ieso.ca

Vice-President, Corporate Relations, Terry Young
terry.young@ieso.ca

General Counsel & Corporate Secretary, Human Resources, Roy Stewart
roy.stewart@ieso.ca

Information & Privacy Commissioner of Ontario

#1400, 2 Bloor St. East, Toronto, ON M4W 1A8
Tel: 416-326-3333
Fax: 416-325-9195
Toll-Free: 800-387-0073
info@ipc.on.ca
www.ipc.on.ca
TTY: 416-325-7539

The IPC is the oversight body for Ontario's three provincial freedom of information & protection of privacy statues, & is responsible for resolving appeals when government organizations refuse to grant access to information; investigating privacy complaints related to government-held information; ensuring government compliance with the acts; conducting research on access & privacy issues & providing advice on proposed government legislation & programs; educating the public on Ontario's access, privacy & personal health information laws & access & privacy issues; investigating complaints related to personal health information; reviewing policies & procedures, & ensuring compliance with the Personal Health Information Protection Act.

Acts Administered:
Freedom of Information & Protection of Privacy Act
Municipal Freedom of Information & Protection of Privacy Act
Personal Health Information Protection Act

Commissioner, Ann Cavoukian
Tel: 416-326-3333
commissioner@ipc.on.ca

Assistant Commissioner, Privacy, Ken Anderson
Tel: 416-326-3942
ken.anderson@ipc.on.ca

Assistant Commissioner, Access, Brian Beamish
Tel: 416-326-3333
brian.beamish@ipc.on.ca

Director, Policy, Michelle Chibba
Tel: 416-326-3966
michelle.chibba@ipc.on.ca

Registrar, Tribunal Services, Robert Binstock
Tel: 416-326-0008
robert.binstock@ipc.on.ca

Ontario Ministry of Infrastructure

Mowat Block, 900 Bay St., 5th Fl., Toronto, ON M7A 1C2
Toll-Free: 888-668-4636
www.moi.gov.on.ca
TTY: 800-239-4224

Acts Administered:
Electricity Act
Green Energy Act
Ministry of Infrastructure Act, 2011
Ontario Infrastructure & Lands Corporation Act
Places to Grow Act
Toronto Waterfront Revitalization Corporation Act

Minister, Hon. Bob Chiarelli
Tel: 416-325-5270
Fax: 416-325-8860
bchiarelli.mpp.co@liberal.ola.org

Deputy Minister, Drew Fagan
Tel: 416-212-0646
Fax: 416-212-0641

Assistant Deputy Minister, Corporate Development Division/Regulatory Affairs & Strategic Policy, John Whitehead
Tel: 416-325-6544
Fax: 416-314-3354
john.whitehead@ontario.ca

Provincial Development Facilitator, Paula Dill
Tel: 416-325-9764
Fax: 416-325-0209
paula.dill@ontario.ca

Parliamentary Assistant, Dipika Damerla
Tel: 416-325-1662
dipika.damerla@ontario.ca

Acting Director, Legal Services, Halyna Perun
Tel: 416-325-6681
Fax: 416-325-1781
halyna.perun2@ontario.ca

Director, Communications Branch, John Whytock
Tel: 416-327-6541
Fax: 416-326-3947
john.whytock@ontario.ca

Associated Agencies, Boards & Commissions:

• **Infrastructure Ontario**
College Park
777 Bay St., 6th Fl.
Toronto, ON M5G 2C8
Tel: 416-327-6008
Fax: 416-326-9291
info@infrastructureontario.ca
www.infrastructureontario.ca
Management of complex infrastructure projects identified in the government's mulit-year capital plan as alternative financing & procurement projects.

• **Ontario Realty Corporation**
#2000, 1 Dundas St. West
Toronto, ON M5G 2L5
Tel: 416-327-3937
Fax: 416-327-1906
Toll-free: 877-863-9672
feedback@ontariorealty.ca
www.ontariorealty.ca
Other Communication: Accounts Payable Fax: 416-327-1834
The Ontario Realty Corporation manages one of the largest real estate portfolios in Canada, consisting of approximately 6,000 buildings and structures and over 80,000 acres of land across the province. The portfolio includes a wide variety of properties ranging from detention centres to office space, courthouses and heritage buildings.

• **Waterfront Toronto**
#1310, 20 Bay St.
Toronto, ON M5J 2N8
Tel: 416-241-1344
Fax: 416-214-4591
info@waterfrontoronto.ca
www.waterfrontoronto.ca

Corporate Development Division
880 Bay St, 5th Flr, Toronto, ON M7A 2C1
Tel: 416-327-7106
Fax: 416-314-3354
www.Energy.gov.on.ca

Assistant Deputy Minister, John Whitehead
Tel: 416-325-6544
john.whitehead@ontario.ca
Acting Director, Business and Resource Planning, Lourdes Valenton
Tel: 416-327-7227
lourdes.valenton@ontario.ca
Director, Service Management, Betty Morgan
Tel: 416-314-3309
betty.morgan@ontario.ca

Infrastructure Policy & Planning Division
Frost Bldg. South, 7 Queen's Park Cres., 6th Fl., Toronto, ON M7A 1Y7
Tel: 416-325-9411
Fax: 416-325-8851

Assistant Deputy Minister, Chris Giannekos
Tel: 416-325-5621
chris.giannekos@ontario.ca
Director, Infrastructure Planning & Budgeting, Adrian Franko
Tel: 416-325-3307
adrian.franko@ontario.ca
Director, Infrastructure Implementation Secretariat, Heather Fraser
Tel: 416-326-3340
heather.fraser@ontario.ca
Director, Infrastructure Economics & Finance Branch, John Gerritsen
Tel: 416-325-6801
john.gerritsen@ontario.ca
Director, Infrastructure Partnerships Branch, Joe Iannace
Tel: 416-325-3359
joe.iannace@ontario.ca
Director, Infrastructure Policy Branch, Kelly Shields
Tel: 416-325-3349
kelly.shields@ontario.ca

Office of the Provincial Development Facilitator
College Park, 777 Bay St. 27th Flr Suite 2704, Toronto, ON M7A 2J8
Tel: 416-325-0835
Fax: 416-325-0209
www.moi.gov.on.ca

Provincial Development Facilitator, Paula Dill
Tel: 416-325-9764
paula.dill@ontario.ca
Project Manager, Linda Tam
Tel: 416-325-0255
linda.tam@ontario.ca

Ontario Growth Secretariat
College Park, #425, 777 Bay St., Toronto, ON M5G 2E5
Tel: 416-325-1210
Fax: 416-325-7405
Toll-Free: 866-479-9781

Assistant Deputy Minister, Victor Severino
Tel: 416-325-5803
victor.severino@ontario.ca
Director, Growth Policy, Planning & Analysis Branch, Tija Dirks
Tel: 416-325-1546
Fax: 416-325-7403
tija.dirks@ontario.ca
Director, Partnerships & Consultation Branch, Hannah Evans
Tel: 416-325-5799
Fax: 416-325-7403
hannah.evans@ontario.ca

Regulatory Affairs and Strategic Policy
Mowat Block, 900 Bay St. 5th Flr, Toronto, ON M7A 2E3
Tel: 416-325-6559
Fax: 416-325-7041
www.Energy.gov.on.ca

Assistant Deputy Minister, John Whitehead
Tel: 416-325-6544
john.whitehead@ontario.ca
Director, Planning and Agency Relations Branch, Alex Killoch
Tel: 416-326-5572
alex.killoch@ontario.ca
Director, Strategic Policy and Research, Kaili Sermat-Harding
Tel: 416-327-5555
kaili.sermat-harding@ontario.ca

Strategic Real Estate Asset Management
College Park, 777 Bay St., 4th Fl., Toronto, ON M5G 2E5
Tel: 416-327-5596
Fax: 416-325-4920

Assistant Deputy Minister, Victoria Vidal-Ribas
Tel: 416-314-4835
victoria.vidal-ribas@ontario.ca
Acting Director, Accommodation & Property Management Policy Branch, Maggie Allan
Tel: 416-212-1167
maggie.allan@ontario.ca
Director, Policy & Planning Branch, Barbara Ko
Tel: 416-327-2840
barbara.ko@ontario.ca
Director, Real Estate Policy Branch, Bruce Singbush
Tel: 416-326-1766
bruce.singbush2@ontario.ca

Office of the Integrity Commissioner

#2101, 2 Bloor St. East, Toronto, ON M4W 1A8
Tel: 416-314-8983
Fax: 416-314-8987
integrity.mail@oico.on.ca
www.oico.on.ca

The Commissioner administers the Member's Integrity Act, 1994 as it applies to members of the Legislative Assembly & Executive Council in Ontario, including the filing of Public Disclosure Statements, & the right to conduct an inquiry if there are reasonable & probable grounds to believe that the Act has been contravened. The Commissioner also has responsiblity under the MPP Compensation Reform Act (Arm's Length Process), 2001 & the Accountability for Expenses Act (Cabinet Ministers & Opposition Leaders), 2002

Commissioner, Lynn Morrison
Tel: 416-314-8983
lynn.morrison@oico.on.ca

Office Assistant, Janelle King
Tel: 416-314-8983
janelle.king@oico.on.ca

Lobbyists Registration Office
#2101, 2 Bloor St. E., Toronto, ON M4W 1A8
Tel: 416-327-4053
Fax: 416-327-4017
lobbyist.mail@oico.on.ca
lobbyist.oico.on.ca

Under the Lobbyists Registration Act, 1998, the Registrar is responsible for administering the lobbyist registration process, ensuring paid lobbyists report their lobbying of public office holders by filing a return; & ensuring public accessibility to the information contained in the lobbyist's registry.
Registrar, Lynn Morrison
Tel: 416-327-4053
lynn.morrison@oico.on.ca

Ontario Ministry of Intergovernmental Affairs

77 Wellesley St. West, Toronto, ON M7A 1N3
Tel: 416-325-4800
Fax: 416-325-4787
www.ontario.ca/en/your_government/ONT06_023584

Acts Administered:
Ministry of Intergovernmental Affairs Act

Minister & Premier, Hon. Dalton McGuinty
Tel: 416-325-7754
Fax: 416-325-7755
dmcguinty.mpp.co@liberal.ola.org

Deputy Minister, Paul Genest
Tel: 416-314-9710
paul.genest@ontario.ca

Assistant Deputy Minister, Economics & Justice, Craig McFadyen
Tel: 416-325-4603
craig.mcfadyen@ontario.ca

Assistant Deputy Minister, Health, Social, Environment & National Institutions, Ernie Bartucci
Tel: 416-325-4804
ernie.bartucci@ontario.ca

Assistant Deputy Minister & Chief of Protocol, Office of International Relations & Protocol, Mary Shenstone
Tel: 416-325-8545
mary.shenstone@ontario.ca

Ontario Ministry of Labour

400 University Ave., 14th Fl., Toronto, ON M7A 1T7
Tel: 416-326-7160
Toll-Free: 800-531-5551
www.labour.gov.on.ca
TTY: 866-567-8893

Advances safe, fair & harmonious workplace practices that are essential to the social & economic well-being of the people of Ontario. Through the ministry's key areas of occupational health & safety, employment rights & responsibilities, labour relations & internal administration, the ministry's mandate is to set, communicate & enforce workplace standards while encouraging greater workplace self-reliance. A range of specialized agencies, boards & commissions assist the ministry in its work.

Acts Administered:
Ambulance Services Collective Bargaining Act
Back to School Act (Hamilton-Wentworth District School Board), 2000
Back to School Act (Simcoe Muskoka Catholic District School Board), 2002
Back to School Act (Toronto & Windsor), 2001
Back to School Act (Toronto Catholic Elementary) & Education & Provincial Schools Negotiations Amendment Act, 2003
City of Toronto Labour Disputes Resolution Act
Control of Exposure to Biological or Chemical Agents Regulations
Crown Employees Collective Bargaining Act, 2011
Designated Substance Regulations (Various)
Employment Protection for Foreign Nationals Act (Live-in Caregivers & Others), 2009
Employment Standards Act, 2011
Fairness for Parents & Employees Act (Teachers' Withdrawal of Services), 1997
Fire Protection & Prevention Act
Hospital Labour Disputes Arbitration Act
Labour Relations Act
Ministry of Labour Act
Occupational Health & Safety Act
Pay Equity Act
Public Sector Dispute Resolution Act
Public Sector Labour Relations Transitions Act
Regulatory Modernization Act, 2007
Rights of Labour Act
SARS Assistance & Recovery Strategy Act, 2003
Toronto Public Transit Service Resumption Act, 2008
Toronto Transit Commission Labour Disputes Resolution Act, 2011
Workplace Hazardous Materials Information System (WHMIS) Regulations
Workplace Safety & Insurance Act
York University Labour Disputes Resolution Act, 2009

Minister, Hon. Linda Jeffrey
Tel: 416-326-7600
Fax: 416-326-1449
ljeffrey.mpp.co@liberal.ola.org

Deputy Minister, Cynthia Morton
Tel: 416-326-7576
Fax: 416-326-0507

Parliamentary Assistant, Laura Albanese
Tel: 416-243-7984
lalbanese.mpp.co@liberal.ola.org

Chief Information Officer, Ken Kawall
Tel: 416-327-1955
Fax: 416-327-3755
ken.kawall@ontario.ca

Chief Prevention Officer, George Gritziotis
Tel: 416-314-6342
george.gritziotis@ontario.ca

Director, Legal Services, Bridget Lynett
Tel: 416-326-7953
Fax: 416-326-7985
bridget.lynett@ontario.ca

Director, Health & Safety Review Project Secretariat, John Vander Doelen
Tel: 416-325-9280
Fax: 416-325-9286
john.vanderdoelen@ontario.ca

Director, Communications & Marketing, Tom Zach
Tel: 416-326-7404
Fax: 416-314-5809
tom.zach@ontario.ca

Deputy Director, Legal Services, Jane Mallen
Tel: 416-326-1350
jane.mallen@ontario.ca

Assistant Director, Communications & Marketing, Kevin McKaye
Tel: 416-326-1814
kevin.mckaye@ontario.ca

Associated Agencies, Boards & Commissions:
• Office of the Employer Advisor
#704, 151 Bloor St. West.
Toronto, ON M5S 1S4
Tel: 416-327-0020
Fax: 416-327-0726
Toll-free: 800-387-0774
www.employeradviser.ca
Advise & represent employers with fewer than 100 employees in relation to worker's compensation issues at no cost to the employer.
• Office of the Worker Advisor
#1300, 123 Edward St.
Toronto, ON M5G 1E2
Tel: 416-325-8570
Fax: 416-325-4830
Toll-free: 800-435-8980
www.owa.gov.on.ca
• Ontario Labour Relations Board (OLRB)
505 University Ave., 2nd Fl.
Toronto, ON M5G 2P1
Tel: 416-326-7500
Fax: 416-326-7531
Toll-free: 877-339-3335
TTY: 416-212-7036
www.olrb.gov.on.ca
• Pay Equity Commission
#300, 180 Dundas St. West
Toronto, ON M7A 2S6
Tel: 416-314-1896
Fax: 416-314-8741
Toll-free: 800-387-8813
www.payequity.gov.on.ca
• Workplace Safety & Insurance Appeals Tribunal
505 University Ave., 7th Fl.
Toronto, ON M5G 2P2
Tel: 416-314-8800
Fax: 416-326-5164
Toll-free: 888-618-8846
TTY: 416-314-1787
www.wsiat.on.ca
• Workplace Safety & Insurance Board
200 Front St. West
Toronto, ON M5V 3J1
Tel: 416-344-1000
Fax: 416-344-4684
Toll-free: 800-387-0750
TTY: 800-387-0050
wsibcomm@wsib.on.ca; prevention@wsib.on.ca (training programs)
www.wsib.on.ca
Other Communication: eServices Inquiries, Phone: 1-888-243-1569; Forms Order Line: 416-344-3862; Collections, Phone: 1-800-268-0929
The Workplace Safety & Insurance Board is involved in Ontario's occupational health & safety system. The Board's responsibilities are as follows: administering no-fault workplace insurance in Ontario for employers & workers; providing disability benefits; monitoring the quality of healthcare; & assisting workers who have been injured on the job or persons who have contracted an occupational disease in an early & safe return to work.

Economics & Transportation I & IT Cluster
400 University Ave., 9th Fl., Toronto, ON M7A 1T7
Chief Information Officer, Ken Kawall
Tel: 416-327-1955
ken.kawall@ontario.ca

Internal Administrative Services Division
400 University Ave., 14th Fl., Toronto, ON M7A 1T7
Tel: 416-326-7586
Fax: 416-326-5809
Assistant Deputy Minister & Chief Administrative Officer, Mike Anderson
Tel: 416-326-7305
Fax: 416-326-5809
Mike.Anderson@ontario.ca
Director, Finance & Administration, Susan Flanagan
Tel: 416-326-7271
Fax: 416-326-9069
susan.flanagan@ontario.ca

Operations Division
400 University Ave., 14th Fl., Toronto, ON M7A 1T7
Tel: 416-326-7606
Fax: 416-212-4455
Assistant Deputy Minister, Sophie Dennis
Tel: 416-326-7665
sophie.dennis@ontario.ca

Acting Director, Employment Practices, Rakhra Kanchan
Tel: 416-326-7004
Kanchan.Rakhra@ontario.ca
Director, Divisional Learning Unit, Don Hall
Tel: 905-577-1238
don.hall@ontario.ca
Director, Occupational Health & Safety, Renu Kulendran
Tel: 416-326-7866
Fax: 416-326-7242
renu.kulendran@ontario.ca
Acting Director, Information Management & Analysis, Jody Young
Tel: 416-326-9615
jody.young@ontario.ca
Provincial Coordinator, Specialized Professional Services, Gabriel Mansour
Tel: 416-326-1404
gabriel.mansour@ontario.ca

Policy & Dispute Resolution Services Division
400 University Ave., 14th Fl., Toronto, ON M7A 1T7
Tel: 416-326-7558
Fax: 416-326-7599
Assistant Deputy Minister, Kevin J. Wilson
Tel: 416-326-7555
kevin.j.wilson@ontario.ca
Acting Director, Employment, Labour & Corporate Policy, David Beaulieu
Tel: 416-326-7641
david.beaulieu@ontario.ca
Acting Director, Jobs Protection Office, Bob Onyschuk
Tel: 613-260-8363
bob.onyschuk@ontario.ca
Director, Health & Safety Policy Branch, Maria Papoutsis
Tel: 416-326-7628
maria.papoutsis@ontario.ca
Director, Dispute Resolution Services, Reg Pearson
Tel: 416-326-7322
reg.pearson@ontario.ca
Director, Strategic Alignment Project, Richard Prial
Tel: 416-326-7617
prial.richard@ontario.ca

Regional Offices
Central East
#1600, 5001 Yonge St., Toronto, ON M7A 0A3
Tel: 647-777-5005
Fax: 647-777-5010
Regional Director, Ken Fox
Tel: 647-777-5112
ken.fox@ontario.ca
Central West
#400, 1290 Central Pkwy. West, Mississauga, ON L5C 4R3
Tel: 416-235-5330
Fax: 416-235-5355
Toll-Free: 877-202-0008
TTY: 866-567-8893
Regional Director, Jody Young
Tel: 905-615-6543
jody.young@ontario.ca
Eastern
Preston Sq., 347 Preston St., 4th Fl., Ottawa, ON K1S 3J4
Tel: 613-228-8050
Fax: 613-727-2900
Regional Director, Sandra Lawson
Tel: 613-727-2844
Fax: 613-727-2900
sandra.lawson@ontario.ca
Northern
#301, 159 Cedar St., Sudbury, ON P3E 6A5
Tel: 705-564-7400
Fax: 705-670-7435
Toll-Free: 800-461-6325
TTY: 866-567-8893
Regional Director, Peter Augruso
Tel: 705-564-7433
peter.augruso@ontario.ca
Western
119 King St. West, 13th Fl., Hamilton, ON L8P 4Y7
Tel: 905-577-6221
Fax: 905-577-1200
Toll-Free: 800-263-6906
Regional Director, Filomena Savoia
Tel: 905-577-1238
filomena.savoia@ontario.ca

Ontario Ministry of Municipal Affairs & Housing

College Park, 777 Bay St., 17th Fl., Toronto, ON M5G 2E5
Tel: 416-585-7041
Fax: 416-585-6470
Toll-Free: 866-220-2290
mininfo@ontario.ca
www.mah.gov.on.ca
TTY: 866-220-2290
Other Communication: TTY: 416-585-6991
Responsible for providing provincial leadership in defining the framework for governance, finances & management for the local government systems; as well as leadership in the development & administration of the legislative & policy framework for land use planning. It is also responsible for providing the operational, policy & accountability framework for local government to fund & administer social housing; policy & program instruments to create a competitive marketplace for rental housing; & the regulatory framework for buildings.
Acts Administered:
Barrie-Innisfil Boundary Adjustment Act, 2009
Building Code Act
City of Greater Sudbury Act
City of Hamilton Act
City of Kawartha Lakes Act
City of Ottawa Act
City of Toronto Act, 2006
Commercial Tenancies Act
Designation of the Oak Ridges Moraine Area
Development Charges Act
Elderly Person's Housing Aid Act
Geographic Township of Creighton-Davies Act
Greenbelt Act
Housing Development Act
Housing Services Act, 2011
Line Fences Act
Ministry of Municipal Affairs & Housing Act
Municipal Act
Municipal Affairs Act
Municipal Arbitrations Act
Municipal Conflict of Interest Act
Municipal Corporations Quieting Orders Act
Municipal Elections Act
Municipal Extra-Territorial Tax Act
Municipal Franchises Act
Municipal Tax Assistance Act
Municipalities that are Required to Prepare & Adopt Official Plan Amendments
OC Transpo Payments Act
Oak Ridges Moraine Conservation Act
Oak Ridges Moraine Conservation Plan
Oak Ridges Moraine Protection Act, 2001
Ontario Mortgage & Housing Corporation Act
Ontario Municipal Employees Retirement System Act, 2006
Ontario Planning & Development Act
Planning Act
Public Utilities Act
Regional Municipality of Peel Act, 2005
Residential Tenancies Act, 2006
Road Access Act
Shoreline Property Assistance Act
Social Housing Reform Act
Statute Labour Act
Tax Sales Confirmation Act
Territorial Division Act
Toronto Islands Residential Community Stewardship Act
Town of Haldimand Act
Town of Moosonee Act
Town of Norfolk Act

Minister, Hon. Kathleen Wynne
Tel: 416-585-7000
minister.mah@ontario.ca; kwynne.mpp.co@liberal.ola.org

Deputy Minister, William Forward
Tel: 416-585-7100
william.forward@ontario.ca

Parliamentary Assistant, Housing, Mario Sergio
Tel: 416-743-7272
msergio.mpp@liberal.ola.org

Parliamentary Assistant, Municipal Affairs, David Zimmer
Tel: 416-733-7878
dzimmer.mpp.co@liberal.ola.org

Chief Information Officer & Assistant Deputy Minister, Soussan Tabari
Tel: 416-326-8216
Fax: 416-325-8371
soussan.tabari@ontario.ca

Director, Communications, Jodi Melnychuk

Tel: 416-585-6900
jodi.melnychuk@ontario.ca

Executive Assistant, Communications Branch, Lina Minniti
Tel: 416-585-7105
Fax: 416-585-6227
lina.minniti@ontario.ca

Associated Agencies, Boards & Commissions:
• **Building Code Commission (BCC)**
777 Bay St., 2nd Fl.
Toronto, ON M5G 2E5
Tel: 416-585-6666
Fax: 416-585-7531
www.mah.gov.on.ca/Page7394.aspx
Works with the municipal & building sectors & consumer groups to improve & streamline the building regulatory system. This leads to efficient development & more construction jobs, while protecting public safety. The Branch administers the Building Code Act (BCA) & the Ontario Building Code (OBC), which govern the construction of new buildings & the renovation & maintenance of existing buildings. It provides enforcement officials & other building code users with advice & information so that they can apply building code requirements more consistently.
• **Building Materials Evaluation Commission (BMEC)**
777 Bay St., 2nd Fl.
Toronto, ON M5G 2E5
Tel: 416-585-4234
Fax: 416-585-7531
www.mah.gov.on.ca/Page8295.aspx

Business Management Division
Tel: 416-585-7209
Fax: 416-585-6191
Assistant Deputy Minister, Pam Skinner
Tel: 416-585-6670
Fax: 416-585-6191
pam.skinner@ontario.ca
Director, Controllership & Financial Planning, Jim Cassimatis
Tel: 416-585-7693
Fax: 416-585-7328
jim.cassimatis@ontario.ca
Director, Legal Services, Joanne Davies
Tel: 416-585-6551
Fax: 416-585-4003
joanne.davies@ontario.ca
Director, Ontario Internal Audit, Community Services Audit Service Team, David W. Johnston
Tel: 416-585-6550
david.w.johnston@ontario.ca
Director, Human Resources Strategies Branch, Diane Phillipson
Tel: 416-585-6742
Fax: 416-585-7259
diane.phillipson@ontario.ca
Director, Corporate Planning, Karen Rodman
Tel: 416-585-7321
Fax: 416-585-7643
karen.rodman@ontario.ca

Housing Division
Tel: 416-585-6238
Fax: 416-585-6800
Assistant Deputy Minister, Janet Hope
Tel: 416-585-6755
janet.hope@ontario.ca
Director, Housing Programs Branch, Rob Cressman
Tel: 416-585-7021
rob.cressman@ontario.ca
Director, Housing Funding & Risk Management Branch, Keith Extrance
Tel: 416-585-7524
keith.extance@ontario.ca
Director, Housing Policy, Melissa Thomson
Tel: 416-585-6400
Fax: 416-585-7607
melissa.thomson@ontario.ca

Local Government & Planning Policy Division
Tel: 416-585-6320
Fax: 416-585-6463
Assistant Deputy Minister, Dana Richardson
Tel: 416-585-6320
Fax: 416-585-6463
dana.richardson@ontario.ca
Director, Provincial Planning Policy Branch, Audrey Bennett
Tel: 416-585-6072
Fax: 416-585-6870
audrey.bennett@ontario.ca
Director, Municipal Finance Policy Branch, Trevor Bingler
Tel: 416-585-6951
Fax: 416-585-6315
trevor.bingler@ontario.ca
Director, Intergovernmental Relations & Partnerships Branch, Diane McArthur-Rodgers
Tel: 416-585-6047
Fax: 416-585-7638
diane.mcarthur-rodgers@ontario.ca
Director, Local Government Policy Branch, Ralph Walton
Tel: 416-585-7260
Fax: 416-585-7638
ralph.walton@ontario.ca

Municipal Services Division
Fax: 416-585-6445
Assistant Deputy Minister, Elizabeth Harding
Tel: 416-585-6427
Fax: 416-585-6445
liz.harding@ontario.ca
Acting Director, Building & Development Branch, James Douglas
james.douglas@ontario.ca
Acting Director, Municipal Programs & Education Branch, Donna Simmonds
Tel: 416-585-7226
Fax: 416-585-7292
donna.simmonds@ontario.ca

Municipal Services Offices
Municipal Services Offices
Central
777 Bay St., 2nd Fl., Toronto, ON M5G 2E5
Tel: 416-585-6226
Fax: 416-585-6882
Toll-Free: 800-668-0230
Regional Director, Larry Clay
Tel: 416-585-7264
Fax: 416-585-6882
larry.clay@ontario.ca
Eastern
Rockwood House, 8 Estate Lane, Postal Bag 2500, Kingston, ON K7M 9A8
Tel: 613-545-2100
Fax: 613-548-6822
Toll-Free: 800-267-9438
Regional Director, Vincent Fabilli
Tel: 613-545-2133
Fax: 613-548-6822
vincent.fabiilli@ontario.ca
Northeastern
#401, 159 Cedar St., Sudbury, ON P3E 6A5
Tel: 705-564-0120
Fax: 705-564-6863
Toll-Free: 800-461-1193
Regional Director, Lynn Buckham
Tel: 705-564-6858
Fax: 705-564-6863
lynn.buckham@ontario.ca
Northwestern
#223, 435 James St. South, Thunder Bay, ON P7E 6S7
Tel: 807-475-1651
Fax: 807-475-1196
Toll-Free: 800-465-5027
Acting Regional Director, Lynn Buckingham
Tel: 807-475-1187
Fax: 807-475-1196
lynn.buckham@ontario.ca
Western
659 Exeter Rd., 2nd Fl., London, ON N6E 1L3
Tel: 519-873-4020
Fax: 519-873-4018
Toll-Free: 800-265-4736
Regional Director, Micheline Riopelle
Tel: 519-873-4037
Fax: 519-873-4018
micheline.riopelle@ontario.ca

Office of the Chief Information Officer, Community Services I & IT Cluster
Mowat Block, 900 Bay St., 3rd Fl., Toronto, ON M7A 1L2
Tel: 416-325-4598
Fax: 416-325-8371

Ontario Ministry of Natural Resources (MNR)

Whitney Block, #6630, 99 Wellesley St. West, 6th Fl., Toronto, ON M7A 1W3
Toll-Free: 800-667-1940
www.mnr.gov.on.ca
The MNR manages & protects natural resources in the province for wise use. Working with environmental organizations, private industries, fish & game associations, researchers, & other government agencies, the MNR is responsible for the following areas: science & information resources; forest management; fish & wildlife management; land & waters management; Ontario Parks; aviation & forest fire management; & geographic information.
Acts Administered:
Aggregate Resources Act
Algonquin Forestry Authority Act
An Act for the Settlement of certain Questions between the Governments of Canada & Ontario respecting Indian Reserve Lands
An Act to Confirm the title of the Government of Canada to certain Lands & Indian Lands
Arboreal Emblem Act
Avian Emblem Act
Beds of Navigable Waters Act
Conservation Authorities Act
Conservation Bodies Land Regulation
Conservation Land Act
Crown Forest Sustainability Act
Designation of Parks
Duffins Rouge Agricultural Preserve Act, 2005
Endangered Species Act, 2007
Endangered Species Regulation
Far North Act
Fish & Wildlife Conservation Act
Fish Inspection Act
Fisheries Loans Act
Forest Fires Prevention Act
Forestry Act
Forestry Workers Lien for Wages Act
Freshwater Fish Marketing Act (Ontario)
Gas & Oil Leases Act
Guides in Quetico Provincial Park
Heritage Hunting & Fishing Act, 2002
Indian Lands Act
Indian Lands Agreement (1986) Confirmation Act, 2010
Industrial & Mining Lands Compensation Act
Kawartha Highlands Signature Site Park Act
Lake of the Woods Control Board Act
Lakes & Rivers Improvement Act
Mineral Emblem Act
Mining Act
Mining in Provincial Parks
Ministry of Natural Resources Act
Niagara Escarpment Planning & Development Act
North Georgian Bay Recreational Reserve Act
Oil, Gas & Salt Resources Act
Ontario Geographic Names Board Act
Ottawa River Water Powers Act
Possession, Buying & Selling of Wildlife
Professional Foresters Act
Provincial Parks & Conservation Reserves Act
Public Lands Act
Seine River Diversion Act
Surveyors Act
Surveys Act
Wild Rice Harvesting Act
Wilderness Areas Act
Wildlife Management Units
Wildlife Schedules
Wildlife in Captivity

Minister, Hon. Michael Gravelle
Tel: 416-314-2301
Fax: 416-325-5316
minister.mnr@ontario.ca; mgravelle.mpp.co@liberal.ola.org

Deputy Minister, David O'Toole
Tel: 416-314-2150
Fax: 416-314-2159
david.o'toole@ontario.ca

Parliamentary Assistant, Mike Colle
Tel: 416-781-2395
mcolle.mpp.co@liberal.ola.org

Commissioner, Mining & Lands, Linda Kamerman
Tel: 416-314-2322
Fax: 416-314-2327
linda.kamerman@ontario.ca

Director, Communications, David Ayotte
Tel: 416-314-2119
Fax: 416-314-2102
david.ayotte@ontario.ca

Director, Legal Services, Anne Marie Gutierrez
Tel: 416-314-2025
Fax: 416-314-2030
annemarie.gutierrez@ontario.ca

Director, Ontario Internal Audit, Resources & Labour Audit Service Team, Ray Masse
Tel: 416-314-9208
Fax: 416-314-9220
ray.masse@ontario.ca

Associated Agencies, Boards & Commissions:

• Academic & Experience Requirements Committee of the Association of Ontario Land Surveyors (AERC)
1043 McNicoll Ave.
Toronto, ON M1W 3W6
Tel: 416-491-9020
Fax: 416-491-2576

• Algonquin Forestry Authority - Huntsville
222 Main St. West
Huntsville, ON P1H 1Y1
Tel: 705-789-9647
Fax: 705-789-3353
info@algonquinforestry.on.ca
www.algonquinforestry.on.ca
Ensures the viability of the local forest industry while preserving the soil & water resources, fish & wildlife habitat & recreational areas in the park.

• Algonquin Forestry Authority - Pembroke
Victoria Centre
84 Isabella St., 2nd Fl.
Pembroke, ON K8A 5S5
Tel: 613-735-0173
Fax: 613-735-4192
info@algonquinforestry.on.ca
www.algonquinforestry.on.ca

• Association of Ontario Land Surveyors
1043 McNicoll Ave.
Toronto, ON M1W 3W6
Tel: 416-491-9020
Fax: 416-491-2576

• Ontario Fish & Wildlife Heritage Commission
Robinson Pl.
300 Water St.
PO Box 7000
Peterborough, ON K9J 8M5
Tel: 705-755-1905
Fax: 705-755-1900

• Ontario Geographic Names Board
Robinson Place
300 Water St., 2nd Fl.
PO Box 7000
Peterborough, ON K9J 8M5
Tel: 705-755-2134
The Board investigates the background of geographic names & recommends names to be used on maps.

• Ontario Moose & Bear Allocation Advisory Committee
PO Box 964
Sioux Lookout, ON P8T 1B3
Tel: 807-737-2615
Fax: 807-737-4173
An independent advisory committee to allocate moose & bear hunting opportunities provided by the Ministry of Natural Resources within the tourism industry in a manner which is ecologically sustainable & supports the economic viability of the industry in general & specific tourist establishments.

• Ottawa River Regulation Planning Board / Commission de planification de la régularisation de la rivière des Outaouais
351 St Joseph Blvd.
Hull, QC J8Y 3Z5
Tel: 613-994-7079
Toll-free: 800-778-1246
secretariat@ottawariver.ca
www.ottawariver.ca
Established under the terms of a Canada-Ontario-Québec Agreement, it is responsible for the preparation & continuing review of policies, guidelines & criteria for the integrated management of the principal reservoirs of the Ottawa River Basin in order to reduce flood damages along the river, its tributaries & in the Montréal area; it is also responsible for the operation & coordination of inflow forecasting, flow routing & optimization models that will reduce flood damages while having the least possible impact on users of the basin.

• Rabies Advisory Committee
Trent University Science Complex
PO Box 4840
Peterborough, ON K9J 8N8
Tel: 705-755-2270
Established in 1979 it advises the Minister on the development of suitable vaccines against rabies & an effective system for vaccinating wild animals.

• Shibogama Interim Planning Board
PO Box 105
Wunnumin, ON P0V 2Z0
Tel: 807-442-2559
Fax: 807-442-2627
Advises the province on land use & resource development in an 11,131-square-kilometre area south of Big Trout Lake in northwestern Ontario.

• Windigo Interim Planning Board
PO Box 299
Sioux Lookout, ON P8T 1A3
Tel: 807-737-1585
Fax: 807-737-3133
Advises the province on land use & resource development in two areas totalling 15,959 square kilometres south of Big Trout Lake.

Niagara Escarpment Commission (NEC)
232 Guelph St., Georgetown, ON L7G 4B1
Tel: 905-877-5191
Fax: 905-873-7452
Responsible for implementing the Niagara Escarpment Planning & Development Act, which is designed to maintain the escarpment & surrounding area as a continuous natural environment & to ensure that all new development in the escarpment area is compatible with provincial goals of environmental protection & conservation. The commission is also the main source of information on the Niagara Escarpment & the Niagara Escarpment Plan.
Chair, Don Scott
Tel: 905-877-5594
Fax: 905-873-7452
don.scott@ontario.ca
Director, Mark Frawley
Tel: 905-877-4810
Fax: 905-873-7452
mark.frawley@ontario.ca

Corporate Management Division
Whitney Block, #6540, 99 Wellesley St., 6th Fl., Toronto, ON M7A 1W3
Tel: 416-314-1900
Fax: 416-314-1994
Assistant Deputy Minister, David Lynch
Tel: 416-314-1939
Fax: 416-314-1994
david.lynch@ontario.ca
Other Communications: Alternate Phone: 705-755-2700
Director, Corporate Finance & Controllership Branch, Brian Baker
Tel: 705-755-1857
brian.baker@ontario.ca
Director, Services & Infrastructure Management Branch, Larry Davis
Tel: 705-755-2532
Fax: 705-755-2508
300 Water St., 3rd Fl.
PO Box 7000
Peterborough, ON K9J 8M5 Canada
Director, Strategic Human Resources Business Branch, Pat Freistatter
Tel: 705-755-3131
pat.freistatter@ontario.ca
300 Water St., 3rd Fl.
PO Box 7000
Peterborough, ON K9J 8M5 Canada
Manager, Franch Language Services, Land & Resources Cluster, Louise Gagnon
Tel: 416-212-4274
louise.gagnon@ontario.ca
Project Manager, Provincial 2, 4, 5-T Coordinating Office, Amanda Holmes
Tel: 705-755-5641
amanda.holmes@ontario.ca

Forestry Division
Roberta Bondar Pl., #400, 70 Foster Dr., Sault Ste. Marie, ON P6A 6V5
Fax: 705-945-5977
Toll-Free: 800-667-1940
Acting Assistant Deputy Minister, Kathleen McFadden
Tel: 705-945-6660
bill.thornton@ontario.ca
Acting Director, Business Development Branch, Wayne Barnes
Tel: 705-945-6795
wayne.barnes@ontario.ca
Director, Operations Branch, David Hayhurst
Tel: 705-945-5733
david.hayhurst@ontario.ca
Director, Forest Tenure & Economics Branch, Mark Speers
Tel: 705-945-6636
mark.speers@ontario.ca

Office of the Chief Information Officer, Land and Resources I&IT Cluster
Whitney Block, 99 Wellesley, 6th Flr Rm 6601, Toronto, ON M7A 1W3
Fax: 416-314-6091
Chief Information Officer, Robert Hollis
Tel: 416-314-1528
robert.hollis@ontario.ca
Acting Director, Organizational Performance, Judy Tomarin
Tel: 416-212-7560
judy.tomarin@ontario.ca
Head, Business Solutions Services, Patrick Chung
Tel: 416-212-4821
patrick.hung@ontario.ca
Head, Strategy Information and Program Management, Doug Green
Tel: 519-826-3236
doug.green@ontario.ca
Head, Service Management, Uwe Helmer
Tel: 519-826-5160
uwe.helmer@ontario.ca
Acting Manager, Business & Financial Services, Glenn Wetherall
Tel: 519-826-4769
glenn.wetherall@ontario.ca

Policy Division
#6540, 99 Wellesley St. West, Toronto, ON M7A 1W3
Fax: 416-314-1994
Toll-Free: 800-667-1940
Provides assistance, advice & direction to ministry staff at all levels, on a variety of compliance & law enforcement matters. The branch is responsible for the development, coordination & delivery of an Integrated Provincial Compliance Program which focuses on the promotion, monitoring & enforcement aspects of compliance.
Assistant Deputy Minister, Rosalyn Lawrence
Tel: 416-314-6131
rosalyn.lawrence@ontario.ca
Director, Aboriginal Branch, Karan Aquino
Tel: 705-755-1996
Fax: 705-755-1372
karan.aquino@ontario.ca
Director, Biodiversity Branch & Renewable Energy Program, Eric Boysen
Tel: 705-755-5999
Fax: 705-755-2901
eric.boysen@ontario.ca
Director, Strategic Policy & Economics Branch, Craig Brown
Tel: 416-314-1923
Fax: 416-314-1948
craig.brown@ontario.ca
Director, Natural Heritage, Lands & Protected Spaces Branch, Ray Pichette
Tel: 705-755-1241
Fax: 705-755-1971
ray.pichette@ontario.ca
Director, Species at Risk Branch, Marc Rondeau
Tel: 416-314-1819
Fax: 705-755-5483
marc.rondeau@ontario.ca
Director, Forests Branch, Chris M. Walsh
Tel: 705-945-6653
Fax: 705-945-6667
chris.m.walsh@ontario.ca

Provincial Services Division
#6540, 99 Wellesley St. West, Toronto, ON M7A 1W3
Tel: 416-326-9504
The ministry's local presence in communities across the province, delivering integrated programs on resource management through 3 regions & 25 districts. The division delivers programs on provincial enforcement, native affairs, fisheries, forests & provincial lands, in addition to resources such as finance, facilities & engineering infrastructure, equipment & vehicles.
Assistant Deputy Minister, Tracey Mill
Tel: 416-326-9502
tracey.mill@ontario.ca
Director, Enforcement Branch, Lois Deacon
Tel: 705-755-1750
Fax: 705-755-1757
lois.deacon@ontario.ca
Director, Ontario Parks, Bradley Fauteux
Tel: 705-755-1702
Fax: 705-755-1701
bradley.fauteux@ontario.ca
Other Communications: Web Site: www.ontarioparks.com
Director, Fish & Wildlife Services Branch, Mike Morencie
Tel: 519-873-4609
Fax: 705-755-1901
mike.morencie@ontario.ca
Director, Aviation, Forest Fire & Emergency Services Branch, Al Tithecott
Tel: 705-945-5937
al.tithecott@ontario.ca

Regional Operations Division
#6610, 99 Wellesley St. West, Toronto, ON M7A 1W3
Fax: 416-314-2629
Toll-Free: 800-667-1940
Other Communication: Peterborough Fax: 705-755-5073
Acting Assistant Deputy Minister, Carrie Hayward
Tel: 416-314-2621
carrie.hayward@ontario.ca
Director, Far North Branch (South Porcupine), Dianne Corbett
Tel: 705-235-1284
Fax: 705-235-1106
dianne.corbett@ontario.ca
Director, Integration Branch, Dan Marinigh
Tel: 705-755-1620

Fax: 705-755-1201
dan.marinigh@ontario.ca

Regional Offices
Northeast Region
Ontario Government Complex, 5520 Hwy. 101 East, PO Box 3020, South Porcupine, ON P0N 1H0
Tel: 705-235-1157
Fax: 705-235-1246
Regional Director, Ginette Brindle
Tel: 705-235-1153
Fax: 705-235-1226
ginette.brindle@ontario.ca
Northwest Region
Ontario Government Bldg., #221A, 435 James St. South, Thunder Bay, ON P7E 6S8
Tel: 807-475-1261
Fax: 807-473-3023
Regional Director, Allan Willcocks
Tel: 807-475-1264
allan.willcocks@ontario.ca
District Manager, Kim Groenendyk
Tel: 807-887-5013
kim.groenendyk@ontario.ca
Southern Region
Robinson Place, South Tower, 300 Water St., 4th Fl. South, PO Box 7000, Peterborough, ON K9J 8M5
Tel: 705-755-2000
Fax: 705-755-3233
Acting Regional Director, Jane Ireland
Tel: 705-755-3235
jane.ireland@ontario.ca
District Manager, Debbie Pella Keen
Tel: 905-713-7372
debbie.pellakeen@ontario.ca
District Manager, Kenneth Durst
Tel: 613-258-8201
ken.durst@ontario.ca
District Manager, Rick Watchorn
Tel: 613-732-5520
rick.watchorn@ontario.ca

Science & Information Resources Division
Roberta Bondar Pl., #400, 70 Foster Dr., Sault Ste Marie, ON P6A 6V5
Tel: 705-755-2000
Fax: 705-755-2802
Toll-Free: 800-667-1940
The division leads the development & application of scientific knowledge, information management systems & information technologies in support of the Ministry mandate. The division is responsible for ensuring operational decision-making requirements of the Ministry are supported by sound science & reliable data, by providing accurate, relevant & timely information to manage resources in an ecologically sustainable manner.
Assistant Deputy Minister, Frank Kennedy
Tel: 705-945-6703
Fax: 705-755-2802
frank.kennedy@ontario.ca
Acting Director, Science & Information Branch, Cameron Mack
Tel: 705-755-1909
Fax: 705-945-6527
cameron.mack@ontario.ca
Director, Geographic Information Branch, Brian Maloney
Tel: 705-755-2204
Fax: 705-755-1640
brian.j.maloney@ontario.ca
Director, Applied Research & Development Branch, Anne Neary
Tel: 705-755-2807
Fax: 705-755-2802
anne.neary@ontario.ca

Ontario Ministry of Northern Development & Mines

159 Cedar St., Sudbury, ON P3E 6A5
Fax: 416-327-0651
Toll-Free: 888-415-9845
www.mndm.gov.on.ca
TTY: 866-349-1388
Other Communication: Sudbury Phone: 705-670-5755, Fax: 705-670-5818
Secondary Address: #5630, 99 Wellesley St. West, 5th Fl. Whitney Block
Toronto, ON M7A 1W3
Fax: 416-327-0665
The Ministry of Northern Development & Mines is the only regional ministry within the government & plays a central role in northern affairs. MNDM supports the mineral industry by providing it with valuable information about the province's geology. It also delivers & administers Ontario's Mining Act to improve the investment climate for mineral development. The ministry has a two-fold mandate, to promote northern economic development & support mineral sector competitiveness. The ministry is developing an initiative to help Ontario's Far North communities attract environmentally sound development, work with First Nation communities, partner ministries, the federal government, the mineral sector & private sector stakeholders to create opportunities for residents to help First Nation communities become more self-reliant. The ministry works with the Northern Ontario Heritage Fund Corporation & with the Ontario Northland Transportation Commission to bring much-needed service improvements to the northeast.
Acts Administered:
Forestry Workers Lien for Wages Act
Mining Act
Ministry of Northern Development, Mines & Forestry Act
Northern Forest Tenure Modernization Act, 2011
Northern Ontario Grow Bonds Corporation Act
Northern Ontario Grow Bonds Corporation Repeal Act, 2011
Northern Ontario Heritage Fund Act
Northern Services Boards Act
Ontario Northland Transportation Commission Act
Professional Geoscientists Act

Minister, Hon. Rick Bartolucci
Tel: 416-327-0633
Fax: 416-327-0665
ndmminister@ontario.ca; rbartolucci.mpp.co@liberal.ola.org
Whitney Block
5630 - 99 Wellesley St. West, 5th Fl.
Toronto, ON M7A 1W3

Deputy Minister, George Ross
Tel: 416-212-2701
george.ross@ontario.ca

Parliamentary Assistant, Bill Mauro
Tel: 807-623-9237
bill.mauro@ontario.ca
Whitney Block
5630 - 99 Wellesley St. West, 5th Fl.
Toronto, ON M7A 1W3

Chief of Staff, Joanne Campea
Tel: 416-327-1208
joanne.campea@ontario.ca
Whitney Block
5630 - 99 Wellesley St. West, 5th Fl.
Toronto, ON M7A 1W3

Director, Corporate Policy Secretariat, Alison Drummond
Tel: 416-327-0302
Fax: 416-327-0634
alison.drummond@ontario.ca

Director, Legal Services, Andrew Macdonald
Tel: 416-327-0640
Fax: 416-327-0646
andrew.macdonald@ontario.ca

Director, Ontario Internal Audit, Resources & Labour Audit Service Team, Ray Masse
Tel: 416-314-9208
ray.masse@ontario.ca

Director, Communications Services Branch, Fadia Mishrigi
Tel: 416-327-0687
Fax: 416-327-0664
fadia.mishrigi@ontario.ca

Associated Agencies, Boards & Commissions:
• Ontario Northland
555 Oak St. East
North Bay, ON P1B 8L3
Tel: 705-472-4500
Fax: 705-472-4267
Toll-free: 800-363-7512
info@ontarionorthland.ca
www.ontarionorthland.ca
• Owen Sound Transportation Company Ltd.
717875, Hwy. 6
Owen Sound, ON N4K 5N7
Tel: 519-376-8740
Toll-free: 800-265-3163
www.ontarioferries.com

Corporate Management Division
#704, 159 Cedar St., Sudbury, ON P3E 6A5
Tel: 705-564-7438
Fax: 705-564-7447
Assistant Deputy Minister & Chief Adminstrative Officer, Don Ignacy
Tel: 705-564-7443
Fax: 705-564-7447
don.ignacy@ontario.ca
Director, Human Resources Business Unit, Cleo Degagne
Tel: 705-564-7445
Fax: 705-564-7942
cleo.degagne@ontario.ca

Mines & Minerals Division
Willet Green Miller Centre, 933 Ramsey Lake Rd., Sudbury, ON P3E 6B5
Tel: 705-670-5755
Fax: 705-670-5818
Toll-Free: 888-415-9845
The Mines & Minerals Division works to generate new wealth & benefits for the residents of Ontario by providing basic geological information gathering & interpretation in support of Ontario's exploration, mine development & mining sectors & the administration of Ontario's Mining Act in a fair & consistent fashion. Collects, analyzes & publishes valuable information about the state of the mining & mineral industries, as well as specific information about the location & quality of mineral deposits. The field staff throughout the province provide consultative services to the industry through all phases of the mining sequence, & include resident geologists, mining recorders & mineral development officers.
Acting Assistant Deputy Minister, Cindy Blancher-Smith
Tel: 705-670-5820
Fax: 705-670-5818
cindy.blancher-smith@ontario.ca
Director, Aboriginal Relations Branch, Bernie Hughes
Tel: 705-670-5743
Fax: 705-670-5818
bernie.hughes@ontario.ca
Acting Director, Diamond Sector Unit, Marc Leroux
Tel: 705-670-5609
Fax: 705-670-5818
marc.leroux@ontario.ca
Director, Mining Act Modernization, Robert Merwin
Tel: 705-670-5627
Fax: 416-327-0634
robert.merwin@ontario.ca
Senior Manager, Mining Lands Section, Roy Denomme
Tel: 705-670-5840
Fax: 705-475-1120
roy.denomme@ontario.ca

Mineral Development & Lands Branch
Willet Green Miller Centre, 933 Ramsey Lake Rd., Level B4, Sudbury, ON P3E 6B5
Tel: 705-670-5787
Fax: 705-670-5803
Toll-Free: 888-415-9845
Acting Director, Rob Ferguson
Tel: 705-670-5784
rob.ferguson@ontario.ca
Manager, Mineral Exploration & Development Section, Stephen DeVos
Tel: 705-670-5795
stephen.devos@ontario.ca
Manager, Mine Rehabilitation, Inspection & Compliance, Leslie Cooper
Tel: 705-670-5790
leslie.cooper@ontario.ca
Manager, Strategic Support Unit, Bruce Pollard
Tel: 705-670-3003
bruce.pollard@ontario.ca

Ontario Geological Survey
Willet Green Miller Centre, 933 Ramsey Lake Rd., Level B6, Sudbury, ON P3E 6B5
Tel: 705-670-5758
Fax: 705-670-5818
Toll-Free: 888-415-9845
Director, Dr. Andy Fyon
Tel: 705-670-5924
andy.fyon@ontario.ca
Senior Manager, Geoscience Laboratories, Ed Debicki
Tel: 705-670-5643
ed.debicki@ontario.ca
Senior Manager, Precambrian Geoscience, Jack Parker
Tel: 705-670-5976
jack.parker@ontario.ca
Senior Manager, Resident Geologist Program, Jim Ireland
Tel: 705-670-5955
jim.ireland@ontario.ca
Acting Manager, Sedimentary Geoscience, Derek Armstrong
Tel: 705-670-5913
derek.armstrong@ontario.ca

Northern Development Division
Roberta Bondar Place, #200, 70 Foster Dr., Sault Ste Marie, ON P6A 6V8
Tel: 705-945-5900
Fax: 705-945-5931
Toll-Free: 800-461-2287
Other Communication: Delivery of Government Services: 705-945-5904
Responsible for promoting business, industrial, community & regional economic development & diversification; improving access to social & health services for northerners; planning & coordinating an integrated transportation system to meet private & commercial transportation needs at local, regional & provincial levels; coordinating the policies & programs of other ministries to

ensure the special needs of northerners are addressed by government.
Assistant Deputy Minister, Cal McDonald
Tel: 705-564-7569
Fax: 705-945-5932
cal.mcdonald@ontario.ca
Executive Director, Northern Ontario Heritage Fund Corporation, Bruce Strapp
Tel: 705-945-6734
Fax: 705-564-7447
bruce.strapp@ontario.ca
Director, Transportation, Trade & Investment Branch, Faye Johnson
Tel: 705-945-5903
Fax: 705-564-7597
faye.johnson@ontario.ca
Director, Regional Economic Development Branch, Helen Mulc
Tel: 705-564-7134
Fax: 705-564-7582
helen.mulc@ontario.ca
Director, Strategic Coordination & Planning Branch, Lisa Zanetti
Tel: 705-564-7016
lisa.zanetti@ontario.ca
Kenora
#104, 810 Robertson St., Kenora, ON P9N 4J2
Tel: 807-468-2937
Fax: 807-468-2930
Manager, Christine Hansen
Tel: 807-468-2938
christine.hansen@ontario.ca
North Bay
#203, 447 McKeown Ave., North Bay, ON P1B 9S9
Tel: 705-494-4045
Fax: 705-494-4069
Manager, Moe Dorie
Tel: 705-494-4176
moe.dorie@ontario.ca
Sault Ste. Marie
Roberta Bondar Place, #200, 70 Foster Dr., Sault Ste Marie, ON P6A 6V8
Tel: 705-945-5914
Fax: 705-945-5931
Manager, Denis Rochon
Tel: 705-356-3004
denis.rochon@ontario.ca
Sudbury
#601, 159 Cedar St., Sudbury, ON P3E 6A5
Tel: 705-564-7517
Fax: 705-564-7583
Manager, Murray Morello
Tel: 705-564-7519
murray.morello@ontario.ca
Thunder Bay
#332, 435 James St. South, Thunder Bay, ON P7E 6L3
Tel: 807-475-1648
Fax: 807-475-1589
Manager, Dale Willis
Tel: 807-475-1573
dale.willis@ontario.ca
Timmins
5520 Hwy. 101 East, PO Box 3060, South Porcupine, ON P0N 1H0
Tel: 705-235-1664
Fax: 705-235-1660
Manager, Brian Pountney
Tel: 705-235-1654
brian.pountney@ontario.ca

Office of the Chief Information Officer, Land & Resources I&IT Cluster
Whitney Block, #6601, 99 Wellesley St. West, 6th Fl., Toronto, ON M7A 1W3
Chief Information Officer, Robert Hollis
Tel: 416-314-1528
robert.hollis@ontario.ca
Acting Director, Organizational Performance, Judy Tomarin
Tel: 416-212-7560
judy.tomarin@ontario.ca
Head, Business Solutions Services, Patrick Chung
Tel: 416-212-4821
patrick.chung@ontario.ca
Head, Strategy, Information & Program Management, Doug Green
Tel: 519-826-3236
doug.green@ontario.ca
Head, Service Management, Uwe Helmer
Tel: 519-826-5160
uwe.helmer@ontario.ca
Acting Manager, Business & Financial Services, Glenn Wetherall
Tel: 519-826-4769
glenn.wetherall@ontario.ca

Ring of Fire Secretariat
Willet Green Miller Centre, 933 Ramsey Lake Rd., Level B2, Sudbury, ON P3E 6B5
Tel: 705-670-5755
Fax: 705-670-5818
Toll-Free: 888-415-9845
Assistant Deputy Minister, Christine Kaszycki
Tel: 705-670-5877
christine.kaszycki@ontario.ca
Director, Aboriginal Community & Stakeholder Relations, Harvey Yesno
Tel: 807-475-1587
harvey.yesno@ontario.ca
Senior Policy Advisor, Enviromental Assessment & Land Use Planning, Ariane Heisey
Tel: 416-327-0110
ariane.heisey@ontario.ca

Office of the Ombudsman

Bell Trinity Sq., South Tower, 483 Bay St., 10th Fl., Toronto, ON M5G 2C9
Tel: 416-586-3300
Fax: 416-586-3485
Toll-Free: 800-263-1830
info@ombudsman.on.ca
www.ombudsman.on.ca
TTY: 866-411-4211
Other Communication: Ligne sans frais: 1-800-387-2620 (Français)

An impartial body independent of government that investigates & resolves complaints about the administrative actions & decisions of provincial government organizations such as ministries, boards, agencies, commissions & tribunals. The Ombudsman is an Officer of the provincial Legislature & has jurisdiction over all provinical government organizations as an office of last resort. All available complaint & appeal procedures whenever possible should be used before the Ombudsman conducts an investigation. The Ombudsman decides cases based on independent investigations & works to find solutions that are acceptable to everyone involved. Services are free & confidential & are available in English, French or any other language.

Acts Administered:
Ombudsman Act

Ombudsman, André Marin
Tel: 416-586-3300

Executive Administrative Assistant, Denise Salmon
Tel: 416-586-3300
www.ombudsman.on.ca

Ontario Power Generation

700 University Ave., Toronto, ON M5G 1X6
Tel: 416-592-2555
Toll-Free: 877-592-2555
webmaster@opg.com
www.opg.com
Other Communication: Media Relations Email: media@opg.com; Investor Relations Email: investor.relations@opg.com

Mandate is to meet Ontario's requirements for electricity so as to result in the greatest overall benefit to the community & the lowest cost to the consumer, while operating in a safe & environmentally responsible manner. Assets include 3 nuclear generating stations, 5 fossil generating stations, 64 hydroelectric stations, 3 wind generating stations.

Chair, Hon. Jake Epp

President & Chief Executive Officer, Tom Mitchell

Chief Financial Officer, Donn Hanbridge

Senior Vice-President, Business Services & Information Technology, Robert Boguski

Executive Vice-President, Corporate Affairs, Bruce Boland

Executive Vice-President, Hydro, John Murphy

Senior Vice-President, Human Resources & Chief Ethics Officer, Barb Keenan

Senior Vice-President, Law & General Counsel, David Brennan

Chief Nuclear Officer, Wayne Robbins

Ontario Ministry of Tourism & Culture

Hearst Block, 900 Bay St., 9th Fl., Toronto, ON M7A 2E1
Tel: 416-326-9326
Fax: 416-314-7854
Toll-Free: 800-668-2746
www.mtc.gov.on.ca
TTY: 416-325-5807
Other Communication: Ontario Travel Information: 1-800-668-2746; Toll-Free TTY: 1-866-700-0040

Acts Administered:
AGO Act
Arts Council Act
Asian Heritage Act
Celebration of Portuguese Heritage Act
Centennial Centre of Science & Technology Act
Dutch Heritage Month Act
Emancipation Day Act
Foreign Cultural Objects Immunity from Seizure Act
George R. Gardiner Museum of Ceramic Art Act
German Pioneers Day Act
Historical Parks Act
Hotel Registration of Guests Act
Hummingbird Performing Arts Centre Corporation Act
Innkeepers Act
Irish Heritage Day Act
Italian Heritage Month Act
McMichael Canadian Art Collection Act
Metropolitan Toronto Convention Centre Act
Ministry of Citizenship & Culture Act
Ministry of Tourism & Recreation Act
Niagara Parks Act
Ontario Heritage Act
Ontario Place Corporation Act
Ontario Wine Week Act
Ottawa Convention Centre Corporation Act
Public Libraries Act
Royal Ontario Museum Act
Science North Act
South Asian Heritage Act
St. Lawrence Parks Commission Act
Status of Ontario Artists Act
Tartan Act
Ukrainian Heritage Day Act
United Empire Loyalists' Day Act

Minister, Hon. Michael Chan
Tel: 416-326-9326
Fax: 416-314-7854
mchan.mpp.co@liberal.ola.org

Acting Deputy Minister, Steven Davidson
Tel: 416-314-7846
steven.davidson@ontario.ca

Parliamentary Assistant, Tourism, Kim Craitor
Tel: 416-325-3715
Fax: 416-326-1712
kim.craitor@ontario.ca

Parliamentary Assistant, Culture & Sport, Michael Coteau
Tel: 416-494-6856
mcoteau.mpp.co@liberal.ola.org

Acting Director, Communications, Jennifer E. Lang
Tel: 416-212-3929
Fax: 416-325-5968
jennifer.lang@ontario.ca

Associated Agencies, Boards & Commissions:
- **Art Gallery of Ontario**
317 Dundas St. West
Toronto, ON M5T 1G4
Tel: 416-977-0414
Fax: 416-979-6669
www.ago.net
- **Conservation Review Board**
400 University Ave. 4th Fl.
Toronto, ON M7A 2R9
Tel: 416-314-7137
Fax: 416-314-7175
conservation.review.board@ontario.ca
www.crb.gov.on.ca
- **McMichael Canadian Art Collection**
10365 Islington Ave.
Kelinburg, ON L0J 1C0
Tel: 905-893-1121
Fax: 905-893-2588
www.mcmichael.com

• Metro Toronto Convention Centre Corporation (MTCC)
255 Front St. West
Toronto, ON M5V 2W6
Tel: 416-585-8120
Fax: 416-585-8198
info@mtccc.com; sales@mtccc.com
www.mtccc.com

• Minister's Advisory Council for Arts & Culture
400 University Ave., 5th Fl.
Toronto, ON M7A 2R9
Tel: 416-314-8321
Fax: 416-314-7091
macac@ontario.ca

• Niagara Parks Commission
Oak Hall Administration Bldg.
7400 Portage Rd. South
PO Box 150
Niagara Falls, ON L2E 6T2
Tel: 905-356-2241
Fax: 905-354-6041
Toll-free: 877-642-7275
www.niagaraparks.com

• Ontario Arts Council
151 Bloor St. West, 5th Fl.
Toronto, ON M5S 1T6
Tel: 416-961-1660
Fax: 416-961-7796
www.arts.on.ca

• Ontario Heritage Trust (OHT)
10 Adelaide St. East
Toronto, ON M5C 1J3
Tel: 416-325-5000
Fax: 416-325-5071
www.heritagetrust.on.ca
For more than three decades, the Ontario Heritage Trust has preserved, protected & promoted Ontario's rich & varied heritage. The Trust celebrates the people, places & events that have influenced & continue to shape our culture. As Ontario's lead heritage agency, the Trust's work extends to every corner of the province.

• Ontario Library Service - North / Service des bibliothèques de l'Ontario - Nord
334 Regent St.
Sudbury, ON P3C 4E2
Tel: 705-675-6467
Fax: 705-675-2285
Toll-free: 800-461-6348
www.olsn.ca

• Ontario Media Development Corporation (OMDC)
South Tower
#501, 175 Bloor St. East
Toronto, ON M4W 3R8
Tel: 416-314-6858
Fax: 416-314-6876
mail@omdc.on.ca
www.omdc.on.ca
Formerly the Ontario Film Development Corporation (OFDC).

• Ontario Place Corporation
955 Lake Shore Blvd. West
Toronto, ON M6K 3B9
Tel: 416-314-9900
Fax: 416-314-9992
www.ontarioplace.com

• Ontario Science Centre
770 Don Mills Rd.
Toronto, ON M3C 1T3
Tel: 416-696-1000
Fax: 416-696-3124
www.ontariosciencecentre.ca

• Ontario Tourism Marketing Partnership Corporation
#900,10 Dundas St. East
Toronto, ON M7A 2A1
Tel: 416-212-0757
Fax: 416-325-6004
Toll-free: 800-668-2746
www.ontariotravel.net

• Ontario Trillium Foundation
800 Bay St., 5th Fl.
Toronto, ON M5S 3A9
Tel: 416-963-4927
Fax: 416-963-8781
Toll-free: 800-263-2887
TTY: 416-963-7905
trillium@trilliumfoundation.org
www.trilliumfoundation.org
The Ontario Trillium Foundation is an agency of the Ministry of Culture. Grants are provided to eligible not-for-profit & charitable organizations in the areas of arts & culture, sports and recreation, human & social services, & the environment.

• Ottawa Convention Centre
55 Colonel By Dr.
Ottawa, ON K1N 9J2
Tel: 613-563-1984
Fax: 613-563-7646
www.ottawaconventioncentre.com

• Royal Botanical Gardens
680 Plains Rd. West
Burlington, ON L7T 4H4
Tel: 905-527-1158
Fax: 905-577-0375
Toll-free: 800-694-4769
www.rbg.ca

• Royal Ontario Museum (ROM)
100 Queen's Park Cres.
Toronto, ON M5S 2C6
Tel: 416-586-5549
Fax: 416-586-5685
info@rom.on.ca
www.rom.on.ca

• Science North
100 Ramsey Lake Rd.
Sudbury, ON P3E 5S9
Tel: 705-522-3701
Fax: 705-522-4954
www.sciencenorth.ca

• Southern Ontario Library Service
#902, 111 Peter St.
Toronto, ON M5V 2H1
Tel: 416-961-1669
Fax: 416-961-5122
Toll-free: 800-387-5765
www.sols.org

• St. Lawrence Parks Commission
RR#1
Morrisburg, ON K0C 1X0
Tel: 613-543-3704
Fax: 613-543-2847
Toll-free: 800-437-2233
TTY: 613-543-4181
www.parks.on.ca
The St. Lawrence Parks Commission is an Ontario provincial agency established in 1955 to provide recreation, tourism, cultural & educational opportunities for residents of Ontario & visitors to the province through the presentation & interpretation of historical attractions & the development & operation of parks, campgrounds, scenic parkways & recreational areas.

Culture Division
#1800, 401 Bay St., Toronto, ON M7A 0A7
Tel: 416-314-7265
Fax: 416-314-7461

Assistant Deputy Minister, Kevin Finnerty
Tel: 416-314-7262
kevin.finnerty@ontario.ca
Director, Programs & Services Branch, Peter Armstrong
Tel: 416-314-7342
peter.armstrong@ontario.ca
Director, Culture & Strategic Policy Branch, Donna Ratchford
Tel: 416-212-7646
donna.ratchford@ontario.ca
Acting Director, Culture Agencies Branch, Suzanne Rowe Knight
Tel: 416-327-4305
suzanne.roweknight@ontario.ca

Office of the Chief Information Officer, Community Services I & IT Cluster
Mowat Block, 900 Bay St., 3rd Fl., Toronto, ON M7A 1L2
Assistant Deputy Minister & Chief Information Officer, Soussan Tabari
Tel: 416-326-8216
soussan.tabari@ontario.ca
Director, Case & Grants Management Solutions, Sanaul Haque
Tel: 416-585-6746
sanaul.haque@ontario.ca
Director, I-Access Solutions Branch, Sanjay Madan
Tel: 416-325-2264
sanjay.madan@ontario.ca
Director, Strategic Planning & Business Relationship Management Branch, Lolita Singh
Tel: 416-326-7942
lolita.singh@ontario.ca
Head, Data Collection & Decision Support Solutions Branch, Michael Villani
Tel: 416-212-9709
michael.villani@ontario.ca

Ontario Internal Audit, Culture & Innovation Audit Service Team
College Park, 777 Bay St., 25th Fl., Toronto, ON M5G 2E5
Tel: 416-326-0800
Fax: 416-326-1712

Ontario Seniors' Secretariat
#601C, 777 Bay St., 6th Fl., Toronto, ON M7A 2J4
Tel: 416-326-7076
Fax: 416-326-7078
www.ontarioseniors.ca

Minister Responsible, Hon. Linda Jeffrey
Tel: 416-326-7600
ljeffrey.mpp.co@liberal.ola.org
Parliamentary Assistant, Joe Dickson
Tel: 905-427-2060
jdickson.mpp.co@liberal.ola.org
Assistant Deputy Minister, Juanita Dobson
Tel: 416-326-7069
Fax: 416-326-7079
juanita.dobson@ontario.ca
Director, Retirement Homes Project, Abby Katz Starr
Tel: 416-325-2649
abby.katzstarr@ontario.ca
Manager, Policy Initiatives, Elizabeth Esteves
Tel: 416-326-7064
elizabeth.esteves@ontario.ca
Acting Content Coordinator, Public Education & Awareness, Justin Saynaraine
Tel: 416-325-7853
justin.saynaraine@ontario.ca

Sport, Recreation & Community Programs
College Park, 777 Bay St., 23rd Fl., Toronto, ON M7A 1S5
Tel: 416-326-4371
Fax: 416-314-6301

Assistant Deputy Minister, Phil Malcolmson
Tel: 416-212-8995
phil.malcolmson@ontario.ca
Director, Sport, Recreation & Community Programs Branch, Rick Beaver
Tel: 416-314-7696
rick.beaver@ontario.ca
Manager, Strategic Development, Gillian Steeve
Tel: 416-326-4370
gillian.steeve@ontario.ca

Tourism Planning & Operations Division
Hearst Block, 900 Bay St., 10th Fl., Toronto, ON M7A 2E2
Acting Assistant Deputy Minister, Brian Lemire
Tel: 416-325-2861
brian.lemire@ontario.ca
General Manager, Fort William Historical Park, Sergio Buonocore
Tel: 807-473-2341
sergio.buonocore@ontario.ca
Other Communications: URL: www.fwhp.ca
General Manager, Huronia Historical Parks, Jan Gray
Tel: 705-528-7690
jan.gray@ontario.ca
Other Communications: URL: www.hhp.on.ca
Director, Tourism Agencies Branch, Dean Hustwick
Tel: 416-326-9579
dean.hustwick@ontario.ca
Director, Ontario Place Revitalization Branch, Sevaun Palvetzian
Tel: 416-212-4861
sevaun.palvetzian@ontario.ca

Tourism Policy & Development Division
Hearst Block, 900 Bay St., 10th Fl., Toronto, ON M7A 2E1
Tel: 416-326-9326
Fax: 416-325-6985
www.tourism.gov.on.ca

Assistant Deputy Minister, Richard McKinnell
Tel: 416-325-6961
richard.mckinnell@ontario.ca
Director, Investment & Development Office, Michael Langford
Tel: 416-314-7105
Fax: 416-327-2506
michael.langford@ontario.ca
Acting Director, Tourism Policy & Research, Diane Wise
Tel: 416-325-6055
Fax: 416-314-7341
diane.wise@ontario.ca
Manager, Sports, Culture & Tourism Partnerships Secretariat, Karen L. Drake
Tel: 416-314-1685
karen.l.drake@ontario.ca
Acting Grants Administration Officer, Product Development & Investment Services, Joan Marquis
Tel: 416-326-6894
joan.marquis@ontario.ca

Regional & Corporate Services Division
400 University Ave., 2nd Fl., Toronto, ON M7A 2R9
Tel: 416-314-7311
Fax: 416-314-7313

Assistant Deputy Minister & Chief Administrative Officer, Robert M. Montgomery
robert.m.montgomery@ontario.ca
Acting Director, Legal Services, James Girling
Tel: 416-314-7022

Fax: 416-314-7038
james.girling@ontario.ca
Acting Director, Regional Services Branch, Tom Chrzan
Tel: 416-314-6680
Fax: 416-314-6686
tom.chrzan@ontario.ca
Director, Corporate Resources Branch, Heather Taylor
Tel: 416-325-6135
Fax: 416-314-4968
heather.taylor@ontario.ca
Central Region
400 University Ave., 4th Fl., Toronto, ON M7A 2R9
Tel: 416-314-6044
Fax: 416-314-2024
Toll-Free: 877-395-4105

Manager, Tom Chrzan
Tel: 416-314-6682
tom.chrzan@ontario.ca
East Region
347 Preston St., 4th Fl., Ottawa, ON K1S 3J4
Tel: 613-742-3360
Fax: 613-742-5300
Toll-Free: 800-267-9340

Manager, Valerie Andrews
Tel: 613-742-3366
valerie.andrews@ontario.ca
North Region
#334, 435 James St. South, Thunder Bay, ON P7E 6S7
Tel: 807-475-1683
Fax: 807-475-1297
Toll-Free: 800-465-6861

Manager, Elaine Lynch
Tel: 807-475-1635
elaine.lynch@ontario.ca
West Region
#405, 30 Duke St. West, Kitchener, ON N2H 3W5
Fax: 519-578-1632
Toll-Free: 800-265-2189

Acting Manager, Kathy Glaser
Tel: 519-571-6051
kathy.glaser@ontario.ca

Ontario Ministry of Training, Colleges & Universities

Mowat Block, 900 Bay St., 14th Fl., Toronto, ON M7A 1L2
Tel: 416-325-2929
Fax: 416-325-6348
Toll-Free: 800-387-5514
information.met@ontario.ca
www.tcu.gov.on.ca
TTY: 800-263-2892

Acts Administered:
Algoma University Act
Apprenticeship & Certification Act, 1998
Colleges Collective Bargaining Act, 2008
Education Act (in part)
Higher Education Quality Council of Ontario Act
Ministry of Training, Colleges & Universities Act
Ontario College of Art & Design University Act
Ontario College of Trades & Apprenticeship Act
Ontario Colleges of Applied Arts & Technology Act, 2002
Ontario Labour Mobility Act
Post-secondary Education Choice & Excellence Act, 2000
Private Career Colleges Act, 2005
Trades Qualification & Apprenticeship Act
University Expropriation Powers Act
University Foundations Act, 1992
University of Ontario Institute of Technology Act

Minister, Hon. Glen Murray
Tel: 416-326-1600
Fax: 416-326-1656
gmurray.mpp.co@liberal.ola.org

Deputy Minister, Deborah Newman
Tel: 416-314-9244
Fax: 416-314-7117
deborah.newman@ontario.ca

Parliamentary Assistant, Kevin Flynn

Chief Information Officer/Assistant Deputy Minister, Soussan Tabari
Tel: 416-326-8216
Fax: 416-325-8371
soussan.tabari@ontario.ca

Director, Communications, Heather Wright
Tel: 416-325-2944
Fax: 416-212-4158
heather.wright@ontario.ca

Team Lead, Change Management Office, Charmaine Charles
Tel: 416-325-9231
charmaine.charles@ontario.ca

Manager, Brian Fleming Research & Learning Library, Simon Loban
Tel: 416-325-2654
Fax: 416-325-4235
simon.loban@ontario.ca

Associated Agencies, Boards & Commissions:
• Ontario Graduate Scholarship Program Selection Board
189 Red River Rd., 4th Fl.
PO Box 4500
Thunder Bay, ON P7B 6G9
Tel: 807-343-7257
Fax: 807-343-7278
Toll-free: 800-465-3957
www.osap.gov.on.ca
Provides advice & recommendations to the minister concerning the policies & administration of the Ontario Graduate Scholarship program & selects successful candidates for funding under the program.
• Ontario Student Assistance Appeal Board
Mowat Block
900 Bay St., 7th Fl.
Toronto, ON M7A 1L2
Tel: 416-314-0714
Fax: 416-325-3096
• Post-secondary Education Quality Assessment Board
#1511, 2 Carlton St.
Toronto, ON M5B 1J3
Tel: 416-212-1230
Fax: 416-212-6620
peqab.ca

Corporate Management & Services Division
Mowat Block, #342 - 900 Bay St., Toronto, ON M7A 1L2
Tel: 416-325-2772
Fax: 416-325-2778
Assistant Deputy Minister/Chief Administrative Officer, David Fulford
Tel: 416-325-2773
david.fulford@ontario.ca
Director, Legal Services, John Calcott
Tel: 416-325-2399
Fax: 416-325-2410
john.calcott@ontario.ca
Director, Strategic Human Resources, Sandra Diprospero
Tel: 416-325-4511
Fax: 416-327-9043
sandra.diprospero@ontario.ca
Director, Internal Audit Services, Education Audit Service Team, Warren McCay
Tel: 416-212-4814
Fax: 416-325-1120
warren.mccay@ontario.ca
Director, Corporate Coordination, Russell Riddell
Tel: 416-326-6662
Fax: 416-314-0558
russell.riddell@ontario.ca
Team Lead Procurement, Corporate Finance and Services, Dasha Hubschmann
Tel: 416-326-1822
dasha.hubschmann@ontario.ca

Employment & Training Division
Fax: 416-325-2995
Toll-Free: 888-562-4769
Assistant Deputy Minister, Laurie LeBlanc
Tel: 416-325-2989
laurie.leblanc@ontario.ca
Director, Service Standards & Accountability Branch, Todd Kilpatrick
Tel: 416-325-2751
todd.kilpatrick@ontario.ca
Director, Business & Systems Management Branch, Robert Lowry
Tel: 416-325-4056
Fax: 416-314-0499
robert.lowry@ontario.ca
Director, Service Delivery Branch, Barbara Simmons
Tel: 416-314-4268
Fax: 416-325-6162
barbara.simmons@ontario.ca
Director, Strategic Oversight Office, Andrew Tang
Tel: 416-212-6222
andrew.tang@ontario.ca

Post-secondary Education Division
Tel: 416-325-2199
Fax: 416-326-3256
Assistant Deputy Minister, Nancy Naylor
Tel: 416-325-2116
nancy.naylor@ontario.ca
Director, Post-secondary Accountability Branch, Martin Hicks
Tel: 416-325-1815
martin.hicks@ontario.ca
Director, Post-secondary Finance & Information Management Branch, Didem Proulx
didem.proulx@ontario.ca
Director, Student Financial Assistance Branch, Noah Morris
Tel: 416-325-2853
Fax: 416-325-3096
noah.morris@ontario.ca
Director, Private Career Colleges Branch, Allan Scott
Tel: 416-314-9474
allan.scott@ontario.ca

Strategic Policy & Programs Division
Assistant Deputy Minister, Marie-Lison Fougère
Tel: 416-212-5420
marie-lison.fougere@ontario.ca
Director, Programs Branch, Virginia Hatchette
Tel: 416-326-5849
virginia.hatchette@ontario.ca
Director, Research & Planning Branch, Chris Monahan
Tel: 416-325-4034
chris.monahan@ontario.ca
Director, Strategic Policy & Initiatives Branch, Ellen Passmore
Tel: 416-326-6023
ellen.passmore@ontario.ca

Ontario Ministry of Transportation (MTO)

Ferguson Block, 77 Wellesley St. West, 3rd Fl., Toronto, ON M7A 1Z8
Tel: 416-235-4686
Fax: 905-704-2001
Toll-Free: 800-268-4686
www.mto.gov.on.ca
TTY: 905-704-2426
Other Communication: TTY Toll Free: 1-866-471-8929; Driver and Vehicle Licensing: 1-800-387-3445; Road Test Booking: 1-888-570-6110
The Ministry performs the following functions: planning, designing & building highways; performing environmental assessments; rehabilitating existing highways to increase their efficiency & safety; performing ongoing highway maintenance; developing standards, operational guidelines & policies relating to highways; & researching & introducing new technologies for more effective highway management. MTO commits to providing & promoting transportation services in a way that sustains a healthful environment through the Ministry's Statement of Environmental Values. The Ministry applies & integrates environmental concerns, along with prevailing social, economic, scientific & other considerations when conducting its business activities.
Acts Administered:
Airports Act
Bluewater Bridge Act
Bridges Act
Capital Investment Plan Act
Dangerous Goods Transportation Act
Highway 407 Act
Highway 407 East Completion Act
Highway Memorials for Fallen Police Officers Act
Highway Traffic Act
Improving Customer Service for Road Users Act
Local Roads Boards Act
Ministry of Transportation Act
Motor Vehicle Transportation Act
Motorized Snow Vehicles Act
Northern Transportation Commission Act
Off-Road Vehicles Act
Ontario Highway Transport Board Act
Ontario Transportation Development Corporation Act
Photo Card Act
Public Service Works on Highways Act
Public Transportation & Highway Improvement Act
Public Vehicles Act
Railways Act
Rainbow Bridge Act
Shortline Railways Act
Statute Labour Act (part)
Toll Bridges Act
Toronto Area Transit Operating Authority Act
Township of Pelee Act
Urban Transportation Development Corporation Ltd. Act

Minister, Hon. Bob Chiarelli
Tel: 416-327-9200
Fax: 416-327-9188
bchiarelli.mpp.co@liberal.ola.org

Deputy Minister, Carol Layton
Tel: 416-327-9162
carol.layton@ontario.ca

Parliamentary Assistant, Vic Dhillon

Tel: 905-796-8669
vdhillon.mpp.co@liberal.ola.org

Director, Communications, Kimberley Bates
Tel: 416-327-2117
Fax: 416-327-2591
kimberley.bates@ontario.ca

Director, Legal Services, Mary Gersht
Tel: 416-235-4406
Fax: 416-235-4924
mary.gersht@ontario.ca

Associated Agencies, Boards & Commissions:

• Metrolinx
#600, 20 Bay St.
Toronto, ON M5J 2W3
Tel: 416-869-3200
Fax: 416-869-3525
Toll-free: 888-438-6646
TTY: 800-387-3652
www.gotransit.com

• Ontario Highway Transport Board
151 Bloor St. West, 10th Fl.
Toronto, ON M5S 2T5
Tel: 416-326-6732
Fax: 416-326-6738
ohtb@mto.gov.on.ca
www.ohtb.gov.on.ca

Corporate Services Division
Garden City Tower, 301 St. Paul St., 6th Fl., St Catharines, ON L2R 7R4
Tel: 905-704-2693
Fax: 905-704-2445

Assistant Deputy Minister, Mike Goodale
Tel: 905-704-2701
mike.goodale@ontario.ca
Director, Finance, Jill Hughes
Tel: 905-704-2702
jill.hughes@ontario.ca
Director, Facilities & Business Services, Lesley Spinney
Tel: 905-704-2727
Director, Strategic Human Resources, Maria Tejeda
Tel: 905-704-2043
maria.tejeda@ontario.ca
Manager, Procurement and Costing Office, Beth Bertone
Tel: 905-704-2717
beth.bertone@ontario.ca
Manager, Emergency Management and Planning, Noris Bot
Tel: 905-704-2463
noris.bot@ontario.ca
Acting Manager, Freeedom of Information and Privacy Office, Janet Dadufalza
Tel: 416-212-1923
janet.dadufalza@ontario.ca
Manager, Financial Planning and Strategies Office, Ian Freeman
Tel: 905-704-2722
ian.freeman@ontario.ca
Manager, French Language Services, Louise Gagnon
Tel: 416-212-4274
louise.gagnon@ontario.ca
Manager, Facility Management Office - Downsview, Facilities & Business Services, Carolyn Johnstone
Tel: 416-235-5200
carolyn.johnstone@ontario.ca
Manager, Facility Management Office - St Catharines, Facilities & Business Services, Carolyn Johnstone
Tel: 905-704-2588
carolyn.johnstone@ontario.ca
Manager, Fleet Management, Facilities & Business Services, Shaf Khan
Tel: 905-704-2968
shaf.khan@ontario.ca
Manager, Controllership Office, Finance, Michelle Pasqua
Tel: 905-704-2476
michelle.pasqua@ontario.ca
Acting Manager, Resources Management, Strategic Human Resources, Liz Salter
Tel: 905-704-2132
liz.salter@ontario.ca
Manager, Customer Service, Facilities & Business Services, Ather Shabbar
Tel: 905-704-3242
ather.shabbar@ontario.ca

Labour & Transportation I&IT Cluster
400 University Ave., 9th Fl., Toronto, ON M7A 1T7
Tel: 416-327-3754
Fax: 416-327-3755

Chief Information Officer, Ken Kawall
Tel: 416-327-1955
Fax: 416-327-3755
ken.kawall@ontario.ca
Director, Strategic & Resources Planning, Michael Anderson
Tel: 416-327-5314
michael.anderson@ontario.ca
Director, Highways & Economics Solutions Branch, Howard Bertrand
Tel: 905-704-2488
howard.bertrand@ontario.ca
Director, Service Management, Dani Danyluk
Tel: 905-704-2834
dani.danyluk@ontario.ca
Director, Road User Safety Solutions Branch, Bob Stephens
Tel: 416-235-5209
Fax: 416-235-5658
bob.stephens@ontario.ca
Director, Architecture, Information Management and Labour Solutions Branch, Daniel Young
Tel: 416-326-3181
daniel.young@ontario.ca
Director, RUS Modernization IT Branch, Harp Ahluwalia
Tel: 416-235-6689
harp.ahluwalia@ontario.ca
Director, Service Management, Dani Danyluk
Tel: 905-704-2834
dani.danyluk@ontario.ca
Senior Manager, Enterprise Solutions Office, Road User Safety Solutions Branch, David Biensch
Tel: 416-235-5302
david.biensch@ontario.ca
Senior Manager, Solutions Engineering Office, Road User Safety Solutions Branch, Fan Cheng
Tel: 416-235-3880
fan.cheng@ontario.ca
Senior Manager, Application Services Office, Highways and Economics Solutions, Laura Munari
Tel: 905-704-2618
laura.munari@ontario.ca
Manager, Cluster Organizational Performance Office, Kathy Mareski
Tel: 416-235-4395
mohamed.safir@ontario.ca
Manager, Systems Development, Road User Safety Solutions Branch, Mohamed Safir
Tel: 416-235-4395
mohamed.safir@ontario.ca
Senior Manager, Modernizations Solutions, RUS Modernization, Craig Batten
Tel: 416-235-4496
craig.batten@ontario.ca
Senior Manager, PMO, Project Quality and Support, RUS Modernization, Vesna Nikolic
Tel: 416-235-4636
vesna.nikolic@ontario.ca
Manager, Service Strategy and Design, Service Management, Real Martin
Tel: 905-704-2615
real.martin@ontario.ca
Manager, Service Transition, Service Management, Julian Stiles
Tel: 905-704-2611

Policy & Planning Division
Ferguson Block, 77 Wesley St., 3rd Fl., Toronto, ON M7A 1Z8
Tel: 416-327-8521
Fax: 416-327-8746

Assistant Deputy Minister, John Lieou
Tel: 416-327-8521
john.lieou@ontario.ca
Director, Transportation Planning, Patricia Boeckner
Tel: 905-585-7238
Fax: 905-704-2445
patricia.boeckner@ontario.ca
Director, Transportation Policy, Linda McAusland
Tel: 416-585-7177
Fax: 905-704-2445
linda.mcausland@ontario.ca
Director, Transit Policy, Andrew Posluns
Tel: 416-585-7347
Fax: 905-704-2445
andrew.posluns@ontario.ca
Director, Strategic Policy & Transportation, Economics, David Ward
Tel: 416-212-1893
Fax: 905-704-2445
david.ward@ontario.ca
Director, Aboriginal Relations Branch, Bob Goulais
Tel: 416-585-7329
bob.goulais@ontario.ca
Acting Manager, Division Services and Program Management, Sandy Hand
Tel: 416-585-7137
sandy.hand@ontario.ca
Manager, Policy Priorties and Coordination, Strategic Policy and Transportation Economics, Jennifer Bailey
Tel: 416-212-1916
jennifer.bailey@ontario.ca
Manager, Strategic Initiatives and Federal, Provincial Relations Office, Strategic Policy and Transportation Economics, David Ward
Tel: 416-212-1893
David.ward@ontario.ca
Manager, Transportation Economics Office, Strategic Policy and Transportation Economics, William Denning
Tel: 416-212-1903
william.denning@ontario.ca
Manager, Provincial Transit Policy, Kevin Pal
Tel: 416-585-7360
kevin.pal@ontario.ca
Manager, Regional Transit Policy, Chris Burke
Tel: 416-585-7352
chris.burke@ontario.ca
Manager, Transit Infrastructure Policy Office, Gregory Tokarz
Tel: 416-585-7386
greg.tokarz@ontario.ca
Manager, Provincial Planning, Transportation Planning, Joe Perrotta
Tel: 416-585-7255
joe.perrotta@ontario.ca
Manager, Goods Movement,Transportation Policy, James Perttula
Tel: 416-585-7116
james.perttula@ontario.ca
Manager, Passenger and Municipal Policy Office, Robert Cantafio
Tel: 416-585-7205
robert.cantafio@ontario.ca
Manager, Sustainable Transportation Policy Office, Suzanne Adamkowski
Tel: 416-585-7270
suzanne.adamkowski@ontario.ca

Provincial Highways Management Division
Ferguson Block, 77 Wellesley St. West, 3rd Fl., Toronto, ON M7A 1Z8
Tel: 416-327-9044
Fax: 416-327-9226

Assistant Deputy Minister, Gerry Chaput
Tel: 416-327-9044
Fax: 416-327-9226
gerry.chaput@ontario.ca
Acting Executive Director, Asset Management & Director, Highway Standards Branch, Steve Cripps
Tel: 905-704-2299
Fax: 905-704-2562
steve.cripps@ontario.ca
Acting Director, Investment Strategies Branch, Dino Bagnariol
Tel: 905-704-2044
Fax: 905-704-2626
dino.bagnariol@ontario.ca
Director, Contract Management & Operations Branch, Paul M. Leocoarer
Tel: 905-704-2601
Fax: 905-704-2030
paul.lecoarer@ontario.ca
Director, Highway Standards Branch, Steve Cripps
Tel: 905-704-2194
steve.cripps@ontario.ca
Director, Windsor Border Initiatives Implementation Group (BIIG), Fausto Natarelli
Tel: 416-326-6876
Fax: 416-326-7056
fausto.natarelli@ontario.ca
Manager, Division Services Office, Cindy Lucas
Tel: 905-704-2473
cindy.lucas@ontario.ca

Central
Atrium Tower, 1201 Wilson Ave., Downsview, ON M3M 1J8
Tel: 416-235-5412
Fax: 416-235-5266

Regional Director, Lou Politano
Tel: 416-235-5400
Fax: 416-235-5266
lou.politano@ontario.ca

Eastern
1355 John Counter Blvd., PO Box 4000, Kingston, ON K7L 5A3
Tel: 613-545-4711
Fax: 613-545-4786
Toll-Free: 800-267-0295

Regional Director, Kathryn Moore
Tel: 613-545-4600
kathryn.moore@ontario.ca

Northeastern
Ontario Government Bldg., 447 McKeown Ave., 1st Fl., North Bay, ON P1B 9S9
Tel: 705-472-7900
Fax: 705-497-5422
Toll-Free: 800-461-9547

Regional Director, Eric Doidge
Tel: 705-497-5500
eric.doidge@ontario.ca

Northwestern
615 James St. South, Thunder Bay, ON P7E 6P6
Tel: 807-473-2000
Fax: 807-473-2157
Toll-Free: 800-465-5034

Regional Director, Ian Smith
Tel: 807-473-2050
Fax: 807-473-2165
ian.smith@ontario.ca
Western
659 Exeter Rd., 4th Fl., London, ON N6E 1L3
Tel: 519-873-4335
Fax: 519-873-4236
Toll-Free: 800-265-6072

Regional Director, Ann Baldwin
Tel: 519-873-4333
Fax: 519-873-4236
ann.baldwin@ontario.ca

Road User Safety Division
Bldg A, #191, 1201 Wilson Ave., Downsview, ON M3M 1J8
Tel: 416-235-2999
Fax: 416-235-4153

The division sets safety standards, develops policies, legislation & regulation, & educates road users about road user safety. Responsibilities include evaluating the effectiveness of safety measures, inspecting, monitoring & enforcing compliance with standards, testing, licenses & drivers, & registering vehicles. Through public education, legislation & enforcement, the government strives to ensure all motorists take responsibility for their driving behaviour. The Assistant Deputy Minister, Road User Safety, is responsible for the co-ordination of all Road User Safety activities for the province & acts as the Registrar of Motor Vehicles for Ontario.

Assistant Deputy Minister, Rob Fleming
Tel: 416-235-4453
Fax: 416-235-4153
rob.fleming@ontario.ca
Director, Licencing Services, Paul Brown
Tel: 416-235-4392
Fax: 416-235-5139
paul.h.brown@ontario.ca
Director, RUS Modernization Project, Linda Dunstall
Tel: 416-235-4628
linda.dunstall@ontario.ca
Director, Regional Operations, Tony Foster
Tel: 416-235-3526
tony.foster@ontario.ca
Director, Safety Policy & Education, Heidi Francis
Tel: 416-235-4050
Fax: 416-235-5139
heidi.francis@ontario.ca
Director, Program Development & Evaluation, Paul Harbottle
Tel: 416-235-4199
paul.harbottle@ontario.ca
Director, Carrier Safety & Enforcement, Peter Hurst
Tel: 416-235-2501
paul.harbottle@ontario.ca
Director, Service Delivery Partnerships, Kim Lambert
Tel: 416-235-5312
kim.lambert@ontario.ca
Director, Oranizational Development, Shelley Unterlander
Tel: 416-235-4769
shelley.unterlander@ontario.ca
Manager, Driver Programs Office, Angela Litrenta
Tel: 416-235-5130
angela.litrenta@ontario.ca

Ontario Women's Directorate (OWD)

777 Bay St., 6th Fl., Toronto, ON M7A 2J4
Tel: 416-314-0300
Fax: 416-314-0247
Toll-Free: 866-510-5902
owd@ontario.ca
www.citizenship.gov.on.ca/owd
TTY: 416-314-0258

A division of the Ministry of Citizenship and Immigration, the OWD focuses upon the following issues related to women: social, economic & justice-related concerns. The main activities of the OWD are preventing violence against women & promoting women's economic independence.

Minister Responsible, Hon. Laurel Broten
Tel: 416-212-7432
Fax: 416-212-7431
lbroten.mpp.co@liberal.ola.org

Parliamentary Assistant, Teresa Piruzza
Tel: 519-977-7191
tpiruzza.mpp.ca@liberal.ola.org

Executive Director, Susan Seaby
Tel: 416-314-1850
Fax: 416-314-0247
susan.seaby@ontario.ca

Manager, Stakeholder Relations & Policy Development, Suzanne Hastie
Tel: 416-314-1783
Fax: 416-314-0255
suzanne.hastie@ontario.ca

Workplace Safety & Insurance Board

200 Front St. West, Ground Fl., Toronto, ON M5V 3J1
Tel: 416-344-1000
Fax: 416-344-4684
Toll-Free: 800-387-0750
www.wsib.on.ca
TTY: 800-387-0050

Chair, Elizabeth Witmer

President & Chief Executive Officer, David Marshall
Tel: 416-344-4009

Government of Prince Edward Island

Seat of Government: Island Information Service, PO Box 2000, Charlottetown, PE C1A 7N8
Tel: 902-368-4000
island@gov.pe.ca
www.gov.pe.ca
Other Communication: Tourism Information, Toll-Free Phone: 1-800-463-4734

The Province of Prince Edward Island entered Confederation on July 1, 1873. It has an area of 5,683.91 km2, with a population of 140,204, according to the 2011 national census.

Office of the Lieutenant Governor

Government House, PO Box 846, Charlottetown, PE C1A 7L9
Tel: 902-368-5480
Fax: 902-368-5481
www.gov.pe.ca/olg

The Honourable H. Frank Lewis was sworn in as the 41st Lieutenant Governor of Prince Edward Island by the Chief Justice of the Supreme Court of Prince Edward Island at Province House on August 15, 2011.

Lieutenant Governor, Hon. H. Frank Lewis
Tel: 902-368-5480
Fax: 902-368-5481
hflewis@gov.pe.ca

Executive Assistant, Cindy Cheverie
ccheverie@gov.pe.ca

Administrative Assistant, Krista Rodd
klrodd@gov.pe.ca

Office of the Premier

Shaw Bldg., 95 Rochford St. South, 5th Fl., PO Box 2000, Charlottetown, PE C1A 7N8
Tel: 902-368-4501
Fax: 902-368-6118
www.gov.pe.ca/premier

Honourable Robert W.J. Ghiz is the thirty-first Premier of Prince Edward Island. In the October 2011 provincial election, he secured his second majority government.

Premier, Prince Edward Island; President, Executive Council; Minister Responsible, Intergovernmental Affairs; Minister Responsible, Acadian & Francophone Affairs; Leader, Liberal Party of Prince Edward Island, Hon. Robert W.J. Ghiz
Tel: 902-368-4400
Fax: 902-386-4416
premier@gov.pe.ca; robert.ghiz@liberal.pe.ca
Social Media:
www.facebook.com/pages/Robert-Ghiz-PEI-Premier/1174119 11662012

Deputy Premier, Prince Edward Island; Minister, Agriculture, Hon. George T. Webster
Tel: 902-368-4820
Fax: 902-368-4846
gtwebster@gov.pe.ca; george.webster@liberal.pe.ca

Chief of Staff, Allan V. Campbell
Tel: 902-368-4400
Fax: 902-368-4416
avcampbell@gov.pe.ca

Director, Communications & Legislative Affairs, Geoff Townsend
Tel: 902-368-4400
gatownsend@gov.pe.ca

Executive Assistant, Ian "Tex" MacDonald
Tel: 902-368-4400
Fax: 902-368-4416
ilmacdonald@gov.pe.ca

Executive Council

Shaw Bldg., 5th Fl., PO Box 2000, Charlottetown, PE C1A 7N8
Tel: 902-368-4502
Fax: 902-368-6118
www.gov.pe.ca/ec

The Executive Council of Prince Edward Island is made up of Ministers of the Crown. The role of the Executive Council is to decide upon the policy & direction that the government will take & to advise the Lieutenant Governor. Consisting of Ministers of the Crown, the Executive Council advises the Lieutenant Governor on the policy & direction which the government will take.

President, Executive Council; Premier, Prince Edward Island; Minister Responsible, Intergovernmental Affairs; Acadian & Francophone Affairs; Aboriginal Affairs; Leader, Liberal Party of Prince Edward Island, Hon. RobertW.J. Ghiz
Tel: 902-368-4400
Fax: 902-368-4416
premier@gov.pe.ca; robert.ghiz@liberal.pe.ca
Social Media:
www.facebook.com/pages/Robert-Ghiz-PEI-Premier/1174119 11662012
Note: Web Site: www.gov.pe.ca/premier(Office of the Premier)
Office of the Premier of Prince Edward Island, Shaw Bldg.
95 Rochford St. South, 5th Fl.
PO Box 2000
Charlottetown, PE C1A 7N8

Minister, Agriculture & Forestry; Deputy Premier, Prince Edward Island, Hon. George T. Webster
Tel: 902-368-4820
Fax: 902-368-4846
gtwebster@gov.pe.ca; george.webster@liberal.pe.ca
Other Communications: Department Phone: 902-368-4880; Fax: 902-368-4857
Note: Web Site: www.gov.pe.ca/agriculture (Department of Agriculture)
Department of Agriculture, Jones Bldg.
11 Kent St., 5th Fl.
PO Box 2000
Charlottetown, PE C1A 7N8

Minister, Fisheries, Aquaculture, & Rural Development, Hon. Ron W. MacKinley
Tel: 902-368-5120
Toll-free: 877-407-0187
Fax: 902-368-5385
rwmackinley@gov.pe.ca; ron.mackinley@liberal.pe.ca
Other Communications: Department Phone: 902-838-0910; Fax: 902-838-0975
Social Media:
www.facebook.com/pages/Ron-MacKinley/60342728811
Note: Web Site: www.gov.pe.ca/fard (Department of Fisheries, Aquaculture, & Rural Development)
Department of Fisheries, Aquaculture, & Rural Development
548 Main St.
PO Box 1180
Montague, PE C0A 1R0

Minister, Health & Wellness, Hon. Doug W. Currie
Tel: 902-368-5152
Fax: 902-368-4910
dwcurrie@gov.pe.ca; doug.currie@liberal.pe.ca
Other Communications: Department Phone: 902-368-6414; Fax: 902-368-4121
Social Media: www.twitter.com/DougCurrie, www.facebook.com/doug.w.currie
Note: Web Sites: www.gov.pe.ca/health (Department of Health & Wellness); www.dougcurrie.ca (Personal Website)
Department of Health & Wellness
105 Rochford St.,North, 4th Fl.
PO Box 2000
Charlottetown, PE C1A 7N8

Minister, Finance, Energy & Municipal Affairs, Hon. Wesley J. Sheridan
Tel: 902-368-4050
Fax: 902-368-6575
wjsheridan@gov.pe.ca; wes.sheridan@liberal.pe.ca
Other Communications: Department Phone: 902-368-4000; Fax: 902-368-5544
Social Media:

www.facebook.com/profile.php?id=100002547484282&ref=ts
Note: Web Site: www.gov.pe.ca/finance (Department of Finance & Municipal Affairs)
Department of Finance &Municipal Affairs, Shaw Bldg.
95 Rochford St. South, 2nd Fl.
PO Box 2000
Charlottetown, PE C1A 7N8

Minister, Community Services & Seniors; Minister Responsible, Status of Women, Hon. Valerie E. Docherty
Tel: 902-368-4330
Toll-free: 866-594-3777
Fax: 902-368-4348
vedocherty@assembly.pe.ca; valerie.docherty@liberal.pe.ca
Other Communications: Department Phone: 902-620-3777; Fax:902-368-4740
Social Media:
www.facebook.com/profile.php?id=100002087193589
Note: Web Site: www.gov.pe.ca/sss (Department of Community Services, Seniors, & Labour)
Department of Community Services, Seniors, & Labour, Jones Bldg.
11 Kent St., 2nd Fl.
PO Box 2000
Charlottetown, PE C1A 7N8

Minister, Environment, Labour & Justice; Attorney General, Hon. Janice A. Sherry
Tel: 902-368-4930
Fax: 902-368-4974
jasherry@gov.pe.ca; janice.sherry@liberal.pe.ca
Other Communications: Department Phone: 902-368-5000; Fax: 902-368-5830
Social Media:
www.facebook.com/people/Janice-Sherry/100002079465746
Note: Web Site: www.gov.pe.ca/eef (Department of Environment, Energy, & Forestry)
Department ofEnvironment, Energy, & Forestry, Jones Bldg.
11 Kent St., 4th Fl.
PO Box 2000
Charlottetown, PE C1A 7N8

Minister, Transportation & Infrastructure Renewal, Hon. Robert S. Vessey
Tel: 902-368-4801
Fax: 902-368-5277
rsvessey@gov.pe.ca; robert.vessey@liberal.pe.ca
Other Communications: Department Phone: 902-368-5100; Fax: 902-368-5395
Note: Web Site: www.gov.pe.ca/tir (Department of Transportation & Infrastructure Renewal)
Department ofTransportation & Infrastructure Renewal, Jones Bldg.
11 Kent St., 3rd Fl.
PO Box 2000
Charlottetown, PE C1A 7N8

Minister, Tourism & Culture, Hon. Robert L. Henderson
Tel: 902-368-5540
Fax: 902-368-5277
rlhenderson@assembly.pe.ca;
robert.henderson@liberal.pe.ca
Social Media:
www.facebook.com/profile.php?id=100001965683516
Note: Web Site:www.gov.pe.ca/tourism (Department of Tourism & Culture)
Department of Tourism & Culture
PO Box 2000
Charlottetown, PE C1A 7N8

Minister, Education & Early Childhood Development, Hon. J. Alan McIsaac
Tel: 902-368-4330
Fax: 902-368-4348
jamcisaac@assembly.pe.ca; alan.mcisaac@liberal.pe.ca
Other Communications: Department Phone: 902-438-4130; Fax: 902-438-4062
Social Media:
www.facebook.com/profile.php?id=100001892659368
Note: Web Sites: www.gov.pe.ca/eecd (Department of Education & Early Childhood Development); www.gov.pe.ca/jps (Department of Justice & PublicSafety)
Department ofEducation & Early Childhood Development, Holman Centre
#101, 250 Water St.
Charlottetown, PE C1N 1B6

Minister, Innovation & Advanced Learning, Hon. Allen F. Roach
allen.roach@liberal.pe.ca
Other Communications: Department Phone: 902-368-4240; Fax: 902-368-4242
Social Media:
www.facebook.com/profile.php?id=100002417155344
Note: Web Site: www.gov.pe.ca/ia (Department of Innovation & Advanced Learning)
Department of Innovation & Advanced Learning, Shaw Bldg.
105 Rochford St., 5thFl.
PO Box 2000
Charlottetown, PE C1A 7N8

Executive Council Office
Shaw Bldg., 5th Fl., PO Box 2000, Charlottetown, PE C1A 7N8
Tel: 902-368-4000
www.gov.pe.ca/eco
It is the responsibility of the Executive Council Office to provide administrative services & advice to the Executive Council. Advice & support are also offered to the government's departments & agencies.
The Executive Council Office supports the Acadian & Francophone Community. A key activitiy is the assistance given to departments & agencies in planning & delivering French language programs & services.
Another important activity of the Executive Council Office is the provision of research & analysis on intergovernmental affairs. Advice is given related to social & economic policies.
The Executive Office is also involved in the coordination of traditional ceremonial or legal requirements, such as the swearing into office of Members of Cabinet or the Lieutenant Governor.
Premier, Prince Edward Island; President, Executive Council; Minister Responsible, Intergovernmental Affairs; Minister Responsible, Acadian & Francophone Affairs; Leader, Liberal Party of Prince Edward Island, Hon. Robert W.J. Ghiz
Tel: 902-368-4400
Fax: 902-368-4416
premier@gov.pe.ca; robert.ghiz@liberal.pe.ca
Social Media:
www.facebook.com/pages/Robert-Ghiz-PEI-Premier/117411911662012
Note: Web Site: www.gov.pe.ca/premier (Office of the Premier)
Clerk of the Executive Council; Secretary to Cabinet, Rory Beck
Tel: 902-368-4502
Fax: 902-368-6118
rbeck@gov.pe.ca
Chief, Protocol & Events, Mary Ellen E. Moerike
Tel: 902-368-4501
Fax: 902-368-6118
memoerike@gov.pe.ca
Deputy Minister, Intergovernmental Affairs, Sandy Stewart
Tel: 902-368-4502
Fax: 902-368-6118
swstewart@gov.pe.ca
Assistant Deputy Minister, Acadian & Francophone Affairs, Aubrey Cormier
Tel: 902-368-6337
Fax: 902-368-6118
arcormier@gov.pe.ca
Director, Acadian & Francophone Affairs, Diane Arsenault
Tel: 902-368-4872
Fax: 902-368-4857
dianearsenault@gov.pe.ca
Director, Intergovernmental Affairs, Rochelle Gallant
Tel: 902-368-4415
Fax: 902-368-6118
rgallant@gov.pe.ca

Operations Committee
Shaw Bldg., 5th Fl., PO Box 2000, Charlottetown, PE C1A 7N8
Tel: 902-368-4305
Fax: 902-368-6118
The Operations Committee coordinates the legislative development process. All proposed legislation, regulations, & amendments to regulations are reviewed & analyzed prior to submission to the Executive Council for approval.
Secretary, Operations Committee, Matt McGuire
Tel: 902-368-4407
Fax: 902-368-6118
mdmcguire@gov.pe.ca

Policy Board Committee
Shaw Bldg., 5th Fl., PO Box 2000, Charlottetown, PE C1A 7N8
Tel: 902-368-4502
Fax: 902-368-6118
Secretary to the Policy Board, Wendy MacDonald
Tel: 902-620-3457
Fax: 902-368-6118
wimacdonald@gov.pe.ca

Treasury Board Committee
Shaw Bldg., 95 Rochford St. South, 3rd Fl., PO Box 2000, Charlottetown, PE C1A 7N8
The Executive Council Act established the Treasury Board as a committee of the Executive Council. The Board advises the Executive Council about budgetary & financial matters & the management of the Public Service.
Secretary to the Treasury Board, Doug Clow, CA
Tel: 902-368-4052
Fax: 902-368-6575
dmclow@gov.pe.ca
Treasury Officer, Margaret Simpson
Tel: 902-368-4140
Fax: 902-368-4077

Prince Edward Island Legislative Assembly

Province House, 165 Richmond St., 1st Fl., PO Box 2000, Charlottetown, PE C1A 7N8
Tel: 902-368-5970
Fax: 902-368-5175
Toll-Free: 877-315-5518
legislativelibrary@assembly.pe.ca
www.assembly.pe.ca
The Legislative Assembly of Prince Edward Island consists of the lawmakers & the offices & officials who support their work.

Director, Security & Sergeant-at-Arms, W/O Al J. McDonald
Tel: 902-368-5976
Fax: 902-368-5175
ajmcdonald@assembly.pe.ca

Committee Clerk, Melissa M. Keefe
Tel: 902-620-3764
Fax: 902-368-5175
mmkeefe@assembly.pe.ca

Office of the Clerk
Province House, 165 Richmond St., 1st Fl., PO Box 2000, Charlottetown, PE C1A 7N8
Tel: 902-368-5970
Fax: 902-368-5175
The Clerk of the Legislative Assembly is responsible for providing administrative support to the Speaker, the House, & its members. Decisions of the House are recorded by the Clerk & published in the Journals of the Legislative Assembly of Prince Edward Island.
Clerk of the Legislative Assembly, Charles MacKay
Tel: 902-368-5970
Fax: 902-368-5175
chmackay@assembly.pe.ca
Clerk of Committees & Clerk Assistant, Marian Johnston
Tel: 902-368-5972
Fax: 902-368-5175
majohnston@assembly.pe.ca
Administrative Officer, Cheryl Stead
Tel: 902-368-5970
Fax: 902-368-5175
chstead@assembly.pe.ca

Office of the Conflict of Interest Commissioner
Province House, 165 Richmond St., 1st Fl., PO Box 2000, Charlottetown, PE C1A 7N8
Tel: 902-368-5970
Fax: 902-368-5175
The Conflict of Interest Commissioner is an independent officer of the Legislative Assembly who administers the Conflict of Interest Act. To enhance public confidence in the Legislative Assembly, the Conflict of Interest Act ensures that Ministers & Members reconcile their private & public interests & conduct their responsibilities with integrity.
Commisioner, Conflict of Interest, Neil Robinson
anrobinson@assembly.pe.ca

Government Members' Office (Liberal)
Coles Bldg., 175 Richmond St., 2nd Fl., PO Box 2890, Charlottetown, PE C1A 8C5
Tel: 902-368-4330
Fax: 902-368-4348
Administrative support to government backbenchers is provided by the Government Members' Office.
Premier, Prince Edward Island; Leader, Liberal Party of Prince Edward Island; President, Executive Council; Minister Responsible, Intergovernmental Affairs; Minister Responsible, Acadian & Francophone Affairs, Hon. Robert W.J. Ghiz
Tel: 902-368-4400
Fax: 902-368-4416
premier@gov.pe.ca; robert.ghiz@liberal.pe.ca
Social Media:
www.facebook.com/pages/Robert-Ghiz-PEI-Premier/117411911662012
Note: Web Site: www.gov.pe.ca/premier (Office of the Premier)
Government House Leader; Member, Legislative Assembly, Sonny Gallant
Tel: 902-368-4330
Fax: 902-368-4348
sjgallant@assembly.pe.ca;sonny.gallant@liberal.pe.ca
Social Media:
www.facebook.com/people/Sonny-Gallant/100001793535144
Office Manager, Hazel Gallant
Tel: 902-368-4341

Fax: 902-368-4348
hggallant@assembly.pe.ca
Researcher, Kathy Paugh
Tel: 902-368-4330
Fax: 902-368-4348
kjpaugh@gov.pe.ca

Hansard Office
J. Angus MacLean Bldg., 94 Great George St., 2nd Fl., PO Box 774, Charlottetown, PE C1A 7L3
Tel: 902-368-5371
Fax: 902-368-5175
The published daily debates of Members in the House & in committees are known as Hansard. Staff of the Hansard Office transcribes, publishes, & indexes the debates.
Manager, Hansard, Jeff Bursey
jrbursey@assembly.pe.ca

Office of the Information & Privacy Commissioner
J. Angus MacLean Bldg., 180 Richmond St., 2nd Fl., PO Box 2000, Charlottetown, PE C1A 7K7
Tel: 902-368-4099
Fax: 902-368-5947
The Information & Privacy Commissioner is appointed by the Legislature for a five year term. The Commissioner, who is an independent officer of the Legislative Assembly, reports annually to the Speaker of the Legislative Assembly about the work of the Office.
The Commissioner accepts Requests for Review from persons who are not satisfied with responses as a result of access to information requests made under the Freedom of Information & Protection of Privacy Act. Upon conclusion of a review, the order of the Information & Privacy Commissioner is final. Applicants, the public body, or a third party may only apply to the Supreme Court of Prince Edward Island for judicial review.
The Commissioner also conducts investigations related to privacy complaints.
Commissioner, Information & Privacy, Maria C. MacDonald
Tel: 902-368-4099
Fax: 902-368-5947
mariamacdonald@gov.pe.ca

Legislative Library & Research Service
Coles Bldg., 175 Richmond St., 1st Fl., PO Box 2000, Charlottetown, PE C1A 7N8
Tel: 902-620-3765
Fax: 902-620-3975
Opened in 2008, the Legislative Library supports members, committees, & house officers in their work. Non-partisan reports are provided by the research service.
Research Librarian, Laura Morrell
Tel: 902-620-3765
Fax: 902-368-5175
lemorrell@assembly.pe.ca
Research Officer, Ryan Reddin
Tel: 902-620-3766
Fax: 902-368-5175
rmreddin@assembly.pe.ca

Office of the Official Opposition (Progressive Conservative)
Coles Bldg., 175 Richmond St., 3rd Fl., PO Box 338, Charlottetown, PE C1A 7K7
Tel: 902-368-4360
Fax: 902-368-4377
The Official Opposition raises concerns of Islanders & holds the government accountable for its policies & promises.
Leader, Official Opposition, Hon. Olive Crane
Tel: 902-368-4360
Fax: 902-368-4377
omcrane@assembly.pe.ca
Advisor, Communications & Research, Iris Phillips
Tel: 902-368-4358
Fax: 902-368-4377
iephillips@assembly.pe.ca
Researcher, Andrew Halliday
Tel: 902-368-7554
Fax: 902-368-4377
amhalliday@assembly.pe.ca
Press Secretary, Sheryl MacAulay
semacaulay@assembly.pe.ca

Office of the Speaker
Province House, 165 Richmond St., 1st Fl., PO Box 2000, Charlottetown, PE C1A 7N8
Tel: 902-368-4310
Fax: 902-368-4473
At the beginning of each new General Assembly, a Speaker of the Legislative Assembly is elected by secret ballot. The following Members of the Legislative Assembly are ineligible to be the Speaker: the Premier, the Leader of the Opposition & leaders of other political parties in the Assembly, & Members of the Executive Council.
Administrative Assistant, Speaker's Office, Barbara O'Donnell
Tel: 902-368-4310
Fax: 902-368-4473
baodonnell@assembly.pe.ca

Sixty-fourth General Assembly - Prince Edward Island

Province House, 165 Richmond St., 1st Fl., PO Box 2000, Charlottetown, PE C1A 7N8
Tel: 902-368-5970
Fax: 902-368-5175
Toll-Free: 877-315-5518
www.assembly.pe.ca
Last Provincial General Election: October 3, 2011.
Next Provincial General Election (scheduled under the province's fixed-date legislation): October 2015.
Party Standings (October 2011):
Liberal: 22;
Progressive Conservative 5;
Total: 27.
Salaries, Indemnities & Allowances (April 2010):
A Member of the Legislative Assembly's salary is $65,344.
In addition to this basic salary for each Member of the Legislative Assembly are the following additional salaries:
Premier $71,094 (total $136,438);
Ministers $45,688 (total $111,032);
Speaker $38,474 (total $103,818);
Deputy Speaker $19,237 (total $84,581);
Leader of the Opposition $45,688 (total $111,032);
Government House Leader $12,337 (total $77,681);
Opposition House Leader $4,339 (total $69,683);
Government Whip & Opposition Whip $3,659 (total $69,003);
Non-Ministerial Members of Executive Council Committees $5,996 (total $71,340);
Leader of a Third Party $16,764 (total $82,108).
The following is a list of Members of the Legislative Assembly, with their electoral district number & name, number of persons enumerated in the district for the 2011 provincial general election, party affiliation, & contact information. The general address for all Members of the Legisla tive Assembly is as follows: PO Box 2000, Charlottetown PE, C1A 7N8.
Member, Legislative Assembly, James Aylward
Constituency: District #6 - Stratford -Kinlock *No. of Constituents:* 4,702, Progressive Conservative
Tel: 902-368-4360
jamesaylward@peipcparty.ca
PO Box 338
Charlottetown, PE C1A 7K7
Member, Legislative Assembly, Hon. Carolyn Bertram
Constituency: District #18 - Rustico - Emerald *No. of Constituents:* 3,867, Liberal
Tel: 902-368-5250
Fax: 902-368-4121
cibertram@gov.pe.ca; carolyn.bertram@liberal.pe.ca
Other Communications: Constituency Phone: 902-963-2700 or902-964-2015
Shaw Bldg.
105 Rochford St., 4th Fl.
PO Box 2000
Charlottetown, PE C1A 7N8
Member, Legislative Assembly, Paula Biggar
Constituency: District #23 - Tyne Valley - Linkletter *No. of Constituents:* 3,436, Liberal
Tel: 902-368-4330
Fax: 902-368-4348
pjbiggar@assembly.pe.ca; paula.biggar@liberal.pe.ca
Other Communications: Constituency Phone: 902-831-2686 or902-436-5066
Social Media: www.twitter.com/pjbiggar, www.facebook.com/paula.biggar, www.linkedin.com/pub/paula-biggar/17/13a/392
Coles Bldg.
175 Richmond St., 2nd Fl.
PO Box 2890
Charlottetown, PE C1A 8C5
Member, Legislative Assembly, Hon. Richard Brown
Constituency: District #12 - Charlottetown - Victoria Park *No. of Constituents:* 3,168, Liberal
Tel: 902-368-6410
Fax: 902-368-6488
rebrown@gov.pe.ca; richard.brown@liberal.pe.ca
Other Communications: Constituency Phone: 902-566-4560
Social Media: www.facebook.com/profile.php?id=712491160
Jones Bldg.
11Kent St., 4th Fl.
PO Box 2000
Charlottetown, PE C1A 7N8
Member, Legislative Assembly, Hon. Kathleen Casey
Constituency: District #14 - Charlottetown - Lewis Point *No. of Constituents:* 3,905, Liberal
Tel: 902-368-4310
Fax: 902-368-4473
kmcasey@assembly.pe.ca; kathleen.casey@liberal.pe.ca
Other Communications: Constituency Phone: 902-566-5036
Social Media: www.facebook.com/profile.php?id=100001926175864, www.linkedin.com/pub/kathleen-casey/9/a84/134
ProvinceHouse
165 Richmond St., 1st Fl.
PO Box 2000
Charlottetown, PE C1A 1J1
Member, Legislative Assembly; Leader, Opposition, Hon. Olive Crane
Constituency: District #7 - Morell - Mermaid *No. of Constituents:* 3,217, Progressive Conservative
Tel: 902-368-4360
Fax: 902-368-4377
omcrane@assembly.pe.ca; olivecrane@peipcparty.ca
Social Media: www.twitter.com/olivecrane, www.facebook.com/OliveCrane, www.linkedin.com/pub/olive-crane/2a/abb/58
Coles Bldg.
175 RichmondSt., 3rd Fl.
PO Box 338
Charlottetown, PE C1A 7K7
Member, Legislative Assembly; Minister, Health & Wellness; Minister Responsible, Aboriginal Affairs, Hon. Doug W. Currie
Constituency: District #11 - Charlottetown - Parkdale *No. of Constituents:* 3,333, Liberal
Tel: 902-368-5152
Fax: 902-368-4910
dwcurrie@gov.pe.ca;doug.currie@liberal.pe.ca
Other Communications: Constituency Phone: 902-566-4160
Social Media: www.twitter.com/DougCurrie, www.facebook.com/doug.w.currie
Note: Web Sites: www.dougcurrie.ca (Personal Website); www.gov.pe.ca/health(Department of Health & Wellness)
Shaw Bldg.
950 Rochford St., 4th Fl.
PO Box 2000
Charlottetown, PE C1A 7N8
Member, Legislative Assembly; Minister, Community Services, Seniors. & Labour; Minister Responsible, Status of Women, Hon. Valerie E. Docherty
Constituency: District #17 - Kellys Cross - Cumberland *No. of Constituents:* 4,229, Liberal
Tel: 902-368-4330
Fax: 902-368-4348
vedocherty@assembly.pe.ca; valerie.docherty@liberal.pe.ca
Other Communications: Constituency Phone: 902-675-4215
Social Media: www.facebook.com/profile.php?id=100002087193589
Note: Web Site: www.gov.pe.ca/sss(Department of Community Services, Seniors, & Labour)
Coles Bldg.
175 Richmond St. 2nd Fl.
PO Box 2890
Charlottetown, PE C1A 8C5
Member, Legislative Assembly, Bush Dumville
Constituency: District #15 - West Royalty - Springvale *No. of Constituents:* 4,176, Liberal
Tel: 902-368-4330
Fax: 902-368-4348
sfdumville@assembly.pe.ca; bush.dumville@liberal.pe.ca
Other Communications: Constituency Phone: 902-566-5150
Social Media: www.facebook.com/profile.php?id=100002345233840
ColesBldg.
175 Richmond St., 2nd Fl.
PO Box 2890
Charlottetown, PE C1A 8C5
Member, Legislative Assembly; Government House Leader, Sonny Gallant
Constituency: District #24 - Evangeline - Miscouche *No. of Constituents:* 2,634, Liberal
Tel: 902-368-4330
Fax: 902-368-4348
sjgallant@assembly.pe.ca; sonny.gallant@liberal.pe.ca
Other Communications: Constituency Phone:902-854-3214
Social Media: www.facebook.com/people/Sonny-Gallant/100001793535144
Coles Bldg.
175 Richmond St., 2nd Fl.
PO Box 2890
Charlottetown, PE C1A 8C5
Member, Legislative Assembly; Premier, Prince Edward Island; President, Executive Council; Minister Responsible, Intergovernmental Affairs; Minister Responsible, Acadian &Francophone Affairs; Leader, Liberal Party of Prince Edward Island, Hon. Robert W.J. Ghiz
Constituency: District #13 - Charlottetown - Brighton *No. of Constituents:* 3,042, Liberal
Tel: 902-368-4400
Fax: 902-368-4416
premier@gov.pe.ca; robert.ghiz@liberal.pe.ca
www.gov.pe.ca/premier (Office of the Premier)
Other Communications: Constituency Phone: 902-566-4832
Social Media: www.facebook.com/pages/Robert-Ghiz-PEI-Premier/117411911662012
Shaw Bldg.
95 Rochford St., 5th Fl.

PO Box 2000
Charlottetown, PE C1A 7N8

Member, Legislative Assembly, Hon. Gerard Greenan
Constituency: District #22 - Summerside - St. Eleanors *No. of Constituents:* 4,343, Liberal
Tel: 902-368-4330
Fax: 902-368-4348
lggreenan@assembly.pe.ca; gerard.greenan@liberal.pe.ca
Other Communications: Constituency Phone: 902-436-4788
Social Media: www.twitter.com/gerardgreenan, www.facebook.com/gerardgreenan
ColesBldg.
175 Richmond St., 2nd Fl.
PO Box 2890
Charlottetown, PE C1A 8C5

Member, Legislative Assembly; Minister, Tourism & Culture, Hon. Robert L. Henderson
Constituency: District #25 - O'Leary - Inverness *No. of Constituents:* 3,293, Liberal
Tel: 902-368-4330
Fax: 902-368-4348
rlhenderson@assembly.pe.ca; robert.henderson@liberal.pe.ca
www.gov.pe.ca/tourism (Department ofTourism & Culture)
Other Communications: Constituency Phone: 902-859-2955
Social Media: www.facebook.com/profile.php?id=100001965683516
Coles Bldg.
175 Richmond St., 2nd Fl.
PO Box 2890
Charlottetown, PE C1A 8C5

Member, Legislative Assembly, Colin LaVie
Constituency: District #1 - Souris - Elmira *No. of Constituents:* 3,112, Progressive Conservative
Tel: 902-368-4360
colinlavie@peipcparty.ca
Social Media: www.facebook.com/profile.php?id=100002620587903
PO Box 338
Charlottetown, PE C1A 7K7

Member, Legislative Assembly; Minister of Fisheries, Aquaculture, & Rural Development, Hon. Ron W. MacKinley
Constituency: District #16 - Cornwall - Meadowbank *No. of Constituents:* 3,770, Liberal
Tel: 902-368-5120
Fax: 902-368-5385
rwmackinley@gov.pe.ca;ron.mackinley@liberal.pe.ca
Other Communications: Constituency Phone: 902-566-6600
Social Media: www.facebook.com/pages/Ron-MacKinley/60342728811
Note: Web Site: www.gov.pe.ca/fard (Department of Fisheries, Aquaculture, & RuralDevelopment)
Jones Bldg.
11 Kent St., 3rd Fl.
PO Box 2000
Charlottetown, PE C1A 7N8

Member, Legislative Assembly, Charles McGeoghegan
Constituency: District #4 - Belfast - Murray River *No. of Constituents:* 3,146, Liberal
Tel: 902-368-4330
Fax: 902-368-4348
cemcgeoghegan@assembly.pe.ca; charlie.mcgeoghegan@liberal.pe.ca
Other Communications: Constituency Phone:902-962-4020
Social Media: www.facebook.com/profile.php?id=100002798127012
Coles Bldg.
175 Richmond St., 2nd Fl.
Charlottetown, PE C1A 1H8

Member, Legislative Assembly; Minister, Education & Early Childhood Development; Minister, Justice & Public Safety; Attorney General, Hon. J. Alan McIsaac
Constituency: District #5 - Vernon River - Stratford *No. of Constituents:* 3,373, Liberal
Tel: 902-368-4330
Fax: 902-368-4348
jamcisaac@assembly.pe.ca; alan.mcisaac@liberal.pe.ca
Other Communications: Constituency Phone: 902-569-2200
Social Media: www.facebook.com/profile.php?id=100001892659368
Note: Web Sites: www.gov.pe.ca/eecd(Department of Education & Early Childhood Development); www.gov.pe.ca/jps (Department of Justice & Public Safety)
Coles Bldg.
175 Richmond St., 2nd Fl.
Charlottetown, PE C1A 1H8

Member, Legislative Assembly, Robert Mitchell
Constituency: District #10 - Charlottetown - Sherwood *No. of Constituents:* 3,676, Liberal
Tel: 902-368-4330
Fax: 902-368-4348
rjmitchell@gov.pe.ca; robert.mitchell@liberal.pe.ca
Other Communications: Constituency Phone: 902-566-3973
Social Media: www.facebook.com/profile.php?id=625801979
Coles Bldg.
175 Richmond St., 2nd Fl.
PO Box 2890
Charlottetown, PE C1A 8C5

Member, Legislative Assembly, Pat Murphy
Constituency: District #26 - Alberton - Roseville *No. of Constituents:* 3,450, Liberal
Tel: 902-368-4330
Fax: 902-368-4348
pwmurphy@assembly.pe.ca; pat.murphy@liberal.pe.ca
Other Communications: Constituency Phone: 902-853-4393
Social Media: www.facebook.com/pwmurphy
Coles Bldg.
175Richmond St., 2nd Fl.
PO Box 2890
Charlottetown, PE C1A 8C5

Member, Legislative Assembly, Steven Myers
Constituency: District #2 - Georgetown - St.Peters *No. of Constituents:* 3,542, Progressive Conservative
Tel: 902-368-4360
stevenmyers@peipcparty.ca
PO Box 338
Charlottetown, PE C1A 7K7

Member, Legislative Assembly, Hal Perry
Constituency: District #27 - Tignish - Palmer Road *No. of Constituents:* 2,880, Progressive Conservative
Tel: 902-368-4360
halperry@peipcparty.ca
PO Box 338
Charlottetown, PE C1A 7K7

Member, Legislative Assembly; Minister, Innovation & Advanced Learning, Hon. Allen F. Roach
Constituency: District #3 - Montague - Kilmur *No. of Constituents:* 3.132, Liberal
allen.roach@liberal.pe.ca
www.gov.pe.ca/ia (Dept. of Innovation & Advanced Learning)
Other Communications: Constituency Phone: 902-838-5406
Social Media: www.facebook.com/profile.php?id=100002417155344

Member, Legislative Assembly; Minister, Finance & Municipal Affairs, Hon. Wesley J. Sheridan
Constituency: District #20 - Kensington - Malpeque *No. of Constituents:* 4,275, Liberal
Tel: 902-368-4050
Fax: 902-368-6575
wjsheridan@gov.pe.ca; wes.sheridan@liberal.pe.ca
Other Communications: Constituency Phone: 902-836-7000
Social Media: www.facebook.com/profile.php?id=100002547484282&ref=ts
Shaw Bldg.
95 Rochford St., 2nd Fl.
PO Box 2000
Charlottetown, PE C1A 7N8

Member, Legislative Assembly; Minister, Environment, Energy, & Forestry, Hon. Janice A. Sherry
Constituency: District #21 - Summerside - Wilmot *No. of Constituents:* 3,874, Liberal
Tel: 902-368-4930
Fax: 902-368-4974
jasherry@gov.pe.ca; janice.sherry@liberal.pe.ca
Other Communications: Constituency Phone: 902-436-2588
Social Media: www.facebook.com/people/Janice-Sherry/100002079465746
Jones Bldg.
11 Kent St., 2nd Fl.
PO Box 2000
Charlottetown, PE C1A 7N8

Member, Legislative Assembly; Minister, Transportation & Infrastructure Renewal, Hon. Robert S. Vessey
Constituency: District #9 - York - Oyster Bed *No. of Constituents:* 4,537, Liberal
Tel: 902-368-4801
Fax: 902-368-5277
rsvessey@gov.pe.ca;robert.vessey@liberal.pe.ca
Other Communications: Constituency Phone: 902-672-2774
Note: Web Site: www.gov.pe.ca/tir (Department of Transportation & InfrastructureRenewal)
Shaw Bldg.
105 Rochford St., 3rd Fl.
PO Box 2000
Charlottetown, PE C1A 7N8

Member, Legislative Assembly, Buck Watts
Constituency: District #8 - Tracadie - Hillsborough Park *No. of Constituents:* 3,710, Liberal
Tel: 902-368-4330
Fax: 902-368-4348
fdwatts@assembly.pe.ca; buck.watts@liberal.pe.ca
Other Communications: Constituency Phone: 902-566-6551
Social Media: www.facebook.com/profile.php?id=100002411296559
Coles Bldg.
175Richmond St., 2nd Fl.
PO Box 2890
Charlottetown, PE C1A 8C5

Member, Legislative Assembly; Deputy Premier, Prince Edward Island; Minister, Agriculture, Hon. George T. Webster
Constituency: District #19 - Borden - Kinkora *No. of Constituents:* 4,145, Liberal
Tel: 902-368-4820
Fax: 902-368-4846
gtwebster@gov.pe.ca;george.webster@liberal.pe.ca
www.gov.pe.ca/agriculture (Department of Agriculture)
Other Communications: Constituency Phone: 902-887-3185
Jones Bldg.
11 Kent St., 5th Fl.
PO Box 2000
Charlottetown, PE C1A 7N8

Prince Edward Island Government Departments & Agencies

Prince Edward Island Department of Agriculture & Forestry

Jones Bldg., 11 Kent St., PO Box 2000, Charlottetown, PE C1A 7N8

Tel: 902-368-4880
Fax: 902-368-4857
www.gov.pe.ca/agriculture

Prince Edward Island's Department of Agriculture provides programs & services to farmers. Programs are developed within the context of the Sustainable Resource Policy, which protects the province's land, water, & air.
The following are some examples of program categories: AgriFlexibility; Buy PEI;, Crop Production; Food Safety, Biosecurity, & Traceability; Forestry; Innovation & Applied Research; Laboratory Services; Livestock; Organic; & Training.

Acts Administered:
Agricultural Crop Rotation Act
Agricultural Insurance Act
Agricultural Products Standards Act
Agrologists Act
Animal Health & Protection Act
Artificial Insemination Act
Companion Animal Protection Act
Dairy Industry Act
Dairy Producers Act
Dog Act
Environmental Protection Act
Farm Machinery Dealers & Vendors Act
Farm Practices Act
Farm Registration & Farm Organization Funding Act
Fire Prevention Act
Forest Management Act
Gasoline Tax Act
Grain Elevators Corporation Act
Lands Protection Act, P.E.I.
Livestock Community Auction Sales Act
Natural Areas Protection Act
Natural Products Marketing Act
Occupational Health & Safety Act
PEI Farm Safety Code of Practice
Pesticides Control Act
Planning Act
Plant Health Act
Public Forest Council Act
Real Property Assessment Act
Real Property Tax Act
Revenue Tax Axt
Smoke Free Places Act
Stray Livestock Act
Veterinary Profession Act
Weed Control Act
Women's Institute Act

Minister, Agriculture; Deputy Premier, Prince Edward Island, Hon. George T. Webster
Tel: 902-368-4820
Fax: 902-368-4846
gtwebster@gov.pe.ca; george.webster@liberal.pe.ca
Other Communications: Department Phone: 902-368-4880; Fax:902-368-4857

Deputy Minister, John MacQuarrie
Tel: 902-368-4830
Fax: 902-368-4846
jamacquarrie@gov.pe.ca

Communications Officer, Kim Devine
Tel: 902-368-5286
Fax: 902-368-5830
kmdevine@gov.pe.ca

Associated Agencies, Boards & Commissions:

• Agricultural Insurance Corporation
29 Indigo Cres.
PO Box 1600
Charlottetown, PE C1A 7N3
Tel: 902-368-4842
Fax: 902-368-6677
www.gov.pe.ca/growingforward
Production insurance is administered by the Prince Edward Island Agricultural Insurance Corporation. It provides production risk protection to producers who may sustain crop losses due to natural hazards.
Programs administered by the Corporation are as follows: AgriStability, AgriInvest, AgriInsurance, & AgriRecovery.
• Farm Practices Review Board
The Farm Practices Review Board is responsible for reviewing concerns from the public about farm practices.
• Grain Elevators Corporation
7 Gerald McCarville Dr.
PO Box 250
Kensington, PE C0B 1M0
Tel: 902-836-8935
Fax: 902-836-8926
www.peigec.com
The Prince Edward Island Grain Elevators Corporation is a leader in the province's cereal & protein sector.
For growers who want the pooled return, the Corporation operates grain marketing pools. Producers may also sell part of their crop to the Corporation at daily market prices.
Grain & products marketed throughout Prince Edward Island & Atlantic Canada.
• Marketing Council

Agriculture Policy & Regulatory Division
Jones Bldg., 11 Kent St., 5th Fl., Charlottetown, PE C1A 7N8

The Agriculture Policy & Regulatory Division oversees areas such as the following: research; administration of industry development programs; community pastures; on-farm food safety; food quality; marketing legislation; domestic & foreign trade; traceability; foreign animal disease; & emergency preparedness.
Director, Agriculture Policy & Regulatory Division, Shane Murphy
Tel: 902-620-3084
srmurphy@gov.pe.ca
Manager, Agriculture Regulatory Programs, Brian Matheson
Tel: 902-368-5087
Fax: 902-368-4857
bgmatheson@gov.pe.ca
Acting Manager, Farm Practices Review Board, Michael J Delaney
Tel: 902-836-8929
Fax: 902-836-8926
mjdelaney@peigec.com
Administrative Director, 4-H, Emily Brown
Tel: 902-368-4836
Fax: 902-368-6289
eabrown@gov.pe.ca
(Acting) Officer, Marketing Council, Murray Myles
Tel: 902-569-7575
Fax: 902-569-7745
mamyles@gov.pe.ca

Agriculture Resource Division
Research Station, University Ave., PO Box 1600, Charlottetown, PE C1A 7N3
Tel: 902-368-4145
Fax: 902-368-5661
The Agriculture Resource Division delivers sustainable resource & farm extension programs & services.
Director, Agriculture Resource Division, Tracy Wood
Tel: 902-368-5645
Fax: 902-368-5661
tmwood@gov.pe.ca
Manager, Agriculture Information, Sandra MacKinnon
Tel: 902-368-5647
Fax: 902-368-5729
sjmackinnon@gov.pe.ca
Manager, Agriculture Innovation, Lynda MacSwain
Tel: 902-368-4815
Fax: 902-368-5729
lemacswain@gov.pe.ca
Manager, Sustainable Agriculture Resources, Barry Thompson
Tel: 902-368-6366
Fax: 902-368-5661
blthompson@gov.pe.ca

Corporate & Financial Services Division
Jones Bldg., 11 Kent St., 5th Fl., PO Box 2000, Charlottetown, PE C1A 7N8
Tel: 902-368-4880
Fax: 902-368-4857
Financial, administrative, & human resources services are provided by the Corporate & Financial Services Division.
Director, Corporate & Financial Services, Jerry Gavin
Tel: 902-368-5741
Fax: 902-368-4857
jpgavin@gov.pe.ca
Manager, Human Resources, Tory Kennedy
Tel: 902-368-6694
Fax: 902-368-4857
tkkennedy@gov.pe.ca
Officer, Financial Services, Janet Doyle
Tel: 902-368-4837
Fax: 902-368-4857
jedoyle@gov.pe.ca
Manager, PEI Agricultural Insurance Corporation, David Aiton
Tel: 905-368-4843
Fax: 902-368-6677
draiton@gov.pe.ca

Forests, Fish, & Wildlife Division
J. Frank Gaudet Tree Nursery, 183 Upton Rd., PO Box 2000, Charlottetown, PE C1A 7N8
Tel: 902-368-4700
Fax: 902-368-4713
The Forests, Fish, & Wildlife Division oversees the following programs & services: the provincial forests; the private forest program; production development; resource inventory & modelling; & wildlife & fish.
Director, Forests, Fish, & Wildlife, Kate E. MacQuarrie
Tel: 902-368-4705
Fax: 902-368-4713
kemacquarrie@gov.pe.ca
Senior Manager, Forests, Fish, & Wildlife, Dan McAskill
Tel: 902-368-6730
Fax: 902-368-4713
jdmcaskill@gov.pe.ca
Manager, Private Forests, Brian Brown
Tel: 902-368-6431
Fax: 902-368-4713
bmbrown@gov.pe.ca
Manager, Production Development, Bill Butler
Tel: 902-368-4711
Fax: 902-368-4713
wabutler@gov.pe.ca
Manager, Public Lands, Jon Hutchinson
Tel: 902-368-4707
Fax: 902-368-4713
pjhutchinson@gov.pe.ca
Manager, Fish & Wildlife, Gerald MacDougall
Tel: 902-368-5111
Fax: 902-368-4713
dgmacdougall@gov.pe.ca
Inventory Forester, Resource Inventory & Modelling, Mike Montigny
Tel: 902-368-4709
mmontigny@gov.pe.ca

Prince Edward Island Analytical Laboratories
Research Station, University Ave., PO Box 1600, Charlottetown, PE C1A 7N3
Tel: 902-368-4190
Prince Edward Island Analytical Laboratories include the Dairy Laboratory, the Soil, Feed, & Water Chemistry Testing Laboratory, & the Water Microbiology Laboratory.
The Dairy Laboratory works in support of the Prince Edward Island Dairy Industry Act & Regulations. It also provides services to VALACTA in Prince Edward Island, Nova Scotia, & New Brunswick.
The Soil, Feed, & Water Chemistry Testing Laboratory provides analytical information for farmers & the public.
Manager, Prince Edward Island Laboratories, Anna Marie MacFarlane
Tel: 902-368-4190
Fax: 902-368-4486
ammacfarlane@gov.pe.ca
Supervisor, Soil, Feed, & Water Chemistry Testing Laboratory, Lori C. Connolly-Brine
Tel: 902-368-5671
Fax: 902-368-6299
lcconnolly@gov.pe.ca
Supervisor, Dairy Laboratory & Water Microbiology Laboratory; Mass Spectrometry Technologist, April M. Driscoll
Tel: 902-314-2811
amdriscoll@gov.pe.ca
Diagnostician, Plant Disease, Marleen Clark
Tel: 902-836-8922
Fax: 902-836-8921
mmclark@gov.pe.ca

Office of the Auditor General

Shaw Bldg., 105 Rochford St. North, 2nd Fl., Charlottetown, PE C1A 7N8
Tel: 902-368-4520
Fax: 902-368-4598
www.assembly.pe.ca
Accountability & best practices in government operations are promoted by the Office of the Auditor General. Independent audits & examinations are conducted by the Office of the Auditor General for the Legislative Assembly of Prince Edward Island.

Auditor General, Colin P. Younker, CA
Tel: 902-368-4520
Fax: 902-368-4598
cpyounker@gov.pe.ca

Audit Director, B. Jane MacAdam, CA
Tel: 902-368-4524
Fax: 902-368-4598
bjmacadam@gov.pe.ca

Audit Director, Scott Messervey, CA, MPA
Tel: 902-368-4518
Fax: 902-368-4598
dsmesservey@gov.pe.ca

Prince Edward Island Department of Community Services & Seniors

Jones Bldg., 11 Kent St., 2nd Fl., PO Box 2000, Charlottetown, PE C1A 7N8
Tel: 902-620-3777
Fax: 902-368-4740
Toll-Free: 866-594-3777
www.gov.pe.ca/sss
The Department of Community Services, Seniors, & Labour strives to develop healthy & self-reliant individuals & to support vulnerable members of the province. Programs & services are offered to promote social & economic prosperity & the creation of work environments that contribute to a safe, healthy, & engaged workforce.
Acts Administered:
Adoption Act
Advisory Council on the Status of Women Act
Blind Workers' Compensation Act
Child Protection Act
Employment Standards Act
Family & Child Services Act (Repealed)
Health Authorities' Employees Act (Repealed)
Housing Corporation Act
Labour Act
North American Labour Cooperation Agreement Implementation Act
Occupational Health & Safety Act
Pay Equity Act
Rehabilitation of Disabled Persons Act
Social Assistance Act
Social Work Act
Youth Employment Act

Minister, Community Services, Seniors & Labour; Minister Responsible, Status of Women, Hon. Valerie E. Docherty
Tel: 902-368-4330
Toll-free: 866-594-3777
Fax: 902-368-4348
vedocherty@assembly.pe.ca;valerie.docherty@liberal.pe.ca
Social Media:
www.facebook.com/profile.php?id=100002087193589

Deputy Minister, Carol Ann Duffy
Tel: 902-368-6520
Fax: 902-368-4740
secameron@gov.pe.ca

Communications Officer, Amber Nicholson
Tel: 902-620-3409
Fax: 902-894-0242
amnicholson@gov.pe.ca

Associated Agencies, Boards & Commissions:
• Advisory Council on the Status of Women
Sherwood Business Centre
161 St. Peter's Rd., Main Level
PO Box 2000
Charlottetown, PE C1A 7N8
Tel: 902-368-4510
Fax: 902-368-3269
peistatusofwomen@eastlink.ca
www.gov.pe.ca/acsw
The Prince Edward Island Advisory Council on the Status of Women consists of nine members. Members are appointed by government to serve on the government advisory agency. The Council advises the Minister Responsible for the Status of Women & works to support equality & the participation of women in economic, political, legal, & cultural activities.
• Employment Standards Board
Sherwood Business Centre
161 St. Peters Rd., 2nd Fl.
Charlottetown, PE C1A 7N8
www.gov.pe.ca/sss

The Employment Standards Board listens to appeals from employers regarding alleged violations of the Employment Standards Act. The Employment Standards Board is also responsible for presenting recommendations about the Minimum Wage Order to the Lieutenant Governor in Council.

• **Labour Relations Board**
Sherwood Business Centre
161 St. Peters Rd., 2nd Fl.
PO Box 2000
Charlottetown, PE C1A 7N8
Tel: 902-368-5550
Fax: 902-368-5476
Toll-free: 800-333-4362
www.gov.pe.ca/sss
The Labour Relations Board works to resolve applications received from labour or management, in accordance with Prince Edward Island's Labour Act.

• **Workers Compensation Appeal Tribunal (WCAT)**
161 St. Peters Rd., 1st Fl.
PO Box 2000
Charlottetown, PE C1A 7N8
Established under Prince Edward Island's Worker's Compensation Act, the Workers Compensation Appeal Tribunal operates as an independent quasi-judicial administrative tribunal. Workers or employers who are dissatisfied with a decision made by the Internal Reconsideration Officer can appeal it through the Workers Compensation Appeal Tribunal. The appeal body is the last level of appeal for workers' compensation matters.
The Office of the Workers Compensation Appeal Tribunal Coordinator is responsible for administrative duties related to the tribunal. The coordinator attends all hearings, but is not part of the decision making process.

Child & Family Services Division
Jones Bldg., 11 Kent St., 2nd Fl., PO Box 2000, Charlottetown, PE C1A 7N8
Tel: 902-368-5294
The Child & Family Services Division offers a wide range of programs & services to care for Prince Edward Island's children & families. Examples of programs include child protection, foster care, & adoption services.
Director, Child & Family Services, Rona Smith
Tel: 902-368-5396
Fax: 902-368-4258
ronasmith@gov.pe.ca
Provincial Coordinator, Child Protection, Maureen G. MacEwen
Tel: 902-368-6161
Fax: 902-620-3362
mgmacewen@gov.pe.ca
Coordinator, Prevention & Residential Services, Child Protection & Youth Services, Barry L. Chandler
Tel: 902-368-6180
Fax: 902-620-3362
blchandler@gov.pe.ca
Coordinator, Family Violence Prevention & Community Development, Premier's Action Committee on Family ViolencePrevention, Dr. Wendy Verhoek-Oftedahl
Tel: 902-368-6712
Fax: 902-368-6169
wverhoekoftedahl@gov.pe.ca

Housing, Seniors & Corporate Support
Jones Bldg., 11 Kent St., 2nd Fl., PO Box 2000, Charlottetown, PE C1A 7N8
Fax: 902-894-0242
The Corporate & Financial Services Division is responsible for the following areas: finance, administration, human resources, communications, French language services, intergovernmental & external relations, records information management, & emergency social services.
Director, Seniors & Corporate Support, W. Lorne Clow
Tel: 902-368-6109
Fax: 902-894-0242
wlclow@gov.pe.ca
Manager, Financial Services & Audit, Sonya L. Cobb
Tel: 902-620-3408
Fax: 902-894-0242
slcobb@gov.pe.ca
Coordinator, Corporate Support, Jennifer Burgess
Tel: 902-368-5199
Fax: 902-894-0242
jmburgess@gov.pe.ca
Coordinator, Provincial Housing, Bill Fleming
Tel: 905-368-5779
Fax: 902-894-5471
bhfleming@gov.pe.ca

Interministerial Women's Secretariat
Sullivan Bldg., 16 Fitzroy St., 1st Fl., PO Box 2000, Charlottetown, PE C1A 7N8
Tel: 902-368-6494
Fax: 902-569-7798
The role of the Interministerial Women's Secretariat is to assist the Minister Responsible for the Status of Women to protect & promote gender equality.
Director, Michelle Harris-Genge
Tel: 902-368-5557
Fax: 902-892-0242
mdharris-genge@gov.pe.ca
Director, Interministerial Women's Secretariat, Michelle Harris-Genge
Tel: 902-368-5557
Fax: 902-569-7798
mdharris-genge@gov.pe.ca

Social Programs
Jones Bldg., 11 Kent St., 2nd Fl., PO Box 2000, Charlottetown, PE C1A 7N8
The Social Programs & Housing Division provides services related to social assistance, disability support, & housing.
Director, Social Programs, Bob D. Creed
Tel: 902-368-6446
Fax: 902-620-3553
bdcreed@gov.pe.ca
Coordinator, Social Assistance & Disability Support Programs (East), Rhea M. Jenkins
Tel: 902-368-5904
Fax: 902-368-6443
rmjenkins@ihis.org
Coordinator, Social Assistance & Disability Support Programs (West), Pat W. MacDonald
Tel: 902-888-8149
Fax: 902-888-8398
pwmacdonald@ihis.org

Prince Edward Island Department of Education & Early Childhood Development

Holman Centre, #101, 250 Water St., Summerside, PE C1N 1B6
Tel: 902-438-4130
Fax: 902-438-4062
www.gov.pe.ca/education
Other Communication: Charlottetown Phone: 902-368-4600
Prince Edward Island's Department of Education & Early Childhood Development offers programs & services for children from birth to the conclusion of twelfth grade.
Acts Administered:
Child Care Facilities Act
Island Regulatory & Appeals Commission Act
School Act
Teachers' Superannuation Act

Minister, Education & Early Childhood Development; Minister, Justice & Public Safety; Attorney General, Hon. J. Alan McIsaac
Tel: 902-368-4330
Fax: 902-368-4348
jamcisaac@assembly.pe.ca; alan.mcisaac@liberal.pe.ca
Social Media:
www.facebook.com/profile.php?id=100001892659368

Deputy Minister, Dr. Alex (Sandy) MacDonald
Tel: 902-438-4876
Fax: 902-438-4150
agmacdonald@edupe.ca

Coordinator, Communications, Major Stewart
Tel: 902-438-4873
Fax: 902-438-4150
mbstewart@gov.pe.ca

Associated Agencies, Boards & Commissions:

• **Children's Secretariat**
c/o Sarah Henry, Education & Early Childhood Development
161 St. Peters Rd.
PO Box 2000
Charlottetown, PE C1A 7N8
Prince Edward Island's Children's Secretariat consists of government & community representatives. They strive to improve outcomes for children to age eight, in areas such as healthy child development & public education.

• **Eastern School District**
PO Box 8600
Charlottetown, PE C1A 8V7
Tel: 902-368-6990
Fax: 902-368-6960
www.edu.pe.ca/esd
The Eastern School District consists of 36 schools. Education is offered to students from kindergarten to grade 12.

• **French Language School Board / La Commission scolaire de langue française de l'Îlw-du-Prince-Édouard**
1596, rte 124
Abram-Village, PE C0B 2E0
Tel: 902-854-2975
Fax: 902-854-2981
cslf@edu.pe.ca
www.edu.pe.ca/cslf
Prince Edward Island's French Language School Board administers six schools.

• **Prince Edward Island Athletic Association (PEISAA)**
#101, 250 Water St.
Summerside, PE C1N 1B6
Tel: 902-438-4846
Fax: 902-438-4884
www.peisaa.pe.ca
The Prince Edward Island Athletic Association was established as the governing body for all school sports in the province. The association is a member of the Canadian School Sport Federation & is affiliated with the National Federation of State High School Athletic Associations.

• **Western School Board of Prince Edward Island**
Summerside Office
272 MacEwen Dr.
Summerside, PE C1N 2P7
Tel: 902-888-8400
Fax: 902-888-8449
www.edu.pe.ca/wsb
Other Communication: Elmsdale Office, Phone: 902-853-8602, Fax: 902-853-8679
The Western School Board oversees twenty-one schools situated in the western region of Prince Edward Island.

Administration & Corporate Services Division
#101. 250 Water St., Summerside, PE C1N 1B6
Tel: 902-438-4819
Fax: 902-438-4874
The Administration & Corporate Services Division oversees the following areas: finance & school board operations; program evaluation & student assessment; research & corporate services; technology in education; human resources; & the Office of the Registrar.
Senior Director, Administration & Corporate Services, Terry Keefe
Tel: 902-438-4880
Fax: 902-438-4874
tekeefe@gov.pe.ca
Director, Finance & School Board Operations, Gordon MacFadyen
Tel: 902-438-4882
Fax: 902-438-4874
gsmacfadyen@gov.pe.ca
Manager, Research & Corporate Services, Robin Phillips
Tel: 902-438-4837
Fax: 902-438-4874
Manager, Human Resources, Tanya Tynski
Tel: 902-438-4881
Fax: 902-438-4874
tmtynski@gov.pe.ca
Manager, Program Evaluation & Student Assessment, Cindy Wood
Tel: 902-438-4904
Fax: 902-438-4889
clwood@gov.pe.ca
Registrar & Coordinator, International Education, Nancy Desrosiers
Tel: 902-438-4827
Fax: 902-438-4062
ndesrosiers@gov.pe.ca
Coordinator, Information Management, Mark DeMone
Tel: 902-438-4839
Fax: 902-438-4874
mxdemone@gov.pe.ca
Coordinator, Education Technology, Edward MacLean
Tel: 902-438-4834
Fax: 902-438-4874
edmaclean@gov.pe.ca

Learning & Early Childhood Development Division
Holman Centre, 250 Water St., Summerside, PE C1N 1B6
Tel: 902-438-4816
Fax: 902-438-4874
The Public Education Branch is responsible for the following services: early childhood development & kindergarten; child & student services; & English & French programs.
Senior Director, Learning & Early Childhood Development, Imelda Arsenault
Tel: 902-438-4879
Fax: 902-438-4150
imarsenault@edu.pe.ca
Director, French Programs, Guy Albert
Tel: 902-438-4155
Fax: 902-438-4884
gcalbert@edu.pe.ca
Director, Child & Student Services, Glenn Edison
Tel: 902-438-4886
Fax: 902-438-4884
ggedison@edu.pe.ca
Director, English Programs, Kathy McDonald
Tel: 902-438-4870
Fax: 902-438-4062
kmmcdonald@edu.pe.ca
Manager, Early Childhood Development & Kindergarten, Carolyn Simpson
Tel: 902-438-4883

Fax: 902-438-4884
cesimpson@edu.pe.ca
Coordinator, Elementary Education, Sheila Barnes
Tel: 902-438-4800
Fax: 902-438-4062
sebarnes@edu.pe.ca
Coordinator, Autism, Marlene Breitenbach
Tel: 902-569-7792
Fax: 902-368-4622
mmbreitenbach@edu.pe.ca
Coordinator, Student Services, Sterling Carruthers
Tel: 902-438-4134
Fax: 902-438-4062
sdcarruthers@edu.pe.ca
Coordinator, Healthy Child Development, Sarah Henry
Tel: 902-438-4843
Fax: 902-438-4874
skhenry@edu.pe.ca
Coordinator, Secondary Education, Mike Leslie
Tel: 902-438-4801
Fax: 902-438-4062
mjleslie@edu.pe.ca
Coordinator, Community Information, Melanie Melanson
Tel: 902-438-4842
Fax: 902-438-4874
mdmelanson@edu.pe.ca
Administrator, English as an Additional Language, Janet Perry-Payne
Tel: 902-620-3735
Fax: 902-620-3737
jlpayne@edu.pe.ca

Elections Prince Edward Island

J. Angus MacLean Bldg., 94 Great George St., 1st Fl., PO Box 774, Charlottetown, PE C1A 7L3
Tel: 902-368-5895
Fax: 902-368-6500
Toll-Free: 888-234-8783
www.electionspei.ca

Elections Prince Edward Island provides information to electors & candidates. Guided by the Canadian Charter of Rights & Freedoms, Elections Prince Edward Island works to ensure that electors & candidates have the opportunity to exercise their democratic right.

Chief Electoral Officer, Lowell Croken
Tel: 902-368-5898
Fax: 902-368-6500
ljcroken@gov.pe.ca

Deputy Chief Electoral Officer, Norma E. Palmer-Bowers
Tel: 902-368-5895
Fax: 902-368-6500
nepalmer@gov.pe.ca

Manager, Election Operations, Judy Richard
Tel: 902-620-3709
Fax: 902-368-6500
jgrichard@gov.pe.ca

Prince Edward Island Department of Environment, Labour & Justice

Shaw Bldg. South, 95 Rochford St., 4th Fl., PO Box 2000, Charlottetown, PE C1A 7N8
Tel: 902-620-3774
Fax: 902-368-4242
rryder@gov.pe.ca
www.gov.pe.ca/jps

Acts Administered:
Affidavits Act
Age of Majority Act
Agriculture Crop Rotation Act
Amusement Devices Act
Ancient Burial Grounds Act
Appeals Act
Apportionment Act
Arbitration Act
Auctioneers Act
Automobile Junk Yards Act
Bailable Proceedings Act
Beverage Containers Act
Boilers & Pressure Vessels Act
Business Practices Act
Canada-United Kingdom Judgments Recognition Act
Canadian Judgments (Enforcement) Act
Cemeteries Act
Charities Act
Child Status Act
Co-operative Associations Act
Collection Agencies Act
Commorientes Act
Companies Act
Consumer Protection Act
Consumer Reporting Act
Contributory Negligence Act
Controverted Elections (Provincial) Act
Coroners Act
Coroners Act (Repealed)
Correctional Services Act
Court Reporters Act
Court Security Act
Credit Unions Act
Crown Proceedings Act
Custody Jurisdiction & Enforcement Act
Defamation Act
Dependants of a Deceased Person Relief Act
Designation of Beneficiaries Under Benefit Plans Act
Direct Sellers Act
Electrical Inspection Act
Electronic Commerce Act
Electronic Evidence Act
Elevators & Lifts Act
Emergency 911 Act
Emergency Measures Act
Emergency Measures Act
Emergency Measures Act (Repealed)
Energy Corporation Act
Environmental Protection Act
Escheats Act
Evidence Act
Extra-Provincial Corporations Registration Act
Factors Act
Family Law Act
Fatal Accidents Act
Films Act
Fire Prevention Act
Fire Prevention Act
Floral Hills Memorial Gardens Administration Act
Foreign Resident Corporations Act
Forest Management Act
Franchises Act
Frauds on Creditors Act
Freedom of Information & Protection of Privacy Act
Frustrated Contracts Act
Garage Keepers' Lien Act
Garnishee Act
Gift Cards
Gulf Trust Corporation Act
Habeas Corpus Act
Human Rights Act
Institute of Man & Resources Act
Insurance Act
Intercountry Adoption (Hague Convention) Act
Interjurisdictional Support Orders Act
International Commercial Arbitration Act
International Sale of Goods Act
International Trusts Act
Interpretation Act
Interprovincial Subpoena Act
Investigation of Titles Act
Islander Day
Judgment & Execution Act
Judicature Act
Judicial Review Act
Jury Act
Landlord & Tenant Act
Legal Profession Act
Licensing Act (Repealed)
Lightning Rod Act
Limited Partnerships Act
Maintenance Enforcement Act
Mechanics' Lien Act
Mineral Resources Act
Natural Areas Protection Act
Occupiers' Liability Act
Oil & Natural Gas Act
PEI Firefighters Long Service Medal Act
PEI Firefighters Long Service Medal Act
Partnership Act
Partnership Act
Perpetuities Act
Personal Property Security Act
Pesticides Control Act
Police Act
Police Act (Repealed)
Power Engineers Act
Powers of Attorney Act
Prearranged Funeral Services Act
Premium Tax Act
Private Investigators & Security Guards Act
Probate Act
Probation Act
Provincial Administrator of Estates Act
Provincial Building Code Act
Provincial Court Act
Public Accounting & Auditing Act
Public Accounting & Auditing Act (Repealed)
Public Forest Council Act
Public Trustee Act
Quieting Titles Act
Real Estate Trading Act
Real Property Act
Reciprocal Enforcement of Judgments Act
Reciprocal Enforcement of Maintenance Orders Act (Repealed)
Renewable Energy Act
Retail Business Holidays Act
Rural Community Fire Companies Act
Sale of Goods Act
Securities Act
Securities Act (Repealed)
Sheriffs Act
Statute of Frauds
Statute of Limitations
Store Hours Act
Summary Proceedings Act
Supreme Court Act (Repealed)
Supreme Court Reporters Act (Renamed)
Survival of Actions Act
Time Uniformity Act
Time in Public Offices Act (Repealed)
Transboundary Pollution (Reciprocal Access) Act
Trespass to Property Act
Truck Operators' Remuneration Act
Trust & Fiduciary Companies Act
Trustee Act
Unclaimed Articles Act
Unconscionable Transactions Relief Act
Uniformity Commissioners Act
Unsightly Property Act
Variation of Trusts Act
Vendors & Purchasers Act
Victims of Crime Act
Victims of Family Violence Act
Volunteers Liability Act
Warehousemen's Lien Act
Wildlife Conservation Act
Winding-up Act
Young Offenders (P.E.I.) Act (Renamed)
Youth Justice Act

Minister, Environment, Labour & Justice, Hon. Janice A. Sherry
Tel: 902-368-6410
Fax: 902-368-6488
jasherry@gov.pe.ca; janice.sherry@liberal.pe.ca
Social Media:
www.facebook.com/people/Janice-Sherry/100002079465746

Deputy Minister & Deputy Attorney General, Shauna Sullivan Curley, Q.C.
Tel: 902-368-5152
Fax: 902-368-4910
sscurley@gov.pe.ca

Officer, Communications, Kim Devine
Tel: 902-368-5286
Fax: 902-368-5830
kmdevine@gov.pe.ca

Associated Agencies, Boards & Commissions:
• Environmental Advisory Council
PO Box 2000
Charlottetown, PE C1A 7N8
The Environmental Advisory Council advises the Minister responsible for the environment about environmental concerns. Members of the council are appointed by the Lieutenant Governor in Council.
• Office of the Police Commissioner
114 Kent St.
PO Box 427
Charlottetown, PE C1A 7K7
Tel: 902-368-7200
Fax: 902-368-1123
Toll-free: 877-541-7204
www.policecommissioner.pe.ca
The Office of the Police Commissioner investigates & resolves complaints about the unprofessional conduct of police, other than the RCMP. Under the Police Act, a person who is 18 years of age & over, who has been directly affected by the conduct of municipal police officer, may make a complaint. The Office of the Police Commissioner also handles complaints about a chief of a municipal police service, a director or instructing officer at the Atlantic Police Academy, or a security police officer at the University of Prince Edward Island. The independent statutory office works to carry out its mission in a timely & impartial manner.
Persons must call the Office of the Police Commissioner to book an appointment.

• Prince Edward Island Energy Corporation
Jones Bldg.
11 Kent St., 4th Fl.
PO Box 2000
Charlottetown, PE C1A 7N8
The Prince Edward Island Energy Corporation promotes the development, generation, transmission, & distribution of energy in an economic & efficient manner.
• Public Forest Council (PFC)
c/o PEI Department of Environment, Energy, & Forestry
Forestry Division
PO Box 2000
Charlottetown, PE C1A 7N8
Fax: 902-368-4713
publicforest@gov.pe.ca
www.gov.pe.ca/eef/PFC
The Public Forest Council is made up of six private sector members & three public sector members, who are appointed by the Lieutenant Governor in Council. Council members foster discussion about the potential for provincial woodlands. The council is especially interested in non-traditional, non-consumptive uses of public forests.
• Species at Risk Advisory Committee
The Species at Risk Advisory Committee performs the following tasks: assessing the province's wildlife resources; advising the Minister of Environment, Energy, & Forestry about the species that should be listed at risk; analyzing the effects of land use on wildlife & their habitat; & making recommendations about the conservation of wildlife & its habitat.

Administrative Services Division
Jones Bldg., 11 Kent St., 4th Fl., PO Box 2000, Charlottetown, PE C1A 7N8
Tel: 902-368-5000
Fax: 902-368-5830
Administrative services, human resources, & finances are the responsibilities of this division.
Director, Administrative Services, Mary Kinsman
Tel: 902-368-5032
Fax: 902-368-5830
makinsman@gov.pe.ca

Community & Correctional Services Division
109 Water St., Summerside, PE C1N 1A8
Tel: 902-432-2847
Fax: 902-432-2851
www.gov.pe.ca/jps
The Community & Correctional Services Division provides community & custody programs to contribute to the rehabilitation of youth & adult offenders. The division also offers the following services: research; policy development; support services to the courts & victims of crime; crime prevention programs; & public education.
The work of the Community & Correctional Services Division is conducted by the following sections: Community Programs; Correctional Programs; Victim Services; & Clinical Services.
Director, Community & Correctional Services, John R. Picketts
Tel: 902-432-2850
Fax: 902-432-2851
jrpicketts@gov.pe.ca
Provincial Manager, Community Services, Karen MacDonald
Tel: 902-368-5295
Fax: 902-368-4579
kamacdonald@gov.pe.ca
Provincial Manager, Victim Services, Susan Maynard
Tel: 902-368-4584
Fax: 902-368-4514
smaynard@gov.pe.ca
Provincial Manager, Correctional Programs, Donna Myers
Tel: 902-569-7683
Fax: 902-569-7711
dfmyers@gov.pe.ca
Manager, Prince Edward Island Youth Centre, Shannon L. Ellis
Tel: 902-888-8256
Fax: 902-888-8247
slellis@gov.pe.ca
Manager, Youth Justice Services (West), Paula Finkle
Tel: 902-888-8254
Fax: 902-888-8214
plfinkle@gov.pe.ca
Manager, Clinical Services, Dr. Edward F. Hansen
Tel: 902-569-7684
Fax: 902-368-5644
efhansen@gov.pe.ca
Manager, Provincial Correctional Centre, Kim Kempton
Tel: 902-368-4885
Fax: 902-368-5834
kjkempton@gov.pe.ca
Manager, Youth Justice Services (East), Glenda L. Lutes
Tel: 902-368-4578
Fax: 902-368-4579
gllutes@gov.pe.ca
Manager, Prince Correctional Centre, Gordon Roche
Tel: 902-888-8209
Fax: 902-888-8464
gmroche@gov.pe.ca
Manager, Corporate Services, Denise M. Spenceley
Tel: 902-569-7681
Fax: 902-569-7711
dmspenceley@gov.pe.ca
Manager, Probation Services, Gary Trainor
Tel: 902-368-4697
Fax: 902-368-4579
gjtrainor@gov.pe.ca

Community Safety & Justice Policy
Shaw Bldg., 105 Rochford St., 4th Fl., Charlottetown, PE C1A 7N8
Tel: 902-368-6620
Fax: 902-368-5335
www.gov.pe.ca/jps
The Policy, Policing, & Crime Prevention Division is comprised of the following sections: Justice Resource Service; Policing Services; & Access & Privacy Services.
The Justice Resource Service supports government & community organizations in justice issues, with a focus on community & social development.
The Police Act is administerd by the Policing Services Section.
The Access & Privacy Services Section offers advice regarding the operation of the Freedom of Information & Protection of Privacy (FOIPP) Act & its regulations.
Director, Community Safety & Justice Policy, Erin Mitchell
Tel: 902-368-6619
Fax: 902-368-5335
etmitchell@gov.pe.ca
Provincial Manager, Access & Privacy Services, Kathryn Dickson
Tel: 902-569-0568
Fax: 902-368-4096
kedickson@gov.pe.ca
Manager, Policing Services, Gordon Garrison
Tel: 902-368-4823
Fax: 902-368-5335
gagarrison@gov.pe.ca
Manager, Justice Resource Service, Jill Lightwood
Tel: 902-368-4583
Fax: 902-368-4096
jlightwood@gov.pe.ca
Coordinator, Planning & Communications, Policy, Policing, & Crime Prevention, Joanne MacKinnon
Tel: 902-368-5010
Fax: 902-368-5335
jymackinnon@gov.pe.ca

Consumer, Labour, & Financial Services
Shaw Bldg., 95 Rochford St., 4th Fl., PO Box 2000, Charlottetown, PE C1A 7N8
Tel: 902-368-4550
Fax: 902-368-5283
www.gov.pe.ca/jps
The Consumer, Corporate, & Insurance Division consists of the following sections: Consumer Affairs; Corporations; Securities; Firearms Office; & Insurance & Real Estate.
The Consumer Affairs section administers the Lottery Schemes Order. It also responds to complaints & inquiries from consumers.
The Corporations section handles the registration of partnerships & business names. It also oversees the incorporation of companies, non-profit corporations, co-operatives, & credit unions.
The Securities Act is administered & enforced by the Securities Division.
The Gun Control Program is administered by the Firearms Office, in accordance with the Criminal Code of Canada & the federal Firearms Act. The Firearms Office is also responsible for the administration of the Private Investigators & Security Guards Act.
Under the supervision of the Superintendent of Insurance, the Insurance & Real Estate section administers the Fire Prevention Act, the Insurance Act, the Premium Tax Act, & the Real Estate Trading Act.
Director, Consumer, Labour & Financial Services, Katharine Tummon
Tel: 902-368-4542
Fax: 902-368-5283
kptummon@gov.pe.ca
Superintendent, Insurance, Robert Bradley
Tel: 902-368-6478
Fax: 902-368-5283
rabradley@gov.pe.ca
Chair, Employment Standards Board, Donald G. MacCormac
Tel: 902-368-5550
Toll-free: 800-333-4362
Fax: 902-368-5476
Corporations Officer, Corporation Section, Joan MacKay
Tel: 902-368-4509
Fax: 902-368-5283
jmmakday@gov.pe.ca
Compliance Officer, Consumer Affairs Section, Linda Peters
Tel: 902-368-5653
Fax: 902-368-5283
lmpeters@gov.pe.ca
Capital Markets Contact, Securities Section, Janice Callbeck
Tel: 902-368-6288
Fax: 902-368-5283
jccallbeck@gov.pe.ca
Manager, Labour & Industrial Relations, Faye M. Martin
Tel: 902-569-0545
Toll-free: 866-333-4362
Fax: 902-368-5476
fmmartin@gov.pe.ca

Crown Attorneys Office
197 Richmond St., Charlottetown, PE C1A 1J3
Tel: 902-368-4595
Fax: 902-368-5812
www.gov.pe.ca/jps
It is the responsibility of the Crown Attoneys Office to prosecute criminal cases under provincial statutes & the Criminal Code of Canada.
Director, Crown Attorneys Office, Cyndria L. Wedge
Tel: 902-368-5073
Fax: 902-368-5812
clwedge@gov.pe.ca
Senior Crown Attorney, Summerside Location, David P. O'Brien, QC
Tel: 902-888-8047
Fax: 902-888-8224
dpobrien@gov.pe.ca
243 Harbour Dr.
Summerside, PE C1N 5R1
Senior Crown Attorney, Charlottetown Location, Gerald Quinn, QC
Tel: 902-368-5076
Fax: 902-368-5812
gkquinn@gov.pe.ca

Environment
Jones Bldg., 11 Kent St., 4th Fl., PO Box 2000, Charlottetown, PE C1A 7N8
Tel: 902-368-5044
Fax: 902-368-5830
Toll-Free: 866-368-5044
The Environment Division oversees programs that protect the province's environement, including the following elements: groundwater; inland surface water & coastal estuaries; drinking water; the ozone layer; & air quality.
The division is also involved in waste management activities, such as the handling of litter, beverage containers, hazardous wastes, used oil, petroleum storage tanks, lead-acid batteries, tires, & derelict vehicles.
Director, Environment, Jim Young, P.Eng
Tel: 902-368-5034
Fax: 902-368-5830
jjyoung@gov.pe.ca
Manager, Climate Change & Air Management, Erin Taylor
Tel: 902-368-6111
Fax: 902-368-5830
eotaylor@gov.pe.ca
Manager, Administrative & Customer Services, Roxanne Larter
Tel: 902-368-5561
Fax: 902-368-5526
rmlarter@gov.pe.ca
Manager, Inspection Services, Glenda MacKinnon-Peters, P.Eng.
Tel: 902-368-4874
Fax: 902-368-5526
gcmackinnon-peters@gov.pe.ca
Manager, Watershed & Subdivision Planning, Bruce Raymond
Tel: 902-368-5054
Fax: 902-368-5830
bgraymond@gov.pe.ca
Manager, Drinking Water, Land, & Systems Protection, George Somers
Tel: 902-368-5046
Fax: 902-368-5830
ghsomers@gov.pe.ca
Manager, Environmental Land Management, Greg Wilson
Tel: 902-368-5274
Fax: 902-368-5830
gbwilson@gov.pe.ca
Chief, Safety Standards, Alan Robison
Tel: 902-368-4892
Fax: 902-368-5526
amrobison@gov.pe.ca
Chief Engineer, Building Standards, Garth Simmons
Tel: 902-569-7746
Fax: 902-368-5830
gssimmons@gov.pe.ca
Chief Officer, Boiler & Pressure Vessel, Plumbing & Propane Inspection, Steve Townsend
Tel: 902-368-5567

Fax: 902-368-5526
srtownsend@gov.pe.ca
Coordinator, Pesticide Monitoring & Control, Thane Clarke
Tel: 902-368-5599
Fax: 902-368-5830
ktclarke@gov.pe.ca
Coordinator, Alternative Land Use Services (ALUS) Program, Shawn Hill
Tel: 902-620-3725
Fax: 902-368-5830
sjhill@gov.pe.ca
Environmental & Regulatory Coordinator, Barrie Jackson
Tel: 902-368-5173
Fax: 902-368-5830
bajackson@gov.pe.ca

Legal Aid
40 Great George St., PO Box 2000, Charlottetown, PE C1A 7N8
www.gov.pe.ca/jps
The Legal Aid program in Prince Edward Island is staffed by lawyers who offer direct assistance to legal aid clients in the areas of family & criminal law. In order to be eligible for these legal services, potential clients are required to take a financial means test.
Funding of the family legal aid program is provided by the province of Prince Edward Island & the Prince Edward Island Law Foundation. Prince Edward Island & Canada fund the criminal legal aid program.
Director, Legal Aid, W. Kent Brown, Q.C.
Tel: 902-368-6043
Fax: 902-368-6122
wkbrown@gov.pe.ca
Administrative Officer, Legal Aid, Jackie M. Hamm
Tel: 902-368-6016
Fax: 902-368-6122
jmhamm@gov.pe.ca
Criminal Legal Aid, Charlottetown Location, Brenda J. Picard, Q.C.
Tel: 902-368-6043
Fax: 902-368-6122
bjpicard@gov.pe.ca
Family Legal Aid, Charlottetown Location, Leslie A. Collins
Tel: 902-368-6540
Fax: 902-620-3083
lacollins@gov.pe.ca
Criminal Legal Aid, Summerside Location, Patricia L. Cheverie, Q.C.
Tel: 902-888-8219
Fax: 902-438-4071
tlcheverie@gov.pe.ca
Family Legal Aid, Summerside Location, Michelle L. Arsenault
Tel: 902-888-8066
Fax: 902-438-4071
miarsenault@gov.pe.ca

Legal & Court Services Division
Shaw Bldg., 95 Rochford St., 4th Fl., Charlottetown, PE C1A 7N8
Tel: 902-368-6522
Fax: 902-368-4563
www.gov.pe.ca/jps
The Legal & Court Services Division consists of the following sections: Office of the Public Trustee & Public Guardian; Court Services; Legal Services; Law Enforcement; & Family Law.
The Office of the Public Trustee & Public Guardian administers the Provincial Administrator of Estates Act & the Public Trustee Act.
The Court Services Section oversees court personnel & services, while the Legal Services Section handles legal services to the provincial government's departments & agencies.
The Law Enforcement Section is headed by the Commanding Officer of the RCMP, the Provincial Police Force. Police protection throughout the province is handled by the RCMP, except for the areas of Borden-Carleton, Charlottetown, Kensington, St. Eleanors, & Summerside which have municipal police forces.
The following programs & services are administered by the Family Law Section: Parent Education Program, Family Court Counsellors' Office, Child Support Guidelines Office, Administrative Recalculation Office, & the Maintenance Enforcement Program.
Director, Legal & Court Services, Barrie L. Grandy, QC
Tel: 902-368-4554
Fax: 902-368-4563
blgrandy@gov.pe.ca
Public Trustee & Guardian, Office of the Public Trustee & Public Guardian, Mark L. Gallant, LLB
Tel: 902-368-4552
Fax: 902-368-5335
mgallant@gov.pe.ca
Public Guardian, Office of the Public Trustee & Public Guardian, Judy Harper
Tel: 902-368-6506
Fax: 902-368-5335
jaharper@gov.pe.ca
Prothonotary & Registrar, Court Services Section, Charles P. Thompson, O.C.
Tel: 902-368-6669
Fax: 902-368-0266
cpthompson@gov.pe.ca
Chief Superintendent & Commanding Officer, RCMP, Law Enforcement Section, Tracy Hardy
Tel: 902-566-7132
Fax: 902-566-7235
tracy.hardy@rcmp-grc.gc.ca
Chief Sheriff, Court Services Section, Ron Dowling
Tel: 902-368-6055
Fax: 902-368-6571
rjdowling@gov.pe.ca
Chief Provincial Court Clerk, Court Services Section, Kevin Gotell
Tel: 902-368-6693
Fax: 902-368-6210
Manager, Family Law Section, Loretta Coady MacAulay
Tel: 902-368-4886
Fax: 902-368-6474
llmacaulay@gov.pe.ca
Manager, Legal Services Section, Terri MacPherson, Q.C.
Tel: 902-368-5145
Fax: 902-368-4563
tamacpherson@gov.pe.ca
Manager, Court Services & Deputy Registrar, Court Services Section, Judy A. Turpin
Tel: 902-368-6005
Fax: 902-368-6210
jaturpin@gov.pe.ca
Director, Maintenance Enforcement Program, Family Law Section, Norma Reardon
Tel: 902-368-6499
Fax: 902-368-6934
nireardon@gov.pe.ca
Coordinator, Parent Education Program, Family Law Section, Gordon Ritchie
Tel: 902-368-4333
Toll-free: 877-203-8828
Fax: 902-368-6934
giritchie@gov.pe.ca
Coordinator, Family Court Counsellors' Office, Family Law Section, Ron Stanley
Tel: 902-836-8924
Fax: 902-368-6934
rdstanley@gov.pe.ca
Trial Coordinator, Supreme Court of Prince Edward Island, Court Services Section, Shelley Young Brennan
Tel: 902-368-6023
Fax: 902-368-6123
sdyoung@gov.pe.ca
Administrative Recalculation Officer, Family Law Section, Sharon Fortier
Tel: 902-368-4109
Fax: 902-368-6934
safortier@gov.pe.ca
Child Support Guidelines Officer, Charlottetown Location, Family Law Section, Angelie C. Murnaghan
Tel: 902-368-6658
Fax: 902-368-6934
acmurnaghan@gov.pe.ca
Child Support Guidelines Officer, Summerside Location, Family Law Section, Barbara Richard
Tel: 902-888-8188
Fax: 902-888-8222
bmrichard@gov.pe.ca

Legislative Counsel
J. Angus MacLean Bldg., 180 Richmond St., PO Box 2000, Charlottetown, PE C1A 7N8
www.gov.pe.ca/jps
The Legislative Counsel is responsible for the following duties: drafting statutes & regulations; revising statutes, & producing loose-leaf updates of the consolidations of statutes & regulations.
Chief Legislative Counsel, Shawn Flynn
Tel: 902-368-5284
Fax: 902-368-5176
sbflynn@gov.pe.ca
Legislative Counsel, Janet Christian
Tel: 902-368-4295
Fax: 902-368-5176
jmchristian@gov.pe.ca
Legislative Counsel, Peter F. Allison
Tel: 902-368-4553
Fax: 902-368-5176
ptallison@gov.pe.ca
Legislative Editor, Kent W. Walker
Tel: 902-368-4269
Fax: 902-368-5176
kwwalker@gov.pe.ca

Policy & Administration Division
Shaw Bldg., 105 Rochford St., 4th Fl., PO Box 2000, Charlottetown, PE C1A 7N8
Tel: 902-368-4865
Fax: 902-368-5335
www.gov.pe.ca/jps
The Policy & Administration Division provides financial administration & human resource management services for the Department of Justice & Public Safety.
Director, Policy & Administration, Kevin Barnes, CA
Tel: 902-368-4865
Fax: 902-368-4224
kcbarnes@gov.pe.ca
Manager, Financial Administration, Barry Gosby
Tel: 902-368-4897
Fax: 902-368-5335
bbgosby@gov.pe.ca
Manager, Human Resource Management, Michael Ready
Tel: 902-569-0549
Fax: 902-368-4224
mcready@gov.pe.ca

Office of Public Safety
National Bank Tower, #600, 134 Kent St., 6th Fl., PO Box 2000, Charlottetown, PE C1A 7N8
Tel: 902-894-0385
Fax: 902-368-6362
www.gov.pe.ca/jps
The Office of Public Safety includes the following sections: 911 Administration Office; Emergency Measures Organization; Fire Marshal's Office; & the Office for Business Continuity Management Planning.
Director, Office of Public Safety, Aaron Campbell
Tel: 902-894-0385
Fax: 902-368-6362
acampbell@gov.pe.ca
Provincial Coordinator, 911 Call Answer & Transfer Service, Pat J. Kelly
Tel: 902-894-0299
Fax: 902-368-6362
pjkelly@gov.pe.ca
Provincial Emergency Management Coordinator, Emergency Measures Organization, Tanya Mullally
Tel: 902-368-5980
Fax: 902-368-6362
tlmullally@gov.pe.ca
Coordinator, Civic Addressing, 911 Call Answer & Transfer Service, D. Steven Dickie
Tel: 902-368-6361
Fax: 902-368-6362
dsdickie@gov.pe.ca
Fire Marshal, Fire Marshal's Office, David Rossiter
Tel: 902-368-4869
Fax: 902-368-5526
derossiter@gov.pe.ca
Project Manager, Maritime Radio Project, Larry Avery
Tel: 902-368-4073
Fax: 902-368-6362
jlavery@gov.pe.ca
Communications Officer, Office of Public Safety, Connie McNeill
Tel: 902-894-0374
Fax: 902-368-6362
cbmcneill@gov.pe.ca
Senior Business Continuity Planner, Office for Business Continuity Management Planning, Brian McFeely
Tel: 902-438-4174
Fax: 902-432-2659
bcmcfeely@gov.pe.ca
Deputy Fire Marshal, Fire Marshal's Office, Robert Arsenault
Tel: 902-368-4893
Fax: 902-368-5526
robarsenault@gov.pe.ca

Prince Edward Island Department of Finance, Energy & Municipal Affairs

Shaw Bldg., 95 Rochford St. South, 2nd Fl., PO Box 2000, Charlottetown, PE C1A 7N8
Tel: 902-368-4000
Fax: 902-368-5544
www.gov.pe.ca/finance
The Department of Finance & Municipal Affairs facilitates the management of the Government of Prince Edward Island's human & financial resources.
Acts Administered:
Charlottetown Area Municipalities Act
City of Summerside Act
Civil Service Act
Civil Service Superannuation Act
Community Development Equity Tax Credit Act
Condominium Act
Deposit Receipt (Winding-up) Act
Environment Tax Act
Financial Administration Act
Financial Corporation Capital Tax Act

Gasoline Tax Act
Health Tax Act
Income Tax Act
Lands Protection Act, P.E.I.
Lotteries Commission Act
Maritime Provinces Harness Racing Commission Act
Municipal Boundaries Act
Municipal Debenture Guarantee Act
Municipalities Act
Northumberland Strait Crossing Act
Planning Act
Public Purchasing Act
Public Sector Pay Reduction Act
Queen's Printer Act
Real Property Assessment Act
Real Property Tax Act
Real Property Transfer Tax Act
Registry Act
Revenue Administration Act
Revenue Tax Act
Statistics Act
Tobacco Tax Act

Minister, Finance & Municipal Affairs, Hon. Wesley J. Sheridan
Tel: 902-368-4050
Fax: 902-368-6575
wjsheridan@gov.pe.ca; wes.sheridan@liberal.pe.ca
Social Media:
www.facebook.com/profile.php?id=100002547484282&ref=ts

Deputy Minister, Doug Clow, CA
Tel: 902-368-4201
Fax: 902-368-6661
dmclow@gov.pe.ca

Officer, Communications, Jennifer MacDonald-Donovan
Tel: 902-620-3679
Fax: 902-368-6575
jwmacdonald@gov.pe.ca

Associated Agencies, Boards & Commissions:
• Office of the Child & Youth Services Commissioner
Homan Bldg.
#101, 250 Water St.
Summerside, PE C1N 1B6
Tel: 902-438-4872
Fax: 902-438-4874
www.gov.pe.ca/childandyouth
The Child & Youth Services Commissioner deals with issues that affect children & youth in Prince Edward Island. The following legislation in Prince Edward Island affects children & youth: Child Protection Act; Mental Health Act; School Act; & Youth Justice Act.
• Commission on the Land & Local Governance
Aubin Arsenault Bldg.
3 Brighton Rd.
Charlottetown, PE C1A 8T6
www.gov.pe.ca/landandlocalgovernance
• Public Service Commission (PSC)
Shaw Bldg. North
105 Rochford St., 1st Fl.
PO Box 2000
Charlottetown, PE C1A 7N8
Tel: 902-368-4080
Fax: 902-368-4383
www.gov.pe.ca/psc
The independent & impartial agency coordinates human resources in the public sector of Prince Edward Island. All government departments & agencies, health authorities, & other public sector employers are served by Prince Edward Island's Public Service Commission. Examples of services include recruitment, selection, occupational health & safety, payroll & benefits administration, & the employee assistant program.

Communications Prince Edward Island
Shaw Bldg., 95-105 Rochford St., 5th Fl., Charlottetown, PE C1A 7N8
www.gov.pe.ca/finance
Communications PEI provides provincial government departments, agencies, & crown corporations with a variety of communication services, such as graphic design, video & radio production, photography services, & mail services.
Assistant Deputy Minister, Communications Prince Edward Island, Matt McGuire
Tel: 902-368-4407
Fax: 902-368-6118
mdmcguire@gov.pe.ca
Director, Strategic & Corporate Communications, Patricia Devine
Tel: 902-368-5513
pdevine@gov.pe.ca
Queen's Printer & Manager, Document Publishing Centre & PEI Mail, Mike Fagan
Tel: 902-368-5192
Fax: 902-368-5168
ssccoles@gov.pe.ca
Manager, Strategic Marketing & Graphic Design, Sheri Coles
Tel: 902-368-6326
Fax: 902-569-7543
ssccoles@gov.pe.ca
Manager, Communications, Jean Doherty
Tel: 902-569-0548
jmdoherty@gov.pe.ca
Manager, Multimedia Services, Peter MacPhee
Tel: 902-368-6322
Fax: 902-368-5641
pwmacphee@gov.pe.ca
Officer, Corporate Communications, Heather Robinson
Tel: 902-620-3144
hrobinson@gov.pe.ca

Office of the Comptroller
Shaw Bldg., 95 Rochford St., 2nd Fl., PO Box 2000, Charlottetown, PE C1A 7N8
Tel: 902-368-4201
Fax: 902-368-6661
www.gov.pe.ca/finance
The Office of the Comptroller carries out the following responsibilities: operating the government's corporate accounting system; providing advice related to financial management; administering the corporate procurement service for departments & agencies; managing a corporate fleet information system; & producing the province's public accounts.
Comptroller, Doug Clow, CA
Tel: 902-368-4201
Fax: 902-368-6661
dmclow@gov.pe.ca
Manager, Procurement Services, Ian K. Burge
Tel: 902-368-4041
Fax: 902-368-5171
ikburge@gov.pe.ca
Manager, Accounting, Doug H. Carr, FCGA
Tel: 902-368-4014
Fax: 902-368-6661
dhcarr@gov.pe.ca
Manager, Risk Management & Insurance Section, Linus Kelly
Tel: 902-368-6165
Fax: 902-368-6243
lmkelly@gov.pe.ca
Manager, Administration Services, Lane Pineau
Tel: 902-569-7559
Fax: 902-368-6661
lepineau@gov.pe.ca
Administrator, Financial System Administration, Helen Clow
Tel: 902-368-4012
Fax: 902-368-6661
nhclow@gov.pe.ca
Supervisor, Accounts Payable, Theresa A. DesRoches
Tel: 902-368-4067
Fax: 902-368-6661
tadesroches@gov.pe.ca
Budget Analyst, Investment Section, Alan Silliker, CA
Tel: 902-569-7666
Fax: 902-368-4077
agsilliker@gov.pe.ca

Economics, Statistics, & Federal Fiscal Relations Division
Shaw Bldg., 95 Rochford St., 2nd Fl., PO Box 2000, Charlottetown, PE C1A 7N8
Tel: 902-368-4030
Fax: 902-368-4034
www.gov.pe.ca/finance
The Economics, Statistics, & Federal Fiscal Relations Division is engaged in the following activities: offering economic policy, statistical, tax, & fiscal advice; providing a liaison with the federal government & the other provinces on fiscal arrangements; & responding to queries regarding statistical information.
Director, Economics, Statistics, & Federal Fiscal Relations, Nigel Burns
Tel: 902-368-4181
Fax: 902-368-4034
ndburns@gov.pe.ca
Economist, Tax Policy, Brad Binns
Tel: 902-368-4984
Fax: 902-368-4034
bjbinns@gov.pe.ca
Economist, Statistics, Colin Mosley
Tel: 902-368-4035
Fax: 902-368-4034
cdmosley@gov.pe.ca
Economist, Fiscal, Meaghan A. Zwicker
Tel: 902-368-4032
Fax: 902-368-4034
mazwicker@gov.pe.ca

Energy & Minerals Division
Jones Bldg., 4th Fl., Charlottetown, PE C1A 7N8
Tel: 902-894-0288
Fax: 902-894-0290
The Energy & Minerals Division is engaged in the following activities: developing & managing energy policies & programs; overseeing the development of mineral resources; & supporting gas exploration.
Director, Energy & Minerals, Wayne MacQuarrie
Tel: 902-894-0289
Fax: 902-894-0290
dwmacquarrie@gov.pe.ca
Manager, Office Of Energy Efficiency, Mike Proud
Tel: 902-620-3792
Fax: 902-620-3796
mpproud@gov.pe.ca
Officer, Sustainable Operations Program, George Meggison
Tel: 902-620-3793
Fax: 902-620-3796
gemeggison@gov.pe.ca

Fiscal Management Division
Shaw Bldg., 95 Rochford St. South, 3rd Fl., PO Box 2000, Charlottetown, PE C1A 7N8
Tel: 902-368-5802
Fax: 902-368-4077
www.gov.pe.ca/finance
The Fiscal Management Division has the following roles: administering pensions & benefits; offering administrative support & financial analysis to the Treasury Board, & ensuring that public funds are budgeted & monitored properly.
Executive Director, Fiscal Management, Jim Miles, CA
Tel: 902-368-6278
Fax: 902-368-4077
jamiles@gov.pe.ca
Manager, Pensions & Benefits, Terry Hogan
Tel: 902-368-4002
Fax: 902-620-3096
tmhogan@gov.pe.ca
Budget Analyst, Budgement Management Section, George W. Mason, CA, FCMA
Tel: 902-620-3351
Fax: 902-368-4077
gwmason@gov.pe.ca
Officer, Treasury, Margaret Simpson
Tel: 902-368-4140
Fax: 902-368-4077
mrmacewen@gov.pe.ca

Information Technology Shared Services Division
Shaw Bldg., 95-105 Rochford St., 2nd Fl., PO Box 2000, Charlottetown, PE C1A 7N8
Tel: 902-368-6160
Fax: 902-368-6575
www.gov.pe.ca/finance
Information Technology Shared Services consists of the following sections: Client Services; Information Technology Infrastructure Support; Corporate, Operations, Finance & Policy Planning; Business Systems; & Enterprise Architecture Services.

Director, Enterprise Architecture Services, Scott Cudmore
Tel: 902-569-7510
Fax: 902-569-7632
fscudmore@gov.pe.ca
Director, Corporate, Operations, Finance & Policy Planning, Randy Francis
Tel: 902-569-7611
Fax: 902-620-3503
drfrancis@gov.pe.ca
Director, Infrastructure, Edmund Malone
Tel: 902-368-4111
Fax: 902-368-4716
emmalone@gov.pe.ca
Director, Business Application Services, Carol A. Mayne
Tel: 902-368-4126
Fax: 902-368-5444
camayne@gov.pe.ca

Municipal Affairs & Provincial Planning Division
3 Brighton Rd., PO Box 2000, Charlottetown, PE C1A 7N8
Tel: 902-620-3558
Fax: 902-569-7545
www.gov.pe.ca/finance
Municipal Affairs acts as the liaison with municipalities & municipal interest groups on municipal matters. Consulting services are available regarding governance, administration, operations, & municipal land use planning.
Provincial Planning works in accordance with Prince Edward Island's Planning Act & Lands Protection Act related to land use & development in the province. Efforts are made to achieve sustainable development in the province.
Director, Municipal Affairs & Provincial Planning, Albert MacDonald
Tel: 902-368-5582
Fax: 902-569-7545
Manager, Land Use & Local Governance, Implementation, Christine MacKinnon
Tel: 902-368-5282

Fax: 902-569-7545
cgmackinnon@gov.pe.ca
Manager, Municipal Affairs, Samantha J. Murphy
Tel: 902-368-5892
Fax: 902-569-7545
sjmurphy@gov.pe.ca
Senior Provincial Planner, Acting Manager, Dale McKeigan
Tel: 902-620-3634
Fax: 902-569-7545
dfmckeigan@gov.pe.ca

Taxation & Property Records Division
Shaw Bldg., 95 Rochford St., 1st Fl., PO Box 2000, Charlottetown, PE C1A 7N8
Tel: 902-368-4070
Fax: 902-368-6164
www.gov.pe.ca/finance

The role of the Taxation & Property Records Division is to ensure equity in the collection of provincial tax revenues & in the production of both provincial & municipal real property assessment rolls. Services are coordinated with federal, provincial, & municipal governments.
Provincial Tax Commissioner, Elizabeth (Beth) Gaudet
Tel: 902-368-5686
Fax: 902-368-6584
eagaudet@gov.pe.ca
Manager, Tax Compliance Services, Mary Hennessey, CA
Tel: 902-368-4174
Fax: 902-368-6584
mihennessey@gov.pe.ca

Prince Edward Island Department of Fisheries, Aquaculture, & Rural Development

548 Main St., PO Box 1180, Montague, PE C0A 1R0
Tel: 902-838-0910
Fax: 902-838-0975
Toll-Free: 877-407-0187
www.gov.pe.ca/fard

The Department of Fisheries, Aquaculture, & Rural Development is guided by the following federal legislation: Aboriginal Communal Fishing Licences Regulations; Atlantic Fishery Regulations, 1985; Canada's Species at Risk Act; Federal Fisheries Act; Fishery Health Protection Regulations; Fishery (General) Regulations; Management of Contaminated Fisheries Regulations; Maritime Provinces Fishery Regulations; & the Navigable Waters Protection Act. The department carries out its mission through its divisions.
The Marine Fisheries & Seafood Services Division provides information to clients & advocates on behalf of the marine fisheries industry.
The Aquaculture Division offers assistance to the aquaculture & estuarial shellfish fisheries.
The Rural Development Division serves rural clients through community development & the delivery of employment programs.
Access PEI offers provincial government programs, services, & information to residents of Prince Edward Island. Examples of Access PEI's services include purchasing a fishing license or obtaining a drivers license.
Acts Administered:
Fish Inspection Act
Fisheries Act

Minister, Fisheries, Aquaculture, & Rural Developmen, Hon. Ron W. MacKinley
Tel: 902-838-0976
Toll-free: 877-407-0187
Fax: 902-838-0972
rwmackinley@gov.pe.ca
Social Media:
www.facebook.com/pages/Ron-MacKinley/60342728811

Deputy Minister, Fisheries, Aquaculture, & Rural Development, Richard Gallant
Tel: 902-838-0983
Toll-free: 877-407-0187
Fax: 902-838-0972
rkgallant@gov.pe.ca

Officer, Communications, Kim Devine
Tel: 902-368-5286
Fax: 902-368-5830
kmdevine@gov.pe.ca

Aquaculture Division
548 Main St., Montague, PE C0A 1R0
Tel: 902-838-0828
Fax: 902-838-0975
Toll-Free: 877-407-0187

The Aquaculture Division delivers the following services: advice & information to the provinces's aquaculture industry; financial programs to assist in aquaculture development; & biological & technical services to the shellfish & finfish sectors on the Island.
Director, Aquaculture Division, Neil MacNair
Tel: 902-838-0685
Toll-free: 877-407-0187
Fax: 902-838-0975
ngmacnair@gov.pe.ca
Aquaculture Biologist, Kim Gill
Tel: 902-838-0859
Fax: 902-838-0975
klgill@gov.pe.ca
Aquaculture Biologist, Aaron Ramsay
Tel: 902-838-0827
Fax: 902-838-0975
apramsay@gov.pe.ca
Mussel Technician, Brian Gillis
Tel: 902-838-0895
Fax: 902-838-0975
blgillis@gov.pe.ca
Shellfish Technician, Gary Smith
Tel: 902-838-5287
Fax: 902-838-0975
gbsmith@gov.pe.ca

Marine Fisheries & Seafood Services Division
548 Main St., PO Box 1180, Montague, PE C0A 1R0
Tel: 902-838-0612
Fax: 902-838-0975
Toll-Free: 877-407-0187

The Marine Fisheries & Seafood Services Division is engaged in the following activities: advocating for Prince Edward Island's fishing industry; offering programs to support new technology & value-added processing of seafood; supporting development of emerging species; undertaking biological research in support of major fish species; issuing licences for fish buying, fish peddling, & fish processing; managing & maintaining shellfish launching sites around the province; enforcing regulations under Prince Edward Island's Fish Inspection Act & Fisheries Act; overseeing the dead mammal removal program from the province's shore line; & compiling statistics about the fishing industry.
Director, Marine Fisheries & Seafood Service, Barry MacPhee
Tel: 902-838-0625
Toll-free: 877-407-0187
Fax: 902-838-0975
jbmacphee@gov.pe.ca
Manager, Marine Fisheries, David MacEwen
Tel: 902-838-0635
Fax: 902-838-0975
dgmacewen@gov.pe.ca
Manager, Seafood Services, David McGuire
Tel: 902-838-0691
Fax: 902-838-0975
dpmcguire@gov.pe.ca
Lobster Biologist, Robert MacMillan
Tel: 902-838-0699
Fax: 902-838-0975
rjmacmillan@gov.pe.ca
Fisheries Technician, Michelle Dixon
Tel: 902-838-0819
Fax: 902-838-0975
madixon@gov.pe.ca
Officer, Program Statistics, Cheryl Campbell
Tel: 902-838-0826
Fax: 902-838-0975
cherylcampbell@gov.pe.ca

Rural Development Division
548 Main St., PO Box 1180, Montague, PE C0A 1R0
Tel: 902-838-0910
Fax: 902-838-0975

The responsibilities of the Rural Development Division are as follows: implementing action items in the Rural Action Plan; overseeing the delivery of the Island Community Fund; & ensuring the effectiveness of the Seasonal Hiring Centre & the Employment Development Agency.
Director, Rural Development, Brian Schmeisser
Tel: 902-838-0662
Fax: 902-838-0975
beschmeisser@gov.pe.ca
Community Development Officer, Giselle Bernard
Tel: 902-854-3680
Fax: 902-854-3099
gbbernard@gov.pe.ca
Community Development Officer, Eastern Kings, Chris Blaisdell
Tel: 902-687-7083
Fax: 902-687-7091
cwblaisdell@gov.pe.ca
Community Development Officer, Southern Kings, Stephen Lewis
Tel: 902-838-0618
Fax: 902-838-0975
sjlewis@gov.pe.ca
Community Development Officer, East Prince, Kellie Mulligan
Tel: 902-887-3975
Fax: 902-887-2400
kamulligan@gov.pe.ca
Community Development Officer, Rural Queens, Nancy Murphy
Tel: 902-894-0347
Fax: 902-368-5542
nkmurphy@gov.pe.ca
Community Development Officer, West Prince, Brenda Profit
Tel: 902-853-0104
Fax: 902-853-3839
bfprofit@gov.pe.ca

Single Window Service / Access PEI
548 Main St., PO Box 1180, Montague, PE C0A 1R0
Tel: 902-838-0910
Fax: 902-838-0975
www.gov.pe.ca/accesspei
TTY: 877-407-0187

Prince Edward Island Provincial Government services are available at government service centres, known as Access PEI locations. At the eight Access PEI centres across Prince Edward Island, citizens obtain information about the Provincial Government & its programs.
The Access PEI Centres are situated in the following places:
Alberton (902-853-8622);
Charlottetown (902-368-5200);
Montague (902-838-0600);
O'Leary (902-859-8800);
Souris' Johnny Ross Young Service Centre (902-687-7000);
Summerside (902-888-8000;
Tignish (902-882-7351); &
Wellington (902-854-7250).
Director, Access PEI / Single Window Service, Tim G. Garrity
Tel: 902-838-0651
Fax: 902-838-0975
tggarrity@gov.pe.ca
Manager, Access PEI Summerside & PEI Wellington, Cindy Lou Andrews
Tel: 902-888-8001
Fax: 902-888-8306
clandrews@gov.pe.ca; accesspeisummerside@gov.pe.ca
Other Communications: Access PEI Wellington: accesspeiwellington@gov.pe.ca
Access PEISummerside
120 Harbour Dr.
Summerside, PE C1N 5L2
Manager, Access PEI Montague & Access PEI Souris, Eleanor Avery
Tel: 902-687-7050
Fax: 902-687-7091
emavery@gov.pe.ca; accesspeimontague@gov.pe.ca
Other Communications: Access PEI Souris, E-mail: accesspeisouris@gov.pe.ca
Access PEI Souris, JohnnyRoss Young Services Centre
15 Green St.
PO Box 550
Souris, PE C0A 2B0
Manager, Access PEI Alberton, Access PEI O'Leary, & Access PEI Tignish, Martha Dawson
Tel: 902-859-8801
Fax: 902-859-8709
accesspeialberton@gov.pe.ca; accesspeioleary@gov.pe.ca
Other Communications: Access PEI Tignish
E-mail:accesspeitignish@gov.pe.ca
Access PEI O'Leary
45 East Dr.
PO Box 8
O'Leary, PE C0B 1V0
Manager, Access PEI Charlottetown, Paulette Gallant
Tel: 902-368-6847
Fax: 902-569-7560
plgallant@gov.pe.ca; accesspeicharlottetown@gov.pe.ca
Other Communications: Access PEI Charlottetown, Fax: 902-569-7560
Access PEI Charlottetown, Highway SafetyBldg.
33 Riverside Dr.
PO Box 2000
Charlottetown, PE C1A 7N8

Prince Edward Island Department of Health & Wellness

105 Rochford St. North, 4th Fl., PO Box 2000, Charlottetown, PE C1A 7N8
Tel: 902-368-6414
Fax: 902-368-4121
www.gov.pe.ca/health/index.php3

The Department of Health & Wellness carries out the following responsibilities: ensuring quality health care to the citizens of Prince Edward Island; providing leadership in policy, programs, & operations; maintaining & improving the health of citizens; playing a leadership role in innovation; coordinating the implementation of the Healthy Living Strategy; providing regulatory services to the health system; acting as a central contact for Aboriginal organizations; & promoting cooperation on governmental matters related to Aboriginal affairs.
Acts Administered:
Adult Protection Act

Archaeological Sites Protection Act (Repealed)
Archaeology Act
Change of Name Act
Change of Name Act (Repealed)
Chiropractic Act
Chiropractic Act (Repealed)
Community Care Facilities & Nursing Homes Act
Community Hospital Authorities Act (Repeal)
Consent to Treatment &d Health Care Directives Act
Dental Profession Act
Denturists Act
Dietitians Act
Dispensing Opticians Act
Donation of Food Act
Drug Cost Assistance Act
Health & Community Services Act (Repealed)
Health & Community Services Reorganization Act (Repeal)
Health Services Act (Repealed)
Health Services Act
Health Services Payment Act
Hospital & Diagnostic Services Insurance Act
Hospitals Act
Hospitals Act (Repealed)
Human Tissue Donation Act
Licensed Nursing Assistants Act (Repealed)
Licensed Practical Nurses Act
Long-Term Care Subsidization
Marriage Act
Medical Act
Mental Health Act
Mental Health Act (Repealed)
Nurses Act (repealed)
Occupational Therapists Act
Optometry Act
Pharmaceutical Information Act
Pharmacy Act
Physiotherapy Act
Premarital Health Examination Act (Repealed)
Provincial Health Number Act
Psychologists Act
Psychologists Act (Repealed)
Public Health Act
Registered Nurses Act
Smoke-free Places Act
Tobacco Sales & Access Act
Vital Statistics Act
Welfare Assistance Act (Renamed)
White Cane Act

Minister, Health & Wellness; Minister Responsible, Aboriginal Affairs, Hon. Doug W. Currie
Tel: 902-368-5152
Fax: 902-368-4910
dwcurrie@gov.pe.ca; doug.currie@liberal.pe.ca
www.dougcurrie.ca
Social Media: www.twitter.com/DougCurrie, www.facebook.com/doug.w.currie

Deputy Minister, Dr. Michael Mayne
Tel: 902-368-5290
Fax: 902-368-4121
mbmayne@gov.pe.ca

Communications Officer & Citizen Engagement Strategist, Beth P. Johnston
Tel: 902-368-5512
Fax: 902-368-4224
pjohnston@gov.pe.ca

Associated Agencies, Boards & Commissions:
• Prince Edward Island Pharmacy Board
Trans Canada Hwy.
PO Box 89
Crapaud, PE C0A 1J0
Tel: 902-658-2780
Fax: 902-658-2198
peipharm@pei.aibn.com
www.napra.org
The Prince Edward Island Pharmacy Board regulates the practice of pharmacy in Prince Edward Island. Its goal is to promote high standards of pharmaceutical service for the welfare of the public.

Aboriginal Affairs Secretariat
Shaw Bldg., 105 Rochford St. North, 4th Fl., Charlottetown, PE
www.gov.pe.ca/aboriginalaffairs
The Aboriginal Affairs Secretariat coordinates & manages Aboriginal Affairs for the provincial government. Specific duties include developing policy, negotiating with the federal government & organizations representing the Mi'kmaq & other Aboriginal people, & managing federal-provincial agreements.
Director, Aboriginal Affairs Secretariat, Dr. Helen E. Kristmanson
Tel: 902-368-5378
Fax: 902-368-4224
hekristmanson@gov.pe.ca
Policy Analyst, Andrew Ramsay
Tel: 902-368-6583
Fax: 902-368-4224

Chief Public Health Office
Sullivan Bldg., 16 Fitzroy St., 2nd Fl., Charlottetown, PE C1A 7N8
The Chief Health Office administers & enforces the Public Health Act. The office also delivers services in the following areas: environmental health, epidemiology, reproductive care, & vital statistics.
Chief Health Officer, Dr. Heather G. Morrison
Tel: 902-368-4996
Fax: 902-620-3354
hgmorrison@gov.pe.ca
Deputy Chief Health Officer, Dr. Lamont Sweet
Tel: 902-368-4996
Fax: 902-620-3354
lesweet@ihis.org
Coordinator, Provincial Infection Control Program, Stacey L. Burns
Tel: 902-368-4934
Fax: 902-620-3354
slburns@ihis.org
Coordinator, Communicable Disease & Immunization, Anne M. Neatby
Tel: 902-368-6114
Fax: 902-620-3354
amneatbty@ihis.org
Coordinator, Infection Control Services, Corrine A. Rowswell
Tel: 902-368-6190
Fax: 902-620-3354
carowswell@ihis.org
Manager, Environmental Health, Joe Bradley
Tel: 902-368-4792
Fax: 902-368-6468
joebradley@ihis.org
Manager, Vital Statistics, Thelma A. Johnston
Tel: 902-838-0884
Fax: 902-838-0883
tajohnston@ihis.org
Provincial Epidemiologist, Dr. Carolyn J. Sanford
Tel: 902-368-4964
Fax: 902-620-3354
cjsanford@gov.pe.ca

Finance & Corporate Management Division
Shaw Bldg., 105 Rochford St. North, 4th Fl., PO Box 2000, Charlottetown, PE C1A 7N8
The Finance & Corporate Management Division supports the Department of Health & Wellness in the areas of finances, human resources, communications, & the administration of the Freedom of Information & Protection of Privacy Act.
Director, Finance & Corporate Management Division, Kevin Barnes, CA
Tel: 902-368-4865
Fax: 902-368-4224
kcbarnes@gov.pe.ca
Manager, Financial Services & Administration, Barry Gosby
Tel: 902-368-4897
Fax: 902-368-5335
bbgosby@gov.pe.ca
Manager, Human Resources, Michael Ready
Tel: 902-569-0549
Fax: 902-368-4224
mcready@gov.pe.ca
Coordinator, Freedom of Information & Protection of Privacy Act; Communications Officer, Autumn Tremere
Tel: 902-368-5610
Fax: 902-368-4224
agtremere@gov.pe.ca

Health System Planning & Development Division
Sullivan Bldg., 16 Fitzroy St., 3rd Fl., Charlottetown, PE C1A 7N8
The Health System Planning & Development Division supports the Department of Health & Wellness. It includes the Health Recruitment & Retention section.
Manager, Health Recruitment & Retention, Marney MacRae
Tel: 902-620-3874
Fax: 902-620-3875
mjmacrae@gov.pe.ca
Coordinator, Physician Recruitment, Sheila MacLean
Tel: 902-368-6302
Fax: 902-620-3875
smmaclean@gov.pe.ca
Consultant, Pharmacy, Roy Cairns
Tel: 902-368-4907
Fax: 902-368-4905
brcairns@gov.pe.ca
Consultant, Dietetic Services, Diane M. Clow
Tel: 902-368-6262
Fax: 902-569-7656
mdclow@ihis.org
Consultant, Community Care Facilities & Nursing Homes, Mary P. MacSwain
Tel: 902-368-4953
Fax: 902-569-7656
mpmacswain@ihis.org
Legislative Specialist, Nichola M. Hewitt
Tel: 902-368-6681
Fax: 902-620-3081
nmhewitt@gov.pe.ca
Planner & Policy Analyst, Shaun MacNeill
Tel: 902-368-6117
Fax: 902-368-4224
smacneill@gov.pe.ca

Sport, Recreation, & Healthy Living Division
Shaw Bldg., 105 Rochford St. North, 4th Fl., PO Box 2000, Charlottetown, PE
The main role of the Sport, Recreation & Healthy Living Division is to encourage citizens of Prince Edward Island to be active. Sport, recreation, & other physical activities are promoted. Consultation services & grants are available for community, regional, & provincial groups.
Director, Sport, Recreation, & Healthy Living, John Morrison
Tel: 902-894-0283
Fax: 902-368-4224
jwmorris@gov.pe.ca
Officer, Health Promotion & Chronic Disease Prevention, Laraine Poole
Tel: 902-368-4926
Fax: 902-620-3081
lfpoole@gov.pe.ca
Coordinator, Central Region, Sport, Recreation, & Healthy Living, Francois R. Caron
Tel: 902-432-2706
Fax: 902-888-8023
frcaron@gov.pe.ca
Coordinator, Eastern Region, Sport, Recreation, & Healthy Living, Neil A. Kinsman
Tel: 902-687-7041
Fax: 902-368-4224
nakinsman@gov.pe.ca
Coordinator, Western Region, Sport, Recreation, & Healthy Living, Joanne P. Wallace
Tel: 902-859-8861
Fax: 902-859-8709
jpwallace@gov.pe.ca

Health PEI

16 Garfield St., PO Box 2000, Charlottetown, PE C1A 7N8
Tel: 902-368-6130
Fax: 902-368-6136
healthinput@gov.pe.ca
www.healthpei.ca
When the Health Services Act was proclaimed in 2010, Health PEI took on responsibility for the operation & delivery of health services in the province.
The main goals of Health PEI are to improve access to quality health care across Prince Edward Island & to develop more consistent standards & practices for health services

Chief Executive Officer, Keith Dewar
Tel: 902-368-4935
Fax: 902-368-4974
kdewar@gov.pe.ca

Chair, Leo Steven
Tel: 902-368-5810
Fax: 902-368-5835
lsteven@gov.pe.ca

Vice-Chair, Gordon MacKay

Administrative Assistant, Barb Buell
Tel: 902-368-4637
Fax: 902-368-4974
healthpeiboard@gov.pe.ca

Community Hospitals & Primary Health Care Division
16 Garfield St., 1st Fl., Charlottetown, PE C1A 6A5
Executive Director, Community Hospitals & Primary Health Care, Deborah Bradley
Tel: 902-368-6157
Fax: 902-569-0579
mdbradley@gov.pe.ca
Director, Primary Care Networks & Chronic Desease Prevention & Management, Marilyn A. Barrett
Tel: 902-569-7640
Fax: 902-569-0579
mabarrett@gov.pe.ca
Director, Public Health, Kathy Jones
Tel: 902-894-0247

Fax: 902-569-0579
kljones@gov.pe.ca
Director, Mental Health & Addictions, Margaret Kennedy
Tel: 902-368-6197
Fax: 902-569-0579
mmkennedy@gov.pe.ca
Administrator, Community Hospitals East, Terry S. Campbell
Tel: 902-687-7150
Fax: 902-687-7175
tscampbell@gov.pe.ca
Administrator, Community Hospitals West, Andrew MacDougall
Tel: 902-368-5773
Fax: 902-368-6764
asmacdougall@gov.pe.ca

Corporate Development & Innovation Division
16 Garfield St., 2nd Fl., Charlottetown, PE C1A 6A5
Executive Director, Corporate Development & Innovation, Pamela Trainor
Tel: 902-368-5804
Fax: 902-368-4969
pjtrainor@gov.pe.ca
Director, Quality & Access Management, Joanne Donahoe
Tel: 902-368-5815
Fax: 902-368-4969
jmdonahoe@gov.pe.ca
Director, Human Resources, Glen Doyle
Tel: 902-368-6257
Fax: 902-368-4969
grdoyle@gov.pe.ca
Director, Strategy & Performance, Una Hassenstein
Tel: 902-368-4932
Fax: 902-368-4969
uehassenstein@gov.pe.ca

Financial Services Division
16 Garfield St., 1st Fl., Charlottetown, PE C1A 6A5
Executive Director, Financial Services, Denise Lewis Fleming
Tel: 902-368-6125
Fax: 902-368-6136
dmlewis@gov.pe.ca
Director, Fiscal Planning, Analysis, & Audit, Kellie C. Hawes
Tel: 902-569-0506
Fax: 902-368-6136
kchawes@ihis.org
Director, Materials Management, Deborah Steeves
Tel: 902-894-2097
Fax: 902-894-2384
dasteeves@ihis.org
Comptroller, Accounting Services, Pat G. Ryan
Tel: 902-368-4921
Fax: 902-368-6136
pgryan@gov.pe.ca

Health Information Management Division
16 Garfield St., 1st Fl., Charlottetown, PE C1A 6A5
The Health Information Management Division oversees the following areas: eHealth implementation; eHealth operations; eHealth strategy; health information; IM & IT planning; & privacy & information access.
Executive Director, Health Information Management, Liam Whitty
Tel: 902-620-3165
Fax: 902-368-6136
lwhitty@gov.pe.ca
Project Manager, iEHR & eHealth Project Implementation, Brenda Campbell
Tel: 902-368-6517
Fax: 902-620-3061
bccampbell@gov.pe.ca
Coordinator, Privacy & Information Access, Marina Fay
Tel: 902-368-4942
Fax: 902-368-4969
mafay@ihis.org
Information Technology Architect, Jackie Irwin
Tel: 902-620-3229
Fax: 902-368-6136
jrirwin@gov.pe.ca

Home-Based & Long-Term Care Division
16 Garfield St., 1st Fl., Charlottetown, PE C1A 6A5
Executive Director, Home-Based & Long-Term Care, Cecil Villard
Tel: 902-894-0337
Fax: 902-368-6136
cfvillard@gov.pe.ca
Director, Home Care, Mary Sullivan
Tel: 902-888-8005
Fax: 902-432-2610
mksullivan@gov.pe.ca
Administrator, Long Term Care, East, Jean Fallis
Tel: 902-838-0643
Fax: 902-838-5294
njfallis@gov.pe.ca
Administrator, Long Term Care, East Prince, Gayle Lamont
Tel: 902-888-8350
Fax: 902-888-8369
gdlamont@gov.pe.ca
Administrator, Long Term Care, Queens, Andrew MacDougall
Tel: 902-368-5773
Fax: 902-368-6764
asmacdougall@gov.pe.ca
Administrator, Long Term Care, West Prince, John Martin
Tel: 902-859-8734
Fax: 902-859-8774
jmartin@gov.pe.ca
Coordinator, Provincial Geriatric Services, Elaine Campbell
Tel: 902-432-2861
Fax: 902-432-2859
eecampbell@ihis.org
Consultant, Seniors' Mental Health Services, Debye Macdonald Connolly
Tel: 902-368-4602
Fax: 902-368-6136
damacdonald-connolly@ihis.org

Medical Affairs Division
16 Garfield St., 2nd Fl., Charlottetown, PE C1A 6A5
Executive Director, Medical Affairs, Dr. Richard Wedge
Tel: 902-368-6261
Fax: 902-620-3072
rhwedge@gov.pe.ca
Manager, Physician Services, Johanne Irwin
Tel: 902-368-6736
Fax: 902-620-3072
jcirwin@gov.pe.ca
PHC Medical Director, Summerside, Dr. Andre Celliers
acelliers@ihis.org
PHC Medical Director, West Prince, Dr. Gil Grimes
gcgrimes@gov.pe.ca
PHC Medical Director, Kings, Dr. David Hambly
jdhambly@ihis.org
PHC Medical Director, Queens, Dr. Alf Morais
Tel: 902-569-7625
Fax: 902-620-3072
jamorais@ihis.org

Prince County Hospital (PCH)
65 Boates Ave., PO Box 3000, Summerside, PE C1N 2A9
Tel: 902-438-4200
Fax: 902-438-4511
www.healthpei.ca/pch
Executive Director, Prince County Hospital, Arlene Gallant-Bernard
Tel: 902-438-4514
Fax: 902-438-4381
algallant-bernard@gov.pe.ca
Director, Hospital Services, Cynthia Bryanton
Tel: 902-438-4519
Fax: 902-438-4381
clbryanton@gov.pe.ca
Director, Administration & Support Services, Margie Kays
Tel: 902-438-4530
Fax: 902-438-4381
mrkays@gov.pe.ca
Director, Medical Services, Dr. Wassim Salamoun
Tel: 902-438-4518
Fax: 902-438-4381
wsalamoun@ihis.org
Director, Nursing Services, Brenda Worth
Tel: 902-438-4516
Fax: 902-438-4381
baworth@gov.pe.ca

Provincial Clinical Services Division
16 Garfield St., 3rd Fl., Charlottetown, PE C1A 6A5
Executive Director, Provincial Clinical Services, Jamie MacDonald
Tel: 902-894-2277
Fax: 902-894-2276
jamiemacdonald@ihis.org
Director, Provincial Diagnostic Imaging Services, Theresa Callaghan
Tel: 902-894-2979
Fax: 902-894-2416
tkcallaghan@gov.pe.ca
Manager, Provincial Pharmacare Program, Faye E. Campbell
Tel: 902-368-6338
Fax: 902-368-4905
fecampbell@ihis.org
Manager, Emergency Health Services, Alan Toombs
Tel: 902-368-6719
Fax: 902-368-6136
altoombs@gov.pe.ca
Coordinator, Pharmaceutical Information Program, Kelly Drummond
Tel: 902-620-3762
Fax: 902-368-4905
ktdrummond@gov.pe.ca

Queen Elizabeth Hospital
60 Riverside Dr., PO Box 6600, Charlottetown, PE C1A 8T5
Tel: 902-894-2111
Fax: 902-894-2416
www.healthpei.ca/index.php3?number=1020318&lang=E
TTY: 902-894-2204
Executive Director, Rick Adams
Tel: 902-894-2351
Fax: 902-894-2416
radams@gov.pe.ca
Director, Nursing Services, Marion H. Dowling
Tel: 902-894-2356
Fax: 902-894-2926
mhdowling@gov.pe.ca
Director, Medical Services, Dr. Rosemary Henderson
Tel: 902-894-2411
Fax: 902-894-2416
rfhenderson@gov.pe.ca
Director, Hospital Services, Kelley Rayner
Tel: 902-894-2364
Fax: 902-894-0138
kjrayner@gov.pe.ca
Director, Support Services, David J. White
Tel: 902-894-2353
Fax: 902-894-2416
jdwhite@gov.pe.ca

Prince Edward Island Human Rights Commission

53 Water St., PO Box 2000, Charlottetown, PE C1A 7N8
Tel: 902-368-4180
Fax: 902-368-4236
Toll-Free: 800-237-5031
www.peihumanrights.ca

The Prince Edward Island Human Rights Act is administered & enforced by the Prince Edward Island Human Rights Commission.
The Commission receives, investigates, & settles & makes rulings on complaints. Other tasks of the Commission include the development of public information & educational programs & the provision of advice to the government about human rights issues.

Chair, Anne Nicholson
Tel: 902-368-4180
Fax: 902-368-4236

Commissioner, Arthur Currie, Q.C.
Tel: 902-368-4180
Fax: 902-368-4236

Commissioner, George Lyle
Tel: 902-368-4180
Fax: 902-368-4236

Commissioner, John Rogers
Tel: 902-368-4180
Fax: 902-368-4236

Commissioner, Lou Ann Thomson
Tel: 902-368-4180
Fax: 902-368-4236

Executive Director, Greg Howard
Tel: 902-368-4134
Fax: 902-368-4236
ghoward@peihumanrights.ca

Human Rights Officer, Wendy Baker
Tel: 902-368-4180
Fax: 902-368-4236
wbaker@peihumanrights.ca

Administrative / Intake Officer, R. Lorraine Buell
Tel: 902-368-4180
Fax: 902-368-4236
lbuell@peihumanrights.ca

Prince Edward Island Department of Innovation & Advanced Learning

Shaw Bldg., 105 Rochford St., 5th Fl., PO Box 2000, Charlottetown, PE C1A 7N8
Tel: 902-368-4240
Fax: 902-368-4242
www.gov.pe.ca/ial

The role of Prince Edward Island's Department of Innovation & Advanced Learning is to manage the implementation of The Island Prosperity Strategy, A Focus for Change. This is the provincial government's economic strategy. It is the goal of the government to improve post-secondary opportunities for Islanders to ensure a strong workforce prepared for the present economy.
Acts Administered:
Apprenticeship & Trades Qualification Act

Area Industrial Commission Act
Business Development Inc. Act, P.E.I. (Repealed)
Employment Development Agency Act
Hairdressers Act
Holland College Act
Innovation PEI Act
Island Investment Development Act
Labour Mobility Act
Lending Agency Act
Maritime Economic Cooperation Act
Maritime Provinces Higher Education Commission Act
Maritime Provinces Higher Education Commission Act (Repealed)
Prince Edward Island Science & Technology Corporation Act (Repealed)
Private Training Schools Act
Student Financial Assistance Act
University Act

Minister, Innovation & Advanced Learning, Hon. Allen F. Roach
allen.roach@liberal.pe.ca
Social Media: www.facebook.com/profile.php?id=100002417155344

Deputy Minister, Melissa MacEachern
Tel: 902-368-4250
Fax: 902-368-5277
mamaceachern@gov.pe.ca

Associated Agencies, Boards & Commissions:

• Anne of Green Gables Licensing Authority Inc.
94 Euston
PO Box 910
Charlottetown, PE C1A 7L9
Tel: 902-569-7787
Fax: 902-368-6301
kobaker@gov.pe.ca; aggla@bellnet.ca
Other Communication: Toronto Office, Phone: 416-971-7473
The Anne of Green Gables Licensing Authority Inc. controls the use of Anne of Green Gables & related trademarks, protects the integrity of Anne images, & preserves the legacy of L.M. Montgomery & her works. The authority is jointly owned by the Province of Prince Edward Island, Ruth Macdonald, & David Macdonald.

• BIO FOOD TECH
101 Belvedere Ave.
PO Box 2000
Charlottetown, PE C1A 7N8
Tel: 902-368-5548
Fax: 902-368-5549
Toll-free: 877-368-5548
biofoodtech@biofoodtech.ca
www.biofoodtech.ca
Formerly known as the PEI Food Technology Centre, BIO FOOD TECH operates as a contract research & analytical services company. It serves companies & entrepreneurs in the food & bioprocessing sectors.

• Charlottetown Area Development Corporation (CADC)
4 Pownal St.
PO Box 786
Charlottetown, PE C1A 7L9
Tel: 902-892-5341
Fax: 902-368-1935
www.cadcpei.com
The Charlottetown Area Development Corporation operates as a self-financed entity that aims to attract private sector development to the Greater Charlottetown area. To carry out its work, the Charlottetown Area Development Corporation partners with the Province of Prince Edward Island, the City of Charlottetown, & the Town of Stratford.

• Charlottetown Civic Centre Management Inc.
46 Kensington Rd.
Charlottetown, PE C1A 5H7
Tel: 902-629-6600
Fax: 902-629-6650
www.civiccentre.pe.ca
The Charlottetown Civic Centre is a multi-purpose facility.

• Innovation PEI
94 Euston St.
PO Box 910
Charlottetown, PE C1A 7L9
Tel: 902-368-6300
Fax: 902-368-6301
Toll-free: 800-563-3734
www.innovationpei.com
Innovation PEI strives to advance economic development in Prince Edward Island. It promotes small business development, business improvement, employment creation, research, innovation, market access, & trade. Through the Island Prosperity Strategy, Innovation PEI focuses upon the following sectors: renewable energy, aerospace, information technology, & bioscience.

• Island Investment Development Inc. (IIDI)
94 Euston St., 2nd Fl.
Charlottetown, PE C1A 7M8
Tel: 902-620-3628
Fax: 902-368-5886
peinominee@gov.pe.ca
www.gov.pe.ca/immigration
The Island Investment Development Inc. is a crown corporation. Its business name is Immigration Services. The organization oversees the Prince Edward Island Provincial Nominee Program.

• Prince Edward Island Lending Agency
Homburg Financial Tower
98 Fitzroy St., 2nd Fl.
Charlottetown, PE C1A 1R7
Tel: 902-368-6200
Fax: 902-368-6201
Assistance is provided by the Lending Agency to new & growing businesses. Loans are available for organizations with export potential in the following industries: agriculture, fisheries & aquaculture, tourism, manufacturing & processing, information technology, & small business.

• Summerside Regional Development Corporation Ltd. (SRDC)
268 Water St.
Summerside, PE C1N 1B6
Tel: 902-436-2246
Fax: 902-436-9269
acroken@srdcpei.com
www.summersidewaterfront.com
Formerly known as the Summerside Waterfront Development Corporation, the Summerside Regional Development Corporation works to facilitate economic development in Summerside & the surrounding region. Shareholders of the corporation include the Province of Prince Edward Island, the City of Summerside, & the Greater Summerside Development Inc.

Finance & Administration Division
105 Rochford St., Charlottetown, PE C1A 7N8
Tel: 902-368-5878
Fax: 902-368-7087
Responsibilities include financial management, administration, the Prince Edward Island Business Development Inc., & human resource management.
Director, Finance & Administration, Shannon Burke, CA
Tel: 902-368-5875
Fax: 902-268-7087
slburke@gov.pe.ca
Controller, Department of Innovaton & Advanced Learning, Jean Kimpton, CMA
Tel: 902-894-0343
Fax: 902-368-6255
jakimpton@gov.pe.ca
Controller, Crowns, Brad Colwill, CA
Tel: 902-894-0373
Fax: 902-368-5756
bccolwill@gov.pe.ca
Manager, Human Resources, Leah Eldershaw
Tel: 902-368-5876
Fax: 902-368-7087
ljelders@gov.pe.ca
Coordinator, FOIPP; Officer, Human Resources, Camilla McAleer
Tel: 902-368-5869
Fax: 902-368-5756
ccmcaleer@gov.pe.ca

Population Secretariat
Atlantic Technology Centre, 90 University Ave., Charlottetown, PE C1A 4K9
Tel: 902-620-3656
Fax: 902-368-4252
populationsecretariat@gov.pe.ca
www.gov.pe.ca/ial/popsec
The Population Secretariat promotes Prince Edward Island as a welcoming place to live. The Secretariat works to attract immigrants & former Islanders, & to retain youth & immigrants.
Director, Population Secretariat, Jane Mallard
Tel: 902-569-7556
Fax: 902-368-4252
jmallard@gov.pe.ca
Officer, Attraction & Promotion, Isabelle Dasylva-Gill
Tel: 902-569-7539
Fax: 902-368-4252
idasylvagill@gov.pe.ca
Officer, Policy, Research, & Planning, Erin Docherty
Tel: 902-368-5127
Fax: 902-368-4252
ecdocherty@gov.pe.ca
Officer, Settlement, Joey Jeffrey
Tel: 902-368-4861
Fax: 902-368-4252
jajeffrey@gov.pe.ca
Officer, Retention, Ian G. Lane
Tel: 902-368-5368
Fax: 902-368-4252
iglane@gov.pe.ca

Post-Secondary & Continuing Education
Atlantic Technology Centre, #212, 90 University Ave., 2nd Fl., Charlottetown, PE C1A 4K9
Director, Post-Secondary & Continuing Education, Susan A. MacKenzie
Tel: 902-368-4615
Fax: 902-368-6144
samackenzie@gov.pe.ca
Manager, Apprenticeship Training, Susan LeFort
Tel: 902-368-4625
Fax: 902-368-6144
sflefort@gov.pe.ca
Manager, GED & Private Training Schoolsl Literacy Secretariat, Barbara Macnutt
Tel: 902-368-6286
Fax: 902-368-6144
bemacnutt@edu.pe.ca
Senior Officer, Financial Services, Don Currie
Tel: 902-368-4604
Fax: 902-368-6144
dscurrie@gov.pe.ca

SkillsPEI
Atlantic Technology Centre, #212, 90 University Ave., Charlottetown, PE C1A 4K9
Tel: 902-368-4260
Fax: 902-368-6340
Toll-Free: 877-491-4766
Skills PEI manages the delivery of training & skills development programs. The programming is funded by the Labour Market Agreement & the Canada-Prince Edward Island Labour Market Development Agreement. Examples of programs include Training PEI, Employ PEI, Self Employ PEI, Community Internship, Immigrant Work Experience, & Labour Market Partnerships. SkillsPEI offices are located across Prince Edward Island.
Director, SkillsPEI, Birt MacKinnon
Tel: 902-368-4244
Fax: 902-368-6580
bwmackinnon@gov.pe.ca
Director, Labour Market Unit, Scot MacDonald
Tel: 902-368-6521
Fax: 902-368-6340
dsmacdonald@gov.pe.ca
Manager, Service Delivery, Kings & Queens County, Blair Aitken
Tel: 902-368-4178
Fax: 902-368-6580
abaitken@gov.pe.ca
Manager, Service Delivery, Prince County, Mary Hunter
Tel: 902-438-4110
Fax: 902-438-4096
mehunter@gov.pe.ca
Manager, Labour Mobility, Jeannie Pitts
Tel: 902-368-5825
Fax: 902-368-6340
jpitts@gov.pe.ca
Coordinator, Provincial Employment, Heather Berrigan
Tel: 902-368-5908
Fax: 902-368-5909
heberrigan@gov.pe.ca
Coordinator, Passport to Employment Program, Maitland MacIsaac
Tel: 902-368-4466
Fax: 902-368-5909
mamacisaac@gov.pe.ca
Coordinator, Foreign Qualifications Recognition Project, Rebecca Murphy
Tel: 902-620-3082
Fax: 902-368-6340
romurphy@gov.pe.ca

Prince Edward Island Liquor Control Commission (PEILCC)

3 Garfield St., PO Box 967, Charlottetown, PE C1A 7M4
Tel: 902-368-5710
Fax: 902-368-5735
www.peilcc.ca
Under the authority of the Liquor Control Act & Regulations, the Prince Edward Island Liquor Control Commission is responsible for managing the distribution of alcohol & regulating the sale & purchase of all alcoholic beverages. The crown corporation also administers the operation of nineteen retail liquor stores across the province. Licenses are issued by the commission for dining rooms, clubs, lounges, special premises, military canteens, & caterers & waiters.

Chief Executive Officer, Brooke MacMillan
Tel: 902-368-5720

Fax: 902-368-5735
jbmacmillan@gov.pe.ca

Director, Sales & Marketing, Fred J. MacDonald
Tel: 902-368-5715
Fax: 902-368-5735
fjmacdonald@gov.pe.ca

Director, Finance & Retail Operations, Wendy L. MacDonald, CA
Tel: 902-368-5126
Fax: 902-368-5395
wlmacdonald@gov.pe.ca

Director, Licensing & Security, James C. MacLeod
Tel: 902-368-5714
Fax: 902-368-5735
jcmacleod@gov.pe.ca

Director, Purchasing & Distribution, David Stewart
Tel: 902-368-5721
Fax: 902-368-5735
dlstewart@gov.pe.ca

Prince Edward Island Regulatory & Appeals Commission (IRAC) / Commission de réglementation et d'appels

National Bank Tower, #501, 134 Kent St., PO Box 577, Charlottetown, PE C1A 7L1

Tel: 902-892-3501
Fax: 902-566-4076
Toll-Free: 800-501-6268
info@irac.pe.ca
www.irac.pe.ca

Prince Edward Island's Regulatory & Appeals Commission was established in 1991, with the amalgamation of the Office of the Director of Residential Property, the Public Utilities Commission, & the Land Use Commission.
Operating under the authority of the Island Regulatory & Appeals Commission Act, the Regulatory & Appeals Commission works at arms-length from the provincial government to administer statutes dealing with economic regulation. The quasi-judicial tribunal also listens to appeals dealing with property & revenue sales tax, land use, & unsightly premises.
The Regulatory & Appeals Commission reports to the Legislative Assembly of Prince Edward Island through the Minister of Education & Early Childhood Development.

Acts Administered:
Electric Power Act
Environmental Protection Act
Insurance Act
Lands Protection Act
Petroleum Products Act
Renewable Energy Act
Water & Sewerage Act

Director, Land, Corporate & Appellate Services Division, Eileen Callaghan
mecallaghan@irac.pe.ca

Director, Residential Rental Property, Cathy Flanagan
cflanagan@irac.pe.ca

Director, Technical & Regulatory Services Division, Allison MacEwen
amacewen@irac.pe.ca

Prince Edward Island Department of Tourism & Culture

PO Box 2000, Charlottetown, PE C1A 7N8

Tel: 902-368-5540
Fax: 902-368-5277
tpswitch@gov.pe.ca
www.gov.pe.ca/tourism

Prince Edward Island's Department of Tourism & Culture is engaged in the following activities: promoting tourism & special events; facilitating product development; managing infrastructure projects such as parks & golf courses; providing library services; promoting historic preservation & documentation; & encouraging cultural development.

Acts Administered:
Archives & Records Act
Archives Act (Repealed)
Confederation Birthplace Act (Repealed)
Fathers of Confederation Buildings Act
Heritage Places Protection Act
Highway Advertisements Act (Repealed)
Highway Signage Act
Liquor Control Act
Lucy Maud Montgomery Foundation Act
Museum Act
National Park Act
Public Libraries Act
Recreation Development Act
Tourism Industry Act
Tourism PEI Act
Tourism PEI Act
Trails Act

Minister, Tourism & Culture, Hon. Robert L. Henderson
Tel: 902-368-5540
Fax: 902-368-5277
rlhenderson@assembly.pe.ca;
robert.henderson@liberal.pe.ca
Social Media:
www.facebook.com/profile.php?id=100001965683516

Deputy Minister, David Mackenzien
Tel: 902-368-5956
dmack@gov.pe.ca

Communications Officer, Andrew Spraque
Tel: 902-368-5535
Fax: 902-894-0342
asgsprague@gov.pe.ca

Associated Agencies, Boards & Commissions:

• Museum & Heritage Foundation
Beaconsfield Historic House
2 Kent St.
Charlottetown, PE C1A 1M6
Tel: 902-368-6600
Fax: 902-368-6608
mhpei@gov.pe.ca
www.peimuseum.com; www.gov.pe.ca/peimhf
Governed by the Museum Act, the Prince Edward Island Museum & Heritage Foundation operates as a Schedule B Provincial Crown Corporation. The mandate of the registered charitable corporation is to collect, preserve, & interpret Prince Edward Island's human & natural heritage.
The following seven provincial museums & heritage sites across Prince Edward Island are administered by the organization for the benefit & enjoyment of the people of the province & tourists: Elmira Railway Museum; Basin Head Fisheries Museum; Orwell Corner Historic Village & Agricultural Museum; Beaconsfield Historic House; Eptek Art & Culture Centre; The Acadian Museum of Prince Edward Island; & Green Park Shipbuilding Museum & Yeo House. There are more than 90,000 artifacts in the Provincial Collection, which are the responsibility of the Foundation.

• Tourism Advisory Council of Prince Edward Island (TAC)
Shaw Bldg., 3rd Fl.
Rochford St.
PO Box 2000
Charlottetown, PE C1A 7N8
Tel: 902-368-5907
www.peitac.com
An industry advisory board to the Minister of Tourism & Culture, Prince Edward Island's Tourism Advisory Council features nineteen members. Members include senior provincial & federal government members & industry stakeholders who discuss the challenges of the tourism industry.
The Tourism Advisory Council works to ensure growing revenues in the tourism industry. To achieve this goal, the council partners with the Tourism Industry Association of PEI, Tourism PEI, & the Atlantic Canada Opportunities Agency.
The Minister of Tourism & Culture receives advice from the council about research initiatives, product development, & marketing.

Corporate Services Division
PO Box 2000, Charlottetown, PE C1A 7N8

Activities of the Corporate Services Division include financial services, administration, human resources, insurance matters, records management, & the operation of provincial parks & golf courses.

Director, Corporate Services, Kevin Jenkins, CA
Tel: 902-368-5874
Fax: 902-894-0342
wkjenkin@gov.pe.ca

General Manager, Provincial Golf Courses, Ryan Garrett
Tel: 902-368-4238
Fax: 902-894-0342
ragarrett@gov.pe.ca

Manager, Provincial Parks, Shane Arbing
Tel: 902-368-4404
Fax: 902-894-0342
sdarbing@gov.pe.ca

Manager, Financial Services, Beecher D. Gillis, CMA
Tel: 902-368-5932
Fax: 902-894-0342
bdgillis@gov.pe.ca

Manager, Human Resources, Danny McLaughlin
Tel: 902-368-5520
Fax: 902-368-0342
djmclaughlin@gov.pe.ca

Controller, Jennifer De Coursey, CA
Tel: 902-368-4084
Fax: 902-894-0342
jbdecourse@gov.pe.ca

Coordinator, Records Information, Lorianne McCormack
Tel: 902-569-7597
lxmccormack@gov.pe.ca

Consumer Sales & Customer Relationship Management Division
PO Box 2000, Charlottetown, PE C1A 7N8

Tel: 902-368-6316
Fax: 902-368-4438

The Consumer Sales & Customer Relationship Management Division is involved in the operation of Visitor Information & Call Centres, as well as the Central Reservation System & Integrated Tourism Solution Technology.

Manager, Call Centre, Jennifer Bernard
Tel: 902-437-8570
Fax: 902-437-8536
jfbernard@gov.pe.ca

Manager, Visitor Services, Heather Pollard
Tel: 368-444-1570
Fax: 902-368-4438
hlpollard@gov.pe.ca

Culture, Heritage, & Libraries Division
Sullivan Bldg., 16 Fitzroy St., 1st Fl., PO Box 2000, Charlottetown, PE C1A 7N8

Tel: 902-368-4787
Fax: 902-368-4663

The Culture, Heritage, & Libraries Division acts as a liaison between the Prince Edward Island provincial government & organizations that represent the library, heritage, & cultural sectors.

Director, Culture, Heritage, & Libraries, Harry Holman
Tel: 902-368-4784
Fax: 902-368-4663
htholman@gov.pe.ca

Provincial Librarian, Public Library Service, Kathleen Eaton
Tel: 902-961-7316
Fax: 902-961-7322
keeaton@gov.pe.ca

Provincial Archivist, Public Archives & Records Offices, Jill MacMicken-Wilson
Tel: 902-368-4351
Fax: 902-368-6327
jswilson@gov.pe.ca

Francophone Cultural Affairs Officer, Culture & Heritage, Cecile Arsenault
Tel: 902-854-7265
Fax: 902-854-7255
ccarsenault@gov.pe.ca

Heritage Officer, Charlotte Stewart
Tel: 902-368-5940
Fax: 902-368-4663
clstewart@gov.pe.ca

Marketing Communications Division
Shaw Bldg., 95-105 Rochford St., 3rd Fl., PO Box 2000, Charlottetown, PE C1A 7N8

The role of the Marketing Communications Division is the promotion of Prince Edward Island as an excellent tourist destination.

Director, Marketing & Communications, Brenda Gallant
Tel: 902-368-6066
Fax: 902-368-4438
bgallant@gov.pe.ca

Acting Manager, Advertising & Publicity, Robert Ferguson
Tel: 902-368-5522
Fax: 902-368-4438
rnfergus@gov.pe.ca

Manager, Trade & Sales, Craig Sulis
Tel: 902-368-5754
Fax: 902-368-4438
cdsulis@gov.pe.ca

Information Officer, Advertising & Publicity, Carol Johnston
Tel: 902-368-4447
Fax: 902-368-4438
cajohnston@gov.pe.ca

Editorial & Marketing Officer, Alison MacDougall
Tel: 902-368-6343
Fax: 902-368-4438
alimacdougall@gov.pe.ca

Coordinator, Publications, Paul Baglole
Tel: 902-368-6334
Fax: 902-368-4438
pnbaglol@gov.pe.ca

Coordinator, Print & Photography; Marketing Officer, Interactive Media, Marc C. Dagenais
Tel: 902-368-5882
Fax: 902-368-4438
mcdagenais@gov.pe.ca

Coordinator, Fulfilment, Harold McGuigan
Tel: 902-368-4452
Fax: 902-368-4459
hjmcguig@gov.pe.ca

Museum & Heritage Foundation
Shaw Bldg., 95-105 Rochford St., 3rd Fl., PO Box 2000, Charlottetown, PE C1A 7N8
The role of the Marketing Communications Division is the promotion of Prince Edward Island as an excellent tourist destination.
Chair, Harry Kielly
Tel: 902-368-6600
Fax: 902-368-6608
Executive Director, Dr. David Keenlyside
Tel: 902-368-6601
Fax: 902-368-6608
clkeenlyside@gov.pe.ca
Business Administrator, Mary Paguet
Tel: 902-368-6602
Fax: 902-368-6608
mmpaguet@gov.pe.ca

Strategy, Evaluation & Industry Investment
The Strategy, Evaluation, & Industry Investment Division works with regional tourism associations to help them prosper. Overseeing the development of support programs is a key activity.
The division is also responsible for the management of regulatory affairs related to the Highway Signage Act & the Tourism Industry Act. Examples of these responsibilities include special event signage, on-premise signage, licensing, & occupancy reports.
Advocating for the interests of the tourism industry is another part of the mandate for The Strategy, Evaluation, & Industry Investment Division. The division has represented the tourism industry in areas such as the Atlantic Gateway Initiative & land use issues.
Director, Chris K. Jones
Tel: 902-368-6342
Fax: 902-368-4438
ckjones@gov.pe.ca
Manager, Evaluation, Measurement, & Business Intelligence Unit, Brian Dunn
Tel: 902-368-4237
Fax: 902-368-4438
bjdunn@gov.pe.ca
Manager, Product Development, Investment, & Regulatory Affairs Unit, Janet Wood
Tel: 902-368-5508
Fax: 902-368-4438
jewood@gov.pe.ca
Senior Research Analyst, Evaluation, Measurement, & Business Intelligence Unit, Sharon Chuu
Tel: 902-368-6321
Fax: 902-368-4438
schuu@gov.pe.ca
Registrar, Signage, Product Development, Investment, & Regulatory Affairs Unit, Hubert MacIsaac
Tel: 902-368-4398
Fax: 902-368-6568
hamacisaac@gov.pe.ca

Prince Edward Island Department of Transportation & Infrastructure Renewal

Jones Bldg., 11 Kent St., 3rd Fl., PO Box 2000, Charlottetown, PE C1A 7N8
Tel: 902-368-5100
Fax: 902-368-5395
www.gov.pe.ca/tir
Prince Edward Island's Department of Transportation & Infrastructure Renewal maintains & enhances transportation systems & services throughout the province to ensure the safe & efficient movement of people, goods, & services.
The department also works to provide necessary infrastructure for the efficient operation of government. The department is therefore involved in crown land management & building construction & maintenance.
Acts Administered:
Architects Act
Closing of Roads Regulations
Crown Building Corporation Act
Dangerous Goods (Transportation) Act
Engineering Profession Act
Expropriation Act
Highway Access Regulations
Highway Traffic Act
Land Survey Act
Land Survey Act (Repealed)
Land Surveyors Act
Off-Highway Vehicle Act
Public Utility Easement (Fees) Regulation
Public Works Act
Roads Act
Vehicle Weights & Dimensions Regulations

Minister, Transportation & Infrastructure Renewal, Hon. Robert S. Vessey
Tel: 902-368-4801
Fax: 902-368-5277
rsvessey@gov.pe.ca; robert.vessey@liberal.pe.ca

Deputy Minister, Brian Douglas
Tel: 902-368-5130
Fax: 902-368-5385
bwdouglas@gov.pe.ca

Communications Officer, Mary Moszynski
Tel: 902-368-5112
Fax: 902-368-5385
mamoszynski@gov.pe.ca

Associated Agencies, Boards & Commissions:
• Island Waste Management Corporation (IWMC)
110 Watts Ave.
Charlottetown, PE C1E 2C1
Tel: 902-894-0330
Fax: 902-894-0331
Toll-free: 888-280-8111
reception@iwmc.pe.ca; info@iwmc.pe.ca
www.iwmc.pe.ca
The Island Waste Management Corporation is a provincial Crown Corporation that was formed in 1999, according to the Environmental Act R.S.P.E.I. 1988, Cap. E-9. Conducting business throughout Prince Edward Island, the corporation administers & provides solid waste management services to both commercial & residential sectors.
One of the Island Waste Management Corporation's successful environmental programs is Waste Watch. Everyone in Prince Edward Island must separate waste into one of three categories: compost, marketable recyclable material, & waste. Waste Watch Drop-Off Centres also accept household hazardous waste free of charge.
In addition to operating the Waste Watch Drop-Off Centres, the Island Waste Management Corporation also operates or oversees the following facilities: Central Compost Facility, East Prince Waste Management Facility, & the Energy from Waste Facility.

Capital Projects Division
Jones Bldg., 11 Kent St., 3rd Fl., Charlottetown, PE C1A 7N8
The following sections make up the Capital Projects Division: Engineering Services; Highway Construction; Materials Lab; & Planning & Design. Staff take care of the design & construction of highways & building infrastructure.
Director, Capital Projects Division; Chief Engineer, Stephen J. Yeo, P.Eng.
Tel: 902-368-5105
Fax: 902-368-5425
sjyeo@gov.pe.ca
Senior Manager, Materials Lab, Terry Kelly, P.Eng.
Tel: 902-676-7979
Fax: 902-676-7994
jtkelly@gov.pe.ca
Manager, Design & Bridge Maintenance, Darrell Evans, P.Eng.
Tel: 902-569-0578
Fax: 902-368-5395
djevans@gov.pe.ca
Manager, Engineering Services, Dan MacDonald
Tel: 902-368-5158
Fax: 902-368-5425
wdmacdonald@gov.pe.ca
Engineer, Traffic Operations, Alan Aitken, P.Eng.
Tel: 902-368-5006
Fax: 902-368-5425
aaaitken@gov.pe.ca
Regional Engineer, Eastern Highway Construction, Matt Collins, P.Eng.
Tel: 902-652-8998
Fax: 902-652-8981
mscollins@gov.pe.ca
Regional Engineer, Central Highway Construction, Mark Sherren, P.Eng.
Tel: 902-368-6195
Fax: 902-368-5425
mesherren@gov.pe.ca

Finance & Human Resources Division
Jones Bldg., 11 Kent St., 2nd Fl., Charlottetown, PE C1A 7N8
Tel: 902-368-5100
Fax: 902-368-5395
The fiscal matters & human resources issues of the Department of Transportation & Infrastructure Renewal are handled by the Finance & Human Resources Division.
Director, Finance & Human Resource Division, Wendy L. MacDonald, CA
Tel: 902-368-5126
Fax: 902-368-5395
wlmacdonald@gov.pe.ca
Manager, Human Resources, Anne MacAulay
Tel: 902-620-3356
Fax: 902-894-0368
ammacaulay@gov.pe.ca

Highway Maintenance Division
Park St. & Riverside Dr. Provincial Headquarters, PO Box 2000, Charlottetown, PE C1A 7N8
Tel: 902-368-5090
Fax: 902-368-6244
The Highway Maintenance Division is responsible for the upkeep of the total provincial highway system.
Director, Highway Maintenance Division, Darren Chaisson, P.Eng
Tel: 902-368-5103
Fax: 902-368-6244
ddchaisson@gov.pe.ca
Manager, Fleet, Mechanical Branch, Wilfred J. MacDonald
Tel: 902-368-5222
Fax: 902-368-5994
wjmacdonald@gov.pe.ca
Manager, Inventory Control, Provincial Headquarters, Robert A. MacKinnon
Tel: 902-368-4746
Fax: 902-368-6244
ramackinnon@gov.pe.ca
Superintendent, Western Highway Maintenance, Mike Berrigan
Tel: 902-888-8282
Fax: 902-888-8291
mjberrigan@gov.pe.ca
Superintendent, Central Highway Maintenance, Gordie Lund
Tel: 902-368-5172
Fax: 902-368-6244
gllund@gov.pe.ca
Superintendent, Eastern Highway Maintenance, Gerard F. Morrison
Tel: 902-652-8971
Fax: 902-652-8978
gfmorrison@gov.pe.ca

Highway Safety Division
33 Riverside Dr., Charlottetown, PE C1A 9R9
Tel: 902-368-5228
Fax: 902-368-5236
Safety issues from the province's highways are handled by the Highway Safety Division.
Director, Highway Safety Division, John B. MacDonald
Tel: 902-368-5225
Fax: 902-368-5236
jbmacdonald@gov.pe.ca
Registrar, Motor Vehicles, Graham L. Miner
Tel: 902-368-5223
Fax: 902-368-5236
glminer@gov.pe.ca
Coordinator, Safety, Doug J. MacEwen
Tel: 902-368-5219
Fax: 902-368-5236
djmacewen@gov.pe.ca

Infrastructure Division
#303, 75 Fitzroy St., PO Box 2000, Charlottetown, PE C1A 7N8
Tel: 902-620-3383
Toll-Free: 888-240-4411
cpei-infrastructure@gov.pe.ca
www.gov.pe.ca/tir
Infrastructure is a joint initiative between the Government of Prince Edward Island & the Government of Canada.
Provincial Manager, Infrastructure, Darlene Rhodenizer
Tel: 902-368-6213
Fax: 902-620-3383
dlrhodenizer@gov.pe.ca
Federal Manager, Pat MacAulay
Tel: 902-368-0987
Toll-free: 888-240-4411
Fax: 902-620-3383
pat.macaulay@acoa-apeca.gc.ca
Provincial Project Officer, John Arsenault
Tel: 902-368-4882
Fax: 902-620-3383
jearsenault@gov.pe.ca
Federal Project Officer, Kandace McEntee
Tel: 902-566-7097
Toll-free: 888-240-4411
Fax: 902-620-3383
kandace.mcentee@acoa-apeca.gc.ca

Land & Environment Division
Jones Bldg., 11 Kent St., 3rd Fl., PO Box 2000, Charlottetown, PE C1A 7N8
Tel: 902-368-5221
Fax: 902-368-5395
The Land & Environment Division is responsible for provincial lands. Environmental services are also provided by the Land & Environment Division for projects related to transportation & public works. Staff members ensure compliance with provincial & federal environmental legislation & regulations during highway construction & maintenance projects.

Director, Land & Environment Division, Brian F. Thompson, P.Eng.
Tel: 902-368-5185
Fax: 902-368-5395
bfthompson@gov.pe.ca
Chief Surveyor, David R.J. Morris, P.Eng, PEILS, CLS
Tel: 902-368-5143
Fax: 902-620-3033
drjmorris@gov.pe.ca
Manager, Provincial Land, Leo J. Creamer
Tel: 902-368-5134
Fax: 902-368-5395
jlcreamer@gov.pe.ca
Supervisor, Land Administration, Carol Craswell, BBA
Tel: 902-368-6119
Fax: 902-368-5395
cmcraswell@gov.pe.ca
Supervisor, Provincial Roads, Sharon N. Slauenwhite, BA
Tel: 902-368-6387
Fax: 902-368-5395
snslauenwhite@gov.pe.ca
Environmental Coordinator, Shelley Cole-Arbing
Tel: 902-368-5095
Fax: 902-368-5395
slcole@gov.pe.ca

Public Works & Planning Division
Jones Bldg., 11 Kent St., 3rd Fl., Charlottetown, PE C1A 7N8
Tel: 902-368-5100
Fax: 902-368-5395

The Public Works & Planning Division is engaged in the following activities: analyzing long term transportation requirements; planning & designing construction projects; implementing major projects; & maintaining buildings.
Director, Public Works & Planning, Alan Maynard, P.Eng.
Tel: 902-368-5147
Fax: 902-569-0590
aemaynard@gov.pe.ca
Manager, Planning, Paul Godfrey, P.Eng.
Tel: 902-368-4849
Fax: 902-569-0590
jpgodfrey@gov.pe.ca
Manager, Building Maintenance & Accommodation, Holly Hinds
Tel: 902-368-4854
Fax: 902-368-5395
hahinds@gov.pe.ca
Manager, Building Construction Contract Administration, Kevin Kennedy
Tel: 902-368-5148
Fax: 902-368-5395
kjkennedy@gov.pe.ca
Manager, Building Design & Construction, Tyler Richardson, P.Eng.
Tel: 902-368-4249
Fax: 902-569-0590
ttrichardson@gov.pe.ca

Prince Edward Island Workers Compensation Board (WCB)

14 Weymouth St., PO Box 757, Charlottetown, PE C1A 7L7
Tel: 902-368-5680
Fax: 902-368-5696
Toll-Free: 800-237-5049
www.wcb.pe.ca
Other Communication: Customer Liaison Service, Toll-Free Phone: 1-866-460-3074; Employer Services, Phone: 902-368-5705

The Workers Compensation Board of Prince Edward Island operates as an independent, non-profit organization. Prince Edward Island employers provide funding for the board. Both workers & employers are served by the Workers Compensation Board through the promotion of workplace health & safety & the provision of workplace injury & illness insurance.
Acts Administered:
Occupational Health & Safety Act
Workers Compensation Act

Chief Executive Officer, Sharon Cameron
Tel: 902-368-5688
secameron@wcb.pe.ca

Director, Corporate Development, Bonnie Blakney
Tel: 902-620-3478
blblakney@wcb.pe.ca

Director, Client Services, Wendy McIsaac
Tel: 902-368-5687
wlmcisaac@wcb.pe.ca

Director, Occupational Health & Safety, Bill Reid
Tel: 902-368-5562
bkreid@wcb.pe.ca

Director, Corporate Services, Tammy Turner
Tel: 902-368-4102
teturner@wcb.pe.ca

Manager, Case Management, Dawn Bradley
Tel: 902-368-6044
dbradley@wcb.pe.ca

Manager, Employer Services, Greg MacCallum
Tel: 902-368-5679
ggmaccallum@wcb.pe.ca

Manager, Information Technology Services, Darren MacDonald
Tel: 902-368-5669
dpmacdonald@wcb.pe.ca

Manager, Intake & Entitlement, Kate Marshall
Tel: 902-368-6358
kmarshall@wcb.pe.ca

Manager, Human Resources, Luanne Gallant
Tel: 902-894-0315
lmgallant@wcb.pe.ca

Manager, Facilities & Procurement, Chris Power
Tel: 902-368-4091
cipower@wcb.pe.ca a

Manager, OHS, Ian Rodd
Tel: 902-368-5575
ihrodd@wcb.pe.ca

Gouvernement du Québec / Government of Québec

Siege du gouvernement: Hôtel du Parlement, 1045, rue des Parlementaires, Québec, QC G1A 1A3
Tél: 418-643-7239
Téléc: 418-646-4271
Ligne sans frais: 866-337-8837
www.gouv.qc.ca; www.assnat.qc.ca
La Province de Québec est entrée dans la Confédération le 1ère juillet, 1867. Terre: 1,356,366.78 km2. Population: 7,903,001 (2011)

Cabinet du Lieutenant-gouverneur / Office of the Lieutenant Governor

Édifice André-Laurendeau, 1050, rue des Parlementaires R.C., Québec, QC G1A 1A1
Tél: 418-643-5385
Téléc: 418-644-4677
Ligne sans frais: 866-791-0766
www.lieutenant-gouverneur.qc.ca
Rôles constitutionnels et cérémoniels: le lieutenant-gouverneur a des pouvoirs constitutionnels d'un chef d'État et est le fonctionnaire exécutif en chef de la province; il/elle donne une suite légale à la politique déterminée par le gouvernement en ce qui concerne la nomination du premier ministre, et les membres du Conseil exécutif, la convocation, la prorogation et la dissolution de l'Assemblée nationale, la ratification des décrets du gouvernement, et la nomination des juges des cours de la province; il/elle occupe le plus haut rang protocolaire du Québec et il/elle a préséance sur tous les membres de la famille royale, à l'exception de Sa Majesté qu'il/elle représente

Lieutenant-gouverneur, L'hon. Pierre Duchesne

Secrétaire général et aide de camp principal, Michel Demers, Col. (Ret'd)

Adjoint exécutif, Felipe Marquez

Adjointe administrative, Francine Royer

Cabinet du premier ministre / Office of the Premier

Édifice Honoré-Mercier, 835, boul René-Lévesque est, 3e étage, Québec, QC G1A 1B4
Tél: 418-643-5321
Téléc: 418-643-3924
www.premier-ministre.gouv.qc.ca
Autre numéros: Alternative Phone: 514-873-3411; Alternative Fax: 514-873-6769

Premier ministre/Premier, L'hon. Pauline Marois, PQ
Tél: 418-643-5321
Téléc: 418-646-1854
pauline.marois@assnat.qc.ca

Secrétaire général/Secretary General, Michel Bonsaint
Tél: 418-643-7355
sec.general@assnat.qc.ca

Attaché de presse, Hugo D'Amours
Tél: 418-643-5321
communications-pm@mce.gouv.qc.ca

Ministère du Conseil exécutif / Executive Council

875, Grande Allée est, Québec, QC G1R 4Y8
Tél: 418-646-3021
Téléc: 418-528-9242
www.mce.gouv.qc.ca
Autre numéros: Montréal: 514-873-7029

Premier ministre, Ministre responsable des dossiers jeunesse, L'hon. Pauline Marois
Tél: 418-643-5321
Téléc: 418-643-3924
pauline.marois@assnat.qc.ca

Vice-première ministre & Ministre, L'Agriculture, des Pêcheries et de l'Alimentation, Ministre responsable de la région del'Abitibi-Témiscamingue, L'hon. François Gendron
Tél: 418-643-7295
Téléc: 418-643-4318
fgendron-abou@assnat.qc.ca

Ministre responsable de l'Administration gouvernementale, Président du Conseil du trésor, Ministre responsable de la région duSaguenay-Lac-Saint-Jean, L'hon. Stéphane Bédard
Tél: 418-649-2319
Téléc: 418-643-4804
sbedard-chic@assnat.qc.ca

Ministre des Finances et de l'Économie, Président du Comité ministériel de la prospérité et du développement régional, L'hon. Nicolas Marceau
Tél: 418-644-1417
Téléc: 418-646-7804
nmarceau-rous@assnat.qc.ca

Ministre du Travail, de l'Emploi et de la Solidarité sociale, Présidente du Comité ministériel de la solidarité, Ministre responsable de la Condition féminine, Ministre responsable de la région de la Capitale-Nationale etChaudière-Appalaches, L'hon. Agnès Maltais
Tél: 418-644-1042
Téléc: 418-646-4491
amaltais-tasc@assnat.qc.ca

Ministre responsable des Institutions démocratiques et de la Participation citoyenne, Président du Comité ministériel de l'identité, Ministre responsable de la région de la Mauricie, L'hon. Bernard Drainville
Tél: 418-643-5611
Téléc: 418-646-7812
bdrainville-mavi@assnat.qc.ca

Ministre, Justice, Président du Comité de législation, L'hon. Bertrand St-Arnaud
Tél: 418-646-7508
Téléc: 418-643-0616
bstarnaud-chmb@assnat.qc.ca

Ministre, Famille, Ministre responsable de la région de Laval et de la région des Laurentides, L'hon. Nicole Léger
Tél: 418-643-2301
Téléc: 418-643-3325
nleger-pat@assnat.qc.ca

Ministre, Éducation, du Loisir et du Sport, Ministre responsable de la région de la Montérégie, L'hon. Marie Malavoy
Tél: 418-646-4283
Téléc: 418-644-9697
mmalavoy-tail@assnat.qc.ca

Ministre des Relations internationales, de la Francophonie et du Commerce extérieur, Président du Comité ministériel de la région métropolitaine, Ministre responsable de la région deMontréal, L'hon. Jean-François Lisée

Ministre, Transports, Ministre des Affaires municipales, des Régions et de l'Occupation du territoire, L'hon. Sylvain Gaudreault
Tél: 418-646-7647
Téléc: 418-646-7801
sgaudreault-jonq@assnat.qc.ca

Ministre, Ressources naturelles, L'hon. Martine Ouellet
Tél: 418-644-0751
Téléc: 418-646-7810
martineouellet@assnat.qc.ca

Ministre délégué aux Affaires intergouvernementales canadiennes et à la Gouvernance souverainiste, Ministre responsable de la région de la Côte-Nord et de la région du Nord du Québec, L'hon. Alexandre Cloutier
Tél: 418-644-0901
Téléc: 418-528-9534
acloutier-lsj@assnat.qc.ca

Ministre de la Santé et des Services sociaux, Ministre responsable des Aînés, Ministre responsable de la région del'Estrie, L'hon. Réjean Hébert
Tél: 418-266-7171
Téléc: 418-266-7197
ministre@msss.gouv.qc.ca

Ministre déléguée à la Santé publique et à la Protection de la jeunesse, Ministre responsable de la région de Lanaudière, L'hon. Véronique Hivon
Tél: 418-644-1598
Téléc: 418-644-9697
vhivon-joli@assnat.qc.ca

Ministre, Culture et des Communications, L'hon. Maka Kotto
Tél: 418-646-2128
Téléc: 418-644-3712
mkotto-bour@assnat.qc.ca

Ministre, Sécurité publique, Ministre responsable de la région de l'Outaouais, L'hon. Stéphane Bergeron
Tél: 418-644-9368
Téléc: 418-646-6640
sbedard-chic@assnat.qc.ca

Ministre, Enseignement supérieur, de la Recherche, de la Science et de la Technologie, Ministre responsable de la région du Centre-du-Québec, L'hon. Pierre Duchesne

Ministre, Immigration et des Communautés culturelles, Ministre responsable de la Charte de la langue française, L'hon. Diane De Courcy
Tél: 418-644-2128
Téléc: 418-528-0829
cabinet@micc.gouv.qc.ca

Ministre, Développement durable, de l'Environnement, de la Faune et des Parcs, L'hon. Daniel Breton

Ministre responsable des Tourisme, Ministre responsable de la région du Bas-Saint-Laurent, L'hon. Pascal Bérubé
Tél: 418-644-0054
pberube@assnat.qc.ca

Ministre responsable a la, Politique industrielle et à la Banque de développement économique du Québec, L'hon. Élaine Zakaïb

Ministre responsable aux, Régions, Ministre responsable de la région de la Gaspésie-Iles-de-la-Madeleine, L'hon. Gaétan Lelièvre

Ministre délégué aux, Affaires autochtones, L'hon. Élizabeth Larouche

Whip en chef, L'hon. Yves-François Blanchet
Tél: 418-644-1052
Téléc: 418-643-1216
yfblanchet-drum@assnat.qc.ca

Président du, Caucus du gouvernement, L'hon. Marjolain Dufour
Tél: 418-644-0809
Téléc: 418-646-7811
marjolaindufour-rele@assnat.qc.ca

Cabinet du Conseil exécutif / Cabinet Office
Édifice Honoré-Mercier, #2.12A, 835, boul René-Lévesque est, Québec, QC G1A 1B4
Tél: 418-643-7355
Téléc: 418-528-9552
Secrétaire général, Jean St-Gelais
Tél: 418-643-7355
Téléc: 418-528-9552

Comités ministériels / Cabinet Committees
Secrétariat général, Édifice Honoré-Mercier, #2.12A, 835, boul René-Lévesque est, Québec, QC G1A 1B4
Tél: 418-643-7355
Téléc: 418-528-9552
Président, Conseil du trésor, et Ministre responsable de l'Administration gouvernementale, l'hon. Stéphane Bédard
Tel: 418-643-5926
Fax: 418-643-7824
cabinet@sct.gouv.qc.ca
Président, Comité ministériel de l'identité, et Ministre responsable des Institutions démocratiques et de la Participationcitoyenne, l'hon. Bernard Drainville
Tel: 418-643-5611
Fax: 418-646-7812
bdrainville-mavi@assnat.qc.ca
Président, Comité ministériel de la région métropolitaine, et Ministre des Relations internationales, de la Francophonie et du Commerce extérieur, l'hon. Jean-François Lisée
Présidente, Comité ministériel de la solidarité, et Ministre du Travail, de l'Emploi et de la Solidarité sociale, l'hon. Agnès Maltais
Tel: 418-646-6090
Fax: 418-646-6088
amaltais-tasc@assnat.qc.ca
Président, Comité ministériel de la prospérité économique et du développement régional, et Ministre des Finances et del'Économie, l'hon. Nicolas Marceau
Tel: 450-831-8979
Fax: 450-831-2093
nmarceau-rous@assnat.qc.ca
Présidente, Comité des priorités, et Première ministre du Québec, l'hon. Pauline Marois
Tel: 418-643-5321
Fax: 418-646-1854
pauline.marois@assnat.qc.ca
Président, Comité de législation, et Ministre de la justice, l'hon. Bertrand St-Arnaud
Tel: 418-643-4210
Fax: 418-646-0027
ministre@justice.gouv.qc.ca

L'Assemblée nationale / National Assembly

Hôtel du Parlement, 1045, rue des Parlementaires, Québec, QC G1A 1A3
Tél: 418-643-7239
Téléc: 418-646-4271
Ligne sans frais: 866-337-8837
responsable.contenu@assnat.qc.ca
www.assnat.qc.ca

Président de l'Assemblée nationale/Speaker of the National Assembly, Président de la Commission de l'Assemblée nationale, et la Sous-commission de la réforme parlementaire, Jacques Chagnon
Tél: 418-644-0675
Téléc: 418-643-1734
courrier.president@assnat.qc.ca

Première vice-présidente/First Vice-President, Fatima Houda-Pepin
Tél: 418-643-2750
Téléc: 418-643-2942
fhoudapepin@assnat.qc.ca

Deuxième vice-président/Second Vice-President, François Ouimet
Tél: 418-643-2810
Téléc: 418-643-3688
fouimet-marq@assnat.qc.ca

Troisième vice-président/Third Vice-President, François Gendron
Tél: 418-380-2525
Téléc: 418-380-2184
ministre.mapaq@mapaq.gouv.qc.ca

Secrétaire général/Secretary General, Michel Bonsaint
sec.general@assnat.qc.ca

Whip en chef du gouvernement, Yves-François Blanchet
Tél: 418-643-6018
Téléc: 418-643-3325
yfblanchet-drum@assnat.qc.ca

Whip adjoint du gouvernement, Dave Turcotte
Tél: 418-644-1463
dave.turcotte-saje@assnat.qc.ca

Leader parlementaire du gouvernement, Stéphane Bédard
Tél: 418-643-5926
Téléc: 418-643-7824
cabinet@sct.gouv.qc.ca

Leader parlementaire adjoint du gouvernement, Bertrand St-Arnaud
Tél: 418-643-4210
Téléc: 418-646-0027
ministre@justice.gouv.qc.ca

Leader parlementaire adjoint du gouvernement, Mathieu Traversy
Tél: 418-644-1616
Téléc: 418-644-5976
mtraversy-terr@assnat.qc.ca

Président du caucus du gouvernement, Marjolain Dufour
Tél: 418-644-0809
Téléc: 418-643-0183
marjolaindufour-rele@assnat.qc.ca

Cabinet du chef de l'opposition officielle / Office of the Official Opposition (ADQ)
Hôtel du Parlement, #2.89, 1045, rue des Parlementaires, Québec, QC G1A 1A4
Chef de l'opposition officielle/Leader of the Official Opposition, Jean-Marc Fournier
Tél: 418-643-2743
Téléc: 418-643-2502
Leader parlementaire de l'opposition officielle, Robert Dutil
Tél: 418-226-4570
Téléc: 418-227-9664
rdutil-besu@assnat.qc.ca
Whip en chef de l'opposition officielle, Laurent Lessard
Tél: 418-332-3444
Téléc: 418-332-3445
llessard-lotb@assnat.qc.ca
Whip adjointe de l'opposition officielle, Lucie Charlebois
Tél: 418-643-6018
Téléc: 418-643-5462
lcharlebois-soul@assnat.qc.ca
Président du caucus de l'opposition officielle, Geoffrey Kelley
Tél: 514-697-7663
Téléc: 514-697-6499
gkelley-jaca@assnat.qc.ca

Direction de l'Assemblée nationale du Québec / Directorate of the National Assembly of Québec
Directeur et adjoint du secrétaire général, Secrétariat du Bureau, Marc Painchaud
Tél: 418-643-2724
sec.general@assnat.qc.ca
Directrice générale, Affaires juridiques et parlementaries, Ariane Mignolet
Tél: 418-528-0020
Directeur, Travaux parlementaires, François Arsenault
Tél: 418-643-2722
Directrice, Traduction et de l'édition des lois, Louise Auger
Tél: 418-643-2840

Affaires institutionnelles et de la Bibliothèque de l'Assemblée nationale / Institutional Affairs & the Library of the National Assembly
Directeur général, Frédéric Fortin
Tél: 418-646-2383
Directeur, Communications, Jean Dumas
Tél: 418-643-1992
Directeur, Service des ressources documentaires et archives, Jean Chabot
Tél: 418-643-5030
Directeur, Protocole et de l'accueil, Daniel Cloutier
Tél: 418-643-4206
Directeur, Service de la recherche, Jacques Gagnon
Tél: 418-643-4567
Directrice, Éducation à la démocratie parlementaire, Isabelle Giguére
Tél: 418-643-4101
Directeur, Relations interparlementaires et internationales, Dominic Toupin
Tél: 418-643-7391

Secrétariat général adjoint à l'administration / General Secretariat for Administration
Secrétaire général adjoint, Jacques Jobin
Tél: 418-643-6000
Directeur, Service des systèmes informationnels et des réseaux, François Asselin
Tél: 418-643-2725
Directrice, Ressources financières, de l'approvisionnement et de la vérification, Lyne Bergeron
Tél: 418-643-3022
Directeur, Ressources humaines, Serge Bouchard
Tél: 418-644-5444
Directeur, Sécurité, Pierre Duchaine
Tél: 418-644-2783
Directeur, Informatique et des télécommunications, et de la diffusion des débats (par intérim), Claude Dugas
Tél: 418-643-2725
Directeur, Gestion immobilière et des ressources matérielles, Guy L. Huot
Tél: 418-643-1828
Directrice, Service du Journal des débats, Carole Lessard
Tél: 418-643-2890

Les Régions administratives au Québec - Les ministres responsables / Regional Parliamentary Assistants
Abitibi-Témiscamingue, L'hon. Pierre Corbeil
Bas-Saint-Laurent, L'hon. Nathalie Normandeau
Capitale-Nationale, L'hon. Sam Hamad

Centre-du-Québec, L'hon. Laurent Lessard
Chaudière-Appalaches, L'hon. Laurent Lessard
Côte-Nord, L'hon. Serge Simard
Estrie, L'hon. Monique Gagnon-Tremblay
Gaspésie-Iles-de-la-Madeleine, L'hon. Nathalie Normandeau
Laurentides, L'hon. Michelle Courchesne
Lanaudière, L'hon. Michelle Courchesne
Laval, L'hon. Michelle Courchesne
Mauricie, L'hon. Julie Boulet
Montérégie, L'hon. Nicole Ménard
Montréal, L'hon. Raymond Bachand
Nord-du-Québec, L'hon. Pierre Corbeil
Outaouais, L'hon. Norman MacMillan
Saguenay-Lac-Saint-Jean, L'hon. Serge Simard

Quarantième assemblée nationale / Fortieth National Assembly - Québec

Hôtel du Parlement, 1045, rue des Parlementaires, Québec, QC G1A 1A4
Tél: 418-643-7239
Téléc: 418-646-4271
Ligne sans frais: 866-337-8837
www.assnat.qc.ca

La dernière élection générale: le 4 septembre, 2012. Depuis le 21 juin 2011, la composition de l'Assemblée est la suivante: Parti Libéral du Québec (PLQ): 50; Parti québécois (PQ): 54; Coalition Avenir Québec (CAQ): 19; Québec solidaire (QS): 2; Total: 125. Salaires, indemnités, allocations: indemnité annuelle: $85,388 et une allocation de dépenses de $15,538. L'indemnité annuelle des membres de l'Assemblée nationale n'est pas majorée du 1er avril 2010 au 31 mars 2012. En plus, le Premier ministre reçot $89,657, les ministres $64,041, le Leader parlementaire du gouvernement et le Président $64,041, le Chef de l'Opposition officielle $64,041. Par la suite: membre, circonscription, allégeance politique, téléphone & télécopieur, courriel, (Adresse: Hôtel du Parlement, Québec, QC G1A 1A4)

Members

L'hon. Pierre Arcand
Constituency: Mont-Royal *No. of Constituents:* 40 802, Liberal
Tél: 418-521-3911
Téléc: 418-643-4143
ministre@mddep.gouv.qc.ca

Raymond Bachand
Constituency: Outremont *No. of Constituents:* 38 999, Liberal
Tél: 418-643-5270
Téléc: 418-646-1574
ministre@finances.gouv.qc.ca

Denise Beaudoin
Constituency: Mirabel *No. of Constituents:* 55 366, Parti Québécois
Tél: 418-644-1543
Téléc: 418-644-9697
denise.beaudoin-mira@assnat.qc.ca

Stéphane Bédard
Constituency: Chicoutimi *No. of Constituents:* 46 604, Parti Québécois
Tél: 418-643-1275
Téléc: 418-643-1906
sbedard@assnat.qc.ca

Stéphane Bergeron
Constituency: Verchères *No. of Constituents:* 55 111, Parti Québécois
Tél: 418-644-9368
Téléc: 418-646-6640
sbergeron-verc@assnat.qc.ca

L'hon. Lawrence S. Bergman
Constituency: D'Arcy-McGee *No. of Constituents:* 40 224, Liberal
Tél: 418-528-1960
Téléc: 418-643-0183
lbergman-dmg@assnat.qc.ca

Pascal Bérubé
Constituency: Matane-Matapédia *No. of Constituents:* 47 632, Parti Québécois
Tél: 418-644-0054
pberube@assnat.qc.ca

Stéphane Billette
Constituency: Huntingdon *No. of Constituents:* 41 012, Liberal
Tél: 418-644-5992
Téléc: 418-646-8169
sbillette-hunt@assnat.qc.ca

L'hon. Marguerite Blais
Constituency: Saint-Henri—Sainte-Anne *No. of Constituents:* 52 824, CA
Tél: 418-646-7757
Téléc: 418-646-7769
m.blais@aines.gouv.qc.ca

Yves-François Blanchet
Constituency: Johnson *No. of Constituents:* 55 705, Parti Québécois
Tél: 819-474-7770
Téléc: 819-474-4492
Autre numéros: yves-francoisblanchet.deputes.pq.org
Les réseaux sociaux: twitter.com/yfblanchet, www.facebook.com/YvesFrancoisBlanchet

Ghislain Bolduc
Constituency: Mégantic *No. of Constituents:* 38 228, Liberal

L'hon. Yves Bolduc
Constituency: Jean-Talon *No. of Constituents:* 45 899, Liberal
Tél: 418-266-7171
Téléc: 418-266-7197
ministre@msss.gouv.qc.ca

François Bonnardel
Constituency: Granby *No. of Constituents:* 49 239, CA
Tél: 418-528-0407
Téléc: 418-528-9479
fbonnardel-shef@assnat.qc.ca

Marie Bouillé
Constituency: Iberville *No. of Constituents:* 45 476, Parti Québécois
Tél: 418-644-1475
Téléc: 418-646-1085
mbouille-iber@assnat.qc.ca

L'hon. Julie Boulet
Constituency: Laviolette *No. of Constituents:* 35 816, Liberal
Tél: 418-643-4810
Téléc: 418-643-2802
ministre@mess.gouv.qc.ca

Stéphane Le Bouyonnec
Constituency: La Prairie *No. of Constituents:* 40 798, CA

Daniel Breton
Constituency: Sainte-Marie—Saint-Jacques *No. of Constituents:* 41 396, Parti Québécois

Léo Bureau-Blouin
Constituency: Laval-des-Rapides *No. of Constituents:* 53 259, Parti Québécois

Éric Caire
Constituency: La Peltrie *No. of Constituents:* 52 715, CA
Tél: 418-644-0185
Téléc: 418-528-6935
ecaire-lape@assnat.qc.ca

Serge Cardin
Constituency: Sherbrooke *No. of Constituents:* 48 157, Parti Québécois
Tél: 819-791-2863
Téléc: 819-791-2642
Autre numéros: sergecardin.org
Les réseaux sociaux: twitter.com/SergeCardin, www.facebook.com/sergecardin12

Marc Carrière
Constituency: Chapleau *No. of Constituents:* 53 979, Liberal
Tél: 418-528-0390
Téléc: 418-528-5668
mcarriere-chap@assnat.qc.ca

Jacques Chagnon
Constituency: Westmount—Saint-Louis *No. of Constituents:* 39 164, Liberal
Tél: 418-643-2820
Téléc: 418-643-3423
presidentcabinet@assnat.qc.ca

Noëlla Champagne
Constituency: Champlain *No. of Constituents:* 48 438, Parti Québécois
Tél: 418-644-2499
Téléc: 418-528-0427
nchampagne-chmp@assnat.qc.ca

Gilles Chapadeau
Constituency: Rouyn-Noranda—Témiscamingue *No. of Constituents:* 43 609, Parti Québécois
Tél: 819-797-4117
Téléc: 819-797-4147
gilleschapadeau.org
Les réseaux sociaux: twitter.com/abitibichaps, www.facebook.com/pqrnt

Francine Charbonneau
Constituency: Mille-îles *No. of Constituents:* 40 928, Liberal
Tél: 418-644-0866
Téléc: 418-644-5990
fcharbonneau-miil@assnat.qc.ca

L'hon. Lucie Charlebois
Constituency: Soulanges *No. of Constituents:* 45 523, Liberal
Tél: 418-643-6018
Téléc: 418-643-5462
lcharlebois@assnat.qc.ca

Jean-Marie Claveau
Constituency: Dubuc *No. of Constituents:* 39 235, Parti Québécois

Alexandre Cloutier
Constituency: Lac-Saint-Jean *No. of Constituents:* 42 310, Parti Québécois
Tél: 418-644-0901
Téléc: 418-644-2062
acloutier-lsj@assnat.qc.ca

Claude Cousineau
Constituency: Bertrand *No. of Constituents:* 55 362, Parti Québécois
Tél: 418-643-2769
Téléc: 418-644-2121
ccousineau-berr@assnat.qc.ca

Jean D'Amour
Constituency: Rivière-du-Loup-Témiscouata *No. of Constituents:* 50 774, Liberal
Tél: 418-528-2914
Téléc: 418-644-5990
jdamour-rdl@assnat.qc.ca

Hélène Daneault
Constituency: Groulx *No. of Constituents:* 55 818, CA

Françoise David
Constituency: Gouin *No. of Constituents:* 42 737, Independent

Diane De Courcy
Constituency: Crémazie *No. of Constituents:* 45 731, Parti Québécois

Gérard Deltell
Constituency: Chauveau *No. of Constituents:* 55 842, CA
Tél: 418-644-9318
Téléc: 418-528-9479
gdeltell-chau@assnat.qc.ca

Jean-Paul Diamond
Constituency: Maskinongé *No. of Constituents:* 46 544, Liberal
Tél: 418-644-0617
Téléc: 418-646-8169
jpdiamond-mask@assnat.qc.ca

Bernard Drainville
Constituency: Marie-Victorin *No. of Constituents:* 46 534, Parti Québécois
Tél: 418-643-5611
Téléc: 418-646-7812
bdrainville-mavi@assnat.qc.ca

André Drolet
Constituency: Jean-Lesage *No. of Constituents:* 46 480, Liberal
Tél: 418-646-7635
Téléc: 418-528-0425
adrolet-jele@assnat.qc.ca

Christian Dubé
Constituency: Lévis *No. of Constituents:* 46 289, CA

Emmanuel Dubourg
Constituency: Viau *No. of Constituents:* 40 350, Liberal
Tél: 418-646-7648
Téléc: 514-728-2759
edubourg-viau@assnat.qc.ca

Pierre Duchesne
Constituency: Borduas *No. of Constituents:* 55 140, Parti Québécois

Jacques Duchesneau
Constituency: Saint-Jérôme *No. of Constituents:* 53 163, CA

Marjolain Dufour
Constituency: René-Lévesque *No. of Constituents:* 34 357, Parti Québécois
Tél: 418-644-0809
Téléc: 418-646-7811
marjolaindufour-rele@assnat.qc.ca

L'hon. Robert Dutil
Constituency: Beauce-Sud *No. of Constituents:* 47 510, Liberal
Tél: 418-643-2112
Téléc: 418-646-6168
ministre@msp.gouv.qc.ca

Luc Ferland
Constituency: Ungava *No. of Constituents:* 25 587, Parti Québécois
Tél: 418-644-1363
Téléc: 418-528-0439
lferland-unga@assnat.qc.ca

L'hon. Jean-Marc Fournier
Constituency: Saint-Laurent *No. of Constituents:* 52 694, Liberal
Tél: 418-643-4210
Téléc: 418-646-0027
ministre@justice.gouv.qc.ca

Diane Gadoury-Hamelin
Constituency: Masson *No. of Constituents:* 47 376, Parti Québécois

Maryse Gaudreault
Constituency: Hull *No. of Constituents:* 51 134, Liberal
Tél: 418-644-9954
Téléc: 418-643-0595
mgaudreault-hull.assnat.qc.ca

Sylvain Gaudreault
Constituency: Jonquière *No. of Constituents:* 44 983, Parti Québécois
Tél: 418-646-7647
Téléc: 418-646-7801
sgaudreault-jonq@assnat.qc.ca

Henri-François Gautrin
Constituency: Verdun *No. of Constituents:* 47 068, Liberal
Tél: 418-646-7497

Téléc: 418-643-0241
hfgautrin-verd@assnat.qc.ca
François Gendron
Constituency: Abitibi-Ouest *No. of Constituents:* 34 942, Parti Québécois
Tél: 418-644-1007
Téléc: 418-644-1368
fgendron@assnat.qc.ca
Daniel Goyer
Constituency: Deux-Montagnes *No. of Constituents:* 46 706, Parti Québécois
Tél: 450-983-4820
Téléc: 514-666-0522
danielgoyer@danielgoyer.com
Autre numéros: www.danielgoyer.com
Les réseaux sociaux: www.facebook.com/danielgoyerpq
L'hon. Sam Hamad
Constituency: Louis-Hébert *No. of Constituents:* 43 737, Liberal
Tél: 418-643-6980
Téléc: 418-643-2033
ministre@mtq.gouv.qc.ca
Réjean Hébert
Constituency: Saint-François *No. of Constituents:* 54 567, Parti Québécois
Véronique Hivon
Constituency: Joliette *No. of Constituents:* 55 602, Parti Québécois
Tél: 418-644-1598
Téléc: 418-644-9697
vhivon-joli@assnat.qc.ca
Fatima Houda-Pepin
Constituency: La Pinière *No. of Constituents:* 57 359, Liberal
Tél: 418-643-2750
Téléc: 418-643-2942
fhoudapepin@assnat.qc.ca
Alexandre Iraca
Constituency: Papineau *No. of Constituents:* 55 636, Liberal
L'hon. Yolande James
Constituency: Nelligan *No. of Constituents:* 56 205, Liberal
Tél: 418-643-2181
Téléc: 418-643-2640
ministre.famille@mfa.gouv.qc.ca
L'hon. Geoffrey Kelley
Constituency: Jacques-Cartier *No. of Constituents:* 43 693, Liberal
Tél: 418-646-7627
Téléc: 418-643-0595
gkelley@assnat.qc.ca
Amir Khadir
Constituency: Mercier *No. of Constituents:* 39 413, QS
Tél: 418-644-1430
Téléc: 418-643-0624
akhadir-merc@assnat.qc.ca
Maka Kotto
Constituency: Bourget *No. of Constituents:* 48 318, Parti Québécois
Tél: 418-646-2128
Téléc: 418-646-8166
mkotto-bour@assnat.qc.ca
Charlotte L'Écuyer
Constituency: Pontiac *No. of Constituents:* 47 605, Liberal
Tél: 418-644-0679
Téléc: 418-528-5668
clecuyer-pont@assnat.qc.ca
Élizabeth Larouche
Constituency: Abitibi-Est *No. of Constituents:* 32 780, Parti Québécois
Autre numéros: elizabethlarouche.org
Guy Leclair
Constituency: Beauharnois *No. of Constituents:* 44 923, Parti Québécois
Tél: 418-644-7844
Téléc: 418-528-7410
guy.leclair-beau@assnat.qc.ca
François Legault
Constituency: L'Assomption *No. of Constituents:* 50 105, CA
Nicole Léger
Constituency: Pointe-aux-Trembles *No. of Constituents:* 40 534, Parti Québécois
Tél: 418-643-2301
Téléc: 418-643-3325
nleger-pat@assnat.qc.ca
Gaetan Lelièvre
Constituency: Gaspé *No. of Constituents:* 30 971, Parti Québécois
L'hon. Laurent Lessard
Constituency: Lotbinière-Frontenac *No. of Constituents:* 53 521, Liberal
Tél: 418-691-2050
Téléc: 418-643-1795
ministre@mamrot.gouv.qc.ca
Sylvain Lévesque
Constituency: Vanier-Les Rivières *No. of Constituents:* 54 376, CA
Jean-François Lisée
Constituency: Rosemont *No. of Constituents:* 50 789, Parti Québécois
Marie Malavoy
Constituency: Taillon *No. of Constituents:* 50 442, Parti Québécois
Tél: 418-646-4283
Téléc: 418-644-9697
mmalavoy-tail@assnat.qc.ca
Agnès Maltais
Constituency: Taschereau *No. of Constituents:* 48 822, Parti Québécois
Tél: 418-644-1042
Téléc: 418-646-4991
amaltais-tasc@assnat.qc.ca
Nicolas Marceau
Constituency: Rousseau *No. of Constituents:* 59 297, Parti Québécois
Tél: 418-644-1417
Téléc: 418-646-7804
nmarceau-rous@assnat.qc.ca
Jacques Marcotte
Constituency: Portneuf *No. of Constituents:* 39 672, CA
Yvon Marcoux
Constituency: Vaudreuil *No. of Constituents:* 55 715, Liberal
Tél: 418-646-7623
Téléc: 418-528-5668
ymarcoux-vaud@assnat.qc.ca
Pauline Marois
Constituency: Charlevoix-Côte-de-Beaupré *No. of Constituents:* 50 309, Parti Québécois
Tél: 418-643-2743
Téléc: 418-643-2957
pauline.marois@assnat.qc.ca
Pierre Marsan
Constituency: Robert-Baldwin *No. of Constituents:* 53 622, Liberal
Tél: 418-646-5554
Téléc: 418-643-9127
pmarsan-roba@assnat.qc.ca
Donald Martel
Constituency: Nicolet-Bécancour *No. of Constituents:* 39 036, CA
Tél: 819-386-7786
nicoletbecancour@coalitionavenirquebec.org
Les réseaux sociaux: www.facebook.com/MartelD.coalition
Scott McKay
Constituency: Repentigny *No. of Constituents:* 49 587, Parti Québécois
Tél: 450-581-6102
Téléc: 450-581-9173
smckay-asso@assnat.qc.ca
L'hon. Nicole Ménard
Constituency: Laporte *No. of Constituents:* 45 665, Liberal
Tél: 418-528-8063
Téléc: 418-528-8066
ministre@tourisme.gouv.qc.ca
L'hon. Pierre Moreau
Constituency: Châteauguay *No. of Constituents:* 48 456, Liberal
Tél: 418-646-5950
Téléc: 418-528-0981
ministre.saic@mce.gouv.qc.ca
Norbert Morin
Constituency: Côte-du-Sud *No. of Constituents:* 50 610, Liberal
Tél: 418-644-0513
Téléc: 418-644-8589
nmorin-mois@assnat.qc.ca
Martine Ouellet
Constituency: Vachon *No. of Constituents:* 47 213, Parti Québécois
Tél: 418-644-0751
Téléc: 418-646-7810
martineouellet@assnat.qc.ca
Guy Ouellette
Constituency: Chomedey *No. of Constituents:* 56 049, Liberal
Tél: 418-644-4050
Téléc: 418-646-7385
gouellette-chom@assnat.qc.ca
François Ouimet
Constituency: Marquette *No. of Constituents:* 43 974, Liberal
Tél: 418-643-2810
Téléc: 418-643-3688
fouimet-marq@assnat.qc.ca
Gilles Ouimet
Constituency: Fabre *No. of Constituents:* 46 182, Liberal
Tél: 514-360-1577
gillesouimet@plq.org
Les réseaux sociaux: twitter.com/GilOuimet
Sylvain Pagé
Constituency: Labelle *No. of Constituents:* 46 760, Parti Québécois
Tél: 418-528-1349
Téléc: 418-528-7185
spage@assnat.qc.ca
Pierre Paradis
Constituency: Brome-Missisquoi *No. of Constituents:* 54 216, Liberal
Tél: 418-644-0551
Téléc: 418-646-6684
pparadis-brmi@assnat.qc.ca
Émilien Pelletier
Constituency: Saint-Hyacinthe *No. of Constituents:* 56 453, Parti Québécois
Tél: 418-644-5283
Téléc: 418-646-7815
epelletier-sahy@assnat.qc.ca
Irvin Pelletier
Constituency: Rimouski *No. of Constituents:* 43 453, Parti Québécois
Tél: 418-644-1386
Téléc: 418-644-7851
ipelletier-rimo@assnat.qc.ca
Marc Picard
Constituency: Chutes-de-la-Chaudière *No. of Constituents:* 53 779, Independent
Tél: 418-528-1694
Téléc: 418-528-6935
mpicard-cdlc@assnat.qc.ca
Robert Poeti
Constituency: Marguerite-Bourgeoys *No. of Constituents:* 51 309, Liberal
Carole Poirier
Constituency: Hochelaga-Maisonneuve *No. of Constituents:* 40 331, Parti Québécois
Tél: 418-644-1629
Téléc: 418-646-7810
cpoirier@assnat.qc.ca
Suzanne Proulx
Constituency: Sainte-Rose *No. of Constituents:* 48 392, Parti Québécois
Daniel Ratthé
Constituency: Blainville *No. of Constituents:* 56 226, Parti Québécois
Tél: 418-644-1444
Téléc: 418-646-7804
dratthe-blai@assnat.qc.ca
Pierre Reid
Constituency: Orford *No. of Constituents:* 39 941, Liberal
Tél: 418-644-3944
Téléc: 418-646-0516
preid-orfo@assnat.qc.ca
Jeannine Richard
Constituency: Îles-de-la-Madeleine *No. of Constituents:* 10882, Parti Québécois
Tél: 418-986-1340
Téléc: 418-986-1370
jerichard@tlb.sympatico.ca
Autre numéros: jeanninerichard.org
Les réseaux sociaux: twitter.com/JeRichard_PQ, www.facebook.com/JeannineRichard.PQdesIles
Lorraine Richard
Constituency: Duplessis *No. of Constituents:* 38 084, Parti Québécois
Tél: 418-643-2446
Téléc: 418-644-3219
lorrainerichard-dupl@assnat.qc.ca
Roland Richer
Constituency: Argenteuil *No. of Constituents:* 43 010, Parti Québécois
Filomena Rotiroti
Constituency: Jeanne-Mance-Viger *No. of Constituents:* 47 660, Liberal
Tél: 418-646-5743
Téléc: 418-644-5990
frotiroti-jmv@assnat.qc.ca
Jean Rousselle
Constituency: Vimont *No. of Constituents:* 43 688, Liberal
Tél: 450-933-5151
jeanrousselle@plq.org
Nathalie Roy
Constituency: Montarville *No. of Constituents:* 51 332, CA
Sylvain Roy
Constituency: Bonaventure *No. of Constituents:* 35 993, Parti Québécois
Sylvie Roy
Constituency: Arthabaska *No. of Constituents:* 57 447, CA
Tél: 418-728-3236
arthabaska@coalitionavenirquebec.org
Les réseaux sociaux: www.facebook.com/sylvie.roy.coalition
Rita de Santis
Constituency: Bourassa-Sauvé *No. of Constituents:* 47 239,

Liberal
Tél: 514-360-4351
Sébastien Schneeberger
Constituency: Drummond-Bois-Francs *No. of Constituents:* 49 098, Independent
Tél: 819-475-7336
drummondboisfranc@coalitionavenirquebec.org
Les réseaux sociaux:
www.facebook.com/Schneeberger.coalition
Gerry Sklavounos
Constituency: Laurier-Dorion *No. of Constituents:* 45 912, Liberal
Tél: 418-644-5987
Téléc: 418-644-5977
gsklavounos-lado@assnat.qc.ca
André Spénard
Constituency: Beauce-Nord *No. of Constituents:* 41 417, CA
Danielle St-Amand
Constituency: Trois-Rivières *No. of Constituents:* 43 178, Liberal
Tél: 418-528-0413
Téléc: 418-646-8169
dstamand-trri@assnat.qc.ca
Bertrand St-Arnaud
Constituency: Chambly *No. of Constituents:* 44 424, Parti Québécois
Tél: 418-646-7508
Téléc: 418-643-0616
bstarnaud-chmb@assnat.qc.ca
Michelyne C. St-Laurent
Constituency: Montmorency *No. of Constituents:* 53 692, CA
Tél: 581-996-1093
montmorency@coalitionavenirquebec.org
Les réseaux sociaux: www.facebook.com/StLaurent.coalition
L'hon. Christine St-Pierre
Constituency: Acadie *No. of Constituents:* 48 015, Liberal
Tél: 418-380-2310
Téléc: 418-380-2311
ministre@mcccf.gouv.qc.ca
Marc Tanguay
Constituency: LaFontaine *No. of Constituents:* 40 387, Liberal
Tél: 514-648-1007
Téléc: 514-648-4559
marc.tanguay-lafo@assnat.qc.ca
L'hon. Lise Thériault
Constituency: Anjou-Louis-Riel *No. of Constituents:* 43 699, Liberal
Tél: 418-643-5297
Téléc: 418-644-0003
ministre@travail.gouv.qc.ca
Alain Therrien
Constituency: Sanguinet *No. of Constituents:* 37 686, Parti Québécois
Mathieu Traversy
Constituency: Terrebonne *No. of Constituents:* 53 500, Parti Québécois
Tél: 418-644-1616
Téléc: 418-644-5976
mtraversy-terr@assnat.qc.ca
Denis Trottier
Constituency: Roberval *No. of Constituents:* 44 887, Parti Québécois
Tél: 418-644-0707
Téléc: 418-646-7801
dtrottier-robe@assnat.qc.ca
Denise Trudel
Constituency: Charlesbourg *No. of Constituents:* 52 174, Liberal
Luc Trudel
Constituency: Saint-Maurice *No. of Constituents:* 36 530, Parti Québécois
Dave Turcotte
Constituency: Saint-Jean *No. of Constituents:* 57 938, Parti Québécois
Tél: 418-644-1463
Téléc: 418-646-7798
dave.turcotte-saje@assnat.qc.ca
Stéphanie Vallée
Constituency: Gatineau *No. of Constituents:* 55 199, Liberal
Tél: 418-644-5980
Téléc: 418-528-5668
svallee-gati@assnat.qc.ca
Karine Vallières
Constituency: Richmond *No. of Constituents:* 56 530, Liberal
L'hon. Dominique Vien
Constituency: Bellechasse *No. of Constituents:* 42 282, Liberal
Tél: 418-266-7181
Téléc: 418-266-7199
ministre.deleguee@msss.gouv.qc.ca
André Villeneuve
Constituency: Berthier *No. of Constituents:* 55 343, Parti Québécois
Tél: 418-644-1399
Téléc: 418-646-7801
avilleneuve-berh@assnat.qc.ca
L'hon. Kathleen Weil
Constituency: Notre-Dame-de-Grâce *No. of Constituents:* 39 351, Liberal
Tél: 418-644-2128
Téléc: 418-528-0829
cabinet@micc.gouv.qc.ca
Élaine Zakaïb
Constituency: Richelieu *No. of Constituents:* 43 874, Parti Québécois

Directeur, Direction des communications, Jean Dumas
Tél: 418-643-1992
communications@assnat.qc.ca
Édifice Jean-Antoine-Panet
1020, rue des Parlementaires, 2e étage
Québec, QC G1A 1A3 Canada

Ministères et organismes du gouvernement du Québec / Québec Government Departments & Agencies

Agences, Conseils et Commissions Associés/ Associated Agencies, Boards & Commissions:

• Commission municipale du Québec / Québec Municipal Commission
Mezzanine, aile Chauveau
10, rue Pierre-Olivier-Chauveau
Québec, QC G1R 4J3
Tél: 418-691-2014
Téléc: 418-644-4676
Ligne sans frais: 866-353-6767
cmq@mamr.gouv.qc.ca
www.cmq.gouv.qc.ca
CMQ est un tribunal et un organisme administratif, d'enquête et de conseil, spécialisé en matière municipale.
• Régie du logement du Québec / Québec Rental Board
Pyramide Ouest
#2095, 5199, rue Sherbrooke est
Montréal, QC H1T 3X1
Tél: 514-873-2245
Téléc: 514-864-8077
Ligne sans frais: 800-683-2245
www.rdl.gouv.qc.ca
Autres numéros: Montréal, Laval & Longueuil: 514-873-2245
• Société d'habitation du Québec / Housing Québec
Aile St-Amable
1054, rue Louis-Alexandre-Taschereau, 3e étage
Québec, QC G1R 5E7
Tél: 418-643-4035
Téléc: 418-643-2533
Ligne sans frais: 800-463-4315
www.habitation.gouv.qc.ca

Secrétariat aux affaires autochtones / Aboriginal Affairs

905, av Honoré-Mercier, 1er étage, Québec, QC G1R 5M6
Tél: 418-643-3166
Téléc: 418-646-4918
www.autochtones.gouv.qc.ca

Ministre responsable, L'hon. Élizabeth Larouche
Tél: 418-646-9131
Téléc: 418-646-9487
ministre.autochtones@mce.gouv.qc.ca
Note: Ministre responsable des Affaires autochtones; Comité ministériel du développement social,éducatif et culturel

Secrétariat aux affaires intergouvernementales canadiennes / Canadian Intergovernmental Affairs Secretariat

875, Grande Allée est, 3e étage, Québec, QC G1R 4Y8
Tél: 418-643-4011
Téléc: 418-528-0052
www.saic.gouv.qc.ca

Ministre responsable, Alexandre Cloutier
Tél: 418-646-5950
Téléc: 418-528-0981
acloutier-lsj@assnat.qc.ca
Note: Ministre responsable des Affaires intergouvernementales canadiennes et de la Francophonie canadienne; et Ministreresponsable de la Réforme des institutions démocratiques et de l'Accès à l'information

Secrétaire général associé, Affaires intergouvernementales canadiennes, Yves Castonguay
Tél: 418-646-9562

Secrétaire adjointe, Suzanne Lévesque

Secrétaire adjointe, Francophonie canadienne, Sylvie Lachance
Tél: 418-643-4060

Responsable, Bureau du Secrétaire général associé/Responsable de l'accès à l'information, Cynthia Jean

Directeur, Réflexion stratégique, Simon Carmichael
Tél: 418-646-2483

Directeur, Politiques institutionnelles et constitutionnelles, Michel Frédérick
Tél: 418-528-0919

Directeur, Affaires économiques, culturelles et sociales, Artur J. Pires
Tél: 418-646-5914
Moncton
Bureau du Québec dans les Provinces atlantiques, #510, 777, rue Main, 5e étage, Moncton, NB E1C 1E9
Tél: 506-857-9851
Téléc: 506-857-9883
bqmoncton@mce.gouv.qc.ca
Chef de poste, Richard Barrette
Ottawa
Bureau du Québec à Ottawa, #300, 81 rue Metcalfe, 3e étage, Ottawa, ON K1P 6K7
Tél: 613-238-5322
Téléc: 613-563-9137
bqottawa@mce.gouv.qc.ca
Toronto
Bureau du Québec à Toronto, #1504, 20 rue Queen ouest, CP 13, Toronto, ON M5H 3S3
Tél: 416-977-6060
Téléc: 416-596-1407
bqtoronto@mce.gouv.qc.ca
Chef de poste, Paul-Arthur Huot
Vancouver
Antenne de Vancouver, #780, 789 rue Pender ouest, Vancouver, BC V6C 1H2
Tél: 604-682-3500
Téléc: 604-682-6670
vancouver@mce.gouv.qc.ca
Sous la responsabilité du Bureau du Québec à Toronto
Responsable, Paul-Arthur Huot

Ministère des Affaires municipales, des Régions et de l'Occupation du territoire / Municipal Affairs, Regions & Land Occupancy

Aile Chaveau, 10, rue Pierre-Olivier-Chauveau, 3e étage, Québec, QC G1R 4J3
Tél: 418-691-2019
Téléc: 418-643-7385
communications@mamrot.gouv.qc.ca
www.mamrot.gouv.qc.ca
A la charge de conseiller le gouvernement & d'assurer la coordination interministérielle dans ces domaines; a pour mission de favoriser la mise en place & le maintien d'un cadre de vie & de services municipaux de qualité pour des citoyens/citoyennes; le développement des régions & des milieux ruraux; & le progrès & le rayonnement de la métropole; intervient auprès des municipalités locales, régionales de comté, des communautés métropolitaines de Montréal & de Québec, & de l'administration régionale Kativik
Acts Administered:
Code municipal du Québec
Loi concernant la Ville de Schefferville
Loi concernant la consultation des citoyens sur la réorganisation territoriale
Loi concernant la négociation d'ententes relatives à la réduction des coûts de main-d'oeuvre dans le secteur municipal
Loi concernant la réglementation municipale des édifices publics
Loi concernant les droits sur les mutations immobilières
Loi instituant le fonds spécial de financement des activités locales
Loi modifiant de nouveau diverses dispositions législatives concernant le domaine municipal
Loi portant réforme de l'organisation territoriale municipale des régions métropolitaines de Montréal, de Québec et de l'Outaouais
Loi sur Immobilière SHQ
Loi sur l'aide municipale à la protection du public aux traverses de chemin de fer
Loi sur l'aménagement et l'urbanisme
Loi sur l'exercice de certaines compétences municipales dan certaines agglomérations
Loi sur l'expropriation
Loi sur l'instruction publique
Loi sur l'instruction publique pour les autochtones cris, inuits et naskapis

Loi sur l'interdiction de subventions municipales
Loi sur l'organisation territoriale municipale
Loi sur la Commission municipale
Loi sur la Communauté métropolitaine de Montréal
Loi sur la Communauté métropolitaine de Québec
Loi sur la Régie du logement
Loi sur la Société Innovatech du grand Montréal
Loi sur la Société d'habitation du Québec
Loi sur la Société du Parc industriel et portuaire de Bécancour
Loi sur la Société québécoise d'assainissement des eaux
Loi sur la conservation du patrimoine naturel
Loi sur la conservation et la mise en valeur de la faune
Loi sur la fiscalité municipale
Loi sur la police
Loi sur la qualité de l'environnement
Loi sur le Ministère de l'Agriculture, des Pêcheries et de l'Alimentation
Loi sur le Ministère du Développement durable, de l'Environnement et des Parcs
Loi sur le développement de la région de la Baie-James
Loi sur le régime de retraite des élus municipaux
Loi sur le traitement des élus municipaux
Loi sur les abus préjudiciables à l'agriculture
Loi sur les cités et villes
Loi sur les compétences municipales
Loi sur les conseils intermunicipaux de transport dans la région de Montréal
Loi sur les cours municipales
Loi sur les dettes et les emprunts municipaux
Loi sur les espèces menacées ou vulnérables
Loi sur les immeubles industriels municipaux
Loi sur les impôts
Loi sur les régimes de retraite des maires et des conseillers des municipalités
Loi sur les sociétés d'économie mixte dans le secteur municipal
Loi sur les sociétés de transport en commun
Loi sur les travaux municipaux
Loi sur les villages Nordiques et l'Administration régionale Kativik
Loi sur les villages cris et le village Naskapi
Loi sur les élections et les référendums dans les municipalités

Ministre, L'hon. Sylvain Gaudreault
Tél: 418-691-2050
Téléc: 418-643-1795
ministre@mamrot.gouv.qc.ca

Sous-ministre, Sylvain Boucher
Tél: 418-691-2040
Téléc: 418-643-7708

Sous-ministre adjoint, Métropole, Claire Deronzier
Tél: 514-873-8395

Sous-ministre adjoint, Infrastructures & finances municipales, Frédéric Guay
Tél: 418-691-2040

Sous-ministre adjointe, Territoires, Linda Morin
Tél: 418-691-2040

Sous-ministre adjoint, Politiques, Jérôme Unterberg
Tél: 418-691-2040

Secrétariat général, Stéphanie Jourdain
Tél: 418-691-2040

Directeur, Affaires juridiques, Nicolas Paradis
Tél: 418-691-2022

Infrastructures et finances municipales / Infrastructures & Municipal Financing
Sous-ministre adjoint, Frédéric Guay
Tél: 418-691-2040
Directeur général, Infrastructures, Pierre Aubé
Tél: 418-691-2005
Directeur général, Finances municipales, Jean Monfet
Tél: 418-691-2007

Métropole / Metropolitan Regions
800, rue du Square-Victoria, bureau 2.17, CP 83, Montréal, QC H4Z 1B7
Tél: 514-873-8246
Téléc: 514-864-7082
Sous-ministre adjoint, Claire Deronzier
Tél: 514-873-8395
Directeur, Développement régional & métropolitain, Hubert De Nicolini
Tél: 514-873-6992
Directrice métropolitaine, Aménagement et des affaires municipales, Lucie Tremblay
Tél: 514-873-8246

Politiques / Policy
Sous-ministre adjoint, Jérôme Unterberg
Tél: 418-691-2040
Directrice générale, Urbanisme/Aménagement du territoire, Marie-Lise Côté
Tél: 418-691-2015
Directeur général, Fiscalité, Bernard Guay
Tél: 418-691-2035
Directeur, Évaluation foncière, Luc Sauvageau
Tél: 418-691-2044
Directrice générale, Politiques, Jocelyn Savoie
Tél: 418-691-2015 ext: 352

Services à la gestion / Administrative Services
Directeur général, Raymond Sarrazin
Tél: 418-691-2015
Directrice (par intérim), Ressources humaines/Performance organisationnelle, Kathleen Dumont
Tél: 418-691-2025
Directrice, Ressources financières et matérielles, Sylvie Plante
Tél: 418-691-2001

Territoires / Regions
Sous-ministre adjointe, Linda Morin
Tél: 418-691-2040
Directeur général, Information territoriale, Dominique Jodoin
Tél: 418-691-2088
Directrice générale, Affaires territoriales, Marie-Claude Samuel
Directeur, Géomatique, et de la statistique, Sylvain Goulet
Directeur, Économie numérique, Daniel Roberge
Directeur (par intérim), Régional, rural, et de l'économie sociale, Yannick Routhier
Tél: 418-691-2078

Abitibi-Témiscamingue
#105, 170, av Principale, 1er étage, Rouyn-Noranda, QC J9X 4P7
Tél: 819-763-3582
Téléc: 819-763-3803
dr.abitibi-temis@mamrot.gouv.qc.ca
Directeur, Denis Moffet
Tél: 519-763-3582

Bas-Saint-Laurent
337, rue Moreault, 2e étage, Rimouski, QC G5L 1P4
Tél: 418-727-3629
Téléc: 418-727-3537
dr.bas-st-laur@mamrot.gouv.qc.ca
Directeur, Gilles Julien
Tél: 418-727-3629

Capitale-Nationale
Aile Chauveau, 10, rue Pierre-Olivier-Chauveau, 3e étage, Québec, QC G1R 4J3
Tél: 418-691-2016
Téléc: 418-643-2206
dr.capnat@mamrot.gouv.qc.a
Directeur, Jean Dionne
Tél: 418-691-2060

Centre-du-Québec
le Chauveau, 62, rue Saint-Jean-Baptiste, #S-05, Québec, QC G6P 4E3
Tél: 819-752-2453
Téléc: 819-795-3673
dr.centre-quebec@mamrot.gouv.qc.a
Directeur, Gaétan Désilets
Tél: 819-752-2453

Chaudière-Appalaches
#102, 1100, boul Frontenac est, Thetford Mines, QC G6G 6H1
Tél: 418-338-4624
Téléc: 418-338-1908
dr.chaud-app@mamrot.gouv.qc.ca
Directrice, Danie Croteau
Tél: 418-338-4624

Côte-Nord
625, boul Laflèche, #RC-708, Baie-Comeau, QC G5C 1C5
Tél: 418-295-4241
Téléc: 418-295-4955
dr.cotenord@mamrot.gouv.qc.ca
Directeur, Jacques Tremblay
Tél: 418-295-4241

Estrie
#4.04, 200, rue Belvédère nord, Sherbrooke, QC J1H 4A9
Tél: 819-820-3244
Téléc: 819-820-3979
dr.estrie@mamrot.gouv.qc.ca
Directeur, Pierre Poulin
Tél: 819-820-3244

Gaspésie—Iles-de-la-Madeleine
#10B, 500, av Daigneault, Chandler, QC G0C 1K0
Tél: 418-689-5024
Téléc: 418-689-4823
dr.gaspe-ilesmad@mamrot.gouv.qc.ca
Directeur, Michel Gionest
Tél: 418-689-5024

Lanaudière
#3200, 40, rue Gauthier sud, Joliette, QC J6E 4J4
Tél: 450-752-8080
Téléc: 450-752-8087
dr.lanaudiere@mamrot.gouv.qc.ca
Directeur, Jean Ouellet
Tél: 450-752-8060

Laurentides
#210, 161, rue de la Gare, Saint-Jérôme, QC J7Z 2B9
Tél: 450-569-7646
Téléc: 450-569-3131
dr.laurentides@mamrot.gouv.qc.ca
Directeur, Jean Ouellet
Tél: 450-569-7646

Mauricie
#321, 100, rue Laviolette, 3e étage, Trois-Rivières, QC G9A 5S9
Tél: 819-371-6653
Téléc: 819-371-6953
dr.mauricie@mamrot.gouv.qc.ca
Directeur, Pierre Robert
Tél: 819-371-6653

Montérégie
#403, 201, place Charles-Le Moyne, Longueuil, QC J4K 2T5
Tél: 450-928-5670
Téléc: 450-928-5673
dr.monteregie@mamrot.gouv.qc.ca
Directeur, Robert Sabourin
Tél: 450-926-5670

Nord-du-Québec
#1, 215, 3e Rue, Chibougamau, QC G8P 1N3
Tél: 418-748-7737
Téléc: 418-748-7841
nord-du-quebec@mamrot.gouv.qc.ca
Directeur, Richard Leclerc
Tél: 418-748-7738

Outaouais
#9.300, 170, rue de l'Hôtel-de-Ville, Gatineau, QC J8X 4C2
Tél: 819-772-3006
Téléc: 819-772-3989
dr.outaouais@mamrot.gouv.qc.ca
Directeur (par intérim), Yannick Gignac
Tél: 819-772-3006

Saguenay—Lac-Saint-Jean
227, rue Racine est, #RC.03, Chicoutimi, QC G7H 7B4
Tél: 418-698-3523
Téléc: 418-698-3526
dr.sag-lac@mamrot.gouv.qc.ca
Directeur, Jean Dionne
Tél: 418-698-3523

Ministère de l'Agriculture, des Pêcheries et de l'Alimentation (MAPAQ) / Agriculture, Fisheries & Food

200, ch Sainte-Foy, Québec, QC G1R 4X6
Tél: 418-380-2110
Ligne sans frais: 888-222-6272
www.mapaq.gouv.qc.ca

Le Ministère influence et appuie l'essor de l'industrie bioalimentaire québécoise dans une perspective de développement durable; réalise des interventions en production, transformation, commercialisation & consommation des produits agricoles, marins & alimentaires; & joue un rôle important en matière de recherche & de développement, d'enseignement & de formation

Acts Administered:
Code municipal du Québec/Municipal Code of Québec (certain sections)
La Charte de la Ville de Sherbrooke/The Charter of the City of Sherbrooke (certain sections)
La Charte de la Ville de Trois-Rivières/The Charter of the City of Trois-Rivières (certain sections)
La Charte de la ville de Québec/The Charter of the City of Québec (certain sections)
Loi sur l'acquisition de terres agricoles par des non-résidants/An Act governing the acquisition of farm land by non-residents
Loi sur l'aquaculture commerciale/ An Act respecting commercial aquaculture
Loi sur l'assurance-prêts agricoles et forestiers/An Act respecting farm-loan insurance & forestry-loan insurance
Loi sur l'assurance-récolte/Crop Insurance Act
Loi sur l'assurance-stabilisation des revenus agricoles/An Act respecting farm income stabilization insurance
Loi sur l'école de laiterie et les écoles moyennes d'agriculture/An Act respecting the École de laiterie & intermediate agricultural schools
Loi sur la commercialisation des produits marins/An Act respecting the marketing of marine products
Loi sur la conservation et la mise en valeur de la faune/An Act respecting the conservation & development of wildlife
Loi sur la protection des animaux pur sang/Thoroughbred Cattle Act
Loi sur la protection des plantes/Plant Protection Act

Loi sur la protection sanitaire des animaux/Animal Health Protection Act
Loi sur la transformation des produits marins/The Marine Products Processing Act
Loi sur le Mérite national de la restauration et de l'alimentation/Restaurant Merit Act
Loi sur le financement de la pêche commerciale/Maritime Fisheries Credit Act
Loi sur le ministère de l'Agriculture, des Pêcheries et de l'Alimentation/An Act respecting the Ministère de l'Agriculture, des Pêcheries et de l'Alimentation
Loi sur le mérite national de la pêche et de l'aquaculture/Fishermen's Merit Act
Loi sur les abus préjudiciables à l'agriculture/Agricultural Abuses Act
Loi sur les appellations réservées et les termes valorisants
Loi sur les cités et villes/Cities & Towns Act (certain sections)
Loi sur les producteurs agricoles/Farm Producers Act
Loi sur les produits agricoles, les produits marins et les aliments/Farm, Food & Fishery Products Act
Loi sur les produits alimentaires/Food Products Act
Loi sur les pêcheries commerciales et la récolte commerciale de végétaux aquatiques
Loi sur les races animales du Patrimoine agricole du Qu ébec
Loi sur les sociétés agricoles et laitières/An Act respecting farmers' & dairymen's associations
Loi sur les sociétés d'horticulture/Horticultural Societies Act
Loi sur les terres agricoles du domaine de l'État/An Act respecting agricultural lands in the domain of the state
Ordre national du mérite agricole/Agricultural Merit Act

Ministre, L'hon François Gendron
Tél: 418-380-2525
Téléc: 418-380-2184
ministre.mapaq@mapaq.gouv.qc.ca

Sous-ministre, Norman Johnston
Tél: 418-380-2136
Téléc: 418-380-2171

Sous-ministre associée, Transformation Alimentaire Québec, Dominique Fortin
Tél: 418-380-2136
Téléc: 418-380-2171

Agences, Conseils et Commissions Associés/ Associated Agencies, Boards & Commissions:

• Commission de protection du territoire agricole du Québec / Agricultural Land Preservation Commission
200, ch Ste-Foy, 2e étage
Québec, QC G1R 4X6
Tél: 418-643-3314
Téléc: 418-643-2261
Ligne sans frais: 800-667-5294
info@cptaq.gouv.qc.ca
www.cptaq.gouv.qc.ca

• La financière agricole de Québec
1400, boul de la Rive-Sud
Saint-Romuald, QC G6W 8K7
Tél: 418-838-5602
Téléc: 418-833-3871
Ligne sans frais: 800-749-3646
financiereagricole@fadq.qc.ca
www.financiereagricole.qc.ca

• Régie des marchés agricoles et alimentaires du Québec / Québec Agriculture & Food Marketing Board
201, boul Crémazie est, 5e étage
Montréal, QC H2M 1L3
Tél: 514-873-4024
Téléc: 514-873-3984
www.rmaaq.gouv.qc.ca

Pêches et aquaculture commerciales / Commercial Fishing & Aquaculture
Sous-ministre adjointe, Hélène Vincent
Tel: 418-380-2136
Fax: 418-380-2171
Directeur, Analyses et politiques, Abdoul Aziz Niang
Tel: 418-380-2100 ext: 338
Fax: 418-380-2182

Directions régionales/Regional Offices
Directions régionales/Regional Offices
Côte-Nord
466, av Arnaud, Sept-îles, QC G4R 3B1
Tél: 418-964-8521
Téléc: 418-964-8744
drcn@mapag.gouv.qc.ca

Directeur régional, Alain Côté
Estuaire et eaux intérieures
460, boul Louis-Fréchette, RC, Nicolet, QC J3T 1Y2
Tél: 819-293-5677
Téléc: 819-293-8519
dreei@mapaq.gouv.qc.ca

Directeur régional, Denis Lacerte
Gaspésie
#205, 96, montée de Sandy Beach, Gaspé, QC G4X 2V6
Tél: 418-368-7630
Téléc: 418-360-8851
drg@mapaq.gouv.qc.ca

Directeur régional, Marcel Roussy
îles-de-la-Madeleine
Édifice Réjean-Richard, 101-125, ch du Parc, Cap-aux-Meules, QC G4T 1B3
Tél: 418-986-2098
Téléc: 418-986-4421
drim@mapaq.gouv.qc.ca

Directeur régional, Donald Arseneau

Transformation Alimentaire Québec / Food Processing Québec
Sous-ministre associé, Dominique Fortin
Tel: 418-380-2136
Fax: 418-380-2171
Directeur (par intérim), Amélioration de la compétitivité & analyses stratégiques, Denis Desrosiers
Directrice, Développement des marchés intérieurs & affaires ministérielles, France St-Onge
Tel: 514-873-4147 ext: 522
Directeur (par intérim), Développement des marchés extérieurs & entreprises, Bernard Houle
Tel: 514-873-4147 ext: 524
bernard.houle@mapaq.gouv.qc.ca

Développement régional et développement durable / Regional Development/Sustainable Development
Sous-ministre adjoint, Michel Bonneau
Coordinateur, Opérations régionales, Sylvain Tremblay
Directeur, Soutien à l'enregistrement & remboursement des taxes, François Michaud
Directrice, Appui au développement des entreprises et de l'aménagement du territoire, Hélène Doddridge
Directeur, Agroenvironnement et développement durable, Michel Riendeau
Abitibi-Témiscamingue - Nord-du-Québec
#2.01, 180, boul Rideau, Rouyn-Noranda, QC J9X 1N9
Tél: 819-763-3287
Téléc: 819-763-3359

Directrice régionale, Line Charland
Montérégie - Secteur Est
#3300, 1355, rue Johnson ouest, Saint-Hyacinthe, QC J2S 8W7
Tél: 450-778-6530
Téléc: 450-778-6540

Directeur régional, Jean-Pierre Lessard
Capitale Nationale
#RC.22, 1685, boul Wilfrid-Hamel ouest, Québec, QC G1N 3Y7
Tél: 418-643-0033
Téléc: 418-644-8263

Directrice régionale, Suzanne Pilote
Saguenay—Lac-Saint-Jean
801, ch du Pont-Taché nord, Alma, QC G8B 5W2
Tél: 418-662-6457
Téléc: 418-668-8694
Ligne sans frais: 866-727-6584

Directeur régional, Sylvie Denis

Santé animale & inspection des aliments / Animal Health & Food Inspection
dgsaia@mapaq.gouv.qc.ca
Sous-ministre adjointe, Madeleine Fortin
Tel: 418-380-2136
Fax: 418-380-2171
Directeur, Inspection des aliments - Secteur Est et Ouest, Guy Caron
Directeur, Inspection des aliments, Michel Houle
Directrice, Coordination administrative et Services à la clientèle, Michèle Lavoie
Tel: 418-380-2100
Fax: 418-380-2169
Directrice, Laboratoire d'expertises et d'analyses alimentaires, Ginette Levesque
Tel: 418-266-4440
Fax: 418-266-4438
dleaa@mapaq.gouv.qc.ca
#C 2.105, 2700, rue Einstein
Sainte-Foy, QC G1P 3W8 Canada
Directeur, Inspection des viandes, Claude Rivard
Tel: 418-380-2100
Fax: 418-380-2169
Directeur, Développement et réglementation, Geneviève Rousseau

Directions régionales/Regional Offices
Directions régionales/Regional Offices
Bas-Saint-Laurent - Gaspésie - Iles-de-la-Madeleine - Saguenay - Lac Saint Jean
#2, 1600, rue Bersimis, Chicoutimi, QC G7K 1H9
Tél: 418-698-3530
Téléc: 418-698-3533

Directrice régionale, Johanne Martel
Laurentides - Outaouais - Abitibi-Témiscamingue
Galeries de Buckingham, 999, rue Dollard, Gatineau, QC J8L 3E6
Tél: 819-986-8985
Téléc: 819-986-9793

Directrice régionale, Joanne Twigg
Mauricie - Centre-du-Québec - Estrie
#55, 5195, boul des Forges, Trois-Rivières, QC G8Y 4Z3
Tél: 819-475-8506
Téléc: 819-371-4907

Directeur régional, Guy Caron
Montréal - Laval - Lanaudière
201, boul Crémazie est, 2e étage, Montréal, QC H2M 1L4
Tél: 514-873-8101
Téléc: 514-873-9994

Directeur régional (par intérim), Guy Caron
Québec - Chaudière-Appalaches
#C RC.245, 2700, rue Einstein, Québec, QC G1P 3W8
Tél: 418-643-6140
Téléc: 418-644-6327

Directeur régional, Laurent Bolduc

Ministère de la Culture, des Communications & de la Condition féminine / Culture, Communications & the Status of Women

225, Grande Allée est, Québec, QC G1R 5G5
Ligne sans frais: 888-380-8882
www.mcccf.gouv.qc.ca

Acts Administered:
Charte de la langue française
Loi sur Bibliothèque et archives nationales du Québec
Loi sur la Société de développement des entreprises culturelles
Loi sur la Société de la Place des Arts de Montréal
Loi sur la Société de télédiffusion du Québec
Loi sur la Société du Grand Théâtre de Québec
Loi sur la programmation éducative
Loi sur le Conseil des arts et des lettres du Québec
Loi sur le Conservatoire de musique et d'art dramatique du Québec
Loi sur le Musée des beaux-arts de Montréal
Loi sur le cinéma
Loi sur le développement des entreprises québécoises dans le domaine du livre
Loi sur le ministère de la Culture et des Communications
Loi sur le statut professionnel des artistes des arts visuels, des métiers d'art et de la littérature et sur leurs contrats avec les diffuseurs
Loi sur le statut professionnel et les conditions d'engagement des artistes de la scène, du disque et du cinéma
Loi sur les archives
Loi sur les biens culturels
Loi sur les concours artistiques, littéraires et scientifiques
Loi sur les musées nationaux

Ministre, L'hon. Maka Kotto
Tél: 418-380-2310
Téléc: 418-380-2311
ministre@mcccf.gouv.qc.ca

Sous-ministre, Rachel Laperriere
Tél: 418-380-2330
Téléc: 418-380-2391

Sous-ministre adjointe, Secrétariat à la condition féminine, Thérèse Mailloux
Tél: 418-646-8395
Téléc: 418-643-4991
therese.mailloux@mcccf.gouv.qc.ca

Responsable, Planification stratégique, Jacques Laflamme
Tél: 418-380-2362
Téléc: 418-380-2345
jacques.laflamme@mcccf.gouv.qc.ca

Responsable, Secrétariat à la diversité culturelle, Dave Atkinson
Tél: 418-380-2372
Téléc: 418-380-2340
dave.atkinson@mcccf.gouv.qc.ca

Directrice, Communications & affaires publiques, Colette Duval
Tél: 418-380-2363
Téléc: 418-380-2364
colette.duval@mcccf.gouv.qc.ca

Directeur, Affaires juridiques, Daniel Morin
Tél: 418-643-3747 ext: 208
Téléc: 418-646-6849

Directeur, Planification stratégique et évolution organisationnelle, Jacques Laflamme

Directrice, Bureau de la sous-ministre, Sophie Magnan

Directeur général, Administration, Denis Charland

Directeur, Technologies de l'information, Louis Guilbault
Tél: 418-380-2312
Téléc: 418-380-2314
louis.guilbault@mcccf.gouv.qc.ca

Directrice, Ressources humaines, gestion immobilière et communication interne, Marc Tremblay
Tél: 418-380-2358
Téléc: 418-380-2364

Directeur, Financement des sociétés d'État, Patrick Tessier

Directeur, Ressources financières et matérielles, Geneviève Vézina
Tél: 418-380-2301
Téléc: 418-380-2302
genevieve.vezina@mcccf.gouv.qc.ca

Directeur général, Interventions régionales et immobilisations, Jean Bissonnette

Directeur, Immobilisations et intégration des arts à l'architecture, Martin Pineault

Action territoriale
Sous-ministre adjointe, Louis Vallée
Tél: 418-380-2330
Téléc: 418-380-2392
louis.vallee@mcccf.gouv.qc.ca
Directeur générale, Interventions régionales et immobilisations, Jean Bissonnette
Tél: 418-380-2348
Téléc: 418-380-2349
jean.bissonnette@mcccf.gouv.qc.ca
Directrice, Coordination des programmes, Richard Saint-Pierre
Directeur, Affaires internationales & Relations intergouvernementales, Michel Lafleur
Tél: 418-380-2335
Téléc: 418-380-2340
michel.lafleur@mcccf.gouv.qc.ca
Abitibi-Témiscamingue et Nord-du-Québec
#450, 19, rue Perreault ouest, Rouyn-Noranda, QC J9X 6N5
Tél: 819-763-3517
Téléc: 819-763-3382
dratnq@mcccf.gouv.qc.ca
Directrice, Monik Duhaime
monik.duhaime@mcccf.gouv.qc.ca
Bas-St-Laurent
337, rue Moreault, # RC-12, Rimouski, QC G5L 1P4
Tél: 418-727-3650
Téléc: 418-727-3824
drbsl@mcccf.gouv.qc.ca
Directeur (par intérim), Louis Landry
Capitale-Nationale
Bloc C, RC, 225, Grande-Allée est, Québec, QC G1R 5G5
Tél: 418-380-2346
Téléc: 418-380-2347
dcn@mcccf.gouv.qc.ca
Directeur, Claude Fleury
Tél: 418-380-2346 ext: 703
Chaudière-Appalaches
51, rue du Mont-Marie, Lévis, QC G6V 0C3
Tél: 418-838-9886
Téléc: 418-838-1485
drca@mcccf.gouv.qc.ca
Directrice, Nicole Champagne
Tél: 418-838-9886 ext: 0
nicole.champagne@mcccf.gouv.qc.ca
Côte-Nord
#1.806, 625, boul Laflèche, Baie-Comeau, QC G5C 1C5
Tél: 418-295-4979
Téléc: 418-295-4070
drcn@mcccf.gouv.qc.ca
Directrice, Françoise Aubry
francoise.aubry@mcccf.gouv.qc.ca
Estrie
#410, 225, rue Frontenac, Sherbrooke, QC J1H 1K1
Tél: 819-820-3007
Téléc: 819-820-3930
dre@mcccf.gouv.qc.ca
Directrice, Jocelyne Jacques
Tél: 819-820-3012
jocelyne.jacques@mcccf.gouv.qc.ca
Gaspésie—Iles-de-la-Madeleine
146, av de Grand-Pré, Bonaventure, QC G0C 1E0
Tél: 418-534-4431
Téléc: 418-534-4564
drgim@mcccf.gouv.qc.ca
Directrice, Hélène Latérière
helene.lateriere@mcccf.gouv.qc.ca
Laval, Lanaudière et les Laurentides
#200, 300, rue Sicard, Sainte-Thérèse, QC J7E 3X5
Tél: 450-430-3737
Téléc: 450-430-2475
drlll@mcccf.gouv.qc.ca
Directeur, Gilbert Lepage
Tél: 450-430-2271
Mauricie et Centre-du-Québec
#315, 100, rue Laviolette, Trois-Rivières, QC G9A 5S9
Tél: 819-387-6001
Téléc: 819-371-6984
drmcq@mcccf.gouv.qc.ca
Directeur (par interim), Jean Bissonnette
Montérégie
#500, 2, boul Desaulniers, Saint-Lambert, QC J4P 1L2
Tél: 450-671-1231
Téléc: 450-671-3884
drmonter@mcccf.gouv.qc.ca
Directrice, Annie Goudreault
annie.goudreault@mcccf.gouv.qc.ca
Montréal
#600, 480, boul St-Laurent, Montréal, QC H2Y 3Y7
Tél: 514-873-2255
Téléc: 514-864-2448
dm@mcccf.gouv.qc.ca
Directrice, Hélène Binette
Outaouais
#4.140, 170, rue de l'Hôtel-de-Ville, 4e étage, Gatineau, QC J8X 4C2
Tél: 819-772-3002
Téléc: 819-772-3950
dro@mcccf.gouv.qc.ca
Directrice, Anne-Marie Gendron
Tél: 819-772-3282
anne-marie.gendron@mcccf.gouv.qc.ca
Saguenay—Lac-Saint-Jean
202, rue Jacques-Cartier est, Chicoutimi, QC G7H 6R8
Tél: 418-698-3500
Téléc: 418-698-3522
drslstj@mcccf.gouv.qc.ca
Directeur, Réjean Goudreault
rejean.goudreault@mcccf.gouv.qc.ca

Politiques, patrimoine, muséologie & communications / Policy, Heritage, Museology & Communication
Sous-ministre adjoint, France Dionne
Tél: 418-380-2330
Téléc: 418-380-2331
france.dionne@mcccf.gouv.qc.ca
Directeur général, Centre de conservation du Québec, René Bouchard
Tél: 418-643-7001
Téléc: 418-646-5419
Directeur général, Politiques de culture & de communications, Daniel Cloutier
Tél: 418-380-2365 ext: 636
Téléc: 418-380-2340
daniel.cloutier@mcccf.gouv.qc.ca
Directrice, Patrimoine et muséologie, Danielle Dubé
Tél: 418-380-2352
Téléc: 418-380-2336
Directrice, Médias & télécommunications, Louise Gingras
Tél: 418-380-2307
Téléc: 418-380-2316
louise.gingras@mcccf.gouv.qc.ca
Directrice, Développement des services, Francine Lalonde
Tél: 418-380-2333
Téléc: 418-380-2324
francine.lalonde@mcccf.gouv.qc.ca
Directrice, Lectorat & politiques, Giles Simard
Responsable, Secrétariat à la condition socioéconomique des artistes, Gaétan Patenaude
Tél: 418-380-2322 ext: 737
Téléc: 418-380-2345
gaetan.pateneaude@mcccf.gouv.qc.ca

Secrétariat à la Condition féminine / Status of Women Secretariat
#905, av Honoré-Mercier, 3e étage, Québec, QC G1R 5M6
Tél: 418-643-9052
Téléc: 418-643-4991
www.scf.gouv.qc.ca
Ministre responsable, l'hon. Agnès Maltais
Sous-ministre adjointe, Thérèse Mailloux
Tél: 418-646-8395
Téléc: 418-643-4991
Directrice, Régionalisation, Michèle Grenier
Directrice, Coordination et de l'administration, Gina Morency
Tél: 418-644-4417
Téléc: 418-643-4991

Bibliothèque et Archives nationales du Québec (BAnQ) / National Library & Archives of Québec
475, boul De Maisonneuve est, Montréal, QC H2L 5C4
Tél: 514-873-1100
Téléc: 514-873-9312
Ligne sans frais: 800-363-9028
www.banq.qc.ca
Président-directeur générale, Guy Berthiaume

Commission des biens culturels du Québec / Québec Cultural Property Commission
Bloc A-RC, 225, Grande Allée est, Québec, QC G1R 5G5
Tél: 418-643-8378
Téléc: 418-643-8591
info@cbcq.gouv.qc.ca
www.cbcq.gouv.qc.ca
Président, Yves Lefebvre
Vice-présidente, Ann Mundy

Conseil des arts et des lettres du Québec
79, boul René-Lévesque est, 3e étage, Québec, QC G1R 5N5
Tél: 418-643-1707
Téléc: 418-643-4558
Ligne sans frais: 800-897-1707
info@calq.gouv.qc.ca
www.calq.gouv.qc.ca
Secondary Address: 500, Place d'Armes, 15e étage Montréal, QC H2Y 2W2 Canada
Président et Directeur général, Yvan Gauthier

Musée d'art contemporain de Montréal (MACM) / Montréal Museum of Contemporary Art
185, rue Ste-Catherine ouest, Montréal, QC H2X 3X5
Tél: 514-847-6226
Téléc: 514-847-6290
info@macm.org
www.macm.org
Directrice Générale, Paulette Gagnon

Musée de la civilisation / Museum of Civilisation
85, rue Dalhousie, CP 155 B, Québec, QC G1K 7A6
Tél: 418-643-2158
Téléc: 418-646-9705
Ligne sans frais: 866-710-8031
mcqweb@mcq.org
www.mcq.org
Présidente, Margaret Delisle
Directrice générale, Danielle Poiré

Musée national des beaux-arts du Québec
Parc des Champs-de-Bataille, 1, av Wolfe-Montcalm, Québec, QC G1R 5H3
Tél: 418-643-2150
Téléc: 418-646-3330
Ligne sans frais: 866-220-2150
webmestre@mnba.qc.ca
www.mnba.qc.ca
Directrice générale, Sylvie Desjardins
Tél: 418-644-6460 ext: 222
sylvie.desjardins@mnba.qc.ca
Conseillère juridique, Louise Pradet-Jobin
Tél: 418-644-6460 ext: 444
Téléc: 418-644-1067
louise.jobin@mnba.qc.ca

Régie du cinéma / Film Board
#100, 390, rue Notre-Dame ouest, Montréal, QC H2Y 1T9
Tél: 514-873-2371
Téléc: 514-873-8874
Ligne sans frais: 800-463-2463
regieducinema@rcq.gouv.qc.ca
www.rcq.gouv.qc.ca
Présidente, France Boucher
Directeur, Planification & communications, Robert Arthur

Secrétariat à la politique linguistique / French Language Board
225 Grande-Allée est, 4e étage, Québec, QC G1R 5G5
Tél: 418-643-4248
Téléc: 418-646-7832
info@spl.gouv.qc.ca
www.spl.gouv.qc.ca
Sous-ministre associé responsable de l'application de la politique linguistique, Jacques Gosselin

Société de développement des entreprises culturelles (SODEC) / Arts & Cultural Enterprise Development Commission
#800, 215, rue Saint-Jacques, Montréal, QC H2Y 1M6
Tél: 514-841-2200
Téléc: 514-841-8606
Ligne sans frais: 800-363-0401
info@sodec.gouv.qc.ca
www.sodec.gouv.qc.ca
Secondary Address: 36 1/2, rue St-Pierre
Québec, QC G1K 3Z6 Canada
Téléc: 418-643-8918
capitale@sodec.gouv.qc.ca
Président, François Macerola
Directeur des affaires juridiques & Secrétaire, Jean Valois
Directrice générale, Contrôle & gestion financière, Carole Hamelin

Société de la Place des Arts de Montréal / Montréal Place des Arts Corporation
260, boul de Maisonneuve ouest, Montréal, QC H2X 1Y9
Tél: 514-285-4200
Téléc: 514-285-1968
info@pda.qc.ca
www.pda.qc.ca
Présidente-Directrice générale, Marie Lavigne

Société de télédiffusion du Québec (Télé-Québec) / Radio-Québec
1000, rue Fullum, Montréal, QC H2K 3L7
Tél: 514-521-2424
Téléc: 514-873-2601
Ligne sans frais: 800-361-4362
info@telequebec.tv
www.telequebec.tv
Présidente-directrice générale, Michèle Fortin

Société du Grand Théâtre de Québec / Grand Theatre of Québec
269, boul René-Lévesque est, Québec, QC G1R 2B3
Tél: 418-643-8111
gtq@grandtheatre.qc.ca
www.grandtheatre.qc.ca
Président-directeur général, Marcel Dallaire

Ministère du Développement durable, de l'Environnement, de la Faune, et des Parcs / Sustainable Development, Environment, Wildlife & Parks

Édifice Marie-Guyart, 675, boul René-Lévesque est, 29e étage, Québec, QC G1R 5V7
Tél: 418-521-3830
Téléc: 418-646-5974
Ligne sans frais: 800-561-1616
info@mddep.gouv.qc.ca
www.mddep.gouv.qc.ca
A pour mission d'assurer la protection de l'environnement & des écosystèmes naturels; de promouvoir le développement durable & d'assurer à la population un environnement sain en harmonie avec le développement économique & le progrès social du Québec
Acts Administered:
Agricultural Operations Regulation, 2002
Groundwater Catchment Regulation, 2002
Land Protection & Rehabilitation Regulation, 2003
Loi portant restrictions à l'élevage de porcs/Act to Impose Restrictions on Pig Farming, 2002
Loi portant sur la délimitation de la ligne des hautes eaux du Fleuve Saint-Laurent sur le territoire de la municipalité régionale de comté de la Côte-de-Beaupré/An Act to delimit the high water mark of the St. LawrenceRiver in the territory of Municipa
Loi sur la Société des établissements de plein air du Québec
Loi sur la Société québécoise de récupération et de recyclage
Loi sur la conservation du patrimoine naturel/Natural Heritage Conservation Act
Loi sur la conservation et la mise en valeur de la faune/Act respecting the Conservation & Development of Wildlife (in part)
Loi sur la protection des arbres/Tree Protection Act
Loi sur la provocation artificielle de la pluie/Act respecting the artificial inducement of rain
Loi sur la qualité de l'environnement/Environment Quality Act
Loi sur la sécurité des barrages/Dam Safety Act
Loi sur la vente et la distribution de bière et de boissons gazeuses dans des contenants à remplissage unique/Act respecting the Sale & Distribution of Beer & Soft Drinks in Non-returnable Containers
Loi sur le Parc Forillon et des environs
Loi sur le développement durable
Loi sur le ministère du Développement durable, de l'Environnement et des Parcs
Loi sur le parc de la Mauricie et ses environs
Loi sur le parc marin du Saguenay—Saint-Laurent
Loi sur le régime des eaux/Watercourses Act
Loi sur les espèces menacées ou vulnérables/Act respecting Threatened or Vulnerable Species
Loi sur les parcs
Loi sur les pesticides/Pesticides Act
Loi sur les villages cris et le village naskapi/The Cree Villages and the Naskapi Village Act
Loi visant la préservation des ressources en eau/Water Resources Preservation Act
Pesticides Management Code, 2003
Regulation Respecting Waste Water Disposal Systems for Isolated Dwellings
Regulation respecting Compensation for Municipal Services Provided to Recover & Reclaim Residual Materials
Regulation respecting Environmental Impact Assessments & review applicable to part of Northeastern Québec
Regulation respecting Halocarbons
Regulation respecting Hazardous Materials
Regulation respecting Hot Mix Asphalt Plants
Regulation respecting Industrial Depollution Attestations
Regulation respecting Motor Vehicle Traffic in Certain Fragile Environments
Regulation respecting Permits & Certificates for the Sale & Use of Pesticides
Regulation respecting Pits & Quarries
Regulation respecting Prevention of Water Pollution in Livestock Operations
Regulation respecting Public Swimming & Wading Pools
Regulation respecting Pulp & Paper Mills
Regulation respecting Sanitary Conditions in Industrial or other Camps
Regulation respecting Snow Elimination Sites
Regulation respecting Solid Waste
Regulation respecting Used Tire Storage
Regulation respecting Waterworks & Sewer Services
Regulation respecting certain bodies for the protection of the environment and social milieu of the territory of James Bay and Northern Québec
Regulation respecting the Application of the Environment Quality Act
Regulation respecting the Artificial Inducement of Rain
Regulation respecting the Burial of Contaminated Soils
Regulation respecting the Liquid Effluents of Petroleum Refineries
Regulation respecting the Quality of Drinking Water
Regulation respecting the Quality of the Atmosphere
Regulation respecting the Recovery & Reclamation of Discarded Paint Containers & Paints
Regulation respecting the Recovery & Reclamation of Used Oils, Oil or Fluid Containers & Used Filters
Regulation respecting the Water Property in the Domain of the State, 2003
Regulation respecting the environmental and social impact assessment and review procedure applicable to the territory of James Bay and Northern Québec
Regulation respecting the environmental impact assessment and review applicable to a part of the northeastern Québec region
Regulation respecting threatened or vulnerable plant species and their habitats
Rules of internal management of the James Bay Advisory Committee on the Environment
Rules of internal management of the Katívik Environmental Advisory Committee

Ministre, L'hon. Daniel Breton
Tél: 418-521-3911
Téléc: 418-643-4143

Sous-ministre, Diane Jean
Tél: 418-521-3861 ext: 401
Téléc: 418-643-3619

Directeur du Cabinet, François Émond
Tél: 418-521-3911

Sous-ministre adjointe, Services à la gestion & au milieu terrestre, Brigitte Portelance

Sous-ministre adjoint, Changements climatiques, à l'air & à l'eau, Charles Larochelle

Sous-ministre adjoint, Développement durable, Léopold Gaudreau

Sous-ministre adjoint, Expertise hydrique, analyse et évaluations environnementales, Jacques Dupoint

Sous-ministre adjoint, Analyse & expertise régionales/Centre de contrôle environnemental du Québec, Michel Rousseau

Secrétaire générale et Directrice, Vérification interne, Caroline Drouin
Tél: 418-521-3810
Téléc: 418-646-4762

Directeur, Bureau des renseignements, de l'accès à l'information et des plaintes sur la qualité des services, Lise Rodrigues

Directrice, Affaires juridiques, Monique Rousseau
Tél: 418-521-3816 ext: 454
Téléc: 418-646-0908

Directeur, Communications, Jérôme Thibaudeau

Agences, Conseils et Commissions Associés/ Associated Agencies, Boards & Commissions:

• **Bureau d'audiences publiques sur l'environnement (BAPE) / Environmental Public Hearing Board**
Édifice Lomer-Gouin
#2.10, 575, rue Saint-Amable
Québec, QC G1R 6A6
Tél: 418-643-7447
Téléc: 418-643-9474
Ligne sans frais: 800-463-4732
communication@bape.gouv.qc.ca
www.bape.gouv.qc.ca
• **Comité consultatif de l'environnement Kativik (CCEK) / Kativik Environmental Advisory Committee**
CP 930
Kuujjuaq, QC J0M 1C0
Tél: 819-964-2961
Téléc: 819-964-0694
• **Société des établissements en plein air du Québec (SÉPAQ)**
Place de la Cité, Tour Cominar
#250, 2640, boul Laurier, 2e étage
Québec, QC G1V 5C2
Tel: 418-890-6527
Fax: 418-528-6025
Toll-free: 800-665-6527
inforeservation@sepaq.com
www.sepaq.com
• **Société québécoise de récupération et de recyclage (RECYC-QUÉBEC)**
#200, 420, boul Charest est
Québec, QC G1K 8M4
Tél: 418-643-0394
Téléc: 418-643-6507
Ligne sans frais: 866-523-8290
info@recyc-quebec.gouv.qc.ca
www.recyc-quebec.gouv.qc.ca
Autres numéros: Infoline: 1-800-807-0678; Montréal: 514-351-7835

Analyses environnementales et aux technologies de l'information / Environmental Analysis & Information Technology
Sous-ministre adjoint, Michel Gagnon
Directeur général, Technologies de l'information, Yvan Déry
Directeur général, Centre d'expertise en analyse environnementale du Québec, Guy Chouinard
Directeur, Solutions d'affaires, Yvan Béliveau
Directeur, Laboratoire des pollutions industrielles; Analyse et de l'étude de la qualité du milieu, Claude Laliberté
Directeur, Accréditation etdes relations externes, Louis Martel
Directeur, Technologies et de l'exploitation, Patrice Tremblay
Directrice, Pilotage des systèmes et de l'assistance aux utilisateurs, Céline Villeneuve

Analyse et expertise régionales / Regional Analysis & Expertise
Édifice Marie-Guyart, 675, boul René-Lévesque est, 30e étage, Québec, QC G1R 5V7
Tél: 418-521-3861
Téléc: 418-646-1800
La mission est d'assurer l'analyse & la délivrance d'autorisations environnementales & d'offrir une expertise professionnelle en matière d'environnement
Sous-ministre adjoint, Michel Rousseau
Tél: 418-521-3861
Téléc: 418-646-1800
Baie-Comeau
20, boul Comeau, Baie-Comeau, QC G4Z 3A8
Tél: 418-294-8888
Téléc: 418-294-8018
cote-nord@mddep.gouv.qc.ca
Directeur, Alain Gaudreault
Gatineau
#7.340, 170, rue de l'Hôtel-de-Ville, Gatineau, QC J8X 4C2
Tél: 819-772-3434
Téléc: 819-772-3952
outaouais@mddep.gouv.qc.ca
Directeur, Marc Dubreuil

Laval
850, boul Vanier, Laval, QC H7C 2M7
Tél: 450-661-2008
Téléc: 450-661-2217
laval@mddep.gouv.qc.ca
Directeur, Pierre Robert
Longueuil
201, Place Charles-Le Moyne, 2e étage, Longueuil, QC J4K 2T5
Tél: 450-928-7607
Téléc: 450-928-7625
monteregie@mddep.gouv.qc.ca
Directeur adjoint, Pierre Paquin
Montréal
#3860, 5199, rue Sherbrooke est, Montréal, QC H1T 3X9
Tél: 514-873-3636
Téléc: 514-873-5662
montreal@mddep.gouv.qc.ca
Directeur, Pierre Robert
Nicolet
1579, boul Louis-Fréchette, Nicolet, QC J3T 2A5
Tél: 819-293-4122
Téléc: 819-293-8322
centre-du-quebec@mddep.gouv.qc.ca
Directeur, Luc St-Martin
Québec
#100, 1175, boul Lebourgneuf, Québec, QC G2K 0B7
Tél: 418-644-8844
Téléc: 418-646-1214
capitale-nationale@mddep.gouv.qc.ca
Directrice, Isabelle Olivier
Repentigny
100, boul Industriel, Repentigny, QC J6A 4X6
Tél: 450-654-4355
Téléc: 450-654-6131
lanaudiere@mddep.gouv.qc.ca
Directeur, Pierre Robert
Rimouski
212, av Belzile, Rimouski, QC G5L 3C3
Tél: 418-727-3511
Téléc: 418-727-3849
bas-saint-laurent@mddep.gouv.qc.ca
Directeur, Jean-Marie Dionne
Rouyn-Noranda
180, boul Rideau, 1er étage, Rouyn-Noranda, QC J9X 1N9
Tél: 819-763-3333
Téléc: 819-763-3202
abitibi-temiscamingue@mddep.gouv.qc.ca
Directrice, Édith van de Walle
Saguenay
3950, boul Harvey, 4e étage, Saguenay, QC G7X 8L6
Tél: 418-695-7883
Téléc: 418-695-7897
saguenay-lac-saint-jean@mddep.gouv.qc.ca
Directrice, Édith Tremblay
Sainte-Anne-des-Monts
124, 1re av ouest, Sainte-Anne-des-Monts, QC G4V 1C5
Tél: 418-763-3301
Téléc: 418-763-7810
gaspesie-iles-de-la-madeleine@mddep.gouv.qc.ca
Directeur, Jean-Marie Dionne
Sainte-Marie
#200, 675, rte Cameron, Sainte-Marie, QC G6E 3V7
Tél: 418-386-8000
Téléc: 418-386-8080
chaudiere-appalaches@mddep.gouv.qc.ca
Directrice, Isabelle Olivier
Sainte-Thérèse
#80, 300, rue Sicard, Sainte-Thérèse, QC J7E 3X5
Tél: 450-433-2220
Téléc: 450-433-1315
laurentides@mddep.gouv.qc.ca
Directeur, Pierre Robert
Sept-Îles
818, boul Laure, Sept-Îles, QC G4R 1Y8
Tél: 418-964-8888
Téléc: 418-964-8023
cote-nord@mddep.gouv.qc.ca
Directeur, Alain Gaudreault
Sherbrooke
770, rue Goretti, Sherbrooke, QC J1E 3H4
Tél: 819-820-3882
Téléc: 819-820-3958
estrie@mddep.gouv.qc.ca
Directeur, Pierre Paquin
Trois-Rivières
#102, 100, rue Laviolette, Trois-Rivières, QC G9A 5S9
Tél: 819-371-6581
Téléc: 819-371-6987
mauricie@mddep.gouv.qc.ca
Directeur, Luc St-Martin

Changements climatiques, de l'air et de l'eau / Climate Change
675, boul René-Lévesque est, 30e étage, Québec, QC G1R 5V7
Tél: 418-521-3861
Téléc: 418-643-9990
Sous-ministre adjoint, Charles Larochelle
Tél: 418-521-3868
Téléc: 418-646-4920
Directeur, Politiques de l'eau, Marcel Gaucher
Directeur, Politiques de la qualité de l'atmosphère, Michel Goulet
Directrice, Bureau des changements climatiques, Geneviève Moisan
Directrice, Relations intergouvernementales, Danielle Pronovost

Centre de contrôle environnemental du Québec
Édifice Marie-Guyart, 675, boul René-Lévesque est, 30e étage, Québec, QC G1R 5V7
Tél: 418-521-3861
Téléc: 418-646-1800
Baie-Comeau
20, boulevard Comeau, Baie-Comeau, QC G4Z 3A8
Tél: 418-294-8888
Téléc: 418-294-8018
cote-nord@mddep.gouv.qc.ca
Directrice, Nathalie Chouinard
Gatineau
 # 7.340, 170, rue de l'Hôtel-de-Ville, Gatineau, QC J8X 4C2
Tél: 819-772-3434
Téléc: 819-772-3952
outaouais@mddep.gouv.qc.ca
Directeur, Alexandre Iracà
Nicolet
1579, boul Louis-Fréchette, Nicolet, QC J3T 2A5
Tél: 819-293-4122
Téléc: 819-293-8322
centre-du-quebec@mddep.gouv.qc.ca
Directeur, Pierre Boucher
Rimouski
212, av Belzile, Rimouski, QC G5L 3C3
Tél: 418-727-3511
Téléc: 418-727-3849
bas-saint-laurent@mddep.gouv.qc.ca
Directeur, Jules Boulanger
Rouyn-Noranda
180, boul Rideau, 1er étage, Rouyn-Noranda, QC J9X 1N9
Tél: 819-763-3333
Téléc: 819-763-3202
abitibi-temiscamingue@mddep.gouv.qc.ca
Directrice (par intérim), Hélène Iracà
Saguenay
3950, boul Harvey, 4e étage, Saguenay, QC G7X 8L6
Tél: 418-695-7883
Téléc: 418-695-7897
saguenay-lac-saint-jean@mddep.gouv.qc.ca
Directeur, Daniel Labrecque
Sainte-Marie
#200, 675, rte Cameron, Sainte-Marie, QC G6E 3V7
Tél: 418-386-8000
Téléc: 418-386-8080
chaudiere-appalaches@mddep.gouv.qc.ca
Directeur, Jean-Marc Lachance
Sherbrooke
770, rue Goretti, Sherbrooke, QC J1E 3H4
Tél: 819-820-3882
Téléc: 819-820-3958
estrie@mddep.gouv.qc.ca
Directeur, Émile Grieco
Montréal
#3860, 5199, rue Sherbrooke est, Montréal, QC H1T 3X9
Tél: 514-873-3636
Téléc: 514-873-5662
montreal@mddep.gouv.qc.ca
Directrice (par intérim), Hélène Proteau

Développement durable / Sustainable Development
Tél: 418-521-3861
Téléc: 418-646-5883
Sous-ministre adjoint, Léopold Gaudreau
Tél: 418-521-3861
Téléc: 418-646-5883
Directeur, Patrimoine écologique et des parcs, Patrick Beauchesne
Tél: 418-521-3907
Téléc: 418-646-6169
Directrice, Suivi de l'état de l'environnement, Linda Tapin
Tél: 418-521-3820
Téléc: 418-643-9591
Directeur, Bureau de Coordination du développement durable, Luc Vézina
Tél: 418-521-3848
Téléc: 418-646-6169

Expertise hydrique et aux évaluations environnementales / Water & Environmental Assessments
Sous-ministre adjoint, Jacques Dupont
Tél: 418-521-3861
Téléc: 418-643-7812
Directeur général, Centre d'expertise hydrique du Québec, Yvon Gosselin
Directrice, Expertise hydriques, Paula Bergeron
Directeur, Sécurité des barrages, Michel Dolbec
Directrice, Évaluations environnementales, Marie-Josée Lizotte
Directrice, Bureau de coordination sur les évaluations stratégiques, Yvon Maranda
Directrice, Domaine hydrique de l'État, Peter Stevenson

Services à la gestion & au milieu terrestre / Administrative Services & Earth Environment
Tél: 418-521-3861
Téléc: 418-643-9990
Sous-ministre adjoint et directrice générale (par intérim), Brigitte Portelance
Tél: 418-521-3861
Téléc: 418-643-9990
Directrice, Ressources humaines, Sylvie Beaulieu
Tél: 418-521-3811
Téléc: 418-646-6498
Directeur, Analyse et des instruments économiques, André G. Bernier
Directeur, Matières résiduelles & lieux contaminés, Mario Bérubé
Tél: 418-521-3950
Téléc: 418-644-3386
Directeur, Secteur agricole & pesticides, Didier Bicchi
Tél: 418-521-3950
Téléc: 418-644-8562
Directeur, Ressources financières et matérielles, Sophie Boisvert

Ministère du Développement économique, de l'Innovation et de l'Exportation / Economic Development, Innovation & Export Trade

710, place D'Youville, 3e étage, Québec, QC G1R 4Y4
Tél: 418-691-5950
Téléc: 418-644-0118
Ligne sans frais: 866-680-1884
www.mdeie.gouv.qc.ca

A pour mission de soutenir le développement économique, l'innovation & l'exportation; d'offrir des services-conseils; de promouvoir l'image du Québec à l'étranger auprès des investisseurs

Acts Administered:
Loi favorisant l'augmentation du capital des petites et moyennes entreprises/An Act to promote the capitalization of small and medium-sized businesses
Loi sur Investissement Québec/An Act respecting Investissement Québec
Loi sur l'aide au développement des coopérative et des personnes morales sans but lucratif/An Act respecting assistance for the development of cooperatives and non-profit legal persons
Loi sur la Régie des installations olympiques
Loi sur la Société Innovatech Québec et Chaudière-Appalaches/An Act respecting Société Innovatech Québec et Chaudière-Appalaches
Loi sur la Société Innovatech Régions ressources/An Act respecting Société Innovatech Régions ressources
Loi sur la Société Innovatech du Grand Montréal/An Act respecting the Société Innovatech du Grand Montréal
Loi sur la Société Innovatech du sud du Québec/An Act respecting the Société Innovatech du sud du Québec
Loi sur la Société des alcools du Québec/An Act respecting the Société des alcools du Québec
Loi sur la Société du Centre des congrès de Québec
Loi sur la Société du Palais de Congrès de Montréal
Loi sur la Société du parc industriel et portuaire de Bécancour/An Act respecting the Société du parc industriel et portuaire de Bécancour
Loi sur le Centre de recherche industriel du Québec/An Act respecting the Centre de recherche industrielle du Québec
Loi sur le ministère des Relations internationales/An Act respecting the Ministère des Relations internationales
Loi sur le ministère du Développement économique, de l'Innovation et de l'Esportation
Loi sur les concours artistiques, littéraires et scientifiques/An Act respecting artistic, literary and scientific competitions
Loi sur les coopératives/Cooperatives Act
Loi sur les heures et les jours d'admission dans les établissements commerciaux/An Act respecting hours and days of admission to commercial establishments
Loi sur les matériaux de rembourrage et les articles rembourrés/An Act respecting stuffing and upholstered and stuffed articles
Loi sur les sociétés de placement dans l'entreprise québécoise

Ministre, L'hon. Sam Hamad

Sous-ministre, Christyne Tremblay

Directrice (par intérim), Affaires juridiques, Christian Caron

Directeur, Accords internationaux et mandit spécial, Patrick Muzzi

Directeur, Politique commerciale, Jean-François Raymond

Directrice, Communications, Johanne Pelletier

Directeur, Vérification interne, Jacques St-Pierre

Service, Stratégies et des communications, Lynda Cloutier

Secrétaire générale, Geneviève Masse

Agences, Conseils et Commissions Associés/ Associated Agencies, Boards & Commissions:

• Centre de recherche industrielle du Québec (CRIQ) / Industrial Research Centre of Québec
333, rue Franquet
Québec, QC G1P 4C7
Tél: 418-659-1550
Téléc: 418-652-2251
Ligne sans frais: 800-667-2386
infocriq@criq.qc.ca
www.criq.qc.ca
Recherche industrielle appliquée; services de RD pour des entreprises

• Fonds québécois de la recherche sur la nature et les technologies / Québec Fund for Research on Nature and Technologies
#450, 140, Grande Allée est
Québec, QC G1R 5M8
Tél: 418-643-8560
Téléc: 418-643-1451
info@fqrnt.gouv.qc.ca
www.fqrnt.gouv.qc.ca

• Fonds québécois de la recherche sur la société et la culture / Québec Fund for Research on Society and Culture
#470, 140, Grande Allée est
Québec, QC G1R 5M8
Tél: 418-643-7582
Téléc: 418-644-5248
fqrsc@fqrsc.gouv.qc.ca
www.fqrsc.gouv.qc.ca

• Fonds de la recherche en santé du Québec / Québec Health Research Fund
#800, 500, rue Sherbrooke ouest
Montréal, QC H3A 3C6
Tél: 514-873-2114
Téléc: 514-873-8768
www.frsq.gouv.qc.ca

• Investissement Québec / Investment Québec
#500, 1200, rte de l'Église
Québec, QC G1V 5A3
Tél: 418-643-5172
Ligne sans frais: 866-870-0437
www.investquebec.com

• Innovatech Québec
#410, 888, rue St-Jean
Québec, QC G1R 5H6
Tél: 418-528-9770
Téléc: 418-528-9783
Ligne sans frais: 866-605-1676
www.innovatechquebec.com

Affaires économiques internationales (AEI) / International Economic Affairs
Sous-ministre adjoint, Jean Séguin
Directeur général, Export Québec, Alain Proulx
Directeur, Occasions d'affaires mondiales, Chantal Castonguay
Directrice, Asie-Pacifique et Océanie, Marie-ève Jean
Directeur, Amérique du Nord et Europe, Yves Lafortune
Directrice, Information, promotion, et investissements internationaux, Isabelle Phaneuf
Directeur, Amérique latine, Afrique et Moyen-Orient, Rafaël Sanchez

Bureau de la Capitale-Nationale / National Capital Office

Industries stratégiques (IS) / Strategic Industries
Sous-ministre adjointe, Suzanne Lévesque
Directeur général, Développement des industries, Marc Leduc
Directeur, Équipements de transport, Martin Aubé
Directrice, Biens de consommation, Marie-Annick Drouin
Directeur, Commence et construction, Pierre A. Forgues
Directrice, Technologies de l'information et des communications, Diane Hastie
Directrice, Santé et biotechnologies, Michèle Houpert
Directeur, Technologies vertes et entreprises de service, Gaétan Poiré

Politiques économiques (PE) / Economic Policies
Sous-ministre adjoint et directeur (par intérim), Politiques économiques, Alain Veilleux
Directrice, Développement de l'entrepreneuriat, Lyne Fournier
Directeur, Développement des coopératives, Michel Jean
Directrice, Analyse économique, Denise Lacroix
Directeur, Évaluation de programmes et planification stratégique, François Maxime Langlois

Projets économiques majeurs et sociétés d'État (PEMSE) / Major Economic Projects & Crown Corporations
Sous-ministre adjoint, Mario Bouchard
Directeur général, Interventions stratégiques, Pierre Dupont
Directeur, Produits industriels, Clément Drolet
Directrice, FDE et programmes, Lise Mathieu
Directrice, Interventions financières, Michèle Robert
Directrice, Coordination, analyse et sociétés d'État, Lisette Seyer
Directeur, Projets économiques, Frédéric Simard

Recherche, innovation et science citoyenne (RISC) / Research, Innovation, & Social Science
Sous-ministre adjoint et directeur général (par intérim), Reserche Québec, Jean Belzile
Directeur, Financement des infrastructures de recherche, Gaston Beaudoin
Directrice, Collaborations internationales, Marie-Josée Blais
Directeur, Recherche industrielle, Marco Blouin
Directeur (par intérim), Recherche universitaire & collégiale, Martin Doyon
Directrice, Promotion de la science citoyenne, Christian Desbiens
Directrice, Coordination & concertation, Marie-Odile Koch
Directrice, Soutien à l'innovation technologique et sociale, Monique La Rue
Directeur, Politiques & analyses, Mawana Pongo

Services à la gestion / Administrative Services
Directrice générale, Carole Lafond
Directrice, Ressources humaines et matérielles, Nicole Lévesque
Directeur, Ressources informationnelles, Guy Leclerc
Directeur, Ressources financières, Francis Mathieu

Services aux entreprises et affaires territoriales (SEAT) / Business Services & Territorial Affairs
Sous-ministre adjoint, Jean-Marc Sauvé
Directeur général, Affaires économiques métropolitaines, Mario Limoges
Directeur, Pôles et créneaux d'excellence, Xavier Fonteneau
Directrice (par intérim), Coordination régionale, Michèle Robert
Directeur, Développement des entreprises, Bertrand Verbruggen

Abitibi-Témiscamingue
#202, 170, av Principale, Rouyn-Noranda, QC J9X 4P7
Tél: 819-763-3561
Téléc: 819-763-3462
Ligne sans frais: 866-463-6642
Directeur, Yves Drolet

Bas-St-Laurent
#RC 04, 337, rue Moreault, Rimouski, QC G5L 1P4
Tél: 418-727-3577
Téléc: 418-727-3640
Ligne sans frais: 866-463-6642
Directeur, Denis Goulet

Capitale-Nationale
900, place d'Youville, 3e étage, Québec, QC G1R 3P7
Tél: 418-691-5824
Téléc: 418-643-4099
Ligne sans frais: 866-463-6642
Directeur, Jean-François Talbot

Centre-du-Québec
Édifice provincial, #1.03, 62, rue Saint-Jean-Baptiste, Victoriaville, QC G6P 4E3
Tél: 819-752-9781
Téléc: 819-758-4306
Ligne sans frais: 866-463-6642
Directeur, Vincent Bourassa

Chaudière-Appalaches
#1, 1055, boul Vachon nord, Sainte-Marie, QC G6E 1M4
Tél: 418-386-8677
Téléc: 418-386-8037
Ligne sans frais: 866-463-6642
Directeur, Roch Delagrave

Côte-Nord
#RC 711, 625, boul Laflèche, Baie-Comeau, QC G5C 1C5
Tél: 418-589-4349
Téléc: 418-295-4199
Ligne sans frais: 866-463-6642
Directeur, Jacques Chiasson

Estrie
#4.05, 200, rue Belvédère nord, Sherbrooke, QC J1H 4A9
Tél: 819-820-3731
Téléc: 819-820-3929
Ligne sans frais: 866-463-6642
Directeur, Robert Fortin

Gaspésie/Iles-de-la-Madeleine
#10-A, 500, av Daigneault, CP 1360, Chandler, QC G0C 1K0
Tél: 418-689-1200
Téléc: 418-689-4108
Ligne sans frais: 866-463-6642
Directeur, Roger Cyr

Lanaudière
#3300, 40, rue Gauthier sud, Joliette, QC J6E 4J4
Tél: 450-752-8050
Téléc: 450-752-8064
Ligne sans frais: 866-463-6642
Directeur, Éric Lescarbeault

Laurentides
#C-3.35, 85, rue de Martigny, Saint-Jérôme, QC J7Y 3R8
Tél: 450-569-3031
Téléc: 450-569-3039
Ligne sans frais: 866-463-6642
Directrice, Jocelyn Bianki

Laval
#RC 30, 705, ch du Trait-Carré, Laval, QC H7N 1B3
Tél: 450-680-6175
Téléc: 450-972-3090
Ligne sans frais: 866-463-6642
Directeur, Serge Thériault

Mauricie
Édifice Capitanal, #114, 100, rue Laviolette, Trois-Rivières, QC G9A 5S9
Tél: 819-371-6617
Téléc: 819-371-6960
Ligne sans frais: 866-463-6642
Directeur, Denis Hébert

Montérégie
#101, 201, place Charles-Le Moyne, Longueuil, QC J4K 2T5
Tél: 450-928-7645
Téléc: 450-928-7465
Ligne sans frais: 866-463-6642
Directeur, Jacques La Rue

Montréal
380, rue Saint-Antoine ouest, 5e étage, Montréal, QC H2Y 3X7
Tél: 514-499-2550
Téléc: 514-873-9913
Ligne sans frais: 866-463-6642
Directeur, Daniel Gagné

Nord-du-Québec
333, 3e rue, Chibougamau, QC G8P 1N4
Tel: 418-748-6681
Fax: 418-748-6698
Toll-Free: 866-463-6642
Directeur (par intérim), Stéphane Bergeron

Outaouais
#7.200, 170, rue de l'Hôtel-de-Ville, Gatineau, QC J8X 4C2
Tél: 819-772-3219
Téléc: 819-772-3968
Ligne sans frais: 866-463-6642
Directeur, Jeffrey MacHan

Saguenay/Lac-Saint-Jean
#2.05, 3950, boul Harvey, 2e étage, Jonquière, QC G7X 8L6
Tél: 418-695-7971
Téléc: 418-695-7870
Ligne sans frais: 866-463-6642
Directeur (par intérim), Stéphane Bergeron

Commission des droits de la personne et des droits de la jeunesse / Commission for Human Rights & the Rights of Youth

360, rue St-Jacques, 2e étage, Montréal, QC H2Y 1P5
Tél: 514-873-5146
Téléc: 514-873-6032
Ligne sans frais: 800-361-6477
accueil@cdpdj.qc.ca
www.cdpdj.qc.ca

A pour mission d'assurer la promotion et le respect des droits et libertés affirmés par la Charte des droits et libertés de la personne, par la Loi sur la protection de la jeunesse, et par la Loi sur les jeunes contrevenants

Président, Gaétan Cousineau

Vice-présidente, Renée Dupuis

Ministère de l'Éducation, du Loisir et du Sport / Education, Leisure & Sports

1035, rue De La Chevrotière, 28e étage, Québec, QC G1R 5A5
Tél: 418-643-7095
Téléc: 418-646-6561
Ligne sans frais: 866-747-6626
www.mels.gouv.qc.ca

Acts Administered:
Charte de la langue française/Charter of the French language
Loi concernant le transfert de la propriété d'un immeuble à la Commission scolaire de Montréal et modifiant la Loi sur l'instruction publique/Act respecting the transfer of the ownership of an immovable to the Commissionscolaire de Montréal & amending t
Loi concernant les conditions d'utilisation d'immeubles de la Commission des écoles protestantes du Grand Montréal par la Commission des écoles catholiques de Montréal/Act respecting conditions governing the use ofimmovables of the Protestant School Boa
Loi du mérite scolaire/Scholastic Merit Act
Loi favorisant la conclusion d'ententes dans le secteur de l'éducation/Act to foster labour agreements in the education sector
Loi modifiant diverses dispositions législatives dans le secteur de l'éducation concernant la confessionnalité/Act to amend various legislative provisions respecting education as regards confessional matters
Loi sur l'Institut de tourisme et d'hôtellerie du Québec/Act respecting the Institut de tourisme et d'hôtellerie du Québec
Loi sur l'Université du Québec/Act respecting the Université du Québec
Loi sur l'accréditation et le financement des associations d'élèves ou d'étudiants/Act respecting the accreditation and financing of students' associations
Loi sur l'aide financière aux études/Act respecting financial assistance for education expenses
Loi sur l'enseignement privé/Act respecting private education
Loi sur l'instruction publique pour les autochtones cris, inuits et naskapis/Education Act for Cree, Inuit and Naskapi Native Persons
Loi sur l'instruction publique/Education Act
Loi sur l'élection des premiers commissaires des commissions scolaires nouvelles et modifiant diverses dispositions législatives/Act respecting the election of the first commissioners of the new school boards and amendingvarious legislative provisions
Loi sur l'École de laiterie et les écoles moyennes d'agriculture/Act respecting the École de laiterie and intermediate agricultural schools
Loi sur la Commission d'évaluation de l'enseignement collégial/Act respecting the Commission d'évaluation de l'enseignement collégial
Loi sur le Conseil supérieur de l'éducation/Act respecting the Institut de tourisme et d'hôtellerie du Québec
Loi sur le ministère de l'Éducation, du Loisir et du Sport/Act respecting the Ministère de l'Éducation, du Loisir et du Sport
Loi sur les collèges d'enseignement général et professionnel/General and Vocational Colleges Act
Loi sur les fondations universitaires/Act respecting university foundations
Loi sur les investissements universitaires/Univeristy Investments Act
Loi sur les élections scolaires/Act respecting school elections
Loi sur les établissements d'enseignement de niveau universitaire/Act respecting educational institutions at the university level

Ministre, L'hon. Marie Malavoy
Tél: 418-644-0664
Téléc: 418-646-7551
marie.malavoy@mels.gouv.qc.ca

Sous-ministre, Bernard Matte
Tél: 418-643-3810
Téléc: 418-644-4591

Directeur, Secrétariat aux affaires religieuses, Roger Boisvert
Tél: 418-643-7070 ext: 399
Téléc: 418-644-7142

Directrice, Accès à l'information et plaintes, Manon Boisvert
Tél: 418-646-5324 ext: 602

Directeur, Affaires juridiques, Daniel Morin
Tel: 418-643-3747 ext: 208
Fax: 418-646-6849

Directrice, Secrétariat général, Stéphanie Vachon
Tél: 418-643-3810 ext: 392

Directrice, Condition féminine, Raymonde Villemure
Tél: 418-643-3810 ext: 369

Directeur, Vérification interne, Christian Boivin
Tél: 418-643-8194 ext: 220

Directrice, Communications, Mireille Dubé
Tél: 418-528-2265 ext: 297

Sous-ministre adjoint, Services à la communauté anglophone & Affaires autochtones, Leo La France
Tél: 514-873-3788 ext: 544

Sous-ministre adjointe, Réseaux, Manuelle Oudar
Tél: 418-643-3810

Sous-ministre adjointe, Formation professionnelle, technique & continue, Brigitte Guay
Tél: 418-643-3810 ext: 609

Sous-ministre adjointe, Enseignement supérieur, Christiane Piché

Sous-ministre adjoint, Politiques, recherche et statistiques, Gilles Charland
Tél: 418-643-3810 ext: 376

Sous-ministre adjoint, Services en soutien à la mission & aide financière aux études, Raymond Lesage
Tél: 418-643-3810 ext: 603

Sous-ministre adjoint, Loisir et sport, Jean-Guy Ouellette
Tél: 418-646-6018 ext: 363

Agences, Conseils et Commissions Associés/ Associated Agencies, Boards & Commissions:

• Commission consultative de l'enseignement privé / Advisory Committee on Private Education
1035, rue de la Chevrotière, 14e étage
Québec, QC G1R 5A5
Tél: 418-646-1249
Téléc: 418-643-7752
commission.consultative@mels.gouv.qc.ca
Autres numéros: Téléphone poste: 2503
• Commission de l'éducation en langue anglaise / Advisory Board on English Education
600, rue Fullum, 9e étage
Montréal, QC H2K 4L1
Tél: 514-873-5656
Téléc: 514-864-4181
cela-abee@mels.gouv.qc.ca
www.mels.gouv.qc.ca/cela/anglais.htm
• Commission d'évaluation de l'enseignement collégial / College Teachers Assessment Commission
800, place d'Youville, 18e étage
Québec, QC G1R 5P4
Tél: 418-643-9938
Téléc: 418-643-9019
info@ceec.gouv.qc.ca
www.ceec.gouv.qc.ca
• Comité-conseil sur les programmes d'études
1035, de la Chevrotière, 17e étage
Québec, QC G1R 5A5
Tél: 418-646-0133
Téléc: 418-643-0056
ccpe@mels.gouv.qc.ca
www.ccpe.gouv.qc.ca
• Conseil supérieur de l'éducation / Superior Council of Education
#180, 1175, av Lavigerie
Québec, QC G1V 5B2
Tél: 418-643-3850
Téléc: 418-644-2530
panorama@cse.gouv.qc.ca
www.cse.gouv.qc.ca

Financement et dirigeante Réseau de l'information / Funding & Leadership Information Network
Sous-ministre adjoint, Fernand Archambault
Directeur Général, Gouvernance et gestion des ressources informationnelles dans les réseaux, Bernard Chartier
Directeur Général, Financement et équipement, enseignement supérieur, Pierre Boutet
Directeur Général, Financement et équipement, Éducation préscolaire, enseignement primaire et secondaire, René Lepage
Directeur, Politiques et operations budgétaires, Serge Dupéré
Directrice, Équipement, Hélène Guenette
Directeur, Programmation budgétaire et financement, Jean Leroux
Directeur, Systèmes et contrôle, Pierre Larochelle
Directeur, Équipement scolaire, Gilles Marchand
Directrice, Opérations financières aux réseaux, Catherine Tremblay

Administration et aide financière aux études / Adminsitration & Student Financial Aid
1035, rue De La Chevrotière, Québec, QC G1R 5A5
Tél: 418-643-3750
Ligne sans frais: 877-643-3750
www.afe.gouv.qc.ca
Sous-ministre adjoint, Raymond Lesage
Tél: 418-644-3810 ext: 603
Téléc: 418-528-0779
Directrice, Services administratifs, Nicole Martel
Directeur, Service de planification & programmes, Robert Sasseville
Tél: 418-643-6276 ext: 601
Directrice, Gestion des prêts, Suzanne Gingras
Tél: 418-646-5115 ext: 628
Directeur, Systéms d'information, Mario Pellerin
Directeur, Infrastructures technologiques, Stéphane Lehoux
Directeur, Technologies de l'information, Gilles Bélanger
Directrice, Planification, architecture et soutien aux projets, Suzie Dion
Directrice, Services à la clientèle et de l'attribution, Nathalie Surprenant
Directrice, Ressources humaines, Yola Dubé
Directrice, Ressources financiéres, Joëlle Jobin
Directeur, Affaires internationales et canadiennes, Francis Gauthier
Directrice, Pilotage des systèmes ministériels, Anne-Marie Carpentier

Éducation préscolaire, enseignement primaire et secondaire et régions / Preschool, Elementary & Secondary School Education
Sous-ministre adjoint, Alain Veilleux
Tél: 418-643-3810
Téléc: 418-644-2131
Directrice, Services de soutien aux élèves, Denise Gosselin
Tél: 418-266-0156 ext: 356
Directeur, Services à l'enseignement, Guy Dumais
Tél: 418-643-3452 ext: 315
Directeur, Service aux communautés culturelles, Christian Rousseau
Tel: 514-873-3744 ext: 531
Directrice, Programmes, Catherine Dupont
Tél: 418-644-5240 ext: 252
Téléc: 418-528-8023
Directrice, Adaptation scolaire, Anne Robitaille
Tél: 418-646-7000
Téléc: 418-644-5914
Directeur, Sanction des études, Jean-Guy Hamel
Tél: 418-644-0905 ext: 223
Téléc: 418-644-6909
Directrice, Évaluation, Linda Drouin
Tél: 514-864-1896
Téléc: 514-873-2571
Directrice, Ressources didactiques, Lise Gagnon
Tél: 418-643-3452 ext: 315

Formation professionnelle et technique et formation continue / Professional & Technical Training & Continuing Education
Sous-ministre adjointe, Brigitte Guay
Tél: 418-643-3810 ext: 609
Téléc: 418-644-4591
Directrice, Éducation des adultes & action communautaire, Geneviève Leblanc
Directrice, Formation continue et soutien, Sonia Léveillé
Tél: 418-646-1536 ext: 232
Directeur, Gestion sectorielle des ressources, Laurent Mercier
Tél: 418-646-4225 ext: 234
Directrice, Planification et coordination sectorielles, Julie Lévesque
Tél: 418-646-9477 ext: 377
Directrice, Programmes et la veille sectorielle, Nora Desrochers
Tél: 418-646-4215 ext: 228
Directeur, Direction adjointe, Laurence Mosseray
Directeur, Formation professionnelle et technique, Daniel Desbiens
Directeur, Gestion stratégique de l'offre de formation, Jean-Marc Bissonnette

Réseaux / Networks
Sous-ministre adjointe, Manuelle Oudar
Tél: 418-643-3810
Téléc: 418-646-9220
Directrice, Enseignement privé, Maryse Malenfant
Tél: 418-646-3939 ext: 255
Directeur, Relations du travail du personnel professionnel et de soutien, Richard Bernier
Tél: 418-646-9000 ext: 340
Directeur, Relations du travail, Éric Bergeron
Tél: 418-646-9000 ext: 340

Directrice (par intérim), Relations du travail-personnel enseignant, Pascal Poulin
Tél: 418-646-9000 ext: 340
Directrice, Conditions de travail du personnel d'encadrement, Françoise Dion
Tél: 418-646-9000 ext: 340
Directrice, Politiques et relations interministérielles, Josée Bourdages
Directrice, Statistiques et information décisionnelle, Myriam Proulx
Tél: 418-528-7693
Directeur, Indicateurs et statistiques, Vacant
Chef de service, Information décisionnelle et géomatique, Julie Gauvin

Régions / Regions
Directeur général, Régions, Guylaine Larose
Tel: 418-643-7498 ext: 237
Fax: 418-646-8419
Abitibi-Témiscamingue/Nord-du-Québec
215, boul Rideau, 1er étage, Rouyn-Noranda, QC J9X 5Y6
Tél: 819-763-3001
Téléc: 819-763-3017
dr-08@mels.gouv.qc.ca
Directrice régionale, Louise Bilodeau
Bas-Saint-Laurent/Gaspésie/Iles-de-la-Madeleine
355, boul Saint-Germain ouest, 2e étage, Rimouski, QC G5L 0A5
Tél: 418-727-3600
Téléc: 418-727-3557
dr-01@mels.gouv.qc.ca
Directeur régional, Gérard Bédard
Capitale-Nationale/Chaudière-Appalaches
1020, rte de l'Église, 3e étage, Québec, QC G1V 3V9
Tél: 418-643-7934
Téléc: 418-643-0972
dr-03@mels.gouv.qc.ca
Directeur, Guy Larose
Côte-Nord
#201, 106, rue Napoléon, Sept-îles, QC G4R 3L7
Tél: 418-964-8420
Téléc: 418-964-8504
dr09-si@mels.gouv.qc.ca
Directrice, Suzanne Côté
Estrie
#3.05, 200, rue Belvédère nord, Sherbrooke, QC J1H 4A9
Tél: 819-820-3382
Téléc: 819-820-3947
dr-05@mels.gouv.qc.ca
Directeur régional, Roger Tremblay
Laval/Laurentides/Lanaudière
#200, 300, rue Sicard, Sainte-Thérèse, QC J7E 3X5
Tél: 450-430-3611
Téléc: 450-430-4005
dr-061@mels.gouv.qc.ca
Directeur régionale, Daniel Parent
Mauricie/Centre-du-Québec
Édifice Capitanal, #213, 100, rue Laviolette, Trois-Rivières, QC G9A 5S9
Tél: 819-371-6711
Téléc: 819-971-6075
dr-04@mels.gouv.qc.ca
Autre numéros: Email: dr-17@mels.gouv.qc.ca
Directrice régionale, Carole Gaudet
Montérégie
Édifice Montval, 201, place Charles-Le Moyne, 6e étage, Longueuil, QC J4K 2T5
Tél: 450-928-7438
Téléc: 450-928-7451
dr-062@mels.gouv.qc.ca
Directrice régionale, Lise Langlois
Montréal
600, rue Fullum, 10e étage, Montréal, QC H2K 4L1
Tél: 514-873-4630
Téléc: 514-873-0620
dr-063@mels.gouv.qc.ca
Directeur régional, Francis Culée
Outaouais
170, rue de l'Hôtel-de-Ville, 4e étage, Gatineau, QC J8X 4C2
Tél: 819-772-3382
Téléc: 819-772-3955
dr-07@mels.gouv.qc.ca
Directrice régionale, Louise Lafontaine
Saguenay/Lac-Saint-Jean
2220, rue St-David, Jonquière, QC G7X 0L3
Tél: 418-695-7982
Téléc: 418-695-7990
dr-02@mels.gouv.qc.ca
Directeur régional, Jean-François Coulombe

Loisir et sport / Sport & Recreation
Sous-ministre adjoint, Jean-Guy Ouellette
Tél: 418-646-6018 ext: 363
Téléc: 418-644-9474
Directeur, Bureau des grands projets, Robert Bédard
Tél: 418-646-6137 ext: 365
Directeur, Gestion administrative et contrôles des programmes, Normand Fauchon
Directeur, Promotion de la sécurité, Michel Fafard
Directrice, Sport, loisir et activité physique, France Vigneault
Tél: 418-646-6142 ext: 361

Services à la communauté anglophone, affaires autochtones & Plan Nord / Anglophone Services, Aboriginal Affairs & Northern Plan
Sous-ministre adjoint, Directeur, Politiques & projets, Leo La France
Tél: 514-873-3788 ext: 544
Directrice, Affaires autochtones et Plan Nord, Francis Paradis
Directeur, Services à la communauté anglophone, Paul Rémillard

Directeur général des Élections du Québec / Chief Electoral Officer of Québec

Édifice René-Lévesque, 3460, rue de La Pérade, Québec, QC G1X 3Y5
Tél: 418-528-0422
Téléc: 418-643-7291
Ligne sans frais: 888-353-2846
info@electionsquebec.qc.ca
www.electionsquebec.qc.ca
TTY: 418-646-0644

Acts Administered:
Loi sur la consultation populaire/Referendum Act
Loi sur les élections et les référendums dans les municipalités/An Act respecting Elections & Referendums in Municipalities
Loi sur les élections scolaires
Loi électorale du Québec/Election Act

Directeur général, Président de la commission de la représentation électorale, Jacques Drouin
Tél: 418-646-3569

Adjoint au président, Secretaire, Denis Fontaine
Tél: 418-646-6072

Ministre de l'Enseignement supérieur, de la Recherche, de la Science et de la Technologie / Higher Education, Research, Science & Technology

Ministre, Pierre Duchesne
Tél: 418-643-3810
Téléc: 418-646-1526

Sous-ministre, Christine Tremblay

Sous-ministre, Jean Belzile

Ministre, L'hon. Agnès Maltais
Tél: 418-646-6090
Téléc: 418-646-6088
amaltais-tasc@assnat.qc.ca

Sous-ministre, Brigitte Pelletier
Tél: 418-646-0425 ext: 441

Directrice, Soutien à la gouvernance, et Direction de la vérification interne et des enquêtes administratives (par intérim), Michelle Coudé
Tél: 418-646-0425 ext: 380

Directeur, Bureau de la sous-ministre, Patrick Grenier

Directeur, Affaires juridiques, Mélanie Paradis

Assurance parentale et relations avec les citoyens / Parental Insurance & Citizen Relations
Sous-ministre adjoint, Jacques Duguay
Tél: 418-646-0425 ext: 464
Directrice, Secrétariat Entraide - Secteurs public et parapublic, Pascale Despins
Tél: 418-646-0425 ext: 867
Directrice, Régions de l'ouest du Québec, Diane Labelle
Tél: 450-928-7505 ext: 237
Directrice, Île-de-Montréal, Dannie Mailloux
Tél: 514-873-4313 ext: 252
Directeur, Régions de l'est du Québec, Michel Mailloux
Tél: 418-646-8066 ext: 253
Directeur, Bureau des renseignements et plaintes, Laurence Mosseray
Tél: 418-646-0425 ext: 422
Directrice, Révision et recours administratifs, Esther Quirion
Tél: 418-646-0425 ext: 617

Services à la gestion / Management Services
Sous-ministre adjoint, Normand Légaré
Tél: 418-646-0425 ext: 355
Directeur, Centre ministériel d'expertise en gestion de projets, Jean-Pierre Bélanger
Tél: 418-646-0425 ext: 339
Directeur, Systèmes de l'emploi et de la solidarité sociale, Marc Blanchard
Tél: 418-646-0425 ext: 810
Directrice, Systèmes partagés et assurance parentale, Jasmine Dion
Tél: 418-643-7868
Directeur, Gouverne des technologies de l'information, Denis Gagnon
Tél: 418-646-0425 ext: 867

Emploi-Québec / Employment Québec
425, rue St-Amable, #RC 175, Québec, QC G1R 4Z1
Tél: 418-643-4721
Ligne sans frais: 888-643-4721
emploiquebec.net
Sous-ministre associé et secrétaire générale de la CPMT, Johanne Bourassa

Opérations / Operations
Sous-ministre adjointe, Diane Landriault
Tél: 514-873-0800 ext: 389
Directrice générale adjointe, île-de-Montréal, Johanne Beaulieu
Tél: 514-725-5221 ext: 210
Directeur général adjointe, Opérations du Nord et de l'Est, Marian Lavoie
Tél: 418-646-0425 ext: 886
Directeur générale adjointe, Opérations du Sud et de l'Ouest, Lorraine St-Cyr
Tél: 514-873-0800 ext: 387

Mesures, services et soutien / Measures, Services & Support
Directrice générale adjointe, Martine Bégin
Tél: 418-646-0425 ext: 484

Services corporatifs / Corporate Services
Directeur général adjointe, Michel Lalande
Tél: 514-873-0800 ext: 355

Politiques & l'analyse stratégique / Policy & Strategic Analysis
Sous-ministre adjointe, Marie-Renée Roy
Tél: 418-646-0425 ext: 370
Directrice générale adjoint, Recherche, évaluation et suivi de la performance, Patricia Caris
Tél: 418-646-0425 ext: 312
Directeur général adjoint, Planification, politiques et relations intergouvernementales, Guy Dumais
Tél: 418-646-0425 ext: 625
Directeur général adjoint, Secrétariat à l'action communautaire autonome et aux initiatives sociales, Daniel Jean
Tél: 418-646-9270 ext: 657

Ministère de la Famille / Family

425, rue Saint-Amable, 1er étage, Québec, QC G1R 4Z1
Ligne sans frais: 877-216-6202
www.mfa.gouv.qc.ca
A la suite de la formation du nouveau Conseil des ministres, le 19 septembre 2012, le volet Aînés relève désormais du ministère de la Santé et des Services sociaux.
Acts Administered:
Loi favorisant l'établissement d'un régime de retraite à l'intention d'employés oeuvrant dans le domaine des services de garde à l'enfance/An Act to facilitate the establishment of a Pension Plan for employees working inChildcare Services
Loi sur le ministère de la Famille, des Aînés et de la Condition féminine/An Act respecting the Ministère de la Famille, des Aînés et de la Condition féminine
Loi sur les prestations familiales/An Act respecting Family Benefits
Loi sur les services de garde éducatifs à l'enfance/Educational Childcare Act

Ministre, Famille, L'hon. Nicole Léger
Tél: 418-643-2181
Téléc: 418-643-2640
ministre.famille@mfa.gouv.qc.ca

Sous-ministre, Line Bérubé
Tél: 418-646-4680
Téléc: 418-646-4903

Secretaire générale, Sylvain Pelletier
Tél: 418-528-6689

Agences, Conseils et Commissions Associés/ Associated Agencies, Boards & Commissions:

• Comité national d'éthique sur le vieillissement et les changements démographiques / National Ethics Committee on Aging & Demographic Changes
#700, 875, Grande Allée est, 5e étage
Québec, QC G1R 5W5
Tél: 418-643-0098
Téléc: 418-643-0082
jacques.vaillancourt@mfa.gouv.qc.ca

• Curateur public du Québec / Québec Public Trustee
600, boul René-Lévesque ouest
Montréal, QC H3B 4W9
Tél: 514-873-4074
Téléc: 514-873-5033
Ligne sans frais: 800-363-9020
www.curateur.gouv.qc.ca

Ministre, L'hon. Raymond Bachand
Tél: 418-643-5270
Téléc: 418-646-1574

Ministre délégué aux finances, Alain Paquet

Sous-ministre, Luc Monty
Tél: 418-643-5738
Téléc: 418-528-5546

Sous-ministre associé, Éric Ducharme

Sous-ministre adjoint, Politiques économiques & fiscales, Carl Gauthier
Tél: 418-691-2214
Téléc: 418-646-6688

Sous-ministre adjoint, Politiques relatives aux institutions financières et au droit corporatif, Richard Boivin
Tél: 418-646-7563
Téléc: 418-646-7610

Sous-ministre adjointe, Droit fiscal & la fiscalité, Josée Morin
Tél: 418-691-2261
Téléc: 418-644-1666

Sous-ministre adjoint, Politique budgétaire, Simon Bergeron

Contrôleur, Finances et comptabilité gouvernementale, Simon-Pierre Falardeau

Droit fiscal et la fiscalité / Fiscal Law & Taxation
Sous-ministre adjointe, Josée Morin
Tél: 418-691-2236
Téléc: 418-644-5262
Directeur, Impôts des entreprises, Agathe Simard
Directrice, Impôts des particuliers, Lyse Gauthier
Directrice, Taxes, Lyne Dussault

Financement, gestion de la dette et opérations financières / Financing, Debt Management & Financial Transactions
Sous-ministre adjoint, Bernard Turgeon
Tél: 418-643-5738
Directeur général, Opérations bancaires et financières, François Tardif
Directeur général, Financement et gestion de la dette, Alain Bélanger
Directrice, Financement des organismes publics et de la documentation financière, Nathalie Parenteau
Directeur général, Prévisions financières et des relations avec les agences de crédit, Gino Ouellet
Directeur, Gestion de l'encaisse, Renaud Raymond
Directeur, Gestion des risques, Éric Deschênes
Directeur, Analyse et des prévisions du service de la dette, Jean-Charles Doucet
Directeur, Gestion des fonds et des paiements, Harold Garneau
Directrice, Gestion de la dette et de l'ingénierie financière, Marie-Pierre Hillinger
Directeur, Comptabilité et du bureau des dépôts et consignations, Michel Breault
Directrice, Produits d'épargne et du suivi des transactions financières, Isabelle Blackburn
Sous-ministre adjoint, Politiques fédérales-provinciales et financières, Patrick Déry
Directrice, Relations fédérales-provinciales, Marie-Claude Lavallée
Directeur, Projets spéciaux, Martin Guérard

Politique budgétaire et économique / Budgetary & Economic Policy
Sous-ministre adjoint, Luc Monty
Directeur général, Simon Bergeron
Directeur général, Analyse et de la prévision économiques, Marc Sirois
Directeur général, Organisation financière et du suivi des opérations budgétaires et non budgétaires, Jacques Caron
Directeur général, Politiques locales et autochtones et de l'optimisation des revenus, Marc Grandisson
Directeur, Économie québécoise et canadienne, Michel Dionne
Directeur, Analyse et de la prévision des dépenses et de la tarification, Richard Masse

Politiques économiques et fiscales / Economic & Fiscal Policy
Sous-ministre adjoint, Carl Gauthier
Directeur général, Politiques aux entreprises, Éric Ducharme
Directeur général, Politiques aux particuliers, Éric Fournier
Directeur, Développement économique, Brigitte Bazin
Directeur, Études économiques et fiscales et taxes de vente, David Bahan
Directeur, Mesures structurantes, Luc Bilodeau
Directeur, Politique sociale, Gilbert Fontaine
Directeur, Taxation des particuliers, Jean-Pierre Simard
Directeur, Taxation des entreprises, Bertrand Cayouette

Politiques relatives aux institutions financières et au droit corporatif / Policy Regarding Financial Institutions & Corporations
Sous-ministre adjoint, Richard Boivin
Directeur général, Pierre Rhéaume
Directeur, Encadrement du secteur financier, François Bouchard

Directeur, Développement du secteur financier et des personnes morales, Martin Landry

Commission de la fonction publique / Public Service Commission

800, place D'Youville, 7e étage, Québec, QC G1R 3P4
Tél: 418-643-1425
Téléc: 418-643-7264
Ligne sans frais: 800-432-0432
cfp@cfp.gouv.qc.ca
www.cfp.gouv.qc.ca

Présidente, Christiane Barbe

Hydro-Québec

75, boul René-Lévesque ouest, Montréal, QC H2Z 1A4
Tél: 514-289-2211
www.hydroquebec.com

Président, Conseil d'administration, Michael Louis Turcotte

Président-directeur général, Thierry Vandal

Vice-présidente exécutive, Affaires corporatives & Secrétaire générale, Marie-José Nadeau

Vice-président exécutif, Technologie, Élie Saheb

Président, Hydro-Québec TransÉnergie, André Boulanger

Président, Hydro-Québec Production, Richard Cacchione

Président, Hydro-Québec Équipement & services partagés, Réal Laporte
Président-directeur général, Thierry Vandal

Subsidiaries/Filiales
Subsidiaries/Filiales

Société d'énergie de la Baie-James (SEBJ) / James Bay Energy
888, de Maisonneuve est, 6e étage, Montréal, QC H2L 5B2
Tél: 514-286-2020
www.hydroquebec.com/sebj
Président-directeur général, Réal Laporte
Directeur, Projets de l'Eastmain, Normand Béchard

Ministère de l'Immigration et des Communautés culturelles / Immigration & Cultural Communities

Édifice Gérald-Godin, 360, rue McGill, Montréal, QC H2Y 2E9

Tél: 514-864-9191
Téléc: 514-864-2899
Ligne sans frais: 877-864-9191
www.micc.gouv.qc.ca
TTY: 514-864-8158
Autre numéros: Téléscripteur: 1-866-227-5968

Acts Administered:
Loi sur l'immigration au Québec/An act respecting immigration to Québec
Loi sur le ministère de l'Immigration et des Communautés culturelles/An act respecting the ministère de l'Immigration et des Communautés culturelles

Ministre, L'hon Diane De Courcy
Tél: 418-644-2128
Téléc: 418-528-0829
cabinet@micc.gouv.qc.ca

Sous-ministre, Robert Baril
Tél: 514-873-9450

Directeur, Affaires juridiques, Mélanie Paradis
Tél: 514-873-7484
Téléc: 514-873-2354

Directrice, Affaires publiques et communications, Hélène Saint-Pierre
Tél: 514-873-8624
Téléc: 514-873-7349

Secrétaire général, Paul Rémillard
Tél: 514-873-3464
Téléc: 514-864-2255

Directeur, Vérification interne, Manon Beauregard
Tél: 514-864-9896
Téléc: 514-864-2255

Agences, Conseils et Commissions Associés/ Associated Agencies, Boards & Commissions:

• Conseil des relations interculturelles (CRI)
#10.04, 500, boul René-Lévesque ouest
Montréal, QC H2Z 1W7
Tél: 514-873-5634
Téléc: 514-873-3469
info@conseilinterculturel.gouv.qc.ca
www.conseilinterculturel.gouv.qc.ca

Performance et francisation
Sous-ministre adjoint à la Performance et à la Francisation, Yvan Turcotte
Tél: 514-873-5942
Commissaire aux plaintes, Qualité des services, Hélène Lavallée
Tél: 514-873-3533
Directeur général, Francisation, Jacques Leroux
Tél: 514-864-3511
Directeur, Systèmes de l'information, François Mongrain
Tél: 514-873-2396
Téléc: 514-873-8180
Directrice, Ressources humaines, Dominique Laniel
Tél: 514-873-7172
Directeur, Ressources financières et matérielles, Denis Lazure
Tél: 514-873-1565
Directeur, Registraire et évaluation, Gilles Boileau
Tél: 514-864-2639
Directrice, Formation, Danièle Noël
Tél: 514-873-3663
Directrice, Développement, Luc Boisvert
Tél: 514-873-9393
Téléc: 514-864-2079
Directrice, Technologies et soutien aux utilisateurs, Stéphanie Laliberté
Tél: 514-873-1533
Téléc: 514-873-8180
Directrice, Recherche et analyse prospective, Anne-Marie Fadel
Tél: 514-864-9812
Directrice, Amélioration continue de la qualité, Odette Guertin
Tél: 514-873-2324
Directrice, Planification, Anne-Michéle Meggs
Tél: 514-873-2324

Immigration / Immigration
Sous-ministre adjoint, Robert Baril
Tél: 514-873-0706
Téléc: 514-873-0453
Directeur général, Opérations, Éric Gervais
Tél: 514-873-2446
Directrice, Politiques et programmes d'immigration, Marie-Josée Lemay
Tél: 514-873-5914
Directeur, Prospection et promotion, Bernard Roy
Tél: 514-873-5914
Directeur, Immigration économique — International, Owen-John Peate
Tél: 514-873-2812
Directeur (par intérim), Immigration économique — Québec, Fanny Marcoux
Tél: 514-864-1165
Directrice, Immigration familiale & humanitaire, Chantal Drolet
Tél: 514-864-9305
Directrice, Courrier et encaissement et de l'évaluation comparative, Michèle Langlois
Tél: 514-864-9097

Intégration / Integration
Sous-ministre adjointe, Claire Deronzier
Tél: 514-864-3404
Directrice générale, Intervention territoriale, Louise Boucher
Tél: 418-646-1605

Directeur général, Politiques et programmes d'intégration et d'interculturalisme, Martine Faille
Tél: 514-873-6440
Téléc: 514-864-4695
Directrice générale, Opérations régionales, Charlotte Poirier
Tél: 514-864-2345
Téléc: 514-864-3597
Directeur, Partenariats, François Bouchard
Tél: 514-864-2345
Directrice, Authentification, de l'évaluation professionnelle et de la révision administrative, Lyn Fleury
Tél: 514-864-2022
Téléc: 514-873-8701
Directrice, Politiques et programmes d'intégration sociale et économique, Jacinthe Michaud
Tél: 514-873-6440
Directeur, Mobilité professionnelle et services aux entreprises, François Plourde
Tél: 514-864-8352
Immigration-Québec - Capitale-Nationale/Est-de-Québec
Édifice Bois-Fontaine, 930, ch Sainte-Foy, RC, Québec, QC G1S 2L4
Tél: 418-643-1435
Téléc: 418-646-7460
Ligne sans frais: 888-643-1435
direction.quebec@micc.gouv.qc.ca
www.immigration-quebec.gouv.qc.ca
Directeur régionale, Yvon Doyle
Tél: 418-646-1605
Téléc: 418-646-0783
Immigration-Québec - Estrie/Mauricie/Centre-du-Québec
202, rue Wellington nord, Sherbrooke, QC J1H 5C6
Tél: 819-820-3606
Téléc: 819-820-3213
Ligne sans frais: 888-879-4288
direction.estrie@micc.gouv.qc.ca
www.immigration-quebec.gouv.qc.ca
Directrice régionale, Chantal Lussier
Tél: 819-820-3600
Immigration-Québec - Laval, Laurentides et Lanaudière
1438, boul Daniel-Johnson, Laval, QC H7N 4B5
Tél: 450-687-1220
Téléc: 450-687-7327
Ligne sans frais: 800-375-7426
direction.drlll@micc.gouv.qc.ca
www.immigration-quebec.gouv.qc.ca
Directeur régional, Serge Tétreault
Tél: 450-687-9080
Immigration-Québec - Montérégie
2, boul Desaulniers, 3e étage, Saint-Lambert, QC J4P 1L2
Tél: 450-466-4461
Téléc: 450-466-4481
Ligne sans frais: 888-287-5819
direction.monteregie@micc.gouv.qc.ca
www.immigration-quebec.gouv.qc.ca
Directeur régional, Guy Gagnon
Tél: 450-466-4025
Immigration-Québec - Outaouais/Abitibi-Témiscamingue/Nord-du-Québec
#100, 227, rue Montcalm, Gatineau, QC J8Y 3B9
Tél: 819-246-3212
Téléc: 819-246-3314
direction.outaouais@micc.gouv.qc.ca
www.immigration-quebec.gouv.qc.ca
Directrice régionale, Dominic Vaillancourt
Tél: 819-246-3212

Ministère de la Justice / Justice

Édifice Louis-Philippe-Pigeon, 1200, rte de l'Église, Québec, QC G1V 4M1
Tél: 418-643-5140
Ligne sans frais: 866-536-5140
informations@justice.gouv.qc.ca
www.justice.gouv.qc.ca

Acts Administered:
Charte des droits et libertés de la personne/Charter of Human Rights & Freedoms (in part)
Code civil du Québec/Civil Code of Québec
Code de la sécurité routière/Highway Safety Code (in part)
Code de procédure civile/Code of Civil Procedure
Code de procédure pénale/Code of Penal Procedure
Code des professions/Professional Code
Code du travail/Labour Code
Convention des Nations Unies sur les contrats de vente internationale de marchandises/An Act respecting the United Nations Convention on Contracts for the International Sale of Goods
Jugements rendus par la Cour suprême du Canada sur la langue des lois et d'autres actes de nature législative/An Act respecting the Judgements rendered in the Supreme Court of Canada on the language of statutes & otherinstruments of a legislative nature
Loi assurant l'application de l'entente sur l'entraide judiciaire entre la France et le Québec/An Act to secure the carrying out of the Entente between France & Québec respecting mutual aid in judicial matters
Loi concernant la loi constitutionnelle de 1982/An Act respecting Constitution Act, 1982
Loi concernant le cadre juridique des technologies de l'information/An Act to establish a Legal framework for information technology
Loi d'interprétation/Interpretation Act
Loi médicale/Medical Act
Loi sur l'acupuncture/An Act respecting Acupuncture
Loi sur l'aide aux victimes d'actes criminels/An Act respecting Assistance for victims of crime
Loi sur l'aide juridique/Legal Aid Act
Loi sur l'exécution réciproque d'ordonnances alimentaires/An Act respecting Reciprocal enforcement of maintenance orders
Loi sur l'indemnisation des victimes d'actes criminels/Crime Victims Compensation Act
Loi sur l'optométrie/Optometry Act
Loi sur la Société québécoise d'information juridique/An Act respecting the Société québécoise d'information juridique
Loi sur la chiropratique/Chiropractic Act
Loi sur la denturologie/Denturologists Act
Loi sur la division territoriale/Territorial Division Act (in part)
Loi sur la justice administrative/An Act respecting Administrative Justice
Loi sur la liberté des cultes/Freedom of Worship Act
Loi sur la pharmacie/Pharmacy Act
Loi sur la podiatrie/Podiatry Act
Loi sur la presse/Press Act
Loi sur la protection de la jeunesse/Youth Protection Act (in part)
Loi sur la protection du consommateur/Consumer Protection Act
Loi sur la réforme du cadastre québécois/An Act to promote the Reform of the cadastre in Québec
Loi sur la transparence et l'éthique en matière de lobbyisme/Lobbying transparency and Ethics Act
Loi sur le Recueil des lois et des règlements du Québec
Loi sur le barreau/An Act respecting the Barreau
Loi sur le drapeau et les emblèmes du Québec/An Act respecting the Flag and emblems of Québec
Loi sur le ministère de la Justice/An Act respecting the Ministère de la Justice
Loi sur le notariat/Notarial Act
Loi sur le paiement de certaines amendes/An Act respecting the Payment of certain fines
Loi sur le paiement de certains témoins/An Act respecting Payment of certain Crown witnesses
Loi sur le recours collectif/An Act respecting the Class Action
Loi sur le recouvrement de certaines créances/An Act respecting the collection of certain debts
Loi sur les agences des voyages/Travel Agents Act
Loi sur les agronomes/Agrologists Act
Loi sur les architectes/Architects Act
Loi sur les arpenteurs-géomètres/Land Surveyors Act
Loi sur les arrangements préalables de services funéraires et de sépulture/An Act respecting Prearranged funeral services and sepultures
Loi sur les aspects civils de l'enlèvement international et interprovincial d'enfants/An Act respecting Civil aspects of international and interprovincial child abduction
Loi sur les audioprothésistes/Hearing-aid Acousticians Act
Loi sur les chimistes professionnels/Professional Chemists Act
Loi sur les commissions d'enquête/An Act respecting Public inquiry commissions
Loi sur les comptables agréés/Chartered Accountants Act
Loi sur les cours municipales/An Act respecting the Municipal courts
Loi sur les dentistes/Dental Act
Loi sur les employés publics/Public Officers Act
Loi sur les huissiers de justice/Court Bailiffs Act
Loi sur les infirmières et infirmiers/Nurses Act
Loi sur les ingénieurs forestiers/Forest Engineers Act
Loi sur les ingénieurs/Engineers Act
Loi sur les journaux et autres publications/Newspaper Declaration Act
Loi sur les jurés/Jurors Act
Loi sur les maisons de désordre/Disorderly Houses Act
Loi sur les médecins vétérinaires/Veterinary Surgeons Act
Loi sur les opticiens d'ordonnance/Dispensing Opticians Act
Loi sur les privilèges des magistrats/Magistrate's Privileges Act
Loi sur les renvois à la Cour d'appel/Court of Appeal Reference Act
Loi sur les règlements/Regulations Act (in part)
Loi sur les sages-femmes/Midwives Act
Loi sur les salaires d'officiers de justice/An Act respecting the Salaries of officers of Justice
Loi sur les shérifs/Sheriffs' Act
Loi sur les sténographes/Stenographers' Act
Loi sur les substituts du procureur général/An Act respecting Attorney General's Prosecutors
Loi sur les technologues en radiologie/Radiology Technologists Act
Loi sur les tribunaux judiciaires/Courts of Justice Act
Loi visant à favoriser le civisme/An Act to promote Good citizenship

Ministre, L'hon. Bernard St-Arnaud
Tél: 418-643-4210
Téléc: 418-646-0027
ministre@justice.gouv.qc.ca

Sous-ministre, Nathalie G. Drouin
Tél: 418-643-4090

Directrice, Bureau du sous-ministre, Andrée Giguère
Tél: 418-643-4090 ext: 205

Directeur, Communications, Jean Guay

Directrice, Vérification interne, Francine Asselin
Tél: 418-643-8372 ext: 202

Directeur général, Système intégré d'information de justice, Michel Chandonnet

Agences, Conseils et Commissions Associés/ Associated Agencies, Boards & Commissions:

• Commission des services juridiques / Legal Services Commission
Tour de l'Est
#1404, 2, Complexe Desjardins
Montréal, QC H5B 1B3
Tél: 514-873-3562
Téléc: 514-873-8762
info@csj.qc.ca
www.csj.qc.ca/
• Conseil de la justice administrative / Administrative Justice Council
#RC-01, 575, rue Saint-Amable
Québec, QC G1R 2G4
Tél: 418-644-6279
Téléc: 418-528-8471
Ligne sans frais: 888-848-2581
courrier@cja.gouv.qc.ca
www.cja.gouv.qc.ca
• Conseil de la magistrature
#5.12, 300, boul Jean-Lesage
Québec, QC G1K 8K6
Tél: 418-644-2196
Téléc: 418-528-1581
information@cm.gouv.qc.ca
www.cm.gouv.qc.ca
• Directeur de l'état civil / Vital Statistics
2535, boul Laurier
Québec, QC G1V 5C5
Tél: 418-643-3900
Téléc: 418-646-3255
Ligne sans frais: 800-567-3900
etatcivil@gouv.qc.ca
www.etatcivil.gouv.qc.ca
Autres numéros: Montréal: 514/864-3900, Fax: 514/864-4563
• Fonds d'aide aux recours collectifs
#10.30, 1, rue Notre-Dame est
Montréal, QC H2Y 1B6
Tél: 514-393-2087
Téléc: 514-864-2998
farc@justice.gouv.qc.ca
• Office des professions du Québec / Occupations Board
• Société québécoise d'information juridique / Judicial Information Society of Québec
715, carré Victoria, 8e étage
Montréal, QC H2Y 2H7
Tél: 514-842-8741
Téléc: 514-844-8984
Ligne sans frais: 800-363-6718
info@soquij.qc.ca
www.soquij.qc.ca
• Tribunal administratif du Québec / Administrative Tribunal of Québec
575, rue Saint-Amable
Québec, QC G1R 5R4
Tél: 418-643-3418
Téléc: 418-643-5335
www.taq.gouv.qc.ca
Autres numéros: EMail: tribunal.administratif@taq.gouv.qc.ca

Affaires juridiques et législatives / Judicial & Legislative Affairs
Sous-ministre associée, Anne Trotier
Tél: 418-643-4228
Téléc: 418-644-0420
Directrice générale adjointe, Activités juridiques, Danielle Parent
Tél: 418-643-4228 ext: 207
Directrice générale adjointe, Affaires économiques et territoriales, France Fradette
Directeur général associé, Affaires contentieuses, Jean-Yves Bernard

Directrice générale associée, Litige et Droit public, Judith Sauvé
Directeur, Réseaux et Affaires gouvernementales, Françios Bélanger

Services à l'organisation / Administrative Services
Sous-ministre associé, Vacant
Tél: 418-643-4314
Directeur général associé, Personnel et administration, Sylvie St-Pierre
Directeur général associé, Ressources informationnelles, Michel Lapointe

Services de justice et des registres / Judicial Services & Registries
Sous-ministre associée, France Lynch
Tél: 418-644-7700 ext: 202
Téléc: 418-528-9539
Directrice générale associée, Services judiciaires de la Métropole, Marcelle Beaulieu
Directrice générale associée, Services judiciaires de la Capitale-Nationale et des régions, Chantal Couturier
Directrice, Soutien aux activités judiciaires, Francine Des Roches
Directeur, Gestion immobilière, Donald Tremblay
Directeur, Centre administratif et judiciaire, Gaétan Rancourt
Directrice générale associée, Registres et la certification, Suzanne Potvin Plamondon
Directeur, Soutien à la gestion, Patrice Blackburn

Office des professions du Québec / Occupations Board

800, place D'Youville, 10e étage, Québec, QC G1R 5Z3
Tél: 418-643-6912
Téléc: 418-643-0973
Ligne sans frais: 800-643-6912
courrier@opq.gouv.qc.ca
www.opq.gouv.qc.ca

Acts Administered:
Code des professions/Professional Code
Loi médicale/Medical Act
Loi sur l'acupuncture/An Act respecting Acupuncture
Loi sur l'optométrie/Optometry Act
Loi sur la chiropratique/Chiropractic Act
Loi sur la denturologie/Denturologists Act
Loi sur la pharmacie/Pharmacy Act
Loi sur la podiatrie/Podiatry Act
Loi sur le Barreau/An Act respecting the Barreau de Québec
Loi sur le notariat/Notarial Act
Loi sur les Technologues en imagerie médicale et en radio-oncologie/Act respecting medical imaging technologists & radiation oncology technologists
Loi sur les agronomes/Agrologists Act
Loi sur les architectes/Architects Act
Loi sur les arpenteurs-géomètres/Land Surveyors Act
Loi sur les audioprothésistes/Hearing-aid Acousticians Act
Loi sur les chimistes professionnels/Professional Chemists Act
Loi sur les comptables agrées/Chartered Accountants Act
Loi sur les dentistes/Dental Act
Loi sur les géologues/Geologists Act
Loi sur les infirmières et les infirmiers/Nurses Act
Loi sur les ingénieurs forestiers/Forest Engineers Act
Loi sur les ingénieurs/Engineers Act
Loi sur les médecins vétérinaires/Veterinary Surgeons Act
Loi sur les opticiens d'ordonnances/Dispensing Opticians Act
Loi sur les sages-femmes/Midwives Act

Président, Jean Paul Dutrisac
Tél: 418-643-6912

Vice-présidente, Christiane Gagnon

Directeur, Affaires juridiques, Jean-François Paquet

Directrice, Recherche & analyse, Hélène Dubois

Directeur, Services administratifs, Jacques Laflamme

Le Protecteur du Citoyen / Ombudsman

#1.25, 525, boul René-Lévesque est, Québec, QC G1R 5Y4
Tél: 418-643-2688
Téléc: 418-643-8759
Ligne sans frais: 800-463-5070
protecteur@protecteurducitoyen.qc.ca
www.protecteurducitoyen.qc.ca
TTY: 866-410-0901
Secondary Address: #1000, 1080, côte du Beaver Hull, 10e étage
Montréal, QC H2Z 1S8
Téléc: 514-873-4640

Protectrice du citoyen, Raymonde Saint-Germain

Vice-protecteur, Prévention & innovation, Marc-André Dowd

Directeur, Ressources humaines & l'administration, Marcel Domingue

Registraire des entreprises

787, boul Lebourgneuf, Québec, QC G2J 1C3
Tél: 418-644-4545
Téléc: 418-528-5703
Ligne sans frais: 877-644-4545
registre@servicesquebec.gouv.qc.ca
www.registreentreprises.gouv.qc.ca
TTY: 800-361-9596
2050, rue De Bleury, #RC 10
Montréal, QC H3A 2J5

Acts Administered:
Charte de la Ville de Québec/Charter of Ville de Québec
Code civil du Québec/Civil Code of Québec
Code de procédure civile/Civil Code of Québec
Code du travail/Labour Code
Code municipal du Québec/Municipal Code of Québec
Loi concernant les services de transport par taxi
Loi constituant Capital régional et cooperatif Desjardins
Loi constituant Fondaction, le Fonds de développement de la Confédération des syndicats nationaux pour la coopération et l'emploi
Loi constituant le Fonds de solidarité des travailleurs du Québec
Loi sur la constitution de certaines Églises/Québec Church Incorporation Act
Loi sur la liquidation des compagnies/Winding Up Act
Loi sur la publicité légale des entreprises/An Act respecting the Legal Publicity of enterprises
Loi sur le courtage immobilier
Loi sur le ministère de la Culture et des Communications
Loi sur le registraire des entreprises/An Act respecting the Entreprise registrar
Loi sur les assurances/Québec Act respecting insurance
Loi sur les cités et villes/Cities & Towns Act
Loi sur les clubs de chasse et de pêche/Québec Fish and Game Clubs Act
Loi sur les clubs de récréation/Québec Amusement Clubs Act
Loi sur les compagnies de cimetière catholiques romains/Québec Act respecting Roman Catholic cemetery corporations
Loi sur les compagnies de cimetière/Québec Cemetery Companies Act
Loi sur les compagnies de flottage/Québec Timber-Driving Companies Act
Loi sur les compagnies de gaz, d'eau et d'électricité/Québec Gas, Water and Electricity Companies Act
Loi sur les compagnies de télégraphe et de téléphone/Québec Telegraph and Telephone Companies Act
Loi sur les compagnies minières Québec/Québec Mining Companies Act
Loi sur les compagnies/Québec Companies Act
Loi sur les coopératives de services financiers/Québec Act respecting financial services cooperatives
Loi sur les coopératives/Québec Cooperatives Act
Loi sur les corporations religieuses/Québec Religious Corporations Act
Loi sur les fabriques/Québec Act respecting fabriques
Loi sur les pouvoirs spéciaux des personnes morales
Loi sur les services de santé et les services sociaux pour les autochtones cris/Act respecting health services & social services for Native persons
Loi sur les services de santé et les services sociaux/Québec Act respecting health services & social services
Loi sur les sociétés agricoles et laitières/Québec Act respecting farmers' and dairymen's associations
Loi sur les sociétés d'horticulture/Québec Horticultural Societies Act
Loi sur les sociétés de fiducie et les sociétés d'épargne/Québec Act respecting trust companies and savings companies
Loi sur les sociétés de transport en commun
Loi sur les sociétés nationales de bienfaisance/Qué National Benefit Societies Act
Loi sur les sociétés préventives de cruauté envers les animaux/Québec Act respecting societies for the prevention of cruelty to animals
Loi sur les syndicats professionnels/Québec Professional Syndicates Act
Loi sur les Évêques catholiques romains/Québec Roman Catholic Bishops Act

Ministre responsable, L'hon. Robert Dutil
Tél: 418-652-6835
Téléc: 418-643-7379

Ministère des Relations internationales / International Relations

Édifice Hector-Fabre, 525, boul Réne-Lévesque est, Québec, QC G1R 5R9
Tél: 418-649-2300
Téléc: 418-649-2656
www.mri.gouv.qc.ca
Secondary Address: 380, rue St-Antoine ouest
Montréal, QC H2Y 3X7
Téléc: 514-873-7468

Acts Administered:
Loi sur l'immigration au Québec/An act respecting immigration to Québec
Loi sur le ministère de l'Immigration et des Communautés culturelles/An act respecting the ministère de l'Immigration et des Communautés culturelles

Ministre, L'hon. Jean-François Lisée
Tél: 418-649-2319
Téléc: 418-643-4804

Sous-ministre, Michel Audet
Tél: 418-649-2335
Téléc: 418-649-2667

Directeur, Communications & affaires publiques, Gilles Beaulé
Tél: 418-649-2333

Directeur, Affaires bilatérales, Jean-Stéphane Bernard
Tél: 418-649-2335

Directrice, Politiques & affaires francophones & multilatérales, Vacant
Tél: 418-649-2400 ext: 560

Directeur, Protocole & missions, Claude Pinault
Tél: 418-649-2346
Téléc: 418-649-2657

Directeur, Administration, Bernard Dubois
Tél: 418-649-2666

Administration / Administration
Directeur général, Bernard Dubois
Tél: 418-649-2666
Directeur, Ressources humaines, Anouk Gagné
Tél: 418-649-2339
Directeur, Ressources financières, Sylvain Berniere
Tél: 418-649-2316
Directeur (par intérim), Gestion immobilière, Bernard Dubois
Tél: 418-649-2337
Directeur, Ressources informationnelles, David Beardsell
Tél: 418-649-2326
Directeur, Technologies, Bruno Légaré
Tél: 418-649-2400 ext: 570

Affaires bilatérales / Bilateral Affairs
Directeur, Jean-Stéphane Bernard
Tél: 418-649-2335

Amérique du Nord / North America

Amérique latine et Antilles / Latin America and Caribbean
Directrice, Christina Vigna

États-Unis / United States
Directeur, États-Unis, Jean Saintonge
Tél: 418-649-2310

Bureaux à l'étranger/Offices Abroad
Bureaux à l'étranger/Offices Abroad
Atlanta, GA, USA
Délégation du Québec à Atlanta, #3240, 191 Peachtree St. NE, Atlanta, GA 30303 USA
Tél: 404-584-2995
Téléc: 404-584-2089
qc.atlanta@mri.gouv.qc.ca
Chef de poste, Joane Boyer
Boston, MA, USA
One Boston Place, #3850, 201 Washington St., Boston, MA 02108 USA
Tél: 617-482-1193
Téléc: 617-482-1195
qc.boston@mri.gouv.qc.ca
Chef de poste, Marie-Claude Francoeur
Chicago, IL, USA
Délégation du Québec à Chicago, #3650, 444 N Michigan Ave., Chicago, IL 60611 USA
Tél: 312-645-0932
Téléc: 312-645-0542
qc.chicago@mri.gouv.qc.ca
Chef de poste, Éric Marquis

Los Angeles, CA, USA
Délégation du Québec à Los Angeles, #720, 10940 Wilshire Blvd., Los Angeles, CA 90024 USA
Tél: 310-824-4173
Téléc: 310-824-7759
qc.losangeles@mri.gouv.qc.ca
Chef de poste, Alain Houde
Mexico City, Mexico
Délégation générale du Québec, Avenida Taine 411, Colonia Bosques de Chapultepec, Mexico, DF 11580 Mexico
qc.mexico@mri.gouv.qc.ca
Autre numéros: Téléphone: 52-55-1100-4330; Fax: 52-55-1100-4331
Chef de poste, Christiane Pelchat
New York, NY, USA
Délégation générale du Québec, One Rockefeller Plaza, 26the Fl., New York, NY 10020-2102 USA
Tél: 212-843-0950
Téléc: 212-376-8983
qc.newyork@mri.gouv.qc.ca
Chef de poste (par intérim), Manon Boucher
Washington, DC, USA
Bureau du Québec à Washington, #450, 805 15th St. NW, Washington, DC 20005 USA
Tél: 202-659-8990
Téléc: 202-659-5654
qc.washington@mri.gouv.qc.ca
Chef de poste, Alain Olivier

Asie-Pacifique / Asia-Pacific
Directrice, Asie-Pacifique, Juliette Champagne
Tél: 418-649-2662

Bureaux à l'étranger/Offices Abroad
Bureaux à l'étranger/Offices Abroad
Beijing, Chine
Ambassade du Canada, 19, Dongzhimenwai Dajie, Dist. de Chaoyang, Beijing, 100600 China
rene.milot@international.gc.ca
Autre numéros: Tél: 86 10 5139 4445 poste 3600; Téléc: 86 10 6532 1304
Chef de poste, François Gaudreau
Hong Kong, Chine
Bureau d'immigration, Exchange Square, Tower 1, 8, Connaught Pl., Central, 10th Fl., Hong Kong
biq.hkong@micc.gouv.qc.ca
Autre numéros: Téléphone: 852-2810-7183; Télécopieur: 852 2845 3889
Mumbai, Inde
Bureau du Québec à Mumbai, Fort House, 221, Dr. D.N. Rd., 6e étage, Mumbai, MH 400 001 India
qc.mumbai@mri.gouv.qc.ca
Autre numéros: Téléphone: 91-22-6749-4444; Télécopieur: 91-22-6749-4454
Séoul, Korea
Antenne du Québec, 5F, Leema Bldg., 146-1, Soosong-dong, Jongno-gu, Séoul, 110-755 Korea
qc.seoul@mri.gouv.qc.ca
Autre numéros: Téléphone: 82-2-3703-7700; Télécopieur: 82-2-732-5175
Chef de poste, Chungyoll Yoo
Shanghai, Chine
a/s Consulat général du Canada, Shanghai Centre, #604, West Tower, 1376 Nanjing Xi Rd., Shanghai, 200040 Chine
qc.shanghai@mri.gouv.qc.ca
Autre numéros: Téléphone: 86-21-3279-2800, poste 3600; Télécopieur: 86-21-3279-2801
Chef de poste (par intérim), François Gaudreau
Taipei, Taïwan
Antenne du Québec, Quartier XinYi, 1, rue Song Zhi, 6e étage, Taipei, 11047 Taïwan
qc.taipei@mri.gouv.qc.ca
Autre numéros: Téléphone: 886-2-8789-3556; Télécopieur: 886-2-8789-2898
Chef de poste, Michael Chen
Tokyo, Japon
Délégation générale du Québec, Shiroyama JT Trust Tower, 32e étage, 4-3-1 Toranomon, Minato-Ku, Tokyo, 105-6032 Japan
qc.tokyo@mri.gouv.qc.ca
Autre numéros: Téléphone: 81-3-5733-4001; Télécopieur: 81-3-5472-6721
Chef de poste, Claude-Yves Charron

Europe

Europe de l'Ouest et du Nord - Institutions européennes / Western & Northern Europe
Directrice (par intérim), Europe de l'Ouest & du Nord -Institutions européennes, Élisa Valentin
Tél: 418-649-2669
Téléc: 418-649-2421
Directrice, Solidarité internationale/Haïti et Afrique subsaharienne, Marjolaine Ricard
Tél: 418-649-2341
Directeur, Europe méditerranéenne et est/Maghreb et Moyen-Orient, Bernard Denault
Tél: 418-649-2343

Europe méditerranéenne et de l'Est - Maghreb et Moyen-Orient / Mediterranean and Eastern Europe
Directeur, Europe méditerranéenne et de l'Est - Maghreb et Moyen-Orient, Bernard Denault

Bureaux à l'étranger/Offices Abroad
Bureaux à l'étranger/Offices Abroad
Barcelone, Espagne
Bureau du Québec, Avinguda Diagonal, 420, 3er 1a, Barcelone, 08037 Espagne
qc.barcelone@mri.gouv.qc.ca
Autre numéros: Téléphone: 34-93-476-42-5; Télécopieur: 34-93-476-47-74
Chef de poste, Majolaine Ricard
Berlin, Allemagne
Bureau du Québec, Pariser Platz 6A, Berlin, 10117 Allemagne
qc.berlin@mri.gouv.qc.ca
Autre numéros: Téléphone: 49-30-5900646-0; Télécopieur: 49-30-5900646-29
Chef de poste, Serge Vaillancourt
Bruxelles, Belgique
Délégation générale du Québec, 46, av des Arts, 7e étage, Bruxelles, 1000 Belgique
qc.bruxelles@mri.gouv.qc.ca
Autre numéros: Téléphone: 32-2-512-00-36; Télécopieur: 32-2-514-26-41
Chef de poste, Christos Sirros
Londres, Angleterre
Délégation générale du Québec, 59 Pall Mall, Londres, SW1Y 5JH Royaume-Uni
qc.londres@mri.gouv.qc.ca
Autre numéros: Téléphone: 44-207-766-5900; Télécopieur: 44-207-930-7938
Chef de poste, Pierre Boulanger
Milan, Italie
Antenne économique du Québec, #337, 1 via Manfredo Camperio, 3e étage, Milan, 20123 Italie
qc.milan@mri.gouv.qc.ca
Autre numéros: Téléphone: 39-02-8052-210; Télécopieur: 39-02-72016399
Moscou, Russie
Ambassade du Canada, 23 Starokonyushenny Pereulok, Moscou, 119002 Russie
qc.moscou@mri.gouv.qc.ca
Autre numéros: Téléphone: +7 495-925-6894; Télécopieur: +7 495-925-6051
Chef de poste, Nicolas Fresne
Munich, Allemagne
Délégation générale du Québec, Karl-Scharnagl-Ring 6, Munich, 80539 Allemagne
qc.munich@mri.gouv.qc.ca
Autre numéros: Téléphone: 49-89-2554931-0; Télécopieur: 49-89-21019473
Chef de poste, Charles Villiers
Paris, France
Délégation générale du Québec, 66, rue Pergolèse, Paris, 75116 France
qc.paris@mri.gouv.qc.ca
Autre numéros: Téléphone: 33-1-40-67-85-00; Télécopieur: 33-1-40-67-85-19
Chef de poste, Michel Robitaille
Rome, Italie
Délégation du Québec, #5, 16 via Delle Quattro Fontane, 2e étage, Rome, 00184 Italie
qc.rome@mri.gouv.qc.ca
Autre numéros: Téléphone: 39-06-4203-4501, poste 54301; Télécopieur: 39-06-4203-4502
Chef de poste, Amalia Daniela Renosto
Stockholm, Suède
Bureau d'Investissement Québec à Stockholm, Klarabergsgatan 23, 6e étage, CP 16129, Stockholm, 103 23 Suède
Autre numéros: Téléphone: 46-8-453-30-37; Télécopieur: 46-8-453-30-16

Afrique / Africa

Solidarité international - Haïti et Afrique subsaharienne / Haïti & Sub-Saharan Africa
Directeur, Donald Leblanc

Centrale et Amérique du Sud / Central and South America

Bureaux à l'étranger/Offices Abroad
Bureaux à l'étranger/Offices Abroad
Santiago, Chile
Edificio World Trade Center, Neuva Tajamar 481, Torre Norte, Oficina 904, Santiago
qc.santiago@mri.gouv.qc.ca
Autre numéros: Télé: 56 2 350 4255
Sao Paulo, Brésil
Avenida Engenheiro Luis Carlos Berrini, 1511, CJ 151 e 152, 15e Andar, Sao Paulo, 04571-011 Brésil
qc.saopaulo@mri.gouv.qc.ca
Autre numéros: Télé: +55 11 5505 0444; Téléc: +55 11 5505 0445

Politiques et affaires francophones et multilatérales / Policy and Francophone and Multilateral Affairs
Directrice générale, Vacant
Tél: 418-649-2335
Directeur, Planification et politiques, Roger Ménard
Tél: 418-649-2305
Directeur adjoint, Analyses, Claude Trudelle
Tél: 418-649-2428
Directeur, Organisations internationales, Daniel Lacroix
Tél: 418-649-2320
Téléc: 418-649-2403
Directeur, Engagements internationaux, Patrice Bachand
Tél: 418-649-2411
Directrice, Francophonie, Régine Lavoie
Tél: 418-649-2444

Ministère des Ressources naturelles / Natural Resources

880, ch Sainte-Foy, Québec, QC G1S 4X4
Tél: 418-627-8600
Téléc: 418-644-6513
Ligne sans frais: 866-248-6936
services.clientele@mrnf.gouv.qc.ca
www.mrn.gouv.qc.ca

Acts Administered:
Lands in the Domain of the State Designated for Development of Wildlife Resources Regulation
Loi approuvant la convention de la Baie-James et du nord québécois/An Act approving the Agreement concerning James Bay and Northern Québec
Loi approuvant la convention du nord-est québécois/An Act approving the Northeastern Québec Agreement
Loi assurant la mise en oeuvre de l'entente concernant une nouvelle relation entre le gouvernement du Québec et les Cris du Québec/An Act to ensure the implementation of the Agreement Concerning a New Relationship Betweenthe Government of Québec and the
Loi concernant les droits sur les mines/Mining Duties Act
Loi de 1994 sur la convention concernant les oiseaux migrateurs
Loi favorisant la réforme du cadastre québécois/An Act to promote the reform of the cadastre in Québec
Loi favorisant le crédit forestier par les institutions privées/An Act to promote forest credit by private institutions
Loi sur Hydro-Québec/Hydro-Québec Act
Loi sur l'exportation de l'électricité/An Act respecting the exportation of electric power
Loi sur la Régie de l'énergie/An Act respecting the Régie de l'énergie
Loi sur la conservation et la mise en valeur de la faune/Act respecting the conservation and development of wildlife
Loi sur la division territoriale/Territorial Division Act
Loi sur la société Eeyou de la Baie-James/An Act respecting the James Bay Eeyou Corporation
Loi sur la société de développement autochtone de la Baie James/An Act respecting the James Bay Native Development Corporation
Loi sur la société nationale de l'amiante/An Act respecting the Société nationale de l'amiante
Loi sur le cadastre/Cadastre Act
Loi sur le crédit forestier/Forestry Credit Act
Loi sur le développement et l'organisation municipale de la région de la Baie-James/James Bay Region Development and Municipal Organization Act
Loi sur le ministère des ressources naturelles et de la faune/An Act respecting the Ministère des Ressources naturelles et de la Faune
Loi sur le mode de paiement des services d'électricité et de gaz dans certains immeubles/An Act respecting the mode of payment for electric and gas service in certain buildings
Loi sur le programme d'aide aux Inuits bénéficiaires de la convention de la Baie-James et du nord québécois pour leurs activités de chasse, de pêche et de piégeage/An Act respecting the support program for Inuitbeneficiaries of the James Bay and Norther
Loi sur le régime des eaux/Watercourses Act

Loi sur le régime des terres dans les territoires de la Baie-James et du Nouveau-Québec/An Act respecting the land regime in the James Bay and New Québec territories
Loi sur les Pêches
Loi sur les arpentages/An Act respecting land survey
Loi sur les bureaux de la publicité des droits/An Act respecting registry offices
Loi sur les clubs de chasse et de pêche/Fish and Game Clubs Act
Loi sur les compagnies de flottage/Timber-Driving Companies Act
Loi sur les droits de chasse et de pêche dans les territoires de la Baie James et du Nouveau-Québec/An Act respecting hunting and fishing rights in the James Bay and New Québec territories
Loi sur les espèces menacées ou vulnérables/An Act respecting threatened or vulnerable species
Loi sur les forêts/Forest Act
Loi sur les mesurers de bois/Cullers Act
Loi sur les mines/Mining Act
Loi sur les systèmes municipaux et les systèmes privés d'électricité/An Act respecting municipal and private electric power systems
Loi sur les terres du domaine de l'état/An Act respecting the lands in the domain of the State
Loi sur les titres de propriété dans certains districts électoraux/An Act respecting land titles in certain electoral districts
Regulation respecting aquaculture and the sale of fish
Regulation respecting wildlife habitats
Regulation respecting wildlife sanctuaries
Règlement sur l'application de dispositions législatives par les agents de protection de la faune/Regulation respecting enforcement of certain legislative & regulatory provisions respecting protection of environment bywildlife protection officers
Règlement sur le domaine hydrique de l'État/Regulation respecting the water property in the domain of the State
Règlement sur les produits pétroliers/Petroleum Products Regulation
Règlement sur les zones d'exploitation contrôlée de chasse et de pêche/Regulation respecting hunting & fishing controlled zones

Ministre, L'hon. Martine Ouellet

Ministre délégué, L'hon. Patrick Déry

Sous-ministre, Patrick Déry
Tél: 418-627-6370
Téléc: 418-643-1443

Directeur général, Administration/Connaissance géographique, Ubald Gagné
Tél: 418-627-6260
Téléc: 418-646-2614

Sous-ministre associé, Opérations régionales, Pierre Grenier
Tél: 418-627-6354
Téléc: 418-646-0042

Directeur, Bureau du sous-ministre et serétariat, Démosthène Blasi

Directrice, Évaluation et vérification, Renée Brassard

Directeur, Communications, Pierre Buist

Directrice, Affaires juridiques, Lise Proulx

Agences, Conseils et Commissions Associés/ Associated Agencies, Boards & Commissions:

• Agence de l'efficacité énergétique / Energy Efficiencies Agency
5700, 4e av ouest
Québec, QC G1H 6R1
Tél: 418-627-6379
Téléc: 418-643-5828
Ligne sans frais: 877-727-6655
efficaciteenergetique@mrnf.gouv.qc.ca
www.efficaciteenergetique.mrnf.gouv.qc.ca
Promotes the efficient use of all forms of energy, in all sectors of activity, for the benefit of the people of Québec. The Agency achieves this through demonstration projects, which highlight new technologies, new approaches or new applications that save energy; design, management & evaluation of energy efficient programs; information, training & educational materials; technical & organizational support for export of products & services; review, commentary on proposed amendments to applicable laws & regulations.

• Comité conjoint de chasse, de pêche et de piégeage / Hunting, Fishing & Trapping Joint Committee
#C220, 383 rue Saint-Jacques
Montréal, QC H2Y 1N9
Tél: 514-284-2151
Téléc: 514-284-0039
infohftcc@cccpp-hftcc.com
www.cccpp-hftcc.com

• Fondation de la faune du Québec / Québec Wildlife Foundation
Place Iberville II
#420, 1175, av Lavigerie
Québec, QC G1V 4P1
Tél: 418-644-7926
Téléc: 418-643-7655
Ligne sans frais: 877-639-0742
ffq@fondationdelafaune.qc.ca
www.fondationdelafaune.qc.ca
Non-profit organization whose mission is to enhance the value & promote the conservation of wildlife & its habitats.

• Hydro Québec
75, boul René-Lévesque ouest
Montréal, QC H2Z 1A4
Tél: 514-385-7252
Ligne sans frais: 800-790-2424
www.hydroquebec.com
Autres numéros: Residential Customer Service: 1-888-385-7252; TTY: 711; Persons with a visual impairment: 1-888-385-7252

• Régie de l'énergie / Energy Regulation Board
Tour de la Bourse
#2.55, 800, Place Victoria
Montréal, QC H4Z 1A2
Tél: 514-873-2452
Téléc: 514-873-2070
Ligne sans frais: 888-873-2452
secretariat@regie-energie.qc.ca
www.regie-energie.qc.ca
An economic regulation agency, its mission is to reconcile the public interest, consumer protection, & fair treatment of the electricity carrier & distributors.

• Société de développement de la Baie James (SDBJ) / James Bay Development Society
110, boul Matagami
CP 970
Matagami, QC J0Y 2A0
Tél: 819-739-4717
Téléc: 819-739-4329
mat@sdbj.gouv.qc.ca
www.sdbj.gouv.qc.ca
Developed in 1971, this organization uses its resources & vast knowledge of the territory, contributors, & development projects to promote & maintain activities in the James Bay area, with a perspective of integrated economic development & harmonious cohabitation with territorial residents.

Énergie / Energy
#B401, 5700, 4e av ouest, Québec, QC G1H 6R1
Tél: 418-627-6377
Téléc: 418-643-0701
Le gouvernement québécois prévoit le lancement des projets hydoélectriques représentant 4,500 MW, qui susciteront des investissements de l'ordre de 25m de dollars, et la création d'environ 70,000 emplois sur six ans. Il mise sur le développement du potential existant d'énergie éolienne, avec l'objectif de 4,000 MW d'ici 2015, et prend plusieurs moyens afin de renforcer la sécurité des approvisionnements en pétrole et gaz naturel
Sous-ministre associé, Mario Gosselin
Directrice générale, Électricité, Julie Grignon
Tél: 418-627-6386 ext: 819
Directeur général, Hydrocarbures et Bioarburants, Alain Lefebvre
Tél: 418-627-6385 ext: 825
Directeur général (par intérim), Efficacité et innovation énergétiques, J. E. Alain Daneau
Directeur, Grands projets et réglementation, Philippe-Pierre Nazon

Faune Québec / Wildlife Québec
RC-120, 880, ch Sainte-Foy, Québec, QC G1S 4X4
Tél: 418-627-8652
Sous-ministre associée, Nathalie Camden
Tél: 418-627-8652 ext: 400
Directeur général, Protection de la faune, Guy Nadeau
Tél: 418-627-8688 ext: 751
Directeur, Expertise sur la faune et ses habitats, Pierre Bérubé
Tél: 418-627-8694 ext: 741
Directeur, Développement socio-économique, partenariats et éducation, Jacob Martin-Malus
Tél: 418-627-8691 ext: 736
Chef, Réglementation, tarification et permis, Lucie Aubin

Foncier Québec / Québec Lands
5700, 4e av ouest, Québec, QC G1H 6R1
Tél: 418-643-3582
Téléc: 418-528-8721
Ligne sans frais: 866-226-0977
assistance.clientele@mrnf.registrefoncier.gouv.qc.ca
Sous-ministre associée, Louise Ouellet
Tél: 418-627-6252 ext: 308
Téléc: 418-643-3954
Directeur général, Arpentage et cadastre, Julien Arsenault
Tél: 418-627-6267
Téléc: 418-646-7405
Directeur général, Clientèle et technologies d'affaires, Marc Lainé
Directrice générale, Registre Foncier, Line Drouin
Tél: 418-627-6264 ext: 380
Forestier en chef, Gérard Szaraz
Sous-ministre associé (par intérim), Directeur, Dévelopment stratégique, Marc Plante
Directeur, Calcul des possibilités forestiéres, Jean Girard

Forêt Québec / Québec Forests
880, ch Ste-Foy, #RC 120, Québec, QC G1S 4X4
Tél: 418-627-8652
Téléc: 418-528-1278
foretquebec@mrnf.gouv.qc.ca
Sous-ministre associé, Richard Savard
Sous-ministre associé/Forestier en chef, Gérard Szaraz
Directrice, Orientations stratégiques et administration, Francis Forcier
Directeur, Bureau de la coordination du régime forestier, Alain Sénéchal
Directrice générale, Connaissance et gestion de l'information forestière, Elisabeth Bossert
Directeur, Recherche forestière, Robert Jobidon
Directeur, Gestion de l'information forestière, Denis Robitaille
Directeur, Inventaires forestiers, Luc Tellier
Directeur général, Attribution des bois et développement industriel, Réal Paris
Directeur, Développement de l'industrie et des produits forestiers, André Denis
Directeur, Gestion des stocks ligneux, Réal Paris
Directeur général, Aménagement durable des forêts/Bureau de mise en marché des bois, Mario Gibeault
Directeur, Évaluations économiques et opérations financières, Jean-Pierre Adam
Directeur, Aménagement et environnement forestiers, Ronald Brizard
Directeur, Opérations territoriales de mise en marché, François Trottier

Mines
Centre de service des Mines, 1685, boul Wilfrid Hamel ouest, 1er étage, Québec, QC G1N 3Y7
Tél: 418-627-6278
Téléc: 418-644-8960
Ligne sans frais: 800-363-7233
service.mines@mrnf.gouv.qc.ca
Sous-ministre associé, Mines, Robert Marquis
Tél: 418-627-8652
Directeur général (par intérim), Géologie Québec, Robert Giguère
Tél: 819-354-4514 ext: 232
Directrice générale, Gestion du milieu minier, Lucie Ste-Croix
Tél: 418-627-6292 ext: 538
Directeur général, Développement de l'industrie minérale, Renée Garon
Tél: 418-627-6292 ext: 505
Abitibi-Témiscamingue
70, av Québec, Rouyn-Noranda, QC J9X 6R1
Tél: 819-763-3388
Téléc: 819-763-3186
Directeur (par intérim), Jean-Pierre Lessard
Bas-Saint-Laurent
#207, 92, 2e rue ouest, Rimouski, QC G5L 8B3
Tél: 418-727-3710
Téléc: 418-727-3735
Directeur, Dominic Gagnon
Capitale-Nationale—Chaudière-Appalaches
8400, av Sous-le-Vent, Charny, QC G6X 3S9
Tél: 418-832-7222
Téléc: 418-832-1827
Directeur, André Jutras
Mauricie—Centre-du-Québec
#207, 100 rue Laviolette, Trois-Rivières, QC G9A 5S9
Tél: 819-371-6151
Téléc: 819-371-6978
Ligne sans frais: 866-821-4625
Directeur, Réjean Rioux
Côte-Nord
456, av Arnaud, 1er étage, Sept-îles, QC G4R 3B1
Tél: 418-964-8300
Téléc: 418-964-8506
cote-nord@mrnf.gouv.qc.ca
Directeur, David Erdely

Estrie—Montréal—Montérégie
770, rue Goretti, Sherbrooke, QC J1E 3H4
Tél: 819-820-3883
Téléc: 819-820-3747
Directeur, Claude Beauchemin
Gaspésie—Iles-de-la-Madeleine
124, 1re Avenue ouest, Sainte-Anne-des-Monts, QC G4V 1C5
Tél: 418-763-3302
Téléc: 418-764-2378
Directeur (par intérim), Dominic Gagnon
Laval—Lanaudière—Laurentides
#1.50B, 999, rue Nobel, Saint-Jérôme, QC J7Z 7A3
Tél: 450-569-3113
Téléc: 450-469-7568
Directeur (par intérim), Benoît Levert
Nord-du-Québec
1121, boul Industriel, CP 159, Lebel-sur-Quévillon, QC J0Y 1X0
Tél: 819-755-4838
Téléc: 819-755-3541
nord-du-quebec@mrnf.gouv.qc.ca
Directeur, Michel Bergeron
Outaouais
#RC 100, 16, impasse de la Gare-Talon, Gatineau, QC J8T 0B1
Tél: 819-246-4827
Téléc: 819-246-5049
outaouais@mrnf.gouv.qc.ca
Directeur, Benoît Levert
Saguenay—Lac-Saint-Jean
3950, boul Harvey, 4e étage, Jonquière, QC G7X 8L6
Tél: 418-695-8125
Téléc: 418-695-8436
saguenay-lac-saint-jean@mrnf.gouv.qc.ca
Directrice (par intérim), Jasmin Larouche
Sous-ministre associé, Opérations régionale, Jean-Sylvain Lebel

Directeur générale, Pépinières et stations piscicoles, Daniel Richard
Directeur générale, Developpement et coordination des opérations régionales, François Provost
Abitibi-Témiscamingue
70, av Québec, Rouyn-Noranda, QC J9X 6R1
Tél: 819-763-3388
Téléc: 819-763-3216
abitibi-temiscamingue@mrnf.gouv.qc.ca
Directeur général, Martin Gingras
Bas-Saint-Laurent
#207, 92, 2e Rue ouest, Rimouski, QC G5L 8B3
Tél: 418-727-3710
Téléc: 418-727-3735
bas-saint-laurent@mrnf.gouv.qc.ca
Directeur général, Paul St-Laurent
Capitale-Nationale—Chaudières-Appalaches
#1.14, 1685, boul Wilfrid Hamel ouest, Québec, QC G1N 3Y7
Tél: 418-643-4680
Téléc: 418-644-8960
capitale-nationale@mrnf.gouv.qc.ca
Autre numéros: chaudiere-appalaches@mrnf.gouv.qc.ca
Directrice générale, Cécile Tremblay
Côte-Nord
#RC 702, 625, boul Laflèche, Baie-Comeau, QC G5C 1C5
Tél: 418-295-4676
Téléc: 418-295-4682
cote-nord.@mrnf.gouv.qc.ca
Directeur général (par intérim), Linda Tremblay
Gaspésie—Iles-de-la-Madeleine
195, boul Perron est, Caplan, QC G0C 1H0
Tél: 418-388-2125
Téléc: 418-388-2444
gaspesie-iles-de-la-madeleine@mrnf.gouv.qc.ca
Directeur général, Bernard Landry
Mauricie—Centre-du-Québec
#207, 100, rue Laviolette, Trois-Rivières, QC G9A 5S9
Tél: 418-371-6151
Téléc: 418-371-6978
Ligne sans frais: 866-821-4625
mauricie@mrnf.gouv.qc.ca
Autre numéros: centreduquebec@mrnf.gouv.qc.ca
Directeur général, Alain Simard
Estrie—Montréal—Montérégie et Laval—Lanaudière—Laurentides
545, boul Crémazie est, 8e étage, Montréal, QC H2M 2V1
Tél: 514-873-2140
Téléc: 514-873-8983
estrie@mrnf.gouv.qc.ca
Autre numéros: montreal@mrnf.gouv.qc.ca; monteregie@mrnf.gouv.qc.ca; laval@mrnf.gouv.qc.ca; lanaudiere@mrnf.gouv.qc.ca; laurentides@mrnf.gouv.qc.ca
Directeur général, André B. Lemay

Nord-du-Québec
1121, boul Industriel, CP 159, Lebel-sur-Quévillon, QC J0Y 1X0
Tél: 819-755-4838
Téléc: 819-755-3541
nord-du-quebec@mrnf.gouv.qc.ca
Directeur général, Guy Hétu
Outaouais
#RC 100, 16, impasse de la Gare-Talon, Gatineau, QC J8T 0B1
Tél: 819-246-4827
Téléc: 819-246-5049
outaouais@mrnf.gouv.qc.ca
Directeur général, Pierre Ménard
Saguenay—Lac-Saint-Jean
3950, boul Harvey, 3e étage, Jonquière, QC G7X 8L6
Tél: 418-695-8125
Téléc: 418-695-8133
saguenay-lac-saint-jean@mrnf.gouv.qc.ca
Directeur général, Alain Thibeault

Territoire
#A313, 5700, 4e av ouest, Québec, QC G1H 6R1
Tél: 418-627-6256
Téléc: 418-528-2075

Le Ministère favorise une utilisation du territoire qui rejoint les préoccupations économiques, sociales & environnementales des Québécois
Sous-ministre associé (par intérim), Plan Nord et Territoire, Patrick Déry
Tél: 418-627-6370 ext: 357
Directeur général, Affaires stratégiques et territoire, André Auclair
Tél: 418-627-6256 ext: 312
Directrice, Coordination du Plan Nord, Andrée Bélanger
Tél: 418-627-6368 ext: 295
Directeur, Environnement et Coordination, Marcel Grenier
Tél: 418-627-6256 ext: 312
Directeur, Affaires autochtones, François Dupuis
Tél: 418-627-6254 ext: 309
Directeur (par intérim), Politiques et Intégité du territoire, Benoit Trudel
Tél: 418-627-6362 ext: 260

Revenu Québec / Revenue Québec

Direction des relations publiques/Communications, 3800, rue de Marly, Québec, QC G1X 4A5
Tél: 418-652-6831
Téléc: 418-646-0167
www.revenu.gouv.qc.ca
Secondary Address: 150, rue Ste-Catherine ouest
Complexe Desjardins
Montréal, QC H5B 1A7
Téléc: 514-873-7502

Acts Administered:
Loi concernant l'application de la Loi sur les impôts/Act respecting the application of the Taxation Act
Loi concernant l'impôt sur le tabac/Tobacco Tax Act
Loi concernant la taxe sur les carburants/Fuel Tax Act
Loi facilitant le paiement des pensions alimentaires/Act to facilitate the payment of support
Loi favorisant le développement et la reconnaissance des compétences de la main d'oeuvre/Act to promote workforce skills development and recognition(in part)
Loi sur l'aide aux personnes et aux familles (partiellement)/Individual and Family Assistance Act (in part)
Loi sur la Régie de l'assurance maladie du Québec (partiellement)/Act respecting the Régie de l'assurance-maladie du Québec (in part)
Loi sur la Société d'habitation du Québec (partiellement)/Act respecting the Société d'habitation du Québec (in part)
Loi sur la fiscalité municipale/Act respecting municipal taxation (in part)
Loi sur la taxe d'accise (partiellement)/Excise Tax Act (in part)
Loi sur la taxe de vente du Québec/Act respecting the Québec Sales Tax
Loi sur le Régime de rentes du Québec (partiellement)/Act respecting the Québec Pension Plan (in part)
Loi sur le ministère du Revenu/Act respecting the Ministère du Revenu
Loi sur le remboursement d'impôts fonciers/Act respecting real estate tax refund
Loi sur les centres financiers internationaux (partiellement)/Act respecting international financial centres (in part)
Loi sur les impôts/Taxation Act
Loi sur les licences/Licenses Act
Loi sur les normes du travail (partiellement)/Act respecting labour standards (in part)

Ministre, L'hon. Nicolas Marceau
Tél: 514-482-0199
Téléc: 514-482-9985
cabinet@mrq.gouv.qc.ca

Président-directeur général, Gilles Paquin
Tél: 418-652-6833
Téléc: 418-577-5030

Président du conseil d'administration, Florent Gagné

Vice-président du conseil d'administration, Pierre Roy

Bureau de président-directeur général / Office of the President/Director General
Président-directeur général, Gilles Paquin
Tél: 418-652-6833
Téléc: 418-577-5030
Vice-présidente et directrice générale, Traitement des plaintes et de l'éthique, Joseé Morin

Centre de perception fiscale et des biens non réclamés / Tax Collection
3800, rue de Marly, Secteur 6-4-3, Québec, QC G1X 4A5
Le rôle du Centre est de recouvrer les créances de la clientèle de Revenu Québec
Vice-président et directeur général, Recouvrement, François T. Tremblay
Directeur principal, Services administratifs et techniques, Marcel Turgeon
Directeur régional, Laval-Laurentides-Lanaudière, Claude Benny
Directeur régional, Capitale-Nationale et autres régions, Martin Breton
Directeur régional, Outaouais, Alain Gamache
Directrice régionale, Montérégie, Claire Garceau
Directeur régional, Montréal, Lucien Larrivée

Législation & enquêtes / Legislation & Investigations
3800, rue de Marly, Secteur 5-1-9, Québec, QC G1X 4A5
Tél: 418-652-6844
Téléc: 418-643-9381
Vice-président & Directeur général, Législation, enquêtes & Registraire des entreprises, André Legault
Directeur principal, Enquêtes et de l'inspection, Yves Trudel
Chef du Service (par intérim), Enquêtes informatiques, Serge Leblanc
Directrice, Oppositions de Montréal, Louise Haspect
Directeur, Oppositions de Québec, Denis Morin
Directeur (par intérim), Accès à l'information et du contrôle de qualité, Michel Perreault
Directrice, Services administratifs & informatiques, Ginette St-Laurent

Planification, administration et recherche / Planning, Administration & Research
3800, rue de Marly, Secteur 3-4-4, Québec, QC G1X 4A5
Vice-président & Directeur général, Daniel Prud'homme
Directeur Principal, Recherche et Innovation, Gilles Bernard
Directeur principal, Services administratifs et gestion des renseignements, Alain Gagnon
Directeur principal, Planification stratégique & gestion des revenus, Éric Maranda
Chef du Service, Expertise, de la reddition de comptes et de la qualité du registre, Valérie Dran
Directeur, Paie et avantages sociaux, Claude Hogue
Directeur, Bureau de la lutte contre l'évasion fiscale, Sami Jabbour
Directrice, Santé et mieux-être au travail, Danielle Rheault
Directrice, Études économiques, fiscales et statistiques, Sylvie Thomas

Traitement et des Technologies / Data Processing & Technologies
3800, rue de Marly, Secteur 6-2-9, Québec, QC G1X 4A5
Vice-président & Directeur général, Jean-Marie Lévesque
Directeur principal, Solutions informatiques pour les entreprises, Marco Beaulieu
Directeur principal, Solutions informatiques de recouvrement et d'administration, Daniel Forest
Directeur principal, Solutions informatiques pour les particuliers, Denis Légaré
Chef du Service, Processus de traitement massif, Richard Grenier

Particuliers / Individuals Directorate
Vice-président & Directrice générale, Particuliers, Hajib Amachi
Directeur principal (par intérim), Services à la clientèle des particuliers, Normand Bilodeau
Directeur régional (par intérim), Services à la clientèle des particuliers - Centre et Sud du Québec, Pierre Donais
Directrice principale, Pensions alimentaires, Silvy Tremblay
Directrice, Cotisation des particuliers, Céline Goyette
Directeur régional, Services à la clientèle des particuliers - Nord et Ouest du Québec, Hugo Martel-Fiset
Directrice régionale, Services à la clientèle des particuliers - Montréal, Michelle Page-Melançon
Directrice régionale, Services à la clientèle des particuliers - Capitale-Nationale et Est du Québec, Chantal Poirier

Registre des Entreprises / Businesses Directorate
Vice-présidente & Directrice générale, Entreprises, Carole Imbeault
Directeur principal, Contrôle fiscal des entreprises, Gilbert Caccia
Directeur principal, Relations avec la clientèle des entreprises, Denis Gendron
Directeur principal, Soutien opérationnel et du développement des compétences, Danny Pagé
Directeur (par intérim), Bureau de Toronto, Patrick Ulysse
Directrice régionale, Vérification des entreprises - Laval, Camelia Attya
Directeur régional, Vérification des entreprises - Montréal, Pierre Leclerc
Directrice régionale, Vérification des entreprises - Capitale-Nationale et autres régions, Pierre Montreuil

Ministère de la Santé et des Services sociaux / Health & Social Services

Direction des communications, 1075, ch Sainte-Foy, 16e étage, Québec, QC G1S 2M1
Tél: 418-643-9395
Téléc: 418-643-4768
regisseur.web@msss.gouv.qc.ca
www.msss.gouv.qc.ca

Acts Administered:
Loi assurant l'exercice des droits des personnes handicapées/An Act to secure the handicapped in the exercise of their rights
Loi assurant la mise en oeuvre de la Convention sur la protection des enfants et la coopération en matière d'adoption internationale et modifiant diverses dispositions législatives en matière d'adoption/An Act to implementthe Convention on Protection of
Loi assurant le maintien des services essentiels dans le secteur de la santé et des services sociaux/An Act to ensure that essential services are maintained in the health and social services sector
Loi concernant les unités de négociation dans le secteur des affaires sociales/An Act respecting bargaining units in the social affairs sector
Loi sur Héma-Québec et sur le Comité d'hémovigilance/An Act respecting Héma-Québec and the haemovigilance committee
Loi sur l'Institut national de Santé publique du Québec/An Act respecting the Institut national de Santé publique du Québec
Loi sur l'administration publique/Public Administration Act
Loi sur l'assurance-hospitalisation/Hospital Insurance Act
Loi sur l'assurance-maladie/Health Insurance Act
Loi sur l'assurance-médicaments/An Act respecting prescription drug insurance
Loi sur l'équilibre budgétaire du réseau public de la santé et des services sociaux/An Act to provide for balanced budgets in the public health and social services network
Loi sur la Régie de l'assurance-maladie du Québec/An Act respecting the Régie de l'assurance-maladie du Québec
Loi sur la protection de la jeunesse/Youth Protection Act
Loi sur la protection de la santé publique/Public Health Protection Act
Loi sur la protection des personnes dont l'état mental présente un danger pour elles-mêmes ou pour autrui/An Act respecting the protection of persons whose mental state presents a danger to themselves or to others
Loi sur la santé publique/Public Health Act
Loi sur le Commissaire à la santé et au bien-être/An Act respecting the Health and Welfare Commissioner
Loi sur le Conseil médical du Québec/An Act respecting the Conseil médical du Québec
Loi sur le Protecteur des usagers en matière de santé et de services sociaux/An Act respecting the Health and Social Services Ombudsman
Loi sur le ministère de la Santé et des Services Sociaux/An Act respecting the Ministède la Santé des Services sociaux
Loi sur le tabac/Tobacco Act
Loi sur les activités cliniques et de recherche en matière de procréation assistée
Loi sur les agences de développement de réseaux locaux de services de santé et de services sociaux/An Act respecting local health and social services network development agencies
Loi sur les cimetières non-Catholiques/Non-Catholic Cemeteries Act
Loi sur les inhumations et les exhumations/Burial Act
Loi sur les laboratoires médicaux, la conservation des organes, des tissus, des gamètes et des embryons, les services ambulanciers et la disposition des cadavres/An Act respecting medical laboratories, organ, tissue, gameteand embryo conservation
Loi sur les sages-femmes/Midwives Act
Loi sur les services de santé et les services sociaux pour les autochtones cris/An Act respecting health services and social services for Cree Native persons
Loi sur les services de santé et les services sociaux/An Act respecting health services and social services

Ministre, Santé et des services sociaux et Ministre responsable des aînés, L'hon. Dr Réjean Hébert
Tél: 418-266-7171
Téléc: 418-266-7197
ministre@msss.gouv.qc.ca

Ministre déléguée, Santé publique et à la Protection de la jeunesse, L'hon. Véronique Hivon
Tél: 418-266-7181
Téléc: 418-266-7199
Ministre.deleguee@msss.gouv.qc.ca

Sous-ministre, Jacques Cotton
Tél: 418-266-8989
Téléc: 418-266-8990

Directrice, Cabinet du ministre, France Amyot
Tél: 418-266-7171

Directeur, Cabinet du ministre délégué, Monique Richard
Tél: 418-266-7181

Agences, Conseils et Commissions Associés/ Associated Agencies, Boards & Commissions:

• Agence d'évaluation des technologies et des modes d'intervention en santé (AETMIS) / Technology Assessment & Health Solutions Agency
#10.083, 2021, av Union
Montréal, QC H3A 2S9
Tél: 514-873-2563
Téléc: 514-873-1369
www.aetmis.gouv.qc.ca
• Bureau des projets Centres hospitaliers universitaires de Montréal, CHUM, CUSM et CHU Sainte-Justine / Project Office for the Modernization of Montréal's University Health Centres CHUM, MUHC and Sainte-Justine UHC
#10.049, 2021, rue Union
Montréal, QC H3A 2S9
Tél: 514-864-9883
Téléc: 514-873-7362
info.construction3chu@msss.gouv.qc.ca
www.construction3chu.msss.gouv.qc.ca
• Secrétariat à l'accès aux services en langue anglaise et aux communautés ethnoculturelles / English Language & Ethnocultural Communities Services Secretariat
#1.03, 201 boul Crémazie est, 1er étage
Montréal, QC H2M 1L2
Tél: 514-873-5163
Téléc: 514-873-9876
www.msss.gouv.qc.ca/ministere/saslacc
• Conseil du médicament / Medication Council
#100, 1195, av Lavigerie, 1er étage
Québec, QC G1V 4N3
Tél: 418-644-8103
Téléc: 418-644-8120
cdm@cdm.gouv.qc.ca
www.cdm.gouv.qc.ca
• Commissaire à la santé et du bien-être / Health & Welfare Commission
#700, 1020, rte de l'Église
Québec, QC G1V 3V9
Tél: 418-643-3040
Téléc: 418-644-0654
csbe@csbe.gouv.qc.ca
www.csbe.gouv.qc.ca
• Corporation d'hébergement du Québec / Long Term Care Facilities Corporation of Québec
2535, boul Laurier, 5e étage
Québec, QC G1V 4M3
Tél: 418-644-3600
Téléc: 418-644-3609
clientele.sante@siq.gouv.qc.ca
www.chq.gouv.qc.ca
• Institut national de santé publique du Québec / National Public Health Institute of Québec
945, av Wolfe
Québec, QC G1V 5B3
Tél: 418-650-5115
Téléc: 418-646-9328
info@inspq.qc.ca
www.inspq.qc.ca
Autres numéros: Poste: 5336
• Office des personnes handicapées du Québec / Office for Handicapped Persons
309, rue Brock
Drummondville, QC J2B 1C5
Téléc: 819-475-8753
Ligne sans frais: 800-567-1465
TTY: 800-567-1477
michael.magner@ophq.gouv.qc.ca
www.ophq.gouv.qc.ca
• Urgences-santé Québec / Emergency Health Services Québec
3232, rue Bélanger
Montréal, QC H1Y 3H5
Tél: 514-723-5600
info@urgences-sante.qc.ca
www.urgences-sante.qc.ca
• Régie de l'assurance maladie du Québec / Québec Health Insurance Board
1125, Grande Allée ouest
Québec, QC G1S 1E7
Tél: 418-646-4636
www.ramq.gouv.qc.ca

Cabinet du Sous-ministre / Office of the Deputy Minister
Sous-ministre, Jacques Cotton
Tél: 418-266-8989
Directrice, Relations ministérielles et réseau et de la vérification interne, Domonique Breton
Tél: 418-266-8989
Directeur, Affaires juridiques, Jean-Paul Dupré
Tél: 418-266-8950
Directeur, Secrétariat général, André Giguère
Tél: 418-266-8989
Directeur, Service de l'accès à l'information et de la propriété intellectuelle, Claude Lamarre
Tél: 418-266-7005
Directeur, Direction québécoise de cancéroogie, Jean Latreille
Tél: 418-266-6940
Directrice adjointe, Vérification interne, Isabelle Savard
Tél: 418-266-8989
Directrice, Communications, Michèle St-Jean
Tél: 418-266-8905

Coordination, financement, immobilisations et budget / Coordination, funding & capital budget
Sous-ministre associé, Michel Fontaine
Tél: 418-266-8850
Directeur général adjointe, Budget et des politiques des financement, François Dion
Tél: 418-266-5965
Directeur général adjointe, Coordination et aux ententes de gestion, Pierre Laflamme
Tél: 418-266-5812
Directeur général adjointe, Investissements, Sylvain Périgny
Tél: 418-266-5830
Directeur, Gestion budgétaire et comptable ministérielle, André Bolduc
Tél: 418-266-5986
Directeur, Gestion financière - réseau, Guylaine Lajoie
Tél: 418-266-5920
Directeur, Ressources matérielles, François Lamarre
Tél: 418-266-8760
Directeur, Allocation des ressources, Vacant
Tél: 418-266-7111
Directeur, Ententes de gestion, Vacant
Tél: 418-266-5980
Directeur, Secrétariat à l'accès aux services en langue anglaise et aux communautés culturelles, Ronald McNeil
Tél: 514-873-2292
Directeur (par intérim), Affaires autochtones, ethnoculturelles et régions nordiques, Louise Rondeau
Tél: 418-266-7128
Directeur, Relations institutionnelles, Martin Simard
Tél: 418-266-5800
Directeur, Inspection, Jean-François Therrien
Tél: 418-643-6084
Directrice, Investissements du financement, Marlène Sinclair
Tél: 418-266-5850
Directeur, Gestion intégrée de l'information, Alain Saucier
Tél: 418-266-8399
Directrice, Logistique sociosanitaire, Caroline Imbeau
Tél: 418-266-5835
Directeur, Expertise et de la normalisation, Pierre Gauthier
Tél: 418-266-5956

Planification, performance et qualité / Planning, Performance and Quality
Sous-ministre adjoint, Luc Castonguay
Tél: 418-266-5990
Directeur général adjointe, Performance, Éric Fournier
Tél: 418-266-7025
Directrice, Qualité, Sylvie Bernier
Tél: 418-266-7505
Directeur, Évaluation, Vacant
Tél: 418-266-7030
Directeur, Études et des analyses, Harold Côté
Tél: 418-266-7025
Directrice, Planification et orientations stratégiques, Andrée Quenneville, 2010-09-13
Tél: 418-266-7088
Directrice, Recherche, innovation et transfert des connaissances, Manon St-Pierre
Tél: 418-266-7056

Directrice, Affaires pharmaceutiques et du médicament, Hélène Beaulieu
Tél: 418-266-8810
Directrice, Affaires intergouvernementales et de la coopération internationale, Anne Marcoux
Tél: 418-266-8740

Personnel réseau et ministériel / Personal & Corporate Network
Sous-ministre adjointe, Édith Lapointe
Tél: 418-266-8400
Directeur général adjointe, Relations de travail et professionnelles, Alexandre Hubert
Tél: 418-266-8408
Directeur, Planification de la main-d'oeuvre et du soutien au changement, Gilles Le Beau
Tél: 418-266-8835
Directrice, Analyse et du soutien informationnel, Marie-Pierre Legault
Tél: 418-266-8457
Directeur, Personnel syndiqué, Charles Provencher
Tél: 514-873-1800
Directeur, Professionels de la santé et personnel d'encadrement, Yves Lapointe
Tél: 418-266-8420
Directeur, Ressources humaines ministérielles, Claude Tremblay
Tél: 418-266-8710
Directeur, Personnel horsétablissement et de la classification réseau, Luc Bouchard
Tél: 418-266-8410

Santé publique / Public Health
Sous-ministre adjoint, Horacio Arruda
Tél: 514-873-1587
Directrice, Planification, évaluation et développement en santé publique, Lyne Jobin
Tél: 418-266-6780
Directeur, Développement des individus et de l'environnement social, André Dontigny
Tél: 418-266-6714
Directrice, Prévention des maladies chroniques et des traumatismes, Marie Rochette
Tél: 418-266-6750
Directrice, Protection de la santé publique, Danielle Auger
Tél: 514-864-2755
Directrice (par intérim), Surveillance de l'état de santé, Lyne Jobin
Tél: 418-266-6780

Services de santé et médecine universitaire / Health Services & Academic Medicine
Sous-ministre adjoint, Services de santé et médecine universitaire, Jean Rodrigue
Tél: 418-266-6930
Directrice, Main d'oeuvre médicale, Isabelle Savard
Tél: 418-266-6975
Directeur (par intérim), Organisation des services médicaux et technologiques, Yves Jalbert
Tél: 418-266-6946
Directrice, Services médicaux généraux, Jeannine Auger
Tél: 418-266-5827
Directeur, Affaires universitaires, Louis R. Dufresne
Tél: 418-266-7500
Directrice, Organisation des services de première ligne intégrés, Yolaine Galarneau
Tél: 418-266-6976
Directeur, Santé mentale, André Delorme
Tél: 418-266-6835
Directeur nationale, Urgences, services de traumatologie & services préhospitaliers d'urgence, Daniel Lefrançois
Tél: 418-266-5811
Directeur, Biovigilance, Yves Jalbert
Tél: 418-266-6946
Directeur, Soins infirmiers, Danielle Fleury
Tél: 418-266-8485

Services sociaux / Social Services
Sous-ministre adjoint, Sylvain Gagnon
Tél: 418-266-6800
Directeur général adjointe, Personnes ayant une déficience, des dépendances et de la coordination du soutien à domicile, Vacant
Tél: 418-266-6818
Directrice générale, Personnes âgées, Chantal Maltais
Tél: 418-266-6818
Directrice, Secrétariat à l'adoption internationale, Luce de Bellefeuille
Tél: 514-873-4747
Directeur (par intérim), Services sociaux généraux/Activités communautaires, Mario Frechette
Tél: 418-266-6936
Directrice (par intérim), Jeunes et des familles, Natalie Rosebush
Tél: 418-226-6840
Directrice, Dépendances et de l''itinérance, Lynne Duguay
Tél: 418-266-6830

Directrice, Presonnes ayant une déficience, Josette Chouinard
Tél: 418-266-6874

Technologies de l'information / Information Technology
Sous-ministre associée, Technologies de l'information, Lise Verrault
Tél: 418-266-8770
Directeur général adjoint, Projets, Vacant
Tél: 418-266-8770
Directeur, Relations d'affaires avec les clientèles, Clermont Saucier
Tél: 418-266-6935
Directeur (par intérim), Relations avec les partenaires et les mandataires, Clermont Saucier
Tél: 418-266-6935
Directrice, Sécurité des technologies de l'information, Sonia Roy
Tél: 418-266-6935
Directeur, Service financiers & administratif, Philippe Moss
Tél: 418-266-7118
Directeur, Soutien ministériel & infrastructures communes, Michel Rochette
Tél: 418-266-2287

Secrétariat aux aînés / Seniors
Sous-ministre adjointe, Secrétariat aux aînés, Catherine Ferembach
Tél: 418-643-7811
Directrice, Dévelopment stratégique et des innovations Aînés, Élise Paquette
Tél: 418-643-0837
Directrice, Dévelopment des programmes et des partenariats Aînés, Marie-Josée Poulin
Tél: 418-643-2859

Commission de la santé et de la sécurité du travail du Québec (CSST) / Québec Occupational Health & Safety Commission

524, rue Bourdages, CP 1200 Terminus postal, Québec, QC G1K 7E2
Tél: 418-266-4850
Téléc: 418-266-4669
Ligne sans frais: 866-302-2778
www.csst.qc.ca

A pour mission de soutenir aux travailleurs & aux employeurs dans leurs démarches pour éliminer les dangers présents dans leur milieu de travail, inspecter des lieux de travail, & promouvoir la santé & sécurité du travail

Président & Chef de la direction, Michel Després

Vice-présidente, Partenariat et l'expertise-conseil, Claude Sicard

Vice-présidente, Administration, communications & relations publiques, Carole Théberge

Vice-président, Finances, André Beauchemin

Vice-président, Opérations, Gaétan Thériault

Ministère de la Sécurité publique / Ministry of Public Security

Tour des Laurentides, 2525, boul Laurier, 5e étage, Québec, QC G1V 2L2
Tél: 418-643-2112
Téléc: 418-646-6168
Ligne sans frais: 866-644-6826
www.securitepublique.gouv.qc.ca
Secondary Address: #11.39, 10, rue Saint-Antoine est
Bureau de Montréal
Montréal, QC H2Y 1A2
Téléc: 514-873-6597

A pour mission d'assurer la sécurité publique au Québec
Acts Administered:
Loi sur la Société des alcools du Québec/An Act respecting the Société des alcools du Québec (partially administered by MSP)
Loi sur la Société des loteries du Québec/An Act respecting the Société des loteries du Québec (partially administered by the MSP)
Loi sur la police/Police Act
Loi sur la propriété des bicyclettes/Bicycle Ownership Act
Loi sur la recherche des causes et des circonstances des décès/An Act respecting the determination of the causes & circumstances of death
Loi sur la sécurité civile/Civil Protection Act
Loi sur la sécurité dans les sports/An Act respecting safety in sports
Loi sur la sécurité incendie/Fire Safety Act
Loi sur le ministère de la Sécurité publique/An Act respecting the Ministère de la Sécurité publique
Loi sur le régime syndical applicable à la Sûreté du Québec/An Act respecting the Syndical Plan of the Sûreté du Québec
Loi sur le système correctionnel du Québec/An Act respecting the Québec correctional system
Loi sur les agences d'investigation ou de sécurité/An Act respecting detectives or security agencies
Loi sur les bombes lacrymogènes/Act respecting tear bombs
Loi sur les coffrets de sûreté/Safe-Deposit Boxes Act
Loi sur les courses/An Act respecting racing
Loi sur les explosifs/An Act respecting explosives
Loi sur les infractions en matière de boissons alcooliques/An Act respecting offences relating to Alcoholic Beverages
Loi sur les loteries, les concours publicitaires et les appareils d'amusement/An Act respecting lotteries, publicity, contests & amusement machines
Loi sur les permis d'alcool/An Act respecting liquor permits
Loi sur les services correctionnels/An Act respecting correctional services
Loi sur les villages nordiques et l'Administration régionale Kativik/An Act respecting Northern Villages & the Kativik Regional Government (partially administered by the MSP)

Ministre, L'hon. Stéphane Bergeron
Tél: 418-643-2112
Téléc: 418-646-6168
ministre@msp.gouv.qc.ca
Note: www.securitepublique.gouv.qc.ca

Sous-ministre, Martin Prud'homme

Directrice de cabinet, Sandra Boucher
Tél: 418-643-2112
Téléc: 418-646-6168

Directrice, Exécutive, Liette Abel-Normandin

Directeur, Vérification interne, enquêtes & inspection, Sylvain Ayotte
Tél: 418-644-6777

Directeur, Affaires autotchones, Richard Coleman

Directeur, Affaires juridiques, Michèle Durocher

Directeur, Communications, André Ménard

Directrice, Secrétariat général, Katia Petit

Directeur, Laboratoire de sciences juridiciaires et de médecine légale, Yves (Bob) Dufour

Agences, Conseils et Commissions Associés/ Associated Agencies, Boards & Commissions:

• **Bureau du coroner / Office of the Coroner**
Édifice le Delta 2
#390, 2875, boul Laurier
Québec, QC G1V 5B1
Tél: 418-643-1845
Téléc: 418-643-6174
Ligne sans frais: 866-312-7051
clientele.coroner@msp.gouv.qc.ca
www.coroner.gouv.qc.ca
• **Comité de déontologie policière / Police Ethics Committee**
Tour du Saint-Laurent
#A-200, 2525, boul Laurier, 2e étage
Québec, QC G1V 4Z6
Tél: 418-646-1936
Téléc: 418-528-0987
comite.deontologie@msp.gouv.qc.ca
www.deontologie-policiere.gouv.qc.ca
• **Commissaire à la déontologie policière / Police Ethics Commissioner**
#1-40, 1200, rte de l'Église
Québec, QC G1V 4Y9
Tél: 418-643-7897
Téléc: 418-528-9473
Ligne sans frais: 877-237-7897
deontologie-policiere.quebec@msp.gouv.qc.ca
www.deontologie-policiere.gouv.qc.ca
• **Commissariat des incendies / Fire Commissioner**
455, rue Dupont
Québec, QC G1K 6N2
Tél: 418-529-5706
Téléc: 418-529-9922
cdelage@notarius.net
www.securitepublique.gouv.qc.ca/securite-incendie.html
• **Commission québecoise des libérations conditionnelles / Parole Board**
#1.32A, 300, boul Jean-Lesage
Québec, QC G1R 8K6
Tél: 418-646-8300
Téléc: 418-643-7217
cqlc@msp.gouv.qc.ca
www.cqlc.gouv.qc.ca

• Direction générale de la Sûreté du Québec / Provincial Police
1701, rue Parthenais
Montréal, QC H2K 3S7
Tél: 514-598-4141
Téléc: 514-598-4242
www.surete.qc.ca
• École nationale de police du Québec / National Police School of Québec
350, rue Marguerite-d'Youville
Nicolet, QC J3T 1X4
Tél: 819-293-8631
Téléc: 819-293-8630
courriel@enpq.qc.ca
www.enpq.qc.ca
• École nationale des pompiers du Québec / Québec National Fire Fighters School
#3.08, 2800, boul Saint-Martin ouest
Laval, QC H7T 2S9
Tél: 450-680-6800
Téléc: 450-680-6818
Ligne sans frais: 866-680-3677
www.enpq.gouv.qc.ca
• Régie des alcools, des courses et des jeux / Liquor, Gaming & Racing Board
560, boul Charest est
Québec, QC G1K 3J3
Tél: 418-643-7667
Téléc: 418-643-5971
Ligne sans frais: 800-363-0320
www.racj.gouv.qc.ca

Affaires policières / Police Services
Tél: 418-643-3500
Téléc: 418-643-0275
Sous-ministre associé & directeur général, Yves Morency
Adjointe au Sous-ministre associé, Catherine Fournier
Directrice générale adjointe, Sylvie Tousignant
Tél: 418-646-6777 ext: 601
Téléc: 418-644-0132
Directeur, Protection des personnalités, Martin Maranda
Directeur, Prévention et de l'organisation policière, Ghislain Lebrun
Directeur (intéim), Sécurité de l'état, Jérome Gagnon
Directeur, Sécurité dans les palais de justice, Michel Trotier

Services à la gestion / Management Services
Sous-minstre associée & Directrice générale, Liette Larivée
Adjoint au Sous-minstre associée, Geneviève Lamothe
Directeur, Ressources humaines, Luc Gadbois
Directeur, Gestion immobilière, Jean Leclerc
Directrice & Directrice (part intérim), Ressources financières et matérielles/Planification et des politiques, Lucie Picard
Directeur, Technologies de l'information, Abdelaziz Younsi

Sécurité civile et Sécurité incendie / Public Safety & Fire Services
Sous-ministre associé & directeur général, Guy Laroche
Tél: 418-643-3500
Téléc: 418-643-0275
Directeur, Opérations, Éric Houde
Tél: 418-646-6777 ext: 400
Téléc: 418-646-5426
Directeur (par intérim), Prévention et de la planification, Raynald Chassé
Directeur (par intérim), Service de l'analyse et des politiques, Marc Morin
2525, boul Laurier, 6e étage
Sainte-Foy, QC G1V 2L2 Canada
Directeur, Rétablissement, Denis Landry
Tél: 418-646-6638
Téléc: 418-646-6628
Bas-Saint-Laurent, Gaspésie et Iles-de-la-Madeleine
#60, 70, rue Saint-Germain est, Rimouski, QC G5L 7J9
Tel: 418-727-3589
Fax: 418-727-3643
securite.civile01@msp.gouv.qc.ca
Directeur, Jacques Bélanger
Capitale-Nationale, Chaudière Appalaches et Nunavik
#200, 1122, Grande-Allée ouest, Québec, QC G1S 1E5
Tél: 418-643-3244
Téléc: 418-644-2080
securite.civile03@msp.gouv.qc.ca
Directrice, France-Sylvie Loisel
Estrie et Montérégie
165, rue Jacques-Cartier nord, Saint-Jean-sur-Richelieu, QC J3B 6S9
Tél: 450-346-3200
Téléc: 450-346-5856
securite.civile16@msp.gouv.qc.ca
Directrice, Christine Savard
Mauricie et Centre-du-Québec
4000, rue Louis-Pinard, Trois-Rivières, QC G8Y 4L9
Tel: 819-371-6703
Fax: 819-371-6983
securite.civile04@msp.gouv.qc.ca
Directeur, Sébastien Doire
Montréal, Laval, Lanaudière et Laurentides
RC #23, 5100, rue Sherbrooke est, Montréal, QC H1V 3R9
Tél: 514-873-1300
Téléc: 514-864-8654
securite.civile06@msp.gouv.qc.ca
Autre numéros: securite.civile13@msp.gouv.qc.ca; securite.civile14@msp.gouv.qc.ca; securite.civile15@msp.gouv.qc.ca
Directeur, Louis Métivier
Outaouais, Abitibi-Témiscamingue et Nord-du-Québec
817, boul St-René ouest, Gatineau, QC J8T 8M3
Tel: 819-772-3737
Fax: 819-772-3954
securite.civile07@msp.gouv.qc.ca
Directeur, Jacques Viger
Saguenay-Lac-Saint-Jean et Côte-Nord
RC #01, 3950, boul Harvey, Saguenay, QC G7X 8L6
Tel: 418-695-7872
Fax: 418-695-7875
securite.civile02@msp.gouv.qc.ca
Directeur, Pierre Dassylva

Services correctionnels / Correctional Services
Sous-ministre associé, Johanne Beausoleil
Directeur général adjointe, Programmes et sécurité, Jean-François Longtin
Directrice principale, Programmes et à la sécurité, Élaine Raza
Directeur, Administration, Robert Beaulieu
Tél: 418-646-6777 ext: 500
Téléc: 418-643-3426
Directrice, Recherche, Johanne Lévesque
Tél: 418-646-6767 ext: 500
Téléc: 418-646-6228
Directrice, Conseil à l'organisation, Marlène Langlois
Tél: 418-646-6777 ext: 500
Téléc: 418-644-5645
Abitibi-Témiscamingue, Nord-du-Québec
851, 3e Rue est, Amos, QC J9T 2T4
Tel: 819-444-5222
Fax: 819-444-5298
Directrice, Sylvie Messier
Bas-Saint-Laurent
200, rue des Négociants, Rimouski, QC G5M 1B6
Tel: 418-727-3534
Fax: 418-727-3799
Directeur, Michel Levasseur
Côte-Nord
73, av Mance, Baie-Comeau, QC G4Z 1N1
Tel: 418-294-8646
Fax: 418-294-8853
Toll-Free: 866-640-3026
Directeur, Gérald Murray-Chevrier
Estrie
1055, rue Talbot, Sherbrooke, QC J1G 2P3
Tel: 819-820-3100
Fax: 819-820-3964
Directrice, Kathleen Carroll
Gaspésie-Iles-de-la-Madeleine
#206, 484, Hôtel-de-Ville, Chandler, QC G0C 1K0
Tel: 418-689-4947
Fax: 418-689-2478
Directrice, Suzanne Bourget
suzanne.bourget@msp.gouv.qc.ca
Mauricie—Centre-du-Québec
7 600, boul Parent, Trois-Rivières, QC G9A 5E1
Tel: 819-372-1311
Fax: 819-371-6979
Toll-Free: 866-292-6281
Directeur, Jacques Damphousse
Montérégie
75, boul Poliquin, Sorel-Tracy, QC J3P 7Z5
Tel: 450-742-0471
Fax: 450-742-8399
Directrice, Céline Jacques
Montréal
#11.87, 10, rue Saint-Antoine est, Montréal, QC H2Y 1A2
Tel: 514-864-1800
Fax: 514-873-9362
Directeur, Pierre Couture
Outaouais
75, rue Saint-François, Gatineau, QC J9A 1B4
Tel: 819-772-3065
Fax: 819-772-3076
Toll-Free: 866-466-7603
Directeur (par intérim), Denis Briand
Saguenay—Lac-Saint-Jean
237, rue Price est, Saguenay, QC G7H 2E5
Tel: 418-698-3841
Fax: 418-690-8560
Directrice, Josée Desjardins

Sûreté du Québec / Québec Provincial Police
Directeur général, Richard Deschesnes
Tél: 514-598-4488
Chef de cabinet, Mario Lacroix
Président, Autorité disciplinaire, Gaston Bellemare
Directeur, Realtions avec les municipalités et des communications, Daniel Cauchy
Directeur (par intérim), Audit, Guy Léger

Services Québec

Bureau de la qualité, 800, place D'Youville, 20e étage, Québec, QC G1R 3P4
Tél: 418-644-4545
Ligne sans frais: 877-644-4545
www.gouv.qc.ca/portail/quebec/servicesquebec/
TTY: 800-361-9596
Autre numéros: Montréal: 514-644-4545

Présidente, Monique L. Bégin

Président-directeur général (par intérim) et vice-président, Développement des services et au partenariat, Pierre E. Rodrigue

Vice-présidente, Relations avec les citoyens et les entreprises, Jean Audet

Directrice générale, Secrétariat, de l'administration et des communications, Réjeanne Lachance

Directeur, Vérification interne, André Bélanger

Directeur, État civil, Reno Bernier

Directrice, Services juridiques, Manon Godin

Les Publications du Québec
#500, 1000 rte de l'Église, Québec, QC G1V 3V9
Tél: 418-643-5150
Téléc: 418-643-6177
Ligne sans frais: 800-463-2100
publicationsduquebec@cspq.gouv.qc.ca
www.publicationsduquebec.gouv.qc.ca
Abitibi-Témiscamingue-Nord-du-Québec
RC #01, 255, av Principale, Rouyn-Noranda, QC J9X 7G9
Tél: 418-643-0599
Bas-Saint-Laurent
#195B, av Léonidas sud, Rimouski, QC G5L 1S7
Tél: 418-727-3950
Capitale-Nationale
787, boul Lebourneuf, Québec, QC G2J 1C3
Tél: 418-643-0599
Centre-du-Québec
RC #16, 270, rue Lindsay, Drummondville, QC J2B 1G3
Tél: 450-928-8798
Chaudière-Appalaches
44, rte du Président-Kennedy, Lévis, QC G6V 6C5
Tél: 418-643-0599
Côte-Nord
280, av Arnaud, Sept-Iles, QC G4R 3A7
Tél: 418-295-4047
Estrie
RC #02, 200, rue Belvédère nord, Sherbrooke, QC J1H 4A9
Tél: 418-820-3164
Gaspésie-Iles-de-la-Madeleine
39-5, montée Sandy Beach, Gaspé, QC G4X 2W4
Tél: 418-360-8086
Lanaudière
RC #20, 450, rue Saint-Louis, Joliette, QC J6E 2Y8
Tél: 514-873-9670
Laurentides
Galeries des Laurentides, #1503C, 500, boul des Laurentides, Saint-Jérôme, QC J7Z 4M2
Tél: 514-873-9670
Laval
1796, boul des Laurentides, Laval, QC H7M 2P6
Tél: 514-873-9670
Mauricie
3225, boul Saint-Jean, Trois-Rivières, QC G9B 2M1
Tél: 450-928-8798
Montérégie
#105, 174, boul Sainte-Foy, Longueuil, QC J4J 1W7
Tél: 450-928-8798
Montréal
RC #10, 2050, rue De Bleury, Montréal, QC H3A 2J5
Tél: 514-873-9670
Outaouais
RC #120, 170, rue de l'Hôtel-de-Ville, Gatineau, QC J8X 4C2
Tél: 514-873-9670
Saguenay—Lac-Saint-Jean
2655, boul du Royaume, Jonquière, QC G7S 4S9
Tél: 418-695-8140

Ministère du Tourisme / Tourism Québec

#400, 900, boul René-Lévesque est, Québec, QC G1R 2B5
Tél: 418-643-5959
Téléc: 418-646-8723
Ligne sans frais: 800-482-2433
www.tourisme.gouv.qc.ca

Acts Administered:
Loi sur l'Institut de tourisme et d'hôtellerie du Québec
Loi sur l'aide au développement touristique
Loi sur le ministère du Tourisme
Loi sur les établissements d'hébergement touristique

Ministre, L'hon. Pascal Bérubé

Sous-ministre, Suzanne Giguère
Tél: 418-643-5959 ext: 503

Secrétariat, David Belgue
Tél: 418-643-5959 ext: 349

Directeur, Affaires juridiques, Christian Caron

Directeur, Communications, Pierre Tessier

Agences, Conseils et Commissions Associés/ Associated Agencies, Boards & Commissions:

• Palais des congrès de Montréal
159, rue Saint-Antoine ouest, 9é étage
Montréal, QC H2Z 1H2
Tél: 514-871-8122
Téléc: 514-871-9389
Ligne sans frais: 800-268-8122
info@congresmtl.com
congresmtl.com

• Société du Centre des congrès de Québec / Québec City Convention Centre
1000, boul René-Lévesque est
Québec, QC G1R 5T8
Tél: 418-644-4000
Téléc: 418-644-6455
Ligne sans frais: 888-679-4000
www.convention.qc.ca

Administration / Administration
Directrice générale, Clémence Verret
Tél: 418-643-5959 ext: 330
Directeur, Ressources informationelles, Denis Archambault
Directeur, Ressources financières & matérielles, Sylvain Bergeron
Directrice, Ressources humaines, Valérie Lévesque

Accueil et à l'hébergement touristiques / Tourist Accommodations
Sous-ministre adjointe, Elizabeth MacKay
Directrice, Suzanne Asselin
Directeur, Croisières internationales, François Belzile

Marketing et clientèles touristiques / Marketing & Tourism Consumers
Sous-ministre adjoint, Georges Vacher
Tél: 514-873-7977 ext: 560
Directeur général, Services à la clientèle touristique, Sylvain Lacombe
Directrice générale, Marketing, Sylvie Quenneville
Directeur, Stratégie et de la mise en marché, Alain Dupont
Directeur, Opérations, Julien Cormier
Directrice, Renseignements par téléphone et Internet, Brigitte Hernando
Directrice, Centre d'affaires électroniques, Michèle Morel

Partenariat et du soutien aux enterprises / Partnership & Company Support
Directeur générale, Louis Germain
Directeur, Partenariat et des programmes d'aide financière, François Côté
Directeur, Soutien au développement des enterprises, Steeve Martel

Planification et du développement des stratégies / Planning & Development Strategies
Directeur général, Patrick Dubé

Ministère des Transports (MTQ) / Transportation

700, boul René-Lévesque est, 28e étage, Québec, QC G1R 5H1
Tél: 418-643-6980
Téléc: 418-643-2033
Ligne sans frais: 888-355-0511
communications@mtq.gouv.qc.ca
www.mtq.gouv.qc.ca
Autre numéros: Au Québec: 5-1-1
Secondary Address: 500, boul René-Lévesque ouest, 16e étage
Montréal, QC H4Z 1W7
Téléc: 514-864-2836

Acts Administered:
Code de la sécurité routière/Highway Safety Code
Loi concernant la Compagnie de gestion de Matane inc./Act respecting the Compagnie de gestion de Matane Inc.
Loi concernant les partenariats en matière d'infrastructures de transport/Act respecting transport infrastructure partnerships
Loi concernant les propriétaires et exploitants de véhicules lourds/Act respecting owners and operators of heavy vehicles

Loi concernant les services de transport par taxi/Act respecting transportation services by taxi
Loi interdisant l'affichage publicitaire le long de certaines voies de circulation/Act to prohibit commercial advertising along certain thoroughfares
Loi sur l'Agence métropolitaine de transport/Act respecting the Agence métropolitaine de transport
Loi sur l'assurance automobile/Automobile Insurance Act
Loi sur l'expropriation/Expropriation Act
Loi sur la Société de l'assurance automobile du Québec/Act respecting the Société de l'assurance automobile du Québec
Loi sur la Société des traversiers du Québec/Act respecting the Société des Traversiers du Québec
Loi sur la Société du port ferroviaire de Baie-Comeau-Hauterive/Act respecting the Société du port ferroviaire de Baie-Comeau-Hauterive
Loi sur la publicité au long des routes/Roadside Advertising Act
Loi sur la sécurité du transport terrestre guidé/Act to ensure safety in guided land transportation
Loi sur la voirie/Act respecting roads
Loi sur le Ministère des Transports/Act respecting the Ministère des Transports
Loi sur les chemins de fer/Railway Act
Loi sur les conseils intermunicipaux de transport dans la région de Montréal/Act respecting intermunicipal boards of transport in the area of Montréal
Loi sur les sociétés de transport en commun/Act respecting public transit authorities
Loi sur les transports instituant la Commission des transports du Québec/Transport Act established by the Commission des transports du Québec
Loi sur les transports/Transport Act
Loi sur les véhicules hors route/Act respecting off-highway vehicles

Ministre, L'hon. Sylvain Gaudreault
Tél: 418-643-6980

Directeur, Cabinet du ministre, Thierry St-Cyr
Tél: 418-643-6980

Agences, Conseils et Commissions Associés/ Associated Agencies, Boards & Commissions:

• Agence métropolitaine de transport
700, rue De La Gauchetière Ouest, 26e étage
Montréal, QC H3B 5M2
Tél: 514-287-2464
www.amt.qc.ca

• Commission de la capitale nationale du Québec
Edifice Hector-Fabre
525 boul René-Lévesque Est, RC
Québec, QC G1R 5S9
Tél: 418-528-0773
Téléc: 418-528-0833
Ligne sans frais: 800-442-0773
commission@capitale.gouv.qc.ca
www.capitale.gouv.qc.ca

• Commission des transports du Québec / Québec Transport Commission
200, ch Sainte-Foy, 7e étage
Québec, QC G1R 5V5
Téléc: 418-644-8034
Ligne sans frais: 888-461-2433
www.ctq.gouv.qc.ca

• Société de l'assurance automobile du Québec (SAAQ)
333, boul Jean-Lesage
CP 19600 Terminus
Québec, QC G1K 8J6
Tél: 418-643-7620
Téléc: 418-644-0339
Ligne sans frais: 800-361-7620
TTY: 800-565-7763
courrier@saaq.gouv.qc.ca
www.saaq.gouv.qc.ca

• Société des traversiers du Québec / Ferries Québec
250, rue Saint-Paul
Québec, QC G1K 9K9
Tél: 418-643-2019
Téléc: 418-643-7308
stq@traversiers.gouv.qc.ca
www.traversiers.gouv.qc.ca

• Société du port ferroviaire Baie-Comeau-Hauterive / Baie-Comeau-Hauterive Railway Station
18, rte Maritime
Baie-Comeau, QC G4Z 2L6
Tél: 418-296-6785
Téléc: 418-296-2377
societeduport@globetrotter.net
www.sopor.ca

Bureau de la sous-ministre / Office of the Deputy Minister
Sous-ministre, Dominique Savoie
Tél: 418-643-6740
Directrice, Bureau de la sous-ministre, Julie Bissonnette
Tél: 418-643-6740

Infrastructures et technologies / Infrastructure & Technologies
Directrice générale et sous-ministre adjointe, Anne-Marie Leclerc
Tél: 418-528-0808
Directeur, Structures, Daniel Bouchard
Tél: 418-643-6906
Directeur, Soutien aux opérations, Éric Breton
Tél: 418-643-9298
Directeur, Parcs routiers, Claude Marquis
Tél: 418-646-8301
Directeur, Environnement et recherche, Christian Therrien
Tél: 418-643-8326
Directeur, Laboratoire des chaussées, Guy Tremblay
Tél: 418-643-6618

Politiques et sécurité en transport / Transportation Policy & Security
Directeur général et sous-ministre adjoint, André Meloche
Tél: 418-528-0808
Directeur, Transport routier des marchandises, Benoît Cayouette
Tél: 418-528-0631
Directrice, Transport terrestre des personnes, France Dompierre
Tél: 418-644-0324
Directrice, Transport maritime, aérien et ferroviaire, Josée Hallé
Tél: 418-643-1864
Directeur, Sécurité en transport, Claude Morin
Tél: 418-643-1564

Services à la gestion et de la surveillance des marchés / Administrative Services & Market Oversight
Directrice générale et directrice (par intérim), Contrats et ressources matérielles, Josée Dupont
Tél: 418-528-0808
Directrice générale adjointe, Ressources humaines financières et informationnelles, Danièle Cantin
Tél: 418-646-9934
Directrice, Enquêtes et analyse de marché, Chantale Brouillet
Tél: 418-643-6840
Directeur, Planification budgétaire et expertise immobilière, Raymond Cloutier
Tél: 418-644-2182
Directrice, Gestion financière et information, Brigitte Duchesne
Tél: 418-646-9932
Directrice, Ressources humaines, Mireille Parent
Tél: 418-646-4157
Directeur, Technologies de l'information, Louis Potvin
Tél: 418-643-4431

Territoires / Territories
Directeur général et sous-ministre adoint, André Caron
Tél: 418-528-0808
Directrice générale adjointe, Planification et de la coordination territoriale, Chantal Gingras
Tél: 514-864-1850
Directrice générale adjointe, Projets stratégiques, Ginette Sylvain
Tél: 514-864-1850
Directeur, Programmation, ressources, et opérations, Mario Bergeron
Tél: 418-643-7726
Directeur, Projet Turcot, Alain Marc Dubé
Tél: 514-873-3838
Directeur, Planification et suivi des projets, Fadi Moubayed
Tél: 514-864-1730
Directeur, Projets routiers et de transport collectif, Maroun Shaneen
Tél: 514-873-7781
Directrice, Gouvernance des projets stratégiques et des partenariats public-privé, Sandra Sultana
Tél: 514-873-4377

Abitibi-Témiscamingue
80, av Québec, Rouyn-Noranda, QC J9X 6R1
Tél: 819-763-3271
Téléc: 819-763-3493
dat@mtq.gouv.qc.ca

Directeur régional, Yves Coutu
Tél: 819-763-3237

Bas-Saint-Laurent—Gaspésie—îles-de-la-Madeleine
#101, 92, 2e rue ouest, Rimouski, QC G5L 8E6
Tél: 418-727-3674
Téléc: 418-727-3673
dtbgi@mtq.gouv.qc.ca

Directeur régional, Richard Dionne
Tél: 418-727-3674
Capitale-Nationale
475, boul de l'Atrium, 2e étage, Québec, QC G1H 7H9
Tél: 418-643-1911
Téléc: 418-646-0003
dcnat@mtq.gouv.qc.ca

Directeur régional, Jean-François Saulnier
Tél: 418-380-2003
Chaudière-Appalaches
1156, boul de la Rive-Sud, Saint-Romuald, QC G6W 5M6
Tél: 418-839-5581
Téléc: 418-834-7338
dtca@mtq.gouv.qc.ca

Directeur régional, Richard Charpentier
Tél: 418-839-5581
Côte-Nord
#110, 625, boul Laflèche, Baie-Comeau, QC G5C 1C5
Tél: 418-295-4765
Téléc: 418-295-4766
cotenord@mtq.gouv.qc.ca

Directeur régional, Michel Bérubé
Tél: 418-295-4778
Est-de-la-Montérégie
201, place Charles-Lemoyne, 5e étage, Longueuil, QC J4K 2T5
Tél: 450-677-3413
Téléc: 450-442-1317
dtem@mtq.gouv.qc.ca

Directeur régional, Daniel Donais
Tél: 450-677-8974
Estrie
#2.02, 200, rue Belvédère nord, Sherbrooke, QC J1H 4A9
Tél: 819-820-3280
Téléc: 819-820-3118
dte@mtq.gouv.qc.ca

Directeur régional, Gilles Bourque
Tél: 819-820-3280
île-de-Montréal
500, boul René-Lévesque ouest, 12e étage, CP 5, Montréal, QC H2Z 1W7
Tél: 514-873-7781
Téléc: 514-864-3867
dtim@mtq.gouv.qc.ca

Directeur régional (par intérim), Maroun Shaneen
Tél: 514-873-7781
Laurentides-Lanaudière
222, rue Saint-Georges, 2e étage, Saint-Jérôme, QC J7Z 4Z9
Tél: 450-569-3057
Téléc: 450-569-3072
dll@mtq.gouv.qc.ca

Directrice régional, Sylvie Laroche
Tél: 450-569-7414
Laval-Mille-îles
1725, boul Le Corbusier, Laval, QC H7S 2K7
Tél: 450-680-6330
Téléc: 450-973-4959
dtlmi@mtq.gouv.qc.ca

Directrice régionale, Odile Béland
Tél: 450-680-6333
Mauricie—Centre-du-Québec
100, rue Laviolette, 4e étage, Trois-Rivières, QC G9A 5S9
Tél: 819-371-6896
Téléc: 819-371-6136
dmcq@mtq.gouv.qc.ca

Directeur régional, Jean Douville
Tél: 819-371-6896
Ouest-de-la-Montérégie
#200, 180, boul d'Anjou, Châteauguay, QC J6K 1C4
Tél: 450-698-3400
Téléc: 450-698-3452
dtom@mtq.gouv.qc.ca

Directrice régional, Joceline Béland
Tél: 450-698-3400
Outaouais
#5.110, 170, rue de l'Hôtel-de-Ville, Gatineau, QC J8X 4C2
Tél: 819-772-3849
Téléc: 819-772-3338
dto@mtq.gouv.qc.ca

Directeur général, Jacques Henry
Tél: 819-772-3107
Saguenay—Lac-Saint-Jean—Chibougamau
3950, boul Harvey, Jonquière, QC G7X 8L6
Tél: 418-695-7916
Téléc: 418-695-7926
dt.slsjc@mtq.gouv.qc.ca

Directeur régional, Donald Turgeon
Tél: 418-695-7916

Ministère du Travail / Labour

200, ch Sainte-Foy, 5e étage, Québec, QC G1R 5S1
Tél: 418-644-4545
Téléc: 418-528-0559
Ligne sans frais: 800-643-4817
www.travail.gouv.qc.ca

Acts Administered:
Acts administered by Labour Agencies
Code du travail/Labour Code
Commission de l'équité salariale
Commission de la construction du Québec
Commission de la santé et de la sécurité du travail
Commission des lésions professionelles
Commission des normes du travail
Conseil consultatif du travail et de la main-d'oeuvre
Loi assurant l'exercice des droits des personnes handicapées/Act to secure the handicapped in the exercise of their rights
Loi sur l'indemnisation des victimes d'amiantose ou de silicose dans les mines et les carrières/Act respecting compensation - victims of asbestos or silicosis in mines & quarries
Loi sur l'économie de l'énergie dans le bâtiment/Act respecting the conservation of energy in buildings
Loi sur l'équité salariale/Pay Equity Act
Loi sur la distribution du gaz/Gas distribution Act
Loi sur la fête nationale/National Holiday Act
Loi sur la santé et la sécurité du travail/Occupational Health & Safety Act
Loi sur la sécurité dans les édifices publics/Public Buildings Safety Act
Loi sur le Conseil consultatif du travail et de la main-d'ouvre/Act respecting the Conseil consultatif du travail et de la main d'oeuvre
Loi sur le bâtiment /Building Act
Loi sur le ministère du Travail/Act respecting the Ministère du travail
Loi sur le régime de négociation des conventions collectives dans les secteurs public et parapublic/Act respecting the process of negotiating of the collective agreements in the public & parapublic sectors
Loi sur les accidents du travail et les maladies professionnelles/Act respecting accidents at work & professional illness or sickness
Loi sur les appareils sous pression/Act respecting pressure vessels
Loi sur les décrets de convention collective/Act respecting Collective Agreement Decrees
Loi sur les mécaniciens de machines fixes/Master Pipe Mechanics Act
Loi sur les normes du travail/Act respecting Labour Standards
Loi sur les relations du travail, la formation professionnelle et la gestion de la main-d'ouvre dans l'industrie de la construction/Act Respecting Labour Relations, Vocational Training, and Manpower Management in theConstruction Industry
Loi sur les relations du travail, la formation professionnelle et la gestion de la main-d'ouvre dans l'industrie de la construction/Act respecting labour relations vocational training & manpower management in theconstruction industry
Loi sur les syndicats professionnels/Professional Syndicates Act
Régie du bâtiment du Québec

Ministre, L'hon. Agnès Maltais
Tél: 418-643-5297
Téléc: 418-644-0003
ministre@travail.gouv.qc.ca

Sous-ministre, Brigitte Pelletier
Tél: 418-643-2902
Téléc: 418-643-0735

Directeur, Communications, Gervais Fortier
Tél: 418-646-2642

Directeur, Cabinet du ministre, Pierre Châteauvert
Tél: 418-643-5297

Directrice, Affaires juridiques, Mélanie Paradis

Directeur, Comité consultatif du travail et de la main-d'oeuvre, Fernand Matteau

Directeur, Bureau du sous-ministre, Olivier Simard

Agences, Conseils et Commissions Associés/ Associated Agencies, Boards & Commissions:

• Commission de la construction du Québec / Québec Construction Commission
3530, rue Jean-Talon ouest
Montréal, QC H3R 2G3
Tél: 514-341-7740
Téléc: 514-341-6354
Ligne sans frais: 888-842-8282
www.ccq.org

• Commission de l'équité salariale / Pay Equity Commission
200, ch Ste-Foy, 4e étage
Québec, QC G1R 6A1
Tél: 418-528-8765
Téléc: 418-528-6999
Ligne sans frais: 888-528-8765
equite.salariale@ces.gouv.qc.ca
www.ces.gouv.qc.ca

• Commission des lésions professionnelles / Work-Related Injuries Commission
#700, 900, Place d'Youville
Québec, QC G1R 3P7
Tél: 418-644-7777
Téléc: 418-644-6443
Ligne sans frais: 800-463-1591
www.clp.gouv.qc.ca
Administrative tribunal that is the last recourse for employers or workers who contest a decision made by the Commission de la santé et de la sécurité du travail.

• Commission des normes du travail / Labour Standards Commission
Hall Est
400, boul Jean-Lesage, 7e étage
Québec, QC G1K 8W1
Tél: 418-644-0817
Téléc: 418-643-5132
Ligne sans frais: 800-563-9058
www.cnt.gouv.qc.ca

• Commission des relations du travail / Labour Relations Commission
900, boul René-Lévesque est, 5e étage
Québec, QC G1R 6C9
Tél: 418-643-3208
Téléc: 418-643-8946
Ligne sans frais: 866-864-3646
crtm@crt.gouv.qc.ca
www.crt.gouv.qc.ca

• Commission de la santé et de la sécurité du travail (CSST) / Occupational Health & Safety Commission
425, rue du Pont
CP 4900 Terminus
Québec, QC G1K 7S6
Tél: 418-266-4000
Téléc: 418-266-4015
Ligne sans frais: 888-999-2778
www.csst.qc.ca
Autres numéros: Ile-de-Montréal: 514-906-3000; Address: Tour Sud, 1, complexe Desjardins, 31e étage, CP 3, Succursale Place-Desjardins, Montréal, QC, H5B 1H1

• Conseil consultatif du travail et de la main d'oeuvre / Advisory Council on Labour & Manpower
#9.400, 500, boul René-Lévesque ouest
Montréal, QC H2Z 1W7
Tél: 514-873-2880
Téléc: 514-873-1129
cctm@cctm.gouv.qc.ca
www.cctm.gouv.qc.ca

• Conseil des services essentiels du Québec / Essential Services Council
#9.100, 500, boul René-Lévesque ouest, 9e étage
CP 38
Montréal, QC H2Z 1W7
Tél: 514-873-7246
Téléc: 514-873-3839
Ligne sans frais: 800-337-7246
info@cses.gouv.qc.ca
www.cses.gouv.qc.ca

• Régie du bâtiment du Québec / Québec Construction Companies Board
545, boul Crémazie est, 4e étage
Montréal, QC H2M 2V2
Tél: 514-873-0976
Téléc: 514-864-2903
Ligne sans frais: 800-361-0761
crc@rbq.gouv.qc.ca
www.rbq.gouv.qc.ca

Politiques et recherche / Policy & Research
Sous-ministre adjoint, Normand Pelletier
Directeur, Politiques du travail, Steeve Audet
Directeur, Information sur le travail, Charles Bélanger
Directeur (par intérim), Recherche et innovation en milieu de travail, Martine Poulin

Relations du travail / Labour Relations
Sous-ministre adjointe, Suzanne Thérien

Directeur générale, Daniel Cholette
Directeur (par intérim), Médiation-conciliation & prévention (Montréal), Robert Dupuis
Directeur, Médiation-conciliation, prévention & arbitrage (Québec), Jean Poirier
Directeur, Bureau d'évaluation médicale, Dr André Perron

Secrétariat du Conseil du trésor / Treasury Board

875, Grande Allée est, 5e étage, secteur 500, Québec, QC G1R 5R8
Tél: 418-643-1529
Téléc: 418-643-9226
Ligne sans frais: 866-552-5158
communication@sct.gouv.qc.ca
www.tresor.gouv.qc.ca

Ministre responsable de l'Administration gouvernementale & Présidente du Conseil du trésor, et ministre responsable de la région du Saguenay-Lac-Saint-Jean, L'hon. Stéphane Bédard
Tél: 418-643-5926
Téléc: 418-643-7824
cabinet@sct.gouv.qc.ca

Secrétaire, Yves Ouellet
Tél: 418-643-1977
Téléc: 418-643-6494
communication@sct.gouv.qc.ca

Greffière, Marie-Claude Rioux
Tél: 418-643-0875 ext: 420

Directrice, Vérification interne, Anne DeBlois
Tél: 418-643-0875 ext: 416

Directrice, Affaires juridiques, Josée De Bellefeuille
Tél: 418-643-0875 ext: 426

Directrice, Communications, Francine Tremblay
Tél: 418-643-0875 ext: 405

Agences, Conseils et Commissions Associés/ Associated Agencies, Boards & Commissions:

• **Infrastructure Québec / Infrastructure**
#408, 1050, boul René-Lévesque est
Québec, QC G1R 4X3
Tél: 418-646-6097
Téléc: 418-528-7155
communications@infra.gouv.qc.ca
www.infra.gouv.qc.ca
• **Commission administrative des régimes de retraite et d'assurances (Québec) / Retirement & Insurance Planning Commission**
475, rue Saint-Amable
Québec, QC G1R 5X3
Tél: 418-643-4881
Téléc: 418-644-3839
Ligne sans frais: 800-463-5533
www.carra.gouv.qc.ca
• **Commission de la fonction publique (Québec) / Public Service Commission**
800, Place d'Youville, 7e étage
Québec, QC G1R 3P4
Tél: 418-643-1425
Téléc: 418-643-7264
Ligne sans frais: 800-432-0432
cfp@cfp.gouv.qc.ca
www.cfp.gouv.qc.ca
The Commission works towards the following goals: to ensure equal access for all citizens to the public service; to ensure the competence of persons recruited & promoted; & to guarantee the fairness of decisions in human resources management.

Administration

Directeur général, Yvan Bouchard
Directeur, Technologies, Clément Côté
Directeur, Ressources financières et matérielles, Frédérick Doyon
Directeur, Développement des systèmes d'information, Alexandre Mailhot
Directeur, Ressources humaines, France Normand

Performance

Directrice générale, Debra Dollard
Tél: 418-643-0875 ext: 414

Sous-secrétariat au personnel de la fonction publique / Public Personnel

Secrétaire associé, Guy Mercier
Tél: 418-643-0875 ext: 460
Directeur général, Relations de travail, Rhéal St-Pierre
Tél: 418-643-0875 ext: 460
Directrice générale, Politiques de gestion des ressources humaines, Jocelyne Tremblay
Tél: 418-643-0875 ext: 466
Directeur, Relations professionnelles, Daniel Beaupré
Tél: 418-643-0875 ext: 461
Directeur, Développement des persones et des organisations, Carl Bergeron
Tél: 418-643-0875 ext: 466
Directrice, Planification de la main-d'oeuvre & de l'information de gestion, Marie-Claude Corbeil-Gravel
Tél: 418-643-0875 ext: 469
Directrice, Pilotage des systèmes, Denise Coulombe
Tél: 418-643-0875 ext: 472
Directeur, Classification & rémunération, secteur fonction publique, Jean-Olivier Ferron
Tél: 418-643-0875 ext: 485
Directrice, Santé des personnes au travail, Chantal Gagnon
Tél: 418-643-0875 ext: 464
Directrice, Gestion de main-d'oeuvre, Denise Roy
Tél: 418-643-0875 ext: 468

Sous-secrétariat aux marchés publics / Public Markets

Tél: 418-643-1529
Téléc: 418-643-9226
marches.publics@sct.gouv.qc.ca
Secrétaire associé, Julie Blackburn
Tél: 418-643-0875 ext: 490
Directeur général, Bureau de gouvernance des grandes infrastructures publiques, Bernard Buteau
Tél: 418-643-0875 ext: 494
Directeur général, Services à la gestion contractuelle, Louis Morneau
Tél: 418-643-0875 ext: 490
Directeur général, Politiques de marchés publics, Marc Samson
Tél: 418-643-0875 ext: 493
Directrice, Services d'information à la gestion contractuelle, Doris Blanchet
Tél: 418-643-0875 ext: 490
Directrice, Gouvernance des projets d'infrastructure, Karine Gosselin
Tél: 418-643-0875 ext: 498
Directrice, Formation sur les marchés publics, Pauline Larouche
Tél: 418-646-6171
Directeur, Tarification & accords sur les marchés publics, Bruno Doutriaux Rianderie
Directeur, Analyse & vérification aux contrats, Étienne Sabourin
Directeur, Réglementation & politiques de gestion contractuelle, Robert Villeneuve
Tél: 418-643-0875 ext: 493

Sous-secrétariat aux politiques budgétaires et aux programmes / Budget Policies & Programs

Secrétaire associée, Clément D'Astous
Tél: 418-643-0875 ext: 450
Directeur général, Politiques & opérations budgétaires, Jacques Fortin
Tél: 418-643-0875 ext: 451
Directeur général, Programmes administratifs, sociaux & de santé, Jean-François Lachaine
Tél: 418-643-0875 ext: 453
Directeur général, Programmes économiques, éducatifs & culturels, Yves Lessard
Tél: 418-643-0875 ext: 455
Directeur, Programmes économiques, Anne Boucher
Tél: 418-643-0875 ext: 455
Directeur, Programmes sociaux & de santé, Serge Garon
Tél: 418-643-0875 ext: 453
Directrice, Programmes administratifs, Danielle Hubert
Tél: 418-643-0875 ext: 454
Directeur, Études & analyses en dépenses publiques, Carl Lessard
Tél: 418-643-0875 ext: 450
Directeur, Analyses des investissements en infrastructures & technologies de l'information, Jean Léveillé
Tél: 418-643-0875 ext: 453
Directrice, Opérations de prévisions & de suivi des dépenses, Claire Rainville
Tél: 418-643-0875 ext: 451
Directrice, Programmes éducatifs & culturels, Stéphane Tousignant
Tél: 418-643-0875 ext: 456

Sous-secrétariat aux politiques de rémunération & coordination intersectorielle des négociations / Compensation Policies & Sectoral Coordination Negotiations

Secrétaire associée, Dominique Gauthier
Tél: 418-643-0875 ext: 480
Directeur général, Régimes collectifs et d l'actuariat, Michel Montour
Tél: 418-643-0875 ext: 482
Directeur général, Politiques de rémunération, Charles Duclos
Tél: 418-643-0875 ext: 482
Directeur, Politiques de rémunération & conditions de travail, Bruno Côté
Tél: 418-643-0875 ext: 480
Directrice, Analyse & comparaison de marché en rémunération, Brigitte Dufort
Tél: 418-643-0875 ext: 481
Directeur, Actuariat, Michel Groulx
Tél: 418-643-0875 ext: 483
Directeur, Coordination intersectorielle des négociations & organismes publics, Robert Lessard
Tél: 418-643-0875 ext: 482
Directrice, Régimes collectifs, Isabelle Marcotte
Tél: 418-643-0875 ext: 482

Sous-secrétariat aux ressources informationnelles et bureau du dirigeant principal de l'information / Information Resources & Office of the Chief Information Officer

Secrétaire associé, Denis Garon
Tél: 418-643-0875 ext: 500
Directeur général, Encadrement des ressources informationnelles et du patrimoine numérique, Marcel Boudreault
Tél: 418-643-0875 ext: 501
Directeur général, Encadrement du portefeuille gouvernementa des projets en ressources informationnelles, Bertrand Lauzon
Tél: 418-643-0875 ext: 514
Directrice générale, Gouvernance et de la gestion des ressources informationnelles, Suzanne Létourneau
Tél: 418-643-0875 ext: 507
Directeur, Projets stratégiques et des services communs, Martin Lachance
Tél: 418-643-0875 ext: 510
Directeur, Architecture et des orientations technologiques, Patrice Di Marcantonio
Tél: 418-643-0875 ext: 504
Directeur, Sécurité et de la préservation du patrimoine numérique, Réal Martineau
Tél: 418-643-0875 ext: 506
Directeur, Vision gouvernementale et des orientations stratégiques, Gérald Nedeau

Vérificateur général du Québec / Auditor General

750, boulevard Charest est, 3e étage, Québec, QC G1K 9J6
Tél: 418-691-5900
Téléc: 418-644-4460
verificateur.general@vgq.gouv.qc.ca
www.vgq.gouv.qc.ca
Secondary Address: #1910, 770, rue Sherbrooke ouest
Montréal, QC H3A 1G1 Canada
Téléc: 514-873-7665
Le Vérificateur général du Québec a pour mission de favoriser par la vérification le contrôle parlementaire sur les fonds et autres biens publics.

Vérificateur général (par intérim), Michel Samson
Tél: 418-691-5901 ext: 400

Vérificateur général adjoint, Commissaire au développement durable, Jean Cinq-Mars

Vérificateur général adjointe, Attestation financière, Diane Bergeron

Vérificateur général adjoint, Attestation financière, Marcel Couture

Vérificateur général adjoint, Optimisation des ressources et services linguistiques, Marc Ouellet

Government of Saskatchewan

Seat of Government: Regina, SK S4S 0B3
www.gov.sk.ca
The Province of Saskatchewan entered Confederation on September 1, 1905. It has an area of 588,276.09 km2, & the StatsCan census population in 2011 was 1,033,381.

Office of the Lieutenant Governor

Government House, 4607 Dewdney Ave., Regina, SK S4T 1B7
Tel: 306-787-4070
Fax: 306-787-7716
lgo@ltgov.sk.ca
www.ltgov.sk.ca
Other Communication: Authentication of Documents, Phone: 306-787-2951
The position of the Lieutenant Governor is apolitical & non-partisan. Her Honour the Honourable Vaughn Solomon Schofield, Lieutenant Governor of Saskatchewan, is the representative of The Queen in Saskatchewan.
Some responsibilities of the Lieutenant Governor are as follows: presiding over the swearing in of the Premier, cabinet ministers, & the Chief Justice of Saskatchewan; delivering the Speech from the Throne; giving Royal Assent to acts of the Legislative

Assembly; participating in commemorative ceremonies & provincial celebrations; & honouring achievements.

Lieutenant Governor of Saskatchewan, Hon. Vaughn Solomon Schofield
Note: The Lieutenant Governor's full title is Her Honour the Honourable Vaughn Solomon Schofield, Lieutenant Governor of Saskatchewan

Executive Director & Private Secretary, Heather Salloum
hsalloum@ltgov.sk.ca

Office Manager & Itinerary Coordinator, Patricia Langston
Tel: 306-787-6510
Fax: 306-787-7716
plangston@ltgov.sk.ca

Manager, Communications, Carolyn Speirs
Tel: 306-787-6460
Fax: 306-787-7716
cspeirs@ltgov.sk.ca

Coordinator, Congratulatory Messages, Peg St. Godard

Office of the Premier

Legislative Building, #226, 2405 Legislative Dr., Regina, SK S4S 0B3
Tel: 306-787-9433
Fax: 306-787-0885
www.premier.gov.sk.ca

In November 2011, Brad Wall was re-elected Premier of Saskatchewan.

Premier; President, Executive Council; Minister, Intergovernmental Affairs, Hon. Brad Wall
premier@gov.sk.ca
Social Media: twitter.com/PremierBradWall, www.facebook.com/PremierBradWall

Executive Assistant to the Premier, Everett Hindley
Everett.Hindley@gov.sk.ca

Executive Secretary to the Premier, Ruth Gaura
Ruth.Gaura@gov.sk.ca

Legislative Secretary to the Premier for First Nations Engagement, Rob Norris, Saskatchewan Party
Tel: 306-933-7852
Fax: 306-933-7869
rnorris@mla.legassembly.sk.ca
www.robnorris.org
Social Media: twitter.com/RobNorris_SP, www.facebook.com/RobNorrisSP

Executive Council

Communications Services, Executive Council, #130, 3085 Albert St., Regina, SK S4S 0B1
Tel: 306-787-6276
Fax: 306-787-6123
commserv@gov.sk.ca
www.gov.sk.ca/executive-council

Appointed by the Premier of Saskatchewan, each cabinet minister is responsible for a ministry or portfolio.

The Provincial Cabinet of Saskatchewan

Premier; President, Executive Council; Minister, Intergovernmental Affairs, Hon. Brad Wall
Tel: 306-787-9433
Fax: 306-787-0885
premier@gov.sk.ca
www.premier.gov.sk.ca
Social Media: twitter.com/PremierBradWall, www.facebook.com/PremierBradWall
#226, 2405 Legislative Dr.
Regina, SK S4S0B3

Deputy Premier; Minister, Finance, Hon. Ken Krawetz
Tel: 306-787-6060
Fax: 306-787-6055
minister.fin@gov.sk.ca
Office of the Minister of Finance, Legislative Building
#312, 2405 LegislativeDr.
Regina, SK S4S 0B3

Minister, Economy; Minister Responsible, Global Transporation Hub; Minister Responsible, SK Power Corporation, Enterprise SK, Innovation SK, Uranium Development Partnership, & SK ResearchCouncil, Hon. Bill Boyd
Tel: 306-787-0804
Fax: 306-798-2009
Bill.Boyd@gov.sk.ca
Office of the Minister of Economy, Legislative Building
#340, 2405 Legislative Dr.
Regina, SK S4S 0B3

Minister, Social Services; Minister Responsible, Status of Women, Hon. June Draude
Tel: 306-787-3661
Fax: 306-787-0656
minister.ss@gov.sk.ca
Office of the Minister of Social Services,Legislative Building
#303, 2405 Legislative Dr.
Regina, SK S4S 0B3

Minister, Highways & Infrastructure; Minister Responsible, Saskatchewan Telecommunications; Minister Responsible, Saskatchewan Transportation Company; Minister Responsible, InformationServices Corporation; Minister Responsible, Saskatchewan Gaming Corp., Hon. Don McMorris
Tel: 306-787-6447
Fax: 306-787-1736
minister.hi@gov.sk.ca
Social Media: twitter.com/dmcmorrissp, www.facebook.com/DonMcMorrisSP
Office of the Minister of Highways & Infrastructure, Legislative Building
#302, 2405 LegislativeDr.
Regina, SK S4S 0B3

Minister, Advanced Education; Minister, Labour Relations & Workplace Safety; Minister Responsible, Saskatchewan Workers' Compensation Board, Hon. Don Morgan, Q.C.
Tel: 306-787-0613
Fax: 306-787-6946
minister.ae@gov.sk.ca
Social Media: www.facebook.com/pages/Don-Morgan/48835718931?sk=info
Office of the Minister of Advanced Education / Labour Relation & Workplace Safety, Legislative Bldg.
#361, 2405 Legislative Dr.
Regina, SK S4S 0B3

Minister, Crown Investments; Minister Responsible, Saskatchewan Government Insurance; Minister Responsible, Saskatchewan Liquor & Gaming Authority, Hon. Donna Harpauer
Tel: 306-787-7339
Fax: 306-798-3140
minister.cc@gov.sk.ca
Social Media: www.facebook.com/pages/Donna-Harpauer/60494388240
Office of the Minister of Crown Investments, Legislative Building
#322, 2405 Legislative Dr.
Regina, SK S4S 0B3

Minister, Health, Hon. Dustin Duncan
Tel: 306-787-7345
Fax: 306-787-0237
minister.he@gov.sk.ca
Social Media: twitter.com/dustin_duncan
Office of the Minister of Health, Legislative Building
#204, 2405 Legislative Dr.
Regina, SK S4S0B3

Minister, Justice & Attorney General; Deputy Government House Leader, Hon. Gordon Wyant, Q.C.
Tel: 306-787-5353
Fax: 306-787-1232
minister.ju@gov.sk.ca
Social Media: twitter.com/GordWyant
Office of the Minister of Justice &Attorney General, Legislative Building
#355, 2405 Legislative Dr.
Regina, SK S4S 0B3

Minister Responsible, Energy & Resources; Minister Responsible, Tourism Saskatchewan; Minister Responsible, Trade; Minister Responsible, SaskEnergy Incorporated, Hon. Tim McMillan
Tel: 306-787-9124
Fax: 306-787-0395
minister.er@gov.sk.ca
Social Media: www.facebook.com/timmcmillanmla
Office of the Minister Responsible, Energy & Resources / Tourism Saskatchewan, Legislative Building
#346, 2405 Legislative Dr.
Regina, SK S4S 0B3

Minister, Environment; Minister Responsible, Saskatchewan Watershed Authority; Minister Responsible, Saskatchewan Water Corporation, Hon. Ken Cheveldayoff
Tel: 306-787-0393
Fax: 306-798-1669
minister.env@gov.sk.ca
Social Media: www.facebook.com/pages/Ken-Cheveldayoff/52760912740
Office of the Minister of the Environment, Legislative Building
#315, 2405 Legislative Dr.
Regina, SK S4S 0B3

Minister, Government Relations; Minister Responsible, First Nations, Métis, & Northern Affairs, Hon. Jim Reiter
Tel: 306-787-6100
Fax: 306-787-0399
minister.gr@gov.sk.ca
Social Media: twitter.com/jim_reiter, www.facebook.com/pages/Jim-Reiter/207539405959289
Office of the Ministerof Government Relations, Legislative Building
#348, 2405 Legislative Dr.
Regina, SK S4S 0B3

Minister, Education, Hon. Russ Marchuk
Tel: 306-787-7360
Fax: 306-798-0263
minister.edu@gov.sk.ca
Social Media: twitter.com/marchuk_mla
Office of the Minister of Education, Legislative Building
#307, 2405 Legislative Dr.
Regina, SK S4S 0B3

Minister, Agriculture; Minister Responsible, Saskatchewan Crop Insurance Corporation, Hon. Lyle Stewart
Tel: 306-787-0338
Fax: 306-787-0630
minister.ag@gov.sk.ca
Social Media: www.facebook.com/group.php?gid=182442928469194
Office of the Minister ofAgriculture, Legislative Building
#334, 2405 Legislative Dr.
Regina, SK S4S 0B3

Minister, Central Services; Minister Responsible, Public Service Commission; Minister Responsible, LeanInitiative, Hon. Nancy Heppner
Tel: 306-787-0942
Fax: 306-787-8677
minister.gs@gov.sk.ca
Office of the Minister Central Services, Legislative Building
#306, 2405 Legislative Dr.
Regina, SK S4S 0B3

Minister Responsible, Corrections & Policing, Hon. Christine Tell
Tel: 306-787-4377
Fax: 306-787-5331
minister.cp@gov.sk.ca
Social Media: www.facebook.com/christinetellsp
Office of the Minister Responsible, Corrections & Policing,Legislative Building
#345, 2405 Legislative Dr.
Regina, SK S4S 0B3

Minister Responsible, Rural & Remote Health, Hon. Randy Weekes
Tel: 306-798-9014
Fax: 306-798-9013
minister.rrhe@gov.sk.ca
Social Media: www.facebook.com/pages/Randy-Weekes-MLA/356610274367735?sk=info
Office of the Minister Responsible for Rural & Remote Health,Legislative Building
#208, 2405 Legislative Dr.
Regina, SK S4S 0B3

Minister, Parks, Culture, & Sport; Minister Responsible, Provincial Capital Commission, Hon. Kevin Doherty
Tel: 306-787-0354
Fax: 306-798-0264
minister.pcs@gov.sk.ca
Social Media: www.facebook.com/KevinDohertyforReginaNorthEast, ca.linkedin.com/pub/kevin-doherty/21/125/6b1
Office of the Minister,Parks, Culture, & Sport, Legislative Building
#38, 2405 Legislative Dr.
Regina, SK S4S 0B3

Cabinet Planning
Legislative Building, #37, 2405 Legislative Dr., Regina, SK S4S 0B3
Tel: 306-787-6344
Fax: 306-787-0012
cpu.ec@gov.sk.ca

The Cabinet Planning branch is involved in the following activities: offering research & advice about ministry & sectoral plans & policy proposals; providing policy analysis & secretariat support to the Premier, members of the Executive Council, & the Committee on Planning & Priorities; & participating in inter-ministry & inter-agency working groups.

Associate Deputy Minister, Wolfgang Langenbacher
Senior Policy Advisor, Nancy Cherney
Tel: 306-787-1301
Senior Policy Advisor, Greg Elliott
Senior Policy Advisor, Gord Sisson
Tel: 306-787-6308
Assistant Research Officer, David Cundall

Cabinet Secretariat
Legislative Building, #145, 2405 Legislative Dr., Regina, SK S4S 0B3
Tel: 306-787-9636
Fax: 306-787-8299
cabsec.ec@gov.sk.ca

The Cabinet Secretariat has the following responsibilities: supporting the Premier & President of the Executive Council;

offering administrative support to the Cabinet; maintaining public records & employment contracts.
Cabinet Secretary; Clerk, Executive Council; Registrar, Regulations, Fredrick D. (Rick) Mantey
Tel: 306-787-9630
Cabinet Officer, Cabinet Documents, Leta Lys
Tel: 306-787-9537
Cabinet Officer, Legislation, Regulations, & Proclamations, Shelley Nelson
Tel: 306-787-9636
Cabinet Officer, Orders in Council & Crown Employment, Deanna Schmidt
Tel: 306-787-6343

Communications Services
#130, 3085 Albert St., Regina, SK S4S 0B1
Tel: 306-787-6276
Fax: 306-787-6123
commserv@gov.sk.ca
The Communications Services branch administers the Communications Procurement Policy to government ministries, agencies, & Crowns. The Executive Director of Communications oversees communications to ensure information is provided to the media & the public in a timely & effective manner. Media relations staff provide assistance in the preparation & distribution of news releases.
Executive Director, Communications, Kathy Young
Tel: 306-787-0425
Fax: 306-787-0883
Kathy.Young@gov.sk.ca
Legislative Building
#110, 2405 Legislative Dr.
Regina, SK S4S 0B3
Director, Interactive Strategy & Operations, Andrew Clarke
Tel: 306-541-6984
Fax: 306-787-6123
andrew.clarke@gov.sk.ca
Director, Communication Services, Colleen Opseth
Tel: 306-530-8401
Fax: 306-787-6123
colleen.opseth@gov.sk.ca
Director, Media Services, Leanne Persicke
Tel: 306-787-2127
Fax: 306-787-8233
Legislative Building
#110, 2405 Legislative Dr.
Regina, SK S4S 0B3
Director, Interactive Communications, Derek Robinson
Tel: 306-787-0906
Fax: 306-787-0883
derek.robinson@gov.sk.ca
Legislative Building
#110, 2405 Legislative Dr.
Regina, SK S4S 0B3
Officer, Media Relations, James Parker
Tel: 306-787-1321
Communications Advisor; Industry Consultant, Emily Armer
Tel: 306-550-6194
Fax: 306-787-6123
emily.armer@gov.sk.ca
Interactive Advisor; Industry Consultant, Jeff Armstead
Tel: 306-520-7705
Fax: 306-787-6123
jeff.armstead@gov.sk.ca
Print Advisor; Industry Consultant, Glenn Zaran
Tel: 306-787-5306
Fax: 306-787-6123
glenn.zaran@gov.sk.ca

Corporate Services
Legislative Building, #32, 2405 Legislative Dr., Regina, SK S4S 0B3
Tel: 306-787-7448
Fax: 306-787-0097
admin.ec@gov.sk.ca
The Corporate Services branch of the Executive Council oversees the following areas: the ministry's budget; expense claims of cabinet ministers & ministry staff; human resource services; & information technology.
Executive Director, Corporate Services, Bonita Cairns
Tel: 306-787-6351
Fax: 306-787-0097
bonita.cairns@gov.sk.ca
Manager, Financial Services, Patty Hoyer
Tel: 306-787-1634
Officer, Administration, Sharon Amyotte
Tel: 306-787-7449
Fax: 306-787-0097
sharon.amyotte@gov.sk.ca

Office of the Deputy Minister to the Premier
Legislative Building, #135, 2405 Legislative Dr., Regina, SK S4S 0B3
Tel: 306-787-6337
Fax: 306-787-8338
dmo.ec@gov.sk.ca
The Office of the Deputy Minister to the Premier carries out the following key functions: supporting the Premier; providing coordination between the Cabinet, ministries, agencies, & Crown corporations; & handling appointments of senior executives for ministries.
Deputy Minister to the Premier, Doug Moen
Tel: 306-787-6338
Fax: 306-787-8338
Doug.Moen@gov.sk.ca
Coordinator, Executive Resourcing, Sheree Ruller
Tel: 306-787-2059
Fax: 306-787-8337
Executive Assistant, Kylie Head
Tel: 306-787-6421
Fax: 306-787-8338
kylie.head@gov.sk.ca

Intergovernmental Affairs
1919 Saskatchewan Dr., Regina, SK S4P 4H2
Tel: 306-787-8003
www.ops.gov.sk.ca
The Government of Saskatchewan's Intergovernmental Affairs manages the province's relationships with Canadian provincial & territorial governments, federal governments, & international jurisdictions.
The mission of Intergovernmental Affairs involves promoting the province's interests, securing access to markets for products from Saskatchewan, handling official protocol, managing the provincial honours & awards program, & overseeing Francophone affairs.
Associate Deputy Minister, Wes Jickling
Tel: 306-787-4220
Fax: 306-787-0973
Wes.Jickling@gov.sk.ca
Legislative Building
#14, 2405 Legislative Dr.
Regina, SK S4S 0B3
Chief of Protocol, Jason Quilliam
Tel: 306-787-3109
Fax: 306-787-1269
jason.quilliam@gov.sk.ca
Executive Director, Trade Policy, Robert Donald
Tel: 306-787-8910
Fax: 306-787-7317
Robert.Donald@gov.sk.ca
Executive Director, International Relations, Jacqueline Messer-Lepage
Tel: 306-787-7855
Fax: 306-787-7317
jacqueline.messerlepage@gov.sk.ca
Executive Director, Canadian Intergovernmental Relations, Ashley Metz
Tel: 306-787-7515
Fax: 306-787-7317
Ashley.Metz@gov.sk.ca
Executive Director, Francophone Affairs, Charles-Henri Warren
Tel: 306-787-8035
Fax: 306-787-6352
charleshenri.warren@gov.sk.ca

Premier's Correspondence Unit
Legislative Building, #3, 2405 Legislative Dr., Regina, SK S4S 0B3
Tel: 306-787-6347
Fax: 306-787-0885
premier@gov.sk.ca
Daily correspondence to & from the Premier is administered. The unit also processes requests for photographs of the Premier.
Director, Premier's Correspondence, Bonnie Krajewski-Riel
Tel: 306-787-0492
Fax: 306-787-0885
bonnie.krajewski-riel@gov.sk.ca
Assistant Director, Sylvia O'Callaghan
Tel: 306-787-7148
Fax: 306-787-0885
Manager, Systems, Wendy Milne
Tel: 306-787-6346
Fax: 306-787-0885

Provincial Secretary
Legislative Building, #28, 2405 Legislative Dr., Regina, SK S4S 0B3
Tel: 306-787-1636
Fax: 306-787-0012
The Provincial Secretary reports to the Premier. The work of the Provincial Secretary is to assist the Premier with protocol, events, & French language services.
Provincial Secretary, Hon. Wayne Elhard
wayne.elhard@gov.sk.ca
Administrative Assistant, Jade Hopkins
jade.hopkins@gov.sk.ca

Legislative Assembly of Saskatchewan

Office of the Clerk, Legislative Building, #239, 2405 Legislative Dr., Regina, SK S4S 0B3
info@legassembly.sk.ca
www.legassembly.sk.ca
Other Communication: Library Reference Questions, E-mail: reference@legassembly.sk.ca
The Legislative Assembly oversees the government & performs three major roles: a legislative role, an inquiry role, & a financial role.
Members of the Assembly may include the Premier, the Leader of the Opposition, House Leaders, & Whips. Officers of the House include the Speaker, Clerks, & the Sargeant-at-Arms. Some major legislative services are legislative library services, visitor services, the production of parliamentary publications, & communication & technology services.

Speaker, Legislative Assembly, Hon. Dan D'Autremont
Tel: 306-787-2282
Fax: 306-787-2283
speaker@legassembly.sk.ca
Social Media:
www.facebook.com/pages/Dan-DAutremont/63773726250?sk=info
Legislative Building
#129, 2405 Legislative Dr.
Regina, SK S4S 0B3

Clerk, Greg Putz
Tel: 306-787-2335
Fax: 306-787-0408
gputz@legassembly.sk.ca

Law Clerk; Parliamentary Counsel, Kenneth S. Ring, Q.C.
Tel: 306-787-2298
Fax: 306-787-1246
kring@legassembly.sk.ca
Legislative Building
#225, 2405 Legislative Dr.
Regina, SK S4S 0B3

Sargeant-at-Arms, Patrick Shaw
Tel: 306-787-8798
Legislative Building
#128, 2405 Legislative Dr.
Regina, SK S4S 0B3

Executive Director, Member & Corporate Services, Lynn Jacobson
Tel: 306-787-6477
Fax: 306-787-1558
ljacobson@legassembly.sk.ca
Legislative Building
#123, 2405 Legislative Dr.
Regina, SK S4S 0B3

Director, Financial Services, Dawn Court
Tel: 306-787-2384
Fax: 306-798-2085
dcourt@legassembly.sk.ca
Legislative Building
#123, 2405 Legislative Dr.
Regina, SK S4S 0B3

Director, Visitor Services, Lorraine DeMontigny
Tel: 306-787-5357
Fax: 306-787-8217
ldemontigny@legassembly.sk.ca
Legislative Building
#122, 2405 Legislative Dr.
Regina, SK S4S 0B3

Director, Parliamentary Publications, Lenni Frohman
Tel: 306-787-1924
Fax: 306-787-1556
lfrohman@legassembly.sk.ca
Walter Scott Building
#110, 3085 Albert St.
Regina, SK S4S 0B1

Director, Member Services, Brad Gurash
Tel: 306-787-2338
Fax: 306-787-1558
bgurash@legassembly.sk.ca
Legislative Building
#119, 2405 Legislative Dr.
Regina, SK S4S 0B3

Director, Human Resources, Ginette Michaluk

Tel: 306-787-1734
Fax: 306-787-1558
gmichaluk@legassembly.sk.ca
Legislative Building
#123, 2405 Legislative Dr.
Regina, SK S4S 0B3

Chief Technology Officer, Darcy Hislop
Tel: 306-787-8071
Fax: 306-787-4278
dhislop@legassembly.sk.ca
Legislative Building
#33, 2405 Legislative Dr.
Regina, SK S4S 0B3

Legislative Librarian, Melissa Bennett
Tel: 306-787-2277
Fax: 306-787-1772
mbennett@legassembly.sk.ca
Office of the Legislative Librarian, Legislative Building
#234, 2405 Legislative Dr.
Regina, SK S4S 0B3

Government Caucus Office (Saskatchewan Party)
Legislative Building, #203, 2405 Legislative Dr., Regina, SK S4S 0B3
Tel: 306-787-4300
Fax: 306-787-3174
Toll-Free: 888-708-7780
info@skcaucus.com
www.skcaucus.com

Hon. Brad Wall was first elected Premier of Saskatchewan in the 2007 provincial election. The Saskatchewan Party was re-elected in the November 2011 provincial election.

Premier; President, Executive Council; Minister, Intergovernmental Affairs; Leader, Saskatchewan Party, Hon. Brad Wall
Constituency: Swift Current
Tel: 306-787-9433
Fax: 306-787-0885
bwall@mla.legassembly.sk.ca
www.bradwall.ca; www.premier.gov.sk.ca
Social Media: twitter.com/PremierBradWall, www.facebook.com/PremierBradWall

Deputy Premier; Minister, Finance, Hon. Ken Krawetz
Constituency: Canora-Pelly
Tel: 306-787-6060
Fax: 306-787-6055
kkrawetz@mla.legassembly.sk.ca
www.kenkrawetz.ca

Caucus Chair, Saskatchewan Party, Doreen Eagles
Constituency: Estevan
Tel: 306-787-4300
Fax: 306-787-3174
deagles@mla.legassembly.sk.ca

Government House Leader, Jeremy Harrison
Constituency: Meadow Lake
Tel: 306-787-4300
Toll-free: 877-234-6669
Fax: 306-787-3174
jharrison@mla.legassembly.sk.ca; jharrisonmla@sasktel.net
www.jeremyharrison.ca

Deputy Government House Leader; Minister, Justice & Attorney General, Hon. Gordon Wyant, Q.C.
Constituency: Saskatoon Northwest
Tel: 306-787-5353
Fax: 306-787-1232
gwyant@mla.legassembly.sk.ca
Social Media: twitter.com/GordWyant

Government Whip, Greg Ottenbreit
Constituency: Yorkton
Tel: 306-787-4300
Fax: 306-787-3174
gottenbreit@mla.legassembly.sk.ca
www.gregottenbreit.ca
Social Media: twitter.com/GregOttMLA

Deputy Government Whip, Gene Makowsky
Constituency: Regina Dewdney
Tel: 306-787-4300
Fax: 306-787-3174
gmakowsky@mla.legassembly.sk.ca
www.genemakowsky.ca
Social Media: www.facebook.com/GeneAMakowsky

Chief of Staff, Gerald Proctor
Tel: 306-787-4300
Fax: 306-787-3174
gproctor@skcaucus.com

Opposition Caucus Office (New Democratic Party)
Legislative Building, #265, 2405 Legislative Dr., Regina, SK S4S 0B3
Tel: 306-787-7388
Fax: 306-787-6247
caucus@ndpcaucus.sk.ca
www.ndpcaucus.sk.ca

Dwain Lingenfelter resigned as the leader of Saskatchewan's New Democratic Party after he lost his seat in the November 2011 provincial election. John Nilson, a veteran Member of the Legislative Assembly, took over as the interim leader of the party. In the process to select a new leader, Nilson remains neutral. New Democratic Party members will elect a new leader on March 9, 2013.

Interim Leader, Official Opposition; Interim Leader, New Democratic Party, John Nilson, Q.C.
Constituency: Regina Lakeview
Tel: 306-787-0939
Fax: 306-787-6247
jnilson@mla.legassembly.sk.ca; j.nilson.mla@sasktel.net

Deputy Leader, Opposition, Buckley Belanger
Constituency: Athabasca
Tel: 306-833-3200
Fax: 306-833-2622
bbelanger@mla.legassembly.sk.ca

Caucus Chair, New Democratic Party, David Forbes
Constituency: Saskatoon Centre
Tel: 306-787-0975
Fax: 306-787-6247
dforbes@mla.legassembly.sk.ca; dforbesmla@sasktel.net
www.davidforbesmla.ca
Social Media: www.facebook.com/electDavidForbes

Deputy Caucus Chair, New Democratic Party, Danielle Chartier
Constituency: Saskatoon Riversdale
Tel: 306-787-1900
Fax: 306-787-6247
dchartier@mla.legassembly.sk.ca
www.daniellechartier.ca
Social Media: twitter.com/RiversdaleMLA

House Leader, Opposition, Warren McCall
Constituency: Regina Elphinstone-Centre
Tel: 306-787-8276
Fax: 306-787-6247
wmccall@mla.legassembly.sk.ca; warren.mccall@sasktel.net
Social Media: ca.linkedin.com/pub/warren-mccall/19/2a7/672

Deputy House Leader, Opposition, Cathy Sproule
Constituency: Saskatoon Nutana
Tel: 306-787-9999
Fax: 306-787-6247
csproule@mla.legassembly.sk.ca;
SaskatoonNutana@ndpcaucus.sk.ca
www.cathysproule.com
Social Media: twitter.com/@cathysproule, www.facebook.com/group.php?gid=173288332783856, ca.linkedin.com/pub/cathy-sproule/16/ab8/7b3

Opposition Whip, Doyle Vermette
Constituency: Cumberland
Tel: 306-787-6340
Fax: 306-787-6247
dvermette@mla.legassembly.sk.ca

Deputy Opposition Whip, Cam Broten
Constituency: Saskatoon Massey Place
Tel: 306-787-0230
Fax: 306-787-6247
cbroten@mla.legassembly.sk.ca; cbroten.mla@sasktel.net
Social Media: twitter.com/cambroten, www.facebook.com/cambrotenndp?ref=ts

Chief of Staff, Carolyn Rebeyka
Tel: 306-787-1907
Fax: 306-787-6247
crebeyka@ndpcaucus.sk.ca

Director, Communications, Erin Morrison
Tel: 306-787-6349
Fax: 306-787-6247
emorrison@ndpcaucus.sk.ca

Director, Human Resources & Administration, Cheryl Stecyk
Tel: 306-787-7389
Fax: 306-787-6247
cstecyk@ndpcaucus.sk.ca

Chair, Standing Committee on Crown & Central Agencies, Greg Brkich
Tel: 306-787-430
Fax: 306-787-3174
gbrkich@mla.legassembly.sk.ca

Chair, Standing Committee on the Economy, Don Toth
Tel: 306-787-4300
Fax: 306-798-3174
dtoth@mla.legassembly.sk.ca

Chair, Standing Committee on House Services, Hon. Dan D'Autremont
Tel: 306-787-2282
Fax: 306-787-2283
ddautremont@mla.legassembly.sk.ca
Social Media: www.facebook.com/pages/Dan-DAutremont/63773726250?sk=info

Chair, Standing Committee on Human Services, Delbert Kirsch
Tel: 306-787-4300
Fax: 306-787-3174
dkirsch@mla.legassembly.sk.ca

Chair, Standing Committee on Intergovernmental Affairs & Justice, Warren Michelson
Tel: 306-787-4300
Fax: 306-787-3174
wmichelson@mla.legassembly.sk.ca
Social Media: www.facebook.com/WarrenMichelson

Member, Standing Committee on Private Bills, Buckley Belanger
Tel: 306-833-3200
Fax: 306-833-2622
bbelanger@mla.legassembly.sk.ca

Chair, Standing Committee on Privileges, Hon. Dan D'Autremont
Tel: 306-787-2282
Fax: 306-787-2283
ddautremont@mla.legassembly.sk.ca
Social Media: www.facebook.com/pages/Dan-DAutremont/63773726250?sk=info

Chair, Standing Committee on Public Accounts, Trent Wotherspoon
Tel: 306-787-0077
Fax: 306-787-6247
twotherspoon@mla.legassembly.sk.ca
Social Media: twitter.com/WotherspoonT

Principal Clerk, Iris Lang
Tel: 306-787-1743
Fax: 306-798-9650
ilang@legassembly.sk.ca

Senior Committee Clerk, Kathy Burianyk
Tel: 306-787-4989
Fax: 306-798-9650
kburianyk@legassembly.sk.ca

Twenty-seventh Legislature - Saskatchewan

2405 Legislative Dr., Regina, SK S4S 0B3
www.legassembly.sk.ca
Other Communication: Legislative Library, Phone: 306-787-2276

Last General Election: November 7, 2011.
Party Standings (September 2012):
Saskatchewan Party: 49 seats;
New Democratic Party: 9 seats;
Total 58.
Salaries & Allowances of Members (April 2012):
Member of the Legislative Assembly, Annual Indemnity $91,800.
Additional Allowances:
Premier $66,766 (total $158,566);
Deputy Premier $53,414 (total $145,214);
Speaker $46,738 (total $138,538);
Minister $46,738 (total $138,538);
Leader of the Opposition $46,738 (total $138,538);
Leader of the Third Party $23,368 (total $115,168;
Government House Leader $6,830 (total $98,630);
Opposition House Leader $13,659 (total $105,459);
Third Party House Leader $6,830 (total $98,630);
Government Whip $13,659 (total $105,459);
Opposition Whip $13,659 (total $105,459);
Third Party Whip $6,830 (total $98,630);
Government Caucus Chair $13,659 (total $105,459);
Opposition Caucus Chair $13,659 (total $105,459);
Third Party Caucus Chair $6,830 (total $98,630).
The following is a list of members, with their constituency, the number of electors in the constituency for the 2011 general election, party affiliation, & contact information:

Members of the Legislative Assembly of Saskatchewan

Buckley Belanger
Constituency: Athabasca *No. of Constituents:* 6,511, New Democratic Party
Tel: 306-833-3200
Fax: 306-833-2622
bbelanger@mla.legassembly.sk.ca
Other Communications: Constituency Phone: 306-833-3200, Fax: 306-833-2622
ConstituencyOffice
PO Box 310
Ile-A-La-Crosse, SK S0M 1C0

Bob Bjornerud
Constituency: Melville-Saltcoats *No. of Constituents:* 9,131, Saskatchewan Party
Tel: 306-787-4300
Fax: 306-787-3174
bbjornerud@mla.legassembly.sk.ca; bjornerud@sasktel.net
www.bobbjornerud.ca
Other Communications: Constituency Phone: 306-728-3882, Fax: 306-728-3883
ConstituencyOffice
113 - 3rd Ave. West
PO Box 3215
Melville, SK S0A 2P0

SK Power Corporation, Enterprise SK, Innovation SK, Uranium DevelopmentPartnership, & SK Research Council, Hon. Bill Boyd
Constituency: Kindersley *No. of Constituents:* 9,980, Saskatchewan Party
Tel: 306-787-0804

Fax: 306-798-2009
bboyd@mla.legassembly.sk.ca
Other Communications: Constituency Phone: 306-463-4480, Fax: 306-463-6873
Constituency Office
116C Main St.
PO Box 490
Kindersley, SK S0L1S0

Fred Bradshaw
Constituency: Carrot River Valley *No. of Constituents:* 10,340, Saskatchewan Party
Tel: 306-787-4300
Fax: 306-787-3174
fbradshaw@mla.legassembly.sk.ca
Other Communications: Constituency Phone: 306-768-3977, Fax: 306-768-3979
Constituency Office
29 Main St.
PO Box 969
Carrot River, SK S0E 0L0

Greg Brkich
Constituency: Arm River-Watrous *No. of Constituents:* 10,129, Saskatchewan Party
Tel: 306-787-4300
Fax: 306-787-3174
gbrkich@mla.legassembly.sk.ca
www.gregbrkich.ca
Other Communications: Constituency Phone: 306-567-2843, Fax:306-567-3259
Constituency Office
102 Washington St.
PO Box 1077
Davidson, SK S0G 1A0

Cam Broten
Constituency: Saskatoon Massey Place *No. of Constituents:* 11,520, New Democratic Party
Tel: 306-787-0230
Fax: 306-787-6247
cbroten@mla.legassembly.sk.ca; cbroten.mla@sasktel.net
www.cambrotenmla.ca
Other Communications: Constituency Phone: 306-384-7200, Fax:306-384-4280
Social Media: twitter.com/cambroten, www.facebook.com/cambrotenndp?ref=ts
Constituency Office
511 - 33rd St. West, Unit F
Regina, SK S7L 0V7

Jennifer Campeau
Constituency: Saskatoon Fairview *No. of Constituents:* 8,488, Saskatchewan Party
Tel: 306-787-4300
Fax: 306-787-3174
jcampeau@mla.legassembly.sk.ca
Other Communications: Constituency Phone: 306-974-4125, Fax: 306-974-4128
Social Media: www.facebook.com/JenCampeau
Constituency Office
#16, 15 WorobetzPl.
Saskatoon, SK S7L 6R4

Danielle Chartier
Constituency: Saskatoon Riversdale *No. of Constituents:* 8,388, New Democratic Party
Tel: 306-787-1900
Fax: 306-787-6247
dchartier@mla.legassembly.sk.ca
www.daniellechartier.ca
Other Communications: Constituency Phone: 306-244-5167,306-244-6070
Social Media: twitter.com/RiversdaleMLA
Constituency Office
1030 Ave. L South
Saskatoon, SK S7M 2J5

Saskatchewan Water Corporation, Hon. Ken Cheveldayoff
Constituency: Saskatoon Silver Springs *No. of Constituents:* 16,180, Saskatchewan Party
Tel: 306-787-0393
Fax: 306-798-1669
kcheveldayoff@mla.legassembly.sk.ca; minister.env@gov.sk.ca
www.cheveldayoff.com
Other Communications: Constituency Phone: 306-651-7100, Fax: 306-651-6008
Social Media: www.facebook.com/pages/Ken-Cheveldayoff/52760912740
Constituency Office
1106A Central Ave.
Saskatoon, SK S7N 2H1

Herb Cox
Constituency: The Battlefords *No. of Constituents:* 9,528, Saskatchewan Party
Tel: 306-787-4300
Fax: 306-787-3174
hcox@mla.legassembly.sk.ca
Other Communications: Constituency Phone: 306-445-5195, Fax: 306-445-5196
Constituency Office
1991 - 100th St. North
NorthBattleford, SK S9A 0X2

Hon. Dan D'Autremont
Constituency: Cannington *No. of Constituents:* 9,876, Saskatchewan Party
Tel: 306-787-2282
Fax: 306-787-2283
ddautremont@mla.legassembly.sk.ca; speaker@legassembly.sk.ca
www.dandautremont.ca
Other Communications: Constituency Phone: 306-443-2420, Fax: 306-443-2269
Social Media: www.facebook.com/pages/Dan-DAutremont/63773726250?sk=info
Constituency Office
303 Hwy. 361
PO Box 130
Alida, SK S0C 0B0

Mark Docherty
Constituency: Regina Coronation Park *No. of Constituents:* 10,038, Saskatchewan Party
Tel: 306-787-4300
Fax: 306-787-3174
mdocherty@mla.legassembly.sk.ca
www.markdocherty.ca
Other Communications: Constituency Phone: 306-359-3624, Fax: 306-359-3630
Social Media: twitter.com/dochertymark
Constituency Office
3120 AvonhurstDr.
Regina, SK S4R 3J7

Hon. Kevin Doherty
Constituency: ReginaNortheast *No. of Constituents:* 10,657, Saskatchewan Party
Tel: 306-787-0354
Fax: 306-798-0264
kdoherty@mla.legassembly.sk.ca
Other Communications: Constituency Phone: 306-525-5568, Fax: 306-525-5680
Social Media: www.facebook.com/KevinDohertyforReginaNorthEast, ca.linkedin.com/pub/kevin-doherty/21/125/6b1
Constituency Office
#105, 438 Victoira Ave. East
Regina, SK S4N 0N7

Larry Doke
Constituency: Cut Knife-Turtleford *No. of Constituents:* 8,363, Saskatchewan Party
Tel: 306-787-4300
Fax: 306-787-3174
ldoke@mla.legassembly.sk.ca
Other Communications: Constituency Phone: 306-893-2619, Fax: 306-893-2660
Constituency Office
#6, 116 - 1st Ave.West
PO Box 850
Maidstone, SK S0M 1M0

Hon. June Draude
Constituency: Kelvington-Wadena *No. of Constituents:* 9,509, Saskatchewan Party
Tel: 306-787-3661
Fax: 306-787-0656
jdraude@mla.legassembly.sk.ca; minister.ss@gov.sk.ca
www.junedraude.ca
Other Communications: Constituency Phone: 306-338-3973, Fax: 306-338-3977
Constituency Office
110 Main St.
PO Box 369
Wadena, SK S0A 4J0

Hon. Dustin Duncan
Constituency: Weyburn-Big Muddy *No. of Constituents:* 9,784, Saskatchewan Party
Tel: 306-787-7345
Fax: 306-787-0237
dduncan@mla.legassembly.sk.ca; minister.he@gov.sk.ca
Other Communications: Constituency Phone: 306-842-4810, Fax:306-842-4811
Social Media: twitter.com/dustin_duncan
Constituency Office
35 - 5th St. NE
Weyburn, SK S4H 0Y9

Doreen Eagles
Constituency: Estevan *No. of Constituents:* 10,148, Saskatchewan Party
Tel: 306-787-4300
Fax: 306-787-3174
deagles@mla.legassembly.sk.ca
Other Communications: Constituency Phone: 306-634-7311, Fax: 306-634-7332
Constituency Office
1108 - 4th St.
Estevan, SK S4A 0W7

Hon. Wayne Elhard
Constituency: Cypress Hills *No. of Constituents:* 10,041, Saskatchewan Party
Tel: 306-787-1636
Fax: 306-787-0012
welhard@mla.legassembly.sk.ca
www.wayneelhard.ca
Other Communications: Constituency Phone: 306-295-3688, Fax: 306-295-3699
ConstituencyOffice
401 Redcoat Dr.
PO Box 308
Eastend, SK S0N 0T0

David Forbes
Constituency: Saskatoon Centre *No. of Constituents:* 7,409, New Democratic Party
Tel: 306-787-0975
Fax: 306-787-6247
dforbes@mla.legassembly.sk.ca; dforbesmla@sasktel.net
www.davidforbesmla.ca
Other Communications: Constituency Phone: 306-244-3555, Fax:306-244-3602
Social Media: www.facebook.com/electDavidForbes
Constituency Office
904D - 22nd St. West
Saskatoon, SK S7M 0S1

Saskatchewan Liquor & Gaming Authority, Hon. Donna Harpauer
Constituency: Humboldt *No. of Constituents:* 10,636, Saskatchewan Party
Tel: 306-787-7339
Fax: 306-798-3140
dharpauer@mla.legassembly.sk.ca; minister.cc@gov.sk.ca
www.donnaharpauer.ca
Other Communications: Constituency Phone & Fax: 306-682-5141
Social Media: www.facebook.com/pages/Donna-Harpauer/60494388240
Constituency Office
632 - 9th St.
PO Box 2950
Humboldt, SK S0K 2A0

Jeremy Harrison
Constituency: Meadow Lake *No. of Constituents:* 9,638, Saskatchewan Party
Tel: 306-787-4300
Toll-free: 877-234-6669
Fax: 306-787-3174
jharrison@mla.legassembly.sk.ca; jharrisonmla@sasktel.net
www.jeremyharrison.ca
Other Communications: Constituency Phone: 306-236-6669, Fax:306-236-6744
Constituency Office
201 - 2nd St. West
PO Box 848
Meadow Lake, SK S9X 1Y6

Glen Hart
Constituency: Last Mountain-Touchwood *No. of Constituents:* 10,086, Saskatchewan Party
Tel: 306-787-4300
Toll-free: 877-723-4488
Fax: 306-787-3174
ghart@mla.legassembly.sk.ca; ghart.mla@sasktel.net
www.glenhart.ca
Other Communications: Constituency Phone: 306-723-4421, Fax:306-723-4654
Constituency Office
402 Stanley St.
PO Box 309
Cupar, SK S0G 0Y0

Hon. Nancy Heppner
Constituency: Martensville *No. of Constituents:* 13,371, Saskatchewan Party
Tel: 306-787-0942
Fax: 306-787-8677
nheppner@mla.legassembly.sk.ca; minister.gs@gov.sk.ca
www.nancyheppner.com
Other Communications: Constituency Phone: 306-225-2280, Fax: 306-225-2149
Constituency Office
99 - 4th St.
PO Box 830
Hague, SK S0K 1X0

Darryl Hickie
Constituency: Prince Albert Carlton *No. of Constituents:* 9,588, Saskatchewan Party
Tel: 306-787-4300
Fax: 306-787-3174
dhickie@mla.legassembly.sk.ca
www.darrylhickie.ca
Other Communications: Constituency Phone: 306-922-4676, Fax: 306-922-4674

Constituency Office
#4, 3041 ShermanDr.
Prince Albert, SK S6V 7B7

Bill Hutchinson
Constituency: Regina South *No. of Constituents:* 11,622, Saskatchewan Party
Tel: 306-787-4300
Fax: 306-787-3174
bhutchinson@mla.legassembly.sk.ca
www.billhutchinson.ca
Other Communications: Constituency Phone: 306-205-2067, Fax: 306-205-2069
Constituency Office
#6, 4420 AlbertSt.
Regina, SK S4S 6B6

D.F. (Yogi) Huyghebaert
Constituency: Wood River *No. of Constituents:* 10,005, Saskatchewan Party
Tel: 306-787-4300
Fax: 306-787-3174
yhuyghebaert@mla.legassembly.sk.ca; mlawoodriver@sasktel.net
www.mlawoodriver.ca
Other Communications: Constituency Phone: 306-642-4744; Fax: 306-642-4515
Constituency Office
200 Centre St.
PO Box 2097
Assiniboia, SK S0H 0B0

Victoria Jurgens
Constituency: Prince Albert Northcote *No. of Constituents:* 8,124, Saskatchewan Party
Tel: 306-787-4300
Fax: 306-787-3174
vjurgens@mla.legassembly.sk.ca
www.mlajurgens.ca
Other Communications: Constituency Phone: 306-922-4220, Fax: 306-922-4221
Social Media: twitter.com/MLAJurgens
Constituency Office
#5A, 598 - 15th St.East
Prince Albert, SK S6V 1G2

Delbert Kirsch
Constituency: Batoche *No. of Constituents:* 10,189, Saskatchewan Party
Tel: 306-787-4300
Fax: 306-787-3174
dkirsch@mla.legassembly.sk.ca
Other Communications: Constituency Phone: 306-256-3930, Fax:306-256-3924
Constituency Office
115 Main St.
PO Box 308
Cudworth, SK S0K 1B0

Hon. Ken Krawetz
Constituency: Canora-Pelly *No. of Constituents:* 9,906, Saskatchewan Party
Tel: 306-787-6060
Fax: 306-787-6055
kkrawetz@mla.legassembly.sk.ca; minister.fin@gov.sk.ca
www.kenkrawetz.ca
Other Communications: Constituency Phone: 306-563-4425,Fax: 306-563-5752
Constituency Office
219 Main St.
PO Box 838
Canora, SK S0A 0L0

Greg Lawrence
Constituency: Moose Jaw Wakamow *No. of Constituents:* 9,599, Saskatchewan Party
Tel: 306-787-4300
Fax: 306-787-3174
glawrence@mla.legassembly.sk.ca
Other Communications: Constituency Phone: 306-694-1001, Fax: 306-691-0486
Social Media: www.facebook.com/group.php?gid=132422373482663, ca.linkedin.com/pub/greg-lawrence/54/854/499
Constituency Office
404B Lillooet St.West
Moose Jaw, SK S6H 7T1

Gene Makowsky
Constituency: Regina Dewdney *No. of Constituents:* 10,546, Saskatchewan Party
Tel: 306-787-4300
Fax: 306-787-3174
gmakowsky@mla.legassembly.sk.ca
www.genemakowsky.ca
Other Communications: Constituency Phone: 306-545-4363, Fax: 306-545-4370
Social Media: www.facebook.com/GeneAMakowsky
ConstituencyOffice
#105, 438 Victoria Ave. East
Regina, SK S4N 0N7

Hon. Russ Marchuk
Constituency: Regina Douglas Park *No. of Constituents:* 10,846, Saskatchewan Party
Tel: 306-787-7360
Fax: 306-798-0263
rmarchuk@mla.legassembly.sk.ca; minister.edu@gov.sk.ca
www.russmarchuk-mla.com
Other Communications: Constituency Phone: 306-352-1797, Fax:306-352-1824
Social Media: twitter.com/marchuk_mla
Constituency Office
#105, 438 Victoria Ave. East
Regina, SK S4N 0N7

Warren McCall
Constituency: Regina Elphinstone-Centre *No. of Constituents:* 6,313, New Democratic Party
Tel: 306-787-8276
Fax: 306-787-6247
wmccall@mla.legassembly.sk.ca; warren.mccall@sasktel.net
Other Communications: Constituency Phone: 306-352-2002, Fax:306-352-2065
Social Media: ca.linkedin.com/pub/warren-mccall/19/2a7/672
Constituency Office
2900 - 5th Ave.
Regina, SK S4T 0L6

Trade; Minister Responsible, SaskEnergy Incorporated, Hon. Tim McMillan
Constituency: Lloydminster *No. of Constituents:* 10,693, Saskatchewan Party
Tel: 306-787-9124
Fax: 306-787-0395
tmcmillan@mla.legassembly.sk.ca; minister.er@gov.sk.ca
Other Communications: Constituency Phone: 306-825-4477, Fax: 306-825-4473
Social Media: www.facebook.com/timmcmillanmla
Constituency Office
4910B - 49th St.
Lloydminster, SK S9V 0M3

Saskatchewan Transportation Company; MinisterResponsible, Information Services Corporation; Minister Responsible, Saskatchewan Gaming Corp., Hon. Don McMorris
Constituency: Indian Head-Milestone *No. of Constituents:* 11,352, Saskatchewan Party
Tel: 306-787-6447
Fax: 306-787-1736
dmcmorris@mla.legassembly.sk.ca; minister.hi@gov.sk.ca
www.donmcmorris.ca
Other Communications: Constituency Phone: 306-771-2733, Fax:306-771-2574
Social Media: twitter.com/dmcmorrissp, www.facebook.com/DonMcMorrisSP
Constituency Office
125 Railway St.
PO Box 720
Balgonie, SK S0G 0E0

Paul Merriman
Constituency: Saskatoon Sutherland *No. of Constituents:* 9,939, Saskatchewan Party
Tel: 306-787-4300
Fax: 306-787-3174
pmerriman@mla.legassembly.sk.ca
Other Communications: Constituency Phone: 306-244-5623, Fax: 306-244-5626
Social Media: www.facebook.com/saskpartypaul
Constituency Office
#211, 3521 - 8th St.East
Saskatoon, SK S7H 0W5

Warren Michelson
Constituency: Moose Jaw North *No. of Constituents:* 10,614, Saskatchewan Party
Tel: 306-787-4300
Fax: 306-798-3174
wmichelson@mla.legassembly.sk.ca
www.warrenmichelson.ca
Other Communications: Constituency Phone:306-692-8884, Fax: 306-692-8872
Social Media: www.facebook.com/WarrenMichelson
Constituency Office
326B High St. West
Moose Jaw, SK S6H 1S9

Scott Moe
Constituency: Rosthern-Shellbrook *No. of Constituents:* 11,022, Saskatchewan Party
Tel: 306-787-4300
Toll-free: 855-793-3422
Fax: 306-787-3174
smoe@mla.legassembly.sk.ca
www.scott-moe.com
Other Communications: Constituency Phone: 306-747-3422, Fax: 306-747-3472
Social Media: www.facebook.com/group.php?gid=182365048474566
Constituency Office
34 Main St.
Shellbrook, SK S0J 2E0

Saskatchewan Workers' Compensation Board, Hon. Don Morgan, Q.C.
Constituency: Saskatoon Southeast *No. of Constituents:* 16,343, Saskatchewan Party
Tel: 306-787-0613
Fax: 306-787-6946
dmorgan@mla.legassembly.sk.ca; minister.ae@gov.sk.ca
www.donmorgan.ca
Other Communications: Constituency Phone: 306-955-4755, Fax: 306-955-4765
Social Media: www.facebook.com/pages/Don-Morgan/48835718931?sk=info
Constituency Office
#109, 3502 Taylor St. East
Saskatoon, SK S7H 5H9

John Nilson, Q.C.
Constituency: Regina Lakeview *No. of Constituents:* 11,161, New Democratic Party
Tel: 306-787-0939
Fax: 306-787-6247
jnilson@mla.legassembly.sk.ca;j.nilson.mla@sasktel.net
Other Communications: Constituency Phone: 306-751-7740, Fax: 306-585-2030
Constituency Office
3831A Albert St.
Regina, SK S4S 3R4

Rob Norris
Constituency: Saskatoon Greystone *No. of Constituents:* 11,295, Saskatchewan Party
Tel: 306-787-4300
Fax: 306-787-3174
rnorris@mla.legassembly.sk.ca
www.robnorris.org
Other Communications: Constituency Phone: 306-933-7852,Fax: 306-933-7869
Social Media: twitter.com/RobNorris_SP, www.facebook.com/RobNorrisSP
Constituency Office
#5, 2720 - 8th St. East
Saskatoon, SK S7H 0V8

Greg Ottenbreit
Constituency: Yorkton *No. of Constituents:* 10,961, Saskatchewan Party
Tel: 306-787-4300
Fax: 306-787-3174
gottenbreit@mla.legassembly.sk.ca
www.gregottenbreit.ca
Other Communications: Constituency Phone: 306-783-7275, Fax: 306-787-3174
Social Media: twitter.com/GregOttMLA
ConstituencyOffice
#29A Broadway St. East
Yorkton, SK S3N 0K4

Roger Parent
Constituency: Saskatoon Meewasin *No. of Constituents:* 10,458, Saskatchewan Party
Tel: 306-787-4300
Fax: 306-787-3174
rparent@mla.legassembly.sk.ca
Other Communications: Constituency Phone: 306-652-4607, Fax:: 306-652-4614
Social Media: www.facebook.com/rogerparentmla
Constituency Office
96 - 33rd St. East, BayC
PO Box 26068
Saskatoon, SK S7K 8C1

Kevin Phillips
Constituency: Melfort *No. of Constituents:* 9,880, Saskatchewan Party
Tel: 306-787-4300
Fax: 306-787-3174
kphillips@mla.legassembly.sk.ca
Other Communications: Constituency Phone: 306-752-9500, Fax: 306-752-9005
Constituency Office, Melfort Mall
1121Main St., Bay 14
PO Box 2800
Melfort, SK S0E 1A0

Hon. Jim Reiter
Constituency: Rosetown-Elrose *No. of Constituents:* 9,892, Saskatchewan Party
Tel: 306-787-6100
Fax: 306-787-0399
jreiter@mla.legassembly.sk.ca;minister.gr@gov.sk.ca
www.jimreiter.ca
Other Communications: Constituency Phone: 306-882-4105, Fax: 306-882-4108
Social Media: twitter.com/jim_reiter, www.facebook.com/pages/Jim-Reiter/207539405959289
Constituency Office
215 Main St.

PO Box 278
Rosetown, SK S0L 2V0
Laura Ross
Constituency: Regina Qu'Appelle Valley *No. of Constituents:* 14,660, Saskatchewan Party
Tel: 306-787-4300
Fax: 306-787-3174
lross@mla.legassembly.sk.ca
Other Communications: Constituency Phone: 306-545-6333, Fax: 306-545-6112
Constituency Office
4519 RochdaleBlvd.
Regina, SK S4X 4R3
Cathy Sproule
Constituency: Saskatoon Nutana *No. of Constituents:* 11,843, New Democratic Party
Tel: 306-787-9999
Fax: 306-787-6247
csproule@mla.legassembly.sk.ca;
SaskatoonNutana@ndpcaucus.sk.ca
www.cathysproule.com
Other Communications: Constituency Phone:306-664-6101, Fax: 306-665-5633
Social Media: twitter.com/@cathysproule,
www.facebook.com/group.php?gid=173288332783856,
ca.linkedin.com/pub/cathy-sproule/16/ab8/7b3
Constituency Office
621A Main St.
Saskatoon, SK S7H 0J8
Warren Steinley
Constituency: Regina Walsh Acres *No. of Constituents:* 9,382, Saskatchewan Party
Tel: 306-787-4300
Fax: 306-787-3174
wsteinley@mla.legassembly.sk.ca
www.warrensteinley.com
Other Communications: Constituency Phone: 306-565-3881, Fax: 306-565-3893
Social Media: twitter.com/WSteinley_SP,
www.facebook.com/group.php?gid=102220736527442
Constituency Office
6845 RochdaleBlvd.
Regina, SK S4X 2Z2
Hon. Lyle Stewart
Constituency: Thunder Creek *No. of Constituents:* 11,112, Saskatchewan Party
Tel: 306-787-0338
Fax: 306-787-0630
lstewart@mla.legassembly.sk.ca;minister.ag@gov.sk.ca
www.lylestewart.ca
Other Communications: Constituency Phone: 306-693-3229, 306-693-3251
Social Media:
www.facebook.com/group.php?gid=182442928469194
Constituency Office
#207, 310 Main St. North
Moose Jaw, SK S6H 3K1
Hon. Christine Tell
Constituency: Regina Wascana Plains *No. of Constituents:* 15,809, Saskatchewan Party
Tel: 306-787-4377
Fax: 306-787-5331
ctell@mla.legassembly.sk.ca;
ChristineTellMLA@accesscomm.ca
www.christinetell.com
Other Communications: ConstituencyPhone: 306-205-2126, Fax: 306-205-2127
Social Media: www.facebook.com/christinetellsp
Constituency Office
2318B Assiniboine Ave. East
Regina, SK S4V 2P5
Corey Tochor
Constituency: Saskatoon Eastview *No. of Constituents:* 11,637, Saskatchewan Party
Tel: 306-787-4300
Fax: 306-787-3174
ctochor@mla.legassembly.sk.ca
www.coreytochormla.com
Other Communications: Constituency Phone: 306-384-2011, Fax: 306-384-2229
Social Media: www.facebook.com/public/Corey-Tochor
Constituency Office
#1, 3012 Louise St.
Saskatoon, SK S7J 3L8
Don Toth
Constituency: Moosomin *No. of Constituents:* 10,345, Saskatchewan Party
Tel: 306-787-4300
Toll-free: 888-255-8684
Fax: 306-798-3174
dtoth@mla.legassembly.sk.ca; dtoth@sasktel.net
www.dontoth.ca
Other Communications: Constituency Phone: 306-435-3329, Fax:306-435-3921
Constituency Office
624 Main St.
PO Box 1038
Moosomin, SK S0G 3N0
Doyle Vermette
Constituency: Cumberland *No. of Constituents:* 8,726, New Democratic Party
Tel: 306-787-6340
Fax: 306-787-6247
dvermette@mla.legassembly.sk.ca
Other Communications: Constituency Phone: 306-425-2525, Fax: 306-425-2885
Constituency Office
251La Ronge Ave.
PO Box 192
La Ronge, SK S0J 1L0
Hon. Brad Wall
Constituency: Swift Current *No. of Constituents:* 10,911, Saskatchewan Party
Tel: 306-787-9433
Fax: 306-787-0885
bwall@mla.legassembly.sk.ca
www.bradwall.ca; www.premier.gov.sk.ca
Other Communications: Constituency Phone:306-778-2429, Fax: 306-778-3614
Social Media: twitter.com/PremierBradWall,
www.facebook.com/PremierBradWall
Constituency Office
233 Central Ave. North
Swift Current, SK S9H 0L3
Hon. Randy Weekes
Constituency: Biggar *No. of Constituents:* 10,758, Saskatchewan Party
Tel: 306-798-9014
Fax: 306-798-9013
rweekes@mla.legassembly.sk.ca;
randyweekes.mla@accesscomm.ca
www.randyweekes.ca
Other Communications: ConstituencyPhone: 306-948-4880, Fax: 306-948-4882
Social Media:
www.facebook.com/pages/Randy-Weekes-MLA/356610274367735?sk=info
Constituency Office
106 - 3rd Ave. West
PO Box 1413
Biggar, SK S0K 0M0
Nadine Wilson
Constituency: Saskatchewan Rivers *No. of Constituents:* 10,240, Saskatchewan Party
Tel: 306-787-4300
Fax: 306-798-3174
nwilson@mla.legassembly.sk.ca; saskrivers@sasktel.net
www.nadinewilson.ca
Other Communications: Constituency Phone: 306-763-0615, Fax: 306-763-2503
Social Media:
www.facebook.com/pages/Nadine-Wilson/49297133345?v=info
ConstituencyOffice
Box 4, Site 16, RR#5
Prince Albert, SK S6V 5R3
Trent Wotherspoon
Constituency: Regina Rosemont *No. of Constituents:* 9,713, New Democratic Party
Tel: 306-787-0077
Fax: 306-787-6247
twotherspoon@mla.legassembly.sk.ca
www.trentwotherspoon.com
Other Communications: Constituency Phone: 306-565-2444, Fax:306-565-2952
Social Media: twitter.com/WotherspoonT
Constituency Office
#700E, 4400 - 4th Ave.
Regina, SK S4T 0H8
Hon. Gordon Wyant, Q.C.
Constituency: Saskatoon Northwest *No. of Constituents:* 10,380, Saskatchewan Party
Tel: 306-787-5353
Fax: 306-787-1232
gwyant@mla.legassembly.sk.ca;minister.ju@gov.sk.ca
Other Communications: Constituency Phone: 306-934-2847, Fax: 306-934-2867
Social Media: twitter.com/GordWyant
Constituency Office
75B Lenore Dr.
Saskatoon, SK S7K 7Y1

Saskatchewan Government Departments & Agencies

Saskatchewan Advanced Education (AE)

1945 Hamilton St., Regina, SK S4P 2C8
Tel: 306-787-9478
aeeinquiry@gov.sk.ca
www.aee.gov.sk.ca
Other Communication: SaskJobs: saskjobs@gov.sk.ca; General Educational Development: GED@sasked.gov.sk.ca

The Ministry strives to create a vital, educated & skilled workforce by focussing on the following areas: retaining educated & skilled workers in Saskatchewan; providing educational & training programs to develop a skilled workforce; & promoting the province's opportunities to attract educated & skilled workers from outside Saskatchewan & Canada. In November 2007, a new provincial government resulted in the reorganization of provincial government ministries. An expanded Ministry of Advanced Education, Employment & Labour was formed, & was subsequently changed to Advanced Education, Employment & Immigration.

Acts Administered:
Apprenticeship & Trade Certification Act
Post-Secondary Education & Skills Training Act
Private Vocational Schools Regulation Act
Regional Colleges Act
Saskatchewan Indian Institute of Technologies Act
Saskatchewan Institute of Applied Science & Technology Act
Student Assistance & Student Aid Fund Act
University of Regina Act
University of Saskatchewan Act

Minister, Advanced Education; Minister, Labour Relations & Workplace Safety; Minister Responsible, Saskatchewan Workers' Compensation Board, Hon. Don Morgan, Q.C.
Tel: 306-787-0613
Fax: 306-787-6946
minister.ae@gov.sk.ca
Social Media:
www.facebook.com/pages/Don-Morgan/48835718931?sk=info
Minister'sOffice, Ministry of Advanced Education, Legislative Building
#361, 2405 Legislative Dr.
Regina, SK S4S 0B3

Deputy Minister, Advanced Education, Louise Greenberg
Tel: 306-787-4855
Fax: 306-798-0975
louise.greenberg@gov.sk.ca

Assistant Deputy Minister, Employment, Immigration and Training, Rupen Pandya
Tel: 306-787-6846
Fax: 306-798-0975
Rupen.Pandya@gov.sk.ca

Assistant Deputy Minister, Post Secordary Education, David Boehm
Tel: 306-787-0835
Fax: 306-798-0975

Assistant Deputy Minister, Corporate and Support Services, Karen Allen
Tel: 306-787-5654
Fax: 306-787-7392

Executive Director, Marketing & Communications, Herman Hulshof
Tel: 306-787-9715
Fax: 306-798-5021
Herman.Hulshof@gov.sk.ca

Director, Public Affairs, Rikki Bote
Tel: 306-787-4156
Fax: 306-798-5021
Rikki.Bote@gov.sk.ca

Associated Agencies, Boards & Commissions:
• **Saskatchewan Apprenticeship & Trade Certification Commission**
2140 Hamilton St.
Regina, SK S4P 2E3
Tel: 306-787-2444
Fax: 306-787-5105
Toll-free: 877-363-0536
apprenticeship@gov.sk.ca
www.saskapprenticeship.ca

Advanced Education & Student Services
Assistant Deputy Minister, David Boehm
Tel: 306-787-0835

Fax: 306-798-0975
david.boehm@gov.sk.ca
Executive Director, Program Innovation, Ted Amendt
Tel: 306-787-5984
Fax: 306-787-7182
Ted.Amendt@gov.sk.ca
Executive Director, Student Financial Assistance, Tammy Bloor Cavers
Tel: 306-787-2044
Fax: 306-787-7537
Tammy.BloorCavers@gov.sk.ca
Executive Director, Quality Assurance, Ann Lorenzen
Tel: 306-787-2267
Fax: 306-798-3379
Ann.Lorenzen@gov.sk.ca
Executive Director, Public Institutions & Infrastructure, Dion McGrath
Tel: 306-787-7974
Fax: 306-798-3159
Dion.McGrath@gov.sk.ca
Director, Public Institutions & Infrasturcture, Brent Brownlee
Tel: 306-787-7027
Fax: 306-798-3159
Brent.Brownlee@gov.sk.ca
Director, Program Innovation, Tim Caleval
Tel: 306-787-8131
Fax: 306-787-7182
Tim.Caleval@gov.sk.ca
Director, Public Institutions & Infrasturcture, Heather George
Tel: 306-787-5900
Fax: 306-798-3159
Heather.George@gov.sk.ca
Director, Income Support, Rose-Ann Hamer
Tel: 306-787-0692
Fax: 306-787-0760
Rose-Ann.Hamer@gov.sk.ca
Director, Private Vocational Schools, Darlene Heska-Willard
Tel: 306-787-5457
Fax: 306-798-3379
Darlene.Heska-Willard@gov.sk.ca
Director, Business & Information Technology Services, Ron Kitchen
Tel: 306-787-6231
Fax: 306-787-7537
ron.kitchen@gov.sk.ca
Director, Program Innovation, Jim Seiferling
Tel: 306-787-0477
Fax: 306-787-7182
Jim.Seiferling@gov.sk.ca
Director, Strategic Initiatives, Kirk Wosminity
Tel: 306-787-8064
Fax: 306-787-7537
Kirk.Wosminity@gov.sk.ca

Can-Sask Career & Employment Services
1945 Hamilton St., 8th Fl., Regina, SK S4P 2C8
Tel: 306-787-0701
Fax: 306-798-5022
www.aeei.gov.sk.ca/career-employment/

Executive Director, Jan Morgan
Tel: 306-787-1626
Fax: 306-798-5022
Jan.Morgan@gov.sk.ca
Director, Jan Kot
Tel: 306-787-8458
Fax: 306-798-5022
Jan.Kot@gov.sk.ca
Regional Director, North West Region, Pat Bauer
Tel: 306-446-7890
Fax: 306-446-8707
Pat.Bauer@gov.sk.ca
Regional Director, Centre Region, Chris Broten
Tel: 306-933-5780
Fax: 306-933-7801
Chris.Broten@gov.sk.ca
Regional Director, South West Region, Dennis Schafer
Tel: 306-787-2352
Fax: 306-798-0079
Dennis.Schafer@gov.sk.ca
Regional Director, South East Region, Darcy Smycniuk
Tel: 306-786-5808
Fax: 306-786-1541
Darcy.Smycniuk@gov.sk.ca
Regional Director, North East Region, Penny Sommervill
Tel: 306-953-2203
Fax: 306-953-2763
Penny.Sommervill@gov.sk.ca

Corporate Services
1945 Hamilton St., 14th Fl., Regina, SK S4P 2C8
Tel: 306-787-3920
Fax: 306-787-7392

Executive Director, Karen Allen
Tel: 306-787-5654
Fax: 306-787-7392
Karen.Allen@gov.sk.ca
Director, Financial Planning, Scott Giroux
Tel: 306-787-3501
Fax: 306-787-7392
Scott.Giroux@gov.sk.ca
Director, Financial Operations, Candace Malowany
Tel: 306-787-7384
Fax: 306-787-7392
Candace.Malowany@gov.sk.ca
Director, Audit Services Unit, Duane Rieger
Tel: 306-787-1421
Fax: 306-798-0016
Duane.Rieger@gov.sk.ca
Director, Financial Planning & Business Systems, Brian Schwab
Tel: 306-787-4209
Fax: 306-787-7392
Brian.Schwab@gov.sk.ca
Director, Support Services & Accommodations, Tim Selinger
Tel: 306-798-5902
Fax: 306-798-0193
Tim.Selinger@gov.sk.ca

Immigration Services
1945 Hamilton St., 7th Fl., Regina, SK S4P 2C8
Tel: 306-798-7467
Fax: 306-933-7901
immigration@gov.sk.ca
www.immigration.gov.sk.ca

Acting Director, Policy & Program Support, Eric Johansen
Tel: 306-787-0254
Fax: 306-798-3405
Eric.Johansen@gov.sk.ca
Acting Director, Immigration Policy, Anne McRorie
Tel: 306-798-5904
Fax: 306-798-0713
Anne.McRorie@gov.sk.ca
Director, Community Partnerships & Settlement, Tim Helfrich
Tel: 306-798-2381
Fax: 306-798-0713
Tim.Helfrich@gov.sk.ca
Director, Program Integrity/Saskatchewan Immigrant Nominee Program, Kirk Westgard
Tel: 306-787-0370
Fax: 306-798-0713
Kirk.Westgard@gov.sk.ca
Acting Office Manager, Thera Lovelace
Tel: 306-787-2206
Fax: 306-798-0713
Thera.Lovelace@gov.sk.ca

Policy & Planning
1945 Hamilton St., 15th Fl., Regina, SK S4P 2C8
Tel: 306-787-5663
Fax: 306-787-5870

Executive Director, Linda Smith
Tel: 306-787-2984
Fax: 306-787-5870
Linda.Smith@gov.sk.ca; linda.smith@pnrha.ca
Other Communications: Alternate Email: linda.smith@hrha.sk.ca
Director, Strategic Policy, Karen Banks
Tel: 306-787-4347
Fax: 306-787-5870
Karen.Banks@gov.sk.ca
Director, Economic/Labour Market Information & Analysis, Lorraine Beckman
Tel: 306-787-5626
Fax: 306-787-5870
Lorraine.Beckman@gov.sk.ca
Director, Policy & Intergovernmental, Mary Didowycz
Tel: 306-787-6224
Fax: 306-787-5870
Mary.Didowycz@gov.sk.ca
Director, Privacy Coordinator, Jan Gray
Tel: 306-787-2638
Fax: 306-787-5870
Jan.Gray@gov.sk.ca

Saskatchewan Agriculture (AG)

Walter Scott Bldg., 3085 Albert St., Regina, SK S4S 0B1
Toll-Free: 866-457-2377
aginfo@gov.sk.ca
www.agriculture.gov.sk.ca

The Ministry's mandate is to foster, in partnership with individuals, communities, industry, & government, a commercially viable, self-sufficient, & sustainable agricultural sector in Saskatchewan. The Ministry addresses needs of individual farmers & ranchers, encourages & develops higher value production & processing, & promotes sustainable economic development in rural areas of the province. Some responsibilities are as follows: agri-business development through provision of agriculture-based business experts & technical support; agricultural research to promote development & diversification; corporate services to support the Information Technology Office & the Rural Economic Co-operative Development; crop development; financial programs; inspection & administration of regulations for food & crop protection, animal disease surveillance, environmental reviews, licenses, registrations, & complaint resolution; irrigation development; promotion of sustainable use of Crown land; livestock development; provision of food safety, quality, policy, regulatory, market & business development programs; policy analysis, strategies, & agricultural information services; & delivery of Saskatchewan Crop Insurance Corporation programs & services.

Acts Administered:
Agri-Food Act, 2004
Agri-Food Innovation Act
Agricultural Credit Corporation of Saskatchewan Act
Agricultural Equipment Dealerships Act
Agricultural Implements Act
Agricultural Operations Act
Agricultural Safety Net Act
Agricultural Societies Act
Agrologists Act, 1994
Animal Identification Act
Animal Products Act
Animal Protection Act, 1999
Apiaries Act
Bacterial Ring Rot Control Regulations
Cattle Marketing Deductions Act, 1998
Crop Insurance Act
Crop Payments Act
Department of Agriculture, Food & Rural Revitilization Act
Disease of Animals Act
Dutch Elm Disease Control Regulations
Expropriation (Rehabilitation Projects) Act
Farm Financial Stability Act
Farmers' Counselling & Assistance Act
Farming Communities Land Act
Government Organization Act
Grain Charges Limitation Act
Horned Cattle Purchases Act
Irrigation Act
Land Bank Repeal & Temporary Provisions Act
Leafcutting Beekeepers Registration Act
Line Fence Act
Milk Control Act, 1992
On-farm Quality Assurance Programs Act
Pastures Act
Pest Control Act
Pest Control Products (Saskatchewan) Act
Prairie Agricultural Machinery Institute Act, 1999
Provincial Lands Act
Sale or Lease of Certain Lands Act
Saskatchewan 4-H Foundation Act
Saskatchewan Farm Security Act
Saskatchewan Wetland Conservation Corporation Land Regulation
Soil Drifting Control Act
Stray Animals Act
Vegetable, Fruit & Honey Sales Act
Veterinarians Act, 1987
Veterinary Services Act
Weed Control Act

Minister, Agriculture; Minister Responsible, Saskatchewan Crop Insurance Corporation, Hon. Lyle Stewart
Tel: 306-787-0338
Fax: 306-787-0630
minister.ag@gov.sk.ca
Social Media:
www.facebook.com/group.php?gid=182442928469194
Office of the Minister of Agriculture, Legislative Bldg.
#334, 2405Legislative Dr.
Regina, SK S4S 0B3

Deputy Minister, Agriculture, Alanna Koch
Tel: 306-787-5170
Fax: 306-787-2393
alanna.koch@gov.sk.ca

Assistant Deputy Minister, Rick Burton
Tel: 306-787-8077
Fax: 306-787-2393
rick.burton@gov.sk.ca

Assistant Deputy Minister, Nithi Govindasamy
Tel: 306-787-5247
Fax: 306-787-2393
nithi.govindasamy@gov.sk.ca

Executive Director, Corporate Services, Raymond Arscott
Tel: 306-787-5211
Fax: 306-787-0600
raymond.arscott@gov.sk.ca

Executive Director, Policy, Scott Brown
Tel: 306-787-5961
Fax: 306-787-5134
Scott.Brown@gov.sk.ca

Director, Regional Services, Lee Auten
Tel: 306-787-5018
Fax: 306-787-9623
lee.auten@gov.sk.ca

Director, Irrigation, John Babcock
Tel: 306-787-8711
Fax: 306-787-9623
John.Babcock@gov.sk.ca

Director, Crops, Doug Billett
Tel: 306-787-8061
Fax: 306-787-0428
doug.billett@gov.sk.ca

Director, Lands, Wally Hoehn
Tel: 306-787-1045
Fax: 306-787-5180
Wally.Hoehn@gov.sk.ca

Director, Agriculture Research, Abdul Jalil
Tel: 306-787-5960
Fax: 306-787-2654
abdul.jalil@gov.sk.ca

Director, Livestock, Paul Johnson
Tel: 306-787-6423
Fax: 306-787-1315
paul.johnson@gov.sk.ca;
paul.johnson@saskatoonhealthregion.ca

Director, Communications, Donna Rehirchuk
Tel: 306-787-5389
Fax: 306-787-0216
Donna.Rehirchuk@gov.sk.ca

Director, Financial Programs, Tom Schwartz
Tel: 306-787-6395
Fax: 306-798-3042
tom.schwartz@gov.sk.ca

Associated Agencies, Boards & Commissions:
• **Agri-Food Council**
#302, 3085 Albert St.
Regina, SK S4S 0B1
Tel: 306-787-5978
Fax: 306-787-5134
corey.ruud@gov.sk.ca
www.agriculture.gov.sk.ca/Agri-Food-Council
The Agri-Food Council is an independent board appointed by the provincial government. The Council is accountable to the Minister of Agriculture for the supervision of all agencies established under The Agri-Food Act, 2004.
• **Agricultural Implements Board**
#202, 3085 Albert St.
Regina, SK S4S 0B1
Tel: 306-787-4693
Fax: 306-787-1315
• **Farm Stress Unit**
#125, 3085 Albert St.
Regina, SK S4S 0B1
Tel: 306-787-5196
Fax: 306-798-3042
Toll-free: 800-667-4442
• **Farmland Security Board**
#207, 3988 Albert St.
Regina, SK S4S 3R1
Tel: 306-787-5047
Fax: 306-787-8599
• **Prairie Agricultural Machinery Institute (PAMI)**
Hwy 5 West
PO Box 1150
Humboldt, SK S0K 2A0
Tel: 306-682-2555
Fax: 306-682-5080
Toll-free: 800-567-7264
humboldt@pami.ca
www.pami.ca
PAMI works for the advancement of technology in agriculture through research and development.
• **Saskatchewan Crop Insurance Corporation**
484 Prince William Dr.
PO Box 3000
Melville, SK S0A 2P0
Tel: 306-728-7200
Fax: 306-728-7202
Toll-free: 888-935-0000
customer.service@scic.gov.sk.ca
www.saskcropinsurance.com
The provincial Crown Corporation provides responsive & flexible risk management tools. Crop insurance programs are as follows: Multi-Peril Insurance; Organic Insurance; Forage Insurance; & Weather Based Insurance.
• **Saskatchewan Egg Producers (SEP)**
496 Hoffer Dr.
PO Box 1263
Regina, SK S4P 3B8
Tel: 306-924-1505
Fax: 306-924-1515
sep@saskegg.ca
www.saskegg.ca
• **Saskatchewan Lands Appeal Board (SLAB)**
#202, 3085 Albert St.
Regina, SK S4S 0B1
Tel: 306-787-4693
Fax: 306-787-1315
Donald.Brooks@gov.sk.ca
• **Saskatchewan Milk Marketing Board (SMMB)**
444 McLeod St.
Regina, SK S4N 4Z3
Tel: 306-949-6999
Fax: 306-949-2605
www.saskmilk.ca
• **Saskatchewan Sheep Development Board**
2213C Hanselman Crt.
Saskatoon, SK S7L 6A8
Tel: 306-933-5200
Fax: 306-933-7182
sheepdb@sasktel.net; gordsheepdb@sasktel.net
www.sksheep.com
• **Saskatchewan Turkey Producers Marketing Board**
502 - 45th St. West, 2nd Fl.
Saskatoon, SK S7L 6H2
Tel: 306-931-1050
Fax: 306-931-2825
saskaturkey@sasktel.net
The STP manages the supply management system in Saskatchewan & raises levies in order to submit their own levy to the Canadian Turkey Marketing Agency (CTMA). The STP negotiates the province's quota levels with the CTMA, negotiates price levels with local processors, & develops a long-term strategy for the turkey industry in Saskatchewan.

Saskatchewan Archives Board

University of Regina, 3303 Hillsdale St., PO Box 1665, Regina, SK S4P 3C6
Tel: 306-787-4068
Fax: 306-787-1197
info.regina@archives.gov.sk.ca
www.saskarchives.com
Secondary Address: 3 Campus Dr.
Murray Bldg., University of Saskatchewan
Saskatoon, SK S7N 5A4 Canada
Fax: 306-933-7305
info.saskatoon@archives.gov.sk.ca

The Saskatchewan Archives is a joint university-government agency, which was established under legislation. The Archives collects official records of the Government of Saskatchewan, as well as documentary material from local government & private sources.

Minister-in-charge, Hon. Nancy Heppner
Tel: 306-787-0642
Fax: 306-787-1197
minister.cs@gov.sk.ca

Chair, Trevor Powell
Tel: 306-585-0390
Fax: 306-787-1975

Provincial Archivist, Linda B. McIntyre
Tel: 306-798-4018
Fax: 306-787-1975
lmcintyre@archives.gov.sk.ca

Chief Archivist/Production Coordinator, Reference Services Unit, Saskatoon, Nadine Charabin
Tel: 306-933-8321
ncharabin@archives.gov.sk.ca

Manager, Records Processing, Jeremy Mohr
Tel: 306-787-5803
Fax: 306-798-0333
jmohr@archives.gov.sk.ca

Manager, Appraisal, Acquisition & Collections Management, Trina Gillis
Tel: 306-787-0452
tgillis@archives.gov.sk.ca

Manager, Information Management, Anna Stoszek
Tel: 306-787-0700
astoszek@archives.gov.sk.ca

Director, Archival Programs & Information Management, Lenora Toth
Tel: 306-787-4741
ltoth@archives.gov.sk.ca

Saskatchewan Assessment Management Agency (SAMA)

#200, 2201 - 11th Ave., Regina, SK S4P 0J8
Tel: 306-924-8000
Fax: 306-924-8070
Toll-Free: 800-667-7262
info.request@sama.sk.ca
www.sama.sk.ca

SAMA is an independent agency with responsibility to develop & maintain the province's assessment policies, standards & procedures, audit assessments, & review & confirm municipal assessment rolls & provide property valuation services to local governments (municipalities & school boards).

Chair, Neal Hardy

Chief Executive Officer, Irwin Blank
Tel: 306-924-8046
Fax: 306-924-8060

Managing Director, Finance, George Dobni
Tel: 306-924-8025
Fax: 306-924-8060

Managing Director, Assessment Services, Brad Korbo
Tel: 306-924-8017
Fax: 306-924-8070

Managing Director, Administration, Betty Rogers
Tel: 306-924-8032
Fax: 306-924-8060

Managing Director, Quality Assurance, Gordon Senz
Tel: 306-924-8008
Fax: 306-924-8067

Managing Director, Technical Standards & Policy, Steve Suchan
Tel: 306-924-8024
Fax: 306-924-8060

Provincial Auditor Saskatchewan

#1500, 1920 Broad St., Regina, SK S4P 3V2
Tel: 306-787-6398
Fax: 306-787-6383
info@auditor.sk.ca
www.auditor.sk.ca

The Provincial Auditor is the auditor of public money managed by the Government of Saskatchewan. The Provincial Auditor Act gives the Provincial Auditor the responsibility, authority, and independence to audit and publicly report on all government organizations.

Provincial Auditor, Bonnie Lysyk
Tel: 306-787-6366
Fax: 306-787-6383
lysyk@auditor.sk.ca

Deputy Provincial Auditor, Education, Ed Montgomery
Tel: 306-787-6389
Fax: 306-787-6383
montgomery@auditor.sk.ca

Deputy Provincial Auditor, Finance & Crown Corporations, Judy Ferguson
Tel: 306-787-6372
Fax: 306-787-6383
ferguson@auditor.sk.ca

Deputy Provincial Auditor, Gaming & Insurance, Mike Heffernan
Tel: 306-787-6364
Fax: 306-787-6383
heffernan@auditor.sk.ca

Deputy Provincial Auditor, Health, Mobashar Ahmad
Tel: 306-787-6387
Fax: 306-787-6383
ahmad@auditor.sk.ca

Administrative Services Manager, Deann Dickin
Tel: 306-787-6377
Fax: 306-787-6383
dickin@auditor.sk.ca

Accommodation Services Division
The Municipal Relations Division strengthens Saskatchewan communities by providing the legal framework, organizational support, financial assistance & other services for the operation of municipalities. Working in partnership with municipal organizations & other communities, the Division encourages cooperation, understanding & self-reliance.
Assistant Deputy Minister, Asset Management, Allen Mullen
Tel: 306-787-8018
Fax: 306-798-0370
allen.mullen@gov.sk.cas
Assistant Deputy Minister, Facility Management, Richard Murray
Tel: 306-787-9586
Fax: 306-798-0371
richard.murray@gov.sk.ca
Director, Sustainability & Energy Management, Howard Arndt
Tel: 306-787-2033
Fax: 306-787-1980
Howard.Arndt@gov.sk.ca
Director, Pricing & Data Management Services, Garth Belanger
Tel: 306-787-9680
Fax: 306-787-1980
garth.belanger@gov.sk.ca
Director, Real Estate Services, Alf Bernstein
Tel: 306-787-6959
Fax: 306-787-1980
alf.bernstein@gov.sk.ca
Director, Infrastructure Support Services, Dave Bryanton
Tel: 306-787-0959
Fax: 306-787-2019
Dave.Bryanton@gov.sk.ca
Director, Project Delivery North, Ivan Francis
Tel: 306-933-5676
Fax: 306-933-6999
ivan.francis@gov.sk.ca
Director, Capital & Infrastructure Management, Todd Godfrey
Tel: 306-787-2253
Fax: 306-787-1980
todd.godfrey@gov.sk.ca
Director, Project Delivery South, Paul Nepper
Tel: 306-787-0990
Fax: 306-798-0370
paul.nepper@gov.sk.ca
Director, Strategic Portfolio Management, Loreen Porter
Tel: 306-787-4241
Fax: 306-787-1980
loreen.porter@gov.sk.ca

Saskatchewan Central Services (CS)

1920 Rose St., Regina, SK S4P 0A9
Tel: 306-787-6911
Fax: 306-787-1061
GSReception@gs.gov.sk.ca
www.cs.gov.sk.ca

In May 2012, Central Services replaced the Ministry of Government Services in Saskatchewan. The new organization manages government operations. In a re-organization of the Cabinet, Nancy Heppner was named the new Minister of Central Services, as well as the Minister responsible for the Public Service Commission, the Information Technology Office, & the Lean Initiative.
Acts Administered:
Canadian Information Processing Society of Saskatchewan Act, 2005
Information Technology Office Regulations, December 2004

Minister, Central Services; Minister Responsible, Public Service Commission; Minister Responsible, Lean Initiative, Hon. Nancy Heppner
Tel: 306-787-0942
Fax: 306-787-8677
minister.cs@gov.sk.ca
Office of the Minister CentralServices, Legislative Building
#306, 2405 Legislative Dr.
Regina, SK S4S 0B3

Deputy Minister, Central Services, Ron Dedman
Tel: 306-787-6520
Fax: 306-787-6547
ron.dedman@gov.sk.ca

Senior Advisor to the Deputy Minister of Central Services, Don Wincherauk

Associated Agencies, Boards & Commissions:
• Public Service Commission (PSC)
2350 Albert St.
Regina, SK S4P 4A6
Tel: 306-787-7853
Toll-free: 866-319-5999
inquiry@psc.gov.sk.ca
www.psc.gov.sk.ca
The human resource agency for the Government of Saskatchewan is the Public Service Commission.
The following are some services delivered by the Commission: classifying positions; recruiting & selecting employees; providing a mentorship program & professional development opportunities; offering anti-harassment resources & information about ethics & conduct; participating in labour relations; providing payroll tasks; offering an employee & family assistance program; & providing a long service recognition program.
The Commission is guided by The Public Service Act, 1998 & The Public Service Regulations 1999, as it serves more than 12,000 government employees.

Commercial Services Division
Tel: 306-787-8942
Fax: 306-787-1061
www.gs.gov.sk.ca/commercial/
Executive Director, Greg Lusk
Tel: 306-787-7842
Fax: 306-787-1061
Greg.Lusk@gov.sk.ca
Acting Director, Telecommunications, Cindy Cullen
Tel: 306-787-6899
Fax: 306-798-0371
cindy.cullen@gov.sk.ca
Director, Mail Services, Carol Halvorson
Tel: 306-787-6866
Fax: 306-787-1873
carol.halvorson@gov.sk.ca
Director, Executive Air Services, Chris Olsen
Tel: 306-787-7717
Fax: 306-787-1424
chris.oleson@gov.sk.ca
Director, CVA Business Process & Systems Implementation, Paul Radigan
Tel: 306-787-9046
Fax: 306-787-1061
paul.radigan@gov.sk.ca
Director, Air Ambulance Services, Lee Smith
Tel: 306-933-6501
Fax: 306-933-5490
Lee.Smith@gov.sk.ca; lee.smith2@gov.sk.ca

Corporate Support Services Division
Tel: 306-787-6945
Fax: 306-798-0700
Assistant Deputy Minister, Debbie Koshman
Tel: 306-787-1071
Fax: 306-798-0700
debbie.koshman@gov.sk.ca
Director, Purchasing Branch, Rob Isbister
Tel: 306-787-6005
Fax: 306-787-3023
rob.isbister@gov.sk.ca
Director, Internal Audit/Planning & Policy, Patrick Lumb
Tel: 306-787-1139
Fax: 306-798-0700
patrick.lumb@gov.sk.ca
Director, Risk Management Services, Glynn Mitchell
Tel: 306-787-9280
Fax: 306-798-0700
glynn.mitchell@gov.sk.ca
Director, Financial Services Branch, Shelley Reddekopp
Tel: 306-787-4468
Fax: 306-798-0700
shelley.reddekopp@gov.sk.ca

Communications
1920 Rose St., Regina, SK S4P 0A9
Tel: 306-787-4015
Fax: 306-798-0371
longservice@gov.sk.ca
Executive Director, Communications, Robin Campese
Tel: 306-787-5959
Fax: 306-798-0371
robin.campese@gov.sk.ca
Manager, Communications, Art Newton
Tel: 306-787-2215
Fax: 306-798-2602
art.newton@gov.sk.ca
Coordinator, Marketing, Valerie Rideout
Tel: 306-787-5586
Fax: 306-798-0371
valerie.rideout@gov.sk.ca

Corporate Services
1920 Rose St., Regina, SK S4P 0A9
Tel: 306-787-6945
Fax: 306-798-0700
Assistant Deputy Minister, Shelley Reddekopp
Tel: 306-787-4468
Fax: 306-798-0700
shelley.reddekopp@gov.sk.ca
Director, Information Management, Todd Godfrey
Tel: 306-787-2253
Fax: 306-798-0700
todd.godfrey@gov.sk.ca
Director, Purchasing, Rob Isbister
Tel: 306-787-6005
Fax: 306-787-3023
rob.isbister@gov.sk.ca
Director, Administrative Services, Dana Kachur
Tel: 306-787-9164
Fax: 306-798-0700
dana.kachur@gov.sk.ca
Director, Internal Audit, Patrick Lumb
Tel: 306-787-1139
Fax: 306-798-0700
patrick.lumb@gov.sk.ca
Director, Risk Management Services, Glynn Mitchell
Tel: 306-787-9280
Fax: 306-798-0700
glynn.mitchell@gov.sk.ca
Director, Financial Services, Rebecca Sengmany
Tel: 306-798-2602
Fax: 306-798-0700
Rebecca.Sengmany@gov.sk.ca

Corporate Projects Group
1855 Victoria Ave., 7th Fl., Regina, SK S4P 3T2
Executive Director, Corporate Projects, Lisa Boire
Tel: 306-787-2264
lisa.boire@gov.sk.ca
Manager, Lean Initiative, Mark Anderson
Tel: 306-787-7506
mark.anderson@gov.sk.ca

Government Services
1920 Rose St., Regina, SK S4P 0A9
Tel: 306-787-6911
Fax: 306-787-1061
GSReception@gs.gov.sk.ca
Accommodation & commercial services are handled by this unit.
Acts Administered:
Architects Act, 1996
Interior Designers Act
Public Works & Services Act
Purchasing Act, 2004
Assistant Deputy Minister, Project Management & Delivery, Allen Mullen
Tel: 306-787-8018
Fax: 306-798-0370
allen.mullen@gov.sk.ca
#1420, 1855 Victoria Ave.
Regina, SK S4P 3T2 Canada
Assistant Deputy Minister, Property Management, Richard Murray
Tel: 306-787-9586
Fax: 306-798-0371
richard.murray@gov.sk.ca
#1420, 1855 Victoria Ave.
Regina, SK S4P 3T2 Canada
Executive Director, Commercial Services, Greg Lusk
Tel: 306-787-7842
Fax: 306-787-1061
Greg.Lusk@gov.sk.ca
#1420, 1855 Victoria Ave.
Regina, SK S4P 3T2 Canada
Director, Pricing & Data Management Services, Garth Belanger
Tel: 306-787-9680
Fax: 306-787-1980
garth.belanger@gov.sk.ca
#1420, 1855 Victoria Ave.
Regina, SK S4P 3T2 Canada
Director, Realty, Alf Bernstein
Tel: 306-787-6959
Fax: 306-787-1980
alf.bernstein@gov.sk.ca
#1420, 1855 Victoria Ave.
Regina, SK S4P 3T2 Canada
Director, Infrastructure Support, Dave Bryanton
Tel: 306-787-0959
Fax: 306-787-2019
Dave.Bryanton@gov.sk.ca
#1420, 1855 Victoria Ave.
Regina, SK S4P 3T2 Canada
Director, Sustainability, Rob Clarke
Tel: 306-787-6332
Fax: 306-787-1980
Rob.Clarke@gov.sk.ca
#1420, 1855 Victoria Ave.
Regina, SK S4P 3T2 Canada
Director, Mail Services, Carol Halvorson
Tel: 306-787-6866
Fax: 306-787-1873
carol.halvorson@gov.sk.ca
#1420, 1855 Victoria Ave.
Regina, SK S4P 3T2 Canada
Director, Protective Services, Glynn Mitchell
Tel: 306-787-9280
Fax: 306-787-9495
glynn.mitchell@gov.sk.ca

#1420, 1855 Victoria Ave.
Regina, SK S4P 3T2 Canada
Director, Executive Air Services, Chris Oleson
Tel: 306-787-7717
Fax: 306-787-1424
chris.oleson@gov.sk.ca
#1420, 1855 Victoria Ave.
Regina, SK S4P 3T2 Canada
Director, Strategic Portfolio Management, Loreen Porter
Tel: 306-787-4241
Fax: 306-787-1980
loreen.porter@gov.sk.ca
#1420, 1855 Victoria Ave.
Regina, SK S4P 3T2 Canada
Director, Central Vehicle Agency Business Process & Systems Implementation, Paul Radigan
Tel: 306-787-9046
Fax: 306-787-1061
paul.radigan@gov.sk.ca
#1420, 1855 Victoria Ave.
Regina, SK S4P 3T2 Canada
Director, Air Ambulance Services, Lee Smith
Tel: 306-933-6501
Fax: 306-933-5480
Lee.Smith@gov.sk.ca
#1420, 1855 Victoria Ave.
Regina, SK S4P 3T2 Canada

Information Technology Office
2101 Scarth St., 8th Fl., Regina, SK S4P 2H9
Tel: 306-787-5000
inquiries@ito.gov.sk.ca; itoservicedesk@gov.sk.ca
www.ito.gov.sk.ca

The work of the Information Technology Office is guided by The Information Technology Office Regulations, December 2004 & The Canadian Information Processing Society of Saskatchewan Act, 2005.
The following are some of the programs & services of the Information Technology Office: the procurement of information technology goods & services; corporate services, such as planning & communications; customer support; leadership on issues related to enterprise architecture; application management services; & operations such as the help desk.

Associate Deputy Minister Responsible for Information Technology, Robert Guillaume
Tel: 306-787-2210
Fax: 306-787-5718
Robert.Guillaume@gov.sk.ca
Assistant Deputy Minister, Corporate Services, Tim Kealey
Tel: 306-787-9302
Fax: 306-787-5718
Tim.Kealey@gov.sk.ca
Chief Technology Officer, Doug Quail
Tel: 306-787-2540
Fax: 306-787-5718
Executive Director, Supply Chain Management, Ken Esplen
Tel: 306-787-8892
Fax: 306-798-0313
Ken.Esplen@gov.sk.ca
Executive Director, Support Services, Kelly Fuessel
Tel: 306-787-7894
Fax: 306-798-0355
kelly.fuessel@gov.sk.ca
Executive Director, Application Management Services, Joe Przepiorka
Tel: 306-798-3286
Fax: 306-787-5454
Joe.Przepiorka@gov.sk.ca
Executive Director, Customer Services, Bonnie Schmidt
Tel: 306-798-2307
Fax: 306-787-5718
bonnie.schmidt@gov.sk.ca

Saskatchewan Corrections & Policing (CPSP)

1874 Scarth St., Regina, SK S4P 4B3
Tel: 306-787-7872
communicationsCPSP@gov.sk.ca
www.cpsp.gov.sk.ca

The Ministry of Corrections, Public Safety & Policing promotes safe communities in Saskatchewan. Adult correction & young offender programs & services are delivered that serve individuals in conflict with the law. Public safety is also addressed through the following programs & services: protection & emergency planning & communication; monitoring of building standards; fire prevention & disaster assistance programs; & licensing & inspections services.

Acts Administered:
Amusement Ride Safety Act
Boiler & Pressure Vessel Act, 1999
Correctional Services Act
Electrical Licensing Act
Emergency 911 System Act
Emergency Planning Act
Fire Prevention Act, 1992
Gas Licensing Act
Passenger & Freight Elevator Act
Uniform Building & Accessibility Standards Act
Youth Justice Administration Act

Minister Responsible, Corrections & Policing, Hon. Christine Tell
Tel: 306-787-4377
Fax: 306-787-5331
minister.cp@gov.sk.ca
Social Media: www.facebook.com/christinetellsp
Office of the Minister Responsible, Corrections & Policing, Legislative Building
#345, 2045 LegislativeDr.
Regina, SK S4S 0B3

Deputy Minister, Corrections & Policing, Dale McFee
Tel: 306-787-8065
Fax: 306-798-0270
dale.mcfee@gov.sk.ca

Executive Director, Strategic Policy, Karen Lautsch
Tel: 306-787-7344
Fax: 306-798-0270
karen.lautsch@gov.sk.ca

Director, Information Management & Public Safety Telecommunications, Cathy Drader
Tel: 306-787-9512
Fax: 306-787-6979
Cathy.Drader@gov.sk.ca

Director, Communications & Media Relations, Judy Orthner
Tel: 306-787-5883
Fax: 306-787-3874
judy.orthner@gov.sk.ca

Director, Communications (Justice & Attorney General), Linsay Rabyj
Tel: 306-787-0775
Fax: 306-787-3874
Linsay.Rabyj@gov.sk.ca

Associated Agencies, Boards & Commissions:
• Saskatchewan Police College (SkPC)
217 College West Bldg., University of Regina
3737 Wascana Pkwy.
Regina, SK S4S 0A2
Tel: 306-787-8870
Fax: 306-787-8876
www.uregina.ca/police
• Saskatchewan Police Commission
1850 - 1881 Scarth St.
Regina, SK S4P 4K9
Tel: 306-787-6518
Fax: 306-787-0136
www.cpsp.gov.sk.ca/Saskatchewan-Police-Commission
The Commission promotes crime prevention, improved police relationships with communities, & effective policing throughout Saskatchewan by working closely with police services & Boards of Police Commissioners.

Adult Corrections
Tel: 306-787-8958
Fax: 306-787-0676
www.cpsp.gov.sk.ca/Corrections

Executive Director, Tammy Kirkland
Tel: 306-787-3573
Fax: 306-787-0676
Tammy.Kirkland@gov.sk.ca
Director, Health Services, Syd Bolt
Tel: 306-787-2676
Fax: 306-787-0676
Syd.Bolt@gov.sk.ca
Director, Policy & Planning, Fred Burch
Tel: 306-787-3242
Fax: 306-787-0676
Fred.Burch@gov.sk.ca
Director, Strategic Business & Information Technology, Rick Davis
Tel: 306-787-3640
Fax: 306-787-0676
Rick.Davis@gov.sk.ca
Director, Community Corrections, Carol Fiedelleck
Tel: 306-787-3572
Fax: 306-787-0676
Carol.Fiedelleck@gov.sk.ca
Director, Security & Intelligence, Julien Hulet
Tel: 306-798-8159
Fax: 306-787-0676
Julien.Hulet@gov.sk.ca
Director, Finance, John Igbokwe
Tel: 306-787-3599
Fax: 306-787-0676
John.Igbokwe@gov.sk.ca
Director, Program Development & Therapeutic Services, Brian Rector
Tel: 306-787-3892
Fax: 306-787-0676
Brian.Rector@gov.sk.ca
Director, Institutional Operations, Heather Scriver
Tel: 306-787-3571
Fax: 306-787-0676
heather.scriver@gov.sk.ca
Director, Community Facilities, Dana Wilkins
Tel: 306-798-0988
Fax: 306-787-0676
Dana.Wilkins@gov.sk.ca

Custody Programs
Tel: 306-787-1352
Fax: 306-798-0012

Policing & Community Safety Division
1850 - 1881 Scarth St., Regina, SK S4P 4K9
Tel: 306-787-6518
Fax: 306-787-0136
pisg@justice.gov.sk.ca
www.cpsp.gov.sk.ca/Police-Services-Division

Executive Director, Murray Sawatsky
Tel: 306-787-6534
Murray.Sawatsky@gov.sk.ca
Director, Aboriginal Policing Service, Bernadette Aubichon
Tel: 306-953-3466
Fax: 306-953-2537
bernadette.aubichon@gov.sk.ca
Director, Program & Finance, Terry Hawkes
Tel: 306-787-1150
Fax: 306-787-0136
Terry.Hawkes@gov.sk.ca
Director, Strategic Policy Development, Richard Peach
Tel: 306-787-9292
Fax: 306-787-0136
Richard.Peach@gov.sk.ca
Director, Financial Services, Trevor Wowk
Tel: 306-787-8608
Fax: 306-787-0136
Director, David Horn
Tel: 306-787-0400
Fax: 306-798-7700
David.Horn@gov.sk.ca
Director, Saskatchewan Witness Protection Program, Randy Koroluk
Tel: 306-798-0262
Fax: 306-798-7700
Randy.Koroluk@gov.sk.ca
Director, Seizure of Criminal Property, Don Perron
Tel: 306-798-8155
Fax: 306-798-7700
Don.Perron@gov.sk.ca
Senior Investigator, Safer Communities & Neighbourhoods Investigation Unit, Blair Ritchie
Tel: 306-933-8373
Fax: 306-933-8392
Blair.Ritchie@gov.sk.ca

Young Offender Programs
Tel: 306-787-5699
Fax: 306-787-0676
www.cpsp.gov.sk.ca/yo

Executive Director, Bob Kary
Tel: 306-787-4701
Fax: 306-787-0676
bob.kary@gov.sk.ca
Director, Custody Programs, Constance Hourie
Tel: 306-787-9237
Fax: 306-787-0676
Constance.Hourie@gov.sk.ca
Director, Community Youth Services, Kim Gurnsey
Tel: 306-787-1394
Fax: 306-787-0676
Kim.Gurnsey@gov.sk.ca
Director, Program Development & Therapeutic Services, Brian Rector
Tel: 306-787-3892
Fax: 306-787-0676
brian.rector@gov.sk.ca
Director, Financial Services, Gaylene Weir
Tel: 306-787-0721
Fax: 306-787-0676
Gaylene.Weir@gov.sk.ca

Regional Offices
Central Region
#903, 122 3rd Ave. North, Saskatoon, SK S7K 2H6
Tel: 306-933-6052
Fax: 306-964-1103

Regional Director, Harry Smith
Tel: 306-933-7438

Fax: 306-964-1103
Harry.Smith@gov.sk.ca
Director, Clinical Services, Dean Carey
Tel: 306-933-7435
Fax: 306-964-1103
Dean.Carey@gov.sk.ca
Northeast Region
PO Box 3003, Prince Albert, SK S6V 6G1
Tel: 306-953-2643
Fax: 306-953-2649
Toll-Free: 866-397-7826
Regional Director, Fraser Denton
Tel: 306-953-2583
Fax: 306-953-2649
Regional Director, Jarrett Parker
Tel: 306-953-3192
Fax: 306-953-2649
Jarrett.Parker@gov.sk.ca
South Region
2045 Broad St., 5th Fl., Regina, SK S4P 3T7
Tel: 306-787-9137
Fax: 306-787-5559
Regional Director, Rick Bereti
Tel: 306-787-3695
Fax: 306-787-5559
Rick.Bereti@gov.sk.ca
Director, Clinical Services, Jamie Smith
Tel: 306-787-8643
Fax: 306-787-7546
Jamie.Smith@gov.sk.ca

Crown Investments Corporation of Saskatchewan (CIC)

#400, 2400 College Ave., Regina, SK S4P 1C8
Tel: 306-787-6851
Fax: 306-787-8125
www.cicorp.sk.ca

The holding company for the commercial Crown corporations of Saskatchewan is the Crown Investments Corporation.
The key functions of the Corporation are as follows: assisting the boards of Crown corporations to strengthen governance; overseeing the direction of Crown corporations to improve performance & acountability; managing CIC Asset Management Inc. & the Gradworks program; & overseeing funds established with the administrative coordination or financial assistance of the government.

Minister, Crown Investments; Minister Responsible, Saskatchewan Government Insurance; Minister Responsible, Saskatchewan Liquor & Gaming Authority, Hon. Donna Harpauer
Tel: 306-787-7339
Fax: 306-798-3140
minister.cc@gov.sk.ca
Social Media: www.facebook.com/pages/Donna-Harpauer/60494388240
Officeof the Minister of Crown Investments, Legislative Building
#322, 2405 Legislative Dr.
Regina, SK S4S 0B3

President & Chief Executive Officer, Dick Carter
Tel: 306-787-4553
Fax: 306-787-8125
dcarter@cicorp.sk.ca

Vice-President, Asset Management, Rae Haverstock
Tel: 306-787-6773
Fax: 306-787-6926
rhaverstock@cicorp.sk.ca

Vice-President, Special Projects, Van Isman
Tel: 306-787-9356
Fax: 306-787-8125
visman@cicorp.sk.ca

Vice-President, Special Projects, Karen Layng
Tel: 306-777-5719
karen.layng@sasktel.com

Executive Director, Regulatory Affairs, Denise Batters
Tel: 306-787-3118
Fax: 306-787-8125
dbatters@cicorp.sk.ca

Executive Director, Capital Pension & Benefits Administration, Ken Klein
Tel: 306-787-5948
Fax: 306-787-5798
ken.klein@capitalpension.com

Crown Sector Initiatives Division
#400, 2400 College Ave., Regina, SK S4P 1C8
Tel: 306-787-6471
Fax: 306-787-8125
Director, Major Projects, Guy Roy
Tel: 306-787-8573
Fax: 306-787-8125
groy@cicorp.sk.ca
Director, Crown Sector Initiatives, Peter Wyant
Tel: 306-787-5754
Fax: 306-787-8125
pwyant@cicorp.sk.ca

Finance & Administration Division
#400, 2400 College Ave., Regina, SK S4P 1C8
Tel: 306-787-5937
Fax: 306-787-8030
Chief Financial Officer & Senior Vice-President, Blair Swystun
Tel: 306-787-9085
Fax: 306-787-8030
bswystun@cicorp.sk.ca
Director, Performance Management & Financial Analysis, Cindy Ogilvie
Tel: 306-787-6246
Fax: 306-787-8030
cogilvie@cicorp.sk.ca
Corporate Controller, Accounting & Projects, John Amundson
Tel: 306-787-2132
Fax: 306-787-8030
jamundson@cicorp.sk.ca
Manager, Internal Audit, Bina Bilkhu
Tel: 306-787-7470
Fax: 306-787-4813
bbilkhu@cicorp.sk.ca
Manager, Information Technology, Krzysztof Stoszek
Tel: 306-787-7254
Fax: 306-787-8030
kstoszek@cicorp.sk.ca
Analyst, Corporate Planning, Erin Connelly
Tel: 306-787-3415
Fax: 306-787-0294
econnelly@cicorp.sk.ca

Human Resource Policy, Governance, & Legal Division
#400, 2400 College Ave., Regina, SK S4P 1C8
Tel: 306-787-5915
Fax: 306-787-0294
Executive Director, Human Resource Policy, Governance, & Legal Division, James Hoffman
Tel: 306-787-0474
Fax: 306-787-0294
jhoffman@cicorp.sk.ca
Executive Director, Crown Sector Human Resources, Nancy Croll
Tel: 306-787-1257
Fax: 306-787-8125
ncroll@cicorp.sk.ca
Senior Vice President; General Counsel, Doug Kosloski
Tel: 306-787-5892
Fax: 306-787-0294
dkosloski@cicorp.sk.ca
Director, Corporate Secretariat, Wendy Dean
Tel: 306-787-5985
Fax: 306-787-0294
wdean@cicorp.sk.ca
Manager, Compensation & Labour Relations, Brian Gyoerick
Tel: 306-787-0381
Fax: 306-787-8125
bgyoerick@cicorp.sk.ca
Program Coordinator, Gradworks, Dana Callele
Tel: 306-787-7351
Fax: 306-787-0294
dcallele@cicorp.sk.ca

Saskatchewan Economy (ECON)

#300, 2103 - 11th Ave., Regina, SK S4P 3Z8
www.economy.gov.sk.ca

Saskatchewan's Ministry of the Economy was created in May 2012 to reflect the provincial government's economic growth agenda. The new ministry incoporates economic functions of the government such as energy & resources, Enterprise Saskatchewan, & Tourism Saskatchewan.

Minister, Economy; Minister Responsible, Global Transporation Hub; Minister Responsible, SK Power Corporation, Enterprise SK, Innovation SK, Uranium Development Partnership, & SK ResearchCouncil, Hon. Bill Boyd
Tel: 306-787-0804
Fax: 306-798-2009
Bill.Boyd@gov.sk.ca
Minister's Office, Ministry of Economy, Legislative Building
#340, 2405 Legislative Dr.
Regina, SK S4S 0B3

Deputy Minister, Kent Campbell
Tel: 306-787-9580
Fax: 306-787-2159
kent.campbell@gov.sk.ca

Associated Agencies, Boards & Commissions:
• Surface Rights Board of Arbitration
113 - 2nd Ave. East
PO Box 1597
Kindersley, SK S0L 1S0
Tel: 306-463-5447
Fax: 306-463-5449
surfacerightsboard@gov.sk.ca
www.er.gov.sk.ca/surfacerights
Governed by The Surface Rights Acquisition and Compensation Act, the Surface Rights Board of Arbitration is a last resort when an occupant or landowner & an oil, gas or potash operator are unable to reach an agreement.

Energy & Resources (ER)
#300, 2103 - 11th Ave., Regina, SK S4P 3Z8
Tel: 306-787-2528
www.er.gov.sk.ca

To build an innovative, diversified, & sustainable economy for Saskatchewan, the Energy & Resources unit develops, implements, & promotes policies & programs related to the province's energy, mineral, & forestry sectors.
The following mineral resource databases are available: Saskatchewan Mineral Assessment Database; Saskatchewan Mineral Deposit Index; & Saskatchewan Kimberlite Indicator Minerals.

Minister Responsible, Energy & Resources; Minister Responsible, Tourism Saskatchewan; Minister Responsible, Trade; Minister Responsible, SaskEnergy Incorporated, Hon. Tim McMillan
Tel: 306-787-9124
Fax: 306-787-0395
minister.er@gov.sk.ca
Social Media: www.facebook.com/timmcmillanmla
Office of the Minister Responsible, Energy & Resources / Tourism Saskatchewan, Legislative Building
#346, 2405 Legislative Dr.
Regina, SK S4S 0B3
Assistant Deputy Minister, Petroleum & Natural Gas, Ed Dancsok
Tel: 306-787-2591
Fax: 306-787-2478
Ed.Dancsok@gov.sk.ca
Assistant Deputy Minister, Revenue & Corporate Services, Twyla MacDougall
Tel: 306-787-6717
Fax: 306-787-3872
twyla.macdougall@gov.sk.ca
Assistant Deputy Minister, Minerals, Lands, & Resource Policy, Hal Sanders
Tel: 306-787-3524
Fax: 306-787-2198
Hal.Sanders@gov.sk.ca
Executive Director, Lands & Mineral Tenure, Doug MacKnight
Tel: 306-787-2082
Fax: 306-798-0047
Doug.Macknight@gov.sk.ca
Executive Director, Energy Policy, Floyd Wist
Tel: 306-787-2477
Fax: 306-787-2198
Floyd.Wist@gov.sk.ca
Director, Audit & Collections, Beverly Deglau
Tel: 306-787-5347
Fax: 306-798-2158
Beverly.Deglau@gov.sk.ca
Director, Revenue & Financial Services, Glen Downton
Tel: 306-787-2830
Fax: 306-787-0083
Glen.Downton@gov.sk.ca
Director, Public Affairs, Bob Ellis
Tel: 306-787-8983
Fax: 306-787-2198
robert.ellis@gov.sk.ca
Director, Petroleum Royalties, Mike Ferguson
Tel: 306-787-2605
Fax: 306-787-2478
Mike.Ferguson@gov.sk.ca
Director, Process Renewal & Infrastructure Management Enhancement, Danette Flegel
Tel: 306-798-3068
Fax: 306-787-3872
Danette.Flegel@gov.sk.ca
Director, Petroleum Development, Todd Han
Tel: 306-787-2221
Fax: 306-787-2478
Todd.Han@gov.sk.ca
Director, Mineral Policy, Cory Hughes
Tel: 306-787-3628

Fax: 306-787-2198
Cory.Hughes@gov.sk.ca
Director, Petroleum Data Management & Compliance, Bruce Lerner
Tel: 306-798-9507
Fax: 306-787-3872
Bruce.Lerner@gov.sk.ca
Director, Petroleum Tenure, Paul Mahnic
Tel: 306-787-5385
Fax: 306-787-0620
Paul.Mahnic@gov.sk.ca
Director, Corporate Planning, Renewal, & External Relations, Cam Pelzer
Tel: 306-787-2378
Fax: 306-787-3872
Cam.Pelzer@gov.sk.ca
Director, Engineering Services, Bert West
Tel: 306-787-2318
Fax: 306-787-2478
Bert.West@gov.sk.ca
Chief Geologist, Gary Delaney
Tel: 306-787-1160
Fax: 306-787-1284
Gary.Delaney@gov.sk.ca

Enterprise Saskatchewan
#200, 3085 Albert St., Regina, SK S4S 0B1
Tel: 306-787-4484
Fax: 306-798-0629
invest@gov.sk.ca
www.enterprisesaskatchewan.ca
Enterprise Saskatchewan promotes investment in the province. The following are some of the programs & services offered: Invest in Saskatchewan Program; Small Business Loans Association Program; Ethanol Fuel Grant Program; Business Infosource; Inventory of Major Projects in Saskatchewan; Saskatchewan Manufacturers Guide; Saskbiz.ca; & the Aborignal Business Directory.
Minister, Economy; Minister Responsible, Global Transporation Hub; Minister Responsible, SK Power Corporation, Enterprise SK, Innovation SK, Uranium Development Partnership, & SK ResearchCouncil, Hon. Bill Boyd
Tel: 306-787-0804
Fax: 306-798-2009
Bill.Boyd@gov.sk.ca
Office of the Minister of Economy, Legislative Building
#340, 2405 Legislative Dr.
Regina, SK S4S 0B3
Chief Financial Officer, Investment & Corporate Services, Denise Haas
Tel: 306-787-2756
Fax: 306-798-0629
denise.haas@enterprisesask.ca
Vice-President, Sector Development, Tony Baumgartner
Tel: 306-787-3435
Fax: 306-787-3989
Tony.Baumgartner@enterprisesask.ca
Vice-President, Entrepreneurial Development Services, Ernest Heapy
Tel: 306-787-2561
Fax: 306-787-7559
Ernest.Heapy@enterprisesask.ca
Vice-President, Competitiveness & Strategy, Angela Schmidt
Tel: 306-933-8223
Fax: 306-933-8244
Angela.Schmidt@enterprisesask.ca
Director, Business Services Improvement, Joseph Carson
Tel: 306-787-8865
Fax: 306-787-3989
Joe.Carson@enterprisesask.ca
Director, Economic Analysis & Strategy, Bryan Dilling
Tel: 306-933-7599
Fax: 306-933-8244
Bryan.Dilling@enterprisesask.ca
Director, Investment Attraction, Alex Fallon
Tel: 306-933-7210
Fax: 306-933-8244
Alex.Fallon@enterprisesask.ca
Director, Resources, Kim Lonsdale
Tel: 306-933-7164
Fax: 306-933-8244
Kim.Lonsdale@enterprisesask.ca
Director, Sector & Regional Policy, Michael Mitchell
Tel: 306-787-0572
Fax: 306-787-3989
Michael.Mitchell@enterprisesask.ca
Director, Corporate Services & Financial Programs, Andrea Terry Munro
Tel: 306-787-8024
Fax: 306-798-0796
andrea.terrymunro@enterprisesask.ca
Director, Advanced Technology & Services, Bill Spring
Tel: 306-787-2225
Fax: 306-787-3989
Bill.Spring@enterprisesask.ca

Tourism Saskatchewan
#189, 1621 Albert St., Regina, SK S4P 2S5
Toll-Free: 877-237-2273
Tourism Saskatchewan promotes Saskatchewan as a vacation destination. Services include tourism development, marketing, & visitor services.
Visitor Reception Centres are located at the following places: Langenburg, near the Manitoba border (306-743-6256); Fleming, near the Manitoba border (306-435-4576); Maple Creek, near the Alberta border (306-662-5472); Lloydminster, near the Alberta border (306-825-8690); & North Portal, at the USA border crossing (306-927-6271).
Minister Responsible, Energy & Resources; Minister Responsible, Tourism Saskatchewan; Minister Responsible, Trade; Minister Responsible, SaskEnergy Incorporated, Hon. Tim McMillan
Tel: 306-787-9124
Fax: 306-787-0395
minister.er@gov.sk.ca
Social Media: www.facebook.com/timmcmillanmla
Office of the Minister Responsible, Energy & Resources / Tourism Saskatchewan, Legislative Building
#346, 2405 Legislative Dr.
Regina, SK S4S 0B3

Saskatchewan Education (ED)

2220 College Ave., Regina, SK S4P 4V9
linquiry@gov.sk.ca
www.education.gov.sk.ca
The Ministry provides programs & services in the following key areas: early learning & child care, the prekindergarten to grade 12 education system, & the Provincial Library. In November 2007, a new provincial government resulted in the reorganization of provincial government ministries. The work of Saskatchewan Learning was merged into a newly named ministry. Ken Krawetz was named the Minister of Education.
Acts Administered:
Child Care Act (jointly with Social Services)
Education Act
Government Organization Act
League of Educational Administrators, Directors & Superintendents Act
Libraries Co-operation Act
Public Libraries Act
Registered Music Teachers Act
Teachers' Dental Plan Act
Teachers' Federation Act
Teachers' Life Insurance (Government Contributory) Act
Teachers' Superannuation & Disability Benefits Act

Minister, Education, Hon. Russ Marchuk
Tel: 306-787-7360
Fax: 306-798-0263
minister.edu@gov.sk.ca
Social Media: twitter.com/marchuk_mla
Minister's Office, Ministry of Education, Legislative Building
#307, 2405 Legislative Dr.
Regina, SK S4S 0B3

Deputy Minister, Education, Cheryl Senecal
Tel: 306-787-2471
Fax: 306-787-1300
cheryl.senecal@gov.sk.ca

Assistant Deputy Minister, Donna Johnson
Tel: 306-787-6056
Fax: 306-787-1300
donna.johnson@gov.sk.ca

Assistant Deputy Minister, Greg Miller
Tel: 306-787-3222
Fax: 306-787-1300
greg.miller@gov.sk.ca

Executive Director, Ministry Renewal, Elaine Caswell
Tel: 306-787-6052
Fax: 306-787-2265
Elaine.Caswell@gov.sk.ca

Executive Director, Communications, Tasha Lupanko
Tel: 306-787-5609
Fax: 306-798-2045
tasha.lupanko@gov.sk.ca

Executive Director, Corporate Services, Lori Mann
Tel: 306-787-3520
Fax: 306-798-5042
lori.mann@gov.sk.ca

Associated Agencies, Boards & Commissions:

• **Teachers' Superannuation Commission**
#129, 3085 Albert St.
Regina, SK S4S 0B1
Tel: 306-787-6440
Fax: 306-787-1939
Toll-free: 877-364-8202
mail@stsc.gov.sk.ca
www.stsc.gov.sk.ca

Early Years
Tel: 306-787-2004
Fax: 306-787-0277
Executive Director, Lois Zelmer
Tel: 306-787-0765
Fax: 306-787-0277
Lois.Zelmer@gov.sk.ca
Director, Early Childhood Education, Kathy Abernethy
Tel: 306-787-6158
Fax: 306-787-0277
Kathy.Abernethy@gov.sk.ca
Director, Early Learning & Child Care, Brenda Dougherty
Tel: 306-787-3858
Fax: 306-787-0277
Brenda.Dougherty@gov.sk.ca
Director, Regional Child Care Services, Cindy Jeanes
Tel: 306-787-3750
Fax: 306-798-3146
Cindy.Jeanes@gov.sk.ca
Director, Early Childhood Development & Intregrated Services, Gail Russell
Tel: 306-787-8301
Fax: 306-787-0277
Gail.Russell@gov.sk.ca

Information Management & Support
#128, 1621 Albert St., Regina, SK S4P 2S5
Tel: 306-787-2494
Fax: 306-787-0035
Executive Director, Joylene Campbell
Joylene.Campbell@gov.sk.ca

Infrasturcture & Education Funding
Tel: 306-787-3341
Fax: 306-787-5059
Director, Infrastructure, Mike Back
Tel: 306-787-7856
Fax: 306-798-0787
Mike.Back@gov.sk.ca
Director, Education Funding, Clint Repski
Tel: 306-787-4658
Fax: 306-787-5059
Clint.Repski@gov.sk.ca

Provincial Library & Literacy Office
409A Park St., Regina, SK S4N 5B2
Tel: 306-787-2976
Fax: 306-787-2029
srp.adm@prov.lib.sk.ca
www.education.gov.sk.ca/Provincial-Library
Other Communication: Literacy Office: www.education.gov.sk.ca/literacy
Provincial Librarian, Brett Waytuck
Tel: 306-787-2972
Fax: 306-787-2029
Brett.Waytuck@gov.sk.ca
Director, Library Accountability & Administration, Barbara Bulat
Tel: 306-787-6032
Fax: 306-787-2029
barbara.bulat@gov.sk.ca
Director, Public Library Planning, Stephanie Hall
Tel: 306-787-3005
Fax: 306-787-2029
stephanie.hall@gov.sk.ca

Strategic Policy
Tel: 306-787-6769
Fax: 306-798-2572
Executive Director, Rosanne Glass
Tel: 306-787-3897
Fax: 306-798-2572
Rosanne.Glass@gov.sk.ca; rosanne.glass@saskatoonhealthregion.ca
Southern Region
1831 College Ave., 3rd Fl., Regina, SK S4P 4V5
Fax: 306-787-6139
Regional Director, Darlene Thompson
Tel: 306-787-6075
Fax: 306-787-6139
Darlene.Thompson@gov.sk.ca
Central Region
122 3rd Ave. North, 8th Fl., Saskatoon, SK S7K 2H6
Fax: 306-933-7469
Regional Director, Crandall Hrynkiw

Northern Region
Mistasinihk Place, #2200 1328 La Ronge Ave., PO Box 5000, La Ronge, SK S0J 1L0
Tel: 306-425-4380
Fax: 306-425-4383
Toll-Free: 800-667-4380
Regional Director, Daryl Arnott
Tel: 306-425-4382

Elections Saskatchewan

1702 Park St., Regina, SK S4N 6B2
Tel: 306-787-4000
Fax: 306-787-4052
Toll-Free: 877-958-8683
info@elections.sk.ca
www.elections.sk.ca
Other Communication: Toll-Free Fax: 1-866-678-4052

Acting Chief Electoral Officer, Dave Wilkie
Tel: 306-787-4027
Toll-free: 877-958-8683
dwilkie@elections.sk.ca

Chief Operating Officer, Saundra Arberry
Tel: 306-787-4061
Toll-free: 866-247-5404
sarberry@elections.sk.ca

Manager, Information Technology, Jeff Livingstone
Tel: 306-787-9327
Toll-free: 866-250-2263
jlivingstone@elections.sk.ca

Manager, Election Finances, Brent Nadon
Tel: 306-787-4017
Toll-free: 866-249-7186
bnadon@elections.sk.ca

Communications, Daniel Bodgon
Tel: 306-787-7355
Toll-free: 855-220-7355
dbogdon@elections.sk.ca

Student Achievement & Supports
Executive Director, Simone Gareau
Tel: 306-787-5632
Fax: 306-787-3164
Simone.Gareau@gov.sk.ca
Director, Learning Program (French), Lucie Anderson
Tel: 306-787-6089
Fax: 306-787-3164
Lucie.Anderson@gov.sk.ca
Director, Assessment & Accountability, Michelle Belisle
Tel: 306-787-6053
Fax: 306-787-9178
Other Communications: URL: www.education.gov.sk.ca/programs-services
Director, Learning Program (English), Gerry Craswell
Tel: 306-787-5974
Fax: 306-787-2223
Gerry.Craswell@gov.sk.ca
Director, Supports for Learning, Sharon Yuzdepski
Tel: 306-787-6025
Fax: 306-787-2223
Sharon.Yuzdepski@gov.sk.ca

Corporate & Financial Services
Tel: 306-787-8178
Fax: 306-787-2198
Assistant Depty Minister, Twyla MacDougall
Tel: 306-787-6717
Fax: 306-787-3872
twyla.macdougall@gov.sk.ca
Director, Revenue Operations & Audit Services, Dale Amundson
Tel: 306-787-5343
Fax: 306-798-2158
dale.amundson@gov.sk.ca
Director, Planning, Evaluation & External Relations, Cam Pelzer
Tel: 306-787-2378
Fax: 306-787-2198
Cam.Pelzer@gov.sk.ca
Director, Process Renewal & Infrastructure Management Enhancement (PRIME) Project, Jeff Ritter
Tel: 306-787-0999
Fax: 306-787-3872
Jeff.Ritter@gov.sk.ca
Director, Administrative & Financial Services, Doreen Yurkoski
Tel: 306-787-1612
Fax: 306-787-3872
doreen.yurkoski@gov.sk.ca
Assistant Director, Revenue Operations, Glen Downton
Tel: 306-787-2830
Fax: 306-787-0083
glen.downton@gov.sk.ca

Minerals, Lands & Policy
Tel: 306-787-8178
Fax: 306-787-2198
Assistant Deputy Minister, Hal Sanders
Tel: 306-787-3524
Fax: 306-787-2198
Hal.Sanders@gov.sk.ca
Executive Director, Lands & Development Services, Doug MacKnight
Tel: 306-787-2082
Fax: 306-787-7338
Doug.Macknight@gov.sk.ca
Executive Director, Energy Policy, Floyd Wist
Tel: 306-787-2477
Fax: 306-787-2198
Floyd.Wist@gov.sk.ca
Director, Energy Economics, Mike Balfour
Tel: 306-787-2479
Fax: 306-787-2198
Mike.Balfour@gov.sk.ca
Director, Regulatory Affairs, Jane Chapco
Tel: 306-787-9637
Fax: 306-787-7338
Jane.Chapco@gov.sk.ca; jane.chapco2@gov.sk.ca
Director, Saskatchewan Geological Survey, Gary Delaney
Tel: 306-787-1160
Fax: 306-787-1284
gary.delaney@gov.sk.ca
Director, Mines, Mike Detharet
Tel: 306-787-2139
Fax: 306-798-0047
Mike.Detharet@gov.sk.ca
Director, Mineral Policy, Cory Hughes
Tel: 306-787-3628
Fax: 306-787-2198
Cory.Hughes@gov.sk.ca
Director, Energy Development & Climate Change, Howard Loseth
Tel: 306-787-3379
Fax: 306-787-2198
Howard.Loseth@gov.sk.ca
Acting Director, Petroleum Geology, Melinda Yurkowski
Tel: 306-787-0650
Fax: 306-787-4608
melinda.yurkowski@gov.sk.ca

Petroleum & Natural Gas Division
Tel: 306-787-2592
Fax: 306-787-2478
Assistant Deputy Minister, Ed Dancsok
Tel: 306-787-2591
Fax: 306-787-2478
Ed.Dancsok@gov.sk.ca
Director, Petroleum Development, Todd Han
Tel: 306-787-2221
Fax: 306-787-2478
todd.han@gov.sk.ca
Director, Petroleum Royalties, Mike Ferguson
Tel: 306-787-2605
Fax: 306-787-2478
mike.ferguson@gov.sk.ca
Director, Petroleum Tenure Branch, Paul Mahnic
Tel: 306-787-5385
Fax: 306-787-0620
Paul.Mahnic@gov.sk.ca
Director, Petroleum Statistics, Darwin Roske
Tel: 306-787-2607
Fax: 306-787-8236
darwin.roske@gov.sk.ca
Director, Engineering Services Branch, Steve Rymes
Tel: 306-787-2318
Fax: 306-787-2478
Steve.Rymes@gov.sk.ca

Saskatchewan Environment (ENV)

3211 Albert St., 2nd Fl., Regina, SK S4S 5W6
Tel: 306-787-2584
Fax: 306-787-9544
Toll-Free: 800-567-4224
Centre.Inquiry@gov.sk.ca
www.environment.gov.sk.ca
Other Communication: Parkwatch Line: 1-800-667-1788; Firewatch Line: 1-800-667-9660; Spill Control Centre: 1-800-667-7525; TIP (Turn in Poachers: 1-800-667-7561
Saskatchewan Environment protects & mananges the province's environmental & natural resources by offering the following programs & services: compliance & enforcement to protect the public's interests in the management of air, land, water & natural resources; protection & management of forest ecosystems; wildfire management; Green Strategy; environmental assessment; legislation, & policies to ensure that Crown land is used in ways that respect environmental, economic & social values; fishing & fisheries management; hunting management; licensing & guiding the trapping industry; protection of wildlife; recycling; waste management; & water resource & treatment plant operations management.
Acts Administered:
Assiniboine Slopes Provincial Ecological Reserves Regulations
Buffalograss Ecological Reserve Regulations
Captive Wildlife Regulations
Clean Air Act
Clean Air Regulation
Commercial Activities Regulations
Commercial Fishing Production Incentive Regulations
Conservation Easements Act
Crown Resource Lands Regulations, 1989
Dog Training Regulations
Drainage Control Regulations
Dutch Elm Disease Regulations
Ecological Reserves Act
Environmental Assessment Act
Environmental Management & Protection Act, 2002
Environmental Spill Control Regulations
Fisheries Act
Fisheries Regulations
Forest Resources Management Act
Forest Resources Management Regulations
Forestry Professions Act
Government Land Reserves Regulation
Grasslands National Park Act
Groundwater Regulations
Halocarbon Control Regulations
Hazardous Substances & Dangerous Goods Regulations
Historic Sites Regulations
Indian Treaty Obligations Regulations
Litter Control Act
Mineral Industry Environmental Protection Regulations
Municipal Refuse Management Regulations
Natural Resources Act
Open Seasons Game Regulations
Outfitter & Guide Regulations, 1996
Ozone-Depleting Substances Control Regulations
PCB Waste Storage Regulations
Park Land Reserve Regulations
Park Land Reserves Regulations
Parks Act
Parks Regulations
Potash Refining Air Emissions Regulations
Prairie & Forest Fires Act, 1982
Provincial Ecological Reserves Regulation
Provincial Lands Act
Provincial Lands Regulations
Qu'Appelle Coulee Provincial Ecological Reserves Regulations
Recreation Site Regulations, 1991
Representative Area Ecological Reserve Regulations
Reservoir Development Area Regulations
Reservoir Development Area Regulations
Resource Protection & Development Services Regulations
Sale or Lease of Certain Lands Act
Saskatchewan Watershed Authority Act 2005
Scrap Tire Management Regulations
State of the Environment Report Act
Surface Lease Agreement Regulations: Beaverlodge, Cigar Lake, Cluff Lake, Jolu Project, Key Lake, Konuto Project, McArthur River Operation, McClean Lake, Midwest Joint, Rabbit Lake
Surface Rights Regulations (Grasslands Park, Komis Project, Parks Lake Uranium Mining, Seabee)
Treaty Land Entitlement Withdrawal Regulations
Used Oil Collection Regulations
Waste Electronic Equipment Regulations
Waste Paint Management Regulations
Water Appeal Board Act
Water Regulations
Wild Rice Regulations
Wild Species at Risk Regulations
Wildlife Act, 1998
Wildlife Habitat Lands Designation Regulations
Wildlife Habitat Lands Disposition & Alteration Regulations
Wildlife Habitat Protection Act
Wildlife Landowner Assistance Regulations, 1991
Wildlife Management Zones & Special Areas Boundaries Regulations, 1990
Wildlife Regulations, 1981
Withdrawal of Land from Forests; Historical Interest Regulations

Minister, Environment; Minister Responsible, Saskatchewan Watershed Authority; Minister Responsible, Hon. Ken Cheveldayoff
Tel: 306-787-0393
Fax: 306-787-1669
minister.env@gov.sk.ca
Social Media: www.facebook.com/pages/Ken-Cheveldayoff/52760912740
Office of the Minister of the Environment,Legislative Building #315, 2405 Legislative Dr.
Regina, SK S4S 0B3

Deputy Minister, Environment, Liz Quarshie
Tel: 306-787-2930
Fax: 306-787-2947
liz.quarshie@gov.sk.ca

Executive Director, Strategic Planning & Performance Improvement, Greg Leake
Tel: 306-787-5511
Fax: 306-787-2947

Director, Communications Services, Dorma Everett
Tel: 306-787-2770
Fax: 306-787-3941
Everett.Dorma@gov.sk.ca

Manager, Correspondence, Krista Campbell
Tel: 306-787-5796
Fax: 306-787-3941
krista.campbell@gov.sk.ca

Associated Agencies, Boards & Commissions:

• Saskatchewan Conservation Data Centre
3211 Albert St.
Regina, SK S4S 5W6
Tel: 306-787-9038
Fax: 306-787-9544
www.biodiversity.sk.ca
The SKCDC was formed as a co-operative venture between the province, The Nature Conservancy USA & The Nature Conservancy of Canada. The SKCDC gathers, interprets & distributes scientific information on the ecological status of provincial wild species & communities. The SKCDC is committed to conserving biological diversity; producing scientific reports & being the provincial clearinghouse for threatened & endangered species information.

• Water Appeal Board
#217, 3085 Albert St.
Regina, SK S4S 0B1
Tel: 306-798-7462
Fax: 306-787-8558
www.gov.sk.ca/wb

Environmental Protection & Audit Division
3211 Albert St., 5th Fl., Regina, SK S4S 5W6
Tel: 306-787-2947
Protects human health & ecosystem integrity.
Assistant Deputy Minister, Environmental Protection & Audit, Mark Wittrup
Tel: 306-787-5419
Fax: 306-787-2947
mark.wittrup@gov.sk.ca
Chief Engineer, Technical Resources Branch, Kevin McCullum
Tel: 306-787-2739
Fax: 306-787-2947
Kevin.McCullum@gov.sk.ca
Executive Director, Municipal Branch, Sam Ferris
Tel: 306-787-6193
Fax: 306-787-0197
sam.ferris@gov.sk.ca
Executive Director, Industrial Branch, Wes Kotyk
Tel: 306-933-6542
Fax: 306-933-8442
Wes.Kotyk@gov.sk.ca
Executive Director, Wildfire Management Branch, Steve Roberts
Tel: 306-953-2206
Fax: 306-953-3575
Steve.Roberts@gov.sk.ca
Director, Environmental Assessment Branch, Tareq Al Zabet
Tel: 306-787-1023
Fax: 306-787-0930
tareq.alzabet@gov.sk.ca
Acting Director, Wildfire Support Section, Daryl Jessop
Tel: 306-953-3472
Fax: 306-953-3670
Daryl.Jessop@gov.sk.ca
Director, Wildfire Management Operations Section, Curtis Lee
Tel: 306-953-3429
Fax: 306-953-3575
Curtis.Lee@gov.sk.ca
Director, Environmental Protection Services Section, Thon Phommavong
Tel: 306-787-9986
Fax: 306-787-0197
Thon.Phommavong@gov.sk.ca
Director, Aviation Operations, Denis Renaud
Tel: 306-425-4586
Fax: 306-425-4538
Denis.Renaud@gov.sk.ca

Environmental Support Division
3211 Albert St., 5th Fl., Regina, SK S4S 5W6
Fax: 306-787-2947
Assistant Deputy Minister, Environmental Support, Lori Uhersky
Tel: 306-787-5737
Fax: 306-787-2947
lori.uhersky@gov.sk.ca
Acting Assistant Deputy Minister, Donna Johnson
Tel: 306-787-5737
Fax: 306-787-2947
Donna.Johnson@gov.sk.ca
Chief Information Officer, Information Management & Geomatics Services, Kevin Saunderson
Tel: 306-798-3901
Fax: 306-787-3913
Kevin.Saunderson@gov.sk.ca
Acting Executive Director, Finance & Administration, Laurel Welsh
Tel: 306-787-2484
Fax: 306-787-8441
Laurel.Welsh@gov.sk.ca
Director, Climate Change, Kim Graybiel
Tel: 306-787-0114
Fax: 306-787-0024
Kim.Graybiel@gov.sk.ca
Director, Financial Management, Susan Loewen
Tel: 306-787-7609
Fax: 306-787-8441
Susan.Loewen@gov.sk.ca
Director, Aboriginal Affairs, Jennifer McKillop
Tel: 306-787-9643
Fax: 306-787-0197
Jennifer.Mckillop@gov.sk.ca
Acting Director, Financial & Property Management, Zachery Solomon
Tel: 306-798-3904
Fax: 306-787-8441
zachery.solomon@gov.sk.ca

Resource Management & Compliance Division
3211 Albert St., 5th fl., Regina, SK S4S 5W6
Fax: 306-787-2947
Assistant Deputy Minister, Resource Management & Compliance, Kevin Murphy
Tel: 306-787-8567
Fax: 306-787-2947
Kevin.Murphy@gov.sk.ca
Executive Director, Compliance & Field Services, Kevin Callele
Tel: 306-787-3388
Fax: 306-787-3913
Kevin.Callele@gov.sk.ca
Executive Director, Fish & Wildlife, Lyle Saigeon
Tel: 306-787-2309
Fax: 306-787-9544
Lyle.Saigeon@gov.sk.ca
Executive Director, Forest Service, Bob Wynes
Tel: 306-953-2491
Fax: 306-953-2360
Bob.Wynes@gov.sk.ca
Director, Lands, Todd Olexson
Tel: 306-953-2586
Fax: 306-953-2684
Todd.Olexson@gov.sk.ca
Director, Field Services, Brent Webster
Tel: 306-446-7424
Fax: 306-446-7464
Brent.Webster@gov.sk.ca

Regional Operations
Beauval Compliance Area
Lavoie St., PO Box 280, Beauval, SK S0M 0G0
Tel: 306-288-4710
Fax: 306-288-4717
Compliance Manager, Dennis Daigneault
Tel: 306-288-4713
Fax: 306-288-4717
Dennis.Daigneault@gov.sk.ca
La Ronge Compliance Area
Mistasinihk Place, #1100 - 1328 La Ronge Ave., PO Box 5000, La Ronge, SK S0J 1L0
Tel: 306-425-4234
Fax: 306-425-2580
Compliance Manager, Daryl Minster
Tel: 306-425-4244
Fax: 306-425-2580
Daryl.Minter@gov.sk.ca
Meadow Lake Compliance Area
#1, 101 Railway Pl., Meadow Lake, SK S9X 1X6
Tel: 306-236-7557
Fax: 306-236-7677
Acting Compliance Manager, Marc Painchaud
Tel: 306-236-9833
Fax: 306-236-7677
Marc.Painchaud@gov.sk.ca
Prince Albert Compliance Area
800 Central Ave., PO Box 3003, Prince Albert, SK S6V 6G1
Tel: 306-953-2322
Fax: 306-953-2321
Compliance Manager, Bill Zimmer
Tel: 306-953-2945
Fax: 306-953-2999
Bill.Zimmer@gov.sk.ca
Saskatoon Compliance Area
112 Research Dr., Saskatoon, SK S7N 3R3
Tel: 306-933-6240
Fax: 306-933-5773
Compliance Manager, Doug Robinson
Tel: 306-933-7929
Fax: 306-933-5773
Swift Current Compliance Area
350 Cheadle St. West, PO Box 5000, Swift Current, SK S9H 4G3
Tel: 306-778-8205
Fax: 306-778-8212
Compliance Manager, Bob Roberts
Tel: 306-778-8644
Fax: 306-778-8212
bob.roberts@gov.sk.ca
Yorkton Compliance Area
120 Smith St. East, Yorkton, SK S3N 3V3
Fax: 306-786-5716
Compliance Manager, Phil Decker
Tel: 306-786-1692
Fax: 306-786-5716
Phil.Decker@gov.sk.ca

SaskEnergy Incorporated

1777 Victoria Ave., Regina, SK S4P 4K5
Tel: 306-777-9225
Toll-Free: 800-567-8899
www.saskenergy.com
Other Communication: Emergency & safety Line: 1-888-700-0427; Line Locates: 1-866-828-4888
The provincial Crown corporation provides natural gas to residential, farm, commercial, & industrial customers in 92% of Saskatchewan's communities.
Acts Administered:
SaskEnergy Act

Minister Responsible, Energy & Resources; Minister Responsible, Tourism Saskatchewan; Minister Responsible, Trade; Minister Responsible, SaskEnergy Incorporated, Hon. Tim McMillan
Tel: 306-787-9124
Fax: 306-787-0395
minister.er@gov.sk.ca
Social Media: www.facebook.com/timmcmillanmla
Office of the Minister Responsible Energy & Resources / SaskEnergy Incorporated
#346, 2405 Legislative Dr.
Regina, SK S4S 0B3

Chair, Rob Pletch
Tel: 306-777-9901

Vice-President, General Counsel & Corporate Secretary, Mark Guillet
Tel: 306-777-9427
Fax: 306-565-3332
mguillet@saskenergy.com

Corporate Support
Fax: 306-777-9561
Vice-President, Colleen Huber
Tel: 306-777-9660
chuber@saskenergy.com

Distribution Utility
Tel: 306-777-9994
Fax: 306-522-2217
Executive Vice-President, Dean Reeve
Tel: 306-777-9402
Fax: 306-522-2217
dreeve@saskenergy.com
Executive Director, Distribution Customer Service, Randy Greggains
Tel: 306-777-9233
Fax: 306-522-2217
rgreggains@saskenergy.com

Finance
Fax: 306-777-9070
Vice-President & Chief Financial Officer, Dennis Terry
Tel: 306-777-9417
dterry@saskenergy.com

Gas Supply & Business Development
Tel: 306-777-9354
Fax: 306-569-3522
Senior Vice-President, Daryl Posehn
Tel: 306-777-9567
Fax: 306-569-3522
dposehn@saskenergy.com

Human Resources
Fax: 306-781-7050

Vice-President, Robert Haynes
Tel: 306-777-9405
rhaynes@saskenergy.com

Saskatchewan Finance (FI)

2350 Albert St., Regina, SK S4P 4A6
Tel: 306-787-6768
Fax: 306-787-0241
communications@finance.gov.sk.ca
www.finance.gov.sk.ca
Other Communication: General Tax Inquiries: 1-800-667-6102
The Ministry of Finance manages the financing, revenue, & expenses of the provincial government. The following are some of the duties performed by the department: administering provincial taxes, grant, & refund programs; managing banking, investment, & public debt functions; providing financial & policy analysis; offering economic forecasting & economic & social statistics; producing the provincial budget; assisting the government in the management of public monies; & managing governmental pension & benefit plans.
Acts Administered:
Certified General Accountants Act, 1994
Certified Management Accountants Act (not yet proclaimed)
Certified Management Consultants Act
Chartered Accountants Act, 1986
Corporation Capital Tax Act
Federal-Provincial Agreements Act
Financial Administration Act, 1993
Fuel Tax Act, 2000
Home Energy Loan Act
Income Tax Act
Income Tax Act, 2000
Insurance Premiums Tax Act
Liquor Board Superannuation Act
Liquor Consumption Tax Act
Management Accountants Act
Members of the Legislative Assembly Benefits Act
Motor Vehicle Insurance Premiums Tax Act
Municipal Employees' Pension Act
Municipal Financing Corporation Act
Provincial Auditor Act
Provincial Sales Tax Act
Public Employees Pension Plan Act
Public Service Superannuation Act
Revenue & Financial Services Act
Saskatchewan Development Fund Act
Saskatchewan Pension Annuity Fund Act
Saskatchewan Pension Plan Act
Statistics Act
Superannuation (Supplementary Provisions) Act
Tabling of Documents Act, 1991
Tobacco Tax Act, 1998

Minister, Finance; Deputy Premier, Hon. Ken Krawetz
Tel: 306-787-6060
Fax: 306-787-6055
minister.fin@gov.sk.ca
Legislative Building
#312, 2405 Legislative Dr.
Regina, SK S4S 0B3

Deputy Minister, Education, Clare Isman
Tel: 306-787-6621
Fax: 306-787-7155
clare.isman@gov.sk.ca

Executive Director, Personnel Policy Secretariat, Tor Veltheim
Tel: 306-787-3101
Fax: 306-798-0386
Tor.Veltheim@gov.sk.ca

Director, Financial Services, Louise Usick
Tel: 306-787-6530
Fax: 306-787-6576
Louise.Usick@gov.sk.ca

Manager, Public Relations, Brian Miller
Tel: 306-787-6605
Fax: 306-787-7155
brian.miller@gov.sk.ca

Associated Agencies, Boards & Commissions:
• Board of Revenue Commissioners
#480, 2151 Scarth St.
Regina, SK S4P 2H8
Tel: 306-787-6221
Fax: 306-787-1610
www.gov.sk.ca/BRC
Any write-off or cancellation of monies owing to the Crown is subject to prior approval of the Board of Revenue Commissioners as delegated by the Treasury Board. The Board has the power to hear & determine appeals respecting taxes imposed or assessed pursuant to & by virtue of any taxing enactment & respecting other monies claimed to be due & payable to the Crown where the right of taking appeal to the Board is given by any statute.
• Municipal Employees' Pension Commission
#1000, 1801 Hamilton St.
Regina, SK S4P 4W3
Fax: 306-787-8822
www.peba.gov.sk.ca/MEPP/mepp_commission.htm
The Municipal Employees' Pension Commission is responsible for the administration of the Municipal Employees' Pension Fund.
• Municipal Financing Corporation of Saskatchewan (MFC)
2350 Albert St., 6th Fl.
Regina, SK S4P 4A6
Tel: 306-787-8150
Fax: 306-787-8493
www.gov.sk.ca/mfc
The MFC, established in 1969 under the authority of The Municipal Financing Corporation Act, makes capital funds available to the financing of sewer & water, school, hospital, & other vital municipal construction projects.
• Saskatchewan Development Fund Corporation
#400, 2400 College Ave.
Regina, SK S4P 1C8
Tel: 306-787-1645
Fax: 306-787-8125
www.cicorp.sk.ca/funds/saskatchewan_development_fund_corp
The Saskatchewan Development Fund is a low risk investment fund that provides income & long-term investment growth to Saskatchewan residents. The Fund is administered by the Saskatchewan Development Fund Corporation. Since 1983, the Fund no longer sells new shares to the public.
• Saskatchewan Pension Plan
PO Box 5555
Kindersley, SK S0L 1S0
Tel: 306-463-5410
Fax: 306-463-3500
Toll-free: 800-667-7153
www.saskpension.com

Budget Analysis Division

Tel: 306-787-6742
Associate Deputy Minister, Taxation & Intergovernmental Affairs Branch, Kirk McGregor
Tel: 306-787-6731
Fax: 306-787-7003
kirk.mcgregor@gov.sk.ca
Assistant Deputy Minister, Treasury Board, Denise Macza
Tel: 306-787-6780
Fax: 306-787-3982
Denise.Macza@gov.sk.ca
Executive Director, Economic & Fiscal Policy Branch, Joanne Brockman
Tel: 306-787-6743
Fax: 306-787-1426
joanne.brockman@gov.sk.ca
Executive Director, Estimates, Al Dennett
Tel: 306-787-6726
Fax: 306-787-3982
Al.Dennett@gov.sk.ca
Director, Performance Management Branch, Raelynn Douglas
Tel: 306-787-7762
Fax: 306-787-3982
Raelynn.Douglas@gov.sk.ca

Provincial Comptroller's Division

Tel: 306-787-6353
Fax: 306-787-9720
Provincial Comptroller, Terry Paton
Tel: 306-787-9254
Fax: 306-787-9720
Terry.Paton@gov.sk.ca

Public Employees Benefits Agency

1000 - 1801 Hamilton St., Regina, SK S4P 4W3
Tel: 306-787-2992
Fax: 306-787-8822
peba@peba.gov.sk.ca
www.peba.gov.sk.ca
Assistant Deputy Minister, Brian L. Smith
Tel: 306-787-6757
Fax: 306-798-0065
brian.smith@peba.gov.sk.ca

Revenue Division

Tel: 306-787-6645
Fax: 306-787-0776
Toll-Free: 800-667-6102
Assistant Deputy Minister, Margaret Johannsson
Tel: 306-787-6685
Fax: 306-787-0241
margaret.johannsson@gov.sk.ca
Director, Provincial Sales Tax (PST) Branch, Rob Dobson
Tel: 306-787-7785
Fax: 306-798-3045
rob.dobson@gov.sk.ca; rob.dobson2@gov.sk.ca
Director, Audit Branch, Brent Herbert
Tel: 306-787-7784
Fax: 306-798-3045
Brent.Hebert@gov.sk.ca
Director, Revenue Programs Branch, Doug Lambert
Tel: 306-787-4600
Fax: 306-787-0241
Doug.Lambert@gov.sk.ca
Director, Revenue Operations Branch, Kelly Laurans
Tel: 306-787-7788
Fax: 306-787-6653
kelly.laurans@gov.sk.ca

Treasury & Debt Management Division

Tel: 306-787-6752
Fax: 306-787-8493
Assistant Deputy Minister, Rae Haverstock
Tel: 306-787-9473
Fax: 306-787-8493
Executive Director, Cash & Debt Management Branch, Jim Fallows
Tel: 306-787-3923
Fax: 306-787-8493
jim.fallows@gov.sk.ca
Executive Director, Capital Markets Branch, Vacant
Tel: 306-787-6753
Fax: 306-787-8493
Director, Liability & Risk Management, Carla Brown
Tel: 306-787-9474
Fax: 306-787-8493
carla.brown@gov.sk.ca
Director, Investments, Doug Dorsch
Tel: 306-787-3905
Fax: 306-787-8493
Doug.Dorsch@gov.sk.ca

Saskatchewan Gaming Corporation (SaskGaming)

1880 Saskatchewan Dr., 3rd Fl., Regina, SK S4P 0B2
Tel: 306-787-1590
www.casinoregina.com/corporate
SaskGaming was created by The Saskatchewan Gaming Corporation Act in 1994, in order to establish & operate casinos across the province.

Minister, Highways & Infrastructure; Minister Responsible, Saskatchewan Telecommunications; Minister Responsible, Saskatchewan Transportation Company; Minister Responsible, Information Services Corporation; MinisterResponsible, Saskatchewan Gaming Corp., Hon. Don McMorris
Tel: 306-787-6447
Fax: 306-787-1736
minister.hi@gov.sk.ca
Social Media: twitter.com/dmcmorrissp, www.facebook.com/DonMcMorrisSP
Legislative Building
#302, 2405 Legislative Dr.
Regina, SK S4S 0B3

President/Chief Executive Officer, Twyla Meredith
Tel: 306-787-1291
Fax: 306-787-1444
twyla.meredith@saskgaming.com

Senior Vice-President, Finance & Administration, Tony Coppola
Tel: 306-798-0998
Fax: 306-798-0824
tony.coppola@saskgaming.com

Senior Vice-President, Operations, Gerry Fischer
Tel: 306-787-1483
Fax: 306-787-5880
gerry.fischer@saskgaming.com

Vice-President, Corporate Risk & Compliance, Bob Arlint
Tel: 306-787-2353
Fax: 306-798-2308
bob.arlint@saskgaming.com

Vice-President, Marketing, Susan Flett
Tel: 306-787-1356
Fax: 306-787-0639
susan.flett@saskgaming.com

Vice-President, Communications & Community Relations, Michelle Hunter
Tel: 306-787-2263
Fax: 306-787-4880
michelle.hunter@saskgaming.com

Vice-President, Human Resources, Blaine Pilatzke
Tel: 306-787-1401

Fax: 306-798-0449
blaine.pilatzke@saskgaming.com

Saskatchewan Government Insurance (SGI)

2260 - 11th Ave., Regina, SK S4P 0J9
Tel: 306-751-1200
Fax: 306-787-7477
Toll-Free: 800-667-8015
sgiinquiries@sgi.sk.ca
www.sgi.sk.ca
Other Communication: Customer Service Centre: 1-800-667-9868

Operating in twenty claims centres in Saskatchewan communities, SGI sells property & casualty insurance products. One of SGI's operations is The Saskatchewan Auto Fund, the province's compulsory auto insurance program. The Auto Fund administers the driver's licensing & vehicle registration system.

Minister, Crown Investments; Minister Responsible, Saskatchewan Government Insurance; Minister Responsible, Saskatchewan Liquor & Gaming Authority, Hon. Donna Harpauer
Tel: 306-787-7339
Fax: 306-798-3140
minister.cc@gov.sk.ca
Social Media: www.facebook.com/pages/Donna-Harpauer/60494388240
Legislative Building
#322, 2405 Legislative Dr.
Regina, SK S4S 0B3

Chair, Board of Directors, Warren Sproule

President/Chief Executive Officer, Andrew Cartmell
Tel: 306-751-1717
Fax: 306-525-6040
acartmell@sgi.sk.ca

Chief Financial Officer, Jeff Stepan
Tel: 306-775-6004
jstepan@sgi.sk.ca

Chief Internal Auditor, Kevin Taylor
Tel: 306-751-1781
ktaylor@sgi.sk.ca

Vice-President, Auto Fund, Sherry Wolf
Tel: 306-751-1646
swolf@sgi.sk.ca

Vice-President, Canadian Operations, John Dobie
Tel: 306-751-1597
jdobie@sgi.sk.ca

Vice-President, Claims & Salvage, Earl Cameron
Tel: 306-751-1705
ecameron@sgi.sk.ca

Vice-President, Product Management, Don Thompson
Tel: 306-751-1585
dthompson@sgi.sk.ca

Vice-President, Systems & Facilities, Dwain Wells
Tel: 306-775-6093
dwells@sgi.sk.ca

Vice-President, Underwriting, Randy Heise
Tel: 306-751-1653
rheise@sgicanada.ca

Assistant Vice-President, Corporate Affairs & Planning, Barbara Cross
Tel: 306-751-1652
Fax: 306-525-6040
bcross@sgi.sk.ca

Assistant Vice-President, Human Resources & Corporate Services, Tamara Erhardt
Tel: 306-775-6994
Fax: 306-347-0089
terhardt@sgi.sk.ca

Assistant Vice-President, Marketing & Communications, Tim Kydd
Tel: 306-775-6739
tkydd@sgi.sk.ca

Saskatchewan Government Relations (GR)

1855 Victoria Ave., Regina, SK S4P 3T2
Tel: 306-787-8885
www.gr.gov.sk.ca

Municipal relations, public safety, & First Nations, Métis, & northern affairs are the main responsibilities of the Ministry of Government Relations. The Ministry aims to ensure effective governance, to provide emergency management programs, & to fulfill obligations under Treaty Land Entitlement.

Acts Administered:
Assessment Appraisers Act
Assessment Management Agency Act
Border Areas Act
Cities Act
City of Lloydminster Act
Community Planning Profession Act
Controverted Municipal Elections Act
Cutknife Reference Act
Department of Rural Development Act
Department of Urban Affairs Act (except clause 7(b) which is assigned to the Minister of Social Services)
Flin-Flon Extension of Boundaries Act, 1952
Local Government Election Act
Local Improvements Act, 1993
Municipal Board Act
Municipal Debenture Repayment Act
Municipal Development & Loan (Saskatchewan) Act
Municipal Expropriation Act
Municipal Grants Act
Municipal Industrial Development Corporations Act
Municipal Tax Sharing (Potash) Act
Municipalities Act
Municipality Improvements Assistance (Saskatchewan) Act
Northern Municipalities Act, 2010
Planning & Development Act, 2010
Rural Development Act
Rural Municipal Administrators Act
Subdivisions Act
Tax Enforcement Act
Time Act
Uniform Building & Accessibility Standards Act (the UBAS Act)
Urban Municipal Administrators Act
Urban Municipality Act

Minister, Government Relations; Minister Responsible, First Nations, Métis, & Northern Affairs, Hon. Jim Reiter
Tel: 306-787-6100
Fax: 306-787-0399
minister.gr@gov.sk.ca
Social Media: twitter.com/jim_reiter, www.facebook.com/pages/Jim-Reiter/207539405959289
Office of the Minister of Government Relations, LegislativeBuilding
#348, 2405 Legislative Dr.
Regina, SK S4S 0B3

Deputy Minister, Government Relations, Alan Hilton
Tel: 306-787-1925
Fax: 306-787-1987
Alan.Hilton@gov.sk.ca

Assistant Deputy Minister, Keith Comstock
Tel: 306-787-5765
Fax: 306-787-1987
Keith.Comstock@gov.sk.ca

Associated Agencies, Boards & Commissions:
• Saskatchewan Municipal Board (SMB)
#480, 2151 Scarth St.
Regina, SK S4P 2H8
Tel: 306-787-6221
Fax: 306-787-1610
info@smb.gov.sk.ca
www.smb.gov.sk.ca

Central Management Services
#1410, 1855 Victoria Ave., Regina, SK S4P 3T2
Tel: 306-787-0325
Fax: 306-787-4161

Executive Director, Central Management Services, Wanda Lamberti
Tel: 306-787-1640
Fax: 306-787-4161
Wanda.Lamberti@gov.sk.ca
Director, Financial Planning, Marj Abel
Tel: 306-787-4172
Fax: 306-787-4161
Marj.Abel@gov.sk.ca
Director, Financial Services, Janie Markewich
Tel: 306-787-6408
Fax: 306-787-4161
janie.markewich@gov.sk.ca
Manager, Corporate Planning, Garett Murray
Tel: 306-798-6093
Fax: 306-787-4161
Garett.Murray@gov.sk.ca

Communications
#1530, 1855 Victoria Ave., Regina, SK S4P 3T2
Tel: 306-787-4181

Executive Director, Communications, Jeff Welke
Tel: 306-787-6156
Fax: 306-787-4181
jeff.welke@gov.sk.ca
Co-Director, Communications, Bob Ellis
Tel: 306-787-2709
Fax: 306-787-4181
robert.ellis@gov.sk.ca
Co-Director, Communications, Nicole Fellinger
Tel: 306-787-2687
Fax: 306-787-4181
Nicole.Fellinger@gov.sk.ca
Manager, Content & Internet Coordinator, Lorrie Guillaume
Tel: 306-787-4340
Fax: 306-787-4181
Lorrie.Guillaume@gov.sk.ca

Community Planning
#420, 1855 Victoria Ave., Regina, SK S4P 3T2
Tel: 306-787-9411
Fax: 306-798-0194

Executive Director, Community Planning, Ralph Leibel
Tel: 306-787-7672
Fax: 306-798-0194
Ralph.Leibel@gov.sk.ca
Director, Community Planning (Regina), Barry Braitman
Tel: 306-787-2893
Fax: 306-798-0194
Barry.Braitman@gov.sk.ca
Director, Community Planning (Saskatoon), Len Kowalko
Tel: 306-933-6118
Fax: 306-933-7720
Len.Kowalko@gov.sk.ca
#978, 122 - 3rd Ave. North, 9th Fl.
Saskatoon, SK S7K 2H6

First Nations, Métis, & Northern Affairs (FNMR)
#1020, 1855 Victoria Ave., Regina, SK S4P 3T2
Tel: 306-787-6680
Fax: 306-798-0083

The organization strives to improve the economic & social circumstances for First Nations & Métis people & northerners. The following are programs & services offered: First Nations & Métis Community Initiative; First Nations & Métis Women's Initiative; Treaty Land Entitlement; Northern Development Fund; Northern Saskatchewan Environmental Quality; & Mineral Surface Lease Agreements.

Minister, Government Relations; Minister Responsible, First Nations, Métis, & Northern Affairs, Hon. Jim Reiter
Tel: 306-787-6100
Fax: 306-787-0399
minister.gr@gov.sk.ca
Social Media: twitter.com/jim_reiter, www.facebook.com/pages/Jim-Reiter/207539405959289
Office of the Minister Responsible, First Nations, Métis, &Northern Affairs, Legislative Building
#348, 2405 Legislative Dr.
Regina, SK S4S 0B3
Assistant Deputy Minister, First Nations, Métis, & Northern Affairs, Hon. James Froh
Tel: 306-787-7405
Fax: 306-798-0083
James.Froh@gov.sk.ca
Assistant Deputy Minister, Northern Affairs, Giselle Marcotte
Tel: 306-425-4204
Fax: 306-425-4349
Giselle.Marcotte@gov.sk.ca
Executive Director, Lands & Consultation, Trisha Delormier-Hill
Tel: 306-787-6681
Fax: 306-798-0004
Trisha.Delormier-Hill@gov.sk.ca
Executive Director, Relationship & Policy, Alethea Foster
Tel: 306-787-5176
Fax: 306-787-5832
Alethea.Foster@gov.sk.ca
Executive Director, Northern Regional Economic Development, Doug Howorko
Tel: 306-798-5167
Fax: 306-787-6014
Doug.Howorko2@gov.sk.ca
Executive Director, Northern Social Development, Mark LaRocque
Tel: 306-787-6400
Fax: 306-787-6014
Mark.LaRocque@gov.sk.ca
Executive Director, Strategic Initiatives, Seonaid MacPherson
Tel: 306-787-8142
Fax: 306-798-0083
Seonaid.MacPherson@gov.sk.ca
Executive Director, Northern Industry & Resource Development, Richard Turkheim
Tel: 306-787-2143
Fax: 306-787-6014
Richard.Turkheim@gov.sk.ca

Director, Finance, Accountability & Corporate Services, Kerry Gray
Tel: 306-787-2123
Fax: 306-798-0004
Kerry.Gray@gov.sk.ca
Director, Communications, Cathe Offet
Tel: 306-787-5701
Fax: 306-798-0083
Cathe.Offet@gov.sk.ca
Director, Gaming Trust & Grants, Sam Swan
Tel: 306-787-1695
Fax: 306-798-0004
Sam.Swan@gov.sk.ca

Grant Administration & Financial Management
#410, 1855 Victoria Ave., Regina, SK S4P 3T2
Tel: 306-787-8808
Fax: 306-787-3641
Executive Director, Grant Administration & Financial Management, Kathy Rintoul
Tel: 306-787-8887
Fax: 306-787-3641
Kathy.Rintoul@gov.sk.ca
Director, New Deal Secretariat, Teri Kitney
Tel: 306-787-9699
Fax: 306-787-3641
teri.kitney@gov.sk.ca
Director, Grant Administration, Kyle Toffan
Tel: 306-787-7994
Fax: 306-787-3641
kyle.toffan@gov.sk.ca

Northern Municipal Services
Mistasinihk Pl., #2700, 1328 La Ronge Ave., PO Box 5000, La Ronge, SK S0J 1L0
Tel: 306-425-4320
Fax: 306-425-2401
Toll-Free: 800-663-1555
Northern Municipal Services administers the Northern Municipal Account. Administrative support & operational assistance are given to Saskatchewan's northern municipalities through municipal management functions, training, & advisory services.
Executive Director, Northern Municipal Services, Brad Henry
Tel: 306-425-4322
Fax: 306-425-2401
brad.henry@gov.sk.ca
Manager, Northern Municipal Administration, Colleen Digness
Tel: 306-425-4325
Fax: 306-425-2401
Colleen.Digness@gov.sk.ca
PO Box 69
Buffalo Narrows, SK S0M 0J0
Manager, Financial Services, Ken Kowalczyk
Tel: 306-425-4328
Fax: 306-425-2401
ken.kowalczyk@gov.sk.ca
PO Box 69
Buffalo Narrows, SK S0M 0J0
Northern District Planner, Dee Johns
Tel: 306-425-6642
Fax: 306-425-2401
Dee.Johns@gov.sk.ca
PO Box 69
Buffalo Narrows, SK S0M 0J0

Policy Development
#1540, 1855 Victoria Ave., Regina, SK S4P 3T2
Tel: 306-787-2653
Fax: 306-787-5822
Executive Director, Policy Development, John Edwards
Tel: 306-787-2665
Fax: 306-787-5822
john.edwards2@gov.sk.ca
Director, Property Assessment & Taxation, Norm Magnin
Tel: 306-787-2895
Fax: 306-787-5822
Norm.Magnin@gov.sk.ca
Director, Legislation & Regulations, Rod Nasewich
Tel: 306-798-7048
Fax: 306-787-5822
Rod.Nasewich@gov.sk.ca
Manager, Policy Analysis, Ryan Cossitt
Tel: 306-787-2780
Fax: 306-787-5822
Ryan.Cossitt@gov.sk.ca

Provincial Disaster Assistance Program (PDAP)
PO Box 227, Regina, SK S4P 2Z6
Tel: 306-787-7800
Fax: 306-798-2318
Toll-Free: 866-632-4033
Assistance is provided to recover from natural disasters such as tornadoes, plow winds, flooding, & other severe weather. The Provincial Disaster Assistance Program serves the following people & organizations of Saskatchewan: residents, communual organizations, agricultural operations, nonprofit organizations, small businesses, parks, & communities.
Executive Director, Provincial Disaster Assistance Program, Margaret Anderson
Tel: 306-798-8470
Fax: 306-798-6356
Margaret.Anderson@gov.sk.ca
Director, Policy, Kevin Roche
Tel: 306-798-8020
Fax: 306-798-2318
Kevin.Roche@gov.sk.ca
Manager, Program, Tamie Folwark
Tel: 306-798-0590
Fax: 306-798-2318
Tamie.Folwark@gov.sk.ca
Manager, Finances, Noel McAvena
Tel: 306-798-0583
Fax: 306-798-2318
noel.mcavena@gov.sk.ca
Manager, Contracts, Lee Moyse
Tel: 306-787-9532
Fax: 306-798-2318
lee.moyse@gov.sk.ca

Strategy & Sector Relations
#1010, 1855 Victoria Ave., Regina, SK S4P 3T2
Tel: 306-798-2568
Executive Director, Strategy & Sector Relations, Sheldon Green
Tel: 306-787-7883
Fax: 306-798-2568
Sheldon.Green@gov.sk.ca
Director, Strategy & Sector Relations, Randy McAfee
Tel: 306-787-9641
Fax: 306-798-2568
randy.mcafee@gov.sk.ca
Manager, Sector Relations, Dustin Austman
Tel: 306-787-2740
Fax: 306-798-2568
Dustin.Austman@gov.sk.ca
Manager, Strategic Initiatives, Chris Gunningham
Tel: 306-787-4984
Fax: 306-798-2568
Chris.Gunningham@gov.sk.ca

Saskatchewan Health (HE)

T.C. Douglas Bldg., 3475 Albert St., Regina, SK S4S 6X6
Tel: 306-787-0146
Toll-Free: 800-667-7766
info@health.gov.sk.ca
www.health.gov.sk.ca
Other Communication: Family Health Benefits: 1-800-266-0695; HealthLine: 1-877-800-0002; Health Registration / Health Card: 1-800-667-7551; Prescription Drug Plan: 1-800-667-7581
Saskatchewan Health offers the following programs & services: continuing care to help people live independently; e-health & information systems for access to medical information; emergency services; health benefits; recruitment & retention of healthcare providers; promotion of mental health & treatment for mental illness & addictions; personal health services; prescription drug coverage; public health programs; privacy of health information; services for people with long term disabilities or illnesses; surgery & diagnostics initiatives; & vital statistics.
Acts Administered:
Ambulance Act
Cancer Agency Act
Change of Name Act, 1995
Chiropody Profession Act
Chiropractic Act, 1994
Dental Care Act
Dental Disciplines Act
Department of Health Act
Dietitians Act
Emergency Medical Aid Act
Fetal Alcohol Syndrome Awareness Day Act
Health Districts Act
Health Facilities Licensing Act
Health Information Protection Act
Health Quality Control Act
Hearing Aid Act
Hearing Aid Sales & Services Act
Hospital Standards Act
Housing & Special-care Homes Act
Human Tissue Gift Act
Licensed Practical Nurses Act
Medical & Hospitalization Tax Repeal Act
Medical Laboratory Licensing Act, 1994
Medical Laboratory Technologists Act, 1994
Medical Profession Act, 1981
Medical Radiation Technologists Act, 1994
Mental Health Services Act
Midwifery Act
Mutual Medical & Hospital Benefit Associations Act
Naturopathy Act
Occupational Therapists Act, 1997
Opthalmic Dispensers Act
Optometry Act, 1985
Paramedics Act
Personal Care Homes Act
Pharmacy Act, 1996
Physical Therapists Act, 1998
Podiatry Act
Prescription Drugs Act
Prostate Cancer Awareness Month Act
Psychologists Act
Public Health Act
Regional Health Services Act
Registered Nurses Act, 1988
Registered Psychiatric Nurses Act
Residential Services Act
Respiratory Therapists Act
Saskatchewan Health Research Foundation Act
Saskatchewan Medical Care Insurance Act
Senior Citizens' Heritage Program Act
Speech Language Pathologists & Audiologists Act
Tobacco Control Act
Tobacco Damages & Health Care Costs Recovery Act
Vital Statistics Act, 1995
White Cane Act
Youth Drug Detoxification & Stabilization Act

Minister, Health, Hon. Dustin Duncan
Tel: 306-787-7345
Fax: 306-787-0237
minister.he@gov.sk.ca
Social Media: twitter.com/dustin_duncan
Office of the Minister of Health, Legislative Building
#204, 2405 Legislative Dr.
Regina, SK S4S0B3

Minister Responsible, Rural & Remote Health, Hon. Randy Weekes
Tel: 306-798-9014
Fax: 306-798-9013
minister.rrhe@gov.sk.ca
Social Media:
www.facebook.com/pages/Randy-Weekes-MLA/356610274367735?sk=info
Office of the Minister Responsible for Rural & Remote Health, Legislative Building
#208, 2405 LegislativeDr.
Regina, SK S4S 0B3

Deputy Minister, Dan Florizone
Tel: 306-787-3041
Fax: 306-787-4533
dan.florizone@health.gov.sk.ca

Associate Deputy Minister, Max Hendricks
Tel: 306-787-4695
Fax: 306-787-4533
max.hendricks@health.gov.sk.ca

Assistant Deputy Minister, Lauren Donnelly
Tel: 306-787-0513
Fax: 306-787-4533
lauren.donnelly@health.gov.sk.ca

Executive Director, Physician Leadership & Organizational Development, Brad Havervold
Tel: 306-787-0716
Fax: 306-787-2974
Bhavervold@health.gov.sk.ca

Executive Director, Saskatchewan Surgical Initiative, Mark Wyatt
Tel: 306-787-3153
Fax: 306-798-3367
mark.wyatt@gov.sk.ca

Director, Patient Safety Unit, Valerie Phillips
Tel: 306-787-3542
vphillips@health.gov.sk.ca

Associated Agencies, Boards & Commissions:
• **Health Quality Council**
241, 111 Research Dr.
Saskatoon, SK S7N 3R2
Tel: 306-668-8810
Fax: 306-668-8820
info@hqc.sk.ca
www.hqc.sk.ca
• **Saskatchewan Health Research Foundation**
#253, 111 Research Dr.
Saskatoon, SK S7N 3R2
Tel: 306-975-1680
Fax: 306-975-1688
Toll-free: 800-975-1699
www.shrf.ca

Acute & Emergency Services

Tel: 306-787-3204
Fax: 306-787-6113
www.health.gov.sk.ca/acute-emergency

Executive Director, Deborah Jordan
Tel: 306-787-7854
Fax: 306-787-6113
djordan@health.gov.sk.ca
Acting Director, Research & Clinical Pathway Development, Gwendolyn Friedrich
Tel: 306-787-3656
Fax: 306-787-6113
gfriedrich@health.gov.sk.ca
Acting Director, Cancer Services & EMS, Jason Liggett
Tel: 306-787-1101
Fax: 306-787-6113
jliggett@health.gov.sk.ca
Acting Director, Cancer Services & EMS, Patrick O'Byrne
Tel: 306-787-3219
Fax: 306-787-6113
pobyrne@health.gov.sk.ca

Communications Branch

Tel: 306-787-3696
Fax: 306-787-8310
Toll-Free: 800-667-7766
www.health.gov.sk.ca/communications

Executive Director, Kimberly Kratzig
Tel: 306-787-8433
Fax: 306-787-8310
kimberly.kratzig@gov.sk.ca
Program Services, Joan Petrie
Tel: 306-787-2743
Fax: 306-787-8310
joan.petrie@gov.sk.ca
Correspondence & Internal Communications, Karen Prokopetz
Tel: 306-787-2036
Fax: 306-787-8310
karen.prokopetz@gov.sk.ca
Regional Services, Lorri Thacyk
Tel: 306-787-7296
Fax: 306-787-8310
lorri.thacyk@gov.sk.ca

Community Care Branch

Tel: 306-787-7239
Fax: 306-787-7095
www.health.gov.sk.ca/community-care

Executive Director, Roger Carriere
Tel: 306-787-6092
Fax: 306-787-7095
rcarriere@health.gov.sk.ca
Director, Program Support Unit A, Linda Restau
Tel: 306-787-7901
Fax: 306-787-7095
lrestau@health.gov.sk.ca
Director, Program Support Unit B, Heather Murray
Tel: 306-787-3236
Fax: 306-787-7095
Director, Mental Health & Addictions, Kathy Willerth
Tel: 306-787-5020
Fax: 306-787-7095
kwillerth@health.gov.sk.ca

Drug Plan & Extended Benefits Branch

Tel: 306-787-3317
Fax: 306-787-8679
www.health.gov.sk.ca/drugplan-extendedbenefits

Executive Director, Kevin Wilson
Tel: 306-787-3301
Fax: 306-787-8679
kwilson@health.gov.sk.ca
Director, Business Unit, Morley Machin
Tel: 306-787-3031
mmachin@health.gov.sk.ca
Director, Pharmaceutical Services, Tracey Smith
Tel: 306-787-3305
Fax: 306-787-8679
tsmith@health.gov.sk.ca
Acting Director, Operations Unit, Susan Yee
Tel: 306-787-9268
Fax: 306-787-8679
syee@health.gov.sk.ca

Financial Services Branch

Tel: 306-787-4923
Fax: 306-787-0218
www.health.gov.sk.ca/financial-services

Executive Director, Ted Warawa
Tel: 306-787-5006
Fax: 306-787-0218
ted.warawa@gov.sk.ca
Director, Financial Management & Internal Audit, Garth Herbert
Tel: 306-787-7738
Fax: 306-787-0218
gherbert@health.gov.sk.ca
Director, Regional Financial Services Unit, Jeannette Lowe
Tel: 306-787-0050
Fax: 306-787-0218
jlowe@health.gov.sk.ca
Director, Budget & Financial Planning, Brenda Russell
Tel: 306-787-5025
Fax: 306-787-0218
brussell@health.gov.sk.ca

Health Registration

Fax: 306-787-8951
Toll-Free: 800-667-7551
www.health.gov.sk.ca/health-registration

Vital Statistics Unit is responsible for the issuance of provincial birth, marriage & death certificates. Fee for each certificate is $20.00.

Director, Pat Cambridge
Tel: 306-787-3249
Fax: 306-787-8951
pcambridge@health.gov.sk.ca
#100, 1942 Hamilton St.
Regina, SK S4P 4W2 Canada

Medical Services Branch

Tel: 306-787-3475
Fax: 306-787-3761
Toll-Free: 800-667-7523
www.health.gov.sk.ca/medical-services

Executive Director, Shaylene Salazar
Tel: 306-787-3423
Fax: 306-787-3761
ssalazar@health.gov.sk.ca
Director, Professional Review & Quality Management, Perry Behl
Tel: 306-787-3442
Fax: 306-787-3761
pbehl@health.gov.sk.ca
Director, Operations & Client Services, Lori St. Dennis
Tel: 306-787-3425
Fax: 306-787-3761
lstdennis@health.gov.sk.ca
Director, Management Services/Policy & Regional Programs, June Schultz
Tel: 306-798-2655
Fax: 306-787-3761
jschultz@health.gov.sk.ca

Primary Health Services Branch

Fax: 306-787-0890
www.health.gov.sk.ca/primary-health-services

Executive Director, Donna Magnusson
Tel: 306-787-0875
Fax: 306-787-0890
dmagnusson@health.gov.sk.ca
Director, Margaret Baker
Tel: 306-787-0670
Fax: 306-787-8697
mbaker@health.gov.sk.ca
Director, Fay Schuster
Tel: 306-787-5058
Fax: 306-787-0890
fschuster@health.gov.sk.ca
Director, Operations, Primary Health Care Redesign, Andrea Wagner
Tel: 306-798-7491
Fax: 306-787-0890
awagner1@health.gov.sk.ca

Population Health Branch

Tel: 306-787-8847
Fax: 306-787-3237
www.health.gov.sk.ca/population-health

Chief Medical Health Officer, Dr. Moira McKinnon
Tel: 306-787-4722
Fax: 306-787-3237
Deputy Chief Medical Health Officer, Dr. Saqib Shabab
Tel: 306-787-4722
Fax: 306-787-3237
Chief Population Health Epidemiologist, Dr. Valerie Mann
Tel: 306-787-4086
Fax: 306-787-3823
vmann@health.gov.sk.ca
Executive Director, Rick Trimp
Tel: 306-787-8847
Fax: 306-787-3237
rtrimp@health.gov.sk.ca
Director, Health Promotion, Tami Denomie
Tel: 306-787-7110
Fax: 306-787-3823
tami.denomie@health.gov.sk.ca
Director, Epidemiology & Research, Winanne Downey
Tel: 306-787-7625
Fax: 306-787-3237
Director, Corporate Services, Paul Leech
Tel: 306-787-6544
Fax: 306-787-3237
pleech@health.gov.sk.ca
Director, Environmental Health, Tim Macaulay
Tel: 306-787-7128
Fax: 306-787-3237
tmacaulay@health.gov.sk.ca
Director, Disease Prevention, Jim Myres
Tel: 306-787-1580
Fax: 306-787-3823
jim.myres@health.gov.sk.ca

Risk & Relationship Management

Tel: 306-787-3143
Fax: 306-787-2974
www.health.gov.sk.ca/risk-and-relationship-management
Other Communication: Alternate Phone: 306-787-3150

Acting Executive Director, Jacqueline Messer-Lepage
Tel: 306-787-2137
Fax: 306-787-2974
jmesserlepage@health.gov.sk.ca
Director, Intergovernmental, First Nations & Métis Relations, Randy Passmore
Tel: 306-787-3155
Fax: 306-787-4534
randy.passmore@health.gov.sk.ca
Director, Regional Planning & Support, Lori Hutchison Hunter
Tel: 306-787-7954
Fax: 306-787-2974
lhutchison@health.gov.sk.ca
Director, Operations, Health & Emergency Management, Garnet Matchett
Tel: 306-787-3179
Fax: 306-798-3093
gmatchett@health.gov.sk.ca
Director, Governance & Policy, David Smith
Tel: 306-787-0297
Fax: 306-787-2974
David.Smith@gov.sk.ca; dsmith@health.gov.sk.ca
Other Communications: Alt Email: david.smith@saskatoonhealthregion.ca

Saskatchewan Disease Control Laboratory
5 Research Dr., Regina, SK S4S 0A4

Tel: 306-787-3131
Fax: 306-787-1525
www.health.gov.sk.ca/lab

Executive Director, Rick Trimp
Tel: 306-787-3129
Fax: 306-787-1525
rtrimp@health.gov.sk.ca
Medical Director, Dr. Greg Horsman
Tel: 306-787-8316
Fax: 306-787-1525
ghorsman@health.gov.sk.ca
Director, Environmental Services, Dr. Phillip Bailey
Tel: 306-787-3140
Fax: 306-787-1525
pbailey@health.gov.sk.ca
Director, Immunoserology & Virology, Niki Coffin
Tel: 306-798-4153
Fax: 306-787-1525
ncoffin@health.gov.sk.ca
Director, Screening & Reference Testing, Jeff Eichhorst
Tel: 306-787-3284
Fax: 306-798-0955
jeichhorst@health.gov.sk.ca
Director, Operations, Joyce Kirsch
Tel: 306-787-9404
Fax: 306-787-1525
joyce.kirsch@health.gov.sk.ca
Director, Bacteriology, Dr. Christine Turenne
Tel: 306-798-4154
Fax: 306-787-1525
cturenne@health.gov.sk.ca
Director, Administration, Debra Ulrich
Tel: 306-787-3033
Fax: 306-787-1525
dulrich@health.gov.sk.ca

Strategy & Innovation Branch

Tel: 306-787-0769
Fax: 306-787-2974
www.health.gov.sk.ca/strategic-planning-branch

Executive Director, Pauline M. Rousseau
Tel: 306-787-3951
Fax: 306-787-2974
Director, Health System Quality & Efficiency Management, Trish Livingstone
Tel: 306-787-3146
Fax: 306-787-2974
tlivingstone@health.gov.sk.ca
Director, Capital Asset Planning, Richard Moen
Tel: 306-787-3232
Fax: 306-787-2974
rmoen@health.gov.sk.ca

Director, Health System Planning, Kathleen Peterson
Tel: 306-787-3163
Fax: 306-787-2974
kpeterson@health.gov.sk.ca

Workforce Planning Branch
Tel: 306-787-3152
Fax: 306-798-0023
www.health.gov.sk.ca/workforce-planning

Executive Director, Ron Knaus
Tel: 306-787-6672
Fax: 306-798-0023
rknaus@health.gov.sk.ca

Chief Nursing Officer, Lynn Digney-Davis
Tel: 306-787-7195
Fax: 306-798-0023
ldigneydavis@health.gov.sk.ca

Director, Planning & Provincial Recruitment Projects, Andy Churko
Tel: 306-787-3072
Fax: 306-798-0023
achurko@health.gov.sk.ca

Director, Programs & Resource Development, Sandra Cripps
Tel: 306-787-5693
Fax: 306-798-0023
scripps@health.gov.sk.ca

Saskatchewan Highways & Infrastructure (HI)

Victoria Tower, 1855 Victoria Ave., Regina, SK S4P 3T2
Tel: 306-787-4800
communications@highways.gov.sk.ca
www.highways.gov.sk.ca
Other Communication: Road Information Hotline: 306-933-8333

The Ministry of Highways & Infrastructure is concerned with transportation in Saskatchewan as it relates to the social & economic development of the province. Business areas include ministry services & standards information, plning & policy development, & regional services.

The following are some programs & services offered through the Ministry: Urban Highway Connector Program; Adopt a Highway; Assistance to Motorists; Preservation Program; & Community Airport Partnership Program. In May 2012, Don McMorris became the new Minister of Highways & Infrastructure. He is also the Minister Responsible for SaskBuilds. SaskBuilds is a new government agency that plans, designs, funds, & implements infrastructure projects for the government as well as third-party projects that are government funded, such as hospitals & schools.

Acts Administered:
Dangerous Goods Transportation Act
Engineering & Geoscience Professions Act
Highway Traffic Act
Highways & Transportation Act, 1997
Railway Act
Sand & Gravel Act

Minister, Highways & Infrastructure; Minister Responsible, Saskatchewan Telecommunications; Minister Responsible, Saskatchewan Transportation Company; Minister Responsible, Information Services Corporation; MinisterResponsible, Saskatchewan Gaming Corp., Hon. Don McMorris
Tel: 306-787-6447
Fax: 306-787-1736
minister.hi@gov.sk.ca
Social Media: twitter.com/dmcmorrissp, www.facebook.com/DonMcMorrisSP
Minister's Office, Legislative Building
#302, 2405 Legislative Dr.
Regina, SK S4S 0B3

Deputy Minister, Highways & Infrastructure, Rob Penny
Tel: 306-787-4949
Fax: 306-787-9777
Rob.Penny@gov.sk.ca

Associated Agencies, Boards & Commissions:

• **Global Transportation Hub Authority**
#350, 1777 Victoria Ave.
Regina, SK S4P 4K5
Tel: 306-787-4842
Fax: 306-798-4600
www.gtha.ca
The Hub Authority was created in June 2009, & is the primary agency in charge of planning, developing, constructing & promoting the Global Transportation Hub - a transportation & logistics centre encompassing 2,000 acres of serviced land.

• **Saskatchewan Grain Car Corporation**
#1210, 1855 Victoria Ave.
Regina, SK S4P 3T2
Tel: 306-787-1137
Fax: 306-798-0931
www.sgcc.gov.sk.ca
The SGCC works with farmers, community groups, shippers, & railroads to maximize the efficiency and effectiveness of transporting grain across the province.

• **Saskatchewan Highway Traffic Board**
1550 Saskatchewan Dr.
Regina, SK S4P 0E4
Tel: 306-775-6674
contactus@highwaytrafficboard.sk.ca
www.highwaytrafficboard.sk.ca
The Highway Traffic Board's mandate is to establish & to administer legislation relating to the safe & legal operations of private vehicles, the bus-truck industry & the short line rail industry in Saskatchewan, where specifically legislated to do so.

Ministry Services & Standards Division
Victoria Tower, #1200, 1855 Victoria Ave., Regina, SK S4P 3T2
Tel: 306-787-4904

Responsibilities of the Ministry Services & Standards Division include budgeting, financial reporting, information management, technical standards, enterprise risk management, performance management, & administrative services related to land management.

Assistant Deputy Minister, Ministry Services & Standards, Jennifer Ehrmantraut
Tel: 306-787-4859
Fax: 306-787-9777
Jennifer.Ehrmantraut@gov.sk.ca

Executive Director, Technical Standards, Dave Stearns
Tel: 306-787-2295
Fax: 306-787-4836

Director, Earth Sciences & Research, Magdy Beshara
Tel: 306-787-4922
Fax: 306-787-4582
Magdy.Beshara@gov.sk.ca

Director, Financial Services, Gary Diebel
Tel: 306-787-4794
Fax: 306-787-8700
Gary.Diebel@gov.sk.ca

Director, Corporate Support, Wayne Gienow
Tel: 306-787-1355
Fax: 306-787-8700
wayne.gienow@gov.sk.ca

Director, Design & Traffic Engineering, Sukhy Kent
Tel: 306-787-4945
Fax: 306-787-4836
Sukhy.Kent@gov.sk.ca

Director, Preservation & Operations Standards, Frass Len
Tel: 306-933-5226
Fax: 306-933-7090

Director, Construction Standards, Bill Pacholka
Tel: 306-787-4917
Fax: 306-787-4836
Bill.Pacholka@gov.sk.ca

Director, Bridge Standards, Howard Yea
Tel: 306-787-4830
Fax: 306-787-4836
Howard.Yea@gov.sk.ca

Manager, Forecasting, Judy A. Adams
Tel: 306-787-4796
Fax: 306-787-8700
Judy.Adams@gov.sk.ca

Manager, Property Rights & Registration, Neil Daku
Tel: 306-787-4884
Fax: 306-787-4100
Neil.Daku@gov.sk.ca

Manager, IT Systems, Robert Gee
Tel: 306-787-4824
Fax: 306-787-8700
Robert.Gee@gov.sk.ca

Manager, TLE & Property Preservation, Peter Gennutt
Tel: 306-787-4045
Fax: 306-787-4100
Peter.Gennutt@gov.sk.ca

Planning & Policy Division
Tel: 306-787-4904

Assistant Deputy Minister, George Stamatinos
Tel: 306-787-5028
Fax: 306-787-9777
george.stamatinos@gov.sk.ca

Executive Director, Systems Planning & Management, Miranda Carlberg
Tel: 306-787-0825
Fax: 306-787-3963
Miranda.Carlberg@gov.sk.ca

Executive Director, Strategic Planning & Policy, Harold Hugg
Tel: 306-787-5311
Fax: 306-787-3963
Harold.Hugg@gov.sk.ca

Acting Director, Legislation & Administration, Miranda Carlberg
Tel: 306-964-1210
Fax: 306-933-5188
Miranda.Carlberg@gov.sk.ca

Director, Strategic Municipal Policy, Wayne Gienow
Tel: 306-787-1355
Fax: 306-787-3963
wayne.gienow@gov.sk.ca

Director, Provincial Transportation Infrastructure, Andrew Liu
Tel: 306-787-4784
Fax: 306-787-3963
Andrew.Liu@gov.sk.ca

Director, Strategic Business Planning, Cathy Lynn Borbely
Tel: 306-787-4787
Fax: 306-787-3963
CathyLynn.Borbely@gov.sk.ca

Director, Multimodal, Trade & Logistics, Michael Makowsky
Tel: 306-787-7664
Fax: 306-787-3963
Michael.Makowsky@gov.sk.ca

Acting Director, Rail Services, Ed Zsombor
Tel: 306-787-5847
Fax: 306-787-3963
Ed.Zsombor@gov.sk.ca

Saskatchewan Human Rights Commission (SHRC)

Saskatoon Office, Sturdy Stone Bdg., #816, 122 - 3 Ave. North, 8th Fl., Saskatoon, SK S7K 2H6
Tel: 306-933-5952
Fax: 306-933-7863
Toll-Free: 800-667-9249
shrc@gov.sk.ca
www.shrc.gov.sk.ca
TTY: 306-373-2119
Secondary Address: #301, 1942 Hamilton St.
Regina, SK S4P 2C5
Fax: 306-787-0454
shrc@shrc.gov.sk.ca
Other Communication: Toll Free Phone: 1-800-667-8577; Telewriter: 306-787-8550

The Saskatchewan Human Rights Commission promotes & protects individual dignity & equal rights by discouraging & eliminating discrimination. The Commission's guide is The Saskatchewan Human Rights Code. The following are the principle functions of the Commission: approving equity programs; educating people & promoting human rights laws in Saskatchewan; & investigating complaints of discrimination.

Minister Responsible, Hon. Gordon Wyant, Q.C.
Tel: 306-787-5353
Fax: 306-787-1232
minister.ju@gov.sk.ca

Chief Commissioner, Hon. David M. Arnot
Tel: 306-933-7796
Fax: 306-933-7863
David.Arnot@gov.sk.ca

Manager, Finance & Administration, Sue Lake
Tel: 306-787-2704
Fax: 306-787-0454
Sue.Lake@gov.sk.ca

Manager, Operations, Rebecca McLellan
Tel: 306-787-2394
Fax: 306-787-0454
Rebecca.McLellan@gov.sk.ca

Manager, Human Resources, Brenda Rorke
Tel: 306-933-8285
Fax: 306-933-7863
brenda.rorke@gov.sk.ca

Information & Privacy Commissioner of Saskatchewan

#503, 1801 Hamilton St., Regina, SK S4P 4B4
Tel: 306-787-8350
Fax: 306-798-1603
Toll-Free: 877-748-2298
webmaster@oipc.sk.ca
www.oipc.sk.ca

Commissioner, R. Gary Dickson, Q.C.
Tel: 306-787-8350
Fax: 306-798-1603
gdickson@oipc.sk.ca

Information Services Corporation of Saskatchewan (ISC)

#300, 10 Research Dr., Regina, SK S4S 7J7
Tel: 306-798-0641
Toll-Free: 866-275-4721
www.isc.ca

The ISC is a provincial Crown corporation responsible for the administration of land titles, vital statistics, survey, personal property & corporate registeries, & related geographic information.

Minister, Highways & Infrastructure; Minister Responsible, Saskatchewan Telecommunications; Minister Responsible, Saskatchewan Transportation Company; Minister Responsible, Information Services Corporation; MinisterResponsible, Saskatchewan Gaming Corp., Hon. Don McMorris
Tel: 306-787-6447
Fax: 306-787-1736
minister.hi@gov.sk.ca
Social Media: twitter.com/dmcmorrissp, www.facebook.com/DonMcMorrisSP
Legislative Building
#302, 2405 Legislative Dr.
Regina, SK S4S0B3

President/Chief Executive Officer, Jeff Stusek
Tel: 306-787-1364
Fax: 306-787-9220
jeff.stusek@isc.ca

Vice-President, Operations, Ken Budzak
Tel: 306-787-9631
Fax: 306-787-9220
ken.budzak@isc.ca

Vice-President, Marketing & Business Development, Bryan Burnett
Tel: 306-798-8755
Fax: 306-787-9220
bryan.burnett@isc.ca

Vice-President, Finance & Administration, Charlene Gavel
Tel: 306-798-8760
Fax: 306-787-9220
charlene.gavel@isc.ca

Vice-President & General Counsel, Corporate Affairs, Kathy Hillman-Weir
Tel: 306-787-7299
Fax: 306-798-4125
kathy.hillman-weir@isc.ca

Saskatchewan Justice & Attorney General (JU)

1874 Scarth St., Regina, SK S4P 4B3
Tel: 306-787-8971
communications@justice.gov.sk.ca
www.justice.gov.sk.ca

Acts Administered:
Aboriginal Courtworkers Commission Act
Absconding Debtors Act
Administration of Estates Act
Adult Guardianship & Co-decision-making Act
Age of Majority Act
Agreements of Sale Cancellation Act
Alberta-Saskatchewan Boundary Act, 1939
Arbitration Act, 1992
Assignment of Wages Act
Attachments of Debts Act
Auctioneers Act
Builders' Lien Act
Business Corporations Act
Business Names Registration Act
Canada-United Kingdom Judgements Enforcement Act
Canadian Institute of Management (Saskatchewan Division) Act
Cemeteries Act, 1999
Change of Name Act, 1995
Charitable Fundraising Businesses Act
Children's Law Act, 1997
Choses in Action Act
Class Actions Act
Closing-out Sales Act
Co-operatives Act, 1996
Collection Agents Act
Commercial Liens Act
Commissioners for Oaths Act
Companies Act
Companies Winding Up Act
Condominium Property Act, 1993
Constituency Boundaries Act, 1993
Constitutional Questions Act
Consumer & Commercial Affairs Act
Consumer Protection Act
Contributory Negligence Act
Coroners Act, 1999
Cost of Credit Disclosure Act 2002
Court Jurisdiction & Proceedings Transfer Act
Court Officials Act, 1984
Court Reporting Act
Court Security Act
Court of Appeal Act, 2000
Credit Reporting Act
Credit Union Act, 1985 (Mainly Repealed)
Credit Union Act, 1998
Creditors' Relief Act
Criminal Enterprise Suppression Act
Crown Employment Contracts Act
Crown Suits (Costs) Act
Department of Justice Act
Dependants' Relief Act, 1996
Direct Sellers Act
Distress Act
Electronic Information & Documents Act, 2000
Enforcement of Canadian Judgements Conventions Act (NYP)
Enforcement of Foreign Arbitral Awards Act, 1996
Enforcement of Foreign Judgements Act
Enforcement of Judgements Act, 2002
Enforcement of Maintenance Orders Act, 1997
Equality of Status of Married Persons Act
Escheats Act
Evidence Act
Executions Act
Exemptions Act
Expropriation Act
Expropriation Procedure Act
Factors Act
Family Maintenance Act, 1997
Family Property Act
Fatal Accidents Act
Federal Courts Act
Film & Video Classification Act
Fraudulent Preferences Act
Freedom of Information & Protection of Privacy Act
Frustrated Contracts Act
Funeral & Cremation Services Act
Guarantee Companies Securities Act
Gunshot & Stab Wounds Mandatory Reporting Act
Health Care Directives & Substitute Health Care Decision Makers Act
Home Owners' Protection Act
Homesteads Act, 1989
Hotel Keepers Act
Improvements Under Mistake of Title Act
Income Trust Liability Act
Interjurisdictional Support Orders Act
International Child Abduction Act, 1996
International Commercial Arbitration Act
International Interests in Mobile Aircraft Equipment Act (NYP)
International Protection of Adults Act (NYP)
International Sale of Goods Act
Interpretation Act, 1995
Interprovincial Subpoena Act
Intestate Succession Act, 1996
Judges' Orders Enforcement Act
Judgments Extension Act
Jury Act, 1998
Justice of the Peace Act, 1988
Land Contracts (Actions) Act
Land Information Services Facilitation Act
Land Surveyors & Professional Surveyors Act
Land Surveys Act, 2000
Land Titles Act, 2000
Landlord & Tenant Act
Language Act
Law Reform Commission Act
Legal Aid Act
Legal Profession Act, 1990
Libel & Slander Act
Limitation of Civil Rights Act
Limitations Act
Local Authority Freedom of Information & Protection of Privacy Act
Lord's Day (Saskatchewan) Act
Mandatory Testing & Disclosure (Bodily Substances) Act
Marriage Act, 1995
Marriage Settlement Act
Members' Conflict of Interest Act
Mentally Disordered Persons Act
Missing Persons & Presumption of Death Act
Mortgage Brokerages & Mortgage Administrators Act
Motor Dealers Act
Municipal Hail Insurance Act
Names of Homes Act
New Generation Co-operatives Act
Non-Profit Corporations Amendment Act, 2005
Non-profit Corporations Act, 1995
Notaries Public Act
Ombudsman & Children's Advocate Act
Parents' Maintenance Act
Partnership Act
Pawned Property (Recording) Act
Payday Loans Act (NYP)
Penalties & Forfeitures Act
Pension Benefits Act, 1992
Personal Property Security Act, 1993
Powers of Attorney Act, 2002
Pre-judgement Interest Act
Privacy Act
Proceedings Against the Crown Act
Professional Corporations Act
Provincial Court Act, 1998
Provincial Mediation Board Act
Public Guardian & Trustee Act
Public Inquiries Act
Public Utilities Easements Act
Queen's Bench Act, 1998
Queen's Counsel Act
Queen's Printer Act
Real Estate Act
Reciprocal Enforcement of Judgments Act, 1996
Recovery of Possession of Land Act
Referendum & Plebiscite Act
Registered Plan (Retirement Income) Exemption Act
Regulations Act, 1995
Religious Societies Land Act
Residential Tenancies Act
Revised Statutes Act, 1979
Sale of Goods Act
Sales on Consignment Act
Saskatchewan Financial Services Commission Act
Saskatchewan Human Rights Code
Saskatchewan Insurance Act
Securities Act, 1988
Securities Act, 1988
Seizure of Criminal Property Act
Settlement of International Investment Disputes Act
Slot Machine Act
Small Claims Act, 1997
Statutes & Regulations Revision Act
Summary Offences Procedure Act, 1990
Survival of Actions Act
Survivorship Act, 1993
Thresher Employees Act
Threshers' Lien Act
Ticket Sales Act
Trading Stamp Act
Traffic Safety Court of Saskatchewan Act, 1988
Trespass to Property Act
Trust & Loan Corporations Act, 1997
Trustee Act, 2009
Trusts Convention Implementation Act
Unconscionable Transactions Relief Act
Variation of Trusts Act
Victims of Crime Act, 1995
Victims of Domestic Violence Act
Vital Statistics Act, 2009
Vital Statistics Administration Transfer Act
Wills Act, 1996
Woodmen's Lien Act

Minister, Justice & Attorney General; Deputy Government House Leader, Hon. Gordon Wyant, Q.C.
Tel: 306-787-5353
Fax: 306-787-1232
minister.ju@gov.sk.ca
Social Media: twitter.com/GordWyant
Office of the Minister of Justice & Attorney General, Legislative Buiding
#355,2405 Legislative Dr.
Regina, SK S4S 0B3

Deputy Minister, Justice; Deputy Attorney General, Gerald Tegart
Tel: 306-787-5352
Fax: 306-787-3874
gerald.tegart@gov.sk.ca

Executive Director, Civil Law Division, Rick Hischebett
Tel: 306-787-6642
Fax: 306-787-0581
Rick.Hischebett@gov.sk.ca
Other Communications: URL: www.justice.gov.sk.ca/civillaw

Executive Director, Policy, Planning & Evaluation, Betty Ann Pottruff, Q.C.
Tel: 306-787-8954
Fax: 306-787-9008
bettyann.pottruff@gov.sk.ca

Executive Director, Corporate Services, Dave Tulloch
Tel: 306-787-5472
Fax: 306-787-5830
dave.tulloch@gov.sk.ca; dave.tulloch3@gov.sk.ca

Director, Financial & Resource Planning, Mindy Gudmundson
Tel: 306-787-5580
Fax: 306-787-5830
mindy.gudmundson@gov.sk.ca

Director, Assurance & Financial Reporting, Brad Gurash
Tel: 306-798-5112
Fax: 306-787-5830
brad.gurash2@gov.sk.ca

Director, Communications, Linsay Rabyj
Tel: 306-787-0775
Fax: 306-787-3874
Linsay.Rabyj@gov.sk.ca

Associated Agencies, Boards & Commissions:
• **Automobile Injury Appeal Commission**
#504, 2400 College Ave.
Regina, SK S4P 1C8
Tel: 306-798-5545
Fax: 306-798-5540
Toll-free: 866-798-5544
aiac@gov.sk.ca
www.autoinjuryappeal.sk.ca
• **Law Reform Commission of Saskatchewan**
c/o University of Saskatchewan, College of Law
#209, 15 Campus Drive
Saskatoon, SK S7N 5A6
Tel: 306-966-1625
Fax: 306-966-5900
director.research@sasklawreform.com
www.lawreformcommission.sk.ca
The Law Reform Commission of Saskatchewan was established by An Act to Establish a Law Reform Commission, proclaimed in force in November, 1973, and began functioning in February of 1974.
• **Office of Residential Tenancies (ORT)**
#120, 2151 Scarth St.
Regina, SK S4P 2H8
Tel: 306-787-2699
Fax: 306-787-5574
Toll-free: 888-215-2222
Other Communication: Toll-Free Fax: 1-888-867-7776
• **Provincial Mediation Board**
#120, 2151 Scarth St.
Regina, SK S4P 2H8
Tel: 306-787-5387
Fax: 306-787-5574
Toll-free: 877-787-5408
www.justice.gov.sk.ca/PMB
Other Communication: Toll-Free Fax: 1-888-867-7776
The Provincial Mediation Board provides budgeting advice and counselling to individuals with personal debt problems. It may be able to arrange repayment plans with creditors. The Board also deals with problems of debtors related to property tax arrears, eviction of commercial tenants and residential mortgage foreclosures.
• **Public & Private Rights Board**
#323, 3085 Albert St.
Regina, SK S4S 0B1
Tel: 306-787-4071
Fax: 306-787-0088
www.justice.gov.sk.ca/publicandprivaterightsboard
• **Saskatchewan Film & Video Classification Board**
#500, 1919 Saskatchewan Dr.
Regina, SK S4P 4H2
Tel: 306-787-5550
Fax: 306-787-9779
Toll-free: 888-374-4636
www.justice.gov.sk.ca/filmandvideoclassification
On October 1, 1997, an agreement between the province of British Columbia and Saskatchewan came into effect, under which the British Columbia Film Classification Office will classify all new theatrical releases and adult videos on behalf of the Saskatchewan Film and Video Classification Board.
• **Saskatchewan Financial Services Commission (SFSC)**
#601, 1919 Saskatchewan Dr.
Regina, SK S4P 4H2
Tel: 306-787-5645
Fax: 306-787-5899
www.sfsc.gov.sk.ca
The Saskatchewan Financial Services Commission (SFSC) protects consumer and public interests and supports economic well-being through responsive financial marketplace regulation. The SFSC enhances consumer protection through licensing, registration, audit, complaint handling and enforcement activities pursuant to various provincial statutes.
• **Saskatchewan Human Rights Commission (SHRC)**
#301, 1942 Hamilton St.
Regina, SK S4P 2C5
Tel: 306-787-2530
Fax: 306-787-0454
Toll-free: 800-667-8577
TTY: 306-787-8550
shrc@gov.sk.ca
www.shrc.gov.sk.ca
• **Saskatchewan Legal Aid Commission**
#502, 201 - 21 St. East
Saskatoon, SK S7K 0B8
Tel: 306-933-5300
Fax: 306-933-6764
Toll-free: 800-667-3764
www.legalaid.sk.ca
The Saskatchewan Legal Aid Commission provides legal services to persons and organizations for criminal and civil matters where those persons and organizations are financially unable to secure these services from their own resources. The organization has been in existence since 1974.
• **Saskatchewan Public Complaints Commission**
#300, 1919 Saskatchewan Dr.
Regina, SK S4P 4H2
Tel: 306-787-6519
Fax: 306-787-6528
Toll-free: 866-256-6194
www.publiccomplaintscommission.ca
The Public Complaints Commission (PCC) is a five-person, non-police body appointed by the government. It is responsible for ensuring that both the public and police receive a fair and thorough investigation of a complaint against the police or an investigation of a possible criminal offence by a police officer.
• **Saskatchewan Review Board**
#200, 520 Spadina Cres.
Saskatoon, SK S7K 2P3
Tel: 306-933-5156
Fax: 306-933-5725
lfulawka@sasktel.net
www.justice.gov.sk.ca/saskatchewanreviewboard
The Saskatchewan Review Board was established under the Criminal Code of Canada to review decisions & orders regarding an accused person, where a verdict of not criminally responsible by reason of mental disorder or unfit to stand trial on account of mental disorder has been made.

Community Justice Division
Tel: 306-787-5096
Fax: 306-787-0078
www.justice.gov.sk.ca/communityservicesdivision
Executive Director & Executive Director, Community Services, Jan Turner
Tel: 306-787-5112
Fax: 306-787-0078
jan.turner@gov.sk.ca; jan.turner@saskatoonhealthregion.ca
Executive Director, Aboriginal Courtworker Program, Chris LaFontaine
Tel: 306-787-6470
Fax: 306-787-0078
chris.lafontaine@gov.sk.ca
Chief Coroner, R. Kent Stewart
Tel: 306-787-5541
Fax: 306-787-5503
kent.stewart@gov.sk.ca; ocoroner@gov.sk.ca
Other Communications: URL: www.justice.gov.sk.ca/officeofthechiefcoroner
Director, Interpersonal Violence & Abuse Unit, Linda Selin
Tel: 306-787-8657
Fax: 306-787-0078
Linda.Selin@gov.sk.ca
Director, Victims Services, Pat Thiele
Tel: 306-787-6707
Fax: 306-787-0081
patrick.thiele@gov.sk.ca
Assistant Director, Aboriginal & Northern Justice Initiations Branch, Rhonda Hueser
Tel: 306-953-2352
Fax: 306-953-2353
Rhonda.Hueser@gov.sk.ca

Courts & Civil Justice Division
Tel: 306-787-5359
Fax: 306-787-8737
Assistant Deputy Minister, Ken Acton
Tel: 306-787-0991
Fax: 306-787-8737
ken.acton@gov.sk.ca
Executive Legal Officer & Registrar, Court of Appeal, Melanie Baldwin
Tel: 306-787-5382
Fax: 306-787-5815
lschwann@sasklawcourts.ca
Executive Director, Court Services, Linda Bogard
Tel: 306-787-5680
Fax: 306-787-8737
linda.bogard@gov.sk.ca
Director, Dispute Resolution Office, Glen Gardner
Tel: 306-787-5749
Fax: 306-787-0088
glen.gardner@gov.sk.ca
Director, Family Justice Services/Maintenance Enforcement Office, Lionel McNabb
Tel: 306-787-1650
Fax: 306-787-1420
lionel.mcnabb@gov.sk.ca

Public Law Division
Tel: 306-787-8389
Executive Director, Susan Amrud, Q.C.
Tel: 306-787-8990
susan.amrud@gov.sk.ca
Chief Legislative Crown Counsel, Legislative Drafting, Ian Brown, Q.C.
Tel: 306-787-9346
Fax: 306-787-9111
ian.brown@gov.sk.ca
Director, Aboriginal Law, Mitch McAdam
Tel: 306-787-7846
Fax: 306-787-9111
Mitch.McAdam@gov.sk.ca
Director, Constitutional Law Branch, Graeme G. Mitchell, Q.C.
Tel: 306-787-8385
Fax: 306-787-9111
graeme.mitchell@gov.sk.ca
Manager, Queen's Printer, Marilyn Lustig-McEwen
Tel: 306-787-9345
Toll-free: 800-226-7302
Fax: 306-798-0835
marilyn.lustig-mcewen@gov.sk.ca
Other Communications: URL: www.qp.gov.sk.ca

Public Prosecutions Division
Tel: 306-787-5490
Fax: 306-787-8878
www.justice.gov.sk.ca/publicprosecutionsdivision
Executive Director, Daryl Rayner, Q.C.
Tel: 306-787-5490
Fax: 306-787-8878
Director, Financial & Information Services, Shari Parisian
Tel: 306-787-8943
Fax: 306-787-8878
Director, Appeals, Dean Sinclair
Tel: 306-787-5490
Fax: 306-787-8878

Regulatory Services Division
Tel: 306-787-8995
Fax: 306-787-5830
Assistant Deputy Minister, Rod Cook
Tel: 306-787-7869
Fax: 306-787-5830
Rod.Crook@gov.sk.ca
Public Guardian & Trustee, Ronald J. Kruzeniski, Q.C.
Tel: 306-787-5427
Fax: 306-787-5065
ron.kruzeniski@gov.sk.ca
Director, Information Management Branch, Cathy Drader
Tel: 306-787-9512
Fax: 306-787-6979
Cathy.Drader@gov.sk.ca
Director, Consumer Protection Branch, Eric Greene
Tel: 306-787-2952
Fax: 306-787-9779
Eric.Greene@gov.sk.ca
Other Communications: Alternate Phone: 306-787-8607
Executive Director, Access & Privacy Branch, Duane Mombourquette
Tel: 306-787-6428
Fax: 306-798-4064
Duane.Mombourquette@gov.sk.ca

Saskatchewan Labour Relations & Workplace Safety (LRWS)

#300, 1870 Albert St., Regina, SK S4P 4W1
Tel: 306-787-7404
webmaster@lab.gov.sk.ca
www.lrws.gov.sk.ca
The Ministry is responsible for labour standards, labour support services, labour relations, mediation, occupational health & safety, & workers' advocacy.
Acts Administered:
Building Trades Protection Act
Construction Industry Labour Relations Act, 1992
Employment Agencies Act
Labour Standards Act
Mines Regulation
Occupational Health & Safety Act, 1993
Occupational Health & Safety Regulations, 1996
Public Interest Discolsure Act
Public Service Essential Service Act
Radiation Health & Safety Act, 1985
Radiation Health & Safety Regulations
Trade Union Act
Worker's Compensation Act
Worker's Compensation Act Exclusion Regulations
Worker's Compensation General Regulations, 1985

Minister, Advanced Education; Minister, Labour

Relations & Workplace Safety; Minister Responsible, Saskatchewan Workers' Compensation Board, Hon. Don Morgan, Q.C.
Tel: 306-787-0613
Fax: 306-787-6946
minister.ae@gov.sk.ca
Social Media:
www.facebook.com/pages/Don-Morgan/48835718931?sk=info
Office of theMinister of Advanced Education / Labour Relation & Wokoplace Safety, Legislative Bldg.
#361, 2405 Legislative Dr.
Regina, SK S4S 0B3

Deputy Minister, Labour Relations & Workplace Safety, Mike Carr
Tel: 306-787-7424
Fax: 306-798-5190
Mike.Carr@gov.sk.ca

Executive Director, Corporate Services (Shared Services), Karen Allen
Tel: 306-787-5654
Fax: 306-787-7392
karen.allen@gov.sk.ca

Executive Director, Central Services, Laurier Donais
Tel: 306-787-8078
Fax: 306-798-5190
laurier.donais@gov.sk.ca

Executive Director, Labour Relations & Mediation, Doug Forseth
Tel: 306-787-9106
Fax: 306-787-1064
doug.forseth@gov.sk.ca

Acting Executive Director, Marketing & Communications (Shared Services), Rikki Bote
Tel: 306-787-4156
Fax: 306-798-5021
rikki.bote@gov.sk.ca

Associated Agencies, Boards & Commissions:

• **Labour Relations Board**
#1600, 1920 Broad St.
Regina, SK S4P 3V2
Tel: 306-787-2406
Fax: 306-787-2664
www.sasklabourrelationsboard.com
An independent, quasi-judicial tribunal charged with the responsibility of adjudicating disputes that arise under The Trade Union Act, The Construction Industry Labour Relations Act, 1992 & The Health Labour Relations Reorganization Act

• **Minimum Wage Board**
#400, 1870 Albert St.
Regina, SK S4P 4W1
www.aeei.gov.sk.ca/minimum-wage-board-review-reporting
Makes recommendations respecting minimum employment standards including: the minimum wage, minimum age, maximum work periods, maximum rates for room & board & minimum rest periods.

• **Office of the Worker's Advocate**
#300, 1870 Albert St.
Regina, SK S4P 4W1
Tel: 306-787-2456
Fax: 306-787-0249
Toll-free: 877-787-2456
www.lrws.gov.sk.ca/wao
The Office of the Worker's Advocate provides free assistance to workers who are experiencing difficulties with workers' compensation claims. The Office offers information about the following programs & services: wage loss, benefits, survivor's benefits, medical aid, rehabilitation, & retraining. Working with advocacy groups & unions, The Office of the Worker's Advocate strives to improve service to injured workers. Workers' Compensation Board (WCB) decisions about claims can be reviewed & appealed.

• **Saskatchewan Workers' Compensation Board**
#200, 1881 Scarth St.
Regina, SK S4P 4L1
Tel: 306-787-4370
Fax: 306-787-7582
Toll-free: 800-667-7590
TTY: 888-844-7773
internet_clientsvc@wcbsask.com
www.wcbsask.com
Other Communication: Injury Reports: 1-800-787-9288; Employer Inquiries: reainquiry@wcbsask.com; Health Care Provider Inquiries: internet_healthcare@wcbsask.com; Appeal Fax: 306-787-1116

Labour Standards
Tel: 306-787-2438
Fax: 306-787-4780
Toll-Free: 800-667-1783
www.lrws.gov.sk.ca/ls

Executive Director, Greg Tuer
Tel: 306-787-2432
Fax: 306-787-4780
greg.tuer@gov.sk.ca

Director, Compliance & Investigations (Saskatoon), Glen McRorie
Tel: 306-933-5087
Fax: 306-787-4780
glen.mcrorie@gov.sk.ca

Director, Legal & Education Services, Daniel Parrott
Tel: 306-787-9454
Fax: 306-787-4780
daniel.parrott@gov.sk.ca

Occupational Health & Safety Division
Tel: 306-787-4496
Fax: 306-787-2208
Toll-Free: 800-567-7233
www.lrws.gov.sk.ca/ohs

Executive Director, Glennis Bihun
Tel: 306-787-4481
Fax: 306-787-2208
glennis.bihun@gov.sk.ca

Chief Mines Inspector, Mines Safety, Neil Crocker
Tel: 306-933-5106
Fax: 306-933-7339
neil.crocker@gov.sk.ca

Director, Health Services, Rita Coshan
Tel: 306-787-4539
Fax: 306-787-2208
rita.coshan@gov.sk.ca

Director, Safety Services, Jennifer Fabian
Tel: 306-787-0486
Fax: 306-787-2208
jennifer.fabian@gov.sk.ca

Director, Radiation Safety, Wayne Tiefenbach
Tel: 306-787-4538
Fax: 306-787-2208
Wayne.Tiefenbach@gov.sk.ca

Saskatchewan Liquor & Gaming Authority (SLGA)

2500 Victoria Ave., PO Box 5054, Regina, SK S4P 3M3
Tel: 306-787-4213
inquiry@slga.gov.sk.ca
www.slga.gov.sk.ca

The Treasury Board Crown Corporation is responsible for the distribution, control, & regulation of liquor & most gaming across Saskatchewan.

Minister, Crown Investments; Minister Responsible, Saskatchewan Government Insurance; Minister Responsible, Saskatchewan Liquor & Gaming Authority, Hon. Donna Harpauer
Tel: 306-787-7339
Fax: 306-798-3140
minister.cc@gov.sk.ca
Social Media:
www.facebook.com/pages/Donna-Harpauer/60494388240
Legislative Building
#322, 2405 Legislative Dr.
Regina, SK S4S 0B3

President & Chief Executive Officer, Barry Lacey
Tel: 306-787-1737
Fax: 306-787-8439
blacey@slga.gov.sk.ca

Director, Human Resources Branch, Leeann Pillipow-Kautz
Tel: 306-798-8483
Fax: 306-787-7336

Ombudsman Saskatchewan

#150, 2401 Saskatchewan Dr., Regina, SK S4P 4H8
Tel: 306-787-6211
Fax: 306-787-9090
Toll-Free: 800-667-7180
ombreg@ombudsman.sk.ca
www.ombudsman.sk.ca
Other Communication: Saskatoon e-mail: ombsktn@ombudsman.sk.ca
Secondary Address: 315 - 25th St. East Saskatoon, SK S7K 0L4 Canada

The Ombudsman is an Officer of the Legislative Assembly with the authority to investigate complaints received from members of the public who believe the government administration has dealt with them unfairly. Government administration includes any department, branch, board, agency or commission responsible to the Crown & any public servant in Saskatchewan. The Ombudsman was established by the Ombudsman & Children's Advocate Act.

Ombudsman, Kevin Fenwick, Q.C.
Tel: 306-787-6211
Fax: 306-787-9090
ombreg@ombudsman.sk.ca

Deputy Ombudsman, Regina Office, Janet Mirwaldt
Tel: 306-787-6142
jmirwaldt@ombudsman.sk.ca

Deputy Ombudsman, Saskatoon Office, Joni Sereda
Tel: 306-933-8165
Fax: 306-933-8406
jsereda@ombudsman.sk.ca

Saskatchewan Opportunities Corporation (SOCO)

Innovation Place, #114, 14 Innovation Blvd., Saskatoon, SK S7N 2X8
Tel: 306-933-6295
Fax: 306-933-8215
saskatoon@innovationplace.com
www.innovationplace.com/corporate.php

The Opportunities Corporation aims to support Saskatchewan's technology sector through the development and operation of research parks.

Minister Responsible, Hon. Donna Harpauer
Tel: 306-787-0341
Fax: 306-787-6946
minister.aeei@gov.sk.ca

President/Chief Executive Officer, Doug Tastad
Tel: 306-933-6258
Fax: 306-933-8215
tastad@innovationplace.com

Chief Financial Officer & Vice-President, Finance & Administration, Charlene Callander
Tel: 306-787-8534
Fax: 306-787-8601
ccallander@innovationplace.com

Chief Operating Officer & Vice-President, Research Park Operations, Ken Loeppky
Tel: 306-787-5706
Fax: 306-787-8601
kloeppky@innovationplace.com

Vice-President, Corporate Relations, Austin Beggs
Tel: 306-933-7464
Fax: 306-933-8215
austin@innovationplace.com

Saskatchewan Parks, Culture, & Sport (PCS)

1919 Saskatchewan Dr., 4th Fl., Regina, SK S4P 4H2
Tel: 306-787-5729
Fax: 306-798-0033
Toll-Free: 800-205-7070
info@tpcs.gov.sk.ca
www.pcs.gov.sk.ca
Other Communication: Park Watch (Emergency & Security Issues), Toll-Free Phone: 1-800-667-1788

The Ministry is concerned with Saskatchewan's quality of life, tourism, & economic growth.
The following are some of the goals of the Ministry of Parks, Culture, & Sport: to enhance the province's parks by offering recreational activities & focussing upon natural resources that appeal to residents & visitors; to conserve heritage resources & ecosystems; to protect the province's history & culture; to promote Saskatchewan's cultural & artistic communities; & to encourage residents to be healthy & active through participation in sports & recreational events.
Some of the programs & services available through the Ministry include the Developers' Online Screening Tool, the provision of Archaeological/Palaeontological Permits, the maintenance of the Saskatchewan Register of Heritage Property, the operation of the Royal Saskatchewan Museum, competitive games information, the operation of the Canadian Sport Centre Saskatchewan, & the Active Families Benefit.
Ministry publications available through the provincial government's publication centre include the annual *Parks GuideA Physically Active Saskatchewan: A Strategy to get Saskatchewan People in Motion*& *Conserving Your Historic Places.*

Acts Administered:
Active Families Benefit Act
Arts Board Act, 1997
Arts Professions Act
Communications Network Corporations Act
Culture & Recreation Act, 1993
Doukhobors of Canada C.C.U.B. Trust Fund Act

Film Employment Tax Credit Act
Grasslands National Park Act
Heritage Property Act
Holocaust Memorial Day Act
Interprovincial Lotteries Act, 1984
Jean-Louis Légaré Act
Meewasin Valley Authority Act
Multiculturalism Act
Parks Act
Regional Parks Act, 1979
Royal Saskatchewan Museum Act
Saskatchewan Gaming Corporation Act - Part IV Community Initiatives Fund
Saskatchewan Heritage Foundation Act
Tourism Authority Act
Wakamow Valley Authority Act
Wanuskewin Heritage Park Act 1997
Wascana Centre Act
Western Development Museum Act

Minister, Parks, Culture, & Sport; Minister Responsible, Provincial Capital Commission, Hon. Kevin Doherty
Tel: 306-787-0354
Fax: 306-798-0264
minister.pcs@gov.sk.ca
Social Media:
www.facebook.com/KevinDohertyforReginaNorthEast, ca.linkedin.com/pub/kevin-doherty/21/125/6b1
Office of the Minister, Parks, Culture, & Sport, LegislativeBuilding
#38, 2405 Legislative Dr.
Regina, SK S4S 0B3

Deputy Minister, Parks, Culture, & Sport, Wynne Young
Tel: 306-787-5050
Fax: 306-798-0033
Wynne.Young@gov.sk.ca

Associate Deputy Minister, Parks, Culture, & Sport; Chief Executive Officer, Provincial Capital Commission, Lin Gallagher
Tel: 306-798-3905
Fax: 306-798-0033
Lin.Gallagher@gov.sk.ca

Manager, Executive Services, Wendy Searcy
Tel: 306-787-1062
Fax: 306-798-0033
Wendy.Searcy@gov.sk.ca

Associated Agencies, Boards & Commissions:
• Conexus Arts Centre
200A Lakeshore Dr.
Regina, SK S4S 7L3
Tel: 306-565-4500
Toll-free: 800-667-8497
cac.admin@conexusartscentre.ca
www.conexusartscentre.ca
Other Communication: Box Office, Phone: 306-525-9999
Formerly known as the Saskatchewan Centre of the Arts, the Conexus Arts Centrs is a performing arts & theatre complex. The Centre's mandate is to provide facilities, services, & programs to educate & entertain the people of Saskatchewan.
• Provincial Capital Commission (PCC)
4607 Dewdney Ave.
Regina, SK S4T 1B7
Tel: 306-787-9261
www.opcc.gov.sk.ca
The Provincial Capital Commission aims to provide education about the history of Saskatchewan. The Commission creates tourism & economic development opportunities, through the preservation & promotion of the province's heritage & culture.
The following Acts & Regulations guide the work of the Provincial Capital Commission:
Air, Army, Sea, & Navy League Cadets Recognition Day Act;
Archives Act, 2004;
Culture & Recreation Act, 1993;
Government House Foundation Regulations;
Heritage Property Act;
Historic Properties Foundations Act;
Provincial Capital Commission Regulations;
National Peacekeepers Recognition Day Act;
Recognition of John George Diefenbaker Day Act;
Recognition of Telemiracle Week Act;
Saskatchewan Centre of the Arts Act, 2000;
Saskatchewan Heritage Foundation Act;
Tartan Day Act;
Tommy Douglas Day Act;
Wascana Centre Act.

• Wascana Centre Authority
2900 Wascana Dr.
PO Box 7111
Regina, SK S4P 3S7
Tel: 306-522-3661
Fax: 306-565-2742
wca@wascana.ca
www.wascana.ca
The Wascana Centre is committed to the conservation of the environment, the enhancement of educational & research opportunities, the improvement of recreational facilities, & the advancement of cultural arts. The Centre's vision, mission, & mandate are guided by The Wascana Centre Act.
• Western Development Museum (WDM)
Curatorial Centre
2935 Melville St,
Saskatoon, SK S7J 5A6
Tel: 306-934-1400
Fax: 306-934-4467
Toll-free: 800-363-6345
info@wdm.ca; curatorial@wdm.ca
www.wdm.ca
Other Communication: Moose Jaw WDM, Phone: 306-693-5989; North Battleford WDM, Phone: 306-445-8033; Saskatoon WDM, Phone: 306-931-1910; Yorkton WDM, Phone: 306-783-8361
There are locations in Moose Jaw (50 Diefenbaker Dr., Moose Jaw, SK S6J 1L9), North Battleford (PO Box 183, Hwy. 16 & 40, North Battleford SK S9A 2Y1), Saskatoon (2610 Lorne Ave. South, Saskatoon, SK S7J 0S6), & Yorkton (PO Box 98, Hwy. 16 West, Yorkton, SK S3N 2V6).

Communications
1919 Saskatchewan Dr., 4th Fl., Regina, SK S4P 4H2
Tel: 306-787-0346
Fax: 306-798-0033
Other Communication: Inquiry Line: 306-787-5729; Marketing, Phone: 306-787-7828, Fax: 306-798-0033
Director, Communications, Jennifer Johnson
Tel: 306-787-0619
Fax: 306-798-0033
jennifer.johnson@gov.sk.ca
Manager, Communications, Linda Smith
Tel: 306-787-3506
Fax: 306-798-0033
Linda.Smith@gov.sk.ca
Executive Coordinator, Helen Petrovitch
Tel: 306-787-0346
Fax: 306-798-0033
Helen.Petrovitch@gov.sk.ca
Coordinator, Website, Steve Tompkins
Tel: 306-787-5164
Fax: 306-798-0033
steve.tompkins@gov.sk.ca

Operations Division
Tel: 306-798-0697
Fax: 306-798-0033
Associate Deputy Minister, Operations, Lin Gallagher
Tel: 306-798-3905
Fax: 306-798-3905
Lin.Gallagher@gov.sk.ca
Director, Heritage Conservation, Carlos Germann
Tel: 306-787-5772
Fax: 306-787-0069
Carlos.Germann@gov.sk.ca
Director, Corporate Services, Melinda Leibel
Tel: 306-787-5896
Fax: 306-787-0033
Melinda.Leibel@gov.sk.ca
Executive Director, Park Services Operations, Cindy MacDonald
Tel: 306-787-0731
Fax: 306-787-7000
Cindy.MacDonald@gov.sk.ca
Manager, Garth Pugh
Tel: 306-787-4188
Fax: 306-787-0069
Garth.Pugh@gov.sk.ca

Cultural Planning & Development
1919 Saskatchewan Dr., 2nd Fl., Regina, SK S4P 4H2
Tel: 306-787-5877
Fax: 306-798-3177
Other Communication: Policy Analysis, Phone: 306-787-6880, Fax: 306-798-3177
It is the goal of the Ministry to increase the social & economic benefits of culture. The Ministry is guided by the following plan in its decision-making related to cultural policy: *Pride of Saskatchewan: A Policy Where Culture, Community & Commerce Meet.*
The following programs & events are supported by the Ministry: artsVest Saskatchewan; Creative Industry Growth & Sustainability; Culture on the Go; Culture Days; & Prairie Scene.

Exeuctive Director, Cultural Planning & Development, Gerald Folk
Tel: 306-787-8527
Fax: 306-798-3177
gerry.folk@gov.sk.ca
Analyst, Culture & Heritage, Shannon Chernick
Tel: 306-787-1360
Fax: 306-798-3177
shannon.chernick@gov.sk.ca
Analyst, Policy, Grace Hrycyshen
Tel: 306-787-8580
Fax: 306-798-3177
grace.hrycyshen@gov.sk.ca
Director, Harold Bryant
Tel: 306-787-2813
Fax: 306-787-2820
Harold.Bryant@gov.sk.ca

Operations
1919 Saskatchewan Dr., 4th Fl., Regina, SK S4P 4H2
Tel: 306-798-0697
Fax: 306-787-0033
Other Communication: Heritage Conservation, Phone: 306-787-2817, Fax: 306-787-0069
Responsibilities of the Operations division include corporate services, heritage conservation, oversight of the Saskatchewan Heritage Foundation & the Royal Saskatchewan Museum, & park services.
Heritage conservation involves the protection of the province's heritage legacy, through inventories, research, & consultative services. Resources are available to help municipalities manage their historic places. One program is known as Main Street Saskatchewan, which works to revitalize historic downtown commercial districts.
The Saskatchewan Heritage Foundation was established by provincial legislation as an agent of the Crown. Its mission is to conserve heritage resources for the benefit of present & future generations.
The Royal Saskatchewan Museum in Regina presents Saskatchewan's geological & natural history, as well as a look at First Nations' cultures of the past & present.
Saskatchewan has a provincial parks & protected areas network. The Ministry provides programs & services to conserve, protect, & enhance the province's natural & cultural resources in its parks & protected areas.
Executive Director, Park Services, Cindy MacDonald
Tel: 306-787-0731
Toll-free: 800-205-7070
Fax: 306-787-7000
Cindy.MacDonald@gov.sk.ca
www.saskparks.net
Other Communications: Parks Service, Phone: 306-787-8676, Fax: 306-787-7000
Social Media: www.facebook.com/saskparks
Park Services Operations
3211 Albert St., 2ndFl.
Regina, SK S4S 5W6
Director, Royal Saskatchewan Museum, Harold Bryant
Tel: 306-787-2813
Fax: 306-787-2820
Harold.Bryant@gov.sk.ca
www.royalsaskmuseum.ca
Other Communications: Royal Saskatchewan Museum, Phone: 306-787-2815
Social Media: twitter.com/royalsaskmuseum, www.facebook.com/Royal.Saskatchewan.Museum
Royal Saskatchewan Museum
2445 Albert St.
Regina, SK S4P 4W7
Director, Heritage Conservation, Carolos Germann
Tel: 306-787-5772
Fax: 306-787-0069
Carlos.Germann@gov.sk.ca
Heritage Conservation
1919 Saskatchewan Dr., 9th Fl.
Regina, SK S4P 4H2
Director, Southern Park Operations & Planning, Marty Halpape
Tel: 306-787-7621
Fax: 306-787-7000
Marty.Halpape@gov.sk.ca
Southern Park Operations & Planning
3211 Albert St., 2nd Fl.
Regina, SK S4S 5W6
Director, Facilities, Park Services, Bob Lalonde
Tel: 306-787-2783
Fax: 306-787-4218
Bob.Lalonde@gov.sk.ca
Facilities, Park Services
3211 Albert St., 2nd Fl.
Regina, SK S4S 5W6
Director, Corporate Services, Melinda Leibel
Tel: 306-787-5896
Fax: 306-798-0033
Melinda.Leibel@gov.sk.ca
Corporate Services
1919 Saskatchewan Dr., 4th Fl.
Regina, SK S4P 4H2

Director, Park Management Services, Bob McEachern
Tel: 306-787-2948
Fax: 306-787-7000
Bob.McEachern@gov.sk.ca
Park Management Services
3211 Albert St., 2nd Fl.
Regina, SK S4S 5W6
Director, Northern Park Operations & Planning, Randy Zielke
Tel: 306-953-2884
Fax: 306-953-2502
Randy.Zielke@gov.sk.ca
Northern Park Operations & Planning, L.F. McIntosh Building
800 Central Ave., 6th Fl.
PO Box 3003
Prince Albert, SK S6V 6G1
Senior Project Manager, Facilities, Park Services, Byron Davis
Tel: 306-787-3035
Fax: 306-787-4218
Byron.Davis@gov.sk.ca
Facilities, Park Services
3211 Albert St., 2nd Fl.
Regina, SK S4S 5W6
Manager, Business Development & Leasing, Park Management Services, Kevin Engel
Tel: 306-787-1285
Fax: 306-787-7000
Kevin.Engel@gov.sk.ca
Park Management Services
3211 Albert St., 2nd Fl.
Regina, SK S4S 5W6
Manager, Research & Collections, Royal Saskatchewan Museum, Ray Poulin
Tel: 306-787-2801
Fax: 306-787-2645
ray.poulin@gov.sk.ca
Royal Saskatchewan Museum
2340 Albert St.
Regina, SK S4P 2V7
Manager, Saskatchewan Heritage Foundation, Garth Pugh
Tel: 306-787-4188
Fax: 306-787-0069
Garth.Pugh@gov.sk.ca
Saskatchewan Heritage Foundation
1919 Saskatchewan Dr., 9th Fl.
Regina, SK S4P 4H2
Manager, Exhibits & Public Programs, Royal Saskatchewan Museum, John Snell
Tel: 306-787-2811
Fax: 306-787-2645
john.snell@gov.sk.ca
Other Communications: Public Programs, Phone: 306-787-9054
Royal Saskatchewan Museum
2445 Albert St.
Regina, SK S4P4W7
Manager, Visitor Experiences, Park Services, Mary-Anne Wihak
Tel: 306-787-7826
Fax: 306-787-7000
Mary-Anne.Wihak@gov.sk.ca
Visitor Experiences, Park Services
3211 Albert St., 2nd Fl.
Regina, SK S4S 5W6
Curator of Palaeontology, Royal Saskatchewan Museum Fossil Research Station, Tim Tokaryk
Tel: 306-295-4701
Fax: 306-295-4702
Tim.Tokaryk@gov.sk.ca
Royal Saskatchewan Museum Fossil Research Station
1 T-Rex Dr.
PO Box 460
Eastend, SK S0N0T0
Senior Archaeologist, Nathan Friesen
Tel: 306-787-5774
Fax: 306-787-0069
Nathan.Friesen@gov.sk.ca
Heritage Conservation
1919 Saskatchewan Dr., 9th Fl.
Regina, SK S4P 4H2
Heritage Architect, Patricia Glanville
Tel: 306-787-1588
Fax: 306-787-0069
Heritage Conservation
1919 Saskatchewan Dr., 9th Fl.
Regina, SK S4P 4H2

Policy, Planning, & Evaluation
1919 Saskatchewan Dr., 4th Fl., Regina, SK S4P 4H2
Tel: 306-787-0346
Fax: 306-798-0033

The Policy, Planning, & Evaluation unit carries out the following functions: provision of professional development activities to assist in the policy & program decision-making process; performance of primary research & evaluation studies; provision of technical assistance to external consultants; & analysis of secondary data to support policy & program development.

Executive Director, Policy, Planning, & Evaluation, Leanne Thera
Tel: 306-798-8762
Fax: 306-798-0033
Leanne.Thera@gov.sk.ca
Director, Strategic Alignment, Nancy Martin
Tel: 306-787-2834
Fax: 306-798-0033
nancy.martin@gov.sk.ca
Project Manager, Colin McAllister
Tel: 306-787-8448
Fax: 306-798-3177
Manager, Legislative Services, Janet Peters
Tel: 306-787-4967
Fax: 306-798-0033
Janet.Peters@gov.sk.ca
Senior Policy Analyst, Denise Hildebrand
Tel: 306-787-8170
Fax: 306-798-0033
denise.hildebrand@gov.sk.ca

Sport, Recreation, & Stewardship
1919 Saskatchewan Dr., 9th Fl., Regina, SK S4P 4H2
Tel: 306-787-7451
Fax: 306-787-0069

Ministry staff work with a variety of organizations to ensure that Saskatchewan's citizens have access to sports & recreational programs & services.
Consultative & technical services are also available through the Ministry for the staging of multi-sport competitive games in the province, such as the Saskatchewan Summer & Winter Games, the Saskatchewan Indian Summer & Winter Games, the Northern Games & Cultural Festival, & the 55+ Senior Games.

Executive Director, Sport, Recreation, & Stewardship, Darin Banadyga
Tel: 306-787-0685
Fax: 306-787-0069
Darin.Banadyga@gov.sk.ca
Senior Policy Analyst, Nancy Porter
Tel: 306-787-3828
Fax: 306-787-0069
Nancy.Porter@gov.sk.ca
Senior Policy Analyst, Elizabeth Verrall
Tel: 306-787-5734
Fax: 306-787-0069
Elizabeth.Verrall@gov.sk.ca

Tourism Initiatives
1919 Saskatchewan Dr., 2nd Fl., Regina, SK S4P 4H2
Tel: 306-787-8985
Fax: 306-798-3177

Executive Director, Ken Dueck
Tel: 306-787-7871
Fax: 306-798-3177
Ken.Dueck@gov.sk.ca
Executive Coordinator, Mag Massier
Tel: 306-787-8985
Fax: 306-798-3177
Mag.Massier@gov.sk.ca
Senior Policy Analyst, Tyler Lloyd
Tel: 306-787-5728
Fax: 306-798-3177
Tyler.Lloyd@gov.sk.ca
Tourism Analyst, Travis McLellan
Tel: 306-787-5946
Fax: 306-798-3177
Travis.McLellan@gov.sk.ca
Tourism Analyst, Spencer Roberton
Tel: 306-787-7741
Fax: 306-798-0033
Spencer.Roberton@gov.sk.ca

Saskatchewan Power Corporation (SaskPower)

2025 Victoria Ave., Regina, SK S4P 0S1
Tel: 306-566-3306
Fax: 800-757-6937
Toll-Free: 888-757-6937
www.saskpower.com
Other Communication: Media phone: 306-536-2886

A Crown Corporation which provides services to over 439,000 customers over 652,000 square kilometres of diverse terrain in Saskatchewan; operates 15 generating facilities including, four base-load thermal stations, seven hydroelectric stations, three gas-fired peaking stations, & the Cypress Wind Power facility; capacity of 3,655 megawatts. The SaskPower Environmental policy maintains a commitment to environmental responsibility. The policy includes compliance with relevant environmental legislation, regulations & corporate environmental committees; continual improvement of environmental management systems & prevention of pollution. SaskPower's management system is ISO 14001 registered.

Minister Responsible, Hon. Bill Boyd
Tel: 306-787-0341
Fax: 306-787-6946
minister.aeei@gov.sk.ca

President/Chief Executive Officer, NorthPoint Energy Solutions, Robert Watson
Tel: 306-566-3103

Chief Information Officer & Vice-President, Corporate Information & Technology, Tom Kindred
Tel: 306-566-2146
tkindred@saskpower.com

Chief Financial Officer & Vice-President, Corporate & Financial Services, Sandeep Kalra
Tel: 306-566-2620
skalra@saskpower.com

Vice-President, Planning, Environment & Regulatory Affairs, Guy Bruce
Tel: 306-566-2386
gbruce@saskpower.com

Vice-President, Corporate Relations, Kevin Doherty
Tel: 306-566-3581
kdoherty@saskpower.com

Vice-President, Power Production, John Lebersback
Tel: 306-566-3228
jlebersback@saskpower.com

Vice-President, Transmission & Distribution, Mike Marsh
Tel: 306-566-3271
mmarsh@saskpower.com

Vice-President, Customer Services, Judy May
Tel: 306-566-2161

Vice-President, Clean Coal Technology, Michael Monea
Tel: 306-566-3132
mmonea@saskpower.com

Vice-President, Law, Land & Regulatory Affairs, Rachelle Verret Morphy
Tel: 306-566-3139
rverretmor@saskpower.com

Saskatchewan Research Council (SRC)

#125, 15 Innovation Blvd., Saskatoon, SK S7N 2X8
Tel: 306-933-5400
Fax: 306-933-7446
info@src.sk.ca
www.src.sk.ca

Research activities include: gas emissions testing; indoor environment testing; groundwater pesticides testing; indoor air quality & source testing for rayon & asbestos; spray drift research; vegetation studies for range, forestry, conservation; aquatic monitoring & assessment methods; climate impact assessment for environmental economic & urban stormwater management; development of plant bioassays for assessing the effects of hazardous materials in aquatic ecosystems; radiochemistry, chromatographic analysis, water analysis; parenting verification centre for the Canadian livestock industry; develops the optimum engine & fuel system for natural gas operation; bioprocessing technology; emulsions research; studies to support mineral exploration; analyses various sample material used in mineral exploration; geoenvironmental research. SRC's Biofuels Test Centre opened in September, 2006.

President/Chief Executive Officer, Dr. Laurier Schramm
Tel: 306-933-5402
schramm@src.sk.ca; presidentsoffice@src.sk.ca

Chief Financial Officer, Crystal Nett
Tel: 306-933-8111
Fax: 306-933-7519
crystal.nett@src.sk.ca

Vice-President, Organizational Effectiveness, Toby Arnold
Tel: 306-933-5479
Fax: 306-933-7896
arnold@src.sk.ca

Vice-President, Environment, Joe Muldoon
Tel: 306-933-5439
Fax: 306-933-7299
muldoon@src.sk.ca

Vice-President, Mining & Minerals, Craig Murray
Tel: 306-933-5482
Fax: 306-933-7446
murray@src.sk.ca

Vice-President, Business Ventures & Communications, Wanda Nyirfa

Tel: 306-933-5400
Fax: 306-933-7519
advertising@src.sk.ca; media@src.sk.ca

Vice-President, Energy, Ernie S. Pappas
Tel: 306-787-9351
Fax: 306-787-8811
pappas@src.sk.ca

Vice-President, Agriculture & Biotechnology, Phillip Stephan
Tel: 306-933-8199
Fax: 306-933-7662
stephan@src.sk.ca

Saskatchewan Social Services (SS)

1920 Broad St., Regina, SK S4P 3V6
Tel: 306-787-3700
Toll-Free: 866-221-5200
socialservicesinquiry@gov.sk.ca
www.socialservices.gov.sk.ca
TTY: 306-787-7283
Other Communication: Income Assistance: 306-798-0660; Media inquiries: 306-787-3686; Staus of Women Office: 306-787-7401

The Ministry works with citizens in the following areas: income support; child & family services; supports for persons with disabilities; affordable housing; economic independence; & active involvement in the labour market & the community. In November 2007, a new provincial government resulted in the reorganization of provincial government ministries. The work of Saskatchewan Community Resources was merged into a newly named ministry. Donna Harpauer was named the Minister of Social Services.

Acts Administered:
Adoption Act
Child & Family Services Act
Child Care Act
Condominium Property Act, 1993
Department of Social Services Act
Donation of Food Act
Emergency Protection for Victims of Child Sexual Abuse & Exploitation Act
Intercountry Adoption (Hague Convention) Implementation Act
Landlord & Tenant Act
Rehabilitation Act
Residential Services Act
Saskatchewan Assistance Act
Saskatchewan Housing Corporation Act
Saskatchewan Income Plan Act
Social Workers Act

Minister, Social Services; Minister Responsible, Status of Women, Hon. June Draude
Tel: 306-787-3661
Fax: 306-787-0656
minister.ss@gov.sk.ca
Minister's Office, Ministry of Social Services, Legislative Building
#303, 2405Legislative Dr.
Regina, SK S4S 0B3

Deputy Minister, Ken Acton
Tel: 306-787-3491
Fax: 306-787-1032
ken.acton@gov.sk.ca

Executive Director, Communications, Trish Alcorn
Tel: 306-787-0916
Fax: 306-787-8669
Trish.Alcorn@gov.sk.ca

Director, Child & Family Services (South Service Area), Janice Krumenacker
Tel: 306-787-9109
Fax: 306-787-4940
janice.krumenacker@gov.sk.ca

Director, Child & Family Services (Centre Service Area), Garry Prediger
Tel: 306-933-6075
Fax: 306-933-5665
Garry.Prediger@gov.sk.ca

Corporate Services Division

Tel: 306-787-3984
Fax: 306-787-1032

Assistant Deputy Minister, Alan Syhlonyk
Tel: 306-787-7348
Fax: 306-787-1032
Alan.Syhlonyk@gov.sk.ca
Executive Director, Enterprise Projects & Risk Management, Lorne Brown
Tel: 306-787-3940
Fax: 306-798-2118
Lorne.Brown@gov.sk.ca
Executive Director, Status of Women Office, Pat Faulconbridge
Tel: 306-787-7423
Fax: 306-787-2058
Pat.Faulconbridge@gov.sk.ca
Acting Executive Director, Strategic Policy, Glenda Francis
Tel: 306-787-1338
Fax: 306-787-3650
glenda.francis@gov.sk.ca
Executive Director, Finance & Administration, Miriam Myers
Tel: 306-787-8666
Fax: 306-787-6825
Miriam.Myers@gov.sk.ca
Director, Information Technology Services, Sharon Amorth
Tel: 306-787-4173
Fax: 306-798-2118
Sharon.Amorth@gov.sk.ca
Director, Risk Management & Business Improvement, Maury Harvey
Tel: 306-787-6097
Fax: 306-798-5550
maury.harvey@gov.sk.ca
Director, Enterprise Projects, Ron MacLeod
Tel: 306-787-5241
Fax: 306-798-2118
ron.macleod@gov.sk.ca
Director, Financial Planning, Lori Mann
Tel: 306-787-1911
Fax: 306-787-6825
lori.mann2@gov.sk.ca
Director, Child & Family Policy, Janet Mitchell
Tel: 306-787-1533
Fax: 306-787-3650
Janet.Mitchell@gov.sk.ca
Director, Financial Services, Cathy Myres
Tel: 306-787-3575
Fax: 306-787-1600
cathy.myres@gov.sk.ca; C.Myres@gov.sk.ca
Other Communications: Alternate phone: 306-787-1804
Director, Housing Finance, Rachel Ratch
Tel: 306-787-4961
Fax: 306-787-8571
Director, Benefits Policy, Doug Scott
Tel: 306-787-0626
Fax: 306-787-3650
Doug.Scott@gov.sk.ca
Director, Community-Based Organization Contract Management, Gail Stuermer
Tel: 306-787-9105
Fax: 306-787-8203
Gail.Stuermer@gov.sk.ca
Director, Persons with Disabilities Policy, Tara Truemner
Tel: 306-787-3621
Fax: 306-787-3650
Tara.Truemner@gov.sk.ca
Director, Accommodation Services, Dale Von Hagen
Tel: 306-787-1383
Fax: 306-798-0077
Dale.VonHagen@gov.sk.ca
Director, Housing Policy, Shauna Wouters
Tel: 306-787-6118
Fax: 306-787-3650
Shauna.Wouters@gov.sk.ca

Child & Family Services Division

Tel: 306-787-7010
Fax: 306-787-1032

Executive Director, Program & Service Design, Lynn Allan
Tel: 306-798-4118
Fax: 306-787-0925
Lynn.Allan@gov.sk.ca
Executive Director, Child & Family Service Delivery, Andrea Brittin
Tel: 306-787-3652
Fax: 306-787-0925
andrea.brittin@gov.sk.ca
Executive Director, Child & Family Community Services, Wayne Phaneuf
Tel: 306-787-5481
Fax: 306-787-0925
Wayne.Phaneuf@gov.sk.ca
Director, Child & Family Community Services, Karen Wasylenka
Tel: 306-787-5698
karen.wasylenka@gov.sk.ca

Income Assistance & Disability Services Division

Tel: 306-787-1032

Assistant Deputy Minister, Bob Wihidal
Tel: 306-787-7357
Fax: 306-787-1032
Bob.Wihlidal@gov.sk.ca
Executive Director, Income Assistance Service Delivery, Jeff Redekop
Tel: 306-787-9013
Fax: 306-787-4450
Jeff.Redekop@gov.sk.ca
Executive Director, Community Living Service Delivery, Beverly Smith
Tel: 306-787-1951
Fax: 306-787-4450
Beverly.Smith@gov.sk.ca
Executive Director, Linkin Enterprise, Lynn Tullach
Tel: 306-787-1967
Fax: 306-787-1032
lynn.tulloch@gov.sk.ca
Executive Director, Program & Service Division, Gord Tweed
Tel: 306-787-0015
Fax: 306-787-3650
gord.tweed@gov.sk.ca

Housing Division

Tel: 306-787-4177
Fax: 306-798-3110
Toll-Free: 800-667-7567
www.socialservices.gov.sk.ca/housing

Assistant Deputy Minister, Don Allen
Tel: 306-787-4174
Fax: 306-787-1032
Don.Allen@gov.sk.ca
Executive Director, Program & Service Design, Eileen Badiuk
Tel: 306-787-7288
Fax: 306-798-3110
Eileen.Badiuk@gov.sk.ca
Executive Director, Housing Network, Dianne Baird
Tel: 306-787-8569
Fax: 306-798-3110
Dianne.Baird@gov.sk.ca
Executive Director, Housing Development, Tim Gross
Tel: 306-787-1008
Fax: 306-798-3110
Tim.Gross@gov.sk.ca

Saskatchewan Telecommunications (SaskTel)

2121 Saskatchewan Dr., 7th Fl., Regina, SK S4P 4C3
Tel: 306-777-3737
Toll-Free: 800-727-5835
corporate.comments@sasktel.sk.ca
www.sasktel.com

The provincial Crown Corporation delivers full service telecommunications to the people of Saskatchewan. Services are as follows: competitive voice, data, dial-up, & high speed internet; entertainment & multimedia services; security; web hosting; text & messaging services; & cellular & wireless data services.

Minister, Highways & Infrastructure; Minister Responsible, Saskatchewan Telecommunications; Minister Responsible, Saskatchewan Transportation Company; Minister Responsible, Information Services Corporation; MinisterResponsible, Saskatchewan Gaming Corp., Hon. Don McMorris
Tel: 306-787-6447
Fax: 306-787-1736
minister.hi@gov.sk.ca
Social Media: twitter.com/dmcmorrissp, www.facebook.com/DonMcMorrisSP
Legislative Building
#302, 2405 Legislative Dr.
Regina, SK S4S0B3

Chair, Grant Kook
Tel: 306-777-2201

President/Chief Executive Officer, Ron Styles
Tel: 306-777-2200
ron.styles@sasktel.sk.ca

Chief Financial Officer, Mike Anderson
Tel: 306-777-3185

Chief Technology Officer, Kym Wittal
Tel: 306-777-4504

Chief Information Officer, John Hill
Tel: 306-777-2327
john.hill@gov.sk.ca

Vice-President, Human Resources & Corporate Services, Doug Burnett
Tel: 306-777-2283

Vice-President, Customer Service (Sales), Ken Keesey
Tel: 306-931-5915

Senior Director, Corporate Communications, Darcee MacFarlane
Tel: 306-777-4441

Vice-President, Corporate Counsel, Regulatory Affairs & Partnership Development, John Meldrum
Tel: 306-777-2223

Vice-President, Marketing, Stacey Sandison
Tel: 306-777-3670

Saskatchewan Transportation Company (STC)

1717 Saskatchewan Dr., Regina, SK S4P 2E2
Tel: 306-787-3347
Fax: 306-787-1633
info@stcbus.com
www.stcbus.com

The STC was established in 1946 to provide safe, affordable & accessible freight and passenger bus service throughout Saskatchewan.

Minister, Highways & Infrastructure; Minister Responsible, Saskatchewan Telecommunications; Minister Responsible, Saskatchewan Transportation Company; Minister Responsible, Information Services Corporation; MinisterResponsible, Saskatchewan Gaming Corp., Hon. Don McMorris
Tel: 306-787-6447
Fax: 306-787-1736
minister.hi@gov.sk.ca
Social Media: twitter.com/dmcmorrissp, www.facebook.com/DonMcMorrisSP
Legislative Building
#302, 2405 Legislative Dr.
Regina, SK S4S 0B3

President/Chief Executive Officer, Shawn Grice
Tel: 306-787-2116
Fax: 306-798-4754
sgrice@stcbus.com

Chief Operating Officer, Customer Services/Maintenance, Phil Bohay
Tel: 306-787-7302
Fax: 306-787-1633
pbohay@stcbus.com

Acting Chief Financial Officer, Jason Sherwin
Tel: 306-787-8189
Fax: 306-787-3429
jsherwin@stcbus.com

Saskatchewan Water Corporation (SaskWater)

#200, 111 Fairford St. East, Moose Jaw, SK S6H 1C8
Fax: 306-694-3207
Toll-Free: 888-230-1111
comm@saskwater.com; customerservice@saskwater.com
www.saskwater.com
Other Communication: SaskWater Customer Emergencies: 1-800-667-5799

SaskWater, a provincial Crown corporation, is Saskatchewan's water utility service provider. Lines of business are as follows: supply of potable & non-potable water; treatment & management of wastewater; & certified operations & maintenance. SaskWater is responsible for designing, building, & operating transmission, regional, & stand-alone water supply & wastewater systems. All systems must meet regulatory requirements.
Acts Administered:
Saskatchewan Water Corporation Act, 2002

Minister Responsible, Hon. Ken Cheveldayoff
Tel: 306-787-0393
Fax: 306-787-1669
minister.env@gov.sk.ca
Social Media:
www.facebook.com/pages/Ken-Cheveldayoff/52760912740
Office of the Minister, Legislative Building
#315, 2405 Legislative Dr.
Regina, SK S4S 0B3

President, Doug Matthies
Tel: 306-694-3903
Fax: 306-694-3207
doug.matthies@saskwater.com

Vice-President, Business Development & Corporate Services Division, Marie Alexander
Tel: 306-694-3916
Fax: 306-694-3207
marie.alexander@saskwater.com

Vice-President, Operations & Engineering, Jeff Mander
Tel: 306-694-3880
Fax: 306-694-3207
jeff.mander@saskwater.com

Saskatchewan Watershed Authority (SWA)

111 Fairford St. East, Moose Jaw, SK S6H 7X9
Tel: 306-694-3900
Fax: 306-694-3944
comm@swa.ca
www.swa.ca
Other Communication: Provincial Water Inquiry Line: 866-727-5420

Saskatchewan Watershed Authority is a Crown corporation that is responsible for managing water resources in Saskatchewan. The Authority works to ensure reliable water supplies & safe drinking water sources.
The following regulations are administered by the Saskatchewan Watershed Authority: Conservation & Development; Drainage Control; Ground Water; & Reservoir Development Area.
Acts Administered:
Conservation & Development Act
Saskatchewan Watershed Authority Act, 2005
The Water Power Act
Watershed Associations Act

Minister, Environment; Minister Responsible, Saskatchewan Watershed Authority; Minister Responsible, Saskatchewan Water Corporation, Hon. Ken Cheveldayoff
Tel: 306-787-0393
Fax: 306-787-1669
minister.env@gov.sk.ca
Social Media:
www.facebook.com/pages/Ken-Cheveldayoff/52760912740
Office of theMinister, Legislative Building
#315, 2405 Legislative Dr.
Regina, SK S4S 0B3

President, Wayne Dybvig
Tel: 306-694-7739
Fax: 306-694-3991
wayne.dybvig@swa.ca

Vice-President, Corporate Services, Bob Carles
Tel: 306-694-7737
Fax: 306-694-3465
bob.carles@swa.ca

Executive Director, Dam Safety & Major Structures, Bill Duncan
Tel: 306-694-3990
Fax: 306-694-3944
bill.duncan@swa.ca

Executive Director, Integrated Water Services, Jim Gerhart
Tel: 306-694-3952
Fax: 306-694-3944
jim.gerhart@swa.ca

Executive Director, Policy & Communications, Dale Hjertaas
Tel: 306-787-0726
Fax: 306-787-0780
dale.hjertaas@swa.ca

Director, Hydrology & Groundwater Services, John Fahlman
Tel: 306-694-3954
Fax: 306-694-3944
john.fahlman@swa.ca

Director, Business Information & Technology Systems, Jan Franken
Tel: 306-694-3961
Fax: 306-694-3465
jan.franken@swa.ca

Director, Policy & Risk Management, Terry Hanley
Tel: 306-787-9982
Fax: 306-787-0780
terry.hanley@swa.ca

Director, Parnerships & Plan Implementation, Tom Harrison
Tel: 306-694-3973
Fax: 306-694-3616
tom.harrison@swa.ca

Director, Financial Services, Irene Hrynkiw
Tel: 306-694-3960
Fax: 306-694-3465
irene.hrynkiw@swa.ca

Director, Human Resources & Workplace Services, Joe Maciag
Tel: 306-694-3878
Fax: 306-694-3465
joe.maciag@swa.ca

Director, Licensing & Water Use, Jim Waggoner
Tel: 306-694-3966
Fax: 306-694-3944
jim.waggoner@swa.ca

Saskatchewan Workers' Compensation Board

#200, 1881 Scarth St., Regina, SK S4P 4L1
Tel: 306-787-4370
Fax: 306-787-4311
Toll-Free: 800-667-7590
internet_clientsvc@wcbsask.com
www.wcbsask.com
Other Communication: Injury Reports: 1-800-787-9288; Employer Inquiries: reainquiry@wcbsask.com; Health Care Provider Inquiries: internet_healthcare@wcbsask.com; Appeal Fax: 306-787-1116
Secondary Address: 129 Third Ave. North
Saskatoon, SK S7K 2H6
Fax: 306-787-4311

The Saskatchewan's Workers' Compensation Board was created by the following provincial legislation in Saskatchewan: the Workers' Compensation Act 1979, General Regulations, & Exclusion Regulations. The Board is an independent body that administers a no-fault compensation system to protect employers and workers against the result of work injuries. The WCB provides financial protection, medical benefits. & rehabilitation services to injured workers & their dependents in cases of injury or death arising from, & in the course of, employment.

Minister, Advanced Education; Minister, Labour Relations & Workplace Safety; Minister Responsible, Saskatchewan Workers' Compensation Board, Hon. Don Morgan, Q.C.
Tel: 306-787-0613
Fax: 306-787-6946
minister.ae@gov.sk.ca
Social Media:
www.facebook.com/pages/Don-Morgan/48835718931?sk=info
Office of theMinister of Advanced Education / Labour Relation & Workplace Safety, Legislative Bldg.
#361, 2405 Legislative Dr.
Regina, SK S4S 0B3

Chairman, David Eberle
Tel: 306-787-4379
Fax: 306-787-0213

Chief Executive Officer, Peter Federko
Tel: 306-787-7398
Fax: 306-787-0213
pfederko@wcbsask.com

Vice-President, Human Resources & Team Support, Donna Kane
Tel: 306-787-4440
Fax: 306-787-0213
dkane@wcbsask.com

Vice-President, Prevention, Finance & Information Technology, Gail Kruger
Tel: 306-787-2475
Fax: 306-787-0213
gkruger@wcbsask.com

Vice-President, Operations, Graham Topp
Tel: 306-787-4371
Fax: 306-787-7582
gtopp@wcbsask.com

Government of the Yukon Territory

Seat of Government: PO Box 2703, Whitehorse, YT Y1A 2C6
Tel: 867-667-5811
Toll-Free: 800-661-0408
www.gov.yk.ca
TTY: 867-393-7460

The Yukon was created as a separate territory June 13, 1898. It has an area of 474,711.02 km2, & StatsCan's census in 2011 showed the population was 32,897. A federally appointed commissioner (similar to a provincial lieutenant-governor) oversees federal interests in the territory, but the day-to-day operation of the government rests with the wholly elected executive council (cabinet). The territorial legislature has power to make acts on generally all matters of a local nature in the territory, including the imposition of local taxes, property & civil rights & the administration of justice, education & health & social services. Legislative powers vested in the provinces but not available to the territory include control of unoccupied Crown land, renewable & non-renewable resources (except wildlife &

sport fisheries) & the power to amend the Yukon Act, a federal statute.

Office of the Commissioner

Closeleigh Manor, 1098 First Ave., Whitehorse, YT Y1A 0C1
Tel: 867-667-5121
Fax: 867-393-6201
commissioner@gov.yk.ca
www.commissioner.gov.yk.ca

The Yukon Territory is governed by a commissioner appointed for a 5-year term by the federal government, a government leader, an executive council which functions as a cabinet, & a legislative assembly. The Yukon Act provides for the establishment of a commissioner & the elected legislative assembly.

Commissioner, Hon. Doug Phillips

Executive Assistant, Lyndsey Hamilton
Tel: 867-667-5121
lyndsey.hamilton@gov.yk.ca

Office of the Premier

2071 Second Ave., PO Box 2703, Whitehorse, YT Y1A 1B2
Tel: 867-667-8660
Fax: 867-393-6252
premier@gov.yk.ca
www.yukonpremier.ca

Darrell Pasloski was elected Leader of the Yukon Party on May 28, 2011. He was first sworn in as Premier on June 11, 2011. In the general election of October 11, 2011, The Honourable Darrell Pasloski was elected to the Yukon Legislative Assembly.

Premier, Yukon Territory; Leader, Yukon Party; Minister Responsible, Executive Council Office; Member, Legislative Assembly, Hon. Darrell Pasloski, Yukon Party
Tel: 867-667-8660
Fax: 867-393-6252
premier@gov.yk.ca;darrell.pasloski@gov.yk.ca
Social Media: www.twitter.com/bsp82, www.facebook.com/TeamYukon, ca.linkedin.com/pub/darrell-pasloski/18/943/975

Principal Secretary & Chief of Staff, Gordon Steele
Tel: 867-667-5842
gordon.steele@gov.yk.ca

Senior Cabinet Communications Advisor, Elaine Schiman
Tel: 867-633-7961
elaine.schiman@gov.yk.ca

Director, John Gunter, 2011-11-01
Tel: 867-667-5073
john.gunter@gov.yk.ca

Executive Council

#2071, 2nd Ave., Whitehorse, YT Y1A 2C6
Tel: 867-667-5393
Fax: 867-393-6214
eco@gov.yk.ca

The Executive Council of Yukon Territory is selected by the Honourable Darrell Pasloski, Premier. Members of Yukon's cabinet are members of the Yukon Party, following its victory in the October 2011 general election.

Acts Administered:
Cabinet & Caucus Employees Act
Conflict of Interest Act
Cooperation in Governance Act
Corporate Governance Act
First Nations (Yukon) Self-Government Act
Flag Act
Floral Emblem Act
Government Organisation Act
Intergovernmental Agreements Act
Languages Act
Official Tree Act
Plebiscite Act
Public Inquiries Act
Raven Act
Statistics Act
Waters Act (jointly with Environment & Energy, Mines & Resources)
Yukon Act (Canada)
Yukon Environmental & Socio-Economic Assessment Act
Yukon Land Claim Final Agreements Act
Yukon Tartan Act

Premier, Yukon Territory; Minister Responsible, Executive Council Office; Leader, Yukon Party; Member, Legislative Assembly, Hon. Darrell Pasloski
Tel: 867-667-8660
Fax: 867-393-6252
premier@gov.yk.ca;darrell.pasloski@gov.yk.ca
www.yukonpremier.ca
Social Media: www.twitter.com/bsp82, www.facebook.com/TeamYukon, ca.linkedin.com/pub/darrell-pasloski/18/943/975

Executive Council Office
Tel: 867-667-5393
Fax: 897-393-6252

Deputy Minister & Cabinet Secretary, Joe MacGillivray
Tel: 867-667-5866
Fax: 867-393-6214
joe.macgillivray@gov.yk.ca
Assistant Deputy Minister, Governance Liaison/ Capacity Development, John Burdek
Tel: 867-456-6840
Fax: 867-456-6833
john.burdek@gov.yk.ca
Assistant Deputy Minister, Corporate Services, Janet Mann
Tel: 867-667-5866
janet.mann@gov.yk.ca
Assistant Deputy Minister, Land Claims & Implementation Secretariat/First Nations Relations, Karyn Armour
Tel: 867-667-8566
Fax: 867-667-3599
karyn.armour@gov.yk.ca
Director, Intergovernmental Relations, Andrea Buckley
Tel: 867-667-5744
Fax: 867-393-6202
andrea.buckley@gov.yk.ca
Director, Government Audit Services, John Gunter
Tel: 867-667-5073
Fax: 867-456-6522
john.gunter@gov.yk.ca
Director, Implementation, Michael Hale
Tel: 867-667-8797
Fax: 867-667-3599
michael.hale@gov.yk.ca
Director, Policy & Planning, Karen Hougen-Bell
Tel: 867-667-8201
karen.hougen-bell@gov.yk.ca
Director, Policy, Administration & Communication, Al Jones
Tel: 867-667-8523
Fax: 867-667-3599
al.jones@gov.yk.ca
Director, First Nation Relations, Cheryl McLean
Tel: 867-667-5801
Fax: 867-667-3599
cheryl.mclean@gov.yk.ca
Director, Development Assessment, Diane Reed
Tel: 867-393-6431
Fax: 867-667-3216
diane.reed@gov.yk.ca
Acting Director, Bureau of Statistics, Diane Reed
Tel: 867-667-5463
Fax: 867-393-6203
diane.reed@gov.yk.ca
Senior Government Representative, Intergovernmental Relations Office, Vacant
Tel: 613-234-3206
Fax: 613-563-9602
#707, 350 Sparks St.
Ottawa, ON K1R 7S8 Canada
Acting Chief of Protocol, Kerri Scholz
Tel: 867-667-5875
Fax: 867-563-9602
kerri.scholz@gov.yk.ca
Manager, Youth Directorate, Gord Kurzynski
Tel: 867-667-8213
Fax: 867-393-6341
gord.kurzynski@gov.yk.ca
Manager, Yukon Water Board, Carola Scheu
Tel: 867-456-3984
Fax: 867-456-3890
carola.scheu@gov.yk.ca

Government Inquiry Office
Yukon Government Administration Building, 2071 Second Ave., PO Box 2703, Whitehorse, YT Y1A 2C6
Tel: 867-667-5811
information@gov.yk.ca
www.gov.yk.ca/contactus.html
TTY: 867-393-7460
Other Communication: Alternate Phone: 867-667-5812

Yukon Legislative Assembly

PO Box 2703, Whitehorse, YT Y1A 2C6
Tel: 867-667-5498
Fax: 867-393-6280
yla@gov.yk.ca
www.legassembly.gov.yk.ca

Acts Administered:
Cabinet & Caucus Employees Act
Child & Youth Advocate Act
Conflict of Interest (Members & Ministers) Act
Elections Act
Electoral District Boundaries Act
Legislative Assembly Act
Ombudsman Act
Yukon Day Act

Clerk, Floyd McCormick
Tel: 867-667-5494
Fax: 867-393-6280
floyd.mccormick@gov.yk.ca

Speaker, David Laxton
Tel: 867-667-5662
Fax: 867-393-6280
david.laxton@gov.yk.ca

Sergeant-at-Arms, Rudy Couture

Deputy Sergeant-at-Arms, Doris McLean

Deputy Speaker, Patti McLeod

Deputy Clerk, Linda Kolody
Tel: 867-667-5499
linda.kolody@gov.yk.ca

Receptionist/Finance Clerk, Dawn-Alena Brown
Tel: 867-667-5498
dawn-alena.brown@gov.yk.ca

Government Caucus Office (Yukon Party)
PO Box 31113, Whitehorse, YT Y1A 5P7
Tel: 867-668-6505
www.yukonparty.ca, www.yukongovernmentcaucus.ca
Leader, Darrell Pasloski
darrell.paslowki@gov.yk.ca

Office of the Official Opposition (New Democratic Party)
P.O. Box 31516, Whitehorse, YT Y1A 6K8
Tel: 867-668-2203
www.yukonndp.ca

In September 2009, Elizabeth Hanson became the leader of Yukon's New Democratic Party. After the New Democratic Party won six seats in the general election of October 11, 2011, Hanson became Leader of the Official Opposition.

Leader, Official Opposition; Member, Legislative Assembly, Liz Hanson
Constituency: Whitehorse Centre, New Democratic Party
Tel: 867-393-7059
Fax: 867-393-6499
elizabeth.hanson@yla.gov.yk.ca
www.yukonndp.ca/liz
Social Media: www.twitter.com/lizhansonndp, www.facebook.com/lizhansonMLA, ca.linkedin.com/pub/elizabeth-hanson/39/a51/4a4
Yukon Legislative Assembly
PO Box 2703
Whitehorse, YT Y1A 2C6

Office of the Leader of the Third Party (Liberal Party)
#183, 108 Elliott St., Whitehorse, YT Y1A 6C4
Tel: 867-667-4748
info@ylp.ca
www.ylp.ca

Following the general election of October 2011, Darius Elias was named the interim leader of the Yukon Liberal party. He is the MLA for Vuntut Gwitchin, & one of two Liberals elected in the October 2011 election.

Interim Leader, Yukon Liberal Party; Member, Legislative Assembly, Darius Elias, Liberal
Tel: 867-456-6710
Fax: 867-393-7444
darius.elias@yla.gov.yk.ca
Yukon Legislative Assembly
PO Box 2703
Whitehorse, YT Y1A 2C6

Standing Committees of the Legislature
Members' Services Board; Rules, Elections & Privileges; Public Accounts; Statutory Instruments; Appointments to Major Government Boards & Committees

Thirty-third Legislative Assembly - Yukon Territory

Yukon Legislative Assembly Office, 2071 Second Ave., PO Box 2703, Whitehorse, YT Y1A 2C6
Tel: 867-667-5498

Last General Election: October 11, 2011.
Percentage of eligible voters who cast a ballot in the October 2011 general election: 76.2%.
Party Standings (October 2011):
Yukon Party 11;
New Democratic Party 6;
Liberal Party 2;
Total Seats 19.
Party Leaders: Yukon Party Hon. Darrell Pasloski, Premier;

New Democratic Party Elizabeth Hanson, Official Opposition Leader;
Liberal Party Darius Elias, Third Party Leader.
Salaries, Indemnities, & Allowances (2011-2012):
Members' indemnity $69,531, plus $13,171 expense allowances for both Whitehorse & rural members;
Minister's salary $37,439;
Premier's salary $16,046;
Leader of the Official Opposition's salary $37,439;
Leader of the Third Party's salary $16,046;
Speaker's salary $26,743;
Deputy Speaker's salary $10,697.
Members of the 33rd Legislative Assembly are listed with their constituency, number of electors on the list for the most recent election, party affiliation, & contact information. The address for all Members of the Yukon Legislative Assembly is as follows: PO Box 2703, Whitehorse, YT, Y1A 2C6.
Acts Administered:
Cabinet & Caucus Employees Act (jointly with Executive Council Office)
Child & Youth Advocate Act
Conflict of Interest (Members & Ministers) Act (jointly with Executive Council Office)
Elections Act
Electoral District Boundaries Act, 2002
Legislative Assembly Act
Legislative Assembly Retirement Allowances Act
Ombudsman Act
Yukon Day Act

Member, Legislative Assembly, Kevin Barr
Constituency: Mount Lorne - Southern Lakes *No. of Constituents:* 1,374, New Democratic Party
Tel: 867-393-7050
Fax: 867-393-6499
kevin.barr@yla.gov.yk.ca
www.yukonndp.ca/kevin
Social Media: www.facebook.com/KevinBarrYNDP

Member, Legislative Assembly, Hon. Brad Cathers
Constituency: Lake Laberge *No. of Constituents:* 1,272, Yukon Party
Tel: 867-667-8625
Fax: 867-456-6741
brad.cathers@gov.yk.ca; brad@bradcathers.ca
www.bradcathers.ca
Social Media: www.twitter.com/BradCathers, www.facebook.com/pages/Brad-Cathers-MLA/163755667012676

Member, Legislative Assembly, Hon. Currie Dixon
Constituency: Copperbelt North *No. of Constituents:* 1,543, Yukon Party
Tel: 867-667-5800
Fax: 867-393-6252
currie.dixon@gov.yk.ca
www.bradcathers.ca
Social Media: www.twitter.com/curriedixon

Member, Legislative Assembly; Interim Leader, Yukon Liberal Party, Darius Elias
Constituency: VuntutGwitchin *No. of Constituents:* 154, Liberal
Tel: 867-456-6710
Fax: 867-393-7444
darius.elias@yla.gov.yk.ca

Member, Legislative Assembly, Hon. Doug Graham
Constituency: Porter Creek North *No. of Constituents:* 1,289, Yukon Party
Tel: 867-667-5800
Fax: 867-393-6252
doug.graham@gov.yk.ca

Member, Legislative Assembly; Leader, Official Opposition, Liz Hanson
Constituency: WhitehorseCentre *No. of Constituents:* 1,249, New Democratic Party
Tel: 867-393-7059
Fax: 867-393-6499
elizabeth.hanson@yla.gov.yk.ca
www.yukonndp.ca/liz
Social Media: www.twitter.com/lizhansonndp, www.facebook.com/lizhansonMLA, ca.linkedin.com/pub/elizabeth-hanson/39/a51/4a4

Member, Legislative Assembly, Stacey Hassard
Constituency: Pelly-Nisutlin *No. of Constituents:* 748, Yukon Party
Tel: 867-667-5800
Fax: 867-393-6252
stacey.hassard@gov.yk.ca

Member, Legislative Assembly, Hon. Wade Istchenko
Constituency: Kluane *No. of Constituents:* 888, Yukon Party
Tel: 867-667-5800
Fax: 867-393-6252
wade.istchenko@gov.yk.ca
Social Media: www.facebook.com/groups/219916094720643

Member, Legislative Assembly, Hon. Scott Kent
Constituency: Riverdale North *No. of Constituents:* 1,313, Yukon Party
Tel: 867-667-5800
Fax: 867-393-6252
scott.kent@gov.yk.ca; scott@yukonparty.ca
Social Media: www.facebook.com/pages/Scott-Kent-Riverdale-North/287536247929989

Member, Legislative Assembly, David Laxton
Constituency: Porter Creek Centre *No. of Constituents:* 1,055, Yukon Party
Tel: 867-667-5800
Fax: 867-393-6252
david.laxton@gov.yk.ca
Social Media: www.facebook.com/pages/David-Laxton/159369217480362

Member, Legislative Assembly, Patti McLeod
Constituency: Watson Lake *No. of Constituents:* 845, Yukon Party
Tel: 867-667-5800
Fax: 867-393-6252
patti.mcleod@gov.yk.ca
Social Media: www.facebook.com/pages/Patti-McLeod-for-MLA/223446187711079

Member, Legislative Assembly, Lois Moorcroft
Constituency: Copperbelt South *No. of Constituents:* 1,283, New Democratic Party
Tel: 867-393-7050
Fax: 867-393-6499
lois.moorcroft@yla.gov.yk.ca
www.yukonndp.ca/lois
Social Media: www.facebook.com/LoisMoorcroftNDP

Member, Legislative Assembly, Hon. Mike Nixon
Constituency: Porter Creek South *No. of Constituents:* 810, Yukon Party
Tel: 867-667-5800
Fax: 867-393-6252
mike.nixon@gov.yk.ca; mikenixon@yukonparty.ca
www.votemikenixon.com
Social Media: www.twitter.com/nixon_mike, www.facebook.com/group.php?gid=264844376862257

Member, Legislative Assembly; Premier, Yukon Territory; Minister Responsible, Executive Council Office; Leader, Yukon Party, Hon. Darrell Pasloski
Constituency: Mountainview *No. of Constituents:* 1,382, Yukon Party
Tel: 867-393-7053
Fax: 867-393-6252
darrell.pasloski@gov.yk.ca; premier@gov.yk.ca
www.yukonpremier.ca
Other Communications: Premier's Office, Phone: 867-667-8660; Fax: 393-6252
Social Media: www.twitter.com/bsp82, www.facebook.com/TeamYukon, ca.linkedin.com/pub/darrell-pasloski/18/943/975

Member, Legislative Assembly, Sandy Silver
Constituency: Klondike *No. of Constituents:* 1,319, Liberal
Tel: 867-393-7007
Fax: 867-393-7444
sandy.silver@yla.gov.yk.ca

Member, Legislative Assembly, Jan Stick
Constituency: Riverdale South *No. of Constituents:* 1,387, New Democratic Party
Tel: 867-393-7021
Fax: 867-393-6499
jan.stick@yla.gov.yk.ca
www.yukonndp.ca/jan
Social Media: www.twitter.com/janstickndp, www.facebook.com/janstickYNDP

Member, Legislative Assembly; Deputy Premier, Yukon Territory, Hon. Elaine Taylor
Constituency: Whitehorse West *No. of Constituents:* 961, Yukon Party
Tel: 867-667-8641
Fax: 867-939-2652
elaine.taylor@gov.yk.ca;elainetaylor@yukonparty.ca
Social Media: www.facebook.com/pages/Elaine-Taylor/135880316425564

Member, Legislative Assembly, Jim Tredger
Constituency: Mayo-Tatchun *No. of Constituents:* 916, New Democratic Party
Tel: 867-393-7050
Fax: 867-393-6499
jim.tredger@yla.gov.yk.ca; Jim@YukonNDP.ca
www.yukonndp.ca/jim
Social Media: www.facebook.com/JimTredgerNDP

Member, Legislative Assembly, Kate White
Constituency: Takhini-KopperKing *No. of Constituents:* 1,552, New Democratic Party
Tel: 867-393-7001
Fax: 867-393-6499
kate.white@yla.gov.yk.ca
www.yukonndp.ca/kate
Social Media: www.twitter.com/MsKateWhite, www.facebook.com/KateWhiteNDP

Yukon Territory Government Departments & Agencies

Yukon Child & Youth Advocate Office

19 - 2070, 2nd Ave., Whitehorse, YT Y1A 1B1
Tel: 867-456-5575
Fax: 867-456-5574
Toll-Free: 800-661-0408
www.ycao.ca

Executive Director, Daniel Seems
Tel: 506-444-6291
dan.seems@gnb.ca

Director, Michel Albert
Tel: 506-444-5053
michel.albert@gnb.ca

Manager, Trade Development, Gail Legresley
Tel: 506-453-8747
gail.legresley@gnb.ca

Manager, Trade Development, Suzanne Turmel
Tel: 506-444-5107
suzanne.turmel@gnb.ca

Yukon Community Services

PO Box 2703, Whitehorse, YT Y1A 2C6
Tel: 867-667-5811
Fax: 867-393-6295
Toll-Free: 800-661-0408
inquiry@gov.yk.ca
www.community.gov.yk.ca
TTY: 867-393-7460

The main purpose of the department is to serve Yukoners & their communities by providing access to services to strengthen communities. The department focuses on community affairs & municipal relations within government on behalf of Yukon communities & acts as a liaison between community groups & government departments.
Acts Administered:
Animal Protection Act (jointly with Energy, Mines & Resources)
Area Development Act
Assessment & Taxation Act
Boiler & Pressure Vessels Act
Builder's Lien Act
Building Standards Act
Business Corporations Act
Cemeteries & Burial Sites Act
Certified General Accountants Act
Certified Management Accountants Act
Chartered Accountants Act
Chiropractors Act
Choses in Action Act (jointly with Department of Justice)
Civil Emergency Measures Act
Consumers Protection Act
Cooperative Associations Act
Dawson Municipal Election (2006) Act
Dental Profession Act
Denturists Act
Dog Act
Electrical Protection Act
Elevator & Fixed Conveyances Act
Emergency Medical Aid Act
Employment Agencies Act
Employment Standards Act
Engineering Profession Act
Factors Act
Fire Prevention Act
First Nation Indemnification (Fire Management) Act
Forest Protection Act (jointly with Department of Energy, Mines & Resources)
Funeral Directors Act
Garage Keepers Lien Act
Gas Burning Devices Act
Gasoline Handling Act
Health Professions Act
Home Owner's Grant Act
Insurance Act
International Commercial Arbitration Act
International Sale of Goods Act
Landlord & Tenant Act
Licensed Practical Nurses Act
Lottery Licensing Act
Medical Profession Act
Miner's Lien Act
Motor Vehicles Act (jointly with Highways & Public Works)
Municipal Act
Municipal Finance & Community Grants Act
Municipal Loans Act
Noise Prevention Act
Optometrists Act
Partnership & Business Name Act

Pawnbrokers & Second-Hand Dealers Act
Personal Property Security Act
Pharmacists Act
Private Investigators & Security Guards Act
Public Libraries Act
Real Estate Agents Act
Recreation Act
Registered Nurses Profession Act
Sales of Goods Act
Seniors Property Tax Deferment Act
Societies Act
Subdivision Act
Trustee Act
Warehouse Keepers Lien Act
Warehouse Receipts Act
Whitehorse Streets & Lanes Ordinance
Yukon Foundation Act

Minister, Elaine Taylor, Hon.
Tel: 867-667-8641
Fax: 867-393-6252
elaine.taylor@gov.yk.ca

Deputy Minister, Harvey Brooks
Tel: 867-456-6512
Fax: 867-633-7957
harvey.brooks@gov.yk.ca

Director, Communications, Matt King
Tel: 867-456-6580
Fax: 867-393-6404
matt.king@gov.yk.ca

Director, Corporate Policy, Caitlin Kerwin
Tel: 867-456-5524
Fax: 867-393-6404
caitlin.kerwin@gov.yk.ca

Director, Finance, Systems & Administration, Christine Mahar
Tel: 867-667-5311
Fax: 867-393-6264
christine.mahar@gov.yk.ca

Director, Human Resources, Les Hudson
Tel: 867-667-5667
Fax: 867-393-6933
Les.Hudson@gov.yk.ca

Associated Agencies, Boards & Commissions:

- **Assessment Appeal Board**
Tel: 867-668-6598
Fax: 867-633-2640
- **Driver Control Board**
2130 Second Ave., 3rd Fl.
PO Box 2703
Whitehorse, YT Y1A 2C6
Tel: 867-667-5111
Fax: 867-667-3609
dcb@gov.yk.ca
www.community.gov.yk.ca/dcb
Other Communication: 800-661-0408 (ext. 5111)
- **Yukon Lottery Commission**
312 Wood St.
Whitehorse, YT Y1A 2E6
Tel: 867-633-7890
Fax: 867-668-7561
lotteriesyukon@gov.yk.ca
www.lotteriesyukon.com

Safety Resources
91790 Alaska Hwy., Whitehorse, YT Y1A 5X7
Fax: 867-456-6567

Community Development
The branch assists, advises & organizes municipal & unincorporated communities, provides funding by administering the comprehensive municipal grants & grants in lieu of taxes, assesses properties, collects property taxes & administers the Rural Electrification & Telecommunication program & the Home Owner Grant program. The branch collaborates with communities for the planning, design, & construction of land development projects & includes residential, rural residential, commercial, industrial, & cottage lots. The branch is responsible for regulatory approvals & design, managing construction capital works projects, such as upgrading roads, water & sewage treatment facilities & solid waste disposal sites & assists communities in developing land use plans, working closely with the Yukon Municipal Board & the Association of Yukon Communities. The branch is responsible for the operation of Yukon Government owned facilities for water supply & distribution, sewage treatment & solid waste disposal.
Assistant Deputy Minister, Paul Moore
Tel: 867-667-3534
Fax: 867-393-6216
paul.moore@gov.yk.ca

Emergency Measures Organization (EMO)
Combined Services Bldg., 2nd Fl., 60 Norseman Rd, Airport, Whitehorse, YT Y1A 2C6
Tel: 867-667-5220
Fax: 867-393-6266
Toll-Free: 800-661-0408
emo.yukon@gov.yk.ca
www.community.gov.yk.ca/emo
Responsible for coordinating the Territory's preparedness for, response to, & recovery from, major emergencies & disasters. EMO provides authority to ensure that contingency plans are in place to deal with foreseeable risks & hazards. The Yukon EMO is divided into 13 geographical preparedness areas, mirroring the RCMP detachment boundaries. Eight of these areas have incorporated Municipalities that have appointed a Municipal EMO Coordinator to chair the local Emergency Planning Committee. In the remaining areas, the Emergency Measures Branch appoints a co-ordinator.
Manager, Michael Templeton
Tel: 867-667-5220
Fax: 867-393-6266
michael.templeton@gov.yk.ca
Finance/Admin. Assistant, Arthur MacMaster
Tel: 867-667-5220
Fax: 867-393-6266
arthur.macmaster@gov.yk.ca

Consumer Services & Information Development
Berska Bldg., 2nd Fl., 307 Black St., Whitehorse, YT
Fax: 867-393-6943
Assistant Deputy Minister, Dan Boyd
Tel: 867-667-5486
Fax: 867-393-6251
dan.boyd@gov.yk.ca

Protective Services
91790 Alaska Hwy., Whitehorse, YT Y1A 5X7
Fax: 867-456-6567
Assistant Deputy Minister, Rick Smith
Tel: 867-393-7409
rick.smith@gov.yk.ca

Emergency Medical Services
Yukon Electrical Bldg., #200, 1100 First Ave., Whitehorse, YT
www.community.gov.yk.ca/ems

Fire Marshal's Office
91790 Alaska Hwy., Whitehorse, YT Y1A 5X7
Tel: 867-667-5811
Fax: 867-667-3165
inquiry@gov.yk.ca
www.community.gov.yk.ca/fireprotection/contact.html
The Fire Marshal's Office works to reduce the loss of life & property due to fire & is responsible for public education & fire fighter training, as well as for funding & administering volunteer fire departments in Yukon unincorporated communities. Staff carry out fire & life safety inspections on hotels, motels, public assembly buildings, schools, day care centers, homes for special care, restaurants, etc. throughout Yukon. The Office inspects & permits underground fuel storage tank installations.
Director of Fire & Life Safety/Fire Marshal, Dennis Berry
Tel: 867-667-5217
Fax: 867-667-3165
dennis.berry@gov.yk.ca

Wildlife Fire Management
91790 Alaska Hwy., Whitehorse, YT Y1A 5X7
Tel: 867-456-3845
Fax: 867-667-3191
www.community.gov.yk.ca/firemanagement

Yukon Development Corporation (YDC)

#2 Miles Canyon Rd., PO Box 5920, Whitehorse, YT Y1A 6S7
Tel: 867-393-5337
Fax: 867-393-5401
www.ydc.yk.ca
The Yukon Development Corporation (YDC) assists with implementation of energy policies from the Department of Energy, Mines & Resources, by designing & delivering related energy programs. YDC facilitates the generation, production, transmission & distribution of energy in a manner consistent with sustainable development. YDC has investments in electricity & related energy infrastructure & acts as the primary vehicle for delivery of territorial energy programs & services. YDC owns two subsidiary corporations, Yukon Energy Corporation, YEC, & the Energy Solutions Centre Inc., ESC. YEC is the primary producer & transmitter of electrical energy in the territory & operates under the Yukon Utilities Board & the Public Utilities Act. ESC provides technical services, promotes efficiency & renewable energy technologies, co-ordinates & delivers federal & territorial energy programs to households, businesses, institutions, First Nation & public governments.
Acts Administered:
Yukon Development Corporation Act

Minister responsible, Brad Cathers
Tel: 867-667-8625
Fax: 867-456-6741
brad.cathers@gov.yk.ca

Chief Executive Officer, David Morrison
Tel: 867-393-5400
Fax: 867-393-5401
david.morrison@gov.yk.ca

Yukon Economic Development

PO Box 2703, Whitehorse, YT Y1A 2C6
Tel: 867-393-7191
Fax: 867-393-6412
Toll-Free: 800-661-0408
ecdev@gov.yk.ca
www.economicdevelopment.gov.yk.ca
The Department works with the Yukon business community & with other governments to support business development, trade & investment opportunities, & partnerships for the development of the Yukon economy. It co-ordinates & facilitates the Yukon Government's economic development agenda. The Department is focused on creating a positive business climate in Yukon & is committed to First Nation business development in the territory. Economic Development markets Yukon as a great place to do business.

Minister, Currie Dixon, Hon.
Tel: 867-667-5800
Fax: 867-393-6252
currie.dixon@gov.yk.ca

Deputy Minister, Harvey Brooks
Tel: 867-393-7191
Fax: 867-667-3159
harvey.brooks@gov.yk.ca

Assistant Deputy Minister, Operations, Terry Hayden
Tel: 867-456-3912
Fax: 867-667-3159
terry.hayden@gov.yk.ca

Director, Finance & Information Services, Karen Mason
Tel: 867-667-5933
Fax: 867-393-7199
karen.mason@gov.yk.ca

Director, Policy, Planning & Research, Stephen Rose
Tel: 867-667-8416
Fax: 867-393-6412
stephen.rose@gov.yk.ca

Executive Assistant to the Minister, Valerie Boxall
Tel: 867-667-8628
Fax: 867-393-7400
valerie.boxall@gov.yk.ca

Executive Assistant to the Deputy Minister, Judith Voswinkel
Tel: 867-393-7191
Fax: 867-667-3159
judith.voswinkel@gov.yk.ca

Business & Economic Research
Fax: 867-393-6412
economics@gov.yk.ca
www.economics.gov.yk.ca
Provides research, analysis & reports to support a broad understanding of the economy & the assessment of its impacts on Yukon's fiscal position, budgetary projections & financial decision making.
Acting Director, Clint Ireland
Tel: 867-667-8011
clint.ireland@gov.yk.ca

Business & Industry Development
PO Box 2703 F-2, Whitehorse, YT Y1A 2C6
Tel: 867-456-3920
Fax: 867-393-6944
investyukon@gov.yk.ca
www.economicdevelopment.gov.yk.ca/bidb.html
Other Communication: business.trade@gov.yk.ca
Director, Barbara Dunlop
Tel: 867-667-3430
Fax: 867-393-6944
barbara.dunlop@gov.yk.ca

Coporate Planning & Economic Policy
#209, 212 Main St., Whitehorse, YT
Tel: 867-456-3914
Fax: 867-393-6412
www.economicdevelopment.gov.yk.ca/cpepb.html

Regional Economic Development
308 Wood St., 2nd Fl., Whitehorse, YT
Tel: 867-456-3991
red@gov.yk.ca
Director, Bert Perry
Tel: 867-667-8853
bert.perry@gov.yk.ca

Film & Sound Commission
Closeleigh Manor, 101 Elliott St., PO Box 2703, Whitehorse, YT Y1A 2C6
Tel: 867-667-5400
Fax: 867-393-7040
info@reelyukon.com
www.reelyukon.com
Other Communication: 800-661-0408, ext. 5400 (toll-free)
Film & Sound Commissioner, Film & Sound Commission, Barbara Dunlop
Tel: 867-667-5400
Fax: 867-393-7040

Yukon Education

PO Box 2703, Whitehorse, YT Y1A 2C6
Tel: 867-667-5141
Fax: 867-393-6254
contact.education@gov.yk.ca
www.education.gov.yk.ca
Other Communication: 800-661-0408, ext. 5141 (toll-free)
The Yukon has 28 public schools (14 in Whitehorse, 14 in other communities) & two private schools. The public schools are administered directly by the Department of Education, although elected school council officials are gradually assuming more powers under the 1990 Education Act, & may evolve into school boards in the near future. In 1996, the Yukon Francophone School Board was created, becoming Yukon's first school board. Curriculum is largely based on that of British Columbia, with flexibility for locally developed courses, particularly from a First Nations perspective (approximately one-third of the Yukon's students are of First Nations ancestry). Instruction is English-based for the majority of students. French & Aboriginal languages are widely offered as second language instruction. French Immersion & French First Language education is offered in Whitehorse.
Acts Administered:
Apprentice Training Act
Canada Student Loans Act (federal)
Education Act
Labour Mobility Amendments Act
Occupational Training Act
School Trespass Act
Students' Financial Assistance Act
Teaching Profession Act
Trade Schools Regulation Act
Yukon College Act

Minister, Scott Kent, Hon.
Tel: 867-667-5800
Fax: 867-393-6252
scott.kent@gov.yk.ca

Deputy Minister, Pamela Hine
Tel: 867-667-5126
pamela.hine@gov.yk.ca

Director, Human Resources Services, Dick Chambers
Tel: 867-667-5808
dick.chambers@gov.yk.ca

Director, Finance & Administration, Cyndy Dekuysscher
Tel: 867-667-5701
cyndy.dekuysscher@gov.yk.ca

Director, Policy, Planning & Evaluation, Ann MacDonald
Tel: 867-667-8181
ann.macdonald@gov.yk.ca

Advanced Education
PO Box 2703, Whitehorse, YT Y1A 2C6
Tel: 867-667-5131
Fax: 867-667-8555
contact.education@gov.yk.ca
www.education.gov.yk.ca/advanceded
Assistant Deputy Minister, Brent Slobodin
Tel: 867-667-5129
brent.slobodin@gov.yk.ca
Director, Apprenticeship Training, Judy Thrower
Tel: 867-667-5133
judy.thrower@gov.yk.ca
Director, Labour Market Programs & Services, Shawn Kitchen
Tel: 867-667-5727
shawn.kitchen@gov.yk.ca

Education Support Services
Fax: 867-393-6254
www.education.gov.yk.ca/ess/index.html
Director, Finance & Administration, Cyndy Dekuysscher
Tel: 867-667-5701
cyndy.dekuysscher@gov.yk.ca
Director, Human Resources, Dick Chambers
Tel: 867-667-5808
dick.chambers@gov.yk.ca
Director, Policy, Planning & Evaluation, Ann MacDonald
Tel: 867-667-8181
Fax: 867-456-6788
ann.macdonald@gov.yk.ca

Public Schools Branch
PO Box 2703, Whitehorse, YT Y1A 2C6
Tel: 867-667-5068
Fax: 867-393-6339
www.education.gov.yk.ca/psb
Assistant Deputy Minister, Christie Whitley
Tel: 867-667-5127
christie.whitley@gov.yk.ca
President, Yukon College, Karen Barnes, Dr.
Tel: 867-668-8704
kbarnes@yukoncollege.yk.ca
500 College Dr.
PO Box 2799
Whitehorse, YT Y1A 5K4
Superintendent, Penny Prysnuk
Tel: 867-667-3747
penny.prysnuk@gov.yk.ca
Superintendent, Greg Storey
Tel: 867-667-3722
greg.storey@gov.yk.ca
Superintendent, Mike Woods
Tel: 867-667-5180
mike.woods@gov.yk.ca
Director, Yukon College, Jacqueline Bedard
Tel: 867-456-8619
jaqueline.bedard@gov.yk.ca
Director, First Nations Programs & Partnerships, Edmund Schultz
Tel: 867-393-6905
Fax: 867-456-6766
edmund.schultz@gov.yk.ca
Director, Native Language Centre, John Ritter
Tel: 867-668-8820
Toll-free: 877-414-9652
Fax: 867-668-8825
john.ritter@gov.yk.ca
PO Box 2799
Whitehorse, YT Y1A 5K4
Director, Programs & Services, Elizabeth Lemay
Tel: 867-667-8238
Fax: 867-393-6339
elizabeth.lemay@gov.yk.ca
Coordinator, Francophone Partnerships, Yann Herry
Tel: 867-667-8610
Fax: 867-393-6366
yann.henry@gov.yk.ca
Coordinator, Primary Programs, Jeanette McCrie
Tel: 867-667-5186
jeanette.mccrie@gov.yk.ca

Yukon Energy, Mines & Resources

PO Box 2703, Whitehorse, YT Y1A 2C6
Tel: 867-667-3130
Fax: 867-456-3965
Toll-Free: 800-661-0408
emr@gov.yk.ca
www.emr.gov.yk.ca
TTY: 867-393-7460
The territory has extensive mineral deposits, oil & gas potential, with two producing gas wells, which rank among the top producing wells in Canada, forest reserves & local manufacturing of wood products, such as furniture, wood laminate stock & lumber. The territory has abundant & diverse energy resources due to the presence of fossil fuel reserves, numerous lakes & rivers, windy & mountainous terrain, broad forest cover & sunny conditions. The Yukon is one of the few places left in Canada where Crown land can be obtained for agricultural purposes.
Acts Administered:
Agricultural Products Acts
Agriculture Development Act
Animal Health Act (jointly with Environment)
Animal Protection Act (jointly with Community Services)
Area Development Act
Brands Act
Economic Development Act (jointly with Economic Development)
Energy Conservation Assistance Act
Forest Protection Act (jointly with Community Services)
Lands Act
Oil & Gas Act
Oil & Gas Disposition Regulations
Oil & Gas Drilling & Production Regulations
Oil & Gas Geoscience & Exploration Regulations
Oil & Gas Licence Administration Regulations
Placer Mining Act
Pounds Act
Quartz Mining Act
Subdivision Act
Territorial Lands (Yukon) Act
Waters Act (jointly with Environment & the Executive Council Office)

Minister, Brad Cathers, Hon.
Tel: 867-667-8625
Fax: 867-456-6741
brad.cathers@gov.yk.ca

Deputy Minister, Angus Robertson
Tel: 867-667-5417
Fax: 867-393-7167
angus.robertson@gov.yk.ca

Assistant Deputy Minister, Energy, Corporate Policy & Communications, Shirley Abercrombie
Tel: 867-667-3187
Fax: 867-393-7421
shirley.abercrombie@gov.yk.ca

Executive Director, Yukon Placer Secretariat, Robert Thomson
Tel: 867-667-3136
Fax: 867-667-3632
robert.thomson@gov.yk.ca

Director, Corporate Services, Ross McLachlan
Tel: 867-456-3960
Fax: 867-456-3965
ross.mclachlan@gov.yk.ca

Director, Communications, Mark Roberts
Tel: 867-667-5307
Fax: 867-393-7421
mark.roberts@gov.yk.ca

Agriculture
Tel: 867-667-5838
Fax: 867-393-6222
agriculture@gov.yk.ca
www.emr.gov.yk.ca/agriculture/index.html
Other Communication: 800-661-0408, ext. 5838 (toll-free)
Director, Tony Hill
tony.hill@gov.yk.ca

Assessment & Abandoned Mines
Assessment Centre, #2C, 4114 4th Ave., Whitehorse, YT Y1A 2C6
Tel: 867-393-7098
Fax: 867-456-6780
yukonabandonedmines@gov.yk.ca
www.emr.gov.yk.ca
Other Communication: 800-661-0408, ext. 7098 (toll-free)
Director, Stephen Mead
Tel: 867-393-6904
stephen.mead@gov.yk.ca

Client Services & Inspections
www.emr.gov.yk.ca/csi/index.html
Director, Robert Thomson
Tel: 867-667-3136
Fax: 867-667-3199
robert.thomson@gov.yk.ca

Forestry
Mile 918 Alaska Hwy., PO Box 2703, Whitehorse, YT Y1A 2C6
Tel: 867-456-3999
Fax: 867-667-3138
forestry@gov.yk.ca
www.emr.gov.yk.ca/forestry
Acting Director, Pat MacDonell
Tel: 867-633-7917
patrick.macdonnell@gov.yk.ca

Human Resources
230-300 Main St., PO Box 2703, Whitehorse, YT Y1A 2C6
Tel: 867-667-3007
Fax: 867-393-7422
www.emr.gov.yk.ca/hr
Other Communication: 800-661-0408, ext. 3007 (toll-free)

Director, Ingrid Fawcus
Tel: 867-667-3549
ingrid.fawcus@gov.yk.ca

Land Services
#320, 300 Main St., Whitehorse, YT Y1A 2C6
Tel: 867-667-5215
www.emr.gov.yk.ca/lands
Director, Land Planning, George Stetkiewicz
Tel: 867-667-3530
Fax: 867-393-6340
george.stetkiewicz@gov.yk.ca
Manager, Programs & Policy Support, Mike Draper
Tel: 867-667-3185
Fax: 867-393-6340
mike.draper@gov.yk.ca
Manager, Land Use, Marg White
Tel: 867-667-3173
Fax: 867-667-3214
marg.white@gov.yk.ca
Manager, Land Client Services, John Cole
Tel: 867-667-5882
Fax: 867-667-3214
john.cole@gov.yk.ca

Library
Elijah Smith Building, #335, 300 Main St., Whitehorse, YT Y1A 2B5
Tel: 867-667-3111
Fax: 867-456-3888
emrlibrary@gov.yk.ca
www.emr.gov.yk.ca/library
Manager, Aimee Ellis
Tel: 867-667-3108
aimee.ellis@gov.yk.ca

Mining
#400, 211 Main St., Whitehorse, YT Y1A 2B2
Tel: 867-633-7952
Fax: 867-456-3899
mining@gov.yk.ca
www.emr.gov.yk.ca/mining
Other Communication: 800-661-0408, ext. 7952 (toll-free)
Director, Mineral Resources, Bob Holmes
Tel: 867-667-3126
robert.holmes@gov.yk.ca

Oil & Gas Mineral Resources
#300, 211 Main St., Whitehorse, YT Y1A 2B2
Tel: 867-667-5087
Fax: 867-393-6262
oilandgas@gov.yk.ca
www.emr.gov.yk.ca/oilandgas
Other Communication: 800-661-0408, ext. 5087 (toll-free)
Assistant Deputy Minister, Greg Komaromi
Tel: 867-667-3011
Director, Brian Love
Tel: 867-667-3566
brian.love@gov.yk.ca

Yukon Geological Survey
Elijah Smith Building, #102-300 Main St., Whitehorse, YT
Tel: 867-667-5097
Fax: 867-393-6262
oilandgas@gov.yk.ca
www.emr.gov.yk.ca/oilandgas
Other Communication: 800-661-0408, ext. 5087 (toll-free)
Also located at the Professional Building at 2099-2nd Ave.
Director, Carolyn Relf
Tel: 867-667-8892
carolyn.relf@gov.yk.ca

Yukon Environment

PO Box 2703, Whitehorse, YT Y1A 2C6
Tel: 867-667-5652
Fax: 867-393-7197
environment.yukon@gov.yk.ca
www.env.gov.yk.ca
Other Communication: 800-661-0408, ext. 5652 (toll-free)

The department is responsible for legislation, regulations licensing, management, policies, programs, services, education & information regarding the natural environment in three program areas: fish & wildlife, environmental protection & assessment & parks & protection areas. The department's branches educate resource users & the general public, develop & enforce policies, regulations, & legislation & assist other departments in the sustainable use & management of the territory's natural resources. The department supports land claims negotiations & assists in implementing land claims agreements. The department represents the Yukon government at national & global environmental forums on issues such as climate change & biodiversity conservation.Through the Environmental Awareness Fund the government provides funding to assist registered non-government organizations to promote environmental education or awareness, resource planning & sustainable development in the Yukon.

Acts Administered:
Activities Requiring Environmental Assessment (Inclusion List) Regulations
Administrative Regulation
Air Emissions Regulations
Animal Health Act (jointly with Energy, Mines & Resources)
Beverage Container Regulation
Campground Regulations
Coal River Springs Ecological Reserve
Comprehensive Study List Regulation
Concession & Compensation Review Board Regulations
Conservation Fund Regulations
Contaminated Sites Regulations
Coordination of Environmental Assessment Procedures & Requirement Regulations
Designated Materials
Environment Act
Establish Ni'iinlii Njik (Fishing Branch) Ecological Reserve
Establish Ni'iinlii Njik (Fishing Branch) Wilderness Preserve
Exclusion List Regulation
Game Farm Regulations
Game Management Sub-zone Regulations
Herschel Island Nature Preserve
Herschel Island Park Regulations
Law List Regulation
Mackenzie River Basin Agreement Act
Outfitting Concession Area Boundary Regulations
Ozone Depleting Substances & Other Halocarbons Regulation
Parks & Land Certainty Act
Pesticides Regulations
Recycling Fund Regulation
Solid Waste Regulations
Special Waste Regulations
Spills Regulations
Storage Tank Regulations
Tombstone Territorial Park Regulations
Trapping Concession Area Boundary Regulations
Trapping Regulations
Waters Act (jointly with Energy, Mines & Resources & the Executive Council Office)
Waters Regulation
Wilderness Tourism Licensing Act
Wildlife Act
Wildlife Sanctuary Regulation
Yukon Council on the Economy & the Environment Regulation
Yukon River Basin & Alsek River Basin Agreements Act

Minister, Currie Dixon, Hon.
Tel: 867-667-5800
Fax: 867-393-6252
currie.dixon@gov.yk.ca

Deputy Minister, Kelvin Leary
Tel: 867-667-5460
Fax: 867-393-6213
kelvin.leary@gov.yk.ca

Associated Agencies, Boards & Commissions:
• **Alsek Renewable Resource Council (ARRC)**
PO Box 2077
Haines Junction, YT Y0B 1L0
Tel: 867-634-2524
Fax: 867-634-2527
www.alsekrrc.ca/www.alsekrrc.ca
A voice for local community members in managing renewable resources, such as fish, wildlife and forests, ARRC was formed in 1995 with the signing of the Champagne & Aishihik First Nations (CAFN) Final Agreement.
• **Carcross/ Tagish Renewable Resource Council**
PO Box 70
Tagish, YT Y0B 1T0
Tel: 867-399-4923
Fax: 867-399-4978
carcrosstagishrrc@gmail.com
• **Carmacks Renewable Resource Council**
PO Box 122
Carmacks, YT Y0B 1C0
Tel: 867-863-6838
Fax: 867-863-6429
carmacksrrc@northwestel.net
Other Communication: www.yfwmb.ca/rrc/carmacks
• **Dan Keyi Renewable Resource Council**
PO Box 50
Burwash Landing, YT Y0B 1V0
Tel: 867-841-5820
Fax: 867-841-5821
dankeyirrc@northwestel.net
• **Dawson District Renewable Resource Council**
PO Box 1380
Dawson City, YT Y0B 1G0
Tel: 867-993-6976
Fax: 867-993-6093
dawsonrrc@northwestel.net
www.yfwmb.ca/rrc/dawson
• **Laberge Renewable Resource Council**
#202, 102 Copper Rd.
Whitehorse, YT Y1A 2Z6
labergerrc@northwestel.net
• **Mayo District Renewable Resources Council**
PO Box 249
Mayo, YT Y0B 1M0
Tel: 867-996-2942
Fax: 867-996-2948
mayorrc@yknet.yk.ca
• **North Yukon Renewable Resources Council**
PO Box 80
Old Crow, YT Y0B 1N0
Tel: 867-966-3034
Fax: 867-966-3036
vgrrc@yknet.yk.ca
www.yfwmb.ca/rrc/northyukon
• **Selkirk Renewable Resources Council**
PO Box 32
Pelly Crossing, YT Y0B 1P0
Tel: 867-537-3937
Fax: 867-537-3939
selkirkrrc@yknet.yk.ca
www.yfwmb.ca/rrc/selkirk
• **Teslin Renewable Resource Council**
PO Box 186
Teslin, YT Y0A 1B0
Tel: 867-390-2323
Fax: 867-390-2919
teslinrrc@northwestel.net
www.yfwmb.ca/rrc/teslin
• **Yukon Fish & Wildlife Management Board**
106 Main St., 2nd Fl.
Whitehorse, YT Y1A 5P7
Tel: 867-667-3754
Fax: 867-393-6947
officemanager@yfwmb.ca
www.yfwmb.ca
The Board focuses its efforts on territorial policies, legislation & other measures to help guide management of fish & wildlife, conserve habitat & enhance the renewable resources economy. The Board influences management decisions through public education & by making recommendations to Yukon, Federal and First Nations governments. Recommendations & positions are based on the best technical, traditional & local information available.
• **Yukon Land Use Planning Council**
#201, 307 Jarvis St.
Whitehorse, YT Y1A 2H3
Tel: 867-667-7397
Fax: 867-667-4624
ylupc@planyukon.ca
www.planyukon.ca/
The Yukon Land Use Planning Council assists government & Yukon First Nationsto co-ordinate efforts to conduct community based regional land use planning. This planning is necessary to resolve land use & resource conflicts. The plans ensure that use of lands & resources is consistent with social, cultural, economic & environmental values. These plans build upon traditional knowledge & experience of the residents of each region.

Climate Change Secretariat
Tel: 867-456-5544
Fax: 867-456-5543
Toll-Free: 800-661-0408
ClimateChange@gov.yk.ca
Other Communication: www.env.gov.yk.ca/monitoringenvironment/climate_change_secretariat.php
The Secretariat has the lead role in ensuring Yukon government actions support a healthy & resilient Yukon in a changing climate. It strives to identify needs, opportunities & priorities; promote & support action; & monitor & report on progress.
Director, Eric Schroff
Tel: 867-633-7971
eric.schroff@gov.yk.ca

Conservation Officer Services
Tel: 867-667-8005
Fax: 867-393-6206
Toll-Free: 800-661-0408
coservicesgov.yk.ca
www.env.gov.yk.ca/branches/conservation_officer_services.php
Other Communication: T.I.P. line: 800-661-0525
The Branch provides environmental education, environmental youth camps & projects, provides hunting, fishing & trapping licences, provides hunter & trapper education, resource management support, wildlife safety for the public & provides enforcement & compliance.
Director, John Russell
Tel: 867-667-5786
Fax: 867-393-6206
john.russell@gov.yk.ca

Corporate Services
Tel: 867-667-5652
Fax: 867-393-7197
Toll-Free: 800-661-0408
environmentyukon@gov.yk.ca
www.env.gov.yk.ca/branches/corporate_services.php
Provides support services to the Department of Environment.
Director, Mindy Crayford
Tel: 867-667-8486
Fax: 867-393-7012
mindy.crayford@gov.yk.ca
Manager, Client Services, Dee Balsam
Tel: 867-667-5797
Fax: 867-393-7197
dee.balsam@gov.yk.ca
Manager, Information Management & Technology, Beth Hawkings
Tel: 867-667-8137
Fax: 867-393-7003
beth.hawkings@gov.yk.ca
Manager, Financial Services Branch, Darrell Branch
Tel: 867-667-5160
Fax: 867-393-6219
darrell.branch@gov.yk.ca
Manager, Communications, Dennis Senger
Tel: 867-667-5237
Fax: 867-393-6213
dennis.senger@gov.yk.ca

Environmental Programs
Tel: 867-667-5683
Fax: 867-393-6213
Toll-Free: 800-661-0408
envprot@gov.yk.ca
www.env.gov.yk.ca/branches/environmental_programs.php
Formed in 1994, the Branch is responsible for development of regulations & standards under the Environment Act & programs associated with everyday waste management, contaminated sites, air quality & pesticides. The Branch is also responsible for monitoring & inspection of permits, spill cleanup & environmental assessments of development projects, recycling education & promotion, public education & awareness.
Director, Jon Bowen
Tel: 867-667-8177
Fax: 867-393-6213
jon.bowen@gov.yk.ca

Fish & Wildlife
Tel: 867-667-5715
Fax: 867-393-6405
Toll-Free: 800-661-0408
fish.wildlife@gov.yk.ca
www.env.gov.yk.ca/branches/fish_wildlife.php
The Branch maintains the ecosystem based on sound management of fish, wildlife & their habitats, preserves the sustainability of fish & wildlife populations, works with First Nations & community relations to preserve & enhance the ecosystem, develops management plans, provides policy & planning, collects, assesses & disseminates natural resource data & provides public education for resource users.
Director, Dan Lindsey
Tel: 867-667-5715
Fax: 867-393-6405
dan.lindsey@gov.yk.ca

Human Resources
10 Burns Rd., Whitehorse, YT
Fax: 867-393-7012

Parks
PO Box 2703 V-4, Whitehorse, YT Y1A 2C6
Tel: 867-667-5648
Fax: 867-393-6223
Toll-Free: 800-661-0408
yukon.parks@gov.yk.ca
www.environmentyukon.gov.yk.ca/parks/parks.html
Director, Erik Val
Tel: 867-667-5639
Fax: 867-393-6223
erik.val@gov.yk.ca

Policy & Planning
10 Burns Rd., Whitehorse, YT
Fax: 867-393-6213

Water Resources
Tel: 867-667-3171
Fax: 867-667-3195
Toll-Free: 800-661-0408
water.resources@gov.yk.ca
www.env.gov.yk.ca/monitoringenvironment/aboutwaterresources.php
Director, Kevin McDonnell
Tel: 867-667-3145
Fax: 867-667-3195
kevin.mcdonnell@gov.yk.ca
Manager, Richard Janowicz
Tel: 867-667-3223
richard.janowicz@gov.yk.ca

Yukon Finance

PO Box 2703, Whitehorse, YT Y1A 2C6
Tel: 867-667-5343
Fax: 867-393-6217
fininfo@gov.yk.ca
www.finance.gov.yk.ca

Acts Administered:
Appropriation Acts
Banking Agency Guarantee Act
Faro Mine Loan Act
Financial Administration Act
Fireweed Fund Act
Fuel Oil Tax Act
Income Tax Act
Insurance Premium Tax Act
Interim Supply Appropriation Acts
Liquor Tax Act
Taxpayer Protection Act
Tobacco Tax Act
Yukon Development Corporation Loan Guarantee Act

Minister, Darrell Pasloski
Tel: 867-667-8660
Fax: 867-393-6252
premier@gov.yk.ca

Deputy Minister, David Hrycan
Tel: 867-667-3571
Fax: 867-393-6217
david.hrycan@gov.yk.ca

Director, Finance & Administration, Bill Curtis
Tel: 867-667-5276
Fax: 867-393-6217
bill.curtis@gov.yk.ca

Financial Operations & Taxation
Fax: 867-393-6217
Assistant Deputy Minister, Clarke Laprarie
Tel: 867-667-5355
Fax: 867-393-6217
clarke.laprarie@gov.yk.ca
Comptroller, Accounting & Policy, Miko Miyahara
Tel: 867-667-5375
miko.miyahara@gov.yk.ca
Acting Director, Financial Systems, Alan Houston
Tel: 867-667-5278
Fax: 867-393-6217
alan.houston@gov.yk.ca
Director, Investments & Debt Services, Elaine Carlyle
Tel: 867-667-5346
elaine.carlyle@gov.yk.ca
Director, Taxation, Gerald Gagnon
Tel: 867-667-3074
Fax: 867-456-6709

Fiscal Relations & Management Board Secretariat
Fax: 867-393-6355
Director, Budgets, Christina Frisch
Tel: 867-667-5277
Fax: 867-393-6355
Director, Fiscal Relations, Tim Shoniker
Tel: 867-667-5303
Fax: 867-393-6355
Director, Management Board Secretariat, Jim Connell
Tel: 867-667-3542
jim.connell@gov.yk.ca

Yukon Health & Social Services

PO Box 2703, Whitehorse, YT Y1A 2C6
Tel: 867-667-3673
Fax: 867-667-3096
hss@gov.yk.ca
www.hss.gov.yk.ca
Committed to quality health & social services for Yukoners by helping individuals acquire the skills to live responsible, healthy & independent lives; & providing a range of accessible, affordable services that assist individuals, families & communities to reach their full potential.
Acts Administered:
Adult Protection & Decision-Making Act
Canadian Blood Agency/Canadian Blood Services Indemnification Act
Canadian Council for Donation & Transplantation Indemnifiction Act
Care Consent Act
Change of Name Act
Child & Family Services Act
Child Care Act
Children's Act
Decision Making, Support & Protection to Adults Act
Health Act
Health Care Insurance Plan Act
Hospital Act
Hospital Insurance Services Act
Intercountry Adoption (Hague Convention) Act
Marriage Act
Mental Health Act
Pioneer Utility Grant Act
Public Health & Safety Act
Regulations to Establish Butylnitrite as Regulated Matter
Rehabilitation Services Act
Rubbish Disposal
Seniors' Income Supplement Act
Sewage Disposal Systems Regulations
Smoke-Free Places Act
Social Assistance Act
Travel for Medical Treatment Act
Vital Statistics Act
Young Persons Offences Act
Youth Criminal Justice Act (Canada; jointly with Justice)
Yukon Family Services Association Rent Guarantee Act

Minister, Doug Graham, Hon.
Tel: 867-667-5800
Fax: 867-393-6252
doug.graham@gov.yk.ca

Deputy Minister, Stuart Whitley
Tel: 867-667-5770
Fax: 867-667-3096
stuart.whitley@gov.yk.ca

Associated Agencies, Boards & Commissions:
• Health & Social Service Council
This advisory body makes recommendations to the government relating to issues of health, social services, education & justice.
• Yukon Child Care Board
This advisory body makes recommendations to the Minister of Health & Social Services, on any issues that pertain to child care.

Continuing Care
307 Black St., Whitehorse, YT Y1A 2N1
Tel: 867-667-5945
www.hss.gov.yk.ca/continuing.php
Other Communication: 800-661-0408, ext. 5945 (toll-free)
Provides residential, home care & regional therapy services for the citizens of the Yukon Territory.
Assistant Deputy Minister, Cathy Morton-Bielz
Tel: 867-667-8922
Fax: 867-456-6545
cathy.morton-bielz@gov.yk.ca
Director, Safety & Clinical Excellence, Nancy Kidd
Tel: 867-667-8750
Fax: 867-456-6545
nancy.kidd@gov.yk.ca
Director, Extended Care, Willy Shippey
willy.shippey@gov.yk.ca
Director, Care & Community, Liris Smith
Tel: 867-456-6839
liris.smith@gov.yk.ca

Coporate Services
www.hss.gov.yk.ca/corporate.php
Plays a key role in ensuring that Yukon residents have accurate, up-to-date information about the territory's health & social programs, services & systems.
Assistant Deputy Minister, Birgitte Hunter
Tel: 867-667-8309
Fax: 867-393-6457
birgitte.hunter@gov.yk.ca
Director, Finance, Systems & Administration, Warren Holland
warren.holland@wgh.yk.ca
Director, Policy & Program Development, Brian Kitchen
Tel: 867-667-5688
Fax: 867-667-3096
brian.kitchen@gov.yk.ca
Director, Corporate Strategic Initiatives & Priorities, Cynthia Lyslo
Tel: 867-667-5673
cynthia.lyslo@gov.yk.ca
Director, Quality & Risk Management, Karen Archbell
Tel: 867-667-5943
karen.archbell@gov.yk.ca

Health Services
Financial Plaza, 204 Lambert St., 4th Fl., Whitehorse, YT Y1A 3T2
Fax: 867-393-6486
www.hss.gov.yk.ca/healthservices.php
Responsible for a variety of health care, disease prevention & treatment services which assist eligible Yukon residents in attaining maximum individual independence within their community.

Assistant Deputy Minister, Health Services, Sherri Wright
Tel: 867-667-5689
Fax: 867-667-3096
Director, Insured Health & Hearing Services, Paul Gudatis
Tel: 867-667-5209
Fax: 867-393-6486
Director, Community Nursing, Joy Kajiwara
Tel: 867-667-8324
Fax: 867-667-8338
Director, Community Health Programs, Cathy Stannard
Tel: 867-667-8340
Fax: 867-456-6502
cathy.stannard@gov.yk.ca

Social Services
www.hss.gov.yk.ca/socialservices.php
Consists of Adult Community Services, Alcohol & Drug Services, Family & Children's Services, Regional Services, Senior Services, Seniors & Elder Abuse, Services for People With Disabilities, & Social Assistance.
Assistant Deputy Minister, Dorothea Warren
dorothea.warren@gov.yk.ca
Director, Family & Children's Services, Elaine Schroeder
Acting Director, Michele McDonnell
Tel: 867-667-3705
Fax: 867-393-6926
michele.mcdonnell@gov.yk.ca
Supervisor, Dale Gordon
Tel: 867-393-6913
Fax: 867-667-8471
dale.gordon@gov.yk.ca
Supervisor, Marg Render
Tel: 867-667-5819
Fax: 867-667-5669
marg.render@gov.yk.ca
Manager, Community Audit Services Unit, Tim Brady
Tel: 867-667-5691
Fax: 867-393-6278
Manager, Seniors' Services/ Adult Protection, Kelly Cooper
Tel: 867-456-3948
Fax: 867-393-6926
Acting Manager, Program Management, Sandy Schmidt
Tel: 867-667-5056
Fax: 867-667-8471

Yukon Highways & Public Works

PO Box 2703, Whitehorse, YT Y1A 2C6
Tel: 867-393-7193
Fax: 867-393-6218
Toll-Free: 800-661-0408
hpw-info@gov.yk.ca
www.hpw.gov.yk.ca
TTY: 867-393-7460

The Department of Highways & Public Works is responsible for ensuring safe & efficient public highways, airstrips, buildings & information systems.

Acts Administered:
Access to Information & Protection of Privacy Act
Dangerous Goods Transportation Act
Highways Act
Languages Act
Motor Vehicles Act (jointly with Community Services)
Public Printing Act

Minister, Wade Istchenko, Hon.
Tel: 867-667-5800
Fax: 867-393-6252
wade.istchenko@gov.yk.ca

Deputy Minister, Mike Johnson
Tel: 867-667-3732
Fax: 867-393-6218
mike.johnson@gov.yk.ca

Director, Policy & Communications, Kendra Black
Tel: 867-667-5436
Fax: 867-393-6218
kendra.black@gov.yk.ca

Director, Finance, Jacqueline McBride-Dickson
Tel: 867-667-5410
Fax: 867-667-8231
jackie.mcbride-dixon@gov.yk.ca

Director, Human Resources, Carolyn MacDonald
Tel: 867-667-5156
Fax: 867-667-3685
carolyn.macdonald@gov.yk.ca

Aviation
Tel: 867-634-2450
Fax: 867-634-2131
aviation@gov.yk.ca
Other Communication: 800-661-0408, ext. 2450 (toll-free)

Corporate Services
Tel: 867-667-5128
Other Communication: 800-661-0408, ext. 5128 (toll-free)
Assistant Deputy Minister, Leslie Anderson
Tel: 867-667-5128
Fax: 867-393-6218
leslie.anderson@gov.yk.ca
Senior Advisor, Transporation Maintenance, Catherine Harwood
Tel: 867-667-5761
Fax: 867-667-3648
catherine.harwood@gov.yk.ca

Information & Communications Technology
Tel: 867-667-5397
Fax: 867-667-5304
Other Communication: 800-661-0408, ext. 5397 (toll-free)
Assistant Deputy Minister, Siegfried Fuchsbichler
Tel: 867-667-3712
Fax: 867-667-5304
siegfried.fuchsbichler@gov.yk.ca
Deputy Chief Information Officer, Chris Bookless
Tel: 867-456-6781
Fax: 867-667-5304
chris.bookless@gov.yk.ca
Director, Project Director, Records Program Improvement Initiative, David Downing
Tel: 867-667-8329
david.downing@gov.yk.ca
Director, Technology Infrastructure & Operations, Shane Horsnell
Tel: 867-667-5396
Fax: 867-393-6200
shane.horsnell@gov.yk.ca
Acting Director, Space Planning, Sheila Stockton
Tel: 867-667-3064
Fax: 867-667-5349
sheila.stockton@gov.yk.ca
Director, Facilities Management, Lynn Standing
Tel: 867-667-3589
Fax: 867-393-7039
lynn.standing@gov.yk.ca

Property Management Agency
Tel: 867-667-5879
Fax: 867-667-5349
Other Communication: 800-661-0408, ext. 5879 (toll-free)
Manager, Finance & Administration, Faye Doiron
Tel: 867-667-3706
faye.doiron@gov.yk.ca
Director, Facilities Management & Regional Services, Lynn Standing
Tel: 867-667-3589
Fax: 867-393-7039
lynn.standing@gov.yk.ca

Community & Correctional Service
Prospector Building, 301 Jarvis St., PO Box 2703, Whitehorse, YT Y1A 2C6
Tel: 867-393-7077
Fax: 867-393-6326
Toll-Free: 800-661-0408
justice@gov.yk.ca
Provides programs & services for victims & offenders, & has as its primary goal the safe integration of offenders into communities as law-abiding citizens.
Director, Jeff Ford
Tel: 867-667-5868
jeff.ford@gov.yk.ca
Director, Tricia Ratel
Tel: 867-667-8294
Fax: 867-393-6326
tricia.ratel@gov.yk.ca

Supply Services
Tel: 867-667-5432
Fax: 867-667-2958
hpw-info@gov.yk.ca
Other Communication: 800-661-0408, ext. 5432 (toll-free)
Director, Carl Rumscheidt
Tel: 867-667-5289
Fax: 867-667-2958
carl.rumscheidt@gov.yk.ca
Manager, Procurement Services, David Knight
Tel: 867-393-6387
Fax: 867-667-2958
david.knight@gov.yk.ca
Manager, Queen's Printer, Jo Pond
Tel: 867-667-3585
Fax: 867-393-6210
jo.pond@gov.yk.ca

Transportation
Other Communication: 800-661-0408, ext. 7193 (toll-free)
Assistant Deputy Minister, Allan Nixon
Tel: 867-667-5196
Fax: 867-393-6218
allan.nixon@gov.yk.ca
Director, Transportation Maintenance, Don Hobbis
Tel: 867-667-5761
Director, Transportation Engineering, Robin Walsh
Tel: 867-633-7928
Fax: 867-393-6447
Director, Transport Services Branch, Vern Janz
Tel: 867-667-5833
Fax: 867-667-5799

Driver Control Board
307 Black St., Whitehorse, YT Y1A 2C6
Tel: 867-667-5111
Fax: 867-667-3609
dcb@gov.yk.ca
www.community.gov.yk.ca/dcb

Yukon Housing Corporation

410H Jarvis St., PO Box 2703, Whitehorse, YT Y1A 2H5
Tel: 867-667-5759
Fax: 867-667-3664
Toll-Free: 800-661-0408
ykhouse@housing.yk.ca
www.housing.yk.ca/

Links families, communities & the housing industry with programs & services that work to support the housing needs of Yukoners.

Acts Administered:
Government Employee Housing Plan Act
Housing Corporation Act
Housing Development Act

Minister responsible, Scott Kent, Hon.
Tel: 867-667-5800
Fax: 867-393-6252
scott.kent@gov.yk.ca

President, Ron Macmillan
Tel: 867-667-5155
Fax: 867-393-6274
ron.macmillan@gov.yk.ca

Director, Systems & Administration, Mark Davey
Tel: 867-667-8773
Fax: 867-393-6399
mark.davey@gov.yk.ca

Director, Capital Development, Mike Fraser
Tel: 867-456-6190
Fax: 867-393-6441
mike.fraser@gov.yk.ca

Director, Policy & Communications, JoAnne Harach
Tel: 867-456-6802
Fax: 867-393-6274
joanne.harach@gov.yk.ca

Director, Community & Industry Partnering, Allyn Lyon
Tel: 867-667-3773
Fax: 867-393-6441
allyn.lyon@gov.yk.ca

Director, Program Delivery, Marc Perreault
Tel: 867-393-7154
marc.perreault@gov.yk.ca

Director, Human Resources, Sue Richards
Tel: 867-667-8272
Fax: 867-393-6933
sue.richards@gov.yk.ca

Yukon Justice

Andrew Philipsen Law Centre, 2134 Second Ave., PO Box 2703, Whitehorse, YT Y1A 2C6
Tel: 867-667-3033
Fax: 867-393-5790
jus.msb@gov.yk.ca
www.justice.gov.yk.ca

Acts Administered:
Adult Protection & Decision-Making Act
Age of Majority Act
Arbitration Act
Auxiliary Police Act
Canadian Charter of Rights & Freedoms (Canada) Act
Choices in Action Act
Collection Act
Condominium Act
Conflict of Laws (Traffic Accidents) Act
Constitutional Questions Act
Consumers Protection Act
Continuing Consolidation of Statutes Act
Contributory Negligence Act
Coroners Act

Corrections Act
Court of Appeal Act
Creditor's Relief Act
Crime Prevention & Victim Services Trust Act
Decision Making, Support & Protection to Adults Act (jointly with Health & Social Services)
Defamation Act
Department of Justice Act
Dependant's Relief Act
Devolution of Real Property Act
Distress Act
Electronic Evidence Act
Electronic Registration (Department of Public Statutes) Act
Enactment Republication Act
Enduring Power of Attorney Act
Estate Administration Act
Evidence Act
Executions Act
Exemptions Act
Expropriation Act
Family Property & Support Act
Family Violence Prevention Act
Fatal Accidents Act
Fine Option Act
Foreign Arbitral Awards Act
Fraudulent Preferences & Conveyances Act
Frustrated Contracts Act
Garnishee Act
Human Rights Act
Human Tissue Gift Act
Interjurisdictional Support Orders Act
International Child Abduction (Hague Convention) Act
Interpretation Act
Interprovincial Subpoena Act
Judicature Act
Jury Act
Land Titles Act
Legal Profession Act
Legal Services Society Act
Limitation of Actions Act
Lord's Day Act
Maintenance & Custory Orders Enforcement Act
Maintenance Enforcement Act
Married Women's Property Act
Mediation Board Act
Notaries Act
Perpetuities Act
Presumption of Death Act
Public Guardian & Trustee Act
Public Utilities Act
Reciprocal Enforcement of Judgements Act
Reciprocal Enforcement of Judgements UK Act
Reciprocal Enforcement of Maintenance Orders Act
Recording of Evidence Act
Regulations Act
Retirement Plan Beneficiaries Act
Safer Communities & Neighbours Act
Small Claims Court Act
Spousal Tort Immunity Abolition Act
Summary Convictions Act
Supreme Court Act
Survival of Actions Act
Survivorship Act
Tenants in Common Act
Territorial Court Act
Torture Prohibitation Act
Variation of Trusts Act
Victims of Crime Act
Wills Act
Youth Criminal Justice Act (Canada) (jointly with Health & Social Services)

Minister, Mike Nixon
Tel: 867-667-5800
Fax: 867-393-6252
mike.nixon@gov.yk.ca

Deputy Minister, Dennis Cooley
Tel: 867-667-5959
Fax: 867-393-5790
jus.dm@gov.yk.ca

Director, Finance, Systems & Administration, Luda Ayzenberg
Tel: 867-667-5615
Fax: 867-667-5790
luda.ayzenberg@gov.yk.ca

Director, Policy & Communications, Dan Cable
Tel: 867-667-3508
Fax: 867-677-5790
dan.cable@gov.yk.ca

Director, Human Resources, Brian Farrell
Tel: 867-667-5105

Executive Assistant to the Deputy Minister, Charmaine Hall
Tel: 867-667-5959
Fax: 867-667-5790
charmaine.hall@gov.yk.ca

Executive Assistant to the Minister, Christopher Young
Tel: 867-633-7973
Fax: 867-393-7400
christopher.young@gov.yk.ca

Associated Agencies, Boards & Commissions:

• **Law Society of Yukon - Executive**
#202, 302 Steele St.
Whitehorse, YT Y1A 2C5
Tel: 867-668-4231
Fax: 867-667-7556
info@lawsocietyyukon.com
www.lawsocietyyukon.com
This regulatory society serves & protects the public interest in the administration of justice.

• **Law Society of Yukon - Discipline Committee**
#202, 302 Steele St.
Whitehorse, YT Y1A 3W8
Tel: 867-668-4231
Fax: 867-667-7556
lsy@yknet.yk.ca
www.lawsocietyyukon.com
This adjudicative committee conducts inquiries/investigations into matters regarding the conduct of a member or a student-at-law.

• **Yukon Human Rights Commission**
#101, 9010 Quartz St.
Whitehorse, YT Y1A 2Z5
Tel: 867-667-6226
Fax: 867-667-2662
Toll-free: 800-661-0535
humanrights@yhrc.yk.ca
www.yhrc.yk.ca
The Commission administers the Human Rights Act, hears complaints & arranges for adjudication if required. Promotes & coordinates public education & research programs in the area of human rights.

• **Yukon Human Rights Board of Adjudication**
#202, 407 Black St.
Whitehorse, YT Y1A 2N2
Tel: 867-667-5412
Fax: 867-633-6952
beyondwords@northwestel.net
As part of the human rights complaint process, the Commission may ask for a decision from the Human Rights Board of Adjudication, which is independent of the Yukon Human Rights Commission.

• **Yukon Judicial Council**
PO Box 31222
Whitehorse, YT Y1A 5P7
Tel: 867-667-5438
Fax: 867-393-6400
courtservices@gov.yk.ca
www.yukoncourts.ca/courts/territorial/judicialcouncil.html
The Council makes recommendations respecting appointments of judges& justices, & deals with formal complaints respecting judges & justices. It makes recommendations respecting the efficiency, uniformity & quality of judicial services provided by the Territorial Court or the Justice of the Peace Court. It also performs other duties requested by the Minister.

• **Yukon Law Foundation**
PO Box 31789
Whitehorse, YT Y1A 6L3
Tel: 867-668-4231
Fax: 867-667-7556
lsy@yknet.yk.ca
www.yukonlawfoundation.com

• **Yukon Legal Services Society/Legal Aid**
#203, 2131 - 2nd Ave.
Whitehorse, YT Y1A 1C3
Tel: 867-667-5210
Fax: 867-667-8649
Toll-free: 800-661-0408
legalaid@yknet.yk.ca
www.legalaid.yk.ca
Other Communication: 1-800-661-0408, extension 5210 (Yukon only); administration@legalaid.yk.ca

• **Yukon Utilities Board**
#19, 1114 - 1st Ave.
PO Box 31728
Whitehorse, YT Y1A 6L3
Tel: 867-667-5058
Fax: 867-667-5059
yub@utilitiesboard.yk.ca
This regulatory board consists of three to five members appointed by the Government of Yukon. It receives its mandate from the Public Utilities Act & Regulations.

Community Justice & Public Safety Branch
Prospector Building, 301 Jarvis St., 2nd Fl., Whitehorse, YT Y1A 2C6
Tel: 867-393-7077
Fax: 867-393-6326
cjps@gov.yk.ca

Assistant Deputy Minister, Robert Riches
Tel: 867-393-7077
Fax: 867-393-6326
robert.riches@gov.yk.ca
Chief Coroner, Coroner's Service, Sharon Hanley
Tel: 867-667-5317
Fax: 867-456-6826
sharon.hanley@gov.yk.ca
Director, Special Projects & Partnerships, Sandi Gleason
Tel: 867-667-3656
Fax: 867-393-6326
sandi.gleason@gov.yk.ca

Legal & Regulatory Services
PO Box 2703, Whitehorse, YT Y1A 2C6
Tel: 867-667-5764
Fax: 867-393-6379
legalservices@gov.yk.ca

Assistant Deputy Minister, Thomas Ullyett
Tel: 867-667-3469
Fax: 867-393-6379
thomas.ullyett@gov.yk.ca

Court Services
PO Box 2703 J-3, Whitehorse, YT Y1A 2C6
Tel: 867-667-5441
Fax: 867-393-6212
Toll-Free: 800-661-0408
courtservices@gov.yk.ca

Aboriginal Law Group
Andrew A. Philipsen Law Centre, 2130 Second Avenue (3rd floor), PO Box 2703 J-2E, Whitehorse, YT Y1A 2C6
Tel: 867-667-5630
alq@gov.yk.ca

Yukon Liquor Corporation

9031 Quartz Rd., Whitehorse, YT Y1A 4P9
Tel: 867-667-5245
Fax: 867-393-6306
yukon.liquor@gov.yk.ca
www.ylc.yk.ca

Acts Administered:
Liquor Act
Public Lotteries Act

Minister responsible, Scott Kent, Hon.
Tel: 867-667-5800
Fax: 867-393-6252
scott.kent@gov.yk.ca

President, Ron MacMillan
Tel: 867-667-5155

Vice-President, Virginia Labelle
Tel: 867-667-5708
virginia.labelle@gov.yk.ca

Director, Retail Sales & Territorial Agent Services, Allison Briden
Tel: 867-667-8924
allison.briden@gov.yk.ca

Director, Finance, Systems & Administration, Mark Davey
Tel: 867-667-8773
mark.davey@gov.yk.ca

Director, Purchasing & Distribution, Geoff Dixon
Tel: 867-667-5244
geoff.dixon@gov.yk.ca

Director, Licensing & Social Responsibility, Terry Grabowski
Tel: 867-667-8926
terry.grabowski@gov.yk.ca

Director, Policy & Communications, JoAnne Harach
Tel: 867-456-6802
joanne.harach@gov.yk.ca

Director, Human Resources, Sue Richards
Tel: 867-667-8272
sue.richards@gov.yk.ca

Yukon Ombudsman & Privacy Commissioner

#201, 211 Hawkins St., Whitehorse, YT Y1A 2C6
Tel: 867-667-8468
Fax: 867-667-8469
info@ombudsman.yk.ca
www.ombudsman.yk.ca/ombudsman/
Other Communication: 800-661-0408, ext. 8468

Yukon Public Service Commission

Yukon Government Administration Building, #2071-2nd Ave., PO Box 2703, Whitehorse, YT Y1A 2C6
Tel: 867-667-5653
Fax: 867-667-5755
Toll-Free: 800-661-0408
PSCWebsite@gov.yk.ca
www.psc.gov.yk.ca
TTY: 867-667-5864

This central agency has a mandate to provide human resource advice & support services to Yukon government departments & employees, to act as the employer on behalf of the Yukon government & to establish & maintain human resource legislation, policies & collective agreements.
Acts Administered:
Education Labour Relations Act
Public Sector Compensation Restraint Act
Public Servants Superannuation Act
Public Service Act
Public Service Group Insurance Benefit Plan Act
Public Service Labour Relations Act
Retirement Plan Beneficiaries Act
Territorial Court Judiciary Pension Plan Act

Commissioner, Catharine Read
Tel: 867-667-5252
Fax: 867-393-6919
catharine.read@gov.yk.ca

Director, Corporate Human Resource Services, Martha Kenney
Tel: 867-667-5250
Fax: 867-667-5755
martha.kenney@gov.yk.ca

Director, Finance & Administration, Bonnie Love
Tel: 867-667-5861
Fax: 867-667-6705
bonnie.love@gov.yk.ca

Director, Employee Compensation, Terry Kinney
Tel: 867-667-5251
Fax: 867-667-6705
terry.kinney@gov.yk.ca

Director, Policy, Planning & Communication, Deborah McNevin
Tel: 867-667-3537
Fax: 867-667-6705
deborah.mcnevin@gov.yk.ca

Director, Staff Relations, Megan Slobodin
Tel: 867-667-5201
Fax: 867-393-6919
megan.slobodin@gov.yk.ca

Director, Human Resource Management, Felix Vogt
Tel: 867-667-8222
Fax: 867-667-6705
felix.vogt@gov.yk.ca

Staff Development
Hougen's Center, #3106, 3rd Avenue, 3rd Fl.
Tel: 867-667-8198
Fax: 867-393-6920

Acting Director, Tracey Johnson
Tel: 867-667-8267
tracey.johnson@gov.yk.ca

Yukon Tourism & Culture

100 Hanson St., Whitehorse, YT Y1A 2C6
Tel: 867-667-5036
Fax: 867-667-3546
www.tc.gov.yk.ca/

The department focuses on business, tourism, cultural industries & technology/telecommunications to develop & promote economic capacity & entrepreneurial skills to stimulate economy.

The department works with the Yukon's diverse arts communities to foster creativity & quality of life & with heritage interests to preserve & interpret heritage resources.
Acts Administered:
Archives Act
Arts Act
Arts Centre Act
Historical Resources Act
Hotels & Tourist Establishments Act
Scientists & Explorers Act

Minister, Mike Nixon, Hon.
Tel: 867-667-5800
Fax: 867-393-6252
mike.nixon@gov.yk.ca

Deputy Minister, Joy Waters
Tel: 867-667-5430
Fax: 867-667-8844

Corporate Services
Provides a range of central support services within the Department of Tourism & Culture. These include human resources, information technology, administration, information management, & finance.
Director, Lucy Coulthard
Tel: 867-667-3009
lucy.coulthard@gov.yk.ca

Cultural Services
Tel: 867-667-8589
Toll-Free: 800-661-0408
TTY: 867-393-6456

Dedicated to the preservation, development, interpretation of Yukon's heritage resources & to fostering the growth & mpact of the territory's visual, literary, & performing arts.
Private Records Archivist, Yukon Archives, Lesley Buchan
Tel: 867-667-5641
lesley.buchan@gov.yk.ca
Territorial Archivist, Ian Burnett
Tel: 867-667-5275
ian.burnett@gov.yk.ca
Yukon Archeologist, Ruth Gotthardt
Tel: 867-667-5983
ruth.gotthardt@gov.yk.ca
Yukon Archeologist, Greg Hare
Tel: 867-667-3771
greg.hare@gov.yk.ca
Acting Manager, Brian Groves
Tel: 867-667-3582
brian.groves@gov.yk.ca
Manager, Heritage Resources, Jeff Hunston
Tel: 867-667-5363
jeff.hunston@gov.yk.ca
Director, Cultural Services, Rick Lemaire
Tel: 867-667-8592
rick.lemaire@gov.yk.ca
Manager, Historic Sites, Doug Olynyk
Tel: 867-667-5295
doug.olynyk@gov.yk.ca
Manager, Arts, Laurel Parry
Tel: 867-667-5264
laurel.parry@gov.yk.ca
Development Assessment Archeologist, Christian Thomas
Tel: 867-456-6102
christian.thomas@gov.yk.ca
Acting Manager, Stacie Zaychuk
Tel: 867-667-3516
stacie.zatchuk@gov.yk.ca
Yukon Paleontologist, Grant Zazula
Tel: 867-667-8089
grant.zazula@gov.yk.ca

Policy & Communications
Tel: 867-667-8304
Fax: 867-393-8844
Toll-Free: 800-661-0408
Provides legislative & policy support for Tourism & Culture & coordinates the communications efforts of the department.
Director, Jonathan Parker
Tel: 867-667-3016
jonathan.parker@gov.yk.ca

Tourism & Culture
Tel: 867-667-3053
Toll-Free: 800-661-0408
Engages in tourism marketing, product development, & research in order to bring the scenic natural beauty and rich & diverse cultural heritage of Yukon to the attention of potential visitors.
Supervisor, Digital Assets & Photography, Marten Berkman
Tel: 867-667-5434
marten.berkman@gov.yk.ca
Manager, Product & Research Development, Robert Clark
Tel: 867-667-5632
robert.clark@gov.yk.ca
Director, Pierre Germain
Tel: 867-667-3087
pierre.germain@gov.yk.ca

Yukon Women's Directorate

#1, 404 Hason St., Whitehorse, YT Y1A 1Y8
Tel: 867-667-3030
Fax: 867-393-6270
www.womensdirectorate.gov.yk.ca

Acts Administered:
Yukon Advisory Council on Women's Issues Act

Minister responsible, Elaine Taylor
Tel: 867-667-8641
elaine.taylor@gov.yk.ca

Director, Shauna Curtin
Tel: 867-667-5182
shauna.curtin@gov.yk.ca

Manager, Administration & Finance, Lorie Larose
Tel: 867-667-3026
lorie.larose@gov.yk.ca

Yukon Workers' Compensation Health & Safety Board (YWCHSB)

401 Strickland St., Whitehorse, YT Y1A 5N8
Tel: 867-667-5645
Fax: 867-393-6279
Toll-Free: 800-661-0443
worksafe@gov.yk.ca
wcb.yk.ca/

The Yukon Workers' Compensation Health & Safety Board (YWCHSB) administers workers' compensation & occupational health & safety in the Yukon.
Acts Administered:
Day of Mourning for Victims of Workplace Injuries Act
Occupational Health & Safety Act
Spousal Compensation Act
Workplace Hazardous Materials Information System (WHMIS) Regulations

Minister responsible, Doug Graham
Tel: 867-667-5800
Fax: 867-393-6252
doug.graham@gov.yk.ca

President & Chief Executive Officer, Valerie Royle
Tel: 867-667-8983
Fax: 867-393-6419
valerie.royle@gov.yk.ca

Vice President & Chief Financial Officer, Jim Stephens
Tel: 867-667-8210
jim.stephens@gov.yk.ca

Director, Human Resources, Ryan Sikkes
Tel: 867-667-8190
ryan.sikkes@gov.yk.ca

Director, Social Marketing & Communications, Mark Hill
Tel: 867-667-8695
mark.hill@gov.yk.ca

Director, Occupational Health & Safety, Kurt Dieckmann
Tel: 867-667-3726
kurt.dieckmann@gov.yk.ca

Director, Assessments, Clarence Timmons
Tel: 867-667-5831
clarence.timmons@gov.yk.ca

Acting Director, Claimant Services, Michael McBride
Tel: 867-667-8186
michael.mcbride@gov.yk.ca

The Queen & Royal Family

The House of Windsor

In 1917 the late King George V, by Proclamation, changed the House name of the Royal Family from Saxe-Coburg-Gotha to the House of Windsor.

THE QUEEN. - Elizabeth the Second, (Elizabeth Alexandra Mary, of Windsor) by the Grace of God, of the United Kingdom, Canada and Her other Realms and Territories Queen; Head of the Commonwealth, Defender of the Faith, Succeeded to the throne February 6th, 1952 , and was crowned June 2nd, 1953, at Westminster Abbey. Her Majesty, the elder daughter of the late King George VI and Queen Elizabeth The Queen Mother, was born at 17 Bruton St., London, W.1, on April 21st, 1926, married November 20th, 1947, H.R.H. The Prince Philip, Duke of Edinburgh, K.G., K.T., O.M., G.B.E., A.C., Q.S.O.

THE CHILDREN of Queen Elizabeth and H.R.H. The Prince Philip, Duke of Edinburgh are:

H.R.H. Prince Charles Philip Arthur George, Prince of Wales and Earl of Chester, Duke of Cornwall and Duke of Rothesay, Earl of Carrick and Baron Renfrew, Lord of the Isles, and Great Steward of Scotland, K.G., K.T., G.C.B., O.M., A.K., Q.S.O., A.D.C., born November 14th, 1948. Married July 29th, 1981. Marriage dissolved 1996. The Lady Diana Spencer (died August 31st, 1997) and has issue. Prince William, Prince of Wales and Duke of Cambridge, born June 21st, 1982 (married April 29, 2011, Kate Middleton, H.R.H. Duchess of Cambridge) and Prince Henry of Wales, born September 15th, 1984. Prince Charles married April 9th, 2005 Mrs. Camilla Parker Bowles (H.R.H. The Duchess of Cornwall).

H.R.H. The Princess Royal, Anne Elizabeth Alice Louise, K.G., K.T., G.C.V.O., Q.S.O., born August 15th, 1950. Married 1st November 14th, 1973 Captain Mark Anthony Peter Phillips, C.V.O., A.D.C. and has issue. Peter Phillips born November 15th, 1977 and Zara Phillips born May 15th, 1981. Marriage dissolved 1992. Married 2nd December 12th, 1993 Commodore Timothy James Hamilton Laurence, M.V.O., R.N.

H.R.H. The Prince Andrew Albert Christian Edward, K.C.V.O., A.D.C., Duke of York, Earl of Inverness and Baron Killyleagh, born February 19th, 1960, married July 23rd, 1986 Miss Sarah Margaret Ferguson and has issue, Princess Beatrice of York, born August 8th, 1988, and Princess Eugenie of York, born March 23rd, 1990. Marriage dissolved 1996.

H.R.H. The Prince Edward Antony Richard Louis, K.C.V.O., Earl of Wessex, and Viscount Severn, born March 10th, 1964, married June 19, 1999 Miss Sophie Rhys-Jones.

THE LATE GEORGE VI. - George VI succeeded to the Throne December 11th, 1936; and was crowned at Westminster Abbey, May 12th, 1937. Second son of King George V and Queen Mary, he was born at York Cottage, Sandringham, on December 14th, 1895, married, April 26th, 1923, Lady Elizabeth Bowes-Lyon, daughter of the Earl and Countess of Strathmore and Kinghorne. As Heir Presumptive succeeded to the Throne on the abdication of Edward VIII.

QUEEN ELIZABETH, THE QUEEN MOTHER - born August 4th, 1900, daughter of the 14th Earl of Strathmore and Kinghorne; married, April 26th, 1923. Died March 30th, 2002.

THE ISSUE of the late King George VI and Queen Elizabeth are:

The reigning Sovereign, Elizabeth the Second (elder daughter).

The Princess Margaret (Rose), Countess of Snowdon, C.I., G.C.V.O., born August 21st, 1930, married Antony Charles Robert Armstrong-Jones, G.C.V.O., (since created Earl of Snowdon) May 6th, 1960, and has issue, Viscount Linley, born November 3rd, 1961 and the Lady Sarah Frances Elizabeth Armstrong-Jones, born May 1st, 1964. Marriage dissolved 1978. Died February 9th, 2002.

SUCCESSION-The order stands:

The Prince of Wales
Prince William of Wales
Prince Henry of Wales
The Duke of York
Princess Beatrice of York
Princess Eugenie of York
The Earl of Wessex
The Lady Louise Mountbatten-Windsor
The Princess Royal
Mr. Peter Phillips
Miss Zara Phillips
Viscount Linley
The Hon. Charles Armstrong-Jones
The Hon. Margarita Armstrong-Jones
The Lady Sarah Chatto
Master Samuel Chatto
Master Arthur Chatto
The Duke of Gloucester
Earl of Ulster
The Lady Davina Windsor
The Lady Rose Windsor
The Duke of Kent
The Lady Marina Charlotte Windsor
The Lady Amelia Windsor
The Lady Helen Taylor
Master Columbus Taylor
Master Cassius Taylor
Miss Eloise Taylor
The Lord Frederick Windsor
The Lady Gabriella Windsor
Princess Alexandra, The Hon. Lady Ogilvy
Mr. James Ogilvy
Master Alexander Ogilvy
Miss Flora Ogilvy
Mrs. Paul Mowatt
Master Christian Mowatt
Miss Zenouska Mowatt
The Earl of Harewood

NOTES

1. The Sucession is governed by the Act of Settlement 1701 (12 & 13 Will 3 c 2) which limits the succession to the Throne to the heirs, being Protestants, of Princess Sophia of Hanover, granddaughter of King James I. Section 6 (4) of the Legitimacy Act of 1959 (ôNothing in this Act affects the succession to the Throneö) is also relevant.
2. Earl of St. Andrews & Prince Michael of Kent were excluded from the succession to the Throne on marriage to Roman Catholics, & Lord Downpatrick & the Lord Nicholas Windsor on conversion to Roman Catholicism.

HER MAJESTY'S HOUSEHOLD

Lord Chamberlain, The Lord Peel, G.C.V.O.
Private Secretary to The Queen, The Rt. Hon. Sir Christopher Geidt, K.C.V.O., O.B.E.
Keeper of the Privy Purse, Sir Alan Reid
The Lord Chamberlain has the general supervision of the Royal Household.

The Commonwealth

The Commonwealth is a voluntary association of 54 independent member countries representing over 1.8 billion people around the world - in Africa, the Americas, Asia, the Caribbean, Europe & the Pacific. It promotes good governance, democracy, sustainable economic & social development, the rule of law & human rights. These & other principles are enshrined in the Harare Commonwealth Declaration of 1991.

There are three principal international organizations of the Commonwealth:

THE COMMONWEALTH SECRETARIAT
Marlborough House, Pall Mall, London SW1Y 5HX, UK, +44 (0)20 7747 6500; Fax: +44 (0)20 7930 0827, Email: info@commonwealth.int, URL: www.thecommonwealth.org
Rt. Hon. Kamalesh Sharma (India), Commonwealth Secretary-General
Mmasekgoa Masire-Mwamba, Commonwealth Deputy Secretary-General
Steve Cutts, Commonwealth Assistant Secretary-General, Corporate Affairs
Richard Uku, Official Spokesperson, Director, Communicaitons & Public Affairs, 44 (0)20 7747 6380, r.uku@commonwealth.int

THE COMMONWEALTH FOUNDATION
Marlborough House, Pall Mall, London SW1Y 5HY, UK, +44 (0)20 7830 3783; Fax: +44 (0)20 7839 8157, URL: www.commonwealthfoundation.com

THE COMMONWEALTH OF LEARNING (COL)
#1200-1055 West Hastings, Vancouver BC V6E 2E9, 604-775-8200; Fax: 604-775-8210, Email: info@col.org, URL: www.col.org
The Commonwealth of Learning's focus is in strengthening institutions in developing Commonwealth countries that are striving to provide affordable education to larger numbers of their citizens.

Member States

(showing capital, population (2011-2012) & date of membership. Dates for Australia, Canada & New Zealand are those on which Dominion Status was acquired):

Antigua & Barbuda - St. John's; 89,612; Nov. 1, 1981
Australia - Canberra; 22,620,600; Jan. 1, 1901
- External territories: Norfolk Island, Coral Sea Islands Territory, Australian Antarctic Territory, Heard Island & McDonald Islands, Cocos (Keeling) Islands, Christmas Island, Territory of Ashmore & Cartier Islands

The Bahamas - Nassau; 347,176; July 10, 1973
Bangladesh - Dhaka; 150,493,658; Mar. 26, 1972
Barbados - Bridgetown; 273,925; Nov. 30, 1966
Belize - Belmopan; 356,600; Sept. 21, 1981
Botswana - Gaborone; 2,030,738; Sept. 30, 1966
Brunei Darussalam - Bandar Seri Begawan; 405,938; Feb. 23, 1984
Cameroon - Yaoundé; 20,030,362; May 20, 1995
Canada - Ottawa; 34,482,779; July 1, 1867
Cyprus - Nicosia; 1,116,564; Oct. 1, 1961
Dominica - Roseau; 67,675; Nov. 3, 1978
Fiji Islands - Suva; 868,406; Oct. 10, 1997 N.B. Fiji Islands was suspended from the councils of the Commonwealth in May 2000 following the overthrow of its democratically elected government.
The Gambia - Banjul; 1,776,103; Feb. 18, 1965
Ghana - Accra; 24,965,816; Mar. 6, 1957
Grenada - St. George's; 104,890; Feb. 7, 1974
Guyana - Georgetown; 756,040; Feb. 23, 1966
India - New Delhi; 1,241,491,960; Jan. 26, 1947
Jamaica - Kingston; 2,709,300; Aug. 6, 1962
Kenya - Nairobi; 41,609,728; Dec. 12, 1963
Kiribati - Tarawa; 101,093; July 12, 1979
Lesotho - Maseru; 2,193,843; Oct. 4, 1966
Malawi - Lilongwe; 15,380,888; July 6, 1964
Malaysia - Kuala Lumpur; 28,859,154; Aug. 31, 1957
Maldives - Malé; 320,081; July 26, 1982
Malta - Valletta; 419,000; Mar. 31, 1964
Mauritius - Port Louis; 1,286,051; Mar. 12, 1968
Mozambique - Maputo; 23,929,708; June 25, 1995
Namibia - Windhoek; 2,324,004; Mar. 21, 1990
Nauru - Nauru; 9,378; Jan. 31, 1968 [Special Member as of July 1, 2005]
New Zealand - Wellington; 4,405,200; Sept. 26, 1907 - Includes the territories of Tokelau & the Ross Dependency (Antarctic). Self-governing countries in free association with New Zealand: Cook Islands & Niue.
Nigeria - Abuja; 162,470,737; Oct. 1, 1960
Pakistan - Islamabad; 176,745,364; Mar. 23, 1989 (previously member 1947-1972; rejoined in 1989) N.B. Pakistan was suspended from participation in the councils of the Commonwealth in October1999 following a military coup.
Rwanda - Kigali; 10,942,950; Nov. 2009
Papua New Guinea - Port Moresby; 7,013,829; Sept. 16, 1975
St. Kitts & Nevis - Basseterre; 50,726; Sept. 19, 1983
St. Lucia - Castries; 176,000; Feb. 22, 1979
St. Vincent & The Grenadines - Kingstown; 103,537; Oct. 27, 1979
Samoa - Apia; 183,874; June 1, 1970
Seychelles - Victoria; 86,000; June 18, 1976
Sierra Leone - Freetown; 5,997,486; Apr. 27, 1961
Singapore - Singapore; 5,183,700; Aug. 9, 1965
Solomon Islands - Honiara; 552,267; July 7, 1978
South Africa - Pretoria; 50,586,757; 1931 - Left Commonwealth 1961, rejoined 1994
Sri Lanka - Colombo; 20,869,000; Feb. 4, 1948
Swaziland - Mbabane; 1,067,773; Sept. 6, 1968
Tonga - Nuku'alofa; 104,509; June 4, 1970
Trinidad & Tobago - Port of Spain; 1,346,350; Aug. 31, 1962
Tuvalu - Funafuti; 9,847; Oct. 1, 1978
Uganda - Kampala; 34,509,205; Oct. 9, 1962
United Kingdom- London; 62,641,000
- Overseas territories: Anguilla, Bermuda, British Antarctic Territory, British Indian Ocean Territory, British Virgin Islands, Cayman Islands, Falkland Islands, Gibraltar, Montserrat, Pitcairn, Henderson, Ducie & Oeno Islands, St. Helena & St. Helena Dependencies (Ascension & Tristan da Cunha), South Georgia & the South Sandwich Islands, & Turks & Caicos Islands

United Republic of Tanzania - Dar es Salaam; 46,218,486; Dec. 9, 1961
Vanuatu - Port Vila; 245,619; July 30, 1980
Zambia - Lusaka; 13,474,959; Oct. 24, 1964

La Francophonie

ORGANISATION INTERNATIONALE DE LA FRANCOPHONIE
Secrétariat général, 19-21, av Bosquet, 75007 Paris, France 1-44-11-12-50; Téléc: 1-44-11-12-80; URL: www.francophonie.org
Abdou Diouf (Sénégal), Secrétaire général

Member States

(showing member name, population (2010-2011), national holiday):

Albanie (République d'), 3,169 M, 11 janvier et 28 novembre
Andorre (Principauté), 0,870 M, 8 septembre
Arménie (République d'), 3,090 M, 23 août
Belgique (Royaume de), 10,698 M, 21 juillet
Bénin (République du), 9,212 M, 1er août
Bulgarie (République de), 7,497 M, 3 mars
Burkina Faso, 16,287 M, 11 décembre
Burundi (République du), 8,519 M, 1er juillet
Cambodge (Royaume du), 15,053 M, 7 janvier - 17 avril
Cameroun (République du), 19,958 M, 20 mai
Canada, 34,483 M, 1er juillet
Canada - Nouveau-Brunswick (Province du), 0,751 M, 15 août
Canada - Québec (Province du), 7,903 M, 24 juin
Cap-Vert (République du), 0,513 M, 5 juillet
Centrafricaine (République), 4,506 M, 1er décembre
Chypre, 0,880 M, 1er octobre
Communauté française de Belgique (Wallonie-Bruxelles), 4,505 M, 27 septembre

Comores (Union des), 0,691 M, 6 juillet
Congo (République du), 3,759 M, 15 août
Congo (République démocratique du Congo), 67,827 M, 30 juin
Côte d'Ivoire (République de), 21,571 M, 7 août
Djibouti (République de), 0,879 M, 27 juin
Dominique (Commonwealth de la), 0,067 M, 3 novembre
Égypte (République arabe d'), 84,474 M, 23 juillet
France (République française), 62,637 M, 14 juillet
Gabon (République gabonaise), 1,501 M, 17 août
Ghana, 24,333 M, 6 mars
Grèce, 11,183 M, 25 mars
Guinée (République de), 10,324 M, 2 octobre
Guinée-Bissau (République de), 1,647 M, 24 septembre
Guinée-équatoriale (République de), 0,693 M, 12 octobre
Haïti (République d'), 10,188 M, 1er janvier
Laos (République démocratique populaire Lao), 6,436 M, 2 décembre
Liban (République libanaise), 4,255 M, 22 novembre
Luxembourg (Grand-Duché de), 0,492 M, 23 juin
Macédonie (ARY), 2,043 M, 8 septembre
Madagascar (République de), 20,146 M, 26 juin
Mali (République du), 13,323 M, 22 septembre
Maroc (Royaume du), 32,381 M, 30 juillet
Maurice (République de), 1,297 M, 12 mars
Mauritanie (République islamique de), 3,366 M, 28 novembre
Moldavie, 3,576 M, 27 août
Monaco (Principauté de), 0,033 M, 19 novembre
Niger (République du), 15,891 M, 18 décembre
Roumanie, 21,190 M, 1er décembre
Rwanda (République rwandaise), 10,943 M, 1er juillet
Sainte-Lucie, 0,174 M, 22 février
Sao Tomé et Principe (République démocratique de), 0,165 M, 12 juillet
Sénégal (République du), 12,861 M, 4 avril
Seychelles (République des), 0,085 M, 18 juin
Suisse (Confédération), 7,597 M, 1er août
Tchad (République du), 11,506 M, 11 janvier
Togo (République du), 6,780 M, 13 janvier et 27 avril
Tunisie (République tunisienne), 10,374 M, 20 mars
Vanuatu (République de), 0,246 M, 30 juillet
Vietnam (République socialiste du), 89,029 M, 2 septembre

Canadian Permanent Missions Abroad

Canadian Joint Delegation to NATO (North Atlantic Treaty Organization)
Léopold III Blvd., Brussels, 1110 Belgium
11-322-707-7100, Fax: 11-322-707-7148,
bnato@international.gc.ca
www.europe.forces.gc.ca/sites/page-eng.asp?page=7777
His Excellency Y. Brodeur, Ambassador & Permanent Representative of Canada
Vice-Admiral R. Davidson, Military Representative of Canada CMM, CD

Mission of Canada to the European Union, Brussels
2, av de Tervuren, Brussels, 1040 Belgium
322-741-06-60, Fax: 322-741-06-29,
breu@international.gc.ca
www.canadainternational.gc.ca/eu-ue/index.aspx
His Excellency H. David Plunkett, Ambassador
A. Hausser, Minister-Counsellor & Deputy Head of Mission
T. Mawhinney, Counsellor, Political Affairs

NORAD (North American Aerospace Defense Command)
NORAD Public Affairs, Peterson AFB, #B-016, 250 Vandenberg, Colorado Springs, 80914-3808 USA
719-554-6889,
noradpa@norad.mil, pa@forces.gc.ca
www.norad.mil
Charles H. Jacoby, Jr., Commander, Gen. USA
J.A.J. Parent, Deputy Commander-in-Chief, Lt. Gen. Cdn. Forces OMM, CD

Organization for Economic Cooperation & Development
2, rue André Pascal, Paris, F-75775 France
331-45-24-82-00, Fax: 331-45-24-85-00,
www.oecd.org
Angel Gurría, Secretary-General
Gabriela Ramos, Chief of Staff

Permanent Mission of Canada to the Organization of American States
501 Pennsylvania Ave. NW, Washington, DC 20001 USA
202-682-1768, Fax: 202-682-7264,
wshdc-prmoas@international.gc.ca
www.international.gc.ca/americas-ameriques/oas-oea/permanent_mission_permanente.aspx
Allan B. Culham, Permanent Representative of Canada

UN: Permanent Delegation of Canada to the UN Educational, Scientific & Cultural Organization
5, rue Constantine, Paris, 75007 France
331-44-43-25-71, Fax: 331-44 43-25-79,
pesco@international.gc.ca
www.canadainternational.gc.ca/unesco/index.aspx
His Excellency Jean-Pierre Blackburn, Ambassador & Permanent Delegate
Michèle Stanton-Jean, Counsellor & Representative of the Quebec Government

UN: Permanent Mission of Canada to the Food & Agriculture Organization (FAO)
FAO, Via Zara 30, Rome, 00198 Italy
39-06-854-441, Fax: 39-06-85444-2930,
www.fao.org
J. Fox, Permanent Representative
A. Heuchan, Minister-Counsellor, Development
D. Price, Deputy Permanent Representative
E. Robinson, Alternate Permanent Representative

UN: Permanent Mission of Canada to the International Civil Aviation Organization
ICAO, #1535, 999, rue Université, Montréal, QC H3C 5J9 Canada
514-954-8219, Fax: 514-954-6077,
icaohq@icao.int, library@icao.int
www.icao.int
Raymond Benjamin, Secretary General
Roberto Kobeh González, President of the Council

UN: Permanent Mission of Canada to the International Organizations in Vienna
Laurenzerberg 2, Vienna, A-1010 Austria
431-531-38-3001, Fax: 431-531-38-3903,
vperm@international.gc.ca
www.unvienna.org/unov
His Excellency John Barrett, Permanent Representative & Ambassador
S. Caza, Counsellor & Alternate Permanent Representative

UN: Permanent Mission of Canada to the Office of the UN, The Conference on Disarmament
5, av de l'Ariana, Geneva, 1202 Switzerland
41-22-919-9200, Fax: 41-22-919-9233,
genev@international.gc.ca
www.international.gc.ca/genev/index.aspx
His Excellency John Gero, Permanent Representative & Ambassador to the World Trade Organization
Her Excellency Elissa Goldberg, Permanent Representative & Ambassador to the United Nations & the Conference on Disarmament
M. Grinius, Permanent Representative & Ambassador
A. LeClaire Christie, Minister-Counsellor & Deputy Permanent Representative

UN: Permanent Mission of Canada to the United Nations
One Dag Hammarskjold Plaza, 885 Second Ave., 14th Fl., New York, NY 10017 USA
212-848-1100, Fax: 212-848-1195,
prmny@international.gc.ca
www.canadainternational.gc.ca/prmny-mponu/index.aspx
His Excellency Guillermo E. Rishchynski, Permanent Representative & Ambassador
His Excellency Gilles Rivard, Ambassador & Deputy Permanent Representative

UN: Permanent Mission of Canada to the United Nations Centre for Human Settlements (Habitat)
PO Box 1013, Nairobi, 00621 Kenya
254-20-366-3000, Fax: 254-20-366-3900,
nrobi@international.gc.ca
www.unhabitat.org
R. Hynes, Permanent Representative

UN: Permanent Mission of Canada to the United Nations Environment Programme
PO Box 1013, Nairobi, 00621 Kenya
254-20-366-3000, Fax: 254-20-366-3900,
nrobi@international.gc.ca
www.unep.org
R. Hynes, Permanent Representative

Diplomatic & Consular Representatives in Canada

Islamic State of Afghanistan
Embassy of Afghanistan in Ottawa, 240 Argyle Ave., Ottawa, ON K2P 1B9
613-563-4223, Fax: 613-563-4962,
contact@afghanemb-canada.net
www.afghanemb-canada.net
His Excellency Barna Karimi, Ambassador, b.karimi@afghanembassy.ca
Kaihan Ahadi, First Secretary
Abdullah Sabet Mushahed, Third Secretary
Sharif Ghalib, Senior Political Advisor

Republic of Albania
Embassy of Albania (to Canada), #302, 130 Albert St., Ottawa, ON K1P 5G4
613-236-4114, Fax: 613-236-0804
Her Excellency Elida Petoshati, Ambassador
Taip Sulko, Minister-Counsellor

People's Democratic Republic of Algeria
Embassy of Algeria, 500 Wilbrod St., Ottawa, ON K1N 6N2
613-789-8505, Fax: 613-789-1406,
Info@embassyalgeria.ca, ambalgcan@rogers.com
www.ambalgott.com
His Excellency Smail Benamara, Ambassador
Nakhla Kechacha, Minister-Counsellor
Mohammed Bennecer, Counsellor
Nora Derradji, First Secretary

Principality of Andorra
Two United Nations Plaza, 25th Fl., New York, NY 10017 USA
212-750-8064, Fax: 212-750-6630,
andorra@un.int, rmaples@andorraun.org
His Excellency Narcis Casal de Fonsdeviela, Ambassador

Republic of Angola
189 Laurier Ave. East, Ottawa, ON K1N 6P1
613-234-1152, Fax: 613-234-1179,
info@embangola-can.org
www.embangola-can.org
His Excellency Agostinho Tavares Da Silva Neto, Ambassador
Sandra Marisa A. Lobato, First Secretary
Matilde Pedro Zeferino Antonio, Second Secretary

Argentina
Embassy of the Argentine Republic, 81 Metcalfe St., 7th Fl., Ottawa, ON K1P 6K7
613-236-2351, Fax: 613-235-2659,
ecana@mrecic.gov.ar
www.argentina-canada.net
Jose Nestor Ureta, Minister & Chargé d'affaires
Gerardo Ezequiel Bompadre, Minister
Ruben Oscar Gonzalez, Alternate Representative
Martin Leonardo Soto, Second Secretary

Republic of Armenia
7 Delaware Ave., Ottawa, ON K2P 0Z2
613-234-3710, Fax: 613-234-3444,
armcanadaembassy@mfa.am, armconsottawa@mfa.am
www.armembassycanada.ca
His Excellency Armen Yeganian, Ambassador
Lusine Movsisyan, First Secretary
Aram Hakobyan, Attaché

Commonwealth of Australia
Australian High Commission, #710, 50 O'Connor St., Ottawa, ON K1P 6L2
613-236-0841, Fax: 613-216-1321,
Her Excellency Louise Helen Hand, High Commissioner
Kerryn Maree MacCaulay, Permanent Representative
Bruce Geoffrey Soar, Deputy Head of Mission
Gregory Peter Ryan, First Secretary & Consul
Geraldine Anne Taylor, Second Secretary
Wing Commander Russell John Page, Defence Advisor

Republic of Austria
Embassy of Austria, 445 Wilbrod St., Ottawa, ON K1N 6M7
613-789-1444, Fax: 613-789-3431,
ottawa-ob@bmeia.gv.at
www.bmeia.gv.at/en/embassy/ottawa.html
His Excellency Werner Brandstetter, Ambassador
Ulrike Butschek, Minister & Deputy Head of Mission
Karin Pregler, First Secretary & Consul
Brig. Gen. Harald Gollinger, Defence, Military & Air Attaché

Republic of Azerbaijan
Embassy of Azerbaijan (to Canada), #904, 275 Slater St., Ottawa, ON K1P 5H9
613-288-0497, Fax: 613-230-8089, azerbaijan@azembassy.ca
www.azembassy.ca
His Excellency Farid Shafiyev, Ambassador
Eljan Habibzade, First Secretary
Tural Ganjaliyev, Second Secretary
Goshgar Zeynalov, Attaché

Commonwealth of The Bahamas
High Commission for the Commonwealth of The Bahamas, #1313, 50 O'Connor St., Ottawa, ON K1P 6L2
613-232-1724, Fax: 613-232-0097, www.bahighco.ca
Donna Elena Lowe, Counsellor & Chargé d'Affaires
Gordon J. Feeney, Honorary Consul (Toronto)

Kingdom of Bahrain
Embassy of Bahrain (to Canada), 3502 International Dr. NW, Washington, DC 20008 USA
202-342-0741, Fax: 202-362-2192,
Her Excellency Huda Ezra Ebrahim Nonoo, Ambassador

People's Republic of Bangladesh
Bangladesh High Commission, #1250, 340 Albert St., Ottawa, ON K1R 7Y6
613-236-0138, Fax: 613-567-3213, bangla@rogers.com
www.bdhc.org
His Excellency Kamrul Ahsan, High Commissioner
Ishrat Jahan Ahmed, Counsellor
Dewan Mahmudul Haque, First Secretary
Aparna Rani Paul, Second Secretary

Barbados
High Commission for Barbados, #470, 55 Metcalfe St., Ottawa, ON K1P 6L5
613-236-9517, Fax: 613-230-4362, ottawa@foreign.gov.bb
His Excellency Edward E. Greaves, High Commissioner
Christobelle Elaine Reece, Counsellor
Kereeta Nicole Whyte, First Secretary

Republic of Belarus
#600, 130 Albert St., Ottawa, ON K1P 5G4
613-233-9994, Fax: 613-233-8500, canada@mfa.gov.by
canada.mfa.gov.by
Roman Sobolev, Counsellor & Chargé d'Affaires
Igor Zalomai, First Secretary & Consul

Kingdom of Belgium
#820, 360 Albert St., Ottawa, ON K1R 7X7
613-236-7267, Fax: 613-236-7882, ottawa@diplobel.fed.be
www.diplomatie.be/ottawa
His Excellency Bruno Andreas Maria van der Pluijm, Ambassador
Patrick Hubert M. Stevens, Counsellor
Julien Pierre Francois Lecomte, First Secretary & Deputy Head of Mission
Jonas Valerius Juliana de Meyer, Second Secretary

Belize
High Commission for Belize, 2535 Massachusetts Ave. NW, Washington, DC 20008 USA
202-332-9636, Fax: 202-332-6888, ww.embassyofbelize.org
N. Bob Dhillon, Honorary Consul General (Calgary)
David Smiling, Honorary Consul (Vancouver)

Republic of Benin
Embassy of Benin, 58 Glebe Ave., Ottawa, ON K1S 2C3
613-233-4429, Fax: 613-233-8952, amba.benin@yahoo.ca
www.benin.ca
His Excellency Honoré Théodore Ahimakin, Ambassador
Yellonou Bai Marguerite Sinzogan, Minister-Counsellor

Bhutan
Royal Bhutanese Embassy, 763 United Nations Plaza, 1st Ave., New York, NY 10017 USA
212-682-2268, Fax: 212-661-0551, ww.bhutan.gov.bt
His Excellency Lhatu Wangchuk, Ambassador
Graham David (Sam) Blyth, Honorary Consul (Toronto)

Republic of Bolivia
Embassy of the Plurinational State of Bolivia, #416, 130 Albert St., Ottawa, ON K1P 5G4
613-236-5730, Fax: 613-236-8237,
His Excellency Edgar Jose Torrez Mosqueira, Ambassador
Claudia Maria Alexis Rocabado Mrden, First Secretary
Walter Estenssoro Borda, Honorary Consul General (Montréal)

Bosnia & Herzegovina
Embassy of Bosnia & Herzegovina, #805, 130 Albert St., Ottawa, ON K1P 5G4
613-236-0028, Fax: 613-236-1139, embassyofbih@bellnet.ca
www.bhembassy.ca
His Excellency Biljana Gutic-Bjelica, Ambassador
Mithat Pasic, Counsellor

Republic of Botswana
High Commission for Botswana (to Canada): c/o Republic of Botswana, 1531 - 1533 New Hampshire Ave. NW, Washington, DC 20036 USA
202-244-4990, Fax: 202-244-4164, www.botswanaembassy.org
Her Excellency Tebelelo Seretse, Ambassador
Sophie Heidi Mautle, Minister-Counsellor & Deputy Head of Mission, smautle@botswanaembassy.org
Game Selepeng, First Secretary
Marinah Tshepe, Second Secretary, Administration

Federative Republic of Brazil
Embassy of Brazil, 450 Wilbrod St., Ottawa, ON K1N 6M8
613-237-1090, Fax: 613-237-6144, brasemb.ottawa@itamaraty.gov.br
www.brasembottawa.org
His Excellency Piragibe dos Santos Tarrago, Ambassador
Paulo Roberto Amora Alavrenga, Minister-Counsellor
Paulo Eduardo Borda de Carvalho Silos, First Secretary
Renato Barros de Aguiar Leonardi, Second Secretary

Brunei Darussalam
High Commission of Brunei Darussalam, 395 Laurier Ave. East, Ottawa, ON K1N 6R4
613-234-5656, Fax: 613-234-4397,
Nadiah Ahmad Rafie, Second Secretary & Acting High Commissioner
Hasnan Osman, Third Secretary

Republic of Bulgaria
Embassy of the Republic of Bulgaria, 325 Stewart St., Ottawa, ON K1N 6K5
613-789-3215, Fax: 613-789-3524, embassy.ottawa@mfa.bg
www.mfa.bg/en/40
His Excellency Evgueni Stefanov Stoytchev, Ambassador
Zlati Guerguiev Katzarski, Minister & Chargé d'affaires
Ivan Ventzeslavov Anchev, Counsellor
Emilia Stefanova, Counsellor

Burkina-Faso
Embassy of Burkina-Faso, 48 Range Rd., Ottawa, ON K1N 8J4
613-238-4796, Fax: 613-238-3812, info@burkinafaso.ca, burkina.faso@sympatico.ca
www.burkinafaso.ca
Her Excellency Juliette Bonkoungou Yameogo, Ambassador
Charles Karosy Bamouni, Counsellor, Communications & Culture
Maxime Sib, Counsellor, Economic Affairs

Republic of Burundi
Embassy of Burundi, #815, 325 Dalhousie St., Ottawa, ON K1N 7G2
613-789-0414, Fax: 613-789-9537, ambabottawa@yahoo.ca
www.ambabucanada.com
Else Nizigama Ntamagiro, First Counsellor & Chargé d'Affaires
Howard Crosner, Honorary Consul (Toronto)

Kingdom of Cambodia
Embassy of Cambodia, 327 East 58 St., New York, NY 10022 USA
212-336-0777, Fax: 212-759-7672, cambodia@un.int
www.cambodiaun.org
His Excellency Dr. Sea Kosal, Ambassador
His Excellency Mengeang Nay, Ambassador & Deputy Permanent Representative
Ngoun Sokveng, First Secretary
Heng Pisal, Second Secretary

Republic of Cameroon
Cameroon High Commission, 170 Clemow Ave., Ottawa, ON K1S 2B4
613-236-1522, Fax: 613-236-3885, cameroun@rogers.com
www.hc-cameroon-ottawa.org
His Excellency Solomon Azoh-Mbi Anu'A-Gheyle, High Commissioner
Jean Bosco Etoa Etoa, Counsellor, Cultural Affairs
Labarang Abdoullahi, First Secretary
Ntaribo Ashu Agborngah, First Secretary, Administration & Consular Affairs

Republic of Cape Verde
Embassy of Cape Verde (to Canada), 3415 Massachusetts Ave. NW, Washington, DC 20007 USA
202-965-6820, Fax: 202-965-1207, cveisabel@caboverdeus.net; cveioliveira@caboverdeus.net
www.embcv-usa.gov.cv
Her Excellency Maria de Fátima Lima de Veiga, Ambassador
Daniel Oliveira, Minister-Counsellor & Deputy Chief of Mission
Maria Semedo, First Secretary

Central African Republic
Embassy of Central African Republic (to Canada), 1618 - 22nd St. NW, Washington, DC 20008 USA
202-483-7800, Fax: 202-332-9893,
His Excellency Stanislas Moussa-Kembe, Ambassador

Republic of Chad
Embassy of Chad (to Canada), 2401 Massachusetts Ave., NW, Washington, DC 20008 USA
202-462-4009, Fax: 202-265-1937, embassyofchad.info
His Excellency Adam Bechir Mahamoud, Ambassador
Hamid Takane Youssouf, First Counsellor
N-Bashir Nurane, Counsellor
Tchouli Gombo, First Secretary

Republic of Chile
Embassy of Chile, #1413, 50 O'Connor St., Ottawa, ON K1P 6L2
613-235-4402, Fax: 613-235-1176, echileca@chile.ca, bdelafuente@minrel.gov.cl
www.chile.ca
His Excellency Roberto Cristian Ibarra, Ambassador
Francisco Javier Costa Lobo, Alternate Representative
Claudio Alejandro Espinoza Burgos, Alternate Representative
Fernando Patricio Oritz Acheritogaray, Alternate Representative
Marcos Manuel Correa Letelier, First Secretary & Deputy Head of Mission

People's Republic of China
Embassy of China, 515 St. Patrick St., Ottawa, ON K1N 5H3
613-789-3434, Fax: 613-789-1911, chinaemb_ca@mfa.gov.cn
ca.china-embassy.org
His Excellency Junsai Zhang, Ambassador
Yiqun He, Minister-Counsellor
Shan Jiang, Minister-Counsellor
Jin Liu, Minister-Counsellor & Deputy Head of Mission
Lanchun Zhang, Minister-Counsellor
Wenzhi Zhou, Minister-Counsellor

Republic of Colombia
Embassy of Colombia, #1002, 360 Albert St., Ottawa, ON K1R 7X7
613-230-3760, Fax: 613-230-4416, embajada@embajadacolombia.ca
www.embajadacolombia.ca
Her Excellency Clemencia Forero-Ucros, Ambassador
Cesar Felipe Gonzalez-Hernandez, Minister, ministro@embajadacolombia.ca
Elizabeth Cadena-Fernández, Minister-Counsellor
Monica Beltran-Espitia, Counsellor, Consular & Cultural Affairs, consul@embajadacolombia.ca

Union of the Comoros
c/o Permanent Mission of the Comoros to the UN, #418, 866 UN Plaza, New York, NY 10017 USA
212-750-1637, Fax: 212-750-1657, comoros@un.int
www.un.int/comoros
His Excellency Kaambi Roubani, Ambassador
S. Bélair, Permanent Representative
Richard Lande, Honorary Consul General (Burlington)

Democratic Republic of the Congo
18 Range Rd., Ottawa, ON K1N 8J3
613-230-6391, Fax: 613-230-1945,
His Excellency Dominique Kilufya Kamfwa, Ambassador
Augustin Mulumbwe Katumba, Attaché

Republic of the Congo
Embassy of the Congo (to Canada), 1720-16th Street, NW, Washington, DC 20009 USA
202-726-5500, Fax: 202-726-1860, info@ambacongo-us.org
www.ambacongo-us.org
His Excellency Serge Mombouli, Ambassador
Sylvain Bayalama, Minister-Counsellor
Jacqueline Malanda-Bakouetela, Counsellor
Stephane B. Mamaty, Counsellor

Republic of Costa Rica
Embassy of Costa Rica, #701, 350 Sparks St., Ottawa, ON K1R 7S8
613-562-2855, Fax: 613-562-2582, embcr@costaricaembassy.com
www.costaricaembassy.com
His Excellency Luis Carlos Delgado Murillo, Ambassador
Francisco J. Chacon Hernandez, Minister-Counsellor & Consul General, fchacon@costaricaembassy.com
Eliana Villalobos Cárdenas, Minister-Counsellor, evillalobos@costaricaembassy.com
Natalia Chaves Ballestero, Counsellor, nchaves@costaricaembassy.com

Republic of Côte d'Ivoire
Embassy of Côte d'Ivoire, 9 Marlborough Ave., Ottawa, ON K1N 8E6
613-236-9919, Fax: 613-563-8287, info@canada.diplomatie.gouv.ci
www.canada.diplomatie.gouv.ci
His Excellency N'Goran Kouame, Ambassador
Eric Camille N'Dry, First Counsellor
Lydie Ipe, Counsellor
Logoue Richard Koukougnon, Counsellor

Republic of Croatia / Hrvatska
Embassy of Croatia, 229 Chapel St., Ottawa, ON K1N 7Y6
613-562-7820, Fax: 613-562-7821, croemb.ottawa@mvpei.hr
ca.mfa.hr
His Excellency Veselko Grubisic, Ambassador
Irena Cacic, Counsellor
Mario Martinec, Second Secretary
Ljubinko Matesic, Consul General (Mississauga)

Republic of Cuba
Embassy of Cuba, 388 Main St., Ottawa, ON K1S 1E3
613-563-0141, Fax: 613-563-0068, cuba@embacubacanada.net
www.cubadiplomatica.cu/canada
Her Excellency Teresita de Jesús Vicente Sotolongo, Ambassador
Antonio Rodríguez Varcárcel, Minister-Counsellor, mconsejero@embacubacanada.net
Jesús Milián, Counsellor, cubavig@embacubacanada.net
Ofelia Perera Ibañez, Economic Counsellor, ecounsellor@embacubacanada.net

Republic of Cyprus
High Commission of the Repulic of Cyprus, 2211 R St. NW, Washington, DC 20008 USA
202-462-5772, Fax: 202-483-6710, info@cyprusembassy.net
www.cyprusembassy.net
His Excellency Pavlos Anastasiades, Ambassador
Olympia Neocleous, Deputy Chief of Mission, neocleous@cyprusembassy.net
Nicholaos T. Manolis, First Secretary, manolis@cyprusembassy.net
Neophytos J. Constantinou, Second Secretary & Consul, constantinou@cyprusembassy.net

Czech Republic
Embassy of the Czech Republic, 251 Cooper St., Ottawa, ON K2P 0G2
613-562-3875, Fax: 613-562-3878, ottawa@embassy.mzv.cz
www.mzv.cz/ottawa
His Excellency Karel Žebrakovský, Ambassador
Robert Tripes, Minister-Counsellor
Jan Beroun, Counsellor
Ivana Krahulcova, Counsellor

Kingdom of Denmark
Royal Danish Embassy, #450, 47 Clarence St., Ottawa, ON K1N 9K1
613-562-1811, Fax: 613-562-1812, ottamb@um.dk
canada.um.dk
His Excellency Erik Vilstrup Lorenzen, Ambassador
Christen Krogh, Counsellor & Deputy Head of Mission

Republic of Djibouti
c/o Embassy of the Republic of Djibouti, #515, 1156 - 15th St. NW, Washington, DC 20005 USA
202-331-0270, Fax: 202-331-0302, elisabethdembil@yahoo.ca
dj.embassyinformation.com
His Excellency Roble Olhaye, Ambassador
Issa Daher Bouraleh, Counsellor
Elizabeth K. Dembil, Honorary Consul General (Montréal)

Commonwealth of Dominica
See: Organization of the Eastern Caribbean States

Dominican Republic
#418, 130 Albert St., Ottawa, ON K1P 5G4
613-569-9893, Fax: 613-569-8673, info@drembassy.org
www.drembassy.org
His Excellency Jose del Carmen Ureña, Ambassador, jurena@drembassy.org
Ricardo Alberto Almonte Arias, Minister-Counsellor
Briunny Garabito Segura, Minister-Counsellor
Glenis Regina Guzman Felipe, Minister-Counsellor
Ana Melba Rosario Arias, Minister-Counsellor
Dulce Ileana e Rosario de la Maza

Republic of Ecuador
Embassy of Ecuador, #316, 50 O'Connor St., Ottawa, ON K1P 6L2
613-563-8206, 613-563-4286, Fax: 613-235-5776, embassy@embassyecuador.ca
www.embassyecuador.ca
His Excellency Dr. Andres Teran-Parral, Ambassador
Hilda Sisalema, Minister & Chargé d´Affaires
Gonzalo González, Counsellor, Commercial

Arab Republic of Egypt
Embassy of the Arab Republic of Egypt, 454 Laurier Ave. East, Ottawa, ON K1N 6R3
613-234-4931, Fax: 613-234-9347, egyptemb@sympatico.ca
www.mfa.gov.eg
His Excellency Wael Ahmed Kamal Aboul Magd, Ambassador
Mohamed Naguib Hussein Fakhry, Minister
Yasser Mahmoud Abed, Counsellor
Mohamed Zakaria H. Elghazawy, Second Secretary

Republic of El Salvador
Embassy of El Salvador, 209 Kent St., Ottawa, ON K2P 1Z8
613-238-2939, Fax: 613-238-6940,
His Excellency Oscar Mauricio Duarte Granados, Ambassador
Ana Coralia Mejia de Morot-Gaudry, Minister-Counsellor
Vladimir Solorzano Pena, Counsellor

Equatorial Guinea
c/o Permanent Mission of the Republic of Equatorial Guinea to the United Nations, New York, NY 10017 USA
212-223-2324, Fax: 212-223-2366,
His Excellency Anatolio Ndong Mba, Ambassador

Eritrea
Embassy of the State of Eritrea, 1708 New Hampshire Ave, NW, Washington, DC 20009 USA
202-319-1991, Fax: 202-319-1304, embassyeritrea@embassyeritrea.org
www.embassyeritrea.org
Semere Ghebremariam Ogbamicael, Consul (Toronto)

Embassy of the Republic of Estonia
Embassy of Estonia, #210, 260 Dalhousie St., Ottawa, ON K1N 7E4
613-789-4222, Fax: 613-789-9555, embassy.ottawa@mfa.ee
www.estemb.ca
Her Excellency Marina Kaljurand, Ambassador
Riho Kruuv, Chargé d'affaires
Laas Leivat, Honorary Consul General (Toronto)

Democratic Republic of Ethiopia
Embassy of Federal Democratic Republic of Ethiopia, 3506 International Drive, NW, Washington, DC 20008 USA
202-364-1200, Fax: 202-587-0195, ethiopia@ethiopianembassy.org
www.ethiopianembassy.org
His Excellency Girma Birru Beda, Ambassador
Tefera Mekonnen Tefera, Permanent Representative
Michael Tobias Babisso, Consul General (Toronto)

European Union
Delegation of the European Commission to Canada, 150 Metcalf St., Ottawa, ON K2P 1P1
613-238-6464, Fax: 613-238-5191, delegation-canada@ec.europa.eu
www.delcan.ec.europa.eu
Matthias Brinkmann, Ambassador & Head of Delegation
Manfred Edgar G. Auster, Minister-Counsellor
Maurizio Cellini, First Counsellor, Economic, Commercial & Trade
José Antonio Torres Lacasa, First Counsellor, Political & Public Affairs

Fiji
Embassy of Fiji (to Canada), 2000 M St. NW, Washington, DC 20036 USA
202-337-8320, Fax: 202-466-8325, info@fijiembassy.com
www.fijiembassydc.com
His Excellency Winston Thompson, High Commissioner
Sakiusa Rabuka, Counsellor

Republic of Finland
Embassy of Finland, #850, 55 Metcalfe St., Ottawa, ON K1P 6L5
613-288-2233, Fax: 613-288-2244, embassy@finland.ca
www.finland.ca
His Excellency Charles Murto, Ambassador
Petri Ensio Kruuti, Minister-Counsellor

French Republic
Embassy of France, 42 Sussex Dr., Ottawa, ON K1M 2C9
613-789-1795, Fax: 613-562-3735, politique@ambafrance-ca.org
www.ambafrance-ca.org
His Excellency Philippe Zeller, Ambassador
Frédéric Michel Régis Kaplan, Minister-Counsellor, Economics & Trade
Philippe Marie C. Carlevan, Counsellor, Science & Technology
Karine Gonnet, Counsellor, Legal
Thomas Henri A. Michelon, Counsellor, Culture
Cyril Pierre Henri Pinel, Counsellor

Gabonese Republic
Embassy of Gabon, 4 Range Rd., Ottawa, ON K1N 8J5
613-232-5301, Fax: 613-232-6916, ambgabon@sprint.ca
gabonembassycanada.org
François Ebibi Mba, Chargé d'affaires
Johanna Rose Mamiaka, Counsellor
Vénance Mbingt-Abdoulaye, Counsellor

Republic of the Gambia
High Commission for Gambia (to Canada): c/o Gambia Embassy, #240, Georgetown Plaza, Washington, DC 20007 USA
202-785-1399, Fax: 202-342-0240, info@gambiaembassy.us
www.gambiaembassy.us
His Excellency Alieu Momodou Ngum, High Commissioner
Baboucarr Jallow, Minister-Counsellor & Deputy Chief of Mission

Republic of Georgia
Embassy of Georgia, #2101, 150 Metcalfe St., Ottawa, ON K2P 1P1
613-421-0460, Fax: 613-680-0394
Malkhaz Mikeladze, Minister & Chargé d'Affaires
Beka Dvali, Senior Counsellor & Consul
His Excellency Vasil Sikharulidze, Ambassador

Embassy of the Federal Republic of Germany
Embassy of Germany, 1 Waverley St., Ottawa, ON K2P 0T8
613-232-1101, Fax: 613-594-9330, info@ottawa.diplo.de
www.ottawa.diplo.de
Embassy wants people excluded for the Embassy and Consulates General due to constant changes.
His Excellency Werner Wendt, Ambassador

Republic of Ghana
High Commission for Ghana, 1 Clemow Ave., Ottawa, ON K1S 2A9
613-236-0871, Fax: 613-236-0874, ghanacom@ghc-ca.com
www.ghc-ca.com
His Excellency Samuel Valis-Akyianu, High Commissioner Designate
Kwaasi Obeng-Koranteng, Acting High Commissioner
Louis Kwame Obeng, Minister-Counsellor & Head of Chancery
Adisa Yakubu, Counsellor, Political & Economic Affairs

Hellenic Republic
Embassy of Greece, 80 MacLaren St., Ottawa, ON K2P 0K6
613-238-6271, Fax: 613-238-5676, embassy@greekembassy.ca, gremb.otv@mfa.gr
www.greekembassy.ca
His Excellency Eleftherios Anghelopoulos, Ambassador
Iliana Andritsou, Alternate Representative
Lambros Kakissis, Counsellor
Athanasia Papatriantafyllou, First Secretary

Grenada
See: Organization of the Eastern Caribbean States

Republic of Guatemala
Embassy of Guatemala, #1010, 130 Albert St., Ottawa, ON K1P 5G4
613-233-7237, Fax: 613-233-0135, embassy1@embaguate-canada.com
www.embaguate-canada.com
His Excellency Georges de la Roche du Ronzet Plihal, Ambassador
Martha Aida Rogelia Argueta Molina, First Secretary & Consul
Sandra Refugio Cruz Ordonez, Third Secretary

Republic of Guinea
Embassy of Guinea, 483 Wilbrod St., Ottawa, ON K1N 6N1
613-789-8444, Fax: 613-789-7560
His Excellency Anatolio Ndong Mba, Ambassador
Hawa Diakité, Counsellor & Chargé d'Affaires
Aïssata Sow, Second Counsellor
Mory Sidibe, First Secretary

Republic of Guinea-Bissau
c/o Permanent Mission of the Republic of Guinea-Bissau to the United Nations, #400F, 800 Second Ave., New York, NY 10017 USA
917-770-5598, Fax: 212-856-9820

Republic of Guyana
High Commission for the Republic of Guyana, Burnside Bldg., #309, 151 Slater St., Ottawa, ON K1P 5H3
613-235-7249, Fax: 613-235-1447, guyanahcott@rogers.com
www.guyanamissionottawa.org
His Excellency Harry Narine Nawbatt, High Commissioner
Satyawattie Sawh, Honorary Consul General (Toronto)
Tyrone Emanuel Ramroop, Consul (Toronto)

Republic of Haiti
Embassy of Haiti, #1110, 85 Albert St., Ottawa, ON K1P 6A4
613-235-7249, Fax: 613-235-1447,
His Excellency O. Andre Frantz Liautaud, Ambassador
Marie Michel Geralde Carre Alerte, Minister-Counsellor
Carlo Severe, Minister-Counsellor
Marie Jose Justinvil, Counsellor

Holy See
Apostolic Nunciature, Rockcliffe Park, 724 Manor Ave., Ottawa, ON K1M 0E3
613-746-4914, Fax: 613-746-4786, apostolic.nunciature@rogers.com
His Excellency The Most Re Luigi Ventura, Apostolic Nuncio
Monsignor Maurizio Bravi, Counsellor

Republic of Honduras
Embassy of Honduras, #805, 151 Slater St., Ottawa, ON K1P 5H3
613-233-8900, Fax: 613-232-0193, correo@embassyhonduras.ca
www.embassyhonduras.ca
Her Excellency Sofia Lastenia Cerrato Rodriguez, Ambassador
Luis Francisco Bogran Moncada, Minister-Counsellor
Guillermo Javier Valladares Lainez, Minister-Counsellor
Ivonne Bonilla Medina, Counsellor

Republic of Hungary
Embassy of the Republic Hungary, 299 Waverley St., Ottawa, ON K2P 0V9
613-230-2717, Fax: 613-230-7560, mission.ott@mfa.gov.hu
www.mfa.gov.hu/kulkepviselet/CA/hu
His Excellency Laszlo Csaba Pordany, Ambassador
Lajos Olah, First Secretary & Deputy Head of Mission
Éva Simon, Attaché & Consul
André Molnar, Honorary Consul General (Vancouver)

Republic of Iceland
Embassy of Iceland, #710, 360 Albert St., Ottawa, ON K1R 7X7
613-482-1944, Fax: 613-482-1945, icemb.ottawa@utn.stjr.is
www.iceland.is/iceland-abroad/ca
His Excellency Thordur Aegir Oskarsson, Ambassador
Kristin Eva Jansson Sigurdardottir, Second Secretary

Republic of India
High Commission of India, 10 Springfield Rd., Ottawa, ON K1M 1C9
613-744-3751, Fax: 613-744-0913, hicomind@hciottawa.ca
www.hciottawa.ca
Her Excellency Narinder Chauhan, Acting High Commissioner
Manmohan Singh, Counsellor, Community Affairs
Vineeta Sharma, Counsellor, Political & Consular
B.S. Saini, First Secretary & Head of Chancery
Vijay Kumar, Second Secretary, Commerce

Republic of Indonesia / Republik Indonesia
55 Parkdale Ave., Ottawa, ON K1Y 1E5
613-724-1100, Fax: 613-724-1105, info@indonesia-ottawa.org
www.indonesia-ottawa.org
Her Excellency Dienne Hardianti Moehario, Ambassador
Suprio Utomo Nadir, Deputy Chief of Mission
Fientje M. Suebu, Minister-Counsellor, Information & Social/Cultural Affairs
Cicilia Rusdiharini, Minister-Counsellor, Political Affairs
Raden Hikmat Moeljawan, Counsellor, Economic Affairs

Islamic Republic of Iran
www.iranembassy.ca
Canada suspended diplomatic relations with Iran in September 2012, closing the Canadian embassy in Iran & expelling all Iranian diplomats from Canada, citing human rights abuses as the reason.

Republic of Iraq
Embassy of Iraq, 215 McLeod St., Ottawa, ON K2P 0Z8
613-236-9177, Fax: 613-236-9641, media@iraqembassy.ca
www.iraqembassy.ca
His Excellency Dr. Abdulrahman Hamid Al-Hussaini, Ambassador
Saad Abdulhadi M. A. Al-Khafaji, Second Secretary & Vice-Consul
Suhair Hussein A. Al-Nassrawe, Second Secretary
Firas Raad Mahmoud Al-Doury, Third Secretary
Sinan Aziz Naqi Alsheikh, Third Secretary

Republic of Ireland
Embassy of Ireland, #1105, 130 Albert St., Ottawa, ON K1P 5G4
613-233-6281, Fax: 613-233-5835, embassyofireland@rogers.com
His Excellency John Raymond Bassett, Ambassador
Hilary Reilly, Deputy Head of Mission

State of Israel
Embassy of Israel, #1005, 50 O'Connor St., Ottawa, ON K1P 6L2
613-567-6450, Fax: 613-567-8978, info@ottawa.mfa.gov.il
www.embassyofisrael.ca
Her Excellency Miriam Ziv, Ambassador
Eliaz Luf, Minister-Counsellor
Joshua Krasna, Counsellor
Liliane Haim, First Secretary & Consul
Yosef Tal Aviram, Second Secretary
Eyal Weisler, Second Secretary

Italian Republic
Embassy of Italy, 275 Slater St., 21st Fl., Ottawa, ON K1P 5H9
613-232-2401, Fax: 613-233-1484, ambasciata.ottawa@esteri.it
www.ambottawa.esteri.it/ambasciata_ottawa
His Excellency Andrea Meloni, Ambassador
Nicola Lener, Minister-Counsellor & Deputy Head of Mission
Giovanni Maria de Vita, Counsellor
Maria Michela Laroccia, First Secretary

Ivory Coast
See: Republic of Côte d'Ivoire

Jamaica
Jamaican High Commission, #1000, 151 Slater St., Ottawa, ON K1P 5H3
613-233-9311, Fax: 613-233-0611, hc@jhcottawa.ca
www.jhcottawa.ca
Her Excellency Sheila Ivoline Sealy-Monteith, High Commissioner
Laura Anne McNeil, Counsellor
Seth George Christian Ramocan, Consul General (Toronto)

Japan
Embassy of Japan, 255 Sussex Dr., Ottawa, ON K1N 9E6
613-241-8541, Fax: 613-241-2232, infocul@ot.mofa.go.jp
www.ca.emb-japan.go.jp
His Excellency Kaoru Ishikawa, Ambassador
Fumio Yawata, Minister & Deputy Head of Mission
Hitoshi Ozawa, Minister
Mariko Murakoshi, Counsellor
Hidetaka Nishimura, Counsellor
Yuji Sekiguchi, Counsellor

Hashemite Kingdom of Jordan
Embassy of Jordan, #701, 100 Bronson Ave., Ottawa, ON K1R 6G8
613-238-8090, Fax: 613-232-3341, ottawa@fm.gov.jo
www.embassyofjordan.ca
His Excellency Basheer F.Zoubi, Ambassador
Dr. Bashar Abu Taleb, Deputy Head of Mission
Adli Q.Al-Khaledi, First Secretary & Consul

Republic of Kazakhstan
Embassy of the Republic of Kazakhstan, #1603-1604, 150 Metcalfe St. Ottawa, ON K2P 1P1
613-695-8055, Fax: 613-695-8755, kazakhembassy@gmail.com
www.kazembassy.ca
His Excellency Konstantin Zhigalov, Ambassador
Askar Kuttykadim, Minister-Counsellor
Daniyar Seidaliyev, Counsellor
Nurlan Zhanbatyrov, Second Secretary
Artem Kuzmin, Third Secretary

Republic of Kenya
High Commission for Kenya, 415 Laurier Ave. East, Ottawa, ON K1N 6R4
613-563-1773, Fax: 613-233-6599, kenyahighcommission@rogers.com
www.kenyahighcommission.ca
His Excellency Simon Waynonyi Nabukwesi, High Commissioner
Mohamednur Mohamed Adan, First Counsellor
Alice Njambi Kinyungu, Counsellor
Enock Ndemo Aroni, Second Secretary
Victor Nthenge Musembi, Third Secretary

Democratic People's Republic of Korea
Permanent Mission of Democratic People's Republic of Korea to the UN, 820 Second Ave., 13th Fl., New York, NY 10017 USA
212-972-3105, Fax: 212-972-3154,
His Excellency Son Ho Sin, Ambassador
Je Ryong Hong, Counsellor

Republic of Korea
Embassy of Korea, 150 Boteler St., Ottawa, ON K1N 5A6
613-244-5010, Fax: 613-244-5034, canada@mofat.go.kr
can-ottawa.mofat.go.kr
His Excellency Cho Hee-yong, Ambassador
Bongwoo Ko, Minister-Counsellor
Song Oh, Minister
Heon-Jun Kim, Counsellor
Chong Suk Park, Counsellor
Keonki Roh, Counsellor

State of Kuwait
Embassy of Kuwait, 333 Sussex Dr., Ottawa, ON K1N 1J9
613-780-9999, Fax: 613-780-9905, info@embassyofkuwait.com
www.embassyofkuwait.ca
His Excellency Ali Al-Sammak, Ambassador
Anas E. A. H. E. Al Saloom, Third Secretary
Hadi M. M. F. Alsubaie, Third Secretary

Kyrgyz Republic
Embassy of the Kyrgyz Republic, 2360 Masachussets. Ave. NW, Washington, DC 20008 USA
202-449-9822, Fax: 202-386-7550, consul@kgembassy.org
www.kyrgyzembassy.org
His Excellency Muktar Djumaliev, Ambassador
Arslan Anarbaev, Minister-Counsellor
Uslan Djusupov, Minister-Counsellor
Zhanybek Eraliev, First Secretary
Ruslan Bekbolotov, Second Secretary

Laos
The Embassy of the Lao People's Democratic Republic (to Canada), 2222 S St. NW, Washington, DC 20008 USA
202-332-6416, Fax: 202-332-4923, laoemb@erols.com
www.laoembassy.com
His Excellency Seng Soukhathivong, Ambassador
Bouapha Phommaseng, First Secretary
Thongmoon Phongphailath, First Secretary

Embassy of the Republic of Latvia
Embassy of Latvia, #1200, 350 Sparks St., Ottawa, ON K1R 7S8
613-238-6014, Fax: 613-238-7044, embassy.canada@mfa.gov.lv, consulate.canada@mfa.gov.lv
www.mfa.gov.lv/ottawa
His Excellency Juris Audarins, Ambassador
Egija Eglite, Third Secretary

Lebanese Republic
Embassy of Lebanon, 640 Lyon St., Ottawa, ON K1S 3Z5
613-236-5825, Fax: 613-232-1609, info@lebanonembassy.ca
www.lebanonembassy.ca
Sami Haddad, Chargé d'affaires
Daniel El Haiby, Permanent Representative
Souleiman Eid, Alternate Representative

Kingdom of Lesotho
High Commission for the Kingdom of Lesotho, #1820, 130 Albert St., Ottawa, ON K1P 5G4
613-234-0770, Fax: 613-234-5665, lesotho.ottawa@bellnet.ca, lesotho-ottawa@foreign.gov.ls
www.lesothocanada.gov.ls
Her Excellency Dr. 'Mathabo Tsepa, High Commissioner
Pulane Christina Lechesa, Counsellor & Head of Chancery, lechesap@foreign.gov.ls

Republic of Liberia
Embassy of the Republic of Liberia, 5201, 16th St. NW, Washington, DC 20011 USA
202-723-0437, Fax: 202-723-0436, www.liberianembassyus.org
His Excellency Jeremiah C. Sulunteh, Ambassador

Libya
Embassy of Libya, #1000, 81 Metcalfe St., Ottawa, ON K1P 6K7
613-842-7519, Fax: 613-842-8627, info@libyanembassy.ca
www.libyanembassy.ca
Sulaiman A. Mohamed, Counsellor & Chargé d'Affaires
Ghada Jenbaz, Alternate Representative
Khalifa Alghuwel, First Secretary
Eman O. A. Ali, Third Secretary
Hesham M.R. Huwisa, Third Secretary

Liechtenstein
See: Swiss Confederation

Embassy of the Republic of Lithuania
Embassy of Lithuania, #1600, 150 Metcalfe St., Ottawa, ON K2P 1P1
613-567-5458, Fax: 613-567-5315, ottawa@lithuanianembassy.ca
www.ca.mfa.lt
His Excellency Vytautas Žalys, Ambassador
Jonas Skardinskas, Minister
Vilija Jatkoniene, Counsellor

Grand Duchy of Luxembourg
Embassy of Luxembourg (to Canada), 2200 Massachusetts Ave. NW, Washington, DC 20008 USA
202-265-4171, Fax: 202-328-8270, luxembassy.was@mae.etat.lu
washington.mae.lu
His Excellency Jean-Louis Wolzfeld, Ambassador, jean-louis.wolzfeld@mae.etat.lu
Olivier Baldauff, Deputy Chief of Mission, olivier.baldauff@mae.etat.lu

Republic of Macedonia
Embassy of the Republic of Macedonia, #1006, 130 Albert St., Ottawa, ON K1P 5G4
613-234-3882, Fax: 613-233-1852, ottawa@mfa.gov.mk, emb.macedonia.ottawa@sympatico.ca
www3.sympatico.ca/emb.macedonia.ottawa
His Excellency Ljuben Tevdovski, Ambassador
Konstantin Dorakovski, Minister-Counsellor
Dragan Gjurchevski, Consul General

Republic of Madagascar
Embassy of Madagascar, 3 Raymond St., Ottawa, ON K1R 1A3
613-537-0505, Fax: 613-537-2882, ambamadcanada@bellnet.ca
www.madagascar-embassy.ca
His Excellency Simon Constant Horace, Ambassador
Soloheriniaina Eric Ratsimbazafy, First Counsellor
Tsitohaina Hasina A. Randrianarizao, Counsellor
Clara Randrianjara, Counsellor
Philippe Velo, Counsellor

Republic of Malawi
High Commission for Malawi, #1000, 1029 Vermont Ave., Washington, DC 20005 USA
202-721-0270, Fax: 202-721-0288, malawidc@aol.com
www.malawiembassy-dc.org
His Excellency Steve Matenje, Ambassador
Jane Nankwenya, Deputy Chief of Mission, jane.nankwenya@malawiembassy-dc.org
Rhino Mchenga, Counsellor & Head of Chancery, rhino.mchenga@malawiembassy-dc.org

Malaysia
High Commission of Malaysia, 60 Boteler St., Ottawa, ON K1N 8Y7
613-241-5182, Fax: 613-241-5214, mwottawa@kln.gov.my
Her Excellency Hayati Binti Ismail, High Commissioner
Yong Heng Lim, Permanent Representative
Suraya Binti Ahmad Pauzi, First Secretary
Rozalah Binti Hashim, Second Secretary

Republic of Maldives
c/o Permanent Mission of the Republic of Maldives to the United Nations, #400E, 800 Second Ave., New York, NY 10017 USA
212-599-6194, Fax: 212-661-6405, www.maldivesmission.com
His Excellency Ahmed Sareer, Ambassador
Amin Javed Faizal, Counsellor, Human Rights & Humanitarian Affairs
J. Salim Waheed, First Secretary, Economic & Financial Affairs, JSWaheed@MaldivesMission.com
Hassan Hussain Shihab, First Secretary, Hassan@maldivesmission.com
Fathimath Liusha, Third Secretary, Liusha@maldivesmission.com

Republic of Mali
Embassy of Mali, 50 Goulburn Ave., Ottawa, ON K1N 8C8
613-232-1501, Fax: 613-232-7429, ambassadedumali@rogers.com
www.ambamalicanada.org
Her Excellency Ami Diallo Traor, Ambassador
Boubacar Ballo, First Counsellor
Amadou Ba, Second Counsellor
Diawoye Diabate, Second Counsellor

Republic of Malta
High Commission for Malta (to Canada); c/o Embassy of Malta, 2017 Connecticut Ave. NW, Washington, DC 20008 USA
202-462-3611, Fax: 202-387-5470, maltaembassy.washington@gov.mt
Denis Grech, Chargé d'affaires
Ruth Mary Farrugia, Consul General (Toronto)

Republic of the Marshall Islands
2433 Massachusetts Ave. NW, Washington, DC 20008 USA
202-234-5414, Fax: 202-232-3236,
His Excellency Banny De Brum, Ambassador

Islamic Republic of Mauritania
Permanent Mission of the Islamic Republic of Mauritania, 116 East 38th St., New York, NY 10016 USA
212-252-0113, Fax: 212-252-0175, mauritania@un.int
His Excellency Ahmed Ould Teguedi, Ambassador
Sidati Ould Cheikh, First Counsellor
Maata Ould Mohamed, First Counsellor
Bettah Ould Mohamed, Second Counsellor

Republic of Mauritius
High Commission for Mauritius (to Canada): c/o Embassy of Mauritius, #441, 4301 Connecticut Ave. NW, Washington, DC 20008 USA
202-244-1491, Fax: 202-966-0983, mauritius.embassy@verizon.net
washington.mauritius.gov.mu
His Excellency Somduth Soborun, High Commissioner
Joyker Nayeck, First Secretary & Deputy Head of Mission
S. Gaffar, Second Secretary

United Mexican States
Embassy of Mexico, #1000, 45 O'Connor St., Ottawa, ON K1P 1A4
613-233-8988, Fax: 613-235-9123, info@embamexcan.com
embamex.sre.gob.mx/canada
His Excellency Francisco Javier Barrio Terrazas, Ambassador
Antonio Curzio Gutierrez, Minister
Guillermo Fonseca Leal, Minister
Gabriel Jimenez Romero, Minister
Carlos Enrique Lopez Araiza Genis, Minister
Ernesto Meldonado Garza, Minister
Carlos Jesus Pinera Gonzalez, Minister
Luis Gerardo Sanchez Maleno, Minister

Republic of Moldova
2101 S St. NW, Washington, DC 20008 USA
202-667-1130, Fax: 202-667-1204, washington@mfa.md
www.sua.mfa.md
His Excellency His Excellency Igor Muntaenu, Ambassador
Sergiu Luca, First Secretary
Nicolae Popa, Second Secretary

Principality of Monaco
Embassy of the Principality of Monaco, 3400 International Drive, NW, Washington, DC 20008 USA
202-234-1530, Fax: 202-244-7656, info@monacodc.org
monacodc.org/canadahome.html
His Excellency Gilles Noghès, Ambassador
Jean-Claude Bachand, Honorary Consul General (Montréal)
Bernard Lette, Honorary Consul General (Toronto)
Jacques Becker, Honorary Consul (Vancouver)

Mongolia
Embassy of Mongolia, #503, 151 Slater St., Ottawa, ON K1P 5H3
613-569-3830, Fax: 613-569-3916, ottawa@mfat.gov.mn, mail@mongolembassy.org
ottawa.mfat.gov.mn
His Excellency Zalaa-Uul Tundevdorj, Ambassador
Eldev-Ochir Lkhagvaa, Minister-Counsellor
Batzorig Enkhbold, Third Secretary

Montenegro
Embassy of the Republic of Montenegro, 1610 New Hampshire Ave., Washington, DC
202-234-6108, Fax: 202-234-6109,
His Excellency Srdan Darmanovic, Ambassador
Lt. Col. Velibor Bakrac, Military, Naval & Air Attaché
Kaare Glenne Foy, Honorary Consul (Vancouver)

Montserrat
See: Organization of the Eastern Caribbean States

Kingdom of Morocco
Embassy of Morocco, 38 Range Rd., Ottawa, ON K1N 8J4
613-236-7391, Fax: 613-236-6164, info@ambamaroc.ca, sifamaot@bellnet.ca
www.ambamaroc.ca
Her Excellency Nouzha Chekrouni, Ambassador
Amina Rabhi, Minister
Nadya Talmi, Minister-Counsellor
Mohamed Ait Bihi, Counsellor
Ahmed Amine Bahnini, Counsellor

Republic of Mozambique
High Commission of the Republic of Mozambique to Canada, 1525 New Hampshire Ave. NW, Washington, DC 20036 USA
202-293-7146, Fax: 202-835-0245, mozambvisa@aol.com
www.embamoc-usa.org
Her Excellency Amélia Narciso Matos Sumbana, High Commissioner
Antonio Pinto, Permanent Representative
Eduardo Candido Albino Zaqueu, Counsellor
Antonio Tauzene, Second Secretary

Myanmar
Embassy of the Republic of the Union of Myanmar, #902/903, 85 Range Rd., Ottawa, ON K1N 8J6
613-232-9990, Fax: 613-232-6999, meottawa@rogers.com
www.mofa.gov.mm/myanmarmissions/canada.html
His Excellency Kyaw Tin, Ambassador
Aung Ba Kyu, Minister-Counsellor
Than Htwe, Counsellor
Yee Mon Khine, Second Secretary

Republic of Namibia
High Commission for Namibia (to Canada), 1605 New Hampshire Ave. NW, Washington, DC 20009 USA
202-986-0540, Fax: 202-986-0443, info@namibianembassyusa.org
www.namibianembassyusa.org
His Excellency Martin Andjaba, High Commissioner
Omari Rashi Nundu, Alternate Representative
Ulrich Freddie Gaoseb, Counsellor

Kingdom of Nepal
Embassy of Nepal, 408 Queen St., Ottawa, ON K1R 5A7
613-680-5513, Fax: 613-422-5149, nepalembassy@rogers.com
nepalembassy.ca
His Excellency His Excellency Bhoj Raj Ghimire, Ambassador
Tara Prasad Pokarhel, Minister-Counsellor

Revati Raman Paudel, Second Secretary

Kingdom of the Netherlands

Royal Netherlands Embassy, #2020, 350 Albert St., Ottawa, ON K1R 1A4

613-237-5031, Fax: 613-237-6471,
nlgovott@netcom.ca
www.netherlandsembassy.ca

His Excellency Wilhelm Julius Petrus Geerts, Ambassador
Rochus Johannes Pieter Pronk, Minister & Deputy Head of Mission
Janke Sytske de Vries, Counsellor
Martinus Wilhelmus Maria Olde Monnikhof, Counsellor
Peter John van Mechelen, Counsellor

New Zealand

New Zealand High Commission, Clarica Centre, #727, 99 Bank St., Ottawa, ON K1P 6G3

613-238-5991, Fax: 613-238-5707,
info@nzhcottawa.org
www.nzembassy.com/canada

His Excellency Andrew Needs, High Commissioner
Winton Alexander Holmes, Counsellor
Lesley Jane McConnel, Counsellor
Michael Kelvin Pannett, Counsellor

Republic of Nicaragua

Embassy of Nicaragua, 1627 New Hampshire Ave. NW, Washington, DC 20009 USA

202-939-6570, Fax: 202-939-6545

His Excellency Francisco Obadiah Campbell Hooker, Ambassador
Armando Jose Alaniz Noguera, Defence, Military & Air Attaché
Robert Douglas Sirrs, Honorary Consul (Whitby)

Republic of Niger

Embassy of Niger, 38 Blackburn Ave., Ottawa, ON K1N 8A3

613-232-4291, Fax: 613-230-9808,
ambanigeracanada@rogers.com
www.ambanigeracanada.ca

Her Excellency Fadjimata Maman Sidibe, Ambassador

Federal Republic of Nigeria

Nigeria High Commission, 295 Metcalfe St., Ottawa, ON K2P 1R9

613-236-0521, Fax: 613-236-0529,
chancery@nigeriahcottawa.com
www.nigeriahcottawa.com

His Excellency Chief Ojo Uma Maduekwe, High Commissioner
Charles Nduka Onianwa, Deputy High Commissioner
Ladi Grace Kanginwa, MInister-Counsellor
Yacouba Mahamane, Minister-Counsellor

Kingdom of Norway

Royal Norwegian Embassy, 150 Metcalfe St., Ottawa, ON K2P 1P1

613-238-6571, Fax: 613-238-2765,
emb.ottawa@mfa.no
www.emb-norway.ca

Her Excellency Mona Elisabeth Brøther, Ambassador
Tobias F. Svenningsen, Minister-Counsellor & Chargé d'affaires
Øystein Bell, First Secretary, Administrative & Consular Affairs
Inger Elisabeth Meyer, First Secretary

Sultanate of Oman

Embassy of Oman (to Canada), 2535 Belmont Rd. NW, Washington, DC 20008 USA

202-387-1980, Fax: 202-745-4933,
www.omani.info

Her Excellency Hunaina Sultan Ahmed Al Mughairy, Ambassador
Dorian Mihai, Minister-Counsellor
Raluca Truscanu, First Secretary
Claudiu Adrian Grigoras, Third Secretary

Organization of the Eastern Caribbean States (OECS)

High Commission for the Countries of the Eastern Caribbean States, #700, 130 Albert St., Ottawa, ON K1P 5G4

613-236-8952, Fax: 613-236-3042,
www.oecs.org

Includes: Anguilla, Antigua & Barbuda, British Virgin Islands, Commonwealth of Dominica, Grenada, Montserrat, Saint Christopher (Saint Kitts) & Nevis, Saint Lucia, Saint Vincent & the Grenadines
His Excellency Brendon Browne, High Commissioner

Islamic Republic of Pakistan

High Commission for Pakistan, Burnside Bldg., 10 Range Rd., Ottawa, ON K1N 8J3

613-238-7881, Fax: 613-238-7296,
parepottawa@rogers.com
www.pakmission.ca

His Excellency Mian Gul Akbar Zeb, High Commissioner
Nazia Khalid, Counsellor
Samina Mehtab, First Secretary
Adeel Ahmad Khan, Third Secretary

Republic of Panama

Embassy of Panama, #300, 130 Albert St., Ottawa, ON K1P 5G4

613-236-7177, Fax: 613-236-5775,
info@embassyofpanama.ca
www.embassyofpanama.ca

His Excellency Jorge H. Miranda Corona, Ambassador
Juventino Caballero Aparicio, Third Secretary

Papua New Guinea

High Commission of Papua New Guinea (to Canada), #805, 1779 Massachusetts Ave. NW, Washington, DC 20036 USA

202-745-3680, Fax: 202-745-3679,
info@pngembassy.org
www.pngembassy.org

His Excellency Evan Jeremy Paki, High Commissioner
David R. Beatty, Honoraru Consul (Toronto)

Republic of Paraguay

Embassy of Paraguay, #501, 151 Slater St., Ottawa, ON K1P 5H3

613-567-1283, Fax: 613-567-1679,
embassy@embassyofparaguay.ca
www.embassyofparaguay.ca

His Excellency Manuel Schaerer Kanonnikoff, Ambassador
Raúl Montiel Gastó, Counsellor & Chargé d'Affaires, rmontiel@embassyofparaguay.ca
Alberto Giménez Gauna, Second Secretary, Consular Section, embassy@embassyofparaguay.ca

Republic of Peru

Embassy of Peru, #1901, 130 Albert St., Ottawa, ON K1P 5G4

613-238-1777, Fax: 613-232-3062,
emperuca@bellnet.ca
www.embassyofperu.ca

His Excellency Jose Antonio Raymundo Bellina Acevedo, Ambassador
Roberto Rafael Max Rodriguez Arnillas, Minister & Deputy Head of Mission
Luis Miguel Picardo Martinez, Alternate Representative
Walter Milenko Vojvodic Vargas, Alternate Representative
Claudia Giuliana Betalleluz Otiura, Counsellor

Republic of the Philippines

Embassy of the Philippines, #606, 130 Albert St., Ottawa, ON K1P 5G4

613-233-1121, Fax: 613-233-4165,
embassyofphilippines@rogers.com
philembassy.ca

His Excellency Leslie B. Gatan, Ambassador
Abraham R. Estavillo, Deputy Head of Mission
Neil Frank R. Ferrier, Minister & Consul General
Eric Gerardo E. Tamayo, First Secretary & Consul
Flerida Ann Camille P. Mayo, First Secretary & Consul
Porfirio M Mayo Jr., First Secretary & Consul

Republic of Poland

Embassy of Poland, 443 Daly Ave., Ottawa, ON K1N 6H3

613-789-0468, Fax: 613-789-1218,
ottawa@ottawa.polemb.net; ottawa.info@msz.gov.pl
www.ottawa.polemb.net

His Excellency Zenon Kosiniak-Kamysz, Ambassador
Jaroslaw Kurek, Minister-Counsellor, Head of Political & Economic Unit
Dariusz Manczyk, Minister-Counsellor, Economic Affairs
Wlodzimierz Leszczynski, Trade Commissioner, Head of Trade & Investment Promotion Section

Portuguese Republic

Embassy of Portugal, 645 Island Park Dr., Ottawa, ON K1Y 0B8

613-729-0883, Fax: 613-729-4236,
embportugal@ottawa.dgaccp.pt

His Excellency Pedro Luis Baptista Moitinho de Almeida, Ambassador
Col. Antonio Carlos de Amorim Temporao, Defence Attaché

State of Qatar

Embassy of Qatar, 150 Metcalfe Street, 8th Floor, Ottawa, ON K2P 1P1

613-241-4917, Fax: 613-241-3304

His Excellency His Excellency Salem Mubarak Sh. S. Al-Shafi, Ambassador
Hussain Ali S. Al-Fadhala, First Secretary
Khater Mohammed K. I. Al-Khater, Second Secretary

Romania

Embassy of Romania, 655 Rideau St., Ottawa, ON K1N 6A3

613-789-3709, Fax: 613-789-4365,
romania@romanian-embassy.com
ottawa.mae.ro

Her Excellency Elena Stefoi, Ambassador
Dorian Mihai, Minister-Counsellor, Consular Affairs, dmihai@romanian-embassy.com
Raluca Truscanu, First Secretary, Press & Cultural Affairs, rtruscanu@romanian-embassy.com
Adrian Grigoras, Third Secretary, agrigoras@romanian-embassy.com

Russian Federation

Embassy of the Russian Federation, 285 Charlotte St., Ottawa, ON K1N 8L5

613-235-4341, Fax: 613-236-6342,
rusemb@intranet.ca
www.russianembassy.net

His Excellency Georgy Mamedov, Ambassador
Petr Plikhin, Minister-Counsellor
Vladimir Karpov, Senior Counsellor
Vladimir Lapshin, Senior Counsellor & Head of Economic Section
Leonid Savinov, Counsellor
Sergey Strokov, Agricultural Division
Igor Girenko, Counsellor & Head of Bilateral Section
Anton Vannovskiy, Counsellor, Science & Education Division

Republic of Rwanda

#404, 294 Albert St., Ottawa, ON K1P 6E6

613-569-5420, Fax: 613-569-5421,
generalinfo@ambarwaottawa.ca
www.canada.embassy.gov.rw

Her Excellency Edda Mukabagwiza, Ambassador
Shakilla Umutoni Kazimbaya, First Counsellor
Fixer Eugene Ngoga, First Counsellor
Eric Rutsindintwarane, First Secretary

Saint Kitts & Nevis

See: Organization of the Eastern Caribbean States

Saint Lucia

See: Organization of the Eastern Caribbean States

Saint Vincent & the Grenadines

See: Organization of the Eastern Caribbean States

Samoa

Samoa High Commission, #400J, 800 Second Ave., New York, NY 10017 USA

212-599-6196, Fax: 212-599-0797,
samoa@un.int
samoa.usembassy.gov

His Excellency Ali'ioaiga Feturi Elisaia, High Commissioner

Republic of San Marino

c/o Permanent Mission of the Republic of San Marino to the United Nations, 327 East 50th St., New York, NY 10022 USA

212-751-1234, Fax: 212-751-1436

His Excellency Damiano Beleffi, Ambassador

Democratic Republic of Sao Tomé & Principe

1211 Conneticut Ave., NW Suite 300, Washington, DC 20036 USA

202-775-2075, Fax: 202-775-2077,

His Excellency Ovidio Manuel Barbosa Pequeno, Ambassador
Domingos Ferreira, First Secretary

Kingdom of Saudi Arabia

Royal Embassy of Saudi Arabia, 201 Sussex Dr., Ottawa, ON K1N 1K6

613-237-4100, Fax: 613-237-0567

His Excellency Osamah A. Al Sanosi Ahmad, Ambassador
Talal Mohammed B.A. Kabli, Permanent Representative
Yousuf Rashad A. Abuaish, Minister
Saleh Kh. S. Alfaiz, Counsellor

Republic of Senegal

Embassy of Senegal, 57 Marlborough Ave., Ottawa, ON K1N 8E8

613-238-6392, Fax: 613-238-2695,
ambassn@sympatico.ca
www.ambsencanada.org

Mamadou Ndiaye, Minister-Counsellor & Chargé d'affaires
Saiba Sylla, First Counsellor
Aliou Diouf, Second Counsellor

Republic of Serbia

Embassy of Serbia, 17 Blackburn Ave., Ottawa, ON K1N 8A2 Canada

613-233-6289, Fax: 613-233-7850,
diplomat@serbianembassy.ca
www.serbianembassy.ca

His Excellency Zoran Veljic, Ambassador, ambassador@serbianembassy.ca
Djordje Ciklovan, Minister-Counsellor, ciklovan@serbianembassy.ca
Dejan Kostic, First Secretary, diaspora@serbianembassy.ca

Republic of Seychelles
High Commission for Seychelles (to Canada), #400C, 800 Second Ave., New York, NY 10017 USA
212-972-1785, Fax: 212-972-1786, seychelles@un.int
www.mfa.gov.sc
His Excellency Roland Jean Jumeau, High Commissioner
Gérard le Chêne, Honorary Consul (Montréal)

Republic of Sierra Leone
High Commission for Sierra Leone (to Canada), 1701 - 19th St. NW, Washington, DC 20009 USA
202-939-9261, Fax: 202-483-1793, embassyofsierraleone.net
His Excellency Bockari Kortu Stevens, High Commissioner
Alan Charles Edmund Logan, First Counsellor
Sheku Mesali, First Secretary
Saspo Ibrahim Sankoh, First Secretary

Republic of Singapore
c/o Permanent Mission of the Republic of Singapore to the UN, 231 East 51st St., New York, NY 10022 USA
212-826-0840, Fax: 212-826-2964, singpm_nyc@sgmfa.gov.sg
www.mfa.gov.sg/content/mfa/overseasmission/newyork.html
His Excellency Albert Chua, High Commissioner
Mark Neo, Minister-Counsellor & Deputy Permanent Representative

Slovak Republic / Slovenská Republika
Embassy of the Slovak Republic, 50 Rideau Terrace, Ottawa, ON K1M 2A1
613-749-4442, Fax: 613-749-4989, emb.ottawa@mzv.sk
www.mzv.sk/ottawa
His Excellency Milan Kollár, Ambassador, milan.kollar@mzv.sk
Martin Barton, Counsellor & Deputy Head of Mission, martin.barton@mzv.sk
Ján Galoci, First Secretary, Trade & Economic Section, jan.galoci@mzv.sk

Republic of Slovenia
Embassy of Slovenia, #2200, 150 Metcalfe St., Ottawa, ON K2P 1P1
613-565-5781, Fax: 613-565-5783, vot@gov.si
ottawa.embassy.si/en
Luca Kovacec, Third Secretary & Chargé d'Affaires
Alojzij Krapez, Permanent Representative
Klemen Ferjan, Alternate Representative

Solomon Islands
High Commission c/o Permanent Mission to the U.N., #400L, 800 - 2 Ave., New York, NY 10017 USA
212-599-6192, Fax: 212-661-8925
His Excellency Collin David Beck, High Commissioner
Ashwant Ashish Kumar Dwivedi, Honorary Consul (Vancouver)

Republic of South Africa
High Commission for South Africa, 15 Sussex Dr., Ottawa, ON K1M 1M8
613-744-0330, Fax: 613-741-1639, rsafrica@southafrica-canada.ca
www.southafrica-canada.ca
His Excellency Membathisi Mphumzi S. Mdladlana, High Commissioner
Livhuwani Lawrence Nemukula, Minister
Diedre Viljoen, Minister
Aneshwaren Maistry, Counsellor

Kingdom of Spain
Embassy of Spain, 74 Stanley Ave., Ottawa, ON K1M 1P4
613-747-2252, Fax: 613-744-1224, emb.ottawa@maec.es
www.maec.es
His Excellency CarlosGomez-Mugica Sanz, Ambassador
Juan Antonio Martin Burgos, Deputy Head of Mission
Juan Claudio de Ramon Jacob-Ernst, Counsellor
José Garcia Molina, Counsellor
Javier Tena Garcia, Counsellor

Democratic Socialist Republic of Sri Lanka
High Commission of the Democratic Socialist Republic of Sri Lanka, #1204, 333 Laurier Ave. West, Ottawa, ON K1P 1C1
613-233-8449, Fax: 613-238-8448, slhcit@rogers.com
www.srilankahcottawa.org
Her Excellency Chitranganee Wagiswara, High Commissioner
Lional Premasiri, Deputy High Commissioner
Sumith Dassanayake, Minister-Counsellor
Anzul Jhan, Counsellor

Republic of The Sudan
Embassy of The Sudan, 354 Stewart St., Ottawa, ON K1N 6K8
613-235-4000, Fax: 613-235-6880, sudanembassy-canada@rogers.com
www.sudanembassy.ca
His Excellency Musa Abdelrahim Mohamed, Ambassador
Osman Abufatima Adam Mohammed, Deputy Head of Mission
Robert Ring Ring Aguek, Counsellor

Republic of Suriname
Embassy of Suriname (to Canada), Van Ness Center, #460, 4301 Connecticut Ave. NW, Washington, DC 20008 USA
202-244-7488, Fax: 202-244-5878, www.surinameembassy.org
His Excellency Subhas-Chandra Mungra, Ambassador
Michiel Glenn Raafenberg, Counsellor & Deputy Chief of Mission
Humbert Ewald Eersel, Counsellor

Kingdom of Swaziland
High Commission for Swaziland, 1712 New Hampshire Ave., Washington, DC 20009 USA
202-234-5002, Fax: 202-234-8254, swziland@un.int
His Excellency Abednego Mandla Ntshanegase, High Commissioner
Douglas Frederick Litchfield, Permanent Representative
Lindiwe Cynthia Trizah Kunene, First Secretary

Embassy of Sweden
Embassy of Sweden, Mercury Court, 377 Dalhousie St., Ottawa, ON K1N 9N8
613-244-8200, Fax: 613-241-2277, sweden.ottawa@foreign.ministry.se
www.swedenabroad.com/en-GB/Embassies/Ottawa
Her Excellency Teppo Tauriainen, Ambassador
David Lunderquist, Counsellor
Annica White, First Secretary,Administration & Consular Affairs

Switzerland
Embassy of Switzerland, 5 Marlborough Ave., Ottawa, ON K1N 8E6
613-235-1837, Fax: 613-563-1394, vertretung@ott.rep.admin.ch
www.eda.admin.ch/canada
His Excellency Ulrich Lehner, Ambassador
Barbara Schedler Fischer, Deputy Head of Mission
Nicolas Bruhl, Minister-Counsellor
Johann Christoph Ebell, Counsellor

Syrian Arab Republic
The Syrian embassy was closed in May 2012, following a coordinated effort between Canada, the USA, UK, France, Italy, Spain, Germany, & Australia to expel all Syrian diplomats from those countries. The expulsion was in response to the ongoing Syrian civil war.

Tanzania
High Commission of the United Republic of Tanzania, 50 Range Rd., Ottawa, ON K1N 8J4
613-232-1500, Fax: 613-232-5184, contact@tzrepottawa.ca
www.tzrepottawa.ca
His Excellency Alex C. Massinda, High Commissioner
Joseph Edward Sokoine, Minister & Head of Chancery
Richard Andrew Tibandebage, Minister
Paul James Makelele, Second Secretary0

Kingdom of Thailand
Royal Thai Embassy, 180 Island Park Dr., Ottawa, ON K1Y 0A2
613-722-4444, Fax: 613-722-6624, contact@thaiembassy.ca
www.thaiembassy.ca
His Excellency Udomphol Ninnad, Ambassador
Narong Boonsatheanwong, Minister-Counsellor
Muhamadlutfee Useng, First Secretary, Consular Affairs
Nopakhun Luichant, First Secretary, International Organizations, Political, & Economic Affairs
Ruamporn RidthiprasartFirst Secretary, Protocol, Press, Cultural, & Educational Affairs
Thanaporn Mailaeied, Second Secretary, Administrative & Accounting

Democratic Republic of Timor-Leste
Embassy of Timor-Leste, #504, 4201 Connecticut Ave. NW, Washington, DC 20008 USA
202-966-3202, Fax: 202-966-3205, info@timorlesteembassy.org
Www.timorlesteembassy.org
His Excellency Constâncio da Conceição Pinto, Ambassador

Republic of Togo
Embassy of Togo, 12 Range Rd., Ottawa, ON K1N 8J3
613-238-5916, Fax: 613-235-6425,
Paneybesse Alli, First Secretary & Chargé d'Affaires

Kingdom of Tonga
High Commission for the Kingdom of Tonga, 250 East 51st St., New York, NY 10022 USA
917-369-1025, Fax: 917-369-1024
His Excellency Sonatane Tua Taumoepeau Tupou, High Commissioner

Republic of Trinidad & Tobago
High Commission for Trinidad & Tobago, 200 First Ave., 3rd Fl., Ottawa, ON K1S 2G6
613-232-2418, Fax: 613-232-4349, ottawa@ttmissions.com
www.ttmissions.com
His Excellency Philip Buxo, High Commissioner
Keith Ronald Kerwood, Counsellor
Cindy Shivani Maharaj, Second Secretary

Republic of Tunisia
Embassy of Tunisia, 515 O'Connor St., Ottawa, ON K1S 3P8
613-237-0330, Fax: 613-237-7939,
Hatem Boujemaa, Counsellor & Chargé d'Affaires
Borhene El Kamel, Counsellor

Republic of Turkey
Embassy of Turkey, 197 Wurtemburg St., Ottawa, ON K1N 8L9
613-244-2470, Fax: 613-789-3442, embassy.ottawa@mfa.gov.tr
turkishembassy.com
Gulcan Akoguz, First Counsellor & Chargé d'Affaires
Ferüdün Baser, Counsellor
Bahri Batu, Counsellor
Serdar Ulker, Counsellor

Republic of Turkmenistan
2207 Massachussets Ave. NW, Washington, DC 20008 USA
202-588-1500, Fax: 202-588-0697, turkmenembassyus@verizon.net
turkmenistanembassy.org
His Excellency Meret B. Orazov, Ambassador

Republic of Uganda
High Commission for Uganda, 231 Cobourg St., Ottawa, ON K1N 8J2
613-789-7797, Fax: 613-789-8909, uhc@ugandahighcommission.com
www.ugandahighcommission.com
His Excellency George Marino Abola, High Commissioner
John Wycliffe Kabbs Twijuke, Permanent Representative
Margaret Lucy Kyogire, Minister-Counsellor & Deputy Head of Mission
Elizabeth Beatrice Wamanga, Minister-Counsellor

Republic of Ukraine
Embassy of Ukraine, 310 Somerset St. West, Ottawa, ON K2P 0J9
613-230-2961, Fax: 613-230-2400, emb_ca@ukremb.ca
www.ukremb.ca
Marko O. Shevchenko, Chargé d'Affaires
Natalia I. Holub, First Secretary, Ukrainian community, press & cultural affairs
Mykhailo Khomenko, First Secretary, Economic Affairs
Oksana Kovslovska, First Secretary, Economic Affairs
Heorhii I. Zakraiavskiy, First Secretary, Consular Affairs

United Arab Emirates
Embassy of the United Arab Emirates, 125 Boteler St., Ottawa, ON K1N 0A4
613-565-7272, Fax: 613-565-8007, reception@uae-embassy.com
www.uae-embassy.ae/Embassies/ca
His Excellency Mohammed Saif Helal Al Shehhi, Ambassador
Aysha Alhamili, Permanent Representative
Rashed Ali Sultan A. Alkaabi, Alternate Representative
Ali Rashed Ahmed Rashed Almazrouei, Third Secretary

United Kingdom of Great Britain & Northern Ireland
British High Commission, 80 Elgin St., Ottawa, ON K1P 5K7
613-237-1530, Fax: 613-232-0738, ukincanada.fco.gov.uk

His Excellency Andrew John Pocock CMG, High Commissioner
Corin Jean Stella Robertson, Deputy High Commissioner
Mark Bernard Hugh Rodmell, Permanent Representative
Liliana Biglou, Counsellor
David James Kilby, Counsellor

United States of America
Embassy of USA, PO Box 866 B, 490 Sussex Dr., Ottawa, ON K1P 5T1
613-238-5335, Fax: 613-688-3088,
ottawacons@state.gov, ottawareference@state.gov
canada.usembassy.gov
His Excellency David Jacobson, Ambassador
Jim Nealon, Deputy Head of Mission
Samuel Vincent Brock, Minister-Counsellor
Susan Rose Crystal, Minister-Counsellor
Sylvia Dolores Johnson, Minister-Counsellor
James Dinneen Nealon, Minister-Counsellor
Scott Richard Reynolds, Minister-Counsellor
Christopher Rober Riche, Minister-Counsellor
Sue Ellen Saarino, Minister-Counsellor
Richard Steffens, Minister-Counsellor

Oriental Republic of Uruguay
Embassy of Uruguay, #1905, 130 Albert St., Ottawa, ON K1P 5G4
613-234-2727, Fax: 613-233-4670,
embassy@embassyofuruguay.ca
www.embassyofuruguay.ca
His Excellency Elbio Oscar Rosselli Frieri, Ambassador
Jesus Jorge Iglesias Villoz, Permanent Representative
Alejandro Ramon Rodriguez Cotro, Second Secretary

Republic of Uzbekistan
1746 Massachusetts Ave. NW, Washington, DC 20036 USA
202-887-5300, Fax: 202-293-6804,
info@uzbekistan.org
www.uzbekistan.org
His Excellency Ilhom Nematov, Ambassador
Umid Shadiev, Attaché
Durbek Amanov, Consul General

Bolivarian Republic of Venezuela
Embassy of Venezuela, 32 Range Rd., Ottawa, ON K1N 8J4
613-235-5151, Fax: 613-235-3205,
info.canada@misionvenezuela.org
www.misionvenezuela.org
Ana Carolina Rodriguez de Febres-Cordero, Minister-Counsellor & Chargé d'affaires
David Alfonzo Blanco Carrero, Permanent Representative
Yrasema Rafaela Sanchez Duran, Second Secretary

Socialist Republic of Vietnam
Embassy of Vietnam, 55 MacKay St., Ottawa, ON K1M 2B2
613-236-0772, Fax: 613-236-2704,
vietem-inter@uniserve.com
www.vietem-ca.com
His Excellency Sy Vuong Ha Le, Ambassador
Viet Dung Vu, Minister-Counsellor
Trong Luong Dinh, Counsellor
Ke Tuan Ha, Counsellor,
Van Quyen Nguyen, Counsellor
Linh Chi Vu Thi, Counsellor

Republic of Yemen
Embassy of the Republic of Yemen, 54 Chamberlain Ave., Ottawa, ON K1S 1V9
613-729-6627, Fax: 613-729-8915,
yeminfo@yemenembassy.ca
www.yemenembassy.ca
His Excellency Khaled Mahfoodh Abdulla Bahah, Ambassador, ambassador@yemenembassy.ca
Ahmed Ali Al-Emad, Deputy Head of Mission, ahmed3mad@yahoo.com
Bashir Mohamed Ali Kasim, bashir_makasim@yahoo.com
Loai Yahia Al-Eryani, cultural@yemenembassy.ca, commercial@yemenembassy.ca

Republic of Zambia
High Commission for Zambia (to Canada), #205, 151 Slater St., Ottawa, ON K1B 5H3
613-232-4400, Fax: 613-232-4410,
zhc.ottawa@bellnet.ca
www.zambiahighcommission.ca
His Excellency Bobby Mbunji Samakai, High Commissioner
Sylvia Bambala Chalikosa, Deputy High Commissioner
Friday Chilufya, First Secretary
Hilda Kafumukache Musunsa, First Secretary
Emmah Cheelo Hamweetwa, Second Secretary
Jennifer Konjela Manda, Third Secretary

Republic of Zimbabwe
Embassy for the Republic of Zimbabwe, 332 Somerset St. West, Ottawa, ON K2P 0J9
613-421-1242, Fax: 613-422-7403,
info@zimottawa.com
www.zimbabweembassy.ca
Her Excellency Florence Zano Chideya, Ambassador
Admire Hwata, Counsellor & Head of Chancery
Barbara Chimhandamba, Counsellor
Epiphania Kwari, Second Secretary
Dorcas Mugadza, Third Secretary

Canadian Diplomatic & Consular Representatives Abroad

Islamic State of Afghanistan
Canadian Embassy, House 256, Street 15, Wazir-Akbar-Khan, Kabul, Afghanistan
93-0-799-742-800, Fax: 93-0-799-742-805,
kabul@international.gc.ca
www.afghanistan.gc.ca/canada-afghanistan
His Excellency Glenn Davidson, Ambassador
S. Whiting, Minister-Counsellor & Deputy Head of Mission
K. O'Brien, Counsellor, Immigration
J. Myles, First Secretary, Development

Republic of Albania
See: Italian Republic

People's Democratic Republic of Algeria
Canadian Embassy, PO Box 646, 18 Mustapha Khalef St., Ben Aknoun, Algers, 16306 Algeria
011-213-7008-3000, Fax: 011-213-7008-3070,
alger@international.gc.ca
www.canadainternational.gc.ca/algeria-algerie/
Her Excellency Geneviève des Rivières, Ambassador
G. Dobner, Counsellor, Political & Economic
Lyne Forcier, Counsellor, Administration, & Consul
P. St-Germain, Counsellor, Immigration
A. Dubois, Consul & Senior Trade Commissioner
Sophie Goulet, Trade Commissioner, Environmental Industries, alger-td@international.gc.ca

Principality of Andorra
See: Kingdom of Spain

People's Republic of Angola
See: Republic of Zimbabwe

Anguilla
See: Barbados

Antigua & Barbuda
See: Barbados

Argentine Republic
Canadian Embassy, Tagle 2828, Buenos Aires, C1425EEH Argentine
54-11-4808-1000, Fax: 54-11-4808-1111,
bairs-webmail@international.gc.ca
www.canadainternational.gc.ca/argentina-argentine
Her Excellency G. Kutz, Ambassador
T. Hera, Counsellor, Political & Economic
D. Jorgensen, Counsellor, Immigration
Ana Fisher, Trade Commissioner, Environmental Industries, bairs-commerce@international.gc.ca

Republic of Armenia
See: Russian Federation

Aruba
See: Republic of Venezuela

Commonwealth of Australia
Canadian High Commission, Commonwealth Ave., Canberra, ACT 2600 Australia
61-2-6270-4000, Fax: 61-2-6270-3585,
cnbra@international.gc.ca
www.canadainternational.gc.ca/australia-australie
His Excellency Michael Small, High Commissioner
D. McKinnon, Deputy High Commissioner
K. O'Brien, Counsellor, Immigration
R. Coleman, Counsellor, Commercial
Angela Dark, Trade Commissioner, Environmental Industries, sydny-td@international.gc.ca

Republic of Austria
Canadian Embassy, Laurenzerberg 2, Vienna, A-1010 Austria
43-1-531-38-3000, Fax: 43-1-531-38-3321,
vienn@international.gc.ca
www.canadainternational.gc.ca/austria-autriche
His Excellency John Barrett, Ambassador & Permanent Representative
M. Desbois, Counsellor, Immigration
C. Miranda, Counsellor, Economic
Roland Rossi, Trade Commissioner, Environmental Industries

Republic of Azerbaijan
See: Republic of Turkey

Commonwealth of the Bahamas
See: Jamaica

State of Bahrain
See: Kingdom of Saudi Arabia

People's Republic of Bangladesh
Canadian High Commission, GPO Box 569, Dhaka, 1212 Bangladesh
88-2-988-7091, Fax: 88-2-882-3043,
dhaka@international.gc.ca
www.canadainternational.gc.ca/bangladesh
As of April 2012 the Visa & Immigration Section at the Canadian High Commission in Bangladesh is closed; services have been transferred to the Canadian High Commission in Singapore.
Her Excellency Heather Cruden, High Commissioner
J. Durno, Counsellor, Development
J. Beninger, First Secretary, Development
Mortoza Tarafder, Trade Commissioner, Environmental Industries, mortoza.tarafder@international.gc.ca

Barbados
Canadian High Commission, PO Box 404, Bishops Court Hill, Bridgetown, BB11000 Barbados
246-429-3550, Fax: 246-429-3780,
bdgtn@international.gc.ca
www.canadainternational.gc.ca/barbados-barbade
Her Excellency Ruth Archibald, High Commissioner
L. Clément, Minister-Counsellor
J. P. Hamel, Counsellor, Commercial
M. Mostovac, Counsellor, Development
Tammy Brathwaite, Trade Commissioner, Environmental Industries, bdgtn-td@international.gc.ca

Republic of Belarus
See: Republic of Poland

Kingdom of Belgium
Canadian Embassy, 2, av de Tervuren, Brussels, 1040 Belgium
32-2-741-0611, Fax: 32-2-741-0643,
bru@international.gc.ca
www.canadainternational.gc.ca/belgium-belgique
His Excellency Denis Robert, Ambassador
Arif Keshani, Counsellor, Administration, & Consul
A. Vary, Counsellor, Commercial
S. Hijal, First Secretary
Fabienne De Kimpe, Trade Commissioner, Environmental Industries, bru.td-infocentre@international.gc.ca

Belize
See: Republic of Guatemala

Republic of Benin
See: Republic of Côte d'Ivoire

Bermuda
See: United States of America c/o New York City Office

Bhutan
See: Republic of India

Republic of Bolivia
See: Republic of Peru

Bosnia & Herzegovina
See: Republic of Hungary

Republic of Botswana
See: Republic of Zimbabwe

Federative Republic of Brazil
Canadian Embassy, SES-Av. das Naçes - Qd. 803 - Lote 16, Brasilia, D.F., 70410-900 Brazil
55-61-424-5400, Fax: 55-61-424-5490,
brsla@international.gc.ca
www.canadainternational.gc.ca/brazil-bresil
His Excellency Jamal Khokhar, Ambassador
K. Asselin, Counsellor, Political
N. Neale, Counsellor, Economic
D. Millward, Counsellor, Administration, & Consul
Mariangela Lima, Trade Commissioner, Environmental Industries, infocentre.brazil@international.gc.ca

Brunei Darussalam
Canadian High Commission, PO Box 2808, Bandar Seri Begawan, BS8675 Brunei Darussalam
673-2-220-043, Fax: 673-2-220-040,
bsbgn@international.gc.ca
www.canadainternational.gc.ca/brunei_darussalam
His Excellency Marcel Gaumond, High Commissioner
Nurul Salwani Sabtu, Trade Commissioner, Environmental Industries, bsbgn-td@international.gc.ca

Republic of Bulgaria
See: Republic of Romania
Limited Consular & Visa services are offered at the Canadian Consulate in Sofia: 7, Pozitano Str., Sofia, 1301 Bulgaria; 359-2-969-97-10

Burkina-Faso
Canadian Embassy, PO Box 548, Ouagadougou 01, 316, Ave. Professeur Joseph Ki-Zerbo, Kadiogo, Burkina-Faso
226-50-31-18-94, Fax: 226-50-31-19-00,
ouaga@international.gc.ca
www.canadainternational.gc.ca/burkinafaso
His Excellency Ivan Roberts, Ambassador
R. Pelletier, Counsellor, Development
C. Bedard, First Secretary, Administration, & Consul
Adama Soro, Trade Commissioner, Environmental Industries

Republic of Burundi
See: Republic of Kenya

Kingdom of Cambodia
See: Kingdom of Thailand

Republic of Cameroon
Canadian High Commission, Immeuble SCI-TOM (formerly Stamatiades), PO Box 572 , Yaoundé, Cameroon
011-237-2223-2311, Fax: 011-237-2222-1090,
yunde@international.gc.ca
His Excellency Benoit Pierre Laramee, High Commissioner
D. Giroux, Counsellor, Administration, & Consul
L. P. Sylvestre, Counsellor, Political
Jude Bijingsi, Trade Commissioner, Environmental Industries, yunde-td@international.gc.ca

Republic of Cape Verde
See: Republic of Senegal

Cayman Islands
See: Jamaica

Central African Republic
See: Republic of Cameroon

Republic of Chad
See: Republic of Cameroon

Republic of Chile
Canadian Embassy, Cassilla 139, Correo 10, Santiago, Chile
56-2-652-3800, Fax: 56-2-652-3912,
stago@international.gc.ca
www.canadainternational.gc.ca/chile-chili
Her Excellency Patricia Fuller, Ambassador
E. Coulombe, Counsellor, Political
P. Furesz, Counsellor, Commercial
R. Hur, Counsellor, Immigration
Margot Edwards, Trade Commissioner, Environmental Industries, santiago.commerce@international.gc.ca

People's Republic of China
Canadian Embassy, 19 Dong Zhi Men Wai St., Chao Yang Dist., Beijing, 100600 China
011-86-10-5139-4000, Fax: 011-86-10-5139-4454,
bejing@international.gc.ca
www.canadainternational.gc.ca/china-chine
His Excellency David Mulroney, Ambassador
D. McMullen, Minister, Commercial
S. Taylor, Minister
L. Dumas, Minister-Counsellor, Immigration
M. Kruger, Minister-Counsellor
F. Li, Minister-Counsellor
T. Khan, Counsellor, Development
C. Vervaet, Counsellor, Agriculture & Agri-food
Lee Kane, Trade Commissioner, Environmental Industries, infocentrechina@international.gc.ca

Republic of Colombia
Canadian Embassy, Apartado Aereo 110067, Bogota, Colombia
57-1-657-9800, Fax: 57-1-657-9912,
bgota@international.gc.ca
www.canadainternational.gc.ca/colombia-colombie
His Excellency T. Martin, Ambassador
M. Bolick, Counsellor, Immigration
S. Cohen, Counsellor, Political & Economic
J. P. Hamel, Counsellor, Commercial
J. Tabah, Counsellor, Development
Claudia Paola Gutierrez Chaves, Trade Commissioner, Environmental Industries, bgota-td@international.gc.ca

Islamic Federal Republic of the Comoros
See: United Republic of Tanzania

Democratic Republic of Congo
Canadian Embassy to the Democratic Republic of Congo, PO Box 8341 , Kinshasa, Democratic Republic of Congo
011-243-996-021-500, Fax: 011-243-996-021-510,
knsha@international.gc.ca
www.canadainternational.gc.ca/congo
His Excellency Jean-Carol Pelletier, Ambassador
B. Grundison, Minister-Counsellor, Immigration
L. F. Beaudet, Counsellor, Administration, & Consul
J. Crowley, Counsellor, Political Affairs
M. Tache, Counsellor, Development
C.J. Scott, Trade Commissioner, Environmental Industries, knsha-td@international.gc.ca

Republic of Congo
See: Democratic Republic of Congo

Cook Islands
See: New Zealand

Republic of Costa Rica
Canadian Embassy, Apartado Postal 351-1007 Centro Colon, San José, Costa Rica
011-506-2242-4400, Fax: 011-506-2242-4410,
sjcra@international.gc.ca
www.canadainternational.gc.ca/costa_rica
His Excellency C. MacKay, Ambassador
L. Beaulne, Counsellor
J. Kimmell, Counsellor, Administration
E. Wang, Counsellor, Commercial
Adolfo Quesada, Trade Commissioner, Environmental Industries, sjcra-td@international.gc.ca

Republic of Côte d'Ivoire
Canadian Embassy, Immeuble Trade Centre, 23, av Nogues, 6th & 7th Fls., Le Plateau, Abidjan, 01 Ivory Coast
011-225-20-30-07-00, Fax: 011-225-20-30-07-20,
abdjn@international.gc.ca
www.canadainternational.gc.ca/cotedivoire
Her Excellency C. de Varennes, Ambassador
F. Jacques, Counsellor, Political & Economic
J. Kimmell, Counsellor, Administration
L. Martel, Counsellor & Consul
Laetitia Gadegbeku, Trade Commissioner, Environmental Industries, laetitia.gadegbeku@international.gc.ca

Republic of Croatia
Prilaz Gjure Dezelica #4, Zagreb, 10 000 Croatia
385-1-488-1200, Fax: 385-1-488-1230,
zagrb@international.gc.ca
www.canadainternational.gc.ca/croatia-croatie
His Excellency Edwin Loughlin, Ambassador
D. Fairchild, Counsellor & Consul
Bill McCrimmon, Counsellor & Consul
Synthia Dodig, Trade Commissioner, Environmental Industries, synthia.dodig@international.gc.ca

Republic of Cuba
Canadian Embassy, Calle 30, No. 518, Esquina 7a, Miramar, Havana, Cuba
53-7-204-2516, Fax: 53-7-204-9772,
havan@international.gc.ca
www.canadainternational.gc.ca/cuba
His Excellency Matthew Levin, Ambassador
G. Perreault, Counsellor, Immigration
V. Sorel, Counsellor, Administration, & Consul
Francisco Rodriguez, Trade Commissioner, Environmental Industries, havan-td@international.gc.ca

Republic of Cyprus
See: Hellenic Republic

Czech Republic
Canadian Embassy, Muchova 6, 160 00, Prague, 6 Czech Republic
011-420-272-101-800, Fax: 011-420-272-101-898,
prgue@international.gc.ca
www.canadainternational.gc.ca/czech-tcheque
Her Excellency Valerie Raymond, Ambassador

Kingdom of Denmark
Canadian Embassy, Kr. Bernikowsgade 1, Copenhagen, DK-1105 Denmark
45-33-48-32-00, Fax: 45-33-48-32-20,
copen@international.gc.ca
www.canadainternational.gc.ca/denmark-danemark
His Excellency André François Giroux, Ambassador
K. Girtel, Counsellor, Political
David Horup, Trade Commissioner, Environmental Industries, copen-td@international.gc.ca

Republic of Djibouti
The Embassy of Canada, Place Lagarde, Djibouti, 1188 Djibouti
addis@international.gc.ca
www.canadainternational.gc.ca/ethiopia-ethiopie
The Republic of Djibouti is also represented by the Embassy of Canada to Ethiopia.
M. Angers, Counsellor, Development
K. Gupta, Counsellor, Political
Scott Munro, Counsellor, Administration, & Consul
I. Hentic, First Secretary, Development
C. Berard, Second Secretary, Development

Commonwealth of Dominica
See: Barbados

Dominican Republic
Canadian Embassy, PO Box 2054, Santo Domingo, Dominican Republic
809-262-3100, Fax: 809-262-3155,
sdmgo@international.gc.ca
www.canadainternational.gc.ca/dominican_republic-republique_dominicaine
His Excellency Todd Kuiack, Ambassador
E. Gelinas, Counsellor, Commercial
Counsellor, Immigration
N. Cloutier, First Secretary, Administration, & Consul
T. DosSantos, First Secretary, Border Services
Regis Batista-Lemaire, Trade Commissioner, Environmental Industries, regis.batista@international.gc.ca

Republic of Ecuador
PO Box 17-11-6512, Quito, Ecuador
593-2-2455-499, Fax: 593-2-2277-672,
quito@international.gc.ca
www.canadainternational.gc.ca/ecuador-equateur
His Excellency Andrew Shisko, Ambassador
M. Bolick, Counsellor, Immigration
C. Lapointe, Counsellor
N. Nincevic, First Secretary, Immigration
R. Kuffner, Second Secretary & Vice-Consul
Patricia Bustamante, Trade Commissioner, Environmental Industries, quito-td@international.gc.ca

Arab Republic of Egypt
Canadian Embassy, PO Box 57, 26 Kamel El Shenawy St., Garden City, Cairo, Egypt
011-20-2-2791-8700, Fax: 011-20-2-2791-8860,
cairo@international.gc.ca
www.canadainternational.gc.ca/egypt-egypte
His Excellency David Drake, Ambassador
J. Rose, Counsellor, Immigration
A. M. McNeal, First Secretary, Immigration
S. Erlichman, Second Secretary, Immigration
Joseph Tadros, Trade Commissioner, Environmental Industries, cairo-td@international.gc.ca

Republic of El Salvador
Canadian Embassy, Edificio Centro Financiero Gigante, Alameda Roosevelt y 63 Avenida Sur, Nivel Lobby 2, Loca, San Salvador, El Salvador
503-2279-4655, Fax: 503-2279-0765,
ssal@international.gc.ca
www.canadainternational.gc.ca/el_salvador-salvador
Her Excellency Marianick Tremblay , Ambassador
Romeo Calderon, Trade Commissioner, Environmental Industries, romeo.calderon@international.gc.ca

England
See: United Kingdom of Great Britain & Northern Ireland

Republic of Equatorial Guinea
See: Gabonese Republic

Eritrea
See: Republic of Sudan

Republic of Estonia
Office of the Canadian Embassy, Toom Kooli 13, 2nd Fl., Tallinn, 0100 Estonia
372-627-3311, Fax: 372-627-3312,
tallinn@canada.ee
www.canadainternational.gc.ca/baltic_states-pays_baltes

His Excellency John Morrison, Ambassador (located in Riga, Latvia)

Federal Democratic Republic of Ethiopia
Canadian Embassy, PO Box 1130, Addis Ababa, Ethiopia
251-1-71-30-22, Fax: 251-1-71-30-33, addis@international.gc.ca
Her Excellency M. Lévesque, Ambassador
I. Trites, Counsellor & Consul
E. Wega, Counsellor, Development
I. Hentic, First Secretary, Development
Telahun Workeneh, Trade Commissioner, Environmental Industries, telahun.workeneh@international.gc.ca

European Union
The Mission of Canada to the European Union, 2, av de Tervuren, Brussels, 1040 Belgium
322-741-0660, Fax: 322-741-0629, breu@international.gc.ca
www.canadainternational.gc.ca/eu-ue
His Excellency David Plunkett, Ambassador
Alain Hausser, Deputy Head of Mission
Clare Barry, Counsellor, International Criminal Operations
Catherine Dickson, Counsellor & Section Head, Trade, Investment & Science, & Technology
Lorraine Diguer, Counsellor & Section Head, Political Affairs, Foreign & Security Policy, & Public Affairs
Tina Milanetti, Counsellor & Section Head, Agriculture, Fisheries, & Environment
Pierre Paquet, Counsellor, Border Services
Unnati Vasavada, Counsellor, Immigration & Asylum Policies

Faroe Islands
See: Kingdom of Denmark

Fiji
See: New Zealand

Republic of Finland
Canadian Embassy, PO Box 779, Helsinki, FIN-00101 Finland
358-9-228-530, Fax: 358-9-2285-3385, hsnki@international.gc.ca
www.canadainternational.gc.ca/finland-finlande
His Excellency Chris Shapardanov, Ambassador
A. Arnott, Minister
S. Chase, Counsellor, Commercial
D. Cochrane, Counsellor, Immigration
Seppo Vihersaari, Trade Commissioner, Environmental Industries, seppo.vihersaari@international.gc.ca

French Guyana
See: French Republic

French Polynesia
See: New Zealand

French Republic
Canadian Embassy, 35 - 37, av Montaigne, Paris, 75008 France
33-1-44-43-29-00, Fax: 33-1-44-43-29-99, paris@international.gc.ca
www.international.gc.ca/france
S. Lyle, Acting High Commissioner
K. Butler, Minister & Deputy Head of Mission
S. Scrimshaw, Minister & Deputy Head of Mission
F. Béland, Minister-Counsellor, Administration, & Consul General
L. Blais, Minister-Counsellor, Political & Public Affairs
R. Campbell, Minister-Counsellor
R. Gilbert, Minister-Counsellor, Immigration
J. D. Ieraci, Minister-Counsellor, Economic & Commercial
Yannick Dheilly, Trade Commissioner, Environmental Industries, france-td@international.gc.ca

Gabonese Republic
See: Republic of Cameroon

Republic of the Gambia
See: Republic of Senegal

Republic of Georgia
See: Republic of Turkey

Federal Republic of Germany
Canadian Embassy, Leipziger Platz 17, Berlin, D-10117 Germany
011-49-30-20-312-0, Fax: 011-49-30-20-312-590, brlin@international.gc.ca; brlin-pa@international.gc.ca
www.kanada.de
His Excellency Peter M. Boehm, Ambassador
E. Walsh, Minister
T. Marr, Minister-Counsellor, Commecial & Economic
Ardnt Ulland, Trade Commissioner, Environmental Industries, deutschland.commerce@international.gc.ca

Republic of Ghana
Canadian High Commission, PO Box 1639, 42 Independence Ave., Accra, Ghana
011-233-21-211521, Fax: 011-233-21-211523, accra@international.gc.ca
www.canadainternational.gc.ca/ghana
Her Excellency Trudy Kernighan, High Commissioner
D. Arsenault, Counsellor, Development
David Dix, Counsellor, Consul, & Senior Trade Commissioner, david.dix@international.gc.ca
M. Giralt, Counsellor, Immigration

Hellenic Republic
Canadian Embassy, 4 Ioannou Ghennadiou St., Athens, 115 21 Greece
30-210-727-3400, Fax: 30-210-727-3480, athns@international.gc.ca
www.canadainternational.gc.ca/greece-grece
His Excellency Robert Peck, Ambassador & High Commissioner to Cyprus
H. Edwards, Counsellor, Immigration
B. Fournier, Counsellor, Administration, & Consul
E. Skoulas, Counsellor, Commercial
A. Stewart, Counsellor, Political
Marguerita Niada, Trade Commissioner, Environmental Industries, marguerita.niada@international.gc.ca

Greenland
See: Kingdom of Denmark

Grenada
See: Barbados

Guadeloupe
See: Barbados

Guam
See: Republic of the Philippines

Republic of Guatemala
Canadian Embassy, PO Box 400, Guatemala City, 1001 Guatemala
502-2363-4348, Fax: 502-2365-1210, gtmla@international.gc.ca
www.canadainternational.gc.ca/guatemala
His Excellency H. Rousseau, Ambassador & High Commissioner to Belize
A. Lotfijou, Counsellor & Consul
C. McKinney, Counsellor, Immigration
N. Samson, Counsellor, Commercial
J. Tretiak, First Secretary
Christine Luttmann, Trade Commissioner, Environmental Industries, gtmla-td@international.gc.ca

Guinea
See: Republic of Senegal

Republic of Guinea-Bissau
See: Republic of Senegal

Republic of Guyana
Canadian High Commission, PO Box 10880, Georgetown, Guyana
011-592-227-2081, Fax: 011-592-225-8380, grgtn@international.gc.ca
www.canadainternational.gc.ca/guyana
His Excellency David Devine, High Commissioner
A. M. Alvarez Tello, Counsellor, Administration
Nicole Johnson, Trade Commissioner, Environmental Industries, nicole.johnson@international.gc.ca

Republic of Haiti
PO Box 826, Delmas Rd., Port-au-Prince, Haiti
509-2249-9000, Fax: 509-2249-9920, prnce@international.gc.ca
www.canadainternational.gc.ca/haiti
His Excellency Henri-Paul Normandin, Ambassador
J. F. Hubert-Rouleau, Counsellor, Immigration
J. J. Renaud, Counsellor, Administration
D. Rossetti, Counsellor, Development
Emmanuel Choute, Trade Commissioner, Environmental Industries, emmanuel.choute@international.gc.ca

Holy See
Canadian Embassy, Via Della Conciliazione, 4-D, Rome, 00193 Italy
011-39-06-6830-7316, Fax: 011-39-06-6880-6283, vatcn@international.gc.ca
www.canadainternational.gc.ca/holy_see-saint_siege
Her Excellency Anne Leahy, Ambassador, anne.leahy@international.gc.ca
Roberto Benardi, Public Affairs Assistant, roberto.benardi@international.gc.ca

Republic of Honduras
Canadian Embassy, PO Box 3552, Tegucigalpa, Honduras
011-504-232-4551, Fax: 011-504-239-7769, tglpa@international.gc.ca, sjcra@international.gc.ca
www.canadainternational.gc.ca/costa_rica
His Excellency C. MacKay, Ambassador

Hong Kong
See: People's Republic of China

Republic of Hungary
Canadian Embassy, Ganz U. 12-14, Budapest, 1027 Hungary
011-36-1-392-3360, Fax: 011-36-1-392-3390, bpest@international.gc.ca
www.canadainternational.gc.ca/hungary-hongrie
Her Excellency Tamara Guttman, Ambassador
C. Bedard, Counsellor & Consul
S. Bubic, Counsellor, Commercial
B. Ebel, Counsellor
Zsuzsanna Kovács-Mátyus, Trade Commissioner, Environmental Industries, zsuzsanna.kovacs-matyus@international.gc.ca

Republic of Iceland
PO Box 1510, Reykjavik, 121 Iceland
354-575-6500, Fax: 354-575-6501, rkjvk@international.gc.ca
www.canadainternational.gc.ca/iceland-islande
His Excellency Alan Bones, Ambassador
Brynhildur Magnusdottir, Trade Commissioner, Environmental Industries, brynhildur.magnusdottir@international.gc.ca

Republic of India
Canadian High Commission, 50-F, 7/8 Shantipath, Chanakyapuri, New Delhi, 110021 India
011-91-11-4178-2000, Fax: 011-91-11-4178-2020, delhi@international.gc.ca
www.canadainternational.gc.ca/india-inde
His Excellency Stewart Beck, High Commissioner
J. Nickel, Deputy High Commissioner
S. Frank, Minister
S. Wilshaw, Minister, Commercial
S. Robertson, Minister-Counsellor
Yasmine Dubash, Trade Commissioner, Environmental Industries, india.commerce@international.gc.ca

Republic of Indonesia
Canadian Embassy, PO Box 8324/JKS.MP, Jakarta, 12083 Indonesia
011-62-21-2550-7800, Fax: 011-62-21-2550-7811, jkrta@international.gc.ca
www.canadainternational.gc.ca/indonesia-indonesie
His Excellency Mackenzie Clugston, Ambassador
G. Menard, Counsellor, Immigration
C. Parker, Counsellor, Development
T. Reynolds, Counsellor, Commercial
J. Yendall, Counsellor, Political
Dian Martosoebroto, Trade Commissioner, Environmental Industries, dian.martosoebroto@international.gc.ca

Islamic Republic of Iran
Canada suspended diplomatic relations with Iran in September 2012, citing human rights abuses as the reason. Consular responsibility for Iran was assigned to the Embassy of Canada in Ankara, Turkey.

Republic of Iraq
See: Hashemite Kingdom of Jordan

Republic of Ireland
Canadian Embassy, 7-8 Wilton Terrace, Dublin 2, Ireland
353-1-234-4000, Fax: 353-1-234-4101, dubln@international.gc.ca
www.canadainternational.gc.ca/ireland-irlande
His Excellency Loyola Hearn, Ambassador
A. Arnott, Minister-Counsellor, Immigration
L. Zadravetz, First Secretary, Immigration
S. Lee, Second Secretary, Immigration
Gerry Mongey, Trade Commissioner, Environmental Industries, gerry.mongey@international.gc.ca

State of Israel
Canadian Embassy, PO Box 9442, 3 Nirim St., 4th Fl., Tel Aviv, 67060 Israel
011-972-3-636-3300, Fax: 011-972-3-636-3380, taviv@international.gc.ca
www.canadainternational.gc.ca/israel
His Excellency Paul Hunt, Ambassador
B. Berger, Counsellor, Commercial

A. Brown, Counsellor, Political
J. P. Cliché, Counsellor, Immigration
D. Keating, Counsellor, Administration, & Consul
Mona Ashkar, Trade Commissioner, Environmental Industries, taviv-td@international.gc.ca

Italian Republic
Canadian Embassy, Villa Grazioli, Via Salaria 243, Rome, 00199 Italy
011-39-06-85444-1, Fax: 011- 39-06-85444-3947, rome@international.gc.ca
www.canadainternational.gc.ca/italy-italie
His Excellency James Fox, Ambassador
A. Heuchan, Minister-Counsellor, Development
R. Jansen, Minister-Counsellor, Political & Public Affairs
E. Kamarianakis, Minister-Counsellor, Commercial
Patrizia Giuliotti, Trade Commissioner, Environmental Industries, ital-td@international.gc.ca

Ivory Coast
See: Republic of Côte d'Ivoire

Jamaica
Canadian High Commission, PO Box 1500, 3 West Kings House Rd., Kingston, 10 Jamaica
876-926-1500-7, Fax: 876-511-3494, kngtn@international.gc.ca
www.canadainternational.gc.ca/jamaica-jamaique
D. Fox, Acting High Commissioner
A. Blouin, Counsellor, Immigration
C. Duggan, Counsellor, Political
M. Legault, Counsellor, Development
N. Rowe, Counsellor, Health & Social Affairs
Yasmin Chong, Trade Commissioner, Environmental Industries, yasmin.chong@international.gc.ca

Japan
Canadian Embassy, 3-38 Akasaka, 7-chome, Minato-ku, Tokyo, 107-8503 Japan
011-81-3-5412-6200, Fax: 011-81-3-5412-6303, tokyo@international.gc.ca, jpn.commerce@international.gc.ca
www.canadainternational.gc.ca/japan-japon
His Excellency Jonathan T. Fried, Ambassador
R. Derouin, Minister & Deputy Head of Mission
P. Thoppil, Minister, Commercial
L. Sustersich, Minister-Counsellor & Consul
Stéphane Beaulieu, Trade Commissioner, Environmental Industries, jpn.commerce@international.gc.ca

Hashemite Kingdom of Jordan
Canadian Embassy, PO Box 815403, Amman, 11180 Jordan
011-962-6-520-3300, Fax: 011-962-6-520-3390, amman@international.gc.ca
www.canadainternational.gc.ca/jordan-jordanie
His Excellency Mark Gwozdecky, Ambassador
J. L. Bastien, Counsellor & Consul
P. Boulanger, Counsellor, Commercial
E. King, Counsellor, Political
G. Watson, Counsellor, Immigration
Wafa Herzallah, Trade Commissioner, Environmental Industries, wafa.herzallah@international.gc.ca

Republic of Kazakhstan
Canadian Embassy, #410, 6 Sary-Arka St., Astana, 010000 Kazakhstan
7-7172-7903-64, Fax: 7-7172-7903-69, almat@international.tc.ca
www.canadainternational.gc.ca/kazakhstan
His Excellency Stephen Millar, Ambassador
P. Coolen, Cousellor
David Mallette, Counsellor
C. Peters, Counsellor

Republic of Kenya
Canadian High Commission, PO Box 1013, Limuru Rd., Gigiri, Nairobi, 00621 Kenya
254-20-366-3000, Fax: 254-20-366-3900, nrobi@international.gc.ca
www.canadainternational.gc.ca/kenya
His Excellency David Collins, High Commissioner
B. Grundison, Minister-Counsellor, Immigration
M. Boyd, Counsellor, Development
J. Narraway, Counsellor, Administration
E. Savoie, Counsellor, Political
D. Verbiwski, Counsellor, Commercial
Benjamin Wamahiu, Trade Commissioner, Environmental Industries, benjamin.wamahiu@international.gc.ca

Republic of Kiribati
See: New Zealand

Democratic People's Republic of Korea
See: Republic of Korea

Republic of Korea
Canadian Embassy, 16-1 Jeong-dong, Jung-gu, Seoul, Korea
82-2-3783-6000, Fax: 82-2-3783-6239, seoul@international.gc.ca
www.canadainternational.gc.ca/korea-coree
His Excellency D. Chatterson, Ambassador
M. Danagher, Minister-Counsellor, Commercial
G. Dean, Counsellor, Political & Economic
R. Ulrich, Counsellor, Agrilcutire & Agri-food
E. Yu, Counsellor, Administration, & Consul
T. Venerus, Counsellor, Immigration
Young Jin Kim, Trade Commissioner, Environmental Industries, yougjin.kim@international.gc.ca

Kosovo
See: Republic of Croatia

State of Kuwait
Canadian Embassy, PO Box 25281, Safat, Kuwait City, 13113 Kuwait
965-2256-3025, Fax: 965-2256-0173, kwait@international.gc.ca
www.canadainternational.gc.ca/kuwait-koweit
His Excellency Douglas George, Ambassador
C. Mapendere, Counsellor, Commercial
M. Bose, First Secretary, Administration, & Consul
Yolande Lansing, Trade Commissioner, Environmental Industries, martin.barratt@international.gc.ca

Kyrgyz Republic
See: Republic of Kazakhstan

Lao People's Democratic Republic
See: Thailand

Republic of Latvia
Canadian Embassy, 20/22 Baznicas St., 6th Fl., Riga, LV-1010 Latvia
011-6371-6781-3945, Fax: 011-6371-6781-3960, riga@international.gc.ca
www.canadainternational.gc.ca/baltic_states-pays_baltes
His Excellency John Morrison, Ambassador
Irena Cirpuse, Trade Commissioner, Environmental Industries, irena.cirpuse@international.gc.ca

Lebanese Republic
Canadian Embassy, Coolrite Bldg., 43 Jal El Dib Hwy., Beirut, 60163 Lebanon
011-961-4-713-900, Fax: 011-961-4-710-595, berut@international.gc.ca
www.canadainternational.gc.ca/lebanon-liban
Her Excellency Hilary Childs-Adams, Ambassador
J. Jonk, Counsellor, Immigration
A. Kapellas, Counsellor, Political
Grace Dib, Trade Commissioner, Environmental Industries, berut-td@international.gc.ca

Kingdom of Lesotho
See: Republic of South Africa

Republic of Liberia
See: Republic of Côte d'Ivoire

Libya
Canadian Embassy, PO Box 93392, Tripoli Tower 1, 7th Fl., Tripoli, Libya
218-21-335-1633, Fax: 218-21-335-1630, trpli@international.gc.ca
www.canadainternational.gc.ca/libya-libye
J. Hill, Chargé d'Affaires
M. Doleh, Counsellor, Commercial
F. Jarvis, Counsellor, Administration, & Consul
C. Bloodworth, First Secretary, Political
Hesham Ganem, Trade Commissioner, Environmental Industries, trpli-td@international.gc.ca

Principality of Liechtenstein
See: Swiss Confederation

Republic of Lithuania
Office of the Canadian Embassy, Business Center 2000, Jogailos St. 4, 7th Fl., Vilnius, LT-01116 Lithuania
370-5249-0950, Fax: 370-5249-7865, vilnius@canada.lt
www.canadainternational.gc.ca/baltic_states-pays_baltes
His Excellency John Morrison, Ambassador (located in Rita, Latvia)
Egle Jurkeviciene, Trade Commissioner, Environmental Industries

Grand Duchy of Luxembourg
See: Kingdom of Belgium

Macao
See: People's Republic of China

Republic of Macedonia
See: Serbia

Democratic Republic of Madagascar
See: United Republic of Tanzania

Republic of Malawi
See: Republic of Mozambique

Federation of Malaysia
Canadian High Commission, PO Box 10990, Kuala Lumpur, 50732 Malaysia
011-60-3-2718-3333, Fax: 011-60-3-2718-3399, klmpr@international.gc.ca
www.canadainternational.gc.ca/malaysia-malaisie
His Excellency Randolph Mank, High Commissioner
R. Burley, Counsellor
H. Michaud, First Secretary, Immigration
M. Fortier, Second Secretary
Sharon Fam, Trade Commissioner, Environmental Industries, sharon.fam@international.gc.ca

Republic of Maldives
See: Democratic Socialist Republic of Sri Lanka

Republic of Mali
Canadian Embassy, Route de Koulikoro, Bamako, 99999 Mali
223-2021-2236, Fax: 223-2021-4362, bmakog@international.gc.ca
www.canadainternational.gc.ca/mali
His Excellency L. de Lorimier, Ambassador
D. Nadeau, First Secretary, Administration, & Vice-Consul
J. Jakobiec, Second Secretary, Development
Ernest Akpoue, Trade Commissioner, Environmental Industries, ernest.akpoue@international.gc.ca

Republic of Malta
See: Italian Republic

Marshall Islands
See: Republic of the Philippines

Martinique
See: Barbados

Islamic Republic of Mauritania
See: Kingdom of Morocco

Republic of Mauritius
See: Republic of South Africa

United Mexican States
Canadian Embassy, Apartado Postal 105-05, Mexico City, 06141 Mexico
011-52-57-24-7900, Fax: 011-52-57-24-7980, mxico@international.gc.ca
www.canadainternational.gc.ca/mexico-mexique
Her Excellency Sara Hradecky, Ambassador
G. Boissé, Minister-Counsellor, Immigration
G. Martin, Minister-Counsellor
W. Robson, Minister-Counsellor, Commercial & Economic
José-Antonio Rivas, Trade Commissioner, Environmental Industries, mexico.commerce@international.gc.ca

Federated States of Micronesia
See: Republic of The Philippines

Republic of Moldova
See: Republic of Romania

Principality of Monaco
See: French Republic

Mongolian People's Republic
The Canadian Embassy, #603-607, Central Tower, Sukhbaatar Square-2, Sukhbaatar District, Horoo-8 Ulaanbaatar, 14200 Mongolia
011-976-11-328-285, Fax: 011-976-11-328-289, ulaan@international.gc.ca
www.canadainternational.gc.ca/mongolia-mongolie
His Excellency Gregory Goldhawk, Ambassador

M. Berdichevsky, First Secretary
Maxim Berdichevsky, Senior Trade Commissioner, Environmental Industries, ulaantd@international.gc.ca

Montenegro
See: Serbia

Montserrat
See: Barbados

Kingdom of Morocco
Canadian Embassy, PO Box 709, Rabat-Agdal, Morocco
212-37-68-74-00, Fax: 212-37-68-74-30, rabat@international.gc.ca
www.canadainternational.gc.ca/morocco-maroc
His Excellency Christopher Wilkie, Ambassador
Eric Marin, Counsellor, Administration, & Consul
A. Potvin, Counsellor, Commercial
J. Roberge-Binovec, Counsellor, Immigration
C. St-louis, Counsellor, Political
Asmae Amrouche, Trade Commissioner, Environmental Industrie, rabat-td@international.gc.ca

Republic of Mozambique
Canadian High Commission, PO Box 1578, 1138, Kenneth Kaunda Ave., Maputo, Mozambique
011-258-21-492-623, Fax: 011-258-21-492-667, mputo@international.gc.ca
www.canadainternational.gc.ca/mozambique
His Excellency Alain Latulippe, High Commissioner
B. Giacomin, Counsellor, Commercial
R. Gregoire, Counsellor, Immigration
M. A. Lorrain, Counsellor & Consul
S. Lane, Counsellor, Development
Lurdes Magneli, Trade Commissioner, Environmental Industries, lurdes.magneli@international.gc.ca

Union of Myanmar
See: Kingdom of Thailand

Republic of Namibia
See: Republic of South Africa

Nauru
See: Commonwealth of Australia

Kingdom of Nepal
Canadian Embassy to Nepal, c/o Canadian Cooperation Office, PO Box 4574, Kathmandu, Nepal
011-977-1- 441-5193, Fax: 011-977-1-441-0422, cco@canadanepal.org
www.cconepal.org.np/embassy/canada.php
His Excellency Stewart Beck, High Commissioner (located in New Delhi, India)
Ed Doe, Counsellor, Development, & Consul

Kingdom of the Netherlands
Canadian Embassy, Sophialaan 7, The Hague, 2514 JP The Netherlands
011-31-70-311-1600, Fax: 011-31-70-311-1620, hague@international.gc.ca, info@canada.nl
www.canadainternational.gc.ca/netherlands-pays_bas
His ExcellencyJames Lambert, Ambassador
A. Flanagan Whalen, Counsellor, Political Affairs
G. F. Whalen, Counsellor & Alternate Permanent Representative
R. Pudifin, First Secretary, Science & Technology
G. Owens, Second Secretary, Administration, & Consul
Judith Baguley, Trade Commissioner, Environmental Industries, hague-td@international.gc.ca

Netherlands Antilles
See: Republic of Venezuela

New Caledonia
See: Commonwealth of Australia

New Zealand
Canadian High Commission, PO Box 8047, 125 The Terrace, Level 11, Wellington, 6143 New Zealand
64-4-473-9577, Fax: 64-4-471-2082, wlgtn@international.gc.ca
www.canadainternational.gc.ca/new_zealand-nouvelle_zelande
Her Excellency Caroline Chrétien, High Commissioner
S. Szukits, Counsellor
Pierre Delorme, Senior Trade Commissioner, Environmental Industries, aklnd@international.gc.ca

Republic of Nicaragua
Canadian Embassy, Apartado Postal 25, Managua, Nicaragua
011-505-268-0433, Fax: 011-505-268-0437, mngua@international.gc.ca
www.canadainternational.gc.ca/costa_rica
His Excellency C. MacKay, Ambassador (located in Costa Rica)

Republic of the Niger
Canadian Embassy, PO Box 362 , Niamey, Niger
011-227-75-36-86/87, Fax: 011-227-75-31-07, niamy@international.gc.ca
Her Excellency C. de Varennes, Ambassador (located in Côte d'Ivoire)

Federal Republic of Nigeria
Canadian High Commission, PO Box 5144, 15 Bobo St., Maitama, Abuja, Nigeria
011-234-9-413-9910, Fax: 011-234-9-413-9911, abuja@international.gc.ca
www.canadainternational.gc.ca/nigeria
His Excellency Chris Cooter, High Commissioner
C. DesRoches, Counsellor, Political
Lucky Idedia, Trade Commissioner, Environmental Industries, lucky.idedia@international.gc.ca

Niue
See: New Zealand

Northern Ireland
See: United Kingdom of Great Britain & Northern Ireland

Northern Marianas
See: Commonwealth of Australia

Kingdom of Norway
Canadian Embassy, Wergelandsveien 7, Oslo, N-0244 Norway
47-2299-5300, Fax: 47-2299-5301, oslo@international.gc.ca
www.canadainternational.gc.ca/norway-norvege
G. Norman, Chargé d'affaires
A. Arnott, Minister
D. Dix, Counsellor, Commercial, & Consul
E. Panitcherska, Counsellor & Consul
S. Headland, Second Secretary
John Winterbourne, Trade Commissioner, Environmental Industries, john.winterbourne@international.gc.ca

Sultanate of Oman
See: Kingdom of Saudi Arabia

Islamic Republic of Pakistan
Canadian High Commission, PO Box 1042, Islamabad, 44000 Pakistan
92-51-208-6000, Fax: 92-51-208-6900, isbad@international.gc.ca
www.canadainternational.gc.ca/pakistan
His Excellency Ross Hynes, High Commissioner
R. Gossen-Ehsani, Counsellor, Development
K. O'Brien, Immigration
S. Sears-Carter, Counsellor, Administration
R. Webb, Counsellor, Commercial
Athar Moeen Khan, Trade Commissioner, Environmental Industries, athar.khan@international.gc.ca

Palau
See: Republic of the Philippines

Republic of Panama
Apartado Postal 0832-2446, Estafata World Trade Centre, Panama City, Panama
011-507-294-2500, Fax: 011-507-294-2514, panam@international.gc.ca
www.canadainternational.gc.ca/panama
Her Excellency S. Cesaratto, Ambassador Designate
K. Burkell, Counsellor, Commercial
B. Wickens, Counsellor, Administration, & Consul
Luis Cedeno, Trade Commissioner, Environmental Industries, panam.commerce@international.gc.ca

Papua New Guinea
See: Commonwealth of Australia

Republic of Paraguay
See: Argentine Republic

Republic of Peru
Canadian Embassy, Casilla 18-1126, Calle Bolognesi 228, Miraflores, Lima, Peru
011-511-319-3200, Fax: 011-511-446-4912, lima@international.gc.ca
www.canadainternational.gc.ca/peru-perou
Her Excellency Patricia Fortier, Ambassador
A. Chevrier, Counsellor, Development
C. Lord, Counsellor, Immigration
M. Pawsey, Counsellor, Administration, & Consul
B. St-Jean, Counsellor, Political
S. Shaddick, Counsellor, Commercial
Alexandra Laverdure, Trade Commissioner, Environmental Industries, lima.commerce@international.gc.ca

Republic of the Philippines
Canadian Embassy, PO Box 2098, Makati Central Post Office, Makati City, 1261 Philippines
011-63-2-857-9000, Fax: 011-63-2-843-1082, manil@international.gc.ca
www.canadainternational.gc.ca/philippines
His Excellency Christopher Thornley, Ambassador
C. Bailey, Minister-Counsellor
S. Chapman, Counsellor, Administration, & Consul General
J. Christoff, Counsellor, Political & Economic
K. Francis, Counsellor, Immigration
K. L. Gerrits, Counsellor, Commercial
Ramon Yazon, Trade Commissioner, Environmental Industries, infocentre-manila@international.gc.ca

Republic of Poland
Canadian Embassy, ul. Jana Matejiki 1/5, Warsaw, 00-481 Poland
48-22-584-3100, Fax: 48-22-584-3192, wsaw@international.gc.ca
www.canadainternational.gc.ca/poland-pologne
His Excellency D. Costello, Ambassador
G. Houlahan, Counsellor, Commercial
A. Luhowy, Counsellor, Immigration
J. Mills, Counsell, Administration, & Consul
J. Stovel, Counsellor, Political Affairs
Rouslan Kats, Trade Commissioner, Environmental Industries, wsaw-td@international.gc.ca

Portuguese Republic
Canadian Embassy, Avenida da Liberdade, 196-200, 3rd Fl., Lisbon, 1269-121 Portugal
351-21-316-4600, Fax: 351-21-316-4691, lsbon@international.gc.ca
www.canadainternational.gc.ca/portugal
Her Excellency Anne-Marie Bourcier, Ambassador
Carlos Lindo da Silva, Trade Commissioner, Environmental Industries, lsbon-td@international.gc.ca

Puerto Rico
See: United States of America

State of Qatar
See: State of Kuwait

Republic of Palau
See: Republic of the Philippines

Republic of Romania
Canadian Embassy, 1-3 Tuberozelor Str., Bucharest, 011411 Romania
40-21-307-5000, Fax: 40-21-307-5010, bucst@international.gc.ca
www.canadainternational.gc.ca/romania-roumanie
His Excellency P. Beaulne, Ambassador
N. Brousseau, Counsellor, Political
R. Gregoire, Counsellor, Immigration
S. McCollum, Counsellor, Administration, & Consul
R. Merifield, Counsellor, Commercial
Octavian Bonea, Trade Commissioner, Environmental Industries, bucst-td@international.gc.ca

Russian Federation
Canadian Embassy, 23 Starokonyushenny Pereulok, Moscow, 119002 Russian Federation
011-7-495-925-6000, Fax: 011-7-495-925-6025, mosco@international.gc.ca
www.canadainternational.gc.ca/russia-russie
His Excellency John C. Sloan, Ambassador
L. Sarty, Minister-Counsellor & Deputy Head of Mission
A. Weichert, Minister-Counsellor
J. Furych, Counsellor, Agriculture & Agri-food
M. Felisiak, Counsellor, Administration, & Consul
Laura Lumsden, Trade Commissioner, Environmental Industries, rus.commerce@international.gc.ca

Rwandese Republic
Canadian Embassy, PO Box 1117, Kigali, Rwanda
011-250-573-210, Fax: 011-250-572-719, kgali@international.gc.ca
www.canadainternational.gc.ca/kenya/offices-bureaux/contact-rwanda-contactez.aspx
His Excellency David Collins, Ambassador (located in Kenya)
K. Guay, Second Secretary, Development
W. Minaker, Second Secretary, Development
Benjamin Wamahiu, Trade Commissioner, Environmental Industries, benjamin.wamahiu@international.gc.ca

Saint Kitts & Nevis
See: Barbados

Saint Lucia
See: Barbados

Saint Vincent & the Grenadines
See: Barbados

Samoa
See: New Zealand

Republic of San Marino
See: Italian Republic

Democratic Republic of Sao Tome & Principe
See: Cameroon

Kingdom of Saudi Arabia
Canadian Embassy, PO Box 94321, Riyadh, 11693 Saudi Arabia
966-1-488-2288, Fax: 966-1-488-1997,
ryadh@international.gc.ca
www.canadainternational.gc.ca/saudi_arabia-arabie_saoudite
His Excellency D. Chatterson, Ambassador
C. Andeel, Counsellor, Administration, & Consul
R. Dubuc, Counsellor, Commercial
M. Eichhorst, Counsellor, Immigration
Ali El Hadidi, Trade Commissioner, Environmental Industries, ryadh-td@international.gc.ca

Scotland
See: United Kingdom of Great Britain & Northern Ireland

Republic of Senegal
Canadian Embassy, PO Box 3373, Dakar, Senegal
011-221-33-889-4700, Fax: 011-221-33-889-4720,
dakar@international.gc.ca
www.canadainternational.gc.ca/senegal
His Excellency P. Calderwood, Ambassador
M. Gagnon, Counsellor, Development
N. Gervais, Counsellor, Administration, & Consul
S. Elkateb, Counsellor, Political
I. Ouellet, Counsellor, Immigration
C. Rojas-Arbulú, Counsellor, Commercial
Aminata Ly Faye, Trade Commissioner, Environmental Industries, aminata.ly@international.gc.ca

Serbia
Canadian Embassy, Kneza Milosa 75, Belgrade, 111711 Serbia
011-381-11-306-3000, Fax: 011-381-11-306-3042,
bgrad@international.gc.ca
www.canadainternational.gc.ca/serbia-serbie
Visa & Immigration services are now offered at the Canadian Embassy in Vienna, Austria.
His Excellency R. Waschuk, Ambassador
J. Gobeil, Counsellor, Administration, & Consul
J. Martone, Counsellor
B. Popa, Counsellor
K. Rex, Counsellor
Djurdjevka Ceramilac, Trade Commissioner, Environmental Industries, djurdjevka.ceramilac@international.gc.ca

Republic of Seychelles
See: United Republic of Tanzania

Republic of Sierra Leone
See: Republic of Côte d'Ivoire

Republic of Singapore
Canadian High Commission, PO Box 845, Singapore, 901645 Singapore
011-65-6854-5900, Fax: 011-65-6854-5930,
spore@international.gc.ca
www.canadainternational.gc.ca/singapore-singapour
His Excellency David Sevigny, High Commissioner
P. Nesbitt, Minister-Counsellor
Fumiko Kitano, Second Secretary (Commercial) & Trade Commissioner
E. Baldwin-Jones, Counsellor, Political
R. Borowyk, Counsellor, Commercial
G. Bozak, Counsellor, Agriculture & Agri-Food
C. Guimond, Counsellor, Immigration
Paula Murphy-Ives, Trade Commissioner, Environmental Industries, spore-td@international.gc.ca

Slovak Republic
Embassy of Canada, Mostova 2, Bratislava, 811 02 Slovak Republic
011-421-259-204-031, Fax: 011-421-254-434-227,
brtsv@international.gc.ca
www.canadainternational.gc.ca/czech-tcheque
Her Excellency Valerie Raymond, Ambassador (located in Prague, Czech Republic)
Milan Harustiak, Trade Commissioner, Environmental Industries, milan.harustiak@international.gc.ca

Republic of Slovenia
See: Republic of Hungary

Solomon Islands
See: Commonwealth of Australia

Somali Democratic Republic
See: Republic of Kenya

Republic of South Africa
Canadian High Commission, Private Bag X13, Hatfield, Pretoria, 0028 South Africa
011-27-12-422-3000, Fax: 011-27-12-422-3052,
pret@international.gc.ca
www.canadainternational.gc.ca/southafrica-afriquedusud
Her Excellency Adèle Dion, High Commissioner
R. Gregoire, Counsellor, Immigration
G. White, Counsellor, Political
C. Bradley, First Secretary
K. Mollica, First Secretary, Development
Trindard Makunike, Trade Commissioner, Environmental Industries, jobrg@international.gc.ca

Kingdom of Spain
Canadian Embassy, Torre Espacio, Paseo de la Castellana 259D, Madrid, 28046 Spain
011-34-91-382-8400, Fax: 011-34-91-382-8490,
mdrid@international.gc.ca
www.canadainternational.gc.ca/spain-espagne
His Excellency Graham Shantz, Ambassador (also to Andorra)
D. Dubien, Counsellor, Commercial
R. Letourneau, Counsellor, Administration, & Consul
I. Savard, Counsellor, Political Affairs
Amaya Jauregui, Trade Commissioner, Environmental Industries, espana@international.gc.ca

Democratic Socialist Republic of Sri Lanka
Canadian High Commission, PO Box 1006, Colombo, 7 Sri Lanka
011-94-11-522-6232, Fax: 011-94-11-522-6299,
clmbo@international.gc.ca
www.canadainternational.gc.ca
R. Bale, Acting High Commissioner
B. Hudson, Counsellor, Immigration
M. Foster, Counsellor, Political & Economic
P. Heroux, Counsellor, Development
G. Welton, Counsellor, Administration
Megan Foster, Senior Trade Commissioner, Environmental Industries, megan.foster@international.gc.ca

Republic of The Sudan
Canadian Embassy, 29 Africa Rd., Block 56, Khartouom, 10503 Sudan
011-249-156-550-500, Fax: 011-249-156-550-501,
khrtm@international.gc.ca
www.canadainternational.gc.ca/sudan_south_sudan-soudan_so udan_du_sud/embassy-ambassade.aspx
L. Charette, Chargé d'Affaires
M. Callan, Counsellor, Development
A. Kumar, First Secretary, Political
A. Scotti, First Secretary, Administration, & Consul
Joseph Tadros, Trade Commissioner, Environmental Industries, cairo-td@international.gc.ca

Republic of Suriname
See: Republic of Guyana

Kingdom of Swaziland
See: Republic of Mozambique

Kingdom of Sweden
Canadian Embassy, PO Box 16129, Stockholm, 103 23 Sweden
46-8-453-3000, Fax: 46-8-453-3016,
stkhm@international.gc.ca
www.canadainternational.gc.ca/sweden-suede
His Excellency Kenneth Macartney, Ambassador
A. Arnott, Minister
F. Bourdon, Counsellor
R. Flanagan, Counsellor, Administration, & Consul
C. Pilon, Counsellor, Commercial
Inga-Lill Olsson, Trade Commissioner, Environmental Industries, stkhm-commerce@international.gc.ca

Swiss Confederation
Canadian Embassy, Kirchenfeldstrasse 88, Bern, CH-3005 Switzerland
011-41-31-357-3200, Fax: 011-41-31-357-3210,
bern@international.gc.ca
www.canadainternational.gc.ca/switzerland-suisse
Her Excellency Roberta Santi, Ambassador (and to Liechtenstein)
J. Coulombe, Counsellor, Administration, & Consul
A. Dube, Counsellor, Commercial
C. Schwenger, Counsellor, Public Affairs

Syrian Arab Republic
The Canadian Embassy in Syria was closed in May 2012, following a coordinated effort between Canada, the USA, UK, France, Italy, Spain, Germany, & Australia to suspend diplomatic relations with Syria in response to the ongoing Syrian civil war.

Taiwan
Canadian Trade Office, Taipei 6F, No. 1 SongZhi Rd., Taipei, Xinyi District, 11047, Taiwan
011-886-2-2544-3000, Fax: 011-886-2-2544-3592,
taipei@international.gc.ca
www.canada.org.tw/taiwan
B. Arkinstall, Director, Consular & Administration
A. Edwards, Director, Trade & Investment
J. Reeve, Director, General Relations
J. Radonic, Deputy Director, Visas & Immigration
Vanessa Chen, Trade Commissioner, Environmental Industries, vanessa.chen@international.gc.ca

Republic of Tajikistan
See: Republic of Kazakhstan

United Republic of Tanzania
Canadian High Commission, PO Box 1022 , Dar-es-Salaam, Tanzania
011-255-22-216-3300, Fax: 011-255-22-211-6897,
dslam@international.gc.ca
www.canadainternational.gc.ca/tanzania-tanzanie
His Excellency Robert Orr, High Commissioner
P. McCullagh, Minister-Counsellor, Development
M. A. Jacques, Counsellor, Administration
C. McQueen, Counsellor, Political & Economic
Florence Mndolwa, Trade Commissioner, Environmental Industries, florence.mndolwa@international.gc.ca

Kingdom of Thailand
Canadian Embassy, PO Box 2090, Bangkok, 10501 Thailand
66-2636-0540, Fax: 66-2636-0566,
bngkk@international.gc.ca
www.canadainternational.gc.ca/thailand-thailande
His Excellency Steve Birch, High Commissioner
W. Bazett, Counsellor, Immigration
P. Kitnikone, Counsellor, Commercial
J. May, Counsellor, Political
S. Roy, Counsellor, Administration & Consul General
Ekasit Chunlakittiphan, Trade Commissioner, Environmental Industries, ekasit.chunlakittiphan@international.gc.ca

Republic of Togo
See: Republic of Ghana

Kingdom of Tonga
See: New Zealand

Republic of Trinidad & Tobago
Canadian High Commission, PO Box 1246, Port of Spain, Trinidad & Tobago, West Indies
868-622-6232, Fax: 868-628-2581,
pspan@international.gc.ca
www.canadainternational.gc.ca/trinidad_and_tobago-trinite_et_to bago
Her Excellency Karen L. McDonald, High Commissioner
C. Joseph, Counsellor, Immigration
L. Morel-à-l'Huissier, Political & Economic
L. Steinburg, Counsellor, Administration
Michaeline Narcisse, Trade Commissioner, Environmental Industries, michaeline.narcisse@international.gc.ca

Republic of Tunisia
Canadian Embassy, PO Box 48, Les Berges du Lac, Tunis, 1053 Tunisia
216-71-104-000, Fax: 216-71-104-191,
tunis@international.gc.ca
www.canadainternational.gc.ca/tunisia-tunisie
His Excellency Ariel Delouya, Ambassador
A. Bilodeau, Counsellor, Political
E. Gentile, Counsellor, Immigration
D. McFarlane, Counsellor, Administration, & Consul
E. Sum Wah, Counsellor, Commercial, & Vice-Consul
Lassaad Bourguiba, Trade Commissioner, Environmental Industries, lassaad.bourguiba@international.gc.ca

Republic of Turkey
Canadian Embassy, Cinnah Caddesi 58, Cankaya, Ankara, 06690 Turkey
011-90-312-409-2700, Fax: 90-312-312-409-2810, ankra@international.gc.ca
www.canadainternational.gc.ca/turkey-turquie
His Excellency John Holmes, Ambassador
J. Davison, Counsellor
P. Laurin, Counsellor, Immigration
D. Marion, Counsellor, Administration, & Consul
P. Rozek, Counsellor
Akin Kosetorunu, Trade Commissioner, Environmental Industries, ankra-td@international.gc.ca

Turkmenistan
See: Republic of Turkey

Turks & Caicos Islands
See: Jamaica

Republic of Tuvalu
See: New Zealand

Republic of Uganda
See: Republic of Kenya

Ukraine
Canadian Embassy, 31 Yaroslaviv Val, Kyiv, 1901 Ukraine
380-44-590-3100, Fax: 380-44-590-3134, kyiv@international.gc.ca
www.canadainternational.gc.ca/ukraine
His Excellency Troy Lulashnyk, Ambassador
S. Auger, Counsellor, Immigration
C. Bilyk, Counsellor, Commercial
N. Cmoc, Counsellor, Development
S. Landry, Counsellor, Administration, & Consul
G. Lemermeyer, Counsellor, Political Affairs
Yury Mardak, Trade Commissioner, Environmental Industries, yury.mardak@international.gc.ca

United Arab Emirates
The Canadian Embassy, PO Box 6970, Abu Dhabi, United Arab Emirates
971-2-694-0300, Fax: 971-2-694-0399, abdbi@international.gc.ca
www.canadainternational.gc.ca/uae-eau
His Excellency Kenneth Lewis, Ambassador
S. Ahmed, Counsellor, Commercial
P. Bedard, Counsellor, Administration, & Consul
M. Eichhorst, Counsellor, Immigration
S. Nagi, Counsellor, Political
Imad Arafat, Trade Commissioner, Environmental Industries, uae-eau.infocentre@international.gc.ca

United Kingdom of Great Britain & Northern Ireland
Canadian High Commission, MacDonald House, One Grosvenor Sq., London, W1K 4AB United Kingdom
011-44-20-7258-6600, Fax: 011-44-20-7258-6333, ldn@international.gc.ca
www.canadainternational.gc.ca/united_kingdom-royaume_uni
His Excellency Gordon Campbell, High Commissioner
S. Gregson, Deputy High Commissioner
A. Arnott, Minister
M. Fletcher, Minister-Counsellor
B. Parrott, Minister-Counsellor, Economic & Commercial
D. Proudfoot, Minister-Counsellor, Political & Public Affairs
Daniel Tibbetts, Trade Commissioner, Environmental Industries, ldn-td@international.gc.ca

United States of America
Canadian Embassy, 501 Pennsylvannia Ave. NW, Washington, DC 20001 USA
202-682-1740, Fax: 202-682-7726, wshdc@international.gc.ca
www.canadainternational.gc.ca/washington
His Excellency Gary Doer, Ambassador
Deborah Lyons, Deputy Head of Mission
Deanna Horton, Minister, Congressional, Public, & Intergovernmental Affairs
Sheila Riordon, Minister, Political
Paul Robertson, Minister, Economic
Mario Bot, Minister-Counsellor & Head of Chancery
M.Gen. Nicolas Matern, Commander CDLS(W) & Canadian Defence Attaché
Benjamin Eliasoph, Trade Commissioner, Environmental Industries & Technology, wshdc.infocentre@international.gc.ca

Eastern Republic of Uruguay
Canadian Embassy, #102, Plaza Independencia 749, C.P. 11100, Montevideo, Uruguay
598-2-902-2030, Fax: 598-2-902-2029, mvdeo@international.gc.ca
www.canadainternational.gc.ca/uruguay
Her Excellency C. Poulin, Ambassador
L. Moore, Counsellor, Administration, & Consul
Patricia Wilson, Trade Commissioner, Environmental Industries, patricia.wilson@international.gc.ca

Republic of Uzbekistan
See: Russian Federation

Republic of Vanuatu
See: Commonwealth of Australia

Republic of Venezuela
Canadian Embassy, Apartado Postal 62302, Caracas, 1060A Venezuela
011-58-212-600-3000, Fax: 011-58-212-263-8326, crcas@international.gc.ca
www.canadainternational.gc.ca/venezuela
His Excellency, P. Gibbard, Ambassador
A. Power, Counsellor, Administration, & Consul
M. Cooke, Counsellor, Political
A. Luhowy, Counsellor, Immigration
Guy Salesse, Counsellor, Commercial
Daniela Oyague, Trade Commissioner, Environmental Industries, crcas-td@international.gc.ca

Socialist Republic of Vietnam
Canadian Embassy, 31 Huong Vuong St., Hanoi, Vietnam
011-84-4-3734-5000, Fax: 011-84-4-3734-5049, hanoi@international.gc.ca
www.canadainternational.gc.ca/vietnam
Her Excellency Deborah Chatsis, Ambassador
J. Donnelly, Counsellor, Political
L. Dumas, Counsellor, Immigration
F. Lasalle, Counsellor, Commercial
F. Lesueur, Counsellor, Administration, & Consul
Dang-Anh Thu, Trade Commissioner, Environmental Industries, vietnam-infocentre@international.gc.ca

Virgin Islands (British)
See: Barbados

Virgin Islands (USA)
See: United States of America

Wales
See: United Kingdom of Great Britain & Northern Ireland

West Bank & Gaza Strip
Canadian Representative Office, PO Box 18604, Jerusalem 91184
972-2-297-8430, Fax: 972-2-297-8446, rmlah@international.gc.ca
www.canadainternational.gc.ca/west_bank_gaza-cisjordanie_bande_de_gaza
Chris Greenshields, Representative of Canada
M. Rymek, Chargé d'affaires
A. Bilodeau, Counsellor, Political & Economic
G. Ptolemy, Counsellor, Administration
M. Samper, Counsellor, Development
S. Leduc, First Secretary
Hussein Hirji, Trade Commissioner, Environmental Industries, rmlahtd@international.gc.ca

Republic of Yemen
See: Kingdom of Saudi Arabia

Republic of Zambia
Canadian High Commission, PO Box 31313, Lusaka, 10101 Zambia
260-1-25-08-33, Fax: 260-1-25-41-76, lsaka@international.gc.ca
www.canadainternational.gc.ca/tanzania-tanzanie
Apart from the Canadian High Commission office in Zambia, Canada is also represented by the Canadian High Commission in Dar-es-Salaam, Tanzania.
His Excellency Robert Orr, High Commissioner (located in Tanzania)
S. Landry, First Secretary & Consul
Solomon Milimbo, Trade Commissioner, Environmental Industries, solomon.milimbo@international.gc.ca

Republic of Zimbabwe
Canadian Embassy, 14240 Salisbury Township, Harare, Zimbabwe
011-263-425-2181, Fax: 011-263-425-2186, hrare@international.gc.ca
www.canadainternational.gc.ca/zimbabwe
Her Excellency Lisa Stadelbauer, Ambassador
D. De Rose, Counsellor, Immigration
V. Fuller, Counsellor, Administration, & Consul
B. Giacomin, Counsellor, Commercial
A. Paul, Counsellor, Development
Denis Langois, Senior Trade Commissioner, Environmental Industries, hrare-td@international.gc.ca

SECTION 8
GOVERNMENT/MUNICIPAL

Listings in this section are arranged by province and are as current as possible at time of publication. For appointments made and results of elections held after publication, please refer to Canada's Information Resource Centre (CIRC), if your library subscribes to this online database. Each provincial section includes a district map, notes concerning local government structure and elections, and the following categories:

Counties & Municipal Districts

Major Municipalities

Other Municipalities

ALBERTA

The major legislation concerning municipal government in Alberta is the Municipal Government Act.

Municipal government in Alberta is rural, urban or specialized. Rural municipal governments are organized into Municipal Districts, with Specialized Municipalities created to meet the unique needs of a specific municipality. Elected councils are responsible for the welfare and interests of the municipalities. Two other rural categories are Improvement Districts and Special Areas, which are geographically large, sparsely populated areas for which the provincial government levies and collects all taxes and provides services.

Urban municipalities include Summer Villages, Villages, Towns and Cities. These are fully autonomous municipal units, each with an elected council. They are responsible for providing all municipal services within their corporate limits and for levying taxes and rates.

In addition to the above forms of municipal government there are eight Metis Settlements established under the Metis Settlements Act.

Types of Municipalities that may be formed:

- Municipal District: A majority of the buildings used as dwellings are on parcels of land with an area of at least 1,850 square metres and there is a population of 1,000 or more.
- Village: A majority of the buildings are on parcels of land smaller than 1,850 square metres and there is a population of 300 or more.
- Town: A majority of the buildings are on parcels of land smaller than 1,850 square metres and there is a population of 1,000 or more.
- City: A majority of the buildings are on parcels of land smaller than 1,850 square metres and there is a population of 10,000 or more.

Specialized Municipality: An area in which the Minister is satisfied that a type of municipality (as listed above) does not meet the needs of the proposed municipality; to provide for a form of local government that, in the opinion of the Minister, will provide for the orderly development of the municipality to a type of municipality (as listed above), or to another form of specialized municipality; an area in which the Minister is satisfied for any other reason that it is appropriate in the circumstances to form a specialized municipality.

Incorporation and changes in status are determined by the Lieutenant Governor in Council (Provincial Cabinet) on the recommendation of the Minister of Municipal Affairs. It is not necessary to change status by reason of population change. Elections are held in October. Terms of office are three years (2013, 2016, etc.).

Reproduced with the permission of Natural Resources Canada, 2012

Alberta

Counties & Municipal Districts in Alberta

Acadia No. 34
P.O. Box 30
Acadia Valley, AB T0J 0A0
Tel: 403-972-3808; *Fax:* 403-972-3833
md34@mdacadia.ab.ca
www.mdacadia.ab.ca
Municipal Type: Municipal District
Incorporated: Dec. 9, 1913 *Area:* 1,076.26 sq km
Population in 2011: 495
Next Election: Oct. 21, 2013 (3 year terms)
Dwight Meers, Reeve
councillor.meers@mdacadia.ab.ca
Gary E. Peers, Municipal Administrator
cao@mdcadia.ab.ca

Athabasca County No. 12
3602 - 48 Ave.
Athabasca, AB T9S 1M8
Tel: 780-675-2273; *Fax:* 780-675-5512
info@athabascacounty.com
www.athabascacounty.com
Municipal Type: Municipal District
Incorporated: Dec. 18, 1913 *Area:* 6,126.43 sq km
Population in 2011: 7,662
Next Election: Oct. 21, 2013 (3 year terms)
Note: Incorporated as a municipal district on Dec. 14, 1914.
David Yurdiga, Reeve
dyurdiga@athabascacounty.com
Gary Buchanan, CAO
gbuchanan@athabascacounty.com

Beaver County
P.O. Box 140
Ryley, AB T0B 4A0
Tel: 780-663-3730; *Fax:* 780-663-3602
administration@beaver.ab.ca
www.beaver.ab.ca
Municipal Type: Municipal District
Incorporated: Feb. 1, 1943 *Area:* 3,319.1 sq km
Population in 2011: 5,689
Next Election: Oct. 21, 2013 (3 year terms)
Robert Young, Reeve
division1@mcsnet.ca
Bob Beck, CAO
bbeck@beaver.ab.ca

Big Lakes
P.O. Box 239
5305 -56 ST.
High Prairie, AB T0G 1E0
Tel: 780-523-5955; *Fax:* 780-523-4227
biglakes@mdbiglakes.ca
www.mdbiglakes.ca
Municipal Type: Municipal District
Incorporated: Dec. 18, 1913 *Area:* 13,892.91 sq km
Population in 2011: 5,912
Next Election: Oct. 21, 2013 (3 year terms)
Note: Incorporated as a municipal district on Jan. 1, 1995.
Alvin Billings, Reeve

Bighorn No. 8
P.O. Box 310
2 Heart Mountain Drive
Exshaw, AB T0L 2C0
Tel: 403-673-3611; *Fax:* 403-673-3895
bighorn@mdbighorn.ca
www.mdbighorn.ca
Municipal Type: Municipal District
Incorporated: April 1, 1945 *Area:* 2,767.94 sq km
Population in 2011: 1,341
Next Election: Oct. 21, 2013 (3 year terms)
Note: Incorporated as a municipal district on Jan. 1, 1988.
Dene Cooper, Reeve
Martin Buckley, CAO
martin.buckley@mdbighorn.ca

Birch Hills
P.O. Box 157
Wanham, AB T0H 3P0
Tel: 780-694-3793; *Fax:* 780-694-3788
irenec@birchhillscounty.com
www.birchhillscounty.com
Municipal Type: Municipal District
Incorporated: Dec. 18, 1913 *Area:* 2,856.69 sq km
Population in 2011: 1,582
Next Election: Oct. 21, 2013 (3 year terms)
Warren Smith, Reeve
Irene Cooper, CAO

Bonnyville No. 87
P.O. Box 1010
4905 - 50 Ave.
Bonnyville, AB T9N 2J7
Tel: 780-826-3171; *Fax:* 780-826-4524
kkalinski@md.bonnyville.ab.ca
www.md.bonnyville.ab.ca
Municipal Type: Municipal District
Incorporated: Dec. 14, 1914 *Area:* 6,057.44 sq km
Population in 2011: 11,191
Next Election: Oct. 21, 2013 (3 year terms)
Ryan Poole, CAO
rpoole@md.bonnyville.ab.ca
Ed Rondeau, Reeve

Brazeau County
P.O. Box 77
5516 Industrial Rd.
Drayton Valley, AB T7A 1R1
Tel: 780-542-7777; *Fax:* 780-542-7770
krobinson@brazeau.ab.ca
www.brazeau.ab.ca
Municipal Type: Municipal District
Incorporated: Dec. 18, 1913 *Area:* 3,015.83 sq km
Population in 2011: 7,201
Next Election: Oct. 21, 2013 (3 year terms)
Note: Incorporated as a municipal district on Dec. 13, 1915.
Ron McCullough, CAO
rmccullough@brazeau.ab.ca
Wes Tweedle, Reeve

Camrose County No. 22
3755 - 43 Ave.
Camrose, AB T4V 3S8
Tel: 780-672-4446; *Fax:* 780-672-1008
county@county.camrose.ab.ca
www.county.camrose.ab.ca
Municipal Type: County
Incorporated: Dec. 23, 1912 *Area:* 3,331.98 sq km
County or District: Camrose No. 22; *Population in 2011:* 7,721
Next Election: Oct. 21, 2013 (3 year terms)
Note: Incorporated as a municipal district on Jan. 1, 1944.
Steven Gerlitz, Administrator
sgerlitz@county.camrose.ab.ca
Don L. Gregorwich, Reeve

Cardston County
P.O. Box 580
1050 Main Street
Cardston, AB T0K 0K0
Tel: 403-653-4977; *Fax:* 403-653-1126
office@cardstoncounty.com
www.cardstoncounty.com
Municipal Type: Municipal District
Incorporated: Dec. 18, 1913 *Area:* 3,414.87 sq km
Population in 2011: 4,167
Next Election: Oct. 21, 2013 (3 year terms)
Note: Incorporated as a municipal district on Jan. 1, 1946.
Lloyd Kearl, Reeve
Murray Millward, CAO
murray@cardstoncounty.com

Clear Hills County No. 21
P.O. Box 240
Worsley, AB T0H 3W0
Tel: 780-685-3925; *Fax:* 780-685-3960
info@clearhillscounty.ab.ca
www.clearhillscounty.ab.ca
Municipal Type: Municipal District
Incorporated: Dec. 18, 1913 *Area:* 15,112.69 sq km
Population in 2011: 2,801
Next Election: Oct. 21, 2013 (3 year terms)
Note: Incorporated as a municipal district on Jan. 1, 1995.
Miron Croy, Reeve
Allan Rowe, CAO
allan@clearhillscounty.ab.ca

Clearwater County
P.O. Box 550
4340 - 47th Ave.
Rocky Mountain House, AB T4T 1A4
Tel: 403-845-4444; *Fax:* 403-845-7330
admin@county.clearwater.ab.ca
www.county.clearwater.ab.ca
Municipal Type: Municipal District
Incorporated: April 1, 1945 *Area:* 18,691.65 sq km
Population in 2011: 12,278
Next Election: Oct. 21, 2013 (3 year terms)
Note: Incorporated as a municipal district on Jan. 1, 1985.
Ron Leaf, County Manager
rleaf@county.clearwater.ab.ca
Pat Alexander, Reeve
Joe Baker, Manager, Planning / West Country
jbaker@county.clearwater.ab.ca
Kim Nielsen, Manager, Agricultural Services
knielsen@county.clearwater.ab.ca
Marshall Morton, Manager, Public Works
mmorton@county.clearwater.ab.ca

Crowsnest Pass
P.O. Box 600
Blairmore, AB T0K 0E0
Tel: 403-562-8833; *Fax:* 403-563-5474
reception@crowsnestpass.com
www.town.crowsnestpass.ab.ca
Municipal Type: Regional Municipality
Incorporated: Jan. 1, 1979 *Area:* 373.07 sq km
Population in 2011: 5,565
Provincial Electoral District(s): Livingstone-Macleod
Federal Electoral District(s): Macleod
Next Election: Oct. 21, 2013 (3 year terms)
Bruce Decoux, Mayor
Kevin Robins, CAO
cao@crowsnestpass.com

Cypress County
816 - 2nd Ave.
Dunmore, AB T1B 0K3
Tel: 403-526-2888; *Fax:* 403-526-8958
cypress@cypress.ab.ca
www.cypress.ab.ca
Municipal Type: Municipal District
Incorporated: Dec. 18, 1913 *Area:* 13,166.13 sq km
Population in 2011: 7,214
Next Election: Oct. 21, 2013 (3 year terms)
Note: Incorporated as a municipal district on Jan. 1, 1985.
Lutz Perschon, County Manager
lutz@cypress.ab.ca
Darcy Geigle, Reeve
403-834-2244, Fax: 403-834-2270
dgeigle@xplornet.com

Fairview No. 136
P.O. Box 189
10957-91 Ave.
Fairview, AB T0H 1L0
Tel: 780-835-4903; *Fax:* 780-835-3131
mdinfo@medfairview.ab.ca
www.mdfairview.com
Municipal Type: Municipal District
Incorporated: Dec. 18, 1913 *Area:* 1,390.66 sq km
Population in 2011: 1,673
Next Election: Oct. 21, 2013 (3 year terms)
Note: Incorporated as a municipal district on Dec. 9, 1914.
Ernie Newman, Reeve
fcseedplant@wispernet.ca
Ben Boettcher, CAO
ben@mdfairview.ab.ca

Flagstaff County
P.O. Box 358
4202-50th St.
Sedgewick, AB T0B 4C0
Tel: 780-384-4100; *Fax:* 780-384-3635
county@flagstaff.ab.ca
www.flagstaff.ab.ca
Other Information: Toll-Free: 1-877-387-4100
Municipal Type: County
Incorporated: Dec. 9, 1912 *Area:* 4,066.92 sq km
Population in 2011: 3,244
Next Election: Oct. 21, 2013 (3 year terms)
Henry Hays, Reeve
780-888-2242
Shelly Armstrong, CAO
sarmstrong@flagstaff.ab.ca

Foothills No. 31
P.O. Box 5605
309 Macleod Trail
High River, AB T1V 1M7
Tel: 403-652-2341; *Fax:* 403-652-7880
mdfthlls@mdfoothills.com
www.mdfoothills.com
Other Information: Emergencies: 1-888-808-3722
Municipal Type: Municipal District
Incorporated: Dec. 23, 1912 *Area:* 3,643.6 sq km
Population in 2011: 21,258
Next Election: Oct. 21, 2013 (3 year terms)
Note: Incorporated as a municipal district on Jan. 1, 1944.
Harry Riva Cambrin, Municipal Manager
hrc@mdfoothills.com

Roy McLean, Reeve
council@mdfoothills.com
Graham Clark, Fire Chief, Protective Services
graham.clark@mdfoothills.com
Tom Gillis, Director, Public Works & Engineering
tom.gillis@mdfoothills.com
Nasir Sheikh, Municipal Engineer
nasir.sheikh@mdfoothills.com
Judy Gordon, Coordinator, Planning & Development
judy.gordon@mdfoothills.com
Marilyn Gordon-Cooper, Contact, Property Tax & Utilities Department
marilyn.gordon-cooper@mdfoothills.com
Heather Hemingway, Contact, Environment Committee
heather.hemingway@mdfoothills.com
Ken McKay, Contact, Building Safety Codes & Bylaw Enforcement
ken.mckay@mdfoothills.com

Forty Mile County No. 8
P.O. Box 160
303 Main St.
Foremost, AB T0K 0X0
Tel: 403-867-3530; *Fax:* 403-867-2242
info@fortymile.ab.ca
www.40mile.ca
Municipal Type: County
Incorporated: Dec. 9, 1912 *Area:* 7,229.84 sq km
Population in 2011: 3,336
Next Election: Oct. 21, 2013 (3 year terms)
Tom Thacker, Reeve
403-545-2477
Dale Brown, Administrator
dale@fortymile.ab.ca

Grande Prairie No. 1
10001 - 84 Ave.
Clairmont, AB T0H 0W0
Tel: 780-532-9722; *Fax:* 780-539-9880
info@countygp.ab.ca
www.countygp.ab.ca
Municipal Type: County
Incorporated: Dec. 9, 1912 *Area:* 5,883.92 sq km
Population in 2011: 20,347
Next Election: Oct. 21, 2013 (3 year terms)
Note: Incorporated as a county on Jan. 1, 1951.
W.A. Rogan, County Administrator
brogan1@countygp.ab.ca
Everett McDonald, Reeve
John Simpson, Director, Planning
780-513-3950
plan@countygp.ab.ca
Everett Cooke, Fire Chief
780-567-5590
fire@countygp.ab.ca
Steve Madden, Manager, Environment
780-532-7393
Herb Pfau, Superintendent, Public Works
780-532-7393
pubwks@countygp.ab.ca

Greenview No. 16
P.O. Box 1079
Valleyview, AB T0H 3N0
Tel: 780-524-7600
www.mdgreenview.ab.ca
Other Information: Toll-Free Phone: 1-888-524-7601
Municipal Type: Municipal District
Incorporated: Jan. 1, 1969 *Area:* 32,994.14 sq km
Population in 2011: 5,299
Next Election: Oct. 21, 2013 (3 year terms)
Note: Incorporated as a municipal district on Jan. 1, 1994.
Janis Simpkins, Reeve
780-524-4491
ward5councillor@mdgreenview.ab.ca
Doug Cavers, Chief Administrative Officer

Jasper
P.O. Box 520
Jasper, AB T0E 1E0
Tel: 780-852-3356; *Fax:* 780-852-4019
j.cooper@town.jasper.ab.ca
www.jasper-alberta.com
Municipal Type: Regional Municipality
Incorporated: Aug. 31, 1995 *Area:* 925.52 sq km
Population in 2011: 4,051
Next Election: Oct. 21, 2013 (3 year terms)
Note: Incorporated as a specialized municipality on July 20, 2001.
Richard Ireland, Mayor
rireland@town.jasper.ab.ca
George Krefting, Municipal Manager
gkrefting@town.jasper.ab.ca

Kneehill County
P.O. Box 400
Three Hills, AB T0M 2A0
Tel: 403-443-5541; *Fax:* 403-443-5115
office@kneehillcounty.com
www.kneehillcounty.com
Municipal Type: Municipal District
Incorporated: Dec. 9, 1912 *Area:* 3,380.04 sq km
Population in 2011: 4,921
Next Election: Oct. 21, 2013 (3 year terms)
Carol Calhoun, Reeve
Kevin Miner, CAO
kevincao@kneehillcounty.com

Lac La Biche County
P.O. Box 1679
Lac La Biche, AB T0A 2C0
Tel: 780-623-1747; *Fax:* 780-623-2039
main.office@laclabichecounty.com
www.laclabichecounty.com
Other Information: Toll-Free: 1-877-806-5632
Municipal Type: County
Incorporated: Aug. 1, 2007
Population in 2011: 8,402
Provincial Electoral District(s): Lac La Biche-St. Paul
Federal Electoral District(s): Fort McMurray-Athabasca
Next Election: Oct. 21, 2013 (3 year terms)
Note: The Town of Lac La Biche & Lakeland County amalgamated on August 1, 2007 to create Lac La Biche County.
Peter Kirylchuk, Mayor
780-623-7732, Fax: 780-623-7720
Lucien Cloutier, County Clerk
lucien.cloutier@laclabichecounty.com

Lac Ste. Anne County
P.O. Box 219
4928 Langston St.
Sangudo, AB T0E 2A0
Tel: 780-785-3411; *Fax:* 780-785-2359
lsac@gov.lacsteanne.ab.ca
www.gov.lacsteanne.ab.ca
Other Information: Toll-Free: 1-866-880-5722
Municipal Type: Municipal District
Incorporated: Jan. 1, 1944 *Area:* 2,842.46 sq km
Population in 2011: 10,260
Next Election: Oct. 21, 2013 (3 year terms)
Lloyd Giebelhaus, Reeve
Len Szybunka, County Manager
lszybunka@gov.lacsteanne.ab.ca

Lacombe County
RR#3
Lacombe, AB T4L 2N3
Tel: 403-782-6601; *Fax:* 403-782-3820
info@lacombecounty.com
www.lacombecounty.com
Municipal Type: County
Incorporated: Jan. 1, 1944 *Area:* 2,777.26 sq km
County or District: Lacombe No. 14; *Population in 2011:* 10,312
Next Election: Oct. 21, 2013 (3 year terms)
Note: Incorporated as a county on Jan. 1, 1961.
Terry Hager, County Commissioner
thager@lacombecounty.com
Terry Engen, Reeve
Keith Boras, Manager, Agriculture Services
kboras@lacombecounty.com
Dale Freitag, Manager, Planning Services
dfreitag@lacombecounty.com
Julian Veuger, County Constable, Disaster Services
jveuger@lacombecounty.com
Dale Freitaq, Planner & Development Officer
dfreitaq@lacombecounty.com
Dale Kary, Project Coordinator, Public Works
dkary@lacombecounty.com
Phil Lodermeier, Supervisor, Public Works
plodermeier@lacombecounty.com

Lamont County
Administration Bldg.
5303 - 50 Ave.
Lamont, AB T0B 2R0
Tel: 780-895-2233; *Fax:* 780-895-7404
countyinfo@lamontcounty.ca
www.lamontcounty.ca
Other Information: Toll-Free: 1-877-895-2233
Municipal Type: County
Incorporated: Dec. 23, 1912 *Area:* 2,400.78 sq km
County or District: Lamont No. 30; *Population in 2011:* 3,872
Next Election: Oct. 21, 2013 (3 year terms)
Note: Incorporated as a county on Jan. 1, 1968.
Wayne Woldanski, Reeve
wayne.w@lamontcounty.ca
Allan Harvey, CAO
allan.h@tclamont.ca

Leduc County
#101, 1101 - 5 St.
Nisku, AB T9E 2X3
Tel: 780-955-3555; *Fax:* 780-955-3444
shaunaf@leduc-county.com
www.leduc-county.com
Other Information: Toll free: 1-800-379-9052
Municipal Type: County
Incorporated: Jan. 1, 1944 *Area:* 2,610.25 sq km
County or District: Leduc No. 25; *Population in 2011:* 13,541
Next Election: Oct. 21, 2013 (3 year terms)
Note: Incorporated as a county on Jan. 1, 1964.
Doug Wright, County Manager
780-955-6400
dougw@leduc-county.com
John Whaley, Reeve
Michael MacLean, Director, Public Works & Engineering
780-955-6416
michael@leduc-county.com
Phil Newman, Director, Planning & Development
780-955-6413
phil@leduc-county.com
Dean Ohnysty, Director, Parks & Recreation
780-955-4535
dean@leduc-county.com
Garett Broadbent, Director, Agricultural Services
780-955-6404
garett@leduc-county.com
Bob Galloway, Chief, Fire
780-955-7099
bobg@leduc-county.com
Deryld Dublanko, Manager, Maintenance & Materials Supply
780-955-2469
deryld@leduc-county.com
Janis Fong, Manager, Public Works & Infrastructure
Des Mryglod, Manager, Engineering
Dave McPhee, Officer, Utilities
780-955-4541
dave@leduc-county.com

Lesser Slave River No. 124
P.O. Box 722
Slave Lake, AB T0G 2A0
Tel: 780-849-4888; *Fax:* 780-849-4939
md124@md124.ca
www.md124.ca
Municipal Type: Municipal District
Incorporated: Jan. 1, 1969 *Area:* 10,075.88 sq km
Population in 2011: 2,929
Next Election: Oct. 21, 2013 (3 year terms)
Note: Incorporated as a municipal district on Jan. 1, 1995.
Denny Garratt, Reeve
denny1@telusplanet.net
Allan Winarski, CAO
allan.winarski@md124.ca

Lethbridge County
#100, 905 - 4 Ave. South
Lethbridge, AB T1J 4E4
Tel: 403-328-5525; *Fax:* 403-328-5602
mailbox@lethcounty.ca
www.county.lethbridge.ab.ca
Municipal Type: County
Incorporated: Jan. 1, 1954 *Area:* 2,839.28 sq km
County or District: Lethbridge No. 26; *Population in 2011:* 10,061
Next Election: Oct. 21, 2013 (3 year terms)
Note: Incorporated as a county on Jan 1, 1964.
Lorne Hickey, Reeve
lhickey@lethcounty.ca
Dennis Shigematsu, County Manager
dshigematsu@lethcounty.ca

Mackenzie County
P.O. Box 640
4511 - 46 Ave.
Fort Vermilion, AB T0H 1N0
Tel: 780-927-3718; *Fax:* 780-927-4266
office@mackenziecounty.com
www.mackenziecounty.com
Other Information: Toll Free: 1-877-927-0677
Municipal Type: Regional Municipality
Incorporated: Jan. 1, 1995 *Area:* 80,484.42 sq km
Population in 2011: 10,927
Next Election: Oct. 21, 2013 (3 year terms)

Note: Incorporated as a specialized municipality on June 23, 1999. Name changed from The Municipal District of Mackenzie No. 23 to Mackenzie County in 2007.
William (Bill) Kostiw, CAO
780-841-1801
bkostiw@mackenziecounty.com
Gregory Alan Newman, Reeve
780-927-3807
greg@mackenziecounty.com

Minburn County No. 27
P.O. Box 550
4909-50 St.
Vegreville, AB T9C 1R6
Tel: 780-632-2082; *Fax:* 780-632-6296
info@minburncounty.ab.ca
www.minburncounty.ab.ca
Municipal Type: County
Incorporated: Jan. 30, 1942 *Area:* 2,911.14 sq km
County or District: Minburn No. 27; *Population in 2011:* 3,278
Next Election: Oct. 21, 2013 (3 year terms)
Note: Incorporated as a county on Jan. 1, 1965.
Eric Anderson, Reeve
David Marynowich, Manager

Mountain View County
P.O. Box 100
1408 Twp Rd. 320
Didsbury, AB T0M 0W0
Tel: 403-335-3311; *Fax:* 403-335-9207
info@mountainviewcounty.com
www.mountainviewcounty.com
Other Information: Toll Free Phone: 1-877-264-9754
Municipal Type: County
Incorporated: Dec. 9, 1912 *Area:* 3,804.43 sq km
Population in 2011: 12,359
Next Election: Oct. 21, 2013 (3 year terms)
Note: Incorporated as a county on Jan. 1, 1961.
Doug Plamping, CAO
doug.plamping@mountainviewcounty.com
Albert Kemmere, Reeve
Steve McInnis, Director, Operational Services
steve.mcinnis@mountainviewcounty.com
Tony Martens, Director, Legislative & Community Services
tony.martens@mountainviewcounty.com
Jeff Holmes, Manager, Agriculture & Parks Services
jeff.holmes@mountainviewcounty.com

Newell County No. 4
P.O. Box 130
707 - 2nd Ave. East
Brooks, AB T1R 1B2
Tel: 403-362-3266; *Fax:* 403-362-8681
administration@countyofnewell.ab.ca
www.countyofnewell.ab.ca
Municipal Type: County
Incorporated: Feb. 10, 1948 *Area:* 5,903.47 sq km
Population in 2011: 6,786
Next Election: Oct. 21, 2013 (3 year terms)
Note: Incorporated as a county on Jan. 1, 1953.
Kevin Stephenson, CAO
stephensonk@countyofnewell.ab.ca
Molly Douglass, Reeve

Northern Lights No. 22
P.O. Box 10
#600, 7th Ave. NW
Manning, AB T0H 2M0
Tel: 780-836-3348; *Fax:* 780-836-3663
info@mdnorth22.ab.ca, mdnorth22@mdnorth22.ab.ca
www.mdnorth22.ab.ca
Municipal Type: Municipal District
Incorporated: Dec. 18, 1913 *Area:* 20,745.45 sq km
Population in 2011: 4,117
Next Election: Oct. 21, 2013 (3 year terms)
Note: Incorporated as a municipal district on April 1, 1995.
Edward Kamieniecki, Reeve
Theresa Van Oort, CAO
cao@mdnorth22.ab.ca

Northern Sunrise County
P.O. Box 1300
Peace River, AB T8S 1Y9
Tel: 780-624-0013; *Fax:* 780-624-0023
general@northernsunrise.net
www.northernsunrise.net
Municipal Type: Municipal District
Incorporated: Dec. 18, 1913 *Area:* 21,141.25 sq km
Population in 2011: 1,791
Next Election: Oct. 21, 2013 (3 year terms)
Note: Incorporated as a municipal district on April 1, 1994.
Carolyn Kolebaba, Reeve
Bob Miles, CAO
ramiles@northernsunrise.net

Opportunity No. 17
P.O. Box 60
Wabasca, AB T0G 2K0
Tel: 780-891-3778; *Fax:* 780-891-4283
general_inquiries@mdopportunity.ab.ca
www.mdopportunity.ab.ca
Municipal Type: Municipal District
Incorporated: Dec. 18, 1913 *Area:* 29,140.78 sq km
Population in 2011: 3,074
Next Election: Oct. 21, 2013 (3 year terms)
Note: Incorporated as a municipal district on Aug. 1, 1995.
Paul Sinclair, Reeve
Dennis M. Egyedy, MD, Chief Administrative Officer
cao@mdopportunity.ab.ca

Paintearth County No. 18
P.O. Box 509
Castor, AB T0C 0X0
Tel: 403-882-3211; *Fax:* 403-882-3560
glucas@countypaintearth.ca
www.countypaintearth.ca
Municipal Type: County
Incorporated: Dec. 8, 1913 *Area:* 3,287.24 sq km
County or District: Paintearth No. 18; *Population in 2011:* 2,029
Next Election: Oct. 21, 2013 (3 year terms)
Note: Incorporated as a county on Jan. 1, 1962.
George Glazier, Reeve
gglazier@countypaintearth.ca
Tarolyn Peach, CAO
tpeach@countypaintearth.ca

Parkland County
53109A Sec Hwy. 779
Parkland County, AB T7Z 1R1
Tel: 780-968-8888; *Fax:* 780-968-8413
inquiries@parklandcounty.com
www.parklandcounty.com
Other Information: Toll Free: 1-888-880-0858
Municipal Type: County
Incorporated: March 1, 1918 *Area:* 2,392.61 sq km
Population in 2011: 30,568
Next Election: Oct. 21, 2013 (3 year terms)
Note: Incorporated as a county on Jan. 1, 1969.
Pat Vincent, CAO
780-968-8411
pvincent@parklandcounty.com
Rodney Shaigec, Mayor
rshaigec@parklandcounty.com
Mark Cardinal, Manager, Agricultural Services
mcardinal@parklandcounty.com
Andy Haden, Manager, Planning & Development Services
ahaden@parklandcounty.com
Rob McGowan, Manager, Engineering Services
rmcgowan@parklandcounty.com
Daryl Phillips, Manager, Public Works
dphillips@parklandcounty.com
Ken Saulit, Manager, Protective Services
ksaulit@parklandcounty.com
Ken Van Buul, Manager, Recreation & Parks Services
kvanbuul@parklandcounty.com
Janette Szucs, Coordinator, Purchasing
jszucs@parklandcounty.com
Trent Tompkins, Coordinator, Solid Waste
ttompkins@parklandcounty.com
Kevin Bryant, Supervisor, Utilities & Waste Services
kbryant@parklandcounty.com
Brian Rimmer, Supervisor, Environmental Services
brimmer@parklandcounty.com
Grace Horsfield, Officer, Development
ghorsfield@parklandcounty.com

Peace No. 135
P.O. Box 34
Berwyn, AB T0H 0E0
Tel: 780-338-3845; *Fax:* 780-338-2222
mdpeace@wispernet.ca
www.mdpeace.com
Municipal Type: Municipal District
Incorporated: Dec. 11, 1916 *Area:* 851.92 sq km
Population in 2011: 1,344
Next Election: Oct. 21, 2013 (3 year terms)
Veronica Bliska, Reeve
Lyle McKen, CAO
780-338-3845

Pincher Creek No. 9
P.O. Box 279
Pincher Creek, AB T0K 1W0
Tel: 403-627-3130; *Fax:* 403-627-5070
info@mdpinchercreek.ab.ca
www.mdpinchercreek.ab.ca
Municipal Type: Municipal District
Incorporated: Jan. 1, 1944 *Area:* 3,482.26 sq km
Population in 2011: 3,158
Next Election: Oct. 21, 2013 (3 year terms)
Rodney Cyr, Reeve
bhammond@mdpinchercreek.ab.ca
Wendy Kay, CAO
wkay@mdpinchercreek.ab.ca

Ponoka County
4205 Hwy. 2A
Ponoka, AB T4J 1V9
Tel: 403-783-3333; *Fax:* 403-783-6965
ponokacounty@ponokacounty.com
www.ponokacounty.com
Municipal Type: County
Incorporated: Jan. 1, 1944 *Area:* 2,807.94 sq km
County or District: Ponoka No. 3; *Population in 2011:* 8,856
Next Election: Oct. 21, 2013 (3 year terms)
Note: Incorporated as a county on July 1, 1999.
Charlie Cutforth, CAO
charliecutforth@ponokacounty.com
Gordon Svenningsen, Reeve

Provost No. 52
P.O. Box 300
Provost, AB T0B 3S0
Tel: 780-753-2434; *Fax:* 780-753-6432
mdprovost@mdprovost.ca
www.mdprovost.ca
Municipal Type: Municipal District
Incorporated: Dec. 9, 1912 *Area:* 3,625.2 sq km
Population in 2011: 2,288
Next Election: Oct. 21, 2013 (3 year terms)
Allan Murray, Reeve
780-753-6531
Tyler Lawrason, Administrator
tlawrason@mdprovost.ca

Ranchland No. 66
P.O. Box 1060
Nanton, AB T0L 1R0
Tel: 403-646-3131; *Fax:* 403-646-3141
admin@ranchland66.com
www.mdranchland.ca
Municipal Type: Municipal District
Incorporated: Jan. 1, 1969 *Area:* 2,639.16 sq km
Population in 2011: 79
Next Election: Oct. 21, 2013 (3 year terms)
Note: Incorporated as a municipal district on Jan. 1, 1995.
Harry Streeter, Reeve
Gregory Brkich, CAO
cao@ranchland66.com

Red Deer County
Red Deer County Centre
38106 Range Rd. 275
Red Deer County, AB T4S 2L9
Tel: 403-350-2150; *Fax:* 403-346-9840
info@rdcounty.ca
http://rdcounty.ca
Municipal Type: County
Incorporated: Jan. 1, 1944 *Area:* 4,002.58 sq km
Population in 2011: 18,351
Next Election: Oct. 21, 2013 (3 year terms)
Note: Incorporated as a county on Jan. 1, 1963.
Curtis Herzberg, County Manager
cherzberg@reddeercounty.ab.ca
Jim Wood, Mayor
403-350-2152
Harry Harker, Director, Planning & Development
hharker@reddeercounty.ab.ca
Ric Henderson, Director, Community & Protective Services
rhenderson@reddeercounty.ab.ca
Frank Peck, Director, Operations Services
fpeck@reddeercounty.ab.ca
Cliff Fuller, Fire Chief
cfuller@reddeercounty.ab.ca
Don Bardonnex, Manager, Fire Services
dbardonnex@reddeercounty.ab.ca
Joe D'Onofrio, Manager, Land
jd'onofrio@reddeercounty.ab.ca
Linda Henrickson, Manager, Rural Planning
lhenrickson@reddeercounty.ab.ca
Johan van der Bank, Manager, Urban Planning
jvanderbank@reddeercounty.ab.ca

Marty Campbell, Coordinator, Engineering
mcampbell@reddeercounty.ab.ca
Jo-Ann Symington, Coordinator, Community Services
jsymington@reddeercounty.ab.ca
Andrew Treu, Coordinator, Environmental Services
atreu@reddeercounty.ab.ca
Donna Trottier, Coordinator, Conservation
Dawna Barnes, Specialist, Community Development
dbarnes@reddeercounty.ab.ca
Art Preachuk, Fieldman, Agricultural Services
apreachuk@reddeercounty.ab.ca

Rocky View County
911 - 32 Ave. NE
Calgary, AB T2E 6X6
Tel: 403-230-1401; *Fax:* 403-277-5977
comments@rockyview.ca
www.rockyview.ca
Municipal Type: Municipal District
Incorporated: Feb. 1, 1943 *Area:* 4,014.89 sq km
Population in 2011: 36,461
Next Election: Oct. 21, 2013 (3 year terms)
Robert Coon, CAO
rcoon@rockyview.ca
Lois Habberfield, Reeve
council@rockyview.ca
Brian Jobson, Director, Transportation Services
bjobson@gov.mdrockyview.ab.ca
Frank Misura, Manager, Development/Utility Services
Linda Ratzlaff, Coordinator, Policy Planning
403-520-8166
Tim Dietzler, Fieldman, Agriculture
403-520-1271

Saddle Hills County
P.O. Box 69
Spirit River, AB T0H 3G0
Tel: 780-864-3760; *Fax:* 780-864-3904
admin@saddlehills.ab.ca
www.saddlehills.ab.ca
Municipal Type: Municipal District
Incorporated: April 1, 1945 *Area:* 5,836.94 sq km
Population in 2011: 2,288
Next Election: Oct. 21, 2013 (3 year terms)
Note: Incorporated as a municipal district on Jan. 1, 1995.
Tim Stone, Reeve
council@saddlehills.ab.ca
Dianne Nellis, CAO
dnellis@saddlehills.ab.ca

St. Paul County No. 19
5015 - 49 Ave.
St Paul, AB T0A 3A4
Tel: 780-645-3301; *Fax:* 780-645-3104
countysp@county.stpaul.ab.ca
www.county.stpaul.ab.ca
Municipal Type: Municipal District
Incorporated: Jan. 30, 1942 *Area:* 3,297.74 sq km
Population in 2011: 5,831
Next Election: Oct. 21, 2013 (3 year terms)
Steve Upham, Reeve
Sheila Kitz, CAO
skitz@county.stpaul.ab.ca

Smoky Lake County
P.O. Box 310
Smoky Lake, AB T0A 3C0
Tel: 780-656-3730; *Fax:* 780-656-3768
county@smokylakecounty.ab.ca
www.smokylakecounty.ab.ca
Other Information: toll free: 888-656-3730
Municipal Type: Municipal District
Incorporated: May 3, 1922 *Area:* 3,412.81 sq km
Population in 2011: 3,910
Next Election: Oct. 21, 2013 (3 year terms)
Dareld Cholak, Reeve
dcholak@smokylakecounty.ab.ca
Cory Ollikka, CAO
collika@smokylakecounty.ab.ca

Smoky River No. 130
P.O. Box 210
Falher, AB T0H 1M0
Tel: 780-837-2221; *Fax:* 780-837-2453
rtherriault@mdsmokyriver.com
www.mdsmokyriver.com
Municipal Type: Municipal District
Incorporated: Dec. 18, 1913 *Area:* 2,842.82 sq km
Population in 2011: 2,126
Next Election: Oct. 21, 2013 (3 year terms)
Note: Incorporated as a municipal district on Jan. 1, 1952.
Robert Brochu, Reeve
Lucien G. Turcotte, CAO
lturcotte@mdsmokyriver.com

Spirit River No. 133
P.O. Box 389
Spirit River, AB T0H 3G0
Tel: 780-864-3500; *Fax:* 780-864-4303
mdsr133@mdspiritriver.ab.ca
www.mdspiritriver.ab.ca
Municipal Type: Municipal District
Incorporated: Dec. 18, 1913 *Area:* 684.14 sq km
Population in 2011: 713
Next Election: Oct. 21, 2013 (3 year terms)
Note: Incorporated as a municipal district on Dec. 11, 1916.
Stanley W. Bzowy, Reeve
Kelly Hudson, CAO
mdsr133@mdspiritriver.ab.ca

Starland County
P.O. Box 249
Morrin, AB T0J 2B0
Tel: 403-772-3793; *Fax:* 403-772-3807
info@starlandcounty.com
www.starlandcounty.com
Municipal Type: Municipal District
Incorporated: Dec. 9, 1912 *Area:* 2,557.7 sq km
Population in 2011: 2,057
Next Election: Oct. 21, 2013 (3 year terms)
J. Barrie Hoover, Reeve
bhoover@starlandcounty.com
Ross D. Rawlusyk, CAO
ross@starlandcounty.com

Stettler County No. 6
P.O. Box 1270
Stettler, AB T0C 2L0
Tel: 403-742-4441; *Fax:* 403-742-1277
info@stettlercounty.ca
www.stettler.net
Municipal Type: Municipal District
Incorporated: Dec. 9, 1912 *Area:* 4,008.72 sq km
Population in 2011: 5,089
Next Election: Oct. 21, 2013 (3 year terms)
Wayne Nixon, Reeve
Tim Fox, CAO
tfox@stettlercounty.ca

Strathcona County
2001 Sherwood Dr.
Sherwood Park, AB T8A 3W7
Tel: 780-464-8111; *Fax:* 780-464-8050
info@strathcona.ab.ca
www.strathcona.ab.ca
Municipal Type: Regional Municipality
Incorporated: Jan. 1, 1962 *Area:* 1,179.43 sq km
Population in 2011: 92,490
Next Election: Oct. 21, 2013 (3 year terms)
Note: Incorporated as a specialized municipality on Jan. 1, 1996.
Robyn W. Singleton, Q.C., Chief Commissioner
780-464-8100
singleton@strathcona.ab.ca
Linda Osinchuk, Mayor
Peter Vana, Associate Commissioner, Infrastructure & Planning Services
780-464-8188
vana@strathcona.ab.ca
Denise Exton, Associate Commissioner, Community Services
780-464-8291
exton@strathcona.ab.ca

Sturgeon County
9613 - 100 St.
Morinville, AB T8R 1L9
Tel: 780-939-4321; *Fax:* 780-939-3003
sturgeonmail@sturgeoncounty.ab.ca
www.sturgeoncounty.ab.ca
Other Information: Toll free: 1-866-939-9303
Municipal Type: Municipal District
Incorporated: Feb. 1, 1943 *Area:* 2,108.9 sq km
Population in 2011: 19,578
Next Election: Oct. 21, 2013 (3 year terms)
Case Van Herk, County Commissioner
780-939-8345
cvanherk@sturgeoncounty.ab.ca
Donald Rigney, B.Sc., MBA, Mayor
780-921-3041, Fax: 780-921-3041
drigney@sturgeoncounty.ab.ca
Ian McKay, General Manager, Infrastructure Services
780-939-8337
imckay@sturgeoncounty.ab.ca
Peter Tarnawsky, General Manager, Public Services
780-939-8344
ptarnawsky@sturgeoncounty.ab.ca
Bart Clark, Manager, Protective Services
780-939-0600
bclark@sturgeoncounty.ab.ca
Collin Steffes, Manager, Planning & Development
780-939-8275
csteffes@sturgeoncounty.ab.ca
Roy Lidgren, Manager, Transportation Services
780-939-8250
rlidgern@sturgeoncounty.ab.ca
Quentin Bochar, Manager, Agriculture Services
780-939-8325
qbochar@sturgeoncounty.ab.ca
Mike Hittinger, Coordinator, Municipal Conservation
780-939-8339
nwaci@sturgeoncounty.ab.ca

Taber
4900B - 50 St.
Taber, AB T1G 1T2
Tel: 403-223-3541; *Fax:* 403-223-1799
dkrizsan@mdtaber.ab.ca
www.mdtaber.ab.ca
Municipal Type: Municipal District
Incorporated: April 1, 1945 *Area:* 4,204.38 sq km
Population in 2011: 6,851
Next Election: Oct. 21, 2013 (3 year terms)
T. Brian Brewin, Reeve
Derrick Krizsan, Municipal Administrator

Thorhild County No. 7
P.O. Box 10
Thorhild, AB T0A 3J0
Tel: 780-398-3741; *Fax:* 780-398-3748
angela@thorhildcounty.com
www.thorhildcounty.com
Municipal Type: County
Incorporated: Jan. 1, 1955 *Area:* 1,998.38 sq km
County or District: Thorhild No. 7; *Population in 2011:* 3,417
Next Election: Oct. 21, 2013 (3 year terms)
Charles Newell, Reeve
cnewell@mcsnet.ca
Angela Bilski, County Manager
angela@thorhildcounty.com

Two Hills County No. 21
P.O. Box 490
Two Hills, AB T0B 4K0
Tel: 780-657-3358; *Fax:* 780-657-3504
rjorgensen@thcounty.ab.ca
www.thcounty.ab.ca
Municipal Type: County
Incorporated: Jan. 1, 1944 *Area:* 2,630.95 sq km
County or District: Two Hills No. 21; *Population in 2011:* 3,160
Next Election: Oct. 21, 2013 (3 year terms)
Note: Incorporated as a county on Jan. 1, 1963.
Allen Sayler, Reeve
asayler@thcounty.ab.ca
Robert Jorgensen, CAO
rjorgensen@thcounty.ab.ca

Vermilion River County
P.O. Box 69
4912 - 50 Ave.
Kitscoty, AB T0B 2P0
Tel: 780-846-2244; *Fax:* 780-846-2716
county24@telusplanet.net
www.vermilion-river.com
Municipal Type: Municipal District
Incorporated: Jan. 1, 1944 *Area:* 5,518.71 sq km
Population in 2011: 7,905
Next Election: Oct. 21, 2013 (3 year terms)
Note: Name changed from Vermilion River No. 24 County on Sept. 13, 2006.
Rhonda King, County Administrator
780-846-3303
rking@county24.com
Richard Van Ee, Reeve
780-853-2730

Vulcan County
P.O. Box 180
Vulcan, AB T0L 2B0
Tel: 403-485-2241; *Fax:* 403-485-2920
administration@vulcancounty.ab.ca
www.vulcancounty.ab.ca
Municipal Type: County
Incorporated: April 1, 1945 *Area:* 5,430.06 sq km
County or District: Vulcan County; *Population in 2011:* 3,875

Next Election: Oct. 21, 2013 (3 year terms)
Note: Incorporated as a county on Jan. 1, 1951.
David Schneider, Reeve
Leo Ludwig, County Administrator
cao@vulcancounty.ab.ca

Wainwright No. 61
717 - 14 Ave.
Wainwright, AB T9W 1B3
Tel: 780-842-4454; *Fax:* 780-842-2463
info@mdwainwright.ca
www.mdwainwright.ca
Municipal Type: Municipal District
Incorporated: Jan. 30, 1942 *Area:* 4,154.74 sq km
Population in 2011: 4,138
Next Election: Oct. 21, 2013 (3 year terms)
Bob Barss, Reeve
Kelly Buchinski, Municipal Administrator
admin@mdwainwright.ca

Warner County No. 5
P.O. Box 90
Warner, AB T0K 2L0
Tel: 403-642-3635; *Fax:* 403-642-3631
county5@countyofwarner5.ab.ca
www.countyofwarner5.ab.ca
Municipal Type: Municipal District
Incorporated: Dec. 9, 1912
Population in 2011: 3,841
Next Election: Oct. 21, 2013 (3 year terms)
Robert Jones, Reeve
div5_wa@countyofwarner5.ab.ca
Shawn Hathaway, CAO
administrator@countyofwarner5.ab.ca

Westlock County
10336 - 106 St.
Westlock, AB T7P 2G1
Tel: 780-349-3346; *Fax:* 780-349-2012
info@westlockcounty.com
www.westlockcounty.com
Municipal Type: Municipal District
Incorporated: Feb. 1, 1943 *Area:* 3,174.6 sq km
Population in 2011: 7,644
Next Election: Oct. 21, 2013 (3 year terms)
Charles Navratil, Reeve
780-349-2818
Edward LeBlanc, CAO
eleblanc@westlockcounty.com

Wetaskiwin County No. 10
P.O. Box 6960
Wetaskiwin, AB T9A 2G5
Tel: 780-352-3321; *Fax:* 780-352-3486
fcoutney@county.wetaskiwin.ab.ca
www.county.wetaskiwin.ab.ca
Other Information: Toll Free: 1-800-661-4125
Municipal Type: County
Incorporated: Dec. 13, 1915 *Area:* 3,130.9 sq km
County or District: Wetaskiwin No. 10; *Population in 2011:* 10,866
Next Election: Oct. 21, 2013 (3 year terms)
Note: Incorporated as a county on Jan. 1, 1958.
Frank Coutney, County Administrator
fcoutney@county.wetaskiwin.ab.ca
Garry Dearing, Reeve
Ken Carlson, Director, Disaster Services
780-361-6340
kcarlson@county.wetaskiwin.ab.ca
Dave Dextraze, Director, Public Works
780-361-6230
ddextraze@county.wetaskiwin.ab.ca
Steve Majek, Director, Agricultural Services
780-361-6226
smajek@county.wetaskiwin.ab.ca

Wheatland County
Hwy. 1, RR#1
Strathmore, AB T1P 1J6
Tel: 403-934-3321; *Fax:* 403-934-4889
admin@wheatlandcounty.ca
www.wheatlandcounty.ca
Municipal Type: County
Incorporated: April 1, 1945 *Area:* 4,550.92 sq km
Population in 2011: 8,285
Next Election: Oct. 21, 2013 (3 year terms)
Note: Incorporated as a county on Jan. 1, 1961.
Ben Armstrong, Reeve
ben.armstrong@wheatlandcounty.ca
Jennifer Deak, County Manager
jennifer.deak@wheatlandcounty.ca

Willow Creek No. 26
P.O. Box 550
Claresholm, AB T0L 0T0
Tel: 403-625-3351; *Fax:* 403-625-3886
md26@mdwillowcreek.com
www.mdwillowcreek.com
Other Information: Toll free: 1-888-337-3351
Municipal Type: Municipal District
Incorporated: Jan. 1, 1944 *Area:* 4,560.22 sq km
Population in 2011: 5,107
Next Election: Oct. 21, 2013 (3 year terms)
Henry Van Hierden, Reeve
403-553-2015
Cynthia Vizzutti, Administrator

Wood Buffalo
9909 Franklin Ave.
Fort McMurray, AB T9H 2K4
Tel: 780-743-7000; *Fax:* 780-743-7028
communications@woodbuffalo.ab.ca
www.woodbuffalo.ab.ca
Other Information: Toll Free: 1-800-973-9663
Municipal Type: Regional Municipality
Incorporated: April 1, 1995 *Area:* 63,342.89 sq km
Population in 2011: 65,565
Next Election: Oct. 21, 2013 (3 year terms)
Kelly Kloss, Acting CAO
780-743-7023
kelly.kloss@woodbuffalo.ab.ca
Melissa Blake, Mayor
Wes Holodniuk, Manager, Operations & Maintenance
780-743-7931, Fax: 780-799-5909
wes.holodniuk@woodbuffalo.ab.ca
Salem Abushawashi, Superintendent, Fort Chipewyan
780-697-3600
salem.abushawashi@woodbuffalo.ab.ca
Guy Jette, Acting Superintendent, Operations & Facilities Maintenance
780-799-7486
guy.jette@woodbuffalo.ab.ca
Darcy Elder, Superintendent, Infrastructure
780-799-7475
darcy.elder@woodbuffalo.ab.ca
Michel Savard, Superintendent, Environment
780-799-7490
michel.savard@woodbuffalo.ab.ca
Dwayne Harvie, Project Engineer
780-743-7855
dwayne.harvie@woodbuffalo.ab.ca

Woodlands County
P.O. Box 60
Whitecourt, AB T7S 1N3
Tel: 780-778-8400; *Fax:* 780-778-8402
admin@woodlands.ab.ca
www.woodlands.ab.ca
Other Information: Toll free: 1-888-870-6315
Municipal Type: Municipal District
Incorporated: Jan. 1, 1969 *Area:* 7,668.11 sq km
Population in 2011: 4,306
Next Election: Oct. 21, 2013 (3 year terms)
Note: Incorporated as a municipal district on Jan. 1, 1994.
Jim Rennie, Reeve
jim.rennie@woodlands.ab.ca
Luc Mercier, CAO
luc.mercier@woodlands.ab.ca

Yellowhead County
2716 - 1st Ave.
Edson, AB T7E 1N9
Tel: 780-723-4800; *Fax:* 780-723-5066
info@yellowheadcounty.ab.ca
www.yellowheadcounty.ab.ca
Other Information: Toll Free Phone: 1-800-665-6030
Municipal Type: Municipal District
Incorporated: Jan. 1, 1994 *Area:* 22,303.82 sq km
Population in 2011: 10,469
Next Election: Oct. 21, 2013 (3 year terms)
Jack Ramme, CAO
jack.ramme@yellowheadcounty.ab.ca
Gerald Soroka, Mayor
gsoroka@yellowheadcounty.ab.ca

Major Municipalities in Alberta

Airdrie
400 Main St. SE
Airdrie, AB T4B 3C3
Tel: 403-948-8800; *Fax:* 403-948-6567
information.systems@airdrie.ca
www.airdrie.ca
Municipal Type: City
Incorporated: Sept. 10, 1909 *Area:* 33.10 sq km
Population in 2011: 42,564
Provincial Electoral District(s): Airdrie-Chestermere
Federal Electoral District(s): Wild Rose
Next Election: Oct. 21, 2013 (3 year terms)
Note: Incorporated as a city on Jan. 1, 1985.
Peter Brown, Mayor
mayor@airdrie.ca
George Keene, City Manager
george.keen@airdrie.ca
Mark Locking, Director, Engineering & Public Works
Jeff Greene, City Planner & Team Leader
403-948-8848
planning.development@airdrie.ca
Dave Rimes, Leader, Parks
403-948-8402
parks@airdrie.ca
Mary Grace Curtis, Coordinator, Recycling & Composting
780-948-0246
environmental.services@airdrie.ca
Darryl Wolski, Coordinator, Solid Waste
403-948-0246
pubwrks@airdrie.ca

Beaumont
5600 - 49 St.
Beaumont, AB T4X 1A1
Tel: 780-929-8782; *Fax:* 780-929-8729
admin@town.beaumont.ab.ca
www.town.beaumont.ab.ca
Municipal Type: City
Incorporated: Jan. 1, 1973 *Area:* 10.5 sq km
Population in 2011: 13,284
Provincial Electoral District(s): Leduc-Beaumont-Devon
Federal Electoral District(s): Edmonton-Mill Woods-Beaumont
Next Election: Oct. 21, 2013 (3 year terms)
Note: Incorporated as a town on Jan 1, 1980.
Marc Landry, General Manager
marc.landry@town.beaumont.ab.ca
Camille Bérubé, Mayor

Brooks
P.O. Box 880
201 - 1 Ave. West
Brooks, AB T1R 0Z6
Tel: 403-362-3333; *Fax:* 403-362-4787
admin@brooks.ca
www.brooks.ca
Municipal Type: City
Incorporated: July 14, 1910 *Area:* 17.7 sq km
Population in 2011: 13,676
Provincial Electoral District(s): Strathmore-Brooks
Federal Electoral District(s): Medicine Hat
Next Election: Oct. 21, 2013 (3 year terms)
Note: Incorporated as a city on Sept. 1, 2005.
Kevin Stephenson, City Manager
kstephenson@brooks.ca
Martin Shields, Mayor
mshields@brooks.ca
Neil Hollands, Director, Engineering & Property Services
nhollands@brooks.ca
Kevin Swanson, Director, Protective Services
403-362-2331
Terry Walsh, Director, Parks & Recreation
twalsh@brooks.ca
Maurice Landry, Manager, Development Services
mlandry@brooks.ca
Bill Prentice, Manager, Public Works
403-362-3146
bprentice@brooks.ca
Gord Shaw, Manager, Planning Services
gshaw@brooks.ca

Calgary
P.O. Box 2100 M
800 Macleod Trail SE
Calgary, AB T2P 2M5
Tel: 403-268-2489; *Fax:* 403-538-6111
www.calgary.ca
Other Information: TTY: 403-268-4889

Municipal Type: City
Incorporated: Nov. 7, 1884 *Area:* 726.5 sq km
Population in 2011: 1,096,833
Provincial Electoral District(s): Cal.-Bow; Cal.-Buffalo; Cal.-Cross; Cal.-Currie; Cal.-Egmont; Cal.-East; Cal.-Elbow; Cal.-Fish Creek; Cal.-Foothills; Cal.-Fort; Cal.-Glenmore; Cal.-Hays; Cal.-Lougheed; Cal.-McCall; Cal.-Mackay; Cal.-Montrose; Cal.-Mountain View; Cal.-North Hill; Cal.-Nose Hill; Cal.-Shaw; Cal.-Varsity; Cal.-West
Federal Electoral District(s): Calgary Centre; Calgary Centre-North; Calgary East; Calgary Northeast; Calgary-Nose Hill; Calgary Southeast; Calgary Southwest; Calgary West; Macleod; Wild Rose
Next Election: Oct. 21, 2013 (3 year terms)
Note: Incorporated as a city on Jan. 1, 1894.
Sue Gray, City Clerk
403-268-5861, Fax: 403-268-2362
cityclerk@calgary.ca
Naheed K. Nenshi, Mayor
403-268-5622, Fax: 403-268-8130
themayor@calgary.ca
Dale Hodges, Alderman, Ward(s): 1
403-268-2445, Fax: 403-268-8091
Frederick Gordon Lowe, Alderman, Ward(s): 2
403-268-2430, Fax: 403-268-3823
Jim Stevenson, Alderman, Ward(s): 3
403-268-2430, Fax: 403-268-8091
Gael MacLeod, Alderman, Ward(s): 4
403-268-2430, Fax: 403-268-8091
Ray Jones, Alderman, Ward(s): 5
403-268-2430, Fax: 403-268-3823
Richard Pootmans, Alderman, Ward(s): 6
403-268-2430, Fax: 403-268-8091
Druh Farrell, Alderman, Ward(s): 7
403-268-2475, Fax: 403-268-3823
John Mar, Alderman, Ward(s): 8
403-268-2430, Fax: 403-268-3823
Gian-Carlo Carra, Alderman, Ward(s): 9
403-268-2430, Fax: 403-268-8091
Andre Chabot, Alderman, Ward(s): 10
403-268-2430, Fax: 403-268-3823
Brian Pincott, Alderman, Ward(s): 11
403-268-2430, Fax: 403-268-8091
Shane A. Keating, Alderman, Ward(s): 12
403-268-2430, Fax: 403-268-4673
Diane Colley-Urquhart, Alderman, Ward(s): 13
403-268-2430, Fax: 403-268-8091
Peter Demong, Alderman, Ward(s): 14
403-268-1653, Fax: 403-268-3823
George McLauchlan, Director, Human Resources
403-268-2201, Fax: 403-268-4680
Stuart Dalgleish, Director & City Assessor
403-268-4609, Fax: 403-268-8278
J. Bernie Trahan, Director, Fleet Services
403-268-1122, Fax: 403-266-2496
btrahan@calgary.ca
Anne Charlton, Director, Parks
403-268-3888
Mac Logan, General Manager, Transportation
Mary Axworthy, Director, Land Use Planning & Policy
David L. Day, Director, Environmental & Safety Management
403-268-3668
Dave Griffiths, Director, Waste & Recycling Services
Allyn Humber, Director, Water Services
403-268-2702
waterworks@calgary.ca
Ian Norris, Director, Transportation Infrastructure
403-974-4876
Wolf Keller, Director, Water Resources
403-268-6752
Jack Beaton, Chief of Police
403-206-5900
W. Bruce Burrell, Fire Chief
403-287-4255, Fax: 403-243-1490
Tom Sampson, Deputy Chief, Calgary Emergency Management Agency
tom.sampson@calgary.ca
Owen Tobert, P.Eng., City Manager
owens.tobert@calgary.ca
Rolin Stanley, General Manager, Planning Development & Assessment
403-268-2601
Rob Pritchard, General Manager, Utilities & Environmental Protection
403-268-2042, Fax: 403-537-3023
Erika Hargesheimer, General Manager, Community & Protective Services
403-268-5636
Sharon E. Young, Manager, Environmental & Safety Management
403-268-4699

Bruce Cullen, Manager, Infrastructure & Information Services

Camrose

City Hall
5204 - 50 Ave.
Camrose, AB T4V 0S8
Tel: 780-672-4426; *Fax:* 780-672-2469
admin@camrose.ca
www.camrose.ca
Municipal Type: City
Incorporated: May 4, 1905 *Area:* 31.14 sq km
Population in 2011: 17,286
Provincial Electoral District(s): Wetaskiwin-Camrose
Federal Electoral District(s): Crowfoot
Next Election: Oct. 21, 2013 (3 year terms)
Note: Incorporated as a city on Jan. 1, 1955.
Damian Herle, Manager, Corporate & Protective Services
Marshall Chalmers, Mayor
admin@camrose.ca
Diane Urkow, Manager, Financial Services
Brian Hamblin, P.Eng., City Manager
bhamblin@camrose.ca
Jeremy Enarson, Acting City Engineer, Engineering Services
Chris Clarkson, Director, Parks
780-672-9195
Jim Kupka, Director, Public Works
780-672-5513
Darrell Kambeitz, Police Chief
Peter Krich, Fire Chief/Deputy Director, Emergency Management
Brenda Hisey, Director, Planning & Development
780-672-4428
Doug Delmage, Chief Building Inspector
780-672-4428

Canmore

902 - 7 Ave.
Canmore, AB T1W 3K1
Tel: 403-678-1500; *Fax:* 403-678-1524
info@canmore.ca
www.canmore.ca
Municipal Type: City
Incorporated: Jan. 1, 1965 *Area:* 68.9 sq km
Population in 2011: 12,288
Provincial Electoral District(s): Banff-Cochrane
Federal Electoral District(s): Wild Rose
Next Election: Oct. 21, 2013 (3 year terms)
Note: Incorporated as a town on June 1, 1966.
Don Kochan, CAO
donkochan@canmore.ca
Ron Casey, Mayor
mayor@canmore.ca
Don Kochan, Director, Environmental Services
donkochan@canmore.ca
Doug Townsend, Manager, Facilities
403-678-1586
Kevin Van Vliet, Manager, Engineering
403-678-1545, Fax: 403-678-1534

Chestermere

105 Marina Rd.
Chestermere, AB T1X 1V7
Tel: 403-207-7050; *Fax:* 403-569-0512
town@chestermere.ca
www.chestermere.ca
Municipal Type: City
Incorporated: April 1, 1977 *Area:* 8.91 sq km
Population in 2011: 14,824
Provincial Electoral District(s): Airdrie-Chestermere
Federal Electoral District(s): Crowfoot
Next Election: Oct. 21, 2013 (3 year terms)
Note: Incorporated as a town on March 1, 1993.
Terry Hurlbut, CAO
403-207-7070
thurlbut@chestermere.ca
Patricia Matthews, Mayor
403-207-7073
pmatthews@chestermere.ca
Patrick Bergen, Councillor
Heather Davies, Councillor
Stewart Hutchinson, Councillor
Kelsey Johnson, Councillor
Terry Leighton, Councillor
Christopher Steeves, Councillor

Cochrane

P.O. Box 10
101 Ranche House Rd.
Cochrane, AB T4C 2K8
Tel: 403-851-2505; *Fax:* 403-851-2581
cochrane@cochrane.ca
www.cochrane.ca
Municipal Type: City
Incorporated: June 17, 1903 *Area:* 30.03 sq km
Population in 2011: 17,580
Provincial Electoral District(s): Banff-Cochrane
Federal Electoral District(s): Wild Rose
Next Election: Oct. 21, 2013 (3 year terms)
Note: Incorporated as a town on Feb. 15, 1971.
Julian deCocq, Clerk
julian.decocq@cochrane.ca
Truper McBride, Mayor
truper.mcbride@cochrane.ca
Jim Anderson, Director, Operational Services
403-851-2560
jim.anderson@cochrane.ca
Lori Leipnitz, Director, Corporate Services
403-851-2510
lori.leipnitz@cochrane.ca
Ian Smith, Director, Community & Protective Services
403-851-2530
ian.smith@cochrane.ca
Frank Wesseling, Director, Planning & Engineering
403-851-2570
frank.wesseling@cochrane.ca
Elise Harnick, Engineer, Subdivision & Development
403-851-2575
elise.harnick@cochrane.ca

Cold Lake

5513 - 48 Ave.
Cold Lake, AB T9M 1A1
Tel: 780-594-4494; *Fax:* 780-594-3480
city@coldlake.com
www.coldlake.com
Municipal Type: City
Incorporated: Dec. 31, 1953 *Area:* 59.3 sq km
Population in 2011: 13,839
Provincial Electoral District(s): Bonnyville-Cold Lake
Federal Electoral District(s): Westlock-St. Paul
Next Election: Oct. 21, 2013 (3 year terms)
Note: Incorporated as a city on Oct. 1, 2000.
Gordon Frank, CAO
gfrank@coldlake.com
Craig Copeland, Mayor
Allan Weiss, Chief, Fire
780-594-4494
Carry Grant, Manager, Operations
780-594-3776
cgrant@coldlake.com
George McIntosh, Foreman, Utilities
780-639-3604
wtp@coldlake.com
John McLean, Foreman, Parks & Facilities
780-594-3776
parks@coldlake.com
Kevin Nagoya, Director, Public Works & Infrastructure

Edmonton

City Hall
1 Sir Winston Churchill Sq., 3rd Fl.
Edmonton, AB T5J 2R7
Fax: 780-496-8210
311@edmonton.ca
www.edmonton.ca
Other Information: Telephone: 311 in Edmonton; or 780-442-5311
Municipal Type: City
Incorporated: Jan. 9, 1892 *Area:* 684.37 sq km
Population in 2011: 812,201
Provincial Electoral District(s): Ed.-Beverly-Clareview; Ed.-Calder; Ed.-Castle Downs; Ed.-Centre; Ed.-Decore; Ed.-Ellerslie; Ed.-Glenora; Ed.-Gold Bar; Ed.-Highlands-Norwood; Ed.-Manning; Ed.-McClung; Ed.-Meadowlark; Ed.-Mill Creek; Ed.-Mill Woods; Ed.-Riverview; Ed.-Rutherford; Ed.-Strathcona; Ed.-Whitemud
Federal Electoral District(s): Edmonton Centre; Edmonton East; Edmonton-Leduc; Edmonton-Mill Woods-Beaumont; Edmonton-Sherwood Park; Edmonton-Spruce Grove; Edmonton-St. Albert; Edmonton-Strathcona
Next Election: Oct. 21, 2013 (3 year terms)
Note: Incorporated as a city on Oct. 08, 1904.
David Edey, General Manager, Corporate Services
780-496-7201, Fax: 780-496-8854
david.edey@edmonton.ca
Stephen Mandel, Mayor
780-496-8100, Fax: 780-496-8292
Linda Sloan, Councillor, Ward(s): 1
780-496-8122, Fax: 780-496-8113
linda.sloan@edmonton.ca
Kim Krushell, Councillor, Ward(s): 2
780-496-8128, Fax: 780-496-8113
kim.krushell@edmonton.ca

Dave Loken, Councillor, Ward(s): 3
dave.loken@edmonton.ca
Ed Gibbons, Councillor, Ward(s): 4
ed.gibbons@edmonton.ca
Karen Leibovici, Councillor, Ward(s): 5
780-496-8120, Fax: 780-496-8113
karen.leibovici@edmonton.ca
Jane Batty, Councillor, Ward(s): 6, Fax: 780-496-8113
jane.batty@edmonton.ca
Tony Caterina, Councillor, Ward(s): 7
780-496-8333, Fax: 780-496-8113
tony.caterina@edmonton.ca
Ben Henderson, Councillor, Ward(s): 8
780-496-8146, Fax: 780-496-8113
ben.henderson@edmonton.ca
Bryan Anderson, Councillor, Ward(s): 9
780-496-8130, Fax: 780-496-8113
bryan.anderson@edmonton.ca
Don Iveson, Councillor, Ward(s): 10
780-496-8132, Fax: 780-496-8113
don.iveson@edmonton.ca
Kerry Diotte, Councillor, Ward(s): 11, Fax: 780-496-8113
kerry.diotte@edmonton.ca
Amarjeet Sohi, Councillor, Ward(s): 12
780-496-8148, Fax: 780-496-8113
amarjeet.sohi@edmonton.ca
Simon Farbrother, City Manager
780-496-8231, Fax: 780-496-8220
simon.farbrother@edmonton.ca
David Wiun, City Auditor
780-496-8315, Fax: 780-496-8062
david.wiun@edmonton.ca
Mike Boyd, Police Chief
780-421-3333
Dave Galea, Director, Office of Emergency Preparedness
780-944-6420, Fax: 780-496-3062
david.galea@edmonton.ca
Doug Costigan, Director, Asset Management & Public Works, Parks Branch
780-496-4956, Fax: 780-496-4978
doug.costigan@edmonton.ca
John Hodgson, Manager, Drainage Services
780-496-5658, Fax: 780-496-3629
Gerald W. Goodall, Consultant, Corporate Services, Materials Management Branch
780-496-3729, Fax: 780-496-5015
gerry.goodall@edmonton.ca
Audra Jones, Director, Transportation Planning
780-496-1790, Fax: 780-496-4287
Gary Klassen, General Manager, Planning & Development
780-496-6050, Fax: 780-496-6916
gary.klassen@edmonton.ca
Bob Boutilier, General Manager, Transportation
780-496-2808, Fax: 780-496-2803
transportation@edmonton.ca
Linda Cochrane, General Manager, Community Services
780-496-5804, Fax: 780-577-3525
linda.cochrane@edmonton.ca
Joyce Tustian, General Manager, Deputy City Manager's Office
780-442-6356, Fax: 780-496-8220
joyce.tustian@edmonton.ca
Mary Pat Barry, Manager, Deputy City Manager's Office, Communications Branch
780-496-8191, Fax: 780-496-4877
marypat.barry@edmonton.ca
Peter Muller, EMT-P, ABCP, Emergency Management Officer (Planning), Office of Emergency Preparedness
780-496-1530, Fax: 780-496-3062
peter.muller@edmonton.ca
Grant Pearsell, Director, Asset Management & Public Works, Parks Branch
780-496-6080, Fax: 780-496-5636
grant.pearsell@edmonton.ca
Garth Clyburn, Planner II, Planning & Development, Planning & Policy Branch
780-496-6209, Fax: 780-496-6299
garth.clyburn@edmonton.ca
Roy Neehall, Manager, Waste Management
780-496-5405, Fax: 780-496-5657

Fort Saskatchewan

10005 - 102 St.
Fort Saskatchewan, AB T8L 2C5
Tel: 780-992-6200; *Fax:* 780-998-4774
lrosen@fortsask.ca
www.fortsask.ca
Municipal Type: City
Incorporated: March 1, 1899 *Area:* 48.12 sq km
Population in 2011: 19,051
Provincial Electoral District(s): Fort Saskatchewan-Vegreville
Federal Electoral District(s): Edmonton-Sherwood Park
Next Election: Oct. 21, 2013 (3 year terms)
Note: Incorporated as a city on July 1, 1985.
Lorna Rosen, City Manager
Gale Katchur, Mayor
John Rop, Treasurer
Scott Mack, Director, Planning
780-992-6573
smack@fortsask.ca
Todd Burge, Manager, Corporate Services
780-992-6255
tburge@fortsask.ca
Richard Hobson, Manager, Community & Protective Services
780-992-6205, Fax: 780-992-0192
rhobson@fortsask.ca
Dave Worman, Manager, Planning & Public Works
780-992-6207
dworman@fortsask.ca
Ken Lura, Superintendent, Public Works
780-992-6247
klura@fortsask.ca
Gale Katchur, Contact, Environmental Awareness Committee
gkatchur@fortsask.ca

Grande Prairie

P.O. Box 4000
10205 - 98 St.
Grande Prairie, AB T8V 6V3
Tel: 780-538-0300; *Fax:* 780-538-0746
www.cityofgp.com
Municipal Type: City
Incorporated: April 30, 1914 *Area:* 61.08 sq km
Population in 2011: 55,032
Provincial Electoral District(s): Grande Prairie-Smoky; Grande Prairie-Wapiti
Federal Electoral District(s): Peace River
Next Election: Oct. 21, 2013 (3 year terms)
Note: Incorporated as a city on Jan. 1, 1958.
Bill Given, Mayor
bgiven@cityofgp.com
Greg Scerbak, City Manager
780-538-0312, Fax: 780-814-7560
gscerbak@cityofgp.com
Janette Ferguson, City Clerk
780-538-0314, Fax: 780-539-1056
jferguson@cityofgp.com
Frank Daskewech, Director, Public Works
780-538-0350, Fax: 780-538-4667
fdaskewech@cityofgp.com
Ken Anderson, Director, Financial Services
780-538-0302, Fax: 780-539-1056
kanderson@cityofgp.com
Josy Burrough, Manager, Parks
780-538-0476, Fax: 780-532-7588
jburrough@cityofgp.com
Michael MacIntyre, Planning Manager, Development Services
780-538-0440, Fax: 780-538-0746
mmacintyre@cityofgp.com
Valerie Norris-Kirk, Development Coordinator, Development Services
780-513-5236, Fax: 780-538-0746
vnorrisk@cityofgp.com
Uli Wolf, Solid Waste Services Supervisor, Aquatera Utilities Inc.
780-538-0360, Fax: 780-830-7060
uwolf@aquatera.ca
Amy Horne, Recycling Coordinator, Aquatera Utilities Inc.
780-538-0452, Fax: 780-830-7060
ahorne@aquatera.ca
Mark Simpson, Operations Coordinator, Aquatera Utilities Inc.
780-538-0442, Fax: 780-830-7430
msimpson@aquatera.ca
Dan Lemieux, Sr. Deputy Fire Chief
780-538-0398, Fax: 780-538-0395
dlemieux@cityofgp.com

High River

309B MacLeod Trail SW
High River, AB T1V 1Z5
Tel: 403-652-2110; *Fax:* 403-652-2396
info@highriver.ca
www.highriver.ca
Municipal Type: City
Incorporated: Dec. 5, 1901 *Area:* 14.27 sq km
Population in 2011: 12,920
Provincial Electoral District(s): Highwood
Federal Electoral District(s): Macleod
Next Election: Oct. 21, 2013 (3 year terms)
Note: Incorporated as a town on Feb. 12, 1906.
Harry Harker, Town Manager
Emile Blokland, Mayor

Lacombe

5432 - 56 Ave.
Lacombe, AB T4L 1E9
Tel: 403-782-6666; *Fax:* 403-782-5655
webmaster@lacombe.ca
www.lacombe.ca
Municipal Type: City
Incorporated: July 28, 1896 *Area:* 18.24 sq km
Population in 2011: 11,707
Provincial Electoral District(s): Lacombe-Ponoka
Federal Electoral District(s): Wetaskiwin
Next Election: Oct. 21, 2013 (3 year terms)
Note: Incorporated as a town on May 5, 1902.
Ken Kendall, CAO
kkendall@town.lacombe.ab.ca
Steve Christie, Mayor

Leduc

1 Alexandra Park
Leduc, AB T9E 4C4
Tel: 780-980-7177; *Fax:* 780-980-7127
info@leduc.ca
www.leduc.ca
Municipal Type: City
Incorporated: Dec. 15, 1899 *Area:* 36.97 sq km
Population in 2011: 24,279
Provincial Electoral District(s): Leduc-Beaumont-Devon
Federal Electoral District(s): Edmonton-Leduc
Next Election: Oct. 21, 2013 (3 year terms)
Note: Incorporated as a city on Sept. 01, 1983.
Laura Knoblock, City Clerk
lknoblock@leduc.ca
Greg Krischke, Mayor
mayor@leduc.ca
Linda Kyluik, Treasurer
Paul Benedetto, City Manager
pbenedetto@leduc.ca
Kevin Cole, Director, Public Services
Doug Parrish, Director, Planning & Development
780-980-7124
dparrish@leduc.ca
Rick Sereda, Fire Chief & Director, Protective Services
Allan Yamashita, City Engineer & General Manager, Operations

Lethbridge

City Hall
910 - 4 Ave. South
Lethbridge, AB T1J 0P6
Tel: 403-329-7355; *Fax:* 403-320-7575
info@lethbridge.ca
www.lethbridge.ca
Municipal Type: City
Incorporated: Nov. 29, 1890 *Area:* 121.97 sq km
Population in 2011: 83,417
Provincial Electoral District(s): Lethbridge-East; Lethbridge-West
Federal Electoral District(s): Lethbridge
Next Election: Oct. 21, 2013 (3 year terms)
Note: Incorporated as a city on May 9, 1906.
Dianne Nemeth, City Clerk
403-320-3821, Fax: 403-320-7575
dnemeth@lethbridge.ca
Rajko Dodic, Mayor
403-320-3823, Fax: 403-320-7575
mayor@lethbridge.ca
Bob Babki, Aldermen, Fax: 403-320-7575
Jeff Carlson, Aldermen
403-360-7550, Fax: 403-320-7575
aldermancarlson@gmail.com
Faron Ellis, Aldermen, Fax: 403-320-7575
Liz Iwaskiw, Aldermen, Fax: 403-320-7575
Joe Mauro, Aldermen, Fax: 403-320-7575
Bridget Mearns, Aldermen, Fax: 403-320-7575
Ryan Parker, Aldermen
403-380-4848, Fax: 403-320-7575
aldermanryanparker@gmail.com
Tom Wickersham, Aldermen
403-381-1521, Fax: 403-381-1571
thwicker@gmail.com
Garth Sherwin, B.Comm., CA, City Manager
gsherwin@lethbridge.ca
Douglas Hudson, Q.C., City Solicitor
dhudson@lethbridge.ca
Brian Cornforth, Fire Chief
403-320-3800, Fax: 403-327-3503
astrandlund@lethbridge.ca
Tom McKenzie, Police Chief
403-327-2210, Fax: 403-328-6999
Byron Buzunis, M.Eng., PMP, P.Eng., Urban Construction Manager
403-320-3975

Kathy Hopkins, Director, Community Services
403-320-3015, Fax: 403-380-2512
khopkins@lethbridge.ca
Warren Andrews, Manager, Public Operations
wandrews@lethbridge.ca
Kevin Viergutz, Manager, Transportation Operations
kviergutz@lethbridge.ab.ca
Bary Beck, Director, Corporate Initiatives
Jody Meli, Manager, Corporate & Community Relations
jmeli@lethbridge.ca
John King, Manager, Transit
403-320-3884, Fax: 403-380-3876
jking@lethbridge.ca
Craig Milley, Manager, Purchasing
403-320-3961
cmilley@lethbridge.ca
Kevin Theodore, Manager, Waste & Recycling
403-320-3088
ktheodore@lethbridge.ab.ca
Don Bulpitt, Manager, Water & Wastewater Operations
dbulpitt@lethbridge.ca
Kevin Jensen, Coordinator, Parks
403-330-5108
kjensen@lethbridge.ab.ca
George Kuhl, Senior Planner, Development Services
403-327-3926, Fax: 403-327-6571
gkuhl@lethbridge.ca

Lloydminster
City Hall
4420 - 50 Ave.
Lloydminster, AB T9V 0W2
Tel: 780-875-6184; *Fax:* 780-871-8345
jkeeley@lloydminster.ca
www.lloydminster.ca
Municipal Type: City
Incorporated: Nov. 25, 1903 *Area:* 24.19 sq km
Population in 2011: 18,032
Provincial Electoral District(s): Vermilion-Lloydminster
Federal Electoral District(s): Vegreville-Wainwright
Next Election: Oct. 21, 2013 (3 year terms)
Note: Population figure represents both the Alberta & Saskatchewan populations. Incorporated as a city on Jan. 1, 1958.
Jeff Mulligan, Mayor
mayor@lloydminster.ca
Beth Kembel, City Clerk
780-871-8328
bkembel@lloydminster.ca
Glenn Carroll, City Manager
780-871-8326
gcarroll@lloydminster.ca
Diane Beecroft, Treasurer
780-875-6184
dbeecroft@lloydminster.ca
Adam Homes, Deputy CAO, Infrastructure Services
780-875-8332
ahomes@lloydminster.ca
Ken Coleman, Deputy CAO, Community Services
780-875-4529
kcoleman@lloydminster.ca
Don Newlin, Deputy CAO, Finance
780-871-8330
dnewlin@lloydminster.ca
Brent Stasiuk, Deputy CAO, Protective Services
780-874-9054
bstasiuk@lloydminster.ca

Medicine Hat
City Hall
580 - 1 St. SE
Medicine Hat, AB T1A 8E6
Tel: 403-529-8115; *Fax:* 403-529-8182
clerk@medicinehat.ca
www.medicinehat.ca
Municipal Type: City
Incorporated: May 31, 1894 *Area:* 112.01 sq km
Population in 2011: 60,005
Provincial Electoral District(s): Cypress-Medicine Hat; Medicine Hat
Federal Electoral District(s): Medicine Hat
Next Election: Oct. 21, 2013 (3 year terms)
Note: Incorporated as a city on May 9, 1906.
Dave Leflar, City Clerk
403-529-8234, Fax: 403-529-8182
davlef@medicinehat.ca
Normand Boucher, Mayor
403-529-8181, Fax: 403-529-8182
mayor@medicinehat.ca; norbou@medicinehat.ca
Ted Clugston, Aldermen
403-526-8760
tedclu@medicinehat.ca
Wayne Craven, Aldermen, Fax: 403-529-8182
waycra@medicinehat.ca
Robert C. Dumanowski, Aldermen
John Hamill, Aldermen
403-526-7196, Fax: 403-529-8282
johham@medicinehat.ca
Graham Kelly, Aldermen
403-527-1891, Fax: 403-528-2453
gldarops@shaw.ca
Les Pearson, Aldermen
lespea@medicinehat.ca
Jeremy Thompson, Aldermen
403-504-5647, Fax: 403-526-1422
jertho@medicinehat.ca
Phil Turnbull, Aldermen
Gerry Labas, COO
403-529-8222
gerlab@medicinehat.ca
John Hughes, City Solicitor
403-529-8350
johhug@medicinehat.ca
Andy McGrogan, Police Chief
403-529-8410, Fax: 403-529-8444
Ron Robinson, Fire Chief
403-502-8006, Fax: 403-526-1352
Albert Bizio, Commissioner, Public Services
403-529-8229
albbiz@medicinehat.ca
Don Knutson, Acting Commissioner, Corporate Services
403-529-8231
onknu@medicinehat.ca
John Komanchuk, Commissioner, Development & Infrastructure
403-529-8354
johjo@medicinehat.ca
Dwight Brown, General Manager, Planning, Building & Development Services
Dale Descoteau, General Manager, Information & Computer Services
403-529-8108
daldes@medicinehat.ca
John Fedoruk, General Manager, Environmental Utilities
403-529-8176, Fax: 403-528-4955
eu@medicinehat.ca
Tony Klauwers, General Manager, Municipal Works
Grant MacKay, General Manager, Human Resources
403-529-8239
gramac@medicinehat.ca
Dave Panabaker, General Manager, Gas Utility
403-529-8288
davepan@medicinehat.ca
Ron Webb, General Manager, Community Development
403-529-8310
ronweb@medicinehat.ca
Les Wickenheiser, General Manager, Corporate Asset Management
403-529-8327
leswic@medicinehat.ca
Kendall Woodacre, General Manager, Electric Utility
403-502-8081
kenwoo@medicinehat.ca
R. Vizbar, General Manager, Parks & Outdoor Recreation
403-529-8312, Fax: 403-527-4798
parks@medicinehat.ca
Russ Smith, Manager, Environment Management
403-529-8188
russmi@medicinhat.ca
Frank Wetsch, Manager, Water & WasteWater Treatment
403-529-8227
S. Schentag, Coordinator, Recycling Development
403-502-8593
Ron Davis, Officer, Health & Safety
403-529-8359
rondav@medicine-hat.ca

Okotoks
P.O. Box 20 Main
5 Elizabeth St.
Okotoks, AB T1S 1K1
Tel: 403-938-4404; *Fax:* 403-938-7387
info@okotoks.ca
www.okotoks.ca
Municipal Type: City
Incorporated: Oct. 25, 1899 *Area:* 18.55 sq km
Population in 2011: 24,511
Provincial Electoral District(s): Highwood
Federal Electoral District(s): Macleod
Next Election: Oct. 21, 2013 (3 year terms)
Note: Incorporated as a town on June 1, 1904.
Rick Quail, Municipal Manager
403-938-8900
municipalmanager@okotoks.ca
Bill Robertson, Mayor
mayor@okotoks.ca
Ken Thevenot, Fire Chief
403-938-4066
fire@okotoks.ca
Marley Oness, Municipal Engineer
403-938-8930
municipalengineer@okotoks.ca
Dave Robertson, Manager, Operations
403-938-8952
operations@okotoks.ca

Red Deer
City Hall
P.O. Box 5008
4914 - 48th Ave.
Red Deer, AB T4N 3T4
Tel: 403-342-8111; *Fax:* 403-346-6195
feedback@reddeer.ca
www.reddeer.ca
Municipal Type: City
Incorporated: May 31, 1894 *Area:* 69.23 sq km
Population in 2011: 90,564
Provincial Electoral District(s): Red Deer-North; Red Deer-South
Federal Electoral District(s): Red Deer
Next Election: Oct. 21, 2013 (3 year terms)
Note: Incorporated as a city on March 25, 1913.
Craig Curtis, City Manager
403-342-8156, Fax: 403-342-8365
craig.curtis@reddeer.ca
Morris Flewwelling, Mayor
403-342-8154, Fax: 403-342-8365
mayor@reddeer.ca
Buck Buchanan, Councillor
403-343-6550, Fax: 403-346-6195
buck.buchanan@reddeer.ca
Paul Harris, Councillor
Cindy Jefferies, Councillor
403-302-3706, Fax: 403-346-6195
cindy.jefferies@reddeer.ca
Lynne Mulder, Councillor
403-341-6418, Fax: 403-346-6195
lynne.mulder@reddeer.ca
Chris Stephan, Councillor
Tara Veer, Councillor
403-358-3568, Fax: 403-340-7466
tara.veer@reddeer.ca
Frank Wong, Councillor
403-347-6514, Fax: 403-346-6195
frank.wong@reddeer.ca
Dianne Wyntjes, Councillor
Lorraine Poth, Director, Corporate Services
lorraine.poth@reddeer.ca
Don Simpson, City Solicitor
Brian Simpson, Superintendent, RCMP
rcmp@reddeer.ca
Paul Goranson, Director, Development Services
403-342-8162, Fax: 403-342-8211
paul.goranson@reddeer.ca
Colleen Jensen, Director, Community Services
403-342-8323, Fax: 403-342-8222
communityservices@reddeer.ca
Scott Cameron, Manager, Social Planning
403-342-8100
communityservices@reddeer.ca
Frank Colosimo, Manager, Public Works
403-342-8238, Fax: 403-343-7074
publicworks@reddeer.ca
Kevin Joll, Manager, Transit
403-342-8225, Fax: 403-342-8116
transit@reddeer.ca
Paul Meyette, Director, Planning Division
Rod Risling, Manager, Assessment & Taxation
assessment@reddeer.ca
Greg Scott, Manager, Recreation, Parks & Culture
403-342-8159, Fax: 403-342-8222
Dave Matthews, Supervisor, Planning & Technical Services
Tom Marstaller, Superintendent, Environmental Services
403-342-8238, Fax: 403-343-7074
publicworks@reddeer.ca

St. Albert
5 St. Anne St.
St. Albert, AB T8N 3Z9
Tel: 780-459-1500; *Fax:* 780-460-2394
stalbert@st-albert.net
www.stalbert.ca

Municipal Type: City
Incorporated: Dec. 7, 1899 *Area:* 35.04 sq km
Population in 2011: 61,466
Provincial Electoral District(s): Spruce Grove-Sturgeon-St. Albert; St. Albert
Federal Electoral District(s): Edmonton-St. Albert
Next Election: Oct. 21, 2013 (3 year terms)
Note: Incorporated as a city on Jan. 1, 1977.
Bill Holtby, City Manager
780-459-1607, Fax: 780-459-1591
bholtby@st-albert.net
Nolan Crouse, Mayor
780-459-1606, Fax: 780-459-1591
mayor@st-albert.net
Len Bracko, Councillor
780-458-6478, Fax: 780-418-2961
len@bracko.ca
Wes Broadhead, Councillor
Cathy Heron, Councillor
Roger Lemieux, Councillor
780-460-7223, Fax: 780-651-6147
jrcl@shaw.ca
Cam MacKay, Councillor
Malcolm Parker, Councillor
Gail Barrington-Moss, General Manager, Community & Protective Services
N. Jamieson, General Manager, Planning & Engineering Services
D. Screpnek, General Manager, Corporate Services
B. Treidler, General Manager, Business & Strategic Services
C. Cundy, Director, Planning & Development
D. Irving, Manager, Planning
S. Laarhuis, Chief Legislative Officer
Tracy Young, Administrative Resources Coordinator, Fire & Emergency Medical Services
780-458-2020, Fax: 780-459-7636

Spruce Grove
315 Jespersen Ave.
Spruce Grove, AB T7X 3E8
Tel: 780-962-2611; *Fax:* 780-962-2526
info@sprucegrove.org
www.sprucegrove.org
Municipal Type: City
Incorporated: March 14, 1907 *Area:* 26.4 sq km
Population in 2011: 26,171
Provincial Electoral District(s): Spruce Grove-Sturgeon-St. Albert
Federal Electoral District(s): Edmonton-Spruce Grove
Next Election: Oct. 21, 2013 (3 year terms)
Note: Incorporated as a city on March 1, 1986.
Doug Lagore, City Manager
dlagore@sprucegrove.org
Stuart Houston, Mayor
shouston@sprucegrove.org
Kathy Chan, Treasurer
Ken Luck, Director, FCSS & Recreation
Jackie Araujo, General Manager, Community Services
780-962-7617
David Hales, General Manager, Planning & Infrastructure
780-962-7622
Robert Kosterman, Chief, Fire
780-962-4496
Jeff Mustard, Superintendent, Engineering
780-962-7624
Paul Hanlan, Supervisor, Planning & Development
Jane Holmes, Coordinator, Sustainable Development

Stony Plain
4905 - 51 Ave.
Stony Plain, AB T7Z 1Y1
Tel: 780-963-2151; *Fax:* 780-963-2197
info@stonyplain.com
www.stonyplain.com
Municipal Type: City
Incorporated: March 14, 1907 *Area:* 35.61 sq km
Population in 2011: 15,051
Provincial Electoral District(s): Stony Plain
Federal Electoral District(s): Edmonton-Spruce Grove
Next Election: Oct. 21, 2013 (3 year terms)
Note: Incorporated as a town on Dec. 10, 1908
Thomas Goulden, Manager
780-963-8584, Fax: 780-963-2197
t.goulden@stonyplain.com
Ken Lemke, Mayor
780-963-6310
k.lemke@stonyplain.com

Strathmore
680 Westchester Rd.
Strathmore, AB T1P 1J1
Tel: 403-934-3133; *Fax:* 403-934-4713
Lindan@strathmore.ca
www.strathmore.ca
Municipal Type: City
Incorporated: March 20, 1908 *Area:* 15.59 sq km
Population in 2011: 12,305
Provincial Electoral District(s): Strathmore-Brooks
Federal Electoral District(s): Crowfoot
Next Election: Oct. 21, 2013 (3 year terms)
Note: Incorporated as a town on July 6, 1911.
Dwight Stanford, CAO
dwights@strathmore.ca
Steve Grajczyk, Mayor
council@strathmore.ca

Sylvan Lake
4926 - 50th Ave.
Sylvan Lake, AB T4S 1A1
Tel: 403-887-2141; *Fax:* 403-887-3660
tsl@sylvanlake.ca
www.sylvanlake.ca
Municipal Type: City
Incorporated: Dec. 30, 1912 *Area:* 10.83 sq km
Population in 2011: 12,327
Provincial Electoral District(s): Innisfail-Sylvan Lake
Federal Electoral District(s): Red Deer
Next Election: Oct. 21, 2013 (3 year terms)
Note: Incorporated as a town on May 20, 1946.
Archie Grover, Acting CAO
403-887-2141
Susan Samson, Mayor
ssamson@sylvanlake.ca

Wetaskiwin
P.O. Box 6210
4705 - 50th Ave.
Wetaskiwin, AB T9A 2E9
Tel: 780-361-4400; *Fax:* 780-352-0930
reception@wetaskiwin.ca
www.wetaskiwin.ca
Other Information: Toll Free Phone: 1-800-989-6899
Municipal Type: City
Incorporated: Dec. 4, 1899 *Area:* 16.74 sq km
Population in 2011: 12,525
Provincial Electoral District(s): Wetaskiwin-Camrose
Federal Electoral District(s): Wetaskiwin
Next Election: Oct. 21, 2013 (3 year terms)
Note: Incorporated as a city on May 9, 1906.
Ted Gillespie, City Manager
Bill Elliot, Mayor
mayor@wetaskiwin.ca
Merlin Klassen, Fire Chief
780-361-4429, Fax: 780-352-6261
fireservices@wetaskiwin.ca

Other Municipalities in Alberta

Acme
P.O. Box 299
Acme, AB T0M 0A0
Tel: 403-546-3783; *Fax:* 403-546-3014
clerk@acme.ca
www.acme.ca
Municipal Type: Village
Incorporated: July 7, 1910 *Area:* 2.47 sq km
Population in 2011: 653
Provincial Electoral District(s): Olds-Didsbury-Three Hills
Federal Electoral District(s): Crowfoot
Next Election: Oct. 21, 2013 (3 year terms)
Bruce McLeod, Mayor
Sue Schmidt, Municipal Clerk
acme@airenet.com

Alberta Beach
P.O. Box 278
Alberta Beach, AB T0E 0A0
Tel: 780-924-3181; *Fax:* 780-924-3313
abofficea@albertabeach.com
www.albertabeach.com
Municipal Type: Village
Incorporated: Aug. 23, 1920 *Area:* 1.98 sq km
Population in 2011: 865
Provincial Electoral District(s): Whitecourt-Ste. Anne
Federal Electoral District(s): Yellowhead
Next Election: Oct. 21, 2013 (3 year terms)
Note: Status changed to a village on Nov. 25, 1998.
Lou Hudon, Mayor
Dan Kanuka, Assessor
780-939-3310

Alix
P.O. Box 87
4849 - 50 St.
Alix, AB T0C 0B0
Tel: 403-747-2495; *Fax:* 403-747-3663
info@villageofalix.ca; cao@villageofalix.ca
www.villageofalix.ca
Municipal Type: Village
Incorporated: June 3, 1907 *Area:* 3.15 sq km
Population in 2011: 830
Provincial Electoral District(s): Lacombe-Ponoka
Federal Electoral District(s): Wetaskiwin
Next Election: Oct. 21, 2013 (3 year terms)
Curtis Peterson, Mayor
403-747-2414
Lyle Wack, CAO

Alliance
P.O. Box 149
Alliance, AB T0B 0A0
Tel: 780-879-3911; *Fax:* 780-879-2235
info@villageofalliance.ca
www.villageofalliance.ca
Municipal Type: Village
Incorporated: Aug. 26, 1918 *Area:* 0.64 sq km
Population in 2011: 174
Provincial Electoral District(s): Battle River-Wainwright
Federal Electoral District(s): Vegreville-Wainwright
Next Election: Oct. 21, 2013 (3 year terms)
Muriel Fankhanel, Mayor
Laura Towers, Administrator

Amisk
P.O. Box 72
Amisk, AB T0B 0B0
Tel: 780-856-3980; *Fax:* 780-856-3980
amiskvil@telusplanet.net
www.amisk.ca
Municipal Type: Village
Incorporated: Jan. 1, 1956 *Area:* 0.76 sq km
Population in 2011: 207
Provincial Electoral District(s): Battle River-Wainwright
Federal Electoral District(s): Vegreville-Wainwright
Next Election: Oct. 21, 2013 (3 year terms)
Arnold Nordin, Mayor
Kathy Ferguson, Municipal Administrator

Andrew
P.O. Box 180
5021 - 50 St.
Andrew, AB T0B 0C0
Tel: 780-365-3687; *Fax:* 780-365-2061
pat@villageofandrew.net
www.villageofandrew.net
Municipal Type: Village
Incorporated: June 24, 1930 *Area:* 1.23 sq km
Population in 2011: 379
Provincial Electoral District(s): Fort Saskatchewan-Vegreville
Federal Electoral District(s): Vegreville-Wainwright
Next Election: Oct. 21, 2013 (3 year terms)
Eldon Feniac, Mayor
edon@villageofandrew.net
Pat Skoreyko, CAO
pat@villageofandrew.net

Argentia Beach
P.O. Box 100
Ma-Me-O Beach, AB T0C 1X0
Tel: 780-586-2494; *Fax:* 780-586-3567
svadminoffice@xplornet.com
Municipal Type: Summer Village
Incorporated: Jan. 1, 1967 *Area:* 0.69 sq km
Population in 2011: 15
Provincial Electoral District(s): Drayton Valley-Calmar
Federal Electoral District(s): Wetaskiwin
Next Election: Summer 2013 (3 year terms)
Denis Rowley, Mayor
Sylvia Roy, CAO
Jacques Thériault, Conseillers et Districts, Ward(s): la Pointe

Arrowwood
P.O. Box 36
22 Center St.
Arrowwood, AB T0L 0B0
Tel: 403-534-3821; *Fax:* 403-534-3821
vlgarrw@telusplanet.net
www.villageofarrowwood.ca
Municipal Type: Village
Incorporated: May 13, 1926 *Area:* 0.66 sq km

Population in 2011: 188
Provincial Electoral District(s): Little Bow
Federal Electoral District(s): Macleod
Next Election: Oct. 21, 2013 (3 year terms)
Matt Crane, Mayor
Ted Oakes, Village Administrator

Athabasca
4705 - 49 Ave.
Athabasca, AB T9S 1B7
Tel: 780-675-2063; *Fax:* 780-675-4242
town@town.athabasca.ab.ca
www.town.athabasca.ab.ca
Municipal Type: Town
Incorporated: May 18, 1905 *Area:* 16.98 sq km
Population in 2011: 2,990
Provincial Electoral District(s): Athabasca-Redwater
Federal Electoral District(s): Fort McMurray-Athabasca
Next Election: Oct. 21, 2013 (3 year terms)
Note: Incorporated as a town on Aug. 4, 1913.
Roger Morrill, Mayor
Doug Topinka, CAO

Banff
P.O. Box 1260
Banff, AB T1L 1A1
Tel: 403-762-1200; *Fax:* 403-762-1260
comments@banff.ca
www.banff.ca
Municipal Type: Town
Incorporated: Jan. 1, 1990 *Area:* 4.85 sq km
Population in 2011: 7,584
Provincial Electoral District(s): Banff-Cochrane
Federal Electoral District(s): Wild Rose
Next Election: Oct. 21, 2013 (3 year terms)
Robert Earl, Town Manager
403-762-1203
robert.earl@banff.ca
Karen Sorensen, Mayor

Barnwell
P.O. Box 159
Barnwell, AB T0K 0B0
Tel: 403-223-4018; *Fax:* 403-223-2373
barnwell@platinum.ca
Municipal Type: Village
Incorporated: Jan. 1, 1980 *Area:* 0.9 sq km
Population in 2011: 771
Provincial Electoral District(s): Cardston-Taber-Warner
Federal Electoral District(s): Medicine Hat
Next Election: Oct. 21, 2013 (3 year terms)
Delbert Bodnarek, Mayor
Wendy Bateman, Administrator

Barons
P.O. Box 129
Barons, AB T0L 0G0
Tel: 403-757-3633; *Fax:* 403-757-2599
barons@figment.ca
Municipal Type: Village
Incorporated: May 6, 1910 *Area:* 0.68 sq km
Population in 2011: 315
Provincial Electoral District(s): Little Bow
Federal Electoral District(s): Lethbridge
Next Election: Oct. 21, 2013 (3 year terms)
Ronald Gorzitza, Mayor
Laurie Beck, CAO

Barrhead County No. 11
5306-49 Street
Barrhead, AB T7N 1N5
Tel: 780-674-3331; *Fax:* 780-674-2777
countybarrhead@phrd.ab.ca
www.barrhead.ca
Municipal Type: Town
Incorporated: Nov. 14, 1927 *Area:* 8.1 sq km
Population in 2011: 6,096
Provincial Electoral District(s): Barrhead-Morinville-Westlock
Federal Electoral District(s): Yellowhead
Next Election: Oct. 21, 2013 (3 year terms)
Note: Proclaimed as a town on Nov. 26, 1946.
Brian Schultz, Mayor
bdschultz@barrhead.ca
Martin Taylor, CAO
mtaylor@barrhead.ca
Bill Lee, Reeve
780-584-2323
Mark Oberg, County Manager
moberg@phrd.ab.ca

Barrhead
P.O. Box 4189
Barrhead, AB T7N 1A2
Tel: 780-674-3301; *Fax:* 780-674-5648
town@barrhead.ca
www.barrhead.ca
Municipal Type: Town
Incorporated: Nov. 14, 1927 *Area:* 8.1 sq km
Population in 2011: 4,432
Provincial Electoral District(s): Barrhead-Morinville-Westlock
Federal Electoral District(s): Yellowhead
Next Election: Oct. 21, 2013 (3 year terms)
Note: Proclaimed as a town on Nov. 26, 1946.

Bashaw
P.O. Box 510
Bashaw, AB T0B 0H0
Tel: 780-372-3911; *Fax:* 780-372-2335
admin@townofbashaw.com
www.townofbashaw.com
Municipal Type: Town
Incorporated: Aug. 18, 1911 *Area:* 2.84 sq km
Population in 2011: 873
Provincial Electoral District(s): Lacombe-Ponoka
Federal Electoral District(s): Crowfoot
Next Election: Oct. 21, 2013 (3 year terms)
Note: Incorporated as a town on May 1, 1964.
Robert (Bob) Cammidge, Mayor
Rosemary Wittevrongel, CAO
rwittevrongel@townofbashaw.com

Bassano
P.O. Box 299
Bassano, AB T0J 0B0
Tel: 403-641-3788; *Fax:* 403-641-2585
townbass@telus.net
www.bassano.ca
Municipal Type: Town
Incorporated: Dec. 28, 1909 *Area:* 5.16 sq km
Population in 2011: 1,282
Provincial Electoral District(s): Strathmore-Brooks
Federal Electoral District(s): Medicine Hat
Next Election: Oct. 21, 2013 (3 year terms)
Note: Incorporated as a town on Jan. 16, 1911.
Tom Rose, Mayor
Sabine Nasse, CAO
basscao@telus.net

Bawlf
P.O. Box 40
Bawlf, AB T0B 0J0
Tel: 780-373-3797; *Fax:* 780-373-3798
vilbawlf@syban.net
www.bawlf.com
Municipal Type: Village
Incorporated: Oct. 12, 1906 *Area:* 0.96 sq km
Population in 2011: 403
Provincial Electoral District(s): Battle River-Wainwright
Federal Electoral District(s): Crowfoot
Next Election: Oct. 21, 2013 (3 year terms)
Gordon Blatz, Mayor
780-373-3733
gblatz@bawlf.com
Lynn Horbasenko, Village Manager
LHorbasenko@bawlf.com

Beaverlodge
P.O. Box 30
Beaverlodge, AB T0H 0C0
Tel: 780-354-2201; *Fax:* 780-354-2207
ivan@beaverlodge.ca
www.beaverlodge.ca
Municipal Type: Town
Incorporated: July 31, 1929 *Area:* 5.58 sq km
Population in 2011: 2,365
Provincial Electoral District(s): Grande Prairie-Wapiti
Federal Electoral District(s): Peace River
Next Election: Oct. 21, 2013 (3 year terms)
Note: Incorporated as a town on Jan. 24, 1956.
Ivan Hegland, Town Manager
ivan@beaverlodge.ca
Leona Hanson, Mayor
leona@coaction.ca

Beiseker
P.O. Box 349
Beiseker, AB T0M 0G0
Tel: 403-947-3774; *Fax:* 403-947-2146
beiseker@beiseker.com
www.beiseker.com
Municipal Type: Village
Incorporated: Feb. 23, 1921 *Area:* 2.84 sq km
Population in 2011: 785
Provincial Electoral District(s): Airdrie-Chestermere
Federal Electoral District(s): Crowfoot
Next Election: Oct. 21, 2013 (3 year terms)
Bruce T. Rowe, Mayor
Jo-Anne Lambert, CAO
gpeckham@beiseker.com

Bentley
P.O. Box 179
Bentley, AB T0C 0J0
Tel: 403-748-4044; *Fax:* 403-748-3213
vlgben@telusplanet.net
www.town.bentley.ab.ca
Municipal Type: Town
Incorporated: March 17, 1915 *Area:* 2.3 sq km
Population in 2011: 1,073
Provincial Electoral District(s): Rocky Mountain House
Federal Electoral District(s): Wetaskiwin
Next Election: Oct. 21, 2013 (3 year terms)
Note: Incorporated as a town on Jan. 1, 2001.
Joan Dickau, Mayor
Elizabeth Smart, CAO
liz.bentley@telus.net

Berwyn
P.O. Box 250
Berwyn, AB T0H 0E0
Tel: 780-338-3922; *Fax:* 780-338-2224
vberwynadmin@sebernet.com
www.berwyn.govoffice.com
Municipal Type: Village
Incorporated: Nov. 28, 1936 *Area:* 1.66 sq km
Population in 2011: 526
Provincial Electoral District(s): Dunvegan-Central Peace
Federal Electoral District(s): Peace River
Next Election: Oct. 21, 2013 (3 year terms)
Ron Longtin, Mayor
RonLongtin@wispernet.ca
Mike Rudkin, Municipal Administrator
vberwyn@serbernet.com

Betula Beach
P.O. Box 161
Seba Beach, AB T0E 2B0
Tel: 780-797-2455
svbetula@telusplanet.net
Municipal Type: Summer Village
Incorporated: Jan. 1, 1960 *Area:* 0.18 sq km
Population in 2011: 10
Provincial Electoral District(s): Stony Plain
Federal Electoral District(s): Yellowhead
Next Election: Summer 2013 (3 year terms)
Rob Dickie, Mayor
Linda Bolton, Administrator

Big Valley
P.O. Box 236
29 - 1 Ave. South
Big Valley, AB T0J 0G0
Tel: 403-876-2269; *Fax:* 403-876-2223
villagebigvalley@libs.prl.ab.ca; info@villagebigvalley.ca
www.villagebigvalley.ca
Municipal Type: Village
Incorporated: July 28, 1914 *Area:* 1.84 sq km
Population in 2011: 364
Provincial Electoral District(s): Drumheller-Stettler
Federal Electoral District(s): Crowfoot
Next Election: Oct. 21, 2013 (3 year terms)
Rick Kargaard, Mayor
Corinne Feusi, CAO

Birch Cove
P.O. Box 7
#19, RR 1
Gunn, AB T0E 1A0
Tel: 780-446-1426
devans@birchcove.ca
www.albertasummervillages.org
Municipal Type: Summer Village
Incorporated: Dec. 31, 1988 *Area:* 0.29 sq km
Population in 2011: 45
Provincial Electoral District(s): Whitecourt-Ste. Anne
Federal Electoral District(s): Yellowhead
Next Election: Summer 2013 (3 year terms)
Steven Tymafichuk, Mayor
Dennis Evans, Administrator

Birchcliff
#104, 4505 - 50 Ave.
Sylvan Lake, AB T4S 1W2
Tel: 403-887-2822; *Fax:* 403-887-2897
fivesv@telusplanet.net
Municipal Type: Summer Village
Incorporated: Jan. 1, 1972 *Area:* 0.98 sq km
Population in 2011: 112
Provincial Electoral District(s): Rocky Mountain House
Federal Electoral District(s): Wetaskiwin
Next Election: Summer 2013 (3 year terms)
Joyce Megson, Mayor
Myra Reiter, Administrator

Bittern Lake
P.O. Box 5
300 Rail Way Ave.
Bittern Lake, AB T0C 0L0
Tel: 780-672-7373; *Fax:* 780-672-2353
vobl@syban.net
www.villageofbitternlake.ca
Municipal Type: Village
Incorporated: Nov. 21, 1904 *Area:* 6.64 sq km
Population in 2011: 224
Provincial Electoral District(s): Wetaskiwin-Camrose
Federal Electoral District(s): Crowfoot
Next Election: Oct. 21, 2013 (3 year terms)
Ken Feth, Mayor
Theresa Fuller, CAO

Black Diamond
P.O. Box 10
Black Diamond, AB T0L 0H0
Tel: 403-933-4348; *Fax:* 403-933-5865
info@town.blackdiamond.ab.ca
www.town.blackdiamond.ab.ca
Municipal Type: Town
Incorporated: May 8, 1929 *Area:* 3.21 sq km
Population in 2011: 2,373
Provincial Electoral District(s): Foothills-Rocky View
Federal Electoral District(s): Macleod
Next Election: Oct. 21, 2013 (3 year terms)
Note: Incorporated as a town on Jan 1, 1956.
Sharlene Brown, Mayor
Leonard Smith, Town Manager

Blackfalds
P.O. Box 220
5018 Waghorn St.
Blackfalds, AB T0M 0J0
Tel: 403-885-4677; *Fax:* 403-885-4610
info@blackfalds.com
www.blackfalds.com
Municipal Type: Town
Incorporated: June 17, 1904 *Area:* 8.4 sq km
Population in 2011: 6,300
Provincial Electoral District(s): Lacombe-Ponoka
Federal Electoral District(s): Wetaskiwin
Next Election: Oct. 21, 2013 (3 year terms)
Note: Incorporated as a town on April 1, 1980.
Melodie Stol, Mayor
melodie@blackfalds.com
Corinne Newman, CAO
corinne@blackfalds.com

Bon Accord
P.O. Box 779
5025-50 Ave
Bon Accord, AB T0A 0K0
Tel: 780-921-3550; *Fax:* 780-921-3585
townoffice@town.bonaccord.ab.ca
www.town.bonaccord.ab.ca
Municipal Type: Town
Incorporated: Jan. 1, 1964 *Area:* 2.11 sq km
Population in 2011: 1,488
Provincial Electoral District(s): Athabasca-Redwater
Federal Electoral District(s): Westlock-St. Paul
Next Election: Oct. 21, 2013 (3 year terms)
Note: Incorporated as a town on Nov. 20, 1979.
Randy Boyd, Mayor
boyd@town.bonaccord.ab.ca
Vicky Zinyk, Town Manager
cao@town.bonaccord.ab.ca

Bondiss
724 Baptiste Dr.
West Baptiste, AB T9S 1R8
Tel: 780-675-9270; *Fax:* 780-675-9526
tomaszyk@mcsnet.ca
Municipal Type: Summer Village
Incorporated: Jan. 1, 1983 *Area:* 1.33 sq km
Population in 2011: 106
Provincial Electoral District(s): Athabasca-Redwater
Federal Electoral District(s): Fort McMurray-Athabasca
Next Election: Summer 2013 (3 year terms)
Murray Olsen, Mayor
Edwin Tomaszyk, CAO
Marc Losier, Director, Design & Construction
city.operationalservices@bathurst.ca

Bonnyville
P.O. Box 1006
4917 - 49 Ave.
Bonnyville, AB T9N 2J7
Tel: 780-826-3496; *Fax:* 780-826-4806
admin@town.bonnyville.ab.ca
www.town.bonnyville.ab.ca
Other Information: Toll free: 1-866-826-3496
Municipal Type: Town
Incorporated: Sept. 19, 1929 *Area:* 14.1 sq km
Population in 2011: 6,216
Provincial Electoral District(s): Bonnyville-Cold Lake
Federal Electoral District(s): Westlock-St. Paul
Next Election: Oct. 21, 2013 (3 year terms)
Note: Proclaimed as a town on Feb. 3, 1948.
Mark Power, CAO
mpower@town.bonnyville.ab.ca
Ernie Isley, Mayor

Bonnyville Beach
P.O. Box 6439
Bonnyville, AB T9N 2G9
Tel: 780-826-2925; *Fax:* 780-812-2904
svbbeach@mcsnet.ca
Municipal Type: Summer Village
Incorporated: Jan 1, 1958 *Area:* 0.38 sq km
Population in 2011: 95
Provincial Electoral District(s): Bonnyville-Cold Lake
Federal Electoral District(s): Westlock-St. Paul
Next Election: Summer 2013 (3 year terms)
Chuck Dechene, Mayor
Lionel P. Tercier, Administrator
Robert Langlais, Fire Chief
506-548-0439
city.fire@bathurst.ca

Botha
P.O. Box 160
Botha, AB T0C 0N0
Tel: 403-742-5079; *Fax:* 403-742-6586
vlbotha@xplornet.com
Municipal Type: Village
Incorporated: Sept. 5, 1911 *Area:* 1.09 sq km
Population in 2011: 175
Provincial Electoral District(s): Drumheller-Stettler
Federal Electoral District(s): Crowfoot
Next Election: Oct. 21, 2013 (3 year terms)
Josie Hunter, Mayor
Michelle Renschler, CAO

Bow Island
P.O. Box 100
Bow Island, AB T0K 0G0
Tel: 403-545-2522; *Fax:* 403-545-6642
townoffice@bowisland.com
www.bowisland.com
Municipal Type: Town
Incorporated: June 14, 1910 *Area:* 5.92 sq km
Population in 2011: 2,025
Provincial Electoral District(s): Cypress-Medicine Hat
Federal Electoral District(s): Medicine Hat
Next Election: Oct. 21, 2013 (3 year terms)
Note: Incorporated as a town on Feb. 1, 1912.
Gordon Reynolds, Mayor
mayor@bowisland.com
Anna-Marie Bridge, Town Manager
anna-marie@bowisland.com

Bowden
P.O. Box 338
Bowden, AB T0M 0K0
Tel: 403-224-3395; *Fax:* 403-224-2244
admin@town.bowden.ab.ca
www.town.bowden.ab.ca
Municipal Type: Town
Incorporated: June 17, 1904 *Area:* 1.9 sq km
Population in 2011: 1,241
Provincial Electoral District(s): Innisfail-Sylvan Lake
Federal Electoral District(s): Red Deer
Next Election: Oct. 21, 2013 (3 year terms)
Note: Incorporated as a town on Sept. 1, 1981.
Robb Stuart, Mayor
bowdenmayor@gmail.com
Lori Conkin, CAO
cao@town.bowden.ab.ca

Boyle
P.O. Box 9
Boyle, AB T0A 0M0
Tel: 780-689-3643; *Fax:* 780-689-3998
admin@villageofboyle.com
www.villageofboyle.com
Municipal Type: Village
Incorporated: Dec. 31, 1953 *Area:* 4.1 sq km
Population in 2011: 916
Provincial Electoral District(s): Athabasca-Redwater
Federal Electoral District(s): Fort McMurray-Athabasca
Next Election: Oct. 21, 2013 (3 year terms)
Don Radmanovich, Mayor
Charlie Ashbey, CAO

Breton
P.O. Box 480
4916 - 50 Ave.
Breton, AB T0C 0P0
Tel: 780-696-3636; *Fax:* 780-696-3590
vbreton@telusplanet.net
www.village.breton.ab.ca
Municipal Type: Village
Incorporated: Jan. 1, 1957 *Area:* 1.73 sq km
Population in 2011: 496
Provincial Electoral District(s): Drayton Valley-Calmar
Federal Electoral District(s): Wetaskiwin
Next Election: Oct. 21, 2013 (3 year terms)
Janet Young, Mayor

Bruderheim
P.O. Box 280
Bruderheim, AB T0B 0S0
Tel: 780-796-3731; *Fax:* 780-796-3037
info@bruderheim.ca
www.bruderheim.ca
Municipal Type: Town
Incorporated: May 29, 1908 *Area:* 4.23 sq km
Population in 2011: 1,155
Provincial Electoral District(s): Fort Saskatchewan-Vegreville
Federal Electoral District(s): Vegreville-Wainwright
Next Election: Oct. 21, 2013 (3 year terms)
Note: Incorporated as a town on Sept. 17, 1980.
Karl Hauch, Mayor
Tim Duhamel, CAO
duhamel@strathcona.ab.ca

Burnstick Lake
P.O. Box 1555
Cochrane, AB T4C 1B5
Tel: 403-932-3866; *Fax:* 403-932-6652
rickbutler@pathcom.ca
www.burnsticklakesummervillage.ca
Municipal Type: Summer Village
Incorporated: Dec. 31, 1991 *Area:* 0.18 sq km
Population in 2011: 16
Provincial Electoral District(s): Rocky Mountain House
Federal Electoral District(s): Wild Rose
Next Election: Summer 2013 (3 year terms)
Harold Esche, Mayor
Harold Northcott, Administrator

Calmar
P.O. Box 750
Calmar, AB T0C 0V0
Tel: 780-985-3604; *Fax:* 780-985-3039
info@calmar.ca
www.town.calmar.ab.ca
Municipal Type: Town
Incorporated: Jan. 1, 1949 *Area:* 4.34 sq km
Population in 2011: 1,970
Provincial Electoral District(s): Drayton Valley-Calmar
Federal Electoral District(s): Wetaskiwin
Next Election: Oct. 21, 2013 (3 year terms)
Note: Incorporated as a town on Jan. 19, 1954.
Don Faulkner, Mayor
dfaulkner@calmar.ca
Kathy Rodberg, Town Manager
krodberg@calmar.ca

Carbon
P.O. Box 249
Carbon, AB T0M 0L0
Tel: 403-572-3244; *Fax:* 403-572-3778
admincarbon@wildroseinternet.ca
Municipal Type: Village
Incorporated: Nov. 18, 1912 *Area:* 2 sq km
Population in 2011: 592
Provincial Electoral District(s): Olds-Didsbury-Three Hills

Federal Electoral District(s): Crowfoot
Next Election: Oct. 21, 2013 (3 year terms)
Valorie Reed, Mayor
Debra Grosfield, Municipal Administrator
caocarbon@wildroseinternet.ca

Cardston
P.O. Box 280
Cardston, AB T0K 0K0
Tel: 403-653-3366; *Fax:* 403-653-2499
info@cardston.ca
www.cardston.ca
Municipal Type: Town
Incorporated: Dec. 29, 1898 *Area:* 8.64 sq km
Population in 2011: 3,580
Provincial Electoral District(s): Cardston-Taber-Warner
Federal Electoral District(s): Lethbridge
Next Election: Oct. 21, 2013 (3 year terms)
Note: Incorporated as a town on July 2, 1901.
Rick Schow, Mayor
Marian Carlson, Administrator
marian@cardston.ca

Carmangay
P.O. Box 130
Carmangay, AB T0L 0N0
Tel: 403-643-3595; *Fax:* 403-643-2007
villagec@telusplanet.net
Municipal Type: Village
Incorporated: Jan. 20, 1910 *Area:* 1.86 sq km
Population in 2011: 367
Provincial Electoral District(s): Little Bow
Federal Electoral District(s): Macleod
Next Election: Oct. 21, 2013 (3 year terms)
Kim Nichols, Mayor
Carolyn Erb, Administrator

Caroline
P.O. Box 148
Caroline, AB T0M 0M0
Tel: 403-722-3781; *Fax:* 403-722-4050
administration@caroline.ca
www.caroline.ca
Municipal Type: Village
Incorporated: Dec. 31, 1951 *Area:* 1.98 sq km
Population in 2011: 501
Provincial Electoral District(s): Rocky Mountain House
Federal Electoral District(s): Wild Rose
Next Election: Oct. 21, 2013 (3 year terms)
Laura Cudmore, Mayor
Brian Irmen, CAO
Mary Hughes, Technician, Solid Wastes Recycling
403-329-7367
mhughes@lethbridge.ca

Carstairs
P.O. Box 370
Carstairs, AB T0M 0N0
Tel: 403-337-3341; *Fax:* 403-337-3343
admin@town.carstairs.ab.ca
www.carstairs.ca
Municipal Type: Town
Incorporated: May 15, 1903 *Area:* 5 sq km
Population in 2011: 3,442
Provincial Electoral District(s): Olds-Didsbury-Three Hills
Federal Electoral District(s): Wild Rose
Next Election: Oct. 21, 2013 (3 year terms)
Note: Incorporated as a town on Sept. 1, 1966.
Lance Colby, Mayor
Carl McDonnell, CAO
carlm@carstairs.ca

Castle Island
11318 - 10th Ave.
Edmonton, AB T6J 6S9
Tel: 780-431-9712; *Fax:* 780-431-0882
svoffice@telusplanet.net
Municipal Type: Summer Village
Incorporated: Jan. 1, 1955 *Area:* 0.05 sq km
Population in 2011: 19
Provincial Electoral District(s): Whitecourt-Ste. Anne
Federal Electoral District(s): Yellowhead
Next Election: Summer 2013 (3 year terms)
Cornelia Helland, Mayor
Anita Blais, Administrator

Castor
P.O. Box 479
Castor, AB T0C 0X0
Tel: 403-882-3215; *Fax:* 403-882-2700
sandi@townofcastor.ca
www.castor.ca
Municipal Type: Town
Incorporated: Nov. 26, 1909 *Area:* 2.72 sq km
Population in 2011: 932
Provincial Electoral District(s): Battle River-Wainwright
Federal Electoral District(s): Crowfoot
Next Election: Oct. 21, 2013 (3 year terms)
Note: Incorporated as a town on June 27, 1910.
Gerry DeVloo, Mayor
Michael Yakielashek, CAO

Cereal
P.O. Box 160
Cereal, AB T0J 2J0
Tel: 403-326-3823
vofc@telusplanet.net
Municipal Type: Village
Incorporated: Aug. 19, 1914 *Area:* 0.95 sq km
Population in 2011: 134
Provincial Electoral District(s): Drumheller-Stettler
Federal Electoral District(s): Crowfoot
Next Election: Oct. 21, 2013 (3 year terms)
Allen Buetter, Mayor
Mary Ann Salik, Administrator

Champion
P.O. Box 367
Champion, AB T0L 0R0
Tel: 403-897-3833; *Fax:* 403-897-2250
champvil@wildroseinternet.ca
Municipal Type: Village
Incorporated: May 27, 1911 *Area:* 0.88 sq km
Population in 2011: 378
Provincial Electoral District(s): Little Bow
Federal Electoral District(s): Macleod
Next Election: Oct. 21, 2013 (3 year terms)
Richard Ellis, Mayor
Amy Rupp, Administrator

Chauvin
P.O. Box 160
Chauvin, AB T0B 0V0
Tel: 780-858-3881; *Fax:* 780-858-2125
vchauvin@cciwireless.ca
www.villagechauvin.ca
Municipal Type: Village
Incorporated: Dec. 30, 1912 *Area:* 2.32 sq km
Population in 2011: 334
Provincial Electoral District(s): Battle River-Wainwright
Federal Electoral District(s): Vegreville-Wainwright
Next Election: Oct. 21, 2013 (3 year terms)
Christine Smith, Mayor
Shelly McMann, Municipal Administrator
vchauvin@wy-com.ca

Chipman
P.O. Box 176
4816-50 St.
Chipman, AB T0B 0W0
Tel: 780-363-3982; *Fax:* 780-363-2386
chipmanab@mcsnet.ca
www.chipmanab.ca
Municipal Type: Village
Incorporated: Oct. 21, 1913 *Area:* 0.62 sq km
Population in 2011: 284
Provincial Electoral District(s): Fort Saskatchewan-Vegreville
Federal Electoral District(s): Vegreville-Wainwright
Next Election: Oct. 21, 2013 (3 year terms)
Jim Palmer, Mayor
Pat Tomkow, Village Clerk

Claresholm
P.O. Box 1000
221-45 Ave w
Claresholm, AB T0L 0T0
Tel: 403-625-3381; *Fax:* 403-625-3869
clares@telusplanet.net
www.townofclaresholm.com
Municipal Type: Town
Incorporated: May 30, 1903 *Area:* 8.3 sq km
Population in 2011: 3,758
Provincial Electoral District(s): Livingstone-Macleod
Federal Electoral District(s): Macleod
Next Election: Oct. 21, 2013 (3 year terms)
Note: Incorporated as a town on Aug. 31, 1905.
David Moore, Mayor
david.moore@townofclaresholm.com
Kris Holbeck, CAO
kris.holbeck@townofclaresholm.com

Clive
P.O. Box 90
Clive, AB T0C 0Y0
Tel: 403-784-3366; *Fax:* 403-784-2012
cliveab@platinum.ca
www.clive.ca
Municipal Type: Village
Incorporated: Jan. 9, 1912 *Area:* 2.12 sq km
Population in 2011: 675
Provincial Electoral District(s): Lacombe-Ponoka
Federal Electoral District(s): Wetaskiwin
Next Election: Oct. 21, 2013 (3 year terms)
Anita Gillard, Mayor
Karen Kane, CAO

Clyde
P.O. Box 190
Clyde, AB T0G 0P0
Tel: 780-348-5356; *Fax:* 780-348-5699
admin@villageofclyde.ca
www.villageofclyde.ca
Municipal Type: Village
Incorporated: Jan. 28, 1914 *Area:* 1.36 sq km
Population in 2011: 503
Provincial Electoral District(s): Barrhead-Morinville-Westlock
Federal Electoral District(s): Westlock-St. Paul
Next Election: Oct. 21, 2013 (3 year terms)
Wayne Wilcox, Mayor
mayor@villageofclyde.ca
Melanie Beastall, CAO
cao@villageofclyde.ca

Coaldale
1920 - 17 St.
Coaldale, AB T1M 1M1
Tel: 403-345-1300; *Fax:* 403-345-1311
admin@coaldale.ca
www.coaldale.ca
Municipal Type: Town
Incorporated: Dec. 27, 1919 *Area:* 7.95 sq km
Population in 2011: 7,493
Provincial Electoral District(s): Little Bow
Federal Electoral District(s): Lethbridge
Next Election: Oct. 21, 2013 (3 year terms)
Note: Incorporated as a town on Jan. 7, 1952.
Leo Ludwig, Towm Manager
lludwig@coaldale.ca
Kim Craig, Mayor

Coalhurst
P.O. Box 456
Coalhurst, AB T0L 0V0
Tel: 403-381-3033; *Fax:* 403-381-2924
main@town.coalhurst.ab.ca
www.town.coalhurst.ab.ca
Municipal Type: Town
Incorporated: Dec. 17, 1913 *Area:* 1.64 sq km
Population in 2011: 1,963
Provincial Electoral District(s): Little Bow
Federal Electoral District(s): Lethbridge
Next Election: Oct. 21, 2013 (3 year terms)
Note: Incorporated as a town on June 1, 1995.
Dennis Cassie, Mayor
cassiefamily@shaw.ca
R. Kim Hauta, CAO
rkhauta@town.coalhurst.ab.ca

Consort
P.O. Box 490
Consort, AB T0C 1B0
Tel: 403-577-3623; *Fax:* 403-577-2024
consort@xplornet.com
www.village.consort.ab.ca
Municipal Type: Village
Incorporated: Sept. 23, 1912 *Area:* 2.63 sq km
Population in 2011: 689
Provincial Electoral District(s): Drumheller-Stettler
Federal Electoral District(s): Crowfoot
Next Election: Oct. 21, 2013 (3 year terms)
Wayne Walker, Mayor
wwalker@xplorenet.com
Monique Jeffrey, CAO
mjeffrey@netago.ca

Coronation
P.O. Box 219
Coronation, AB T0C 1C0
Tel: 403-578-3679; *Fax:* 403-578-3020
admin@town.coronation.ab.ca
www.town.coronation.ab.ca
Municipal Type: Town
Incorporated: Dec. 16, 1911 *Area:* 3.73 sq km

Population in 2011: 947
Provincial Electoral District(s): Battle River-Wainwright
Federal Electoral District(s): Crowfoot
Next Election: Oct. 21, 2013 (3 year terms)
Note: Incorporated as a town on April 29, 1912.
Dawna Elliott, Mayor
Sandra Kulyk, Town Manager

Coutts
P.O. Box 236
Coutts, AB T0K 0N0
Tel: 403-344-3848; *Fax:* 403-344-4360
vilcoutt@telus.net
www.villagecoutts.ab.ca
Municipal Type: Village
Incorporated: Jan. 1, 1960 *Area:* 0.98 sq km
Population in 2011: 277
Provincial Electoral District(s): Cardston-Taber-Warner
Federal Electoral District(s): Lethbridge
Next Election: Oct. 21, 2013 (3 year terms)
Thomas Butler, Mayor
Lori Rolfe, CAO

Cowley
P.O. Box 40
Cowley, AB T0K 0P0
Tel: 403-628-3808; *Fax:* 403-628-2807
vilocow@shaw.ca
Municipal Type: Village
Incorporated: Aug. 16, 1906 *Area:* 1.4 sq km
Population in 2011: 236
Provincial Electoral District(s): Livingstone-Macleod
Federal Electoral District(s): Macleod
Next Election: Oct. 21, 2013 (3 year terms)
Garry Hackler, Mayor
Laurie Wilgosh, Administrator
wilgosh@shaw.ca

Cremona
P.O. Box 10
Cremona, AB T0M 0R0
Tel: 403-637-3762; *Fax:* 403-637-2101
admin@village.cremona.ab.ca
www.village.cremona.ab.ca
Municipal Type: Village
Incorporated: Jan. 1, 1955 *Area:* 0.68 sq km
Population in 2011: 457
Provincial Electoral District(s): Olds-Didsbury-Three Hills
Federal Electoral District(s): Wild Rose
Next Election: Oct. 21, 2013 (3 year terms)
Leslie Abrams, Mayor
Terry Lofstrom, CAO

Crossfield
P.O. Box 500
Crossfield, AB T0M 0S0
Tel: 403-946-5565; *Fax:* 403-946-4523
town@crossfieldalberta.com
www.crossfieldalberta.com
Municipal Type: Town
Incorporated: June 3, 1907 *Area:* 4.8 sq km
Population in 2011: 2,853
Provincial Electoral District(s): Foothills-Rocky View
Federal Electoral District(s): Wild Rose
Next Election: Oct. 21, 2013 (3 year terms)
Note: Incorporated as a town on Aug. 1, 1980.
Nathan Anderson, Mayor
Cheryl Skelly, CAO
cheryls@crossfieldalberta.com

Crystal Springs
256 Grandview, RR#1
Westerose, AB T0C 2V0
Tel: 780-586-3522; *Fax:* 780-586-2037
crystalsprings@xplornet.com
www.svcrystalsprings.ca
Municipal Type: Summer Village
Incorporated: Jan. 1, 1957 *Area:* 0.58 sq km
Population in 2011: 90
Provincial Electoral District(s): Drayton Valley-Calmar
Federal Electoral District(s): Wetaskiwin
Next Election: Summer 2013 (3 year terms)
Walter Schlese, Mayor
780-586-2555
Sylvia Roy, CAO

Czar
P.O. Box 30
Czar, AB T0B 0Z0
Tel: 780-857-3740; *Fax:* 780-857-2353
villczar@xplornet.com

Municipal Type: Village
Incorporated: Nov. 12, 1917 *Area:* 1.18 sq km
Population in 2011: 167
Provincial Electoral District(s): Battle River-Wainwright
Federal Electoral District(s): Vegreville-Wainwright
Next Election: Oct. 21, 2013 (3 year terms)
Angela Large, Mayor
Tricia Strang, Administrator

Daysland
P.O. Box 610
Daysland, AB T0B 1A0
Tel: 780-374-3767; *Fax:* 780-374-2455
daystown@telusplanet.net
www.daysland.com
Municipal Type: Town
Incorporated: April 23, 1906 *Area:* 1.75 sq km
Population in 2011: 807
Provincial Electoral District(s): Battle River-Wainwright
Federal Electoral District(s): Vegreville-Wainwright
Next Election: Oct. 21, 2013 (3 year terms)
Note: Incorporated as a town on April 2, 1907.
Jim Martin, Mayor
Sari-Anne Doolaege, CAO

Delburne
P.O. Box 341
Delburne, AB T0M 0V0
Tel: 403-749-3606; *Fax:* 403-749-2800
village@delburne.ca
www.delburne.ca
Municipal Type: Village
Incorporated: Jan. 17, 1913 *Area:* 1.32 sq km
Population in 2011: 830
Provincial Electoral District(s): Innisfail-Sylvan Lake
Federal Electoral District(s): Red Deer
Next Election: Oct. 21, 2013 (3 year terms)
Ray Reckseidler, Mayor
ray.reckseidler@delburne.ca
Karen Fegan, CAO
karen.fegan@delburne.ca

Delia
P.O. Box 206
218 Main Street
Delia, AB T0J 0W0
Tel: 403-364-3787; *Fax:* 403-364-2089
delia@netago.ca
Municipal Type: Village
Incorporated: July 20, 1914 *Area:* 1.31 sq km
Population in 2011: 186
Provincial Electoral District(s): Drumheller-Stettler
Federal Electoral District(s): Crowfoot
Next Election: Oct. 21, 2013 (3 year terms)
Gordon Isaac, Mayor
Caroline Siverson, CAO
cao.delia@netago.ca

Devon
1 Columbia Ave. West
Devon, AB T9G 1A1
Tel: 780-987-8300; *Fax:* 780-987-4778
www.town.devon.ab.ca
Municipal Type: Town
Incorporated: Dec. 31, 1949 *Area:* 8.63 sq km
Population in 2011: 6,510
Provincial Electoral District(s): Leduc-Beaumont-Devon
Federal Electoral District(s): Edmonton-Leduc
Next Election: Oct. 21, 2013 (3 year terms)
Note: Incorporated as a town on Feb. 24, 1950.
Tony Kulbisky, CAO
780-987-8301
Anita Marie Fisher, Mayor

Dewberry
P.O. Box 30
Dewberry, AB T0B 1G0
Tel: 780-847-3053; *Fax:* 780-847-3057
dewberry@hmsinet.ca; ecodew@hmsinet.ca
www.villageofdewberry.ca
Municipal Type: Village
Incorporated: Jan. 1, 1957 *Area:* 0.84 sq km
Population in 2011: 201
Provincial Electoral District(s): Vermilion-Lloydminster
Federal Electoral District(s): Vegreville-Wainwright
Next Election: Oct. 21, 2013 (3 year terms)
Sherry Johnson, Acting Sec.-Treas.
Headley Dennill, Mayor

Didsbury
P.O. Box 790
Didsbury, AB T0M 0W0
Tel: 403-335-3391; *Fax:* 403-335-9794
iquiries@didsbury.ca
www.didsbury.ca
Municipal Type: Town
Incorporated: Dec. 24, 1901 *Area:* 5.47 sq km
Population in 2011: 4,957
Provincial Electoral District(s): Olds-Didsbury-Three Hills
Federal Electoral District(s): Wild Rose
Next Election: Oct. 21, 2013 (3 year terms)
Note: Incorporated as a town on Sept. 27, 1906.
Brian Wittal, Mayor
bwittal@didsbury.ca
Roy Brown, CAO
rbrown@didsbury.ca

Donalda
P.O. Box 160
Donalda, AB T0B 1H0
Tel: 403-883-2345; *Fax:* 403-883-2022
vdonalda@telusplanet.net
www.village.donalda.ab.ca
Municipal Type: Village
Incorporated: Dec. 30, 1912 *Area:* 0.99 sq km
Population in 2011: 259
Provincial Electoral District(s): Drumheller-Stettler
Federal Electoral District(s): Crowfoot
Next Election: Oct. 21, 2013 (3 year terms)
Bruce Gartisde, Mayor
Joan Kapiniak, CAO
cao@village.donalda.ab.ca

Donnelly
P.O. Box 200
Donnelly, AB T0H 1G0
Tel: 780-925-3835; *Fax:* 780-925-2100
vilofdon@serbernet.com
www.villageofdonelly.drackir.com
Municipal Type: Village
Incorporated: Jan. 1, 1956 *Area:* 1.04 sq km
Population in 2011: 305
Provincial Electoral District(s): Dunvegan-Central Peace
Federal Electoral District(s): Peace River
Next Election: Oct. 21, 2013 (3 year terms)
Charles Doyle, Mayor
Rita Therriault, Administrator

Drayton Valley
P.O. Box 6837
5120 - 52nd St.
Drayton Valley, AB T7A 1A1
Tel: 780-514-2200; *Fax:* 780-542-5753
info@town.draytonvalley.ab.ca
www.town.draytonvalley.ab.ca
Municipal Type: Town
Incorporated: Jan. 1, 1956 *Area:* 12.27 sq km
Population in 2011: 7,049
Provincial Electoral District(s): Drayton Valley-Calmar
Federal Electoral District(s): Yellowhead
Next Election: Oct. 21, 2013 (3 year terms)
Note: Incorporated as a town on June 1, 1956.
Manny Deol, Town Manager
mdeol@town.draytonvalley.ab.ca
Mohammed (Moe) Hamdon, Mayor
mayor@town.draytonvalley.ab.ca

Drumheller
703 - 2nd Ave. West
Drumheller, AB T0J 0Y3
Tel: 403-823-6300; *Fax:* 403-823-7739
rmroman@dinosaurvalley.com
www.dinosaurvalley.com
Municipal Type: Town
Incorporated: May 15, 1913 *Area:* 107.93 sq km
Population in 2011: 8,029
Provincial Electoral District(s): Drumheller-Stettler
Federal Electoral District(s): Crowfoot
Next Election: Oct. 21, 2013 (3 year terms)
Note: Incorporated as a town on March 2, 1916.
Ray Romanetz, CAO
rmroman@dinosaurvalley.com
Terry Yemen, Mayor

Duchess
P.O. Box 158
Duchess, AB T0J 0Z0
Tel: 403-378-4452; *Fax:* 403-378-3860
administration@villageofduchess.com
www.villageofduchess.com

Municipal Type: Village
Incorporated: May 12, 1921 *Area:* 1.89 sq km
Population in 2011: 992
Provincial Electoral District(s): Strathmore-Brooks
Federal Electoral District(s): Medicine Hat
Next Election: Oct. 21, 2013 (3 year terms)
Anthony Steidel, Mayor
Yvonne Cosh

Eckville
P.O. Box 578
Eckville, AB T0M 0X0
Tel: 403-746-2171; *Fax:* 403-746-2900
info@eckville.com
www.eckville.com
Municipal Type: Town
Incorporated: Nov. 3, 1921 *Area:* 1.58 sq km
Population in 2011: 1,125
Provincial Electoral District(s): Rocky Mountain House
Federal Electoral District(s): Wetaskiwin
Next Election: Oct. 21, 2013 (3 year terms)
Note: Incorporated as a town on July 1, 1966.
Helen Posti, Mayor
Therese Kleeberger, Administrator
admin@eckville.com

Edberg
P.O. Box 160
Edberg, AB T0B 1J0
Tel: 780-877-3999; *Fax:* 780-877-2562
vledberg@syban.net
www.villageofedberg.com
Municipal Type: Village
Incorporated: Feb. 4, 1930 *Area:* 0.36 sq km
Population in 2011: 168
Provincial Electoral District(s): Lacombe-Ponoka
Federal Electoral District(s): Crowfoot
Next Election: Oct. 21, 2013 (3 year terms)
Lorne Klevgaard, Mayor
Patrick Risk, CAO

Edgerton
P.O. Box 57
Edgerton, AB T0B 1K0
Tel: 780-755-3933; *Fax:* 780-755-3750
info@edgerton-oasis.ca
www.edgerton-oasis.ca
Municipal Type: Village
Incorporated: Sept. 11, 1917 *Area:* 1.22 sq km
Population in 2011: 317
Provincial Electoral District(s): Battle River-Wainwright
Federal Electoral District(s): Vegreville-Wainwright
Next Election: Oct. 21, 2013 (3 year terms)
Barbara L. Sjoquist, Mayor
Al Gordon, CAO

Edson
P.O. Box 6300
605 - 50th St.
Edson, AB T7E 1T7
Tel: 780-723-4401; *Fax:* 780-723-8617
civiccentre@townofedson.ca
www.townofedson.ca
Municipal Type: Town
Incorporated: Jan. 9, 1911 *Area:* 29.54 sq km
Population in 2011: 8,475
Provincial Electoral District(s): West Yellowhead
Federal Electoral District(s): Yellowhead
Next Election: Oct. 21, 2013 (3 year terms)
Note: Incorporated as a town on Sept. 21, 1911.
Clarence Joly, CAO
clarencej@townofedson.ca
Greg Pasychny, Mayor

Elk Point
P.O. Box 448
Elk Point, AB T0A 1A0
Tel: 780-724-3810; *Fax:* 780-724-2762
town@elkpoint.ca
www.elkpoint.ca
Municipal Type: Town
Incorporated: May 31, 1938 *Area:* 4.88 sq km
Population in 2011: 1,412
Provincial Electoral District(s): Lac La Biche-St. Paul
Federal Electoral District(s): Westlock-St. Paul
Next Election: Oct. 21, 2013 (3 year terms)
Note: Incorporated as a town on Jan. 1, 1962.
Parrish Tung, Mayor
parrish.tung@elkpoint.ca
Myron J. Goyan, Manager
mjgoyan@elkpoint.ca

Elnora
P.O. Box 629
Elnora, AB T0M 0Y0
Tel: 403-773-3922; *Fax:* 403-773-3173
elnoravl@platinum.ca
www.villageofelnora.com
Municipal Type: Village
Incorporated: July 22, 1929 *Area:* 0.69 sq km
Population in 2011: 313
Provincial Electoral District(s): Innisfail-Sylvan Lake
Federal Electoral District(s): Red Deer
Next Election: Oct. 21, 2013 (3 year terms)
Rob Aellen, Mayor
Michelle White, Administrator

Empress
P.O. Box 159
Empress, AB T0J 1E0
Tel: 403-565-3938; *Fax:* 403-565-2010
voe14@telus.net
www.villageofempress.com
Municipal Type: Village
Incorporated: Feb. 5, 1914 *Area:* 1.75 sq km
Population in 2011: 188
Provincial Electoral District(s): Drumheller-Stettler
Federal Electoral District(s): Medicine Hat
Next Election: Oct. 21, 2013 (3 year terms)
Roderick L. Briggs, Mayor
Darran Dick, CAO
darran.dick@gov.ab.ca

Fairview
P.O. Box 730
10209 - 109 St.
Fairview, AB T0H 1L0
Tel: 780-835-5461; *Fax:* 780-835-3576
municipalsecretary@fairview.ca
www.fairview.ca
Municipal Type: Town
Incorporated: March 28, 1929 *Area:* 9.65 sq km
Population in 2011: 3,162
Provincial Electoral District(s): Dunvegan-Central Peace
Federal Electoral District(s): Peace River
Next Election: Oct. 21, 2013 (3 year terms)
Note: Incorporated as a town on April 25, 1949.
Martin Taylor, CAO
cao@fairview.ca
Gordon MacLeod, Mayor
mayor@fairview.ca

Falher
P.O. Box 155
Falher, AB T0H 1M0
Tel: 780-837-2247; *Fax:* 780-837-2647
info@town.falher.ab.ca
www.town.falher.ab.ca
Municipal Type: Town
Incorporated: Sept. 05, 1923 *Area:* 2.87 sq km
Population in 2011: 1,075
Provincial Electoral District(s): Dunvegan-Central Peace
Federal Electoral District(s): Peace River
Next Election: Oct. 21, 2013 (3 year terms)
Note: Incorporated as a town on Jan. 1, 1955.
Adele Parker, CAO
aparker@town.falher.ab.ca
Margaret Tardif, Mayor
mtardif@town.falher.ab.ca

Ferintosh
P.O. Box 160
Ferintosh, AB T0B 1M0
Tel: 780-877-3767; *Fax:* 780-877-2338
ferintosh@mailhub.ca
www.ferintosh.info
Municipal Type: Village
Incorporated: Jan. 9, 1911 *Area:* 0.62 sq km
Population in 2011: 181
Provincial Electoral District(s): Lacombe-Ponoka
Federal Electoral District(s): Crowfoot
Next Election: Oct. 21, 2013 (3 year terms)
Marvin Jassman, Mayor
Patrick Risk, CAO

Foremost
P.O. Box 159
Foremost, AB T0K 0X0
Tel: 403-867-3733; *Fax:* 403-867-2031
vlg4most@telusplanet.net
www.foremostalberta.com
Municipal Type: Village
Incorporated: Dec. 31, 1950 *Area:* 1.74 sq km
Population in 2011: 526
Provincial Electoral District(s): Cypress-Medicine Hat
Federal Electoral District(s): Medicine Hat
Next Election: Oct. 21, 2013 (3 year terms)
Kenneth R. Kultgen, Mayor
Kelly Calhoun, Municipal Administrator

Forestburg
P.O. Box 210
Forestburg, AB T0B 1N0
Tel: 780-582-3668; *Fax:* 780-582-2233
forestburg@persona.ca
www.forestburg.ca
Municipal Type: Village
Incorporated: Aug. 21, 1919 *Area:* 2.19 sq km
Population in 2011: 831
Provincial Electoral District(s): Battle River-Wainwright
Federal Electoral District(s): Vegreville-Wainwright
Next Election: Oct. 21, 2013 (3 year terms)
Robert Frizzell, Mayor
Debra Moffatt, CAO

Fort Macleod
P.O. Box 1420
Fort MacLeod, AB T0L 0Z0
Tel: 403-553-4425; *Fax:* 403-553-2426
administration@fortmacleod.com
www.fortmacleod.com
Other Information: Toll free: 1-877-622-5366
Municipal Type: Town
Incorporated: Dec. 31, 1892 *Area:* 23.34 sq km
Population in 2011: 3,117
Provincial Electoral District(s): Livingstone-Macleod
Federal Electoral District(s): Macleod
Next Election: Oct. 21, 2013 (3 year terms)
R. Shawn Patience, Mayor
mayor@fortmacleod.com
Barry Elliott, Municipal Manager
manager@fortmacleod.com

Fox Creek
P.O. Box 149
102 Kaybob Drive
Fox Creek, AB T0H 1P0
Tel: 780-622-3896; *Fax:* 780-622-4247
info@town.fox-creek.ab.ca
www.fox-creek.ca
Municipal Type: Town
Incorporated: July 19, 1967 *Area:* 11.54 sq km
Population in 2011: 1,969
Provincial Electoral District(s): Grande Prairie-Smoky
Federal Electoral District(s): Yellowhead
Next Election: Oct. 21, 2013 (3 year terms)
Leora MacKinnon, Mayor
leora@foxcreek.ca
Ken Gwozdz, CAO
cao@foxcreek.ca

Gadsby
P.O. Box 80
Gadsby, AB T0C 1K0
Tel: 403-574-3793; *Fax:* 403-574-2369
vgadsby@telusplanet.net
Municipal Type: Village
Incorporated: May 6, 1910 *Area:* 0.82 sq km
Population in 2011: 25
Provincial Electoral District(s): Drumheller-Stettler
Federal Electoral District(s): Crowfoot
Next Election: Oct. 21, 2013 (3 year terms)
Fred Entwisle, Mayor
Lavonne Smith, CAO

Galahad
P.O. Box 66
Galahad, AB T0B 1R0
Tel: 780-583-3741; *Fax:* 780-583-2230
office@villageofgalahad.net
www.villagofgalahad.ca
Municipal Type: Village
Incorporated: March 5, 1918 *Area:* 0.6 sq km
Population in 2011: 119
Provincial Electoral District(s): Battle River-Wainwright
Federal Electoral District(s): Vegreville-Wainwright
Next Election: Oct. 21, 2013 (3 year terms)
Sheryl Fossen, Mayor
Brent Hoyland, Assistant CAO
gpoyser@flagstaff.ab.ca

Ghost Lake
P.O. Box 5754
High River, AB T1V 1P3
Tel: 403-652-4636; *Fax:* 403-206-7209
admin@ghostlake.ca
www.ghostlake.ca
Municipal Type: Summer Village
Incorporated: Dec. 31, 1953 *Area:* 0.63 sq km
Population in 2011: 81
Provincial Electoral District(s): Banff-Cochrane
Federal Electoral District(s): Wild Rose
Next Election: Summer 2013 (3 year terms)
Richard Elvey, Mayor
403-881-2276
Sharon Plett, CAO

Gibbons
P.O. Box 68
4807 - 50 Ave.
Gibbons, AB T0A 1N0
Tel: 780-923-3331; *Fax:* 780-923-3691
town@gibbons.ca
www.gibbons.ca
Municipal Type: Town
Incorporated: Jan. 1, 1959 *Area:* 6.46 sq km
Population in 2011: 3,030
Provincial Electoral District(s): Athabasca-Redwater
Federal Electoral District(s): Westlock-St. Paul
Next Election: Oct. 21, 2013 (3 year terms)
Note: Incorporated as a town on April 1, 1977.
Maisie Metrunec, Town Manager
mmetrunec@gibbons.ca
William H. Nimmo, Mayor
gov@gibbons.ca

Girouxville
P.O. Box 276
Girouxville, AB T0H 1S0
Tel: 780-323-4270; *Fax:* 780-323-4110
girouxvl@telusplanet.net
Municipal Type: Village
Incorporated: Dec. 31, 1951 *Area:* 0.58 sq km
Population in 2011: 266
Provincial Electoral District(s): Dunvegan-Central Peace
Federal Electoral District(s): Peace River
Next Election: Oct. 21, 2013 (3 year terms)
Carmen Ewing, Mayor
Estelle Girard, Municipal Administrator

Glendon
P.O. Box 177
Glendon, AB T0A 1P0
Tel: 780-635-3807; *Fax:* 780-635-2100
glendon@mcsnet.ca
Municipal Type: Village
Incorporated: Jan. 1, 1956 *Area:* 1.98 sq km
Population in 2011: 486
Provincial Electoral District(s): Bonnyville-Cold Lake
Federal Electoral District(s): Westlock-St. Paul
Next Election: Oct. 21, 2013 (3 year terms)
John Larry Lofstrand, Mayor
Paula Mack, CAO

Glenwood
Main Ave
Glenwood, AB T0k 2R0
Tel: 403-626-3233; *Fax:* 403-626-3234
admin@glenwood.ca
www.glenwood.ca
Municipal Type: Village
Incorporated: Jan. 1, 1961 *Area:* 1.46 sq km
Population in 2011: 287
Provincial Electoral District(s): Cardston-Taber-Warner
Federal Electoral District(s): Macleod
Next Election: Oct. 21, 2013 (3 year terms)
Doral Lybbert, Mayor
Brad Salmon, CAO

Golden Days
605-2nd Ave.
MA-ME O Beach, AB T0k 1x0
Tel: 780-586-2494; *Fax:* 780-586-3567
svoffice@telusplanet.net
Municipal Type: Summer Village
Incorporated: Jan. 1, 1965 *Area:* 2.27 sq km
Population in 2011: 141
Provincial Electoral District(s): Drayton Valley-Calmar
Federal Electoral District(s): Wetaskiwin
Next Election: Summer 2013 (3 year terms)
Randal Kay, Mayor
Sylvia Roy, Administrator

Grande Cache
P.O. Box 300
Grande Cache, AB T0E 0Y0
Tel: 780-827-3362; *Fax:* 780-827-2406
admin@grandecache.ca
www.grandecache.ca
Municipal Type: Town
Incorporated: Sept. 1, 1966 *Area:* 35.48 sq km
Population in 2011: 4,319
Provincial Electoral District(s): West Yellowhead
Federal Electoral District(s): Yellowhead
Next Election: Oct. 21, 2013 (3 year terms)
Louise Krewusik, Mayor
Darren Ottaway, CAO
darren.ottaway@grandecache.ca

Grandview
P.O. Box 100
603 - 2nd Ave.
Ma-Me-O Beach, AB T0C 1X0
Tel: 780-586-2494; *Fax:* 780-586-3567
svadminoffice@xplornet.com
www.grandview.com
Municipal Type: Summer Village
Incorporated: Jan. 1, 1967 *Area:* 0.8 sq km
Population in 2011: 108
Provincial Electoral District(s): Drayton Valley-Calmar
Federal Electoral District(s): Wetaskiwin
Next Election: Summer 2013 (3 year terms)
Don Davidson, Mayor
Sylvia Roy, CAO

Granum
P.O. Box 88
Granum, AB T0L 1A0
Tel: 403-687-3822; *Fax:* 403-687-2285
tmgr.townofgranum@shaw.ca
www.townofgranum.ca
Municipal Type: Town
Incorporated: July 12, 1904 *Area:* 1.87 sq km
Population in 2011: 447
Provincial Electoral District(s): Livingstone-Macleod
Federal Electoral District(s): Macleod
Next Election: Oct. 21, 2013 (3 year terms)
Note: Incorporated as a town on Nov. 7, 1910.
Gerald Brown, Mayor
Interim Mayor
Larry Flexhaug, Municipal Administrator
cao.townofgranum@shaw.ca

Grimshaw
P.O. Box 377
Grimshaw, AB T0H 1W0
Tel: 780-332-4626; *Fax:* 780-332-1250
wjohnson@grimshaw.ca
www.grimshaw.ca
Municipal Type: Town
Incorporated: Feb. 18, 1930 *Area:* 7.21 sq km
Population in 2011: 2,515
Provincial Electoral District(s): Dunvegan-Central Peace
Federal Electoral District(s): Peace River
Next Election: Oct. 21, 2013 (3 year terms)
Note: Incorporated as a town on Feb. 2, 1953.
Brian Allen, Mayor
Wendy Johnson, CAO
wjohnson@grimshaw.ca

Gull Lake
P.O. Box 5
RR#1, Site 2
Lacombe, AB T4L 2N1
Tel: 403-784-2966; *Fax:* 888-241-6027
admin@summervillageofgulllake.com
www.summervillageofgulllake.com
Municipal Type: Summer Village
Incorporated: Sept. 1, 1993 *Area:* 0.7 sq km
Population in 2011: 122
Provincial Electoral District(s): Rocky Mountain House
Federal Electoral District(s): Wetaskiwin
Next Election: Summer 2013 (3 year terms)
Rick Assinger, Mayor
assinger@telus.net
Harold Northcott, CAO
admin@summervillageofgulllake.com

Half Moon Bay
#90B Hewlett Park Landing
Sylvan Lake, AB T4S 2J3
Tel: 403-887-2822; *Fax:* 403-887-2897
fivesv@telusplanet.net
Municipal Type: Summer Village
Incorporated: Jan. 1, 1978 *Area:* 0.17 sq km
Population in 2011: 38
Provincial Electoral District(s): Rocky Mountain House
Federal Electoral District(s): Wetaskiwin
Next Election: Summer 2013 (3 year terms)
Edward (Ted) Hiscock, Mayor
Myra Reiter, Administrator

Halkirk
P.O. Box 126
Halkirk, AB T0C 1M0
Tel: 403-884-2464; *Fax:* 403-884-2113
halkirk@wildroseinternet.ca
Municipal Type: Village
Incorporated: Feb. 10, 1912 *Area:* 0.65 sq km
Population in 2011: 121
Provincial Electoral District(s): Battle River-Wainwright
Federal Electoral District(s): Crowfoot
Next Election: Oct. 21, 2013 (3 year terms)
Dale Kent, Mayor
Doris Cordel, Village Administrator

Hanna
P.O. Box 430
Hanna, AB T0J 1P0
Tel: 403-854-4433; *Fax:* 403-854-2772
admin@hanna.ca
www.hanna.ca
Municipal Type: Town
Incorporated: Dec. 31, 1912 *Area:* 8.39 sq km
Population in 2011: 2,673
Provincial Electoral District(s): Drumheller-Stettler
Federal Electoral District(s): Crowfoot
Next Election: Oct. 21, 2013 (3 year terms)
Note: Incorporated as a town on April 14, 1914.
Mark Nikota, Mayor
Geraldine Gervais, CAO
ggervais.cao@hanna.ca

Hardisty
P.O. Box 10
Hardisty, AB T0B 1V0
Tel: 780-888-3623; *Fax:* 780-888-2200
town.office@hardisty.ca
www.hardisty.ca
Municipal Type: Town
Incorporated: Dec. 11, 1906 *Area:* 5.48 sq km
Population in 2011: 639
Provincial Electoral District(s): Battle River-Wainwright
Federal Electoral District(s): Vegreville-Wainwright
Next Election: Oct. 21, 2013 (3 year terms)
Note: Incorporated as a town on Nov. 9, 1910.
Kevin O'Grady, Mayor
Alan Parkin, CAO
alanparkin@hardisty.ca

Hay Lakes
P.O. Box 40
Hay Lakes, AB T0B 1W0
Tel: 780-878-3200; *Fax:* 780-878-3897
haylakes@syban.net
www.villageofhaylakes.com
Municipal Type: Village
Incorporated: April 17, 1928 *Area:* 0.58 sq km
Population in 2011: 425
Provincial Electoral District(s): Leduc-Beaumont-Devon
Federal Electoral District(s): Crowfoot
Next Election: Oct. 21, 2013 (3 year terms)
Steve Nickoleff, Mayor
Heather Nadeau, Municipal Administrator

Heisler
P.O. Box 60
Heisler, AB T0B 2A0
Tel: 780-889-3774; *Fax:* 780-889-2280
administration@villageofheisler.ca
www.villageofheisler.ca
Municipal Type: Village
Incorporated: July 27, 1920 *Area:* 0.75 sq km
Population in 2011: 151
Provincial Electoral District(s): Battle River-Wainwright
Federal Electoral District(s): Vegreville-Wainwright
Next Election: Oct. 21, 2013 (3 year terms)
Shean Maciborski, Mayor
Brenda Loesch, CAO

High Level
10511 - 103 St.
High Level, AB T0H 1Z0
Tel: 780-926-2201; *Fax:* 780-926-2899
town@highlevel.ca
www.highlevel.ca

Municipal Type: Town
Incorporated: June 1, 1965 *Area:* 31.99 sq km
Population in 2011: 3,641
Provincial Electoral District(s): Peace River
Federal Electoral District(s): Peace River
Next Election: Oct. 21, 2013 (3 year terms)
Dean Krause, CAO
780-821-4001
dkrause@highlevel.ca
Peter Ernst, Mayor
780-926-4878
mayor@highlevel.ca

High Prairie
P.O. Box 179
High Prairie, AB T0G 1E0
Tel: 780-523-3388; *Fax:* 780-523-5930
reception@highprairie.ca
www.highprairie.ca
Municipal Type: Town
Incorporated: April 6, 1945 *Area:* 6.39 sq km
Population in 2011: 2,600
Provincial Electoral District(s): Lesser Slave Lake
Federal Electoral District(s): Fort McMurray-Athabasca
Next Election: Oct. 21, 2013 (3 year terms)
Note: Incorporated as a town on Jan. 10, 1950.
Rick Dumont, Mayor
mayor@highprairie.ca
Christopher J. Parker, Town Manager
cao@highprairie.ca

Hill Spring
P.O. Box 40
Hill Spring, AB T0K 1E0
Tel: 403-626-3876; *Fax:* 403-626-2333
office@hillspring.ca
www.hillspring.ca
Municipal Type: Village
Incorporated: Jan. 1, 1961 *Area:* 1.11 sq km
Population in 2011: 186
Provincial Electoral District(s): Cardston-Taber-Warner
Federal Electoral District(s): Macleod
Next Election: Oct. 21, 2013 (3 year terms)
Monte Christensen, Mayor
office@hillspring.ca
Kurtis Pratt, CAO
kurtispratt@raymond.ca

Hines Creek
P.O. Box 421
Hines Creek, AB T0H 2A0
Tel: 780-494-3690; *Fax:* 780-494-3605
stacey@hinescreek.com
www.hinescreek.com
Other Information: Other Phone: 780-494-3690
Municipal Type: Village
Incorporated: Dec. 31, 1951 *Area:* 4.37 sq km
Population in 2011: 380
Provincial Electoral District(s): Dunvegan-Central Peace
Federal Electoral District(s): Peace River
Next Election: Oct. 21, 2013 (3 year terms)
Ashley Zavisha, Mayor
ashley@zavishamills.com
Leila Sumner, Municipal Manager
lsumner@hinescreek.com

Hinton
131 Civic Centre Rd., 2nd Fl.
Hinton, AB T7V 2E5
Tel: 780-865-6000; *Fax:* 780-865-5706
bkreiner@town.hinton.ab.ca
www.hinton.ca
Municipal Type: Town
Incorporated: Nov. 1, 1956 *Area:* 25.76 sq km
Population in 2011: 9,640
Provincial Electoral District(s): West Yellowhead
Federal Electoral District(s): Yellowhead
Next Election: Oct. 21, 2013 (3 year terms)
Bernie Kreiner, Town Manager
bkreiner@hinton.ca
Glenn Taylor, Mayor
mayor@hinton.ca

Holden
P.O. Box 357
Holden, AB T0B 2C0
Tel: 780-688-3928; *Fax:* 780-688-2091
vholden@telusplanet.net
www.village.holden.ab.ca
Municipal Type: Village
Incorporated: April 14, 1909 *Area:* 1.7 sq km
Population in 2011: 381
Provincial Electoral District(s): Fort Saskatchewan-Vegreville
Federal Electoral District(s): Vegreville-Wainwright
Next Election: Oct. 21, 2013 (3 year terms)
Christine Mackay, Mayor
Katherine Whiteside, CAO

Horseshoe Bay
P.O. Box 1053
5837 - 44 Ave.
St Paul, AB T0A 3A0
Tel: 780-724-4422; *Fax:* 780-724-4422
d_smereka@telus.net
www.svhorseshoebay.ca
Municipal Type: Summer Village
Incorporated: Jan. 1, 1985 *Area:* 1.04 sq km
Population in 2011: 37
Provincial Electoral District(s): Lac La Biche-St. Paul
Federal Electoral District(s): Westlock-St. Paul
Next Election: Summer 2013 (3 year terms)
Gary Burns, Mayor
780-645-4609
g_burns@telus.net
Darlene Smereka, Administrator
dsmereka@county.stpaul.ab.ca

Hughenden
P.O. Box 26
Hughenden, AB T0B 2E0
Tel: 780-856-3830; *Fax:* 780-856-2034
hughenden@xplornet.com
Municipal Type: Village
Incorporated: Dec. 27, 1917 *Area:* 0.78 sq km
Population in 2011: 230
Provincial Electoral District(s): Battle River-Wainwright
Federal Electoral District(s): Vegreville-Wainwright
Next Election: Oct. 21, 2013 (3 year terms)
Aaron Gramlich, Mayor
hughenden@xplorenet.com
Lawrence Komaranky, CAO
hughendencao@xplornet.com

Hussar
P.O. Box 100
Hussar, AB T0J 1S0
Tel: 403-787-3766; *Fax:* 403-787-2560
hussar@myipplus.net
Municipal Type: Village
Incorporated: April 20, 1928 *Area:* 1.05 sq km
Population in 2011: 176
Provincial Electoral District(s): Strathmore-Brooks
Federal Electoral District(s): Crowfoot
Next Election: Oct. 21, 2013 (3 year terms)
Bruce Kaufman, Mayor
Tracy Anderson, CAO

Hythe
P.O. Box 219
Hythe, AB T0H 2C0
Tel: 780-356-3888; *Fax:* 780-356-2009
admin@hythe.ca
www.hythe.ca
Municipal Type: Village
Incorporated: Aug. 31, 1929 *Area:* 4.12 sq km
Population in 2011: 820
Provincial Electoral District(s): Grande Prairie-Wapiti
Federal Electoral District(s): Peace River
Next Election: Oct. 21, 2013 (3 year terms)
Gary Burgess, Mayor
mayor@hythe.ca
Greg Gayton, Administrator

Innisfail
4943 - 53 St.
Innisfail, AB T4G 1A1
Tel: 403-227-3376; *Fax:* 403-227-4045
townhall@innisfail.ca
www.townofinnisfail.com
Municipal Type: Town
Incorporated: Dec. 15, 1899 *Area:* 13.02 sq km
Population in 2011: 7,876
Provincial Electoral District(s): Innisfail-Sylvan Lake
Federal Electoral District(s): Red Deer
Next Election: Oct. 21, 2013 (3 year terms)
Note: Incorporated as a town on Nov. 20, 1903.
Helen Dietz, Town Manager
helen.dietz@innisfail.ca
Jim Romane, Mayor
mayor@innisfail.ca

Innisfree
P.O. Box 69
Innisfree, AB T0B 2G0
Tel: 780-592-3886; *Fax:* 780-592-3729
inisfree@telus.net
www.villageofinnisfree.com
Municipal Type: Village
Incorporated: March 11, 1911 *Area:* 1.27 sq km
Population in 2011: 220
Provincial Electoral District(s): Vermilion-Lloydminster
Federal Electoral District(s): Vegreville-Wainwright
Next Election: Oct. 21, 2013 (3 year terms)
Ron Konieczny, Mayor
Lori Leibel, Municipal Administrator
lorileibel@telus.net

Irma
P.O. Box 419
Irma, AB T0B 2H0
Tel: 780-754-3665; *Fax:* 780-754-3668
jfenton@irma.ca
www.villageofirma.com
Municipal Type: Village
Incorporated: May 30, 1912 *Area:* 1.11 sq km
Population in 2011: 457
Provincial Electoral District(s): Battle River-Wainwright
Federal Electoral District(s): Vegreville-Wainwright
Next Election: Oct. 21, 2013 (3 year terms)
Douglas Coubrough, Mayor
780-754-3077
Jackie Fenton, CAO
780-754-2160
Jackie@villageofirma.ca

Irricana
P.O. Box 100
Irricana, AB T0M 1B0
Tel: 403-935-4672; *Fax:* 403-935-4270
irricana@irricana.com
www.irricana.com
Municipal Type: Town
Incorporated: June 9, 1911 *Area:* 3.18 sq km
Population in 2011: 1,162
Provincial Electoral District(s): Airdrie-Chestermere
Federal Electoral District(s): Crowfoot
Next Election: Oct. 21, 2013 (3 year terms)
Note: Incorporated as a town on June 9, 2005.
Joshua Taylor, Mayor
jtaylor@irricana.com
Alvin Melton, CAO
cao@irricana.com

Island Lake
10511-109 ST.
Westlock, AB T7P 1A9
Tel: 780-349-3651; *Fax:* 780-349-5194
gmbancroft@shaw.ca
www.myislandlakesouth.com
Municipal Type: Summer Village
Incorporated: Jan. 1, 1958 *Area:* 1.45 sq km
Population in 2011: 243
Provincial Electoral District(s): Athabasca-Redwater
Federal Electoral District(s): Fort McMurray-Athabasca
Next Election: Summer 2013 (3 year terms)
Bob Yontz, Mayor
Marion Bancroft, CAO

Island Lake South
10511 - 109th St.
Westlock, AB T7P 1A9
Tel: 780-349-3651; *Fax:* 780-349-5194
gmbancroft@shaw.ca
www.myislandlakesouth.com
Municipal Type: Summer Village
Incorporated: Jan. 1, 1983 *Area:* 0.63 sq km
Population in 2011: 72
Provincial Electoral District(s): Athabasca-Redwater
Federal Electoral District(s): Fort McMurray-Athabasca
Next Election: Summer 2013 (3 year terms)
Jim Sandmaier, Mayor
Garth Bancroft, Administrator

Itaska Beach
5515 - 44 Ave., #A
Wetaskiwin, AB T9A 0C8
Tel: 780-312-0928; *Fax:* 780-401-3161
cao@extremesolutions.org
www.itaska.ca
Municipal Type: Summer Village
Incorporated: June 30, 1953 *Area:* 0.28 sq km
Population in 2011: 20
Provincial Electoral District(s): Drayton Valley-Calmar

Federal Electoral District(s): Wetaskiwin
Next Election: Summer 2013 (3 year terms)
Ralph Johnston, Mayor
rbjohns@telusplanet.net
June Boyda, CAO
cao@extremesolutions.org

Jarvis Bay
90B Hewlett Park Landing
Sylvan Lake, AB T4S 1W2
Tel: 403-887-2822; *Fax:* 403-887-2897
fivesv@telusplanet.net
Municipal Type: Summer Village
Incorporated: Jan. 1, 1986 *Area:* 0.55 sq km
Population in 2011: 203
Provincial Electoral District(s): Innisfail-Sylvan Lake
Federal Electoral District(s): Red Deer
Next Election: Summer 2013 (3 year terms)
Bob Thomlinson, Mayor
Myra Reiter, Administrator

Kapasiwin
P.O. Box 9
Kapasiwin, AB T0E 2Y0
Tel: 780-892-2684
gckapa@cruzinternet.com
www.kapasiwinalberta.com
Municipal Type: Summer Village
Incorporated: Oct. 25, 1913 *Area:* 0.31 sq km
Population in 2011: 10
Provincial Electoral District(s): Stony Plain
Federal Electoral District(s): Yellowhead
Next Election: Summer 2013 (3 year terms)
Note: Incorporated as a summer village on Sept. 01, 1993.
Brent Baim, Mayor
George Jones, Administrator

Killam
P.O. Box 189
Killam, AB T0B 2L0
Tel: 780-385-3977; *Fax:* 780-385-2120
tkillam@telusplanet.net
www.town.killam.ab.ca
Municipal Type: Town
Incorporated: Dec. 29, 1906 *Area:* 4.53 sq km
Population in 2011: 981
Provincial Electoral District(s): Battle River-Wainwright
Federal Electoral District(s): Vegreville-Wainwright
Next Election: Oct. 21, 2013 (3 year terms)
Note: Incorporated as a town on May 1, 1965.
H.L. (Bud) James, Mayor
bjames@town.killam.ab.ca
Kimberly Borgel, CAO
cao@town.killam.ab.ca

Kitscoty
P.O. Box 128
Kitscoty, AB T0B 2P0
Tel: 780-846-2221; *Fax:* 780-846-2213
kitscoty@ruralsurf.net
Municipal Type: Village
Incorporated: March 22, 1911 *Area:* 1.54 sq km
Population in 2011: 846
Provincial Electoral District(s): Vermilion-Lloydminster
Federal Electoral District(s): Vegreville-Wainwright
Next Election: Oct. 21, 2013 (3 year terms)
Daryl Frank, Mayor
Harold Trew, CAO

Lakeview
P.O. Box 190
Seba Beach, AB T0E 2B0
Tel: 780-797-3863; *Fax:* 780-797-3800
svseba@telusplanet.net
Municipal Type: Summer Village
Incorporated: Oct. 25, 1913 *Area:* 0.33 sq km
Population in 2011: 26
Provincial Electoral District(s): Stony Plain
Federal Electoral District(s): Yellowhead
Next Election: Summer 2013 (3 year terms)
Earle Robertson, Mayor
Susan H. Evans, CAO

Lamont
P.O. Box 330
Lamont, AB T0B 2R0
Tel: 780-895-2010; *Fax:* 780-895-2595
tom.m@tclamont.ca
www.lamont.ca
Municipal Type: Town
Incorporated: June 14, 1910 *Area:* 4.59 sq km
Population in 2011: 1,753
Provincial Electoral District(s): Fort Saskatchewan-Vegreville
Federal Electoral District(s): Vegreville-Wainwright
Next Election: Oct. 21, 2013 (3 year terms)
Note: Incorporated as a town on May 31, 1968.
Denis Durand, Mayor
Tom Miller, CAO

Larkspur
10511-109 St.
Westlock, AB T2P 1A9
Tel: 780-349-3651; *Fax:* 780-349-5194
gmbancroft@shaw.ca
www.myislandlakesouth.com
Municipal Type: Summer Village
Incorporated: Jan. 1, 1985 *Area:* 0.22 sq km
Population in 2011: 38
Provincial Electoral District(s): Barrhead-Morinville-Westlock
Federal Electoral District(s): Westlock-St. Paul
Next Election: Summer 2013 (3 year terms)
Frank Atkinson, Mayor
Marion Bankroft, CAO
gmbancroft@shaw.ca

Legal
P.O. Box 390
Legal, AB T0G 1L0
Tel: 780-961-3773; *Fax:* 780-961-4133
main@town.legal.ab.ca
www.town.legal.ab.ca
Municipal Type: Town
Incorporated: Feb. 20, 1914 *Area:* 2.55 sq km
Population in 2011: 1,225
Provincial Electoral District(s): Barrhead-Morinville-Westlock
Federal Electoral District(s): Westlock-St. Paul
Next Election: Oct. 21, 2013 (3 year terms)
Note: Incorporated as a town on Jan. 1, 1998.
Albert St. Jean, Mayor
astjean@town.legal.ab.ca
Robert Proulx, Administrator
rproulx@town.legal.ab.ca

Linden
P.O. Box 213
Linden, AB T0M 1J0
Tel: 403-546-3888; *Fax:* 403-546-2112
cao@linden.ca
www.linden.ca
Municipal Type: Village
Incorporated: Jan. 1, 1964 *Area:* 2.56 sq km
Population in 2011: 725
Provincial Electoral District(s): Olds-Didsbury-Three Hills
Federal Electoral District(s): Crowfoot
Next Election: Oct. 21, 2013 (3 year terms)
Darwin Moon, Mayor
Joanne Weller, Municipal Administrator

Lomond
P.O. Box 268
Lomond, AB T0L 1G0
Tel: 403-792-3611; *Fax:* 403-792-3300
voflom@keltech.ab.ca
Municipal Type: Village
Incorporated: Feb. 16, 1916 *Area:* 1.28 sq km
Population in 2011: 173
Provincial Electoral District(s): Little Bow
Federal Electoral District(s): Macleod
Next Election: Oct. 21, 2013 (3 year terms)
Brad Koch, Mayor
bkoch@telusplanet.net
Tracy Doram, CAO

Longview
P.O. Box 147
Longview, AB T0L 1H0
Tel: 403-558-3922; *Fax:* 403-558-3743
info@village.longview.ab.ca
www.village.longview.ab.ca
Other Information: Other Email: office-manager@village.longview.ab.ca
Municipal Type: Village
Incorporated: Jan. 1, 1964 *Area:* 1.09 sq km
Population in 2011: 307
Provincial Electoral District(s): Highwood
Federal Electoral District(s): Macleod
Next Election: Oct. 21, 2013 (3 year terms)
Ivor McCorquindale, Mayor
mayor@village.longview.ab.ca
Leslie Fitzgerald, CAO
cao@village.longview.ab.ca

Lougheed
P.O. Box 5
Lougheed, AB T0B 2V0
Tel: 780-386-3970; *Fax:* 780-386-2136
villageoflougheed@xplorenet.com
www.villageoflougheed.com
Municipal Type: Village
Incorporated: Nov. 7, 1911 *Area:* 1.13 sq km
Population in 2011: 233
Provincial Electoral District(s): Battle River-Wainwright
Federal Electoral District(s): Vegreville-Wainwright
Next Election: Oct. 21, 2013 (3 year terms)
Debra Smith, Mayor
lardebsm@xplorenet.com
Linda Felske, Acting CAO
lougheedassist@xplornet.com

Ma-Me-O Beach
P.O. Box 100
603 - 2 Ave.
Ma-Me-O Beach, AB T0C 1X0
Tel: 780-586-2494; *Fax:* 780-586-3567
information@svofficepl.com
www.svofficepl.com
Municipal Type: Summer Village
Incorporated: Dec. 31, 1948 *Area:* 0.65 sq km
Population in 2011: 113
Provincial Electoral District(s): Drayton Valley-Calmar
Federal Electoral District(s): Wetaskiwin
Next Election: Summer 2013 (3 year terms)
Don Fleming, Mayor
780-437-4101
Sylvia Roy, Administrator
sylvia.roy@svofficepl.com

Magrath
P.O. Box 520
Magrath, AB T0K 1J0
Tel: 403-758-3212; *Fax:* 403-758-6333
wade@magrath.ca
www.townofmagrath.ca
Municipal Type: Town
Incorporated: Aug. 20, 1901 *Area:* 4.97 sq km
Population in 2011: 2,217
Provincial Electoral District(s): Cardston-Taber-Warner
Federal Electoral District(s): Lethbridge
Next Election: Oct. 21, 2013 (3 year terms)
Note: Incorporated as a town on July 24, 1907.
Russ Barnett, Mayor
Wade Alston, CAO
wade@magrath.ca
Sunni-Jeanne Walker, Mayor
sonnij@telus.net
John Brodrick, CAO
jbrodrick@manning.ca

Manning
P.O. Box 125
Manning, AB T0H 2M0
Tel: 780-836-3606; *Fax:* 780-836-3570
info@manning.ca
www.manning.ca
Municipal Type: Town
Incorporated: Dec. 31, 1951 *Area:* 3.42 sq km
Population in 2011: 1,164
Provincial Electoral District(s): Peace River
Federal Electoral District(s): Peace River
Next Election: Oct. 21, 2013 (3 year terms)
Note: Incorporated as a town on Jan. 1, 1957.

Mannville
P.O. Box 180
5127 - 50th St.
Mannville, AB T0B 2W0
Tel: 780-763-3500; *Fax:* 780-763-3643
info@mannville.com; cao@mannville.com
www.mannville.com
Municipal Type: Village
Incorporated: Dec. 29, 1906 *Area:* 2.15 sq km
Population in 2011: 803
Provincial Electoral District(s): Vermilion-Lloydminster
Federal Electoral District(s): Vegreville-Wainwright
Next Election: Oct. 21, 2013 (3 year terms)
Al Good, Mayor
council@mannville.com

Marwayne
P.O. Box 113
Marwayne, AB T0B 2X0
Tel: 780-847-3962; *Fax:* 780-847-3324
marwayne@hmsinet.ca
www.village.marwayne.ab.ca

Municipal Type: Village
Incorporated: Dec. 31, 1952 *Area:* 1.15 sq km
Population in 2011: 612
Provincial Electoral District(s): Vermilion-Lloydminster
Federal Electoral District(s): Vegreville-Wainwright
Next Election: Oct. 21, 2013 (3 year terms)
Jenelle Saskiw, Mayor
marwayne@hmsinet.ca
Joanne Horton, Administrative Officer
cao.marwayne@hmsinet.ca

Mayerthorpe
P.O. Box 420
Mayerthorpe, AB T0E 1N0
Tel: 780-786-2416; *Fax:* 780-786-4590
admin@mayerthorpe.ca
www.mayerthorpe.ca
Municipal Type: Town
Incorporated: March 5, 1927 *Area:* 4.78 sq km
Population in 2011: 1,398
Provincial Electoral District(s): Whitecourt-Ste. Anne
Federal Electoral District(s): Yellowhead
Next Election: Oct. 21, 2013 (3 year terms)
Note: Incorporated as a town on March 20, 1961.
Doug McDermid, Mayor
Kim Connell, CAO
cao@mayerthorpe.ca

McLennan
P.O. Box 356
19 - 1st Ave. NW
McLennan, AB T0H 2L0
Tel: 780-324-3065; *Fax:* 780-324-2288
twnmcl@serbernet.com
www.townofmclennan.com
Municipal Type: Town
Incorporated: Feb. 1, 1944 *Area:* 3.58 sq km
Population in 2011: 809
Provincial Electoral District(s): Dunvegan-Central Peace
Federal Electoral District(s): Peace River
Next Election: Oct. 21, 2013 (3 year terms)
Note: Incorporated as a town on Feb. 11, 1948.
Donald Regier, Mayor
Lorraine Willier, CAO

Mewatha Beach
10511 - 109th St.
Westlock, AB T7P 1A9
Tel: 780-349-3651; *Fax:* 780-349-5194
gmbancroft@shaw.ca
www.mymewathabeach.com
Municipal Type: Summer Village
Incorporated: Jan. 1, 1978 *Area:* 0.78 sq km
Population in 2011: 79
Provincial Electoral District(s): Athabasca-Redwater
Federal Electoral District(s): Fort McMurray-Athabasca
Next Election: Summer 2013 (3 year terms)
Barry J. Walker, Mayor
Garth Bancroft, Administrator
gmbancroft@shaw.ca

Milk River
P.O. Box 270
Milk River, AB T0K 1M0
Tel: 403-647-3773; *Fax:* 403-647-3772
main@milkriver.ca
www.milkriver.ca
Municipal Type: Town
Incorporated: July 11, 1916 *Area:* 2.39 sq km
Population in 2011: 811
Provincial Electoral District(s): Cardston-Taber-Warner
Federal Electoral District(s): Lethbridge
Next Election: Oct. 21, 2013 (3 year terms)
Note: Incorporated as a town on Feb. 7, 1956.
Terry Michaelis, Mayor
main@milkriver.ca
Mario Berthiaume, CAO
cao@milkriver.ca

Millet
P.O. Box 270
Millet, AB T0C 1Z0
Tel: 780-387-4554; *Fax:* 780-387-4459
millet@millet.ca
www.millet.ca
Municipal Type: Town
Incorporated: June 17, 1903 *Area:* 3.74 sq km
Population in 2011: 2,092
Provincial Electoral District(s): Wetaskiwin-Camrose
Federal Electoral District(s): Wetaskiwin
Next Election: Oct. 21, 2013 (3 year terms)
Note: Incorporated as a town on Sept. 1, 1983.
Robert E. Lorenson, Mayor
Teri Pelletier, CAO
cao@millet.ca

Milo
P.O. Box 65
Milo, AB T0L 1L0
Tel: 403-599-3883; *Fax:* 403-599-2201
vilmilo@wildroseinternet.ca
www.villageofmilo.ca
Municipal Type: Village
Incorporated: May 7, 1931 *Area:* 0.48 sq km
Population in 2011: 122
Provincial Electoral District(s): Little Bow
Federal Electoral District(s): Macleod
Next Election: Oct. 21, 2013 (3 year terms)
Rafael Zea, Mayor
Kwabena Oduro-Kontoh, Municipal Administrator
kodurokontoh@gmail.com

Minburn
P.O. Box 65
Minburn, AB T0B 3B0
Tel: 780-593-3939; *Fax:* 780-593-3944
vminburn@telus.net
Municipal Type: Village
Incorporated: June 24, 1919 *Area:* 0.73 sq km
Population in 2011: 105
Provincial Electoral District(s): Vermilion-Lloydminster
Federal Electoral District(s): Vegreville-Wainwright
Next Election: Oct. 21, 2013 (3 year terms)
Nick W. Marusiak, Mayor
Karen McQuarrie, CAO

Morinville
10125 - 100 Ave.
Morinville, AB T8R 1L6
Tel: 780-939-4361; *Fax:* 780-939-5633
treaume@morinville.ca
www.morinville.ca
Municipal Type: Town
Incorporated: Aug. 24, 1901 *Area:* 11.34 sq km
Population in 2011: 8,569
Provincial Electoral District(s): Barrhead-Morinville-Westlock
Federal Electoral District(s): Westlock-St. Paul
Next Election: Oct. 21, 2013 (3 year terms)
Note: Incorporated as a town on April 21, 1911.
R. Lloyd Bertschi, Mayor
mayor@morinville.ca
Debbie Oyarzun, CAO
doyarzun@morinville

Morrin
P.O. Box 149
Morrin, AB T0J 2B0
Tel: 403-772-3870; *Fax:* 403-772-2123
morrin@netago.ca
Municipal Type: Village
Incorporated: April 16, 1920 *Area:* 0.82 sq km
Population in 2011: 245
Provincial Electoral District(s): Drumheller-Stettler
Federal Electoral District(s): Crowfoot
Next Election: Oct. 21, 2013 (3 year terms)
Suzanne Lacher, Mayor
Annette Plachner, CAO

Mundare
P.O. Box 348
5128 - 50 St.
Mundare, AB T0B 3H0
Tel: 780-764-3929; *Fax:* 780-764-2003
info@mundare.ca
www.mundare.ca
Municipal Type: Town
Incorporated: March 6, 1907 *Area:* 3 sq km
Population in 2011: 855
Provincial Electoral District(s): Fort Saskatchewan-Vegreville
Federal Electoral District(s): Vegreville-Wainwright
Next Election: Oct. 21, 2013 (3 year terms)
Note: Incorporated as a town on Jan. 4, 1951.
Michael Saric, Mayor
msaric@mundare.ca
Colin Zyla, CAO
cao@mundare.ca

Munson
P.O. Box 10
Munson, AB T0J 2C0
Tel: 403-823-6987; *Fax:* 403-823-9883
munson@netago.ca
Municipal Type: Village
Incorporated: May 5, 1911 *Area:* 2.6 sq km
Population in 2011: 204
Provincial Electoral District(s): Drumheller-Stettler
Federal Electoral District(s): Crowfoot
Next Election: Oct. 21, 2013 (3 year terms)
Scott Dudley, Mayor
Lyle Cawiezel, Administrator

Myrnam
P.O. Box 278
5007 - 50th St.
Myrnam, AB T0B 3K0
Tel: 780-366-3910; *Fax:* 780-366-2246
vmyrnam@mcsnet.ca
www.myrnam.info
Municipal Type: Village
Incorporated: Aug. 22, 1930 *Area:* 2.76 sq km
Population in 2011: 370
Provincial Electoral District(s): Lac la Biche-St. Paul
Federal Electoral District(s): Vegreville-Wainwright
Next Election: Oct. 21, 2013 (3 year terms)
Edward Sosnowski, Mayor
Gary Dupuis, Administrator

Nakamun Park
13 Grandin Rd.
St Albert, AB T8N 3B2
Tel: 780-460-7226; *Fax:* 780-419-2476
hmarsh@telusplanet.net
www.svnakamun.com
Municipal Type: Summer Village
Incorporated: Jan. 1, 1966 *Area:* 0.41 sq km
Population in 2011: 36
Provincial Electoral District(s): Whitecourt-Ste. Anne
Federal Electoral District(s): Yellowhead
Next Election: Summer 2013 (3 year terms)
Janice Baker, Mayor
780-482-2728
Hilda Marsh, CAO
hmarsh@telusplanet.net

Nampa
P.O. Box 69
Nampa, AB T0H 2R0
Tel: 780-322-3852; *Fax:* 780-322-2100
office@nampa.ca
www.nampa.ca
Municipal Type: Village
Incorporated: Jan. 1, 1958 *Area:* 1.86 sq km
Population in 2011: 362
Provincial Electoral District(s): Peace River
Federal Electoral District(s): Peace River
Next Election: Oct. 21, 2013 (3 year terms)
Klaus Noruchat, Mayor
khn@serbernet.com
Ray Coad, CAO
cao@nampa.ca

Nanton
P.O. Box 609
Nanton, AB T0L 1R0
Tel: 403-646-2029; *Fax:* 403-646-2653
cao@nanton.ca
www.nanton.ca
Municipal Type: Town
Incorporated: June 22, 1903 *Area:* 4.25 sq km
Population in 2011: 2,132
Provincial Electoral District(s): Livingstone-Macleod
Federal Electoral District(s): Macleod
Next Election: Oct. 21, 2013 (3 year terms)
Note: Incorporated as a town on Aug. 9, 1907.
John J. Blake, Mayor
Brad Mason, CAO
cao@town.nanton.ab.ca

New Norway
P.O. Box 60
New Norway, AB T0B 3L0
Tel: 780-855-3915; *Fax:* 780-855-3916
admin@villageofnewnorway.ca
www.villageofnewnorway.ca
Municipal Type: Village
Incorporated: May 6, 1910 *Area:* 1.12 sq km
Population in 2011: 283
Provincial Electoral District(s): Lacombe-Ponoka
Federal Electoral District(s): Crowfoot
Next Election: Oct. 21, 2013 (3 year terms)
Tonya Ratushniak, Mayor
Dirk Bannister, CAO

Nobleford
P.O. Box 67
906 Highway Ave.
Nobleford, AB T0L 1S0
Tel: 403-824-3555; *Fax:* 403-824-3553
admin@village.nobleford.ab.ca
www.village.nobleford.ab.ca
Municipal Type: Village
Incorporated: Feb. 28, 1918 *Area:* 1.17 sq km
Population in 2011: 1,000
Provincial Electoral District(s): Little Bow
Federal Electoral District(s): Lethbridge
Next Election: Oct. 21, 2013 (3 year terms)
Marguerite Wobicke, Mayor
Kirk Hofman, CAO
caohofman@village.nobleford.ab.ca

Norglenwold
90B Hewlett Park Landing
Sylvan Lake, AB T4S 2J3
Tel: 403-887-2822; *Fax:* 403-887-2897
fivesv@telusplanet.net
Municipal Type: Summer Village
Incorporated: Jan. 1, 1965 *Area:* 0.67 sq km
Population in 2011: 232
Provincial Electoral District(s): Innisfail-Sylvan Lake
Federal Electoral District(s): Red Deer
Next Election: Summer 2013 (3 year terms)
Carol McMillan, Mayor
Myra Reiter, Administrator

Norris Beach
P.O. Box 100
Ma-Me-O Beach, AB T0C 1X0
Tel: 780-586-2494; *Fax:* 780-586-3567
information@svofficepl.com
www.svofficepl.com
Municipal Type: Summer Village
Incorporated: Dec. 31, 1988 *Area:* 0.16 sq km
Population in 2011: 46
Provincial Electoral District(s): Drayton Valley-Calmar
Federal Electoral District(s): Wetaskiwin
Next Election: Summer 2013 (3 year terms)
Bruce Fowlie, Mayor
Sylvia Roy, Administrator
sylvia.roy@svofficepl.com

Olds
4512 - 46 St.
Olds, AB T4H 1R5
Tel: 403-556-6981; *Fax:* 403-556-6537
admin@olds.ca
www.olds.ca
Municipal Type: Town
Incorporated: May 26, 1896 *Area:* 11.05 sq km
Population in 2011: 8,235
Provincial Electoral District(s): Olds-Didsbury-Three Hills
Federal Electoral District(s): Wild Rose
Next Election: Oct. 21, 2013 (3 year terms)
Note: Incorporated as a town on July 01, 1905.
Judy Dahl, Mayor
403-507-4114
mayor@olds.ca
Norman McInnis, CAO
mclnnis@olds.ca

Onoway
P.O. Box 540
Onoway, AB T0E 1V0
Tel: 780-967-5338; *Fax:* 780-967-3226
info@onoway.com
www.onoway.com
Municipal Type: Town
Incorporated: June 25, 1923 *Area:* 3.34 sq km
Population in 2011: 1,039
Provincial Electoral District(s): Whitecourt-Ste. Anne
Federal Electoral District(s): Yellowhead
Next Election: Oct. 21, 2013 (3 year terms)
Note: Incorporated as a town on Sept. 1, 2005.
Dale Krasnow, Mayor
Wendy Wildman, Interim CAO
cao@onoway.com

Oyen
P.O. Box 360
Oyen, AB T0J 2J0
Tel: 403-664-3511; *Fax:* 403-664-3712
townoffice@townofoyen.com
www.townofoyen.com
Municipal Type: Town
Incorporated: Jan. 17, 1913 *Area:* 4.93 sq km
Population in 2011: 973
Provincial Electoral District(s): Drumheller-Stettler
Federal Electoral District(s): Crowfoot
Next Election: Oct. 21, 2013 (3 year terms)
Note: Incorporated as a town on Sept. 1, 1965.
Paul Christianson, Mayor
Herman Minderlein, Administrator
cao@townofoyen.com

Paradise Valley
P.O. Box 24
Paradise Valley, AB T0B 3R0
Tel: 780-745-2287; *Fax:* 780-745-2287
villageofpv@mcsnet.ca
Municipal Type: Village
Incorporated: Jan. 1, 1964 *Area:* 0.57 sq km
Population in 2011: 174
Provincial Electoral District(s): Vermilion-Lloydminster
Federal Electoral District(s): Vegreville-Wainwright
Next Election: Oct. 21, 2013 (3 year terms)
Curtis Schneider, Mayor
Connie Wilkinson, Municipal Administrator
villageofpv@mcsnet.ca

Parkland Beach
P.O. Box 130
Rimbey, AB T0C 2J0
Tel: 403-843-2055; *Fax:* 888-470-2762
admin@parklandbeachsv.ca
Municipal Type: Summer Village
Incorporated: Jan. 1, 1984 *Area:* 0.93 sq km
Population in 2011: 124
Provincial Electoral District(s): Lacombe-Ponoka
Federal Electoral District(s): Wetaskiwin
Next Election: Summer 2013 (3 year terms)
Larry Scheible, Mayor
Marilee Yakunin, Chief Administrative Officer
admin@parklandbeachsv.ca

Peace River
P.O. Box 6600
9911 - 100 St.
Peace River, AB T8S 1S4
Tel: 780-624-2574; *Fax:* 780-624-4664
info@peaceriver.net
http://peaceriver.net
Municipal Type: Town
Incorporated: June 2, 1914 *Area:* 24.87 sq km
Population in 2011: 6,744
Provincial Electoral District(s): Peace River
Federal Electoral District(s): Peace River
Next Election: Oct. 21, 2013 (3 year terms)
Note: Incorporated as a town on Dec. 1, 1919.
Norma MacQuarrie, CAO
nmacquarrie@peaceriver.net
Lorne Mann, Mayor
780-624-8384

Pelican Narrows
P.O. Box 7878
Bonnyville, AB T9N 2J2
Tel: 780-826-5907; *Fax:* 780-826-2804
plapointe@mcsnet.ca
Municipal Type: Summer Village
Incorporated: July 1, 1979 *Area:* 0.7 sq km
Population in 2011: 162
Provincial Electoral District(s): Bonnyville-Cold Lake
Federal Electoral District(s): Westlock-St.Paul
Next Election: Summer 2013 (3 year terms)
Robert Hornseth, Mayor
Padey Lapointe, Administrator

Penhold
P.O. Box 10
1 Waskasoo Ave.
Penhold, AB T0M 1R0
Tel: 403-886-4567; *Fax:* 403-886-4039
community1@townofpenhold.ca
www.townofpenhold.ca
Municipal Type: Town
Incorporated: May 4, 1904 *Area:* 2.35 sq km
Population in 2011: 2,375
Provincial Electoral District(s): Innisfail-Sylvan Lake
Federal Electoral District(s): Red Deer
Next Election: Oct. 21, 2013 (3 year terms)
Note: Incorporated as a town on Sept. 1, 1980.
Dennis Cooper, Mayor
Rick Binnendyk, Chief Administrative Officer
cao@townofpenhold.ca

Picture Butte
P.O. Box 670
Picture Butte, AB T0K 1V0
Tel: 403-732-4555; *Fax:* 403-732-4334
info@picturebutte.ca
www.picturebutte.ca
Municipal Type: Town
Incorporated: Feb. 4, 1943 *Area:* 2.9 sq km
Population in 2011: 1,650
Provincial Electoral District(s): Little Bow
Federal Electoral District(s): Lethbridge
Next Election: Oct. 21, 2013 (3 year terms)
Note: Incorporated as a town on Jan. 1, 1960.
Terry Kerkhoff, Mayor
tkerkhoff@picturebutte.ca
Audrey Mortensen, Chief Administrative Officer
audrey@picturebutte.ca

Pincher Creek
P.O. Box 159
Pincher Creek, AB T0K 1W0
Tel: 403-627-3156; *Fax:* 403-627-4784
reception@pinchercreek.ca
www.pinchercreek.ca
Municipal Type: Town
Incorporated: Aug. 18, 1898 *Area:* 8.84 sq km
Population in 2011: 3,685
Provincial Electoral District(s): Livingstone-Macleod
Federal Electoral District(s): Macleod
Next Election: Oct. 21, 2013 (3 year terms)
Note: Incorporated as a town on May 12, 1906.
Ernie Olsen, Mayor
Laurie Wilgosh, Chief Administrative Officer
laurie@pinchercreek.ca

Point Alison
4323 - 49A St.
Edmonton, AB T6L 6J5
Tel: 780-462-6372
thomtom@telus.net
www.pointalison.com
Municipal Type: Summer Village
Incorporated: Dec. 31, 1950 *Area:* 0.16 sq km
Population in 2011: 15
Provincial Electoral District(s): Stony Plain
Federal Electoral District(s): Yellowhead
Next Election: Summer 2013 (3 year terms)
C. Gordon Wilson, Mayor
Tom Thompson, Administrator
thomtom@telus.net

Ponoka
5102 - 48 Ave.
Ponoka, AB T4J 1P7
Tel: 403-783-4431; *Fax:* 403-783-6745
town@ponoka.org
www.ponoka.org
Municipal Type: Town
Incorporated: Oct. 19, 1900 *Area:* 13.05 sq km
Population in 2011: 6,773
Provincial Electoral District(s): Lacombe-Ponoka
Federal Electoral District(s): Wetaskiwin
Next Election: Oct. 21, 2013 (3 year terms)
Note: Incorporated as a town on Oct. 15, 1904.
Larry L. Henkelman, Mayor
Brad Watson, Chief Administrative Officer
bwatson@ponoka.org

Poplar Bay
P.O. Box 100
Ma-Me-O Beach, AB T0C 1X0
Tel: 780-586-2494; *Fax:* 780-586-3567
information@svofficepl.com
www.svofficepl.com
Municipal Type: Summer Village
Incorporated: Jan. 1, 1967 *Area:* 0.76 sq km
Population in 2011: 80
Provincial Electoral District(s): Drayton Valley-Calmar
Federal Electoral District(s): Wetaskiwin
Next Election: Summer 2013 (3 year terms)
Kevin D. Davies, Mayor
Sylvia Roy, Chief Administrative Officer
sylvia.roy@svofficepl.com

Provost
P.O. Box 449
Provost, AB T0B 3S0
Tel: 780-753-2261; *Fax:* 780-753-6889
info@townofprovost.ca
www.provost.ca
Municipal Type: Town
Incorporated: Jan. 20, 1910 *Area:* 4.93 sq km

Population in 2011: 2,041
Provincial Electoral District(s): Battle River-Wainwright
Federal Electoral District(s): Vegreville-Wainwright
Next Election: Oct. 21, 2013 (3 year terms)
Note: Incorporated as a town on Dec. 29, 1952.
Kenneth E. (Ken) Knox, Mayor
Judy Larson, Administrator
administrator@townofprovost.ca

Rainbow Lake
P.O. Box 149
Rainbow Lake, AB T0H 2Y0
Tel: 780-956-3934; *Fax:* 780-956-3570
admin@rainbowlake.ca
www.rainbowlake.ca
Municipal Type: Town
Incorporated: Sept. 1, 1966 *Area:* 11.04 sq km
Population in 2011: 870
Provincial Electoral District(s): Peace River
Federal Electoral District(s): Peace River
Next Election: Oct. 21, 2013 (3 year terms)
Rose Cretney, Mayor
Rosemary Offrey, Chief Administrative Officer
roffrey@rainbowlake.ca

Raymond
P.O. Box 629
15 Broadway St.
Raymond, AB T0K 2S0
Tel: 403-752-3322; *Fax:* 403-752-4379
contact@raymond.ca
www.raymond.ca
Municipal Type: Town
Incorporated: May 30, 1902 *Area:* 4.75 sq km
Population in 2011: 3,743
Provincial Electoral District(s): Cardston-Taber-Warner
Federal Electoral District(s): Lethbridge
Next Election: Oct. 21, 2013 (3 year terms)
Note: Incorporated as a town on July 1, 1903.
George Bohne, Mayor
bohne@raymond.ca
J. Scott Barton, Chief Administrative Officer
scottbarton@raymond.ca

Redcliff
P.O. Box 40
Redcliff, AB T0J 2P0
Tel: 403-548-3618; *Fax:* 403-548-6623
redcliff@town.redcliff.ab.ca
www.town.redcliff.ab.ca
Municipal Type: Town
Incorporated: Oct. 29, 1910 *Area:* 10.51 sq km
Population in 2011: 5,588
Provincial Electoral District(s): Cypress-Medicine Hat
Federal Electoral District(s): Medicine Hat
Next Election: Oct. 21, 2013 (3 year terms)
Note: Incorporated as a town on Aug. 5, 1912.
Robert Hazelaar, Mayor
mayor@town.redcliff.ab.ca
David Wolanski, Municipal Manager
davidw@town.redcliff.ab.ca

Redwater
P.O. Box 397
Redwater, AB T0A 2W0
Tel: 780-942-3519; *Fax:* 780-942-4321
www.redwater.ca
Municipal Type: Town
Incorporated: Dec. 31, 1949 *Area:* 7.95 sq km
Population in 2011: 1,915
Provincial Electoral District(s): Athabasca-Redwater
Federal Electoral District(s): Westlock-St. Paul
Next Election: Oct. 21, 2013 (3 year terms)
Note: Incorporated as a town on Dec. 31, 1950.
Mel Smith, Mayor
mayor@redwater.ca
Deb Hamilton, Town Manager

Rimbey
P.O. Box 350
4938 - 50th Ave.
Rimbey, AB T0C 2J0
Tel: 403-843-2113; *Fax:* 403-843-6599
rtown@rimbey.com
www.rimbey.com
Municipal Type: Town
Incorporated: June 13, 1919 *Area:* 11.34 sq km
Population in 2011: 2,378
Provincial Electoral District(s): Lacombe-Ponoka
Federal Electoral District(s): Wetaskiwin
Next Election: Oct. 21, 2013 (3 year terms)
Note: Incorporated as a town on Dec. 13, 1948.
Sheldon Ibbotson, Mayor
mayor@rimbey.com
Tony Goode, Chief Administrative Officer
tony@rimbey.com

Rochon Sands
1 Hall St.
Rochon Sands, AB T0C 3B0
Tel: 403-742-4717; *Fax:* 403-742-4771
info@rochonsands.net
www.rochonsands.net
Municipal Type: Summer Village
Incorporated: May 17, 1929 *Area:* 2.32 sq km
Population in 2011: 84
Provincial Electoral District(s): Drumheller-Stettler
Federal Electoral District(s): Crowfoot
Next Election: Summer 2013 (3 year terms)
Wayne Miller, Mayor
Alan Willis, Village Administrator
info@rochonsands.net

Rocky Mountain House
P.O. Box 1509
Rocky Mountain House, AB T4T 1B2
Tel: 403-845-2866; *Fax:* 403-845-3230
town@rockymtnhouse.com
www.rockymtnhouse.com
Municipal Type: Town
Incorporated: May 15, 1913 *Area:* 12.44 sq km
Population in 2011: 6,933
Provincial Electoral District(s): Rocky Mountain House
Federal Electoral District(s): Wetaskiwin
Next Election: Oct. 21, 2013 (3 year terms)
Note: Incorporated as a town on Aug. 31, 1939.
Fred Nash, Mayor
Todd Becker, Town Manager
tbecker@rockymtnhouse.com

Rockyford
P.O. Box 294
Rockyford, AB T0J 2R0
Tel: 403-533-3950; *Fax:* 403-533-3744
loism_village@rockyford.ca
www.rockyford.ca
Municipal Type: Village
Incorporated: March 28, 1919 *Area:* 1.05 sq km
Population in 2011: 325
Provincial Electoral District(s): Strathmore-Brooks
Federal Electoral District(s): Crowfoot
Next Election: Oct. 21, 2013 (3 year terms)
Darcy J. Burke, Mayor
dburke@rockyford.ca
Lois Mountjoy, Administrator

Rosalind
P.O. Box 181
Rosalind, AB T0B 3Y0
Tel: 780-375-3996; *Fax:* 780-375-3997
rosalindvillage@xplornet.com
www.villageofrosalind.ca
Municipal Type: Village
Incorporated: Jan. 1, 1966 *Area:* 0.59 sq km
Population in 2011: 190
Provincial Electoral District(s): Battle River-Wainwright
Federal Electoral District(s): Crowfoot
Next Election: Oct. 21, 2013 (3 year terms)
James McTavish, Mayor
Nancy Friend, Chief Administrative Officer

Rosemary
P.O. Box 128
Rosemary, AB T0J 2W0
Tel: 403-378-4246; *Fax:* 403-378-3144
rosemary.admin@eidnet.org
www.myrosemary.org
Municipal Type: Village
Incorporated: Dec. 31, 1951 *Area:* 0.56 sq km
Population in 2011: 342
Provincial Electoral District(s): Strathmore-Brooks
Federal Electoral District(s): Medicine Hat
Next Election: Oct. 21, 2013 (3 year terms)
Don L. Gibb, Mayor
dgibb@eidnet.org
Margaret Loewen, Chief Administrative Officer

Ross Haven
P.O. Box 7
Site 19, RR#1
Gunn, AB T0E 1A0
Tel: 780-967-1426; *Fax:* 780-702-6743
d.evans@xplornet.com
Municipal Type: Summer Village
Incorporated: Jan. 1, 1962 *Area:* 0.7 sq km
Population in 2011: 137
Provincial Electoral District(s): Whitecourt-Ste. Anne
Federal Electoral District(s): Yellowhead
Next Election: Summer 2013 (3 year terms)
Kelly Demkiw, Mayor
Dennis Evans, Municipal Administrator

Rycroft
P.O. Box 360
Rycroft, AB T0H 3A0
Tel: 780-765-3652; *Fax:* 780-765-2002
rycroft@rycroft.ca
www.rycroft.ca
Municipal Type: Village
Incorporated: March 15, 1944 *Area:* 1.69 sq km
Population in 2011: 628
Provincial Electoral District(s): Dunvegan-Central Peace
Federal Electoral District(s): Peace River
Next Election: Oct. 21, 2013 (3 year terms)
Whitney Burback, Mayor
wburback@rycroft.ca
Norma Maxwell, Interim Chief Administrative Officer
nmaxwell@rycroft.ca

Ryley
P.O. Box 230
Ryley, AB T0B 4A0
Tel: 780-663-3653; *Fax:* 780-663-3541
info@ryley.ca
www.ryley.ca
Municipal Type: Village
Incorporated: April 2, 1910 *Area:* 1.97 sq km
Population in 2011: 497
Provincial Electoral District(s): Fort Saskatchewan-Vegreville
Federal Electoral District(s): Vegreville-Wainwright
Next Election: Oct. 21, 2013 (3 year terms)
Jorge Mendoza, Mayor
j.mendoza@ryley.ca
Emily House, Chief Administrative Officer
cao@ryley.ca

St. Paul
P.O. Box 1480
St. Paul, AB T0A 3A0
Tel: 780-645-4481; *Fax:* 780-645-5076
townhall@town.stpaul.ab.ca
www.town.stpaul.ab.ca
Municipal Type: Town
Incorporated: June 14, 1912 *Area:* 6.86 sq km
Population in 2011: 5,400
Provincial Electoral District(s): Lac La Biche-St. Paul
Federal Electoral District(s): Westlock-St. Paul
Next Election: Oct. 21, 2013 (3 year terms)
Note: Incorporated as a town on Dec. 15, 1936.
Glenn Andersen, Mayor
glksand@gmail.com
Ronald O. Boisvert, Chief Administrative Officer
rboisvert@town.stpaul.ab.ca

Sandy Beach
P.O. Box 63
Site 1, RR#1
Onoway, AB T0E 1V0
Tel: 780-967-2873; *Fax:* 780-967-2813
svsandyb@xplornet.ca
Municipal Type: Summer Village
Incorporated: Jan. 1, 1956 *Area:* 2.43 sq km
Population in 2011: 223
Provincial Electoral District(s): Whitecourt-Ste. Anne
Federal Electoral District(s): Yellowhead
Next Election: Summer 2013 (3 year terms)
Gordon Drybrough, Mayor
gordon@canniff.ca
Wendy Wildman, Chief Administrative Officer

Seba Beach
P.O. Box 190
Seba Beach, AB T0E 2B0
Tel: 780-797-3863; *Fax:* 780-797-3800
svseba@telusplanet.net
www.sebabeach.ca
Municipal Type: Summer Village
Incorporated: Aug. 2, 1920 *Area:* 0.66 sq km
Population in 2011: 143
Provincial Electoral District(s): Stony Plain
Federal Electoral District(s): Yellowhead
Next Election: Summer 2013 (3 year terms)
Doug Thomas, Mayor
Susan H. Evans, Chief Administrative Officer

Sedgewick
P.O. Box 129
Sedgewick, AB T0B 4C0
Tel: 780-384-3504; *Fax:* 780-384-3545
sedgewick@persona.ca
www.sedgewick.ca
Municipal Type: Town
Incorporated: March 6, 1907 *Area:* 2.6 sq km
Population in 2011: 857
Provincial Electoral District(s): Battle River-Wainwright
Federal Electoral District(s): Vegreville-Wainwright
Next Election: Oct. 21, 2013 (3 year terms)
Note: Incorporated as town on May 1, 1966.
Helen Marie Whitten, Mayor
sedgewick.mayor@eastlink.ca
Thelma Rogers, Chief Administrative Officer
sedgewick.cao@persona.ca

Sexsmith
9927 - 100 St.
Sexsmith, AB T0H 3C0
Tel: 780-568-3681; *Fax:* 780-568-2200
www.sexsmith.ca
Municipal Type: Town
Incorporated: April 12, 1929 *Area:* 3.43 sq km
Population in 2011: 2,418
Provincial Electoral District(s): Grande Prairie-Smoky
Federal Electoral District(s): Peace River
Next Election: Oct. 21, 2013 (3 year terms)
Note: Incorporated as a town on Oct. 15, 1979.
Carolyn Gaunt, Town Manager
cagaunt@sexsmith.ca
Claude Lagace, Mayor

Silver Beach
P.O. Box 619
4917 Hankin St.
Thorsby, AB T0C 2P0
Tel: 780-789-3935; *Fax:* 780-789-3779
hwynne@village.thorsby.ab.ca
www.sbalberta.ca
Municipal Type: Summer Village
Incorporated: Dec. 31, 1953 *Area:* 0.66 sq km
Population in 2011: 52
Provincial Electoral District(s): Drayton Valley-Calmar
Federal Electoral District(s): Wetaskiwin
Next Election: Summer 2013 (3 year terms)
Brad Clough, Mayor
Harold Wynne, Chief Administrative Officer

Silver Sands
P.O. Box 8
Alberta Beach, AB T0E 0A0
Tel: 780-924-3024; *Fax:* 780-924-3025
administration@wildwillowenterprises.com
www.wildwillowenterprises.com
Municipal Type: Summer Village
Incorporated: Jan. 1, 1969 *Area:* 2.35 sq km
Population in 2011: 85
Provincial Electoral District(s): Whitecourt-Ste. Anne
Federal Electoral District(s): Yellowhead
Next Election: Summer 2013 (3 year terms)
Bernie Poulin, Mayor
bpoulin@xplornet.com
Wendy Wildman, Chief Administrative Officer

Slave Lake
P.O. Box 1030
Slave Lake, AB T0G 2A0
Tel: 780-849-8000; *Fax:* 780-849-2633
town@slavelake.ca
www.slavelake.ca
Municipal Type: Town
Incorporated: Jan. 1, 1961 *Area:* 14.18 sq km
Population in 2011: 6,782
Provincial Electoral District(s): Lesser Slave Lake
Federal Electoral District(s): Fort McMurray-Athabasca
Next Election: Oct. 21, 2013 (3 year terms)
Note: Incorporated as a town on Aug. 2, 1965.
Karina Pillay-Kinnee, Mayor
karina@slavelake.ca
Brian Vance, Chief Administrative Officer
brian@slavelake.ca

Smoky Lake
P.O. Box 460
Smoky Lake, AB T0A 3C0
Tel: 780-656-3674; *Fax:* 780-656-3675
fcss@smokylake.ca
www.smokylake.ca
Municipal Type: Town
Incorporated: March 26, 1923 *Area:* 4.2 sq km
Population in 2011: 1,022
Provincial Electoral District(s): Athabasca-Redwater
Federal Electoral District(s): Westlock-St. Paul
Next Election: Oct. 21, 2013 (3 year terms)
Note: Incorporated as a town on Feb. 1, 1962.
Hank Holowaychuk, Mayor
mayor@smokylake.ca
R. Dean Pickering, Chief Administrative Officer
cao@smokylake.ca

South Baptiste
724 Baptiste Dr.
West Baptiste, AB T9S 1R8
Tel: 780-675-9270; *Fax:* 780-675-9526
tomaszyk@mcsnet.ca
www.southbaptiste.com
Municipal Type: Summer Village
Incorporated: Jan. 1, 1983 *Area:* 1.05 sq km
Population in 2011: 52
Provincial Electoral District(s): Athabasca-Redwater
Federal Electoral District(s): Fort McMurray-Athabaska
Next Election: Summer 2013 (3 year terms)
Steve Hamilton, Mayor
Edwin Tomaszyk, Chief Administrative Officer

South View
P.O. Box 8
Alberta Beach, AB T0E 0A0
Tel: 780-924-3024; *Fax:* 780-924-3025
administration@wildwillowenterprises.com
www.wildwillowenterprises.com
Municipal Type: Summer Village
Incorporated: Jan. 1, 1970 *Area:* 0.69 sq km
Population in 2011: 35
Provincial Electoral District(s): Whitecourt-Ste. Anne
Federal Electoral District(s): Yellowhead
Next Election: Summer 2013 (3 year terms)
Sandra Benford, Mayor
Wendy Wildman, Chief Administrative Officer
administration@wildwillowenterprises.com

Spirit River
P.O. Box 130
Spirit River, AB T0H 3G0
Tel: 780-864-3998; *Fax:* 780-864-3433
clerk@townofspiritriver.ca
www.townofspiritriver.ca
Municipal Type: Town
Incorporated: June 13, 1916 *Area:* 2.81 sq km
Population in 2011: 1,025
Provincial Electoral District(s): Dunvegan-Central Peace
Federal Electoral District(s): Peace River
Next Election: Oct. 21, 2013 (3 year terms)
Note: Incorporated as a town on Sept. 18, 1951.
Allan J. Georget, Mayor
ageorget@atb.com
Lloyd Johnston, Chief Administrative Officer
manager@townofspiritriver.ca

Spring Lake
990 Bauer Ave.
Spring Lake, AB T7Z 2S9
Tel: 780-963-4211; *Fax:* 780-963-4260
villageoffice@springlakealberta.com
www.springlakealberta.com
Municipal Type: Village
Incorporated: Jan. 1, 1959 *Area:* 2.12 sq km
Population in 2011: 533
Provincial Electoral District(s): Stoney Plain
Federal Electoral District(s): Edmonton-Spruce Grove
Next Election: Oct. 21, 2013 (3 year terms)
Note: Incorporated as a village on Jan. 1, 1999.
Don Dobing, Mayor
Emily House, Chief Administrative Officer
emily@springlakealberta.com

Standard
P.O. Box 249
Standard, AB T0J 3G0
Tel: 403-644-3968; *Fax:* 403-644-2284
cao@standardab.ca
www.standardab.ca
Municipal Type: Village
Incorporated: April 29, 1922 *Area:* 2.34 sq km
Population in 2011: 379
Provincial Electoral District(s): Strathmore-Brooks
Federal Electoral District(s): Crowfoot
Next Election: Oct. 21, 2013 (3 year terms)
Donald Cuthill, Mayor
dwcutts@standardab.ca
Leah Jensen, Chief Administrative Officer

Stavely
P.O. Box 249
Stavely, AB T0L 1Z0
Tel: 403-549-3761; *Fax:* 403-549-3743
stavely@platinum.ca
www.stavely.ca
Municipal Type: Town
Incorporated: Oct. 16, 1903 *Area:* 1.62 sq km
Population in 2011: 505
Provincial Electoral District(s): Livingstone-Macleod
Federal Electoral District(s): Macleod
Next Election: Oct. 21, 2013 (3 year terms)
Note: Incorporated as a town on May 25, 1912.
Barry Johnson, Mayor
Sheryl Fath, Municipal Administrator

Stettler
P.O. Box 280
Stettler, AB T0C 2L0
Tel: 403-742-8305; *Fax:* 403-742-1404
townoffice@stettler.net
www.stettler.net
Municipal Type: Town
Incorporated: June 30, 1906 *Area:* 9.5 sq km
Population in 2011: 5,748
Provincial Electoral District(s): Drumheller-Stettler
Federal Electoral District(s): Crowfoot
Next Election: Oct. 21, 2013 (3 year terms)
Note: Incorporated as a town on Nov. 23, 1906.
Dick Richards, Mayor
dick_richards@cooperators.ca
Robert Stoutenberg, Chief Administrative Officer
robs@stettler.net

Stirling
P.O. Box 360
229 Fourth Ave.
Stirling, AB T0K 2E0
Tel: 403-756-3379; *Fax:* 403-756-2262
stirl_ng@telus.net
Municipal Type: Village
Incorporated: Sept. 3, 1901 *Area:* 2.64 sq km
Population in 2011: 1,090
Provincial Electoral District(s): Cardston-Taber-Warner
Federal Electoral District(s): Lethbridge
Next Election: Oct. 21, 2013 (3 year terms)
Jason Edwards, Mayor
J. Scott Barton, Chief Administrative Officer
scottbarton@raymond.ca

Strome
P.O. Box 179
5025 - 50th St.
Strome, AB T0B 4H0
Tel: 780-376-3558; *Fax:* 780-376-3557
strome@syban.net
www.villageofstrome.com
Municipal Type: Village
Incorporated: Feb. 3, 1910 *Area:* 0.92 sq km
Population in 2011: 228
Provincial Electoral District(s): Battle River-Wainwright
Federal Electoral District(s): Vegreville-Wainwright
Next Election: Oct. 21, 2013 (3 year terms)
Bruce Curtis, Mayor
Connie Prendergast, Administrative Clerk

Sunbreaker Cove
90B Hewlett Park Landing
Sylvan Lake, AB T4S 2J3
Tel: 403-887-2822; *Fax:* 403-887-2897
fivesv@telusplanet.net
Municipal Type: Summer Village
Incorporated: Dec. 31, 1990 *Area:* 0.49 sq km
Population in 2011: 69
Provincial Electoral District(s): Rocky Mountain House
Federal Electoral District(s): Wetaskiwin
Next Election: Summer 2013 (3 year terms)
Bill Carr, Mayor
Myra Reiter, Administrator
fivesv@telusplanet.net

Sundance Beach
P.O. Box 658
Thorsby, AB T0C 2P0
Tel: 780-789-3935; *Fax:* 780-789-3779
hwynne@thorsby.ca
Municipal Type: Summer Village
Incorporated: Jan. 1, 1970 *Area:* 0.42 sq km
Population in 2011: 82
Provincial Electoral District(s): Drayton Valley-Calmar
Federal Electoral District(s): Wetaskiwin
Next Election: Summer 2013 (3 year terms)

Peter Pellatt, Mayor
Harold Wynne, Chief Administrative Officer

Sundre
P.O. Box 420
Sundre, AB T0M 1X0
Tel: 403-638-3551; *Fax:* 403-638-2100
townmail@sundre.com
www.sundre.com
Municipal Type: Town
Incorporated: Dec. 31, 1949 *Area:* 7.65 sq km
Population in 2011: 2,610
Provincial Electoral District(s): Rocky Mountain House
Federal Electoral District(s): Wild Rose
Next Election: Oct. 21, 2013 (3 year terms)
Note: Incorporated as a town on Jan. 1, 1956.
Annette Clews, Mayor
annetteclews@gmail.com
Ryan Leuzinger, Interim Chief Administrative Officer
ryan.l@sundre.com

Sunrise Beach
P.O. Box 63
Site 1, RR#1
Onoway, AB T0E 1V0
Tel: 780-967-2873; *Fax:* 780-967-2813
svsandyb@xplornet.ca
Municipal Type: Summer Village
Incorporated: Dec. 31, 1988 *Area:* 1.72 sq km
Population in 2011: 149
Provincial Electoral District(s): Whitecourt-Ste. Anne
Federal Electoral District(s): Yellowhead
Next Election: Summer 2013 (3 year terms)
Cindy MacDonald, Mayor
cindysvsunrisebeach@hotmail.com
Wendy Wildman, Chief Administrative Officer

Sunset Beach
724 Baptiste Dr.
West Baptiste, AB T9S 1R8
Tel: 780-675-3270; *Fax:* 780-675-9526
sunsetbeach@mcsnet.ca
Municipal Type: Summer Village
Incorporated: May 1, 1977 *Area:* 0.99 sq km
Population in 2011: 44
Provincial Electoral District(s): Athabasca-Redwater
Federal Electoral District(s): Fort McMurray-Athabasca
Next Election: Summer 2013 (3 year terms)
Mark Lindskoog, Mayor
mlindskoog@nichollandakers.com
Edwin Tomaszyk, Chief Administrative Officer
tomaszyk@mcsnet.ca

Sunset Point
13 Grandin Rd.
St. Albert, AB T8N 3B2
Tel: 780-460-7226; *Fax:* 780-419-2476
hmarsh@telusplanet.net
Municipal Type: Summer Village
Incorporated: Jan. 1, 1959 *Area:* 1.11 sq km
Population in 2011: 221
Provincial Electoral District(s): Whitecourt-Ste. Anne
Federal Electoral District(s): Yellowhead
Next Election: Summer 2013 (3 year terms)
Elizabeth Morrison, Mayor
Hilda Marsh, Chief Administrative Officer

Swan Hills
P.O. Box 149
Swan Hills, AB T0G 2C0
Tel: 780-333-4477; *Fax:* 780-333-4547
town@townofswanhills.com
www.townofswanhills.com
Municipal Type: Town
Incorporated: Sept. 1, 1959 *Area:* 25.44 sq km
Population in 2011: 1,465
Provincial Electoral District(s): Barrhead-Morinville-Westlock
Federal Electoral District(s): Yellowhead
Next Election: Oct. 21, 2013 (3 year terms)
Mark Pickering, Mayor
mark.pickering@townofswanhills.com
Douglas Borg, Interim Chief Administrative Officer
doug.borg@townofswanhills.com

Taber
4900A - 50 St.
Taber, AB T1G 1T1
Tel: 403-223-5500; *Fax:* 403-223-5530
town@taber.ca
www.taber.ca
Municipal Type: Town
Incorporated: March 15, 1905 *Area:* 15.09 sq km
Population in 2011: 8,104
Provincial Electoral District(s): Cardston-Taber-Warner
Federal Electoral District(s): Medicine Hat
Next Election: Oct. 21, 2013 (3 year terms)
Note: Incorporated as a town on July 1, 1907.
Gordon Frank, CAO
town@taber.ca
Ray Bryant, Mayor
mayor@taber.ca

Thorsby
P.O. Box 297
Thorsby, AB T0C 2P0
Tel: 780-789-3935; *Fax:* 780-789-3779
hwynne@thorsby.ca
www.village.thorsby.ab.ca
Municipal Type: Village
Incorporated: Dec. 31, 1949 *Area:* 2.92 sq km
Population in 2011: 797
Provincial Electoral District(s): Drayton Valley-Calmar
Federal Electoral District(s): Wetaskiwin
Next Election: Oct. 21, 2013 (3 year terms)
Barry Rasch, Mayor
Harold Wynne, Chief Administrative Officer

Three Hills
P.O. Box 610
Three Hills, AB T0M 2A0
Tel: 403-443-5822; *Fax:* 403-443-2616
info@threehills.ca
www.threehills.ca
Municipal Type: Town
Incorporated: June 14, 1912 *Area:* 5.63 sq km
Population in 2011: 3,198
Provincial Electoral District(s): Olds-Didsbury-Three Hills
Federal Electoral District(s): Crowfoot
Next Election: Oct. 21, 2013 (3 year terms)
Note: Incorporated as a town on Jan. 1, 1929.
Timothy J. Shearlaw, Mayor
Jack Ramsden, Town Manager
jramsden@threehills.ca

Tilley
P.O. Box 155
Tilley, AB T0J 3K0
Tel: 403-377-2203; *Fax:* 403-377-2234
village.tilley@eidnet.org
Municipal Type: Village
Incorporated: May 9, 1940 *Area:* 0.62 sq km
Population in 2011: 352
Provincial Electoral District(s): Strathmore-Brooks
Federal Electoral District(s): Medicine Hat
Next Election: Oct. 21, 2013 (3 year terms)
John Timko, Mayor
john.timko@tyson.com
Jeannette Zahn, Chief Administrative Officer

Tofield
P.O. Box 30
Tofield, AB T0B 4J0
Tel: 780-662-3269; *Fax:* 780-662-3929
tofield@supernet.ab.ca
www.tofieldalberta.ca
Municipal Type: Town
Incorporated: Sept. 9, 1907 *Area:* 6.01 sq km
Population in 2011: 2,182
Provincial Electoral District(s): Fort Saskatchewan-Vegreville
Federal Electoral District(s): Vegreville-Wainwright
Next Election: Oct. 21, 2013 (3 year terms)
Note: Incorporated as a town on Sept. 10, 1909.
Nabil Chehayeb, Mayor
Cindy Neufeld, CAO
cneufeld@tofieldalberta.ca

Trochu
P.O. Box 340
Trochu, AB T0M 2C0
Tel: 403-442-3085; *Fax:* 403-442-2528
secretary@town.trochu.ab.ca
www.town.trochu.ab.ca
Municipal Type: Town
Incorporated: May 5, 1911 *Area:* 2.82 sq km
Population in 2011: 1,072
Provincial Electoral District(s): Olds-Didsbury-Three Hills
Federal Electoral District(s): Crowfoot
Next Election: Oct. 21, 2013 (3 year terms)
Note: Incorporated as a town on Aug. 1, 1962.
Barry Kletke, Mayor
Maureen Malaka, Chief Administrative Officer

Turner Valley
P.O. Box 330
Turner Valley, AB T0L 2A0
Tel: 403-933-4944; *Fax:* 403-933-5377
admin@turnervalley.ca
www.turnervalley.ca
Municipal Type: Town
Incorporated: Feb. 25, 1930
Population in 2011: 2,167
Provincial Electoral District(s): Foothills-Rocky View
Federal Electoral District(s): Macleod
Next Election: Oct. 21, 2013 (3 year terms)
Note: Incorporated as a town on Sept.1, 1977.
Kelly Tuck, Mayor
kellyt@turnervalley.ca
Leslie Fitzgerald, Chief Administrative Officer
cao@turnervalley.ca

Two Hills
P.O. Box 630
Two Hills, AB T0B 4K0
Tel: 780-657-3395; *Fax:* 780-657-2158
info@townoftwohills.com
www.townofhills.com
Municipal Type: Town
Incorporated: June 4, 1929 *Area:* 3.31 sq km
Population in 2011: 1,379
Provincial Electoral District(s): Lac La Biche-St. Paul
Federal Electoral District(s): Vegreville-Wainwright
Next Election: Oct. 21, 2013 (3 year terms)
Note: Incorporated as a town on Jan. 1, 1955.
Elaine Sorochan, Mayor
Elsie Howanyk, Chief Administrative Officer
cao@townoftwohills.com

Val Quentin
P.O. Box 7
Site 19, RR#1
Gunn, AB T0E 1A0
Tel: 780-446-1426
d.evans@xplornet.com
Municipal Type: Summer Village
Incorporated: Jan. 1, 1966 *Area:* 0.3 sq km
Population in 2011: 157
Provincial Electoral District(s): Whitecourt-Ste. Anne
Federal Electoral District(s): Yellowhead
Next Election: Summer 2013 (3 year terms)
Bob Lehman, Mayor
Dennis Evans, Chief Administrative Officer

Valleyview
P.O. Box 270
Valleyview, AB T0H 3N0
Tel: 780-524-5150; *Fax:* 780-524-2727
valvadmn@telusplanet.net
http://valleyview.govoffice.com
Municipal Type: Town
Incorporated: Jan. 1, 1955 *Area:* 4.57 sq km
Population in 2011: 1,761
Provincial Electoral District(s): Grande Prairie-Smoky
Federal Electoral District(s): Peace River
Next Election: Oct. 21, 2013 (3 year terms)
Note: Incorporated as a town on Feb. 5, 1957.
Frank Besinger, Twon Manager
Vern Lymburner, Mayor

Vauxhall
P.O. Box 509
Vauxhall, AB T0K 2K0
Tel: 403-654-2174; *Fax:* 403-654-4110
cao@town.vauxhall.ab.ca
www.town.vauxhall.ab.ca
Municipal Type: Town
Incorporated: Dec. 31, 1949 *Area:* 2.88 sq km
Population in 2011: 1,288
Provincial Electoral District(s): Little Bow
Federal Electoral District(s): Medicine Hat
Next Election: Oct. 21, 2013 (3 year terms)
Note: Incorporated as a town on Jan. 1, 1961.
Gordon Brown, Mayor
Barbara Miller, Chief Administrative Officer
bmiller@town.vauxhall.ab.ca

Vegreville
P.O. Box 640
Vegreville, AB T9C 1R7
Tel: 780-632-2606; *Fax:* 780-632-3088
vegtown@vegreville.com
www.vegreville.com
Municipal Type: Town
Incorporated: April 4, 1906 *Area:* 13.49 sq km
Population in 2011: 5,717

Provincial Electoral District(s): Fort Saskatchewan-Vegreville
Federal Electoral District(s): Vegreville-Wainwright
Next Election: Oct. 21, 2013 (3 year terms)
Note: Incorporated as a town on Aug 15, 1906.
Richard N. Coleman, Mayor
Jody Quickstad, Town Manager
jquickstad@vegreville.com

Vermilion
5021 - 49th Ave.
Vermilion, AB T9X 1X1
Tel: 780-853-5358; *Fax:* 780-853-4910
townofvermilion@vermilion.ca
www.vermilion.ca
Municipal Type: Town
Incorporated: Feb. 17, 1906 *Area:* 13.69 sq km
Population in 2011: 3,930
Provincial Electoral District(s): Vermilion-Lloydminster
Federal Electoral District(s): Vegreville-Wainwright
Next Election: Oct. 21, 2013 (3 year terms)
Note: Incorporated as a town on Aug. 27, 1906.
Bruce Marriott, Mayor
bgmarr@telusmail.net
Dion Pollard, Town Manager
dpollard@vermilion.ca

Veteran
P.O. Box 439
Veteran, AB T0C 2S0
Tel: 403-575-3954; *Fax:* 403-575-3954
veteran@veterancable.net
Municipal Type: Village
Incorporated: June 30, 1914 *Area:* 0.84 sq km
Population in 2011: 249
Provincial Electoral District(s): Drumheller-Stettler
Federal Electoral District(s): Crowfoot
Next Election: Oct. 21, 2013 (3 year terms)
Pat Gorcak, Mayor
psgorcak@veterancable.net
Debbie Johnstone, Chief Administrative Officer

Viking
P.O. Box 369
Viking, AB T0B 4N0
Tel: 780-336-3466; *Fax:* 780-336-2660
www.town.viking.ab.ca
Municipal Type: Town
Incorporated: Feb. 5, 1909 *Area:* 3.76 sq km
Population in 2011: 1,041
Provincial Electoral District(s): Vermilion-Lloydminster
Federal Electoral District(s): Vegreville-Wainwright
Next Election: Oct. 21, 2013 (3 year terms)
Note: Incorporated as a town on Nov. 10, 1952.
Marlene Grandinetti, Mayor
Rod Krips, Chief Administrative Officer
rod.krips@town.viking.ab.ca

Vilna
P.O. Box 10 Mainstreet
Vilna, AB T0A 3L0
Tel: 780-636-3964; *Fax:* 780-636-3022
info@historicvilna.ca
Municipal Type: Village
Incorporated: June 23, 1923 *Area:* 0.9 sq km
Population in 2011: 249
Provincial Electoral District(s): Lac La Biche-St. Paul
Federal Electoral District(s): Westlock-St. Paul
Next Election: Oct. 21, 2013 (3 year terms)
Donald Romanko, Mayor
pdromanko@yahoo.com
Earla Wagar, Interim Chief Administrative Officer

Vulcan
P.O. Box 360
Vulcan, AB T0L 2B0
Tel: 403-485-2417; *Fax:* 403-485-2914
vulcan@townofvulcan.ca
www.town.vulcan.ab.ca
Municipal Type: Town
Incorporated: Dec. 23, 1912 *Area:* 6.58 sq km
Population in 2011: 1,836
Provincial Electoral District(s): Little Bow
Federal Electoral District(s): Macleod
Next Election: Oct. 21, 2013 (3 year terms)
Note: Incorporated as a town on Jun 15, 1921.
Howard Dirks, Mayor
Alcide Cloutier, Chief Administrative Officer
acloutier@townofvulcan.ca

Wabamun
P.O. Box 240
5217 - 52 St.
Wabamun, AB T0E 2K0
Tel: 780-892-2699; *Fax:* 780-892-2669
admin@wabamun.ca
www.wabamun.ca
Municipal Type: Village
Incorporated: July 18, 1912 *Area:* 3.24 sq km
Population in 2011: 661
Provincial Electoral District(s): Stony Plain
Federal Electoral District(s): Yellowhead
Next Election: Oct. 21, 2013 (3 year terms)
William F. Purdy, Mayor
Linda Hannah, Chief Administrator Officer
cao@wabamun.ca

Wainwright
1018 - 2 Ave.
Wainwright, AB T9W 1R1
Tel: 780-842-3381; *Fax:* 780-842-2898
info@wainwright.ca
www.wainwright.ca
Municipal Type: Town
Incorporated: March 25, 1909 *Area:* 8.55 sq km
Population in 2011: 5,925
Provincial Electoral District(s): Battle River-Wainwright
Federal Electoral District(s): Vegreville-Wainwright
Next Election: Oct. 21, 2013 (3 year terms)
Note: Incorporated as town on July 14, 1910.
Norm Coleman, Mayor
Ray Poulin, Chief Administrative Officer
rpoulin@wainwright.ca

Waiparous
P.O. Box 19554
RPO South Cranston
Calgary, AB T3M 0N5
Tel: 403-652-4636; *Fax:* 403-206-7209
admin@waiparous.ca
www.waiparous.ca
Municipal Type: Summer Village
Incorporated: Jan. 1, 1986 *Area:* 0.41 sq km
Population in 2011: 42
Provincial Electoral District(s): Banff-Cochrane
Federal Electoral District(s): Wild Rose
Next Election: Summer 2013 (3 year terms)
Shirley Begg, Mayor
403-932-2611
Sharon Plett, Administrator
403-554-5515, Fax: 403-206-7209

Warburg
P.O. Box 29
5212 - 50 Ave.
Warburg, AB T0C 2T0
Tel: 780-848-2841; *Fax:* 780-848-2296
villageofwarburg@wildroseinternet.ca
www.villageofwarburg.ab.ca
Municipal Type: Village
Incorporated: Dec. 31, 1953 *Area:* 2.08 sq km
Population in 2011: 789
Provincial Electoral District(s): Drayton Valley-Calmar
Federal Electoral District(s): Wetaskiwin
Next Election: Oct. 21, 2013 (3 year terms)
Dawson Kohl, Mayor
Christine Pankewitz, Municipal Administrator

Warner
P.O. Box 88
Warner, AB T0K 2L0
Tel: 403-642-3877; *Fax:* 403-642-2011
vowarner@shockware.com
www.warner.ca
Municipal Type: Village
Incorporated: Nov. 12, 1908 *Area:* 1.15 sq km
Population in 2011: 331
Provincial Electoral District(s): Cardston-Taber-Warner
Federal Electoral District(s): Lethbridge
Next Election: Oct. 21, 2013 (3 year terms)
Jon Hood, Mayor
Lisa C. Carroll, Chief Administrative Officer

Waskatenau
P.O. Box 99
5008 - 51st St.
Waskatenau, AB T0A 3P0
Tel: 780-358-2208; *Fax:* 780-358-2208
info@waskatenau.ca
www.waskatenau.ca
Municipal Type: Village
Incorporated: May 19, 1932 *Area:* 0.6 sq km
Population in 2011: 255
Provincial Electoral District(s): Athabasca-Redwater
Federal Electoral District(s): Westlock-St. Paul
Next Election: Oct. 21, 2013 (3 year terms)
Casey Caron, Mayor
Bernice Macyk, Chief Administrative Officer

Wembley
P.O. Box 89
Wembley, AB T0H 3S0
Tel: 780-766-2269; *Fax:* 780-766-2868
office@wembley.ca
www.wembley.ca
Municipal Type: Town
Incorporated: Jan. 3, 1928 *Area:* 3.63 sq km
Population in 2011: 1,383
Provincial Electoral District(s): Grande Prairie-Wapiti
Federal Electoral District(s): Peace River
Next Election: Oct. 21, 2013 (3 year terms)
Note: Incorporated as a town on Aug. 1, 1980.
Chris Turnmire, Mayor
clturnmire@telus.net
Lori Parker, Chief Administrative Officer
admin@wembley.ca

West Baptiste
945 Baptiste Dr.
West Baptiste, AB T9S 1R8
Tel: 780-675-3900; *Fax:* 780-675-4174
viviandriver@mcsnet.ca
Municipal Type: Summer Village
Incorporated: Jan. 1, 1983 *Area:* 0.6 sq km
Population in 2011: 52
Provincial Electoral District(s): Athabasca-Redwater
Federal Electoral District(s): Fort McMurray-Athabasca
Next Election: Summer 2013 (3 year terms)
Keith Wilson, Mayor
wilsonkd@shaw.ca
Vivian Driver, Administrator
viviandriver@mcsnet.ca

West Cove
P.O. Box 7
Site 19, RR#1
Gunn, AB T0E 1A0
Tel: 780-446-1426
d.evans@xplornet.com
Municipal Type: Summer Village
Incorporated: Jan. 1, 1963 *Area:* 1.21 sq km
Population in 2011: 121
Provincial Electoral District(s): Whitecourt-Ste. Anne
Federal Electoral District(s): Yellowhead
Next Election: Summer 2013 (3 year terms)
David Breton, Mayor
Dennis Evans, Municipal Administrator

Westlock
10003 - 106 St.
Westlock, AB T7P 2K3
Tel: 780-349-4444; *Fax:* 780-349-4436
info@westlock.ca
www.westlock.ca
Municipal Type: Town
Incorporated: March 13, 1916 *Area:* 9.64 sq km
Population in 2011: 4,823
Provincial Electoral District(s): Barrhead-Morinville-Westlock
Federal Electoral District(s): Westlock-St. Paul
Next Election: Oct. 21, 2013 (3 year terms)
Note: Incorporated as a town on Jan. 7, 1947.
Bruce Lennon, Mayor
blennon@westlock.ca
Darrell Garceau, Town Manager
dgarceau@westlock.ca

Whispering Hills
10511 - 109 St.
Westlock, AB T7P 1A9
Tel: 780-349-3651; *Fax:* 780-349-5194
gmbancroft.@shaw.ca
www.mywhisperinghills.com
Municipal Type: Summer Village
Incorporated: Jan. 1, 1983 *Area:* 1.73 sq km
Population in 2011: 108
Provincial Electoral District(s): Athabasca-Redwater
Federal Electoral District(s): Fort McMurray-Athabasca
Next Election: Summer 2013 (3 year terms)
Dennis Irving, Mayor
Garth Bancroft, Administrator

White Sands
P.O. Box 119
Stettler, AB T0C 2L0
Tel: 403-742-8305; *Fax:* 403-742-1404
townoffice@stettler.net
www.stettler.net
Municipal Type: Summer Village
Incorporated: Jan. 1, 1980 *Area:* 1.6 sq km
Population in 2011: 91
Provincial Electoral District(s): Drumheller-Stettler
Federal Electoral District(s): Crowfoot
Next Election: Summer 2013 (3 year terms)
Lorne Thurston, Mayor
kathyandlorne@yahoo.ca
Greg Switenky, Chief Administrative Officer
403-742-8305
gswitenky@stettler.net

Whitecourt
P.O. Box 509
5004 - 52 Ave.
Whitecourt, AB T7S 1N6
Tel: 780-778-2273; *Fax:* 780-778-2062
administration@whitecourt.ca
www.whitecourt.ca
Municipal Type: Town
Incorporated: Jan. 1, 1959 *Area:* 26.14 sq km
Population in 2011: 9,605
Provincial Electoral District(s): Whitecourt-Ste. Anne
Federal Electoral District(s): Yellowhead
Next Election: Oct. 21, 2013 (3 year terms)
Note: Incorporated as a town on Aug. 15, 1961.
Peter Smyl, CAO
petersmyl@whitecourt.ca
Trevor Thain, Mayor
780-778-0909
trevorthain@whitecourt.ca

Willingdon
P.O. Box 210
Willingdon, AB T0B 4R0
Tel: 780-367-2337; *Fax:* 780-367-2167
vilwil@rjvnet.ca
Municipal Type: Village
Incorporated: Aug. 31, 1928 *Area:* 0.97 sq km
Population in 2011: 275
Provincial Electoral District(s): Lac La Biche-St. Paul
Federal Electoral District(s): Vegreville-Wainwright
Next Election: Oct. 21, 2013 (3 year terms)
Lillian Bezovie, Mayor
Elsie Howanyk, Chief Administrative Officer
cao@townoftwohills.com

Yellowstone
P.O. Box 8
Alberta Beach, AB T0E 0A0
Tel: 780-924-3024; *Fax:* 780-924-3025
administration@wildwillowenterprises.com
www.wildwillowenterprises.com
Municipal Type: Summer Village
Incorporated: Jan. 1, 1965 *Area:* 0.28 sq km
Population in 2011: 124
Provincial Electoral District(s): Whitecourt-Ste. Anne
Federal Electoral District(s): Yellowhead
Next Election: Summer 2013 (3 year terms)
Alice Solesbury, Mayor
Wendy Wildman, Chief Administrative Officer

Youngstown
P.O. Box 99
Youngstown, AB T0J 3P0
Tel: 403-779-3873; *Fax:* 403-779-3875
ytown@xplornet.com
Municipal Type: Village
Incorporated: March 8, 1913 *Area:* 1 sq km
Population in 2011: 178
Provincial Electoral District(s): Drumheller-Stettler
Federal Electoral District(s): Crowfoot
Next Election: Oct. 21, 2013 (3 year terms)
Robert Blagen, Mayor
Emma Garlock, Municipal Administrator

Improvement Districts

Improvement District No. 12 (Jasper National Park)
Municipal Services Branch
10155 - 102 St., 17th Fl.
Edmonton, AB T5J 4L4
Tel: 780-427-2225; *Fax:* 780-420-1016
lgsmail@gov.ab.ca
Municipal Type: Improvement Districts
Incorporated: April 1, 1945 *Area:* 10,181.58 sq. km
Population in 2011: 34
Faye Sheridan, ID Manager
faye.sheridan@gov.ab.ca

Improvement District No. 13 (Elk Island)
Municipal Services Branch
10155 - 102 St., 17th Fl.
Edmonton, AB T5J 4L4
Tel: 780-427-2225; *Fax:* 780-420-1016
lgsmail@gov.ab.ca
Municipal Type: Improvement Districts
Incorporated: April 1, 1958 *Area:* 165.28 sq. km
Population in 2011: 10
Faye Sheridan, ID Manager
faye.sheridan@gov.ab.ca

Improvement District No. 24 (Wood Buffalo)
Municipal Services Branch
10155 - 102 St., 17th Fl.
Edmonton, AB T5J 4L4
Tel: 780-427-2225; *Fax:* 780-420-1016
lgsmail@gov.ab.ca
Municipal Type: Improvement Districts
Incorporated: Jan. 1, 1967 *Area:* 165.28 sq km.
Population in 2011: 590
Faye Sheridan, ID Manager
faye.sheridan@gov.ab.ca
Faye Sheridan, ID Manager
faye.sheridan@gov.ab.ca

Improvement District No. 25 (Willmore Wilderness)
Municipal Services Branch
10155 - 102 St., 17th Fl.
Edmonton, AB T5J 4L4
Tel: 780-427-2225; *Fax:* 780-420-1016
lgsmail@gov.ab.ca
Municipal Type: Improvement Districts
Incorporated: Jan. 2, 1994 *Area:* 4,604.97 sq. km

Improvement District No. 4 (Waterton)
Municipal Services Branch
10155 - 102 St., 17th Fl.
Edmonton, AB T5J 4L4
Tel: 403-752-3322; *Fax:* 403-752-4379
lgsmail@gov.ab.ca
Municipal Type: Improvement Districts
Incorporated: Jan. 1, 1944 *Area:* 480.58 sq. km
Population in 2011: 88
Rick Reeves, Chairperson
J. Scott Barton, Chief Administrative Officer
scottbarton@raymond.ca

Improvement District No. 9 (Banff)
Municipal Services Branch
10155 - 102 St., 17th Fl.
Edmonton, AB T5J 4L4
Tel: 780-720-1994; *Fax:* 780-665-7369
lgsmail@gov.ab.ca
Municipal Type: Improvement Districts
Incorporated: April 1, 1945 *Area:* 6,782.26 sq. km
Population in 2011: 1,175
Rick Werner, Chairperson
rick.werner@skilouise.com
J. Scott Barton, Chief Administrative Officer
scottbarton@raymond.ca

Kananaskis Improvement District
P.O. Box 70
Kananaskis, AB T0L 2H0
Tel: 403-591-7774; *Fax:* 403-591-7123
tammi.pretty@gov.ab.ca
www.kananaskisid.ca
Municipal Type: Improvement Districts
Incorporated: April 1, 1945 *Area:* 4,210.72 sq km
Population in 2011: 249
Dan DeSantis, Chairperson
ddesantis@deltahotels.com
Shawn Polley, Chief Administrative Officer
shawn.polley@gov.ab.ca

Metis Settlement in Alberta

Buffalo Lake
P.O. Box 16
Caslan, AB T0A 0R0
Tel: 780-689-2170; *Fax:* 780-689-2024
hbylan@buffalolakemetis.com
Municipal Type: Metis Settlement
Stan Delorme, Chairperson
Harold Blyan, Administrator
hblyan@buffalolakemetis.com

East Prairie
P.O. Box 1289
High Prairie, AB T0G 1E0
Tel: 780-523-2594; *Fax:* 780-523-2777
jhaggerty@eastprairiemetis.ca
Municipal Type: Metis Settlement
Robert L'Hirondelle, Chairperson
Harry Supernault, Administrator
hsupernault@eastprairiemetis.ca

Elizabeth
P.O. Box 420
Cold Lake, AB T9M 1P1
Tel: 780-594-5026; *Fax:* 780-594-5452
ems@jetnet.ab.ca
Municipal Type: Metis Settlement
Allan Wells, Chairperson
emscon@incentre.net
Jeanette Calliou, Administrator
emscouncil@jetnet.ab.ca

Fishing Lake
General Delivery
Sputinow, AB T0A 3G0
Tel: 780-943-2202; *Fax:* 780-943-2575
www.fishinglakems.ca
Municipal Type: Metis Settlement
Lorne Dustow, Chairperson
Margaret Daniels, Administrator

Gift Lake
P.O. Box 60
Gift Lake, AB T0G 1B0
Tel: 780-767-3794; *Fax:* 780-767-3888
glms@telus.net
Municipal Type: Metis Settlement
Hector Lamouche, Chairperson
Gerry Peardon, Administrator
gerrygl@telus.net

Kikino
General Delivery
Kikino, AB T0A 2B0
Tel: 780-623-7868; *Fax:* 780-623-7080
kiadmin@telus.net
Municipal Type: Metis Settlement
Floyd Thompson, Chairperson
Roger Littlechilds, Administrator
kikinoranch@mcsnet.ca

Paddle Prairie
P.O. Box 58
Paddle Prairie, AB T0H 2W0
Tel: 780-981-2227; *Fax:* 780-981-3737
reception@paddleprairie.com
Municipal Type: Metis Settlement
Greg Calliou, Chairperson
Darla Wanuch, Administrator
darla@paddleprairie.com

Peavine
P.O. Box 238
High Prairie, AB T0G 1E0
Tel: 780-523-2557; *Fax:* 780-523-2626
Municipal Type: Metis Settlement
Ken Noskey, Chairperson
ken.noskey@peavinemetis.com
Fahim Haque, Administrator
fahim.haque@peavinemetis.com

BRITISH COLUMBIA

Incorporated municipalities in British Columbia include Villages, Towns, Cities, and District Municipalities as well as one Indian Government District, a Resort Municipality, and an Island Municipality. Twenty-seven regional districts provide services to unincorporated areas and member municipalities.

Municipal elections in all municipalities are held on the third Saturday of November. Terms of office are three years (2014, 2017, etc.).

Legislation: The Local Government Act, excluding the City of Vancouver, which is regulated under the provisions of the Vancouver Charter.

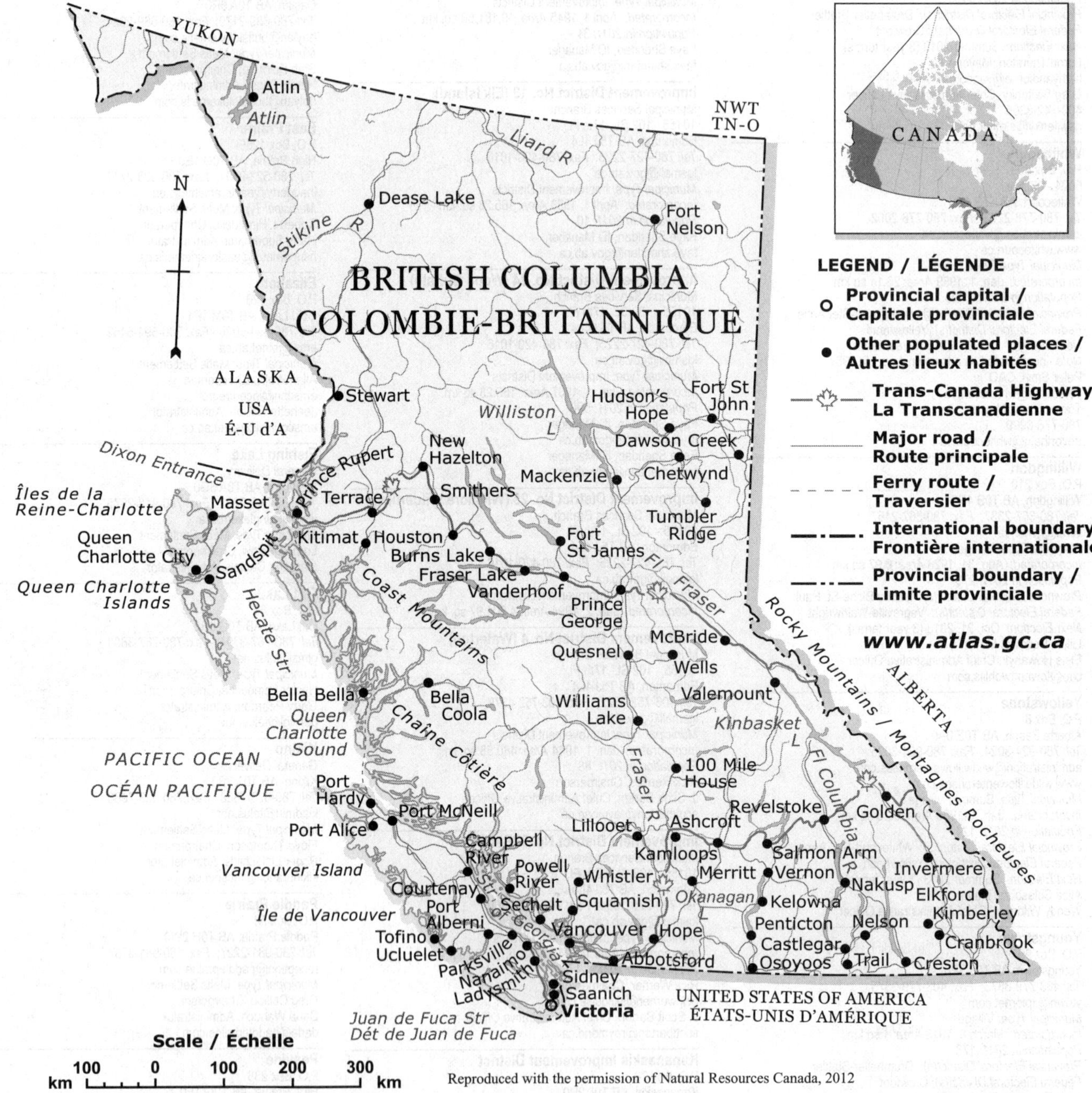

Reproduced with the permission of Natural Resources Canada, 2012

British Columbia

Counties & Municipal Districts in British Columbia

Alberni-Clayoquot

3008 - 5 Ave.
Port Alberni, BC V9Y 2E3
Tel: 250-720-2700; *Fax:* 250-723-1327
mailbox@acrd.bc.ca
www.acrd.bc.ca
Municipal Type: Regional Districts
Incorporated: April 21, 1966 *Area:* 6,596.58 sq km
Population in 2011: 31,061
Next Election: Nov. 15, 2014 (3 year terms)
Note: Member municipalities: Port Alberni; Tofino; Ucluelet.
Glenn Wong, Chair
250-724-4847, Fax: 250-724-4847
glwong@telus.net; chairperson@acrd.bc.ca
Russell Dyosn, Chief Administrative Officer
250-720-2705
rdyson@acrd.bc.ca
Wendy Thompson, Deputy Corporate Officer
250-720-2706
wendy.thomson@acrd.bc.ca
Teri Fong, Manager, Finance
250-720-2707
teri.fong@acrd.bc.ca
Mike Irg, Manager, Planning & Development
250-720-2710
mirg@acrd.bc.ca
Tracy Bond, Secretary
250-720-2700
tbond@acrd.bc.ca
John Thomas, Bamfield Water System
250-720-2718
Joe Daley, Millstream Water System
250-726-7351

Bulkley-Nechako

P.O. Box 820
37, 3rd Ave.
Burns Lake, BC V0J 1E0
Tel: 250-692-3195; *Fax:* 250-692-3305
inquiries@rdbn.bc.ca
www.rdbn.bc.ca
Other Information: Toll Free Phone: 1-800-320-3339
Municipal Type: Regional Districts
Incorporated: Feb. 1, 1966 *Area:* 73,440.95 sq km
Population in 2011: 39,208
Next Election: Nov. 15, 2014 (3 year terms)
Note: Member municipalities: Smithers; Fort St. James; Housten; Vanderhoof; Burns Lake; Fraser Lake; Granisle; Telkwa.
Lance Hamblin, Chair
250-845-7849
chair@rdbn.bc.ca
Gail Chapman, Chief Administrative Officer
250-692-3195, Fax: 250-692-3305
gail.chapman@rdbn.bc.ca
Jason Llewellyn, Director, Planning
jason.llewellyn@rdbn.bc.ca
Janine Dougall, Director, Environmental Services
250-692-3195
janine.dougall@rdbn.bc.ca
Hans Berndorff, C.A., Administrator, Financial Services
hans.berndorff@rdbn.bc.ca
Richard Wainwright, C.A., Chief Building Inspector
richard.wainwright@rdbn.bc.ca
Corrine Swenson, C.A., Regional Strategic Development Analyst, Community Economic Development
richard.wainwright@rdbn.bc.ca
Rory McKenzie, Supervisor, Field Operations, Environmental Services
rory.mckenzie@rdbn.bc.ca

Capital Regional District

625 Fisgard St.
Victoria, BC V8W 1R7
Tel: 250-360-3000
www.crd.bc.ca
Other Information: Mailing address: PO Box 1000, Victoria, BC V8W 2S6
Municipal Type: Regional Districts
Incorporated: Feb. 1, 1966 *Area:* 2,341.02 sq km
Population in 2011: 359,991
Next Election: Nov. 15, 2014 (3 year terms)
Note: Member municipalities: Central Saanich; Colwood; Esquimalt; Highlands; Langford; Metchosin; North Saanich; Oak Bay; Saanich; Sidney; Sooke; Victoria; View Royal.
Geoff Young, Board Chair
250-385-5711, Fax: 250-361-0348
Diana Lokken, General Manager, Corporate Services
250-360-3010
Larissa Hutcheson, General Manager, Environmental Sustainability
250-360-3085
Jack Hull, General Manager, Integrated Water Services
250-474-9604
Robert Lapham, General Manager, Planning & Protective Services
250-360-3285
Andy Orr, Senior Manager, Corporate Communications
250-360-3229
Dan Telford, Senior Manager, Environmental Engineering
250-360-3064
Glenn Harris, Senior Manager, Environmental Protection
250-360-3090
Russ Smith, Senior Manager, Environmental Resource Management
250-360-3083
Tim Tanton, Senior Manager, Infrasturcture Engineering
250-474-9611
Maurice Rachwalski, Senior Manager, Health & Capital Planning Strategies
250-360-3114
Ian Hennigar, Senior Manager, Peninsula Recreation Commission/Panorama Recreation
250-655-2170
Margaret Misek-Evans, Senior Manager, Regional Planning
250-360-3244
Ted Robbins, Senior Manager, Water Management
250-360-3061
Stewart Irwin, Senior Manager, Water Quality
250-474-9603
Gordon Joyce, Senior Manager, Watershep Protection
250-474-9621

Cariboo

180 North 3rd Ave., #D
Williams Lake, BC V2G 2A4
Tel: 250-392-3351; *Fax:* 250-392-2812
mailbox@cariboord.bc.ca
www.cariboord.bc.ca
Other Information: Toll Free Phone: 1-800-665-1636
Municipal Type: Regional Districts
Incorporated: July 9, 1968 *Area:* 80,629.34 sq km
Population in 2011: 62,392
Next Election: Nov. 15, 2014 (3 year terms)
Note: Member municipalities: 100 Mile House; Quesnel; Wells; Williams Lake.
Al Richmond, Chairperson
arichmond@cariboord.bc.ca
Janis Bell, Chief Administrative Officer
jbell@cariboord.bc.ca
Rick Hodgson, Deputy Chief Administrative Officer
rhodgson@cariboord.bc.ca
Alice Johnston, Corporate Officer
ajohnston@cariboord.bc.ca
Scott Reid, Chief Financial Officer
sreid@cariboord.bc.ca
Graham Barbour, Chief Building Official
gbarbour@cariboord.bc.ca
Mitch Minchau, Manager, Utilities/Solid Waste Management
mminchau@cariboord.bc.ca
Rick Brundrige, Manager, Planning Services
rbrundrige@cariboord.bc.ca
Darron Campbell, Manager, Community Services/Recreation/Airports
dcampbell@cariboord.bc.ca
Rowena Bastien, Manager, Protective Services
rbastien@cariboord.bc.ca

Central Coast

P.O. Box 186
626 Cliff St.
Bella Coola, BC V0T 1C0
Tel: 250-799-5291; *Fax:* 250-799-5750
info@ccrd-bc.ca
www.ccrd-bc.ca
Municipal Type: Regional Districts
Incorporated: July 16, 1968 *Area:* 24,556.35 sq km
Population in 2011: 3,206
Next Election: Nov. 15, 2014 (3 year terms)
Brian Lande, Chair
Joy MacKay, Chief Administrative Officer
cao@ccrd-bc.ca
Donna Mikkelson, Chief Financial Officer
cfo@ccrd-bc.ca
Stephen Waugh, Emergency Program Coordinator
epc@ccrd-bc.ca

Central Kootenay

P.O. Box 590
202 Lakeside Dr.
Nelson, BC V1L 5R4
Tel: 250-352-6665; *Fax:* 250-352-9300
info@rdck.bc.ca
www.rdck.bc.ca
Other Information: Toll Free Phone: 1-800-268-7325
Municipal Type: Regional Districts
Incorporated: Nov. 30, 1965 *Area:* 22,130.72 sq km
Population in 2011: 58,441
Next Election: Nov. 15, 2014 (3 year terms)
Note: Member municipalities: Castlegar; Creston; Kaslo; Nakusp; Nelson; New Denver; Salmo; Silverton; Slocan.
John Kettle, Chair
250-428-5560, Fax: 250-428-5567
jrkettlejgalt@ shaw.ca
Jim Gustafson, Chief Administrative Officer
250-352-8152
jgustafson@rdck.bc.ca
Grant Roeland, Chief Financial Officer
250-352-8150
groeland@rdck.bc.ca
Ann Fisher, Human Resources/Corporate Safety Officer
250-352-8193
afisher@rdck.bc.ca
Joe Chirico, General Manager, Community Services
250-352-8158
jchirico@rdck.bc.ca
Dawn Attorp, General Manager, Corporate Administration
250-352-8167
dattorp@rdck.bc.ca
Uli Wolf, General Manager, Environmental Services
250-352-8163
uwolf@rdck.bc.ca
David Oosthuizen, Manager, Information Technology Services
250-352-8188

Central Okanagan

1450 KLO Rd.
Kelowna, BC V1W 3Z4
Tel: 250-763-4918; *Fax:* 250-763-0606
info@cord.bc.ca
www.cord.bc.ca
Municipal Type: Regional Districts
Incorporated: Aug. 24, 1967 *Area:* 2,904.01 sq km
Population in 2011: 179,839
Next Election: Nov. 15, 2014 (3 year terms)
Note: Member municipalities: Kelowna; West Kelowna; Lake Country; Peachland.
Robert Hobson, Chair
250-469-6224
rhobson@cord.bc.ca
Harold Reay, Chief Administrative Officer
Marilyn Rilkoff, Director, Administration & Finance
250-469-6242
finance@cord.bc.ca
Dan Plamondon, Director, Development Services
250-868-5227
planning@cord.bc.ca
Robert Fine, Director, Economic Development Commission
250-469-6280
info@investkelowna.com
Chris Radford, Director, Environmental Services
250-469-6241
engineer@cord.bc.ca
Murray Kopp, Director, Parks Services
Peter Rotheisler, Manager, Regional Waste Reduction Office
250-469-6250, Fax: 250-762-7011
recycle@cord.bc.ca
Cary Berger, Manager, Police Services
250-470-6212, Fax: 250-470-7011

Columbia-Shuswap

P.O. Box 978
781 Marine Park Dr. NE
Salmon Arm, BC V1E 4P1
Tel: 250-832-8194; *Fax:* 250-832-3375
enquiries@csrd.bc.ca
www.csrd.bc.ca
Other Information: Toll Free Phone: 1-888-248-2773
Municipal Type: Regional Districts
Incorporated: Nov. 30, 1965 *Area:* 29,003.97 sq km
Population in 2011: 50,512
Next Election: Nov. 15, 2014 (3 year terms)
Note: Member municipalities: Golden; Revelstoke; Sicamous; Salmon Arm.
Ron Oszust, Chair
Charles Hamilton, Chief Administrative Officer
250-832-8194
admin@csrd.bc.ca, chamilton@csrd.bc.ca

Robyn Cyr, Economic development Officer/Film Commissioner
250-833-5928
rcyr@csrd.bc.ca
Gerald Christie, Manager, Development Services
250-833-5919
gchristie@csrd.bc.ca
Gary Holte, Manager, Environment & Engineering Services
250-833-5935
gholte@csrd.bc.ca
Peter Jarman, Manager, Finance & Information Technology
250-833-5908
pjarman@csrd.bc.ca
Jack Blair, Co-ordinator, Fire Services
250-833-5945
jblair@csrd.bc.ca
Hamish Kassa, Co-ordinator, Environment Services
250-833-5942
hkassa@csrd.bc.ca
Terry Langois, Co-ordinator, Water Systems
250-833-5941
tlanglois@csrd.bc.ca
Ben Van Nostrand, Co-ordinator, Waste Management
250-833-5940
bvannostrand@csrd.bc.ca

Comox Valley
600 Comox Rd.
Courtenay, BC V9N 3P6
Tel: 250-334-6000; *Fax:* 250-334-4358
administration@comoxvalleyrd.ca
www.comoxvalleyrd.ca
Other Information: Toll Free Phone: 1-800-331-6007
Municipal Type: Regional Districts
Incorporated: Aug. 19, 1965 *Area:* 20,013.48 sq km
Population in 2011: 63,538
Next Election: Nov. 15, 2014 (3 year terms)
Note: Member municipalities: Comox; Courtenay; Cumberland.
Edwin Grieve, Chair
edwingrieve@shaw.ca
Debra Oakman, Chief Administrative Officer
Beth Dunlop, Corporate Financial Officer
James Warren, Corporate Legislative Officer
Ian Smith, General Manager, Community Services
Kevin Lorette, General Manager, Property Service Branch
Leigh Carter, General Manager, Public Affairs/Information Systems Branch
Will Hwang, Executive Manager, Human Resources
Geoff Garbutt, Manager, Strategic & Long Range Planning

Cowichan Valley
175 Ingram St.
Duncan, BC V9L 1N8
Tel: 250-746-2500
cvrd@cvrd.bc.ca
www.cvrd.bc.ca
Other Information: Toll Free Phone: 1-800-665-3955
Municipal Type: Regional Districts
Incorporated: Sept. 26, 1967 *Area:* 3,473.12 sq km
Population in 2011: 80,332
Next Election: Nov. 15, 2014 (3 year terms)
Note: Member municipalities: Duncan; Ladysmith; Lake Cowichan; North Cowichan.
Gerry Giles, Chair
chairperson@cvrd.bc.ca
Warren Jones, Chief Administrative Officer
250-746-2510
wjones@cvrd.bc.ca
Mark Kueber, General Manager, Corporate Services
250-746-2571
mkueber@cvrd.bc.ca
Brian Dennison, General Manager, Engineering & Environment
250-746-2532
bdennison@cvrd.bc.ca
Ron Austen, General Manager, Parks, Recreation & Culture
250-746-2635
rausten@cvrd.bc.ca
Tom R. Anderson, General Manager, Planning & Development
250-746-2601
tanderson@cvrd.bc.ca
Sybille Sanderson, Acting General Manager, Public Safety
250-746-2562
ssanderson@cvrd.bc.ca

East Kootenay
19 - 24 Ave. South
Cranbrook, BC V1C 3H8
Tel: 250-489-2791; *Fax:* 250-489-3498
info@rdek.bc.ca
www.rdek.bc.ca
Other Information: Toll Free Phone: 1-888-478-7335
Municipal Type: Regional Districts
Incorporated: Nov. 30, 1965 *Area:* 27,560.49 sq km
Population in 2011: 56,685
Next Election: Nov. 15, 2014 (3 year terms)
Note: Member municipalities: Canal Flats; Cranbrook; Kimberley; Fernie; Sparwood; Elkford; Invermere; Radium Hot Springs.
Scott Manjak, Chair
Lee-Ann Crane, Chief Administrative Officer
lcrane@rdek.bc.ca
Shawn Tomlin, Chief Financial Officer
stomlin@rdek.bc.ca
Dan McNeill, Manager, Building & Protective Services
dmcneill@rdek.bc.ca
Loree Duczek, Manager, Communications
lduczek@rdek.bc.ca
Shannon Moskal, Manager, Community Services
smoskal@rdek.bc.ca
Brian Funke, Manager, Engineering Services
bfunke@rdek.bc.ca
Kevin Paterson, Manager, Environmental Services
kpaterson@rdek.bc.ca
Lori Engler, Manager, Human Resources
lengler@rdek.bc.ca
Andrew McLeod, Manager, Planning & Development Services
amcleod@rdek.bc.ca

Fraser Valley
#1, 45950 Cheam Ave.
Chilliwack, BC V2P 1N6
Tel: 604-702-5000; *Fax:* 604-792-9684
info@fvrd.bc.ca
www.fvrd.com
Other Information: Toll Free Phone: 1-800-528-0061
Municipal Type: Regional Districts
Incorporated: Dec. 12, 1995 *Area:* 13,361.74 sq km
Population in 2011: 277,593
Next Election: Nov. 15, 2014 (3 year terms)
Note: Member municipalities: Abbotsford; Chilliwack; Hope; Kent; Mission; Harrison Hot Springs.
Patricia Ross, Chair
pross@fvrd.bc.ca
Gerald H. Kingston, Chief Administrative Officer
gkingston@fvrd.bc.ca
George Murray, General Manager, Finance
604-702-5033
gmurray@fvrd.bc.ca
Doug Joinson, Manager, Communications & Information Services
djoinson@fvrd.bc.ca
Mike Phelan, Manager, Finance
mphelan@fvrd.bc.ca
Tareq Islam, P.Eng., Director, Engineering
604-702-5026
tislam@fvrd.bc.ca
Lance Lilley, Planner, Watershed
llilley@fvrd.bc.ca

Fraser-Fort George
155 George St.
Prince George, BC V2L 1P8
Tel: 250-960-4400
district@rdffg.bc.ca
www.rdffg.bc.ca
Other Information: Toll Free Phone: 1-800-667-1959
Municipal Type: Regional Districts
Incorporated: March 8, 1967 *Area:* 50,705.84 sq km
Population in 2011: 91,879
Next Election: Nov. 15, 2014 (3 year terms)
Note: Member municipalities: McBride; Mackenzie; Prince George; Valemount.
Art Kaehn, Chair
akaehn@rdffg.bc.ca
Terry Burgess, Vice-Chair
tburgess@rdffg.bc.ca
Reneé McCloskey, Manager, External Relations
250-960-4453

Kitimat-Stikine
#300, 4545 Lazelle Ave.
Terrace, BC V8G 4E1
Tel: 250-615-6100; *Fax:* 250-635-9222
info@rdks.bc.ca
www.rdks.bc.ca
Other Information: Toll Free Phone: 1-800-663-3208
Municipal Type: Regional Districts
Incorporated: Sept. 14, 1967 *Area:* 91,917.88 sq km
Population in 2011: 37,361
Next Election: Nov. 15, 2014 (3 year terms)
Note: Member municipalities: Kitimat; Terrace; Stewart; Hazelton; New Hazelton.
Harry Nyce, Board Chair
Robert Marcellin, Administrator
Verna Wickie, Treasurer
Lori Stark, Confidential Secretary to the Board
Andrew Webber, Manager, Planning & Economic Development
awebber@rdks.bc.ca
Roger Tooms, Manager, Works & Services
rtooms@rdks.bc.ca
Ken Newman, Planner
knewman@rdks.bc.ca
Ted Pellegrino, Planner
tpellegrino@rdks.bc.ca

Kootenay Boundary
#202, 843 Rossland Ave.
Trail, BC V1R 4S8
Tel: 250-368-9148; *Fax:* 250-368-3990
Other Information: Toll Free Phone: 1-800-355-7352 (BC only)
Municipal Type: Regional Districts
Incorporated: Feb. 22, 1966 *Area:* 8,095.63 sq km
Population in 2011: 31,138
Next Election: Nov. 15, 2014 (3 year terms)
Note: Member municipalities: Fruitvale; Grand Forks; Greenwood; Midway; Montrose; Rossland; Trail; Warfield.
Marguerite Rotvold, Chair
rotvoldrdkb@shaw.ca
John MacLean, Chief Administrative Officer
jmaclean@rdkb.com
Sig Dreher, Chief Building & Plumbing Official
jmaclean@rdkb.com
Elaine Kumar, Director, Corporate Administration
ekumar@rdkb.com
Alan Stanley, Director, Environmental Services
astanley@rdkb.com
Gerry Gardner, Director, Finance
ggardner@rdkb.com
Mark Andison, Director, Planning & Development
mandison@rdkb.com
Dale Green, Manager, Information Services
dgreen@rdkb.com

Metro Vancouver
4330 Kingsway
Burnaby, BC V5H 4G8
Tel: 604-432-6200; *Fax:* 604-436-6901
icentre@metrovancouver.org
www.metrovancouver.org
Municipal Type: Regional Districts
Incorporated: June 29, 1967 *Area:* 2,877.36 sq km
Population in 2011: 2,313,328
Next Election: Nov. 15, 2014 (3 year terms)
Note: Member municipalities: Anmore; Belcarra; Bowen Island; Burnaby; Coquitlam; Delta; Langley; Lions Bay; New Westminster; North Vancouver; Pitt Meadows; Port Coquitlam; Port Moody; Richmond; Surrey; Vancouver; West Vancouver; White Rock
Lois Jackson, Chair
Johnny Carline, Chief Administrative Officer/Commissioner
Delia Laglagaron, Deputy Chief Administrative Officer/Deputy Commissioner
Jim Rusnak, Chief Financial Officer
Heather Shoemaker, Manager, Corporate Relations
Greg Smith, Manager, Corporate Services
Tim Jervis, P.Eng., Manager, Engineering & Construction
Linda Shore, Manager, Human Resources
Malcolm Graham, Manager, Labour Relations
Doug Humphris, P.Eng., Manager, Operations & Maintenance
Tovio Allas, Manager, Policy & Planning
Don Littleford, Manager, Regional Housing
Mitch Sokalski, Acting Manager, Regional Parks

Mount Waddington
P.O. Box 729
2044 McNeill Rd.
Port McNeill, BC V0N 2R0
Tel: 250-956-3301; *Fax:* 250-956-3232
info@rdmw.bc.ca
www.rdmw.bc.ca
Other Information: Alternate Phone: 250-956-3161
Municipal Type: Regional Districts
Incorporated: June 13, 1966 *Area:* 20,288.19 sq km
Population in 2011: 11,506
Next Election: Nov. 15, 2014 (3 year terms)
Note: Member municipalities: Alert Bay; Port Alice; Port Hardy; Port McNeill.
Al Huddlestan, Chair
chair@rdmw.bc.ca
Greg Fletcher, Administrator
Joe MacKenzie, Treasurer
Neil Smith, Manager, Economic Development/Parks
Patrick Donaghy, Manager, Operations
Jeff Long, Manager, Planning
Bonnie Danyk, Financial Clerk
Paddy Hinton, Supervisor, Parks

Nanaimo
6300 Hammond Bay Rd.
Nanaimo, BC V9T 6N2
Tel: 250-390-4111; *Fax:* 250-390-4163
corpsrv@rdn.bc.ca
www.rdn.bc.ca
Other Information: Toll Free Phone: 1-877-607-4111
Municipal Type: Regional Districts
Incorporated: Aug. 24, 1967 *Area:* 2,034.93 sq km
Population in 2011: 146,574
Next Election: Nov. 15, 2014 (3 year terms)
Note: Member municipalities: Nanaimo; Lantzville; Parksville; Qualicum Beach.
Joseph Stanhope, Chair
jstanhope@shaw.ca
Carol Mason, Chief Administrative Officer
250-390-4111
Neil Connelly, General Manager, Community Services
250-390-6510
John Finnie, General Manager, Regional & Community Utilities
250-390-6560
Wendy Idema, Acting General Manager, Finance & Information Services
250-390-4111
widema@rdn.bc.ca
Tom Osborne, General Manager, Recreation & Parks Services
recparks@rdn.bc.ca
Paul Thorkelsson, General Manager, Development Services
250-390-6530
Dennis Trudeau, General Manager, Transportation & Solid Waste
250-390-6565

North Okanagan
9848 Aberdeen Rd.
Coldstream, BC V1B 2K9
Tel: 250-550-3700; *Fax:* 250-550-3701
info@nord.ca
www.nord.ca
Municipal Type: Regional Districts
Incorporated: Nov. 9, 1965 *Area:* 7,511.94 sq km
Population in 2011: 81,237
Next Election: Nov. 15, 2014 (3 year terms)
Note: Member municipalities: Enderby; Armstrong; Spallumcheen; Vernon; Coldtream; Lumby.
Herman Halvorson, Chair
Christy Malden, Executive Assistant to the Administrator
250-550-3752
christy.malden@rdno.ca
David Sewell, Chief Financial Officer
250-550-3724
pat.luscombe@rdno.ca
Pat Luscombe, Chief Building Inspector
250-550-3724
pat.luscombe@rdno.ca
Leah Mellott, Acting General Manager, Corporate & Electoral Area Services
250-550-3722
leah.mellott@rdno.ca
Al McNiven, General Manager, Greater Vernon Parks, Recreation & Culture
250-550-3664
Ron Baker, Manager, Comunity Protective Services
doug.buchholz@rdno.ca
Nicole Kohnert, Regional Manager, Engineering Services
250-550-3674
nicole.kohnert@rdno.ca
Dale Danallanko, Manager, Recycling & Disposal Facilities Operations
250-550-3744
dale.danallanko@rdno.ca
Al Cotsworth, Manager, Utilities
250-550-3674
al.cotsworth@rdno.ca
Renee Clark, Manager, Water Quality
250-550-3747
renee.clark@rdno.ca
Greg Routley, Planner, Development Services
250-550-3734
greg.routley@rdno.ca
Marnie Skobalski, Planner, Development Services
250-550-3737
marnie.skobalski@rdno.ca

Northern Rockies
P.O. Box 399
5319 - 50th Ave. South
Fort Nelson, BC V0C 1R0
Tel: 250-774-2541; *Fax:* 250-774-6794
justask@northernrockies.ca
www.northernrockies.ca
Municipal Type: Regional Districts
Incorporated: Oct. 31, 1987 *Area:* 85,148.87 sq km
Population in 2011: 5,578
Next Election: Nov. 15, 2014 (3 year terms)
Note: Member municipality: Fort Nelson.
Bill Streeper, Mayor
Randy McLean, Chief Administrative Officer
250-774-2541
admin@northernrockies.ca
Doug Tofte, Community Resource & Planning Officer
Jaylene Arnold, Economic Development & Tourism Officer
Erin La Vale, Human Resources, Safety & Research Officer
Jack Stevenson, Director, Community Development & Planning
250-774-2541
ecdev@northernrockies.ca
Harvey Woodland, Director, Recreation
250-774-2541
rec@northernrockies.ca
Ross Coupé, Manager
Heather Cosman, Manager, Corporate
Danielle Morin, Manager, Recreation Program

Okanagan-Similkameen
101 Martin St.
Penticton, BC V2A 5J9
Tel: 250-492-0237
info@rdos.bc.ca
www.rdos.bc.ca
Other Information: Toll Free Phone: 1-877-610-3737
Municipal Type: Regional Districts
Incorporated: March 4, 1966 *Area:* 10,412.64 sq km
Population in 2011: 80,742
Next Election: Nov. 15, 2014 (3 year terms)
Note: Member municipalities: Penticton; Summerland; Oliver; Osoyoos; Princeton; Keremeos.
Dan Ashton, Chair
Bill Newell, Chief Administrative Officer
250-492-0237
info@rdos.bc.ca
Mark Woods, Manager, Community Services
250-490-4132
mwoods@rdos.bc.ca
Donna Butler, Manager, Development Services
250-490-4109
dbutler@rdos.bc.ca
Warren Everton, BA, CMA, Manager, Finance
250-490-4105
Patty Tracy, Manager, Human Resources
250-490-4138
pderkach@rdos.bc.ca
Tim Bouwmeester, Manager, Information Services
Doug French, P.Eng., Manager, Public Works
250-490-4103

Peace River
P.O. Box 810
1981 Alaska Ave.
Dawson Creek, BC V1G 4H8
Tel: 250-784-3200; *Fax:* 250-784-3201
prrd.dc@prrd.bc.ca
prrd.bc.ca
Other Information: Toll-Free Phone: 1-800-670-7773
Municipal Type: Regional Districts
Incorporated: Oct. 31, 1987 *Area:* 117,761.07 sq km
Population in 2011: 60,082
Next Election: Nov. 15, 2014 (3 year terms)
Note: Member municipalities: Dawson Creek; Fort St. John; Chetwynd; Hudson's Hope; Tumbler Ridge; Pouce Coupe; Taylor.
Karen Goodings, Chair
Fred Banham, Chief Administrative Officer
250-784-3208
Kim French, Chief Financial Officer
250-784-3221
Faye Salisbury, Corporate Officer
250-784-3216
Bruce Simard, General Manager, Development Services
250-784-3204
Shannon Anderson, General Manager, Environmental Services
250-784-3203
Trish Morgan, Manager, Community Services
250-784-3218
Jeff Rahn, Manager, Solid Waste Services
250-784-3226

Powell River
5776 Marine Ave.
Powell River, BC V8A 2M4
Tel: 604-483-3231; *Fax:* 604-483-2229
administration@powellriverrd.bc.ca
www.powellriverrd.bc.ca
Municipal Type: Regional Districts
Incorporated: Dec. 19, 1967 *Area:* 5,092.05 sq km
Population in 2011: 19,906
Next Election: Nov. 15, 2014 (3 year terms)
Note: Member municipality: Powell River.
Colin Palmer, Chair
Malcolm Fraser, Chief Administrative Officer
Sean McGinn, Manager, Community Services
Linda Greenan, Manager, Financial Services
Shawn Gullette, Foreman, Parks & Properties
Don Turner, Senior Planner

Skeena-Queen Charlotte
100 - 1st Ave. East
Prince Rupert, BC V8J 1A6
Tel: 250-624-2002; *Fax:* 250-627-8493
musgrave@sqcrd.bc.ca
www.sqcrd.bc.ca
Other Information: Toll Free Phone: 1-888-301-2002
Municipal Type: Regional Districts
Incorporated: Aug. 17, 1967 *Area:* 19,871.85 sq km
Population in 2011: 18,784
Next Election: Nov. 15, 2014 (3 year terms)
Note: Member municipalities: Prince Rupert; Port Edward; Queen Charlotte; Port Clemens; Masset.
Barry Pages, Chair
250-626-3995, Fax: 250-626-5503
bpages@mhtv.ca
Joan Merrick, Chief Administrative Officer
Jennifer Robb, Treasurer

Squamish-Lillooet
P.O. Box 219
1350 Aster St.
Pemberton, BC V0N 2L0
Tel: 604-894-6371; *Fax:* 604-894-6526
info@slrd.bc.ca
www.slrd.bc.ca
Other Information: Toll Free Phone: 1-800-298-7753
Municipal Type: Regional Districts
Incorporated: Oct. 3, 1968 *Area:* 16,353.66 sq km
Population in 2011: 38,171
Next Election: Nov. 15, 2014 (3 year terms)
Note: Member municipalities: Squamish; Whistler; Pemberton; Lillooet.
Susan Gimse, Chair
604-894-6371
sgimse@telus.net
Dennis Back, Chief Administrative Officer
604-894-6371
dback@slrd.bc.ca
Leslie Lloyd, Director, Administrative Services
604-894-6371
llloyd@slrd.bc.ca
Suzanne Lafrance, Director, Finance
604-894-6371
slafrance@slrd.bc.ca
Steven Olmstead, Manager, Planning & Development
604-894-6371
Janis Netzel, Director, Utilities & Environmental Services
604-894-6371
rdsouza@slrd.bc.ca

Strathcona
#301, 990 Cedar St.
Campbell River, BC V9W 7Z8
Tel: 250-830-6700; *Fax:* 250-830-6710
administration@strathconard.ca
www.strathconard.ca
Other Information: Toll Free Phone: 1-877-830-2990
Municipal Type: Regional Districts
Incorporated: Feb. 15, 2008 *Area:* 22,000 sq km
Population in 2011: 43,252
Next Election: Nov. 15, 2014 (3 year terms)
Note: Member municipalities: Campbell River; Gold River; Sayward; Tahsis; Zeballos.
Craig Anderson, Chair
250-283-2202
dabear10@cablerocket.com
B. Reardon, Chief Administrative Officer
J. Rohne, Manager, Facilities
Y. Bienvenu, Manager, Facilities Services
D. Christenson, Manager, Financial Services
L. Parker, Manager, Operations
S. Bullock, Manager, Programs

Sunshine Coast
1975 Field Rd.
Sechelt, BC V0N 3A1
Tel: 604-885-6800; *Fax:* 604-885-7909
info@scrd.ca
www.scrd.ca
Other Information: Toll Free Phone: 1-800-687-5753
Municipal Type: Regional Districts
Incorporated: Jan. 4, 1967 *Area:* 3,778.08 sq km
Population in 2011: 28,619
Next Election: Nov. 15, 2014 (3 year terms)
Note: Member municipalities: Sechelt; Gibsons.
Garry Nohr, Chair
John France, Chief Administrative Officer
Randy Brown, Manager, Human Resources
randy.brown@scrd.ca
Angie Legault, Manager, Legislative Services
David Rafael, Senior Planner
604-885-6804
david.rafael@scrd.ca

Thompson-Nicola
#300, 465 Victoria St.
Kamloops, BC V2C 2A9
Tel: 250-377-8673; *Fax:* 250-372-5048
admin@tnrd.bc.ca
www.tnrd.bc.ca
Other Information: Toll Free Phone: 1-877-377-8673
Municipal Type: Regional Districts
Incorporated: Nov. 24, 1967 *Area:* 44,475.73 sq km
Population in 2011: 128,473
Next Election: Nov. 15, 2014 (3 year terms)
Note: Member municipalities: Ashcroft; Barriere; Cache Creek; Chase; Clearwater; Clinton; Kamloops; Logan Lake; Lytton; Merritt; Sun Peaks.
Peter Milobar, Chair
mayor@kamloops.ca
Greg Toma, Chief Administrative Officer
250-377-8673
gtoma@tnrd.bc.ca
Vicci Weller, Executive Director, Film Commission
250-377-7058
vweller@tnrd.bc.ca
Lyle Huntley, Clerk/Director, Corporate & Community Services
250-377-7052
lhuntley@tnrd.bc.ca
Regina Sadilkova, Director, Development Services
250-377-7060
rsadilkova@tnrd.bc.ca
Peter Hughes, Director, Environmental Services
phughes@tnrd.bc.ca
Sukh Gill, Director/Deputy Administrator, Finance & Information Technology
250-377-8673
sgill@tnrd.bc.ca
Kevin Kierans, Director, Libraries
250-374-8866
kevink@tnrdlib.bc.ca
Ron Popoff, Manager, Building Inspection Services
250-377-7062
rpopoff@tnrd.bc.ca
Don May, Manager, Environmental Health Services
250-377-7057
dmay@tnrd.bc.ca
Bob Finley, Manager, Planning Services
250-377-7062
bfinley@tnrd.bc.ca
Arden Bolton, Manager, Utility Services
250-377-7056
abolton@tnrd.bc.ca

Major Municipalities in British Columbia

Abbotsford
32315 South Fraser Way
Abbotsford, BC V2T 1W7
Tel: 604-853-2281; *Fax:* 604-853-1934
www.abbotsford.ca; twitter.com/City_Abbotsford
Other Information: Toll Free Phone: 1-866-853-2281
Municipal Type: City
Incorporated: Jan. 1, 1995 *Area:* 359.36 sq km
County or District: Fraser Valley; *Population in 2011:* 133,497
Provincial Electoral District(s): Abbotsford-Mission; Abbotsford South; Abbotsford West
Federal Electoral District(s): Abbotsford
Next Election: Nov. 15, 2014 (3 year terms)
Bruce Banman, Mayor
mayor@abbotsford.ca
Les Barkman, Councillor
lbarkman@abbotsford.ca
Henry Braun, Councillor
Simon Gibson, Councillor
sgibson@abbotsford.ca
Mohindar (Moe) Gill, Councillor
mgill@abbotsford.ca
Dave Loewen, Councillor
dfloewen@abbotsford.ca
Bill MacGregor, Councillor
bmacgregor@abbotsford.ca
Patricia Ross, Councillor
pross@abbotsford.ca
John Smith, Councillor
jgsmith@abbotsford.ca
Bill Flitton, City Clerk
604-864-5603
bflitton@abbotsford.ca
Frank Pizzuto, City Manager
604-864-5501
fpizzuto@abbotsford.ca
Jim Gordon, P.Eng., General Manager, Engineering & Regional Utilities
604-864-5514
eng-info@abbotsford.ca
Mike Pastro, General Manager, Airport
604-864-5651
mpastro@abbotsford.ca
Patricia Soanes, General Manager, Finance & Corporate Services
604-864-5524, Fax: 604-853-7968
finance-info@abbotsford.ca
Mark Taylor, General Manager, Parks, Recreation & Culture
604-859-3134
prcoffice@abbotsford.ca
Jay Teichroeb, General Manager, Economic Development/Development Services
604-864-5586
econdev@abbotsford.ca
Karen Sinclair, Director, Strategic Planning & Business Improvement
604-865-5640
ksinclair@abbotsford.ca
Don Beer, Fire Chief
604-853-3566
fire-info@abbotsford.ca
Bob Rich, Chief Constable, Abbotsford Police Department
604-859-5225, Fax: 604-859-4812

Burnaby
4949 Canada Way
Burnaby, BC V5G 1M2
Tel: 604-294-7944
postmaster@burnaby.ca
www.city.burnaby.bc.ca
Municipal Type: City
Incorporated: Sept. 22, 1892 *Area:* 89.12 sq km
County or District: Metro Vancouver; *Population in 2011:* 223,218
Provincial Electoral District(s): Burnaby-Edmonds; Burnaby North; Burnaby-Willingdon
Federal Electoral District(s): Burnaby-Douglas; Burnaby-New Westminster
Next Election: Nov. 15, 2014 (3 year terms)
Derek Corrigan, Mayor
604-294-7340
Pietro Calendino, Councillor
604-614-7379
pietro.calendino@burnaby.ca
Richard Chang, Councillor
richard.chang@burnaby.ca
Sav Dhaliwal, Councillor
604-420-8188, Fax: 604-420-8133
sav.dhaliwal@burnaby.ca
Dan Johnston, Councillor
778-228-6714
dan.johnston@burnaby.ca
Colleen Jordan, Councillor
604-970-8117
cjordan@comsavings.com
Anne Kang, Councillor
604-346-6732, Fax: 604-439-1576
anne.kang@burnaby.ca
Paul McDonell, Councillor
paul.mcdonell@burnaby.ca
Nick Volkow, Councillor
778-228-6713, Fax: 604-437-1169
nick.volkow@burnaby.ca
Debbie R. Comis, City Clerk
604-294-7290, Fax: 604-294-7537
Robert H. Moncur, City Manager
604-294-7101
Chad Turpin, Deputy City Manager
Lambert Chu, Director, Engineering
604-294-7460
D. Ellenwood, Director, Parks, Recreation & Cultural Services
604-294-7450
parks@burnaby.ca
Denise Jorgeonson, Director, Finance
604-294-7002, Fax: 604-294-7544
Basil Luksun, Director, Planning & Building
604-294-7400, Fax: 604-294-7220
B.R. Rose, City Solicitor
Patrick Shek, P.Eng, Chief Building Inspector
Bob Cook, Fire Chief
604-294-7195

Campbell River
301 St. Ann's Rd.
Campbell River, BC V9W 4C7
Tel: 250-286-5700
info@campbellriver.ca
www.campbellriver.ca
Municipal Type: City
Incorporated: June 24, 1947 *Area:* 143.48 sq km
County or District: Strathcona; *Population in 2011:* 31,186
Provincial Electoral District(s): North Island
Federal Electoral District(s): Vancouver Island North
Next Election: Nov. 15, 2014 (3 year terms)
Walter Jakeway, Mayor
Andrew Adams, Councillor
councillor.adams@campbellriver.ca
Ron Kerr, Councillor
Ryan Mennie, Councillor
councillor.mennie@campbellriver.ca
Claire Moglove, Councillor
councillor.moglove@campbellriver.ca
Larry Samson, Councillor
Mary Storry, Councillor
councillor.storry@campbellriver.ca
Peter Wipper, City Clerk
250-286-5707
peter.wipper@campbellriver.ca
Andy Laidlaw, City Manager
250-286-5740
andy.laidlaw@campbellriver.ca
Laura Ciarniello, General Manager, Corporate Services
250-286-5759
laura.ciarniello@campbellriver.ca
Ross Milnthorp, General Manager, Parks, Recreation & Culture
250-286-5797
ross.milnthorp@campbellriver.ca
Dave Morris, General Manager, Facilities & Supply Management
250-286-5739
dave.morris@campbellriver.ca
Ron Neufeld, General Manager, Operations Services
250-286-5765
ron.neufeld@campbellriver.ca
Andrew Bailey, Manager, Facilities - Property
250-286-5709
andrew.bailey@campbellriver.ca
Ross Blackwell, Manager, Land Use
250-286-5748
ross.blackwell@campbellriver.ca
Drew Hadfield, Manager, Transportation
250-286-5783
drew.hadfield@campbellriver.ca
Jason Hartley, Manager, Capital Works
250-286-5790
jason.hartley@campbellriver.ca
Warren Kalyn, Manager, Information Services
250-286-5716
warren.kalyn@campbellriver.ca
Jennifer Peters, Manager, Utilities
250-286-5730
jennifer.peters@campbellriver.ca
Amber Zirnhelt, Manager, Sustainability
250-286-5742
amber.zirnhelt@campbellriver.ca
Carrie Jacobs, RCMP Municipal Manager
250-286-5611
carrie.jacobs@campbellriver.ca
Dean Spry, Fire Chief
250-286-6266
dean.spry@campbellriver.ca

Chilliwack
8550 Young Rd
Chilliwack, BC V2P 8A4
Tel: 604-792-9311; *Fax:* 604-795-8443
www.chilliwack.com
Municipal Type: City
Incorporated: Jan. 1, 1980 *Area:* 260.19 sq km
County or District: Fraser Valley; *Population in 2011:* 77,936

Provincial Electoral District(s): Chilliwack-Kent, Chilliwack-Sumas
Federal Electoral District(s): Chilliwack-Fraser Canyon
Next Election: Nov. 15, 2014 (3 year terms)
Sharon Gaetz, Mayor
604-793-2900, Fax: 604-792-2561
Sue Attrill, Councillor
Ken Huttema, Councillor
Jason Lum, Councillor
Stewart McLean, Councillor
Kenneth Popove, Councillor
Chuck Stam, Councillor
Peter Monteith, Chief Administrative Officer
604-793-2903, Fax: 604-792-2561
Jerry Spencer, General Manager/Deputy Chief Administrative Officer, Community Development
604-792-9311, Fax: 604-795-8443
Janet Demarcke, Manager, Environmental Services
604-792-2907, Fax: 604-795-8443
Erik Leidekker, Manager, Information Technology
604-793-2912, Fax: 604-793-1812
Ryan Mulligan, Manager, Civic Facilities
604-793-2704, Fax: 604-792-2583
Rod Sanderson, Manager, Transportation & Drainage
604-793-2907
Karen Stanton, Manager, Long Range Planning
604-793-2906
Gillian Villeneuve, Manager, Development Planning
604-793-2779
Paul Whitehouse, Manager, Purchasing
604-793-2809, Fax: 604-795-2963
David Blain, Director, Engineering
604-793-2907, Fax: 604-793-2285
Robert Carnegie, Director, Corporate Services
604-793-2986, Fax: 604-793-2715
Kurt Houlden, Director, Planning & Strategic Initiatives
604-793-2906
Glen MacPherson, Director, Public Works
604-792-2810, Fax: 604-793-2997
Gordon Pederson, Director, Parks, Recreation & Culture
604-793-2996, Fax: 604-793-8443
Kathleen Fraser, Deputy Director, Finance
604-792-9311, Fax: 604-795-8443
Rick Ryall, Fire Chief
604-792-8713, Fax: 604-702-5087

Colwood

3300 Wishart Rd.
Victoria, BC V9C 1R1
Tel: 250-478-5541; *Fax:* 250-478-7516
generalinquiry@colwood.ca
colwood.ca
Municipal Type: City
Incorporated: June 24, 1985 *Area:* 17.76 sq km
County or District: Capital; *Population in 2011:* 16,093
Provincial Electoral District(s): Esquimalt-Metchosin
Federal Electoral District(s): Esquimalt-Juan de Fuca
Next Election: Nov. 15, 2014 (3 year terms)
Carol Hamilton, Mayor
mayor@colwood.bc.ca
Judith Cullington, Councillor
250-391-8772
judith@cullington.ca
Cynthia Day, Councillor
250-474-5687
councillorday@shaw.ca
Gordie Logan, Councillor
250-478-3630
councillor@telus.net
Shari Lukens, Councillor
Teresa Harvey, Councillor
Shaun Wysiecki, Councillor
250-415-7535
shaun@shaunw.ca
Ross McPhee, Chief Administrative Officer
rmcphee@colwood.ca
Dan Brazier, Manager, Public Works
250-474-4133, Fax: 250-474-6977
dbrazier@colwood.ca
Michael Baxter, Director, Engineering
mbaxter@colwood.ca
Alan Haldenby, Director, Planning
ahaldenby@colwood.ca
Jennifer Reed, Acting Director, Finance
jreed@colwood.ca
Flo Pikula, Chief Building Inspector
fpikula@colwood.ca
Russ Cameron, Fire Chief
250-478-8321, Fax: 250-478-8032
rcameron@colwood.bc.ca

Comox

Town Hall
1809 Beaufort Ave.
Comox, BC V9M 1R9
Tel: 250-339-2202; *Fax:* 250-339-7110
town@comox.ca
www.comox.ca
Municipal Type: City
Incorporated: Jan. 14, 1946 *Area:* 15.16 sq km
County or District: Comox Valley; *Population in 2011:* 13,627
Provincial Electoral District(s): Comox Valley
Federal Electoral District(s): Vancouver Island North
Next Election: Nov. 15, 2014 (3 year terms)
Paul Ives, Mayor
250-339-9109
pives@comox.ca
Patti Fletcher, Councillor
250-339-6683
pfletcher@comox.ca
Ken Grant, Councillor
250-339-1355
kgrant@comox.ca
Tom Grant, Councillor
250-339-7761
tgrant@comox.ca
Hugh MacKinnon, Councillor
250-339-0661
hmackinnon@comox.ca
Barbara Price, Councillor
Maureen Swift, Councillor
Richard Kanigan, Chief Administrative Officer
Donald Jacquest, Director, Finance
Jim Stevenson, Director, Recreation
250-339-2255
Allan Fraser, Superintendent, Parks
250-339-2421
Glenn Westendorp, Superintendent, Public Works
250-339-5410, Fax: 250-890-0698
Marvin Kamenz, Municipal Planner
250-339-1118
Gord Schreiner, Fire Chief
250-339-2432, Fax: 250-339-1988

Coquitlam

3000 Guildford Way
Coquitlam, BC V3B 7N2
Tel: 604-927-3000
feedback@coquitlam.ca
www.coquitlam.ca
Municipal Type: City
Incorporated: July 25, 1891 *Area:* 121.69 sq km
County or District: Metro Vancouver; *Population in 2011:* 126,456
Provincial Electoral District(s): Coquitlam-Maillardville
Federal Electoral District(s): New Westminster-Coquitlam; Port Moody-Westwood-Port Coquitlam
Next Election: Nov. 15, 2014 (3 year terms)
Richard Stewart, Mayor
604-927-3001
rstewart@coquitlam.ca
Brent Asmundson, Councillor
604-616-6331
basmundson@coquitlam.ca
Doug Macdonell, Councillor
604-505-5574
dmacdonell@coquitlam.ca
Neal Nicholson, Councillor
604-218-1398
nnicholson@coquitlam.ca
Terry O'Neil, Councillor
Mae Reid, Councillor
604-464-0414
mreid@coquitlam.ca
Linda Reimer, Councillor
604-617-1490
lreimer@coquitlam.ca
Selina Robinson, Councillor
604-729-0702
srobinson@coquitlam.ca
Lou Sekora, Councillor
604-941-7916
lsekora@coquitlam.ca
Jay Gilbert, City Clerk
604-927-3013
Peter Steblin, City Manager
604-927-2006
managersoffice@coquitlam.ca
Sheena Macleod, Treasurer & Manager, Financial Services
604-927-3031
Lori MacKay, General Manager, Parks, Recreation & Culture Services
604-927-3538
prcs@coquitlam.ca
Jim McIntyre, General Manager, Planning & Development
604-927-3400, Fax: 604-927-3405
planninganddevelopment@coquitlam.ca
Bill Susak, General Manager, Engineering & Public Works
604-927-2504, Fax: 604-927-3505
engineeringandpublicworks@coquitlam.ca
Karen Basi, Manager, Emergency Programs
604-927-3481
Michelle Hunt, Manager, Corporate Planning
604-927-3531, Fax: 604-927-3015
Ron Price, Manager, Human Resources
604-927-3070

Courtenay

830 Cliffe Ave.
Courtenay, BC V9N 2J7
Tel: 250-334-4441; *Fax:* 250-334-4241
info@courtenay.ca
www.courtenay.ca
Municipal Type: City
Incorporated: Jan. 1, 1915 *Area:* 26.68 sq km
County or District: Comox Valley; *Population in 2011:* 24,099
Provincial Electoral District(s): Comox Valley
Federal Electoral District(s): Vancouver Island North
Next Election: Nov. 15, 2014 (3 year terms)
Larry Jangula, Mayor
Jon Ambler, Councillor
250-334-3458
jambler@courtenay.ca
Bill Anglin, Councillor
Doug Hillan, Councillor
250-334-4441
dhillian@courtenay.ca
Ronna-Rae Leonard, Councillor
250-334-4441
rleonard@courtenay.ca
Manno Theos, Councillor
250-334-4441
mtheos@courtenay.ca
Starr Winchester, Councillor
Sandy Gray, City Administrator
sgray@courtenay.ca
Peter Crawford, Director, Planning Services
planning@courtenay.ca
Kevin Lagan, Director, Operational Services
Tillie Manthey, Director, Financial Services
finance@courtenay.ca
Lis Pedersen, Director, Human Resources
John Ward, Director, Corporate Services
Randy Wiwchar, Director, Community Services

Cranbrook

40 - 10th Ave. South
Cranbrook, BC V1C 2M8
Tel: 250-426-4211; *Fax:* 250-426-4026
info@cranbrook.ca
www.cranbrook.ca
Other Information: Toll Free Phone: 1-800-728-2726
Municipal Type: City
Incorporated: Nov. 1, 1905 *Area:* 25.14 sq km
County or District: East Kootenay; *Population in 2011:* 19,319
Provincial Electoral District(s): East Kootenay
Federal Electoral District(s): Kootenay-Columbia
Next Election: Nov. 15, 2014 (3 year terms)
Wayne Stetski, Mayor
Angus Davis, Councillor
Sharon Cross, Councillor
Denise Pallesen, Councillor
Diana J. Scott, Councillor
Gerry Warner, Councillor
Bob Whetham, Councillor
Marnie Dueck, Municipal Clerk
dueck@cranbrook.ca
Will Pearce, Chief Administrative Officer
pearce@cranbrook.ca
Diane Butz, Director, Leisure Services
butz@crankbook.ca
Roy Hales, Director, Corporate Services
hales@cranbrook.ca
Joe McGowan, Director, Public Works
mcgowan@cranbrook.ca
Wayne Price, Director, Fire & Emergency Services
price@crankbook.ca
Wayne Staudt, CA, Director, Finance & Computer Services
staudt@crankbook.ca
Chris Zettel, Corporate Communications Officer
zettel@cranbrook.ca
Jamie Hodge, City Engineer
hodge@cranbrook.ca

Wayne Price, Coordinator, Emergency Program
price@cranbrook.ca

Dawson Creek

P.O. Box 150
10105 - 12A St.
Dawson Creek, BC V1G 4G4
Tel: 250-784-3600; *Fax:* 250-782-3203
admin@dawsoncreek.ca
www.dawsoncreek.ca
Other Information: General Fax: 250-782-3352
Municipal Type: City
Incorporated: May 26, 1936 *Area:* 22.32 sq km
County or District: Peace River; *Population in 2011:* 11,583
Provincial Electoral District(s): Peace River South
Federal Electoral District(s): Prince George-Peace River
Next Election: Nov. 15, 2014 (3 year terms)
Mike Bernier, Mayor
250-784-3616, Fax: 250-782-3203
mayorbernier@dawsoncreek.ca
Sue Kenny, Councillor
250-782-2511
skenny@dawsoncreek.ca
Duncan Malkinson, Councillor
Terry McFadyen, Councillor
250-782-2237
tmcfadyen@dawsoncreek.ca
Charlie Parslow, Councillor
Cheryl Shuman, Councillor
250-782-5323
cshuman@dawsoncreek.ca
Shaely Wilbur, Councillor
Jim Chute, Chief Administrative Officer
250-784-3613
jchute@dawsoncreek.ca
Shelly Woolf, Chief Financial Officer
250-784-3611
swoolf@dawsoncreek.ca
Greg Dobrowolski, Manager, Special Projects
250-784-3619
gdobrowolski@dawsoncreek.ca
Chante Patterson Elden, Manager, recreation Facilities
250-782-2229
celden@dawsoncreek.ca
Darcy Perrin, Manager, Parks Facilities
250-784-3632
rharmon@dawsoncreek.ca
Jim Chute, Director, Community Services
250-784-3605
breynard@dawsoncreek.ca
Brenda Ginter, Director, Corporate Administration
250-784-3614
bginter@dawsoncreek.ca
Kevin Henderson, Director, Infrastructure & Sustainable Development
250-784-3622
khenderson@dawsoncreek.ca
Gordon (Shorty) Smith, Fire Chief
250-784-3635
shorty@dawsoncreek.ca

Fort St. John

10631 - 100 St.
Fort St John, BC V1J 3Z5
Tel: 250-787-8150; *Fax:* 250-787-8181
info@fortstjohn.ca
www.fortstjohn.ca
Municipal Type: City
Incorporated: Dec. 31, 1947 *Area:* 22.74 sq km
County or District: Peace River; *Population in 2011:* 18,609
Provincial Electoral District(s): Peace River North
Federal Electoral District(s): Prince George-Peace River
Next Election: Nov. 15, 2014 (3 year terms)
Lori Ackerman, Mayor
Trevor Bolin, Councillor
250-262-7334
tbolin@fortstjohn.ca
Bruce Christensen, Councillor
250-787-2202
bchristensen@forststjohn.ca
Dan Davies, Councillor
250-787-5847
ddavies@fortstjohn.ca
Larry Evans, Councillor
250-785-2416
levans@fortstjohn.ca
Gord Klassen, Councillor
Bryon Stewart, Councillor
Dianne Hunter, City Manager
citymanager@fortstjohn.ca
Sarah Cockerill, Director, Community Services
scockerill@fortstjohn.ca
Don Demers, Director, Public Works & Utilities
ddemers@fortstjohn.ca
Grace Fika, Director, Corporate Affairs & Human Resources
gfika@fortstjohn.ca
Horacio Galanti, Director, Planning & Engineering
hgalanti@fortstjohn.ca
Janet Prestley, Director, Legislative & Administrative Services
jprestley@fortstjohn.ca
Jim Rogers, Director, Facilities & Protective Services
jrogers@forststjohn.ca
Laura Sanders, Director, Finance
lsanders@forststjohn.ca
Victor Shopland, Director, Infrastructure & Capital Works
vshopland@forststjohn.ca
Fred Burrows, Fire Chief
250-785-4333, Fax: 250-785-0080
fburrows@fortstjohn.ca

Kamloops

City Hall
7 Victoria St. West
Kamloops, BC V2C 1A2
Tel: 250-828-3311
info@kamloops.ca
www.kamloops.ca
Municipal Type: City
Incorporated: Oct. 17, 1967 *Area:* 297.3 sq km
County or District: Thompson-Nicola; *Population in 2011:* 85,678
Provincial Electoral District(s): Kamloops; Kamloops-North Thompson
Federal Electoral District(s): Kamloops-Thompson-Cariboo
Next Election: Nov. 15, 2014 (3 year terms)
Peter Milobar, Mayor
250-828-3495
mayor@kamloops.ca
Nancy Bepple, Councillor
250-828-3494
nbepple@kamloops.ca
Donovan Cavers, Councillor
Ken Christian, Councillor
Nelly Dever, Councillor
Tina Lange, Councillor
250-372-0902
tlange@kamloops.ca
Arjun Singh, Councillor
Marg Spina, Councillor
250-372-0440
mspina@kamloops.ca
Patricia Wallace, Councillor
250-828-3494
pwallace@kamloops.ca
Randy H. Diehl, Chief Administrative Officer
250-828-3498
rdiehl@kamloops.ca
David Duckworth, Director, Public Works & Sustainability
250-828-3348
publicworks@kamloops.ca
Sally Edwards, Director, Finance & Information Technology
250-828-3413
finance@kamloops.ca
Len Hrycan, Director, Community & Corporate Affairs
250-828-3455
legislate@kamloops.ca
Byron McCorkell, Director, Parks, Recreation & Culture Services
250-828-3400
parks@kamloops.ca
David A. Trawin, Director, Development & Engineering Services
250-828-2561
devadmin@kamloops.ca
Neill Moroz, Fire Chief, Fire & Rescue Services
250-372-5131, Fax: 250-372-1447
fireinfo@kamloops.ca

Kelowna

City Hall
1435 Water St.
Kelowna, BC V1Y 1J4
Tel: 250-469-8500; *Fax:* 250-862-3399
ask@kelowna.ca
www.kelowna.ca
Municipal Type: City
Incorporated: May 4, 1905 *Area:* 211.69 sq km
County or District: Central Okanagan; *Population in 2011:* 117,312
Provincial Electoral District(s): Kelowna-Mission; Kelowna-Lake Country; Westside-Kelowna
Federal Electoral District(s): Kelowna-Lake Country; Okanagan-Coquihalla
Next Election: Nov. 15, 2014 (3 year terms)
Walter Gray, Mayor
mayorandcouncil@kelowna.ca
Colin Basran, Councillor
Andre F. Blanleil, Councillor
ablanleil@andres1.com
Maxine DeHart, Councillor
Gail Given, Councillor
Robert Douglas Hobson, Councillor
robert.hobson@cord.bc.ca
Mohini Singh, Councillor
Luke Stack, Councillor
lstack@kelowna.ca
Gerry Zimmermann, Councillor
Stephen Fleming, Clerk
cityclerk@kelowna.ca
Ronald Mattiussi, City Manager
Paul Macklem, General Manager, Corporate Sustainability
Jim Paterson, General Manager, Community Sustainability
John Vos, General Manager, Community Services
Signe Bagh, Director, Policy & Planning
Mo Bayat, Director, Development Services
William J. Berry, Director, Design & Construction Services
Randy Cleveland, Director, Infrastructure Planning
Charlene Covington, Director, Human Resources
Joe Creron, Director, Civic Operations
Jim Gabriel, Director, Recreation & Cultural Services
Shelley Gambacort, Director, Land Use Management
Doug Gilchrist, Director, Real Estate & Building Services
David Graham, Director, Strategic Initiatives
Keith Grayston, Director, Financial Services
Rob Mayne, Director, Corporate Services
Carla Stephens, Director, Community & Media Relations
Ron W. Westlake, Director, Regional Services
Steve Kinsey, Fire Chief

Langford

877 Goldstream Ave., 2nd Fl.
Victoria, BC V9B 2X8
Tel: 250-478-7882
www.cityoflangford.ca
Municipal Type: City
Incorporated: Dec. 8, 1992 *Area:* 39.55 sq km
County or District: Capital; *Population in 2011:* 29,228
Provincial Electoral District(s): Malahat-Juan de Fuca
Federal Electoral District(s): Esquimalt-Juan de Fuca
Next Election: Nov. 15, 2014 (3 year terms)
Stewart Young, Mayor
Denise Blackwell, Councillor
Matt Sahlstrom, Councillor
Lanny Seaton, Councillor
Winnie Sifert, Councillor
Lillian Szpak, Councillor
Roger Wade, Councillor
Lindy Kaercher, Deputy Clerk
Steve Ternent, Acting Administrator
John Manson, City Engineer
Matthew Baldwin, City Planner

Langley

20399 Douglas Cres.
Langley, BC V3A 4B3
Tel: 604-514-2800; *Fax:* 604-530-4371
www.city.langley.bc.ca
Municipal Type: City
Incorporated: March 15, 1955 *Area:* 10.22 sq km
County or District: Metro Vancouver; *Population in 2011:* 25,081
Provincial Electoral District(s): Langley
Federal Electoral District(s): Langley
Next Election: Nov. 15, 2014 (3 year terms)
Peter Fassbender, Mayor
Jack Arnold, Councillor
Dave Hall, Councillor
Teri James, Councillor
Gayle Martin, Councillor
Ted Schaffer, Councillor
Rosemary Wallace, Councillor
Francis Cheung, Chief Administrative Officer
Patty Gilfillan, Chief Bylaw Enforcement Officer
Carolyn Bonnick, Manager/Corporate Officer, Legislative Services
Judy Hale, Manager, Human Resources
Kim Hilton, Director, Recreation, Culture & Community Services
Darrin W. Leite, Director, Corporate Services
Gerald Minchuk, Director, Development Services & Economic Development
Gary Vlieg, Director, Engineering, Parks & Environment
Rory Thompson, Fire Chief

Nanaimo
455 Wallace St.
Nanaimo, BC V9R 5J6
Tel: 250-754-4251
legislativeservices.office@nanaimo.ca
www.nanaimo.ca
Municipal Type: City
Incorporated: Dec. 24, 1874 *Area:* 89.3 sq km
County or District: Nanaimo; *Population in 2011:* 83,810
Provincial Electoral District(s): Nanaimo-Parksville; Nanaimo
Federal Electoral District(s): Nanaimo-Cowichan; Nanaimo-Alberni
Next Election: Nov. 15, 2014 (3 year terms)
John Ruttan, Mayor
250-755-4400
john.ruttan@nanaimo.ca
George Anderson, Councillor
William Leslie (Bill) Bestwick, Councillor
250-753-7065
bill.bestwick@nanaimo.ca
Diane Brennan, Councillor
Ted Greves, Councillor
250-729-0714
ted.greves@nanaimo.ca
Diana Johnstone, Councillor
250-754-9996
diana.johnstone@nanaimo.ca
Jim Kipp, Councillor
250-753-5212
jim.kipp@nanaimo.ca
Bill McKay, Councillor
Fred Pattje, Councillor
250-758-7575
fred.pattje@nanaimo.ca
Alastair (Al) Kenning, City Manager
250-755-4401
alastair.kenning@nanaimo.ca
Doug Holmes, Assistant City Manager/General Manager, Corporate Services
250-755-4488
doug.holmes@nanaimo.ca
Tom Hickey, General Manager, Community Services
250-756-5301
tom.hickey@nanaimo.ca
Ted Swabey, General Manager, Development Services
250-755-4451
ted.swabey@nanaimo.ca
Jeff Ritchie, Senior Manager, Parks
250-755-7503
jeff.ritchie@nanaimo.ca
Brian Denbigh, Manager, Roads & Traffic Services
250-756-5303
John Elliot, Manager, Utilities
250-756-5305
john.elliot@nanaimo.ca
Kurtis Felker, Manager, Purchasing & Stores
250-756-5317
kurtis.felker@nanaimo.ca
Gary Franssen, Manager, Sanitation, Recycling & Cemeteries
250-756-5307
gary.franssen@nanaimo.ca
Joan Harrison, Manager, Legislative Services
506-755-4489
joan.harrison@nanaimo.ca
Rick Kroeker, Manager, Occupational Health & Rehabilitation
250-755-4508
rick.kroeker@nanaimo.ca
Bob Prokopenko, Manager, Engineering Services
250-755-4495
bob.prokopenko@nanaimo.ca
Brian Clemens, Director, Finance
250-755-4431
brian.clemens@nanaimo.ca
Richard Harding, Director, Parks, Recreation & Culture
250-755-7516
richard.harding@nanaimo.ca
Terry Hartley, Director, Human Resources
250-755-4427
terry.hartley@nanaimo.ca
Andrew Tucker, Director, Planning
250-755-4450
andrew.tucker@nanaimo.ca
Jeff Lott, Superintendent & Officer-in-Charge, Nanaimo RCMP Detachment
250-754-2345
jeff.lott@nanaimo.ca
Ron Lambert, Fire Chief
250-755-4555
ron.lambert@nanaimo.ca

New Westminster
511 Royal Ave.
New Westminster, BC V3L 1H9
Tel: 604-521-3711; *Fax:* 604-521-3895
postmaster@newwestcity.ca
www.city.new-westminster.bc.ca
Municipal Type: City
Incorporated: July 16, 1860 *Area:* 15.41 sq km
County or District: Metro Vancouver; *Population in 2011:* 65,976
Provincial Electoral District(s): New Westminster
Federal Electoral District(s): Burnaby-New Westminster; New Westminster-Coquitlam
Next Election: Nov. 15, 2014 (3 year terms)
Wayne Wright, Mayor
604-527-4522, Fax: 604-527-4594
wwright@newwestcity.ca
Jonathan Cote, Councillor
778-773-1364
jcote@newwestcity.ca
Bill Harper, Councillor
778-227-4869
bharper@newwestcity.ca
Jamie McEvoy, Councillor
604-522-9114
jmcevoy@newwestcity.ca
Betty McIntosh, Councillor
778-773-0546
bmcintosh@newwestcity.ca
Chuck Puchmayr, Councillor
Lorrie Williams, Councillor
604-521-3416, Fax: 604-523-3416
lwilliams@newwestcity.ca
Paul Daminato, City Administrator
pdaminato@newwestcity.ca
Rod Carle, General Manager, Electric Utility
rcarle@newwestcity.ca
Joan Burgess, Director, Human Resources
jburgess@newwestcity.ca
Dean Gibson, Director, Parks, Culture & Recreation
dgibson@newwestcity.ca
Gary Holowatiuk, Director, Finance & Information Technology
gholowatiuk@newwestcity.ca
Jim Lowrie, Director, Engineering Services
jlowrie@newwestcity.ca
Rick Page, Director, Legislative Services & Communications
rpage@newwestcity.ca
Lisa Spitale, Director, Development Services
lspitale@newwestcity.ca
Dave Jones, Police Chief, Police Services
djones@nwpolice.org
Tim Armstrong, Fire Chief, Fire & Rescue Services
tarmstrong@newwestcity.ca

North Vancouver
141 - 14 St. West
North Vancouver, BC V7M 1H9
Tel: 604-985-7761; *Fax:* 604-985-9417
info@cnv.org
www.cnv.org
Municipal Type: City
Incorporated: May 13, 1907 *Area:* 11.85 sq km
County or District: Metro Vancouver; *Population in 2011:* 48,196
Provincial Electoral District(s): N. Vancouver-Lonsdale; N. Vancouver-Seymour; W. Vancouver-Capilano; W. Vancouver-Garibaldi
Federal Electoral District(s): North Vancouver
Next Election: Nov. 15, 2014 (3 year terms)
Darrell R. Mussatto, Mayor
604-998-3280
dmussatto@cnv.org
Don Bell, Councillor
Pam Bookham, Councillor
604-986-5560
pbookham@cnv.org
Rod Clark, Councillor
604-351-8166
rclark@cnv.org
Linda Buchanan, Councillor
Guy Heywood, Councillor
604-988-5325
gheywood@cnv.org
Craig Keating, Councillor
604-984-7485, Fax: 604-904-7968
ckeating@cnv.org
Robyn Anderson, City Clerk
604-990-4233, Fax: 604-990-4202
randerson@cnv.org
Ken Tollstam, City Manager
604-990-4243, Fax: 604-985-5971
ktollstam@cnv.org
Francis Caouette, Director, Corporate Services
604-990-4221, Fax: 604-985-7492
fcaouette@cnv.org
Isabel Gordon, Director, Finance
604-983-7387, Fax: 604-985-1573
igordon@cnv.org
Susan Ney, Acting Director, Human Resources
604-990-4241, Fax: 604-985-9149
sney@cnv.org
Richard White, Director, Community Development
604-990-4215, Fax: 604-985-0576
rwhite@cnv.org
Wolfgang Beier, Manager, Purchasing
604-983-7392, Fax: 604-985-1573
wbeier@cnv.org
Navin Chad, Manager, Financial Planning
604-983-7320, Fax: 604-985-1573
nchand@cnv.org
Janice Irwin, Manager, Financial Services
604-983-7300, Fax: 604-985-1573
jirwin@cnv.org
Nikii Hoglund, Manager, Operations
604-983-7388, Fax: 604-987-5379
nhoglund@cnv.org
Mike Hunter, Manager, Environment & Parks
604-983-7335, Fax: 604-985-8439
mhunter@cnv.org
Percy Melville, Manager, Inspections
604-983-7375, Fax: 604-985-0576
pmelville@cnv.org
David Nelson, Manager, Information Technology
604-983-7318, Fax: 604-985-7492
dnelson@cnv.org
Connie Rabold, Manager, Communications
604-983-7383, Fax: 604-985-5971
crabold@cnv.org
Glenn Stainton, Manager, City Facilities
604-983-7305, Fax: 604-985-1573
gstainton@cnv.org
Steven Ono, City Engineer
604-983-7336, Fax: 604-985-8439
sono@cnv.org
Emilie K. Adin, City Planner
604-982-3922, Fax: 604-985-0576
Barrie Penman, Fire Chief
604-904-5201, Fax: 604-980-8544
bpenman@cnv.org

Parksville
P.O. Box 1390
100 Jensen Ave. East
Parksville, BC V9P 2H3
Tel: 250-248-6144; *Fax:* 250-248-6650
www.parksville.ca
Municipal Type: City
Incorporated: June 19, 1945 *Area:* 14.6 sq km
County or District: Nanaimo; *Population in 2011:* 11,977
Provincial Electoral District(s): Nanaimo-Parksville
Federal Electoral District(s): Nanaimo-Alberni
Next Election: Nov. 15, 2014 (3 year terms)
Chris R. Burger, Mayor
250-954-4661
cburger@parksville.ca
Al Greir, Councillor
250-248-1285
hockeypuck1@shaw.ca
Marc Lefebvre, Councillor
250-248-2292
janetmarc@shaw.ca
Peter Morrison, Councillor
Bill Neufeld, Councillor
Sue E. Powell, Councillor
250-951-1082
kfsue@shaw.ca
Carrie J. Powell-Davidson, Councillor
250-954-3758
cpowelldavidson@shaw.ca
Fred Manson, Chief Administrative Officer
250-954-4666
fmanson@city.parksville.bc.ca
Lucy Butterworth, Director, Finance
250-954-3063
lbutterworth@parksville.ca
Debbie Comis, Director, Administrative Services
250-954-3068
dcomis@parksville.ca
Robert Harary, Director, Engineering & Operations
250-951-2477
rharary@parksville.ca

Gayle Jackson, Director, Community Planning
250-954-4656
gjackson@city.parksville.bc.ca
Doug Banks, Fire Chief
250-954-4671
dbanks@parksville.ca

Penticton

171 Main St.
Penticton, BC V2A 5A9
Tel: 250-490-2400; *Fax:* 250-490-2402
www.penticton.ca
Municipal Type: City
Incorporated: Jan. 1, 1909 *Area:* 42.02 sq km
County or District: Okanagan-Similkameen; *Population in 2011:* 32,877
Provincial Electoral District(s): Penticton-Okanagan Valley
Federal Electoral District(s): Okanagan-Coquihalla
Next Election: Nov. 15, 2014 (3 year terms)
Dan Ashton, Mayor
250-809-2540
Wesley Hopkin, Councillor
Andrew Jakubeit, Councillor
250-809-2397
Helena Konanz, Councillor
Garry Litke, Councillor
250-809-2021
Judy Sentes, Councillor
250-490-6446
John Vassilaki, Councillor
250-490-1034
Annette Antoniak, Chief Administrative Officer
250-490-2407
Douglas Leahy, Chief Financial Officer/Treasurer, Accounting & Finance
250-490-2413
Chuck Loewen, General Manager, Recreation
250-490-2445
Cathy Ingram, Manager, Purchasing
250-490-2555
Gillian Kenny, Manager, Human Resources
250-490-2470
Ken Kunka, Manager, Building & Permitting
250-490-2505
Dave Lieskovsky, Manager, Facilities
250-490-2433
Eric Livolsi, Manager, Electric Utility
250-490-2537
Peter Ord, Manager, Museum
250-490-2452
Len Robson, Manager, Public Works
250-490-2500
Kristin Wilkes, Manager, Information Technology
250-490-2499
Anthony Haddad, Director, Development Services
250-490-2520
Mitch Moroziuk, Director, Operations
250-490-2515
Brent Edge, Supervisor, Water
brent.edge@penticton.ca
Berne Udala, Supervisor, Water Quality
250-490-2564
Carolyn Stewart, Environmental Coordinator, Water Treatment Plant
250-490-2562
Wayne Williams, Fire Chief
250-490-2309

Pitt Meadows

Municipal Hall
12007 Harris Rd.
Pitt Meadows, BC V3Y 2B5
Tel: 604-465-5454; *Fax:* 604-465-2404
info@pittmeadows.bc.ca
www.pittmeadows.bc.ca
Municipal Type: City
Incorporated: April 25, 1914 *Area:* 85.38 sq km
County or District: Metro Vancouver; *Population in 2011:* 17,736
Provincial Electoral District(s): Maple Ridge-Pitt Meadows
Federal Electoral District(s): Pitt Meadows-Maple Ridge-Mission
Next Election: Nov. 15, 2014 (3 year terms)
Note: Effective Jan. 1, 2007, Pitt Meadows' designation was changed from a district to a city.
Deb Walters, Mayor
Bruce Bell, Councillor
bbell@pittmeadows.bc.ca
Doug Bing, Councillor
dbing@pittmeadows.bc.ca
Janis Elkerton, Councillor
Tracy Miyashita, Councillor
tmiyashita@pittmeadows.bc.ca
David Murray, Councillor
Gwen O'Connell, Councillor
goconnell@pittmeadows.bc.ca
Jake Rudolph, Chief Administrative Officer
604-465-2413
Kelly Swift, General Manager, Community Development, Parks & Recreation
604-467-7337
Laurie Darcus, Director, Corporate Services
604-465-2449
Kim Grout, Director, Operations & Development Services
604-465-2428
Lorna Jones, Director, Human Resources & Communications
604-465-2448
Don Jolley, Fire Chief, Protective Services
604-465-2401
Dave Walsh, Superintendent, RCMP
604-463-6251

Port Alberni

4850 Argyle St.
Port Alberni, BC V9Y 1V8
Tel: 250-723-2146; *Fax:* 250-723-1003
citypa@portalberni.ca
www.portalberni.ca
Municipal Type: City
Incorporated: Oct. 28, 1967 *Area:* 19.92 sq km
County or District: Alberni-Clayoquot; *Population in 2011:* 17,743
Provincial Electoral District(s): Alberni-Qualicum
Federal Electoral District(s): Nanaimo-Alberni
Next Election: Nov. 15, 2014 (3 year terms)
John Douglas, Mayor
Hira Chopra, Councillor
250-723-7629
citypa@portalberni.ca
Rob Cole, Councillor
John Douglas, Councillor
250-720-2822
jmdouglas56@hotmail.com
Wendy Lee Kerr, Councillor
Jack McLeman, Councillor
250-723-5851
jmcln@shaw.ca
Cindy Solda, Councillor
250-723-7139
cindysolda@me.com
Dan Washington, Councillor
Davina Sparrow, City Clerk
250-720-2810
davina_sparrow@portalberni.ca
Ken Watson, City Manager
250-720-2824
ken_watson@portalberni.ca
Scott Kenny, Director, Parks & Recreation
250-720-2507
scott_kenny@portalberni.ca
Jean McIntosh, Director
250-720-2501
jean_mcintosh@portalberni.ca
Cathy Rothwell, Director, Finance
250-720-2821
cathy_rothwell@portalberni.ca
Randy Fraser, Superintendent, Streets
250-720-2845
randy_fraser@portalberni.ca
Brian Mousley, Superintendent, Utilities
250-720-2849
brian_mousley@portalberni.ca
Guy Cicon, City Engineer
250-720-2838
guy_cicon@port-alberni.ca
Scott Smith, City Planner
250-720-2808
scott_smith@port-alberni.ca
Tim Pley, Fire Chief
250-720-2540
tim_pley@portalberni.ca

Port Coquitlam

2580 Shaughnessy St.
Port Coquitlam, BC V3C 2A8
Tel: 604-927-5411; *Fax:* 604-927-5360
info@portcoquitlam.ca
www.portcoquitlam.ca
Municipal Type: City
Incorporated: March 7, 1913 *Area:* 28.85 sq km
County or District: Metro Vancouver; *Population in 2011:* 56,342
Provincial Electoral District(s): Port Coquitlam-Burke Mountain
Federal Electoral District(s): Port Moody-Westwood-Port Coquitlam
Next Election: Nov. 15, 2014 (3 year terms)
Greg Moore, Mayor
604-927-5410, Fax: 604-927-5331
mooreg@portcoquitlam.ca
Mike Forrest, Councillor
604-942-6289, Fax: 604-464-6280
forrestm@portcoquitlam.ca
Darrell Penner, Councillor
604-941-9823, Fax: 604-941-9887
pennerd@portcoquitlam.ca
Silas Dean Washington, Councillor
Brad West, Councillor
604-313-9185, Fax: 604-927-5331
westb@portcoquitlam.ca
Michael Wright, Councillor
604-942-8897, Fax: 604-942-8744
wrightm@portcoquitlam.ca
Susan Rauh, CMC, Corporate Officer/City Clerk
604-927-5421, Fax: 604-927-5402
corporateoffice@portcoquitlam.ca
Tony Chong, P. Eng., Chief Administrative Officer
604-927-5410, Fax: 604-927-5331
chongt@portcoquitlam.ca
Mindy Smith, Director, Corporate Services
604-927-5211, Fax: 604-927-5402
smithm@portcoquitlam.ca
Kathleen Vincent, Director, Legislative & Administrative Services
604-927-5335
vincentk@portcoquitlam.ca
Igor Zahynacz, P. Eng., Director, Engineering & Operations
604-927-5453
zahynaczi@portcoquitlam.ca
Karen Laustrup, Manager, Purchasing
604-927-5430, Fax: 604-927-5408
laustrupk@portcoquitlam.ca
Brian North, Manager, Revenues & Collections
604-927-5426, Fax: 604-927-5401
northb@portcoquitlam.ca
Pardeep Purewal, Manager, Communications & Administrative Services
604-927-5335, Fax: 604-927-5331
purewalp@portcoquitlam.ca
Robin Wishart, Manager, Information Services
604-927-5302, Fax: 604-927-5403
wishartr@portcoquitlam.ca
Terry Hochstetter, Acting Fire Chief
604-927-5494
hochstettert@portcoquitlam.ca

Port Moody

P.O. Box 36
100 Newport Dr.
Port Moody, BC V3H 3E1
Tel: 604-469-4500; *Fax:* 604-469-4550
info@cityofportmoody.com
www.cityofportmoody.com
Municipal Type: City
Incorporated: March 11, 1913 *Area:* 25.62 sq km
County or District: Metro Vancouver; *Population in 2011:* 32,975
Provincial Electoral District(s): Port Moody-Westwood
Federal Electoral District(s): Port Moody-Westwood-Port Coquitlam; New Westminster-Coquitlam
Next Election: Nov. 15, 2014 (3 year terms)
Mike Clay, Mayor
Diana Dilworth, Councillor
604-469-4516
ddilworth@portmoody.ca
Bob Elliot, Councillor
604-469-4586
belliott@portmoody.ca
Rick Glumac, Councillor
Gerry Nuttall, Councillor
604-469-4517
gnuttall@portmoody.ca
Zoe Royer, Councillor
Rosemary Small, Councillor
Colleen Rohde, City Clerk/Acting City Manager
604-469-4519
citymanager@portmoody.ca
Ron Higo, Director, Community Services
Paul Rockwood, Director, Corporate Services
Lynne Russell, Director, Library Services
Jim Weber, Acting Director, Development Services
Mary De Paoli, Manager, Planning
604-469-4540
planning@portmoody.ca
Devin Jain, Manager, Cultural Services
D. Kidd, Manager, Operations
J. LaCroix, Manager, Recreation
Angie Parnell, Manager, Human Resources

Julie Pavey, Manager, Parks & Environmental Services
Cory Day, City Engineer
Brad Parker, Chief Constable, Police Services
Remo Faedo, Fire Chief
pmfd.info@portmoody.ca

Powell River
6910 Duncan St.
Powell River, BC V8A 1V4
Tel: 604-485-6291; *Fax:* 604-485-2913
info@cdpr.bc.ca
www.powellriver.ca
Municipal Type: City
Incorporated: Oct. 15, 1955 *Area:* 29.77 sq km
County or District: Powell River; *Population in 2011:* 13,165
Provincial Electoral District(s): Powell River-Sunshine Coast
Federal Electoral District(s): West Vancouver-Sunshine Coast-Sea to Sky Country
Next Election: Nov. 15, 2014 (3 year terms)
Dave Formosa, Mayor
Russell Brewer, Councillor
Debbie Dee, Councillor
604-485-0342
ddee@cdpr.bc.ca
Maggie Hathaway, Councillor
604-485-1249
mhathaway@cdpr.bc.ca
Myrna Leishman, Councillor
Chris McNaughton, Councillor
604-483-9597
cmcnaughton@cdpr.bc.ca
Jim Palm, Councillor
604-483-3171
jpalm@cdpr.bc.ca
Marie Claxton, City Clerk
604-485-8601, Fax: 604-485-8628
Stan Westby, Chief Administrative Officer
604-485-8601, Fax: 604-485-8628
Dave Douglas, Director, Financial Services
604-485-8617, Fax: 604-485-8644
finance@cdpr.bc.ca
Bill Reid, Director, Parks, Recreation & Culture
604-485-2891, Fax: 604-485-2162
breid@cdpr.bc.ca
Tor Birtig, Manager, Operational Division
604-485-6291, Fax: 604-485-2913
tbirtig@cdpr.bc.ca
Mike Elvy, Manager, Arena & Sport
604-485-2891, Fax: 604-485-2162
parksrec@cdpr.bc.ca
Barb Mohan, Manager, Human Resources
604-485-8638, Fax: 604-485-2913
Regina Sadilkova, Manager, Development Services
604-485-8612, Fax: 604-485-2913
Lynda Sowerby, Manager, Accounting Services
604-485-8617, Fax: 604-485-8644
lsowerby@cdpr.bc.ca
Vacant, City Engineer
Charlie Kregel, Chief Librarian, Fire & Emergency Services
604-485-8661, Fax: 604-485-5320
ckregel@powellriverlibrary.ca
Dan Ouellette, Fire Chief/Director, Fire & Emergency Services
604-485-4431

Prince George
City Hall
1100 Patricia Blvd.
Prince George, BC V2L 3V9
Tel: 250-561-7600
cityclerk@city.pg.bc.ca
princegeorge.ca
Municipal Type: City
Incorporated: March 6, 1915 *Area:* 316 sq km
County or District: Fraser-Fort George; *Population in 2011:* 71,974
Provincial Electoral District(s): Pr. George-Mt. Robson; Pr. George N.; Pr. George-Omineca
Federal Electoral District(s): Prince George-Peace River; Cariboo-Prince George
Next Election: Nov. 15, 2014 (3 year terms)
Shari Green, Mayor
mayor@city.pg.bc.ca
Frank Everitt, Councillor
Garth Frizzell, Councillor
250-613-2363
garthfrizzell@citynotice.ca
Lyn Hall, Councillor
Albert Koehler, Councillor
Murry Krause, Councillor
murry.krause@cinhs.org
Brian Skakun, Councillor
Cameron Stolz, Councillor
250-640-5299
cameron@cameronstolz.ca
Dave Wilbur, Councillor
councillordavewilbur@shaw.ca
Derek Bates, City Manager
250-561-7607, Fax: 250-561-0183
Walter Babicz, Corporate Officer/Manager, Legislative Services
250-561-7605, Fax: 250-561-0283
Dan Milburn, Acting Director, Planning & Development Contracts
250-561-7614, Fax: 250-561-7721
Kathleen Soltis, Director, Corporate Services
250-561-7630, Fax: 250-561-7759
Colleen Van Mook, Director, Community Services
250-561-7675, Fax: 250-561-7718
Rob Whitwham, Director, Public Safety & Civic Facilities
250-561-7608, Fax: 250-561-0183
Dan Adamson, Manager, Environment
250-561-7698, Fax: 250-561-7721
Frank Blues, Asset Manager, Downtown Projects
250-561-7503, Fax: 250-561-7721
Scott Bone, Manager, Supply & Fleet Services
250-561-7511, Fax: 250-612-5603
Marco Fornari, Manager, Utilities
250-561-7573, Fax: 250-561-7519
Sandra Stibrany, Manager, Financial Services
250-561-7677, Fax: 250-561-7724
Flavio Viola, Manager, Parks & Solid Waste Services
250-561-7575, Fax: 250-612-5612
Dave Dyer, Chief Engineer
250-561-7663, Fax: 250-561-7721
Glenn Stanker, Engineer, Transportation
250-561-7757
John Lane, Fire Chief
250-561-7667, Fax: 250-561-7703

Prince Rupert
424 - 3rd Ave. West
Prince Rupert, BC V8J 1L7
Tel: 250-627-0934; *Fax:* 250-627-0999
cityhall@princerupert.ca
www.princerupert.ca
Municipal Type: City
Incorporated: March 10, 1910 *Area:* 54.9 sq km
County or District: Skeena-Queen Charlotte; *Population in 2011:* 12,508
Provincial Electoral District(s): North Coast
Federal Electoral District(s): Skeena-Bulkley Valley
Next Election: Nov. 15, 2014 (3 year terms)
Jack Mussallem, Mayor
250-627-0939
Anna Ashley, Councillor
Judy Carlick-Pearson, Councillor
Gina Garon, Councillor
Nelson Kinney, Councillor
250-624-9116
Jennifer Rice, Councillor
Joy Thorkelson, Councillor
250-624-6048
Gord Howie, City Manager
Z. Krekic, City Planner
R. Grodecki, Corporate Administrator
Dan Rodin, Chief Financial Officer
250-627-0935, Fax: 250-627-0918
drodin@princerupert.ca
Bill Horne, General Manager, Engineering, Public Works & Development Services
bill.horne@princerupert.ca
Rudy Kelly, Director, Recreation & Community Services
rudy.kelly@princerupert.ca
Keith Cameron, Manager, Engineering Services
keith.cameron@princerupert.ca
Garin Gardiner, Manager, Operations
garin.gardiner@princerupert.ca
Calvin Grav, Manager, Aquatic
calvin.grav@princerupert.ca
Christine Yew, Manager, Budgets & Accounting
250-627-0921, Fax: 250-627-0918
cyew@princerupert.ca
Dave Mckenzie, Fire Chief
250-624-5115
dave.mckenzie@princerupert.ca

Richmond
6911 No. 3 Rd.
Richmond, BC V6Y 2C1
Tel: 604-276-4000
www.richmond.ca
Other Information: TTY: 604-276-4311
Municipal Type: City
Incorporated: Nov. 10, 1879 *Area:* 128.76 sq km
County or District: Metro Vancouver; *Population in 2011:* 190,473
Provincial Electoral District(s): Richmond-Centre; Richmond E.; Richmond-Steveston
Federal Electoral District(s): Richmond; Delta-Richmond East
Next Election: Nov. 15, 2014 (3 year terms)
Malcolm D. Brodie, Mayor
mayorandcouncillors@richmond.ca
Chak Kwong Au, Councillor
Linda Barnes, Councillor
Derek Dang, Councillor
Evelina Halsey-Brandt, Councillor
Ken Johnston, Councillor
Bill McNulty, Councillor
Linda McPhail, Councillor
Harold Steves, Councillor
David Weber, Director, City Clerk's Office
604-276-4007, Fax: 604-278-5139
George Duncan, Chief Administrative Officer
604-276-4336, Fax: 604-276-4222
administratorsoffice@richmond.ca
Mike Kirk, Deputy Chief Administrative Officer, Corporate Services
604-276-4147
corporateservices@richmond.ca
Cathryn Carlile, General Manager, Community Services
604-276-4068
cathryn.carlile@richmond.ca
Phyllis Carlyle, General Manager, Law & Community Safety
604-276-4104
phyllis.carlyle@richmond.ca
Jeff Day, P.Eng., General Manager, Project Development & Facility Management
604-276-4019
jeff.day@richmond.ca
Joe Erceg, General Manager, Planning & Development
604-276-4214
planningdevelopment@richmond.ca
Robert Gonzalez, P. Eng., General Manager, Engineering & Public Works
604-276-4150
robert.gonzalez@richmond.ca
Andrew Nazareth, General Manager, Business & Finance Services
604-276-4095
finance@richmond.ca
Dave Semple, General Manager, Parks & Recreation
604-233-3350
dave.semple@richmond.ca
Allan Cameron, Director, Information Technology
604-276-4096
Jerry Chong, Director, Finance
604-276-4064, Fax: 604-276-4162
Jane Fernyhough, Director, Arts, Culture & Heritage Services
604-276-4288
jane.fernyhough@richmond.ca
Mike Pellant, Director, Human Resources
604-276-4105
hr@richmond.ca
Dave Semple, Director, Operations
604-244-1206
dave.semple@richmond.ca
Greg Buss, Chief Librarian
604-231-6418
greg.buss@rpl.richmond.bc.ca
William (John) McGowan, Fire Chief
604-303-2719
fire@richmond.ca
Sherrdean Turley, N.C.O. in Charge of Strategic Communications
604-765-4779, Fax: 604-207-4716

Salmon Arm
P.O. Box 40
500 - 2nd Ave. NE
Salmon Arm, BC V1E 4N2
Tel: 250-803-4000; *Fax:* 250-803-4041
cityhall@salmonarm.ca
www.salmonarm.ca
Municipal Type: City
Incorporated: May 15, 1905 *Area:* 155.36 sq km
County or District: Columbia-Shuswap; *Population in 2011:* 17,464
Provincial Electoral District(s): Shuswap
Federal Electoral District(s): Okanagan-Shuswap
Next Election: Nov. 15, 2014 (3 year terms)
Nancy Cooper, Mayor
Debbie Cannon, Councillor
dcannon@salmonarm.ca
Chad Eliason, Councillor
celiason@salmonarm.ca

Alan Harrison, Councillor
aharrison@salmonarm.ca
Ken Jamieson, Councillor
kjamieson@salmonarm.ca
Marg Kentel, Councillor
Denise Reimer, Councillor
Carl Bannister, Chief Administrative Officer
cbannistser@salmonarm.ca
Monica Dalziel, Director, Corporate Services
mdalziel@salmonarm.ca
Dale McTaggart, Director, Engineering & Public Works
dmctaggart@salmonarm.ca
Corey Paiement, Director, Development Services
cpaiement@salmonarm.ca
Betty Hiebert, Manager, Financial Services
bhiebert@salmonarm.ca
Maurice Roy, Manager, Permits/Licensing
mroy@salmonarm.ca
John Rosenberg, Manager, Public Works
jrosenberg@salmonarm.ca
Donna Shultz, Manager, Human Resources
dshultz@salmonarm.ca
Brad Shirley, Fire Chief
250-803-4060
bshirley@salmonarm.ca

Sidney

Municipal Hall
2440 Sidney Ave.
Sidney, BC V8L 1Y7
Tel: 250-656-1184; *Fax:* 250-655-4508
www.sidney.ca
Municipal Type: City
Incorporated: Sept. 30, 1952 *Area:* 5.04 sq km
County or District: Capital; *Population in 2011:* 11,178
Provincial Electoral District(s): Saanich N. & the Islands
Federal Electoral District(s): Saanich-Gulf Islands
Next Election: Nov. 15, 2014 (3 year terms)
Larry Cross, Mayor
250-656-4201
Tim Chad, Councillor
Melissa Hailey, Councillor
Mervyn Lougher-Goodey, Councillor
250-656-7303
Marilyn Loveless, Councillor
250-479-6898
Cliff McNeil-Smith, Councillor
250-655-9632
Kenny Podmore, Councillor
250-655-4631
Steve Price, Councillor
250-655-4077
Murray Clarke, Chief Administrative Officer/Corporate Administrator
250-656-1139
Rob Hall, P.Eng., Director, Engineering & Works
250-656-4502
Randy Humble, Director, Development Services
250-655-5418
Valla Tinney, Director, Corporate Services
250-655-5409
Pete Harrison, Manager, Operations
250-656-1034
Andrew Hicik, Manager, Finance
250-655-5410
Peter Payerl, Manager, Information Technology
250-655-5422
Wendy Taylor, Manager
250-656-1139
Mike van der Linden, Manager, Engineering
250-655-5416
Shari Holmes-Saltzman, Municipal Planner
250-655-5419
Jim Marshall, Senior Building Official
250-655-5412
Dan Holder, Fire Chief
250-655-5421

Surrey

14245 - 56th Ave.
Surrey, BC V3X 3A2
Tel: 604-591-4011; *Fax:* 604-591-8731
www.surrey.ca
Municipal Type: City
Incorporated: Nov. 10, 1879 *Area:* 317.19 sq km
County or District: Metro Vancouver; *Population in 2011:* 468,251
Provincial Electoral District(s): Surrey-Cloverdale; Surrey-Green Timbers; Surrey-Newton; Surrey-Panorama Ridge; Surrey-Tynehead; Surrey-Whalley; Surrey-White Rock
Federal Electoral District(s): Surrey North; South Surrey-White Rock-Cloverdale; Newton-North Delta; Fleetwood-Port Kells
Next Election: Nov. 15, 2014 (3 year terms)
Dianne L. Watts, Mayor
604-591-4126, Fax: 604-591-5175
Tom Gill, Councillor
604-591-4634
tsgill@surrey.ca
Bruce Hayne, Councillor
Linda Hepner, Councillor
604-591-4626
lmhepner@surrey.ca
Marvin Hunt, Councillor
604-591-4635
jmhunt@surrey.ca
Mary Martin, Councillor
604-591-4622
mmartin@surrey.ca
Barinder Rasode, Councillor
604-591-4011
bkrasode@surrey.ca
H. Barbara Steele, Councillor
604-591-4623
hbsteele@surrey.ca
Judy Villeneuve, Councillor
604-591-4625
javilleneuve@surrey.ca
Jane Sullivan, City Clerk
604-591-4132
clerkswebmail@surrey.ca
Murray Dinwoodie, City Manager
604-591-4122, Fax: 604-591-4357
Laurie Cavan, General Manager, Parks, Recreation & Culture
604-598-5760, Fax: 604-598-5781
Shaun Greffard, General Manager, Investment & Intergovernmental Relations
604-591-4571, Fax: 604-594-3055
spgreffard@surrey.ca
Vincent Lalonde, P.Eng., General Manager, Engineering
604-591-4314, Fax: 604-591-8693
Jean Lamontagne, General Manager, Planning & Development
604-591-4441, Fax: 604-591-2507
Nicola Webb, General Manager, Human Resources
604-591-4846, Fax: 604-591-4517
Vivienne Wilke, General Manager, Finance & Technology
604-591-4235, Fax: 604-591-3654
financeinquiry@surrey.ca
Jeff Arason, P. Eng., Manager, Utilities
604-591-4367
Jamie Boan, P. Eng., Manager, Transportation
604-591-4514
Sam Chauhan, Manager, Operational Health & Safety
604-591-4658
Sam Lau, P. Eng., Acting Manager, Land Development
604-591-4276
Violet McGregor, CMA, C.P.P., Manager, Purchasing & Payments
604-591-4011
Gerry McKinnon, Manager, Operations
604-590-7211
Sheila McKinnon, Manager, Arts
604-591-5127
Mary Ann Smith, Senior Economic Development Officer
604-591-4333
masmith@surrey.ca
Craig MacFarlane, City Solicitor
Beth Barlow, Chief Librarian
604-598-7304
babarlow@surrey.ca
Len Garis, Fire Chief
604-541-4011
W. Fraser MacRae, Assistant Commissioner/Officer in Charge, RCMP Surrey Detachment
604-599-0502, Fax: 604-599-8894

Terrace

3215 Eby St.
Terrace, BC V8G 2X8
Tel: 250-635-6311; *Fax:* 250-638-4777
cityhall@terrace.ca
www.terrace.ca
Municipal Type: City
Incorporated: Dec. 31, 1927 *Area:* 41.52 sq km
County or District: Kitimat-Stikine; *Population in 2011:* 11,486
Provincial Electoral District(s): Skeena
Federal Electoral District(s): Skeena-Bulkley Valley
Next Election: Nov. 15, 2014 (3 year terms)
David Pernarowski, Mayor
dpernarowski@terrace.ca
Bruce Bidgood, Councillor
bbidgood@terrace.ca
Lynne Christiansen, Councillor
lchristiansen@terrace.ca
James Cordeiro, Councillor
Marylin Davies, Councillor
Brian Downie, Councillor
bdownie@terrace.ca
Stacey Tyers, Councillor
Alisa Thompson, Interim Clerk
250-638-4721
athompson@terrace.ca
Heather Nunn, Interim Chief Administrative Officer
250-638-4722
hnunn@terrace.ca
Ron Bowles, Director, Finance
205-638-4725
rbowles@terrace.ca
Herb Dusdal, Director, Public Works
250-615-4030
hdusdal@terrace.ca
Marvin Kwiatkowski, Director, Development Services
250-615-4041
mkwiatkowski@terrace.ca
Brad Hansen, Manager, Information Systems Manager
250-638-4701
bhansen@terrace.ca
David Block, City Planner
250-615-4028
dblock@terrace.ca
Lisa Teggarty, Deputy Treasurer
rbowles@terrace.ca
John Klie, Fire Chief
250-638-4742
jklie@terrace.ca
Dana Hart, Officer in Charge, RCMP Terrace Detachment
250-638-7400
Lyle Marleau, Foreman, Environmental Health
250-635-6871
lmarleau@terrace.ca

Vancouver

453 West 12th Ave.
Vancouver, BC V5Y 1V4
Tel: 604-873-7000
info@vancouver.ca
www.vancouver.ca
Other Information: Telephone locally: 311; TTY: 711
Municipal Type: City
Incorporated: November 15, 2008 *Area:* 114.71 sq km
County or District: Metro Vancouver; *Population in 2011:* 603,502
Provincial Electoral District(s): Vancouver Burrard; Vanc.-Fraserview; Vanc.-Hastings; Vanc.-Kensington; Vanc.-Kingsway; Vanc.-Langara; Vanc.-Mt. Pleasant; Vanc.-Point Grey; Vanc.-Quilchena; Vanc.-Fairview
Federal Electoral District(s): Vancouver Centre; Vancouver East; Vancouver-Kingsway; Vancouver Quadra; Vancouver South
Next Election: Nov. 15, 2014 (3 year terms)
Gregor Robertson, Mayor
604-873-7621, Fax: 604-873-7685
gregor.robertson@vancouver.ca
George Affleck, Councillor
604-633-9992, Fax: 604-633-9360
george.affleck@npavancouver.ca
Elizabeth Ball, Councillor
604-633-9992, Fax: 604-633-9360
elizabeth.ball@npavancouver.ca
Adriane Carr, Councillor
778-886-4560
abettervancouver@gmail.com
Heather Deal, Councillor
604-873-7242, Fax: 604-873-7750
clrdeal@vancouver.ca
Kerry Jang, Councillor
604-873-7246, Fax: 604-873-7750
clrjang@vancouver.ca
Raymond P. Louie, Councillor
604-873-7243, Fax: 604-873-7750
clrlouie@vancouver.ca
Geoff Meggs, Councillor
604-873-7249, Fax: 604-873-7750
clrmeggs@vancouver.ca
Andrea Reimer, Councillor
604-873-7241, Fax: 604-873-7750
clrreimer@vancouver.ca
Tim Stevenson, Councillor
604-873-7247, Fax: 604-873-7750
clrstevenson@vancouver.ca
Tony Tang, Councillor
604-568-6913
tony.tang@votevision.ca.ca
Marg Coulson, City Clerk

Penny Ballem, City Manager
Ken Bayne, General Manager, Business Planning & Services
ken.bayne@vancouver.ca
Patrice Impey, General Manager & Chief Financial Officer, Financial Services Group
Peter Judd, General Manager, Engineering Services
Peter Kuran, Acting General Manager, Board of Parks & Recreation
John McKearney, General Manager & Fire Chief, Fire & Rescue Services
604-873-7000
vfrscommunications@vancouver.ca
David McLellan, General Manager, Community Services
david.mclellan@vancouver.ca
Garrick Bradshaw, Director, Facilities Design & Management
Frances J. Connell, Director, Legal Services
Annette Klein, Director, Operational Information & Planning
Richard Newirth, Managing Director, Cultural Services
Kevin Wallinger, Director
Jim Chu, Chief Constable, Vancouver Police Department
604-717-3321

Vernon

3400 - 30th St.
Vernon, BC V1T 5E6
Tel: 250-545-1361; *Fax:* 250-545-7876
admin@vernon.ca
www.vernon.ca
Municipal Type: City
Incorporated: Dec. 30, 1892 *Area:* 94.2 sq km
County or District: North Okanagan; *Population in 2011:* 38,150
Provincial Electoral District(s): Okanagan-Vernon
Federal Electoral District(s): Okanagan-Shuswap; Vancouver Island North
Next Election: Nov. 15, 2014 (3 year terms)
Robert Sawatzky, Mayor
mayor@vernon.ca
Juliette Cunningham, Councillor
Catherine Lord, Councillor
Patrick Nicol, Councillor
pnicol@vernon.ca
Mary-Jo O'Keefe, Councillor
mokeefe@vernon.ca
Brian Quiring, Councillor
Bob Spiers, Councillor
bspiers@vernon.ca
Patti Bridal, City Clerk & Manager, Corporate Services
Leon Gous, Chief Administrative Officer
250-550-3515
lgous@vernon.ca
Kevin Bertles, Manager, Finance
Rob Dickinson, Manager, Engineering
Kim Flick, Manager, Planning, Development & Engineering Services
Shirley Koenig, Manager, Operations
Tony Kopp, Manager, Utilities
250-549-6757
James Rice, Manager, Public Works
jrice@vernon.ca
Ed Stranks, Manager, Engineering Development
Keith Green, Fire Chief
250-550-3561
fire@vernon.ca

Victoria

1 Centennial Sq.
Victoria, BC V8W 1P6
Tel: 250-385-5711; *Fax:* 250-361-0214
publicsrv@victoria.ca
www.victoria.ca
Municipal Type: City
Incorporated: Aug. 2, 1862 *Area:* 19.68 sq km
County or District: Capital Regional District; *Population in 2011:* 80,017
Provincial Electoral District(s): Victoria-Beacon Hill; Victoria-Hillside; Oak Bay-Gordon Head. In Greater Victoria: Esquimalt-Metchosin; Saanich South; Saanich North & the Islands; and Malahat-Juan de Fuca
Federal Electoral District(s): Victoria
Next Election: Nov. 15, 2014 (3 year terms)
Dean Fortin, Mayor
250-361-0200, Fax: 250-361-0348
Marianne Alto, Councillor
250-361-0216
malto@victoria.ca
Chris Coleman, Councillor
250-361-0223
ccoleman@victoria.ca
Shellie Gudgeon, Councillor
Lisa Helps, Councillor
Ben Isitt, Councillor
Pamela Madoff, Councillor
250-361-0221
pmadoff@victoria.ca
Charlayne Thornton-Joe, Councillor
250-361-0219
cthornton-joe@victoria.ca
Geoff Young, Councillor
250-361-0220
gyoung@victoria.ca
Gail Stephens, City Manager
250-361-0202
Kevin Greig, General Manager, Corporate Services
250-361-0247
Jocelyn Jenkyns, General Manager, Victoria Conference Centre
250-361-1000
Peter Sparanese, General Manager, Operations
250-361-0292
Deborah Day, Director, Planning & Development
250-361-0511
Wael (Bill) Fanous, Director, Internal Audit & Risk Management
250-361-0524
Kate Friars, Director, Parks, Recreation & Community Development
250-361-0355
Trina Harrison, Director, Human Resources
250-361-0229
Katie Josephson, Director, Communications
250-361-0210
Dwayne Kalynchuk, Director, Engineering & Public Works
250-361-0522
Pete Sparanese, Acting Director, Sustainability
250-361-0292
Brenda Warner, Director, Finance
250-361-0597
Robert Woodland, Director, Legislative & Regulatory Services
250-361-0203
Ed Robertson, Assistant Director, Public Works
250-361-0457
John Sturdy, Assistant Director, Utilities & Facilities
250-361-0531
Scott Clark, Manager, Information Systems
250-361-0265
Rebecca Chow, Manager, Health & Safety
250-361-0574
Mark Hayden, Manager, Bylaw & Licensing Services
250-361-0592
Glen Oberg, Manager, Supply Management Services
250-361-0271
Don Schaffer, Manager, Legislative Services
250-361-0549
Janice Schmidt, Manager, Corporate Planning & Policy
250-361-0543
John Basey, City Solicitor
250-361-0588, Fax: 250-361-0348
Doug Angrove, Fire Chief
250-920-3353
Jamie Graham, Chief Constable
250-995-7217

White Rock

15322 Buena Vista Ave.
White Rock, BC V4B 1Y6
Tel: 604-541-2100; *Fax:* 604-541-2118
whiterockcouncil@city.whiterock.bc.ca
www.city.whiterock.bc.ca
Municipal Type: City
Incorporated: April 15, 1957 *Area:* 5.16 sq km
County or District: Metro Vancouver; *Population in 2011:* 19,339
Provincial Electoral District(s): Surrey-White Rock
Federal Electoral District(s): South Surrey-White Rock-Cloverdale
Next Election: Nov. 15, 2014 (3 year terms)
Wayne Baldwin, Mayor
Mary-Wade Anderson, Councillor
mwade-anderson@city.whiterock.bc.ca
Alan Campbell, Councillor
acampbell@city.whiterock.bc.ca
Helen Fathers, Councillor
hfathers@city.whiterock.bc.ca
Louise Hutchinson, Councillor
Grant Meyer, Councillor
gmeyer@city.whiterock.bc.ca
Larry Robinson, Councillor
Tracey Arthur, City Clerk
604-541-2212
tarthur@city.whiterock.bc.ca
Peggy Clark, Chief Administrative Officer
604-541-2133, Fax: 604-541-9348
pclark@city.whiterock.bc.ca
Sandra Kurylo, Director, Financial Services
604-541-2111
skurylo@city.whiterock.bc.ca
Rob Thompson, Director, Municipal Operations
604-541-2181
rthompson@city.whiterock.bc.ca
Paul Stanton, Director, Development Services
604-541-2142
pstanton@city.whiterock.bc.ca
Sylvia Yee, Acting Director, Development Services
604-541-2173
syee@city.whiterock.bc.ca
Jacquie Johnstone, Director, Human Resources
604-541-2157
jjohnstone@city.whiterock.bc.ca
Chris Zota, Manager, Information Technology
604-541-2113
czota@city.whiterock.bc.ca
Phil Lemire, Fire Chief
604-541-2122
plemire@city.whiterock.bc.ca
Lesli Roseberry, White Rock RCMP Detachment Commander
604-541-5101
lesli.roseberry@rcmp-grc.gc.ca

Williams Lake

450 Mart St.
Williams Lake, BC V2G 1N3
Tel: 250-392-2311; *Fax:* 250-392-4408
corporateservices@williamslake.ca
www.williamslake.ca
Municipal Type: City
Incorporated: March 15, 1929 *Area:* 33.11 sq km
County or District: Cariboo; *Population in 2011:* 10,832
Provincial Electoral District(s): Cariboo North; Cariboo South
Federal Electoral District(s): Cariboo-Prince George
Next Election: Nov. 15, 2014 (3 year terms)
Kerry Cook, Mayor
250-392-2311
mayor@williamslake.ca
Ivan Bonnell, Councillor
Geoff Bourdon, Councillor
gbourdon@williamslake.ca
Danica Hughes, Councillor
Surinderpal Rathor, Councillor
Laurie Walters, Councillor
lwalters@williamslake.ca
Sue Zacharias, Councillor
szacharias@williamslake.ca
Brian Carruthers, Chief Administrative Officer
250-392-1763
bcarruthers@williamslake.ca
Geoff Goodall, General Manager, Planning & Operations
250-392-1766
ggoodall@williamslake.ca
Kevin Goldfuss, Director, Municipal Services
250-392-1783
kgoldfuss@williamslake.ca
Geoff Goodall, Director, Development Services
250-392-1766
ggoodall@williamslake.ca
Patricia Higgins, Director, Financial Services
250-392-1762
phiggins@williamslake.ca
Randy Isfeld, Director/Fire Chief, Protective Services
250-392-1779
risfeld@williamslake.ca
Geoff Paynton, Director, Community Services
250-392-1786
gpaynton@williamslake.ca
Cindy Bouchard, Manager, Legislative Services
cbouchard@williamslake.ca
Joe Engelberts, Manager, Water/Sewer Division
jengelberts@williamslake.ca

Other Municipalities in British Columbia

100 Mile House

P.O. Box 340
385 South Birch Ave.
100 Mile House, BC V0K 2E0
Tel: 250-395-2434; *Fax:* 250-395-3625
district@dist100milehouse.bc.ca
www.100milehouse.com
Municipal Type: District
Incorporated: July 27, 1965 *Area:* 51.34 sq km
County or District: Cariboo; *Population in 2011:* 1,886
Provincial Electoral District(s): Cariboo South
Federal Electoral District(s): Kamloops-Thomson-Cariboo
Next Election: Nov. 15, 2014 (3 year terms)

Mitch Campsall, Mayor
mcampsall@dist100milehouse.bc.ca
Roy Scott, Chief Administrative Officer, Corporate Administration
rscott@dist100milehouse.bc.ca

Alert Bay
P.O. Box 2800
15 Maple Rd.
Alert Bay, BC V0N 1A0
Tel: 250-974-5213; *Fax:* 250-974-5470
officeclerk@alertbay.ca
www.alertbay.ca
Municipal Type: Village
Incorporated: Jan. 14, 1946 *Area:* 1.78 sq km
County or District: Mount Waddington; *Population in 2011:* 445
Provincial Electoral District(s): North Island
Federal Electoral District(s): Vancouver Island North
Next Election: Nov. 15, 2014 (3 year terms)
Michael Berry, Mayor
Madeline McDonald, Chief Administrative Officer

Anmore
2697 Sunnyside Rd.
Anmore, BC V3H 3C8
Tel: 604-469-9877; *Fax:* 604-469-0537
village.hall@anmore.com
www.anmore.com
Municipal Type: Village
Incorporated: Dec. 7, 1987 *Area:* 27.42 sq km
County or District: Metro Vancouver; *Population in 2011:* 2,092
Provincial Electoral District(s): Port Moody-Westwood
Federal Electoral District(s): Port Moody-Westwood-Port Coquitlam
Next Election: Nov. 15, 2014 (3 year terms)
Heather Anderson, Mayor
604-469-0929
heather.m.anderson@telus.net
Howard Carley, Chief Administrative Officer
howard.carley@anmore.com

Armstrong
P.O. Box 40
3570 Bridge St.
Armstrong, BC V0E 1B0
Tel: 250-546-3023; *Fax:* 250-546-3710
info@cityofarmstrong.bc.ca
www.cityofarmstrong.bc.ca
Municipal Type: Town
Incorporated: March 31, 1913 *Area:* 5.24 sq km
County or District: North Okanagan; *Population in 2011:* 4,815
Provincial Electoral District(s): Shuswap
Federal Electoral District(s): Okanagan-Shuswap
Next Election: Nov. 15, 2014 (3 year terms)
Chris Pieper, Mayor
250-550-7239
mayor@cityofarmstrong.bc.ca; cpieper@telus.net
Patti Ferguson, Chief Administrative Officer

Ashcroft
P.O. Box 129
Ashcroft, BC V0K 1A0
Tel: 250-453-9161; *Fax:* 250-453-9664
admin@ashcroftbc.ca
www.ashcroftbc.ca
Other Information: Toll Free Phone: 1-877-453-9161
Municipal Type: Village
Incorporated: June 27, 1952 *Area:* 51.45 sq km
County or District: Thompson-Nicola; *Population in 2011:* 1,628
Provincial Electoral District(s): Cariboo South
Federal Electoral District(s): Chilliwack-Fraser Canyon
Next Election: Nov. 15, 2014 (3 year terms)
Andy Anderson, Mayor
250-453-9161, Fax: 250-453-9664
council@ashcroftbc.ca
Michelle Allen, Chief Administrative Officer

Barriere
P.O. Box 219
4936 Barriere Town Rd.
Barriere, BC V0E 1E0
Tel: 250-672-9751; *Fax:* 250-672-9708
inquiry@districtofbarriere.com
www.districtofbarriere.com
Other Information: Toll Free Phone: 1-866-672-9751
Municipal Type: District
Incorporated: Dec. 4 2007 *Area:* 6.17 sq km
County or District: Thompson-Nicola; *Population in 2011:* 1,773
Provincial Electoral District(s): Lower North Thompson
Federal Electoral District(s): Kamloops-Thompson-Cariboo
Next Election: Nov. 15, 2014 (3 year terms)
Bill Humphreys, Mayor
Colleen Hannigan, Chief Administrative Officer
250-672-9751
channigan@districtofbarriere.com

Belcarra
4084 Bedwell Bay Rd.
Belcarra, BC V3H 4P8
Tel: 604-937-4100; *Fax:* 604-939-5034
belcarra@belcarra.ca
www.belcarra.ca
Municipal Type: Village
Incorporated: Aug. 22, 1979 *Area:* 5.46 sq km
County or District: Metro Vancouver; *Population in 2011:* 644
Provincial Electoral District(s): Port Moody-Westwood
Federal Electoral District(s): Port Moody-Westwood-Port Coquitlam
Next Election: Nov. 15, 2014 (3 year terms)
Ralph E. Drew, Mayor
604-937-0143
rdrew@belcarra.ca
Lynda Floyd, Chief Administrative Officer
604-937-4101
lfloyd@belcarra.ca

Bowen Island
981 Artisan Lane
Bowen Island, BC V0N 1G0
Tel: 604-947-4255; *Fax:* 604-947-0193
bim@bimbc.ca
www.bimbc.ca
Municipal Type: Island Municipality
Incorporated: Dec. 4, 1999 *Area:* 49.94 sq km
County or District: Metro Vancouver; *Population in 2011:* 3,402
Provincial Electoral District(s): West Vancouver-Garibaldi
Federal Electoral District(s): West Vancouver-Sunshine Coast-Sea to Sky Country
Next Election: Nov. 15, 2014 (3 year terms)
Jack A. Adelaar, Mayor
Brent Mahood, Chief Administrative Officer
bmahood@bimbc.ca

Burns Lake
P.O. Box 570
Burns Lake, BC V0J 1E0
Tel: 250-692-7587; *Fax:* 250-692-3059
village@burnslake.org
www.burnslake.org
Other Information: Fire Hall Phone: 250-692-3664
Municipal Type: Village
Incorporated: Dec. 6, 1923 *Area:* 7.17 sq km
County or District: Bulkley-Nechako; *Population in 2011:* 2,029
Provincial Electoral District(s): Bulkley Valley-Stikine
Federal Electoral District(s): Skeena-Bulkley Valley
Next Election: Nov. 15, 2014 (3 year terms)
Luke Strimbold, Mayor
Sheryl Worthing, Chief Administrative Officer

Cache Creek
P.O. Box 7
Cache Creek, BC V0K 1H0
Tel: 250-457-6237; *Fax:* 250-457-9192
admin@cachecreek.info
www.cachecreekvillage.com
Municipal Type: Village
Incorporated: Nov. 28, 1967 *Area:* 10.57 sq km
County or District: Thompson-Nicola; *Population in 2011:* 1,040
Provincial Electoral District(s): Cariboo South
Federal Electoral District(s): Chilliwack-Fraser Canyon
Next Election: Nov. 15, 2014 (3 year terms)
John Ranta, Mayor
bigjohn4@telus.net
Leslie Lloyd, Chief Administrative Officer

Canal Flats
P.O. Box 159
8853 Grainger Rd.
Canal Flats, BC V0B 1B0
Tel: 250-349-5462; *Fax:* 250-349-5460
village@canalflats.ca
www.canalflats.com
Municipal Type: Village
Incorporated: June 29, 2004 *Area:* 10.84 sq km
County or District: East Kootenay; *Population in 2011:* 715
Provincial Electoral District(s): Columbia River-Revelstoke
Federal Electoral District(s): Kootenay-Columbia
Next Election: Nov. 15, 2014 (3 year terms)
Ute Juras, Mayor
Brian Woodward, Chief Administrative Officer

Castlegar
460 Columbia Ave.
Castlegar, BC V1N 1G7
Tel: 250-365-7227; *Fax:* 250-365-4810
www.castlegar.ca
Municipal Type: Town
Incorporated: Jan. 1, 1974 *Area:* 19.8 sq km
County or District: Central Kootenay; *Population in 2011:* 7,816
Provincial Electoral District(s): West Kootenay-Boundary
Federal Electoral District(s): British Columbia Southern Interior
Next Election: Nov. 15, 2014 (3 year terms)
Lawrence Chernoff, Mayor
John Malcolm, Chief Administrative Officer

Central Saanich
1903 Mt. Newton Cross Rd.
Saanichton, BC V8M 2A9
Tel: 250-652-4444; *Fax:* 250-652-0135
www.centralsaanich.ca
Municipal Type: District
Incorporated: Dec. 12, 1950 *Area:* 41.42 sq km
County or District: Capital; *Population in 2011:* 15,936
Provincial Electoral District(s): Saanich North & the Islands
Federal Electoral District(s): Saanich-Gulf Islands
Next Election: Nov. 15, 2014 (3 year terms)
Alastair Bryson, Mayor
John Garrison, Councillor
250-514-4217
Carl Jensen, Councillor
Zeb King, Councillor
Adam Olsen, Councillor
778-426-1000
Cathie Ounsted, Councillor
Terry Siklenka, Councillor
250-508-8313
Susan Brown, Municipal Clerk
Gary C. Nason, Administrator
Nirmal Bhattacharya, P.Eng., Municipal Engineer, Public Works & Operationss
Bruce Greig, Planner
Ron French, Fire Chief
250-544-4227

Chase
P.O. Box 440
826 Okanagan Ave.
Chase, BC V0E 1M0
Tel: 250-679-3238; *Fax:* 250-679-3070
chase@chasebc.ca
www.chasebc.ca
Municipal Type: Village
Incorporated: April 22, 1969 *Area:* 3.75 sq km
County or District: Thompson-Nicola; *Population in 2011:* 2,495
Provincial Electoral District(s): Kamloops-North Thompson
Federal Electoral District(s): Okanagan-Shuswap
Next Election: Nov. 15, 2014 (3 year terms)
Ron Anderson, Mayor
Martin Dalsin, Chief Administrative Officer
mdalsin@chasebc.ca

Chetwynd
P.O. Box 357
5400 North Access Rd.
Chetwynd, BC V0C 1J0
Tel: 250-401-4100; *Fax:* 250-401-4101
d-chet@gochetwynd.com
www.gochetwynd.com
Municipal Type: District
Incorporated: Sept. 25, 1962 *Area:* 64.32 sq km
County or District: Peace River; *Population in 2011:* 2,635
Provincial Electoral District(s): Peace River South
Federal Electoral District(s): Prince George-Peace River
Next Election: Nov. 15, 2014 (3 year terms)
Merlin Nichols, Mayor
Doug Fleming, Chief Administrative Officer
250-401-4103
dfleming@gochetwynd.com

Clearwater
P.O. Box 157
132 Clearwater Station Rd.
Clearwater, BC V0E 1N0
Tel: 250-674-2257; *Fax:* 250-674-2173
admin@districtofclearwater.com
www.districtofclearwater.com
Municipal Type: District
Incorporated: Dec. 7 2007 *Area:* 60 sq km
County or District: Thompson-Nicola; *Population in 2011:* 2,331
Provincial Electoral District(s): Kamloops-North Thompson
Federal Electoral District(s): Kamloops-Thompson-Cariboo
Next Election: Nov. 15, 2014 (3 year terms)
John Harwood, Mayor

Leslie Groulx, Interim Chief Administrative Officer
lgroulx@docbc.ca

Clinton
P.O. Box 309
1423 Cariboo Hwy.
Clinton, BC V0K 1K0
Tel: 250-459-2261; *Fax:* 250-459-2227
admin@village.clinton.bc.ca
www.village.clinton.bc.ca
Municipal Type: Village
Incorporated: July 16, 1963 *Area:* 4.36 sq km
County or District: Thompson-Nicola; *Population in 2011:* 636
Provincial Electoral District(s): Cariboo South
Federal Electoral District(s): Kamloops-Thompson-Cariboo
Next Election: Nov. 15, 2014 (3 year terms)
Jim Rivett, Mayor
mayor@village.clinton.bc.ca
Heidi Frank, Chief Administrative Officer
250-459-2261
hfrank@village.clinton.bc.ca

Coldstream
9901 Kalamalka Rd.
Coldstream, BC V1B 1L6
Tel: 250-545-5304; *Fax:* 250-545-4733
info@districtofcoldstream.ca
www.districtofcoldstream.ca
Municipal Type: District
Incorporated: Dec. 21, 1906 *Area:* 67.25 sq km
County or District: North Okanagan; *Population in 2011:* 10,214
Provincial Electoral District(s): Okanagan-Vernon
Federal Electoral District(s): Okanagan-Shuswap
Next Election: Nov. 15, 2014 (3 year terms)
Jim Garlick, Mayor
250-307-9490
Michael Stamhuis, P. Eng, Chief Administrative Officer
mstamhuis@district.coldstream.bc.ca

Creston
P.O. Box 1339
#238, 10th Ave. North
Creston, BC V0B 1G0
Tel: 250-428-2214; *Fax:* 250-428-9164
info@creston.ca
www.creston.ca
Municipal Type: Town
Incorporated: May 14, 1924 *Area:* 8.48 sq km
County or District: Central Kootenay; *Population in 2011:* 5,306
Provincial Electoral District(s): Nelson-Creston
Federal Electoral District(s): Kootenay-Columbia
Next Election: Nov. 15, 2014 (3 year terms)
Ron Toyota, Mayor
ron.toyota@creston.ca
Lou Varela, Town Manager

Cumberland
P.O. Box 340
2673 Dunsmuir Ave.
Cumberland, BC V0R 1S0
Tel: 250-336-2291; *Fax:* 250-336-2321
www.cumberlandbc.net
Municipal Type: Village
Incorporated: Jan. 1, 1898 *Area:* 29.13 sq km
County or District: Comox Valley; *Population in 2011:* 3,398
Provincial Electoral District(s): Comox Valley
Federal Electoral District(s): Vancouver Island North
Next Election: Nov. 15, 2014 (3 year terms)
Leslie Baird, Mayor
Dave Durrant, Chief Administrative Officer
ddurrant@cumberlandbc.net

Delta
4500 Clarence Taylor Cres.
Delta, BC V4K 3E2
Tel: 604-946-4141
www.corp.delta.bc.ca
Municipal Type: District
Incorporated: Nov. 10, 1879 *Area:* 183.7 sq km
County or District: Metro Vancouver; *Population in 2011:* 99,863
Provincial Electoral District(s): Delta North; Delta South
Federal Electoral District(s): Delta-Richmond East; Newton-North Delta
Next Election: Nov. 15, 2014 (3 year terms)
Lois E. Jackson, Mayor
604-946-3210, Fax: 604-946-6055
mayor@corp.delta.bc.ca
Sylvia Bishop, Councillor
Robert Campbell, Councillor
604-948-0623
rcampbell@corp.delta.bc.ca
Scott Hamilton, Councillor
604-599-9261
shamilton@corp.delta.bc.ca
Jeannie Kanakos, Councillor
Bruce McDonald, Councillor
604-596-8345
bmcdonald@corp.delta.bc.ca
Ian L. Paton, Councillor
Angila Bains, Municipal Clerk
604-946-3220, Fax: 604-946-3390
clerks@corp.delta.bc.ca
George Harvie, Chief Administrative Officer
604-946-3212, Fax: 604-946-3864
cao@corp.delta.bc.ca
Ken Kuntz, Director, Parks, Recreation & Culture
604-952-3000, Fax: 604-946-4693
park-rec@corp.delta.bc.ca
Steven Lan, Director, Engineering
604-946-3260, Fax: 604-946-7492
engineering@corp.delta.bc.ca
Thomas Leathem, Director, Community Planning & Development
604-946-3380
com-pln-dev@corp.delta.bc.ca
Sean McGill, Director, Human Resources & Corporate Planning
604-946-3246
human-resources@corp.delta.bc.ca
Karl Preuss, CA, Director, Finance
604-946-3230, Fax: 604-946-3962
finance@corp.delta.bc.ca
Mike Brotherston, Manager, Climate Action & Environment
604-946-3253
cae@corp.delta.bc.ca
Greg Vanstone, Municipal Solicitor
604-952-3138
legalservices@corp.delta.bc.ca
Dan Copeland, Fire Chief
604-946-8541, Fax: 604-946-0436
fire@corp.delta.bc.ca
Jim Cessford, Chief Constable
604-946-4411, Fax: 604-946-3729
officechiefconstable@deltapolice.ca

Duncan
200 Craig St.
Duncan, BC V9L 1W3
Tel: 250-746-6126; *Fax:* 250-746-6129
duncan@duncan.ca
www.duncan.ca
Municipal Type: Town
Incorporated: March 4, 1912 *Area:* 2.05 sq km
County or District: Cowichan Valley; *Population in 2011:* 4,932
Provincial Electoral District(s): Cowichan-Ladysmith
Federal Electoral District(s): Nanaimo-Cowichan
Next Election: Nov. 15, 2014 (3 year terms)
Phil Kent, Mayor
250-709-0186
mayor@duncan.ca
Tom Ireland, Chief Administrative Officer
tireland@duncan.ca

Elkford
P.O. Box 340
Elkford, BC V0B 1H0
Tel: 250-865-4000; *Fax:* 250-865-4001
info@elkford.ca
www.elkford.ca
Municipal Type: District
Incorporated: July 16, 1971 *Area:* 101.59 sq km
County or District: East Kootenay; *Population in 2011:* 2,523
Provincial Electoral District(s): East Kootenay
Federal Electoral District(s): Kootenay-Columbia
Next Election: Nov. 15, 2014 (3 year terms)
Dean McKerracher, Mayor
mayor@elkford.ca
Corien L. Speaker, Chief Administrative Officer
cspeaker@elkford.ca

Enderby
P.O. Box 400
619 Cliff Ave.
Enderby, BC V0E 1V0
Tel: 250-838-7230; *Fax:* 250-838-6007
enderbycity@sunwave.net
www.enderby.com; cityofenderby.com
Municipal Type: Village
Incorporated: March 1, 1905 *Area:* 4.23 sq km
County or District: North Okanagan; *Population in 2011:* 2,932
Provincial Electoral District(s): Shuswap
Federal Electoral District(s): Okanagan-Shuswap
Next Election: Nov. 15, 2014 (3 year terms)
Howie Cyr, Mayor
Barry Gagnon, Chief Administrative Officer
bgagnon@sunwave.net

Esquimalt
1229 Esquimalt Rd.
Victoria, BC V9A 3P1
Tel: 250-414-7100; *Fax:* 250-414-7111
www.esquimalt.ca
Municipal Type: Township
Incorporated: Sept. 1, 1912 *Area:* 7.04 sq km
County or District: Capital; *Population in 2011:* 16,209
Provincial Electoral District(s): Esquimalt-Metchosin
Federal Electoral District(s): Esquimalt-Juan de Fuca
Next Election: Nov. 15, 2014 (3 year terms)
Barbara Desjardins, Mayor
250-883-1944
Meagan Brame, Councillor
250-285-0660
Dave Hodgins, Councillor
Lynda Hundleby, Councillor
250-383-3759
Bob McKie, Councillor
Tim Morrison, Councillor
David Schinbein, Councillor
Laurie Hurst, Chief Administrative Officer
250-414-7133
Karen Blakely, Chief Financial Officer & Director, Financial Services
250-414-7141
Scott Hartman, Director, Parks & Recreation
250-412-8509
Jeff Miller, Director, Engineering & Public Works
250-414-7147
Barbara Snyder, Director, Development Services
250-414-7146
Wayne Martin, Manager, Public Works
Trevor Parkes, Senior Planner, Development Services
David Ward, Fire Chief
250-414-7125

Fernie
P.O. Box 190
#501, 3rd Ave.
Fernie, BC V0B 1M0
Tel: 250-423-6817; *Fax:* 250-423-3034
cityhall@fernie.ca
www.fernie.ca
Municipal Type: Town
Incorporated: July 28, 1904 *Area:* 16.05 sq km
County or District: East Kootenay; *Population in 2011:* 4,448
Provincial Electoral District(s): East Kootenay
Federal Electoral District(s): Kootenay-Columbia
Next Election: Nov. 15, 2014 (3 year terms)
Mary Giuliano, Mayor
Allan Chabot, Chief Administrative Officer
250-423-2225
allan.chabot@fernie.ca

Fort Nelson
P.O. Box 399
5319 - 50th Ave.
Fort Nelson, BC V0C 1R0
Tel: 250-774-2541
justask@northernrockies.ca
www.northernrockies.ca
Municipal Type: Town
Incorporated: Oct. 31, 1987 *Area:* 13.26 sq km
County or District: Northern Rockies; *Population in 2011:* 3,902
Provincial Electoral District(s): Peace River North
Federal Electoral District(s): Prince George-Peace River
Next Election: Nov. 15, 2014 (3 year terms)
Bill Streeper, Mayor
mayor@northernrockies.org
Randy McLean, Chief Administrative Officer
admin@northernrockies.ca

Fort St. James
P.O. Box 640
477 Stuart Dr. West
Fort St James, BC V0J 1P0
Tel: 250-996-8233; *Fax:* 250-996-2248
www.stuartnechako.ca/fort-st-james
Municipal Type: District
Incorporated: Dec. 19, 1952 *Area:* 22.1 sq km
County or District: Bulkley-Nechako; *Population in 2011:* 1,691
Provincial Electoral District(s): Prince George-Omineca
Federal Electoral District(s): Skeena-Buckley Valley
Next Election: Nov. 15, 2014 (3 year terms)
Rob MacDougall, Mayor
Kevin Crook, Chief Administrative Officer
cao@fortstjames.ca

Fraser Lake
P.O. Box 430
210 Carrier Cres.
Fraser Lake, BC V0J 1S0
Tel: 250-699-6257; *Fax:* 250-699-6469
village@fraserlake.ca
www.fraserlake.ca
Municipal Type: Village
Incorporated: Sept. 27, 1966 *Area:* 3.9 sq km
County or District: Bulkley-Nechako; *Population in 2011:* 1,167
Provincial Electoral District(s): Prince George-Omineca
Federal Electoral District(s): Skeena-Bulkley Valley
Next Election: Nov. 15, 2014 (3 year terms)
Dwayne Lindstrom, Mayor
Clinton Mauthe, Director, Corporate Affairs

Fruitvale
P.O. Box 370
1947 beaver St.
Fruitvale, BC V0G 1L0
Tel: 250-367-7551; *Fax:* 250-367-9267
www.village.fruitvale.bc.ca
Municipal Type: Village
Incorporated: Nov. 4, 1952 *Area:* 36.86 sq km
County or District: Kootenay Boundary; *Population in 2011:* 2,016
Provincial Electoral District(s): West Kootenay-Boundary
Federal Electoral District(s): British Columbia Southern Interior
Next Election: Nov. 15, 2014 (3 year terms)
Patricia-Lynn Cecchini, Mayor
Lila Cresswell, Chief Administrative Officer

Gibsons
P.O. Box 340
474 South Fletcher Rd.
Gibsons, BC V0N 1V0
Tel: 604-886-2274; *Fax:* 604-886-9735
info@gibsons.ca
www.gibsons.ca
Municipal Type: Town
Incorporated: March 4, 1929 *Area:* 4.33 sq km
County or District: Sunshine Coast; *Population in 2011:* 4,437
Provincial Electoral District(s): Powell River-Sunshine Coast
Federal Electoral District(s): West Vancouver-Sunshine Coast-Sea to Sky Country
Next Election: Nov. 15, 2014 (3 year terms)
Wayne Rowe, Mayor
Wayne Waycheshen, Chief Administrative Officer
wwaycheshen@gibsons.ca

Gold River
P.O. Box 610
499 Muchalat Dr.
Gold River, BC V0P 1G0
Tel: 250-283-2202; *Fax:* 250-283-7500
villageofgoldriver@cablerocket.com
www.goldriver.ca
Municipal Type: Village
Incorporated: Aug. 26, 1965 *Area:* 10.51 sq km
County or District: Strathcona; *Population in 2011:* 1,267
Provincial Electoral District(s): North Island
Federal Electoral District(s): Vancouver Island North
Next Election: Nov. 15, 2014 (3 year terms)
Craig Anderson, Mayor
Larry Plourde, Chief Administrative Officer
grlplourde@cablerocket.com

Golden
P.O. Box 350
Golden, BC V0A 1H0
Tel: 250-344-2271; *Fax:* 250-344-6577
enquiries@town.golden.bc.ca
www.town.golden.bc.ca
Municipal Type: Town
Incorporated: June 26, 1957 *Area:* 11.02 sq km
County or District: Columbia-Shuswap; *Population in 2011:* 3,701
Provincial Electoral District(s): Columbia River-Revelstoke
Federal Electoral District(s): Kootenay-Columbia
Next Election: Nov. 15, 2014 (3 year terms)
Christina Benty, Mayor
christina.benty@golden.ca
Viv Thoss, Council Clerk
council.clerk@golden.ca
David Allen, Chief Administrative Officer
cao@town.golden.bc.ca

Grand Forks
P.O. Box 220
7217 - 4th St.
Grand Forks, BC V0H 1H0
Tel: 250-442-8266; *Fax:* 250-442-8000
info@city.grandforks.bc.ca
www.city.grandforks.bc.ca
Municipal Type: Town
Incorporated: April 15, 1897 *Area:* 10.44 sq km
County or District: Kootenay Boundary; *Population in 2011:* 3,985
Provincial Electoral District(s): West Kootenay-Boundary
Federal Electoral District(s): British Columbia Southern Interior
Next Election: Nov. 15, 2014 (3 year terms)
Brian Taylor, Mayor
btaylor@grandforks.ca
Lynne Burch, Chief Administrative Officer
lburch@grandforks.ca

Granisle
P.O. Box 128
Granisle, BC V0J 1W0
Tel: 250-697-2248; *Fax:* 250-697-2306
www.granisle.net
Municipal Type: Village
Incorporated: June 29, 1971 *Area:* 40.21 sq km
County or District: Bulkley-Nechako; *Population in 2011:* 303
Provincial Electoral District(s): Bulkley Valley-Stikine
Federal Electoral District(s): Skeena-Buckley Valley
Next Election: Nov. 15, 2014 (3 year terms)
Linda McGuire, Mayor
Gilles Archambault, Chief Administrative Officer
250-697-2428

Greenwood
P.O. Box 129
202 Government Ave.
Greenwood, BC V0H 1J0
Tel: 250-445-6644; *Fax:* 250-445-6441
greenwoodcity@shaw.ca
www.greenwoodcity.com
Municipal Type: Village
Incorporated: July 12, 1897 *Area:* 2.52 sq km
County or District: Kootenay Boundary; *Population in 2011:* 708
Provincial Electoral District(s): West Kootenay-Boundary
Federal Electoral District(s): British Columbia Southern Interior
Next Election: Nov. 15, 2014 (3 year terms)
Nipper Kettle, Mayor
Gerald A. Henke, Administrator

Harrison Hot Springs
P.O. Box 160
495 Hot Springs Rd.
Harrison Hot Springs, BC V0M 1K0
Tel: 604-796-2171; *Fax:* 604-796-2192
info@harrisonhotsprings.ca
www.harrisonhotsprings.ca
Municipal Type: Village
Incorporated: May 27, 1949 *Area:* 5.47 sq km
County or District: Fraser Valley; *Population in 2011:* 1,468
Provincial Electoral District(s): Chilliwack-Kent
Federal Electoral District(s): Chilliwack-Fraser Canyon
Next Election: Nov. 15, 2014 (3 year terms)
Leo Facio, Mayor
mayor@harrisonhotsprings.ca
Ted Tisdale, Chief Administrative Officer
ttisdale@harrisonhotsprings.ca

Hazelton
P.O. Box 40
Hazelton, BC V0J 1Y0
Tel: 250-842-5991; *Fax:* 250-842-5152
info@village.hazelton.bc.ca
www.village.hazelton.bc.ca
Municipal Type: Village
Incorporated: Feb. 15, 1956 *Area:* 2.85 sq km
County or District: Kitimat-Stikine; *Population in 2011:* 270
Provincial Electoral District(s): Bulkley Valley-Stikine
Federal Electoral District(s): Skeena-Bulkley Valley
Next Election: Nov. 15, 2014 (3 year terms)
Alice Maitland, Mayor
amaitland@village.hazelton.bc.ca
Kelly Mattson, Administrator
administrator@village.hazelton.bc.ca

Highlands
1980 Millstream Rd.
Victoria, BC V9B 6H1
Tel: 250-474-1773; *Fax:* 250-474-3677
www.highlands.bc.ca
Municipal Type: District
Incorporated: Dec. 7, 1993 *Area:* 37.87 sq km
County or District: Capital; *Population in 2011:* 2,120
Provincial Electoral District(s): Malahat-Juan de Fuca
Federal Electoral District(s): Esquimalt-Juan de Fuca
Next Election: Nov. 15, 2014 (3 year terms)
Jane Mendum, Mayor
jmendum@highlands.ca
Christopher D. Coates, Administrator
ccoates@highlands.ca

Hope
325 Wallace St.
Hope, BC V0X 1L0
Tel: 604-869-5671; *Fax:* 604-869-2275
info@hope.ca
www.hope.ca
Municipal Type: District Municipality
Incorporated: April 6, 1929 *Area:* 41.42 sq km
County or District: Fraser Valley; *Population in 2011:* 5,969
Provincial Electoral District(s): Yale-Lillooet
Federal Electoral District(s): Chilliwack-Fraser Canyon
Next Election: Nov. 15, 2014 (3 year terms)
Susan Ann Johnston, Mayor
Earl Rowe, Town Manager
erowe@hope.ca

Houston
P.O. Box 370
3367 - 12th St.
Houston, BC V0J 1Z0
Tel: 250-845-2238; *Fax:* 250-845-3429
doh@houston.ca
www.houston.ca
Municipal Type: District
Incorporated: March 4, 1957 *Area:* 72.83 sq km
County or District: Bulkley-Nechako; *Population in 2011:* 3,147
Provincial Electoral District(s): Bulkley Valley-Stikine
Federal Electoral District(s): Skeena-Buckley Valley
Next Election: Nov. 15, 2014 (3 year terms)
Bill Holmberg, Mayor
bholmberg@finning.ca
Linda Poznikoff, Chief Administrative Officer
poznikoff@houston.ca

Hudson's Hope
P.O. Box 330
9904 Dudley Dr.
Hudson's Hope, BC V0C 1V0
Tel: 250-783-9901; *Fax:* 250-783-5741
www.hudsonshope.ca
Municipal Type: District
Incorporated: Nov. 16, 1965 *Area:* 869.43 sq km
County or District: Peace River; *Population in 2011:* 970
Provincial Electoral District(s): Peace River North
Federal Electoral District(s): Prince George-Peace River
Next Election: Nov. 15, 2014 (3 year terms)
Karen Anderson, Mayor
mayor@hudsonshope.ca
Mike Carter, Acting Chief Administrative Officer/Director, Public Works
mike@hudsonshope.ca

Invermere
P.O. Box 339
914 - 8th Ave.
Invermere, BC V0A 1K0
Tel: 250-342-9281; *Fax:* 250-342-2934
info@invermere.net
www.invermere.net
Municipal Type: District
Incorporated: May 22, 1951 *Area:* 10.18 sq km
County or District: East Kootenay; *Population in 2011:* 2,955
Provincial Electoral District(s): Columbia River-Revelstoke
Federal Electoral District(s): Kootenay-Columbia
Next Election: Nov. 15, 2014 (3 year terms)
Gerry Taft, Mayor
mayor@invermere.net
Christopher Prosser, Cheif Administrative Officer
cao@invermere.net

Kaslo
P.O. Box 576
312 Fourth St.
Kaslo, BC V0G 1M0
Tel: 250-353-2311; *Fax:* 250-353-7767
village@netidea.com
www.kaslo.ca
Municipal Type: Village
Incorporated: Aug. 14, 1893 *Area:* 2.8 sq km
County or District: Central Kootenay; *Population in 2011:* 1,026
Provincial Electoral District(s): Nelson-Creston
Federal Electoral District(s): British Columbia Southern Interior
Next Election: Nov. 15, 2014 (3 year terms)

Greg Lay, Mayor
Rae Sawyer, Chief Administrative Officer
kasloclerk@netidea.com

Kent

P.O. Box 70
7170 Cheam Ave.
Agassiz, BC V0M 1A0
Tel: 604-796-2235; *Fax:* 604-796-9854
www.district.kent.bc.ca
Municipal Type: District
Incorporated: Jan. 1, 1895 *Area:* 166.51 sq km
County or District: Fraser Valley; *Population in 2011:* 5,664
Provincial Electoral District(s): Chilliwack-Kent
Federal Electoral District(s): Chilliwack-Fraser Canyon
Next Election: Nov. 15, 2014 (3 year terms)
John Van Laerhoven, Mayor
Wallace Mah, Chief Administrative Officer
wmah@district.kent.bc.ca

Keremeos

P.O. Box 160
702 - 4th St.
Keremeos, BC V0X 1N0
Tel: 250-499-2711; *Fax:* 250-499-5477
town@keremeos.ca
www.keremeos.ca
Municipal Type: Village
Incorporated: Oct. 30, 1956 *Area:* 2.11 sq km
County or District: Okanagan-Similkameen; *Population in 2011:* 1,330
Provincial Electoral District(s): Yale-Lillooet
Federal Electoral District(s): British Columbia Southern Interior
Next Election: Nov. 15, 2014 (3 year terms)
Manfred Bauer, Mayor
Joni Heinrich, Chief Administrative Officer
cao@keremeos.ca

Kimberley

340 Spokane St.
Kimberley, BC V1A 2E8
Tel: 250-427-5311; *Fax:* 250-427-5252
info@city.kimberley.bc.ca; operations@city.kimberley.bc.ca
www.city.kimberley.bc.ca
Municipal Type: Town
Incorporated: March 29, 1944 *Area:* 58.31 sq km
County or District: East Kootenay; *Population in 2011:* 6,652
Provincial Electoral District(s): Columbia River-Revelstoke
Federal Electoral District(s): Kootenay-Columbia
Next Election: Nov. 15, 2014 (3 year terms)
Ron McRae, Mayor
mayor@city.kimberley.bc.ca
Al Mulholland, Chief Administrative Officer
amulholland@city.kimberley.bc.ca
George Stratton, Chief Corporate Administrative Officer
gstratton@city.kimberley.bc.ca

Kitimat

270 City Centre
Kitimat, BC V8C 2H7
Tel: 250-632-8900; *Fax:* 250-632-4995
feedback@kitimat.ca
www.kitimat.ca
Municipal Type: District
Incorporated: March 31, 1953 *Area:* 242.63 sq km
County or District: Kitimat-Stikine; *Population in 2011:* 8,335
Provincial Electoral District(s): Skeena
Federal Electoral District(s): Skeena-Bulkley Valley
Next Election: Nov. 15, 2014 (3 year terms)
Joanne Monaghan, Mayor
Walter McLellan, Municipal Clerk
250-632-8914
Ron Poole, Municipal Manager
250-632-8916
Steve Christiansen, Treasurer
250-632-8909

Ladysmith

Town Hall
P.O. Box 220 Main
410 Esplanade
Ladysmith, BC V9G 1A2
Tel: 250-245-6400; *Fax:* 250-245-6411
info@ladysmith.ca
www.ladysmith.ca
Municipal Type: Town
Incorporated: June 3, 1904 *Area:* 12.18 sq km
County or District: Cowichan Valley; *Population in 2011:* 7,921
Provincial Electoral District(s): Cowichan-Ladysmith
Federal Electoral District(s): Nanaimo-Cowichan
Next Election: Nov. 15, 2014 (3 year terms)
Robert Hutchins, Mayor
rhutchins@ladysmith.ca
Ruth E. Malli, City Manager
rmalli@ladysmith.ca

Lake Country

10150 Bottom Wood Lake Rd.
Lake Country, BC V4V 2M1
Tel: 250-766-5650; *Fax:* 250-766-0116
admin@lakecountry.bc.ca; customerservice@lakecountry.bc.ca
www.lakecountry.bc.ca
Municipal Type: District
Incorporated: May 2, 1995 *Area:* 122.16 sq km
County or District: Central Okanagan; *Population in 2011:* 11,708
Provincial Electoral District(s): Kelowna-Lake Country
Federal Electoral District(s): Kelowna-Lake Country
Next Election: Nov. 15, 2014 (3 year terms)
James Baker, Mayor
baker@lakecountry.bc.ca
Alberto De Feo, Chief Administrative Officer
250-766-6671

Lake Cowichan

P.O. Box 860
39 South Shore Rd.
Lake Cowichan, BC V0R 2G0
Tel: 250-749-6681; *Fax:* 250-749-3900
general@lakecowichan.ca
www.town.lakecowichan.bc.ca
Municipal Type: Town
Incorporated: Aug. 19, 1944 *Area:* 8.25 sq km
County or District: Cowichan Valley; *Population in 2011:* 2,948
Provincial Electoral District(s): Cowichan-Ladysmith
Federal Electoral District(s): Nanaimo-Cowichan
Next Election: Nov. 15, 2014 (3 year terms)
Ross Forrest, Mayor
rforrest@town.lakecowichan.bc.ca
Joseph A. Fernandez, Chief Administrative Officer
jfernandez@lakecowichan.ca

Langley

20338 - 65 Ave.
Langley, BC V2Y 3J1
Tel: 604-534-3211
info@tol.ca
www.tol.ca
Municipal Type: Township
Incorporated: April 26, 1873 *Area:* 306.93 sq km
County or District: Metro Vancouver; *Population in 2011:* 104,177
Provincial Electoral District(s): Fort Langely-Aldergrove
Federal Electoral District(s): Langley
Next Election: Nov. 15, 2014 (3 year terms)
Rick Green, Mayor
rgreen@tol.ca
Bev Dornan, Councillor
bdornan@tol.ca
Steve Ferguson, Councillor
sferguson@tol.ca
Charlie Fox, Councillor
cfox@tol.ca
Bob Long, Councillor
blong@tol.ca
Kim Richter, Councillor
krichter@tol.ca
Dan Sheel, Councillor
Michelle Sparrow, Councillor
Grant Ward, Councillor
gward@tol.ca
Eric Britton, Township Clerk/Manager, Legislative Services
Mark Bakken, Administrator
604-533-6115
Ramin Sefi, Acting General Manager, Community Development
604-533-6034
cdinfo@tol.ca
Jason Winslade, General Manager, Corporate Administration & Community Services
Colin Wright, General Manager, Engineering
604-532-7300
enginfo@tol.ca
Christine Corfe, Director, Corporate Administration
604-533-6015, Fax: 604-533-6010
ccorfe@tol.bc.ca
Shannon Harvey-Renner, Director, Human Resources
604-533-6061
hrinfo@tol.ca
David Leavers, Director, Recreation, Culture & Parks
604-533-6068
prinfo@tol.ca
Hilary Tsikayi, Director, Finance
604-533-6022
fininfo@tol.ca
Doug Wade, Fire Chief
604-532-7500
fireinfo@tol.ca
Janice Armstrong, Superintendent, RCMP
604-532-3200
langleyrcmp@rcmp-grc.gc.ca

Lantzville

P.O. Box 100
7192 Lantzville Rd.
Lantzville, BC V0R 2H0
Tel: 250-390-4006; *Fax:* 250-390-5188
district@lantzville.ca
www.lantzville.ca
Municipal Type: District
Incorporated: June 25, 2003 *Area:* 27.87 sq km
County or District: Nanaimo; *Population in 2011:* 3,601
Provincial Electoral District(s): Nanaimo-Parksville
Federal Electoral District(s): Nanaimo-Alberni
Next Election: Nov. 15, 2014 (3 year terms)
Jack de Jong, Mayor
Twyla Graff, Chief Administrative Officer
twyla@lantzville.ca

Lillooet

P.O. Box 610
615 Main St.
Lillooet, BC V0K 1V0
Tel: 250-256-4289; *Fax:* 250-256-4288
cityhall@lillooetbc.com
www.lillooetbc.com
Municipal Type: District
Incorporated: Dec. 31, 1946 *Area:* 27.83 sq km
County or District: Squamish-Lillooet; *Population in 2011:* 2,322
Provincial Electoral District(s): Yale-Lillooet
Federal Electoral District(s): Chilliwack-Fraser Canyon
Next Election: Nov. 15, 2014 (3 year terms)
Ted Anchor, Mayor
Grant Loyer, Chief Administrative Officer
gloyer@lillooetbc.com

Lions Bay

P.O. Box 141
400 Centre Rd.
Lions Bay, BC V0N 2E0
Tel: 604-921-9333; *Fax:* 604-921-6643
reception@lionsbay.ca
www.lionsbay.ca
Municipal Type: Village
Incorporated: Dec. 17, 1970 *Area:* 2.55 sq km
County or District: Metro Vancouver; *Population in 2011:* 1,318
Provincial Electoral District(s): West Vancouver-Garibaldi
Federal Electoral District(s): West Vancouver-Sunshine Coast-Sea to Sky Country
Next Election: Nov. 15, 2014 (3 year terms)
Brenda Broughton, Mayor
mayor.broughton@lionsbay.ca
Rory Mandryk, Village Manager
admin@lionsbay.ca

Logan Lake

P.O. Box 190
1 Opal Dr.
Logan Lake, BC V0K 1W0
Tel: 250-523-6225; *Fax:* 250-523-6678
districtofloganlake@loganlake.ca
www.loganlake.ca
Municipal Type: District
Incorporated: Nov. 10, 1970 *Area:* 325.4 sq km
County or District: Thompson-Nicola; *Population in 2011:* 2,073
Provincial Electoral District(s): Yale-Lillooet
Federal Electoral District(s): Okanagan-Coquihalla
Next Election: Nov. 15, 2014 (3 year terms)
Marlon Dosch, Mayor
mdosch@loganlake.ca
Wayne Vollrath, Chief Administrative Officer
wvollrath@loganlake.ca

Lumby

P.O. Box 430
1775 Glencaird St.
Lumby, BC V0E 2G0
Tel: 250-547-2171; *Fax:* 250-547-6894
info@lumby.ca
www.lumby.ca
Municipal Type: Village
Incorporated: Dec. 20, 1955 *Area:* 5.27 sq km
County or District: North Okanagan; *Population in 2011:* 1,731
Provincial Electoral District(s): Okanagan-Vernon

Federal Electoral District(s): Okanagan-Shuswap
Next Election: Nov. 15, 2014 (3 year terms)
Kevin Acton, Mayor
mayor@lumby.ca
Frank Kosa, Village Administrator
fkosa@lumby.ca

Lytton
P.O. Box 100
380 Main St.
Lytton, BC V0K 1Z0
Tel: 250-455-2355; *Fax:* 250-455-2142
hotspot@lytton.ca
www.lytton.ca
Municipal Type: Village
Incorporated: May 3, 1945 *Area:* 6.71 sq km
County or District: Thompson-Nicola; *Population in 2011:* 228
Provincial Electoral District(s): Yale-Lillooet
Federal Electoral District(s): Chilliwack-Fraser Canyon
Next Election: Nov. 15, 2014 (3 year terms)
Jessoa Lightfoot, Mayor
jlightfoot@lytton.ca
Ian Hay, Administrator
ian@lytton.ca

Mackenzie
P.O. Box 340
1 Mackenzie Blvd.
Mackenzie, BC V0J 2C0
Tel: 250-997-3221; *Fax:* 250-997-5186
info@district.mackenzie.bc.ca
www.district.mackenzie.bc.ca
Municipal Type: District
Incorporated: May 19, 1966 *Area:* 159.09 sq km
County or District: Fraser-Fort George; *Population in 2011:* 3,507
Provincial Electoral District(s): Prince George North
Federal Electoral District(s): Prince George-Peace River
Next Election: Nov. 15, 2014 (3 year terms)
Stephanie Killam, Mayor
Mark Fercho, Chief Administrative Officer
mark@district.mackenzie.bc.ca

Maple Ridge
11995 Haney Pl.
Maple Ridge, BC V2X 6A9
Tel: 604-463-5221; *Fax:* 604-467-7329
enquiries@mapleridge.ca
www.mapleridge.ca
Municipal Type: District
Incorporated: Sept. 12, 1874 *Area:* 265.79 sq km
County or District: Metro Vancouver; *Population in 2011:* 76,052
Provincial Electoral District(s): Maple Ridge-Pitt Meadows; Maple Ridge-Mission
Federal Electoral District(s): Pitt Meadows-Maple Ridge-Mission
Next Election: Nov. 15, 2014 (3 year terms)
Ernie Daykin, Mayor
edaykin@mapleridge.ca
Cheryl Ashlie, Councillor
cashlie@mapleridge.ca
Judy Dueck, Councillor
jdueck@mapleridge.ca
Al Hogarth, Councillor
ahogarth@mapleridge.ca
Linda King, Councillor
lking@mapleridge.ca
Mike Morden, Councillor
mmorden@mapleridge.ca
Craig Speirs, Councillor
cspeirs@mapleridge.ca
Jim Rule, Chief Administrative Officer
604-463-5221
jrule@mapleridge.ca
John Bastaja, Chief Information Officer
604-467-7479
jbastaja@mapleridge.ca
Paul Gill, General Manager, Corporate & Financial Services
pgill@mapleridge.ca
Frank Quinn, General Manager, Public Works & Development Services
fquinn@mapleridge.ca
Kelly Swift, General Manager, Community Development, Parks & Recreation Services
kswift@mapleridge.ca
David Boag, Director, Parks & Facilities
604-467-7344
dboag@mapleridge.ca
Russ Carmichael, Director, Engineering Operations
604-467-7363
Liz Holitzki, Director, Licences, Permits & Bylaws
604-467-7370
lholitzki@mapleridge.ca
Wendy McCormick, Director, Recreation
604-467-7328
wmccormick@mapleridge.ca
Jane Pickering, Director, Planning
604-467-7471
jpickering@mapleridge.ca
Sue Wheeler, Director, Community Services
604-467-7308
swheeler@mapleridge.ca
Fred Armstrong, Manager, Corporate Communications
farmstrong@mapleridge.ca
Chuck Goddard, Manager, Development & Environmental Services
604-466-4336
cgoddard@mapleridge.org
Ceri Marlo, P.Eng., Manager, Legislative Services
604-467-7482
cmarlo@mapleridge.ca
Peter Grootendorst, Fire Chief
604-476-3056
pgrootendorst@mapleridge.ca
Dave Walsh, Superintendent, Police Services
604-463-6251

Masset
P.O. Box 68
Masset, BC V0T 1M0
Tel: 250-626-3995; *Fax:* 250-626-3968
vom@mhtv.ca
www.massetbc.com
Municipal Type: Village
Incorporated: May 11, 1961 *Area:* 19.45 sq km
County or District: Skeena-Queen Charlotte; *Population in 2011:* 884
Provincial Electoral District(s): North Coast
Federal Electoral District(s): Skeena-Bulkley Valley
Next Election: Nov. 15, 2014 (3 year terms)
Andrew Merilees, Mayor
Trevor Jarvis, Chief Administrative Officer

McBride
P.O. Box 519
100 Robson Centre
McBride, BC V0J 2E0
Tel: 250-569-2229; *Fax:* 250-569-3276
www.mcbride.ca
Municipal Type: Village
Incorporated: April 7, 1932 *Area:* 4.43 sq km
County or District: Fraser-Fort George; *Population in 2011:* 586
Provincial Electoral District(s): Prince George-Mount Robson
Federal Electoral District(s): Prince George-Peace River
Next Election: Nov. 15, 2014 (3 year terms)
Michael Frazier, Mayor
Eliana Clements, Chief Administrative Officer

Merritt
P.O. Box 189
2185 Voght St.
Merritt, BC V1K 1B8
Tel: 250-378-4224; *Fax:* 250-378-2600
info@merritt.ca
www.merritt.ca
Municipal Type: Town
Incorporated: April 1, 1911 *Area:* 24.94 sq km
County or District: Thompson-Nicola; *Population in 2011:* 6,998
Provincial Electoral District(s): Yale-Lillooet
Federal Electoral District(s): Okanagan-Coquihalla
Next Election: Nov. 15, 2014 (3 year terms)
Susan Roline, Mayor
mayorroline@merritt.ca
Matt Noble, Chief Administrative Officer/Clerk
mnoble@merritt.ca

Metchosin
4450 Happy Valley Rd.
Victoria, BC V9C 3Z3
Tel: 250-474-3167; *Fax:* 250-474-6298
info@metchosin.ca
www.metchosin.ca
Municipal Type: District
Incorporated: Dec. 3, 1984 *Area:* 71.32 sq km
County or District: Capital; *Population in 2011:* 4,803
Provincial Electoral District(s): Esquimalt-Metchosin
Federal Electoral District(s): Esquimalt-Juan de Fuca
Next Election: Nov. 15, 2014 (3 year terms)
John Ranns, Mayor
jranns@metchosin.ca
Rachel Parker, Clerk
rparker@metchosin.ca
Joe Martignago, Chief Administrative Officer
cao@metchosin.ca

Midway
P.O. Box 160
661 Eighth Ave.
Midway, BC V0H 1M0
Tel: 250-449-2222; *Fax:* 250-449-2258
midwaybc@shaw.ca
www.midwaybc.ca
Municipal Type: Village
Incorporated: May 25, 1967 *Area:* 12.16 sq km
County or District: Kootenay Boundary; *Population in 2011:* 674
Provincial Electoral District(s): West Kootenay-Boundary
Federal Electoral District(s): British Columbia Southern Interior
Next Election: Nov. 15, 2014 (3 year terms)
Randy Kappes, Mayor
Jim Madder, Administrator
jfmadder@shaw.ca

Mission
P.O. Box 20
8645 Stave Lake St.
Mission, BC V2V 4L9
Tel: 604-820-3700; *Fax:* 604-820-3715
info@mission.ca
www.mission.ca
Municipal Type: District
Incorporated: June 2, 1892 *Area:* 225.78 sq km
County or District: Fraser Valley; *Population in 2011:* 36,426
Provincial Electoral District(s): Maple Ridge-Mission
Federal Electoral District(s): Pitt Meadows-Maple Ridge-Mission
Next Election: Nov. 15, 2014 (3 year terms)
Ted Adlem, Mayor
Dave Hensman, Councillor
Jeff Jewel, Councillor
Tony Luck, Councillor
Jenny Stevens, Councillor
jennystevens@shaw.ca
Nelson Tilbury, Councillor
Glenn Robertson, Chief Administrative Officer
604-820-3704
grobertson@mission.ca
Kim Allan, Director, Forest Management
604-820-3764
kallan@mission.ca
Ken Bjorgaard, Director, Finance
kbjorgaard@mission.ca
Rick Bomhof, Director, Engineering & Public Works
604-820-3739
rbomhof@mission.ca
Sharon Fletcher, Director, Planning
604-820-3730
sfletcher@mission.ca
Ray Herman, Director, Parks, Recreation & Culture
604-820-5355
rherman@mission.ca
Beverly Endersby, Manager, Inspection Services
604-820-3732
bendersby@mission.ca
Michael Giesbrecht, Manager, Purchasing & Stores
604-820-3756
mgiesbrecht@mission.ca
Ian Fitzpatrick, Fire Chief
604-820-5390
ifitzpatrick@mission.ca

Montrose
P.O. Box 510
565 - 11th Ave.
Montrose, BC V0G 1P0
Tel: 250-367-7234; *Fax:* 250-367-7288
montvill@telus.net
www.montrose.ca
Municipal Type: Village
Incorporated: June 22, 1956 *Area:* 1.53 sq km
County or District: Kootenay Boundary; *Population in 2011:* 1,030
Provincial Electoral District(s): West Kootenay-Boundary
Federal Electoral District(s): British Columbia Southern Interior
Next Election: Nov. 15, 2014 (3 year terms)
Joe Danchuk, Mayor
Kevin Chartres, Chief Administrative Officer

Nakusp
P.O. Box 280
91 - 1st St. NW
Nakusp, BC V0G 1R0
Tel: 250-265-3689; *Fax:* 250-265-3788
info@nakusp.com
www.nakusp.com
Municipal Type: Village
Incorporated: Nov. 24, 1964 *Area:* 8 sq km
County or District: Central Kootenay; *Population in 2011:* 1,569

Provincial Electoral District(s): Nelson-Creston
Federal Electoral District(s): Kootenay-Columbia
Next Election: Nov. 15, 2014 (3 year terms)
Karen Hamling, Mayor
khamling@nakusp.com
Linda Tynan, Acting Chief Administrative Officer
ltynan@nakusp.com

Nelson
#101, 310 Ward St.
Nelson, BC V1L 5S4
Tel: 250-352-5511; *Fax:* 250-352-2131
www.nelson.ca
Municipal Type: Town
Incorporated: March 18, 1897 *Area:* 11.72 sq km
County or District: Central Kootenay; *Population in 2011:* 10,230
Provincial Electoral District(s): Nelson-Creston
Federal Electoral District(s): British Columbia Southern Interior
Next Election: Nov. 15, 2014 (3 year terms)
John Dooley, Mayor
250-354-9615
Kevin Cormack, City Manager
250-352-8203

New Denver
P.O. Box 40
115 Slocan Ave.
New Denver, BC V0G 1S0
Tel: 250-358-2316; *Fax:* 250-358-7251
office@newdenver.ca
www.newdenver.ca
Municipal Type: Village
Incorporated: Jan. 12, 1929 *Area:* 1.1 sq km
County or District: Central Kootenay; *Population in 2011:* 504
Provincial Electoral District(s): Nelson-Creston
Federal Electoral District(s): British Columbia Southern Interior
Next Election: Nov. 15, 2014 (3 year terms)
Ann Bunka, Mayor
Carol Gordon, Chief Administrative Officer

New Hazelton
P.O. Box 340
3026 Bowser St.
New Hazelton, BC V0J 2J0
Tel: 250-842-6571; *Fax:* 250-842-6077
info@newhazelton.ca
www.newhazelton.ca
Municipal Type: District
Incorporated: Dec. 15, 1980 *Area:* 25.64 sq km
County or District: Kitimat-Stikine; *Population in 2011:* 666
Provincial Electoral District(s): Bulkley Valley-Stikine
Federal Electoral District(s): Skeena-Bulkley Valley
Next Election: Nov. 15, 2014 (3 year terms)
Gail Lowry, Mayor
Donny van Dyk, Chief Administrative Officer
donny@newhazelton.ca

North Cowichan
P.O. Box 278
7030 Trans Canada Hwy.
Duncan, BC V9L 3X4
Tel: 250-746-3100; *Fax:* 250-746-3133
info@northcowichan.bc.ca
www.northcowichan.bc.ca
Municipal Type: District
Incorporated: June 18, 1873 *Area:* 193.66 sq km
County or District: Cowichan Valley; *Population in 2011:* 28,807
Provincial Electoral District(s): Cowichan-Ladysmith
Federal Electoral District(s): Nanaimo-Cowichan
Next Election: Nov. 15, 2014 (3 year terms)
Jon Lefebure, Mayor
council@northcowichan.bc.ca
Ruth Hartmann, Councillor
John Koury, Councillor
Barb Lines, Councillor
Kate Marsh, Councillor
Al Siebring, Councillor
Jennifer Woike, Councillor
Dave Devana, Chief Administrative Officer
Mark O. Ruttan, Deputy Chief Administrative Officer/Director
ruttan@northcowichan.bc.ca
Bruce L. Oliphant, Chief Building Inspector
oliphant@northcowichan.ca
Mark Frame, Director, Finance
frame@northcowichan.bc.ca
Scott Mack, Director, Planning & Development
John Mackay, Director, Engineering
Ernie Mansueti, Director, Parks & Recreation
mansueti@northcowichan.bc.ca

North Saanich
1620 Mills Rd.
North Saanich, BC V8L 5S9
Tel: 250-656-0781; *Fax:* 250-656-3155
admin@northsaanich.ca
www.northsaanich.ca
Municipal Type: District
Incorporated: Aug. 19, 1965 *Area:* 37.14 sq km
County or District: Capital; *Population in 2011:* 11,089
Provincial Electoral District(s): Saanich North & the Islands
Federal Electoral District(s): Saanich-Gulf Islands
Next Election: Nov. 15, 2014 (3 year terms)
Alice Finall, Mayor
250-656-6668
Dunstan Browne, Councillor
250-655-4811
Ted Daly, Councillor
Conny McBride, Councillor
Elsie McMurphy, Councillor
Craig Mearns, Councillor
250-656-1173
Celia Stock, Councillor
Rob Buchanan, Chief Administrative Officer
250-655-5452
rbuchan@northsaanich.ca
Curt Kingsley, Manager, Corporate Services
250-655-5453
ckingsley@northsaanich.ca
Mark Brodrick, Director, Planning & Community Services
250-655-5471
mbrodrick@northsaanich.ca
Patrick O'Reilly, Director, Infrastructure Services
250-655-5461
poreilly@northsaanich.ca
Patricia Roberts, Director, Financial Services
250-655-5495
proberts@northsaanich.ca
Gary Wilton, Director, Emergency Services
250-661-0223
gwilton@northsaanich.ca

North Vancouver
355 West Queens Rd.
North Vancouver, BC V7N 4N5
Tel: 604-990-2311
infoweb@dnv.org
www.dnv.org
Municipal Type: District Municipality
Incorporated: Aug. 10, 1891 *Area:* 160.67 sq km
County or District: Metro Vancouver; *Population in 2011:* 84,412
Provincial Electoral District(s): N. Vancouver-Lonsdale; N. Vancouver-Seymour; W. Vancouver-Capilano; W. Vancouver-Garibaldi
Federal Electoral District(s): North Vancouver; West Vancouver-Sunshine Coast-Sea to Sky Country
Next Election: Nov. 15, 2014 (3 year terms)
Richard Walton, Mayor
604-990-2208
rwalton@dnv.org; council@dnv.org
Roger Bassam, Councillor
rbassam@dnv.org
Robin Hicks, Councillor
rhicks@dnv.org
Mike Little, Councillor
mlittle@dnv.org
Doug Mackay-Dunn, Councillor
dmackay-dunn@dnv.org
Lisa Muri, Councillor
lmuri@dnv.org
Alan Nixon, Councillor
anixon@dnv.org
David Stuart, Chief Administrative Officer
604-990-2209
stuartd@dnv.org
Brian Bydwell, Director, Planning, Permits & Bylaws
604-990-2387
bydwellb@dnv.org
Nicole Deveaux, Director, Financial Services
604-990-2233
deveauxn@dnv.org
Jozsef Dioszeghy, P.Eng., Director, Environment, Parks & Engineering
604-990-3885
dioszeghyj@dnv.org
Ian Forsyth, Director, The Arts Office
604-980-3559
ian.forsyth@nvoca.ca
Gavin Joyce, Director, Corporate Services
604-990-2416
joyceg@dnv.org
Dorit Mason, Director, North Shore Emergency Management Office
604-983-7440
dmason@cnv.org
Heather Scoular, Director, Library Services
604-990-5800
scoularh@nvdpl.ca
Heather Turner, Director, Recreation
604-983-6306
turnerh@northvanrec.com
Allen Lynch, Manager, North Shore Recycling Program
604-984-9730
allen@nsrp.bc.ca
Doug Trussler, Fire Chief
604-990-3651
dtrussler@dnv.org
Tonia Enger, Superintendent, North Vancouver RCMP Detachment
604-985-1311
Brian O'Connor, Medical Health Officer

Health Department

Oak Bay
2167 Oak Bay Ave.
Victoria, BC V8R 1G2
Tel: 250-598-3311; *Fax:* 250-598-9108
obcouncil@oakbay.ca
www.oakbaybc.org
Municipal Type: District
Incorporated: July 2, 1906 *Area:* 10.38 sq km
County or District: Capital; *Population in 2011:* 18,015
Provincial Electoral District(s): Oak Bay-Gordon Head
Federal Electoral District(s): Victoria
Next Election: Nov. 15, 2014 (3 year terms)
Nils Jensen, Mayor
Pam Copley, Councillor
Cairine Green, Councillor
John Herbert, Councillor
Michelle Kirby, Councillor
Kevin Murdoch, Councillor
Tara Ney, Councillor
Loranne Hilton, Clerk
Mark Brennan, Administrator
Patricia A. Walker, Treasurer & Collector
Lorna Curtis, Director, Parks & Recreation
250-592-7275
Dave Marshall, Director, Engineering Services
Roy Thomassen, Director, Building & Planning
Janet Barclay, Manager, Recreation Program Services
Lorne Middleton, Manager, Parks Services
250-592-7275
Phil Barnett, Superintendent, Public Works
250-598-4501
Gerry Adam, Fire Chief
250-592-9121
Derek Egan, Interim Chief Constable
250-592-2424
Police Services

Oliver
P.O. Box 638
35016 - 97th St.
Oliver, BC V0H 1T0
Tel: 250-485-6200; *Fax:* 250-498-4466
admin@oliver.ca
www.oliver.ca
Municipal Type: Town
Incorporated: Dec. 31, 1945 *Area:* 4.95 sq km
County or District: Okanagan-Similkameen; *Population in 2011:* 4,824
Provincial Electoral District(s): Penticton-Okanagan Valley
Federal Electoral District(s): British Columbia Southern Interior
Next Election: Nov. 15, 2014 (3 year terms)
Ronald Hovanes, Mayor
Tom Szalay, Municipal Manager
tszalay@oliver.ca

Osoyoos
P.O. Box 3010
8707 Main St.
Osoyoos, BC V0H 1V0
Tel: 250-495-6515; *Fax:* 250-495-2400
tosoyoos@osoyoos.ca
www.osoyoos.ca
Municipal Type: Town
Incorporated: Jan. 14, 1946 *Area:* 8.76 sq km
County or District: Okanagan-Similkameen; *Population in 2011:* 4,845
Provincial Electoral District(s): Penticton-Okanagan Valley
Federal Electoral District(s): British Columbia Southern Interior
Next Election: Nov. 15, 2014 (3 year terms)

Stu Wells, Mayor
swells@osoyoos.ca
Barry Romanko, Chief Administrative Officer
bromanko@osoyoos.ca

Peachland
5806 Beach Ave.
Peachland, BC V0H 1X7
Tel: 250-767-2647; *Fax:* 250-767-3433
ppalmer@peachland.ca
www.peachland.ca
Municipal Type: District
Incorporated: Jan. 1, 1909 *Area:* 15.98 sq km
County or District: Central Okanagan; *Population in 2011:* 5,200
Provincial Electoral District(s): Okanagan-Westside
Federal Electoral District(s): Okanagan-Coquihalla
Next Election: Nov. 15, 2014 (3 year terms)
Keith Fielding, Mayor
250-767-2770
mayor@peachland.ca
Elsie Lemke, Chief Administrative Officer
elemke@peachland.ca

Pemberton
P.O. Box 100
7400 Prospect St.
Pemberton, BC V0N 2L0
Tel: 604-894-6135; *Fax:* 604-894-6136
www.pemberton.ca
Municipal Type: Village
Incorporated: July 20, 1956 *Area:* 4.45 sq km
County or District: Squamish-Lillooet; *Population in 2011:* 2,369
Provincial Electoral District(s): West Vancouver-Garibaldi
Federal Electoral District(s): Chilliwack-Fraser Canyon
Next Election: Nov. 15, 2014 (3 year terms)
Jordan Sturdy, Mayor
jsturdy@pemberton.ca
Daniel Sailland, Chief Administrative Officer
dsailland@pemberton.ca

Port Alice
P.O. Box 130
1061 Marine Dr.
Port Alice, BC V0N 2N0
Tel: 250-284-3391; *Fax:* 250-284-3416
info@portalice.ca
www.portalice.ca
Municipal Type: Village
Incorporated: June 16, 1965 *Area:* 7.65 sq km
County or District: Mount Waddington; *Population in 2011:* 805
Provincial Electoral District(s): North Island
Federal Electoral District(s): Vancouver Island North
Next Election: Nov. 15, 2014 (3 year terms)
Jan Allen, Mayor
Gail Lind, Chief Administrative Officer

Port Clements
P.O. Box 198
36 Cedar Ave. West
Port Clements, BC V0T 1R0
Tel: 250-557-4295; *Fax:* 250-557-4568
office@portclements.com
www.portclements.com
Municipal Type: Village
Incorporated: Dec. 31, 1975 *Area:* 13.59 sq km
County or District: Skeena-Queen Charlotte; *Population in 2011:* 378
Provincial Electoral District(s): North Coast
Federal Electoral District(s): Skeena-Bulkley Valley
Next Election: Nov. 15, 2014 (3 year terms)
Wally Cheer, Mayor
Heather Nelson-Smith, Clerk/Treasurer
heather@portclements.com

Port Edward
P.O. Box 1100
770 Pacific Ave.
Port Edward, BC V0V 1G0
Tel: 250-628-3667; *Fax:* 250-628-9225
info@portedward.ca
www.portedward.ca
Municipal Type: District
Incorporated: June 29, 1966 *Area:* 168.12 sq km
County or District: Skeena-Queen Charlotte; *Population in 2011:* 544
Provincial Electoral District(s): North Coast
Federal Electoral District(s): Skeena-Bulkley Valley
Next Election: Nov. 15, 2014 (3 year terms)
Dave MacDonald, Mayor
Ron Bedard, Chief Administrative Officer

Port Hardy
P.O. Box 68
7360 Columbia St.
Port Hardy, BC V0N 2P0
Tel: 250-949-6665; *Fax:* 250-949-7433
general@porthardy.ca
www.porthardy.ca
Municipal Type: District
Incorporated: May 5, 1966 *Area:* 40.81 sq km
County or District: Mount Waddington; *Population in 2011:* 4,008
Provincial Electoral District(s): North Island
Federal Electoral District(s): Vancouver Island North
Next Election: Nov. 15, 2014 (3 year terms)
Bev Parnham, Mayor
mayor@porthardy.ca
Rick Davidge, Chief Administrative Officer
rickd@porthardy.ca
Deb Clipperton, Director, Financial Services
dclipperton@porthardy.ca
Gloria LeGal, Director, Corporate Services
gloria@porthardy.ca

Port McNeill
P.O. Box 728
1775 Grenville Pl.
Port McNeill, BC V0N 2R0
Tel: 250-956-3111; *Fax:* 250-956-4300
reception.portmcneill@telus.net
www.town.portmcneill.bc.ca
Municipal Type: Town
Incorporated: Feb. 18, 1966 *Area:* 7.74 sq km
County or District: Mount Waddington; *Population in 2011:* 2,505
Provincial Electoral District(s): North Island
Federal Electoral District(s): Vancouver Island North
Next Election: Nov. 15, 2014 (3 year terms)
Gerry Furney, Mayor
mayor.portmcneill@telus.net
Albert Sweet, BA CA, Administrator/Treasurer/Collector
pmfinance@telus.net

Pouce Coupé
P.O. Box 190
5011 - 49 Ave.
Pouce Coupe, BC V0C 2C0
Tel: 250-786-5794; *Fax:* 250-786-5257
admin@poucecoupe.ca
www.poucecoupe.ca
Municipal Type: Village
Incorporated: Jan. 5, 1932 *Area:* 2.06 sq km
County or District: Peace River; *Population in 2011:* 738
Provincial Electoral District(s): Peace River South
Federal Electoral District(s): Prince George-Peace River
Next Election: Nov. 15, 2014 (3 year terms)
Larry Fynn, Mayor
mayor@poucecoupe.ca
Karen P. Mellor, Chief Administrative Officer
cao@poucecoupe.ca

Princeton
P.O. Box 670
169 Bridge St.
Princeton, BC V0X 1W0
Tel: 250-295-3135; *Fax:* 250-295-3477
admin@princeton.ca
www.princeton.ca
Municipal Type: Town
Incorporated: Sept. 11, 1951 *Area:* 10.25 sq km
County or District: Okanagan-Similkameen; *Population in 2011:* 2,724
Provincial Electoral District(s): Yale-Lillooet
Federal Electoral District(s): British Columbia Southern Interior
Next Election: Nov. 15, 2014 (3 year terms)
Fred Thomas, Mayor
Patrick Robins, Chief Administrative Officer

Qualicum Beach
P.O. Box 130
#201, 660 Primrose St.
Qualicum Beach, BC V9K 1S7
Tel: 250-752-6921; *Fax:* 250-752-1243
qbtown@qualicumbeach.com
www.qualicumbeach.com
Municipal Type: Town
Incorporated: May 5, 1942 *Area:* 18 sq km
County or District: Nanaimo; *Population in 2011:* 8,687
Provincial Electoral District(s): Alberni-Qualicum
Federal Electoral District(s): Nanaimo-Alberni
Next Election: Nov. 15, 2014 (3 year terms)
Teunis Westbroek, Mayor
mayor@qualicumbeach.com
Mark D. Brown, Chief Administrative Officer
markb@qualicumbeach.com

Queen Charlotte
P.O. Box 580
903A Oceanview Dr.
Queen Charlotte, BC V0T 1S0
Tel: 250-559-4765; *Fax:* 250-559-4742
office@queencharlotte.ca
www.queencharlotte.ca
Municipal Type: Village
Incorporated: Dec. 7, 2005 *Area:* 37.28 sq km
County or District: Skeena-Queen Charlotte; *Population in 2011:* 944
Provincial Electoral District(s): North Coast
Federal Electoral District(s): Skeena-Bulkley Valley
Next Election: Nov. 15, 2014 (3 year terms)
Carol Kulesha, Mayor
250-559-4634
Bill Beamish, Chief Administrative Officer
250-559-4765

Quesnel
410 Kinchant St.
Quesnel, BC V2J 7J5
Tel: 250-992-2111; *Fax:* 250-992-2206
cityhall@quesnel.ca
www.quesnel.ca
Municipal Type: Town
Incorporated: March 21, 1928 *Area:* 35.34 sq km
County or District: Cariboo; *Population in 2011:* 10,007
Provincial Electoral District(s): Cariboo North
Federal Electoral District(s): Cariboo-Prince George
Next Election: Nov. 15, 2014 (3 year terms)
Mary Sjostrom, Mayor
msjostrom@quesnel.ca
John Brisco, Councillor
Michael Cave, Councillor
mikecave@shaw.ca
Ed Coleman, Councillor
Scott Elliot, Councillor
Laurey Roodenburg, Councillor
l_roodenburg@yahoo.ca
Sushil Thepar, Councillor
thaparquesnel@gmail.com
John Stecyk, City Manager
jstecyk@quesnel.ca
Jeff Norburn, General Manager, Community Services
jnorburn@quesnel.ca
Kari Bolton, Director, Finance
kbolton@quesnel.ca
Ken Coombs, Acting Director, Public Works & Engineering
kcoombs@quesnel.ca
Tanya Turner, Planner
tturner@quesnel.ca
Chris Coben, Superintendent, Utilities
ccoben@quesnel.ca
Alec Darragh, Supervisor, Parks & Solid Waste
adarragh@quesnel.ca
Sylvian Gauthier, Fire Department
sgauthier@quesnel.ca

Radium Hot Springs
P.O. Box 340
Radium Hot Springs, BC V0A 1M0
Tel: 250-347-6455; *Fax:* 250-347-9068
www.radiumhotsprings.ca
Municipal Type: Village
Incorporated: Dec. 10, 1990 *Area:* 6.31 sq km
County or District: East Kootenay; *Population in 2011:* 777
Provincial Electoral District(s): Columbia River-Revelstoke
Federal Electoral District(s): Kootenay Columbia
Next Election: Nov. 15, 2014 (3 year terms)
Dee Conklin, Mayor
mayor@radiumhotsprings.ca
Mark Read, Chief Administrative Officer/Clerk/Approving Officer
mark.read@radiumhotsprings.ca

Revelstoke
P.O. Box 170
216 Mackenzie Ave.
Revelstoke, BC V0E 2S0
Tel: 250-837-2161; *Fax:* 250-837-4930
www.cityofrevelstoke.com
Municipal Type: Town
Incorporated: March 1, 1899 *Area:* 31.9 sq km
County or District: Columbia-Shuswap; *Population in 2011:* 7,139
Provincial Electoral District(s): Columbia River-Revelstoke
Federal Electoral District(s): Kootenay-Columbia
Next Election: Nov. 15, 2014 (3 year terms)
David Raven, Mayor
david.raven@revelstoke.ca

Tim Palmer, Chief Adminsitrative Officer/Director, Corporate Administration

Rossland
P.O. Box 1179
1899 Columbia Ave.
Rossland, BC V0G 1Y0
Tel: 250-362-7396; *Fax:* 250-362-5451
cityhall@rossland.ca
www.rossland.ca
Municipal Type: Town
Incorporated: March 18, 1897 *Area:* 57.97 sq km
County or District: Kootenay Boundary; *Population in 2011:* 3,556
Provincial Electoral District(s): West Kootenay-Boundary
Federal Electoral District(s): British Columbia Southern Interior
Next Election: Nov. 15, 2014 (3 year terms)
Greg Granstrom, Mayor
250-362-5527
Victor Kumar, Chief Administrative Officer
250-362-2324

Saanich
770 Vernon Ave.
Victoria, BC V8X 2W7
Tel: 250-475-1775
www.saanich.ca
Municipal Type: District Municipality
Incorporated: Dec. 12, 1950 *Area:* 103.44 sq km
County or District: Capital; *Population in 2011:* 109,752
Provincial Electoral District(s): Oak Bay-Gordon Head; Saanich N. & the Islands; Saanich S.
Federal Electoral District(s): Esquimalt-Juan de Fuca; Saanich-Gulf Islands; Victoria
Next Election: Nov. 15, 2014 (3 year terms)
Frank Leonard, Mayor
250-475-5510
mayor@saanich.ca; council@saanich.ca
Susan Brice, Councillor
Judy Brownoff, Councillor
jbrownof@telus.net
Vic Derman, Councillor
Paul Gerrard, Councillor
Dean Murdock, Councillor
dean.murdock@telus.net
Vicki Sanders, Councillor
vicki_sanders@telus.net
Nichola Wade, Councillor
Leif Wergeland, Councillor
wergeland@shaw.ca
Tim Wood, Administrator
250-475-5555, Fax: 250-475-5440
tim.wood@saanich.ca
Bonnie Cole, Director, Corporate Services
bonnie.cole@saanich.ca
Colin Doyle, Director, Engineering
250-475-5575, Fax: 250-475-5450
colin.doyle@saanich.ca
Doug Henderson, Director, Parks & Recreation
250-475-5421, Fax: 250-475-5411
doug.henderson@saanich.ca
Sharon Hvozdanski, Director, Planning
250-475-5470, Fax: 250-475-5430
sharon.hvozdanski@saanich.ca
Carrie M. MacPhee, Director, Legislative Services
carrie.macphee@saanich.ca
Paul Murray, Director, Finance
250-475-5521, Fax: 250-475-5429
paul.murray@saanich.ca
Donavon (Von) Bishop, Manager, Development & Municipal Facilities
von.bishop@saanich.ca
Dwayne Halldorson, Manager, Underground Services
250-475-5574, Fax: 250-475-5450
dwayne.halldorson@saanich.ca
Jim Hemstock, Manager, Transportation
250-475-5464, Fax: 250-475-5450
jim.hemstock@saanich.ca
Mike Ippen, Manager, Public Works
250-475-5494, Fax: 250-475-5487
mike.ippen@saanich.ca
Alan Keiser, Manager, Water Works
250-475-5494, Fax: 250-475-5487
alan.keiser@saanich.ca
Quenton Lehmann, Manager, Recreation
250-475-5452, Fax: 250-475-5411
quenton.lehmann@saanich.ca
Cory Manton, Manager, Forestry, Horticulture & Natural Areas
250-475-5488
cory.manton@saanich.ca
Dave McAra, Manager, Solid Waste Services
250-475-5432, Fax: 250-475-5590
david.mcara@saanich.ca
Adriane Pollard, Manager, Environmental Services
250-475-5494, Fax: 250-475-5430
adriane.pollard@saanich.ca
Anne Topp, Manager, Community Planning
250-475-5494, Fax: 250-457-5430
anne.topp@saanich.ca
Michael Burgess, Fire Chief
Mike Chadwick, Chief Constable
250-475-4321, Fax: 250-475-6138
community@saanichpolice.ca

Salmo
P.O. Box 1000
423 Davies Ave.
Salmo, BC V0G 1Z0
Tel: 250-357-9433; *Fax:* 250-357-9633
salvil@telus.net
salmo.ca
Municipal Type: Village
Incorporated: Oct. 30, 1946 *Area:* 2.38 sq km
County or District: Central Kootenay; *Population in 2011:* 1,139
Provincial Electoral District(s): Nelson-Creston
Federal Electoral District(s): British Columbia Southern Interior
Next Election: Nov. 15, 2014 (3 year terms)
Ann Henderson, Mayor
Scott Sommerville, Chief Administrative Officer

Sayward
P.O. Box 29
601 Kelsey Way
Sayward, BC V0P 1R0
Tel: 250-282-5512; *Fax:* 250-282-5511
www.sayward.ca
Municipal Type: Village
Incorporated: June 27, 1968 *Area:* 4.72 sq km
County or District: Strathcona; *Population in 2011:* 317
Provincial Electoral District(s): North Island
Federal Electoral District(s): Vancouver Island North
Next Election: Nov. 15, 2014 (3 year terms)
John MacDonald, Mayor
westie@saywardvalley.net
Colum McCready, Chief Administrative Officer/Chief Financial Officer
cao@saywardvalley.net

Sechelt
P.O. Box 129
5797 Cowrie St., 2nd Fl.
Sechelt, BC V0N 3A0
Tel: 604-885-1986; *Fax:* 604-885-7591
info@sechelt.ca
www.sechelt.ca
Municipal Type: District Municipality
Incorporated: Feb. 15, 1956 *Area:* 39.71 sq km
County or District: Sunshine Coast; *Population in 2011:* 9,291
Provincial Electoral District(s): Powell River-Sunshine Coast
Federal Electoral District(s): West Vancouver-Sunshine Coast-Sea to Sky Country
Next Election: Nov. 15, 2014 (3 year terms)
Darren Inkster, Mayor
inkster@sechelt.ca
Doug Hockley, Councillor
Tom Lamb, Councillor
Alice Lutes, Councillor
lutes@sechelt.ca
Chris Moore, Councillor
Fred Taylor, Councillor
taylor@sechelt.ca
Darnelda Siegers, Councillor
Rob Brenner, Chief Administrative Officer
rbremner@sechelt.ca
Mike Shanks, Councillor

Sicamous
P.O. Box 219
446 Main St.
Sicamous, BC V0E 2V0
Tel: 250-836-2477; *Fax:* 250-836-4314
cityhall@sicamous.ca
www.sicamous.ca
Municipal Type: District
Incorporated: Dec. 4, 1989 *Area:* 14.68 sq km
County or District: Columbia-Shuswap; *Population in 2011:* 2,441
Provincial Electoral District(s): Shuswap
Federal Electoral District(s): Okanagan-Shuswap
Next Election: Nov. 15, 2014 (3 year terms)
Darrell Trouton, Mayor
mayor@sicamous.ca
Alan Harris, Chief Administrative Officer
aharris@sicamous.ca

Silverton
P.O. Box 14
421 Lake Ave.
Silverton, BC V0G 2B0
Tel: 250-358-2472; *Fax:* 250-358-2321
administration@silverton.ca
www.silverton.ca
Municipal Type: Village
Incorporated: May 6, 1930 *Area:* 0.44 sq km
County or District: Central Kootenay; *Population in 2011:* 195
Provincial Electoral District(s): Nelson-Creston
Federal Electoral District(s): British Columbia Southern Interior
Next Election: Nov. 15, 2014 (3 year terms)
Kathy Provan, Mayor
mayor@silverton.ca
Elaine Rogers, Acting Chief Administrative Officer
cfo@silverton.ca

Slocan
P.O. Box 50
503 Slocan Ave.
Slocan, BC V0G 2C0
Tel: 250-355-2277; *Fax:* 250-355-2666
info@villageofslocan.ca
www.slocancity.com
Other Information: Toll Free Phone: 1-866-355-2023
Municipal Type: Village
Incorporated: June 1, 1901 *Area:* 0.75 sq km
County or District: Central Kootenay; *Population in 2011:* 296
Provincial Electoral District(s): Nelson-Creston
Federal Electoral District(s): British Columbia Southern Interior
Next Election: Nov. 15, 2014 (3 year terms)
Madeline Perriere, Mayor
Jack Richardson, Chief Administrative Officer

Smithers
P.O. Box 879
1027 Aldous St.
Smithers, BC V0J 2N0
Tel: 250-847-1600; *Fax:* 250-847-1601
general@smithers.ca
www.smithers.ca
Municipal Type: Town
Incorporated: Oct. 6, 1921 *Area:* 15.69 sq km
County or District: Bulkley-Nechako; *Population in 2011:* 5,404
Provincial Electoral District(s): Bulkley Valley-Stikine
Federal Electoral District(s): Skeena-Bulkley Valley
Next Election: Nov. 15, 2014 (3 year terms)
Taylor Bachrach, Mayor
Deborah Sargent, Chief Administrative Officer

Sooke
2205 Otter Point Rd.
Sooke, BC V9Z 1J2
Tel: 250-642-1634; *Fax:* 250-642-0541
info@sooke.ca
www.sooke.ca
Municipal Type: District
Incorporated: Dec. 7, 1999 *Area:* 50.01 sq km
County or District: Capital; *Population in 2011:* 11,435
Provincial Electoral District(s): Malahat-Juan de Fuca
Federal Electoral District(s): Esquimalt-Juan de Fuca
Next Election: Nov. 15, 2014 (3 year terms)
Wendal Milne, Mayor
Evan Parliament, Chief Administrative Officer
eparliament@sooke.ca

Spallumcheen
4144 Spallumcheen Way
Spallumcheen, BC V0E 1B6
Tel: 250-546-3013; *Fax:* 250-546-8878
mail@spallumcheentwp.bc.ca
www.spallumcheentwp.bc.ca
Municipal Type: Township
Area: 254.9 sq km
County or District: North Okanagan; *Population in 2011:* 5,055
Provincial Electoral District(s): Shuswap
Federal Electoral District(s): Okanagan-Shuswap
Next Election: Nov. 15, 2014 (3 year terms)
Janice Brown, Mayor
mayor@spallumcheentwp.bc.ca
Lynda Shykora, Chief Administrative Officer

Sparwood
P.O. Box 520
136 Spruce Ave.
Sparwood, BC V0B 2G0
Tel: 250-425-6271; *Fax:* 250-425-7277
sparwood@sparwood.bc.ca
www.sparwood.bc.ca
Municipal Type: District
Incorporated: Oct. 6, 1964 *Area:* 177.71 sq km
County or District: East Kootenay; *Population in 2011:* 3,667
Provincial Electoral District(s): East Kootenay
Federal Electoral District(s): Kootenay-Columbia
Next Election: Nov. 15, 2014 (3 year terms)
Lois Halko, Acting Mayor
Terry Melcer, Chief Administrative Officer/Director, Corporate Services
tmelcer@sparwood.bc.ca

Squamish
P.O. Box 310
37955 Second Ave.
Squamish, BC V0N 3G0
Tel: 604-892-5217; *Fax:* 604-892-1083
www.squamish.ca
Municipal Type: District
Incorporated: May 18, 1948 *Area:* 106.11 sq km
County or District: Squamish-Lillooet; *Population in 2011:* 17,158
Provincial Electoral District(s): West Vancouver-Garibaldi
Federal Electoral District(s): West Vancouver-Sunshine Coast-Sea to Sky Country
Next Election: Nov. 15, 2014 (3 year terms)
Rob Kirkham, Mayor
Susan Chapelle, Councillor
Patricia Heintzman, Councillor
Ted C. Prior, Councillor
Doug Race, Councillor
drace@squamish.ca
Bryan Raiser, Councillor
Ron Sander, Councillor
Kevin Ramsay, Chief Administrative Officer
604-892-5217
kramsay@squamish.ca
Mark Caulton, Acting Chief Operator, Waterworks
mcaulton@squamish.ca
Wayne Chadwick, Acting Chief Operator, Wastewater Treatment Plant
wchadwick@squamish.ca
Robin Arthurs, General Manager, Corporate Services
rarthurs@squamish.ca
Cameron Chalmers, General Manager, Community Services
604-815-5000
cchalmers@squamish.ca
Linda Glenday, General Manager, Protective & Support Services
lglenday@squamish.ca .
Joanne Greenless, General Manager, Financial Services
jgreenlees@squamish.ca
Chris Bishop, Acting Manager, Planning & Building
cbishop@squamish.ca
Bob Smith, Manager, Operations
bsmith@squamish.ca
Jim Lang, Coordinator, Emergency Program
jlang@squamish.ca
Russ Inouye, Acting Fire Chief
rinouye@squamish.ca

Stewart
P.O. Box 460
705 Brightwell St.
Stewart, BC V0T 1W0
Tel: 250-636-2251; *Fax:* 250-636-2417
info@districtofstewart.com
www.districtofstewart.com
Municipal Type: District
Incorporated: May 16, 1930 *Area:* 571.5 sq km
County or District: Kitimat-Stikine; *Population in 2011:* 494
Provincial Electoral District(s): North Coast
Federal Electoral District(s): Skeena-Bulkley Valley
Next Election: Nov. 15, 2014 (3 year terms)
Galina Durant, Mayor
mayor@districtofstewart.com
Douglas Jay, Chief Administrative Officer

Summerland
P.O. Box 159
11321 Henry Ave.
Summerland, BC V0H 1Z0
Tel: 250-494-6451; *Fax:* 250-494-1415
info@summerland.ca
www.summerland.ca
Municipal Type: District
Incorporated: Dec. 21, 1906 *Area:* 73.88 sq km
County or District: Okanagan-Similkameen; *Population in 2011:* 11,280
Provincial Electoral District(s): Okanagan-Westside
Federal Electoral District(s): Okanagan-Coquihalla
Next Election: Nov. 15, 2014 (3 year terms)
Janice Perrino, Mayor
Lloyd Christopherson, Councillor
Robert Hacking, Councillor
Bruce Hallquist, Councillor
Orv Robson, Councillor
Martin Van Alphen, Councillor
Peter Waterman, Councillor
Don DeGagne, Chief Administrative Officer
ddegagne@summerland.ca
Don Darling, Director, Engineering & Public Works
ddarling@summerland.ca
Dale McDonald, Director, Parks & Recreation
dmacdonald@summerland.ca
Ian McIntosh, Director, Development Services
imcintosh@summerland.ca
Ken Ostraat, Director, Finance
kostraat@summerland.ca
Dave Hill, Superintendent, Public Works
dhill@summerland.ca
Scott Lee, Superintendent, Water Operations
slee@summerland.ca
Glenn Noble, Fire Chief
gnoble@summerland.ca

Sun Peaks
P.O. Box 1002
#106, 3270 Village Way
Sun Peaks, BC V0E 5N0
Tel: 250-578-2020; *Fax:* 250-578-2023
admin@sunpeaksmunicipality.ca
sunpeaksmunicipality.ca
Municipal Type: Mountain Resort Village
Incorporated: June 28, 2010 *Area:* 40.86 sq km
County or District: Thompson-Nicola; *Population in 2011:* 371
Provincial Electoral District(s): Kamloops-North Thompson
Federal Electoral District(s): Kamloops-Thompson-Cariboo
Next Election: Nov. 2014 (3 year terms)
Al Raine, Mayor
Bob Bremmer, Chief Administrative Officer

Tahsis
P.O. Box 219
Tahsis, BC V0P 1X0
Tel: 250-934-6344
reception@villageoftahsis.com
www.villageoftahsis.com
Municipal Type: Village
Incorporated: June 17, 1970 *Area:* 5.73 sq km
County or District: Strathcona; *Population in 2011:* 316
Provincial Electoral District(s): North Island
Federal Electoral District(s): Vancouver Island North
Next Election: Nov. 15, 2014 (3 year terms)
Judith Schooner, Mayor
mayor@villageoftahsis.com
Harmony Nielsen, Corporate Officer, Corporate Administration
hnielsen@villageoftahsis.com

Taylor
P.O. Box 300
10007 - 100A St.
Taylor, BC V0C 2K0
Tel: 250-789-3392; *Fax:* 250-789-3543
www.districtoftaylor.com
Municipal Type: District
Incorporated: Aug. 23, 1958 *Area:* 16.61 sq km
County or District: Peace River; *Population in 2011:* 1,373
Provincial Electoral District(s): Peace River South
Federal Electoral District(s): Prince George-Peace River
Next Election: Nov. 15, 2014 (3 year terms)
Fred S. Jarvis, Mayor
Charlette LcLeod, Administrator
cmcleod@districtoftaylor.com

Telkwa
P.O. Box 220
1704 Riverside St.
Telkwa, BC V0J 2X0
Tel: 250-846-5212; *Fax:* 250-846-9572
info@telkwa.com
www.telkwa.com
Municipal Type: Village
Incorporated: July 18, 1952 *Area:* 6.56 sq km
County or District: Bulkley-Nechako; *Population in 2011:* 1,350
Provincial Electoral District(s): Bulkley Valley-Stikine
Federal Electoral District(s): Skeena-Bulkley Valley
Next Election: Nov. 15, 2014 (3 year terms)
Carman Graf, Mayor
Kim Martinsen, Chief Administrative Officer

Tofino
P.O. Box 9
121 Third St.
Tofino, BC V0R 2Z0
Tel: 250-725-3229; *Fax:* 250-725-3775
office@tofino.ca
www.tofino.ca
Municipal Type: District
Incorporated: Feb. 5, 1932 *Area:* 10.54 sq km
County or District: Alberni-Clayoquot; *Population in 2011:* 1,876
Provincial Electoral District(s): Alberni-Qualicum
Federal Electoral District(s): Nanaimo-Alberni
Next Election: Nov. 15, 2014 (3 year terms)
Perry Schmunk, Mayor
Braden Smith, Chief Administrative Officer
bsmith@tofino.ca

Trail
1394 Pine Ave.
Trail, BC V1R 4E6
Tel: 250-364-1262; *Fax:* 250-364-0830
info@trail.ca
www.trail.ca
Municipal Type: Town
Incorporated: June 14, 1901 *Area:* 34.78 sq km
County or District: Kootenay Boundary; *Population in 2011:* 7,681
Provincial Electoral District(s): West Kootenay-Boundary
Federal Electoral District(s): British Columbia Southern Interior
Next Election: Nov. 15, 2014 (3 year terms)
Dieter Bogs, Mayor
dbogs@trail.ca
Dave Perehudoff, Chief Administrative Officer/Financial Administrator
dperehudoff@trail.ca

Tumbler Ridge
P.O. Box 100
305 Founders St.
Tumbler Ridge, BC V0C 2W0
Tel: 250-242-4242; *Fax:* 250-242-3993
tradmin@dtr.ca
www.tumblerridge.ca
Municipal Type: District
Incorporated: April 9, 1981 *Area:* 1,574.45 sq km
County or District: Peace River; *Population in 2011:* 2,710
Provincial Electoral District(s): Peace River South
Federal Electoral District(s): Prince George-Peace River
Next Election: Nov. 15, 2014 (3 year terms)
Darwin Wren, Mayor
Barry Elliot, Chief Administrative Officer
250-242-4242

Ucluelet
P.O. Box 999
200 Main St.
Ucluelet, BC V0R 3A0
Tel: 250-726-7744; *Fax:* 250-726-7335
info@ucluelet.ca
www.ucluelet.ca
Municipal Type: District
Incorporated: Feb. 26, 1952 *Area:* 6.55 sq km
County or District: Alberni-Clayoquot; *Population in 2011:* 1,627
Provincial Electoral District(s): Alberni-Qualicum
Federal Electoral District(s): Nanaimo-Alberni
Next Election: Nov. 15, 2014 (3 year terms)
Bill Irving, Mayor
Andrew Yeates, Chief Administrative officer

Valemount
P.O. Box 168
735 Cranberry Lake Rd.
Valemount, BC V0E 2Z0
Tel: 250-566-4435; *Fax:* 250-566-4249
office@valemount.ca
www.valemount.ca
Municipal Type: Village
Incorporated: Dec. 13, 1962 *Area:* 4.96 sq km
County or District: Fraser-Fort George; *Population in 2011:* 1,020
Provincial Electoral District(s): Prince George-Mount Robson
Federal Electoral District(s): Kamloops-Thompson-Cariboo
Next Election: Nov. 15, 2014 (3 year terms)
Andru McCracken, Mayor
mayor@valemount.ca
Tom Dall, Chief Administrative Officer
cao@valemount.ca

Vanderhoof
P.O. Box 900
160 Connaught St.
Vanderhoof, BC V0J 3A0
Tel: 250-567-4711; *Fax:* 250-567-9169
info@district.vanderhoof.ca
www.vanderhoof.ca/district.html
Municipal Type: District
Incorporated: Jan. 22, 1926 *Area:* 54.85 sq km
County or District: Bulkley-Nechako; *Population in 2011:* 4,480
Provincial Electoral District(s): Prince George-Omineca
Federal Electoral District(s): Cariboo-Prince George
Next Election: Nov. 15, 2014 (3 year terms)
Gerry Thiessen, Mayor
mayor@district.vanderhoof.ca
Joe Ukryn, Chief Administrative Officer
cao@district.vanderhoof.ca

View Royal
45 View Royal Ave.
Victoria, BC V9B 1A6
Tel: 250-479-6800; *Fax:* 250-727-9551
www.viewroyal.ca
Municipal Type: Town
Incorporated: Dec. 5, 1988 *Area:* 14.48 sq km
County or District: Capital; *Population in 2011:* 9,381
Provincial Electoral District(s): Esquimalt-Metchosin
Federal Electoral District(s): Esquimalt-Juan de Fuca
Next Election: Nov. 15, 2014 (3 year terms)
Graham Hill, Mayor
mayorandcouncil@town.viewroyal.bc.ca
K. Anema, Chief Administrative Officer

Warfield
555 Schofield Hwy.
Trail, BC V1R 2G7
Tel: 250-368-8202; *Fax:* 250-368-9354
www.warfield.ca
Municipal Type: Village
Incorporated: Dec. 8, 1952 *Area:* 1.9 sq km
County or District: Kootenay Boundary; *Population in 2011:* 1,700
Provincial Electoral District(s): West Kootenay-Boundary
Federal Electoral District(s): British Columbia Southern Interior
Next Election: Nov. 15, 2014 (3 year terms)
Bert Crockett, Mayor
Vince Morelli, CAO/Clerk/Treasurer

Wells
P.O. Box 219
Wells, BC V0K 2R0
Tel: 250-994-3330; *Fax:* 250-994-3331
wells@goldcity.net
www.district.wells.bc.ca
Municipal Type: District
Incorporated: June 29, 1998 *Area:* 159.15 sq km
County or District: Cariboo; *Population in 2011:* 245
Provincial Electoral District(s): Cariboo North
Federal Electoral District(s): Cariboo-Prince George
Next Election: Nov. 15, 2014 (3 year terms)
Robin Sharpe, Mayor
Sundance Topham, Chief Administrative Officer
administrator@district.wells.bc.ca

West Kelowna
2760 Cameron Rd.
West Kelowna, BC V1Z 2T6
Tel: 778-797-1000; *Fax:* 778-797-1001
info@districtofwestkelowna.ca
www.districtofwestkelowna.ca
Municipal Type: District
Incorporated: Dec. 6, 2007 *Area:* 121.4 sq km
County or District: Central Okanagan; *Population in 2011:* 30,892
Provincial Electoral District(s): Westside-Kelowna
Federal Electoral District(s): Okanagan-Coquihalla
Next Election: Nov. 15, 2014 (3 year terms)
Doug Findlater, Mayor
250-801-3814
doug.findlater@districtofwestkelowna.ca
Rick de Jong, Councillor
David Knowles, Councillor
250-801-4479
david.knowles@districtofwestkelowna.ca
Gord Milsom, Councillor
250-801-4781
gord.milsom@districtofwestkelowna.ca
Duane Ophus, Councillor
250-801-5281
duane.ophus@districtofwestkelowna.ca
Bryden Winsby, Councillor
250-801-9557
bryden.winsby@districtofwestkelowna.ca
Carol Zanon, Councillor
250-801-5937
carol.zanon@districtofwestkelowna.ca
Tracey Batten, City Clerk
778-797-2250
Jason Johnson, Chief Administrative Officer
778-797-2210
Jim Zaffino, Chief Financial Officer
778-797-8860
Nancy Henderson, Director, Planning
778-797-8830
Marnie Manders, Director
Gary O'Rourke, Director, Engineering
778-797-8840
Dave Slobodan, Director, Building & Regulatory Services
Linda Langston-Vicioso, Manager, Human Resources
778-797-8890
Lorne Raymond, Manager, Finance
Dallas Johnson, Senior Planner
Wayne Schnitzler, Fire Chief
250-769-1640, Fax: 250-769-4800
Duncan Dixon, Commander, RCMP West Kelowna Detachment
250-768-2880

West Vancouver
750 - 17 St.
West Vancouver, BC V7V 3T3
Tel: 604-925-7000; *Fax:* 604-925-5999
info@westvancouver.ca
www.westvancouver.ca
Municipal Type: District
Incorporated: March 15, 1912 *Area:* 87.13 sq km
County or District: Metro Vancouver; *Population in 2011:* 42,694
Provincial Electoral District(s): N. Vancouver-Lonsdale; W. Vancouver-Capilano; W. Vancouver-Garibaldi
Federal Electoral District(s): West Vancouver-Sunshine Coast-Sea to Sky Country
Next Election: Nov. 15, 2014 (3 year terms)
Michael Smith, Mayor
Mary-Ann Booth, Councillor
Craig Cameron, Councillor
Nora Gambioli, Councillor
Michael Lewis, Councillor
mlewis@westvancouver.ca
Trish Panz, Councillor
tpanz@westvancouver.ca
Bill Soporovich, Councillor
bsoprovich@westvancouver.ca; wsbs@shaw.ca
Grant McRadu, Chief Administrative Officer
604-925-7008
gmcradu@westvancouver.ca
Jenny Benedict, Director, Library Services
604-925-7274
jbenedict@westvanlibrary.ca
Jessica Delaney, Director, Communications
604-925-4736
jdelaney@westvancouver.ca
Raymond Fung, Director, Engineering & Transportation
604-925-7159
rfung@westvancouver.ca
Nina Leemhuis, Director, Financial Services
604-925-7084
nleemhuis@westvancouver.ca
Anne Mooi, Director, Parks & Community Services
604-925-7235
amooi@westvancouver.ca
Bob Sokol, Director, Planning, Lands & Permits
604-925-7058
bsokol@westvancouver.ca
Allen Lynch, Manager, North Shore Recycling Program
604-984-9730, Fax: 604-984-3563
John McMahon, Acting Manager, Roads & Transportation
604-921-2197
jmcmahon@westvancouver.ca
Gareth Rowlands, Acting Manager, Transit
604-985-3500
growlands@westvancouver.ca
Jim Cook, Fire Chief
604-925-7370
jcook@westvancouver.ca

Whistler
4325 Blackcomb Way
Whistler, BC V0N 1B4
Tel: 604-932-5535; *Fax:* 604-935-8109
info@whistler.ca
www.whistler.ca
Municipal Type: Resort Municipality
Incorporated: Sept. 6, 1975 *Area:* 161.71 sq km
County or District: Squamish-Lillooet; *Population in 2011:* 9,824
Provincial Electoral District(s): West Vancouver-Garibaldi
Federal Electoral District(s): West Vancouver-Sunshine Coast-Sea to Sky Country
Next Election: Nov. 15, 2014 (3 year terms)
Nancy Wilhelm-Morden, Mayor
mayorsoffice@whistler.ca
Bill Barrett, Administrator
604-935-8105
bbarrett@whistler.ca

Zeballos
P.O. Box 127
Zeballos, BC V0P 2A0
Tel: 250-761-4229; *Fax:* 250-761-4331
adminzeb@recn.ca
www.zeballos.com
Municipal Type: Village
Incorporated: June 27, 1952 *Area:* 130 sq km
County or District: Strathcona; *Population in 2011:* 125
Provincial Electoral District(s): North Island
Federal Electoral District(s): Vancouver Island North
Next Election: Nov. 15, 2014 (3 year terms)
Edward (Ted) Lewis, Mayor
Holli Bellavie, Chief Administrative Officer

Indian Government District in British Columbia

Sechelt
P.O. Box 740
5555 Sunshine Coast Hwy.
Sechelt, BC V0N 3A0
Tel: 604-885-2273
rbaptiste@secheltnation.net
www.secheltnation.ca
Municipal Type: Metis Settlement
Incorporated: March 17, 1988 *Area:* 10.95 sq km
Population in 2011: 819
Next Election: Nov. 15, 2014 (3 year terms)
Garry Feschuk, Chief
604-885-2273

MANITOBA

All municipalities in Manitoba (except Winnipeg, which is governed by the City of Winnipeg Act) come under authority of the Manitoba Municipal Act.

In Manitoba there are no counties or regional governments; there are only urban and rural municipalities. Incorporation of a new municipality requires a population of at least 1,000 residents and a population density of at least 400 residents per square kilometre for an urban municipality and a population density of less than 400 residents per square kilometre for a rural municipality. Urban municipalities may be called cities, towns, villages or urban municipalities. The population requirement for a city is at least 7,500 residents.

All municipal elections are held every four years (October 2014, October 2018, etc.).

Reproduced with the permission of Natural ResourcesCanada, 2012

Manitoba

Major Municipalities in Manitoba

Brandon
410 - 9th St.
Brandon, MB R7A 6A2
Tel: 204-729-2186; *Fax:* 204-729-8244
cityclerk@brandon.ca
www.brandon.ca
Municipal Type: City
Incorporated: May 3, 1882 *Area:* 76.89 sq km
Population in 2011: 46,061
Provincial Electoral District(s): Brandon East; Brandon West
Federal Electoral District(s): Brandon-Souris
Next Election: Oct. 22, 2014 (4 year terms)
Conrad R. Arvisais, City Clerk
204-729-2207, Fax: 204-729-0975
c.arvisais@brandon.ca
Shari Decter Hirst, Mayor
mayor@brandon.ca
Jeff Fawcett, Councillor, Ward(s): 1. Assiniboine
Corey Roberts, Councillor, Ward(s): 2. Rosser
Murray Blight, Councillor, Ward(s): 3. Victoria
Jeff Harwood, Councillor, Ward(s): 4. University
James McCrae, Councillor, Ward(s): 5. Meadows
Garth Rice, Councillor, Ward(s): 6. South Centre
Shawn Berry, Councillor, Ward(s): 7. Linden Lanes
Stephen Montague, Councillor, Ward(s): 8. Richmond
Len Isleifson, Councillor, Ward(s): 9. Riverview
Jan Chaboyer, Councillor, Ward(s): 10. Green Acres
Grant McMillan, General Manager & City Treasurer, Corporate Services
204-729-2209
g.mcmillan@brandon.ca
Brian MacRae, City Manager
204-729-2204, Fax: 204-729-0975
b.macrae@brandon.ca
Brent Dane, Fire Chief
204-729-2404, Fax: 204-729-2153
b.dane@brandon.ca
Rick Bailey, Director, Public Works
r.bailey@brandon.ca
Brian Kayes, Director, Emergency Coordination
best@brandon.ca
Jeff Roziere, Director, Sanitation
204-573-6480
j.roziere@brandon.ca
Cathy Snelgrove, General Manager, Operations
204-729-2145, Fax: 204-729-2191
c.snelgrove@brandon.ca
Ted Snure, General Manager & City Engineer, Development Services
204-729-2214, Fax: 204-725-3235
t.snure@brandon.ca
Ian Christiansen, Manager, Engineering Services & Water Resources
i.christiansen@brandon.ca
Sandy Trudel, Officer, Economic Development
s.trudel@brandon.ca
Vivianne Lockerby, CPP, Supervisor, Purchasing
v.lockerby@brandon.ca

Flin Flon
20 - 1st Ave.
Flin Flon, MB R8A 0T7
Tel: 204-684-7511; *Fax:* 204-681-7530
mkolt@city.flinflon.mb.ca
www.cityofflinflon.com
Municipal Type: City
Incorporated: Jan. 1, 1933 *Area:* 13.88 sq km
Population in 2011: 5,592
Provincial Electoral District(s): Flin Flon
Federal Electoral District(s): Churchill
Next Election: Oct. 22, 2014 (4 year terms)
Note: Flin Flon straddles a provincial boundary. The population shown represents Manitoba (5,594) & Saskatchewan (242) figures.
George Fontaine, Mayor
Mark Kolt, Chief Administrative Officer

Portage La Prairie
97 Saskatchewan Ave. East
Portage la Prairie, MB R1N 0L8
Tel: 204-239-8337; *Fax:* 204-239-1532
swilliams@city-plap.com
www.city-plap.com
Municipal Type: City
Incorporated: Jan. 3, 1907 *Area:* 24.67 sq km
Population in 2011: 12,996
Provincial Electoral District(s): Portage la Prairie
Federal Electoral District(s): Portage-Lisgar
Next Election: Oct. 22, 2014 (4 year terms)
Earl Porter, Mayor
eporter@city-plap.com
Brent Budz, Councillor
bbudz@city-plap.com
Liz Driedger, Councillor
ldriedger@city-plap.com
Ryan Espey, Councillor
respey@city-plap.com
Irvine Ferris, Councillor
iferris@city-plap.com
Brent Froese, Councillor
bfroese@city-plap.com
Diane Stasiuk, Councillor
dstasiuk@city-plap.com
Dale Lyle, City Manager
Kelly Braden, Director, Operations
204-239-8350, Fax: 204-857-7275
kbraden@city-plap.com
Kathy McGregor, Administrative Assistant, Economic & Community Development
kmcgregor@city-plap.com
Phil Carpenter, Chief, Fire & Emergency
204-239-8340, Fax: 204-239-5154
sharont@city-plap.com
Doug Campbell, Manager, Water Treatment
204-239-8373
dcampbell@city-plap.com
Dave Green, Manager, Parks
204-239-8325
dgreen@city-plap.com
Ian Milne, Manager, Engineering
204-239-8349
imilne@city-plap.com
Brian Taylor, Manager, Public Works
204-239-8352
btaylor@city-plap.com
Wayne Wall, Manager, Water Pollution Control Facility
204-239-8359
wwall@city-plap.com

Selkirk
200 Eaton Ave.
Selkirk, MB R1A 0W6
Tel: 204-785-4900; *Fax:* 204-482-5448
cityofselkirk@cityofselkirk.com
www.cityofselkirk.com
Municipal Type: City
Incorporated: June 5, 1882 *Area:* 24.87 sq km
Population in 2011: 9,834
Provincial Electoral District(s): Selkirk
Federal Electoral District(s): Selkirk-Interlake
Next Election: Oct. 22, 2014 (4 year terms)
Larry Johannson, Mayor
Randy Borsa, Chief Administrative Officer

Steinbach
225 Reimer Ave.
Steinbach, MB R5G 2J1
Tel: 204-326-9877; *Fax:* 204-346-6235
info@steinbach.ca
www.steinbach.ca
Municipal Type: City
Incorporated: Jan. 3, 1946 *Area:* 25.57 sq km
Population in 2011: 13,524
Provincial Electoral District(s): Steinbach
Federal Electoral District(s): Provencher
Next Election: Oct. 22, 2014 (4 year terms)
Chris Goertzen, Mayor
John Fehr, Councillor
Earl Funk, Councillor
Cari Penner, Councillor
Susan Penner, Councillor
Jac Siemens, Councillor
Michael Zwaagstra, Councillor
Jack Kehler, Chief Administrative Officer

Thompson
226 Mystery Lake Rd.
Thompson, MB R8N 1S6
Tel: 204-677-7910; *Fax:* 204-677-7981
rpatrick@city.thompson.mb.ca
www.thompson.ca
Municipal Type: City
Incorporated: Jan. 5, 1970 *Area:* 17.18 sq km
Population in 2011: 12,829
Provincial Electoral District(s): Thompson
Federal Electoral District(s): Churchill
Next Election: Oct. 22, 2014 (4 year terms)
Tim Johnston, Mayor
204-677-7920, Fax: 204-677-7920
johnston@thompson.ca
Brad Evenson, Councillor
Erin Stewart, Councillor
Stella Locker, Councillor
Charlene Lafreniere, Councillor
Judy Kolada, Councillor
Dennis Fenske, Councillor
Penny Byer, Councillor
Luke Robinson, Councillor
Eric Stewart, Councillor
Randy Patrick, Chief Administrative Officer
Ian Thompson, Fire Chief
204-677-7915
fchief@city.thompson.mb.ca
Gary Ceppetelli, Director, Planning & Community Development
gceppetelli@city.thompson.mb.ca
Wayne Koversky, Director, Public Works
koversky@city.thompson.mb.ca
Mike Webb, Technician, Water & Sewer
mwebb@city.thompson.mb.ca
Ken Ament, Technician, Buildings & Roads
kament@city.thompson.mb.ca
Joyce Kopp, Agent, Purchasing
jkopp@city.thompson.mb.ca

Winkler
185 Main St.
Winkler, MB R6W 1B4
Tel: 204-325-9524; *Fax:* 204-325-5915
admin@cityofwinkler.ca
www.cityofwinkler.ca
Municipal Type: City
Incorporated: Jan. 6, 1954 *Area:* 17.01 sq km
Population in 2011: 10,670
Provincial Electoral District(s): Pembina
Federal Electoral District(s): Portage-Lisgar
Next Election: Oct. 22, 2014 (4 year terms)
Martin Harder, Mayor
mayor@cityofwinkler.ca
Dave Burgess, Chief Administrative Officer

Winnipeg
City Hall
510 Main St.
Winnipeg, MB R3B 1B9
Tel: 204-986-6432; *Fax:* 204-947-3452
www.winnipeg.ca
Other Information: Phone or Fax: 311 for information on city services
Municipal Type: City
Incorporated: Nov. 8, 1873 *Area:* 464.01 sq km
Population in 2011: 633,617
Provincial Electoral District(s): Assibonia; Burrows; Charleswood; Concordia; Elmwood; Ft. Garry-Riverview; Ft. Rouge; Ft. Whyte; Inkster; Kildonan; Kirkfield Park; Logan; Minto; Point Douglas; Radisson; Riel; River East; River Heights; Rossmere; Seine River; Southdale; St. Boniface; St. James; St. Johns; St. Norbert; St. Vital; The Maples; Transcona; Tuxedo; Tyndall Park; Wollseley
Federal Electoral District(s): Charleswood-St. James-Assiniboia; Elmwood-Transcona; Kildonan-St. Paul; Saint Boniface; Winnipeg Centre; Winnipeg North; Winnipeg South; Winnipeg South Centre
Next Election: Oct. 22, 2014 (4 year terms)
Richard Kachur, City Clerk
204-986-2428, Fax: 204-947-3452
Sam Katz, Mayor
204-986-2171, Fax: 204-949-0566
feedback@winnipeg.ca
John Orlikow, Councillor, Ward(s): River Heights-Fort Garry
204-986-5236, Fax: 204-986-3725
Devi Sharma, Councillor, Ward(s): Old Kildonan
Mike Pagtakhan, Councillor, Ward(s): Point Douglas
204-986-8401, Fax: 204-986-3531
Paula Havixbeck, Councillor, Ward(s): Charleswood-Tuxedo
Gord Steeves, Councillor, Ward(s): St. Vital
204-986-5088, Fax: 204-986-3725
Scott Fielding, Councillor, Ward(s): St. James-Brooklands
204-986-5848, Fax: 204-986-4320
Ross Eadie, Councillor, Ward(s): Mynarski
Grant Nordman, Councillor, Ward(s): St. Charles
204-986-5920, Fax: 204-986-7359
Thomas Steen, Councillor, Ward(s): Elmwood-East Kildonan
Jenny Gerbasi, Councillor, Ward(s): Fort Rouge-East Fort Garry
204-986-5878, Fax: 204-986-5636
Jeff Browaty, Councillor, Ward(s): North Kildonan
204-986-5196, Fax: 204-986-3725
Daniel Vandal, Councillor, Ward(s): St. Boniface
204-986-5206, Fax: 204-986-3725

Harvey Smith, Councillor, Ward(s): Daniel McIntyre
204-986-5951, Fax: 204-986-7000
Justin Swandel, Councillor, Ward(s): St. Norbert
204-986-6824, Fax: 204-986-3725
Russ Wyatt, Councillor, Ward(s): Transcona
204-986-8087, Fax: 204-986-4530
Jo-Anne Ferrier, City Treasurer
Michael P. Ruta, Deputy CAO/CFO
Glen Laubenstein, Chief Administrative Officer
Jim Brennan, Chief, Winnipeg Fire Paramedic Service
Keith McCaskill, Chief of Police, Winnipeg Police Service
Linda Black, Director, Corporate Support Services
Nelson Karpa, Director, Assessment & Taxation
Bill Larkin, Director, Public Works
Kelly Kjartanson, Manager, Environmental Standards
Barry MacBride, Director, Water & Waste
Deepak Joshi, Director, Planning, Property & Development
Dave Wardrop, Director, Winnipeg Transit
Clive Wightman, Director, Community Services
Brad Sacher, Manager, Transportation
Dave Domke, Manager, Parks & Open Space

Other Municipalities in Manitoba

Altona
P.O. Box 1630
111 Centre Ave. East
Altona, MB R0G 0B0
Tel: 204-324-6468; *Fax:* 204-324-1550
info@townofaltona.com
www.townofaltona.com
Municipal Type: Town
Incorporated: Jan. 1, 1956 *Area:* 9.39 sq km
Population in 2011: 4,088
Provincial Electoral District(s): Emerson
Federal Electoral District(s): Portage-Lisgar
Next Election: Oct. 22, 2014 (4 year terms)
Melvin H. Klassen, Mayor
Russ Phillips, Chief Administrative Officer

Arborg
P.O. Box 159
337 River Rd.
Arborg, MB R0C 0A0
Tel: 204-376-2647; *Fax:* 204-376-5379
townofarborg@mymts.net
www.townofarborg.com
Municipal Type: Town
Incorporated: 1964 *Area:* 2.26 sq km
Population in 2011: 1,152
Provincial Electoral District(s): Interlake
Federal Electoral District(s): Selkirk-Interlake
Next Election: Oct. 22, 2014 (4 year terms)
Randy Sigurdson, Mayor
Lorraine Bardarson, Chief Administrative Officer

Beausejour
P.O. Box 1427
639 Park Ave.
Beausejour, MB R0E 0C0
Tel: 204-268-7550; *Fax:* 204-268-3107
townoffice@townofbeausejour.com
www.townofbeausejour.com
Municipal Type: Town
Incorporated: Jan. 2, 1912 *Area:* 5.35 sq km
Population in 2011: 3,126
Provincial Electoral District(s): Lac du Bonnet
Federal Electoral District(s): Selkirk-Interlake
Next Election: Oct. 22, 2014 (4 year terms)
Brad Saluk, Mayor
Jack Douglas, Chief Administrative Officer

Benito
P.O. Box 369
126 Main St.
Benito, MB R0L 0C0
Tel: 204-539-2634; *Fax:* 204-539-2221
benitov@mts.net
community.svcn.mb.ca/benito
Municipal Type: Village
Incorporated: Jan. 4, 1941 *Area:* 0.92 sq km
Population in 2011: 377
Provincial Electoral District(s): Swan River
Federal Electoral District(s): Dauphin-Swan River-Marquette
Next Election: Oct. 22, 2014 (4 year terms)
Marion Meadows, Mayor
Patricia Ellingson, Chief Administrative Officer

Binscarth
P.O. Box 54
116 Russell St.
Binscarth, MB R0J 0G0
Tel: 204-532-2223; *Fax:* 204-532-2153
vilbins@mts.net
www.binscarth.mb.com
Municipal Type: Village
Incorporated: Jan. 2, 1917 *Area:* 1.52 sq km
Population in 2011: 425
Provincial Electoral District(s): Russell
Federal Electoral District(s): Dauphin-Swan River-Marquette
Next Election: Oct. 22, 2014 (4 year terms)
Dale Sawchuk, Mayor
Sandra Birch, Chief Administrative Officer

Birtle
P.O. Box 70
678 Main St.
Birtle, MB R0M 0C0
Tel: 204-842-3234; *Fax:* 204-842-3496
cao@birtle.ca
www.town.birtle.mb.ca
Municipal Type: Town
Incorporated: Jan. 3, 1884 *Area:* 14.25 sq km
Population in 2011: 664
Provincial Electoral District(s): Russell
Federal Electoral District(s): Dauphin-Swan River-Marquette
Next Election: Oct. 22, 2014 (4 year terms)
James Vinie, Mayor
Debbie Jensen, Chief Administrative Officer

Boissevain
P.O. Box 490
420 South Railway
Boissevain, MB R0K 0E0
Tel: 204-534-2433; *Fax:* 204-534-3710
boissevain@mts.net
www.boissevain.ca
Municipal Type: Town
Incorporated: 1906 *Area:* 2.77 sq km
Population in 2011: 1,572
Provincial Electoral District(s): Arthur-Virden
Federal Electoral District(s): Brandon-Souris
Next Election: Oct. 22, 2014 (4 year terms)
M. Edward Anderson, Mayor
Lloyd Leganchuk, Chief Administrative Officer

Bowsman
P.O. Box 244
105 - 2nd St.
Bowsman, MB R0L 0H0
Tel: 204-238-4351; *Fax:* 204-238-4292
bowsman@mts.net
Municipal Type: Village
Incorporated: Jan. 7, 1949 *Area:* 2.63 sq km
Population in 2011: 298
Provincial Electoral District(s): Swan River
Federal Electoral District(s): Dauphin-Swan River-Marquette
Next Election: Oct. 22, 2014 (4 year terms)
Leanne Hutman, Mayor
Patti Simpson, Chief Administrative Officer

Carberry
P.O. Box 130
316 - 4th Ave.
Carberry, MB R0K 0H0
Tel: 204-834-6600; *Fax:* 204-834-6604
town@townofcarberry.ca
www.townofcarberry.ca
Municipal Type: Town
Incorporated: Jan. 1, 1905 *Area:* 4.79 sq km
Population in 2011: 1,669
Provincial Electoral District(s): Turtle Mountain
Federal Electoral District(s): Brandon-Souris
Next Election: Oct. 22, 2014 (4 year terms)
Wayne Blair, Mayor
Brent McMillan, Chief Administrative Officer

Carman
P.O. Box 160
12 - 2nd Ave. SW
Carman, MB R0G 0J0
Tel: 204-745-2443; *Fax:* 204-745-2903
info@townofcarman.com
www.townofcarman.com
Municipal Type: Town
Incorporated: Jan. 1, 1905 *Area:* 4.12 sq km
Population in 2011: 3,027
Provincial Electoral District(s): Carman
Federal Electoral District(s): Portage-Lisgar
Next Election: Oct. 22, 2014 (4 year terms)
Bob Mitchell, Mayor
Cheryl Young, Chief Administrative Officer

Cartwright
P.O. Box 9
485 Curwen St.
Cartwright, MB R0K 0L0
Tel: 204-529-2363; *Fax:* 204-529-2288
colleen@cartwrightmb.ca
www.cartwrightmb.ca
Municipal Type: Village
Incorporated: Jan. 5, 1948 *Area:* 1.86 sq km
Population in 2011: 308
Provincial Electoral District(s): Turtle Mountain
Federal Electoral District(s): Brandon-Souris
Next Election: Oct. 22, 2014 (4 year terms)
Bruce Leadbeater, Mayor
Colleen Mullin, Chief Administrative Officer

Churchill
P.O. Box 459
180 LaVerendrye Blvd.
Churchill, MB R0B 0E0
Tel: 204-675-8871; *Fax:* 204-675-2934
townofchurchill@churchill.ca
www.churchill.ca
Municipal Type: Town
Incorporated: Jan. 4, 1997 *Area:* 53.96 sq km
Population in 2011: 813
Provincial Electoral District(s): Rupertsland
Federal Electoral District(s): Churchill
Next Election: Oct. 22, 2014 (4 year terms)
Michael Spence, Mayor
Albert Meijering, Chief Executive Officer

Crystal City
P.O. Box 310
26 South Railway Ave.
Crystal City, MB R0K 0N0
Tel: 204-873-2591; *Fax:* 204-873-2459
crystalcity@inetlink.ca
www.crystalcitymb.ca
Municipal Type: Village
Incorporated: Dec. 4, 1947 *Area:* 2.84 sq km
Population in 2011: 384
Provincial Electoral District(s): Turtle Mountain
Federal Electoral District(s): Portage-Lisgar
Next Election: Oct. 22, 2014 (4 year terms)
William (Bill) McKitrick, Mayor
Alexis Gardiner, Chief Administrative Officer

Dauphin
100 Main St. South
Dauphin, MB R7N 1K3
Tel: 204-622-3200; *Fax:* 204-622-3290
info@dauphin.ca
www.dauphin.ca
Municipal Type: Town
Incorporated: Jan. 7, 1898 *Area:* 12.65 sq km
Population in 2011: 8,251
Provincial Electoral District(s): Dauphin-Roblin
Federal Electoral District(s): Dauphin-Swan River-Marquette
Next Election: Oct. 22, 2014 (4 year terms)
Eric B. Irwin, Mayor
Brad D. Collett, Chief Administrative Officer

Deloraine
P.O. Box 510
102 Broadway St. South
Deloraine, MB R0M 0M0
Tel: 204-747-2655; *Fax:* 204-747-2927
deloraine@deloraine.org
www.deloraine.org
Municipal Type: Town
Incorporated: Jan. 6, 1904 *Area:* 2.25 sq km
Population in 2011: 977
Provincial Electoral District(s): Arthur-Virden
Federal Electoral District(s): Brandon-Souris
Next Election: Oct. 22, 2014 (4 year terms)
Brian Franklin, Mayor
Debbie Adams, Chief Administrative Officer

Dunnottar
P.O. Box 321
44 Whytewold Rd.
Matlock, MB R0C 2B0
Tel: 204-389-4962; *Fax:* 204-389-4966
info@dunnottar.ca
www.dunnottar.ca
Municipal Type: Village
Area: 2.79 sq km
Population in 2011: 696

Provincial Electoral District(s): Interlake
Federal Electoral District(s): Selkirk-Interlake
Next Election: July 25, 2014 (4 year terms)
Richard Gamble, Mayor
Janice M. Thevenot, Chief Administrative Officer

Elkhorn
P.O. Box 280
10 Grange St.
Elkhorn, MB R0M 0N0
Tel: 204-845-2161; *Fax:* 204-845-2312
info@elkhorn.mb.ca
www.elkhorn.mb.ca
Municipal Type: Village
Incorporated: Jan. 2, 1906 *Area:* 2.73 sq km
Population in 2011: 471
Provincial Electoral District(s): Arthur-Virden
Federal Electoral District(s): Brandon-Souris
Next Election: Oct. 22, 2014 (4 year terms)
Roland Gagnon, Mayor
Garth Mitchell, Chief Administrative Officer

Emerson
P.O. Box 340
104 Church St.
Emerson, MB R0A 0L0
Tel: 204-373-2002; *Fax:* 204-373-2486
info@townofemerson.com
www.townofemerson.com
Municipal Type: Town
Incorporated: Nov. 3, 1879 *Area:* 22.28 sq km
Population in 2011: 671
Provincial Electoral District(s): Emerson
Federal Electoral District(s): Provencher
Next Election: Oct. 22, 2014 (4 year terms)
Wayne Arseny, Mayor
Jeannette Sabourin, Chief Administrative Officer

Erickson
P.O. Box 40
45 Main St.
Erickson, MB R0J 0P0
Tel: 204-636-2431; *Fax:* 204-636-2516
ericksonadmin@mts.net
www.townerickson.ca
Municipal Type: Town
Incorporated: Jan. 5, 1953 *Area:* 1.3 sq km
Population in 2011: 487
Provincial Electoral District(s): Russell
Federal Electoral District(s): Dauphin-Swan River-Marquette
Next Election: Oct. 22, 2014 (4 year terms)
Val Soltys, Mayor
Kat Bridgeman, Chief Administrative Officer

Ethelbert
P.O. Box 185
5 - 2nd St.
Ethelbert, MB R0L 0T0
Tel: 204-742-3301; *Fax:* 204-742-3228
ethelbert@mts.net
Municipal Type: Village
Incorporated: Jan. 1, 1950 *Area:* 2.47 sq km
Population in 2011: 275
Provincial Electoral District(s): Swan River
Federal Electoral District(s): Dauphin-Swan River-Marquette
Next Election: Oct. 22, 2014 (4 year terms)
Mercil (Mitch) Michaluk, Mayor
Libby Moroz, Chief Administrative Officer

Gilbert Plains
P.O. Box 39
114 Main St. North
Gilbert Plains, MB R0L 0X0
Tel: 204-548-2761; *Fax:* 204-548-2473
townofgp@mts.net
www.gilbertplains.com
Municipal Type: Town
Incorporated: July 1, 1906 *Area:* 2.66 sq km
Population in 2011: 811
Provincial Electoral District(s): Dauphin-Roblin
Federal Electoral District(s): Dauphin-Swan River-Marquette
Next Election: Oct. 22, 2014 (4 year terms)
Lyle Smith, Mayor
Janice Lagoski, Chief Administrative Officer

Gillam
P.O. Box 100
323 Railway Ave.
Gillam, MB R0B 0L0
Tel: 204-652-3150; *Fax:* 204-652-3199
information@townofgillam.com
www.townofgillam.com
Municipal Type: Town
Area: 1,996.35 sq km
Population in 2011: 1,704
Provincial Electoral District(s): Rupertsland
Federal Electoral District(s): Churchill
Next Election: Oct. 22, 2014 (4 year terms)
James Goymer, Mayor
Jackie Clayton, Chief Administrative Officer

Gladstone
P.O. Box 25
14 Dennis St.
Gladstone, MB R0J 0T0
Tel: 204-385-2332; *Fax:* 204-385-2391
info@gladstone.ca
www.gladstone.ca
Municipal Type: Town
Incorporated: Jan. 1, 1882 *Area:* 2.43 sq km
Population in 2011: 879
Provincial Electoral District(s): Ste. Rose
Federal Electoral District(s): Dauphin-Swan River-Marquette
Next Election: Oct. 22, 2014 (4 year terms)
Eileen Clarke, Mayor
Louise E. Blair, Chief Administrative Officer

Glenboro
P.O. Box 190
618 Railway Ave.
Glenboro, MB R0K 0X0
Tel: 204-827-2083; *Fax:* 204-827-2123
gcdc@glenboro.com
www.glenboro.com
Municipal Type: Village
Incorporated: Jan. 1, 1950 *Area:* 2.68 sq km
Population in 2011: 645
Provincial Electoral District(s): Turtle Mountain
Federal Electoral District(s): Brandon-Souris
Next Election: Oct. 22, 2014 (4 year terms)
Robert Jewsbury, Mayor
Eric Plaetinck, Chief Administrative Officer

Grand Rapids
P.O. Box 301
200 Grand Rapids Dr.
Grand Rapids, MB R0C 1E0
Tel: 204-639-2260; *Fax:* 204-639-2475
towngra@xplornet.ca
Municipal Type: Town
Incorporated: Jan. 2, 1962 *Area:* 85.95 sq km
Population in 2011: 239
Provincial Electoral District(s): Swan River
Federal Electoral District(s): Churchill
Next Election: Oct. 22, 2014 (4 year terms)
John Morrisseau, Mayor
Karen Turner, Chief Administrative Officer

Grandview
P.O. Box 219
531 Main St.
Grandview, MB R0L 0Y0
Tel: 204-546-5250; *Fax:* 204-546-5269
townofgv@mts.net
www.grandviewmanitoba.net
Municipal Type: Town
Incorporated: Jan. 1, 1905 *Area:* 2.87 sq km
Population in 2011: 859
Provincial Electoral District(s): Dauphin-Roblin
Federal Electoral District(s): Dauphin-Swan River-Marquette
Next Election: Oct. 22, 2014 (4 year terms)
Tom Bohun, Mayor
Sharon Dalgleish, Chief Administrative Officer

Gretna
P.O. Box 280
612 - 7th St.
Gretna, MB R0G 0V0
Tel: 204-327-5578; *Fax:* 204-327-5458
info@gretna.ca
www.gretna.ca
Municipal Type: Town
Incorporated: Jan. 6, 1886 *Area:* 2.79 sq km
Population in 2011: 556
Provincial Electoral District(s): Emerson
Federal Electoral District(s): Portage-Lisgar
Next Election: Oct. 22, 2014 (4 year terms)
Mark Ratzlaff, Mayor
Michele Sawatzky, Chief Administrative Officer

Hamiota
P.O. Box 100
75 Maple Ave. East
Hamiota, MB R0M 0T0
Tel: 204-764-3050; *Fax:* 204-764-3055
info@hamiota.com
www.hamiota.com
Municipal Type: Town
Incorporated: 1907 *Area:* 3.38 sq km
Population in 2011: 868
Provincial Electoral District(s): Russell
Federal Electoral District(s): Dauphin-Swan River-Marquette
Next Election: Oct. 22, 2014 (4 year terms)
Larry Oakden, Mayor
Tom Mollard, Chief Administrative Officer

Hartney
P.O. Box 339
209 Airdrie St.
Hartney, MB R0M 0X0
Tel: 204-858-2429; *Fax:* 204-858-2681
hartney@mts.net
Municipal Type: Town
Incorporated: Jan. 1, 1905 *Area:* 2.45 sq km
Population in 2011: 415
Provincial Electoral District(s): Arthur-Virden
Federal Electoral District(s): Brandon-Souris
Next Election: Oct. 22, 2014 (4 year terms)
Lori Taylor, Mayor
Brad Coe, Chief Administrative Officer

Killarney - Turtle Mountain
P.O. Box 10
415 Broadway Ave.
Killarney, MB R0K 1G0
Tel: 204-523-7247; *Fax:* 204-523-4637
info@killarney.ca
www.killarney.ca
Municipal Type: Municipality
Incorporated: Jan. 1, 1882 *Area:* 925.13 sq km
Population in 2011: 3,233
Provincial Electoral District(s): Turtle Mountain
Federal Electoral District(s): Brandon-Souris
Next Election: Oct. 22, 2014 (4 year terms)
Note: The municipalities of Killarney & Turtle Mountain amalgamated to form one entity effective Jan. 1, 2007.
Rick Pauls, Mayor
Jim Dowsett, Chief Administrative Officer

Lac du Bonnet
P.O. Box 339
84 - 2nd St.
Lac du Bonnet, MB R0E 1A0
Tel: 204-345-8693; *Fax:* 204-345-8694
townldb@mts.net
www.lacdubonnet.com
Municipal Type: Town
Incorporated: Jan. 4, 1947 *Area:* 2.25 sq km
Population in 2011: 1,328
Provincial Electoral District(s): Lac du Bonnet
Federal Electoral District(s): Provencher
Next Election: Oct. 22, 2014 (4 year terms)
Bill Campbell, Mayor
Colleen L. Johnson, Chief Administrative Officer

Leaf Rapids
Town Centre Complex
P.O. Box 340
Leaf Rapids, MB R0B 1W0
Tel: 204-473-2436; *Fax:* 204-473-2566
administrator@townofleafrapids.ca
www.townofleafrapids.ca
Municipal Type: Town
Incorporated: Jan. 5, 1976 *Area:* 1,272.87 sq km
Population in 2011: 453
Provincial Electoral District(s): Flin Flon
Federal Electoral District(s): Churchill
Next Election: Oct. 22, 2014 (4 year terms)
Geraldine Cockerill, Mayor
Pat Horsley, Chief Administrative Officer

Lynn Lake
P.O. Box 100
503 Sherritt Ave.
Lynn Lake, MB R0B 0W0
Tel: 204-356-2418; *Fax:* 204-356-8297
info@lynnlake.ca
www.lynnlake.ca
Municipal Type: Town
Incorporated: 1950 *Area:* 910.23 sq km
Population in 2011: 482
Provincial Electoral District(s): Flin Flon

Federal Electoral District(s): Churchill
Next Election: Oct. 22, 2014 (4 year terms)
Sean Maher, Mayor
Floyd Buhler, Chief Administrative Officer

MacGregor
P.O. Box 190
27 Hampton St. East
MacGregor, MB R0H 0R0
Tel: 204-685-2211; *Fax:* 204-685-2616
office@macgregor.ca
www.macgregor.ca
Municipal Type: Town
Incorporated: Jan. 4, 1947 *Area:* 2.13 sq km
Population in 2011: 963
Provincial Electoral District(s): Turtle Mountain
Federal Electoral District(s): Portage-Lisgar
Next Election: Oct. 22, 2014 (4 year terms)
William Wiebe, Mayor
Valorie Unrau, Chief Administrative Officer

Manitou
P.O. Box 280
261 Main St.
Manitou, MB R0G 1G0
Tel: 204-242-2515; *Fax:* 204-242-3281
manitou@goinet.ca
www.townofmanitou.ca
Municipal Type: Town
Incorporated: 1897 *Area:* 2.94 sq km
Population in 2011: 808
Provincial Electoral District(s): Pembina
Federal Electoral District(s): Portage-Lisgar
Next Election: Oct. 22, 2014 (4 year terms)
Jake Goertzen, Mayor
Wes Unrau, Chief Administrative Officer

McCreary
P.O. Box 267
436 - 2nd Ave.
McCreary, MB R0J 1B0
Tel: 204-835-2341; *Fax:* 204-835-2658
mccreary@mts.net
www.exploremccreary.com
Municipal Type: Village
Incorporated: Jan. 4, 1964 *Area:* 1.7 sq km
Population in 2011: 472
Provincial Electoral District(s): Ste. Rose
Federal Electoral District(s): Dauphin-Swan River-Marquette
Next Election: Oct. 22, 2014 (4 year terms)
Linda Cripps, Mayor
Wendy Turko, Chief Administrative Officer

Melita
P.O. Box 364
79 Main St.
Melita, MB R0M 1L0
Tel: 204-522-3413; *Fax:* 204-522-3587
tofmel@mts.net
www.melitamb.ca
Municipal Type: Town
Incorporated: Jan. 2, 1906 *Area:* 2.96 sq km
Population in 2011: 1,069
Provincial Electoral District(s): Arthur-Virden
Federal Electoral District(s): Brandon-Souris
Next Election: Oct. 22, 2014 (4 year terms)
Robert Walker, Mayor
Julie Chase, Chief Administrative Officer

Minitonas
P.O. Box 9
311 Main St.
Minitonas, MB R0L 1G0
Tel: 204-525-4461; *Fax:* 204-525-4857
rmmin@minitonas.ca
minitonas.ca
Municipal Type: Town
Incorporated: Jan. 5, 1948 *Area:* 2.01 sq km
Population in 2011: 522
Provincial Electoral District(s): Swan River
Federal Electoral District(s): Dauphin-Swan River-Marquette
Next Election: Oct. 22, 2014 (4 year terms)
Henry Barkowski, Mayor
Carolyn Gordon, Chief Administrative Officer

Minnedosa
P.O. Box 426
103 Main St. South
Minnedosa, MB R0J 1E0
Tel: 204-867-2727; *Fax:* 204-867-2686
minnedosa@mts.net
Municipal Type: Town
Incorporated: Jan. 5, 1948 *Area:* 15.26 sq km
Population in 2011: 2,587
Provincial Electoral District(s): Minnedosa
Federal Electoral District(s): Dauphin-Swan River-Marquette
Next Election: Oct. 22, 2014 (4 year terms)
Ray Orr, Mayor
Ken Jenkins, Chief Administrative Officer

Morden
#100, 195 Stephen St.
Morden, MB R6M 1V3
Tel: 204-822-4434; *Fax:* 204-822-6494
tmorden@mordenmb.com
www.mordenmb.com
Municipal Type: Town
Incorporated: Jan. 1, 1882 *Area:* 16.39 sq km
Population in 2011: 7,812
Provincial Electoral District(s): Pembina
Federal Electoral District(s): Portage-Lisgar
Next Election: Oct. 22, 2014 (4 year terms)
Ken Wiebe, Mayor
Ernie Epp, Chief Administrative Officer

Morris
P.O. Box 28
#1, 380 Stampede Grounds
Morris, MB R0G 1K0
Tel: 204-746-2531; *Fax:* 204-746-6009
tomorris@mts.net
www.town.morris.mb.ca
Municipal Type: Town
Incorporated: Jan. 2, 1883 *Area:* 6.1 sq km
Population in 2011: 1,797
Provincial Electoral District(s): Morris
Federal Electoral District(s): Provencher
Next Election: Oct. 22, 2014 (4 year terms)
Gavin van der Linde, Mayor
Brigitte Doerksen, Chief Administrative Officer

Neepawa
P.O. Box 339
275 Hamilton St.
Neepawa, MB R0J 1H0
Tel: 204-476-7600; *Fax:* 204-476-7624
neepawa@wcgwave.ca
www.neepawa.ca
Municipal Type: Town
Incorporated: Jan. 2, 1883 *Area:* 17.57 sq km
Population in 2011: 3,629
Provincial Electoral District(s): Ste. Rose
Federal Electoral District(s): Dauphin-Swan River-Marquette
Next Election: Oct. 22, 2014 (4 year terms)
Ron Forsman, Mayor
Allison Bardsley, Chief Administrative Officer

Niverville
P.O. Box 267
86 Main St.
Niverville, MB R0A 1E0
Tel: 204-388-4600; *Fax:* 204-388-6110
cao@whereyoubelong.ca
www.whereyoubelong.ca
Municipal Type: Town
Incorporated: Jan. 4, 1969 *Area:* 8.79 sq km
Population in 2011: 3,540
Provincial Electoral District(s): Steinbach
Federal Electoral District(s): Provencher
Next Election: Oct. 22, 2014 (4 year terms)
Greg Fehr, Mayor
mayor@whereyoubelong.ca
G. Jim Buys, Chief Administrative Officer

Notre Dame de Lourdes
P.O. Box 89
55 Rodgers St.
Notre Dame de Lourdes, MB R0G 1M0
Tel: 204-248-7290; *Fax:* 204-248-7289
villagend@mts.net
www.notre-dame-de-lourdes.ca
Municipal Type: Village
Incorporated: Jan. 3, 1963 *Area:* 2.58 sq km
Population in 2011: 683
Provincial Electoral District(s): Carman
Federal Electoral District(s): Portage-Lisgar
Next Election: Oct. 22, 2014 (4 year terms)
Denis Bibault, Mayor
Jean Gaultier, Chief Administrative Officer

Oak Lake
P.O. Box 100
293 - 2nd Ave. West
Oak Lake, MB R0M 1P0
Tel: 204-855-2423; *Fax:* 204-855-2836
cao_sifton@mymts.net
www.oaklakeandarea.com
Municipal Type: Town
Incorporated: Jan. 3, 1907 *Area:* 2.73 sq km
Population in 2011: 383
Provincial Electoral District(s): Arthur-Virden
Federal Electoral District(s): Brandon-Souris
Next Election: Oct. 22, 2014 (4 year terms)
Jeffrey Sigurdson, Mayor
Mary Smith, Chief Administrative Officer

Pilot Mound
P.O. Box 39
219 Broadway Ave.
Pilot Mound, MB R0G 1P0
Tel: 204-825-2587; *Fax:* 204-825-2362
vlgpm@mts.net
www.pilotmound.com
Municipal Type: Town
Incorporated: May 4, 1904 *Area:* 2.7 sq km
Population in 2011: 635
Provincial Electoral District(s): Turtle Mountain
Federal Electoral District(s): Portage-Lisgar
Next Election: Oct. 22, 2014 (4 year terms)
R. Brent Checkley, Mayor
Doris F. Heaver, Chief Administrative Officer

Plum Coulee
P.O. Box 36
253 Main Ave.
Plum Coulee, MB R0G 1R0
Tel: 204-829-3419; *Fax:* 204-829-3436
pcoulee@mts.net
www.townofplumcoulee.com
Municipal Type: Town
Incorporated: Jan. 6, 1901 *Area:* 2.48 sq km
Population in 2011: 843
Provincial Electoral District(s): Emerson
Federal Electoral District(s): Portage-Lisgar
Next Election: Oct. 22, 2014 (4 year terms)
Archie Heinrichs, Mayor
Susan Stein, Chief Administrative Officer

Powerview - Pine Falls
P.O. Box 220
277B Main St.
Powerview, MB R0E 1P0
Tel: 204-367-8483; *Fax:* 204-367-4747
munclerk@mts.net
www.powerview-pinefalls.com
Municipal Type: Town
Incorporated: Jan. 2, 1951 *Area:* 5.05 sq km
Population in 2011: 1,314
Provincial Electoral District(s): Lac du Bonnet
Federal Electoral District(s): Provencher
Next Election: Oct. 22, 2014 (4 year terms)
Gordon Watson, Mayor
Margaret Bonekamp, Chief Administrative Officer

Rapid City
P.O. Box 130
410 - 3rd Ave.
Rapid City, MB R0K 1W0
Tel: 204-826-2679; *Fax:* 204-826-2652
rapcity@mts.net
www.rapidcitymb.ca
Municipal Type: Town
Incorporated: Jan. 2, 1883 *Area:* 5.38 sq km
Population in 2011: 417
Provincial Electoral District(s): Minnedosa
Federal Electoral District(s): Dauphin-Swan River-Marquette
Next Election: Oct. 22, 2014 (4 year terms)
Orest Woloski, Mayor
Kim Moyer, Chief Administrative Officer

Rivers
P.O. Box 520
670 - 2nd Ave.
Rivers, MB R0K 1X0
Tel: 204-328-5250; *Fax:* 204-328-5374
rivers@mts.net
www.townofrivers.mb.ca
Municipal Type: Town
Incorporated: Jan. 4, 1913 *Area:* 7.97 sq km
Population in 2011: 1,189
Provincial Electoral District(s): Minnedosa

Federal Electoral District(s): Brandon-Souris
Next Election: Oct. 22, 2014 (4 year terms)
Todd Gill, Mayor
Dennis Higginson, Chief Administrative Officer

Riverton
P.O. Box 250
56 Laura Ave.
Riverton, MB R0C 2R0
Tel: 204-378-2281; *Fax:* 204-378-5616
vilofriv@mts.net
Municipal Type: Village
Incorporated: Jan. 2, 1951 *Area:* 1.11 sq km
Population in 2011: 538
Provincial Electoral District(s): Interlake
Federal Electoral District(s): Selkirk-Interlake
Next Election: Oct. 22, 2014 (4 year terms)
Colin Bjarnason, Mayor
Nadine Eyjolfson, Chief Administrative Officer

Roblin
P.O. Box 730
125 - 1st Ave. NW
Roblin, MB R0L 1P0
Tel: 204-937-8333; *Fax:* 204-937-4382
toroblin@mts.net
www.roblinmanitoba.com
Municipal Type: Town
Incorporated: Jan. 4, 1913 *Area:* 3.79 sq km
Population in 2011: 1,774
Provincial Electoral District(s): Dauphin-Roblin
Federal Electoral District(s): Dauphin-Swan River-Marquette; Brandon-Souris
Next Election: Oct. 22, 2014 (4 year terms)
Betty Nykyforak, Mayor
Twyla Ludwig, Chief Administrative Officer

Rossburn
P.O. Box 70
43 Main St. North
Rossburn, MB R0J 1V0
Tel: 204-859-2762; *Fax:* 204-859-2022
town.rsb@mts.net
www.town.rossburn.mb.ca
Municipal Type: Town
Incorporated: Jan. 4, 1913 *Area:* 3.43 sq km
Population in 2011: 552
Provincial Electoral District(s): Russell
Federal Electoral District(s): Dauphin-Swan River-Marquette
Next Election: Oct. 22, 2014 (4 year terms)
Shirley Kalyniuk, Mayor
Kerry Lawless, Chief Administrative Officer

Russell
P.O. Box 10
178 Main St. North
Russell, MB R0J 1W0
Tel: 204-773-2253; *Fax:* 204-773-3370
town@russellmb.com
www.russellmb.com
Municipal Type: Town
Incorporated: Jan. 4, 1913 *Area:* 3.15 sq km
Population in 2011: 1,669
Provincial Electoral District(s): Russell
Federal Electoral District(s): Dauphin-Swan River-Marquette
Next Election: Oct. 22, 2014 (4 year terms)
Chris Radford, Mayor
Wally R. Melnyk, Chief Administrative Officer

Ste. Anne
30 Dawson Rd., Unit B
Ste. Anne, MB R5H 1B5
Tel: 204-422-5293; *Fax:* 204-422-5459
town@steannemb.ca
www.steannemb.ca
Municipal Type: Town
Incorporated: Jan. 3, 1963 *Area:* 4.19 sq km
Population in 2011: 1,626
Provincial Electoral District(s): La Verendrye
Federal Electoral District(s): Provencher
Next Election: Oct. 22, 2014 (4 year terms)
Bernard Vermette, Mayor
Nicole Champagne, Chief Administrative Officer

St. Claude
P.O. Box 249
12 - 1st St.
St Claude, MB R0G 1Z0
Tel: 204-379-2382; *Fax:* 204-379-2072
stclaude@mts.net
www.stclaude.ca
Municipal Type: Village
Incorporated: Jan. 3, 1963 *Area:* 1.8 sq km
Population in 2011: 590
Provincial Electoral District(s): Carman
Federal Electoral District(s): Portage-Lisgar
Next Election: Oct. 22, 2014 (4 year terms)
Norman Carter, Mayor
204-379-2720
Simone Dupasquier, Chief Administrative Officer

St. Lazare
P.O. Box 100
100 Chartier Ave. West
St Lazare, MB R0M 1Y0
Tel: 204-683-2241; *Fax:* 204-683-2317
laz_ell@mts.net
stlazare-ellice.com
Municipal Type: Village
Incorporated: Jan. 1, 1950 *Area:* 2.91 sq km
Population in 2011: 254
Provincial Electoral District(s): Russell
Federal Electoral District(s): Dauphin-Swan River-Marquette
Next Election: Oct. 22, 2014 (4 year terms)
Martin Dupont, Mayor
Richard W. Fouillard, Chief Administrative Officer

St. Pierre-Jolys
P.O. Box 218
555 Hébert St.
St. Pierre-Jolys, MB R0A 1V0
Tel: 204-433-7832; *Fax:* 204-433-7053
st-pierre-jolys@mts.net
www.stpierrejolys.com
Municipal Type: Village
Incorporated: Jan. 4, 1947 *Area:* 2.6 sq km
Population in 2011: 1,099
Provincial Electoral District(s): Morris
Federal Electoral District(s): Provencher
Next Election: Oct. 22, 2014 (4 year terms)
Denis Fillion, Mayor
Rachelle Tessier, Chief Administrative Officer

Ste. Rose du Lac
P.O. Box 445
722 Central Ave.
Ste. Rose du Lac, MB R0L 1S0
Tel: 204-447-2229; *Fax:* 204-447-2875
sterose@mts.net
www.town.sterosedulac.mb.ca
Municipal Type: Town
Incorporated: Jan. 5, 1920 *Area:* 2.53 sq km
Population in 2011: 1,023
Provincial Electoral District(s): Ste. Rose
Federal Electoral District(s): Dauphin-Swan River-Marquette
Next Election: Oct. 22, 2014 (4 year terms)
Rene L. Maillard, Mayor
Marlene M. Bouchard, Chief Administrative Officer

Snow Lake
P.O. Box 40
113 Elm St.
Snow Lake, MB R0B 1M0
Tel: 204-358-2551; *Fax:* 204-358-2112
snowlake@mts.net
www.snowlake.com
Municipal Type: Town
Incorporated: 1947 *Area:* 1,211.89 sq km
Population in 2011: 723
Provincial Electoral District(s): Flin Flon
Federal Electoral District(s): Churchill
Next Election: Oct. 22, 2014 (4 year terms)
Clarence Fisher, Mayor
Jeff Precourt, Chief Administrative Officer

Somerset
P.O. Box 187
307 - 3rd St.
Somerset, MB R0G 2L0
Tel: 204-744-2171; *Fax:* 204-744-2618
somerset@mts.net
Municipal Type: Village
Incorporated: Jan. 2, 1962 *Area:* 2.45 sq km
Population in 2011: 439
Provincial Electoral District(s): Carman
Federal Electoral District(s): Portage-Lisgar
Next Election: Oct. 22, 2014 (4 year terms)
Gilbert Mabon, Mayor
Linda Talbot, Chief Administrative Officer

Souris
P.O. Box 518
100 - 2nd St. South
Souris, MB R0K 2C0
Tel: 204-483-5200; *Fax:* 204-483-5203
tnsouris@mts.net
www.sourismanitoba.com
Municipal Type: Town
Incorporated: Jan. 6, 1904 *Area:* 3.64 sq km
Population in 2011: 1,837
Provincial Electoral District(s): Minnedosa
Federal Electoral District(s): Brandon-Souris
Next Election: Oct. 22, 2014 (4 year terms)
Darryl Jackson, Mayor
Charlotte Parham, Chief Administrative Officer

Stonewall
P.O. Box 250
293 Main St.
Stonewall, MB R0C 2Z0
Tel: 204-467-7979; *Fax:* 204-467-7999
info@stonewall.ca
www.stonewall.ca
Municipal Type: Town
Incorporated: Jan. 4, 1908 *Area:* 6.02 sq km
Population in 2011: 4,536
Provincial Electoral District(s): Lakeside
Federal Electoral District(s): Selkirk-Interlake
Next Election: Oct. 22, 2014 (4 year terms)
Ross Thompson, Mayor
Robert Potter, Chief Administrative Officer

Swan River
P.O. Box 879
135 - 5th Ave. North
Swan River, MB R0L 1Z0
Tel: 204-734-4586; *Fax:* 204-734-5166
main@townsr.ca
www.swanrivermanitoba.ca
Municipal Type: Town
Incorporated: Jan. 4, 1908 *Area:* 6.78 sq km
Population in 2011: 3,907
Provincial Electoral District(s): Swan River
Federal Electoral District(s): Dauphin-Swan River-Marquette
Next Election: Oct. 22, 2014 (4 year terms)
Glen McKenzie, Mayor
Shirley Bateman, Chief Administrative Officer

Teulon
P.O. Box 69
44 - 4 Ave. SE
Teulon, MB R0C 3B0
Tel: 204-886-2314; *Fax:* 204-886-3918
teulon@mts.net
www.teulon.ca
Municipal Type: Town
Incorporated: Jan. 4, 1919 *Area:* 3.2 sq km
Population in 2011: 1,124
Provincial Electoral District(s): Lakeside
Federal Electoral District(s): Selkirk-Interlake
Next Election: Oct. 22, 2014 (4 year terms)
Bert Campbell, Mayor
Grant MacAulay, Chief Administrative Officer

The Pas
P.O. Box 870
81 Edwards Ave.
The Pas, MB R9A 1K8
Tel: 204-627-1100; *Fax:* 204-623-5506
randis@townofthepas.ca
www.thepasarea.com
Municipal Type: Town
Incorporated: Jan. 2, 1912 *Area:* 47.83 sq km
Population in 2011: 5,513
Provincial Electoral District(s): The Pas
Federal Electoral District(s): Churchill
Next Election: Oct. 22, 2014 (4 year terms)
Alan McLauchlan, Mayor
Randi Salamanowicz, Chief Administrative Officer

Treherne
P.O. Box 30
215 Broadway St.
Treherne, MB R0G 2V0
Tel: 204-723-2044; *Fax:* 204-723-2719
treherneinfo@mts.net
www.treherne.ca
Municipal Type: Town
Incorporated: Jan. 5, 1948 *Area:* 1.96 sq km
Population in 2011: 616
Provincial Electoral District(s): Carman

Federal Electoral District(s): Portage-Lisgar
Next Election: Oct. 22, 2014 (4 year terms)
James Knockaert, Mayor
Jackie Jenkinson, Chief Administrative Officer

Virden
P.O. Box 310
236 Wellington St. West
Virden, MB R0M 2C0
Tel: 204-748-2440; *Fax:* 204-748-2501
virden_cao@mts.net
virden.cimnet.ca
Municipal Type: Town
Incorporated: Jan. 6, 1904 *Area:* 8.56 sq km
Population in 2011: 3,114
Provincial Electoral District(s): Arthur-Virden
Federal Electoral District(s): Brandon-Souris
Next Election: Oct. 22, 2014 (4 year terms)
Jeff McConnell, Mayor
Rhonda Stewart, Chief Administrative Officer

Waskada
P.O. Box 40
33 Railway Ave.
Waskada, MB R0M 2E0
Tel: 204-673-2401; *Fax:* 204-673-2663
waskadan@mts.net
www.waskada.ca
Municipal Type: Village
Incorporated: Jan. 7, 1949 *Area:* 0.77 sq km
Population in 2011: 183
Provincial Electoral District(s): Arthur-Virden
Federal Electoral District(s): Brandon-Souris
Next Election: Oct. 22, 2014 (4 year terms)
Gary Williams, Mayor
Diane Woodworth, Chief Administrative Officer

Wawanesa
P.O. Box 278
106 - 4th St.
Wawanesa, MB R0K 2G0
Tel: 204-824-2244; *Fax:* 204-824-2244
vwawa@mts.net
www.wawanesa.ca
Municipal Type: Village
Incorporated: Jan. 6, 1909 *Area:* 2.26 sq km
Population in 2011: 562
Provincial Electoral District(s): Minnedosa
Federal Electoral District(s): Brandon-Souris
Next Election: Oct. 22, 2014 (4 year terms)
Bruce Gullett, Mayor
Leonard Plett, Chief Administrative Officer

Winnipeg Beach
P.O. Box 160
29 Robinson Ave.
Winnipeg Beach, MB R0C 3G0
Tel: 204-389-2698; *Fax:* 204-389-2019
info@winnipegbeach.ca
www.winnipegbeach.ca
Municipal Type: Village
Incorporated: Jan. 5, 1914 *Area:* 3.88 sq km
Population in 2011: 1,011
Provincial Electoral District(s): Gimli
Federal Electoral District(s): Selkirk-Interlake
Next Election: July 25, 2014 (4 year terms)
Tony Pimentel, Mayor
Doreen Steg, Chief Administrative Officer

Winnipegosis
P.O. Box 370
130 - 2nd St.
Winnipegosis, MB R0L 2G0
Tel: 204-656-4791; *Fax:* 204-656-4751
vofwinnipegosis@mts.net
www.winnipegosis.ca
Municipal Type: Village
Incorporated: Jan. 6, 1915 *Area:* 2.5 sq km
Population in 2011: 647
Provincial Electoral District(s): Swan River
Federal Electoral District(s): Dauphin-Swan River-Marquette
Next Election: Oct. 22, 2014 (4 year terms)
Dan Brown, Mayor
Jackie Patterson, Chief Administrative Officer

Rural Municipality

Albert
P.O. Box 70
14 Morris St.
Tilston, MB R0M 2B0
Tel: 204-686-2271; *Fax:* 204-686-2335
rmalbert@xplornet.com
Municipal Type: Rural Municipality
Incorporated: Jan. 3, 1946 *Area:* 769.55 sq km
Population in 2011: 323
Provincial Electoral District(s): Arthur-Virden
Federal Electoral District(s): Brandon-Souris
Next Election: Oct. 22, 2014 (4 year terms)
Tom Campbell, Reeve
Trudy Murray, Chief Administrative Officer

Alexander
P.O. Box 100
104058 Provincial Trunk Hwy. 11
St Georges, MB R0E 1V0
Tel: 204-367-6170; *Fax:* 204-367-2257
info@rmalexander.com
Municipal Type: Rural Municipality
Incorporated: Jan. 2, 1945 *Area:* 1,568.66 sq km
Population in 2011: 2,983
Provincial Electoral District(s): Lac du Bonnet; Selkirk
Federal Electoral District(s): Provencher; Brandon-Souris; Selkirk-Interlake
Next Election: Oct. 22, 2014 (4 year terms)
Ed Arnold, Reeve
Scott Spicer, Chief Administrative Officer

Alonsa
P.O. Box 127
20 Railway Ave.
Alonsa, MB R0H 0A0
Tel: 204-767-2054; *Fax:* 204-767-2044
rmalonsa@inetlink.ca
Municipal Type: Rural Municipality
Area: 2,977.50 sq km
Population in 2011: 1,270
Provincial Electoral District(s): Ste. Rose
Federal Electoral District(s): Dauphin-Swan River-Marquette
Next Election: Oct. 22, 2014 (4 year terms)
Stan Asham, Reeve
Pamela Sul, Chief Administrative Officer

Archie
P.O. Box 67
202 Qu'Appelle St.
McAuley, MB R0M 1H0
Tel: 204-722-2053; *Fax:* 204-722-2027
rmarchie@mts.net
Municipal Type: Rural Municipality
Incorporated: Jan. 2, 1883 *Area:* 577.68 sq km
Population in 2011: 325
Provincial Electoral District(s): Russell
Federal Electoral District(s): Dauphin-Swan River-Marquette
Next Election: Oct. 22, 2014 (4 year terms)
Wendy Davidson, Reeve
Nicole Webb, Chief Administrative Officer

Argyle
P.O. Box 40
132 - 2nd St. North
Baldur, MB R0K 0B0
Tel: 204-535-2176; *Fax:* 204-535-2505
rmofargyle@inetbiz.ca
Municipal Type: Rural Municipality
Incorporated: Jan. 1, 1882 *Area:* 770.44 sq km
Population in 2011: 1,071
Provincial Electoral District(s): Turtle Mountain
Federal Electoral District(s): Brandon-Souris; Selkirk-Interlake
Next Election: Oct. 22, 2014 (4 year terms)
Bob Conibear, Reeve
Janine Wiebe, Chief Administrative Officer

Armstrong
P.O. Box 69
55 Hwy. 17
Inwood, MB R0C 1P0
Tel: 204-278-3377; *Fax:* 204-278-3437
rmofarmstrong@highspeedcrow.ca
Municipal Type: Rural Municipality
Incorporated: Dec. 5, 1944 *Area:* 1,864.96 sq km
Population in 2011: 1,835
Provincial Electoral District(s): Interlake
Federal Electoral District(s): Selkirk-Interlake
Next Election: Oct. 22, 2014 (4 year terms)
Garry Wasylowski, Reeve
Carole Oppermann, Chief Administrative Officer

Arthur
P.O. Box 429
138 Main St.
Melita, MB R0M 1L0
Tel: 204-522-3263; *Fax:* 204-522-8706
rmarthur@mts.net
Municipal Type: Rural Municipality
Area: 765.77 sq km
Population in 2011: 413
Provincial Electoral District(s): Arthur-Virden
Federal Electoral District(s): Brandon-Souris
Next Election: Oct. 22, 2014 (4 year terms)
James Trewin, Reeve
Sandra Anderson, Chief Administrative Officer

Bifrost
P.O. Box 70
329 River Rd.
Arborg, MB R0C 0A0
Tel: 204-376-2391; *Fax:* 204-376-2742
bifrost@mts.net
Municipal Type: Rural Municipality
Incorporated: Jan. 4, 1908 *Area:* 1,642.58 sq km
Population in 2011: 2,976
Provincial Electoral District(s): Interlake
Federal Electoral District(s): Selkirk-Interlake
Next Election: Oct. 22, 2014 (4 year terms)
Harold J. Foster, Reeve
R. Kim Dalton, Chief Administrative Officer

Birtle
P.O. Box 70
678 Main St.
Birtle, MB R0M 0C0
Tel: 204-842-3403; *Fax:* 204-842-3496
cao@birtle.ca
Municipal Type: Rural Municipality
Incorporated: Jan. 3, 1884 *Area:* 849.13 sq km
Population in 2011: 632
Provincial Electoral District(s): Russell
Federal Electoral District(s): Dauphin-Swan River-Marquette
Next Election: Oct. 22, 2014 (4 year terms)
Roger Wilson, Reeve
Debbie Jensen, Chief Administrative Officer

Blanshard
P.O. Box 179
10 Cochrane St.
Oak River, MB R0K 1T0
Tel: 204-566-2146; *Fax:* 204-566-2126
blanshardrm@inetlink.ca
www.rmofblanshard.ca
Municipal Type: Rural Municipality
Incorporated: Jan. 3, 1884 *Area:* 578.98 sq km
Population in 2011: 526
Provincial Electoral District(s): Russell
Federal Electoral District(s): Dauphin-Swan River-Marquette
Next Election: Oct. 22, 2014 (4 year terms)
Brent Fortune, Reeve
Diane Kuculym, Chief Administrative Officer

Brenda
P.O. Box 40
33 Railway Ave.
Waskada, MB R0M 2E0
Tel: 204-673-2401; *Fax:* 204-673-2663
waskadan@mts.net
Municipal Type: Rural Municipality
Area: 766 sq km
Population in 2011: 469
Provincial Electoral District(s): Arthur-Virden
Federal Electoral District(s): Brandon-Souris
Next Election: Oct. 22, 2014 (4 year terms)
Duncan Stewart, Reeve
Diane Woodworth, Chief Administrative Officer

Brokenhead
P.O. Box 490
72013 Rd. 42 East
Beausejour, MB R0E 0C0
Tel: 204-268-6700; *Fax:* 204-268-1504
rmbroken@granite.mb.ca
www.granite.mb.ca/erdc/brokenhead/main.html
Municipal Type: Rural Municipality
Incorporated: Jan. 2, 1900 *Area:* 750.54 sq km
Population in 2011: 4,635
Provincial Electoral District(s): Lac du Bonnet
Federal Electoral District(s): Selkirk-Interlake
Next Election: Oct. 22, 2014 (4 year terms)
Glen Dudek, Reeve
Christine Hutlet, Chief Administrative Officer

Cameron
P.O. Box 399
209 Airdrie St.
Hartney, MB R0M 0X0
Tel: 204-858-2590; *Fax:* 204-858-2681
hartney@mts.net
Municipal Type: Rural Municipality
Incorporated: Jan. 6, 1897 *Area:* 759.15 sq km
Population in 2011: 420
Provincial Electoral District(s): Arthur-Virden
Federal Electoral District(s): Brandon-Souris
Next Election: Oct. 22, 2014 (4 year terms)
Wayne Drummond, Reeve
Brad Coe, Chief Administrative Officer

Cartier
P.O. Box 117
28 Provincial Rd. 248 South
Elie, MB R0H 0H0
Tel: 204-353-2214; *Fax:* 204-353-2335
anne@rm-cartier.mb.ca
www.rm-cartier.mb.ca
Municipal Type: Rural Municipality
Incorporated: Jan. 5, 1914 *Area:* 553.42 sq km
Population in 2011: 3,153
Provincial Electoral District(s): Morris
Federal Electoral District(s): Portage-Lisgar
Next Election: Oct. 22, 2014 (4 year terms)
Roland Rasmussen, Reeve
Anne Burns, Chief Administrative Officer

Clanwilliam
P.O. Box 40
45 Main St.
Erickson, MB R0J 0P0
Tel: 204-636-2431; *Fax:* 204-636-2516
erikclan@mts.net
Municipal Type: Rural Municipality
Incorporated: Jan. 3, 1884 *Area:* 354.01 sq km
Population in 2011: 414
Provincial Electoral District(s): Russell
Federal Electoral District(s): Dauphin-Swan River-Marquette
Next Election: Oct. 22, 2014 (4 year terms)
Victor Baraniuk, Reeve
Kat Bridgeman, Chief Administrative Officer

Coldwell
P.O. Box 90
35 Main St.
Lundar, MB R0C 1Y0
Tel: 204-762-5421; *Fax:* 204-762-5177
coldwell@mts.net
Municipal Type: Rural Municipality
Incorporated: Jan. 4, 1913 *Area:* 901.84 sq km
Population in 2011: 1,351
Provincial Electoral District(s): Lakeside
Federal Electoral District(s): Selkirk-Interlake
Next Election: Oct. 22, 2014 (4 year terms)
Brian Sigfusson, Reeve
Nicole Christensen, Chief Administrative Officer

Cornwallis
P.O. Box 10 500
RR#5
Brandon, MB R7A 5Y5
Tel: 204-725-8686; *Fax:* 204-725-3659
info@gov.cornwallis.mb.ca
www.gov.cornwallis.mb.ca
Municipal Type: Rural Municipality
Incorporated: Jan. 3, 1884 *Area:* 500.82 sq km
Population in 2011: 4,378
Provincial Electoral District(s): Minnedosa
Federal Electoral District(s): Brandon-Souris
Next Election: Oct. 22, 2014 (4 year terms)
Reg Atkinson, Reeve
Donna Anderson, Chief Administrative Officer

Daly
P.O. Box 538
645 - 2nd Ave.
Rivers, MB R0K 1X0
Tel: 204-328-7410; *Fax:* 204-328-4431
rmdaly@mts.net
www.townofrivers.mb.ca
Municipal Type: Rural Municipality
Area: 562.44 sq km
Population in 2011: 830
Provincial Electoral District(s): Minnedosa
Federal Electoral District(s): Brandon-Souris
Next Election: Oct. 22, 2014 (4 year terms)
Evan Smith, Reeve
Lorne Green, Chief Administrative Officer

Dauphin
P.O. Box 574
Hwy. 20A East
Dauphin, MB R7N 2V4
Tel: 204-638-4531; *Fax:* 204-638-7598
rmofdphn@mts.net
Municipal Type: Rural Municipality
Area: 1,516.1 sq km
Population in 2011: 2,200
Provincial Electoral District(s): Dauphin-Roblin
Federal Electoral District(s): Dauphin-Swan River-Marquette
Next Election: Oct. 22, 2014 (4 year terms)
Dennis Forbes, Reeve
Marlene Durston, Chief Administrative Officer

De Salaberry
P.O. Box 40
466 Sabourin St.
St Pierre Jolys, MB R0A 1V0
Tel: 204-433-7406; *Fax:* 204-433-7063
info@rmdesalaberry.mb.ca
www.rmdesalaberry.mb.ca
Municipal Type: Rural Municipality
Incorporated: Jan. 2, 1883 *Area:* 670.29 sq km
Population in 2011: 3,450
Provincial Electoral District(s): Morris
Federal Electoral District(s): Provencher
Next Election: Oct. 22, 2014 (4 year terms)
Ron Musick, Reeve
Luc Lahaie, Chief Administrative Officer

Dufferin
P.O. Box 100
12 - 2nd Ave. SW
Carman, MB R0G 0J0
Tel: 204-745-2301; *Fax:* 204-745-6348
rmduff@mts.net
Municipal Type: Rural Municipality
Incorporated: Feb. 7, 1880 *Area:* 915.72 sq km
Population in 2011: 2,394
Provincial Electoral District(s): Carman
Federal Electoral District(s): Portage-Lisgar
Next Election: Oct. 22, 2014 (4 year terms)
Shawn McCutcheon, Reeve
Sharla Murray, Chief Administrative Officer

East St. Paul
#1, 3021 Bird's Hill Rd.
East St Paul, MB R2E 1A7
Tel: 204-668-8112; *Fax:* 204-668-1987
administration.department@eaststpaul.com
www.eaststpaul.com
Municipal Type: Rural Municipality
Incorporated: May 2, 1916 *Area:* 42.1 sq km
Population in 2011: 9,046
Provincial Electoral District(s): Springfield
Federal Electoral District(s): Kildonan-St. Paul
Next Election: Oct. 22, 2014 (4 year terms)
Jerome Mauws, Chief Administrative Officer
Lawrence Morris, Reeve

Edward
P.O. Box 100
58 Railway Ave.
Pierson, MB R0M 1S0
Tel: 204-634-2231; *Fax:* 204-634-2479
rmofedw@inethome.ca
Municipal Type: Rural Municipality
Incorporated: Jan. 1, 1905 *Area:* 769.14 sq km
Population in 2011: 574
Provincial Electoral District(s): Arthur-Virden
Federal Electoral District(s): Brandon-Souris
Next Election: Oct. 22, 2014 (4 year terms)
Ralph Wang, Reeve
Audrey Bird, Chief Administrative Officer

Ellice
P.O. Box 100
100 Chartier Ave. West
St. Lazare, MB R0M 1Y0
Tel: 204-683-2241; *Fax:* 204-683-2317
laz_ell@mts.net
Municipal Type: Rural Municipality
Incorporated: Jan. 2, 1883 *Area:* 572.74 sq km
Population in 2011: 392
Provincial Electoral District(s): Russell
Federal Electoral District(s): Dauphin-Swan River-Marquette
Next Election: Oct. 22, 2014 (4 year terms)
Guy Huberdeau, Reeve
Richard W. Fouillard, Chief Administrative Officer

Elton
Forest, MB R0K 0W0
Tel: 204-728-7834; *Fax:* 204-725-1865
elton@inetlink.ca
Municipal Type: Rural Municipality
Incorporated: Jan. 2, 1883 *Area:* 571.85 sq km
Population in 2011: 1,257
Provincial Electoral District(s): Minnedosa
Federal Electoral District(s): Brandon-Souris
Next Election: Oct. 22, 2014 (4 year terms)
Jim Boyd, Reeve
Kathleen E.I. Steele, Chief Administrative Officer

Eriksdale
P.O. Box 10
10 Main St.
Eriksdale, MB R0C 0W0
Tel: 204-739-2666; *Fax:* 204-739-2073
admin@eriksdale.com
www.eriksdale.com
Municipal Type: Rural Municipality
Incorporated: Jan. 6, 1904 *Area:* 784.76 sq km
Population in 2011: 846
Provincial Electoral District(s): Interlake
Federal Electoral District(s): Selkirk-Interlake
Next Election: Oct. 22, 2014 (4 year terms)
Arne Lindell, Reeve
Arlene Brandson Darknell, Chief Administrative Officer

Ethelbert
P.O. Box 115
5 Railway Ave. North
Ethelbert, MB R0L 0T0
Tel: 204-742-3212; *Fax:* 204-742-3642
rmethelbert@inetlink.ca
Municipal Type: Rural Municipality
Incorporated: Jan. 1, 1905 *Area:* 1,134.5 sq km
Population in 2011: 354
Provincial Electoral District(s): Swan River
Federal Electoral District(s): Dauphin-Swan River-Marquette
Next Election: Oct. 22, 2014 (4 year terms)
Art Potoroka, Reeve
Loretta Woytkiewicz, Chief Administrative Officer

Fisher
P.O. Box 280
30 Tache St.
Fisher Branch, MB R0C 0Z0
Tel: 204-372-6393; *Fax:* 204-372-8470
rmoffisher@mts.net
Municipal Type: Rural Municipality
Incorporated: Jan. 2, 1945 *Area:* 1,481.35 sq km
Population in 2011: 1,704
Provincial Electoral District(s): Interlake
Federal Electoral District(s): Selkirk-Interlake
Next Election: Oct. 22, 2014 (4 year terms)
Richard Hyde, Reeve
Linda Podaima, Chief Administrative Officer

Franklin
P.O. Box 66
115 Waddell Ave.
Dominion City, MB R0A 0H0
Tel: 204-427-2557; *Fax:* 204-427-2224
rmfrank@mts.net
Municipal Type: Rural Municipality
Area: 953.34 sq km
Population in 2011: 1,768
Provincial Electoral District(s): Emerson
Federal Electoral District(s): Dauphin-Swan River-Marquette; Provencher
Next Election: Oct. 22, 2014 (4 year terms)
Greg Janzen, Reeve
Tracey French, Chief Administrative Officer

Gilbert Plains
P.O. Box 220
201 Main St. North
Gilbert Plains, MB R0L 0X0
Tel: 204-548-2326; *Fax:* 204-548-2564
rmofgilbertplains@mts.net
www.gilbertplains.com
Municipal Type: Rural Municipality
Incorporated: Jan. 3, 1901 *Area:* 1,048.14 sq km
Population in 2011: 812
Provincial Electoral District(s): Dauphin-Roblin
Federal Electoral District(s): Dauphin-Swan River-Marquette
Next Election: Oct. 22, 2014 (4 year terms)
Gary Momotiuk, Reeve
Susan Boyachek, Chief Administrative Officer

Gimli
P.O. Box 1246
62 - 2nd St.
Gimli, MB R0C 1B0
Tel: 204-642-6650; *Fax:* 204-642-6660
gimli@rmgimli.com
www.gimli.ca
Municipal Type: Rural Municipality
Incorporated: Jan. 7, 1887 *Area:* 319.25 sq km
Population in 2011: 5,845
Provincial Electoral District(s): Gimli
Federal Electoral District(s): Selkirk-Interlake
Next Election: Oct. 22, 2014 (4 year terms)
Lynn Greenberg, Reeve
Joann King, Chief Administrative Officer

Glenella
P.O. Box 10
50 Main St. North
Glenella, MB R0J 0V0
Tel: 204-352-4281; *Fax:* 204-352-4100
rmofglen@inetlink.ca
Municipal Type: Rural Municipality
Incorporated: Jan. 5, 1920 *Area:* 497.14 sq km
Population in 2011: 522
Provincial Electoral District(s): Ste. Rose
Federal Electoral District(s): Dauphin-Swan River-Marquette
Next Election: Oct. 22, 2014 (4 year terms)
Derek Klassen, Reeve
Wendy Wutzke, Chief Administrative Officer

Glenwood
P.O. Box 487
100 - 2nd St. South
Souris, MB R0K 2C0
Tel: 204-483-2822; *Fax:* 204-483-2062
rmglenwood@mts.net
Municipal Type: Rural Municipality
Incorporated: 1883 *Area:* 577.58 sq km
Population in 2011: 602
Provincial Electoral District(s): Minnedosa
Federal Electoral District(s): Brandon-Souris
Next Election: Oct. 22, 2014 (4 year terms)
M.E. (Sandy) Sanderson, Reeve
Lisa Greig, Chief Administrative Officer

Grahamdale
P.O. Box 160
23 Government Rd.
Moosehorn, MB R0C 2E0
Tel: 204-768-2858; *Fax:* 204-768-3374
info@grahamdale.ca
www.grahamdale.ca
Municipal Type: Rural Municipality
Incorporated: Jan. 2, 1945 *Area:* 2,384.62 sq km
Population in 2011: 1,354
Provincial Electoral District(s): Interlake
Federal Electoral District(s): Selkirk-Interlake
Next Election: Oct. 22, 2014 (4 year terms)
Diane Price, Reeve
Shelly Schwitek, Chief Administrative Officer

Grandview
P.O. Box 340
531 Main St.
Grandview, MB R0L 0Y0
Tel: 204-546-5080; *Fax:* 204-546-5089
rmgra@inetlink.ca
www.rmofgrandview.ca
Municipal Type: Rural Municipality
Incorporated: Jan. 3, 1901 *Area:* 1,152.5 sq km
Population in 2011: 649
Provincial Electoral District(s): Dauphin-Roblin
Federal Electoral District(s): Dauphin-Swan River-Marquette
Next Election: Oct. 22, 2014 (4 year terms)
Clifford Kutzan, Reeve
Sharon Storozuk, Chief Administrative Officer

Grey
P.O. Box 99
34 Main St. North
Elm Creek, MB R0G 0N0
Tel: 204-436-2014; *Fax:* 204-436-2543
rmofgrey@mts.net
www.rmofgrey.ca
Municipal Type: Rural Municipality
Incorporated: Jan. 2, 1906 *Area:* 958.49 sq km
Population in 2011: 2,025
Provincial Electoral District(s): Carman
Federal Electoral District(s): Portage-Lisgar
Next Election: Oct. 22, 2014 (4 year terms)
Ted Tkachyk, Reeve
Kim Gibson, Chief Administrative Officer

Hamiota
P.O. Box 100
45 Maple Ave. East
Hamiota, MB R0M 0T0
Tel: 204-764-3050; *Fax:* 204-764-3055
info@hamiota.com
www.hamiota.com
Municipal Type: Rural Municipality
Incorporated: 1906 *Area:* 572.38 sq km
Population in 2011: 420
Provincial Electoral District(s): Russell
Federal Electoral District(s): Dauphin-Swan River-Marquette
Next Election: Oct. 22, 2014 (4 year terms)
Randy Lints, Reeve
Tom Mollard, Chief Administrative Officer

Hanover
P.O. Box 1720
28 Westland Dr.
Steinbach, MB R5G 1N4
Tel: 204-326-4488; *Fax:* 204-326-4830
www.hanovermb.ca
Municipal Type: Rural Municipality
Incorporated: Jan. 7, 1881 *Area:* 740.31 sq km
Population in 2011: 14,026
Provincial Electoral District(s): Steinbach
Federal Electoral District(s): Provencher
Next Election: Oct. 22, 2014 (4 year terms)
Stan Toews, Reeve
Douglas E. Cavers, Chief Administrative Officer

Harrison
P.O. Box 220
108 Main St.
Newdale, MB R0J 1J0
Tel: 204-849-2107; *Fax:* 204-849-2190
rmharris@inetbiz.ca
www.rmofharrison.com
Municipal Type: Rural Municipality
Incorporated: Jan. 2, 1883 *Area:* 476.73 sq km
Population in 2011: 864
Provincial Electoral District(s): Russell
Federal Electoral District(s): Dauphin-Swan River-Marquette
Next Election: Oct. 22, 2014 (4 year terms)
Murray Davies, Reeve
Donna Memryk, Chief Administrative Officer

Headingley
#1, 126 Bridge Rd.
Headingley, MB R4H 1G9
Tel: 204-837-5766; *Fax:* 204-831-7207
dwhite@rmofheadingley.ca
www.rmofheadingley.ca
Municipal Type: Rural Municipality
Incorporated: Jan. 4, 1992 *Area:* 106.96 sq km
Population in 2011: 3,215
Provincial Electoral District(s): Morris
Federal Electoral District(s): Charleswood-St. James-Assiniboia
Next Election: Oct. 22, 2014 (4 year terms)
Wilfred R. Taillieu, Reeve
Chris Fulsher, Chief Administrative Officer

Hillsburg
P.O. Box 1180
130 - 2nd Ave. NW
Roblin, MB R0L 1P0
Tel: 204-937-2155; *Fax:* 204-937-3317
rmhills@mts.net
Municipal Type: Rural Municipality
Incorporated: Jan. 2, 1912 *Area:* 656.76 sq km
Population in 2011: 426
Provincial Electoral District(s): Dauphin-Roblin
Federal Electoral District(s): Dauphin-Swan River-Marquette
Next Election: Oct. 22, 2014 (4 year terms)
Robert Misko, Reeve
Robin Perchaluk, Chief Administrative Officer

Kelsey
P.O. Box 578
264 Fischer Ave.
The Pas, MB R9A 1K6
Tel: 204-623-7474; *Fax:* 204-623-4546
rmkelsey@mts.net
Municipal Type: Rural Municipality
Incorporated: Jan. 7, 1944 *Area:* 867.64 sq km
Population in 2011: 2,272
Provincial Electoral District(s): Flin Flon; The Pas
Federal Electoral District(s): Churchill
Next Election: Oct. 22, 2014 (4 year terms)
Rod Berezowecki, Reeve
Jerry Hlady, Chief Administrative Officer

La Broquerie
P.O. Box 130
123 Simard St.
La Broquerie, MB R0A 0W0
Tel: 204-424-5251; *Fax:* 204-424-5193
labroquerie@rmlabroquerie.ca
www.labroquerie.com
Municipal Type: Rural Municipality
Incorporated: Jan. 2, 1883 *Area:* 578.2 sq km
Population in 2011: 5,198
Provincial Electoral District(s): Emerson
Federal Electoral District(s): Provencher
Next Election: Oct. 22, 2014 (4 year terms)
Claude Lussier, Reeve
Roger Bouvier, Chief Administrative Officer

Lac du Bonnet
P.O. Box 100
4187 Provincial Trunk Hwy. 317
Lac du Bonnet, MB R0E 1A0
Tel: 204-345-2619; *Fax:* 204-345-6716
rmldb@mts.net
www.lacdubonnet.com
Municipal Type: Rural Municipality
Incorporated: Jan. 2, 1917 *Area:* 1,100.17 sq km
Population in 2011: 2,671
Provincial Electoral District(s): Lac du Bonnet
Federal Electoral District(s): Provencher
Next Election: Oct. 22, 2014 (4 year terms)
Karl Gugenheimer, Reeve
Donna Tschetter, Chief Administrative Officer

Lakeview
P.O. Box 100
101 Main St.
Langruth, MB R0H 0N0
Tel: 204-445-2243; *Fax:* 204-445-2162
rmlakeview@mts.net
Municipal Type: Rural Municipality
Incorporated: Jan. 5, 1920 *Area:* 567.87 sq km
Population in 2011: 311
Provincial Electoral District(s): Ste. Rose
Federal Electoral District(s): Dauphin-Swan River-Marquette
Next Election: Oct. 22, 2014 (4 year terms)
Philip Thordarson, Reeve
Ron Brown, Chief Administrative Officer

Langford
P.O. Box 280
275 Hamilton St.
Neepawa, MB R0J 1H0
Tel: 204-476-7600; *Fax:* 204-476-7624
langford@westman.wave.ca
Municipal Type: Rural Municipality
Area: 561.95 sq km
Population in 2011: 767
Provincial Electoral District(s): Ste. Rose
Federal Electoral District(s): Dauphin-Swan River-Marquette
Next Election: Oct. 22, 2014 (4 year terms)
Kathy Jasienczyk, Reeve
Allison Bardsley, Chief Administrative Officer

Lansdowne
P.O. Box 141
302 Lansdowne Ave.
Arden, MB R0J 0B0
Tel: 204-368-2202; *Fax:* 204-368-2278
rmlansdowne@inetlink.ca
Municipal Type: Rural Municipality
Incorporated: Jan. 3, 1884 *Area:* 766.29 sq km
Population in 2011: 723
Provincial Electoral District(s): Ste. Rose
Federal Electoral District(s): Dauphin-Swan River-Marquette
Next Election: Oct. 22, 2014 (4 year terms)
Richard Funk, Reeve
Tracey Winthrop-Meyers, Chief Administrative Officer

Lawrence
P.O. Box 220
714 Main St.
Rorketon, MB R0L 1R0
Tel: 204-732-2333; *Fax:* 204-732-2557
rmlaw@inetlink.ca
Municipal Type: Rural Municipality
Incorporated: Jan. 5, 1914 *Area:* 761.64 sq km
Population in 2011: 456
Provincial Electoral District(s): Dauphin-Roblin
Federal Electoral District(s): Dauphin-Swan River-Marquette
Next Election: Oct. 22, 2014 (4 year terms)
Fred Taylor, Reeve

Vacant, Chief Administrative Officer

Lorne
P.O. Box 10
307 - 3rd St.
Somerset, MB R0G 2L0
Tel: 204-744-2133; *Fax:* 204-744-2349
rmlorne@inetlink.ca
Municipal Type: Rural Municipality
Incorporated: Jan. 5, 1880 *Area:* 906.82 sq km
Population in 2011: 1,884
Provincial Electoral District(s): Carman
Federal Electoral District(s): Portage-Lisgar
Next Election: Oct. 22, 2014 (4 year terms)
Aurel Pantel, Reeve
Shannon Gaultier, Chief Administrative Officer

Louise
P.O. Box 310
26 South Railway Ave. East
Crystal City, MB R0K 0N0
Tel: 204-873-2591; *Fax:* 204-873-2459
rmlouise@inetlink.ca
Municipal Type: Rural Municipality
Incorporated: Jan. 5, 1880 *Area:* 932.67 sq km
Population in 2011: 913
Provincial Electoral District(s): Turtle Mountain
Federal Electoral District(s): Portage-Lisgar
Next Election: Oct. 22, 2014 (4 year terms)
Kenneth S. Buchanan, Reeve
Alexis Gardiner, Chief Administrative Officer

Macdonald
P.O. Box 100
161 Mandan Dr.
Sanford, MB R0G 2J0
Tel: 204-736-2255; *Fax:* 204-736-4335
info@rmofmacdonald.com
rmofmacdonald.com
Municipal Type: Rural Municipality
Incorporated: Jan. 7, 1881 *Area:* 1,156.62 sq km
Population in 2011: 6,280
Provincial Electoral District(s): Morris
Federal Electoral District(s): Portage-Lisgar
Next Election: Oct. 22, 2014 (4 year terms)
Rodney Burns, Reeve
W. Tom Raine, Chief Administrative Officer

McCreary
P.O. Box 338
432 - 1st Ave.
McCreary, MB R0J 1B0
Tel: 204-835-2309; *Fax:* 204-835-2649
rmmccreary@inetlink.ca
Municipal Type: Rural Municipality
Incorporated: Jan. 6, 1909 *Area:* 522.69 sq km
Population in 2011: 476
Provincial Electoral District(s): Ste. Rose
Federal Electoral District(s): Dauphin-Swan River-Marquette
Next Election: Oct. 22, 2014 (4 year terms)
Larry McLauchlan, Reeve
Margaret I. Roncin, Chief Administrative Officer

Miniota
P.O. Box 70
111 Sarah Ave.
Miniota, MB R0M 1M0
Tel: 204-567-3683; *Fax:* 204-567-3807
miniota@mts.net
Municipal Type: Rural Municipality
Incorporated: 1900 *Area:* 832.75 sq km
Population in 2011: 871
Provincial Electoral District(s): Russell
Federal Electoral District(s): Dauphin-Swan River-Marquette
Next Election: Oct. 22, 2014 (4 year terms)
Olive McKean, Reeve
Tina Collier, Chief Administrative Officer

Minitonas
P.O. Box 9
311 Main St.
Minitonas, MB R0L 1G0
Tel: 204-525-4461; *Fax:* 204-525-4857
rmmin@mts.net
Municipal Type: Rural Municipality
Incorporated: Jan. 3, 1901 *Area:* 1,197.67 sq km
Population in 2011: 996
Provincial Electoral District(s): Swan River
Federal Electoral District(s): Dauphin-Swan River-Marquette
Next Election: Oct. 22, 2014 (4 year terms)
Michael McIntosh, Reeve
Carolyn Gordon, Chief Administrative Officer

Minto
P.O. Box 247
49 Main St. South
Minnedosa, MB R0J 1E0
Tel: 204-867-3865; *Fax:* 204-867-1937
rmminto@mts.net
Municipal Type: Rural Municipality
Incorporated: Jan. 5, 1903 *Area:* 363.65 sq km
Population in 2011: 644
Provincial Electoral District(s): Minnedosa
Federal Electoral District(s): Brandon-Souris; Dauphin-Swan River-Marquette
Next Election: Oct. 22, 2014 (4 year terms)
Calvin Jacobson, Reeve
Aaren Robertson, Chief Administrative Officer

Montcalm
P.O. Box 300
46 - 1st St. East
Letellier, MB R0G 1C0
Tel: 204-737-2271; *Fax:* 204-737-2326
montcalm@mts.net
Municipal Type: Rural Municipality
Incorporated: Jan. 1, 1882 *Area:* 469.41 sq km
Population in 2011: 1,309
Provincial Electoral District(s): Emerson
Federal Electoral District(s): Provencher
Next Election: Oct. 22, 2014 (4 year terms)
Roger Vermette, Reeve
Mitch Duval, Chief Administrative Officer

Morris
P.O. Box 518
207 Main St. North
Morris, MB R0G 1K0
Tel: 204-746-2642; *Fax:* 204-746-8801
rmmorris@mts.net
Municipal Type: Rural Municipality
Incorporated: Jan. 5, 1880 *Area:* 1,041.15 sq km
Population in 2011: 2,999
Provincial Electoral District(s): Morris
Federal Electoral District(s): Provencher
Next Election: Oct. 22, 2014 (4 year terms)
Ralph Groening, Reeve
Michelle Robert, Chief Administrative Officer

Morton
P.O. Box 490
420 South Railway
Boissevain, MB R0K 0E0
Tel: 204-534-2433; *Fax:* 204-534-3710
boissevain@mts.net
Municipal Type: Rural Municipality
Area: 1,089.88 sq km
Population in 2011: 698
Provincial Electoral District(s): Arthur-Virden
Federal Electoral District(s): Brandon-Souris
Next Election: Oct. 22, 2014 (4 year terms)
Robert J.D. McCallum, Reeve
Lloyd Leganchuk, Chief Administrative Officer

Mossey River
P.O. Box 80
100 - 2nd Ave. East
Fork River, MB R0L 0V0
Tel: 204-657-2331; *Fax:* 204-657-2202
rmmossey@inetlink.ca
Municipal Type: Rural Municipality
Incorporated: Jan. 2, 1906 *Area:* 1,123.06 sq km
Population in 2011: 539
Provincial Electoral District(s): Swan River
Federal Electoral District(s): Dauphin-Swan River-Mossey River
Next Election: Oct. 22, 2014 (4 year terms)
Ron Kostyshyn, Reeve
Linda Rosteski, Chief Administrative Officer

Mountain
P.O. Box 155
200 Drury Ave.
Birch River, MB R0L 0E0
Tel: 204-236-4222; *Fax:* 204-236-4773
rmmountn@mts.net
Municipal Type: Rural Municipality
Area: 2607.69 sq km
Population in 2011: 1,104
Provincial Electoral District(s): Swan River
Federal Electoral District(s): Dauphin-Swan River-Marquette
Next Election: Oct. 22, 2014 (4 year terms)
Robert Hanson, Reeve
Norman Bruce, Chief Administrative Officer

Mystery Lake
P.O. Box 189 Main
Airport Rd. South
Thompson, MB R8N 1N1
Tel: 204-677-4075; *Fax:* 204-778-7642
lgdmystlake@mymts.net
Municipal Type: Local Goverment District
Incorporated: Jan. 1, 1956 *Area:* 3,464.06 sq km
Population in 2011: 10
Next Election: Oct. 22, 2014 (4 year terms)
Corinne Stewart, Resident Administrator & Acting Chief Administrative Officer

North Cypress
P.O. Box 130
316 - 4th Ave.
Carberry, MB R0K 0H0
Tel: 204-834-6600; *Fax:* 204-834-6604
north.cypress@rmofnorthcypress.ca
www.rmofnorthcypress.ca
Municipal Type: Rural Municipality
Incorporated: Jan. 1, 1882 *Area:* 1,199.92 sq km
Population in 2011: 1,860
Provincial Electoral District(s): Turtle Mountain
Federal Electoral District(s): Brandon-Souris
Next Election: Oct. 22, 2014 (4 year terms)
Ralph Oliver, Reeve
Brent McMillan, Chief Administrative Officer

North Norfolk
P.O. Box 190
27 Hampton St. East
MacGregor, MB R0H 0R0
Tel: 204-685-2211; *Fax:* 204-685-2616
office@northnorfolk.ca
northnorfolk.ca
Municipal Type: Rural Municipality
Incorporated: Jan. 1, 1882 *Area:* 1,158.76 sq km
Population in 2011: 2,799
Provincial Electoral District(s): Turtle Mountain
Federal Electoral District(s): Portage-Lisgar
Next Election: Oct. 22, 2014 (4 year terms)
Neil Christoffersen, Reeve
Valorie Unrau, Chief Administrative Officer

Oakland
P.O. Box 28
1 Main St.
Nesbitt, MB R0K 1P0
Tel: 204-824-2666; *Fax:* 204-824-2374
rm_of_oakland@hotmail.com
Municipal Type: Rural Municipality
Incorporated: Jan. 2, 1883 *Area:* 575.21 sq km
Population in 2011: 1,056
Provincial Electoral District(s): Minnedosa
Federal Electoral District(s): Brandon-Souris; Portage Lisgar
Next Election: Oct. 22, 2014 (4 year terms)
David B. Inkster, Reeve
Marlene Biles, Chief Administrative Officer

Ochre River
P.O. Box 40
206 MacKenzie Ave.
Ochre River, MB R0L 1K0
Tel: 204-733-2423; *Fax:* 204-733-2259
rmochre@inetlink.ca
www.mts.net/~rmochre
Municipal Type: Rural Municipality
Incorporated: Jan. 3, 1901 *Area:* 535.59 sq km
Population in 2011: 945
Provincial Electoral District(s): Dauphin-Roblin
Federal Electoral District(s): Dauphin-Swan River-Marquette
Next Election: Oct. 22, 2014 (4 year terms)
Clinton Cleave, Reeve
Pat Nichols, Chief Administrative Officer

Odanah
P.O. Box 1197
49 Main St. South
Minnedosa, MB R0J 1E0
Tel: 204-867-3282; *Fax:* 204-867-1937
rmminto@mts.net
Municipal Type: Rural Municipality
Incorporated: Jan. 2, 1883 *Area:* 380.25 sq km
Population in 2011: 533
Provincial Electoral District(s): Minnedosa
Federal Electoral District(s): Dauphin-Swan River-Marquette
Next Election: Oct. 22, 2014 (4 year terms)
James A. Andersen, Reeve
Aaren Robertson, Chief Administrative Officer

Park
P.O. Box 190
43 Gateway St.
Onanole, MB R0J 1N0
Tel: 204-848-7614; *Fax:* 204-848-2082
admin@rmpark.org
www.rmpark.org
Municipal Type: Rural Municipality
Incorporated: Jan. 6, 1954 *Area:* 793.38 sq km
Population in 2011: 935
Provincial Electoral District(s): Dauphin-Roblin; Russell
Federal Electoral District(s): Dauphin-Swan River-Marquette
Next Election: Oct. 22, 2014 (4 year terms)
Craig Atkinson, Reeve
Chad Davies, Chief Administrative Officer

Pembina
P.O. Box 189
315 Main St.
Manitou, MB R0G 1G0
Tel: 204-242-2838; *Fax:* 204-242-2798
admin@rmofpembina.com
www.rmofpembina.com
Municipal Type: Rural Municipality
Incorporated: Jan. 4, 1890 *Area:* 1,114.76 sq km
Population in 2011: 1,561
Provincial Electoral District(s): Pembina
Federal Electoral District(s): Portage-Lisgar
Next Election: Oct. 22, 2014 (4 year terms)
Kim Taylor, Reeve
Judy D. Young, Chief Administrative Officer

Pinawa
P.O. Box 100
36 Burrows Rd.
Pinawa, MB R0E 1L0
Tel: 204-753-5100; *Fax:* 204-753-2770
info@pinawa.com
www.pinawa.com
Municipal Type: Local Goverment District
Incorporated: Jan. 3, 1963 *Area:* 128.47 sq km
Population in 2011: 1,444
Next Election: Oct. 22, 2014 (4 year terms)
Blair Skinner, Mayor
Gary Hanna, Resident Administrator

Piney
P.O. Box 48
6092 Boundary St.
Vassar, MB R0A 2J0
Tel: 204-437-2284; *Fax:* 204-437-2556
martin_rmpiney@wiband.ca
www.rmofpiney.mb.ca
Municipal Type: Rural Municipality
Area: 2,433.77 sq km
Population in 2011: 1,720
Provincial Electoral District(s): Emerson
Federal Electoral District(s): Provencher
Next Election: Oct. 22, 2014 (4 year terms)
Duane Boutang, Reeve
Martin Van Osch, Chief Administrative Officer

Pipestone
P.O. Box 99
401 - 3rd Ave.
Reston, MB R0M 1X0
Tel: 204-877-3327; *Fax:* 204-877-3999
admin@rmofpipestone.com
www.rmofpipestone.com
Municipal Type: Rural Municipality
Incorporated: Jan. 6, 1897 *Area:* 1,147.35 sq km
Population in 2011: 1,447
Provincial Electoral District(s): Arthur-Virden
Federal Electoral District(s): Brandon-Souris
Next Election: Oct. 22, 2014 (4 year terms)
Ross Tycoles, Reeve
June Greggor, Chief Administrative Officer

Portage la Prairie
35 Tupper St. South
Portage la Prairie, MB R1N 1W7
Tel: 204-857-3821; *Fax:* 204-239-0069
info@rmofportage.ca
www.rmofportage.ca
Municipal Type: Rural Municipality
Incorporated: Jan. 4, 1879 *Area:* 1,964.32 sq km
Population in 2011: 6,525
Provincial Electoral District(s): Portage la Prairie; Carman
Federal Electoral District(s): Portage-Lisgar; Selkirk-Interlake
Next Election: Oct. 22, 2014 (4 year terms)
Kam Blight, Reeve
Daryl Hrehirchuk, Chief Administrative Officer

Reynolds
P.O. Box 46
46044 Hwy. 11
Hadashville, MB R0E 0X0
Tel: 204-426-5305; *Fax:* 204-426-5552
rmreynol@mts.net
www.rmofreynolds.com
Municipal Type: Rural Municipality
Incorporated: Jan. 2, 1945 *Area:* 3,573.31 sq km
Population in 2011: 1,285
Provincial Electoral District(s): La Verendrye; Lac du Bonnet
Federal Electoral District(s): Provencher
Next Election: Oct. 22, 2014 (4 year terms)
David Turchyn, Reeve
Holly Krysko, Chief Administrative Officer

Rhineland
P.O. Box 270
72 - 2nd St. NE
Altona, MB R0G 0B0
Tel: 204-324-5357; *Fax:* 204-324-1516
rhineland@mts.net
Municipal Type: Rural Municipality
Incorporated: Jan. 3, 1884 *Area:* 953.42 sq km
Population in 2011: 4,373
Provincial Electoral District(s): Emerson
Federal Electoral District(s): Portage-Lisgar
Next Election: Oct. 22, 2014 (4 year terms)
Grant Heinrichs, Reeve
Michael Rempel, Chief Administrative Officer

Ritchot
352 Main St.
St. Adolphe, MB R5A 1B9
Tel: 204-883-2293; *Fax:* 204-883-2674
municipaloffice@ritchot.com
www.ritchot.com
Municipal Type: Rural Municipality
Incorporated: Jan. 4, 1890 *Area:* 333.53 sq km
Population in 2011: 5,478
Provincial Electoral District(s): La Verendrye; Morris
Federal Electoral District(s): Provencher; Winnipeg South
Next Election: Oct. 22, 2014 (4 year terms)
Robert Stefaniuk, Mayor
Florence May, Chief Administrative Officer

Riverside
P.O. Box 126
110 Rea St.
Dunrea, MB R0K 0S0
Tel: 204-776-2113; *Fax:* 204-776-2228
riverside@mts.net
www.rmriverside.ca
Municipal Type: Rural Municipality
Area: 577.34 sq km
Population in 2011: 780
Provincial Electoral District(s): Turtle Mountain
Federal Electoral District(s): Brandon-Souris; Provencher; Kildonan-St. Paul
Next Election: Oct. 22, 2014 (4 year terms)
Lonn Dunlop, Reeve
Lori Bessant, Chief Administrative Officer

Roblin
P.O. Box 9
485 Curwen St.
Cartwright, MB R0K 0L0
Tel: 204-529-2363; *Fax:* 204-529-2288
www.cartwrightroblin.ca
Municipal Type: Rural Municipality
Incorporated: Jan. 4, 1902 *Area:* 716.15 sq km
Population in 2011: 932
Provincial Electoral District(s): Turtle Mountain
Federal Electoral District(s): Brandon-Souris; Dauphin-Swan River-Marquette
Next Election: Oct. 22, 2014 (4 year terms)
Tom Mowbray, Reeve
Colleen Mullin, Chief Administrative Officer

Rockwood
P.O. Box 902
285 Main St.
Stonewall, MB R0C 2Z0
Tel: 204-467-2272; *Fax:* 204-467-5329
info@rockwood.ca
www.rockwood.ca
Municipal Type: Rural Municipality
Incorporated: Jan. 7, 1881 *Area:* 1,199.76 sq km
Population in 2011: 7,964
Provincial Electoral District(s): Lakeside
Federal Electoral District(s): Selkirk-Interlake
Next Election: Oct. 22, 2014 (4 year terms)
Jim Campbell, Reeve
L. Grant Thorsteinson, Chief Administrative Officer

Roland
P.O. Box 119
45 - 3rd St.
Roland, MB R0G 1T0
Tel: 204-343-2061; *Fax:* 204-343-2001
rmroland@pmcnet.ca
Municipal Type: Rural Municipality
Incorporated: Jan. 4, 1908 *Area:* 485.06 sq km
Population in 2011: 1,058
Provincial Electoral District(s): Carman
Federal Electoral District(s): Portage-Lisgar
Next Election: Oct. 22, 2014 (4 year terms)
Brian Coates, Reeve
Kristi Olson, Chief Administrative Officer

Rosedale
P.O. Box 100
282 Hamilton St.
Neepawa, MB R0J 1H0
Tel: 204-476-5414; *Fax:* 204-476-5431
rosedale@mts.net
Municipal Type: Rural Municipality
Incorporated: Jan. 3, 1884 *Area:* 865.58 sq km
Population in 2011: 1,627
Provincial Electoral District(s): Ste. Rose
Federal Electoral District(s): Dauphin-Swan River-Marquette
Next Election: Oct. 22, 2014 (4 year terms)
Edward Levandoski, Reeve
Karen McDonald, Chief Administrative Officer

Rossburn
P.O. Box 100
39 Main St. North
Rossburn, MB R0J 1V0
Tel: 204-859-2779; *Fax:* 204-859-2959
rsbrm@mts.net
Municipal Type: Rural Municipality
Incorporated: Jan. 3, 1884 *Area:* 679.29 sq km
Population in 2011: 494
Provincial Electoral District(s): Russell
Federal Electoral District(s): Dauphin-Swan River-Marquette
Next Election: Oct. 22, 2014 (4 year terms)
Ed Mychasiw, Reeve
Marianne Choptuik, Chief Administrative Officer

Rosser
P.O. Box 131
Provincial Rd. 221
Rosser, MB R0H 1E0
Tel: 204-467-5711; *Fax:* 204-467-5958
info@rmofrosser.com
www.rmofrosser.com
Municipal Type: Rural Municipality
Incorporated: Jan. 1, 1893 *Area:* 441.43 sq km
Population in 2011: 1,352
Provincial Electoral District(s): Lakeside
Federal Electoral District(s): Selkirk-Interlake
Next Election: Oct. 22, 2014 (4 year terms)
Frances Smee, Chief Administrative Officer
Beverley Wells, Reeve

Russell
P.O. Box 220
362 Main St. North
Russell, MB R0J 1W0
Tel: 204-773-2294; *Fax:* 204-773-3841
rmrussel@mts.net
Municipal Type: Rural Municipality
Incorporated: Jan. 1, 1882 *Area:* 567.83 sq km
Population in 2011: 459
Provincial Electoral District(s): Russell
Federal Electoral District(s): Dauphin-Swan River-Marquette
Next Election: Oct. 22, 2014 (4 year terms)
Robert W. Muir, Reeve
Nicole Burdeniuk, Chief Administrative Officer

St. Andrews
P.O. Box 130
500 Railway Ave.
Clandeboye, MB R0C 0P0
Tel: 204-738-2264; *Fax:* 204-738-2500
info@rmofstandrews.com
www.rmofstandrews.com
Municipal Type: Rural Municipality
Incorporated: Jan. 5, 1880 *Area:* 752.7 sq km
Population in 2011: 11,875
Provincial Electoral District(s): Gimli
Federal Electoral District(s): Selkirk-Interlake
Next Election: Oct. 22, 2014 (4 year terms)

Don Forfar, Reeve
Sue Sutherland, Chief Administrative Officer

Ste. Anne
141 Central Ave.
Ste. Anne, MB R5H 1C3
Tel: 204-422-5929; *Fax:* 204-422-9723
info@rmofsteanne.com
www.rmofsteanne.com
Municipal Type: Rural Municipality
Incorporated: Feb. 3, 1881 *Area:* 477.65 sq km
Population in 2011: 4,686
Provincial Electoral District(s): La Verendrye
Federal Electoral District(s): Provencher
Next Election: Oct. 22, 2014 (4 year terms)
Art Bergmann, Reeve
A.T. (Loni) Eskildsen, Chief Administrative Officer

St. Clements
P.O. Box 2
1043 Kittson Rd.
East Selkirk, MB R0E 0M0
Tel: 204-482-3300; *Fax:* 204-482-3098
info@rmofstclements.com
www.rmofstclements.com
Municipal Type: Rural Municipality
Incorporated: July 7, 1883 *Area:* 728.67 sq km
Population in 2011: 10,505
Provincial Electoral District(s): Selkirk
Federal Electoral District(s): Selkirk-Interlake
Next Election: Oct. 22, 2014 (4 year terms)
Steve Strang, Reeve
DJ Sigmundson, Chief Administrative Officer

St. François Xavier
1060 Hwy. 26
St François Xavier, MB R4L 1A5
Tel: 204-864-2092; *Fax:* 204-864-2390
info@rm-stfrancois.mb.ca
www.rm-stfrancois.mb.ca
Municipal Type: Rural Municipality
Incorporated: Jan. 5, 1880 *Area:* 204.55 sq km
Population in 2011: 1,240
Provincial Electoral District(s): Morris
Federal Electoral District(s): Portage-Lisgar
Next Election: Oct. 22, 2014 (4 year terms)
Roger Poitras, Reeve
Robert Poirier, Chief Administrative Officer

St. Laurent
P.O. Box 220
436 St. Laurent Veterans Memorial Rd.
St Laurent, MB R0C 2S0
Tel: 204-646-2259; *Fax:* 204-646-2705
rmstlaur@mts.net
www.rmofstlaurent.ca
Municipal Type: Rural Municipality
Incorporated: Jan. 1, 1882 *Area:* 462.51 sq km
Population in 2011: 1,305
Provincial Electoral District(s): Lakeside
Federal Electoral District(s): Selkirk-Interlake
Next Election: Oct. 22, 2014 (4 year terms)
Earl Zotter, Reeve
Diana Friesen, Chief Administrative Officer

Ste. Rose
P.O. Box 30
630 Central Ave.
Ste. Rose du Lac, MB R0L 1S0
Tel: 204-447-2633; *Fax:* 204-447-2278
rmstrose@mymts.net
www.sterose.ca
Municipal Type: Rural Municipality
Incorporated: Nov. 7, 1902 *Area:* 626.03 sq km
Population in 2011: 771
Provincial Electoral District(s): Ste. Rose
Federal Electoral District(s): Dauphin-Swan River-Marquette
Next Election: Oct. 22, 2014 (4 year terms)
Maurice Maguet, Reeve
Michelle Denys, Chief Administrative Officer

Saskatchewan
P.O. Box 9
435 - 3rd Ave.
Rapid City, MB R0K 1W0
Tel: 204-826-2515; *Fax:* 204-826-2274
rmsk@mts.net
Municipal Type: Rural Municipality
Incorporated: Jan. 2, 1883 *Area:* 563.73 sq km
Population in 2011: 570
Provincial Electoral District(s): Minnedosa
Federal Electoral District(s): Dauphin-Swan River-Marquette
Next Election: Oct. 22, 2014 (4 year terms)
Robert Sharpe, Reeve
Lois Sharpe, Chief Administrative Officer

Shell River
P.O. Box 998
213 - 2nd Ave. NW
Roblin, MB R0L 1P0
Tel: 204-937-4430; *Fax:* 204-937-8496
shellrvr@mts.net
www.rm.shellriver.mb.ca
Municipal Type: Rural Municipality
Incorporated: Jan. 3, 1884 *Area:* 735.12 sq km
Population in 2011: 1,084
Provincial Electoral District(s): Dauphin-Roblin
Federal Electoral District(s): Dauphin-Swan River-Marquette
Next Election: Oct. 22, 2014 (4 year terms)
Albert Nabe, Reeve
Dione Cherneski, Chief Administrative Officer

Shellmouth - Boulton
P.O. Box 110
118 Main St.
Inglis, MB R0J 0X0
Tel: 204-564-2589; *Fax:* 204-564-2643
rmosb@mts.net
Municipal Type: Rural Municipality
Incorporated: Jan. 6, 1999 *Area:* 1,095.07 sq km
Population in 2011: 930
Provincial Electoral District(s): Russell
Federal Electoral District(s): Dauphin-Swan River-Marquette
Next Election: Oct. 22, 2014 (4 year terms)
Alvin Zimmer, Reeve
Cindy Marzoff, Chief Administrative Officer

Shoal Lake
P.O. Box 278
306 Elm St.
Shoal Lake, MB R0J 1Z0
Tel: 204-759-2565; *Fax:* 204-759-2740
shoalake@goinet.ca
www.shoallake.ca
Municipal Type: Rural Municipality
Area: 568.18 sq km
Population in 2011: 1,229
Provincial Electoral District(s): Russell
Federal Electoral District(s): Dauphin-Swan River-Marquette
Next Election: Oct. 22, 2014 (4 year terms)
Donald Yanick, Reeve
Nadine Gapka, Chief Administrative Officer

Sifton
P.O. Box 100
293 - 2nd Ave. West
Oak Lake, MB R0M 1P0
Tel: 204-855-2423; *Fax:* 204-855-2836
cao_sifton@mts.net
Municipal Type: Rural Municipality
Incorporated: Jan. 3, 1884 *Area:* 768.11 sq km
Population in 2011: 789
Provincial Electoral District(s): Arthur-Virden
Federal Electoral District(s): Brandon-Souris; Dauphin-Swan River-Marquette
Next Election: Oct. 22, 2014 (4 year terms)
Rick Plaisier, Reeve
Mary Smith, Chief Administrative Officer

Siglunes
P.O. Box 370
38 Main St.
Ashern, MB R0C 0E0
Tel: 204-768-2641; *Fax:* 204-768-2301
siglunes@mts.net
Municipal Type: Rural Municipality
Incorporated: Jan. 2, 1917 *Area:* 837.42 sq km
Population in 2011: 1,360
Provincial Electoral District(s): Interlake
Federal Electoral District(s): Selkirk-Interlake
Next Election: Oct. 22, 2014 (4 year terms)
Barry Zacharias, Reeve
William Hildebrand, Chief Administrative Officer

Silver Creek
P.O. Box 130
307 Main St.
Angusville, MB R0J 0A0
Tel: 204-773-2449; *Fax:* 204-773-3101
silcreek@mts.net
Municipal Type: Rural Municipality
Incorporated: Jan. 3, 1884 *Area:* 525.46 sq km
Population in 2011: 460
Provincial Electoral District(s): Russell
Federal Electoral District(s): Dauphin-Swan River-Marquette
Next Election: Oct. 22, 2014 (4 year terms)
Fred Dunn, Reeve
Cheryl Mernyk, Chief Administrative Officer

South Cypress
P.O. Box 219
618 Railway Ave.
Glenboro, MB R0K 0X0
Tel: 204-827-2252; *Fax:* 204-827-2123
caormsc@mts.net
Municipal Type: Rural Municipality
Incorporated: Jan. 7, 1881 *Area:* 1,095.08 sq km
Population in 2011: 838
Provincial Electoral District(s): Turtle Mountain
Federal Electoral District(s): Brandon-Souris
Next Election: Oct. 22, 2014 (4 year terms)
Earl E. Malyon, Reeve
Eric C. Plaetinck, Chief Administrative Officer

South Norfolk
P.O. Box 30
180 Broadway St.
Treherne, MB R0G 2V0
Tel: 204-723-2044; *Fax:* 204-723-2719
treherne@mts.net
Municipal Type: Rural Municipality
Area: 726.76 sq km
Population in 2011: 1,125
Provincial Electoral District(s): Carman
Federal Electoral District(s): Portage-Lisgar
Next Election: Oct. 22, 2014 (4 year terms)
Craig Spencer, Reeve
Jackie Jenkinson, Chief Administrative Officer

Springfield
P.O. Box 219
628 Main St.
Oakbank, MB R0E 1J0
Tel: 204-444-3321; *Fax:* 204-444-2137
ltetrault@rmofspringfield.ca
www.rmofspringfield.ca
Municipal Type: Rural Municipality
Incorporated: Jan. 4, 1873 *Area:* 1,100.81 sq km
Population in 2011: 14,069
Provincial Electoral District(s): Springfield
Federal Electoral District(s): Provencher; Selkirk-Interlake
Next Election: Oct. 22, 2014 (4 year terms)
Jim McCarthy, Reeve
Laurent Tétrault, Chief Administrative Officer

Stanley
#100, 379 Stephen St.
Morden, MB R6M 1V1
Tel: 204-822-6251; *Fax:* 204-822-3596
info@rmofstanley.ca
www.rmofstanley.ca
Municipal Type: Rural Municipality
Incorporated: Nov. 7, 1890 *Area:* 835.59 sq km
Population in 2011: 8,256
Provincial Electoral District(s): Pembina
Federal Electoral District(s): Portage-Lisgar
Next Election: Oct. 22, 2014 (4 year terms)
Art Petkau, Reeve
Rick Klippenstein, Chief Administrative Officer

Strathclair
P.O. Box 160
127 Veterans Way
Strathclair, MB R0J 2C0
Tel: 204-365-2196; *Fax:* 204-365-2056
strathrm@inetbiz.ca
Municipal Type: Rural Municipality
Incorporated: Jan. 3, 1884 *Area:* 539.96 sq km
Population in 2011: 744
Provincial Electoral District(s): Russell
Federal Electoral District(s): Dauphin-Swan River-Marquette
Next Election: Oct. 22, 2014 (4 year terms)
Ken Wozney, Reeve
Shelley Glenn, Chief Administrative Officer

Strathcona
P.O. Box 100
101 Albert St. East
Belmont, MB R0K 0C0
Tel: 204-537-2241; *Fax:* 204-537-2364
caostrathcona@inethome.ca
Municipal Type: Rural Municipality
Incorporated: Jan. 2, 1906 *Area:* 485.56 sq km
Population in 2011: 643
Provincial Electoral District(s): Turtle Mountain

Federal Electoral District(s): Brandon-Souris
Next Election: Oct. 22, 2014 (4 year terms)
Dennis Schram, Reeve
Carolyn Davies, Chief Administrative Officer

Stuartburn
P.O. Box 59
108 Main St. North
Vita, MB R0A 2K0
Tel: 204-425-3218; *Fax:* 204-425-3513
612rm@mts.net
Municipal Type: Rural Municipality
Incorporated: Jan. 4, 1997 *Area:* 1,161.65 sq km
Population in 2011: 1,535
Provincial Electoral District(s): Emerson
Federal Electoral District(s): Provencher
Next Election: Oct. 22, 2014 (4 year terms)
Jim Swidersky, Reeve
Jennifer Blatz, Chief Administrative Officer

Swan River
P.O. Box 610
216 Main St. West
Swan River, MB R0L 1Z0
Tel: 204-734-3344; *Fax:* 204-734-3701
ruralm@mts.net
www.rmofswanriver.com
Municipal Type: Rural Municipality
Incorporated: Jan. 3, 1901 *Area:* 1,719.58 sq km
Population in 2011: 2,546
Provincial Electoral District(s): Swan River
Federal Electoral District(s): Dauphin-Swan River-Marquette
Next Election: Oct. 22, 2014 (4 year terms)
Lorne Henkelman, Reeve
Debbie Reich, Chief Administrative Officer

Taché
P.O. Box 100
1294 Dawson Rd.
Lorette, MB R0A 0Y0
Tel: 204-878-3321; *Fax:* 204-878-9977
info@rmtache.ca
Municipal Type: Rural Municipality
Incorporated: Jan. 5, 1880 *Area:* 581.52 sq km
Population in 2011: 10,284
Provincial Electoral District(s): La Verendrye
Federal Electoral District(s): Provencher
Next Election: Oct. 22, 2014 (4 year terms)
William Danylchuk, Reeve
Dan Poersch, Chief Administrative Officer

Thompson
P.O. Box 190
531 Norton Ave.
Miami, MB R0G 1H0
Tel: 204-435-2114; *Fax:* 204-435-2067
rmthompson@cici.mb.ca
Municipal Type: Rural Municipality
Incorporated: Jan. 6, 1909 *Area:* 528.57 sq km
Population in 2011: 1,397
Provincial Electoral District(s): Carman
Federal Electoral District(s): Portage-Lisgar
Next Election: Oct. 22, 2014 (4 year terms)
Jason Vanstone, Reeve
Diane Chatwin, Chief Administrative Officer

Victoria
P.O. Box 40
130 Broadway St.
Holland, MB R0G 0X0
Tel: 204-526-2423; *Fax:* 204-526-2028
office@rmofvictoria.com
rmofvictoria.com
Municipal Type: Rural Municipality
Incorporated: Jan. 4, 1902 *Area:* 697.63 sq km
Population in 2011: 1,119
Provincial Electoral District(s): Carman
Federal Electoral District(s): Portage-Lisgar
Next Election: Oct. 22, 2014 (4 year terms)
Harold W. Purkess, Reeve
Ivan Bruneau, Chief Administrative Officer

Victoria Beach
#303, 960 Portage Ave.
Winnipeg, MB R3G 0R4
Tel: 204-774-4263; *Fax:* 204-774-9834
vicbeach@mts.net
Municipal Type: Rural Municipality
Incorporated: Jan. 4, 1902 *Area:* 20.28 sq km
Population in 2011: 374
Provincial Electoral District(s): Selkirk
Federal Electoral District(s): Selkirk-Interlake
Next Election: July 25, 2014 (4 year terms)
Tom Farrell, Reeve
Raymond Moreau, Chief Administrative Officer

Wallace
P.O. Box 2200
305 Nelson St. West
Virden, MB R0M 2C0
Tel: 204-748-1239; *Fax:* 204-748-3450
don.wallace@mts.net
Municipal Type: Rural Municipality
Incorporated: Jan. 6, 1909 *Area:* 1,148.75 sq km
Population in 2011: 1,526
Provincial Electoral District(s): Arthur-Virden
Federal Electoral District(s): Brandon-Souris
Next Election: Oct. 22, 2014 (4 year terms)
Vacant, Reeve
Don Stephenson, Chief Administrative Officer

West St. Paul
3550 Main St.
West St Paul, MB R4A 5A3
Tel: 204-338-0306; *Fax:* 204-334-9362
info@weststpaul.com
www.weststpaul.com
Municipal Type: Rural Municipality
Incorporated: Jan. 7, 1916 *Area:* 87.66 sq km
Population in 2011: 4,932
Provincial Electoral District(s): Gimli
Federal Electoral District(s): Kildonan-St. Paul
Next Election: Oct. 22, 2014 (4 year terms)
Bruce Henley, Reeve
Brent Olynyk, Chief Administrative Officer

Westbourne
P.O. Box 150
Hwy. 16 West
Gladstone, MB R0J 0T0
Tel: 204-385-2388; *Fax:* 204-385-2780
info@rmwestbourne.mb.ca
Municipal Type: Rural Municipality
Incorporated: Jan. 2, 1877 *Area:* 1,261.79 sq km
Population in 2011: 1,878
Provincial Electoral District(s): Ste. Rose
Federal Electoral District(s): Dauphin-Swan River-Marquette
Next Election: Oct. 22, 2014 (4 year terms)
David Single, Reeve
Patricia McCaskill, Municipal Administrator

Whitehead
P.O. Box 107
517 - 2nd Ave.
Alexander, MB R0K 0A0
Tel: 204-752-2261; *Fax:* 204-752-2129
rmwhitehead@mts.net
Municipal Type: Rural Municipality
Incorporated: Jan. 2, 1883 *Area:* 562.82 sq km
Population in 2011: 1,533
Provincial Electoral District(s): Minnedosa
Federal Electoral District(s): Brandon-Souris
Next Election: Oct. 22, 2014 (4 year terms)
Wayne D. Dobbie, Reeve
John B. MacLellan, Chief Administrative Officer

Whitemouth
P.O. Box 248
47 Railway Ave.
Whitemouth, MB R0E 2G0
Tel: 204-348-2221; *Fax:* 204-348-2576
rmwhite@mymts.net
www.rmwhitemouth.com
Municipal Type: Rural Municipality
Incorporated: Jan. 1, 1905 *Area:* 703.02 sq km
Population in 2011: 1,548
Provincial Electoral District(s): Lac du Bonnet
Federal Electoral District(s): Provencher
Next Election: Oct. 22, 2014 (4 year terms)
Kevin Lavallee, Reeve
kevin@rmwhitemouth.com
Jenny Peterson, Chief Administrative Officer

Whitewater
P.O. Box 53
201 South Railway St.
Minto, MB R0K 1M0
Tel: 204-776-2172; *Fax:* 204-776-2252
cao@whitewaterrm.ca
whitewaterrm.ca
Municipal Type: Rural Municipality
Incorporated: Jan. 6, 1897 *Area:* 584.25 sq km
Population in 2011: 645
Provincial Electoral District(s): Minnedosa
Federal Electoral District(s): Brandon-Souris
Next Election: Oct. 22, 2014 (4 year terms)
Blair Woods, Reeve
Lisa Scott, Chief Administrative Officer

Winchester
P.O. Box 387
129 Broadway St. North
Deloraine, MB R0M 0M0
Tel: 204-747-2572; *Fax:* 204-747-2883
pamela@winchester.ca
Municipal Type: Rural Municipality
Area: 725.58 sq km
Population in 2011: 508
Provincial Electoral District(s): Arthur-Virden
Federal Electoral District(s): Brandon-Souris
Next Election: Oct. 22, 2014 (4 year terms)
Michael Dillabough, Reeve
Pamela Hainsworth, Chief Administrative Officer

Woodlands
P.O. Box 10
57 Railway Ave.
Woodlands, MB R0C 3H0
Tel: 204-383-5679; *Fax:* 204-383-5169
rmwdlds1@mts.net
www.rmwoodlands.info
Municipal Type: Rural Municipality
Incorporated: Jan. 5, 1880 *Area:* 1,160.45 sq km
Population in 2011: 3,521
Provincial Electoral District(s): Lakeside
Federal Electoral District(s): Selkirk-Interlake
Next Election: Oct. 22, 2014 (4 year terms)
Donald Walsh, Reeve
Lynn Kauppila, Chief Administrative Officer

Woodworth
P.O. Box 148
220 Cornwall St.
Kenton, MB R0M 0Z0
Tel: 204-838-2317; *Fax:* 204-838-2000
rmwdwo@inetlink.ca
Municipal Type: Rural Municipality
Incorporated: Jan. 2, 1883 *Area:* 817.84 sq km
Population in 2011: 860
Provincial Electoral District(s): Arthur-Virden
Federal Electoral District(s): Brandon-Souris
Next Election: Oct. 22, 2014 (4 year terms)
Denis Carter, Reeve
Carol-Ann Brethour, Chief Administrative Officer

NEW BRUNSWICK

The provincial government of New Brunswick provides all services of a municipal nature for the rural area of the province while municipalities provide these services to their residents. For the rural area, an advisory committee may be elected at public meetings biennially to assist and advise the Minister. Municipal councils are elected to look after the affairs of the municipalities.

Acts of the legislature governing municipalities are the Municipalities Act, the Municipal Assistance Act, the Community Planning Act, the Assessment Act, the Municipal Capital Borrowing Act, the Municipal Elections Act, and the Control of Municipalities Act.

Population requirements for incorporation of municipalities are 10,000 for cities and 1,500 for towns. There are no specified requirements for villages.

Municipal elections are held every four years on the second Monday in May (May 2012, May 2016, etc.).

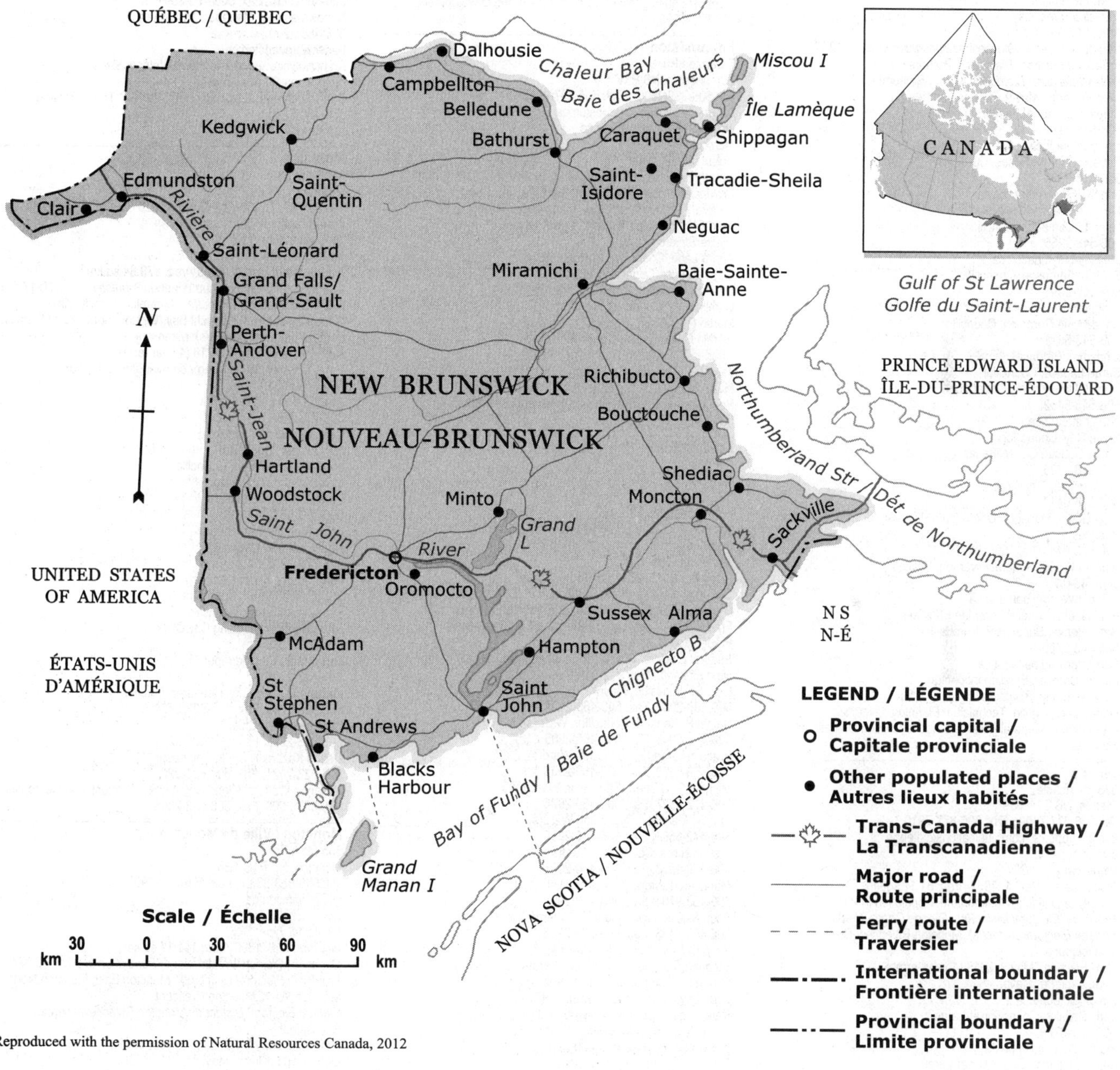

New Brunswick

Major Municipalities in New Brunswick

Bathurst
150 St. George St.
Bathurst, NB E2A 1B5
Tel: 506-548-0400; *Fax:* 506-548-0581
city@bathurst.ca
www.bathurst.ca
Municipal Type: City
Area: 91.55 sq km
County or District: Gloucester; *Population in 2011:* 12,275
Provincial Electoral District(s): Bathurst
Federal Electoral District(s): Acadie-Bathurst
Next Election: May 9, 2016 (4 year terms)
Stephen J. Brunet, Mayor
506-548-2171
city@bathurst.ca
Robert (Bob) Anderson, Councillor
506-548-3536
bobelva@nb.sympatico.ca
Michelle Branch, Councillor
Hugh L. Comeau, Councillor
506-548-2255
2868@nb.sympatico.ca
Scott A. Ferguson, Councillor
506-547-8993
scott.ferguson@nbed.nb.ca
Anne-Marie Gammon, Councillor
506-545-6821
amgammon@nbnet.nb.ca
Serge Lagacé, Councillor
Daniel (Danny) Roy, Councillor
506-545-5452
city@bathurst.ca
Susie Roy, Councillor
André Doucet, City Manager
506-548-0733
Lola Doucet, City Clerk
506-548-0417
Paul Godin, Manager, Operational Planning (acting), Operational Services
506-548-0444, Fax: 506-548-0581
Vincent Wood, General Foreman, Utilities
506-548-0444
Vincent.Wood@bathurst.ca
Paul Godin, General Foreman Engineer
Barry Veniot, Supervisor, Purchasing
506-548-0700
Barry.Veniot@bathurst.ca
Lucien Cormier, Building Inspector
Lucien.Cormier@bathurst.ca
Donald McLaughlin, Technician, Planning
Dave Moran, General Foreman, Above Ground Operational Services

Dieppe
333, av Acadie
Dieppe, NB E1A 1G9
Tel: 506-877-7900; *Fax:* 506-877-7910
info@dieppe.ca, communications@dieppe.ca
www.dieppe.ca
Municipal Type: City
Incorporated: Jan. 1, 1952 *Area:* 51.17 sq km
County or District: Westmorland; *Population in 2011:* 23,310
Provincial Electoral District(s): Dieppe Centre-Lewisville
Federal Electoral District(s): Moncton-Riverview-Dieppe; Beauséjour
Next Election: May 9, 2016 (4 year terms)
Yvon Lapierre, Mayor
mayor@dieppe.ca
Jody Dallaire, Councillor-at-Large
506-387-8738
jody.dallaire@dieppe.ca
Jean J. Gaudet, Councillor-at-Large
506-854-8409
jean.gaudet@dieppe.ca
Jordan E. Nowlan, Councillor-at-Large
Jean-Marc Brideau, Councillor, Ward(s): 1
Jean-Claude Cormier, Councillor, Ward(s): 2
Paul N. Belliveau, Councillor, Ward(s): 3
506-855-2637
paul.belliveau@dieppe.ca
Ernest Thibodeau, Councillor, Ward(s): 4
Roger J. LeBlanc, Councillor, Ward(s): 5
506-850-1604
roger.leblanc@dieppe.ca
Pierre LaForest, Assistant Chief Administrative Officer/City Clerk
Pierre.laForest@dieppe.ca
Nicole Rioux, Treasurer
Jacques LeBlanc, Director, Public Works
Isabelle LeBlanc, Director, Communications
communications@dieppe.ca
Luc St-Jules, Director, Municipal Buildings and Environment
luc.stjules@dieppe.ca
Charles LeBlanc, Fire Chief, Fire Department
506-877-7970
charles.leblanc@dieppe.ca
Nicole Melanson, Coordinator, Planning and Development
506-877-7855

Edmundston
7 Canada Rd.
Edmundston, NB E3V 1T7
Tel: 506-739-4636; *Fax:* 506-737-6902
communication@edmundston.ca
www.ville.edmundston.nb.ca
Municipal Type: City
Area: 106.92 sq km
County or District: Madawaska; *Population in 2011:* 16,032
Provincial Electoral District(s): Edmundston-Saint-Basile
Federal Electoral District(s): Madawaska-Restigouche
Next Election: May 9, 2016 (4 year terms)
Cyrille Simard, Mayor
André Lang, Councillor, Ward(s): 1
Guy A. Voyer, Councillor, Ward(s): 1
Denis M. Pelletier, Councillor, Ward(s): 2
Camille Roy, Councillor, Ward(s): 2
Martin (Tin) Albert, Councillor, Ward(s): 3
Gérald G. Morneault, Councillor, Ward(s): 3
Charles E. Fournier, Councillor, Ward(s): 4
Jean-Guy Marquis, Councillor, Ward(s): 4
Marc Michaud, Acting Chief Administrative Officer
Paul Dionne, Director, Public Works and Environment
506-739-2103

Fredericton
City Hall
P.O. Box 130
397 Queen St.
Fredericton, NB E3B 4Y7
Tel: 506-460-2020; *Fax:* 506-460-2042
www.fredericton.ca
Municipal Type: City
Incorporated: 1848 *Area:* 130.68 sq km
County or District: York; *Population in 2011:* 56,224
Provincial Electoral District(s): Fredericton-Lincoln; Fredericton-Silverwood; Fredericton-Fort Nashwaak; Fredericton-Nashwaaksis
Federal Electoral District(s): Fredericton
Next Election: May 9, 2016 (4 year terms)
Brad S. Woodside, Mayor
506-460-2085, Fax: 506-460-2134
Daniel R. Keenan, Councillor, Ward(s): 1
506-472-6046, Fax: 506-460-2905
Bruce N. Grandy, Councillor, Ward(s): 2
506-459-5378, Fax: 506-460-2905
Michael G. O'Brien, Councillor, Ward(s): 3
506-472-4527, Fax: 506-460-2905
Eric W. Megarity, Councillor, Ward(s): 4
506-472-6594, Fax: 506-460-2905
Steven Hicks, Councillor, Ward(s): 5
506-458-1973, Fax: 506-460-2905
Marilyn K. Kerton, Councillor, Ward(s): 6
506-453-9704, Fax: 506-460-2905
Scott McConaghy, Councillor, Ward(s): 7
506-450-9183, Fax: 506-460-2905
Greg Ericson, Councillor, Ward(s): 8
Stephen A. Chase, Councillor, Ward(s): 9
506-455-0711, Fax: 506-460-2905
Leah Levac, Councillor, Ward(s): 10
Kate Rogers, Councillor, Ward(s): 11
David A.J. Kelly, Councillor, Ward(s): 12
506-458-8518, Fax: 506-460-2905
Pamela G. Hargrove, City Clerk
pam.hargrove@fredericton.ca
Marven Grant, City Treasurer & Director, Financial Services
marven.grant@fredericton.ca
Bruce A. Noble, City Solicitor
bruce.noble@fredericton.ca
Paul R. Stapleton, City Administrator
cityadmin@fredericton.ca
Barry MacKnight, Police Chief & Director, Emergency Measures Organization
506-460-2300
policechief@fredericton.ca
Philip E. Toole, Fire Chief & Deputy Director, Emergency Measures Organization
506-460-2500
fire@fredericton.ca
Jane Blakely, Director, Corporate Services
jane.blakely@fredericton.ca
W. Frank Flanagan, Director, Development Services
planning@fredericton.ca
Murray Jamer, P.Eng., Director, Engineering & Public Works
publicworks@fredericton.ca
Wayne Tallon, Director, Community Services
wayne.tallon@fredericton.ca
Ken Forrest, Manager, Policy & Planning
506-460-2110, Fax: 506-460-2894
Sandy MacNeill, Manager, Transit
506-460-2200
transit@fredericton.ca
Andy Holyoke, Superintendent, Water & Sewer
publicworks@fredericton.ca
Brian Cochrane, Superintendent, Parks & Trees Division
506-460-2230
recreation@fredericton.ca

Miramichi
141 Henry St.
Miramichi, NB E1V 2N5
Tel: 506-623-2200; *Fax:* 506-623-2201
jim.lamkey@miramichi.org
www.miramichi.org
Municipal Type: City
Incorporated: Jan. 1, 1995 *Area:* 179.84 sq km
County or District: Northumberland; *Population in 2011:* 17,811
Provincial Electoral District(s): Miramichi-Bay du Vin; Miramichi-Centre; Miramichi Bay-Neguac; Southwest Miramichi
Federal Electoral District(s): Miramichi
Next Election: May 9, 2016 (4 year terms)
Gerry Cormier, Mayor, gerry.cormier@miramichi.org
506-773-5054
Joan M. Cripps, Councillor
506-773-4996
joan.cripps@miramichi.org
Billy Fleiger, Councillor
John Winston Foran, Councillor
Lisa L. Harris, Councillor
Brian J. King, Councillor
506-773-6543
Brian.King@miramichi.org
Nancy Lordon, Councillor
506-778-3932
nancy.lordon@miramichi.org
Peggy M. McLean, Councillor
Shelly A. Williams, Councillor
Rhonda Haining, Acting City Clerk
506-623-2208
David Dick, City Manager
506-623-2205
Darlene O'shea, City Treasurer, Finance
506-623-2200, Fax: 506-623-2434
Ian Gavet, Fire Chief
506-623-2225, Fax: 506-623-2226
Csaba Kazamer, Clerk, Engineering
506-623-2021, Fax: 506-623-2201
Suzanne Watters, Clerk, Community Wellness and Recreation
506-623-2300, Fax: 506-623-2306

Moncton / Ville de Moncton
655 Main St.
Moncton, NB E1C 1E8
Tel: 506-853-3333; *Fax:* 506-389-5904
info@moncton.ca
www.moncton.ca
Municipal Type: City
Incorporated: 1890 *Area:* 141.17 sq km
County or District: Westmorland; *Population in 2011:* 69,074
Provincial Electoral District(s): Moncton East; Moncton North; Moncton West; Moncton Crescent
Federal Electoral District(s): Moncton-Riverview-Dieppe; Beauséjour
Next Election: May 9, 2016 (4 year terms)
George H. LeBlanc, Mayor
506-856-4343, Fax: 506-853-3553
info.mayor@moncton.ca
Dawn Arnold, Councillor at Large
Pierre A. Boudreau, Councillor at Large
pierre.boudreau@moncton.ca
Shawn Crossman, Councillor, Ward(s): 1
Paulette Thériault, Councillor, Ward(s): 1
paulette.theriault@moncton.ca
Merrill A. Henderson, Councillor, Ward(s): 2
merrill.henderson@moncton.ca
Charles Leger, Councillor, Ward(s): 2
Daniel Bourgeois, Councillor, Ward(s): 3
daniel.bourgeois@moncton.ca

Brian A. Hicks, Councillor, Ward(s): 3
brian.hicks@moncton.ca
René (Pepsi) Landry, Councillor, Ward(s): 4
rene.landry@moncton.ca
Paul A. Pellerin, Councillor, Ward(s): 4
paul.pellerin@moncton.ca
Jacques Dubé, City Manager, Legislative Support
506-843-3498, Fax: 506-859-4225
John Martin, City Treasurer & CFO
506-853-3566
john.martin@moncton.ca
Anne Caron, City Solicitor
Eric Arsenault, Fire Chief
506-857-8800, Fax: 506-856-4353
info.fire@moncton.ca
B. Butler, Constable, Codiac Regional RCMP
Bill Budd, Director, District Planning
C. Despres, Director, Corporate Planning & Policy Development
506-859-2608
info.support@moncton.ca
D. Morehouse, Director, Engineering Operations
info.engineering@moncton.ca
A. Richard, Director, Design & Construction
S. Sparks, Director, Building Inspection
info.inspection@moncton.ca
Paul Thomson, Director, Corporate Communications
info.communications@moncton.ca
Kevin Silliker, Director, Economic Development
506-853-3516
Tanya Carter, Manager, Purchasing
506-853-3535
info.purchasing@moncton.ca
Catherine Dallaire, General Manager, Corporate Services
catherine.dallaire@moncton.ca
Donald MacLellan, General Manager, Community Safety Services
don.maclellan@moncton.ca
Rod Higgins, General Manager, Parks and Leisure Services
rod.higgins@moncton.ca

Quispamsis

P.O. Box 21085
12 Landing Ct.
Quispamsis, NB E2E 4Z4
Tel: 506-849-5778; *Fax:* 506-849-5799
quispamsis@quispamsis.ca
www.quispamsis.ca
Municipal Type: City
Area: 57.06 sq km
County or District: Kings; *Population in 2011:* 17,886
Provincial Electoral District(s): Quispamsis
Federal Electoral District(s): Fundy Royal; Saint John
Next Election: May 9, 2016 (4 year terms)
Murray Driscoll, Mayor
506-849-5992
mayor@quispamsis.ca
Gary D. Clark, Councillor
506-847-3700
Lisa Loughery, Councillor
506-849-6165
Kirk R. Miller, Councillor
506-847-3700
Libby O'Hara, Councillor
506-847-5078
Emil T. Olsen, Councillor
506-847-5197
J. Pierre Rioux, Councillor
506-847-4925
Beth Thompson, Councillor
506-849-2852
Catherine Snow, Clerk
506-849-5738
Jo-Anne McGraw, Town Treasurer
506-849-5738
Chris Vriezen, Superintendent, Utility
506-849-5734
cvriezen@quispamsis.ca
Phil Shedd, Superintendent, Works
506-849-5742
pshedd@quispamsis.ca
Margie McGrath, Secretary, Planning Advisory Committee
506-849-5745
mmcgrath@quispamsis.ca
Paul Kirkpatrick, Fleet Foreman, Kennebecasis Valley Fire Dept.
506-849-5726
Gary Losier, Director, Engineering & Works
506-849-5749
glosier@quispamsis.ca

Riverview

30 Honour House Ct.
Riverview, NB E1C3Y9
Tel: 506-387-2020; *Fax:* 506-387-2033
www.townofriverview.ca
Municipal Type: City
Area: 33.88 sq km
County or District: Albert; *Population in 2011:* 19,128
Provincial Electoral District(s): Riverview
Federal Electoral District(s): Moncton-Riverview-Dieppe; Fundy Royal
Next Election: May 9, 2016 (4 year terms)
Ann Seamans, Mayor
506-386-1703
Lana Hansen, Councillor, Ward(s): 1
Ian A Macdonald, Councillor, Ward(s): 2
506-386-8756
imacdonald@town.riverview.nb.ca
Russell Hayward, Councillor, Ward(s): 3
Wayne Bennett, Councillor, Ward(s): 4
506-386-3295
wbennett@townofriverview.ca
Cecile Cassista, Councillor at Large
Andrew J. Leblanc, Councillor at Large
Tom Toner, Councillor at Large
David Muir, Chief Administrative Officer
506-387-2021
Denyse Richard, Deputy Town Clerk
506-387-2043
Robert Higson, Director, Finance
506-387-2023
Tina Smith, Director, Human Resources
506-387-2163
Cole Gerry, Director, Parks, Recreation & Community Relations
506-387-2031
Denis Pleau, Chief, Fire & Rescue
506-387-2201
rivefire@nbnet.nb.ca
Michel Ouellet, Director, Works & Engineering
506-387-2220

Rothesay

70 Hampton Rd.
Rothesay, NB E2E 5L5
Tel: 506-848-6600; *Fax:* 506-848-6677
info@rothesay.ca
www.rothesay.ca
Municipal Type: City
Incorporated: Jan. 1, 1998 *Area:* 34.73 sq km
County or District: Kings; *Population in 2011:* 11,947
Provincial Electoral District(s): Rothesay
Federal Electoral District(s): Saint John; Fundy Royal
Next Election: May 9, 2016 (4 year terms)
William J. (Bill) Bishop, Mayor
506-847-8607, Fax: 506-849-4121
BillBishop@rothesay.ca
Matt Alexander, Councillor
Patricia Gallagher Jette, Councillor
506-847-3028, Fax: 506-849-3029
patgallagherjette@rothesay.ca
Nancy E. Grant, Councillor
Peter J. Lewis, Councillor
Blair R. MacDonald, Councillor
506-847-2724, Fax: 506-849-5933
blairmacdonald@rothesay.ca
Bill McGuire, Councillor
Miriam J. Wells, Councillor
Mary Jane Banks, Clerk
MaryJaneBanks@rothesay.ca
Susan Johnson, Treasurer, Operations
susanjohnson@rothesay.ca
Charles Jensen, Director, Recreation
charlesjensen@rothesay.ca
Gay Drescher, Director, Development Services
gaydrescher@rothesay.ca
Corinne Bexson, Senior GIS Technician, Engineering
corrinebexson@rothesay.ca

Saint John

City Hall
P.O. Box 1971
15 Market Sq.
Saint John, NB E2L 4L1
Tel: 506-649-6000
inquiries@saintjohn.ca
www.saintjohn.ca
Municipal Type: City
Incorporated: May 18, 1785 *Area:* 315.49 sq km
County or District: Saint John; *Population in 2011:* 70,063
Provincial Electoral District(s): Saint John East; Saint John Harbour; Saint John Portland; Saint John Lancaster; Saint John-Fundy
Federal Electoral District(s): Saint John
Next Election: May 9, 2016 (4 year terms)
Mel K. Norton, Mayor
Shirley McAlary, Councillor at Large
Shelley M. Rinehart, Deputy Mayor
Bill Farren, Councillor, Ward(s): 1
506-674-8102
bill.farren@saintjohn.ca
Greg J. Norton, Councillor, Ward(s): 1
Susan Fullerton, Councillor, Ward(s): 2
John Mackenzie, Councillor, Ward(s): 2
Donna Reardon, Councillor, Ward(s): 3
Donnie Snook, Councillor, Ward(s): 3
donnie.snook@saintjohn.ca
David Merrithew, Councillor, Ward(s): 4
Ray Strowbridge, Councillor, Ward(s): 4
J. Patrick Woods, City Manager
506-658-2913, Fax: 506-658-2802
citymanager@saintjohn.ca
Greg Yeomans, Commissioner, Finance & Administrative Services
506-658-2951, Fax: 506-649-7901
finance@saintjohn.ca
William Edwards, Commissioner, Transportation & Environment Services
506-658-2911, Fax: 506-632-6199
municipaloperations@saintjohn.ca
Jacqueline Hamilton, Commissioner, Strategic Services
strategicservices@saintjohn.ca
Margaret Totten, Manager, Tourism Saint John
506-658-2990, Fax: 506-632-6118
visitsj@saintjohn.ca
John Nugent, City Solicitor
506-658-2860, Fax: 506-649-7939
legal@saintjohn.ca
Allen Bodechon, Police Chief
506-648-3200, Fax: 506-648-3304
police@saintjohn.ca
Rob Simonds, Fire Chief
506-658-2910, Fax: 506-658-2916
fire@saintjohn.ca
Shayne Galbraith, Director, Works
506-658-2852
works@saintjohn.ca
Peter J. Hanlon, P.Eng., Manager, Water & Sewerage Services
506-658-2811, Fax: 506-658-4740
waterandsewerage@cityofsaintjohn.com
David Logan, Purchasing Agent, Material & Fleet Management
506-658-2930, Fax: 506-658-4742
mat-man@saintjohn.ca

Other Municipalities in New Brunswick

Alma

8 School St.
Alma, NB E4H 1L2
Tel: 506-887-6123; *Fax:* 506-887-6124
almavill@nb.aibn.com
Municipal Type: Village
Area: 47.64 sq km
County or District: Albert; *Population in 2011:* 232
Provincial Electoral District(s): Albert
Federal Electoral District(s): Fundy Royal
Next Election: May 9, 2016 (4 year terms)
Herta Kirstin Shortt, Mayor
Louise Butland, Clerk-Treasurer

Aroostook

383 Main St.
Aroostook, NB E7H 2Z4
Tel: 506-273-6443; *Fax:* 506-273-3025
varoostk@nb.aibn.com
Municipal Type: Village
Area: 2.24 sq km
County or District: Victoria; *Population in 2011:* 351
Provincial Electoral District(s): Victoria-Tobique
Federal Electoral District(s): Tobique-Mactaquac
Next Election: May 9, 2016 (4 year terms)
Marven C. Demmings, Mayor

Atholville

247, rue Notre-Dame
Atholville, NB E3N 4T1
Tél: 506-789-2944; *Téléc:* 506-789-2925
lyssa@nb.aibn.com
www.atholville.net
Entité municipal: Village
Incorporation: 1966 *Area:* 10.25 sq km
Comté ou district: Restigouche; *Population au 2011:* 1,237

Circonscription(s) électorale(s) provinciale(s): Campbellton-Restigouche Centre
Circonscription(s) électorale(s) fédérale(s): Madawaska-Restigouche
Prochaines élections: May 9, 2016 (4 year terms)
Michel Soucy, Mayor
Lyssa Leclerc, Clerk-Administrator

Baker Brook
3677, rue Principale, #A
Baker Brook, NB E7A 1V3
Tél: 506-258-3030; *Téléc:* 506-258-3017
villagebakerbrook@nb.aibn.com
Entité municipal: Village
Area: 12.4 sq km
Comté ou district: Madawaska; *Population au 2011:* 645
Circonscription(s) électorale(s) provinciale(s): Madawaska-les-Lacs
Circonscription(s) électorale(s) fédérale(s): Madawaska-Restigouche
Prochaines élections: May 9, 2016 (4 year terms)
Francine Caron, Mayor

Balmoral
CP 2531
1447, av des Pionniers
Balmoral, NB E8E 2W7
Tél: 506-826-6060; *Téléc:* 506-826-6037
vilbal@nbnet.nb.ca
www.balmoralnb.com
Entité municipal: Village
Incorporation: 1972 *Area:* 43.51 sq km
Comté ou district: Restigouche; *Population au 2011:* 1,719
Circonscription(s) électorale(s) provinciale(s): Dalhousie-Restigouche-East
Circonscription(s) électorale(s) fédérale(s): Madawaska-Restigouche
Prochaines élections: May 9, 2016 (4 year terms)
Charles Bernard, Mayor
Gilles LePage, Clerk-Administrator

Bas-Caraquet
8185, rue St-Paul
Bas-Caraquet, NB E1W 6C4
Tél: 506-726-2776; *Téléc:* 506-726-2770
vilbasca@nbnet.nb.ca
www.bascaraquet.com
Entité municipal: Village
Area: 31 sq km
Comté ou district: Gloucester; *Population au 2011:* 1,380
Circonscription(s) électorale(s) provinciale(s): Caraquet
Circonscription(s) électorale(s) fédérale(s): Acadie-Bathurst
Prochaines élections: May 9, 2016 (4 year terms)
Agnès Doiron, Mairesse
Richard Frigault, Gérant

Bath
161 School St.
Bath, NB E7J 1C3
Tel: 506-278-5293; *Fax:* 506-278-5932
bath@nbnet.nb.ca
Municipal Type: Village
Area: 2.03 sq km
County or District: Carleton; *Population in 2011:* 532
Provincial Electoral District(s): Carleton
Federal Electoral District(s): Tobique-Mactaquac
Next Election: May 9, 2016 (4 year terms)
Troy F.J. Stone, Mayor
Christa Walton, Clerk

Belledune
P.O. Box 1006
2330 Main St.
Belledune, NB E8G 2X9
Tel: 506-522-3700; *Fax:* 506-522-3704
bell001@nbnet.nb.ca
www.belledune.com
Municipal Type: Village
Incorporated: Jan. 1, 1968 *Area:* 189.03 sq km
County or District: Gloucester; *Population in 2011:* 1,548
Provincial Electoral District(s): Nigadoo-Chaleur
Federal Electoral District(s): Miramichi
Next Election: May 9, 2016 (4 year terms)
Ron Bourque, Mayor
Brenda Cormier, Clerk-Treasurer

Beresford
#2, 855, rue Principale
Beresford, NB E8K 1T3
Tél: 506-542-2727; *Téléc:* 506-542-2702
beresfor@nbnet.nb.ca
Entité municipal: Town
Area: 19.2 sq km
Comté ou district: Gloucester; *Population au 2011:* 4,351
Circonscription(s) électorale(s) provinciale(s): Nigadoo-Chaleur
Circonscription(s) électorale(s) fédérale(s): Acadie-Bathurst
Prochaines élections: May 9, 2016 (4 year terms)
Paul Losier, Mayor
Norval Godin, Administrateur

Bertrand
#1, 651, boul des Acadiens
Bertrand, NB E1W 1G5
Tél: 506-726-2442; *Téléc:* 506-726-2449
bertrand@nb.aibn.com
Entité municipal: Village
Area: 46.45 sq km
Comté ou district: Gloucester; *Population au 2011:* 1,137
Circonscription(s) électorale(s) provinciale(s): Caraquet
Circonscription(s) électorale(s) fédérale(s): Acadie-Bathurst
Prochaines élections: May 9, 2016 (4 year terms)
Yvon Godin, Maire
Mélanie Arseneau, Chief Administrative Officer

Blacks Harbour
65 Wallace Cove Rd.
Blacks Harbour, NB E5H 1G9
Tél: 506-456-4870; *Téléc:* 506-456-4872
blkhvill@nbnet.nb.ca
www.villageofblacksharbour.com
Entité municipal: Village
Area: 8.9 sq km
Comté ou district: Charlotte; *Population au 2011:* 982
Circonscription(s) électorale(s) provinciale(s): Charlotte
Circonscription(s) électorale(s) fédérale(s): New Brunswick Southwest
Prochaines élections: May 9, 2016 (4 year terms)
Terry James, Mayor
Deanna Hunter, Manager

Blackville
12 South Bartholomew Road
Blackville, NB E9B 1N2
Tel: 506-843-6337; *Fax:* 506-843-6043
blackvl@nb.sympatico.ca
www.villageofblackville.com
Municipal Type: Village
Area: 21.73 sq km
County or District: Northumberland; *Population in 2011:* 990
Provincial Electoral District(s): Southwest Miramichi
Federal Electoral District(s): Miramichi
Next Election: May 9, 2016 (4 year terms)
Harold (Hal) Peter Muck, Mayor
Kurt Marks, Clerk-Administrator

Bouctouche
211, boul Irving
Bouctouche, NB E4S 3K6
Tél: 506-743-7260; *Téléc:* 506-743-7261
ville@bouctouche.ca
www.bouctouche.org
Entité municipal: Town
Area: 18.34 sq km
Comté ou district: Kent; *Population au 2011:* 2,423
Circonscription(s) électorale(s) provinciale(s): Kent
Circonscription(s) électorale(s) fédérale(s): Beauséjour
Prochaines élections: May 9, 2016 (4 year terms)
Aldéo Saulnier, Maire
Marc Landry, Gérant-Greffier

Cambridge-Narrows
Municipal Bldg.
6 Municipal Lane
Cambridge-Narrows, NB E4C 4P4
Tel: 506-488-3155; *Fax:* 506-488-1018
office@nbnet.nb.ca
www.cambridge-narrows.ca
Municipal Type: Village
Area: 106.94 sq km
County or District: Queens; *Population in 2011:* 620
Provincial Electoral District(s): Grand Lake-Gagetown
Federal Electoral District(s): New Brunswick Southwest
Next Election: May 9, 2016 (4 year terms)
Blair C. Cummings, Mayor
Alexis Trebble, Clerk

Campbellton
Campbellton City Centre
P.O. Box 100
76 Water St.
Campbellton, NB E3N 3G1
Tel: 506-789-2700; *Fax:* 506-759-7403
manon.cloutier@campbellton.org
www.campbellton.org
Municipal Type: Town
Incorporated: 1889 *Area:* 18.66 sq km
County or District: Restigouche; *Population in 2011:* 7,385
Provincial Electoral District(s): Campbellton-Restigouche Centre
Federal Electoral District(s): Madawaska-Restigouche
Next Election: May 9, 2016 (4 year terms)
Bruce N. MacIntosh, Mayor
mayor@campbellton.org
Monique Cormier, Clerk
monique.cormier@campbellton.org

Canterbury
199 Main St.
Canterbury, NB E6H 1M6
Tel: 506-279-6248; *Fax:* 506-279-9019
Municipal Type: Village
Area: 5.34 sq km
County or District: York; *Population in 2011:* 331
Provincial Electoral District(s): Woodstock
Federal Electoral District(s): Tobique-Mactaquac
Next Election: May 9, 2016 (4 year terms)
Elaine B. English, Mayor
Cara Hatton, Clerk

Cap-Pelé
33, ch St-André
Cap-Pelé, NB E4N 1Z4
Tél: 506-577-2030; *Téléc:* 506-577-2035
cappele@nb.aibn.com
www.cap-pele.com
Entité municipal: Village
Incorporation: 1969 *Area:* 23.78 sq km
Comté ou district: Westmorland; *Population au 2011:* 2,256
Circonscription(s) électorale(s) provinciale(s): Shediac-Cap-Pelé
Circonscription(s) électorale(s) fédérale(s): Beauséjour
Prochaines élections: May 9, 2016 (4 year terms)
Debbie Dodier, Mairesse
Stéphane Dallaire, Administrateur/Greffier
stephane.dallaire@cappele.com

Caraquet
CP 5695
10, rue du Colisée
Caraquet, NB E1W 1B7
Tél: 506-726-2727; *Téléc:* 506-726-2660
caraquet@nbnet.nb.ca
www.ville.caraquet.nb.ca
Entité municipal: Town
Incorporation: Nov. 15, 1961 *Area:* 68.26 sq km
Comté ou district: Gloucester; *Population au 2011:* 4,169
Circonscription(s) électorale(s) provinciale(s): Caraquet
Circonscription(s) électorale(s) fédérale(s): Acadie-Bathurst
Prochaines élections: May 9, 2016 (4 year terms)
Kevin J. Haché, Maire
Lucien Sonier, Directeur général
luciensonier@nb.aibn.com

Centreville
836 Central St.
Centreville, NB E7K 2E7
Tel: 506-276-3671; *Fax:* 506-276-9891
clerk@nbnet.nb.ca
www.villageofcentreville.ca
Municipal Type: Village
Area: 2.69 sq km
County or District: Carleton; *Population in 2011:* 542
Provincial Electoral District(s): Carleton
Federal Electoral District(s): Tobique-Mactaquac; New Brunswick Southwest
Next Election: May 9, 2016 (4 year terms)
Gary R. Thomas, Mayor
Teresa Burtt, Administrator

Charlo
614, rue Chaleur
Charlo, NB E8E 2G6
Tél: 506-684-7850; *Téléc:* 506-684-7855
vcharlo@nbnet.nb.ca
www.villagecharlo.com
Entité municipal: Village
Incorporation: 1966 *Area:* 30.75 sq km
Comté ou district: Restigouche; *Population au 2011:* 1,324
Circonscription(s) électorale(s) provinciale(s): Dalhousie-Restigouche East

Circonscription(s) électorale(s) fédérale(s): Madawaska-Restigouche
Prochaines élections: May 9, 2016 (4 year terms)
Jason Carter, Maire
Joanne McIntyre Levesque, Administrateur

Chipman
#1, 10 Civic Ct.
Chipman, NB E4A 2H9
Tel: 506-339-6601; *Fax:* 506-339-6197
mail@chipmannb.org
www.chipmannb.com
Municipal Type: Village
Area: 19.58 sq km
County or District: Queens; *Population in 2011:* 1,236
Provincial Electoral District(s): Grand Lake-Gagetown
Federal Electoral District(s): Fredericton
Next Election: May 9, 2016 (4 year terms)
Edward L. Farris, Mayor
Susan Kennedy, Clerk

Clair
809E, rue Principale
Clair, NB E7A 2H7
Tél: 506-992-6030; *Téléc:* 506-992-6041
vgeclair@nbnet.nb.ca
www.villagedeclair.com
Entité municipal: Village
Area: 10.46 sq km
Comté ou district: Madawaska; *Population au 2011:* 857
Circonscription(s) électorale(s) provinciale(s): Madawaska-les-Lacs
Circonscription(s) électorale(s) fédérale(s): Madawaska-Restigouche
Prochaines élections: May 9, 2016 (4 year terms)
Pierre Michaud, Maire
Nicole Michaud, Greffière-Trés.

Dalhousie
#1, 111 Hall St.
Dalhousie, NB E8C 1X2
Tel: 506-684-7600; *Fax:* 506-684-7613
reception@dalhousienb.com
www.dalhousienb.com
Municipal Type: Town
Incorporated: 1905 *Area:* 14.51 sq km
County or District: Restigouche; *Population in 2011:* 3,512
Provincial Electoral District(s): Dalhousie-Restigouche East
Federal Electoral District(s): Madawaska-Restigouche
Next Election: May 9, 2016 (4 year terms)
Clem Tremblay, Mayor

Doaktown
8 Miramichi St.
Doaktown, NB E9C 1C8
Tel: 506-365-7970; *Fax:* 506-365-7111
doaktown@nbnet.nb.ca
www.doaktown.com
Municipal Type: Village
Area: 28.74 sq km
County or District: Northumberland; *Population in 2011:* 793
Provincial Electoral District(s): Southwest Miramichi
Federal Electoral District(s): Miramichi
Next Election: May 9, 2016 (4 year terms)
Beverly K. Gaston, Mayor
Marilyn E. Price, Clerk-Administrator
marilyn.price@nb.aibn.com

Dorchester
4984 Main St.
Dorchester, NB E4K 2Z1
Tel: 506-379-3030; *Fax:* 506-379-3033
vilofdor@nb.sympatico.ca
www.dorchester.ca
Municipal Type: Village
Area: 5.74 sq km
County or District: Westmorland; *Population in 2011:* 1,167
Provincial Electoral District(s): Tantramar
Federal Electoral District(s): Beauséjour
Next Election: May 9, 2016 (4 year terms)
Jerome Simon Bear, Mayor
Simonne Malenfant-Edgett, Clerk-Treasurer

Drummond
1412, ch Tobique
Drummond, NB E3Y 1H7
Tél: 506-475-4000; *Téléc:* 506-475-4010
vildrum@nb.sympatico.ca
www.sn2000.nb.ca/comp/drummond
Entité municipal: Village
Area: 8.91 sq km
Comté ou district: Victoria; *Population au 2011:* 775
Circonscription(s) électorale(s) provinciale(s): Grand Falls-Drummond-Saint-André
Circonscription(s) électorale(s) fédérale(s): Tobique-Mactaquac
Prochaines élections: May 9, 2016 (4 year terms)
Cyril Rioux, Maire
Annie Gagné, Administratrice

Eel River Crossing
CP 159
20, rue Savoie
Eel River Crossing, NB E8E 1T8
Tél: 506-826-6080; *Téléc:* 506-826-6088
voerc@nbnet.nb.ca
Entité municipal: Village
Area: 17.43 sq km
Population au 2011: 1,209
Circonscription(s) électorale(s) provinciale(s): Dalhousie-Restigouche East
Circonscription(s) électorale(s) fédérale(s): Madawaska-Restigouche
Prochaines élections: May 9, 2016 (4 year terms)
Denis D. Savoie, Maire
Kim Bujold, Administrateure

Florenceville-Bristol
4724 Juniper Rd.
Bristol, NB E7L 2W9
Tel: 506-392-6013; *Fax:* 506-392-5211
vbristol@nb.sympatico.ca
www.florencevillebristol.ca
Municipal Type: Village
Incorporated: 2008
County or District: Carleton; *Population in 2011:* 1,639
Provincial Electoral District(s): Carleton
Federal Electoral District(s): Tobique-Mactaquac
Next Election: May 9, 2016 (4 year terms)
Note: The villages of Florenceville & Bristol amalgamated to create the municipality of Florenceville-Bristol.
Karl E. Curtis, Mayor
Nancy Shaw, Chief Administrative Officer

Fredericton Junction
102 Wilsey Rd.
Fredericton Junction, NB E5L 1W7
Tel: 506-368-2628; *Fax:* 506-368-1900
fredjct@nbnet.nb.ca
www.frederictonjunction.com
Municipal Type: Village
Area: 23.86 sq km
County or District: Sunbury; *Population in 2011:* 752
Provincial Electoral District(s): New Maryland-Sunbury West
Federal Electoral District(s): New Brunswick Southwest
Next Election: May 9, 2016 (4 year terms)
Gary W. Mersereau, Mayor
Jocelyn Nason, Clerk

Gagetown
68 Babbit St.
Gagetown, NB E5M 1C8
Tel: 506-488-3567; *Fax:* 506-488-3543
gagetnvl@nbnet.nb.ca
www.villageofgagetown.ca
Municipal Type: Village
Incorporated: 1966 *Area:* 49.48 sq km
County or District: Queens; *Population in 2011:* 698
Provincial Electoral District(s): Grand Lake-Gagetown
Federal Electoral District(s): New Brunswick Southwest
Next Election: May 9, 2016 (4 year terms)
Michael Blaney, Mayor
Connie May, Clerk-Administrator

Grand Bay-Westfield
P.O. Box 3001
609 River Valley Dr.
Grand Bay-Westfield, NB E5K 4V3
Tel: 506-738-6400; *Fax:* 506-738-6424
sgautreau@town.grandbay-westfield.nb.ca
www.town.grandbay-westfield.nb.ca
Municipal Type: Town
Incorporated: 1998 *Area:* 59.73 sq km
County or District: Kings; *Population in 2011:* 5,117
Provincial Electoral District(s): Fundy-River Valley
Federal Electoral District(s): New Brunswick Southwest
Next Election: May 9, 2016 (4 year terms)
Grace Losier, Mayor
losier@town.grandbay-westfield.nb.ca
Sandra M. Gautreau, Town Manager & Clerk
smgautreau2002@yahoo.ca

Grand Falls / Grand-Sault
#200, 131, rue Pleasant
Grand-Sault, NB E3Z 1G6
Tél: 506-475-7777; *Téléc:* 506-475-7779
tgf@nbnet.nb.ca
www.grandfalls.com
Entité municipal: Town
Area: 18.06 sq km
Comté ou district: Victoria; *Population au 2011:* 5,706
Circonscription(s) électorale(s) provinciale(s): Grand Falls-Drummond-Saint-André
Circonscription(s) électorale(s) fédérale(s): Tobique-Mactaquac
Prochaines élections: May 9, 2016 (4 year terms)
Richard Keeley, Mayor
Peter Michaud, Chief Administrative Officer-Clerk
petergf@nb.aibn.com

Grand Manan
#4, 1021 rte 776
Grand Manan, NB E5G 4E5
Tel: 506-662-7059; *Fax:* 506-662-7060
grandmanan@villageofgrandmanan.com
www.villageofgrandmanan.com
Municipal Type: Village
Incorporated: May 8, 1995 *Area:* 150.78 sq km
County or District: Charlotte; *Population in 2011:* 2,377
Provincial Electoral District(s): Charlotte-The Isles
Federal Electoral District(s): New Brunswick Southwest
Next Election: May 9, 2016 (4 year terms)
Dennis Clifton Greene, Mayor
dennisgreene@villageofgrandmanan.com
Rob MacPherson, Chief Administrative Officer
Melanie Frost, Clerk/Assistant Treasurer

Grande-Anse
393, rue Acadie
Grande-Anse, NB E8N 1E2
Tél: 506-732-3242; *Téléc:* 506-732-3217
grande-anse@i-web.net
www.grande-anse.net
Entité municipal: Village
Incorporation: 1968 *Area:* 24.42 sq km
Comté ou district: Gloucester; *Population au 2011:* 738
Circonscription(s) électorale(s) provinciale(s): Caraquet
Circonscription(s) électorale(s) fédérale(s): Acadie-Bathurst
Prochaines élections: May 9, 2016 (4 year terms)
Yves Létourneau, Maire
Rhéal Paulin, Administrateur

Hampton
P.O. Box 1066
27 Centennial Rd.
Hampton, NB E5N 8H1
Tel: 506-832-6065; *Fax:* 506-832-6098
brenda.collings@nb.aibn.com
www.townofhampton.ca
Municipal Type: Town
Area: 21 sq km
County or District: Kings; *Population in 2011:* 4,292
Provincial Electoral District(s): Hampton-Kings
Federal Electoral District(s): Fundy Royal
Next Election: May 9, 2016 (4 year terms)
Kenneth A. Chorley, Mayor
hampton@nbnet.nb.ca
Brenda Collings, Chief Administrative Officer
Megan O'Brien Harrison, Clerk & Development Officer
megan.obrienharrison@nb.aibn.com

Hartland
#1, 31 Orser St.
Hartland, NB E7P 1R4
Tel: 506-375-4357; *Fax:* 506-375-8265
hartland@nbnet.nb.ca
www.town.hartland.nb.ca
Municipal Type: Town
Area: 9.63 sq km
County or District: Carleton; *Population in 2011:* 947
Provincial Electoral District(s): Carleton
Federal Electoral District(s): Tobique-Mactaquac
Next Election: May 9, 2016 (4 year terms)
J. Craig Melanson, Mayor
Judy Dee, Clerk

Harvey
58 Hanselpacker Rd.
Harvey, NB E6K 1A3
Tel: 506-366-6240; *Fax:* 506-366-6242
village.harvey@rogers.com
www.village.harvey-station.nb.ca
Municipal Type: Village
Incorporated: Nov. 9, 1966 *Area:* 2.46 sq km
County or District: York; *Population in 2011:* 363

Provincial Electoral District(s): York
Federal Electoral District(s): New Brunswick Southwest
Next Election: May 9, 2016 (4 year terms)
Winston Gamblin, Mayor
Amber Binney, Clerk
506-366-6240, Fax: 506-366-6242

Hillsborough
#1, 2849 Main St.
Hillsborough, NB E4H 2X7
Tel: 506-734-3733; *Fax:* 506-734-3711
hillsborough@rogers.com
www.villageofhillsborough.ca
Municipal Type: Village
Incorporated: 1966 *Area:* 12.98 sq km
County or District: Albert; *Population in 2011:* 1,350
Provincial Electoral District(s): Albert
Federal Electoral District(s): Fundy Royal
Next Election: May 9, 2016 (4 year terms)
Patrick E. Armstrong, Mayor
Shari Collins, Administrator-Clerk

Kedgwick
114, rue Notre-Dame
Kedgwick, NB E8B 1H8
Tél: 506-284-2160; *Téléc:* 506-284-2859
villkedg@nbnet.nb.ca
www.village.kedgwick.nb.ca
Entité municipal: Village
Area: 4.28 sq km
Comté ou district: Restigouche; *Population au 2011:* 993
Circonscription(s) électorale(s) provinciale(s):
Restigouche-La-Vallée
Circonscription(s) électorale(s) fédérale(s):
Madawaska-Restigouche
Prochaines élections: May 9, 2016 (4 year terms)
Jean Paul (JP) Savoie, Maire
Suzanne J. Cyr, Greffière

Lac-Baker
69, rue De La Pointe
Lac Baker, NB E7A 1J1
Tél: 506-992-6060; *Téléc:* 506-992-6061
lacbacac@nbnet.nb.ca
Entité municipal: Village
Area: 4.02 sq km
Comté ou district: Madawaska; *Population au 2011:* 719
Circonscription(s) électorale(s) provinciale(s):
Madawaska-les-Lacs
Circonscription(s) électorale(s) fédérale(s):
Madawaska-Restigouche
Prochaines élections: May 9, 2016 (4 year terms)
Jean-Marc Nadeau, Mayor
Doris Blanchard, Supervisor

Lamèque
CP 2037
28, rue de l'Hôpital
Lamèque, NB E8T 3N4
Tél: 506-344-3222; *Téléc:* 506-344-3266
info@lameque.ca
www.lameque.ca
Entité municipal: Town
Area: 12.45 sq km
Comté ou district: Gloucester; *Population au 2011:* 1,432
Circonscription(s) électorale(s) provinciale(s):
Lamèque-Shippagan-Miscou
Circonscription(s) électorale(s) fédérale(s): Acadie-Bathurst
Prochaines élections: May 9, 2016 (4 year terms)
Réginald Paulin, Maire
Henri-Paul Guignard, Administrateur
hplameque@nb.aibn.com

Le Goulet
1295, rue Principale
Le Goulet, NB E8S 2E9
Tél: 506-336-3272; *Téléc:* 506-336-3281
villagelegoulet@nb.aibn.com
www.legoulet.peninsuleacadienne.ca
Entité municipal: Village
Incorporation: May 12, 1986 *Area:* 5.46 sq km
Comté ou district: Gloucester; *Population au 2011:* 817
Circonscription(s) électorale(s) provinciale(s):
Lamèque-Shippagan-Miscou
Circonscription(s) électorale(s) fédérale(s): Acadie-Bathurst
Prochaines élections: May 9, 2016 (4 year terms)
Wilfred Roussel, Maire
Line Roussel, Sec.-trés. adjointe

Maisonnette
1512, rue Châtillon
Maisonnette, NB E8N 1S4
Tél: 506-726-2717; *Téléc:* 506-726-2718
maisonet@nbnet.nb.ca
www.maisonnette.ca
Entité municipal: Village
Incorporation: May 12, 1986 *Area:* 12.88 sq km
Comté ou district: Gloucester; *Population au 2011:* 573
Circonscription(s) électorale(s) provinciale(s): Caraquet
Circonscription(s) électorale(s) fédérale(s): Acadie-Bathurst
Prochaines élections: May 9, 2016 (4 year terms)
Jason Godin, Maire
Lynne-Andrée Galarneau, Greffière

McAdam
146 Saunders Rd.
McAdam, NB E6J 1L2
Tel: 506-784-2293; *Fax:* 506-784-1402
villageofmcadam@nb.aibn.com
www.mcadamnb.com
Municipal Type: Village
Area: 14.47 sq km
County or District: York; *Population in 2011:* 1,284
Provincial Electoral District(s): York
Federal Electoral District(s): New Brunswick Southwest
Next Election: May 9, 2016 (4 year terms)
Frank M. Carroll, Mayor
Ann Donahue, Clerk-Treasurer

Meductic
320 Rte. 165
Meductic, NB E6H 1J5
Tel: 506-272-2098; *Fax:* 506-272-1883
villageofmeductic@nb.aibn.com
Municipal Type: Village
Area: 5.57 sq km
County or District: York; *Population in 2011:* 270
Provincial Electoral District(s): Woodstock
Federal Electoral District(s): Tobique-Mactaquac
Next Election: May 9, 2016 (4 year terms)
Lance Royden Graham, Mayor
Pamela Grant, Clerk-Treasurer

Memramcook
540, rue Centrale
Memramcook, NB E4K 3S6
Tél: 506-758-4078; *Téléc:* 506-758-4079
village@memramcook.com
www.memramcook.com/English/index.html
Entité municipal: Village
Incorporation: 1995 *Area:* 185.71 sq km
Comté ou district: Westmorland; *Population au 2011:* 4,831
Circonscription(s) électorale(s) provinciale(s):
Memramcook-Lakeville-Dieppe
Circonscription(s) électorale(s) fédérale(s): Beauséjour
Prochaines élections: May 9, 2016 (4 year terms)
Donald Oscar LeBlanc, Maire
Monique Bourque, Secrétaire Municipale
monique@memramcook.com

Millville
39 Howland Ridge Rd.
Millville, NB E6E 1Y3
Tel: 506-463-2719; *Fax:* 506-463-8262
villageofmillville@nb.aibn.com
Municipal Type: Village
Area: 12.16 sq km
County or District: York; *Population in 2011:* 307
Provincial Electoral District(s): York North
Federal Electoral District(s): Tobique-Mactaquac
Next Election: May 9, 2016 (4 year terms)
Beverly Herbert Forbes, Mayor
Karen Cooney, Clerk-Treasurer

Minto
420 Pleasant Dr.
Minto, NB E4B 2T3
Tel: 506-327-3383; *Fax:* 506-327-3041
minto@nb.aibn.com
www.village.minto.nb.ca
Municipal Type: Village
Area: 31.53 sq km
County or District: Sunbury-Queens; *Population in 2011:* 2,505
Provincial Electoral District(s): Grand Lake-Gagetown
Federal Electoral District(s): Fredericton
Next Election: May 9, 2016 (4 year terms)
Eric G. Barnett, Mayor
Trila McKenelley, Clerk-Administrator

Nackawic
115 Otis Dr.
Nackawic, NB E6G 2P1
Tel: 506-575-2241; *Fax:* 506-575-2035
townhall@nackawic.com
www.nackawic.com
Municipal Type: Town
Area: 8.4 sq km
County or District: York; *Population in 2011:* 1,049
Provincial Electoral District(s): York North
Federal Electoral District(s): Tobique-Mactaquac
Next Election: May 9, 2016 (4 year terms)
Nancy A. Cronkhite, Mayor
Duncan Walker, Chief Administrative Officer
506-575-2241
duncan.walker@nackawic.com

Néguac
#1, 1175, rue Principale
Néguac, NB E9G 1T1
Tél: 506-776-3950; *Téléc:* 506-776-3975
village@nbnet.nb.ca
www.neguac.com
Entité municipal: Village
Incorporation: Aug. 23, 1967 *Area:* 26.69 sq km
Comté ou district: Northumberland; *Population au 2011:* 1,678
Circonscription(s) électorale(s) provinciale(s): Miramichi Bay-Neguac
Circonscription(s) électorale(s) fédérale(s): Miramichi
Prochaines élections: May 9, 2016 (4 year terms)
Georges Rhéal Savoie, Maire
Albertine Savoie, Administrateur
village.denis@nb.aibn.com

New Maryland
584 New Maryland Hwy.
New Maryland, NB E3C 1K1
Tel: 506-451-8508; *Fax:* 506-450-1605
office@vonm.ca
www.vonm.ca
Municipal Type: Village
Incorporated: 1991 *Area:* 21.23 sq km
County or District: York; *Population in 2011:* 4,232
Provincial Electoral District(s): New Maryland-Sunbury West
Federal Electoral District(s): Fredericton; New Brunswick Southwest
Next Election: May 9, 2016 (4 year terms)
Judy E. Wilson-Shee, Mayor
mayor@vonm.ca
Cynthia Geldart, Chief Administrative Officer-Clerk
cynthia.geldart@vonm.ca

Nigadoo
#1, 385, rue Principale
Nigadoo, NB E8K 3R6
Tél: 506-542-2626; *Téléc:* 506-542-2678
nigadoov@nbnet.nb.ca
www.acadie-bathurst.com
Entité municipal: Village
Incorporation: 1967 *Area:* 7.69 sq km
Comté ou district: Gloucester; *Population au 2011:* 952
Circonscription(s) électorale(s) provinciale(s): Nigadoo-Chaleur
Circonscription(s) électorale(s) fédérale(s): Acadie-Bathurst
Prochaines élections: May 9, 2016 (4 year terms)
Gilberte Boudreau, Mairesse
Aline Morrison, Secrétaire

Norton
P.O. Box 335
Norton, NB E5T 1J7
Tel: 506-839-3011; *Fax:* 506-839-3015
vnorton@nbnet.nb.ca
Municipal Type: Village
Area: 75.35 sq km
County or District: Kings; *Population in 2011:* 1,301
Provincial Electoral District(s): Hampton-Kings; Kings East
Federal Electoral District(s): Fundy Royal; New Brunswick Southwest
Next Election: May 9, 2016 (4 year terms)
Juliana Catherine Booth, Mayor
Anita Pollock, Clerk-Treasurer

Oromocto
4 Doyle Dr.
Oromocto, NB E2V 2V3
Tel: 506-357-4400; *Fax:* 506-357-2266
gengov@oromocto.ca
www.oromocto.ca
Municipal Type: Town
Area: 22.37 sq km
County or District: Sunbury; *Population in 2011:* 8,932
Provincial Electoral District(s): Oromocto

Federal Electoral District(s): Fredericton
Next Election: May 9, 2016 (4 year terms)
Robert (Bob) Edward Powell, Mayor
Dick Isabelle, Chief Administrative Officer-Clerk

Paquetville
1094, rue du Parc
Paquetville, NB E8R 1J4
Tél: 506-764-2500; *Téléc:* 506-764-2504
Entité municipal: Village
Incorporation: 1966 *Area:* 9.4 sq km
Comté ou district: Gloucester; *Population au 2011:* 706
Circonscription(s) électorale(s) provinciale(s): Centre-Péninsule-Saint-Sauveur
Circonscription(s) électorale(s) fédérale(s): Acadie-Bathurst
Prochaines élections: May 9, 2016 (4 year terms)
André Gozzo, Maire
Marie-Louise (Loulou) Blanchard, Greffière & Secrétaire

Perth-Andover
1131 West Riverside Dr.
Perth-Andover, NB E7H 5G5
Tel: 506-273-4959; *Fax:* 506-273-4947
info@perth-andover.com
www.perth-andover.com
Municipal Type: Village
Incorporated: 1966 *Area:* 8.89 sq km
County or District: Victoria; *Population in 2011:* 1,778
Provincial Electoral District(s): Victoria-Tobique
Federal Electoral District(s): Tobique-Mactaquac
Next Election: May 9, 2016 (4 year terms)
Terrence Peter Ritchie, Mayor
Daniel Dionne, Chief Administrative Officer
dan.dionne@perth-andover.com

Petit-Rocher
582, rue Principale
Petit-Rocher, NB E8J 1S5
Tél: 506-542-2686; *Téléc:* 506-542-2708
petit-rocher@nb.aibn.com
www.acadie-bathurst.com
Entité municipal: Village
Area: 4.49 sq km
Comté ou district: Gloucester; *Population au 2011:* 1,908
Circonscription(s) électorale(s) provinciale(s): Nigadoo-Chaleur
Circonscription(s) électorale(s) fédérale(s): Acadie-Bathurst
Prochaines élections: May 9, 2016 (4 year terms)
Luc Desjardins, Maire
Guy Clavette, Gérant

Petitcodiac
P.O. Box 2507
63 Main St.
Petitcodiac, NB E4Z 6H4
Tel: 506-756-3140; *Fax:* 506-756-3142
vop@nbnet.nb.ca
www.petitcodiac.ca
Municipal Type: Village
Area: 17.22 sq km
County or District: Westmorland; *Population in 2011:* 1,429
Provincial Electoral District(s): Petitcodiac
Federal Electoral District(s): Fundy Royal
Next Election: May 9, 2016 (4 year terms)
Gerald A.W. Gogan, Mayor
Janice Conley, Clerk

Plaster Rock
159 Main St.
Plaster Rock, NB E7G 2H2
Tel: 506-356-6070; *Fax:* 506-356-6081
vilprock@nb.aibn.com
www.plasterrockvillage.com
Municipal Type: Village
Area: 3.09 sq km
County or District: Victoria; *Population in 2011:* 1,135
Provincial Electoral District(s): Victoria-Tobique
Federal Electoral District(s): Tobique-Mactaquac
Next Election: May 9, 2016 (4 year terms)
Alexis D. Fenner, Mayor
Patty St. Peter, Chief Administrative Officer
506-356-6071
clerkpr@nb.aibn.com

Pointe-Verte
375, rue Principale
Pointe-Verte, NB E8J 2S8
Tél: 506-542-2606; *Téléc:* 506-542-2638
pverte@nbnet.nb.ca
www.acadie-bathurst.com
Entité municipal: Village
Area: 13.79 sq km
Comté ou district: Gloucester; *Population au 2011:* 976
Circonscription(s) électorale(s) provinciale(s): Nigadoo-Chaleur
Circonscription(s) électorale(s) fédérale(s): Acadie-Bathurst
Prochaines élections: May 9, 2016 (4 year terms)
Daniel Guitard, Maire
Marie-Eve Cyr, Directrice generale

Port Elgin
41 East Main St.
Port Elgin, NB E4M 2X8
Tel: 506-538-2120; *Fax:* 506-538-2126
prtelgin@nbnet.nb.ca
www.villageofportelgin.com
Municipal Type: Village
Incorporated: 1922 *Area:* 2.61 sq km
County or District: Westmorland; *Population in 2011:* 418
Provincial Electoral District(s): Tantramar
Federal Electoral District(s): Beauséjour
Next Election: May 9, 2016 (4 year terms)
Judy E. Scott, Mayor
Sonia M. Wells, Clerk-Treasurer

Rexton
#1, 79 Main St.
Rexton, NB E4W 1Z9
Tel: 506-523-6921; *Fax:* 506-523-7383
villageofrexton@nb.aibn.com
www.villageofrexton.com
Municipal Type: Village
Incorporated: Nov. 9, 1966 *Area:* 6.14 sq km
County or District: Kent; *Population in 2011:* 818
Provincial Electoral District(s): Kent
Federal Electoral District(s): Beauséjour
Next Election: May 9, 2016 (4 year terms)
David L. Hanson, Mayor
Barry Glencross, General Manager

Richibucto
9235, rue Main
Richibucto, NB E4W 4B4
Tél: 506-523-7870; *Téléc:* 506-523-7850
vtrcto@nbnet.nb.ca
www.richibucto.org
Entité municipal: Town
Incorporation: 1967 *Area:* 11.83 sq km
Comté ou district: Kent; *Population au 2011:* 1,286
Circonscription(s) électorale(s) provinciale(s): Rogersville-Kouchibouguac
Circonscription(s) électorale(s) fédérale(s): Beauséjour
Prochaines élections: May 9, 2016 (4 year terms)
Roger Doiron, Mayor
Gilles Belleau, Gérant

Riverside-Albert
5823 King St.
Riverside-Albert, NB E4H 4B4
Tel: 506-882-3022; *Fax:* 506-882-3016
villra@nbnet.nb.ca
www.bay-of-fundy.com/riverside-albert
Municipal Type: Village
Area: 3.41 sq km
County or District: Albert; *Population in 2011:* 353
Provincial Electoral District(s): Albert
Federal Electoral District(s): Fundy Royal
Next Election: May 9, 2016 (4 year terms)
C. Dale Elliot, Mayor
Deborah Murray, Clerk

Rivière-Verte
78, rue Principale
Rivière-Verte, NB E7C 2T8
Tél: 506-263-1060; *Téléc:* 506-263-1065
evelyne@nbnet.nb.ca
Entité municipal: Village
Area: 7 sq km
Comté ou district: Madawaska; *Population au 2011:* 744
Circonscription(s) électorale(s) provinciale(s): Restigouche-La-Vallée
Circonscription(s) électorale(s) fédérale(s): Madawaska-Restigouche
Prochaines élections: May 9, 2016 (4 year terms)
Michel Leblond, Maire
Evelyn Therrien, Greffière

Rogersville
#2, 28, rue de l'École
Rogersville, NB E4Y 1V7
Tél: 506-775-2080; *Téléc:* 506-775-2090
rogervil@nbnet.nb.ca
www.rogersville.info
Entité municipal: Village
Incorporation: Nov. 9, 1966 *Area:* 7.23 sq km
Comté ou district: Kent; *Population au 2011:* 1,170
Circonscription(s) électorale(s) provinciale(s): Rogersville-Kouchibouguac
Circonscription(s) électorale(s) fédérale(s): Miramichi
Prochaines élections: May 9, 2016 (4 year terms)
Pierrette F. Robichaud, Mairesse
Hélène LeBlanc, Greffière & Administratrice

Sackville
P.O. Box 6191
110 East Main St.
Sackville, NB E4L 1G6
Tel: 506-364-4930; *Fax:* 506-364-4976
b.carroll@sackville.com
www.sackville.com
Municipal Type: Town
Incorporated: Jan. 1903 *Area:* 74.32 sq km
County or District: Westmorland; *Population in 2011:* 5,558
Provincial Electoral District(s): Tantramar
Federal Electoral District(s): Beauséjour
Next Election: May 9, 2016 (4 year terms)
Robert D. Berry, Mayor
Eric Mourant, Chief Administrative Officer
e.mourant@sackville.com
Rhonda Tower, Clerk
r.tower@sackville.com

Saint-André
438, rue Lévesque
Saint-André, NB E3Y 3C7
Tél: 506-473-7580; *Téléc:* 506-473-7585
Entité municipal: Village
Area: 3.72 sq km
Comté ou district: Madawaska; *Population au 2011:* 819
Circonscription(s) électorale(s) provinciale(s): Grand Falls-Drummond-Saint-André
Circonscription(s) électorale(s) fédérale(s): Tobique-Mactaquac
Prochaines élections: May 9, 2016 (4 year terms)
Allain Desjardins, Maire
Gisèle Ouellette, Sec.-Tres.

Saint-Antoine
4599, rue Principale
Saint-Antoine, NB E4V 1P8
Tél: 506-525-4020; *Téléc:* 506-525-4027
village@village.stantoine.nb.ca
www.village.stantoine.nb.ca
Entité municipal: Village
Area: 6.43 sq km
Comté ou district: Kent; *Population au 2011:* 1,770
Circonscription(s) électorale(s) provinciale(s): Kent South
Circonscription(s) électorale(s) fédérale(s): Beauséjour
Prochaines élections: May 9, 2016 (4 year terms)
Roseline M. Maillet, Mairesse
Bernadine Maillet-LeBlanc, Directrice générale
berniem@village.stantoine.nb.ca

Saint-François-de-Madawaska
2033, rue Commerciale
Saint-François-de-Madawaska, NB E7A 1B3
Tél: 506-992-6050; *Téléc:* 506-992-6049
munstf@nb.aibn.com
Entité municipal: Village
Area: 6.34 sq km
Comté ou district: Madawaska; *Population au 2011:* 630
Circonscription(s) électorale(s) provinciale(s): Madawaska-les-Lacs
Circonscription(s) électorale(s) fédérale(s): Madawaska-Restigouche
Prochaines élections: May 9, 2016 (4 year terms)
Gérard Cyr, Maire
Colette Lévesque, Greffière

Saint-Hilaire
2190, rue Centrale
Saint-Hilaire, NB E3V 4W1
Tél: 506-258-3307; *Téléc:* 506-258-1802
Entité municipal: Village
Area: 5.67 sq km
Comté ou district: Madawaska; *Population au 2011:* 290
Circonscription(s) électorale(s) provinciale(s): Madawaska-les-Lacs
Circonscription(s) électorale(s) fédérale(s): Madawaska-Restigouche
Prochaines élections: May 9, 2016 (4 year terms)
Roland Dube, Maire
Oscar Roussel, Maire
Dave Cowan, Directeur général
506-358-6005, Fax: 506-358-6010
dave.cowan@saintisidore.ca

Saint-Isidore
3906, boul des Fondateurs
Saint-Isidore, NB E8M 1C2
Tel: 506-358-6005; *Fax:* 506-358-6010
villasti@nbnet.nb.ca
www.saintisidore.ca
Municipal Type: Village
Incorporated: June 1, 1991 *Area:* 22.58 sq km
Population in 2011: 748
Provincial Electoral District(s): Centre-Péninsule-Saint-Sauveur
Federal Electoral District(s): Acadie-Bathurst
Next Election: May 9, 2016 (4 year terms)

Saint-Léolin
117, rue des Prés
Saint-Léolin, NB E8N 2P9
Tél: 506-732-3266; *Téléc:* 506-732-3267
stleolin@nb.aira.com
www.villagesaintleolin.ca
Entité municipal: Village
Area: 19.78 sq km
Comté ou district: Gloucester; *Population au 2011:* 488
Circonscription(s) électorale(s) provinciale(s): Caraquet
Circonscription(s) électorale(s) fédérale(s): Acadie-Bathurst
Prochaines élections: May 9, 2016 (4 year terms)
Mathieu Chayer, Maire
Gérard Battah, Administrateur

Saint-Léonard
108, rue du Pont
Saint-Léonard, NB E7E 1Y1
Tél: 506-423-3111; *Téléc:* 506-423-3115
sleonard@nbnet.nb.ca
www.saint-leonard.ca
Entité municipal: Town
Incorporation: 1920 *Area:* 5.2 sq km
Comté ou district: Madawaska; *Population au 2011:* 1,343
Circonscription(s) électorale(s) provinciale(s):
Restigouche-La-Vallée
Circonscription(s) électorale(s) fédérale(s):
Madawaska-Restigouche
Prochaines élections: May 9, 2016 (4 year terms)
Carmel St-Amand, Maire
Charles Boucher, Directeur général

Saint-Louis-de-Kent
83, rue Beauséjour, #A
Saint-Louis-de-Kent, NB E4X 1A6
Tél: 506-876-3420; *Téléc:* 506-876-3477
vstlouis@nbnet.nb.ca
www.st-louis-de-kent.ca
Entité municipal: Village
Area: 2 sq km
Comté ou district: Kent; *Population au 2011:* 930
Circonscription(s) électorale(s) provinciale(s):
Rogersville-Kouchibouguac
Circonscription(s) électorale(s) fédérale(s): Beauséjour
Prochaines élections: May 9, 2016 (4 year terms)
Danielle Andrée Dugas, Mairesse
Léo-Paul Frigault, Administrateur

Saint-Quentin
10, rue Deschênes
Saint-Quentin, NB E8A 1M1
Tél: 506-235-2425; *Téléc:* 506-235-1952
ville@saintquentin.nb.ca
www.saintquentin.nb.ca
Entité municipal: Town
Incorporation: 1947 *Area:* 4.3 sq km
Comté ou district: Restigouche; *Population au 2011:* 2,095
Circonscription(s) électorale(s) provinciale(s):
Restigouche-La-Vallée
Circonscription(s) électorale(s) fédérale(s):
Madawaska-Restigouche
Prochaines élections: May 9, 2016 (4 year terms)
Note: Proclaimed as a town in 1992.
Rodrique Levesque, Maire
Suzanne Coulombe, Greffière

St. Andrews
212 Water St.
St. Andrews, NB E5B 1B4
Tel: 506-529-5120; *Fax:* 506-529-5183
thenderson@townofstandrews.ca
www.townofstandrews.ca
Municipal Type: Town
Area: 8.35 sq km
County or District: Charlotte; *Population in 2011:* 1,889
Provincial Electoral District(s): Charlotte-Campobello
Federal Electoral District(s): New Brunswick Southwest
Next Election: May 9, 2016 (4 year terms)
Stanley M. Choptainy, Mayor
W. Timothy Henderson, Chief Administrative Officer & Development Officer

Sainte-Anne-de-Madawaska
75, rue Principale
Sainte-Anne-de-Madawaska, NB E7E 1A8
Tél: 506-445-2449; *Téléc:* 506-445-2405
Entité municipal: Village
Area: 9.21 sq km
Comté ou district: Madawaska; *Population au 2011:* 1,002
Circonscription(s) électorale(s) provinciale(s):
Restigouche-La-Vallée
Circonscription(s) électorale(s) fédérale(s):
Madawaska-Restigouche
Prochaines élections: May 9, 2016 (4 year terms)
Guy Bellefleur, Maire
Lise Deschênes, Clerk-Très.

Sainte-Marie-Saint-Raphaël
1541, boul de la Mer
Sainte-Marie-Saint-Raphaël, NB E8T 1P5
Tél: 506-344-3210; *Téléc:* 506-344-3213
smsr@nbnet.nb.ca
www.ste-marie-st-raphael.ca
Entité municipal: Village
Incorporation: May 12, 1986 *Area:* 15.61 sq km
Comté ou district: Gloucester; *Population au 2011:* 955
Circonscription(s) électorale(s) provinciale(s):
Lamèque-Shippagan-Miscou
Circonscription(s) électorale(s) fédérale(s): Acadie-Bathurst
Prochaines élections: May 9, 2016 (4 year terms)
Henri Pierre Duguay, Maire
Denis Ducharme, Directeur général

St. George
1 School St.
St George, NB E5C 3N2
Tel: 506-755-4320; *Fax:* 506-755-4329
stgeonb@nbnet.nb.ca
www.town.stgeorge.nb.ca
Municipal Type: Town
Incorporated: Oct. 17, 1904 *Area:* 16.13 sq km
County or District: Charlotte; *Population in 2011:* 1,543
Provincial Electoral District(s): Charlotte-The Isles
Federal Electoral District(s): New Brunswick Southwest
Next Election: May 9, 2016 (4 year terms)
Daniel Joseph Henry, Mayor
Ross A. Norman, Manager

St. Martins
#2, 73 Main St.
St Martins, NB E5R 1B4
Tel: 506-833-2010; *Fax:* 506-833-2008
vilstmar@nbnet.nb.ca
www.stmartinscanada.com
Municipal Type: Village
Incorporated: Nov. 9, 1967 *Area:* 2.29 sq km
County or District: Saint John; *Population in 2011:* 314
Provincial Electoral District(s): Saint John-Fundy
Federal Electoral District(s): Fundy-Royal
Next Election: May 9, 2016 (4 year terms)
Bette Ann M. Chatterton, Mayor
Sandra Roy, Clerk

St. Stephen
73 Milltown Blvd.
St Stephen, NB E3L 1G5
Tel: 506-466-7700; *Fax:* 506-466-7701
jflewelling@town.ststephen.nb.ca
www.town.ststephen.nb.ca
Municipal Type: Town
County or District: Charlotte; *Population in 2011:* 4,817
Provincial Electoral District(s): Charlotte-Campobello
Federal Electoral District(s): New Brunswick Southwest
Next Election: May 9, 2016 (4 year terms)
John B. Quartermain, Mayor
Joan Flewelling, Clerk

Salisbury
56, rue Douglas
Salisbury, NB E4J 3E3
Tel: 506-372-3230; *Fax:* 506-372-3225
vilsalisbury@nb.aibn.com
www.salisburynb.ca
Municipal Type: Village
Incorporated: 1966 *Area:* 13.68 sq km
County or District: Westmorland; *Population in 2011:* 2,208
Provincial Electoral District(s): Petitcodiac
Federal Electoral District(s): Fundy Royal
Next Election: May 9, 2016 (4 year terms)
Terry A. Keating, Mayor
Pamela Cochrane, Clerk-Administrator

Shediac
#300, 290, rue Main
Shediac, NB E4P 2E3
Tél: 506-532-7000; *Téléc:* 506-532-6156
info@shediac.org
www.shediac.org
Entité municipal: Town
Area: 11.97 sq km
Comté ou district: Westmorland; *Population au 2011:* 6,053
Circonscription(s) électorale(s) provinciale(s): Shediac-Cap-Pelé
Circonscription(s) électorale(s) fédérale(s): Beauséjour
Prochaines élections: May 9, 2016 (4 year terms)
Jacques Leblanc, Mayor
Jeannette Bourque, Greffière

Shippagan
200, av Hôtel de Ville
Shippagan, NB E8S 1M1
Tél: 506-336-3900; *Téléc:* 506-336-3901
shipadm@nbnet.nb.ca
www.ville.shippagan.com
Entité municipal: Town
Incorporation: 1947 *Area:* 9.94 sq km
Comté ou district: Gloucester; *Population au 2011:* 2,603
Circonscription(s) électorale(s) provinciale(s):
Lamèque-Shippagan-Miscou
Circonscription(s) électorale(s) fédérale(s): Acadie-Bathurst
Prochaines élections: May 9, 2016 (4 year terms)
Note: Proclaimed as a town in 1958.
Tilmon Mallet, Maire
Nathalie Robichaud, Clerk
nathalie.robichaud@shippagan.com

Stanley
20 Main St.
Stanley, NB E6B 1A2
Tel: 506-367-3245; *Fax:* 506-367-0006
vstanley@nbnet.nb.ca
www.villageofstanley.com
Municipal Type: Village
Area: 17.34 sq km
County or District: York; *Population in 2011:* 419
Provincial Electoral District(s): York North
Federal Electoral District(s): Tobique-Mactaquac
Next Election: May 9, 2016 (4 year terms)
Mark A.J. Foreman, Mayor
Lorna Pinnock, Clerk-Administrator

Sussex
524 Main St.
Sussex, NB E4E 3E4
Tel: 506-432-4540; *Fax:* 506-432-4566
townofsussex@sussex.ca
www.sussex.ca
Municipal Type: Town
Incorporated: 1904 *Area:* 9.03 sq km
County or District: Kings; *Population in 2011:* 4,312
Provincial Electoral District(s): Kings East
Federal Electoral District(s): Fundy Royal
Next Election: May 9, 2016 (4 year terms)
Marc Thorne, Mayor
Paul Maguire, Clerk-Treasurer
paul.maguire@sussex.ca

Sussex Corner
1067 Main St.
Sussex Corner, NB E4E 3A1
Tel: 506-433-5184; *Fax:* 506-433-3785
sussex.corner@nb.aibn.com
www.sussexcorner.com
Municipal Type: Village
Incorporated: 1966 *Area:* 9.43 sq km
County or District: Kings; *Population in 2011:* 1,495
Provincial Electoral District(s): Kings East
Federal Electoral District(s): Fundy Royal
Next Election: May 9, 2016 (4 year terms)
Steven G. Gillies, Mayor
Don Smith, Clerk-Treasurer

Tide Head
6 Mountain St.
Tide Head, NB E3N 4J9
Tel: 506-789-6550; *Fax:* 506-789-6553
viltide@nb.sympatico.ca
www.tidehead.ca
Municipal Type: Village
Area: 19.57 sq km
County or District: Restigouche; *Population in 2011:* 1,036
Provincial Electoral District(s): Campbellton-Restigouche Centre
Federal Electoral District(s): Madawaska-Restigouche
Next Election: May 9, 2016 (4 year terms)
Randy Hunter, Mayor

Christine Babcock, Clerk-Administrator

Tracadie-Sheila
CP 3600 Main
3620, rue Principale
Tracadie-Sheila, NB E1X 1G5
Tél: 506-394-4020; *Téléc:* 506-394-4025
info@tracadie-sheila.ca
www.tracadie-sheila.ca
Entité municipal: Town
Incorporation: Jan. 1, 1992 *Area:* 24.64 sq km
Comté ou district: Gloucester; *Population au 2011:* 4,933
Circonscription(s) électorale(s) provinciale(s): Tracadie-Sheila
Circonscription(s) électorale(s) fédérale(s): Acadie-Bathurst
Prochaines élections: May 9, 2016 (4 year terms)
Aldéoda Losier, Maire
Denis Poirier, Directeur général

Tracy
4435 Heritage Dr.
Tracy, NB E5L 1C1
Tel: 506-368-2878; *Fax:* 506-368-1014
Municipal Type: Village
Area: 29.36 sq km
County or District: Sunbury; *Population in 2011:* 611
Provincial Electoral District(s): New Maryland-Sunbury West
Federal Electoral District(s): New Brunswick-Southwest
Next Election: May 9, 2016 (4 year terms)
Dale W. Mowry, Mayor
Susan Phillips, Clerk

Woodstock
824 Main St.
Woodstock, NB E7M 2E8
Tel: 506-325-4600; *Fax:* 506-325-4308
townhall@town.woodstock.nb.ca
www.town.woodstock.nb.ca
Municipal Type: Town
Incorporated: 1856 *Area:* 13.41 sq km
County or District: Carleton; *Population in 2011:* 5,254
Provincial Electoral District(s): Woodstock
Federal Electoral District(s): Tobique-Mactaquac
Next Election: May 9, 2016 (4 year terms)
Arthur L. Slipp, Mayor
Ken Harding, Chief Administrative Officer
ken.harding@town.woodstock.nb.ca

NEWFOUNDLAND & LABRADOR

The provincial government of Newfoundland and Labrador exercises control over the activities of all municipalities in accordance with the Executive Council Act and the Municipal Affairs Act. Under the provisions of the Municipalities Act, the Department exercises a certain degree of financial and administrative control over all municipalities with the exception of the cities of St. John's, Corner Brook and Mount Pearl. The towns incorporated under the Municipalities Act do not require ministerial approval of their annual budgets, but the Department employs Municipal Analysts to oversee municipal activities. The province assumes responsibility for public health, welfare and law enforcement which are elsewhere generally considered to be municipal functions.

The cities and towns incorporated in Newfoundland are authorized to levy taxes and to provide a wide range of municipal services and to make appropriate bylaws or regulations for the implementation and administration of these services.

City and town councils in Newfoundland are elected on the last Tuesday in September every four years (2013, 2017, etc.).

Newfoundland & Labrador

Major Municipalities in Newfoundland & Labrador

Conception Bay South
106 Conception Bay Hwy.
Conception Bay South, NL A1W 3A5
Tel: 709-834-6500; *Fax:* 709-834-8337
jmiller@conceptionbaysouth.ca
www.conceptionbaysouth.ca
Municipal Type: City
Incorporated: Sept. 1, 1971 *Area:* 59.27 sq km
Population in 2011: 24,848
Provincial Electoral District(s): Conception Bay South; Topsail
Federal Electoral District(s): St. John's East; Avalon
Next Election: Sept. 24, 2013 (4 year terms)
Woodrow French, Mayor
WFrench@conceptionbaysouth.ca
Rex Hillier, Councillor, Ward(s): 1
Stephen Tessier, Councillor, Ward(s): 2
Ken McDonald, Councillor, Ward(s): 3
Kirk Younden, Councillor, Ward(s): 4
Kenneth George, Councillor, Ward(s): at large
Beverly Rowe, Councillor, Ward(s): at large
Keith Arns, CAO
709-834-6506
karns@conceptionbaysouth.ca
Elaine Mitchell, Director, Planning
709-834-6553
Ron Franey, Director, Public Works
709-834-6523
Dave Tibbo, Director, Recreation & Leisure Services
709-834-6534
Todd Brophy, Fire Chief, Fire Department
709-834-6543

Corner Brook
City Hall
P.O. Box 1080
Corner Brook, NL A2H 6E1
Tel: 709-637-1500; *Fax:* 709-637-1625
cityhall@cornerbrook.com
www.cornerbrook.com
Municipal Type: City
Incorporated: April 27, 1955 *Area:* 148.27 sq km
Population in 2011: 19,886
Provincial Electoral District(s): Humber East; Humber West
Federal Electoral District(s): Humber-St. Barbe-Baie Verte
Next Election: Sept. 24, 2013 (4 year terms)
Note: City Hall is located on Mount Bernard Ave. at Main St.
Neville Greeley, Mayor
709-637-1537, Fax: 709-637-1543
ngreeley@cornerbrook.com
Leo Bruce, Councillor
lbruce@cornerbrook.com
Priscilla Boutcher, Councillor
pboutcher@cornerbrook.com
Donna Francis, Councillor
dfrancis@cornerbrook.com
Charlie Renouf, Councillor
crenouf@cornerbrook.com
Linda Chaisson, Councillor
lchaisson@cornerbrook.com
Marina Redmond, City Clerk
709-637-1534
mredmond@cornerbrook.com
Michael Dolter, CAO
709-637-1532
mdolter@cornerbrook.com
Neville Wheaton, Fire Chief
709-637-1615
nmwheaton@cornerbrook.com
Paul Barnable, Director, Community Services
709-637-1548, Fax: 709-637-1514
pbarnable@cornerbrook.com
Gerry Cole, Supervisor, Recreational Services
709-637-1232
gcole@cornerbrook.com
Trina Burden, Business Resource Manager
709-637-1558
tburden@cornerbrook.com
Steve May, Director, Operational Services
709-637-1541, Fax: 709-637-1502
smay@cornerbrook.com
Todd Pickett, Land Management Officer
709-637-1544
tpickett@cornerbrook.com
Colleen Humphries, Supervisor, Planning
709-637-1553
chumphries@cornerbrook.com
James Warford, P.Eng., Coordinator, Engineering Services
709-637-1626
jwarford@cornerbrook.com
Keith Costello, Superintendent, Water & Sewer
709-637-1595
kcostello@cornerbrook.com
Barry Ellsworth, Manager, Public Works
709-637-1509
bellsworth@cornerbrook.com
Percy Joyce, Officer, Land Management
709-637-1544
pjoyce@cornerbrook.com
Deon Rumbolt, Supervisor, Development & Inspection
709-637-1552
drumbolt@cornerbrook.com
Rhea Hutchings, Sustainable Development Officer, Operational Services
709-637-1574
rhutchings@cornerbrook.com
Craig Kennedy, Superintendent, Public Works
709-637-1607
ckennedy@cornerbrook.com

Grand Falls-Windsor
P.O. Box 439
Grand Falls-Windsor, NL A2A 2J8
Tel: 709-489-0412; *Fax:* 709-489-0465
jrowsell@grandfallswindsor.com
www.grandfallswindsor.com
Municipal Type: City
Incorporated: Jan. 1, 1991 *Area:* 54.48 sq km
Population in 2011: 13,725
Provincial Electoral District(s): Grand Falls-Buchans; Windsor-Springdale
Federal Electoral District(s): Bonavista-Gander-Grand Falls-Windsor
Next Election: Sept. 24, 2013 (4 year terms)
Allan Hawkins, Mayor
mayor@grandfallswindsor.com
Anne Blackmore, Deputy Mayor
Darren Finn, Councillor
Bruce Moores, Councillor
Jean Buffett-Mercer, Councillor
Amy Coady-Davis, Councillor
Roger Barnett, Councillor
Michael Pinsent, Town Manager
709-487-0407, Fax: 709-292-0018
mpinsent@grandfallswindsor.com
Jeff Saunders, Director, Engineering Works
709-489-0427, Fax: 709-489-0465
jsaunders@grandfallswindsor.com
Vince J. McKenzie, Fire Chief
709-489-0431, Fax: 709-489-0885
firechief@grandfallswindsor.com
Dave Nichols, Director, Parks & Recreation
709-489-0450, Fax: 709-489-0454
dnichols@grandfallswindsor.com
Robert Thompson, Supervisor, Engineering & Works
709-489-0421, Fax: 709-489-0467
rthompson@grandfallswindsor.com
Mark Kelly, Clerk, Purchasing
709-489-0422, Fax: 709-489-0465
purchasing@grandfallswindsor.com

Mount Pearl
3 Centennial St.
Mount Pearl, NL A1N 1G4
Tel: 709-748-1006; *Fax:* 709-748-1150
info@mtpearl.nf.ca
www.mountpearl.ca
Municipal Type: City
Incorporated: Jan. 11, 1955 *Area:* 15.75 sq km
Population in 2011: 24,284
Provincial Electoral District(s): Mount Pearl; Waterford Valley
Federal Electoral District(s): St. John's South-Mount Pearl
Next Election: Sept. 24, 2013 (4 year terms)
Randy Simms, Mayor
rsimms@mountpearl.ca
Jim Locke, Deputy Mayor
jlocke@mountpearl.ca
Lucy Stoyles, Councillor
lstoyless@mountpearl.ca
John Walsh, Councillor
jwalsh@mountpearl.ca
Paul Lane, Councillor
plane@mountpearl.ca
Paula Tessier, Councillor
ptessier@mountpearl.ca
Dave Aker, Councillor
daker@mountpearl.ca
Michele Peach, CAO
709-748-1025
mpeach@mountpearl.ca
Mona Lewis, Deputy City Clerk
709-748-1032
mlewis@mountpearl.ca
Stephen Jewczyk, Director, Planning & Development
709-748-1029
sjewczyk@mountpearl.ca
Scott Lush, Director, Infrastructure & Public Works
709-748-1028
slush@mountpearl.ca
Brian Chmarney, Director, Community Services
709-748-1027
bchmarney@mountpearl.ca
Bronda Aylward, Director, Economic Development
709-748-1096
baylward@mountpearl.ca
Jason Silver, Director, Corporate Services
709-748-1026
jsilver@mountpearl.ca
Norm Snelgrove, Manager, Finance
709-748-1159
nsnelgrove@mountpearl.ca
Colleen Butler, Manager, Human Resources
709-748-1095
cbutler@mountpearl.ca
Blair Tilley, Superintendent, Municipal Enforcement
709-748-1068
btilley@mountpearl.ca

Paradise
28 McNamara Dr.
Paradise, NL A1L 0A6
Tel: 709-782-1400; *Fax:* 709-782-3601
info@townofparadise.ca
www.townofparadise.ca
Municipal Type: City
Incorporated: Feb. 1, 1992 *Area:* 29.24 sq km
Population in 2011: 17,695
Provincial Electoral District(s): Conception Bay East & Bell Island; Topsail
Federal Electoral District(s): St. John's East; Bonavista-Gander-Grand Falls-Windsor; Labrador
Next Election: Sept. 24, 2013 (4 year terms)
Ralph Wiseman, Mayor
rwiseman@townofparadise.ca
Allan English, Deputy Mayor, Councillor
aenglish@townofparadise.ca
Dan Bobbett, Councillor
dbobbett@townofparadise.ca
Sterling Willis, Councillor
swillis@townofparadise.ca
Vince Burton, Councillor
vburton@townofparadise.ca
Deborah Quilty, Councillor
dquilty@townofparadise.ca
Rodney Cumby, CAO
rcumby@townofparadise.ca
Terrilynn Smith, Director, Corporate Services
tlsmith@townofparadise.ca
Alton Glenn, Director, Planning and Protective Services
aglenn@townofparadise.ca
Jason Collins, Director, Recreation and Leisure Services
jcolins@townofparadise.ca

St. John's
City Hall
P.O. Box 908
10 New Gower St.
St. John's, NL A1C 5M2
Tel: 709-754-2489; *Fax:* 709-576-7688
council@stjohns.ca
www.stjohns.ca
Other Information: 311 for city services
Municipal Type: City
Incorporated: Aug. 7, 1921 *Area:* 446.04 sq km
Population in 2011: 106,172
Provincial Electoral District(s): Kilbride; Signal Hill-Quidi Vidi; St. J. Centre; St. J. East; St. J. North; St. J. South; St. J. West; Virginia Waters; Mount Pearl North; Cape St. Francis
Federal Electoral District(s): St. John's East; St. John's South-Mount Pearl
Next Election: Sept. 24, 2013 (4 year terms)
Dennis O'Keefe, Mayor
709-576-8477, Fax: 709-576-8250
dokeefe@stjohns.ca

Shannie Duff, Deputy Mayor & Councillor
709-576-8583, Fax: 709-576-8474
sduff@stjohns.ca
Gerry Colbert, Councillor at Large
709-576-7689, Fax: 709-576-8474
gcolbert@stjohns.ca
Sheilagh O'Leary, Councillor at Large
709-576-8567, Fax: 709-576-8474
soleary@stjohns.ca
Tom Hann, Councillor at Large
709-576-8219, Fax: 709-576-8474
thann@stjohns.ca
Sandy Hickman, Councillor at Large
709-576-8045, Fax: 709-576-8474
shickman@stjohns.ca
Danny Breen, Councillor, Ward(s): 1
709-576-2332, Fax: 709-576-8474
dbreen@stjohns.ca
Frank Galgay, Councillor, Ward(s): 2
709-576-8577, Fax: 709-576-8474
fgalgay@stjohns.ca
Bruce Tilley, Councillor, Ward(s): 3
709-576-8643, Fax: 709-576-8474
btilley@stjohns.ca
Debbie Hanlon, Councillor, Ward(s): 4
709-576-2383, Fax: 709-576-8474
dhanlon@stjohns.ca
Wally Collins, Councillor, Ward(s): 5
709-576-8584, Fax: 709-576-8474
wcollins@stjohns.ca
Neil Martin, City Clerk, Director & Associate Commissioner, Corporate Services
709-576-8446, Fax: 709-576-8474
Robert Bishop, C.A., Treasurer & Director, Finance
709-576-8696, Fax: 709-576-8564
Ronald Penney, City Solicitor & City Manager
709-576-8557, Fax: 709-576-8561
legal@stjohns.ca
Walt Mills, Director, Engineering
709-576-8658, Fax: 709-576-8625
David Blackmore, Director, Building & Property Management
709-576-8701, Fax: 709-576-8160
Kevin Breen, Director, Human Resources
709-576-8213, Fax: 709-576-8575
Jill Brewer, Director, Recreation
709-576-8405, Fax: 709-576-8469
Cliff Johnston, Director, Planning
709-576-8383, Fax: 709-576-8625
Elizabeth Lawrence, Director, Economic Development, Tourism & Culture
709-576-8203, Fax: 709-576-8246
Paul Mackey, Director, Public Works & Parks
709-576-8303, Fax: 709-576-8026
Jim Clarke, Manager, Streets & Parks
709-576-8541, Fax: 709-576-8026
P.J. (Jim) Ford, Manager, Regulatory Services
709-576-8294, Fax: 709-576-8160
Gareth Griffiths, C.E.T., Manager, Real Estate Services
709-576-8440, Fax: 709-576-8561
Kevin Gushue, Manager, Tourism Development
709-567-8545, Fax: 709-576-8246
Geraldine King, Manager, Environmental Initiatives
709-576-8613, Fax: 709-576-8625
Joe Sampson, Manager, Development
Bob Wilson, Manager, Energy Efficiency
709-576-8238, Fax: 709-576-8160
Robin King, Transportation Engineer
709-576-8232, Fax: 709-576-8625

Other Municipalities in Newfoundland & Labrador

Admiral's Beach
P.O. Box 196
Admiral's Beach, NL A0B 3A0
Tel: 709-521-2671; *Fax:* 709-521-2671
Municipal Type: Town
Incorporated: Jan. 16, 1968 *Area:* 24.42 sq km
Population in 2011: 153
Provincial Electoral District(s): Placentia & St. Mary's
Federal Electoral District(s): Avalon
Next Election: Sept. 24, 2013 (4 year terms)
Keith Guitar, Mayor
Mary Dobbin, Clerk

Anchor Point
P.O. Box 117
Anchor Point, NL A0K 1A0
Tel: 709-456-2011; *Fax:* 709-456-2364
anchorpoint@nf.aibn.com
Municipal Type: Town
Incorporated: Sept. 10, 1974 *Area:* 2.41 sq km
Population in 2011: 326
Provincial Electoral District(s): St. Barbe
Federal Electoral District(s): Humber-St. Barbe-Baie Verte
Next Election: Sept. 24, 2013 (4 year terms)
Gerry Gros, Mayor
Sharon Gaulton, Clerk

Appleton
PO Box 31, Site 4
Appleton, NL A0G 2K0
Tel: 709-679-2289; *Fax:* 709-679-5552
townofappleton@personainternet.com
Municipal Type: Town
Incorporated: Feb. 27, 1962 *Area:* 6.39 sq km
Population in 2011: 622
Provincial Electoral District(s): Gander
Federal Electoral District(s): Bonavista-Gander-Grand Falls-Windsor
Next Election: Sept. 24, 2013 (4 year terms)
Derm Flynn, Mayor
Pat Barnes, Clerk

Aquaforte
General Delivery
Aquaforte, NL A0A 1A0
Tel: 709-363-2618
townofaqauaforte@hotmail.com
Municipal Type: Town
Incorporated: April 25, 1972 *Area:* 6.82 sq km
Population in 2011: 83
Provincial Electoral District(s): Ferryland
Federal Electoral District(s): Avalon
Next Election: Sept. 24, 2013 (4 year terms)
Carol Ann Case, Mayor
Kathleen Hayes, Clerk

Arnold's Cove
P.O. Box 70
Arnolds Cove, NL A0B 1A0
Tel: 709-463-2323; *Fax:* 709-463-2326
townofarnoldscove@nf.aibn.com
www.townofarnoldscove.com
Municipal Type: Town
Incorporated: June 3, 1967 *Area:* 4.93 sq km
Population in 2011: 990
Provincial Electoral District(s): Bellevue
Federal Electoral District(s): Avalon
Next Election: Sept. 24, 2013 (4 year terms)
Thomas Osbourne, Mayor
Wayne Slade, Clerk

Avondale
P.O. Box 59
Avondale, NL A0A 1B0
Tel: 709-229-4201; *Fax:* 709-229-4446
townofavondale@persona.ca
Municipal Type: Town
Incorporated: Nov. 26, 1974 *Area:* 29.93 sq km
Population in 2011: 636
Provincial Electoral District(s): Harbour Main-Whitbourne
Federal Electoral District(s): Avalon
Next Election: Sept. 24, 2013 (4 year terms)
Bern Hickey, Mayor
Jennifer Lewis, Clerk

Badger
P.O. Box 130
Badger, NL A0H 1A0
Tel: 709-539-2406; *Fax:* 709-539-5262
townofbadger@gmail.com
Municipal Type: Town
Incorporated: Sept. 24, 1963 *Area:* 1.96 sq km
Population in 2011: 793
Provincial Electoral District(s): Grand Falls-Buchans
Federal Electoral District(s): Bonavista-Gander-Grand Falls-Windsor
Next Election: Sept. 24, 2013 (4 year terms)
Michael Patey, Mayor
Pansy Hurley, Clerk

Baie Verte
P.O. Box 218
Baie Verte, NL A0K 1B0
Tel: 709-532-8222; *Fax:* 709-532-4134
info@townofbaieverte.ca
www.townofbaieverte.ca
Municipal Type: Town
Incorporated: April 29, 1958 *Area:* 371.07 sq km
Population in 2011: 1,370
Provincial Electoral District(s): Baie Verte
Federal Electoral District(s): Humber-St. Barbe-Baie Verte
Next Election: Sept. 24, 2013 (4 year terms)
Gerald Acreman, Mayor
Angela Furey, Clerk

Baine Harbour
General Delivery
Baine Harbour, NL A0E 1A0
Tel: 709-443-2980; *Fax:* 709-443-2355
Municipal Type: Town
Incorporated: Dec. 1, 1970 *Area:* 4.82 sq km
Population in 2011: 137
Provincial Electoral District(s): Burin-Placentia West
Federal Electoral District(s): Random-Burin-St. George's
Next Election: Sept. 24, 2013 (4 year terms)
Harold Kenway, Mayor
Dinah Smith, Clerk

Bauline
2 Brook Path
Bauline, NL A1K 1E9
Tel: 709-335-2483; *Fax:* 709-335-2053
baulinetowncouncil@nf.aibn.com
Municipal Type: Town
Incorporated: July 1, 1988 *Area:* 15.95 sq km
Population in 2011: 397
Provincial Electoral District(s): Cape St. Francis
Federal Electoral District(s): St. John's East
Next Election: Sept. 24, 2013 (4 year terms)
Christopher Dredge, Mayor
Raylene Manning, Clerk

Bay Bulls
P.O. Box 70
Bay Bulls, NL A0A 1C0
Tel: 709-334-3454; *Fax:* 709-334-3477
townofbaybulls@nf.aibn.com
www.baybulls.com
Municipal Type: Town
Incorporated: Jan. 1, 1986 *Area:* 30.74 sq km
Population in 2011: 1,283
Provincial Electoral District(s): Ferryland
Federal Electoral District(s): Avalon
Next Election: Sept. 24, 2013 (4 year terms)
Harold Mullowney, Mayor
Janet O'Brien, Clerk

Bay de Verde
P.O. Box 10
Bay de Verde, NL A0A 1E0
Tel: 709-587-2260; *Fax:* 709-587-2049
towncouncilbdv@persona.ca
www.baydeverde.com
Municipal Type: Town
Incorporated: Aug. 22, 1950 *Area:* 13.28 sq km
Population in 2011: 398
Provincial Electoral District(s): Trinity-Bay de Verde
Federal Electoral District(s): Avalon
Next Election: Sept. 24, 2013 (4 year terms)
Gerald Murphy, Mayor
Molly Walsh, Clerk

Bay L'Argent
P.O. Box 29
Bay L'Argent, NL A0E 1B0
Tel: 709-461-2606; *Fax:* 709-461-2608
townofbaylargent@nf.aibn.com
Municipal Type: Town
Incorporated: July 13, 1971 *Area:* 3.56 sq km
Population in 2011: 285
Provincial Electoral District(s): Bellevue
Federal Electoral District(s): Random-Burin-St. George's
Next Election: Sept. 24, 2013 (4 year terms)
Rhonda Baker, Mayor
Viola Pardy, Clerk

Bay Roberts
P.O. Box 114
Bay Roberts, NL A0A 1G0
Tel: 709-786-2126; *Fax:* 709-786-2128
shawe@town.bayroberts.nf.ca
www.bayroberts.com
Municipal Type: Town
Incorporated: Feb. 17, 1951 *Area:* 23.92 sq km
Population in 2011: 5,818
Provincial Electoral District(s): Port de Grave
Federal Electoral District(s): Avalon
Next Election: Sept. 24, 2013 (4 year terms)
Glenn Littlejohn, Mayor
glennlittlejohn@bayroberts.com
Shirley Hawe, Clerk

Baytona
P.O. Box 29
Baytona, NL A0G 2J0
Tel: 709-659-6101; *Fax:* 709-659-6101
thetownofbaytona@eastlink.ca
Municipal Type: Town
Incorporated: Aug. 1, 1975 *Area:* 15.38 sq km
Population in 2011: 264
Provincial Electoral District(s): Lewisporte
Federal Electoral District(s): Bonavista-Gander-Grand Falls-Windsor
Next Election: Sept. 24, 2013 (4 year terms)
Rex Quinlan, Mayor
Patsy Lewis, Clerk

Beachside
112 Bayview Rd.
Beachside, NL A0J 1T0
Tel: 709-267-5251; *Fax:* 709-267-5251
Municipal Type: Town
Incorporated: July 7, 1961 *Area:* 2.61 sq km
Population in 2011: 150
Provincial Electoral District(s): Baie Verte
Federal Electoral District(s): Humber-St. Barbe-Baie Verte
Next Election: Sept. 24, 2013 (4 year terms)
Ada Locke, Mayor
Robert Stone, Clerk

Bellburns
General Delivery
Bellburns, NL A0K 1H0
Tel: 709-898-2468; *Fax:* 709-898-2442
Municipal Type: Town
Incorporated: May 13, 1969 *Area:* 7.39 sq km
Population in 2011: 62
Provincial Electoral District(s): St. Barbe
Federal Electoral District(s): Humber-St. Barbe-Baie Verte
Next Election: Sept. 24, 2013 (4 year terms)
Baxter House, Mayor
Pauline House, Clerk

Belleoram
P.O. Box 29
Belleoram, NL A0H 1B0
Tel: 709-881-6161; *Fax:* 709-881-6161
belloeam1946@yahoo.ca
Municipal Type: Town
Incorporated: March 19, 1946 *Area:* 2.1 sq km
Population in 2011: 409
Provincial Electoral District(s): Fortune Bay-Cape La Hune
Federal Electoral District(s): Random-Burin-St. George's
Next Election: Sept. 24, 2013 (4 year terms)
Steward May, Mayor
Evelyn Savoury, Clerk

Birchy Bay
P.O. Box 40
Birchy Bay, NL A0G 1E0
Tel: 709-659-3221; *Fax:* 709-659-2121
office@birchybay.ca
Municipal Type: Town
Incorporated: Aug. 27, 1974 *Area:* 49.52 sq km
Population in 2011: 566
Provincial Electoral District(s): Lewisporte
Federal Electoral District(s): Bonavista-Gander-Grand Falls-Windsor
Next Election: Sept. 24, 2013 (4 year terms)
Seymour Quinlan, Mayor
Cynthia Baker, Clerk

Bird Cove
67 Michael's Dr.
Bird Cove, NL A0K 1L0
Tel: 709-247-2256; *Fax:* 709-247-2254
tobc@nf.aibn.com
Municipal Type: Town
Incorporated: April 15, 1977 *Area:* 9.39 sq km
Population in 2011: 182
Provincial Electoral District(s): St. Barbe
Federal Electoral District(s): Humber-St. Barbe-Baie Verte
Next Election: Sept. 24, 2013 (4 year terms)
Richard May, Mayor
Wanda Pittman, Clerk

Bishop's Cove
P.O. Box 36
Bishop's Cove, NL A0A 3X0
Tel: 709-589-2195
Municipal Type: Town
Incorporated: June 24, 1969 *Area:* 1.89 sq km
Population in 2011: 275
Provincial Electoral District(s): Port de Grave
Federal Electoral District(s): Avalon
Next Election: Sept. 24, 2013 (4 year terms)
Lori Ann King, Mayor
Irene Menchions, Clerk

Bishop's Falls
P.O. Box 310
Bishops Falls, NL A0H 1C0
Tel: 709-258-6581; *Fax:* 709-258-6346
info@bishopsfalls.com
Municipal Type: Town
Incorporated: Nov. 1, 1961 *Area:* 28.12 sq km
Population in 2011: 3,341
Provincial Electoral District(s): Exploits
Federal Electoral District(s): Bonavista-Gander-Grand Falls-Windsor
Next Election: Sept. 24, 2013 (4 year terms)
Robert Hobbs, Mayor
Randy Drover, Clerk

Bonavista
P.O. Box 279
Bonavista, NL A0C 1B0
Tel: 709-468-7816; *Fax:* 709-468-2495
town.bonavista@nf.sympatico.ca
Municipal Type: Town
Incorporated: Nov. 24, 1964 *Area:* 31.5 sq km
Population in 2011: 3,589
Provincial Electoral District(s): Bonavista South
Federal Electoral District(s): Bonavista-Gander-Grand Falls-Windsor
Next Election: Sept. 24, 2013 (4 year terms)
Elizabeth Fitzgerald, Mayor
David Hiscock, Clerk

Botwood
P.O. Box 490
Botwood, NL A0H 1E0
Tel: 709-257-2839; *Fax:* 709-257-3330
botwoodtowncouncil@nf.aibn.com
www.town.botwood.nl.ca
Municipal Type: Town
Incorporated: June 21, 1960 *Area:* 15.05 sq km
Population in 2011: 3,008
Provincial Electoral District(s): Exploits
Federal Electoral District(s): Bonavista-Gander-Grand Falls-Windsor
Next Election: Sept. 24, 2013 (4 year terms)
Jerry Dean, Mayor
Audrey Rowsell, Clerk

Branch
P.O. Box 129
Branch, NL A0B 1E0
Tel: 709-338-2920; *Fax:* 709-338-2921
townofbranch@nf.aibn.com
Municipal Type: Town
Incorporated: May 17, 1966 *Area:* 16.15 sq km
Population in 2011: 247
Provincial Electoral District(s): Placentia & St. Mary's
Federal Electoral District(s): Avalon
Next Election: Sept. 24, 2013 (4 year terms)
Priscilla Corcoran Mooney, Mayor
Augustine Power, Clerk

Brent's Cove
General Delivery
Brents Cove, NL A0K 1R0
Tel: 709-661-5301; *Fax:* 709-661-5216
Municipal Type: Town
Incorporated: April 12, 1966 *Area:* 1.02 sq km
Population in 2011: 181
Provincial Electoral District(s): Baie Verte
Federal Electoral District(s): Humber-St. Barbe-Baie Verte
Next Election: Sept. 24, 2013 (4 year terms)
Ellen Butler, Clerk
Richard Andrews, Mayor

Brighton
General Delivery
Brighton, NL A0J 1B0
Tel: 709-263-7391; *Fax:* 709-263-7391
Other Information: townofbrighton@hotmail.com
Municipal Type: Town
Incorporated: Jan. 1, 1986 *Area:* 2.23 sq km
Population in 2011: 171
Provincial Electoral District(s): Windsor-Springdale
Federal Electoral District(s): Humber-St. Barbe-Baie Verte
Next Election: Sept. 24, 2013 (4 year terms)
Lindy Fudge, Mayor
Jane Fudge, Clerk

Brigus
P.O. Box 220
Brigus, NL A0A 1K0
Tel: 709-528-4588; *Fax:* 709-528-4588
brigus@eastlink.ca
www.brigus.net
Municipal Type: Town
Incorporated: July 21, 1964 *Area:* 11.57 sq km
Population in 2011: 750
Provincial Electoral District(s): Harbour Main-Whitbourne
Federal Electoral District(s): Avalon
Next Election: Sept. 24, 2013 (4 year terms)
Byron Rodway, Mayor
709-528-3201
byronrodway@personainternet.com
Wayne Rose, Town Clerk & Manager

Bryant's Cove
PO Box 5, Site 3
Bryant's Cove, NL A0A 3P0
Tel: 709-596-2291; *Fax:* 709-596-0015
Other Information: bryantscove@eastlink.ca
Municipal Type: Town
Incorporated: July 29, 1977 *Area:* 4.87 sq km
Population in 2011: 396
Provincial Electoral District(s): Port de Grave
Federal Electoral District(s): Avalon
Next Election: Sept. 24, 2013 (4 year terms)
Kim Sheppard, Mayor
Michelle Antle, Clerk

Buchans
P.O. Box 190
Buchans, NL A0H 1G0
Tel: 709-672-3972; *Fax:* 709-672-3702
townofbuchans@nf.aibn.com
Municipal Type: Town
Incorporated: April 24, 1963 *Area:* 4.88 sq km
Population in 2011: 696
Provincial Electoral District(s): Grand Falls-Buchans
Federal Electoral District(s): Bonavista-Gander-Grand Falls-Windsor
Next Election: Sept. 24, 2013 (4 year terms)
Derm Corbett, Mayor
David Whalen, Clerk

Burgeo
P.O. Box 220
Burgeo, NL A0N 2H0
Tel: 709-886-2250; *Fax:* 709-886-2166
townofburgeo@bbsict.ca
Municipal Type: Town
Incorporated: June 17, 1950 *Area:* 31.34 sq km
Population in 2011: 1,464
Provincial Electoral District(s): Burgeo & La Poile
Federal Electoral District(s): Random-Burin-St. George's
Next Election: Sept. 24, 2013 (4 year terms)
Gerald MacDonald, Mayor
Michael Ballard, Clerk

Burin
P.O. Box 370
Burin, NL A0E 1E0
Tel: 709-891-1760; *Fax:* 709-891-2069
townofburin@eastlink.ca
www.burincanada.com
Municipal Type: Town
Incorporated: July 18, 1950 *Area:* 34.05 sq km
Population in 2011: 2,424
Provincial Electoral District(s): Burin-Placentia West; Grand Bank
Federal Electoral District(s): Random-Burin-St. George's
Next Election: Sept. 24, 2013 (4 year terms)
Kevin Lundrigan, Mayor
Beth Hanrahan, Clerk
bhanrahan@persona.ca

Burlington
General Delivery
Burlington, NL A0K 1S0
Tel: 709-252-2607; *Fax:* 709-252-2161
mbartlett@townofburlington.ca
www.townofburlington.ca
Municipal Type: Town
Incorporated: Oct. 20, 1953 *Area:* 4.1 sq km
Population in 2011: 349
Provincial Electoral District(s): Baie Verte
Federal Electoral District(s): Humber-St. Barbe-Baie Verte
Next Election: Sept. 24, 2013 (4 year terms)
George Kelly, Mayor
gkelly@townofburlington.ca
Mary Lou Bartlett, Clerk

Burnt Islands
P.O. Box 39
Burnt Islands, NL A0M 1B0
Tel: 709-698-3512; *Fax:* 709-698-3512
townofburntislands@hotmail.com
Municipal Type: Town
Incorporated: Oct. 31, 1975 *Area:* 9.52 sq km
Population in 2011: 651
Provincial Electoral District(s): Burgeo & La Poile
Federal Electoral District(s): Random-Burin-St. George's
Next Election: Sept. 24, 2013 (4 year terms)
Alfred Taylor, Mayor
Linda Thorne, Clerk

Campbellton
P.O. Box 70
Campbellton, NL A0G 1L0
Tel: 709-261-2300; *Fax:* 709-261-2375
townofcampbellton@nf.aibn.com
Municipal Type: Town
Incorporated: Oct. 21, 1972 *Area:* 35.71 sq km
Population in 2011: 520
Provincial Electoral District(s): Lewisporte
Federal Electoral District(s): Bonavista-Gander-Grand Falls-Windsor
Next Election: Sept. 24, 2013 (4 year terms)
Maisie Clarke, Mayor
Gail Osmond, Clerk

Cape Broyle
P.O. Box 69
Cape Broyle, NL A0A 1P0
Tel: 709-432-2288; *Fax:* 709-432-2794
townofcapebroyle@nf.aibn.com
Municipal Type: Town
Incorporated: Jan. 1, 1990 *Area:* 10.05 sq km
Population in 2011: 506
Provincial Electoral District(s): Ferryland
Federal Electoral District(s): Avalon
Next Election: Sept. 24, 2013 (4 year terms)
Donald Graham, Mayor
Wendy Duggan, Clerk

Cape St. George
876 Oceanview Drive
Cape St George, NL A0N 1T1
Tel: 709-644-2290; *Fax:* 709-644-2291
townofcapestgeorge@eastlink.ca
Municipal Type: Town
Incorporated: June 24, 1969 *Area:* 33.46 sq km
Population in 2011: 949
Provincial Electoral District(s): Port au Port
Federal Electoral District(s): Random-Burin-St. George's
Next Election: Sept. 24, 2013 (4 year terms)
Peter Fenwick, Mayor
Ina Renouf, Clerk

Carbonear
P.O. Box 999
Carbonear, NL A1Y 1C5
Tel: 709-596-3831; *Fax:* 709-596-5021
info@carbonear.ca
www.carbonear.ca
Municipal Type: Town
Incorporated: July 13, 1948 *Area:* 11.81 sq km
Population in 2011: 4,739
Provincial Electoral District(s): Carbonear-Harbour Grace
Federal Electoral District(s): Avalon
Next Election: Sept. 24, 2013 (4 year terms)
Sam Slade, Mayor
Cathy Somers, Clerk
csomers@@nf.aibn.com

Carmanville
P.O. Box 239
Carmanville, NL A0G 1N0
Tel: 709-534-2814; *Fax:* 709-534-2425
townofcarmanville@nf.aibn.com
Municipal Type: Town
Incorporated: March 29, 1955 *Area:* 43.08 sq km
Population in 2011: 737
Provincial Electoral District(s): Bonavista North
Federal Electoral District(s): Bonavista-Gander-Grand Falls-Windsor
Next Election: Sept. 24, 2013 (4 year terms)
Sam Winsor, Mayor
Dianne Goodyear, Clerk

Cartwright
P.O. Box 129
Cartwright, NL A0K 1V0
Tel: 709-938-7259; *Fax:* 709-938-7454
shopkins@nf.aibn.com
Municipal Type: Town
Incorporated: Oct. 10, 1956 *Area:* 3.27 sq km
Population in 2011: 516
Provincial Electoral District(s): Cartwright-L'Anse au Clair
Federal Electoral District(s): Labrador
Next Election: Sept. 24, 2013 (4 year terms)
Rosetta Holwell, Mayor
Shirley Hopkins, Clerk

Centreville-Wareham-Trinity
P.O. Box 130
Centreville, NL A0G 4P0
Tel: 709-678-2840; *Fax:* 709-678-2536
townofcentreville@nf.aibn.com
Municipal Type: Town
Incorporated: Jan. 1, 1992 *Area:* 37.25 sq km
Population in 2011: 1,161
Provincial Electoral District(s): Bonavista North
Federal Electoral District(s): Bonavista-Gander-Grand Falls-Windsor
Next Election: Sept. 24, 2013 (4 year terms)
Churence Rogers, Mayor
Gertrude Brown, Clerk

Chance Cove
P.O. Box 133
Chance Cove, NL A0B 1K0
Tel: 709-460-4151; *Fax:* 709-460-5580
townofchancecove@nf.aibn.com
Municipal Type: Town
Incorporated: Feb. 8, 1972 *Area:* 18.2 sq km
Population in 2011: 282
Provincial Electoral District(s): Bellevue
Federal Electoral District(s): Avalon
Next Election: Sept. 24, 2013 (4 year terms)
Edgar Crann, Mayor
Glenis Rowe, Clerk

Change Islands
P.O. Box 67
Change Islands, NL A0G 1R0
Tel: 709-621-4181; *Fax:* 709-621-3202
townclerk@changeislands.ca
www.changeislands.ca
Municipal Type: Town
Incorporated: Oct. 16, 1951 *Area:* 5.31 sq km
Population in 2011: 257
Provincial Electoral District(s): Twillingate & Fogo
Federal Electoral District(s): Bonavista-Gander-Grand Falls-Windsor
Next Election: Sept. 24, 2013 (4 year terms)
Stephen Brinson, Mayor
709-621-3401
Sherry Diamond, Clerk

Channel-Port aux Basques
P.O. Box 67
Port aux Basques, NL A0G 1R0
Tel: 709-621-4181; *Fax:* 709-621-3202
townclerk@changeislands.ca
www.portauxbasques.ca
Municipal Type: Town
Incorporated: Nov. 6, 1945 *Area:* 38.77 sq km
Population in 2011: 4,170
Provincial Electoral District(s): Burgeo & La Poile
Federal Electoral District(s): Random-Burin-St. George's
Next Election: Sept. 24, 2013 (4 year terms)
Stephen Brinson, Mayor
Sherry Diamond, Clerk

Chapel Arm
68 Main Rd.
Chapel Arm, NL A0B 1L0
Tel: 709-592-2720; *Fax:* 709-592-2800
ppretty@eastlink.ca
Municipal Type: Town
Incorporated: Nov. 24, 1970 *Area:* 28.17 sq km
Population in 2011: 468
Provincial Electoral District(s): Bellevue
Federal Electoral District(s): Avalon
Next Election: Sept. 24, 2013 (4 year terms)
Larry Reid, Mayor
Phyllis Pretty, Clerk

Charlottetown
P.O. Box 151
Charlottetown, NL A0K 5Y0
Tel: 709-949-0299; *Fax:* 709-949-0377
ctown@nf.aibn.com
Municipal Type: Town
Incorporated: March 4, 1988 *Area:* 30.53 sq km
Population in 2011: 308
Provincial Electoral District(s): Cartwright-L'Anse au Clair
Federal Electoral District(s): Bonavista-Gander-Grand Falls-Windsor; Labrador
Next Election: Sept. 24, 2013 (4 year terms)
Charmaine Powell, Mayor
Zillah Kippenhuck, Clerk

Clarenville
99 Pleasant St.
Clarenville, NL A5A 1V9
Tel: 709-466-7937; *Fax:* 709-466-2276
info@clarenville.net
www.clarenville.net
Municipal Type: Town
Incorporated: June 12, 1951 *Area:* 140.79 sq km
Population in 2011: 6,036
Provincial Electoral District(s): Trinity North
Federal Electoral District(s): Random-Burin-St.George's
Next Election: Sept. 24, 2013 (4 year terms)
Fred Best, Mayor
Marie Blackmore, Clerk

Clarke's Beach
P.O. Box 159
Clarkes Beach, NL A0A 1W0
Tel: 709-786-3993; *Fax:* 709-786-3994
joanwilcox@nf.aibn.com
Municipal Type: Town
Incorporated: Aug. 24, 1965 *Area:* 12.71 sq km
Population in 2011: 1,396
Provincial Electoral District(s): Harbour Main-Whitbourne
Federal Electoral District(s): Avalon
Next Election: Sept. 24, 2013 (4 year terms)
Betty Moore, Mayor
Joan Wilcox, Clerk

Coachman's Cove
General Delivery
Coachmans Cove, NL A0K 1X0
Tel: 709-253-5161; *Fax:* 709-253-5161
Municipal Type: Town
Incorporated: Nov. 24, 1970 *Area:* 18.15 sq km
Population in 2011: 92
Provincial Electoral District(s): Baie Verte
Federal Electoral District(s): Humber-St. Barbe-Baie Verte
Next Election: Sept. 24, 2013 (4 year terms)
Martin Breen, Mayor
Johanna Breen, Clerk

Colinet
P.O. Box 8
Colinet, NL A0B 1M0
Tel: 709-521-2300; *Fax:* 709-521-2482
Municipal Type: Town
Incorporated: Sept. 24, 1974 *Area:* 6.23 sq km
Population in 2011: 110
Provincial Electoral District(s): Placentia & St. Mary's
Federal Electoral District(s): Avalon
Next Election: Sept. 24, 2013 (4 year terms)
Linda Hearn, Mayor
Marie Bonia, Clerk

Colliers
P.O. Box 84
Colliers, NL A0A 1Y0
Tel: 709-229-4333; *Fax:* 709-229-4033
townofcolliers@nl.aibn.com
Municipal Type: Town
Incorporated: Oct. 31, 1972 *Area:* 26.16 sq km
Population in 2011: 651
Provincial Electoral District(s): Harbour Main-Whitbourne
Federal Electoral District(s): Avalon
Next Election: Sept. 24, 2013 (4 year terms)
Waneta Whelan, Clerk
Patrick L. Phillips, Mayor

Come By Chance
P.O. Box 89
Come By Chance, NL A0B 1N0
Tel: 709-542-3240; *Fax:* 709-542-3121
townofcbc@xplornet.com
Municipal Type: Town
Incorporated: July 22, 1969 *Area:* 41.16 sq km
Population in 2011: 247

Provincial Electoral District(s): Bellevue
Federal Electoral District(s): Avalon
Next Election: Sept. 24, 2013 (4 year terms)
Joan Cleary, Mayor
Stephanie Eddy, Clerk

Comfort Cove-Newstead
P.O. Box 10
Comfort Cove, NL A0G 3K0
Tel: 709-244-4125; *Fax:* 709-244-4122
ccntown@eastlink.ca
Municipal Type: Town
Incorporated: Oct. 24, 1967 *Area:* 29.83 sq km
Population in 2011: 451
Provincial Electoral District(s): Lewisporte
Federal Electoral District(s): Bonavista-Gander-Grand Falls-Windsor
Next Election: Sept. 24, 2013 (4 year terms)
Stanley Reid, Mayor
Mona Lane, Clerk

Conception Harbour
P.O. Box 128
Conception Harbour, NL A0A 1Z0
Tel: 709-229-4781; *Fax:* 709-229-0432
charbour@eastlink.ca
Municipal Type: Town
Incorporated: Oct. 31, 1972 *Area:* 21.62 sq km
Population in 2011: 697
Provincial Electoral District(s): Harbour Main-Whitbourne
Federal Electoral District(s): Avalon
Next Election: Sept. 24, 2013 (4 year terms)
John Curran, Mayor
Lillian Connors, Clerk

Conche
P.O. Box 59
Conche, NL A0K 1Y0
Tel: 709-622-4531; *Fax:* 709-622-4491
townofconche@nf.aibn.com
Municipal Type: Town
Incorporated: Sept. 13, 1960 *Area:* 9.09 sq km
Population in 2011: 181
Provincial Electoral District(s): The Straits & White Bay North
Federal Electoral District(s): Humber-St. Barbe-Baie Verte
Next Election: Sept. 24, 2013 (4 year terms)
Gary Carroll, Mayor
Alice Flynn, Clerk

Cook's Harbour
P.O. Box 69
Cooks Harbour, NL A0K 1Z0
Tel: 709-249-3111; *Fax:* 709-249-4105
r.short@nf.aibn.com
Municipal Type: Town
Incorporated: Oct. 10, 1956 *Area:* 1.95 sq km
Population in 2011: 76
Provincial Electoral District(s): The Straits & White Bay North
Federal Electoral District(s): Humber-St. Barbe-Baie Verte
Next Election: Sept. 24, 2013 (4 year terms)
Barry Decker, Mayor
Regina Short, Clerk

Cormack
280 Veteran'S Dr.
Cormack, NL A8A 2R4
Tel: 709-635-7025; *Fax:* 709-635-7363
townofcormack@nf.aibn.com
Municipal Type: Town
Incorporated: April 14, 1964 *Area:* 135.23 sq km
Population in 2011: 605
Provincial Electoral District(s): Humber Valley
Federal Electoral District(s): Humber-St.Barbe-Baie Verte
Next Election: Sept. 24, 2013 (4 year terms)
Melvin Rideout Sr., Mayor
Cynthia Fry, Clerk

Cottlesville
P.O. Box 10
Cottlesville, NL A0G 1S0
Tel: 709-629-3505; *Fax:* 709-629-7411
vecassell@yahoo.ca
www.cottlesville.com
Municipal Type: Town
Incorporated: Oct. 24, 1972 *Area:* 11.17 sq km
Population in 2011: 272
Provincial Electoral District(s): Twillingate & Fogo
Federal Electoral District(s): Bonavista-Gander-Grand Falls-Windsor
Next Election: Sept. 24, 2013 (4 year terms)
Larry Peddle, Mayor
Shelly Abbott, Clerk

Cow Head
P.O. Box 40
Cow Head, NL A0K 2A0
Tel: 709-243-2446; *Fax:* 709-243-2590
townofcowhead@eastlink.ca
www.cowhead.ca
Municipal Type: Town
Incorporated: Feb. 1, 1964 *Area:* 17.84 sq km
Population in 2011: 475
Provincial Electoral District(s): St. Barbe
Federal Electoral District(s): Humber-St. Barbe-Baie Verte
Next Election: Sept. 24, 2013 (4 year terms)
Garland Hutchings, Mayor
Ruth Payne, Clerk

Cox's Cove
P.O. Box 100
Coxs Cove, NL A0L 1C0
Tel: 709-688-2900; *Fax:* 709-688-2929
coxcove@eastlink.ca
Municipal Type: Town
Incorporated: Nov. 11, 1969 *Area:* 7.21 sq km
Population in 2011: 660
Provincial Electoral District(s): Bay of Islands
Federal Electoral District(s): Humber-St. Barbe-Baie Verte
Next Election: Sept. 24, 2013 (4 year terms)
Tony Oxford, Mayor
Tonya Sheppard, Clerk

Crow Head
P.O. Box 250
Crow Head, NL A0G 4M0
Tel: 709-884-5651; *Fax:* 709-884-2344
Municipal Type: Town
Incorporated: Sept. 13, 1960 *Area:* 2.98 sq km
Population in 2011: 203
Provincial Electoral District(s): Twillingate & Fogo
Federal Electoral District(s): Bonavista-Gander-Grand Falls-Windsor
Next Election: Sept. 24, 2013 (4 year terms)
Meta J. Hamlyn, Clerk
John Hamlyn, Mayor

Cupids
P.O. Box 99
Cupids, NL A0A 2B0
Tel: 709-528-4428; *Fax:* 709-528-4430
townofcupids@eastlink.ca
Municipal Type: Town
Incorporated: April 13, 1965 *Area:* 11.02 sq km
Population in 2011: 761
Provincial Electoral District(s): Harbour Main-Whitbourne
Federal Electoral District(s): Avalon
Next Election: Sept. 24, 2013 (4 year terms)
Ivy King, Clerk
Ronald Laracy, Mayor

Daniel's Harbour
P.O. Box 68
Daniels Harbour, NL A0K 2C0
Tel: 709-898-2300; *Fax:* 709-898-2311
townofdanielshr@eastlink.ca
Municipal Type: Town
Incorporated: March 9, 1965 *Area:* 8.19 sq km
Population in 2011: 265
Provincial Electoral District(s): St. Barbe
Federal Electoral District(s): Humber-St. Barbe-Baie Verte
Next Election: Sept. 24, 2013 (4 year terms)
Melda Hann, Clerk
Ross Humber, Mayor

Deer Lake
6 Crescent St.
Deer Lake, NL A8A 1E9
Tel: 709-635-2451; *Fax:* 709-635-5857
deerlake@nf.aibn.com
www.town.deerlake.nf.ca
Municipal Type: Town
Incorporated: May 27, 1950 *Area:* 73.23 sq km
Population in 2011: 4,995
Provincial Electoral District(s): Humber Valley
Federal Electoral District(s): Humber-St. Barbe-Baie Verte
Next Election: Sept. 24, 2013 (4 year terms)
Kimberley Reid, Clerk
Dean Ball, Mayor

Dover
P.O. Box 10
Dover, NL A0G 1X0
Tel: 709-537-2139; *Fax:* 709-537-2190
townofdover@persona.ca
Municipal Type: Town
Incorporated: July 13, 1971 *Area:* 11.55 sq km
Population in 2011: 673
Provincial Electoral District(s): Terra Nova
Federal Electoral District(s): Bonavista-Gander-Grand Falls-Windsor
Next Election: Sept. 24, 2013 (4 year terms)
Wendy Elms, Clerk
Tony R. Keats, Mayor

Duntara
P.O. Box 15
Duntara, NL A0C 1M0
Tel: 709-447-3106; *Fax:* 709-447-3107
Municipal Type: Town
Incorporated: Nov. 14, 1961 *Area:* 17.78 sq km
Population in 2011: 46
Provincial Electoral District(s): Bonavista South
Federal Electoral District(s): Bonavista-Gander-Grand Falls-Windsor
Next Election: Sept. 24, 2013 (4 year terms)

Eastport
P.O. Box 119
Eastport, NL A0G 1Z0
Tel: 709-677-2161; *Fax:* 709-677-2144
cynthia@eastport.ca
www.eastport.ca
Municipal Type: Town
Incorporated: Oct. 20, 1959 *Area:* 18.64 sq km
Population in 2011: 482
Provincial Electoral District(s): Terra Nova
Federal Electoral District(s): Bonavista-Gander-Grand Falls-Windsor
Next Election: Sept. 24, 2013 (4 year terms)
Genevieve Squire, Mayor
Cynthia Bull, Clerk

Elliston
P.O. Box 115
Elliston, NL A0C 1N0
Tel: 709-468-2649; *Fax:* 709-468-2867
town_elliston@yahoo.ca
www.rootcellars.com
Municipal Type: Town
Incorporated: June 15, 1965 *Area:* 10.05 sq km
Population in 2011: 337
Provincial Electoral District(s): Bonavista South
Federal Electoral District(s): Bonavista-Gander-Grand Falls-Windsor
Next Election: Sept. 24, 2013 (4 year terms)
Gary Baker, Mayor
Wendy Baker, Clerk

Embree
P.O. Box 81
General Delivery
Embree, NL A0G 2A0
Tel: 709-535-8712; *Fax:* 709-535-8716
Municipal Type: Town
Incorporated: Sept. 28, 1971 *Area:* 18.16 sq km
Population in 2011: 691
Provincial Electoral District(s): Lewisporte
Federal Electoral District(s): Bonavista-Gander-Grand Falls-Windsor
Next Election: Sept. 24, 2013 (4 year terms)
Donald Bennett, Mayor
Verma Bursey, Clerk

Englee
P.O. Box 160
Englee, NL A0K 2J0
Tel: 709-866-2711; *Fax:* 709-866-2357
dorisenglee@nf.aibn.com
Municipal Type: Town
Incorporated: Dec. 23, 1948 *Area:* 28.76 sq km
Population in 2011: 583
Provincial Electoral District(s): The Straits & White Bay North
Federal Electoral District(s): Humber-St. Barbe-Baie Verte
Next Election: Sept. 24, 2013 (4 year terms)
Rudy Porter, Mayor
Doris Randell, Clerk

English Harbour East
P.O. Box 21
General Delivery
English Harbour East, NL A0E 1M0
Tel: 709-245-4346; *Fax:* 709-245-4556
Municipal Type: Town
Incorporated: Feb. 5, 1974 *Area:* 3.2 sq km
Population in 2011: 147
Provincial Electoral District(s): Bellevue

Federal Electoral District(s): Random-Burin-St. George's
Next Election: Sept. 24, 2013 (4 year terms)
Janet Rideout, Mayor
Dorothy Evans, Clerk

Fermeuse
General Delivery
Fermeuse, NL A0A 2G0
Tel: 709-363-2400; *Fax:* 709-363-2308
townoffermeuse@gmail.com
Municipal Type: Town
Incorporated: Nov. 28, 1967 *Area:* 38.73 sq km
Population in 2011: 323
Provincial Electoral District(s): Ferryland
Federal Electoral District(s): Avalon
Next Election: Sept. 24, 2013 (4 year terms)
Perry Oates, Mayor
Mary Kenny, Clerk

Ferryland
P.O. Box 75
Ferryland, NL A0A 2H0
Tel: 709-432-2127; *Fax:* 709-432-2209
town.ferryland@nf.aibn.com
Municipal Type: Town
Incorporated: Oct. 19, 1971 *Area:* 13.62 sq km
Population in 2011: 465
Provincial Electoral District(s): Ferryland
Federal Electoral District(s): Avalon
Next Election: Sept. 24, 2013 (4 year terms)
Leo Moriarty, Mayor
Doris Kavanagh, Clerk

Flatrock
663 Wind Gap Rd.
Flatrock, NL A1K 1C7
Tel: 709-437-6312; *Fax:* 709-437-6311
townmanager@nf.aibn.ca
www.townofflatrock.com
Municipal Type: Town
Incorporated: Oct. 31, 1975 *Area:* 18.12 sq km
Population in 2011: 1,457
Provincial Electoral District(s): Cape St. Francis
Federal Electoral District(s): St. John's East
Next Election: Sept. 24, 2013 (4 year terms)
Kevin Butt, Mayor
Rita Farrell, Clerk

Fleur de Lys
General Delivery
Fleur de Lys, NL A0K 2M0
Tel: 709-253-3131; *Fax:* 709-253-2146
fleurdelys@nf.aibn.com
Municipal Type: Town
Incorporated: April 18, 1967 *Area:* 39.77 sq km
Population in 2011: 265
Provincial Electoral District(s): Baie Verte
Federal Electoral District(s): Humber-St. Barbe-Baie Verte
Next Election: Sept. 24, 2013 (4 year terms)
Millie Walsh, Mayor
Esther Lewis, Clerk

Flower's Cove
P.O. Box 149
Flowers Cove, NL A0K 2N0
Tel: 709-456-2124; *Fax:* 709-456-2086
townofflowerscove@nf.aibn.net
Municipal Type: Town
Incorporated: Dec. 12, 1961 *Area:* 7.64 sq km
Population in 2011: 308
Provincial Electoral District(s): The Straits & White Bay North
Federal Electoral District(s): Humber-St. Barbe-Baie Verte
Next Election: Sept. 24, 2013 (4 year terms)
Keith Billard, Mayor
Bruce Way, Clerk

Fogo Island
P.O. Box 2
6 Centre Island Rd. South, Hwy. 333
Fogo Island Centre, NL A0G 2X0
Tel: 709-266-1320; *Fax:* 709-266-1323
info@townoffogoisland.ca
www.townoffogoisland.ca
Municipal Type: Town
Incorporated: March 1, 2011 *Area:* 237.65 sq km
Population in 2011: 2,395
Provincial Electoral District(s): The Isles of Notre Dame
Federal Electoral District(s): Bonavista-Gander-Grand Falls-Windsor
Next Election: Sept. 24, 2013 (4 year terms)
Note: Effective Dec. 2010, the towns of Fogo, Joe Batt's Arm-Barr'd Islands-Shoal Bay, Seldom-Little Seldom, Tilting & Fogo Island Region amalgamated to form the new Town of Fogo Island.
Gerald Foley, Mayor
Blanche Bennett, Clerk
townclerk@townoffogoisland.ca

Forteau
P.O. Box 99
Forteau, NL A0K 2P0
Tel: 709-931-2241; *Fax:* 709-931-2037
gflynn2006@hotmail.com
Municipal Type: Town
Incorporated: Dec. 7, 1971 *Area:* 7.44 sq km
Population in 2011: 429
Provincial Electoral District(s): Cartwright-L'Anse au Clair
Federal Electoral District(s): Labrador
Next Election: Sept. 24, 2013 (4 year terms)
Reginald Hancock, Mayor
Gail Flynn, Clerk

Fortune
P.O. Box 159
Fortune, NL A0E 1P0
Tel: 709-832-2810; *Fax:* 709-832-2210
fortune@nf.aibn.com
Municipal Type: Town
Incorporated: Sept. 3, 1946 *Area:* 54.85 sq km
Population in 2011: 1,442
Provincial Electoral District(s): Grand Bank
Federal Electoral District(s): Random-Burin-St. George's
Next Election: Sept. 24, 2013 (4 year terms)
Charles Penwell, Mayor
Norma Stacey, Clerk

Fox Cove-Mortier
PO Box 17, Site 25, RR#1
Fox Cove-Mortier, NL A0E 1E0
Tel: 709-891-1500; *Fax:* 709-891-1999
Municipal Type: Town
Incorporated: June 2, 1970 *Area:* 25.6 sq km
Population in 2011: 333
Provincial Electoral District(s): Burin-Placentia West
Federal Electoral District(s): Random-Burin-St. George's
Next Election: Sept. 24, 2013 (4 year terms)
Wanda Antle, Mayor
Gladys Kavanagh, Clerk

Fox Harbour
P.O. Box 64
Fox Harbour PB, NL A0B 1V0
Tel: 709-227-2271; *Fax:* 709-227-2271
Municipal Type: Town
Incorporated: Oct. 13, 1964 *Area:* 19.78 sq km
Population in 2011: 270
Provincial Electoral District(s): Placentia & St. Mary's
Federal Electoral District(s): Avalon
Next Election: Sept. 24, 2013 (4 year terms)
John Maher, Mayor
Patricia Quilty, Clerk

Frenchman's Cove
P.O. Box 20
Frenchman's Cove, NL A0E 1R0
Tel: 709-826-2190; *Fax:* 709-826-2190
townoffrenchmanscove@persona.ca
Municipal Type: Town
Incorporated: May 28, 1974 *Area:* 68.55 sq km
Population in 2011: 172
Provincial Electoral District(s): Grand Bank; Bay of Islands
Federal Electoral District(s): Humber-St. Barbe-Baie Verte; Random-Burin-St. George's
Next Election: Sept. 24, 2013 (4 year terms)
Leah Sperry, Mayor
Corina Thorne, Clerk

Gallants
General Delivery
Gallants, NL A0L 1G0
Tel: 709-646-2115; *Fax:* 709-646-2627
marion21@xplornet.ca
Municipal Type: Town
Incorporated: Aug. 16, 1966 *Area:* 6.34 sq km
Population in 2011: 59
Provincial Electoral District(s): Humber West
Federal Electoral District(s): Random-Burin-St. George's
Next Election: Sept. 24, 2013 (4 year terms)
James Collier, Mayor
Marion Collier, Clerk

Gambo
P.O. Box 250
Gambo, NL A0G 1T0
Tel: 709-674-4476; *Fax:* 709-674-5399
lgtownofgambo@nf.aibn.com
www.townofgambo.com
Municipal Type: Town
Incorporated: July 10, 1962 *Area:* 92.07 sq km
Population in 2011: 1,984
Provincial Electoral District(s): Terra Nova
Federal Electoral District(s): Bonavista-Gander-Grand Falls-Windsor
Next Election: Sept. 24, 2013 (4 year terms)
Peter Lush, Mayor
Jean Blackwood, Acting Town Clerk & Manager

Gander
100 Elizabeth Dr.
Gander, NL A1V 1G7
Tel: 709-651-2930; *Fax:* 709-256-5809
info@gandercanada.com
www.gandercanada.com
Municipal Type: Town
Incorporated: Dec. 28, 1954 *Area:* 104.25 sq km
Population in 2011: 11,054
Provincial Electoral District(s): Gander
Federal Electoral District(s): Bonavista-Gander-Grand Falls-Windsor
Next Election: Sept. 24, 2013 (4 year terms)
Claude Elliott, Mayor
Garry Brown, Town Clerk & Director, Finance

Garnish
P.O. Box 70
Garnish, NL A0E 1T0
Tel: 709-826-2330; *Fax:* 709-826-2173
townclerk@eastlink.ca
Municipal Type: Town
Incorporated: Aug. 25, 1971 *Area:* 39.11 sq km
Population in 2011: 545
Provincial Electoral District(s): Grand Bank
Federal Electoral District(s): Random-Burin-St. George's
Next Election: Sept. 24, 2013 (4 year terms)
Reuben Noseworthy, Mayor
Ruth Cluett, Clerk

Gaskiers-Point La Haye
P.O. Box 434
St Marys, NL A0B 3B0
Tel: 709-525-2430; *Fax:* 709-525-2431
townofgaskiers@nf.aibn.com
Municipal Type: Town
Incorporated: Aug. 25, 1970 *Area:* 23.81 sq km
Population in 2011: 233
Provincial Electoral District(s): Placentia & St. Mary's
Federal Electoral District(s): Avalon
Next Election: Sept. 24, 2013 (4 year terms)
Pearl Kielly, Mayor
Jeanette Critch, Clerk

Gaultois
P.O. Box 101
Gaultois, NL A0H 1N0
Tel: 709-841-6546; *Fax:* 709-841-3521
Other Information: townofgaultois@hotmail.com
Municipal Type: Town
Incorporated: Jan. 1, 1962 *Area:* 4.33 sq km
Population in 2011: 179
Provincial Electoral District(s): Fortune Bay-Cape La Hune
Federal Electoral District(s): Random-Burin-St. George's
Next Election: Sept. 24, 2013 (4 year terms)
Gordon Hunt, Mayor
Sylvin Rose, Clerk

Gillams
P.O. Box 3968
RR#2
Corner Brook, NL A2H 6B9
Tel: 709-783-2800; *Fax:* 709-783-2800
townofgillams@nf.aibn.com
Municipal Type: Town
Incorporated: Aug. 17, 1971 *Area:* 6.7 sq km
Population in 2011: 407
Provincial Electoral District(s): Bay of Islands
Federal Electoral District(s): Humber-St. Barbe-Baie Verte
Next Election: Sept. 24, 2013 (4 year terms)
Newton Pritchett, Mayor
Shelly Penny, Clerk

Glenburnie-Birchy Head-Shoal Brook
General Delivery
Birchy Head, NL A0K 1K0
Tel: 709-453-7220; *Fax:* 709-453-7220
Municipal Type: Town
Incorporated: Sept. 1, 1978 *Area:* 6.57 sq km
Population in 2011: 258
Provincial Electoral District(s): Humber Valley
Federal Electoral District(s): Humber-St. Barbe-Baie Verte
Next Election: Sept. 24, 2013 (4 year terms)
Marilyn Wight, Mayor
Myrna Hynes, Clerk

Glenwood
P.O. Box 130
Glenwood, NL A0G 2K0
Tel: 709-679-2159; *Fax:* 709-679-5470
Municipal Type: Town
Incorporated: June 12, 1962 *Area:* 6.92 sq km
Population in 2011: 791
Provincial Electoral District(s): Gander
Federal Electoral District(s): Bonavista-Gander-Grand Falls-Windsor
Next Election: Sept. 24, 2013 (4 year terms)
Darren Bursey, Mayor
Susan Gillingham, Clerk

Glovertown
P.O. Box 224
Glovertown, NL A0G 2L0
Tel: 709-533-2351; *Fax:* 709-533-2225
jperry@personainternet.com
www.glovertown.net
Municipal Type: Town
Incorporated: Dec. 28, 1954 *Area:* 70.33 sq km
Population in 2011: 2,122
Provincial Electoral District(s): Terra Nova
Federal Electoral District(s): Bonavista-Gander-Grand Falls-Windsor
Next Election: Sept. 24, 2013 (4 year terms)
David Saunders, Mayor
Joanne Perry, Clerk

Goose Cove East
P.O. Box 208
Goose Cove, NL A0K 4S0
Tel: 709-454-8393; *Fax:* 709-454-8393
Municipal Type: Town
Incorporated: Oct. 19, 1971 *Area:* 2.69 sq km
Population in 2011: 211
Provincial Electoral District(s): The Straits & White Bay North
Federal Electoral District(s): Humber-St. Barbe-Baie Verte
Next Election: Sept. 24, 2013 (4 year terms)
Marie Reardon, Mayor
Patricia Reardon, Clerk

Grand Bank
P.O. Box 640
56 Main St.
Grand Bank, NL A0E 1W0
Tel: 709-832-1600; *Fax:* 709-832-1636
townofgrandbank@townofgrandbank.net
www.townofgrandbank.com
Municipal Type: Town
Incorporated: Dec. 28, 1943 *Area:* 16.97 sq km
Population in 2011: 2,415
Provincial Electoral District(s): Grand Bank
Federal Electoral District(s): Random-Burin-St. George's
Next Election: Sept. 24, 2013 (4 year terms)
Darrell LeFosse, Mayor
Cathy Follett, Town Clerk & Treas.

Grand Le Pierre
P.O. Box 35
Grand Le Pierre, NL A0E 1Y0
Tel: 709-662-2702; *Fax:* 709-662-2076
Municipal Type: Town
Incorporated: June 17, 1969 *Area:* 153.59 sq km
Population in 2011: 260
Provincial Electoral District(s): Bellevue
Federal Electoral District(s): Random-Burin-St. George's
Next Election: Sept. 24, 2013 (4 year terms)
Willoughby Bolt, Mayor
Rhonda Bolt, Clerk

Greenspond
P.O. Box 100
Greenspond, NL A0G 2N0
Tel: 709-269-3111; *Fax:* 709-269-3191
greenspond@eastlink.ca
Municipal Type: Town
Incorporated: Aug. 15, 1951 *Area:* 2.85 sq km
Population in 2011: 305
Provincial Electoral District(s): Bonavista North
Federal Electoral District(s): Bonavista-Gander-Grand Falls-Windsor
Next Election: Sept. 24, 2013 (4 year terms)
Kevin Blackwood, Mayor
Derrick Bragg, Clerk

Hampden
P.O. Box 9
Hampden, NL A0K 2Y0
Tel: 709-455-4212; *Fax:* 709-455-2117
townofhampden@eastlink.ca
Municipal Type: Town
Incorporated: Dec. 8, 1959 *Area:* 32.97 sq km
Population in 2011: 457
Provincial Electoral District(s): Humber Valley
Federal Electoral District(s): Humber-St. Barbe-Baie Verte
Next Election: Sept. 24, 2013 (4 year terms)
Jerry Martin, Mayor
Ruth Jenkins, Clerk

Hant's Harbour
P.O. Box 40
Hants Harbour, NL A0B 1Y0
Tel: 709-586-2741; *Fax:* 709-586-2680
Municipal Type: Town
Incorporated: Oct. 13, 1970 *Area:* 32.31 sq km
Population in 2011: 346
Provincial Electoral District(s): Trinity-Bay de Verde
Federal Electoral District(s): Avalon
Next Election: Sept. 24, 2013 (4 year terms)
Donald G. Green, Mayor
Doris J. Short, Clerk

Happy Adventure
PO Box 1, Site 2
Happy Adventure, NL A0G 1Z0
Tel: 709-677-2593; *Fax:* 709-677-2594
happyadventure@aibn.com
Municipal Type: Town
Incorporated: May 10, 1960 *Area:* 9.62 sq km
Population in 2011: 219
Provincial Electoral District(s): Terra Nova
Federal Electoral District(s): Bonavista-Gander-Grand Falls-Windsor
Next Election: Sept. 24, 2013 (4 year terms)
James Warren, Mayor
Kim Babstock, Clerk

Happy Valley-Goose Bay
P.O. Box 40 B
Happy Valley-Goose Bay, NL A0P 1E0
Tel: 709-896-3321; *Fax:* 709-896-9454
townclerk@happyvalley-goosebay.com
www.happyvalley-goosebay.com
Municipal Type: Town
Incorporated: March 15, 1955 *Area:* 305.85 sq km
Population in 2011: 7,552
Provincial Electoral District(s): Lake Melville
Federal Electoral District(s): Labrador
Next Election: Sept. 24, 2013 (4 year terms)
Leo Abbass, Mayor
labbass@cdli.ca
Valerie Sheppard, Clerk
townclerk@happyvalley-goosebay.com

Harbour Breton
P.O. Box 130
Harbour Breton, NL A0H 1P0
Tel: 709-885-2354; *Fax:* 709-885-2095
bernice@harbourbreton.com
www.harbourbreton.com
Municipal Type: Town
Incorporated: Dec. 16, 1952 *Area:* 13.74 sq km
Population in 2011: 1,711
Provincial Electoral District(s): Fortune Bay-Cape La Hune
Federal Electoral District(s): Random-Burin-St. George's
Next Election: Sept. 24, 2013 (4 year terms)
Eric Skinner, Mayor
Bernice Herritt, Clerk

Harbour Grace
P.O. Box 310
Harbour Grace, NL A0A 2M0
Tel: 709-596-3631; *Fax:* 709-596-1991
thg@nf.sympatico.ca
www.hrgrace.ca
Municipal Type: Town
Incorporated: July 10, 1945 *Area:* 33.71 sq km
Population in 2011: 3,131
Provincial Electoral District(s): Carbonear-Harbour Grace
Federal Electoral District(s): Avalon
Next Election: Sept. 24, 2013 (4 year terms)
Don Coombs, Mayor
Lester Forward, Clerk

Harbour Main-Chapel Cove-Lakeview
P.O. Box 40
Harbour Main, NL A0A 2P0
Tel: 709-229-6822; *Fax:* 709-229-6234
hmcouncil@eastlink.ca
Municipal Type: Town
Incorporated: June 1, 1965 *Area:* 21.05 sq km
Population in 2011: 1,083
Provincial Electoral District(s): Harbour Main-Whitbourne
Federal Electoral District(s): Avalon
Next Election: Sept. 24, 2013 (4 year terms)
Raymond Parsley, Mayor
Marian Hawco, Clerk

Hare Bay
P.O. Box 130
Hare Bay BB, NL A0G 2P0
Tel: 709-537-2187; *Fax:* 709-537-2987
Municipal Type: Town
Incorporated: Oct. 20, 1964 *Area:* 34.06 sq km
Population in 2011: 1,031
Provincial Electoral District(s): Terra Nova
Federal Electoral District(s): Bonavista-Gander-Grand Falls-Windsor
Next Election: Sept. 24, 2013 (4 year terms)
James Payne, Mayor
George R. Collins, Clerk

Hawke's Bay
P.O. Box 33
Hawkes Bay, NL A0K 3B0
Tel: 709-248-5216; *Fax:* 709-248-5201
hbcouncil@nf.aibn.com
Municipal Type: Town
Incorporated: Aug. 21, 1956 *Area:* 46.55 sq km
Population in 2011: 338
Provincial Electoral District(s): St. Barbe
Federal Electoral District(s): Humber-St. Barbe-Baie Verte
Next Election: Sept. 24, 2013 (4 year terms)
Lloyd Bennett, Mayor
Emily Smith, Clerk

Heart's Content
P.O. Box 31
Hearts Content, NL A0B 1Z0
Tel: 709-583-2491; *Fax:* 709-583-2226
townofheartscontent@persona.ca
Municipal Type: Town
Incorporated: Aug. 25, 1967 *Area:* 62.81 sq km
Population in 2011: 375
Provincial Electoral District(s): Trinity-Bay de Verde
Federal Electoral District(s): Avalon
Next Election: Sept. 24, 2013 (4 year terms)
Donald Blundon, Mayor
Alice Cumby, Clerk

Heart's Delight-Islington
P.O. Box 129
Hearts Delight, NL A0B 2A0
Tel: 709-588-2708; *Fax:* 709-588-2235
heartsdelightislington@persona.ca
Municipal Type: Town
Incorporated: Oct. 24, 1972 *Area:* 27.27 sq km
Population in 2011: 704
Provincial Electoral District(s): Trinity-Bay de Verde
Federal Electoral District(s): Avalon
Next Election: Sept. 24, 2013 (4 year terms)
Denzil Sheppard, Mayor
Emily Harnum, Clerk

Heart's Desire
P.O. Box 10
Hearts Desire, NL A0B 2B0
Tel: 709-588-2280; *Fax:* 709-588-2343
townofheartsdesire@persona.ca
Municipal Type: Town
Incorporated: Sept. 28, 1971 *Area:* 17.27 sq km
Population in 2011: 223
Provincial Electoral District(s): Trinity-Bay de Verde
Federal Electoral District(s): Avalon
Next Election: Sept. 24, 2013 (4 year terms)
Patrick Coombs, Mayor
Eleanor Andrews, Clerk

Hermitage-Sandyville
P.O. Box 160
Hermitage, NL A0H 1S0
Tel: 709-883-2343; *Fax:* 709-883-2150
jsimms@nf.aibn.com
www.hermitage-sandyville.ca
Municipal Type: Town
Incorporated: Oct. 22, 1960 *Area:* 28.91 sq km
Population in 2011: 450
Provincial Electoral District(s): Fortune Bay-Cape La Hune
Federal Electoral District(s): Random-Burin-St. George's
Next Election: Sept. 24, 2013 (4 year terms)
Douglas Rose, Mayor
Josephine (Josie) Rideout Simms, Town Manager

Holyrood
P.O. Box 100
Holyrood, NL A0A 2R0
Tel: 709-229-7252; *Fax:* 709-229-7269
cturnbull@townofholyrood.com
www.townofholyrood.com
Municipal Type: Town
Incorporated: March 23, 1969 *Area:* 125.57 sq km
Population in 2011: 1,995
Provincial Electoral District(s): Conception Bay South
Federal Electoral District(s): Avalon
Next Election: Sept. 24, 2013 (4 year terms)
Gary Goobie, Mayor
Marie Searle, CAO-Clerk

Hopedale
P.O. Box 189
Hopedale, NL A0P 1G0
Tel: 709-933-3864; *Fax:* 709-933-3800
towncouncilhopedale@nf.aibn.com
Municipal Type: Town
Incorporated: Sept. 30, 1969 *Area:* 3.36 sq km
Population in 2011: 556
Provincial Electoral District(s): Torngat Mountains
Federal Electoral District(s): Labrador
Next Election: Sept. 24, 2013 (4 year terms)
Judy Dicker, Mayor
Jullian Mistuk, Clerk

Howley
P.O. Box 40
Howley, NL A0K 3E0
Tel: 709-635-5555; *Fax:* 709-635-5850
Municipal Type: Town
Incorporated: Feb. 4, 1958 *Area:* 19.91 sq km
Population in 2011: 221
Provincial Electoral District(s): Humber Valley
Federal Electoral District(s): Humber-St. Barbe-Baie Verte
Next Election: Sept. 24, 2013 (4 year terms)
Calvin Samms, Mayor
Blanche Gilley, Clerk

Hughes Brook
P.O. Box 2527
RR#2
Corner Brook, NL A2H 6B9
Tel: 709-783-2921; *Fax:* 709-783-2921
Municipal Type: Town
Incorporated: July 25, 1975 *Area:* 1.6 sq km
Population in 2011: 231
Provincial Electoral District(s): Bay of Islands
Federal Electoral District(s): Humber-St. Barbe-Baie Verte
Next Election: Sept. 24, 2013 (4 year terms)
Maurice Osborne, Mayor
Gloria Loder, Clerk

Humber Arm South
General Delivery
Benoits Cove, NL A0L 1A0
Tel: 709-789-2981; *Fax:* 709-789-2918
humberarmsouth@nf.aibn.com
Municipal Type: Town
Incorporated: June 15, 1971 *Area:* 65.05 sq km
Population in 2011: 1,681
Provincial Electoral District(s): Bay of Islands
Federal Electoral District(s): Humber-St. Barbe-Baie Verte
Next Election: Sept. 24, 2013 (4 year terms)
Arch Mitchell, Mayor
Marion Evoy, Clerk

Indian Bay
General Delivery
Indian Bay, NL A0G 2V0
Tel: 709-678-2727; *Fax:* 709-678-2727
Municipal Type: Town
Incorporated: Oct. 19, 1971 *Area:* 86.24 sq km
Population in 2011: 174
Provincial Electoral District(s): Bonavista North
Federal Electoral District(s): Bonavista-Gander-Grand Falls-Windsor
Next Election: Sept. 24, 2013 (4 year terms)
Ronald Collins, Mayor
Thomas Easton, Clerk

Irishtown-Summerside
P.O. Box 2795
RR#2
Corner Brook, NL A2H 6B9
Tel: 709-783-2146; *Fax:* 709-783-2146
Municipal Type: Town
Incorporated: Jan. 1, 1991 *Area:* 11.89 sq km
Population in 2011: 1,428
Provincial Electoral District(s): Bay of Islands
Federal Electoral District(s): Humber-St. Barbe-Baie Verte
Next Election: Sept. 24, 2013 (4 year terms)
Ralph Loder, Mayor
Rita Blanchard, Clerk

Isle aux Morts
P.O. Box 110
Isle-aux-Morts, NL A0M 1J0
Tel: 709-698-3441; *Fax:* 709-698-3449
townhalliam@nf.aibn.com
Municipal Type: Town
Incorporated: Nov. 5, 1956 *Area:* 7.66 sq km
Population in 2011: 619
Provincial Electoral District(s): Burgeo & La Poile
Federal Electoral District(s): Random-Burin-St. George's
Next Election: Sept. 24, 2013 (4 year terms)
Raymond LeFrense, Mayor
Lydia Francis, Clerk

Jackson's Arm
P.O. Box 10
Jacksons Arm, NL A0K 3H0
Tel: 709-459-3122; *Fax:* 709-459-3173
info@townofjacksonsarm.com
Municipal Type: Town
Incorporated: June 19, 1982 *Area:* 7.02 sq km
Population in 2011: 323
Provincial Electoral District(s): Humber Valley
Federal Electoral District(s): Humber-St. Barbe-Baie Verte
Next Election: Sept. 24, 2013 (4 year terms)
Claude Jones, Mayor
Carmel Wicks, Clerk

Keels
P.O. Box 20
Keels, NL A0C 1R0
Tel: 709-447-3127; *Fax:* 709-447-6186
Municipal Type: Town
Incorporated: June 14, 1966 *Area:* 6.54 sq km
Population in 2011: 61
Provincial Electoral District(s): Bonavista South
Federal Electoral District(s): Bonavista-Gander-Grand Falls-Windsor
Next Election: Sept. 24, 2013 (4 year terms)
Annie Fitzgerald, Mayor
Crystal Taylor, Clerk

King's Cove
General Delivery
Kings Cove, NL A0C 1S0
Tel: 709-447-4361; *Fax:* 709-448-2004
Municipal Type: Town
Incorporated: June 14,1966 *Area:* 21.48 sq km
Population in 2011: 111
Provincial Electoral District(s): Bonavista South
Federal Electoral District(s): Bonavista-Gander-Grand Falls-Windsor; Humber-St. Barbe-Baie Verte; Labrador
Next Election: Sept. 24, 2013 (4 year terms)
Tom Maddox, Mayor
Gerald Barron, Clerk

King's Point
P.O. Box 10
Kings Point, NL A0J 1H0
Tel: 709-268-3838; *Fax:* 709-268-3856
d.snow@eastlink.ca
Municipal Type: Town
Incorporated: Oct. 1, 1957 *Area:* 46.31 sq km
Population in 2011: 675
Provincial Electoral District(s): Baie Verte
Federal Electoral District(s): Humber-St. Barbe-Baie Verte
Next Election: Sept. 24, 2013 (4 year terms)
Ed Wright, Mayor
Don Snow, Clerk

Kippens
2 Juniper Ave.
Kippens, NL A2N 3H8
Tel: 709-643-5281; *Fax:* 709-643-9773
kippens@nf.aibn.com
www.kippens.ca
Municipal Type: Town
Incorporated: Dec. 31, 1968 *Area:* 14.32 sq km
Population in 2011: 1,815
Provincial Electoral District(s): Port au Port
Federal Electoral District(s): Random-Burin-St. George's
Next Election: Sept. 24, 2013 (4 year terms)
Cator Best, Mayor
Debbie Cormier, Acting Clerk

L'Anse au Clair
P.O. Box 83
L'Anse au Clair, NL A0K 3K0
Tel: 709-931-2481; *Fax:* 709-931-2488
townoflanseauclair@hotmail.com
Municipal Type: Town
Incorporated: June 2, 1970 *Area:* 61.92 sq km
Population in 2011: 192
Provincial Electoral District(s): Cartwright-L'Anse au Clair
Federal Electoral District(s): Labrador
Next Election: Sept. 24, 2013 (4 year terms)
Nath Moores, Mayor
Loretta Griffin, Clerk

L'Anse au Loup
P.O. Box 101
L'Anse au Loup, NL A0K 3L0
Tel: 709-927-5573; *Fax:* 709-927-5263
lanseauloup@nf.aibn.com
www.lanseauloup.ca
Municipal Type: Town
Incorporated: April 11, 1975 *Area:* 3.48 sq km
Population in 2011: 550
Provincial Electoral District(s): Cartwright-L'Anse au Clair
Federal Electoral District(s): Labrador; Random-Burin-St. George's
Next Election: Sept. 24, 2013 (4 year terms)
Headley Ryland, Mayor
Lawrence Normore, Town Clerk, Manager & Officer, Community Economic Development

La Scie
P.O. Box 130
La Scie, NL A0K 3M0
Tel: 709-675-2266; *Fax:* 709-675-2168
townoflascie@eastlink.ca
Municipal Type: Town
Incorporated: May 25, 1955 *Area:* 29.14 sq km
Population in 2011: 899
Provincial Electoral District(s): Baie Verte
Federal Electoral District(s): Humber-St. Barbe-Baie Verte
Next Election: Sept. 24, 2013 (4 year terms)
Clyde Saunders, Mayor
Rowena Morey, Clerk

Labrador City
P.O. Box 280
Labrador City, NL A2V 2K5
Tel: 709-944-5537; *Fax:* 709-944-2810
www.labradorwest.com
Municipal Type: Town
Incorporated: June 27, 1961 *Area:* 38.83 sq km
Population in 2011: 7,367
Provincial Electoral District(s): Labrador West
Federal Electoral District(s): Labrador
Next Election: Sept. 24, 2013 (4 year terms)
Janice Barnes, Mayor
Diane Gear, Town Clerk

Lamaline
P.O. Box 40
Lamaline, NL A0E 2C0
Tel: 709-857-2341; *Fax:* 709-857-2210
barbking70@hotmail.com
Municipal Type: Town
Incorporated: April 24, 1963 *Area:* 81.69 sq km
Population in 2011: 286
Provincial Electoral District(s): Grand Bank
Federal Electoral District(s): Random-Burin-St. George's
Next Election: Sept. 24, 2013 (4 year terms)
Maureen Fleming, Mayor
Barbara King, Clerk

Lark Harbour
P.O. Box 40
Lark Harbour, NL A0L 1H0
Tel: 709-681-2270; *Fax:* 709-681-2900

Municipal Type: Town
Incorporated: Jan. 22, 1974 *Area:* 12.92 sq km
Population in 2011: 510
Provincial Electoral District(s): Bay of Islands
Federal Electoral District(s): Humber-St. Barbe-Baie Verte
Next Election: Sept. 24, 2013 (4 year terms)
John Parsons, Mayor
Debra Park, Clerk
Louise Darrigan, Co-Clerk

Lawn
P.O. Box 29
Lawn, NL A0E 2E0
Tel: 709-873-2439; *Fax:* 709-873-3006
townoflawn@nf.aibn.com
Municipal Type: Town
Incorporated: Sept. 30, 1952 *Area:* 3.61 sq km
Population in 2011: 672
Provincial Electoral District(s): Grand Bank
Federal Electoral District(s): Random-Burin-St. George's
Next Election: Sept. 24, 2013 (4 year terms)
William Lockyer, Mayor
Ruth M. Bennett, Clerk

Leading Tickles
P.O. Box 39
Leading Tickles West, NL A0H 1T0
Tel: 709-483-2180; *Fax:* 709-483-2185
leadingtickles@nf.aibn.com
www.leadingtickles.ca
Municipal Type: Town
Incorporated: July 11, 1961 *Area:* 26.73 sq km
Population in 2011: 337
Provincial Electoral District(s): Exploits
Federal Electoral District(s): Bonavista-Gander-Grand Falls-Windsor
Next Election: Sept. 24, 2013 (4 year terms)
Harry Hallet, Mayor
Doreen Haggett, Clerk

Lewin's Cove
P.O. Box 40
Lewins Cove, NL A0E 2G0
Tel: 709-894-4777; *Fax:* 709-894-4952
townoflewinscove@bellaliant.com
Municipal Type: Town
Incorporated: May 1, 1973 *Area:* 6.52 sq km
Population in 2011: 555
Provincial Electoral District(s): Grand Bank
Federal Electoral District(s): Random-Burin-St. George's
Next Election: Sept. 24, 2013 (4 year terms)
William Wakeley, Mayor
Barbara Mullett, Clerk

Lewisporte
P.O. Box 219
Lewisporte, NL A0G 3A0
Tel: 709-535-2737; *Fax:* 709-535-2695
elaine@lewisportecanada.com
www.lewisportecanada.com
Municipal Type: Town
Incorporated: July 2, 1946 *Area:* 36.91 sq km
Population in 2011: 3,483
Provincial Electoral District(s): Lewisporte
Federal Electoral District(s): Bonavista-Gander-Grand Falls-Windsor
Next Election: Sept. 24, 2013 (4 year terms)
Brian Peckford, Mayor
Elaine Bursey, Clerk
elaine@lewisportecanada.com

Little Bay
P.O. Box 39
Little Bay, NL A0J 1J0
Tel: 709-267-3200; *Fax:* 709-267-3200
Municipal Type: Town
Incorporated: April 19, 1966 *Area:* 1.45 sq km
Population in 2011: 108
Provincial Electoral District(s): Baie Verte
Federal Electoral District(s): Humber-St. Barbe-Baie Verte; Random-Burin-St. George's
Next Election: Sept. 24, 2013 (4 year terms)
Bronson Webber, Mayor
Jamie Winsor, Clerk

Little Bay East
P.O. Box 15
Little Bay East, NL A0E 2J0
Tel: 709-461-2724; *Fax:* 709-461-2724
Municipal Type: Town
Incorporated: April 27, 1979 *Area:* 1.48 sq km
Population in 2011: 130
Provincial Electoral District(s): Bellevue
Federal Electoral District(s): Random-Burin-St. George's
Next Election: Sept. 24, 2013 (4 year terms)
Earl Thornhill, Mayor
Gail Clarke, Clerk

Little Bay Islands
P.O. Box 64
Little Bay Islands, NL A0J 1K0
Tel: 709-626-3511; *Fax:* 709-626-3512
lbtowncouncil@eastlink.ca
Municipal Type: Town
Incorporated: Oct. 25, 1955 *Area:* 7.16 sq km
Population in 2011: 97
Provincial Electoral District(s): Baie Verte
Federal Electoral District(s): Humber-St. Barbe-Baie Verte
Next Election: Sept. 24, 2013 (4 year terms)
Kelly Roberts, Clerk
Perry Locke, Mayor

Little Burnt Bay
P.O. Box 40
Little Burnt Bay, NL A0G 3B0
Tel: 709-535-6415; *Fax:* 709-535-6490
lbbtowncouncil@bellaliant.com
Municipal Type: Town
Incorporated: Sept. 19, 1975 *Area:* 8.5 sq km
Population in 2011: 294
Provincial Electoral District(s): Lewisporte
Federal Electoral District(s): Bonavista-Gander-Grand Falls-Windsor
Next Election: Sept. 24, 2013 (4 year terms)
Laverne Suppa, Mayor
Maisie Wells, Clerk

Logy Bay-Middle Cove-Outer Cove
744 Logy Bay Rd.
Logy Bay, NL A1K 3B5
Tel: 709-726-7930; *Fax:* 709-726-2178
office@lbmcoc.ca
Municipal Type: Town
Incorporated: Sept. 1, 1986 *Area:* 16.98 sq km
Population in 2011: 2,098
Provincial Electoral District(s): Cape St. Francis
Federal Electoral District(s): St. John's East
Next Election: Sept. 24, 2013 (4 year terms)
John Kennedy, Mayor
Richard Roache, Clerk

Long Harbour-Mount Arlington Heights
P.O. Box 40
Long Harbour, NL A0B 2J0
Tel: 709-228-2920; *Fax:* 709-228-2900
towncouncil@longharbour.net
Municipal Type: Town
Incorporated: Oct. 22, 1968 *Area:* 18.41 sq km
Population in 2011: 298
Provincial Electoral District(s): Bellevue
Federal Electoral District(s): Avalon
Next Election: Sept. 24, 2013 (4 year terms)
Gary Keating, Mayor
Harriet Bruce, Clerk

Lord's Cove
General Delivery
Lord's Cove, NL A0E 2C0
Tel: 709-857-2316; *Fax:* 709-857-2031
Municipal Type: Town
Incorporated: May 17, 1966 *Area:* 30.91 sq km
Population in 2011: 175
Provincial Electoral District(s): Grand Bank
Federal Electoral District(s): Random-Burin-St. George's
Next Election: Sept. 24, 2013 (4 year terms)
Eileen Harnett, Acting Clerk

Lourdes
P.O. Box 29
Lourdes, NL A0N 1R0
Tel: 709-642-5812; *Fax:* 709-642-5812
townoflourdes@yahoo.ca
Municipal Type: Town
Incorporated: July 17, 1969 *Area:* 8.1 sq km
Population in 2011: 532
Provincial Electoral District(s): Port au Port
Federal Electoral District(s): Random-Burin-St. George's
Next Election: Sept. 24, 2013 (4 year terms)
Henry Gaudon, Mayor
Angela Young, Clerk

Lumsden
P.O. Box 100
Lumsden, NL A0G 3E0
Tel: 709-530-2309; *Fax:* 709-530-2144
townoflumsden@nf.aibn.com
www.lumsdennl.ca
Municipal Type: Town
Incorporated: April 16, 1968 *Area:* 20.43 sq km
Population in 2011: 545
Provincial Electoral District(s): Bonavista North
Federal Electoral District(s): Bonavista-Gander-Grand Falls-Windsor
Next Election: Sept. 24, 2013 (4 year terms)
Danny Gibbons, Mayor
Jeanie Stokes, Clerk

Lushes Bight-Beaumont-Beaumont North
P.O. Box 40
Beaumont, NL A0J 1A0
Tel: 709-264-3271; *Fax:* 709-264-3191
townoflushesbightbeaumont@nf.aibn.com
Municipal Type: Town
Incorporated: Oct. 15, 1968 *Area:* 34.38 sq km
Population in 2011: 220
Provincial Electoral District(s): Windsor-Springdale
Federal Electoral District(s): Humber-St. Barbe-Baie Verte
Next Election: Sept. 24, 2013 (4 year terms)
Clyde Croucher, Mayor
Joan Pittman, Clerk

Main Brook
P.O. Box 130
Main Brook, NL A0K 3N0
Tel: 709-865-6561; *Fax:* 709-865-3279
townofmainbrook@nf.aibn.com
Municipal Type: Town
Incorporated: June 1, 1948 *Area:* 28.51 sq km
Population in 2011: 265
Provincial Electoral District(s): The Straits & White Bay North
Federal Electoral District(s): Humber-St. Barbe-Baie Verte
Next Election: Sept. 24, 2013 (4 year terms)
Leander Pilgrim, Mayor
Karen Pilgrim, Clerk

Makkovik
P.O. Box 132
Makkovik, NL A0P 1J0
Tel: 709-923-2221; *Fax:* 709-923-2126
townmanager@makkovik.ca
Municipal Type: Town
Incorporated: April 7, 1970 *Area:* 1.97 sq km
Population in 2011: 361
Provincial Electoral District(s): Torngat Mountains
Federal Electoral District(s): Labrador
Next Election: Sept. 24, 2013 (4 year terms)
Herbert R. Jacque, Mayor
Doreen Winters, Clerk

Mary's Harbour
P.O. Box 134
Mary's Harbour, NL A0K 3P0
Tel: 709-921-6281; *Fax:* 709-921-6255
maryshbr@nf.aibn.com
Municipal Type: Town
Incorporated: April 11, 1975 *Area:* 38.16 sq km
Population in 2011: 383
Provincial Electoral District(s): Cartwright-L'Anse au Clair
Federal Electoral District(s): Labrador
Next Election: Sept. 24, 2013 (4 year terms)
Larry Rumbolt, Mayor
Sheena Rumbolt, Clerk

Marystown
P.O. Box 1118
Marystown, NL A0E 2M0
Tel: 709-279-1661; *Fax:* 709-279-2862
info@townofmarystown.ca
www.townofmarystown.ca
Municipal Type: Town
Incorporated: Dec. 18, 1951 *Area:* 61.97 sq km
Population in 2011: 5,506
Provincial Electoral District(s): Burin-Placentia West
Federal Electoral District(s): Random-Burin-St. George's
Next Election: Sept. 24, 2013 (4 year terms)
Sam Synard, Mayor
ssynard@townofmarystown.ca
Dennis P. Kelly, Clerk & Manager
dkelly@townofmarystown.ca

Massey Drive
85 Massey Dr.
Massey Drive, NL A2H 7A2
Tel: 709-634-2742; *Fax:* 709-634-2899
townmasseydr@nf.aibn.com
Municipal Type: Town
Incorporated: Sept. 28, 1971 *Area:* 2.48 sq km
Population in 2011: 1,412
Provincial Electoral District(s): Humber East
Federal Electoral District(s): Humber-St. Barbe-Baie Verte
Next Election: Sept. 24, 2013 (4 year terms)
Gord Davis, Mayor
Rodger Hunt, Town Manager/Clerk

McIvers
P.O. Box 4375
RR#2
Corner Brook, NL A2H 6B9
Tel: 709-688-2603; *Fax:* 709-688-2680
mciverscouncil@eastlink.ca
Municipal Type: Town
Incorporated: June 15, 1971 *Area:* 12.06 sq km
Population in 2011: 546
Provincial Electoral District(s): Bay of Islands
Federal Electoral District(s): Humber-St. Barbe-Baie Verte
Next Election: Sept. 24, 2013 (4 year terms)
Warren Blanchard, Mayor
Bernice E. Parsons, Clerk

Meadows
P.O. Box 3529
RR#2
Corner Brook, NL A2H 6B9
Tel: 709-783-2339; *Fax:* 709-783-2501
townofmeadows@nf.aibn.com
Municipal Type: Town
Incorporated: Jan. 13, 1970 *Area:* 3.79 sq km
Population in 2011: 649
Provincial Electoral District(s): Bay of Islands
Federal Electoral District(s): Humber-St. Barbe-Baie Verte
Next Election: Sept. 24, 2013 (4 year terms)
Kenneth March, Mayor
Joy Taylor, Clerk

Middle Arm
P.O. Box 51
Middle Arm, NL A0K 3R0
Tel: 709-252-2521; *Fax:* 709-252-2521
townofmiddlearm@nf.aibn.com
Municipal Type: Town
Incorporated: Nov. 29, 1966 *Area:* 25.19 sq km
Population in 2011: 476
Provincial Electoral District(s): Baie Verte
Federal Electoral District(s): Avalon; Humber-St. Barbe-Baie Verte
Next Election: Sept. 24, 2013 (4 year terms)
Nevil Robinson, Mayor
Loretta Budgell, Clerk

Miles Cove
General Delivery
Miles Cove, NL A0J 1L0
Tel: 709-652-3685; *Fax:* 709-652-3695
Municipal Type: Town
Incorporated: Sept. 22, 1970 *Area:* 4.03 sq km
Population in 2011: 137
Provincial Electoral District(s): Windsor-Springdale
Federal Electoral District(s): Humber-St. Barbe-Baie Verte
Next Election: Sept. 24, 2013 (4 year terms)
Melvin Morey, Mayor
Gloria Reid, Clerk

Millertown
P.O. Box 56
Millertown, NL A0H 1V0
Tel: 709-852-6216; *Fax:* 709-852-5431
townofmillertown@nf.aibn.com
Municipal Type: Town
Incorporated: Dec. 15, 1959 *Area:* 3.24 sq km
Population in 2011: 99
Provincial Electoral District(s): Grand Falls-Buchans
Federal Electoral District(s): Bonavista-Gander-Grand Falls-Windsor
Next Election: Sept. 24, 2013 (4 year terms)
Kevin Greene, Mayor
Eileen M. Scott, Clerk

Milltown-Head of Bay D'Espoir
P.O. Box 70
Milltown, NL A0H 1W0
Tel: 709-882-2232; *Fax:* 709-882-2636
townofmill@bellaliant.com
Municipal Type: Town
Incorporated: Dec. 16, 1952 *Area:* 25.02 sq km
Population in 2011: 789
Provincial Electoral District(s): Fortune Bay-Cape La Hune
Federal Electoral District(s): Random-Burin-St. George's
Next Election: Sept. 24, 2013 (4 year terms)
Georgina Brushett, Mayor
Kimberly Kendell, Clerk

Ming's Bight
P.O. Box 59
Mings Bight, NL A0K 3S0
Tel: 709-254-6516; *Fax:* 709-254-6516
townmingsbight@xplornet.ca
Municipal Type: Town
Incorporated: June 6, 1970 *Area:* 3.78 sq km
Population in 2011: 333
Provincial Electoral District(s): Baie Verte
Federal Electoral District(s): Humber-St. Barbe-Baie Verte
Next Election: Sept. 24, 2013 (4 year terms)
Danny Regular, Mayor
Glenda Regular, Clerk

Morrisville
P.O. Box 19
Morrisville, NL A0H 1W0
Tel: 709-882-2831; *Fax:* 709-882-2831
Municipal Type: Town
Incorporated: June 1, 1971 *Area:* 14.26 sq km
Population in 2011: 117
Provincial Electoral District(s): Fortune Bay-Cape La Hune
Federal Electoral District(s): Random-Burin-St. George's
Next Election: Sept. 24, 2013 (4 year terms)
Helen Kendell, Mayor
Karl Kendell, Clerk

Mount Carmel-Mitchell's Brook-St. Catherines
General Delivery
Mount Carmel, NL A0B 2M0
Tel: 709-521-2040; *Fax:* 709-521-2258
Municipal Type: Town
Incorporated: Oct. 6, 1970 *Area:* 61.55 sq km
Population in 2011: 358
Provincial Electoral District(s): Placentia & St. Mary's
Federal Electoral District(s): Avalon
Next Election: Sept. 24, 2013 (4 year terms)
Kim Mercer, Mayor
Geraldine Nolan, Clerk

Mount Moriah
P.O. Box 31
Mount Moriah, NL A0L 1J0
Tel: 709-785-5232; *Fax:* 709-785-5332
mtmoriahtowncouncil@nf.aibn.com
Municipal Type: Town
Incorporated: Oct. 12, 1971 *Area:* 15.71 sq km
Population in 2011: 785
Provincial Electoral District(s): Bay of Islands
Federal Electoral District(s): Humber-St. Barbe-Baie Verte
Next Election: Sept. 24, 2013 (4 year terms)
James Gillam, Mayor
Carol Skeard, Clerk

Musgrave Harbour
P.O. Box 159
Musgrave Harbour, NL A0G 3J0
Tel: 709-655-2119; *Fax:* 709-655-2064
musgravetowncouncil@nf.aibn.com
www.musgraveharbour.com
Municipal Type: Town
Incorporated: Jan. 1, 1954 *Area:* 69.94 sq km
Population in 2011: 1,053
Provincial Electoral District(s): Bonavista North
Federal Electoral District(s): Bonavista-Gander-Grand Falls-Windsor
Next Election: Sept. 24, 2013 (4 year terms)
Raymond Stokes, Mayor
Sharla Abbott, Clerk

Musgravetown
P.O. Box 129
Musgravetown, NL A0C 1Z0
Tel: 709-467-2726; *Fax:* 709-467-2109
townofmusg@nf.aibn.com
Municipal Type: Town
Incorporated: March 1, 1974 *Area:* 13.63 sq km
Population in 2011: 556
Provincial Electoral District(s): Terra Nova
Federal Electoral District(s): Bonavista-Gander-Grand Falls-Windsor
Next Election: Sept. 24, 2013 (4 year terms)
Jim Brown, Mayor
Linda Fitzgerald, Clerk

Nain
P.O. Box 400
Nain, NL A0P 1L0
Tel: 709-922-2842; *Fax:* 709-922-2295
towncouncilnain@nf.aibn.com
Municipal Type: Town
Incorporated: Nov. 24, 1970 *Area:* 94.58 sq km
Population in 2011: 1,188
Provincial Electoral District(s): Torngat Mountains
Federal Electoral District(s): Labrador
Next Election: Sept. 24, 2013 (4 year terms)
Sarah Erickson, Mayor
Karen Dicker, Clerk

New Perlican
P.O. Box 130
New Perlican, NL A0B 2S0
Tel: 709-583-2500; *Fax:* 709-583-2554
townofnewperlican@persona.ca
Municipal Type: Town
Incorporated: Sept. 28, 1971 *Area:* 24.47 sq km
Population in 2011: 210
Provincial Electoral District(s): Trinity-Bay de Verde
Federal Electoral District(s): Avalon
Next Election: Sept. 24, 2013 (4 year terms)
Linda Moyles, Mayor
Courtney Clarke, Clerk

New-Wes-Valley
P.O. Box 64
Badgers Quay, NL A0G 1B0
Tel: 709-536-2010; *Fax:* 709-536-3481
new-wes-valley@nf.aibn.com
www.townofnewwesvalley.com
Municipal Type: Town
Incorporated: Jan. 1, 1992 *Area:* 133.59 sq km
Population in 2011: 2,265
Provincial Electoral District(s): Bonavista North
Federal Electoral District(s): Bonavista-Gander-Grand Falls-Windsor
Next Election: Sept. 24, 2013 (4 year terms)
Grant Burry, Mayor
Harry Winter, Clerk & Manager

Nipper's Harbour
P.O. Box 10
Nippers Harbour, NL A0K 3T0
Tel: 709-255-3151; *Fax:* 709-255-3151
Municipal Type: Town
Incorporated: Nov. 10, 1964 *Area:* 1.93 sq km
Population in 2011: 128
Provincial Electoral District(s): Baie Verte
Federal Electoral District(s): Humber-St. Barbe-Baie Verte
Next Election: Sept. 24, 2013 (4 year terms)
Ted Noble, Mayor
Beth Prole, Clerk

Norman's Cove-Long Cove
P.O. Box 70
Normans Cove, NL A0B 2T0
Tel: 709-592-2490; *Fax:* 709-592-2106
townofnclc@eastlink.ca
Municipal Type: Town
Incorporated: June 2, 1970 *Area:* 19.98 sq km
Population in 2011: 720
Provincial Electoral District(s): Bellevue
Federal Electoral District(s): Avalon
Next Election: Sept. 24, 2013 (4 year terms)
Eva Bennett, Mayor
Dianne Hudson, Clerk

Norris Arm
P.O. Box 70
Norris Arm, NL A0G 3M0
Tel: 709-653-2519; *Fax:* 709-653-2163
norrisarm@gmail.com
www.norrisarm.com
Municipal Type: Town
Incorporated: April 20, 1971 *Area:* 41.49 sq km
Population in 2011: 912
Provincial Electoral District(s): Lewisporte
Federal Electoral District(s): Bonavista-Gander-Grand Falls-Windsor
Next Election: Sept. 24, 2013 (4 year terms)
Chris Manuel, Mayor
Beverly Peyton, Clerk

Norris Point
P.O. Box 119
Norris Point, NL A0K 3V0
Tel: 709-458-2896; *Fax:* 709-458-2883
norrispointcouncil@nf.aibn.com
www.norrispoint.ca
Municipal Type: Town
Incorporated: Oct. 25, 1960 *Area:* 4.91 sq km
Population in 2011: 685
Provincial Electoral District(s): St. Barbe
Federal Electoral District(s): Humber-St. Barbe-Baie Verte
Next Election: Sept. 24, 2013 (4 year terms)
Howard Neil, Mayor
mayor@norrispoint.ca
Regina Organ, Clerk

North River
P.O. Box 104
North River, NL A0A 3C0
Tel: 709-786-6216; *Fax:* 709-786-1955
Municipal Type: Town
Incorporated: Aug. 11, 1964 *Area:* 4.32 sq km
Population in 2011: 562
Provincial Electoral District(s): Harbour Main-Whitbourne
Federal Electoral District(s): Avalon; Labrador
Next Election: Sept. 24, 2013 (4 year terms)
Sheila Power, Mayor
Sheila Hall, Clerk

North West River
P.O. Box 100
North West River, NL A0P 1M0
Tel: 709-497-8533; *Fax:* 709-497-8228
manager@townofnwr.ca
www.townofnwr.ca
Municipal Type: Town
Incorporated: March 11, 1958 *Area:* 3.2 sq km
Population in 2011: 553
Provincial Electoral District(s): Lake Melville
Federal Electoral District(s): Labrador
Next Election: Sept. 24, 2013 (4 year terms)
Lowell Barkman, Mayor

Northern Arm
P.O. Box 2006
Northern Arm, NL A0H 1E0
Tel: 709-257-3482; *Fax:* 709-257-3482
ella@townofnorthernarm.ca
www.townofnorthernarm.ca
Municipal Type: Town
Incorporated: July 18, 1972 *Area:* 25.64 sq km
Population in 2011: 397
Provincial Electoral District(s): Exploits
Federal Electoral District(s): Bonavista-Gander-Grand Falls-Windsor
Next Election: Sept. 24, 2013 (4 year terms)
Deanna Gail Hancock, Mayor
Ella Humphries, Clerk

Old Perlican
P.O. Box 39
Old Perlican, NL A0A 3G0
Tel: 709-587-2266; *Fax:* 709-587-2261
townofoldperlican@persona.ca
Municipal Type: Town
Incorporated: March 30, 1971 *Area:* 14.47 sq km
Population in 2011: 661
Provincial Electoral District(s): Trinity-Bay de Verde
Federal Electoral District(s): Avalon
Next Election: Sept. 24, 2013 (4 year terms)
Harry Strong, Mayor
Judi Barter, Clerk

Pacquet
General Delivery
Pacquet, NL A0K 3X0
Tel: 709-251-5496; *Fax:* 709-251-5497
pacquet@eastlink.ca
Municipal Type: Town
Incorporated: June 12, 1962 *Area:* 14.48 sq km
Population in 2011: 184
Provincial Electoral District(s): Baie Verte
Federal Electoral District(s): Humber-St. Barbe-Baie Verte
Next Election: Sept. 24, 2013 (4 year terms)
Morris Geenham, Mayor
Janet Sacrey, Clerk

Parker's Cove
General Delivery
Parker's Cove, NL A0E 1H0
Tel: 709-443-2216; *Fax:* 709-443-2216
council@eatlink.ca
Municipal Type: Town
Incorporated: Jan. 25, 1966 *Area:* 4.85 sq km
Population in 2011: 301
Provincial Electoral District(s): Burin-Placentia West
Federal Electoral District(s): Random-Burin-St. George's
Next Election: Sept. 24, 2013 (4 year terms)
Cyril Synard, Mayor
Jeanette Murphy, Clerk

Parson's Pond
P.O. Box 39
Parsons Pond, NL A0K 3Z0
Tel: 709-243-2564; *Fax:* 709-243-2500
towncouncilpp@nf.aibn.com
Municipal Type: Town
Incorporated: March 29, 1966 *Area:* 12.63 sq km
Population in 2011: 383
Provincial Electoral District(s): St. Barbe
Federal Electoral District(s): Humber-St. Barbe-Baie Verte
Next Election: Sept. 24, 2013 (4 year terms)
Brenda Biggin, Mayor
Joan Parsons, Clerk

Pasadena
18 Tenth Ave.
Pasadena, NL A0L 1K0
Tel: 709-686-2075; *Fax:* 709-686-2507
pasadena@nf.aibn.com
www.town.pasadena.nf.ca
Municipal Type: Town
Incorporated: Oct. 25, 1955 *Area:* 49.16 sq km
Population in 2011: 3,352
Provincial Electoral District(s): Humber East
Federal Electoral District(s): Humber-St. Barbe-Baie Verte
Next Election: Sept. 24, 2013 (4 year terms)
Jim Merrigan, Mayor
bmercer@nf.aibn.com
Jim Merrigan, Clerk & Manager
jimmerrigan@nf.aibn.com

Peterview
P.O. Box 10
Peterview, NL A0H 1Y0
Tel: 709-257-2926; *Fax:* 709-257-2926
townofpeterview@nf.aibn.com
Municipal Type: Town
Incorporated: June 12, 1962 *Area:* 6.72 sq km
Population in 2011: 809
Provincial Electoral District(s): Exploits
Federal Electoral District(s): Bonavista-Gander-Grand Falls-Windsor
Next Election: Sept. 24, 2013 (4 year terms)
James Samson, Mayor
Venus Samson, Clerk

Petty Harbour-Maddox Cove
P.O. Box 434
Petty Harbour, NL A0A 3H0
Tel: 709-368-3959; *Fax:* 709-368-3994
ncostello@phmc.nf.net
www.pettyharbourmaddoxcove.ca
Municipal Type: Town
Incorporated: March 25, 1969 *Area:* 4.51 sq km
Population in 2011: 924
Provincial Electoral District(s): Ferryland
Federal Electoral District(s): St. John's South-Mount Pearl
Next Election: Sept. 24, 2013 (4 year terms)
Nath Hutchings, Mayor
Noreen Costello, Clerk

Pilley's Island
P.O. Box 70
Pilleys Island, NL A0J 1M0
Tel: 709-652-3555; *Fax:* 709-652-3852
pilleysisland@nf.aibn.com
Municipal Type: Town
Incorporated: April 11, 1975 *Area:* 34.67 sq km
Population in 2011: 301
Provincial Electoral District(s): Windsor-Springdale
Federal Electoral District(s): Humber-St. Barbe-Baie Verte
Next Election: Sept. 24, 2013 (4 year terms)
Fern Roberts, Mayor
Paulette Callahan, Clerk

Pinware
P.O. Box 37
Pinware, NL A0K 5S0
Tel: 709-927-5422; *Fax:* 709-927-5422
Municipal Type: Town
Incorporated: May 18, 1978 *Area:* 4.37 sq km
Population in 2011: 107
Provincial Electoral District(s): Cartwright-L'Anse au Clair
Federal Electoral District(s): Labrador
Next Election: Sept. 24, 2013 (4 year terms)
Joanne Dorey, Mayor
Gina Winslow, Clerk

Placentia
P.O. Box 99
Placentia, NL A0B 2Y0
Tel: 709-227-2151; *Fax:* 709-227-2323
townofplacentia@placentia.ca
www.placentia.ca
Municipal Type: Town
Incorporated: Nov. 6, 1945 *Area:* 58.05 sq km
Population in 2011: 3,643
Provincial Electoral District(s): Placentia & St. Mary's
Federal Electoral District(s): Avalon
Next Election: Sept. 24, 2013 (4 year terms)
William P. Hogan, Mayor
wph@placentia.ca
Ed O'Keefe, Clerk

Point au Gaul
P.O. Box 11
Point au Gaul, NL A0E 2C0
Tel: 709-857-2514
Municipal Type: Town
Incorporated: Jan. 4, 1966 *Area:* 3.84 sq km
Population in 2011: 97
Provincial Electoral District(s): Grand Bank
Federal Electoral District(s): Random-Burin-St. George's
Next Election: Sept. 24, 2013 (4 year terms)
Elizabeth Hillier, Mayor
Theresa Dodge, Clerk

Point Lance
P.O. Box 15
Point Lance, NL A0B 1E0
Tel: 709-338-2186; *Fax:* 709-338-2186
j_power@xplornet.ca
Municipal Type: Town
Incorporated: Dec. 7, 1971 *Area:* 29.14 sq km
Population in 2011: 120
Provincial Electoral District(s): Placentia & St. Mary's
Federal Electoral District(s): Avalon
Next Election: Sept. 24, 2013 (4 year terms)
Melvin Careen, Mayor
Jane Power, Clerk

Point Leamington
P.O. Box 39
Point Leamington, NL A0H 1Z0
Tel: 709-484-3421; *Fax:* 709-484-3556
ptleamington@nf.aibn.com
Municipal Type: Town
Incorporated: Aug. 25, 1970 *Area:* 28.81 sq km
Population in 2011: 619
Provincial Electoral District(s): Exploits
Federal Electoral District(s): Bonavista-Gander-Grand Falls-Windsor
Next Election: Sept. 24, 2013 (4 year terms)
Roosevelt Thompson, Mayor
Patricia Lanning, Clerk

Point May
P.O. Box 19
Point May, NL A0E 2C0
Tel: 709-857-2640; *Fax:* 709-857-2640
janicehaley@hotmail.com
Municipal Type: Town
Incorporated: Dec. 4, 1962 *Area:* 64.89 sq km
Population in 2011: 233
Provincial Electoral District(s): Grand Bank
Federal Electoral District(s): Random-Burin-St. George's
Next Election: Sept. 24, 2013 (4 year terms)
Janice Haley, Clerk

Point of Bay
P.O. Box 9
Point of Bay, NL A0H 2A0
Tel: 709-257-3171; *Fax:* 709-257-3192
Municipal Type: Town
Incorporated: April 18, 1967 *Area:* 21.94 sq km
Population in 2011: 159
Provincial Electoral District(s): Exploits
Federal Electoral District(s): Bonavista-Gander-Grand Falls-Windsor
Next Election: Sept. 24, 2013 (4 year terms)
Clarence Sparkes, Mayor
Sybil Boone, Clerk

Pool's Cove
P.O. Box 10
Pools Cove, NL A0H 2B0
Tel: 709-665-3371; *Fax:* 709-665-3372
Municipal Type: Town
Incorporated: Nov. 25, 1969 *Area:* 2.64 sq km
Population in 2011: 182
Provincial Electoral District(s): Fortune Bay-Cape La Hune
Federal Electoral District(s): Random-Burin-St. George's
Next Election: Sept. 24, 2013 (4 year terms)
Melvin Perham, Mayor
Sharon May, Clerk

Port Anson
General Delivery
Port Anson, NL A0J 1N0
Tel: 709-652-3683; *Fax:* 709-652-3680
townofportanson@hotmail.com
Municipal Type: Town
Incorporated: Dec. 12, 1961 *Area:* 7.69 sq km
Population in 2011: 165
Provincial Electoral District(s): Windsor-Springdale
Federal Electoral District(s): Humber-St. Barbe-Baie Verte
Next Election: Sept. 24, 2013 (4 year terms)
Shawn Burton, Mayor
Grace Burton, Clerk

Port au Choix
P.O. Box 89
Port au Choix, NL A0K 4C0
Tel: 709-861-3409; *Fax:* 709-861-3061
portauchoix@nf.aibn.com
Municipal Type: Town
Incorporated: July 26, 1966 *Area:* 35.61 sq km
Population in 2011: 839
Provincial Electoral District(s): St. Barbe
Federal Electoral District(s): Humber-St. Barbe-Baie Verte
Next Election: Sept. 24, 2013 (4 year terms)
Carolyn Lavers, Mayor
Annette Payne, Clerk

Port au Port East
P.O. Box 160
Port au Port East, NL A0N 1T0
Tel: 709-648-2731; *Fax:* 709-648-9481
townofp.a.p.e@cablerocket.com
Municipal Type: Town
Incorporated: Dec. 16, 1952 *Area:* 24.76 sq km
Population in 2011: 598
Provincial Electoral District(s): Port au Port
Federal Electoral District(s): Random-Burin-St. George's
Next Election: Sept. 24, 2013 (4 year terms)
Eileen Hann, Mayor
Joanne Ryan, Clerk

Port au Port West-Aguathuna-Felix Cove
P.O. Box 89
Aguathuna, NL A0N 1T0
Tel: 709-648-2891; *Fax:* 709-648-9292
papwaf@nf.aibn.com
Municipal Type: Town
Incorporated: Oct. 6, 1970 *Area:* 16.72 sq km
Population in 2011: 447
Provincial Electoral District(s): Port au Port
Federal Electoral District(s): Random-Burin-St. George's
Next Election: Sept. 24, 2013 (4 year terms)
Vanessa Glasgow, Clerk

Port Blandford
P.O. Box 70
Port Blandford, NL A0C 2G0
Tel: 709-543-2170; *Fax:* 709-543-2153
vgreening@nf.aibn.com
www.portblandford.com
Municipal Type: Town
Incorporated: Sept. 28, 1971 *Area:* 50.56 sq km
Population in 2011: 483
Provincial Electoral District(s): Terra Nova
Federal Electoral District(s): Bonavista-Gander-Grand Falls-Windsor
Next Election: Sept. 24, 2013 (4 year terms)
Reginald Penney, Mayor
Vida Greening, Town Clerk & Manager

Port Hope Simpson
P.O. Box 130
Port Hope Simpson, NL A0K 4E0
Tel: 709-960-0236; *Fax:* 709-960-0387
porthopesimpson@nf.aibn.com
Municipal Type: Town
Incorporated: May 1, 1973 *Area:* 32.52 sq km
Population in 2011: 441
Provincial Electoral District(s): Cartwright-L'Anse au Clair
Federal Electoral District(s): Labrador
Next Election: Sept. 24, 2013 (4 year terms)
Margaret Burden, Mayor
Michelle Clarke, Clerk

Port Kirwan
PO Box 40, Site 2
Port Kirwan, NL A0A 2G0
Tel: 709-363-2207
Municipal Type: Town
Incorporated: June 15, 1965 *Area:* 9.19 sq km
Population in 2011: 65
Provincial Electoral District(s): Ferryland
Federal Electoral District(s): Avalon
Next Election: Sept. 24, 2013 (4 year terms)
Eugene Brothers, Mayor
Dana Boland, Clerk

Port Rexton
P.O. Box 55
Port Rexton, NL A0C 2H0
Tel: 709-464-2006; *Fax:* 709-464-2006
portrexton@bellaliant.com
Municipal Type: Town
Incorporated: April 22, 1969 *Area:* 11.78 sq km
Population in 2011: 338
Provincial Electoral District(s): Trinity North
Federal Electoral District(s): Bonavista-Gander-Grand Falls-Windsor
Next Election: Sept. 24, 2013 (4 year terms)
Alvin Piercey, Mayor
Lois Long, Clerk

Port Saunders
P.O. Box 39
Port Saunders, NL A0K 4H0
Tel: 709-861-3105; *Fax:* 709-861-2137
townofportsaunders@nf.aibn.com
Municipal Type: Town
Incorporated: Aug. 21, 1956 *Area:* 38.81 sq km
Population in 2011: 697
Provincial Electoral District(s): St. Barbe
Federal Electoral District(s): Humber-St. Barbe-Baie Verte
Next Election: Sept. 24, 2013 (4 year terms)
Tony Ryan, Mayor
Judy Quinlan, Clerk
Helen Hamlyn, Co-clerk

Portugal Cove South
PO Box 8, Site 11
Trepassey, NL A0A 4B0
Tel: 709-438-2092; *Fax:* 709-438-2092
townofpcs@live.ca
Municipal Type: Town
Incorporated: Aug. 6, 1963 *Area:* 1.14 sq km
Population in 2011: 160
Provincial Electoral District(s): Ferryland
Federal Electoral District(s): Avalon
Next Election: Sept. 24, 2013 (4 year terms)
Clarence Molloy, Mayor
Ida Perry, Clerk

Portugal Cove-St Philip's
1119 Thorburn Rd.
Portugal Cove-St Philips, NL A1M 1T6
Tel: 709-895-8000; *Fax:* 709-895-3780
pcsp@pcsp.ca
www.pcsp.ca
Municipal Type: Town
Incorporated: Feb. 1, 1992 *Area:* 57.35 sq km
Population in 2011: 7,366
Provincial Electoral District(s): Conception Bay East & Bell Island
Federal Electoral District(s): St. John's East
Next Election: Sept. 24, 2013 (4 year terms)
Bill Fagan, Mayor
Judy Squires, Town Clerk & Treas.

Postville
P.O. Box 74
Postville, NL A0P 1N0
Tel: 709-479-9830; *Fax:* 709-479-9888
communitycouncil@nf.aibn.com
Municipal Type: Town
Incorporated: Aug. 1, 1975 *Area:* 1.96 sq km
Population in 2011: 206
Provincial Electoral District(s): Torngat Mountains
Federal Electoral District(s): Labrador
Next Election: Sept. 24, 2013 (4 year terms)
Diane Gear, Mayor
Melanie Gear, Clerk

Pouch Cove
P.O. Box 59
Pouch Cove, NL A0A 3L0
Tel: 709-335-2848; *Fax:* 709-335-2840
pouchcove@nf.aibn.com
www.pouchcove.ca
Municipal Type: Town
Incorporated: Dec. 22, 1970 *Area:* 58.34 sq km
Population in 2011: 1,866
Provincial Electoral District(s): Cape St. Francis
Federal Electoral District(s): St. John's East
Next Election: Sept. 24, 2013 (4 year terms)
Sarah Patten, Mayor
709-335-2464
Kim Osmond, Clerk

Raleigh
P.O. Box 119
Raleigh, NL A0K 4J0
Tel: 709-452-4461; *Fax:* 709-452-2135
townofraleigh@nf.aibn.com
Municipal Type: Town
Incorporated: Oct. 2, 1973 *Area:* 11.12 sq km
Population in 2011: 201
Provincial Electoral District(s): The Straits & White Bay North
Federal Electoral District(s): Humber-St. Barbe-Baie Verte
Next Election: Sept. 24, 2013 (4 year terms)
Millicent Taylor, Mayor
Angela Taylor, Clerk

Ramea
P.O. Box 69
Ramea, NL A0N 2J0
Tel: 709-625-2280; *Fax:* 709-625-2010
rameatowncouncil@nf.aibn.com
Municipal Type: Town
Incorporated: March 20, 1951 *Area:* 1.89 sq km
Population in 2011: 280
Provincial Electoral District(s): Fortune Bay-Cape La Hune
Federal Electoral District(s): Random-Burin-St. George's
Next Election: Sept. 24, 2013 (4 year terms)
Minnie Organ, Clerk
Lloyd Rossiter, Mayor

Red Bay
P.O. Box 108
Red Bay, NL A0K 4K0
Tel: 709-920-2197; *Fax:* 709-920-2103
redbaytowncouncil@nf.aibn.com
Municipal Type: Town
Incorporated: May 22, 1973 *Area:* 1.58 sq km
Population in 2011: 194
Provincial Electoral District(s): Cartwright-L'Anse au Clair
Federal Electoral District(s): Labrador
Next Election: Sept. 24, 2013 (4 year terms)
Wade Earle, Mayor
Liz Yetman, Clerk

Red Harbour
General Delivery
Red Harbour PB, NL A0E 2R0
Tel: 709-443-2599; *Fax:* 709-443-2599
townofredhr@yahoo.ca
Municipal Type: Town
Incorporated: Nov. 9, 1969 *Area:* 11.35 sq km
Population in 2011: 191
Provincial Electoral District(s): Burin-Placentia West
Federal Electoral District(s): Random-Burin-St. George's
Next Election: Sept. 24, 2013 (4 year terms)
Kevin Paddle, Clerk

Reidville
2 Community Sq.
Reidville, NL A8A 2V7
Tel: 709-635-5232; *Fax:* 709-635-4498
townofreidville@nf.aibn.com
www.reidville-nl.ca
Municipal Type: Town
Incorporated: Oct. 3, 1975 *Area:* 58.41 sq km
Population in 2011: 474
Provincial Electoral District(s): Humber Valley
Federal Electoral District(s): Humber-St. Barbe-Baie Verte
Next Election: Sept. 24, 2013 (4 year terms)
Helen Reid, Mayor
Connie Reid, Clerk

Rencontre East
P.O. Box 56
Rencontre East, NL A0H 2C0
Tel: 709-848-3171; *Fax:* 709-848-4194
Municipal Type: Town
Incorporated: Feb. 8, 1972 *Area:* 2.62 sq km

Population in 2011: 141
Provincial Electoral District(s): Fortune Bay-Cape La Hune
Federal Electoral District(s): Random-Burin-St. George's
Next Election: Sept. 24, 2013 (4 year terms)
Tom Caines, Mayor
Barbara Caines, Clerk

Renews-Cappahayden
P.O. Box 40
Renews, NL A0A 3N0
Tel: 709-363-2500; *Fax:* 709-363-2143
townofrenewscappahayden@nf.aibn.com
Municipal Type: Town
Incorporated: Sept. 19, 1967 *Area:* 127.84 sq km
Population in 2011: 310
Provincial Electoral District(s): Ferryland
Federal Electoral District(s): Avalon
Next Election: Sept. 24, 2013 (4 year terms)
Donna Dinn, Mayor
Susan Perry, Clerk

Rigolet
P.O. Box 69
Rigolet, NL A0P 1P0
Tel: 709-947-3382; *Fax:* 709-947-3360
sherri.wolfrey@rigolet.ca
www.thebigland.ca
Municipal Type: Town
Incorporated: Jan. 7, 1977 *Area:* 3.61 sq km
Population in 2011: 306
Provincial Electoral District(s): Torngat Mountains
Federal Electoral District(s): Labrador
Next Election: Sept. 24, 2013 (4 year terms)
Max Pottle, Acting Mayor
Sherri Wolfrey, Town Clerk

River of Ponds
P.O. Box 10
River of Ponds, NL A0K 4M0
Tel: 709-225-3161; *Fax:* 709-225-3162
Municipal Type: Town
Incorporated: May 26, 1970 *Area:* 4.69 sq km
Population in 2011: 228
Provincial Electoral District(s): St. Barbe
Federal Electoral District(s): Humber-St. Barbe-Baie Verte
Next Election: Sept. 24, 2013 (4 year terms)
Eric Patey, Mayor
Cynthia Wheaton, Clerk

Riverhead
P.O. Box 426
St Marys, NL A0B 3B0
Tel: 709-525-2600; *Fax:* 709-525-2106
Municipal Type: Town
Incorporated: Dec. 20, 1966 *Area:* 105.6 sq km
Population in 2011: 212
Provincial Electoral District(s): Placentia & St. Mary's
Federal Electoral District(s): Avalon
Next Election: Sept. 24, 2013 (4 year terms)
Gloria White, Mayor
Anne Lee, Clerk

Robert's Arm
P.O. Box 10
Roberts Arm, NL A0J 1R0
Tel: 709-652-3331; *Fax:* 709-652-3079
townofrobertsarm@eastlink.ca
Municipal Type: Town
Incorporated: Sept. 7, 1954 *Area:* 35.79 sq km
Population in 2011: 807
Provincial Electoral District(s): Windsor-Springdale
Federal Electoral District(s): Humber-St. Barbe-Baie Verte
Next Election: Sept. 24, 2013 (4 year terms)
Lloyd Coulbourne, Mayor
Stephanie Ryan, Clerk

Rocky Harbour
P.O. Box 24
Rocky Harbour, NL A0K 4N0
Tel: 709-458-2376; *Fax:* 709-458-2293
rockyharbour@msn.com
www.rockyharbour.ca
Municipal Type: Town
Incorporated: April 5, 1966 *Area:* 12.08 sq km
Population in 2011: 979
Provincial Electoral District(s): St. Barbe
Federal Electoral District(s): Humber-St. Barbe-Baie Verte
Next Election: Sept. 24, 2013 (4 year terms)
Walter Nicolle, Mayor
Kay Reid, Clerk

Roddickton-Bide Arm
P.O. Box 10
Roddickton, NL A0K 4P0
Tel: 709-457-2413; *Fax:* 709-457-2663
roddickton@nf.aibn.com
Municipal Type: Town
Incorporated: April 7, 1953 *Area:* 47.71 sq km
Population in 2011: 1,057
Provincial Electoral District(s): The Straits & White Bay North
Federal Electoral District(s): Humber-St. Barbe-Baie Verte
Next Election: Sept. 24, 2013 (4 year terms)
Raymond Norman, Mayor
Denise Adams, Clerk

Rose Blanche-Harbour Le Cou
P.O. Box 159
Rose Blanche, NL A0M 1P0
Tel: 709-956-2540; *Fax:* 709-956-2541
townofroseblanche@nf.aibn.com
Municipal Type: Town
Incorporated: Aug. 25, 1971 *Area:* 4.44 sq km
Population in 2011: 118
Provincial Electoral District(s): Burgeo & La Poile
Federal Electoral District(s): Random-Burin-St. George's
Next Election: Sept. 24, 2013 (4 year terms)
Christine Nussey, Mayor
Tammy Farrell, Clerk

Rushoon
General Delivery
Rushoon, NL A0E 2S0
Tel: 709-443-2572; *Fax:* 709-443-2572
townofrushoon@bellaliant.com
Municipal Type: Town
Incorporated: Jan. 18, 1966 *Area:* 6.15 sq km
Population in 2011: 288
Provincial Electoral District(s): Burin-Placentia West
Federal Electoral District(s): Random-Burin-St. George's
Next Election: Sept. 24, 2013 (4 year terms)
Jill Mulrooney, Mayor
Jacqueline Gaulton, Clerk

St. Alban's
P.O. Box 10
St Albans, NL A0H 2E0
Tel: 709-538-3132; *Fax:* 709-538-3683
st.albans@nf.aibn.com
www.stalbans.ca
Municipal Type: Town
Incorporated: Sept. 1, 1953 *Area:* 20.85 sq km
Population in 2011: 1,233
Provincial Electoral District(s): Fortune Bay-Cape La Hune
Federal Electoral District(s): Random-Burin-St. George's
Next Election: Sept. 24, 2013 (4 year terms)
Rodney Kendall, Mayor
Genevieve Tremblett, Clerk & Manager

St. Anthony
P.O. Box 430
St Anthony, NL A0K 4S0
Tel: 709-454-3454; *Fax:* 709-454-4154
stanthony@nf.aibn.com
www.town.stanthony.nf.ca
Municipal Type: Town
Incorporated: July 18, 1945 *Area:* 37.02 sq km
Population in 2011: 2,418
Provincial Electoral District(s): The Straits & White Bay North
Federal Electoral District(s): Humber-St. Barbe-Baie Verte
Next Election: Sept. 24, 2013 (4 year terms)
Ernest Simms, Mayor
Wallace Green, Clerk

St. Bernard's-Jacques Fontaine
P.O. Box 70
St Bernards, NL A0E 2T0
Tel: 709-461-2257; *Fax:* 709-461-2179
townofsbjf@eastlink.ca
Municipal Type: Town
Incorporated: Nov. 21, 1967 *Area:* 16.44 sq km
Population in 2011: 470
Provincial Electoral District(s): Bellevue
Federal Electoral District(s): Random-Burin-St. George's
Next Election: Sept. 24, 2013 (4 year terms)
Clifford Allen, Mayor
Pauline Smith, Clerk

St. Brendan's
P.O. Box 43
St Brendans, NL A0G 3V0
Tel: 709-669-4271; *Fax:* 709-669-4271
Municipal Type: Town
Incorporated: Sept. 1, 1953 *Area:* 10.14 sq km
Population in 2011: 147
Provincial Electoral District(s): Terra Nova
Federal Electoral District(s): Bonavista-Gander-Grand Falls-Windsor
Next Election: Sept. 24, 2013 (4 year terms)
Rita White, Clerk

St. Bride's
General Delivery
St Brides, NL A0B 2Z0
Tel: 709-337-2160; *Fax:* 709-337-2160
Municipal Type: Town
Incorporated: May 2, 1972 *Area:* 5.84 sq km
Population in 2011: 308
Provincial Electoral District(s): Placentia & St. Mary's
Federal Electoral District(s): Avalon
Next Election: Sept. 24, 2013 (4 year terms)
Eugene Manning, Mayor
Joan Morrissey, Clerk

St. George's
P.O. Box 250
St Georges, NL A0N 1Z0
Tel: 709-647-3283; *Fax:* 709-647-3180
townofstgeorges@nf.aibn.com
www.townofstgeorges.com
Municipal Type: Town
Incorporated: May 18, 1965 *Area:* 25.83 sq km
Population in 2011: 1,207
Provincial Electoral District(s): St. George's-Stephenville East
Federal Electoral District(s): Random-Burin-St. George's
Next Election: Sept. 24, 2013 (4 year terms)
Fintan Alexander, Mayor
Ray Chant, Clerk

St. Jacques-Coomb's Cove
P.O. Box 102
English Harbour West, NL A0H 1M0
Tel: 709-888-6141; *Fax:* 709-888-6102
sjcctc@gmail.com
Municipal Type: Town
Incorporated: Nov. 15, 1971 *Area:* 83.76 sq km
Population in 2011: 618
Provincial Electoral District(s): Fortune Bay-Cape La Hune
Federal Electoral District(s): Random-Burin-St. George's
Next Election: Sept. 24, 2013 (4 year terms)
Max Taylor, Mayor
Frances Courtney, Clerk

St. Joseph's
P.O. Box 9
St Josephs, NL A0B 3A0
Tel: 709-521-2440; *Fax:* 709-521-2440
Municipal Type: Town
Incorporated: Aug. 18, 1970 *Area:* 32.31 sq km
Population in 2011: 115
Provincial Electoral District(s): Placentia & St. Mary's
Federal Electoral District(s): Avalon
Next Election: Sept. 24, 2013 (4 year terms)
Anthony Healey, Mayor
Maureen Healey, Clerk

St. Lawrence
P.O. Box 128
St Lawrence, NL A0E 2V0
Tel: 709-873-2222; *Fax:* 709-873-3352
townofstlawrence@nf.aibn.com
www.discoverstlawrence.com
Municipal Type: Town
Incorporated: Nov. 15, 1949 *Area:* 35.5 sq km
Population in 2011: 1,244
Provincial Electoral District(s): Grand Bank
Federal Electoral District(s): Random-Burin-St. George's
Next Election: Sept. 24, 2013 (4 year terms)
Wayde Rowsell, Mayor
Gregory Quirke, Clerk

St. Lewis
P.O. Box 106
St. Lewis, NL A0K 4W0
Tel: 709-939-2282; *Fax:* 709-939-2210
Municipal Type: Town
Incorporated: July 17, 1981 *Area:* 9.25 sq km
Population in 2011: 207
Provincial Electoral District(s): Cartwright-L'Anse au Clair
Federal Electoral District(s): Labrador
Next Election: Sept. 24, 2013 (4 year terms)
Annie Rumbolt, Mayor
Lorraine Poole, Clerk

St. Lunaire-Griquet
P.O. Box 9
St Lunaire-Griquet, NL A0K 2X0
Tel: 709-623-2323; *Fax:* 709-623-2170
stlunaire.griquet@nf.aibn.com
Municipal Type: Town
Incorporated: June 10, 1958 *Area:* 16.68 sq km
Population in 2011: 661
Provincial Electoral District(s): The Straits & White Bay North
Federal Electoral District(s): Humber-St. Barbe-Baie Verte
Next Election: Sept. 24, 2013 (4 year terms)
Gerald Hillier, Mayor
Linda Hillier, Clerk

St. Mary's
P.O. Box 348
St Marys, NL A0B 3B0
Tel: 709-525-2586; *Fax:* 709-525-2587
theresap@nf.aibn.com
Municipal Type: Town
Incorporated: Dec. 13, 1966 *Area:* 37.05 sq km
Population in 2011: 439
Provincial Electoral District(s): Placentia & St. Mary's
Federal Electoral District(s): Avalon
Next Election: Sept. 24, 2013 (4 year terms)
Joseph Dillon, Mayor
Theresa Power, Clerk

St. Pauls
P.O. Box 9
St Pauls, NL A0K 4Y0
Tel: 709-243-2279; *Fax:* 709-243-2299
Municipal Type: Town
Incorporated: July 30, 1968 *Area:* 5.35 sq km
Population in 2011: 258
Provincial Electoral District(s): St. Barbe
Federal Electoral District(s): Humber-St. Barbe-Baie Verte
Next Election: Sept. 24, 2013 (4 year terms)
Jerry Bennett, Mayor
Monica Pittman, Clerk

St. Shott's
General Delivery
St Shotts, NL A0A 3R0
Tel: 709-438-2694; *Fax:* 709-438-2617
Municipal Type: Town
Incorporated: May 21, 1963 *Area:* 1.14 sq km
Population in 2011: 81
Provincial Electoral District(s): Placentia & St. Mary's
Federal Electoral District(s): Avalon
Next Election: Sept. 24, 2013 (4 year terms)
Patrick Hewitt, Mayor
Elizabeth Hewitt, Clerk

St. Vincent's-St. Stephen's-Peter's River
P.O. Box 39
St Vincents, NL A0B 3C0
Tel: 709-525-2540; *Fax:* 709-525-2110
svstpr@nf.aibn.com
Municipal Type: Town
Incorporated: Aug. 1, 1971 *Area:* 87.5 sq km
Population in 2011: 340
Provincial Electoral District(s): Placentia & St. Mary's
Federal Electoral District(s): Avalon
Next Election: Sept. 24, 2013 (4 year terms)
Gus Stamp, Mayor
Marilyn Gibbons, Clerk

Salmon Cove
P.O. Box 240
Salmon Cove, NL A0A 3S0
Tel: 709-596-2101; *Fax:* 709-596-1170
townofsalmoncove@nf.aibn.com
Municipal Type: Town
Incorporated: Aug. 27, 1974 *Area:* 4.21 sq km
Population in 2011: 695
Provincial Electoral District(s): Carbonear-Harbour Grace
Federal Electoral District(s): Avalon
Next Election: Sept. 24, 2013 (4 year terms)
Roy Rose, Mayor
Juanita Korpan, Clerk

Salvage
General Delivery
Salvage, NL A0G 3X0
Tel: 709-677-3535; *Fax:* 709-677-3535
Municipal Type: Town
Incorporated: Oct. 24, 1972 *Area:* 15.86 sq km
Population in 2011: 136
Provincial Electoral District(s): Terra Nova
Federal Electoral District(s): Bonavista-Gander-Grand Falls-Windsor
Next Election: Sept. 24, 2013 (4 year terms)
Dave Brown, Mayor
Beverly Hunter, Clerk

Sandringham
43-47Main St.
Sandringham, NL A0G 3Y0
Tel: 709-677-2317; *Fax:* 709-677-2317
townofsandringham@yahoo.ca
Municipal Type: Town
Incorporated: April 30, 1968 *Area:* 9.6 sq km
Population in 2011: 274
Provincial Electoral District(s): Terra Nova
Federal Electoral District(s): Bonavista-Gander-Grand Falls-Windsor
Next Election: Sept. 24, 2013 (4 year terms)
Glenn Arnold, Mayor
Audrey Penney, Clerk

Sandy Cove
PO Box 37, Site 8
Eastport, NL A0G 1Z0
Tel: 709-677-2731; *Fax:* 709-677-2731
sandycove@nf.sympatico.ca
www3.nf.sympatico.ca/sandycove
Municipal Type: Town
Incorporated: Sept. 18, 1956 *Area:* 9.01 sq km
Population in 2011: 132
Provincial Electoral District(s): Terra Nova; The Straits & White Bay North
Federal Electoral District(s): Bonavista-Gander-Grand Falls-Windsor; Humber-St. Barbe-Baie Verte
Next Election: Sept. 24, 2013 (4 year terms)
Tony Parsons, Mayor
Anne Benger, Clerk

Seal Cove Fortune Bay
P.O. Box 156
Seal Cove Fortune Bay, NL A0H 2G0
Tel: 709-851-4431; *Fax:* 709-851-6174
sealcovecc@nf.aibn.com
Municipal Type: Town
Incorporated: Jan. 25, 1972 *Area:* 2.42 sq km
Population in 2011: 263
Provincial Electoral District(s): Fortune Bay-Cape La Hune
Federal Electoral District(s): Random-Burin-St. George's
Next Election: Sept. 24, 2013 (4 year terms)
Junior Abbott, Mayor
Emily Loveless, Clerk

Seal Cove White Bay
P.O. Box 119
Seal Cove White Bay, NL A0K 5E0
Tel: 709-531-2550; *Fax:* 709-531-2551
sealcovewb@nf.aibn.com
Municipal Type: Town
Incorporated: Dec. 16, 1958 *Area:* 10.79 sq km
Population in 2011: 304
Provincial Electoral District(s): Baie Verte
Federal Electoral District(s): Humber-St. Barbe-Baie Verte
Next Election: Sept. 24, 2013 (4 year terms)
Winston May, Mayor
Vanessa Osbourne, Clerk

Small Point-Adam's Cove-Blackhead-Broad Cove
P.O. Box 160
Broad Cove, NL A0A 1L0
Tel: 709-598-2610; *Fax:* 709-598-2618
towncouncil@eastlink.ca
Municipal Type: Town
Incorporated: Oct. 24, 1972 *Area:* 22.22 sq km
Population in 2011: 389
Provincial Electoral District(s): Tinity-Bay de Verde
Federal Electoral District(s): Avalon
Next Election: Sept. 24, 2013 (4 year terms)
Leslie Grover, Mayor
Dana Reid, Clerk

South Brook
P.O. Box 63
South Brook, NL A0J 1S0
Tel: 709-657-2206; *Fax:* 709-657-2202
townofsbrk@yahoo.ca
Municipal Type: Town
Incorporated: July 6, 1965 *Area:* 9.07 sq km
Population in 2011: 487
Provincial Electoral District(s): Windsor-Springdale
Federal Electoral District(s): Humber-St. Barbe-Baie Verte
Next Election: Sept. 24, 2013 (4 year terms)
Paul Mills, Mayor
Michelle Morey, Clerk

South River
P.O. Box 40
South River, NL A0A 3W0
Tel: 709-786-6761; *Fax:* 709-786-6760
townofsouthriver@persona.com
Municipal Type: Town
Incorporated: June 7, 1966 *Area:* 6.06 sq km
Population in 2011: 655
Provincial Electoral District(s): Harbour Main-Whitbourne
Federal Electoral District(s): Avalon
Next Election: Sept. 24, 2013 (4 year terms)
Arthur Petten, Mayor
Terrie Lynn Aisien, Town Clerk & Manager

Southern Harbour
P.O. Box 10
Southern Harbour PB, NL A0B 3H0
Tel: 709-463-2329; *Fax:* 709-463-2208
twnsouthernharbour@nf.aibn.com
Municipal Type: Town
Incorporated: Aug. 20, 1968 *Area:* 5.41 sq km
Population in 2011: 534
Provincial Electoral District(s): Bellevue
Federal Electoral District(s): Avalon
Next Election: Sept. 24, 2013 (4 year terms)
Joan Hickey, Mayor
Bernadette Power, Clerk

Spaniard's Bay
P.O. Box 190
Spaniards Bay, NL A0A 3X0
Tel: 709-786-3568; *Fax:* 709-786-7273
spaniardsbay@persona.ca
www.townofspaniardsbay.ca
Municipal Type: Town
Incorporated: June 8, 1965 *Area:* 65.73 sq km
Population in 2011: 2,622
Provincial Electoral District(s): Port de Grave
Federal Electoral District(s): Avalon
Next Election: Sept. 24, 2013 (4 year terms)
John W. Drover, Mayor
Tony Ryan, Clerk & Manager

Springdale
P.O. Box 57
Springdale, NL A0J 1T0
Tel: 709-673-3439; *Fax:* 709-673-4969
townoffice.springdale@nf.aibn.com
www.townofspringdale.ca
Municipal Type: Town
Incorporated: Oct. 23, 1961 *Area:* 17.6 sq km
Population in 2011: 2,907
Provincial Electoral District(s): Windsor-Springdale
Federal Electoral District(s): Humber-St. Barbe-Baie Verte
Next Election: Sept. 24, 2013 (4 year terms)
Harvey Tizzard, Mayor
Daphne Earle, Clerk & Manager

Steady Brook
P.O. Box 117
Steady Brook, NL A2H 2N2
Tel: 709-634-7601; *Fax:* 709-634-7547
townoffice@steadybrook.com
www.steadybrook.com
Municipal Type: Town
Incorporated: April 7, 1953 *Area:* 1.22 sq km
Population in 2011: 408
Provincial Electoral District(s): Humber East
Federal Electoral District(s): Humber-St. Barbe-Baie Verte
Next Election: Sept. 24, 2013 (4 year terms)
Donna Thistle, Mayor
Robert Gosse, Clerk & Manager
townclerk@steadybrook.com

Stephenville
P.O. Box 420
Stephenville, NL A2N 2Z5
Tel: 709-643-8360; *Fax:* 709-643-2770
manager@town.stephenville.nf.ca
www.town.stephenville.nf.ca
Municipal Type: Town
Incorporated: Oct. 1, 1952 *Area:* 35.69 sq km
Population in 2011: 6,719
Provincial Electoral District(s): St. George's-Stephenville East; Port au Port
Federal Electoral District(s): Random-Burin-St. George's
Next Election: Sept. 24, 2013 (4 year terms)
Tom O'Brien, Mayor
mayor@town.stephenville.nf.ca
Carolyn Lindstone, Clerk

Stephenville Crossing
P.O. Box 68
Stephenville Crossing, NL A0N 2C0
Tel: 709-646-2600; *Fax:* 709-646-2065
yyounge@nf.aibn.com
Municipal Type: Town
Incorporated: Oct. 20, 1958 *Area:* 31.2 sq km
Population in 2011: 1,875
Provincial Electoral District(s): St. George's-Stephenville East
Federal Electoral District(s): Random-Burin-St. George's
Next Election: Sept. 24, 2013 (4 year terms)
Leona Webb, Mayor
Yvonne Young, Clerk

Summerford
P.O. Box 59
Summerford, NL A0G 4E0
Tel: 709-629-3419; *Fax:* 709-629-7532
townofsummerford@nf.aibn.com
www.townofsummerford.com
Municipal Type: Town
Incorporated: Sept. 28, 1971 *Area:* 16.06 sq km
Population in 2011: 853
Provincial Electoral District(s): Twillingate & Fogo
Federal Electoral District(s): Bonavista-Gander-Grand Falls-Windsor
Next Election: Sept. 24, 2013 (4 year terms)
Clayton LeDrew, Mayor
Vicky Anstey, Clerk

Sunnyside Trinity Bay
P.O. Box 89
Sunnyside, NL A0B 3J0
Tel: 709-472-4506; *Fax:* 709-472-4182
townofsunnyside@eastlink.ca
Municipal Type: Town
Incorporated: March 10, 1970 *Area:* 37.95 sq km
Population in 2011: 452
Provincial Electoral District(s): Bellevue
Federal Electoral District(s): Bonavista-Gander-Grand Falls-Windsor
Next Election: Sept. 24, 2013 (4 year terms)
Robert Snook, Mayor
G. Philip Smith, Clerk

Terra Nova
1 River Road
Terra Nova, NL A0C 1L0
Tel: 709-265-6543; *Fax:* 709-265-6533
townofterranova@nf.aibn.com
Municipal Type: Town
Incorporated: Sept. 13, 1960 *Area:* 2.46 sq km
Population in 2011: 83
Provincial Electoral District(s): Terra Nova
Federal Electoral District(s): Bonavista-Gander-Grand Falls-Windsor
Next Election: Sept. 24, 2013 (4 year terms)
Paul Noseworthy, Mayor
Tracie Crocker, Clerk

Terrenceville
P.O. Box 100
Terrenceville, NL A0E 2X0
Tel: 709-662-2204; *Fax:* 709-662-2071
terrancevilletownoffice@nf.aibn.com
Municipal Type: Town
Incorporated: Aug. 15, 1972 *Area:* 14.5 sq km
Population in 2011: 530
Provincial Electoral District(s): Bellevue
Federal Electoral District(s): Random-Burin-St. George's
Next Election: Sept. 24, 2013 (4 year terms)
Sheila Cox, Mayor
Joan Rideout, Clerk

Tilt Cove
P.O. Box 22
Tilt Cove, NL A0K 3M0
Tel: 709-675-2641
Municipal Type: Town
Incorporated: March 4, 1969 *Area:* 3.1 sq km
Population in 2011: 5
Provincial Electoral District(s): Baie Verte
Federal Electoral District(s): Humber-St. Barbe-Baie Verte
Next Election: Sept. 24, 2013 (4 year terms)
Donald Collins, Mayor
Margaret Collins, Clerk

Torbay
P.O. Box 1160
Torbay, NL A1K 1K4
Tel: 709-437-6532; *Fax:* 709-437-1309
dchaplin@torbay.ca
www.town.torbay.nf.ca
Municipal Type: Town
Incorporated: Oct. 24, 1972 *Area:* 34.88 sq km
Population in 2011: 7,397
Provincial Electoral District(s): Cape St. Francis
Federal Electoral District(s): St. John's East
Next Election: Sept. 24, 2013 (4 year terms)
Robert Codner, Mayor
Dawn Chaplin, CAO-Clerk
dchaplin@town.torbay.nf.ca

Traytown
1 Poplar Lane
Traytown, NL A0G 4K0
Tel: 709-533-2156; *Fax:* 709-533-2155
traytown@thezone.net
Municipal Type: Town
Incorporated: June 15, 1971 *Area:* 13.31 sq km
Population in 2011: 283
Provincial Electoral District(s): Terra Nova
Federal Electoral District(s): Bonavista-Gander-Grand Falls-Windsor
Next Election: Sept. 24, 2013 (4 year terms)
Leo Tulk, Mayor
Sarah Patten, Clerk

Trepassey
P.O. Box 129
Trepassey, NL A0A 4B0
Tel: 709-438-2641; *Fax:* 709-438-2749
jill@townoftrepassey.com
Municipal Type: Town
Incorporated: Aug. 1, 1967 *Area:* 55.81 sq km
Population in 2011: 570
Provincial Electoral District(s): Ferryland
Federal Electoral District(s): Avalon
Next Election: Sept. 24, 2013 (4 year terms)
Dennis Pearce, Mayor
Jill McNeil, Clerk

Trinity
P.O. Box 42
Trinity, NL A0C 2S0
Tel: 709-464-3836; *Fax:* 709-464-3836
counciltrinity@netscape.net
Municipal Type: Town
Incorporated: May 13, 1969 *Area:* 12.92 sq km
Population in 2011: 137
Provincial Electoral District(s): Trinity North; Bonavista North
Federal Electoral District(s): Bonavista-Gander-Grand Falls-Windsor
Next Election: Sept. 24, 2013 (4 year terms)
Jim Miller, Mayor
Linda Sweet, Clerk

Trinity Bay North
P.O. Box 91
Port Union, NL A0C 2J0
Tel: 709-469-2571; *Fax:* 709-469-3444
tbn@personainternet.com
www.trinitybaynorth.com
Municipal Type: Town
Incorporated: Jan. 1, 2005 *Area:* 14.28 sq km
Population in 2011: 1,827
Provincial Electoral District(s): Bonavista South
Federal Electoral District(s): Bonavista-Gander-Grand Falls-Windsor
Next Election: Sept. 24, 2013 (4 year terms)
Note: Effective Jan. 1, 2005, the towns of Catalina, Port Union, & Melrose amalgamated to form the new town of Trinity Bay North. Little Catalina was included on Oct. 1, 2010.
Brendan Peters, Mayor
Valerie Rogers, Clerk

Triton
P.O. Box 10
Triton, NL A0J 1V0
Tel: 709-263-2264; *Fax:* 709-263-2381
townoftriton@eastlink.ca
www.townoftriton.ca
Municipal Type: Town
Incorporated: March 11, 1958 *Area:* 7.55 sq km
Population in 2011: 998
Provincial Electoral District(s): Windsor-Springdale
Federal Electoral District(s): Humber-St. Barbe-Baie Verte
Next Election: Sept. 24, 2013 (4 year terms)
Jason Roberts, Mayor
Sandy Windsor, Clerk

Trout River
P.O. Box 89
Trout River, NL A0K 5P0
Tel: 709-451-5376; *Fax:* 709-451-2127
townoftroutriver@nf.aibn.com
Municipal Type: Town
Incorporated: April 12, 1966 *Area:* 5.91 sq km
Population in 2011: 576
Provincial Electoral District(s): Humber Valley
Federal Electoral District(s): Humber-St. Barbe-Baie Verte
Next Election: Sept. 24, 2013 (4 year terms)
Gertrude Hann, Mayor
Shelly Emily Butler, Clerk

Twillingate
P.O. Box 220
Twillingate, NL A0G 4M0
Tel: 709-884-2438; *Fax:* 709-884-5278
Municipal Type: Town
Incorporated: Jan. 1, 1992 *Area:* 25.74 sq km
Population in 2011: 2,268
Provincial Electoral District(s): Twillingate & Fogo
Federal Electoral District(s): Bonavista-Gander-Grand Falls-Windsor
Next Election: Sept. 24, 2013 (4 year terms)
Gordon Noseworthy, Mayor
David Burton, Clerk

Upper Island Cove
P.O. Box 149
Upper Island Cove, NL A0A 4E0
Tel: 709-589-2503; *Fax:* 709-589-2522
townofuic@nf.aibn.com
Municipal Type: Town
Incorporated: Oct. 19, 1965 *Area:* 7.85 sq km
Population in 2011: 1,594
Provincial Electoral District(s): Port de Grave
Federal Electoral District(s): Avalon
Next Election: Sept. 24, 2013 (4 year terms)
George Adams, Mayor
Neil Shute, Clerk

Victoria
P.O. Box 130
Victoria, NL A0A 4G0
Tel: 709-596-3783; *Fax:* 709-596-5020
townofvictoria@nf.aibn.com
Municipal Type: Town
Incorporated: July 1, 1971 *Area:* 17.64 sq km
Population in 2011: 1,764
Provincial Electoral District(s): Carbonear-Harbour Grace
Federal Electoral District(s): Avalon
Next Election: Sept. 24, 2013 (4 year terms)
Arthur Burke, Mayor
Sharon Snooks, Clerk

Wabana
P.O. Box 1229
Wabana, NL A0A 4H0
Tel: 709-488-2990; *Fax:* 709-488-3181
council@bellisland.net
www.bellisland.net
Municipal Type: Town
Incorporated: Aug. 28, 1950 *Area:* 14.5 sq km
Population in 2011: 2,346
Provincial Electoral District(s): Conception Bay East & Bell Island
Federal Electoral District(s): St. John's East
Next Election: Sept. 24, 2013 (4 year terms)
Gary Gosine, Mayor
Ben Noseworthy, Clerk
bennoseworthy@townofwabana.net

Wabush
P.O. Box 190
Wabush, NL A0R 1B0
Tel: 709-282-5696; *Fax:* 709-282-5142
info@wabush.ca
www.labradorwest.com
Municipal Type: Town
Incorporated: April 11, 1967 *Area:* 46.25 sq km
Population in 2011: 1,861
Provincial Electoral District(s): Labrador West
Federal Electoral District(s): Labrador
Next Election: Sept. 24, 2013 (4 year terms)
Ronald Barron, Mayor
Brian Hudson, Clerk
townclerk@wabush.ca

West St. Modeste
P.O. Box 78
West St Modeste, NL A0K 5S0
Tel: 709-927-5583; *Fax:* 709-927-5898
sandraodell@hotmail.com
Municipal Type: Town
Incorporated: Aug. 1, 1975 *Area:* 7.78 sq km
Population in 2011: 120
Provincial Electoral District(s): Cartwright-L'Anse au Clair
Federal Electoral District(s): Labrador
Next Election: Sept. 24, 2013 (4 year terms)
Agnes Pike, Mayor
Sandra O'Dell, Clerk

Westport
P.O. Box 29
Westport, NL A0K 5R0
Tel: 709-224-5501; *Fax:* 709-224-5501
Municipal Type: Town
Incorporated: July 18, 1967 *Area:* 5.13 sq km
Population in 2011: 220
Provincial Electoral District(s): Baie Verte
Federal Electoral District(s): Humber-St. Barbe-Baie Verte
Next Election: Sept. 24, 2013 (4 year terms)
Maxwell Warren, Mayor
Peggy Randell, Clerk

Whitbourne
P.O. Box 119
Whitbourne, NL A0B 3K0
Tel: 709-759-2780; *Fax:* 709-759-2016
whit.towncouncil@eastlink.ca
Municipal Type: Town
Incorporated: April 16, 1968 *Area:* 21.41 sq km
Population in 2011: 916
Provincial Electoral District(s): Harbour Main-Whitbourne
Federal Electoral District(s): Avalon
Next Election: Sept. 24, 2013 (4 year terms)
Lloyd Gosse, Mayor
Crystal Peddle, Clerk

Whiteway
Main St.
Whiteway, NL A0B 3L0
Tel: 709-588-2948; *Fax:* 709-588-2985
townofwhiteway@eastlink.ca
Municipal Type: Town
Incorporated: Oct. 3, 1975 *Area:* 22.64 sq km
Population in 2011: 293
Provincial Electoral District(s): Trinity-Bay de Verde
Federal Electoral District(s): Avalon
Next Election: Sept. 24, 2013 (4 year terms)
Craig Whalen, Mayor
Melinda Legge, Clerk

Winterland
P.O. Box 10
Winterland, NL A0E 2Y0
Tel: 709-279-3701; *Fax:* 709-279-3702
townofwinterland@hotmail.com
Municipal Type: Town
Incorporated: Nov. 24, 1970 *Area:* 54.34 sq km
Population in 2011: 363
Provincial Electoral District(s): Grand Bank
Federal Electoral District(s): Random-Burin-St. George's
Next Election: Sept. 24, 2013 (4 year terms)
Ches Kenway, Mayor
Marlyese Simms, Clerk

Winterton
P.O. Box 59
Winterton, NL A0B 3M0
Tel: 709-583-2010; *Fax:* 709-583-2099
wintertontowncouncil@persona.ca
Municipal Type: Town
Incorporated: April 15, 1964 *Area:* 10.52 sq km
Population in 2011: 484
Provincial Electoral District(s): Trinity-Bay de Verde
Federal Electoral District(s): Avalon
Next Election: Sept. 24, 2013 (4 year terms)
Jim Harnum, Mayor
Adella Green, Clerk

Witless Bay
P.O. Box 130
Witless Bay, NL A0A 4K0
Tel: 709-334-3407; *Fax:* 709-334-2377
townofwitlessbay@nf.aibn.com
Municipal Type: Town
Incorporated: Jan. 1, 1986 *Area:* 17.49 sq km
Population in 2011: 1,179
Provincial Electoral District(s): Ferryland
Federal Electoral District(s): Avalon
Next Election: Sept. 24, 2013 (4 year terms)
Patrick Curran, Mayor
Geraldine Caul, Clerk

Woodstock
19 Park St.
Woodstock, NL A0K 5X0
Tel: 709-251-3176; *Fax:* 709-251-3176
townofwoodstock@nf.aibn.com
Municipal Type: Town
Incorporated: Sept. 29, 1970 *Area:* 10.09 sq km
Population in 2011: 190
Provincial Electoral District(s): Baie Verte
Federal Electoral District(s): Humber-St. Barbe-Baie Verte
Next Election: Sept. 24, 2013 (4 year terms)
Terry Decker, Mayor
Norma Mitchell, Clerk

Woody Point
P.O. Box 100
Woody Point, NL A0K 1P0
Tel: 709-453-2273; *Fax:* 709-453-2270
woodypoint@nf.aibn.com
www.townofwoodypoint.ca
Municipal Type: Town
Incorporated: March 27, 1956 *Area:* 2.91 sq km
Population in 2011: 281
Provincial Electoral District(s): Humber Valley
Federal Electoral District(s): Humber-St. Barbe-Baie Verte
Next Election: Sept. 24, 2013 (4 year terms)
Ken Thomas, Mayor
Heather Coates, Clerk

York Harbour
136-138 Main St.
York Harbour, NL A0L 1L0
Tel: 709-681-2280; *Fax:* 709-681-2799
yorkharbourcouncil@nf.aibn.com
Municipal Type: Town
Incorporated: June 27, 1972 *Area:* 3.9 sq km
Population in 2011: 347
Provincial Electoral District(s): Bay of Islands
Federal Electoral District(s): Humber-St. Barbe-Baie Verte
Next Election: Sept. 24, 2013 (4 year terms)
Marie Byrne, Mayor
Michelle Sheppard, Clerk

NORTHWEST TERRITORIES

LEGISLATION: Cities, Towns and Villages Act; Hamlets Act; Charter Communities Act; Effective August 4, 2005, establishment of Tlicho Community Governments as a result of implementation of the Tlicho Self-Government and Land Claim; Settlements Act; Property Assessment and Taxation Act; Local Authorities Elections Act; Fire Protection Act; Civil Emergencies Act; Commissioner's Lands Act; Planning Act; Religious Societies Lands Act; Senior Citizens and Disabled Persons Property Tax Relief Act.

Incorporation as a city, town or village is determined by the value of all assessable land. Incorporation values: Village, $10 million; Town, $50 million; City, $200 million. All tax-based. Hamlets and Charter Communities may request tax-based status.

Local Authorities Elections: three years for cities, towns and villages; two years/staggered terms for hamlets and settlements; two to three years for charter communities. The Minister may extend or shorten terms on applications. Except for settlement councils, heads of councils are elected by separate ballot. First nations conduct their own electoral process.

Heads of Councils: Mayor, K'wati, Ehk'Wahtide, Chief, Chairperson.

First Nations provide municipal services as the main governing authority in several communities.

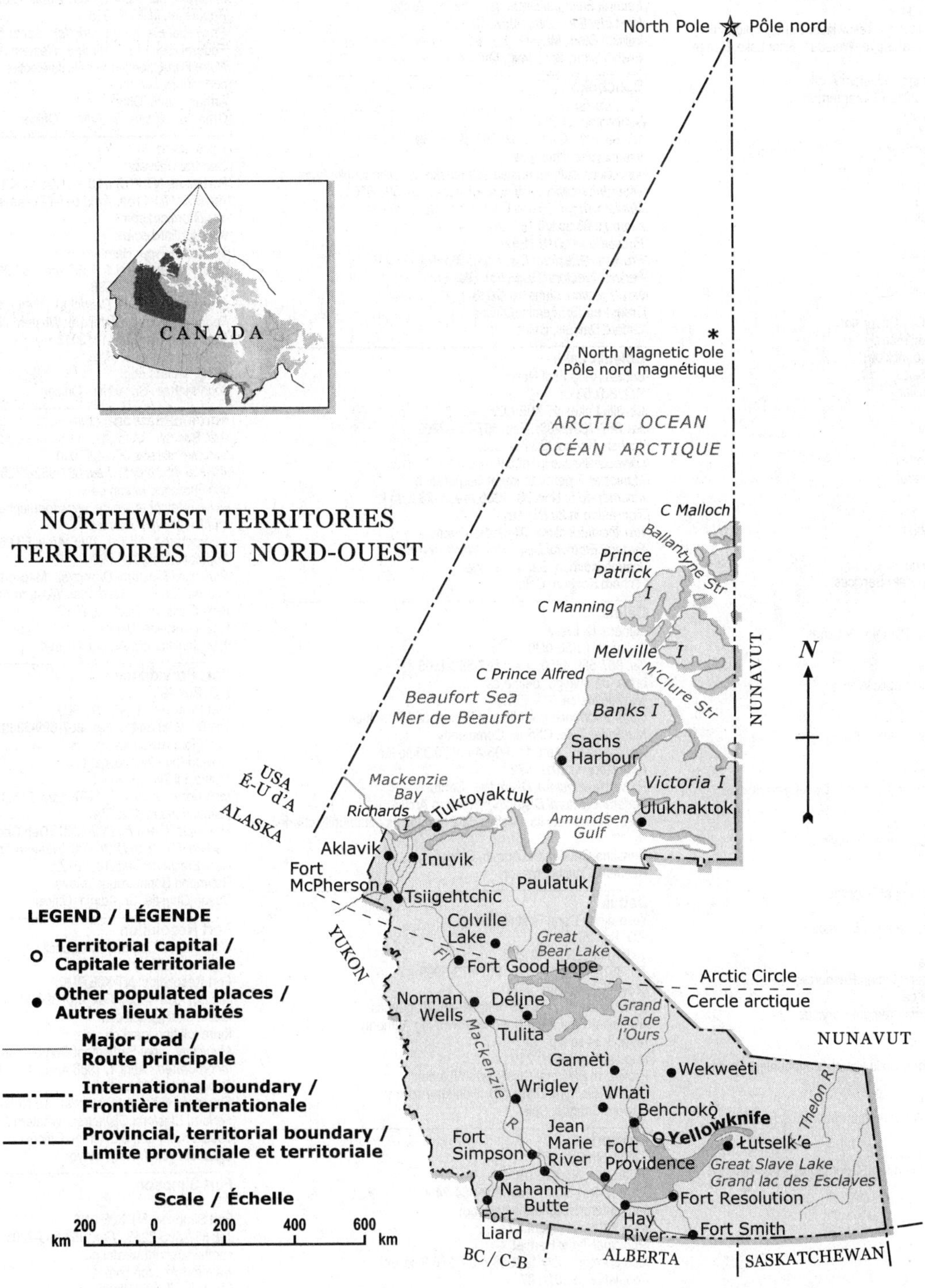

Northwest Territories

Major Municipalities in Northwest Territories

Yellowknife
P.O. Box 580
4807 - 52 St.
Yellowknife, NT X1A 2N4
Tel: 867-920-5600; *Fax:* 867-920-5649
cityclerk@yellowknife.ca
www.yellowknife.ca
Municipal Type: City
Incorporated: Jan. 1, 1970 *Area:* 105.22 sq km
Population in 2011: 19,234
Provincial Electoral District(s): Yellowknife South; Yellowknife Centre; Frame Lake; Great Slave; Weledeh; Kam Lake, Range Lake
Federal Electoral District(s): Western Arctic
Next Election: Oct. 15, 2012 (3 year terms)
Gordon Van Tighem, Mayor
gvantighem@yellowknife.ca
Lydia Bardak, City Councillor
lbardak@yellowknife.ca
Bob Brooks, City Councillor
bbrooks@yellowknife.ca
Paul Falvo, City Councillor
pfalvo@yellowknife.ca
Mark Heyck, City Councillor
mheyck@yellowknife.ca
Amanda Mallon, City Councillor
amallon@yellowknife.ca
Shelagh Montgomery, City Councillor
smontgomery@yellowknife.ca
Cory Vanthuyne, City Councillor
cvanthuyne@yellowknife.ca
David Wind, City Councillor
dwind@yellowknife.ca
Debbie Gillard, City Clerk
867-920-5646
debbie.gillard@yellowknife.ca
Max Hall, City Administrator
867-920-5624
mhall@yellowknife.ca
Darcy Hernblad, Fire Chief
867-766-5501
dhernblad@yellowknife.ca
Carl Bird, Director, Corporate Services
867-920-5666
cbird@yellowknife.ca
Jeffrey Humble, Director, Planning & Lands
867-920-5633
jhumble@yellowknife.ca
Dennis Kefalas, Director, Public Works
867-920-5639
dkefalas@yellowknife.ca
Dennis Marchiori, Director, Public Safety
867-920-5661
dmarchiori@yellowknife.ca
Peter Neugebauer, Director, Economic Development
867-920-5660
pneugebauer@yellowknife.ca
Grant White, Director, Community Services
867-920-5636
gwhite@yellowknife.ca
Kerry Penney, Manager, Legal Services
kpenney@yellowknife.ca
Nalini Naidoo, Manager, Planning & Lands
867-920-5675
nnaidoo@yellowknife.ca
Marie Couturier, Manager, Human Resources
mcouturier@yellowknife.ca
Clem Hand, Manager, Procurement Services
867-920-5617
chand@yellowknife.ca
Bruce Underhay, Manager, Solid Waste Management Facility
867-669-3404
bunderhay@yellowknife.ca
Sharolynn Woodward, Manager, Information Technology
867-920-5651
swoodward@yellowknife.ca
Dennis Althouse, Superintendent, Operations & Maintenance
867-766-5512
dalthouse@yellowknife.ca

Other Municipalities in Northwest Territories

Aklavik
P.O. Box 88
Aklavik, NT X0E 0A0
Tel: 867-978-2351; *Fax:* 867-978-2434
saoaklavik@permafrost.com
www.aklavik.ca
Other Information: Additional Phone: 867-978-2361
Municipal Type: Hamlet
Incorporated: Jan. 1, 1974 *Area:* 8.16 sq km
Population in 2011: 633
Provincial Electoral District(s): Mackenzie Delta
Federal Electoral District(s): Western Arctic
Next Election: Dec. 10, 2012
William Storr, Mayor
Evelyn Storr, Sr. Admin. Officer

Behchokò
P.O. Box 68
Behchokò, NT X0E 0Y0
Tel: 867-392-6500; *Fax:* 867-392-6139
finance@behchoko.ca
www.tlicho.ca/communities/behchoko, www.behchoko.lgant.ca
Other Information: Additional Phone: 867-392-6561
Municipal Type: Tlicho Community Government
Area: 75.08 sq km
Population in 2011: 1,926
Provincial Electoral District(s): Monfwi
Federal Electoral District(s): Western Arctic
Next Election: June 10, 2013
Craig Yeo, Sr. Admin. Officer
Clifford Daniels, Chief

Colville Lake
Behdzi Ahda First Nation
P.O. Box 53
Colville Lake, NT X0E 0L0
Tel: 867-709-2200; *Fax:* 867-709-2202
Joseph_Kochon@airware.ca
www.colvillelake.lgant.ca
Municipal Type: Settlement Corporation
Incorporated: Nov. 30, 1995 *Area:* 128.3 sq km
Population in 2011: 149
Provincial Electoral District(s): Sahtu
Federal Electoral District(s): Western Arctic
Joseph Kochon, Band Manager
Richard Kochon, Chief

Déline
General Delivery
Deline, NT X0E 0G0
Tel: 867-589-4800; *Fax:* 867-589-4106
erma_baton@gov.deline.ca
www.deline.ca
Other Information: Additional Phone: 867-589-3604
Municipal Type: Charter Community
Incorporated: April 1, 1993 *Area:* 79.33 sq km
Population in 2011: 472
Provincial Electoral District(s): Sahtu
Federal Electoral District(s): Western Arctic
Note: Déline sets its election date through its community charter.

Christina Gaudet, Sr. Admin. Officer
Raymond Tutcho, Mayor

Dettah
Yellowknife Dene First Nation
P.O. Box 2514
Yellowknife, NT X1A 2P8
Tel: 867-873-4307; *Fax:* 867-873-5969
ceo@ykdene.com
www.ykdene.com, www.dettahandndilo.lgant.ca
Municipal Type: First Nations/Governing Authority
Area: 1.34 sq km
Population in 2011: 210
Provincial Electoral District(s): Weledeh
Federal Electoral District(s): Western Arctic
Edward Sangris, Chief

Enterprise
526 Robin Rd.
Enterprise, NT X0E 0R1
Tel: 867-984-3491; *Fax:* 867-984-3400
sao_enterprise@northwestel.net
www.enterprise.lgant.ca
Municipal Type: Hamlet
Incorporated: July 1, 1988 *Area:* 286.9 sq km
Population in 2011: 87
Provincial Electoral District(s): Deh Cho
Federal Electoral District(s): Western Arctic
Next Election: Dec. 10, 2012
Allan Flamand, Mayor
Peter Groenen, Sr. Admin Officer

Fort Good Hope
K'asho Got'ine Charter Community
P.O. Box 80
Fort Good Hope, NT X0E 0H0
Tel: 867-598-2231; *Fax:* 867-598-2024
greglaboucan@hotmail.com
www.fortgoodhope.lgant.ca
Other Information: Additional Phone: 867-598-2232
Municipal Type: Charter Community
Incorporated: April 1, 1995 *Area:* 52.82 sq km
Population in 2011: 515
Provincial Electoral District(s): Sahtu
Federal Electoral District(s): Western Arctic
Note: Fort Good Hope sets its election date through its community charter.
Arthur Tobac, Chief
Greg Labourcan, Sr. Admin. Officer

Fort Liard
General Delivery
Fort Liard, NT X0G 0A0
Tel: 867-770-4104; *Fax:* 867-770-4004
sao@fortliard.com
www.fortliard.com
Municipal Type: Hamlet
Incorporated: April 1, 1987 *Area:* 67.96 sq km
Population in 2011: 536
Provincial Electoral District(s): Nahendeh
Federal Electoral District(s): Western Arctic
Next Election: Dec. 10, 2012
Julie Capot-Blanc, Mayor
myr@fortliard.com
John McKee, Sr. Admin. Officer

Fort McPherson
P.O. Box 57
Fort McPherson, NT X0E 0J0
Tel: 867-952-2428; *Fax:* 867-952-2725
sao@fortmcpherson.ca
www.fortmcpherson.ca, www.fortmcpherson.lgant.ca
Municipal Type: Hamlet
Incorporated: Nov. 1, 1986 *Area:* 53.06 sq km
Population in 2011: 792
Provincial Electoral District(s): Mackenzie Delta
Federal Electoral District(s): Western Arctic
Next Election: Dec. 10, 2012
Hazel Nerysoo, Mayor
Troy Jenkins, Sr. Admin. Officer

Fort Providence
P.O. Box 290
Fort Providence, NT X0E 0L0
Tel: 867-699-3441; *Fax:* 867-699-3360
sao@fortprovidence.ca
www.fortprovidence.lgant.ca
Municipal Type: Hamlet
Incorporated: Jan. 1, 1987 *Area:* 256.33 sq km
Population in 2011: 734
Provincial Electoral District(s): Deh Cho
Federal Electoral District(s): Western Arctic
Next Election: Dec. 10, 2012
Raymond Bonnetrouge, Mayor
Susan Christie, Sr. Admin. Officer

Fort Resolution
c/o Deninoo Community Council
General Delivery
Fort Resolution, NT X0E 0M0
Tel: 867-394-4556; *Fax:* 867-394-5415
tausia.sao@gmail.com
fortresolution.lgant.ca
Municipal Type: Settlement Corporation
Incorporated: April 1, 1988 *Area:* 455.06 sq km
Population in 2011: 474
Provincial Electoral District(s): Tu Nedhe
Federal Electoral District(s): Western Arctic
Tausia Kaitu-Lal, Sr. Admin. Officer
Elizabeth Ann Mckay, Mayor

Fort Simpson
P.O. Box 438
Fort Simpson, NT X0E 0N0
Tel: 867-695-2253; *Fax:* 867-695-2005
saoftsim@northwestel.net
www.fortsimpson.com
Municipal Type: Village
Incorporated: Jan. 1, 1973 *Area:* 78.32 sq km

Population in 2011: 1,238
Provincial Electoral District(s): Nahendeh
Federal Electoral District(s): Western Arctic
Next Election: Oct. 15, 2012 (3 year terms)
John Ivey, Senior Administrative Officer
Sean Whelly, Mayor
mayor@fortsimpson.com

Fort Smith
P.O. Box 147
174 McDougal Rd.
Fort Smith, NT X0E 0P0
Tel: 867-872-8400; *Fax:* 867-872-8401
bblack@fortsmith.ca
www.fortsmith.ca
Municipal Type: Town
Incorporated: Oct. 1, 1966 *Area:* 92.79 sq km
Population in 2011: 2,093
Provincial Electoral District(s): Thebacha
Federal Electoral District(s): Western Arctic
Next Election: Oct. 15, 2012 (3 year terms)
Jane Hobart, Mayor
Brenda Black, Sr. Admin. Officer

Gamèti
Gameti First Nation
P.O. Box 1
Gameti, NT X0E 1R0
Tel: 867-997-3441; *Fax:* 867-997-3411
sao@gameti.org
www.tlicho.ca/communities/gameti, www.gameti.lgant.ca
Municipal Type: Tlicho Community Government
Incorporated: Aug. 4, 2005 *Area:* 9.18 sq km
Population in 2011: 253
Provincial Electoral District(s): Monfwi
Federal Electoral District(s): Western Arctic
Next Election: June 10, 2013
Eddie Chocolate, Chief
Gregory Morash, Sr. Admin. Officer

Hay River
73 Woodland Dr.
Hay River, NT X0E 1G1
Tel: 867-874-6522; *Fax:* 867-874-3237
molenkamp@hayriver.com
www.hayriver.com
Municipal Type: Town
Incorporated: June 16, 1963 *Area:* 132.58 sq km
Population in 2011: 3,606
Provincial Electoral District(s): Hay River North; Hay River South
Federal Electoral District(s): Western Arctic
Next Election: Oct. 15, 2012 (3 year terms)
Kelly Schofield, Mayor
Terry Molenkemp, Sr. Admin Officer
molenkamp@hayriver.com

Hay River Reserve - K'atlodeeche First Nation
Katlodeechee First Nation
P.O. Box 3060
Hay River, NT X0E 1G0
Tel: 867-874-6701; *Fax:* 867-874-3229
kfnceo@katlodeeche.com
www.hayriverreserve.lgant.ca
Municipal Type: Reserve
Area: 134.21 sq km
Population in 2011: 292
Provincial Electoral District(s): Deh Cho
Federal Electoral District(s): Western Arctic
Roy Fabien, Chief
Scotty Edgerton, Band Manager

Inuvik
P.O. Box 1160
2 Firth St.
Inuvik, NT X0E 0T0
Tel: 867-777-8600; *Fax:* 867-777-8601
sao@town.inuvik.nt.ca
www.inuvik.ca
Municipal Type: Town
Incorporated: Jan. 1, 1979 *Area:* 49.76 sq km
Population in 2011: 3,463
Provincial Electoral District(s): Inuvik Twin Lakes; Inuvik Boot Lake
Federal Electoral District(s): Western Arctic
Next Election: Oct. 15, 2012 (3 year terms)
Denny Rodgers, Mayor
dlindsay@town.inuvik.nt.ca
Grant Hood, Sr. Admin. Officer

Jean Marie River
TthedzedK'edili First Nation
General Delivery
Fort Simpson, NT X0E 0N0
Tel: 867-809-2000; *Fax:* 867-809-2002
sao@jmrfn.ca
www.jmrfn.ca, www.jeanmarieriver.lgant.ca
Municipal Type: First Nations/Governing Authority
Area: 37.26 sq km
Population in 2011: 64
Provincial Electoral District(s): Nahendeh
Federal Electoral District(s): Western Arctic
Stanley Sanguez, Chief
Tammy Neal, Band Manager

Kakisa
Ka'a'gee Tu First Nation
P.O. Box 4428
Hay River, NT X0E 1G4
Tel: 867-825-2000; *Fax:* 867-825-2002
R_landry@airware.ca
www.kakisa.lgant.ca
Municipal Type: First Nations/Governing Authority
Area: 94.82 sq km
Population in 2011: 45
Provincial Electoral District(s): Deh Cho
Federal Electoral District(s): Western Arctic
Lloyd Chicot, Chief
Ruby Landry, Council Manager

Lutsel K'e
Lutsel K'e Dene Band
P.O. Box 28
Lutselk'e, NT X0E 1A0
Tel: 867-370-7000; *Fax:* 867-370-3010
cyberia@mts.net
www.lutselke.lgant.ca
Municipal Type: First Nations/Governing Authority
Area: 43.01 sq km
Population in 2011: 295
Provincial Electoral District(s): Tu Nedhe
Federal Electoral District(s): Western Arctic
Antoine Michel, Chief
Ray Griffith, Sr. Admin. Officer & Band Manager

Nahanni Butte
Nahanni Butte First Nation
General Delivery
Fort Simpson, NT X0E 0N0
Tel: 867-602-2900; *Fax:* 867-602-2910
manager@nahadeh.org
nahannibutte.lgant.ca
Municipal Type: First Nations/Governing Authority
Area: 78.96 sq km
Population in 2011: 102
Provincial Electoral District(s): Nahendeh
Federal Electoral District(s): Western Arctic
Fred Tesou, Chief

Norman Wells
P.O. Box 5
Norman Wells, NT X0E 0V0
Tel: 867-587-3700; *Fax:* 867-587-3701
townmgr@normanwells.com
www.normanwells.com
Municipal Type: Town
Incorporated: April 12, 1992 *Area:* 93.28 sq km
Population in 2011: 727
Provincial Electoral District(s): Sahtu
Federal Electoral District(s): Western Arctic
Next Election: Oct. 15, 2012 (3 year terms)
Dudley C. Johnson, Mayor
Ian Fremantle, Town Manager
townmgr@normanwells.com

Paulatuk
P.O. Box 98
Paulatuk, NT X0E 1N0
Tel: 867-580-3531; *Fax:* 867-580-3703
hopaulatuk@hotmail.com
www.paulatuk.lgant.ca
Municipal Type: Hamlet
Incorporated: April 1, 1987 *Area:* 66.76 sq km
Population in 2011: 313
Provincial Electoral District(s): Nunakput
Federal Electoral District(s): Western Arctic
Next Election: Dec. 10, 2012
Ray Ruben, Mayor
Debbie Gordon-Ruben, Sr. Admin. Officer

Sachs Harbour
General Delivery
P.O. Box 90
Sachs Harbour, NT X0E 0Z0
Tel: 867-690-4351; *Fax:* 867-690-4802
hamlet_sachs@airware.ca
sachsharbour.lgant.ca
Municipal Type: Hamlet
Incorporated: April 1, 1986 *Area:* 290.94 sq km
Population in 2011: 112
Provincial Electoral District(s): Nunakput
Federal Electoral District(s): Western Arctic
Next Election: Dec. 10, 2012
Priscilla Haogak, Mayor
Jackie Coultier, Sr. Admin. Officer

Trout Lake
Sambaa K'e Dene Band
P.O. Box 10
Trout Lake, NT X0E 1Z0
Tel: 867-206-2800; *Fax:* 867-206-2828
manager@sambaake.org
troutlake.lgant.ca
Municipal Type: First Nations/Governing Authority
Area: 119.42 sq km
Population in 2011: 92
Provincial Electoral District(s): Nahendeh
Federal Electoral District(s): Western Arctic
Dolphus Jumbo, Chief
Ruby Jumbo, Sr. Admin. Officer

Tsiigehtchic
General Delivery
Tsiigehtchic, NT X0E 0B0
Tel: 867-953-3201; *Fax:* 867-953-3302
sao@tsiigehtchic.ca
www.tsiigehtchic.lgant.ca
Municipal Type: Charter Community
Incorporated: June 21, 1993 *Area:* 48.98 sq km
Population in 2011: 143
Provincial Electoral District(s): Mackenzie Delta
Federal Electoral District(s): Western Arctic
Note: Tsiigehtchic sets its election date through its community charter.
Frederick Blake, Chief
Carolyn Lennie, Sr. Admin. Officer

Tuktoyaktuk
P.O. Box 120
Tuktoyaktuk, NT X0E 1C0
Tel: 867-977-2286; *Fax:* 867-977-2110
tuksao@netkaster.ca
www.tuktoyaktuk.lgant.ca
Municipal Type: Hamlet
Incorporated: April 1, 1970 *Area:* 11.07 sq km
Population in 2011: 854
Provincial Electoral District(s): Nunakput
Federal Electoral District(s): Western Arctic
Next Election: Dec. 10, 2012
Mervin Gruben, Mayor
Tom Matus, Sr. Admin. Officer

Tulita
General Delivery
P.O. Box 91
Tulita, NT X0E 0K0
Tel: 867-588-4471; *Fax:* 867-588-4908
sao@hamletoftulita.ca
www.tulita.lgant.ca
Other Information: Alt 867-588-4351
Municipal Type: Hamlet
Incorporated: April 1, 1984 *Area:* 51.74 sq km
Population in 2011: 478
Provincial Electoral District(s): Sahtu
Federal Electoral District(s): Western Arctic
Next Election: Dec. 10, 2012
Danny Yakeleya, Mayor
Brad Carlson, Sr. Admin. Officer

Ulukhaktok
P.O. Box 157
Ulukhaktok, NT X0E 0S0
Tel: 867-396-8000; *Fax:* 867-396-8001
ulukhaktok_sao@airware.ca
www.ulukhaktok.lgant.ca
Municipal Type: Hamlet
Incorporated: April 1, 1984 *Area:* 124.43 sq km
Population in 2011: 402
Provincial Electoral District(s): Nunakput
Federal Electoral District(s): Western Arctic
Next Election: Dec. 10, 2012
Note: Formerly known as Holman.

Janet Kanayok, Mayor
Lena Egotak, Sr. Admin. Officer

Wekweeti

Community Government of Wekweeti
P.O. Box 69
Wekweeti, NT X1A 1W0
Tel: 867-713-2010; *Fax:* 867-713-2030
saowekweti@netkaster.ca
www.tlicho.ca/communities/wekweeti, www.weweeti.lgant.ca
Municipal Type: Tlicho Community Government
Incorporated: Aug. 4, 2005 *Area:* 14.66 sq km
Population in 2011: 141
Provincial Electoral District(s): Monfwi
Federal Electoral District(s): Western Arctic
Next Election: June 10, 2013
Charlie Football, Chief
Grace Angel, Sr. Admin. Officer

Whatì

Community Government of Whati
P.O. Box 71
Whatì, NT X0E 1P0
Tel: 867-573-3401; *Fax:* 867-573-3018
sao@whati.ca
www.tlicho.ca/communities/whati, www.whati.lgant.ca
Municipal Type: Tlicho Community Government
Incorporated: Aug. 4, 2005 *Area:* 15.18 sq km
Population in 2011: 492
Provincial Electoral District(s): Monfwi
Federal Electoral District(s): Western Arctic
Next Election: June 10, 2013
Alfonz Nitsiza, Chief
Grant Scott, Sr. Admin. Officer

Wrigley

Pehdzeh Ki First Nation
General Delivery
Wrigley, NT X0E 1E0
Tel: 867-581-3321; *Fax:* 867-581-3329
bandmanager@pehdzehki.ca
www.whati.lgant.ca
Other Information: Additional Phone: 867-581-3581
Municipal Type: First Nations/Governing Authority
Area: 55.83 sq km
Population in 2011: 133
Provincial Electoral District(s): Nahendeh
Federal Electoral District(s): Western Arctic
Tim Lennie, Chief

NOVA SCOTIA

Nova Scotia is geographically divided into 18 counties. Twelve of these constitute separate municipalities (three are regional municipalities). The remaining six are each divided into two districts and each of these constitutes a separate municipality. Thus there are 21 rural municipalities. Within each of these areas are 31 autonomous incorporated towns and other local organizations with limited jurisdiction, including school boards, boards of school trustees, village commissions, local service commissions, rural fire districts and other special purpose forms.

Incorporation of a town is governed by the Municipal Government Act, Sections 383 to 393 (dissolution is governed by Sections 394 to 402).

The organization of municipalities and villages is governed by the Municipal Government Act. Additional regulation is provided by the Municipal Finance Corporation Act.

All general and special municipal elections, including elections for school board members, are governed by the Municipal Elections Act, 1979. The term of office for mayors, councillors, aldermen, and elective school board members is four years. Elections take place on the third Saturday in October in every fourth year (October 2012, 2016, etc.).

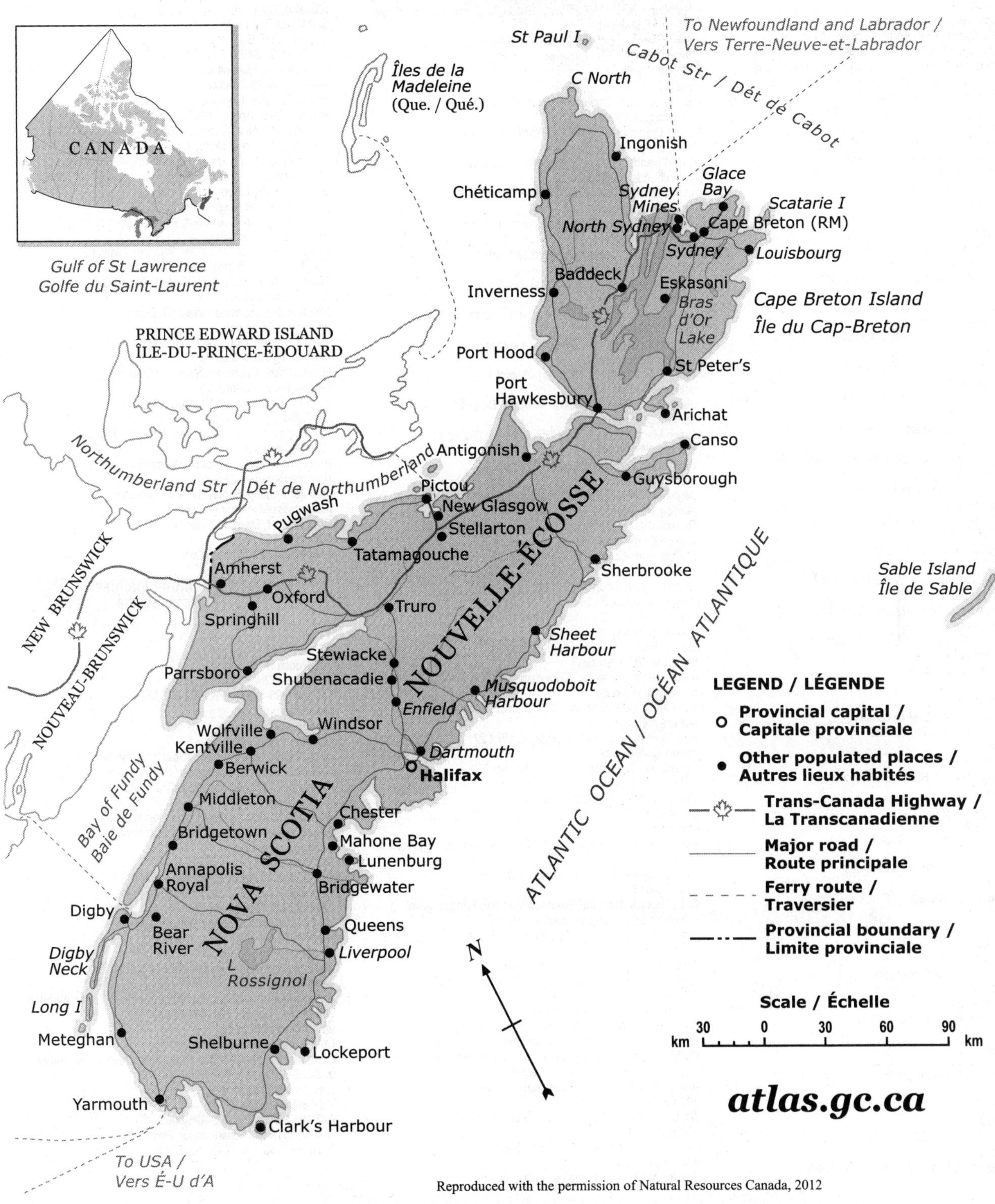

Reproduced with the permission of Natural Resources Canada, 2012

Nova Scotia

Counties & Municipal Districts in Nova Scotia

Cape Breton
Civic Centre
320 Esplanade
Sydney, NS B1P 7B9
Tel: 902-563-5005; *Fax:* 902-564-0481
cbrm@cbrm.ns.ca
www.cbrm.ns.ca
Municipal Type: Regional Municipality
Incorporated: Aug. 1, 1995 *Area:* 2,433.33 sq km
County or District: Cape Breton; *Population in 2011:* 97,398
Provincial Electoral District(s): Cape Breton Centre; Cape Breton East; Cape Breton North; Cape Breton Nova; Cape Breton South; Cape Breton-The Lakes
Federal Electoral District(s): Cape Breton-Canso; Sydney-Victoria
Next Election: Oct. 20, 2012 (4 year terms)
John W. Morgan, Mayor, Fax: 902-563-5585
jwmorgan@cbrm.ns.ca
Brian Lahey, Councillor, Ward(s): District 1
blahey@cbrm.ns.ca
Kevin Saccary, Councillor, Ward(s): District 2
ksaccary@cbrm.ns.ca
Lee McNeil, Councillor, Ward(s): District 3
lmcneil@cbrm.ns.ca
George MacDonald, Councillor, Ward(s): District 4
gmmacdonald@cbrm.ns.ca
Darren Bruckschwaiger, Councillor, Ward(s): District 5
drbruckschwaiger@cbrm.ns.ca
Kim Desveaux, Councillor, Ward(s): District 6
kadesveaux@cbrm.ns.ca
Jim MacLeod, Councillor, Ward(s): District 7
jmacleod@cbrm.ns.ca
Ray Paruch, Councillor, Ward(s): District 8
frparuch@cbrm.ns.ca
Tom Wilson, Councillor, Ward(s): District 9
twilson@cbrm.ns.ca
Derek Mombourquette, Councillor, Ward(s): District 10
dcmombourquette@cbrm.ns.ca
Dave LeBlanc, Councillor, Ward(s): District 11
dfleblanc@cbrm.ns.ca
Claire Detheridge, Councillor, Ward(s): District 12
mcdetheridge@cbrm.ns.ca
Mae Rowe, Councillor, Ward(s): District 13
mjrowe@cbrm.ns.ca
Gordon MacLeod, Councillor, Ward(s): District 14
gmacleod@cbrm.ns.ca
Clarence Prince, Councillor, Ward(s): District 15
cprince@cbrm.ns.ca
Wesley Stubbert, Councillor, Ward(s): District 16
wstubbert@cbrm.ns.ca
Bernie White, Municipal Clerk
902-563-5010
bjwhite@cbrm.ns.ca
Jerry Ryan, Chief Administrative Officer
Robin B. Campbell, Regional Solicitor
902-563-5045
rbcampbell@cbrm.ns.ca
Angus Fleming, Director, Human Resources
902-563-5058
acfleming@cbrm.ns.ca
Doug Foster, Director, Planning
902-563-5070
dbfoster@cbrm.ns.ca
Bernie MacKinnon, Director, Fire Services
902-563-5132
Edgar MacLeod, Police Chief
902-563-5095
eamacleod@cbrmps.cape-breton.ns.ca
Marie Walsh, Director, Finance
902-563-5014
Fred Brooks, Sr. Manager, Recreation
902-563-5510
ftbrooks@cbrm.ns.ca
Francis Campbell, Manager, Solid Waste
902-563-5182
solidwaste@cbrm.ns.ca

Halifax Regional Municipality
P.O. Box 1749
1841 Argyle St.
Halifax, NS B3J 3A5
Tel: 902-490-4000; *Fax:* 902-490-4208
www.halifax.ca
Other Information: Toll Free Phone: 1-800-835-6428
Municipal Type: Regional Municipality
Incorporated: April 1, 1996 *Area:* 5,490.18 sq km
Population in 2011: 390,096
Provincial Electoral District(s): Bedford-Birch Cove; Cole Harbour; Cole Harbour-Eastern Passage; Dartmouth E.; Dartmouth N.; Dartmouth S.-Portland Valley; Eastern Shore; Hlfx Atlantic; Hlfx Chebucto; Hlfx Citadel-Sable Island; Hlfx-Clayton Park; Hlfx Fairview; Hlfx Needham; Hammonds Plains-Upper Sackville; Preston; Sackville-Cobequid; Timberlea-Prospect; Waverly-Fall River-Beaver Bank
Federal Electoral District(s): Central Nova; Cumberland-Colchester-Musquodoboit Valley; Dartmouth-Cole Harbour; Halifax; Halifax West; Sackville-Eastern Shore; South Shore-St. Margaret's
Next Election: Oct. 20, 2012 (4 year terms)
Peter J. Kelly, M.B.A., Mayor
902-490-4010
kellyp@halifax.ca
Steve Streatch, Councillor, Ward(s): District 1
streats@halifax.ca
Barry Dalrymple, Councillor, Ward(s): District 2
barry.dalrymple@halifax.ca
David Hendsbee, Councillor, Ward(s): District 3
david.hendsbee@halifax.ca
Lorelei Nicoll, Councillor, Ward(s): District 4
lorelei.nicoll@halifax.ca
Gloria McCluskey, Councillor, Ward(s): District 5
mcclusg@halifax.ca
Darren Fisher, Councillor, Ward(s): District 6
darren.fisher@halifax.ca
Bill Karsten, Councillor, Ward(s): District 7
karsteb@halifax.ca
Jackie Barkhouse, Councillor, Ward(s): District 8
barkhoj@halifax.ca
Jim Smith, Councillor, Ward(s): District 9
smithj@halifax.ca
Mary Wile, Councillor, Ward(s): District 10
wilema@halifax.ca
Jerry Blumenthal, Councillor, Ward(s): District 11
blumenj@halifax.ca
Dawn Marie Sloane, Councillor, Ward(s): District 12
sloaned@halifax.ca
Sue Uteck, Councillor, Ward(s): District 13
utecks@halifax.ca
Jennifer Watts, Councillor, Ward(s): District 14
jennifer.watts@halifax.ca
Russell Walker, Councillor, Ward(s): District 15
walkerr@halifax.ca
Debbie Hum, Councillor, Ward(s): District 16
humd@halifax.ca
Linda Mosher, Councillor, Ward(s): District 17
mosherl@halifax.ca
Stephen Adams, Councillor, Ward(s): District 18
adamss@halifax.ca
Brad Johns, Councillor, Ward(s): District 19
brad.johns@halifax.ca
Robert (Bob) P. Harvey, Councillor, Ward(s): District 20
harveyb@halifax.ca
Tim Outhit, Councillor, Ward(s): District 21
outhitt@halifax.ca
Reg Rankin, Councillor, Ward(s): District 22
rankinr@halifax.ca
Peter Lund, Councillor, Ward(s): District 23
peter.lund@halifax.ca
Cathy Mellett, Acting Municipal Clerk
902-490-4210
clerks@halifax.ca
Larry Munroe, Municipal Auditor General, Business Systems & Control
Richard Butts, Chief Administrative Officer
902-490-6430
Brad Anguish, Director, Business Planning & Information Management & Harbour Solutions Project
Frank Beazley, Chief, Halifax Regional Police
902-490-6500
James Cooke, C.G.A., Director, Finance
Mary Ellen Donovan, B.Sc., LL.B., Director, Legal Services
902-490-4226
Bill Mosher, Chief Director, Fire & Emergency Services
Catherine Mullally, Director, Human Resources
Ken Reashor, Director, Transportation & Public Works
Phillip Townsend, Director, Infrastructure & Asset Management
Vacant, Director, Community Development
Alan Brady, Manager, Wastewater Treatment
302-835-9566
Jim Donovan, Project Manager, Economic Strategy
902-490-1742
Gord Helm, Manager, Solid Waste Resources
902-490-6606
Shaune MacKinlay, Manager, Public Affairs
John P. Sheppard, P.Eng., Manager, Environmental Engineering Services
902-490-6958, Fax: 902-490-4858
sheppaj@halifax.ca
John Sibbald, Coordinator, Pollution Prevention
902-490-5527
sibbalj@halifax.ca
Carl Yates, Manager, Halifax Water
902-490-4827, Fax: 902-490-4808
general.manager@hrwc.ca

Queens
P.O. Box 1264
249 White Point Rd.
Liverpool, NS B0T 1K0
Tel: 902-354-3453; *Fax:* 902-354-7473
info@regionofqueens.com
www.regionofqueens.com
Municipal Type: Regional Municipality
Incorporated: April 1, 1996 *Area:* 2,386.58 sq km
County or District: Queens; *Population in 2011:* 10,917
Provincial Electoral District(s): Queens
Federal Electoral District(s): South Shore-St. Margaret's
Next Election: Oct. 20, 2012 (4 year terms)
John G. Leefe, Mayor
jleefe@regionofqueens.com
Darlene Norman, Councillor, Ward(s): District 1
ross.surf@ns.sympatico.ca
Sheldon Brannen, Councillor, Ward(s): District 2
sheldonbrannen@gmail.com
Owen Hamlin, Councillor, Ward(s): District 3
mrh@ns.sympatico.ca
Bruce Inglis, Councillor, Ward(s): District 4
bruceinglis@live.ca
Mervin Hartlen, Councillor, Ward(s): District 5
m.hartlen@eastlink.ca
Randi Dickie, Councillor, Ward(s): District 6
randidickie@eastlink.ca
John Croft, Councillor, Ward(s): District 7
jfcroft@ns.sympatico.ca
R. Douglas Adams, Councillor, Ward(s): District 8
radams@eastlink.ca
Peter Waterman, Councillor, Ward(s): District 9
pmwaterman@eastlink.ca
Jennifer Keating-Hubley, Director, Finance
jkeating@regionofqueens.com
Brad Rowter, Director, Finance
902-354-3455
browter@regionofqueens.com

Major Municipalities in Nova Scotia

Truro
P.O. Box 427
695 Prince St.
Truro, NS B2N 5C5
Tel: 902-895-4484; *Fax:* 902-893-0501
town@truro.ca
www.truro.ca
Municipal Type: City
Incorporated: May 6, 1875 *Area:* 37.63 sq km
County or District: Colchester; *Population in 2011:* 12,059
Provincial Electoral District(s): Truro-Bible Hill
Federal Electoral District(s): Cumberland-Colchester-Musquodoboit Valley
Next Election: Oct. 20, 2012 (4 year terms)
W.R. (Bill) Mills, Mayor
902-893-2438
Diane Bennett Cook, Councillor, Ward(s): 1
Raymond Tynes, Councillor, Ward(s): 1
Charles Cox, Councillor, Ward(s): 2
Brian Kinsman, Councillor, Ward(s): 2
Sharron Byers, Councillor, Ward(s): 3
Greg MacArthur, Councillor, Ward(s): 3
Jim Langille, Chief Administrative Officer
jlangille@truro.ca
Andrew McKinnon, Director, Public Works & Traffic Authority
902-895-4243, Fax: 902-893-6091
amackinnon@truro.ca
Chuck Roberts, Senior Engineer
Doug MacKenzie, Director, Parks & Recreation Committee
902-893-6078, Fax: 902-893-6099
dmackenzie@truro.ca
Tom Bremner, Chief, Fire
902-895-8645, Fax: 902-895-8063
Juanita Bigelow, Administrator, Planning
902-895-1148, Fax: 902-893-6091

Other Municipalities in Nova Scotia

Amherst
P.O. Box 516
5 Ratchford St.
Amherst, NS B4H 4A1
Tel: 902-667-3352; *Fax:* 902-667-3356
www.town.amherst.ns.ca
Municipal Type: Town
Incorporated: Dec. 18, 1889 *Area:* 12.02 sq km
County or District: Cumberland; *Population in 2011:* 9,717
Provincial Electoral District(s): Cumberland North
Federal Electoral District(s):
Cumberland-Colchester-Musquodoboit Valley
Next Election: Oct. 20, 2012 (4 year terms)
Gregory D. Herrett, CA, Chief Administrative Officer
902-667-6513, Fax: 902-667-2090
gherrett@town.amherst.ns.ca
Rebecca Purdy, Mayor
902-667-6510
rpurdy@amherst.ca

Annapolis Royal
P.O. Box 310
285 St. George St.
Annapolis Royal, NS B0S 1A0
Tel: 902-532-2043; *Fax:* 902-532-7443
admin@annapolisroyal.com
www.annapolisroyal.com
Municipal Type: Town
Incorporated: Nov. 29, 1892 *Area:* 2.04 sq km
County or District: Annapolis; *Population in 2011:* 481
Provincial Electoral District(s): Annapolis
Federal Electoral District(s): West Nova
Next Election: Oct. 20, 2012 (4 year terms)
Phil Roberts, Mayor
Amery Boyer, Chief Administrative Officer
cao@annapolisroyal.com

Antigonish
274 Main St.
Antigonish, NS B2G 2C4
Tel: 902-863-1312; *Fax:* 902-863-9201
www.townofantigonish.ca
Municipal Type: Town
Incorporated: Jan. 9, 1889 *Area:* 5.15 sq km
County or District: Antigonish; *Population in 2011:* 4,524
Provincial Electoral District(s): Antigonish
Federal Electoral District(s): Central Nova
Next Election: Oct. 20, 2012 (4 year terms)
Carl Chisholm, Mayor
T. Wadden, Chief Administrative Officer

Aylesford
P.O. Box 91
Aylesford, NS B0P 1C0
Tel: 902-847-0827; *Fax:* 902-847-0827
aylesfordvillage@eastlink.ca
Municipal Type: Village
County or District: Kings;
Provincial Electoral District(s): Kings West
Federal Electoral District(s): West Nova
Next Election: Oct. 20, 2012 (4 year terms)
Rhonda Carey, Chair
Trudie Spinney, Clerk-Treasurer

Baddeck
P.O. Box 63
Baddeck, NS B0E 1B0
Tel: 902-295-3666; *Fax:* 902-295-1729
webmasters@vccaps.com
www.baddeck.com
Municipal Type: Village
Area: 2.08 sq km
County or District: Victoria; *Population in 2011:* 769
Provincial Electoral District(s): Victoria-The Lakes
Federal Electoral District(s): Sydney-Victoria
Next Election: Oct. 20, 2012 (4 year terms)
Eddie Keeling, Chair
Erin Bradley, Clerk-Treasurer

Berwick
P.O. Box 130
236 Commercial St.
Berwick, NS B0P 1E0
Tel: 902-538-8068; *Fax:* 902-538-3724
general@town.berwick.ns.ca
www.town.berwick.ns.ca
Municipal Type: Town
Incorporated: May 25, 1923 *Area:* 6.8 sq km
County or District: Kings; *Population in 2011:* 2,454
Provincial Electoral District(s): Kings West
Federal Electoral District(s): West Nova
Next Election: Oct. 20, 2012 (4 year terms)
John P. Prall, Mayor
902-583-4008
mayor@town.berwick.ns.ca
Bob Ashley, Chief Administrative Officer
902-583-4007
bashley.berwick@gmail.com

Bible Hill
67 Pictou Rd.
Bible Hill, NS B2N 2R9
Tel: 902-893-8083; *Fax:* 902-897-0430
office@biblehill.ca
www.biblehill.ca
Municipal Type: Village
County or District: Colchester; *Population in 2011:* 5,500
Provincial Electoral District(s): Truro-Bible Hill
Federal Electoral District(s):
Cumberland-Colchester-Musquodoboit Valley
Next Election: Oct. 20, 2012 (4 year terms)
Robert Christianson, Clerk-Treas.
chris@biblehill.ca
Tom Burke, Chair

Bridgetown
P.O. Box 609
271 Granville St.
Bridgetown, NS B0S 1C0
Tel: 902-665-4637; *Fax:* 902-665-5011
bridgetown@ns.sympatico.ca
www.town.bridgetown.ns.ca
Municipal Type: Town
Incorporated: Sept. 15, 1897 *Area:* 3.54 sq km
County or District: Annapolis; *Population in 2011:* 949
Provincial Electoral District(s): Annapolis
Federal Electoral District(s): West Nova
Next Election: Oct. 20, 2012 (4 year terms)
Darrell Hiltz, Chief Administrative Officer
Robert Fowler, Mayor

Bridgewater
60 Pleasant St.
Bridgewater, NS B4V 3X9
Tel: 902-543-4651; *Fax:* 902-543-6876
admin@town.bridgewater.ns.ca
www.town.bridgewater.ns.ca
Municipal Type: Town
Incorporated: Feb. 13, 1899 *Area:* 13.6 sq km
County or District: Lunenburg; *Population in 2011:* 8,241
Provincial Electoral District(s): Lunenburg West
Federal Electoral District(s): South Shore-St. Margaret's
Next Election: Oct. 20, 2012 (4 year terms)
Carroll Publicover, Mayor
Ken Smith, Town Manager

Canning
P.O. Box 9
2229 North Ave.
Canning, NS B0P 1H0
Tel: 902-582-3768; *Fax:* 902-582-3068
village.canning@xcountry.tv
www.canningnovascotia.ca
Municipal Type: Village
County or District: Kings;
Provincial Electoral District(s): Kings North
Federal Electoral District(s): Kings-Hants
Next Election: Oct. 20, 2012 (4 year terms)
Kim MacQuarrie, Chair
kpphalen@hotmail.com
Gloria Porter, Clerk-Treasurer

Canso
P.O. Box 189
11 Telegraph St.
Canso, NS B0H 1H0
Tel: 902-366-2525; *Fax:* 902-366-3093
michelle@townofcanso.com
www.townofcanso.com
Municipal Type: Town
Incorporated: May 14, 1901 *Area:* 5.42 sq km
County or District: Guysborough; *Population in 2011:* 806
Provincial Electoral District(s): Guysborough-Sheet Harbour
Federal Electoral District(s): Cape Breton-Canso
Next Election: Oct. 20, 2012 (4 year terms)
Frank Fraser, Mayor
mayor@townofcanso.com
Michelle Hart, Town Clerk-Treas.
mhart@townofcanso.com

Chester
P.O. Box 620
Chester, NS B0J 1J0
Tel: 902-275-4482; *Fax:* 902-275-2021
admin@chesterareans.ca
www.chesterareans.ca
Municipal Type: Village
County or District: Lunenburg;
Provincial Electoral District(s): Chester-St.Margaret's
Federal Electoral District(s): South Shore-St. Margaret's
Next Election: Oct. 20, 2012 (4 year terms)
Tony Howlett, Chair
Iris Tolliver, Clerk-Treas.

Clark's Harbour
P.O. Box 160
2648 Main St.
Clarks Harbour, NS B0W 1P0
Tel: 902-745-2390; *Fax:* 902-745-1772
www.clarksharbour.com
Municipal Type: Town
Incorporated: March 4, 1919 *Area:* 2.9 sq km
County or District: Shelburne; *Population in 2011:* 820
Provincial Electoral District(s): Shelburne
Federal Electoral District(s): South Shore-St. Margaret's
Next Election: Oct. 20, 2012 (4 year terms)
Leigh B. Stoddart, Mayor
leighstoddart@eastlink.ca
Brian Crowell, Clerk-Treasurer
briancrowell@eastlink.ca

Cornwallis Square
P.O. Box 129
1415 Country Home Rd., Cambridge
Waterville, NS B0P 1V0
Tel: 902-538-0325; *Fax:* 902-538-1683
Municipal Type: Village
County or District: Kings;
Provincial Electoral District(s): Kings North
Federal Electoral District(s): Kings-Hants
Next Election: Oct. 20, 2012 (4 year terms)
George Foote, Chair
Bill Farrell, Clerk-Treas.

Digby
P.O. Box 579
147 First Ave.
Digby, NS B0V 1A0
Tel: 902-245-4769; *Fax:* 902-245-2121
www.digby.ca
Municipal Type: Town
Incorporated: Feb. 28, 1890 *Area:* 3.14 sq km
County or District: Digby; *Population in 2011:* 2,152
Provincial Electoral District(s): Digby-Annapolis
Federal Electoral District(s): West Nova
Next Election: Oct. 20, 2012 (4 year terms)
Ben Cleveland, Mayor
Tom Ossinger, Chief Administrative Officer
eossinger@digby.ca

Freeport
P.O. Box 31
Freeport, NS B0V 1B0
Tel: 902-839-2144
Municipal Type: Village
County or District: Digby;
Provincial Electoral District(s): Digby-Annapolis
Federal Electoral District(s): West Nova
Next Election: Oct. 20, 2012 (4 year terms)
Peter Morehouse, Chair
Vacant, Clerk-Treasurer

Greenwood
P.O. Box 1068
904 Central Ave.
Greenwood, NS B0P 1N0
Tel: 902-765-8788; *Fax:* 902-765-4369
greenwoodns@eastlink.ca
www.greenwoodnovascotia.com
Municipal Type: Village
County or District: Kings;
Provincial Electoral District(s): Kings West
Federal Electoral District(s): West Nova
Next Election: Oct. 20, 2012 (4 year terms)
Note: As of 2011, Statistics Canada shows that the Designated Place known as Kingston - Greenwood has an area of 14.50 sq km, & a population of 6,595.
Don MacDonald, Chair
902-765-2894
Marian Elsworth, Clerk-Treasurer

Hantsport
P.O. Box 399
20 Main St.
Hantsport, NS B0P 1P0
Tel: 902-684-3211; *Fax:* 902-684-3227
www.hantsportnovascotia.com
Municipal Type: Town
Incorporated: April 1, 1895 *Area:* 2.13 sq km
County or District: Hants; *Population in 2011:* 1,159
Provincial Electoral District(s): Hants West
Federal Electoral District(s): Kings-Hants
Next Election: Oct. 20, 2012 (4 year terms)
Jeffrey Lawrence, Chief Administrative Officer
H. Wayne Folker, Mayor
mayor@hantsportnovascotia.com

Havre Boucher
1318 Cape Jack Rd.
Havre Boucher, NS B0P 1P0
Tel: 902-234-3088
www.havreboucher.com
Municipal Type: Village
County or District: Antigonish;
Provincial Electoral District(s): Antigonish
Federal Electoral District(s): Central Nova
Next Election: Oct. 20, 2012 (4 year terms)
Chuck Tibbo, Chair
Raymond Carpenter, Clerk

Hebbville
47 Catidian Pl., RR#4
Bridgewater, NS B4V 2W3
Tel: 902-543-5786; *Fax:* 902-543-7006
Municipal Type: Village
County or District: Lunenburg;
Provincial Electoral District(s): Lunenburg West
Federal Electoral District(s): South Shore-St. Margaret's
Next Election: Oct. 20, 2012 (4 year terms)
Glen Whitehouse, Chair
Vernon Cornish, Clerk-Treasurer

Kentville
354 Main St.
Kentville, NS B4N 1K6
Tel: 902-679-2500; *Fax:* 902-679-2375
info@town.kentville.ns.ca
www.town.kentville.ns.ca
Municipal Type: Town
Incorporated: May 1, 1886 *Area:* 17.35 sq km
County or District: Kings; *Population in 2011:* 6,094
Provincial Electoral District(s): Kings North
Federal Electoral District(s): Kings-Hants
Next Election: Oct. 20, 2012 (4 year terms)
David Corkum, Mayor
dcorkum@kentville.ca
Keith Robichaud, Chief Administrative Officer
cao@kentville.ca

Kings County
P.O. Box 100
87 Cornwallis St.
Kentville, NS B4N 3W3
Tel: 902-678-6141; *Fax:* 902-678-9279
inquiry@county.kings.ns.ca
www.county.kings.ns.ca
Municipal Type: Municipality
Incorporated: April 17, 1879 *Area:* 2,122.18 sq km
County or District: Kings; *Population in 2011:* 60,589
Provincial Electoral District(s): Kings North; Kings South; Kings West
Federal Electoral District(s): Kings-Hants; West Nova
Next Election: Oct. 20, 2012 (4 year terms)
Diana Brothers, Warden
902-690-6132
warden.brothers@county.kings.ns.ca
Jim Taylor, Councillor, Ward(s): District 1
councillor.taylor@county.kings.ns.ca
Janet Newton, Councillor & Deputy Warden, Ward(s): District 2
councillor.newton@county.kings.ns.ca
Dick Killam, Councillor, Ward(s): District 3
councillor.killam@county.kings.ns.ca
Fred Whalen, Councillor, Ward(s): District 4
councillor.whalen@county.kings.ns.ca
Wayne Atwater, Councillor, Ward(s): District 5
councillor.atwater@county.kings.ns.ca
Diana Brothers, Councillor, Ward(s): District 6
councillor.brothers@county.kings.ns.ca
Dale Lloyd, Councillor, Ward(s): District 8
councillor.lloyd@county.kings.ns.ca
Basil Hall, Councillor, Ward(s): District 9
councillor.hall@county.kings.ns.ca
Chris Parker, Councillor, Ward(s): District 10
councillor.parker@county.kings.ns.ca
Eric Smith, Councillor, Ward(s): District 11
councillor.smith@county.kings.ns.ca
Mike Ennis, Councillor, Ward(s): District 12
902-542-5217
councillor.ennis@county.kings.ns.ca
Vacant, Municipal Clerk
Bob Ashley, Chief Administrative Officer
902-690-6131, Fax: 902-678-9279
bashley@county.kings.ns.ca
Trish Javorek, Manager, Development & Building Services
902-690-6167
pjavorek@county.kings.ns.ca
Kathleen Leslie, Manager, Information Technology
902-690-6155, Fax: 902-690-6165
kleslie@county.kings.ns.ca
Scott Quinn, Manager, Engineering & Public Works
902-690-6194
squinn@county.kings.ns.ca
Ben Sivak, Manager, Planning
902-690-6102
bsivak@county.kings.ns.ca
Gary Smith, Manager, Protective Services
902-690-6117
gsmith@county.kings.ns.ca
Bob Suffron, Coordinator, Parks & Open Spaces
902-690-6153
bsuffron@county.kings.ns.ca

Kingston
P.O. Box 254
671 Main St.
Kingston, NS B0P 1R0
Tel: 902-765-2800; *Fax:* 902-765-0807
info@kingstonnovascotia.ca
www.kingstonnovascotia.ca
Municipal Type: Village
Incorporated: 1957
County or District: Kings;
Provincial Electoral District(s): Kings West
Federal Electoral District(s): West Nova
Next Election: Oct. 20, 2012 (4 year terms)
Note: As of 2011, Statistics Canada shows that the Designated Place known as Kingston - Greenwood has an area of 14.50 sq km, & a population of 6,595.
Jaki Fraser, Chair
902-584-3501
Kelly Rice, Clerk-Treasurer

Lawrencetown
P.O. Box 38
12 Prince St.
Lawrencetown, NS B0S 1M0
Tel: 902-584-3559; *Fax:* 902-584-3878
villagelawrencetown@ns.aliantzinc.ca
www.lawrencetownnovascotia.com
Municipal Type: Village
Area: 5.62 sq km
County or District: Annapolis; *Population in 2011:* 625
Provincial Electoral District(s): Annapolis
Federal Electoral District(s): West Nova
Next Election: Oct. 20, 2012 (4 year terms)
Jaki Fraser, Chair
902-584-3501
jaki@ns.sympatico.ca
Kelly Rice, Clerk-Treasurer

Lockeport
P.O. Box 189
26 North St.
Lockeport, NS B0T 1L0
Tel: 902-656-2216; *Fax:* 902-656-2935
townoflockeport@ns.sympatico.ca
www.lockeport.ns.ca
Municipal Type: Town
Incorporated: Feb. 26, 1907 *Area:* 2.32 sq km
County or District: Shelburne; *Population in 2011:* 588
Provincial Electoral District(s): Shelburne
Federal Electoral District(s): South Shore-St. Margaret's
Next Election: Oct. 20, 2012 (4 year terms)
Darian Huskilson, Mayor
902-875-7747
Joyce Y. Young, Clerk-Treas.

Lunenburg
P.O. Box 129
119 Cumberland St.
Lunenburg, NS B0J 2C0
Tel: 902-634-4410; *Fax:* 902-634-4416
explorelunenburg@ns.sympatico.ca
www.explorelunenburg.ca
Municipal Type: Town
Incorporated: Oct. 29, 1888 *Area:* 4.01 sq km
County or District: Lunenburg; *Population in 2011:* 2,313
Provincial Electoral District(s): Lunenburg
Federal Electoral District(s): South Shore-St. Margaret's
Next Election: Oct. 20, 2012 (4 year terms)
Laurence Mawhinney, Mayor
lmawhinney@explorelunenburg.ca
Beatrice Renton, Town Manager & Clerk
brenton@explorelunenburg.ca

Mahone Bay
P.O. Box 530
493 Main St.
Mahone Bay, NS B0J 2E0
Tel: 902-624-8327; *Fax:* 902-624-8069
Municipal Type: Town
Incorporated: March 31, 1919 *Area:* 3.13 sq km
County or District: Lunenburg; *Population in 2011:* 943
Provincial Electoral District(s): Lunenburg
Federal Electoral District(s): South Shore-St. Margaret's
Next Election: Oct. 20, 2012 (4 year terms)
Jim Wentzell, Chief Administrative Officer
C. Joseph Feeney, Mayor
cjfeeney@ns.sympatico.ca

Middleton
P.O. Box 340
131 Commercial St.
Middleton, NS B0S 1P0
Tel: 902-825-4841; *Fax:* 902-825-6460
www.town.middleton.ns.ca
Municipal Type: Town
Incorporated: May 31, 1909 *Area:* 5.44 sq km
County or District: Annapolis; *Population in 2011:* 1,749
Provincial Electoral District(s): Annapolis
Federal Electoral District(s): West Nova
Next Election: Oct. 20, 2012 (4 year terms)
Clayton MacMurty, Chief Administrative Officer
cao@town.middleton.ns.ca
Calvin Eddy, Mayor
callyn@ns.sympatico.ca

Mulgrave
P.O. Box 129
457 MacLeod St.
Mulgrave, NS B0E 2G0
Tel: 902-747-2243; *Fax:* 902-747-2585
info@townofmulgrave.ca
www.townofmulgrave.ca
Municipal Type: Town
Incorporated: Dec. 1, 1923 *Area:* 17.81 sq km
County or District: Guysborough; *Population in 2011:* 794
Provincial Electoral District(s): Guysborough-Sheet Harbour
Federal Electoral District(s): Cape Breton-Canso
Next Election: Oct. 20, 2012 (4 year terms)
Marney Simmons, Mayor
902-747-2662
J. Hugh Landry, Chief Administrative Officer
902-747-2243
hugh.landry@townofmulgrave.ca

New Glasgow
P.O. Box 7
111 Provost St.
New Glasgow, NS B2H 5E1
Tel: 902-755-7788; *Fax:* 902-755-6242
newglasgow@newglasgow.ca
www.newglasgow.ca
Municipal Type: Town
Incorporated: May 6, 1875 *Area:* 9.93 sq km
County or District: Pictou; *Population in 2011:* 9,562
Provincial Electoral District(s): Pictou Centre
Federal Electoral District(s): Central Nova
Next Election: Oct. 20, 2012 (4 year terms)
Barrie MacMillan, Mayor
902-752-4550, Fax: 902-755-6242
barrie.macmillan@newglasgow.ca
Lisa M. MacDonald, Chief Administrative Officer
902-755-8333
lisa.macdonald@newglasgow.ca

New Minas
9209 Commercial St.
New Minas, NS B4N 3G1
Tel: 902-681-6972; *Fax:* 902-681-0779
newminas@ns.aliantzinc.ca
www.newminas.com
Municipal Type: Village
Incorporated: Sept. 1, 1968
County or District: Kings; *Population in 2011:* 4,000
Provincial Electoral District(s): Kings South

Federal Electoral District(s): Kings-Hants
Next Election: Oct. 20, 2012 (4 year terms)
Dave Chaulk, Chair
902-681-2387
dchaulk@av.eastlink.ca
Terry Silver, Clerk-Treasurer
902-681-0292
newminas@ns.sympatico.ca

Oxford
P.O. Box 338
105 Lower Main St.
Oxford, NS B0M 1P0
Tel: 902-447-2170; *Fax:* 902-447-2485
dwhite@town.oxford.ns.ca
www.town.oxford.ns.ca
Municipal Type: Town
Incorporated: April 19, 1904 *Area:* 10.76 sq km
County or District: Cumberland; *Population in 2011:* 1,151
Provincial Electoral District(s): Cumberland South
Federal Electoral District(s):
Cumberland-Colchester-Musquodoboit Valley
Next Election: Oct. 20, 2012 (4 year terms)
Lloyd Jenkins, Mayor
ljenkins@townofoxford.ns.ca
Darrell White, Chief Administrative Officer
dwhite@town.oxford.ns.ca

Parrsboro
P.O. Box 400
4030 Eastern Ave.
Parrsboro, NS B0M 1S0
Tel: 902-254-2036; *Fax:* 902-254-2313
town@town.parrsboro.ns.ca
www.town.parrsboro.ns.ca
Municipal Type: Town
Incorporated: July 15, 1889 *Area:* 14.88 sq km
County or District: Cumberland; *Population in 2011:* 1,305
Provincial Electoral District(s): Cumberland South
Federal Electoral District(s):
Cumberland-Colchester-Musquodoboit Valley
Next Election: Oct. 20, 2012 (4 year terms)
Dawn McCully, Mayor
J. Raymond Hickey, Chief Administrative Officer

Pictou
P.O. Box 640
40 Water St.
Pictou, NS B0K 1H0
Tel: 902-485-4372; *Fax:* 902-485-8110
town.pictou@north.nsis.com
www.townofpictou.com
Municipal Type: Town
Incorporated: May 4, 1874 *Area:* 7.94 sq km
County or District: Pictou; *Population in 2011:* 3,437
Provincial Electoral District(s): Pictou West
Federal Electoral District(s): Central Nova
Next Election: Oct. 20, 2012 (4 year terms)
Joseph F. Hawes, Mayor
902-485-6025
joe.hawes@townofpictou.ca
Scott Conrad, Chief Administrative Officer
902-485-4372
scott.conrad@townofpictou.com

Port Hawkesbury
#1, 606 Reeves St.
Port Hawkesbury, NS B9A 2R7
Tel: 902-625-2746; *Fax:* 902-625-0040
www.townofporthawkesbury.ca
Municipal Type: Town
Incorporated: Jan. 22, 1889 *Area:* 8.11 sq km
County or District: Inverness; *Population in 2011:* 3,366
Provincial Electoral District(s): Inverness
Federal Electoral District(s): Cape Breton-Canso
Next Election: Oct. 20, 2012 (4 year terms)
W.J. (Billy Joe) MacLean, Mayor
902-625-1800
billyjoe.maclean@townofporthawkesbury.ca
Maria Freimanis, Chief Administrative Officer
902-625-7890
maria.freimanis@townofhawkesbury.ca

Port Williams
P.O. Box 153
1045 Main St.
Port Williams, NS B0P 1T0
Tel: 902-542-4411; *Fax:* 902-542-4566
villageoffice@ns.aliantzinc.ca
www.portwilliams.com
Municipal Type: Village
County or District: Kings;
Provincial Electoral District(s): Kings North
Federal Electoral District(s): Kings-Hants
Next Election: Oct. 20, 2012 (4 year terms)
Kim Cogswell, Vice-Chair
kimcogswell@eastlink.ca
Vacant, Clerk

Pugwash
P.O. Box 220
124 Water St.
Pugwash, NS B0K 1L0
Tel: 902-243-2946; *Fax:* 902-243-2126
villagecommission@pugwashvillage.com
www.pugwashvillage.com
Municipal Type: Village
Area: 9.83 sq km
County or District: Cumberland; *Population in 2011:* 744
Provincial Electoral District(s): Cumberland North
Federal Electoral District(s):
Cumberland-Colchester-Musquodoboit Valley
Next Election: Oct. 20, 2012 (4 year terms)
Rod Benjamin, Chair
Lisa Betts, Clerk-Treas.
lisabetts@pugwashvillage.com

River Hebert
2724 Taylor Rd.
River Hebert, NS B0L 1G0
Tel: 902-251-2250
Municipal Type: Village
County or District: Cumberland;
Provincial Electoral District(s): Cumberland South
Federal Electoral District(s):
Cumberland-Colchester-Musquodoboit Valley
Next Election: Oct. 20, 2012 (4 year terms)
Dale Porter, Chair
Judy Jollymore, Clerk-Treas.

St. Peter's
P.O. Box 452
60 Deny St.
St. Peters, NS B0E 3B0
Tel: 902-535-2155; *Fax:* 902-535-2330
info@visitstpeters.com
www.visitstpeters.com
Municipal Type: Village
County or District: Richmond; *Population in 2011:* 800
Provincial Electoral District(s): Richmond
Federal Electoral District(s): Cape Breton-Canso
Next Election: Oct. 20, 2012 (4 year terms)
Esther McDonnell, Chair
Rena Burke, Clerk-Treasurer

Shelburne
P.O. Box 670
168 Water St.
Shelburne, NS B0T 1W0
Tel: 902-875-2991; *Fax:* 902-875-3932
shelburnetown@ns.aliantzinc.ca
www.town.shelburne.ns.ca
Municipal Type: Town
Incorporated: April 4, 1907 *Area:* 9 sq km
County or District: Shelburne; *Population in 2011:* 1,686
Provincial Electoral District(s): Shelburne
Federal Electoral District(s): South Shore-St. Margaret's
Next Election: Oct. 20, 2012 (4 year terms)
Al Delaney, Mayor
902-875-4747
mayordelaney@town.shelburne.ns.ca
Rhonda Henneberry, Chief Administrative Officer
rhenneberry@town.shelburne.ca

Springhill
P.O. Box 1000
43 Main St.
Springhill, NS B0M 1X0
Tel: 902-597-3751; *Fax:* 902-597-3637
www.town.springhill.ns.ca
Municipal Type: Town
Incorporated: March 30, 1889 *Area:* 11.15 sq km
County or District: Cumberland; *Population in 2011:* 3,868
Provincial Electoral District(s): Cumberland South
Federal Electoral District(s):
Cumberland-Colchester-Musquodoboit Valley
Next Election: Oct. 20, 2012 (4 year terms)
Allen Dill, Mayor
Donald F. Tabor, Chief Administrative Officer
dtabor@townofspringhill.ns.ca

Stellarton
P.O. Box 2200
250 Foord St.
Stellarton, NS B0K 1S0
Tel: 902-752-2114; *Fax:* 902-755-4105
townoffice@town.stellarton.ns.ca
www.stellarton.ca
Municipal Type: Town
Incorporated: Oct. 22, 1889 *Area:* 8.99 sq km
County or District: Pictou; *Population in 2011:* 4,485
Provincial Electoral District(s): Pictou Centre
Federal Electoral District(s): Central Nova
Next Election: Oct. 20, 2012 (4 year terms)
Joe Gennoe, Mayor
mayor@town.stellarton.ns.ca
Joyce Eaton, Clerk-Treas.
jeaton@town.stellarton.ns.ca

Stewiacke
P.O. Box 8
295 George St.
Stewiacke, NS B0N 2J0
Tel: 902-639-2231; *Fax:* 902-639-2221
sdorey@stewiacke.net
www.stewiacke.net
Municipal Type: Town
Incorporated: Aug. 30, 1906 *Area:* 17.67 sq km
County or District: Colchester; *Population in 2011:* 1,438
Provincial Electoral District(s): Colchester-Musqodoboit Valley
Federal Electoral District(s):
Cumberland-Colchester-Musquodoboit Valley
Next Election: Oct. 20, 2012 (4 year terms)
Dereck Rhoddy, Mayor
drhoddy@stewiacke.net
Sheldon Dorey, Chief Administrative Officer
sdorey@stewiacke.net

Tatamagouche
P.O. Box 119
423 Main St.
Tatamagouche, NS B0K 1V0
Tel: 902-657-3696
www.tatamagouchetoday.com
Municipal Type: Village
Area: 8.04 sq km
County or District: Colchester; *Population in 2011:* 752
Provincial Electoral District(s): Colchester North
Federal Electoral District(s):
Cumberland-Colchester-Musquodoboit Valley
Next Election: Oct. 20, 2012 (4 year terms)
Marilyn Ebsary, Clerk-Treasurer
Dale Semple, Chair

Tiverton
P.O. Box 16
RR#1
Tiverton, NS B0V 1G0
Tel: 902-839-2369
www.hometowncanada.com/ns/Tiverton.html
Municipal Type: Village
County or District: Digby;
Provincial Electoral District(s): Digby-Annapolis
Federal Electoral District(s): West Nova
Next Election: Oct. 20, 2012 (4 year terms)
Mary Cossaboom, Clerk-Treasurer
Woodrow Outhouse, Chair

Trenton
P.O. Box 328
120 Main St.
Trenton, NS B0K 1X0
Tel: 902-752-5311; *Fax:* 902-752-0090
trenton@town.trenton.ns.ca
www.town.trenton.ns.ca
Other Information: www.facebook.com/TrentonNS
Municipal Type: Town
Incorporated: March 18, 1911 *Area:* 6 sq km
County or District: Pictou; *Population in 2011:* 2,616
Provincial Electoral District(s): Pictou Centre
Federal Electoral District(s): Central Nova
Next Election: Oct. 20, 2012 (4 year terms)
Glen MacKinnon, Mayor
glen.mackinnon@sobeys.com
Cathy MacGillivary, Chief Administrative Officer
cabugden@town.trenton.ns.ca

Westport
The Spouter Inn
P.O. Box 1192
263 Water St.
Westport, NS B0V 1H0
Tel: 902-839-2219; *Fax:* 902-839-2219

Municipal Type: Village
County or District: Digby;
Provincial Electoral District(s): Digby-Annapolis
Federal Electoral District(s): West Nova
Next Election: Oct. 20, 2012 (4 year terms)
Glenda Welch, Chair
Caroline Norwood, Clerk-Treasurer

Westville
P.O. Box 923
2042 Queen St.
Westville, NS B0K 2A0
Tel: 902-396-1500; *Fax:* 902-396-3986
www.westville.ca
Municipal Type: Town
Incorporated: Aug. 20, 1894 *Area:* 14.39 sq km
County or District: Pictou; *Population in 2011:* 3,798
Provincial Electoral District(s): Pictou East
Federal Electoral District(s): Central Nova
Next Election: Oct. 20, 2012 (4 year terms)
Roger McKay, Mayor
rmackay@westville.ca
Scott Fraser, Chief Administrative Officer
sfraser@westville.ca

Weymouth
P.O. Box 121
5108 Hwy. 1
Weymouth, NS B0W 3T0
Tel: 902-837-4976
village@weymouthnovascotia.com
www.weymouthnovascotia.com
Municipal Type: Village
County or District: Digby;
Provincial Electoral District(s): Digby-Annapolis
Federal Electoral District(s): West Nova
Next Election: Oct. 20, 2012 (4 year terms)
Murray Betts, Clerk-Treas.
Suzanne MacLean, Chair

Windsor
P.O. Box 158
100 King St.
Windsor, NS B0N 2T0
Tel: 902-798-2275; *Fax:* 902-798-5679
info@town.windsor.ns.ca
www.town.windsor.ns.ca
Municipal Type: Town
Incorporated: April 4, 1878 *Area:* 9.06 sq km
County or District: Hants; *Population in 2011:* 3,785
Provincial Electoral District(s): Hants West
Federal Electoral District(s): Kings-Hants
Next Election: Oct. 20, 2012 (4 year terms)
Paul Beazley, Mayor
pbeazley@town.windsor.ns.ca
Louis Coutinho, Chief Administrative Officer
902-798-6675
lcoutinho@town.windsor.ns.ca

Wolfville
359 Main St.
Wolfville, NS B4P 1A1
Tel: 902-542-5767; *Fax:* 902-542-4789
www.town.wolfville.ns.ca
Municipal Type: Town
Incorporated: March 4, 1893 *Area:* 6.45 sq km
County or District: Kings; *Population in 2011:* 4,269
Provincial Electoral District(s): Kings South
Federal Electoral District(s): Kings-Hants
Next Election: Oct. 20, 2012 (4 year terms)
Robert A. (Bob) Stead, Mayor
Rachel Turner, Interim Chief Administrative Officer
902-542-8842, Fax: 902-542-4789
rturner@wolfville.ca

Yarmouth
400 Main St.
Yarmouth, NS B5A 1G2
Tel: 902-742-8565; *Fax:* 902-742-6244
www.yarmouth-town.com
Municipal Type: Town
Incorporated: Aug. 6, 1890 *Area:* 10.56 sq km
County or District: Yarmouth; *Population in 2011:* 6,761
Provincial Electoral District(s): Yarmouth
Federal Electoral District(s): West Nova
Next Election: Oct. 20, 2012 (4 year terms)
Charles Crosby, Mayor
mayor.mooney@townofyarmouth.ca
Jeffrey Gushue, Chief Administrative Officer
902-742-8565, Fax: 902-742-6244
cao@townofyarmouth.ca

Rural Municipality

Annapolis County
P.O. Box 100
752 George St.
Annapolis Royal, NS B0S 1A0
Tel: 902-532-2331; *Fax:* 902-532-2096
info@annapoliscounty.ns.ca
www.annapoliscounty.ns.ca
Municipal Type: Rural Municipality
Incorporated: April 17, 1879 *Area:* 3,184.97 sq km
County or District: Annapolis; *Population in 2011:* 20,756
Provincial Electoral District(s): Annapolis; Digby-Annapolis
Federal Electoral District(s): West Nova
Next Election: Oct. 20, 2012 (4 year terms)
Reg Ritchie, Warden
902-532-3137
rritchie@annapoliscounty.ns.ca
Marilyn Wilkins, Councillor, Ward(s): 1
mwilkins@ns.sympatico.ca
Brian Connell, Councillor, Ward(s): 2
mwilkins@ns.sympatico.ca
R. Wayne Fowler, Councillor, Ward(s): 3
Brenda Orchard, Chief Administrative Officer
902-532-3130
admin@annapoliscounty.ns.ca
Carolyn Young, Clerk & Executive Assistant
cyoung@annapoliscounty.ns.ca
Stephen McInnis, Director
902-532-3141
smcinnis@annapoliscounty.ns.ca

Antigonish County
285 Beech Hill Rd.
Antigonish, NS B2G 0B4
Tel: 902-863-1117; *Fax:* 902-863-5751
clerk@antigonishcounty.ns.ca
www.antigonishcounty.ns.ca
Municipal Type: Rural Municipality
Incorporated: April 17, 1879 *Area:* 1,457.82 sq km
County or District: Antigonish; *Population in 2011:* 19,589
Provincial Electoral District(s): Antigonish
Federal Electoral District(s): Central Nova
Next Election: Oct. 20, 2012 (4 year terms)
Herbert J. DeLorey, Warden & Councillor, Ward(s): 8. Tracadie/Monastery
warden@antigonishcounty.ns.ca
Mary MacLellan, Councillor, Ward(s): 1. Arisaig
Donnie MacDonald, Councillor, Ward(s): 2
Jerome Grant, Councillor, Ward(s): 3. St. Joseph's
Vaughan Chisholm, Councillor, Ward(s): 4. Fringe Area West
Rémi Deveau, Councillor, Ward(s): 5. Pomquet
Owen McCarron, Councillor, Ward(s): 6. St. Andrew's
Angus Bowie, Councillor, Ward(s): 7. Heatherton
Havre Boucher, Councillor, Ward(s): 9. Havre Boucher
Bill MacFarlane, Councillor, Ward(s): 10. Fringe Area South
Alan J. Bond, Clerk & Treasurer
clerk@antigonishcounty.ns.ca
John Bain, Director & Development Officer, Eastern District Planning Commission
902-625-5364
jdbain@edpc.ca
Michael O'Leary, Director, Public Works
902-863-5004
publicworks@antigonishcounty.ns.ca
Michael O'Leary, Director, Public Works
902-863-5004
solidwaste@antigonishcounty.ns.ca

Argyle District
P.O. Box 10
27 Courthouse St.
Tusket, NS B0W 3M0
Tel: 902-648-2311; *Fax:* 902-648-0367
admin@munargyle.com
www.munargyle.com
Municipal Type: Rural Municipality
Incorporated: April 17, 1879 *Area:* 1,527.1 sq km
County or District: Yarmouth; *Population in 2011:* 8,252
Provincial Electoral District(s): Argyle
Federal Electoral District(s): West Nova
Next Election: Oct. 20, 2012 (4 year terms)
Aldric D'Entremont, Warden & Councillor, Ward(s): 8. West Pubnico
902-762-2195
Alain Muise, Chief Administrative Officer
902-648-3293
admuise@munargyle.com

Barrington District
P.O. Box 100
2447 Hwy. 3
Barrington, NS B0W 1E0
Tel: 902-637-2015; *Fax:* 902-637-2075
www.barringtonmunicipality.com
Municipal Type: Rural Municipality
Incorporated: April 17, 1879 *Area:* 631.94 sq km
County or District: Shelburne; *Population in 2011:* 6,994
Provincial Electoral District(s): Shelburne
Federal Electoral District(s): South Shore-St. Margaret's
Next Election: Oct. 20, 2012 (4 year terms)
George El-Jakl, Warden
Brian Holland, Clerk
mobclerk@eastlink.ca

Chester District
P.O. Box 369
151 King St.
Chester, NS B0J 1J0
Tel: 902-275-3554; *Fax:* 902-275-4771
administration@district.chester.ns.ca
www.chester.ca
Municipal Type: Rural Municipality
Incorporated: April 17, 1879 *Area:* 1,120.75 sq km
County or District: Lunenburg; *Population in 2011:* 10,599
Provincial Electoral District(s): Chester-St. Margaret's
Federal Electoral District(s): South Shore-St. Margaret's
Next Election: Oct. 20, 2012 (4 year terms)
Allen Webber, Warden
awebber@district.chester.ns.ca
Floyd Shatford, Deputy Warden
fshatford@district.chester.ns.ca
Marshal Hector, Councillor, Ward(s): 1
mhector@district.chester.ns.ca
Brad Armstrong, Councillor, Ward(s): 3
barmstrong@chester.ca
Allen Webber, Councillor, Ward(s): 4
awebber@chester.ca
Robert Myra, Councillor, Ward(s): 5
myra@chester.ca
Cheryl Scott, Councillor, Ward(s): 6
cscott@chester.ca
Sharon Church-Cornelius, Councillor, Ward(s): 6
scornelius@chester.ca
Erin Beaudin, Chief Administrative Officer
ebeaudin@chester.ca
Pam Myra, Municipal Clerk
pmyra@chester.ca
Matthew Davidson, Director, Public Works
902-275-1312
Bruce Forest, Director, Solid Waste
bforest@chester.ca
Cliff Gall, Director, Information Services
cgall@chester.ca
Steve Graham, Treasurer & Director, Finance
sgraham@chester.ca
Chad Haughn, Director, Recreation & Parks
chaughn@chester.ca
Geoff MacDonald, Planning Director
902-275-2599
gmacdonald@chester.ca
Karen Newton, Development Officer
knewton@chester.ca
Arden Weagle, Fire Inspector
aweagle@chester.ca
Earl Woodworth, Building Inspector
ewoodworth@chester.ca

Clare District
P.O. Box 458
1185 Hwy. 1
Little Brook, NS B0W 1Z0
Tel: 902-769-2031; *Fax:* 902-769-3773
council@municipality.clare.ns.ca
www.clarenovascotia.com
Municipal Type: Rural Municipality
Incorporated: April 17, 1879 *Area:* 852.82 sq km
County or District: Digby; *Population in 2011:* 8,319
Provincial Electoral District(s): Clare
Federal Electoral District(s): West Nova
Next Election: Oct. 20, 2012 (4 year terms)
Jean Melanson, Warden & Councillor, Ward(s): 8
jeanmelanson@gmail.com
Connie Saulnier, Chief Administrative Officer

Colchester County

P.O. Box 697
1 Church St.
Truro, NS B2N 5E7
Tel: 902-897-3160; *Fax:* 902-895-9983
www.colchester.ca
Other Information: 866-728-5144 (toll-free)
Municipal Type: Rural Municipality
Incorporated: April 17, 1879 *Area:* 3,627.69 sq km
County or District: Colchester; *Population in 2011:* 50,968
Provincial Electoral District(s): Colchester-Musqudoboit Valley; Colchester North; Truro-Bible Hill
Federal Electoral District(s): Cumberland-Colchester-Musquodoboit Valley
Next Election: Oct. 20, 2012 (4 year terms)
Bob Taylor, Mayor
mayor@colchester.ca
Ron Cavanaugh, Deputy Mayor, Ward(s): 8
councillordistrict8@colchester.ca
Christine Blair, Councillor, Ward(s): 1
councillordistrict1@colchester.ca
Bill Masters, Councillor, Ward(s): 2
councillordistrict2@colchester.ca
Gerald Buott, Councillor, Ward(s): 3
councillordistrict3@colchester.ca
Mike Cooper, Councillor, Ward(s): 4
councillordistrict4@colchester.ca
Glen Edwards, Councillor, Ward(s): 5
councillordistrict5@colchester.ca
Karen MacKenzie, Councillor, Ward(s): 6
councillordistrict6@colchester.ca
Jimmie Le Fresne, Councillor, Ward(s): 7
councillordistrict7@colchester.ca
Dan McDougall, Chief Administrative Officer
dmcdougall@colchester.ca
Crawford Macpherson, Director, Community Development
902-897-3170
cmacpherson@colchester.ca
Bruce Purchase, Director, Corporate Services
bpurchase@colchester.ca
Ramesh Ummat, Director, Public Works
rummat@colchester.ca
Wayne Wamboldt, Director, Public Works
wwamboldt@colchester.ca

Cumberland County

E.D. Fullerton Municipal Bldg.
P.O. Box 428
1395 Blair Lake Rd., RR#6
Amherst, NS B4H 3Y4
Tel: 902-667-2313; *Fax:* 902-667-1352
info@cumberlandcounty.ns.ca
www.cumberlandcounty.ns.ca
Other Information: Toll Free Phone: 1-888-756-6262
Municipal Type: Rural Municipality
Incorporated: April 17, 1879 *Area:* 4,271.14 sq km
County or District: Cumberland; *Population in 2011:* 31,353
Provincial Electoral District(s): Cumberland North; Cumberland South
Federal Electoral District(s): Cumberland-Colchester-Musquodoboit Valley
Next Election: Oct. 20, 2012 (4 year terms)
Keith Hunter, Warden & Councillor, Ward(s): 3
khunter@cumberlandcounty.ns.ca
Gerald Read, Councillor, Ward(s): 2
gread@cumberlandcounty.ns.ca
Allison Gillis, Councillor, Ward(s): 3
agillis@cumberlandcounty.ns.ca
Ron MacNutt, Councillor, Ward(s): 5
rmacnutt@cumberlandcounty.ns.ca
Kathy Redmond, Councillor, Ward(s): 6
kredmond@cumberlandcounty.ns.ca
Phillip Donkin, Councillor, Ward(s): 7
pdonkin@cumberlandcounty.ns.ca
Ernest Gilbert, Councillor, Ward(s): 7
egilbert@cumberlandcounty.ns.ca
John Reid, Councillor, Ward(s): 7
jreid@cumberlandcounty.ns.ca
Ratchford Merriam, Councillor, Ward(s): 7
rmerriam@cumberlandcounty.ns.ca
Rennie Bugley, Chief Administrative Officer
rbugley@cumberlandcounty.ns.ca
Shelley Hoeg, Executive Assistant
shoeg@cumberlandcounty.ns.ca
Steve Ferguson, Director, Policy & Research
sferguson@cumberlandcounty.ns.ca
Penny Henneberry, Director, Planning & Development
phenneberry@cumberlandcounty.ns.ca
Andrew MacDonald, Director, Finance & Administration
amacdonald@cumberlandcounty.ns.ca
Robert Streatch, Director, Public Works
902-667-3029
rstreatch@cumberlandcounty.ns.ca

Digby District

P.O. Box 429
Digby, NS B0V 1A0
Tel: 902-245-4777; *Fax:* 902-245-5748
www.digbydistrict.ca
Municipal Type: Rural Municipality
Incorporated: April 17, 1879 *Area:* 1,655.93 sq km
County or District: Digby; *Population in 2011:* 7,463
Provincial Electoral District(s): Digby-Annapolis
Federal Electoral District(s): West Nova
Next Election: Oct. 20, 2012 (4 year terms)
Linda Gregory, Warden
warden.mundigby@tartannet.ns.ca
Linda Fraser, Chief Administrative Officer
lfraser@municipality.digby.ns.ca

Guysborough District

Municipal Bldg.
P.O. Box 79
33 Pleasant St.
Guysborough, NS B0H 1N0
Tel: 902-533-3705; *Fax:* 902-533-2749
district@modg.ca
www.municipality.guysborough.ns.ca
Municipal Type: Rural Municipality
Incorporated: April 17, 1879 *Area:* 2,111.42 sq km
County or District: Guysborough; *Population in 2011:* 8,143
Provincial Electoral District(s): Guysborough-Sheet Harbour
Federal Electoral District(s): Cape Breton-Canso
Next Election: Oct. 20, 2012 (4 year terms)
Lloyd P. Hines, Warden
lhines@modg.ca
Barry Carrollll, Chief Administrative Officer
902-533-3705
bcarroll@modg.ca

Hants East District

P.O. Box 190
2361 Hwy. 2, Milford
Shubenacadie, NS B0N 2H0
Tel: 902-758-2299; *Fax:* 902-758-3497
info@easthants.ca
www.easthants.ca
Municipal Type: Rural Municipality
Incorporated: April 17, 1879 *Area:* 1,787.64 sq km
County or District: Hants; *Population in 2011:* 22,111
Provincial Electoral District(s): Hants East
Federal Electoral District(s): Kings-Hants
Next Election: Oct. 20, 2012 (4 year terms)
John Patterson, Warden & Councillor, Ward(s): 13
Fred Bannister, Councillor, Ward(s): 1. Enfield
fbannister@easthants.ca
Norval Mitchell, Councillor, Ward(s): 2. Elmsdale
nmitchell@easthants.ca
Willy Versteeg, Councillor, Ward(s): 3. Milford
wversteeg@easthants.ca
Pam MacInnis, Councillor, Ward(s): 4. Shubenacadie
pmacinnis@easthants.ca
Keith Ryno, Councillor, Ward(s): 5. Maitland
kryhno@easthants.ca
Wayne Greene, Councillor, Ward(s): 6. Noel
wgreene@easthants.ca
John A. MacDonald, Councillor, Ward(s): 6. Noel
jamacdonald@easthants.ca
Greg Grant, Councillor, Ward(s): 8. Gore
ggrant@easthants.ca
Eldon Hebb, Councillor, Ward(s): 9. Nine Mile River
ehebb@easthants.ca
Jim D. Smith, Councillor, Ward(s): 10. Enfield/Horne Settlement
jdsmith@easthants.ca
Eleanor Roulston, Councillor, Ward(s): 11. Rawdon
eroulston@easthants.ca
Rosanne Bland, Councillor, Ward(s): 11. Rawdon
rbland@easthants.ca
Connie Nolan, Chief Administrative Officer
902-883-7098
cnolan@easthants.ca
Janice VanTol, Executive Assitant & Deputy Clerk
902-883-7098
jvantol@easthants.ca
Lew Landers, P.Eng., Director, Engineering Services
llanders@easthants.ca
Terry Matheson, MA Sc.E., Officer, Environmental Compliance
tmatheson@easthants.ca
Andrea Trask, Coordinator & Educator, Waste Reduction
atrask@easthants.ca
John Woodford, Director, Planning & Development
902-758-2715
jwoodford@easthants.ca
Heidi Achenbach, Manager, Solid Waste
902-758-2299
hachenbach@easthants.ca
Jim Ashley, Manager, Public Works
jashley@easthants.ca
Mike Brown, Centre Foreman, Solid Waste Management
902-261-2178
Edward McQuillan, Operator, Water Distribution
emcquillan@easthants.ca

Hants West District

Windsor-West Hants Industrial Park
P.O. Box 3000
76 Morrison Dr.
Windsor, NS B0N 2T0
Tel: 902-798-8391; *Fax:* 902-798-8553
west.hants@westhants.ca
www.westhants.ca
Municipal Type: Rural Municipality
Incorporated: April 17, 1879 *Area:* 1,238.12 sq km
County or District: Hants; *Population in 2011:* 14,165
Provincial Electoral District(s): Hants West
Federal Electoral District(s): Kings-Hants
Next Election: Oct. 20, 2012 (4 year terms)
Richard B. Dauphinee, Warden & Councillor, Ward(s): 6
902-798-4908
admin@westhants.ca
Reed W. Allen, Councillor, Ward(s): 1
rallen@ns.sympatico.ca
Shirley Pineo, Councillor, Ward(s): 2
councillorpineo@eastlink.ca
Randall Matheson, Councillor, Ward(s): 2
matheson007@eastlink.ca
Thomas Brown, Councillor, Ward(s): 2
councillorthomasb@gmail.com
Gary Cochrane, Councillor, Ward(s): 2
garycochrane@eastlink.ca
Gloria Shanks, Councillor, Ward(s): 7
gkshanks@ns.sympatico.ca
Rick Gaudet, Councillor, Ward(s): 8
rickgaudet@eastlink.ca
Pam Ainslie, Councillor, Ward(s): 8
painslie@eastlink.ca
Cheryl Chislett, Chief Administrative Officer
cao@westhants.ca
Lynn Davis, Director, Planning
902-798-6900
ldavis@windsorwesthantsplanning.ns.ca
Paul DeMont, Operator, Water Treatment
drc@westhants.ca
Christine McClare, Coordinator, Waste Reduction
waste@westhants.ca
Rick Sherrard, Director, Public Works
public.works@westhants.ca

Inverness County

Municipal Bldg.
P.O. Box 179
375 Main St.
Port Hood, NS B0E 2W0
Tel: 902-787-2274; *Fax:* 902-787-3110
www.invernesscounty.ca
Municipal Type: Rural Municipality
Incorporated: April 17, 1879 *Area:* 3,830.4 sq km
County or District: Inverness; *Population in 2011:* 17,947
Provincial Electoral District(s): Guysborough-Sheet Harbour; Inverness; Victoria-The Lakes
Federal Electoral District(s): Cape Breton-Canso; Sydney-Victoria
Next Election: Oct. 20, 2012 (4 year terms)
Duart MacAulay, Warden & Councillor, Ward(s): 4
duartmaca@ns.sympatico.ca
Daniel Boudreau, Councillor, Ward(s): 1
Gloria Leblanc, Councillor, Ward(s): 2
James Mustard, Councillor, Ward(s): 3
Susan Mallette, Councillor, Ward(s): 5
Dwayne MacDonald, Councillor, Ward(s): 6
Joe O'Connor, Chief Administrative Officer
joe.oconnor@invernesscounty.ca
Joe O'Connor, Director, Public Works
902-787-3502, Fax: 902-787-2339
invworks@ns.sympatico.ca
William Gillis, Officer, Bylaw Enforcement

Lunenburg District
P.O. Box 200
210 Aberdeen Rd.
Bridgewater, NS B4V 2W8
Tel: 902-543-8181; *Fax:* 902-543-7123
admin@municipality.lunenburg.ca
www.lunenburgdistrict.com
Municipal Type: Rural Municipality
Incorporated: April 17, 1879 *Area:* 1,759.14 sq km
County or District: Lunenburg; *Population in 2011:* 25,118
Provincial Electoral District(s): Chester-St. Margaret's
Lunenburg; Lunenburg West
Federal Electoral District(s): South Shore-St. Margaret's
Next Election: Oct. 20, 2012 (4 year terms)
Don Downe, Mayor
902-543-5357
Martin Bell, Deputy Mayor
902-543-5357
Martin Bell, Deputy Mayor
902-543-5357
Milton Countway, Councillor
Frank Fawson, Councillor
Erik Hustvedt, Councillor
Cathy Moore, Councillor
Lee Nauss, Councillor
Basil Oickle, Councillor
Sandra Statton, Councillor
John Veinot, Councillor
April Whynot-Lohnes, Municipal Clerk
902-541-1323
Tammy Wilson, Chief Administrative Officer
902-541-1320
twilson@modl.ca
Jim Annand, Manager, Solid Waste Operations
902-541-1325
jannand@modl.ca
Laura Barkhouse, Coordinator, Trails
902-541-1352
lbarkhouse@modl.ca
Jeff Merrill, Planner, Planning & Development
902-541-1340
jmerrill@modl.ca
Norma Schiefer, Officer, Development
902-541-1334
nschiefer@modl.ca
Roger Stein, Municipal Engineer & Director, Engineering
Kevin Wentzell, Supervisor, Compost Plant
902-543-0151
kwentzell@modl.ca

Pictou County
P.O. Box 910
46 Municipal Dr.
Pictou, NS B0K 1H0
Tel: 902-485-4311; *Fax:* 902-485-6475
cmacintosh@county.pictou.ns.ca
www.county.pictou.ns.ca
Municipal Type: Rural Municipality
Incorporated: April 17, 1879 *Area:* 2,845.26 sq km
County or District: Pictou; *Population in 2011:* 45,643
Provincial Electoral District(s): Pictou Centre; Pictou East;
Pictou West
Federal Electoral District(s): Central Nova
Next Election: Oct. 20, 2012 (4 year terms)
Ronald Baillie, Warden & Councillor, Ward(s): 4
normabaillie@northnovacable.ca
Kelly McVicar, Councillor, Ward(s): 2
kmcvicar@county.pictou.ns.ca
Edward MacMaster, Councillor
edwardmacmaster@county.pictou.ns.ca
Robert Parker, Councillor, Ward(s): 5
rparker@county.pictou.ns.ca
Jim Turple, Councillor, Ward(s): 6
jturple@county.pictou.ns.ca
David Parker, Councillor, Ward(s): 7
dparker@county.pictou.ns.ca
Leonard Fraser, Councillor, Ward(s): 8
lfraser@county.pictou.ns.ca
Lori Kilburn, Councillor, Ward(s): 9
lkilburn@county.pictou.ns.ca
Allister MacDonald, Councillor, Ward(s): 10
amacdonald@county.pictou.ns.ca
Andy Thompson, Councillor, Ward(s): 11
athompson@county.pictou.ns.ca
Chester Dewar, Councillor, Ward(s): 12
cdewar@county.pictou.ns.ca
Randy Palmer, Councillor, Ward(s): 13
rpalmer@county.pictou.ns.ca
Fielding Smith, Councillor, Ward(s): 13
fsmith@county.pictou.ns.ca
Brian Cullen, Chief Administrative Officer
bcullen@county.pictou.ns.ca
Carol MacKenzie, Manager, Waste Reduction Program
902-396-1495
cmackenzie@pcwastemgmt.com

Richmond County
P.O. Box 120
2357 Hwy. 206
Arichat, NS B0E 1A0
Tel: 902-226-2400; *Fax:* 902-226-1510
ldigout@richmondcounty.ca
www.richmondcounty.ca
Municipal Type: Rural Municipality
Incorporated: April 17, 1879 *Area:* 1,244.24 sq km
County or District: Richmond; *Population in 2011:* 9,293
Provincial Electoral District(s): Richmond
Federal Electoral District(s): Cape Breton-Canso
Next Election: Oct. 20, 2012 (4 year terms)
John Boudreau, Warden
902-226-3380, Fax: 902-226-1510
jboudreau@richmondcounty.ca
Warren Olsen, Chief Adminstrative Officer
902-226-3970, Fax: 902-226-2824
wolsen@richmondcounty.ca

St. Mary's District
P.O. Box 296
16 Main St.
Sherbrooke, NS B0J 3C0
Tel: 902-522-2049; *Fax:* 902-522-2309
council@saint-marys.ca
www.saint-marys.ca
Municipal Type: Rural Municipality
Incorporated: April 17, 1879 *Area:* 1,909.59 sq km
County or District: Guysborough; *Population in 2011:* 2,354
Provincial Electoral District(s): Guysborough-Sheet Harbour
Federal Electoral District(s): Central Nova
Next Election: Oct. 20, 2012 (4 year terms)
David Clark, Warden
902-522-2049, Fax: 902-522-2309
dp.clark@nis.sympatico.ca
David Gillis, Clerk-Treasurer
902-522-2049, Fax: 902-522-2309
davidgillis@munet.ns.ca

Shelburne District
P.O. Box 280
136 Hammond Rd.
Shelburne, NS B0T 1W0
Tel: 902-875-3083; *Fax:* 902-875-1278
ademings@municipalityofshelburne.ca
Municipal Type: Rural Municipality
Incorporated: April 17, 1879 *Area:* 1,818.49 sq km
County or District: Shelburne; *Population in 2011:* 4,408
Provincial Electoral District(s): Shelburne
Federal Electoral District(s): South Shore-St. Margaret's
Next Election: Oct. 20, 2012 (4 year terms)
Vacant, Warden
902-875-3544
Penny Smith, Clerk
902-875-3544

Victoria County
P.O. Box 370
495 Chebucto St.
Baddeck, NS B0E 1B0
Tel: 902-295-3231; *Fax:* 902-295-3331
heather.maclean@countyvictoria.ns.ca
www.countyvictoria.ns.ca
Municipal Type: Rural Municipality
Incorporated: April 17, 1879 *Area:* 2,870.85 sq km
County or District: Victoria; *Population in 2011:* 7,115
Provincial Electoral District(s): Victoria-The Lakes
Federal Electoral District(s): Sydney-Victoria
Next Election: Oct. 20, 2012 (4 year terms)
Bruce Morrison, Warden
902-565-8229, Fax: 902-295-1311
bruce.morrison@countyvictoria.ns.ca
Alexander (Sandy) W. Hudson, Chief Administrative Officer
902-295-3660, Fax: 902-295-3331
sandy.hudson@countyvictorian.ns.ca

Yarmouth District
P.O. Box 21
932, Hwy 1
Hebron, NS B0W 1X0
Tel: 902-742-7159; *Fax:* 902-742-3164
admin@district.yarmouth.ns.ca
www.district.yarmouth.ns.ca
Municipal Type: Rural Municipality
Incorporated: April 17, 1879 *Area:* 585.27 sq km
County or District: Yarmouth; *Population in 2011:* 10,105
Provincial Electoral District(s): Yarmouth
Federal Electoral District(s): West Nova
Next Election: Oct. 20, 2012 (4 year terms)
Leland Anthony, Warden & Councillor, Ward(s): 7
warden@district.yarmouth.ns.ca
Murray Goodwin, Deputy Warden & Councillor, Ward(s): 2
murray@district.yarmouth.ns.ca
John Cunningham, Councillor, Ward(s): 1
johnc@district.yarmouth.ns.ca
Ken Crosby, Councillor, Ward(s): 3
kenc@district.yarmouth.ns.ca
Trevor Cunningham, Councillor, Ward(s): 5
trevor@district.yarmouth.ns.ca
Heather MacDonald, Councillor, Ward(s): 4
heather@district.yarmouth.ns.ca
Ken Moses, Chief Administrative Officer
cao@district.yarmouth.ns.ca
Trudy LeBlanc, Deputy Chief Administrative Officer
trudy@district.yarmouth.ns.ca
Greg Shay, Director, Finance
greg@district.yarmouth.ns.ca

NUNAVUT

The Department of Community and Government Services has legislative responsibility for 27 Territorial Acts and Regulations. These Acts include: Area Development; Business Licenses; Cities, Town and Villages; Civil Emergency Measures; Commissioner's Land; Community Employees Benefits Program Transfer; Conflict of Interest; Consumer Protection; Curfew; Dog; Film Classification; Fire Prevention; Hamlet; Homeowners Property; Local Authorities Election; Lotteries; Pawnbrokers and Second-hand Dealers; Planning; Property Assessments and Taxation; Real Estate Agents Licensing; Religious Societies; Residential Tenancies; Technical Standards and Safety; Senior Citizens and Disabled Persons Property Tax Relief Act; Settlement; Western Canada Lottery.

Incorporation as a city, town or village is determined by the value of all assessable land. Incorporation values: Village, $10 million; Town, $50 million; City, $200 million, all tax-based. Hamlets may request tax-based status. There is one city and 24 hamlets in Nunavut.

There is no fixed schedule for elections, but they are typically held every four to five years (2013, 2017, etc).

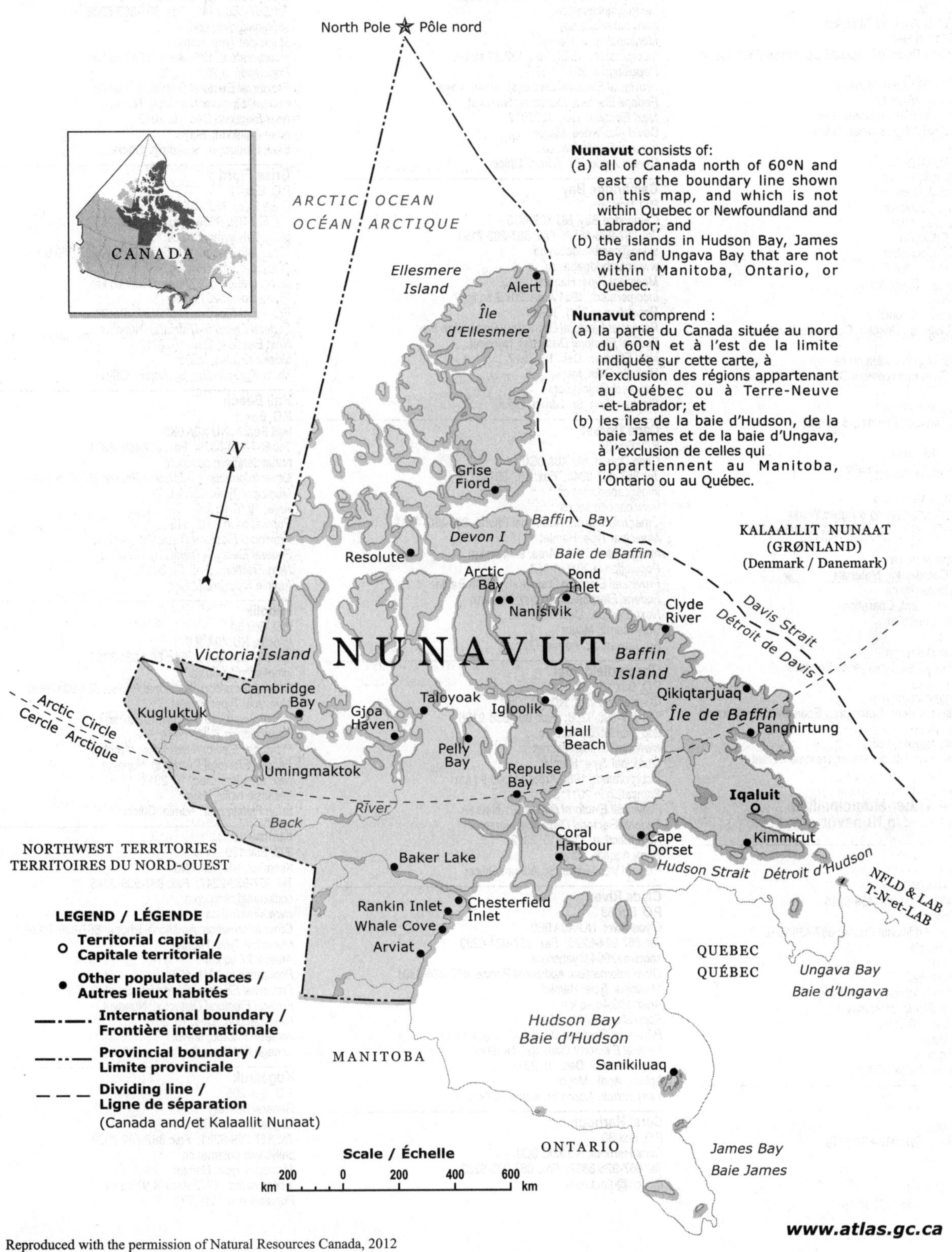

North Pole
Pôle nord
CANADA
ARCTIC OCEAN
OCÉAN ARCTIQUE
Nunavut consists of:
(a) all of Canada north of 60°N and east of the boundary line shown on this map, and which is not within Quebec or Newfoundland and Labrador; and
(b) the islands in Hudson Bay, James Bay and Ungava Bay that are not within Manitoba, Ontario, or Quebec.
Nunavut comprend :
(a) la partie du Canada située au nord du 60°N et à l'est de la limite indiquée sur cette carte, à l'exclusion des régions appartenant au Québec ou à Terre-Neuve -et-Labrador; et
(b) les îles de la baie d'Hudson, de la baie James et de la baie d'Ungava, à l'exclusion de celles qui appartiennent au Manitoba, l'Ontario ou au Québec.
Ellesmere Island
Île d'Ellesmere
Alert
N
Grise Fiord
Baffin Bay
Baie de Baffin
Devon I
Resolute
KALAALLIT NUNAAT
(GRØNLAND)
(Denmark / Danemark)
Arctic Bay
Pond Inlet
Nanisivik
Clyde River
Davis Strait
Détroit de Davis
Victoria Island
NUNAVUT
Baffin Island
Cambridge Bay
Kugluktuk
Arctic Circle
Cercle Arctique
Taloyoak
Gjoa Haven
Igloolik
Qikiqtarjuaq
Île de Baffin
Pangnirtung
Hall Beach
Pelly Bay
Umingmaktok
Repulse Bay
Iqaluit
Back River
NORTHWEST TERRITORIES
TERRITOIRES DU NORD-OUEST
Coral Harbour
Cape Dorset
Kimmirut
Baker Lake
Hudson Strait
Détroit d'Hudson
NFLD & LAB
T-N-et-LAB
LEGEND / LÉGENDE
Territorial capital / Capitale territoriale
Other populated places / Autres lieux habités
International boundary / Frontière internationale
Provincial boundary / Limite provinciale
Dividing line / Ligne de séparation
(Canada and/et Kalaallit Nunaat)
Rankin Inlet
Chesterfield Inlet
Whale Cove
Arviat
QUEBEC
QUÉBEC
Ungava Bay
Baie d'Ungava
Hudson Bay
Baie d'Hudson
MANITOBA
Sanikiluaq
Scale / Échelle
200 0 200 400 600
km km
ONTARIO
James Bay
Baie James
www.atlas.gc.ca

Nunavut

Major Municipalities in Nunavut

Iqaluit
P.O. Box 460
Iqaluit, NU X0A 0H0
Tel: 867-979-5600; *Fax:* 867-979-5922
info@city.iqaluit.nu.ca
www.city.iqaluit.nu.ca
Municipal Type: City
Incorporated: 2001 *Area:* 52.34 sq km
Population in 2011: 6,699
Provincial Electoral District(s): Iqaluit East; Iqaluit West; Iqaluit Centre
Federal Electoral District(s): Nunavut
Next Election: Oct. 15, 2012
Note: Formerly known as Frobisher Bay.
John Hussey, Chief Administration Officer
867-979-5666
j.hussey@city.iqaluit.nu.ca
Elisapee Sheutiapik, Mayor
mayor@city.iqaluit.nu.ca
Mary Akpalialuk, Councillor
Jimmy Kilabuk, Councillor
Natsiq Kango, Councillor
Mat Knicklebein, Councillor
Simon Nattaq, Councillor
Mary Ekho Wilman, Councillor
David Ell, Councillor
Romeyn Stevenson, Councillor
John Mabberi-Mudonyi, Director, Corporate Services
867-979-5675
j.mabberi-mudonyi@city.iqaluit.nu.ca
Doug Vincent, Chief Enforcement Officer
867-979-6363
d.vincent@city.iqaluit.nu.ca
Michèle Bertol, Director, Planning & Lands
867-979-6363
m.bertol@city.iqaluit.nu.ca
Amy Elgersma, Director, Recreation
867-979-5616
a.elgersma@city.iqaluit.nu.ca
Vacant, Director, Engineering & Public Works
Meagan Leach, Director, Engineering & Sustainability
867-979-6363
m.leach@city.iqaluit.nu.ca
Sean Tiessen, Coordinator, Materials
s.tiessen@city.iqaluit.nu.ca
Vacant, Superintendent, Operations
Geneva Chislett, Controller
867-979-5610
g.chislett@city.iqaluit.nu.ca
Walter Oliver, Fire Chief, Emergency Services
867-976-5657
w.oliver@city.iqaluit.nu.ca
Joamie Eegeesiak, Officer, Community Economic Development
867-979-6363
j.eegeesiak@city.iqaluit.nu.ca
Rob Hogan, Foreman, Utilidor Water Treatment Plant
867-975-8509

Other Municipalities in Nunavut

Arctic Bay
General Delivery
Arctic Bay, NU X0A 0A0
Tel: 867-439-8483; *Fax:* 867-439-8916
sao_ab@qiniq.com
Other Information: Additional Phone: 867-439-9918
Municipal Type: Hamlet
Area: 247.5 sq km
Population in 2011: 823
Provincial Electoral District(s): Quttiktuq
Federal Electoral District(s): Nunavut
Next Election: Dec. 10, 2012
Andrew Taqtu, Mayor
mayor_ab@qiniq.com
Joeli Qamanirq, Sr. Admin. Officer

Arviat
P.O. Box 150
Arviat, NU X0C 0E0
Tel: 867-857-2841; *Fax:* 867-857-2519
arviatsao@qiniq.com
www.arviat.ca
Municipal Type: Hamlet
Incorporated: 1977 *Area:* 132 sq km
Population in 2011: 2,318
Provincial Electoral District(s): Arviat
Federal Electoral District(s): Nunavut
Next Election: Dec. 10, 2012
Note: Formerly known as Eskimo Point.
Bob Leonard, Mayor
Ed Murphy, Sr. Admin. Officer

Baker Lake
P.O. Box 149
Baker Lake, NU X0C 0A0
Tel: 867-793-2874; *Fax:* 867-793-2509
bledo@netkaster.ca
www.bakerlake.org
Municipal Type: Hamlet
Incorporated: 1977 *Area:* 182.22 sq km
Population in 2011: 1,872
Provincial Electoral District(s): Baker Lake
Federal Electoral District(s): Nunavut
Next Election: Dec. 10, 2012
David Aksawnee, Mayor
blmayor@netkaster.ca
Dennis Zettler, Sr. Admin. Officer

Cambridge Bay
P.O. Box 16
Cambridge Bay, NU X0B 0C0
Tel: 867-983-4650; *Fax:* 867-983-2193
sking@cambridgebay.ca
www.cambridgebay.ca
Municipal Type: Hamlet
Incorporated: 1984 *Area:* 202.2 sq km
Population in 2011: 1,608
Provincial Electoral District(s): Cambridge Bay
Federal Electoral District(s): Nunavut
Next Election: Dec. 10, 2012
Michelle Gillis, Mayor
mayorycb@qiniq.com
Stephen King, Sr. Admin. Officer

Cape Dorset
P.O. Box 30
Cape Dorset, NU X0A 0C0
Tel: 867-897-8943; *Fax:* 867-897-8030
info@capedorset.ca
www.capedorset.ca
Other Information: Additional Phone: 867-897-8981
Municipal Type: Hamlet
Incorporated: 1982 *Area:* 9.74 sq km
Population in 2011: 1,363
Provincial Electoral District(s): South Baffin
Federal Electoral District(s): Nunavut
Next Election: Dec. 10, 2012
Cary Merritt, Mayor
Art Stewart, Sr. Admin. Officer

Chesterfield Inlet
P.O. Box 10
Chesterfield Inlet, NU X0C 0B0
Tel: 867-898-9206; *Fax:* 867-898-9108
edo_hamlet@qiniq.com
www.chesterfieldinlet.net
Municipal Type: Hamlet
Incorporated: 1980 *Area:* 141.08 sq km
Population in 2011: 313
Provincial Electoral District(s): Nanulik
Federal Electoral District(s): Nunavut
Next Election: Dec. 10, 2012
Harry Aqqark, Mayor
Richard Van Horne, Sr. Admin. Officer

Clyde River
P.O. Box 89
Clyde River, NU X0A 0E0
Tel: 867-924-6220; *Fax:* 867-924-6293
saoclyde2004@yahoo.ca
Other Information: Additional Phone: 867-924-6301
Municipal Type: Hamlet
Area: 106.48 sq km
Population in 2011: 934
Provincial Electoral District(s): Uqqummiut
Federal Electoral District(s): Nunavut
Next Election: Dec. 10, 2012
Apiusie Apak, Mayor
Terry Kalluk, Acting Sr. Admin. Officer

Coral Harbour
P.O. Box 30
Coral Harbour, NU X0C 0C0
Tel: 867-925-8867; *Fax:* 867-925-8233
munch@qiniq.com
Municipal Type: Hamlet
Area: 137.83 sq km
Population in 2011: 834
Provincial Electoral District(s): Nanulik
Federal Electoral District(s): Nunavut
Next Election: Dec. 10, 2012
Jerry Pianiyuk, Mayor
Ronald Ladd, Sr. Admin. Officer

Gjoa Haven
P.O. Box 200
Gjoa Haven, NU X0B 1J0
Tel: 867-360-7141; *Fax:* 867-360-6309
saogjoa@qiniq.com
Municipal Type: Hamlet
Incorporated: 1981 *Area:* 28.47 sq km
Population in 2011: 1,279
Provincial Electoral District(s): Nattilik
Federal Electoral District(s): Nunavut
Next Election: Dec. 10, 2012
Allen Aqlukkaq, Mayor
Enuk Pauloosie, Sr. Admin. Officer

Grise Fiord
P.O. Box 77
Grise Fiord, NU X0A 0J0
Tel: 867-980-9959; *Fax:* 867-980-9052
gfsao@nv.sympatico.ca
Other Information: Additional Phone: 867-980-9060
Municipal Type: Hamlet
Incorporated: 1987 *Area:* 332.7 sq km
Population in 2011: 130
Provincial Electoral District(s): Quttiktuq
Federal Electoral District(s): Nunavut
Next Election: Dec. 10, 2012
Meeka Kigutak, Mayor
Marty Kuluguaqtuq, Sr. Admin. Officer

Hall Beach
P.O. Box 3
Hall Beach, NU X0A 0K0
Tel: 867-928-8829; *Fax:* 867-928-8871
hbhamlet@sympatico.ca
Other Information: Additional Phone: 867-928-8945
Municipal Type: Hamlet
Area: 16.52 sq km
Population in 2011: 546
Provincial Electoral District(s): Amittuq
Federal Electoral District(s): Nunavut
Next Election: Dec. 10, 2012
Ammie Kipsigak, Mayor

Igloolik
P.O. Box 30
Igloolik, NU X0A 0L0
Tel: 867-934-8940; *Fax:* 867-934-8757
igloolik@magma.ca
Other Information: Additional Phone: 867-934-8830
Municipal Type: Hamlet
Incorporated: 1976 *Area:* 102.87 sq km
Population in 2011: 1,454
Provincial Electoral District(s): Amittuq
Federal Electoral District(s): Nunavut
Next Election: Dec. 10, 2012
Lucassie Ivalu, Mayor
Brian Fleming, Sr. Admin. Officer

Kimmirut
P.O. Box 120
Kimmirut, NU X0A 0N0
Tel: 867-939-2247; *Fax:* 867-939-2045
cedkimm@qiniq.com
www.kimmirut.ca
Other Information: Additional Phone: 867-939-2002
Municipal Type: Hamlet
Area: 2.27 sq km
Population in 2011: 455
Provincial Electoral District(s): South Baffin
Federal Electoral District(s): Nunavut
Next Election: Dec. 10, 2012
Jamesie Kootoo, Mayor
Akeego Ikkidluak, Sr. Admin. Officer

Kugaaruk
P.O. Box 205
General Delivery
Kugaaruk, NU X0B 1K0
Tel: 867-769-6281; *Fax:* 867-769-6069
pellybay@polarnet.ca
Municipal Type: Hamlet
Incorporated: 1972 *Area:* 4.97 sq km
Population in 2011: 771

Provincial Electoral District(s): Akulliq
Federal Electoral District(s): Nunavut
Next Election: Dec. 10, 2012
Note: Formerly known as Pelly Bay.
Makabe Nartok, Mayor
Andre Larabie, Sr. Admin. Officer

Kugluktuk
P.O. Box 271
Kugluktuk, NU X0B 0E0
Tel: 867-982-6500; *Fax:* 867-982-3060
saokug@qiniq.com
Other Information: Additional Phone: 867-982-6505
Municipal Type: Hamlet
Incorporated: 1981 *Area:* 549.61 sq km
Population in 2011: 1,450
Provincial Electoral District(s): Kugluktuk
Federal Electoral District(s): Nunavut
Next Election: Dec. 10, 2012
Note: Formerly known as Coppermine.
Ernie Bernhardt, Mayor
Derrick Power, Sr. Admin. Officer

Pangnirtung
P.O. Box 253
Pangnirtung, NU X0A 0R0
Tel: 867-473-8953; *Fax:* 867-473-8832
pang_sao@qiniq.com
Municipal Type: Hamlet
Incorporated: 1972 *Area:* 7.54 sq km
Population in 2011: 1,425
Provincial Electoral District(s): Pangnirtung
Federal Electoral District(s): Nunavut
Next Election: Dec. 10, 2012
Moses Qarpik, Mayor
Ron Mongeau, Sr. Admin. Officer

Pond Inlet
P.O. Box 180
Pond Inlet, NU X0A 0S0
Tel: 867-899-8934; *Fax:* 867-899-8940
hamletpond_sao@qiniq.com
www.pondinlet.ca
Other Information: Additional Phone: 867-899-8935
Municipal Type: Hamlet
Area: 173.36 sq km
Population in 2011: 1,549
Provincial Electoral District(s): Tunnuniq
Federal Electoral District(s): Nunavut
Next Election: Dec. 10, 2012
Jaykolasie Killiktee, Mayor
Mike Richards, Sr. Admin. Officer

Qikiqtarjuaq
P.O. Box 4
Qikiqtarjuaq, NU X0A 0B0
Tel: 867-927-8832; *Fax:* 867-927-8120
munQik@qiniq.com
Other Information: Additional Phone: 867-927-8178
Municipal Type: Hamlet
Area: 130.65 sq km
Population in 2011: 520
Provincial Electoral District(s): Uqqummiut
Federal Electoral District(s): Nunavut
Next Election: Dec. 10, 2012
Note: Formerly Broughton Island.
Hannah Audlakiak, Mayor
Qikmayor@qiniq.com
Rick Van Horne, Sr. Admin. Officer

Rankin Inlet
P.O. Box 310
Rankin Inlet, NU X0C 0G0
Tel: 867-645-2895; *Fax:* 867-645-2146
sao@rankininlet.ca
www.rankininlet.net
Municipal Type: Hamlet
Incorporated: 1975 *Area:* 20.24 sq km
Population in 2011: 2,266
Provincial Electoral District(s): Rankin Inlet North; Rankin Inlet South/Whale Cove
Federal Electoral District(s): Nunavut
Next Election: Dec. 10, 2012
Pujjutt Towtongie, Mayor
Hilda Price, Sr. Admin. Officer

Repulse Bay
P.O. Box 10
Repulse Bay, NU X0C 0H0
Tel: 867-462-4014; *Fax:* 867-462-4411
saorepulse@qiniq.com
Municipal Type: Hamlet
Incorporated: 1978 *Area:* 423.74 sq km
Population in 2011: 945
Provincial Electoral District(s): Akulliq
Federal Electoral District(s): Nunavut
Next Election: Dec. 10, 2012
Donaty Milortok, Mayor
Bob Aymont, Sr. Admin. Officer

Resolute Bay
P.O. Box 60
Resolute Bay, NU X0A 0V0
Tel: 867-252-3616; *Fax:* 867-252-3749
hamletsao@qiniq.com
Other Information: Additional Phone: 867-252-3689
Municipal Type: Hamlet
Incorporated: 1987 *Area:* 116.89 sq km
Population in 2011: 214
Provincial Electoral District(s): Quttiktuq
Federal Electoral District(s): Nunavut
Next Election: Dec. 10, 2012
Ludy Pudluk, Mayor
Josh Hunter, Sr. Admin. Officer

Sanikiluaq
General Delivery
Sanikiluaq, NU X0A 0W0
Tel: 867-266-7900; *Fax:* 867-266-8903
sanisao@qiniq.com
Other Information: Additional Phone: 867-266-7901
Municipal Type: Hamlet
Incorporated: 1976 *Area:* 114.98 sq km
Population in 2011: 812
Provincial Electoral District(s): Hudson Bay
Federal Electoral District(s): Nunavut
Next Election: Dec. 10, 2012
Joe Aragutina, Mayor
Thomas Kutluk, Sr. Admin. Officer

Taloyoak
P.O. Box 8
Taloyoak, NU X0B 1B0
Tel: 867-561-6341; *Fax:* 867-561-5057
hamoftal@qiniq.com
www.polarnet.ca/~taloyoak
Municipal Type: Hamlet
Incorporated: 1981 *Area:* 37.65 sq km
Population in 2011: 899
Provincial Electoral District(s): Nattilik
Federal Electoral District(s): Nunavut
Next Election: Dec. 10, 2012
Note: Formerly known as Spence Bay.
Tommy Aiyout, Mayor
Stephen King, Sr. Admin. Officer

Whale Cove
P.O. Box 120
Whale Cove, NU X0C 0J0
Tel: 867-896-9961; *Fax:* 867-896-9109
saowc@qiniq.com
Municipal Type: Hamlet
Incorporated: 1976 *Area:* 283.65 sq km
Population in 2011: 407
Provincial Electoral District(s): Rankin Inlet South/Whale Cove
Federal Electoral District(s): Nunavut
Next Election: Dec. 10, 2012
Percy Kabloona, Mayor

ONTARIO

There are two types of municipal government structure in Ontario: two-tier municipalities, which consist of upper-tier municipalities, known as either regions or counties, plus their constituent lower-tier municipalities; and single-tier municipalities.

One-half of Ontario's population lives in the single-tier cities of Toronto, Ottawa and Hamilton and in areas with a regional system of government. The regional system was created for the more densely populated areas of this province. Regions have more servicing responsibilities than a county, and while there are variations, services usually provided by regions include arterial roads, transit, policing, sewer and water systems, waste disposal, region-wide land use planning and development, health and social services. Lower-tier municipalities within regions are generally responsible for local roads, fire protection, tax collection, garbage collection, recreation and local land use planning. All municipalities in a region participate in the regional system.

Counties exist only in southern Ontario. Lower-tier municipalities (known as cities, towns, villages, townships) within counties provide the majority of municipal services to their residents. The services provided by county governments are usually limited to arterial roads, health and social services and county land use planning. Local municipalities raise taxes for their own purposes, as well as for upper-tier and school board purposes.

Generally, membership of the upper-tier council comprises representatives from the lower tiers, although heads of council can be directly elected.

Single-tier municipalities exist across Ontario and include separated municipalities that are located within a county but are not part of the county for municipal purposes (e.g. City of Windsor, Town of Smiths Falls, Township of Pelee). Single-tier municipalities also include all northern municipalities (e.g. City of Thunder Bay, Town of Blind River, Township of Cockburn Island). Single-tier municipalities also include those former counties or regional municipalities that have amalgamated into single-tier municipalities (e.g. Municipality of Chatham-Kent, County of Prince Edward, County of Brant, City of Kawartha Lakes, City of Toronto, City of Hamilton, City of Ottawa, City of Greater Sudbury, Haldimand County, Norfolk County). Single-tier municipalities have responsibilities for their residents.

The more populated areas are incorporated into municipalitites; only 40,000 people (not including aboriginal peoples on reserves) live in areas not incorporated as municipalities. Services in the northern regions have been structured to optimize efficiencies in service delivery. District Social Service Administration Boards deliver core services in social assistance, child care and social housing, and may also provide optional health services, land ambulances and public health. Some services in a limited number of unincorporated areas are provided by local service boards and local roads which are funded by the province.

Under the Municipal Elections Act, local government elections are held on the fourth Monday in October, for a four-year term (2014, 2018, etc.). The preliminary list of electors is compiled by the Municipal Property Assessment Corporation from assessment and other data. The Municipal Elections Act provides for alternative methods of voting, including touch screen, vote by mail, vote by telephone, and internet voting.

Reproduced with the permission of Natural Resources Canada, 2012

Ontario

Counties & Municipal Districts in Ontario

Brant
P.O. Box 160
26 Park Ave.
Burford, ON N0E 1A0
Tel: 519-449-2451; *Fax:* 519-449-2454
brant@county.brant.on.ca
www.brant.ca
Other Information: Toll Free Phone: 1-888-250-2297
Municipal Type: County
Incorporated: Jan. 1, 1999 *Area:* 843.1 sq km
Population in 2011: 35,638
Provincial Electoral District(s): Brant
Federal Electoral District(s): Brant
Next Election: Oct. 27, 2014 (4 year terms)
Ron Eddy, Mayor
Steve Schmitt, Councillor, Ward(s): 1
John Wheat, Councillor, Ward(s): 1
Roy Haggart, Councillor, Ward(s): 2
Shirley Simons, Councillor, Ward(s): 2
Cliff Atfield, Councillor, Ward(s): 3
Murray Powell, Councillor, Ward(s): 3
Robert Chambers, Councillor, Ward(s): 4
Kevin Hodge, Councillor, Ward(s): 4
Brian Coleman, Councillor, Ward(s): 5
Joan Gatward, Councillor, Ward(s): 5
Jayne Carman, Clerk & Coordinator, Council Committee
Don Glassford, Chief Administrative Officer
Heather Mifflin, Treasurer
Fran Bell, Director, Corporate Services
Cynthia Compeau, Director, Public Works
David Johnston, Director, Development Services
Paul Boissonneault, Fire Chief
Kathy Ballantyne, Manager, Parks & Facilities
Alex Davidson, Manager, Water Division
Lee Robinson, Manager, Infrastructure Services
Ed Sharp, Manager, Environmental Services
Mike Tout, Manager, Roads Operations

Bruce
P.O. Box 70
30 Park St.
Walkerton, ON N0G 2V0
Tel: 519-881-1291; *Fax:* 519-881-1619
www.brucecounty.on.ca
Municipal Type: County
Area: 4,079.17 sq km
Population in 2011: 66,102
Next Election: Oct. 27, 2014 (4 year terms)
Mike Smith, Warden & Councillor, Ward(s): Saugeen Shores
Paul Eagleson, Councillor, Ward(s): Arran-Elderslie
David Inglis, Councillor, Ward(s): Brockton
Mitch Twolan, Councillor, Ward(s): Huron-Kinloss
Larry Kraemer, Councillor, Ward(s): Kincardine
Milt McIver, Councillor, Ward(s): Northern Bruce Peninsula
Bill Goetz, Councillor, Ward(s): South Bruce
John Close, Councillor, Ward(s): South Bruce Peninsula
J. Wayne Jamieson, Chief Administrative Officer
wjamieson@brucecounty.on.ca
Bettyanne Cobean, C.M.O., Clerk-Treasurer, Corporate Services
bcobean@brucecounty.on.ca
Doug Harris, Director, Human Resources
Chris LaForest, Director, Planning
Terry Sanderson, Director, Social Services & Social Housing
Doug Smith, Director, Emergency Services
Brian Knox, County Engineer

Dufferin
51 Zina St.
Orangeville, ON L9W 1E5
Tel: 519-941-2816; *Fax:* 519-941-4565
info@dufferincounty.on.ca; treasury@dufferincounty.on.ca
www.dufferincounty.on.ca
Other Information: Toll-Free Phone: 1-877-941-6991
Municipal Type: County
Incorporated: Jan. 24, 1881 *Area:* 1,485.58 sq km
Population in 2011: 56,881
Next Election: Oct. 27, 2014 (4 year terms)
Warren Maycock, Warden & Councillor, Ward(s): Orangeville
warden@dufferincounty.on.ca
Don MacIver, Councillor, Ward(s): Amaranth
Walter Kolodziechuk, Councillor, Ward(s): Amaranth
John Oosterhof, Councillor, Ward(s): East Luther Grand Valley
Bill Hill, Councillor, Ward(s): Melancthon
Darren White, Councillor, Ward(s): Melancthon
Ken McGhee, Councillor, Ward(s): Mono
Laura Ryan, Councillor, Ward(s): Mono
Rhonda Campbell Moon, Councillor, Ward(s): Mulmur
Paul Mills, Councillor, Ward(s): Mulmur
Rob Adams, Councillor, Ward(s): Orangeville
Ken Bennington, Councillor, Ward(s): Shelburne
Ed Crewson, Councillor, Ward(s): Shelburne
Pam Hillock, Clerk & Director, Corporate Services
clerk@dufferincounty.on.ca
Sonya Pritchard, Chief Administrative Officer
cao@dufferincounty.on.ca
Alan Selby, Treasurer
treasurer@dufferincounty.on.ca
Trevor Lewis, Director, Public Works
directorofpublicworks@dufferincounty.on.ca
Michael A. Giles, Chief Building Official
cbo@dufferincounty.on.ca
Mark Bialkowski, Manager, Human Resources
hr@dufferincounty.on.ca
Melissa Kovacs-Reid, Coordinator, Waste Management
wastemgmt@dufferincounty.on.ca
Shara Bagnell, Officer, Health & Safety
health&safety@dufferincounty.on.ca

Durham
P.O. Box 623
605 Rossland Rd. East
Whitby, ON L1N 6A3
Tel: 905-668-7711; *Fax:* 905-668-9963
info@durham.ca; cishelp@durham.ca (Corporate Information)
www.durham.ca
Other Information: Toll-Free Phone: 1-800-372-1102
Municipal Type: Regional Municipality
Incorporated: Jan. 1, 1974 *Area:* 2,523.15 sq km
Population in 2011: 608,124
Next Election: Oct. 27, 2014 (4 year terms)
Roger Anderson, Regional Chair & Chief Executive Officer, Councillor, Fax: 905-668-1567
chair@durham.ca
Shaun Collier, Councillor, Ward(s): Ajax
Colleen Jordan, Councillor, Ward(s): Ajax
Debbie Bath, Councillor, Ward(s): Brock
Adrian Foster, Councillor, Ward(s): Clarington
Mary Novak, Councillor, Ward(s): Clarington
Willie Woo, Councillor, Ward(s): Clarington
John R. Aker, Councillor, Ward(s): Oshawa
Bob Chapman, Councillor, Ward(s): Oshawa
Nancy Diamond, Councillor, Ward(s): Oshawa
Amy England, Councillor, Ward(s): Oshawa
Tito-Dante Marimpietri, Councillor, Ward(s): Oshawa
John Neal, Councillor, Ward(s): Oshawa
Nester Pidwerbecki, Councillor, Ward(s): Oshawa
Jennifer O'Connell, Councillor, Ward(s): Pickering 1
Bill McLean, Councillor, Ward(s): Pickering 2
Peter Rodrigues, Councillor, Ward(s): Pickering 3
Bobbie Drew, Councillor, Ward(s): Scugog
Jack Ballinger, Councillor, Ward(s): Uxbridge
Lorne Earle Coe, Councillor, Ward(s): Whitby
Joe Drumm, Councillor, Ward(s): Whitby
Don Mitchell, Councillor, Ward(s): Whitby
Patricia M. Madill, Regional Clerk, Fax: 905-668-9963
clerks@durham.ca
Garry H. Cubitt, M.S.W., Chief Administrative Officer
cao@durham.ca
R. Jim Clapp, Treasurer/Commissioner, Finance Department, Fax: 905-666-6256
Cliff Curtis, Commissioner, Works Department, Fax: 905-668-2051
works@durham.ca
Hugh A. Drouin, Commissioner, Social Services Department, Fax: 905-666-6219
socserv@durham.ca
Alex L. Georgieff, Commissioner, Planning Department, Fax: 905-666-6208
planning@durham.ca
Garth S. Johns, Commissioner, Human Resources, Fax: 905-666-3327
Robert J. Kyle, Commissioner, Health Department & Medical Officer of Health, Fax: 905-666-3327
health@durham.ca
Pat W. Olive, Commissioner, Economic Development & Tourism 800-413-0017, Fax: 905-666-6228
business@durham.ca; tourism@durham.ca
Ivan Ciuciura, Director, Durham Emergency Management Office 905-430-2792, Fax: 905-430-8635
demo@durham.ca
Sherri Munns-Audet, Director, Corporate Communications, Fax: 905-668-1468
corporatecommunications@durham.ca
Ted Galinis, General Manager, Durham Region Transit, Fax: 905-666-6193
transit@durham.ca

Elgin
450 Sunset Dr.
St Thomas, ON N5R 5V1
Tel: 519-631-1460; *Fax:* 519-633-7661
www.elgin-county.on.ca
Municipal Type: County
Incorporated: 1852 *Area:* 1,880.84 sq km
Population in 2011: 87,461
Next Election: Oct. 27, 2014 (4 year terms)
Note: Restructuring of the county occurred in 1998.
Dave Mennill, Warden & Councillor, Ward(s): Malahide
Jack Couckuyt, Councillor, Ward(s): Aylmer
Paul Ens, Councillor, Ward(s): Bayham
David Marr, Councillor, Ward(s): Central Elgin
Bill Walters, Councillor, Ward(s): Central Elgin
Cameron McWilliam, Councillor, Ward(s): Dutton/Dunwich
Jim Jenkins, Councillor, Ward(s): Malahide
James McIntyre, Councillor, Ward(s): Southwold
Bernie Wiehle, Councillor, Ward(s): West Elgin
Mark G. McDonald, Chief Administrative Officer
mmcdonald@elgin-county.on.ca
Rob Bryce, Director, Human Resources
Jim Bundschuh, Director, Financial Services
jbundschuh@elgin-county.on.ca
Brian Masschaele, Director, Community & Cultural Services
bmasschaele@elgin-county.on.ca
Clayton Watters, Director, Engineering Services

Essex
360 Fairview Ave. West
Essex, ON N8M 1Y6
Tel: 519-776-6441; *Fax:* 519-776-4455
www.countyofessex.on.ca
Other Information: Planning Department, Fax: 519-776-1253
Municipal Type: County
Incorporated: 1999 *Area:* 1,851.34 sq km
Population in 2011: 388,782
Next Election: Oct. 27, 2014 (4 year terms)
Tom Bain, Warden & Councillor, Ward(s): Lakeshore
tbain@lakeshore.ca
Gary McNamara, Deputy Warden & Councillor, Ward(s): Tecumseh
gmcnamara@tecumseh.ca
Wayne Hurst, Councillor, Ward(s): Amherstburg
519-736-7646
whurst@amherstburg.ca
Ron Sutherland, Councillor, Ward(s): Amerstburg
519-736-8092
rsutherland@amherstburg.ca
Ron McDermott, Councillor, Ward(s): Essex
519-776-8150
rmcdermott@essex.ca
Richard Meloche, Councillor, Ward(s): Essex
519-776-5726
rmeloche@essex.ca
Nelson Santos, Councillor, Ward(s): Kingsville
519-733-9936
nsantos@kingsville.ca
Tamara Stomp, Councillor, Ward(s): Kingsville
519-733-5254
stomp@mnsi.net
Al Fazio, Councillor, Ward(s): Lakeshore
519-728-0490
afazio@lakeshore.ca
Ken Antaya, Councillor, Ward(s): LaSalle
mayor@town.lasalle.on.ca
Mark Carrick, Councillor, Ward(s): LaSalle
mcarrick@town.lasalle.on.ca
John Peterson, Councillor, Ward(s): Leamington
519-322-8470
jpaterson@leamington.ca
Charles Wright, Councillor, Ward(s): Leamington
519-324-5455
cwright@leamington.ca
Cheryl Hardcastle, Councillor, Ward(s): Tecumseh
519-817-4864
chardcastle@tecumseh.ca
Mary S. Brennan, Clerk & Director, Council Services
Brian Gregg, Chief Administrative Officer
Robert Maisonville, Director, Corporate Services & Treasurer
Greg Schlosser, Director, Human Resources
Bill King, Manager, Planning Services
Tom Bateman, County Engineer
Phillip Berthiaume, Planner, Emergency Measures

Frontenac
2069 Battersea Rd., RR#1
Glenburnie, ON K0H 1S0
Tel: 613-548-9400; *Fax:* 613-546-8460
info@frontenaccounty.ca
www.frontenaccounty.ca

Municipal Type: County
Incorporated: Jan. 1, 1998 *Area:* 3,672.49 sq km
Population in 2011: 149,738
Next Election: Oct. 27, 2014 (4 year terms)
Gary Davison, Warden & Councillor, Ward(s): South Frontenac
sfmayor@frontenaccounty.ca
Janet Gutowski, Deputy Warden & Councillor, Ward(s): Central Frontenac
John Purden, Councillor, Ward(s): Central Frontenac
Denis Doyle, Councillor, Ward(s): Frontenac Islands
David Jones, Councillor, Ward(s): Frontenac Islands
Bud Clayton, Councillor, Ward(s): North Frontenac
John Inglis, Councillor, Ward(s): North Frontenac
John McDougall, Councillor, Ward(s): South Frontenac
Liz Savill, Chief Administrative Officer & Clerk
Marian Van Bruinessen, Treasurer
Paul Charbonneau, Director, Emergency & Transportation Services & Chief, Paramedics
Joe Gallivan, Manager, Sustainability Planning
Anne Marie Young, Manager, Economic Development

Grey

County Administration Bldg.
595 Ninth Ave. East
Owen Sound, ON N4K 3E3
Tel: 519-376-2205
www.greycounty.ca
Other Information: Toll-Free Phone: 1-800-567-4739
Municipal Type: County
Incorporated: Jan. 1, 1852 *Area:* 4,508.12 sq km
Population in 2011: 92,568
Next Election: Oct. 27, 2014 (4 year terms)
Arlene Wright, Warden & Councillor
warden@grey.ca
Bob Pringle, Mayor, Councillor, Ward(s): Chatsworth
bob.pringle@grey.ca
Terry McKay, Deputy Mayor & Councillor, Ward(s): Chatsworth
terry.mckay@grey.ca
Alan Barfoot, Mayor, Councillor, Ward(s): Georgian Bluffs
alan.barfoot@grey.ca
Dwight Burley, Deputy Mayor & Councillor, Ward(s): Georgian Bluffs
dwight.burley@grey.ca
Wayne Fitzgerald, Mayor, Councillor, Ward(s): Grey Highlands
wayne.fitzgerald@grey.ca
Paul McQueen, Deputy Mayor & Councillor, Ward(s): Grey Highlands
paul.mcqueen@grey.ca
Kathi Maskell, Mayor, Councillor, Ward(s): Hanover
kathi.maskell@grey.ca
Bob White, Deputy Mayor & Councillor, Ward(s): Hanover
bob.white@grey.ca
Francis Richardson, Mayor, Councillor, Ward(s): Meaford
francis.richardson@grey.ca
Harley Greenfield, Deputy Mayor & Councillor, Ward(s): Meaford
harley.greenfield@grey.ca
Deborah Haswell, Mayor, Councillor, Ward(s): Owen Sound
deb.haswell@grey.ca
Arlene Wright, City / County Councillor, Councillor, Ward(s): Owen Sound
arlene.wright@grey.ca
Brian Milne, Mayor, Councillor, Ward(s): Southgate
brian.milne@grey.ca
Norman Jack, Deputy Mayor & Councillor, Ward(s): Southgate
norman.jack@grey.ca
Ellen Anderson, Mayor, Councillor, Ward(s): The Blue Mountains
ellen.anderson@grey.ca
Duncan McKinlay, Deputy Mayor & Councillor, Ward(s): The Blue Mountains
duncan.mckinlay@grey.ca
Kevin Eccles, Mayor, Councillor, Ward(s): West Grey
kevin.eccles@grey.ca
John Bell, Deputy Mayor & Councillor, Ward(s): West Grey
john.bell@grey.ca
Sharon Vokes, C.M.O., County Clerk & Director, Council Services
svokes@greycounty.ca
Lance Thurston, Chief Administrative Officer
lance.thurston@grey.ca
Kevin Weppler, Director, Finance
kevin.weppler@grey.ca
Barb Fedy, BA, Director, Social Services
barb.fedy@grey.ca
Geoff Hogan, BSc, Director, Information Technology
geoff.hogan@grey.ca
Randy Scherzer, BES, MCIP, RPP, Director, Planning & Development
randy.scherzer@grey.ca
Grant McLevy, Director, Human Resources
grant.mclevy@grey.ca; employment@grey.ca

Haldimand

Cayuga Administration Bldg.
45 Munsee St. North
Cayuga, ON N0A 1E0
Tel: 905-318-5932; *Fax:* 905-772-3542
www.haldimandcounty.on.ca
Municipal Type: County
Incorporated: Jan. 1, 2001 *Area:* 1,251.58 sq km
Population in 2011: 44,876
Provincial Electoral District(s): Haldimand-Norfolk
Federal Electoral District(s): Haldimand-Norfolk
Next Election: Oct. 27, 2014 (4 year terms)
Ken Hewitt, Mayor
khewitt@haldimandcounty.on.ca
Leroy Bartlett, Councillor, Ward(s): 1
lbartlett@haldimandcounty.on.ca
Fred Morison, Councillor, Ward(s): 2
fmorison@haldimandcounty.on.ca
Craig Grice, Councillor, Ward(s): 3
cgrice@haldimandcounty.on.ca
Tony Dalimonte, Councillor, Ward(s): 4
tdalimonte@haldimandcounty.on.ca
Rob Shirton, Councillor, Ward(s): 5
rshirton@haldimandcounty.on.ca
Lorne Boyko, Councillor, Ward(s): 6
lpboyko@haldimandcounty.on.ca
Evelyn Eichenbaum, Clerk
eeichenbaum@haldimandcounty.on.ca
Donald Boyle, Chief Administrative Officer
dboyle@haldimandcounty.on.ca
Karen General, General Manager, Corporate Services
kgeneral@haldimandcounty.on.ca
Hugh Hanly, General Manager, Community Services
hhanly@haldimandcounty.on.ca
Craig Manley, General Manager, Planning & Economic Development
cmanley@haldimandcounty.on.ca
Paul Mungar, Director, Environemtnal Services & Fleet & Facility Asset Management
pmungar@haldimandcounty.on.ca

Haliburton

P.O. Box 399
11 Newcastle St.
Minden, ON K0M 2K0
Tel: 705-286-1333; *Fax:* 705-286-4829
aballe@county.haliburton.on.ca
www.haliburtoncounty.ca
Other Information: Toll-Free: 1-866-886-8815
Municipal Type: County
Incorporated: Jan. 1, 2001 *Area:* 4,025.27 sq km
Population in 2011: 17,026
Next Election: Oct. 27, 2014 (4 year terms)
Murray Fearrey, Warden & Councillor, Ward(s): Dysart et al
mfearrey@dysartetal.ca
Carol Moffatt, Councillor, Ward(s): Algonquin Highlands
cmoffatt@algonquinhighlands.ca
Liz Danielsen, Councillor, Ward(s): Algonquin Highlands
ldanielsen@algonquinhighlands.ca
Bill Davis, Councillor, Ward(s): Dysart et al
billdavis@dysartetal.ca
Dave Burton, Councillor, Ward(s): Highlands East
dburton@highlandseast.ca
Suzanne Partridge, Councillor, Ward(s): Highlands East
spartridge@highlandseast.ca
Barb Reid, Councillor, Ward(s): Minden Hills
breid@mindenhills.ca
Cheryl Murdoch, Councillor, Ward(s): Minden Hills
705-286-1701
Jim Wilson, County Clerk & Chief Administrative Officer
jwilson@county.haliburton.on.ca
Laura Janke, Treasurer
ljanke@county.haliburton.on.ca
Pat Kennedy, Director, Emergency Services
pkennedy@county.haliburton.on.ca
Doug Ray, Director, Public Works
dray@county.haliburton.on.ca
Robert Smith, Director, Economic Development & Tourism
rsmith@county.haliburton.on.ca
Jane Tousaw, Director, Planning
jtousaw@county.haliburton.on.ca
Roy Haig, Manager, Engineering & 911 Services
rhaig@county.haliburton.on.ca
Jim Young, Manager, Operations
jyoung@county.haliburton.on.ca

Halton

1151 Bronte Rd.
Oakville, ON L6M 3L1
Tel: 905-825-6000; *Fax:* 905-825-9010
accesshalton@halton.ca
www.halton.ca
Other Information: Toll-Free Phone: 1-866-442-5866; TTY: 905-827-9833
Municipal Type: Regional Municipality
Incorporated: Jan. 1, 1974 *Area:* 967.17 sq km
Population in 2011: 501,669
Next Election: Oct. 27, 2014 (4 year terms)
Gary Carr, Regional Chair, Councillor
905-825-6115, Fax: 905-825-8273
gary.carr@halton.ca
Rick Goldring, Councillor, Ward(s): Burlington Mayor
Rick Craven, Councillor, Ward(s): Burlington 1
Marianne Meed Ward, Councillor, Ward(s): Burlington 2
John Taylor, Councillor, Ward(s): Burlington 3
Jack Dennison, Councillor, Ward(s): Burlington 4
Paul Sharman, Councillor, Ward(s): Burlington 5
Blair Lancaster, Councillor, Ward(s): Burlington 6
Rick Bonnette, Councillor, Ward(s): Halton Hills Mayor
Clark Somerville, Councillor, Ward(s): Halton Hills 1 & 2
Jane Fogal, Councillor, Ward(s): Halton Hills 3 & 4
Gordon Krantz, Councillor, Ward(s): Milton Mayor
Tony Lambert, Councillor, Ward(s): Milton 1, 6, 7, 8
Colin Best, Councillor, Ward(s): Milton 2, 3, 4, 5
Rob Burton, Councillor, Ward(s): Oakville Mayor
Alan Johnston, Councillor, Ward(s): Oakville 1
Cathy Duddeck, Councillor, Ward(s): Oakville 2
F. Keith Bird, Councillor, Ward(s): Oakville 3
Allan Elgar, Councillor, Ward(s): Oakville 4
Jeff Knoll, Councillor, Ward(s): Oakville 5
Tom Adams, Councillor, Ward(s): Oakville 6
Susan Lathan, Regional Clerk & Director, Council Services
regionalclerk@halton.ca; susan.lathan@halton.ca
Pat Moyle, Chief Administrative Officer
J.E. MacCaskill, Regional Treasurer & Commissioner, Corporate Services
Mark Meneray, Commissioner, Legislative & Planning Services & Corporate Counsel
Robert Nosal, Commissioner & Medical Officer of Health
S. Wolfson, Commissioner, Social & Community Services
M. Zamojc, Commissioner, Public Works

Hastings

County Administration Bldg.
P.O. Box 4400
235 Pinnacle St.
Belleville, ON K8N 3A9
Tel: 613-966-1319; *Fax:* 613-966-2574
www.hastingscounty.com
Other Information: Toll-Free Phone: 1-800-510-3306
Municipal Type: County
Incorporated: 1850 *Area:* 5,977.64 sq km
Population in 2011: 134,934
Next Election: Oct. 27, 2014 (4 year terms)
Jo-Anne Albert, Warden & Councillor, Ward(s): Tweed
albertj@hastingscounty.com
Bernice Jenkins, Councillor, Ward(s): Bancroft
Bonnie Adams, Councillor, Ward(s): Carlow/Mayo
Owen Ketcheson, Councillor, Ward(s): Centre Hastings
Norm Clark, Councillor, Ward(s): Deseronto
Carl Tinney, Councillor, Ward(s): Faraday
Ron Emond, Councillor, Ward(s): Hastings Highlands
Dave Golem, Councillor, Ward(s): Limerick
Bob Sager, Councillor, Ward(s): Madoc
Terry Clemens, Councillor, Ward(s): Marmora & Lake
Rodney Cooney, Councillor, Ward(s): Stirling-Rawdon
Wanda Donaldson, Councillor, Ward(s): Tudor & Cashel
Rick Phillips, Councillor, Ward(s): Tyendinaga
Dan McCaw, Councillor, Ward(s): Wollaston
James Pine, Chief Administrative Officer & Clerk
pinej@hastingscounty.com
Sue Horwood, Treasurer, Director, Finance, Asset Management & Services
Shaune Lightfoot, Director, Human Resources
Brian McComb, Director, Planning

Huron

1 Court House Sq.
Goderich, ON N7A 1M2
Tel: 519-524-8394; *Fax:* 519-524-2044
huronadmin@huroncounty.ca
www.huroncounty.ca
Other Information: Toll-Free Phone: 1-888-524-8394 (in 519 area)
Municipal Type: County
Area: 3,396.68 sq km

Population in 2011: 59,100
Next Election: Oct. 27, 2014 (4 year terms)
Neil Vincent, Warden & Councillor, Ward(s): North Huron
Ben Van Diepenbeek, Councillor, Ward(s): Ashfield-Colborne-Wawanosh
Neil Rintoul, Councillor, Ward(s): Ashfield-Colborne-Wawanosh
Paul Klopp, Councillor, Ward(s): Bluewater
Tyler Hessel, Councillor, Ward(s): Bluewater
Jim Ginn, Councillor, Ward(s): Central Huron
David Jewitt, Councillor, Ward(s): Central Huron
Brian Barnim, Councillor, Ward(s): Central Huron
Deb Shewfelt, Councillor, Ward(s): Goderich
John Grace, Councillor, Ward(s): Goderich
Art Versteeg, Councillor, Ward(s): Howick
Bernie MacLellan, Councillor, Ward(s): Huron East
Joe Steffler, Councillor, Ward(s): Huron East
Bill Siemon, Councillor, Ward(s): Huron East
Paul Gowing, Councillor, Ward(s): Morris-Turnberry
Dave Riach, Councillor, Ward(s): North Huron
George Robertson, Councillor, Ward(s): South Huron
Jim Dietrich, Councillor, Ward(s): South Huron
David Frayne, Councillor, Ward(s): South Huron
Barbara Wilson, Clerk
Dave Laurie, Director, Public Works
Scott Tousaw, Director, Planning & Development
Nancy Cameron, Medical Officer of Health

Lambton

P.O. Box 3000
789 Broadway St.
Wyoming, ON N0N 1T0
Tel: 519-845-0801; *Fax:* 519-845-3160
www.lambtononline.com
Other Information: Toll-Free Phone: 1-866-324-6912
Municipal Type: County
Incorporated: 1853 *Area:* 3,001.7 sq km
Population in 2011: 126,199
Next Election: Oct. 27, 2014 (4 year terms)
Steve Arnold, Warden & Councillor, Ward(s): St. Clair
sarnold1@rogers.blackberry.net
Lonny Napper, Deputy Warden & Councillor, Ward(s): Plympton-Wyoming
lnapper@xcelco.on.ca
Don McGugan, Councillor, Ward(s): Brooke-Alvinston
jdmcgugan@hotmail.com
William (Bill) Bilton, Councillor, Ward(s): Dawn-Euphemia
mayor@dawneuphemia.on.ca
Jim Burns, Councillor, Ward(s): Enniskillen
jim.burns@county-lambton.on.ca
Bill Weber, Councillor, Ward(s): Lambton Shores
bweber@lambtonshores.ca
Elizabeth Davis-Dagg, Councillor, Ward(s): Lambton Shores
edavis-dagg@lambtonshores.ca
Ian Veen, Councillor, Ward(s): Oil Springs
ianveen1@hotmail.com
John McCharles, Councillor, Ward(s): Petrolia
johnnyremax@bellnet.ca
Dick Kirkland, Councillor, Ward(s): Point Edward
dkirkland@villageofpointedward.com
Mike Bradley, Councillor, Ward(s): Sarnia
mayor@sarnia.ca
David Boushy, Councillor, Ward(s): Sarnia
d.boushy@cogeco.ca
Anne Marie Gillis, Councillor, Ward(s): Sarnia
sarcouncillor@gmail.com
Jim Foubister, Councillor, Ward(s): Sarnia
jfoubister1@cogeco.ca
Bev MacDougall, Councillor, Ward(s): Sarnia
bevmacdougall@ebtech.net
Peter Gilliland, Councillor, Ward(s): St. Clair
pgillila@rivernet.net
Todd Case, Councillor, Ward(s): Warwick
cases@execulink.com
Ronald G. Van Horne, Chief Administrative Officer
ron.vanhorne@county-lambton.on.ca
Andrew Taylor, Acting General Manager, Public Health Services
Jim Kutyba, P.Eng., General Manager, Infrastructure & Development Services
jim.kutyba@county-lambton.on.ca
Robert Tremain, General Manager, Cultural Services
robert.tremain@county-lambton.on.ca
Jason Cole, P.Eng., Manager, Public Works
jason.cole@county-lambton.on.ca

Lanark

County Administration Bldg.
P.O. Box 37
99 Christie Lake Rd.
Perth, ON K7H 3E2
Tel: 613-267-4200; *Fax:* 613-267-2964
info@county.lanark.on.ca
www.county.lanark.on.ca
Other Information: Toll-Free Phone: 1-888-952-6275
Municipal Type: County
Incorporated: Jan. 1st 1998 *Area:* 2,979.14 sq km
Population in 2011: 65,667
Next Election: Oct. 27, 2014 (4 year terms)
Sharon Mousseau, Warden & Councillor, Ward(s): Beckwith
Richard Kidd, Councillor, Ward(s): Beckwith Township
rkidd@ripnet.com
Wendy Leblanc, Councillor, Ward(s): Carleton Place
wendyjleblanc@gmail.com
Ed Sonnenburg, Councillor, Ward(s): Carleton Place
e.sonnenburg@rogers.com
Aubrey Churchill, Councillor, Ward(s): Drummond/North Elmsley
achurchill@storm.ca
Gail Code, Councillor, Ward(s): Drummond/North Elmsley
gmcconnell@ripnet.com
Peter McLaren, Councillor, Ward(s): Lanark Highlands
p.mclarenfarms@sympatico.ca
Brian Stewart, Councillor, Ward(s): Lanark Highlands
brian_stewart@sympatico.ca
John Levi, Councillor, Ward(s): Mississippi Mills
johnlevi.mm@gmail.com
Val Wilkinson, Councillor, Ward(s): Mississippi Mills
vwilkinson@storm.ca
Bill Dobson, Councillor, Ward(s): Montague
bdobson@ripnet.com
Pat Dolan, Councillor, Ward(s): Montague
pdolan.montague@bell.net
John Fenik, Councillor, Ward(s): Perth
jfenik@cogeco.ca
John Gemmell, Councillor, Ward(s): Perth
jgemmell2@cogeco.ca
Keith Kerr, Councillor, Ward(s): Tay Valley Township
kmkk@ripnet.com
Susan Freeman, Councillor, Ward(s): Tay Valley Township
susan@cysh.ca
Cathie Ritchie, Clerk
clerk@county.lanark.on.ca
Peter Wagland, Chief Administrative Officer
cao@county.lanark.on.ca
Kurt Greaves, Treasurer & Director, Finance
Lisa Crosbie-Larmon, Director, Human Resources
Nancy Green, Director, Social Services
Sam Law, Director, Information Technology

Lennox & Addington

P.O. Box 1000
97 Thomas St. East
Napanee, ON K7R 3S9
Tel: 613-354-4883; *Fax:* 613-354-3112
www.lennox-addington.on.ca
Municipal Type: County
Area: 2,776.48 sq km
Population in 2011: 41,824
Next Election: Oct. 27, 2014 (4 year terms)
Henry Hogg, Warden & Councillor, Ward(s): Addington Highlands
613-336-0227
warden@lennox-addington.on.ca
Bill Cox, Councillor, Ward(s): Addington Highlands
613-336-8491
Roger Cole, Councillor, Ward(s): Greater Napanee
613-354-7634
Gordon Schermerhorn, Councillor, Ward(s): Greater Napanee
613-354-0429
Bill Lowry, Councillor, Ward(s): Loyalist
613-583-2412
Ric Bresee, Councillor, Ward(s): Loyalist
613-634-5544
Doug Bearance, Councillor, Ward(s): Stone Mills
613-375-8874
Eric Smith, Councillor, Ward(s): Stone Mills
613-379-2366
Larry Keech, Chief Administrative Officer & Clerk
lkeech@lennox-addington.on.ca
Mark Schjerning, Chief, Emergency Services
Bill Bishop, Director, Human Resources
bbishop@lennox-addington.on.ca
Brian Elo-Shepherd, Director, Social Services
Mary Anne Evans, Director, Information Services
mevans@lennox-addington.on.ca
Stephen Fox, Director, Financial & Physical Services
sfox@lennox-addington.on.ca

Stephen Paul, Manager, Economic Development

Middlesex

399 Ridout St. North
London, ON N6A 2P1
Tel: 519-434-7321; *Fax:* 519-434-0638
www.middlesex.ca
Municipal Type: County
Area: 3,317.15 sq km
Population in 2011: 439,151
Next Election: Oct. 27, 2014 (4 year terms)
Joanne Vanderheyden, Warden & Councillor, Ward(s): Thames Centre
519-434-7321
David Bolton, Councillor, Ward(s): Adelaide Metcalfe
Paul Hodgins, Councillor, Ward(s): Lucan Biddulph
Al Edmondson, Councillor, Ward(s): Middlesex Centre
Clare Bloomfield, Councillor, Ward(s): Middlesex Centre
Don Whipway, Councillor, Ward(s): North Middlesex
Chuck Hall, Councillor, Ward(s): North Middlesex
Doug Reycraft, Councillor, Ward(s): Southwest Middlesex
Vance Blackmore, Councillor, Ward(s): Southwest Middlesex
Brad Richards, Councillor, Ward(s): Strathroy Caradoc
Jim Maudsley, Councillor, Ward(s): Thames Centre
Marcel Meyer, Councillor, Ward(s): Thames Centre
Kathy Bunting, Clerk
Bill Rayburn, Chief Administrative Officer
Jim Gates, Treasurer
Sally Bennett, Director, Social Services
Steve Evans, Director, Planning & Economic Development
Neal Roberts, Director, Emergency Services
Chris Traini, County Engineer
Doug Spettigue, Human Resource Officer
John Trott, Woodlands Conservation Officer & Weed Inspector

Muskoka

70 Pine St.
Bracebridge, ON P1L 1N3
Tel: 705-645-2231; *Fax:* 705-645-5319
info@muskoka.on.ca
www.muskoka.on.ca
Other Information: Toll-Free Phone: 1-800-461-4210 (In 705 area code)
Municipal Type: Regional Municipality
Incorporated: Jan. 1, 1971 *Area:* 3,890.24 sq km
Population in 2011: 57,047
Next Election: Oct. 27, 2014 (4 year terms)
John Klinck, District Chair & Councillor, Ward(s): Gravenhurst
jklinck@muskoka.on.ca
Scott Young, Deputy Chair & Councillor, Ward(s): Bracebridge
Graydon Smith, Councillor, Ward(s): Bracebridge
Steven Clement, Councillor, Ward(s): Bracebridge
Lori-Lynn Giaschi-Pacini, Councillor, Ward(s): Bracebridge
Larry Braid, Councillor, Ward(s): Georgian Bay
Mike Kennedy, Councillor, Ward(s): Georgian Bay
Paul Wiancko, Councillor, Ward(s): Georgian Bay
Paisley Donaldson, Councillor, Ward(s): Gravenhurst
Sandy Cairns, Councillor, Ward(s): Gravenhurst
Bob Colhoun, Councillor, Ward(s): Gravenhurst
Rosemary King, Councillor, Ward(s): Gravenhurst
Claude Doughty, Councillor, Ward(s): Huntsville
Scott Aitchison, Councillor, Ward(s): Huntsville
Fran Coleman, Councillor, Ward(s): Huntsville
Brian Thompson, Councillor, Ward(s): Huntsville
Bob Young, Councillor, Ward(s): Lake of Bays
Shane Baker, Councillor, Ward(s): Lake of Bays
Bob Lacroix, Councillor, Ward(s): Lake of Bays
Alice Murphy, Councillor, Ward(s): Muskoka Lakes
Allen Edwards, Councillor, Ward(s): Muskoka Lakes
Phil Harding, Councillor, Ward(s): Muskoka Lakes
Ruth-Ellen Nishikawa, Councillor, Ward(s): Muskoka Lakes
Debbie Crowder, District Clerk
Jim Green, Chief Administrative Officer
Stephen Cairns, Commissioner, Finance & Corporate Services
Marg French, Commissioner, Planning Economic Development
Rick Williams, Commissioner, Community Services
705-645-2100
Tony White, Commissioner, Engineering & Public Works
705-645-6764
Geoff Bache, Director, Environmental Services
Terri Burton, Director, Emergency Services
Herman Clemens, Director, Water & Sewer Operations
Anna Landry, Director, Human Resources
alandry@muskoka.on.ca

Niagara
P.O. Box 1042
2201 St. David's Rd.
Thorold, ON L2V 4T7
Tel: 905-685-1571; *Fax:* 905-687-4977
www.niagararegion.ca
Other Information: Toll-Free Phone: 1-800-263-7215; TTY: 905-984-3613
Municipal Type: Regional Municipality
Incorporated: Jan. 1, 1970 *Area:* 1,854.17 sq km
Population in 2011: 431,346
Next Election: Oct. 27, 2014 (4 year terms)
Gary Burroughs, Regional Chair & Councillor, Ward(s): Niagara-on-the-Lake
Douglas Martin, Councillor, Ward(s): Fort Erie
905-871-1600
John Teal, Councillor, Ward(s): Fort Erie
905-871-5796
Bob Bentley, Councillor, Ward(s): Grimsby
905-945-9634
Debbie M. Zimmerman, Councillor, Ward(s): Grimsby
905-945-9516
Bill Hodgson, Councillor, Ward(s): Lincoln
905-562-4464
Mark Bylsma, Councillor, Ward(s): Lincoln
905-562-0064
Jim Diodati, Councillor, Ward(s): Niagara Falls
905-356-7521
Barbara Greenwood, Councillor, Ward(s): Niagara Falls
905-358-7226
Bart Meaves, Councillor, Ward(s): Niagara Falls
289-241-3785
Selina Volpeti, Councillor, Ward(s): Niagara Falls
905-358-0333
Dave Eke, Councillor, Ward(s): Niagara-on-the-Lake
905-468-7320
Dave Lepp, Councillor, Ward(s): Niagara on the Lake
905-468-2980
Dave Augustyn, Councillor, Ward(s): Pelham
905-892-2607
Brian Baty, Councillor, Ward(s): Pelham
905-892-5317
Vance Badawey, Councillor, Ward(s): Port Colborne
905-835-2900
David Barrick, Councillor, Ward(s): Port Colborne
905-328-5126
Brian McMullan, Councillor, Ward(s): St Catharines
905-688-5600
Alan Caslin, Councillor, Ward(s): St Catharines
289-407-0137
Brian Heit, Councillor, Ward(s): St Catharines
905-935-8377
Ronna Katzman, Councillor, Ward(s): St Catharines
905-688-1993
Andrew Petrowski, Councillor, Ward(s): St Catharines
289-241-6098
Tim Rigby, Councillor, Ward(s): St Catharines
905-328-8508
D. Bruce Timms, Councillor, Ward(s): St Catharines
905-934-6816
Ted Luciani, Councillor, Ward(s): Thorold
905-227-8733
Henry D'Angela, Councillor, Ward(s): Thorold
905-227-8298
April Jeffs, Councillor, Ward(s): Wainfleet
905-834-9052
Barry Sharpe, Councillor, Ward(s): Welland
905-735-1700
Cindy Forster, Councillor, Ward(s): Welland
905-714-7999
George Marshall, Councillor, Ward(s): Welland
905-734-4851
Douglas Joyner, Councillor, Ward(s): West Lincoln
905-957-4926
Kevin Bain, Regional Clerk
905-685-4225
Michael Trojan, Chief Administrative Officer
Gord Lockyer, Treasurer & Director, Financial Management & Reporting
Brian Hutchings, Commissioner, Corporate Services
Cathy Cousins, Acting Commissioner, Community Services
Patrick Robson, Commissioner, Integrated Community Planning
Valerie Jaeger, Commissioner, Public Health & Medical Officer of Health
Ken Bothers, Commissioner, Public Works
Andrew Pollock, Director, Waste Management Services
Denise Papaiz, Senior Manager, Corporate Communications
905-685-4225

Norfolk
50 Colborne St. South
Simcoe, ON N3Y 4N5
Tel: 519-426-5870; *Fax:* 519-426-8573
www.norfolkcounty.on.ca
Other Information: Delhi Customer Service Ctr., Phone: 519-582-2100
Municipal Type: County
Incorporated: Jan. 1, 2001 *Area:* 1,606.91 sq km
Population in 2011: 62,175
Provincial Electoral District(s): Haldimand-Norfolk
Federal Electoral District(s): Haldimand-Norfolk
Next Election: Oct. 27, 2014 (4 year terms)
Dennis Travale, Mayor
dennis.travale@norfolkcounty.ca
Betty Chanyi, Councillor, Ward(s): 1
betty.chanyi@norfolkcounty.ca
Roger Geysens, Councillor, Ward(s): 2
roger.geysens@norfolkcounty.ca
Michael J. Columbus, Councillor, Ward(s): 3
michael.columbus@norfolkcounty.ca
Jim Oliver, Councillor, Ward(s): 4
jim.oliver@norfolkcounty.ca
Peter Black, Councillor, Ward(s): 5
peter.black@norfolkcounty.ca
Charlie Luke, Councillor, Ward(s): 5
charlie.luke@norfolkcounty.ca
John Wells, Councillor, Ward(s): 6
john.wells@norfolkcounty.ca
Harold Sonnenberg, Councillor, Ward(s): 7
harold.sonnenberg@norfolkcounty.ca
Beverley D. Wood, Clerk & Manager, Council Services
bev.wood@norfolkcounty.ca
Keith Robicheau, County Manager
keith.robicheau@norfolkcounty.ca
John Ford, Treasurer & Manager, Financial Services
john.ford@norfolkcounty.ca
Christopher D. Baird, CET, CMMIII, Ec.D., General Manager, Planning & Economic Development
chris.baird@norfolkcounty.ca
Eric R. D'Hondt, P.Eng., General Manager, Public Works & Environmental Services, Fax: 519-582-4571
eric.dhondt@norfolkcounty.ca
Frank Gelinas, General Manager, Corporate Services
frank.gelinas@norfolkcounty.ca
Kevin Lichach, General Manager, Community Services
Patti Moore, General Manager, Health & Social Services
patti.moore@haldimand-norfolk.org
Bob Fields, Manager, Environmental Services
bob.fields@norfolkcounty.ca
John Hamilton, Manager, Engineering
john.hamilton@norfolkcounty.ca
Marlene L. Ireland, Manager, Fleets & Facilities
marlene.ireland@norfolkcounty.ca
Terry Dicks, Fire Chief
519-426-4115, Fax: 519-426-4140
terry.dicks@norfolkcounty.ca

Northumberland
555 Courthouse Rd.
Cobourg, ON K9A 5J6
Tel: 905-372-3329; *Fax:* 905-372-1746
www.northumberlandcounty.ca
Other Information: Toll-Free Phone: 1-800-354-7050
Municipal Type: County
Area: 1,902.97 sq km
Population in 2011: 82,126
Next Election: Oct. 27, 2014 (4 year terms)
Mark Lovshin, Warden & Councillor, Ward(s): Hamilton
lovshinm@northumberlandcounty.ca
Dalton McDonald, Councillor, Ward(s): Alnwick/Haldimand
mcdonaldd@northumberlandcounty.ca
Mark Walas, Councillor, Ward(s): Brighton
walasm@northumberlandcounty.ca
Gil Brocanier, Councillor, Ward(s): Cobourg
BrocanierG@northumberlandcounty.ca
Marc Coombs, Councillor, Ward(s): Cramahe
coombsm@northumberlandcounty.ca
Linda Thompson, Councillor, Ward(s): Hamilton
mayor@porthope.ca
Hector Macmillan, Councillor, Ward(s): Trent Hills
macmillanh@northumberlandcounty.ca
Diane Cane, CMO, County Clerk
caned@northumberlandcounty.ca
Bill Pyatt, Chief Administrative Officer
pyattb@northumberlandcounty.ca
Jennifer Moore, Treasurer & Director, Finance
moorej@northumberlandcounty.ca
James Rogers, By-Law Officer, Forest Conservation
705-799-2470
Ken Stubbings, Coordinator, Emergency Management
stubbingsk@northumberlandcounty.ca

Peel
70 Peel Centre Dr.
Brampton, ON L6T 4B9
Tel: 905-791-7800; *Fax:* 905-791-7871
info@peelregion.ca
www.peelregion.ca
Other Information: Toll-Free Phone: 1-888-919-7800
Municipal Type: Regional Municipality
Incorporated: Oct. 15, 1973 *Area:* 1,242.40 sq km
Population in 2011: 1,296,814
Next Election: Oct. 27, 2014 (4 year terms)
Emil Kolb, Regional Chair & Councillor
905-791-7800, Fax: 905-791-2567
Susan Fennell, Mayor & Councillor, Ward(s): Brampton
susan.fennell@brampton.ca
Elaine Moore, Councillor, Ward(s): Brampton 1 & 5
elaine.moore@brampton.ca
Paul Palleschi, Councillor, Ward(s): Brampton 2 & 6
paul.palleschi@brampton.ca
John Sanderson, Councillor, Ward(s): Brampton 3 & 4
john.sanderson@brampton.ca
Sandra Hames, Councillor, Ward(s): Brampton 7 & 8
sandra.hames@brampton.ca
Gael Miles, Councillor, Ward(s): Brampton 7 & 8
gael.miles@brampton.ca
John Sprovieri, Councillor, Ward(s): Brampton 9 & 10
john.sprovieri@brampton.ca
Marolyn Morrison, Mayor, Ward(s): Caledon
marolyn.morrison@caledon.ca
Richard Paterak, Councillor, Ward(s): Caledon 1
richard.paterak@caledon.ca
Allan Thompson, Councillor, Ward(s): Caledon 2
allan.thompson@caledon.ca
Richard Whitehead, Councillor, Ward(s): Caledon 3 & 4
r.whitehead@sympatico.ca
Patti Foley, Councillor, Ward(s): Caledon 5
patti.foley@caledon.ca
Hazel McCallion, Mayor & Councillor, Ward(s): Mississauga
mayor@mississauga.ca
Jim Tovey, Councillor, Ward(s): Mississauga 1
jim.tovey@mississauga.ca
Patricia Mullin, Councillor, Ward(s): Mississauga 2
pat.mullin@mississauga.ca
Chris Fonseca, Councillor, Ward(s): Mississauga 3
chris.fonseca@mississauga.ca
Frank Dale, Councillor, Ward(s): Mississauga 4
frank.dale@mississauga.ca
Ron Starr, Councillor, Ward(s): Mississauga 6
ron.starr@mississauga.ca
Nando Iannicca, Councillor, Ward(s): Mississauga 7
nando.iannicca@mississauga.ca
Katie Mahoney, Councillor, Ward(s): Mississauga 8
katie.mahoney@mississauga.ca
Pat Saito, Councillor, Ward(s): Mississauga 9
pat.saito@mississauga.ca
Sue McFadden, Councillor, Ward(s): Mississauga 10
sue.mcfadden@mississauga.ca
George Carlson, Councillor, Ward(s): Mississauga 11
george.carlson@mississauga.ca
Carol Reid, Regional Clerk
David Szwarc, Chief Administrative Officer
Norma Trim, Chief Financial Officer & Commissioner, Corporate Services
Kent Gillespie, Commissioner, Employee & Business Services
Dan Labrecque, Commissioner, Public Works
Janette Smith, Commissioner, Health Services
Janet Menard, Commissioner, Human Services
David Mowat, Medical Officer of Health
Arvin Prasad, Director, Planning Policy & Research
Norman Lee, Director, Waste Management

Perth
Courthouse
1 Huron St.
Stratford, ON N5A 5S4
Tel: 519-271-0531; *Fax:* 519-271-6265
www.perthcounty.ca
Municipal Type: County
Incorporated: Jan. 1850 *Area:* 2,218.41 sq km
Population in 2011: 75,112
Next Election: Oct. 27, 2014 (4 year terms)
Note: Restructuring occurred in Jan. 1998.
Julie Behrns, Warden & Councillor, Ward(s): North Perth
Vince Judge, Councillor, Ward(s): North Perth
519-291-3877
Meredith Schneider, Councillor, Ward(s): North Perth
519-343-2849

Ian Forrest, Councillor, Ward(s): Perth East
519-595-4031
Bob McMillan, Councillor, Ward(s): Perth East
519-656-2839
Rhonda Ehgoetz, Councillor, Ward(s): Perth East
519-393-6888
Robert Wilhelm, Councillor, Ward(s): Perth South
519-225-2304
James Aitcheson, Councillor, Ward(s): Perth South
519-393-5298
Walter McKenzie, Councillor, Ward(s): West Perth
519-348-4236
Bill French, Councillor, Ward(s): West Perth
519-348-8749
Kerri Ann O'Rourke, Clerk
Bill Arthur, Chief Administrative Officer
barthur@perthcounty.ca
Renato Pullia, Treasurer & Director, Corporate Services
rpullia@perthcounty.ca
Matt Ash, Director, Public Works
mash@perthcounty.ca
Dave Hanly, Director, Planning & Development
dhanly@perthcounty.ca
Linda Rockwood, Director, Emergency Medical Services
lrockwood@perthcounty.ca
Cliff Eggleton, Manager, EMS Operations
ceggleton@perthcounty.ca
Ann McKnight Duralia, Manager, Human Resources
amcknight@perthcounty.ca

Peterborough
County Court House
470 Water St.
Peterborough, ON K9H 3M3
Tel: 705-743-0380; *Fax:* 705-876-1730
www.county.peterborough.on.ca
Other Information: Toll-Free Phone: 1-800-710-9586
Municipal Type: County
Area: 3,805.71 sq km
Population in 2011: 134,933
Next Election: Oct. 27, 2014 (4 year terms)
James Jones, Warden & Councillor, Ward(s): Douro-Dummer
dumnews@nexicom.net
Douglas Pearcy, Councillor, Ward(s): Asphodel-Norwood
dpearcy@accel.net
Joseph Crowley, Councillor, Ward(s): Asphodel-Norwood
jwcrowley2010@gmail.com
John Fallis, Councillor, Ward(s): Cavan Monaghan
jbfallis@nexicom.net
Scott McFadden, Councillor, Ward(s): Cavan Monaghan
smcfadden@cavanmonaghan.net
Karl Moher, Councillor, Ward(s): Douro-Dummer
kmoher@nexicom.net
Janet Clarkson, Councillor, Ward(s): Galway-Cavendish & Harvey
gallery@baysideboutique.com
Ron Windover, Councillor, Ward(s): Galway-Cavendish & Harvey
windover@bell.net
Ronald Gerow, Councillor, Ward(s): Havelock-Belmont-Methuen
ron.gerow@sympatico.ca
Andy Sharpe, Councillor, Ward(s): Havelock-Belmont-Methuen
2andysharpe@gmail.com
Jim Whelan, Councillor, Ward(s): North Kawartha
reeve@northkawartha.on.ca
Barry Rand, Councillor, Ward(s): North Kawartha
dreeve@northkawartha.on.ca
David Nelson, Councillor, Ward(s): Otonabee-South Monaghan
dnelson@nexicom.net
Joe Taylor, Councillor, Ward(s): Otonabee-South Monaghan
jtaylor@osmtownship.ca
Mary Smith, Councillor, Ward(s): Smith-Ennismore-Lakefield
mjsmith@peterboro.net
Andy Mitchell, Councillor, Ward(s): Smith-Ennismore-Lakefield
mmitchell12@sympatico.ca
Sally Saunders, Clerk
ssaunders@county.peterborough.on.ca
Gary King, Chief Administrative Officer & Deputy Clerk
gking@county.peterborough.on.ca
John Butler, Treasurer
jbutler@county.peterborough.on.ca
Chris Bradley, Director, Public Works
cbradley@county.peterborough.on.ca
Patti Kraft, Director, Human Resources
pkraft@county.peterborough.on.ca
Bryan Weir, Director, Planning
bweir@county.peterborough.on.ca
Sheridan Graham, General Manager, Strategic Services & Corporate Projects
sgraham@county.peterborough.on.ca
Laurie Westaway, Manager, Environmental Services
lwestaway@county.peterborough.on.ca
Bill Linnen, Manager, Operations
blinnen@county.peterborough.on.ca
Bob English, Chief, Emergency Medical Services (EMS)
benglish@county.peterborough.on.ca
Mark Cross, Specialist, Waste Diversion Operations
mcross@county.peterborough.on.ca

Prince Edward
332 Main St.
Picton, ON K0K 2T0
Tel: 613-476-2148; *Fax:* 613-476-8356
council@pecounty.on.ca
www.pecounty.on.ca
Municipal Type: County
Incorporated: Jan. 1, 1998 *Area:* 1,050.14 sq km
Population in 2011: 25,258
Provincial Electoral District(s): Prince Edward-Hastings
Federal Electoral District(s): Prince Edward-Hastings
Next Election: Oct. 27, 2014 (4 year terms)
Peter Mertensn, Mayor
pmertens@pecounty.on.ca
Bev Campbell, Councillor, Ward(s): 1 - Picton
bcampbell@pecounty.on.ca
Brian Marisett, Councillor, Ward(s): 1 - Picton
bmarisett@pecounty.on.ca
Barry Turpin, Councillor, Ward(s): 2 - Bloomfield
bturpin@pecounty.on.ca
Jim Dunlop, Councillor, Ward(s): 3 - Wellington
jdunlop@pecounty.on.ca
Janice Maynard, Councillor, Ward(s): 4 - Ameliasburgh
jmaynard@pecounty.on.ca
Dianne O'Brien, Councillor, Ward(s): 4 - Ameliasburgh
dobrien@pecounty.on.ca
Nick Nowitski, Councillor, Ward(s): 4 - Ameliasburgh
nnowitski@pecounty.on.ca
Jamie Forrester, Councillor, Ward(s): 5 - Athol
jforrester@pecounty.on.ca
Heather Campbell, Councillor, Ward(s): 6 - Hallowell
hcampbell@pecounty.on.ca
Keith MacDonald, Councillor, Ward(s): 6 - Hallowell
kmacdonald@pecounty.on.ca
Alec Lunn, Councillor, Ward(s): 7 - Hillier
alunn@pecounty.on.ca
Robert Quaiff, Councillor, Ward(s): 8 - North Marysburgh
rquaiff@pecounty.on.ca
Barbara Proctor, Councillor, Ward(s): 9 - South Marysburgh
bproctor@pecounty.on.ca
Kevin Gale, Councillor, Ward(s): 10 - Sophiasburgh
kgale@pecounty.on.ca
Terry Shortt, Councillor, Ward(s): 10 - Sophiasburgh
tshortt@pecounty.on.ca
Victoria Leskie, Clerk
vleskie@pecounty.on.ca
Gerry Murphy, Acting Chief Administrative Officer & Commissioner, Planning Services
gmurphy@pecounty.on.ca
James Hepburn, Treasurer
jhepburn@pecounty.on.ca
Barry Braun, Commissioner, Recreation, Parks, & Culture Department
bbraun@pecounty.on.ca
Robert McAuley, Commissioner, Public Works Department
rmcauley@pecounty.on.ca
Susan Turnbull, Commissioner, Corporate Services & Finance
sturnbull@pecounty.on.ca
Kimberly Pierce, Manager, Human Resources, Corporate Services & Finance
kpierce@pecounty.on.ca
Scott Manlow, Fire Chief
smanlow@pecounty.on.ca

Renfrew
9 International Dr.
Pembroke, ON K8A 6W5
Tel: 613-735-7288; *Fax:* 613-735-2081
info@countyofrenfrew.on.ca
www.countyofrenfrew.on.ca
Other Information: Toll-Free Phone: 1-800-273-0183
Municipal Type: County
Incorporated: June 8, 1861 *Area:* 7,403.46 sq km
Population in 2011: 101,326
Next Election: Oct. 27, 2014 (4 year terms)
Bob Sweet, Warden & Councillor, Ward(s): Petawawa
warden@countyofrenfrew.on.ca
Raye-Anne Briscoe, Councillor, Ward(s): Admaston/Bromley
613-432-2885
Walter Stack, Councillor, Ward(s): Arnprior
613-623-4231
Jennifer Murphy, Councillor, Ward(s): Bonnechere Valley
613-628-3101
Norm Lentz, Councillor, Ward(s): Brudenell, Lyndoch, & Raglan
613-758-2061
Dave Thompson, Councillor, Ward(s): Deep River
613-584-2000
Peter Emon, Councillor, Ward(s): Greater Madawaska
613-752-2222
Tammy Stewart, Councillor, Ward(s): Head, Clara & Maria
613-586-2526
Robert A. Johnston, Councillor, Ward(s): Horton
613-432-6271
Janice Visneskie, Councillor, Ward(s): Killaloe, Hagarty & Richards
613-757-2300
Dick Rabishaw, Councillor, Ward(s): Laurentian Hills
613-584-3114
Jack Wilson, Councillor, Ward(s): Laurentian Valley
613-735-6291
David Shulist, Councillor, Ward(s): Madawaska Valley
613-756-2747
Mary Campbell, Councillor, Ward(s): McNab/Braeside
613-623-5756
Harold Weckworth, Councillor, Ward(s): North Algona Wilberforce
613-628-2080
Audrey R. Green, Councillor, Ward(s): Renfrew
613-432-4848
Jim Hutton, Chief Administrative Officer & Clerk
James D. Kutschke, CA, Treasurer & Deputy Clerk
jkutschke@countyofrenfrew.on.ca
Bruce Beakley, Director, Human Resources
Dave Darch, Director, Public Works & Engineering
Michael Nolan, Director, Emergency Services
Jeff Muzzi, Manager, Forestry Services
613-735-3204
jmuzzi@countyofrenfrew.on.ca

Simcoe
County of Simcoe Administration Centre
1110 Hwy. 26
Midhurst, ON L0L 1X0
Tel: 705-735-6901; *Fax:* 705-719-4626
info@simcoe.ca
www.simcoe.ca
Other Information: Toll-Free Phone: 1-800-263-3199
Municipal Type: County
Incorporated: Jan. 1, 1850 *Area:* 4,840.56 sq km
Population in 2011: 446,063
Next Election: Oct. 27, 2014 (4 year terms)
Cal Patterson, Warden & Councillor, Ward(s): Wasaga Beach
cal.patterson@simcoe.ca
Mary Small Brett, Councillor, Ward(s): Adjala-Tosorontio
mary.smallbrett@simcoe.ca
Tom Walsh, Councillor, Ward(s): Adjala-Tosorontio
tom.walsh@simcoe.ca
Doug White, Councillor, Ward(s): Bradford West Gwillimbury
doug.white@simcoe.ca
Rob Keffer, Councillor, Ward(s): Bradford West Gwillimbury
rob.keffer@simcoe.ca
Ken Ferguson, Councillor, Ward(s): Clearview
ken.ferguson@simcoe.ca
Alicia Savage, Councillor, Ward(s): Clearview
alicia.savage@simcoe.ca
Sandra Cooper, Councillor, Ward(s): Collingwood
sandra.cooper@simcoe.ca
Rick Lloyd, Councillor, Ward(s): Collingwood
rick.lloyd@simcoe.ca
Terry Dowdall, Councillor, Ward(s): Essa
terry.dowdall@simcoe.ca
Sandie Macdonald, Councillor, Ward(s): Essa
sandie.macdonald@simcoe.ca
Barb Baguley, Councillor, Ward(s): Innisfil
barb.baguley@simcoe.ca
Dan Davidson, Councillor, Ward(s): Innisfil
dan.davidson@simcoe.ca
Gord McKay, Councillor, Ward(s): Midland
gord.mckay@simcoe.ca
Stephan Kramp, Councillor, Ward(s): Midland
stephan.kramp@simcoe.ca
Mike MacEachern, Councillor, Ward(s): New Tecumseth
mike.maceachern@simcoe.ca
Rick Milne, Councillor, Ward(s): New Tecumseth
rick.milne@simcoe.ca
Harry Huges, Councillor, Ward(s): Oro-Medonte
harry.hughes@simcoe.ca
Ralph Hough, Councillor, Ward(s): Oro-Medonte
ralph.hough@simcoe.ca
Gerry Marshall, Councillor, Ward(s): Penetanguishene
gerry.marshall@simcoe.ca

Patrick Marion, Councillor, Ward(s): Penetanguishene
patrick.marion@simcoe.ca
Bill Duffy, Councillor, Ward(s): Ramara
bill.duffy@simcoe.ca
Basil Clarke, Councillor, Ward(s): Ramara
basil.clarke@simcoe.ca
Mike Burkett, Councillor, Ward(s): Severn
mike.burkett@simcoe.ca
Judith Cox, Councillor, Ward(s): Severn
judith.cox@simcoe.ca
Linda Collins, Councillor, Ward(s): Springwater
linda.collins@simcoe.ca
Tony Hope, Councillor, Ward(s): Springwater
dan.mclean@simcoe.ca
Scott Warnock, Councillor, Ward(s): Tay
scott.warnock@simcoe.ca
Bill Rawson, Councillor, Ward(s): Tay
bill.rawson@simcoe.ca
Ray Millar, Councillor, Ward(s): Tiny
ray.millar@simcoe.ca
George Lawrence, Councillor, Ward(s): Tiny
george.lawrence@simcoe.ca
David Foster, Councillor, Ward(s): Wasaga Beach
david.foster@simcoe.ca
Brenda Clark, Clerk
brenda.clark@simcoe.ca
Mark Aitken, Chief Administrative Officer
Craig Elliott, General Manager, Finance & Administration
craig.elliott@simcoe.ca
Rick Newlove, General Manager, Engineering, Planning & Environment
rick.newlove@simcoe.ca
Jane Sinclair, General Manager, Health & Emergency Services
jane.sinclair@simcoe.ca
Terry Talon, General Manager, Social & Community Services
terry.talon@simcoe.ca
Dawn Hipwell, Director, Procurement, Fleet & Property
dawn.hipwell@simcoe.ca
Jim Hunter, Director, Transportation Construction
jim.hunter@simcoe.ca
Bryan MacKell, Director, Planning, Development & Tourism
bryan.macKell@simcoe.ca
Michael Moffatt, Director, Human Resources
michael.moffatt@simcoe.ca

Waterloo

Regional Administration Bldg.
P.O. Box 9051 C
150 Frederick St.
Kitchener, ON N2G 4J3
Tel: 519-575-4400; *Fax:* 519-575-4481
regionalinquiries@region.waterloo.on.ca
www.region.waterloo.on.ca
Other Information: Phone, Regional Councillors: 519-575-4581
Municipal Type: Regional Municipality
Incorporated: Jan. 1, 1973 *Area:* 1,368.64 sq km
Population in 2011: 507,096
Next Election: Oct. 27, 2014 (4 year terms)
Ken Seiling, Regional Chair & Councillor
519-575-4585, Fax: 519-575-4440
kseiling@regionofwaterloo.ca
Doug Craig, Councillor, Ward(s): Cambridge
dcraig@regionofwaterloo.ca
Jane Brewer, Councillor, Ward(s): Cambridge
jbrewer@regionofwaterloo.ca
Claudette Millar, Councillor, Ward(s): Cambridge
cmillar@regionofwaterloo.ca
Carl Zehr, Councillor, Ward(s): Kitchener
czhr@regionofwaterloo.ca
Tom Galloway, Councillor, Ward(s): Kitchener
tgalloway@regionofwaterloo.ca
Jean Haalboom, Councillor, Ward(s): Kitchener
jhaalboom@regionofwaterloo.ca
Geoff Lorentz, Councillor, Ward(s): Kitchener
glorentz@regionofwaterloo.ca
Jim Wideman, Councillor, Ward(s): Kitchener
jwideman@regionofwaterloo.ca
Rob Deutschmann, Councillor, Ward(s): North Dumfries
rdeutschmann@regionofwaterloo.ca
Brenda Halloran, Councillor, Ward(s): Waterloo
bhalloran@regionofwaterloo.ca
Jane Mitchell, Councillor, Ward(s): Waterloo
jmitchell@regionofwaterloo.ca
Sean Strickland, Councillor, Ward(s): Waterloo
sstrickland@regionofwaterloo.ca
Ross Kelterborn, Councillor, Ward(s): Wellesley
rkelterborn@regionofwaterloo.ca
Les Armstrong, Councillor, Ward(s): Wilmot
lesarmstrong@regionofwaterloo.ca
Todd Cowan, Councillor, Ward(s): Woolwich
tcowan@regionofwaterloo.ca

Kris Fletcher, Regional Clerk & Director, Council & Administrative Services
Mike Murray, Chief Administrative Officer
Larry Ryan, Chief Financial Officer
Rob Horne, Commissioner, Planning, Housing & Community Services
Thomas Schmidt, Commissioner, Transportation & Environmental Services
Michael Schuster, Commissioner, Social Services
Penny Smiley, Commissioner, Human Resources
Gary Sosnoski, Commissioner, Corporate Resources
Jon Arsenault, Director, Waste Management
Debra Arnold, Director, Legal Services & Regional Solicitor
Lucille Bish, Director, Community Services
Amanda Kutler, Director, Community Planning
Eric Gillespie, Director, Transit Services
Nancy Kodousek, Director, Water Services
Ellen McGaghey, Director, Facilities Management & Fleet Services
Graham Vincent, Director, Transportation Planning
Liana Nolan, Medical Officer of Health

Wellington

74 Woolwich St.
Guelph, ON N1H 3T9
Tel: 519-837-2600; *Fax:* 519-837-1909
finance@county.wellington.on.ca (Treasury)
www.wellington.ca
Other Information: Toll-Free Phone: 1-800-663-0750
Municipal Type: County
Incorporated: Jan. 1, 1852 *Area:* 2,656.66 sq km
Population in 2011: 208,360
Next Election: Oct. 27, 2014 (4 year terms)
Note: The council of the County of Wellington is comprised of the mayors of its seven municipalities, plus nine elected county ward councillors.
Chris White, Warden & Councillor, Ward(s): Guelph/Eramosa
warden@wellington.ca
Joanne Ross-Zuj, Councillor, Ward(s): Centre Wellington
Lou Maieron, Councillor, Ward(s): Erin
Bruce Whale, Councillor, Ward(s): Mapleton
George Bridge, Councillor, Ward(s): Minto
Dennis Lever, Councillor, Ward(s): Puslinch
Raymond Trout, Councillor, Ward(s): Wellington North
Mark MacKenzie, Councillor, Ward(s): 1
John Green, Councillor, Ward(s): 2
Gary Williamson, Ward(s): 3
Linda White, Ward(s): 4
Jean Innes, Councillor, Ward(s): 5
Shawn Watters, Councillor, Ward(s): 6
Don McKay, Councillor, Ward(s): 7
Gordon Tosh, Councillor, Ward(s): 8
Ken Chapman, Councillor, Ward(s): 9
Donna Bryce, County Clerk
donnab@wellington.ca
Scott Wilson, Chief Administrative Officer
scottw@wellington.ca
Craig Dyer, Treasurer
craigd@county.wellington.on.ca
Andrea Lawson, Administrator, Human Resources, Fax: 519-837-8882
andreal@county.wellington.on.ca
Heather Burke, Director, Housing
heatherb@wellington.ca; wghsinfo@wellington.ca
Gary Cousins, Director, Planning, Fax: 519-823-1694
garyc@wellington.ca
Luisa Della Croce, Director, Child Care Services
luisad@wellington.ca
Linda Dickson, Coordinator, Community Emergency Management
519-846-8058, Fax: 519-846-8482
lindad@wellington.ca
Rob Johnson, Coordinator, Forestry

York

17250 Yonge St.
Newmarket, ON L3Y 6Z1
Tel: 905-895-1231; *Fax:* 905-895-1238
info@york.ca; twgeneral@york.ca (Transportation & Works)
www.york.ca
Other Information: Toll-Free Phone: 1-877-464-9675
Municipal Type: Regional Municipality
Incorporated: Jan. 1, 1971 *Area:* 1,761.84 sq km
Population in 2011: 1,032,524
Next Election: Oct. 27, 2014 (4 year terms)
Bill Fisch, Regional Chair & Councillor
regional.chair@york.ca
Geoff Dawe, Councillor, Ward(s): Aurora
Virginia Hackson, Councillor, Ward(s): East Gwillimbury
Robert Grossi, Councillor, Ward(s): Georgina
Danny Wheeler, Councillor, Ward(s): Georgina
Steve Pellegrini, Councillor, Ward(s): King
Frank Scarpitti, Councillor, Ward(s): Markham
Jack Heath, Councillor, Ward(s): Markham
Jim Jones, Councillor, Ward(s): Markham
Gordon Landon, Councillor, Ward(s): Markham
Joe Li, Councillor, Ward(s): Markham
A.J. (Tony) Van Bynen, Councillor, Ward(s): Newmarket
John Taylor, Councillor, Ward(s): Newmarket
David Barrow, Councillor, Ward(s): Richmond Hill
Brenda Hogg, Councillor, Ward(s): Richmond Hill
Vito Spatafora, Councillor, Ward(s): Richmond Hill
Maurizio Bevilacqua, Councillor, Ward(s): Vaughan
Michael Di Biase, Councillor, Ward(s): Vaughan
Deb Schulte, Councillor, Ward(s): Vaughan
Gino Rosati, Councillor, Ward(s): Vaughan
Wayne Emmerson, Councillor, Ward(s): Whitchurch-Stouffville
Denis Kelly, Regional Clerk
regionalclerk@york.ca
Bruce Macgregor, Chief Administrative Officer
Bill Hughes, Regional Treasurer & Commissioner, Finance
Jim Davidson, Commissioner, Corporate Services
Kathleen Llewellyn-Thomas, Commissioner, Transportation Services
Erin Mahoney, Commissioner, Environmental Services
Adelina Urbanski, Commissioner, Community & Health Services
John Walker, Acting Commissioner, Planning & Development Services
Patrick Casey, Director, Corporate Communications
patrick.casey@york.ca
Karen Close, Director, Human Resources
Karim Kurji, Medical Officer of Health & Director, Public Health Programs

Major Municipalities in Ontario

Barrie

P.O. Box 400
70 Collier St.
Barrie, ON L4M 4T5
Tel: 705-726-4242; *Fax:* 705-739-4243
cityinfo@barrie.ca
www.barrie.ca; www.facebook.com/cityofbarrie
Other Information: TTY: 705-792-7910; Council Info: 705-739-4204
Municipal Type: City
Incorporated: 1853 *Area:* 76.99 sq km
County or District: Simcoe; *Population in 2011:* 135,711
Provincial Electoral District(s): Barrie
Federal Electoral District(s): Barrie
Next Election: Oct. 27, 2014 (4 year terms)
Jeff Lehman, Mayor
705-792-7900
officeofthemayor@barrie.ca
Bonnie J. Ainsworth, Councillor, Ward(s): 1
bainsworth@barrie.ca
Lynn M. Strachan, Councillor, Ward(s): 2
lstrachan@barrie.ca
Doug Shipley, Councillor, Ward(s): 3
dshipley@barrie.ca
Barry J. Ward, Councillor, Ward(s): 4
bward@barrie.ca
Peter Silveira, Councillor, Ward(s): 5
psilveira@barrie.ca
Michael Prowse, Councillor, Ward(s): 6
mprowse@barrie.ca
John Brassard, Councillor, Ward(s): 7
jbrassard@barrie.ca
Jennifer Robinson, Councillor, Ward(s): 8
psilveira@barrie.ca
Brian H. Jackson, Councillor, Ward(s): 9
bjackson@barrie.ca
Alexander Nuttall, Councillor, Ward(s): 10
anuttall@barrie.ca
Dawn McAlpine, City Clerk
705-739-4204
Jon Babulic, Chief Administrative Officer
Ed Archer, CMA, General Manager, Corporate Services
Richard Forward, M.Sc., P.Eng., General Manager, Infrastructure, Development & Culture Division
J.W. (Jim) Sales, General Manager, Community Operations
G. Allison, Director, Building Services & Chief Building Official
Sandy Coulter, B.Sc., Acting Director, Operations - Water, Wastewater & Environmental
Dave Friary, Acting Director, Operations - Roads, Parks & Fleet Operations
Hany Kirolos, Director, Strategy & Economic Development
Wendell McArthur, Director, Engineering
Debbie McKinnon, Director, Finance
Barbara Roth, Director, Leisure, Transit & Facilities

J. Taylor, Director, Planning Services Department
John Lynn, Fire Chief
Bruce L. Griffin, Community Emergency Planner

Belleville
City Hall
169 Front St.
Belleville, ON K8N 2Y8
Tel: 613-968-6481; *Fax:* 613-967-3206
www.city.belleville.on.ca
Other Information: TTY: 613-967-3768
Municipal Type: City
Area: 246.76 sq km
County or District: Hastings; *Population in 2011:* 49,454
Provincial Electoral District(s): Prince Edward-Hastings
Federal Electoral District(s): Prince Edward-Hastings
Next Election: Oct. 27, 2014 (4 year terms)
Neil R. Ellis, Mayor
613-967-3267, Fax: 613-967-3209
mayor.ellis@city.belleville.on.ca
Egerton Boyce, Councillor, Ward(s): 1
councillor.boyce@city.belleville.on.ca
Pat Culhane, Councillor, Ward(s): 1
councillor.culhane@city.belleville.on.ca
Jodie Jenkins, Councillor, Ward(s): 1
councillor.jenkins@city.belleville.on.ca
Tom Lafferty, Councillor, Ward(s): 1
councillor.lafferty@city.belleville.on.ca
Jack Miller, Councillor, Ward(s): 1
councillor.miller@city.belleville.on.ca
Garnet Thompson, Councillor, Ward(s): 1
councillor.thompson@city.belleville.on.ca
Taso Christopher, Councillor, Ward(s): 2
councillor.christopher@city.belleville.on.ca
Jackie Denyes, Councillor, Ward(s): 2
councillor.denyes@city.belleville.on.ca
Julie C. Oram, City Clerk & Director, Corporate Services
613-967-3271
joram@city.belleville.on.ca
Rick Kester, Chief Administrative Officer
rkester@city.belleville.on.ca
Brian Cousins, Director, Finance & Treasurer
bcousins@city.belleville.on.ca
Mark Fluhrer, Director, Recreation Culture & Community Services
mfluhrer@city.belleville.on.ca
Rod Bovay, Acting Director, Engineering & Development Services
rbovay@city.belleville.on.ca
John Martin, Director, Human Resources
jmartin@city.belleville.on.ca
Brad Wilson, Director, Environmental & Operational Services
bwilson@city.belleville.on.ca
Ted Marecak, Chief Building Official
tmarecak@city.belleville.on.ca
Rhéaume Chaput, Fire Chief
rchaput@city.belleville.on.ca
Peter Hodgson, Manager, Transit Operations
phodgson@city.belleville.on.ca
Art MacKay, Manager, Policy Planning
amackay@city.belleville.on.ca
Pat McNulty, Manager, Transportation
pmcnulty@city.belleville.on.ca
Richard Reinert, Manager, Environmental Services (Water Operations)
rreinert@city.belleville.on.ca

Brampton
2 Wellington St. West
Brampton, ON L6Y 4R2
Tel: 905-874-2000; *Fax:* 905-874-2119
cityhall@brampton.ca; tourism@brampton.ca (Tourism)
www.brampton.ca
Other Information: E-mail, Economic Development: edo@brampton.ca
Municipal Type: City
Incorporated: Jan. 1, 1974 *Area:* 266.71 sq km
County or District: Peel Reg. Mun.; *Population in 2011:* 523,911
Provincial Electoral District(s): Bramalea-Gore-Malton; Brampton Springdale; Brampton West; Brampton South-Mississauga
Federal Electoral District(s): Bramalea-Gore-Malton; Brampton Springdale; Brampton West; Mississauga-Brampton South
Next Election: Oct. 27, 2014 (4 year terms)
Susan Fennell, Mayor
mayor@brampton.ca
Grant Gibson, City Councillor, Ward(s): 1 & 5
grant.gibson@brampton.ca
John Hutton, City Councillor, Ward(s): 2 & 6
john.hutton@brampton.ca
Bob Callahan, City Councillor, Ward(s): 3 & 4
bob.callahan@brampton.ca
Sandra Hames, City Councillor, Ward(s): 7 & 8
sandra.hames@brampton.ca
Vicky Dhillon, City Councillor, Ward(s): 9 & 10
vicky.dhillon@brampton.ca
Elaine Moore, Regional Councillor, Ward(s): 1 & 5
elaine.moore@brampton.ca
Paul Palleschi, Regional Councillor, Ward(s): 2 & 6
paul.palleschi@brampton.ca
John Sanderson, Regional Councillor, Ward(s): 3 & 4
john.sanderson@brampton.ca
Gael Miles, Regional Councillor, Ward(s): 7 & 8
gael.miles@brampton.ca
John Sprovieri, Regional Councillor, Ward(s): 9 & 10
john.sprovieri@brampton.ca
Peter Fay, City Clerk
905-874-2100, Fax: 905-874-2119
cityclerksoffice@brampton.ca
Deborah Dubenofsky, City Manager
Mo Lewis, Commissioner, Finance
John Corbett, Commissioner, Planning, Design & Development
Dennis Cutajar, Commissioner, Economic Development & Communications
Jamie Lowery, Commissioner, Community Services
Tom Mulligan, Commissioner, Works & Transportation
Julian Patteson, Commissioner, Buildings & Property Management
Kathy Zammit, Commissioner, Corporate Services

Brantford
City Hall
P.O. Box 818
100 Wellington Sq.
Brantford, ON N3T 2M3
Tel: 519-759-4150
webmaster@brantford.ca
www.brantford.ca
Municipal Type: City
Incorporated: May 31, 1877 *Area:* 72.47 sq km
County or District: Brant; *Population in 2011:* 93,650
Provincial Electoral District(s): Brant
Federal Electoral District(s): Brant
Next Election: Oct. 27, 2014 (4 year terms)
Chris Friel, Mayor
cfriel@brantford.ca
Larry M. Kings, Councillor, Ward(s): 1
lkings@brantford.ca
Jan C. Vander Stelt, Councillor, Ward(s): 1
jvanderstelt@brantford.ca
Vince Bucci, Councillor, Ward(s): 2
vbucci@brantford.ca
John K. Utley, Councillor, Ward(s): 2
jutley@brantford.ca
Debi Dignan-Rumble, Councillor, Ward(s): 3
ddignan-rumble@brantford.ca
Dan McCreary, Councillor, Ward(s): 3
dmccreary@brantford.ca
Richard Carpenter, Councillor, Ward(s): 4
rcarpenter@brantford.ca
Dave Wrobel, Councillor, Ward(s): 4
dwrobel@brantford.ca
Marguerite Ceschi-Smith, Councillor, Ward(s): 5
mceschi-smith@brantford.ca
David E. Neumann, Councillor, Ward(s): 5
dneumann@brantford.ca
Charlene Touzel, Acting City Clerk
ctouzel@brantford.ca
Ted Salisbury, Chief Administrative Officer & General Manager, Community Development Services
Greg Dworak, Acting General Manager, Engineering & Operational Services
Dan Temprile, General Manager, Public Health, Safety, & Social Services

Brighton
P.O. Box 189
35 Alice St.
Brighton, ON K0K 1H0
Tel: 613-475-0670; *Fax:* 613-475-3453
general@brighton.ca
www.brighton.ca
Other Information: Phone, Public Works & Planning: 613-475-1162
Municipal Type: City
Area: 222.52 sq km
County or District: Northumberland; *Population in 2011:* 10,928
Provincial Electoral District(s): Northumberland-Quinte West
Federal Electoral District(s): Northumberland-Quinte West
Next Election: Oct. 27, 2014 (4 year terms)
Mark Walas, Mayor
mayor@brighton.ca
Craig Kerr, Councillor
ckerr@brighton.ca
John Martinello, Councillor
jmartinello@brighton.ca
Thomas Rittwage, Councillor
trittwage@brighton.ca
Emily Rowley, Councillor
erowley@brighton.ca
Mary Tadman, Councillor
mtadman@brighton.ca
Mike Vandertoorn, Councillor
mvandertoorn@brighton.ca
Gayle J. Frost, Chief Administrative Officer
gfrost@brighton.ca
Andrew Drzewiecki, Director, Public Works & Development
adrzewiecki@brighton.ca
Jim Millar, Director, Parks & Recreation
millar@brighton.ca
Linda Widdifield, Director, Finance & Administrative Services
linda@brighton.ca
Lloyd Hutchinson, Fire Chief
lhutchinson@brighton.ca

Brockville
Victoria Bldg.
P.O. Box 5000
1 King St. West
Brockville, ON K6V 7A5
Tel: 613-342-8772; *Fax:* 613-342-8780
info@brockville.com; tourism@brockvillechamber.com
www.brockville.com
Municipal Type: City
Area: 20.74 sq km
County or District: Leeds & Grenville; *Population in 2011:* 21,870
Provincial Electoral District(s): Leeds-Grenville
Federal Electoral District(s): Leeds-Grenville
Next Election: Oct. 27, 2014 (4 year terms)
David L. Henderson, Mayor
themayor@brockville.com
Jason Baker, Councillor
jwbaker@rogers.blackberry.net
David E. Beatty, Councillor
dbeatty@canarm.ca
Leigh Z. Bursey, Councillor
leighbursey@gmail.com
Jeffery Earle, Councillor
jearle@brockville.com
Jane Fullerton, Councillor
jane@mentoringmatters.ca
Larry F. Journal, Councillor
ljournal@cogeco.ca
Mike Kalivas, Councillor
mkalivas@ripnet.com
David D. LeSueur, Councillor
dlesueur@cogeco.ca
Mary Jane McFall, Councillor
mjm@tmlegal.ca
Sandra M. Seale, City Clerk
sseale@brockville.com
Bob Casselman, City Manager
bcasselman@brockville.com
Donna Cyr, Director, Finance
dcyr@brockville.com
Jim Baker, Director, Human Resources
jbaker@brockville.com
David C. Paul, Director, Economic Development
dpaul@brockville.com
Maureen Pascoe Merkley, Director, Planning
mpmerkley@brockville.com
Peter Raabe, Director, Environmental Services
praabe@brockville.com
Harry Jones, Fire Chief
hjones@brockville.com

Burlington
City Hall
P.O. Box 5013
426 Brant St.
Burlington, ON L7R 3Z6
Tel: 905-335-7600; *Fax:* 905-335-7881
cob@burlington.ca
www.burlington.ca
Other Information: Toll-Free Phone: 1-877-213-3609
Municipal Type: City
Incorporated: 1914 *Area:* 185.74 sq km
County or District: Halton Regional Municipality; *Population in 2011:* 175,779
Provincial Electoral District(s):

Ancaster-Dundas-Flamborough-Westdale; Burlington; Halton
Federal Electoral District(s): Burlington; Halton; Ancaster-Dundas-Flamborough-Westdale
Next Election: Oct. 27, 2014 (4 year terms)
Note: Incorporated as a city in 1974.
Rick Goldring, Mayor
905-335-7607, Fax: 905-335-7708
mayor@burlington.ca
Rick Craven, Councillor, Ward(s): 1
cravenr@burlington.ca
Marianne Meed Ward, Councillor, Ward(s): 2
meedwardm@burlington.ca
John Taylor, Councillor, Ward(s): 3
taylorj@burlington.ca
Jack Dennison, Councillor, Ward(s): 4
dennisonj@burlington.ca
Paul Sharman, Councillor, Ward(s): 5
sharmanp@burlington.ca
Blair Lancaster, Councillor, Ward(s): 6
lancasterb@burlington.ca
Kim Phillips, City Clerk
905-335-7698, Fax: 905-335-7881
cityclerks@burlington.ca; phillipsk@burlington.ca
Scott Stewart, Acting City Manager
stewarts@burlington.ca

Cambridge

P.O. Box 669
50 Dickson St.
Cambridge, ON N1R 5W8
Tel: 519-623-1340; *Fax:* 519-740-3011
questions@cambridge.ca; csd@cambridge.ca (Community Svs.)
www.cambridge.ca
Other Information: E-mail, Corporate Services: corpserv@cambridge.ca
Municipal Type: City
Incorporated: Jan. 1973 *Area:* 112.86 sq km
County or District: Waterloo Regional Municipality; *Population in 2011:* 126,748
Provincial Electoral District(s): Cambridge
Federal Electoral District(s): Cambridge
Next Election: Oct. 27, 2014 (4 year terms)
Doug Craig, Mayor
mayor@cambridge.ca; council@cambridge.ca
Donna Reid, City Councillor, Ward(s): 1
reidd@cambridge.ca
Rick Cowsill, City Councillor, Ward(s): 2
cowsillr@cambridge.ca
Karl Kiefer, City Councillor, Ward(s): 3
kieferk@cambridge.ca
Ben Tucci, City Councillor, Ward(s): 4
tuccib@cambridge.ca
Pam Wolf, City Councillor, Ward(s): 5
wolfp@cambridge.ca
Gary Price, City Councillor, Ward(s): 6
priceg@cambridge.ca
Frank Monteiro, City Councillor, Ward(s): 7
monteirof@cambridge.ca
Nicholas Ermeta, City Councillor, Ward(s): 8
ermetan@cambridge.ca
Jane Brewer, Regional Councillor
bjane@regionofwaterloo.ca
Claudette Millar, Regional Councillor
mclaudette@regionofwaterloo.ca
Alex Mitchell, City Clerk
519-740-4680
clerks@cambridge.ca
Jim King, Chief Administrative Officer
519-740-4683
cao@cambridge.ca
Janet Babcock, Commisssioner, Planning Services
Steven Fairweather, Commisssioner, Corporate Services
George Elliott, Commisssioner, Transportation & Public Works
Kent McVittie, Commisssioner, Community Services
Bill Chesney, Fire Chief

Clarence-Rockland

1560 Laurier St.
Rockland, ON K4K 1P7
Tel: 613-446-6022; *Fax:* 613-446-1497
www.clarence-rockland.com
Municipal Type: City
Incorporated: Jan. 1, 1998 *Area:* 296.53 sq km
County or District: Prescott & Russell; *Population in 2011:* 23,185
Provincial Electoral District(s): Glengarry-Prescott-Russell
Federal Electoral District(s): Glengarry-Prescott-Russell
Next Election: Oct. 27, 2014 (4 year terms)
Note: Amalgamation of the Town of Rockland and the Township of Clarence.
Marcel Guibord, Mayor
613-446-0240
mguibord@xplornet.com
Michel Thivierge, Councillor, Ward(s): 1
André Henrie, Councillor, Ward(s): 2
Bernard Payer, Councillor, Ward(s): 3
Raymond Serrurier, Councillor, Ward(s): 4
Guy Félio, Councillor, Ward(s): 5
Guy Desjardins, Councillor, Ward(s): 6
René Campeau, Councillor, Ward(s): 7
Diane Choinière, Councillor, Ward(s): 8
Monique Ouellet, Clerk
mouellet@clarence-rockland.com
Chantal McLean-Leroux, Treasurer
cmcleanleroux@clarence-rockland.com
Thérèse Lefaivre, Director, Community Services
tlefaivre@clarence-rockland.com
Michael Michaud, Director, Planning
mmichaud@clarence-rockland.com
Yves Rivard, Director, By-law Enforcement
yrivard@clarence-rockland.com
Yves Rousselle, Director, Physical Services
yrousselle@clarence-rockland.com
Pierre Sabourin, Fire Chief
psabourin@clarence-rockland.com
Denis Longpré, Manager, Environment
dlongpre@clarence-rockland.com

Cornwall

P.O. Box 877
360 Pitt St.
Cornwall, ON K6H 5T9
Tel: 613-932-6252; *Fax:* 613-932-8145
www.cornwall.ca
Municipal Type: City
Incorporated: 1834 *Area:* 61.52 sq km
County or District: Stormont, Dundas & Glengarry; *Population in 2011:* 46,340
Provincial Electoral District(s): Stormont-Dundas-South Glengarry
Federal Electoral District(s): Stormont-Dundas-South Glengarry
Next Election: Oct. 27, 2014 (4 year terms)
Note: Incorporated as a city in 1945.
Bob Kilger, Mayor
mayor@cornwall.ca
Denis Carr, Councillor
dcarr@cornwall.ca
Bernadette Clément, Councillor
bclement@cornwall.ca
Maurice Dupelle, Councillor
mdupelle@cornwall.ca
Syd Gardiner, Councillor
sgardiner@cornwall.ca
Glen Grant, Councillor
gggrant@cornwall.ca
Elaine MacDonald, Councillor
emacdonald@cornwall.ca
David Murphy, Councillor
dmurphy@cornwall.ca
Leslie O'Shaugnessy, Councillor
loshaughnessy@cornwall.ca
André Rivette, Councillor
arivette@cornwall.ca
Denis Thibault, Councillor
dthibault@cornwall.ca
Denise Labelle-Gelinas, City Clerk
Paul Fitzpatrick, Chief Administrative Officer
Maureen Adams, General Manager, Financial Services
Stephen Alexander, General Manager, Planning, Parks & Recreation Services
Norm Levac, General Manager, Infrastructure & Municipal Works
Jean Cousineau, Division Manager, Municipal Works
Morris McCormick, Division Manager, Environment
Len Tapp, Division Manager, Transit
Mark Boileau, Manager, Economic Development
Myles Cassidy, Fire Chief & Manager, Emergency Services
Patrick Carrière, Supervisor, Waste Water Treatment Facility
Owen O'Keefe, Supervisor, Water Purification Plant

Elliot Lake

45 Hillside Dr. North
Elliot Lake, ON P5A 1X5
Tel: 705-848-2287
www.cityofelliotlake.com
Municipal Type: City
Area: 698.12 sq km
County or District: Algoma District; *Population in 2011:* 11,348
Provincial Electoral District(s): Algoma-Manitoulin
Federal Electoral District(s): Algoma-Manitoulin-Kapuskasing
Next Election: Oct. 27, 2014 (4 year terms)
Rick Hamilton, Mayor
Al Collett, Councillor
Tom Farquhar, Councillor
Sandy Finamore, Councillor
Norman Mann, Councillor
Chris Patrie, Councillor
Ken Rastin, Councillor
Lesley Sprague, City Clerk
Rob deBortoli, Chief Administrative Officer
Dawn Halcrow, Director, Finance
Paul Officer, Fire Chief

Greater Napanee

P.O. Box 97
124 John St.
Napanee, ON K7R 3L4
Tel: 613-354-3351; *Fax:* 613-354-6545
info@greaternapanee.com; roads@greaternapanee.com
www.greaternapanee.com
Other Information: E-mail, Programs: recreation@greaternapanee.com
Municipal Type: City
Area: 459.71 sq km
County or District: Lennox-Addington; *Population in 2011:* 15,511
Provincial Electoral District(s): Lanark-Frontenac-Lennox & Addington
Federal Electoral District(s): Lanark-Frontenac-Lennox & Addington
Next Election: Oct. 27, 2014 (4 year terms)
Gord Schermerhorn, Mayor
613-354-0429
Roger Cole, Deputy Mayor & Councillor
613-354-7634
Michael Schenk, Councillor, Ward(s): 1
Shane Grant, Councillor, Ward(s): 2
Marg Isbester, Councillor, Ward(s): 3
Bill Pierson, Councillor, Ward(s): 4
Shaune Lucas, Councillor, Ward(s): 5
Rebecca Murphy, Clerk & Director, Corporate & Legal Services
rmurphy@greaternapanee.com
Raymond Callery, Chief Administrative Officer
rcallery@greaternapanee.com
Vern Amey, Director, Public Works
vamey@greaternapanee.com
Mark Day, Director, Finance & Treasurer
mday@greaternapanee.com
Kevin Hill, Director, Parks, Recreation & Culture
khill@greaternapanee.com
Charles McDonald, Director, Development Services
cmcdonald@greaternapanee.com
Terry Gervais, Fire Chief
tgervais@greaternapanee.com
Ron Vankoughnet, Supervisor, Roads & Landfill

Greater Sudbury / Grand Sudbury

Tom Davies Square
P.O. Box 5000 A
200 Brady St.
Sudbury, ON P3A 5P3
Tel: 705-671-2489; *Fax:* 705-671-8118
www.greatersudbury.ca
Other Information: Phone, Local Calls: 3-1-1
Municipal Type: City
Incorporated: Jan. 1, 2001 *Area:* 3,200.56 sq km
Population in 2011: 160,274
Provincial Electoral District(s): Nickel Belt; Sudbury
Federal Electoral District(s): Nickel Belt; Sudbury
Next Election: Oct. 27, 2014 (4 year terms)
Marianne Matichuk, Mayor
705-674-4455, Fax: 705-673-3096
mayor@greatersudbury.ca
Joe Cimino, Councillor, Ward(s): 1
joe.cimino@greatersudbury.ca
Jacques Barbeau, Councillor, Ward(s): 2
jacques.barbeau@greatersudbury.ca
Claude Berthiaume, Councillor, Ward(s): 3
claude.berthiaume@greatersudbury.ca
Evelyn Dutrisac, Councillor, Ward(s): 4
claude.berthiaume@greatersudbury.ca
Ron Dupuis, Councillor, Ward(s): 5
ron.dupuis@greatersudbury.ca
André Rivest, Councillor, Ward(s): 6
andre.rivest@greatersudbury.ca
Dave Kilgour, Councillor, Ward(s): 7
dave.kilgour@greatersudbury.ca
Fabio Belli, Councillor, Ward(s): 8
fabio.belli@greatersudbury.ca
Doug Craig, Councillor, Ward(s): 9
doug.craig@greatersudbury.ca

Frances Caldarelli, Councillor, Ward(s): 10
frances.caldarelli@greatersudbury.ca
Terry Kett, Councillor, Ward(s): 11
terry.kett@greatersudbury.ca
Joscelyne Landry-Altmann, Councillor, Ward(s): 12
joscelyne.landry-altmann@greatersudbury.ca
Angie Hache, City Clerk
705-674-4455, Fax: 705-671-8118
angie.hache@greatersudbury.ca
Doug Nadorozny, Chief Administrative Officer
doug.nadorozny@greatersudbury.ca
Lorella M. Hayes, B.Comm., CA, Chief Financial Officer & Treasurer
lorella.hayes@greatersudbury.ca
Greg Clausen, P. Eng, General Manager, Infrastructure Services
greg.clausen@greatersudbury.ca
Bill Lautenbach, General Manager, Growth & Development
bill.lautenbach@greatersudbury.ca
Catherine Matheson, General Manager, Community Development
catherine.matheson@greatersudbury.ca
Bruno Mangiardi, Chief Information Officer
bruno.mangiardi@greatersudbury.ca
Tim P. Beadman, Chief, Emergency Services
tim.beadman@greatersudbury.ca
Marc Leduc, Fire Chief
marc.leduc@greatersudbury.ca
Nick Benkovich, Director, Water & Wastewater
nick.benkovich@greatersudbury.ca
Robert Falcioni, Director, Roads & Transportation
robert.falcioni@greatersudbury.ca
Guido Mazza, Director, Building Services
guido.mazza@greatersudbury.caa
Roger Sauvé, Director, Greater Sudbury Transit
roger.sauve@greatersudbury.ca
Kevin Shaw, Director, Engineering Services
kevin.shaw@greatersudbury.ca

Guelph
City Hall
1 Carden St.
Guelph, ON N1H 3A1
Tel: 519-822-1260; *Fax:* 519-763-1269
info@guelph.ca; communications@guelph.ca
www.guelph.ca
Other Information: TTY: 519-826-9771
Municipal Type: City
Incorporated: 1879 *Area:* 86.72 sq km
County or District: Wellington; *Population in 2011:* 121,688
Provincial Electoral District(s): Guelph; Wellington-Halton Hills
Federal Electoral District(s): Guelph; Wellington-Halton Hills
Next Election: Oct. 27, 2014 (4 year terms)
Karen Farbridge, Mayor
519-837-5643, Fax: 519-822-8277
mayor@guelph.ca
Bob Bell, Councillor, Ward(s): 1
bob.bell@guelph.ca
Jim J. Furfaro, Councillor, Ward(s): 1
jim.furfaro@guelph.ca
Ian Findlay, Councillor, Ward(s): 2
ian.findlay@guelph.ca
Andy Van Hellemond, Councillor, Ward(s): 2
andy.vanhellemond@guelph.ca
June Hofland, Councillor, Ward(s): 3
june.hofland@guelph.ca
Maggie Laidlaw, Councillor, Ward(s): 3
maggie.laidlaw@guelph.ca
Cam Guthrie, Councillor, Ward(s): 4
cam.guthrie@guelph.ca
Gloria Kovach, Councillor, Ward(s): 4
gloria.kovach@guelph.ca
Lise Burcher, Councillor, Ward(s): 5
lise.burcher@guelph.ca
Leanne Piper, Councillor, Ward(s): 5
leanne.piper@guelph.ca
Todd Dennis, Councillor, Ward(s): 6
todd.dennis@guelph.ca
Karl Wettstein, Councillor, Ward(s): 6
karl.wettstein@guelph.ca
Lois Giles, City Clerk & Director, Information Services
clerks@guelph.ca
Ann Pappert, Chief Administrative Officer
administration@guelph.ca
Margaret Neubauer, Chief Financial Officer
finance@guelph.ca; margaret.neubauer@guelph.ca
Mark Amorosi, Executive Director, Human Resources & Legal Services
mark.amorosi@guelph.ca
Janet Laird, Executive Director, Environmental Services
janet.laird@guelph.ca
Derek McCaughan, Executive Director, Operations
operations@guelph.ca
Shawn Armstrong, General Manager, Emergency Services

Hamilton
Hamilton City Centre
P.O. Box 2040 LCD1
#220, 77 James St. North
Hamilton, ON L8R 2K3
Tel: 905-546-2489; *Fax:* 905-546-2095
askCITY@hamilton.ca; communications@hamilton.ca
www.hamilton.ca
Other Information: E-mail, Dev.: economicdevelopment@hamilton.ca
Municipal Type: City
Incorporated: 1846 *Area:* 1,117.21 sq km
Population in 2011: 519,949
Provincial Electoral District(s): Ancaster-Dundas-Flamborough-Westdale; Hamilton Centre; Hamilton East-Stoney Creek; Hamilton Mountain; Niagara West-Glanbrook
Federal Electoral District(s): Hamilton Centre; Hamilton East-Stoney Creek; Hamilton Mountain; Niagara West-Glanbrook; Ancaster-Dundas-Flamborough-Westdale
Next Election: Oct. 27, 2014 (4 year terms)
Note: Incorporated as a city on Jan. 1, 2001.
Bob Bratina, Mayor
mayor@hamilton.ca
Brian McHattie, Councillor, Ward(s): 1
brian.mchattie@hamilton.ca
Jason Farr, Councillor, Ward(s): 2
jason.farr@hamilton.ca
Bernie Morelli, Councillor, Ward(s): 3
bernie.morelli@hamilton.ca
Sam Merulla, Councillor, Ward(s): 4
sam.merulla@hamilton.ca
Chad Collins, Councillor, Ward(s): 5
chad.collins@hamilton.ca
Tom Jackson, Councillor, Ward(s): 6
tom.jackson@hamilton.ca
Scott Duvall, Councillor, Ward(s): 7
scott.duvall@hamilton.ca
Terry Whitehead, Councillor, Ward(s): 8
terry.whitehead@hamilton.ca
Brad Clark, Councillor, Ward(s): 9
brad.clark@hamilton.ca
Maria Pearson, Councillor, Ward(s): 10
maria.pearson@hamilton.ca
Brenda Johnson, Councillor, Ward(s): 11
brenda.johnson@hamilton.ca
Lloyd Ferguson, Councillor, Ward(s): 12
lloyd.ferguson@hamilton.ca
Russ Powers, Councillor, Ward(s): 13
russ.powers@hamilton.ca
Robert Pasuta, Councillor, Ward(s): 14
robert.pasuta@hamilton.ca
Judi Partridge, Councillor, Ward(s): 15
judi.partridge@hamilton.ca
Rose Caterini, City Clerk
clerk@hamilton.ca
Chris Murray, City Manager
905-540-5420
Roberto Rossini, General Manager, Finance & Corporate Services
Jim Kay, General Manager, Hamilton Emergency Services
Tim McCabe, General Manager, Planning & Economic Development
Joe-Anne Priel, General Manager, Community Services
Scott Stewart, C.E.T., General Manager, Public Works

Huntsville
37 Main St. East
Huntsville, ON P1H 1A1
Tel: 705-789-1751; *Fax:* 705-789-6689
administration@huntsville.ca
www.huntsville.ca
Other Information: TTY: 705-789-1768
Municipal Type: City
Area: 703.23 sq km
County or District: Muskoka Dist. Mun.; *Population in 2011:* 19,056
Provincial Electoral District(s): Parry Sound-Muskoka
Federal Electoral District(s): Parry Sound-Muskoka
Next Election: Oct. 27, 2014 (4 year terms)
Claude Doughty, Mayor
mayor@huntsville.ca
Scott Aitchison, District & Town Councillor/Deputy Mayor
Fran Coleman, District & Town Councillor
Brian Thompson, District & Town Councillor
Tim Withey, Councillor, Ward(s): Brunel
John Davis, Councillor, Ward(s): Chaffey
Karin Terziano, Councillor, Ward(s): Huntsville
Det Schumacher, Councillor, Ward(s): Stisted/Stephenson/Port Sydney
Chris Zanetti, Councillor, Ward(s): Stisted/Stephenson/Port Sydney
Kathleen Gilchrist, Municipal Clerk
Kelly Pender, Chief Administrative Officer
Dianne Leeder, Treasurer
Brian Crozier, Director, Community Services
Mike Gooch, Director, Building & Chief Building Official
Steve Hernen, Director, Protective Services & Fire Chief
Steve Keeley, Director, Public Works
Colleen MacDonald, Manager, Parks & Cemeteries
Lisa Smith, Manager, Human Resources

Kawartha Lakes
P.O. Box 9000
26 Francis St.
Lindsay, ON K9V 5R8
Tel: 705-324-9411; *Fax:* 705-324-8110
info@city.kawarthalakes.on.ca
www.city.kawarthalakes.on.ca
Other Information: Toll-Free Phone: 1-888-822-2225
Municipal Type: City
Incorporated: Jan. 1, 2001 *Area:* 3,059.47 sq km
Population in 2011: 73,214
Provincial Electoral District(s): Haliburton-Kawartha Lakes-Brock
Federal Electoral District(s): Haliburton-Kawartha Lakes-Brock
Next Election: Oct. 27, 2014 (4 year terms)
Note: Formerly the County of Victoria.
Ric McGee, Mayor
rmcgee@city.kawarthalakes.on.ca
John Macklem, Councillor, Ward(s): 1
jmacklem@city.kawarthalakes.on.ca
Emmett Yeo, Councillor, Ward(s): 2
eyeo@city.kawarthalakes.on.ca
David Hodgson, Councillor, Ward(s): 3
dhodgson@city.kawarthalakes.on.ca
Glenn Campbell, Councillor, Ward(s): 4
gcampbell@city.kawarthalakes.on.ca
Stephen Strangway, Councillor, Ward(s): 5
sstrangway@city.kawarthalakes.on.ca
Doug Elmslie, Councillor, Ward(s): 6
delmslie@city.kawarthalakes.on.ca
Brian Junkin, Councillor, Ward(s): 7
bjunkin@city.kawarthalakes.on.ca
Donna Villemaire, Councillor, Ward(s): 8
dvillemaire@city.kawarthalakes.on.ca
Andy Luff, Councillor, Ward(s): 9
aluff@city.kawarthalakes.on.ca
Pat Dunn, Councillor, Ward(s): 10
pdunn@city.kawarthalakes.on.ca
Patrick O'Reilly, Councillor, Ward(s): 11
poreilly@city.kawarthalakes.on.ca
Gord James, Councillor, Ward(s): 12
gjames@city.kawarthalakes.on.ca
Pat Warren, Councillor, Ward(s): 13
pwarren@city.kawarthalakes.on.ca
Ron Ashmore, Councillor, Ward(s): 14
rashmore@city.kawarthalakes.on.ca
Gerald McGregor, Councillor, Ward(s): 15
gmcgregor@city.kawarthalakes.on.ca
Heather Stauble, Councillor, Ward(s): 16
hstauble@city.kawarthalakes.on.ca
Judy Currins, City Clerk
Albert Horsman, Chief Administrative Officer
Rudy Huisman, Director, Financial Services
rhuisman@city.kawarthalakes.on.ca
Michelle Hendry, Director, Public Works
mhendry@city.kawarthalakes.on.ca
Ron Taylor, Director, Development Services
rtaylor@city.kawarthalakes.on.ca
Bob Knight, Director, Health & Social Services
bknight@city.kawarthalakes.on.ca
Kevin Williams, Director, Community Services
kwilliams@city.kawarthalakes.on.ca
Mark Pankhurst, Fire Chief
mpankhurst@city.kawarthalakes.on.ca

Kenora
1 Main St. South
Kenora, ON P9N 3X2
Tel: 807-467-2000; *Fax:* 807-467-2009
service@kenora.ca
www.kenora.ca
Municipal Type: City
Area: 210.91 sq km
County or District: Kenora District; *Population in 2011:* 15,348
Provincial Electoral District(s): Kenora-Rainy River

Federal Electoral District(s): Kenora
Next Election: Oct. 27, 2014 (4 year terms)
David S. Canfield, Mayor
dcanfield@kenora.ca
Charito V. Drinkwalter, Councillor
cdrinkwalter@kenora.ca
Ron Lunny, Councillor
rlunny@kenora.ca
Rod McKay, Councillor
rmckay@kenora.ca
Rory McMillan, Councillor
rmcmillan@kenora.ca
Louie Roussin, Councillor
lroussin@kenora.ca
Sharon L. Smith, Councillor
ssmith@kenora.ca
Joanne L. McMillin, Clerk
jmcmillin@kenora.ca
Karen Brown, Chief Administrative Officer
kbrown@kenora.ca
Charlotte Edie, Treasurer
cedie@kenora.ca
Warren Brinkman, Manager, Emergency Services
wbrinkman@kenora.ca
Sharen McDowall, Manager, Human Resources
smcdowall@kenora.ca
Colleen Neil, Manager, Recreation
cneil@kenora.ca
Rick Perchuk, Manager, Operations
rperchuk@kenora.ca
Mike Mostow, Supervisor, Fleet & Solid Waste
mmostow@kenora.ca
Warren Ortlieb, Supervisor, Sewer & Water
wortlieb@kenora.ca
Kevin Robertson, Chief Building Official
krobertson@kenora.ca
Marco Vogrig, Municipal Engineer
mvogrig@kenora.ca

Kingston
City Hall
216 Ontario St.
Kingston, ON K7L 2Z3
Tel: 613-546-0000; *Fax:* 613-546-5232
www.cityofkingston.ca
Other Information: TTY: 613-546-4889
Municipal Type: City
Incorporated: Jan. 1, 1998 *Area:* 450.39 sq km
County or District: Frontenac; *Population in 2011:* 123,363
Provincial Electoral District(s): Kingston & the Islands
Federal Electoral District(s): Kingston & the Islands
Next Election: Oct. 27, 2014 (4 year terms)
Mark Gerretsen, Mayor
mgerretsen@cityofkingston.ca
Rick Downes, Councillor, Ward(s): Cataraqui District
rdownes@cityofkingston.ca
Lisa Osanic, Councillor, Ward(s): Collins-Bayridge District
losanic@cityofkingston.ca
Jeff Scott, Councillor, Ward(s): Countryside District
jscott@cityofkingston.ca
Rob Hutchinson, Councillor, Ward(s): King's Town District
rhutchison@cityofkingston.ca
Sandy Berg, Councillor, Ward(s): Kingscourt-Strathcona District
sberg@cityofkingston.ca
Dorothy Hector, Councillor, Ward(s): Lakeside District
dhector@cityofkingston.ca
Kevin George, Councillor, Ward(s): Loyalist-Cataraqui District
kgeorge@cityofkingston.ca
Brian Reitzel, Councillor, Ward(s): Pittsburgh District
breitzel@cityofkingston.ca
Liz Schell, Councillor, Ward(s): Portsmouth District
lschell@cityofkingston.ca
Bill Glover, Councillor, Ward(s): Sydenham District
bglover@cityofkingston.ca
Bryan Paterson, Councillor, Ward(s): Trillium District
bpaterson@cityofkingston.ca
Jim Neill, Councillor, Ward(s): Williamsville District
jneill@cityofkingston.ca
John Bolognone, City Clerk
Gerard Hunt, Chief Administrative Officer
Desiree Kennedy, Treasurer & Director, Financial Services
Cynthia Beach, Commissioner, Sustainability & Growth
Denis Leger, Commissioner, Transportation, Properties & Emergency Services
Lanie Hurdle, Commissioner, Community Services & Director, Recreation & Leisure Services
Paul MacLatchy, Director, Strategy, Environment, & Communications
Mark Van Buren, Director, Engineering
Damon Wells, Director, Public Works
Terry Willing, Director, Building & Licensing
Harold Tulk, Fire Chief
John Cross, Manager, Emergency Planning
John Giles, Manager, Solid Waste
George Wallace, Project Manager, Sustainability & Growth

Kingsville
2021 Division Rd. North
Kingsville, ON N9Y 2Y9
Tel: 519-733-2305; *Fax:* 519-733-8108
www.kingsville.ca
Municipal Type: City
Incorporated: 1874 *Area:* 246.84 sq km
County or District: Essex; *Population in 2011:* 21,362
Provincial Electoral District(s): Essex
Federal Electoral District(s): Essex
Next Election: Oct. 27, 2014 (4 year terms)
Note: Incorporated as a town in 1901. Restructuring occurred in 1999.
Nelson Santos, Mayor
nsantos@kingsville.ca
Tamara Stomp, Deputy Mayor & Councillor
stomp@mnsi.net
Ron Colasanti, Councillor
ronaldcolasanti@gmail.com
Gord Queen, Councillor
pgordonqueen@msn.com
Bob Peterson, Councillor
rpeterson9@cogeco.ca
Sandi McIntyre, Councillor
sandygmcintyre@hotmail.com
Gail Stiffler, Councillor
g.stiffler@sympatico.ca
Ruth Orton-Pert, Clerk & Director, Corporate Services
rorton-pert@kingsville.ca
Dan DiGiovanni, Chief Administrative Officer
ddigiovanni@kingsville.ca
Sandra Ingratta, Director, Financial Services
singratta@kingsville.ca
Andrew Plancke, C.E.T., Director, Municipal Services
aplancke@kingsville.ca
Michael Arthur, Chief Building Official
marthur@kingsville.ca
Bob Kissner, Fire Chief
bkissner@kingsville.ca
Andy Coghill, Manager, Public Works
acoghill@kingsville.ca
Dan Wood, Manager, Parks & Recreation
dwood@kingsville.ca

Kitchener
City Hall
P.O. Box 1118
200 King St. West
Kitchener, ON N2G 4G7
Tel: 519-741-2345
www.kitchener.ca
Other Information: TTY: 1-866-969-9994
Municipal Type: City
Incorporated: June 9, 1912 *Area:* 136.89 sq km
County or District: Waterloo Regional Municipality; *Population in 2011:* 219,153
Provincial Electoral District(s): Kitchener Centre; Kitchener-Waterloo; Waterloo-Wellington
Federal Electoral District(s): Kitchener Centre; Kitchener-Waterloo; Kitchener-Conestoga
Next Election: Oct. 27, 2014 (4 year terms)
Carl Zehr, Mayor
519-741-2300
mayor@kitchener.ca
Scott Davey, Councillor, Ward(s): 1
scott.davey@kitchener.ca
Berry Vrbanovic, Councillor, Ward(s): 2
berryv@kitchener.ca
John Gazzola, Councillor, Ward(s): 3
john.gazzola@kitchener.ca
Yvonne Fernandes, Councillor, Ward(s): 4
yvonne.fernandes@kitchener.ca
Kelly Galloway, Councillor, Ward(s): 5
kelly.galloway@kitchener.ca
Paul Singh, Councillor, Ward(s): 6
paul.singh@kitchener.ca
Bil Ioannidis, Councillor, Ward(s): 7
bil.ioannidis@kitchener.ca
Zyg Janecki, Councillor, Ward(s): 8
zyg.janecki@kitchener.ca
Frank Etherington, Councillor, Ward(s): 9
frank.etherington@kitchener.ca
Daniel Glenn-Graham, Councillor, Ward(s): 10
dan.glenn-graham@kitchener.ca
Carla Ladd, Chief Administrative Officer
carla.ladd@kitchener.ca
Dan Chapman, City Treasurer & General Manager, Financial Services
Pauline Houston, General Manager, Community Services
Troy Speck, General Manager, Corporate Services
Jeff Willmer, General Manager, Development & Technical Services
Grant Murphy, Director, Engineering Services
Alain Pinard, Director, Planning
Mike Seiling, Director, Building
Tim Beckett, Fire Chief
519-741-2495
Colin Goodeve, Committee Administrator

Environmental Committee, Dept. of Corporate Services

London
City Hall
P.O. Box 5035
300 Dufferin Ave.
London, ON N6A 4L9
Tel: 519-661-4500; *Fax:* 519-661-4892
webmaster@london.ca
www.london.ca
Municipal Type: City
Incorporated: 1855 *Area:* 420.57 sq km
County or District: Middlesex; *Population in 2011:* 366,151
Provincial Electoral District(s): London-Fanshawe; Elgin-Middlesex-London; London North Centre; London West
Federal Electoral District(s): London-Fanshawe; Elgin-Middlesex-London; London North Centre; London West
Next Election: Oct. 27, 2014 (4 year terms)
Joe Fontana, Mayor
jfontana@london.ca
Bud Polhill, Councillor, Ward(s): 1
bpolhill@london.ca
Bill Armstrong, Councillor, Ward(s): 2
barmstro@london.ca
Joe Swan, Councillor, Ward(s): 3
jswan@london.ca
Stephen Orser, Councillor, Ward(s): 4
sorser@london.ca
Joni Baechler, Councillor, Ward(s): 5
jbaechle@london.ca
Nancy Ann Branscombe, Councillor, Ward(s): 6
nbransco@london.ca
Matt Brown, Councillor, Ward(s): 7
mbrown@london.ca
Paul Hubert, Councillor, Ward(s): 8
phubert@london.ca
Dale Henderson, Councillor, Ward(s): 9
dhenders@london.ca
Paul Van Meerbergen, Councillor, Ward(s): 10
pvanmeer@london.ca
Denise Brown, Councillor, Ward(s): 11
dbrown@london.ca
Harold Usher, Councillor, Ward(s): 12
husher@london.ca
Judy Bryant, Councillor, Ward(s): 13
jbryant@london.ca
Sandy White, Councillor, Ward(s): 14
sawhite@london.ca
Cathy Saunders, City Clerk
csaunder@london.ca
Jeff Fielding, Chief Administrative Officer
jfielding@london.ca
Martin Hayward, City Treasurer & Chief Financial Officer
Joseph Edward, Chief Technology Officer
jedward@london.ca
Veronica McAlea Major, Chief Human Resources Officer
vmcaleamajor@london.ca
Ross Fair, Executive Director, Community Services
rfair@london.ca
Patrick McNally, P.Eng., Executive Director, Planning, Environmental & Engineering Services
William Coxhead, Director, Parks & Recreation
bcoxhead@london.ca
Ronald Standish, Director, Wastewater & Treatment
rstandis@london.ca
Jay Stanford, Director, Environmental Programs & Solid Waste
jstanfor@london.ca

Markham
Markham Civic Centre
101 Town Centre Blvd.
Markham, ON L3R 9W3
Tel: 905-477-7000; *Fax:* 905-479-7771
customerservice@markham.ca; webmaster@markham.ca
www.markham.ca
Other Information: Customer Service: 905-477-5530
Municipal Type: City
Incorporated: Jan. 1, 1971 *Area:* 212.58 sq km
County or District: York Reg. Mun.; *Population in 2011:* 301,709

Provincial Electoral District(s): Markham-Unionville; Oak Ridges-Markham; Thornhill
Federal Electoral District(s): Markham-Unionville; Oak Ridges-Markham; Thornhill
Next Election: Oct. 27, 2014 (4 year terms)
Frank Scarpitti, Mayor
905-475-4702
fscarpitti@markham.ca
Jack Heath, Deputy Mayor & Regional Councillor
905-475-4872
jheath@markham.ca
Jim Jones, Regional Councillor
905-479-7757
jjones@markham.ca
Gordon Landon, Regional Councillor
905-415-7534
glandon@markham.ca
Joe Li, Regional Councillor
905-479-7749
joeli@markham.ca
Valerie Burke, Councillor, Ward(s): 1
vburke@markham.ca
Howard Shore, Councillor, Ward(s): 2
hshore@markham.ca
Don Hamilton, Councillor, Ward(s): 3
dhamilton@markham.ca
Carolina Moretti, Councillor, Ward(s): 4
cmoretti@markham.ca
Colin Campbell, Councillor, Ward(s): 5
ccampbell@markham.ca
Alan Ho, Councillor, Ward(s): 6
alan.ho@markham.ca
Logan Kanapathi, Councillor, Ward(s): 7
lkanapathi@markham.ca
Alex Chiu, Councillor, Ward(s): 8
achiu@markham.ca
Kimberly Kitteringham, Town Clerk
905-475-4729
kkitteringham@markham.ca
John Livey, Chief Administrative Officer
905-479-7755
jlivey@markham.ca
Joel Lustig, Treasurer
905-475-4715
jlustig@markham.ca
Jim Baird, Commissioner, Development Services
905-475-4875
jbaird@markham.ca
Brenda Librecz, Commissioner, Community & Fire Services
905-479-7761
blibrecz@markham.ca
Andy Taylor, Commissioner, Corporate Services
905-475-4705
ataylor@markham.ca
Nasir Kenea, Chief Information Officer
905-475-4733
nkenea@markham.ca
Bill Snowball, Fire Chief, Fire & Emergency Services
905-305-5982
bsnowball@markham.ca
Alan Brown, Director, Engineering
905-415-7507
abrown@markham.ca
Sharon Laing, Director, Human Resources
905-475-4725
slaing@markham.ca
Peter Loukes, Director, Operations
905-475-4894
ploukes@markham.ca
Tim Moore, Director, Building Standards
905-475-4712
tmoore@markham.ca
Claudia Marsales, Senior Manager, Waste Management & Environment
cmarsales@markham.ca

Mississauga

Civic Centre
300 City Centre Dr.
Mississauga, ON L5B 3C1
Tel: 905-615-4311; *Fax:* 905-615-4081
public.info@mississauga.ca
www.mississauga.ca
Other Information: TTY: 905-896-5151
Municipal Type: City
Incorporated: Jan. 1, 1974 *Area:* 288.53 sq km
County or District: Peel Reg. Mun.; *Population in 2011:* 713,443
Provincial Electoral District(s): Bramalea-Gore-Malton; Mississauga-Brampton South; Mississauga-Erindale; Mississauga East-Cooksville; Mississauga South; Mississauga-Streetsville
Federal Electoral District(s): Bramalea-Gore-Malton; Mississauga-Brampton South; Mississauga-Erindale; Mississauga East-Cooksville; Mississauga South; Mississauga-Streetsville
Next Election: Oct. 27, 2014 (4 year terms)
Hazel McCallion, Mayor
mayor@mississauga.ca
Jim Tovey, Councillor, Ward(s): 1
jim.tovey@mississauga.ca
Patricia Mullin, Councillor, Ward(s): 2
pat.mullin@mississauga.ca
Chris Fonseca, Councillor, Ward(s): 3
chris.fonseca@mississauga.ca
Frank Dale, Councillor, Ward(s): 4
frank.dale@mississauga.ca
Ron Starr, Councillor, Ward(s): 6
ron.starr@mississauga.ca
Nando Iannicca, Councillor, Ward(s): 7
nando.iannicca@mississauga.ca
Katie Mahoney, Councillor, Ward(s): 8
katie.mahoney@mississauga.ca
Pat Saito, Councillor, Ward(s): 9
pat.saito@mississauga.ca
Sue McFadden, Councillor, Ward(s): 10
sue.mcfadden@mississauga.ca
George Carlson, Councillor, Ward(s): 11
george.carlson@mississauga.ca
Crystal Greer, City Clerk & Director, Legislative Services
Janice Baker, City Manager & Chief Administrative Officer
city.manager@mississauga.ca
Brenda Breault, Commissioner, Corporate Services, & Treasurer

Paul Mitcham, Commissioner, Community Services
Martin Powell, Commissioner, Transportation & Works
Ed Sajecki, Commissioner, Planning & Building
John McDougall, Fire Chief

Newmarket

P.O. Box 328
395 Mulock Dr.
Newmarket, ON L3Y 4X7
Tel: 905-895-5193; *Fax:* 905-953-5100
info@newmarket.ca
www.newmarket.ca
Municipal Type: City
Incorporated: 1857 *Area:* 38.08 sq km
County or District: York Regional Municipality; *Population in 2011:* 79,978
Provincial Electoral District(s): Newmarket-Aurora
Federal Electoral District(s): Newmarket-Aurora
Next Election: Oct. 27, 2014 (4 year terms)
Note: Incorporated as a town in 1880.
Tony Van Bynen, Mayor
905-898-2876, Fax: 905-953-5102
mayor@newmarket.ca
John Taylor, Regional Councillor
jtaylor@newmarket.ca
Tom Vegh, Councillor, Ward(s): 1
tomvegh@gmail.com
Dave Kerwin, Councillor, Ward(s): 2
dkerwin@newmarket.ca
Jane Twinney, Councillor, Ward(s): 3
jtwinney@newmarket.ca
Tom Hempen, Councillor, Ward(s): 4
thempen@newmarket.ca
Joe Sponga, Councillor, Ward(s): 5
jsponga@newmarket.ca
Maddie Di Muccio, Councillor, Ward(s): 6
mdimuccio@newmarket.ca
Chris Emanuel, Councillor, Ward(s): 7
cemanuel@newmarket.ca
Anita Moore, Clerk & Director, Legislative Services
Robert N. Shelton, Chief Administrative Officer
Mike Mayes, Treasurer & Director, Financial Services
finance@newmarket.ca
Robert Dixon, Commissioner, Corporate & Financial Services
Robert Prentice, Commissioner, Community Services
Wanda Bennett, Director, Corporate Communications
communications@newmarket.ca
Lynn Georgeff, Director, Human Resources
Brian Jones, Director, Public Works Services
Jim Koutroubis, Director, Engineering Services
engineering@newmarket.ca
Ian McDougall, Director, Recreation & Culture Services
Rick Nethery, BES, MCIP, RPP, Director, Planning
905-953-5321, Fax: 905-953-5140
planning@newmarket.ca
David Potter, Chief Building Official
buildings@newmarket.ca

Niagara Falls

City Hall
P.O. Box 1023
4310 Queen St.
Niagara Falls, ON L2E 6X5
Tel: 905-356-7521; *Fax:* 905-356-9083
www.niagarafalls.ca
Municipal Type: City
Incorporated: Jan. 1, 1904 *Area:* 209.58 sq km
County or District: Niagara Reg. Mun.; *Population in 2011:* 82,997
Provincial Electoral District(s): Niagara Falls
Federal Electoral District(s): Niagara Falls
Next Election: Oct. 27, 2014 (4 year terms)
Jim Diodati, Mayor
jdiodati@niagarafalls.ca
Wayne Thomson, City Councillor
wthomson@niagarafalls.ca
Victor Pietrangelo, City Councillor
vpietrangelo@niagarafalls.ca
Carolynn Ioannoni, City Councillor
ioannoni@niagarafalls.ca
Vince A. Kerrio, City Councillor
kerrio@overlookingthefalls.com s
Wayne Gates, City Councillor
wgates@niagarafalls.ca
Joyce Morocco, City Councillor
joycemorocco@niagarafalls.ca
Janice Wing, City Councillor
jwing@niagarafalls.ca
Bart Maves, City Councillor
wmaves@cogeco.ca
Dean Iorfida, City Clerk & Director, Council Services
diorfida@niagarafalls.ca
Ken Todd, Chief Administrative Officer
ktodd@niagarafalls.ca
Serge Felicetti, Director, Business Development
sfelicetti@niagarafalls.ca
Alex Herlovitch, Director, Planning & Development
planning@niagarafalls.ca
Geoffrey Holman, Director, Municipal Works
Lee Smith, Fire Chief
Lee Smith, Fire Chief

Fire Dept.

North Bay

City Hall
P.O. Box 360
200 McIntyre St. East
North Bay, ON P1B 8H8
Tel: 705-474-0400; *Fax:* 705-495-4353
info@cityofnorthbay.ca
www.city.north-bay.on.ca
Other Information: Toll-Free Phone: 1-800-465-1882
Municipal Type: City
Incorporated: 1925 *Area:* 314.91 sq km
County or District: Nipissing District; *Population in 2011:* 53,651
Provincial Electoral District(s): Nipissing
Federal Electoral District(s): Nipissing-Timiskaming
Next Election: Oct. 27, 2014 (4 year terms)
Al McDonald, Mayor
mayor@cityofnorthbay.ca
Peter Chirico, Councillor
peter.chirico@cityofnorthbay.ca
Mike Anthony, Councillor
mike.anthony@cityofnorthbay.ca
Mac Bain, Councillor
mac.bain@cityofnorthbay.ca
Sean Lawlor, Councillor
sean.lawlor@cityofnorthbay.ca
George Maroosis, Councillor
george.maroosis@cityofnorthbay.ca
Judy Koziol, Councillor
judy.koziol@cityofnorthbay.ca
Chris Mayne, Councillor
chris.mayne@cityofnorthbay.ca
Dave Mendicino, Councillor
dave.mendicino@cityofnorthbay.ca
Daryl Vaillancourt, Councillor
daryl.vaillancourt@cityofnorthbay.ca
Tanya Vrebosch Merry, Councillor
tanya.vrebosch-merry@cityofnorthbay.ca
Cathy Conrad, City Clerk
cathy.conrad@cityofnorthbay.ca
Dave Linkie, Chief Administration Officer
dave.linkie@cityofnorthbay.ca
Margaret Karpenko, Chief Financial Officer & Treasurer
margaret.karpenko@cityofnorthbay.ca
Jerry Knox, Managing Director, Community Services
jerry.knox@cityofnorthbay.ca

Alan Korell, Managing Director, Engineering, Environmental & Works
alan.korell@cityofnorthbay.ca
David Euler, Director, Sewer & Water
david.euler@cityofnorthbay.ca
Jamie Houston, Director, Parks, Recreation, & Leisure Services
jamie.houston@cityofnorthbay.ca
Lea Janisse, Director, Human Resources
lea.janisse@cityofnorthbay.ca
John Severino, Manager, Environmental Services
john.severino@cityofnorthbay.ca
Dorothea Carvell, Manager, Transit
dorothea.carvell@cityofnorthbay.ca
Joe Germano, Manager, Road & Traffic
joe.germano@cityofnorthbay.ca
Ian Kilgour, Manager, Planning Services
ian.kilgour@cityofnorthbay.ca
Shawn Killins, Chief Building Official
shawn.killins@cityofnorthbay.ca
Peter Leckie, City Solicitor
peter.leckie@cityofnorthbay.ca
Grant Love, Fire Chief
grant.love@cityofnorthbay.ca

Oakville

1225 Trafalgar Rd.
Oakville, ON L6J 5A6
Tel: 905-845-6601; *Fax:* 905-815-2025
publicinquiry@oakville.ca; communications@oakville.ca
www.oakville.ca
Other Information: TTY: 905-338-4200
Municipal Type: City
Incorporated: May 27, 1857 *Area:* 138.56 sq km
County or District: Halton Regional Municipality; *Population in 2011:* 182,520
Provincial Electoral District(s): Halton; Oakville
Federal Electoral District(s): Halton; Oakville
Next Election: Oct. 27, 2014 (4 year terms)
Rob Burton, Mayor, Fax: 905-815-2001
mayor@oakville.ca
Alan Johnston, Town & Regional Councillor, Ward(s): 1
ajohnston@oakville.ca
Ralph Robinson, Town Councillor, Ward(s): 1
rrobinson@oakville.ca
Cathy Duddeck, Town & Regional Councillor, Ward(s): 2
cduddeck@oakville.ca
Pam Damoff, Town Councillor, Ward(s): 2
pdamoff@oakville.ca
F. Keith Bird, Town & Regional Councillor, Ward(s): 3
kbird@oakville.ca
Dave Gittings, Town Councillor, Ward(s): 3
dgittings@oakville.ca
Allan Elgar, Town & Regional Councillor, Ward(s): 4
aelgar@oakville.ca
Roger Lapworth, Town Councillor, Ward(s): 4
rlapworth@oakville.ca
Jeff Knoll, Town & Regional Councillor, Ward(s): 5
jknoll@oakville.ca
Marc Grant, Town Councillor, Ward(s): 5
mgrant@oakville.ca
Tom Adams, Town & Regional Councillor, Ward(s): 6
tadams@oakville.ca
Max Khan, Town Councillor, Ward(s): 6
mkhan@oakville.ca
Cathie Best, Town Clerk
clerks@oakville.ca; cbest@oakville.ca
Ray Green, Chief Administrative Officer
rgreen@oakville.ca
Patricia Elliott-Spencer, M.B.A., CMA, Treasurer & Director, Finance
pelliott-spencer@oakville.ca; finance@oakville.ca
David Bloomer, Commissioner, Infrastructure & Transportation Services
dbloomer@oakville.ca
Jane Clohecy, Commissioner, Planning & Development Services
jclohecy@oakville.ca; planning@oakville.ca
Gord Lalonde, Commissioner, Corporate Services
glalonde@oakville.ca
Domenic Lunardo, Commissioner, Community Services
dlunardo@oakville.ca
Elizabeth Bourns, Director, Human Resources
ebourns@oakville.ca; humanresources@oakville.ca
Barry Cole, Director, Transit Services
bcole@oakville.ca; transit@oakville.ca
Daniel Cozzi, P.Eng., Director, Roads & Works Operations
dcozzi@oakville.ca
Darnell Lambert, C.E.T., Director, Engineering & Construction
dlambert@oakville.ca
Chris Mark, Director, Parks & Open Space
cmark@oakville.ca; parks@oakville.ca
Cindy Toth, Director, Environmental Policy
ctoth@oakville.ca; environment@oakville.ca
Sheldon Switzer, Director, Building Services & Chief Building Official
sswitzer@oakville.ca; building@oakville.ca
John McNeil, Manager, Forestry & Cemetery Services
jmcneil@oakville.ca; forestry@oakville.ca
Richard Boyes, Fire Chief
rboyes@oakville.ca; fire@oakville.ca

Orillia

Administration Office
#300, 50 Andrew St. South
Orillia, ON L3V 7T5
Tel: 705-325-1311; *Fax:* 705-325-5178
corporate@city.orillia.on.ca
www.orillia.ca
Municipal Type: City
Incorporated: 1867 *Area:* 28.61 sq km
County or District: Simcoe; *Population in 2011:* 30,586
Provincial Electoral District(s): Simcoe North
Federal Electoral District(s): Simcoe North
Next Election: Oct. 27, 2014 (4 year terms)
Note: Incorporated as a town in 1875 & as a city in 1969.
Angelo Orsi, Mayor
mayor@city.orillia.on.ca
Donald W. Jenkins, Councillor, Ward(s): 1
Patrick F. Kehoe, Councillor, Ward(s): 1
Pete Bowen, Councillor, Ward(s): 2
Linda Murray, Councillor, Ward(s): 2
Michael Fogarty, Councillor, Ward(s): 3
Paul Spears, Councillor, Ward(s): 3
Andrew Hill, Councillor, Ward(s): 4
Tony Madden, Councillor, Ward(s): 4
Gayle Jackson, City Clerk
clerks@orillia.ca; gjackson@orillia.ca
Bob Ripley, Interim City Manager/Treasurer
treas@orillia.ca
Lori Bolton, Director, Human Resources
lbolton@orillia.ca
Peter Dance, Director, Public Works
publicworks@orillia.ca; pdance@orillia.ca
Ray Merkley, Director, Parks & Recreation
parks@orillia.ca; rmerkley@orillia.ca
Craig Metcalf, Director, Culture & Heritage
cmetcalf@orillia.ca
Ian Sugden, Director, Planning & Development
planning@orillia.ca; isugden@orillia.ca
Ralph Dominell, Fire Chief
ofd@orillia.ca; rdominelli@orillia.ca
Kelly Smith, Chief Building Official
ksmith@orillia.ca
Jack Green, Manager, Transportation
jgreen@orillia.ca
Andrew Schell, Manager, Environmental Services
aschell@orillia.ca
Percival Thomas, Manager, Water & Wastewater Systems
pthomas@orillia.ca

Oshawa

City Hall
50 Centre St. South
Oshawa, ON L1H 3Z7
Tel: 905-436-3311; *Fax:* 905-436-5642
service@oshawa.ca
www.oshawa.ca
Other Information: Toll-Free Phone: 1-800-667-4292; TTY: 905-436-5627
Municipal Type: City
Incorporated: March 8, 1924 *Area:* 145.67 sq km
County or District: Durham Reg. Mun.; *Population in 2011:* 149,607
Provincial Electoral District(s): Whitby-Oshawa; Oshawa
Federal Electoral District(s): Whitby-Oshawa; Oshawa
Next Election: Oct. 27, 2014 (4 year terms)
John Henry, Mayor
jhenry@oshawa.ca
John Aker, Regional Councillor
jaker@oshawa.ca
Bob Chapman, Regional Councillor
bchapman@oshawa.ca
Nancy Diamond, Regional Councillor
ndiamond@oshawa.ca
Amy England, Regional Councillor
aengland@oshawa.ca
Tito-Dante Marimpietri, Regional Councillor
tdmarimpietri@oshawa.ca
John Neal, Regional Councillor
jneal@oshawa.ca
Nester Pidwerbecki, Regional Councillor
npidwerbecki@oshawa.ca
Roger Bouma, City Councillor
rbouma@oshawa.ca
Doug Sanders, City Councillor
dsanders@oshawa.ca
Bruce Wood, City Councillor
bwood@oshawa.ca
Sandra Kranc, City Clerk, Fax: 905-436-5697
service@oshawa.ca
Bob Duignan, City Manager
905-436-3311, Fax: 905-436-5623
Chris Brown, Director, Finance Services, Fax: 905-436-5664
Garth Johns, Interim Commissioner, Community Services Department
Tom Hodgins, Commissioner, Development Services Department
Rick Stockman, Commissioner, Corporate Services Department
Ron Foster, Auditor General
905-436-5688, Fax: 905-436-5652
rfoster@oshawa.ca
Tracy Adams, Director, Corporate Communications & Marketing
Jamie Bronsema, Director, Strategic & Business Services
Jacqueline Long, Director, Human Resource Services
humanresources@oshawa.ca
Gary Carroll, Director, Engineering Services
Denyse Morrissey, Director, Recreation & Culture Services
recreation@oshawa.ca
Craig Kelly, Director, Works & Transportation Services
Paul Ralph, Director, Planning Services
Mike Leonard, Chief Building Official
buildings@oshawa.ca
Steve Meringer, Fire Chief

Ottawa

City Hall
110 Laurier Ave. West
Ottawa, ON K1P 1J1
Tel: 613-580-2400; *Fax:* 613-560-1380
info@ottawa.ca
www.ottawa.ca
Other Information: Toll Free Phone: 1-866-261-9799; or 311
Municipal Type: City
Incorporated: Jan. 1, 1855 *Area:* 2,778.13 sq km
Population in 2011: 883,391
Provincial Electoral District(s): Glengarry-Prescott-Russell; Nepean-Carleton; Ottawa Centre; Ottawa South; Ottawa-Vanier; Ottawa West-Nepean; Ottawa-Orléans; Carleton-Mississippi Mills
Federal Electoral District(s): Glengarry-Prescott-Russell; Nepean-Carleton; Ottawa Centre; Ottawa South; Ottawa-Vanier; Ottawa West-Nepean; Ottawa-Orléans; Carleton-Mississippi Mills
Next Election: Oct. 27, 2014 (4 year terms)
Jim Watson, Mayor
613-580-2496
jim.watson@ottawa.ca
Bob Monette, Councillor, Ward(s): 1 - Orléans
613-580-2471
bob.monette@ottawa.ca
Rainer Bloess, Councillor, Ward(s): 2 - Innes
613-580-2472
rainer.bloess@ottawa.ca
Jan Harder, Councillor, Ward(s): 3 - Barrhaven
613-580-2473
jan.harder@ottawa.ca
Marianne Wilkinson, Councillor, Ward(s): 4 - Kanata North
613-580-2474
marianne.wilkinson@ottawa.ca
Eli El-Chantiry, Councillor, Ward(s): 5 - West Carleton-March
613-580-2475
eli.el-chantiry@ottawa.ca
Shad Qadri, Councillor, Ward(s): 6 - Stittsville-Kanata West
613-580-2476
shad.qadri@ottawa.ca
Mark Taylor, Councillor, Ward(s): 7 - Bay
613-580-2477
mark.taylor@ottawa.ca
Rick Chiarelli, Councillor, Ward(s): 8 - College
613-580-2478
rick.chiarelli@ottawa.ca
Keith Egli, Councillor, Ward(s): 9 - Knoxdale-Merivale
613-580-2479
ward9@ottawa.ca
Diane Deans, Councillor, Ward(s): 10 - Gloucester-Southgate
613-580-2480
diane.deans@ottawa.ca
Tim Tierney, Councillor, Ward(s): 11 - Beacon Hill-Cyrville
613-580-2481
tim.tierney@ottawa.ca
Mathieu Fleury, Councillor, Ward(s): 12 - Rideau-Vanier
613-580-2482
mathieu.fleury@ottawa.ca

Peter Clark, Councillor, Ward(s): 13 - Rideau-Rockcliffe
613-580-2483
peter.clark@ottawa.ca
Diane Holmes, Councillor, Ward(s): 14 - Somerset
613-580-2484
diane.holmes@ottawa.ca
Katherine Hobbs, Councillor, Ward(s): 15 - Kitchissippi
613-580-2485
katherine.hobbs@ottawa.ca
Maria McRae, Councillor, Ward(s): 16 - River
613-580-2486
maria.mcrae@ottawa.ca
David Chernushenko, Councillor, Ward(s): 17 - Capital
613-580-2487
david.chernushenko@ottawa.ca
Peter Hume, Councillor, Ward(s): 18 - Alta Vista
613-580-2488
peter.hume@ottawa.ca
Stephen Blais, Councillor, Ward(s): 19 - Cumberland
613-580-2489
stephen.blais@ottawa.ca
Doug Thompson, Councillor, Ward(s): 20 - Osgoode
613-580-2490
doug.thompson@ottawa.ca
Scott Moffatt, Councillor, Ward(s): 21 - Rideau-Goulbourn
613-580-2491
scott.moffatt@ottawa.ca
Steve Desroches, Councillor, Ward(s): 22 - Gloucester-South
613-580-2751
steve.desroches@ottawa.ca
Allan Hubley, Councillor, Ward(s): 23 - Kanata South
613-580-2752
allan.hubley@ottawa.ca
M. Rick O'Connor, City Clerk & Solicitor
Kent Kirkpatrick, City Manager
Marian Simulik, City Treasurer
Steve Kanellakos, Deputy City Manager
Nancy Schepers, Deputy City Manager
Chris Day, Chief, Corporate Communications
Catherine Frederick, Director, Human Resources
Donna L. Gray, Director, Organizational Development & Performance
Guy Michaud, Director, Information Technology & Chief Information Officer
Johanne Levesque, Director, Community Sustainability
Wayne Newell, Director, Infrastructure Services
Aaron Burry, General Manager, Community & Social Services
Dan Chenier, General Manager, Parks, Recreation & Cultural Service
Susan Jones, General Manager, Emergency & Protective Services
John Manconi, General Manager, Public Works
Alain Mercier, General Manager, Transit Services
John Moser, General Manager, Planning & Growth Management

Dixon A. Weir, General Manager, Environmental Services
Isra Levy, Medical Officer of Health
Michel Chevalier, Manager, Wastewater & Drainage Operations
Felice Petti, Manager, Strategic & Environmental Services
Tammy Rose, Manager, Drinking Water Services

Fire Department

Owen Sound

City Hall
808 - 2nd Ave. East
Owen Sound, ON N4K 2H4
Tel: 519-376-1440; *Fax:* 519-371-0511
cityadmin@e-owensound.com;
communityservices@e-owensound.com
www.owensound.ca
Municipal Type: City
Incorporated: Jan. 1, 2001 *Area:* 24.22 sq km
County or District: Grey; *Population in 2011:* 21,688
Provincial Electoral District(s): Bruce-Grey-Owen Sound
Federal Electoral District(s): Bruce-Grey-Owen Sound
Next Election: Oct. 27, 2014 (4 year terms)
Deborah Haswell, Mayor
David Adair, Councillor
Ian C. Boddy, Councillor
Jan Chamberlain, Councillor
Peter Lemon, Councillor
Jim McManaman, Councillor
Colleen Purdon, Councillor
Bill Twaddle, Councillor
Arlene Wright, City & County Councillor
Marion Koepke, C.M.O., City Clerk
mkoepke@owensound.ca
Jim Harrold, City Manager
Wayne Ritchie, CGA, Director, Financial Services
writchie@e-owensound.com
Pam Coulter, Director, Community Services
pcoulter@e-owensound.com
Glen Henry, C.M.O., Director, Corporate Services
ghenry@owensound.ca
John D. Johnston, C.E.T., Director, Operations
jdjohnson@e-owensound.com
Steve Furness, Manager, Economic Development & Tourism
business@e-owensound.com
Chris Webb, P.Eng., Manager, Engineering Services
Ed Nowak, Fire Chief
enowak@e-owensound.com

Pembroke

1 Pembroke St. East
Pembroke, ON K8A 3J5
Tel: 613-735-6821; *Fax:* 613-735-3660
pembroke@pembroke.ca
www.pembroke.ca
Municipal Type: City
Incorporated: 1877 *Area:* 14.35 sq km
County or District: Renfrew; *Population in 2011:* 14,360
Provincial Electoral District(s): Renfrew-Nipissing-Pembroke
Federal Electoral District(s): Renfrew-Nipissing-Pembroke
Next Election: Oct. 27, 2014 (4 year terms)
Note: Incorporated as a city in 1971.
Ed Jacyno, Mayor
Ronald Gervais, Deputy Mayor & Councillor, Councillor
Dan Callaghan, Councillor
Bob Hackett, Councillor
Patricia Lafreniere, Councillor
Terry O'Neill, Councillor
Les Scott, Councillor
Gary Severin, Councillor
Colonel Towriss, Councillor
Terry Lapierre, Chief Administrative Officer
tlapierre@pembroke.ca
LeeAnn McIntyre, Treasurer
lmcintyre@pembroke.ca
Susan Ellis, Manager, Economic Development, Recreation, & Tourism
sellis@pembroke.ca
Colleen Sauriol, Coordinator, Emergency Management
csauriol@pembroke.ca
Douglas Sitland, Manager, Operations
dsitland@pembroke.ca
Daniel Herback, Fire Chief
dherback@pembroke.ca
Robert Hughes, Chief Building Official
rhughes@pembroke.ca
Ron Conroy, Supervisor, Parks & Facilities
rconroy@pembroke.ca
Chris Mantha, Supervisor, Roads & Fleet
cmantha@pembroke.ca
Curtis Mick, Supervisor, Water & Sewer
cmick@pembroke.ca

Peterborough

500 George St. North
Peterborough, ON K9H 3R9
Tel: 705-742-7777; *Fax:* 705-742-4138
cityptbo@peterborough.ca; clerk@peterborough.ca
www.peterborough.ca
Other Information: E-mail, Human Resources: hr@peterborough.ca
Municipal Type: City
Incorporated: 1850 *Area:* 58.40 sq km
County or District: Peterborough; *Population in 2011:* 78,698
Provincial Electoral District(s): Peterborough
Federal Electoral District(s): Peterborough
Next Election: Oct. 27, 2014 (4 year terms)
Daryl Bennett, Mayor
dbennett@peterborough.ca
Dan McWilliams, Councillor, Ward(s): 1 - Otonabee
dmcwilliams@peterborough.ca
Lesley Parnell, Councillor, Ward(s): 1 - Otonabee
lparnell@peterborough.ca
Henry Clarke, Councillor, Ward(s): 2 - Monaghan
hclarke@peterborough.ca
Jack Doris, Councillor, Ward(s): 2 - Monaghan
jdoris@peterborough.ca
Bill J. Juby, Councillor, Ward(s): 3 - Town
bjuby@peterborough.ca
Dean Pappas, Councillor, Ward(s): 3 - Town
dpappas@peterborough.ca
Keith G. Riel, Councillor, Ward(s): 4 - Ashburnham
kriel@peterborough.ca
Len Vass, Councillor, Ward(s): 4 - Ashburnham
lvass@peterborough.ca
Andrew Beamer, Councillor, Ward(s): 5 - Northcrest
arbeamer@peterborough.ca
Bob Hall, Councillor, Ward(s): 5 - Northcrest
bhall@peterborough.ca
Nancy Wright-Laking, City Clerk
nwright-laking@peterborough.ca
Brian Horton, Chief Administrative Officer
cao@peterborough.ca
Sandra Clancy, Director, Corporate Services
sclancy@peterborough.ca
Ken Doherty, Director, Community Services
kdoherty@peterborough.ca
Malcolm Hunt, Director, Planning & Development Services
mhunt@peterborough.ca
Wayne Jackson, Director, Utility Services & Deputy CAO
wjackson@peterborough.ca
Trent Gervais, Fire Chief

Pickering

1 The Esplanade
Pickering, ON L1V 6K7
Tel: 905-420-2222
info@cityofpickering.com; customercare@cityofpickering.com
www.cityofpickering.com
Other Information: Toll-Free Phone: 1-866-683-2760; TTY: 905-420-1739
Municipal Type: City
Incorporated: 1849 *Area:* 231.59 sq km
County or District: Durham Reg. Mun.; *Population in 2011:* 88,721
Provincial Electoral District(s): Ajax-Pickering; Pickering-Scarborough East
Federal Electoral District(s): Ajax-Pickering; Pickering-Scarborough East
Next Election: Oct. 27, 2014 (4 year terms)
Note: Incorporated as a town in 1974 & as a city in 2000.
Dave Ryan, Mayor
905-420-4600, Fax: 905-420-6064
mayor@cityofpickering.com
Jennifer O'Connell, Regional Councillor, Ward(s): 1
jenniferoconnell@sympatico.ca
Kevin Ashe, City Councillor, Ward(s): 1
Bill McLean, Regional Councillor, Ward(s): 2
bmclean@cityofpickering.com
Doug Dickerson, City Councillor, Ward(s): 2
ddickerson@cityofpickering.com
Peter Rodrigues, Regional Councillor, Ward(s): 3
prodrigues@cityofpickering.com
David Pickles, City Councillor, Ward(s): 3
dpickles@cityofpickering.com
Debbie Shields, City Clerk
dshields@cityofpickering.com
Tony Prevedel, Chief Administrative Officer
cao@cityofpickering.com
Gilles A. Paterson, Treasurer & Director, Corporate Services
905-420-4634
gpaterson@cityofpickering.com
Everett Buntsma, Director, Community Services
905-420-4624
ebuntsma@cityofpickering.com
Neil Carroll, Director, Planning & Development
905-420-4617
ncarroll@cityofpickering.com
Thomas E. Melymuk, Director, Office of Sustainability
905-420-4636
tmelymuk@cityofpickering.com
Richard W. Holborn, Division Head, Engineering Services Division
90-542-2049
rholborn@cityofpickering.com
Jennifer Parent, Division Head, Human Resources
905-420-2160
Stephen Reynolds, Division Head, Culture & Recreation
905-420-4620
sreynolds@cityofpickering.com
William T. Douglas, Fire Chief
905-839-9968, Fax: 905-839-6327
fire@cityofpickering.com
Kyle Bentley, Chief Building Official
905-420-2070
kbentley@cityofpickering.com
Paul Bigioni, City Solicitor
905-420-2048
pbigioni@cityofpickering.com

Port Colborne

66 Charlotte St.
Port Colborne, ON L3K 3C8
Tel: 905-835-2900; *Fax:* 905-834-5746
www.portcolborne.ca
Municipal Type: City
Incorporated: 1870 *Area:* 121.97 sq km
County or District: Niagara Reg. Mun.; *Population in 2011:*

18,424
Provincial Electoral District(s): Welland
Federal Electoral District(s): Welland
Next Election: Oct. 27, 2014 (4 year terms)
Note: Incorporated as a town in 1918 & as a city in 1966.
Vance Badawey, Mayor, Fax: 905-835-2969
mayor@portcolborne.ca
David Barrick, Regional Councillor
david.barrick@niagararegion.ca
David B. Elliott, Councillor, Ward(s): 1
daveelliott@portcolborne.ca
Bill Steele, Councillor, Ward(s): 1
billsteele@portcolborne.ca
Yvon A. Doucet, Councillor, Ward(s): 2
yvondoucet@portcolborne.ca
Angie Desmarais, Councillor, Ward(s): 2
angiedesmarais@portcolborne.ca
Frank M. Danch, Councillor, Ward(s): 3
frankdanch@portcolborne.ca
Bea Kenny, Councillor, Ward(s): 3
beakenny@portcolborne.ca
Ron Bodner, Councillor, Ward(s): 4
ronbodner@portcolborne.ca
Barbara Butters, Councillor, Ward(s): 4
barbarabutters@portcolborne.ca
Ashley Grigg, City Clerk
ashleygrigg@portcolborne.ca
Carrie McIntosh, Chief Administrative Officer
carriemcintosh@portcolborne.ca
Dan Aquilina, Director, Planning & Development
danaquilina@portcolborne.ca
Ron Hanson, Director, Engineering & Operations
hanson@portcolborne.cane.ca
Peter Senese, Director, Community & Corporate Services
petersenese@portcolborne.ca
Stephen Thompson, General Manager, Economic Development, Tourism & Marketing
stephenthompson@portcolborne.ca
Thomas Cartwright, Fire Chief
firechief@portcolborne.ca
Ernie Cronier, Chief Building Official
erniecronier@portcolborne.ca
Randy Chamberlain, Coordinator, Health & Safety
randychamberlain@portcolborne.ca
Rick Marshall, Coordinator, Human Resources
rickmarshall@portcolborne.ca
Darlene Suddard, Coordinator, Water & Waste Water Compliance
darlenesuddard@portcolborne.ca

Quinte West

P.O. Box 490
7 Creswell Dr.
Trenton, ON K8V 5R6
Tel: 613-392-2841; *Fax:* 613-392-5608
www.city.quintewest.on.ca
Other Information: Toll-Free Phone: 1-866-485-2841
Municipal Type: City
Incorporated: Jan. 1, 1998 *Area:* 493.85 sq km
County or District: Hastings; *Population in 2011:* 43,086
Provincial Electoral District(s): Northumberland-Quinte West
Federal Electoral District(s): Northumberland-Quinte West
Next Election: Oct. 27, 2014 (4 year terms)
Note: Amalgamation of the former municipalities of Trenton, Sidney, Murray & Frankford.
John R. Williams, Mayor
Sally Freeman, Councillor, Ward(s): 1 - Trenton
613-965-6769
Fred Kuypers, Councillor, Ward(s): 1 - Trenton
613-392-8588
Leslie Roseblade, Councillor, Ward(s): 1 - Trenton
613-394-3492
Bob Wannamaker, Councillor, Ward(s): 1 - Trenton
613-392-8548
Doug Whitney, Councillor, Ward(s): 1 - Trenton
613-392-4779
Terry R.F. Cassidy, Councillor, Ward(s): 2 - Sidney
613-395-2031
Ron Hamilton, Councillor, Ward(s): 2 - Sidney
613-392-5369
Don Kuntze, Councillor, Ward(s): 2 - Sidney
613-962-6122
Paul Kyte, Councillor, Ward(s): 2 - Sidney
613-967-2134
Jim Alyea, Councillor, Ward(s): 3 - Murray
613-475-1519
Jim Harrison, Councillor, Ward(s): 3 - Murray
613-392-9437
Keith Reid, Councillor, Ward(s): 4 - Frankford
613-398-7991
DonnaLee Craig, Clerk & Manager, Corporate Services
Gary Dyke, Chief Administrative Officer
David Clazie, Treasurer & Director, Corporate & Financial Services
Chris Angelo, Director, Public Works & Environmental Services
Charlie Murphy, Director, Planning & Development Services
Tim Colasante, Manager, Engineering Services
Matt Tracey, Manager, Water & Wastewater
Tim Osborne, Manager, Human Resources
Phillip Lappan, Chief Building Official
John Whelan, Fire Chief

Richmond Hill

225 East Beaver Creek Rd.
Richmond Hill, ON L4B 3P4
Tel: 905-771-8800; *Fax:* 905-771-2500
www.richmondhill.ca
Municipal Type: City
Incorporated: 1873 *Area:* 100.89 sq km
County or District: York Reg. Mun.; *Population in 2011:* 185,541
Provincial Electoral District(s): Richmond Hill; Oak Ridges-Markham
Federal Electoral District(s): Richmond Hill; Oak Ridges-Markham
Next Election: Oct. 27, 2014 (4 year terms)
Dave Barrow, Mayor
officemayor@richmondhill.ca
Brenda Hogg, Regional & Local Councillor
bhogg@richmondhill.ca
Vito Spatafora, Regional & Local Councillor
vspatafora@richmondhill.ca
Greg Beros, Councillor, Ward(s): 1
gberos@richmondhill.ca
Carmine Perrelli, Councillor, Ward(s): 2
cperrelli@richmondhill.ca
Catro Liu, Councillor, Ward(s): 3
cliu@richmondhill.ca
Lynn Foster, Councillor, Ward(s): 4
lfoster@richmondhill.ca
Nick Papa, Councillor, Ward(s): 5
npapa@richmondhill.ca
Godwin Chan, Councillor, Ward(s): 6
gchan@richmondhill.ca
D. McLarty, Town Clerk
clerks@richmondhill.ca
Joan Anderton, Chief Administrative Officer
cao@richmondhill.ca
David Dexter, Treasurer & Director, Financial Services
revenue@richmondhill.ca; budget@richmondhill.ca
A. Bassios, Commissioner, Planning
planning@richmondhill.ca
Italo Brutto, Commissioner, Environment & Infrastructure Services
905-771-8830
eis@richmondhill.ca
Dean Miller, Commissioner, Corporate & Financial Services
905-771-2497
dmiller@richmondhill.ca
J. DeVries, Director, Building Services, & Chief Building Official
D. Joslin, Director, Recreation & Culture
P. Lee, Director, Planning Policy

St. Catharines

City Hall
P.O. Box 3012
50 Church St.
St Catharines, ON L2R 7C2
Tel: 905-688-5600; *Fax:* 905-682-3631
info@stcatharines.ca
www.stcatharines.ca
Other Information: TTY: 905-688-4889
Municipal Type: City
Incorporated: 1876 *Area:* 96.11 sq km
County or District: Niagara Reg. Mun.; *Population in 2011:* 131,400
Provincial Electoral District(s): St. Catharines; Welland
Federal Electoral District(s): St. Catharines; Welland
Next Election: Oct. 27, 2014 (4 year terms)
Brian McMullan, Mayor
Jeff Burch, Councillor, Ward(s): 1. Merritton
Jennifer Stevens, Councillor, Ward(s): 1. Merritton
Matthew J. Harris, Councillor, Ward(s): 2. St. Andrew's
Joseph Kushner, Councillor, Ward(s): 2. St. Andrew's
Peter Secord, Councillor, Ward(s): 3. St. Georges
Greg Washuta, Councillor, Ward(s): 3. St. Georges
Mark Elliott, Councillor, Ward(s): 4. St. Patricks
Mathew D. Siscoe, Councillor, Ward(s): 4. St. Patricks
Dawn Dodge, Councillor, Ward(s): 5. Grantham
Bill Phillips, Councillor, Ward(s): 5. Grantham
Len Stack, Councillor, Ward(s): 6. Port Dalhousie
Bruce Williamson, Councillor, Ward(s): 6. Port Dalhousie
Bonnie Nistico-Dunk, City Clerk
Colin Briggs, Chief Administrative Officer
Shelley Chemnitz, Director, Financial Management Services
fms@stcatharines.ca
Paul Chapman, Director, Planning Services
Richard Lane, Director, Recreation & Community Services
rcs@stcatharines.ca
Mark Mehlenbacher, Director, Fire & Emergency Management Services
fs@stcatharines.ca
Paul Mustard, Director, Transportation & Environmental Services
tes@stcatharines.ca
David Oakes, Director, Economic Development & Tourism Services
edt@stcatharines.ca
Nicole Auty, City Solicitor

St. Thomas

City Hall
P.O. Box 520
545 Talbot St.
St Thomas, ON N5P 3V7
Tel: 519-631-1680
www.city.st-thomas.on.ca
Municipal Type: City
Incorporated: March 4, 1881 *Area:* 35.48 sq km
County or District: Elgin; *Population in 2011:* 37,905
Provincial Electoral District(s): Elgin-Middlesex-London
Federal Electoral District(s): Elgin-Middlesex-London
Next Election: Oct. 27, 2014 (4 year terms)
Heather Jackson-Chapman, Mayor
hchapman@city.st-thomas.on.ca
Lori Baldwin-Sands, Alderman
loribaldwinsands@live.com
Gord Campbell, Alderman
jcampbell384@rogers.com
Mark Cosens, Alderman
mark@markyourx.com
Tom Johnston, Alderman
tomjohnston@execulink.com
Jeff Kohler, Alderman
jkohler67@live.com
David Warden, Alderman
warden_dave@hotmail.com
Sam Yusuf, Alderman
sam@samyusuf.ca
Wendell Graves, City Clerk
wgraves@city.st-thomas.on.ca
Bill Day, City Treasurer
bday@city.st-thomas.on.ca
Graham Dart, Director, Human Resources
gdart@city.st-thomas.on.ca
John Dewancker, Director, Environmental Services, & City Engineer
jdewancker@city.st-thomas.on.ca
Patrick Keenan, Director, Planning
pkeenan@city.st-thomas.on.ca
Brian Clement, Manager, Engineering
bclement@city.st-thomas.on.ca
Edward Soldo, Manager, Operations & Compliance
esoldo@city.st-thomas.on.ca
Ross Tucker, Director, Parks & Recreation
rtucker@city.st-thomas.on.ca
Rob Broadbent, Fire Chief
rbroadbent@city.st-thomas.on.ca
Leon Bach, Chief Building Official
lbach@city.st-thomas.on.ca
Cyril McCready, Supervisor, Water & Wastewater
cmccready@city.st-thomas.on.ca
Dave White, Supervisor, Roads & Transportation
dwhite@city.st-thomas.on.ca

Sarnia

City Hall
P.O. Box 3018
255 North Christina St.
Sarnia, ON N7T 7N2
Tel: 519-332-0330
clerks@sarnia.ca; bylaws@sarnia.ca; legal@sarnia.ca
www.sarnia.ca
Other Information: TTY: 519-332-2664
Municipal Type: City
Incorporated: May 7, 1914 *Area:* 164.63 sq km
County or District: Lambton; *Population in 2011:* 72,366
Provincial Electoral District(s): Sarnia-Lambton
Federal Electoral District(s): Sarnia-Lambton
Next Election: Oct. 27, 2014 (4 year terms)
Mike Bradley, Mayor
mayor@sarnia.ca
Dave Boushy, City / County Councillor
dave.boushy@sarnia.ca

Jim Foubister, City / County Councillor
jim.foubister@sarnia.ca
Anne Marie Gillis, City / County Councillor
sarcouncillor@gmail.com
Bev MacDougall, City / County Councillor
bevmacdougall@ebtech.net
Andy Bruziewicz, City Councillor
andybruziewicz@hotmail.com
Terry Burrell, City Councillor
terry@terryburrell.ca
Mike Kelch, City Councillor
mjkelch@mac.com
Jon McEachran, City Councillor
jonmceachran@hotmail.com
Brian Knott, Clerk & Solicitor
brian.knott@sarnia.ca
Lloyd Fennell, City Manager
lloyd.fennell@sarnia.ca
Brian McKay, Director, Finance
finance@.sarnia.ca; brian.mckay@sarnia.ca
Kim Bresee, Director, Planning & Building
planning@sarnia.ca; kim.bresee@sarnia.ca
Ian Smith, Director, Community Services
comserv@sarnia.ca; ian.smith@sarnia.ca
Jim Stevens, Director, Transit
transit@sarnia.ca; jim.stevens@sarnia.ca
Peter Hungerford, Manager, Economic Development & Corporate Planning
economic@sarnia.ca; peter.hungerford@sarnia.ca
Chris Armstrong, Manager, Human Resources
hr@sarnia.ca; chris.armstrong@sarnia.ca
Andre Morin, City Engineer
engineer@sarnia.ca; andre.morin@sarnia.ca
Doug Robertson, Superintendent, Public Works Department
doug.robertson@sarnia.ca
Pat Cayen, Fire Chief, Fire Rescue Services
firerescue@sarnia.ca; pat.cayen@sarnia.ca

Sault Ste. Marie
Civic Centre
P.O. Box 580
99 Foster Dr.
Sault Ste Marie, ON P6A 5N1
Tel: 705-759-2500; *Fax:* 705-759-2310
webmaster@cityssm.on.
www.cityssm.on.ca
Municipal Type: City
Incorporated: 1912 *Area:* 221.71 sq km
County or District: Algoma District; *Population in 2011:* 75,141
Provincial Electoral District(s): Sault Ste. Marie
Federal Electoral District(s): Sault Ste. Marie
Next Election: Oct. 27, 2014 (4 year terms)
Debbie Amaroso, Mayor
mayor.amaroso@cityssm.on.ca
Steve Butland, Councillor, Ward(s): 1
s.butland@cityssm.on.ca
Paul Christian, Councillor, Ward(s): 1
p.christian@cityssm.on.ca
Susan Myers, Councillor, Ward(s): 2
s.myers@cityssm.on.ca
Terry Sheehan, Councillor, Ward(s): 2
t.sheehan@cityssm.on.ca
Pat Mick, Councillor, Ward(s): 3
p.mick@cityssm.on.ca
Brian Watkins, Councillor, Ward(s): 3
ab.watkins@cityssm.on.ca
Rick Niro, Councillor, Ward(s): 4
r.niro@cityssm.on.ca
Lou Turco, Councillor, Ward(s): 4
l.turco@cityssm.on.ca
Marchy Bruni, Councillor, Ward(s): 5
m.bruni@cityssm.on.ca
Frank Fata, Councillor, Ward(s): 5
f.fata@cityssm.on.ca
Joe Krmpotich, Councillor, Ward(s): 6
j.krmpotich@cityssm.on.ca
Frank Manzo, Councillor, Ward(s): 6
Malcolm White, City Clerk
705-759-5388
cityclerk@cityssm.on.ca
Joseph M. (Joe) Fratesi, B.A., LL.B., Chief Administrative Officer
705-759-5347
j.fratesi@cityssm.on.ca
William Freiburger, Treasurer & Commissioner, Finance
705-759-5349
b.freiburger@cityssm.on.ca
Nicholas J. Apostle, Commissioner, Community Services
n.apostle@cityssm.on.ca
Jerry Dolcetti, Commissioner, Engineering & Planning
j.dolcetti@cityssm.on.ca
John R. Luszka, Commissioner, Human Resources
j.luszka@cityssm.on.ca
Larry Girardi, Commissioner, Public Works & Transportation
l.girardi@cityssm.on.ca
Kim Streich-Poser, Commissioner, Social Services
k.streich-poser@cityssm.on.ca
Nuala Kenny, City Solicitor
n.kenny@cityssm.on.ca
Marcel Provenzano, Fire Chief
m.provenzano@cityssm.on.ca

Stratford
City Hall
P.O. Box 818
1 Wellington St.
Stratford, ON N5A 6W1
Tel: 519-271-0250; *Fax:* 519-273-5041
general@city.stratford.on.ca
www.city.stratford.on.ca
Other Information: TTY: 519-271-5241
Municipal Type: City
Incorporated: 1854 *Area:* 25.28 sq km
County or District: Perth; *Population in 2011:* 30,886
Provincial Electoral District(s): Perth-Wellington
Federal Electoral District(s): Perth-Wellington
Next Election: Oct. 27, 2014 (4 year terms)
Note: Incorporated as a city in 1886.
Daniel Mathieson, Mayor
519-271-2783
dmathieson@city.stratford.on.ca
Brad Beatty, Councillor
bbeatty@city.stratford.on.ca
George Brown, Councillor
gbrowny1@gmail.com
Tom Clifford, Councillor
tclifford@brownclimatecare.com
Keith Culliton, Councillor
CBL@cullitonbrothers.com
Bonnie Henderson, Councillor
bonnie48henderson@yahoo.ca
Frank Mark, Councillor
frank.mark@schaeffler.com
Kerry McManus, Councillor
kmcmanus@city.stratford.on.ca
Paul Nickel, Councillor
nickel@sympatico.ca
Martin Ritsma, Councillor
martinritsma@gmail.com
Karen Smythe, Councillor
k.smythe@rogers.com
Joan Thomson, Clerk
clerks@city.stratford.on.ca
Ronald R. Shaw, Chief Administrative Officer
cao@city.stratford.on.ca
Larry Appel, Director, Economic Development
lappel@city.stratford.on.ca
George Bowa, Director, Engineering & Public Works
Barbara Dembek, Director, Building & Planning
David St. Louis, Director, Community Services
Bill Tigert, Director, Social Services
Rick Young, Fire Chief
Jeff Bannon, City Planner
Randy Mattice, Economic Development Officer

Temiskaming Shores
Temiskaming Shores Administration Office
P.O. Box 2050
325 Farr Ave.
Haileybury, ON P0J 1K0
Tel: 705-672-3363; *Fax:* 705-672-3200
www.temiskamingshores.ca
Municipal Type: City
Incorporated: Jan. 1, 2004 *Area:* 177 sq km
County or District: Timiskaming District; *Population in 2011:* 10,400
Provincial Electoral District(s): Timiskaming-Cochrane
Federal Electoral District(s): Nipissing-Timiskaming
Next Election: Oct. 27, 2014 (4 year terms)
Note: Amalgamation of the Town of Haileybury, the Town of New Liskeard & the Township of Dymond.
Carman Kidd, Mayor
Bob Hobbs, Councillor
Doug Jelly, Councillor
Mike McArthur, Councillor
Jamie Morrow, Councillor
Brian Thornton, Councillor
Danny Whalen, Councillor
Sue Weiss, Clerk
Christopher W. Oslund, City Manager
Laura Lee McLeod, Treasurer
Dan Harvey, Acting Director, Public Works
Tammie Caldwell, Director, Leisure Services
James Sheppard, Manager, Public Works Operations
David Treen, Manager, Environmental & Engineering Services
Tim Uttley, Fire Chief

Thorold
Thorold City Hall
P.O. Box 1044
3540 Schmon Pkwy.
Thorold, ON L2V 4A7
Tel: 905-227-6613; *Fax:* 905-227-5590
secr@thorold.com (Administrative Assistant)
www.thorold.com
Other Information: E-mail, Deputy City Clerk: depclerk@thorold.com
Municipal Type: City
Incorporated: 1798 *Area:* 83 sq km
County or District: Niagara Reg. Mun.; *Population in 2011:* 17,931
Provincial Electoral District(s): Welland
Federal Electoral District(s): Welland
Next Election: Oct. 27, 2014 (4 year terms)
Note: Incorporated as a village in 1850, as a town in 1875, as a new town (amalgamating the Township of Thorold & the Town of Thorold) in 1970, & as a city in 1975.
Ted Luciani, Mayor
mayor@thorold.com
Henry D'Angela, Regional Councillor
Arlene Arch, Councillor
councillorarch@cogeco.ca
Becky Day, Councillor
beckyday@hotmail.com
Jennifer Ferry, Councillor
jenniferlynnferry@gmail.com
Mike Murphy, Councillor
m__murphy7@sympatico.ca
Sergio Paone, Councillor
spaone@cogeco.ca
Norbert Preiner, Councillor
norbert.preiner@ncdsb.com
Tim Whalen, Councillor
twhalen1@cogeco.ca
Shawn Wilson, Councillor
councillorshawnwilson@gmail.com
Susan M. Daniels, AMCT, City Clerk
clerk@thorold.com
Frank A. Fabiano, Chief Administrative Officer
adm@thorold.com
Maria J. Mauro, Director, Finance
finance@thorold.com
Adele Arbour, Director, Planning & Building Services
aarbour@thorold.com
Mike Sauchuk, Director, Operations
905-227-3535
theoreng@thorold.com
Jeff Menard, A.Sc.T., B.Tech, Chief Building Official
jmenard@thorold.com
Dave Akrigg, Manager, Parks, Cemetary & Arena Operations
905-227-1911
dave@thorold.com

Thunder Bay
City Hall
P.O. Box 800
500 Donald St. East
Thunder Bay, ON P7C 5K4
Tel: 807-625-2230; *Fax:* 807-623-5468
cityinfo@thunderbay.ca
www.thunderbay.ca
Other Information: TTY: 807-625-2230
Municipal Type: City
Incorporated: Jan 1, 1970 *Area:* 328.48 sq km
County or District: Thunder Bay District; *Population in 2011:* 108,359
Provincial Electoral District(s): Thunder Bay-Superior North; Thunder Bay-Atikokan
Federal Electoral District(s): Thunder Bay-Rainy River; Thunder Bay-Superior North
Next Election: Oct. 27, 2014 (4 year terms)
Keith Hobbs, Mayor
Iain Angus, Councillor at Large
Ken Boshcoff, Councillor at Large
Larry Hebert, Councillor at Large
Rebecca Johnson, Councillor at Large
Aldo. V. Ruberto, Councillor at Large
Andrew Foulds, Ward Councillor, Ward(s): Current River
Trevor Giertuga, Ward Councillor, Ward(s): McIntyre
Paul Pugh, Ward Councillor, Ward(s): McKellar
Linda Rydholm, Ward Councillor, Ward(s): Neebing
Mark Bentz, Ward Councillor, Ward(s): Northwood
Brian McKinnon, Ward Councillor, Ward(s): Red River

Joe Virdiramo, Ward Councillor, Ward(s): Westfort
John S. Hannam, City Clerk
807-623-2238, Fax: 807-623-5468
jhannam@thunderbay.ca
Tim Commisso, City Manager
807-625-2224, Fax: 807-623-1164
tcommisso@thunderbay.ca
Carol Busch, C.G.A., Treasurer & General Manager, Finance
807-625-2242
cbusch@thunderbay.ca
Greg Alexander, General Manager, Community Services
807-625-2315, Fax: 807-623-3292
galexander@thunderbay.ca
Rosalie Evans, General Manager, Corporate Services & City Solicitor
807-625-2405, Fax: 807-623-2256
revans@thunderbay.ca
Alan Fydirchuk, General Manager, Facilities & Fleet
807-684-2774, Fax: 807-345-1909
afydirchuk@thunderbay.ca
Darrell Matson, General Manager, Transportation & Works
dmatson@thunderbay.ca
Mark Smith, General Manager, Development Services
807-625-2544, Fax: 807-625-2206
msmith@thunderbay.ca
Norm Gale, Chief, Emergency Medical Services
807-625-3259, Fax: 807-625-2698
ngale@thunderbay.ca
John Hay, Fire Chief
jhay@thunderbay.ca
Brad Loroff, Manager, Transit
807-684-2187
bloroff@thunderbay.ca
Alan Hjorth, Manager, Human Resources
807-625-2585, Fax: 807-625-3585
ahjorth@thunderbay.ca
Karen Lewis, Manager, Corporate Communications & Strategic Initiatives
807-625-3859, Fax: 807-625-0181
klewis@thunderbay.ca
Kerri Marshall, Manager, Environment
807-625-2836, Fax: 807-625-3588
kmarshall@thunderbay.ca
Pat Mauro, Manager, Engineering
807-625-3022, Fax: 807-625-3588
pmauro@thunderbay.ca

Timmins
220 Algonquin Blvd. East
Timmins, ON P4N 1B3
Tel: 705-264-1331; *Fax:* 705-360-2674
www.timmins.ca
Municipal Type: City
Incorporated: 1973 *Area:* 2,961.58 sq km
County or District: Cochrane District; *Population in 2011:* 43,165
Provincial Electoral District(s): Timmins-James Bay
Federal Electoral District(s): Timmins-James Bay
Next Election: Oct. 27, 2014 (4 year terms)
Thomas B. Laughren, Mayor
mayor@timmins.ca
Gary Scripnick, Councillor, Ward(s): 1
gary.scripnick@timmins.ca
John P. Curley, Councillor, Ward(s): 2
john.curley@timmins.ca
Noella C. Rinaldo, Councillor, Ward(s): 3
noella.rinaldo@timmins.ca
Pat Bamford, Councillor, Ward(s): 4
pat.bamford@timmins.ca
Steven L. Black, Councillor, Ward(s): 5
steven.black@timmins.ca
Michael J.J. Doody, Councillor, Ward(s): 5
michael.doody@timmins.ca
Todd Lever, Councillor, Ward(s): 5
todd.lever@timmins.ca
Andrew Marks, Councillor, Ward(s): 5
andrew.marks@timmins.ca
R. Jack Watson, Clerk
Joe Torlone, Chief Administrative Officer
cao@timmins.ca
Bernie Christian, City Treasurer
Luc Duval, Director, Public Works & Engineering
David Laneville, Director, Information Technology
Mike Pintar, Fire Chief

Toronto
City Hall
100 Queen St. West
Toronto, ON M5H 2N2
Tel: 416-392-2489; *Fax:* 416-338-0685
311@toronto.ca
www.toronto.ca
Other Information: In Toronto: 311; TTY: 416-338-0889
Municipal Type: City
Incorporated: March 6, 1834 *Area:* 630.18 sq km
Population in 2011: 2,615,060
Provincial Electoral District(s): Beaches-East York; To.-Danforth; Davenport; Don V. East; Don V. West; Eglinton-Lawrence; Etob. Centre; Etob.-Lakeshore; Etob. North; Parkdale-High Park; St. Paul's; Scarb.-Agincourt; Scarb. Centre; Scarb. Southwest; Scarb.-Guildwood; Scarb.-Rouge River; To. Centre; Trinity-Spadina; Willowdale; York Centre; York South-Weston; York West
Federal Electoral District(s): Beaches-East York; Davenport; Don V. East; Don V. West; Eglinton-Lawrence; Etob. Centre; Etob.-Lakeshore; Etob. North; Parkdale-High Park; St. Paul's; Scarb.-Agincourt; Scarb. Centre; Scarb. Southwest; Scarb.-Guildwood; Scarb.-Rouge River; To. Centre; To.-Danforth; Trinity-Spadina; Willowdale; York Centre; York South-Weston, York West
Next Election: Oct. 27, 2014 (4 year terms)
Note: Incorporated as a city on Jan. 1, 1998, & comprising the 6 former municipalities of: Etobicoke; North York; York; East York; Scarborough; & Old Toronto
Rob Ford, Mayor
mayor_ford@toronto.ca
Vincent Crisanti, Councillor, Ward(s): 1 - Etobicoke North
councillor_crisanti@toronto.ca
Doug Ford, Councillor, Ward(s): 2 - Etobicoke North
councillor_dford@toronto.ca
Doug Holyday, Councillor, Ward(s): 3 - Etobicoke Centre
councillor_holyday@toronto.ca
Gloria Lindsay Luby, Councillor, Ward(s): 4 - Etobicoke Centre
councillor_lindsay_luby@toronto.ca
Peter Milczyn, Councillor, Ward(s): 5 - Etobicoke-Lakeshore
councillor_milczyn@toronto.ca
Mark Grimes, Councillor, Ward(s): 6 - Etobicoke-Lakeshore
councillor_grimes@toronto.ca
Giorgio Mammoliti, Councillor, Ward(s): 7 - York West
councillor_mammoliti@toronto.ca
Anthony Perruzza, Councillor, Ward(s): 8 - York West
councillor_perruzza@toronto.ca
Maria Augimeri, Councillor, Ward(s): 9 - York Centre
councillor_augimeri@toronto.ca
James Pasternak, Councillor, Ward(s): 10 - York Centre
councillor_pasternak@toronto.ca
Frances Nunziata, Councillor, Ward(s): 11 - York South-Weston
councillor_nunziata@toronto.ca
Frank Di Giorgio, Councillor, Ward(s): 12 - York South-Weston
councillor_digiorgio@toronto.ca
Sarah Doucette, Councillor, Ward(s): 13 - Parkdale-High Park
councillor_doucette@toronto.ca
Gord Perks, Councillor, Ward(s): 14 - Parkdale-High Park
councillor_perks@toronto.ca
Josh Colle, Councillor, Ward(s): 15 - Eglinton-Lawrence
councillor_colle@toronto.ca
Karen Stintz, Councillor, Ward(s): 16 - Eglinton-Lawrence
councillor_stintz@toronto.ca
Cesar Palacio, Councillor, Ward(s): 17 - Davenport
councillor_palacio@toronto.ca
Ana Bailao, Councillor, Ward(s): 18 - Davenport
councillor_bailao@toronto.ca
Mike Layton, Councillor, Ward(s): 19 - Trinity-Spadina
councillor_layton@toronto.ca
Adam Vaughan, Councillor, Ward(s): 20 - Trinity-Spadina
councillor_vaughan@toronto.ca
Joe Mihevc, Councillor, Ward(s): 21 - St. Paul's
councillor_mihevc@toronto.ca
Josh Matlow, Councillor, Ward(s): 22 - St. Paul's
councillor_matlow@toronto.ca
John Filion, Councillor, Ward(s): 23 - Willowdale
councillor_filion@toronto.ca
David Shiner, Councillor, Ward(s): 24 - Willowdale
councillor_shiner@toronto.ca
Jaye Robinson, Councillor, Ward(s): 25 - Don Valley West
councillor_robinson@toronto.ca
John Parker, Councillor, Ward(s): 26 - Don Valley West
councillor_parker@toronto.ca
Kristyn Wong-Tam, Councillor, Ward(s): 27 - Toronto Centre-Rosedale
councillor_wongtam@toronto.ca
Pam McConnell, Councillor, Ward(s): 28 - Toronto Centre-Rosedale
councillor_mcconnell@toronto.ca
Mary Fragedakis, Councillor, Ward(s): 29 - Toronto-Danforth
councillor_fragedakis@toronto.ca
Paula Fletcher, Councillor, Ward(s): 30 - Toronto-Danforth
councillor_fletcher@toronto.ca
Janet Davis, Councillor, Ward(s): 31 - Beaches-East York
councillor_davis@toronto.ca
Mary-Margaret McMahon, Councillor, Ward(s): 32 - Beaches-East York
councillor_mcmahon@toronto.ca
Shelley Carroll, Councillor, Ward(s): 33 - Don Valley East
councillor_carroll@toronto.ca
Denzil Minnan-Wong, Councillor, Ward(s): 34 - Don Valley East
councillor_minnan-wong@toronto.ca
Michelle Berardinetti, Councillor, Ward(s): 35 - Scarborough Southwest
councillor_berardinetti@toronto.ca
Gary Crawford, Councillor, Ward(s): 36 - Scarborough Southwest
councillor_crawford@toronto.ca
Michael Thompson, Councillor, Ward(s): 37 - Scarborough Centre
councillor_thompson@toronto.ca
Glenn De Baeremaeker, Councillor, Ward(s): 38 - Scarborough Centre
councillor_debaeremaeker@toronto.ca
Mike Del Grande, Councillor, Ward(s): 39 - Scarborough-Agincourt
councillor_delgrande@toronto.ca
Norm Kelly, Councillor, Ward(s): 40 - Scarborough-Agincourt
councillor_kelly@toronto.ca
Chin Lee, Councillor, Ward(s): 41 - Scarborough-Rouge River
councillor_lee@toronto.ca
Raymond Cho, Councillor, Ward(s): 42 - Scarborough-Rouge River
councillor_cho@toronto.ca
Paul Ainslie, Councillor, Ward(s): 43 - Scarborough East
councillor_ainslie@toronto.ca
Ron Moeser, Councillor, Ward(s): 44 - Scarborough East
councillor_moeser@toronto.ca
Ulli S. Watkiss, City Clerk
416-392-8010, Fax: 416-392-2980
Joseph Pennachetti, City Manager
416-392-3551, Fax: 416-392-1827
Cam Weldon, Chief Financial Officer & Deputy City Manager
416-392-8773, Fax: 416-397-5236
Richard Butts, Deputy City Manager
416-338-7200, Fax: 416-392-4540
Sue Corke, Deputy City Manager
416-338-7205, Fax: 416-395-0388
Bruce L. Anderson, Executive Director, Human Resources
416-397-4112, Fax: 416-392-1524
Ann Borooah, Executive Director, Toronto Building, & Chief Building Official
416-397-4446, Fax: 416-397-4383
Jim Hart, Executive Director, Municipal Licensing & Standards
416-392-8445, Fax: 416-397-5463
Gary Wright, Executive Director, City Planning, & Chief Planner
416-392-8772, Fax: 416-392-8115
Phil Brown, General Manager, Shelter, Support, & Housing Administration
416-392-7885, Fax: 416-392-0548
Lou Di Gironimo, General Manager, Toronto Water
416-392-8200, Fax: 416-302-4540
Bruce K. Farr, General Manager, Emergency Medical Services, & EMS Chief
416-397-9240, Fax: 416-392-2115
Heather MacVicar, General Manager, Employment & Social Services
416-392-8952, Fax: 416-392-4214
Brenda Patterson, General Manager, Parks, Forestry, & Recreation
416-392-8182, Fax: 416-392-8565
parks@toronto.ca
Geoff Rathbone, General Manager, Solid Waste Management Services
416-392-4715, Fax: 416-392-4754
William (Bill) Stewart, General Manager, Fire Services & Fire Chief
416-338-9051, Fax: 416-338-9060
Gary Welsh, General Manager, Transportation Services
416-392-8431, Fax: 416-392-4455
Anna Kinastowski, City Solicitor
416-392-0080, Fax: 416-397-5624
David McKeown, Medical Officer of Health
416-338-7820, Fax: 416-392-0713

Vaughan
2141 Major Mackenzie Dr.
Vaughan, ON L6A 1T1
Tel: 905-832-2281; *Fax:* 905-832-8535
clerks@vaughan.ca; humanresources@vaughan.ca
www.vaughan.ca
Other Information: Phone (Automated): 905-832-8585

Municipal Type: City
Incorporated: Jan. 1, 1971 *Area:* 273.58 sq km
County or District: York Regional Municipality; *Population in 2011:* 288,201
Provincial Electoral District(s): Vaughan; Thornhill
Federal Electoral District(s): Vaughan; Thornhill
Next Election: Oct. 27, 2014 (4 year terms)
Maurizio Bevilacqua, Mayor
mayor@vaughan.ca
Michael Di Biase, Regional Councillor
michael.dibiase@vaughan.ca
Gino Rosati, Regional Councillor
gino.rosati@vaughan.ca
Deb Schulte, Regional Councillor
deb.schulte@vaughan.ca
Marilyn Iafrate, Councillor, Ward(s): 1
marilyn.iafrate@vaughan.ca
Tony Carella, Councillor, Ward(s): 2
tony.carella@vaughan.ca
Rosanna Defrancesca, Councillor, Ward(s): 3
rosanna.defrancesca@vaughan.ca
Sandra Yeung Racco, Councillor, Ward(s): 4
sandra.racco@vaughan.ca
Alan Shefman, Councillor, Ward(s): 5
alan.shefman@vaughan.ca
Jeffrey A. Abrams, City Clerk
jeffrey.abrams@vaughan.ca
Clayton Harris, City Manager
clayton.harris@vaughan.ca
Barbara Cribbett, Treasurer & Commissioner, Finance
Janice Atwood-Petkovski, Commissioner, Legal & Administrative Services
Marlon Kallideen, Commissioner, Community Services
marlon.kallideen@vaughan.ca
Paul Jankowski, Commissioner, Engineering & Public Works
John Zipay, Commissioner, Planning
john.mackenzie@vaughan.ca
Marjie Fraser, Director, Parks & Forestry Operations
parks@vaughan.ca
Jack Graziosi, Director, Engineering Services
jack.graziosi@vaughan.ca
Leo Grellette, Director, Building Standards
leo.grellette@vaughan.ca
Andrew D. Pearce, Director, Development & Transportation Engineering
andrew.pearce@vaughan.ca
Mary Reali, Director, Recreation & Culture
rec@vaughan.ca
Madeline Zito, Director, Corporate Communications
madeline.zito@vaughan.ca
Gregory R. Senay, Fire Chief
firerescue@vaughan.ca

Waterloo

City Hall
100 Regina St. South
Waterloo, ON N2J 4A8
Tel: 519-886-1550; *Fax:* 519-747-8500
www.city.waterloo.on.ca
Other Information: TTY Toll Free: 1-866-786-3941
Municipal Type: City
Incorporated: Jan. 15, 1857 *Area:* 64.1 sq km
County or District: Waterloo Regional Municipality; *Population in 2011:* 98,780
Provincial Electoral District(s): Kitchener-Waterloo
Federal Electoral District(s): Kitchener-Waterloo
Next Election: Oct. 27, 2014 (4 year terms)
Note: Incorporated as a town in 1876 & as a city on Jan 1, 1948.
Brenda Halloran, Mayor
brenda.halloran@waterloo.ca
Scott Witmer, Councillor, Ward(s): 1
scott.witmer@waterloo.ca
Karen Scian, Councillor, Ward(s): 2
karen.scian@waterloo.ca
Angela Veith, Councillor, Ward(s): 3
angela.vieth@waterloo.ca
Diane Freeman, Councillor, Ward(s): 4
diane.freeman@waterloo.ca
Mark Whaley, Councillor, Ward(s): 5
mark.whaley@waterloo.ca
Jeff Henry, Councillor, Ward(s): 6
jeff.henry@waterloo.ca
Melissa Durrell, ouncillor, Ward(s): 7
melissa.durrell@waterloo.ca
Susan Greatrix, City Clerk
519-747-8705, Fax: 519-747-8510
Tim Anderson, Chief Administrative Officer
519-747-8702, Fax: 519-747-8500
Bob Mavin, Chief Financial Officer
bob.mavin@waterloo.ca
David Calder, General Manager, Corporate Services
Cameron Rapp, General Manager, Development Services
David Smith, General Manager, Recreation & Leisure Services
Mark Dykstra, Director, Environment & Parks Services
Bill Garibaldi, Director, Water Services
Phil Hewitson, Director, Transportation
Patti McKague, Director, Corporate Communications
Murray Kieswetter, Manager, Parks Operations
519-747-8607, Fax: 519-886-5788
Mary Thorpe, Manager, Human Resources
John DeHooge, Fire Chief

Welland

60 East Main St.
Welland, ON L3B 3X4
Tel: 905-735-1700; *Fax:* 905-732-1919
www.welland.ca
Municipal Type: City
Incorporated: July 24, 1858 *Area:* 81.09 sq km
County or District: Niagara Regional Municipality; *Population in 2011:* 50,631
Provincial Electoral District(s): Welland
Federal Electoral District(s): Welland
Next Election: Oct. 27, 2014 (4 year terms)
Note: Incorporated as a town on Jan. 1, 1878 & as a city on July 1, 1917.
Barry Sharpe, Mayor
mayor@welland.ca
Mark Carl, Councillor, Ward(s): 1
mark.carl@welland.ca
Mary Ann Grimaldi, Councillor, Ward(s): 1
maryann.grimaldi@welland.ca
Frank Campion, Councillor, Ward(s): 2
frank.campion@welland.ca
David McLeod, Councillor, Ward(s): 2
david.mcleod@welland.ca
Dan Fortier, Councillor, Ward(s): 3
dan.fortier@welland.ca
Paul Grenier, Councillor, Ward(s): 3
paul.grenier@welland.ca
Pat Chiocchio, Councillor, Ward(s): 4
pat.chiocchio@welland.ca
Tony Dimarco, Councillor, Ward(s): 4
tony.dimarco@welland.ca
Rocky G. Létourneau, Councillor, Ward(s): 5
rocky.letourneau@welland.ca
Michael Petrachenko, Councillor, Ward(s): 5
michael.petrachenko@welland.ca
Jim Larouche, Councillor, Ward(s): 6
jim.larouche@welland.ca
Bob Wright, Councillor, Ward(s): 6
bob.wright@welland.ca
Christine Mintoff, City Clerk
clerk@welland.ca
Craig A. Stirtzinger, City Manager
craig.stirtzinger@welland.ca
Kristine Douglas, Treasurer & General Manager, Financial & Corporate Services
kristine.douglas@welland.ca
Bill Fenwick, General Manager, Parks, Facilities & Leisure Services
bill.fenwick@welland.ca
Sal Iannello, General Manager, Engineering, Public Works, & Transportation Svs.
sal.iannello@welland.ca
Rosanne Mantesso, General Manager, Human Resources
rosanne.mantesso@welland.ca
Donald Thorpe, General Manager, Planning & Development Services
don.thorpe@welland.ca
Dan Degazio, Manager, Economic Development
Mike Mantesso, Chief Building Official
mike.mantesso@welland.ca
Denys Prevost, Fire Chief
denys.prevost@welland.ca

Windsor

City Hall
P.O. Box 1607
350 City Hall Sq. West
Windsor, ON N9A 6S1
Fax: 519-255-6868
311@city.windsor.on.ca; hrdiv@city.windsor.on.ca (HR Dept.)
www.citywindsor.ca
Other Information: Phone: 311; Toll Free Phone: 1-877-746-4311
Municipal Type: City
Incorporated: 1854 *Area:* 146.91 sq km
County or District: Essex; *Population in 2011:* 210,891
Provincial Electoral District(s): Windsor-Tecumseh; Windsor-West
Federal Electoral District(s): Windsor-Tecumseh; Windsor-West
Next Election: Oct. 27, 2014 (4 year terms)
Note: Incorporated as a town in 1858 & as a city in 1892.
Eddie Francis, Mayor
mayoro@city.windsor.on.ca
Drew Dilkens, Councillor, Ward(s): 1
ddilkens@city.windsor.on.ca
Ronald Jones, Councillor, Ward(s): 2
rjones@city.windsor.on.ca
Fulvio Valentinis, Councillor, Ward(s): 3
fvalentinis@city.windsor.on.ca
Alan Halberstadt, Councillor, Ward(s): 4
ahalberstadt@city.windsor.on.ca
Ed Sleiman, Councillor, Ward(s): 5
esleiman@city.windsor.on.ca
Jo-Anne Gignac, Councillor, Ward(s): 6
joagignac@city.windsor.on.ca
Percy Hatfield, Councillor, Ward(s): 7
phatfield@city.windsor.on.ca
Bill (Biagio) Marra, Councillor, Ward(s): 8
bmarra@city.windsor.on.ca
Hilary Payne, Councillor, Ward(s): 9
hpayne@city.windsor.on.ca
Al Maghneih, Councillor, Ward(s): 10
amaghnieh@city.windsor.on.ca
Valerie Critchley, City Clerk
519-255-6868
clerks@city.windsor.on.ca
Helga Reidel, Chief Administrative Officer
519-255-6349
caodept@city.windsor.on.ca
Michael Duben, General Manager, Community & Protective Services
Dev Tyagi, General Manager, Public Works
pubwork@city.windsor.on.ca
Ronna Warsh, General Manager, Social & Health Services
socserv@city.windsor.on.ca
Thom Hunt, MCIP, RPP, City Planner
thunt@city.windsor.on.ca
Mario Sonego, P. Eng., City Engineer
engineeringdept@city.windsor.on.ca
David T. Fields, Fire Chief, Windsor Fire & Rescue Service
519-253-6573, Fax: 519-255-6832
Josette Eugeni, Manager, Transportation Planning
Bill Lacasse, Manager, Lou Romano Water Reclamation Plant
519-253-7217
Jack MacRae, Manager, Little River Pollution Control Plant
519-948-1751
Jim Yanchula, MCIP, RPP, Manager, Urban Design & Community Development
jyanchula@city.windsor.on.ca
David Fields, Fire Chief
Glenn Stannard, Chief of Police
Ronna Warsh, General Manager
Allen Heimann, Medical Officer of Health

Woodstock

City Hall
P.O. Box 1539
500 Dundas St.
Woodstock, ON N4S 7W5
Tel: 519-539-1291
aash@city.woodstock.on.ca (Assistant to Mayor & CAO)
www.city.woodstock.on.ca
Municipal Type: City
Incorporated: Jan. 1, 1851 *Area:* 43.79 sq km
County or District: Oxford; *Population in 2011:* 37,754
Provincial Electoral District(s): Oxford
Federal Electoral District(s): Oxford
Next Election: Oct. 27, 2014 (4 year terms)
Note: Incorporated as a city on July 1, 1901.
Pat Sobeski, Mayor
mayor@city.woodstock.on.ca
Deb A. Tait, City / County Councillor
519-421-7449
dtait@city.woodstock.on.ca

Sandra J. Talbot, City / County Councillor
519-788-0639
stalbot@city.woodstock.on.ca
Bill M. Bes, City Councillor
bbes@city.woodstock.on.ca
Ron Fraser, City Councillor
rfraser@city.woodstock.on.ca
Jim Northcott, City Councillor
519-539-3698
jnorthcott@city.woodstock.on.ca
Paul D. Plant, City Councillor
pplant@city.woodstock.on.ca
Louise Gartshore, City Clerk
lgartshore@city.woodstock.on.ca
David Creery, Chief Administrative Officer
dcreery@city.woodstock.on.ca
Patrice Hilderley, Treasurer
philderley@city.woodstock.on.ca
Len Magyar, Commissioner, Development
lmagyar@city.woodstock.on.ca
Bob McFarland, Director, Community Services
bmcfarland@city.woodstock.on.ca
Harold deHaan, City Engineer
hdehaan@city.woodstock.on.ca
Filippo D'Emilio, Engineer, Development
fdemilio@city.woodstock.on.ca
Scott Tegler, Fire Chief
stegler@city.woodstock.on.ca
Laird Crooks, Manager, Human Resources
lcrooks@city.woodstock.on.ca
Alex Piggott, Superintendent, Works
apiggott@city.woodstock.on.ca
Terry Harrington, Supervisor, Water Distribution
tharrington@city.woodstock.on.ca
Dan Major, Supervisor, Parks
dmajor@city.woodstock.on.ca

Other Municipalities in Ontario

Addington Highlands
P.O. Box 89
Flinton, ON K0H 1P0
Tel: 613-336-2286; *Fax:* 613-336-2847
www.addingtonhighlands.ca
Municipal Type: Township
Area: 1,288.47 sq km
County or District: Lennox & Addington; *Population in 2011:* 2,532
Provincial Electoral District(s): Lanark-Frontenac-Lennox & Addington
Federal Electoral District(s): Lanark-Frontenac-Lennox & Addington
Next Election: Oct. 27, 2014 (4 year terms)
Henry Hogg, Reeve
henryh@sympatico.ca
Jack Pauhl, Clerk
clerk@addingtonhighlands.ca

Adelaide Metcalfe
2340 Egremont Dr., RR#5
Strathroy, ON N7G 3H6
Tel: 519-247-3687; *Fax:* 519-247-3411
info@adelaidemetcalfe.on.ca
www.adelaidemetcalfe.on.ca
Municipal Type: Township
Incorporated: Jan. 1, 2001 *Area:* 331.26 sq km
County or District: Middlesex; *Population in 2011:* 3,028
Provincial Electoral District(s): Lambton-Kent-Middlesex
Federal Electoral District(s): Lambton-Kent-Middlesex
Next Election: Oct. 27, 2014 (4 year terms)
Note: Amalgamation of the former Township of Adelaide & the Township of Metcalfe.
David Bolton, Reeve
mayor@adelaidemetcalfe.on.ca
Fran Urbshott, Clerk, Administrator, & Treasurer
fran@adelaidemetcalfe.on.ca

Adjala-Tosorontio
7855 Sideroad 30, RR#1
Alliston, ON L9R 1V1
Tel: 705-434-5055; *Fax:* 705-434-5051
www.townshipadjtos.on.ca
Municipal Type: Township
Incorporated: Jan. 1, 1994 *Area:* 372.33 sq km
County or District: Simcoe; *Population in 2011:* 10,603
Provincial Electoral District(s): Simcoe-Grey
Federal Electoral District(s): Simcoe-Grey
Next Election: Oct. 27, 2014 (4 year terms)
Note: Amalgamation of the former Township of Adjala & the former Township of Tosorontio.
Tom Walsh, Mayor
905-729-2132
twalsh@townshipadjtos.on.ca
Mary Small Brett, Deputy Mayor & Councillor
519-941-5828
marysmallbrett@sympatico.ca
Floyd Pinto, Councillor, Ward(s): 1
905-936-9616
marysmallbrett@sympatico.ca
Ambrose J. Keenan, Councillor, Ward(s): 2
905-729-3361
tundraathome@295.ca
Doug Little, Councillor, Ward(s): 3
705-435-9020
dlittle@townshipadjtos.on.ca
Tom Gauley, Councillor, Ward(s): 4
705-435-1437
tomlisegauley@rogers.com
Scott W. Anderson, Councillor, Ward(s): 5
705-424-0769
scott@andersonward5.ca
Barbara Kane, Clerk
bkane@townshipadjtos.on.ca
Eric Wargel, Chief Administrative Officer
ewargel@townshipadjtos.on.ca
Dorthy Bulman, Treasurer & Deputy Clerk
dbulman@townshipadjtos.on.ca
Jacquie Tschekalin, Director, Planning
jtschekalin@townshipadjtos.on.ca

Admaston/Bromley
477 Stone Rd., RR#2
Renfrew, ON K7V 3Z5
Tel: 613-432-2885; *Fax:* 613-432-4052
www.admastonbromley.com
Municipal Type: Township
Incorporated: Jan. 1, 2000 *Area:* 520.5 sq km
County or District: Renfrew; *Population in 2011:* 2,844
Provincial Electoral District(s): Renfrew-Nipissing-Pembroke
Federal Electoral District(s): Renfrew-Nipissing-Pembroke
Next Election: Oct. 27, 2014 (4 year terms)
Note: Amalgamation of Admaston Township & Bromley Township.
Raye-Anne Briscoe, Mayor
613-432-5728
Beverly Briscoe, Clerk-Treasurer
bbriscoe@admastonbromley.com

Ajax
65 Harwood Ave. South
Ajax, ON L1S 2H9
Tel: 905-683-4550; *Fax:* 905-683-1061
contactus@townofajax.com; info@townofajax.com
www.townofajax.com
Other Information: Corporate Communications: 905-619-2529, ext. 3362
Municipal Type: Town
Incorporated: 1955 *Area:* 67.09 sq km
County or District: Durham Regional Municipality; *Population in 2011:* 109,600
Provincial Electoral District(s): Ajax-Pickering
Federal Electoral District(s): Ajax-Pickering
Next Election: Oct. 27, 2014 (4 year terms)
Steve Parish, Mayor
905-619-2529, Fax: 905-683-9450
steve.parish@townofajax.com
Shaun Collier, Regional Councillor, Ward(s): 1 & 2
shaun.collier@townofajax.com
Colleen Jordan, Regional Councillor, Ward(s): 3 & 4
colleen.jordan@townofajax.com
Marilyn Crawford, Councillor, Ward(s): 1
Renrick Ashby, Councillor, Ward(s): 2
renrick.ashby@townofajax.com
Joanne Dies, Councillor, Ward(s): 3
joanne.dies@townofajax.com
Pat Brown, Councillor, Ward(s): 4
pat.brown@townofajax.com
Brian J. Skinner, Chief Administrative Officer
brian.skinner@townofajax.com
Rob Ford, Director, Finance & Treasurer
rob.ford@townofajax.com
John Fleck, Director, Human Resource Services
905-619-2529
Dave Meredith, Director, Operations & Environmental Services
operations@townofajax.com

Alberton
#B2, RR#1
Fort Frances, ON P9A 3M2
Tel: 807-274-6053; *Fax:* 807-274-8449
alberton@jam21.net
www.alberton.ca
Municipal Type: Township
Area: 115.3 sq km
County or District: Rainy River District; *Population in 2011:* 864
Provincial Electoral District(s): Kenora-Rainy River
Federal Electoral District(s): Thunder Bay-Rainy River; Ancaster-Dundas-Flamborough-Westdale
Next Election: Oct. 27, 2014 (4 year terms)
Michael Hammond, Reeve
Dawn Hayes, CAO & Clerk-Treasurer

Alfred & Plantagenet
P.O. Box 350
205 Old Hwy. 17
Plantagenet, ON K0B 1L0
Tel: 613-673-4797; *Fax:* 613-673-4812
www.alfred-plantagenet.com
Municipal Type: Township
Incorporated: Jan. 1, 1997 *Area:* 391.68 sq km
County or District: Prescott & Russell; *Population in 2011:* 9,196
Provincial Electoral District(s): Glengarry-Prescott-Russell
Federal Electoral District(s): Glengarry-Prescott-Russell
Next Election: Oct. 27, 2014 (4 year terms)
Note: Amalgamation of the Township of Alfred, the Village of Alfred, the Township of North Plantagenet & the Village of Plantagenet.
Jean-Yves Lalonde, Mayor
jean-yves.lalonde@sympatico.ca
Marc Daigneault, Chief Administrative Officer & Clerk

Algoma
c/o Algoma District Svs. Administration Bd.
1 Collver Rd., RR#1
Thessalon, ON P0R 1L0
Tel: 705-842-3370; *Fax:* 705-842-3747
www.adsab.on.ca
Municipal Type: District
Area: 48,734.66 sq km
Population in 2011: 115,870
Provincial Electoral District(s): Algoma-Manitoulin
Federal Electoral District(s): Algoma-Manitoulin-Kapuskasing
Keith Bell, Chief Administrative Officer
kbell@adsab.on.ca

Algonquin Highlands
1123 North Shore Rd., RR#2
Minden, ON K0M 1J1
Tel: 705-489-2379; *Fax:* 705-489-3491
info@algonquinhighlands.ca
www.algonquinhighlands.ca
Other Information: Phone, Dorset Satellite Office: 705-766-2211
Municipal Type: Township
Area: 1,002.12 sq km
County or District: Haliburton; *Population in 2011:* 2,156
Provincial Electoral District(s): Haliburton-Kawartha Lakes-Brock
Federal Electoral District(s): Haliburton-Kawartha Lakes-Brock
Next Election: Oct. 27, 2014 (4 year terms)
Carol Moffat, Reeve
cmoffatt@algonquinhighlands.ca
Angela Bird, Clerk & Chief Administrative Officer
abird@algonquinhighlands.ca

Alnwick-Haldimand
P.O. Box 70
10836 County Rd. No. 2
Grafton, ON K0K 2G0
Tel: 905-349-2822; *Fax:* 905-349-3259
alnhald@alnwickhaldimand.ca
www.alnwickhaldimand.ca
Other Information: Phone, Roseneath Satellite Office: 905-352-3949
Municipal Type: Township
Area: 398.08 sq km
County or District: Northumberland; *Population in 2011:* 6,617
Provincial Electoral District(s): Northumberland-Quinte West
Federal Electoral District(s): Northumberland-Quinte West
Next Election: Oct. 27, 2014 (4 year terms)
Dalton McDonald, Mayor
905-349-2747
mayor@alnwickhaldimand.ca
Robin van de Moosdyk, A.M.C.T., Clerk
rvandemoosdyk@alnwickhaldimand.ca

Amaranth
374028 - 6th Line, RR#7
Orangeville, ON L9W 2Z3
Tel: 519-941-1007; *Fax:* 519-941-1802
township@amaranth-eastgary.ca
www.amaranth-eastgary.ca
Municipal Type: Township
Incorporated: Jan. 2, 1854 *Area:* 264.35 sq km
County or District: Dufferin; *Population in 2011:* 3,963

Provincial Electoral District(s): Dufferin-Caledon
Federal Electoral District(s): Dufferin-Caledon
Next Election: Oct. 27, 2014 (4 year terms)
Don MacIver, Mayor
519-925-3457
mayor.maciver@hotmail.com
Susan M. Stone, A.M.C.T., Chief Administrative Officer & Clerk-Treasurer
suestone@amaranth-eastgary.ca

Amherstburg
271 Sandwich St. South
Amherstburg, ON N9V 2A5
Tel: 519-736-0012; *Fax:* 519-736-5403
www.amherstburg.ca
Other Information: TTY: 519-736-9860
Municipal Type: Town
Incorporated: 1851 *Area:* 185.65 sq km
County or District: Essex; *Population in 2011:* 21,556
Provincial Electoral District(s): Essex
Federal Electoral District(s): Essex
Next Election: Oct. 27, 2014 (4 year terms)
Note: Incorporated as a town in 1878.
Wayne Hurst, Mayor
519-736-7646
whurst@amherstburg.ca
Carolyn Davies, Councillor
cdavies@amherstburg.ca
Bart DiPasquale, Councillor
bdipasquale@amherstburg.ca
Robert (Bob) Pillon, Councillor
rpillon@amherstburg.ca
Diane Pouget, Councillor
dpouget@amherstburg.ca
Ron Sutherland, Councillor
rsutherland@amherstburg.ca
John Sutton, Councillor
jsutton@amherstburg.ca
Brenda Percy, Clerk/Manager of Council & Legislative Services
bpercy@amherstburg.ca
Pam Malott, Chief Administrative Officer
pmalott@amherstburg.ca
Lou Zarlenga, P.Eng, Manager, Public Works
Antonietta Giofu, P.Eng, Engineer, Environmental Services
Dwayne Grondin, Superintendent, Sewer & Watermain
Todd Hewitt, Superintendent, Roads

Armour
Municipal Office
P.O. Box 533
56 Ontario St.
Burks Falls, ON P0A 1C0
Tel: 705-382-3332; *Fax:* 705-382-2068
info@armourtownship.ca
www.armourtownship.ca
Other Information: Alternative Phone: 705-382-2954
Municipal Type: Township
Area: 164.1 sq km
County or District: Parry Sound District; *Population in 2011:* 1,372
Provincial Electoral District(s): Parry Sound-Muskoka
Federal Electoral District(s): Parry Sound-Muskoka
Next Election: Oct. 27, 2014 (4 year terms)
Bob MacPhail, Reeve
705-636-7678
aberdeen@surenet.net
Wendy Whitwell, Clerk-Administrator
clerk@armourtownship.ca

Armstrong
P.O. Box 546
35 Tenth St.
Earlton, ON P0J 1E0
Tel: 705-563-2375; *Fax:* 705-563-2093
www.armstrongtownship.com
Municipal Type: Township
Area: 90.33 sq km
County or District: Timiskaming District; *Population in 2011:* 1,216
Provincial Electoral District(s): Timiskaming-Cochrane
Federal Electoral District(s): Timmins-James Bay
Next Election: Oct. 27, 2014 (4 year terms)
Jules Gravel, Reeve
Reynald Rivard, Clerk-Treasurer
reynaldrivard@nt.net

Arnprior
P.O. Box 130
105 Elgin St. West
Arnprior, ON K7S 0A8
Tel: 613-623-4231; *Fax:* 613-623-8091
arnprior@arnprior.ca
www.arnprior.ca
Municipal Type: Town
Area: 13.04 sq km
County or District: Renfrew; *Population in 2011:* 8,114
Provincial Electoral District(s): Renfrew-Nipissing-Pembroke
Federal Electoral District(s): Renfrew-Nipissing-Pembroke
Next Election: Oct. 27, 2014 (4 year terms)
Terry Gibeau, Mayor
tgibeau@arnprior.ca
Jacquie Farrow-Lawrence, Town Clerk
jfarrow-lawrence@arnprior.ca

Arran-Elderslie
P.O. Box 70
1925 Bruce Rd. 10
Chesley, ON N0G 1L0
Tel: 519-363-3039; *Fax:* 519-363-2203
areld@bmts.com
www.arran-elderslie.com
Municipal Type: Municipality
Area: 460.13 sq km
County or District: Bruce; *Population in 2011:* 6,810
Provincial Electoral District(s): Bruce-Grey-Owen Sound
Federal Electoral District(s): Bruce-Grey-Owen Sound
Next Election: Oct. 27, 2014 (4 year terms)
Paul Eagleson, Mayor
519-363-3559
Peggy Rouse, Clerk

Ashfield-Colborne-Wawanosh
82133 Council Line, RR#5
Goderich, ON N7A 3Y2
Tel: 519-524-4669; *Fax:* 519-524-1951
www.acwtownship.ca
Municipal Type: Township
Area: 587.07 sq km
County or District: Huron; *Population in 2011:* 5,582
Provincial Electoral District(s): Huron-Bruce
Federal Electoral District(s): Huron-Bruce
Next Election: Oct. 27, 2014 (4 year terms)
Ben Van Diepenbeek, Reeve
519-529-7830
Mark Becker, Administrator & Clerk-Treasurer
clerk@acwtownship.ca

Asphodel-Norwood
P.O. Box 29
2357 County Rd. 45
Norwood, ON K0L 2V0
Tel: 705-639-5343; *Fax:* 705-639-1880
www.asphodelnorwood.com
Municipal Type: Township
Incorporated: 1998 *Area:* 160.85 sq km
County or District: Peterborough; *Population in 2011:* 4,041
Provincial Electoral District(s): Peterborough
Federal Electoral District(s): Peterborough
Next Election: Oct. 27, 2014 (4 year terms)
Note: Amalgamation of the Village of Norwood & the Township of Asphodel.
Doug Pearcy, Reeve
705-639-5510, Fax: 705-639-5388
dpearcy@accel.net
Valerie Przybilla, Chief Administrative Officer, Clerk & Treasurer
valeriep@asphodelnorwood.com

Assiginack
P.O. Box 238
25B Spragge St.
Manitowaning, ON P0P 1N0
Tel: 705-859-3196; *Fax:* 705-859-3010
assiginackinfo@amtelecom.net
www.assiginack.ca
Other Information: Toll-Free Phone: 1-800-540-0179
Municipal Type: Township
Area: 227.44 sq km
County or District: Manitoulin District; *Population in 2011:* 960
Provincial Electoral District(s): Algoma-Manitoulin
Federal Electoral District(s): Algoma-Manitoulin-Kapuskasing
Next Election: Oct. 27, 2014 (4 year terms)
Clyde Rohn, Reeve
Alton Hobbs, Clerk-Treasurer

Athens
P.O. Box 189
1 Main St. West
Athens, ON K0E 1B0
Tel: 613-924-2044; *Fax:* 613-924-2091
athens@ripnet.com
www.athenstownship.ca
Municipal Type: Township
Incorporated: 2001 *Area:* 126.46 sq km
County or District: Leeds & Grenville; *Population in 2011:* 3,118
Provincial Electoral District(s): Leeds-Grenville
Federal Electoral District(s): Leeds-Grenville
Next Election: Oct. 27, 2014 (4 year terms)
Herb Scott, Mayor
613-924-2133
Darlene Noonan, Chief Administrative Officer & Clerk Treasurer

Atikokan
P.O. Box 1330
120 Marks St.
Atikokan, ON P0T 1C0
Tel: 807-597-1234; *Fax:* 807-597-6186
info@atikokan.ca
www.atikokan.ca
Municipal Type: Township
Area: 316.75 sq km
County or District: Rainy River District; *Population in 2011:* 2,787
Provincial Electoral District(s): Thunder Bay-Atikokan
Federal Electoral District(s): Thunder Bay-Rainy River
Next Election: Oct. 27, 2014 (4 year terms)
Dennis Brown, Mayor
denbrown@tbaytel.net
Angela Sharbot, Clerk
angela.sharbot@atikokan.ca

Augusta
3560 County Rd. 26, RR#2
Prescott, ON K0E 1T0
Tel: 613-925-4231; *Fax:* 613-925-3499
www.augusta.ca
Municipal Type: Township
Area: 314.06 sq km
County or District: Leeds & Grenville; *Population in 2011:* 7,430
Provincial Electoral District(s): Leeds-Grenville
Federal Electoral District(s): Leeds-Grenville
Next Election: Oct. 27, 2014 (4 year terms)
Mel Campbell, Reeve
613-342-6962
John Trudgen, Acting Chief Administrative Officer & Clerk

Aurora
P.O. Box 1000
100 John Way West
Aurora, ON L4G 6J1
Tel: 905-727-1375; *Fax:* 905-726-4738
info@aurora.ca
www.aurora.ca
Other Information: Alternative Phone: 905-727-3123; TTY: 905-726-4766
Municipal Type: Town
Area: 49.62 sq km
County or District: York Regional Municipality; *Population in 2011:* 53,203
Provincial Electoral District(s): Newmarket-Aurora
Federal Electoral District(s): Newmarket-Aurora
Next Election: Oct. 27, 2014 (4 year terms)
Geoff Dawe, Mayor
mayor@aurora.ca
John Abel, Councillor
jabel@aurora.ca
Chris Ballard, Councillor
chris@chrisballard.ca
Evelyn Buck, Councillor
ebuck@aurora.ca
Wendy Gaertner, Councillor
wgaertner@aurora.ca
John Gallo, Councillor
jgallo@aurora.ca
Sandra Humphries, Councillor
shumfryes@aurora.ca
Paul Pirri, Councillor
ppirri@aurora.ca
Michael Thompson, Councillor
mthompson@aurora.ca
John D. Leach, Town Clerk & Director, Customer & Legislative Services
905-727-3123
jleach@aurora.ca
Neil Garbe, Chief Administrative Officer
ngarbe@aurora.ca

Aylmer
46 Talbot St. West
Aylmer, ON N5H 1J7
Tel: 519-773-3164; *Fax:* 519-765-1446
www.aylmer.ca
Municipal Type: Town
Area: 6.22 sq km
County or District: Elgin; *Population in 2011:* 7,151
Provincial Electoral District(s): Elgin-Middlesex-London
Federal Electoral District(s): Elgin-Middlesex-London
Next Election: Oct. 27, 2014 (4 year terms)
Jack Couckuyt, Mayor
mayor@town.aylmer.on.ca
Nancie Irving, Clerk & Officer, Lottery Licensing
nirving@town.aylmer.on.ca

Baldwin
P.O. Box 7095
11 Spooner St.
McKerrow, ON P0P 1M0
Tel: 705-869-0225
www.townshipofbaldwin.ca
Municipal Type: Township
Area: 81.82 sq km
County or District: Sudbury District; *Population in 2011:* 551
Provincial Electoral District(s): Algoma-Manitoulin
Federal Electoral District(s): Algoma-Manitoulin-Kapuskasing
Next Election: Oct. 27, 2014 (4 year terms)
Archie Boivin, Reeve
Joan Seidel, Clerk & Treasurer
joanseidel@townshipofbaldwin.ca

Bancroft
P.O. Box 790
24 Flint Ave.
Bancroft, ON K0L 1C0
Tel: 613-332-3331; *Fax:* 613-332-0384
bancroft@town.bancroft.on.ca
www.town.bancroft.on.ca
Municipal Type: Town
Incorporated: 1904 *Area:* 227.84 sq km
County or District: Hastings; *Population in 2011:* 3,888
Provincial Electoral District(s): Prince Edward-Hastings
Federal Electoral District(s): Prince Edward-Hastings
Next Election: Oct. 27, 2014 (4 year terms)
Bernice Jenkins, Mayor
613-332-1041
bjenkins@town.bancroft.on.ca
Barry Wannamaker, Chief Administrative Officer & Clerk
bwannamaker@town.bancroft.on.ca

Bayham
P.O. Box 160
9344 Plank Rd.
Straffordville, ON N0J 1Y0
Tel: 519-866-5521; *Fax:* 519-866-3884
bayham@bayham.on.ca
www.bayham.on.ca
Municipal Type: Municipality
Area: 244.99 sq km
County or District: Elgin; *Population in 2011:* 6,989
Provincial Electoral District(s): Elgin-Middlesex-London
Federal Electoral District(s): Elgin-Middlesex-London
Next Election: Oct. 27, 2014 (4 year terms)
Paul Ens, Mayor
ens@porchlight.ca
Lynda Millard, Clerk
lmillard@bayham.on.ca

Beckwith
1702 - 9th Line, RR#2
Carleton Place, ON K7C 3P2
Tel: 613-257-1539; *Fax:* 613-257-8996
www.twp.beckwith.on.ca
Other Information: Toll-Free Phone: 1-800-535-4532 (in 613 area code)
Municipal Type: Township
Area: 240.12 sq km
County or District: Lanark; *Population in 2011:* 6,986
Provincial Electoral District(s): Lanark-Frontenac-Lennox & Addington
Federal Electoral District(s): Lanark-Frontenac-Lennox & Addington
Next Election: Oct. 27, 2014 (4 year terms)
Richard Kidd, Reeve
613-257-5409
rkidd@ripnet.com
Cynthia Moyle, Chief Administrative Officer
cmoyle@twp.beckwith.on.ca

Billings
Municipal Office
P.O. Box 34
15 Old Mill Rd.
Kagawong, ON P0P 1J0
Tel: 705-282-2611; *Fax:* 705-282-3199
billingsadmin@xplornet.com
www.billingstwp.ca
Municipal Type: Township
Incorporated: 1884 *Area:* 209.15 sq km
County or District: Manitoulin District; *Population in 2011:* 506
Provincial Electoral District(s): Algoma-Manitoulin
Federal Electoral District(s): Algoma-Manitoulin-Kapuskasing
Next Election: Oct. 27, 2014 (4 year terms)
Austin Hunt, Reeve
705-282-2684
Katherine McDonald, Clerk-Treasurer
clerktreasurer@billingstwp.ca

Black River-Matheson
P.O. Box 601
429 Park Lane
Matheson, ON P0K 1N0
Tel: 705-273-2313
reception@blackriver-matheson.com
www.blackriver-matheson.com
Municipal Type: Township
Area: 1,161.67 sq km
County or District: Cochrane District; *Population in 2011:* 2,410
Provincial Electoral District(s): Timiskaming-Cochrane
Federal Electoral District(s): Timmins-James Bay
Next Election: Oct. 27, 2014 (4 year terms)
Mike Milinkovich, Mayor
Heather Smith, Clerk & Treasurer
705-273-2313

Blandford-Blenheim
P.O. Box 100
47 Wilmot St. South
Drumbo, ON N0J 1G0
Tel: 519-463-5347; *Fax:* 519-463-5881
generalmail@twp.bla-ble.on.ca
www.blandfordblenheim.ca
Municipal Type: Township
Area: 382.34 sq km
County or District: Oxford; *Population in 2011:* 7,359
Provincial Electoral District(s): Oxford
Federal Electoral District(s): Oxford
Next Election: Oct. 27, 2014 (4 year terms)
Marion Wearn, Mayor
mwearn@blandfordblenheim.ca
Fran Bell, Chief Administrative Officer & Clerk
fbell@blandfordblenheim.ca

Blind River
P.O. Box 640
11 Hudson St.
Blind River, ON P0R 1B0
Tel: 705-356-2251; *Fax:* 705-356-7343
www.blindriver.ca
Municipal Type: Town
Incorporated: 1906 *Area:* 520.59 sq km
County or District: Algoma District; *Population in 2011:* 3,549
Provincial Electoral District(s): Algoma-Manitoulin
Federal Electoral District(s): Algoma-Manitoulin-Kapuskasing
Next Election: Oct. 27, 2014 (4 year terms)
Sue Jensen, Mayor
sue.jensen@blindriver.ca
Ken Corbiere, Clerk
kencorb@blindriver.ca

Bluewater, Municipality of
P.O. Box 250
14 Mill Ave.
Zurich, ON N0M 2T0
Tel: 519-236-4351; *Fax:* 519-236-4329
www.town.bluewater.on.ca
Other Information: Toll-Free: 1-877-236-4351
Municipal Type: Town
Area: 416.99 sq km
County or District: Huron; *Population in 2011:* 7,044
Provincial Electoral District(s): Huron-Bruce
Federal Electoral District(s): Huron-Bruce
Next Election: Oct. 27, 2014 (4 year terms)
Bill Dowson, Mayor
wjdowson@tcc.on.ca
Lori Wolfe, Chief Administrative Officer & Clerk
l.wolfe@town.bluewater.on.ca

Bonfield
365 Hwy. 531
Bonfield, ON P0H 1E0
Tel: 705-776-2641; *Fax:* 705-776-1154
www.ebonfield.org
Municipal Type: Township
Incorporated: 1975 *Area:* 205.75 sq km
County or District: Nipissing District; *Population in 2011:* 2,016
Provincial Electoral District(s): Nipissing
Federal Electoral District(s): Nipissing-Timiskaming
Next Election: Oct. 27, 2014 (4 year terms)
Randall McLaren, Mayor
rmclaren@ebonfield.org
Lise B. McMillan, A.M.C.T., Administrator, Clerk & Treasurer
lise@ebonfield.org

Bonnechere Valley
P.O. Box 100
49 Bonnechere St. East
Eganville, ON K0J 1T0
Tel: 613-628-3101; *Fax:* 613-628-1336
admin@eganville.com
www.bonnecherevalleytwp.com
Municipal Type: Township
Incorporated: Jan. 1, 2001 *Area:* 589.87 sq km
County or District: Renfrew; *Population in 2011:* 3,763
Provincial Electoral District(s): Renfrew-Nipissing-Pembroke
Federal Electoral District(s): Renfrew-Nipissing-Pembroke
Next Election: Oct. 27, 2014 (4 year terms)
Note: Amalgamation of Eganville Village, Grattan Township, Sebastopol Township & Algona South Township.
Jennifer Murphy, Mayor
613-628-3295
jenniferm@eganville.com
Bryan Martin, Chief Administrative Officer
bryanm@eganville.com

Bracebridge
1000 Taylor Ct.
Bracebridge, ON P1L 1R6
Tel: 705-645-5264; *Fax:* 705-645-1262
www.bracebridge.ca
Other Information: Fax, Public Works: 705-645-7525
Municipal Type: Town
Area: 617.42 sq km
County or District: Muskoka Dist. Mun.; *Population in 2011:* 15,409
Provincial Electoral District(s): Parry Sound-Muskoka
Federal Electoral District(s): Parry Sound-Muskoka
Next Election: Oct. 27, 2014 (4 year terms)
Graydon Smith, Mayor
gsmith@bracebridge.ca
Steve Clement, District Councillor
sclement@bracebridge.ca
Liam Cragg, Councillor
lcragg@bracebridge.ca
Lori-Lynn Giaschi-Pacini, District Councillor
lgiaschi-pacini@bracebridge.ca
Rick Maloney, Councillor
rmaloney@bracebridge.ca
Barb McMurray, Councillor
bmcmurray@bracebridge.ca
Mark Quemby, Councillor
mquemby@bracebridge.ca
Gerry Tryon, Councillor
gtryon@bracebridge.ca
Scott Young, District Councillor
syoung@bracebridge.ca
Lori McDonald, Clerk
lmcdonald@bracebridge.ca
John R. Sisson, Chief Administrative Officer
jsisson@bracebridge.ca
Carol Wakefield, Treasurer
cwakefield@bracebridge.ca
Kim Horrigan, Director, Development Services
khorrigan@bracebridge.ca
Cheryl Kelley, Director, Economic Development
ckelley@bracebridge.ca
Ron Walton, Municipal Engineer
rwalton@bracebridge.ca
Murray Medley, Fire Chief
firechief@bracebridgefire.com

Bradford West Gwillimbury
Administration Centre
P.O. Box 100
100 Dissette St.
Bradford, ON L3Z 2A7
Tel: 905-775-5366; *Fax:* 905-775-0153
www.town.bradfordwestgwillimbury.on.ca

Municipal Type: Town
Incorporated: 1857 *Area:* 201.03 sq km
County or District: Simcoe; *Population in 2011:* 28,077
Provincial Electoral District(s): York-Simcoe
Federal Electoral District(s): York-Simcoe
Next Election: Oct. 27, 2014 (4 year terms)
Note: Incorporated as a town in 1960.
Doug White, Mayor
dwhite@townofbwg.com
Rob Keffer, Deputy Mayor & Councillor
rkeffer@townofbwg.com
Raj Sandhu, Councillor, Ward(s): 1
rsandhu@townofbwg.com
Del Crake, Councillor, Ward(s): 2
dcrake@townofbwg.com
Gary R. Lamb, Councillor, Ward(s): 3
glamb@townofbwg.com
Carl Hordyk, Councillor, Ward(s): 4
chordyk@townofbwg.com
Ron Simpson, Councillor, Ward(s): 5
rsimpson@townofbwg.com
James Leduc, Councillor, Ward(s): 6
jleduc@townofbwg.com
Peter Dykie, Jr., Councillor, Ward(s): 7
pdykie@townofbwg.com
Jay Currier, Chief Administrative Officer
jcurrier@townofbwg.com
Ian Goodfellow, Director, Finance & Treasurer
igoodfellow@townofbwg.com
Debbie Korolnek, Director, Engineering Services
dkorolnek@townofbwg.com
Geoff McKnight, Director, Planning & Development
gmcknight@townofbwg.com
Paul Feehely, Superintendent, Public Works
pfeehely@townofbwg.com
Edward O'Donnell, Supervisor, Water
eodonnell@townofbwg.com
Rick Way, Supervisor, Waste Water
rway@townofbwg.com
Lorne Arscott, Fire Chief
kgallant@townofbwg.com

Brethour
P.O. Box 537
51476 Brethour Rd.
Belle Vallee, ON P0J 1A0
Tel: 705-647-1712; *Fax:* 705-647-6851
brethourtwp@ntl.sympatico.ca
Municipal Type: Township
Area: 82.05 sq km
County or District: Timiskaming District; *Population in 2011:* 129
Provincial Electoral District(s): Timiskaming-Cochrane
Federal Electoral District(s): Timmins-James Bay
Next Election: Oct. 27, 2014 (4 year terms)
Maurice Chabot, Reeve
Pam Bennewies, Clerk-Treasurer

Brock
P.O. Box 10
1 Cameron St. East
Cannington, ON L0E 1E0
Tel: 705-432-2355; *Fax:* 705-432-3487
brock@townshipofbrock.ca
www.townshipofbrock.ca
Other Information: Toll-Free Phone: 1-866-223-7668
Municipal Type: Township
Incorporated: 1973 *Area:* 423.31 sq km
County or District: Durham Reg. Mun.; *Population in 2011:* 11,341
Provincial Electoral District(s): Haliburton-Kawartha Lakes-Brock
Federal Electoral District(s): Haliburton-Kawartha Lakes-Brock
Next Election: Oct. 27, 2014 (4 year terms)
W. Terry Clayton, Mayor
tclayton@townshipofbrock.ca
Debbie Bath, Regional Coucillor
dbath@townshipofbrock.ca
Mike Manchester, Councillor, Ward(s): 1
mmanchester@townshipofbrock.ca
Randy Skinner, Councillor, Ward(s): 2
rskinner@townshipofbrock.ca
Walter Schummer, Councillor, Ward(s): 3
wschummer@townshipofbrock.ca
Keith Shier, Councillor, Ward(s): 4
kshier@townshipofbrock.ca
W.E. Ted Smith, Councillor, Ward(s): 5
tsmith@townshipofbrock.ca
Thomas G. Gettinby, MA, MCIP, RPP, CMO, Chief Administrative Officer & Municipal Clerk
tgettinby@townshipofbrock.ca
Laura Barta, CMA, Treasurer
lbarta@townshipofbrock.ca
Nick Colucci, P.Eng., Director, Public Works
ncolucci@townshipofbrock.ca
Joseph J. Bonura, Chief Building Offical
jbonura@townshipofbrock.ca
Rick Harrison, Chief, Fire
rharrison@townshipofbrock.ca

Brockton
P.O. Box 68
100 Scott St.
Walkerton, ON N0G 2V0
Tel: 519-881-2223
info@brockton.ca
www.brockton.ca
Other Information: Toll-Free Phone: 1-877-885-8084
Municipal Type: Municipality
Incorporated: Jan. 1, 1999 *Area:* 565.07 sq km
County or District: Bruce; *Population in 2011:* 9,432
Provincial Electoral District(s): Huron-Bruce
Federal Electoral District(s): Huron-Bruce
Next Election: Oct. 27, 2014 (4 year terms)
Note: Amalgamation of the Town of Walkerton, Township of Brant, & the Township of Greenock.
David Inglis, Mayor
dinglis@brockton.ca
Debra Roth, Clerk
droth@brockton.ca

Brooke-Alvinston
P.O. Box 28
3236 River St.
Alvinston, ON N0N 1A0
Tel: 519-898-2173; *Fax:* 519-898-5653
info@brookealvinston.com
www.brookealvinston.com
Other Information: Toll-Free Phone, Enforcement Unit: 1-866-344-9119
Municipal Type: Township
Area: 311.3 sq km
County or District: Lambton; *Population in 2011:* 2,548
Provincial Electoral District(s): Lambton-Kent-Middlesex
Federal Electoral District(s): Lambton-Kent-Middlesex
Next Election: Oct. 27, 2014 (4 year terms)
Don McGugan, Mayor
519-847-5606, Fax: 519-847-5607
jdmcgugan@hotmail.com
Cathy Case, Clerk
cathycase@amtelecom.net

Bruce Mines
P.O. Box 220
9180 Hwy. 17 East
Bruce Mines, ON P0R 1C0
Tel: 705-785-3493; *Fax:* 705-785-3170
brucemines@bellnet.ca
www.brucemines.ca
Municipal Type: Town
Incorporated: 1903 *Area:* 6.13 sq km
County or District: Algoma District; *Population in 2011:* 566
Provincial Electoral District(s): Algoma-Manitoulin
Federal Electoral District(s): Sault Ste Marie
Next Election: Oct. 27, 2014 (4 year terms)
Gordon Post, Mayor
Donna Brunke, Town Clerk
dbrunke@bellnet.ca

Brudenell, Lyndoch & Raglan
P.O. Box 40
42 Burnt Bridge Rd.
Palmer Rapids, ON K0J 2E0
Tel: 613-758-2061; *Fax:* 613-758-2235
blrtownship@xplornet.com
www.countyofrenfrew.on.ca
Municipal Type: Township
Incorporated: Jan. 1, 1999 *Area:* 702.77 sq km
County or District: Renfrew; *Population in 2011:* 1,658
Provincial Electoral District(s): Renfrew-Nipissing-Pembroke
Federal Electoral District(s): Renfrew-Nipissing-Pembroke
Next Election: Oct. 27, 2014 (4 year terms)
Norman Lentz, Reeve
Michelle Mantifel, Clerk-Treasurer

Burk's Falls
P.O. Box 160
172 Ontario St.
Burks Falls, ON P0A 1C0
Tel: 705-382-3138; *Fax:* 705-382-2273
villofbf@bellnet.ca
www.burksfalls.net
Municipal Type: Village
Incorporated: 1890 *Area:* 3.12 sq km
County or District: Parry Sound District; *Population in 2011:* 967
Provincial Electoral District(s): Parry Sound-Muskoka
Federal Electoral District(s): Parry Sound-Muskoka
Next Election: Oct. 27, 2014 (4 year terms)
Cathy Still, Reeve
Kim Dunnett, Clerk

Burpee & Mills
RR#1
Evansville, ON P0P 1E0
Tel: 705-282-0624; *Fax:* 705-282-0624
burpeemills@xplornet.com
www.burpeemills.com
Municipal Type: Township
Area: 218.48 sq km
County or District: Manitoulin District; *Population in 2011:* 308
Provincial Electoral District(s): Algoma-Manitoulin
Federal Electoral District(s): Algoma-Manitoulin-Kapuskasing
Next Election: Oct. 27, 2014 (4 year terms)
Ken Noland, Reeve
Bonnie J. Bailey, Clerk-Treasurer

Caledon
Town Hall
6311 Old Church Rd.
Caledon, ON L7C 1J6
Tel: 905-584-2272; *Fax:* 905-584-4325
www.caledon.ca
Other Information: Toll-Free Phone: 1-888-225-3366
Municipal Type: Town
Incorporated: Jan. 1, 1974 *Area:* 687.17 sq km
County or District: Peel Regional Municipality; *Population in 2011:* 59,460
Provincial Electoral District(s): Dufferin-Caledon
Federal Electoral District(s): Dufferin-Caledon
Next Election: Oct. 27, 2014 (4 year terms)
Marolyn Morrison, Mayor
marolyn.morrison@caledon.ca
Richard Paterak, Regional Councillor, Ward(s): 1
richard.paterak@caledon.ca
Allan Thompson, Regional Councillor, Ward(s): 2
allan.thompson@caledon.ca
Richard Whitehead, Regional Councillor, Ward(s): 3 & 4
richard.whitehead@caledon.ca
Patti Foley, Regional Councillor, Ward(s): 5
patti.foley@caledon.ca
Doug Beffort, Area Councillor, Ward(s): 1
doug.beffort@caledon.ca
Gord McClure, Area Councillor, Ward(s): 2
gord.mcclure@caledon.ca
Nick deBoer, Area Councillor, Ward(s): 3 & 4
nick.deboer@caledon.ca
Rob Mezzapelli, Area Councillor, Ward(s): 5
rob.mezzapelli@caledon.ca
Karen Landry, Town Clerk & Director, Administration
Douglas Barnes, Chief Administrative Officer
Ron Kaufman, Chief Financial Officer, Deputy CAO, & Director, Corporate Services
Craig Campbell, Director, Public Works
public.works@caledon.ca
Glenn Middlebrook, Chief Building Official
glenn.middlebrook@caledon.ca
Sara Peckford, Officer, Envrionmental Progress
sara.peckford@caledon.ca
Jeremy Schembri, Coordinator, Energy & Environment
jeremy.schembri@caledon.ca

Callander, Municipality of
P.O. Box 100
280 Main St. North
Callander, ON P0H 1H0
Tel: 705-752-1410; *Fax:* 705-752-3116
www.callander.ca
Municipal Type: Township
Area: 100.96 sq km
County or District: Parry Sound District; *Population in 2011:* 3,864
Provincial Electoral District(s): Nipissing
Federal Electoral District(s): Nipissing-Timiskaming
Next Election: Oct. 27, 2014 (4 year terms)
Note: Formerly North Himsworth Township.
Hector Lavigne, Mayor
705-845-5010
Jeffrey Celentano, Chief Administration Officer & Clerk

Calvin
1355 Peddlers Dr., RR#2
Mattawa, ON P0H 1V0
Tel: 705-744-2700; *Fax:* 705-744-0309
administration@calvintownship.ca
www.calvintownship.ca
Municipal Type: Township
Area: 139.17 sq km
County or District: Nipissing District; *Population in 2011:* 568
Provincial Electoral District(s): Nipissing
Federal Electoral District(s): Nipissing-Timiskaming
Next Election: Oct. 27, 2014 (4 year terms)
Wayne Brown, Mayor
mayor@calvintownship.ca
Lynda Kovacs, Clerk-Treasurer
clerk@calvintownship.ca

Carleton Place
175 Bridge St.
Carleton Place, ON K7C 2V8
Tel: 613-257-6200; *Fax:* 613-257-8170
info@carletonplace.ca; bylaw@carletonplace.ca (Bylaws)
www.carletonplace.ca
Other Information: E-mail, Public Works:
dyoung@carletonplace.ca
Municipal Type: Town
Area: 8.83 sq km
County or District: Lanark; *Population in 2011:* 9,809
Provincial Electoral District(s): Lanark-Frontenac-Lennox & Addington
Federal Electoral District(s): Lanark-Frontenac-Lennox & Addington
Next Election: Oct. 27, 2014 (4 year terms)
Wendy LeBlanc, Mayor
613-257-6206
wendyleblanc@sympatico.ca
Duncan H. Rogers, Clerk
613-257-6211
drogers@carletonplace.ca

Carling
2 West Carling Bay Rd., RR#1
Nobel, ON P0G 1G0
Tel: 705-342-5856; *Fax:* 705-342-9527
www.carlingtownship.ca
Municipal Type: Township
Area: 243.94 sq km
County or District: Parry Sound District; *Population in 2011:* 1,248
Provincial Electoral District(s): Parry Sound-Muskoka
Federal Electoral District(s): Parry Sound-Muskoka
Next Election: Oct. 27, 2014 (4 year terms)
Gord Harrison, Mayor
705-342-5230
gordharrison@carlingtownship.ca
Stephen Kaegi, Chief Administrative Officer & Clerk
cao@carlingtownship.ca

Carlow/Mayo
General Delivery, 3987 Boulter Rd.
Boulter, ON K0L 1G0
Tel: 613-332-1760; *Fax:* 613-332-2175
carlowmayo@hughes.net
www.carlowmayo.ca
Municipal Type: Township
Incorporated: Jan. 1, 2001 *Area:* 388.36 sq km
County or District: Hastings; *Population in 2011:* 892
Provincial Electoral District(s): Prince Edward-Hastings
Federal Electoral District(s): Prince Edward-Hastings
Next Election: Oct. 27, 2014 (4 year terms)
Note: Amalgamation of the former townships of Carlow & Mayo.
Bonnie Adams, Reeve
Arlene Cox, Clerk-Administrator

Casey
P.O. Box 460
Belle Vallee, ON P0J 1A0
Tel: 705-647-7257; *Fax:* 705-647-6373
harlytwp@parolink.net; lise_chhk@parolink.net
harley.ca/casey/index.html
Municipal Type: Township
Incorporated: 1909 *Area:* 80.75 sq km
County or District: Timiskaming District; *Population in 2011:* 374
Provincial Electoral District(s): Timiskaming-Cochrane
Federal Electoral District(s): Timmins-James Bay
Next Election: Oct. 27, 2014 (4 year terms)
Guy Labonté, Reeve
Michel Lachapelle, Clerk-Treasurer

Casselman
P.O. Box 710
751 St. Jean St.
Casselman, ON K0A 1M0
Tel: 613-764-3139; *Fax:* 613-764-5709
info@casselman.ca
www.casselman.ca
Municipal Type: Village
Area: 5.15 sq km
County or District: Prescott & Russell; *Population in 2011:* 3,626
Provincial Electoral District(s): Glengarry-Prescott-Russell
Federal Electoral District(s): Glengarry-Prescott-Russell
Next Election: Oct. 27, 2014 (4 year terms)
Claude Levac, Mayor
maire@casselman.ca
Gilles R. Lortie, Clerk
glortie@casselman.ca

Cavan Monaghan
988 County Rd. 10, RR#3
Millbrook, ON L0A 1G0
Tel: 705-932-2929; *Fax:* 705-932-3458
info@cavanmonaghan.net
www.cavanmonaghan.net
Other Information: Toll-Free Phone: 1-877-906-5556
Municipal Type: Township
Area: 306.13 sq km
County or District: Peterborough; *Population in 2011:* 8,601
Provincial Electoral District(s): Haliburton-Kawartha Lakes-Brock
Federal Electoral District(s): Haliburton-Kawartha Lakes-Brock
Next Election: Oct. 27, 2014 (4 year terms)
Note: Formerly The Corporation of the Township of Cavan-Millbrook-North Monaghan.
John Fallis, Mayor
705-932-5568
jfallis@cavanmonaghan.net
Gail Empey, Clerk
705-932-9326
gempey@cavanmonaghan.net

Central Elgin
450 Sunset Dr.
St Thomas, ON N5R 5V1
Tel: 519-631-4860; *Fax:* 519-631-4036
www.centralelgin.org
Municipal Type: Municipality
Area: 280.22 sq km
County or District: Elgin; *Population in 2011:* 12,743
Provincial Electoral District(s): Elgin-Middlesex-London
Federal Electoral District(s): Elgin-Middlesex-London
Next Election: Oct. 27, 2014 (4 year terms)
Bill Walters, Mayor
519-631-8110
billwalters@amtelecom.net
David Marr, Deputy Mayor & Councillor
grvalley@rogers.com
Dan McNeil, Councillor, Ward(s): 1
dkmcneil@rogers.com
Sally Martyn, Councillor, Ward(s): 2
tcg@execulink.com
Stephen Carr, Councillor, Ward(s): 3
secarr40@yahoo.ca
Russell Matthews, Councillor, Ward(s): 4
russellm@rogers.com
Robert McFarlan, Councillor, Ward(s): 5
rdmcfarlan@rogers.com
Donald N. Leitch, Chief Administrative Officer & Clerk
dleitch@centralelgin.org
Sharon Larmour, Treasurer & Director, Financial Services
slarmour@centralelgin.org
Donald Crocker, Director, Fire & Rescue Services
dcrocker@centralelgin.org
Lloyd Perrin, Director, Physical Services
lperrin@centralelgin.org

Central Frontenac
P.O. Box 89
1084 Elizabeth S.
Sharbot Lake, ON K0H 2P0
Tel: 613-279-2935; *Fax:* 613-279-2422
township@centralfrontenac.com
www.centralfrontenac.com
Municipal Type: Township
Incorporated: Jan. 1, 1998 *Area:* 970.07 sq km
County or District: Frontenac; *Population in 2011:* 4,556
Provincial Electoral District(s): Lanark-Frontenac-Lennox & Addington
Federal Electoral District(s): Lanark-Frontenac-Lennox & Addington
Next Election: Oct. 27, 2014 (4 year terms)
Janet Gutowski, Mayor
613-374-1355
j.gutowski@sympatico.ca
John DuChene, Chief Administrative Officer & Clerk
jduchene@centralfrontenac.com

Central Huron, Municipality of
P.O. Box 400
23 Albert St.
Clinton, ON N0M 1L0
Tel: 519-482-3997; *Fax:* 519-482-9183
www.centralhuron.com
Municipal Type: Township
Incorporated: Jan. 1, 2001 *Area:* 447.6 sq km
County or District: Huron; *Population in 2011:* 7,591
Provincial Electoral District(s): Huron-Bruce
Federal Electoral District(s): Huron-Bruce
Next Election: Oct. 27, 2014 (4 year terms)
Note: Amalgamation of the Town of Clinton, the Township of Hullett, & the Township of Goderich.
Jim Ginn, Reeve
519-524-2522, Fax: 519-524-2755
jginn@centralhuron.com
Brenda MacIsaac, Clerk
clerk@centralhuron.com

Central Manitoulin
P.O. Box 187
6020 Hwy. 542
Mindemoya, ON P0P 1S0
Tel: 705-377-5726; *Fax:* 705-377-5585
centralm@amtelecom.net; centralinspections@amtelecom.net
www.centralmanitoulin.ca
Other Information: E-mail, Economic Dev.:
centralecdev@amtelecom.net
Municipal Type: Township
Area: 431.53 sq km
County or District: Manitoulin District; *Population in 2011:* 1,958
Provincial Electoral District(s): Algoma-Manitoulin
Federal Electoral District(s): Algoma-Manitoulin-Kapuskasing
Next Election: Oct. 27, 2014 (4 year terms)
Gerry Strong, Reeve
cmreeve@eastlink.ca
Ruth Frawley, Chief Administrative Officer & Clerk

Centre Hastings
P.O. Box 900
7 Furnace St.
Madoc, ON K0K 2K0
Tel: 613-473-4030; *Fax:* 613-473-5444
www.centrehastings.com
Municipal Type: Municipality
Area: 222.09 sq km
County or District: Hastings; *Population in 2011:* 4,543
Provincial Electoral District(s): Prince Edward-Hastings
Federal Electoral District(s): Prince Edward-Hastings
Next Election: Oct. 27, 2014 (4 year terms)
Owen Ketcheson, Reeve
613-477-2527
Matt MacDonald, Chief Administrative officer & Clerk
mmacdonald@centrehastings.com

Centre Wellington
P.O. Box 10
1 MacDonald Sq.
Elora, ON N0B 1S0
Tel: 519-846-9691; *Fax:* 519-846-2190
www.centrewellington.ca
Municipal Type: Township
Area: 407.33 sq km
County or District: Wellington; *Population in 2011:* 26,693
Provincial Electoral District(s): Wellington-Halton Hills
Federal Electoral District(s): Wellington-Halton Hills
Next Election: Oct. 27, 2014 (4 year terms)
Joanne Ross-Zuj, Mayor
519-846-0213, Fax: 519-846-2825
Kelly Linton, Councillor, Ward(s): 1
Kirk McElwain, Councillor, Ward(s): 2
Mary Lloyd, Councillor, Ward(s): 3
Fred Morris, Councillor, Ward(s): 4
Walt Visser, Councillor, Ward(s): 5
Steven VanLeeuwen, Councillor, Ward(s): 6
Marion Morris, Clerk
Michael K. Wood, Chief Administrative Officer
Wes Snarr, Chief Financial Officer & Treasurer
Andrew Goldie, Director, Parks & Recreation
Brett Salmon, Director, Planning
Brad Patton, Fire Chief
Ken Elder, Contact, Public Works

Chamberlain
467501 Chamberlain Rd. 5
Englehart, ON P0J 1H0
Tel: 705-544-8088; *Fax:* 705-544-1118
twpchamb@ntl.sympatico.ca
www.twpofchamberlain.com
Municipal Type: Township
Incorporated: 1908 *Area:* 110.13 sq km
County or District: Timiskaming District; *Population in 2011:* 297
Provincial Electoral District(s): Timiskaming-Cochrane
Federal Electoral District(s): Timmins-James Bay
Next Election: Oct. 27, 2014 (4 year terms)
William Dickinson, Reeve
Barbara Cook, Township Clerk-Treasurer

Champlain
948 Pleasant Corners Rd. East
Vankleek Hill, ON K0B 1R0
Tel: 613-678-3003; *Fax:* 613-678-3363
info@champlain.com
www.champlain.ca
Municipal Type: Township
Incorporated: Jan. 1, 1998 *Area:* 207.15 sq km
County or District: Prescott & Russell; *Population in 2011:* 8,573
Provincial Electoral District(s): Glengarry-Prescott-Russell
Federal Electoral District(s): Glengarry-Prescott-Russell
Next Election: Oct. 27, 2014 (4 year terms)
Note: Amalgamation of the Village of L'Orignal, the Township of West Hawkesbury, the Township of Longueuil & the Village of Vankleek Hill.
Gary J. Barton, Mayor
613-678-3101
gary.barton@champlain.ca
Jean Thériault, Chief Administrative Officer & Clerk-Treasurer
jean.theriault@champlain.ca

Chapleau
Civic Centre
P.O. Box 129
20 Pine St.
Chapleau, ON P0M 1K0
Tel: 705-864-1330; *Fax:* 705-864-1824
www.chapleau.ca
Municipal Type: Township
Area: 14.27 sq km
County or District: Sudbury District; *Population in 2011:* 2,116
Provincial Electoral District(s): Algoma-Manitoulin
Federal Electoral District(s): Algoma-Manitoulin-Kapuskasing
Next Election: Oct. 27, 2014 (4 year terms)
Andre Byham, Mayor
mayorbyham@township.chapleau.on.ca
Allan D. Pellow, Chief Administrative Officer
apellow@township.chapleau.on.ca

Chapple
P.O. Box 4
Barwick, ON P0W 1A0
Tel: 807-487-2354; *Fax:* 807-487-2406
info@chapple.on.ca
www.chapple.on.ca
Municipal Type: Township
Area: 529.02 sq km
County or District: Rainy River District; *Population in 2011:* 741
Provincial Electoral District(s): Kenora-Rainy River
Federal Electoral District(s): Thunder Bay-Rainy River
Next Election: Oct. 27, 2014 (4 year terms)
Peter Van Heyst, Reeve
Peggy Johnson, Chief Administrative Officer & Clerk-Treasurer

Charlton & Dack
RR#2
Englehart, ON P0J 1H0
Tel: 705-544-7525; *Fax:* 705-544-2369
dack@ntl.sympatico.ca
www.charltonanddack.com
Municipal Type: Municipality
Incorporated: Jan. 1, 2003 *Area:* 92.33 sq km
County or District: Timiskaming District; *Population in 2011:* 671
Provincial Electoral District(s): Timiskaming-Cochrane
Federal Electoral District(s): Timmins-James Bay
Next Election: Oct. 27, 2014 (4 year terms)
Note: Amalgamation of the Town of Charlton & the Township of Dack.
Wayne Pawson, Reeve

Chatham-Kent
Civic Centre
P.O. Box 640
315 King St. West
Chatham, ON N7M 5K8
Tel: 519-360-1998; *Fax:* 519-436-3237
ckinfo@chatham-kent.ca
www.chatham-kent.ca
Other Information: Toll-Free Phone: 1-800-714-7497
Municipal Type: Municipality
Incorporated: Jan. 1, 1998 *Area:* 2,458.06 sq km
Population in 2011: 103,671
Provincial Electoral District(s): Chatham-Kent-Essex; Lambton-Kent-Middlesex
Federal Electoral District(s): Chatham-Kent-Essex; Lambton-Kent-Middlesex
Next Election: Oct. 27, 2014 (4 year terms)
Note: Formerly the County of Kent.
Randy Hope, Mayor & Chief Executive Officer
519-436-3219, Fax: 519-436-3236
ckmayor@chatham-kent.ca
Bryon Fluker, Councillor, Ward(s): 1 - West Kent
bryon.fluker@chatham-kent.ca
Brian W. King, Councillor, Ward(s): 1 - West Kent
brian.king@chatham-kent.ca
Karen Herman, Councillor, Ward(s): 2 - South Kent
karen.herman@chatham-kent.ca
Art Sterling, Councillor, Ward(s): 2 - South Kent
art.stirling@chatham-kent.ca
Frank Vercouteren, Councillor, Ward(s): 2 - South Kent
frank.vercouteren@chatham-kent.ca
Jim Brown, Councillor, Ward(s): 3 - East Kent
jim.brown@chatham-kent.ca
Steve Pinsonneault, Councillor, Ward(s): 3 - East Kent
steve.pinsonneault@chatham-kent.ca
Joe Faas, Councillor, Ward(s): 4 - North Kent
joe.faas@chatham-kent.ca
Leon Leclair, Councillor, Ward(s): 4 - North Kent
leon.leclair@chatham-kent.ca
Sheldon Parsons, ouncillor, Ward(s): 5 - Wallaceburg
sheldon.parsons@chatham-kent.ca
Jeff Wesley, Councillor, Ward(s): 5 - Wallaceburg
jeff.wesley@chatham-kent.ca
Michael Bondy, Councillor, Ward(s): 6 - Chatham
michael.bondy@chatham-kent.ca
Marjorie Crew, Councillor, Ward(s): 6 - Chatham
marjorie.crew@chatham-kent.ca
Anne Gilbert, Councillor, Ward(s): 6 - Chatham
anne.gilbert@chatham-kent.ca
Bob Myers, Councillor, Ward(s): 6 - Chatham
bob.myers@chatham-kent.ca
Derek Robertson, Councillor, Ward(s): 6 - Chatham
derek.robertson@chatham-kent.ca
Douglas Sulman, Councillor, Ward(s): 6 - Chatham
doug.sulman@chatham-kent.ca
Elinor Mifflin, Clerk
Rob Browning, Chief Administrative Officer
Stuart Wood, CMA, Director, Financial Services & Treasurer
Lucy Brown, General Manager, Health & Family Services
Leo Denys, General Manager, Infrastruture & Engineering Systems
Don Shropshire, General Manager. Community Development & Planning Services

Chatsworth
#316837, Hwy. 6, RR#1
Chatsworth, ON N0H 1G0
Tel: 519-794-3232; *Fax:* 519-794-4499
office@chatsworth.ca
www.chatsworth.ca
Municipal Type: Township
Incorporated: Jan. 1, 2001 *Area:* 595.35 sq km
County or District: Grey; *Population in 2011:* 6,437
Provincial Electoral District(s): Bruce-Grey-Owen Sound
Federal Electoral District(s): Bruce-Grey-Owen Sound
Next Election: Oct. 27, 2014 (4 year terms)
Note: Amalgamation of the Townships of Holland & Sullivan & the Village of Chatsworth.
Bob Pringle, Mayor
519-794-2579
bob.pringle@grey.ca
Will Moore, Chief Administrative Officer & Clerk
519-794-3232
wmoore@chatsworth.ca

Chisholm
2847 Chiswick Line, RR#4
Powassan, ON P0H 1Z0
Tel: 705-724-3526; *Fax:* 705-724-5099
info@chisholm.ca; twpchisholm@ontera.ca
www.chisholm.ca
Other Information: Phone, Public Works: 705-724-5530
Municipal Type: Township
Incorporated: 1912 *Area:* 205.26 sq km
County or District: Nipissing District; *Population in 2011:* 1,263
Provincial Electoral District(s): Nipissing
Federal Electoral District(s): Nipissing-Timiskaming
Next Election: Oct. 27, 2014 (4 year terms)
Leo Jobin, Mayor
Linda M. Ringler, Clerk-Treasurer

Clarington
40 Temperance St.
Bowmanville, ON L1C 3A6
Tel: 905-623-3379; *Fax:* 905-623-6506
info@clarington.net; communications@clarington.net
www.clarington.net
Other Information: Toll-Free Phone: 1-800-563-1195
Municipal Type: Municipality
Area: 611.1 sq km
County or District: Durham Reg. Mun.; *Population in 2011:* 84,548
Provincial Electoral District(s): Durham
Federal Electoral District(s): Durham
Next Election: Oct. 27, 2014 (4 year terms)
Adrian Foster, Mayor
mayor@clarington.net
Mary Novak, Regional Councillor, Ward(s): 1 & 2
mnovak@clarington.net
Willie Woo, Regional Councillor, Ward(s): 3 & 4
wwoo@clarington.net
Joe Neal, Local Councillor, Ward(s): 1
jneal@clarington.net
Ron Hooper, Local Councillor, Ward(s): 2
rhooper@clarington.net
Corinna Trail, Local Councillor, Ward(s): 3
ctraill@clarington.net
Wendy Partner, Local Councillor, Ward(s): 4
wpartner@clarington.net
Patti L. Barrie, Municipal Clerk
pbarrie@clarington.net; clerks@clarington.net
Franklin Wu, Chief Administrative Officer
cao@clarington.net
Nancy Taylor, Treasurer & Director, Finance
ntaylor@clarington.net; finance@clarington.net
Tony Cannella, Director, Engineering Services
tcannella@clarington.net
Joseph Caruana, Director, Community Services
jcaruana@clarington.net
David Crome, Director, Planning Services
dcrome@clarington.net; planning@clarington.net
Fred Horvath, Director, Operations
fhorvath@clarington.net; operations@clarington.net
Marie Marano, Director, Corporate Services
mmarano@clarington.net
Gord Weir, Director, Emergency & Fire Services
gweir@clarington.net

Clearview
P.O. Box 200
217 Gideon St.
Stayner, ON L0M 1S0
Tel: 705-428-6230; *Fax:* 705-428-0288
www.clearview.ca
Municipal Type: Township
Area: 557.32 sq km
County or District: Simcoe; *Population in 2011:* 13,734
Provincial Electoral District(s): Simcoe-Grey
Federal Electoral District(s): Simcoe-Grey
Next Election: Oct. 27, 2014 (4 year terms)
Ken Ferguson, Mayor
kferguson@clearview.ca
Alicia Savage, Deputy Mayor & Councillor
asavage@clearview.ca
Doug Measures, Councillor, Ward(s): 1
dmeasures@clearview.ca
Orville Brown, Councillor, Ward(s): 2
obrown@clearview.ca
Brent Preston, Councillor, Ward(s): 3
mroyal@clearview.ca
Thom Paterson, Councillor, Ward(s): 4
tpaterson@clearview.ca
Robert Walker, Councillor, Ward(s): 5
rwalker@clearview.ca
Deborah Bronée, Councillor, Ward(s): 6
dbronee@clearview.ca

Shawn Davidson, Councillor, Ward(s): 7
sdavidson@clearview.ca
Bob Campbell, Clerk
bcampbell@clearview.ca
Susan McKenzie, Chief Administrative Officer
smckenzie@clearview.ca
Edward Henley, Treasurer
ehenley@clearview.ca
Richard Spraggs, Director, Public Works
rspraggs@clearview.ca
Michael Wynia, Director, Planning & Development
mwynia@clearview.ca
Bob McKean, Fire Chief
bmckean@clearview.ca

Cobalt
P.O. Box 70
18 Silver St.
Cobalt, ON P0J 1C0
Tel: 705-679-8877
www.cobalt.ca
Municipal Type: Town
Area: 2.11 sq km
County or District: Timiskaming District; *Population in 2011:* 1,133
Provincial Electoral District(s): Timiskaming-Cochrane
Federal Electoral District(s): Nipissing-Timiskaming
Next Election: Oct. 27, 2014 (4 year terms)
Tina Sartoretto, Mayor
Steph Palmateer, Chief Administrative Officer & Clerk-Treasurer

Cobourg
55 King St. West
Cobourg, ON K9A 2M2
Tel: 905-372-4301; *Fax:* 905-372-7421
webmaster@cobourg.ca
www.cobourg.ca
Other Information: Toll-Free Phone: 1-888-262-6874
Municipal Type: Town
Area: 22.37 sq km
County or District: Northumberland; *Population in 2011:* 18,519
Provincial Electoral District(s): Northumberland-Quinte West
Federal Electoral District(s): Northumberland-Quinte West
Next Election: Oct. 27, 2014 (4 year terms)
Gil Brocanier, Mayor
gbrocanier@cobourg.ca
Stan Frost, Deputy Mayor & Councillor
sfrost@cobourg.ca
John Henderson, Councillor
jhenderson@cobourg.ca
Miriam Mutton, Councillor
mmutton@cobourg.ca
Forrest Rowden, Councillor
frowden@cobourg.ca
Larry E. Sherwin, Councillor
lsherwin@cobourg.ca
Donna Todd, Councillor
dtodd@cobourg.ca
Lorraine Brace, Municipal Clerk
lbrace@cobourg.ca
Stephen E. Peacock, P.Eng., Chief Administrative Officer
speacock@cobourg.ca
Ian Davey, Director, Corporate Services
idavey@cobourg.ca
Glenn J. McGlashon, Director, Planning & Development Services
gmcglashon@cobourg.ca
Bill Watson, Director, Public Works
bwatson@cobourg.ca

Cochrane
P.O. Box 490
171 Fourth Ave.
Cochrane, ON P0L 1C0
Tel: 705-272-4361; *Fax:* 705-272-6068
townhall@town.cochrane.on.ca
www.town.cochrane.on.ca
Municipal Type: Town
Incorporated: 1910 *Area:* 538.76 sq km
County or District: Cochrane District; *Population in 2011:* 5,340
Provincial Electoral District(s): Timiskaming-Cochrane
Federal Electoral District(s): Timmins-James Bay
Next Election: Oct. 27, 2014 (4 year terms)
Peter Politis, Mayor
peter.politis@town.cochrane.on.ca
Jean-Pierre Ouellette, Chief Administrative Officer & Clerk

Cochrane
Cochrane, ON
www.cdssab.on.ca
Municipal Type: District
Area: 141,247.30 sq km
Population in 2011: 81,122
David Landers, CAO, Cochrane District Social Services Administration Board
705-268-7722, Fax: 705-268-8290
cao@cdssab.on.ca

Cockburn Island
General Delivery
Walford, ON P0P 2E0
Tel: 705-844-2289; *Fax:* 705-844-1101
Municipal Type: Township
Area: 167.6 sq km
County or District: Manitoulin District;
Provincial Electoral District(s): Algoma-Manitoulin
Federal Electoral District(s): Algoma-Manitoulin-Kapuskasing
Next Election: Oct. 27, 2014 (4 year terms)
David Haight, Reeve
Austin Clipperton, Clerk-Treasurer

Coleman
937907 Marsh Bay Rd.
Coleman, ON P0J 1C0
Tel: 705-679-8833; *Fax:* 705-679-8300
toc@ontera.net
www.colemantownship.ca
Municipal Type: Township
Incorporated: 1906 *Area:* 177.6 sq km
County or District: Timiskaming District; *Population in 2011:* 597
Provincial Electoral District(s): Timiskaming-Cochrane
Federal Electoral District(s): Nipissing-Timiskaming
Next Election: Oct. 27, 2014 (4 year terms)
Dan Cleroux, Mayor
danc@ntl.sympatico.ca
Claire Bigelow, Clerk-Treasurer

Collingwood
P.O. Box 157
97 Hurontario St.
Collingwood, ON L9Y 3Z5
Tel: 705-445-1030; *Fax:* 705-445-2448
www.collingwood.ca
Municipal Type: Town
Incorporated: 1858 *Area:* 33.46 sq km
County or District: Simcoe; *Population in 2011:* 19,241
Provincial Electoral District(s): Simcoe-Grey
Federal Electoral District(s): Simcoe-Grey
Next Election: Oct. 27, 2014 (4 year terms)
Sandra Cooper, Mayor
705-445-8451
scooper@collingwood.ca
Rick Lloyd, Deputy Mayor & Councillor
rlloyd@collingwood.ca
Ian Chadwick, Councillor
ichadwick@collingwood.ca
Sandy Cunningham, Councillor
scunningham@collingwood.ca
Mike Edwards, Councillor
medwards@collingwood.ca
Joe Gardhouse, Councillor
jgardhouse@collingwood.ca
Keith Hull, Councillor
khull@collingwood.ca
Kevin Lloyd, Councillor
klloyd@collingwood.ca
Dale West, Councillor
dwest@collingwood.ca
Sara J. Almas, Clerk
salmas@collingwood.ca
Kim Wingrove, Chief Administrative Officer
kwingrove@collingwood.ca
Marjory Leonard, Treasurer
mleonard@collingwood.ca
Ed Houghton, Executive Director, Public Works
ehoughton@collingwood.ca
Larry Irwin, Director, Information Technology
lirwin@collingwood.ca
Bill Plewes, Chief Building Official & Director, Building Services
bplewes@collingwood.ca
Nancy Farrer, Director, Planning Services
nfarrer@collingwood.ca
Donald Green, Manager, Environmental Services
dgreen@collingwood.ca
Wendy Martin, Manager, Parks
wmartin@collingwood.ca
Trent Elyea, Fire Chief
telyea@collingwood.ca

Conmee
19 Holland Rd. West, RR#1
Kakabeka Falls, ON P0T 1W0
Tel: 807-475-5229; *Fax:* 807-475-4793
info@conmee.com
www.conmee.com
Municipal Type: Township
Area: 167.53 sq km
County or District: Thunder Bay District; *Population in 2011:* 764
Provincial Electoral District(s): Thunder Bay-Atikokan
Federal Electoral District(s): Thunder Bay-Rainy River
Next Election: Oct. 27, 2014 (4 year terms)
Kevin Holland, Reeve
Patricia Maxwell, Clerk-Treasurer

Cramahe
P.O. Box 357
1 Toronto St.
Colborne, ON K0K 1S0
Tel: 905-355-2821; *Fax:* 905-355-3430
www.visitcramahe.ca
Other Information: Toll-Free Phone: 1-877-272-4263
Municipal Type: Township
Area: 201.56 sq km
County or District: Northumberland; *Population in 2011:* 6,073
Provincial Electoral District(s): Northumberland-Quinte West
Federal Electoral District(s): Northumberland-Quinte West
Next Election: Oct. 27, 2014 (4 year terms)
Marc Coombs, Mayor
marc.coombs@airnet.ca
Christie Alexander, Chief Administrative Officer & Clerk
christie@cramahetownship.ca

Dawn-Euphemia
4591 Lambton Line, RR#4
Dresden, ON N0P 1M0
Tel: 519-692-5148; *Fax:* 519-692-5511
admin@dawneuphemia.on.ca
www.lambtononline.ca/county_councillors
Municipal Type: Township
Area: 445.05 sq km
County or District: Lambton; *Population in 2011:* 2,049
Provincial Electoral District(s): Lambton-Kent-Middlesex
Federal Electoral District(s): Lambton-Kent-Middlesex
Next Election: Oct. 27, 2014 (4 year terms)
William E. Bilton, Mayor
mayor@dawneuphemia.on.ca
Michael Schnare, Administrator-Clerk

Dawson
P.O. Box 427
211 Fourth St.
Rainy River, ON P0W 1L0
Tel: 807-852-3529; *Fax:* 807-852-3529
Municipal Type: Township
Area: 338.35 sq km
County or District: Rainy River District; *Population in 2011:* 563
Provincial Electoral District(s): Kenora-Rainy River
Federal Electoral District(s): Thunder Bay-Rainy River
Next Election: Oct. 27, 2014 (4 year terms)
Eltjo Wiersema, Reeve
Patrick W. Giles, Clerk-Treasurer

Deep River
P.O. Box 400
100 Deep River Rd.
Deep River, ON K0J 1P0
Tel: 613-584-2000; *Fax:* 613-584-3237
townmail@deepriver.ca
www.deepriver.ca
Municipal Type: Town
Area: 50.84 sq km
County or District: Renfrew; *Population in 2011:* 4,193
Provincial Electoral District(s): Renfrew-Nipissing-Pembroke
Federal Electoral District(s): Renfrew-Nipissing-Pembroke
Next Election: Oct. 27, 2014 (4 year terms)
Dave Thompson, Mayor
Michelle Larose, Chief Administrative Officer & Clerk
mlarose@deepriver.ca

Deseronto
P.O. Box 310
331 Main St.
Deseronto, ON K0K 1X0
Tel: 613-396-2440; *Fax:* 613-396-3141
jcarter@deseronto.ca (Public Works)
www.deseronto.ca
Other Information: E-mail, Economic Dev.: mconger@deseronto.ca
Municipal Type: Town
Incorporated: 1889 *Area:* 2.52 sq km
County or District: Hastings; *Population in 2011:* 1,835

Provincial Electoral District(s): Prince Edward-Hastings
Federal Electoral District(s): Prince Edward-Hastings
Next Election: Oct. 27, 2014 (4 year terms)
Norm Clark, Mayor
nnclark@sympatico.ca
Bryan Brooks, Clerk-Treasurer
bbrooks@deseronto.ca

Dorion
170 Dorion Loop Rd., RR#1
Dorion, ON P0T 1K0
Tel: 807-857-2289; *Fax:* 807-857-2203
office@doriontownship.ca
www.doriontownship.ca
Municipal Type: Township
Area: 212.07 sq km
County or District: Thunder Bay District; *Population in 2011:* 338
Provincial Electoral District(s): Thunder Bay-Superior North
Federal Electoral District(s): Thunder Bay-Superior North
Next Election: Oct. 27, 2014 (4 year terms)
Dave Harris, Reeve
dharris@doriontownship.ca
Helena Tamminen, Clerk-Treasurer
helena@doriontownship.ca

Douro-Dummer
P.O. Box 92
894 South St.
Warsaw, ON K0L 3A0
Tel: 705-652-8392; *Fax:* 705-652-5044
info@dourodummer.on.ca
www.dourodummer.on.ca
Other Information: Toll-Free Phone: 1-800-899-8785
Municipal Type: Township
Area: 458.36 sq km
County or District: Peterborough; *Population in 2011:* 6,805
Provincial Electoral District(s): Peterborough
Federal Electoral District(s): Peterborough
Next Election: Oct. 27, 2014 (4 year terms)
J. Murray Jones, Reeve
705-652-6325, Fax: 705-652-6325
jjones@dourodummer.on.ca
Linda G. Moher, Clerk & Coordinator, Planning
lindamo@dourodummer.on.ca

Drummond-North Elmsley
310 Port Elmsley Rd., RR#5
Perth, ON K7H 3L7
Tel: 613-267-6500; *Fax:* 613-267-2083
admin@drummondnorthelmsley.com
www.drummondnorthelmsley.com
Municipal Type: Township
Incorporated: 1998 *Area:* 364.78 sq km
County or District: Lanark; *Population in 2011:* 7,487
Provincial Electoral District(s): Lanark-Frontenac-Lennox & Addington
Federal Electoral District(s): Lanark-Frontenac-Lennox & Addington
Next Election: Oct. 27, 2014 (4 year terms)
Note: Amalgamation of the Townships of Drummond and North Elmsley.
Aubrey Churchill, Reeve
613-264-8404
Cindy Halcrow, Clerk-Administrator
cindy@drummondnorthelmsley.com

Dryden
30 Van Horne Ave.
Dryden, ON P8N 2A7
Tel: 807-223-1147; *Fax:* 807-223-1126
generalinquiries@dryden.ca
www.dryden.ca
Other Information: Alternative Phone: 807-223-1126
Municipal Type: Town
Area: 65.2 sq km
County or District: Kenora; *Population in 2011:* 7,617
Provincial Electoral District(s): Kenora-Rainy River
Federal Electoral District(s): Kenora
Next Election: Oct. 27, 2014 (4 year terms)
Craig Nuttall, Mayor
cnuttall@dryden.ca
Colleen Brosseau, City Clerk
807-223-1127
cbrosseau@dryden.ca

Dubreuilville
P.O. Box 367
23 Pine St.
Dubreuilville, ON P0S 1B0
Tel: 705-884-2340; *Fax:* 705-884-2626
www.dubreuilville.ca
Municipal Type: Township
Incorporated: 1978 *Area:* 89.57 sq km
County or District: Algoma District; *Population in 2011:* 635
Provincial Electoral District(s): Algoma-Manitoulin
Federal Electoral District(s): Algoma-Manitoulin-Kapuskasing
Next Election: Oct. 27, 2014 (4 year terms)
Louise Perrier, Mayor
lperrier@dubreuilville.ca
Réjean Raymond, Chief Administrative Officer & Clerk
rraymond@dubreuilville.ca

Dutton-Dunwich
P.O. Box 329
199 Currie Rd.
Dutton, ON N0L 1J0
Tel: 519-762-2204; *Fax:* 519-762-2278
htuffin@duttondunwich.on.ca (Office assistant)
www.duttondunwich.on.ca
Municipal Type: Municipality
Area: 294.63 sq km
County or District: Elgin; *Population in 2011:* 3,876
Provincial Electoral District(s): Elgin-Middlesex-London
Federal Electoral District(s): Elgin-Middlesex-London
Next Election: Oct. 27, 2014 (4 year terms)
Cameron McWilliam, Mayor
csmcwilliam@gmail.com
Ken Loveland, Administrator & Clerk-Treasurer
kloveland@duttondunwich.on.ca

Dysart et al
P.O. Box 389
135 Maple Ave.
Haliburton, ON K0M 1S0
Tel: 705-457-1740; *Fax:* 705-457-1964
www.dysartetal.ca
Municipal Type: Township
Incorporated: Jan. 7, 1867 *Area:* 1,474.07 sq km
County or District: Haliburton; *Population in 2011:* 5,966
Provincial Electoral District(s): Haliburton-Kawartha Lakes-Brock
Federal Electoral District(s): Haliburton-Kawartha Lakes-Brock
Next Election: Oct. 27, 2014 (4 year terms)
Murray Fearrey, Reeve
Cheryl Coulson, Chief Administrative Officer & Clerk
ccoulson@dysartetal.ca

Ear Falls
P.O. Box 309
Ear Falls, ON P0V 1T0
Tel: 807-222-3624; *Fax:* 807-222-2384
eftownship@ear-falls.com
www.ear-falls.com
Other Information: E-mail, Public Services & Ops: pdyck@ear-falls.com
Municipal Type: Township
Area: 330.99 sq km
County or District: Kenora District; *Population in 2011:* 1,026
Provincial Electoral District(s): Kenora-Rainy River
Federal Electoral District(s): Kenora
Next Election: Oct. 27, 2014 (4 year terms)
Kevin Kahoot, Mayor
kkahoot@ear-falls.com
Kimberly Ballance, Clerk-Treasurer & Administrator
kballance@ear-falls.com

East Ferris
390 Hwy. 94
Corbeil, ON P0H 1K0
Tel: 705-752-2740
eastferris.ca
Municipal Type: Township
Area: 149.76 sq km
County or District: Nipissing District; *Population in 2011:* 4,512
Provincial Electoral District(s): Nipissing
Federal Electoral District(s): Nipissing-Timiskaming
Next Election: Oct. 27, 2014 (4 year terms)
William Vrebosch, Mayor
John B. Fior, Clerk
john.fior@eastferris.ca

East Garafraxa
374028 6th Line, RR#3
Orton, ON L0N 1N0
Tel: 519-928-5298; *Fax:* 519-941-1802
township@amaranth-eastgary.ca
www.amaranth-eastgary.ca
Other Information: Alternative Phone: 519-941-1007
Municipal Type: Township
Incorporated: Jan. 1, 1869 *Area:* 165.72 sq km
County or District: Dufferin; *Population in 2011:* 2,595
Provincial Electoral District(s): Dufferin-Caledon
Federal Electoral District(s): Dufferin-Caledon
Next Election: Oct. 27, 2014 (4 year terms)
Allen Taylor, Mayor
519-941-4047
Susan M. Stone, AMCT, Chief Administrative Officer & Clerk-Treasurer
suestone@amaranth-eastgary.ca

East Gwillimbury
19000 Leslie St.
Sharon, ON L0G 1V0
Tel: 905-478-4282; *Fax:* 905-478-2808
town@eastgwillimbury.ca; engineering@eastgwillimbury.ca
www.eastgwillimbury.ca
Other Information: Alternate Fax: 905-478-8545
Municipal Type: Town
Incorporated: 1850 *Area:* 245.06 sq km
County or District: York Regional Municipality; *Population in 2011:* 22,473
Provincial Electoral District(s): York-Simcoe
Federal Electoral District(s): York-Simcoe
Next Election: Oct. 27, 2014 (4 year terms)
Virginia Hackson, Mayor
vhackson@eastgwillimbury.ca
John Eaton, Councillor
jeaton@eastgwillimbury.ca
Marlene Johnston, Councillor
mjohnston@eastgwillimbury.ca
Cathy Morton, Councillor
cmorton@eastgwillimbury.ca
Tara Roy-Diclemente, Councillor
troydiclemente@eastgwillimbury.ca
Kathleen Foster, Municipal Clerk
kfoster@eastgwillimbury.ca
Thomas R. Webster, Chief Administrative Officer
twebster@eastgwillimbury.ca
Mark Valcic, General Manager, Corporate & Financial Services & Treasurer
mvalcic@eastgwillimbury.ca
Wayne Hunt, General Manager, Community Programs & Infrastructure
whunt@eastgwillimbury.ca
Don Sinclair, General Manager, Legal & Council Support Services/Town Solicitor
dsinclair@eastgwillimbury.ca
Don Allan, Manager, Engineering Branch
dallan@eastgwillimbury.ca
Carolyn Kellington, Manager, Community Planning & Development Branch
ckellington@eastgwillimbury.ca
Steve Krystal, Manager, Capital Programs & Traffic Engineering Branch
skrystal@eastgwillimbury.ca
Gary Shropshire, Manager, Community Parks & Programs Branch
gshropshire@eastgwillimbury.ca
Tim Gibson, Chief Building Official & Director, Building Approvals & Inspections
tgibson@eastgwillimbury.ca
Christopher Kalimootoo, Director, Engineering & Environmental Services
ckalimootoo@eastgwillimbury.ca
Robin Prentice, Environmental Planner
rprentice@eastgwillimbury.ca

East Hawkesbury
P.O. Box 340
5151 County Rd. 14
St Eugene, ON K0B 1P0
Tel: 613-674-2170; *Fax:* 613-674-2989
www.easthawkesbury.ca
Municipal Type: Township
Incorporated: Jan. 1, 1850 *Area:* 235.09 sq km
County or District: Prescott & Russell; *Population in 2011:* 3,335
Provincial Electoral District(s): Glengarry-Prescott-Russell
Federal Electoral District(s): Glengarry-Prescott-Russell
Next Election: Oct. 27, 2014 (4 year terms)
Robert Kirby, Mayor
613-632-4841, Fax: 613-632-4841
Linda Rozon, Chief Administrative Officer & Clerk-Treasurer
lrozon@easthawkesbury.ca

East Luther Grand Valley
P.O. Box 249
5 Main St. North
Grand Valley, ON L0N 1G0
Tel: 519-928-5652; *Fax:* 519-928-2275
mail@eastluthergrandvalley.ca
www.eastluthergrandvalley.ca
Municipal Type: Township
Incorporated: Dec. 27, 1880 *Area:* 158.2 sq km
County or District: Dufferin; *Population in 2011:* 2,726

Provincial Electoral District(s): Dufferin-Caledon
Federal Electoral District(s): Dufferin-Caledon
Next Election: Oct. 27, 2014 (4 year terms)
Note: Amalgamation of the Township of East Luther & the Village of Grand Valley on Jan. 1, 1995.
John K. Oosterhof, Mayor
519-928-3117
joosterhof@eastluthergrandvalley.ca
Jane M. Wilson, Chief Administrative Officer & Clerk-Treasurer
jwilson@eastluthergrandvalley.ca

East Zorra-Tavistock
P.O. Box 100
90 Loveys St.
Hickson, ON N0J 1L0
Tel: 519-462-2697; *Fax:* 519-462-2961
ezt@twp.ezt.on.ca
www.twp.ezt.on.ca
Municipal Type: Township
Area: 247.42 sq km
County or District: Oxford; *Population in 2011:* 6,836
Provincial Electoral District(s): Oxford
Federal Electoral District(s): Oxford
Next Election: Oct. 27, 2014 (4 year terms)
Don McKay, Mayor
519-532-2500
dmckay@twp.ezt.on.ca
Brenda Junker, Municipal Clerk & Tax Collector
bjunker@twp.ezt.on.ca

Edwardsburgh/Cardinal
P.O. Box 129
18 Centre St.
Spencerville, ON K0E 1X0
Tel: 613-658-3055; *Fax:* 613-658-3445
www.twpec.ca
Other Information: Toll-Free Phone: 1-866-848-9099
Municipal Type: Township
Area: 311.83 sq km
County or District: Leeds & Grenville; *Population in 2011:* 6,959
Provincial Electoral District(s): Leeds-Grenville
Federal Electoral District(s): Leeds-Grenville
Next Election: Oct. 27, 2014 (4 year terms)
Bill Sloane, Mayor
613-802-0797
mayor@twpec.ca
Debra McKinstry, Clerk & Administrator, Planning
dmckinstry@twpec.ca

Elizabethtown-Kitley
6544 New Dublin Rd., RR#2
Addison, ON K0E 1A0
Tel: 613-345-7480; *Fax:* 613-345-7235
mail@elizabethtown-kitley.on.ca
www.elizabethtown-kitley.on.ca
Other Information: Toll-Free Phone: 1-800-492-3175
Municipal Type: Township
Area: 554.24 sq km
County or District: Leeds & Grenville; *Population in 2011:* 9,724
Provincial Electoral District(s): Leeds-Grenville
Federal Electoral District(s): Leeds-Grenville
Next Election: Oct. 27, 2014 (4 year terms)
Jim Pickard, Mayor
613-342-5721
jimpickard@ripnet.com
Earl Brayton, Councillor
613-345-2650
Dan Downey, Councillor
613-275-1460
John Johnston, Councillor
613-342-8952
Susan Prettejohn, Councillor
613-498-2842
Elenor Renaud, Councillor
613-275-2091
Rob Smith, Councillor
613-498-0827
Yvonne L. Robert, Administrator-Clerk
Melanie Kirkby, Director, Finance & Treasurer
Barbara Kalivas, Director, Planning & Development
Dale Kulp, Director, Public Works
Jim Donovan, Fire Chief
613-498-2460
Ray Scissons, Chief Building Official
cbo@elizabethtown-kitley.on.ca

Emo
P.O. Box 520
39 Roy St.
Emo, ON P0W 1E0
Tel: 807-482-2378; *Fax:* 807-482-2741
township@emo.ca
www.emo.ca
Municipal Type: Township
Incorporated: 1899 *Area:* 203.54 sq km
County or District: Rainy River District; *Population in 2011:* 1,252
Provincial Electoral District(s): Kenora-Rainy River
Federal Electoral District(s): Thunder Bay-Rainy River
Next Election: Oct. 27, 2014 (4 year terms)
Vince Sheppard, Mayor
Brenda J. Cooke, Chief Administrative Officer & Clerk-Treasurer

Englehart
P.O. Box 399
61 Fifth Ave.
Englehart, ON P0J 1H0
Tel: 705-544-2244
englehrt@ntl.sympatico.ca
www.englehart.ca
Municipal Type: Town
Incorporated: 1908 *Area:* 3.04 sq km
County or District: Timiskaming District; *Population in 2011:* 1,519
Provincial Electoral District(s): Timiskaming-Cochrane
Federal Electoral District(s): Timmins-James Bay
Next Election: Oct. 27, 2014 (4 year terms)
Nina Wallace, Mayor
Jana Van Oosten, Clerk

Enniskillen
4465 Rokeby Line, RR#1
Petrolia, ON N0N 1R0
Tel: 519-882-2490
www.enniskillen.ca
Municipal Type: Township
Area: 338.18 sq km
County or District: Lambton; *Population in 2011:* 2,930
Provincial Electoral District(s): Sarnia-Lambton
Federal Electoral District(s): Sarnia-Lambton
Next Election: Oct. 27, 2014 (4 year terms)
Jim Burns, Mayor
jim.tara.burns@cogeco.ca
Duncan McTavish, Administrator-Clerk
dmctavish@enniskillen.ca

Erin
5684 Wellington Rd., RR#2
Hillsburgh, ON N0B 1Z0
Tel: 519-855-4407; *Fax:* 519-855-4821
council@erin.ca; cao@erin.ca (Town Manager)
www.erin.ca
Other Information: Toll-Free Phone: 1-877-818-2888
Municipal Type: Town
Incorporated: 1997 *Area:* 296.98 sq km
County or District: Wellington; *Population in 2011:* 10,770
Provincial Electoral District(s): Wellington-Halton Hills
Federal Electoral District(s): Wellington-Halton Hills
Next Election: Oct. 27, 2014 (4 year terms)
Lou Maieron, Mayor, Fax: 519-833-2492
lou.maieron@erin.ca
John Brennan, Councillor
john.brennan@erin.ca
Deb Callaghan, Councillor
deb.callaghan@erin.ca
Barb Tocher, Councillor
barb.tocher@erin.ca
Josie Wintersinger, Councillor
josie.wintersinger@erin.ca
Kathryn Ironmonger, Clerk
Lisa Hass, Town Manager
Sharon Marshall, Director, Finance
Louise Warn, Administrator, Water Compliance
Dan Callaghan, Fire Chief
Andrew Hartholt, Chief Building Official
Larry Van Wyck, Superintendent, Roads

Espanola
#2, 100 Tudhope St.
Espanola, ON P5E 1S6
Tel: 705-869-1540; *Fax:* 705-869-0083
town@town.espanola.on.ca
www.town.espanola.on.ca
Other Information: E-mail, Public Works: jyusko@town.espanola.on.ca
Municipal Type: Town
Incorporated: March 1, 1958 *Area:* 82.37 sq km
County or District: Sudbury District; *Population in 2011:* 5,364
Provincial Electoral District(s): Algoma-Manitoulin
Federal Electoral District(s): Algoma-Manitoulin-Kapuskasing
Next Election: Oct. 27, 2014 (4 year terms)
Mike Lehoux, Mayor
Joel Mackenzie, Clerk-Treasurer & Administrator
jmackenzie@town.espanola.on.ca

Essa
5786 County Rd. 21
Utopia, ON L0M 1T0
Tel: 705-424-9770; *Fax:* 705-424-2367
info@essatownship.on.ca
www.essatownship.on.ca
Other Information: TTY: 705-424-5302
Municipal Type: Township
Incorporated: 1850 *Area:* 279.57 sq km
County or District: Simcoe; *Population in 2011:* 18,505
Provincial Electoral District(s): Simcoe-Grey
Federal Electoral District(s): Simcoe-Grey
Next Election: Oct. 27, 2014 (4 year terms)
Terry Dowdall, Mayor
705-423-1154
tdowdall@essatownship.on.ca
Sandie Macdonald, Deputy Mayor & Councillor
705-424-6844
smacdonald@essatownship.on.ca
Keith White, Councillor, Ward(s): 1
705-424-2727
kwhite@essatownship.on.ca
Michael Smith, Councillor, Ward(s): 2
705-794-3230
msmith@essatownship.on.ca
Ron Henderson, Councillor, Ward(s): 3
705-424-9752
rhenderson@essatownship.on.ca
Bonnie Sander, Clerk
Greg Murphy, Chief Administrative Officer & Manager, Public Works
gmurphy@essatownship.on.ca
Julie Barrett, Treasurer & Deputy Chief Administrative Officer
jbarrett@essatownship.on.ca
Colleen Healey, Manager, Planning & Development
chealey@essatownship.on.ca
Paul Macdonald, Fire Chief
fire@essatownship.on.ca
Heather Rutherford, Chief Building Official
hrutherford@essatownship.on.ca

Essex
33 Talbot St. South
Essex, ON N8M 1A8
Tel: 519-776-7336; *Fax:* 519-776-8811
www.essex.ca
Municipal Type: Town
Incorporated: 1883 *Area:* 277.95 sq km
County or District: Essex; *Population in 2011:* 19,600
Provincial Electoral District(s): Essex
Federal Electoral District(s): Essex
Next Election: Oct. 27, 2014 (4 year terms)
Note: Incorporated as a town in 1890. Restructuring occurred in 1999.
Ron McDermott, Mayor
519-776-8150
rmcdermott@essex.ca
Morley Bowman, Councillor, Ward(s): 1
mbowman@essex.ca
Randy Voakes, Councillor, Ward(s): 1
rvoakes@essex.ca
Richard Meloche, Deputy Mayor & Councillor, Ward(s): 2
rmeloche@essex.ca
Bill Baker, Councillor, Ward(s): 3
bbaker@essex.ca
John Scott, Councillor, Ward(s): 3
jscott@essex.ca
Sherry Bondy, Councillor, Ward(s): 4
sbondy@essex.ca
Cheryl Bondy, Clerk & Deputy-Treasurer
cbondy@essex.ca
Wayne Miller, Chief Administrative Officer
wmiller@essex.ca
Donna Hunter, Director, Finance & Administration & Treasurer
dhunter@essex.ca
Richard Beausoleil, Director, Public Works
rbeausoleil@essex.ca
Chris Nepszy, Director, Infastructure & Development
cnepszy@essex.ca
Ed Pillon, Fire Chief
519-776-6476, Fax: 519-776-7171
epillon@essex.ca
Heather Jablonski, Town Planner
hjablonski@essex.ca

Dan Boudreau, Superintendent, Drainage
dboudreau@essex.ca
Andy Graf, Superintendent, Water
agraf@essex.ca

Evanturel
P.O. Box 209
245453 Hwy. 659
Englehart, ON P0J 1H0
Tel: 705-544-8200; *Fax:* 705-544-8206
www.evanturel.com
Other Information: E-mail, Building: cbo@ntl.sympatico.ca
Municipal Type: Township
Incorporated: Jan. 1, 1904 *Area:* 88.99 sq km
County or District: Timiskaming District; *Population in 2011:* 452
Provincial Electoral District(s): Timiskaming-Cochrane
Federal Electoral District(s): Timmins-James Bay
Next Election: Oct. 27, 2014 (4 year terms)
Jack Briggs, Reeve
Amy Vickery-Menard, Clerk-Treasurer
evanturelclerk@parolink.net

Faraday
P.O. Box 929
29860 Hwy. 28 South
Bancroft, ON K0L 1C0
Tel: 613-332-3638; *Fax:* 613-332-3006
faraday@reztel.net
www.faraday.ca
Municipal Type: Township
Area: 215.23 sq km
County or District: Hastings; *Population in 2011:* 1,468
Provincial Electoral District(s): Prince Edward-Hastings
Federal Electoral District(s): Prince Edward-Hastings
Next Election: Oct. 27, 2014 (4 year terms)
Carl A. Tinney, Reeve
613-332-2050
Brenda Vader, Clerk-Treasurer & Tax Collector

Fauquier-Strickland
P.O. Box 40
25 Grzela Rd.
Fauquier, ON P0L 1G0
Tel: 705-339-2521; *Fax:* 705-339-2421
info@fauquierstrickland.com
fauquierstrickland.com
Municipal Type: Township
Area: 1,013.54 sq km
County or District: Cochrane District; *Population in 2011:* 530
Provincial Electoral District(s): Timmins-James Bay
Federal Electoral District(s): Algoma-Manitoulin-Kapuskasing
Next Election: Oct. 27, 2014 (4 year terms)
Madeleine Tremblay, Reeve
Robert Courchesne, Administrator & Clerk-Treasurer

Fort Erie
1 Municipal Centre Dr.
Fort Erie, ON L2A 2S6
Tel: 905-871-1600; *Fax:* 905-871-4022
www.forterie.on.ca
Other Information: Fax, Corporate Services: 905-871-9984
Municipal Type: Town
Incorporated: 1857 *Area:* 166.35 sq km
County or District: Niagara Regional Municipality; *Population in 2011:* 29,960
Provincial Electoral District(s): Niagara Falls
Federal Electoral District(s): Niagara Falls
Next Election: Oct. 27, 2014 (4 year terms)
Douglas G. Martin, Mayor
905-871-1600
Stephen Passero, Councillor, Ward(s): 1
Richard Shular, Councillor, Ward(s): 2
Bob Steckley, Councillor, Ward(s): 3
John Hill, Councillor, Ward(s): 4
Don Lubberts, Councillor, Ward(s): 5
Paul Collard, Councillor, Ward(s): 6
John Teal, Regional Councillor
Carolyn J. Kett, Town Clerk
H. Schlange, Chief Administrative Officer
Helen Chamberlain, Director, Financial Services
Richard Brady, Director, Community & Development Services
Heather Salter, B.E.S., LL.B., Director, Legal & Legislative Services & Town Solicitor
Ron Tripp, Director, Infrastructure Services
Larry Coplen, Fire Chief & Coordinator, Community Emergency Management
D. Heyworth, Manager, Land Use Policy

Fort Frances
320 Portage Ave.
Fort Frances, ON P9A 3P9
Tel: 807-274-5323; *Fax:* 807-274-8479
town@fort-frances.com
www.fort-frances.com
Municipal Type: Town
Incorporated: 1903 *Area:* 26.85 sq km
County or District: Rainy River District; *Population in 2011:* 7,952
Provincial Electoral District(s): Kenora-Rainy River
Federal Electoral District(s): Thunder Bay-Rainy River
Next Election: Oct. 27, 2014 (4 year terms)
Roy Avis, Mayor
ravis@fort-frances.com
Glenn Treftlin, Clerk
gtreftlin@fort-frances.com

French River, Municipality of / Municipalité de la Rivière des Français
P.O. Box 156
#1, 44 St. Christophe St.
Noëlville, ON P0M 2N0
Tel: 705-898-2294; *Fax:* 705-898-2181
www.frenchriver.ca
Municipal Type: Town
Incorporated: Jan. 1, 1999 *Area:* 734.26 sq km
County or District: Sudbury District; *Population in 2011:* 2,442
Provincial Electoral District(s): Timiskaming-Cochrane; Nickle Belt
Federal Electoral District(s): Nickel Belt
Next Election: Oct. 27, 2014 (4 year terms)
Claude Bouffard, Mayor
cbouffard@frenchriver.ca
Michel V. Monette, CMA, Chief Administrative Officer & Clerk
mmonette@frenchriver.ca

Front of Yonge
P.O. Box 130
1514 County Rd. 2
Mallorytown, ON K0E 1R0
Tel: 613-923-2251; *Fax:* 613-923-2421
admin@frontofyonge.com
www.frontofyonge.com
Other Information: Phone, Public Works: 613-923-5074
Municipal Type: Township
Area: 127.85 sq km
County or District: Leeds & Grenville; *Population in 2011:* 2,680
Provincial Electoral District(s): Leeds-Grenville
Federal Electoral District(s): Leeds-Grenville
Next Election: Oct. 27, 2014 (4 year terms)
Roger Haley, Reeve
rogerhaley@frontofyonge.com
Elaine A. Covey, Clerk
ecovey@frontofyonge.com

Frontenac Islands
P.O. Box 130
Rd. 96
Wolfe Island, ON K0H 2Y0
Tel: 613-385-2216; *Fax:* 613-385-1032
www.municipality.frontenacislands.on.ca
Municipal Type: Township
Incorporated: Jan. 1, 1998 *Area:* 174.99 sq km
County or District: Frontenac; *Population in 2011:* 1,864
Provincial Electoral District(s): Kingston & the Islands
Federal Electoral District(s): Kingston & the Islands
Next Election: Oct. 27, 2014 (4 year terms)
Note: Amalgamation of Howe Island & Wolfe Island.
Dennis Doyle, Mayor
613-385-2763
denisdoyle@kos.net
Terry J. O'Shea, AMCT, Chief Administrative Officer & Clerk
tjoshea@kos.net

Galway-Cavendish-Harvey
P.O. Box 820
701 County Rd. 36, RR#3
Bobcaygeon, ON K0M 1A0
Tel: 705-738-3800; *Fax:* 705-738-3801
www.galwaycavendishharvey.ca
Other Information: Toll-Free Phone: 1-800-374-4009
Municipal Type: Township
Area: 848.26 sq km
County or District: Peterborough; *Population in 2011:* 5,105
Provincial Electoral District(s): Haliburton-Kawartha Lakes-Brock
Federal Electoral District(s): Haliburton-Kawartha Lakes-Brock
Next Election: Oct. 27, 2014 (4 year terms)
Janet Clarkson, Reeve
705-657-9932
jclarkson@galwaycavendishharvey.ca
Lynn Holtz, Clerk
lholtz@galwaycavendishharvey.ca

Gananoque
Town Hall
P.O. Box 100
30 King St. East
Gananoque, ON K7G 2T6
Tel: 613-382-2149; *Fax:* 613-382-8587
www.townofgananoque.com
Municipal Type: Separated for Municipal Purposes Only
Area: 7.01 sq km
County or District: Leeds & Grenville; *Population in 2011:* 5,194
Provincial Electoral District(s): Leeds-Grenville
Federal Electoral District(s): Leeds-Grenville
Next Election: Oct. 27, 2014 (4 year terms)
Erika Demchuk, Mayor
mayor@townofgananoque.ca
Robert W. Small, Chief Administrative Officer
rsmall@gananoque.ca

Gauthier
P.O. Box 65
92 McPherson St.
Dobie, ON P0K 1B0
Tel: 705-568-8951; *Fax:* 705-568-8951
Municipal Type: Township
Area: 88.36 sq km
County or District: Timiskaming District; *Population in 2011:* 123
Provincial Electoral District(s): Timiskaming-Cochrane
Federal Electoral District(s): Timmins-James Bay
Next Election: Oct. 27, 2014 (4 year terms)
Dave Fraser, Reeve
Dianne Quinn, Clerk-Treasurer
quinner@ntl.sympatico.ca

Georgian Bay
99 Lone Pine Rd.
Port Severn, ON L0K 1S0
Tel: 705-538-2337; *Fax:* 705-538-1850
clerks@township.georgianbay.on.ca
www.township.georgianbay.on.ca
Other Information: Toll-Free Phone: 1-800-567-0187
Municipal Type: Township
Area: 535.48 sq km
County or District: Muskoka District Municipality; *Population in 2011:* 2,124
Provincial Electoral District(s): Parry Sound-Muskoka
Federal Electoral District(s): Parry Sound-Muskoka
Next Election: Oct. 27, 2014 (4 year terms)
Larry Braid, Mayor
Susan Boonstra, Clerk
sboonstra@gbtownship.ca

Georgian Bluffs
177964 Grey Rd. 18, RR#3
Owen Sound, ON N4K 5N5
Tel: 519-376-2729; *Fax:* 519-372-1620
office@georgianbluffs.on.ca
www.georgianbluffs.on.ca
Municipal Type: Township
Incorporated: Jan. 1, 2001 *Area:* 603.58 sq km
County or District: Grey; *Population in 2011:* 10,404
Provincial Electoral District(s): Bruce-Grey-Owen Sound
Federal Electoral District(s): Bruce-Grey-Owen Sound
Next Election: Oct. 27, 2014 (4 year terms)
Note: Amalgamation of the Townships of Derby, Keppel & Sarawak.
Alan Barfoot, Mayor
abarfoot@georgianbluffs.on.ca
Dwight Burley, Deputy Mayor & Councillor
dburley@georgianbluffs.on.ca
Carol Barfoot, Councillor
cbarfoot@georgianbluffs.on.ca
Judy Gay, Councillor
jgay@georgianbluffs.on.ca
Robert Lennox, Councillor
rlennox@georgianbluffs.on.ca
Ryan Thompson, Councillor
rthompson@georgianbluffs.on.ca
Tom Wiley, Councillor
twiley@georgianbluffs.on.ca
Bruce Hoffman, Clerk
bhoffman@georgianbluffs.on.ca
Bill White, Chief Administrative Officer
Holly Morrison, Treasurer
hmorrison@georgianbluffs.on.ca
Bill Klingenberg, Chief Building Official
Martin Timmerman, Supervisor, Operations

Georgina
Georgina Civic Centre
26557 Civic Centre Rd., RR#2
Keswick, ON L4P 3G1
Tel: 905-476-4301; *Fax:* 905-476-8100
info@georgina.ca; events@georgina.ca
www.georgina.ca
Other Information: Alternative Phones: 905-722-6516; 705-437-2210
Municipal Type: Town
Area: 287.72 sq km
County or District: York Reg. Mun.; *Population in 2011:* 43,517
Provincial Electoral District(s): York-Simcoe
Federal Electoral District(s): York-Simcoe
Next Election: Oct. 27, 2014 (4 year terms)
Note: Amalgamation of the Village of Keswick, the Township of Georgina & Village of Sutton.
Robert Grossi, Mayor, Fax: 905-476-1475
rgrossi@georgina.ca
Danny Wheeler, Deputy Mayor & Regional Councillor
dwheeler@georgina.ca
Naomi Davison, Councillor, Ward(s): 1
ndavison@georgina.ca
Phil Craig, Councillor, Ward(s): 2
pcraig@georgina.ca
Dave Szollosy, Councillor, Ward(s): 3
dszollosy@georgina.ca
Ken Hackenbrook, Councillor, Ward(s): 4
khackenbrook@georgina.ca
Brad Smockum, Councillor, Ward(s): 5
bsmockum@georgina.ca
Roland Chénier, A.M.C.T., Town Clerk
rchenier@georgina.ca
Robert Magloughlen, Interim Chief Administrative Officer
rmagloughlen@georgina.ca
Rebecca Mathewson, C.G.A., Director, Administrative Services
rmathewson@georgina.ca
Harold Lenters, M.Sc.Pl., MCIP, RPP, Director, Planning & Building
hlenters@georgina.ca
Robert Magloughlen, P.Eng., Director, Engineering & Public Works
rmagloughlen@georgina.ca
Bill O'Neill, C.M.M. III, Director, Emergency Services & Fire Chief
boneill@georgina.ca
Faye Richardson, Director, Parks & Culture
frichardson@georgina.ca
Claire Marsden, C.H.R.P., C.M.M. I, Manager, Human Resources
cmarsden@georgina.ca

Gillies
1092 Hwy. 595, RR#1
South Gillies, ON P0T 1W0
Tel: 807-475-3185; *Fax:* 807-473-0767
gillies@tbaytel.net
www.gilliestownship.ca
Other Information: E-mail, Building: cmaki@xplornet.com
Municipal Type: Township
Area: 92.67 sq km
County or District: Thunder Bay District; *Population in 2011:* 473
Provincial Electoral District(s): Thunder Bay-Atikokan
Federal Electoral District(s): Thunder Bay-Rainy River
Next Election: Oct. 27, 2014 (4 year terms)
Rick Kieri, Reeve
Karen Caren, Clerk-Treasurer
gillies@tbaytel.net

Goderich
Municipal Office, Town Hall
57 West St.
Goderich, ON N7A 2K5
Tel: 519-524-8344; *Fax:* 519-524-7209
townhall@goderich.ca
www.goderich.ca
Municipal Type: Town
Area: 7.91 sq km
County or District: Huron; *Population in 2011:* 7,521
Provincial Electoral District(s): Huron-Bruce
Federal Electoral District(s): Huron-Bruce
Next Election: Oct. 27, 2014 (4 year terms)
Delbert (Deb) Shewfelt, Mayor
519-524-9581
Larry J. McCabe, Clerk-Administrator

Gordon / Barrie Island
P.O. Box 680
29 Noble Side Rd.
Gore Bay, ON P0P 1H0
Tel: 705-282-2702; *Fax:* 705-282-2722
adminoffice@gordonbarrieisland.ca
gordontownship.manitoulin-link.com
Municipal Type: Municipality
Incorporated: Jan. 1, 2009
County or District: Manitoulin District; *Population in 2011:* 526
Provincial Electoral District(s): Algoma-Manitoulin
Federal Electoral District(s): Algoma-Manitoulin-Kapuskasing
Next Election: Oct. 27, 2014 (4 year terms)
Note: Amalgamation of the former Township of Gordon & Allan West & the Township of Barrie Island.
Art Madore, Reeve
Carrie Lewis, Clerk-Treasurer
clerk@gordonbarrieisland.ca

Gore Bay
P.O. Box 590
15 Water St.
Gore Bay, ON P0P 1H0
Tel: 705-282-2420; *Fax:* 705-282-3076
www.gorebay.ca
Other Information: E-mail, Treasury: pbond@gorebay.ca
Municipal Type: Town
Incorporated: 1890 *Area:* 5.27 sq km
County or District: Manitoulin District; *Population in 2011:* 850
Provincial Electoral District(s): Algoma-Manitoulin
Federal Electoral District(s): Algoma-Manitoulin-Kapuskasing
Next Election: Oct. 27, 2014 (4 year terms)
Ron Lane, Mayor
mayor@gorebay.ca
Annette Clarke, Clerk
aclarke@gorebay.ca

Gravenhurst
3 - 5 Pineridge Gate
Gravenhurst, ON P1P 1Z3
Tel: 705-687-3412; *Fax:* 705-687-7016
reception@gravenhurst.ca
www.gravenhurst.ca
Municipal Type: Town
Area: 517.99 sq km
County or District: Muskoka District Municipality; *Population in 2011:* 11,640
Provincial Electoral District(s): Parry Sound-Muskoka
Federal Electoral District(s): Parry Sound-Muskoka
Next Election: Oct. 27, 2014 (4 year terms)
Paisley Donaldson, Mayor
705-689-5659
pdonaldson@gravenhurst.ca
Sandy Cairns, District Councillor
sanmar@cogeco.ca
Bob Colhoun, District Councillor
colhoun@muskoka.com
Rosemary King, District Councillor
rosemary@rosemaryking.net
Heidi Lorenz, Councillor, Ward(s): 1
heidi.lorenz@cogeco.ca
Lola Bratty, Councillor, Ward(s): 2
lola@lolabratty.ca
Joe Donoghue, Councillor, Ward(s): 3
shamrocktrailerpark@gmail.com
Randy Jorgensen, Councillor, Ward(s): 4
randy@randyjorgensen.com
Jeff Watson, Deputy Mayor & Councillor, Ward(s): 5
jwatson17@cogeco.ca
Candace Thwaites, Clerk
D. Weldon, Interim Chief Administrative Officer
Kenneth Watson, Treasurer
kwatson@gravenhurst.ca
D. Broderick, Manager, Recreation, Community Services, & Centennial Ctr. Ops.
S. Lucas, Manager, Development Services
G. Carelton, Manager, Public Works & Operations

Greater Madawaska
P.O. Box 180
1101 Francis St.
Calabogie, ON K0J 1H0
Tel: 613-752-2222; *Fax:* 613-752-2617
admin@greatermadawaska.com
www.townshipofgreatermadawaska.com
Municipal Type: Township
Incorporated: Jan. 1, 2001 *Area:* 1,011.67 sq km
County or District: Renfrew; *Population in 2011:* 2,485
Provincial Electoral District(s): Renfrew-Nipissing-Pembroke
Federal Electoral District(s): Renfrew-Nipissing-Pembroke
Next Election: Oct. 27, 2014 (4 year terms)
Note: Amalgamation of Bagot, Blythfield & Brougham Township & Griffith & Matawatchan Township.
Peter Emon, Reeve
613-752-2922
peteremon@somuchmore.ca
Angela Yolkowskie, Chief Administrative Officer
ayolkowskie@greatermadawaska.com

Greenstone, Municipality of
P.O. Box 70
301 East St.
Geraldton, ON P0T 1M0
Tel: 807-854-1100; *Fax:* 807-854-1947
www.greenstone.ca
Municipal Type: Town
Area: 2,780.99 sq km
County or District: Thunder Bay; *Population in 2011:* 4,724
Provincial Electoral District(s): Thunder Bay-Superior North
Federal Electoral District(s): Thunder Bay-Superior North
Next Election: Oct. 27, 2014 (4 year terms)
Renald Beaulieu, Mayor
Elizabeth (Lisa) Slomke, Clerk
lisa.slomke@greenstone.ca

Grey Highlands, Municipality of
P.O. Box 409
#1, 206 Toronto St. South
Markdale, ON N0C 1H0
Tel: 519-986-2811; *Fax:* 519-986-3643
info@greyhighlands.ca
www.greyhighlands.ca
Other Information: Toll-Free Phone: 1-888-342-4059
Municipal Type: Township
Incorporated: Jan. 1, 2001 *Area:* 880.6 sq km
County or District: Grey; *Population in 2011:* 9,520
Provincial Electoral District(s): Bruce-Grey-Owen Sound
Federal Electoral District(s): Bruce-Grey-Owen Sound
Next Election: Oct. 27, 2014 (4 year terms)
Note: Amalgamation of Flesherton, Artemesia, Euphrasia, Markdale & Osprey.
Wayne Fitzgerald, Mayor
519-986-3898
Debbie Robertson, Clerk
519-986-1216
robertson@greyhighlands.ca

Grimsby
160 Livingston Ave.
Grimsby, ON L3M 4G3
Tel: 905-945-9634; *Fax:* 905-945-5010
www.town.grimsby.on.ca
Municipal Type: Town
Area: 68.94 sq km
County or District: Niagara Reg. Mun.; *Population in 2011:* 25,325
Provincial Electoral District(s): Niagara West-Glanbrook
Federal Electoral District(s): Niagara West-Glanbrook
Next Election: Oct. 27, 2014 (4 year terms)
Robert N. Bentley, Mayor
905-945-2710
bbentley@grimsby.ca
Steve Berry, Alderman, Ward(s): 1
905-945-2578
sberry@grimsby.ca
Dave Wilson, Alderman, Ward(s): 1
905-309-0905
dwilson@grimsby.ca
Dave Kadwell, Alderman, Ward(s): 2
905-945-8259
dkadwell@grimsby.ca
Michelle Seaborn, Alderman, Ward(s): 2
905-945-7963
mseaborn@grimsby.ca
David Finch, Alderman, Ward(s): 3
905-945-7074
dfinch@grimsby.ca
Joanne Johnston, Alderman, Ward(s): 3
905-945-9851
jjohnston@grimsby.ca
Nick DiFlavio, Alderman, Ward(s): 4
905-309-4133
ndiflavio@grimsby.ca
Carolyn Mullins, Alderman, Ward(s): 4
289-235-9460
cmullins@grimsby.ca
Hazel Soady-Easton, Town Clerk
905-309-2003
Keith Vogl, Town Manager
Stephen Gruninger, CGA, Town Treasurer & Director, Finance
Bruce Atkinson, CGA, Director, Recreation, Facilities, & Culture
Robert LeRoux, P.Eng., Director, Public Works
Michael Seaman, Director, Planning

M. Cain, Fire Chief
Brandon Wartman, Manager, EHS Compliance
905-309-2016

Guelph / Eramosa

P.O. Box 700
8348 Wellington Rd. 124
Rockwood, ON N0B 2K0
Tel: 519-856-9951; *Fax:* 519-856-2240
general@get.on.ca
www.get.on.ca
Other Information: Toll-Free Phone: 1-800-267-1465
Municipal Type: Township
Incorporated: Jan. 1, 1999 *Area:* 291.73 sq km
County or District: Wellington; *Population in 2011:* 12,380
Provincial Electoral District(s): Wellington-Halton Hills
Federal Electoral District(s): Wellington-Halton Hills
Next Election: Oct. 27, 2014 (4 year terms)
Note: Amalgamation of the Townships of Guelph, Eramosa, Pilkington & Nichol.
Chris White, Mayor
whitecj@sympatico.ca
Meaghen Reid, Clerk
mreid@get.on.ca
Shawn Armstrong, Fire Chief
519-824-6590
Brad Roelfson, Manager, Property & Leisure Services
broelofson@get.on.ca
Ken Gagnon, Manager, Public Works
kgagnon@get.on.ca
Mark Thorpe, Officer, Bylaw Enforcement
mthorpe@get.on.ca
Mike Newark, Chief Building Official
mnewark@get.on.ca

Halton Hills

1 Halton Hills Dr.
Georgetown, ON L7G 5G2
Tel: 905-873-2600; *Fax:* 905-873-2347
www.haltonhills.ca
Other Information: TTY: 905-873-0644
Municipal Type: Town
Area: 276.26 sq km
County or District: Halton Reg. Mun.; *Population in 2011:* 59,008
Provincial Electoral District(s): Wellington-Halton Hills
Federal Electoral District(s): Wellington-Halton Hills
Next Election: Oct. 27, 2014 (4 year terms)
Rick Bonnette, Mayor
mayor@haltonhills.ca
Clark A. Somerville, Regional Councillor, Ward(s): 1 & 2
clarks@haltonhills.ca
Jane Fogal, Regional Councillor, Ward(s): 3 & 4
janefogal@haltonhills.ca
Jon Hurst, Councillor, Ward(s): 1
jon@haltonhills.ca
Mike O'Leary, Councillor, Ward(s): 1
mikeo@haltonhills.ca
Joan Robson, Councillor, Ward(s): 2
joanr@haltonhills.ca
Bryan Lewis, Councillor, Ward(s): 2
bryanlewis@haltonhills.ca
Moya Johnson, Councillor, Ward(s): 3
moyajohnson@haltonhills.ca
David Kentner, Councillor, Ward(s): 3
davek@haltonhills.ca
Bob Inglis, Councillor, Ward(s): 4
b_inglis@sympatico.ca
Ann Lawlor, Councillor, Ward(s): 4
annl@haltonhills.ca
S. Jones, Town Clerk
D. Perlin, Chief Administrative Officer
Ed DeSousa, Treasurer & Director, Corporate Services
Terry Alyman, Director, Recreation & Parks
John Linhardt, Director, Planning, Development, & Sustainability
Chris Mills, Director, Infrastructure Services & Town Engineer
D. Szybalski, Coordinator, Sustainability

Hamilton

P.O. Box 1060
8285 Majestic Hills Dr.
Cobourg, ON K9A 4W5
Tel: 905-342-2810; *Fax:* 905-342-2818
info@hamiltontownship.ca
www.hamiltontownship.ca
Municipal Type: Township
Area: 256.11 sq km
County or District: Northumberland; *Population in 2011:* 10,702
Provincial Electoral District(s): Northumberland-Quinte West
Federal Electoral District(s): Northumberland-Quinte West
Next Election: Oct. 27, 2014 (4 year terms)
Mark Lovshin, Mayor
mlovshin@cogeco.ca
Isobel Hie, Deputy Mayor & Councillor
ihie@hamiltontownship.ca
Donna Cole, Councillor
dcole@hamiltontownship.ca
John Davison, Councillor
jdavison@hamiltontownship.ca
Gary Woods, Councillor
gwoods@hamiltontownship.ca
Kate Surerus, Clerk
ksurerus@hamiltontownship.ca
Bill Winegard, Interim Chief Administrative Officer
bwinegard@hamiltontownship.ca
Fran Aird, Acting Tax Collector & Treasurer
faird@hamiltontownship.ca
Doug Murray, Director, Public Works
dmurray@hamiltontownship.ca
Ken Clapperton, Fire Chief, Baltimore
baltimorefire@hamiltontownship.ca
Reg Jackson, Fire Chief, Bewdley
bewdleyfire@hamiltontownship.ca
Pete Staples, Fire Chief, Harwood
harwoodfire@hamiltontownship.ca
Scott Jibb, Chief Building Official
sjibb@hamiltontownship.ca
Sandra Stothart, Coordinator, Planning
sstothart@hamiltontownship.ca
Doug Thompson, Manager, Water Operations
dthompson@hamiltontownship.ca

Hanover

341 - 10th St.
Hanover, ON N4N 1P5
Tel: 519-364-2780; *Fax:* 519-364-6456
civic@hanover.ca
www.hanover.ca
Municipal Type: Town
Incorporated: Jan. 1, 2001 *Area:* 9.81 sq km
County or District: Grey; *Population in 2011:* 7,490
Provincial Electoral District(s): Bruce-Grey-Owen Sound
Federal Electoral District(s): Bruce-Grey-Owen Sound
Next Election: Oct. 27, 2014 (4 year terms)
Kathi Maskell, Mayor
kmaskell@hanover.ca
Mike Dunlop, Chief Administrative Officer & Clerk
mdunlop@hanover.ca

Harley

903303 Hanbury Rd., RR#2
New Liskeard, ON P0J 1P0
Tel: 705-647-5439; *Fax:* 705-647-6373
harleytwp@parolink.net
www.harley.ca
Municipal Type: Township
Incorporated: 1904 *Area:* 91.73 sq km
County or District: Timiskaming District; *Population in 2011:* 539
Provincial Electoral District(s): Timiskaming-Cochrane
Federal Electoral District(s): Timmins-James Bay
Next Election: Oct. 27, 2014 (4 year terms)
Pauline Archambault, Reeve
Michel Lachapelle, Clerk-Treasurer

Harris

Site 4-96, RR#3
New Liskeard, ON P0J 1P0
Tel: 705-647-5094; *Fax:* 705-647-0041
harris@ntl.sympatico.ca
Municipal Type: Township
Area: 50.17 sq km
County or District: Timiskaming District; *Population in 2011:* 523
Provincial Electoral District(s): Timiskaming-Cochrane
Federal Electoral District(s): Nipissing-Timiskaming
Next Election: Oct. 27, 2014 (4 year terms)
Martin Auger, Reeve

Hastings Highlands

P.O. Box 130
33011 Hwy. 62 North
Maynooth, ON K0L 2S0
Tel: 613-338-2811; *Fax:* 613-338-3292
office@hastingshighlands.ca
www.hastingshighlands.ca
Other Information: Toll-Free Phone: 1-877-338-2818
Municipal Type: Municipality
Area: 967.34 sq km
County or District: Hastings; *Population in 2011:* 4,168
Provincial Electoral District(s): Prince Edward-Hastings
Federal Electoral District(s): Prince Edward-Hastings
Next Election: Oct. 27, 2014 (4 year terms)
Ronald J. Emond, Mayor
remond@hastingshighlands.ca
Craig Davidson, Chief Administrative Officer & Clerk-Treasurer
cdavidson@hastingshighlands.ca

Havelock-Belmont-Methuen

P.O. Box 10
1 Ottawa St. East
Havelock, ON K0L 1Z0
Tel: 705-778-2308; *Fax:* 705-778-5248
havbelmet@hbmtwp.ca
www.havelockbelmontmethuen.on.ca
Other Information: Toll-Free Phone: 1-877-767-2795
Municipal Type: Township
Area: 526.02 sq km
County or District: Peterborough; *Population in 2011:* 4,523
Provincial Electoral District(s): Peterborough
Federal Electoral District(s): Peterborough
Next Election: Oct. 27, 2014 (4 year terms)
Ronald Gerow, Reeve
705-778-2092
rgerow@hbmtwp.ca
Glenn Girven, Clerk
ggirven@hbmtwp.ca

Hawkesbury

600 Higginson St.
Hawkesbury, ON K6A 1H1
Tel: 613-632-0106
www.hawkesbury.ca
Municipal Type: Town
Area: 9.46 sq km
County or District: Prescott & Russell; *Population in 2011:* 10,551
Provincial Electoral District(s): Glengarry-Prescott-Russell
Federal Electoral District(s): Glengarry-Prescott-Russell
Next Election: Oct. 27, 2014 (4 year terms)
Rene Berthiaume, Mayor
rberthiaume@hawkesbury.ca
Michel A. Beaulne, Councillor
mbeaulne@hawkesbury.ca
André Chamaillard, Councillor
achamaillard@hawkesbury.ca
Alain Fraser, Councillor
afraser@hawkesbury.ca
Johanne Portelance, Councillor
jportelance@hawkesbury.ca
Michel Thibodeau, ouncillor
mthibodeau@hawkesbury.ca
Marc Tourangeau, Councillor
mtourangeau@hawkesbury.ca
Christine Groulx, Clerk
Normand Beaulieu, Chief Administrative Officer & Treasurer
Liette Valade, Director, Recreation & Culture
Gérald Campbell, Superintendent, Public Works
Richard Guertin, Superintendent, Water Treatment Plant
Jean-Claude Miner, Chief Building Official
Ghislain Pigeon, Fire Chief
Danielle Fredette-Thériault, Officer, Human Resources
Manon Belle-Isle, Planner

Head, Clara & Maria

15 Township Hall Rd.
Stonecliffe, ON K0J 2K0
Tel: 613-586-2526; *Fax:* 613-586-2596
twpshcm@xplornet.com
www.townshipsofheadclaramaria.ca
Other Information: Phone, Building Inspection: 613-586-1950
Municipal Type: Township
Area: 727.96 sq km
County or District: Renfrew; *Population in 2011:* 235
Provincial Electoral District(s): Renfrew-Nipissing-Pembroke
Federal Electoral District(s): Renfrew-Nipissing-Pembroke
Next Election: Oct. 27, 2014 (4 year terms)
Tammy Lea Stewart, Reeve
613-586-2750
Melinda Reith, Municipal Clerk

Hearst

Town Hall
P.O. Box 5000
925 Alexandra St.
Hearst, ON P0L 1N0
Tel: 705-362-4341; *Fax:* 705-362-5902
townofhearst@hearst.ca
www.hearst.ca
Municipal Type: Town
Incorporated: 1922 *Area:* 98.67 sq km
County or District: Cochrane District; *Population in 2011:* 5,090
Provincial Electoral District(s): Timmins-James Bay
Federal Electoral District(s): Algoma-Manitoulin-Kapuskasing
Next Election: Oct. 27, 2014 (4 year terms)
Roger Sigouin, Mayor
Claude J. Laflamme, Chief Administrative Officer & Clerk
705-372-2817

Highlands East, Municipality of
P.O. Box 295
County Rd. 648
Wilberforce, ON K0L 3C0
Tel: 705-448-2981; *Fax:* 705-448-2532
www.highlandseast.ca
Municipal Type: Township
Incorporated: Jan. 1, 2001 *Area:* 701.32 sq km
County or District: Haliburton; *Population in 2011:* 3,249
Provincial Electoral District(s): Haliburton-Kawartha Lakes-Brock
Federal Electoral District(s): Haliburton-Kawartha Lakes-Brock
Next Election: Oct. 27, 2014 (4 year terms)
Note: Amalgamation of the Townships of Bicroft, Cardiff, Glamorgan & Monmouth.
Dave Burton, Reeve
705-448-9355
dburton@highlandseast.ca
Irene Cook, CMO, Clerk, Fax: 705-448-3211
icook@highlandseast.ca

Hilliard
P.O. Box 12
RR#3
Thornloe, ON P0J 1S0
Tel: 705-563-2593; *Fax:* 705-563-2593
twphill@ntl.sympatico.ca
Municipal Type: Township
Area: 91.17 sq km
County or District: Timiskaming District; *Population in 2011:* 204
Provincial Electoral District(s): Timiskaming-Cochrane
Federal Electoral District(s): Timmins-James Bay
Next Election: Oct. 27, 2014 (4 year terms)
Morgan Carson, Reeve
Janet Gore, Clerk-Treasurer

Hilton
P.O. Box 205
2983 Base Line
Hilton Beach, ON P0R 1G0
Tel: 705-246-2472; *Fax:* 705-246-0132
admin@hiltontownship.ca; hiltontownship@xplornet.com
www.hiltontownship.ca
Other Information: Phone, Roads: 705-246-1781
Municipal Type: Township
Incorporated: 1883 *Area:* 115.78 sq km
County or District: Algoma District; *Population in 2011:* 261
Provincial Electoral District(s): Algoma-Manitoulin
Federal Electoral District(s): Sault Ste Marie
Next Election: Oct. 27, 2014 (4 year terms)
James See, Reeve
see@hiltontownship.ca
Valerie Obarymskyj, Clerk-Treasurer
clerk@hiltontownship.ca

Hilton Beach
P.O. Box 25
3100 Bowker St.
Hilton Beach, ON P0R 1G0
Tel: 705-246-2242; *Fax:* 705-246-2913
info@hiltonbeach.com
www.hiltonbeach.com
Municipal Type: Village
Area: 2.46 sq km
County or District: Algoma District; *Population in 2011:* 145
Provincial Electoral District(s): Algoma-Manitoulin
Federal Electoral District(s): Sault Ste Marie
Next Election: Oct. 27, 2014 (4 year terms)
Wilfred Stevens, Mayor
Gloria Fischer, Clerk

Hornepayne
P.O. Box 370
68 Front St.
Hornepayne, ON P0M 1Z0
Tel: 807-868-2020; *Fax:* 807-868-2787
www.hornepayne.com/township
Municipal Type: Township
Area: 204.52 sq km
County or District: Algoma District; *Population in 2011:* 1,050
Provincial Electoral District(s): Algoma-Manitoulin
Federal Electoral District(s): Algoma-Manitoulin-Kapuskasing
Next Election: Oct. 27, 2014 (4 year terms)
Gene Belanger, Mayor
Susan Smith, Township Clerk
smith.hpayne@xplornet.com

Horton
2253 Johnston Rd., RR#5
Renfrew, ON K7V 3Z8
Tel: 613-432-6271; *Fax:* 613-432-7298
mjmhorton@xplornet.com
www.hortontownship.ca
Municipal Type: Township
Area: 158.38 sq km
County or District: Renfrew; *Population in 2011:* 2,719
Provincial Electoral District(s): Renfrew-Nipissing-Pembroke
Federal Electoral District(s): Renfrew-Nipissing-Pembroke
Next Election: Oct. 27, 2014 (4 year terms)
Don Eady, Mayor
Mackie J. McLaren, Chief Administrative Officer & Clerk

Howick
P.O. Box 89
Hwy 87
Gorrie, ON N0G 1X0
Tel: 519-335-3208; *Fax:* 519-335-6208
office@town.howick.on.ca
www.town.howick.on.ca
Municipal Type: Township
Area: 287.17 sq km
County or District: Huron; *Population in 2011:* 3,856
Provincial Electoral District(s): Huron-Bruce
Federal Electoral District(s): Huron-Bruce
Next Election: Oct. 27, 2014 (4 year terms)
Art Versteeg, Reeve
versteeg@wightman.ca
Genevieve Scharback, Clerk
clerk@town.howick.on.ca

Hudson
903303 Hanbury Rd., RR#2
New Liskeard, ON P0J 1P0
Tel: 705-647-5439; *Fax:* 705-647-6373
harleytwp@parolink.net
www.hudson.ca
Municipal Type: Township
Area: 90.46 sq km
County or District: Timiskaming District; *Population in 2011:* 476
Provincial Electoral District(s): Timiskaming-Cochrane
Federal Electoral District(s): Nipissing-Timiskaming
Next Election: Oct. 27, 2014 (4 year terms)
Larry Craig, Reeve
Michel Lachapelle, Clerk-Treasurer

Huron East, Municipality of
P.O. Box 610
72 Main St. South
Seaforth, ON N0K 1W0
Tel: 519-527-0160; *Fax:* 519-527-2561
webmaster@huroneast.com
www.huroneast.com
Other Information: Toll-Free Phone: 1-888-868-7513
Municipal Type: Town
Incorporated: Jan. 1, 2001 *Area:* 669.16 sq km
County or District: Huron; *Population in 2011:* 9,264
Provincial Electoral District(s): Huron-Bruce
Federal Electoral District(s): Huron-Bruce
Next Election: Oct. 27, 2014 (4 year terms)
Note: Amalgamation of the Town of Seaforth, the Village of Brussels, & the Townships of Grey, McKillop and Tuckersmith.
Bernie MacLellan, Mayor
519-233-7489, Fax: 519-233-3405
mayor@huroneast.com
Brad Knight, Clerk-Administrator
bknight@huroneast.com

Huron Shores
P.O. Box 460
7 Bridge St.
Iron Bridge, ON P0R 1H0
Tel: 705-843-2033; *Fax:* 705-843-2035
email@huronshores.ca
www.huronshores.ca
Municipal Type: Municipality
Area: 455.33 sq km
County or District: Algoma District; *Population in 2011:* 1,723
Provincial Electoral District(s): Algoma-Manitoulin
Federal Electoral District(s): Algoma-Manitoulin-Kapuskasing
Next Election: Oct. 27, 2014 (4 year terms)
Lionel Reeves, Mayor
Deborah Tonelli, AMCT, Administrator-Clerk

Huron-Kinloss
P.O. Box 130
21 Queen St.
Ripley, ON N0G 2R0
Tel: 519-395-3735; *Fax:* 519-395-4107
info@huronkinloss.com
www.huronkinloss.com
Municipal Type: Township
Incorporated: 1999 *Area:* 440.59 sq km
County or District: Bruce; *Population in 2011:* 6,790
Provincial Electoral District(s): Huron-Bruce
Federal Electoral District(s): Huron-Bruce
Next Election: Oct. 27, 2014 (4 year terms)
Note: Amalgamation of the Village of Lucknow & the Townships of Ripley-Huron & Kinloss.
Mitch Twolan, Mayor
519-395-0717
mitch.twolan@remax-lx.ca
Sonya Watson, Clerk
clerk@huronkinloss.com

Ignace
P.O. Box 248
34 Hwy. 17 West
Ignace, ON P0T 1T0
Tel: 807-934-2202; *Fax:* 807-934-2864
ecdev@tbaytel.net
www.town.ignace.on.ca
Municipal Type: Township
Incorporated: 1908 *Area:* 72.66 sq km
County or District: Kenora District; *Population in 2011:* 1,202
Provincial Electoral District(s): Kenora-Rainy River
Federal Electoral District(s): Kenora
Next Election: Oct. 27, 2014 (4 year terms)
Lee Kennard, Mayor
elkennard@yahoo.com
Wayne Hanchard, Administrator & Treasurer
admintreasurer@tbaytel.net

Ingersoll
130 Oxford St., 2nd Fl.
Ingersoll, ON N5C 2V5
Tel: 519-485-0120; *Fax:* 519-485-3543
www.ingersoll.ca
Municipal Type: Town
Area: 12.9 sq km
County or District: Oxford; *Population in 2011:* 12,146
Provincial Electoral District(s): Oxford
Federal Electoral District(s): Oxford
Next Election: Oct. 27, 2014 (4 year terms)
Ted J. Comiskey, Mayor
mayor@ingersoll.ca
Fred Freeman, Deputy Mayor & Councillor
ffreeman@ingersoll.ca
John F. Fortner, Councillor
jfortner@ingersoll.ca
Gord Lesser, Councillor
glesser@ingersoll.ca
Dave McLeod, Councillor
dmcleod@ingersoll.ca
Cathy Mott, Councillor
cmott@ingersoll.ca
Kristy Van Kooten-Bossence, Councillor
kvankootenbossence@ingersoll.ca
Marsha Paley, Clerk & Deputy Chief Administrative Officer
clerks@ingersoll.ca
James Timlin, Chief Administrative Officer
jtimlin@ingersoll.ca
Gary Seitz, Treasurer & Director, Finance
Gene McLaren, Director, Engineering Services
Bonnie Ward, Director, Parks & Recreation
Darell Parker, Fire Chief & Deputy Chief Administrative Officer

Innisfil
2101 Innisfil Beach Rd.
Innisfil, ON L9S 1A1
Tel: 705-436-3710; *Fax:* 705-436-7120
www.innisfil.ca
Municipal Type: Town
Incorporated: 1850 *Area:* 284.18 sq km
County or District: Simcoe; *Population in 2011:* 33,079
Provincial Electoral District(s): York Simcoe
Federal Electoral District(s): York-Simcoe; Barrie
Next Election: Oct. 27, 2014 (4 year terms)
Barb Baguley, Mayor
bbaguley@innisfil.ca
Dan Davidson, Deputy Mayor & Councillor
ddavidson@innisfil.ca
Doug Lougheed, Councillor, Ward(s): 1
dlougheed@innisfil.ca

Richard Simpson, Councillor, Ward(s): 2
rsimpson@innisfil.ca
Ken Simpson, Councillor, Ward(s): 3
ksimpson@innisfil.ca
Rod Boynton, Councillor, Ward(s): 4
rboynton@innisfil.ca
Bill Loughead, Councillor, Ward(s): 5
bloughead@innisfil.ca
Maria Baier, Councillor, Ward(s): 6
mbaierinnisfil.ca
Lynn Dollin, Councillor, Ward(s): 7
ldollin@innisfil.ca
Jason Reynar, Clerk & Director, Legal Services
John Skorobohacz, Chief Administrative Officer
Lockie Davis, Chief Financial officer & Director, Finance & Customer Service
Michelle Collette, Director, Human Resources
Kerry Columbus, Director, Community Services
Susan Downs, Director, Strategic Planning
Jim Zimmerman, Director, Infrastructure & Engineering Services
Ross Cotton, Manager, Planning
R. Wayne Young, Manager, Operational Services
Randy Smith, Fire Chief

Iroquois Falls

P.O. Box 230
253 Main St.
Iroquois Falls, ON P0K 1G0
Tel: 705-232-5700; *Fax:* 705-232-4241
www.iroquoisfalls.com
Municipal Type: Town
Area: 599.43 sq km
County or District: Cochrane District; *Population in 2011:* 4,595
Provincial Electoral District(s): Timiskaming-Cochrane
Federal Electoral District(s): Timmins-James Bay
Next Election: Oct. 27, 2014 (4 year terms)
Gilles Forget, Mayor
mayor@iroquoisfalls.com
Michel S. Morrissette, Administrator-Clerk
morrissm@iroquoisfalls.com

James

P.O. Box 10
372 Third St.
Elk Lake, ON P0J 1G0
Tel: 705-678-2237; *Fax:* 705-678-2495
elklake@ntl.sympatico.ca
www.elklake.ca
Municipal Type: Township
Incorporated: 1909 *Area:* 86.19 sq km
County or District: Timiskaming District; *Population in 2011:* 424
Provincial Electoral District(s): Timiskaming-Cochrane
Federal Electoral District(s): Timmins-James Bay
Next Election: Oct. 27, 2014 (4 year terms)
Terry Fiset, Reeve
Myrna J. Hayes, Clerk-Treasurer

Jocelyn

RR#1
Richards Landing, ON P0R 1J0
Tel: 705-246-2025; *Fax:* 705-246-3282
jocelynt@soonet.ca
Municipal Type: Township
Area: 131.37 sq km
County or District: Algoma District; *Population in 2011:* 237
Provincial Electoral District(s): Algoma-Manitoulin
Federal Electoral District(s): Sault Ste Marie
Next Election: Oct. 27, 2014 (4 year terms)
Mark Henderson, Reeve
Janet Boucher, Clerk

Johnson

P.O. Box 160
1 Johnson Dr.
Desbarats, ON P0R 1E0
Tel: 705-782-6601; *Fax:* 705-782-6780
johnsontwp@bellnet.ca
www.johnsontwp.ca
Municipal Type: Township
Area: 119.67 sq km
County or District: Algoma District; *Population in 2011:* 750
Provincial Electoral District(s): Algoma-Manitoulin
Federal Electoral District(s): Sault Ste Marie
Next Election: Oct. 27, 2014 (4 year terms)
Ted Hicks, Mayor
705-782-6348
Ruth Kelso, Clerk & Chief Administrative Officer

Joly

P.O. Box 519
871 Forest Lake Rd.
Sundridge, ON P0A 1Z0
Tel: 705-384-5428; *Fax:* 705-384-0845
twpjoly@on.aibn.com
Municipal Type: Township
Area: 193.82 sq km
County or District: Parry Sound District; *Population in 2011:* 284
Provincial Electoral District(s): Parry Sound-Muskoka
Federal Electoral District(s): Parry Sound-Muskoka
Next Election: Oct. 27, 2014 (4 year terms)
Mario Campese, Reeve
Gerry Whittington, Chief Administrative Officer & Clerk

Kapuskasing

Civic Centre
88 Riverside Dr.
Kapuskasing, ON P5N 1B3
Tel: 705-335-2341; *Fax:* 705-337-1741
townkap@ntl.sympatico.ca
www.kapuskasing.ca
Municipal Type: Town
Incorporated: 1921 *Area:* 83.98 sq km
County or District: Cochrane District; *Population in 2011:* 8,196
Provincial Electoral District(s): Timmins-James Bay
Federal Electoral District(s): Algoma-Manitoulin-Kapuskasing
Next Election: Oct. 27, 2014 (4 year terms)
Alan Spacek, Mayor
Yvan Brousseau, Chief Administrative Officer

Kearney

P.O. Box 38
8 Main St.
Kearney, ON P0A 1M0
Tel: 705-636-7752; *Fax:* 705-636-0527
kearney1@vianet.ca
www.townofkearney.com
Municipal Type: Town
Incorporated: 1908 *Area:* 529.5 sq km
County or District: Parry Sound District; *Population in 2011:* 841
Provincial Electoral District(s): Parry Sound-Muskoka
Federal Electoral District(s): Parry Sound-Muskoka
Next Election: Oct. 27, 2014 (4 year terms)
Paul Tomlinson, Mayor
kearneytomlinson@gmail.com
Yvonne Aubichon, Clerk Administrator
clerkadministrator@townofkearney.com

Kenora

Kenora District Services Board Admin Office
#1, 211 Princess St.
Dryden, ON P8N 3L5
Tel: 807-223-2100; *Fax:* 807-223-6500
kdsb@kdsb.on.ca
www.kdsb.on.ca
Municipal Type: District
Area: 407,192.66 sq km
Population in 2011: 64,419
Phil Vinet, Chair, Kenora District Services Board of Directors, & Councillor
Dan McNeill, Chief Administrative Officer, Kenora District Services Board
dmcneill@kdsb.on.ca

Kerns

903303 Hanbury Rd., RR#2
New Liskeard, ON P0J 1P0
Tel: 705-647-5439; *Fax:* 705-647-6373
harleytwp@parolink.net
www.kerns.ca
Municipal Type: Township
Incorporated: 1904 *Area:* 90.44 sq km
County or District: Timiskaming District; *Population in 2011:* 359
Provincial Electoral District(s): Timiskaming-Cochrane
Federal Electoral District(s): Timmins-James Bay
Next Election: Oct. 27, 2014 (4 year terms)
Terry Phillips, Reeve
Michel Lachapelle, Clerk-Treasurer

Killaloe, Hagarty & Richards

P.O. Box 39
1 John St.
Killaloe, ON K0J 2A0
Tel: 613-757-2300; *Fax:* 613-757-3634
info@khrtownship.ca
www.killaloe-hagarty-richards.ca
Municipal Type: Township
Incorporated: July 1, 2000 *Area:* 395.91 sq km
County or District: Renfrew; *Population in 2011:* 2,402
Provincial Electoral District(s): Renfrew-Nipissing-Pembroke
Federal Electoral District(s): Renfrew-Nipissing-Pembroke
Next Election: Oct. 27, 2014 (4 year terms)
Note: Amalgamation of the Township of Hagarty & Richards & the former Village of Killaloe.
Janice Visneskie, Mayor
moorevisneskie@hotmail.com
Lorna Hudder, Chief Administrative Officer & Clerk-Treasurer
lhudder@khrtownship.ca

Killarney, Municipality of

32 Commissioner St.
Killarney, ON P0M 2A0
Tel: 705-287-2424; *Fax:* 705-287-2660
townkill@vianet.on.ca
www.municipality.killarney.on.ca
Other Information: Toll-Free Phone: 1-888-597-2721
Municipal Type: Town
Incorporated: Jan. 1, 1999 *Area:* 1,513.58 sq km
County or District: Sudbury District; *Population in 2011:* 505
Provincial Electoral District(s): Algoma-Manitoulin
Federal Electoral District(s): Nickel Belt
Next Election: Oct. 27, 2014 (4 year terms)
Morgan Pitfield, Mayor
Candy Beavais, Clerk-Treasurer

Kincardine

1475 Conc. 5, RR#5
Kincardine, ON N2Z 2X6
Tel: 519-396-3468; *Fax:* 519-396-8288
ssmith@kincardine.net
www.kincardine.net
Municipal Type: Municipality
Area: 537.65 sq km
County or District: Bruce; *Population in 2011:* 11,174
Provincial Electoral District(s): Huron-Bruce
Federal Electoral District(s): Huron-Bruce
Next Election: Oct. 27, 2014 (4 year terms)
Larry Kraemer, Mayor
519-395-3130
mayor@kincardine.net
Anne Eadie, Deputy Mayor & Councillor
519-396-6927
aeadie@brucetelecom.com
Ron Coristine, Councillor at Large
519-396-5458
ronc@tnt21.com
Maureen Couture, Councillor at Large
519-395-3629
ronc@tnt21.com
Kenneth Craig, Councillor at Large
519-396-8767
kencraig@bmts.com
Jacqueline Faubert, Councillor, Ward(s): 1
519-396-7240
jfauberb@sfu.ca
Mike Leggett, Councillor, Ward(s): 1
519-396-4529
ff1221@tnt21.com
Candy Hewitt, Councillor, Ward(s): 2
519-395-2461
candyhewitt@hotmail.com
Randy Roppel, Councillor, Ward(s): 3
519-368-7792
Donna MacDougall, Clerk & Acting Chief Administrative Officer
clerk@kincardine.net; cao@kincardine.net
Brenda French, Treasurer
519-396-3468
treasurer@kincardine.net
Michele Barr, Manager, Building & Planning
cbo@kincardine.net
Jim O'Rourke, Manager, Public Works
pwmgr@kincardine.net
Jamie MacKinnon, Fire Chief
kinfirechief@bmts.com
Steve Murray, Coordinator, Community Services
smurray@kincardine.net
Roberta Trelford, Coordinator, Community Emergency Management, & Health & Safety
kinfirecemc@bmts.com
Donna Hardman, Compliance Officer, Public Works
519-396-4660
dhardman@bmts.com

King

2075 King Rd.
King City, ON L7B 1A1
Tel: 905-833-5321; *Fax:* 905-833-2300
online@king.ca
www.king.ca
Municipal Type: Township
Incorporated: 1850 *Area:* 333.04 sq km
County or District: York Reg. Mun.; *Population in 2011:* 19,899
Provincial Electoral District(s): Oak Ridges-Markham;

York-Simcoe
Federal Electoral District(s): Oak Ridges-Markham; York-Simcoe
Next Election: Oct. 27, 2014 (4 year terms)
Steve Pellegrini, Mayor
spellegrini@king.ca
Cleve Mortelliti, Councillor, Ward(s): 1
cmortelliti@king.ca
Peter Grandilli, Councillor, Ward(s): 2
pgrandilli@king.ca
Linda Pabst, Councillor, Ward(s): 3
lpabst@king.ca
Bill Cober, Councillor, Ward(s): 4
bcober@king.ca
Debbie Schaefer, Councillor, Ward(s): 5
dschaefer@king.ca
Avia Eek, Councillor, Ward(s): 6
aeek@king.ca
Kathryn Smyth, Clerk
ksmyth@king.ca
Susan Plamondon, Chief Administrative Officer
splamondon@king.ca
Jeff Schmidt, Director, Finance
jschmidt@king.ca
Judy Laplante, Director, Engineering & Development
jlaplante@king.ca
David Clark, Director, Parks, Recreation & Culture
dclark@king.ca
Marilyn Loan, Manager, Human Resources
mloan@king.ca
Gaspare Ritacca, Manager, Planning & Development
gritacca@king.ca
Bryan Burbidge, Fire Chief
bburbidge@king.ca
Jamie Smyth, Community Development Officer
jsmyth@king.ca

Kirkland Lake

P.O. Box 1757
3 Kirkland St. West
Kirkland Lake, ON P2N 3P4
Tel: 705-567-9361; *Fax:* 705-567-3535
edd@tkl.ca
www.discoverkl.ca
Municipal Type: Town
Incorporated: 1972 *Area:* 262.24 sq km
County or District: Timiskaming District; *Population in 2011:* 8,133
Provincial Electoral District(s): Timiskaming-Cochrane
Federal Electoral District(s): Timmins-James Bay
Next Election: Oct. 27, 2014 (4 year terms)
Note: Formerly known as the Township of Teck.
William Enouy, Mayor
bill.enouy@tkl.ca
Jo Ann Ducharme, Clerk, Department of Corporate Services
joann.ducharme@tkl.ca

La Vallée

P.O. Box 99
56 Church Rd.
Devlin, ON P0W 1C0
Tel: 807-486-3452; *Fax:* 807-486-3863
lavalley@nwonet.net
www.lavallee.ca
Municipal Type: Township
Area: 237.26 sq km
County or District: Rainy River District; *Population in 2011:* 988
Provincial Electoral District(s): Kenora-Rainy River
Federal Electoral District(s): Thunder Bay-Rainy River
Next Election: Oct. 27, 2014 (4 year terms)
Ross Donaldson, Reeve
Sylvia Smeeth, Municipal Clerk

Laird

3 Pumpkin Point Rd., RR#4
Echo Bay, ON P0S 1C0
Tel: 705-248-2395; *Fax:* 705-248-1138
lairdtwp@soonet.ca
www.lairdtownship.ca
Municipal Type: Township
Incorporated: 1891 *Area:* 101.77 sq km
County or District: Algoma District; *Population in 2011:* 1,057
Provincial Electoral District(s): Algoma-Manitoulin
Federal Electoral District(s): Sault Ste Marie
Next Election: Oct. 27, 2014 (4 year terms)
Richard (Dick) Beitz, Mayor
Phyllis L. MacKay, Clerk-Treasurer, Tax Collector, & License Issuing Officer

Lake of Bays

1012 Dwight Beach Rd., RR#1
Dwight, ON P0A 1H0
Tel: 705-635-2272; *Fax:* 705-635-2132
contact@lakeofbays.on.ca
www.lakeofbays.on.ca
Other Information: Toll-Free Phone: 1-877-566-0005
Municipal Type: Township
Incorporated: 1971 *Area:* 671.46 sq km
County or District: Muskoka Dist. Mun.; *Population in 2011:* 3,284
Provincial Electoral District(s): Parry Sound-Muskoka
Federal Electoral District(s): Parry Sound-Muskoka
Next Election: Oct. 27, 2014 (4 year terms)
Note: Amalgamation of the former Townships of Franklin, Ridout, McLean & Sinclair/Finlayson.
Bob Young, Mayor
705-635-1845
ryoung@lakeofbays.on.ca
Don Chevalier, Chief Administrative Officer & Treasurer

Lake of the Woods

P.O. Box 427
211 Fourth St.
Rainy River, ON P0W 1L0
Tel: 807-852-3529; *Fax:* 807-852-3529
www.lakeofthewoods.ca
Municipal Type: Township
Incorporated: Jan. 1, 1998 *Area:* 751.17 sq km
County or District: Rainy River District; *Population in 2011:* 296
Provincial Electoral District(s): Kenora-Rainy River
Federal Electoral District(s): Thunder Bay-Rainy River
Next Election: Oct. 27, 2014 (4 year terms)
Note: Amalgamation of the Township of Morson & McCrosson-Tovell.
Valerie Pizey, Mayor
Patrick W. Giles, Clerk-Treasurer
gllesp@tbaytel.net

Lakeshore

419 Notre Dame Rd.
Belle River, ON N0R 1A0
Tel: 519-728-2700; *Fax:* 519-728-9530
webmaster@lakeshore.ca
www.lakeshore.ca
Municipal Type: Town
Incorporated: 1999 *Area:* 530.32 sq km
County or District: Essex; *Population in 2011:* 34,546
Provincial Electoral District(s): Essex
Federal Electoral District(s): Essex
Next Election: Oct. 27, 2014 (4 year terms)
Note: Amalgamation of the former Town of Belle River & the former Townships of Maidstone, Rochester, Tilbury North & Tilbury West.
Tom Bain, Mayor
tbain@lakeshore.ca
Al Fazio, Deputy Mayor & Councillor
afazio@lakeshore.ca
Len Janisse, Councillor, Ward(s): 1
ljanisse@lakeshore.ca
Dave Monk, Councillor, Ward(s): 2
dmonk@lakeshore.ca
Charles W. McLean, Councillor, Ward(s): 3
cmclean@lakeshore.ca
Steven Bezaire, Councillor, Ward(s): 4
sbezaire@lakeshore.ca
Dan Diemer, Councillor, Ward(s): 5
ddiemer@lakeshore.ca
Linda McKinlay, Councillor, Ward(s): 6
lmckinlay@lakeshore.ca
Mary Masse, Town Clerk
mmasse@lakeshore.ca
Kirk Foran, Acting Chief Administrative Officer & Director, Corporate Services
kforan@lakeshore.ca
Sylvia Rammelaere, Director, Finance & Performance Service
srammelaere@lakeshore.ca
Lee Holling, Director, Community & Development Services
lholling@lakeshore.ca
Tom Touralias, Director, Engineering & Infrastructure Services
ttouralias@lakeshore.ca
Chuck Chevalier, Manager, Public Works
cchevalier@lakeshore.ca
Kim Darroch, Manager, Development Services
kdarroch@lakeshore.ca
Tony DiCiocco, Manager, Engineering Services
tdiciocco@lakeshore.ca
Tony Francisco, Manager, Environmental Services
tfrancisco@lakeshore.ca
Don Williamson, Fire Chief
dwilliamson@lakeshore.ca

Maureen Lesperance, Coordinator, Planning
mlesperance@lakeshore.ca

Lambton Shores

P.O. Box 610
7883 Amtelecom Pkwy.
Forest, ON N0N 1J0
Tel: 519-786-2335; *Fax:* 519-786-2135
administration@lambtonshores.ca
www.lambtonshores.ca
Other Information: Toll-Free Phone: 1-877-786-2335
Municipal Type: Municipality
Incorporated: 2001 *Area:* 331.08 sq km
County or District: Lambton; *Population in 2011:* 10,656
Provincial Electoral District(s): Lambton-Kent-Middlesex
Federal Electoral District(s): Lambton-Kent-Middlesex
Next Election: Oct. 27, 2014 (4 year terms)
Note: Amalgamation of the Towns of Bosanquet & Forest, & the Villages of Thedford, Arkona & Grand Bend.
Bill Weber, Mayor
519-238-1313
bweber@lambtonshores.ca
Elizabeth Davis-Dagg, Deputy Mayor & Councillor
519-899-2535
edavis-dagg@lambtonshores.ca
Dave Maguire, Councillor, Ward(s): 1
dmaguire@lambtonshores.ca
Doug Bonesteel, Councillor, Ward(s): 2
dbonesteel@lambtonshores.ca
Lorie Scott, Councillor, Ward(s): 3
lscott@lambtonshores.ca
Ruth Illman, Councillor, Ward(s): 4
rillman@lambtonshores.ca
Martin Underwood, Councillor, Ward(s): 5
munderwood@lambtonshores.ca
Doug Cook, Councillor, Ward(s): 6
dcook@lambtonshores.ca
John Russell, Councillor, Ward(s): 7
jrussell@lambtonshores.ca
Carol McKenzie, Clerk
cpmckenzie@lambtonshores.ca
John Byrne, Chief Administrative Officer
jbyrne@lambtonshores.ca
Janet Ferguson, Treasurer
jferguson@lambtonshores.ca
Peggy Van Mierlo-West, Director, Community Services
pvmwest@lambtonshores.ca
Patti Richardson, Planner
prichardson@lambtonshores.ca
Allan Little, Superintendent, Drainage, & Construction Inspector
alittle@lambtonshores.ca

Lanark Highlands

P.O. Box 340
75 George St.
Lanark, ON K0G 1K0
Tel: 613-259-2398; *Fax:* 613-259-2291
mailbag@lanarkhighlands.ca
www.lanarkhighlands.ca
Other Information: Toll-Free Phone: 1-800-239-4695
Municipal Type: Township
Incorporated: July 1, 1997 *Area:* 1,033.3 sq km
County or District: Lanark; *Population in 2011:* 5,128
Provincial Electoral District(s): Lanark-Frontenac-Lennox & Addington
Federal Electoral District(s): Lanark-Frontenac-Lennox & Addington
Next Election: Oct. 27, 2014 (4 year terms)
Note: Amalgamation of North West Lanark Township & Darling Township.
Peter McLaren, Mayor
Ross Trimble, Chief Administrative Officer & Clerk
rtrimble@lanarkhighlands.ca

Larder Lake

P.O. Box 40
13 Godfrey St.
Larder Lake, ON P0K 1L0
Tel: 705-643-2158; *Fax:* 705-643-2311
www.larderlake.net
Municipal Type: Township
Area: 228.73 sq km
County or District: Timiskaming District; *Population in 2011:* 684
Provincial Electoral District(s): Timiskaming-Cochrane
Federal Electoral District(s): Timmins-James Bay
Next Election: Oct. 27, 2014 (4 year terms)
Patricia Bodick, Reeve
Jim Roman, Clerk-Treasurer
jroman@ntl.sympatico.ca

LaSalle
5950 Malden Rd.
Lasalle, ON N9H 1S4
Tel: 519-969-7770; *Fax:* 519-969-4469
webmaster@town.lasalle.on.ca
www.town.lasalle.on.ca
Municipal Type: Town
Incorporated: 1924 *Area:* 65.25 sq km
County or District: Essex; *Population in 2011:* 28,643
Provincial Electoral District(s): Essex
Federal Electoral District(s): Essex
Next Election: Oct. 27, 2014 (4 year terms)
Note: Dissolved into Township of Sandwich West in 1959. Status & name change to Town of LaSalle in 1991.
Ken Antaya, Mayor
mayor@town.lasalle.on.ca
Mark Carrick, Deputy Mayor & Councillor
mcarrick@town.lasalle.on.ca
Marc Bondy, Councillor
mbondy@town.lasalle.on.ca
Terry Burns, Councillor
tburns@town.lasalle.on.ca
Sue Desjarlais, Councillor
sdesjarl@town.lasalle.on.ca
Crystal B. Meloche, Councillor
cmeloche@town.lasalle.on.ca
Ray Renaud, Councillor
rrenaud@town.lasalle.on.ca
Brenda Andreatta, Clerk
bandreat@town.lasalle.on.ca
Kevin Miller, Chief Administrative Officer
kmiller@town.lasalle.on.ca
Joe Milicia, Treasurer
jmilicia@town.lasalle.on.ca
Larry Silani, Director, Planning & Development Services
lsilani@town.lasalle.on.ca
Robert Hayes, P. Eng, Town Engineer
rhayes@town.lasalle.on.ca

Latchford
P.O. Box 10
10 Main St.
Latchford, ON P0J 1N0
Tel: 705-676-2416; *Fax:* 705-676-2121
www.latchford.ca
Municipal Type: Town
Incorporated: 1907 *Area:* 153.27 sq km
County or District: Timiskaming District; *Population in 2011:* 387
Provincial Electoral District(s): Timiskaming-Cochrane
Federal Electoral District(s): Nipissing-Timiskaming
Next Election: Oct. 27, 2014 (4 year terms)
George Lefebvre, Mayor
glefebvre@latchford.ca
Jaime Allen, Municipal Clerk
jallen@latchford.ca

Laurentian Hills
34465 Hwy. 17, RR#1
Deep River, ON K0J 1P0
Tel: 613-584-3114; *Fax:* 613-584-3285
info@laurentianhills.ca
www.laurentianhills.ca
Municipal Type: Town
Incorporated: Jan. 1, 2000 *Area:* 640.37 sq km
County or District: Renfrew; *Population in 2011:* 2,811
Provincial Electoral District(s): Renfrew-Nipissing-Pembroke
Federal Electoral District(s): Renfrew-Nipissing-Pembroke
Next Election: Oct. 27, 2014 (4 year terms)
Note: Amalgamation of the United Townships of Rolph, Buchanan, Wylie & McKay & the Village of Chalk River.
Richard Rabishaw, Mayor
mayor@laurentianhills.ca
Wayne T. Kirby, Chief Administrative Officer & Clerk
cao@laurentianhills.ca

Laurentian Valley
460 Witt Rd., RR#4
Pembroke, ON K8A 6W5
Tel: 613-735-6291; *Fax:* 613-735-5820
laurentian@laurvall.on.ca
www.laurentianvalleytwsp.on.ca
Municipal Type: Township
Incorporated: Jan. 1, 2000 *Area:* 552.44 sq km
County or District: Renfrew; *Population in 2011:* 9,657
Provincial Electoral District(s): Renfrew-Nipissing-Pembroke
Federal Electoral District(s): Renfrew-Nipissing-Pembroke
Next Election: Oct. 27, 2014 (4 year terms)
Note: Amalgamation of the former Townships of Stafford-Pembroke & Alice & Fraser.
Jack Wilson, Mayor
613-732-9281
John Baird, Chief Administrative Officer & Clerk

Leamington
111 Erie St. North
Leamington, ON N8H 2Z3
Tel: 519-326-5761; *Fax:* 519-326-2481
info@leamington.ca
www.leamington.ca
Other Information: E-mail, Public Works: publicworks@leamington.ca
Municipal Type: Municipality
Incorporated: 1874 *Area:* 261.92 sq km
County or District: Essex; *Population in 2011:* 28,403
Provincial Electoral District(s): Chatham-Kent-Essex
Federal Electoral District(s): Chatham-Kent-Essex
Next Election: Oct. 27, 2014 (4 year terms)
Note: Incorporated as a town in 1890. Restructuring occurred in 1999.
John Paterson, Mayor
519-326-5761
councilmembers@leamington.ca
Charlie Wright, Deputy Mayor & Councillor
Rick Atkin, Councillor
Chris Chopchik, Councillor
John Jacobs, Councillor
Hilda MacDonald, Councillor
Larry Verbeke, Councillor
Brian R. Sweet, B.A., LL.B, Municipal Clerk, Corporate Counsel & Director, Corporate Services
clerk@leamington.ca
William J. Marck, B.A., LL.B, Chief Administrative Officer
bmarck@leamington.ca
Cheryl L. Horrobin, B.Comm, CA, AMCT, Director, Finance & Business Services
Tracey Pillon-Abbs, Director, Development Services
Robert Sharon, Director, Community Services
Chuck Parsons, Fire Chief
Bechara Daher, Manager, Building Services
Allan Botham, Manager, Engineering
Cameron McKay, Manager, Public Works
Kit Woods, Manager, Environmental Services
Gary Foisy, Superintendent, Water Services

Leeds & Grenville
#100, 25 Central Ave. West
Brockville, ON K6V 4N6
Tel: 613-342-3840; *Fax:* 613-342-2101
www.uclg.ca
Other Information: Toll-Free Phone: 1-800-770-2170
Municipal Type: United County
Area: 3,350.18 sq km
Population in 2011: 99,306
Next Election: Oct. 27, 2014 (4 year terms)
Mel Campbell, Warden & Councillor, Ward(s): Augusta Township
Herb Scott, Councillor, Ward(s): Athens Township
William Sloan, Councillor, Ward(s): Edwardsburgh/Cardinal Township
Jim Pickard, Councillor, Ward(s): Elizabethtown-Kitley Township
Roger Haley, Councillor, Ward(s): Front of Yonge Township
Bruce Bryan, Councillor, Ward(s): Leeds & the Thousand Islands

J. Douglas Struthers, Councillor, Ward(s): Merrickville-Wolford
David Gordon, Councillor, Ward(s): North Grenville Municipality
Ronald E. Holman, Councillor, Ward(s): Rideau Lakes Township
William (Bill) L. Thake, Councillor, Ward(s): Westport
Lesley Todd, Clerk
Steven Silver, Chief Administrative Officer
Nigel White, Treasurer & Director, Corporate Services
Leslie Shepherd, Director, Works, Planning Services & Asset Management
Alison Tutak, Director, Human Services
James Alexander (Sandy) Hay, County Planner
Ann Weir, Manager, Economic Development
Dan Chevrier, Manager, Emergency Medical Services (EMS) Division
Kristen Hobbs, Manager, Human Resources
Geoff McVey, Manager, Forest

Leeds & The Thousand Islands
P.O. Box 129
1233 Prince St.
Lansdowne, ON K0E 1L0
Tel: 613-659-2415
www.townshipleeds.on.ca
Other Information: Toll-Free Phone: 1-866-220-2327
Municipal Type: Township
Incorporated: Jan. 1, 2001 *Area:* 607.18 sq km
County or District: Leeds & Grenville; *Population in 2011:* 9,277
Provincial Electoral District(s): Leeds-Grenville
Federal Electoral District(s): Leeds-Grenville
Next Election: Oct. 27, 2014 (4 year terms)
Note: Amalgamation of Front of Leeds & Lansdowne, Rear of Leeds & Lansdowne & Front of Escott.
Bruce Bryan, Mayor
bbryan@townshipleeds.on.ca
Vanessa Latimer, AMCT, Clerk
vanessa@townshipleeds.on.ca

Limerick
89 Limerick Lake Rd., RR#2
Gilmour, ON K0L 1W0
Tel: 613-474-2863; *Fax:* 613-474-0478
assistant@township.limerick.on.ca
www.township.limerick.on.ca
Municipal Type: Township
Incorporated: 1887 *Area:* 200.59 sq km
County or District: Hastings; *Population in 2011:* 352
Provincial Electoral District(s): Prince Edward-Hastings
Federal Electoral District(s): Prince Edward-Hastings
Next Election: Oct. 27, 2014 (4 year terms)
David Golem, Reeve
613-474-0803
Jennifer Trumble, Clerk-Treasurer
613-474-2863
clerk@township.limerick.on.ca

Lincoln
4800 South Service Rd.
Beamsville, ON L0R 1B1
Tel: 905-563-8205; *Fax:* 905-563-6566
info@lincoln.ca
www.lincoln.ca
Municipal Type: Town
Incorporated: Jan. 1, 1970 *Area:* 162.86 sq km
County or District: Niagara Reg. Mun.; *Population in 2011:* 22,487
Provincial Electoral District(s): Niagara West-Glanbrook
Federal Electoral District(s): Niagara West-Glanbrook
Next Election: Oct. 27, 2014 (4 year terms)
Note: Amalgamation of the Town of Beamsville, the Township of Clinton, & part of the Township of Louth.
Bill Hodgson, Mayor
bhodgson@lincoln.ca
Dianne Rintjema, Councillor, Ward(s): 1
drintjema@lincoln.ca
Robert Foster, Councillor, Ward(s): 1
rfoster@lincoln.ca
John A. Kralt, Councillor, Ward(s): 2
jkralt@lincoln.ca
John D. Pachereva, Councillor, Ward(s): 2
jdpachereva@lincoln.ca
Robert Condotta, Councillor, Ward(s): 3
rcondotta@lincoln.ca
Dave A. Thomson, Councillor, Ward(s): 3
Geoffrey Barlow, Councillor, Ward(s): 4
gbarlow@lincoln.ca
Wayne MacMillan, Councillor, Ward(s): 4
wmacmillan@lincoln.ca
William J. Kolasa, Clerk & Director, Corporate Services
wkolasa@lincoln.ca
Anne Louise Heron, Chief Administrative Officer
aheron@lincoln.ca
Robert Spadoni, Director, Finance
bspadoni@lincoln.ca
Kathleen Dale, Director, Planning & Development
kdale@lincoln.ca
Doug Kerr, Director, Public Works
dkerr@lincoln.ca
Judy Pease, Director, Community Services
jpease@lincoln.ca
Scott Blake, Fire Chief
sblake@lincoln.ca
Andrew Greenaway, Chief Building Official
agreenaway@lincoln.ca
Greg Lancaster, Manager, Facilities & Parks
glancaster@lincoln.ca

Loyalist
P.O. Box 70
263 Main St.
Odessa, ON K0H 2H0
Tel: 613-386-7351; *Fax:* 613-386-3833
www.loyalisttownship.ca
Municipal Type: Township
Incorporated: 1998 *Area:* 340.02 sq km
County or District: Lennox & Addington; *Population in 2011:* 16,221
Provincial Electoral District(s): Lanark-Frontenac-Lennox & Addington
Federal Electoral District(s): Lanark-Frontenac-Lennox & Addington
Next Election: Oct. 27, 2014 (4 year terms)

Note: Amalgamation of the Townships of Ernestown, Amherst Island & the Village of Bath.
Bill Lowry, Mayor
blowry@loyalist.ca
Ric Bresee, Deputy Mayor
rbresee@gmail.com
Duncan Ashley, Councillor, Ward(s): 1 Amherst Island
Ed Daniliunas, Councillor, Ward(s): 2 Bath
Jim Hegadorn, Councillor, Ward(s): 3 Ernestown
John Ibey, Councillor, Ward(s): 3 Ernestown
Penny Porter, Councillor, Ward(s): 3 Ernestown
Brenda Hamilton, Township Clerk
Diane Pearce, Chief Administrative Officer
Alida Moffatt, Director, Finance
Cindy Lawson, Director, Recreation
David Thompson, Director, Engineering Services
Murray Beckel, Chief Building Official & Planner
Wayne Calver, Fire Chief
Ed Adams, Manager, Transportaton & Solid Waste
Lorie McFarland, Manager, Utilities
Brenda Martineau, Coordinator, Employee Relations

Lucan Biddulph
P.O. Box 190
33351 Richmond St., RR#3
Lucan, ON N0M 2J0
Tel: 519-227-4491; *Fax:* 519-227-4998
info@lucanbiddulph.on.ca
www.lucanbiddulph.on.ca
Municipal Type: Township
Incorporated: Jan. 1, 1999 *Area:* 169.15 sq km
County or District: Middlesex; *Population in 2011:* 4,338
Provincial Electoral District(s): Lambton-Kent-Middlesex
Federal Electoral District(s): Lambton-Kent-Middlesex
Next Election: Oct. 27, 2014 (4 year terms)
Note: Amalgamation of the Village of Lucan and the Township of Biddulph.
Paul Hodgins, Mayor
phodgins@lucanbiddulph.on.ca
Lisa deBoer, Clerk
ldeboer@lucanbiddulph.on.ca

MacDonald, Meredith & Aberdeen Additional
P.O. Box 10
208 Church St.
Echo Bay, ON P0S 1C0
Tel: 705-248-2441
twpmacd@onlink.net
www.echobay.ca
Municipal Type: Township
Incorporated: 1899 *Area:* 161.73 sq km
County or District: Algoma District; *Population in 2011:* 1,464
Provincial Electoral District(s): Algoma-Manitoulin
Federal Electoral District(s): Sault Ste Marie
Next Election: Oct. 27, 2014 (4 year terms)
Lynn Watson, Mayor
Lynne Duguay, Clerk

Machar
P.O. Box 70
73 Municipal Rd. North
South River, ON P0A 1X0
Tel: 705-386-7741; *Fax:* 705-386-0765
www.machartownship.net
Municipal Type: Township
Area: 184.38 sq km
County or District: Parry Sound District; *Population in 2011:* 923
Provincial Electoral District(s): Parry Sound-Muskoka
Federal Electoral District(s): Parry Sound-Muskoka
Next Election: Oct. 27, 2014 (4 year terms)
Douglas Maeck, Mayor
Brenda Paul, AMCT, Clerk-Treasurer
bpaulmachar@vianet.ca

Machin
P.O. Box 249
75 Spruce St.
Vermilion Bay, ON P0V 2V0
Tel: 807-227-2633; *Fax:* 807-227-5443
deputyclerk@visitmachin.com
www.visitmachin.com
Municipal Type: Township
Area: 288.85 sq km
County or District: Kenora District; *Population in 2011:* 935
Provincial Electoral District(s): Kenora-Rainy River
Federal Electoral District(s): Kenora
Next Election: Oct. 27, 2014 (4 year terms)
Joe Ruete, Acting Mayor
Tammy Rob, Clerk-Treasurer
clerktreasurer@visitmachin.com

Madawaska Valley
P.O. Box 1000
85 Bay St.
Barrys Bay, ON K0J 1B0
Tel: 613-756-2747; *Fax:* 613-756-0553
info@madawaskavalley.on.ca
www.madawaskavalley.on.ca
Other Information: Toll-Free Phone: 1-866-222-8699
Municipal Type: Township
Incorporated: Jan. 1, 2001 *Area:* 670.11 sq km
County or District: Renfrew; *Population in 2011:* 4,282
Provincial Electoral District(s): Renfrew-Nipissing-Pembroke
Federal Electoral District(s): Renfrew-Nipissing-Pembroke
Next Election: Oct. 27, 2014 (4 year terms)
Note: Amalgamation of Barry's Bay Village, Radcliffe Township & Sherwood, Jones & Burns Township.
David M. Shulist, Mayor
613-756-5200
mayor@madawaskavalley.ca
Pat Pilgrim, C.M.O., Chief Administrative Officer & Clerk
ppilgrim@madawaskavalley.on.ca

Madoc
P.O. Box 503
15651 Hwy. 62, RR#2
Madoc, ON K0K 2K0
Tel: 613-473-2677; *Fax:* 613-473-5580
www.madoc.ca
Other Information: E-mail, Building: building@madoc.ca
Municipal Type: Township
Incorporated: 1850 *Area:* 269.98 sq km
County or District: Hastings; *Population in 2011:* 2,197
Provincial Electoral District(s): Prince Edward-Hastings
Federal Electoral District(s): Prince Edward-Hastings
Next Election: Oct. 27, 2014 (4 year terms)
Robert Sager, Reeve
twpmad@sympatico.ca
W.G. (Bill) Lebow, B.A., AMCT, Clerk Administrator
clerk@madoc.ca

Magnetawan, Municipality of
P.O. Box 70
4304 Hwy. 520
Magnetawan, ON P0A 1P0
Tel: 705-387-3947; *Fax:* 705-387-4875
admin@magnetawan.com
www.magnetawan.com
Other Information: E-mail, Roads: roads@magnetawan.com
Municipal Type: Township
Incorporated: July 4, 1997 *Area:* 523.07 sq km
County or District: Parry Sound District; *Population in 2011:* 1,454
Provincial Electoral District(s): Parry Sound-Muskoka
Federal Electoral District(s): Parry Sound-Muskoka
Next Election: Oct. 27, 2014 (4 year terms)
Sam Dunnett, Mayor
mayor@magnetawan.com
Roger Labelle, Clerk
clerk@magnetawan.com

Malahide
87 John St. South
Aylmer, ON N5H 2C3
Tel: 519-773-5344; *Fax:* 519-773-5334
www.malahide.ca
Municipal Type: Township
Incorporated: Jan. 1, 1998 *Area:* 395.07 sq km
County or District: Elgin; *Population in 2011:* 9,146
Provincial Electoral District(s): Elgin-Middlesex-London
Federal Electoral District(s): Elgin-Middlesex-London
Next Election: Oct. 27, 2014 (4 year terms)
Note: Amalgamation of the Township of Malahide, Village of Springfield & Township of South Dorchester.
Dave Mennill, Mayor
519-773-8850
davemennill@eastlink.ca
Michelle M. Casavecchia, Chief Administrative Officer & Clerk
mcasavecchia@malahide.ca

Manitoulin
Gore Bay, ON

Municipal Type: District
Area: 4,759.74 sq km
Population in 2011: 13,048
Provincial Electoral District(s): Algoma-Manitoulin
Federal Electoral District(s): Algoma-Manitoulin-Kapuskasing
Note: The District incorporates the towns of Gore Bay, & Northeastern Manitoulin & the Islands; communities in the townships of Assiginack, Barrie Isl., Billing, Burpe & Mills, Central Manitoulin, Cockburn Isl., Gordon, & Tehkummah; & 1st Nations reserves

Manitouwadge
1 Mississauga Rd.
Manitouwadge, ON P0T 2C0
Tel: 807-826-3227; *Fax:* 807-826-4592
www.manitouwadge.ca
Municipal Type: Township
Area: 351.97 sq km
County or District: Thunder Bay District; *Population in 2011:* 2,105
Provincial Electoral District(s): Algoma-Manitoulin
Federal Electoral District(s): Algoma-Manitoulin-Kapuskasing
Next Election: Oct. 27, 2014 (4 year terms)
John MacEachern, Mayor
mayor@manitouwadge.ca
Cecile Kerster, Municipal Manager Clerk & Acting Treasurer
ckerster@manitouwadge.ca

Mapleton
P.O. Box 160
7275 Sideroad 3
Drayton, ON N0G 1P0
Tel: 519-638-3313; *Fax:* 519-638-5113
www.mapleton.ca
Other Information: Toll-Free Phone: 1-800-385-7248
Municipal Type: Township
Incorporated: Jan. 1, 1999 *Area:* 534.71 sq km
County or District: Wellington; *Population in 2011:* 9,989
Provincial Electoral District(s): Perth-Wellington
Federal Electoral District(s): Perth-Wellington
Next Election: Oct. 27, 2014 (4 year terms)
Note: Amalgamation of the Townships of Maryborough & Peel & the Village of Drayton.
Bruce Whale, Mayor
519-638-2230
Patty Sinnamon, Chief Administrative Officer & Clerk
psinnamon@town.mapleton.on.ca

Marathon
P.O. Box TM
4 Hemlo Dr.
Marathon, ON P0T 2E0
Tel: 807-229-1340; *Fax:* 807-229-1999
info@marathon.ca; clerk@marathon.ca
www.marathon.ca
Municipal Type: Town
Area: 170.48 sq km
County or District: Thunder Bay District; *Population in 2011:* 3,353
Provincial Electoral District(s): Thunder Bay-Superior North
Federal Electoral District(s): Thunder Bay-Superior North
Next Election: Oct. 27, 2014 (4 year terms)
Rick Dumas, Mayor
mayor@marathon.ca
Brian Tocheri, Chief Administrative Officer & Clerk
cao@marathon.ca

Markstay-Warren, Municipality of
P.O. Box 79
21 Main St. South
Markstay, ON P0M 2G0
Tel: 705-853-4536; *Fax:* 705-853-4964
info@markstay-warren.ca
www.markstay-warren.ca
Other Information: Toll-Free Phone: 1-866-710-1065
Municipal Type: Town
Incorporated: Jan. 1, 1999 *Area:* 510.12 sq km
County or District: Sudbury District; *Population in 2011:* 2,297
Provincial Electoral District(s): Timiskaming-Cochrane
Federal Electoral District(s): Nickel Belt
Next Election: Oct. 27, 2014 (4 year terms)
Note: Amalgamation of the Towns of Warren, Markstay & the Townships of Awrey, Street, Hawley, Loughrin & Henry.
Sonja Flynn, Mayor
sflynn@msdsb.net
Denis Turcot, Chief Administrative Officer & Clerk
dturcot@markstay-warren.ca

Marmora & Lake, Municipality of
P.O. Box 459
12 Bursthall St.
Marmora, ON K0K 2M0
Tel: 613-472-2629; *Fax:* 613-472-5330
www.marmoraandlake.ca
Other Information: Toll-Free Phone: 1-866-518-2282
Municipal Type: Township
Area: 533.75 sq km
County or District: Hastings; *Population in 2011:* 4,074
Provincial Electoral District(s): Prince Edward-Hastings
Federal Electoral District(s): Prince Edward-Hastings
Next Election: Oct. 27, 2014 (4 year terms)
Terry Clemens, Reeve
t.clemens@marmoraandlake.ca

Judy Durbatch, Municipal Clerk
j.durbatch@marmoraandlake.ca

Matachewan
P.O. Box 177
Matachewan, ON P0K 1M0
Tel: 705-565-2274; *Fax:* 705-565-2564
township@ntl.sympatico.ca
www.matachewan.com
Municipal Type: Township
Area: 543.63 sq km
County or District: Timiskaming District; *Population in 2011:* 268
Provincial Electoral District(s): Timiskaming-Cochrane
Federal Electoral District(s): Timmins-James Bay
Next Election: Oct. 27, 2014 (4 year terms)
Beverley Hine, Reeve
Andrew Van Oosten, Chief Administrative Officer & Clerk-Treasurer

Mattawa
P.O. Box 390
160 Water St.
Mattawa, ON P0H 1V0
Tel: 705-744-5611; *Fax:* 705-744-0104
info@mattawa.info
www.mattawa.info
Municipal Type: Town
Area: 3.66 sq km
County or District: Nipissing District; *Population in 2011:* 2,023
Provincial Electoral District(s): Nipissing
Federal Electoral District(s): Nipissing-Timiskaming
Next Election: Oct. 27, 2014 (4 year terms)
Dean Backer, Mayor
Wayne P. Belter, Administrator, Clerk & Treasurer

Mattawan
P.O. Box 610
Mattawa, ON P0H 1V0
Tel: 705-744-5680; *Fax:* 705-744-4141
info@mattawan.info
www.mattawan.info
Municipal Type: Township
Area: 199.52 sq km
County or District: Nipissing District; *Population in 2011:* 162
Provincial Electoral District(s): Nipissing
Federal Electoral District(s): Nipissing-Timiskaming
Next Election: Oct. 27, 2014 (4 year terms)
Peter Murphy, Mayor
Deborah Miller, Clerk

Mattice-Val Côté
P.O. Box 129
500 Hwy. 11
Mattice, ON P0L 1T0
Tel: 705-364-6511; *Fax:* 705-364-6431
mattice@ntl.sympatico.ca
www.nt.net/mattice
Municipal Type: Township
Area: 414.64 sq km
County or District: Cochrane District; *Population in 2011:* 686
Provincial Electoral District(s): Timmins-James Bay
Federal Electoral District(s): Algoma-Manitoulin-Kapuskasing
Next Election: Oct. 27, 2014 (4 year terms)
Jean Louis Brunet, Reeve
Gilbert Brisson, Administrator-Clerk

McDougall
5 Barager Blvd., RR#3
Parry Sound, ON P2A 2W9
Tel: 705-342-5252; *Fax:* 705-342-5573
www.municipalityofmcdougall.com
Municipal Type: Township
Incorporated: May 1, 1872 *Area:* 262.69 sq km
County or District: Parry Sound District; *Population in 2011:* 2,705
Provincial Electoral District(s): Parry Sound-Muskoka
Federal Electoral District(s): Parry Sound-Muskoka
Next Election: Oct. 27, 2014 (4 year terms)
Dale Robinson, Mayor
Tammy Hazzard, Clerk & Secretary

McGarry
P.O. Box 99
27 Webster St.
Virginiatown, ON P0K 1X0
Tel: 705-634-2145; *Fax:* 705-634-2700
admin@mcgarry.ca
www.mcgarry.ca
Municipal Type: Township
Area: 86.05 sq km
County or District: Timiskaming District; *Population in 2011:* 595
Provincial Electoral District(s): Timiskaming-Cochrane
Federal Electoral District(s): Timmins-James Bay
Next Election: Oct. 27, 2014 (4 year terms)
Clermont Lapointe, Reeve
Gary Cunnington, Clerk-Treasurer

McKellar
P.O. Box 69
701 Hwy. 124
McKellar, ON P0G 1C0
Tel: 705-389-2842; *Fax:* 705-389-1244
www.township.mckellar.on.ca
Municipal Type: Township
Incorporated: 1873 *Area:* 177.48 sq km
County or District: Parry Sound District; *Population in 2011:* 1,144
Provincial Electoral District(s): Parry Sound-Muskoka
Federal Electoral District(s): Parry Sound-Muskoka
Next Election: Oct. 27, 2014 (4 year terms)
Peter Hopkins, Reeve
705-389-2842
Shawn Boggs, AMCT, Clerk Administrator

McMurrich-Monteith
P.O. Box 70
31 William St.
Sprucedale, ON P0A 1Y0
Tel: 705-685-7901; *Fax:* 705-685-7393
mcmurric@surenet.net
www.mcmurrichmonteith.com
Municipal Type: Township
Area: 273.33 sq km
County or District: Parry Sound District; *Population in 2011:* 779
Provincial Electoral District(s): Parry Sound-Muskoka
Federal Electoral District(s): Parry Sound-Muskoka
Next Election: Oct. 27, 2014 (4 year terms)
Glynn Robinson, Reeve
705-685-7779
Cheryl Marshall, Clerk

McNab-Braeside
2508 Russett Dr., RR#2
Arnprior, ON K7S 3G8
Tel: 613-623-5756; *Fax:* 613-623-9138
info@mcnabbraeside.com
www.mcnabbraeside.com
Other Information: Toll-Free Phone: 1-800-957-4621
Municipal Type: Township
Incorporated: Jan. 1, 1998 *Area:* 253.87 sq km
County or District: Renfrew; *Population in 2011:* 7,371
Provincial Electoral District(s): Renfrew-Nipissing-Pembroke
Federal Electoral District(s): Renfrew-Nipissing-Pembroke
Next Election: Oct. 27, 2014 (4 year terms)
Note: Amalgamation of Braeside Village & McNab Township.
Mary M. Campbell, Mayor
mcampbell@mcnabbraeside.com
Noreen C. Mellema, CMO, Chief Administrative Officer & Clerk
nmellema@mcnabbraeside.com

Meaford
21 Trowbridge St. West
Meaford, ON N4L 1A1
Tel: 519-538-1060; *Fax:* 519-538-5240
www.meaford.ca
Other Information: Alternate Fax: 519-538-1556
Municipal Type: Municipality
Incorporated: Jan. 1, 2001 *Area:* 588.47 sq km
County or District: Grey; *Population in 2011:* 11,100
Provincial Electoral District(s): Bruce-Grey-Owen Sound
Federal Electoral District(s): Bruce-Grey-Owen Sound
Next Election: Oct. 27, 2014 (4 year terms)
Note: Formerly the Town of Georgian Highlands. Amalgamation of Sydenham, St. Vincent & Meaford.
Francis Richardson, Mayor
519-538-1060
frichardson@meaford.ca
Harley Greenfield, Deputy Mayor & Councillor
519-538-2570
hgreenfield@meaford.ca
Barb Clumpus, Councillor
519-538-3345
bclumpus@meaford.ca
James McIntosh, Councillor
519-538-2306
jmcintosh@meaford.ca
Mike Poetker, Councillor
519-538-4075
mpoetker@meaford.ca
Lynda Stephens, Councillor
519-538-9239
lstephens@meaford.ca
Deborah Young, Councillor
519-379-9646
dyoung@meaford.ca
Pamela Fettes, Clerk
pfettes@meaford.ca
Frank Miele, Chief Administrative Officer
fmiele@meaford.ca
Robert Armstrong, Director, Planning & Building
rarmstrong@meaford.ca
Karen Davies, Director, Human Resources
kdavies@meaford.ca
Stephen Vokes, Director, Operations
svokes@meaford.ca
Rick Carefoot, Chief Building Official
rcarefoot@meaford.ca
Chris Collyer, Chief Operator, Environmental Services
jcollyer@meaford.ca
Steve Nickels, Fire Chief
mmolloy@meaford.ca

Melancthon
157101 Hwy. 10, RR#6
Shelburne, ON L0N 1S9
Tel: 519-925-5525; *Fax:* 519-925-1110
info@melancthontownship.ca
www.melancthontownship.ca
Municipal Type: Township
Incorporated: Jan. 1, 1853 *Area:* 310.88 sq km
County or District: Dufferin; *Population in 2011:* 2,839
Provincial Electoral District(s): Dufferin-Caledon
Federal Electoral District(s): Dufferin-Caledon
Next Election: Oct. 27, 2014 (4 year terms)
Bill Hill, Mayor
519-925-1161
bhill@melancthontownship.ca
Denise B. Holmes, Chief Administrative Officer & Clerk-Treasurer
dholmes@melancthontownship.ca

Merrickville-Wolford
P.O. Box 340
317 Brock St. West
Merrickville, ON K0G 1N0
Tel: 613-269-4791; *Fax:* 613-269-3095
reception@merrickville-wolford.ca
www.merrickville-wolford.ca
Other Information: E-mail, Admin.: admin@merrickville-wolford.ca
Municipal Type: Village
Area: 213.77 sq km
County or District: Leeds-Grenville; *Population in 2011:* 2,850
Provincial Electoral District(s): Leeds-Grenville
Federal Electoral District(s): Leeds-Grenville
Next Election: Oct. 27, 2014 (4 year terms)
J. Douglas Struthers, Mayor
mayor@merrickville-wolford.ca
Jill Eagle, Chief Administrative Officer & Clerk
cao@merrickville-wolford.ca

Middlesex Centre
10227 Ilderton Rd., RR#2
Ilderton, ON N0M 2A0
Tel: 519-666-0190; *Fax:* 519-666-0271
cormans@middlesexcentre.on.ca
www.middlesexcentre.on.ca
Other Information: Toll-Free Phone: 1-800-220-8968
Municipal Type: Township
Incorporated: Jan. 1, 1998 *Area:* 588.05 sq km
County or District: Middlesex; *Population in 2011:* 16,487
Provincial Electoral District(s): Lambton-Kent-Middlesex
Federal Electoral District(s): Lambton-Kent-Middlesex
Next Election: Oct. 27, 2014 (4 year terms)
Note: Amalgamation of the former Townships of Delaware, Lobo, & London.
Al Edmondson, Mayor
edmondson@middlesexcentre.on.ca
Clare Bloomfield, Deputy Mayor
bloomfield@middlesexcentre.on.ca
Stephen Harvey, Councillor, Ward(s): 1
harvey@middlesexcentre.on.ca
John Brennan, Councillor, Ward(s): 2
brennan@middlesexcentre.on.ca
Sharon McMillan, Councillor, Ward(s): 3
mcmillan@middlesexcentre.on.ca
Aina DeViet, Councillor, Ward(s): 4
deviet@middlesexcentre.on.ca
Frank Berze, Councillor, Ward(s): 5
berze@middlesexcentre.on.ca
Stephanie Troyer-Boyd, Clerk
boyds@middlesexcentre.on.ca
Michelle Smibert, Chief Administrative Officer
smibert@middlesexcentre.on.ca

Greg Watterton, Director, Finance & Community Services
watterton@middlesexcentre.on.ca
Maureen A. Looby, Director, Public Works & Engineering
loobym@middlesexcentre.on.ca
Arnie Marsman, Director, Planning & Development Svs., & Chief Building Official
marsmana@middlesexcentre.on.ca
Wayne Shipley, Fire Chief
shipley@middlesexcentre.on.ca
Jim Reeve, Superintendent, Drainage
reevej@middlesexcentre.on.ca
Mauro Castrilli, Coordinator, Transportation
castrilli@middlesexcentre.on.ca
Laura Snobelen, Environmental Technologist
snobelen@middlesexcentre.on.ca

Midland
575 Dominion Ave.
Midland, ON L4R 1R2
Tel: 705-526-4275; *Fax:* 705-526-9971
clerks@midland.ca
www.midland.ca
Other Information: TTY: 705-526-4276, ext. 2824
Municipal Type: Town
Area: 29.09 sq km
County or District: Simcoe; *Population in 2011:* 16,572
Provincial Electoral District(s): Simcoe North
Federal Electoral District(s): Simcoe North
Next Election: Oct. 27, 2014 (4 year terms)
Gordon A. McKay, Mayor
mayor@midland.ca; gmckay@midland.ca
Stephan M. Kramp, Deputy Mayor & Councillor
skramp@midland.ca
Jim Attwood, Councillor, Ward(s): 1
jattwood@midland.ca
Patricia A. File, Councillor, Ward(s): 1
pfile@midland.ca
Zena Pendlebury, Councillor, Ward(s): 1
zpendlebury@midland.ca
Jack H. Charlebois, Councillor, Ward(s): 2
jcharlebois@midland.ca
Bob Jeffery, Councillor, Ward(s): 2
bjeffery@midland.ca
Mike Ross, Councillor, Ward(s): 2
mross@midland.ca
Glen M. Canning, Councillor, Ward(s): 3
gcanning@midland.ca
Karen Desroches, Acting Deputy Clerk
Ted Walker, Chief Administrative Officer
Sue Gignac, Treasurer & Director, Finance
treasury@midland.ca
Shawn Berriault, Director, Public Works
engineering@midland.ca
Wes Crown, Director, Planning & Development
wcrown@midland.ca; planning@midland.ca

Milton
150 Mary St.
Milton, ON L9T 6Z5
Tel: 905-878-7252; *Fax:* 905-878-6995
info@milton.ca
www.milton.ca
Municipal Type: Town
Incorporated: 1857 *Area:* 366.61 sq km
County or District: Halton Regional Municipality; *Population in 2011:* 84,362
Provincial Electoral District(s): Halton
Federal Electoral District(s): Halton
Next Election: Oct. 27, 2014 (4 year terms)
Gordon A. Krantz, Mayor
Tony Lambert, Local & Regional Councillor, Ward(s): South
tonylambert2010@yahoo.com
Colin Best, Local & Regional Councillor, Ward(s): North
Sharon Barkley, Councillor, Ward(s): 1
sharon@sharonbarkley.ca
Greg Nelson, Councillor, Ward(s): 2
Cindy Lunau, Councillor, Ward(s): 3
Rick Malboeuf, Councillor, Ward(s): 4
Arnold Huffman, Councillor, Ward(s): 5
Mike Cluett, Councillor, Ward(s): 6
Rick Di Lorenzo, Councillor, Ward(s): 7
rick@dilorenzo.com
Zeeshan Hamid, Councillor, Ward(s): 8
mail@zhamid.ca
Troy McHarg, Clerk
townclerk@milton.ca
William Mann, P.Eng., Director, Planning & Development
Linda Leeds, Treasurer & Director, Corporate Services
Jennifer Reynolds, Director, Community Services
Brian Ellsworth, P.Eng., Fire Chief

Minden Hills
P.O. Box 359
7 Milne St.
Minden, ON K0M 2K0
Tel: 705-286-1260; *Fax:* 705-286-4917
admin@mindenhills.ca
www.mindenhills.ca
Other Information: Treasury/Bldg./By-law/Planning, Fax: 705-286-6005
Municipal Type: Township
Area: 847.76 sq km
County or District: Haliburton; *Population in 2011:* 5,655
Provincial Electoral District(s): Haliburton-Kawartha Lakes-Brock
Federal Electoral District(s): Haliburton-Kawartha Lakes-Brock
Next Election: Oct. 27, 2014 (4 year terms)
Barb Reid, Reeve
breid@mindenhills.ca
Laura Cunliffe, Clerk
lcunliffe@mindenhills.ca

Minto
5941 Hwy. 89
Harriston, ON N0G 1Z0
Tel: 519-338-2511; *Fax:* 519-338-2005
peg@town.minto.on.ca (Clerical Assistant)
www.town.minto.on.ca
Other Information: E-mail, Treasury: gordon@town.minto.on.ca
Municipal Type: Town
Area: 300.37 sq km
County or District: Wellington; *Population in 2011:* 8,334
Provincial Electoral District(s): Perth-Wellington
Federal Electoral District(s): Perth-Wellington
Next Election: Oct. 27, 2014 (4 year terms)
George Bridge, Mayor
georgeabridge@gmail.com
Bill White, Chief Administrative Officer & Clerk

Mississippi Mills
P.O. Box 400
3131 Old Perth Rd., RR#2
Almonte, ON K0A 1A0
Tel: 613-256-2064; *Fax:* 613-256-4887
town@mississippimills.ca
www.mississippimills.ca
Other Information: Toll-Free Phone: 1-888-779-8666
Municipal Type: Town
Incorporated: Jan. 1, 1998 *Area:* 509.05 sq km
County or District: Lanark; *Population in 2011:* 12,385
Provincial Electoral District(s): Carleton-Mississippi Mills
Federal Electoral District(s): Carleton-Mississippi Mills
Next Election: Oct. 27, 2014 (4 year terms)
Note: Merger of the Town of Almonte with the townships of Ramsay & Pakenham.
John Levi, Mayor
Garry Dalgity, Councillor, Ward(s): Almonte
Rick Minnille, Councillor, Ward(s): Almonte
Bernard Cameron, Councillor, Ward(s): Almonte
Alex Gillis, Councillor, Ward(s): Almonte
Duncan A. Abbott, Councillor, Ward(s): Pakenham
Denzil Ferguson, Councillor, Ward(s): Pakenham
John H. Edwards, Councillor, Ward(s): Ramsay
Shaun J. McLaughlin, Councillor, Ward(s): Ramsay
Paul J. Watters, Councillor, Ward(s): Ramsay
Val Wilkinson, Councillor, Ward(s): Ramsay
Shawna Stone, Town Clerk
sstone@mississippimills.ca
Diane Smithson, Chief Administrative Officer
dsmithson@mississippimills.ca
Rhonda Whitmarsh, Treasurer
rwhitmarsh@mississippimills.ca
Troy Dunlop, Director, Roads & Public Works
tdunlop@mississippimills.ca
Rod Cameron, Manager, Operations
rcameron@mississippimills.ca
Art Brown, Fire Chief
abrown@mississippimills.ca
Sherry Morrison, Chief Building Official
smorrison@mississippimills.ca

Mono
347209 MonoCenter Rd., RR#1
Orangeville, ON L9W 2Y8
Tel: 519-941-3599; *Fax:* 519-941-9490
info@townofmono.com
www.townofmono.com
Municipal Type: Town
Incorporated: June 1, 1999 *Area:* 277.67 sq km
County or District: Dufferin; *Population in 2011:* 7,546
Provincial Electoral District(s): Dufferin-Caledon
Federal Electoral District(s): Dufferin-Caledon
Next Election: Oct. 27, 2014 (4 year terms)
Laura Ryan, Mayor
mayor@townofmono.com
Keith J. McNenly, Chief Administrative Officer & Clerk
keith@townofmono.com

Montague
P.O. Box 755
6547 Roger Stevens Dr.
Smiths Falls, ON K7A 4W6
Tel: 613-283-7478; *Fax:* 613-283-3112
info@township.montague.on.ca
www.township.montague.on.ca
Municipal Type: Township
Area: 277.03 sq km
County or District: Lanark; *Population in 2011:* 3,483
Provincial Electoral District(s): Lanark-Frontenac-Lennox & Addington
Federal Electoral District(s): Lanark-Frontenac-Lennox & Addington
Next Election: Oct. 27, 2014 (4 year terms)
Bill Dobson, Reeve
bdobson@ripnet.com
Katie Valentin, Clerk
kvalentin@township.montague.on.ca

Moonbeam
P.O. Box 330
53 St. Aubin Ave.
Moonbeam, ON P0L 1V0
Tel: 705-367-2244; *Fax:* 705-367-2610
moonbeam@moonbeam.ca
www.moonbeam.ca
Municipal Type: Township
Area: 235.17 sq km
County or District: Cochrane District; *Population in 2011:* 1,101
Provincial Electoral District(s): Timmins-James Bay
Federal Electoral District(s): Algoma-Manitoulin-Kapuskasing
Next Election: Oct. 27, 2014 (4 year terms)
Gilles Audet, Mayor
Carole Gendron, Clerk-Treasurer
cgendron@moonbeam.ca

Moosonee
P.O. Box 727
5 First St.
Moosonee, ON P0L 1Y0
Tel: 705-336-2993; *Fax:* 705-336-2426
www.moosonee.ca
Municipal Type: Town
Area: 555.35 sq km
County or District: Cochrane District; *Population in 2011:* 1,725
Provincial Electoral District(s): Timmins-James Bay
Federal Electoral District(s): Timmins-James Bay
Next Election: Oct. 27, 2014 (4 year terms)
Victor Mitchell, Mayor
Shelley L. Petten, Clerk-Treasurer

Morley
P.O. Box 40
Stratton, ON P0W 1N0
Tel: 807-483-5455; *Fax:* 807-483-5882
morley@nwonet.net
www.townshipofmorley.ca
Municipal Type: Township
Incorporated: 1903 *Area:* 375.61 sq km
County or District: Rainy River District; *Population in 2011:* 474
Provincial Electoral District(s): Kenora-Rainy River
Federal Electoral District(s): Thunder Bay-Rainy River
Next Election: Oct. 27, 2014 (4 year terms)
Gary Gamsby, Reeve
Anna H.M. Boily, CMO, Clerk-Treasurer

Morris-Turnberry
41342 Morris Rd., RR#4
Brussels, ON N0G 1H0
Tel: 519-887-6137; *Fax:* 519-887-6424
morris@scsinternet.com
www.morris-turnberry.on.ca
Municipal Type: Township
Incorporated: Jan. 1, 2001 *Area:* 376.45 sq km
County or District: Huron; *Population in 2011:* 3,413
Provincial Electoral District(s): Huron-Bruce
Federal Electoral District(s): Huron-Bruce
Next Election: Oct. 27, 2014 (4 year terms)
Note: Amalgamation of the Township of Morris & the Township of Turnberry.
Paul Gowing, Mayor
pgowing@hurontel.on.ca
Nancy Michie, Administrator & Clerk-Treasurer
nmichie@morristurnberry.ca

Mulmur
758070 2nd Line East, RR#2
Lisle, ON L0M 1M0
Tel: 705-466-3341; *Fax:* 705-466-2922
info@mulmurtownship.ca
www.mulmurtownship.ca
Other Information: Toll-Free Phone: 1-866-472-0417 (In 519 area code)
Municipal Type: Township
Incorporated: 1851 *Area:* 286.73 sq km
County or District: Dufferin; *Population in 2011:* 3,391
Provincial Electoral District(s): Dufferin-Caledon
Federal Electoral District(s): Dufferin-Caledon
Next Election: Oct. 27, 2014 (4 year terms)
Paul Mills, Mayor
pmills@mulmurtownship.ca
Terry M. Horner, AMCT, Chief Administrative Officer & Clerk
thorner@mulmurtownship.ca

Muskoka Lakes
P.O. Box 129
1 Bailey St.
Port Carling, ON P0B 1J0
Tel: 705-765-3156; *Fax:* 705-765-6755
www.muskokalakes.ca
Municipal Type: Township
Incorporated: Jan. 1971 *Area:* 781.55 sq km
County or District: Muskoka Dist. Mun.; *Population in 2011:* 6,324
Provincial Electoral District(s): Parry Sound-Muskoka
Federal Electoral District(s): Parry Sound-Muskoka
Next Election: Oct. 27, 2014 (4 year terms)
Alice Murphy, Mayor
amurphy@muskokalakes.ca
Cheryl Mortimer, AMCT, Clerk
cmortimer@muskokalakes.ca

Nairn & Hyman
64 McIntyre St.
Nairn Centre, ON P0M 2L0
Tel: 705-869-4232
information@nairncentre.ca
www.nairncentre.ca
Municipal Type: Township
Incorporated: 1896 *Area:* 159.03 sq km
County or District: Sudbury District; *Population in 2011:* 477
Provincial Electoral District(s): Algoma-Manitoulin
Federal Electoral District(s): Algoma-Manitoulin-Kapuskasing
Next Election: Oct. 27, 2014 (4 year terms)
Laurier P. Falldien, Mayor
laurierfalldien@nairncentre.ca
Robert Deschene, Chief Administrative Officer & Clerk-Treasurer

Neebing, Municipality of
4766 Hwy. 61
Thunder Bay, ON P7L 0B5
Tel: 807-474-5331; *Fax:* 807-474-5332
neebing@neebing.org
www.neebing.org
Other Information: Information Phone Line: 807-474-5338
Municipal Type: Town
Area: 875.51 sq km
County or District: Thunder Bay District; *Population in 2011:* 1,986
Provincial Electoral District(s): Thunder Bay-Atikokan
Federal Electoral District(s): Thunder Bay-Rainy River
Next Election: Oct. 27, 2014 (4 year terms)
Ziggy Polkowski, Mayor
Delma Stajkowski, AMCT, Clerk

New Tecumseth
Town Administration Centre
P.O. Box 910
10 Wellington St. East
Alliston, ON L9R 1A1
Tel: 705-435-6219; *Fax:* 705-435-2873
www.town.newtecumseth.on.ca
Other Information: Alternative Phone: 905-729-0057
Municipal Type: Town
Incorporated: Jan. 1991 *Area:* 274.18 sq km
County or District: Simcoe; *Population in 2011:* 30,234
Provincial Electoral District(s): Simcoe-Grey
Federal Electoral District(s): Simcoe-Grey
Next Election: Oct. 27, 2014 (4 year terms)
Mike MacEachern, Mayor
mayor@town.newtecumseth.on.ca
Rick Milne, Deputy Mayor & Councillor
deputymayor@town.newtecumseth.on.ca
Bob Marrs, Councillor, Ward(s): 1
ward.1@town.newtecumseth.on.ca
Jamie Smith, Councillor, Ward(s): 2
ward.2@town.newtecumseth.on.ca
J.J. Paul Whiteside, Councillor, Ward(s): 3
ward.3@town.newtecumseth.on.ca
Fran Sainsbury, Councillor, Ward(s): 4
ward.4@town.newtecumseth.on.ca
Donna Jebb, Councillor, Ward(s): 5
ward.5@town.newtecumseth.on.ca
Richard Norcross, Councillor, Ward(s): 6
ward.6@town.newtecumseth.on.ca
Bruce Haire, Councillor, Ward(s): 7
ward.7@town.newtecumseth.on.ca
Jim Stone, Councillor, Ward(s): 8
ward.8@town.newtecumseth.on.ca
Cheryl McCarroll, Clerk & Manager, Administration
Terri Caron, Chief Administrative Officer
Mark Sirr, Treasurer & Manager, Finance
Eric Chandler, Manager, Planning
Ray Osmond, Manager, Parks, Recreation & Culture
Chad Horan, Manager, Public Works
Hilary McCormack, Manager, Human Resources
John Miller, Manager, Building Standards & Chief Building Official
Rick Vatri, Manager, Engineering
Dan Heydon, Fire Chief

Newbury
P.O. Box 130
22910 Hagerty Rd.
Newbury, ON N0L 1Z0
Tel: 519-693-4941; *Fax:* 519-693-4340
vnewbury@on.aibn.com
www.newbury.ca
Municipal Type: Village
Incorporated: 1873 *Area:* 1.85 sq km
County or District: Middlesex; *Population in 2011:* 447
Provincial Electoral District(s): Lambton-Kent-Middlesex
Federal Electoral District(s): Lambton-Kent-Middlesex
Next Election: Oct. 27, 2014 (4 year terms)
Diane Brewer, Reeve
Betty D. Gordon, Clerk-Treasurer

Niagara-on-the-Lake
P.O. Box 100
1593 Four Mile Creek Rd.
Virgil, ON L0S 1T0
Tel: 905-468-3266; *Fax:* 905-468-2959
webinquiry@notl.org
www.notl.org
Municipal Type: Town
Area: 132.83 sq km
County or District: Niagara Reg. Mun.; *Population in 2011:* 15,400
Provincial Electoral District(s): Niagara Falls
Federal Electoral District(s): Niagara Falls
Next Election: Oct. 27, 2014 (4 year terms)
David Eke, Mayor
deke@notl.org
Dave Lepp, Regional Councillor
dave.lepp@niagararegion.ca
Maria Bau-Coote, Deputy Mayor & Councillor
mbau-coote@notl.org
Jim Collard, Councillor
jcollard@notl.org
Dennis Dick, Councillor
ddick@notl.org
Terry Flynn, Councillor
tflynn@notl.org
Andrea Kaiser, Councillor
akaiser@notl.org
Jamie R. King, Councillor
jking@notl.org
Martin Mazza, Councillor
mmazza@notl.org
Gary Zalepa, Jr., Councillor
gzalepajr@notl.org
Holly Dowd, Town Clerk
hdowd@notl.org
Mike Galloway, Chief Administrative Officer
mgalloway@notl.org
Sheldon Randall, CMA, Director, Corporate Services
srandall@notl.org
Will Walker, Interim Director, Community & Development Services
wwalker@notl.org
Clive Buist, Director, Parks & Recreation
cbuist@notl.org
E. Kuczera, Director, Public Works
ekuczera@notl.org
Greg Warner, Acting Fire Chief
Larry Higgins, Supervisor, Water & Wastewater
lhiggins@notl.org
J. Darren MacKenzie, Superintendent, Irrigation & Drainage
dmackenzie@notl.org

Nipigon
P.O. Box 160
52 Front St.
Nipigon, ON P0T 2J0
Tel: 807-887-3135; *Fax:* 807-887-3564
info@nipigon.net
www.nipigon.net
Other Information: E-mail, Recreation Inquiries: nipigonrec@shaw.ca
Municipal Type: Township
Area: 109.14 sq km
County or District: Thunder Bay District; *Population in 2011:* 1,631
Provincial Electoral District(s): Thunder Bay-Superior North
Federal Electoral District(s): Thunder Bay-Superior North
Next Election: Oct. 27, 2014 (4 year terms)
Richard Harvey, Mayor
richardharvey@nipigon.net
Lindsay Mannila, Chief Administrative Officer

Nipissing
45 Beatty St.
Nipissing, ON P0H 1W0
Tel: 705-724-2144; *Fax:* 705-724-5385
www.nipissingtownship.com
Municipal Type: Township
Area: 387.4 sq km
County or District: Parry Sound District; *Population in 2011:* 1,704
Provincial Electoral District(s): Nipissing; Timiskaming-Cochrane
Federal Electoral District(s): Nipissing-Timiskaming
Next Election: Oct. 27, 2014 (4 year terms)
Pat Haufe, Mayor
705-729-5343
Charles H. Barton, Chief Administrative Officer & Clerk

Nipissing
District Social Services Administration Bd.
P.O. Box 750
200 McIntyre St. East
North Bay, ON P1B 8J8
Municipal Type: District
Area: 17,065.07 sq km
Population in 2011: 84,736
George Maroosis, Chair, District of Nipissing Social Services Administration Board
705-474-2151, Fax: 705-474-0136
Leo Deloyde, CAO, District of Nipissing Social Services Administration Board
705-474-2151, Fax: 705-474-7155
Leo.deloyde@dnssab.on.ca

North Algona Wilberforce
1091 Shaw Woods Rd., RR#1
Eganville, ON K0J 1T0
Tel: 613-628-2080; *Fax:* 613-628-3341
naw@nalgonawil.com
www.nalgonawil.com
Municipal Type: Township
Incorporated: Jan. 1, 1999 *Area:* 378.53 sq km
County or District: Renfrew; *Population in 2011:* 2,873
Provincial Electoral District(s): Renfrew-Nipissing-Pembroke
Federal Electoral District(s): Renfrew-Nipissing-Pembroke
Next Election: Oct. 27, 2014 (4 year terms)
Note: Amalgamation of North Algona Township & Wilberforce Township.
Harold Weckworth, Mayor
Marilyn M. Schruder, Clerk-Treasurer

North Dumfries
1171 Greenfield Rd., RR#4
Cambridge, ON N1R 5S5
Tel: 519-621-0340; *Fax:* 519-623-7641
www.northdumfries.ca
Other Information: Toll-Free Phone: 1-800-563-5595
Municipal Type: Township
Area: 187.22 sq km
County or District: Waterloo Regional Municipality; *Population in 2011:* 9,334
Provincial Electoral District(s): Cambridge
Federal Electoral District(s): Cambridge
Next Election: Oct. 27, 2014 (4 year terms)
Robert Deutschmann, Mayor
519-574-4001
Roger Mordue, Chief Administrative Officer & Clerk
519-621-0340

North Dundas
P.O. Box 489
636 St. Lawrence St.
Winchester, ON K0C 2K0
Tel: 613-774-2105; *Fax:* 613-774-5699
info@northdundas.com
www.northdundas.com
Other Information: Toll-Free Phone: 1-800-795-0437
Municipal Type: Township
Incorporated: Jan. 1, 1998 *Area:* 503.18 sq km
County or District: Stormont, Dundas & Glengarry; *Population in 2011:* 11,225
Provincial Electoral District(s): Stormont-Dundas-South Glengarry
Federal Electoral District(s): Stormont-Dundas-South Glengarry
Next Election: Oct. 27, 2014 (4 year terms)
Note: Amalgamation of the former Townships of Winchester & Mountain & the villages of Chesterville & Winchester.
Eric Duncan, Mayor
613-774-1081
eduncan2@gmail.com
Gerry Boyce, Deputy Mayor
613-989-2330
glboyce@hotmail.com
Allan Armstrong, Councillor
613-774-0752
alarmstrong@bell.net
Tony Fraser, Councillor
613-774-2182
tonyfraser@personainternet.com
John Thompson, Councillor
613-448-2963
jthompsonelect@hotmail.com
Jo-Anne McCaslin, Clerk
613-774-2105
jmccaslin@northdundas.com
Howard F. Smith, Chief Administrative Officer
613-774-2105
hsmith@northdundas.com
John J. Gareau, CA, AMCT, Treasurer
jgareau@northdundas.com
Greg Trizisky, Chief Building Official & Officer, Property Standards
613-774-2105
gtrizisky@northdundas.com
Arden Carruthers, Director, Public Works, & Fire Chief, Morewood
613-774-2105
acarruthers@northdundas.com
Mark Guy, Director, Recreation & Culture
mguy@northdundas.com
Calvin Pol, BES, MCIP, RPP, Director, Planning, Building, & Enforcement
613-774-2105
cpol@northdundas.com
Rob Hunter, Officer, Economic Development & Communications
613-774-2105
rhunter@northdundas.com
Doug Froats, Coordinator, Waste Management
dfroats@northdundas.com
Mike Gruich, Fire Chief, Chesterville
Dan Kelly, Fire Chief, Winchester
Scott Patterson, Fire Chief, Mountain

North Frontenac
P.O. Box 97
6648 Rd. 506
Plevna, ON K0H 2M0
Tel: 613-479-2231; *Fax:* 613-479-2352
info@northfrontenac.ca
www.northfrontenac.com
Other Information: Toll-Free Phone: 1-800-234-3953
Municipal Type: Township
Incorporated: Jan. 1, 1998 *Area:* 1,135.75 sq km
County or District: Frontenac; *Population in 2011:* 1,842
Provincial Electoral District(s): Hastings-Frontenac-Lennox & Addington
Federal Electoral District(s): Lanark-Frontenac-Lennox & Addington
Next Election: Oct. 27, 2014 (4 year terms)
Bud Clayton, Mayor
613-966-9222
dundiggin@xplornet.ca
Jenny Duhamel, Clerk & Manager, Planning
613-479-2231
clerkplanning@northfrontenac.ca

North Glengarry
P.O. Box 700
90 Main St. South
Alexandria, ON K0C 1A0
Tel: 613-525-1110; *Fax:* 613-525-1649
www.northglengarry.ca
Municipal Type: Township
Area: 642.4 sq km
County or District: Stormont, Dundas & Glengarry; *Population in 2011:* 10,251
Provincial Electoral District(s): Glengarry-Prescott-Russell
Federal Electoral District(s): Glengarry-Prescott-Russell
Next Election: Oct. 27, 2014 (4 year terms)
Grant E. Crack, Mayor
613-525-1110, Fax: 613-525-1649
Chris McDonell, Deputy Mayor & Councillor
613-525-1110
Gary Shepherd, Councillor at Large
613-525-1110
Jamie MacDonald, Councillor, Ward(s): Alexandria
613-525-1110
Jim Picken, Councillor, Ward(s): Kenyon
613-525-1110
Eric MacSweyn, Councillor, Ward(s): Lochiel
613-525-1110
Carma Williams, Councillor, Ward(s): Maxville
613-525-1110
Daniel Gagnon, Chief Administrative Officer
613-525-1110
Johanna (Annie) Levac, Treasurer
613-525-1110
André Bachand, Manager, Public Works
613-525-1110
Dean McDonald, Manager, Water Works
613-525-1110
Gerry Murphy, Manager, Planning & By-law Enforcement, & Chief Building Official
613-525-1110
Stephane Ouimet, Director, Recreation
613-525-0614
Manson Barton, Superintendent, Drainage & Beaver Management
613-525-1110

North Grenville
P.O. Box 130
285 County Rd. 44
Kemptville, ON K0G 1J0
Tel: 613-258-9569; *Fax:* 613-258-9620
www.northgrenville.ca
Municipal Type: MN
Incorporated: July 14, 2003 *Area:* 350.14 sq km
County or District: Leeds-Grenville; *Population in 2011:* 15,085
Provincial Electoral District(s): Leeds-Grenville
Federal Electoral District(s): Leeds-Grenville
Next Election: Oct. 27, 2014 (4 year terms)
David Gordon, Mayor
613-258-9569
dgordon@northgrenville.on.ca
Ken Finnerty, Deputy Mayor
613-258-9569
kfinnerty@northgrenville.on.ca
Terry Butler, Councillor
613-258-9569, Fax: 613-258-9620
tbutler@northgrenville.on.ca
Tim Sutton, Councillor
613-258-9569, Fax: 613-258-9620
tsutton@northgrenville.on.ca
Barb Tobin, Councillor
613-258-9569, Fax: 613-258-9620
btobin@northgrenville.on.ca
Cahl Pominville, Clerk & Director, Corporate Services
cpominville@northgrenville.on.ca
Andy Brown, Chief Administrative Officer
abrown@northgrenville.on.ca
Sheila Kehoe, Treasurer
skehoe@northgrenville.on.ca
Karen Dunlop, Director, Public Works
kdunlop@northgrenville.on.ca
Darren Patmore, Director, Parks, Recreation & Culture
dpatmore@northgrenville.on.ca
Forbes Symon, Director, Planning & Development
fsymon@northgrenville.on.ca
Paul Hutt, Fire Chief
phutt@northgrenville.on.ca
Randy Wilkinson, Chief Building Official
rwilkinson@northgrenville.on.ca
Gary Boal, Superintendent, Waste Site
613-258-9677
Doug Scott, Superintendent, Roads
dscott@northgrenville.on.ca
Mark Tenbult, Engineering Technologist
mtenbult@northgrenville.on.ca
Gary Simser, Technician, Regulatory Water / Wastewater Compliance
gsimser@magma.ca

North Huron
P.O. Box 90
274 Josephine St.
Wingham, ON N0G 2W0
Tel: 519-357-3550; *Fax:* 519-357-1110
www.northhuron.ca
Municipal Type: Township
Incorporated: Jan. 1, 2001 *Area:* 178.98 sq km
County or District: Huron; *Population in 2011:* 4,884
Provincial Electoral District(s): Huron-Bruce
Federal Electoral District(s): Huron-Bruce
Next Election: Oct. 27, 2014 (4 year terms)
Note: Amalgamation of the Village of Blyth, the Township of East Wawanosh & the Town of Wingham.
Neil Vincent, Reeve
519-357-2336
nvincent@northhuron.ca
Gary Long, Clerk Administrator
519-357-3550

North Kawartha
P.O. Box 550
280 Burleigh St.
Apsley, ON K0L 1A0
Tel: 705-656-4445; *Fax:* 705-656-4446
d.page@northkawartha.on.ca (Reception)
www.northkawartha.on.ca
Other Information: Toll-Free Phone: 1-800-755-6931
Municipal Type: Township
Area: 765.02 sq km
County or District: Peterborough; *Population in 2011:* 2,289
Provincial Electoral District(s): Haliburton-Kawartha Lakes-Brock
Federal Electoral District(s): Haliburton-Kawartha Lakes-Brock
Next Election: Oct. 27, 2014 (4 year terms)
Jim Whelan, Reeve
reeve@northkawartha.on.ca
Connie Parent, Clerk
c.parent@northkawartha.on.ca

North Middlesex
Administrative Centre
P.O. Box 9
229 Parkhill Main St.
Parkhill, ON N0M 2K0
Tel: 519-294-6244; *Fax:* 519-294-0573
clerk@northmiddlesex.on.ca
www.northmiddlesex.on.ca
Other Information: Toll-Free Phone: 1-888-793-9637
Municipal Type: Municipality
Incorporated: Jan. 1, 2001 *Area:* 597.86 sq km
County or District: Middlesex; *Population in 2011:* 6,658
Provincial Electoral District(s): Lambton-Kent-Middlesex
Federal Electoral District(s): Lambton-Kent-Middlesex
Next Election: Oct. 27, 2014 (4 year terms)
Note: Amalgamation of the Townships of East Williams, West Williams & McGillivray, the Town of Parkhill & the Village of Ailsa Craig.
Don F. Shipway, Mayor
519-293-3219
donshipway@execulink.com
Linda Creaghe, Chief Administrative Officer
519-294-6244
lindacr@northmiddlesex.on.ca

North Perth
330 Wallace Ave. North
Listowel, ON N4W 1L3
Tel: 519-291-2950
town@northperth.ca
www.northperth.ca
Other Information: Toll-Free Phone: 1-888-714-1993
Municipal Type: Municipality
Incorporated: 1998 *Area:* 493.18 sq km
County or District: Perth; *Population in 2011:* 12,631
Provincial Electoral District(s): Perth-Wellington
Federal Electoral District(s): Perth-Wellington
Next Election: Oct. 27, 2014 (4 year terms)
Note: Amalgamation of Elma Township, Town of Listowel & Wallace Township.
Julie Behrns, Mayor
juliebehrns@northperth.ca
Vince Judge, Deputy Mayor & Councillor
vincejudge@northperth.ca
Kenneth Buchanan, Councillor, Ward(s): Elma
kenbuchanan@northperth.ca

Matt Duncan, Councillor, Ward(s): Elma
mattduncan@northperth.ca
David Ludington, Councillor, Ward(s): Elma
davidludington@northperth.ca
Warren Howard, Councillor, Ward(s): Listowel
warrenhoward@northperth.ca
Doug Kellum, Councillor, Ward(s): Listowel
dougkellum@northperth.ca
Matt Richardson, Councillor, Ward(s): Listowel
mattrichardson@northperth.ca
Paul Horn, Councillor, Ward(s): Wallace
paulhorn@northperth.ca
Meredith Schneider, Councillor, Ward(s): Wallace
Patricia Berfelz, Clerk
519-292-2062
pberfelz@northperth.ca
Frances Hale, Treasurer & Director, Finance
519-292-2045, Fax: 519-291-5611
fhale@northperth.ca
Steve Hardie, Director, Parks & Recreation
519-292-2055
shardie@northperth.ca
Mark Hackett, Manager, Environmental Services
519-292-2069
mhackett@northperth.ca
Ed Podniewicz, Chief Building Official & Administrator, Zoning
519-292-2058
epodniewicz@northperth.ca
Ed Smith, Fire Chief
519-291-6825
esmith@northperth.ca

North Stormont
P.O. Box 99
15 Union St.
Berwick, ON K0C 1G0
Tel: 613-984-2821; *Fax:* 613-984-2908
www.northstormont.ca
Other Information: Toll-Free Phone: 1-877-984-2821
Municipal Type: Township
Area: 515.55 sq km
County or District: Stormont, Dundas & Glengarry; *Population in 2011:* 6,775
Provincial Electoral District(s): Stormont-Dundas-South Glengarry
Federal Electoral District(s): Stormont-Dundas-South Glengarry
Next Election: Oct. 27, 2014 (4 year terms)
Dennis Fife, Mayor
613-984-2821, Fax: 613-984-2908
Karen McPherson, Municipal Clerk
613-984-2821, Fax: 613-984-2908

Northeastern Manitoulin & the Islands
P.O. Box 2000
15 Manitowaning Rd.
Little Current, ON P0P 1K0
Tel: 705-368-3500; *Fax:* 705-368-2245
info@townofnemi.on.ca
www.townofnemi.on.ca
Municipal Type: Town
Area: 495.04 sq km
County or District: Manitoulin District; *Population in 2011:* 2,706
Provincial Electoral District(s): Algoma-Manitoulin
Federal Electoral District(s): Algoma-Manitoulin-Kapuskasing
Next Election: Oct. 27, 2014 (4 year terms)
Joe Chapman, Mayor
705-968-0193
jchapman@townofnemi.on.ca
Janet Moore, Clerk
705-368-3500

Northern Bruce Peninsula
56 Lindsay Rd. 5, RR#2
Lion's Head, ON N0H 1W0
Tel: 519-793-3552; *Fax:* 519-793-3823
northernbrucepen@amtelecom.net
www.northbrucepeninsula.ca
Municipal Type: Municipality
Incorporated: Jan. 1999 *Area:* 781.51 sq km
County or District: Bruce; *Population in 2011:* 3,744
Provincial Electoral District(s): Bruce-Grey-Owen Sound
Federal Electoral District(s): Bruce-Grey-Owen Sound
Next Election: Oct. 27, 2014 (4 year terms)
Note: Amalgamation of of the former Townships of St. Edmunds, Lindsay, Eastnor & the Village of Lion's Head.
Milton McIver, Mayor
519-592-3076
mayor.nbp@eastlink.ca
Mary Lynn Standen, Municipal Clerk
519-793-3522
marylynn.nbp@amtelecom.net

Norwich
P.O. Box 100
210 Main St. East
Otterville, ON N0J 1R0
Tel: 519-863-2709; *Fax:* 519-879-6385
www.twp.norwich.on.ca
Other Information: Alternative Phone: 519-879-6568
Municipal Type: Township
Area: 431.28 sq km
County or District: Oxford; *Population in 2011:* 10,721
Provincial Electoral District(s): Oxford
Federal Electoral District(s): Oxford
Next Election: Oct. 27, 2014 (4 year terms)
Donald Doan, Mayor
519-468-5609
ddoan@twp.norwich.on.ca
Pat Lee, Councillor, Ward(s): 1
519-842-9635
plee@twp.norwich.on.ca
Lynne DePlancke, Councillor, Ward(s): 2
519-468-6728
ldeplancke@twp.norwich.on.ca
Russell Jull, Councillor, Ward(s): 3
519-468-5648
rjull@twp.norwich.on.ca
Susan Hampson, Councillor, Ward(s): 4
519-424-9784
shampson@twp.norwich.on.ca
Michael Graves, Chief Administrativve Officer & Clerk
519-879-6568
mgraves@twp.norwich.on.ca
Mike Legge, Treasurer & Director, Finance
519-879-6568
mlegge@twp.norwich.on.ca
Brian Reid, Chief Building Official, Property Standards
519-879-6568
breid@twp.norwich.on.ca
Patrick Hovorka, Director, Community Development Services
519-863-3733
phovorka@twp.norwich.on.ca
Ron Smith, Superintendent, Public Works
519-879-6568
ronsmith@twp.norwich.on.ca
Monica Bratley, Coordinator, Customer Service & Records Management
519-879-6568
mbratley@twp.norwich.on.ca
Jason Brander, Planner
519-539-9800
jbrander@county.oxford.on.ca

O'Connor
RR#1
Kakabeka Falls, ON P0T 1W0
Tel: 807-476-1451; *Fax:* 807-473-0891
twpoconn@tbaytel.net
www.oconnortownship.ca
Municipal Type: Township
Incorporated: January 1, 1907 *Area:* 108.58 sq km
County or District: Thunder Bay District; *Population in 2011:* 685
Provincial Electoral District(s): Thunder Bay-Atikokan
Federal Electoral District(s): Thunder Bay-Rainy River
Next Election: Oct. 27, 2014 (4 year terms)
Ron Nelson, Mayor
807-475-9213
Lorna Buob, Clerk-Treasurer
twpoconn@tbaytel.net

Oil Springs
P.O. Box 22
4591 Oil Springs Line
Oil Springs, ON N0N 1P0
Tel: 519-834-2939; *Fax:* 519-834-2333
oilsprings@ciaccess.com
www.oilsprings.ca
Municipal Type: Village
Incorporated: 1865 *Area:* 8.18 sq km
County or District: Lambton; *Population in 2011:* 704
Provincial Electoral District(s): Sarnia-Lambton
Federal Electoral District(s): Sarnia-Lambton
Next Election: Oct. 27, 2014 (4 year terms)
Ian Veen, Mayor
Christine Poland, Clerk-Treasurer

Oliver Paipoonge, Municipality of
P.O. Box 10
4569 Oliver Rd.
Murillo, ON P0T 2G0
Tel: 807-935-2613; *Fax:* 807-935-2161
sharron.marlyn@oliverpaipoonage.on.ca
www.oliverpaipoonge.on.ca
Municipal Type: Township
Incorporated: Jan. 1, 1998 *Area:* 350.27 sq km
County or District: Thunder Bay District; *Population in 2011:* 5,732
Provincial Electoral District(s): Thunder Bay-Atikokan
Federal Electoral District(s): Thunder Bay-Rainy River
Next Election: Oct. 27, 2014 (4 year terms)
Note: Amalgamation of the Township of Oliver & the Township of Paipoonge.
Lucy Kloosterhuis, Mayor
807-473-5658, Fax: 807-935-2161
lakbusiness@xplornet.com
Jamie Cressman, Chief Administrative Officer & Clerk
807-935-2613, Fax: 807-935-2123
jamie.cressman@oliverpaipoonge.on.ca

Opasatika
P.O. Box 100
50 Government Rd.
Opasatika, ON P0L 1Z0
Tel: 705-369-4531; *Fax:* 705-369-2002
twpopas@persona.ca
www.opasatika.net
Municipal Type: Township
Area: 329.98 sq km
County or District: Cochrane District; *Population in 2011:* 214
Provincial Electoral District(s): Timmins-James Bay
Federal Electoral District(s): Algoma-Manitoulin-Kapuskasing
Next Election: Oct. 27, 2014 (4 year terms)
Françoise Lambert, Mayor
Denis Dorval, Clerk-Treasurer
705-369-4531, Fax: 705-369-2002

Orangeville
87 Broadway St.
Orangeville, ON L9W 1K1
Tel: 519-941-0440; *Fax:* 519-941-9033
info@orangeville.ca
www.orangeville.ca
Other Information: Toll-Free Phone: 1-866-941-0440; TTY: 519-943-0782
Municipal Type: Town
Incorporated: Dec. 22, 1863 *Area:* 15.57 sq km
County or District: Dufferin; *Population in 2011:* 27,975
Provincial Electoral District(s): Dufferin-Caledon
Federal Electoral District(s): Dufferin-Caledon
Next Election: Oct. 27, 2014 (4 year terms)
Note: Incorporated as a town on Dec. 15, 1873.
Rob Adams, Mayor
radams@orangeville.ca
Warren Maycock, Deputy Mayor & Councillor
Sylvia Bradley, Councillor
Gail Campbell, Councillor
Mary Rose, Councillor
Jeremy Williams, Councillor
Scott Wilson, Councillor
Cheryl Johns, Clerk
cjohns@orangeville.ca
Rick Schwarzer, Chief Administrative Officer
rschwarzer@orangeville.ca
Bill McKennan, Treasurer
bmckennan@orangeville.ca
Vern Douglas, Director, Building & By-law Enforcement
vdouglas@orangeville.ca
Patrick D'Almada, Director, Parks & Recreation
pdalmada@orangeville.ca
James Stiver, Director, Planning
jstiver@orangeville.ca
Jack Tupling, Director, Public Works
jtupling@orangeville.ca
Ed Gill, Managing Director, Operations & Transportation
egill@orangeville.ca
Doug Jones, Managing Director, Environmental & Development Services
djones@orangeville.ca
Jennifer Gohn, Manager, Human Resources
jgohn@orangeville.ca
Andy Macintosh, Fire Chief
amacintosh@orangeville.ca

Oro-Medonte
148 Line 7 South
Oro, ON L0L 2X0
Tel: 705-487-2171; *Fax:* 705-487-0133
www.oro-medonte.ca
Municipal Type: Township
Area: 586.65 sq km
County or District: Simcoe; *Population in 2011:* 20,078
Provincial Electoral District(s): Simcoe North
Federal Electoral District(s): Simcoe North
Next Election: Oct. 27, 2014 (4 year terms)

Harry Hughes, Mayor
705-487-2128
Ralph Hough, Deputy Mayor
705-835-2770
Mel Coutanche, Councillor, Ward(s): 1
705-835-5728
Kelly Meyer, Councillor, Ward(s): 2
705-835-2656
Marty Lancaster, Councillor, Ward(s): 3
705-220-5410
John Crawford, Councillor, Ward(s): 4
705-487-3373
Dwight Evans, Councillor, Ward(s): 5
705-325-1653
Doug Irwin, Clerk & Director, Corporate Services
Robin Dunn, Chief Administrative Officer
Paul Gravelle, Treasurer, Deputy CAO, & Director, Finance
Jerry Ball, Director, Transportation & Environmental Services
Shawn Binns, Director, Recreation & Community Services
Donna Hewitt, Director, Corporate & Strategic Initiatives
Andria Leigh, Director, Development Services
Kim Allen, Chief Building Official
Lisa McNiven, Manager, Engineering & Environmental Services
Tamara Obee, Manager, Health & Safety & Human Resources
Brian Roubos, Manager, Transportation Services
Glenn White, Manager, Planning Services
Hugh Murray, Deputy Fire Chief
705-835-5568, Fax: 705-487-0133

Otonabee-South Monaghan

Municipal Office
P.O. Box 70
20 Third St.
Keene, ON K0L 2G0
Tel: 705-295-6852; *Fax:* 705-295-6405
info@osmtownship.ca
www.osmtownship.ca
Other Information: Toll-Free Phone: 1-800-999-4861 (In 705 area code)
Municipal Type: Township
Area: 349.22 sq km
County or District: Peterborough; *Population in 2011:* 6,660
Provincial Electoral District(s): Peterborough
Federal Electoral District(s): Peterborough
Next Election: Oct. 27, 2014 (4 year terms)
David Nelson, Reeve
705-295-4628
dnelson@osmtownship.ca
Heather Scott, Clerk
705-295-6852
hscott@osmtownship.ca

Oxford

P.O. Box 1614
21 Reeve St.
Woodstock, ON N4S 7Y3
Tel: 519-539-9800
www.oxfordcounty.ca
Municipal Type: Restructured County
Area: 2,039.46 sq km
Population in 2011: 105,719
Next Election: Oct. 27, 2014 (4 year terms)
Don McKay, Warden & Councillor, Ward(s): East Zorra-Tavistock
519-539-9800, Fax: 519-421-4712
Marion Wearn, Councillor, Ward(s): Blandford-Blenheim
519-463-5347
Ted J. Comiskey, Councillor, Ward(s): Ingersoll
519-485-0120
Donald Doan, Councillor, Ward(s): Norwich
519-863-2709, Fax: 519-468-3229
David Mayberry, Councillor, Ward(s): South-West Oxford
519-485-0477
John Lessif, Councillor, Ward(s): Tillsonburg
519-688-3009
Pat Sobeski, Councillor, Ward(s): Woodstock
519-539-2382
Deb A. Tait, Councillor, Ward(s): Woodstock
519-421-7449
Sandra J. Talbot, Councillor, Ward(s): Woodstock
519-539-6685, Fax: 519-539-4526
Margaret E. Lupton, Councillor, Ward(s): Zorra
519-485-2490
Michael Bragg, Chief Administrative Officer & Clerk
519-539-9800
Lynn Beath, Director, Public Health & Emergency Services
519-539-9800
Lynn Buchner, Director, Corporate Services
519-539-9800
Robert Walton, Director, Public Works
519-539-9800
Gordon K. Hough, Corporate Manager, Community & Strategic Planning
519-539-9800
Janice Kubiak, Corporate Manager, Human Resources
519-539-9800

Papineau-Cameron

P.O. Box 630
4861 Hwy. 17
Mattawa, ON P0H 1V0
Tel: 705-744-5610; *Fax:* 705-744-0434
www.papineaucameron.ca
Municipal Type: Township
Area: 561.37 sq km
County or District: Nipissing District; *Population in 2011:* 978
Provincial Electoral District(s): Nipissing
Federal Electoral District(s): Nipissing-Timiskaming
Next Election: Oct. 27, 2014 (4 year terms)
Robert Corriveau, Mayor
Sandra J. Morin, Clerk-Treasurer

Parry Sound

52 Seguin St.
Parry Sound, ON P2A 1B4
Tel: 705-746-2101; *Fax:* 705-746-7461
middaugh@townofparrysound.com (Economic Dev. & Leisure Svs.)
www.townofparrysound.com
Municipal Type: Town
Area: 13.33 sq km
County or District: Parry Sound District; *Population in 2011:* 6,191
Provincial Electoral District(s): Parry Sound-Muskoka
Federal Electoral District(s): Parry Sound-Muskoka
Next Election: Oct. 27, 2014 (4 year terms)
Jamie McGarvey, Mayor
jmcgarvey@townofparrysound.com
Rob Mens, Chief Administrative Officer
rmens@townofparrysound.com

Parry Sound

District Social Services Administration Bd.
1 Beechwood Dr., 2nd Fl.
Parry Sound, ON P2A 1J2
Tel: 705-746-7777; *Fax:* 705-746-7783
Municipal Type: District
Area: 9,222.04 sq km
Population in 2011: 42,162
Rick Zanussi, Chair, Parry Sound District Social Services Administration Board
Janet Patterson, Chief Administrative Officer, District Social Service Admin Board
705-746-7777

Pelee

1045 West Shore Rd.
Pelee Island, ON N0R 1M0
Tel: 519-724-2931; *Fax:* 519-724-2470
info@pelee.ca
www.pelee.org
Other Information: Toll-Free Phone: 1-866-889-5203
Municipal Type: Township
Incorporated: 1869 *Area:* 41.79 sq km
County or District: Essex; *Population in 2011:* 171
Provincial Electoral District(s): Essex
Federal Electoral District(s): Essex
Next Election: Oct. 27, 2014 (4 year terms)
Rick Masse, Mayor
Ann Mitchell, Clerk-Treasurer

Pelham

P.O. Box 400
20 Pelham Town Sq.
Fonthill, ON L0S 1E0
Tel: 905-892-2607
www.pelham.ca
Municipal Type: Town
Incorporated: 1970 *Area:* 126.42 sq km
County or District: Niagara Reg. Mun.; *Population in 2011:* 16,598
Provincial Electoral District(s): Niagara West-Glanbrook
Federal Electoral District(s): Niagara West-Glanbrook
Next Election: Oct. 27, 2014 (4 year terms)
Dave Augustyn, Mayor
mayordave@pelham.ca
Larry Clark, Councillor, Ward(s): 1
lclark@pelham.ca
Richard Rybiak, Councillor, Ward(s): 1
rrybiak@pelham.ca
Gary Accursi, Councillor, Ward(s): 2
gaccursi@pelham.ca
Catherine King, Councillor, Ward(s): 2
cking@pelham.ca
John Durley, Councillor, Ward(s): 3
jjdurley@sympatico.ca
Peter Papp, Councillor, Ward(s): 3
ppapp@pelham.ca
Nancy J. Bozzato, Clerk
njbozzato@pelham.ca
Martin Yamich, Chief Administrative Officer
myamich@pelham.ca
Cari Pupo, Treasurer
cpupo@pelham.ca
Craig Larmour, Director, Planning & Development
clarmour@pelham.ca
Keegan Gennings, Chief Building Official & Manager, By-law Enforcement
kgennings@pelham.ca
Jim Phelps, Acting Fire Chief
jphelps@pelham.ca
Alan Mannell, Manager, Engineering
amannell@pelham.ca

Penetanguishene

P.O. Box 5009
10 Robert St. West
Penetanguishene, ON L9M 2G2
Tel: 705-549-7453; *Fax:* 705-549-3743
www.penetanguishene.ca
Other Information: Public Works, Phone: 705-549-7992
Municipal Type: Town
Incorporated: Feb. 22, 1882 *Area:* 25.38 sq km
County or District: Simcoe; *Population in 2011:* 9,111
Provincial Electoral District(s): Simcoe North
Federal Electoral District(s): Simcoe North
Next Election: Oct. 27, 2014 (4 year terms)
Gerry Marshall, Mayor
Holly Bryce, Town Clerk
hbryce@penetanguishene.ca

Perry

P.O. Box 70
1695 Emsdale Rd.
Emsdale, ON P0A 1J0
Tel: 705-636-5941; *Fax:* 705-636-5759
info@townshipofperry.ca; perrylib@ontera.net (library)
www.townshipofperry.ca
Other Information: Public Works Email: publicworks@townshipofperry.ca
Municipal Type: Township
Area: 186.63 sq km
County or District: Parry Sound District; *Population in 2011:* 2,317
Provincial Electoral District(s): Parry Sound-Muskoka
Federal Electoral District(s): Parry Sound-Muskoka
Next Election: Oct. 27, 2014 (4 year terms)
John Dunn, Mayor
705-636-5727
john.dunn@townshipofperry.ca
Beth Morton, Clerk & Planning Administrator
705-636-5941
beth.morton@townshipofperry.ca

Perth

Town Hall
80 Gore St. East
Perth, ON K7H 1H9
Tel: 613-267-3311; *Fax:* 613-267-5635
www.perthcanada.com
Other Information: After hour water & sewer emergencies: 613-267-1072
Municipal Type: Town
Area: 10.36 sq km
County or District: Lanark; *Population in 2011:* 5,840
Provincial Electoral District(s): Lanark-Frontenac-Lennox & Addington
Federal Electoral District(s): Lanark-Frontenac-Lennox & Addington
Next Election: Oct. 27, 2014 (4 year terms)
John Fenik, Mayor
613-267-3311
jfenik@perth.ca
Lauren Walton, Clerk
613-267-3311
lwalton@perth.ca

Perth East

P.O. Box 455
25 Mill St. East
Milverton, ON N0K 1M0
Tel: 519-595-2800; *Fax:* 519-595-2801
township@pertheast.on.ca
www.pertheast.on.ca

Municipal Type: Township
Area: 715.07 sq km
County or District: Perth; *Population in 2011:* 12,028
Provincial Electoral District(s): Perth-Wellinton
Federal Electoral District(s): Perth-Wellington
Next Election: Oct. 27, 2014 (4 year terms)
Note: Amalgamation of North Easthope Township, South Easthope Township, Ellice Township, Village of Milverton & Mornington Township.
Ian Forrest, Mayor
iforrest@pertheast.on.ca
Bob McMillan, Deputy Mayor
mcmillan@cyg.net
Rhonda Ehgoetz, Councillor, Ward(s): Ellice
rhonda.ehgoetz@hotmail.com
Jeremy Matheson, Councillor, Ward(s): Milverton
jmatheson@zehrinsurance.com
Don Brunk, Councillor, Ward(s): Mornington
morningtonward@hotmail.com
Hugh McDermid, Councillor, Ward(s): North Easthope
mcdermid2020hotmail.com
Andrew MacAlpine, Councillor, Ward(s): South Easthope
a.macalpine@sympatico.ca
Theresa Campbell, Municipal Clerk
519-595-2800
tcampbell@pertheast.on.ca
Glenn Schwendinger, Chief Administrative Officer
519-595-2800
Rhonda Fischer, Municipal Treasurer & Manager, Finance Department
519-595-2800
Bill Hunter, Fire Chief
519-595-2800
519-595-2801
Grant Schwartzentruber, Chief Building Official
519-595-2800
Becky Boertien, Manager, Perth East Recreation Complex
519-595-2244, Fax: 519-595-4067
Wes Kuepfer, Manager, Public Works & Parks
519-595-2800
Donna Chaffe, Coordinator, Human Resources
519-595-2800
Martin Feeney, By-law Enforcement Officer & Building & Sewage Inspector
519-595-2800
Geoff VanderBaaren, Planner
519-271-0531

Perth South
3191 Rd. 122
St. Pauls, ON N0K 1V0
Tel: 519-271-0619; *Fax:* 519-271-0647
township@perthsouth.ca
www.perthsouth.ca
Other Information: Toll-Free Phone: 1-866-771-0619
Municipal Type: Township
Area: 393.01 sq km
County or District: Perth; *Population in 2011:* 3,993
Provincial Electoral District(s): Perth-Wellington
Federal Electoral District(s): Perth-Wellington
Next Election: Oct. 27, 2014 (4 year terms)
Note: Amalgamation of Blanshard Township & Downie Township.
Robert Wilhelm, Mayor
519-225-2304
ulchtran@quadro.net
Lizet Scott, Clerk
519-271-0619
lscott@perthsouth.ca

Petawawa
1111 Victoria St.
Petawawa, ON K8H 2E6
Tel: 613-687-5536; *Fax:* 613-687-5973
www.petawawa.ca
Municipal Type: Town
Incorporated: July 1, 1997 *Area:* 164.68 sq km
County or District: Renfrew; *Population in 2011:* 15,988
Provincial Electoral District(s): Renfrew-Nipissing-Pembroke
Federal Electoral District(s): Renfrew-Nipissing-Pembroke
Next Election: Oct. 27, 2014 (4 year terms)
Note: Amalgamation of Petawawa Village & Petawawa Township.
Robert Sweet, Mayor
mayor@petawawa.ca
Tom Mohns, Deputy Mayor & Councillor
tmohns@petawawa.ca
James Carmody, Councillor
jcarmody@petawawa.ca
Frank Cirella, Councillor
fcirella@petawawa.ca
Treena Lemay, Councillor
tlemay@petawawa.ca
Murray Rutz, Councillor
mrutz@petawawa.ca
Theresa Sabourin, Councillor
tsabourin@petawawa.ca
Mitchell Stillman, Chief Administrative Officer & Clerk
Daniel Scissons, Treasurer & Deputy Clerk
Randy Mohns, Chief Building Official
Steve Knott, Fire Chief
Tom Renaud, Supervisor, Public Works
Cyndy Phillips McCann, Coordinator, Economic Development
Karen Cronier, Coordinator, Planning

Petrolia
P.O. Box 1270
411 Greenfield St.
Petrolia, ON N0N 1R0
Tel: 519-882-2350; *Fax:* 519-882-3373
petrolia@town.petrolia.on.ca
www.town.petrolia.on.ca
Other Information: After Hours Emergency, Phone: 519-882-2351
Municipal Type: Town
Area: 12.68 sq km
County or District: Lambton; *Population in 2011:* 5,528
Provincial Electoral District(s): Lambton-Kent-Middlesex
Federal Electoral District(s): Sarnia-Lambton
Next Election: Oct. 27, 2014 (4 year terms)
John McCharles, Mayor
519-882-2455
johnnyremax@bellnet.ca
Dianne Caryn, Chief Administrative Officer & Clerk
dcaryn@town.petrolia.on.ca

Pickle Lake
P.O. Box 340
2 Anne St.
Pickle Lake, ON P0V 3A0
Tel: 807-928-2034; *Fax:* 807-928-2708
reception@picklelake.org
www.picklelake.ca
Other Information: Toll-Free Phone: 1-800-565-9189
Municipal Type: Township
Incorporated: Dec. 1980 *Area:* 255.08 sq km
County or District: Kenora District; *Population in 2011:* 425
Provincial Electoral District(s): Kenora-Rainy River
Federal Electoral District(s): Kenora
Next Election: Oct. 27, 2014 (4 year terms)
Roy Hoffman, Mayor
mayor@picklelake.org
Paul Panciw, Clerk-Treasurer
clerktreasurer@picklelake.org

Plummer Additional
38 Railway Cres., RR#2
Bruce Mines, ON P0R 1C0
Tel: 705-785-3479; *Fax:* 705-785-3135
plumtwsp@onlink.net
www.plummertownship.ca
Municipal Type: Township
Area: 221.31 sq km
County or District: Algoma District; *Population in 2011:* 650
Provincial Electoral District(s): Algoma-Manitoulin
Federal Electoral District(s): Sault Ste Marie
Next Election: Oct. 27, 2014 (4 year terms)
Beth West, Mayor
Vicky Goertzen-Cooke, Clerk-Treasurer

Plympton-Wyoming
P.O. Box 250
546 Niagara St.
Wyoming, ON N0N 1T0
Tel: 519-845-3939; *Fax:* 519-845-0597
feedback@plympton-wyoming.ca
www.plympton-wyoming.com
Other Information: Toll-Free Phone: 1-877-313-3939
Municipal Type: Town
Incorporated: Jan. 1, 2001 *Area:* 318.76 sq km
County or District: Lambton; *Population in 2011:* 7,576
Provincial Electoral District(s): Sarnia-Lambton
Federal Electoral District(s): Sarnia-Lambton
Next Election: Oct. 27, 2014 (4 year terms)
Note: Amalgamation of the Village of Wyoming & the Township of Plympton.
Lonny Napper, Mayor
lnapper@xcelco.on.ca
Caroline DeSchutter, Clerk & Deputy Chief Administrative Officer
cdeschutter@plympton-wyoming.ca

Point Edward
Municipal Office
135 Kendall St.
Point Edward, ON N7V 4G6
Tel: 519-337-3021; *Fax:* 519-337-5963
info@villageofpointedward.com
www.villageofpointedward.com
Municipal Type: Village
Incorporated: 1878 *Area:* 3.27 sq km
County or District: Lambton; *Population in 2011:* 2,034
Provincial Electoral District(s): Sarnia-Lambton
Federal Electoral District(s): Sarnia-Lambton
Next Election: Oct. 27, 2014 (4 year terms)
Dick Kirkland, Mayor
518-344-8755
dkirkland@villageofpointedward.com
Peggy Cramp, Chief Administrative Officer &
519-337-3021
pcramp@villageofpointedward.com

Port Hope
Town Hall
56 Queen St.
Port Hope, ON L1A 3Z9
Tel: 905-885-4544; *Fax:* 905-885-7698
admin@porthope.ca
www.porthope.ca
Municipal Type: Municipality
Incorporated: March 6, 1834 *Area:* 278.97 sq km
County or District: Northumberland; *Population in 2011:* 16,214
Provincial Electoral District(s): Northumberland-Quinte West
Federal Electoral District(s): Northumberland-Quinte West
Next Election: Oct. 27, 2014 (4 year terms)
Linda M. Thompson, Mayor
905-885-4544
mayor@porthope.ca
Jeffrey S. Gilmer, Deputy Mayor & Councillor, Ward(s): 2
905-753-2685
jgilmer@porthope.ca
Rick Austin, Councillor, Ward(s): 1
905-376-9050
raustin@porthope.ca
Mary Lou Ellis, Councillor, Ward(s): 1
905-885-0376
mellis@porthope.ca
Jeff G. Lees, Councillor, Ward(s): 1
905-885-8977
jlees@porthope.ca; jefflees@sympatico.ca
David Turck, Councillor, Ward(s): 1
905-885-8927
dturck@porthope.ca
Greg W. Burns, Councillor, Ward(s): 2
905-797-9616
gburns@porthope.ca
Sue Dawe, Clerk & Director, Corporate Services
905-885-4544
sdawe@porthope.ca
R. Carl Cannon, Chief Administrative Officer
905-885-4544
ccannon@porthope.ca
Liz Araujo, Treasurer & Director, Finance
905-885-4544
laraujo@porthope.ca
Peter Angelo, P.Eng., Director, Public Works
905-885-2431
pangelo@porthope.ca
Rob Collins, Director, Fire & Emergency Services
905-885-5323
rcollins@porthope.ca
Judy Selvig, Director, Economic Development & Tourism
905-885-2431
jselvig@porthope.ca
Karen Sharpe, Director, Parks, Recreation, & Culture
905-753-2230, Fax: 905-753-2434
ksharpe@porthope.ca
Ron Warne, Director, Planning & Development Services
905-885-2431, Fax: 905-885-0507
rwarne@porthope.ca
Ken Andrus, Chief Building Official
905-885-2431
kandrus@porthope.ca
Gina Jackson, Manager, Human Resources
905-885-4544
gjackson@porthope.ca
Sandra Weeks, Coordinator, Communications
905-885-4544
sweeks@porthope.ca

Powassan, Municipality of
P.O. Box 250
466 Main St.
Powassan, ON P0H 1Z0
Tel: 705-724-2813; *Fax:* 705-724-5533
info@powassan.net
www.powassan.net
Municipal Type: Town
Incorporated: Nov. 30, 1904 *Area:* 222.75 sq km
County or District: Parry Sound District; *Population in 2011:* 3,378
Provincial Electoral District(s): Nipissing
Federal Electoral District(s): Nipissing-Timiskaming
Next Election: Oct. 27, 2014 (4 year terms)
Peter McIsaac, Mayor
705-491-0374
pmcisaac@powassan.net
Maureen Lang, Clerk-Treasurer
795-724-2813, Fax: 705-724-5533
mlang@powassan.netet

Prescott
P.O. Box 160
360 Dibble St. West
Prescott, ON K0E 1T0
Tel: 613-925-2812; *Fax:* 613-925-4381
info@prescott.ca
www.prescott.ca
Municipal Type: Town
Area: 4.95 sq km
County or District: Leeds & Grenville; *Population in 2011:* 4,284
Provincial Electoral District(s): Leeds-Grenville
Federal Electoral District(s): Leeds-Grenville
Next Election: Oct. 27, 2014 (4 year terms)
Brett Todd, Mayor
613-925-2812
btodd@prescott.ca
Randy Haller, Chief Administrative Officer & Clerk
613-925-2812, Fax: 613-925-4381
rhaller@prescott.ca

Prescott & Russell
P.O. Box 304
59 Court St.
L'Orignal, ON K0B 1K0
Tel: 613-675-4661; *Fax:* 613-675-2519
support@prescott-russell.on.ca
www.prescott-russell.on.ca
Other Information: Toll-Free Phone: 1-800-667-6307
Municipal Type: United County
Incorporated: 1820 *Area:* 2,001.18 sq km
Population in 2011: 85,381
Next Election: Oct. 27, 2014 (4 year terms)
Jean-Yves Lalonde, Warden & Mayor, Township of Alfred & Plantagenet
613-673-4797, Fax: 613-673-4812
jean-yves.lalonde@sympatico.ca
Gary J. Barton, Council Member & Mayor, Township of Champlain
613-678-3003, Fax: 613-678-3363
gary.barton@champlain.ca
René Berthiaume, Council Member & Mayor, Town of Hawkesbury
613-632-0106, Fax: 613-636-2096
rberthiaume@hawkesbury.ca
Marcel Guibord, Council Member & Mayor, City of Clarence-Rockland
613-446-6022, Fax: 613-446-1497
mguibord@clarence-rockland.com
Robert Kirby, Council Member & Mayor, Township of East Hawkesbury
613-674-2170, Fax: 613-632-4841
Claude Levac, Council Member & Mayor, Village of Casselman
613-764-3139, Fax: 613-764-5709
maire@casselman.ca
François St. Amour, Council Member & Mayor, Nation Municipality
613-764-5444
fstamour@nationmun.ca
Jean-Paul Saint-Pierre, Council Member & Mayor, Township of Russell
613-443-3066, Fax: 613-443-1042
jpstpierre@russell.ca
Stéphane P. Parisien, Chief Administrative Officer & Clerk
613-675-4661
spparisien@prescott-russell.on.ca
Louise Lepage-Gareau, Treasurer
613-675-4661, Fax: 613-675-4547
llgareau@prescott-russell.on.ca
Michel Chrétien, Director, Emergency Services
613-673-5139, Fax: 613-673-1401
mchretien@prescott-russell.on.ca
Marc Clermont, Director, Public Works
613-675-4661, Fax: 613-675-1007
mclermont@prescott-russell.on.ca
Louis Prévost, Director, Planning & Forestry
613-675-4661, Fax: 613-675-1007
lprevost@prescott-russell.on.ca
Jonathan B. Roy, Director, Human Resources
613-675-4661, Fax: 613-675-4547
jbroy@prescott-russell.on.ca
Anne Comtois Lalonde, Administrator, Social Services Management
613-675-4642, Fax: 613-675-2030
aclalonde@prescott-russell.on.ca

Prince
3042 2nd Line West
Sault Ste Marie, ON P6A 6K4
Tel: 705-779-2992; *Fax:* 705-779-2725
www.princetwp.ca
Municipal Type: Township
Area: 84.28 sq km
County or District: Algoma District; *Population in 2011:* 1,031
Provincial Electoral District(s): Algoma Manitoulin
Federal Electoral District(s): Sault Ste Marie
Next Election: Oct. 27, 2014 (4 year terms)
Ken Lamming, Reeve
705-779-2875
kenlamming@sympatico.ca
Peggy Greco, Chief Administrative Officer & Administrator

Puslinch
7404 Wellington Rd. 34, RR#3
Guelph, ON N1H 6H9
Tel: 519-763-1226; *Fax:* 519-763-5846
admin@twp.puslinch.on.ca
www.twp.puslinch.on.ca
Municipal Type: Township
Incorporated: Jan. 1, 1850 *Area:* 214.44 sq km
County or District: Wellington; *Population in 2011:* 7,029
Provincial Electoral District(s): Wellington-Halton Hills
Federal Electoral District(s): Wellington-Halton Hills; Guelph
Next Election: Oct. 27, 2014 (4 year terms)
Dennis Lever, Mayor
226-971-2067
dennisl@wellington.ca
Brenda Law, Chief Administrative Officer & Clerk-Treasurer
519-763-1226
brendal@twp.puslinch.on.ca

Rainy River
P.O. Box 488
Rainy River, ON P0W 1L0
Tel: 807-852-3244; *Fax:* 807-852-3553
rainyriver@tbaytel.net
www.rainyriver.ca
Municipal Type: Town
Incorporated: 1904 *Area:* 2.99 sq km
County or District: Rainy River District; *Population in 2011:* 842
Provincial Electoral District(s): Kenora-Rainy River
Federal Electoral District(s): Thunder Bay-Rainy River
Next Election: Oct. 27, 2014 (4 year terms)
Deborah Ewald, Mayor
Veldron Vogan, Chief Administrative Officer

Rainy River
District Social Services Administration Bd.
450 Scott St.
Fort Frances, ON P9A 1H2
Tel: 807-274-5349; *Fax:* 807-274-0678
Other Information: Toll-Free Phone: 1-800-265-5349
Municipal Type: District
Area: 15,472.94 sq km
Population in 2011: 20,370
Ross Donaldson, Chair, Rainy River District Social Services Administration Board
Donna Dittaro, CAO, Rainy River District Social Services Administration Board
donnad@rrdssab.on.ca

Ramara
Ramara Administration Building
P.O. Box 130
2297 Hwy. 12
Brechin, ON L0K 1B0
Tel: 705-484-5374; *Fax:* 705-484-0441
ramara@ramara.ca
www.ramara.ca
Other Information: Toll-Free Phone: 1-800-663-4054 (for 689 exchange)
Municipal Type: Township
Area: 417.25 sq km
County or District: Simcoe; *Population in 2011:* 9,275
Provincial Electoral District(s): Simcoe North
Federal Electoral District(s): Simcoe North
Next Election: Oct. 27, 2014 (4 year terms)
Bill Duffy, Mayor
705-326-3915
council@ramara.ca
Janice McKinnon, Clerk
705-484-5374
jmckinnon@ramara.ca

Red Lake
P.O. Box 1000
2 Fifth St.
Balmertown, ON P0V 1C0
Tel: 807-735-2096; *Fax:* 807-735-2286
municipality@red-lake.com
www.red-lake.com
Municipal Type: Municipality
Incorporated: July 1, 1998 *Area:* 610.38 sq km
County or District: Kenora District; *Population in 2011:* 4,366
Provincial Electoral District(s): Kenora-Rainy River
Federal Electoral District(s): Kenora
Next Election: Oct. 27, 2014 (4 year terms)
Note: Amalgamation of the former Unorganized Territory of Madsen, the Township of Red Lake, & the Township of Golden.
Phil T. Vinet, Mayor
807-735-2096, Fax: 807-735-2286
Shelly Kocis, Clerk
807-735-2096, Fax: 807-735-2286
shelly@red-lake.com

Red Rock
P.O. Box 447
Red Rock, ON P0T 2P0
Tel: 807-886-2245; *Fax:* 807-886-2793
info@redrocktownship.com
www.redrocktownship.com
Other Information: Phone, Public Works: 807-886-2524
Municipal Type: Township
Area: 62.93 sq km
County or District: Thunder Bay District; *Population in 2011:* 942
Provincial Electoral District(s): Thunder Bay-Superior North
Federal Electoral District(s): Thunder Bay-Superior North
Next Election: Oct. 27, 2014 (4 year terms)
Gary Nelson, Mayor
807-886-2503
Kal Pristanski, CAO, Clerk-Treasurer, Tax Collector, & Commissioner of Oaths
cao@shawbiz.ca

Renfrew
127 Raglan St. South
Renfrew, ON K7V 1P8
Tel: 613-432-4848; *Fax:* 613-432-7245
info@town.renfrew.on.ca
www.town.renfrew.on.ca
Municipal Type: Town
Area: 12.77 sq km
County or District: Renfrew; *Population in 2011:* 8,218
Provincial Electoral District(s): Renfrew-Nipissing-Pembroke
Federal Electoral District(s): Renfrew-Nipissing-Pembroke
Next Election: Oct. 27, 2014 (4 year terms)
Bill Ringrose, Mayor
613-432-4848
bringrose@town.renfrew.on.ca
Kim R. Bulmer, Town Clerk
613-432-4848
kbulmer@town.renfrew.on.ca

Rideau Lakes
1439 County Rd. 8
Delta, ON K0E 1G0
Tel: 613-928-2251; *Fax:* 613-928-3097
info@twprideaulakes.on.ca
www.twprideaulakes.on.ca
Other Information: Toll-Free Phone: 1-800-928-2250
Municipal Type: Township
Incorporated: Jan. 1, 1998 *Area:* 710.25 sq km
County or District: Leeds-Grenville; *Population in 2011:* 10,207
Provincial Electoral District(s): Leeds-Grenville
Federal Electoral District(s): Leeds-Grenville
Next Election: Oct. 27, 2014 (4 year terms)
Note: Amalgamation of the former Townships of North Crosby, South Crosby, Bastard & South Burgess, South Elmsley & the Village of Newboro.
Ron Holman, Mayor
613-283-0724, Fax: 613-283-5517
mayor@twprideaulakes.on.ca

Ron Pollard, Deputy Mayor & Councillor, Ward(s): North Crosby
613-273-5491
pollard.ron@kingston.net
Anders Carson, Councillor, Ward(s): Bastard & South Burgess
613-272-3354
anderscarson77@gmail.com
Rob Dunfield, Councillor, Ward(s): Bastard & South Burgess
613-272-2179
dunfield.robert@gmail.com
Cathy Monck, Councillor, Ward(s): Newboro
613-272-3453
monck.cathy@bell.net
Bob Lavoie, Councillor, Ward(s): North Crosby
613-273-8177
BobLavoie@kingston.net
Linda Carr, Councillor, Ward(s): South Crosby
613-272-2227
councillorlinda@gmail.com
Robert Taylor, Councillor, Ward(s): South Crosby
613-359-5118
robert.roy.taylor@hotmail.ca
Jeff Banks, Councillor, Ward(s): South Elmsley
613-800-2790
jeffbanks@xplornet.com
Paul A.L. Smith, Councillor, Ward(s): South Elmsley
613-283-6265
smith.paul@sympatico.ca
Dianna Bresee, Clerk
613-928-2251
dianna@twprideaulakes.on.ca
Robert Maddocks, Chief Administrative Officer
613-928-2251
cao@twprideaulakes.on.ca
Joseph Whyte, Treasurer
613-928-2251
joe@twprideaulakes.on.ca
Susan Dunfield, Manager, Community & Leisure Services
613-928-2251
susan@twprideaulakes.on.ca
Sheldon Laidman, Manager, Development Services
613-928-2251
slaidman@twprideaulakes.on.ca
Michael Touw, Manager, Public Works & Superintendent, Drainage
613-928-2251
mtouw@twprideaulakes.on.ca
Jay DeBernardi, Fire Chief
613-928-2251
fire.j@twprideaulakes.on.ca

Russell

717 Notre Dame St.
Embrun, ON K0A 1W1
Tel: 613-443-3066; *Fax:* 613-443-1042
info@russell.ca; publicworks.voirie@russell.ca
www.russell.ca
Other Information: Bylaws, E-mail: bylaws.reglements@russell.ca
Municipal Type: Township
Area: 198.96 sq km
County or District: Prescott & Russell; *Population in 2011:* 15,247
Provincial Electoral District(s): Glengarry-Prescott-Russell
Federal Electoral District(s): Glengarry-Prescott-Russell
Next Election: Oct. 27, 2014 (4 year terms)
JP St-Pierre, Mayor
jpstpierre@russell.ca
Éric Bazinet, Councillor
ericbazinet@russell.ca
Craig Cullen, Councillor
craigcullen@russell.ca
Jamie Laurin, Councillor
jlaurin@russell.ca
Pierre Leroux, Councillor
pierreleroux@russell.ca
Ginette Bertrand, Municipal Clerk
clerk.greffe@russell.ca
Jean Leduc, Chief Administrative Officer
Christiane B. Brault, Treasurer & Director, Finance
finances@russell.ca
Millie Bourdeau, Director, Public Safety & Enforcement
Graham Gorman, Director, Environmental Services & Public Utilities
Jacques Lortie, Director, Public Works, Parks, & Recreation
recreation@russell.ca
Dominique Tremblay, Director, Planning & Building
planning.amenagement@russell.ca
Bruce Armstrong, Fire Chief, Russell
Jean-Luc Bourgie, Fire Chief, Embrun

Ryerson

28 Midlothian Rd., RR#1
Burks Falls, ON P0A 1C0
Tel: 705-382-3232; *Fax:* 705-382-3286
admin@ryersontownship.ca
www.ryersontownship.ca
Municipal Type: Township
Area: 186.79 sq km
County or District: Parry Sound District; *Population in 2011:* 634
Provincial Electoral District(s): Parry Sound-Muskoka
Federal Electoral District(s): Parry Sound-Muskoka
Next Election: Oct. 27, 2014 (4 year terms)
Glenn Miller, Reeve
705-382-2898
Judy Kosowan, Chief Administrative Officer & Clerk-Treasurer

Sables-Spanish Rivers

PO Box 5, Site 1, 11 Birch Lake Rd. RR#3
Massey, ON P0P 1P0
Tel: 705-865-2646; *Fax:* 705-865-2736
inquiries@sables-spanish.ca
www.sables-spanish.ca
Municipal Type: Township
Incorporated: July 1998 *Area:* 806.27 sq km
County or District: Sudbury District; *Population in 2011:* 3,075
Provincial Electoral District(s): Algoma-Manitoulin
Federal Electoral District(s): Algoma-Manitoulin-Kapuskasing
Next Election: Oct. 27, 2014 (4 year terms)
Leslie Gamble, Mayor
705-865-2655
Kim Sloss, Clerk-Administrator
705-865-2646, Fax: 705-865-2736
kasloss@sables-spanish.ca

St. Clair

Civic Centre
1155 Emily St.
Mooretown, ON N0N 1M0
Tel: 519-867-2021; *Fax:* 519-867-5509
webmaster@twp.stclair.on.ca; publicworks@twp.stclair.on.ca
www.twp.stclair.on.ca
Other Information: Toll-Free Phone: 1-800-809-0301 (Sombra & Lambton)
Municipal Type: Township
Area: 619.3 sq km
County or District: Lambton; *Population in 2011:* 14,515
Provincial Electoral District(s): Sarnia-Lambton
Federal Electoral District(s): Sarnia-Lambton
Next Election: Oct. 27, 2014 (4 year terms)
Steve Arnold, Mayor
519-381-7440
Peter Gilliland, Deputy Mayor
519-862-3534
Jeff Agar, Councillor, Ward(s): 1
519-862-5062
Patricia Carswell-Alexander, Councillor, Ward(s): 1
519-864-4006
Jim DeGurse, Councillor, Ward(s): 1
519-862-3060
Steve Miller, Councillor, Ward(s): 2
519-677-5676
Darrell Randell, Councillor, Ward(s): 2
519-627-3764
John DeMars, Clerk, Deputy CAO, & Director, Administration
519-867-2021
John Rodey, MCIP, RPP, Chief Administrative Officer
519-867-2021, Fax: 519-867-5509
jrodey@twp.stclair.on.ca
Charles Quenneville, B.Com., CMA, Treasurer
519-867-2024
cquenneville@twp.stclair.on.ca
Gary Hackett, Director, Community Services
ghackett@twp.stclair.on.ca
Roy Dewhirst, Fire Chief
rdewhirst@twp.stclair.on.ca
J. Baranek, Coordinator, Planning
Rick McClemens, Coordinator, Facilities & Parks
rmcclemens@twp.stclair.on.ca

St. Joseph

P.O. Box 187
1669 Arthur St.
Richards Landing, ON P0R 1J0
Tel: 705-246-2625; *Fax:* 705-246-3142
stjosephtownship@bellnet.ca
www.stjosephtownship.com
Municipal Type: Township
Area: 129.18 sq km
County or District: Algoma District; *Population in 2011:* 1,201
Provincial Electoral District(s): Algoma-Manitoulin
Federal Electoral District(s): Sault Ste Marie
Next Election: Oct. 27, 2014 (4 year terms)
Jody Wildman, Mayor
705-246-0616
Carol O. Trainor, A.M.C.T., Clerk Administrator
stjoeadmin@bellnet.ca

St. Marys

P.O. Box 998
175 Queen St. East, 2nd Fl.
St. Marys, ON N4X 1B6
Tel: 519-284-2340; *Fax:* 519-284-3881
www.townofstmarys.com
Municipal Type: Town
Area: 12.48 sq km
County or District: Perth; *Population in 2011:* 6,655
Provincial Electoral District(s): Perth-Wellington
Federal Electoral District(s): Perth-Wellington
Next Election: Oct. 27, 2014 (4 year terms)
Steve Grose, Mayor
519-284-2340
sgrose@town.stmarys.on.ca
Robert Brindley, Chief Administrative Officer
519-284-2340
rbrindley@town.stmarys.on.ca

Saugeen Shores

P.O. Box 820
600 Tomlinson Dr.
Port Elgin, ON N0H 2C0
Tel: 519-832-2008; *Fax:* 519-832-2140
www.saugeenshores.ca
Municipal Type: Town
Area: 170.58 sq km
County or District: Bruce; *Population in 2011:* 12,661
Provincial Electoral District(s): Huron-Bruce
Federal Electoral District(s): Huron-Bruce
Next Election: Oct. 27, 2014 (4 year terms)
Mike Smith, Mayor
mayor@saugeenshores.ca
Luke Charbonneau, Deputy Mayor & Councillor
lcharbonneau@bmts.com
Doug Gowanlock, Vice Deputy Mayor & Councillor
beaglerun@bmts.com
Marcel Legault, Ward(s): Port Elgin
mlegaul@bmts.com
Fred Schildroth, Councillor, Ward(s): Port Elgin
schildrf@bmts.com
Gary R. Brown, Councillor, Ward(s): Saugeen
cargar@bmts.com
Taun Frosst, Councillor, Ward(s): Saugeen
sunset.taun@gmail.com
Diane Huber, Councillor, Ward(s): Southampton
dianehuber@bmts.com
Thead Seaman, Councillor, Ward(s): Southampton
t.j.seaman@bmts.com
Linda White, Clerk
whitel@saugeenshores.ca
Lawrence Allison, Chief Administrative Officer
allisonl@saugeenshores.ca
Lori Sweiger, Treasurer
sweigerl@saugeenshores.ca
Dave Burnside, Director, Engineering Services
burnsided@saugeenshores.ca
Stuart Doyle, Director, Public Works
doyles@saugeenshores.ca
Mike Myatt, Director, Community Services
myattm@saugeenshores.ca
Lynn Worsley, Officer, Human Resources
worsleyl@saugeenshores.ca
Jim Bell, Chief Building Official
bellj@saugeenshores.ca
Phil Eagleson, Fire Chief
shores.fire@bmts.com
Cassie Coulson, Coordinator, Water & Sewer
coulsonc@saugeenshores.ca

Schreiber

P.O. Box 40
204 Alberta St.
Schreiber, ON P0T 2S0
Tel: 807-824-2711; *Fax:* 807-824-3231
executiveassistant@schreiber.ca
www.schreiber.ca
Municipal Type: Township
Area: 36.79 sq km
County or District: Thunder Bay District; *Population in 2011:* 1,126
Provincial Electoral District(s): Thunder Bay-Superior North
Federal Electoral District(s): Thunder Bay-Superior North
Next Election: Oct. 27, 2014 (4 year terms)

Don McArthur, Mayor
807-824-2711
mayor@schreiber.ca
Jon Hall, Clerk & Deputy Treasurer
807-824-2711
clerk@schreiber.ca

Scugog

P.O. Box 780
181 Perry St.
Port Perry, ON L9L 1A7
Tel: 905-985-7346; *Fax:* 905-985-9914
www.scugog.ca
Municipal Type: Township
Area: 474.63 sq km
County or District: Durham Regional Municipality; *Population in 2011:* 21,569
Provincial Electoral District(s): Durham
Federal Electoral District(s): Durham
Next Election: Oct. 27, 2014 (4 year terms)
Chuck Mercier, Mayor
905-985-7346
mayormercier@scugog.ca
Bobbie Drew, Regional Councillor
905-985-7183
bdrew@scugog.ca
Larry Corrigan, Councillor, Ward(s): 1
905-985-7215
lcorrigan@scugog.ca
John Hancock, Councillor, Ward(s): 2
905-985-8083
jhancock@scugog.ca
Jim Howard, Councillor, Ward(s): 3
905-442-0448
jhoward@scugog.ca
Wilma Wotten, Councillor, Ward(s): 4
905-986-4975
wwotten@scugog.ca
Howard Danson, Councillor, Ward(s): 5
905-982-2724
hdanson@scugog.ca
Bev Hendry, Chief Administrative Officer
905-985-7346, Fax: 905-985-9914
T. DeBruijn, Treasurer & Director, Finance
D. Gordon, Director, Community Services
I. Roger, Director, Public Works & Parks
Richard Miller, Fire Chief
905-985-2384

Seguin

5 Humphrey Dr., RR#2
Parry Sound, ON P2A 2W8
Tel: 705-732-4300; *Fax:* 705-732-6347
info@seguin.ca
www.seguin.ca
Other Information: Toll-Free Phone: 1-877-473-4846
Municipal Type: Township
Incorporated: May 8, 1997 *Area:* 586.17 sq km
County or District: Parry Sound District; *Population in 2011:* 3,988
Provincial Electoral District(s): Parry Sound-Muskoka
Federal Electoral District(s): Parry Sound-Muskoka
Next Election: Oct. 27, 2014 (4 year terms)
David Conn, Mayor, Fax: 705-732-2730
connd@rogers.com
Craig Jeffery, Clerk & Officer, Lottery Licensing
cjeffery@seguin.ca

Severn

P.O. Box 159
1024 Hurlwood Lane
Orillia, ON L3V 6J3
Tel: 705-325-2315; *Fax:* 705-327-5818
severn@encode.com
www.townshipofsevern.com
Municipal Type: Township
Incorporated: Jan. 1, 1994 *Area:* 534.78 sq km
County or District: Simcoe; *Population in 2011:* 12,377
Provincial Electoral District(s): Simcoe North
Federal Electoral District(s): Simcoe North
Next Election: Oct. 27, 2014 (4 year terms)
Mike Burkett, Mayor
MBurkett@townshipofsevern.com
Judith Cox, Deputy Mayor
JCox@townshipofsevern.com
Mark Taylor, Councillor, Ward(s): 1
MTaylor@townshipofsevern.com
Jane Dunlop, Councillor, Ward(s): 2
JDunlop@townshipofsevern.com
Ian Crichton, Councillor, Ward(s): 3
ICrichton@townshipofsevern.com
Ron Stevens, Councillor, Ward(s): 4
RStevens@townshipofsevern.com
Rob Ferguson, Councillor, Ward(s): 5
RFerguson@townshipofsevern.com
Henry Sander, Clerk-Treasurer & Director, Corporate Services
705-325-2315
Clayton Cameron, Director, Public Works
Eric Dowell, Director, Fire & Emergency Services
David Parks, Director, Planning & Development
705-325-2315
James Oakley, Chief Building Official
705-325-2315
Rob Martel, Officer, Municipal Law Enforcement

Shelburne

Town of Shelburne Municipal Office
203 Main St. East
Shelburne, ON L0N 1S0
Tel: 519-925-2600; *Fax:* 519-925-6134
www.townofshelburne.on.ca
Municipal Type: Town
Incorporated: March 22, 1879 *Area:* 6.44 sq km
County or District: Dufferin; *Population in 2011:* 5,846
Provincial Electoral District(s): Dufferin-Caledon
Federal Electoral District(s): Dufferin-Caledon
Next Election: Oct. 27, 2014 (4 year terms)
Note: Incorporated as a town on Dec. 31, 1976.
Ed Crewson, Mayor
519-925-2600, Fax: 519-925-6134
John Telfer, AMCT, Chief Administrative Officer & Town Clerk
519-925-2600
jtelfer@townofshelburne.on.ca

Shuniah

420 Leslie Ave.
Thunder Bay, ON P7A 1X8
Tel: 807-683-4545
shuniah@shuniah.org
www.shuniah.org
Municipal Type: Township
Incorporated: 1873 *Area:* 569.18 sq km
County or District: Thunder Bay District; *Population in 2011:* 2,737
Provincial Electoral District(s): Thunder Bay-Superior North
Federal Electoral District(s): Thunder Bay-Superior North
Next Election: Oct. 27, 2014 (4 year terms)
Maria Harding, Reeve
807-983-2276
mharding@tbaytel.net
Wendy Hamlin, Clerk
whamlin@shuniah.org

Sioux Lookout, Municipality of

P.O. Box 158
25 Fifth Ave.
Sioux Lookout, ON P8T 1A4
Tel: 807-737-2700
admin@siouxlookout.ca
www.siouxlookout.ca
Municipal Type: Town
Incorporated: 1912 *Area:* 378.61 sq km
County or District: Kenora District; *Population in 2011:* 5,037
Provincial Electoral District(s): Kenora-Rainy River
Federal Electoral District(s): Kenora
Next Election: Oct. 27, 2014 (4 year terms)
Dennis Leney, Mayor
dleney@siouxlookout.ca
Mary L. MacKenzie, Municipal Clerk
clerk@siouxlookout.ca

Sioux Narrows-Nestor Falls

P.O. Box 417
Sioux Narrows, ON P0X 1N0
Tel: 807-226-5241; *Fax:* 807-226-5712
www.siouxnarrows-nestorfalls.ca
Municipal Type: Township
Area: 1,221.56 sq km
County or District: Kenora District; *Population in 2011:* 720
Provincial Electoral District(s): Kenora-Rainy River
Federal Electoral District(s): Kenora
Next Election: Oct. 27, 2014 (4 year terms)
William (Bill) Thompson, Mayor
Wanda Kabel, Chief Administrative Officer

Smith-Ennismore-Lakefield

P.O. Box 270
1310 Centre Line, RR#4
Bridgenorth, ON K0L 1H0
Tel: 705-292-9507; *Fax:* 705-292-8964
www.smithennismorelakefield.on.ca
Other Information: Toll-Free Phone: 1-877-213-7419 (in 705 area code)
Municipal Type: Township
Area: 318.77 sq km
County or District: Peterborough; *Population in 2011:* 16,846
Provincial Electoral District(s): Peterborough
Federal Electoral District(s): Peterborough
Next Election: Oct. 27, 2014 (4 year terms)
Mary Smith, Reeve
705-652-0784
Andy Mitchell, Deputy Reeve
705-931-4873
Donna Ballantyne, Councillor, Ward(s): Ennismore
705-292-7174
Anita Locke, Councillor, Ward(s): Lakefield
705-652-1086
Sherry Senis, Councillor, Ward(s): Smith
705-657-1166
Angela Chittick, Clerk
705-292-9507
Janice Lavalley, Chief Administrative Officer
705-292-9507
R. Lane Vance, Treasurer & Manager, Financial Services
705-292-9507
Ed Barber, Manager, Recreation
705-292-9507
Stephen Crough, Manager, Public Works
705-292-9507
Robert Lamarre, Manager, Building & Planning
705-292-9507
Gord Jopling, Fire Chief
705-292-7282
Kim Berry, Coordinator, Human Resources
705-292-9507

Smiths Falls

77 Beckwith St. North
Smiths Falls, ON K7A 4T6
Tel: 613-283-4124
info@smithsfalls.ca
www.smithsfalls.ca
Municipal Type: Separated for Municipal Purposes Only
Incorporated: 1854 *Area:* 8.2 sq km
County or District: Lanark; *Population in 2011:* 8,978
Provincial Electoral District(s): Lanark-Frontenac-Lennox & Addington
Federal Electoral District(s): Lanark-Frontenac-Lennox & Addington
Next Election: Oct. 27, 2014 (4 year terms)
Note: Incorporated as a town on Jan. 1, 1883. In Dec. 1902, the Town of Smiths Falls became the Separated Town of Smiths Falls.
Dennis Staples, Mayor
613-283-4124, Fax: 613-283-4764
mayor@smithsfalls.ca
Kerry Costello, Clerk
613-283-4124
kcostello@smithsfalls.ca

Smooth Rock Falls

P.O. Box 249
142 First St.
Smooth Rock Falls, ON P0L 2B0
Tel: 705-338-2717; *Fax:* 705-338-2584
comments@townsrf.ca
www.townofsmoothrockfalls.ca
Municipal Type: Town
Incorporated: 1929 *Area:* 199.79 sq km
County or District: Cochrane District; *Population in 2011:* 1,376
Provincial Electoral District(s): Timmins-James Bay
Federal Electoral District(s): Algoma-Manitoulin-Kapuskasing
Next Election: Oct. 27, 2014 (4 year terms)
Michel Arseneault, Mayor
Luc Denault, Chief Administrative Officer
luc.denault@townsrf.ca

South Algonquin

P.O. Box 217
Hay Creek Rd.
Whitney, ON K0J 2M0
Tel: 613-637-2650; *Fax:* 613-637-5368
southalgonquin@xplornet.com
www.township.southalgonquin.on.ca
Other Information: Toll-Free Phone: 1-888-307-3187
Municipal Type: Township
Area: 871.31 sq km
County or District: Nipissing District; *Population in 2011:* 1,211
Provincial Electoral District(s): Renfrew-Nipissing-Pembroke
Federal Electoral District(s): Renfrew-Nipissing-Pembroke
Next Election: Oct. 27, 2014 (4 year terms)
Jane A.E. Dumas, Mayor
613-637-5261
mayor.tsa@xplornet.ca

Harold Luckasavitch, Clerk-Treasurer
613-637-2650, Fax: 613-637-5368

South Bruce
P.O. Box 540
21 Gordon St. East
Teeswater, ON N0G 2S0
Tel: 519-392-6623; *Fax:* 519-392-6266
clerk@town.southbruce.on.ca
www.town.southbruce.on.ca
Municipal Type: Municipality
Incorporated: 1999 *Area:* 487.17 sq km
County or District: Bruce; *Population in 2011:* 5,685
Provincial Electoral District(s): Huron-Bruce
Federal Electoral District(s): Huron-Bruce
Next Election: Oct. 27, 2014 (4 year terms)
Note: Amalgamation of the Village of Mildmay, the Township of Carrick, the Village of Teeswater, & the Township of Culross.
William Goetz, Mayor
519-367-5509
Sharon Chambers, Chief Administrative Officer & Clerk
519-392-6623

South Bruce Peninsula
P.O. Box 310
315 George St.
Wiarton, ON N0H 2T0
Tel: 519-534-1400; *Fax:* 519-534-4862
admin@southbrucepeninsula.com
www.southbrucepeninsula.com
Other Information: Toll-Free Phone: 1-877-534-1400
Municipal Type: Town
Area: 531.9 sq km
County or District: Bruce; *Population in 2011:* 8,413
Provincial Electoral District(s): Bruce-Grey-Owen Sound
Federal Electoral District(s): Bruce-Grey-Owen Sound
Next Election: Oct. 27, 2014 (4 year terms)
John D. Close, B.SC.(Agri), Mayor
519-534-1589
John.Close@southbrucepeninsula.com
Angie Cathrae, Clerk
519-534-1400
sbpen@bmts.com

South Dundas
P.O. Box 160
4296 County Rd. 31
Williamsburg, ON K0C 2H0
Tel: 613-535-2673; *Fax:* 613-535-2099
mail@southdundas.com
www.southdundas.com
Other Information: Toll-Free Phone: 1-800-265-0619
Municipal Type: Township
Area: 519.98 sq km
County or District: Stormont, Dundas & Glengarry; *Population in 2011:* 10,794
Provincial Electoral District(s): Stormont-Dundas-South Glengarry
Federal Electoral District(s): Stormont-Dundas-South Glengarry
Next Election: Oct. 27, 2014 (4 year terms)
Steven J. Byvelds, Mayor, Fax: 613-535-2746
mayor@southdundas.com
Jim Locke, Deputy Mayor, Fax: 613-652-2233
jp.locke@hotmail.com
Evonne Delegarde, Councillor
evonne_delegarde@hotmail.com
Jim Graham, Councillor
jwg60@xplornet.com
Archie L. Mellan, Councillor
amellan@ripnet.com
Brenda M. Brunt, Clerk
bbrunt@southdundas.com
Stephen McDonald, Chief Administrative Officer
smcdonald@southdundas.com
Shannon Geraghty, Treasurer
sgeraghty@southdundas.com
Hugh Garlough, Manager, Public Works
hgarlough@southdundas.com
Don J.W. Lewis, Manager, Planning & Enforcement
dlewis@southdundas.com
Don W. Lewis, Manager, Recreation
arena@southdundas.com
Chris McDonough, Fire Chief
cmcdonough@southdundas.com

South Frontenac
P.O. Box 100
4432 George St.
Sydenham, ON K0H 2T0
Tel: 613-376-3027; *Fax:* 613-376-6657
admin@township.southfrontenac.on.ca
www.township.southfrontenac.on.ca
Other Information: Toll-Free Phone: 1-800-559-5862
Municipal Type: Township
Incorporated: Jan. 1, 1998 *Area:* 941.28 sq km
County or District: Frontenac; *Population in 2011:* 18,113
Provincial Electoral District(s): Lanark-Frontenac-Lennox & Addington
Federal Electoral District(s): Lanark-Frontenac-Lennox & Addington
Next Election: Oct. 27, 2014 (4 year terms)
Gary Davison, Mayor
613-376-3027, Fax: 613-376-6657
davison4544@yahoo.ca
Del Stowe, Councillor, Ward(s): Bedford
delstowe@yahoo.com
Mark Tinlin, Councillor, Ward(s): Bedford
marktinlin@rideau.net
Allan G. McPhail, Councillor, Ward(s): Loughborough
mcphail@queensu.ca
Ron W. Vandewal, Councillor, Ward(s): Loughborough
lakevalley@kos.net
John R. McDougall, Councillor, Ward(s): Portland
john.mcdougall@xplornet.ca
Bill W.L. Robinson, Councillor, Ward(s): Portland
wlrobinson@bell.net
Cam L. Naish, Councillor, Ward(s): Storrington
camnaish@kingston.net
Larry W. York, Councillor, Ward(s): Storrington
blue@reztel.net
Wayne Orr, Chief Administrative Officer
613-376-3027
worr@township.southfrontenac.on.ca
Deborah Bracken, Treasurer
613-376-3027
dbracken@township.southfrontenac.on.ca
Mark Segsworth, Manager, Public Works
613-376-3027
msegsworth@township.southfrontenac.on.ca
Rick Chesebrough, Fire Chief
613-376-3027
rchesebrough@township.southfrontenac.on.ca
Alan Revill, Chief Building Inspector
613-376-3027
arevill@township.southfrontenac.on.ca
Lindsay Mills, Coordinator, Planning
613-376-3027
lmills@township.southfrontenac.on.ca

South Glengarry
6 Oak St.
Lancaster, ON K0C 1N0
Tel: 613-347-1166
info@southglengarry.com
www.southglengarry.com
Municipal Type: Township
Incorporated: Jan. 1, 1998 *Area:* 604.91 sq km
County or District: Stormont, Dundas & Glengarry; *Population in 2011:* 13,162
Provincial Electoral District(s): Stormont-Dundas-South Glengarry
Federal Electoral District(s): Stormont-Dundas-South Glengarry
Next Election: Oct. 27, 2014 (4 year terms)
Jim McDonell, Mayor, Fax: 613-347-3411
jim.mcdonell@bell.net
Ian McLeod, Deputy Mayor
613-933-5602, Fax: 613-933-2620
ian.mcleod@genivar.com
Trevor Bougie, Councillor
tx_bougie@laurentian.ca
Joyce Gravelle, Councillor
joyceg50@bell.net
Bill McKenzie, Councillor
613-347-3254, Fax: 613-347-3119
Marilyn Lebrun, Clerk
613-347-1166, Fax: 613-347-3411
marilyn@southglengarry.com
Derik Brandt, Chief Administrative Officer
613-347-1166, Fax: 613-347-3411
derik@southglengarry.com
Michel J. Samson, Treasurer & Deputy Clerk
613-347-1166, Fax: 613-347-3411
mike@southglengarry.com
Joanne Haley, General Manager, Community Services
613-347-1166, Fax: 613-347-3411
jhaley@southglengarry.com
Ewen MacDonald, General Manager, Infrastructure Services
613-347-2040, Fax: 613-347-3411
ewen@southglengarry.com
Dwane Crawford, Director, Development
613-347-1166, Fax: 613-347-3411
dwane@southglengarry.com
Shawn Killoran, Director, Water & Wastewater
613-931-3036
shawnkilloran@on.aibn.com
Roger Lapierre, Director, Roads
613-930-3445, Fax: 613-347-3411
roger.southglengarry@bellnet.ca
Gary Poupart, Manager, Property Standards & Enforcement
613-347-1166, Fax: 613-347-3411
gary@southglengarry.com

South Huron
P.O. Box 759
322 Main St. South
Exeter, ON N0M 1S6
Tel: 519-235-0310; *Fax:* 519-235-3304
info@southhuron.ca
www.southhuron.ca
Other Information: Toll-Free: 1-877-204-0747
Municipal Type: Municipality
Incorporated: 2001 *Area:* 425.35 sq km
County or District: Huron; *Population in 2011:* 9,945
Provincial Electoral District(s): Huron-Bruce
Federal Electoral District(s): Huron-Bruce
Next Election: Oct. 27, 2014 (4 year terms)
George Robertson, Mayor
519-235-2030
g.robertson@southhuron.ca
Michael Di Lullo, Clerk & Manager, Corporate Services
519-235-0310
m.dilullo@southhuron.ca

South River
P.O. Box 310
63 Marie St.
South River, ON P0A 1X0
Tel: 705-386-2573
info@southriverontario.com
www.southriverontario.com
Other Information: Public Works, Phone: 705-386-0245
Municipal Type: Village
Incorporated: 1907 *Area:* 4.04 sq km
County or District: Parry Sound District; *Population in 2011:* 1,049
Provincial Electoral District(s): Parry Sound-Muskoka
Federal Electoral District(s): Parry Sound-Muskoka
Next Election: Oct. 27, 2014 (4 year terms)
Jim Coleman, Mayor
Susan Arnold, Administrator & Clerk

South Stormont
P.O. Box 84
2 Mille Roches Rd.
Long Sault, ON K0C 1P0
Tel: 613-534-8889; *Fax:* 613-534-2280
info@southstormont.ca
www.southstormont.ca
Other Information: Toll-Free Phone: 1-800-265-3915
Municipal Type: Township
Area: 447.46 sq km
County or District: Stormont, Dundas & Glengarry; *Population in 2011:* 12,617
Provincial Electoral District(s): Stormont-Dundas-South Glengarry
Federal Electoral District(s): Stormont-Dundas-South Glengarry
Next Election: Oct. 27, 2014 (4 year terms)
Bryan McGillis, Mayor
613-577-0753, Fax: 613-937-3116
mayor@southstormont.ca
Tammy Hart, Deputy Mayor
613-984-2543
tammy.farms@xplornet.com
Barry Brownlee, Councillor
613-537-9753
Richard F. Waldroff, Councillor
613-537-8226, Fax: 613-362-7596
rwaldroff@bell.net
Cindy Woods, Councillor
613-537-2977
cindy_woods@xplornet.com
Betty de Haan, Chief Administrative Officer & Clerk
613-534-8889
betty@southstormont.ca
Johanna Barkley, Treasurer
613-534-8889
johanna@southstormont.ca

Hilton Cryderman, Manager, Building & Development
613-534-8889
hilton@southstormont.ca
Dan Pilon, Manager, Public Works
613-534-8889
dan@southstormont.ca
Roger Desjardins, Fire Chief
613-534-8889
roger@southstormont.ca
Harry Hutchinson, Deputy Chief Building Official & Superintendent, Drainage
613-534-8889
buildinginspector@southstormont.ca
Gord Ramsay, Officer, Law Enforcement
613-534-8889
bylawofficer@southstormont.ca

South-West Oxford
312915 Dereham Line
Mount Elgin, ON N0J 1N0
Tel: 519-485-0477; *Fax:* 519-485-2932
dbarnes@swox.org (Office)
www.swox.org
Other Information: Phone, Works Department: 519-877-2702
Municipal Type: Township
Area: 370.63 sq km
County or District: Oxford; *Population in 2011:* 7,544
Provincial Electoral District(s): Oxford
Federal Electoral District(s): Oxford
Next Election: Oct. 27, 2014 (4 year terms)
David Mayberry, Mayor
519-485-3642
mayor@swox.org
Mary Ellen Greb, Chief Administrative Officer
519-877-2702
cao@swox.org

Southgate
185667 Grey Rd. 9, RR#1
Dundalk, ON N0C 1B0
Tel: 519-923-2110; *Fax:* 519-923-9262
info@town.southgate.on.ca
www.town.southgate.on.ca
Other Information: Toll-Free Phone: 1-888-560-6607
Municipal Type: Township
Incorporated: Jan. 1, 2001 *Area:* 643.95 sq km
County or District: Grey; *Population in 2011:* 7,190
Provincial Electoral District(s): Bruce-Grey-Owen Sound
Federal Electoral District(s): Bruce-Grey-Owen Sound
Next Election: Oct. 27, 2014 (4 year terms)
Note: Amalgamation of the Village of Dundalk, the Township of Proton & the Township of Egremont.
Brian A. Milne, Mayor
519-334-3712, Fax: 519-334-9836
brian.milne@grey.ca
Carol Watson, Clerk
519-923-9262
cwatson@town.southgate.on.ca

Southwest Middlesex, Municipality of
P.O. Box 218
153 McKellar St.
Glencoe, ON N0L 1M0
Tel: 519-287-2015; *Fax:* 519-287-2359
info@southwestmiddlesex.ca
www.southwestmiddlesex.ca
Municipal Type: Township
Incorporated: Jan. 1, 2001 *Area:* 427.92 sq km
County or District: Middlesex; *Population in 2011:* 5,860
Provincial Electoral District(s): Lambton-Kent-Middlesex
Federal Electoral District(s): Lambton-Kent-Middlesex
Next Election: Oct. 27, 2014 (4 year terms)
Note: Amalgamation of the Villages of Glencoe & Wardsville & the Townships of Ekfrid & Mosa.
Doug Reycraft, Mayor
519-287-2015, Fax: 519-287-2359
dreycraft@southwestmiddlesex.ca
Janneke Newitt, Administrator & Clerk
519-287-2015
jnewitt@southwestmiddlesex.ca

Southwold
General Delivery
35663 Fingal Line
Fingal, ON N0L 1K0
Tel: 519-769-2010; *Fax:* 519-769-2837
southwold@twp.southwold.on.ca
www.twp.southwold.on.ca
Municipal Type: Township
Area: 301.71 sq km
County or District: Elgin; *Population in 2011:* 4,494
Provincial Electoral District(s): Elgin-Middlesex-London
Federal Electoral District(s): Elgin-Middlesex-London
Next Election: Oct. 27, 2014 (4 year terms)
James McIntyre, Mayor
519-764-9764
Donna Ethier, Chief Administrative Officer, Clerk, & Deputy Treasurer
cao@twp.southwold.on.ca

Spanish
P.O. Box 70
8 Trunk Rd.
Spanish, ON P0P 2A0
Tel: 705-844-2300; *Fax:* 705-844-2622
info@town.spanish.on.ca
www.town.spanish.on.ca
Municipal Type: Town
Area: 106.02 sq km
County or District: Algoma District; *Population in 2011:* 696
Provincial Electoral District(s): Algoma-Manitoulin
Federal Electoral District(s): Algoma-Manitoulin-Kapuskasing
Next Election: Oct. 27, 2014 (4 year terms)
Note: Formerly the Township of Shedden. Effective Oct. 1, 2004, the name was changed to the Town of Spanish.
Gary Bishop, Mayor
Brent St. Denis, Chief Administrative Officer & Clerk-Treasurer
brent.st.denis@ontera.net

Springwater
Township of Springwater Administrative Ctr.
2231 Nursery Rd.
Minesing, ON L0L 1Y2
Tel: 705-728-4784; *Fax:* 705-728-6957
info@springwater.ca; council@springwater.ca
www.springwater.ca
Municipal Type: Township
Incorporated: Jan. 1, 1994 *Area:* 536.3 sq km
County or District: Simcoe; *Population in 2011:* 18,223
Provincial Electoral District(s): Simcoe-Grey
Federal Electoral District(s): Simcoe-Grey
Next Election: Oct. 27, 2014 (4 year terms)
Linda Collins, Mayor
705-728-4784, Fax: 705-728-6957
linda.collins@springwater.ca
Dan McLean, Deputy Mayor
705-728-4784, Fax: 705-728-6957
dan.mclean@springwater.ca
Dan Clement, Councillor, Ward(s): 1
705-728-4784, Fax: 705-728-6957
dan.clement@springwater.ca
Perry Ritchie, Councillor, Ward(s): 2
705-728-4784, Fax: 705-728-6957
perry.ritchie@springwater.ca
Rick Webster, Councillor, Ward(s): 3
705-728-4784, Fax: 705-728-6957
rick.webster@springwater.ca
Sandy McConkey, Councillor, Ward(s): 4
705-728-4784, Fax: 705-737-4729
sandy.mcconkey@springwater.ca
Jack Hanna, Councillor, Ward(s): 5
705-728-4784, Fax: 705-728-6957
jack.hanna@springwater.ca
John Daly, Clerk & Director, Corporate Services
705-728-4784, Fax: 705-728-6957
Winanne Grant, Chief Administrative Officer
705-728-4784, Fax: 705-728-6957
Laurie Kennard, CA, Treasurer & Director, Finance
705-728-4784
finance@springwater.ca
Ron Belcourt, Director, Recreation Services
705-728-4784
recreation@springwater.ca
Brad Sokach, Director, Public Works
705-728-4784
publicworks@springwater.ca
Tony Van Dam, Director, Fire & Emergency Services
705-728-4784, Fax: 705-726-7223
fire@springwater.ca
Nick Ippolito, Chief Building Official
705-728-4784, Fax: 705-728-2759
building@springwater.ca
Barb Fralick, Manager, Human Resources
705-728-4784, Fax: 705-728-6957
Jennett Mays, Coordinator, Communications
705-728-4784, Fax: 705-728-6957
jennett.mays@springwater.ca
Brent Spagnol, Planner
705-728-4784, Fax: 705-728-6957
planning@springwater.ca

St.-Charles, Municipality of
P.O. Box 70
2 King St. East
St Charles, ON P0M 2W0
Tel: 705-867-2032; *Fax:* 705-867-5789
cta@stcharlesontario.ca; tourism@stcharlesontario.ca
www.stcharlesontario.ca
Other Information: Toll-Free Phone: 1-877-867-2032
Municipal Type: Town
Area: 318.47 sq km
County or District: Sudbury District; *Population in 2011:* 1,282
Provincial Electoral District(s): Timiskaming-Cochrane
Federal Electoral District(s): Nickel Belt
Next Election: Oct. 27, 2014 (4 year terms)
Paul Schoppman, Mayor
mayor@stcharlesontario.ca
Theresa Niemi, Clerk-Treasurer & Administrator

Stirling-Rawdon
P.O. Box 40
14 Demorest Rd.
Stirling, ON K0K 3E0
Tel: 613-395-3380; *Fax:* 613-395-0864
info@stirling-rawdon.com
www.stirling-rawdon.com
Municipal Type: Township
Area: 280.63 sq km
County or District: Hastings; *Population in 2011:* 4,978
Provincial Electoral District(s): Prince Edward-Hastings
Federal Electoral District(s): Prince Edward-Hastings
Next Election: Oct. 27, 2014 (4 year terms)
Rodney Cooney, Mayor
613-395-3947
Kevin Heath, Clerk-Administrator
cao@stirling-rawdon.com

Stone Mills
4504 County Rd. 4
Centreville, ON K0K 1N0
Tel: 613-378-2475; *Fax:* 613-378-0033
caoclerk@stonemills.com
www.stonemills.com
Municipal Type: Township
Incorporated: Jan. 1, 1998 *Area:* 688.28 sq km
County or District: Lennox-Addington; *Population in 2011:* 7,560
Provincial Electoral District(s): Lanark-Frontenac-Lennox & Addington
Federal Electoral District(s): Lanark-Frontenac-Lennox & Addington
Next Election: Oct. 27, 2014 (4 year terms)
Note: Amalgamation of the former Township of Camden East, Township of Sheffield & Village of Newburgh.
Douglas Bearance, Reeve
613-375-8874
bearance@frontenac.net
Darlene Plumley, Chief Administrative Officer & Municipal Clerk
613-378-2475
caoclerk@stonemills.com

Stormont, Dundas & Glengarry
26 Pitt St.
Cornwall, ON K6J 3P2
Tel: 613-932-1515; *Fax:* 613-936-2913
info@sdgcounties.ca
www.sdgcounties.ca
Other Information: Toll-Free Phone: 1-800-267-7158
Municipal Type: United County
Area: 3,306.86 sq km
Population in 2011: 111,164
Next Election: Oct. 27, 2014 (4 year terms)
Steven Byvelds, Warden & Mayor, Ward(s): South Dundas
mayor@southdundas.com
Eric Duncan, Mayor, Ward(s): North Dundas
eduncan2@gmail.com
Gerry Boyce, Deputy Mayor, Ward(s): North Dundas
glboyce@hotmail.com
Grant Crack, Mayor, Ward(s): North Glengarry
613-525-1110
grantcrack@northglengarry.ca
Chris McDonell, Deputy Mayor, Ward(s): North Glengarry
cy.mcdonell@sympatico.ca
Denis Fife, Mayor, Ward(s): North Stormont
613-984-2059
fifeag@plantpioneer.com
Bill McGimpsey, Deputy Mayor, Ward(s): North Stormont
mcgimpsey@ontarioeast.net
James Locke, Deputy Mayor, Ward(s): South Dundas
jp.locke@hotmail.com
Jim McDonell, Mayor, Ward(s): South Glengarry
jim.mcdonell@bell.net

Ian McLeod, Deputy Mayor, Ward(s): South Glengarry
613-933-5602
ian.mcleod@genivar.com
Bryan McGillis, Mayor, Ward(s): South Stormont
mayor@southstormont.ca
Tammy Hart, Deputy Mayor, Ward(s): South Stormont
tammy.farms@xplornet.com
Helen Thomson, Clerk
Tim J. Simpson, Chief Administrative Officer
Vanessa Bennett, Treasurer
Benjamin deHaan, P.Emg., County Engineer
Michael Otis, County Planner

Strathroy-Caradoc

52 Frank St.
Strathroy, ON N7G 2R4
Tel: 519-245-1070; *Fax:* 519-245-6353
general@strathroy-caradoc.ca
www.strathroy-caradoc.ca
Municipal Type: Township
Incorporated: 2001 *Area:* 274.19 sq km
County or District: Middlesex; *Population in 2011:* 20,978
Provincial Electoral District(s): Lambton-Kent-Middlesex
Federal Electoral District(s): Lambton-Kent-Middlesex
Next Election: Oct. 27, 2014 (4 year terms)
Note: Amalgamation of the Town of Strathroy & the Township of Caradoc.
Joanne Vanderheyden, Mayor
519-245-1105, Fax: 519-245-6353
jvanderheyden@strathroy-caradoc.ca
Brad Richards, Deputy Mayor
519-245-1105, Fax: 519-245-6353
brichards@strathroy-caradoc.ca
Marie Baker, Councillor, Ward(s): 1 - Strathroy
519-245-8696, Fax: 519-245-0076
mbaker@strathroy-caradoc.caadoc.ca
John G. Brennan, Councillor, Ward(s): 1 - Strathroy
519-245-2680
jbrennan@strathroy-caradoc.ca
Dave Cameron, Councillor, Ward(s): 1 - Strathroy
dcameron@strathroy-caradoc.ca
Steve Pelkman, Councillor, Ward(s): 1 - Strathroy
519-245-5277
spelkman@strathroy-caradoc.ca
Larry Cowan, Councillor, Ward(s): 2 - Caradoc
lcowan@strathroy-caradoc.ca
Steve Dausett, Councillor, Ward(s): 2 - Caradoc
519-246-1900
sdausett@strathroy-caradoc.ca
Neil Flegel, Councillor, Ward(s): 2 - Caradoc
nflegel@strathroy-caradoc.ca
Angela Toth, Clerk & Director, Corporate Services
519-245-1105, Fax: 224- -
atoth@strathroy-caradoc.ca
Jane McPherson, Treasurer & Director, Financial Services
519-245-1105, Fax: 519-245-2177
jmcpherson@strathroy-caradoc.ca
Tom Gibson, Director, Fire Services & Fire Chief
519-245-1990
tgibson@strathroy-caradoc.ca
Tim Hanna, Director, Recreation & Leisure Services
519-245-1105, Fax: 519-245-9534
thanna@strathroy-caradoc.ca
Mark Harris, Director, Environmental Services
519-245-2010
mharris@strathroy-caradoc.ca
Matthew Stephenson, Director, Building & Waste Services
519-245-1105
mstephenson@strathroy-caradoc.ca
Brad Dausett, Manager, Roads
519-245-1105, Fax: 519-245-6353
bdausett@strathroy-caradoc.ca
Andrew Meyer, Manager, Community Development
519-245-0492, Fax: 519-245-1073
agmeyer@strathroymuseum.ca
Leslie Pommer, Coordinator, Customer Services & Concession
519-245-7557
lpommer@strathroy-caradoc.ca
Paul Hicks, Planner
519-245-1105, Fax: 519-245-6353
phicks@strathroy-caradoc.ca

Strong

P.O. Box 1120
28 Municipal Lane
Sundridge, ON P0A 1Z0
Tel: 705-384-5819; *Fax:* 705-384-5892
www.strongtownship.com
Municipal Type: Township
Area: 158.73 sq km
County or District: Parry Sound District; *Population in 2011:* 1,341
Provincial Electoral District(s): Parry Sound-Muskoka
Federal Electoral District(s): Parry Sound-Muskoka
Next Election: Oct. 27, 2014 (4 year terms)
Christine Ellis, Mayor
705-384-5243
Linda Maurer, Clerk & Treasurer
705-384-5819

Sudbury District

c/o Manitoulin-Sudbury District Services Bd
210 Mead Blvd.
Espanola, ON P5E 1R9

www.msdsb.net
Municipal Type: District
Area: 38,504.53 sq km
Population in 2011: 21,196
Provincial Electoral District(s): Algoma-Manitoulin; Nickel Belt
Federal Electoral District(s): Nickel Belt; Algoma-Manitoulin-Kapuskasing
Les Gamble, Board Chair, Manitoulin-Sudbury District Services Board
705-865-2646
lgamble@msdsb.nett
Fern Dominelli, Chief Administrative Officer, Manitoulin-Sudbury District Svs Bd
705-862-7850, Fax: 705-862-7866
fern.dominelli@msdsb.net; cao@msdsb.net

Sundridge

P.O. Box 129
110 Main St.
Sundridge, ON P0A 1Z0
Tel: 705-384-5316; *Fax:* 705-384-7874
villageoffice@sundridge.ca
www.sundridge.ca
Municipal Type: Village
Incorporated: 1889 *Area:* 2.23 sq km
County or District: Parry Sound District; *Population in 2011:* 985
Provincial Electoral District(s): Parry Sound-Muskoka
Federal Electoral District(s): Parry Sound-Muskoka
Next Election: Oct. 27, 2014 (4 year terms)
Elgin Schneider, Mayor
705-384-5883
elgin28@sympatico.ca
Lillian S. Fowler, Chief Administrative Officer & Clerk
705-384-5316

Tarbutt & Tarbutt Additional

27 Barr Rd. South
Desbarats, ON P0R 1E0
Tel: 705-782-6776; *Fax:* 705-782-4274
tarbutttownship@bellnet.ca
www.tarbutttownship.com
Municipal Type: Township
Incorporated: 1889 *Area:* 52.82 sq km
County or District: Algoma District; *Population in 2011:* 396
Provincial Electoral District(s): Algoma-Manitoulin
Federal Electoral District(s): Sault Ste Marie
Next Election: Oct. 27, 2014 (4 year terms)
Ken Richie, Mayor
705-782-4386
Glenn Martin, Clerk-Treasurer

Tay

P.O. Box 100
450 Park St.
Victoria Harbour, ON L0K 2A0
Tel: 705-534-7248; *Fax:* 705-534-4493
taytownship@tay.ca
www.tay.ca
Municipal Type: Township
Area: 138.93 sq km
County or District: Simcoe; *Population in 2011:* 9,736
Provincial Electoral District(s): Simcoe North
Federal Electoral District(s): Simcoe North
Next Election: Oct. 27, 2014 (4 year terms)
Scott Warnock, Mayor
swarnock@tay.ca
Alison Thomas, Clerk
795-534-7248
athomas@tay.ca

Tay Valley

217 Harper Rd., RR#4
Perth, ON K7H 3C6
Tel: 613-267-5353; *Fax:* 613-264-8516
cao@tayvalleytwp.ca; treasurer@tayvalleytwp.ca
www.tayvalleytwp.ca
Other Information: Toll-Free Phone: 1-800-810-0161
Municipal Type: Township
Area: 527.46 sq km
County or District: Lanark; *Population in 2011:* 5,571
Provincial Electoral District(s): Lanark-Frontenac-Lennox & Addington
Federal Electoral District(s): Lanark-Frontenac-Lennox & Addington
Next Election: Oct. 27, 2014 (4 year terms)
Note: Formerly the Township of Bathurst Burgess Sherbrooke.
Keith Kerr, Reeve
613-267-4025
Amanda Mabo, Clerk & Returning Officer
613-267-5353
clerk@tayvalleytwp.ca

Tecumseh

917 Lesperance Rd.
Tecumseh, ON N8N 1W9
Tel: 519-735-2184; *Fax:* 519-735-6712
info@tecumseh.ca
www.tecumseh.ca
Municipal Type: Town
Incorporated: 1921 *Area:* 94.71 sq km
County or District: Essex; *Population in 2011:* 23,610
Provincial Electoral District(s): Windsor-Tecumseh
Federal Electoral District(s): Windsor-Tecumseh
Next Election: Oct. 27, 2014 (4 year terms)
Note: Restructuring occurred in 1999.
Gary McNamara, Mayor
gmcnamara@tecumseh.ca
Cheryl M. Hardcastle, Deputy Mayor & Councillor
519-818-2047
Marcel (Pat) Blais, Councillor, Ward(s): 1
519-735-2686
Rita Ossington, Councillor, Ward(s): 1
519-735-8251
Guy Dorion, Councillor, Ward(s): 2
519-735-8580
Joe Bachetti, Councillor, Ward(s): 3
519-979-3339
Tania C. Jobin, Councillor, Ward(s): 4
519-791-4213
Laura Moy, Clerk & Director, Staff Services
Tony Haddad, Chief Administrative Officer
Luc Gagnon, Treasurer & Director, Financial Services
Dan Piescic, Director, Public Works & Environmental Services
Shaun Fuerth, Director, Information Systems
Brian Hillman, Director, Planning & Building Services
Doug Pitre, Director, Fire Services
Denis Berthiume, Manager, Water Services
Casey Colthurst, Manager, Parks & Horticulture
Rob Filipov, Manager, Engineering Services
Kerri Rice, Manager, Recreation Programs & Events

Tehkummah

Municipal Building
456 Hwy. 542A
Tehkummah, ON P0P 2C0
Tel: 705-859-3293; *Fax:* 705-859-2605
www.manitoulin-island.com/tehkummah/
Municipal Type: Township
Incorporated: 1881 *Area:* 132.48 sq km
County or District: Manitoulin District; *Population in 2011:* 406
Provincial Electoral District(s): Algoma-Manitoulin
Federal Electoral District(s): Algoma-Manitoulin-Kapuskasing
Next Election: Oct. 27, 2014 (4 year terms)
Gary Brown, Reeve

Temagami

P.O. Box 220
Temagami, ON P0H 2H0
Tel: 705-569-3421; *Fax:* 705-569-2834
visit@temagami.ca; finance@temagami.ca
www.temagami.ca
Other Information: E-mail, Public Works: publicworks@temagami.ca
Municipal Type: Municipality
Incorporated: Jan. 1, 1998 *Area:* 1,906.42 sq km
County or District: Nipissing District; *Population in 2011:* 820
Provincial Electoral District(s): Timiskaming-Cochrane
Federal Electoral District(s): Nipissing-Timiskaming
Next Election: Oct. 27, 2014 (4 year terms)
John Hodgson, Mayor
mayor@temagami.ca
Elaine Gunnell, Municipal Clerk
705-569-3421
clerk@temagami.ca

Terrace Bay
P.O. Box 40
1 Selkirk Ave.
Terrace Bay, ON P0T 2W0
Tel: 807-825-3315; *Fax:* 807-825-9576
info@terracebay.ca
www.terracebay.ca
Municipal Type: Township
Incorporated: Sept. 1, 1947 *Area:* 151.04 sq km
County or District: Thunder Bay District; *Population in 2011:* 1,471
Provincial Electoral District(s): Thunder Bay-Superior North
Federal Electoral District(s): Thunder Bay-Superior North
Next Election: Oct. 27, 2014 (4 year terms)
Note: Incorporated as a municipality on July 1, 1959.
Michael King, Mayor
807-825-3501
m.king@terracebay.ca
Carmelo Notarbartolo, Chief Administrative Officer
807-825-3315
cao@terracebay.ca

Thames Centre
4305 Hamilton Rd.
Dorchester, ON N0L 1G3
Tel: 519-268-7334; *Fax:* 519-268-3928
inquiries@thamescentre.on.ca
www.thamescentre.on.ca
Other Information: Toll-Free Phone: 1-866-425-7306
Municipal Type: Municipality
Incorporated: Jan. 1, 2001 *Area:* 433.8 sq km
County or District: Middlesex; *Population in 2011:* 13,000
Provincial Electoral District(s): Elgin-Middlesex-London
Federal Electoral District(s): Elgin-Middlesex-London
Next Election: Oct. 27, 2014 (4 year terms)
Note: Amalgamation of the former Township of West Nissouri & the Township of North Dorchester.
Jim Maudsley, Mayor
jmaudsley@thamescentre.on.ca
Marcel Meyer, Deputy Mayor
mmeyer@thamescentre.on.ca
Mike Bontje, Councillor, Ward(s): 1
mbontje@thamescentre.on.ca
Chris Patterson, Councillor, Ward(s): 2
cpatterson@thamescentre.on.ca
Angelo Suffoletta, Councillor, Ward(s): 3
asuffoletta@thamescentre.on.ca
Margaret Lewis, Clerk & Manager, Cemetery
519-268-7334, Fax: 519-268-3928
mlewis@thamescentre.on.ca
Greg Borduas, Chief Administrative Officer
519-268-7334, Fax: 519-268-3928
gborduas@thamescentre.on.ca
John Cummings, Treasurer & Director, Financial Services
519-268-7334, Fax: 519-268-3928
jcummings@thamescentre.on.ca
Eric Boere, Director, Environmental Services
519-268-7334, Fax: 519-268-3928
eboere@thamescentre.on.ca
Stewart Findlater, Director, Community Services & Development
519-268-7334, Fax: 519-268-3928
sfindlater@thamescentre.on.ca
Randy Kalan, Fire Chief
519-268-7334
rkalan@thamescentre.on.ca
Dave Murray, Chief Building Official
519-268-7334, Fax: 519-268-3928
dmurray@thamescentre.on.ca
Dave Armstrong, Manager, Information Systems
519-268-7334, Fax: 519-268-3928
darmstrong@thamescentre.on.ca
Matt Jenner, Manager, Roads
519-268-7982
mjenner@thamescentre.on.ca
Liz Murray, Manager, Recreation & Facilities
519-268-7334, Fax: 519-268-3928
lizmurray@thamescentre.on.ca
Jarrod Craven, Superintendent, Environmental Services
519-268-7334, Fax: 519-268-3928
jcraven@thamescentre.on.ca
Dennis Shand, Superintendent, Drainage
519-268-7334, Fax: 519-268-3928
dshand@thamescentre.on.ca

The Archipelago
9 James St.
Parry Sound, ON P2A 1T4
Tel: 705-746-4243; *Fax:* 705-746-7301
www.thearchipelago.on.ca
Municipal Type: Township
Incorporated: April 1, 1980 *Area:* 602.3 sq km
County or District: Parry Sound District; *Population in 2011:* 566
Provincial Electoral District(s): Parry Sound-Muskoka
Federal Electoral District(s): Parry Sound-Muskoka
Next Election: Oct. 27, 2014 (4 year terms)
Note: Amalgamation of the Township of Georgian Bay South Archipelago & the Township of Georgian Bay North Archipelago.
Peter Ketchum, Reeve
416-944-1116
peter.ketchum@sympatico.ca
Stephen Kaegi, Chief Administrative Officer & Clerk
705-746-4243
skaegi@thearchipelago.on.ca

The Blue Mountains
P.O. Box 310
32 Mill St.
Thornbury, ON N0H 2P0
Tel: 519-599-3131; *Fax:* 519-599-7723
info@town.thebluemountains.on.ca
www.thebluemountains.ca
Other Information: Toll-Free Phone: 1-888-258-6867
Municipal Type: Town
Incorporated: Jan. 1, 2001 *Area:* 286.78 sq km
County or District: Grey; *Population in 2011:* 6,453
Provincial Electoral District(s): Simcoe-Grey
Federal Electoral District(s): Simcoe-Grey
Next Election: Oct. 27, 2014 (4 year terms)
Note: Amalgamation of Collingwood & Thornbury.
Ellen Anderson, Mayor
519-599-3131
mayor@thebluemountains.ca
Corrina Giles, Town Clerk
519-599-3131
cgiles@thebluemountains.ca

The Nation
958 Rte. 500 West
Casselman, ON K0A 1M0
Tel: 613-764-5444; *Fax:* 613-764-3310
mmccuaig@nationmun.ca
www.nationmun.ca
Other Information: Toll-Free Phone: 1-800-475-2855
Municipal Type: Municipality
Incorporated: Jan. 1, 1998 *Area:* 657.16 sq km
County or District: Prescott & Russell; *Population in 2011:* 11,668
Provincial Electoral District(s): Glengarry-Prescott-Russell
Federal Electoral District(s): Glengarry-Prescott-Russell
Next Election: Oct. 27, 2014 (4 year terms)
Note: Amalgamation of the Townships of Cambridge, South Plantagenet, Caledonia & the Village of St. Isidore.
François St. Amour, Mayor
fstamour@nationmun.ca
Raymond Lalande, Councillor, Ward(s): 1
613-673-1013
raylalande@nationmun.ca
Marcel Legault, Councillor, Ward(s): 2
613-524-2873
mlegault@nationmun.ca
Danika Bourgeois-Desnoyers, Councillor, Ward(s): 3
dbourgeoisdesnoyers@nationmun.ca
Richard Legault, Councillor, Ward(s): 4
613-443-3000
rlegault@nationmun.ca
Mary J. McCuaig, Chief Administrative Officer & Clerk
613-764-5444, Fax: 613-764-3310
mmccuaig@nationmun.ca
Cécile Lortie, Treasurer
613-764-5444, Fax: 613-764-3310
clortie@nationmun.ca
Marc Legault, Director, Public Works
613-524-2932, Fax: 613-524-1140
marclegault@nationmun.ca
Carol Ann Scott, Director, Recreation
613-524-2529
cscott@nationmun.ca
Todd Bayly, Chief Building Official
613-764-5444, Fax: 613-764-3310
tbayly@nationmun.ca
Jocelyn Ferguson, Manager, LAN
613-764-5444, Fax: 613-764-3310
webmaster@nationmun.ca
Guylain Laflèche, Municipal Planner
613-764-5444, Fax: 613-764-3310
glafleche@nationmun.ca
Yves Roy, Senior Officer, Municipal Law Enforcement Officer
613-524-2932
yvesroy@nationmun.ca
Roger Parent, Coordinator, Landfill Sites
613-524-2932, Fax: 613-524-1140
Doug Renaud, Senior Technician, Water & Sewers
613-524-2740, Fax: 613-524-5379
drenaud@nationmun.ca

The North Shore
P.O. Box 108
1385 Hwy. 17 West
Algoma Mills, ON P0R 1A0
Tel: 705-849-2213; *Fax:* 705-849-2428
www.townshipofthenorthshore.ca
Municipal Type: Township
Incorporated: March 1, 1973 *Area:* 230.79 sq km
County or District: Algoma District; *Population in 2011:* 509
Provincial Electoral District(s): Algoma-Manitoulin
Federal Electoral District(s): Algoma-Manitoulin-Kapuskasing
Next Election: Oct. 27, 2014 (4 year terms)
Note: Incorporated as a township on Dec. 1, 1978.
Randi Condie, Mayor
705-849-2489
mayor.northshore@ontera.net
Brenda Green, Clerk
bgreen@ontera.net

Thessalon
P.O. Box 220
169 Main St.
Thessalon, ON P0R 1L0
Tel: 705-842-2217; *Fax:* 705-842-2572
townthess@bellnet.ca
townthessalon.ca
Municipal Type: Town
Area: 4.37 sq km
County or District: Algoma District; *Population in 2011:* 1,279
Provincial Electoral District(s): Algoma-Manitoulin
Federal Electoral District(s): Algoma-Manitoulin-Kapuskasing
Next Election: Oct. 27, 2014 (4 year terms)
Brent Rankin, Mayor
Robert P. MacLean, Clerk-Treasurer

Thornloe
P.O. Box 30
Main St.
Thornloe, ON P0J 1S0
Tel: 705-563-8303; *Fax:* 705-563-8303
thorn@ntl.sympatico.ca
Municipal Type: Village
Area: 6.49 sq km
County or District: Timiskaming District; *Population in 2011:* 123
Provincial Electoral District(s): Timiskaming-Cochrane
Federal Electoral District(s): Timmins-James Bay
Next Election: Oct. 27, 2014 (4 year terms)
Ron Vottero, Reeve
Janet Gore, Clerk-Treasurer

Thunder Bay
District Social Services Administration Bd.
34 North Cumberland St., 4th Fl.
Thunder Bay, ON P7A 8B9

Municipal Type: District
Area: 103,706.27 sq km
Population in 2011: 146,057
Iain Angus, Chair, District of Thunder Bay Social Services Administration Bd.
807-474-0926, Fax: 807-474-0881
Melissa Harrison, CAO, District of Thunder Bay Social Services Administration Board
807-766-2103, Fax: 807-345-6146

Tillsonburg
200 Broadway St., 2nd Fl.
Tillsonburg, ON N4G 5A7
Tel: 519-842-9200; *Fax:* 519-688-0759
www.tillsonburg.ca
Municipal Type: Town
Incorporated: 1872 *Area:* 22.34 sq km
County or District: Oxford; *Population in 2011:* 15,301
Provincial Electoral District(s): Oxford
Federal Electoral District(s): Oxford
Next Election: Oct. 27, 2014 (4 year terms)
John Lessif, Mayor
jlessif@tillsonburg.ca
Mark Renaud, Deputy Mayor & Councillor
mrenaud@tillsonburg.ca
Dave Beres, Councillor
dberes@tillsonburg.ca
Mel Getty, Councillor
mgetty@tillsonburg.ca
Marty Klein, Councillor
mklein@tillsonburg.ca
Chris (Chrissy) Rosehart, Councillor
crosehart@tillsonburg.ca

Brian Stephenson, Councillor
bstephenson@tillsonburg.ca
Donna Hemeryck, Clerk
dhemeryck@tillsonburg.ca
Kelley Coulter, Chief Administrative Officer
kcoulter@tillsonburg.ca
Darrell Eddington, Director, Finance
deddington@town.tillsonburg.on.ca
Steve Lund, Director, Operations
slund@town.tillsonburg.on.ca
Bryan Drinkwater, Manager, Operations Utility
bdrinkwater@town.tillsonburg.on.ca
Peter Fung, Manager, Engineering
pfung@town.tillsonburg.on.ca
Kelly Batt, Manager, Parks & Facilities
kbatt@town.tillsonburg.on.ca
Geno Vanhaelewyn, Chief Building Official
gvanhaelewyn@tillsonburg.ca
Bob Parsons, Fire Chief
bparsons@town.tillsonburg.on.ca

Timiskaming

District Social Services Administrative Bd.
P.O. Box 310
29 Duncan Ave. North
Kirkland Lake, ON P2N 3H7
Tel: 705-567-9366
Other Information: Toll-Free Phone: 1-888-544-5555
Municipal Type: District
Area: 13,279.88 sq km
Population in 2011: 32,634
Jim Whipple, Chair, District of Timiskaming Social Services Administration Bd.
Don Studholme, CAO, District of Timiskaming Social Services Administration Board
705-567-9366, Fax: 705-567-3908
studholmed@dtssab.com

Tiny

130 Balm Beach Rd. West, RR#1
Perkinsfield, ON L0L 2J0
Tel: 705-526-4204; *Fax:* 705-526-2372
www.tiny.ca
Other Information: Toll-Free Phone: 1-866-939-8469
Municipal Type: Township
Area: 343.19 sq km
County or District: Simcoe; *Population in 2011:* 11,232
Provincial Electoral District(s): Simcoe North
Federal Electoral District(s): Simcoe North
Next Election: Oct. 27, 2014 (4 year terms)
Ray Millar, Mayor
George Lawrence, Deputy Mayor
André Claire, Councillor
Nigel Warren, Councillor
Gibb Wishart, Councillor
Doug Luker, Chief Administrative Officer-Clerk
Doug Taylor, Treasurer & Manager, Administrative Services
Henk Blom, Manager, Public Works
Roger E. Robitaille, Manager, Planning & Development
Randy Smith, Fire Chief
Steven Harvey, Chief Municipal Law Enforcement Officer
705-526-4136

Trent Hills

P.O. Box 1030
66 Front St. South
Campbellford, ON K0L 1L0
Tel: 705-653-1900; *Fax:* 705-653-5203
info@trenthills.ca
www.trenthills.ca
Other Information: Public Works Emergency, Phone: 705-653-2610
Municipal Type: Municipality
Area: 510.83 sq km
County or District: Northumberland; *Population in 2011:* 12,604
Provincial Electoral District(s): Northumberland-Quinte West
Federal Electoral District(s): Northumberland-Quinte West
Next Election: Oct. 27, 2014 (4 year terms)
Hector MacMillan, Mayor
705-653-1900
hector.macmillan@trenthills.ca
Rosemary Kelleher-MacLennan, Deputy Mayor, Ward(s): 1 - Campbellford / Seymour
705-653-3456, Fax: 705-653-5300
rosemary.kelleher-maclennan@trenthills.ca
Eugene Brahaney, Councillor, Ward(s): 1 - Campbellford / Seymour, Fax: 705-653-1879
gene.brahaney@trenthills.ca
William J. Thompson, Councillor, Ward(s): 1 - Campbellford / Seymour
705-653-3540, Fax: 705-653-5360
bill.thompson@trenthills.ca
Meirion Jones, Councillor, Ward(s): 2 - Percy
meirion.jones@trenthills.ca
Kim MacNeil, Councillor, Ward(s): 2 - Percy
kim.macneil@trenthills.ca
Robert Crate, Councillor, Ward(s): 3 - Hastings
bob.crate@trenthills.ca
Marg Montgomery, Clerk
705-653-1900
marg.montgomery@trenthills.ca
Mike Rutter, Chief Administrative Officer
705-653-1900
mike.rutter@trenthills.ca
Shelley Eliopoulos, Treasurer & Director, Finance
705-653-1900
shelleyeli@trenthills.ca
Richard Bolduc, Director, Public Works
705-653-1900
richard.bolduc@trenthills.ca
Jim Peters, Director, Planning & Development
705-653-1900
jim.peters@trenthills.ca
David Rogers, Chief Building Official
705-653-1900
dave.rogers@trenthills.ca
Neil Allanson, Manager, Roads & Urban Services
Scott White, Manager, Water & Wastewater Operations
Joanne Chartrand, Officer, Bylaw Enforcement
705-653-1900
joanne.chartrand@trenthills.ca
Scott Rose, Officer, Community Services
705-653-1900
scott.rose@trenthills.ca
Shari Lang, Coordinator, Health & Safety
705-653-1900
shari.lang@trenthills.ca
Kari Petherick, Coordinator, Human Resources & Special Projects
705-653-1900
kari.petherick@trenthills.ca

Tudor & Cashel

P.O. Box 436
371 Weslemkoon Lake Rd., RR#2
Gilmour, ON K0L 1W0
Tel: 613-474-2583; *Fax:* 613-474-0664
clerk@tudorandcashel.com
www.tudorandcashel.com
Municipal Type: Township
Incorporated: 1869 *Area:* 433.49 sq km
County or District: Hastings; *Population in 2011:* 586
Provincial Electoral District(s): Prince Edward-Hastings
Federal Electoral District(s): Prince Edward-Hastings
Next Election: Oct. 27, 2014 (4 year terms)
Wanda Donaldson, Reeve
613-473-4806
Bernice Crocker, Chief Administrative Officer
613-474-2583
clerk@tudorandcashel.com

Tweed

P.O. Box 729
255 Metcalf St.
Tweed, ON K0K 3J0
Tel: 613-478-2535; *Fax:* 613-478-6457
info@twp.tweed.on.ca
www.twp.tweed.on.ca
Municipal Type: Municipality
Incorporated: 1998 *Area:* 896.98 sq km
County or District: Hastings; *Population in 2011:* 6,057
Provincial Electoral District(s): Prince Edward-Hastings
Federal Electoral District(s): Prince Edward-Hastings
Next Election: Oct. 27, 2014 (4 year terms)
Jo-Anne Albert, Reeve
reeve@twp.tweed.on.ca
Patricia Bergeron, Chief Administrative Officer & Clerk
plb@twp.tweed.on.ca

Tyendinaga

859 Melrose Rd., RR#1
Shannonville, ON K0K 3A0
Tel: 613-396-1944; *Fax:* 613-396-2080
info@tyendinagatownship.com
www.tyendinagatownship.com
Municipal Type: Township
Area: 311.94 sq km
County or District: Hastings; *Population in 2011:* 4,150
Provincial Electoral District(s): Prince Edward-Hastings
Federal Electoral District(s): Prince Edward-Hastings
Next Election: Oct. 27, 2014 (4 year terms)
Rick Phillips, Reeve
613-477-3129
phillipsr@xplornet.ca
Steve Mercer, Clerk-Treasurer
clerk@tyendinagatownship.com

Uxbridge

P.O. Box 190
51 Toronto St. South
Uxbridge, ON L9P 1T1
Tel: 905-852-9181; *Fax:* 905-852-9674
info@town.uxbridge.on.ca
www.town.uxbridge.on.ca
Municipal Type: Township
Incorporated: 1872 *Area:* 420.65 sq km
County or District: Durham Reg. Mun.; *Population in 2011:* 20,623
Provincial Electoral District(s): Durham
Federal Electoral District(s): Durham
Next Election: Oct. 27, 2014 (4 year terms)
Note: Incorporated as a town in 1885, & town became part of Uxbridge Township in 1973.
Gerri Lynn O'Connor, Mayor
905-852-9181
gloconnor@town.uxbridge.on.ca
Jack Ballinger, Regional Councillor
416-320-0585
johnhballinger@gmail.com
Beverly Northeast, Councillor, Ward(s): 1
905-640-3966
bnortheast@powergate.ca
Pat Molloy, Councillor, Ward(s): 2
905-852-9181
pmolloy@town.uxbridge.on.ca
Pat Mikuse, Councillor, Ward(s): 3
905-852-0206
prmikuse@sympatico.ca
Jacob Mantle, Councillor, Ward(s): 4
905-852-9181
jmantle@town.uxbridge.on.ca
Gordon Highet, Councillor, Ward(s): 5
905-852-9181
ghighet@town.uxbridge.on.ca
Debbie Leroux, Clerk
905-852-9181, Fax: 905-852-9674
Ingrid Svelnis, Chief Administrative Officer
905-852-9181, Fax: 905-852-9674
isvelnis@town.uxbridge.on.ca
Alan Shultz, Treasurer
ashultz@town.uxbridge.on.ca
Ben Kester, C.E.T., Director, Public Works
905-852-9181, Fax: 905-852-9674
bkester@town.uxbridge.on.ca
Amanda Ferraro, Manager, Recreation, Culture, & Tourism
905-852-0095
aferraro@town.uxbridge.on.ca
Richard Vandezand, Manager, Development Services
905-852-9181, Fax: 905-852-9674
rvandezande@town.uxbridge.on.ca
Brian Pigozzo, Chief Building Official
905-852-9181, Fax: 905-852-9674
bpigozzo@town.uxbridge.on.ca
Scott Richardson, Fire Chief
srichardson@town.uxbridge.on.ca
Andre Gratton, MLEO (C), C.P.S.O., Supervisor, Municipal Law Enforcement
905-852-9181, Fax: 905-852-9674
agratton@town.uxbridge.on.ca

Val Rita-Harty

P.O. Box 100
2 Eglise Ave.
Val Rita, ON P0L 2G0
Tel: 705-335-6146; *Fax:* 705-337-6292
www.valharty.ca
Municipal Type: Township
Area: 382.64 sq km
County or District: Cochrane District; *Population in 2011:* 817
Provincial Electoral District(s): Timmins-James Bay
Federal Electoral District(s): Algoma-Manitoulin-Kapuskasing
Next Election: Oct. 27, 2014 (4 year terms)
Laurier Bourgeois, Mayor
Christiane Potvin, Clerk-Treasurer

Wainfleet

P.O. Box 40
31940 Hwy. 3
Wainfleet, ON L0S 1V0
Tel: 905-899-3463; *Fax:* 905-899-2340
sluey@township.wainfleet.on.ca
www.wainfleet.ca
Municipal Type: Township
Area: 217.20 sq km
County or District: Niagara Reg. Mun.; *Population in 2011:* 6,356
Provincial Electoral District(s): Welland

Federal Electoral District(s): Welland
Next Election: Oct. 27, 2014 (4 year terms)
April Jeffs, Mayor
905-899-3463, Fax: 905-899-2340
ajeffs@wainfleet.ca
Tanya Lamb, Township Clerk
905-899-3463
tlamb@township.wainfleet.on.ca

Warwick
6332 Nauvoo Rd.
Watford, ON N0M 2S0
Tel: 519-849-3926; *Fax:* 519-849-6136
info@warwicktownship.ca
www.warwicktownship.ca
Municipal Type: Township
Incorporated: 1998 *Area:* 290.2 sq km
County or District: Lambton; *Population in 2011:* 3,717
Provincial Electoral District(s): Lambton-Kent-Middlesex
Federal Electoral District(s): Lambton-Kent-Middlesex
Next Election: Oct. 27, 2014 (4 year terms)
Todd Case, Mayor
Don R. Bruder, Administrator-Treasurer
dbruder@warwicktownship.ca

Wasaga Beach
30 Lewis St.
Wasaga Beach, ON L9Z 1A1
Tel: 705-429-3844; *Fax:* 705-429-7603
www.wasagabeach.com
Municipal Type: Town
Incorporated: 1947 *Area:* 58.43 sq km
County or District: Simcoe; *Population in 2011:* 17,537
Provincial Electoral District(s): Simcoe-Grey
Federal Electoral District(s): Simcoe-Grey
Next Election: Oct. 27, 2014 (4 year terms)
Note: Incorporated as a village in 1951 & as a town in 1974.
Cal Patterson, Mayor
mayor@wasagabeach.com
David Foster, Deputy Mayor & Councillor
deputymayor@wasagabeach.com
Ron Anderson, Councillor
council2@wasagabeach.com
Morley Bercovitch, Councillor
council3@wasagabeach.com
Nina Bifolchi, Councillor
council4@wasagabeach.com
George Watson, Councillor
Stan Wells, Councillor
council5@wasagabeach.com
Twyla Nicholson, Clerk
clerk@wasagabeach.com
George Vadeboncoeur, Chief Administrative Officer
Monica Quinlan, Treasurer
treasurer@wasagabeach.com
Kevin Lalonde, Director, Public Works
publicworksdirector@wasagabeach.com
Gerry Reinders, Manager
parksandfac@wasagabeach.com
Ray Kelso, Manager, Planning & Development
rkelso@wasagabeach.com
Barrie Vickers, Chief Building Officer
cbo@wasagabeach.com
Jenny Legget, Economic Development Officer
edo@wasagabeach.com
Mike McWilliam, Fire & Emergency Management Chief
firechief@wasagabeach.com

Wawa
P.O. Box 500
40 Broadway Ave.
Wawa, ON P0S 1K0
Tel: 705-856-2244; *Fax:* 705-856-2120
info@wawa.cc
www.wawa.cc
Other Information: Toll-Free Phone: 1-800-367-9292
Municipal Type: Township
Area: 417.78 sq km
County or District: Algoma District; *Population in 2011:* 2,875
Provincial Electoral District(s): Algoma-Manitoulin
Federal Electoral District(s): Algoma-Manitoulin-Kapuskasing
Next Election: Oct. 27, 2014 (4 year terms)
Linda Nowicki, Mayor
Chris Wray, Chief Administrative Officer & Clerk-Treasurer
705-856-2244
cwray@wawa.cc

Wellesley
Administration Office
4639 Lobsinger Line, RR#1
St Clements, ON N0B 2M0
Tel: 519-699-4611; *Fax:* 519-699-4540
www.township.wellesley.on.ca
Municipal Type: Township
Area: 277.84 sq km
County or District: Waterloo Regional Municipality; *Population in 2011:* 10,713
Provincial Electoral District(s): Kitchener-Conestoga
Federal Electoral District(s): Kitchener-Conestoga
Next Election: Oct. 27, 2014 (4 year terms)
Ross Kelterborn, Mayor
519-656-2445
kross@region.waterloo.on.ca
Susan Duke, Clerk & Executive Director, Corporate Services
sduke@wellesley.ca

Wellington North
P.O. Box 125
7490 Sideroad 7 West
Kenilworth, ON N0G 2E0
Tel: 519-848-3620
township@wellington-north.com
www.wellington-north.com
Other Information: Toll-Free Phone: 1-866-848-3620
Municipal Type: Township
Incorporated: Jan. 1, 1999 *Area:* 524.38 sq km
County or District: Wellington; *Population in 2011:* 11,477
Provincial Electoral District(s): Perth-Wellington
Federal Electoral District(s): Perth-Wellington
Next Election: Oct. 27, 2014 (4 year terms)
Note: Amalgamation of the Township of Arthur, Arthur Village, the Township of West Luther & the Town of Mount Forest.
Raymond T. Tout, Mayor
519-323-9146
rtout@wellington-north.ca
Dan Yake, Councillor, Ward(s): 1
519-323-2334
dyake@wellington-north.ca
Sherry Burke, Councillor, Ward(s): 2
519-323-2604
sburke@wellington-north.ca
Mark Goetz, Councillor, Ward(s): 3
519-848-3380
mgoetz@wellington-north.ca
Andy Lennox, Councillor, Ward(s): 4
519-848-9948
alennox@wellington-north.ca
Lorraine (Lori) Heinbuch, Chief Administrative Officer & Clerk
519-848-3620
lheinbuch@wellington-north.com
John W. Jeffery, Treasurer
519-848-3620
jjeffery@wellington-north.com
Barry Trood, Director, Public Works
519-848-3620
btrood@wellington-north.com
Darren Jones, Chief Building Official
519-848-3620
djones@wellington-north.com
Dale Clark, Superintendent, Roads
519-848-3620
dclark@wellington-north.com
Mark Van Patter, Senior Planner
519-837-2600
markv@county.wellington.on.ca

West Elgin
P.O. Box 490
22413 Hoskins Line
Rodney, ON N0L 2C0
Tel: 519-785-0560; *Fax:* 519-785-0644
westelgin@westelgin.net
www.westelgin.net
Municipal Type: Municipality
Area: 322.52 sq km
County or District: Elgin; *Population in 2011:* 5,157
Provincial Electoral District(s): Elgin-Middlesex-London
Federal Electoral District(s): Elgin-Middlesex-London
Next Election: Oct. 27, 2014 (4 year terms)
Bernhard Wiehle, Mayor
519-785-0560, Fax: 519-785-0644
bwiehle@sympatico.ca
Norma Bryant, AMCT, Clerk
519-785-0560
nbryant@westelgin.net

West Grey
402813 Grey Rd., RR#2
Durham, ON N0G 1R0
Tel: 519-369-2200; *Fax:* 519-369-5962
info@westgrey.com
www.westgrey.com
Other Information: Toll-Free Phone: 1-800-538-9647
Municipal Type: Municipality
Incorporated: Jan 1, 2001 *Area:* 875.37 sq km
County or District: Grey; *Population in 2011:* 12,286
Provincial Electoral District(s): Bruce-Grey-Owen Sound
Federal Electoral District(s): Bruce-Grey-Owen Sound
Next Election: Oct. 27, 2014 (4 year terms)
Note: Amalgamation of Bentinck, Glenelg, Normanby, Neustadt & Durham.
Kevin Eccles, Mayor
519-799-5476
mayor@westgrey.com
John A. Bell, Deputy Mayor
519-369-6894
deputymayor@westgrey.com
Bev Cutting, Councillor
519-986-4635
bevcutting@westgrey.com
John Eccles, Councillor
519-369-3618
johneccles@westgrey.com
Carol Lawrence, Councillor
519-369-3816
Don Marshall, Councillor
519-369-7221
donmarshall@westgrey.com
David Mollison, Councillor
519-369-5337
davemollison@westgrey.com
Mark Rapke, Councillor
519-986-4498
markrapke@westgrey.com
Rob Thompson, Councillor
519-369-3052
robthompson@westgrey.com
Mark Turner, Clerk
519-369-2200
mturner@westgrey.com
Christine Robinson, Chief Administrative Officer
519-369-2200
robinsonc@westgrey.com
Kerri Mighton, Treasurer & Director, Finance
519-369-2200
kmighton@westgrey.com
Ken Gould, Director, Infrastructure & Public Works
519-369-2200
kgould@westgrey.com

West Lincoln
P.O. Box 400
318 Canborough St.
Smithville, ON L0R 2A0
Tel: 905-957-3346; *Fax:* 905-957-3219
reception@westlincoln.ca
www.westlincoln.ca
Other Information: Toll-Free Phone: 1-800-350-3876; TTY: 905-957-0680
Municipal Type: Township
Incorporated: Jan. 1, 1970 *Area:* 387.72 sq km
County or District: Niagara Reg. Mun.; *Population in 2011:* 13,837
Provincial Electoral District(s): Niagara West-Glanbrook
Federal Electoral District(s): Niagara West-Glanbrook
Next Election: Oct. 27, 2014 (4 year terms)
Note: Amalgamation of the former Townships of South Grimsby, Caistor, & Gainsborough.
Douglas Joyner, Mayor
905-957-4926
djoyner@westlincoln.ca
Eric Leith, Alderman, Ward(s): 1
905-957-1626
eleith@westlincoln.ca
Sue-Ellen Merritt, Alderman, Ward(s): 1
905-869-0939
smerritt@westlincoln.ca
Joann Chechalk, Alderman, Ward(s): 2
905-386-6412
jchechalk@westlincoln.ca
Alexander Micallef, Alderman, Ward(s): 2
289-668-8654
amicallef@westlincoln.ca
Luciano (Lou) Di Leonardo, Alderman, Ward(s): 3
905-957-8435
ldileonardo@westlincoln.ca

John Glazier, Alderman, Ward(s): 3
905-957-1140
jglazier@westlincoln.ca
Carolyn Langley, Clerk
905-957-3346
carolynlangley@westlincoln.ca
Derrick Thomson, Chief Administrative Officer
905-957-3346
dthomson@westlincoln.ca
Stephanie Nagel, Treasurer & Director, Finance
905-957-3346
snagel@westlincoln.ca
Brian Treble, Director, Planning & Building
905-957-3346
btreble@westlincoln.ca
Dennis Fisher, Fire Chief
905-957-3346
dfisher@westlincoln.ca

West Nipissing
Municipal Office
#101, 225 Holditch St.
Sturgeon Falls, ON P2B 1T1
Tel: 705-753-2250; *Fax:* 705-753-3950
www.westnipissingouest.ca
Municipal Type: Municipality
Area: 1,989.57 sq km
County or District: Nipissing District; *Population in 2011:* 14,149
Provincial Electoral District(s): Timiskaming-Cochrane
Federal Electoral District(s): Nickel Belt
Next Election: Oct. 27, 2014 (4 year terms)
Joanne Savage, Mayor
705-753-2250, Fax: 705-753-3950
jsavage@westnipissing.ca
Denise Brisson, Councillor, Ward(s): 1
705-753-3136
dbrisson@westnipissing.ca
Léo Malette, Councillor, Ward(s): 2
705-753-3568
lmalette@westnipissing.ca
Don Fortin, Councillor, Ward(s): 3
705-753-2844
dfortin@westnipissing.ca
Jamie Restoule, Councillor, Ward(s): 4
705-753-9396
jrestoule@westnipissing.ca
Guilles Tessier, Councillor, Ward(s): 5
705-753-3559
gtessier@westnipissing.ca
Paul Finley, Councillor, Ward(s): 6
705-594-2882
pfinley@westnipissing.ca
Normand Roberge, Councillor, Ward(s): 7
705-594-9486
nroberge@westnipissing.ca
Guy Fortier, Councillor, Ward(s): 8
705-594-2301
gfortier@westnipissing.ca
Mélanie Ducharme, Municipal Clerk & Planner
705-753-2250
mducharme@westnipissing.ca
Jean-Pierre (Jay) Barbeau, Chief Administrative Officer
705-753-2250
jbarbeau@westnipissing.ca
Serge Ducharme, Director, Museum
705-753-4716
admin@sturgeonriverhouse.com
Marc Gagnon, Director, Operations
705-753-2250
mgagnon@westnipissing.ca
Stephan Poulin, Director, Economic Development & Community Services
705-753-2250
spoulin@westnipissing.ca
Alain Bazinet, Chief Building Official & Officer, Property Maintenance
705-753-2250
abazinet@westnipissing.ca
Richard Savage, Fire Chief
705-753-1171
rsavage@wnfs.ca
Denis Lafreniere, Manager, Solid Waste
705-753-6913
dlafreniere@westnipissing.ca
Raymond Lortie, Manager, Power Generation
705-753-6364
westnipissingpower@bellnet.ca
Peter Ming, Manager, Water & Wastewater Operations
705-753-6454
pming@westnipissing.ca
Ginette Rochon, Manager, Ancillary Operations
705-753-6939
grochon@westnipissing.ca

West Perth, Municipality of
169 St. David St.
Mitchell, ON N0K 1N0
Tel: 519-348-8429
info@westperth.com
www.westperth.com
Municipal Type: Township
Area: 579.4 sq km
County or District: Perth; *Population in 2011:* 8,919
Provincial Electoral District(s): Perth-Wellington
Federal Electoral District(s): Perth-Wellington
Next Election: Oct. 27, 2014 (4 year terms)
Note: Amalgamation of Fullarton Township, Hibbert Township, Logan Township & the Town of Mitchell.
Walter McKenzie, Mayor
wmckenzie@westperth.com
Susan Cronin, Municipal Clerk
519-348-8429

Westport
P.O. Box 68
30 Bedford St.
Westport, ON K0G 1X0
Tel: 613-273-2191; *Fax:* 613-273-3460
westport@rideau.net
www.village.westport.on.ca
Municipal Type: Village
Incorporated: 1904 *Area:* 1.71 sq km
County or District: Leeds & Grenville; *Population in 2011:* 628
Provincial Electoral District(s): Leeds-Grenville
Federal Electoral District(s): Leeds-Grenville
Next Election: Oct. 27, 2014 (4 year terms)
William (Bill) L. Thake, Mayor
Scott Bryce, Clerk-Treasurer

Whitby
575 Rossland Rd. East
Whitby, ON L1N 2M8
Tel: 905-668-5803; *Fax:* 905-686-7005
www.whitby.ca
Other Information: TTY: 905-430-1942
Municipal Type: Town
Incorporated: 1855 *Area:* 146.52 sq km
County or District: Durham Reg. Mun.; *Population in 2011:* 122,022
Provincial Electoral District(s): Whitby-Oshawa
Federal Electoral District(s): Whitby-Oshawa
Next Election: Oct. 27, 2014 (4 year terms)
Pat Perkins, Mayor
council@whitby.ca
Tracy Hanson, Councillor, Ward(s): 1 - North
Elizabeth Roy, Councillor, Ward(s): 2 - West
Michael G. Emm, Councillor, Ward(s): 3 - Centre
Ken Montague, Councillor, Ward(s): 4 - East
Lorne Earl Coe, Regional Councillor
Joe Drumm, Regional Councillor
Don Mitchell, Regional Councillor
D. Wilcox, Town Clerk
clerks@whitby.ca
R. Petrie, Chief Administrative Officer
Robert B. Short, Director, Planning
planning@whitby.ca
Peter LeBel, Director, Community & Marketing Services
lebelp@whitby.ca
Suzanne Beale, Director, Public Works
engineering@whitby.ca
Sheila McGrory, Manager, Economic Development
905-430-4312
mcgrorys@whitby.ca
Steve Edwards, Manager, Parks, Marina, Long Range Planning, Special Events & Tourism
edwardss@whitby.ca
M. Gerrard, Fire Chief
fire@whitby.ca

Whitchurch-Stouffville
111 Sandiford Dr.
Stouffville, ON L4A 0Z8
Tel: 905-640-1900; *Fax:* 905-640-7957
www.townofws.com
Other Information: Toll-Free Phone: 1-855-642-8696
Municipal Type: Town
Incorporated: 1877 *Area:* 206.74 sq km
County or District: York Reg. Mun.; *Population in 2011:* 37,628
Provincial Electoral District(s): Oak Ridges-Markham
Federal Electoral District(s): Oak Ridges-Markham
Next Election: Oct. 27, 2014 (4 year terms)
Note: Incorporated as a town in 1971, with the amalgamation of Whitchurch Township & the Village of Stouffville.
Wayne Emmerson, Mayor
mayor.emmerson@townofws.ca
Ken Ferdinands, Councillor, Ward(s): 1
ken.ferdinands@townofws.ca
Phil Bannon, Councillor, Ward(s): 2
phil.bannon@townofws.ca
Clyde Smith, Councillor, Ward(s): 3
clyde.smith@townofws.ca
Susanne Hilton, Councillor, Ward(s): 4
susanne.hilton@townofws.ca
Richard Bartley, Councillor, Ward(s): 5
richard.bartley@townofws.ca
Rob Hargrave, Councillor, Ward(s): 6
rob.hargrave@townofws.ca
Michele Kennedy, Clerk
michele.kennedy@townofws.ca
David J. Cash, Cheif Administrative Officer
Marc J. Pourvahidi, Treasurer & Director, Finance
Mike Molinari, P.Eng., Director, Engineering & Capital Projects
Paul Whitehouse, Director
paul.whitehouse@townofws.com
Rob Raycroft, Manager
leisure.services@townofws.com
Andrew McNeely, Manager, Planning Services
andrew.mcneely@townofws.com
Rob McKenzie, Fire Chief

White River
P.O. Box 307
102 Durham St.
White River, ON P0M 3G0
Tel: 807-822-2450; *Fax:* 807-822-2719
info@whiteriver.ca
www.whiteriver.ca
Municipal Type: Township
Area: 96.94 sq km
County or District: Algoma District; *Population in 2011:* 607
Provincial Electoral District(s): Algoma-Manitoulin
Federal Electoral District(s): Algoma-Manitoulin-Kapuskasing
Next Election: Oct. 27, 2014 (4 year terms)
Angelo Bazzoni, Mayor
Marilyn Parent Lethbridge, Clerk Administrator
807-822-2450, Fax: 807-822-2179

Whitestone, Municipality of
General Delivery
21 Church St.
Dunchurch, ON P0A 1G0
Tel: 705-389-2466; *Fax:* 705-389-1855
general@whitestone.ca; confidential@whitestone.ca
www.whitestone.ca
Municipal Type: Township
Incorporated: 2000 *Area:* 946.56 sq km
County or District: Parry Sound District; *Population in 2011:* 918
Provincial Electoral District(s): Parry Sound-Muskoka
Federal Electoral District(s): Parry Sound-Muskoka
Next Election: Oct. 27, 2014 (4 year terms)
Chris Armstrong, Mayor
705-389-3721
mayor.armstrong@whitestone.ca
Liliane Nolan, Chief Administrative Officer & Clerk
705-389-2466
clerk.administrator@whitestone.ca

Whitewater Region
P.O. Box 40
44 Main St.
Cobden, ON K0J 1K0
Tel: 613-646-2282; *Fax:* 613-646-2283
info@whitewaterregion.ca
www.whitewaterregion.ca
Other Information: Toll-Free Phone: 1-877-646-2282
Municipal Type: Township
Incorporated: Jan. 1, 2001 *Area:* 537.96 sq km
County or District: Renfrew; *Population in 2011:* 6,921
Provincial Electoral District(s): Renfrew-Nipissing-Pembroke
Federal Electoral District(s): Renfrew-Nipissing-Pembroke
Next Election: Oct. 27, 2014 (4 year terms)
Note: Amalgamation of Beachburg Village, Cobden Village, Westmeath Township & Ross Township.
Jim Labow, Mayor
613-582-3969, Fax: 613-582-3338
jlabow@whitewaterregion.ca
Donald Rathwell, Reeve
613-646-7924, Fax: 613-646-7417
djr@nrtco.net
Dean Sauriol, Chief Administrative Officer & Clerk
dsauriol@whitewaterregion.ca

Wilmot

60 Snyder's Rd. West
Baden, ON N3A 1A1
Tel: 519-634-8444; *Fax:* 519-634-5522
info@wilmot.ca
www.wilmot.ca
Other Information: Toll-Free Phone: 1-800-469-5576
Municipal Type: Township
Area: 263.73 sq km
County or District: Waterloo Regional Municipality; *Population in 2011:* 19,223
Provincial Electoral District(s): Kitchener-Conestoga
Federal Electoral District(s): Kitchener-Conestoga
Next Election: Oct. 27, 2014 (4 year terms)
Les Armstrong, Mayor, Fax: 519-662-2764
les.armstrong@wilmot.ca
Al Junker, Councillor, Ward(s): 1
519-696-3922
al.junker@wilmot.ca
Peter Roe, Councillor, Ward(s): 2
519-886-6395, Fax: 519-886-6395
peter.roe@wilmot.ca
Barry Fisher, Councillor, Ward(s): 3
519-634-8916
barry.fisher@wilmot.ca
Jeff Gerber, Councillor, Ward(s): 4
519-662-6658
jeff.gerber@wilmot.ca
Mark Murray, Councillor, Ward(s): 4
519-662-2625, Fax: 519-662-2601
mark.murray@wilmot.ca
Barbara McLeod, Director, Clerk's Services
519-634-8444, Fax: 519-634-5522
barb.mcleod@wilmot.ca
Grant Whittington, Chief Administrative Officer
519-634-8444, Fax: 519-634-5522
grant.whittington@wilmot.ca
Rosita Tse, Treasurer & Director, Finance
519-634-8444, Fax: 519-634-5522
rosita.tse@wilmot.ca
Gary Charbonneau, Director, Public Works
519-634-8444, Fax: 519-634-5044
gary.charbonneau@wilmot.ca
Scott Nancekivell, Director, Facilities & Recreation
519-634-8444, Fax: 519-634-5044
scott.nancekivell@wilmot.ca
Harold O'Krafka, Director, Development Services
519-634-8444, Fax: 519-634-5044
harold.okrafka@wilmot.ca
John Ritz, Fire Chief
519-634-8444, Fax: 519-634-5660
john.ritz@wilmot.ca
Doug Robertson, Chief Building Official
519-634-8444, Fax: 519-634-5044
doug.robertson@wilmot.ca
Derek Wallace, Senior Officer, Municipal Law Enforcement
519-634-8444, Fax: 519-634-5522
derek.wallace@wilmot.ca
Andrew Martin, Planner & Officer, Economic Development
519-634-8444, Fax: 519-634-5044
andrew.martin@wilmot.ca

Wollaston

P.O. Box 99
90 Wollaston Lake Rd.
Coe Hill, ON K0L 1P0
Tel: 613-337-5731; *Fax:* 613-337-5789
wollaston@bellnet.ca
www.township.wollaston.on.ca
Municipal Type: Township
Incorporated: 1880 *Area:* 215.22 sq km
County or District: Hastings; *Population in 2011:* 708
Provincial Electoral District(s): Prince Edward-Hastings
Federal Electoral District(s): Prince Edward-Hastings
Next Election: Oct. 27, 2014 (4 year terms)
Dan McCaw, Reeve
613-337-5705
danandedithm@yahoo.ca
Christine FitzSimons, Chief Administrative Officer & Clerk
wollaston@bellnet.ca

Woolwich

P.O. Box 158
24 Church St. West
Elmira, ON N3B 2Z6
Tel: 519-669-1647; *Fax:* 519-669-1820
woolwich.mail@woolwich.ca
www.woolwich.ca
Other Information: Phone from 648 exchange: 519-664-2613
Municipal Type: Township
Incorporated: Jan. 1, 1973 *Area:* 326 sq km
County or District: Waterloo Regional Municipality; *Population in 2011:* 23,145
Provincial Electoral District(s): Kitchener-Conestoga
Federal Electoral District(s): Kitchener-Conestoga
Next Election: Oct. 27, 2014 (4 year terms)
Todd A. Cowan, Mayor
519-669-0591
Julie-Anne Herteis, Councillor, Ward(s): 1
519-669-4740
Allan Poffenroth, Councillor, Ward(s): 1
519-669-8074
Mark Bauman, Councillor, Ward(s): 2
519-664-3318
Bonnie Bryant, Councillor, Ward(s): 3
519-648-3608
Christine Broughton, Clerk & Director, Council & Information Services
519-669-1647
David Brenneman, Chief Administrative Officer
519-669-1647
Richard Petherick, Treasurer & Director, Finance
519-669-1647
Larry Devitt, Director, Recreation & Facilities Services
519-669-1647
Dan Kennaley, Director, Engineering & Planning Services
519-669-1647
Rick Pedersen, Township Fire Chief
519-664-2887
Peter vanderBeek, Chief Building Official
519-669-1647
Barry Baldasaro, Superintendent, Public Works
519-669-1647
Laurel Davies-Snyder, Officer, Economic Development & Tourism
519-669-1647

Zorra

Municipal Office
P.O. Box 306
274620 - 27th Line, RR#3
Ingersoll, ON N5C 3K5
Tel: 519-485-2490; *Fax:* 519-485-2520
admin@zorra.on.ca
www.zorra.on.ca
Other Information: Toll-Free Phone: 1-888-699-3868
Municipal Type: Township
Area: 528.78 sq km
County or District: Oxford; *Population in 2011:* 8,058
Provincial Electoral District(s): Oxford
Federal Electoral District(s): Oxford
Next Election: Oct. 27, 2014 (4 year terms)
Margaret Lupton, Mayor
519-475-4443, Fax: 519-485-2520
mlupton@zorra.on.ca
Karen Graham, Clerk
519-485-2490, Fax: 519-485-2520
kgraham@zorra.on.ca

PRINCE EDWARD ISLAND

Enabling legislation in P.E.I. includes the Charlottetown Area Municipalities Act, the City of Summerside Act, and the Municipalities Act. The first provides governance for three municipalities, the second provides governance for one municipality, and the third provides the framework for 71 municipalities. There are no population considerations for incorporation of a municipality, but a petition must be made by at least 25 residents of an area indicating their desire to incorporate; stating the boundaries of the area, whether it is to be a town or a community, and the services which are to be provided.

Municipal Elections are held every three or four years in November (2011, 2015, etc.).

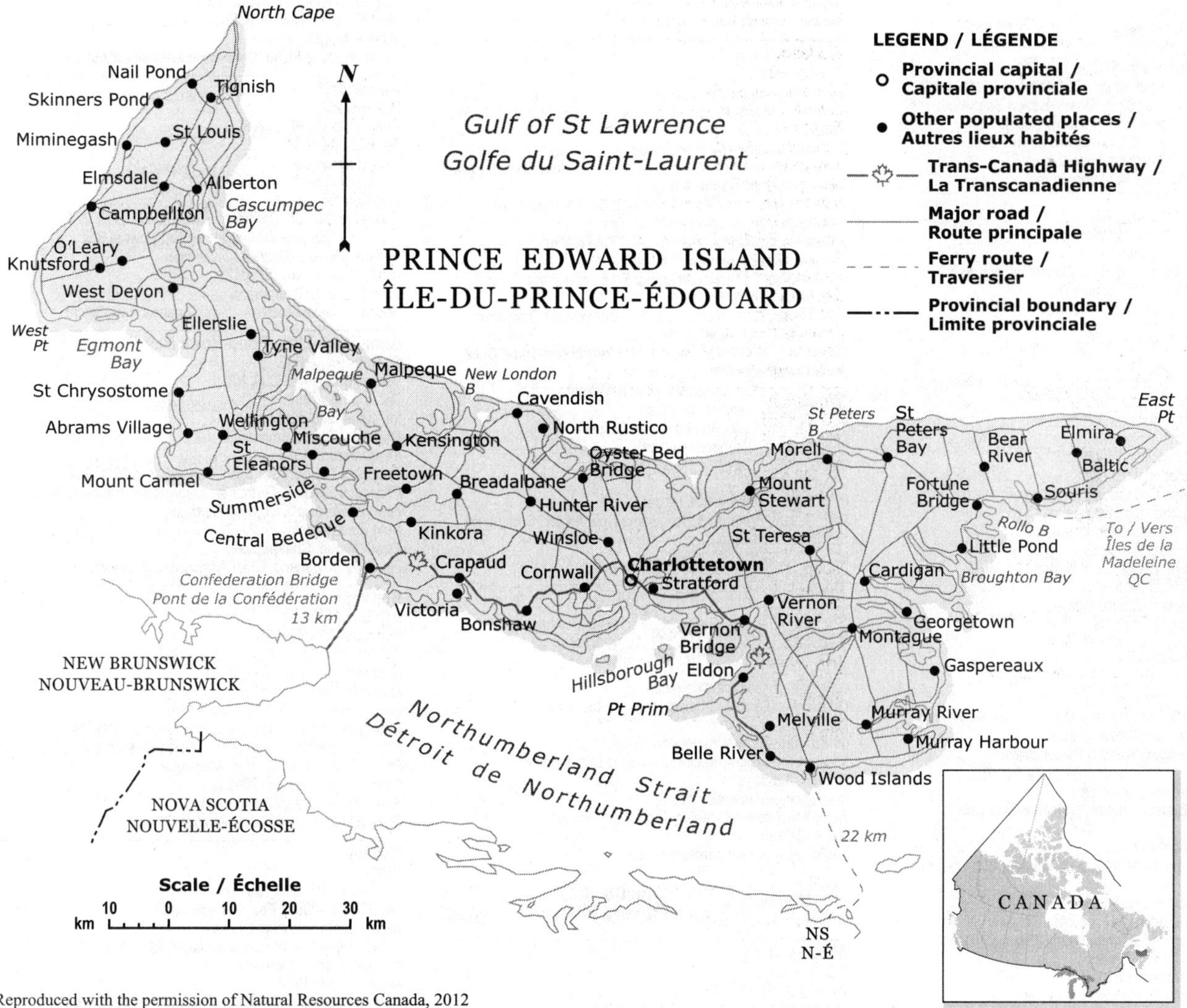

Reproduced with the permission of Natural Resources Canada, 2012

Prince Edward Island

Major Municipalities in Prince Edward Island

Charlottetown
P.O. Box 98
199 Queen St.
Charlottetown, PE C1A 4B7
Tel: 902-566-5548; *Fax:* 902-566-4701
city@city.charlottetown.pe.ca
www.city.charlottetown.pe.ca
Municipal Type: City
Incorporated: 1855 *Area:* 44.33 sq km
County or District: Hillsborough; *Population in 2011:* 34,562
Provincial Electoral District(s): Charlottetown-Sherwood; Charlottetown-Parkdale; Charlottetown-Victoria Park; Charlottetown-Brighton; Charlottetown-Lewis Point
Federal Electoral District(s): Charlottetown
Next Election: Nov. 3, 2014 (4 year terms)
Clifford J. Lee, Mayor
mayor@city.charlottetown.pe.ca
Kim Devine, B.A., Councillor, Ward(s): 1
kdevine@city.charlottetown.pe.ca
Daniel (Danny) J. Redmond, B.A., Councillor, Ward(s): 2
dredmond@city.charlottetown.pe.ca
Rob Lantz, B.Sc., Councillor, Ward(s): 3
rlantz@city.charlottetown.pe.ca
Mitchell G. Tweel, B.A., Councillor, Ward(s): 4
mitchell.tweel@pei.sympatico.ca
Sterling MacFadyen, Deputy Mayor & Councillor, Ward(s): 5
smacfadyen@city.charlottetown.pe.ca
David MacDonald, Councillor, Ward(s): 6
dmacdonald@city.charlottetown.pe.ca
Cecil F. Villard, Councillor, Ward(s): 7
cvillard@city.charlottetown.pe.ca
Peter F. McCloskey, Councillor, Ward(s): 8
pmccloskey@city.charlottetown.pe.ca
Melissa Hilton, B.A., Councillor, Ward(s): 9
mhilton@city.charlottetown.pe.ca
Terence H. Bernard, Councillor, Ward(s): 10
tbernard@city.charlottetown.pe.ca
Roy Main, Chief Administrative Officer
rmain@city.charlottetown.pe.ca
Joseph Coady, Director, Public Services
jcoady@city.charlottetown.pe.ca
Donna Waddell, Director, Corporate Services
dwaddell@city.charlottetown.pe.ca
Phil Handrahan, Director, Fiscal & Development Services
phandrahan@city.charlottetown.pe.ca
Craig Walker, Manager, Water & Sewer Utility
902-629-4014
cwalker@city.charlottetown.pe.ca
Bill Clair, Works Superintendent, Water & Sewer Utility
902-629-4015
bclair@city.charlottetown.pe.ca
Herman Van Omme, Superintendent, Waste Water Treatment Plant
902-628-6647, Fax: 902-628-6684
hvanomme@city.charlottetown.pe.ca
Ron Atkinson, Economic Development Officer, Economic Development, Tourism & Events
ratkinson@city.charlottetown.pe.ca
Dan Hughes, Manager, Human Resources
Don Poole, Manager of Planning, Planning & Development
dpoole@city.charlottetown.pe.ca
Vada Fernandez, Purchasing Officer, Finance
vfernandez@city.charlottetown.pe.ca
Mel Cheverie, Chief Building Inspector, Planning & Development
mcheverie@city.charlottetown.pe.ca
Jim Molyneux, Field Works Coordinator, Public Works
jmolyneux@city.charlottetown.pe.ca
Blair Kinch, Sr. Superintendent, Public Works
bkinch@city.charlottetown.pe.ca
Lance Jones, Streets Maintenance Supervisor, Public Works
ljones@city.charlottetown.pe.ca
Nancy McMinn, Parks Superintendent, Parks & Recreation
nmcminn@city.charlottetown.pe.ca
Scott Ryan, M.B.A., CMA, FCMA, Manager, Finance
sryan@city.charlottetown.pe.ca
Randy MacDonald, Fire Chief, Fire Services
rmacdonald@city.charlottetown.pe.ca
Paul Johnston, Manager, Public Works
902-894-5208
pjohnston@city.charlottetown.pe.ca
Sue Hendricken, Manager, Parks & Recreation
902-368-1025
shendricken@city.charlottetown.pe.ca
Paul Smith, Chief of Police
psmith@city.charlottetown.pe.ca

Summerside
275 Fitzroy St.
Summerside, PE C1N 1H9
Tel: 902-432-1230; *Fax:* 902-436-9296
cityhall@city.summerside.pe.ca
www.city.summerside.pe.ca
Municipal Type: City
Incorporated: 1995 *Area:* 28.36 sq km
County or District: Egmont; *Population in 2011:* 14,751
Provincial Electoral District(s): Wilmot-Summerside; St. Eleanors-Summerside
Federal Electoral District(s): Egmont
Next Election: Nov. 3, 2014 (4 year terms)
Basil Stewart, Mayor
902-432-1244
mayor@city.summerside.pe.ca
Bruce MacDougall, Deputy Mayor & Councillor, Ward(s): 1. St. Eleanors-Bayview
bmacdougall@city.summerside.pe.ca
Frank Costa, Councillor, Ward(s): 2. St. Eleanors-Slemon Park
frank.costa@city.summerside.pe.ca
Peter Holman, Councillor, Ward(s): 3. Summerside-North
peter.holman@city.summerside.pe.ca
Jim Steele, Councillor, Ward(s): 4. Clifton/Market
jim.steele@city.summerside.pe.ca
Ron Dowling, Councillor, Ward(s): 5. Hillcrest-Platte River
rondowling@hotmail.com
Jeff Sullivan, Councillor, Ward(s): 6. Centre East-Downtown
jeff.sullivan@city.summerside.pe.ca
Tina Mundy, Councillor, Ward(s): 7. Greenhouse-Three Oaks
tina.mundy@city.summerside.pe.ca
Cory Thomas, Councillor, Ward(s): 8. Wilmot
cthomas@city.summerside.pe.ca
Terry Murphy, Chief Administrative Officer
tmurphy@city.summerside.pe.ca
Malcolm Millar, Director, Financial Services
902-432-1250
mmillar@city.summerside.pe.ca
Paul Gallant, Program & Scheduling Coordinator, Community Services, Recreation
902-432-1294
pgallant@city.summerside.pe.ca
James Peters, Director, Fire Services
902-432-1224
jpeters@city.summerside.pe.ca
J. David Poirier, Director, Police Services
902-432-1330
dpoirier@city.summerside.pe.ca
Gordon MacFarlane, Director, Human Resources
902-432-1240
gmacfarlane@city.summerside.pe.ca
Michael Thususka, Director, Economic Development
902-432-1255
miket@city.summerside.pe.ca
Aaron MacDonald, Director, Technical Services
902-432-1258
aaronmac@city.summerside.pe.ca

Other Municipalities in Prince Edward Island

Abrams Village
P.O. Box 104
Wellington, PE C0B 2E0
Tel: 902-854-4111; *Fax:* 902-854-2740
Municipal Type: Community
Incorporated: 1974 *Area:* 1.37 sq km
Population in 2011: 267
Provincial Electoral District(s): Evangeline-Miscouche
Federal Electoral District(s): Egmont
Next Election: Nov. 5, 2012
Roger Gallant, Chairperson
Karen Gallant, Chief Administrative Officer

Afton
P.O. Box 836
Cornwall, PE C0A 1H0
Tel: 902-675-3515
afton.cic@gmail.com
Municipal Type: Community
Incorporated: 1974
Population in 2011: 1,222
Provincial Electoral District(s): Tracadie-Fort Augustus
Federal Electoral District(s): Malpeque
Next Election: Nov. 5, 2012
Gina Rankin, Chairperson
Beverley McIsaac, Chief Administrative Officer

Alberton
P.O. Box 153
Alberton, PE C0B 1B0
Tel: 902-853-2720; *Fax:* 902-853-2314
info@townofalberton.ca
www.townofalberton.ca
Municipal Type: Town
Incorporated: May 1913 *Area:* 4.50 sq km
County or District: Egmont; *Population in 2011:* 1,135
Provincial Electoral District(s): Alberton-Miminegash
Federal Electoral District(s): Egmont
Next Election: Nov. 5, 2012
Michael Murphy, Mayor
Susan Wallace-Flynn, Chief Administrative Officer

Alexandra
P.O. Box 2683
Charlottetown, PE C1A 8C3
Tel: 902-569-4760
sgw@hotmail.com
Municipal Type: Community
Incorporated: 1972
County or District: Cardigan; *Population in 2011:* 224
Provincial Electoral District(s): Belfast-Pownal Bay
Federal Electoral District(s): Cardigan
Next Election: Nov. 5, 2012
John Brehaut, Chairperson
Sheila Whiteway-McNeill, Chief Administrative Officer

Annandale-Little Pond-Howe Bay
75 Ross Rd., RR#2
Vernon Bridge, PE C0A 2B0
Tel: 902-583-2865
fm_sutherland@yahoo.ca
Municipal Type: Community
Incorporated: 1975
County or District: Cardigan; *Population in 2011:* 262
Provincial Electoral District(s): Georgetown-Baldwin's Road
Federal Electoral District(s): Cardigan
Next Election: Nov. 5, 2012
Edwin McKie, Chairperson
Florence Sutherland, Chief Administrative Officer

Bedeque
P.O. Box 4109
Bedeque, PE C0B 1C0
Tel: 902-887-2909; *Fax:* 902-887-3226
jlkimmet@pei.sympatico.ca
Municipal Type: Community
Incorporated: 1978 *Area:* 0.68 sq km
County or District: Malpeque; *Population in 2011:* 143
Provincial Electoral District(s): Borden-Kinkora
Federal Electoral District(s): Malpeque
Next Election: Nov. 5, 2012
Karen McLenithan, Chairperson
Dianna Linder, Chief Administrative Officer

Belfast
RR#3
Belle River, PE C0A 1B0
Tel: 902-659-2989; *Fax:* 902-659-2813
belfast.cap@pei.sympatico.ca
www3.pei.sympatico.ca/belfast.cap/public_html
Municipal Type: Community
Incorporated: 1972
County or District: Cardigan; *Population in 2011:* 1,637
Provincial Electoral District(s): Belfast-Pownal Bay
Federal Electoral District(s): Cardigan
Next Election: Nov. 5, 2012
Norman Gillis, Chairperson
Janice MacDonald, Chief Administrative Officer

Bonshaw
599 Riverdale Rd., RR#3
Bonshaw, PE C0A 1C0
Tel: 902-675-3670; *Fax:* 902-368-1239
Municipal Type: Community
Incorporated: 1977
County or District: Malpeque; *Population in 2011:* 218
Provincial Electoral District(s): Crapaud-Hazel Grove
Federal Electoral District(s): Malpeque
Next Election: Nov. 5, 2012
John Jamieson, Chairperson
Dianne Dowling, Chief Administrative Officer
dianne_dowling@hotmail.com

Borden-Carleton
P.O. Box 89
167 Industrial Dr.
Borden-Carleton, PE C0B 1X0
Tel: 902-437-2225; *Fax:* 902-437-2610
bcadmin@borden-carleton.ca
www.borden-carleton.ca
Municipal Type: Community
Incorporated: July 1, 1995 *Area:* 13.16 sq km
County or District: Malpeque; *Population in 2011:* 750
Provincial Electoral District(s): Borden-Kinkora
Federal Electoral District(s): Malpeque
Next Election: Nov. 5, 2012
Fred Leard, Chairperson
Charles McNally, Chief Administrative Officer

Brackley
576 Brackley Point Rd.
Brackley, PE C1E 1Z3
Tel: 902-368-8274
Municipal Type: Community
Incorporated: 1983 *Area:* 8.92 sq km
County or District: Malpeque; *Population in 2011:* 340
Provincial Electoral District(s): Stanhope-East Royalty
Federal Electoral District(s): Malpeque
Next Election: Nov. 5, 2012
Leonard MacCormack, Chairperson
Maureen Cudmore, Chief Administrative Officer
cudmoremo@yahoo.ca

Breadalbane
20 Grafton St.
Breadalbane, PE C0A 1E0
Tel: 902-964-2730
Municipal Type: Community
Incorporated: 1991 *Area:* 12.57 sq km
Population in 2011: 173
Provincial Electoral District(s): Crapaud-Hazel Grove
Federal Electoral District(s): Malpeque
Next Election: Nov. 5, 2012
Dawna MacLeod, Chairperson
Kim MacLeod, Chief Administrative Officer
macleodkim@hotmail.com

Brudenell
415 Brudenell Point Rd., RR#5
Montague, PE C0A 1R0
Tel: 902-838-4160; *Fax:* 902-838-3517
Municipal Type: Community
Incorporated: 1973
County or District: Cardigan; *Population in 2011:* 362
Provincial Electoral District(s): Montague-Kilmuir
Federal Electoral District(s): Cardigan
Next Election: Nov. 5, 2012
Peggy Coffin, Chairperson
Linda Barry, Chief Administrative Officer
lindabarry.brudenell@gmail.com

Cardigan
P.O. Box 40
Cardigan, PE C0A 1G0
Tel: 902-583-2198; *Fax:* 902-583-3198
villageofcardigan@gmail.com
Municipal Type: Community
Incorporated: 1954 Area: 5.28 sq km
County or District: Cardigan; *Population in 2011:* 332
Provincial Electoral District(s): Georgetown-Baldwin's Road
Federal Electoral District(s): Cardigan
Next Election: Nov. 5, 2012
Darlene Stewart, Chairperson
Jimmy Mooney, Chief Administrative Officer

Central Bedeque
246 Walker Ave.
Summerside, PE C1N 5P2
Tel: 902-436-8894
Municipal Type: Community
Incorporated: 1966 *Area:* 1.89 sq km
County or District: Malpeque; *Population in 2011:* 167
Provincial Electoral District(s): Borden-Kinkora
Federal Electoral District(s): Malpeque
Next Election: Nov. 5, 2012
Earl Smith, Chairperson
Douglas MacMurdo, Chief Administrative Officer
doug.macmurdo@ca.gt.com

Central Kings
P.O. Box 10
Bridgetown, RR#5
Cardigan, PE C0A 1G0
Tel: 902-583-2218
Municipal Type: Community
Incorporated: 1975
Population in 2011: 329
Provincial Electoral District(s): Morell-Fortune Bay
Federal Electoral District(s): Cardigan
Next Election: Nov. 5, 2012
Craig Jackson, Chairperson
Micheline Downe, Chief Administrative Officer
michdowne@hotmail.com

Clyde River
P.O. Box 644
Cornwall, PE C0A 1H0
Tel: 902-675-4747
clyderiver.cic@pei.sympatico.ca
Municipal Type: Community
Incorporated: 1974 *Area:* 16.05 sq km
County or District: Malpeque; *Population in 2011:* 576
Provincial Electoral District(s): Crapaud-Hazel Grove
Federal Electoral District(s): Malpeque
Next Election: Nov. 5, 2012
Douglas Gillespie, Chairperson
Bruce Brine, Chief Administrative Officer

Cornwall
P.O. Box 430
Cornwall, PE C0A 1H0
Tel: 902-566-2354; *Fax:* 902-566-5228
town.cornwall@town.cornwall.pe.ca
www.town.cornwall.pe.ca
Municipal Type: Town
Incorporated: 1995 *Area:* 28.2 sq km
County or District: Malpeque; *Population in 2011:* 5,162
Provincial Electoral District(s): North River-Rice Point
Federal Electoral District(s): Malpeque
Next Election: Nov. 3, 2014 (4 year terms)
Glen (Barney) Fullerton, Mayor
902-566-2354
gfullerton@town.cornwall.pe.ca
Kevin McCarville, Chief Administrative Officer
902-566-2354
kmccarville@town.cornwall.pe.ca

Crapaud
P.O. Box 30
Crapaud, PE C0A 1J0
Tel: 902-658-2558
crapaudadmin@pei.aibn.com
Municipal Type: Community
Incorporated: 1950 *Area:* 2.16 sq km
County or District: Malpeque; *Population in 2011:* 345
Provincial Electoral District(s): Crapaud-Hazel Grove
Federal Electoral District(s): Malpeque
Next Election: Nov. 5, 2012
Joanne Harvey, Acting Chairperson
Ann Tompkins, Chief Administrative Officer

Darlington
30 Darlington Rd., RR#4
North Wiltshire, PE C0A 1Y0
Tel: 902-964-2438
wandb@pei.sympatico.ca
Municipal Type: Community
Incorporated: 1983
County or District: Malpeque; *Population in 2011:* 109
Provincial Electoral District(s): Crapaud-Hazel Grove
Federal Electoral District(s): Malpeque
Next Election: Nov. 5, 2012
Warren MacDonald, Chairperson
Bonnie MacDonald, Chief Administrative Officer

Eastern Kings
85 Munns Rd.
Bothwell, PE C0A 1K0
Tel: 902-357-2894; *Fax:* 902-357-2607
easternkingspe@gmail.com
www.easternkingspei.com
Municipal Type: Community
Incorporated: 1974
County or District: Cardigan; *Population in 2011:* 702
Provincial Electoral District(s): Souris-Elmira
Federal Electoral District(s): Cardigan
Next Election: Nov. 5, 2012
Sheila Eastman, Chairperson
Horatio Toledo, Chief Administrative Officer

Ellerslie-Bideford
P.O. Box 13
Ellerslie, PE C0B 1J0
Tel: 902-831-3268
mandj@pei.sympatico.ca
Municipal Type: Community
Incorporated: 1977
County or District: Egmont; *Population in 2011:* 357
Provincial Electoral District(s): Cascumpec-Grand River
Federal Electoral District(s): Egmont
Next Election: Nov. 5, 2012
Myron Hutchinson, Chairperson
Julie Ellisworth-Enman, Chief Administrative Officer

Georgetown
P.O. Box 89
36 Kent St.
Georgetown, PE C0A 1L0
Tel: 902-652-2924; *Fax:* 902-652-2701
georgetown@pei.sympatico.ca
www.georgetown.ca
Municipal Type: Town
Incorporated: 1912 *Area:* 1.65 sq km
County or District: Cardigan; *Population in 2011:* 675
Provincial Electoral District(s): Georgetown-Baldwin's Road
Federal Electoral District(s): Cardigan
Next Election: Nov. 5, 2012
Lewis Lavandier, Mayor
lewis.lavandier@georgetown.ca
Tonya Cameron, Chief Administrative Officer
tonya.cameron@georgetown.ca

Grand Tracadie
York, PE C0A 1P0
Tel: 902-672-3429
Municipal Type: Community
Incorporated: 1984
County or District: Cardigan; *Population in 2011:* 293
Provincial Electoral District(s): Tracadie-Fort Augustus
Federal Electoral District(s): Cardigan
Next Election: Nov. 5, 2012
Kim Meunier, Chairperson
Patsy MacKinnon, Chief Administrative Officer

Greenmount-Montrose
1981 Union Rd., RR#2
Alberton, PE C0B 1B0
Tel: 902-853-3949; *Fax:* 902-853-2583
Municipal Type: Community
Incorporated: 1977
County or District: Egmont; *Population in 2011:* 258
Provincial Electoral District(s): Tignish-DeBlois
Federal Electoral District(s): Egmont
Next Election: Nov. 5, 2012
David Pizio, Chairperson
Donna Gallant, Chief Administrative Officer

Hampshire
RR#2
North Wiltshire, PE C0A 1Y0
Tel: 902-368-1144
Municipal Type: Community
Incorporated: 1974
County or District: Malpeque; *Population in 2011:* 420
Provincial Electoral District(s): North River-Rice Point; Crapaud-Hazel Grove
Federal Electoral District(s): Malpeque
Next Election: Nov. 5, 2012
Florence Nicholson, Chairperson
Gail Stewart, Chief Administrative Officer
tgstewart@hotmail.ca

Hazelbrook
P.O. Box 1023
101 Kent St.
Charlottetown, PE C1A 1M0
Tel: 902-892-5819; *Fax:* 902-892-5760
council@communityofhazelbrook.com
www.communityofhazelbrook.com
Municipal Type: Community
Incorporated: 1974
County or District: Cardigan; *Population in 2011:* 172
Provincial Electoral District(s): Belfast-Pownal Bay; Tracadie-Fort Augustus
Federal Electoral District(s): Cardigan
Next Election: Nov. 5, 2012
Brian Gallant, Chairperson
Ruth Copeland, Chief Administrative Officer

Hunter River
P.O. Box 154
Hunter River, PE C0A 1N0
Tel: 902-621-2170; *Fax:* 902-621-0836
admin.hunter.river@gmail.com
www.peicaps.org/~hunterriver
Municipal Type: Community
Incorporated: 1974 *Area:* 6.08 sq km

County or District: Malpeque; *Population in 2011:* 294
Provincial Electoral District(s): Crapaud-Hazel Grove; Park Corner-Oyster Bed
Federal Electoral District(s): Malpeque
Next Election: Nov. 5, 2012
Paul Ellis, Chairperson
Zoe Kunschner, Chief Administrative Officer

Kensington
P.O. Box 418
55 Victoria St.
Kensington, PE C0B 1M0
Tel: 902-836-3781; *Fax:* 902-836-3741
mail@townofkensington.com;
townmanager@townofkensington.com
www.townofkensington.com
Municipal Type: Town
Incorporated: 1914 *Area:* 3.02 sq km
County or District: Malpeque; *Population in 2011:* 1,496
Provincial Electoral District(s): Kensington-Malpeque
Federal Electoral District(s): Malpeque
Next Election: Nov. 5, 2012
Gordon Coffin, Mayor
mayor@townofkensington.com
Geoff Baker, Chief Administrative Officer
townmanager@townofkensington.com

Kingston
P.O. Box 648
Cornwall, PE C0A 1H0
Tel: 902-675-3670; *Fax:* 902-368-1239
www.kingstoncc.ca
Municipal Type: Community
Incorporated: 1974
County or District: Malpeque; *Population in 2011:* 794
Provincial Electoral District(s): North River-Rice Point; Crapaud-Hazel Grove
Federal Electoral District(s): Malpeque
Next Election: Nov. 5, 2012
Kimberlee Trainor, Chairperson
Dianne Dowling, Chief Administrative Officer
dianne_dowling@hotmail.com

Kinkora
P.O. Box 38
45 Anderson St.
Kinkora, PE C0B 1N0
Tel: 902-887-2868; *Fax:* 902-887-3514
communityofkinkora@bellaliant.com
www.kinkorapei.com
Municipal Type: Community
Incorporated: 1955 *Area:* 3.82 sq km
County or District: Malpeque; *Population in 2011:* 339
Provincial Electoral District(s): Borden-Kinkora
Federal Electoral District(s): Malpeque
Next Election: Nov. 5, 2012
Roger Savoie, Chairperson
Aaron Gauthier, Chief Administrative Officer

Lady Slipper
11703 Rte. 11, RR#2
Tyne Valley, PE C0B 2C0
Tel: 902-831-3496
Municipal Type: Community
Incorporated: 1983
County or District: Egmont; *Population in 2011:* 805
Provincial Electoral District(s): Casumpec-Grand River
Federal Electoral District(s): Egmont
Next Election: Nov. 5, 2012
Julie Smith, Chairperson
Douglas MacLeod, Chief Administrative Officer

Linkletter
211 Glenn Dr.
Linkletter, PE C1N 5N2
Tel: 902-724-0914
communityoflinkletter@gmail.com
Municipal Type: Community
Incorporated: 1972 *Area:* 9.05 sq km
County or District: Egmont; *Population in 2011:* 320
Provincial Electoral District(s): St. Eleanors-Summerside
Federal Electoral District(s): Egmont
Next Election: Nov. 5, 2012
David Linkletter, Chairperson
Brian Morrison, Chief Administrative Officer

Lorne Valley
415 Brudenell Point Rd., RR#5
Montague, PE C0A 1R0
Tel: 902-838-4160
Municipal Type: Community
Incorporated: 1978
County or District: Cardigan; *Population in 2011:* 106
Provincial Electoral District(s): Georgetown-Baldwin's Road
Federal Electoral District(s): Cardigan
Next Election: Nov. 5, 2012
Karen MacLeod, Chairperson
Linda Barry, Chief Administrative Officer
lindabarry.brudenell@gmail.com

Lot 11 & Area
P.O. Box 40
Ellerslie, PE C0B 1J0
Tel: 902-859-3594
www.lot11andarea.org
Municipal Type: Community
Incorporated: 1982
County or District: Egmont; *Population in 2011:* 635
Provincial Electoral District(s): Cascumpec-Grand River
Federal Electoral District(s): Egmont
Next Election: Nov. 5, 2012
Alfred Bridges, Chairperson
Shirley Phillips, Chief Administrative Officer
shirley.phillips@lot11andarea.org

Lower Montague
P.O. Box 821
Montague, PE C0A 1R0
Tel: 902-838-5405; *Fax:* 902-838-3617
administrator@lowermontague.ca
www.lowermontague.ca
Municipal Type: Community
Incorporated: 1974
County or District: Cardigan; *Population in 2011:* 665
Provincial Electoral District(s): Montague-Kilmuir
Federal Electoral District(s): Cardigan
Next Election: Nov. 5, 2012
Scott Annear, Chairperson
Elizabeth Nicholson, Chief Administrative Officer

Malpeque Bay
P.O. Box 405
Kensington, PE C0B 1M0
Tel: 902-836-5029
council@malpequebay.ca
www.malpequebay.ca
Municipal Type: Community
Incorporated: 1973
County or District: Malpeque; *Population in 2011:* 1,029
Provincial Electoral District(s): Kensington-Malpeque
Federal Electoral District(s): Malpeque
Next Election: Nov. 5, 2012
Jimmy Carruthers, Chairperson
Joanne McCarvill, Chief Administrative Officer

Meadowbank
P.O. Box 358
RR#2
Cornwall, PE C0A 1H0
Tel: 902-566-3215
Municipal Type: Community
Incorporated: 1974 *Area:* 9.25 sq km
County or District: Malpeque; *Population in 2011:* 338
Provincial Electoral District(s): North River-Rice Point
Federal Electoral District(s): Malpeque
Next Election: Nov. 5, 2012
Helen MacPhail, Chairperson
Alan MacCormac, Chief Administrative Officer
alanmaccormac@hotmail.com

Miltonvale Park
P.O. Box 38
Winsloe, PE C1E 1Z2
Tel: 902-368-3090; *Fax:* 902-368-1152
admin@miltonvalepark.com
www.miltonvalepark.com
Municipal Type: Community
Incorporated: 1974 *Area:* 35.32 sq km
County or District: Malpeque; *Population in 2011:* 1,153
Provincial Electoral District(s): Winsloe-West Royalty
Federal Electoral District(s): Malpeque
Next Election: Nov. 5, 2012
Betty Pryor, Chairperson
Shari MacDonald, Chief Administrative Officer

Miminegash
11315 Rte. 14
Miminegash, PE C0B 1S0
Tel: 902-882-3223
Municipal Type: Community
Incorporated: 1968 *Area:* 1.85 sq km
County or District: Egmont; *Population in 2011:* 173
Provincial Electoral District(s): Alberton-Miminegash
Federal Electoral District(s): Egmont
Next Election: Nov. 5, 2012
Charlie Murphy, Chairperson
cemurphy@edu.pe.ca
Lou Ann Gallant, Chief Administrative Officer

Miscouche
P.O. Box 70
Miscouche, PE C0B 1T0
Tel: 902-436-4962; *Fax:* 902-436-4963
communityofmiscouche@pei.aibn.com
Municipal Type: Community
Incorporated: 1957 *Area:* 3.34 sq km
County or District: Egmont; *Population in 2011:* 869
Provincial Electoral District(s): Evangeline-Miscouche
Federal Electoral District(s): Egmont
Next Election: Nov. 5, 2012
Wayne Poirier, Chairperson
Judy Gallant, Chief Administrative Officer

Montague
24 Queens Rd.
Montague, PE C0A 1R0
Tel: 902-838-2528; *Fax:* 902-838-3392
townhall@pei.sympatico.ca
www.townofmontaguepei.com
Municipal Type: Town
Incorporated: 1917 *Area:* 3.04 sq km
County or District: Cardigan; *Population in 2011:* 1,895
Provincial Electoral District(s): Montague-Kilmuir
Federal Electoral District(s): Cardigan
Next Election: Nov. 5, 2012
Richard Collins, Mayor
racollins@montaguepei.ca
Andrew Daggett, Chief Administrative Officer
adaggett@montaguepei.ca

Morell
P.O. Box 307
25 Sunset Cres.
Morell, PE C0A 1S0
Tel: 902-961-2900; *Fax:* 902-739-2900
morellcommunity@eastlink.ca
www.morellpei.com
Municipal Type: Community
Incorporated: 1953 *Area:* 1.40 sq km
County or District: Cardigan; *Population in 2011:* 313
Provincial Electoral District(s): Morell-Fortune Bay
Federal Electoral District(s): Cardigan
Next Election: Nov. 5, 2012
Jean Eldershaw, Chairperson
Sharon Laybolt, Chief Administrative Officer

Mount Stewart
P.O. Box 143
Mount Stewart, PE C0A 1T0
Tel: 902-676-2881; *Fax:* 902-731-3111
mountstewart@eastlink.ca
Municipal Type: Community
Incorporated: 1953 *Area:* 1.22 sq km
County or District: Cardigan; *Population in 2011:* 225
Provincial Electoral District(s): Tracadie-Fort Augustus
Federal Electoral District(s): Cardigan
Next Election: Nov. 5, 2012
Connie Doucette, Chairperson
Christine Watts, Chief Administrative Officer

Murray Harbour
P.O. Box 72
Murray Harbour, PE C0A 1V0
Tel: 902-962-3835; *Fax:* 902-962-3835
villoffice@eastlink.ca
www.murrayharbourpei.com
Municipal Type: Community
Incorporated: 1953 *Area:* 4.01 sq km
County or District: Cardigan; *Population in 2011:* 320
Provincial Electoral District(s): Murray River-Gaspereaux
Federal Electoral District(s): Cardigan
Next Election: Nov. 5, 2012
Faye Fraser, Chairperson
Joan Young, Chief Administrative Officer

Murray River
P.O. Box 266
Murray River, PE C0A 1W0
Tel: 902-962-2820; *Fax:* 902-962-3671
mrvillage@isnhighspeed.ca
www.murrayriverpei.com
Municipal Type: Community
Incorporated: 1955 *Area:* 1.43 sq km
County or District: Cardigan; *Population in 2011:* 334
Provincial Electoral District(s): Murray River-Gaspereaux

Federal Electoral District(s): Cardigan
Next Election: Nov. 5, 2012
Anne Petley, Chairperson
mrvillagechair@bellaliant.net
Dianne MacDonald, Chief Administrative Officer

New Haven-Riverdale
599 Riverdale Rd., RR#3
Bonshaw, PE C0A 1C0
Tel: 902-675-3670; *Fax:* 902-368-1239
newhavenriverdalecc.ca
Other Information: Alternate Phone: 902-629-4024
Municipal Type: Community
Incorporated: 1974
County or District: Malpeque; *Population in 2011:* 485
Provincial Electoral District(s): Crapaud-Hazel Grove
Federal Electoral District(s): Malpeque
Next Election: Nov. 5, 2012
Stephen Gould, Chairperson
Dianne Dowling, Chief Administrative Officer
dianne_dowling@hotmail.com

North Rustico
P.O. Box 38
106 Riverside Dr.
North Rustico, PE C0A 1X0
Tel: 902-963-3211; *Fax:* 902-963-3321
info@northrustico.net; northrustico@pei.aibn.com
www.northrustico.net
Municipal Type: Community
Incorporated: 1954 *Area:* 2.45 sq km
County or District: Malpeque; *Population in 2011:* 583
Provincial Electoral District(s): Park Corner-Oyster Bed
Federal Electoral District(s): Malpeque
Next Election: Nov. 5, 2012
Giles Gallant, Chairperson
Patsy Gamauf, Chief Administrative Officer

North Shore
P.O. Box 134 Post Office
York, PE C0A 1P0
Tel: 902-672-1586; *Fax:* 902-672-1766
nscouncil@stanhopecovehead.pe.ca
www.stanhopecovehead.pe.ca
Municipal Type: Community
Incorporated: 1974
County or District: Malpeque; *Population in 2011:* 1,112
Provincial Electoral District(s): Stanhope-East Royalty
Federal Electoral District(s): Malpeque
Next Election: Nov. 5, 2012
Sandy Gallant, Chairperson
argallant@edu.pe.ca
Joanne Smith, Chief Administrative Officer
nscc@pei.aibn.com

North Wiltshire
1605 Kinkora Rd.
North Wiltshire, PE C0A 1Y0
Tel: 902-621-1908
Municipal Type: Community
Incorporated: 1974
County or District: Egmont; *Population in 2011:* 182
Provincial Electoral District(s): Crapaud-Hazel Grove
Federal Electoral District(s): Malpeque
Next Election: Nov. 5, 2012
Robert Bertram, Chairperson
Charlene Waddell, Chief Administrative Officer

Northport
P.O. Box 466
Alberton, PE C0B 1B0
Tel: 902-853-2551
Municipal Type: Community
Incorporated: 1974
County or District: Egmont; *Population in 2011:* 188
Provincial Electoral District(s): Alberton-Miminegash
Federal Electoral District(s): Egmont
Next Election: Nov. 5, 2012
Wendy McNeil, Chairperson
Paula Foley, Chief Administrative Officer

O'Leary
P.O. Box 130
O'Leary, PE C0B 1V0
Tel: 902-859-3311; *Fax:* 902-859-2341
olearyadm@eastlink.ca
Municipal Type: Community
Incorporated: 1951 *Area:* 1.60 sq km
County or District: Egmont; *Population in 2011:* 812
Provincial Electoral District(s): West Point-Bloomfield
Federal Electoral District(s): Egmont
Next Election: Nov. 5, 2012
Nancy Wallace, Chairperson
Beverley Shaw, Chief Administrative Officer

Pleasant Grove
P.O. Box 2
York, PE C0A 1P0
Tel: 902-672-1707
Municipal Type: Community
Incorporated: 1980
County or District: Malpeque; *Population in 2011:* 496
Provincial Electoral District(s): Stanhope-East Royalty
Federal Electoral District(s): Malpeque
Next Election: Nov. 5, 2012
Eugene Doyle, Chairperson
Kim Doyle, Chief Administrative Officer

Resort Municipality
RR#2
Hunter River, PE C0A 1N0
Tel: 902-963-2698; *Fax:* 902-963-2932
resort@pei.aibn.com
Municipal Type: Community
Incorporated: 1990 *Area:* 37.74 sq km
Population in 2011: 266
Provincial Electoral District(s): Park Corner-Oyster Bed
Federal Electoral District(s): Malpeque
Next Election: Nov. 5, 2012
Mel Gass, Chairperson
Brenda MacDonald, Chief Administrative Officers

St. Felix
P.O. Box 22
Tignish, PE C0B 2B0
Tel: 902-882-4015
Municipal Type: Community
Incorporated: 1977
County or District: Egmont; *Population in 2011:* 348
Provincial Electoral District(s): Tignish-DeBlois
Federal Electoral District(s): Egmont
Next Election: Nov. 5, 2012
Claude Gaudette, Chairperson
Joanne Gaudette, Chief Administrative Officer

St. Louis
P.O. Box 40
St. Louis, PE C0B 1Z0
Tel: 902-882-2447
Municipal Type: Community
Incorporated: 1964 *Area:* 0.62 sq km
County or District: Egmont; *Population in 2011:* 51
Provincial Electoral District(s): Alberton-Miminegash; Tignish-DeBlois
Federal Electoral District(s): Egmont
Next Election: Nov. 5, 2012
Everett (Sonny) Wedge, Chairperson
Linda McCue, Chief Administrative Officer

St. Nicholas
3702 St. Nicholas
Miscouche, PE C0B 1T0
Tel: 902-854-2731
Municipal Type: Community
Incorporated: 1991
Population in 2011: 198
Provincial Electoral District(s): Evangeline-Miscouche
Federal Electoral District(s): Egmont
Next Election: Nov. 5, 2012
Pam Dawson, Chairperson
Corina Mundy, Chief Administrative Officer

St. Peter's Bay
P.O. Box 51
St. Peter's Bay, PE C0A 2A0
Tel: 902-961-2268; *Fax:* 902-961-3148
stpeters@eastlink.ca
Municipal Type: Community
Incorporated: 1953 *Area:* 4.24 sq km
County or District: Cardigan; *Population in 2011:* 253
Provincial Electoral District(s): Morell-Fortune Bay
Federal Electoral District(s): Cardigan
Next Election: Nov. 5, 2012
Ron MacInnis, Chairperson
Mary Burge, Chief Administrative Officer

Sherbrooke
P.O. Box 1344
Summerside, PE C1N 4K2
Tel: 902-436-7005; *Fax:* 902-436-9170
Municipal Type: Community
Incorporated: 1972 *Area:* 8.83 sq km
Population in 2011: 172
Provincial Electoral District(s): Wilmot-Summerside
Federal Electoral District(s): Egmont
Next Election: Nov. 5, 2012
Ron Chappell, Chair
Peggy Kilbride, Chief Administrative Officer
peggykilbride@yahoo.ca

Souris
P.O. Box 628
75 Main St.
Souris, PE C0A 2B0
Tel: 902-687-2157; *Fax:* 902-687-4426
town@sourispei.com
www.sourispei.com
Municipal Type: Town
Incorporated: 1910 *Area:* 3.42 sq km
County or District: Cardigan; *Population in 2011:* 1,173
Provincial Electoral District(s): Souris-Elmira
Federal Electoral District(s): Cardigan
Next Election: Nov. 5, 2012
David McDonald, Mayor
902-969-3361
Shelley LaVie, Chief Administrative Officer
902-687-2157
smacinnis@sourispei.com

Souris West
P.O. Box 680
Souris, PE C0A 2B0
Tel: 902-368-6886
Municipal Type: Community
Incorporated: 1972
County or District: Cardigan; *Population in 2011:* 399
Provincial Electoral District(s): Souris-Elmira
Federal Electoral District(s): Cardigan
Next Election: Nov. 5, 2012
Mark Kickham, Chairperson
mekickham@ihis.org
Cathy Williams, Chief Administrative Officer

Stratford
234 Shakespeare Dr.
Stratford, PE C1B 2V8
Tel: 902-569-1995; *Fax:* 902-569-5000
info@town.stratford.pe.ca
townofstratford.ca
Municipal Type: Town
Incorporated: April 1, 1995 *Area:* 22.48 sq km
Population in 2011: 8,574
Provincial Electoral District(s): Glen Stewart-Bellevue Cove
Federal Electoral District(s): Cardigan
Next Election: Nov. 3, 2014 (4 year terms)
David Dunphy, CA, Mayor
902-569-2149
ddunphy@town.stratford.pe.ca
Robert Hughes, P.Eng, Chief Administrative Officer
902-569-6251
rhughes@town.stratford.pe.ca

Tignish
P.O. Box 57
209 Phillip St.
Tignish, PE C0B 2B0
Tel: 902-882-2600; *Fax:* 902-882-2414
administrator@tignish.com
www.tignish.com
Municipal Type: Community
Incorporated: 1952 *Area:* 5.86 sq km
County or District: Egmont; *Population in 2011:* 779
Provincial Electoral District(s): Tignish-DeBlois
Federal Electoral District(s): Egmont
Next Election: Nov. 5, 2012
Gerard LeClair, Chairperson
Karen Gaudet-Gavin, Chief Administrative Officer

Tignish Shore
RR#1
Tignish, PE C0B 2B0
Tel: 902-853-3931
Municipal Type: Community
Incorporated: 1975
Population in 2011: 73
Provincial Electoral District(s): Tignish-DeBlois
Federal Electoral District(s): Egmont
Next Election: Nov. 5, 2012
Ronnie McRae, Chairperson
Donna MacKay, Chief Administrative Officer

Tyne Valley
P.O. Box 39
Tyne Valley, PE C0B 2C0
Tel: 902-831-2038

Municipal Type: Community
Incorporated: 1966 *Area:* 1.74 sq km
County or District: Egmont; *Population in 2011:* 222
Provincial Electoral District(s): Cascumpec-Grand River
Federal Electoral District(s): Egmont
Next Election: Nov. 5, 2012
Kevin Kadey, Chairperson
Marie Barlow, Chief Administrative Officer
marie.barlow@pei.sympatico.ca

Union Road
P.O. Box 20114
161 St. Peters Rd.
Charlottetown, PE C1A 9E3
Tel: 902-566-4097; *Fax:* 902-367-9862
admin@communityofunionroadpei.com
www.communityofunionroadpei.com
Municipal Type: Community
Incorporated: 1977 *Area:* 9.95 sq km
County or District: Malpeque; *Population in 2011:* 235
Provincial Electoral District(s): Georgetown-Baldwin's Road
Federal Electoral District(s): Malpeque
Next Election: Nov. 5, 2012
Fern Yeo, Chairperson
Vicki Cotton, Chief Administrative Officer

Valleyfield
1783 Queens Rd.
Lyndale, PE C0A 1R0
Tel: 902-838-4447; *Fax:* 902-838-3649
Municipal Type: Community
Incorporated: 1974
County or District: Cardigan; *Population in 2011:* 672
Provincial Electoral District(s): Georgetown-Baldwin's Road; Montague-Kilmuir; Belfast-Pownal Bay
Federal Electoral District(s): Cardigan
Next Election: Nov. 5, 2012
Graham Jones, Chairperson
Margaret Campion, Chief Administrative Officer
dmcampion@pei.sympatico.ca

Victoria
P.O. Box 7
Victoria, PE C0A 2G0
Tel: 902-658-2541; *Fax:* 902-658-2541
victoriaadmin@eastlink.ca
Municipal Type: Community
Incorporated: 1951 *Area:* 1.40 sq km
County or District: Malpeque; *Population in 2011:* 104
Provincial Electoral District(s): Crapaud-Hazel Grove
Federal Electoral District(s): Malpeque
Next Election: Nov. 5, 2012
Ben Smith, Chairperson
Hilary Price, Chief Administrative Officer

Warren Grove
P.O. Box 963
Cornwall, PE C0A 1H0
Tel: 902-675-2788
rodr@isnhighspeed.ca
Municipal Type: Community
Incorporated: 1985 *Area:* 10.32 sq km
County or District: Malpeque; *Population in 2011:* 367
Provincial Electoral District(s): North River-Rice Point
Federal Electoral District(s): Malpeque
Next Election: Nov. 5, 2012
Amber Tawil, Chairperson
Rod Raper, Chief Administrative Officer

Wellington
P.O. Box 26
Wellington, PE C0B 2E0
Tel: 902-854-2920
Municipal Type: Community
Incorporated: 1959 *Area:* 1.80 sq km
County or District: Egmont; *Population in 2011:* 409
Provincial Electoral District(s): Cascumpec-Grand River; Evangeline-Miscouche
Federal Electoral District(s): Egmont
Next Election: Nov. 5, 2012
Gilles Painchaud, Chairperson
Claudette Gallant, Chief Administrative Officer

West River
#12, 10 Mutch Dr.
Stratford, PE C1B 1S5
Tel: 902-569-1792; *Fax:* 902-367-1147
Municipal Type: Community
Incorporated: 1974
County or District: Malpeque; *Population in 2011:* 741
Provincial Electoral District(s): North River-Rice Point
Federal Electoral District(s): Malpeque
Next Election: Nov. 5, 2012
Eric MacArthur, Chairperson
Bill Grant, Chief Administrative Officer
bill.grant@bellaliant.net

Winsloe South
465 Winsloe Rd., Rte 223
South Winsloe, PE C1E 2Y2
Tel: 902-368-1444
Municipal Type: Community
Incorporated: 1986 *Area:* 9.63 sq km
County or District: Malpeque; *Population in 2011:* 221
Provincial Electoral District(s): Winsloe-West Royalty
Federal Electoral District(s): Malpeque
Next Election: Nov. 5, 2012
Brian Turner, Chairperson
Joanne Turner, Chief Administrative Officer
joanneturner@eastlink.ca

York
P.O. Box 8910
669 Rte. 25, York Rd.
Charlottetown, PE C0A 1P0
Tel: 902-566-5653; *Fax:* 902-569-1132
Municipal Type: Community
Incorporated: 1986
Population in 2011: 284
Provincial Electoral District(s): Stanhope-East Royalty
Federal Electoral District(s): Malpeque
Next Election: Nov. 5, 2012
Robert Adams, Chairperson
Carolyn Kellough, Chief Administrative Officer
cakellough@hotmail.com

QUÉBEC

Québec legislation recognizes two levels of municipal organization: the local and the regional.

Major municipal reform has reduced the number of local municipalities from nearly 1,400 in 1998 to 1,087 on April 1, 2005. Of this number, 201 towns fall under the jurisdiction of the Cities and Towns Act (RSQ, chap. C-19). Nine of them have over 100,000 inhabitants and account for 53% of the Québec population. The 886 other local municipalities, which go by a variety of designations (township, united township, parish, municipality, village) are governed by the Municipal Code of Québec (RSQ, chap. C-27.1). Québec also has 96 unorganized territories, 39 Indian reserves, 14 Northern villages, eight Cree villages and one Naskapi village.

The regional level of municipal territorial organization includes the Montréal and Québec City metropolitan communities, the 86 regional county municipalities (RCMs), and the Kativik Regional Government. The metropolitan communities and RCMs are made up of local municipalities. RCMs may also include unorganized territories. As for the area under the administration of the Kativik Regional Government, it includes the Northern villages, the Naskapi village and one unorganized territory.

The regional organizations were created to ensure that issues that go beyond local boundaries were handled at the regional or metropolitan level. Although their structures, operation and powers vary, they are based on identical principles. The Montréal and Québec City metropolitan communities are responsible at their level for land use planning, economic development, international economic promotion, artistic and cultural development, regional orientations in public transit, waste management planning, establishing a tax base sharing program, as well as for determining and financing regional facilities, infrastructures, activities, and services. RCMs also meet regional needs, including land use planning and the pooling of services. In addition, they exercise certain powers in the areas of economic development, public security and the environment. The Kativik Regional Government is in charge of local administration, police, transport, communications and labour force training and use, and may also set minimum standards by ordinance for things like house and building construction.

Eight local municipalities belong neither to a metropolitan community nor to one of the regional county municipalities. They do, however, wield some of the same powers as RCMs. This also holds true for six other cities, which although situated within one of the two metropolitan communities, nonetheless exercise certain of the powers of an RCM.

Ten cities are divided into boroughs. The boroughs have consultative and decision-making powers, are responsible for delivering certain neighbourhood services, and are represented by an elected borough council.

Source: Ministère des Affaires municipales, Régions et Occupation du territoire.

Reproduced with the permission of Natural Resources Canada, 2012

Québec

Major Municipalities in Québec

Alma

140, rue St-Joseph
Alma, QC G8B 3R1
Tél: 418-669-5000; *Téléc:* 418-669-5019
info@ville.alma.qc.ca
www.ville.alma.qc.ca
Entité municipal: City
Incorporation: 21 février 2001 *Area:* 202,10 km2
Comtéou district: Lac-St-Jean-Est; *Population au 2011:* 30,904
Circonscription(s) électorale(s) provinciale(s): Lac-Saint-Jean
Circonscription(s) électorale(s) fédérale(s): Jonquière-Alma
Prochaines élections: 1er novembre 2013
Marc Asselin, Maire
418-669-5005, Fax: 418-668-8923
marc.asselin@ville.alma.qc.ca
Lucien Boily, Conseiller, Ward(s): 1
418-669-1070
lucien.boily@ville.alma.qc.ca
Jocelyn Fradette, Conseillère, Ward(s): 2
418-450-1359
jocelyn.fradette@ville.alma.qc.ca
Gilles Girard, Conseiller, Ward(s): 3
418-668-6815
gilles.girard@ville.alma.qc.ca
Frédéric Tremblay, Conseiller, Ward(s): 4
418-668-5014
frederic.tremblay@ville.alma.qc.ca
Gino Villeneuve, Conseiller, Ward(s): 5
418-321-3458
gino.villeneuve@ville.alma.qc.ca
Sylvie Beaumont, Conseillère, Ward(s): 6
418-668-0919
sylvie.beaumont@ville.alma.qc.ca
Pascal Pilote, Conseiller, Ward(s): 7
418-480-1417
pascal.pilote@ville.alma.qc.ca
Alain Fortin, Conseiller, Ward(s): 8
418-669-1083
alain.fortin@ville.alma.qc.ca
Jean Paradis, Greffier
418-669-5001
jean.paradis@ville.alma.qc.ca
Yves Thériault, Trésorier, Trésorerie
418-669-5001
yves.theriault@ville.alma.qc.ca
Jean-Yves Lessard, Directeur
418-669-5001, Fax: 418-669-5180
jeanyves.lessard@ville.alma.qc.ca
Guy Simard, Directeur général
418-669-5001
guy.simard@ville.alma.qc.ca
Bernard Dallaire, Directeur, Prévention des incendies
418-669-5059
bernard.dallaire@ville.alma.qc.ca
Jocelyn Tremblay, Directrice, Loisirs & culture
418-669-5111
jocelyn.tremblay@ville.alma.qc.ca

Amos

182, 1re Rue est
Amos, QC J9T 2G1
Tél: 819-732-3254; *Téléc:* 819-727-9792
master@ville.amos.qc.ca
www.ville.amos.qc.ca
Entité municipal: City
Incorporation: 17 janvier 1987 *Area:* 430,84 km2
Comté ou district: Abitibi; *Population au 2011:* 12,671
Circonscription(s) électorale(s) provinciale(s): Abitibi-Ouest
Circonscription(s) électorale(s) fédérale(s): Abitibi-Témiscamingue
Prochaines élections: 3e novembre 2013
Ulrick Chérubin, Maire
Sébastien D'Astous, Conseiller, Infrastructures & services aux citoyens, Ward(s): 1
Amélie Mercier, Conseillère, Environnement, culture & services à la population, Ward(s): 2
Éric Mathieu, Conseiller, Développement économique, industriel & commercial, Ward(s): 3
Denis Chandonnet, Conseiller, Administration & sports, Ward(s): 4
Benoit Deshaies, Conseiller, Qualité de vie & famille, Ward(s): 5
Julie Cazes, Conseillère, Administration, développement communautaire & social & service à la population, Ward(s): 6
Alain Plante, Greffier
819-732-3254, Fax: 819-727-9792
Gérald Lavoie, Trésorier
819-732-3254, Fax: 819-727-9792
Régis Fortin, Directeur, Service de l'environnement
819-732-3254, Fax: 819-732-9675

Baie-Comeau

19, av Marquette
Baie-Comeau, QC G4Z 1K5
Tél: 418-296-4931; *Téléc:* 418-296-3759
vbc@ville.baie-comeau.qc.ca
www.ville.baie-comeau.qc.ca
Entité municipal: City
Incorporation: 23 juin 1982 *Area:* 371,69 km2
Comté ou district: Manicouagan; *Population au 2011:* 22,113
Circonscription(s) électorale(s) provinciale(s): René-Lévesque
Circonscription(s) électorale(s) fédérale(s): Manicouagan
Prochaines élections: 3e novembre 2013
Christine Brisson, Mairesse
418-296-8109, Fax: 418-296-4194
mairie@ville.baie-comeau.qc.ca
Alain Larouche, Conseiller, Ward(s): Saint-Sacrement
418-589-2107
Richard Bélanger, Conseiller, Ward(s): Mgr-Bélanger
418-589-9979
Denise Arsenault, Conseillère, Ward(s): Trudel
418-589-6795
Carole Deschênes, Conseillère, Ward(s): N.-A.-Labrie
418-589-8734
André Veillette, Conseiller, Ward(s): La Chasse
418-296-6070
Léa Thibault, Conseillère, Ward(s): Saint-Nom-de-Marie
418-296-4654
Reina Savoie Jourdain, Conseillère, Ward(s): Sainte-Amélie
418-296-5231
Régis Deschênes, Conseiller, Ward(s): Saint-Georges
418-296-5989
Lorna Pineault, Greffière
418-296-8898, Fax: 418-296-8194
lpineault@ville.baie-comeau.qc.ca
Danielle Bernatchez, Trésorière
418-296-8128, Fax: 418-296-3759
dbernatchez@ville.baie-comeau.qc.ca
François Corriveau, Directeur général (par intérim)
418-296-8104, Fax: 418-296-8121
jviens@ville.baie-comeau.qc.ca
Jacques Comeau, Directeur, Service des communications
418-296-8142, Fax: 418-296-3759
jcomeau@ville.baie-comeau.qc.ca
François LeBlond, Directeur, Loisirs, sports & vie communautaire
418-296-8358, Fax: 418-296-8399
fleblond@ville.baie-comeau.qc.ca
Ghislain Gauthier, Directeur, Service des travaux publics
418-296-8180, Fax: 418-296-3095
ggauthier@ville.baie-comeau.qc.ca
David Pollock, Maire
514-428-4410
Michael Montagano, Conseiller, Ward(s): 1
514-697-9558
Karin Essen, Conseiller, Ward(s): 2
514-693-5024
Wade Staddon, Conseiller, Ward(s): 3
514-448-1349
Brian Ross, Conseiller, Ward(s): 4
514-865-3176
Roy Baird, Conseiller, Ward(s): 5
514-630-1576
Rhonda Massad, Conseiller, Ward(s): 6
514-830-6694

Beaconsfield

303, boul Beaconsfield
Beaconsfield, QC H9W 4A7
Tél: 514-428-4400; *Téléc:* 514-428-4424
info@beaconsfield.ca
www.beaconsfield.ca
Entité municipal: City
Incorporation: 1er janvier 2006 *Area:* 10,64 km2
Comté ou district: Communauté métropolitaine de Montréal; *Population au 2011:* 19,505
Circonscription(s) électorale(s) provinciale(s): Jacques-Cartier
Circonscription(s) électorale(s) fédérale(s): Lac-Saint-Louis
Prochaines élections: 3e novembre 2013

Beauharnois

#100, 660, rue Ellice
Beauharnois, QC J6N 1Y1
Tél: 450-429-3546; *Téléc:* 450-429-2478
direction.generale@ville.beauharnois.qc.ca
www.ville.beauharnois.qc.ca
Entité municipal: City
Incorporation: 1er janvier 2002 *Area:* 73,05 km2
Comté ou district: Beauharnois-Salaberry; *Population au 2011:* 12,011
Circonscription(s) électorale(s) provinciale(s): Beauharnois
Circonscription(s) électorale(s) fédérale(s): Beauharnois-Salaberry
Prochaines élections: 3e novembre 2013
Claude Haineault, Maire
450-429-3546
Gaëtan Dagenais, Conseiller, Ward(s): 1
Michel Quevillon, Conseiller, Ward(s): 2
Guillaume Lévesque-Sauvé, Conseiller, Ward(s): 3
Patrick Laniel, Conseiller, Ward(s): 4
Jocelyne Rajotte, Conseillère, Ward(s): 5
Bruno Tremblay, Conseiller, Ward(s): 6
Manon Fortier, Greffière
manon.fortier@ville.beauharnois.qc.ca
Alain Gravel, Directeur général
alain.gravel@ville.beauharnois.qc.ca
Guylaine Côte, Trésorière
guylaine.cote@ville.beauharnois.qc.ca
Yves Magnan, Directeur, Travaux publics
450-225-0650
yves.magnan@ville.beauharnois.qc.ca
Richard Plouffe, Directeur, Urbanisme
450-429-3546
richard.plouffe@ville.beauharnois.qc.ca
Jean-Maurice Marleau, Directeur, Service des incendies
450-225-2222
directeur.incendie@ville.beauharnois.qc.ca
Daniel Leblanc, Directeur, Environnement
450-429-3959
daniel.leblanc@ville.beauharnois.qc.ca

Bécancour

1295, av Nicolas-Perrot
Bécancour, QC G9H 1A1
Tél: 819-294-6500; *Téléc:* 819-294-6535
becancour@ville.becancour.qc.ca
www.becancour.net
Entité municipal: City
Incorporation: 17 octobre 1965 *Area:* 434,28 km2
Comté ou district: Bécancour; *Population au 2011:* 12,438
Circonscription(s) électorale(s) provinciale(s): Nicolet-Yamaska
Circonscription(s) électorale(s) fédérale(s): Bas-Richelieu-Nicolet-Bécancour
Prochaines élections: 3e novembre 2013
Maurice Richard, Maire
Fernand Croteau, Conseiller, Ward(s): Bécancour
Gaétane Désilets, Conseillère, Ward(s): Saint-Grégoire
Alain Lévesque, Conseiller, Ward(s): Sainte-Angèle
Guy Richard, Conseiller, Ward(s): Sainte-Gertrude
Mario Gagné, Conseiller, Ward(s): Précieux-Sang
Karl Grondin, Conseiller, Ward(s): Gentilly
France Leclerc, Greffière
Daniel Brunelle, Trésorier
819-294-6500, Fax: 819-294-6535
finances@ville.becancour.qc.ca
Gaston Bélanger, Directeur général

Beloeil

777, rue Laurier
Beloeil, QC J3G 4S9
Tél: 450-467-2835; *Téléc:* 450-464-5445
info@ville.beloeil.qc.ca
www.ville.beloeil.qc.ca
Entité municipal: City
Incorporation: 9e décembre 1903 *Area:* 24 km2
Comté ou district: La Vallée-du-Richelieu; *Population au 2011:* 20,783
Circonscription(s) électorale(s) provinciale(s): Borduas
Circonscription(s) électorale(s) fédérale(s): Chambly-Borduas
Prochaines élections: 3e novembre 2013
Diane Lavoie, Mairesse
450-464-3095
dlavoie@ville.beloeil.qc.ca
Louise Allie, Conseillère, Ward(s): 1
450-446-4201
zoize@hotmail.com
Renée Trudel, Conseillère, Ward(s): 2
514-823-3722
rtrudel@ville.beloeil.qc.ca
Lyse Girard, Conseillère, Ward(s): 3
450-446-8624
lgirard@ville.beloeil.qc.ca
Denis Corriveau, Conseiller, Ward(s): 4
450-464-2435
dcorriveau@ville.beloeil.qc.ca
Guy Bédard, Conseiller, Ward(s): 5
450-446-7837
gbedard@ville.beloeil.qc.ca

Pierre Verret, Conseiller, Ward(s): 6
450-467-0630
pierre-verret@hotmail.com
Lise Touchette, Conseillère, Ward(s): 7
450-467-4645
toulise@videotron.ca
Jean-Yves Labadie, Conseiller, Ward(s): 8
450-446-0347
jylabadie@ville.beloeil.qc.ca
Sylvie Piérard, Greffière
450-467-2835, Fax: 450-464-5445
Cathy Goyette, Directrice, Finances
450-467-2835, Fax: 450-464-5445
Martine Vallières, Directrice générale
450-467-2835, Fax: 450-464-5445
direction@ville.beloeil.qc.ca

Blainville
1000, ch du Plan-Bouchard
Blainville, QC J7C 3S9
Tél: 450-434-5200; *Téléc:* 450-434-8295
accueil@ville.blainville.qc.ca
www.ville.blainville.qc.ca
Entité municipal: City
Incorporation: 1er juillet 1968 *Area:* 54,62 km2
Comté ou district: Thérèse-De Blainville; *Population au 2011:* 53,510
Circonscription(s) électorale(s) provinciale(s): Blainville
Circonscription(s) électorale(s) fédérale(s): Terrebonne-Blainville
Prochaines élections: 3e novembre 2013
François Cantin, Maire
francois.cantin@ville.blainville.qc.ca
Liza Poulin, Conseillère, Ward(s): 1. Fontainebleu
liza.poulin@ville.blainville.qc.ca
Alain Portelance, Conseiller, Ward(s): 2. Côte-Saint-Louis
alain.portelance@ville.blainville.qc.ca
Serge Paquette, Conseiller, Ward(s): 3. Saint-Rédempteur
serge.paquette@ville.blainville.qc.ca
Guy Frigon, Conseiller, Ward(s): 4. Plan-Bouchard
guy.frigon@ville.blainville.qc.ca
Normand Dupont, Conseiller, Ward(s): 5. Notre-Dame-de-l'Assomption
normand.dupont@ville.blainville.qc.ca
Nicole Ruel, Conseillère, Ward(s): 6. Chante-Bois
nicole.ruel@ville.blainville.qc.ca
Louis Lamarre, Conseiller, Ward(s): 7. Hirondelles
louis.lamarre@ville.blainville.qc.ca
Richard Perreault, Conseiller, Ward(s): 8. Alençon
richard.perreault@ville.blainville.qc.ca
François Garand, Conseiller, Ward(s): 9. Renaissance
francois.garand@ville.blainville.qc.ca
Marie-Claude Collin, Conseillère, Ward(s): 10. Blainvillier
marie-claude.collin@ville.blainville.qc.ca
Claude Bertrand, Greffier
Lorraine Barry, Trésorière
Paul Allard, Directeur général

Boisbriand
940, boul de la Grande-Allée
Boisbriand, QC J7G 2J7
Tél: 450-435-1954; *Téléc:* 450-435-6398
www.ville.boisbriand.qc.ca
Entité municipal: City
Incorporation: 1er janvier 1946 *Area:* 26,43 km2
Comté ou district: Thérèse-De Blainville; Communauté métropolitaine de Montréal; *Population au 2011:* 26,816
Circonscription(s) électorale(s) provinciale(s): Groulx
Circonscription(s) électorale(s) fédérale(s): Rivière-des-Mille-Iles
Prochaines élections: 1er novembre 2013
Lucie Mongeau, Greffière
Sylvie St-Jean, Mairesse
sstjean@ville.boisbriand.qc.ca
Michel Lacasse, Directeur général
André Drainville, Directeur, Finances & Trésorerie
Lyne Levert, Conseillers et Districts, Ward(s): 1 Sanche
llevert@ville.boisbriand.qc.ca
Gilles Sauriol, Conseillers et Districts, Ward(s): 2 Du Gué
gsauriol@ville.broisbriand.qc.ca
Robert Frégeau, Conseillers et Districts, Ward(s): 3 Filion
rfregeau@ville.boisbriand.qc.ca
Patrick Thifault, Conseillers et Districts, Ward(s): 4 Dubois
pthifault@ville.boisbriand.qc.ca
Louise Gauthier, Conseillers et Districts, Ward(s): 5 Brosseau
lgauthier@ville.boisbriand.qc.ca
Louise Lemay, Conseillers et Districts, Ward(s): 6 Labelle
llemay@ville.boisbriand.qc.ca
Mario Lavallée, Conseillers et Districts, Ward(s): 7 Desjardins
mlavallee@ville.boisbriand.qc.ca
Marlene Cordato, Conseillers et Districts, Ward(s): 8 Dion
mcordato@ville.boisbriand.qc.ca

Boucherville
500, rue de la Rivière-aux-Pins
Boucherville, QC J4B 2Z7
Tél: 450-449-8100; *Téléc:* 450-655-0086
information@boucherville.ca
www.ville.boucherville.qc.ca
Entité municipal: City
Incorporation: 1er janvier 2006 *Area:* 69,33 km2
Comté ou district: Communauté métropolitaine de Montréal; *Population au 2011:* 40,753
Circonscription(s) électorale(s) provinciale(s): Marguerite-D'Youville
Circonscription(s) électorale(s) fédérale(s): Longueuil—Pierre-Boucher; Verchères—Les Patriotes
Prochaines élections: 3e novembre 2013
Jean Martel, Maire
450-449-8105
mairie@boucherville.ca
Yan Savaria-Laquerre, Conseiller, Ward(s): 1. Pierre-Viger
yan.savaria-laquerre@boucherville.ca
Francine Crevier Bélair, Conseillère, Ward(s): 2. Père-Le Jeune
francine.crevierbelair@boucherville.ca
Alexandra Capone, Conseillère, Ward(s): 3. Sainte Famille
alexandra.capone@boucherville.ca
Anne Barabé, Conseillère, Ward(s): 4. Découvreurs
anne.barabe@boucherville.ca
Dominic Lévesque, Conseiller, Ward(s): 5. Seigneurie
dominic.levesque@boucherville.ca
Magalie Queval, Conseillère, Ward(s): 6. Saint-Louis
magalie.queval@boucherville.ca
Jacqueline Boubane, Conseillère, Ward(s): 7. Mortagne
jacqueline.boubane@boucherville.ca
Lise Roy, Conseillère, Ward(s): 8. Normandie
lise.roy@boucherville.ca
Claude Caron, Greffier
450-449-8605, Fax: 450-655-0086
greffe@boucherville.ca

Brossard
2001, boul Rome
Brossard, QC J4W 3K5
Tél: 450-923-6300; *Téléc:* 450-923-7009
information@brossard.ca
www.ville.brossard.qc.ca
Entité municipal: City
Incorporation: 1er janvier 2006 *Area:* 44,77 km2
Comté ou district: Communauté métropolitaine de Montréal; *Population au 2011:* 79,273
Circonscription(s) électorale(s) provinciale(s): La Pinière
Circonscription(s) électorale(s) fédérale(s): Brossard—La Prairie
Prochaines élections: 3e novembre 2013
Paul Leduc, Maire
450-923-6325
mairie@brossard.ca
Doreen Assaad, Conseillère, Ward(s): 1
450-923-6304
doreen.assaad@brossard.ca
Pierre O'Donoughue, Conseiller, Ward(s): 2
450-923-6304
pierre.odonoughue@brossard.ca
Monique Gagné, Conseillère, Ward(s): 3
450-923-6304
monique.gagne@brossard.ca
Alexandre Plante, Conseiller, Ward(s): 4
450-923-6304
alexandre.plante@brossard.ca
Serge Séguin, Conseiller, Ward(s): 5
450-923-6304
serge.seguin@brossard.ca
Claudio Benedetti, Conseiller, Ward(s): 6
450-923-6304
claudio.benedetti@brossard.ca
Zaki Thomas, Conseiller, Ward(s): 7
450-923-6304
zaki.thomas@brossard.ca
Antoine Assaf, Conseiller, Ward(s): 8
450-923-6304
antoine.assaf@brossard.ca
Pascal Forget, Conseiller, Ward(s): 9
450-923-6304
pascal.forget@brossard.ca
Daniel Lucier, Conseiller, Ward(s): 10
450-923-6304
daniel.lucier@brossard.ca
Diane Lebrun, Greffière
450-923-6305, Fax: 450-923-7009

Candiac
100, boul Montcalm nord
Candiac, QC J5R 3L8
Tél: 450-444-6000; *Téléc:* 450-444-6009
info@ville.candiac.qc.ca
www.ville.candiac.qc.ca
Entité municipal: City
Incorporation: 31 janvier 1957 *Area:* 16,40 km2
Comté ou district: Roussillon; *Population au 2011:* 19,876
Circonscription(s) électorale(s) provinciale(s): La Prairie
Circonscription(s) électorale(s) fédérale(s): Brossard—La Prairie
Prochaines élections: 3e novembre 2013
André J. Côté, Maire
mairie@ville.candiac.qc.ca
Thérèse Gatien, Conseillère, Ward(s): La Promenade
tgatien@ville.candiac.qc.ca
Vincent Chatel, Conseiller, Ward(s): Saint-Laurent
vchatel@ville.candiac.qc.ca
Kevin Vocino, Conseiller, Ward(s): Champlain
kvocino@ville.candiac.qc.ca
Anne Scott, Conseillère, Ward(s): Taschereau
ascott@ville.candiac.qc.ca
Charles-André Fortier, Conseiller, Ward(s): Montcalm
cafortier@ville.candiac.qc.ca
Normand Dyotte, Conseiller, Ward(s): Jean-Leman
ndyotte@ville.candiac.qc.ca
Carole Lemaire, Greffière
450-444-6398, Fax: 450-444-0789
greffe@ville.candiac.qc.ca
David Johnstone, Directeur général
450-444-6006, Fax: 450-444-2480
directiongenerale@ville.candiac.qc.ca
Sylvie Landry, Trésorière
450-444-6018, Fax: 450-444-6009
finances@ville.candiac.qc.ca

Chambly
56, rue Martel
Chambly, QC J3L 1V3
Tél: 450-658-8788; *Téléc:* 450-447-4525
information@ville.chambly.qc.ca
www.ville.chambly.qc.ca
Entité municipal: City
Incorporation: 26 octobre 1848 *Area:* 25,01 km2
Comté ou district: La Vallée-du-Richelieu; *Population au 2011:* 25,571
Circonscription(s) électorale(s) provinciale(s): Chambly
Circonscription(s) électorale(s) fédérale(s): Chambly-Borduas
Prochaines élections: 3e novembre 2013
Denis Lavoie, Maire
450-658-8788
maire@ville.chambly.qc.ca
Denise Grégoire, Conseillère, Ward(s): Canton
450-447-2549
denise.gregoire@cstjean.qc.ca
Normand Perrault, Conseiller, Ward(s): Bassin
450-447-2336, Fax: 514-971-5439
normandperrault@videotron.ca
Lucette Robert, Conseillère, Ward(s): Charles-Michel-de Salaberry
514-799-3575
lucette.robert@usherbrooke.ca
Richard Tetreault, Conseiller, Ward(s): La Petite Rivière
450-658-4282, Fax: 514-891-4282
rtetreault@videotron.qc.ca
Serge Gélinas, Conseiller, Ward(s): Antoine-Louis-Fréchette
514-462-0151
sergelinas01@hotmail.com
Luc Ricard, Conseiller, Ward(s): Louis-Franquet
450-447-1829
lucricard@videotron.ca
Jean Roy, Conseiller, Ward(s): Ruisseau
450-447-6152
jeanrr@hotmail.com
Steeves Demers, Conseiller, Ward(s): Grandes-Terres
514-250-9960
steeves.demers@hotmail.com
Louise Bouvier, Greffière
450-658-8788, Fax: 450-658-4214
greffe@ville.chambly.qc.ca
Jean Lacroix, Directeur général
450-658-8788, Fax: 450-447-4525
jean.lacroix@ville.chambly.qc.ca
Annie Nepton, Directrice & trésorière, Service des finances
450-658-8788, Fax: 450-447-4525
finances@ville.chambly.qc.ca

Châteauguay
5, boul d'Youville
Châteauguay, QC J6J 2P8
Tél: 450-698-3000; *Téléc:* 450-698-3019
info@ville.chateauguay.qc.ca
www.ville.chateauguay.qc.ca
Entité municipal: City
Incorporation: 3e novembre 1975 *Area:* 35,37 km2
Comté ou district: Roussillon; *Population au 2011:* 45,904
Circonscription(s) électorale(s) provinciale(s): Châteauguay
Circonscription(s) électorale(s) fédérale(s): Châteauguay—St-Constant
Prochaines élections: 3e novembre 2013
Nathalie Simon, Mairesse
450-698-3008
mairie@ville.chateauguay.qc.ca
Barry Doyle, Conseiller, Ward(s): 1
450-699-1984
barry.doyle@ville.chateauguay.qc.ca
Pierre Gloutnay, Conseiller, Ward(s): 2
514-706-1582
pierre.gloutnay@ville.chateauguay.qc.ca
Esther Salomon, Conseillère, Ward(s): 3
450-844-0507
esther.salomon@ville.chateauguay.qc.ca
Guillaume Dumas, Conseiller, Ward(s): 4
450-691-3177
guillaume.dumas@ville.chateauguay.qc.ca
Marcel Deschamps, Conseiller, Ward(s): 5
450-699-1120
marcel.deschamps@ville.chateauguay.qc.ca
Michel Gendron, Conseiller, Ward(s): 6
514-829-1986
mike.gendron@ville.chateauguay.qc.ca
Ginette Gendron, Conseillère, Ward(s): 7
450-692-3302
ginette.gendron@ville.chateauguay.qc.ca
Alain Côté, Conseiller, Ward(s): 8
450-692-8877
alain.cote@ville.chateauguay.qc.ca
Paul G. Brunet, Greffier & Directeur général
Manon Tourigny, Trésorière

Côte-Saint-Luc
5801, boul Cavendish
Côte-Saint-Luc, QC H4W 3C3
Tél: 514-485-6800; *Téléc:* 514-485-6963
info@cotesaintluc.org
www.cotesaintluc.org
Entité municipal: City
Incorporation: 1er janvier 2006 *Area:* 7,35 km2
Comté ou district: Communauté métropolitaine de Montréal; *Population au 2011:* 32,321
Circonscription(s) électorale(s) provinciale(s): D'Arcy-McGee
Circonscription(s) électorale(s) fédérale(s): Mount Royal
Prochaines élections: 3e novembre 2013
Anthony Housefather, Maire
514-485-6936
ahousefather@cotesaintluc.org
Sam Goldbloom, Conseiller, Ward(s): 1
514-485-6945
sgoldbloom@cotesaintluc.org
Mike Cohen, Counseiller, Ward(s): 2
mcohen@cotesaintluc.org
Dida Berku, Conseillère, Ward(s): 3
dberku@cotesaintluc.org
Steven Erdelyi, Conseillère, Ward(s): 4
serdelyi@cotesaintluc.org
Allan J. Levine, Conseiller, Ward(s): 5
alevine@cotesaintluc.org
Glenn J. Nashen, Conseiller, Ward(s): 6
gjnashen@cotesaintluc.org
Mitchell Brownstein, Conseiller, Ward(s): 7
mbrownstein@cotesaintluc.org
Ruth Kovac, Conseillère, Ward(s): 8
rkovac@cotesaintluc.org
Jonathan Shecter, Greffier
514-485-6800
jshecter@cotesaintluc.org
Tanya Abramovitch, Directrice générale
tabramovitch@cotesaintluc.org
Raymond LeBlanc, Trésorier
514-485-6922

Cowansville
220, place Municipale
Cowansville, QC J2K 1T4
Tél: 450-263-0141; *Téléc:* 450-263-9357
hoteldeville@ville.cowansville.qc.ca
www.ville.cowansville.qc.ca
Entité municipal: City
Incorporation: 1er janvier 1876 *Area:* 48,79 km2
Comté ou district: Brome-Missisquoi; *Population au 2011:* 12,489
Circonscription(s) électorale(s) provinciale(s): Brome-Missisquoi
Circonscription(s) électorale(s) fédérale(s): Brome-Missisquoi
Prochaines élections: 3e novembre 2013
Arthur Fauteux, Maire
450-263-0141
afauteux@ville.cowansville.qc.ca
Guy Patenaude, Conseiller, Ward(s): Ruiter
450-263-7327
gpatenaude@ville.cowansville.qc.ca
Lucille Robert, Conseillère, Ward(s): Sweetsburg
450-263-3779
lrobert@ville.cowansville.qc.ca
Ghyslain Vallières, Conseiller, Ward(s): Vilas
450-260-5703
gvallières@ville.cowansville.qc.ca
Michel Charbonneau, Conseiller, Ward(s): Bruck
450-266-1146
mcharbonneau@ville.cowansville.qc.ca
Yvon Pepin, Conseiller, Ward(s): Davignon
450-263-1426
ypepin@ville.cowansville.qc.ca
Sylvie Beauregard, Conseillère, Ward(s): Fordyce
450-266-4312
sbeauregard@ville.cowansville.qc.ca
Sandra Ruel, Greffière
Pierre Belle, Trésorier
450-263-0141

Deux-Montagnes
803, ch d'Oka
Deux-Montagnes, QC J7R 1L8
Tél: 450-473-2796; *Téléc:* 450-473-2417
info@ville.deux-montagnes.qc.ca
www.ville.deux-montagnes.qc.ca
Entité municipal: City
Incorporation: 18 août 1921 *Area:* 5,82 km2
Comté ou district: Deux-Montagnes; *Population au 2011:* 17,552
Circonscription(s) électorale(s) provinciale(s): Deux-Montagnes
Circonscription(s) électorale(s) fédérale(s): Rivière-des-Mille-îles
Prochaines élections: 3e novembre 2013
Marc Lauzon, Maire
450-473-8898
mlauzon@ville.deux-montagnes.qc.ca
Suzette Bigras, Conseillère, Ward(s): Grand-Moulin
sbigras@ville.deux-montagnes.qc.ca
Mario Saint-Charles, Conseiller, Ward(s): Lac
mst-charles@ville.deux-montagnes.qc.ca
Tom Whitton, Conseiller, Ward(s): Olympia
twhitton@ville.deux-montagnes.qc.ca
Nathalie Chayer, Conseillère, Ward(s): Gare
nchayer@ville.deux-montagnes.qc.ca
Guillaume Bouvrette, Conseiller, Ward(s): Coteau
gbouvrette@ville.deux-montagnes.qc.ca
James McAllister, Conseiller, Ward(s): Golf
jmcallister@ville.deux-montagnes.qc.ca
Jacques Robichaud, Greffier
450-473-2796, Fax: 450-473-4434
Jean Langevin, Directeur général
450-473-2796, Fax: 450-473-2417
Marie-Josée Boissonneault, Directrice, Finances & Trésorerie, Fax: 450-473-3412

Dolbeau-Mistassini
1100, boul Wallberg
Dolbeau-Mistassini, QC G8L 1G7
Tél: 418-276-0160; *Téléc:* 418-276-8312
hotelville@ville.dolbeau-mistassini.qc.ca
www.ville.dolbeau-mistassini.qc.ca
Entité municipal: City
Incorporation: 17 décembre 1997 *Area:* 296,57 km2
Comté ou district: Maria-Chapdelaine; *Population au 2011:* 14,384
Circonscription(s) électorale(s) provinciale(s): Roberval
Circonscription(s) électorale(s) fédérale(s): Roberval—Lac-St-Jean
Prochaines élections: 3e novembre 2013
Georges Simard, Maire
maire@ville.dolbeau-mistassini.qc.ca
Richard Hébert, Conseiller, Ward(s): 1
r.hebert@bellnet.ca
Claude Ouellet, Conseiller, Ward(s): 2
mairie-greffe@ville.dolbeau-mistassini.qc.ca
Daniel Savard, Conseiller, Ward(s): 3
conseillers@ville.dolbeau-mistassini.qc.ca
Daniel Lambert, Conseiller, Ward(s): 4
conseillers@ville.dolbeau-mistassini.qc.ca
Claire Néron, Conseillère, Ward(s): 5
cneron@mrcmaria.qc.ca
Pierre Lavoie, Conseiller, Ward(s): 6
mairie-greffe@ville.dolbeau-mistassini.qc.ca
André Côté, Greffier
418-276-0160
acote@ville.dolbeau-mistassini.qc.ca
Frédéric Lemieux, Directeur général
418-276-0160
flemieux@ville.dolbeau-mistassini.qc.ca
Suzie Gagnon, Directrice, Finances & trésorier
418-276-0160
sgagnon@ville.dolbeau-mistassini.qc.ca

Dollard-Des-Ormeaux
12001, boul De Salaberry
Dollard-des-Ormeaux, QC H9B 2A7
Tél: 514-684-1010; *Téléc:* 514-684-6894
ville@ddo.qc.ca
www.ville.ddo.qc.ca
Entité municipal: City
Incorporation: 1er janvier 2006 *Area:* 15,20 km2
Comté ou district: Communauté métropolitaine de Montréal; *Population au 2011:* 49,637
Circonscription(s) électorale(s) provinciale(s): Robert-Baldwin
Circonscription(s) électorale(s) fédérale(s): Pierrefonds—Dollard
Prochaines élections: 3e novembre 2013
Ed Janiszewski, Maire
Zoé Bayouk, Conseillère, Ward(s): 1
Errol Johnson, Conseiller, Ward(s): 2
Mickey Max Guttman, Conseiller, Ward(s): 3
Herbert Brownstein, Conseiller, Ward(s): 4
Morris Vesely, Conseiller, Ward(s): 5
Peter Prassas, Conseiller, Ward(s): 6
Alex Bottausci, Conseiller, Ward(s): 7
Colette Gauthier, Conseillère, Ward(s): 8
Chantale Bilodeau, Greffière
514-684-9244
cbilodeau@ddo.qc.ca
Jack Benzaquen, Directeur général
514-684-8060
jbenzaquen@ddo.qc.ca
Caroline Thall, Trésorière
514-684-9391
cthall@ddo.qc.ca

Dorval
60, av Martin
Dorval, QC H9S 3R4
Tél: 514-633-4040; *Téléc:* 514-633-4138
dorval@ville.dorval.qc.ca
www.ville.dorval.qc.ca
Entité municipal: City
Incorporation: 1er janvier 2006 *Area:* 20,64 km2
Comté ou district: Communauté métropolitaine de Montréal; *Population au 2011:* 18,208
Circonscription(s) électorale(s) provinciale(s): Marquette
Circonscription(s) électorale(s) fédérale(s): Notre-Dame-de-Grâce—Lachine
Prochaines élections: 3e novembre 2013
Edgar Rouleau, Maire
erouleau@ville.dorval.qc.ca
Claude Valiquet, Conseiller, Ward(s): 1
cvaliquet@ville.dorval.qc.ca
Michel Hébert, Conseiller, Ward(s): 2
mhebert@ville.dorval.qc.ca
Daniel da Chão, Conseiller, Ward(s): 3
ddachao@ville.dorval.qc.ca
Marc Doret, Conseiller, Ward(s): 4
mdoret@ville.dorval.qc.ca
Heather Allard, Conseillère, Ward(s): 5
hallard@ville.dorval.qc.ca
Margo Heron, Conseillère, Ward(s): 6
mheron@ville.dorval.qc.ca
Colette Gauthier, Greffière
514-633-4142
Robert Bourbeau, Directeur général
514-633-4044
André Girard, Trésorier
514-633-4040

Drummondville
CP 398
415, rue Lindsay
Drummondville, QC J2B 6W3
Tél: 819-478-6550
communications@ville.drummondville.qc.ca
www.ville.drummondville.qc.ca
Entité municipal: City
Incorporation: 7e juillet 2004 *Area:* 249,80 km2
Comté ou district: Drummond; *Population au 2011:* 71,852
Circonscription(s) électorale(s) provinciale(s): Drummond

Circonscription(s) électorale(s) fédérale(s): Drummond
Prochaines élections: 3e novembre 2013
Note: Effective July 7, 2004, the municipalities of St-Charles-de-Drummond & St-Joachim-de-Courval & the cities of St-Nicéphore & Drummondville regrouped to form the new city of Drummondville
Francine Ruest Jutras, Mairesse
mairie@ville.drummondville.qc.ca
Mario Jacques, Conseiller, Ward(s): 1
mjacques@ville.drummondville.qc.ca
Roberto Léveillée, Conseiller, Ward(s): 2
rleveillee@ville.drummondville.qc.ca
Jocelyn Gagné, Conseiller, Ward(s): 3
jgagne@ville.drummondville.qc.ca
Isabelle Marquis, Conseillère, Ward(s): 4
imarquis@ville.drummondville.qc.ca
John Husk, Conseiller, Ward(s): 5
jhusk@ville.drummondville.qc.ca
Marie-Eve Le Gendre, Conseillère, Ward(s): 6
melegendre@ville.drummondville.qc.ca
Alain Martel, Conseiller, Ward(s): 7
amartel@ville.drummondville.qc.ca
Yves Grondin, Conseiller, Ward(s): 8
ygrondin@ville.drummondville.qc.ca
Annick Bellavance, Conseillère, Ward(s): 9
abellavance@ville.drummondville.qc.ca
Vincent Chouinard, Conseiller, Ward(s): 10
vchouinard@ville.drummondville.qc.ca
Philippe Mercure, Conseiller, Ward(s): 11
pmercure@ville.drummondville.qc.ca
Pierre Levasseur, Conseiller, Ward(s): 12
plevasseur@ville.drummondville.qc.ca
Thérèse Cajolet, Greffière
819-478-6554, Fax: 819-478-3363
greffe@ville.drummondville.qc.ca
Claude Proulx, Directeur général
819-478-6557, Fax: 819-478-3363
direction@ville.drummondville.qc.ca
Gilles Bélisle, Trésorier
819-478-6559, Fax: 819-478-3164
tresor@ville.drummondville.qc.ca

Gaspé

25, rue de l'Hôtel-de-Ville
Gaspé, QC G4X 2A5
Tél: 418-368-2104; *Téléc:* 418-368-8532
direction.generale@ville.gaspe.qc.ca
www.ville.gaspe.qc.ca
Entité municipal: City
Incorporation: 1er janvier 1971 *Area:* 1446,95 km2
Comté ou district: La Côte-de-Gaspé; *Population au 2011:* 15,163
Circonscription(s) électorale(s) provinciale(s): Gaspé
Circonscription(s) électorale(s) fédérale(s): Gaspésie—Îles-de-la-Madeleine
Prochaines élections: 3e novembre 2013
François Roussy, Maire
Luc Savage, Conseiller, Ward(s): 1
Charles Aspirault, Conseiller, Ward(s): 2
Nelson O'Connor, Conseiller, Ward(s): 3
Patrice Quenneville, Conseiller, Ward(s): 4
Aline Perry, Conseillère, Ward(s): 5
Ghislain Smith, Conseiller, Ward(s): 6
Doreen Savage, Adjointe de direction, Greffe et services juridiques
greffe@ville.gaspe.qc.ca
Daniel Côté, Coordonnateur municipal, Direction générale et mairie
daniel.cote@ville.gaspe.qc.ca
Yvanne Huet, Adjointe de direction, Finances
serv.administratif@ville.gaspe.qc.ca

Gatineau

CP 1970 Hull
25, rue Laurier
Gatineau, QC J8X 3Y9
Tél: 819-595-2002
info@gatineau.ca
www.ville.gatineau.qc.ca
Entité municipal: City
Incorporation: 1er janvier 2002 *Area:* 344,16 km2
Population au 2011: 265,349
Circonscription(s) électorale(s) provinciale(s): Gatineau; Chapleau; Hull; Papineau; Pontiac
Circonscription(s) électorale(s) fédérale(s): Gatineau
Prochaines élections: 3e novembre 2013
Marc Bureau, Maire
819-595-7100
maire@gatineau.ca
Stefan Psenak, Conseiller, Ward(s): 1. Aylmer
psenak.stefan@gatineau.ca
André Laframboise, Conseiller, Ward(s): 2. Lucerne
laframboise.andre@gatineau.ca
Alain Riel, Conseiller, Ward(s): 3. Deschênes
riel.alain@gatineau.ca
Maxime Tremblay, Conseiller, Ward(s): 4. Plateau-Manoir-des-Trembles
tremblay.maxime@gatineau.ca
Patrice Martin, Conseiller, Ward(s): 5. Wright—Parc-de-la-Montagne
martin.patrice@gatineau.ca
Mireille Apollon, Conseillère, Ward(s): 6. Orée-du-Parc
apollon.mireille@gatineau.ca
Pierre Philion, Conseiller, Ward(s): 7. Saint-Raymond—Vanier
philion.pierre@gatineau.ca
Denise Laferrière, Conseillère, Ward(s): 8. Hull—Val-Tétreau
laferriere.denise@gatineau.ca
Nicole Champagne, Conseillère, Ward(s): 9. Limbour
champagne.nicole@gatineau.ca
Denis Tassé, Conseiller, Ward(s): 10. Touraine
tasse.denis@gatineau.ca
Luc Angers, Conseiller, Ward(s): 11. Pointe-Gatineau
angers.luc@gatineau.ca
Patsy Bouthillette, Conseillère, Ward(s): 12. Carrefour-de-l'Hôpital
bouthillette.patsy@gatineau.ca
Joseph De Sylva, Conseiller, Ward(s): 13. Versant
desylva.joseph@gatineau.ca
Sylvie Goneau, Conseillère, Ward(s): 14. Bellevue
goneau.sylvie@gatineau.ca
Stéphane Lauzon, Conseiller, Ward(s): 15. Lac-Beauchamp
lauzon.stephane@gatineau.ca
Yvon Boucher, Conseiller, Ward(s): 16. Rivière-Blanche
boucher.yvon@gatineau.ca
Luc Montreuil, Conseiller, Ward(s): 17. Masson-Angers
montreuil.luc@gatineau.ca
Maxime Pedneaud-Jobin, Conseiller, Ward(s): 18. Buckingham
pedneaud-jobin.maxime@gatineau.ca
Suzanne Ouellet, Greffière
819-595-7180, Fax: 819-595-7192
ouellet.suzanne@ville.gatineau.qc.ca
Robert F. Weemaes, Directeur général
Marco Lalonde, Directeur, Service des travaux publics
Louise Lavoie, Directrice, Service de l'environnement
Marc Pageau, Directeur, Service des ressources humaines
André Bonneau, Directeur, Service de sécurité incendie
Marie-Claude Martel, Directrice, Service de l'urbanisme et du développement durable
André Barbeau, Directeur, Service des finances
Nicole Dumoulin, Directrice, Service des communications
Mario Harel, Directeur, Service de police

Granby

87, rue Principale
Granby, QC J2G 2T8
Tél: 450-776-8282; *Téléc:* 450-776-8231
communication@ville.granby.qc.ca
www.ville.granby.qc.ca
Entité municipal: City
Incorporation: 1er janvier 2007 *Area:* 156,68 km2
Comté ou district: La Haute-Yamaska; *Population au 2011:* 63,433
Circonscription(s) électorale(s) provinciale(s): Shefford
Circonscription(s) électorale(s) fédérale(s): Shefford
Prochaines élections: 3e novembre 2013
Richard Goulet, Maire
450-776-8228, Fax: 450-378-0010
mairie@ville.granby.qc.ca
Louise B. Comeau, Conseillère, Ward(s): 1
450-378-2645
Éliette Jenneau, Conseillère, Ward(s): 2
450-531-8526
Pierre Breton, Conseiller, Ward(s): 3
450-777-7695
Patrick Girard, Conseiller, Ward(s): 4
450-578-4808
Denis Choinière, Conseiller, Ward(s): 5
Serges Ruel, Conseiller, Ward(s): 6
450-405-4446
Pascal Bonin, Conseiller, Ward(s): 7
450-776-1285
Guy Gaudor, Conseiller, Ward(s): 8
450-379-5949
Yves Pronovost, Conseiller, Ward(s): 9
450-577-2439
Michel Mailhot, Conseiller, Ward(s): 10
450-372-8317
Catherine Bouchard, Greffière
450-776-8275, Fax: 450-776-8278
greffe@ville.granby.qc.ca
Michel Pineault, Directeur général
450-776-8232, Fax: 450-776-8279
direction.generale@ville.granby.qc.ca
Jean-Pierre Renaud, Trésorier
450-776-8287, Fax: 450-776-8384
tresorerie@ville.granby.qc.ca
André Jean, Directeur, Travaux publics
450-776-8366, Fax: 450-776-8370
travaux.publics@ville.granby.qc.ca
Pierre Lacombe, Directeur, Incendies
450-776-8344, Fax: 450-839-0370
incendie@ville.granby.qc.ca
Patrice Faucher, Directeur, Loisir, arts, culture et vie communautaire
450-776-8224
pfaucher@ville.granby.qc.ca
Claude Ouimette, Coordonnateur, Station d'épuration des eaux usées
450-776-8371, Fax: 450-776-8373
epuration@ville.granby.qc.ca

Joliette

614, boul Manseau
Joliette, QC J6E 3E4
Tél: 450-753-8000; *Téléc:* 450-753-8199
www.ville.joliette.qc.ca
Entité municipal: City
Incorporation: 12 novembre 1966 *Area:* 22,36 km2
Comté ou district: Joliette; *Population au 2011:* 19,621
Circonscription(s) électorale(s) provinciale(s): Joliette
Circonscription(s) électorale(s) fédérale(s): Joliette
Prochaines élections: 3e novembre 2013
René Laurin, Maire
450-753-8020
mairie@ville.joliette.qc.ca
Alain Beaudry, Conseiller, Ward(s): 1
Normand-Guy Lépine, Conseiller, Ward(s): 2
Alain Lozeau, Conseiller, Ward(s): 3
Diane Nicoletti, Conseillère, Ward(s): 4
Jean-François Courteau, Conseiller, Ward(s): 5
Yves Liard, Conseiller, Ward(s): 6
Richard Leduc, Conseiller, Ward(s): 7
Pierrick Sylvestre, Greffier
450-753-8030
greffier@ville.joliette.qc.ca
Renald Gravel, Directeur général
450-753-8031
renald.gravel@ville.joliette.qc.ca
France Venne, Directrice, Opérations financières
450-753-8185
service.finances@ville.joliette.qc.ca
François Pépin, Directeur, Travaux publics et services techniques
450-753-8080
francois.pepin@ville.joliette.qc.ca
Terry Rousseau, Directeur, Incendies
450-753-8154
service.incendies@ville.joliette.qc.ca

L'Assomption

399, rue Dorval
L'Assomption, QC J5W 1A1
Tél: 450-589-5671; *Téléc:* 450-589-4512
information@ville.lassomption.qc.ca
www.ville.lassomption.qc.ca
Entité municipal: City
Incorporation: 1er juillet 2000 *Area:* 100,09 km2
Comté ou district: L'Assomption; *Population au 2011:* 20,065
Circonscription(s) électorale(s) provinciale(s): L'Assomption et Rousseau
Circonscription(s) électorale(s) fédérale(s): Repentigny
Prochaines élections: 3e novembre 2013
Louise T. Francoeur, Maire
450-589-5671
lfrancoeur@ville.lassomption.qc.ca
René Langlais, Conseiller, Ward(s): 1. Hector-Charland
rlanglais@ville.lassomption.qc.ca
Micheline Martel-Richard, Conseillère, Ward(s): 2. Wilfrid-Laurier
mmartel@ville.lassomption.qc.ca
Laurette Jobin-Morin, Conseillère, Ward(s): 3. J.-Edouard-Faribault
ljobin@ville.lassomption.qc.ca
Eugène Vincent, Conseiller, Ward(s): 4. L.-Michel-Viger
evincent@ville.lassomption.qc.ca
Nicole Martel, Conseillère, Ward(s): 5. Pierre-LeSueur
nmartel@ville.lassomption.qc.ca
Valérie Couturier, Conseillère, Ward(s): 6. Louis-Laberge
vcouturier@ville.lassomption.qc.ca
Charles Asselin, Conseiller, Ward(s): 7. Albert-Racette
casselin@ville.lassomption.qc.ca

Chantal Bédard, Greffière
greffe@ville.lassomption.qc.ca
Martin Levièvre, Directeur général
directiongenerale@ville.lassomption.qc.ca
Dominique Valiquette, Trésorier
tresorerie@ville.lassomption.qc.ca

L'île-Perrot

110, boul Perrot
L'Ile-Perrot, QC J7V 3G1
Tél: 514-453-1751; *Téléc:* 514-453-2432
ville@ile-perrot.qc.ca
www.ileperrot.qc.ca
Entité municipal: City
Incorporation: 1er juillet 1855 *Area:* 4,86 km2
Comté ou district: Vaudreuil-Soulanges; *Population au 2011:* 10,503
Circonscription(s) électorale(s) provinciale(s): Vaudreuil
Circonscription(s) électorale(s) fédérale(s): Vaudreuil-Soulanges
Prochaines élections: 3e novembre 2013
Marc Roy, Maire
514-453-6975
mroy@ile-perrot.qc.ca
André Legault, Conseiller, Ward(s): 1
514-453-6337
alegault@ile-perrot.qc.ca
Daniel Taillefer, Conseiller, Ward(s): 2
514-453-4774
dtaillefer@ile-perrot.qc.ca
Marcel Rainville, Conseiller, Ward(s): 3
514-902-1352
mrainville@ile-perrot.qc.ca
Michelle L. LeCavalier, Conseillère, Ward(s): 4
514-453-2599
mlecavalier@ile-perrot.qc.ca
René Pinsonneault, Conseiller, Ward(s): 5
514-453-7405
rpinsonneault@ile-perrot.qc.ca
Daniel Leblanc, Conseiller, Ward(s): 6
514-425-0403
dleblanc@ile-perrot.qc.ca
Lucie Coallier, Greffière
514-453-1751
lcoallier@ile-perrot.qc.ca
André Morin, Directeur général
514-453-1751
amorin@ile-perrot.qc.ca
Danielle Rioux, Trésorière
514-453-1751
drioux@ile-perrot.qc.ca

La Prairie

#400, 170, boul Taschereau
La Prairie, QC J5R 5H6
Tél: 450-444-6600; *Téléc:* 450-444-6636
info@ville.laprairie.qc.ca
www.ville.laprairie.qc.ca
Entité municipal: City
Incorporation: 30 mars 1846 *Area:* 43,53 km2
Comté ou district: Roussillon; *Population au 2011:* 23,357
Circonscription(s) électorale(s) provinciale(s): La Prairie
Circonscription(s) électorale(s) fédérale(s): Brossard-La Prairie
Prochaines élections: 3e novembre 2013
Lucie F. Roussel, Mairesse
Donat Serres, Conseiller, Ward(s): 1. Milice
Christian Caron, Conseiller, Ward(s): 2. Christ-Roi
Laurent Blais, Conseiller, Ward(s): 3. Vieux La Prairie
Jacques Bourbonnais, Conseiller, Ward(s): 4. Citière
Yvon Brière, Conseiller, Ward(s): 5. Clairière
Pierre Vocino, Conseiller, Ward(s): 6. Magdeleine
Yves Senécal, Conseiller, Ward(s): 7. Bataille
Suzanne Perron, Conseillère, Ward(s): 8. Briqueterie
Manon Thériault, Greffière
450-444-6625
greffe@ville.laprairie.qc.ca
Jean Bergeron, Directeur général
450-444-6619
dg@ville.laprairie.qc.ca
Nathalie Guérin, Trésorière
450-444-6603
finances@ville.laprairie.qc.ca
Guy Trahan, Directeur, Travaux publics
450-444-6684, Fax: 450-444-6692
tp@ville.laprairie.qc.ca

La Tuque

375, rue St-Joseph
La Tuque, QC G9X 1L5
Tél: 819-523-8200; *Téléc:* 819-523-5419
dg@ville.latuque.qc.ca
www.ville.latuque.qc.ca
Entité municipal: City
Incorporation: 26 mars 2003 *Area:* 28 421,48 km2
Population au 2011: 11,227
Circonscription(s) électorale(s) provinciale(s): Laviolette
Circonscription(s) électorale(s) fédérale(s): St-Maurice-Champlain
Prochaines élections: 3e novembre 2013
Note: Dès le 26 mars 2003, la nouvelle ville de La Tuque regroupe La Tuque, les municipalités de La Croche, La Bostonnais, & Lac-Édouard, le village de Parent, & 8 autres territoires.
Normand Beaudoin, Maire
819-523-8200
mairie@ville.latuque.qc.ca
Sylvie Lachapelle, Conseillère, Ward(s): 1. Parent
819-667-2323, Fax: 819-667-2542
parent@tlb.sympatico.ca
Line Pilote, Conseillère, Ward(s): 2. Croche/Couronee rurale
lpilote@ville.latuque.qc.ca
Luc Martel, Conseiller, Ward(s): 3. Jacques-Buteux
lmartel@ville.latuque.qc.ca
Jean-Marc Dumont, Conseiller, Ward(s): 4. Polyvalente
jdumont@ville.latuque.qc.ca
Jean Duchesneau, Conseiller, Ward(s): 5. Bel-Air—Centre-ville
jduchesneau@ville.latuque.qc.ca
Roch Lepage, Conseiller, Ward(s): 6. Aéroport
rlepage@ville.latuque.qc.ca
Jean-Sébastien Poirier, Greffier
greffe@ville.latuque.qc.ca
Marco Lethiecq, Directeur général
mlethiecq@ville.latuque.qc.ca
Pierre Bouchard, Trésorier
tresorerie@ville.latuque.qc.ca

Lachute

380, rue Principale
Lachute, QC J8H 1Y2
Tél: 450-562-3781; *Téléc:* 450-562-1431
lachute@ville.lachute.qc.ca
www.ville.lachute.qc.ca
Entité municipal: City
Incorporation: 30 avril 1966 *Area:* 111,20 km2
Comté ou district: Argenteuil; *Population au 2011:* 12,551
Circonscription(s) électorale(s) provinciale(s): Argenteuil
Circonscription(s) électorale(s) fédérale(s): Argenteuil-Papineau-Mirabel
Prochaines élections: 3e novembre 2013
Daniel Mayer, Maire
Marcelle L. Louis-Seize, Conseillère, Ward(s): 1
Mario Beaudin, Conseiller, Ward(s): 2
Guy Léger, Conseiller, Ward(s): 3
Stéphane Braney, Conseiller, Ward(s): 4
Guy Desforges, Conseiller, Ward(s): 5
Paul Cleary, Conseiller, Ward(s): 6
Louise Beaulieu, Greffière
450-562-3781
lbeaulieu@ville.lachute.qc.ca
Pierre Gionet, Directeur général
450-562-3781
pgionet@ville.lachute.qc.ca
Nathalie Piret, Trésorière
450-562-3781
npiret@ville.lachute.qc.ca

Laval

Hôtel de Ville
CP 422 St-Martin
1, Place du Souvenir
Laval, QC H7V 3Z4
Tél: 450-978-8000; *Téléc:* 450-978-5943
info@ville.laval.qc.ca
www.ville.laval.qc.ca
Entité municipal: City
Incorporation: 6e août 1965 *Area:* 245,40 km2
Population au 2011: 401,553
Circonscription(s) électorale(s) provinciale(s): Chomedey; Fabre; Laval-des-Rapides; Mille-Iles; Vimont
Circonscription(s) électorale(s) fédérale(s): Laval; Marc-Aurèle-Fortin; Alfred-Pellan; Laval-Les Iles
Prochaines élections: 3e novembre 2013
Gilles Vaillancourt, Maire
Jacques St-Jean, Conseiller, Ward(s): 1. Saint-François
450-666-2509
j.stjean@ville.laval.qc.ca
Sylvie Clermont, Conseillère, Ward(s): 2. Saint-Vincent-de-Paul
450-664-2776
s.clermont@ville.laval.qc.ca
Madeleine Sollazzo, Conseillère, Ward(s): 3. Val-des-Arbres
450-661-8248
info@madeleinesollazzo.com
Michèle des Trois Maisons, Conseillère, Ward(s): 4. Duvernay-Pont-Viau
450-975-2493
m.destroismaisons@ville.laval.qc.ca
Francine Légaré, Conseillère, Ward(s): 5. Marigot
450-661-9730
fr.legare@ville.laval.qc.ca
Claire Le Bel, Conseillère, Ward(s): 6. Concorde-Bois-de-Boulogne
450-663-8039
cl.lebel@ville.laval.qc.ca
Benoit Fradet, Conseiller, Ward(s): 7. Renaud
450-662-4140
b.fradet@ville.laval.qc.ca
Norman Girard, Conseiller, Ward(s): 8. Vimont
450-967-1633
n.girard@ville.laval.qc.ca
Yvon Martineau, Conseiller, Ward(s): 9. Saint-Bruno
450-629-8803
ymartineau@live.ca
Lucie Hill Larocque, Conseiller, Ward(s): 10. Auteuil
450-625-1821
l.hill@ville.laval.qc.ca
Ginette Grisé, Conseillère, Ward(s): 11. Laval-des-Rapides
450-967-7373
g.grise@ville.laval.qc.ca
Jocelyne Guertin, Conseillère, Ward(s): 12. Souvenir-Labelle
450-662-4140
j.guertin@ville.laval.qc.ca
Ginette Legault Bernier, Conseillère, Ward(s): 13. Abord-à-Plouffe
450-681-9468
glbernier@yahoo.com
Basile Angelopoulos, Conseiller, Ward(s): 14. Chomedey
450-662-4140
b.angelopoulos@ville.laval.qc.ca
Alexandre Duplessis, Conseiller, Ward(s): 15. Saint-Martin
514-944-2961
a.duplessis@ville.laval.qc.ca
Pierre Cléroux, Conseiller, Ward(s): 16. Sainte-Dorothée
450-689-7331
p.cleroux@ville.laval.qc.ca
Jean-Jacques Beldié, Conseiller, Ward(s): 17. Laval-les-îles
514-945-4700
j-j.beldie@ville.laval.qc.ca
France Dubreuil, Conseillère, Ward(s): 18. Orée-des-bois
514-239-1396
f.dubreuil@ville.laval.qc.ca
Yvon Bromley, Conseiller, Ward(s): 19. Marc-Aurèle-Fortin
450-628-4799
y.bromley@ville.laval.qc.ca
Martine Beaugrand, Conseillère, Ward(s): 20. Fabreville
450-736-3086
m.beaugrand@ville.laval.qc.ca
Denis Robillard, Conseiller, Ward(s): 21. Sainte-Rose
450-628-3055
d.robillard@ville.laval.qc.ca
Guy Collard, Greffier et secrétaire-trésorier
450-978-3950
Gaétan Turbide, Directeur général
450-978-3676
Robert Cadieux, Directeur, Contentieux
450-978-5866
Gilles Benoit, Directeur, Environnement
450-978-8000
Ernest Lépine, Directeur, Évaluation
450-978-8777
Suzanne Deshaies, Directrice, Finances
450-978-6888
Gérard Poirier, Directeur, Ingénierie
450-680-2999
Jean-Pierre Gariépy, Directeur, Protection des citoyens
450-662-4242
Martin Fiset, Directeur, Ressources humaines
450-978-6560
Lise Poirier, Directrice, Systèmes & technologies
450-662-4040
Michel Toutant, Directeur, Travaux publics
450-978-8000
Sylvain Dubois, Directeur, Urbanisme
450-680-5500
Marc Deblois, Directeur, Vie communautaire, culture et communications
450-978-2900
Martine Lachambre, Vérificateur général
450-978-8715

Lavaltrie
1370, rue Notre-Dame
Lavaltrie, QC J0K 1H0
Tél: 450-586-2921; *Téléc:* 450-586-3939
mairie@ville.lavaltrie.qc.ca
www.ville.lavaltrie.qc.ca
Entité municipal: City
Incorporation: 16 mai 2001 *Area:* 68,61 km2
Comté ou district: D'Autray; *Population au 2011:* 13,267
Circonscription(s) électorale(s) provinciale(s): Berthier
Circonscription(s) électorale(s) fédérale(s): Berthier-Maskinongé
Prochaines élections: 3e novembre 2013
Jean-Claude Gravel, Maire
Michele Dawe, Conseillère, Ward(s): 1. Terrasses
Robert Pellerin, Conseiller, Ward(s): 2. Rivière
Louise Martel, Conseillère, Ward(s): 3. Chemin du Roy
Lynda Pelletier, Conseillère, Ward(s): 4. Érablière
Georges Bonin, Conseiller, Ward(s): 5. Boisé
Sophie Hervieux, Conseillère, Ward(s): 6. Golf
Yves Deguire, Conseiller, Ward(s): 7. Chasse-galerie
Gaétan Bérard, Conseiller, Ward(s): 8. Saint-Antoine
Madeleine Barbeau, Greffière
450-586-2921, Fax: 450-586-3939
mbarbeau@ville.lavaltrie.qc.ca
Yvon Mousseau, Directeur général
450-586-2921, Fax: 450-586-3939
ymousseau@ville.lavaltrie.qc.ca
Réjean Nantais, Trésorier
450-586-2921, Fax: 450-586-4060
tresorerie@ville.lavaltrie.qc.ca
André Houle, Directeur, Travaux publics
450-586-2921, Fax: 450-586-3540
travauxpublics@ville.lavaltrie.qc.ca

Lévis
2175, ch du Fleuve
Lévis, QC G6W 7W9
Tél: 418-839-2002; *Téléc:* 418-839-5548
levis@ville.levis.qc.ca
www.ville.levis.qc.ca
Entité municipal: City
Incorporation: 1er janvier 2002 *Area:* 443,65 km2
Population au 2011: 138,769
Circonscription(s) électorale(s) provinciale(s): Chutes-de-la-Chaudière; Lévis
Circonscription(s) électorale(s) fédérale(s): Lévis-Bellechasse; Lotbinière—Chutes-de-la-Chaudière
Prochaines élections: 3e novembre 2013
Danielle Roy Marinelli, Mairesse
dmarinelli@ville.levis.qc.ca
Mario Fortier, Conseiller, Ward(s): 1
mfortier@ville.levis.qc.ca
Dominique Maranda, Conseillère, Ward(s): 2
dmaranda@ville.levis.qc.ca
Anne Ladouceur, Conseillère, Ward(s): 3
aladouceur@ville.levis.qc.ca
Réjean Lamontagne, Conseiller, Ward(s): 4
rlamontagne@ville.levis.qc.ca
Michel Patry, Conseiller, Ward(s): 5
michel.patry@ville.levis.qc.ca
Michel Turner, Conseiller, Ward(s): 6
mturner@ville.levis.qc.ca
Guy Dumoulin, Conseiller, Ward(s): 7
gdumoulin@ville.levis.qc.ca
Jean-Pierre Bazinet, Conseiler, Ward(s): 8
jpbazinet@ville.levis.qc.ca
Jean-Luc Daigle, Conseiller, Ward(s): 9
jldaigle@ville.levis.qc.ca
Simon Théberge, Conseiller, Ward(s): 10
stheberge@ville.levis.qc.ca
Serge Côté, Conseiller, Ward(s): 11
scote@ville.levis.qc.ca
Janet Jones, Conseillère, Ward(s): 12
jjones@ville.levis.qc.ca
Robert Maranda, Conseiller, Ward(s): 13
rmaranda@ville.levis.qc.ca
Jean-Claude Bouchard, Conseiller, Ward(s): 14
jcbouchard@ville.levis.qc.ca
Ann Jeffrey, Conseillère, Ward(s): 15
ajeffrey@ville.levis.qc.ca
Danielle Bilodeau, Greffière
418-839-2002
levis@ville.levis.qc.ca
Jean Dubé, Directeur général
418-839-2002
jdube@ville.levis.qc.ca
Marcel Rodrigue, Trésorier
418-839-2002, Fax: 418-835-8522
Claude Pelletier, Chef de police
Christian Brière, Directeur, Communications
Claude Guérin, Directeur, Ressources humaines
René Tremblay, Directeur, Culture et des loisirs
Alain Francoeur, Directeur, Travaux publics
Pierre Boulay, Directeur, Environnement
André Matte, Vérificateur général
Robert Cooke, Directeur, Urbanisme
Philippe Meurant, Directrice, Planification et du développement
Yves Després, Directeur, Sécurité incendie

Longueuil
4250, ch de la Savane
Longueuil, QC J3Y 9G4
Tél: 450-463-7000; *Téléc:* 450-463-7403
www.longueuil.ca
Entité municipal: City
Incorporation: 1er janvier 2002 *Area:* 111,50 km2
Population au 2011: 231,409
Circonscription(s) électorale(s) provinciale(s): Marie-Victorin; Taillon; Laporte; Vachon
Circonscription(s) électorale(s) fédérale(s): Saint-Lambert; Longueuil-Pierre-Boucher; Saint-Bruno-Saint Hubert
Prochaines élections: 3e novembre 2013
Caroline St-Hilaire, Mairesse
Michel Desjardins, Conseiller, Ward(s): 1. Vieux-Longueuil
450-463-7081
Sylvie Parent, Conseillère, Ward(s): 2. Vieux-Longueuil
Benôit L'Ecuyer, Conseiller, Ward(s): 3. Vieux-Longueuil
450-468-6650
André Groleau, Conseiller, Ward(s): 4. Vieux-Longueuil
450-748-1015
Albert Beaudry, Conseiller, Ward(s): 5. Vieux-Longueuil
Michel Lanctôt, Conseiller, Ward(s): 6. Vieux-Longueuil
Marie-Lise Sauvé, Conseillère, Ward(s): 7. Vieux-Longueuil
450-448-7777
Manon D. Hénault, Conseillère, Ward(s): 8. Vieux-Longueuil
450-679-0931
Nicole Lafontaine, Conseillère, Ward(s): 9. Vieux-Longueuil
450-928-3616
Claude Jr. Gladu, Conseiller, Ward(s): 10. Vieux-Longueuil
450-651-7959
Johane Fontaine-Deshaies, Conseillère, Ward(s): 11. Vieux-Longueuil
450-677-2157
Monique Bastien, Conseillère, Ward(s): 12. Vieux-Longueuil
Monique Brisson, Conseillère, Ward(s): 13. Vieux-Longueuil
Robert Gladu, Conseiller, Ward(s): 14. Vieux-Longueuil
450-646-7671
Gilles Grégoire, Conseiller, Ward(s): 15. Vieux-Longueuil, Le Moyne
450-671-2149
Mireille Carrière, Conseillère, Ward(s): 16. Greenfield Park
Robert Myles, Conseiller, Ward(s): 17. Greenfield Park
450-465-6703
Michael O'Grady, Conseiller, Ward(s): 18. Greenfield Park
Jacques Lemire, Conseiller, Ward(s): 19. St-Hubert
450-445-2216
Roger Roy, Conseiller, Ward(s): 20. St-Hubert
450-676-8529
Jacques E. Poitras, Conseiller, Ward(s): 21. St-Hubert
Éric Beaulieau, Conseiller, Ward(s): 22. St-Hubert
450-463-7001
Suzanne Lachance, Conseillère, Ward(s): 23. St-Hubert
Nathalie Boisclair, Conseillère, Ward(s): 24. St-Hubert
Lorraine Guay-Boivin, Conseillère, Ward(s): 25. St-Hubert
450-463-7100
Michel Latendresse, Conseiller, Ward(s): 26. St-Hubert
Daniel Carrier, Directeur, Services juridiques
Guy Benedetti, Directeur général
Sylvie Toupin, Directrice, Finances
Pierre Archambault, Directeur, Ressources informationnelles & matérielles
Sylvie Cossette, Directrice, Développement durable et de la planification du territoire
Linda Rivard, Directrice, Communications et relations avec le citoyen
Denis Desroches, Directeur, Service de police
Claude Chevalier, Directeur, Service de sécurité incendie
Alain Cyr, Directeur, Travaux publics
Hélène Ladouceur, Directrice, Urbanisme
Michel Vallée, Directeur, Évaluation
André Lachapelle, Directeur général adjoint, Services administratifs
Alain Desgagné, Directeur, Ressources humaines
Francine Brunette, Vérificatrice générale

Magog
7, rue Principale est
Magog, QC J1X 1Y4
Tél: 819-843-6501; *Téléc:* 819-843-1091
info@ville.magog.qc.ca
www.ville.magog.qc.ca
Entité municipal: City
Incorporation: 9e octobre 2002 *Area:* 145,68 km2
Comté ou district: Memphrémagog; *Population au 2011:* 25,358
Circonscription(s) électorale(s) provinciale(s): Orford
Circonscription(s) électorale(s) fédérale(s): Brome-Missisquoi
Prochaines élections: 3e novembre 2013
Note: Depuis le 9 oct., le canton de Magog, le village d'Omerville & la ville de Magog sont regroupés pour former la nouvelle ville de Magog.
Vicki May Hamm, Mairesse
819-843-2880
vm.hamm@ville.magog.qc.ca
Michel Bombardier, Conseiller, Ward(s): 1. La Rivière
819-843-0370
mbom@cgocable.ca
Yvon Lamontagne, Conseiller, Ward(s): 2. Omerville
819-843-7250
info@ville.magog.qc.ca
Denise Poulin-Marcotte, Conseillère, Ward(s): 3. Des Sommets
819-843-1146
denisepmarcotte@hotmail.com
Olivier Tremblay, Conseiller, Ward(s): 4. Du Marais
819-847-4191
olitremblay@hotmail.com
Robert Ranger, Conseiller, Ward(s): 5. Canton Ouest
819-620-4134
rangerconseiller@live.ca
Jacques Laurendeau, Conseiller, Ward(s): 6. Des Pionniers
819-843-3244
info@ville.magog.qc.ca
Gilbert Kurt Boucher, Conseiller, Ward(s): 7. Centre
819-868-2006
bouc7@sympatico.ca
Nathalie Bélanger, Conseillère, Ward(s): 8. Monseigneur Vel
819-868-0256
nathbel30@hotmail.com
Nathalie Pelletier, Conseillère, Ward(s): 9. Des Marinas
819-868-5126
natp@cgocable.ca
Diane Pelletier, Conseillère, Ward(s): 10. Des Deux lacs
819-570-7597
diane.pelletier@cgocable.ca
Martine Savard, Greffière
819-843-6501
greffe@ville.magog.qc.ca
Armand Comeau, Directeur général
819-843-2880
dg@ville.magog.qc.ca
Anne Couturier, Trésorière
819-843-6501
finances@ville.magog.qc.ca

Mascouche
3034, ch Ste-Marie
Mascouche, QC J7K 1P1
Tél: 450-474-4133; *Téléc:* 450-474-6401
www.ville.mascouche.qc.ca
Entité municipal: City
Incorporation: 1er juillet 1855 *Area:* 107,95 km2
Comté ou district: Les Moulins; *Population au 2011:* 42,491
Circonscription(s) électorale(s) provinciale(s): Masson
Circonscription(s) électorale(s) fédérale(s): Montcalm
Prochaines élections: 3e novembre 2013
Richard Marcotte, Maire
450-474-4133
Normand Pagé, Conseiller, Ward(s): 1. Louis-Hébert
450-966-6326
Lise Gagnon, Conseillère, Ward(s): 2. Laurier
450-474-4501
Jacques Tremblay, Conseiller, Ward(s): 3. Le Gardeur
514-591-8710
Donald Mailly, Conseiller, Ward(s): 4. La Vérendrye
450-966-1413
Sylvain Picard, Conseiller, Ward(s): 5. Du Coteau
450-966-9233
Chantal Laurin, Conseillère, Ward(s): 6. Des Hauts-Bois
450-477-4953
Nathalie Filion, Conseillère, Ward(s): 7. Du Rucher
514-461-3065
Denise Paquette, Conseillère, Ward(s): 8. Du Manoir
450-966-6044
Yvan Laberge, Greffier
450-474-4133
Luc Tremblay, Directeur général
450-474-4133
Michel Gobeil, Trésorier, Finances
450-474-4133

Matane
230, av St-Jérôme
Matane, QC G4W 3A2
Tél: 418-562-2333; *Téléc:* 418-562-4869
mairie@ville.matane.qc.ca
www.ville.matane.qc.ca
Entité municipal: Cité
Incorporation: 26 septembre 2001 *Area:* 214,63 km2
Comté ou district: Matane; *Population au 2011:* 14,462
Circonscription(s) électorale(s) provinciale(s): Matane
Circonscription(s) électorale(s) fédérale(s): Haute-Gaspésie-La Mitis-Matane-Matapédia
Prochaines élections: 3e novembre 2013
Claude Canuel, Maire
mairie@ville.matane.qc.ca
Anick Fortin, Conseiller, Ward(s): 1
418-562-7334
Monique Fournier, Conseillère, Ward(s): 2
colombo@cgocable.ca
Claude Harrison, Conseiller, Ward(s): 3
charrison@globetrotter.net
Mario Hamilton, Conseiller, Ward(s): 4
mhjm@globetrotter.net
Martin Lefrançois, Conseiller, Ward(s): 5
martin@lefrancoisfrancoeur.ca
Steve Girard, Conseiller, Ward(s): 6
418-562-4975
sgirard.matane@globetrotter.net
Nicolas Leclerc, Greffier (par intérim)
n.leclerc@ville.matane.qc.ca
Michel Barriault, Directeur général
418-562-2333
m.barriault@ville.matane.qc.ca
Marie Pelletier, Trésorière
418-562-2333
m.pelletier@ville.matane.qc.ca

Mercier
869, boul St-Jean-Baptiste, 2e étage
Mercier, QC J6R 2L3
Tél: 450-691-6090; *Téléc:* 450-691-6529
info@ville.mercier.qc.ca
www.ville.mercier.qc.ca
Entité municipal: City
Incorporation: 1er juillet 1855 *Area:* 45,89 km2
Comté ou district: Roussillon; *Population au 2011:* 11,584
Circonscription(s) électorale(s) provinciale(s): Châteauguay
Circonscription(s) électorale(s) fédérale(s):
Châteauguay—St-Constant
Prochaines élections: 3e novembre 2013
Jacques Lambert, Maire
450-691-6090
jacques.lambert@ville.mercier.qc.ca
Stéphane Roy, Conseiller, Ward(s): 1
stephane.roy@ville.mercier.qc.ca
Jeannine Breault, Conseillère, Ward(s): 2
jeannine.breault@ville.mercier.qc.ca
Gilles Desponts, Conseiller, Ward(s): 3
gilles.desponts@ville.mercier.qc.ca
Daniel Pilon, Conseiller, Ward(s): 4
daniel.pilon@ville.mercier.qc.ca
Louis Cimon, Conseiller, Ward(s): 5
louis.cimon@ville.mercier.qc.ca
Pierre Hébert, Conseiller, Ward(s): 6
pierre.hebert@ville.mercier.qc.ca
Marc Rouleau, Greffier et directeur général
450-691-6090
marc.rouleau@ville.mercier.qc.ca
Nadia René, Trésorière
450-691-6090
nadia.rene@ville.mercier.qc.ca

Mirabel
14111, rue Saint-Jean
Mirabel, QC J7J 1Y3
Tél: 450-475-8653; *Téléc:* 450-475-7195
communications@ville.mirabel.qc.ca
ville.mirabel.qc.ca
Entité municipal: City
Incorporation: 1er janvier 1971 *Area:* 477,86 km2
Comté ou district: Mirabel; *Population au 2011:* 41,957
Circonscription(s) électorale(s) provinciale(s): Mirabel
Circonscription(s) électorale(s) fédérale(s):
Argenteuil-Papineau-Mirabel
Prochaines élections: 3e novembre 2013
Hubert Meilleur, Maire
Michel Lauzon, Conseiller, Ward(s): 1
Gérald Forget, Conseiller, Ward(s): 2
Jean Bouchard, Conseiller, Ward(s): 3
François Bélanger, Conseiller, Ward(s): 4
Daniel Gauthier, Conseiller, Ward(s): 5
Pierre-Paul Meloche, Conseiller, Ward(s): 6
Luc St-Jean, Conseiller, Ward(s): 7
Guy Laurin, Conseiller, Ward(s): 8
Suzanne Mireault, Greffière
450-475-2002
s.mireault@ville.mirabel.qc.ca
Louis Prud'homme, Directeur général
450-475-2000, Fax: 450-475-2013
l.prud'homme@ville.mirabel.qc.ca
Germain Paquette, Trésorier
450-475-2003
g.paquette@ville.mirabel.qc.ca
Bernard Poulin, Directeur, Communications
450-475-2001
b.poulin@ville.mirabel.qc.ca
Jean Gaudreault, Directeur, Loisirs, la culture et la vie
450-475-8656
j.gaudreault@ville.mirabel.qc.ca
Denis Maurice, Directeur adjoint, Sécurité incendie
450-475-2010
d.maurice@ville.mirabel.qc.ca

Mont-Laurier
485, rue Mercier
Mont-Laurier, QC J9L 3N8
Tél: 819-623-1221; *Téléc:* 819-623-4840
info@villemontlaurier.qc.ca
www.villemontlaurier.qc.ca
Entité municipal: City
Incorporation: 8e janvier 2003 *Area:* 590,64 km2
Comté ou district: Antoine-Labelle; *Population au 2011:* 13,779
Circonscription(s) électorale(s) provinciale(s): Labelle
Circonscription(s) électorale(s) fédérale(s): Laurentides-Labelle
Prochaines élections: 3e novembre 2013
Note: Dès le 8 janvier 2003, la ville de Mont-Laurier regroupe les municipalités de Des Ruisseaux & Saint-Aimé-du-Lac-des-Iles.
Michel Adrien, Maire
Denis Ethier, Conseiller, Ward(s): 1
Frank Crépeau, Conseiller, Ward(s): 2
Jocelyne Cloutier, Conseillère, Ward(s): 3
Benoit Pagé, Conseiller, Ward(s): 4
Louis-Pierre Blais, Conseiller, Ward(s): 5
Lise St-Louis, Conseillère, Ward(s): 6
Blandine Boulianne, Greffière
Jean-Yves Forget, Directeur général
Johanne Nantel, Trésorière

Mont-St-Hilaire
100, rue du Centre-Civique
Mont-Saint-Hilaire, QC J3H 3M8
Tél: 450-467-2854; *Téléc:* 450-467-6460
information@villemsh.ca
www.ville.mont-saint-hilaire.qc.ca
Entité municipal: City
Incorporation: 12 mars 1966 *Area:* 38,96 km2
Comté ou district: La Vallée-du-Richelieu; *Population au 2011:* 18,200
Circonscription(s) électorale(s) provinciale(s): Borduas
Circonscription(s) électorale(s) fédérale(s): Chambly-Borduas
Prochaines élections: 3e novembre 2013
Michel Gilbert, Maire
450-446-9511
michel.gilbert@villemsh.ca
Guy Boulé, Conseiller, Ward(s): 1. Déboulis
450-467-6631
guy.boule@villemsh.ca
Rémi H. Lair, Conseiller, Ward(s): 2. Patriotes
450-536-0960
remi.h.lair@villemsh.ca
André Ricard, Conseiller, Ward(s): 3. Piémont
450-446-5774
andre.ricard@villemsh.ca
Valéry Lapointe, Conseillère, Ward(s): 4. Rouville
450-714-1351
valery.lapointe@villemsh.ca
Jean-Luc Halde, Conseiller, Ward(s): 5. Montagne
450-467-6535
jean-luc.halde@villemsh.ca
Fernand Brillant, Conseiller, Ward(s): 6. Pommeraie
450-467-4699
fernand.brillant@villemsh.ca
Estelle Simard, Greffière
450-467-2854
greffe@villemsh.ca
Vacant, Directeur général
450-467-2854
direction.generale@villemsh.ca
Carmel Constant, Trésorier
450-467-2854
finances@villemsh.ca
Pierre Bergeron, Directeur, Loisir, culture et communication

Montmagny
143, rue St-Jean-Baptiste est
Montmagny, QC G5V 1K4
Tél: 418-248-3361; *Téléc:* 418-248-4870
info@ville.montmagny.qc.ca
www.ville.montmagny.qc.ca
Entité municipal: City
Incorporation: 2e avril 1966 *Area:* 125,76 km2
Comté ou district: Montmagny; *Population au 2011:* 11,491
Circonscription(s) électorale(s) provinciale(s): Montmagny-L'Islet
Circonscription(s) électorale(s) fédérale(s):
Montmagny-L'Islet-Kamouraska-Rivière-du-Loup
Prochaines élections: 3e novembre 2013
Jean-Guy Desrosiers, Maire
Jean-Paul Boivin, Conseiller, Ward(s): 1
Gaston Caron, Conseiller, Ward(s): 2
Michel Coulombe, Conseiller, Ward(s): 3
Michel Mercier, Conseiller, Ward(s): 4
Michel Paquet, Conseiller, Ward(s): 5
Rémy Langevin, Conseiller, Ward(s): 6
Félix Michaud, Greffier
418-248-3362
felix.michaud@ville.montmagny.qc.ca
Bernard Létourneau, Directeur général
418-248-3362
bernard.letourneau@ville.montmagny.qc.ca
André Lévesque, Directeur, Finances et approvisionnement
418-248-3361, Fax: 418-248-8468
finances@ville.montmagny.qc.ca
Yves Chayer, Directeur, Protection contre les incendies
418-248-5813, Fax: 418-248-2266
yves.chayer@ville.montmagny.qc.ca

Montréal
Hôtel de Ville
275, rue Notre-Dame est
Montréal, QC H2Y 1C6
Tél: 514-872-3142; *Téléc:* 514-872-5655
www.ville.montreal.qc.ca
Entité municipal: City
Incorporation: 1er janvier 2002 *Area:* 363,52 km2
Population au 2011: 1,649,519
Circonscription(s) électorale(s) provinciale(s):
Acadie;Anjou;Bourassa-Sauvé;Bourget;Crémazie;D'Arcy McGee;Gouin;Hochelaga-Maisonneuve;Jeanne-Mance-Viger;La Fontaine;Laurier-Dorion;Marguerite-Bourgeoys;Mercier;Marquette;Mont-Royal;Nelligan;Notre-Dame-de-Grâce;Outremont;Pointe-aux-Trembles;Robert-Baldwin;Rosemont;St-Henri-Ste-Anne;St-Laurent;Ste-Marie -St-Jacques;Westmount-St-Louis;Verdun;Viau
Circonscription(s) électorale(s) fédérale(s): Ahuntsic; Bourassa; Hochelaga; Honoré-Mercier; Jeanne-Le Ber; Lac-Saint-Louis; LaSalle-Émard; Laurier-Ste-Marie; Mount Royal; Notre-Dame-de-Grâce-Lachine; Outremont; Papineau; Rosemont-La Petite-Patrie; Westmount-Ville-Marie; St-Laurent-Cartierville; St-Léonard-St-Michel; La Pointe-de-l'Ile; Pierrefonds-Dollard
Prochaines élections: 3e novembre 2013
Gérald Tremblay, Maire
514-872-3101, Fax: 514-872-4059
Yves Saindon, Greffier
514-872-3007
yvessaindon@ville.montreal.qc.ca
Louis Roquet, Directeur général
Robert Lamontagne, Directeur, Finances
Pierre Villeneuve, Directeur (par intérim), Relations avec les citoyens
Jean Yves Hinse, Directeur, Service du capital humain
Jacques Bergeron, Vérificateur général
Jacques Bergeron, CA, MBA, M.Sc., Vérificateur général
Serge Tremblay, Directeur
Jean Yves Hinse, Directeur
Louis Roquet, Directeur général
Marc Parent, Directeur
Élaine Ayotte, Conseillère de la ville, Marie-Victorin, Ward(s): Rosemont—La Petite—Patrie
514-868-3931, Fax: 514-868-3932
Frantz Benjamin, Conseillère de la ville, Saint-Michel, Ward(s): Villeray-St-Michel-Parc-Ext.
514-872-3103, Fax: 514-872-2196
Richard Bergeron, Conseiller de la ville, Jeanne-Mance, Ward(s): Le Plateau-Mont-Royal
514-872-8023, Fax: 514-868-4077
richardbbergeron@ville.montreal.qc.ca
Laurent Blanchard, Conseiller de la ville, Hochelaga, Ward(s): Mercier—Hochelaga-Maisonneuve
514-872-9899, Fax: 514-872-7125
laurentblanchard@ville.montreal.qc.ca
Caroline Bourgeois, Conseillère de la ville, La Pointe-aux-Prairies, Ward(s): Riv.-des-Prairies-Pte-aux-Trem
514-868-4356, Fax: 514-868-4353

Robert Duquette, CA, Vérificateur général adjoint, Optimisation des ressources et conformité réglementair
Étienne Brunet, Conseiller de la ville, Sault-au-Récollet, Ward(s): Ahuntsic-Cartierville
514-872-0430, Fax: 514-868-3324
Serge Vaillancourt, Vérificateur général adjoint, Technologies de l'information, éthique et administration
Daniel Bélanger, Conseiller de la ville, Saint-Paul—Émard, Ward(s): Le Sud-Ouest
514-872-6814, Fax: 514-872-3705
Denis Tremblay, Vérificateur général adjoint, Certification des états financiers Ville et autres organismes municipaux
Maria Calderone, Conseillère de la ville, Rivière-des-Prairies, Ward(s): Riv.-des-Prairies-Pte-aux-Trem
514-868-4052, Fax: 514-872-3709
mariacalderone@ville.montreal.qc.ca
Denis Tremblay, Chef de division, Vérification -Autre organismes municipaux
Jocelyn Ann Campbell, Conseillère de la ville, Saint-Sulpice, Ward(s): Ahuntsic-Cartierville
514-872-2246, Fax: 514-868-3324
jacampbell@ville.montreal.qc.ca
Harout Chitilian, Conseiller de la ville, Bordeaux-Cartierville, Ward(s): Ahuntsic-Cartierville
514-872-2246, Fax: 514-868-3324
Susan Clarke, Conseillère de la ville, Loyola, Ward(s): Côte-des-Neiges-N.-D.-de-Grâce
514-872-4863, Fax: 514-868-3327
Jane Cowell-Poitras, Conseillère de la ville, Ward(s): Lachine
514-634-3471, Fax: 514-634-8164
Mary Deros, Conseillère de la ville, Parc-Extension, Ward(s): Villeray-St-Michel-Parc-Extens
514-872-3103, Fax: 514-872-2196
mderos@ville.montreal.qc.ca
Richard Deschamps, Conseiller de la ville, Sault-St-Louis, Ward(s): LaSalle
514-872-4879, Fax: 514-367-6600
richarddeschamps@ville.montreal.qc.ca
Christian G. Dubois, Conseiller de la ville, Bois-de-Liesse, Ward(s): Pierrefonds-Roxboro
514-624-1488, Fax: 514-624-1415
christiangdubois@ville.montreal.qc.ca
Josée Duplessis, Conseillère de la ville, De Lorimier, Ward(s): Le Plateau-Mont-Royal
514-868-5196, Fax: 514-868-4118
joseeduplessis@ville.montreal.qc.ca
Suzanne Décarie, Conseillère de la ville, Pointe-aux-Trembles, Ward(s): Riv.-des-Prairies-Pte-aux-Trem
514-868-4350, Fax: 514-868-4353
suzannedecarie@ville.montreal.qc.ca
Alvaro Farinacci, Conseiller de la ville, Cecil-P.-Newman, Ward(s): LaSalle
514-367-6208, Fax: 514-367-6600
genesee@qc.aira.com
Sammy Forcillo, Conseiller de la ville, Peter-McGill, Ward(s): Ville-Marie
514-868-5858, Fax: 514-872-8347
sforcillo@ville.montreal.qc.ca
Helen Fotopulos, Conseillère de la ville, Côte-des-Neiges, Conseillers et Districts, Ward(s): Côte-de-Neiges-N.-D.-de-Grâce
hfotopulos@ville.montreal.qc.ca
Véronique Fournier, Conseillère de la ville, St-Henri-Petite-Bourgogne-Pte-St-Charles, Ward(s): Le Sud-Ouest
514-872-6814, Fax: 514-872-3705
Marc-André Gadoury, Conseiller de la ville, Étienne-Desmarteau, Ward(s): Rosemont—La Petite-Patrie
514-872-8390, Fax: 514-868-3932
Jean-Marc Gibeau, Conseiller de la ville, Ovide-Clermont, Ward(s): Montréal-Nord
514-328-4000, Fax: 514-325-4025
jgibeau@ville.montreal.qc.ca
Louise Harel, Conseillère de la ville, Maisonneuve—Longue-Pointe, Ward(s): Mercier-Hochelaga-Maisonneuve
514-872-7123, Fax: 514-872-7125
Andrée Hénault, Conseillère de la ville, Ward(s): Anjou
514-493-8051, Fax: 514-493-8013
ahenault@ville.montreal.qc.ca
Pierre Lampron, Conseiller de la ville, Vieux-Rosemont, Ward(s): Rosemont—La Petite-Patrie
514-868-3907, Fax: 514-868-3932
Elsie Lefebvre, Conseillère de la ville, Villeray, Ward(s): Villeray St-Michel-Parc-Extens
514-872-3103, Fax: 514-872-2196
François Limoges, Conseiller de la ville, Saint-Édouard, Ward(s): Rosemont—La Petite-Patrie
514-872-8234, Fax: 514-868-3932
Pierre Mainville, Conseiller de la ville, Ste-Marie, Ward(s): Ville-Marie
514-868-5169, Fax: 514-868-5963
pierremainville@ville.montreal.qc.ca
Ginette Marotte, Conseillère de la ville, Champlain-L'île-des-Soeurs, Ward(s): Verdun
514-765-7010, Fax: 514-765-7013
ginette.marotte@verdun.ca
Peter McQueen, Conseiller de la ville, Notre-Dame-de-Grâce, Ward(s): Côte-des-Neiges-N.-D.-de-Grâce
514-868-4281, Fax: 514-868-3327
Francesco Miele, Conseiller de la ville, Côte-de-Liesse, Ward(s): Saint-Laurent
514-855-6000, Fax: 514-855-6049
Alex Norris, Conseiller de la ville, Mile End, Ward(s): Le Plateau-Mont-Royal
514-872-8023, Fax: 514-868-4077
Lionel Perez, Conseiller de la ville, Darlington, Ward(s): Côte-des-Neiges-N.-D.-de-Grâce
514-872-4863, Fax: 514-868-3327
Dominic Perri, Conseiller de la ville, St-Léonard-Ouest, Ward(s): Saint-Léonard
514-328-8410, Fax: 514-328-8419
dperri@ville.montreal.qc.ca
Gaëtan Primeau, Conseiller de la ville, Tétreaultville, Ward(s): Mercier—Hochelaga-Maisonneuve
514-872-8241, Fax: 514-872-7125
gaetanprimeau@ville.montreal.qc.ca
François Robillard, Conseiller de la ville, St-Jacques, Ward(s): Ville-Marie
514-868-5178, Fax: 514-872-8347
Marvin Rotrand, Conseiller de la ville, Snowdon, Ward(s): Côte-des-Neiges-N.-D.-de-Grâce
514-872-4863, Fax: 514-868-3327
mrotrand@ville.montreal.qc.ca
Aref Salem, Conseiller de la ville, Norman-McLaren, Ward(s): Saint-Laurent
514-855-6000, Fax: 514-855-6049
Alain Tassé, Conseiller de la ville, Desmarchais-Crawford, Ward(s): Verdun
514-765-7010, Fax: 514-765-7013
alain.tasse@verdun.ca
Clementina Teti-Tomassi, Conseillère de la ville, Marie-Clarac, Ward(s): Montréal-Nord
514-328-4000, Fax: 514-325-4025
clementinatetitomassi@ville.montreal.qc.ca
Émilie Thuillier, Conseillère de la ville, Ward(s): Ahuntsic-Cartierville
514-872-2246, Fax: 514-868-3324
Lyn Thériault, Conseillère de la Ville, Ward(s): Mercier-Hochelaga-Maisonneuve
514-872-7123, Fax: 514-872-7125
lyn.theriault@ville.montreal.qc.ca
Frank Venneri, Conseiller de la ville, François-Perrault, Ward(s): Villeray St-Michel-Parc-Extens
514-872-3103, Fax: 514-872-2196
mfvenneri@ville.montreal.qc.ca
Bertrand A. Ward, Conseiller de la ville, Cap-Saint-Jacques, Ward(s): Pierrefonds-Roxboro
514-624-1053, Fax: 514-624-1415
bward@ville.montreal.qc.ca
Robert L. Zambito, Conseiller de la ville, St-Léonard-Est, Ward(s): Saint-Léonard
514-328-8410, Fax: 514-328-8419
rzambito@ville.montreal.qc.ca
Michael Applebaum, Maire d'arrondissement/Conseiller de la ville, Ward(s): Côte-des-Neiges-N.-D.-de-Grâce
514-872-4863, Fax: 514-868-3327
mapplebaum@ville.montreal.qc.ca
Manon Barbe, Mairesse d'arrondissement/Conseillère de la ville, Ward(s): LaSalle
514-367-6206, Fax: 514-367-6600
mbarbe@ville.montreal.qc.ca
Michel Bissonnet, Maire d'arrondissement/Conseiller de la ville, Ward(s): Saint-Léonard
514-328-8410, Fax: 514-328-8419
Richard Bélanger, Maire d'arrondissement/Conseiller de la ville, Ward(s): L'île-Bizard—Ste-Geneviève
514-620-7592, Fax: 514-620-4543
richardbelanger@ville.montreal.qc.ca
Marie Cinq-Mars, Mairesse d'arrondissement/Conseillère de la ville, Ward(s): Outremont
514-495-6220, Fax: 514-495-6290
mariecinq-mars@ville.montreal.qc.ca
François W. Croteau, Maire d'arrondissement/Conseiller de la ville, Ward(s): Rosemont—La Petite-Patrie
514-868-3934, Fax: 514-868-3932
Claude Dauphin, Maire d'arrondissement/Conseiller de la ville, Ward(s): Lachine
514-634-3471, Fax: 514-634-8164
Alan DeSousa, Maire d'arrondissement/Conseiller de la ville, Ward(s): Saint-Laurent
514-855-6000, Fax: 514-855-6049
adesousa@ville.montreal.qc.ca
Gilles Deguire, Maire d'arrondissement/Conseiller de la ville, Ward(s): Montréal-Nord
514-328-4000, Fax: 514-328-5577
Benoit Dorais, Maire d'arrondissement/Conseiller de la ville, Ward(s): Le Sud-Ouest
514-872-6814, Fax: 514-872-3705
Luc Ferrandez, Maire d'arrondissement/Conseiller de la ville, Ward(s): Le Plateau-Mont-Royal
514-872-8023, Fax: 514-868-4118
Pierre Gagnier, Maire d'arrondissement/Conseiller de la ville, Ward(s): Ahuntsic-Cartierville
514-872-0430, Fax: 514-868-3324
Luis Miranda, Maire d'arrondissement/Conseiller de la ville, Ward(s): Anjou
514-493-8010, Fax: 514-493-8013
lmiranda@ville.montreal.qc.ca
Réal Ménard, Maire d'arrondissement/Conseiller de la ville, Ward(s): Mercier—Hochelaga-Maisonneuve
514-872-8759, Fax: 514-869-4451
Chantal Rouleau, Mairesse d'arrondissement/Conseillère de la ville, Ward(s): Riv.-des-Prairies-Pte-aux-Trem
514-868-4050, Fax: 514-868-4353
Anie Samson, Mairesse d'arrondissement/Conseillère de la ville, Ward(s): Villeray St-Michel-Parc-Extens
514-872-3103, Fax: 514-872-2196
asamson@ville.montreal.qc.ca
Claude Trudel, Maire d'arrondissement/Conseiller de la ville, Ward(s): Verdun
514-765-7010, Fax: 514-765-7013
claude.trudel@verdun.ca
Monique Worth, Mairesse d'arrondissement/Conseillère de la ville, Ward(s): Pierrefonds-Roxboro
514-624-1400, Fax: 514-624-1415
mworth@ville.montreal.qc.ca
Gilles Beaudry, Conseiller d'arrondissement, Ouest, Ward(s): Anjou
514-493-8019, Fax: 514-493-8013
gillesbeaudry@ville.montreal.qc.ca
Paul Beaupré, Conseiller d'arrondissement, Champlain-L'île-des-Soeurs, Ward(s): Verdun
514-765-7010, Fax: 514-765-7013
Dimitrios Jim Beis, Conseiller d'arrondissement, Bois-de-Liesse, Ward(s): Pierrefonds-Roxboro
514-624-1175, Fax: 514-624-1415
Michèle D. Biron, Conseillère d'arrondissement, Norman-McLaren, Ward(s): Saint-Laurent
514-855-6000, Fax: 514-855-6049
Ross Blackhurst, Conseiller d'arrondissement, Sault-St-Louis, Ward(s): LaSalle
514-794-7677, Fax: 514-367-6600
Bernard Blanchet, Conseiller d'arrondissement, J.-Émery-Provost, Ward(s): Lachine
514-634-3471, Fax: 514-634-8164
Mario Blanchet, Conseiller d'arrondissement, La Pointe-aux-Prairies, Ward(s): Riv.-des-Prairies-Pte-aux-Trem
514-868-4350, Fax: 514-868-4353
Carl Boileau, Conseillère d'arrondissement, De Lorimier, Ward(s): Le Plateau-Mont-Royal
514-872-8023, Fax: 514-868-4077
Vincenzo Cesari, Conseiller d'arrondissement, Cecil-P.-Newman, Ward(s): LaSalle
514-367-6216, Fax: 514-367-6600
Andrée Champoux, Conseillère d'arrondissement, Champlain-L'île-des-Soeurs, Ward(s): Verdun
514-765-7010, Fax: 514-765-7013
Jean-François Cloutier, Conseiller d'arrondissement, Fort-Rolland, Ward(s): Lachine
514-634-3471, Fax: 514-634-8164
Catherine Clément-Talbot, Conseillère d'arrondissement, Cap-St-Jacques, Ward(s): Pierrefonds-Roxboro
514-624-1174, Fax: 514-624-1415
catherineclementtalbot@ville.montreal.qc.ca
Maurice Cohen, Conseiller d'arrondissement, Côte-de-Liesse, Ward(s): Saint-Laurent
514-855-6000, Fax: 514-855-6049
mcohen@ville.montreal.qc.ca
Michèle Di Genova Zammit, Conseillère d'arrondissement, Centre, Ward(s): Anjou
514-493-8085, Fax: 514-493-8013
mzammit@ville.montreal.qc.ca
Éric Dugas, Conseiller d'arrondissement, Ste-Geneviève, Ward(s): L'île-Bizard—Ste-Geneviève
514-620-6896, Fax: 514-620-4543
Gilles Déziel, Conseiller d'arrondissement, Pointe-aux-Trembles, Ward(s): Riv.-des-Prairies-Pte-aux-Trem
514-868-4350, Fax: 514-868-4353
Céline Forget, Conseillère d'arrondissement, Joseph-Beaubien, Ward(s): Outremont
514-495-7430, Fax: 514-872-5655

Diane Gibb, Conseillère d'arrondissement, Pierre-Foretier, Ward(s): L'île-Bizard—Ste-Geneviève
514-620-6896, Fax: 514-620-4543
dianegibb@ville.montreal.qc.ca
Ann Guy, Conseillère d'arrondissement, Desmarchais-Crawford, Ward(s): Verdun
514-765-7010, Fax: 514-765-7013
Piper Huggins, Conseillère d'arrondissement, Jeanne-Mance, Ward(s): Le Plateau-Mont-Royal
514-872-8023, Fax: 514-868-4077
Christopher Little, Conseiller d'arrondissement, Denis-Benjamin-Viger, Ward(s): L'île-Bizard—Ste-Geneviève
514-620-6896, Fax: 514-620-4543
littlechristopher@ville.montreal.qc.ca
Louis Moffatt, Conseiller d'arrondissement, Claude-Ryan, Ward(s): Outremont
514-495-6230, Fax: 514-495-6290
louismoffatt@ville.montreal.qc.ca
Ana Nunes, Conseillère d'arrondissement, Jeanne-Sauvé, Ward(s): Outremont
514-495-6228, Fax: 514-495-6290
anunes@ville.montreal.qc.ca
Laura-Ann Palestini, Conseillère d'arrondissement, Sault-St-Louis, Ward(s): LaSalle
514-367-6216, Fax: 514-367-6600
Paul-Yvon Perron, Conseiller d'arrondissement, Est, Ward(s): Anjou
514-493-8017, Fax: 514-493-8013
Marie Potvin, Conseillère d'arrondissement, Robert-Bourassa, Ward(s): Outremont
514-495-6248, Fax: 514-495-6290
marie.potvin@ville.montreal.qc.ca
Lise Poulin, Conseillère d'arrondissement, Canal, Ward(s): Lachine
514-634-3471, Fax: 514-634-8164
Giovanni Rapanà, Conseiller d'arrondissement, Rivière-des-Prairies, Ward(s): Riv.-des-Prairies-Pte-aux-Trem
514-868-5558, Fax: 514-872-3709
Monica Ricourt, Conseiller d'arrondissement, Ovide-Clermont, Ward(s): Montréal-Nord
514-328-4000, Fax: 514-325-4025
François Robert, Conseiller d'arrondissement, Jacques-Bizard, Ward(s): L'île-Bizard—Ste-Geneviève
514-620-6896, Fax: 514-620-4543
francoisrobert@ville.montreal.qc.ca
Chantal Rossi, Conseillère d'arrondissement, Marie-Clarac, Ward(s): Montréal-Nord
514-328-4000, Fax: 514-325-4025
Huguette Roy, Conseil. d'arrondissmnt., St-Henri-Pte-Bourgogne-Pte-St-Charles, Ward(s): Le Sud-Ouest
514-872-6814, Fax: 514-872-3705
Richard Ryan, Conseiller d'arrondissement, Mile End, Ward(s): Le Plateau-Mont-Royal
514-872-8023, Fax: 514-868-4077
André Savard, Conseiller d'arrondissement, Desmarchais-Crawford, Ward(s): Verdun
514-765-7010, Fax: 514-765-7013
Sophie Thiébaut, Conseil. d'arrondissmnt., St-Henri-Pte-Bourgogne-Pte-St-Charles, Ward(s): Le Sud-Ouest
514-872-6814, Fax: 514-872-3705
Lili-Anne Tremblay, Conseillère d'arrondissement, Saint-Léonard-Est, Ward(s): Saint-Léonard
514-328-8410, Fax: 514-328-8419
Josée Troilo, Conseillère d'arrondissement, Cecil-P.-Newman, Ward(s): LaSalle
514-367-6216, Fax: 514-367-6600

Pincourt

919, ch Duhamel
Pincourt, QC J7V 4G8
Tél: 514-453-8981; *Téléc:* 514-453-8401
pincourtinfo@videotron.ca
www.villepincourt.qc.ca
Entité municipal: City
Incorporation: 1er janvier 1950 *Area:* 8,36 km2
Comté ou district: Vaudreuil-Soulanges; *Population au 2011:* 14,305
Circonscription(s) électorale(s) provinciale(s): Vaudreuil
Circonscription(s) électorale(s) fédérale(s): Vaudreuil-Soulanges
Prochaines élections: 3e novembre 2013
Yvan Cardinal, Maire
Stéphane Boyer, Conseiller, Ward(s): 1
Marie-Andrée G. Laliberté, Conseillère, Ward(s): 2
John Kinnear, Conseiller, Ward(s): 3
Michel Pratte, Conseiller, Ward(s): 4
Jim Miron, Conseiller, Ward(s): 5
André D'Aragon, Conseiller, Ward(s): 6
Nicole Drouin, Greffière
514-453-8981
Michel Perrier, Directeur général
514-453-8981, Fax: 514-453-0934
Nathalie Boisvert, Trésorière
514-453-8981

Prévost

2870, boul du Curé-Labelle
Prévost, QC J0R 1T0
Tél: 450-224-8888; *Téléc:* 450-224-8323
info@ville.prevost.qc.ca
www.ville.prevost.qc.ca
Entité municipal: City
Incorporation: 20 janvier 1973 *Area:* 34,32 km2
Comté ou district: La Rivière-du-Nord; *Population au 2011:* 12,171
Circonscription(s) électorale(s) provinciale(s): Prévost
Circonscription(s) électorale(s) fédérale(s): Rivière-du-Nord
Prochaines élections: 3e novembre 2013
Germain Richer, Maire
450-224-8888
maire@ville.prevost.qc.ca
Gaétan Bordeleau, Conseiller, Ward(s): 1
450-224-8888
gbordeleau@ville.prevost.qc.ca
Jean-Pierre Joubert, Conseiller, Ward(s): 2
450-224-8888
jpjoubert@ville.prevost.qc.ca
Diane Berthiaume, Conseillère, Ward(s): 3
450-224-8888
diane.berthiaume@ville.prevost.qc.ca
Claude Leroux, Conseiller, Ward(s): 4
450-224-8888
claude.leroux@ville.prevost.qc.ca
Brigitte Paquette, Conseillère, Ward(s): 5
450-224-8888
brigitte.paquette@ville.prevost.qc.ca
Stéphane Parent, Conseiller, Ward(s): 6
450-224-8888
sparent@ville.prevost.qc.ca
Laurent Laberge, Greffier
450-224-8888
greffe@ville.prevost.qc.ca
Réal Martin, Directeur général
450-224-8888
dg@ville.prevost.qc.ca
Jean-Yves Crispin, Trésorier
450-224-8888
tresor@ville.prevost.qc.ca

Québec

Hôtel de Ville
CP 700 Haute-Ville
2, rue des Jardins
Québec, QC G1R 4S9
Tél: 418-641-6000; *Téléc:* 418-641-6463
renseignements@ville.quebec.qc.ca
www.ville.quebec.qc.ca
Entité municipal: City
Incorporation: 1er janvier 2002 *Area:* 451,79 km2
Population au 2011: 516,622
Circonscription(s) électorale(s) provinciale(s): Charlesbourg-Haute-Saint-Charles; Chauveau; Jean-Lesage; Jean-Talon; La Peltrie; Louis-Hébert; Montmorency; Taschereau; Vanier
Circonscription(s) électorale(s) fédérale(s): Québec; Louis-St-Laurent
Prochaines élections: 3e novembre 2013
Régis Labeaume, Maire
418-641-6434
Sylvain Ouellet, Greffier
418-641-6212
greffearchives@ville.quebec.qc.ca
Alain Marcoux, Directeur général
418-641-6373
directiongenerale@ville.quebec.qc.ca
Jacques Grantham, Directeur, Environnement
418-641-6189
environnement@ville.quebec.qc.ca
Chantale Giguère, Directrice, Rssources humaines
418-641-6234
ressourceshumaines@ville.quebec.qc.ca
Denis Deslauriers, Directeur, Technologies de l'information/télécomm.
418-641-6239
technologies@ville.quebec.qc.ca
Rhonda Rioux, Directrice, Culture
418-641-6181
culture@ville.quebec.qc.ca
Fernand Martin, Directeur, Aménagement du territoire
418-641-6160
amenageterrit@ville.quebec.qc.ca
Marcel Roy, Directeur, Travaux publics
418-641-6240
travauxpublics@ville.quebec.qc.ca
Pierre Huot, Directeur, Évaluation
418-641-6193
evaluation@ville.quebec.qc.ca
Guy Bélanger, Directeur, Loisirs, sports & vie communautaire
418-641-6224
loisirs@ville.quebec.qc.ca
Jean-Yves Tellier, Directeur, Développement économique
418-641-6183
deveconomique@ville.quebec.qc.ca
Daniel Lessard, Directeur, Ingénierie
418-641-6217
ingenierie@ville.quebec.qc.ca
Richard Poitras, Directeur, Protection contre l'incendie
418-641-6231
protectionincendie@ville.quebec.qc.ca
Serge Bélisle, Directeur, Police
418-641-6292
police@ville.quebec.qc.ca
Vacant, Directeur, Communications
418-641-6651
communications@ville.quebec.qc.ca
Daniel Maranda, Directeur, Service des approvisionnements
418-641-6164
approvisionnements@ville.quebec.qc.ca
Gabriel Savard, Directeur, Office du tourisme de Québec
418-522-3511
François Gagnon, Vérificateur général
Serge Giasson, Directeur, Affaires juridiques
418-641-6156
Gilles Noël, Directeur général adjoint, Services de soutien
Suzanne Canac Marquis, Directrice générale adjointe, Développement culturel, touristique, sportif & social
Alain Thériault, Directeur général adjoint (par intérim), Développement durable
Chantale Giguère, Directrice générale adjointe, Sécurité publique
Alain Thériault, Directeur général adjoint, Coordination des arrondissements
Yves Courchesne, Directeur, Services des finances
418-641-6203
finances@ville.quebec.qc.ca
Michel Beauchemin, Directeur
Lisette Lepage, Conseillère, Ward(s): Seigneurial
418-641-6501
Jean-Marie Laliberté, Conseiller, Ward(s): Monts
418-641-6401
Yvon Bussières, Conseiller, Ward(s): Saint-Sacrement-Belvédère
418-641-6101
Simon Brouard, Conseiller, Ward(s): Châtels
418-641-6701
Christiane Bois, Conseillère, Ward(s): Cité-Universitaire
418-641-6301
Richard Côté, Conseiller, Ward(s): Vanier
418-641-6411
Julie Lemieux, Conseillère, Ward(s): Chute-Montmorency
418-641-6501
Michelle Morin-Doyle, Conseillère, Ward(s): Trait-Carré
418-641-6401
Chantal Gilbert, Conseillère, Ward(s): Faubourgs
418-641-6411
Raymond Dion, Conseiller, Ward(s): Loretteville
418-641-6701
Jean Guilbault, Conseiller, Ward(s): Laurentien
418-641-6301
Patrick Pauqet, Conseiller, Ward(s): Neufchâtel
418-641-6201
Marc Simoneau, Conseiller, Ward(s): Robert-Giffard
418-641-6501
Odette Simoneau, Conseillère, Ward(s): Sentiers
418-641-6401
Anne Guérette, Conseillère, Ward(s): Vieux-Québec-Montcalm
418-641-6411
Sylvain Légaré, Conseiller, Ward(s): Val-Bélair
418-641-6411
Francine Lortie, Conseillère, Ward(s): Saint-Louis-Sillery
418-641-6301
François Picard, Conseiller, Ward(s): Lebourgneuf
418-641-6411
Marie France Trudel, Conseillère, Ward(s): Sainte-Thérèse-de-Lisieux
418-641-6501
Denise Trudel, Conseillère, Ward(s): Saint-Rodrigue
418-641-6401
Geneviève Hamelin, Conseillère, Ward(s): Saint-Sauveur
418-641-6411

Steeve Verret, Conseiller, Ward(s): Lac-Saint-Charles—Saint-Émile
418-641-6701
Marie-Josée Savard, Conseillère, Ward(s): Plateau
418-641-6411
Gérald Poirier, Conseiller, Ward(s): Duberger—Les Saules
418-641-6201
Ginette Picard-Lavoie, Conseillère, Ward(s): Maizerets-Lairet
418-641-6411
Denise Tremblay Blanchette, Conseillère, Ward(s): Cap-Rouge
418-641-6301
Suzanne Verrault, Conseillère, Ward(s): Sylvain-Lelièvre
418-641-6411

Repentigny

435, boul Iberville
Repentigny, QC J6A 2B6
Tél: 450-470-3000; *Téléc:* 450-470-3082
communication@ville.repentigny.qc.ca
www.ville.repentigny.qc.ca
Entité municipal: City
Incorporation: 1er juin 2002 *Area:* 68,42 km2
Comté ou district: L'Assomption; *Population au 2011:* 82,000
Circonscription(s) électorale(s) provinciale(s): L'Assomption; Masson
Circonscription(s) électorale(s) fédérale(s): Repentigny
Prochaines élections: 3e novembre 2013
Chantal Deschamps, Mairesse
450-470-3103
deschampsc@ville.repentigny.qc.ca
André Cyr, Conseiller, Ward(s): 1
450-585-3410
cyra@ville.repentigny.qc.ca
Georges Robinson, Conseiller, Ward(s): 2
450-654-9746
robinsong@ville.repentigny.qc.ca
Denyse Peltier, Conseillère, Ward(s): 3
450-581-5733
peltierd@ville.repentigny.qc.ca
Cécile Hénault, Conseillère, Ward(s): 4
450-654-3046
henaultc@ville.repentigny.qc.ca
Éric Laporte, Conseiller, Ward(s): 5
450-581-5026
laportee@ville.repentigny.qc.ca
Sylvain Benoit, Conseiller, Ward(s): 6
514-602-4793
benoits@ville.repentigny.qc.ca
Raymond Hénault, Conseiller, Ward(s): 7
450-581-0319
henaultr@ville.repentigny.qc.ca
Mario Morais, Conseiller, Ward(s): 8
450-654-4018
moraism@ville.repentigny.qc.ca
Serge Gauthier, Conseiller, Ward(s): 9
450-585-6616
gauthiers@ville.repentigny.qc.ca
Luc Gauthier, Conseiller, Ward(s): 10
514-713-8337
gauthierl@ville.repentigny.qc.ca
Francine Payer, Conseillère, Ward(s): 11
450-582-7711
payerf@ville.repentigny.qc.ca
Sylvie Langlois-Brouillette, Conseillère, Ward(s): 12
514-295-8376
langlois-brouillettes@ville.repentigny.qc.ca
Louis-André Garceau, Greffier
450-470-3130
greffe@ville.repentigny.qc.ca
Daniel L'Écuyer, Directeur général
450-470-3110
direction-generale@ville.repentigny.qc.ca
Diane Pelchat, Trésorière
450-470-3200
finance@ville.repentigny.qc.ca
Michel Mailhot, Directeur, Ressources humaines
450-470-3700
ressources-humaines@ville.repentigny.qc.ca
Helen Dion, Directrice, Police (Quartier général)
450-470-3600
securite-publique@ville.repentigny.qc.ca
David Legault, Directeur, Permis, inspections et urbanisme
450-470-3840
permis@ville.repentigny.qc.ca
Denis Larose, Directeur, Incendie
450-470-3620
incendie@ville.repentigny.qc.ca
Sylvie Bouchard, Directrice, Travaux publics
450-470-3800
travaux-publics@ville.repentigny.qc.ca
Vacant, Directeur, Communications
450-470-3140
communication@ville.repentigny.qc.ca
Sylviane DiFolco, Directrice, Loisirs, culture et vie communautaire
450-470-3400
loisirs@ville.repentigny.qc.ca
Ghislain Bélanger, Directeur, Développement économique et services techniques
450-470-3150
belangerg@ville.repentigny.qc.ca

Rimouski

CP 710
205, av de la Cathédrale
Rimouski, QC G5L 7C7
Tél: 418-724-3126; *Téléc:* 418-724-3183
communications@ville.rimouski.qc.ca
www.ville.rimouski.qc.ca
Entité municipal: City
Incorporation: 1er janvier 2002 *Area:* 254,16 km2
Comté ou district: Rimouski-Neigette; *Population au 2011:* 46,860
Circonscription(s) électorale(s) provinciale(s): Rimouski
Circonscription(s) électorale(s) fédérale(s): Rimouski-Neigette-Témiscouata-Les Basques
Prochaines élections: 3e novembre 2013
Éric Forest, Maire
418-724-3126
mairie@ville.rimouski.qc.ca
Marc St-Laurent, Conseiller, Ward(s): 1. Sacré-Coeur
418-722-0326
marc.st-laurent@ville.rimouski.qc.ca
Rodrigue Joncas, Conseiller, Ward(s): 2. Nazareth
418-725-4991
rodrigue.joncas@ville.rimouski.qc.ca
Jennifer Murray, Conseillère, Ward(s): 3. Saint-Germain
418-721-7752
jennifer.murray@ville.rimouski.qc.ca
Denise Banville, Conseillère, Ward(s): 4. Rimouski-Est
418-723-6477
denise.banville@ville.rimouski.qc.ca
Raymond-Marie Murray, Conseiller, Ward(s): 5. Pointe-au-Père
418-724-7250
raymond-marie.murray@ville.rimouski.qc.ca
Donald Bélanger, Conseiller, Ward(s): 6. Sainte-Odile
418-723-3467
donald.belanger@ville.rimouski.qc.ca
Christian Tremblay, Conseiller, Ward(s): 7. Saint-Robert
418-723-8299
christian.tremblay@ville.rimouski.qc.ca
Jean Yves Beaulieu, Conseiller, Ward(s): 8. Terrasse Arthur-Buies
418-722-9372
jeanyves.beaulieu@ville.rimouski.qc.ca
Karol Francis, Conseiller, Ward(s): 9. Saint-Pie-X
418-721-4262
karol.francis@ville.rimouski.qc.ca
Bernard Lepage, Conseiller, Ward(s): 10. Sainte-Blanche/Mont-Lebel
418-735-5611
bernard.lepage@ville.rimouski.qc.ca
Marc Doucet, Greffier
418-724-3125, Fax: 418-724-9795
greffe@ville.rimouski.qc.ca
Jean Matte, Directeur général
418-724-3171, Fax: 418-724-3183
direction.generale@ville.rimouski.qc.ca
Jean-Charles Fournier, Directeur, Service des finances
418-724-3111, Fax: 418-724-3180
finances@ville.rimouski.qc.ca

Rivière-du-Loup

CP 37
65, rue de l'Hôtel-de-Ville
Rivière-du-Loup, QC G5R 3Y7
Tél: 418-867-6700; *Téléc:* 418-862-2817
www.ville.riviere-du-loup.qc.ca
Entité municipal: City
Incorporation: 30 décembre 1998 *Area:* 83,39 km2
Comté ou district: Rivière-du-Loup; *Population au 2011:* 19,447
Circonscription(s) électorale(s) provinciale(s): Rivière-du-Loup
Circonscription(s) électorale(s) fédérale(s): Montmagny-L'Islet-Kamouraska-Rivière-du-Loup
Prochaines élections: 3e novembre 2013
Michel Morin, Maire
418-867-6625
maire@ville.riviere-du-loup.qc.ca
Amélie Dionne, Conseillère, Ward(s): Rivière
Jacques Minville, Conseiller, Ward(s): Fraserville
Sylvie Vignet, Conseillère, Ward(s): Plaine
Gaétan St-Pierre, Conseiller, Ward(s): Estuaire
Denis Tardif, Conseiller, Ward(s): Saint-Patrice
Georges Deschênes, Greffier
418-867-6715
georges.deschenes@ville.riviere-du-loup.qc.ca
Jacques Poulin, Directeur général
418-867-6707
jacques.poulin@ville.riviere-du-loup.qc.ca
Marie Lapointe, Directrice, Finances et Trésorerie
418-867-6711
marie.lapointe@ville.riviere-du-loup.qc.ca
Gérald Tremblay, Directeur, Travaux publics
418-862-2121, Fax: 418-867-6096
gerald.tremblay@ville.riviere-du-loup.qc.ca
Éric Côté, Directeur, Environnement et développement durable
418-867-6663
eric.cote@ville-riviere-du-loup.qc.ca
Benoît Ouellet, Directeur, Loisirs, culture et vie communautaire
418-862-0906
benoit.ouellet@ville.riviere-du-loup.qc.ca

Roberval

851, boul St-Joseph
Roberval, QC G8H 2L6
Tél: 418-275-0202; *Téléc:* 418-275-5031
vroberval@ville.roberval.qc.ca
www.ville.roberval.qc.ca
Entité municipal: City
Incorporation: 23 décembre 1976 *Area:* 168,27 km2
Comté ou district: Le Domaine-du-Roy; *Population au 2011:* 10,227
Circonscription(s) électorale(s) provinciale(s): Roberval
Circonscription(s) électorale(s) fédérale(s): Roberval-Lac-St-Jean
Prochaines élections: 3e novembre 2013
Michel Larouche, Maire
Jocelyn Bouchard, Conseiller, Ward(s): 1
Nancy Guillemette, Conseillère, Ward(s): 2
Gilles Otis, Conseiller, Ward(s): 3
Michèle Claveau, Conseillère, Ward(s): 4
Rémy Leclerc, Conseiller, Ward(s): 5
Jacques Dion, Conseiller, Ward(s): 6
Jean-Guy Tardif, Greffier
jgtardif@ville.roberval.qc.ca
Jeannot Gagnon, Directeur général
jeannotgagnon@ville.roberval.qc.ca
Nancy Boutin, Trésorière
nboutin@ville.roberval.qc.ca

Rosemère

100, rue Charbonneau
Rosemère, QC J7A 3W1
Tél: 450-621-3500; *Téléc:* 450-621-7601
info@ville.rosemere.qc.ca
ville.rosemere.qc.ca
Entité municipal: City
Incorporation: 1er janvier 1947 *Area:* 10,35 km2
Comté ou district: Thérèse-De Blainville; *Population au 2011:* 14,294
Circonscription(s) électorale(s) provinciale(s): Groulx
Circonscription(s) électorale(s) fédérale(s): Marc-Aurèle-Fortin
Prochaines élections: 3e novembre 2013
Hélène Daneault, Mairesse
Normand Bleau, Conseiller, Ward(s): 1
Pierre Roussel, Conseiller, Ward(s): 2
Madeleine Leduc, Conseillère, Ward(s): 3
Normand Corriveau, Conseiller, Ward(s): 4
Eric Westram, Conseiller, Ward(s): 5
Claude Roy, Conseiller, Ward(s): 6
Patrick St-Amour, Greffier
450-621-3500
pstamour@ville.rosemere.qc.ca
Michel Gagné, Directeur général
450-621-3500
mgagne@ville.rosemere.qc.ca
Luce Jacques, Trésorière
450-621-3500
ljacques@ville.rosemere.qc.ca

Rouyn-Noranda

CP 220
100, rue Taschereau est
Rouyn-Noranda, QC J9X 5C3
Tél: 819-797-7110; *Téléc:* 819-797-7108
www.ville.rouyn-noranda.qc.ca
Entité municipal: City
Incorporation: 1er janvier 2002 *Area:* 6435,64 km2
Population au 2011: 41,012
Circonscription(s) électorale(s) provinciale(s): Rouyn-Noranda—Témiscamingue
Circonscription(s) électorale(s) fédérale(s):

Abitibi-Témiscamingue
Prochaines élections: 3e novembre 2013
Mario Provencher, Maire
info@rouyn-noranda.ca
Marc Bibeau, Conseiller, Ward(s): Noranda-Nord/Lac-Dufault
Sylvie Turgeon, Conseillère, Ward(s): Noranda-Ouest
André Philippon, Conseiller, Ward(s): Rouyn-Sud
Yves Gauthier, Conseiller, Ward(s): Centre-Ville
Robert B. Brière, Conseiller, Ward(s): Vieux-Noranda
robertbbriere@royallepage.ca
Bernard Duchesneau, Conseiller, Ward(s): Université
Luc Lacroix, Conseiller, Ward(s): Granada
Philippe Marquis, Conseiller, Ward(s): Marie-Victorin/Du Sourire
André Tessier, Conseiller, Ward(s): Évain
Marcel Maheux, Conseiller, Ward(s): Sud-Ouest
François Cotnoir, Conseiller, Ward(s): Dallaire
Marc Paquin, Conseiller, Ward(s): Nord
paquin2009@gmail.com
Jean Olivier, Conseiller, Ward(s): Bellecombe/McWatters
Yvon Hurtubise, Conseiller, Ward(s): Cadillac
yvon.hurtubise@cablevision.qc.ca
Daniel Samson, Greffier
819-797-7110, Fax: 819-797-7108
Denis Charron, Directeur général
819-797-7110, Fax: 819-797-7108
Hélène Piuze, Directrice, Finances
819-797-7110, Fax: 819-797-7120
Noël Lanouette, Directeur, Travaux publics et services techniques
819-797-7110, Fax: 819-797-7153

Saguenay

CP 129
201, rue Racine est
Chicoutimi, QC G7H 5B8
Tél: 418-698-3000; *Téléc:* 418-541-4524
info@ville.saguenay.qc.ca
www.ville.saguenay.qc.ca
Entité municipal: City
Incorporation: 18 février 2002 *Area:* 1,166 km2
Population au 2011: 144,746
Circonscription(s) électorale(s) provinciale(s): Dubuc; Chicoutimi; Jonquière
Circonscription(s) électorale(s) fédérale(s): Chicoutimi-Le Fjord
Prochaines élections: 3e novembre 2013
Jean Tremblay, Maire
418-698-3330, Fax: 418-541-4510
maire@ville.saguenay.qc.ca
Paul-Roger Cantin, Conseiller, Ward(s): 1
paul-roger.cantin@ville.saguenay.qc.ca
Réjean Laforest, Conseiller, Ward(s): 2
rejean.laforest@ville.saguenay.qc.ca
Sylvie Gaudreault, Conseillère, Ward(s): 3
sylvie.gaudreault@ville.saguenay.qc.ca
Georges Bouchard, Conseiller, Ward(s): 4
georges.bouchard@ville.saguenay.qc.ca
Bernard Noël, Conseiller, Ward(s): 5
bernard.noel@ville.saguenay.qc.ca
Carl Dufour, Conseiller, Ward(s): 6
carl.dufour@ville.saguenay.qc.ca
Claude Tremblay, Conseiller, Ward(s): 7
claude.tremblay@ville.saguenay.qc.ca
Fabien Hovington, Conseiller, Ward(s): 8
fabien.hovington@ville.saguenay.qc.ca
Jean-Yves Provencher, Conseiller, Ward(s): 9
jean-yves.provencher@ville.saguenay.qc.ca
Marc Pettersen, Conseiller, Ward(s): 10
marc.pettersen@ville.saguenay.qc.ca
Marina Larouche, Conseillère, Ward(s): 11
marina.larouche@ville.saguenay.qc.ca
Marcel Jean, Conseiller, Ward(s): 12
marcel.jean@ville.saguenay.qc.ca
Jacques Cleary, Conseiller, Ward(s): 13
jacques.cleary@ville.saguenay.qc.ca
Denis Dahl, Conseiller, Ward(s): 14
denis.dahl@ville.saguenay.qc.ca
Jacques Fortin, Conseiller, Ward(s): 15
jacques.fortin@ville.saguenay.qc.ca
Luc Blackburn, Conseiller, Ward(s): 16
luc.blackburn@ville.saguenay.qc.ca
Martine Gauthier, Conseillère, Ward(s): 17
martine.gauthier@ville.saguenay.qc.ca
Luc Boivin, Conseiller, Ward(s): 18
luc.boivin@ville.saguenay.qc.ca
Jean-Eudes Simard, Conseiller, Ward(s): 19
jean-eudes.simard@ville.saguenay.qc.ca
Caroline Dion, Greffière
418-698-3260, Fax: 418-541-5961
Jean-François Boivin, Directeur général
418-698-3320, Fax: 418-541-4524
Christine Tremblay, Trésorière
418-698-3030, Fax: 418-698-3049
Serges Chamberland, Directeur général adjoint, Opérations
Francine Maltais, Directrice, Arts, culture, communautaire et bibliothèque
418-698-3000, Fax: 418-698-3129
Daniel Larouche, Directeur, Arrondissement de Jonquière
418-698-3356, Fax: 418-546-2058
André Martin, Directeur, Arrondissement de Chicoutimi
418-698-3355, Fax: 418-698-3129
Gaétan Bergeron, Directeur, Arrondissement de La Baie
418-698-3357, Fax: 418-697-5059
Jeannot Allard, Directeur, Communications
418-698-3350, Fax: 418-541-4545
Sylvie Jean, Directrice, Approvisionnements
418-698-3055, Fax: 418-546-2114
Pierre A. Tremblay, Directeur, Ressources informationnelles
418-698-3335, Fax: 418-697-5187
Robert Pépin, Directeur, Affaires juridiques et du greffe
418-698-3260, Fax: 418-541-5961
Denis Coulombe, Directeur, Aménagement du territoire et urbanisme
418-698-3130, Fax: 418-698-1158
Claude Bouchard, Directeur, Hydro-Jonquière
418-698-3370, Fax: 418-546-2068
Jean Morneau, Directeur, Immeubles et équipements motorisés
418-698-3060, Fax: 418-698-3069
Pierre Racine, Directeur, Sports et du plein air
418-698-3000, Fax: 418-699-6095
Carol Girard, Directeur, Sécurité incendie
418-698-3380, Fax: 418-698-3389
Mario Giroux, Directeur, Sécurité publique
418-699-6000, Fax: 418-699-8206
Denis Simard, Directeur, Travaux publics
418-698-3180, Fax: 418-698-3189

Saint-Basile-le-Grand

204, rue Principale
Saint-Basile-le-Grand, QC J3N 1M1
Tél: 450-461-8000; *Téléc:* 450-461-8029
communciations@ville.saint-basile-le-grand.qc.ca
www.ville.saint-basile-le-grand.qc.ca
Entité municipal: City
Incorporation: 15 juin 1871 *Area:* 34,82 km2
Comté ou district: La Vallée-du-Richelieu; *Population au 2011:* 16,736
Circonscription(s) électorale(s) provinciale(s): Chambly
Circonscription(s) électorale(s) fédérale(s): Chambly-Borduas
Prochaines élections: 3e novembre 2013
Bernard Gagnon, Maire
450-461-8000
bernardgagnon@villesblg.ca
Marie Ginette Lafrance, Conseillère
marieginette.lafrance@villesblg.ca
Jacques Fafard, Conseiller
jacques.fafard@villesblg.ca
Norman Perreault, Conseiller
normanperreault@videotron.ca
Maurice Cantin, Conseiller
maurice.cantin@villesblg.ca
Guylaine Yelle, Conseillère
guylaine.yelle@villesblg.ca
Geneviève Desrosiers, Conseillère
genevieve.desrosiers@villesblg.ca
Sophie Deslauriers, Greffière
450-461-8000, Fax: 450-461-8029
greffe@ville.saint-basile-le-grand.qc.ca
Jean-Marie Beaupré, Directeur général
450-461-8000, Fax: 450-461-8039
direction.generale@ville.saint-basile-le-grand.qc.
Normand Lalande, Trésorier
450-461-8000, Fax: 450-653-4394
finances@ville.saint-basile-le-grand.qc.ca
Marc-André Lehoux, Directeur, Loisirs, culture et vie communautaire

Saint-Constant

147, rue St-Pierre
Saint-Constant, QC J5A 2G2
Tél: 450-638-2010; *Téléc:* 450-638-5919
communications@ville.saint-constant.qc.ca
www.ville.saint-constant.qc.ca
Entité municipal: City
Incorporation: 1er juillet 1855 *Area:* 57,04 km2
Comté ou district: Roussillon; *Population au 2011:* 24,980
Circonscription(s) électorale(s) provinciale(s): La Prairie
Circonscription(s) électorale(s) fédérale(s): Châteauguay—St-Constant
Prochaines élections: 3e novembre 2013
Gilles Pepin, Maire
Jonathan Bédard, Conseiller, Ward(s): 1
Pierre Lalonde, Conseiller, Ward(s): 2
Gilles Lapierre, Conseiller, Ward(s): 3
France Hébert, Conseillère, Ward(s): 4
André Sauvé, Conseiller, Ward(s): 5
Ginette Bourget, Conseillère, Ward(s): 6
Pascal Bédard, Conseiller, Ward(s): 7
Mario Arsenault, Conseiller, Ward(s): 8
Sophie Laflammme, Greffière
450-638-2010, Fax: 450-638-5919
greffe@ville.saint-constant.qc.ca
Sylvain Boulianne, Directeur général
450-638-2010, Fax: 450-638-5919
direction_generale@ville.saint-constant.qc.ca
Frédéric Thifault, Trésorier
450-638-2010, Fax: 450-638-4764
finances@ville.saint-constant.qc.ca
Vacant, Responsable, Travaux publics
450-638-2010, Fax: 450-632-0072
travaux_publics@ville.saint-constant.qc.ca
Jean Gariépy, Directeur et chef, Brigade des pompiers
Sylvain Boulianne, Coordonnateur, Mesures d'urgence

Saint-Eustache

145, rue St-Louis
Saint-Eustache, QC J7R 1X9
Tél: 450-974-5000; *Téléc:* 450-974-5229
communications@ville.saint-eustache.qc.ca
www.ville.saint-eustache.qc.ca
Entité municipal: City
Incorporation: 15 janvier 1972 *Area:* 70,61 km2
Comté ou district: Deux-Montagnes; Communauté métropolitaine de Montréal; *Population au 2011:* 44,154
Circonscription(s) électorale(s) provinciale(s): Deux-Montagnes
Circonscription(s) électorale(s) fédérale(s): Rivière-des-Mille-Îles
Prochaines élections: 3e novembre 2013
Pierre Charron, Maire
450-974-5014, Fax: 450-974-5203
maire@ville.saint-eustache.qc.ca
Denis Paré, Conseiller, Ward(s): 1. Vieux-Saint-Eustache
450-472-2533
dpare@ville.saint-eustache.qc.ca
André Biard, Conseiller, Ward(s): 2. Carrefour
450-473-2214
abiard@ville.saint-eustache.qc.ca
Patrice Paquette, Conseiller, Ward(s): 3. Rivière-Nord
450-974-1120
ppaquette@ville.saint-eustache.qc.ca
Daniel Goyer, Conseiller, Ward(s): 4. Des Érables
450-974-9104
dgoyer@ville.saint-eustache.qc.ca
Marc Lamarre, Conseiller, Ward(s): 5. Clair Matin
450-473-4792
mlamarre@ville.saint-eustache.qc.ca
Germain Lalonde, Conseiller, Ward(s): 6. Seigneurie
450-472-5890
glalonde@ville.saint-eustache.qc.ca
Pauline Harrison, Conseillère, Ward(s): 7. Moissons
450-473-8141
pharrison@ville.saint-eustache.qc.ca
Raymond Tessier, Conseiller, Ward(s): 8. Îles
450-472-3951
rtessier@ville.saint-eustache.qc.ca
Nicole Carignan Lefebvre, Conseillère, Ward(s): 9. Plateau-des-Chênes
450-623-5730
ncarignan-lefebvre@ville.saint-eustache.qc.ca
Sylvie Cloutier, Conseillère, Ward(s): 10. Jardins
450-974-9379
scloutier@ville.saint-eustache.qc.ca
Marc Tourangeau, Greffier
Christian Bellemare, Directeur général
450-974-5280, Fax: 450-974-5229
Ginette Lacoix, Trésorière
450-974-5070, Fax: 450-974-5077
Yves Guillemette, Directeur général adjoint
Bastien Morin, Directeur, Services municipaux
450-974-5284, Fax: 450-974-5229
Stéphanie Bouchard, Directrice, Communications
450-974-5220, Fax: 450-974-5223
communications@ville.saint-eustache.qc.ca

Saint-Félicien

CP 7000
1209, boul Sacré-Coeur
Saint-Félicien, QC G8K 2R5
Tél: 418-679-0251; *Téléc:* 418-679-1449
dir.general@ville.stfelicien.qc.ca
www.ville.stfelicien.qc.ca
Entité municipal: City
Incorporation: 12 juin 1996 *Area:* 359,69 km2
Comté ou district: Le Domaine-du-Roy; *Population au 2011:*

10,278
Circonscription(s) électorale(s) provinciale(s): Roberval
Circonscription(s) électorale(s) fédérale(s): Roberval—Lac-St-Jean
Prochaines élections: 3e novembre 2013
Gilles Potvin, Maire
maire@ville.stfelicien.qc.ca
Luc Imbeault, Conseiller, Ward(s): 1
Bernard Boivin, Conseiller, Ward(s): 2
Camil Guy, Conseiller, Ward(s): 3
Luc Gibbons, Conseiller, Ward(s): 4
Sonia Boudreault, Conseiller, Ward(s): 5
Michel Gagnon, Conseiller, Ward(s): 6
Louise Ménard, Greffière
418-679-2100, Fax: 418-679-1449
louise.menard@ville.stfelicien.qc.ca
Mario Ménard, Directeur général (par intérim)
418-679-2100, Fax: 418-679-1449
mmenard@ville.stfelicien.qc.ca
Dany Coudé, Trésorier
418-679-2100, Fax: 418-679-2178
tresorerie@ville.stfelicien.qc.ca
Olivier de Launière, Directeur, Protection contre les incendies
418-679-0313, Fax: 418-679-8217
sincendie@ville.st-felicien.qc.ca
Jacynthe Duplain, Secrétaire administrative, Aménagement et entretien du territoire
418-679-2100, Fax: 418-679-4083
urbanisme@ville.stfelicien.qc.ca

Saint-Georges

11700, boul Lacroix
Saint-Georges, QC G5Y 1L3
Tél: 418-228-5555; *Téléc:* 418-228-3855
www.ville.saint-georges.qc.ca
Entité municipal: City
Incorporation: 26 septembre 2001 *Area:* 199,51 km2
Comté ou district: Beauce-Sartigan; *Population au 2011:* 31,173
Circonscription(s) électorale(s) provinciale(s): Beauce-Sud
Circonscription(s) électorale(s) fédérale(s): Beauce
Prochaines élections: 3e novembre 2013
François Fecteau, Maire
maire@ville.saint-georges.qc.ca
Serge Thomassin, Conseiller, Ward(s): 1
Manon Tousignant, Conseillère, Ward(s): 2
Jean Perron, Conseiller, Ward(s): 3
Irma Quirion, Conseillère, Ward(s): 4
Manon Bougie, Conseillère, Ward(s): 5
Marie-Ève Dutil, Conseillère, Ward(s): 6
Marcel Drouin, Conseiller, Ward(s): 7
Lionel Bisson, Conseiller, Ward(s): 8
Jean McCollough, Greffier
jean.mccollough@ville.saint-georges.qc.ca
Marcel Grondin, Directeur général
marcel.grondin@ville.saint-georges.qc.ca
Isabelle Déchêne, Trésorière

Saint-Hyacinthe

CP 10
700, av de l'Hôtel-de-Ville
Saint-Hyacinthe, QC J2S 5B2
Tél: 450-778-8300; *Téléc:* 450-778-8628
communications@ville.st-hyacinthe.qc.ca
www.ville.st-hyacinthe.qc.ca
Entité municipal: City
Incorporation: 27 décembre 2001 *Area:* 189,11 km2
Comté ou district: Les Maskoutains; *Population au 2011:* 53,236
Circonscription(s) électorale(s) provinciale(s): St-Hyacinthe
Circonscription(s) électorale(s) fédérale(s): St-Hyacinthe—Bagot
Prochaines élections: 3e novembre 2013
Claude Bernier, Maire
450-778-8302, Fax: 450-778-5800
claude.bernier@ville.st-hyacinthe.qc.ca
Donald Côté, Conseiller, Ward(s): 1. Sainte-Rosalie
donald.cote@ville.st-hyacinthe.qc.ca
Sylvain Savoie, Conseiller, Ward(s): 2. Laurier
sylvain.savoie@ville.st-hyacinthe.qc.ca
Louise Arpin, Conseillère, Ward(s): 3. Saint-Joseph
louise.arpin@ville.st-hyacinthe.qc.ca
Bernard Barré, Conseiller, Ward(s): 4. Providence
bernard.barre@ville.st-hyacinthe.qc.ca
André Beauregard, Conseiller, Ward(s): 5. Douville
andre.beauregard@ville.st-hyacinthe.qc.ca
Guylain Coulombe, Conseiller, Ward(s): 6. Saint-Thomas-d'Aquin
guylain.coulombe@ville.st-hyacinthe.qc.ca
Brigitte Sansoucy, Conseillère, Ward(s): 7. Saint-Sacrement
brigitte.sansoucy@ville.st-hyacinthe.qc.ca
Alain Leclerc, Conseiller, Ward(s): 8. Bois-Joli
alain.leclerc@ville.st-hyacinthe.qc.ca
David Bousquet, Conseiller, Ward(s): 9. Sacré-Coeur
david.bousquet@ville.st-hyacinthe.qc.ca
Sylvie Adam, Cascades, Ward(s): 10. Cascades
sylvie.adam@ville.st-hyacinthe.qc.ca
Nicole Dion-Audette, Conseillère, Ward(s): 11. Hertel-Notre-Dame
n.dion-audette@ville.st-hyacinthe.qc.ca
Hélène Beauchesne, Greffière
450-778-8317, Fax: 450-778-2514
Louis Bilodeau, Directeur général
louis.bilodeau@ville.st-hyacinthe.qc.ca
Michel Tradif, OMA, Trésorier
450-778-8306
finances@ville.st-hyacinthe.qc.ca
Chantal Frigon, Directrice générale adjointe
450-778-8304
chantal.frigon@ville.st-hyacinthe.qc.ca
Yvan Gatien, Directeur, Urbanisme
450-778-8321, Fax: 450-778-5820
urbanisme@ville.st-hyacinthe.qc.ca
Daniel Dubois, Directeur, Sécurité incendie
450-778-8550, Fax: 450-778-5853
daniel.dubois@ville.st.hyacinthe.qc.ca

Saint-Jean-sur-Richelieu

CP 1025
188, rue Jacques-Cartier nord
Saint-Jean-sur-Richelieu, QC J3B 7B2
Tél: 450-357-2100; *Téléc:* 450-357-2362
info@ville.saint-jean-sur-richelieu.qc.ca
www.ville.saint-jean-sur-richelieu.qc.ca
Entité municipal: City
Incorporation: 24 janvier 2001 *Area:* 225,61 km2
Comté ou district: Le Haut-Richelieu; *Population au 2011:* 92,394
Circonscription(s) électorale(s) provinciale(s): St-Jean; Iberville
Circonscription(s) électorale(s) fédérale(s): St-Jean
Prochaines élections: 3e novembre 2013
Gilles Dolbec, Maire
450-357-2095, Fax: 450-357-2079
mairie@ville.saint-jean-sur-richelieu.qc.ca
Philippe Lasnier, Conseiller, Ward(s): 1
450-347-1299
p.lasnier@ville.saint-jean-sur-richelieu.qc.ca
Justin Bessette, Conseiller, Ward(s): 2
514-718-5675
j.bessette@ville.saint-jean-sur-richelieu.qc.ca
Gaétan Gagnon, Conseiller, Ward(s): 3
450-347-3209
g.gagnon@ville.saint-jean-sur-richelieu.qc.ca
Jean Fontaine, Conseiller, Ward(s): 4
450-346-3063
j.fontaine@ville.saint-jean-sur-richelieu.qc.ca
Stéphane Legrand, Conseiller, Ward(s): 5
450-545-9515
s.legrand@ville.saint-jean-sur-richelieu.qc.ca
Germain Poissant, Conseiller, Ward(s): 6
450-347-8703
g.poissant@ville.saint-jean-sur-richelieu.qc.ca
Christiane Marcoux, Conseillère, Ward(s): 7
450-347-5277
c.marcoux@ville.saint-jean-sur-richelieu.qc.ca
Marco Savard, Conseiller, Ward(s): 8
450-349-0473
m.savard@ville.saint-jean-sur-richelieu.qc.ca
Yvan Berthelot, Conseiller, Ward(s): 9
450-349-0685
y.berthelot@ville.saint-jean-sur-richelieu.qc.ca
Alain Paradis, Conseiller, Ward(s): 10
450-348-8046
a.paradis@ville.saint-jean-sur-richelieu.qc.ca
Alain Laplante, Conseiller, Ward(s): 11
450-349-1312
a.laplante@ville.saint-jean-sur-richelieu.qc.ca
Robert Cantin, Conseiller, Ward(s): 12
450-349-6661
r.cantin@ville.saint-jean-sur-richelieu.qc.ca
François Lapointe, Greffier
450-357-2077, Fax: 450-357-2362
greffe@ville.saint-jean-sur-richelieu.qc.ca
Daniel Desroches, Directeur général
450-357-2383, Fax: 450-357-2385
Pierre Beauvais, Trésorier
finances@ville.saint-jean-sur-richelieu.qc.ca
Roch Arbour, Directeur, Travaux publics
450-357-2238, Fax: 450-357-2290
Michelle Hébert, Directrice générale adjointe
Serge Boulerice, Directeur, Police
450-359-2529
police@ville.saint-jean-sur-richelieu.qc.ca
Luc Castonguay, Directeur, Urbanisme
urbanisme@ville.saint-jean-sur-richelieu.qc.ca

Saint-Jérôme

#301, 10, rue St-Joseph
Saint-Jérôme, QC J7Z 7G7
Tél: 450-436-1511; *Téléc:* 450-436-6626
info@vsj.ca
www.ville.saint-jerome.qc.ca
Entité municipal: City
Incorporation: 1er janvier 2002 *Area:* 89,37 km2
Comté ou district: La Rivière-du-Nord; *Population au 2011:* 68,456
Circonscription(s) électorale(s) provinciale(s): Prévost
Circonscription(s) électorale(s) fédérale(s): Rivière-du-Nord
Prochaines élections: 3e novembre 2013
Marc Gascon, Maire
450-436-1511
Renée Arsenault, Conseillère, Ward(s): 1
450-592-3469
Guy Lalande, Conseiller, Ward(s): 2
450-438-2021
Bernard Bougie, Conseiller, Ward(s): 3
450-431-7227
Alain Langlois, Conseiller, Ward(s): 4
450-569-2242
Robert Carrière, Conseiller, Ward(s): 5
450-432-5629
Benoît Delage, Conseiller, Ward(s): 6
450-436-6134
Marcel Lachance, Conseiller, Ward(s): 7
450-432-4399
Michel Des Chênes, Conseiller, Ward(s): 8
450-565-0693
Martin Pigeon, Conseiller, Ward(s): 9
450-436-1787
François Boyer, Conseiller, Ward(s): 10
450-224-1148
Tommy Kulczyk, Conseiller, Ward(s): 11
450-432-3700
Manon Labrèche, Conseillère, Ward(s): 12
450-432-2733
Luc Savoie, Conseiller, Ward(s): 13
450-592-3921
Michèle Céclier, Conseillère, Ward(s): 14
450-438-1073
Marcel Bélanger, Greffier
Éric Lachapelle, Directeur général
Johanne Coursol, Trésorière
Fernand Boudreault, Directeur, Travaux publics
Louis Bruneault, Directeur, Police
Marc Lapointe, Directeur, Sécurité incendie
Marc Lapointe, Directeur, Mesures d'urgence
Érick Frigon, Directeur, Ingénierie
Yvan Patenaude, Directeur, Communications
Richard St-Jean, Directeur, Urbanisme

Saint-Lambert

55, avenue Argyle
Saint-Laurent, QC J4P 2H3
Tél: 450-672-444; *Téléc:* 450-672-3732
direction.generale@ville.saint-lambert.qc.ca
www.ville.saint-lambert.qc.ca
Entité municipal: City
Incorporation: 1er janvier 2006 *Area:* 6,43 km2
Population au 2011: 21,555
Circonscription(s) électorale(s) provinciale(s): Laporte
Circonscription(s) électorale(s) fédérale(s): Saint-Lambert
Prochaines élections: 3e novembre 2013
Philippe Brunet, Maire
Myriam Pellerin, Greffière

Saint-Lazare

1960, ch Ste-Angélique
Saint-Lazare, QC J7T 3A3
Tél: 450-424-8000; *Téléc:* 450-455-4712
info@ville.saint-lazare.qc.ca
www.ville.saint-lazare.qc.ca
Entité municipal: City
Incorporation: 29 décembre 1875 *Area:* 67,59 km2
Comté ou district: Vaudreuil-Soulanges; *Population au 2011:* 19,295
Circonscription(s) électorale(s) provinciale(s): Soulanges
Circonscription(s) électorale(s) fédérale(s): Vaudreuil-Soulanges
Prochaines élections: 3e novembre 2013
Pierre Kary, Maire
pkary@ville.saint-lazare.qc.ca
Jean-Pierre Giguère, Conseiller, Ward(s): 1
jpgiguere@ville.saint-lazare.qc.ca
Nathalie Richard, Conseillère, Ward(s): 2
nrichard@ville.saint-lazare.qc.ca

Brigitte Asselin, Conseillère, Ward(s): 3
basselin@ville.saint-lazare.qc.ca
Michel Lambert, Conseiller, Ward(s): 4
mlambert@ville.saint-lazare.qc.ca
Gilbert Arsenault, Conseiller, Ward(s): 5
garsenault@ville.saint-lazare.qc.ca
Jean-Claude Gauthier, Conseiller, Ward(s): 6
jcgauthier@ville.saint-lazare.qc.ca
Nathaly Rayneault, Greffière
François Vaillancourt, Directeur général
fvaillancourt@ville.saint-lazare.qc.ca
Claude La Rue, Directeur, Travaux publics

Saint-Lin-Laurentides

900, 12e av
Saint-Lin-Laurentides, QC J5M 2W2
Tél: 450-439-3130; *Téléc:* 450-439-1525
saint-lin-laurentides.com
Entité municipal: City
Incorporation: 1er mars 2000 *Area:* 117,52 km2
Comté ou district: Montcalm; *Population au 2011:* 17,463
Circonscription(s) électorale(s) provinciale(s): Rousseau
Circonscription(s) électorale(s) fédérale(s): Montcalm
Prochaines élections: 3e novembre 2013
André Auger, Maire
450-439-3130, Fax: 450-439-2876
Luc Cyr, Conseiller, Ward(s): 1
450-439-6588
Mathieu Maisonneuve, Conseiller, Ward(s): 2
450-772-1849
André Malouin, Conseiller, Ward(s): 3
450-439-2352
Patrick Massé, Conseiller, Ward(s): 4
450-891-1423
Jean-Luc Arène, Conseiller, Ward(s): 5
450-431-1465
Pierre Lortie, Conseiller, Ward(s): 6
450-439-8230
Richard Dufort, Greffier & Directeur général
Sylvain Martel, Trésorier
André Héroux, Directeur, Travaux publics
Jean-Pierre Desjardins, Directeur, Incendies

Sainte-Adèle

1381, boul de Sainte-Adèle
Sainte-Adèle, QC J8B 1A3
Tél: 450-229-2921; *Téléc:* 450-229-4179
dirgenerale@ville.sainte-adele.qc.ca
sainte-adele.net
Entité municipal: City
Incorporation: 27 août 1997 *Area:* 122,19 km2
Comté ou district: Les Pays-d'en-Haut; *Population au 2011:* 12,137
Circonscription(s) électorale(s) provinciale(s): Bertrand
Circonscription(s) électorale(s) fédérale(s): Laurentides-Labelle
Prochaines élections: 3e novembre 2013
Réjean Charbonneau, Maire
Nadine Brière, Conseillère, Ward(s): 1
Roch Bédard, Conseiller, Ward(s): 2
Lise Gendron, Conseillère, Ward(s): 3
John Butler, Conseiller, Ward(s): 4
Robert Lagacé, Conseiller, Ward(s): 5
Pierre Morabito, Conseiller, Ward(s): 6
Michel Rousseau, Greffier
Pierre Dionne, Directeur général

Sainte-Anne-des-Plaines

139, boul Ste-Anne
Sainte-Anne-des-Plaines, QC J0N 1H0
Tél: 450-478-0211; *Téléc:* 450-478-5660
info@ville.ste-anne-des-plaines.qc.ca
www.ville.ste-anne-des-plaines.qc.ca
Entité municipal: City
Incorporation: 1er juillet 1855 *Area:* 92,22 km2
Comté ou district: Thérèse-De Blainville; *Population au 2011:* 14,535
Circonscription(s) électorale(s) provinciale(s): Blainville
Circonscription(s) électorale(s) fédérale(s): Terrebonne-Blainville
Prochaines élections: 3e novembre 2013
Guy Charbonneau, Mairesse
Julie Bellerose, Conseillère, Ward(s): 1
France Majeau, Conseiller, Ward(s): 2
Alain Cassista, Conseiller, Ward(s): 3
Denys Gagnon, Conseiller, Ward(s): 4
Mario Gauthier, Conseiller, Ward(s): 5
Stéphane Chouinard, Conseiller, Ward(s): 6
Serge Lepage, Greffier et Directeur général
Christiane Joyal, Trésorière
Paul Fournier, Directeur, Travaux publics

Sainte-Catherine

5465, boul Marie-Victorin
Sainte-Catherine, QC J5C 1M1
Tél: 450-632-0590; *Téléc:* 450-632-3298
information@ville.sainte-catherine.qc.ca
www.ville.sainte-catherine.qc.ca
Entité municipal: City
Incorporation: 30 octobre 1937 *Area:* 9,06 km2
Comté ou district: Roussillon; *Population au 2011:* 16,762
Circonscription(s) électorale(s) provinciale(s): La Prairie
Circonscription(s) électorale(s) fédérale(s): Châteauguay—St-Constant
Prochaines élections: 3e novembre 2013
Jocelyne Bates, Mairesse
Daniel Lamanque, Conseiller, Ward(s): 1
Martin Gélinas, Conseiller, Ward(s): 2
Jocelyne Brossard, Conseillère, Ward(s): 3
Louise Cormier, Conseillère, Ward(s): 4
Michel Béland, Conseiller, Ward(s): 5
Daniel Gagnon, Conseiller, Ward(s): 6
Jacques Foucher, Greffier
Danielle Chevrette, Directrice générale
Serge Courchesne, Trésorier

Sainte-Julie

1580, ch du Fer-à-Cheval
Sainte-Julie, QC J3E 2M1
Tél: 450-922-7111; *Téléc:* 450-922-7108
communications@ville.sainte-julie.qc.ca
www.ville.sainte-julie.qc.ca
Entité municipal: City
Incorporation: 1er juillet 1855 *Area:* 47,78 km2
Comté ou district: Lajemmerais; *Population au 2011:* 30,104
Circonscription(s) électorale(s) provinciale(s): Verchères
Circonscription(s) électorale(s) fédérale(s): Verchères-Les Patriotes
Prochaines élections: 3e novembre 2013
Suzanne Roy, Mairesse
450-922-7053
mairesse@ville.sainte-julie.qc.ca
Isabelle Poulet, Conseillère, Ward(s): 1. Belle-Rivière/Ringuet
André Lemay, Conseiller, Ward(s): 2. Moulin
Donald Savaria, Conseiller, Ward(s): 3. Vallée
Nicole Marchand, Conseillère, Ward(s): 4. Rucher
Mario Lemay, Conseiller, Ward(s): 5. Vieux-Village
Normand Varin, Conseiller, Ward(s): 6. Grand-Coteau
Henri Corbin, Conseiller, Conseillers et Districts, Ward(s): 7. Arc-en-Ciel
Lucie Bisson, Conseillère, Ward(s): 8. Montagne
bissonlucie@videotron.ca
Jean-François Gauthier, Greffier
450-922-7050
greffe@ville.sainte-julie.qc.ca
Pierre Bernardin, Directeur général
450-922-7102
dirgen@ville.sainte-julie.qc.ca
Jean-Pierre Duplin, Trésorier
450-922-7062
finances@ville.sainte-julie.qc.ca
Denyse Journault, Directrice, Communications
450-922-7092
communications@ville.sainte-julie.qc.ca
Pierre-Luc Blanchard, Directeur, Urbanisme
450-922-7142
urbanisme@ville.sainte-julie.qc.ca
Daniel Chagnon, Directeur, Loisirs
450-922-7122
loisirs@ville.sainte-julie.qc.ca

Sainte-Marie

270, av Marguerite-Bourgeoys
Sainte-Marie, QC G6E 3Z3
Tél: 418-387-2301; *Téléc:* 418-387-2454
info@sainte-marie.ca
www.ville.sainte-marie.qc.ca
Entité municipal: City
Incorporation: 15 avril 1978 *Area:* 106,65 km2
Comté ou district: La Nouvelle-Beauce; *Population au 2011:* 12,889
Circonscription(s) électorale(s) provinciale(s): Beauce-Nord
Circonscription(s) électorale(s) fédérale(s): Beauce
Prochaines élections: 3e novembre 2013
Harold Guay, Maire
Christian Laroche, Conseiller, Ward(s): 1
Mélanie Boissonneault, Conseillère, Ward(s): 2
Rosaire Simoneau, Conseiller, Ward(s): 3
Patrice Cossette, Conseiller, Ward(s): 4
Paulin Nappert, Conseiller, Ward(s): 5
Yves Chassé, Conseiller, Ward(s): 6
Hélène Gagné, Greffière
418-387-2301
helene.gagne@ville.sainte-marie.qc.ca
Louis Normand, Directeur général
418-387-2301
Jacques Boutin, Trésorier
418-387-2301
Maurice Mercier, Directeur, Travaux publics
418-387-6111

Sainte-Marthe-sur-le-Lac

3000, ch d'Oka
Sainte-Marthe-sur-le-Lac, QC J0N 1P0
Tél: 450-472-7310; *Téléc:* 450-472-0109
info@ville.sainte-marthe-sur-le-lac.qc.ca
www.sainte-marthe-sur-le-lac.qc.ca
Entité municipal: City
Incorporation: 1er janvier 1960 *Area:* 9,01 km2
Comté ou district: Deux-Montagnes; Communauté métropolitaine de Montréal; *Population au 2011:* 15,689
Circonscription(s) électorale(s) provinciale(s): Mirabel
Circonscription(s) électorale(s) fédérale(s): Rivière-des-Mille-Iles
Prochaines élections: 1er novembre 2013
Sylvie Brunet, Greffière
Sonia Paulus, Mairesse
Valérie Vivier, Trésorière
Marisol Charland, Directrice générale

Sainte-Thérèse

CP 100
6, rue de l'Église
Sainte-Thérèse, QC J7E 4H7
Tél: 450-434-1440; *Téléc:* 450-434-1499
info@sainte-therese.ca
www.ville.sainte-therese.qc.ca
Entité municipal: City
Incorporation: 1er juin 1849 *Area:* 8,62 km2
Comté ou district: Thérèse-De Blainville; *Population au 2011:* 26,025
Circonscription(s) électorale(s) provinciale(s): Groulx
Circonscription(s) électorale(s) fédérale(s): Marc-Aurèle-Fortin
Prochaines élections: 3e novembre 2013
Sylvie Surprenant, Mairesse
mairie@sainte-therese.ca
Denise Perreault-Théberge, Conseillère, Ward(s): 1. Sève
d.perreault-theberge@sainte-therese.ca
Patrick Morin, Conseiller, Ward(s): 2. Verschelden
p.morin@sainte-therese.ca
Marie-Andrée Petelle, Conseillère, Ward(s): 3. Morris
ma.petelle@sainte-therese.ca
Normand Toupin, Conseiller, Ward(s): 4. Chapleau
n.toupin@sainte-therese.ca
Luc Vézina, Conseiller, Ward(s): 5. Lonergan
l.vezina@sainte-therese.ca
Michel Milette, Conseiller, Ward(s): 6. Ducharme
m.milette@sainte-therese.ca
Louis Lauzon, Conseiller, Ward(s): 7 Blanchard
l.lauzon@sainte-therese.ca
Vincent Arseneau, Conseiller, Ward(s): 8. Marie-Thérèse
v.arseneau@sainte-therese.ca
Jean-Luc Berthiaume, Greffier
jl.berthiaume@sainte-therese.ca
Chantal Gauvreau, Directrice générale
450-434-1440, Fax: 450-434-1499
c.gauvreau@sainte-therese.ca
Jean Pierre Gendron, Trésorier
450-434-1440, Fax: 450-434-1499
jp.gendron@sainte-therese.ca

Salaberry-de-Valleyfield

61, rue Ste-Cécile
Salaberry-de-Valleyfield, QC J6T 1L8
Tél: 450-370-4300
communications@ville.valleyfield.qc.ca
www.ville.valleyfield.qc.ca
Entité municipal: City
Incorporation: 24 avril 2002 *Area:* 100,96 km2
Comté ou district: Beauharnois-Salaberry; *Population au 2011:* 40,077
Circonscription(s) électorale(s) provinciale(s): Beauharnois
Circonscription(s) électorale(s) fédérale(s): Beauharnois-Salaberry
Prochaines élections: 3e novembre 2013
Denis Lapointe, Maire
450-370-4801
denis.lapointe@ville.valleyfield.qc.ca
Denis Laître, Conseiller, Ward(s): 1. Grande-île
450-373-0954
denis.laitre@ville.valleyfield.qc.ca
Jean-Marc Rochon, Conseiller, Ward(s): 2. Nitro
450-377-2774
jean-marc.rochon@ville.valleyfield.qc.ca

Louise Sauvé, Conseillère, Ward(s): 3. Georges-Leduc
450-377-8597
louise.sauvé@ville.valleyfield.qc.ca
Robert Savard, Conseiller, Ward(s): 4. Champlain
450-371-1173
robert.savard@ville.valleyfield.qc.ca
Jean-Jacques Leduc, Conseiller, Ward(s): 5. La Baie
450-371-5099
jean-jacques.leduc@ville.valleyfield.qc.ca
Jacques Smith, Conseiller, Ward(s): 6. Robert-Cauchon
450-371-4975
jacques.smith@ville.valleyfield.qc.ca
Pierre-Paul Messier, Conseiller, Ward(s): 7. Jules-Léger
450-373-5459
pierre-paul.messier@ville.valleyfield.qc.ca
Normand Amesse, Conseiller, Ward(s): 8. Saint-Timothée
450-371-6895
normand.amesse@ville.valleyfield.qc.ca
Alain Gagnon, Greffier
450-370-4304, Fax: 450-370-4388
alain.gagnon@ville.valleyfield.qc.ca
Pierre Chevrier, Directeur général
450-370-4800, Fax: 450-370-4343
pierre.chevrier@ville.valleyfield.qc.ca
Jacques Lemieux, CA, OMA, Trésorier
450-370-4320, Fax: 450-370-4316
jacques.lemieux@ville.valleyfield.qc.ca
Michel Ménard, Directeur, Sécurité incendie
450-370-4750, Fax: 450-370-4755
securiteincendie@ville.valleyfield.qc.ca
Denis Larochelle, Directeur, Eau et environnement/Travaux publics
450-370-4820, Fax: 450-370-4370
gestionduterritoire@ville.valleyfield.qc.ca
Danielle Prieur, Coordonnatrice
450-370-4875, Fax: 450-370-4343
communications@ville.valleyfield.qc.ca
René Monette, Directeur, Récréatif et communautaire
450-370-4390, Fax: 450-370-4888
src@ville.valleyfield.qc.ca

Sept-Îles

546, av De Quen
Sept-Îles, QC G4R 2R4
Tél: 418-962-2525; *Téléc:* 418-964-3213
info@ville.sept-iles.qc.ca
www.ville.sept-iles.qc.ca
Entité municipal: City
Incorporation: 12 février 2003 *Area:* 1 969,42 km2
Comté ou district: Sept-Rivières; *Population au 2011:* 25,686
Circonscription(s) électorale(s) provinciale(s): Duplessis
Circonscription(s) électorale(s) fédérale(s): Manicouagan
Prochaines élections: 3e novembre 2013
Note: En 1970, Clarke City est fusionnée à Sept-Iles; le 12 fév., 2003, Moisie & Gallix sont fusionnées à Sept-Iles.
Serge Lévesque, Maire
maire@ville.sept-iles.qc.ca
Gervais Gagné, Conseiller, Ward(s): 1. Ste-Marguerite
district1@ville.sept-iles.qc.ca
Maurice Gagné, Conseiller, Ward(s): 2. Ferland
district2@ville.sept-iles.qc.ca
Jean Masse, Conseiller, Ward(s): 3. L'Anse
district3@ville.sept-iles.qc.ca
Denis Miousse, Conseiller, Ward(s): 4. Marie-Immaculée
district4@ville.sept-iles.qc.ca
Gaby Gauthier, Conseiller, Ward(s): 5. Vieux-Quai
district5@ville.sept-iles.qc.ca
Lorraine Dubuc-Johnson, Conseillère, Ward(s): 6. Mgr-Blanche
district6@ville.sept-iles.qc.ca
Jean-François Martin, Conseiller, Ward(s): 7. Jacques-Cartier
district7@ville.sept-iles.qc.ca
Martial Lévesque, Conseiller, Ward(s): 8. Sainte-Famille
district8@ville.sept-iles.qc.ca
Claude Lessard, Conseiller, Ward(s): 9. Moisie-Plages
district9@ville.sept-iles.qc.ca
Valérie Haince, Greffière
418-964-3205
greffe@ville.sept-iles.qc.ca
Claude Bureau, Directeur général
418-964-3201
directiongenerale@ville.sept-iles.qc.ca
Serge Gagné, Directeur, Finances
418-964-3215
finances@ville.sept-iles.qc.ca
Stéphanie Prévost, Directrice générale
sprevost@cpesi@cgocable.ca

La Corporation de protection de l'environnement de Sept-Iles (CPESI)

Shawinigan

CP 400
550, av de l'Hôtel-de-Ville
Shawinigan, QC G9N 6V3
Tél: 819-536-7200; *Téléc:* 819-536-7255
information@shawinigan.ca
www.shawinigan.ca
Entité municipal: City
Incorporation: 1er janvier 2002 *Area:* 781,81 km2
Population au 2011: 50,060
Circonscription(s) électorale(s) provinciale(s): Saint-Maurice; Laviolette
Circonscription(s) électorale(s) fédérale(s): Saint-Maurice—Champlain
Prochaines élections: 3e novembre 2013
Note: 8 nouveaux districts seront en vigueur lors des élections municipal de nov/09.
Michel Angers, Mairesse
819-536-7211
cabinetdumaire@shawinigan.ca
Josette Allard-Gignac, Conseillère, Ward(s): Almaville
819-537-4727
jallard-gignac@shawinigan.ca
Bernard Cayouette, Conseiller, Ward(s): Boisés
819-835-2874
bcayouette@shawinigan.ca
Alain Lord, Conseiller, Ward(s): Cité
819-539-8462
bcayouette@shawinigan.ca
Jean-Yves Tremblay, Conseiller, Conseillers et Districts, Ward(s): Hêtres
819-536-7211
jytremblay@shawinigan.ca
Serge Aubry, Conseiller, Ward(s): Montagnes
819-539-9474
saubry@shawinigan.ca
Jacques Grenier, Conseiller, Ward(s): Rivière
819-269-2161
jgrenier@shawinigan.ca
Lucie de Bons, Conseillère, Ward(s): Rocher
819-538-7348
ldebons@shawinigan.ca
Pierre Giguère, Conseiller, Ward(s): Val-Mauricie
819-537-6043
pgiguere@shawinigan.ca
Yves Vincent, Greffier
819-536-7211
greffe@shawinigan.ca
Gaétan Béchard, Directeur général
819-536-7211
directiongenerale@shawinigan.ca
Sylvie Lavoie, Directrice, Finances
servicesadministratifs@shawinigan.ca
Réal Beauchamp, Directeur général adjoint
819-536-7211
directiongenerale@shawinigan.ca
Vacant, Directeur, Aménagement et de l'environnement
819-536-7211
urbanisme@shawinigan.ca
François St-Onge, Directeur, Communications
819-536-7211
fstonge@shawinigan.ca
Pierre Godin, Directeur, Travaux publics
819-536-7211
travauxpublics@shawinigan.ca
Robert Y. Desjardins, Directeur, Loisirs, culture et vie communautaire
819-536-7211
loisirs@shawinigan.ca
François Garceau, Directeur, Ressources humaines
ressourceshumaines@shawinigan.ca
Claude Larocque, Directeur, Techniques
819-536-7211
servicestechniques@shawinigan.ca
François Lelièvre, Directeur, Sécurité incendie
819-538-2248
incendie@shawinigan.ca

Sherbrooke

CP 610
191, rue du Palais
Sherbrooke, QC J1H 5H9
Tél: 819-821-5500; *Téléc:* 819-822-6064
www.ville.sherbrooke.qc.ca
Entité municipal: City
Incorporation: 1er janvier 2002 *Area:* 366,00 km2
Population au 2011: 154,601
Circonscription(s) électorale(s) provinciale(s): St-François; Sherbrooke; Orford; Johnson
Circonscription(s) électorale(s) fédérale(s): Sherbrooke
Prochaines élections: 3e novembre 2013
Bernard Sévigny, Maire
819-821-5969, Fax: 819-822-6131
mairie@ville.sherbrooke.qc.ca
Isabelle Sauvé, Greffière
819-821-5500, Fax: 819-822-6064
Claude Marcoux, Directeur général
819-821-5618, Fax: 819-823-5121
Claude Périnet, Directeur général adjoint
François Poulette, Trésorier
819-821-5490, Fax: 819-822-6091
Colette Ouellet, Directrice, Communications
819-821-5572, Fax: 819-823-5153
communications@ville.sherbrooke.qc.ca
Jacques Leduc, Directeur, Ressources humaines
819-821-5677, Fax: 819-822-6086
ressources.humaines@ville.sherbrooke.qc.ca
Gaétan Labbé, Directeur, Protection des incendies
819-821-5514, Fax: 819-821-5516
protection.incendies@ville.sherbrooke.qc.ca
Nicole Bergeron, Conseillère, Ward(s): Brompton
819-846-2757
nicole.bergeron@ville.sherbrooke.qc.ca
Louisda Brochu, Conseiller, Ward(s): Lavigerie
819-565-9954
louida.brochu@ville.sherbrooke.qc.ca
David W. Price, Conseiller, Ward(s): Lennoxville
819-569-9388
david.price@ville.sherbrooke.qc.ca
Serge Paquin, Conseiller, Ward(s): Centre-Sud
819-346-9312
paquin.serge@videotron.ca
Julien Lachance, Conseiller, Ward(s): Saint-Élie
819-566-7886
jlach@videotron.ca
Chantal L'Espérance, Conseillère, Ward(s): Domaine Howard
819-565-8089
chantal.lesperance@ville.sherbrooke.qc.ca
Benoit Dionne, Conseiller, Ward(s): Beauvoir
819-846-4725
dionneb@csrs.qc.ca
Jean-Guy Demers, Conseiller, Ward(s): Desranleau
819-432-2562
jgdemers01@hotmail.com
Mark McLaughlin, Conseiller, Ward(s): Fairview
819-212-5851
mark.mclaughlin@videotron.ca
Pierre Boisvert, Conseiller, Ward(s): Croix-Lumineuse
819-564-8924
pboisvert2005@sympatico.ca
Diane Délisle, Conseillère, Ward(s): Deauville
819-864-4656
ddelisle@abacom.com
Marc Denault, Conseiller, Ward(s): Montcalm
819-565-5555
denaultm@abacom.com
Michel Lamontagne, Conseiller, Ward(s): Moulins
819-846-3257
Rémi Demers, Conseiller, Ward(s): Marie-Rivier
819-565-1066
remi.demers@videotron.qc.ca
William Smith, Conseiller, Ward(s): Uplands
819-569-8175
Robert Y. Pouliot, Conseiller, Ward(s): Ascot
819-563-1848
r.pouliot@bobpouliotinc.ca
Serge Foreste, Conseillère, Ward(s): Rock Forest
819-823-0062
serge.forest@videotron.ca
Nathalie Goguen, Conseillère, Ward(s): Beckett
819-348-1929
nathalie.goguen@videotron.ca
Mariette Fugère, Conseillère, Ward(s): Pin-Solitaire
819-562-7064
mariette.fugere@sympatico.ca
Jean-François Rouleau, Conseiller, Ward(s): Université
819-569-0208
jean-francois.rouleau@ville.sherbrooke.qc.ca
Bruno Vachon, Conseiller, Ward(s): Châteaux-d'Eau
819-212-5688
bruno.vachon@ville.sherbrooke.qc.ca
Pierre Tardif, Conseiller, Ward(s): Carrefour
819-566-7926
pierrectardif@videotron.ca
Roger Labrecque, Conseiller, Ward(s): Quatre-Saisons
819-823-2125
labrecqueniro@videotron.ca

Arrondissement de Brompton

Arrondissement de Fleurimont

Arrondissement de Lennoxville

Arrondissement du Mont-Bellevue

Arrondissement de Rock Forest-Saint-Élie-Deauville

Arrondissement de Jacques-Cartier

Sorel-Tracy

CP 368
71, rue Charlotte
Sorel-Tracy, QC J3P 7K1
Tél: 450-780-5600; *Téléc:* 450-780-5625
info@ville.sorel-tracy.qc.ca
www.ville.sorel.qc.ca
Entité municipal: City
Incorporation: 15 mars 2000 *Area:* 56,58 km2
Comté ou district: Pierre-De Saurel; *Population au 2011:* 34,600
Circonscription(s) électorale(s) provinciale(s): Richelieu
Circonscription(s) électorale(s) fédérale(s):
Bas-Richelieu—Nicolet—Bécancour
Prochaines élections: 3e novembre 2013
Réjean Dauplaise, Maire
Sophie Chevalier, Conseillère, Ward(s): 1. Bourgchemin
450-746-3858
sophie.chevalier@ville.sorel-tracy.qc.ca
André Potvin, Conseiller, Ward(s): 2. Saint-Laurent
450-746-2536
andre.potvin@ville.sorel-tracy.qc.ca
Yvon Bibeau, Conseiller, Ward(s): 3. Saint-Laurent
450-746-8987
yvon.bibeau@ville.sorel-tracy.qc.ca
Corina Bastiani, Conseillère, Ward(s): 4. Vieux-Sorel
450-780-2252
corina.bastiani@ville.sorel-tracy.qc.ca
Alain Maher, Conseiller, Ward(s): 5. Du Faubourg
450-743-8749
alain.maher@ville.sorel-tracy.qc.ca
Gilles Jr. Lemieux, Conseiller, Ward(s): 6. Gouverneurs
450-780-2225
gilles.lemieux@ville.sorel-tracy.qc.ca
Michèle Lacombe-Gauthier, Conseillère, Ward(s): 7. Patriotes
450-746-7710
michele.lacombe@ville.sorel-tracy.qc.ca
Dominique Ouellet, Conseillère, Ward(s): 8. Pierre-De Saurel
450-780-1248
dominique.ouellet@ville.sorel-tracy.qc.ca
René Chevalier, Greffier
450-780-5600
Mario Lazure, Directeur général
450-780-5600
Diane Robillard, Directrice, Finances & Trésorerie
450-780-5600
Alain Rouleau, Directeur, Sécurité incendie
450-780-5600

Terrebonne

775, rue St-Jean-Baptiste
Terrebonne, QC J6W 1B5
Tél: 450-961-2001; *Téléc:* 450-471-4482
information@ville.terrebonne.qc.ca
www.ville.terrebonne.qc.ca
Entité municipal: City
Incorporation: 27 juin 2001 *Area:* 155,44 km2
Comté ou district: Les Moulins; *Population au 2011:* 106,322
Circonscription(s) électorale(s) provinciale(s): Terrebonne; Masson
Circonscription(s) électorale(s) fédérale(s): Terrebonne-Blainville
Prochaines élections: 3e novembre 2013
Jean-Marc Robitaille, Maire
Nathalie Bellavance, Conseillère, Ward(s): 1
Daniel L'Espérance, Conseiller, Ward(s): 2
Marie-Claude Lamarche, Conseillère, Ward(s): 3
Réal Leclerc, Conseiller, Ward(s): 4
Denis Poitras, Conseiller, Ward(s): 5
Michel Morin, Conseiller, Ward(s): 6
Paul Asselin, Conseiller, Ward(s): 7
Marie-Josée Beaupré, Conseillère, Ward(s): 8
Marc Campagna, Conseiller, Ward(s): 9
Frédéric Asselin, Conseiller, Ward(s): 10
Clermont Lévesque, Conseiller, Ward(s): 11
Jean-Luc Labrecque, Conseiller, Ward(s): 12
Sylvain Tousignant, Conseiller, Ward(s): 13
Michel Lefebvre, Conseiller, Conseillers et Districts, Ward(s): 14
Stéphane Berthe, Conseiller, Ward(s): 15
Jean-Guy Sénécal, Conseiller, Ward(s): 16
Denis Bouffard, Greffier
Denis Lévesque, Directeur général
Francine Blain, Trésorière
Guy Dubois, Chef de police
Jacques Bérubé, Directeur, Incendie
Michel Sarrazin, Directeur, Travaux publics

Thetford Mines

CP 489
144, rue Notre-Dame sud
Thetford Mines, QC G6G 5T3
Tél: 418-335-2981; *Téléc:* 418-335-7089
infos@ville.thetfordmines.qc.ca
www.ville.thetfordmines.qc.ca
Entité municipal: City
Incorporation: 17 octobre 2001 *Area:* 224,37 km2
Comté ou district: Des Appalaches; *Population au 2011:* 25,709
Circonscription(s) électorale(s) provinciale(s): Frontenac
Circonscription(s) électorale(s) fédérale(s): Mégantic-L'Érable
Prochaines élections: 3e novembre 2013
Luc Berthold, Maire
Clément Boudreau, Conseiller, Ward(s): 1. Black Lake
418-423-2257
Renaud Legendre, Conseiller, Ward(s): 2. Black Lake-Mitchell/Lacs
418-423-2349
renaudlegendre@hotmail.com
Ghyslain Cliche, Conseiller, Ward(s): 3. Thetford Mines
418-335-9267
ghcliche@hotmail.com
Luc Champagne, Conseiller, Ward(s): 4. Thetford Mines
418-338-2812
Carmen Jalbert-Jacques, Conseillère, Ward(s): 5. Thetford Mines
418-338-1901
cjalbertjacques@sympatico.ca
Louis-Philippe Champagne, Conseiller, Ward(s): 6. Thetford Mines
418-335-7119
lphilchampagne@hotmail.com
Marco Tanguay, Conseiller, Ward(s): 7. Thetford Mines
418-338-8819
tanguaymarco@sympatico.ca
Marc Vachon, Conseiller, Ward(s): 8. Thetford Mines
418-334-0340
marcf.vachon@cgocable.ca
Paul-André Marchand, Conseiller, Ward(s): 9. Thetford-Sud
418-335-9871
paul.marchand@cgocable.ca
Gaétan Vachon, Conseiller, Ward(s): 10. Robertsonville/Pontbriand
418-335-9543
Réjean Martin, Greffier
greffe@ville.thetfordmines.qc.ca
René Soucy, Directeur général
dirgen@ville.thetfordmines.qc.ca
Sylvain Tremblay, Trésorier
s.tremblay@ville.thetfordmines.qc.ca
François Gagnon, Directeur, Sécurité publique
secpub@ville.thetfordmines.qc.ca

Trois-Rivières

CP 368
1325, place de l'Hôtel-de-Ville
Trois-Rivières, QC G9A 5H3
Tél: 819-374-2002; *Téléc:* 819-372-4631
info@v3r.net
www.v3r.net
Entité municipal: City
Incorporation: 1er janvier 2002 *Area:* 288,50 km2
Population au 2011: 131,338
Circonscription(s) électorale(s) provinciale(s): Trois-Rivières; Maskinongé; Champlain
Circonscription(s) électorale(s) fédérale(s): Trois-Rivières
Prochaines élections: 3e novembre 2013
Yves Lévesque, Maire
André Noël, Conseiller, Ward(s): Carmel
anoel@v3r.net
Monique Leclerc, Conseillère, Ward(s): Châteaudun
Marie-Claude Camirand, Conseillère, Ward(s): Chavigny
mccamirand@v3r.net
Fernand Lajoie, Conseiller, Ward(s): Estacades
flajoie@v3r.net
Guy Daigle, Conseiller, Ward(s): Laviolette
gdaigle@v3r.net
René Goyette, Conseiller, Ward(s): Madeleine
rgoyette@v3r.net
Sylvie Tardif, Conseillère, Ward(s): Marie de l'Incarnation
stardif@v3r.net
Marie-Josée Tardif, Conseillère, Ward(s): Plateaux
mjtardif@v3r.net
Michel Veillette, Conseiller, Ward(s): Pointe-du-lac
michel.veillette@v3r.net
Ginette Bellemare, Conseillère, Ward(s): Rigaud
gbellemare@v3r.net
Michel Bronsard, Conseiller, Ward(s): St-Louis-de-France
mbronsard@v3r.net
Catherine Dufresne, Conseillère, Ward(s): Ste-Marguerite
cdufresne@v3r.net
Micheline Courteau, Conseillère, Ward(s): Ste-Marthe
Alain Croteau, Conseiller, Ward(s): Sanctuaire
acroteau@v3r.net
Yves Landry, Conseiller, Ward(s): Terrasses
ylandry@v3r.net
Françoise H. Viens, Conseillère, Ward(s): Vieilles-Forges
fviens@v3r.net
Gilles Poulin, Directeur, Greffe/Services juridiques
819-372-4604, Fax: 819-372-4636
greffe@v3r.net
Michel Byette, Directeur général
819-372-4608, Fax: 819-372-4631
directiongenerale@v3r.net
Daniel Thibault, Directeur général adjoint
France Cinq-Mars, Directrice, Finances
819-374-2002, Fax: 819-372-4630
finances@v3r.net
Éric Chevalier, Directeur, Ressources humaines
819-372-4603, Fax: 819-374-9005
ressourceshumaines@v3r.net
Francis Gobeil, Directeur, Sécurité publique
819-370-6700, Fax: 819-374-3506
policeincendie@v3r.net
Michel Jutras, Directeur, Arts et culture
Pierre Desjardins, Directeur, Aménagement, gestion et développement durable du territoire
819-372-4626, Fax: 819-375-5865
urbanisme@v3r.net
Vincent Fortier, Directeur, Techniques
819-372-4627, Fax: 819-374-6646
Michel Lemieux, Directeur, Loisirs et communautaires
819-372-4621, Fax: 819-374-7133
François Roy, Directeur, Communications
819-372-4602, Fax: 819-374-0210
relationspubliques@v3r.net
Ghislain Lachance, Directeur, Travaux publics
819-379-3733

Val-d'Or

CP 400
855, 2e av
Val-d'Or, QC J9P 4P4
Tél: 819-824-9613; *Téléc:* 819-825-6650
info@ville.valdor.qc.ca
www.ville.valdor.qc.ca
Entité municipal: City
Incorporation: 1er janvier 2002 *Area:* 3 958,13 km2
Comté ou district: La Vallée-de-l'Or; *Population au 2011:* 31,862
Circonscription(s) électorale(s) provinciale(s): Abitibi-Est
Circonscription(s) électorale(s) fédérale(s):
Abitibi-Baie-James-Nunavik-Eeyou
Prochaines élections: 3e novembre 2013
Fernand Trahan, Maire
Suzanne Couture Bordeleau, Conseillère, Ward(s): 1. Lac Blouin-Centre-ville
Michael Prince, Conseiller, Ward(s): 2. Paquinville-Fatima
Pierre Potvin, Conseiller, Ward(s): 3. Belvédère
Céline Brindamour, Conseillère, Ward(s): 4. Sullivan
Gilles Bérubé, Conseiller, Ward(s): 5. Val-Senneville-Vassan
Francis Murphy, Conseiller, Ward(s): 6. Bourlamaque-Louvicourt

Bernard Gauthier, Conseiller, Ward(s): 7. Lemoine-Baie-Carrière

Robert Quesnal, Conseiller, Ward(s): 8. Dubuisson
Sophie Gareau, Greffière
819-824-9613
Guy Faucher, Directeur général
819-824-9613
Chantale Gilbert, Trésorier
819-824-9613
Alain Cloutier, Directeur, Ressources humaines et Communications
819-824-9613
Danny Burbridge, Directeur, Infrastructures urbaines
819-824-9613
Robert Migué, Directeur, Culturel
819-824-9613

Varennes

CP 5000
175, rue Ste-Anne
Varennes, QC J3X 1T5
Tél: 450-652-9888; *Téléc:* 450-652-2655
general@ville.varennes.qc.ca
ville.varennes.qc.ca
Entité municipal: City
Incorporation: 26 août 1972 *Area:* 93,96 km2

Comté ou district: Marguerite-D'Youville; *Population au 2011:* 20,994
Circonscription(s) électorale(s) provinciale(s): Verchères
Circonscription(s) électorale(s) fédérale(s): Verchères-Les Patriotes
Prochaines élections: 3e novembre 2013
Martin Damphousse, Maire
martin.damphousse@ville.varennes.qc.ca
Joël Beauchemin, Conseiller, Ward(s): 1. Guillaudière
joel.beauchemin@ville.varennes.qc.ca
Lyne Beaulieu, Conseillère, Ward(s): 2. Sitière
lyne.beaulieu@ville.varennes.qc.ca
Francis Rinfret, Conseiller, Ward(s): 3. Langloiserie
francis.rinfret@ville.varennes.qc.ca
Denis Le Blanc, Conseiller, Ward(s): 4. Notre-Dame
denis.leblanc@ville.varennes.qc.ca
Bruno Desjarlais, Conseiller, Ward(s): 5. Petite Prairie
bruno.desjarlais@ville.varennes.qc.ca
Natalie Parent, Conseiller, Ward(s): 6. Seigneuries
natalie.parent@ville.varennes.qc.ca
Gaétan Marcil, Conseiller, Ward(s): 7. Saint-Charles
gaetan.marcil@ville.varennes.qc.ca
Brigitte Collin, Conseillère, Ward(s): 8. Martigny
brigitte.collin@ville.varennes.qc.ca
Marc Giard, Greffier
Sébastien Roy, Directeur général
Denise Beauchemin, Trésorière
Denis Guay, Directeur, Travaux publics
Denis Marchand, Directeur, Urbanisme

Vaudreuil-Dorion
#200, 2555, rue Dutrisac
Vaudreuil-Dorion, QC J7V 7E6
Tél: 450-455-3371; *Téléc:* 450-424-8540
courriel@ville.vaudreuil-dorion.qc.ca
www.ville.vaudreuil-dorion.qc.ca
Entité municipal: City
Incorporation: 16 mars 1994 *Area:* 73,18 km2
Comté ou district: Vaudreuil-Soulanges; *Population au 2011:* 33,305
Circonscription(s) électorale(s) provinciale(s): Vaudreuil
Circonscription(s) électorale(s) fédérale(s): Vaudreuil-Soulanges
Prochaines élections: 3e novembre 2013
Guy Pilon, Maire
Claude Beaudoin, Conseiller, Ward(s): 1. Quinchien
François Séguin, Conseiller, Ward(s): 2. Harwood
Robert A. Laurence, Conseiller, Ward(s): 3. Fief-Cavagnal
Denis Vincent, Conseiller, Ward(s): 4. Seigneurie
Rénald Gabriele, Conseiller, Ward(s): 5. Chenaux
Gabriel Parent, Conseiller, Ward(s): 6. Cité-des-Jeunes
Guylène Duplessis, Conseillère, Ward(s): 7. Carrefour
Paul Dumoulin, Conseiller, Ward(s): 8. Baie
Jean St-Antoine, Greffier
Manon Bernard, Directrice générale
Marco Pilo, Trésorier
Luc Duval, Directeur, Travaux publics

Victoriaville
CP 370
1, rue Notre-Dame ouest
Victoriaville, QC G6P 6T2
Tél: 819-758-1571; *Téléc:* 819-758-9292
info@ville.victoriaville.qc.ca
www.ville.victoriaville.qc.ca
Entité municipal: City
Incorporation: 23 juin 1993 *Area:* 81,96 km2
Comté ou district: Arthabaska; *Population au 2011:* 43,462
Circonscription(s) électorale(s) provinciale(s): Arthabaska
Circonscription(s) électorale(s) fédérale(s): Richmond-Arthabaska
Prochaines élections: 3e novembre 2013
Alain Rayes, Maire
819-758-1571
alain.rayes@ville.victoriaville.qc.ca
Caroline Pilon, Conseillère, Ward(s): 1. Parc-de-l'Amitié
819-604-1600
caroline.pilon@ville.victoriaville.qc.ca
Jacques Gagnon, Conseiller, Ward(s): 2. Parc-de-l'Ile
819-758-8511
jacques.gagnon@ville.victoriaville.qc.ca
Jacques Nadeau, Conseiller, Ward(s): 3. Charles-Édouard-Mailhot
819-758-8530
jacques.nadeau@ville.victoriaville.qc.ca
Alexandre Côté, Conseiller, Ward(s): 4. Sainte-Famille
819-357-3272
alexandre.cote@ville.victoriaville.qc.ca
France Auger, Conseillère, Ward(s): 5. Parc-Terre-des-Jeunes
819-758-7330
france.auger@ville.victoriaville.qc.ca
Marc Mortin, Conseiller, Ward(s): 6. Parc-Victoria
819-758-1864
marc.morin@ville.victoriaville.qc.ca
Michel Allard, Conseiller, Ward(s): 7. Sainte-Victoire
819-752-6362
michel.allard@ville.victoriaville.qc.ca
Denis Morin, Conseiller, Ward(s): 8. Arthabaska-Nord
819-357-7821
denis.morin@ville.victoriaville.qc.ca
Gilles Lafontaine, Conseiller, Ward(s): 9. Arthabaska-Ouest
819-357-8712
gilles.lafontaine@ville.victoriaville.qc.ca
Christian Lettre, Conseiller, Ward(s): 10. Arthabaska-Est
819-357-8573
christian.lettre@ville.victoriaville.qc.ca
Jean Poirier, Greffier
819-758-1571
jean.poirier@ville.victoriaville.qc.ca
Martin Lessard, Directeur général
martin.lessard@ville.victoriaville.qc.ca
Yves Fréchette, Trésorier
yves.frechette@ville.victoriaville.qc.ca
Jean Mercier, Directeur, Ressources humaines
819-758-1571
jean.mercier@ville.victoriaville.qc.ca
André Charest, Directeur, Travaux publics
819-758-0651
andre.charest@ville.victoriaville.qc.ca
Jean Demers, Directeur, Gestion du territoire
819-758-1571
jean.demers@ville.victoriaville.qc.ca

Other Municipalities in Québec

Abercorn
10, ch des Églises ouest
Abercorn, QC J0E 1B0
Tél: 450-538-2664; *Téléc:* 450-538-6295
mun.abercorn@vivomail.ca
Entité municipal: Village
Incorporation: 25 juin 1929 *Area:* 27,84 km2
Comté ou district: Brome-Missisquoi; *Population au 2011:* 391
Circonscription(s) électorale(s) provinciale(s): Brome-Missisquoi
Circonscription(s) électorale(s) fédérale(s): Brome-Missisquoi
Prochaines élections: 3e novembre 2013
Jean-Charles Bisonnette, Maire
Danielle Corriveau, Directrice générale

Abitibi
CP 214
571, 1re Rue est
Amos, QC J9T 2H3
Tél: 819-732-5356; *Téléc:* 819-732-9607
mrc@mrcabitibi.qc.ca
www.mrcabitibi.qc.ca
Entité municipal: Regional County Municipality
Population au 2011: 24,354
Note: 17 municipalités & 2 autres territoires.
Jacques Riopel, Préfet
Michel Roy, Directeur général
michel.roy@mrcabitibi.qc.ca

Abitibi-Ouest
#105, 6, 8e Av est
La Sarre, QC J9Z 1N6
Tél: 819-339-5671; *Téléc:* 819-339-5400
mrcao@mrcao.qc.ca
www.mrc.ao.ca
Entité municipal: Regional County Municipality
Population au 2011: 21,003
Note: 21 municipalités & 2 autres territoires.
Daniel Rancourt, Préfet
Nicole Breton, Directrice générale
nicole.breton@lino.com

Acton
CP 99
1037, rue Beaugrand
Acton Vale, QC J0H 1A0
Tél: 450-546-3256; *Téléc:* 450-546-0525
mrc@mrcacton.qc.ca
www.mrcacton.qc.ca
Entité municipal: Regional County Municipality
Population au 2011: 15,381
Huguette St-Pierre-Beaulac, Préfète
Yvan Talbot, Directeur général
yvan.talbot@mrcacton.qc.ca

Acton Vale
1025, rue Boulay
Acton Vale, QC J0H 1A0
Tél: 450-546-2703; *Téléc:* 450-546-4865
actonvale@ville.actonvale.qc.ca
www.ville.actonvale.qc.ca
Entité municipal: Town
Incorporation: 26 janvier 2000 *Area:* 90,88 km2
Comté ou district: Acton; *Population au 2011:* 7,664
Circonscription(s) électorale(s) provinciale(s): Johnson
Circonscription(s) électorale(s) fédérale(s): St-Hyacinthe-Bagot
Prochaines élections: 3e novembre 2013
Éric Charbonneau, Maire
Rita Parent, Greffière

Adstock
35, rue Principale ouest
Adstock, QC G0N 1S0
Tél: 418-422-2135; *Téléc:* 418-422-2134
info@municipaliteadstock.qc.ca
www.municipaliteadstock.qc.ca
Entité municipal: Municipality
Incorporation: 24 octobre 2001 *Area:* 289,220 km2
Comté ou district: Des Appalaches; *Population au 2011:* 2,643
Circonscription(s) électorale(s) provinciale(s): Frontenac
Circonscription(s) électorale(s) fédérale(s): Mégantic-L'Érable
Prochaines élections: 3e novembre 2013
René Gosselin, Maire
Jean-Rock Turgeon, Directeur général

Aguanish
CP 47
106, rte Jacques-Cartier
Aguanish, QC G0G 1A0
Tél: 418-533-2323; *Téléc:* 418-533-2012
munag@xplornet.com
Entité municipal: Municipality
Incorporation: 1er janvier 1957 *Area:* 594,40 km2
Comté ou district: Minganie; *Population au 2011:* 278
Circonscription(s) électorale(s) provinciale(s): Duplessis
Circonscription(s) électorale(s) fédérale(s): Manicouagan
Prochaines élections: 3e novembre 2013
Richard Noël, Maire
Bernard Déraps, Directeur général

Akulivik
CP 50
Akulivik, QC J0M 1V0
Tél: 819-496-2222; *Téléc:* 819-496-2200
www.nvakulivik.ca
Entité municipal: Northern Village
Incorporation: 29 décembre 1979 *Area:* 79,37 km2
Comté ou district: Administration régionale Kativik; *Population au 2011:* 615
Circonscription(s) électorale(s) provinciale(s): Ungava
Circonscription(s) électorale(s) fédérale(s): Abitibi-Baie-James-Nunavik-Eeyou
Prochaines élections: 3e novembre 2013
Lucasi Alayco, Maire
Lydia Nappatuk, Directrice

Albanel
160, rue Principale
Albanel, QC G8M 3J5
Tél: 418-279-5250; *Téléc:* 418-279-3147
info@albanel.ca
www.albanel.ca
Entité municipal: Municipality
Incorporation: 11 avril 1990 *Area:* 195,69 km2
Comté ou district: Maria-Chapdelaine; *Population au 2011:* 2,293
Circonscription(s) électorale(s) provinciale(s): Roberval
Circonscription(s) électorale(s) fédérale(s): Roberval—Lac-Saint-Jean
Prochaines élections: 3e novembre 2013
Évangéline Plourde, Mairesse
Réjean Hudon, Directeur général

Albertville
CP 9
1058, rue Principale
Albertville, QC G0J 1A0
Tél: 418-756-3554; *Téléc:* 418-756-3554
albertville@mrcmatapedia.qc.ca
Entité municipal: Municipality
Incorporation: 29 novembre 1930 *Area:* 104,55 km2
Comté ou district: La Matapédia; *Population au 2011:* 256
Circonscription(s) électorale(s) provinciale(s): Matapédia
Circonscription(s) électorale(s) fédérale(s): Haute-Gaspésie-La Mitis-Matane-Matapédia
Prochaines élections: 3e novembre 2013
Martin Landry, Maire

Claire Sénéchal, Directrice-générale

Alleyn-et-Cawood
10, ch Jondée
Alleyn-et-Cawood, QC J0X 1P0
Tél: 819-467-2941; *Téléc:* 819-467-3133
administration@municipalite.alleyn-et-cawood.qc.ca
Entité municipal: United Township (Cantons)
Incorporation: 1er janvier 1877 *Area:* 346,64 km2
Comté ou district: Pontiac; *Population au 2011:* 168
Circonscription(s) électorale(s) provinciale(s): Pontiac
Circonscription(s) électorale(s) fédérale(s): Pontiac
Prochaines élections: 3e novembre 2013
Charlene Scharf-Lafleur, Mairesse
Annie Beauregard, Directrice générale

Amherst
CP 30
124, rue St-Louis
Amherst, QC J0T 2L0
Tél: 819-687-3355; *Téléc:* 819-687-8430
bdavidson@municipalite.amherst.qc.ca
Entité municipal: Township
Incorporation: 9e mars 1887 *Area:* 260,82 km2
Comté ou district: Les Laurentides; *Population au 2011:* 1,524
Circonscription(s) électorale(s) provinciale(s): Labelle
Circonscription(s) électorale(s) fédérale(s): Laurentides-Labelle
Prochaines élections: 3e novembre 2013
Bernard Lapointe, Maire
Bernard Davidson, Directeur général

Amqui
20, promenade de l'Hôtel-de-Ville
Amqui, QC G5J 1A1
Tél: 418-629-4242; *Téléc:* 418-629-4090
administration@ville.amqui.qc.ca
www.matapedia.net/amqui
Entité municipal: Town
Incorporation: 16 janvier 1991 *Area:* 127,90 km2
Comté ou district: La Matapédia; *Population au 2011:* 6,322
Circonscription(s) électorale(s) provinciale(s): Matapédia
Circonscription(s) électorale(s) fédérale(s): Haute-Gaspésie-La Mitis-Matane-Matapédia
Prochaines élections: 3e novembre 2013
Gaëtan Ruest, Maire
Marie-Claude Gagnon, Greffière

Ange-Gardien
249, rue St-Joseph
Ange-Gardien, QC J0E 1E0
Tél: 450-293-7575; *Téléc:* 450-293-6635
municipalite.ange-gardien@videotron.ca
Entité municipal: Municipality
Incorporation: 31 décembre 1997 *Area:* 89,07 km2
Comté ou district: Rouville; *Population au 2011:* 2,420
Circonscription(s) électorale(s) provinciale(s): Iberville
Circonscription(s) électorale(s) fédérale(s): Shefford
Prochaines élections: 3e novembre 2013
Odette Ménard, Mairesse
Robert Taylor, Directeur général

Angliers
CP 9
14, rue de la Baie Miller
Angliers, QC J0Z 1A0
Tél: 819-949-4351; *Téléc:* 819-949-4351
angliers@lino.com
Entité municipal: Village
Incorporation: 24 mai 1945 *Area:* 378,20 km2
Comté ou district: Témiscamingue; *Population au 2011:* 298
Circonscription(s) électorale(s) provinciale(s):
Rouyn-Noranda-Témiscamingue
Circonscription(s) électorale(s) fédérale(s):
Abitibi-Témiscamingue
Prochaines élections: 3e novembre 2013
Lyne Pine, Mairesse
Micheline Champoux, Directrice générale

Antoine-Labelle
425, rue du Pont
Mont-Laurier, QC J9L 2R6
Tél: 819-623-3485; *Téléc:* 819-623-5052
administration@mrc-antoine-labelle.qc.ca
www.mrc-antoine-labelle.qc.ca
Entité municipal: Regional County Municipality
Population au 2011: 35,159
Note: 17 municipalités & 11 autres territoires.
Roger Lapointe, Préfet
Jackline Williams, Directrice générale

Argenteuil
430, rue Grace
Lachute, QC J8H 1M6
Tél: 450-562-2474; *Téléc:* 450-562-1911
mrc@argenteuil.qc.ca
www.argenteuil.qc.ca
Entité municipal: Regional County Municipality
Population au 2011: 32,117
Note: 9 municipalités.
Ronald Tittlit, Préfet
Marc Carrière, Directeur général
mcarriere@argenteuil.qc.ca

Armagh
CP 87
5, rue de la Salle
Armagh, QC G0R 1A0
Tél: 418-466-2916; *Téléc:* 418-466-2409
www.armagh.ca
Entité municipal: Municipality
Incorporation: 29 décembre 1993 *Area:* 168,15 km2
Comté ou district: Bellechasse; *Population au 2011:* 1,491
Circonscription(s) électorale(s) provinciale(s): Bellechasse
Circonscription(s) électorale(s) fédérale(s): Lévis-Bellechasse
Prochaines élections: 3e novembre 2013
Guylain Chamberland, Maire
Sylvie Vachon, Directrice générale

Arthabaska
40, rte de la Grande-Ligne
Victoriaville, QC G6T 0E6
Tél: 819-752-2444; *Téléc:* 819-752-3623
info@mrc-arthabaska.qc.ca
www.mrc-arthabaska.qc.ca
Entité municipal: Regional County Municipality
Population au 2011: 69,237
Note: 24 municipalités.
Lionel Fréchette, Préfet
Frédérick Michaud, Directeur général

Arundel
2, rue du Village
Arundel, QC J0T 1A0
Tél: 819-687-3991; *Téléc:* 819-687-8760
info@municipalite.arundel.qc.ca
Entité municipal: Township
Incorporation: 1er janvier 1878 *Area:* 64,43 km2
Comté ou district: Les Laurentides; *Population au 2011:* 604
Circonscription(s) électorale(s) provinciale(s): Argenteuil
Circonscription(s) électorale(s) fédérale(s): Laurentides-Labelle
Prochaines élections: 3e novembre 2013
Johanna Earle, Mairesse
Bernice Goulet, Directrice générale

Asbestos
185, rue du Roi
Asbestos, QC J1T 1S4
Tél: 819-879-7171; *Téléc:* 819-879-2343
adm.mun@ville.asbestos.qc.ca
www.ville.asbestos.qc.ca
Entité municipal: Town
Incorporation: 8e décembre 1999 *Area:* 29,55 km2
Comté ou district: Des Sources; *Population au 2011:* 7,096
Circonscription(s) électorale(s) provinciale(s): Richmond
Circonscription(s) électorale(s) fédérale(s):
Richmond-Arthabaska
Prochaines élections: 3e novembre 2013
Hugues Grimard, Maire
adm.mun@ville.asbestos.qc.ca
Georges-André Gagné, Directeur général
gagagne@ville.asbestos.qc.ca

Ascot Corner
5655, rte 112
Ascot-Corner, QC J0B 1A0
Tél: 819-566-5436; *Téléc:* 819-566-8526
ascot.corner@hsfqc.ca
www.ascot-corner.qc.ca
Entité municipal: Municipality
Incorporation: 28 mars 1901 *Area:* 83,38 km2
Comté ou district: Le Haut-St-François; *Population au 2011:* 2,891
Circonscription(s) électorale(s) provinciale(s):
Mégantic-Compton
Circonscription(s) électorale(s) fédérale(s): Compton-Stanstead
Prochaines élections: 3e novembre 2013
Fabien Morin, Maire
Daniel St-Onge, Directeur général
daniel.st-onge@hsfqc.ca

Aston-Jonction
1300, rue Principale
Aston-Jonction, QC G0Z 1A0
Tél: 819-226-3459; *Téléc:* 819-226-3459
mun.astonjonction@lino.com
www.municipalite.aston-jonction.qc.ca
Entité municipal: Municipality
Incorporation: 26 mars 1997 *Area:* 26,43 km2
Comté ou district: Nicolet-Yamaska; *Population au 2011:* 410
Circonscription(s) électorale(s) provinciale(s): Nicolet-Yamaska
Circonscription(s) électorale(s) fédérale(s):
Bas-Richelieu-Nicolet-Bécancour
Prochaines élections: 3e novembre 2013
Pierre Gaudet, Maire
Jacqueline Leblanc, Directrice générale

Auclair
773A, rue du Clocher
Auclair, QC G0L 1A0
Tél: 418-899-2834; *Téléc:* 418-899-6958
info@municipaliteauclair.ca
Entité municipal: Municipality
Incorporation: 1er janvier 1954 *Area:* 106,66 km2
Comté ou district: Témiscouata; *Population au 2011:* 444
Circonscription(s) électorale(s) provinciale(s):
Kamouraska-Témiscouata
Circonscription(s) électorale(s) fédérale(s):
Rimouski-Neigette-Témiscouata-Les-Basques
Prochaines élections: 3e novembre 2013
Jean-Guy Robert, Maire
Ryna St-Pierre, Directrice générale

Audet
CP 27
266, rue Principale
Audet, QC G0Y 1A0
Tél: 819-583-1596; *Téléc:* 819-583-1596
munaudet@axion.ca
Entité municipal: Municipality
Incorporation: 26 novembre 1903 *Area:* 132,86 km2
Comté ou district: Le Granit; *Population au 2011:* 724
Circonscription(s) électorale(s) provinciale(s):
Mégantic-Compton
Circonscription(s) électorale(s) fédérale(s): Mégantic-L'Érable
Prochaines élections: 3e novembre 2013
André Grenier, Maire
France Larochelle, Directrice générale

Aumond
679, rte Principale
Aumond, QC J0W 1W0
Tél: 819-449-4006; *Téléc:* 819-449-7448
mun.aumond@lino.com
Entité municipal: Township
Incorporation: 12 décembre 1877 *Area:* 215,12 km2
Comté ou district: La Vallée-de-la-Gatineau; *Population au 2011:* 725
Circonscription(s) électorale(s) provinciale(s): Gatineau
Circonscription(s) électorale(s) fédérale(s): Pontiac
Prochaines élections: 3e novembre 2013
Denis Charron, Maire
Rénald Mongrain, Directeur général

Aupaluk
CP 4
Aupaluk, QC J0M 1X0
Tél: 819-491-7070; *Téléc:* 819-491-7035
sectre@nvaupaluk.ca
www.nvaupaluk.ca
Entité municipal: Northern Village
Incorporation: 2e février 1980 *Area:* 32,93 km2
Comté ou district: Administration régionale Kativik; *Population au 2011:* 195
Circonscription(s) électorale(s) provinciale(s): Ungava
Circonscription(s) électorale(s) fédérale(s):
Abitibi-Baie-James-Nunavik-Eeyou
Prochaines élections: 3e novembre 2013
David Lucassie, Maire
Jessica Kulula, Directrice générale

Austin
21, ch Millington
Austin, QC J0B 1B0
Tél: 819-843-2388; *Téléc:* 819-843-8211
dg_@municipalite.austin.qc.ca
Entité municipal: Municipality
Incorporation: 5 novembre 1938 *Area:* 72,62 km2
Comté ou district: Memphrémagog; *Population au 2011:* 1,880
Circonscription(s) électorale(s) provinciale(s): Brome-Missisquoi
Circonscription(s) électorale(s) fédérale(s): Brome-Missisquoi
Prochaines élections: 3e novembre 2013
Roger Nicolet, Maire

Anne-Marie Ménard, Directrice générale

Authier
605, av Principale
Authier, QC J0Z 1C0
Tél: 819-782-3093; *Téléc:* 819-782-3203
authier.ao.ca
Entité municipal: Municipality
Incorporation: 20 septembre 1918 *Area:* 139,72 km2
Comté ou district: Abitibi-Ouest; *Population au 2011:* 282
Circonscription(s) électorale(s) provinciale(s): Abitibi Ouest
Circonscription(s) électorale(s) fédérale(s):
Abitibi-Témiscamingue
Prochaines élections: 3e novembre 2013
Pierre Lambert, Maire
Louise Lambert, Directrice générale

Authier-Nord
452, rue Principale
Authier-Nord, QC J0Z 1E0
Tél: 819-782-3914; *Téléc:* 819-782-3914
authier-nord@mrcao.qc.ca
authier-nord.ao.ca
Entité municipal: Municipality
Incorporation: 1er janvier 1983 *Area:* 289,79 km2
Comté ou district: Abitibi-Ouest; *Population au 2011:* 273
Circonscription(s) électorale(s) provinciale(s): Abitibi-Ouest
Circonscription(s) électorale(s) fédérale(s):
Abitibi-Témiscamingue
Prochaines élections: 3e novembre 2013
Alain Gagnon, Maire
Élyse Gagnon, Directrice générale

Avignon
CP 128
470, rue Francoeur
Nouvelle, QC G0C 2E0
Tél: 418-794-2221; *Téléc:* 418-794-2076
info@mrcavignon.com
www.mrcavignon.com
Entité municipal: Regional County Municipality
Incorporation: 18 mars 1981
Population au 2011: 15,246
Note: 11 municipalités & 2 autres territoires.
Bertrand Berger, Préfet
Gaétan Bernatchez, Directeur général
gaetan.bernatchez@mrcavigon.com

Ayer's Cliff
958, rue Main
Ayer's Cliff, QC J0B 1C0
Tél: 819-838-5006; *Téléc:* 819-838-4411
ayerclif@abacom.com
Entité municipal: Village
Incorporation: 24 février 1909 *Area:* 11,15 km2
Comté ou district: Memphrémagog; *Population au 2011:* 1,109
Circonscription(s) électorale(s) provinciale(s): Orford
Circonscription(s) électorale(s) fédérale(s): Compton-Stanstead
Prochaines élections: 3e novembre 2013
Vincent Gérin, Maire
Ghislaine Poulin-Doherty, Directrice générale

Baie-D'Urfé
20410, ch Lakeshore
Baie-D'Urfé, QC H9X 1P7
Tél: 514-457-5324; *Téléc:* 514-457-5671
info@baie-durfe.qc.ca
www.baie-durfe.qc.ca
Entité municipal: Town
Incorporation: 1er janvier 2006 *Area:* 6,70 km2
Population au 2011: 3,850
Circonscription(s) électorale(s) provinciale(s): Jacques-Cartier
Circonscription(s) électorale(s) fédérale(s): Lac-Saint-Louis
Prochaines élections: 3e novembre 2013
Maria Tutino, Mairesse
mtutino@baie-durfe.qc.ca
Nathalie Hadida, Greffière

Baie-des-Sables
CP 39
20, rue du Couvent
Baie-des-Sables, QC G0J 1C0
Tél: 418-772-6218; *Téléc:* 418-772-6455
infobaiedessables@lac-megantic.qc.ca
www.baiedessables.com
Entité municipal: Municipality
Incorporation: 1er janvier 1859 *Area:* 64,54 km2
Comté ou district: Matane; *Population au 2011:* 609
Circonscription(s) électorale(s) provinciale(s): Matane
Circonscription(s) électorale(s) fédérale(s): Haute-Gaspésie-La Mitis-Matane-Matapédia
Prochaines élections: 3e novembre 2013
Denis Santerre, Maire
Adam Coulombe, Directeur général

Baie-du-Febvre
CP 10
298, rte Marie-Victorin
Baie-du-Febvre, QC J0G 1A0
Tél: 450-783-6422; *Téléc:* 450-783-6423
municipalite@baie-du-febvre.net
www.baie-du-febvre.net
Entité municipal: Municipality
Incorporation: 26 mars 1983 *Area:* 96,04 km2
Comté ou district: Nicolet-Yamaska; *Population au 2011:* 1,010
Circonscription(s) électorale(s) provinciale(s): Nicolet-Yamaska
Circonscription(s) électorale(s) fédérale(s):
Bas-Richelieu-Nicolet-Bécancour
Prochaines élections: 3e novembre 2013
Claude Biron, Maire
450-783-6735
Maryse Baril, Directeur général

Baie-James
CP 500
110, boul de Matagami
Matagami, QC J0Y 2A0
Tél: 819-739-2030; *Téléc:* 819-739-2713
municipalite@baie-james.net
municipalite.baie-james.qc.ca
Entité municipal: Municipality
Incorporation: 14 juillet 1971 *Area:* 333 255,55 km2
Population au 2011: 1,303
Circonscription(s) électorale(s) provinciale(s): Ungava
Circonscription(s) électorale(s) fédérale(s):
Abitibi-Baie-James-Nunavik-Eeyou
Prochaines élections: 3e novembre 2013
Gérald Lemoyne, Maire
Stéphane Simard, Greffier

Baie-Johan-Beetz
20, rue Johan-Beetz
Baie-Johan-Beetz, QC G0G 1B0
Tél: 418-539-0125; *Téléc:* 418-539-0205
munbjb@globetrotter.net
Entité municipal: Municipality
Incorporation: 1er janvier 1966 *Area:* 425,31 km2
Comté ou district: Minganie; *Population au 2011:* 81
Circonscription(s) électorale(s) provinciale(s): Duplessis
Circonscription(s) électorale(s) fédérale(s): Manicouagan
Prochaines élections: 3e novembre 2013
Martin Côté, Maire
Sylvain Roy, Directeur général

Baie-Saint-Paul
15, rue Forget
Baie-Saint-Paul, QC G3Z 3G1
Tél: 418-435-2205; *Téléc:* 418-435-2688
ville@baiesaintpaul.com
www.baiesaintpaul.com
Entité municipal: Town
Incorporation: 3e janvier 1996 *Area:* 546,73 km2
Comté ou district: Charlevoix; *Population au 2011:* 7,332
Circonscription(s) électorale(s) provinciale(s): Charlevoix
Circonscription(s) électorale(s) fédérale(s):
Montmorency-Charlevoix-Haute-Côte-Nord
Prochaines élections: 3e novembre 2013
Jean Fortin, Maire
Émilien Bouchard, Greffier

Baie-Ste-Catherine
CP 10
308, rue Leclerc
Baie-Sainte-Catherine, QC G0T 1A0
Tél: 418-237-4241; *Téléc:* 418-237-4223
municipalite@baiestecatherine.com
baiestecatherine.com
Entité municipal: Municipality
Incorporation: 4e novembre 1903 *Area:* 232,16 km2
Comté ou district: Charlevoix-Est; *Population au 2011:* 204
Circonscription(s) électorale(s) provinciale(s): Charlevoix
Circonscription(s) électorale(s) fédérale(s):
Montmorency-Charlevoix-Haute-Côte-Nord
Prochaines élections: 3e novembre 2013
Albert Boulianne, Maire
Brigitte Boulianne, Directrice générale

Baie-Trinité
CP 100
28, rte 138
Baie-Trinité, QC G0H 1A0
Tél: 418-939-2231; *Téléc:* 418-939-2616
municipalite.baie.trinite@globetrotter.net
Entité municipal: Village
Incorporation: 1er janvier 1955 *Area:* 536,33 km2
Comté ou district: Manicouagan; *Population au 2011:* 419
Circonscription(s) électorale(s) provinciale(s): René-Lévesque
Circonscription(s) électorale(s) fédérale(s): Manicouagan
Prochaines élections: 3e novembre 2013
Denis Lejeune, Maire
Manon Comeau, Greffière

Barkmere
CP 11
182, ch de Barkmere
Barkmere, QC J0T 1A0
Tél: 819-687-3373; *Téléc:* 819-687-3383
dg@barkmere.org
www.barkmere.org
Entité municipal: Village
Incorporation: 24 mars 1926 *Area:* 18,07 km2
Comté ou district: Les Laurentides; *Population au 2011:* 58
Circonscription(s) électorale(s) provinciale(s): Argenteuil
Circonscription(s) électorale(s) fédérale(s): Laurentides-Labelle
Prochaines élections: 3e novembre 2013
Luc Trépanier, Maire
Caroline Dion, Directrice générale

Barnston-Ouest
741, ch Hunter
Ayer's Cliff, QC J0B 1C0
Tél: 819-838-4334; *Téléc:* 819-838-1717
barnston.ouest@xittel.ca
barnston-ouest.ca
Entité municipal: Municipality
Incorporation: 1er janvier 1946 *Area:* 97,90 km2
Comté ou district: Coaticook; *Population au 2011:* 591
Circonscription(s) électorale(s) provinciale(s): Orford
Circonscription(s) électorale(s) fédérale(s): Compton-Stanstead
Prochaines élections: 3e novembre 2013
Ghislaine Leblond, Mairesse
Manon Bergeron, Directrice générale

Barraute
CP 299
481, 8e Av
Barraute, QC J0Y 1A0
Tél: 819-734-6574; *Téléc:* 819-734-5186
mun.barraute@cableamos.com
Entité municipal: Municipality
Incorporation: 5e janvier 1994 *Area:* 495,51 km2
Comté ou district: Abitibi; *Population au 2011:* 1,980
Circonscription(s) électorale(s) provinciale(s): Abitibi-Est
Circonscription(s) électorale(s) fédérale(s):
Abitibi-Témiscamingue
Prochaines élections: 3e novembre 2013
Lionel Pelchat, Maire
Richard Nantel, Directeur général

Batiscan
395, rue Principale
Batiscan, QC G0X 1A0
Tél: 418-362-2421; *Téléc:* 418-362-3174
municipalite@batiscan.ca
www.batiscan.ca
Entité municipal: Municipality
Incorporation: 1er juillet 1855 *Area:* 44,02 km2
Comté ou district: Les Chenaux; *Population au 2011:* 940
Circonscription(s) électorale(s) provinciale(s): Champlain
Circonscription(s) électorale(s) fédérale(s):
St-Maurice-Champlain
Prochaines élections: 3e novembre 2013
Christian Fortin, Maire
Johanne Faucher, Directrice générale

Béarn
CP 369
28, 2e rue nord
Béarn, QC J0Z 1G0
Tél: 819-726-4121; *Téléc:* 819-726-2121
dg.bearn@mrctemiscamingue.qc.ca
www.temiscamingue.net/bearn
Entité municipal: Municipality
Incorporation: 3e octobre 1912 *Area:* 566,48 km2
Comté ou district: Témiscamingue; *Population au 2011:* 775
Circonscription(s) électorale(s) provinciale(s):
Rouyn-Noranda-Témiscamingue
Circonscription(s) électorale(s) fédérale(s):
Abitibi-Témiscamingue
Prochaines élections: 3e novembre 2013
Luc Lalonde, Maire
Lynda Gaudet, Directrice générale

Beauce-Sartigan
2727, 6e Av
Saint-Georges, QC G5Y 3Y1
Tél: 418-228-8418; *Téléc:* 418-228-3709
mrcbsart@globetrotter.net
Entité municipal: Regional County Municipality
Population au 2011: 50,962
Note: 16 municipalités.
Luc Lemieux, Préfet
Éric Paquet, Directeur général

Beauceville
540, boul Renault
Beauceville, QC G5X 1N1
Tél: 418-774-9137; *Téléc:* 418-774-9141
beauceville@ville.beauceville.qc.ca
www.ville.beauceville.qc.ca
Entité municipal: Town
Incorporation: 25 février 1998 *Area:* 167,76 km2
Comté ou district: Robert-Cliche; *Population au 2011:* 6,354
Circonscription(s) électorale(s) provinciale(s): Beauce-Nord
Circonscription(s) électorale(s) fédérale(s): Beauce
Prochaines élections: 3e novembre 2013
Luc Provençal, Maire
Madeleine Poulin, Greffière

Beauharnois-Salaberry
#200, 660, rue Ellice
Beauharnois, QC J6N 1Y1
Tél: 450-225-0870; *Téléc:* 450-225-0872
info@mrc-beauharnois-salaberry.com
www.mrc-beauharnois-salaberry.com
Entité municipal: Regional County Municipality
Population au 2011: 61,950
Note: 7 municipalités.
Yves Daoust, Préfet
Linda Phaneuf, Directrice générale
l.phaneuf@mrc-beauharnois-salaberry.com

Beaulac-Garthby
96, rte 112
Beaulac-Garthby, QC G0Y 1B0
Tél: 418-458-2375; *Téléc:* 418-458-1127
municipalitedebeaulac@bellnet.ca
www.beaulac-garthby.com
Entité municipal: Municipality
Incorporation: 15 mars 2000 *Area:* 76,81 km2
Comté ou district: Des Appalaches; *Population au 2011:* 878
Circonscription(s) électorale(s) provinciale(s): Richmond
Circonscription(s) électorale(s) fédérale(s): Mégantic-L'Érable
Prochaines élections: 3e novembre 2013
Loic Lenoir, Maire
Cynthia Gagné, Directrice générale

Beaumont
48, ch du Domaine
Beaumont, QC G0R 1C0
Tél: 418-833-3369; *Téléc:* 418-833-4788
info.generale@municipalite.beaumont.qc.ca
www.municipalitedebeaumont.com
Entité municipal: Municipality
Incorporation: 1er juillet 1855 *Area:* 45,29 km2
Comté ou district: Bellechasse; *Population au 2011:* 2,420
Circonscription(s) électorale(s) provinciale(s): Bellechasse
Circonscription(s) électorale(s) fédérale(s): Lévis-Bellechasse
Prochaines élections: 3e novembre 2013
André Goulet, Maire
Patrice Bissonnette, Directeur général

Beaupré
216, rue Prévost
Beaupré, QC G0A 1E0
Tél: 418-827-4541; *Téléc:* 418-827-3818
mairie@ville.beaupre.qc.ca
www.ville.beaupre.qc.ca
Entité municipal: Town
Incorporation: 23 avril 1928 *Area:* 22,53 km2
Comté ou district: La Côte-de-Beaupré; *Population au 2011:* 3,439
Circonscription(s) électorale(s) provinciale(s): Charlevoix
Circonscription(s) électorale(s) fédérale(s):
Montmorency-Charlevoix-Haute-Côte-Nord
Prochaines élections: 3e novembre 2013
Michel Paré, Maire
Johanne Gagnon, Greffière

Bécancour
#1, 3689, boul Bécancour
Bécancour, QC G9H 3W7
Tél: 819-298-2070; *Téléc:* 819-298-2041
info@mrcbecancour.qc.ca
Entité municipal: Regional County Municipality
Incorporation: 1er janvier 1982
Population au 2011: 20,081
Note: 12 municipalités.
Maurice Richard, Préfet
Laval Dubois, Directeur général
l.dubois@mrcbecancour.qc.ca

Bedford
237, rte 202 est
Canton de Bedford, QC J0J 1A0
Tél: 450-248-7576; *Téléc:* 450-248-0135
canton.bedford@qc.aira.com
www.cantondebedford.ca
Entité municipal: Township
Incorporation: 4e mars 1919 *Area:* 31,06 km2
Comté ou district: Brome-Missisquoi; *Population au 2011:* 699
Circonscription(s) électorale(s) provinciale(s): Brome-Missisquoi
Circonscription(s) électorale(s) fédérale(s): Brome-Missisquoi
Prochaines élections: 3e novembre 2013
Gilles St-Jean, Maire
Linda Payment, Directrice générale

Bedford
1, rue Principale
Bedford, QC J0J 1A0
Tél: 450-248-0550; *Téléc:* 450-248-3220
corpobedford@bellnet.ca
www.bedfordplus.com
Entité municipal: Town
Incorporation: 21 novembre 1866 *Area:* 4,57 km2
Comté ou district: Brome-Missisquoi; *Population au 2011:* 2,684
Circonscription(s) électorale(s) provinciale(s): Brome-Missisquoi
Circonscription(s) électorale(s) fédérale(s): Brome-Missisquoi
Prochaines élections: 3e novembre 2013
Claude Dubois, Maire
Yvon Labonté, Directeur général

Bégin
126, rue Brassard
Bégin, QC G0V 1B0
Tél: 418-672-4270; *Téléc:* 418-672-6161
munbegin@hotmail.com
www.begin.ca
Entité municipal: Municipality
Incorporation: 8e février 1922 *Area:* 191,81 km2
Comté ou district: Le Fjord-du-Saguenay; *Population au 2011:* 868
Circonscription(s) électorale(s) provinciale(s): Dubuc
Circonscription(s) électorale(s) fédérale(s): Jonquière-Alma
Prochaines élections: 3e novembre 2013
Gérald Savard, Maire
Peggy Lemieux, Directrice générale

Belcourt
CP 22
219, rue Communautaire
Belcourt, QC J0Y 2M0
Tél: 819-737-8894; *Téléc:* 819-737-8894
g.m.a@munbelcourt.ca
Entité municipal: Municipality
Incorporation: 24 octobre 1918 *Area:* 411,23 km2
Comté ou district: La Vallée-de-l'Or; *Population au 2011:* 239
Circonscription(s) électorale(s) provinciale(s): Abitibi-Est
Circonscription(s) électorale(s) fédérale(s):
Abitibi-Baie-James-Nunavik-Eeyou
Prochaines élections: 3e novembre 2013
Carol Nolet, Maire
Nathalie Lizotte, Directrice

Bellechasse
100, rue Monseigneur-Bilodeau
Saint-Lazare-de-Bellechasse, QC G0R 3J0
Tél: 418-883-3347; *Téléc:* 418-883-2555
clement@mrcbellechasse.qc.ca
www.mrcbellechasse.qc.ca
Entité municipal: Regional County Municipality
Incorporation: 1er janvier 1982
Population au 2011: 35,318
Note: 20 municipalités.
Hervé Blais, Préfet
Clément Fillion, Directeur général
clement@mrcbellechasse.qc.ca

Belleterre
CP 130
265, 1re av
Belleterre, QC J0Z 1L0
Tél: 819-722-2122; *Téléc:* 819-722-2527
villebelleterre@hotmail.com
Entité municipal: Village
Incorporation: 13 mai 1942 *Area:* 606,33 km2
Comté ou district: Témiscamingue; *Population au 2011:* 298
Circonscription(s) électorale(s) provinciale(s):
Rouyn-Noranda-Témiscamingue
Circonscription(s) électorale(s) fédérale(s):
Abitibi-Témiscamingue
Prochaines élections: 3e novembre 2013
Bruno Boyer, Maire
Liliane Rochon, Directrice générale

Berry
274, rte 399
Berry, QC J0Y 2G0
Tél: 819-732-1815; *Téléc:* 819-732-3289
direction.berry@mrcabitibi.qc.ca
Entité municipal: Municipality
Incorporation: 1er janvier 1982 *Area:* 583,36 km2
Comté ou district: Abitibi; *Population au 2011:* 625
Circonscription(s) électorale(s) provinciale(s): Abitibi-Ouest
Circonscription(s) électorale(s) fédérale(s):
Abitibi-Témiscamingue
Prochaines élections: 3e novembre 2013
Jean-Pierre Naud, Maire
Sandra Boutin, Directrice générale

Berthier-sur-Mer
5, rue du Couvent
Berthier-sur-Mer, QC G0R 1E0
Tél: 418-259-7343; *Téléc:* 418-259-2038
berthier-sur-mer@montmagny.com
www.berthiersurmer.ca
Entité municipal: Municipality
Incorporation: 1er juillet 1855 *Area:* 26,05 km2
Comté ou district: Montmagny; *Population au 2011:* 1,398
Circonscription(s) électorale(s) provinciale(s): Montmagny-L'Islet
Circonscription(s) électorale(s) fédérale(s):
Montmagny-L'Islet-Kamouraska-Rivière-du-Loup
Prochaines élections: 3e novembre 2013
Rosario Bossé, Maire
Suzanne G. Blais, Directrice générale

Berthierville
CP 269
588, rue De Montcalm
Berthierville, QC J0K 1A0
Tél: 450-836-7035; *Téléc:* 450-836-1446
info@ville.berthierville.qc.ca
www.ville.berthierville.qc.ca
Entité municipal: Town
Incorporation: 14 avril 1852 *Area:* 7,20 km2
Comté ou district: D'Autray; *Population au 2011:* 4,091
Circonscription(s) électorale(s) provinciale(s): Berthier
Circonscription(s) électorale(s) fédérale(s): Berthier-Maskinongé
Prochaines élections: 3e novembre 2013
Bernard Grégoire, Maire
Lincoln Le Breton, Greffier

Béthanie
1321, ch de Béthanie
Béthanie, QC J0H 1E1
Tél: 450-548-2826; *Téléc:* 450-548-5693
bethanie@cooptel.qc.ca
municipalite.bethanie.qc.ca
Entité municipal: Municipality
Incorporation: 2e mars 1920 *Area:* 47,29 km2
Comté ou district: Acton; *Population au 2011:* 314
Circonscription(s) électorale(s) provinciale(s): Johnson
Circonscription(s) électorale(s) fédérale(s): St-Hyacinthe-Bagot
Prochaines élections: 3e novembre 2013
Chantal Beauregard Favreau, Mairesse
Heidi Bédard, Directrice générale

Biencourt
CP 70
2, rue St-Marc
Biencourt, QC G0K 1T0
Tél: 418-499-2423; *Téléc:* 418-499-2708
info@biencourt.ca
www.biencourt.ca
Entité municipal: Municipality
Incorporation: 1er janvier 1947 *Area:* 187,80 km2
Comté ou district: Témiscouata; *Population au 2011:* 506
Circonscription(s) électorale(s) provinciale(s): Rimouski
Circonscription(s) électorale(s) fédérale(s):
Rimouski-Neigette-Témiscouata-Les Basques
Prochaines élections: 3e novembre 2013
Daniel Boucher, Maire
Julie Vaillancourt, Directrice générale

Blanc-Sablon
CP 400
1149, boul Dr.-Camille-Marcoux
Lourdes-de-Blanc-Sablon, QC G0G 1W0
Tél: 418-461-2707; *Téléc:* 418-461-2529
mbsablon@globetrotter.net
Entité municipal: Municipality
Incorporation: 1er janvier 1990 *Area:* 254,49 km2
Population au 2011: 1,118
Circonscription(s) électorale(s) provinciale(s): Duplessis
Circonscription(s) électorale(s) fédérale(s): Manicouagan
Prochaines élections: 3e novembre 2013
Anthony Dumas, Maire
Réjean L. Dumas, Directeur général

Blue Sea
CP 99
7, rue Principale
Blue Sea, QC J0X 1C0
Tél: 819-463-2261; *Téléc:* 819-463-4345
info@bluesea.ca
www.bluesea.ca
Entité municipal: Municipality
Incorporation: 31 janvier 1921 *Area:* 76,89 km2
Comté ou district: La Vallée-de-la-Gatineau; *Population au 2011:* 674
Circonscription(s) électorale(s) provinciale(s): Gatineau
Circonscription(s) électorale(s) fédérale(s): Pontiac
Prochaines élections: 3e novembre 2013
Laurent Fortin, Maire
Josée Parsons, Directrice générale

Boileau
702, ch de Boileau
Boileau, QC J0V 1N0
Tél: 819-687-3436; *Téléc:* 819-687-3745
mun.boileau@mrcpapineau.com
www.municipaliteboileau.ca
Entité municipal: Municipality
Incorporation: 8e mars 1882 *Area:* 136,22 km2
Comté ou district: Papineau; *Population au 2011:* 380
Circonscription(s) électorale(s) provinciale(s): Papineau
Circonscription(s) électorale(s) fédérale(s): Argenteuil-Papineau-Mirabel
Prochaines élections: 3e novembre 2013
Henri Gariépy, Maire
Ghyslaine Lauzon, Directrice générale

Bois-des-Filion
375, boul Adophe-Chapleau
Bois-des-Filion, QC J6Z 1H1
Tél: 450-621-1460; *Téléc:* 450-621-8483
ville@ville.bois-des-filion.qc.ca
ville.bois-des-filion.qc.ca
Entité municipal: Town
Incorporation: 1er janvier 1949 *Area:* 4,34 km2
Comté ou district: Thérèse-De Blainville; *Population au 2011:* 9,485
Circonscription(s) électorale(s) provinciale(s): Blainville
Circonscription(s) électorale(s) fédérale(s): Marc-Aurèle-Fortin
Prochaines élections: 3e novembre 2013
Paul Larocque, Maire
Robert L'Africain, Greffière

Bois-Franc
466, rte 105
Bois-Franc, QC J9E 3A9
Tél: 819-449-2252; *Téléc:* 819-449-4407
mun.bois-franc@ireseau.com
www.bois-franc.ca
Entité municipal: Municipality
Incorporation: 17 novembre 1920 *Area:* 73,24 km2
Comté ou district: La Vallée-de-la-Gatineau; *Population au 2011:* 447
Circonscription(s) électorale(s) provinciale(s): Gatineau
Circonscription(s) électorale(s) fédérale(s): Pontiac
Prochaines élections: 3e novembre 2013
Armand Hubert, Maire
Claudette Rochon, Directrice générale

Boischatel
45, rue Bédard
Boischatel, QC G0A 1H0
Tél: 418-822-4500; *Téléc:* 418-822-4512
info@municipalitedeboischatel.ca
www.municipalitedeboischatel.ca
Entité municipal: Municipality
Incorporation: 3e avril 1920 *Area:* 19,64
Comté ou district: La Côte de Beaupré; *Population au 2011:* 6,465
Circonscription(s) électorale(s) provinciale(s): Montmorency
Circonscription(s) électorale(s) fédérale(s): Montmorency-Charlevoix-Haute-Côte-Nord
Prochaines élections: 3e novembre 2013
Yves Germain, Maire
Carl Michaud, Directeur général

Bolton-Est
858, rte Missisquoi
Bolton-Est, QC J0E 1G0
Tél: 450-292-3444; *Téléc:* 450-292-4224
info@boltonest.ca
www.boltonest.ca
Entité municipal: Municipality
Incorporation: 28 décembre 1876 *Area:* 80,78
Comté ou district: Memphrémagog; *Population au 2011:* 910
Circonscription(s) électorale(s) provinciale(s): Brome-Missisquoi
Circonscription(s) électorale(s) fédérale(s): Brome-Missisquoi
Prochaines élections: 3e novembre 2013
Royal Dupuis, Maire
Monique Pépin, Directrice générale (par intérim)

Bolton-Ouest
9, ch Town Hall
Bolton-Ouest, QC J0E 2T0
Tél: 450-242-2704; *Téléc:* 450-242-2705
info@municipalitedeboltonouest.com
www.municipalitedeboltonouest.com
Entité municipal: Municipality
Incorporation: 28 décembre 1876 *Area:* 103,59
Comté ou district: Brome-Missisquoi; *Population au 2011:* 678
Circonscription(s) électorale(s) provinciale(s): Brome-Missisquoi
Circonscription(s) électorale(s) fédérale(s): Brome-Missisquoi
Prochaines élections: 3e novembre 2013
Donald Badger, Maire
Carrol Kralik, Directrice générale

Bonaventure
127, av de Louisbourg
Bonaventure, QC G0C 1E0
Tél: 418-534-2313; *Téléc:* 418-534-4336
adm@bonaventuregaspesie.com
bonaventuregaspesie.com
Entité municipal: Town
Incorporation: 1er janvier 1884 *Area:* 109,20 km2
Comté ou district: Bonaventure; *Population au 2011:* 2,775
Circonscription(s) électorale(s) provinciale(s): Bonaventure
Circonscription(s) électorale(s) fédérale(s): Gaspésie—Îles-de-la-Madeleine
Prochaines élections: 3e novembre 2013
Serge Arsenault, Maire
Rollande Roy, Greffière

Bonaventure
CP 310
51, rue Notre-Dame
New Carlisle, QC G0C 1Z0
Tél: 418-752-6601; *Téléc:* 418-752-6657
mrcbonav@globetrotter.net
www.mrcbonaventure.com
Entité municipal: Regional County Municipality
Incorporation: 8e avril 1981
Population au 2011: 18,000
Note: 13 municipalités & 1 autre territoire.
Jean-Guy Poirier, Préfet
Anne-Marie Flowers, Directrice générale
mrcbonavaflowers@globetrotter.net

Bonne-Espérance
CP 40
100, rue Whiteley
Rivière-Saint-Paul, QC G0G 2P0
Tél: 418-379-2911; *Téléc:* 418-379-2959
bonneesperance@xplornet.com
Entité municipal: Municipality
Incorporation: 1er janvier 1990 *Area:* 721,28 km2
Comté ou district: Le Golfe-du-Saint-Laurent; *Population au 2011:* 732
Circonscription(s) électorale(s) provinciale(s): Duplessis
Circonscription(s) électorale(s) fédérale(s): Manicouagan
Prochaines élections: 3e novembre 2013
Bryce Douglas Fequet, Maire
René Fequet, Directeur général

Bonsecours
691, rte 220
Bonsecours, QC J0E 1H0
Tél: 450-532-3139; *Téléc:* 450-532-3953
mbonsecours@cooptel.qc.ca
www.bonsecours.ca
Entité municipal: Municipality
Incorporation: 20 mars 1905 *Area:* 59,92 km2
Comté ou district: Le Val-St-François; *Population au 2011:* 577
Circonscription(s) électorale(s) provinciale(s): Brome-Missisquoi
Circonscription(s) électorale(s) fédérale(s): Shefford
Prochaines élections: 3e novembre 2013
Cécile Laliberté, Mairesse
Lyne Gaudreau, Directrice générale

Bouchette
CP 59
36, rue Principale
Bouchette, QC J0X 1E0
Tél: 819-465-2555; *Téléc:* 819-465-2318
mun.bouchette@ireseau.com
www.bouchette.ca
Entité municipal: Municipality
Incorporation: 22 mars 1980 *Area:* 131,97 km2
Comté ou district: La Vallée-de-la-Gatineau; *Population au 2011:* 786
Circonscription(s) électorale(s) provinciale(s): Gatineau
Circonscription(s) électorale(s) fédérale(s): Pontiac
Prochaines élections: 3e novembre 2013
Réjean Major, Maire
Claudia Lacroix, Directrice générale

Bowman
214, rte 307
Bowman, QC J0X 3C0
Tél: 819-454-2421; *Téléc:* 819-454-2133
bowman01@mrcpapineau.com
www.bowman.ca
Entité municipal: Municipality
Incorporation: 27 juin 1913 *Area:* 166,99 km2
Comté ou district: Papineau; *Population au 2011:* 677
Circonscription(s) électorale(s) provinciale(s): Papineau
Circonscription(s) électorale(s) fédérale(s): Argenteuil-Papineau-Mirabel
Prochaines élections: 3e novembre 2013
Michel David, Maire
Mylène Groulx, Directrice générale

Brébeuf
217, rte 323
Brébeuf, QC J0T 1B0
Tél: 819-425-9833; *Téléc:* 819-425-6611
secretariat@brebeuf.ca
www.brebeuf.ca
Entité municipal: Parish (Paroisse)
Incorporation: 4e juin 1910 *Area:* 36,71 km2
Comté ou district: Les Laurentides; *Population au 2011:* 1,012
Circonscription(s) électorale(s) provinciale(s): Labelle
Circonscription(s) électorale(s) fédérale(s): Laurentides-Labelle
Prochaines élections: 3e novembre 2013
Ronald Provost, Maire
Pascal Caron, Directeur général

Brigham
118, av des Cèdres
Brigham, QC J2K 4K4
Tél: 450-263-5942; *Téléc:* 450-263-8380
info@brigham.ca
www.brigham.ca
Entité municipal: Municipality
Incorporation: 1er juillet 1855 *Area:* 84,80 km2
Comté ou district: Brome-Missisquoi; *Population au 2011:* 2,457
Circonscription(s) électorale(s) provinciale(s): Brome-Missisquoi
Circonscription(s) électorale(s) fédérale(s): Brome-Missisquoi
Prochaines élections: 3e novembre 2013
Steven Neil, Maire
Jean-François Grandmont, Directeur général

Bristol
32, ch d'Aylmer
Bristol, QC J0X 1G0
Tél: 819-647-5555; *Téléc:* 819-647-2424
info@bristolmunicipality.qc.ca
www.bristolmunicipality.qc.ca
Entité municipal: Municipality
Incorporation: 1er juillet 1855 *Area:* 224,08 km2
Comté ou district: Pontiac; *Population au 2011:* 1,128
Circonscription(s) électorale(s) provinciale(s): Pontiac
Circonscription(s) électorale(s) fédérale(s): Pontiac
Prochaines élections: 3e novembre 2013
Brent Orr, Maire
Christina Peck, Directrice générale

Brome
330, ch Stagecoach
Brome, QC J0E 1K0
Tél: 450-243-0489; *Téléc:* 450-243-1091
bromevillage@axion.ca
Entité municipal: Village
Incorporation: 20 juin 1923 *Area:* 11,75 km2
Comté ou district: Brome-Missisquoi; *Population au 2011:* 271
Circonscription(s) électorale(s) provinciale(s): Brome-Missisquoi

Circonscription(s) électorale(s) fédérale(s): Brome-Missisquoi
Prochaines élections: 3e novembre 2013
L. Thomas Selby, Maire
Paul McKeogh, Directeur général

Brome-Missisquoi
749, rue Principale
Cowansville, QC J2K 1J8
Tél: 450-266-4900; *Téléc:* 450-266-6141
administration@mrcbm.qc.ca
www.brome-missisquoi.ca
Entité municipal: Regional County Municipality
Population au 2011: 55,621
Note: 20 municipalités.
Arthur Fauteux, Préfet
prefet@mrcbm.qc.ca
Robert Desmarais, Directeur général
rdesmarais@mrcbm.qc.ca

Bromont
88, boul de Bromont
Bromont, QC J2L 1A1
Tél: 450-534-2021; *Téléc:* 450-534-1025
ville@bromont.com
www.bromont.com
Entité municipal: Town
Incorporation: 27 janvier 1973 *Area:* 108,36 km2
Comté ou district: Brome-Missisquoi; *Population au 2011:* 7,649
Circonscription(s) électorale(s) provinciale(s): Brome-Missisquoi
Circonscription(s) électorale(s) fédérale(s): Brome-Missisquoi
Prochaines élections: 3e novembre 2013
Pauline Quinlan, Mairesse
Joanne Skelling, Greffière

Brownsburg-Chatham
300, rue de l'Hôtel-de-Ville
Brownsburg-Chatham, QC J8G 3B4
Tél: 450-533-6687; *Téléc:* 450-533-5795
secretariat@brownsburgchatham.ca
www.brownsburgchatham.ca
Entité municipal: Town
Incorporation: 6e octobre 1999 *Area:* 249,31 km2
Comté ou district: Argenteuil; *Population au 2011:* 7,209
Circonscription(s) électorale(s) provinciale(s): Argenteuil
Circonscription(s) électorale(s) fédérale(s):
Argenteuil-Papineau-Mirabel
Prochaines élections: 3e novembre 2013
Georges Dinel, Maire
Marie-Josée Larocque, Greffière

Bryson
CP 190
833, rue Principale
Bryson, QC J0X 1H0
Tél: 819-648-5940; *Téléc:* 819-648-5297
bryson@mrcpontiac.qc.ca
Entité municipal: Municipality
Incorporation: 1er janvier 1873 *Area:* 3,10 km2
Comté ou district: Pontiac; *Population au 2011:* 647
Circonscription(s) électorale(s) provinciale(s): Pontiac
Circonscription(s) électorale(s) fédérale(s): Pontiac
Prochaines élections: 3e novembre 2013
John Griffin, Maire
Tracey Hérault, Directrice générale

Bury
563, rue Main
Bury, QC J0B 1J0
Tél: 819-560-8414; *Téléc:* 819-872-3675
information.bury@hsfqc.ca
www.municipalitedebury.qc.ca
Entité municipal: Municipality
Incorporation: 1er juillet 1855 *Area:* 232,52 km2
Comté ou district: Le Haut-St-François; *Population au 2011:* 1,159
Circonscription(s) électorale(s) provinciale(s):
Mégantic-Compton
Circonscription(s) électorale(s) fédérale(s): Compton-Stanstead
Prochaines élections: 3e novembre 2013
Walter Dougherty, Maire
Suzanne Ménard, Directrice générale

Cacouna
415, rue St-Georges
Cacouna, QC G0L 1G0
Tél: 418-867-1781; *Téléc:* 418-867-5677
municipalite@cacouna.ca
www.cacouna.ca
Entité municipal: Municipality
Incorporation: 22 mars 2006 *Area:* 62,49 km2
Comté ou district: Rivière-du-Loup; *Population au 2011:* 1,939
Circonscription(s) électorale(s) provinciale(s): Rivière-du-Loup
Circonscription(s) électorale(s) fédérale(s):
Montmagny—L'Islet—Kamouraska—Rivière-du-Loup
Prochaines élections: 3e novembre 2013
Ghislaine Daris, Maire
Madeleine Lévesque, Directrice générale

Calixa-Lavallée
771, ch de la Beauce
Calixa-Lavallée, QC J0L 1A0
Tél: 450-583-6470; *Téléc:* 450-583-5508
directeur@calixa-lavallee.ca
www.calixa-lavallee.ca
Entité municipal: Parish (Paroisse)
Incorporation: 24 juillet 1878 *Area:* 32,42 km2
Comté ou district: Marguerite-D'Youville; *Population au 2011:* 504
Circonscription(s) électorale(s) provinciale(s): Verchères
Circonscription(s) électorale(s) fédérale(s): Verchères-Les Patriotes
Prochaines élections: 3e novembre 2013
Claude Jutras, Maire
Alain Beauregard, Directeur général

Campbell's Bay
CP 157
59, rue Leslie
Campbell's Bay, QC J0X 1K0
Tél: 819-648-5811; *Téléc:* 819-648-2045
administration@municipalite.campbellsbay.qc.ca
Entité municipal: Municipality
Incorporation: 23 février 1904 *Area:* 3,08 km2
Comté ou district: Pontiac; *Population au 2011:* 775
Circonscription(s) électorale(s) provinciale(s): Pontiac
Circonscription(s) électorale(s) fédérale(s): Pontiac
Prochaines élections: 3e novembre 2013
William Stewart, Maire
Colleen Larivière, Directrice générale

Cantley
8, ch River
Cantley, QC J8V 2Z9
Tél: 819-827-3434; *Téléc:* 819-827-4328
municipalite@cantley.ca
www.cantley.ca
Entité municipal: Municipality
Incorporation: 1er janvier 1989 *Area:* 134,00 km2
Comté ou district: Les Collines-de-l'Outaouais; *Population au 2011:* 9,888
Circonscription(s) électorale(s) provinciale(s): Gatineau
Circonscription(s) électorale(s) fédérale(s): Pontiac
Prochaines élections: 3e novembre 2013
Steve Harris, Maire
Sylvie Loublier, Greffière

Cap-Chat
CP 279
53, rue Notre-Dame
Cap-Chat, QC G0J 1E0
Tél: 418-786-5537; *Téléc:* 418-786-5540
ville.capchat@globetrotter.net
Entité municipal: Town
Incorporation: 15 mars 2000 *Area:* 183,13 km2
Comté ou district: La Haute-Gaspésie; *Population au 2011:* 2,623
Circonscription(s) électorale(s) provinciale(s): Matane
Circonscription(s) électorale(s) fédérale(s): Haute-Gaspésie-La Mitis-Matane-Matapédia
Prochaines élections: 3e novembre 2013
Judes Landry, Maire
Jacques Fournier, Greffier

Cap-Santé
194, rte 138
Cap-Santé, QC G0A 1L0
Tél: 418-285-1207; *Téléc:* 418-285-0009
villecapsante@globetrotter.net
www.capsante.qc.ca
Entité municipal: Town
Incorporation: 1er juillet 1855 *Area:* 54,38 km2
Comté ou district: Portneuf; *Population au 2011:* 2,996
Circonscription(s) électorale(s) provinciale(s): Portneuf
Circonscription(s) électorale(s) fédérale(s):
Portneuf-Jacques-Cartier
Prochaines élections: 3e novembre 2013
Jean-Yves Nobert, Maire
Jacques Blais, Directeur général

Cap-St-Ignace
850, rte du Souvenir
Cap-Saint-Ignace, QC G0R 1H0
Tél: 418-246-5631; *Téléc:* 418-246-5663
dg@capsaintignace.ca
www.capsaintignace.ca
Entité municipal: Municipality
Incorporation: 1er juillet 1855 *Area:* 227,76 km2
Comté ou district: Montmagny; *Population au 2011:* 3,045
Circonscription(s) électorale(s) provinciale(s): Montmagny-L'Islet
Circonscription(s) électorale(s) fédérale(s):
Montmagny-L'Islet-Kamouraska-Rivière-du-Loup
Prochaines élections: 3e novembre 2013
André Clavet, Maire
Sophie Boucher, Directrice générale

Caplan
CP 360
17, boul Perron est
Caplan, QC G0C 1H0
Tél: 418-388-2075; *Téléc:* 418-388-2429
caplan@globetrotter.net
www.municipalitecaplan.com
Entité municipal: Municipality
Incorporation: 1er janvier 1875 *Area:* 85,05 km2
Comté ou district: Bonaventure; *Population au 2011:* 2,039
Circonscription(s) électorale(s) provinciale(s): Bonaventure
Circonscription(s) électorale(s) fédérale(s):
Gaspésie—Îles-de-la-Madeleine
Prochaines élections: 3e novembre 2013
Doris Boissonnault, Mairesse
Lise Castilloux, Directrice générale

Carignan
2555, ch Bellevue
Carignan, QC J3L 6G8
Tél: 450-658-1066; *Téléc:* 450-658-6079
info@villedecarignan.org
www.villedecarignan.org
Entité municipal: Town
Incorporation: 1er juillet 1855 *Area:* 62,39 km2
Comté ou district: La Vallée-du-Richelieu; *Population au 2011:* 7,966
Circonscription(s) électorale(s) provinciale(s): Chambly
Circonscription(s) électorale(s) fédérale(s): Chambly-Borduas
Prochaines élections: 3e novembre 2013
Louise Lavigne, Mairesse
Rémi Raymond, Greffier

Carleton-sur-Mer
629, boul Perron
Carleton, QC G0C 1J0
Tél: 418-364-7073; *Téléc:* 418-364-6011
direction@carletonsurmer.com
www.carletonsurmer.com
Entité municipal: Town
Incorporation: 4e octobre 2000 *Area:* 214,78 km2
Comté ou district: Avignon; *Population au 2011:* 3,991
Circonscription(s) électorale(s) provinciale(s): Bonaventure
Circonscription(s) électorale(s) fédérale(s):
Gaspésie—Îles-de-la-Madeleine
Prochaines élections: 3e novembre 2013
Denis Henry, Maire
Caroline Asselin, Greffière

Cascapédia-St-Jules
55, rte Gallagher
Cascapédia-Saint-Jules, QC G0C 1T0
Tél: 418-392-4042; *Téléc:* 418-392-6004
cascapediastjules.loisirs@globetrotter.net
Entité municipal: Municipality
Incorporation: 2e juin 1999 *Area:* 168,00 km2
Comté ou district: Bonaventure; *Population au 2011:* 741
Circonscription(s) électorale(s) provinciale(s): Bonaventure
Circonscription(s) électorale(s) fédérale(s):
Gaspésie—Îles-de-la-Madeleine
Prochaines élections: 3e novembre 2013
Pat Saint-Onge, Maire
Susan Legouffe, Directrice générale

Causapscal
1, rue St-Jacques nord
Causapscal, QC G0J 1J0
Tél: 418-756-3444; *Téléc:* 418-756-3344
causapscal@mrcmatapedia.qc.ca
www.causapscal.net
Entité municipal: Town
Incorporation: 31 décembre 1997 *Area:* 163,88 km2
Comté ou district: La Matapédia; *Population au 2011:* 2,458
Circonscription(s) électorale(s) provinciale(s): Matapédia
Circonscription(s) électorale(s) fédérale(s): Haute-Gaspésie-La

Mitis-Matane-Matapédia
Prochaines élections: 3e novembre 2013
Mario Côté, Maire
Jean-Noël Barriault, Directeur général

Cayamant
6, ch Lachapelle
Lac-Cayamant, QC J0X 1Y0
Tél: 819-463-3587; *Téléc:* 819-463-4020
mun.caymant@ireseau.com
Entité municipal: Municipality
Incorporation: 10 octobre 1906 *Area:* 411,13 km2
Comté ou district: La Vallée-de-la-Gatineau; *Population au 2011:* 875
Circonscription(s) électorale(s) provinciale(s): Gatineau
Circonscription(s) électorale(s) fédérale(s): Pontiac
Prochaines élections: 3e novembre 2013
Pierre Pedro Chartrand, Maire
Suzanne Vallières, Directrice générale

Chambord
1526, rue Principale
Chambord, QC G0W 1G0
Tél: 418-342-6274; *Téléc:* 418-342-8438
info@chambord.ca
www.chambord.ca
Entité municipal: Municipality
Incorporation: 8e décembre 1973 *Area:* 157,03 km2
Comté ou district: Le Domaine-du-Roy; *Population au 2011:* 1,773
Circonscription(s) électorale(s) provinciale(s): Roberval
Circonscription(s) électorale(s) fédérale(s):
Roberval-Lac-Saint-Jean
Prochaines élections: 3e novembre 2013
Gérard Savard, Maire
Sylvie Desmeules, Directrice générale

Champlain
CP 250
819, rue Notre-Dame
Champlain, QC G0X 1C0
Tél: 819-295-3979; *Téléc:* 819-295-3032
municipalite.champlain@infoteck.qc.ca
www.municipalite.champlain.qc.ca
Entité municipal: Municipality
Incorporation: 11 décembre 1982 *Area:* 58,59 km2
Comté ou district: Les Chenaux; *Population au 2011:* 1,664
Circonscription(s) électorale(s) provinciale(s): Champlain
Circonscription(s) électorale(s) fédérale(s):
St-Maurice-Champlain
Prochaines élections: 3e novembre 2013
Jean-Robert Barnes, Maire
Jean Houde, Directeur général

Champneuf
12, 6e av nord
Champneuf, QC J0Y 1E0
Tél: 819-754-2053; *Téléc:* 819-754-5749
munichampneuf@cableamos.com
Entité municipal: Municipality
Incorporation: 1er janvier 1964 *Area:* 241,38 km2
Comté ou district: Abitibi; *Population au 2011:* 127
Circonscription(s) électorale(s) provinciale(s): Abitibi-Ouest
Circonscription(s) électorale(s) fédérale(s):
Abitibi-Témiscamingue
Prochaines élections: 3e novembre 2013
Rosaire Guénette, Maire
Josée Beauregard, Directrice générale

Chandler
CP 459
35, rue Commerciale ouest
Chandler, QC G0C 1K0
Tél: 418-689-2221; *Téléc:* 418-689-3073
hdvchan@globetrotter.net
www.villedechandler.com
Entité municipal: Town
Incorporation: 27 juin 2001 *Area:* 424,90 km2
Comté ou district: Le Rocher-Percé; *Population au 2011:* 7,703
Circonscription(s) électorale(s) provinciale(s): Gaspé
Circonscription(s) électorale(s) fédérale(s):
Gaspésie—Îles-de-la-Madeleine
Prochaines élections: 3e novembre 2013
Louisette Langlois, Mairesse
Roch Giroux, Greffier et Directeur général

Chapais
CP 380
145, boul Springer
Chapais, QC G0W 1H0
Tél: 418-745-2511; *Téléc:* 418-745-3871
villedechapais@lino.com
www.villedechapais.com
Entité municipal: Village
Incorporation: 16 novembre 1955 *Area:* 62,78 km2
Population au 2011: 1,610
Circonscription(s) électorale(s) provinciale(s): Ungava
Circonscription(s) électorale(s) fédérale(s):
Abitibi-Baie-James-Nunavik-Eeyou
Prochaines élections: 3e novembre 2013
Steve Gamache, Maire
Yves Blackburn, Greffier

Charette
390, rue St-Édouard
Charette, QC G0X 1E0
Tél: 819-221-2095; *Téléc:* 819-221-3493
municipalitecharette@sogetel.net
Entité municipal: Municipality
Incorporation: 9e février 1918 *Area:* 42,55 km2
Comté ou district: Maskinongé; *Population au 2011:* 993
Circonscription(s) électorale(s) provinciale(s): Maskinongé
Circonscription(s) électorale(s) fédérale(s): Berthier-Maskinongé
Prochaines élections: 3e novembre 2013
Guy Diamond, Maire
Danielle D. Villemure, Directeur général

Charlemagne
84, rue du Sacré-Coeur
Charlemagne, QC J5Z 1W8
Tél: 450-581-2541; *Téléc:* 450-581-0597
info@ville.charlemagne.qc.ca
www.ville.charlemagne.qc.ca
Entité municipal: Town
Incorporation: 13 novembre 1906 *Area:* 1,95 km2
Comté ou district: L'Assomption; *Population au 2011:* 5,853
Circonscription(s) électorale(s) provinciale(s): Masson
Circonscription(s) électorale(s) fédérale(s): Repentigny
Prochaines élections: 3e novembre 2013
Normand Grenier, Maire
Bernard Boudreau, Greffier et Directeur général

Charlevoix
#201, 4, place de l'Église
Baie-Saint-Paul, QC G3Z 1T2
Tél: 418-435-2639; *Téléc:* 418-435-2666
mrc@charlevoix.net
www.mrc-charlevoix.com
Entité municipal: Regional County Municipality
Incorporation: 1er janvier 1982
Population au 2011: 13,338
Note: 6 municipalités & 1 autre territoire.
Dominic Tremblay, Préfet
Karine Horvath, Directrice générale

Charlevoix-Est
172, boul Notre-Dame
Clermont, QC G4A 1G1
Tél: 418-439-3947; *Téléc:* 418-439-2502
direction@mrccharlevoixest.ca
www.mrccharlevoixest.ca
Entité municipal: Regional County Municipality
Incorporation: 1er janvier 1982
Population au 2011: 16,240
Note: 7 municipalités & 2 autres territoires.
Jean-Luc Simard, Préfet
Pierre Girard, Directeur général

Chartierville
27, rue St-Jean-Baptiste
Chartierville, QC J0B 1K0
Tél: 819-560-8522; *Téléc:* 819-560-8523
chartierville@hsfqc.ca
www.chartierville.ca
Entité municipal: Municipality
Incorporation: 1er janvier 1879 *Area:* 139,13 km2
Comté ou district: Le Haut-St-François; *Population au 2011:* 307
Circonscription(s) électorale(s) provinciale(s):
Mégantic-Compton
Circonscription(s) électorale(s) fédérale(s): Compton-Stanstead
Prochaines élections: 3e novembre 2013
Jean Belhumeur, Maire
Maryse Prud'homme, Directrice générale

Château-Richer
8006, av Royale
Château-Richer, QC G0A 1N0
Tél: 418-824-4294; *Téléc:* 418-824-3277
chateau.richer@videotron.ca
www.chateauricher.qc.ca
Entité municipal: Town
Incorporation: 1er juillet 1855 *Area:* 228,99 km2
Comté ou district: La Côte-de-Beaupré; *Population au 2011:* 3,834
Circonscription(s) électorale(s) provinciale(s): Montmorency
Circonscription(s) électorale(s) fédérale(s):
Montmorency-Charlevoix-Haute-Côte-Nord
Prochaines élections: 3e novembre 2013
Frédéric Dancause, Maire
Lucie Gagnon, Greffière

Chazel
752, 1er Avenue ouest
Chazel, QC J0Z 1N0
Tél: 819-333-4758; *Téléc:* 819-333-3818
chazel@mrcao.qc.ca
www.chazel.ao.ca
Entité municipal: Municipality
Incorporation: 19 février 1938 *Area:* 134,57 km2
Comté ou district: Abitibi-Ouest; *Population au 2011:* 289
Circonscription(s) électorale(s) provinciale(s): Abitibi-Ouest
Circonscription(s) électorale(s) fédérale(s):
Abitibi-Témiscamingue
Prochaines élections: 3e novembre 2013
Daniel Favreau, Maire
Sandra Baillargeon, Directrice générale

Chelsea
100, ch d'Old Chelsea
Chelsea, QC J9B 1C1
Tél: 819-827-1124; *Téléc:* 819-827-2672
info@chelsea.ca
www.chelsea.ca
Entité municipal: Municipality
Incorporation: 1er janvier 1875 *Area:* 111,2 km2
Comté ou district: Les Collines-de-l'Outaouais; *Population au 2011:* 6,977
Circonscription(s) électorale(s) provinciale(s): Gatineau
Circonscription(s) électorale(s) fédérale(s): Pontiac
Prochaines élections: 3e novembre 2013
Caryl Green, Maire
Paul St-Louis, Directeur général

Chénéville
63, rue de l'Hôtel-de-Ville
Chénéville, QC J0V 1E0
Tél: 819-428-3583; *Téléc:* 819-428-4838
adm.cheneville@mrcpapineau.com
www.ville.cheneville.qc.ca
Entité municipal: Municipality
Incorporation: 21 août 1996 *Area:* 65,22 km2
Comté ou district: Papineau; *Population au 2011:* 792
Circonscription(s) électorale(s) provinciale(s): Papineau
Circonscription(s) électorale(s) fédérale(s):
Argenteuil-Papineau-Mirabel
Prochaines élections: 3e novembre 2013
Gilles Tremblay, Maire
Suzanne Prévost, Directrice générale

Chertsey
333, av de l'Amitié
Chertsey, QC J0K 3K0
Tél: 450-882-2920; *Téléc:* 450-882-3333
general@municipalite.chertsey.qc.ca
www.municipalite.chertsey.qc.ca
Entité municipal: Municipality
Incorporation: 13 novembre 1991 *Area:* 313,22 km2
Comté ou district: Matawinie; *Population au 2011:* 4,836
Circonscription(s) électorale(s) provinciale(s): Bertrand
Circonscription(s) électorale(s) fédérale(s): Joliette
Prochaines élections: 3e novembre 2013
Jocelyn Gravel, Maire
Pierre Mercier, Directeur général

Chesterville
472, rue de l'Accueil
Chesterville, QC G0P 1J0
Tél: 819-382-2059; *Téléc:* 819-382-2073
info@municipalite.chesterville.qc.ca
Entité municipal: Municipality
Incorporation: 18 décembre 1982 *Area:* 114,89 km2
Comté ou district: Arthabaska; *Population au 2011:* 891
Circonscription(s) électorale(s) provinciale(s): Arthabaska
Circonscription(s) électorale(s) fédérale(s):
Richmond-Arthabaska
Prochaines élections: 3e novembre 2013

Louis Lafleur, Maire
Lise Setlakwe, Directrice générale

Chibougamau
650, 3e rue
Chibougamau, QC G8P 1P1
Tél: 418-748-2688; *Téléc:* 418-748-6562
directiongenerale@ville.chibougamau.qc.ca
www.ville.chibougamau.qc.ca
Entité municipal: Town
Incorporation: 8e novembre 1952 *Area:* 1,041,97 km2
Population au 2011: 7,541
Circonscription(s) électorale(s) provinciale(s): Ungava
Circonscription(s) électorale(s) fédérale(s):
Abitibi-Baie-James-Nunavik-Eeyou
Prochaines élections: 3e novembre 2013
Manon Cyr, Maire
Mario Asselin, Greffier

Chichester
CP 158
75, rue Notre-Dame
Chapeau, QC J0X 1M0
Tél: 819-689-2266; *Téléc:* 819-689-5619
chichester@mrcpontiac.qc.ca
Entité municipal: Township
Incorporation: 1er janvier 1857 *Area:* 225,71 km2
Comté ou district: Pontiac; *Population au 2011:* 368
Circonscription(s) électorale(s) provinciale(s): Pontiac
Circonscription(s) électorale(s) fédérale(s): Pontiac
Prochaines élections: 3e novembre 2013
Donald Gagnon, Maire
Richard Vaillancourt, Directeur général

Chisasibi
CP 150
1, rue Riverside
Chisasibi, QC J0M 1E0
Tél: 819-855-2878; *Téléc:* 819-855-2875
kanatewat4@hotmail.com
www.chisasibi.ca
Entité municipal: Villages Cris
Incorporation: 28 juin 1978 *Area:* 497,80 km2
Circonscription(s) électorale(s) provinciale(s): Ungava
Circonscription(s) électorale(s) fédérale(s):
Abitibi-Baie-James-Nunavik-Eeyou
Davey Bobbish, Maire
Nellie Pashagumeskum, Secrétaire

Chute-aux-Outardes
2, rue de l'École
Chute-aux-Outardes, QC G0H 1C0
Tél: 418-567-2144; *Téléc:* 418-567-4478
directeur@municao.com
www.mrcmanicouagan.qc.ca
Entité municipal: Village
Incorporation: 7e mars 1951 *Area:* 8,31 km2
Comté ou district: Manicouagan; *Population au 2011:* 1,644
Circonscription(s) électorale(s) provinciale(s): René-Lévesque
Circonscription(s) électorale(s) fédérale(s): Manicouagan
Prochaines élections: 3e novembre 2013
Arlette Girard, Mairesse
Rick Tanguay, Directeur général

Chute-Saint-Philippe
592, ch du Progrès
Chute-Saint-Philippe, QC J0W 1A0
Tél: 819-585-3397; *Téléc:* 819-585-4949
dg@chute-saint-philippe.ca
www.chute-saint-philippe.ca
Entité municipal: Municipality
Incorporation: 26 octobre 1940 *Area:* 282,28 km2
Comté ou district: Antoine-Labelle; *Population au 2011:* 892
Circonscription(s) électorale(s) provinciale(s): Labelle
Circonscription(s) électorale(s) fédérale(s): Laurentides-Labelle
Prochaines élections: 3e novembre 2013
Normand St-Amour, Maire
Ginette Ippersiel, Directrice générale

Clarendon
CP 777
C427, rte 148
Shawville, QC J0X 2Y0
Tél: 819-647-3862; *Téléc:* 819-647-3822
clarendon@mrcpontiac.qc.ca
Entité municipal: Municipality
Incorporation: 1er juillet 1855 *Area:* 327,27 km2
Comté ou district: Pontiac; *Population au 2011:* 1,183
Circonscription(s) électorale(s) provinciale(s): Pontiac
Circonscription(s) électorale(s) fédérale(s): Pontiac
Prochaines élections: 3e novembre 2013
John A. Lang, Maire

Ruth Potter Strutt, Directrice générale

Clermont
722, ch des 4e-et-5e-Rangs est
Saint-Vital-de-Clermont, QC J0Z 3M0
Tél: 819-333-6129; *Téléc:* 819-333-3811
clermont@mrcao.qc.ca
www.clermont.ao.ca
Entité municipal: Township
Incorporation: 4e mars 1936 *Area:* 155,89 km2
Comté ou district: Abitibi-Ouest; *Population au 2011:* 482
Circonscription(s) électorale(s) provinciale(s): Abitibi-Ouest
Circonscription(s) électorale(s) fédérale(s):
Abitibi-Témiscamingue
Prochaines élections: 3e novembre 2013
Robert Paquette, Maire
Mélissa Caron, Directrice générale

Clermont
2, rue Maisonneuve
Clermont, QC G4A 1G6
Tél: 418-439-3931; *Téléc:* 418-439-4889
info@ville.clermont.qc.ca
www.ville.clermont.qc.ca
Entité municipal: Town
Incorporation: 16 février 1935 *Area:* 52,99 km2
Comté ou district: Charlevoix-Est; *Population au 2011:* 3,118
Circonscription(s) électorale(s) provinciale(s): Charlevoix
Circonscription(s) électorale(s) fédérale(s):
Montmorency-Charlevoix-Haute-Côte-Nord
Prochaines élections: 3e novembre 2013
Jean-Pierre Gagnon, Maire
Brigitte Harvey, Directrice générale

Clerval
579, 2e rang
Clerval, QC J0Z 1R0
Tél: 819-783-2640; *Téléc:* 819-783-4001
clerval@mrcao.qc.ca
www.clerval.ao.ca
Entité municipal: Municipality
Incorporation: 12 septembre 1927 *Area:* 101,60 km2
Comté ou district: Abitibi-Ouest; *Population au 2011:* 364
Circonscription(s) électorale(s) provinciale(s): Abitibi-Ouest
Circonscription(s) électorale(s) fédérale(s):
Abitibi-Témiscamingue
Prochaines élections: 3e novembre 2013
Suzanne Théberge, Maire
Marielle Gauthier, Directrice générale

Cleveland
292, ch de la Rivière
Cleveland, QC J0B 2H0
Tél: 819-826-3546; *Téléc:* 819-826-2827
cleveland.dir.gen@b2b2c.ca
Entité municipal: Township
Incorporation: 1er juillet 1855 *Area:* 120,82 km2
Comté ou district: Le Val-St-François; *Population au 2011:* 1,609
Circonscription(s) électorale(s) provinciale(s): Richmond
Circonscription(s) électorale(s) fédérale(s):
Richmond-Arthabaska
Prochaines élections: 3e novembre 2013
Pierre Grandmont, Maire
Claudette Lapointe, Directrice générale

Cloridorme
CP 253
472, rte 132
Cloridorme, QC G0E 1G0
Tél: 418-395-2808; *Téléc:* 418-395-2228
dgclori@globetrotter.net
canton-de-cloridorme.com
Entité municipal: Township
Incorporation: 1er janvier 1885 *Area:* 162,10 km2
Comté ou district: La Côte-de-Gaspé; *Population au 2011:* 743
Circonscription(s) électorale(s) provinciale(s): Gaspé
Circonscription(s) électorale(s) fédérale(s):
Gaspésie—Îles-de-la-Madeleine
Prochaines élections: 3e novembre 2013
Jocelyne Huet, Mairesse
Marie Dufresne, Directrice générale

Coaticook
294, rue St-Jacques nord
Coaticook, QC J1A 2R3
Tél: 819-849-9166; *Téléc:* 819-849-4320
secretariat@mrcdecoaticook.qc.ca
www.mrcdecoaticook.qc.ca
Entité municipal: Regional County Municipality
Incorporation: 1er janvier 1982
Population au 2011: 18,847
Note: 12 municipalités.
Réjean Masson, Préfet
secretariat@mrcdecoaticook.qc.ca
Sylvie Harvey, Directrice générale
direction@mrcdecoaticook.qc.ca

Coaticook
150, rue Child
Coaticook, QC J1A 2B3
Tél: 819-849-2721; *Téléc:* 819-849-9669
hoteldeville@ville.coaticook.qc.ca
www.ville.coaticook.qc.ca
Entité municipal: Town
Incorporation: 30 décembre 1998 *Area:* 218,89 km2
Comté ou district: Coaticook; *Population au 2011:* 9,255
Circonscription(s) électorale(s) provinciale(s): St-François
Circonscription(s) électorale(s) fédérale(s): Compton-Stanstead
Prochaines élections: 3e novembre 2013
Bertrand Lamoureux, Maire
administration@ville.coaticook.qc.ca
Luc Marcoux, Conseiller, Ward(s): 1
Sonia Montminy, Conseillère, Ward(s): 2
Sylvain Véronneau, Conseiller, Ward(s): 3
Raynald Drolet, Conseiller, Ward(s): 4
Simon Madore, Conseiller, Ward(s): 5
François Lévesque, Conseiller, Ward(s): 6
Geneviève Dupras, Greffière
819-849-2721, Fax: 819-849-9669
greffe@ville.coaticook.qc.ca
Vincent Tanguay, Directeur général
directeurgeneral@ville.coaticook.qc.ca
Roger Garceau, Trésorier
rogergarceau@ville.coaticook.qc.ca

Colombier
CP 69
568, rue Principale
Colombier, QC G0H 1P0
Tél: 418-565-3343; *Téléc:* 418-565-3289
info@municipalite.colombier.qc.ca
www.municipalite.colombier.qc.ca
Entité municipal: Municipality
Incorporation: 1er janvier 1946 *Area:* 313,20 km2
Comté ou district: La Haute-Côte-Nord; *Population au 2011:* 747
Circonscription(s) électorale(s) provinciale(s): René-Lévesque
Circonscription(s) électorale(s) fédérale(s):
Montmorency-Charlevoix-Haute-Côte-Nord
Prochaines élections: 3e novembre 2013
Jean-Claude Degrace, Maire
Claire Savard, Directrice générale

Compton
3, ch de Hatley
Compton, QC J0B 1L0
Tél: 819-835-5584; *Téléc:* 819-835-5750
muncompton@bellnet.ca
www.compton.ca
Entité municipal: Municipality
Incorporation: 8e décembre 1999 *Area:* 205,72 km2
Comté ou district: Coaticook; *Population au 2011:* 3,112
Circonscription(s) électorale(s) provinciale(s): St-François
Circonscription(s) électorale(s) fédérale(s): Compton-Stanstead
Prochaines élections: 3e novembre 2013
Fernand Veilleux, Maire
Jacques Leblond, Directeur général

Contrecoeur
5000, rte Marie-Victorin
Contrecoeur, QC J0L 1C0
Tél: 450-587-5901; *Téléc:* 450-587-5855
mairie@ville.contrecoeur.qc.ca
www.ville.contrecoeur.qc.ca
Entité municipal: Town
Incorporation: 1er janvier 1976 *Area:* 61,56 km2
Comté ou district: Lajemmerais; *Population au 2011:* 6,252
Circonscription(s) électorale(s) provinciale(s): Verchères
Circonscription(s) électorale(s) fédérale(s): Verchères-Les Patriotes
Prochaines élections: 3e novembre 2013
Suzanne Dansereau, Mairesse
Yves Beaulieu, Directeur général

Cookshire-Eaton
220, rue Principale est
Cookshire, QC J0B 1M0
Tél: 819-560-8585; *Téléc:* 819-875-5311
cookshire-eaton@hsfqc.ca
www.cookshire-eaton.qc.ca
Entité municipal: Town
Incorporation: 24 juillet 2002 *Area:* 297,60 km2
Comté ou district: Le Haut-St-François; *Population au 2011:* 5,171
Circonscription(s) électorale(s) provinciale(s):

Mégantic-Compton
Circonscription(s) électorale(s) fédérale(s): Compton-Stanstead
Prochaines élections: 3e novembre 2013
Noël Landry, Maire
Martin Tremblay, Directeur général

Côte-Nord-du-Golfe-du-St-Laurent
Chevery, QC G0G 1G0
Tél: 418-787-2244; *Téléc:* 418-787-2241
mcngsl@xplornet.com
Entité municipal: Municipality
Incorporation: 22 juin 1963 *Area:* 2783,59 km2
Comté ou district: Le Golfe-du-Saint-Laurent; *Population au 2011:* 971
Circonscription(s) électorale(s) provinciale(s): Duplessis
Circonscription(s) électorale(s) fédérale(s): Manicouagan
Prochaines élections: 3e novembre 2013
Jacques Lareau, Administrateur (par intérim)

Coteau-du-Lac
342, ch du Fleuve
Coteau-du-Lac, QC J0P 1B0
Tél: 450-763-5822; *Téléc:* 450-763-0938
info@coteau-du-lac.com
www.coteau-du-lac.com
Entité municipal: Municipality
Incorporation: 6e février 1982 *Area:* 46,57 km2
Comté ou district: Vaudreuil-Soulanges; *Population au 2011:* 6,842
Circonscription(s) électorale(s) provinciale(s): Soulanges
Circonscription(s) électorale(s) fédérale(s): Vaudreuil-Soulanges
Prochaines élections: 3e novembre 2013
Robert Sauvé, Maire
Claire Blais, Greffière

Courcelles
CP 160
116, av du Domaine
Courcelles, QC G0M 1C0
Tél: 418-483-5540; *Téléc:* 418-483-3540
municipal@telcourcelles.net
www.muncourcelles.qc.ca
Entité municipal: Parish (Paroisse)
Incorporation: 6e avril 1904 *Area:* 92,25 km2
Comté ou district: Le Granit; *Population au 2011:* 1,004
Circonscription(s) électorale(s) provinciale(s): Beauce-Sud
Circonscription(s) électorale(s) fédérale(s): Mégantic-L'Érable
Prochaines élections: 3e novembre 2013
Mario Quirion, Maire
Renée Mathieu, Directrice générale

Crabtree
CP 660
111, 4e Av
Crabtree, QC J0K 1B0
Tél: 450-754-3434; *Téléc:* 450-754-2172
info@municipalitecrabtree.qc.ca
www.municipalitecrabtree.qc.ca
Entité municipal: Municipality
Incorporation: 23 octobre 1996 *Area:* 24,71 km2
Comté ou district: Joliette; *Population au 2011:* 3,887
Circonscription(s) électorale(s) provinciale(s): Joliette
Circonscription(s) électorale(s) fédérale(s): Joliette
Prochaines élections: 3er novembre 2013
Denis Laporte, Maire
Pierre Rondeau, Directeur général

D'Autray
CP 1500
550, rue De Montcalm
Berthierville, QC J0K 1A0
Tél: 450-836-7007; *Téléc:* 450-836-1576
mrcautray@mrcautray.com
www.mrcautray.com
Entité municipal: Regional County Municipality
Incorporation: 1er janvier
Population au 2011: 41,650
Note: 15 municipalités.
Gaétan Gravel, Préfet
Danielle Joyal, Directrice générale

Danville
CP 310
150, rue Water
Danville, QC J0A 1A0
Tél: 819-839-2771; *Téléc:* 819-839-2918
info@villededanville.com
www.villededanville.com
Entité municipal: Town
Incorporation: 17 mars 1999 *Area:* 149,51 km2
Comté ou district: Les Sources; *Population au 2011:* 4,070
Circonscription(s) électorale(s) provinciale(s): Richmond
Circonscription(s) électorale(s) fédérale(s):
Richmond-Arthabaska
Prochaines élections: 3e novembre 2013
Jacques Hémond, Maire
Michel Lecours, Directeur général

Daveluyville
CP 187
337, rue Principale
Daveluyville, QC G0Z 1C0
Tél: 819-367-3395; *Téléc:* 819-367-3550
info@ville.daveluyville.qc.ca
www.ville.daveluyville.qc.ca
Entité municipal: Village
Incorporation: 13 novembre 1901 *Area:* 2,25 km2
Comté ou district: Arthabaska; *Population au 2011:* 96
Circonscription(s) électorale(s) provinciale(s): Nicolet-Yamaska
Circonscription(s) électorale(s) fédérale(s):
Richmond-Arthabaska
Prochaines élections: 3e novembre 2013
Réal Savoie, Directeur général
Gilles Labarre, Maire

Dégelis
369, av Principale
Dégelis, QC G5T 2G3
Tél: 418-853-2332; *Téléc:* 418-853-3464
info@ville.degelis.qc.ca
www.ville.degelis.qc.ca
Entité municipal: Town
Incorporation: 13 décembre 1969 *Area:* 562,84 km2
Comté ou district: Témiscouata; *Population au 2011:* 3,051
Circonscription(s) électorale(s) provinciale(s):
Kamouraska-Témiscouata
Circonscription(s) électorale(s) fédérale(s):
Rimouski-Neigette-Témiscouata-Les Basques
Prochaines élections: 3e novembre 2013
Claude Lavoie, Maire
Bernard Caron, Directeur général

Déléage
175, rte 107, RR#1
Déléage, QC J9E 3A8
Tél: 819-449-1979; *Téléc:* 819-449-7441
reception@deleage.ca
www.deleage.ca
Entité municipal: Municipality
Incorporation: 1er janvier 1881 *Area:* 249,44 km2
Comté ou district: La Vallée-de-la-Gatineau; *Population au 2011:* 1,856
Circonscription(s) électorale(s) provinciale(s): Gatineau
Circonscription(s) électorale(s) fédérale(s): Pontiac
Prochaines élections: 3e novembre 2013
Jean-Paul Barbe, Maire
Emmanuelle Michaud, Directrice générale

Delson
50, rue Ste-Thérèse
Delson, QC J5B 2B2
Tél: 450-632-1050; *Téléc:* 450-632-1571
info@ville.delson.qc.ca
www.ville.delson.qc.ca
Entité municipal: Town
Incorporation: 4e janvier 1918 *Area:* 7,76 km2
Comté ou district: Roussillon; *Population au 2011:* 7,462
Circonscription(s) électorale(s) provinciale(s): La Prairie
Circonscription(s) électorale(s) fédérale(s):
Châteauguay-St-Constant
Prochaines élections: 3e novembre 2013
Gilles Meloche, Maire
Nicole Lafontaine, Greffière

Denholm
419, ch du Poisson-Blanc
Denholm, QC J8N 9C8
Tél: 819-457-2992; *Téléc:* 819-457-9862
info@municipalite.denholm.qc.ca
www.mundenholm.com
Entité municipal: Municipality
Incorporation: 27 février 1924 *Area:* 191,65 km2
Comté ou district: La Vallée-de-la-Gatineau; *Population au 2011:* 572
Circonscription(s) électorale(s) provinciale(s): Gatineau
Circonscription(s) électorale(s) fédérale(s): Pontiac
Prochaines élections: 3e novembre 2013
Pierre Nelson Renaud, Maire
Sandra Bélisle, Directrice générale

Desbiens
CP 9
925, rue Hébert
Desbiens, QC G0W 1N0
Tél: 418-346-5571; *Téléc:* 418-346-5422
administration@ville.desbiens.qc.ca
www.ville.desbiens.qc.ca
Entité municipal: Village
Incorporation: 16 août 1926 *Area:* 10,35 km2
Comté ou district: Lac-St-Jean-Est; *Population au 2011:* 1,053
Circonscription(s) électorale(s) provinciale(s): Lac-St-Jean
Circonscription(s) électorale(s) fédérale(s):
Roberval-Lac-St-Jean
Prochaines élections: 3e novembre 2013
Nicolas Martel, Maire
Michaël Gagnon, Directeur général

Deschaillons-sur-St-Laurent
1596, rte Marie-Victorin
Deschaillons-sur-Saint-Laurent, QC G0S 1G0
Tél: 819-292-2085; *Téléc:* 819-292-3194
mun.deschaillons@qc.aira.com
Entité municipal: Municipality
Incorporation: 23 mai 1990 *Area:* 37,70 km2
Comté ou district: Bécancour; *Population au 2011:* 954
Circonscription(s) électorale(s) provinciale(s): Lotbinière
Circonscription(s) électorale(s) fédérale(s):
Bas-Richelieu-Nicolet-Bécancour
Prochaines élections: 3e novembre 2013
Christian Baril, Maire
France Grimard, Directrice générale

Deschambault-Grondines
CP 220
120, rue St-Joseph
Deschambault, QC G0A 1S0
Tél: 418-286-4511; *Téléc:* 418-286-6511
deschambault@csportneuf.qc.ca
www.municipalite.deschambault.qc.ca
Entité municipal: Municipality
Incorporation: 27 février 2002 *Area:* 123,60 km2
Comté ou district: Portneuf; *Population au 2011:* 2,131
Circonscription(s) électorale(s) provinciale(s): Portneuf
Circonscription(s) électorale(s) fédérale(s):
Portneuf-Jacques-Cartier
Prochaines élections: 3e novembre 2013
Gaston Arcand, Maire
Claire St-Arnaud, Directrice générale

Deux-Montagnes
1, place de la Gare
Saint-Eustache, QC J7R 0B4
Tél: 450-491-1818; *Téléc:* 450-491-3040
info@mrc2m.qc.ca
Entité municipal: Regional County Municipality
Incorporation: 1er janvier 1983
Population au 2011: 95,670
Note: 7 municipalités.
Marc Lauzon, Préfet
Nicole Loiselle, Directrice générale

Disraéli
550, av Jacques-Cartier
Disraéli, QC G0N 1E0
Tél: 418-449-2771; *Téléc:* 418-449-4299
hoteldeville@villededisraeli.com
www.villededisraeli.com
Entité municipal: Town
Incorporation: 19 novembre 1904 *Area:* 6,470 km2
Comté ou district: Les Appalaches; *Population au 2011:* 2,502
Circonscription(s) électorale(s) provinciale(s): Frontenac
Circonscription(s) électorale(s) fédérale(s): Mégantic-L'Érable
Prochaines élections: 3e novembre 2013
André Rodrigue, Maire
Francyne Gagné, Directrice générale

Disraéli
8306, rte 112
Disraéli, QC G0N 1E0
Tél: 418-449-5329; *Téléc:* 418-449-5459
paroissedisraeli@tlb.sympatico.ca
www.paroissedisraeli.com
Entité municipal: Parish (Paroisse)
Incorporation: 1er janvier 1883 *Area:* 93,880 km2
Comté ou district: Les Appalaches; *Population au 2011:* 1,168
Circonscription(s) électorale(s) provinciale(s): Frontenac
Circonscription(s) électorale(s) fédérale(s): Mégantic-L'Érable
Prochaines élections: 3e novembre 2013
André Gosselin, Maire
Caroline Picard, Directrice générale

Dixville
251, rue Parker
Dixville, QC J0B 1P0
Tél: 819-849-3037; *Téléc:* 819-849-9520
bureaumunicipal@dixville.ca
www.dixville.ca
Entité municipal: Municipality
Incorporation: 27 septembre 1995 *Area:* 76,17 km2
Comté ou district: Coaticook; *Population au 2011:* 710
Circonscription(s) électorale(s) provinciale(s):
Mégantic-Compton
Circonscription(s) électorale(s) fédérale(s): Compton-Stanstead
Prochaines élections: 3e novembre 2013
Réal Ouimette, Maire
Mary Brus, Directrice générale

Donnacona
138, av Pleau
Donnacona, QC G3M 1A1
Tél: 418-285-0110; *Téléc:* 418-285-0020
naudb@villededonnacona.com
www.villededonnacona.com
Entité municipal: Town
Incorporation: 21 janvier 1967 *Area:* 20,12 km2
Comté ou district: Portneuf; *Population au 2011:* 6,283
Circonscription(s) électorale(s) provinciale(s): Portneuf
Circonscription(s) électorale(s) fédérale(s):
Portneuf-Jacques-Cartier
Prochaines élections: 3e novembre 2013
Sylvain Germain, Maire
Pierre-Luc Gignac, Greffier

Dosquet
183, rte St-Joseph
Dosquet, QC G0S 1H0
Tél: 418-728-3653; *Téléc:* 418-728-3338
mundosquet@videotron.ca
www.municipalitededosquet.com
Entité municipal: Municipality
Incorporation: 9e février 1918 *Area:* 67,26 km2
Comté ou district: Lotbinière; *Population au 2011:* 887
Circonscription(s) électorale(s) provinciale(s): Lotbinière
Circonscription(s) électorale(s) fédérale(s):
Lotbinière-Chutes-de-la-Chaudière
Prochaines élections: 3e novembre 2013
Yvan Charest, Maire
Paul Fillion, Directeur général

Drummond
436, rue Lindsay
Drummondville, QC J2B 1G6
Tél: 819-477-2230; *Téléc:* 819-477-8442
courriel@mrcdrummond.qc.ca
www.mrcdrummond.qc.ca
Entité municipal: Regional County Municipality
Incorporation: 1er janvier 1982
Population au 2011: 98,681
Note: 18 municipalités.
Francine Ruest Jutras, Préfète
Michel Gagnon, Directeur général
mgagnon@mrcdrummond.qc.ca

Dudswell
76, rue Main
Bishopton, QC J0B 1G0
Tél: 819-560-8484; *Téléc:* 819-884-5777
helene.leroux@hsfqc.ca
Entité municipal: Municipality
Incorporation: 11 octobre 1995 *Area:* 214,76 km2
Comté ou district: Le Haut-St-François; *Population au 2011:*
1,771
Circonscription(s) électorale(s) provinciale(s):
Mégantic-Compton
Circonscription(s) électorale(s) fédérale(s): Compton-Stanstead
Prochaines élections: 3e novembre 2013
Claude Corriveau, Maire
Hélène Leroux, Directrice générale

Duhamel
1890, rue Principale
Duhamel, QC J0V 1G0
Tél: 819-428-7100; *Téléc:* 819-428-1941
dg.duhamel@mrcpapineau.com
www.municipalite.duhamel.qc.ca
Entité municipal: Municipality
Incorporation: 15 août 1936 *Area:* 449,45 km2
Comté ou district: Papineau; *Population au 2011:* 412
Circonscription(s) électorale(s) provinciale(s): Papineau
Circonscription(s) électorale(s) fédérale(s):
Argenteuil-Papineau-Mirabel
Prochaines élections: 3e novembre 2013
David Pharand, Maire
Claire Dinel, Directrice générale

Duhamel-Ouest
361, rte 101 sud
Duhamel-Ouest, QC J9V 1A2
Tél: 819-629-2522; *Téléc:* 819-629-2422
duhamel.ouest@mrctemiscamingue.qc.ca
Entité municipal: Municipality
Incorporation: 20 février 1911 *Area:* 127,61 km2
Comté ou district: Témiscamingue; *Population au 2011:* 828
Circonscription(s) électorale(s) provinciale(s):
Rouyn-Noranda-Témiscamingue
Circonscription(s) électorale(s) fédérale(s):
Abitibi-Témiscamingue
Prochaines élections: 3e novembre 2013
Alain Sarrazin, Maire
Lise Perron, Directrice générale

Dundee
3296, montée Smallman
Dundee, QC J0S 1L0
Tél: 450-264-4674; *Téléc:* 450-264-8044
mun.dundee@sftl.ca
Entité municipal: Township
Incorporation: 1er juillet 1855 *Area:* 94,20 km2
Comté ou district: Le Haut-St-Laurent; *Population au 2011:* 408
Circonscription(s) électorale(s) provinciale(s): Huntingdon
Circonscription(s) électorale(s) fédérale(s):
Beauharnois-Salaberry
Prochaines élections: 3e novembre 2013
Jean Armstrong, Maire
Stéphan Landry, Directeur général

Dunham
CP 70
3777, rue Principale
Dunham, QC J0E 1M0
Tél: 450-295-2418; *Téléc:* 450-295-2182
info@ville.dunham.qc.ca
www.ville.dunham.qc.ca
Entité municipal: Town
Incorporation: 25 septembre 1971 *Area:* 200,99 km2
Comté ou district: Brome-Missisquoi; *Population au 2011:* 3,471
Circonscription(s) électorale(s) provinciale(s): Brome-Missisquoi
Circonscription(s) électorale(s) fédérale(s): Brome-Missisquoi
Prochaines élections: 3e novembre 2013
Jean Guy Demers, Maire
Pierre Loiselle, Greffier

Duparquet
86, rue Principale
Duparquet, QC J0Z 1W0
Tél: 819-948-2266; *Téléc:* 819-948-2466
duparquet@mrcao.qc.ca
www.duparquet.ao.ca
Entité municipal: Village
Incorporation: 13 avril 1933 *Area:* 157,40 km2
Comté ou district: Abitibi-Ouest; *Population au 2011:* 657
Circonscription(s) électorale(s) provinciale(s): Abitibi-Ouest
Circonscription(s) électorale(s) fédérale(s):
Abitibi-Témiscamingue
Prochaines élections: 3e novembre 2013
Gilbert Rivard, Maire
Jacques Taillefer, Greffier

Dupuy
2, av du Chemin-de-Fer
Dupuy, QC J0Z 1X0
Tél: 819-783-2595; *Téléc:* 819-783-2192
dupuy@mrcao.qc.ca
www.dupuy.ao.ca
Entité municipal: Municipality
Incorporation: 20 septembre 1918 *Area:* 123,48 km2
Comté ou district: Abitibi-Ouest; *Population au 2011:* 930
Circonscription(s) électorale(s) provinciale(s): Abitibi-Ouest
Circonscription(s) électorale(s) fédérale(s):
Abitibi-Témiscamingue
Prochaines élections: 3e novembre 2013
Marc-André Côté, Maire
Pascale Lavigne, Greffière

Durham-Sud
CP 70
70, rue de l'Hôtel-de-Ville
Durham-Sud, QC J0H 2C0
Tél: 819-858-2044; *Téléc:* 819-858-2044
mun@durham-sud.com
www.durham-sud.com
Entité municipal: Municipality
Incorporation: 1er novembre 1975 *Area:* 92,02 km2
Comté ou district: Drummond; *Population au 2011:* 1,008
Circonscription(s) électorale(s) provinciale(s): Johnson
Circonscription(s) électorale(s) fédérale(s): Drummond
Prochaines élections: 3e novembre 2013
Michel Noël, Maire
Christiane Bastien, Directrice générale

East Broughton
600, 10e av sud
East Broughton, QC G0N 1H0
Tél: 418-427-2608; *Téléc:* 418-427-3414
municipaliteeastbroughton@bellnet.ca
Entité municipal: Municipality
Incorporation: 5e janvier 1994 *Area:* 9,310 km2
Comté ou district: Les Appalaches; *Population au 2011:* 2,229
Circonscription(s) électorale(s) provinciale(s): Frontenac
Circonscription(s) électorale(s) fédérale(s): Mégantic-L'Érable
Prochaines élections: 3e novembre 2013
Kaven Mathieu, Maire
Normand Laplante, Directeur général

East Farnham
228, rue Principale
East Farnham, QC J2K 4T5
Tél: 450-263-4252; *Téléc:* 450-263-6131
eastfarnham@videotron.ca
www.municipalite.eastfarnham.qc.ca
Entité municipal: Village
Incorporation: 27 août 1914 *Area:* 5,29 km2
Comté ou district: Brome-Missisquoi; *Population au 2011:* 553
Circonscription(s) électorale(s) provinciale(s): Brome-Missisquoi
Circonscription(s) électorale(s) fédérale(s): Brome-Missisquoi
Prochaines élections: 3e novembre 2013
Sylvie D.-Raymond, Mairesse
Madelyn Marcoux, Directrice générale

East Hereford
15, rue de l'Église
East Hereford, QC J0B 1S0
Tél: 819-844-2463; *Téléc:* 819-844-2463
dlrioux@municipalite.easthereford.qc.ca
www.municipalite.easthereford.qc.ca
Entité municipal: Municipality
Incorporation: 1er juillet 1855 *Area:* 71,56 km2
Comté ou district: Coaticook; *Population au 2011:* 306
Circonscription(s) électorale(s) provinciale(s):
Mégantic-Compton
Circonscription(s) électorale(s) fédérale(s): Compton-Stanstead
Prochaines élections: 3e novembre 2013
Richard Belleville, Maire
Diane Lauzon-Rioux, Directrice générale

East-Angus
49, rue Angus nord
East Angus, QC J0B 1R0
Tél: 819-560-8600; *Téléc:* 819-560-8611
info.eastangus@hsfqc.ca
www.ville.east-angus.qc.ca
Entité municipal: Town
Incorporation: 14 mars 1912 *Area:* 8,10 km2
Comté ou district: Le Haut-St-François; *Population au 2011:*
3,741
Circonscription(s) électorale(s) provinciale(s):
Mégantic-Compton
Circonscription(s) électorale(s) fédérale(s): Compton-Stanstead
Prochaines élections: 3e novembre 2013
Robert G. Roy, Maire
Normand Graillon, Directeur général

Eastmain
147, Shabow Meskino
Eastmain, QC J0M 1W0
Tél: 819-977-0211; *Téléc:* 819-977-0281
Entité municipal: Villages Cris
Incorporation: 28 juin 1978 *Area:* 334,70 km2
Population au 2011: 767
Circonscription(s) électorale(s) provinciale(s): Ungava
Circonscription(s) électorale(s) fédérale(s):
Abitibi-Baie-James-Nunavik-Eeyou
Prochaines élections: 3e novembre 2013
Rusty Cheezo, Maire
Vacant, Trésorier

Eastman
160, ch George-Bonnallie
Eastman, QC J0E 1P0
Tél: 450-297-3440; *Téléc:* 450-297-3448
municipaliteeastman@bellnet.ca
www.muneastman.ca
Entité municipal: Municipality
Incorporation: 30 mai 2001 *Area:* 68,87 km2
Comté ou district: Memphrémagog; *Population au 2011:* 1,740
Circonscription(s) électorale(s) provinciale(s): Brome-Missisquoi

Circonscription(s) électorale(s) fédérale(s): Brome-Missisquoi
Prochaines élections: 3e novembre 2013
Gérard Marinovich, Maire
Caroline Rioux, Directrice générale

Egan-Sud
95, rte 105
Egan-Sud, QC J9E 3A9
Tél: 819-449-1702; *Téléc:* 819-449-7423
mun.egansud@ireseau.com
Entité municipal: Municipality
Incorporation: 17 novembre 1920 *Area:* 50,67 km2
Comté ou district: La Vallée-de-la-Gatineau; *Population au 2011:* 542
Circonscription(s) électorale(s) provinciale(s): Gatineau
Circonscription(s) électorale(s) fédérale(s): Pontiac
Prochaines élections: 3e novembre 2013
Neil Gagnon, Maire
Mariette Rochon, Directrice générale

Elgin
933,ch de la 2e Concession
Elgin, QC J0S 2E0
Tél: 450-264-2320; *Téléc:* 450-264-6846
munelgindir.gen@targo.ca
Entité municipal: Township
Incorporation: 1er juillet 1855 *Area:* 69,38 km2
Comté ou district: Le Haut-St-Laurent; *Population au 2011:* 401
Circonscription(s) électorale(s) provinciale(s): Huntingdon
Circonscription(s) électorale(s) fédérale(s): Beauharnois—Salaberry
Prochaines élections: 3e novembre 2013
Deborah Stewart, Mairesse
Danielle Sauvé, Directrice générale

Entrelacs
2351, ch d'Entrelacs
Entrelacs, QC J0T 2E0
Tél: 450-228-2529; *Téléc:* 450-228-4866
info@entrelacs.com
www.entrelacs.com
Entité municipal: Municipality
Incorporation: 1er janvier 1860 *Area:* 51,78 km2
Comté ou district: Matawinie; *Population au 2011:* 906
Circonscription(s) électorale(s) provinciale(s): Bertrand
Circonscription(s) électorale(s) fédérale(s): Joliette
Prochaines élections: 3e novembre 2013
Sylvain Breton, Maire
Ginette Brisebois, Directrice (par intérim)

Escuminac
13, rue de l'Église
Pointe-à-la-Garde, QC G0C 2M0
Tél: 418-788-5644; *Téléc:* 418-788-2613
munescuminac@globetrotter.net
Entité municipal: Municipality
Incorporation: 10 octobre 1907 *Area:* 109,55 km2
Comté ou district: Avignon; *Population au 2011:* 588
Circonscription(s) électorale(s) provinciale(s): Bonaventure
Circonscription(s) électorale(s) fédérale(s): Gaspésie—îles-de-la-Madeleine
Prochaines élections: 3e novembre 2013
Bertrand Berger, Maire
Sylvie Bossé, Directrice générale

Esprit-Saint
121, rue Principale
Esprit-Saint, QC G0K 1A0
Tél: 418-779-2716; *Téléc:* 418-779-2716
muni.esprit@globetrotter.net
www.municipalite.esprit-saint.qc.ca
Entité municipal: Municipality
Incorporation: 13 mai 1972 *Area:* 169,28 km2
Comté ou district: Rimouski-Neigette; *Population au 2011:* 379
Circonscription(s) électorale(s) provinciale(s): Rimouski
Circonscription(s) électorale(s) fédérale(s): Rimouski-Neigette-Témicouata-Les Basques
Prochaines élections: 3e novembre 2013
Marlène Dubé, Mairesse
Diane Ouellet, Directrice générale

Estérel
115, ch Dupuis
Estérel, QC J0T 1E0
Tél: 450-228-3232; *Téléc:* 450-228-3737
info@villedesterel.com
www.villedesterel.com
Entité municipal: Village
Incorporation: 1er janvier 2006 *Area:* 12,06 km2
Comté ou district: Les Pays-d'en-Haut; *Population au 2011:* 199
Circonscription(s) électorale(s) provinciale(s): Bertrand
Circonscription(s) électorale(s) fédérale(s): Laurentides—Labelle
Prochaines élections: 3e novembre 2013
Jean-Pierre Nepveu, Maire
Luc Lafontaire, Directeur général

Farnham
477, rue de l'Hôtel-de-Ville
Farnham, QC J2N 2H3
Tél: 450-293-3178; *Téléc:* 450-293-2989
administration@ville.farnham.qc.ca
www.ville.farnham.qc.ca
Entité municipal: Town
Incorporation: 8e mars 2000 *Area:* 92,53 km2
Comté ou district: Brome-Missisquoi; *Population au 2011:* 8,330
Circonscription(s) électorale(s) provinciale(s): Brome-Missisquoi
Circonscription(s) électorale(s) fédérale(s): Brome-Missisquoi
Prochaines élections: 3e novembre 2013
Josef Hüsler, Maire
Marielle Benoit, Greffière

Fassett
19, rue Gendron
Fassett, QC J0V 1H0
Tél: 819-423-6943; *Téléc:* 819-423-5388
munfassett@mrcpapineau.com
www.village-fassett.com
Entité municipal: Municipality
Incorporation: 1er juillet 1855 *Area:* 13,98 km2
Comté ou district: Papineau; *Population au 2011:* 451
Circonscription(s) électorale(s) provinciale(s): Papineau
Circonscription(s) électorale(s) fédérale(s): Argenteuil-Papineau-Mirabel
Prochaines élections: 3e novembre 2013
Michel Rioux, Maire
Diane Leduc, Directrice générale

Ferland-et-Boileau
CP 260
461, rte 381
Ferland-et-Boilleau, QC G0V 1H0
Tél: 418-676-2282; *Téléc:* 418-676-3092
municipalite@ferlandetboilleau.com
www.ferlandetboilleau.com
Entité municipal: Municipality
Incorporation: 1er janvier 1978 *Area:* 418,85 km2
Comté ou district: Le Fjord-du-Saguenay; *Population au 2011:* 583
Circonscription(s) électorale(s) provinciale(s): Dubuc
Circonscription(s) électorale(s) fédérale(s): Chicoutimi-Le Fjord
Prochaines élections: 3e novembre 2013
Carmen Simard, Mairesse
Sylvie Gagnon, Directrice générale

Ferme-Neuve
125, 12e rue
Ferme-Neuve, QC J0W 1C0
Tél: 819-587-3400; *Téléc:* 819-587-4733
bureau@municipalite.ferme-neuve.qc.ca
www.municipalite.ferme-neuve.qc.ca
Entité municipal: Municipality
Incorporation: 24 décembre 1997 *Area:* 1031,55 km2
Comté ou district: Antoine-Labelle; *Population au 2011:* 2,822
Circonscription(s) électorale(s) provinciale(s): Labelle
Circonscription(s) électorale(s) fédérale(s): Laurentides-Labelle
Prochaines élections: 3e novembre 2013
Gilbert Pilote, Maire
Normand Bélanger, Directeur général

Fermont
CP 2010
100, place Daviault
Fermont, QC G0G 1J0
Tél: 418-287-5411; *Téléc:* 418-287-5413
administration@villedefermont.qc.ca
www.caniapiscau.net
Entité municipal: Town
Incorporation: 15 octobre 1974 *Area:* 497,45 km2
Comté ou district: Caniapiscau; *Population au 2011:* 2,874
Circonscription(s) électorale(s) provinciale(s): Duplessis
Circonscription(s) électorale(s) fédérale(s): Manicouagan
Prochaines élections: 3er novembre 2013
Lise Pelletier, Mairesse
Carolle Bourque, Greffière

Forestville
1, 2e av
Forestville, QC G0T 1E0
Tél: 418-587-2285; *Téléc:* 418-587-6212
forestville@forestville.ca
www.forestville.ca
Entité municipal: Town
Incorporation: 5e janvier 1980 *Area:* 241,73 km2
Comté ou district: La Haute Côte-Nord; *Population au 2011:* 3,270
Circonscription(s) électorale(s) provinciale(s): René-Lévesque
Circonscription(s) électorale(s) fédérale(s): Montmorency-Charlevoix-Haute-Côte-Nord
Prochaines élections: 3e novembre 2013
Micheline Anctil, Mairesse
Jacques Beaulieu, Directeur général

Fort-Coulonge
CP 640
134, rue Principale
Fort-Coulonge, QC J0X 1V0
Tél: 819-683-2259; *Téléc:* 819-683-3627
administration@fortcoulonge.qc.ca
www.fortcoulonge.qc.ca
Entité municipal: Village
Incorporation: 15 décembre 1888 *Area:* 3,44 km2
Comté ou district: Pontiac; *Population au 2011:* 1,377
Circonscription(s) électorale(s) provinciale(s): Pontiac
Circonscription(s) électorale(s) fédérale(s): Pontiac
Prochaines élections: 3e novembre 2013
Raymond Durocher, Maire
Gilles Beaulieu, Directrice générale

Fortierville
198, rue de la Fabrique
Fortierville, QC G0S 1J0
Tél: 819-287-5922; *Téléc:* 819-287-0322
municipalite@fortierville.com
www.fortierville.com
Entité municipal: Municipality
Incorporation: 3e juin 1998 *Area:* 45,53 km2
Comté ou district: Bécancour; *Population au 2011:* 706
Circonscription(s) électorale(s) provinciale(s): Lotbinière
Circonscription(s) électorale(s) fédérale(s): Bas-Richelieu-Nicolet-Bécancour
Prochaines élections: 3e novembre 2013
Normand Gagnon, Maire
Annie Jacques, Directrice générale

Fossambault-sur-le-Lac
145, rue Gingras
Fossambault-sur-le-Lac, QC G0A 3M0
Tél: 418-875-3133; *Téléc:* 418-875-3544
fossam@coopcscf.com
www.fossambault-sur-le-lac.com
Entité municipal: Village
Incorporation: 10 mars 1949 *Area:* 10,96 km2
Comté ou district: La Jacques-Cartier; *Population au 2011:* 1,613
Circonscription(s) électorale(s) provinciale(s): Portneuf
Circonscription(s) électorale(s) fédérale(s): Portneuf-Jacques-Cartier
Prochaines élections: 3e novembre 2013
Jean Laliberté, Maire
Jacques Arsenault, Greffier

Frampton
107, rue Ste-Anne
Frampton, QC G0R 1M0
Tél: 418-479-5363; *Téléc:* 418-479-5364
munframpton@globetrotter.net
www.nouvellebeauce.com/frampton
Entité municipal: Municipality
Incorporation: 1er juillet 1855 *Area:* 150,76 km2
Comté ou district: La Nouvelle-Beauce; *Population au 2011:* 1,393
Circonscription(s) électorale(s) provinciale(s): Beauce-Nord
Circonscription(s) électorale(s) fédérale(s): Beauce
Prochaines élections: 3e novembre 2013
Jacques Soucy, Maire
Josée Audet, Directrice générale

Franklin
1670, rte 202
Franklin, QC J0S 1E0
Tél: 450-827-2538; *Téléc:* 450-827-2640
franklin@qc.aira.com
Entité municipal: Municipality
Incorporation: 31 mars 1973 *Area:* 112,19 km2
Comté ou district: Le Haut-St-Laurent; *Population au 2011:* 1,688
Circonscription(s) électorale(s) provinciale(s): Huntingdon
Circonscription(s) électorale(s) fédérale(s): Beauharnois-Salaberry
Prochaines élections: 3e novembre 2013
Suzanne Yelle Blair, Mairesse
Nancy Westerman, Directrice générale

Franquelin
CP 10
27, rue des Érables
Franquelin, QC G0H 1E0
Tél: 418-296-1406; *Téléc:* 418-296-6946
munic.franq@globetrotter.net
Entité municipal: Municipality
Incorporation: 1er janvier 1978 *Area:* 529,84 km2
Comté ou district: Manicouagan; *Population au 2011:* 324
Circonscription(s) électorale(s) provinciale(s): René-Lévesque
Circonscription(s) électorale(s) fédérale(s): Manicouagan
Prochaines élections: 3e novembre 2013
Michel Lévesque, Maire
Diane Cyr, Directrice générale

Frelighsburg
2, place de l'Hôtel-de-Ville
Frelighsburg, QC J0J 1C0
Tél: 450-298-5133; *Téléc:* 450-298-5557
municipalite@village.frelighsburg.qc.ca
Entité municipal: Municipality
Incorporation: 28 septembre 1985 *Area:* 123,27 km2
Comté ou district: Brome-Missisquoi; *Population au 2011:* 1,094
Circonscription(s) électorale(s) provinciale(s): Brome-Missisquoi
Circonscription(s) électorale(s) fédérale(s): Brome-Missisquoi
Prochaines élections: 3e novembre 2013
Roland Lemaire, Maire
Anne Pouleur, Directrice générale

Frontenac
2430, rue St-Jean
Frontenac, QC G6B 2S1
Tél: 819-583-3295; *Téléc:* 819-583-0855
adm@municipalitefrontenac.qc.ca
www.municipalitefrontenac.qc.ca
Entité municipal: Municipality
Incorporation: 1er janvier 1882 *Area:* 225,71 km2
Comté ou district: Le Granit; *Population au 2011:* 1,650
Circonscription(s) électorale(s) provinciale(s):
Mégantic-Compton
Circonscription(s) électorale(s) fédérale(s): Mégantic-L'Érable
Prochaines élections: 3e novembre 2013
Jean-Denis Cloutier, Maire
Bruno Turmel, Directeur général

Fugèreville
43, rue Principale
Fugèreville, QC J0Z 2A0
Tél: 819-748-3241; *Téléc:* 819-748-2422
dg.fugereville@mrctemiscamingue.qc.ca
Entité municipal: Municipality
Incorporation: 5e février 1904 *Area:* 163,79 km2
Comté ou district: Témiscamingue; *Population au 2011:* 329
Circonscription(s) électorale(s) provinciale(s):
Rouyn-Noranda-Témiscamingue
Circonscription(s) électorale(s) fédérale(s):
Abitibi-Témiscamingue
Prochaines élections: 3e novembre 2013
André Pâquet, Maire
Marguerite Lachance, Directrice générale

Gallichan
207, ch de la Rivière ouest
Gallichan, QC J0Z 2B0
Tél: 819-787-6092; *Téléc:* 819-787-6015
gallichan@mrca.qc.ca
www.gallichan.ao.ca
Entité municipal: Municipality
Incorporation: 1er janvier 1958 *Area:* 73,32 km2
Comté ou district: Abitibi-Ouest; *Population au 2011:* 484
Circonscription(s) électorale(s) provinciale(s): Abitibi-Ouest
Circonscription(s) électorale(s) fédérale(s): Abitibi-Témiscamigue
Prochaines élections: 3e novembre 2013
Émilien Larochelle, Maire
Johanne Shink, Directrice générale

Girardville
180, rue Principale
Girardville, QC G0W 1R0
Tél: 418-258-3293; *Téléc:* 418-258-3473
admin@ville.girardville.qc.ca
ville.girardville.qc.ca
Entité municipal: Municipality
Incorporation: 11 novembre 1921 *Area:* 125,80 km2
Comté ou district: Maria-Chapdelaine; *Population au 2011:*
1,100
Circonscription(s) électorale(s) provinciale(s): Roberval
Circonscription(s) électorale(s) fédérale(s):
Roberval-Lac-St-Jean
Prochaines élections: 3e novembre 2013
Jeanne Savard, Mairesse
Denis Desmeules, Directeur général

Godbout
CP 248
144, rue Pascal-Comeau
Godbout, QC G0H 1G0
Tél: 418-568-7581; *Téléc:* 418-568-7401
mgodbout144@hotmail.com
www.godbout.info
Entité municipal: Village
Incorporation: 1er janvier 1955 *Area:* 204,34 km2
Comté ou district: Manicouagan; *Population au 2011:* 298
Circonscription(s) électorale(s) provinciale(s): René-Lévesque
Circonscription(s) électorale(s) fédérale(s): Manicouagan
Prochaines élections: 3e novembre 2013
Alain Labrie, Maire
Carolle Vallée, Directrice générale

Godmanchester
2282, ch Ridge
Godmanchester, QC J0S 1H0
Tél: 450-264-4116; *Téléc:* 450-264-9749
godmanchester@intermobilex.com
Entité municipal: Township
Incorporation: 1er juillet 1855 *Area:* 138,77 km2
Comté ou district: Le Haut-St-Laurent; *Population au 2011:*
1,417
Circonscription(s) électorale(s) provinciale(s): Huntingdon
Circonscription(s) électorale(s) fédérale(s):
Beauharnois-Salaberry
Prochaines élections: 3e novembre 2013
Pierre Poirier, Maire
Élaine Duhème, Directrice générale

Gore
9, ch Cambria
Lakefield, QC J0V 1K0
Tél: 450-562-2025; *Téléc:* 450-562-5424
dchales@cantondegore.qc.ca
www.cantondegore.qc.ca
Entité municipal: Township
Incorporation: 1er juillet 1855 *Area:* 93,86 km2
Comté ou district: Argenteuil; *Population au 2011:* 1,775
Circonscription(s) électorale(s) provinciale(s): Argenteuil
Circonscription(s) électorale(s) fédérale(s):
Argenteuil-Papineau-Mirabel
Prochaines élections: 3e novembre 2013
Scott Pearce, Maire
Ron Kelley, Directeur général

Gracefield
CP 329
351, rte 105
Gracefield, QC J0X 1W0
Tél: 819-463-3458; *Téléc:* 819-463-4236
infos@gracefield.ca
www.gracefield.ca
Entité municipal: Town
Incorporation: 13 mars 2002 *Area:* 386,95 km2
Comté ou district: La Vallée-de-la-Gatineau; *Population au 2011:*
2,355
Circonscription(s) électorale(s) provinciale(s): Gatineau
Circonscription(s) électorale(s) fédérale(s): Pontiac
Prochaines élections: 3e novembre 2013
Note: Formerly known as Wright-Gracefield-Northfield.
Réal Rochon, Maire
Jean-Marie Gauthier, Greffier

Grand-Métis
70, ch Kempt
Grand-Métis, QC G0J 1Z0
Tél: 418-775-6485; *Téléc:* 418-775-3591
grandmetis@mitis.qc.ca
www.municipalite.grand-metis.qc.ca
Entité municipal: Municipality
Incorporation: 13 septembre 1855 *Area:* 25,85 km2
Comté ou district: La Mitis; *Population au 2011:* 237
Circonscription(s) électorale(s) provinciale(s): Matapédia
Circonscription(s) électorale(s) fédérale(s): Haute-Gaspésie-La
Mitis-Matane-Matapédia
Prochaines élections: 3e novembre 2013
Richard Fournier, Maire
Chantal Tremblay, Directrice générale

Grand-Remous
1508, rte Transcanadienne
Grand-Remous, QC J0W 1E0
Tél: 819-438-2877; *Téléc:* 819-438-2364
info@grandremous.ca
www.grandremous.ca
Entité municipal: Municipality
Incorporation: 29 avril 1937 *Area:* 386,55 km2
Comté ou district: La Vallée-de-la-Gatineau; *Population au 2011:*
1,168
Circonscription(s) électorale(s) provinciale(s): Gatineau
Circonscription(s) électorale(s) fédérale(s): Pontiac
Prochaines élections: 3e novembre 2013
Betty McCarthy, Sec.-Trés.
Gérard Coulombe, Maire

Grand-St-Esprit
5410, rte Principale
Grand-Saint-Esprit, QC J0G 1B0
Tél: 819-289-2410; *Téléc:* 819-289-2029
municipalite@grandsaintesprit.qc.ca
www.grandsaintesprit.qc.ca
Entité municipal: Municipality
Incorporation: 14 mai 1938 *Area:* 28,41 km2
Comté ou district: Nicolet-Yamaska; *Population au 2011:* 471
Circonscription(s) électorale(s) provinciale(s): Nicolet-Yamaska
Circonscription(s) électorale(s) fédérale(s):
Bas-Richelieu-Nicolet-Bécancour
Prochaines élections: 3e novembre 2013
Julien Boudreault, Maire
Caludie Larochelle, Directrice générale

Grande-Rivière
CP 188
108, rue de l'Hôtel de Ville
Grande-Rivière, QC G0C 1V0
Tél: 418-385-2282; *Téléc:* 418-385-2290
villegr@globetrotter.net
www.ville.grande-riviere.qc.ca
Entité municipal: Town
Incorporation: 21 septembre 1974 *Area:* 87,15 km2
Comté ou district: Le Rocher Percé; *Population au 2011:* 3,456
Circonscription(s) électorale(s) provinciale(s): Gaspé
Circonscription(s) électorale(s) fédérale(s):
Gaspésie—îles-de-la-Madeleine
Prochaines élections: 3e novembre 2013
Bernard Stevens, Maire
Éliane Hotton-Beaulieu, Greffière

Grande-Vallée
3, rue St-François-Xavier est
Grande-Vallée, QC G0E 1K0
Tél: 418-393-2161; *Téléc:* 418-393-2274
gvdiane@globetrotter.net
www.grande-vallee.ca
Entité municipal: Municipality
Incorporation: 15 septembre 1927 *Area:* 154,67 km2
Comté ou district: La Côte-de-Gaspé; *Population au 2011:* 1,137
Circonscription(s) électorale(s) provinciale(s): Gaspé
Circonscription(s) électorale(s) fédérale(s):
Gaspésie—îles-de-la-Madeleine
Prochaines élections: 3e novembre 2013
Nathalie Côté, Mairesse
Ghislaine Bouthillette, Directrice générale

Grandes-Piles
630, 4e av
Grandes-Piles, QC G0X 1H0
Tél: 819-538-9708; *Téléc:* 819-538-6947
info@grandespiles.qc.ca
www.grandespiles.qc.ca
Entité municipal: Village
Incorporation: 10 août 1885 *Area:* 115,38 km2
Comté ou district: Mékinac; *Population au 2011:* 361
Circonscription(s) électorale(s) provinciale(s): Laviolette
Circonscription(s) électorale(s) fédérale(s):
St-Maurice-Champlain
Prochaines élections: 3e novembre 2013
Jean-Pierre Ratelle, Maire
Roger Lacaille, Directeur général

Grenville
21, rue Tri-Jean
Grenville, QC J0V 1J0
Tél: 819-242-2146; *Téléc:* 819-242-5891
info@grenville.ca
www.grenville.ca
Entité municipal: Village
Incorporation: 1er janvier 1876 *Area:* 3,05 km2
Comté ou district: Argenteuil; *Population au 2011:* 1,577
Circonscription(s) électorale(s) provinciale(s): Argenteuil
Circonscription(s) électorale(s) fédérale(s):
Argenteuil-Papineau-Mirabel
Prochaines élections: 3e novembre 2013
Ronald Tittlit, Maire
Alain Léveillé, Directeur général

Grenville-sur-la-Rouge
40, rue Maple
Grenville, QC J0V 1J0
Tél: 819-242-8762; *Téléc:* 819-242-9341
info@grenvillesurlarouge.ca
www.grenvillesurlarouge.ca
Entité municipal: Municipality
Incorporation: 24 avril 2002 *Area:* 321,81 km2
Comté ou district: Argenteuil; *Population au 2011:* 2,746
Circonscription(s) électorale(s) provinciale(s): Argenteuil
Circonscription(s) électorale(s) fédérale(s):
Argenteuil-Papineau-Mirabel
Prochaines élections: 3e novembre 2013
John Saywell, Maire
Pascal B. Surprenant, Directeur général

Gros-Mécatina
CP 9
30, rte Mecatina
La Tabatière, QC G0G 1T0
Tél: 418-773-2263; *Téléc:* 418-773-2696
mungrosmecatina@xplornet.com
Entité municipal: Municipality
Incorporation: 1er janvier 1994 *Area:* 961,46 km2
Comté ou district: Le Golfe-du-Saint-Laurent; *Population au 2011:* 499
Circonscription(s) électorale(s) provinciale(s): Duplessis
Circonscription(s) électorale(s) fédérale(s): Manicouagan
Prochaines élections: 3e novembre 2013
Randy Jones, Maire
Rita Collier, Directrice générale

Grosses-Roches
CP 69
122, rue de la Mer
Grosses-Roches, QC G0J 1K0
Tél: 418-733-4273; *Téléc:* 418-733-4273
grossesroches@mrcdematane.qc.ca
Entité municipal: Municipality
Incorporation: 19 août 1939 *Area:* 63,99 km2
Comté ou district: Matane; *Population au 2011:* 411
Circonscription(s) électorale(s) provinciale(s): Matane
Circonscription(s) électorale(s) fédérale(s): Haute-Gaspésie-La Mitis-Matane-Matapédia
Prochaines élections: 3e novembre 2013
Victoire Marin, Mairesse
Linda Imbeault, Directrice générale

Guérin
#101, 516, rue St-Gabriel ouest
Guérin, QC J0Z 2E0
Tél: 819-784-7011; *Téléc:* 819-784-7012
mun.guerin@mrctemiscamingue.qc.ca
Entité municipal: Township
Incorporation: 8e novembre 1911 *Area:* 203,10 km2
Comté ou district: Témiscamingue; *Population au 2011:* 305
Circonscription(s) électorale(s) provinciale(s):
Rouyn-Noranda-Témiscamingue
Circonscription(s) électorale(s) fédérale(s):
Abitibi-Témiscamingue
Prochaines élections: 3e novembre 2013
Maurice Laverdière, Maire
Doris Gauthier, Directrice générale

Ham-Nord
CP 1271
474, rue Principale
Ham-Nord, QC G0P 1A0
Tél: 819-344-2424; *Téléc:* 819-344-2806
info@ham-nord.ca
www.ham-nord.ca
Entité municipal: Township
Incorporation: 1er janvier 1864 *Area:* 101,60 km2
Comté ou district: Arthabaska; *Population au 2011:* 832
Circonscription(s) électorale(s) provinciale(s): Richmond
Circonscription(s) électorale(s) fédérale(s):
Richmond-Arthabaska
Prochaines élections: 3e novembre 2013
François Marcotte, Maire
Aline Lemieux, Directrice générale

Hampden
CP 1055
863, rte 257 nord
Hampden, QC J0B 1Y0
Tél: 819-560-8444; *Téléc:* 819-560-8445
muni.hampden@hsfqc.ca
www.cantonhampden.com
Entité municipal: Township
Incorporation: 1er janvier 1874 *Area:* 110,10 km2
Comté ou district: Le Haut-St-François; *Population au 2011:* 214
Circonscription(s) électorale(s) provinciale(s):
Mégantic-Compton
Circonscription(s) électorale(s) fédérale(s): Compton-Stanstead
Prochaines élections: 3e novembre 2013
Bertrand Prévost, Maire
Diane Carrier, Directrice générale

Harrington
2811, rte 327
Harrington, QC J8G 2T1
Tél: 819-687-2122; *Téléc:* 819-687-8610
r.lacroix@harrington.ca
www.harrington.ca
Entité municipal: Township
Incorporation: 1er juillet 1855 *Area:* 243,87 km2
Comté ou district: Argenteuil; *Population au 2011:* 853
Circonscription(s) électorale(s) provinciale(s): Argenteuil
Circonscription(s) électorale(s) fédérale(s):
Argenteuil-Papineau-Mirabel
Prochaines élections: 3e novembre 2013
Keith Robson, Maire
Robert Lacroix, Directeur général

Hatley
135, rue Main
North Hatley, QC J0B 2C0
Tél: 819-842-2977; *Téléc:* 819-842-2639
info@cantondehatley.ca
www.cantondehatley.ca
Entité municipal: Township
Incorporation: 1er juillet 1855 *Area:* 65,87 km2
Comté ou district: Memphrémagog; *Population au 2011:* 2,003
Circonscription(s) électorale(s) provinciale(s): Orford
Circonscription(s) électorale(s) fédérale(s): Compton-Stanstead
Prochaines élections: 3e novembre 2013
Pierre A. Levac, Maire
Liane Breton, Directrice générale

Hatley
2100, rte 143
Hatley, QC J0B 4B0
Tél: 819-838-5877; *Téléc:* 819-838-4646
hatley@xplornet.com
Entité municipal: Municipality
Incorporation: 27 juillet 1995 *Area:* 66,31 km2
Comté ou district: Memphrémagog; *Population au 2011:* 761
Circonscription(s) électorale(s) provinciale(s): Orford
Circonscription(s) électorale(s) fédérale(s): Compton-Stanstead
Prochaines élections: 3e novembre 2013
Roland Gascon, Directeur général
Jacques de Léséleuc, Maire

Havelock
481, rte 203
Havelock, QC J0S 2C0
Tél: 450-826-4741; *Téléc:* 450-826-4800
mun.havelock@xplornet.com
Entité municipal: Township
Incorporation: 1er avril 1863 *Area:* 87,98 km2
Comté ou district: Le Haut-St-Laurent; *Population au 2011:* 756
Circonscription(s) électorale(s) provinciale(s): Huntingdon
Circonscription(s) électorale(s) fédérale(s):
Beauharnois-Salaberry
Prochaines élections: 3e novembre 2013
Joanne Primeau, Administratrice
Daniel Pilon, Directeur général

Havre-Saint-Pierre
#01, 1235, rue de la Digue
Hâvre-Saint-Pierre, QC G0G 1P0
Tél: 418-538-2717; *Téléc:* 418-538-3439
info@havresaintpierre.com
www.havresaintpierre.com
Entité municipal: Municipality
Incorporation: 1er janvier 1873 *Area:* 3779,89 km2
Comté ou district: Minganie; *Population au 2011:* 3,418
Circonscription(s) électorale(s) provinciale(s): Duplessis
Circonscription(s) électorale(s) fédérale(s): Manicouagan
Prochaines élections: 3e novembre 2013
Berchmans Boudreau, Maire
Danys Jomphe, Directeur général

Hébertville
351, rue Turgeon
Hébertville, QC G8N 1S8
Tél: 418-344-1302; *Téléc:* 418-344-4618
guy@ville.hebertville.qc.ca
www.ville.hebertville.qc.ca
Entité municipal: Municipality
Incorporation: 16 décembre 1972 *Area:* 263,88 km2
Comté ou district: Lac-St-Jean-Est; *Population au 2011:* 2,441
Circonscription(s) électorale(s) provinciale(s): Lac-St-Jean
Circonscription(s) électorale(s) fédérale(s):
Roberval-Lac-St-Jean
Prochaines élections: 3e novembre 2013
Martin Bergeron, Maire
Christian Ouellet, Directeur général

Hébertville-Station
6, rue Tremblay
Hébertville-Station, QC G0W 1T0
Tél: 418-343-3961; *Téléc:* 418-343-2349
dg@hebertville-station.com
hebertville-station.com
Entité municipal: Village
Incorporation: 18 février 1903 *Area:* 33,28 km2
Comté ou district: Lac-St-Jean-Est; *Population au 2011:* 1,216
Circonscription(s) électorale(s) provinciale(s): Lac-St-Jean
Circonscription(s) électorale(s) fédérale(s):
Roberval-Lac-St-Jean
Prochaines élections: 3e novembre 2013
Réal Côté, Maire
Serge Martel, Directeur général

Hemmingford
#3, 505, rue Frontière
Hemmingford, QC J0L 1H0
Tél: 450-247-2050; *Téléc:* 450-247-3283
canton.township@hemmingford.ca
www.hemmingford.ca
Entité municipal: Township
Incorporation: 1er juillet 1855 *Area:* 155,78 km2
Comté ou district: Les Jardins-de-Napierville; *Population au 2011:* 1,747
Circonscription(s) électorale(s) provinciale(s): Huntingdon
Circonscription(s) électorale(s) fédérale(s):
Beauharnois-Salaberry
Prochaines élections: 3e novembre 2013
Paul Viau, Maire
Margaret Hess, Directrice générale

Hemmingford
#5, 505, rue Frontière
Hemmingford, QC J0L 1H0
Tél: 450-247-3310; *Téléc:* 450-247-2389
village@hemmingford.ca
www.hemmingford.ca
Entité municipal: Village
Incorporation: 1er janvier 1878 *Area:* 0,85 km2
Comté ou district: Les Jardins-de-Napierville; *Population au 2011:* 808
Circonscription(s) électorale(s) provinciale(s): Huntingdon
Circonscription(s) électorale(s) fédérale(s):
Beauharnois-Salaberry
Prochaines élections: 3e novembre 2013
Drew Somerville, Maire
Diane Lawrence, Directrice générale

Henryville
165, rue de l'Église
Henryville, QC J0J 1E0
Tél: 450-299-2655; *Téléc:* 450-299-2355
mcchoquette.munihenryville@netc.net
www.municipalite-henryville.com
Entité municipal: Municipality
Incorporation: 15 décembre 1999 *Area:* 64,87 km2
Comté ou district: Le Haut-Richelieu; *Population au 2011:* 1,464
Circonscription(s) électorale(s) provinciale(s): Iberville
Circonscription(s) électorale(s) fédérale(s): Brome-Missisquoi
Prochaines élections: 3e novembre 2013
Serges Lafrance, Maire
Marie-Claude Choquette, Directrice générale

Hérouxville
1060, rue St-Pierre sud
Hérouxville, QC G0X 1J0
Tél: 418-365-7135; *Téléc:* 418-365-7041
herouxville@regionmekinac.com
www.municipalite.herouxville.qc.ca
Entité municipal: Parish (Paroisse)
Incorporation: 13 avril 1904 *Area:* 54,51 km2
Comté ou district: Mékinac; *Population au 2011:* 1,340
Circonscription(s) électorale(s) provinciale(s): Laviolette
Circonscription(s) électorale(s) fédérale(s):
St-Maurice-Champlain
Prochaines élections: 3e novembre 2013
Bernard Thompson, Maire
Denise Cossette, Directrice générale

Hinchinbrooke
1056, ch Brook
Hinchinbrooke, QC J0S 1A0
Tél: 450-264-5353; *Téléc:* 450-264-3787
hinchinbrooke@targo.ca

Entité municipal: Township
Incorporation: 1er juillet 1855 *Area:* 148,95 km2
Comté ou district: Le Haut-St-Laurent; *Population au 2011:* 2,242
Circonscription(s) électorale(s) provinciale(s): Huntingdon
Circonscription(s) électorale(s) fédérale(s): Beauharnois-Salaberry
Prochaines élections: 3e novembre 2013
Normand Crête, Maire
Kevin Neal, Directeur général

Honfleur
320, rue St-Jean
Honfleur, QC G0R 1N0
Tél: 418-885-9195; *Téléc:* 418-885-9195
livro@globetrotter.qc.ca
munhonfleur.net
Entité municipal: Municipality
Incorporation: 5e mars 1915 *Area:* 50,99 km2
Comté ou district: Bellechasse; *Population au 2011:* 765
Circonscription(s) électorale(s) provinciale(s): Bellechasse
Circonscription(s) électorale(s) fédérale(s): Lévis-Bellechasse
Prochaines élections: 3e novembre 2013
Marcel Blais, Maire
Jocelyne G. Paré, Directrice générale

Hope
330, rte 132
Hope, QC G0C 2K0
Tél: 418-752-3212; *Téléc:* 418-752-6986
mun.hope@globetrotter.net
Entité municipal: Township
Incorporation: 1er juillet 1855 *Area:* 71,45 km2
Comté ou district: Bonaventure; *Population au 2011:* 630
Circonscription(s) électorale(s) provinciale(s): Bonaventure
Circonscription(s) électorale(s) fédérale(s): Gaspésie—Îles-de-la-Madeleine
Prochaines élections: 3e novembre 2013
Hazen Whittom, Maire
Nancy Castilloux, Directrice générale

Hope Town
CP 146
209, rte 132 ouest
Hope Town, QC G0C 3C0
Tél: 418-752-2137; *Téléc:* 418-752-3789
hopetown@navigue.com
www.municipalitehopetown.com
Entité municipal: Municipality
Incorporation: 21 novembre 1936 *Area:* 49,80 km2
Comté ou district: Bonaventure; *Population au 2011:* 344
Circonscription(s) électorale(s) provinciale(s): Bonaventure
Circonscription(s) électorale(s) fédérale(s): Gaspésie—Îles-de-la-Madeleine
Prochaines élections: 3e novembre 2013
Lisa Marie MacWhirter, Maire
Gina Mei, Directrice générale

Howick
51, rue Colville
Howick, QC J0S 1G0
Tél: 450-825-2032; *Téléc:* 450-825-0026
municipalite@villagehowick.com
Entité municipal: Village
Incorporation: 29 octobre 1915 *Area:* 0,89 km2
Comté ou district: Le Haut-St-Laurent; *Population au 2011:* 630
Circonscription(s) électorale(s) provinciale(s): Huntingdon
Circonscription(s) électorale(s) fédérale(s): Beauharnois-Salaberry
Prochaines élections: 3e novembre 2013
Denis Loiselle, Maire
Claudette Provost, Directrice générale

Huberdeau
101, rue du Pont
Huberdeau, QC J0T 1G0
Tél: 819-687-8321; *Téléc:* 819-687-8808
info@municipalite.huberdeau.qc.ca
www.municipalite.huberdeau.qc.ca
Entité municipal: Municipality
Incorporation: 8e juin 1926 *Area:* 57,18 km2
Comté ou district: Les Laurentides; *Population au 2011:* 894
Circonscription(s) électorale(s) provinciale(s): Labelle
Circonscription(s) électorale(s) fédérale(s): Laurentides-Labelle
Prochaines élections: 3e novembre 2013
Évelyne Charbonneau, Mairesse
Guylaine Maurice, Directrice générale

Hudson
481, rue Principale
Hudson, QC J0P 1H0
Tél: 450-458-5348; *Téléc:* 450-458-4922
louisev@ville.hudson.qc.ca
www.ville.hudson.qc.ca
Entité municipal: Town
Incorporation: 7e juin 1969 *Area:* 21,62 km2
Comté ou district: Vaudreuil-Soulanges; *Population au 2011:* 5,135
Circonscription(s) électorale(s) provinciale(s): Vaudreuil
Circonscription(s) électorale(s) fédérale(s): Vaudreuil-Soulanges
Prochaines élections: 3e novembre 2013
Michael Elliot, Maire
Louise L.-Villandré, Directrice générale

Huntingdon
23, rue King
Huntingdon, QC J0S 1H0
Tél: 450-264-5389; *Téléc:* 450-264-6826
dg@villehuntingdon.com
www.villehuntingdon.com
Entité municipal: Town
Incorporation: 9e octobre 1848 *Area:* 2,61 km2
Comté ou district: Le Haut-St-Laurent; *Population au 2011:* 2,457
Circonscription(s) électorale(s) provinciale(s): Huntingdon
Circonscription(s) électorale(s) fédérale(s): Beauharnois-Salaberry
Prochaines élections: 3e novembre 2013
Stéphane Gendron, Maire
Denyse Jenneau, Greffière

Inukjuak
CP 234
Inukjuak, QC J0M 1M0
Tél: 819-254-8822; *Téléc:* 819-254-8779
jnaktialuk@nvinukjuak.ca
www.nvinukjuak.ca
Entité municipal: Northern Village
Incorporation: 7e juin 1980 *Area:* 64,45 km2
Comté ou district: Administration régionale Kativik; *Population au 2011:* 1,597
Circonscription(s) électorale(s) provinciale(s): Ungava
Circonscription(s) électorale(s) fédérale(s): Abitibi-Baie-James-Nunavil-Eeyou
Prochaines élections: 7e novembre 2012
Sarollie Weetaluktuk, Mairesse
Caroline Naktialuk, Secrétaire-trésorière

Inverness
CP 129
1799, rte Dublin
Inverness, QC G0S 1K0
Tél: 418-453-2512; *Téléc:* 418-453-2554
info@municipaliteinverness.ca
www.municipaliteinverness.ca
Entité municipal: Municipality
Incorporation: 9e septembre 1998 *Area:* 176,35 km2
Comté ou district: L'Érable; *Population au 2011:* 822
Circonscription(s) électorale(s) provinciale(s): Lotbinière
Circonscription(s) électorale(s) fédérale(s): Mégantic-L'Érable
Prochaines élections: 3e novembre 2013
Gilles St-Pierre, Maire
Sonia Tardif, Directrice générale

Irlande
157, ch Gosford
Irlande, QC G6H 2N7
Tél: 418-428-9216; *Téléc:* 418-428-4262
mundirlande@bellnet.ca
Entité municipal: Municipality
Incorporation: 1er juillet 1855 *Area:* 110,200 km2
Comté ou district: Les Appalaches; *Population au 2011:* 959
Circonscription(s) électorale(s) provinciale(s): Frontenac
Circonscription(s) électorale(s) fédérale(s): Mégantic-L'Érable
Prochaines élections: 3e novembre 2013
Bruno Vézina, Maire
Christiane Laroche, Directrice générale

Ivujivik
CP 20
Ivujivik, QC J0M 1H0
Tél: 819-922-9940; *Téléc:* 819-922-3045
mayorivu@nvivujivik.ca
www.nvivujivik.ca
Entité municipal: Northern Village
Incorporation: 27 juin 1981 *Area:* 36,59 km2
Comté ou district: Kativik; *Population au 2011:* 370
Circonscription(s) électorale(s) provinciale(s): Ungava
Circonscription(s) électorale(s) fédérale(s): Abitibi-Baie-James-Nunavik-Eeyou
Prochaines élections: 7e novembre 2012
Charlie Paningajak, Maire
Johnny Mark, Secrétaire-trésorier

Joliette
632, rue De Lanaudière
Joliette, QC J6E 3M7
Tél: 450-759-2237; *Téléc:* 450-759-2597
info@mrcjoliette.qc.ca
www.mrcjoliette.qc.ca
Entité municipal: Regional County Municipality
Incorporation: 1er janvier 1982
Population au 2011: 63,551
Note: 10 municipalités.
André Hénault, Préfet
prefet@mrcjoliette.qc.ca
Line Laporte, Directrice générale
llaporte@mrcjoliette.qc.ca

Kamouraska
67, av Morel
Kamouraska, QC G0L 1M0
Tél: 418-492-6523; *Téléc:* 418-492-9789
mychelle.levesque@kamouraska.ca
www.kamouraska.ca
Entité municipal: Municipality
Incorporation: 25 avril 1987 *Area:* 40,81 km2
Comté ou district: Kamouraska; *Population au 2011:* 589
Circonscription(s) électorale(s) provinciale(s): Kamouraska-Témiscouata
Circonscription(s) électorale(s) fédérale(s): Montmagny-L'Islet-Kamouraska-Rivière-du-Loup
Prochaines élections: 3e novembre 2013
Claude Langlais, Maire
Mychelle Lévesque, Directrice générale

Kamouraska
CP 1120
425, av Patry
Saint-Pascal, QC G0L 3Y0
Tél: 418-492-1660; *Téléc:* 418-492-2220
info@mrckamouraska.com
www.kamouraska.ca
Entité municipal: Regional County Municipality
Incorporation: 1er janvier 1982
Population au 2011: 21,492
Note: 17 municipalités & 2 autres territoires.
Yvon Soucy, Préfet
Guy Lavoie, Directeur général
glavoie@mrckamouraska.com

Kangiqsualujjuaq
CP 120
Kangiqsualujjuaq, QC J0M 1N0
Tél: 819-337-5271; *Téléc:* 819-337-5200
tannanack@nvkangiqsualujjuaq.ca
www.nvkangiqsualujjuaq.ca
Entité municipal: Northern Village
Incorporation: 2e février 1980 *Area:* 36,23 km2
Comté ou district: Administration régionale Kativik; *Population au 2011:* 874
Circonscription(s) électorale(s) provinciale(s): Ungava
Circonscription(s) électorale(s) fédérale(s): Abitibi-Baie-James-Nunavik-Eeyou
Prochaines élections: 7e novembre 2012
Kitty Annanack, Mairesse
Tommy Annanack, Secrétaire-trésorier

Kangiqsujuaq
CP 60
901, ch Sinaitia
Kangiqsujuaq, QC J0M 1K0
Tél: 819-338-3342; *Téléc:* 819-338-3237
sectreasurer@nvkangiqsujuaq.ca
www.nvkangiqsujuaq.ca
Entité municipal: Northern Village
Incorporation: 20 septembre 1980 *Area:* 12,47 km2
Comté ou district: Administration régionale Kativik; *Population au 2011:* 696
Circonscription(s) électorale(s) provinciale(s): Ungava
Circonscription(s) électorale(s) fédérale(s): Abitibi-Baie-James-Nunavik-Eeyou
Prochaines élections: 7e novembre 2012
Mary A. Pilurtuut, Mairesse
Pasa Kiatainaq, Secrétaire-trésorière

Kangirsuk
CP 90
101, ch Kuuvviliariaq
Kangirsuk, QC J0M 1A0
Tél: 819-935-4388; *Téléc:* 819-935-4287
secreasurer@nvkangirsuk.ca
www.nvkangirsuk.ca
Entité municipal: Northern Village
Incorporation: 17 janvier 1981 *Area:* 58,73 km2
Comté ou district: Administration régionale Kativik; *Population au 2011:* 549
Circonscription(s) électorale(s) provinciale(s): Ungava
Circonscription(s) électorale(s) fédérale(s): Abitibi-Baie-James-Nunavik-Eeyou
Prochaines élections: 7e novembre 2012
Tommy Nassak, Maire
Alec Kudluk, Secrétaire-trésorier

Kawawachikamach
CP 5111
Kawawachikamach, QC G0G 2Z0
Tél: 418-585-2686; *Téléc:* 418-585-3130
kawawa@naskapi.ca
www.naskapi.ca
Entité municipal: Villages Naskapi
Incorporation: 10 septembre 1981 *Area:* 284,7 km2
Comté ou district: Administration régionale Kativik;
Circonscription(s) électorale(s) provinciale(s): Duplessis
Circonscription(s) électorale(s) fédérale(s): Manicouagan
Pillip Einish, Maire
John Mameamskum, Directeur général

Kazabazua
CP 10
30, ch Begley
Kazabazua, QC J0X 1X0
Tél: 819-467-2852; *Téléc:* 819-467-3872
munkaz@qc.aibn.com
www.kazabazua.ca
Entité municipal: Municipality
Incorporation: 1er janvier 1862 *Area:* 175,49 km2
Comté ou district: La Vallée-de-la-Gatineau; *Population au 2011:* 847
Circonscription(s) électorale(s) provinciale(s): Gatineau
Circonscription(s) électorale(s) fédérale(s): Pontiac
Prochaines élections: 3e novembre 2013
Ota Hora, Maire
Pierre Vaillancourt, Directeur général

Kiamika
3, ch Valiquette
Kiamika, QC J0W 1G0
Tél: 819-585-3225; *Téléc:* 819-585-3992
mun.kiamika@tlb.sympatico.ca
www.kiamika.ca
Entité municipal: Municipality
Incorporation: 3e janvier 1898 *Area:* 348,25 km2
Comté ou district: Antoine-Labelle; *Population au 2011:* 772
Circonscription(s) électorale(s) provinciale(s): Labelle
Circonscription(s) électorale(s) fédérale(s): Laurentides-Labelle
Prochaines élections: 3e novembre 2013
Michel Dion, Maire
Josée Lacasse, Directrice générale

Kingsbury
370, rue du Moulin
Kingsbury, QC J0B 1X0
Tél: 819-826-2527; *Téléc:* 819-826-2520
kingsbury@qc.aira.com
Entité municipal: Village
Incorporation: 7e juillet 1896 *Area:* 6,26 km2
Comté ou district: Le Val-St-François; *Population au 2011:* 123
Circonscription(s) électorale(s) provinciale(s): Richmond
Circonscription(s) électorale(s) fédérale(s): Richmond-Arthabaska
Prochaines élections: 3e novembre 2013
Jean Dandurand, Maire
Yves Barthe, Directeur général

Kingsey Falls
CP 270
15, rue Caron
Kingsey Falls, QC J0A 1B0
Tél: 819-363-3810; *Téléc:* 819-363-3819
villedekingseyfalls@kingseyfalls.ca
www.kingseyfalls.ca
Entité municipal: Town
Incorporation: 31 décembre 1997 *Area:* 70,14 km2
Comté ou district: Arthabaska; *Population au 2011:* 2,000
Circonscription(s) électorale(s) provinciale(s): Richmond
Circonscription(s) électorale(s) fédérale(s): Richmond-Arthabaska
Prochaines élections: 3e novembre 2013
Micheline Pinard-Lampron, Mairesse
Gino Dubé, Greffier

Kinnear's Mills
120, rue des Églises
Kinnear's Mills, QC G0N 1K0
Tél: 418-424-3377; *Téléc:* 418-424-3015
munikin@gabskycom.com
www.kinnearsmills.com
Entité municipal: Municipality
Incorporation: 1er juillet 1855 *Area:* 93,18 km2
Comté ou district: Les Appalaches; *Population au 2011:* 369
Circonscription(s) électorale(s) provinciale(s): Frontenac
Circonscription(s) électorale(s) fédérale(s): Mégantic-L'Érable
Prochaines élections: 3e novembre 2013
Paul Vachon, Maire
Claudette Perreault, Directrice générale

Kipawa
15, rue Principale
Kipawa, QC J0Z 2H0
Tél: 819-627-3500; *Téléc:* 819-627-1067
kipawa@mrctemiscamingue.qc.ca
www.kipawa.ca
Entité municipal: Municipality
Incorporation: 1er janvier 1985 *Area:* 47,20 km2
Comté ou district: Témiscamingue; *Population au 2011:* 474
Circonscription(s) électorale(s) provinciale(s): Rouyn-Noranda-Témiscamingue
Circonscription(s) électorale(s) fédérale(s): Abitibi-Témiscamingue
Prochaines élections: 3e novembre 2013
Norman Young, Maire
Danielle Gravelle, Directrice générale

Kuujjuaq
CP 210
528, ch de l'Airport
Kuujjuaq, QC J0M 1C0
Tél: 819-964-2943; *Téléc:* 819-964-2980
mayor@nvkuujjuaq.qc.ca
www.nvkuujjuaq.ca
Entité municipal: Northern Village
Incorporation: 29 décembre 1979 *Area:* 390,33 km2
Comté ou district: Administration régionale Kativik; *Population au 2011:* 2,375
Circonscription(s) électorale(s) provinciale(s): Ungava
Circonscription(s) électorale(s) fédérale(s): Abitibi-Baie-James-Nunavik-Eeyou
Prochaines élections: 7e novembre 2012
Paul Parsons, Maire
Ian D. Robertson, Secrétaire-trésorier

Kuujjuarapik
CP 360
412, av St-Edmund
Kuujjuarapik, QC J0M 1G0
Tél: 819-929-3360; *Téléc:* 819-929-3453
proussel@nkuujjaraapik.ca
Entité municipal: Northern Village
Incorporation: 7e juin 1980 *Area:* 7,46 km2
Comté ou district: Administration régionale Kativik; *Population au 2011:* 657
Circonscription(s) électorale(s) provinciale(s): Ungava
Circonscription(s) électorale(s) fédérale(s): Abitibi-Baie-James-Nunavik-Eeyou
Prochaines élections: 7e novembre 2012
Raymond Mickpegak, Maire
Pierre Roussel, Secrétaire-trésorier

L'Ange-Gardien
870, ch Donaldson
L'Ange-Gardien, QC J8L 0K8
Tél: 819-986-7470; *Téléc:* 819-986-8349
adm@ville.lange-gardien.qc.ca
www.ville.lange-gardien.qc.ca
Entité municipal: Municipality
Incorporation: 17 mai 1979 *Area:* 224,17 km2
Comté ou district: Les Collines-de-l'Outaouais; *Population au 2011:* 5,051
Circonscription(s) électorale(s) provinciale(s): Papineau
Circonscription(s) électorale(s) fédérale(s): Pontiac
Prochaines élections: 3e novembre 2013
Robert Goulet, Maire
Alain Descarreaux, Directeur général

L'Ange-Gardien
6405, av Royale
L'Ange-Gardien, QC G0A 2K0
Tél: 418-822-1555; *Téléc:* 418-822-2526
mun-langegardien@bellnet.ca
www.langegardien.qc.ca
Entité municipal: Parish (Paroisse)
Incorporation: 1er juillet 1855 *Area:* 50,67 km2
Comté ou district: La Côte-de-Beaupré; *Population au 2011:* 3,634
Circonscription(s) électorale(s) provinciale(s): Montmorency
Circonscription(s) électorale(s) fédérale(s): Montmorency-Charlevoix-Haute-Côte-Nord
Prochaines élections: 3e novembre 2013
Pierre Lefrançois, Maire
Lise Drouin, Directrice générale

L'Anse-St-Jean
3, rue du Couvent
L'Anse-Saint-Jean, QC G0V 1J0
Tél: 418-272-2633; *Téléc:* 418-544-3078
info@lanse-saint-jean.ca
www.lanse-saint-jean.ca
Entité municipal: Municipality
Incorporation: 1er janvier 1859 *Area:* 527,06 km2
Comté ou district: Le Fjord-du-Saguenay; *Population au 2011:* 1,208
Circonscription(s) électorale(s) provinciale(s): Dubuc
Circonscription(s) électorale(s) fédérale(s): Chicoutimi-Le Fjord
Prochaines élections: 3e novembre 2013
Claude Boucher, Maire
Marina Gagné, Directrice générale

L'Ascension
CP 30
59, rue de l'Hôtel-de-Ville
L'Ascension, QC J0T 1W0
Tél: 819-275-3027; *Téléc:* 819-275-3489
directiongenerale@municipalite-lascension.qc.ca
www.municipalite-lascension.qc.ca
Entité municipal: Municipality
Incorporation: 23 septembre 1905 *Area:* 342,83 km2
Comté ou district: Antoine-Labelle; *Population au 2011:* 844
Circonscription(s) électorale(s) provinciale(s): Labelle
Circonscription(s) électorale(s) fédérale(s): Laurentides-Labelle
Prochaines élections: 3e novembre 2013
Yves Meilleur, Maire
Hélène Beauchamp, Directrice générale

L'Ascension-de-Notre-Seigneur
CP 100
1000, 1re rue est
L'Ascension-de-Notre-Seigneur, QC G0W 1Y0
Tél: 418-347-3482; *Téléc:* 418-347-4253
normand.desgagne@ville.ascension.qc.ca
www.ville.ascension.qc.ca
Entité municipal: Parish (Paroisse)
Incorporation: 25 février 1919 *Area:* 131,83 km2
Comté ou district: Lac-St-Jean-Est; *Population au 2011:* 1,983
Circonscription(s) électorale(s) provinciale(s): Lac-St-Jean
Circonscription(s) électorale(s) fédérale(s): Roberval-Lac-St-Jean
Prochaines élections: 3e novembre 2013
Louis Ouellet, Maire
Normand Desgagné, Directeur général

L'Ascension-de-Patapédia
CP 9
70, rue Principale
L'Ascension-de-Patapédia, QC G0J 1R0
Tél: 418-299-2024; *Téléc:* 418-299-2027
munlas-d-pat@globetrotter.net
www.matapedialesplateaux.com
Entité municipal: Municipality
Incorporation: 1er janvier 1968 *Area:* 95,38 km2
Comté ou district: Avignon; *Population au 2011:* 190
Circonscription(s) électorale(s) provinciale(s): Bonaventure
Circonscription(s) électorale(s) fédérale(s): Gaspésie—Îles-de-la-Madeleine
Prochaines élections: 3e novembre 2013
Rémi Gallant, Maire
Josiane Boucher, Directrice générale

L'Assomption
300A, rue Dorval
L'Assomption, QC J5W 3A1
Tél: 450-589-2288; *Téléc:* 450-589-9430
mrcinfo@mrclassomption.qc.ca
www.mrclassomption.qc.ca
Entité municipal: Regional County Municipality
Incorporation: 1er janvier 1983

Population au 2011: 119,840
Note: 6 municipalités.
Chantal Deschamps, Préfète
Michel C. Gagnon, Directeur général

L'Avenir
545, rue Principale
L'Avenir, QC J0C 1B0
Tél: 819-394-2422; *Téléc:* 819-394-2222
info@municipalitelavenir.qc.ca
www.municipalitelavenir.qc.ca
Entité municipal: Municipality
Incorporation: 23 décembre 1976 *Area:* 96,47 km2
Comté ou district: Drummond; *Population au 2011:* 1,202
Circonscription(s) électorale(s) provinciale(s): Johnson
Circonscription(s) électorale(s) fédérale(s): Drummond
Prochaines élections: 3e novembre 2013
Jean Parenteau, Maire
Suzie Lemire, Directrice générale

L'Épiphanie
331, rang du Bas-de-l'Achigan
L'Épiphanie, QC J5X 1E1
Tél: 450-588-5547; *Téléc:* 450-588-6050
mun@paroisse-lepiphanie.com
www.paroisse-lepiphanie.com
Entité municipal: Parish (Paroisse)
Incorporation: 1er juillet 1855 *Area:* 55,32 km2
Comté ou district: L'Assomption; *Population au 2011:* 3,296
Circonscription(s) électorale(s) provinciale(s): Rousseau
Circonscription(s) électorale(s) fédérale(s): Repentigny
Prochaines élections: 3e novembre 2013
Denis Lévesque, Maire
Nicole Renaud, Directrice générale

L'Épiphanie
66, rue Notre-Dame
L'Épiphanie, QC J5X 1A1
Tél: 450-588-5515; *Téléc:* 450-588-6171
courrier@ville.lepiphanie.qc.ca
www.ville.lepiphanie.qc.ca
Entité municipal: Town
Incorporation: 30 juin 1967 *Area:* 2,46 km2
Comté ou district: L'Assomption; *Population au 2011:* 5,353
Circonscription(s) électorale(s) provinciale(s): Rousseau
Circonscription(s) électorale(s) fédérale(s): Repentigny
Prochaines élections: 3e novembre 2013
Benoît Verstraete, Maire
Claude Crépeau, Greffier

L'Érable
#300, 1783, av St-Édouard
Plessisville, QC G6L 3S7
Tél: 819-362-2333; *Téléc:* 819-362-9150
info@mrc-erable.qc.ca
www.mrc-erable.qc.ca
Entité municipal: Regional County Municipality
Incorporation: 1er janvier 1982
Population au 2011: 23,366
Note: 11 municipalités.
Donald Langlois, Préfet
Rick Lavergne, Directeur général
rlavergne@mrc-erable.qc.ca

L'île-Cadieux
50, ch de l'île
L'île-Cadieux, QC J7V 8P3
Tél: 450-424-4273; *Téléc:* 450-424-6327
secretaire.ilecadieux@videotron.ca
www.ilecadieux.ca
Entité municipal: Village
Incorporation: 21 mars 1922 *Area:* 0,62 km2
Comté ou district: Vaudreuil-Soulanges; *Population au 2011:* 1105
Circonscription(s) électorale(s) provinciale(s): Vaudreuil
Circonscription(s) électorale(s) fédérale(s): Vaudreuil-Soulanges
Prochaines élections: 3e novembre 2013
Marc-André Léger, Maire
Gisèle Fournier, Directrice générale

L'île-d'Anticosti
CP 119
25B, ch des Forestiers
Port-Menier, QC G0G 2Y0
Tél: 418-535-0311; *Téléc:* 418-535-0381
munanticosti@xplornet.com
www.ile-anticosti.com
Entité municipal: Municipality
Incorporation: 1er janvier 1984 *Area:* 7923,16 km2
Comté ou district: Minganie; *Population au 2011:* 240
Circonscription(s) électorale(s) provinciale(s): Duplessis
Circonscription(s) électorale(s) fédérale(s): Manicouagan
Prochaines élections: 3e novembre 2013
Denis Duteau, Maire
Véronique Rodgers, Directrice générale

L'île-d'Orléans
3896, ch Royal
Sainte-Famille, QC G0A 3P0
Tél: 418-829-1011; *Téléc:* 418-829-2513
info@mrcio.qc.ca
mrcio.qc.ca
Entité municipal: Regional County Municipality
Incorporation: 1er janvier 1982
Population au 2011: 6,711
Note: 6 municipalités.
Jean-Pierre Turcotte, Préfet
Chantale Cormier, Directrice générale

L'île-du-Grand-Calument
CP 130
8, rue Brizard
L'île-du-Grand-Calumet, QC J0X 1J0
Tél: 819-648-5965; *Téléc:* 819-648-2659
ile-du-grand-calumet@mrcpontiac.qc.ca
Entité municipal: Municipality
Incorporation: 1er juillet 1855 *Area:* 130,61 km2
Comté ou district: Pontiac; *Population au 2011:* 731
Circonscription(s) électorale(s) provinciale(s): Pontiac
Circonscription(s) électorale(s) fédérale(s): Pontiac
Prochaines élections: 3e novembre 2013
Paul-Émile Maleau, Maire
Jacques Mantha, Directeur général

L'Isle-aux-Allumettes
CP 100
75, rue Notre-Dame
L'Isle-aux-Allumettes, QC J0X 1M0
Tél: 819-689-2266; *Téléc:* 819-689-5619
lisle-aux-allumettes@mrcpontiac.qc.ca
www.isle-aux-allumettes.com
Entité municipal: Municipality
Incorporation: 30 décembre 1998 *Area:* 190,19 km2
Comté ou district: Pontiac; *Population au 2011:* 1,345
Circonscription(s) électorale(s) provinciale(s): Pontiac
Circonscription(s) électorale(s) fédérale(s): Pontiac
Prochaines élections: 3e novembre 2013
Winston Sunstrum, Maire
Richard Vaillancourt, Directeur général

L'Isle-aux-Coudres
1026, ch des Coudriers
L'Isle-aux-Coudres, QC G0A 3J0
Tél: 418-760-1060; *Téléc:* 418-760-1061
contact@municipaliteiac.ca
Entité municipal: Municipality
Incorporation: 23 août 2000 *Area:* 29,54 km2
Comté ou district: Charlevoix; *Population au 2011:* 1,279
Circonscription(s) électorale(s) provinciale(s): Charlevoix
Circonscription(s) électorale(s) fédérale(s):
Montmorency-Charevoix-Haute-Côte-Nord
Prochaines élections: 3e novembre 2013
Dominic Tremblay, Maire
Johanne Fortin, Directrice générale

L'Isle-Verte
CP 159
141, rue St-Jean-Baptiste
L'Isle-Verte, QC G0L 1K0
Tél: 418-898-2812; *Téléc:* 418-898-2788
guyberube@lisle-verte.ca
www.municipalite.lisle-verte.qc.ca
Entité municipal: Municipality
Incorporation: 9 février 2000 *Area:* 112,33 km2
Comté ou district: Rivière-du-Loup; *Population au 2011:* 1,469
Circonscription(s) électorale(s) provinciale(s): Rivière-du-Loup
Circonscription(s) électorale(s) fédérale(s):
Montmagny-L'Islet-Kamouraska-Rivière-du-Loup
Prochaines élections: 1er novembre 2013
Serge Forest, Maire
Guy Bérubé, Directeur général

L'Islet
284, boul Nilus-Leclerc
L'Islet, QC G0R 2C0
Tél: 418-247-3060; *Téléc:* 418-247-5085
muni-islet@globetrotter.net
www.lislet.com
Entité municipal: Municipality
Incorporation: 1er janvier 2000 *Area:* 119,44 km2
Comté ou district: L'Islet; *Population au 2011:* 3,999
Circonscription(s) électorale(s) provinciale(s): Montmagny-L'Islet
Circonscription(s) électorale(s) fédérale(s):
Montmagny-L'Islet-Kamouraska-Rivière-du-Loup
Prochaines élections: 3e novembre 2013
André Caron, Maire
Colette Lord, Directrice générale

L'Islet
34-A, rue Fortin
Saint-Jean-Port-Joli, QC G0R 3G0
Tél: 418-598-3076; *Téléc:* 418-598-6880
administration@mrclislet.com
www.mrclislet.com
Entité municipal: Regional County Municipality
Incorporation: 1er janvier 1982
Population au 2011: 18,517
Note: 14 municipalités.
Réal Laverdière, Préfet
Michel Pelletier, Directeur général

La Conception
1371, rue du Centenaire
La Conception, QC J0T 1M0
Tél: 819-686-3016; *Téléc:* 819-686-5808
mbrisson@municipalite.laconception.qc.ca
www.municipalite.laconception.qc.ca
Entité municipal: Municipality
Incorporation: 1er janvier 1882 *Area:* 142,61 km2
Comté ou district: Les Laurentides; *Population au 2011:* 1,287
Circonscription(s) électorale(s) provinciale(s): Labelle
Circonscription(s) électorale(s) fédérale(s): Laurentides-Labelle
Prochaines élections: 3e novembre 2013
Maurice Plouffe, Maire
Marie-France Brisson, Directrice générale

La Corne
324, rte 111
La Corne, QC J0Y 1R0
Tél: 819-799-3571; *Téléc:* 819-799-3572
mun.lacorne@cableamos.com
www.lacorne.ca
Entité municipal: Municipality
Incorporation: 2e août 1975 *Area:* 331,54 km2
Comté ou district: Abitibi; *Population au 2011:* 700
Circonscription(s) électorale(s) provinciale(s): Abitibi-Ouest
Circonscription(s) électorale(s) fédérale(s):
Abitibi-Témiscamingue
Prochaines élections: 3e novembre 2013
Michel Lévesque, Maire
Diane St-Pierre, Directrice générale

La Côte-de-Beaupré
3, rue de la Seigneurie
Château-Richer, QC G0A 1N0
Tél: 418-824-3444; *Téléc:* 418-824-3917
info@mrccotedebeaupre.qc.ca
Entité municipal: Regional County Municipality
Incorporation: 1er janvier 1982
Population au 2011: 26,172
Note: 9 municipalités & 2 autres territoires.
Henri Cloutier, Préfet
Jacques Pichette, Directeur général

La Côte-de-Gaspé
#208, 19, rue Adams
Gaspé, QC G4X 1E5
Tél: 418-368-7000; *Téléc:* 418-368-8181
mrc@cotedegaspe.ca
mrc.cotedegaspe.ca
Entité municipal: Regional County Municipality
Incorporation: 1er janvier 1982
Population au 2011: 17,985
Note: 5 municipalités & 2 autres territoires.
François Roussy, Préfet
Pierre R. Charron, Directeur général

La Doré
5000, rue des Peupliers
La Doré, QC G8J 1E8
Tél: 418-256-3545; *Téléc:* 418-256-3496
info@municipalite.ladore.qc.ca
www.municipalite.ladore.qc.ca
Entité municipal: Parish (Paroisse)
Incorporation: 16 mars 1906 *Area:* 280,83 km2
Comté ou district: Le Domaine-du-Roy; *Population au 2011:* 1,453
Circonscription(s) électorale(s) provinciale(s): Roberval
Circonscription(s) électorale(s) fédérale(s):
Roberval-Lac-St-Jean
Prochaines élections: 3e novembre 2013
Jacques Asselin, Maire
René Perron, Directeur général

La Durantaye
539, rue du Piedmont
La Durantaye, QC G0R 1W0
Tél: 418-884-3465; *Téléc:* 418-884-3048
par.ladurantaye@globetrotter.net
www.munladurantaye.qc.ca
Entité municipal: Parish (Paroisse)
Incorporation: 4e août 1910 *Area:* 33,78 km2
Comté ou district: Bellechasse; *Population au 2011:* 722
Circonscription(s) électorale(s) provinciale(s): Bellechasse
Circonscription(s) électorale(s) fédérale(s): Lévis-Bellechasse
Prochaines élections: 3e novembre 2013
Jean-Paul Lacroix, Maire
Cindy Breton, Directrice générale

La Guadeloupe
483, 9e rue est
La Guadeloupe, QC G0M 1G0
Tél: 418-459-3342; *Téléc:* 418-459-3507
dglagua@tlb.sympatico.ca
www.munlaguadeloupe.qc.ca
Entité municipal: Village
Incorporation: 6e août 1929 *Area:* 31,67 km2
Comté ou district: Beauce-Sartigan; *Population au 2011:* 1,787
Circonscription(s) électorale(s) provinciale(s): Beauce-Sud
Circonscription(s) électorale(s) fédérale(s): Beauce
Prochaines élections: 3e novembre 2013
Huguette Plante, Mairesse
Marc-André Doyle, Directeur général

La Haute-Côte-Nord
#101, 26, rue de la Rivière
Les Escoumins, QC G0T 1K0
Tél: 418-233-2102; *Téléc:* 418-233-3010
info@mrchcn.qc.ca
www.mrchcn.qc.ca
Entité municipal: Regional County Municipality
Incorporation: 1er janvier 1982
Population au 2011: 11,546
Note: 8 municipalités & 1 autre territoire.
Pierre Laurencele, Préfet
Alain Tremblay, Directeur général
atremblay@mrchcn.qc.ca

La Haute-Gaspésie
464, boul Ste-Anne ouest
Sainte-Anne-des-Monts, QC G4V 1T5
Tél: 418-763-7791; *Téléc:* 418-763-7737
mrchg.rdeschenes@globetrotter.net
www.hautegaspesie.com
Entité municipal: Regional County Municipality
Incorporation: 18 mars 1981
Population au 2011: 12,088
Note: 8 municipalités & 2 autres territoires.
Allen Cormier, Préfet
Renée Deschênes, Directrice générale

La Haute-Yamaska
#100, 142, rue Dufferin
Granby, QC J2G 4X1
Tél: 450-378-9975; *Téléc:* 450-378-2465
mrc@mrchauteyamaska.qc.ca
www.haute-yamaska.ca
Entité municipal: Regional County Municipality
Incorporation: 3e mars 1982
Population au 2011: 85,042
Note: 9 municipalités.
Pascal Russell, Préfet
Johanne Gaouette, Directrice générale
jgaouette@mrchauteyamaska.qc.ca

La Jacques-Cartier
60, rue St-Patrick
Shannon, QC G0A 4N0
Tél: 418-844-2160; *Téléc:* 418-844-2664
mrcjc@mrc.lajacquescartier.qc.ca
www.mrc.lajacquescartier.qc.ca
Entité municipal: Regional County Municipality
Incorporation: 1er avril 1981
Population au 2011: 36,883
Note: 9 municipalités & 1 autre territoire.
Jacques Marcotte, Préfet
Francine Breton, Directrice générale
fbreton@mrc.lajacquescartier.qc.ca

La Malbaie
280, rue John-Nairne
La Malbaie, QC G5A 1L9
Tél: 418-665-3747; *Téléc:* 418-665-4935
dg@ville.lamalbaie.qc.ca
www.ville.lamalbaie.qc.ca
Entité municipal: Town
Incorporation: 1er décembre 1999 *Area:* 470,57 km2
Comté ou district: Charlevoix-Est; *Population au 2011:* 8,862
Circonscription(s) électorale(s) provinciale(s): Charlevoix
Circonscription(s) électorale(s) fédérale(s): Montmorency-Charlevoix-Haute-Côte-Nord
Prochaines élections: 1er novembre 2013
Lise Lapointe, Mairesse
Caroline Tremblay, Greffière

La Martre
9, av du Phare
La Martre, QC G0E 2H0
Tél: 418-288-5605; *Téléc:* 418-288-5144
lamartre@globetrotter.net
Entité municipal: Municipality
Incorporation: 18 décembre 1923 *Area:* 185,69 km2
Comté ou district: La Haute-Gaspésie; *Population au 2011:* 245
Circonscription(s) électorale(s) provinciale(s): Matane
Circonscription(s) électorale(s) fédérale(s): Haute-Gaspésie-La Mitis-Matane-Matapédia
Prochaines élections: 3er novembre 2013
Claudette Robinson, Mairesse
Marie-Alexandrine Hudon, Directrice générale

La Matapédia
#501, 123, rue Desbiens
Amqui, QC G5J 3P9
Tél: 418-629-2053; *Téléc:* 418-629-3195
administration@mrcmatapedia.qc.ca
www.lamatapedia.com/mrc
Entité municipal: Regional County Municipality
Incorporation: 1er janvier 1982
Population au 2011: 18,573
Note: 18 municipalités & 7 autres territoires.
Chantale Lavoie, Préfète
Mario Lavoie, Directeur général

La Minerve
6, rue Mailloux
La Minerve, QC J0T 1S0
Tél: 819-274-2364; *Téléc:* 819-274-2031
bureau@municipalite.laminerve.qc.ca
www.municipalite.laminerve.qc.ca
Entité municipal: Municipality
Incorporation: 30 décembre 1892 *Area:* 297,78 km2
Comté ou district: Les Laurentides; *Population au 2011:* 1,234
Circonscription(s) électorale(s) provinciale(s): Labelle
Circonscription(s) électorale(s) fédérale(s): Laurentides-Labelle
Prochaines élections: 3e novembre 2013
Vacant, Maire
Pierre Gagnon, Directeur général (par intérim)

La Mitis
300, av du Sanatorium
Mont-Joli, QC G5H 1V7
Tél: 418-775-8445; *Téléc:* 418-775-9303
mrc.mitis@cgocable.ca
www.lamitis.ca
Entité municipal: Regional County Municipality
Incorporation: 1er janvier 1982
Population au 2011: 18,942
Note: 16 municipalités & 2 autres territoires.
Michel Côté, Préfet
Marcel Moreau, Directeur général
mmoreau@mitis.qc.ca

La Morandière
204, rte 397
La Morandière, QC J0Y 1S0
Tél: 819-734-6143; *Téléc:* 819-734-6143
lamo@cableamos.com
www.lamorandiere.ca
Entité municipal: Municipality
Incorporation: 1er janvier 1983 *Area:* 430 km2
Comté ou district: Abitibi; *Population au 2011:* 233
Circonscription(s) électorale(s) provinciale(s): Abitibi-Ouest
Circonscription(s) électorale(s) fédérale(s): Abitibi-Témiscamingue
Prochaines élections: 3e novembre 2013
Guy Lemire, Maire
Sandra Hardy, Directrice générale

La Motte
CP 644
349, ch St-Luc
La Motte, QC J0Y 1T0
Tél: 819-732-2878; *Téléc:* 819-727-4248
municipalite.lamotte@cableamos.com
www.municipalitedelamotte.ca
Entité municipal: Municipality
Incorporation: 30 mai 1921 *Area:* 224,03 km2
Comté ou district: Abitibi; *Population au 2011:* 457
Circonscription(s) électorale(s) provinciale(s): Abitibi-Ouest
Circonscription(s) électorale(s) fédérale(s): Abitibi-Témiscamingue
Prochaines élections: 3e novembre 2013
René Martineau, Maire
Rachel Cossette, Directrice générale

La Nouvelle-Beauce
#B, 700, rue Notre-Dame nord
Sainte-Marie, QC G6E 2K9
Tél: 418-387-3444; *Téléc:* 418-387-7060
mrc.lanouvellebeauce@nouvellebeauce.com
www.nouvellebeauce.com
Entité municipal: Regional County Municipality
Incorporation: 1er janvier 1982
Population au 2011: 35,107
Note: 11 municipalités.
Richard Lehoux, Préfet
Mario Caron, Directeur général
mariocaron@nouvellebeauce.com

La Patrie
18, rue Chartier
La Patrie, QC J0B 1Y0
Tél: 819-560-8535; *Téléc:* 819-888-2697
munilapatrie@hsfqc.ca
www.municipalite.lapatrie.qc.ca
Entité municipal: Municipality
Incorporation: 24 décembre 1997 *Area:* 206,95 km2
Comté ou district: Le Haut-St-François; *Population au 2011:* 749
Circonscription(s) électorale(s) provinciale(s): Mégantic-Compton
Circonscription(s) électorale(s) fédérale(s): Compton-Stanstead
Prochaines élections: 3e novembre 2013
Jacques Blais, Maire
Johanne Latendresse, Directrice générale

La Pêche
1, rue Principale ouest
La Pêche, QC J0X 2W0
Tél: 819-456-2161; *Téléc:* 819-456-4534
tchartrand@villelapeche.qc.ca
www.villelapeche.qc.ca
Entité municipal: Municipality
Incorporation: 1er janvier 1975 *Area:* 597,14 km2
Comté ou district: Les Collines-de-l'Outaouais; *Population au 2011:* 7,619
Circonscription(s) électorale(s) provinciale(s): Gatineau
Circonscription(s) électorale(s) fédérale(s): Pontiac
Prochaines élections: 3e novembre 2013
Robert Bussière, Maire
Charles Ricard, Directeur général

La Pocatière
412, 9e rue
La Pocatière, QC G0R 1Z0
Tél: 418-856-3394; *Téléc:* 418-856-5465
danielle.caron@lapocatiere.ca
www.lapocatiere.ca
Entité municipal: Town
Incorporation: 1er janvier 1960 *Area:* 22,71 km2
Comté ou district: Kamouraska; *Population au 2011:* 4,266
Circonscription(s) électorale(s) provinciale(s): Kamouraska-Témiscouata
Circonscription(s) électorale(s) fédérale(s): Montmagny-L'Islet-Kamouraska-Rivière-du-Loup
Prochaines élections: 3e novembre 2013
Sylvain Hudon, Maire
Danielle Caron, Greffière

La Présentation
772, rue Principale
La Présentation, QC J0H 1B0
Tél: 450-796-2317; *Téléc:* 450-796-1707
lapresentation@mrcmaskoutains.qc.ca
www.municipalitelapresentation.qc.ca
Entité municipal: Parish (Paroisse)
Incorporation: 1er juillet 1855 *Area:* 104,71 km2
Comté ou district: Les Maskoutains; *Population au 2011:* 2,466
Circonscription(s) électorale(s) provinciale(s): Verchères
Circonscription(s) électorale(s) fédérale(s): St-Hyacinthe-Bagot
Prochaines élections: 3e novembre 2013
Claude Roger, Maire
Lise Lapalme, Directrice générale

La Rédemption
CP 39
68, rue Soucy
La Rédemption, QC G0J 1P0
Tél: 418-776-5311; *Téléc:* 418-776-5711
redemption@mitis.qc.ca
www.municipalite.laredemption.qc.ca
Entité municipal: Parish (Paroisse)
Incorporation: 1er janvier 1956 *Area:* 116,29 km2
Comté ou district: La Mitis; *Population au 2011:* 488
Circonscription(s) électorale(s) provinciale(s): Matapédia
Circonscription(s) électorale(s) fédérale(s): Haute-Gaspésie-La Mitis-Matane-Matapédia
Prochaines élections: 3e novembre 2013
Isabelle Dupont, Mairesse
Nadine Roussy, Directrice générale

La Reine
1, 3e av ouest
La Reine, QC J0Z 2L0
Tél: 819-947-5271; *Téléc:* 819-947-5271
lareine@mrcao.qc.ca
www.lareine.ao.ca
Entité municipal: Municipality
Incorporation: 19 septembre 1981 *Area:* 100,01 km2
Comté ou district: Abitibi-Ouest; *Population au 2011:* 340
Circonscription(s) électorale(s) provinciale(s): Abitibi-Ouest
Circonscription(s) électorale(s) fédérale(s): Abitibi-Témiscamingue
Prochaines élections: 3e novembre 2013
Jean-Guy Boulet, Maire
Sylvie Germain, Directrice générale

La Rivière-du-Nord
#200, 161, rue de la Gare
Saint-Jérôme, QC J7Z 2B9
Tél: 450-436-9321; *Téléc:* 450-436-1977
info@mrcrivieredunord.qc.ca
www.mrcrivieredunord.qc.ca
Entité municipal: Regional County Municipality
Incorporation: 1er janvier 1983
Population au 2011: 115,165
Note: 5 municipalités.
Yvon Brière, Préfet
Pierre Godin, Directeur général
pgodindg@mrcrivieredunord.qc.ca

La Sarre
6, 4e av est
La Sarre, QC J9Z 1J9
Tél: 819-333-2282; *Téléc:* 819-333-3090
info@ville.lasarre.qc.ca
www.ville.lasarre.qc.ca
Entité municipal: Town
Incorporation: 19 avril 1980 *Area:* 148,21 km2
Comté ou district: Abitibi-Ouest; *Population au 2011:* 7,719
Circonscription(s) électorale(s) provinciale(s): Abitibi-Ouest
Circonscription(s) électorale(s) fédérale(s): Abitibi-Témiscamingue
Prochaines élections: 3e novembre 2013
Normand Houde, Maire
François Casaubon, Greffier

La Trinité-des-Monts
CP 9
12, rue Principale ouest
La Trinité-des-Monts, QC G0K 1B0
Tél: 418-779-2421; *Téléc:* 418-779-2454
muntrinite@globetrotter.net
trinite-des-monts.qc.ca
Entité municipal: Parish (Paroisse)
Incorporation: 1er janvier 1965 *Area:* 233,09 km2
Comté ou district: Rimouski-Neigette; *Population au 2011:* 256
Circonscription(s) électorale(s) provinciale(s): Rimouski
Circonscription(s) électorale(s) fédérale(s): Rimouski-Neigette-Témiscouata-Les Basques
Prochaines élections: 3e novembre 2013
Fernand Garon, Maire
Jacky Malenfant, Directrice générale

La Vallée-de-l'Or
42, place Hammond
Val-d'Or, QC J9P 3A9
Tél: 819-825-7733; *Téléc:* 819-825-4137
info@mrcvo.qc.ca
www.mrcvo.qc.ca
Entité municipal: Regional County Municipality
Incorporation: 8e avril 1981
Population au 2011: 42,896
Note: 6 municipalités & 5 autres territoires.
Fernand Trahan, Préfet
Louis Bourget, Directeur général
louisbourget@mrcvo.qc.ca

La Vallée-de-la-Gatineau
7, rue de la Polyvalente
Gracefield, QC J0X 1W0
Tél: 819-463-3241; *Téléc:* 819-463-3632
info@mrcvg.qc.ca
www.mrcvg.qc.ca
Entité municipal: Regional County Municipality
Incorporation: 1er janvieer 1983
Population au 2011: 20,530
Note: 17 municipalités & 5 autres territoires.
Pierre Rondeau, Préfet
André Beauchemin, Directeur général
abeauchemin@mrcvg.qc.ca

La Vallée-du-Richelieu
#100, 255, boul Laurier
McMasterville, QC J3G 0B7
Tél: 450-464-0339; *Téléc:* 450-464-3827
info@mrcvr.ca
www.vallee-du-richelieu.ca
Entité municipal: Regional County Municipality
Incorporation: 1er janvier 1982
Population au 2011: 116,773
Note: 13 municipalités.
Gilles Plante, Préfet
Bernard Roy, Directeur général

La Visitation-de-l'île-Dupas
113, rue de l'Église
La Visitation-de-l'île-Dupas, QC J0K 2P0
Tél: 450-836-6019; *Téléc:* 450-836-8266
admin@ile-dupas.ca
Entité municipal: Municipality
Incorporation: 1er juillet 1855 *Area:* 24,86 km2
Comté ou district: D'Autray; *Population au 2011:* 619
Circonscription(s) électorale(s) provinciale(s): Berthier
Circonscription(s) électorale(s) fédérale(s): Joliette
Prochaines élections: 3e novembre 2013
Maurice Désy, Maire
Sylive Toupin, Directrice générale

La Visitation-de-Yamaska
21, rue Principale
La Visitation, QC J0G 1C0
Tél: 450-564-2818; *Téléc:* 450-564-9923
info@lavisitationdeyamaska.net
www.lavisitationdeyamaska.net
Entité municipal: Municipality
Incorporation: 2 février 1899 *Area:* 41,86 km2
Comté ou district: Nicolet-Yamaska; *Population au 2011:* 331
Circonscription(s) électorale(s) provinciale(s): Nicolet-Yamaska
Circonscription(s) électorale(s) fédérale(s): Bas-Richelieu-Nicolet-Bécancour
Prochaines élections: 3e novembre 2013
Sylvain Laplante, Maire
Suzanne Bibeau, Directrice générale

Labelle
1, rue du Pont
Labelle, QC J0T 1H0
Tél: 819-681-3371; *Téléc:* 819-686-3820
info@municipalite.labelle.qc.ca
www.municipalite.labelle.qc.ca
Entité municipal: Municipality
Incorporation: 27 janvier 1973 *Area:* 217,11 km2
Comté ou district: Les Laurentides; *Population au 2011:* 2,445
Circonscription(s) électorale(s) provinciale(s): Labelle
Circonscription(s) électorale(s) fédérale(s): Laurentides-Labelle
Prochaines élections: 3e novembre 2013
Gilbert Brassard, Maire
Claire Coulombe, Directrice générale

Labrecque
3425, rue Ambroise
Labrecque, QC G0W 2S0
Tél: 418-481-2022; *Téléc:* 418-481-1210
municipalite@ville.labrecque.qc.ca
www.ville.labrecque.qc.ca
Entité municipal: Municipality
Incorporation: 6 octobre 1925 *Area:* 147,37 km2
Comté ou district: Lac-St-Jean-Est; *Population au 2011:* 1,215
Circonscription(s) électorale(s) provinciale(s): Lac-St-Jean
Circonscription(s) électorale(s) fédérale(s): Roberval-Lac-St-Jean
Prochaines élections: 3e novembre 2013
Daniel Perron, Maire
Suzanne Couture, Directrice générale

Lac-au-Saumon
CP 98
36, rue Bouillon
Lac-au-Saumon, QC G0J 1M0
Tél: 418-778-3378; *Téléc:* 418-778-3706
lacausaumon@mrcmatapedia.qc.ca
www.lacausaumon.com
Entité municipal: Municipality
Incorporation: 17 décembre 1997 *Area:* 79,74 km2
Comté ou district: La Matapédia; *Population au 2011:* 1,453
Circonscription(s) électorale(s) provinciale(s): Matapédia
Circonscription(s) électorale(s) fédérale(s): Haute-Gaspésie-La Mitis-Matane-Matapédia
Prochaines élections: 3e novembre 2013
Michel Chevarie, Maire
Chantale Gagné, Directrice générale

Lac-aux-Sables
820, rue St-Alphonse
Lac-aux-Sables, QC G0X 1M0
Tél: 418-336-2331; *Téléc:* 418-336-2500
lac-aux-sables@regionmekinac.com
www.lac-aux-sables.qc.ca
Entité municipal: Parish (Paroisse)
Incorporation: 24 avril 1899 *Area:* 285,45 km2
Comté ou district: Mékinac; *Population au 2011:* 1,373
Circonscription(s) électorale(s) provinciale(s): Portneuf
Circonscription(s) électorale(s) fédérale(s): St-Maurice-Champlain
Prochaines élections: 3e novembre 2013
Yvan Hamelin, Maire
Valérie Adm.A. Cloutier, Directrice générale

Lac-Beauport
65, ch du Tour-du-Lac
Lac-Beauport, QC G3B 0A1
Tél: 418-849-7141; *Téléc:* 418-849-0361
info@lacbeauport.net
www.lac-beauport.ca
Entité municipal: Municipality
Incorporation: 1er juillet 1855 *Area:* 62,72 km2
Comté ou district: La Jacques-Cartier; *Population au 2011:* 7,281
Circonscription(s) électorale(s) provinciale(s): Chauveau
Circonscription(s) électorale(s) fédérale(s): Portneuf—Jacques-Cartier
Prochaines élections: 3e novembre 2013
Michel Beaulieu, Maire
Richard Labrecque, Directeur général

Lac-Bouchette
249, rue Principale
Lac-Bouchette, QC G0W 1V0
Tél: 418-348-6306; *Téléc:* 418-348-9477
munilac@lac-bouchette.com
Entité municipal: Municipality
Incorporation: 25 septembre 1971 *Area:* 919,99 km2
Comté ou district: Le Domaine-du-Roy; *Population au 2011:* 1,174
Circonscription(s) électorale(s) provinciale(s): Roberval
Circonscription(s) électorale(s) fédérale(s): Roberval-Lac-St-Jean
Prochaines élections: 3e novembre 2013
Benoît Gélinas, Maire
Jean-Pierre Tremblay, Directeur général

Lac-Brome
122, ch Lakeside
Lac-Brome, QC J0E 1V0
Tél: 450-243-6111; *Téléc:* 450-243-5300
reception@ville.lac-brome.qc.ca
ville.lac-brome.qc.ca
Entité municipal: Town
Incorporation: 2 janvier 1971 *Area:* 209,37 km2
Comté ou district: Brome-Missisquoi; *Population au 2011:* 5,609
Circonscription(s) électorale(s) provinciale(s): Brome-Missisquoi
Circonscription(s) électorale(s) fédérale(s): Brome-Missisquoi
Prochaines élections: 3e novembre 2013
Gilles Decelles, Maire
Alain Roy, Greffier

Lac-Delage
24, rue du Pied-des-Pentes
Lac-Delage, QC G3C 5A4
Tél: 418-848-2417; *Téléc:* 418-848-1948
villelacdelage@ccapcable.com
www.lacdelage.qc.ca
Entité municipal: Village
Incorporation: 11 février 1959 *Area:* 1,46 km2
Comté ou district: La Jacques-Cartier; *Population au 2011:* 598
Circonscription(s) électorale(s) provinciale(s): Chauveau
Circonscription(s) électorale(s) fédérale(s):

Portneuf-Jacques-Cartier
Prochaines élections: 3e novembre 2013
Marc Boiteau, Maire
Guylaine Thibault, Directrice générale

Lac-des-Aigles
CP 70
75, rue Principale
Lac-des-Aigles, QC G0K 1V0
Tél: 418-779-2300; *Téléc:* 418-779-3024
info@lacdesaigles.ca
Entité municipal: Municipality
Incorporation: 1er janvier 1948 *Area:* 85,10 km2
Comté ou district: Témiscouata; *Population au 2011:* 551
Circonscription(s) électorale(s) provinciale(s): Rimouski
Circonscription(s) électorale(s) fédérale(s):
Rimouski-Neigette-Témiscouata-Les Basques
Prochaines élections: 3e novembre 2013
Claude Breault, Maire
Francine Beaulieu, Directrice générale

Lac-des-Écorces
672, boul St-François
Lac-des-Écorces, QC J0W 1H0
Tél: 819-585-4600; *Téléc:* 819-585-4610
dg@lacdesecorces.ca
www.lacdesecorces.ca
Entité municipal: Municipality
Incorporation: 10 octobre 2002 *Area:* 143,59 km2
Comté ou district: Antoine-Labelle; *Population au 2011:* 2,713
Circonscription(s) électorale(s) provinciale(s): Labelle
Circonscription(s) électorale(s) fédérale(s): Laurentides-Labelle
Prochaines élections: 3e novembre 2013
Note: Effective October 10, 2002, the Municipality of Beaux-Rivages, the Village of Lac-des-Écorces & the Village of Val-Barrette amalgamated to create the new Municipality of Beaux-Rivages-Lac-des-Écorces-Val-Barrette. Effective June 21, 2003, name change
Pierre Flamand, Maire
Claude Meilleur, Directeur général

Lac-des-Plages
2053, ch Tour-du-Lac
Lac-des-Plages, QC J0T 1K0
Tél: 819-426-2391; *Téléc:* 819-426-2085
admin@lacdesplages.com
www.lacdesplages.com
Entité municipal: Municipality
Incorporation: 1er janvier 1950 *Area:* 121,78 km2
Comté ou district: Papineau; *Population au 2011:* 522
Circonscription(s) électorale(s) provinciale(s): Papineau
Circonscription(s) électorale(s) fédérale(s):
Argenteuil-Papineau-Mirabel
Prochaines élections: 3e novembre 2013
Josée Simon, Maire
Denis Dagenais, Directeur général

Lac-des-Seize-îles
47, rue de l'Église
Lac-des-Seize-îles, QC J0T 2M0
Tél: 450-226-3117; *Téléc:* 450-226-1461
munlac16iles@qc.aira.com
www.lac-des-seize-iles.ca
Entité municipal: Municipality
Incorporation: 19 février 1914 *Area:* 8,49 km2
Comté ou district: Les Pays-d'en-Haut; *Population au 2011:* 223
Circonscription(s) électorale(s) provinciale(s): Argenteuil
Circonscription(s) électorale(s) fédérale(s):
Argenteuil-Papineau-Mirabel
Prochaines élections: 3e novembre 2013
Luc Lamond, Maire
Luce Bergeron, Directrice générale

Lac-Drolet
685, rue Principale
Lac-Drolet, QC G0Y 1C0
Tél: 819-549-2332; *Téléc:* 819-549-2626
munlacdrolet@axion.ca
www.lacdrolet.ca
Entité municipal: Municipality
Incorporation: 1er janvier 1885 *Area:* 124,94 km2
Comté ou district: Le Granit; *Population au 2011:* 1,071
Circonscription(s) électorale(s) provinciale(s):
Mégantic-Compton
Circonscription(s) électorale(s) fédérale(s): Mégantic-L'Érable
Prochaines élections: 3e novembre 2013
Marielle Fecteau, Mairesse
Maryse Champagne, Directrice générale

Lac-du-Cerf
19, ch de l'Église
Lac-du-Cerf, QC J0W 1S0
Tél: 819-597-2424; *Téléc:* 819-597-4036
taxation@lac-du-cerf.ca
www.lac-du-cerf.info
Entité municipal: Municipality
Incorporation: 1er janvier 1955 *Area:* 78,45 km2
Comté ou district: Antoine-Labelle; *Population au 2011:* 415
Circonscription(s) électorale(s) provinciale(s): Labelle
Circonscription(s) électorale(s) fédérale(s): Laurentides-Labelle
Prochaines élections: 3e novembre 2013
Pauline Ouimet, Mairesse
Jacinthe Valiquette, Directrice générale

Lac-Etchemin
208, 2e Av
Lac-Etchemin, QC G0R 1S0
Tél: 418-625-4521; *Téléc:* 418-625-3175
munetchemin@sogetel.net
www.municipalite.lac-etchemin.qc.ca
Entité municipal: Municipality
Incorporation: 10 octobre 2001 *Area:* 160,57 km2
Comté ou district: Les Etchemins; *Population au 2011:* 4,061
Circonscription(s) électorale(s) provinciale(s): Bellechasse
Circonscription(s) électorale(s) fédérale(s): Lévis-Bellechasse
Prochaines élections: 3e novembre 2013
Harold Gagnon, Maire
Laurent Rheault, Directeur général

Lac-Frontière
22, rue de l'Église
Lac-Frontière, QC G0R 1T0
Tél: 418-245-3553; *Téléc:* 418-245-3552
municipalitelac-frontiere@globetrotter.net
www.lac-frontiere.ca
Entité municipal: Municipality
Incorporation: 7 février 1916 *Area:* 51,33 km2
Comté ou district: Montmagny; *Population au 2011:* 198
Circonscription(s) électorale(s) provinciale(s): Montmagny-L'Islet
Circonscription(s) électorale(s) fédérale(s):
Montmagny-L'Islet-Kamouraska-Rivière-du-Loup
Prochaines élections: 3e novembre 2013
Léon Laverdière, Maire
Dany Robert, Directrice générale

Lac-Mégantic
#200, 5527, rue Frontenac
Lac-Mégantic, QC G6B 1H6
Tél: 819-583-2441; *Téléc:* 819-583-5920
greffier@ville.lac-megantic.qc.ca
www.ville.lac-megantic.qc.ca
Entité municipal: Town
Incorporation: 14 mars 1907 *Area:* 20,33 km2
Comté ou district: Le Granit; *Population au 2011:* 5,932
Circonscription(s) électorale(s) provinciale(s):
Mégantic-Compton
Circonscription(s) électorale(s) fédérale(s): Mégantic-L'Érable
Prochaines élections: 3e novembre 2013
Colette Roy Laroche, Mairesse
Chantal Dion, Greffière

Lac-Poulin
CP 1019
Lac-Poulin, QC G0M 1P0
Tél: 418-228-7585; *Téléc:* 418-222-6931
munlacpoulin@globetrotter.net
Entité municipal: Village
Incorporation: 5 mars 1959 *Area:* 1,08 km2
Comté ou district: Beauce-Sartigan; *Population au 2011:* 134
Circonscription(s) électorale(s) provinciale(s): Beauce-Sud
Circonscription(s) électorale(s) fédérale(s): Beauce
Prochaines élections: 3e novembre 2013
Denis Drouin, Maire
Karina Bélanger, Directrice générale

Lac-Saguay
257A, rte 117
Lac-Saguay, QC J0W 1L0
Tél: 819-278-3972; *Téléc:* 819-278-0260
info@lacsaguay.qc.ca
www.lacsaguay.qc.ca
Entité municipal: Village
Incorporation: 1er juillet 1951 *Area:* 176,26 km2
Comté ou district: Antoine-Labelle; *Population au 2011:* 446
Circonscription(s) électorale(s) provinciale(s): Labelle
Circonscription(s) électorale(s) fédérale(s): Laurentides-Labelle
Prochaines élections: 3e novembre 2013
Francine Asselin-Bélisle, Mairesse
Richard Gagnon, Directeur général

Lac-Saint-Jean-Est
625, rue Bergeron ouest
Alma, QC G8B 1V3
Tél: 418-668-3023; *Téléc:* 418-668-5112
sabin.larouche@mrclac.qc.ca
www.mrclacsaintjeanest.qc.ca
Entité municipal: Regional County Municipality
Incorporation: 1er janvier 1982
Population au 2011: 52,520
Note: 14 municipalités & 4 autres territoires.
André Paradis, Préfet
Sabin Larouche, Directeur général
sabin.larouche@mrclac.qc.ca

Lac-Ste-Marie
CP 97
106, ch de Lac-Ste-Marie
Lac-Sainte-Marie, QC J0X 1Z0
Tél: 819-467-5437; *Téléc:* 819-467-3691
municipalite@lac-sainte-marie.com
www.lac-sainte-marie.com
Entité municipal: Municipality
Incorporation: 1er janvier 1872 *Area:* 211,13 km2
Comté ou district: La Vallée-de-la-Gatineau; *Population au 2011:* 611
Circonscription(s) électorale(s) provinciale(s): Gatineau
Circonscription(s) électorale(s) fédérale(s): Pontiac
Prochaines élections: 3e novembre 2013
Gary Lachapelle, Maire
Yvon Blanchard, Directeur général

Lac-Sergent
1149, ch Tour-du-Lac nord
Lac-Sergent, QC G0A 2J0
Tél: 418-875-4854; *Téléc:* 418-875-3805
lac-sergent@bellnet.ca
www.villelacsergent.com
Entité municipal: Village
Incorporation: 25 février 1921 *Area:* 3,52 km2
Comté ou district: Portneuf; *Population au 2011:* 466
Circonscription(s) électorale(s) provinciale(s): Portneuf
Circonscription(s) électorale(s) fédérale(s):
Portneuf-Jacques-Cartier
Prochaines élections: 3e novembre 2013
Denis Racine, Maire
Josée Brouillette, Directrice générale

Lac-Simon
CP 3550
849, ch du Tour-du-Lac
Chénéville, QC J0V 1E0
Tél: 819-428-3906; *Téléc:* 819-428-3455
mun.lacsimon@mrcpapineau.com
www.lac-simon.net
Entité municipal: Municipality
Incorporation: 1er janvier 1881 *Area:* 96,83 km2
Comté ou district: Papineau; *Population au 2011:* 984
Circonscription(s) électorale(s) provinciale(s): Papineau
Circonscription(s) électorale(s) fédérale(s):
Argenteuil-Papineau-Mirabel
Prochaines élections: 3e novembre 2013
Gaston A. Tremblay, Maire
Jacques Maillé, Directeur général

Lac-St-Joseph
1048, ch Thomas-Maher
Lac-St-Joseph, QC G3N 0B4
Tél: 418-875-3355; *Téléc:* 418-875-0444
villedelacstjoseph@coopcscf.com
www.villelacstjoseph.com
Entité municipal: Village
Incorporation: 10 juin 1936 *Area:* 32,81 km2
Comté ou district: La Jacques-Cartier; *Population au 2011:* 251
Circonscription(s) électorale(s) provinciale(s): Portneuf
Circonscription(s) électorale(s) fédérale(s):
Portneuf-Jacques-Cartier
Prochaines élections: 3e novembre 2013
O'Donnell Bédard, Maire
Vivian Viviers, Directrice générale

Lac-St-Paul
388, rue Principale
Lac-Saint-Paul, QC J0W 1K0
Tél: 819-587-4283; *Téléc:* 819-587-4892
dg@lac-saint-paul.ca
www.lac-saint-paul.ca
Entité municipal: Municipality
Incorporation: 11 septembre 1922 *Area:* 173,06 km2
Comté ou district: Antoine-Labelle; *Population au 2011:* 481
Circonscription(s) électorale(s) provinciale(s): Labelle
Circonscription(s) électorale(s) fédérale(s): Laurentides-Labelle
Prochaines élections: 3e novembre 2013

Claude Ménard, Maire
Suzanne Raymond, Directrice générale

Lac-Supérieur
1281, ch du Lac-Supérieur
Lac-Supérieur, QC J0T 1J0
Tél: 819-681-3370; *Téléc:* 819-688-3010
directiongenerale@muni.lacsuperieur.qc.ca
www.muni.lacsuperieur.qc.ca
Entité municipal: Municipality
Incorporation: 1er janvier 1881 *Area:* 380,36 km2
Comté ou district: Les Laurentides; *Population au 2011:* 1,892
Circonscription(s) électorale(s) provinciale(s): Labelle
Circonscription(s) électorale(s) fédérale(s): Laurentides-Labelle
Prochaines élections: 3e novembre 2013
Daniele Lagarde, Mairesse
Diane Taillon, Directrice générale

Lacolle
1, rue de l'Église sud
Lacolle, QC J0J 1J0
Tél: 450-246-3201; *Téléc:* 450-246-4412
admin@lacolle.com
www.lacolle.com
Entité municipal: Municipality
Incorporation: 13 septembre 2001 *Area:* 49,17 km2
Comté ou district: Le Haut-Richelieu; *Population au 2011:* 2,680
Circonscription(s) électorale(s) provinciale(s): Huntingdon
Circonscription(s) électorale(s) fédérale(s): St-Jean
Prochaines élections: 3e novembre 2013
Yves Duteau, Maire
Jacques Mireault, Directeur général

Laforce
CP 25
703, ch du Village
Laforce, QC J0Z 2J0
Tél: 819-722-2461; *Téléc:* 819-722-2462
dir.genlaforce@mrctemiscamingue.qc.ca
www.laforce.ca
Entité municipal: Municipality
Incorporation: 1er janvier 1979 *Area:* 612,65 km2
Comté ou district: Témiscamingue; *Population au 2011:* 147
Circonscription(s) électorale(s) provinciale(s):
Rouyn-Noranda-Témiscamingue
Circonscription(s) électorale(s) fédérale(s):
Abitibi-Témiscamingue
Prochaines élections: 3e novembre 2013
Gérald Charron, Maire
Daniel Lizotte, Directeur général

Lamarche
100, rue Principale
Lamarche, QC G0W 1X0
Tél: 418-481-2861; *Téléc:* 418-481-1412
mun.lamarche@ville.lamarche.qc.ca
www.ville.lamarche.qc.ca
Entité municipal: Municipality
Incorporation: 1er janvier 1967 *Area:* 94,79 km2
Comté ou district: Lac-St-Jean-Est; *Population au 2011:* 557
Circonscription(s) électorale(s) provinciale(s): Lac-St-Jean
Circonscription(s) électorale(s) fédérale(s):
Roberval-Lac-St-Jean
Prochaines élections: 3e novembre 2013
Claude Bourgault, Maire
Fabienne Girard, Directrice générale

Lambton
230, rue du Collège
Lambton, QC G0M 1H0
Tél: 418-486-7438; *Téléc:* 418-486-7440
dg@munilambton.qc.ca
www.lambton.ca
Entité municipal: Municipality
Incorporation: 23 décembre 1976 *Area:* 106,86 km2
Comté ou district: Le Granit; *Population au 2011:* 1,584
Circonscription(s) électorale(s) provinciale(s):
Mégantic-Compton
Circonscription(s) électorale(s) fédérale(s): Mégantic-L'Érable
Prochaines élections: 3e novembre 2013
Ghislain Bolduc, Maire
Sylvain Carrier, Directeur général

Landrienne
158, av Principale est
Landrienne, QC J0Y 1V0
Tél: 819-732-4357; *Téléc:* 819-732-3866
jperron@landrienne.com
www.landrienne.com
Entité municipal: Township
Incorporation: 15 juillet 1918 *Area:* 276,22 km2
Comté ou district: Abitibi; *Population au 2011:* 977
Circonscription(s) électorale(s) provinciale(s): Abitibi-Ouest
Circonscription(s) électorale(s) fédérale(s):
Abitibi-Témiscamingue
Prochaines élections: 3e novembre 2013
François Lemieux, Maire
Jacques Perron, Directeur général

Lanoraie
57, rue Laroche
Lanoraie, QC J0K 1E0
Tél: 450-887-1100; *Téléc:* 450-836-5221
info@lanoraie.ca
www.municipalite.lanoraie.qc.ca
Entité municipal: Municipality
Incorporation: 6 décembre 2000 *Area:* 102,04 km2
Comté ou district: D'Autray; *Population au 2011:* 4,447
Circonscription(s) électorale(s) provinciale(s): Berthier
Circonscription(s) électorale(s) fédérale(s): Berthier-Maskinongé
Prochaines élections: 3e novembre 2013
Jacinthe Brissette, Mairesse
Michel Dufort, Directeur général

Lantier
CP 39
118, croissant des Trois-Lacs
Lantier, QC J0T 1V0
Tél: 819-326-2674; *Téléc:* 819-326-5204
direction@municipalite.lantier.qc.ca
www.municipalite.lantier.qc.ca
Entité municipal: Municipality
Incorporation: 1er janvier 1948 *Area:* 43,57 km2
Comté ou district: Les Laurentides; *Population au 2011:* 828
Circonscription(s) électorale(s) provinciale(s): Bertrand
Circonscription(s) électorale(s) fédérale(s): Laurentides-Labelle
Prochaines élections: 3e novembre 2013
Richard Forget, Maire
Benoit Charbonneau, Directeur général

Larouche
709, rue Gauthier
Larouche, QC G0W 1Z0
Tél: 418-695-2201; *Téléc:* 418-693-2119
administration@villedelarouche.qc.ca
www.villedelarouche.qc.ca
Entité municipal: Municipality
Incorporation: 21 mars 1922 *Area:* 88 km2
Comté ou district: Le Fjord-du-Saguenay; *Population au 2011:* 1,277
Circonscription(s) électorale(s) provinciale(s): Lac-St-Jean
Circonscription(s) électorale(s) fédérale(s): Jonquière-Alma
Prochaines élections: 3e novembre 2013
Réjean Bédard, Maire
Martin Gagné, Directeur général

Latulipe-et-Gaboury
1B, rue Principale est
Latulipe-et-Gaboury, QC J0Z 2N0
Tél: 819-747-4281; *Téléc:* 819-747-2194
dir.gen_latulipe@mrctemiscamingue.qc.ca
www.latulipeetgaboury.net
Entité municipal: United Township (Cantons)
Incorporation: 18 novembre 1924 *Area:* 298,38 km2
Comté ou district: Témiscamingue; *Population au 2011:* 304
Circonscription(s) électorale(s) provinciale(s):
Rouyn-Noranda-Témiscamingue
Circonscription(s) électorale(s) fédérale(s):
Abitibi-Témiscamingue
Prochaines élections: 3e novembre 2013
Yvon Gingras, Maire
Julie Gilbert, Directrice générale

Launay
843, rue des Pionniers
Launay, QC J0Y 1W0
Tél: 819-796-2545; *Téléc:* 819-796-2546
canton.launay@cableamos.com
Entité municipal: Township
Incorporation: 18 mai 1921 *Area:* 252,44 km2
Comté ou district: Abitibi; *Population au 2011:* 229
Circonscription(s) électorale(s) provinciale(s): Abitibi-Ouest
Circonscription(s) électorale(s) fédérale(s):
Abitibi-Témiscamingue
Prochaines élections: 3e novembre 2013
Rémi Gilbert, Maire
Valérie Normand, Directrice générale

Laurier-Station
121, rue St-André
Laurier-Station, QC G0S 1N0
Tél: 418-728-3852; *Téléc:* 418-728-4801
info@ville.laurier-station.qc.ca
www.ville.laurier-station.qc.ca
Entité municipal: Village
Incorporation: 1er janvier 1951 *Area:* 12,43 km2
Comté ou district: Lotbinière; *Population au 2011:* 2,634
Circonscription(s) électorale(s) provinciale(s): Lotbinière
Circonscription(s) électorale(s) fédérale(s):
Lotbinière-Chutes-de-la-Chaudière
Prochaines élections: 3e novembre 2013
Pierrette Trépanier, Mairesse
Nancy Clavet, Directrice générale

Laurierville
140, rue Grenier
Laurierville, QC G0S 1P0
Tél: 819-365-4646; *Téléc:* 819-365-4200
rgingras@laurierville.ca
www.laurierville.net
Entité municipal: Municipality
Incorporation: 26 novembre 1997 *Area:* 110,62 km2
Comté ou district: L'Érable; *Population au 2011:* 1,454
Circonscription(s) électorale(s) provinciale(s): Lotbinière
Circonscription(s) électorale(s) fédérale(s): Mégantic-L'Érable
Prochaines élections: 3e novembre 2013
Marc Simoneau, Maire
Réjean Gingras, Directeur général

Laval
1, Place du Souvenir
Laval, QC H7V 3Z4
Tél: 450-978-3951; *Téléc:* 450-978-3966
info@ville.laval.qc.ca
www.ville.laval.qc.ca
Entité municipal: Regional County Municipality
Incorporation: 1er juin 1980
Population au 2011: 401,553
Gilles Vaillancourt, Préfet
Guy Collard, Directeur général

Laverlochère
CP 159
11, rue St-Isidore ouest
Laverlochère, QC J0Z 2P0
Tél: 819-765-5111; *Téléc:* 819-765-2564
dg.lave@mrctemiscamingue.qc.ca
www.temiscamingue.net/laverlochere
Entité municipal: Municipality
Incorporation: 3 octobre 1912 *Area:* 107,01 km2
Comté ou district: Témiscamingue; *Population au 2011:* 1,022
Circonscription(s) électorale(s) provinciale(s):
Rouyn-Noranda-Témiscamingue
Circonscription(s) électorale(s) fédérale(s):
Abitibi-Témiscamingue
Prochaines élections: 3e novembre 2013
Daniel Barrette, Maire
Monique Rivest, Directrice générale

Lawrenceville
2100, rue Dandenault
Lawrenceville, QC J0E 1W0
Tél: 450-535-6398; *Téléc:* 450-535-6537
munlaw@cooptel.qc.ca
Entité municipal: Village
Incorporation: 27 avril 1905 *Area:* 17,40 km2
Comté ou district: Le Val-St-François; *Population au 2011:* 652
Circonscription(s) électorale(s) provinciale(s): Brome-Missisquoi
Circonscription(s) électorale(s) fédérale(s): Shefford
Prochaines élections: 3e novembre 2013
Michel Carbonneau, Maire
Ginette Bergeron, Directrice générale

Le Domaine-du-Roy
901, boul St-Joseph
Roberval, QC G8H 2L8
Tél: 418-275-5044; *Téléc:* 418-275-4049
administration@mrcdomaineduroy.ca
www.domaineduroy.ca
Entité municipal: Regional County Municipality
Incorporation: 1er janvier 1983
Population au 2011: 31,870
Note: 9 municipalités & 1 autre territoire.
Bernard Généreux, Préfet
Denis Taillon, Directeur général
dtaillon@mrcdomaineduroy.ca

Le Fjord-du-Saguenay
3110, boul Martel
Saint-Honoré, QC G0V 1L0
Tél: 418-673-1705; *Téléc:* 418-673-7205
mrcdufjord@mrc-fjord.qc.ca
www.mrc-fjord.qc.ca
Entité municipal: Regional County Municipality
Population au 2011: 20,465
Note: 13 municipalités & 3 autres territoires.

Jean-Marie Claveau, Préfet
Christine Dufour, Directrice générale
christine.dufour@mrc-fjord.qc.ca

Le Granit
5090, rue Frontenac
Lac-Mégantic, QC G6B 1H3
Tél: 819-583-0181; *Téléc:* 819-583-5327
administration@mrcgranit.qc.ca
www.mrcgranit.qc.ca
Entité municipal: Regional County Municipality
Incorporation: 26 mai 1982
Population au 2011: 22,259
Note: 20 municipalités.
Maurice Bernier, Préfet
Serge Bilodeau, Directeur général

Le Haut-Richelieu
380, 4e av
Saint-Jean-sur-Richelieu, QC J2X 1W9
Tél: 450-346-3636; *Téléc:* 450-346-8464
info@mrchr.qc.ca
mrchr.qc.ca
Entité municipal: Regional County Municipality
Incorporation: 1er janvier 1982
Population au 2011: 114,344
Note: 14 municipalités.
Gilles Dolbec, Préfet
Joane Saulnier, Directrice générale

Le Haut-St-François
85, rue du Parc
Cookshire, QC J0B 1M0
Tél: 819-875-5451; *Téléc:* 819-875-3135
dominic.provost@hsfqc.ca
www.mrchsf.com
Entité municipal: Regional County Municipality
Incorporation: 1er janvier 1982
Population au 2011: 22,065
Note: 14 municipalités.
Nicole Robert, Préfète
nicole.robert@hsfqc.ca
Dominique Provost, Directeur général

Le Haut-St-Laurent
#400, 10, rue King
Huntingdon, QC J0S 1H0
Tél: 450-264-5411; *Téléc:* 450-264-6885
mrchsl@mrchsl.com
www.mrchsl.com
Entité municipal: Regional County Municipality
Incorporation: 1 janvier 1982
Population au 2011: 21,197
Note: 13 municipalités.
Alain Castagner, Préfet
François Landreville, Directeur général

Le Rocher-Percé
CP 128
129, boul René-Lévesque ouest
Chandler, QC G0C 1K0
Tél: 418-689-4313; *Téléc:* 418-689-5807
mrc@rocherperce.qc.ca
www.mrcrocherperce.qc.ca
Entité municipal: Regional County Municipality
Incorporation: 1 avril 1981
Population au 2011: 17,979
Note: 5 municipalités & 1 autre territoire.
Diane Lebouthillier, Préfet
Mario Grenier, Directeur général
418-689-4017

Le Val-St-François
CP 3160
810, montée du Parc
Richmond, QC J0B 2H0
Tél: 819-826-6505; *Téléc:* 819-826-3484
mrc@val-saint-francois.qc.ca
www.val-saint-francois.qc.ca
Entité municipal: Regional County Municipality
Incorporation: 26 mai 1982
Population au 2011: 29,654
Note: 18 municipalités.
Claude Boucher, Préfet
Manon Fortin, Directrice générale
manon.fortin@val-saint-francois.qc.ca

Lebel-sur-Quévillon
CP 430
500, place Quévillon
Lebel-sur-Quévillon, QC J0Y 1X0
Tél: 819-755-4826; *Téléc:* 819-755-8124
ville@lebel-sur-quevillon.com
www.lebel-sur-quevillon.com
Entité municipal: Town
Incorporation: 6 août 1965 *Area:* 44,74 km2
Population au 2011: 2,159
Circonscription(s) électorale(s) provinciale(s): Ungava
Circonscription(s) électorale(s) fédérale(s):
Abitibi-Baie-James-Nunavik-Eeyou
Prochaines élections: 3e novembre 2013
Gérald Lemoyne, Maire
Réal Lavigne, Greffier

Leclercville
1014, rue de l'Église
Leclercville, QC G0S 2K0
Tél: 819-292-2331; *Téléc:* 819-292-2639
mun.leclercville@videotron.ca
www.munleclercville.qc.ca
Entité municipal: Municipality
Incorporation: 26 janvier 2000 *Area:* 135,40 km2
Comté ou district: Lotbinière; *Population au 2011:* 477
Circonscription(s) électorale(s) provinciale(s): Lotbinière
Circonscription(s) électorale(s) fédérale(s):
Lotbinière-Chutes-de-la-Chaudière
Prochaines élections: 3e novembre 2013
Marcel Richard, Maire
Francine B. Demers, Directrice générale

Lefebvre
186, 10e rang
Lefebvre, QC J0H 2C0
Tél: 819-394-2782; *Téléc:* 819-394-2186
municipalite.lefebvre@xittel.ca
Entité municipal: Municipality
Incorporation: 10 octobre 1922 *Area:* 65,75 km2
Comté ou district: Drummond; *Population au 2011:* 867
Circonscription(s) électorale(s) provinciale(s): Johnson
Circonscription(s) électorale(s) fédérale(s): Drummond
Prochaines élections: 3e novembre 2013
Claude Bahl, Maire
Julie Yergeau, Directrice générale

Lejeune
CP 40
69, rue de la Grande-Coulée
Lejeune, QC G0L 1S0
Tél: 418-855-2428; *Téléc:* 418-855-2428
info@municipalitelejeune.ca
Entité municipal: Municipality
Incorporation: 1er janvier 1964 *Area:* 269,40 km2
Comté ou district: Témiscouata; *Population au 2011:* 286
Circonscription(s) électorale(s) provinciale(s):
Kamouraska-Témiscouata
Circonscription(s) électorale(s) fédérale(s):
Rimouski-Neigette-Témiscouata-Les Basques
Prochaines élections: 3e novembre 2013
Lucie Gilbert, Mairesse
Claudine Castonguay, Directrice générale

Lemieux
530, rue de l'Église
Lemieux, QC G0X 1S0
Tél: 819-283-2506; *Téléc:* 819-283-2029
info@municipalitelemieux.ca
Entité municipal: Municipality
Incorporation: 14 août 1922 *Area:* 74,79 km2
Comté ou district: Bécancour; *Population au 2011:* 304
Circonscription(s) électorale(s) provinciale(s): Lotbinière
Circonscription(s) électorale(s) fédérale(s):
Bas-Richelieu-Nicolet-Bécancour
Prochaines élections: 3e novembre 2013
Jean-Louis Bélisle, Maire
France Hénault, Directrice générale

Léry
1, rue de l'Hôtel-de-Ville
Léry, QC J6N 1E8
Tél: 450-692-6861; *Téléc:* 450-692-6881
villedelery@videotron.ca
Entité municipal: Town
Incorporation: 1er juin 1914 *Area:* 10,98 km2
Comté ou district: Roussillon; *Population au 2011:* 2,307
Circonscription(s) électorale(s) provinciale(s): Châteauguay
Circonscription(s) électorale(s) fédérale(s):
Châteauguay-St-Constant
Prochaines élections: 3e novembre 2013
Yvon Mailhot, Maire

Dale Stewart, Directeur général

Les Appalaches
3830, boul Frontenac ouest
Thetford Mines, QC G6H 2L8
Tél: 418-423-2757; *Téléc:* 418-423-5122
info@mrcdesappalaches.ca
www.mrcdesappalaches.ca
Entité municipal: Regional County Municipality
Incorporation: 1er janvier 1982
Population au 2011: 43,120
Note: 19 municipalités.
Ghislain Hamel, Préfet
Marie-Eve Mercier, Directrice générale
memercier@mrcdesappalaches.ca

Les Basques
#400, 2, rue Jean-Rioux
Trois-Pistoles, QC G0L 4K0
Tél: 418-851-3206; *Téléc:* 418-851-3171
mrc@mrcdesbasques.com
www.mrcdesbasques.com
Entité municipal: Regional County Municipality
Incorporation: 1er avril 1981
Population au 2011: 9,142
Note: 11 municipalités & 1 autre territoire.
Denis Bertin, Préfet
François Gosselin, Directeur général

Les Bergeronnes
CP 158
424, rue de la Mer
Les Bergeronnes, QC G0T 1G0
Tél: 418-232-6244; *Téléc:* 418-232-6602
info@bergeronnes.com
www.bergeronnes.net
Entité municipal: Municipality
Incorporation: 29 décembre 1999 *Area:* 291,89 km2
Comté ou district: La Haute Côte-Nord; *Population au 2011:* 693
Circonscription(s) électorale(s) provinciale(s): René-Lévesque
Circonscription(s) électorale(s) fédérale(s):
Montmorency-Charlevoix-Haute-Côte-Nord
Prochaines élections: 3e novembre 2013
Francis Bouchard, Maire
Lynda Tremblay, Directrice générale

Les Cèdres
1060, ch du Fleuve
Les Cèdres, QC J7T 1A1
Tél: 450-452-4651; *Téléc:* 450-452-4605
dgenerale@ville.lescedres.qc.ca
www.ville.lescedres.qc.ca
Entité municipal: Municipality
Incorporation: 9 mars 1985 *Area:* 78,31 km2
Comté ou district: Vaudreuil-Soulanges; *Population au 2011:* 6,079
Circonscription(s) électorale(s) provinciale(s): Soulanges
Circonscription(s) électorale(s) fédérale(s): Vaudreuil-Soulanges
Prochaines élections: 3e novembre 2013
Géraldine T. Quesnel, Mairesse
Jimmy Poulin, Directeur général

Les Chenaux
630, rue Principale
Saint-Luc-de-Vincennes, QC G0X 3K0
Tél: 819-840-0704; *Téléc:* 819-295-5117
info@mrcdeschenaux.ca
www.mrcdeschenaux.ca
Entité municipal: Regional County Municipality
Incorporation: 1er janvier 2002
Population au 2011: 17,865
Note: 10 municipalités.
Gérard Bruneau, Préfet
Pierre St-Onge, Directeur général
pierre.stonge@mrcdeschenaux.ca

Les Collines-de-l'Outaouais
216, ch Old Chelsea
Chelsea, QC J9B 1J4
Tél: 819-827-0516; *Téléc:* 819-827-4669
gpoulin@mrcdescollines.com
www.mrcdescollines.com
Entité municipal: Regional County Municipality
Incorporation: 4e décembre 1991
Population au 2011: 46,393
Note: 7 municipalités.
Robert Bussière, Préfet
Ghislain Poulin, Directeur général

Les Coteaux
65, rte 338
Les Coteaux, QC J7X 1A2
Tél: 450-267-3531; *Téléc:* 450-267-3532
municipalitedescoteaux@videotron.ca
www.les-coteaux.qc.ca
Entité municipal: Municipality
Incorporation: 18 mai 1994 *Area:* 12,11 km2
Comté ou district: Vaudreuil-Soulanges; *Population au 2011:* 4,568
Circonscription(s) électorale(s) provinciale(s): Soulanges
Circonscription(s) électorale(s) fédérale(s): Vaudreuil-Soulanges
Prochaines élections: 3e novembre 2013
Réal Boisvert, Maire
Claude Madore, Directeur général

Les Éboulements
248, rue du Village
Les Éboulements, QC G0A 2M0
Tél: 418-489-2988; *Téléc:* 418-489-2989
municipalite@leseboulements.com
www.leseboulements.com
Entité municipal: Municipality
Incorporation: 19 septembre 2001 *Area:* 153,99 km2
Comté ou district: Charlevoix; *Population au 2011:* 1,328
Circonscription(s) électorale(s) provinciale(s): Charlevoix
Circonscription(s) électorale(s) fédérale(s): Montmorency-Charlevoix-Haute-Côte-Nord
Prochaines élections: 3e novembre 2013
Bertrand Bouchard, Maire
Linda Gauthier, Directrice générale

Les Escoumins
2, rue Sirois
Les Escoumins, QC G0T 1K0
Tél: 418-233-2766; *Téléc:* 418-233-3273
administration.muni@escoumins.ca
www.escoumins.ca
Entité municipal: Municipality
Incorporation: 5 mai 1863 *Area:* 267,33 km2
Comté ou district: La Haute-Côte-Nord; *Population au 2011:* 2,000
Circonscription(s) électorale(s) provinciale(s): René-Lévesque
Circonscription(s) électorale(s) fédérale(s): Montmorency-Charlevoix-Haute-Côte-Nord
Prochaines élections: 3e novembre 2013
Pierre Laurencelle, Maire
Chantale Otis, Directrice générale

Les Etchemins
1137, rte 277
Lac-Etchemin, QC G0R 1S0
Tél: 418-625-9000; *Téléc:* 418-625-9005
mrcetchemins@sogetel.net
www.mrcetchemins.qc.ca
Entité municipal: Regional County Municipality
Incorporation: 1er janvier 1982
Population au 2011: 17,254
Note: 13 muncipalités.
Hector Provençal, Préfet
Fernand Heppell, Directeur général
fheppell@mrcetchemins.qc.ca

Les Hauteurs
50, rue de l'Église
Les Hauteurs, QC G0K 1C0
Tél: 418-798-8266; *Téléc:* 418-798-4707
leshauteurs@mitis.qc.ca
municipalite.leshauteurs.qc.ca
Entité municipal: Municipality
Incorporation: 7e novembre 1918 *Area:* 105,41 km2
Comté ou district: La Mitis; *Population au 2011:* 524
Circonscription(s) électorale(s) provinciale(s): Matapédia
Circonscription(s) électorale(s) fédérale(s): Haute-Gaspésie-La Mitis-Matane-Matapédia
Prochaines élections: 3e novembre 2013
Noël Lambert, Maire
Diane Bernier, Directrice générale

Les îles-de-la-Madeleine
460, ch Principal
Cap-aux-Meules, QC G4T 1A1
Tel: 418-986-3100; *Fax:* 418-986-6962
jlebreux@muniles.ca
www.muniles.ca
Municipal Type: Municipality
Incorporated: 1er janvier 2002 *Area:* 166,39 km2
Population in 2011: 12,781
Provincial Electoral District(s): îles-de-la-Madeleine
Federal Electoral District(s): Gaspésie—îles-de-la-Madeleine
Next Election: 3e novembre 2013
Joël Arseneau, Maire
Jean-Yves Lebreux, Greffier

Les Jardins-de-Napierville
1767, rue Principale
Saint-Michel, QC J0L 2J0
Tél: 450-454-0559; *Téléc:* 450-454-0560
info@mrcjardinsdenapierville.ca
mrcjardinsdenapierville.ca
Entité municipal: Regional County Municipality
Incorporation: 1er janvier 1982
Population au 2011: 26,234
Circonscription(s) électorale(s) provinciale(s): Huntington
Circonscription(s) électorale(s) fédérale(s): Beauharnois-Salaberry
Note: 11 municipalités.
Michel Lavoie, Préfet
M. Michel Charbonneau, Directeur général
michel.c@cld-jardinsdenapierville.com

Les Laurentides
1255, ch des Lacs
Saint-Faustin-Lac-Carré, QC J0T 1J2
Tél: 819-425-5555; *Téléc:* 819-688-6590
adm@mrclaurentides.qc.ca
www.mrclaurentides.qc.ca
Entité municipal: Regional County Municipality
Incorporation: 1er janvier 1983
Population au 2011: 45,157
Note: 20 municipalités.
Ronald Provost, Préfet
Michel Bélanger, Directeur général
mbelanger@mrclaurentides.qc.ca

Les Maskoutains
805, av du Palais
Saint-Hyacinthe, QC J2S 5C6
Tél: 450-774-3141; *Téléc:* 450-774-7161
admin@mrcmaskoutains.qc.ca
www.mrcmaskoutains.qc.ca
Entité municipal: Regional County Municipality
Incorporation: 1er janvier 1982
Population au 2011: 84,248
Note: 17 municipalités.
Francine Morin, Préfète
Gabriel Michaud, Directeur général

Les Méchins
108, rte des Fonds
Les Méchins, QC G0J 1T0
Tél: 418-729-3952; *Téléc:* 418-729-3585
lesmechins@mrcdematane.qc.ca
www.lesmechins.com
Entité municipal: Municipality
Incorporation: 27 novembre 1982 *Area:* 452 km2
Comté ou district: Matane; *Population au 2011:* 1,107
Circonscription(s) électorale(s) provinciale(s): Matane
Circonscription(s) électorale(s) fédérale(s): Haute-Gaspésie-La Mitis-Matane-Matapédia
Prochaines élections: 3e novembre 2013
Jean-Sébastien Barriault, Maire
Lyne Fortin, Directrice générale

Les Moulins
148, rue St-André
Terrebonne, QC J6W 3C3
Tél: 450-471-9576; *Téléc:* 450-471-8193
info@mrclesmoulins.ca
www.mrclesmoulins.ca
Entité municipal: Regional County Municipality
Incorporation: 1er janvier 1982
Population au 2011: 148,813
Note: 2 municipalités.
Jean-Marc Robitaille, Préfet
Daniel Pilon, Directeur général
dpilon@mrclesmoulins.ca

Les Pays-d'en-Haut
1014, rue Valiquette
Sainte-Adèle, QC J8B 2M3
Tél: 450-229-6637; *Téléc:* 450-229-5203
info@mrcpdh.org
www.mrcpdh.com
Entité municipal: Regional County Municipality
Incorporation: 1er janvier 1983
Population au 2011: 40,331
Note: 10 municipalités.
Charles Garnier, Préfet
Yvan Genest, Directeur général

Les Sources
309, rue Chassé
Asbestos, QC J1T 2B4
Tél: 819-879-6643; *Téléc:* 819-879-5188
mrcdessources@mrcdessources.com
www.mrcdessources.com
Entité municipal: Regional County Municipality
Incorporation: 1er janvier 1982
Population au 2011: 14,756
Note: 7 municipalités.
Jacques Hémond, Préfet
Yvan Provencher, Directeur général

Lingwick
72, rte 108
Lingwick, QC J0B 2Z0
Tél: 819-560-8422; *Téléc:* 819-877-3315
canton.lingwick@hsfqc.ca
www.cantondelingwick.com
Entité municipal: Township
Incorporation: 1er juillet 1855 *Area:* 242,83 km2
Comté ou district: Le Haut-St-François; *Population au 2011:* 399
Circonscription(s) électorale(s) provinciale(s): Mégantic-Compton
Circonscription(s) électorale(s) fédérale(s): Compton-Stanstead
Prochaines élections: 3e novembre 2013
Céline Gagné, Mairesse
Monique Polard, Directrice générale

Litchfield
CP 340
1362, rte 148
Campbell's Bay, QC J0X 1K0
Tél: 819-648-5511; *Téléc:* 819-648-5575
litchfield@mrcpontiac.qc.ca
Entité municipal: Municipality
Incorporation: 1er juillet 1855 *Area:* 178,96 km2
Comté ou district: Pontiac; *Population au 2011:* 456
Circonscription(s) électorale(s) provinciale(s): Pontiac
Circonscription(s) électorale(s) fédérale(s): Pontiac
Prochaines élections: 3e novembre 2013
Michael McCrank, Maire
Jacqueline Brisebois, Directrice générale

Lochaber
164, rte 148 est
Lochaber, QC J0X 3B0
Tél: 819-985-3291; *Téléc:* 819-985-3291
munlochaber@qc.aira.com
Entité municipal: Township
Incorporation: 1er juillet 1855 *Area:* 62,17 km2
Comté ou district: Papineau; *Population au 2011:* 409
Circonscription(s) électorale(s) provinciale(s): Papineau
Circonscription(s) électorale(s) fédérale(s): Argenteuil-Papineau-Mirabel
Prochaines élections: 3e novembre 2013
Georges Leduc, Maire
Marthe Thibaudeau, Directrice générale

Lochaber-Partie-Ouest
#11, 161, rue Galipeau
Thurso, QC J0X 3B0
Tél: 819-985-1553; *Téléc:* 819-985-0790
mun.lochaberouest@mrcpapineau.com
Entité municipal: Township
Incorporation: 20 avril 1891 *Area:* 61,22 km2
Comté ou district: Papineau; *Population au 2011:* 646
Circonscription(s) électorale(s) provinciale(s): Papineau
Circonscription(s) électorale(s) fédérale(s): Argenteuil-Papineau-Mirabel
Prochaines élections: 3e novembre 2013
Michel Labreque, Maire
Alain Hotte, Directeur général

Longue-Pointe-de-Mingan
CP 68
878, ch du Roi
Longue-Pointe-de-Mingan, QC G0G 1V0
Tél: 418-949-2053; *Téléc:* 418-949-2166
munlpm@xplornet.com
Entité municipal: Municipality
Incorporation: 1er janvier 1966 *Area:* 417,60 km2
Comté ou district: Minganie; *Population au 2011:* 479
Circonscription(s) électorale(s) provinciale(s): Duplessis
Circonscription(s) électorale(s) fédérale(s): Manicouagan
Prochaines élections: 3e novembre 2013
Jean-Luc Burgess, Maire
Célyne B.-Loiselle, Directrice générale

Longue-Rive
3, rue de l'Église
Longue-Rive, QC G0T 1Z0
Tél: 418-231-2344; *Téléc:* 418-231-2577
munlonguerive@bellnet.ca
Entité municipal: Municipality
Incorporation: 28 mai 1997 *Area:* 295,35 km2
Comté ou district: La Haute-Côte-Nord; *Population au 2011:* 1,113
Circonscription(s) électorale(s) provinciale(s): René-Lévesque
Circonscription(s) électorale(s) fédérale(s): Montmorency-Charlevoix-Haute-Côte-Nord
Prochaines élections: 3e novembre 2013
Mario Tremblay, Maire
Hélène Boulianne, Sec.-Trés.

Lorraine
33, boul De Gaulle
Lorraine, QC J6Z 3W9
Tél: 450-621-8550; *Téléc:* 450-621-4763
communication@ville.lorraine.qc.ca
www.ville.lorraine.qc.ca
Entité municipal: Town
Incorporation: 4e février 1960 *Area:* 5,96 km2
Comté ou district: Thérèse-De Blainville; *Population au 2011:* 9,479
Circonscription(s) électorale(s) provinciale(s): Blainville
Circonscription(s) électorale(s) fédérale(s): Marc-Aurèle-Fortin
Prochaines élections: 3e novembre 2013
Ramez Ayoub, Maire
450-965-8717
mairie@ville.lorraine.qc.ca
Sylvie Trahan, Greffière
450-621-8550
greffe@ville.lorraine.qc.ca

Lorrainville
CP 218
2, rue St-Jean-Baptiste est
Lorrainville, QC J0Z 2R0
Tél: 819-625-2167; *Téléc:* 819-625-2380
lorrainville@mrctemiscamingue.qc.ca
www.lorrainville.ca
Entité municipal: Municipality
Incorporation: 16 février 1994 *Area:* 85,12 km2
Comté ou district: Témiscamingue; *Population au 2011:* 1,272
Circonscription(s) électorale(s) provinciale(s): Rouyn-Noranda-Témiscamingue
Circonscription(s) électorale(s) fédérale(s): Abitibi-Témiscamingue
Prochaines élections: 3e novembre 2013
Philippe Boutin, Maire
Francyne Bleau, Directrice générale

Lotbinière
7440, rue Marie-Victorin
Lotbinière, QC G0S 1S0
Tél: 418-796-2103; *Téléc:* 418-796-2198
info@municipalite.lotbiniere.qc.ca
www.municipalite.lotbiniere.qc.ca
Entité municipal: Municipality
Incorporation: 1er janvier 1979 *Area:* 78,47 km2
Comté ou district: Lotbinière; *Population au 2011:* 887
Circonscription(s) électorale(s) provinciale(s): Lotbinière
Circonscription(s) électorale(s) fédérale(s): Lotbinière-Chutes-de-la-Chaudière
Prochaines élections: 3e novembre 2013
Maurice Sénécal, Maire
Bernard Lepage, Directeur général

Lotbinière
6375, rue Garneau
Sainte-Croix, QC G0S 2H0
Tél: 418-926-3407; *Téléc:* 418-926-3409
info@mrclotbiniere.org
www.mrclotbiniere.org
Entité municipal: Regional County Municipality
Incorporation: 1 janvier 1982
Population au 2011: 29,617
Note: 18 municipalités.
Maurice Sénécal, Préfet
Daniel Patry, Directeur général
daniel.patry@mrclotbiniere.org

Louiseville
105, av St-Laurent
Louiseville, QC J5V 1J6
Tél: 819-228-9437; *Téléc:* 819-228-2263
directiongenerale@ville.louiseville.qc.ca
www.ville.louiseville.qc.ca
Entité municipal: Town
Incorporation: 31 décembre 1988 *Area:* 62,56 km2
Comté ou district: Maskinongé; *Population au 2011:* 7,517
Circonscription(s) électorale(s) provinciale(s): Maskinongé
Circonscription(s) électorale(s) fédérale(s): Berthier-Maskinongé
Prochaines élections: 3e novembre 2013
Guy Richard, Mairesse
Martine St-Yves, Greffière

Low
4A, ch d'Amour
Low, QC J0X 2C0
Tél: 819-422-3528; *Téléc:* 819-422-3796
info@lowquebec.ca
www.lowquebec.ca
Entité municipal: Township
Incorporation: 1er janvier 1858 *Area:* 259,95 km2
Comté ou district: La Vallée-de-la-Gatineau; *Population au 2011:* 920
Circonscription(s) électorale(s) provinciale(s): Gatineau
Circonscription(s) électorale(s) fédérale(s): Pontiac
Prochaines élections: 3e novembre 2013
Morris O'Connor, Maire
Liette Hickey, Directrice générale

Lyster
2375, rue Bécancour
Lyster, QC G0S 1V0
Tél: 819-389-5787; *Téléc:* 819-389-5981
info@municipalite.lyster.qc.ca
www.municipalite.lyster.qc.ca
Entité municipal: Municipality
Incorporation: 18 septembre 1976 *Area:* 162,35 km2
Comté ou district: L'Érable; *Population au 2011:* 1,628
Circonscription(s) électorale(s) provinciale(s): Lotbinière
Circonscription(s) électorale(s) fédérale(s): Mégantic-L'Érable
Prochaines élections: 3e novembre 2013
Sylvain Labrecque, Maire
Suzie Côté, Directrice générale

Macamic
70, rue Principale
Macamic, QC J0Z 2S0
Tél: 819-782-4604; *Téléc:* 819-782-4283
macamic@mrcao.qc.ca
www.villemacamic.qc.ca
Entité municipal: Town
Incorporation: 6 mars 2002 *Area:* 191,95 km2
Comté ou district: Abitibi-Ouest; *Population au 2011:* 2,734
Circonscription(s) électorale(s) provinciale(s): Abitibi-Ouest
Circonscription(s) électorale(s) fédérale(s): Abitibi-Témiscamingue
Prochaines élections: 3e novembre 2013
Daniel Rancourt, Maire
Denis Bédard, Directeur général

Maddington
86, rte 261 nord
Maddington, QC G0Z 1C0
Tél: 819-367-2577; *Téléc:* 819-367-3137
info@maddington.ca
Entité municipal: Township
Incorporation: 11 janvier 1902 *Area:* 23,38 km2
Comté ou district: Arthabaska; *Population au 2011:* 443
Circonscription(s) électorale(s) provinciale(s): Nicolet-Yamaska
Circonscription(s) électorale(s) fédérale(s): Richmond-Arthabaska
Prochaines élections: 3e novembre 2013
Normand Soucy, Maire
Martine Lebeau, Directrice générale

Malartic
CP 3090
901, rue Royale
Malartic, QC J0Y 1Z0
Tél: 819-757-3611; *Téléc:* 819-757-3084
cmaurice@ville.malartic.qc.ca
www.ville.malartic.qc.ca
Entité municipal: Town
Incorporation: 28 avril 1939 *Area:* 159,31 km2
Comté ou district: La Vallée-de-l'Or; *Population au 2011:* 3,449
Circonscription(s) électorale(s) provinciale(s): Abitibi-Est
Circonscription(s) électorale(s) fédérale(s): Abitibi-Baie-James-Nunavik-Eeyou
Prochaines élections: 3e novembre 2013
André Vezeau, Maire
Claudyne Maurice, Greffière

Mandeville
162, rue Desjardins
Mandeville, QC J0K 1L0
Tél: 450-835-2055; *Téléc:* 450-835-7795
mandeville@intermonde.net
www.mandeville.qc.ca
Entité municipal: Municipality
Incorporation: 20 avril 1904 *Area:* 330,85 km2
Comté ou district: D'Autray; *Population au 2011:* 2,043
Circonscription(s) électorale(s) provinciale(s): Berthier
Circonscription(s) électorale(s) fédérale(s): Joliette
Prochaines élections: 3e novembre 2013
Francine Bergeron, Mairesse
Hélène Plourde, Directrice générale

Manicouagan
768, rue Bossé
Baie-Comeau, QC G5C 1L6
Tél: 418-589-9594; *Téléc:* 418-589-6383
info@mrcmanicouagan.qc.ca
www.mrcmanicouagan.qc.ca
Entité municipal: Regional County Municipality
Incorporation: 1er avril 1981
Population au 2011: 32,012
Note: 8 municipalités & 1 autre territoire.
Christine Brisson, Préfète
Patricia Huet, Directrice générale
patricia.huet@globetrotter.net

Maniwaki
186, rue Principale sud
Maniwaki, QC J9E 1Z9
Tél: 819-449-2800; *Téléc:* 819-449-7078
maniwaki@ville.maniwaki.qc.ca
www.ville.maniwaki.qc.ca
Entité municipal: Town
Incorporation: 15 mars 1904 *Area:* 5,60 km2
Comté ou district: La Vallée-de-la-Gatineau; *Population au 2011:* 3,930
Circonscription(s) électorale(s) provinciale(s): Gatineau
Circonscription(s) électorale(s) fédérale(s): Pontiac
Prochaines élections: 3e novembre 2013
Robert Coulombe, Maire
Andrée Loyer, Greffière

Manseau
200, rue Roux
Manseau, QC G0X 1V0
Tél: 819-356-2450; *Téléc:* 819-356-2721
directiongenerale@manseau.ca
www.manseau.ca
Entité municipal: Municipality
Incorporation: 31 décembre 1997 *Area:* 102,5 km2
Comté ou district: Bécancour; *Population au 2011:* 843
Circonscription(s) électorale(s) provinciale(s): Lotbinière
Circonscription(s) électorale(s) fédérale(s): Bas-Richelieu-Nicolet-Bécancour
Prochaines élections: 3e novembre 2013
Guy St-Pierre, Maire
Nadine Watters, Directrice générale

Mansfield-et-Pontefract
300, rue Principale
Mansfield, QC J0X 1R0
Tél: 819-683-2944; *Téléc:* 819-683-3590
mansfield@personainternet.com
Entité municipal: Municipality
Incorporation: 1er janvier 1868 *Area:* 420,79 km2
Comté ou district: Pontiac; *Population au 2011:* 2,204
Circonscription(s) électorale(s) provinciale(s): Pontiac
Circonscription(s) électorale(s) fédérale(s): Pontiac
Prochaines élections: 3e novembre 2013
Leslie L. Bélair, Maire
Éric Rochon, Directeur général

Marguerite-D'Youville
609, rte Marie-Victorin
Verchères, QC J0L 2R0
Tél: 450-583-3301; *Téléc:* 450-583-3592
info@margueritedyouville.ca
www.margueritedyouville.ca
Entité municipal: Regional County Municipality
Incorporation: 1er janvier 1982
Population au 2011: 74,416
Note: 6 municipalités.
Suzanne Roy, Préfète
Sylvain Berthiaume, Directeur général

Maria
545, boul Perron
Maria, QC G0C 1Y0
Tél: 418-759-3883; *Téléc:* 418-759-3059
munmaria@globetrotter.net
www.mariaquebec.com
Entité municipal: Municipality
Incorporation: 1er juillet 1855 *Area:* 96,34 km2
Comté ou district: Avignon; *Population au 2011:* 2,536
Circonscription(s) électorale(s) provinciale(s): Bonaventure

Circonscription(s) électorale(s) fédérale(s):
Gaspésie—Îles-de-la-Madeleine
Prochaines élections: 3e novembre 2013
Normand Audet, Maire
Gilbert Leblanc, Directeur général

Maria-Chapdelaine
173, boul St-Michel
Dolbeau-Mistassini, QC G8L 4N9
Tél: 418-276-2131; *Téléc:* 418-276-7043
portail@mrcmaria.qc.ca
www.mrcdemaria-chapdelaine.ca
Entité municipal: Regional County Municipality
Incorporation: 1er janvier 1983
Population au 2011: 25,279
Note: 12 municipalités & 2 autres territoires.
Jean-Pierre Boivin, Préfet
Christian Bouchard, Directeur général
cbouchard@mrcmaria.qc.ca

Maricourt
1195, 3e rang nord
Maricourt, QC J0E 1Y0
Tél: 450-532-2243; *Téléc:* 450-532-2246
munmari@cooptel.qc.ca
Entité municipal: Municipality
Incorporation: 1er janvier 1864 *Area:* 62,03 km2
Comté ou district: Le Val-St-François; *Population au 2011:* 497
Circonscription(s) électorale(s) provinciale(s): Johnson
Circonscription(s) électorale(s) fédérale(s): Shefford
Prochaines élections: 3e novembre 2013
Réjean Paquette, Maire
Yves Barthe, Directeur général

Marieville
682, rue Saint-Charles
Marieville, QC J3M 1P9
Tél: 450-460-4444; *Téléc:* 450-460-2770
administration@ville.marieville.qc.ca
www.ville.marieville.qc.ca
Entité municipal: Town
Incorporation: 14 juin 2000 *Area:* 64,25 km2
Comté ou district: Rouville; *Population au 2011:* 10,094
Circonscription(s) électorale(s) provinciale(s): Iberville
Circonscription(s) électorale(s) fédérale(s): Chambly-Borduas
Prochaines élections: 3e novembre 2013
Alain Ménard, Maire
Nancy Forget, Greffière

Marsoui
CP 130
8, rte Principale est
Marsoui, QC G0E 1S0
Tél: 418-288-5552; *Téléc:* 418-288-5104
municipalite.marsoui@globetrotter.net
www.marsoui.com
Entité municipal: Village
Incorporation: 1er janvier 1950 *Area:* 182,95 km2
Comté ou district: La Haute-Gaspésie; *Population au 2011:* 309
Circonscription(s) électorale(s) provinciale(s): Matane
Circonscription(s) électorale(s) fédérale(s): Haute-Gaspésie-La Mitis-Matane-Matapédia
Prochaines élections: 3e novembre 2013
Jovette Gasse, Mairesse
Nancy Leclerc, Directrice générale

Marston
175, rte 263 sud
Marston, QC G0Y 1G0
Tél: 819-583-0435; *Téléc:* 819-583-6604
marston@axion.ca
www.munmarston.qc.ca
Entité municipal: Township
Incorporation: 1er janvier 1874 *Area:* 71,77 km2
Comté ou district: Le Granit; *Population au 2011:* 662
Circonscription(s) électorale(s) provinciale(s):
Mégantic-Compton
Circonscription(s) électorale(s) fédérale(s): Mégantic-L'Érable
Prochaines élections: 3e novembre 2013
Jacques Lalonde, Maire
Francine Veilleux, Directrice générale

Martinville
233, rue Principale est
Martinville, QC J0B 2A0
Tél: 819-835-5390; *Téléc:* 819-835-0171
martinville@qc.aira.com
Entité municipal: Municipality
Incorporation: 21 décembre 1895 *Area:* 48,64 km2
Comté ou district: Coaticook; *Population au 2011:* 469
Circonscription(s) électorale(s) provinciale(s):
Mégantic-Compton
Circonscription(s) électorale(s) fédérale(s): Compton-Stanstead
Prochaines élections: 3e novembre 2013
Réjean Masson, Maire
France Veilleux, Directrice générale

Maskinongé
154, boul Ouest, rte 138
Maskinongé, QC J0K 1N0
Tél: 819-227-2243; *Téléc:* 819-227-2097
fgervais@mun-maskinonge.ca
www.mun-maskinonge.ca
Entité municipal: Municipality
Incorporation: 25 avril 2001 *Area:* 75,98 km2
Comté ou district: Maskinongé; *Population au 2011:* 2,253
Circonscription(s) électorale(s) provinciale(s): Maskinongé
Circonscription(s) électorale(s) fédérale(s): Berthier-Maskinongé
Prochaines élections: 3e novembre 2013
Roger Michaud, Maire
France Gervais, Directrice générale

Maskinongé
651, boul St-Laurent est
Louiseville, QC J5V 1J1
Tél: 819-228-9461; *Téléc:* 819-228-2193
mrcinfo@mrc-maskinonge.qc.ca
www.mrc-maskinonge.qc.ca
Entité municipal: Regional County Municipality
Incorporation: 1er janvier 1982
Population au 2011: 36,286
Note: 17 municipalités.
Robert Lalonde, Préfet
Janyse L. Pichette, Directrice générale

Massueville
CP 90
881, rue Royale
Massueville, QC J0G 1K0
Tél: 450-788-2957; *Téléc:* 450-788-2050
massueville@bas-richelieu.net
www.massueville.net
Entité municipal: Village
Incorporation: 25 mars 1903 *Area:* 1,29 km2
Comté ou district: Pierre-De Saurel; *Population au 2011:* 516
Circonscription(s) électorale(s) provinciale(s): Richelieu
Circonscription(s) électorale(s) fédérale(s):
Bas-Richelieu-Nicolet-Bécancour
Prochaines élections: 3e novembre 2013
Denis Marion, Maire
France Saint-Pierre, Directrice générale

Matagami
CP 160
195, boul Matagami
Matagami, QC J0Y 2A0
Tél: 819-739-2541; *Téléc:* 819-739-4278
matagami@matagami.com
www.matagami.com
Entité municipal: Village
Incorporation: 1er avril 1963 *Area:* 64,75 km2
Population au 2011: 1,526
Circonscription(s) électorale(s) provinciale(s): Ungava
Circonscription(s) électorale(s) fédérale(s):
Abitibi-Baie-James-Nunavik-Eeyou
Prochaines élections: 3e novembre 2013
René Dubé, Maire
Pierre Deslauriers, Greffier

Matane
145, rue Soucy
Matane, QC G4W 2E1
Tél: 418-562-6734; *Téléc:* 418-562-7265
mrcmatane@mrcdematane.qc.ca
Entité municipal: Regional County Municipality
Incorporation: 1er janvier 1982
Population au 2011: 21,786
Note: 11 municipalités & 1 autre territoire.
Yvan Imbeault, Préfet
Line Ross, Directrice générale

Matapédia
CP 207
1, rue de l'Hôtel-de-Ville
Matapédia, QC G0J 1V0
Tél: 418-865-2917; *Téléc:* 418-865-2828
munmata@globetrotter.net
Entité municipal: Parish (Paroisse)
Incorporation: 4e novembre 1905 *Area:* 70,75 km2
Comté ou district: Avignon; *Population au 2011:* 664
Circonscription(s) électorale(s) provinciale(s): Bonaventure
Circonscription(s) électorale(s) fédérale(s):
Gaspésie—Îles-de-la-Madeleine
Prochaines élections: 3e novembre 2013
Louis Michaud, Maire
Carole Bélanger, Directrice générale

Matawinie
3184, 1re Av
Rawdon, QC J0K 1S0
Tél: 450-834-5441; *Téléc:* 450-834-6560
administration@matawinie.org
www.matawinie.org
Entité municipal: Regional County Municipality
Incorporation: 1er janvier 1982
Population au 2011: 49,516
Note: 15 municipalités & 12 autres territoires.
Gaétan Morin, Préfet
Lyne Arbour, Directrice générale

Mayo
CP 2936
20, ch McAlendin
Gatineau, QC J8L 4J7
Tél: 819-986-3199; *Téléc:* 819-986-8881
mun.mayo@mrcpapineau.com
Entité municipal: Municipality
Incorporation: 1er août 1864 *Area:* 72,67 km2
Comté ou district: Papineau; *Population au 2011:* 572
Circonscription(s) électorale(s) provinciale(s): Papineau
Circonscription(s) électorale(s) fédérale(s):
Argenteuil-Papineau-Mirabel
Prochaines élections: 3e novembre 2013
Gaëtan Brunet, Maire
Yves Lafleur, Directeur général

McMasterville
255, boul Constable
McMasterville, QC J3G 6N9
Tél: 450-467-3580; *Téléc:* 450-467-2493
hoteldeville@municipalitemcmasterville.qc.ca
www.mcmasterville.ca
Entité municipal: Municipality
Incorporation: 31 juillet 1917 *Area:* 3,00 km2
Comté ou district: La Vallée-du-Richelieu; *Population au 2011:* 5,615
Circonscription(s) électorale(s) provinciale(s): Borduas
Circonscription(s) électorale(s) fédérale(s): Chambly-Borduas
Prochaines élections: 3e novembre 2013
Gilles Plante, Maire
Lyne Savaria, Directrice générale

Mékinac
560, rue Notre-Dame
Saint-Tite, QC G0X 3H0
Tél: 418-365-5151; *Téléc:* 418-365-7377
mrcmekinac@mrcmekinac.com
www.regionmekinac.com
Entité municipal: Regional County Municipality
Incorporation: 1 janvier 1982
Population au 2011: 12,924
Note: 10 municipalités & 4 autres territoires.
Lucien Mongrain, Préfet
Claude Beaulieu, Directeur général
claude.beaulieu@mrcmekinac.com

Melbourne
1257, rte 243
Melbourne, QC J0B 2B0
Tél: 819-826-3555; *Téléc:* 819-826-3981
melcan@qc.aibn.com
www.melbournecanton.ca
Entité municipal: Township
Incorporation: 1er juillet 1855 *Area:* 170,29 km2
Comté ou district: Le Val-St-François; *Population au 2011:* 1,004
Circonscription(s) électorale(s) provinciale(s): Richmond
Circonscription(s) électorale(s) fédérale(s):
Richmond-Arthabaska
Prochaines élections: 3e novembre 2013
James Johnston, Maire
Cindy Jones, Directrice générale

Memphrémagog
#200, 455, rue MacDonald
Magog, QC J1X 1M2
Tél: 819-843-9292; *Téléc:* 819-843-7295
info@mrcmemphremagog.com
www.mrcmemphremagog.com
Entité municipal: Regional County Municipality
Incorporation: 1er janvier 1982
Population au 2011: 48,551
Note: 17 municipalités.
Gérard Marinovich, Préfet
Guy Jauron, Directeur général
g.jauron@mrcmemphremagog.com

Messines
CP 69
70, rue Principale
Messines, QC J0X 2J0
Tél: 819-465-2323; *Téléc:* 819-465-2943
info@messines.ca
www.messines.ca
Entité municipal: Municipality
Incorporation: 19 août 1921 *Area:* 108,46 km2
Comté ou district: La Vallée-de-la-Gatineau; *Population au 2011:* 1,608
Circonscription(s) électorale(s) provinciale(s): Gatineau
Circonscription(s) électorale(s) fédérale(s): Pontiac
Prochaines élections: 3e novembre 2013
Ronald Cross, Maire
Jim Smith, Directeur général

Métabetchouan—Lac-à-la-Croix
87, rue St-André
Métabetchouan—Lac-à-la-Croix, QC G8G 1A1
Tél: 418-349-2060; *Téléc:* 418-349-2395
bouchard.mario@ville.metabetchouan.qc.ca
www.ville.metabetchouan.qc.ca
Entité municipal: Town
Incorporation: 6 janvier 1999 *Area:* 185,86 km2
Comté ou district: Lac-St-Jean-Est; *Population au 2011:* 4,097
Circonscription(s) électorale(s) provinciale(s): Lac-St-Jean
Circonscription(s) électorale(s) fédérale(s): Roberval-Lac-St-Jean
Prochaines élections: 3e novembre 2013
Lili Simard, Mairesse
Mario Bouchard, Greffier

Métis-sur-Mer
138, rue Principale
Métis-sur-Mer, QC G0J 1S0
Tél: 418-936-3255; *Téléc:* 418-936-3117
metissurmer@mitis.qc.ca
www.ville.metis-sur-mer.qc.ca
Entité municipal: Village
Incorporation: 4 juillet 2002 *Area:* 48,01 km2
Comté ou district: La Mitis; *Population au 2011:* 644
Circonscription(s) électorale(s) provinciale(s): Matapédia
Circonscription(s) électorale(s) fédérale(s): Haute-Gaspésie-La Mitis-Matane-Matapédia
Prochaines élections: 3e novembre 2013
Jean-Pierre Pelletier, Maire
Stéphane Marcheterre, Greffier

Milan
CP 54
403, rang Ste-Marie
Milan, QC G0Y 1E0
Tél: 819-657-4527; *Téléc:* 819-657-2987
munmilan@axion.ca
www.munmilan.qc.ca
Entité municipal: Municipality
Incorporation: 1er juin 1948 *Area:* 130,06 km2
Comté ou district: Le Granit; *Population au 2011:* 270
Circonscription(s) électorale(s) provinciale(s): Mégantic-Compton
Circonscription(s) électorale(s) fédérale(s): Mégantic-L'Érable
Prochaines élections: 3e novembre 2013
Claude Turcotte, Maire
Noëlla Bergeron, Directrice générale

Mille-Isles
1262, ch de Mille-Isles
Mille-Isles, QC J0R 1A0
Tél: 450-438-2958; *Téléc:* 450-438-6157
jringuette@mille-isles.ca
www.mille-isles.ca
Entité municipal: Municipality
Incorporation: 1er juillet 1855 *Area:* 59,98 km2
Comté ou district: Argenteuil; *Population au 2011:* 1,629
Circonscription(s) électorale(s) provinciale(s): Argenteuil
Circonscription(s) électorale(s) fédérale(s): Argenteuil-Papineau-Mirabel
Prochaines élections: 3e novembre 2013
Yvon Samson, Maire
Johanne Ringuette, Directrice générale

Mirabel
14111, rue Saint-Jean
Mirabel, QC J7J 1Y3
Tél: 450-475-8653; *Téléc:* 450-475-7195
communications@ville.mirabel.qc.ca
www.ville.mirabel.qc.ca
Entité municipal: Regional County Municipality
Incorporation: 1er janvier 1985
Population au 2011: 41,957
Note: 1 municipalité.
Hubert Meilleur, Préfet
Suzanne Mireault, Directrice générale
s.mireault@ville.mirabel.qc.ca

Mistissini
187, ch Main
Mistissini, QC G0W 1C0
Tél: 418-923-3461; *Téléc:* 418-923-3115
legislative@mistissini.ca
Entité municipal: Villages Cris
Incorporation: 28 juin 1978 *Area:* 841,10 km2
Circonscription(s) électorale(s) provinciale(s): Ungava
Circonscription(s) électorale(s) fédérale(s): Abitibi-Baie-James-Nunavik-Eeyou
Richard Shecapio, Maire
Thomas Neeposh, Directeur général

Moffet
CP 89
14D, rue Principale
Moffet, QC J0Z 2W0
Tél: 819-747-6116; *Téléc:* 819-747-6117
dg.moffet@mrctemiscamingue.qc.ca
www.moffet.ca
Entité municipal: Municipality
Incorporation: 1er janvier 1953 *Area:* 431,46 km2
Comté ou district: Témiscamingue; *Population au 2011:* 196
Circonscription(s) électorale(s) provinciale(s): Rouyn-Noranda-Témiscamingue
Circonscription(s) électorale(s) fédérale(s): Abitibi-Témiscamingue
Prochaines élections: 3e novembre 2013
Michel Paquette, Maire
Linda Roy, Directrice générale

Mont-Carmel
22, rue de la Fabrique
Mont-Carmel, QC G0L 1W0
Tél: 418-498-2050; *Téléc:* 418-489-2522
direction@mont-carmel.ca
www.mont-carmel.ca
Entité municipal: Municipality
Incorporation: 1er juillet 1855 *Area:* 435,29 km2
Comté ou district: Kamouraska; *Population au 2011:* 1,136
Circonscription(s) électorale(s) provinciale(s): Kamouraska-Témiscouata
Circonscription(s) électorale(s) fédérale(s): Montmagny-L'Islet-Kamouraska-Riviére-du-Loup
Prochaines élections: 3e novembre 2013
Denis Lévesque, Maire
Odile Soucy, Directrice générale

Mont-Joli
40, av de l'Hôtel-de-Ville
Mont-Joli, QC G5H 1W8
Tél: 418-775-7285; *Téléc:* 418-775-6320
mont-joli@ville.mont-joli.qc.ca
www.ville.mont-joli.qc.ca
Entité municipal: Town
Incorporation: 13 juin 2001 *Area:* 22,64 km2
Comté ou district: La Mitis; *Population au 2011:* 6,665
Circonscription(s) électorale(s) provinciale(s): Matapédia
Circonscription(s) électorale(s) fédérale(s): Huate-Gaspésie-La Mitis-Matane-Matapédia
Prochaines élections: 3e novembre 2013
Jean Bélanger, Maire
Yves Sénéchal, Greffier

Mont-St-Grégoire
225, rue St-Joseph
Mont-Saint-Grégoire, QC J0J 1K0
Tél: 450-347-5376; *Téléc:* 450-347-9200
taxes@mmsg.ca
www.mont-saint-gregoire.ca
Entité municipal: Municipality
Incorporation: 21 décembre 1994 *Area:* 79,92 km2
Comté ou district: Le Haut-Richelieu; *Population au 2011:* 3,086
Circonscription(s) électorale(s) provinciale(s): Iberville
Circonscription(s) électorale(s) fédérale(s): St-Jean
Prochaines élections: 3e novembre 2013
Suzanne Boulais, Mairesse
Christianne Pouliot, Directrice générale

Mont-St-Michel
94, rue de l'Église
Mont-Saint-Michel, QC J0W 1P0
Tél: 819-587-3093; *Téléc:* 819-587-3781
mun.mont-st-michel@tlb.sympatico.ca
Entité municipal: Municipality
Incorporation: 11 septembre 1928 *Area:* 137,65 km2
Comté ou district: Antoine-Labelle; *Population au 2011:* 633
Circonscription(s) électorale(s) provinciale(s): Labelle
Circonscription(s) électorale(s) fédérale(s): Laurentides-Labelle
Prochaines élections: 3e novembre 2013
Roger Lapointe, Maire
Lucie Gagnon, Directrice générale

Mont-St-Pierre
CP 9
102, rue Prudent-Cloutier
Mont-Saint-Pierre, QC G0E 1V0
Tél: 418-797-2898; *Téléc:* 418-797-2307
mont-st-pierre@globetrotter.net
www.mont-saint-pierre.ca
Entité municipal: Village
Incorporation: 1er juillet 1947 *Area:* 60,45 km2
Comté ou district: La Haute-Gaspésie; *Population au 2011:* 192
Circonscription(s) électorale(s) provinciale(s): Matane
Circonscription(s) électorale(s) fédérale(s): Haute-Gaspésie-La Mitis-Matane-Matapédia
Prochaines élections: 3e novembre 2013
Jean-Sébastien Cloutier, Maire
Jérôme Émond, Directeur général

Mont-Tremblant
1145, rue de St-Jovite
Mont-Tremblant, QC J8E 1V1
Tél: 819-425-8614; *Téléc:* 819-425-2528
info@villedemont-tremblant.qc.ca
www.villedemont-tremblant.qc.ca
Entité municipal: Town
Incorporation: 22 novembre 2000 *Area:* 235,97 km2
Comté ou district: Les Laurentides; *Population au 2011:* 9,494
Circonscription(s) électorale(s) provinciale(s): Labelle
Circonscription(s) électorale(s) fédérale(s): Laurentides-Labelle
Prochaines élections: 3e novembre 2013
Pierre Pilon, Maire
Isabelle Grenier, Greffière

Montcalm
10, rue de l'Hôtel-de-Ville
Montcalm, QC J0T 2V0
Tél: 819-687-2836
direction@municipalite.montcalm.qc.ca
www.municipalite.montcalm.qc.ca
Entité municipal: Municipality
Incorporation: 6e mars 1907 *Area:* 119,65 km2
Comté ou district: Les Laurentides; *Population au 2011:* 619
Circonscription(s) électorale(s) provinciale(s): Argenteuil
Circonscription(s) électorale(s) fédérale(s): Laurentides-Labelle
Prochaines élections: 3e novembre 2013
Steven Larose, Maire
Lucie Côté, Directrice générale

Montcalm
1540, rue Albert
Sainte-Julienne, QC J0K 2T0
Tél: 450-831-2182; *Téléc:* 450-831-2647
info@mrcmontcalm.com
www.mrcmontcalm.com
Entité municipal: Regional County Municipality
Incorporation: 1er janvier 1982
Population au 2011: 48,378
Note: 11 municipalités.
Danielle Henri Allard, Préfet
Gaétan Hudon, Directeur général

Montcerf-Lytton
18, rue Principale nord
Montcerf-Lytton, QC J0W 1N0
Tél: 819-449-4578; *Téléc:* 819-449-7310
mun.montcerf@ireseau.com
www.montcerf-lytton.com
Entité municipal: Municipality
Incorporation: 19 septembre 2001 *Area:* 358,34 km2
Comté ou district: La Vallée-de-la-Gatineau; *Population au 2011:* 687
Circonscription(s) électorale(s) provinciale(s): Gatineau
Circonscription(s) électorale(s) fédérale(s): Pontiac
Prochaines élections: 3e novembre 2013
Alain Fortin, Maire
Liliane Crytes, Directrice générale

Montebello
550, rue Notre-Dame
Montebello, QC J0V 1L0
Tél: 819-423-5123; *Téléc:* 819-423-5703
mun.montebello@videotron.ca
www.ville.montebello.qc.ca
Entité municipal: Municipality
Incorporation: 29 août 1878 *Area:* 7,85 km2
Comté ou district: Papineau; *Population au 2011:* 978
Circonscription(s) électorale(s) provinciale(s): Papineau
Circonscription(s) électorale(s) fédérale(s):

Argenteuil-Papineau-Mirabel
Prochaines élections: 3e novembre 2013
Pierre Bertrand, Maire
Charles-Guy Beauchamp, Directeur général

Montmagny
159, rue Saint-Louis
Montmagny, QC G5V 1N5
Tél: 418-248-5985; *Téléc:* 418-248-4624
mrc@montmagny.com
www.montmagny.com
Entité municipal: Regional County Municipality
Incorporation: 1er janvier 1982
Population au 2011: 22,877
Note: 14 municipalités.
Jean-Guy Desrosiers, Préfet
Nancy Labrecque, Directrice générale

Montpellier
4, rue du Bosquet
Montpellier, QC J0V 1M0
Tél: 819-428-3663; *Téléc:* 819-428-1221
admin.montpellier@mrcpapineau.com
www.montpellier.ca
Entité municipal: Municipality
Incorporation: 11 octobre 1920 *Area:* 249,16 km2
Comté ou district: Papineau; *Population au 2011:* 986
Circonscription(s) électorale(s) provinciale(s): Papineau
Circonscription(s) électorale(s) fédérale(s):
Argenteuil-Papineau-Mirabel
Prochaines élections: 3e novembre 2013
Pierre Bernier, Maire
Manon Lanthier, Directrice générale (par intérim)

Morin-Heights
567, ch du Village
Morin-Heights, QC J0R 1H0
Tél: 450-226-3232; *Téléc:* 450-226-8786
municipalite@morinheights.com
www.morinheights.com
Entité municipal: Municipality
Incorporation: 1er juillet 1855 *Area:* 55,42 km2
Comté ou district: Les Pays-d'en-Haut; *Population au 2011:* 3,925
Circonscription(s) électorale(s) provinciale(s): Argenteuil
Circonscription(s) électorale(s) fédérale(s):
Argenteuil-Papineau-Mirabel
Prochaines élections: 3e novembre 2013
Timothy Watchorn, Maire
Yves Desmarais, Directeur général

Mulgrave-et-Derry
591, av de Buckingham
Gatineau, QC J8L 2H2
Tél: 819-986-9519; *Téléc:* 819-986-9954
mulgrave-derry@bellnet.ca
Entité municipal: Municipality
Incorporation: 1er janvier 1870 *Area:* 297,74 km2
Comté ou district: Papineau; *Population au 2011:* 246
Circonscription(s) électorale(s) provinciale(s): Papineau
Circonscription(s) électorale(s) fédérale(s):
Argenteuil-Papineau-Mirabel
Prochaines élections: 3e novembre 2013
Michael Kane, Maire
Isabelle Cusson, Directrice générale

Murdochville
CP 1120
635, 5e rue
Murdochville, QC G0E 1W0
Tél: 418-784-2536; *Téléc:* 418-784-2607
dgmurd@globetrotter.net
www.murdochville.com
Entité municipal: Village
Incorporation: 15 juillet 1953 *Area:* 64,68 km2
Comté ou district: La Côte-de-Gaspé; *Population au 2011:* 764
Circonscription(s) électorale(s) provinciale(s): Gaspé
Circonscription(s) électorale(s) fédérale(s):
Gaspésie—îles-de-la-Madeleine
Prochaines élections: 3e novembre 2013
Délisca Ritchie Roussy, Mairesse
Jean-Pierre Cassivi, Greffier

Namur
996, rue du Centenaire
Namur, QC J0V 1N0
Tél: 819-426-2457; *Téléc:* 819-426-3074
dirgeneral.namur@mrcpapineau.com
Entité municipal: Municipality
Incorporation: 1er janvier 1964 *Area:* 57,07 km2
Comté ou district: Papineau; *Population au 2011:* 596
Circonscription(s) électorale(s) provinciale(s): Papineau
Circonscription(s) électorale(s) fédérale(s):
Argenteuil-Papineau-Mirabel
Prochaines élections: 3e novembre 2013
Gilbert Dardel, Maire
Diane Thibault, Directrice générale

Nantes
1244, rue Principale
Nantes, QC G0Y 1G0
Tél: 819-547-3655; *Téléc:* 819-547-3755
munantes@axion.ca
www.munantes.qc.ca
Entité municipal: Municipality
Incorporation: 1er janvier 1874 *Area:* 120,47 km2
Comté ou district: Le Granit; *Population au 2011:* 1,374
Circonscription(s) électorale(s) provinciale(s):
Mégantic-Compton
Circonscription(s) électorale(s) fédérale(s): Mégantic-L'Érable
Prochaines élections: 3e novembre 2013
Bernard Isabel, Maire
Lucie Lortitch, Directrice générale

Napierville
260, rue de l'Église
Napierville, QC J0J 1L0
Tél: 450-245-7210; *Téléc:* 450-245-7691
mun.napierville@qc.aira.com
www.napierville.ca
Entité municipal: Village
Incorporation: 1er janvier 1873 *Area:* 4,53 km2
Comté ou district: Les Jardins-de-Napierville; *Population au 2011:* 3,525
Circonscription(s) électorale(s) provinciale(s): Huntingdon
Circonscription(s) électorale(s) fédérale(s):
Beauharnois-Salaberry
Prochaines élections: 3e novembre 2013
Alain Fredette, Maire
Ginette Leblanc-Pruneau, Directrice générale

Natashquan
CP 99
29, ch d'en-Haut
Natashquan, QC G0G 2E0
Tél: 418-726-3362; *Téléc:* 418-726-3698
muninatashquan@globetrotter.net
www.natashquan.org
Entité municipal: Township
Incorporation: 16 septembre 1907 *Area:* 193,20 km2
Comté ou district: Minganie; *Population au 2011:* 246
Circonscription(s) électorale(s) provinciale(s): Duplessis
Circonscription(s) électorale(s) fédérale(s): Manicouagan
Prochaines élections: 3e novembre 2013
Léonard Landry, Sec.-Trés.
Jacques Landry, Maire

Nédélec
CP 70
33, rue Principale
Nédélec, QC J0Z 2Z0
Tél: 819-784-3311; *Téléc:* 819-784-2126
nedelec@mrctemiscamingue.qc.ca
municipalite.nedelec.qc.ca
Entité municipal: Township
Incorporation: 1er février 1909 *Area:* 369,90 km2
Comté ou district: Témiscamingue; *Population au 2011:* 403
Circonscription(s) électorale(s) provinciale(s):
Rouyn-Noranda-Témiscamingue
Circonscription(s) électorale(s) fédérale(s):
Abitibi-Témiscamingue
Prochaines élections: 3e novembre 2013
Carmen Rivard, Mairesse
Nancy Beaulé, Directrice générale

Némiscau
1, rue Lakeshore
Némiscau, QC J0Y 3B0
Tel: 819-673-2512; *Fax:* 819-673-2542
nation@nemaska.ca
www.nemaska.ca
Municipal Type: Villages Cris
Incorporated: 28 juin 1978 *Area:* 55,40 km2
Provincial Electoral District(s): Ungava
Federal Electoral District(s): Abitibi-Baie-James-Nunavik-Eeyou
Next Election: 3e novembre 2013
Josie Jimiken, Maire
Georges Wapachee, Directeur général

Neuville
230, rue du Père-Rhéaume
Neuville, QC G0A 2R0
Tél: 418-876-2280; *Téléc:* 418-876-3349
mun@ville.neuville.qc.ca
www.ville.neuville.qc.ca
Entité municipal: Town
Incorporation: 2 janvier 1997 *Area:* 72,04 km2
Comté ou district: Portneuf; *Population au 2011:* 3,888
Circonscription(s) électorale(s) provinciale(s): Portneuf
Circonscription(s) électorale(s) fédérale(s):
Portneuf-Jacques-Cartier
Prochaines élections: 3e novembre 2013
Bernard Gaudreau, Maire
Nicole Béland, Greffière

New Carlisle
CP 40
138, boul Gérard-D.-Levesque
New Carlisle, QC G0C 1Z0
Tél: 418-752-3141; *Téléc:* 418-752-3140
newcarlisle@globetrotter.net
www.new-carlisle.com
Entité municipal: Municipality
Incorporation: 1er février 1877 *Area:* 66,12 km2
Comté ou district: Bonaventure; *Population au 2011:* 1,358
Circonscription(s) électorale(s) provinciale(s): Bonaventure
Circonscription(s) électorale(s) fédérale(s):
Gaspésie—îles-de-la-Madeleine
Prochaines élections: 3e novembre 2013
Cyrus Journeau, Maire
Denise Dallain, Directrice générale

New Richmond
99, place Suzanne-Guité
New Richmond, QC G0C 2B0
Tél: 418-392-7000; *Téléc:* 418-392-5331
scyr@villenewrichmond.com
www.villenewrichmond.com
Entité municipal: Town
Incorporation: 1er juillet 1855 *Area:* 168,63 km2
Comté ou district: Bonaventure; *Population au 2011:* 3,810
Circonscription(s) électorale(s) provinciale(s): Bonaventure
Circonscription(s) électorale(s) fédérale(s):
Gaspésie—îles-de-la-Madeleine
Prochaines élections: 3e novembre 2013
Nicole Appleby, Mairesse
Stéphane Cyr, Greffier

Nicolet
180, rue Monseigneur-Panet
Nicolet, QC J3T 1S6
Tél: 819-293-6901; *Téléc:* 819-293-6767
p.genest@ville.nicolet.qc.ca
www.ville.nicolet.qc.ca
Entité municipal: Town
Incorporation: 27 décembre 2000 *Area:* 94,50 km2
Comté ou district: Nicolet-Yamaska; *Population au 2011:* 7,828
Circonscription(s) électorale(s) provinciale(s): Nicolet-Yamaska
Circonscription(s) électorale(s) fédérale(s):
Bas-Richelieu-Nicolet-Bécancour
Prochaines élections: 3e novembre 2013
Alain Drouin, Maire
Monique Corriveau, Greffière

Nicolet-Yamaska
#257, 1, rue de Mgr-Courchesne
Nicolet, QC J3T 2C1
Tél: 819-293-2997; *Téléc:* 819-293-5367
mrcny@mrcnicolet-yamaska.qc.ca
www.mrcnicolet-yamaska.qc.ca
Entité municipal: Regional County Municipality
Incorporation: 1 janvier 1982
Population au 2011: 22,798
Note: 16 municipalités.
Alain Drouin, Préfet
Donald Martel, Directeur général

Nominingue
2110, ch du Tour-du-Lac
Nominingue, QC J0W 1R0
Tél: 819-278-3384; *Téléc:* 819-278-4967
mun.nominingue@tlb.sympatico.ca
www.municipalitenominingue.qc.ca
Entité municipal: Municipality
Incorporation: 30 octobre 1971 *Area:* 308,34 km2
Comté ou district: Antoine-Labelle; *Population au 2011:* 2,019
Circonscription(s) électorale(s) provinciale(s): Labelle
Circonscription(s) électorale(s) fédérale(s): Laurentides-Labelle
Prochaines élections: 3e novembre 2013
Yves Généreux, Maire
Robert Généreux, Directeur général

Normandin
1048, rue St-Cyrille
Normandin, QC G8M 4R9
Tél: 418-274-2004; *Téléc:* 418-274-7171
admin@ville.normandin.qc.ca
www.ville.normandin.qc.ca
Entité municipal: Town
Incorporation: 10 mars 1979 *Area:* 211,96 km2
Comté ou district: Maria-Chapdelaine; *Population au 2011:* 3,137
Circonscription(s) électorale(s) provinciale(s): Roberval
Circonscription(s) électorale(s) fédérale(s): Roberval-Lac-St-Jean
Prochaines élections: 3e novembre 2013
Lucien Guillemette, Maire
Guy Mailloux, Greffier

Normétal
CP 308
59, 1re rue
Normétal, QC J0Z 3A0
Tél: 819-788-2550; *Téléc:* 819-788-2730
normetal@mrcao.qc.ca
www.normetal.ao.ca
Entité municipal: Municipality
Incorporation: 1er janvier 1945 *Area:* 55,89 km2
Comté ou district: Abitibi-Ouest; *Population au 2011:* 856
Circonscription(s) électorale(s) provinciale(s): Abitibi-Ouest
Circonscription(s) électorale(s) fédérale(s): Abitibi-Témiscamingue
Prochaines élections: 3e novembre 2013
Jocelyn Trottier, Maire
Lyne Blanchet, Directrice générale

North Hatley
3125, ch Capelton
North Hatley, QC J0B 2C0
Tél: 819-842-2754; *Téléc:* 819-842-4501
villagenorthhatley@qc.aira.com
www.northhatley.org
Entité municipal: Village
Incorporation: 25 octobre 1897 *Area:* 3,23 km2
Comté ou district: Memphrémagog; *Population au 2011:* 654
Circonscription(s) électorale(s) provinciale(s): Orford
Circonscription(s) électorale(s) fédérale(s): Compton-Stanstead
Prochaines élections: 3e novembre 2013
Michael Page, Maire
Léonard Castagner, Directeur général

Notre-Dame-Auxiliatrice-de-Buckland
4340, rue Principale
Buckland, QC G0R 1G0
Tél: 418-789-3119; *Téléc:* 418-789-3535
buckland@globetrotter.net
Entité municipal: Parish (Paroisse)
Incorporation: 1er janvier 1885 *Area:* 96,32 km2
Comté ou district: Bellechasse; *Population au 2011:* 785
Circonscription(s) électorale(s) provinciale(s): Bellechasse
Circonscription(s) électorale(s) fédérale(s): Lévis-Bellechasse
Prochaines élections: 3e novembre 2013
Juliette Laflamme, Mairesse
Jocelyne Nadeau, Directrice générale

Notre-Dame-de-Bonsecours
220A, rue Bonsecours
Montebello, QC J0V 1L0
Tél: 819-423-5575; *Téléc:* 819-423-5571
mun.ndbonsecours@mrcpapineau.com
www.ndbonsecours.com
Entité municipal: Municipality
Incorporation: 7 mars 1918 *Area:* 265,75 km2
Comté ou district: Papineau; *Population au 2011:* 261
Circonscription(s) électorale(s) provinciale(s): Papineau
Circonscription(s) électorale(s) fédérale(s): Argenteuil-Papineau-Mirabel
Prochaines élections: 3e novembre 2013
Denis Beauchamp, Maire
Suzie Latourelle, Directrice générale

Notre-Dame-de-Ham
25, rue de l'Église
Notre-Dame-de-Ham, QC G0P 1C0
Tél: 819-344-5806; *Téléc:* 819-344-5807
info@notre-dame-de-ham.ca
Entité municipal: Municipality
Incorporation: 7 octobre 1898 *Area:* 32,34 km2
Comté ou district: Arthabaska; *Population au 2011:* 414
Circonscription(s) électorale(s) provinciale(s): Richmond
Circonscription(s) électorale(s) fédérale(s): Richmond-Arthabaska
Prochaines élections: 3e novembre 2013
Diane Lefort, Mairesse
Christiane Leblanc, Directrice générale

Notre-Dame-de-l'île-Perrot
21, rue de l'Église
Notre-Dame-de-l'île-Perrot, QC J7V 8P4
Tél: 514-453-4128; *Téléc:* 514-453-8961
info@ndip.org
www.ndip.org
Entité municipal: Municipality
Incorporation: 14 avril 1984 *Area:* 28,14 km2
Comté ou district: Vaudreuil-Soulanges; *Population au 2011:* 10,620
Circonscription(s) électorale(s) provinciale(s): Vaudreuil
Circonscription(s) électorale(s) fédérale(s): Vaudreuil-Soulanges
Prochaines élections: 3e novembre 2013
Marie-Claude Beaulieu-Nichols, Maire
Katherine-Erika Vincent, Greffière

Notre-Dame-de-la-Merci
1900, montée de la Réserve
Notre-Dame-de-la-Merci, QC J0T 2A0
Tél: 819-424-2113; *Téléc:* 819-424-7347
municipaliteNDM@netaxis.ca
www.municipalitenotredamedelamerci.com
Entité municipal: Municipality
Incorporation: 1er janvier 1950 *Area:* 251,22 km2
Comté ou district: Matawinie; *Population au 2011:* 978
Circonscription(s) électorale(s) provinciale(s): Bertrand
Circonscription(s) électorale(s) fédérale(s): Joliette
Prochaines élections: 3e novembre 2013
Julien Alarie, Maire
Chantal Soucy, Directrice générale

Notre-Dame-de-la-Paix
267, rue Notre-Dame
Notre-Dame-de-la-Paix, QC J0V 1P0
Tél: 819-522-6610; *Téléc:* 819-522-6710
mun.ndlapaix@mrcpapineau.com
www.notredamedelapaix.qc.ca
Entité municipal: Municipality
Incorporation: 3 octobre 1902 *Area:* 105,90 km2
Comté ou district: Papineau; *Population au 2011:* 718
Circonscription(s) électorale(s) provinciale(s): Papineau
Circonscription(s) électorale(s) fédérale(s): Argenteuil-Papineau-Mirabel
Prochaines élections: 3e novembre 2013
Daniel Bock, Maire
Nadine Proulx, Directrice générale

Notre-Dame-de-la-Salette
CP 59
45, rue des Saules
Notre-Dame-de-la-Salette, QC J0X 2L0
Tél: 819-766-2533; *Téléc:* 819-766-2983
salette@muni-ndsalette.qc.ca
www.notredamedelasalette.ca
Entité municipal: Municipality
Incorporation: 17 mai 1979 *Area:* 117,54 km2
Comté ou district: Les Collines-de-l'Outaouais; *Population au 2011:* 757
Circonscription(s) électorale(s) provinciale(s): Papineau
Circonscription(s) électorale(s) fédérale(s): Pontiac
Prochaines élections: 3e novembre 2013
Daniel Malette, Maire
Sylvie Gratton, Directrice générale

Notre-Dame-de-Lorette
22, rue Principale
Notre-Dame-de-Lorette, QC G0W 1B0
Tél: 418-276-1934; *Téléc:* 418-276-1934
muni.lorette@hotmail.com
Entité municipal: Municipality
Incorporation: 1er janvier 1966 *Area:* 225,32 km2
Comté ou district: Maria-Chapdelaine; *Population au 2011:* 189
Circonscription(s) électorale(s) provinciale(s): Roberval
Circonscription(s) électorale(s) fédérale(s): Roberval-Lac-St-Jean
Prochaines élections: 3e novembre 2013
Daniel Tremblay, Maire
Michèle Tremblay, Directrice générale

Notre-Dame-de-Lourdes
830, rue Principale
Lourdes, QC G0S 1T0
Tél: 819-385-4315; *Téléc:* 819-385-4827
info@municipalitelourdes.com
www.municipalitelourdes.com
Entité municipal: Parish (Paroisse)
Incorporation: 7 octobre 1897 *Area:* 83,39 km2
Comté ou district: L'Érable; *Population au 2011:* 700
Circonscription(s) électorale(s) provinciale(s): Lotbinière
Circonscription(s) électorale(s) fédérale(s): Mégantic-L'Érable
Prochaines élections: 3e novembre 2013
Jocelyn Bédard, Maire
Danielle Bédard, Directrice générale

Notre-Dame-de-Lourdes
4050, rue Principale
Notre-Dame-de-Lourdes, QC J0K 1K0
Tél: 450-759-2277; *Téléc:* 450-759-2055
munindl@intermonde.net
www.notredamedelourdes.ca
Entité municipal: Municipality
Incorporation: 28 octobre 1925 *Area:* 35,48 km2
Comté ou district: Joliette; *Population au 2011:* 2,595
Circonscription(s) électorale(s) provinciale(s): Joliette
Circonscription(s) électorale(s) fédérale(s): Joliette
Prochaines élections: 3e novembre 2013
Céline Geoffroy, Maire
Micheline Miron, Directrice générale

Notre-Dame-de-Montauban
555, av des Loisirs
Notre-Dame-de-Montauban, QC G0X 1W0
Tél: 418-336-2640; *Téléc:* 418-336-2353
nd-montauban@regionmekinac.com
www.municipalite.notre-dame-de-montauban.qc.ca
Entité municipal: Municipality
Incorporation: 3 janvier 1976 *Area:* 163,53 km2
Comté ou district: Mékinac; *Population au 2011:* 747
Circonscription(s) électorale(s) provinciale(s): Portneuf
Circonscription(s) électorale(s) fédérale(s): St-Maurice-Champlain
Prochaines élections: 3e novembre 2013
Jean-Guy Lavoie, Maire
Manon Frenette, Directrice générale

Notre-Dame-de-Pontmain
5, rue de l'Église
Notre-Dame-de-Pontmain, QC J0W 1S0
Tél: 819-597-2382; *Téléc:* 819-597-2231
dg@munpontmain.qc.ca
www.munpontmain.qc.ca
Entité municipal: Municipality
Incorporation: 26 janvier 1894 *Area:* 267,92 km2
Comté ou district: Antoine-Labelle; *Population au 2011:* 720
Circonscription(s) électorale(s) provinciale(s): Labelle
Circonscription(s) électorale(s) fédérale(s): Laurentides-Labelle
Prochaines élections: 3e novembre 2013
Lyz Beaulieu, Mairesse
Daisy Constantineau, Directrice générale

Notre-Dame-de-Stanbridge
CP 209
900, rue Principale
Notre-Dame-de-Stanbridge, QC J0J 1M0
Tél: 450-296-4710; *Téléc:* 450-296-5001
notredamedestanbridge@videotron.ca
www.notredamedestanbridge.qc.ca
Entité municipal: Parish (Paroisse)
Incorporation: 21 mars 1889 *Area:* 44,57 km2
Comté ou district: Brome-Missisquoi; *Population au 2011:* 660
Circonscription(s) électorale(s) provinciale(s): Brome-Missisquoi
Circonscription(s) électorale(s) fédérale(s): Brome-Missisquoi
Prochaines élections: 3e novembre 2013
Ginette Simard Gendreault, Maire
Béatrice Travers, Directrice générale

Notre-Dame-des-Anges
260, boul Langelier
Québec, QC G1K 5N1
Tél: 418-529-0931; *Téléc:* 418-524-7162
mamj@mediom.com
Entité municipal: Parish (Paroisse)
Incorporation: 1er juillet 1855 *Area:* 0,06 km2
Population au 2011: 394
Circonscription(s) électorale(s) provinciale(s): Taschereau
Circonscription(s) électorale(s) fédérale(s): Québec
Prochaines élections: 3e novembre 2013
Aline Plante, Administratrice
Colette Huot, Directrice générale

Notre-Dame-des-Bois
35, rte de l'Église
Notre-Dame-des-Bois, QC J0B 2E0
Tél: 819-888-2724; *Téléc:* 819-888-2904
mun.notredamedesbois@axion.ca
www.notredamedesbois.qc.ca
Entité municipal: Municipality
Incorporation: 1er janvier 1877 *Area:* 190,90 km2
Comté ou district: Le Granit; *Population au 2011:* 911
Circonscription(s) électorale(s) provinciale(s): Mégantic-Compton

Circonscription(s) électorale(s) fédérale(s): Mégantic-L'Érable
Prochaines élections: 3e novembre 2013
Jean-Louis Gobeil, Maire
Guylaine Blais, Directrice générale

Notre-Dame-des-Monts
15, rue Principale
Notre-Dame-des-Monts, QC G0T 1L0
Tél: 418-489-2011; *Téléc:* 418-489-2014
municipalitenddm@coopnddm.com
www.notredamedesmonts.com
Entité municipal: Municipality
Incorporation: 11 avril 1935 *Area:* 56,15 km2
Comté ou district: Charlevoix-Est; *Population au 2011:* 815
Circonscription(s) électorale(s) provinciale(s): Charlevoix
Circonscription(s) électorale(s) fédérale(s):
Montmorency-Charlevoix-Haute-Côte-Nord
Prochaines élections: 3e novembre 2013
Jean-Claude Simard, Maire
Marcelle Pedneault, Directrice générale

Notre-Dame-des-Neiges
4, 2e rang Centre
Trois-Pistoles, QC G0L 4K0
Tél: 418-851-3009; *Téléc:* 418-851-3169
admin@notredamedesneiges.qc.ca
www.notredamedesneiges.qc.ca
Entité municipal: Municipality
Incorporation: 1er juillet 1855 *Area:* 92,87 km2
Comté ou district: Les Basques; *Population au 2011:* 1,129
Circonscription(s) électorale(s) provinciale(s): Rivière-du-Loup
Circonscription(s) électorale(s) fédérale(s):
Rimouski-Neigette-Témiscouata-Les Basques
Prochaines élections: 3e novembre 2013
Jean Marie Lafrance, Maire
Danielle Ouellet, Directrice générale

Notre-Dame-des-Pins
CP 40
2790, 1re av
Notre-Dame-des-Pins, QC G0M 1K0
Tél: 418-774-9718; *Téléc:* 418-774-9728
notredamedespins@sogetel.net
www.notredamedespins.qc.ca
Entité municipal: Parish (Paroisse)
Incorporation: 29 juin 1926 *Area:* 24,60 km2
Comté ou district: Beauce-Sartigan; *Population au 2011:* 1,227
Circonscription(s) électorale(s) provinciale(s): Beauce-Sud
Circonscription(s) électorale(s) fédérale(s): Beauce
Prochaines élections: 3e novembre 2013
Pierre Bégin, Maire
Dominique Lamarre, Directrice générale

Notre-Dame-des-Prairies
225, boul Antonio-Barrette
Notre-Dame-des-Prairies, QC J6E 1E7
Tél: 450-759-7741; *Téléc:* 450-759-6255
prairies@notre-dame-des-prairies.org
www.notre-dame-des-prairies.org
Entité municipal: Town
Incorporation: 1er janvier 1957 *Area:* 17,74 km2
Comté ou district: Joliette; *Population au 2011:* 8,868
Circonscription(s) électorale(s) provinciale(s): Joliette
Circonscription(s) électorale(s) fédérale(s): Joliette
Prochaines élections: 3e novembre 2013
Alain Larue, Maire
Sylvie Malo, Greffière

Notre-Dame-des-Sept-Douleurs
6201, ch de l'île
Notre-Dame-des-Sept-Douleurs, QC G0L 1K0
Tél: 418-898-3451; *Téléc:* 418-898-3492
mun_ndsd-ileverte@ileverte.qc.ca
www.ileverte.qc.ca
Entité municipal: Parish (Paroisse)
Incorporation: 1er janvier 1874 *Area:* 11,18 km2
Comté ou district: Rivière-du-Loup; *Population au 2011:* 49
Circonscription(s) électorale(s) provinciale(s): Rivière-du-Loup
Circonscription(s) électorale(s) fédérale(s):
Montmagny-L'Islet-Kamouraska-Rivière-du-Loup
Prochaines élections: 3e novembre 2013
Gilbert Delage, Maire
Denis Cusson, Directeur général

Notre-Dame-du-Bon-Conseil
1428, rte 122
Notre-Dame-du-Bon-Conseil, QC J0C 1A0
Tél: 819-336-5374; *Téléc:* 819-336-2389
vaubin@cgocable.ca
Entité municipal: Parish (Paroisse)
Incorporation: 15 février 1898 *Area:* 86,42 km2
Comté ou district: Drummond; *Population au 2011:* 979
Circonscription(s) électorale(s) provinciale(s): Richmond
Circonscription(s) électorale(s) fédérale(s): Drummond
Prochaines élections: 3e novembre 2013
Michel Bourgeois, Maire
Valérie Aubin, Directrice générale

Notre-Dame-du-Bon-Conseil
541, rue Notre-Dame
Notre-Dame-du-Bon-Conseil, QC J0C 1A0
Tél: 819-336-2744; *Téléc:* 819-336-2030
nb.bonconseil@cgocable.ca
www.notre-dame-du-bon-conseil-village.qc.ca
Entité municipal: Village
Incorporation: 1er janvier 1957 *Area:* 4,22 km2
Comté ou district: Drummond; *Population au 2011:* 1,404
Circonscription(s) électorale(s) provinciale(s): Richmond
Circonscription(s) électorale(s) fédérale(s): Drummond
Prochaines élections: 3e novembre 2013
Yvon Lampron, Maire
Isabelle Dumont, Directrice générale

Notre-Dame-du-Laus
CP 10
66, rue Principale
Notre-Dame-du-Laus, QC J0X 2M0
Tél: 819-767-2247; *Téléc:* 819-767-3102
mun.notre-dame-du-laus@tlb.sympatico.ca
www.notre-dame-du-laus.ca
Entité municipal: Municipality
Incorporation: 1er janvier 1876 *Area:* 866,02 km2
Comté ou district: Antoine-Labelle; *Population au 2011:* 1,518
Circonscription(s) électorale(s) provinciale(s): Labelle
Circonscription(s) électorale(s) fédérale(s): Laurentides-Labelle
Prochaines élections: 3e novembre 2013
Ken Ménard, Maire
Yves Larocque, Directeur général

Notre-Dame-du-Mont-Carmel
3860, rue de l' Hôtel de Ville
Notre-Dame-du-Mont-Carmel, QC G0X 3J0
Tél: 819-375-9856; *Téléc:* 819-373-4045
municipalite@mont-carmel.org
www.mont-carmel.org
Entité municipal: Parish (Paroisse)
Incorporation: 30 décembre 1858 *Area:* 126,61 km2
Comté ou district: Les Chenaux; *Population au 2011:* 5,467
Circonscription(s) électorale(s) provinciale(s): St-Maurice
Circonscription(s) électorale(s) fédérale(s):
St-Maurice-Champlain
Prochaines élections: 3e novembre 2013
Pierre A. Bouchard, Maire
Jean Lachance, Directeur général

Notre-Dame-du-Nord
71, rue Principale nord
Notre-Dame-du-Nord, QC J0Z 3B0
Tél: 819-723-2294; *Téléc:* 819-723-2483
rejean.nddn@mrctemiscamingue.qc.ca
municipalite.notre-dame-du-nord.qc.ca
Entité municipal: Municipality
Incorporation: 23 septembre 1919 *Area:* 103,60 km2
Comté ou district: Témiscamingue; *Population au 2011:* 1,075
Circonscription(s) électorale(s) provinciale(s):
Rouyn-Noranda-Témiscamingue
Circonscription(s) électorale(s) fédérale(s):
Abitibi-Témiscamingue
Prochaines élections: 3e novembre 2013
Mychel Tremblay, Maire
Réjean Pelletier, Directeur général

Notre-Dame-du-Portage
560, rte de la Montagne
Notre-Dame-du-Portage, QC G0L 1Y0
Tél: 418-862-9163; *Téléc:* 418-862-5240
directiongenerale@notre-dame-du-portage.ca
www.municipalite.notre-dame-du-portage.qc.ca
Entité municipal: Municipality
Incorporation: 19 juillet 1856 *Area:* 39,55 km2
Comté ou district: Rivière-du-Loup; *Population au 2011:* 1,193
Circonscription(s) électorale(s) provinciale(s): Rivière-du-Loup
Circonscription(s) électorale(s) fédérale(s):
Montmagny-L'Islet-Kamouraska-Rivière-du-Loup
Prochaines élections: 3e novembre 2013
Louis Vadeboncoeur, Maire
Annie Lemieux, Directrice générale

Notre-Dame-du-Rosaire
144, rue Principale
Notre-Dame-du-Rosaire, QC G0R 2H0
Tél: 418-469-2802; *Téléc:* 418-469-2802
munndr@globetrotter.net
www.notredamedurosaire.com
Entité municipal: Municipality
Incorporation: 18 décembre 1894 *Area:* 158,53 km2
Comté ou district: Montmagny; *Population au 2011:* 384
Circonscription(s) électorale(s) provinciale(s): Montmagny-L'Islet
Circonscription(s) électorale(s) fédérale(s):
Montmagny-L'Islet-Kamouraska-Rivière-du-Loup
Prochaines élections: 3e novembre 2013
Gilles Giroux, Maire
Isabelle Lachance, Directrice générale

Notre-Dame-du-Sacré-Coeur-d'Issoudun
268, rue Principale
Issoudun, QC G0S 1L0
Tél: 418-728-2006; *Téléc:* 418-728-2303
munissoudun@videotron.ca
www.issoudun.qc.ca
Entité municipal: Parish (Paroisse)
Incorporation: 4 janvier 1909 *Area:* 60,81 km2
Comté ou district: Lotbinière; *Population au 2011:* 869
Circonscription(s) électorale(s) provinciale(s): Lotbinière
Circonscription(s) électorale(s) fédérale(s):
Lotbinière-Chutes-de-la-Chaudière
Prochaines élections: 3e novembre 2013
Annie Thériault, Mairesse
Suzanne Therrien-Croteau, Directrice générale

Nouvelle
CP 68
470, rue Francoeur
Nouvelle, QC G0C 2E0
Tél: 418-794-2253; *Téléc:* 418-794-2254
direction@nouvellegaspesie.com
nouvellegaspesie.com
Entité municipal: Municipality
Incorporation: 10 octobre 1907 *Area:* 230,63 km2
Comté ou district: Avignon; *Population au 2011:* 1,689
Circonscription(s) électorale(s) provinciale(s): Bonaventure
Circonscription(s) électorale(s) fédérale(s):
Gaspésie—Îles-de-la-Madeleine
Prochaines élections: 3e novembre 2013
Richard St-Laurent, Maire
Daniel Bujold, Directeur général

Noyan
1312, ch de la Petite-France
Noyan, QC J0J 1B0
Tél: 450-294-2689; *Téléc:* 450-294-2175
renseignements@ville.noyan.qc.ca
www.ville.noyan.qc.ca
Entité municipal: Municipality
Incorporation: 1er juillet 1855 *Area:* 43,79 km2
Comté ou district: Le Haut-Richelieu; *Population au 2011:* 1,297
Circonscription(s) électorale(s) provinciale(s): Iberville
Circonscription(s) électorale(s) fédérale(s): Brome-Missisquoi
Prochaines élections: 3e novembre 2013
Réal Ryan, Maire
Marie-France Saucier, Directrice générale

Ogden
70, ch Ogden
Ogden, QC J0B 3E3
Tél: 819-876-7117; *Téléc:* 819-876-2121
mun.ogden@gmail.com
Entité municipal: Municipality
Incorporation: 23 janvier 1932 *Area:* 75,49 km2
Comté ou district: Memphrémagog; *Population au 2011:* 770
Circonscription(s) électorale(s) provinciale(s): Orford
Circonscription(s) électorale(s) fédérale(s): Compton-Stanstead
Prochaines élections: 3e novembre 2013
Joe Stairs, Maire
Renée Donaldson, Directrice générale

Oka
183, rue des Anges
Oka, QC J0N 1E0
Tél: 450-479-8333; *Téléc:* 450-479-1886
info@municipalite.oka.qc.ca
www.municipalite.oka.qc.ca
Entité municipal: Municipality
Incorporation: 8 septembre 1999 *Area:* 67,21 km2
Comté ou district: Deux-Montagnes; *Population au 2011:* 3,969
Circonscription(s) électorale(s) provinciale(s): Mirabel
Circonscription(s) électorale(s) fédérale(s):
Argenteuil-Papineau-Mirabel
Prochaines élections: 3e novembre 2013
Richard Lalonde, Maire
Marie Daoust, Directrice générale

Orford
2530, ch du Parc
Orford, QC J1X 8R8
Tél: 819-843-3111; *Téléc:* 819-843-2707
info@canton.orford.qc.ca
www.canton.orford.qc.ca
Entité municipal: Township
Incorporation: 1er juillet 1855 *Area:* 135,25 km2
Comté ou district: Memphrémagog; *Population au 2011:* 3,575
Circonscription(s) électorale(s) provinciale(s): Orford
Circonscription(s) électorale(s) fédérale(s): Brome-Missisquoi
Prochaines élections: 3e novembre 2013
Pierre Bastien, Maire
Brigitte Boisvert, Greffière

Ormstown
81, rue Lambton
Ormstown, QC J0S 1K0
Tél: 450-829-2625; *Téléc:* 450-829-4162
ormstown@ormstown.ca
www.ormstown.ca
Entité municipal: Municipality
Incorporation: 26 janvier 2000 *Area:* 142,39 km2
Comté ou district: Le Haut-St-Laurent; *Population au 2011:* 3,595
Circonscription(s) électorale(s) provinciale(s): Huntingdon
Circonscription(s) électorale(s) fédérale(s): Beauharnois-Salaberry
Prochaines élections: 3e novembre 2013
Jacques Lapierre, Maire
Daniel Théroux, Directeur général

Otter Lake
CP 70
15, av Palmer
Otter Lake, QC J0X 2P0
Tél: 819-453-7049; *Téléc:* 819-453-7311
otter-lake@mrcpontiac.qc.ca
www.otterlakequebec.ca
Entité municipal: Municipality
Incorporation: 1er janvier 1877 *Area:* 496,21 km2
Comté ou district: Pontiac; *Population au 2011:* 1,109
Circonscription(s) électorale(s) provinciale(s): Pontiac
Circonscription(s) électorale(s) fédérale(s): Pontiac
Prochaines élections: 3e novembre 2013
Graham Hawley, Maire
Andrea Lafleur, Directrice générale

Otterburn Park
601, ch Ozias-Leduc
Otterburn Park, QC J3H 2M6
Tél: 450-536-0303; *Téléc:* 450-467-8260
info@ville.otterburnpark.qc.ca
www.ville.otterburnpark.qc.ca
Entité municipal: Town
Incorporation: 1er juillet 1855 *Area:* 5,20 km2
Comté ou district: La Vallée-du-Richelieu; *Population au 2011:* 8,450
Circonscription(s) électorale(s) provinciale(s): Borduas
Circonscription(s) électorale(s) fédérale(s): Chambly-Borduas
Prochaines élections: 3e novembre 2013
Vacant, Maire
Julie Waite, Greffière

Oujé-Bougoumou
203, Opemiska Meskino
Oujé-Bougoumou, QC G0W 3C0
Tél: 888-745-3905; *Téléc:* 418-745-3544
tourism@ouje.ca
www.ouje.ca
Entité municipal: Villages Cris
Area: 2,54 km2
Population au 2011: 725
Circonscription(s) électorale(s) provinciale(s): Ungava
Circonscription(s) électorale(s) fédérale(s): Roberval-Lac-St-Jean
Louise Wapachee, Chief

Packington
35A, rue Principale
Packington, QC G0L 1Z0
Tél: 418-853-2269; *Téléc:* 418-853-6427
info@packington.org
www.packington.org
Entité municipal: Parish (Paroisse)
Incorporation: 6 octobre 1925 *Area:* 117,89 km2
Comté ou district: Témiscouata; *Population au 2011:* 595
Circonscription(s) électorale(s) provinciale(s): Kamouraska-Témiscouata
Circonscription(s) électorale(s) fédérale(s): Rimouski-Neigette-Témiscouata-Les Basques
Prochaines élections: 3e novembre 2013
Emilien Beaulieu, Maire
Denis Moreau, Directeur général

Padoue
CP 15
215, rue Beaulieu
Padoue, QC G0J 1X0
Tél: 418-775-8188; *Téléc:* 418-775-8177
padoue@mitis.qc.ca
www.municipalite.padoue.qc.ca
Entité municipal: Municipality
Incorporation: 31 janvier 1911 *Area:* 67,57 km2
Comté ou district: La Mitis; *Population au 2011:* 411
Circonscription(s) électorale(s) provinciale(s): Matapédia
Circonscription(s) électorale(s) fédérale(s): Haute-Gaspésie-La Mitis-Matane-Matapédia
Prochaines élections: 3e novembre 2013
Gilles Laflamme, Maire
Line Fillion, Directrice générale

Palmarolle
CP 309
499, rte 393
Palmarolle, QC J0Z 3C0
Tél: 819-787-2303; *Téléc:* 819-787-2412
palmarolle@mrcao.qc.ca
www.palmarolle.ao.ca
Entité municipal: Municipality
Incorporation: 14 avril 1930 *Area:* 118,36 km2
Comté ou district: Abitibi-Ouest; *Population au 2011:* 1,465
Circonscription(s) électorale(s) provinciale(s): Abitibi-Ouest
Circonscription(s) électorale(s) fédérale(s): Abitibi-Témiscamingue
Prochaines élections: 3e novembre 2013
Marcel Caron, Maire
Claude Marquis, Directeur général

Papineau
266, rue Viger
Papineauville, QC J0V 1R0
Tél: 819-427-6243; *Téléc:* 819-427-8318
info@mrcpapineau.com
www.mrcpapineau.com
Entité municipal: Regional County Municipality
Incorporation: 1er janvier 1983
Population au 2011: 22,541
Note: 24 municipalités.
Paulette Lalande, Préfète
Ghislain Ménard, Directeur général
menard@mrcpapineau.com

Papineauville
#100, 188, rue Jeanne-D'Arc
Papineauville, QC J0V 1R0
Tél: 819-427-5511; *Téléc:* 819-427-5590
papineauville@mrcpapineau.com
www.mun-papineauville.qc.ca
Entité municipal: Municipality
Incorporation: 29 novembre 2000 *Area:* 48,52 km2
Comté ou district: Papineau; *Population au 2011:* 2,165
Circonscription(s) électorale(s) provinciale(s): Papineau
Circonscription(s) électorale(s) fédérale(s): Argenteuil-Papineau-Mirabel
Prochaines élections: 3e novembre 2013
Gilles Clément, Maire
Martine Joanisse, Greffier

Parisville
975, rte Principale ouest
Parisville, QC G0S 1X0
Tél: 819-292-2222; *Téléc:* 819-292-1514
dg@municipalite.parisville.qc.ca
www.municipalite.parisville.qc.ca
Entité municipal: Parish (Paroisse)
Incorporation: 18 mars 1901 *Area:* 36,85 km2
Comté ou district: Bécancour; *Population au 2011:* 528
Circonscription(s) électorale(s) provinciale(s): Lotbinière
Circonscription(s) électorale(s) fédérale(s): Bas-Richelieu-Nicolet-Bécancour
Prochaines élections: 3e novembre 2013
Maurice Grimard, Maire
François Gaudreault, Directeur général

Paspébiac
CP 130
178, 9e rue
Paspébiac, QC G0C 2K0
Tél: 418-752-2277; *Téléc:* 418-752-6566
paspebia@globetrotter.net
www.ville.paspebiac.qc.ca
Entité municipal: Town
Incorporation: 20 août 1997 *Area:* 94,59 km2
Comté ou district: Bonaventure; *Population au 2011:* 3,198
Circonscription(s) électorale(s) provinciale(s): Bonaventure
Circonscription(s) électorale(s) fédérale(s): Gaspésie—îles-de-la-Madeleine
Prochaines élections: 3e novembre 2013
Gino LeBrasseur, Maire
Paul Langlois, Directeur général

Percé
CP 99
137, rte 132 ouest
Percé, QC G0C 2L0
Tél: 418-782-2933; *Téléc:* 418-782-5487
renseignements@ville.perce.qc.ca
www.ville.perce.qc.ca
Entité municipal: Town
Incorporation: 1er janvier 1971 *Area:* 427,94 km2
Comté ou district: Le Rocher-Percé; *Population au 2011:* 3,312
Circonscription(s) électorale(s) provinciale(s): Gaspé
Circonscription(s) électorale(s) fédérale(s): Gaspésie—îles-de-la-Madeleine
Prochaines élections: 3e novembre 2013
Bruno Cloutier, Maire
Gemma Vibert, Greffière

Péribonka
312, rue Édouard-Niquet
Péribonka, QC G0W 2G0
Tél: 418-374-2967; *Téléc:* 418-374-2355
sharvey@peribonka.ca
www.municipalite-peribonka.com
Entité municipal: Municipality
Incorporation: 19 septembre 1908 *Area:* 113,46 km2
Comté ou district: Maria-Chapdelaine; *Population au 2011:* 464
Circonscription(s) électorale(s) provinciale(s): Roberval
Circonscription(s) électorale(s) fédérale(s): Roberval-Lac-St-Jean
Prochaines élections: 3e novembre 2013
Gilbert Goulet, Maire
Steve Harvey, Directeur général

Petit-Saguenay
35, ch du Quai
Petit-Saguenay, QC G0V 1N0
Tél: 418-272-2323; *Téléc:* 418-544-3077
munps@royaume.com
www.petit-saguenay.com
Entité municipal: Municipality
Incorporation: 12 août 1919 *Area:* 328,72 km2
Comté ou district: Le Fjord-du-Saguenay; *Population au 2011:* 727
Circonscription(s) électorale(s) provinciale(s): Dubuc
Circonscription(s) électorale(s) fédérale(s): Chicoutimi-Le Fjord
Prochaines élections: 3e novembre 2013
Thérèse Gaudreault, Maire
Alexis Lavoie, Directeur général

Petite-Rivière-St-François
CP 10
1067, rue Principale
Petite-Rivière-Saint-François, QC G0A 2L0
Tél: 418-760-1050; *Téléc:* 418-760-1051
francined@petiteriviere.com
www.petiteriviere.com
Entité municipal: Municipality
Incorporation: 1er juillet 1855 *Area:* 135,66 km2
Comté ou district: Charlevoix; *Population au 2011:* 744
Circonscription(s) électorale(s) provinciale(s): Charlevoix
Circonscription(s) électorale(s) fédérale(s): Montmorency-Charlevoix-Haute-Côte-Nord
Prochaines élections: 3e novembre 2013
Gérald Maltais, Maire
Francine Dufour, Directrice générale

Petite-Vallée
CP 1067
45, rue Principale
Petite-Vallée, QC G0E 1Y0
Tél: 418-393-2949; *Téléc:* 418-393-2949
bibliopv@globetrotter.qc.ca
Entité municipal: Municipality
Incorporation: 1er janvier 1957 *Area:* 37,83 km2
Comté ou district: La Côte-de-Gaspé; *Population au 2011:* 178
Circonscription(s) électorale(s) provinciale(s): Gaspé
Circonscription(s) électorale(s) fédérale(s): Gaspésie—îles-de-la-Madeleine
Prochaines élections: 3e novembre 2013
Rodrigue Brousseau, Maire
Simon Côté, Directeur général

Piedmont
670, rue Principale
Piedmont, QC J0R 1K0
Tél: 450-227-1888; *Téléc:* 450-227-6716
info@municipalite.piedmont.qc.ca
www.municipalite.piedmont.qc.ca
Entité municipal: Municipality
Incorporation: 22 septembre 1923 *Area:* 23,66 km2
Comté ou district: Les Pays-d'en-Haut; *Population au 2011:* 2,721
Circonscription(s) électorale(s) provinciale(s): Bertrand
Circonscription(s) électorale(s) fédérale(s): Laurentides-Labelle
Prochaines élections: 3e novembre 2013
Clément Cardin, Maire
Gilbert Aubin, Directeur général

Pierre-De Saurel
50, rue du Fort
Sorel-Tracy, QC J3P 7X7
Tél: 450-743-2703; *Téléc:* 450-743-7313
mrc@pierredesaurel.com
www.soreltracyregion.net
Entité municipal: Regional County Municipality
Incorporation: 1er janvier 1982
Population au 2011: 50,900
Note: 12 municipalités.
Raymond Arel, Préfet
Denis Boisvert, Directeur général

Pierreville
CP 300
26, rue Ally
Pierreville, QC J0G 1J0
Tél: 450-568-2139; *Téléc:* 450-568-0689
info@municipalitepierreville.qc.ca
www.pierreville.net
Entité municipal: Municipality
Incorporation: 13 juin 2001 *Area:* 79,54 km2
Comté ou district: Nicolet-Yamaska; *Population au 2011:* 2,176
Circonscription(s) électorale(s) provinciale(s): Nicolet-Yamaska
Circonscription(s) électorale(s) fédérale(s): Bas-Richelieu-Nicolet-Bécancour
Prochaines élections: 3e novembre 2013
André Descôteaux, Maire
Micheline C. Laforce, Directrice générale

Piopolis
403, rue Principale
Piopolis, QC G0Y 1H0
Tél: 819-583-3953; *Téléc:* 819-583-1467
municipalite@piopolis.ca
www.piopolis.ca
Entité municipal: Municipality
Incorporation: 1er janvier 1880 *Area:* 104,14 km2
Comté ou district: Le Granit; *Population au 2011:* 364
Circonscription(s) électorale(s) provinciale(s): Mégantic-Compton
Circonscription(s) électorale(s) fédérale(s): Mégantic-L'Érable
Prochaines élections: 3e novembre 2013
André St-Marseille, Maire
Julie Cloutier, Directrice générale

Plaisance
274, rue Desjardins
Plaisance, QC J0V 1S0
Tél: 819-427-5363; *Téléc:* 819-427-5015
ville.plaisance@videotron.ca
www.ville.plaisance.qc.ca
Entité municipal: Municipality
Incorporation: 31 octobre 1900 *Area:* 42,61 km2
Comté ou district: Papineau; *Population au 2011:* 1,103
Circonscription(s) électorale(s) provinciale(s): Papineau
Circonscription(s) électorale(s) fédérale(s): Argenteuil-Papineau-Mirabel
Prochaines élections: 3e novembre 2013
Paulette Lalande, Mairesse
Benoit Hébert, Directeur général

Plessisville
CP 245
290, rte 165 sud
Plessisville, QC G6L 2Y7
Tél: 819-362-2712; *Téléc:* 819-362-9185
info@paroisseplessisville.com
www.paroisseplessisville.com
Entité municipal: Parish (Paroisse)
Incorporation: 1er juillet 1855 *Area:* 136,29 km2
Comté ou district: L'Érable; *Population au 2011:* 2,678
Circonscription(s) électorale(s) provinciale(s): Arthabaska
Circonscription(s) électorale(s) fédérale(s): Mégantic-L'Érable
Prochaines élections: 3e novembre 2013
Alain Dubois, Maire
Johanne Dubois, Directrice générale

Plessisville
1700, rue St-Calixte
Plessisville, QC G6L 1R3
Tél: 819-362-3284; *Téléc:* 819-362-6421
info@ville.plessisville.qc.ca
www.ville.plessisville.qc.ca
Entité municipal: Town
Incorporation: 27 avril 1855 *Area:* 4,44 km2
Comté ou district: L'Érable; *Population au 2011:* 6,688
Circonscription(s) électorale(s) provinciale(s): Arthabaska
Circonscription(s) électorale(s) fédérale(s): Mégantic-L'Érable
Prochaines élections: 3e novembre 2013
Réal Ouellet, Maire
Jean Marcoux, Dicecteur général

Pohénégamook
1309, rue Principale
Pohénégamook, QC G0L 1J0
Tél: 418-859-2222; *Téléc:* 418-859-3465
info.ville@pohenegamook.net
www.pohenegamook.net
Entité municipal: Town
Incorporation: 3 novembre 1973 *Area:* 351,97 km2
Comté ou district: Témiscouata; *Population au 2011:* 2,770
Circonscription(s) électorale(s) provinciale(s): Kamouraska-Témiscouata
Circonscription(s) électorale(s) fédérale(s): Rimouski-Neigette-Témiscouata-Les Basques
Prochaines élections: 3e novembre 2013
Louise Labonté, Mairesse
Denise Pelletier, Greffière

Pointe-à-la-Croix
CP 159
139, boul Inter-Provincial
Pointe-à-la-Croix, QC G0C 1L0
Tél: 418-788-2011; *Téléc:* 418-788-2916
pointe-a-la-croix@globetrotter.net
www.pointe-a-la-croix.com
Entité municipal: Municipality
Incorporation: 7 mai 1983 *Area:* 394,03 km2
Comté ou district: Avignon; *Population au 2011:* 1,472
Circonscription(s) électorale(s) provinciale(s): Bonaventure
Circonscription(s) électorale(s) fédérale(s): Gaspésie—Iles-de-la-Madeleine
Prochaines élections: 3e novembre 2013
Jean-Paul Audy, Maire
Claude Audet, Directeur général

Pointe-aux-Outardes
471, ch Principal
Pointe-aux-Outardes, QC G0H 1M0
Tél: 418-567-2203; *Téléc:* 418-567-4409
municipalite@pointe-aux-outardes.ca
www.pointe-aux-outardes.ca
Entité municipal: Village
Incorporation: 1er janvier 1964 *Area:* 71,56 km2
Comté ou district: Manicouagan; *Population au 2011:* 1,330
Circonscription(s) électorale(s) provinciale(s): René-Lévesque
Circonscription(s) électorale(s) fédérale(s): Manicouagan
Prochaines élections: 3e novembre 2013
André Lepage, Maire
Dania Hovington, Directrice générale

Pointe-Calumet
300, av Basile-Routhier
Pointe-Calumet, QC J0N 1G2
Tél: 450-473-5930; *Téléc:* 450-473-6571
info@municipalite.pointe-calumet.qc.ca
www.municipalite.pointe-calumet.qc.ca
Entité municipal: Municipality
Incorporation: 12 février 1953 *Area:* 4,89 km2
Comté ou district: Deux-Montagnes; *Population au 2011:* 6,396
Circonscription(s) électorale(s) provinciale(s): Mirabel
Circonscription(s) électorale(s) fédérale(s): Argenteuil-Papineau-Mirabel
Prochaines élections: 3e novembre 2013
Jacques Séguin, Maire
Chantal Pilon, Directrice générale

Pointe-des-Cascades
105, ch du Fleuve
Pointe-des-Cascades, QC J0P 1M0
Tél: 450-455-3414; *Téléc:* 450-455-9671
pointe-des-cascades@videotron.ca
www.pointe-des-cascades.com
Entité municipal: Village
Incorporation: 1er mai 1961 *Area:* 2,66 km2
Comté ou district: Vaudreuil-Soulanges; *Population au 2011:* 1,340
Circonscription(s) électorale(s) provinciale(s): Soulanges
Circonscription(s) électorale(s) fédérale(s): Vaudreuil-Soulanges
Prochaines élections: 3e novembre 2013
Maryse M. Sauvé, Maire
Christiane Cyr, Directrice générale

Pointe-Fortune
694, rue du Tisseur
Pointe-Fortune, QC J0P 1N0
Tél: 450-451-5178; *Téléc:* 450-451-4649
mpf@qc.aira.com
pointefortune.ca
Entité municipal: Village
Incorporation: 28 août 1880 *Area:* 9,09 km2
Comté ou district: Vaudreuil-Soulanges; *Population au 2011:* 542
Circonscription(s) électorale(s) provinciale(s): Soulanges
Circonscription(s) électorale(s) fédérale(s): Vaudreuil-Soulanges
Prochaines élections: 3e novembre 2013
Jean-Pierre Daoust, Maire
Diane Héroux, Directrice générale

Pointe-Lebel
365, rue Granier
Pointe-Lebel, QC G0H 1N0
Tél: 418-589-8073; *Téléc:* 418-589-6154
nadiaptl@globetrotter.net
www.pointe-lebel.com
Entité municipal: Village
Incorporation: 1er janvier 1964 *Area:* 91,16 km2
Comté ou district: Manicouagan; *Population au 2011:* 1,973
Circonscription(s) électorale(s) provinciale(s): René-Lévesque
Circonscription(s) électorale(s) fédérale(s): Manicouagan
Prochaines élections: 3e novembre 2013
Ghislain Beaudin, Maire
Nadia Allard, Directrice générale

Pont-Rouge
212, rue Dupont
Pont-Rouge, QC G3H 1A1
Tél: 418-873-4481; *Téléc:* 418-873-3494
info@ville.pontrouge.qc.ca
www.ville.pontrouge.qc.ca
Entité municipal: Town
Incorporation: 3 janvier 1996 *Area:* 121,02 km2
Comté ou district: Portneuf; *Population au 2011:* 8,723
Circonscription(s) électorale(s) provinciale(s): Portneuf
Circonscription(s) électorale(s) fédérale(s): Portneuf-Jacques-Cartier
Prochaines élections: 3e novembre 2013
Claude Bégin, Maire
Jocelyne Laliberté, Greffière

Pontiac
2024, rte 148
Pontiac, QC J0X 2G0
Tél: 819-455-2401; *Téléc:* 819-455-9756
dirgen@munpontiac.com
www.munpontiac.com
Entité municipal: Municipality
Incorporation: 1er janvier 1975 *Area:* 446,87 km2
Comté ou district: Les Collines-de-l'Outaouais; *Population au 2011:* 5,681
Circonscription(s) électorale(s) provinciale(s): Pontiac
Circonscription(s) électorale(s) fédérale(s): Pontiac
Prochaines élections: 3e novembre 2013
Edward McCann, Maire
Sylvain Bertrand, Directeur général

Pontiac
602, rte 301
Campbell's Bay, QC J0X 1K0
Tél: 819-648-5689; *Téléc:* 819-648-5810
mrc@mrcpontiac.qc.ca
www.mrcpontiac.qc.ca
Entité municipal: Regional County Municipality
Incorporation: 1er janvier 1983
Population au 2011: 14,358
Note: 18 municipalités & 1 autre territoire.
Michael McCrank, Préfet
Rémi Bertrand, Directeur général

Port-Cartier
40, av Parent
Port-Cartier, QC G5B 2G5
Tél: 418-766-2349; *Téléc:* 418-766-3390
directiongenerale@villeport-cartier.com
www.villeport-cartier.com
Entité municipal: Town
Incorporation: 19 février 2003 *Area:* 1073,70 km2
Comté ou district: Sept-Rivières; *Population au 2011:* 6,651
Circonscription(s) électorale(s) provinciale(s): Duplessis

Circonscription(s) électorale(s) fédérale(s): Manicouagan
Prochaines élections: 3e novembre 2013
Laurence Méthot, Mairesse
Andrée Bouffard, Greffière

Port-Daniel—Gascons
494, rte 132
Port-Daniel—Gascons, QC G0C 2N0
Tél: 418-396-5225; *Téléc:* 418-396-5588
municipalitedeport-daniel@globetrotter.net
www.port-daniel-gascons.ca
Entité municipal: Municipality
Incorporation: 17 janvier 2001 *Area:* 305,34 km2
Comté ou district: Le Rocher Percé; *Population au 2011:* 2,453
Circonscription(s) électorale(s) provinciale(s): Bonaventure
Circonscription(s) électorale(s) fédérale(s):
Gaspésie—Îles-de-la-Madeleine
Prochaines élections: 3e novembre 2013
Maurice Anglehart, Maire
Thérèse Roussy, Directrice générale

Portage-du-Fort
CP 130
24, rue de l'Église
Portage-du-Fort, QC J0X 2T0
Tél: 819-647-2767; *Téléc:* 819-647-1910
therault@hotmail.com
Entité municipal: Village
Incorporation: 1er janvier 1863 *Area:* 4,24 km2
Comté ou district: Pontiac; *Population au 2011:* 266
Circonscription(s) électorale(s) provinciale(s): Pontiac
Circonscription(s) électorale(s) fédérale(s): Pontiac
Prochaines élections: 3e novembre 2013
Lynne Cameron, Mairesse
Tracey Hérault, Directrice générale

Portneuf
297, 1re Av
Portneuf, QC G0A 2Y0
Tél: 418-286-3844; *Téléc:* 418-286-4304
vilport@globetrotter.net
www.villedeportneuf.com
Entité municipal: Town
Incorporation: 4 juillet 2002 *Area:* 110,43 km2
Comté ou district: Portneuf; *Population au 2011:* 3,107
Circonscription(s) électorale(s) provinciale(s): Portneuf
Circonscription(s) électorale(s) fédérale(s):
Portneuf-Jacques-Cartier
Prochaines élections: 3e novembre 2013
Nelson Bédard, Maire
France Marcotte, Greffière
Yves Landry, Directeur général

Portneuf
185, rte 138
Cap-Santé, QC G0A 1L0
Tél: 418-285-3744; *Téléc:* 418-285-1703
portneuf@mrc-portneuf.qc.ca
www.portneuf.com
Entité municipal: Regional County Municipality
Incorporation: 1er janvier 1982
Population au 2011: 49,370
Note: 18 municipalités & 3 autres territoires.
Denis Langlois, Préfet
Josée Frenette, Directrice générale

Portneuf-sur-Mer
CP 98
170, rue Principale
Portneuf-sur-Mer, QC G0T 1P0
Tél: 418-238-2642; *Téléc:* 418-238-5319
muniport@bellnet.ca
www.portneuf-sur-mer.ca
Entité municipal: Municipality
Incorporation: 12 septembre 1902 *Area:* 241,23 km2
Comté ou district: La Haute-Côte-Nord; *Population au 2011:* 761
Circonscription(s) électorale(s) provinciale(s): René-Lévesque
Circonscription(s) électorale(s) fédérale(s):
Montmorency-Charlevoix-Haute-Côte-Nord
Prochaines élections: 3e novembre 2013
Jean-Marie Delaunay, Maire
Gontran Tremblay, Directeur général

Potton
CP 330
2, rue de Vale Perkins
Mansonville, QC J0E 1X0
Tél: 450-292-3313; *Téléc:* 450-292-5555
info@potton.ca
www.potton.ca
Entité municipal: Township
Incorporation: 1er juillet 1855 *Area:* 264,10 km2
Comté ou district: Memphrémagog; *Population au 2011:* 1,849
Circonscription(s) électorale(s) provinciale(s): Brome-Missisquoi
Circonscription(s) électorale(s) fédérale(s): Brome-Missisquoi
Prochaines élections: 3e novembre 2013
Jacques Marcoux, Maire
Thierry Gilbert, Directeur général

Poularies
CP 58
990, rue Principale
Poularies, QC J0Z 3E0
Tél: 819-782-5159; *Téléc:* 819-782-5063
poularies@mrcao.qc.ca
poularies.ao.ca
Entité municipal: Municipality
Incorporation: 7 mai 1924 *Area:* 164,95 km2
Comté ou district: Abitibi-Ouest; *Population au 2011:* 679
Circonscription(s) électorale(s) provinciale(s): Abitibi-Ouest
Circonscription(s) électorale(s) fédérale(s):
Abitibi-Témiscamingue
Prochaines élections: 3e novembre 2013
Claude Blais, Maire
Katy Rivard, Directrice générale

Preissac
6, rue des Rapides
Preissac, QC J0Y 2E0
Tél: 819-732-4938; *Téléc:* 819-732-4909
direction@preissac.com
www.preissac.com
Entité municipal: Municipality
Incorporation: 1er janvier 1979 *Area:* 489,50 km2
Comté ou district: Abitibi; *Population au 2011:* 786
Circonscription(s) électorale(s) provinciale(s): Abitibi-Ouest
Circonscription(s) électorale(s) fédérale(s):
Abitibi-Témiscamingue
Prochaines élections: 3e novembre 2013
Huguette Saucier, Mairesse
France Beaulieu, Directrice générale (par intérim)

Price
CP 340
18, rue Fournier
Price, QC G0J 1Z0
Tél: 418-775-2144; *Téléc:* 418-775-2459
price@mitis.qc.ca
www.municipaliteprice.com
Entité municipal: Village
Incorporation: 3 mars 1926 *Area:* 2,35 km2
Comté ou district: La Mitis; *Population au 2011:* 1,673
Circonscription(s) électorale(s) provinciale(s): Matapédia
Circonscription(s) électorale(s) fédérale(s):
Haute-Gaspésie-La-Mitis-Matane-Matapédia
Prochaines élections: 3e novembre 2013
Laurent Emond, Maire
Louise Furlong, Greffière

Princeville
50, rue St-Jacques ouest
Princeville, QC G6L 4Y5
Tél: 819-364-3333; *Téléc:* 819-364-5198
info@villedeprinceville.qc.ca
www.villedeprinceville.qc.ca
Entité municipal: Town
Incorporation: 23 février 2000 *Area:* 198,00 km2
Comté ou district: L'Érable; *Population au 2011:* 5,693
Circonscription(s) électorale(s) provinciale(s): Arthabaska
Circonscription(s) électorale(s) fédérale(s): Mégantic-L'Érable
Prochaines élections: 3e novembre 2013
Gilles Fortier, Maire
Mario Juaire, Greffier

Puvirnituq
CP 150
Puvirnituq, QC J0M 1P0
Tél: 819-988-2825; *Téléc:* 819-988-2751
sec.treasurer@nvpuvirnituq.ca
www.nvpuvirnituq.ca
Entité municipal: Northern Village
Incorporation: 2 septembre 1989 *Area:* 111,00 km2
Comté ou district: Kativik; *Population au 2011:* 1,692
Circonscription(s) électorale(s) provinciale(s): Ungava
Circonscription(s) électorale(s) fédérale(s):
Abitibi-Baie-James-Nunavik-Eeyou
Prochaines élections: 7e novembre 2012
Aisara Kenuajuak, Maire
Sarah Beaulne, Secrétaire-trésorière

Quaqtaq
CP 107
Quaqtaq, QC J0M 1J0
Tél: 819-492-9912; *Téléc:* 819-492-9935
stukkiapik@nvquaqtaq.ca
www.nvquaqtaq.ca
Entité municipal: Northern Village
Incorporation: 1er novembre 1980 *Area:* 26,49 km2
Comté ou district: Kativik; *Population au 2011:* 376
Circonscription(s) électorale(s) provinciale(s): Ungava
Circonscription(s) électorale(s) fédérale(s):
Abitibi-Baie-James-Nunavik-Eeyou
Prochaines élections: 7e novembre 2012
Bobby Putulik, Maire
Sammy Tukkiapik, Secrétaire-trésorier

Racine
348, rue de L'Église
Racine, QC J0E 1Y0
Tél: 450-532-2876; *Téléc:* 450-532-2865
reception@municipalite.racine.qc.ca
www.municipalite.racine.qc.ca
Entité municipal: Municipality
Incorporation: 15 février 1995 *Area:* 107,87 km2
Comté ou district: Le Val-St-François; *Population au 2011:* 1,252
Circonscription(s) électorale(s) provinciale(s): Johnson
Circonscription(s) électorale(s) fédérale(s): Jonquière-Alma
Prochaines élections: 3e novembre 2013
Rene Pelletier, Maire
André Courtemanche, Directeur général

Ragueneau
523, rte 138
Ragueneau, QC G0H 1S0
Tél: 418-567-2345; *Téléc:* 418-567-2344
ragueneau@satcomcolibri.com
www.municipalite.ragueneau.qc.ca
Entité municipal: Parish (Paroisse)
Incorporation: 7 mars 1951 *Area:* 215,92 km2
Comté ou district: Manicouagan; *Population au 2011:* 1,405
Circonscription(s) électorale(s) provinciale(s): René-Lévesque
Circonscription(s) électorale(s) fédérale(s): Manicouagan
Prochaines élections: 3e novembre 2013
Claude Lavoie, Maire
Audrey Morin, Directrice générale

Rapide-Danseur
535, rue du Village
Rapide-Danseur, QC J0Z 3G0
Tél: 819-948-2152; *Téléc:* 819-948-2265
rapide-danseur@mrcao.qc.ca
www.rapide-danseur.ao.ca
Entité municipal: Municipality
Incorporation: 1er janvier 1981 *Area:* 185,18 km2
Comté ou district: Abitibi-Ouest; *Population au 2011:* 312
Circonscription(s) électorale(s) provinciale(s): Abitibi-Ouest
Circonscription(s) électorale(s) fédérale(s):
Abitibi-Témiscamingue
Prochaines élections: 3e novembre 2013
Alain Gagnon, Maire
Mona Cyr, Directrice générale (par intérim)

Rapides-des-Joachims
CP 2-10
48, rue de l'Église
Rapides-des-Joachims, QC J0X 3M0
Tél: 613-586-2532; *Téléc:* 613-586-2720
rapides-des-joachims@mrcpontiac.qc.ca
www.rapidesdesjoachims.ca
Entité municipal: Municipality
Incorporation: 1er janvier 1955 *Area:* 248,92 km2
Comté ou district: Pontiac; *Population au 2011:* 131
Circonscription(s) électorale(s) provinciale(s): Pontiac
Circonscription(s) électorale(s) fédérale(s): Pontiac
Prochaines élections: 3e novembre 2013
James Gibson, Maire
Hélène Larente, Directrice générale

Rawdon
3647, rue Queen
Rawdon, QC J0K 1S0
Tél: 450-834-2596; *Téléc:* 450-834-3031
lmarsh@rawdon.ca
www.rawdon.ca
Entité municipal: Municipality
Incorporation: 28 mai 1998 *Area:* 179,73 km2
Comté ou district: Matawinie; *Population au 2011:* 10,416
Circonscription(s) électorale(s) provinciale(s): Rousseau
Circonscription(s) électorale(s) fédérale(s): Joliette
Prochaines élections: 3e novembre 2013
Jacques Beauregard, Maire
Georges Robitaille, Greffier adjoint

Rémigny
1304, ch de l'Église
Rémigny, QC J0Z 3H0
Tél: 819-761-2421; *Téléc:* 819-761-2421
mun.remigny@mrctemiscamingue.qc.ca
www.municipaliteremigny.qc.ca
Entité municipal: Municipality
Incorporation: 1er janvier 1978 *Area:* 985,03 km2
Comté ou district: Témiscamingue; *Population au 2011:* 279
Circonscription(s) électorale(s) provinciale(s):
Rouyn-Noranda-Témiscamingue
Circonscription(s) électorale(s) fédérale(s):
Abitibi-Témiscamingue
Prochaines élections: 3e novembre 2013
Jocelyn Aylwin, Maire
Josée Dubeau, Directrice générale

Richelieu
200, boul Richelieu
Richelieu, QC J3L 3R4
Tél: 450-658-1157; *Téléc:* 450-658-5096
n.poirier@villederichelieu.org
www.villederichelieu.org
Entité municipal: Town
Incorporation: 15 mars 2000 *Area:* 29,75 km2
Comté ou district: Rouville; *Population au 2011:* 5,467
Circonscription(s) électorale(s) provinciale(s): Chambly
Circonscription(s) électorale(s) fédérale(s): Chambly-Borduas
Prochaines élections: 3e novembre 2013
Jacques Ladouceur, Maire
Nancy Poirier, Greffière

Richmond
745, rue Gouin
Richmond, QC J0B 2H0
Tél: 819-826-3789; *Téléc:* 819-826-2813
admin@ville.richmond.qc.ca
www.ville.richmond.qc.ca
Entité municipal: Town
Incorporation: 29 décembre 1999 *Area:* 7,76 km2
Comté ou district: Le Val-St-François; *Population au 2011:* 3,275
Circonscription(s) électorale(s) provinciale(s): Richmond
Circonscription(s) électorale(s) fédérale(s):
Richmond-Arthabaska
Prochaines élections: 3e novembre 2013
Marc-André Martel, Maire
Daniel Leduc, Directeur général

Rigaud
391, ch de la Mairie
Rigaud, QC J0P 1P0
Tél: 450-451-0869; *Téléc:* 450-451-4227
rigaud@ville.rigaud.qc.ca
www.ville.rigaud.qc.ca
Entité municipal: Municipality
Incorporation: 29 novembre 1995 *Area:* 97,15 km2
Comté ou district: Vaudreuil-Soulanges; *Population au 2011:* 7,346
Circonscription(s) électorale(s) provinciale(s): Soulanges
Circonscription(s) électorale(s) fédérale(s): Vaudreuil-Soulanges
Prochaines élections: 3e novembre 2013
Réal Brazeau, Maire
Hélène Therrien, Greffière

Rimouski-Neigette
#220, 23, rue de l'Évêché ouest
Rimouski, QC G5L 4H4
Tél: 418-724-5154; *Téléc:* 418-725-4567
administration@mrcrimouskineigette.qc.ca
Entité municipal: Regional County Municipality
Incorporation: 26 mai 1982
Population au 2011: 55,095
Note: 10 municipalités & 1 autre territoire.
Gilbert Pigeon, Préfet
Louise Audet, Directrice générale

Ripon
#101, 31, rue Coursol
Ripon, QC J0V 1V0
Tél: 819-983-2000; *Téléc:* 819-983-1327
information@ville.ripon.qc.ca
www.ville.ripon.qc.ca
Entité municipal: Municipality
Incorporation: 3 mai 2000 *Area:* 140,57 km2
Comté ou district: Papineau; *Population au 2011:* 1,522
Circonscription(s) électorale(s) provinciale(s): Papineau
Circonscription(s) électorale(s) fédérale(s):
Argenteuil-Papineau-Mirabel
Prochaines élections: 3e novembre 2013
Luc Desjardins, Maire
Lorraine Sabourin, Directrice générale

Ristigouche-Partie-Sud-Est
35, ch Kempt, RR#2
Matapédia, QC G0J 1V0
Tél: 418-788-5769; *Téléc:* 418-788-2598
ristigouchesudest@globetrotter.net
www.ristigouchesudest.ca
Entité municipal: Township
Incorporation: 30 juin 1906 *Area:* 48,95 km2
Comté ou district: Avignon; *Population au 2011:* 167
Circonscription(s) électorale(s) provinciale(s): Bonaventure
Circonscription(s) électorale(s) fédérale(s):
Gaspésie—îles-de-la-Madeleine
Prochaines élections: 3e novembre 2013
Annette Sénéchal, Mairesse
Suzanne Bourdages, Directrice générale

Rivière-à-Claude
520, rue Principale est
Rivière-à-Claude, QC G0E 1Z0
Tél: 418-797-2422; *Téléc:* 418-797-2455
munirac@globetrotter.net
Entité municipal: Municipality
Incorporation: 18 décembre 1923 *Area:* 155,39 km2
Comté ou district: La Haute-Gaspésie; *Population au 2011:* 130
Circonscription(s) électorale(s) provinciale(s): Matane
Circonscription(s) électorale(s) fédérale(s): Haute-Gaspésie-La Mitis-Matane-Matapédia
Prochaines élections: 3e novembre 2013
Réjean Normand, Maire
Claudine Auclair, Directrice générale

Rivière-à-Pierre
CP 648
830, rue Principale
Rivière-à-Pierre, QC G0A 3A0
Tél: 418-323-2112; *Téléc:* 418-323-2111
rivapier@globetrotter.net
www.riviereapierre.com
Entité municipal: Municipality
Incorporation: 11 octobre 1897 *Area:* 521,31 km2
Comté ou district: Portneuf; *Population au 2011:* 671
Circonscription(s) électorale(s) provinciale(s): Portneuf
Circonscription(s) électorale(s) fédérale(s):
Portneuf-Jacques-Cartier
Prochaines élections: 3e novembre 2013
Ghislaine Noreau, Mairesse
Pascale Bonin, Directrice générale

Rivière-au-Tonnerre
CP 129
473, rue Jacques Cartier
Rivière-au-Tonnerre, QC G0G 2L0
Tél: 418-465-2255; *Téléc:* 418-465-2956
municipaliterivauton@globetrotter.net
Entité municipal: Municipality
Incorporation: 14 décembre 1925 *Area:* 1331,17 km2
Comté ou district: Minganie; *Population au 2011:* 307
Circonscription(s) électorale(s) provinciale(s): Duplessis
Circonscription(s) électorale(s) fédérale(s): Manicouagan
Prochaines élections: 3e novembre 2013
Jeannot Boudreau, Maire
Carmelle Anglehart, Directrice générale

Rivière-Beaudette
663, ch de la Frontière
Rivière-Beaudette, QC J0P 1R0
Tél: 450-269-2931; *Téléc:* 450-269-2815
munrivbeaudette@qc.aira.com
www.riviere-beaudette.com
Entité municipal: Municipality
Incorporation: 17 janvier 1990 *Area:* 19,62 km2
Comté ou district: Vaudreuil-Soulanges; *Population au 2011:* 1,885
Circonscription(s) électorale(s) provinciale(s): Soulanges
Circonscription(s) électorale(s) fédérale(s): Vaudreuil-Soulanges
Prochaines élections: 3e novembre 2013
Patrick Bousez, Maire
Céline Chayer, Directrice générale

Rivière-Bleue
32, rue des Pins est
Rivière-Bleue, QC G0L 2B0
Tél: 418-893-5559; *Téléc:* 418-893-5530
info@riviere-bleue.ca
www.riviere-bleue.ca
Entité municipal: Municipality
Incorporation: 14 juin 1975 *Area:* 179,93 km2
Comté ou district: Témiscouata; *Population au 2011:* 1,299
Circonscription(s) électorale(s) provinciale(s):
Kamouraska-Témiscouata
Circonscription(s) électorale(s) fédérale(s):
Rimouski-Neigette-Témiscouata-Les Basques
Prochaines élections: 3e novembre 2013
Claude H. Pelletier, Maire
Claudie Levasseur, Directrice générale

Rivière-du-Loup
310, rue St-Pierre
Rivière-du-Loup, QC G5R 3V3
Tél: 418-867-2485; *Téléc:* 418-867-3100
administration@mrc-riviere-du-loup.qc.ca
www.mrc-rdl.qc.ca
Entité municipal: Regional County Municipality
Incorporation: 1 janvier 1982
Population au 2011: 34,375
Note: 13 municipalités.
Michel Lagacé, Préfet
Raymond Duval, Directeur général

Rivière-Éternité
418, rte Principale
Rivière-Éternité, QC G0V 1P0
Tél: 418-272-2860; *Téléc:* 418-544-3085
municipalite@riviere-eternite.com
www.riviere-eternite.com
Entité municipal: Municipality
Incorporation: 20 juillet 1974 *Area:* 496,88 km2
Comté ou district: Le Fjord-du-Saguenay; *Population au 2011:* 484
Circonscription(s) électorale(s) provinciale(s): Dubuc
Circonscription(s) électorale(s) fédérale(s): Chicoutimi-Le Fjord
Prochaines élections: 3e novembre 2013
Rémi Gagné, Maire
Denis Houde, Directeur général

Rivière-Héva
CP 60
740, rte St-Paul nord
Rivière-Héva, QC J0Y 2H0
Tél: 819-735-3521; *Téléc:* 819-735-4251
nsavard@mun-r-h.com
Entité municipal: Municipality
Incorporation: 1er janvier 1982 *Area:* 166,09 km2
Comté ou district: La Vallée-de-l'Or; *Population au 2011:* 1,433
Circonscription(s) électorale(s) provinciale(s): Abitibi-Est
Circonscription(s) électorale(s) fédérale(s):
Abitibi-Baie-James-Nunavik-Eeyou
Prochaines élections: 3e novembre 2013
Réjean Guay, Maire
Nathalie Savard, Directrice générale

Rivière-Ouelle
CP 99
106, rue de l'Église
Rivière-Ouelle, QC G0L 2C0
Tél: 418-856-3829; *Téléc:* 418-856-1790
dg@riviereouelle.ca
www.riviereouelle.ca
Entité municipal: Municipality
Incorporation: 1er juillet 1855 *Area:* 54,72 km2
Comté ou district: Kamouraska; *Population au 2011:* 1,058
Circonscription(s) électorale(s) provinciale(s):
Kamouraska-Témiscouata
Circonscription(s) électorale(s) fédérale(s):
Montmagny-L'Islet-Kamouraska-Rivière-du-Loup
Prochaines élections: 3e novembre 2013
Elizabeth Hudon, Mairesse
Adam Ménard, Directeur général

Rivière-Rouge
25, rue L'Annonciation sud
Rivière-Rouge, QC J0T 1T0
Tél: 819-275-2929; *Téléc:* 819-275-3676
greffe@riviere-rouge.ca
www.riviere-rouge.ca
Entité municipal: Town
Incorporation: 18 décembre 2002 *Area:* 463,18 km2
Comté ou district: Antoine-Labelle; *Population au 2011:* 4,645
Circonscription(s) électorale(s) provinciale(s): Labelle
Circonscription(s) électorale(s) fédérale(s): Laurentides-Labelle
Prochaines élections: 3e novembre 2013
Déborah Bélanger, Mairesse
Pierre St-Onge, Greffier

Rivière-St-Jean
116, rue du Quai
Rivière-Saint-Jean, QC G0G 2N0
Tél: 418-949-2464; *Téléc:* 418-949-2489
magpiest-jean@globetrotter.net
Entité municipal: Municipality
Incorporation: 1er janvier 1966 *Area:* 652,54 km2
Comté ou district: Minganie; *Population au 2011:* 239
Circonscription(s) électorale(s) provinciale(s): Duplessis

Circonscription(s) électorale(s) fédérale(s): Manicouagan
Prochaines élections: 3e novembre 2013
Michel Beaudin, Maire
Louise Rodgers, Directrice générale

Robert-Cliche
111A, 107e Rue
Beauceville, QC G5X 2P9
Tél: 418-774-9828; *Téléc:* 418-774-4057
mrc.robert.cliche@beaucerc.com
www.beaucerc.com
Entité municipal: Regional County Municipality
Incorporation: 1 janvier 1982
Population au 2011: 19,288
Note: 10 municipalités.
Jean-Rock Veilleux, Préfet
Gilbert Caron, Directeur général
gilbert.caron@beaucerc.com

Rochebaucourt
20, rue du Chanoine-Girard
Rochebaucourt, QC J0Y 2J0
Tél: 819-754-2083; *Téléc:* 819-754-5417
muniroche@cableamos.com
www.municipalite-rochebaucourt.org
Entité municipal: Municipality
Incorporation: 1er janvier 1983 *Area:* 185,00 km2
Comté ou district: Abitibi; *Population au 2011:* 161
Circonscription(s) électorale(s) provinciale(s): Abitibi-Ouest
Circonscription(s) électorale(s) fédérale(s):
Abitibi-Témiscamingue
Prochaines élections: 3e novembre 2013
Gaby Chiasson Yergeau, Maire
Nathalie Lyrette, Directrice générale

Roquemaure
15, rue Raymond est
Roquemaure, QC J0Z 3K0
Tél: 819-787-6311; *Téléc:* 819-787-6383
roquemaure@mrcao.qc.ca
www.roquemaure.ao.ca
Entité municipal: Municipality
Incorporation: 1er janvier 1952 *Area:* 121,67 km2
Comté ou district: Abitibi-Ouest; *Population au 2011:* 414
Circonscription(s) électorale(s) provinciale(s): Abitibi-Ouest
Circonscription(s) électorale(s) fédérale(s):
Abitibi-Témiscamingue
Prochaines élections: 3e novembre 2013
Léo Pinard, Maire
Annick Lavoie, Directrice générale

Rougemont
61, ch de Marieville
Rougemont, QC J0L 1M0
Tél: 450-469-3790; *Téléc:* 450-469-0309
reception@rougemont.ca
www.rougemont.ca
Entité municipal: Municipality
Incorporation: 26 janvier 2000 *Area:* 44,48 km2
Comté ou district: Rouville; *Population au 2011:* 2,723
Circonscription(s) électorale(s) provinciale(s): Iberville
Circonscription(s) électorale(s) fédérale(s): Shefford
Prochaines élections: 3e novembre 2013
Alain Brière, Maire
Kathia Joseph, Directrice générale

Roussillon
#200, 260, rue Saint-Pierre
Saint-Constant, QC J5A 2A5
Tél: 450-638-1221; *Téléc:* 450-638-4499
admin@mrcroussillon.qc.ca
www.mrcroussillon.qc.ca
Entité municipal: Regional County Municipality
Incorporation: 1er janvier 1982
Population au 2011: 162,187
Note: 11 municipalités.
Nathalie Simon, Préfète
Pierre Largy, Directeur général
p.largy@mrcroussillon.qc.ca

Rouville
#100, 500 rue Desjardins
Marieville, QC J3M 1E1
Tél: 450-460-2127; *Téléc:* 450-460-7169
mrcrouville@on.aira.com
www.mrcrouville.qc.ca
Entité municipal: Regional County Municipality
Incorporation: 1er janvier 1982
Population au 2011: 35,690
Note: 8 municipalités.
Michel Picotte, Préfet
Rosaire Marcil, Directeur général
r.marcil@mrcrouville.qc.ca

Roxton
216, rang Ste-Geneviève
Roxton Falls, QC J0H 1E0
Tél: 450-548-2500; *Téléc:* 450-548-2412
canrox@cooptel.qc.ca
www.cantonderoxton.qc.ca
Entité municipal: Township
Incorporation: 1er juillet 1855 *Area:* 149,07 km2
Comté ou district: Acton; *Population au 2011:* 1,093
Circonscription(s) électorale(s) provinciale(s): Johnson
Circonscription(s) électorale(s) fédérale(s): St-Hyacinthe-Bagot
Prochaines élections: 3e novembre 2013
Stéphane Beauregard, Maire
Deynse Viens, Directrice générale (par intérim)

Roxton Falls
26, rue du Marché
Roxton Falls, QC J0H 1E0
Tél: 450-548-5790; *Téléc:* 450-548-5881
roxton@roxtonfalls.ca
www.roxtonfalls.ca
Entité municipal: Village
Incorporation: 1er janvier 1863 *Area:* 5,25 km2
Comté ou district: Acton; *Population au 2011:* 1,265
Circonscription(s) électorale(s) provinciale(s): Johnson
Circonscription(s) électorale(s) fédérale(s): St-Hyacinthe-Bagot
Prochaines élections: 3e novembre 2013
Jean-Marie Laplante, Maire
Julie Gagné, Directrice générale

Roxton Pond
901, rue St-Jean
Roxton Pond, QC J0E 1Z0
Tél: 450-372-6875; *Téléc:* 450-372-1205
fgiasson@roxtonpond.ca
Entité municipal: Municipality
Incorporation: 17 décembre 1997 *Area:* 102,11 km2
Comté ou district: La Haute-Yamaska; *Population au 2011:* 3,786
Circonscription(s) électorale(s) provinciale(s): Johnson
Circonscription(s) électorale(s) fédérale(s): Shefford
Prochaines élections: 3e novembre 2013
Raymond Loignon, Maire
Francois Giasson, Directeur général

Sacré-Coeur
88, rue Principale nord
Sacré-Coeur, QC G0T 1Y0
Tél: 418-236-4621; *Téléc:* 418-236-9144
s-c@municipalite.sacre-coeur.qc.ca
www.municipalite.sacre-coeur.qc.ca
Entité municipal: Municipality
Incorporation: 30 juin 1976 *Area:* 341,74 km2
Comté ou district: La Haute-Côte-Nord; *Population au 2011:* 1,881
Circonscription(s) électorale(s) provinciale(s): René-Lévesque
Circonscription(s) électorale(s) fédérale(s):
Montmorency-Charlevoix-Haute-Côte-Nord
Prochaines élections: 3e novembre 2013
Gilles Pineault, Maire
Claudia Gauthier, Directrice générale

Sacré-Coeur-de-Jésus
4118, rte 112
East Broughton, QC G0N 1G0
Tél: 418-427-3447; *Téléc:* 418-427-4774
info@sacrecoeurdejesus.qc.ca
www.sacrecoeurdejesus.qc.ca
Entité municipal: Parish (Paroisse)
Incorporation: 11 décembre 1889 *Area:* 103,850 km2
Comté ou district: Les Appalaches; *Population au 2011:* 564
Circonscription(s) électorale(s) provinciale(s): Frontenac
Circonscription(s) électorale(s) fédérale(s): Mégantic-L'Érable
Prochaines élections: 3e novembre 2013
Guy Roy, Maire
Marie-France Létourneau, Directrice générale

Saint-Adalbert
55, rue Principale
Saint-Adalbert, QC G0R 2M0
Tél: 418-356-5271; *Téléc:* 418-356-5317
mstadalb@globetrotter.net
www.saintadalbert.qc.ca
Entité municipal: Municipality
Incorporation: 26 août 1911 *Area:* 213,95 km2
Comté ou district: L'Islet; *Population au 2011:* 536
Circonscription(s) électorale(s) provinciale(s): Montmagny-L'Islet
Circonscription(s) électorale(s) fédérale(s):
Montmagny-L'Islet-Kamouraska-Rivière-du-Loup
Prochaines élections: 3e novembre 2013
René Laverdière, Maire
Magguy Mathault, Directrice générale

Saint-Adelme
CP 39
138, rue Principale
Saint-Adelme, QC G0J 2B0
Tél: 418-733-4044; *Téléc:* 418-733-4111
st-adelme@mrcdematane.qc.ca
www.mrcdematane.qc.ca/stadelme.html
Entité municipal: Parish (Paroisse)
Incorporation: 9 septembre 1933 *Area:* 100,20 km2
Comté ou district: Matane; *Population au 2011:* 485
Circonscription(s) électorale(s) provinciale(s): Matane
Circonscription(s) électorale(s) fédérale(s): Haute-Gaspésie-La Mitis-Matane-Matapédia
Prochaines élections: 3e novembre 2013
Yvan Imbeault, Maire
Annick Hudon, Directrice générale

Saint-Adelphe
150, rue Baillargeon
Saint-Adelphe-de-Champlain, QC G0X 2G0
Tél: 418-322-5721; *Téléc:* 418-322-5434
st-adelphe@regionmekinac.com
www.st-adelphe.qc.ca/
Entité municipal: Parish (Paroisse)
Incorporation: 19 octobre 1891 *Area:* 135,35 km2
Comté ou district: Mékinac; *Population au 2011:* 952
Circonscription(s) électorale(s) provinciale(s): Laviolette
Circonscription(s) électorale(s) fédérale(s):
Saint-Maurice-Champlain
Prochaines élections: 3e novembre 2013
Paul Labranche, Maire
Daniel Bacon, Directeur général

Saint-Adolphe-d'Howard
1881, ch du Village
Saint-Adolphe-d'Howard, QC J0T 2B0
Tél: 819-327-2044; *Téléc:* 819-327-2282
info@stadolphedhoward.qc.ca
www.stadolphedhoward.qc.ca
Entité municipal: Municipality
Incorporation: 1er janvier 1883 *Area:* 144,41 km2
Comté ou district: Les Pays-d'en-Haut; *Population au 2011:* 3,702
Circonscription(s) électorale(s) provinciale(s): Argenteuil
Circonscription(s) électorale(s) fédérale(s):
Argenteuil-Papineau-Mirabel
Prochaines élections: 3e novembre 2013
Pierre Roy, Maire
maire@stadolphedhoward.qc.ca
Richard Daveluy, Directeur général
rdaveluy@stadolphedhoward.qc.ca

Saint-Adrien
1589, rue Principale
Saint-Adrien, QC J0A 1C0
Tél: 819-828-2872; *Téléc:* 819-828-0442
munstadrien@cgocable.ca
st-adrien.com
Entité municipal: Municipality
Incorporation: 1er janvier 1879 *Area:* 97,59 km2
Comté ou district: Les Sources; *Population au 2011:* 490
Circonscription(s) électorale(s) provinciale(s): Richmond
Circonscription(s) électorale(s) fédérale(s):
Richmond-Arthabaska
Prochaines élections: 3e novembre 2013
Pierre Therrien, Maire
Maryse Ducharme, Directrice générale

Saint-Adrien-d'Irlande
152, rue Municipale
Saint-Adrien-d'Irlande, QC G0N 1M0
Tél: 418-335-2585; *Téléc:* 418-335-4040
muadrien@hotmail.com
Entité municipal: Municipality
Incorporation: 1er janvier 1873 *Area:* 52,780 km2
Comté ou district: Les Appalaches; *Population au 2011:* 389
Circonscription(s) électorale(s) provinciale(s): Frontenac
Circonscription(s) électorale(s) fédérale(s): Mégantic-L'Érable
Prochaines élections: 3e novembre 2013
Jessika Lacombe, Mairesse
Ghislaine Leblanc, Directrice générale

Saint-Agapit
1186, rue Principale
Saint-Agapit, QC G0S 1Z0
Tél: 418-888-4620; *Téléc:* 418-888-4791
stagapit@globetrotter.net
st-agapit.qc.ca
Entité municipal: Municipality
Incorporation: 14 avril 1979 *Area:* 65,91 km2
Comté ou district: Lotbinière; *Population au 2011:* 3,567
Circonscription(s) électorale(s) provinciale(s): Lotbinière
Circonscription(s) électorale(s) fédérale(s): Lotbinière-Chutes-de-la-Chaudière
Prochaines élections: 3e novembre 2013
Sylvie Fortin Graham, Mairesse
Isabelle Paré, Directrice générale
isabelle.pare@st-agapit.qc.ca

Saint-Aimé
CP 240
285, rue Bonsecours
Massueville, QC J0G 1K0
Tél: 450-788-2737; *Téléc:* 450-788-3337
staime@bas-richelieu.net
www.saintaime.qc.ca/
Entité municipal: Municipality
Incorporation: 1er juillet 1855 *Area:* 61,33 km2
Comté ou district: Pierre-De Saurel; *Population au 2011:* 505
Circonscription(s) électorale(s) provinciale(s): Richelieu
Circonscription(s) électorale(s) fédérale(s): Bas-Richelieu-Nicolet-Bécancour
Prochaines élections: 3e novembre 2013
Maria Libert, Mairesse
Francine B. Lambert, Directrice générale

Saint-Aimé-des-Lacs
119, rue Principale
Saint-Aimé-des-Lacs, QC G0T 1S0
Tél: 418-439-2229; *Téléc:* 418-439-1475
info@saintaimedeslacs.ca
www.saintaimedeslacs.ca
Entité municipal: Municipality
Incorporation: 1er janvier 1950 *Area:* 101,57 km2
Comté ou district: Charlevoix-Est; *Population au 2011:* 1,073
Circonscription(s) électorale(s) provinciale(s): Charlevoix
Circonscription(s) électorale(s) fédérale(s): Montmorency-Charlevoix-Haute-Côte-Nord
Prochaines élections: 3e novembre 2013
Bernard Maltais, Maire
maire@saintaimedeslacs.ca
Suzanne Gaudreault, Directrice générale

Saint-Aimé-du-Lac-des-Iles
871, chemin Diotte
Saint-Aimé-du-Lac-des-Iles, QC J0W 1J0
Tél: 819-597-2047; *Téléc:* 819-597-2554
munldi@tlb.sympatico.ca
www.saint-aime-du-lac-des-iles.ca
Entité municipal: Municipality
Incorporation: 1er janvier 2006 *Area:* 165,77 km2
Comté ou district: Antoine-Labelle; *Population au 2011:* 778
Circonscription(s) électorale(s) provinciale(s): Labelle
Circonscription(s) électorale(s) fédérale(s): Laurentides-Labelle
Prochaines élections: 3e novembre 2013
François Desjardins, Maire
mairieldi@tlb.sympatico.ca
Gisèle Lépine-Pilotte, Directrice générale
dgldi@tlb.sympatico.ca

Saint-Alban
204, rue Principale
Saint-Alban, QC G0A 3B0
Tél: 418-268-8026; *Téléc:* 418-268-5073
www.st-alban.qc.ca
Entité municipal: Municipality
Incorporation: 31 décembre 1991 *Area:* 150,55 km2
Comté ou district: Portneuf; *Population au 2011:* 1,225
Circonscription(s) électorale(s) provinciale(s): Portneuf
Circonscription(s) électorale(s) fédérale(s): Portneuf-Jacques-Cartier
Prochaines élections: 3e novembre 2013
Lynn Audet, Mairesse
Andrée Gosselin, Directrice générale
a.gosselin@st-alban.qc.ca

Saint-Albert
CP 100
25, rue des Loisirs
Saint-Albert, QC J0A 1E0
Tél: 819-353-3300; *Téléc:* 819-353-3313
stalbert@munstalbert.ca
Entité municipal: Municipality
Incorporation: 1er janvier 1864 *Area:* 70,36 km2
Comté ou district: Arthabaska; *Population au 2011:* 1,526
Circonscription(s) électorale(s) provinciale(s): Richmond
Circonscription(s) électorale(s) fédérale(s): Richmond-Arthabaska
Prochaines élections: 3e novembre 2013
Alain St-Pierre, Maire
Suzanne Corriveau-Crête, Directrice générale

Saint-Alexandre
453, rue St-Denis
Saint-Alexandre, QC J0J 1S0
Tél: 450-346-6641; *Téléc:* 450-346-0538
villedestalexandre@qc.aira.com
www.ville.saint-alexandre.qc.ca
Entité municipal: Municipality
Incorporation: 17 septembre 1988 *Area:* 76,55 km2
Comté ou district: Le Haut-Richelieu; *Population au 2011:* 2,495
Circonscription(s) électorale(s) provinciale(s): Iberville
Circonscription(s) électorale(s) fédérale(s): St-Jean
Prochaines élections: 3e novembre 2013
André Bergeron, Maire
Michèle Bertrand, Directrice générale

Saint-Alexandre-de-Kamouraska
CP 10
629, rte 289
Saint-Alexandre-de-Kamouraska, QC G0L 2G0
Tél: 418-495-2440; *Téléc:* 418-495-2659
stalex.kamouraska@bellnet.ca
www.stalex.kamouraska.qc.ca
Entité municipal: Municipality
Incorporation: 1er juillet 1855 *Area:* 115,95 km2
Comté ou district: Kamouraska; *Population au 2011:* 2,050
Circonscription(s) électorale(s) provinciale(s): Kamouraska-Témiscouata
Circonscription(s) électorale(s) fédérale(s): Montmagny-L'Islet-Kamouraska-Rivière-du-Loup
Prochaines élections: 3e novembre 2013
Luc Chouinard, Maire
Lyne Dumont, Directrice générale
ldumont@stalexkamouraska.com

Saint-Alexandre-des-Lacs
17, rue de l'Église
Saint-Alexandre-des-Lacs, QC G0J 2C0
Tél: 418-778-3532; *Téléc:* 418-778-1315
stalexandre@mrcmatapedia.qc.ca
Entité municipal: Parish (Paroisse)
Incorporation: 1er janvier 1965 *Area:* 92,98 km2
Comté ou district: La Matapédia; *Population au 2011:* 258
Circonscription(s) électorale(s) provinciale(s): Matapédia
Circonscription(s) électorale(s) fédérale(s): Haute-Gaspésie-La Mitis-Matane-Matapédia
Prochaines élections: 3e novembre 2013
Jean-Marc Roy, Maire
Caroline Savoie, Directrice générale

Saint-Alexis
232, rue Principale
Saint-Alexis, QC J0K 1T0
Tél: 450-839-7277; *Téléc:* 450-839-6241
info@st-alexis.com
Entité municipal: Parish (Paroisse)
Incorporation: 1er juillet 1855 *Area:* 36,59 km2
Comté ou district: Montcalm; *Population au 2011:* 790
Circonscription(s) électorale(s) provinciale(s): Rousseau
Circonscription(s) électorale(s) fédérale(s): Montcalm
Prochaines élections: 3e novembre 2013
Adélard Éthier, Maire
Rémy Lanoue, Directeur général

Saint-Alexis
232, rue Principale
Saint-Alexis, QC J0K 1T0
Tél: 450-839-7277; *Téléc:* 450-839-6241
info@st-alexis.com
Entité municipal: Village
Incorporation: 16 novembre 1920 *Area:* 6,60 km2
Comté ou district: Montcalm; *Population au 2011:* 577
Circonscription(s) électorale(s) provinciale(s): Rousseau
Circonscription(s) électorale(s) fédérale(s): Montcalm
Prochaines élections: 3e novembre 2013
Adélard Éthier, Maire
Rémy Lanoue, Directeur général

Saint-Alexis-de-Matapédia
CP 99
190, rue Principale
Saint-Alexis-de-Matapédia, QC G0J 2E0
Tél: 418-299-2030; *Téléc:* 418-299-3011
plateau1@globetrotter.qc.ca
www.matapedialesplateaux.com
Entité municipal: Municipality
Incorporation: 1er juillet 1855 *Area:* 83,37 km2
Comté ou district: Avignon; *Population au 2011:* 548
Circonscription(s) électorale(s) provinciale(s): Bonaventure
Circonscription(s) électorale(s) fédérale(s): Gaspésie—îles-de-la-Madeleine
Prochaines élections: 3e novembre 2013
Guy Gallant, Maire
Lise Pitre, Directrice générale

Saint-Alexis-des-Monts
101, rue de l'Hôtel-de-Ville
Saint-Alexis-des-Monts, QC J0K 1V0
Tél: 819-265-2046; *Téléc:* 819-265-2481
info@saint-alexis-des-monts.ca
www.saint-alexis-des-monts.ca
Entité municipal: Parish (Paroisse)
Incorporation: 21 avril 1984 *Area:* 1153,85 km2
Comté ou district: Maskinongé; *Population au 2011:* 3,046
Circonscription(s) électorale(s) provinciale(s): Maskinongé
Circonscription(s) électorale(s) fédérale(s): Berthier-Maskinongé
Prochaines élections: 3e novembre 2013
Madeleine L. Robert, Mairesse
Sylvie Clément, Directrice générale

Saint-Alfred
9, rte du Cap
Saint-Alfred, QC G0M 1L0
Tél: 418-774-2068; *Téléc:* 418-774-2068
municipalitestalfred@sogetel.net
www.st-alfred.qc.ca
Entité municipal: Municipality
Incorporation: 1er janvier 1950 *Area:* 42,42 km2
Comté ou district: Robert-Cliche; *Population au 2011:* 485
Circonscription(s) électorale(s) provinciale(s): Beauce-Nord
Circonscription(s) électorale(s) fédérale(s): Beauce
Prochaines élections: 3e novembre 2013
Jean-Roch Veilleux, Maire
Diane Jacques, Directrice générale

Saint-Alphonse
127, rue Principale est
Saint-Alphonse, QC G0C 2V0
Tél: 418-388-5214; *Téléc:* 418-388-2435
st-alphonsemuni@globetrotter.net
www.st-alphonsegaspesie.com
Entité municipal: Municipality
Incorporation: 9 mai 1902 *Area:* 113,13 km2
Comté ou district: Bonaventure; *Population au 2011:* 691
Circonscription(s) électorale(s) provinciale(s): Bonaventure
Circonscription(s) électorale(s) fédérale(s): Gaspésie—îles-de-la-Madeleine
Prochaines élections: 3e novembre 2013
Gérard Porlier, Maire
Reina Goulet, Directrice générale

Saint-Alphonse-de-Granby
360, rue Principale
Saint-Alphonse-de-Granby, QC J0E 2A0
Tél: 450-375-4570; *Téléc:* 450-375-4717
infos@st-alphonse.qc.ca
www.st-alphonse.qc.ca
Entité municipal: Parish (Paroisse)
Incorporation: 30 décembre 1890 *Area:* 50,52 km2
Comté ou district: La Haute-Yamaska; *Population au 2011:* 3,125
Circonscription(s) électorale(s) provinciale(s): Brome-Missisquoi
Circonscription(s) électorale(s) fédérale(s): Shefford
Prochaines élections: 3e novembre 2013
Clément Choinière, Maire
Réal Pitt, Directeur général

Saint-Alphonse-Rodriguez
101, rue de la Plage
Saint-Alphonse-Rodriguez, QC J0K 1W0
Tél: 450-883-2264; *Téléc:* 450-883-0833
info@munsar.ca
www.munsar.ca
Entité municipal: Municipality
Incorporation: 1er juillet 1855 *Area:* 101,37 km2
Comté ou district: Matawinie; *Population au 2011:* 3,134
Circonscription(s) électorale(s) provinciale(s): Berthier
Circonscription(s) électorale(s) fédérale(s): Joliette
Prochaines élections: 3e novembre 2013
Robert W. Desnoyers, Maire
François Dauphin, Directeur général

Saint-Amable
575, rue Principale
Saint-Amable, QC J0L 1N0
Tél: 450-649-3555; *Téléc:* 450-922-0728
ville@st-amable.qc.ca
www.st-amable.qc.ca
Entité municipal: Municipality
Incorporation: 13 juin 1921 *Area:* 38,04 km2
Comté ou district: Lajemmerais; *Population au 2011:* 10,870
Circonscription(s) électorale(s) provinciale(s): Verchères
Circonscription(s) électorale(s) fédérale(s):
Verchères-Les-Patriotes
Prochaines élections: 3e novembre 2013
François Gamache, Maire
Carmen McDuff, Directrice générale

Saint-Ambroise
330, rue Gagnon
Saint-Ambroise, QC G7P 2P9
Tél: 418-672-4765; *Téléc:* 418-672-6126
info@st-ambroise.qc.ca
www.st-ambroise.qc.ca
Entité municipal: Municipality
Incorporation: 25 septembre 1971 *Area:* 148,61 km2
Comté ou district: Le Fjord-du-Saguenay; *Population au 2011:* 3,546
Circonscription(s) électorale(s) provinciale(s): Dubuc
Circonscription(s) électorale(s) fédérale(s): Jonquière-Alma
Prochaines élections: 3e novembre 2013
Marcel Claveau, Maire
Michel Perreault, Directeur général

Saint-Ambroise-de-Kildare
CP 57
850, rue Principale
Kildare, QC J0K 1C0
Tél: 450-755-4782; *Téléc:* 450-755-4784
info@saintambroise.ca
www.saintambroisedekildare.qc.ca
Entité municipal: Parish (Paroisse)
Incorporation: 1er juillet 1855 *Area:* 66,89 km2
Comté ou district: Joliette; *Population au 2011:* 3,747
Circonscription(s) électorale(s) provinciale(s): Joliette
Circonscription(s) électorale(s) fédérale(s): Joliette
Prochaines élections: 3e novembre 2013
René Laurin, Maire
Renald Gravel, Directeur général

Saint-Anaclet-de-Lessard
318, rue Principale ouest
Saint-Anaclet, QC G0K 1H0
Tél: 418-723-2816; *Téléc:* 418-723-0436
municipalite@stanaclet.qc.ca
stanaclet.qc.ca
Entité municipal: Parish (Paroisse)
Incorporation: 9 mai 1859 *Area:* 126,26 km2
Comté ou district: Rimouski-Neigette; *Population au 2011:* 3,035
Circonscription(s) électorale(s) provinciale(s): Rimouski
Circonscription(s) électorale(s) fédérale(s):
Rimouski-Neigette-Témiscouata-Les Basques
Prochaines élections: 3e novembre 2013
Francis St-Pierre, Maire
Alain Lapierre, Directeur général

Saint-André
122A, rue Principale
Saint-André-de-Kamouraska, QC G0L 2H0
Tél: 418-493-2085; *Téléc:* 418-493-2373
munand@bellnet.ca
www.standredekamouraska.ca
Entité municipal: Municipality
Incorporation: 14 février 1987 *Area:* 68,94 km2
Comté ou district: Kamouraska; *Population au 2011:* 651
Circonscription(s) électorale(s) provinciale(s):
Kamouraska-Témiscouata
Circonscription(s) électorale(s) fédérale(s):
Montmagny-L'Islet-Kamouraska-Rivière-du-Loup
Prochaines élections: 3e novembre 2013
Gervais Darisse, Maire
Claudine Lévesque, Directrice générale

Saint-André-Avellin
119, rue Principale
Saint-André-Avellin, QC J0V 1W0
Tél: 819-983-2318; *Téléc:* 819-983-2344
info@ville.st-andre-avellin.qc.ca
www.ville.st-andre-avellin.qc.ca
Entité municipal: Municipality
Incorporation: 17 décembre 1997 *Area:* 131,05 km2
Comté ou district: Papineau; *Population au 2011:* 3,702
Circonscription(s) électorale(s) provinciale(s): Papineau
Circonscription(s) électorale(s) fédérale(s):
Argenteuil-Papineau-Mirabel
Prochaines élections: 3e novembre 2013
Thérèse Whissell, Mairesse
Claire Tremblay, Directrice générale

Saint-André-d'Argenteuil
10, rue de la Mairie
Saint-André-d'Argenteuil, QC J0V 1X0
Tél: 450-537-3527; *Téléc:* 450-537-3070
info@saintandredargenteuil.ca
www.saintandredargenteuil.ca
Entité municipal: Municipality
Incorporation: 29 décembre 1999 *Area:* 98,45 km2
Comté ou district: Argenteuil; *Population au 2011:* 3,275
Circonscription(s) électorale(s) provinciale(s): Argenteuil
Circonscription(s) électorale(s) fédérale(s):
Argenteuil-Papineau-Mirabel
Prochaines élections: 3e novembre 2013
André Jetté, Maire
Ronald Baidr, Directeur général

Saint-André-de-Restigouche
CP 4
163, rue Principale
Saint-André-de-Restigouche, QC G0J 2G0
Tél: 418-865-2234; *Téléc:* 418-865-1393
m.st.and.restigouche@globetrotter.net
www.matapedialesplateaux.com
Entité municipal: Municipality
Incorporation: 1er juillet 1855 *Area:* 146,07 km2
Comté ou district: Avignon; *Population au 2011:* 157
Circonscription(s) électorale(s) provinciale(s): Bonaventure
Circonscription(s) électorale(s) fédérale(s):
Gaspésie—Îles-de-la-Madeleine
Prochaines élections: 3e novembre 2013
Doris Deschênes, Mairesse
Blandine Parent, Directrice générale

Saint-André-du-Lac-St-Jean
11, rue du Collège
Saint-André-du-Lac-Saint-Jean, QC G0W 2K0
Tél: 418-349-8167; *Téléc:* 418-349-1019
municipalite@standredulac.qc.ca
Entité municipal: Village
Incorporation: 29 novembre 1969 *Area:* 157,75 km2
Comté ou district: Le Domaine-du-Roy; *Population au 2011:* 488
Circonscription(s) électorale(s) provinciale(s): Lac-St-Jean
Circonscription(s) électorale(s) fédérale(s):
Roberval-Lac-St-Jean
Prochaines élections: 3e novembre 2013
Gabriel Martel, Maire
Maude Tremblay, Directrice générale

Saint-Anicet
335, av Jules-Léger
Saint-Anicet, QC J0S 1M0
Tél: 450-264-2555; *Téléc:* 450-264-2395
saint.anicet@municipalite-saint-anicet.qc.ca
www.municipalite-saint-anicet.qc.ca
Entité municipal: Parish (Paroisse)
Incorporation: 1er juillet 1855 *Area:* 136,25 km2
Comté ou district: Le Haut-St-Laurent; *Population au 2011:* 2,523
Circonscription(s) électorale(s) provinciale(s): Huntingdon
Circonscription(s) électorale(s) fédérale(s):
Beauharnois-Salaberry
Prochaines élections: 3e novembre 2013
Alain Castagner, Maire
Lyne Viau, Directrice générale

Saint-Anselme
134, rue Principale
Saint-Anselme, QC G0R 2N0
Tél: 418-885-4977; *Téléc:* 418-885-9834
municipalite@st-anselme.ca
www.st-anselme.ca
Entité municipal: Municipality
Incorporation: 7 janvier 1998 *Area:* 74,45 km2
Comté ou district: Bellechasse; *Population au 2011:* 3,458
Circonscription(s) électorale(s) provinciale(s): Bellechasse
Circonscription(s) électorale(s) fédérale(s): Lévis-Bellechasse
Prochaines élections: 3e novembre 2013
Michel Bonneau, Maire
Louis Felteau, Directeur général

Saint-Antoine de l'Isle-aux-Grues
107, ch de la Volière
L'Isle-aux-Grues, QC G0R 1P0
Tél: 418-248-8060; *Téléc:* 418-248-7955
municipaliteiag@globetrotter.net
www.isle-aux-grues.com
Entité municipal: Parish (Paroisse)
Incorporation: 1er janvier 1860 *Area:* 26,40 km2
Comté ou district: Montmagny; *Population au 2011:* 146
Circonscription(s) électorale(s) provinciale(s): Montmagny-L'Islet
Circonscription(s) électorale(s) fédérale(s):
Montmagny-L'Islet-Kamouraska-Rivière-du-Loup
Prochaines élections: 3e novembre 2013
Frédéric Poulin, Maire
Hélène Painchaud, Directrice générale

Saint-Antoine-de-Tilly
CP 10
3870, ch de Tilly
Saint-Antoine-de-Tilly, QC G0S 2C0
Tél: 418-886-2441; *Téléc:* 418-886-2075
info@saintantoinedetilly.com
www.saintantoinedetilly.com
Entité municipal: Municipality
Incorporation: 1er juillet 1855 *Area:* 60,29 km2
Comté ou district: Lotbinière; *Population au 2011:* 1,604
Circonscription(s) électorale(s) provinciale(s): Lotbinière
Circonscription(s) électorale(s) fédérale(s):
Lotbinière-Chutes-de-la-Chaudière
Prochaines élections: 3e novembre 2013
Ghislain Daigle, Maire
Diane Laroche, Directrice générale

Saint-Antoine-sur-Richelieu
1060, rue des Ormes
Saint-Antoine-sur-Richelieu, QC J0L 1R0
Tél: 450-787-3497; *Téléc:* 450-787-2852
municipalite@sasr.ca
www.saint-antoine-sur-richelieu.ca
Entité municipal: Municipality
Incorporation: 6 novembre 1982 *Area:* 65,26 km2
Comté ou district: La Vallée-du-Richelieu; *Population au 2011:* 1,659
Circonscription(s) électorale(s) provinciale(s): Verchères
Circonscription(s) électorale(s) fédérale(s): Verchères-Les Patriotes
Prochaines élections: 3e novembre 2013
Martin Lévesque, Maire
Élise Guertin, Directrice générale

Saint-Antonin
CP 340
261, rue Principale
Saint-Antonin, QC G0L 2J0
Tél: 418-862-1056; *Téléc:* 418-862-3268
saintantonin@municipalitedesaintantonin.qc.ca
www.municipalite.saint-antonin.qc.ca
Entité municipal: Parish (Paroisse)
Incorporation: 30 août 1856 *Area:* 182,66 km2
Comté ou district: Rivière-du-Loup; *Population au 2011:* 4,027
Circonscription(s) électorale(s) provinciale(s): Rivière-du-Loup
Circonscription(s) électorale(s) fédérale(s):
Montmagny-L'Islet-Kamouraska-Rivière-du-Loup
Prochaines élections: 3e novembre 2013
Réal Thibault, Maire
Louisiane Dubé, Directrice générale

Saint-Apollinaire
11, rue Industrielle
Saint-Apollinaire, QC G0S 2E0
Tél: 418-881-3996; *Téléc:* 418-881-4152
www.st-apollinaire.com
Entité municipal: Municipality
Incorporation: 6 avril 1974 *Area:* 96,63 km2
Comté ou district: Lotbinière; *Population au 2011:* 5,102
Circonscription(s) électorale(s) provinciale(s): Lotbinière
Circonscription(s) électorale(s) fédérale(s):
Lotbinière-Chutes-de-la-Chaudière
Prochaines élections: 3e novembre 2013
Ginette Moreau, Mairesse
Martine Couture, Directrice générale
martine.couture@st-apollinaire.com

Saint-Armand
444, ch Bradley
Saint-Armand, QC J0J 1T0
Tél: 450-248-2344; *Téléc:* 450-248-3820
starmand@bellnet.ca
www.municipalite.saint-armand.qc.ca
Entité municipal: Municipality
Incorporation: 3 février 1999 *Area:* 84,26 km2
Comté ou district: Brome-Missisquoi; *Population au 2011:* 1,248
Circonscription(s) électorale(s) provinciale(s): Brome-Missisquoi
Circonscription(s) électorale(s) fédérale(s): Brome-Missisquoi
Prochaines élections: 3e novembre 2013
Réal Pelletier, Maire
Jacqueline Chisholm, Directrice générale

Saint-Arsène
#101, 49, rue de l'Église
Saint-Arsène, QC G0L 2K0
Tél: 418-867-2205; *Téléc:* 418-867-2025
directiongenerale@saint-arsene.ca
www.municipalite.saint-arsene.qc.ca
Entité municipal: Parish (Paroisse)
Incorporation: 1er juillet 1855 *Area:* 71,01 km2
Comté ou district: Rivière-du-Loup; *Population au 2011:* 1,253
Circonscription(s) électorale(s) provinciale(s): Rivière-du-Loup
Circonscription(s) électorale(s) fédérale(s):
Montmagny-L'Islet-Kamouraska-Rivière-du-Loup
Prochaines élections: 3e novembre 2013
André Roy, Maire
François Michaud, Directeur général

Saint-Athanase
CP 108
6081, ch de l'Église
Saint-Athanase, QC G0L 2L0
Tél: 418-859-2575; *Téléc:* 418-859-3415
info@saint-athanase.com
www.saint-athanase.com
Entité municipal: Municipality
Incorporation: 1er janvier 1955 *Area:* 289,08 km2
Comté ou district: Témiscouata; *Population au 2011:* 301
Circonscription(s) électorale(s) provinciale(s):
Kamouraska-Témiscouata
Circonscription(s) électorale(s) fédérale(s):
Rimouski-Neigette-Témiscouata-Les Basques
Prochaines élections: 3e novembre 2013
Mario Patry, Maire
Francine Morin, Directrice générale

Saint-Aubert
14, rue des Loisirs
Saint-Aubert, QC G0R 2R0
Tél: 418-598-3368; *Téléc:* 418-598-3369
administration@saint-aubert.net
saint-aubert.net
Entité municipal: Municipality
Incorporation: 1er juillet 1857 *Area:* 97,15 km2
Comté ou district: L'Islet; *Population au 2011:* 1,409
Circonscription(s) électorale(s) provinciale(s): Montmagny-L'Islet
Circonscription(s) électorale(s) fédérale(s):
Montmagny-L'Islet-Kamouraska-Rivière-du-Loup
Prochaines élections: 3e novembre 2013
Germain Robichaud, Maire
Serge Roussel, Directeur général

Saint-Augustin
CP 279
Saint-Augustin, QC G0G 2R0
Tél: 418-947-2404; *Téléc:* 418-947-2533
generaldirector.msa@gmail.com
Entité municipal: Municipality
Incorporation: 1er janvier 1993 *Area:* 1435,82 km2
Population au 2011: 478
Circonscription(s) électorale(s) provinciale(s): Duplessis
Circonscription(s) électorale(s) fédérale(s):
Roberval-Lac-St-Jean
Prochaines élections: 3e novembre 2013
Randy Maurice, Maire
Jackie Gallibois, Directrice générale

Saint-Augustin
686, rue Principale
Saint-Augustin, QC G0W 1K0
Tél: 418-374-2147; *Téléc:* 418-374-2984
mun.sta@derytele.com
www.saint-augustin.net
Entité municipal: Parish (Paroisse)
Incorporation: 14 mai 1925 *Area:* 103,96 km2
Comté ou district: Maria-Chapdelaine; *Population au 2011:* 400
Circonscription(s) électorale(s) provinciale(s): Roberval
Circonscription(s) électorale(s) fédérale(s):
Roberval-Lac-St-Jean
Prochaines élections: 3e novembre 2013
Nicole Fortin, Mairesse
Maud Larouche, Directrice générale

Saint-Augustin-de-Woburn
590, rue St-Augustin
Woburn, QC G0Y 1R0
Tél: 819-544-4211; *Téléc:* 819-544-9236
mun.woburn@axion.ca
Entité municipal: Parish (Paroisse)
Incorporation: 13 janvier 1900 *Area:* 280,80 km2
Comté ou district: Le Granit; *Population au 2011:* 695
Circonscription(s) électorale(s) provinciale(s):
Mégantic-Compton
Circonscription(s) électorale(s) fédérale(s): Mégantic-L'Érable
Prochaines élections: 3e novembre 2013
Steve Charrier, Maire
Gaétane Allard, Directrice générale

Saint-Barnabé
CP 250
70, rue Duguay
Saint-Barnabé, QC G0X 2K0
Tél: 819-264-2085; *Téléc:* 819-264-2079
municipalitest-barnabe@telmilot.net
Entité municipal: Parish (Paroisse)
Incorporation: 1er juillet 1855 *Area:* 58,81 km2
Comté ou district: Maskinongé; *Population au 2011:* 1,179
Circonscription(s) électorale(s) provinciale(s): Maskinongé
Circonscription(s) électorale(s) fédérale(s): Berthier-Maskinongé
Prochaines élections: 3e novembre 2013
René Bourassa, Maire
Denis Gélinas, Directeur général

Saint-Barnabé-Sud
251, rang de Michaudville
Saint-Barnabé-Sud, QC J0H 1G0
Tél: 450-792-3030; *Téléc:* 450-792-3759
munstbarnabesud@mrcmaskoutains.qc.ca
Entité municipal: Municipality
Incorporation: 1er juillet 1855 *Area:* 57,08 km2
Comté ou district: Les Maskoutains; *Population au 2011:* 859
Circonscription(s) électorale(s) provinciale(s): St-Hyacinthe
Circonscription(s) électorale(s) fédérale(s): St-Hyacinthe-Bagot
Prochaines élections: 3e novembre 2013
Richard Leblanc, Maire
Nathalie Audette, Directrice générale

Saint-Barthélemy
1980, rue Bonin
Saint-Barthélémy, QC J0K 1X0
Tél: 450-885-3511; *Téléc:* 450-836-5220
municipalite@saint-barthelemy.ca
www.saint-barthelemy.ca
Entité municipal: Parish (Paroisse)
Incorporation: 1er juillet 1855 *Area:* 98,80 km2
Comté ou district: D'Autray; *Population au 2011:* 1,883
Circonscription(s) électorale(s) provinciale(s): Berthier
Circonscription(s) électorale(s) fédérale(s): Berthier-Maskinongé
Prochaines élections: 3e novembre 2013
Pierre Roy, Maire
Francine Rivest, Directrice générale

Saint-Basile
20, rue St-Georges
Saint-Basile, QC G0A 3G0
Tél: 418-329-2204; *Téléc:* 418-329-2788
greffe@saintbasile.qc.ca
www.saintbasile.qc.ca
Entité municipal: Town
Incorporation: 1er mars 2000 *Area:* 97,69 km2
Comté ou district: Portneuf; *Population au 2011:* 2,463
Circonscription(s) électorale(s) provinciale(s): Portneuf
Circonscription(s) électorale(s) fédérale(s):
Portneuf-Jacques-Cartier
Prochaines élections: 3e novembre 2013
Jean Poirier, Maire
Paulin Leclerc, Directeur général

Saint-Benjamin
CP 100
440, av du Collège
Saint-Benjamin, QC G0M 1N0
Tél: 418-594-8156; *Téléc:* 418-594-6068
munstbenjamin@aclcable.ca
www.st-benjamin.qc.ca
Entité municipal: Municipality
Incorporation: 9 janvier 1897 *Area:* 110,53 km2
Comté ou district: Les Etchemins; *Population au 2011:* 891
Circonscription(s) électorale(s) provinciale(s): Beauce-Sud
Circonscription(s) électorale(s) fédérale(s): Beauce
Prochaines élections: 3e novembre 2013
Martine Boulet, Maire
France Veilleux, Directrice générale

Saint-Benoît-du-Lac
1, rue Principale
Saint-Benoît-du-Lac, QC J0B 2M0
Tél: 819-843-4080; *Téléc:* 819-868-1861
muni.sbl@axion.ca
www.st-benoit-du-lac.com
Entité municipal: Municipality
Incorporation: 16 mars 1939 *Area:* 2,27 km2
Comté ou district: Memphrémagog; *Population au 2011:* 50
Circonscription(s) électorale(s) provinciale(s): Brome-Missisquoi
Circonscription(s) électorale(s) fédérale(s): Brome-Missisquoi
Prochaines élections: 3e novembre 2013
Jacques Duguay, Administrateur

Saint-Benoît-Labre
216, rte 271
Saint-Benoît-Labre, QC G0M 1P0
Tél: 418-228-9250; *Téléc:* 418-228-0518
munstben@globetrotter.net
www.saintbenoitlabre.qc.ca
Entité municipal: Municipality
Incorporation: 4 janvier 1894 *Area:* 83,92 km2
Comté ou district: Beauce-Sartigan; *Population au 2011:* 1,612
Circonscription(s) électorale(s) provinciale(s): Beauce-Sud
Circonscription(s) électorale(s) fédérale(s): Beauce
Prochaines élections: 3e novembre 2013
Marco Marois, Maire
Gaétane Vallée, Directrice générale

Saint-Bernard
CP 70
1512, rue St-Georges
Saint-Bernard, QC G0S 2G0
Tél: 418-475-6060; *Téléc:* 418-475-6069
stbernard@globetrotter.net
Entité municipal: Municipality
Incorporation: 9 mai 1987 *Area:* 87,56 km2
Comté ou district: La Nouvelle-Beauce; *Population au 2011:* 2,131
Circonscription(s) électorale(s) provinciale(s): Beauce-Nord
Circonscription(s) électorale(s) fédérale(s): Beauce
Prochaines élections: 3e novembre 2013
Liboire Lefebrve, Maire
Marie-Eve Parent, Directrice générale

Saint-Bernard-de-Lacolle
116, rang St-Claude
Saint-Bernard-de-Lacolle, QC J0J 1V0
Tél: 450-246-3348; *Téléc:* 450-246-4380
mun.st-bernard-de-lacolle@bellnet.ca
Entité municipal: Parish (Paroisse)
Incorporation: 1er juillet 1855 *Area:* 112,63 km2
Comté ou district: Les Jardins-de-Napierville; *Population au 2011:* 1,477
Circonscription(s) électorale(s) provinciale(s): Huntingdon
Circonscription(s) électorale(s) fédérale(s):
Beauharnois-Salaberry
Prochaines élections: 3e novembre 2013
Robert Duteau, Maire
Daniel Striletsky, Directeur général

Saint-Bernard-de-Michaudville
390, rue Principale
Saint-Bernard-de-Michaudville, QC J0H 1C0
Tél: 450-792-3190; *Téléc:* 450-792-3591
munstbernard@mrcmaskoutains.qc.ca
Entité municipal: Municipality
Incorporation: 31 août 1908 *Area:* 64,80 km2
Comté ou district: Les Maskoutains; *Population au 2011:* 521
Circonscription(s) électorale(s) provinciale(s): Richelieu
Circonscription(s) électorale(s) fédérale(s): St-Hyacinthe-Bagot
Prochaines élections: 3e novembre 2013
Francine Morin, Mairesse
Sylvie Chaput, Directrice générale

Saint-Blaise-sur-Richelieu
795, rue des Loisirs
Saint-Blaise-sur-Richelieu, QC J0J 1W0
Tél: 450-291-5944; *Téléc:* 450-291-3832
info@municipalite.saint-blaise-sur-richelieu.qc.ca
Entité municipal: Municipality
Incorporation: 20 juin 1892 *Area:* 68,42 km2
Comté ou district: Le Haut-Richelieu; *Population au 2011:* 1,837
Circonscription(s) électorale(s) provinciale(s): St-Jean
Circonscription(s) électorale(s) fédérale(s): St-Jean
Prochaines élections: 3e novembre 2013
Jacques Desmarais, Mairesse
Francine Milot, Directrice générale

Saint-Bonaventure
720, rue Plante
Saint-Bonaventure, QC J0C 1C0
Tél: 819-396-2335; *Téléc:* 819-396-2335
st-bonaventure@mrcdrummond.qc.ca
Entité municipal: Municipality
Incorporation: 1er janvier 1867 *Area:* 78,83 km2
Comté ou district: Drummond; *Population au 2011:* 1,017
Circonscription(s) électorale(s) provinciale(s): Nicolet-Yamaska
Circonscription(s) électorale(s) fédérale(s): Drummond
Prochaines élections: 3e novembre 2013
Félicien Cardin, Maire
Claire Côté, Directrice générale

Saint-Boniface
140, rue Guimont
Saint-Boniface, QC G0X 2L0
Tél: 819-535-3811; *Téléc:* 819-535-1242
lgauthier@ville.saint-boniface.ca
Entité municipal: Municipality
Incorporation: 1er janvier 1962 *Area:* 112,12 km2
Comté ou district: Maskinongé; *Population au 2011:* 4,511
Circonscription(s) électorale(s) provinciale(s): St-Maurice
Circonscription(s) électorale(s) fédérale(s): Berthier-Maskinongé
Prochaines élections: 3e novembre 2013
Claude Caron, Maire
Jacques Caron, Directeur général

Saint-Bruno
563, av St-Alphonse
Saint-Bruno, QC G0W 2L0
Tél: 418-343-2303; *Téléc:* 418-343-2662
info@ville.saint-bruno.qc.ca
www.ville.saint-bruno.qc.ca
Entité municipal: Municipality
Incorporation: 12 juillet 1975 *Area:* 77,88 km2
Comté ou district: Lac-St-Jean-Est; *Population au 2011:* 2,636
Circonscription(s) électorale(s) provinciale(s): Lac-St-Jean
Circonscription(s) électorale(s) fédérale(s):
Roberval-Lac-St-Jean
Prochaines élections: 3e novembre 2013
Réjean Bouchard, Maire
Gilles Boudreault, Directeur général

Saint-Bruno-de-Guigues
CP 130
21, rue Principale nord
Saint-Bruno-de-Guigues, QC J0Z 2G0
Tél: 819-728-2186; *Téléc:* 819-728-2404
dg.guigues@mrctemiscamingue.qc.ca
www.temiscamingue.net/guigues
Entité municipal: Municipality
Incorporation: 3 octobre 1912 *Area:* 188,99 km2
Comté ou district: Témiscamingue; *Population au 2011:* 1,100
Circonscription(s) électorale(s) provinciale(s):
Rouyn-Noranda-Témiscamingue
Circonscription(s) électorale(s) fédérale(s):
Abitibi-Témiscamingue
Prochaines élections: 3e novembre 2013
Joanne Larochelle, Maire
Serge Côté, Directeur général

Saint-Bruno-de-Kamouraska
CP 10
4, rue du Couvent
Saint-Bruno-de-Kamouraska, QC G0L 2M0
Tél: 418-492-2612; *Téléc:* 418-492-9076
mun.stbrunokam@globetrotter.net
www.stbrunokam.qc.ca
Entité municipal: Municipality
Incorporation: 1er janvier 1887 *Area:* 186,79 km2
Comté ou district: Kamouraska; *Population au 2011:* 534
Circonscription(s) électorale(s) provinciale(s):
Kamouraska-Témiscouata
Circonscription(s) électorale(s) fédérale(s):
Montmagny-L'Islet-Kamouraska-Rivière-du-Loup
Prochaines élections: 3e novembre 2013
Roger Lavoie, Maire
Constance Gagné, Directrice générale

Saint-Calixte
6230, rue de l'Hôtel-de-Ville
Saint-Calixte, QC J0K 1Z0
Tél: 450-222-2782; *Téléc:* 450-222-2789
lemay@mscalixte.qc.ca
www.municipalite.saint-calixte.qc.ca
Entité municipal: Municipality
Incorporation: 1er juillet 1855 *Area:* 147,68 km2
Comté ou district: Montcalm; *Population au 2011:* 5,934
Circonscription(s) électorale(s) provinciale(s): Rousseau
Circonscription(s) électorale(s) fédérale(s): Montcalm
Prochaines élections: 3e novembre 2013
Louis-Charles Thouin, Maire
Denis Lemay, Directeur général

Saint-Camille
87, rue Desrivières
Saint-Camille, QC J0A 1G0
Tél: 819-828-3222; *Téléc:* 819-828-3723
munstcamille@cgocable.ca
www.saint-camille.ca
Entité municipal: Township
Incorporation: 1er janvier 1860 *Area:* 81,27 km2
Comté ou district: Asbestos; *Population au 2011:* 511
Circonscription(s) électorale(s) provinciale(s): Richmond
Circonscription(s) électorale(s) fédérale(s):
Richmond-Arthabaska
Prochaines élections: 3e novembre 2013
Benoit Bourassa, Maire
Mélisa Camiré, Directrice générale

Saint-Camille-de-Lellis
CP 70
217, rue Principale
Saint-Camille-de-Lellis, QC G0R 2S0
Tél: 418-595-2233; *Téléc:* 418-595-2238
mustcam@sogetel.net
www.saint-camille.net
Entité municipal: Parish (Paroisse)
Incorporation: 11 janvier 1904 *Area:* 252,08 km2
Comté ou district: Les Etchemins; *Population au 2011:* 844
Circonscription(s) électorale(s) provinciale(s): Bellechasse
Circonscription(s) électorale(s) fédérale(s): Lévis-Bellechasse
Prochaines élections: 3e novembre 2013
Adélard Couture, Maire
Nicole Mathieu, Directrice générale

Saint-Casimir
CP 220
220, boul de la Montagne
Saint-Casimir, QC G0A 3L0
Tél: 418-339-2543; *Téléc:* 418-339-3105
st-casimir@infoteck.qc.ca
www.saint-casimir.com
Entité municipal: Municipality
Incorporation: 21 juin 2000 *Area:* 65,93 km2
Comté ou district: Portneuf; *Population au 2011:* 1,500
Circonscription(s) électorale(s) provinciale(s): Portneuf
Circonscription(s) électorale(s) fédérale(s): Portneuf-Jacques Cartier
Prochaines élections: 3e novembre 2013
Dominic Tessier Perry, Maire
René Savard, Directeur général

Saint-Célestin
990, rang du Pays-Brûlé
Saint-Célestin, QC J0C 1G0
Tél: 819-229-3745; *Téléc:* 819-229-1386
info@saint-celestin.net
www.saint-celestin.net
Entité municipal: Municipality
Incorporation: 1er juillet 1864 *Area:* 78,72 km2
Comté ou district: Nicolet-Yamaska; *Population au 2011:* 611
Circonscription(s) électorale(s) provinciale(s): Nicolet-Yamaska
Circonscription(s) électorale(s) fédérale(s):
Bas-Richelieu-Nicolet-Bécancour
Prochaines élections: 3e novembre 2013
Maurice Morin, Maire
Gisèle Plourde, Directrice générale

Saint-Célestin
510, rue Marquis
Saint-Célestin, QC J0C 1G0
Tél: 819-229-3642; *Téléc:* 819-229-1149
info@village-st-celestin.net
www.village-st-celestin.net
Entité municipal: Village
Incorporation: 25 novembre 1896 *Area:* 1,61 km22
Comté ou district: Nicolet-Yamaska; *Population au 2011:* 781
Circonscription(s) électorale(s) provinciale(s): Nicolet-Yamaska
Circonscription(s) électorale(s) fédérale(s):
Bas-Richelieu-Nicolet-Bécancour
Prochaines élections: 3e novembre 2013
Raymond Noël, Maire
Pascale Lamoureux, Directrice générale

Saint-Césaire
1111, av St-Paul
Saint-Césaire, QC J0L 1T0
Tél: 450-469-3108; *Téléc:* 450-469-5275
ville-st-cesaire@bellnet.ca
www.ville.saint-cesaire.qc.ca
Entité municipal: Town
Incorporation: 26 janvier 2000 *Area:* 84,14 km2
Comté ou district: Rouville; *Population au 2011:* 5,686
Circonscription(s) électorale(s) provinciale(s): Iberville
Circonscription(s) électorale(s) fédérale(s): Shefford
Prochaines élections: 3e novembre 2013
Serge Gendron, Maire
Louise Benoît, Greffière

Saint-Charles-Borromée
370, rue de la Visitation
Saint-Charles-Borromée, QC J6E 4P3
Tél: 450-759-4415; *Téléc:* 450-759-3393
info@st-charles-borromee.org
www.st-charles-borromee.org
Entité municipal: Municipality
Incorporation: 1er juillet 1855 *Area:* 18,60 km2
Comté ou district: Joliette; *Population au 2011:* 13,321
Circonscription(s) électorale(s) provinciale(s): Joliette
Circonscription(s) électorale(s) fédérale(s): Joliette
Prochaines élections: 3e novembre 2013
André Hénault, Maire
Denis Girard, Coordonnateur, Génie/Urbanisme
Jacques Fortin, Directeur, Services d'incendie/Protection civile
François Thériault, Directeur général

Saint-Charles-de-Bellechasse
2815, av Royale
Saint-Charles-de-Bellechasse, QC G0R 2T0
Tél: 418-887-6600; *Téléc:* 418-887-6779
munstcha@globetrotter.net
www.saint-charles.ca
Entité municipal: Municipality
Incorporation: 22 décembre 1993 *Area:* 94,73 km2
Comté ou district: Bellechasse; *Population au 2011:* 2,246
Circonscription(s) électorale(s) provinciale(s): Bellechasse
Circonscription(s) électorale(s) fédérale(s): Lévis-Bellechasse
Prochaines élections: 3e novembre 2013
Martin Lapierre, Maire
Denis Labbé, Directeur général

Saint-Charles-de-Bourget
357, 2e rang
Saint-Charles-de-Bourget, QC G0V 1G0
Tél: 418-672-2624; *Téléc:* 418-673-2118
info@stcharlesdebourget.ca
Entité municipal: Municipality
Incorporation: 29 septembre 1885 *Area:* 62,31 km2
Comté ou district: Le Fjord-du-Saguenay; *Population au 2011:* 690
Circonscription(s) électorale(s) provinciale(s): Dubuc
Circonscription(s) électorale(s) fédérale(s): Jonquière-Alma
Prochaines élections: 3e novembre 2013
Michel Ringuette, Maire
Audrey Thibeault, Directrice générale

Saint-Charles-Garnier
CP 39
38, rue Principale
Saint-Charles-Garnier, QC G0K 1K0
Tél: 418-798-4305; *Téléc:* 418-798-4499
stcharles@mitis.qc.ca
www.municipalite.saint-charles-garnier.qc.ca
Entité municipal: Parish (Paroisse)
Incorporation: 1er janvier 1966 *Area:* 83,73 km2
Comté ou district: La Mitis; *Population au 2011:* 271
Circonscription(s) électorale(s) provinciale(s): Matapédia
Circonscription(s) électorale(s) fédérale(s): Haute-Gaspésie-La Mitis-Matane-Matapédia
Prochaines élections: 3e novembre 2013
Jean-Pierre Bélanger, Maire
Josette Bouillon, Directrice générale

Saint-Charles-sur-Richelieu
#101, 405, ch des Patriotes
Saint-Charles-sur-Richelieu, QC J0H 2G0
Tél: 450-584-3484; *Téléc:* 450-584-2965
direction@saint-charles-sur-richelieu.ca
www.saint-charles-sur-richelieu.ca
Entité municipal: Municipality
Incorporation: 22 mars 1995 *Area:* 63,59 km2
Comté ou district: La Vallée-du-Richelieu; *Population au 2011:* 1,643
Circonscription(s) électorale(s) provinciale(s): Verchères
Circonscription(s) électorale(s) fédérale(s):
Verchères-Les-Patriotes
Prochaines élections: 3e novembre 2013
Denis Miller, Maire
Nancy Fortier, Directrice générale

Saint-Christophe-d'Arthabaska
418, av Pie-X
Saint-Christophe-d'Arthabaska, QC G6R 0M9
Tél: 819-357-9031; *Téléc:* 819-357-9087
directiongenerale@saint-christophe-darthabaska.ca
www.saint-christophe-darthabaska.ca
Entité municipal: Parish (Paroisse)
Incorporation: 1er juillet 1855 *Area:* 74,87 km2
Comté ou district: Arthabaska; *Population au 2011:* 2,892
Circonscription(s) électorale(s) provinciale(s): Arthabaska
Circonscription(s) électorale(s) fédérale(s):
Richmond-Arthabaska
Prochaines élections: 3e novembre 2013
Clémence LeMay Verville, Maire
Francine Moreau, Directrice générale

Saint-Chrysostome
624, rue Notre-Dame, 2e étage
Saint-Chrysostome, QC J0S 1R0
Tél: 450-826-3911; *Téléc:* 450-826-0568
dg@mun-sc.ca
www.mun-sc.ca
Entité municipal: Municipality
Incorporation: 29 septembre 1999 *Area:* 99,54 km2
Comté ou district: Le Haut-St-Laurent; *Population au 2011:* 2,522
Circonscription(s) électorale(s) provinciale(s): Huntingdon
Circonscription(s) électorale(s) fédérale(s): Beauharnois-Salaberry
Prochaines élections: 3e novembre 2013
Jocelyne Lefort, Maire
Céline Ouimet, Directrice générale

Saint-Claude
295, rte de l'Église
Saint-Claude, QC J0B 2N0
Tél: 819-845-7795; *Téléc:* 819-845-2479
directrice@st-claude.ca
www.municipalite.st-claude.ca
Entité municipal: Municipality
Incorporation: 15 novembre 1912 *Area:* 120,38 km2
Comté ou district: Le Val-St-François; *Population au 2011:* 1,106
Circonscription(s) électorale(s) provinciale(s): Richmond
Circonscription(s) électorale(s) fédérale(s): Richmond-Arthabaska
Prochaines élections: 3e novembre 2013
Hervé Provencher, Maire
France Lavertu, Directrice générale

Saint-Clément
CP 40
25A, rue St-Pierre
Saint-Clément, QC G0L 2N0
Tél: 418-963-2258; *Téléc:* 418-963-2619
admin@stclement.qc.ca
www.st-clement.ca
Entité municipal: Parish (Paroisse)
Incorporation: 1er janvier 1885 *Area:* 80,44 km2
Comté ou district: Les Basques; *Population au 2011:* 499
Circonscription(s) électorale(s) provinciale(s): Rivière-du-Loup
Circonscription(s) électorale(s) fédérale(s): Rimouski-Neigette-Témiscouata-Les Basques
Prochaines élections: 3e novembre 2013
Richard April, Maire
Line Caron, Directrice générale

Saint-Cléophas
350, rue Principale
Saint-Cléophas, QC G0J 3N0
Tél: 418-536-3023; *Téléc:* 418-536-1349
stcleophas@mrcmatapedia.qc.ca
Entité municipal: Parish (Paroisse)
Incorporation: 19 mai 1921 *Area:* 97,46 km2
Comté ou district: La Matapédia; *Population au 2011:* 334
Circonscription(s) électorale(s) provinciale(s): Matapédia
Circonscription(s) électorale(s) fédérale(s): Haute-Gaspésie-La Mitis-Matane-Matapédia
Prochaines élections: 3e novembre 2013
Jean-Paul Bélanger, Maire
Katie St-Pierre, Directrice générale

Saint-Cléophas-de-Brandon
750, rue Principale
Saint-Cléophas-de-Brandon, QC J0K 2A0
Tél: 450-889-5683; *Téléc:* 450-835-6076
dg@st-cleophas.qc.ca
www.st-cleophas.qc.ca
Entité municipal: Municipality
Incorporation: 7 octobre 1897 *Area:* 14,76 km2
Comté ou district: D'Autray; *Population au 2011:* 276
Circonscription(s) électorale(s) provinciale(s): Berthier
Circonscription(s) électorale(s) fédérale(s): Berthier-Maskinongé
Prochaines élections: 3e novembre 2013
Denis Gamelin, Maire
Chantal Piette, Directrice générale

Saint-Clet
4, rue du Moulin
Saint-Clet, QC J0P 1S0
Tél: 450-456-3363; *Téléc:* 450-456-3879
st-clet@videotron.ca
www.municipalite-st-clet.qc.ca
Entité municipal: Municipality
Incorporation: 31 août 1974 *Area:* 38,61 km2
Comté ou district: Vaudreuil-Soulanges; *Population au 2011:* 1,738
Circonscription(s) électorale(s) provinciale(s): Soulanges
Circonscription(s) électorale(s) fédérale(s): Vaudreuil-Soulanges
Prochaines élections: 3e novembre 2013
Gilles Farand, Maire
Nathalie Pharand, Directrice générale

Saint-Colomban
330, montée de l'Église
Saint-Colomban, QC J5K 1A1
Tél: 450-436-1453; *Téléc:* 450-436-5955
info@st-colomban.qc.ca
www.st-colomban.qc.ca
Entité municipal: Municipality
Incorporation: 1er juillet 1855 *Area:* 94,24 km2
Comté ou district: La Rivière-du-Nord; *Population au 2011:* 13,080
Circonscription(s) électorale(s) provinciale(s): Argenteuil
Circonscription(s) électorale(s) fédérale(s): Rivière-du-Nord
Prochaines élections: 3e novembre 2013
Jacques Labrosse, Maire
Claude Panneton, Directeur général

Saint-Côme
1673, 55e rue
Saint-Côme, QC J0K 2B0
Tél: 450-883-2726; *Téléc:* 450-883-6431
dg@stcomelanaudiere.ca
www.stcomelanaudiere.ca
Entité municipal: Parish (Paroisse)
Incorporation: 1er janvier 1873 *Area:* 167,26 km2
Comté ou district: Matawinie; *Population au 2011:* 2,198
Circonscription(s) électorale(s) provinciale(s): Berthier
Circonscription(s) électorale(s) fédérale(s): Joliette
Prochaines élections: 3e novembre 2013
Jocelyn Breault, Maire
Alice Riopel, Directrice générale

Saint-Côme-Linière
1375, 18e rue
Saint-Côme-Linière, QC G0M 1J0
Tél: 418-685-3825; *Téléc:* 418-685-2566
st-come@globetrotter.net
www.stcomeliniere.com
Entité municipal: Municipality
Incorporation: 13 avril 1994 *Area:* 151,24 km2
Comté ou district: Beauce-Sartigan; *Population au 2011:* 3,274
Circonscription(s) électorale(s) provinciale(s): Beauce-Sud
Circonscription(s) électorale(s) fédérale(s): Beauce
Prochaines élections: 3e novembre 2013
Gabriel Giguère, Maire
Yvan Bélanger, Directeur général

Saint-Cuthbert
CP 100
1891, rue Principale
Saint-Cuthbert, QC J0K 2C0
Tél: 450-836-4852; *Téléc:* 450-836-4833
mairie@st-cuthbert.qc.ca
www.st-cuthbert.qc.ca
Entité municipal: Municipality
Incorporation: 7 janvier 1998 *Area:* 133,71 km2
Comté ou district: D'Autray; *Population au 2011:* 1,839
Circonscription(s) électorale(s) provinciale(s): Berthier
Circonscription(s) électorale(s) fédérale(s): Berthier-Maskinongé
Prochaines élections: 3e novembre 2013
Bruno Vadnais, Maire
Richard Lauzon, Directeur général

Saint-Cyprien
CP 9
101B, rue Collin
Saint-Cyprien, QC G0L 2P0
Tél: 418-963-2730; *Téléc:* 418-963-3490
www.municipalite.saint-cyprien.qc.ca
Entité municipal: Municipality
Incorporation: 1er janvier 1883 *Area:* 136,14 km2
Comté ou district: Rivière-du-Loup; *Population au 2011:* 1,163
Circonscription(s) électorale(s) provinciale(s): Rivière-du-Loup
Circonscription(s) électorale(s) fédérale(s): Montmagny-L'Islet-Kamouraska-Rivière-du-Loup
Prochaines élections: 3e novembre 2013
Michel Lagacé, Maire
Sanny Beaulieu, Greffière
sanny@saintcyprien.ca

Saint-Cyprien
CP 100
399, rue Principale
Saint-Cyprien-des-Etchemins, QC G0R 1B0
Tél: 418-383-5274; *Téléc:* 418-383-5269
corpmun@sogetel.net
www.st-cyprien.qc.ca
Entité municipal: Parish (Paroisse)
Incorporation: 22 février 1918 *Area:* 92,82 km2
Comté ou district: Les Etchemins; *Population au 2011:* 548
Circonscription(s) électorale(s) provinciale(s): Bellechasse
Circonscription(s) électorale(s) fédérale(s): Lévis-Bellechasse
Prochaines élections: 3e novembre 2013
Poste vacant, Maire
Pauline Fortier, Directrice générale

Saint-Cyprien-de-Napierville
121, rang Cyr
Saint-Cyprien-de-Napierville, QC J0J 1L0
Tél: 450-245-3658; *Téléc:* 450-245-7824
www.st-cypriendenapierville.ca
Entité municipal: Parish (Paroisse)
Incorporation: 1er juillet 1855 *Area:* 97,62 km2
Comté ou district: Les Jardins-de-Napierville; *Population au 2011:* 1,869
Circonscription(s) électorale(s) provinciale(s): Huntingdon
Circonscription(s) électorale(s) fédérale(s): Beauharnois-Salaberry
Prochaines élections: 3e novembre 2013
André Tremblay, Maire
Nancy Trottier, Directrice générale
ntrottier@st-cypriendenapierville.ca

Saint-Cyrille-de-Lessard
282, rue Principale
Saint-Cyrille-de-Lessard, QC G0R 2W0
Tél: 418-247-5186; *Téléc:* 418-247-7086
munstcyrille@globetrotter.net
www.st-cyrille-de-lessard.ca
Entité municipal: Parish (Paroisse)
Incorporation: 1er juillet 1855 *Area:* 228,95 km2
Comté ou district: L'Islet; *Population au 2011:* 753
Circonscription(s) électorale(s) provinciale(s): Montmagny-L'Islet
Circonscription(s) électorale(s) fédérale(s): Montmagny-L'Islet-Kamouraska-Rivière-du-Loup
Prochaines élections: 3e novembre 2013
Luc Caron, Maire
Josée Godbout, Directrice générale

Saint-Cyrille-de-Wendover
4055, rue Principale
Saint-Cyrille-de-Wendover, QC J1Z 1C8
Tél: 819-397-4226; *Téléc:* 819-397-5505
municipalite@stcyrille.qc.ca
www.stcyrille.qc.ca
Entité municipal: Municipality
Incorporation: 6 septembre 1905 *Area:* 112,24 km2
Comté ou district: Drummond; *Population au 2011:* 4,389
Circonscription(s) électorale(s) provinciale(s): Richmond
Circonscription(s) électorale(s) fédérale(s): Drummond
Prochaines élections: 3e novembre 2013
Daniel Lafond, Maire
Mario Picotin, Directeur général

Saint-Damase
115, rue St-Étienne
Saint-Damase, QC J0H 1J0
Tél: 450-797-3341; *Téléc:* 450-797-3543
svfrechette@st-damase.qc.ca
www.st-damase.qc.ca
Entité municipal: Municipality
Incorporation: 5 octobre 2001 *Area:* 79,06 km2
Comté ou district: Les Maskoutains; *Population au 2011:* 2,506
Circonscription(s) électorale(s) provinciale(s): St-Hyacinthe
Circonscription(s) électorale(s) fédérale(s): St-Hyacinthe-Bagot
Prochaines élections: 3e novembre 2013
Note: Effective October 10, 2001, the Village & Parish of St-Damase amalgamated to create the Municipality of St-Damase.
Germain Chabot, Maire
Sylvie V. Fréchette, Directrice générale

Saint-Damase-de-L'Islet
CP 10
26, rue du Village est
Saint-Damase-de-L'Islet, QC G0R 2X0
Tél: 418-598-9370; *Téléc:* 418-598-9396
stdamase3@hotmail.com
Entité municipal: Municipality
Incorporation: 9 novembre 1898 *Area:* 259,72 km2
Comté ou district: L'Islet; *Population au 2011:* 591
Circonscription(s) électorale(s) provinciale(s): Montmagny-L'Islet
Circonscription(s) électorale(s) fédérale(s): Montmagny-L'Islet-Kamouraska-Rivière-du-Loup
Prochaines élections: 3e novembre 2013
Paulette Lord, Maire
Dany Marois, Directrice générale

Saint-Damien
6850, ch Montauban
Saint-Damien, QC J0K 2E0
Tél: 888-835-3419; *Téléc:* 450-835-5538
stdamien@intermonde.net
www.st-damien.com
Entité municipal: Parish (Paroisse)
Incorporation: 6 septembre 1870 *Area:* 260,38 km2
Comté ou district: Matawinie; *Population au 2011:* 2,020
Circonscription(s) électorale(s) provinciale(s): Berthier
Circonscription(s) électorale(s) fédérale(s): Joliette
Prochaines élections: 3e novembre 2013
Yves Giard, Mairesse
Josée Tellier, Directrice générale

Saint-Damien-de-Buckland
75, rte St-Gérard
Saint-Damien-de-Buckland, QC G0R 2Y0
Tél: 418-789-2526; *Téléc:* 418-789-2125
info@saint-damien.com
www.saint-damien.com
Entité municipal: Parish (Paroisse)
Incorporation: 20 décembre 1890 *Area:* 85,17 km2
Comté ou district: Bellechasse; *Population au 2011:* 2,071
Circonscription(s) électorale(s) provinciale(s): Bellechasse
Circonscription(s) électorale(s) fédérale(s): Lévis-Bellechasse
Prochaines élections: 3e novembre 2013
Hervé Blais, Maire
Jacques Thibault, Directeur général

Saint-David
16, rue Saint-Charles
Saint-David, QC J0G 1L0
Tél: 450-789-2288; *Téléc:* 450-789-3023
stdavid@bas-richelieu.net
www.stdavid.qc.ca
Entité municipal: Municipality
Incorporation: 1er juillet 1855 *Area:* 91,08 km2
Comté ou district: Pierre-De Saurel; *Population au 2011:* 832
Circonscription(s) électorale(s) provinciale(s): Nicolet-Yamaska
Circonscription(s) électorale(s) fédérale(s):
Bas-Richelieu-Nicolet-Bécancour
Prochaines élections: 3e novembre 2013
Raymond Arel, Maire
Sylvie Letendre, Directrice générale

Saint-David-de-Falardeau
CP 130
140, boul St-David
Saint-David-de-Falardeau, QC G0V 1C0
Tél: 418-673-4647; *Téléc:* 418-673-3266
info@villefalardeau.ca
www.villefalardeau.ca
Entité municipal: Municipality
Incorporation: 1er janvier 1948 *Area:* 379,23 km2
Comté ou district: Le Fjord-du-Saguenay; *Population au 2011:* 2,657
Circonscription(s) électorale(s) provinciale(s): Dubuc
Circonscription(s) électorale(s) fédérale(s): Jonquière-Alma
Prochaines élections: 3e novembre 2013
Jean-Yves Dufour, Maire
Daniel Hudon, Directeur général

Saint-Denis
5, rte 287
Saint-Denis, QC G0L 2R0
Tél: 418-498-2968; *Téléc:* 418-498-2948
www.munstdenis.com
Entité municipal: Parish (Paroisse)
Incorporation: 1er juillet 1855 *Area:* 33,84 km2
Comté ou district: Kamouraska; *Population au 2011:* 503
Circonscription(s) électorale(s) provinciale(s):
Kamouraska-Témiscouata
Circonscription(s) électorale(s) fédérale(s):
Montmagny-L'Islet-Kamouraska-Rivière-du-Loup
Prochaines élections: 3e novembre 2013
Jean Dallaire, Mairesse
Anne Desjardins, Directrice générale
adesjardins@munstdenis.com

Saint-Denis-de-Brompton
CP 120
2050, rue Ernest-Camiré
Saint-Denis-de-Brompton, QC J0B 2P0
Tél: 819-846-2744; *Téléc:* 819-846-0915
mstdenis@videotron.ca
www.saintdenisdebrompton.com
Entité municipal: Parish (Paroisse)
Incorporation: 6 mars 1935 *Area:* 70,25 km2
Comté ou district: Le Val-St-François; *Population au 2011:* 3,402
Circonscription(s) électorale(s) provinciale(s): Johnson
Circonscription(s) électorale(s) fédérale(s): Brome-Missisquoi; Richmond-Arthabaska
Prochaines élections: 3e novembre 2013
Marc Laflamme, Sec.-Trés.
Mike Doyle, Maire

Saint-Denis-sur-Richelieu
599, ch des Patriotes
Saint-Denis-sur-Richelieu, QC J0H 1K0
Tél: 450-787-2244; *Téléc:* 450-787-2635
municipalitedestdenis@bellnet.ca
www.stdenissurrichelieu.ca
Entité municipal: Municipality
Incorporation: 24 décembre 1997 *Area:* 82,20 km2
Comté ou district: La Vallée-du-Richelieu; *Population au 2011:* 2,285
Circonscription(s) électorale(s) provinciale(s): Verchères
Circonscription(s) électorale(s) fédérale(s): Verchères-Les Patriotes
Prochaines élections: 3e novembre 2013
Jacques Villemaire, Maire
Pierre Pétrin, Directeur général

Saint-Didace
380, rue Principale
Saint-Didace, QC J0K 2G0
Tél: 450-835-4184; *Téléc:* 450-835-0602
info@saint-didace.com
www.saint-didace.com
Entité municipal: Parish (Paroisse)
Incorporation: 27 août 1863 *Area:* 99,66 km2
Comté ou district: D'Autray; *Population au 2011:* 593
Circonscription(s) électorale(s) provinciale(s): Berthier
Circonscription(s) électorale(s) fédérale(s): Berthier-Maskinongé
Prochaines élections: 3e novembre 2013
Guy Desjarlais, Maire
André Allard, Directeur général

Saint-Dominique
467, rue Deslandes
Saint-Dominique, QC J0H 1L0
Tél: 450-774-9939; *Téléc:* 450-774-1595
admin@municipalite.saint-dominique.qc.ca
www.municipalite.saint-dominique.qc.ca
Entité municipal: Municipality
Incorporation: 1er juillet 1855 *Area:* 70,16 km2
Comté ou district: Les Maskoutains; *Population au 2011:* 2,327
Circonscription(s) électorale(s) provinciale(s): St-Hyacinthe
Circonscription(s) électorale(s) fédérale(s): St-Hyacinthe-Bagot
Prochaines élections: 3e novembre 2013
Robert Houle, Maire
Diane G. Bélanger, Directrice générale

Saint-Dominique-du-Rosaire
235, rue Principale
Saint-Dominique-du-Rosaire, QC J0Y 2K0
Tél: 819-727-9544; *Téléc:* 819-727-4344
mun.stdomrosaire@cableamos.com
Entité municipal: Municipality
Incorporation: 1er janvier 1978 *Area:* 512,24 km2
Comté ou district: Abitibi; *Population au 2011:* 434
Circonscription(s) électorale(s) provinciale(s): Abitibi-Ouest
Circonscription(s) électorale(s) fédérale(s):
Abitibi-Témiscamingue
Prochaines élections: 3e novembre 2013
Maurice Godbout, Maire
Nathalie Boire, Directrice générale

Saint-Donat
CP 70
194, av du Mont-Comi
Saint-Donat-de-Rimouski, QC G0K 1L0
Tél: 418-739-4634; *Téléc:* 418-739-5003
municipalite@saintdonat.ca
www.saintdonat.ca
Entité municipal: Parish (Paroisse)
Incorporation: 10 mars 1869 *Area:* 93,23 km2
Comté ou district: La Mitis; *Population au 2011:* 890
Circonscription(s) électorale(s) provinciale(s): Matapédia
Circonscription(s) électorale(s) fédérale(s): Haute-Gaspésie-La Mitis-Matane-Matapédia
Prochaines élections: 3e novembre 2013
Michel Côté, Maire
Gil Bérubé, Directeur général

Saint-Donat
490, rue Principale
Saint-Donat, QC J0T 2C0
Tél: 819-424-2383; *Téléc:* 819-424-5020
dg@saint-donat.ca
www.saint-donat.ca
Entité municipal: Municipality
Incorporation: 19 février 1904 *Area:* 361,42 km2
Comté ou district: Matawinie; *Population au 2011:* 4,130
Circonscription(s) électorale(s) provinciale(s): Bertrand
Circonscription(s) électorale(s) fédérale(s): Joliette
Prochaines élections: 3e novembre 2013
Richard Bénard, Maire
Michel Séguin, Directeur général

Saint-Edmond-de-Grantham
1393, rue Notre-Dame-de-Lourdes
Saint-Edmond-de-Grantham, QC J0C 1K0
Tél: 819-395-2562; *Téléc:* 819-395-2666
muned@tellabaie.net
www.st-edmond-de-grantham.qc.ca
Entité municipal: Parish (Paroisse)
Incorporation: 9 février 1918 *Area:* 48,79 km2
Comté ou district: Drummond; *Population au 2011:* 673
Circonscription(s) électorale(s) provinciale(s): Drummond
Circonscription(s) électorale(s) fédérale(s): Drummond
Prochaines élections: 3e novembre 2013
Marie-Andrée Auger, Mairesse
Julie Galarneau, Directrice générale

Saint-Edmond-les-Plaines
561, ch Principale
Saint-Edmond-les-Plaines, QC G0W 2M0
Tél: 418-274-3069; *Téléc:* 418-274-5629
stedmond@destination.ca
www.stedmond.ca
Entité municipal: Municipality
Incorporation: 3 septembre 1938 *Area:* 87,15 km2
Comté ou district: Maria-Chapdelaine; *Population au 2011:* 390
Circonscription(s) électorale(s) provinciale(s): Roberval
Circonscription(s) électorale(s) fédérale(s):
Roberval-Lac-St-Jean
Prochaines élections: 3e novembre 2013
Rodrigue Cantin, Maire
Danielle Bernard, Directrice générale

Saint-Édouard
CP 120
405C, montée Lussier
Saint-Édouard, QC J0L 1Y0
Tél: 450-454-6333; *Téléc:* 450-454-4921
lucieriendeau@intermobilex.com
Entité municipal: Parish (Paroisse)
Incorporation: 1er juillet 1855 *Area:* 52,91 km2
Comté ou district: Les Jardins-de-Napierville; *Population au 2011:* 1,312
Circonscription(s) électorale(s) provinciale(s): Huntingdon
Circonscription(s) électorale(s) fédérale(s):
Beauharnois-Salaberry
Prochaines élections: 3e novembre 2013
Poste vacant, Maire
Poste vacant, Directeur général

Saint-Édouard-de-Fabre
CP 70
620, rue de l'Église
Saint-Édouard-de-Fabre, QC J0Z 1Z0
Tél: 819-634-4441; *Téléc:* 819-634-2646
municipalitefabre@mrctemiscamingue.qc.ca
Entité municipal: Parish (Paroisse)
Incorporation: 3 octobre 1912 *Area:* 216,18 km2
Comté ou district: Témiscamingue; *Population au 2011:* 649
Circonscription(s) électorale(s) provinciale(s):
Rouyn-Noranda-Témiscamingue
Circonscription(s) électorale(s) fédérale(s):
Abitibi-Témiscamingue
Prochaines élections: 3e novembre 2013
Réjean Drouin, Maire
Gérard Pétrin, Directeur général

Saint-Édouard-de-Lotbinière
105, rte Soucy
Saint-Edouard-de-Lotbinière, QC G0S 1Y0
Tél: 418-796-2971; *Téléc:* 418-796-2228
st-edouar@municipalite.st-edouard.qc.ca
www.municipalite.st-edouard.qc.ca
Entité municipal: Parish (Paroisse)
Incorporation: 1er décembre 1862 *Area:* 98,57 km2
Comté ou district: Lotbinière; *Population au 2011:* 1,248
Circonscription(s) électorale(s) provinciale(s): Lotbinière
Circonscription(s) électorale(s) fédérale(s):
Lotbinière-Chutes-de-la-Chaudière
Prochaines élections: 3e novembre 2013
Alain Soucy, Maire
Anna Blondin, Directrice générale

Saint-Édouard-de-Maskinongé
3851, rue Notre-Dame
Saint-Édouard-de-Maskinongé, QC J0K 2H0
Tél: 819-268-2833; *Téléc:* 819-268-2883
municipalitestedouard@telmilot.net
Entité municipal: Municipality
Incorporation: 1er janvier 1950 *Area:* 55,06 km2
Comté ou district: Maskinongé; *Population au 2011:* 774
Circonscription(s) électorale(s) provinciale(s): Maskinongé
Circonscription(s) électorale(s) fédérale(s): Berthier-Maskinongé
Prochaines élections: 3e novembre 2013
Denis Morin, Maire
Sylvie Vallières, Directrice générale

Saint-Élie-de-Caxton
52, ch des Loisirs
Saint-Élie, QC G0X 2N0
Tél: 819-221-2839; *Téléc:* 819-221-4039
saintelie@sogetel.com
www.saint-elie-de-caxton.com
Entité municipal: Municipality
Incorporation: 12 avril 1865 *Area:* 118,75 km2
Comté ou district: Maskinongé; *Population au 2011:* 1,676
Circonscription(s) électorale(s) provinciale(s): Maskinongé
Circonscription(s) électorale(s) fédérale(s): Berthier-Maskinongé
Prochaines élections: 3e novembre 2013
André Garant, Maire
Micheline Allard, Directrice générale

Saint-Éloi
CP 9
183, rue Principale
Saint-Éloi, QC G0L 2V0
Tél: 418-898-2734; *Téléc:* 418-898-2305
st-eloi@st-eloi.qc.ca
www.st-eloi.qc.ca
Entité municipal: Parish (Paroisse)
Incorporation: 1er juillet 1855 *Area:* 67,69 km2
Comté ou district: Les Basques; *Population au 2011:* 311
Circonscription(s) électorale(s) provinciale(s): Rivière-du-Loup
Circonscription(s) électorale(s) fédérale(s):
Rimouski-Neigette-Témiscouata-Les Basques
Prochaines élections: 3e novembre 2013
Mario St-Louis, Maire
Annie Roussel, Directrice générale

Saint-Elphege
245, rang St-Antoine
Saint-Elphege, QC J0G 1J0
Tél: 450-568-0288; *Téléc:* 450-568-0288
mun.stelphege@sogetel.net
Entité municipal: Parish (Paroisse)
Incorporation: 12 mars 1886 *Area:* 40,32 km2
Comté ou district: Nicolet-Yamaska; *Population au 2011:* 292
Circonscription(s) électorale(s) provinciale(s): Nicolet-Yamaska
Circonscription(s) électorale(s) fédérale(s):
Bas-Richelieu-Nicolet-Bécancour
Prochaines élections: 3e novembre 2013
France Dionne, Sec.-Trés.
Gérard Côté, Maire

Saint-Elzéar
CP 40
148, ch Principal
Saint-Elzéar-de-Bonaventure, QC G0C 2W0
Tél: 418-534-2611; *Téléc:* 866-499-8558
muni@saint-elzear.net
www.saint-elzear.org
Entité municipal: Municipality
Incorporation: 1er janvier 1965 *Area:* 198,75 km2
Comté ou district: Bonaventure; *Population au 2011:* 467
Circonscription(s) électorale(s) provinciale(s): Bonaventure
Circonscription(s) électorale(s) fédérale(s):
Gaspésie—Îles-de-la-Madeleine
Prochaines élections: 3e novembre 2013
Damien Arsenault, Maire
Marjolaine St-Pierre, Directrice générale

Saint-Elzéar
672, av Principale
Saint-Elzéar, QC G0S 2J0
Tél: 418-387-2534; *Téléc:* 418-387-4378
munst-elzear@nouvellebeauce.com
Entité municipal: Municipality
Incorporation: 30 novembre 1994 *Area:* 85,12 km2
Comté ou district: La Nouvelle-Beauce; *Population au 2011:* 2,107
Circonscription(s) électorale(s) provinciale(s): Beauce-Nord
Circonscription(s) électorale(s) fédérale(s): Beauce
Prochaines élections: 3e novembre 2013
Richard Lehoux, Maire
Solange Marcoux, Directrice générale

Saint-Elzér-de-Témiscouata
209, rue de l'Église
Saint-Elzér-de-Témiscouata, QC G0L 2W0
Tél: 418-854-7690; *Téléc:* 418-854-3279
admin@saintelzear.ca
Entité municipal: Municipality
Incorporation: 19 novembre 1938 *Area:* 151,54 km2
Comté ou district: Témiscouata; *Population au 2011:* 343
Circonscription(s) électorale(s) provinciale(s):
Kamouraska-Témiscouata
Circonscription(s) électorale(s) fédérale(s):
Rimouski-Neigette-Témiscouata-Les Basques
Prochaines élections: 3e novembre 2013
Réjean Deschênes, Maire
Denise Dubé, Directrice générale

Saint-Émile-de-Suffolk
299, rte des Cantons
Saint-Émile-de-Suffolk, QC J0V 1Y0
Tél: 819-426-2987; *Téléc:* 819-426-3447
admstemile@mrcpapineau.com
www.st-emile-de-suffolk.com
Entité municipal: Municipality
Incorporation: 1er janvier 1881 *Area:* 54,07 km2
Comté ou district: Papineau; *Population au 2011:* 566
Circonscription(s) électorale(s) provinciale(s): Papineau
Circonscription(s) électorale(s) fédérale(s):
Argenteuil-Papineau-Mirabel
Prochaines élections: 3e novembre 2013
Michel Samson, Maire
Gisèle Éthier, Directrice générale

Saint-Éphrem-de-Beauce
#3, 2, rue de la Clinique
Saint-Éphrem-de-Beauce, QC G0M 1R0
Tél: 418-484-5716; *Téléc:* 418-484-2305
munise@telstep.net
Entité municipal: Municipality
Incorporation: 24 décembre 1997 *Area:* 115,35 km2
Comté ou district: Beauce-Sartigan; *Population au 2011:* 2,567
Circonscription(s) électorale(s) provinciale(s): Beauce-Sud
Circonscription(s) électorale(s) fédérale(s): Beauce
Prochaines élections: 3e novembre 2013
Luc Lemieux, Maire
François Fontaine, Directeur général

Saint-Épiphane
280, rue Bernier
Saint-Épiphane, QC G0L 2X0
Tél: 418-862-0052; *Téléc:* 418-862-7753
direction@saint-epiphane.ca
www.saint-epiphane.ca
Entité municipal: Municipality
Incorporation: 1er juillet 1855 *Area:* 82,36 km2
Comté ou district: Rivière-du-Loup; *Population au 2011:* 849
Circonscription(s) électorale(s) provinciale(s): Rivière-du-Loup
Circonscription(s) électorale(s) fédérale(s):
Montmagny-L'Islet-Kamouraska-Rivière-du-Loup
Prochaines élections: 3e novembre 2013
Jean-Pierre Gratton, Maire
Nicolas Dionne, Directrice générale

Saint-Esprit
21, rue Principale
Saint-Esprit, QC J0K 2L0
Tél: 450-831-2114; *Téléc:* 450-839-6070
dg@municipalite-saint-esprit.com
www.municipalite-saint-esprit.com
Entité municipal: Municipality
Incorporation: 1er juillet 1855 *Area:* 54,36 km2
Comté ou district: Montcalm; *Population au 2011:* 1,963
Circonscription(s) électorale(s) provinciale(s): Rousseau
Circonscription(s) électorale(s) fédérale(s): Montcalm
Prochaines élections: 3e novembre 2013
Michel Brisson, Mairesse
Diane Précourt, Directrice générale

Saint-Étienne-de-Beauharnois
489, ch St-Louis
Saint-Étienne-de-Beauharnois, QC J0S 1S0
Tél: 450-225-1000; *Téléc:* 450-225-1011
stetienne@videotron.ca
www.st-etiennedebeauharnois.qc.ca
Entité municipal: Municipality
Incorporation: 1er janvier 1867 *Area:* 41,62 km2
Comté ou district: Beauharnois-Salaberry; *Population au 2011:* 806
Circonscription(s) électorale(s) provinciale(s): Beauharnois
Circonscription(s) électorale(s) fédérale(s):
Beauharnois-Salaberry
Prochaines élections: 3e novembre 2013
Louis Pouliot, Maire
Ginette Prud'Homme, Directrice générale

Saint-Étienne-de-Bolton
9, rang de la Montagne
Saint-Étienne-de-Bolton, QC J0E 2E0
Tél: 450-297-3353; *Téléc:* 450-297-0412
stetiennedebolton@axion.ca
www.sedb.qc.ca
Entité municipal: Municipality
Incorporation: 27 mai 1939 *Area:* 47,99 km2
Comté ou district: Memphrémagog; *Population au 2011:* 534
Circonscription(s) électorale(s) provinciale(s): Brome-Missisquoi
Circonscription(s) électorale(s) fédérale(s): Brome-Missisquoi
Prochaines élections: 3e novembre 2013
Pierre Patry, Maire
Pauline Desautels, Directrice générale

Saint-Étienne-des-Grès
1230, rue Principale
Saint-Étienne-des-Grès, QC G0X 2P0
Tél: 819-535-3113; *Téléc:* 819-535-1246
saint-etienne-des-gres@mun-stedg.qc.ca
www.mun-stedg.qc.ca
Entité municipal: Parish (Paroisse)
Incorporation: 14 avril 1859 *Area:* 103,52 km2
Comté ou district: Maskinongé; *Population au 2011:* 4,217
Circonscription(s) électorale(s) provinciale(s): Maskinongé
Circonscription(s) électorale(s) fédérale(s): Berthier-Maskinongé
Prochaines élections: 3e novembre 2013
Robert Landry, Maire
Nathalie Vallée, Directrice générale

Saint-Eugène
CP 120
1065, rang de l'Église
Saint-Eugène, QC J0C 1J0
Tél: 819-396-3000; *Téléc:* 819-396-3576
municipalite.steugene@xittel.ca
Entité municipal: Municipality
Incorporation: 31 octobre 1879 *Area:* 76,37 km2
Comté ou district: Drummond; *Population au 2011:* 1,131
Circonscription(s) électorale(s) provinciale(s): Drummond
Circonscription(s) électorale(s) fédérale(s): Drummond
Prochaines élections: 3e novembre 2013
Gilles Watier, Maire
Maryse Desbiens, Directrice générale

Saint-Eugène-d'Argentenay
CP 70
439, rue Principale
Saint-Eugène-d'Argentenay, QC G0W 1B0
Tél: 418-276-1787; *Téléc:* 418-276-9356
argentenay@derytele.com
Entité municipal: Municipality
Incorporation: 14 novembre 2009 *Area:* 83,37 km2
Comté ou district: Maria-Chapdelaine; *Population au 2011:* 546
Circonscription(s) électorale(s) provinciale(s): Roberval
Circonscription(s) électorale(s) fédérale(s):
Roberval-Lac-St-Jean
Prochaines élections: 1er novembre 2013
Françoise Boudreault, Mairesse
Karine Ouellet, Directrice générale

Saint-Eugène-de-Guigues
CP 1070
4, rue Notre-Dame ouest
Saint-Eugène-de-Guigues, QC J0Z 3L0
Tél: 819-785-2301; *Téléc:* 819-785-2302
munst-eugene@mrctemiscamingue.qc.ca
Entité municipal: Municipality
Incorporation: 20 novembre 1912 *Area:* 113,02 km2
Comté ou district: Témiscamingue; *Population au 2011:* 454
Circonscription(s) électorale(s) provinciale(s):
Rouyn-Noranda-Témiscamingue
Circonscription(s) électorale(s) fédérale(s):
Abitibi-Témiscamingue
Prochaines élections: 3e novembre 2013
Jacinthe Marcoux, Mairesse
Hugo Bellehumeur, Directeur général

Saint-Eugène-de-Ladrière
155, rue Principale
Saint-Eugène-de-Ladrière, QC G0L 1P0
Tél: 418-869-2582; *Téléc:* 418-869-2582
ladriere@globetrotter.net
www.ladriere.qc.ca
Entité municipal: Parish (Paroisse)
Incorporation: 1er janvier 1962 *Area:* 355,09 km2
Comté ou district: Rimouski-Neigette; *Population au 2011:* 421
Circonscription(s) électorale(s) provinciale(s): Rimouski
Circonscription(s) électorale(s) fédérale(s):

Rimouski-Neigette-Témiscouata-Les Basques
Prochaines élections: 3e novembre 2013
Gilbert Pigeon, Maire
Christiane Berger, Directrice générale

Saint-Eusèbe

222, rue Principale
Saint-Eusèbe, QC G0L 2Y0
Tél: 418-899-2762; *Téléc:* 418-899-0194
admin@sainteusebe.ca
sainteusebe.ca
Entité municipal: Parish (Paroisse)
Incorporation: 5 janvier 1911 *Area:* 120,12 km2
Comté ou district: Témiscouata; *Population au 2011:* 614
Circonscription(s) électorale(s) provinciale(s): Kamouraska-Témiscouata
Circonscription(s) électorale(s) fédérale(s): Rimouski-Neigette-Témiscouata-Les Basques
Prochaines élections: 3e novembre 2013
Gaston Chouinard, Maire
Chantal Bouchard, Directrice générale

Saint-Évariste-de-Forsyth

495, rue Principale
Saint-Évariste-de-Forsyth, QC G0M 1S0
Tél: 418-459-6488; *Téléc:* 418-459-6268
munstevar@tlb.sympatico.ca
www.st-evariste.qc.ca
Entité municipal: Municipality
Incorporation: 1er mars 1870 *Area:* 111,36 km2
Comté ou district: Beauce-Sartigan; *Population au 2011:* 525
Circonscription(s) électorale(s) provinciale(s): Beauce-Sud
Circonscription(s) électorale(s) fédérale(s): Beauce
Prochaines élections: 3e novembre 2013
Gaétan Bégin, Maire
Nathalie Poulin, Directrice générale

Saint-Fabien

CP 9
10, 7e av
Saint-Fabien, QC G0L 2Z0
Tél: 418-869-2950; *Téléc:* 418-869-3265
informations@saintfabien.net
www.saintfabien.net
Entité municipal: Parish (Paroisse)
Incorporation: 1er juillet 1855 *Area:* 128,07 km2
Comté ou district: Rimouski-Neigette; *Population au 2011:* 1,906
Circonscription(s) électorale(s) provinciale(s): Rimouski
Circonscription(s) électorale(s) fédérale(s): Rimouski-Neigette-Témiscouata-Les Basques
Prochaines élections: 3e novembre 2013
Marnie Perreault, Mairesse
Yves Galbrand, Directeur général

Saint-Fabien-de-Panet

195, rue Bilodeau
Saint-Fabien-de-Panet, QC G0R 2J0
Tél: 418-249-4471; *Téléc:* 418-249-4470
munpanet@globetrotter.net
www.stfabiendepanet.com
Entité municipal: Parish (Paroisse)
Incorporation: 26 mars 1907 *Area:* 185,31 km2
Comté ou district: Montmagny; *Population au 2011:* 992
Circonscription(s) électorale(s) provinciale(s): Montmagny-L'Islet
Circonscription(s) électorale(s) fédérale(s): Montmagny-L'Islet-Kamouraska-Rivière-du-Loup
Prochaines élections: 3e novembre 2013
Pierre Thibaudeau, Maire
Julie Lapointe, Directrice générale

Saint-Faustin-Lac-Carré

100, Place de la Mairie
Saint-Faustin-Lac-Carré, QC J0T 1J2
Tél: 819-688-2161; *Téléc:* 819-688-6791
dirgen@munipalite.stfaustin.qc.ca
www.municipalite.stfaustin.qc.ca
Entité municipal: Municipality
Incorporation: 3 janvier 1996 *Area:* 119,86 km2
Comté ou district: Les Laurentides; *Population au 2011:* 3,467
Circonscription(s) électorale(s) provinciale(s): Labelle
Circonscription(s) électorale(s) fédérale(s): Laurentides-Labelle
Prochaines élections: 3e novembre 2013
Pierre Poirier, Maire
Jacques Brisebois, Directeur général

Saint-Félix-d'Otis

455, rue Principale
Saint-Félix-d'Otis, QC G0V 1M0
Tél: 418-544-5543; *Téléc:* 418-544-9122
municipalite@st-felix-dotis.qc.ca
www.st-felix-dotis.qc.ca
Entité municipal: Municipality
Incorporation: 3 octobre 1923 *Area:* 235,94 km2
Comté ou district: Le Fjord-du-Saguenay; *Population au 2011:* 801
Circonscription(s) électorale(s) provinciale(s): Dubuc
Circonscription(s) électorale(s) fédérale(s): Chicoutimi-Le Fjord
Prochaines élections: 3e novembre 2013
Jean-Marie Claveau, Maire
Hélène Gagnon, Directrice générale

Saint-Félix-de-Dalquier

CP 219
41, rue de L'Aqueduc
Saint-Felix-de-Dalquier, QC J0Y 1G0
Tél: 819-727-1732; *Téléc:* 819-727-9685
mun.stfelixdedalquier@cableamos.com
Entité municipal: Municipality
Incorporation: 29 octobre 1932 *Area:* 112,12 km2
Comté ou district: Abitibi; *Population au 2011:* 856
Circonscription(s) électorale(s) provinciale(s): Abitibi-Ouest
Circonscription(s) électorale(s) fédérale(s): Abitibi-Témiscamingue
Prochaines élections: 3e novembre 2013
Luc Pomerleau, Maire
Richard Michaud, Directeur général

Saint-Félix-de-Kingsey

CP 30
1205, rue de l'Église
Saint-Félix-de-Kingsey, QC J0B 2T0
Tél: 819-848-2321; *Téléc:* 819-848-2202
direction.generale@saintfelixdekingsey.ca
Entité municipal: Municipality
Incorporation: 1er juillet 1855 *Area:* 125,38
Comté ou district: Drummond; *Population au 2011:* 1,563
Circonscription(s) électorale(s) provinciale(s): Richmond
Circonscription(s) électorale(s) fédérale(s): Drummond
Prochaines élections: 3e novembre 2013
Joëlle Cardonne, Mairesse
Nancy Lussier, Directrice générale

Saint-Félix-de-Valois

600, ch de Joliette
Saint-Félix-de-Valois, QC J0K 2M0
Tél: 450-889-5589; *Téléc:* 450-889-5259
municipalite@st-felix-de-valois.com
www.st-felix-de-valois.com
Entité municipal: Municipality
Incorporation: 24 décembre 1997 *Area:* 85,79 km2
Comté ou district: Matawinie; *Population au 2011:* 6,029
Circonscription(s) électorale(s) provinciale(s): Berthier
Circonscription(s) électorale(s) fédérale(s): Joliette
Prochaines élections: 3e novembre 2013
Gyslain Loyer, Maire
René Charbonneau, Directeur général

Saint-Ferdinand

821, rue Principale
Saint-Ferdinand, QC G0N 1N0
Tél: 418-428-3480; *Téléc:* 418-428-9724
info@municipalite.saint-ferdinand.qc.ca
www.municipalite.saint-ferdinand.qc.ca
Entité municipal: Municipality
Incorporation: 29 novembre 2000 *Area:* 137,07 km2
Comté ou district: L'Érable; *Population au 2011:* 2,067
Circonscription(s) électorale(s) provinciale(s): Lotbinière
Circonscription(s) électorale(s) fédérale(s): Mégantic-L'Érable
Prochaines élections: 3e novembre 2013
Donald Langlois, Maire
Sylvie Tardif, Directrice générale

Saint-Ferréol-les-Neiges

33, rue de l'Église
Saint-Ferréol-les-Neiges, QC G0A 3R0
Tél: 418-826-2253; *Téléc:* 418-826-0489
info@saintferreollesneiges.qc.ca
www.saintferreollesneiges.qc.ca
Entité municipal: Municipality
Incorporation: 1er juillet 1855 *Area:* 82,28 km2
Comté ou district: La Côte-de-Beaupré; *Population au 2011:* 2,964
Circonscription(s) électorale(s) provinciale(s): Charlevoix
Circonscription(s) électorale(s) fédérale(s): Montmorency-Charlevoix-Haute-Côte-Nord
Prochaines élections: 3e novembre 2013
Germain Tremblay, Maire
François Drouin, Directeur général

Saint-Flavien

177, rue Prinipale
Saint-Flavien, QC G0S 2M0
Tél: 418-728-4190; *Téléc:* 418-728-3775
municipalite@st-flavien.com
www.st-flavien.com
Entité municipal: Municipality
Incorporation: 29 décembre 1999 *Area:* 67,56 km2
Comté ou district: Lotbinière; *Population au 2011:* 1,578
Circonscription(s) électorale(s) provinciale(s): Lotbinière
Circonscription(s) électorale(s) fédérale(s): Lotbinière-Chutes-de-la-Chaudière
Prochaines élections: 3e novembre 2013
Roland Gagnon, Maire
Mario Roy, Directeur général

Saint-Fortunat

156, rue Principale
Saint-Fortunat, QC G0P 1G0
Tél: 819-344-5399; *Téléc:* 819-344-5399
dg.stfortunat@gmail.com
www.st-fortunat.com
Entité municipal: Municipality
Incorporation: 1er janvier 1873 *Area:* 75,520 km2
Comté ou district: Les Appalaches; *Population au 2011:* 280
Circonscription(s) électorale(s) provinciale(s): Richmond
Circonscription(s) électorale(s) fédérale(s): Mégantic-L'Érable
Prochaines élections: 3e novembre 2013
Denis Fortier, Maire
Lise Henri, Directrice générale

Saint-François-d'Assise

457, ch Central
Saint-François-d'Assise, QC G0J 2N0
Tél: 418-299-2066; *Téléc:* 418-299-3037
munstfrs@globetrotter.net
Entité municipal: Municipality
Incorporation: 3 septembre 1926 *Area:* 171,97 km2
Comté ou district: Avignon; *Population au 2011:* 706
Circonscription(s) électorale(s) provinciale(s): Bonaventure
Circonscription(s) électorale(s) fédérale(s): Gaspésie—îles-de-la-Madeleine
Prochaines élections: 1er novembre 2013
Pauline Gallant, Sec.-Trés.
Michaud Ghislain, Maire

Saint-François-de-l'Ile-d'Orléans

337, ch Royal
Saint-François, QC G0A 3S0
Tél: 418-829-3100; *Téléc:* 418-829-1004
info@msfio.ca
www.msfio.ca
Entité municipal: Municipality
Incorporation: 1er juillet 1855 *Area:* 30,76 km2
Comté ou district: L'Ile-d'Orléans; *Population au 2011:* 527
Circonscription(s) électorale(s) provinciale(s): Montmorency
Circonscription(s) électorale(s) fédérale(s): Montmorency-Charlevoix-Haute-Côte-Nord
Prochaines élections: 3e novembre 2013
Lina Labbé, Maire
Marco Langlois, Directeur général

Saint-François-de-la-Rivière-du-Sud

534, ch St-François ouest
St-François-de-la-Riv.-du-Sud, QC G0R 3A0
Tél: 418-259-7228; *Téléc:* 418-259-2056
munist-frs@globetrotter.net
stfrancoisdelarivieredusud.com
Entité municipal: Municipality
Incorporation: 1er juillet 1855 *Area:* 95,49 km2
Comté ou district: Montmagny; *Population au 2011:* 1,596
Circonscription(s) électorale(s) provinciale(s): Montmagny-L'Islet
Circonscription(s) électorale(s) fédérale(s): Montmagny-L'Islet-Kamouraska-Rivière-du-Loup
Prochaines élections: 3e novembre 2013
Yves Laflamme, Maire
Yves Laflamme, Directeur général

Saint-François-de-Sales

541, rue Principale
Saint-François-de-Sales, QC G0W 1M0
Tél: 418-348-6736; *Téléc:* 418-348-9439
municipalite@stfrancoisdesales.qc.ca
Entité municipal: Municipality
Incorporation: 14 mai 1888 *Area:* 200,56 km2
Comté ou district: Le Domaine-du-Roy; *Population au 2011:* 654
Circonscription(s) électorale(s) provinciale(s): Roberval
Circonscription(s) électorale(s) fédérale(s): Roberval-Lac-St-Jean
Prochaines élections: 3e novembre 2013
Louis-Joseph Gagnon, Maire
Renaud Blanchette, Directeur général

Saint-François-du-Lac
CP 60
400, rue Notre-Dame
Saint-François-du-Lac, QC J0G 1M0
Tél: 450-568-2124; *Téléc:* 450-568-7465
municipalite@saint-francois-du-lac.ca
www.saint-francois-du-lac.ca
Entité municipal: Municipality
Incorporation: 31 décembre 1997 *Area:* 63,11 km2
Comté ou district: Nicolet-Yamaska; *Population au 2011:* 1,957
Circonscription(s) électorale(s) provinciale(s): Nicolet-Yamaska
Circonscription(s) électorale(s) fédérale(s):
Bas-Richelieu-Nicolet-Bécancour
Prochaines élections: 3e novembre 2013
Georgette Critchley, Mairesse
Peggy Péloquin, Directrice générale

Saint-François-Xavier-de-Brompton
CP 10
94, rue Principale
St-François-Xavier-de-Brompton, QC J0B 2V0
Tél: 819-845-3954; *Téléc:* 819-845-7711
info@sfxb.qc.ca
www.municipalite.sfxb.qc.ca
Entité municipal: Parish (Paroisse)
Incorporation: 28 décembre 1887 *Area:* 96,11 km2
Comté ou district: Le Val-St-François; *Population au 2011:* 2,101
Circonscription(s) électorale(s) provinciale(s): Johnson
Circonscription(s) électorale(s) fédérale(s):
Richmond-Arthabaska
Prochaines élections: 3e novembre 2013
Claude Sylvian, Maire
Sylvie Champagne, Directrice générale

Saint-François-Xavier-de-Viger
123, rue Principale
Saint-François-Xavier-de-Viger, QC G0L 3C0
Tél: 418-497-2302; *Téléc:* 418-497-2302
munstfrancois@munstfrancoisxv.qc.ca
Entité municipal: Municipality
Incorporation: 1er janvier 1950 *Area:* 110,19 km2
Comté ou district: Rivière-du-Loup; *Population au 2011:* 256
Circonscription(s) électorale(s) provinciale(s): Rivière-du-Loup
Circonscription(s) électorale(s) fédérale(s):
Montmagny-L'Islet-Kamourask-Rivière-du-Loup
Prochaines élections: 3e novembre 2013
Yvon Caron, Maire
Yvette Beaulieu, Directrice générale

Saint-Frédéric
850, rue de l'Hôtel-de-Ville
Saint-Frédéric, QC G0N 1P0
Tél: 418-426-3357; *Téléc:* 418-426-1259
municipal@saint-frederic.com
www.saint-frederic.com
Entité municipal: Parish (Paroisse)
Incorporation: 1er juillet 1855 *Area:* 71,58 km2
Comté ou district: Robert-Cliche; *Population au 2011:* 1,085
Circonscription(s) électorale(s) provinciale(s): Beauce-Nord
Circonscription(s) électorale(s) fédérale(s): Beauce
Prochaines élections: 3e novembre 2013
Henri Gagné, Maire
Cathy Poulin, Directrice générale

Saint-Fulgence
253, rue du Saguenay
Saint-Fulgence, QC G0V 1S0
Tél: 418-674-2588; *Téléc:* 418-673-2116
admin@ville.st-fulgence.qc.ca
www.ville.st-fulgence.qc.ca
Entité municipal: Municipality
Incorporation: 1er mai 1973 *Area:* 354,68 km2
Comté ou district: Le Fjord-du-Saguenay; *Population au 2011:* 1,949
Circonscription(s) électorale(s) provinciale(s): Dubuc
Circonscription(s) électorale(s) fédérale(s): Chicoutimi-Le Fjord
Prochaines élections: 3e novembre 2013
Gilbert Simard, Maire
Daniel Gaudreault, Directeur général

Saint-Gabriel
45, rue Beausoleil
Saint-Gabriel, QC J0K 2N0
Tél: 450-835-2212; *Téléc:* 450-835-9852
mairie@ville.stgabriel.qc.ca
Entité municipal: Town
Incorporation: 17 décembre 1892 *Area:* 2,9 km2
Comté ou district: D'Autray; *Population au 2011:* 2,844
Circonscription(s) électorale(s) provinciale(s): Berthier
Circonscription(s) électorale(s) fédérale(s): Berthier-Maskinongé
Prochaines élections: 3e novembre 2013
Gaétan Gravel, Maire
Michel St-Laurent, Greffier & Directeur général

Saint-Gabriel-de-Brandon
5111, ch du Lac
Saint-Gabriel-de-Brandon, QC J0K 2N0
Tél: 450-835-3494; *Téléc:* 450-835-3495
info@munstgab.com
Entité municipal: Parish (Paroisse)
Incorporation: 30 juin 1864 *Area:* 95,87 km2
Comté ou district: D'Autray; *Population au 2011:* 2,679
Circonscription(s) électorale(s) provinciale(s): Berthier
Circonscription(s) électorale(s) fédérale(s): Berthier-Maskinongé
Prochaines élections: 3e novembre 2013
Roch Desrosiers, Maire
Jeanne Pelland, Directrice générale

Saint-Gabriel-de-Rimouski
248, rue Principale
Saint-Gabriel-de-Rimouski, QC G0K 1M0
Tél: 418-798-4938; *Téléc:* 418-798-4108
stgabriel@mitis.qc.ca
www.municipalite.saint-gabriel-de-rimouski.qc.ca
Entité municipal: Municipality
Incorporation: 7 janvier 1989 *Area:* 132,10 km2
Comté ou district: La Mitis; *Population au 2011:* 1,180
Circonscription(s) électorale(s) provinciale(s): Matapédia
Circonscription(s) électorale(s) fédérale(s): Haute-Gaspésie-La Mitis-Matane-Matapédia
Prochaines élections: 3e novembre 2013
Georges Deschenes, Maire
Martin Norman, Directeur générale

Saint-Gabriel-de-Valcartier
1743, boul Valcartier
Saint-Gabriel-de-Valcartier, QC G0A 4S0
Tél: 418-844-1218; *Téléc:* 418-844-3030
admin@munsgdv.ca
www.saint-gabriel-de-valcartier.ca
Entité municipal: Municipality
Incorporation: 5 octobre 1985 *Area:* 441,17 km2
Comté ou district: La Jacques-Cartier; *Population au 2011:* 2,933
Circonscription(s) électorale(s) provinciale(s): Chauveau
Circonscription(s) électorale(s) fédérale(s):
Portneuf-Jacques-Cartier
Prochaines élections: 3e novembre 2013
Brent Montgomery, Maire
Joan Sheehan, Directrice générale

Saint-Gabriel-Lalemant
12, ave des Érables
Saint-Gabriel-Lalemant, QC G0L 3E0
Tél: 418-852-2801; *Téléc:* 418-852-3390
munstgab@videotron.ca
www.saintgabriellalemant.qc.ca
Entité municipal: Municipality
Incorporation: 27 mai 1939 *Area:* 80,49 km2
Comté ou district: Kamouraska; *Population au 2011:* 799
Circonscription(s) électorale(s) provinciale(s):
Kamouraska-Témiscouata
Circonscription(s) électorale(s) fédérale(s):
Montmagny-L'Islet-Kamouraska-Rivière-du-Loup
Prochaines élections: 3e novembre 2013
Raymond Chouinard, Maire
Kathy Lévesque, Directrice générale

Saint-Gédéon
208, rue De Quen
Saint-Gédéon, QC G0W 2P0
Tél: 418-345-8001; *Téléc:* 418-345-2306
mairie@ville.st-gedeon.qc.ca
www.ville.st-gedeon.qc.ca
Entité municipal: Municipality
Incorporation: 6 décembre 1975 *Area:* 64,17 km2
Comté ou district: Lac-St-Jean-Est; *Population au 2011:* 2,001
Circonscription(s) électorale(s) provinciale(s): Lac-St-Jean
Circonscription(s) électorale(s) fédérale(s):
Roberval-Lac-St-Jean
Prochaines élections: 3e novembre 2013
Jean-Paul Boucher, Maire
Dany Dallaire, Directeur général

Saint-Gédéon-de-Beauce
102 - 1re av sud
Saint-Gédéon-de-Beauce, QC G0M 1T0
Tél: 418-582-3341; *Téléc:* 418-582-6016
stgedeon@globetrotter.net
www.st-gedeon-de-beauce.qc.ca
Entité municipal: Municipality
Incorporation: 12 février 1003 *Area:* 193,45 km2
Comté ou district: Beauce-Sartigan; *Population au 2011:* 2,277
Circonscription(s) électorale(s) provinciale(s): Beauce-Sud
Circonscription(s) électorale(s) fédérale(s): Beauce
Prochaines élections: 3e novembre 2013
Note: Effective October 12, 2003, the Municipality of St-Gédéon-de-Beauce & the Parish of St-Gédéon amalgamated to create the new Municipality of St-Gédéon-de-Beauce.
Eric Lachance, Maire
Pierre-Alain Pelchat, Directeur général

Saint-Georges-de-Clarenceville
1350, ch Middle
Saint-Georges-de-Clarenceville, QC J0J 1B0
Tél: 450-294-2464; *Téléc:* 450-294-2016
st-georges@qc.aira.com
Entité municipal: Municipality
Incorporation: 27 décembre 1989 *Area:* 63,76 km2
Comté ou district: Le Haut-Richelieu; *Population au 2011:* 1,056
Circonscription(s) électorale(s) provinciale(s): Iberville
Circonscription(s) électorale(s) fédérale(s): Brome-Missisquoi
Prochaines élections: 3e novembre 2013
Louis Hak, Maire
Thérèse Lacombe, Directrice générale

Saint-Georges-de-Windsor
485, rue Principale
Saint-Georges-de-Windsor, QC J0A 1J0
Tél: 819-828-2716; *Téléc:* 819-828-0213
mungeorges@cgocable.ca
Entité municipal: Municipality
Incorporation: 30 novembre 2009 *Area:* 126,57 km2
Comté ou district: Les Sources; *Population au 2011:* 911
Circonscription(s) électorale(s) provinciale(s): Richmond
Circonscription(s) électorale(s) fédérale(s):
Richmond-Arthabaska
Prochaines élections: 3e novembre 2013
René Perreault, Maire
Armande Perreault, Directrice générale

Saint-Gérard-Majella
435, rang St-Antoine
Saint-Gérard-Majella, QC J0G 1X0
Tél: 450-789-5777; *Téléc:* 450-789-1188
info@munistgerardmajella.com
Entité municipal: Parish (Paroisse)
Incorporation: 18 février 1907 *Area:* 37,81 km2
Comté ou district: Pierre-De Saurel; *Population au 2011:* 246
Circonscription(s) électorale(s) provinciale(s): Nicolet-Yamaska
Circonscription(s) électorale(s) fédérale(s):
Bas-Richelieu-Nicolet-Bécancour
Prochaines élections: 3e novembre 2013
Charles Lachapelle, Maire
Anny Boisjoli, Directeur général

Saint-Germain
146, rang des Côtes
Saint-Germain, QC G0L 3G0
Tél: 418-492-9771; *Téléc:* 418-492-9772
Entité municipal: Parish (Paroisse)
Incorporation: 29 juin 1893 *Area:* 26,70 km2
Comté ou district: Kamouraska; *Population au 2011:* 280
Circonscription(s) électorale(s) provinciale(s):
Kamouraska-Témiscouata
Circonscription(s) électorale(s) fédérale(s):
Montmagny-L'Islet-Kamouraska-Rivière-du-Loup
Prochaines élections: 3e novembre 2013
Daniel Laplante, Maire
Hélène B.-Bernier, Directrice générale
berubehelene@videotron.ca

Saint-Germain-de-Grantham
233, ch Yamaska
Saint-Germain-de-Grantham, QC J0C 1K0
Tél: 819-395-5496; *Téléc:* 819-395-5200
municipalitestgermain@cgocable.ca
www.st-germain.info
Entité municipal: Municipality
Incorporation: 22 février 1995 *Area:* 86,29 km2
Comté ou district: Drummond; *Population au 2011:* 4,551
Circonscription(s) électorale(s) provinciale(s): Drummond
Circonscription(s) électorale(s) fédérale(s): Drummond
Prochaines élections: 3e novembre 2013
Yvon Nault, Maire
Danielle Smith Gauthier, Directrice générale

Saint-Gervais
CP 9
150, rue Principale
Saint-Gervais, QC G0R 3C0
Tél: 418-887-6116; *Téléc:* 418-887-6312
mungerv@globetrotter.net
www.saint-gervais.ca
Entité municipal: Municipality
Incorporation: 1er juillet 1855 *Area:* 87,23 km2

Comté ou district: Bellechasse; *Population au 2011:* 2,058
Circonscription(s) électorale(s) provinciale(s): Bellechasse
Circonscription(s) électorale(s) fédérale(s): Lévis-Bellechasse
Prochaines élections: 3e novembre 2013
Gilles Nadeau, Maire
Patrick Côté, Directeur général

Saint-Gilbert

110, rue Principale
Saint-Gilbert, QC G0A 3T0
Tél: 418-268-8194; *Téléc:* 418-268-6466
saint-gilbert@globetrotter.net
www.municipalite.saint-gilbert.qc.ca
Entité municipal: Parish (Paroisse)
Incorporation: 27 avril 1893 *Area:* 36,95 km2
Comté ou district: Portneuf; *Population au 2011:* 282
Circonscription(s) électorale(s) provinciale(s): Portneuf
Circonscription(s) électorale(s) fédérale(s):
Portneuf-Jacques-Cartier
Prochaines élections: 3e novembre 2013
Luc Gignac, Maire
Réjeanne Plamondon, Directrice générale

Saint-Gilles

1540, rue Principale
Saint-Gilles, QC G0S 2P0
Tél: 418-888-3198; *Téléc:* 418-888-5145
info@stgilles.net
www.st-gilles.qc.ca
Entité municipal: Parish (Paroisse)
Incorporation: 1er juillet 1855 *Area:* 174,74 km2
Comté ou district: Lotbinière; *Population au 2011:* 2,138
Circonscription(s) électorale(s) provinciale(s): Lotbinière
Circonscription(s) électorale(s) fédérale(s):
Lotbinière-Chutes-de-la-Chaudière
Prochaines élections: 3e novembre 2013
Robert Samson, Maire
Lucie-Marie De Blois, Directrice générale

Saint-Godefroi

CP 157
109C, rte 132
Saint-Godefroi, QC G0C 3C0
Tél: 418-752-6316; *Téléc:* 418-752-6396
stgodefroi@navigue.com
Entité municipal: Township
Incorporation: 16 décembre 1913 *Area:* 60,32 km2
Comté ou district: Bonaventure; *Population au 2011:* 405
Circonscription(s) électorale(s) provinciale(s): Bonaventure
Circonscription(s) électorale(s) fédérale(s):
Gaspésie—îles-de-la-Madeleine
Prochaines élections: 3e novembre 2013
Gérard-Raymond Blais, Maire
Céline Roussy, Directrice générale

Saint-Guillaume

106, rue St-Jean-Baptiste
Saint-Guillaume, QC J0C 1L0
Tél: 819-396-2403; *Téléc:* 819-396-0184
municipalite.st-guillaume@tellabaie.net
www.municipalite-st-guillaume.qc.ca
Entité municipal: Municipality
Incorporation: 8 novembre 1995 *Area:* 86,83 km2
Comté ou district: Drummond; *Population au 2011:* 1,547
Circonscription(s) électorale(s) provinciale(s): Nicolet-Yamaska
Circonscription(s) électorale(s) fédérale(s): Drummond
Prochaines élections: 3e novembre 2013
Jean-Pierre Vallée, Maire
Gaétan Bellerose, Directeur général

Saint-Guy

52, rue Principal
Saint-Guy, QC G0K 1W0
Tél: 418-963-2601; *Téléc:* 418-963-2601
admin@st-guy.qc.ca
Entité municipal: Municipality
Incorporation: 1er janvier 1958 *Area:* 140,09 km2
Comté ou district: Les Basques; *Population au 2011:* 91
Circonscription(s) électorale(s) provinciale(s): Rivière-du-Loup
Circonscription(s) électorale(s) fédérale(s):
Rimouski-Neigette-Témiscouata-Les Basques
Prochaines élections: 3e novembre 2013
Roger Rioux, Maire
Marie-Eve Chouinard, Directrice générale

Saint-Henri

219, rue Commerciale
Saint-Henri, QC G0R 3E0
Tél: 418-882-2401; *Téléc:* 418-882-0302
munhenri@globetrotter.net
www.municipalite.saint-henri.qc.ca
Entité municipal: Municipality
Incorporation: 9 octobre 1976 *Area:* 121,78 km2
Comté ou district: Bellechasse; *Population au 2011:* 5,023
Circonscription(s) électorale(s) provinciale(s): Bellechasse
Circonscription(s) électorale(s) fédérale(s): Lévis-Bellechasse
Prochaines élections: 3e novembre 2013
Yvon Bruneau, Maire
Jacques Risler, Directeur général

Saint-Henri-de-Taillon

401, rue de l'Hôtel-de-Ville
Saint-Henri-de-Taillon, QC G0W 2X0
Tél: 418-347-3243; *Téléc:* 418-347-1138
municipalite@ville.st-henri-de-taillon.qc.ca
www.ville.st-henri-de-taillon.qc.ca
Entité municipal: Municipality
Incorporation: 12 août 1903 *Area:* 62,95 km2
Comté ou district: Lac-St-Jean-Est; *Population au 2011:* 760
Circonscription(s) électorale(s) provinciale(s): Lac-St-Jean
Circonscription(s) électorale(s) fédérale(s):
Roberval-Lac-St-Jean
Prochaines élections: 3e novembre 2013
André Paradis, Maire
Rachel Bourget, Directrice générale

Saint-Herménégilde

776, rue Principale
Saint-Herménégilde, QC J0B 2W0
Tél: 819-849-4443; *Téléc:* 819-849-6924
municipalite@st-hermenegilde.qc.ca
www.st-hermenegilde.qc.ca
Entité municipal: Municipality
Incorporation: 12 octobre 1985 *Area:* 169,90 km2
Comté ou district: Coaticook; *Population au 2011:* 702
Circonscription(s) électorale(s) provinciale(s):
Mégantic-Compton
Circonscription(s) électorale(s) fédérale(s): Compton-Stanstead
Prochaines élections: 3e novembre 2013
Lucie Tremblay, Mairesse
Nathalie Isabelle, Directrice générale

Saint-Hilaire-de-Dorset

847, rue Principale
Saint-Hilaire-de-Dorset, QC G0M 1G0
Tél: 418-459-6872; *Téléc:* 418-459-6882
munsthilaire@hotmail.com
Entité municipal: Parish (Paroisse)
Incorporation: 12 avril 1916 *Area:* 252,52 km2
Comté ou district: Beauce-Sartigan; *Population au 2011:* 50
Circonscription(s) électorale(s) provinciale(s): Beauce-Sud
Circonscription(s) électorale(s) fédérale(s): Beauce
Prochaines élections: 3e novembre 2013
Jérôme Lacroix, Maire
Johanne Jacques, Directrice générale

Saint-Hilarion

306, ch Cartier Nord
Saint-Hilarion, QC G0A 3V0
Tél: 418-457-3463; *Téléc:* 418-457-3805
municipalite@sainthilarion.ca
Entité municipal: Parish (Paroisse)
Incorporation: 1er juillet 1855 *Area:* 97,77 km2
Comté ou district: Charlevoix; *Population au 2011:* 1,181
Circonscription(s) électorale(s) provinciale(s): Charlevoix
Circonscription(s) électorale(s) fédérale(s):
Montmorency-Charlevoix-Haute-Côte-du-Loup
Prochaines élections: 3e novembre 2013
Rosaire Lavoie, Maire
Madeleine Tremblay, Directrice générale

Saint-Hippolyte

2253, ch des Hauteurs
Saint-Hippolyte, QC J8A 1A1
Tél: 450-563-2505; *Téléc:* 450-563-2362
municipalite@saint-hippolyte.ca
www.saint-hippolyte.ca
Entité municipal: Parish (Paroisse)
Incorporation: 1er juillet 1855 *Area:* 121,19 km2
Comté ou district: La Rivière-du-Nord; *Population au 2011:*
8,083
Circonscription(s) électorale(s) provinciale(s): Bertrand
Circonscription(s) électorale(s) fédérale(s): Rivière-du-Nord
Prochaines élections: 3e novembre 2013
Bruno Laroche, Maire
Christiane Côté, Directrice générale

Saint-Honoré

3611, boul Martel
Saint-Honoré, QC G0V 1L0
Tél: 418-673-3405; *Téléc:* 418-673-3871
admin@ville.sthonore.qc.ca
www.ville.sthonore.qc.ca
Entité municipal: Municipality
Incorporation: 16 décembre 1972 *Area:* 189,82 km2
Comté ou district: Le Fjord-du-Saguenay; *Population au 2011:*
5,257
Circonscription(s) électorale(s) provinciale(s): Dubuc
Circonscription(s) électorale(s) fédérale(s): Chicoutimi-Le Fjord
Prochaines élections: 3e novembre 2013
Marie-Luce Demers-Martin, Mairesse
Stéphane Leclerc, Directeur général

Saint-Honoré-de-Shenley

CP 128
499, rue Principale
Saint-Honoré-de-Shenley, QC G0M 1V0
Tél: 418-485-6738; *Téléc:* 418-485-6171
st.honore@tlb.sympatico.ca
www.sthonoredeshenley.com
Entité municipal: Municipality
Incorporation: 19 avril 2000 *Area:* 136,46 km2
Comté ou district: Beauce-Sartigan; *Population au 2011:* 1,610
Circonscription(s) électorale(s) provinciale(s): Beauce-Sud
Circonscription(s) électorale(s) fédérale(s): Beauce
Prochaines élections: 3e novembre 2013
Herman Bolduc, Maire
Edith Quirion, Directrice générale

Saint-Honoré-de-Témiscouata

99, rue Principale
Saint-Honoré-de-Témiscouata, QC G0L 3K0
Tél: 418-497-2588; *Téléc:* 418-497-1656
admin@sainthonoredetemiscouata.ca
www.sainthonoredetemiscouata.ca
Entité municipal: Municipality
Incorporation: 1er janvier 1881 *Area:* 251,58 km2
Comté ou district: Témiscouata; *Population au 2011:* 780
Circonscription(s) électorale(s) provinciale(s):
Kamouraska-Témiscouata
Circonscription(s) électorale(s) fédérale(s):
Rimouski-Neigette-Témiscouata-Les Basques
Prochaines élections: 3e novembre 2013
Marin Lebel, Maire
Lucie April, Directrice générale

Saint-Hubert-Rivière-du-Loup

CP 218
10, rue Saint-Rosaire
Saint-Hubert-Rivière-du-Loup, QC G0L 3L0
Tél: 418-497-3394; *Téléc:* 418-497-1187
mun.st-hubert@sthubertrdl.qc.ca
www.municipalite.saint-hubert-de-riviere-du-loup.qc.ca
Entité municipal: Municipality
Incorporation: 4 janvier 1894 *Area:* 183,99 km2
Comté ou district: Rivière-du-Loup; *Population au 2011:* 1,235
Circonscription(s) électorale(s) provinciale(s): Rivière-du-Loup
Circonscription(s) électorale(s) fédérale(s):
Montmagney-L'Islet-Kamouraska-Rivière-du-Loup
Prochaines élections: 3e novembre 2013
Napoléon Lévesque, Maire
Sylvie Samson, Directrice générale

Saint-Hugues

508, rue Notre-Dame
Saint-Hugues, QC J0H 1N0
Tél: 450-794-2030; *Téléc:* 450-794-2474
munst-huguesdirection@mrcmaskoutains.qc.ca
www.saint-hugues.com
Entité municipal: Municipality
Incorporation: 6 novembre 1982 *Area:* 89,39 km2
Comté ou district: Les Maskoutains; *Population au 2011:* 1,292
Circonscription(s) électorale(s) provinciale(s): St-Hyacinthe
Circonscription(s) électorale(s) fédérale(s): St-Hyacinthe-Bagot
Prochaines élections: 3e novembre 2013
Serge Picard, Maire
Yolande Simoneau, Directrice générale

Saint-Ignace-de-Loyola

25, rue Laforest
Saint-Ignace-de-Loyola, QC J0K 2P0
Tél: 450-836-3376; *Téléc:* 450-836-1400
st.ignace.loyola@intermonde.net
www.stignacedeloyola.qc.ca
Entité municipal: Parish (Paroisse)
Incorporation: 11 février 1897 *Area:* 30,76 km2
Comté ou district: D'Autray; *Population au 2011:* 2,086
Circonscription(s) électorale(s) provinciale(s): Berthier
Circonscription(s) électorale(s) fédérale(s): Berthier-Maskinongé
Prochaines élections: 3e novembre 2013
Jean-Luc Barthe, Maire
Fabrice St-Martin, Directeur général

Saint-Ignace-de-Stanbridge
678, rang de l'Église nord
Saint-Ignace-de-Stanbridge, QC J0J 1Y0
Tél: 450-296-4467; *Téléc:* 450-296-4461
stignace@citenet.net
www.saint-ignace-de-stanbridge.com
Entité municipal: Parish (Paroisse)
Incorporation: 21 mars 1889 *Area:* 69,33 km2
Comté ou district: Brome-Missisquoi; *Population au 2011:* 638
Circonscription(s) électorale(s) provinciale(s): Brome-Missisquoi
Circonscription(s) électorale(s) fédérale(s): Brome-Missisquoi
Prochaines élections: 3e novembre 2013
Albert Santerre, Maire
Mélanie Thibault, Directrice générale

Saint-Irénée
475, rue Principale
Saint-Irénée, QC G0T 1V0
Tél: 418-620-5015; *Téléc:* 418-620-5017
dg@saintirenee.ca
www.saintirenee.ca
Entité municipal: Parish (Paroisse)
Incorporation: 1er juillet 1855 *Area:* 60,29 km2
Comté ou district: Charlevoix-Est; *Population au 2011:* 674
Circonscription(s) électorale(s) provinciale(s): Charlevoix
Circonscription(s) électorale(s) fédérale(s):
Montmorency-Charlevoix-Haute-Côte-Nord
Prochaines élections: 3e novembre 2013
Pierre Boudreault, Maire
Marie-Claude Lavoie, Directrice générale

Saint-Isidore
671, rue St-Régis
Saint-Isidore, QC J0L 2A0
Tél: 450-454-3919; *Téléc:* 450-454-7485
www.municipalite.saint-isidore.qc.ca
Entité municipal: Parish (Paroisse)
Incorporation: 1er juillet 1855 *Area:* 52,00 km2
Comté ou district: Roussillon; *Population au 2011:* 2,581
Circonscription(s) électorale(s) provinciale(s): Châteauguay
Circonscription(s) électorale(s) fédérale(s): Châteauguay-St Constant
Prochaines élections: 3e novembre 2013
Gilles Yelle, Maire
Daniel Vinet, Directeur général
daniel.vinet@municipalite.saint-isidore.qc.ca

Saint-Isidore
128, route Coulombe
Saint-Isidore, QC G0S 2S0
Tél: 418-882-5670; *Téléc:* 418-882-5902
info@saint-isidore.net
www.saint-isidore.net
Entité municipal: Municipality
Incorporation: 22 septembre 1993 *Area:* 101,18 km2
Comté ou district: La Nouvelle-Beauce; *Population au 2011:* 2,947
Circonscription(s) électorale(s) provinciale(s): Beauce-Nord
Circonscription(s) électorale(s) fédérale(s): Beauce
Prochaines élections: 3e novembre 2013
Réal Turgeon, Maire
Louise Trachy, Directrice générale

Saint-Isidore-de-Clifton
66, ch Auckland
Saint-Isidore-de-Clifton, QC J0B 2X0
Tél: 819-658-3637; *Téléc:* 819-658-9070
Bureau.StIsidoredeclifton@hsfqc.ca
www.st-isidore-clifton.qc.ca
Entité municipal: Municipality
Incorporation: 24 décembre 1997 *Area:* 178,43 km2
Comté ou district: Le Haut-St-François; *Population au 2011:* 716
Circonscription(s) électorale(s) provinciale(s):
Mégantic-Compton
Circonscription(s) électorale(s) fédérale(s): Compton-Stanstead
Prochaines élections: 3e novembre 2013
André Perron, Maire
Gaétan Perron, Directeur général

Saint-Jacques
16, rue Maréchal
Saint-Jacques, QC J0K 2R0
Tél: 450-839-3671; *Téléc:* 450-839-2387
info@st-jacques.org
www.st-jacques.org
Entité municipal: Municipality
Incorporation: 20 mai 1998 *Area:* 64,69 km2
Comté ou district: Montcalm; *Population au 2011:* 4,021
Circonscription(s) électorale(s) provinciale(s): Joliette
Circonscription(s) électorale(s) fédérale(s): Montcalm
Prochaines élections: 3e novembre 2013
Pierre Beaulieu, Maire
Josée Favreau, Directrice générale

Saint-Jacques-de-Leeds
355, rue Principale
Saint-Jacques-de-Leeds, QC G0N 1J0
Tél: 418-424-3321; *Téléc:* 418-424-0126
mun.leeds@cableeds.com
www.stjacquesdeleeds.com
Entité municipal: Municipality
Incorporation: 23 septembre 1929 *Area:* 81,830 km2
Comté ou district: Les Appalaches; *Population au 2011:* 711
Circonscription(s) électorale(s) provinciale(s): Frontenac
Circonscription(s) électorale(s) fédérale(s): Mégantic-L'Érable
Prochaines élections: 3e novembre 2013
Philippe Chabot, Maire
Nathalie Laflamme, Directrice générale

Saint-Jacques-le-Majeur-de-Wolfstown
877, rte 263
Saint-Jacques-le-Majeur, QC G0N 1E0
Tél: 418-449-1531; *Téléc:* 418-449-1876
stjacqueslemajeur@hotmail.com
Entité municipal: Parish (Paroisse)
Incorporation: 30 septembre 1909 *Area:* 59,330 km2
Comté ou district: Les Appalaches; *Population au 2011:* 189
Circonscription(s) électorale(s) provinciale(s): Frontenac
Circonscription(s) électorale(s) fédérale(s): Mégantic-L'Érable
Prochaines élections: 3e novembre 2013
Steven Laprise, Maire
France Moisan, Directrice générale

Saint-Jacques-le-Mineur
91, rue Principale
Saint-Jacques-le-Mineur, QC J0J 1Z0
Tél: 450-347-5446; *Téléc:* 450-347-5754
info@sjlm.ca
Entité municipal: Parish (Paroisse)
Incorporation: 1er juillet 1855 *Area:* 65,19 km2
Comté ou district: Les Jardins-de-Napierville; *Population au 2011:* 1,672
Circonscription(s) électorale(s) provinciale(s): Huntingdon
Circonscription(s) électorale(s) fédérale(s):
Beauharnois-Salaberry
Prochaines élections: 3e novembre 2013
Lise Trotter, Mairesse
Jean-Pierre Cayer, Directeur général

Saint-Janvier-de-Joly
729, rue des Loisirs
Saint-Janvier-de-Joly, QC G0S 1M0
Tél: 418-728-2984; *Téléc:* 418-728-2997
joly33065@globetrotter.net
www.municipalitedejoly.com
Entité municipal: Municipality
Incorporation: 1er janvier 1944 *Area:* 109,86 km2
Comté ou district: Lotbinière; *Population au 2011:* 968
Circonscription(s) électorale(s) provinciale(s): Lotbinière
Circonscription(s) électorale(s) fédérale(s):
Lotbinière-Chutes-de-la-Chaudière
Prochaines élections: 3e novembre 2013
Bernard Fortier, Maire
Céline Biron, Directrice générale

Saint-Jean-Baptiste
3041, rue Principale
Saint-Jean-Baptiste, QC J0L 2B0
Tél: 450-467-3456; *Téléc:* 450-467-8813
info@msjb.qc.ca
www.msjb.qc.ca
Entité municipal: Municipality
Incorporation: 1er juillet 1855 *Area:* 75,98 km2
Comté ou district: La Vallée-du-Richelieu; *Population au 2011:* 3,191
Circonscription(s) électorale(s) provinciale(s): 2006uas
Circonscription(s) électorale(s) fédérale(s): Chambly-Borduas
Prochaines élections: 3e novembre 2013
Jacques Durand, Maire
Denis Meunier, Directeur général

Saint-Jean-de-Brébeuf
844, rue de l'Église
Saint-Jean-de-Brébeuf, QC G6G 0A1
Tél: 418-453-7774; *Téléc:* 418-453-2339
stjeandebrebeuf@bellnet.ca
Entité municipal: Municipality
Incorporation: 1er janvier 1946 *Area:* 79,680 km2
Comté ou district: Les Appalaches; *Population au 2011:* 359
Circonscription(s) électorale(s) provinciale(s): Frontenac
Circonscription(s) électorale(s) fédérale(s): Mégantic-L'Érable
Prochaines élections: 3e novembre 2013
Ghyslain Hamel, Maire
Paule Bizier, Directrice générale

Saint-Jean-de-Cherbourg
10, 8e rang
Saint-Jean-de-Cherbourg, QC G0J 2R0
Tél: 418-733-8177; *Téléc:* 418-733-8177
st-jeandecherbourg@mrcdematane.qc.ca
Entité municipal: Parish (Paroisse)
Incorporation: 1er mai 1954 *Area:* 113,23 km2
Comté ou district: Matane; *Population au 2011:* 193
Circonscription(s) électorale(s) provinciale(s): Matane
Circonscription(s) électorale(s) fédérale(s): Haute-Gaspésie-La Mitis-Matane-Matapédia
Prochaines élections: 3e novembre 2013
Jocelyn Bergeron, Maire
Jacinthe Imbeault, Directrice générale

Saint-Jean-de-Dieu
32, rue Principale sud
Saint-Jean-de-Dieu, QC G0L 3M0
Tél: 418-963-3529; *Téléc:* 418-963-2903
stjeandd@intermobilex.com
Entité municipal: Municipality
Incorporation: 1er janvier 1865 *Area:* 151,32 km2
Comté ou district: Les Basques; *Population au 2011:* 1,606
Circonscription(s) électorale(s) provinciale(s): Rivière-du-Loup
Circonscription(s) électorale(s) fédérale(s):
Rimouski-Neigette-Témisouata-Les Basques
Prochaines élections: 3e novembre 2013
Jean-Marie Côté, Maire
Normand Morency, Directeur général

Saint-Jean-de-l'Ile-d'Orléans
8, ch des Côtes
Saint-Jean-de-l'Ile-d'Orléans, QC G0A 3W0
Tél: 418-829-2206; *Téléc:* 418-829-0997
stjeanio@bellnet.ca
Entité municipal: Municipality
Incorporation: 1er juillet 1855 *Area:* 43,64 km2
Comté ou district: L'Ile-d'Orléans; *Population au 2011:* 923
Circonscription(s) électorale(s) provinciale(s): Montmorency
Circonscription(s) électorale(s) fédérale(s):
Montmorency-Charlevoix-Haute-Côte-Nord
Prochaines élections: 3e novembre 2013
Jean-Claude Pouliot, Maire
Lucie Lambert, Directrice générale

Saint-Jean-de-la-Lande
810, rue Principale
Saint-Jean-de-la-Lande, QC G0L 3N0
Tél: 418-853-3703; *Téléc:* 418-853-3475
info@saintjeandelalande.ca
Entité municipal: Municipality
Incorporation: 1er janvier 1965 *Area:* 108,80 km2
Comté ou district: Témiscouata; *Population au 2011:* 310
Circonscription(s) électorale(s) provinciale(s):
Kamouraska—Témiscouata
Circonscription(s) électorale(s) fédérale(s):
Rimouski-Neigette-Témiscouata-Les Basques
Prochaines élections: 3e novembre 2013
Serge Boulet, Maire
Danielle Rousseau, Directrice générale

Saint-Jean-de-Matha
170, rue Ste-Louise
Saint-Jean-de-Matha, QC J0K 2S0
Tél: 450-886-3867; *Téléc:* 450-886-3398
matha@qc.aira.com
www.municipalitestjeandematha.com
Entité municipal: Municipality
Incorporation: 1er juillet 1855 *Area:* 117,01 km2
Comté ou district: Matawinie; *Population au 2011:* 4,335
Circonscription(s) électorale(s) provinciale(s): Berthier
Circonscription(s) électorale(s) fédérale(s): Joliette
Prochaines élections: 3e novembre 2013
Normand Champagne, Maire
Nicole D. Archambault, Directrice générale

Saint-Jean-Port-Joli
7, place de l'Église
Saint-Jean-Port-Joli, QC G0R 3G0
Tél: 418-598-3084; *Téléc:* 418-598-3085
munisjpj@globetrotter.net
www.saintjeanportjoli.com
Entité municipal: Municipality
Incorporation: 1er juillet 1855 *Area:* 68,55 km2
Comté ou district: L'Islet; *Population au 2011:* 3,304
Circonscription(s) électorale(s) provinciale(s): Montmagny-L'Islet
Circonscription(s) électorale(s) fédérale(s):
Montmagny-L'Islet-Kamouraska-Rivière-du-Loup
Prochaines élections: 3e novembre 2013
Jean-Pierre Dubé, Maire
Stéphen Lord, Directeur général

Saint-Joachim
172, rue de l'Église
Saint-Joachim, QC G0A 3X0
Tél: 418-827-3755; *Téléc:* 418-827-8574
dg@saintjoachim.qc.ca
www.saintjoachim.qc.ca
Entité municipal: Parish (Paroisse)
Incorporation: 1er juillet 1855 *Area:* 40,68 km2
Comté ou district: La Côte-de-Beaupré; *Population au 2011:* 1,458
Circonscription(s) électorale(s) provinciale(s): Charlevoix
Circonscription(s) électorale(s) fédérale(s): Montmorency-Charlevoix-Haute-Côte-Nord
Prochaines élections: 3e novembre 2013
Marc Dubeau, Maire
Roger Carrier, Directeur général

Saint-Joachim-de-Shefford
567, 1er rang ouest
Saint-Joachim-de-Shefford, QC J0E 2G0
Tél: 450-539-3201; *Téléc:* 450-539-3145
mairie@st-joachim.ca
www.st-joachim.ca
Entité municipal: Parish (Paroisse)
Incorporation: 10 juin 1884 *Area:* 126,98 km2
Comté ou district: La Haute-Yamaska; *Population au 2011:* 1,171
Circonscription(s) électorale(s) provinciale(s): Johnson
Circonscription(s) électorale(s) fédérale(s): Shefford
Prochaines élections: 3e novembre 2013
René Beauregard, Maire
France Lagrandneur, Directrice générale

Saint-Joseph-de-Beauce
843, av du Palais
Saint-Joseph-de-Beauce, QC G0S 2V0
Tél: 418-397-4358; *Téléc:* 418-397-5715
info@vsjb.ca
www.ville.stjosephdebeauce.qc.ca
Entité municipal: Town
Incorporation: 27 janvier 1999 *Area:* 108,54 km2
Comté ou district: Robert-Cliche; *Population au 2011:* 4,722
Circonscription(s) électorale(s) provinciale(s): Beauce-Nord
Circonscription(s) électorale(s) fédérale(s): Beauce
Prochaines élections: 3e novembre 2013
Michel Cliche, Maire
Danielle Maheu, Greffière

Saint-Joseph-de-Coleraine
88, av St-Patrick
Saint-Joseph-de-Coleraine, QC G0N 1B0
Tél: 418-423-4000; *Téléc:* 418-423-4150
coleraine@bellnet.ca
www.coleraine.qc.ca
Entité municipal: Municipality
Incorporation: 11 novembre 1891 *Area:* 125,11 km2
Comté ou district: Les Appalaches; *Population au 2011:* 1,870
Circonscription(s) électorale(s) provinciale(s): Frontenac
Circonscription(s) électorale(s) fédérale(s): Mégantic-L'Érable
Prochaines élections: 3e novembre 2013
Gilles Gosselin, Maire
Martin Cadorette, Directeur général

Saint-Joseph-de-Ham-Sud
9, ch Gosford sud
Saint-Joseph-de-Ham-Sud, QC J0B 3J0
Tél: 819-877-3258; *Téléc:* 819-877-5121
hamsud@cgocable.ca
www.saint-joseph-de-ham-sud.ca
Entité municipal: Parish (Paroisse)
Incorporation: 1er janvier 1879 *Area:* 150,45 km2
Comté ou district: Les Sources; *Population au 2011:* 225
Circonscription(s) électorale(s) provinciale(s): Richmond
Circonscription(s) électorale(s) fédérale(s): Richmond-Arthabaska
Prochaines élections: 3e novembre 2013
Langevin Gagnon, Maire
Caroline Poirier, Directrice générale

Saint-Joseph-de-Kamouraska
300, rue Principale ouest
Saint-Joseph-de-Kamouraska, QC G0L 3P0
Tél: 418-493-2214; *Téléc:* 418-493-1126
stjosephkam@bellnet.ca
www.stjosephkam.ca
Entité municipal: Parish (Paroisse)
Incorporation: 14 janvier 1924 *Area:* 84,61 km2
Comté ou district: Kamouraska; *Population au 2011:* 418
Circonscription(s) électorale(s) provinciale(s): Kamouraska-Témiscouata
Circonscription(s) électorale(s) fédérale(s): Montmagny-L'Islet-Kamouraska-Rivière-du-Loup
Prochaines élections: 3e novembre 2013
Sylvain Roy, Maire
Charles Montamat, Directeur général

Saint-Joseph-de-Lepage
70, rue de la Rivière
Saint-Joseph-de-Lepage, QC G5H 3N8
Tél: 418-775-4171; *Téléc:* 418-775-3004
stjoseph@mitis.qc.ca
www.municipalite.saint-joseph-de-lepage.qc.ca
Entité municipal: Parish (Paroisse)
Incorporation: 29 septembre 1873 *Area:* 30,27 km2
Comté ou district: La Mitis; *Population au 2011:* 527
Circonscription(s) électorale(s) provinciale(s): Matapédia
Circonscription(s) électorale(s) fédérale(s): Haute-Gaspésie-La Mitis-Matane-Matapédia
Prochaines élections: 3e novembre 2013
Réginald Morissette, Maire
Renée Roy, Directrice générale

Saint-Joseph-de-Sorel
700, rue Montcalm
Saint-Joseph-de-Sorel, QC J3R 1C9
Tél: 450-742-3744; *Téléc:* 450-742-1315
ville@vsjs.ca
www.vsjs.ca
Entité municipal: Village
Incorporation: 1er mai 1907 *Area:* 1,4 km2
Comté ou district: Pierre-De Saurel; *Population au 2011:* 1,677
Circonscription(s) électorale(s) provinciale(s): Richelieu
Circonscription(s) électorale(s) fédérale(s): Bas-Richelieu-Nicolet-Bécancour
Prochaines élections: 3e novembre 2013
Olivar Gravel, Maire
Martin Valois, Directeur général

Saint-Joseph-des-Érables
370A, rang des Érables
Saint-Joseph-des-Érables, QC G0S 2V0
Tél: 418-397-4772; *Téléc:* 418-397-1555
municipalite@stjosephdeserables.com
www.stjosephdeserables.com
Entité municipal: Municipality
Incorporation: 26 novembre 2009 *Area:* 50,01 km2
Comté ou district: Robert-Cliche; *Population au 2011:* 420
Circonscription(s) électorale(s) provinciale(s): Beauce-Nord
Circonscription(s) électorale(s) fédérale(s): Beauce
Prochaines élections: 1er novembre 2013
Louis Jacques, Maire
Mélanie Jacques, Directrice générale

Saint-Joseph-du-Lac
1110, ch Principal
Saint-Joseph-du-Lac, QC J0N 1M0
Tél: 450-623-1072; *Téléc:* 450-623-2889
info@sjdl.qc.ca
www.sjdl.qc.ca
Entité municipal: Municipality
Incorporation: 1er juillet 1855 *Area:* 40,81 km2
Comté ou district: Deux-Montagne; *Population au 2011:* 6,195
Circonscription(s) électorale(s) provinciale(s): Mirabel
Circonscription(s) électorale(s) fédérale(s): Argenteuil-Papineau-Mirabel
Prochaines élections: 3e novembre 2013
Alain Guindon, Maire
Guylaine Comtois, Directrice générale

Saint-Jude
940, rue du Centre
Saint-Jude, QC J0H 1P0
Tél: 450-792-3855; *Téléc:* 450-792-3828
munstjude@mrcmaskoutains.qc.ca
www.saint-jude.ca
Entité municipal: Municipality
Incorporation: 1er juillet 1855 *Area:* 77,36 km2
Comté ou district: Les Maskoutains; *Population au 2011:* 1,235
Circonscription(s) électorale(s) provinciale(s): Richelieu
Circonscription(s) électorale(s) fédérale(s): St-Hyacinthe-Bagot
Prochaines élections: 3e novembre 2013
Yves de Bellefeuille, Maire
Sylvie Beauregard, Directrice générale

Saint-Jules
390, rte Principale
Saint-Jules, QC G0N 1R0
Tél: 418-397-5444; *Téléc:* 418-397-5007
mun.st-jules@axion.ca
www.st-jules.qc.ca
Entité municipal: Parish (Paroisse)
Incorporation: 28 mai 1919 *Area:* 57,08 km2
Comté ou district: Robert-Cliche; *Population au 2011:* 573
Circonscription(s) électorale(s) provinciale(s): Beauce-Nord
Circonscription(s) électorale(s) fédérale(s): Beauce
Prochaines élections: 3e novembre 2013
Ghislaine Doyon, Mairesse
Claire Roy, Directrice générale

Saint-Julien
787, ch St-Julien
Saint-Julien, QC G0N 1B0
Tél: 418-423-4295; *Téléc:* 418-423-2384
municipalite@st-julien.ca
www.st-julien.ca
Entité municipal: Municipality
Incorporation: 1er juillet 1855 *Area:* 82,300 km2
Comté ou district: Les Appalaches; *Population au 2011:* 406
Circonscription(s) électorale(s) provinciale(s): Frontenac
Circonscription(s) électorale(s) fédérale(s): Mégantic-L'Érable
Prochaines élections: 3e novembre 2013
Jacques Laprise, Maire
Réjean Gouin, Directeur géneral

Saint-Juste-du-Lac
CP 38
28, ch Principal
Saint-Juste-du-Lac, QC G0L 3R0
Tél: 418-899-2855; *Téléc:* 418-899-2938
info@saintjustedulac.com
www.saintjustedulac.com
Entité municipal: Municipality
Incorporation: 23 mai 1923 *Area:* 170,11 km2
Comté ou district: Témiscouata; *Population au 2011:* 585
Circonscription(s) électorale(s) provinciale(s): Kamouraska-Témiscouata
Circonscription(s) électorale(s) fédérale(s): Montmagny-L'Islet-Kamouraska-Rivière-du-Loup
Prochaines élections: 3e novembre 2013
Jean-Jacques Bonenfant, Maire
Nicole Dubé-Chouinard, Directrice générale

Saint-Just-de-Bretenières
CP 668
250, rue Principale
Saint-Just-de-Bretenières, QC G0R 3H0
Tél: 418-244-3637; *Téléc:* 418-244-3637
st-just-de-bretenieres@globetrotter.net
www.saintjustdebretenieres.com
Entité municipal: Municipality
Incorporation: 27 mai 1918 *Area:* 132,35 km2
Comté ou district: Montmagny; *Population au 2011:* 709
Circonscription(s) électorale(s) provinciale(s): Montmagny-L'Islet
Circonscription(s) électorale(s) fédérale(s): Lévis-Bellechasse
Prochaines élections: 3e novembre 2013
Réal Bolduc, Maire
Isabelle Simard, Directrice générale

Saint-Justin
1281, rue Gérin
Saint-Justin, QC J0K 2V0
Tél: 819-227-2838; *Téléc:* 819-227-4876
dg@saint-justin.ca
www.saint-justin.ca
Entité municipal: Parish (Paroisse)
Incorporation: 1er juillet 1855 *Area:* 82,46 km2
Comté ou district: Maskinongé; *Population au 2011:* 1,060
Circonscription(s) électorale(s) provinciale(s): Maskinongé
Circonscription(s) électorale(s) fédérale(s): Berthier-Maskinongé
Prochaines élections: 3e novembre 2013
Denis McKinnon, Mairesse
Michel C. Cousineau, Directeur général

Saint-Lambert
CP 86
509, rte 5e-au-8e Rang
Des Méloizes, QC J0Z 1V0
Tél: 819-788-2491; *Téléc:* 819-788-2491
st-lambert@mrcao.qc.ca
www.st-lambert.ao.ca
Entité municipal: Parish (Paroisse)
Incorporation: 14 mai 1938 *Area:* 101,76 km2
Comté ou district: Abitibi-Ouest; *Population au 2011:* 211
Circonscription(s) électorale(s) provinciale(s): Abitibi-Ouest
Circonscription(s) électorale(s) fédérale(s): Abitibi-Témiscamingue
Prochaines élections: 3e novembre 2013
Emilien Rivard, Maire
Nataly Morin, Directrice générale

Saint-Lambert-de-Lauzon
1200, rue du Pont
Saint-Lambert-de-Lauzon, QC G0S 2W0
Tél: 418-889-9715; *Téléc:* 418-889-0660
info@municipalite.saint-lambert-de-lauzon.qc.ca
www.municipalite.saint-lambert-de-lauzon.qc.ca
Entité municipal: Parish (Paroisse)
Incorporation: 1er juillet 1855 *Area:* 107,32 km2
Comté ou district: La Nouvelle-Beauce; *Population au 2011:* 6,177
Circonscription(s) électorale(s) provinciale(s): Beauce-Nord
Circonscription(s) électorale(s) fédérale(s): Lotbinière-Chutes-de-la-Chaudière
Prochaines élections: 3e novembre 2013
François Barret, Maire
Magdalen Blanchet, Directrice générale

Saint-Laurent-de-l'Ile-d'Orléans
1430, ch Royal
St-Laurent-de-l'Ile-d'Orléans, QC G0A 3Z0
Tél: 418-828-2322; *Téléc:* 418-828-2170
stlaurentorleans@videotron.ca
st-laurent.iledorleans.com
Entité municipal: Municipality
Incorporation: 1er juillet 1855 *Area:* 35,32 km2
Comté ou district: L'Ile-d'Orléans; *Population au 2011:* 1,580
Circonscription(s) électorale(s) provinciale(s): Montmorency
Circonscription(s) électorale(s) fédérale(s): Montmorency-Charlevoix-Haute-Côte-Nord
Prochaines élections: 3e novembre 2013
Yves Coulombe, Maire
Claudette Pouliot, Directrice générale

Saint-Lazare-de-Bellechasse
116, rue de la Fabrique
Saint-Lazare-de-Bellechasse, QC G0R 3J0
Tél: 418-883-3841; *Téléc:* 418-883-2551
munstlaz@globetrotter.net
Entité municipal: Municipality
Incorporation: 1er juillet 1855 *Area:* 85,53 km2
Comté ou district: Bellechasse; *Population au 2011:* 1,172
Circonscription(s) électorale(s) provinciale(s): Bellechasse
Circonscription(s) électorale(s) fédérale(s): Lévis-Bellechasse
Prochaines élections: 3e novembre 2013
Martin J. Côté, Maire
Richard Côté, Directeur général

Saint-Léandre
2005, rue de l'Église
Saint-Léandre, QC G0J 2V0
Tél: 418-737-4973; *Téléc:* 418-737-4972
st-leandre@mrcdematane.qc.ca
Entité municipal: Parish (Paroisse)
Incorporation: 20 mars 1912 *Area:* 102,62 km2
Comté ou district: Matane; *Population au 2011:* 402
Circonscription(s) électorale(s) provinciale(s): Matane
Circonscription(s) électorale(s) fédérale(s): Haute-Gaspésie-La Mitis-Matane-Matapédia
Prochaines élections: 3e novembre 2013
Yvon Tremblay, Maire
Guylaine Ouellet, Directrice générale

Saint-Léon-de-Standon
CP 130
100A, rue St-Pierre
Saint-Léon-de-Standon, QC G0R 4L0
Tél: 418-642-5034; *Téléc:* 418-642-2570
mun.st-leon@globetrotter.net
www.stleondestandon.qc.ca
Entité municipal: Parish (Paroisse)
Incorporation: 1er janvier 1874 *Area:* 136,90 km2
Comté ou district: Bellechasse; *Population au 2011:* 1,128
Circonscription(s) électorale(s) provinciale(s): Bellechasse
Circonscription(s) électorale(s) fédérale(s): Lévis-Bellechasse
Prochaines élections: 3e novembre 2013
Bernard Morin, Maire
Michel Lacasse, Directeur général

Saint-Léon-le-Grand
CP 188
277, rue Plourde
Saint-Léon-le-Grand, QC G0J 2W0
Tél: 418-743-2914; *Téléc:* 418-743-2914
stleonlegrand@mrcmatapedia.qc.ca
www.saintleonlegrand.com
Entité municipal: Parish (Paroisse)
Incorporation: 12 août 1903 *Area:* 127,73 km2
Comté ou district: La Matapédia; *Population au 2011:* 970
Circonscription(s) électorale(s) provinciale(s): Matapédia
Circonscription(s) électorale(s) fédérale(s): Haute-Gaspésie-La Mitis-Matane-Matapédia
Prochaines élections: 3e novembre 2013
Steve Lamontagne, Maire
Suzanne Poirier, Directrice générale

Saint-Léon-le-Grand
49, rue de la Fabrique
Saint-Léon-le-Grand, QC J0K 2W0
Tél: 819-228-3236; *Téléc:* 819-228-8088
glessard@st-leon.com
Entité municipal: Parish (Paroisse)
Incorporation: 1er juillet 1855 *Area:* 72,57 km2
Comté ou district: Maskinongé; *Population au 2011:* 992
Circonscription(s) électorale(s) provinciale(s): Maskinongé
Circonscription(s) électorale(s) fédérale(s): Berthier-Maskinongé
Prochaines élections: 3e novembre 2013
Robert Lalonde, Maire
Gabrielle Lessard, Directrice générale

Saint-Léonard-d'Aston
370, rue Principale
Saint-Léonard-d'Aston, QC J0C 1M0
Tél: 819-399-2596; *Téléc:* 819-399-2333
municipalite@saint-leonard-daston.net
www.saint-leonard-daston.net
Entité municipal: Municipality
Incorporation: 13 avril 1994 *Area:* 81,83 km2
Comté ou district: Nicolet-Yamaska; *Population au 2011:* 2,271
Circonscription(s) électorale(s) provinciale(s): Nicolet-Yamaska
Circonscription(s) électorale(s) fédérale(s): Bas-Richelieu-Nicolet-Bécancour
Prochaines élections: 3e novembre 2013
Luc P. Balleux, Maire
Carmelle L. Dupuis, Directrice générale

Saint-Léonard-de-Portneuf
260, rue Pettigrew
Saint-Léonard-de-Portneuf, QC G0A 4A0
Tél: 418-337-6741; *Téléc:* 418-337-6742
saintleonard@derytele.com
www.municipalite.st-leonard.qc.ca
Entité municipal: Municipality
Incorporation: 22 juillet 1899 *Area:* 138,71 km2
Comté ou district: Portneuf; *Population au 2011:* 1,019
Circonscription(s) électorale(s) provinciale(s): Portneuf
Circonscription(s) électorale(s) fédérale(s): Portneuf-Jacques-Cartier
Prochaines élections: 3e novembre 2013
Denis Langlois, Maire
Eddy Alain, Directeur-général

Saint-Liboire
CP 120
21, place Mauriac
Saint-Liboire, QC J0H 1R0
Tél: 450-793-2811; *Téléc:* 450-793-4428
admin@municipalite.st-liboire.qc.ca
www.municipalite.st-liboire.qc.ca
Entité municipal: Municipality
Incorporation: 17 août 1994 *Area:* 72,90 km2
Comté ou district: Les Maskoutains; *Population au 2011:* 3,051
Circonscription(s) électorale(s) provinciale(s): St-Hyacinthe
Circonscription(s) électorale(s) fédérale(s): St-Hyacinthe-Bagot
Prochaines élections: 3e novembre 2013
Denis Chabot, Maire
Lucie Chevrier, Directrice générale

Saint-Liguori
750, rue Principale
Saint-Liguori, QC J0K 2X0
Tél: 450-753-3570; *Téléc:* 450-753-4638
info@saint-liguori.com
Entité municipal: Parish (Paroisse)
Incorporation: 1er juillet 1855 *Area:* 50,91 km2
Comté ou district: Montcalm; *Population au 2011:* 1,976
Circonscription(s) électorale(s) provinciale(s): Joliette
Circonscription(s) électorale(s) fédérale(s): Montcalm
Prochaines élections: 3e novembre 2013
Serge Rivest, Maire
Edith Gagné, Directrice générale

Saint-Louis
765B, rue St-Joseph
Saint-Louis, QC J0G 1K0
Tél: 450-788-2631; *Téléc:* 450-788-2231
mstlouis@mrcmaskoutains.qc.ca
mun-st-louis.qc.ca
Entité municipal: Parish (Paroisse)
Incorporation: 29 août 1881 *Area:* 45,92 km2
Comté ou district: Les Maskoutains; *Population au 2011:* 775
Circonscription(s) électorale(s) provinciale(s): Richelieu
Circonscription(s) électorale(s) fédérale(s): St-Hyacinthe-Bagot
Prochaines élections: 3e novembre 2013
Doris Gosselin, Mairesse
Pascale Dalcourt, Directrice générale

Saint-Louis-de-Blandford
CP 140
80-1, rue Principale
Saint-Louis-de-Blandford, QC G0Z 1B0
Tél: 819-364-7007; *Téléc:* 819-364-2781
info@saint-louis-de-blandford.ca
www.saint-louis-de-blandford.ca
Entité municipal: Parish (Paroisse)
Incorporation: 1er juillet 1855 *Area:* 106,70 km2
Comté ou district: Arthabaska; *Population au 2011:* 903
Circonscription(s) électorale(s) provinciale(s): Lotbinière
Circonscription(s) électorale(s) fédérale(s): Richmond-Arthabaska
Prochaines élections: 3e novembre 2013
Gilles Marchand, Maire
Mélisa Morissette, Directrice générale

Saint-Louis-de-Gonzague
108, rue de l'Église
Ravignan, QC G0R 2L0
Tél: 418-267-5931; *Téléc:* 418-267-5930
munstlouis@sogetel.net
www.st-louisdegonzague.qc.ca
Entité municipal: Municipality
Incorporation: 17 mars 1923 *Area:* 116,36 km2
Comté ou district: Les Etchemins; *Population au 2011:* 421
Circonscription(s) électorale(s) provinciale(s): Bellechasse
Circonscription(s) électorale(s) fédérale(s): Lévis-Bellechasse; Beauharnois-Salaberry
Prochaines élections: 3e novembre 2013
Suzanne Campeau Guenette, Mairesse
Odette Poulin, Directrice générale

Saint-Louis-de-Gonzague
CP 382
140, rue Principale
Saint-Louis-de-Gonzague, QC J0S 1T0
Tél: 450-371-0523; *Téléc:* 450-371-6229
munstlouisdegonzague@intermobilex.com
saint-louis-de-gonzague.com
Entité municipal: Parish (Paroisse)
Incorporation: 1er juillet 1855 *Area:* 78,52 km2
Comté ou district: Beauharnois-Salaberry; *Population au 2011:* 1,389
Circonscription(s) électorale(s) provinciale(s): Beauharnois
Circonscription(s) électorale(s) fédérale(s): Beauharnois-Salaberry
Prochaines élections: 3e novembre 2013
Yves Daoust, Maire
Micheline J.-Carrière, Directrice générale

Saint-Louis-de-Gonzague-du-Cap-Tourmente
CP 460 Haute-Ville
1, rue des Remparts
Québec, QC G1R 4R7
Tél: 418-692-3981; *Téléc:* 418-692-4345
jroberge@globetrotter.net
Entité municipal: Parish (Paroisse)
Incorporation: 1er janvier 1917
Comté ou district: La Côte-de-Beaupré; *Population au 2011:* 18
Circonscription(s) électorale(s) provinciale(s): Charlevoix
Circonscription(s) électorale(s) fédérale(s): Charlevoix-Montmorency-Haute-Côte-Nord
Prochaines élections: 3e novembre 2013
Jacques Roberge, Administrateur

Saint-Louis-du-Ha!-Ha!
95, rue St-Charles
Saint-Louis-du-Ha!-Ha!, QC G0L 3S0
Tél: 418-854-2260; *Téléc:* 418-854-0717
municipalite@saintlouisduhaha.com
www.saintlouisduhaha.com
Entité municipal: Parish (Paroisse)
Incorporation: 14 juillet 1874 *Area:* 114,45 km2
Comté ou district: Témiscouata; *Population au 2011:* 1,318
Circonscription(s) électorale(s) provinciale(s): Kamouraska-Témiscouata
Circonscription(s) électorale(s) fédérale(s): Rimouski-Neigette-Témiscouata-Les Basques
Prochaines élections: 3e novembre 2013
Louiselle Ouellet, Mairesse
Gratien Ouellet, Directeur général

Saint-Luc-de-Bellechasse
115, rue de la Fabrique
Saint-Luc-de-Bellechasse, QC G0R 1L0
Tél: 418-636-2176; *Téléc:* 418-636-2176
munstluc@sogetel.net
www.st-luc-bellechasse.qc.ca

Entité municipal: Municipality
Incorporation: 12 août 1921 *Area:* 160,03 km2
Comté ou district: Les Etchemins; *Population au 2011:* 480
Circonscription(s) électorale(s) provinciale(s): Bellechasse
Circonscription(s) électorale(s) fédérale(s): Lévis-Bellechasse
Prochaines élections: 3e novembre 2013
René Leclerc, Maire
Amélie Gagnon, Directrice générale

Saint-Luc-de-Vincennes
CP 450
660, rue Principale
Saint-Luc-de-Vincennes, QC G0X 3K0
Tél: 819-295-3782; *Téléc:* 819-295-3782
municipalite@stlucdevincennes.com
www.stlucdevincennes.com
Entité municipal: Municipality
Incorporation: 19 janvier 1865 *Area:* 52,73 km2
Comté ou district: Les Chenaux; *Population au 2011:* 591
Circonscription(s) électorale(s) provinciale(s): Champlain
Circonscription(s) électorale(s) fédérale(s):
St-Maurice-Champlain
Prochaines élections: 3e novembre 2013
Jean-Claude Milot, Maire
Manon Shallow, Directrice générale

Saint-Lucien
5350, 7e rang
Saint-Lucien, QC J0C 1N0
Tél: 819-397-4679; *Téléc:* 819-397-2732
lynda.lalancette@municipalite.saint-lucien.qc.ca
Entité municipal: Parish (Paroisse)
Incorporation: 11 novembre 1907 *Area:* 113,61 km2
Comté ou district: Drummond; *Population au 2011:* 1,584
Circonscription(s) électorale(s) provinciale(s): Richmond
Circonscription(s) électorale(s) fédérale(s): Drummond
Prochaines élections: 3e novembre 2013
Suzanne Pinard Lebeau, Mairesse
Lynda Lalancette, Directrice générale

Saint-Ludger
212, rue La Salle
Saint-Ludger, QC G0M 1W0
Tél: 819-548-5408; *Téléc:* 819-548-5743
munstludger@sogetel.net
www.st-ludger.qc.ca
Entité municipal: Municipality
Incorporation: 25 février 1998 *Area:* 124,46 km2
Comté ou district: Le Granit; *Population au 2011:* 1,255
Circonscription(s) électorale(s) provinciale(s): Beauce-Sud
Circonscription(s) électorale(s) fédérale(s): Beauce
Prochaines élections: 3e novembre 2013
Diane Roy, Maire
Julie Létourneau, Directrice générale

Saint-Ludger-de-Milot
739, rue Gaudreault
Saint-Ludger-de-Milot, QC G0W 2B0
Tél: 418-373-2266; *Téléc:* 418-373-2554
administration@ville.st-ludger-de-milot.qc.ca
www.ville.st-ludger-de-milot.qc.ca
Entité municipal: Municipality
Incorporation: 1er janvier 1948 *Area:* 106,81 km2
Comté ou district: Lac-St-Jean-Est; *Population au 2011:* 678
Circonscription(s) électorale(s) provinciale(s): Lac-St-Jean
Circonscription(s) électorale(s) fédérale(s):
Roberval-Lac-St-Jean
Prochaines élections: 3e novembre 2013
Marc Laliberté, Maire
Rita Ouellet, Directrice générale

Saint-Magloire
130, rue Principale
Saint-Magloire, QC G0R 3M0
Tél: 418-257-4421; *Téléc:* 418-257-4422
stmagloire@sogetel.net
www.saint-magloire.com
Entité municipal: Municipality
Incorporation: 1er janvier 1875 *Area:* 208,64 km2
Comté ou district: Les Etchemins; *Population au 2011:* 725
Circonscription(s) électorale(s) provinciale(s): Bellechasse
Circonscription(s) électorale(s) fédérale(s): Lévis-Bellechasse
Prochaines élections: 3e novembre 2013
Marcel Asselin, Maire
Huguette Lavigne, Directrice générale

Saint-Majorique-de-Grantham
1966, boul St-Joseph ouest
Saint-Majorique-de-Grantham, QC J2B 8A8
Tél: 819-478-7058; *Téléc:* 819-478-8479
municipalite.st-majorique@reseauxalliance.com

Entité municipal: Parish (Paroisse)
Incorporation: 13 juillet 1901 *Area:* 57,26 km2
Comté ou district: Drummond; *Population au 2011:* 1,251
Circonscription(s) électorale(s) provinciale(s): Drummond
Circonscription(s) électorale(s) fédérale(s): Drummond
Prochaines élections: 3e novembre 2013
Réjean Rodier, Maire
Hélène Ruel, Directrice générale

Saint-Malachie
610, 7e rue
Saint-Malachie, QC G0R 3N0
Tél: 418-642-2102; *Téléc:* 418-642-2231
munimala@globetrotter.net
www.st-malachie.qc.ca
Entité municipal: Parish (Paroisse)
Incorporation: 1er juin 1874 *Area:* 100,59 km2
Comté ou district: Bellechasse; *Population au 2011:* 1,489
Circonscription(s) électorale(s) provinciale(s): Bellechasse
Circonscription(s) électorale(s) fédérale(s): Lévis-Bellechasse
Prochaines élections: 1er novembre 2013
Hélène Bissonnette, Sec.-Trés. & Directrice générale
Vital Labonté, Maire

Saint-Malo
228, rte 253 sud
Saint-Malo, QC J0B 2Y0
Tél: 819-658-2174; *Téléc:* 819-658-1169
saint-malo@axion.ca
Entité municipal: Municipality
Incorporation: 1er janvier 1870 *Area:* 129,30 km2
Comté ou district: Coaticook; *Population au 2011:* 483
Circonscription(s) électorale(s) provinciale(s):
Mégantic-Compton
Circonscription(s) électorale(s) fédérale(s): Compton-Stanstead
Prochaines élections: 3e novembre 2013
Jacques Madore, Maire
Micheline Robert, Directrice générale

Saint-Marc-de-Figuery
CP 12
10, av Michaud
Saint-Marc-de-Figuery, QC J0Y 1J0
Tél: 819-732-8501; *Téléc:* 819-732-4324
mun.stmard@cableamos.com
Entité municipal: Parish (Paroisse)
Incorporation: 10 novembre 1926 *Area:* 91,10 km2
Comté ou district: Abitibi; *Population au 2011:* 771
Circonscription(s) électorale(s) provinciale(s): Abitibi-Ouest
Circonscription(s) électorale(s) fédérale(s):
Abitibi-Témiscamingue
Prochaines élections: 3e novembre 2013
Jacques Riopel, Maire
Aline Guénette, Directrice générale

Saint-Marc-des-Carrières
965, av Bona-Dussault
Saint-Marc-des-Carrières, QC G0A 4B0
Tél: 418-268-3862; *Téléc:* 418-268-8776
info@villestmarc.com
www.st-marc-des-carrieres.qc.ca
Entité municipal: Town
Incorporation: 24 octobre 1918 *Area:* 16,73 km2
Comté ou district: Portneuf; *Population au 2011:* 2,862
Circonscription(s) électorale(s) provinciale(s): Portneuf
Circonscription(s) électorale(s) fédérale(s):
Portneuf-Jacques-Cartier
Prochaines élections: 3e novembre 2013
Guy Denis, Maire
Maryon Leclerc, Directeur général

Saint-Marc-du-Lac-Long
12, rue de l'Église
Saint-Marc-du-Lac-Long, QC G0L 1T0
Tel: 418-893-2643; *Fax:* 418-893-7228
admin@saintmarcdulaclong.ca
Municipal Type: Parish (Paroisse)
Incorporated: 11 juin 1938 *Area:* 147,16 km2
County or District: Témiscouata; *Population in 2011:* 440
Provincial Electoral District(s): Kamouraska-Témiscouata
Federal Electoral District(s):
Rimouski-Neigette-Témiscouata-Les Basques
Next Election: 3e novembre 2013
Adrien Kennedy, Maire
Karine Plourde, Directrice générale

Saint-Marc-sur-Richelieu
102, rue de la Fabrique
Saint-Marc-sur-Richelieu, QC J0L 2E0
Tél: 450-584-2258; *Téléc:* 450-584-2795
sburelle@ville.saint-marc-sur-richelieu.qc.ca
www.ville.saint.marc-sur-richelleu.qc.ca

Entité municipal: Municipality
Incorporation: 1er juillet 1855 *Area:* 59,51 km2
Comté ou district: Le Vallée-du-Richelieu; *Population au 2011:* 2,050
Circonscription(s) électorale(s) provinciale(s): Verchères
Circonscription(s) électorale(s) fédérale(s): Verchères-Les Patriotes
Prochaines élections: 3e novembre 2013
Jean Murray, Maire
Sylvie Burelle, Directrice générale

Saint-Marcel
48, ch Taché est
Saint-Marcel, QC G0R 3R0
Tél: 418-356-2691; *Téléc:* 418-356-2820
mun.sm@globetrotter.net
www.saintmarcel.qc.ca
Entité municipal: Municipality
Incorporation: 30 juillet 1904 *Area:* 178,86 km2
Comté ou district: L'Islet; *Population au 2011:* 439
Circonscription(s) électorale(s) provinciale(s): Montmagny-L'Islet
Circonscription(s) électorale(s) fédérale(s):
Montmagny-L'Islet-Kamouraska-Rivière-du-Loup
Prochaines élections: 3e novembre 2013
Clément Bernier, Maire
Carole St-Hilaire, Directrice générale

Saint-Marcel-de-Richelieu
117, rue Saint-Louis
Saint-Marcel-de-Richelieu, QC J0H 1T0
Tél: 450-794-2832; *Téléc:* 450-794-1140
munst-marcel@mrcmaskoutains.qc.ca
Entité municipal: Municipality
Incorporation: 1er juillet 1855 *Area:* 50,21 km2
Comté ou district: Les Maskoutains; *Population au 2011:* 543
Circonscription(s) électorale(s) provinciale(s): Nicolet-Yamaska
Circonscription(s) électorale(s) fédérale(s): St-Hyacinthe-Bagot
Prochaines élections: 3e novembre 2013
Yvon Pesant, Maire
Christiane Janelle, Directrice générale

Saint-Marcellin
336, rte 234
Saint-Marcellin, QC G0K 1R0
Tél: 418-798-4382; *Téléc:* 418-798-4383
munstmar@globetrotter.net
www.st-marcellin.qc.ca
Entité municipal: Parish (Paroisse)
Incorporation: 19 novembre 1924 *Area:* 117,01 km2
Comté ou district: Rimouski-Neigette; *Population au 2011:* 323
Circonscription(s) électorale(s) provinciale(s): Rimouski
Circonscription(s) électorale(s) fédérale(s):
Rimouski-Neigette-Témiscouata-Les Basques
Prochaines élections: 3e novembre 2013
Sarto Roy, Maire
Brigitte Rouleau, Directrice générale

Saint-Martin
131, 1e av est
Saint-Martin, QC G0M 1B0
Tél: 418-382-5035; *Téléc:* 418-382-5561
municipalite@st-martin.qc.ca
www.st-martin.qc.ca
Entité municipal: Parish (Paroisse)
Incorporation: 12 octobre 1911 *Area:* 119,34 km2
Comté ou district: Beauce-Sartigan; *Population au 2011:* 2,462
Circonscription(s) électorale(s) provinciale(s): Beauce-Sud
Circonscription(s) électorale(s) fédérale(s): Beauce
Prochaines élections: 3e novembre 2013
Jean-Marc Paquet, Maire
Brigitte Quirion, Directrice générale

Saint-Mathias-sur-Richelieu
300, ch des Patriotes
Saint-Mathias-sur-Richelieu, QC J3L 6Z5
Tél: 450-658-2841; *Téléc:* 450-447-1416
information@st-mathias.org
Entité municipal: Municipality
Incorporation: 1er juillet 1855 *Area:* 48,22 km2
Comté ou district: Rouville; *Population au 2011:* 4,618
Circonscription(s) électorale(s) provinciale(s): Chambly
Circonscription(s) électorale(s) fédérale(s): Chambly-Borduas
Prochaines élections: 3e novembre 2013
Yanik Maheu, Maire
Catherine Chartrand, Directrice général

Saint-Mathieu
299, ch St-Édouard
Saint-Mathieu, QC J0L 2H0
Tél: 450-632-9528; *Téléc:* 450-632-9544
dg@municipalite.saint-mathieu.qc.ca

Entité municipal: Municipality
Incorporation: 1er août 1917 *Area:* 32,27 km2
Comté ou district: Roussillon; *Population au 2011:* 1,879
Circonscription(s) électorale(s) provinciale(s): La Prairie
Circonscription(s) électorale(s) fédérale(s):
Châteauguay-St-Constant
Prochaines élections: 3e novembre 2013
Lise Poissant-Charron, Mairesse
Louise Hébert, Directrice générale

Saint-Mathieu-d'Harricana
203, ch Lanoix
Saint-Mathieu-d'Harricana, QC J0Y 1M0
Tél: 819-727-9557; *Téléc:* 819-727-2052
mun.st-mathieu@cableamos.com
Entité municipal: Municipality
Incorporation: 1er janvier 1943 *Area:* 104,09 km2
Comté ou district: Abitibi; *Population au 2011:* 696
Circonscription(s) électorale(s) provinciale(s): Abitibi-Ouest
Circonscription(s) électorale(s) fédérale(s):
Abitibi-Témiscamingue
Prochaines élections: 3e novembre 2013
Martin Roch, Maire
Kathleen Guévin, Directrice générale

Saint-Mathieu-de-Beloeil
5000, rue des Loisirs
Saint-Mathieu-de-Beloeil, QC J3G 2C9
Tél: 450-467-7490; *Téléc:* 450-467-2999
reception@munstmathbel.ca
www.saint-mathieu-de-beloeil.com
Entité municipal: Municipality
Incorporation: 1er juillet 1855 *Area:* 39,26 km2
Comté ou district: La Vallée-du-Richelieu; *Population au 2011:* 2,624
Circonscription(s) électorale(s) provinciale(s): Borduas
Circonscription(s) électorale(s) fédérale(s): Chambly-Borduas
Prochaines élections: 3e novembre 2013
Michel Aubin, Maire
Doris Parent, Directrice générale

Saint-Mathieu-de-Rioux
41, rue de l'Église
Saint-Mathieu-de-Rioux, QC G0L 3T0
Tél: 418-738-2953; *Téléc:* 418-738-2454
admin@stmathieuderioux.qc.ca
www.st-mathieu-de-rioux.ca
Entité municipal: Parish (Paroisse)
Incorporation: 18 août 1865 *Area:* 102,35 km2
Comté ou district: Les Basques; *Population au 2011:* 678
Circonscription(s) électorale(s) provinciale(s): Rivière-du-Loup
Circonscription(s) électorale(s) fédérale(s):
Rimouski-Neigette-Témiscouata-Les Basques
Prochaines élections: 3e novembre 2013
Réal Côté, Maire
Michelle Lafontaine, Directrice générale

Saint-Mathieu-du-Parc
561, ch Déziel
Saint-Mathieu-du-Parc, QC G0X 1N0
Tél: 819-532-2205; *Téléc:* 819-532-2415
stmathieu@stmathieuduparc.org
www.stmathieuduparc.org
Entité municipal: Municipality
Incorporation: 30 juin 1886 *Area:* 196,45 km2
Comté ou district: Maskinongé; *Population au 2011:* 1,407
Circonscription(s) électorale(s) provinciale(s): St-Maurice
Circonscription(s) électorale(s) fédérale(s): Berthier-Maskinongé
Prochaines élections: 3e novembre 2013
Claude Mayrand, Maire
Sylvian Tousignant, Directeur général

Saint-Maurice
CP 9
2510, rang St-Jean
Saint-Maurice, QC G0X 2X0
Tél: 819-374-4525; *Téléc:* 819-374-9132
municipalite@st-maurice.ca
www.st-maurice.ca
Entité municipal: Parish (Paroisse)
Incorporation: 1er juillet 1855 *Area:* 90,33 km2
Comté ou district: Les Chenaux; *Population au 2011:* 2,775
Circonscription(s) électorale(s) provinciale(s): Champlain
Circonscription(s) électorale(s) fédérale(s):
St-Maurice-Champlain
Prochaines élections: 3e novembre 2013
Gérard Bruneau, Maire
Andrée Neault, Directrice générale

Saint-Maxime-du-Mont-Louis
CP 130
1, 1re av ouest
Saint-Maxime-du-Mont-Louis, QC G0E 1T0
Tél: 418-797-2310; *Téléc:* 418-797-2928
munst-maxime@globetrotter.net
www.municipalitest-maxime.qc.ca
Entité municipal: Municipality
Incorporation: 10 juin 1884 *Area:* 220,38 km2
Comté ou district: La Haute-Gaspésie; *Population au 2011:* 1,118
Circonscription(s) électorale(s) provinciale(s): Matane
Circonscription(s) électorale(s) fédérale(s): Haute-Gaspésie-La Mitis-Matane-Matapédia
Prochaines élections: 3e novembre 2013
Paul-Hébert Bernatchez, Maire
Hilaire Lemieux, Directeur général

Saint-Médard
1B, rue Principale est
Saint-Médard, QC G0L 3V0
Tél: 418-963-6276; *Téléc:* 418-963-6468
admin@st-medard.qc.ca
www.info-basques.com
Entité municipal: Municipality
Incorporation: 1er janvier 1949 *Area:* 67,59 km2
Comté ou district: Les Basques; *Population au 2011:* 222
Circonscription(s) électorale(s) provinciale(s): Rivière-du-Loup
Circonscription(s) électorale(s) fédérale(s):
Rimouski-Neigette-Témiscouata-Les Basques
Prochaines élections: 3e novembre 2013
Diane Marquis, Maire
Andrée O. Beaulieu, Directrice générale

Saint-Michel
1700, rue Principale
Saint-Michel, QC J0L 2J0
Tél: 450-454-4502; *Téléc:* 450-454-7508
stmichel@cstsm.net
Entité municipal: Parish (Paroisse)
Incorporation: 1er juillet 1855 *Area:* 57,36 km2
Comté ou district: Les Jardins-de-Napierville; *Population au 2011:* 2,884
Circonscription(s) électorale(s) provinciale(s): Huntingdon
Circonscription(s) électorale(s) fédérale(s): St-Léonard-St-Michel
Prochaines élections: 3e novembre 2013
Pierre Raymond Cloutier, Maire
Micheline Lemay, Directrice générale

Saint-Michel-de-Bellechasse
129, rte 132 est
Saint-Michel-de-Bellechasse, QC G0R 3S0
Tél: 418-884-2865; *Téléc:* 418-884-2866
munstmic@globetrotter.net
www.saintmicheldebellechasse.com
Entité municipal: Municipality
Incorporation: 1er juillet 1855 *Area:* 53,43 km2
Comté ou district: Bellechasse; *Population au 2011:* 1,816
Circonscription(s) électorale(s) provinciale(s): Bellechasse
Circonscription(s) électorale(s) fédérale(s): Lévis-Bellechasse
Prochaines élections: 3e novembre 2013
Suzanne Côté, Mairesse
Ronald Gonthier, Directeur général

Saint-Michel-des-Saints
441, rue Brassard
Saint-Michel-des-Saints, QC J0K 3B0
Tél: 450-886-4502; *Téléc:* 450-833-6081
info@saintmicheldessaints.com
www.saintmicheldesaints.com
Entité municipal: Municipality
Incorporation: 3 mars 1979 *Area:* 563,72 km2
Comté ou district: Matawinie; *Population au 2011:* 2,201
Circonscription(s) électorale(s) provinciale(s): Berthier
Circonscription(s) électorale(s) fédérale(s): Joliette
Prochaines élections: 3e novembre 2013
Jean-Pierre Bellerose, Maire
Alain Bellerose, Directeur général

Saint-Michel-du-Squatec
CP 280
150, rue St-Joseph
Saint-Michel-du-Squatec, QC G0L 4H0
Tél: 418-855-2185; *Téléc:* 418-855-2935
info@squatec.qc.ca
www.squatec.qc.ca
Entité municipal: Parish (Paroisse)
Incorporation: 16 avril 1928 *Area:* 363,10 km2
Comté ou district: Témiscouata; *Population au 2011:* 1,171
Circonscription(s) électorale(s) provinciale(s):
Kamouraska-Témiscouata
Circonscription(s) électorale(s) fédérale(s):
Rimouski-Neigette-Témiscouata-Les Basques
Prochaines élections: 3e novembre 2013
André Chouinard, Maire
Danielle Albert, Directrice générale

Saint-Modeste
312, rue Principale
Saint-Modeste, QC G0L 3W0
Tél: 418-867-2352; *Téléc:* 418-867-5359
municipalite@saint-modeste.ca
www.municipalite.saint-modeste.qc.ca
Entité municipal: Parish (Paroisse)
Incorporation: 1er juillet 1855 *Area:* 107,91 km2
Comté ou district: Rivière-du-Loup; *Population au 2011:* 1,128
Circonscription(s) électorale(s) provinciale(s): Rivière-du-Loup
Circonscription(s) électorale(s) fédérale(s):
Montmagny-L'Islet-Kamouraska-Rivière-du-Loup
Prochaines élections: 3e novembre 2013
Louis-Marie Bastille, Maire
Alain Vila, Directeur général

Saint-Moïse
CP 8
117-B, rue Principale
Saint-Moïse, QC G0J 2Z0
Tél: 418-776-2833; *Téléc:* 418-776-2835
Other Information: muni.moise@globetrotter.net
Entité municipal: Parish (Paroisse)
Incorporation: 1er janvier 1878 *Area:* 106,83 km2
Comté ou district: La Matapédia; *Population au 2011:* 577
Circonscription(s) électorale(s) provinciale(s): Matapédia
Circonscription(s) électorale(s) fédérale(s): Haute-Gaspésie-La Mitis-Matane-Matapédia
Prochaines élections: 3e novembre 2013
Paul Lepage, Maire
Monique Bouchard, Directrice générale

Saint-Narcisse
353, rue Notre-Dame
Saint-Narcisse, QC G0X 2Y0
Tél: 418-328-8645; *Téléc:* 418-328-4348
municipalite@saint-narcisse.com
Entité municipal: Parish (Paroisse)
Incorporation: 1er juillet 1855 *Area:* 103,49 km2
Comté ou district: Les Chenaux; *Population au 2011:* 1,762
Circonscription(s) électorale(s) provinciale(s): Champlain
Circonscription(s) électorale(s) fédérale(s):
St-Maurice-Champlain
Prochaines élections: 3e novembre 2013
Guy Veillette, Maire
André Carignan, Directeur général

Saint-Narcisse-de-Beaurivage
#1, 508, rue de l'École
Saint-Narcisse-de-Beaurivage, QC G0S 1W0
Tél: 418-475-6842; *Téléc:* 418-475-6880
saintnarcisse@globetrotter.net
www.saintnarcissedebeaurivage.ca
Entité municipal: Parish (Paroisse)
Incorporation: 1er mai 1874 *Area:* 60,83 km2
Comté ou district: Lotbinière; *Population au 2011:* 1,091
Circonscription(s) électorale(s) provinciale(s): Lotbinière
Circonscription(s) électorale(s) fédérale(s):
Lotbinière-Chutes-de-la-Chaudière
Prochaines élections: 3e novembre 2013
Denis Dion, Maire
Dany Lehoux, Directrice générale

Saint-Narcisse-de-Rimouski
7, rue du Pavillon
Saint-Narcisse-de-Rimouski, QC G0K 1S0
Tél: 418-735-2638; *Téléc:* 418-735-6021
informations@saintnarcisse.net
www.saintnarcisse.net
Entité municipal: Parish (Paroisse)
Incorporation: 13 février 1922 *Area:* 166,83 km2
Comté ou district: Rimouski-Neigette; *Population au 2011:* 1,017
Circonscription(s) électorale(s) provinciale(s): Rimouski
Circonscription(s) électorale(s) fédérale(s):
Rimouski-Neigette-Témiscouata-Les Basques
Prochaines élections: 3e novembre 2013
Laurent Proulx, Maire
Gilles Lepage, Directeur général

Saint-Nazaire
199, rue Principale
Saint-Nazaire, QC G0W 2V0
Tél: 418-662-4154; *Téléc:* 418-662-5467
ktremblay@ville.saint-nazaire.ca
www.ville.saint-nazaire.qc.ca
Entité municipal: Municipality
Incorporation: 23 septembre 1905 *Area:* 147,78 km2

Comté ou district: Lac-St-Jean-Est; *Population au 2011:* 2,114
Circonscription(s) électorale(s) provinciale(s): Lac-St-Jean
Circonscription(s) électorale(s) fédérale(s):
Roberval-Lac-St-Jean
Prochaines élections: 3e novembre 2013
Martin Sauvé, Maire
Kathy Tremblay, Directrice générale

Saint-Nazaire-d'Acton
750, rue des Loisirs
Saint-Nazaire-d'Acton, QC J0H 1V0
Tél: 819-392-2347; *Téléc:* 819-392-2039
Entité municipal: Parish (Paroisse)
Incorporation: 8 janvier 1894 *Area:* 57,49 km2
Comté ou district: Acton; *Population au 2011:* 826
Circonscription(s) électorale(s) provinciale(s): Johnson
Circonscription(s) électorale(s) fédérale(s): St-Hyacinthe-Bagot
Prochaines élections: 3e novembre 2013
André Fafard, Maire
Guylaine Bourgoin, Directrice générale
gbourgoin@mun-nazaire.qc.ca

Saint-Nazaire-de-Dorchester
61A, rue Principale
Saint-Nazaire, QC G0R 3T0
Tél: 418-642-1305; *Téléc:* 418-642-2945
mun_st_nazaire@globetrotter.net
www.saint-nazaire-de-dorchester.org
Entité municipal: Parish (Paroisse)
Incorporation: 9 mars 1906 *Area:* 51,43 km2
Comté ou district: Bellechasse; *Population au 2011:* 355
Circonscription(s) électorale(s) provinciale(s): Bellechasse
Circonscription(s) électorale(s) fédérale(s): Lévis-Bellechasse
Prochaines élections: 3e novembre 2013
Claude Lachance, Maire
Francine Brochu, Directrice générale

Saint-Nérée
1990, rte Principale
Saint-Nérée, QC G0R 3V0
Tél: 418-243-2735; *Téléc:* 418-243-2136
muneree@globetrotter.net
www.st-neree.qc.ca
Entité municipal: Parish (Paroisse)
Incorporation: 29 mars 1887 *Area:* 75,73 km2
Comté ou district: Bellechasse; *Population au 2011:* 743
Circonscription(s) électorale(s) provinciale(s): Bellechasse
Circonscription(s) électorale(s) fédérale(s): Lévis-Bellechasse
Prochaines élections: 3e novembre 2013
Clément Vallières, Maire
Michael Couture, Directeur général

Saint-Noël
CP 99
51, rue de l'Église
Saint-Noël, QC G0J 3A0
Tél: 418-776-2936; *Téléc:* 418-776-5521
stnoel@mrcmatapedia.qc.ca
Entité municipal: Village
Incorporation: 2 octobre 1906 *Area:* 45,68 km2
Comté ou district: La Matapédia; *Population au 2011:* 434
Circonscription(s) électorale(s) provinciale(s): Matapédia
Circonscription(s) électorale(s) fédérale(s): Haute-Gaspésie-La Mitis-Matane-Matapédia
Prochaines élections: 3e novembre 2013
Gilbert Sénéchal, Maire
Manon Caron, Directrice générale

Saint-Norbert
2150, rue Principale
Saint-Norbert, QC J0K 3C0
Tél: 450-836-4700; *Téléc:* 450-836-4004
municipalite@saint-norbert.net
www.saint-norbert.net
Entité municipal: Parish (Paroisse)
Incorporation: 1er juillet 1855 *Area:* 77,31 km2
Comté ou district: D'Autray; *Population au 2011:* 1,059
Circonscription(s) électorale(s) provinciale(s): Berthier
Circonscription(s) électorale(s) fédérale(s): Berthier-Maskinongé
Prochaines élections: 3e novembre 2013
André Dauphin, Maire
Martine Laberge, Directrice générale

Saint-Norbert-d'Arthabaska
44, rue Landry
Saint-Norbert-d'Arthabaska, QC G0P 1B0
Tél: 819-369-9318; *Téléc:* 819-369-8686
Entité municipal: Municipality
Incorporation: 30 novembre 1994 *Area:* 113,66 km2
Comté ou district: Arthabaska; *Population au 2011:* 1,185
Circonscription(s) électorale(s) provinciale(s): Arthabaska
Circonscription(s) électorale(s) fédérale(s):
Richmond-Arthabaska
Prochaines élections: 3e novembre 2013
Ghislain Caouette, Maire
Linda Trottier, Directrice générale
ltrottier@saint-norbert-darthabaska.ca

Saint-Octave-de-Métis
201A, rue de l'Église
Saint-Octave-de-Métis, QC G0J 3B0
Tél: 418-775-2996; *Téléc:* 418-775-0099
stoctave@mitis.qc.ca
Entité municipal: Parish (Paroisse)
Incorporation: 25 avril 1908 *Area:* 74,63 km2
Comté ou district: La Mitis; *Population au 2011:* 345
Circonscription(s) électorale(s) provinciale(s): Matapédia
Circonscription(s) électorale(s) fédérale(s): Haute-Gaspésie-La Mitis-Matane-Matapédia
Prochaines élections: 3e novembre 2013
Mylène-Julie Lavoie, Maire
Maxime Richard-Dubé, Directeur général

Saint-Odilon-de-Cranbourne
CP 100
111, rue de l'Hôtel-de-Ville
Saint-Odilon, QC G0S 3A0
Tél: 418-464-4801; *Téléc:* 418-464-4800
info@saint-odilon.qc.ca
www.saint-odilon.qc.ca
Entité municipal: Parish (Paroisse)
Incorporation: 1er juillet 1855 *Area:* 128,77 km2
Comté ou district: Robert-Cliche; *Population au 2011:* 1,459
Circonscription(s) électorale(s) provinciale(s): Beauce-Nord
Circonscription(s) électorale(s) fédérale(s): Beauce
Prochaines élections: 3e novembre 2013
Marc-André Labbé, Maire
Suzie Turcotte, Directrice générale

Saint-Omer
243, rang des Pelletier
Saint-Omer, QC G0R 4R0
Tél: 418-356-5634; *Téléc:* 418-356-5634
municipalitest-omer@globetrotter.net
Entité municipal: Municipality
Incorporation: 1er janvier 1954 *Area:* 125,35 km2
Comté ou district: L'Islet; *Population au 2011:* 310
Circonscription(s) électorale(s) provinciale(s): Montmagny-L'Islet
Circonscription(s) électorale(s) fédérale(s):
Montmagny-L'Islet-Kamouraska-Rivière-du-Loup
Prochaines élections: 3e novembre 2013
Réjeanne Godbout, Mairesse
Lise Bastien, Directrice générale

Saint-Onésime-d'Ixworth
12, rue de l'Église
Saint-Onésime-d'Ixworth, QC G0R 3W0
Tél: 418-856-3018; *Téléc:* 418-856-6626
municipalite@stonesime.com
Entité municipal: Parish (Paroisse)
Incorporation: 13 mai 1895 *Area:* 103,59 km2
Comté ou district: Kamouraska; *Population au 2011:* 559
Circonscription(s) électorale(s) provinciale(s):
Kamouraska-Témiscouata
Circonscription(s) électorale(s) fédérale(s):
Montmagny-L'Islet-Kamouraska-Rivière-du-Loup
Prochaines élections: 3e novembre 2013
Jacques Dionne, Maire
Hélène Lessard, Directrice générale

Saint-Ours
CP 129
2540, rue de l'Immaculée-Conception
Saint-Ours, QC J0G 1P0
Tél: 450-785-2203; *Téléc:* 450-785-2254
Entité municipal: Village
Incorporation: 17 avril 1991 *Area:* 58,50 km2
Comté ou district: Pierre-De Saurel; *Population au 2011:* 1,721
Circonscription(s) électorale(s) provinciale(s): Richelieu
Circonscription(s) électorale(s) fédérale(s):
Bas-Richelieu-Nicolet-Bécancour
Prochaines élections: 3e novembre 2013
Robert Tremblay, Maire
Pierre Dion, Directeur général
pdion@pierredesaurel.com

Saint-Pacôme
CP 370
27, rue St-Louis
Saint-Pacôme, QC G0L 3X0
Tél: 418-852-2356; *Téléc:* 418-852-2977
stpacome@bellnet.ca
www.st-pacome.ca
Entité municipal: Municipality
Incorporation: 5 janvier 1980 *Area:* 29,31 km2
Comté ou district: Kamouraska; *Population au 2011:* 1,658
Circonscription(s) électorale(s) provinciale(s):
Kamouraska-Témiscouata
Circonscription(s) électorale(s) fédérale(s):
Montmagny-L'Islet-Kamouraska-Rivière-du-Loup
Prochaines élections: 3e novembre 2013
Gervais Lévesque, Maire
Fréderic Lee, Directeur général

Saint-Pamphile
3, rte Elgin sud
Saint-Pamphile, QC G0R 3X0
Tél: 418-356-5501; *Téléc:* 418-356-5502
pamphile@globetrotter.qc.ca
www.saintpamphile.ca
Entité municipal: Town
Incorporation: 21 janvier 1888 *Area:* 136,80 km2
Comté ou district: L'Islet; *Population au 2011:* 2,685
Circonscription(s) électorale(s) provinciale(s): Montmagny-L'Islet
Circonscription(s) électorale(s) fédérale(s):
Montmagny-L'Islet-Kamouraska-Rivière-du-Loup
Prochaines élections: 3e novembre 2013
Réal Laverdière, Maire
Richard Pelletier, Directeur général

Saint-Pascal
CP 250
405, rue Taché
Saint-Pascal, QC G0L 3Y0
Tél: 418-492-2312; *Téléc:* 418-492-9862
hoteldeville@villestpascal.com
www.villesaintpascal.qc.ca
Entité municipal: Town
Incorporation: 1er mars 2000 *Area:* 57,75 km2
Comté ou district: Kamouraska; *Population au 2011:* 3,490
Circonscription(s) électorale(s) provinciale(s):
Kamouraska-Témiscouata
Circonscription(s) électorale(s) fédérale(s):
Montmagny-L'Islet-Kamouraska-Rivière-du-Loup
Prochaines élections: 3e novembre 2013
Renald Bernier, Maire
Louise Saint-Pierre, Greffière

Saint-Patrice-de-Beaurivage
530, rue Principale
Saint-Patrice-de-Beaurivage, QC G0S 1B0
Tél: 418-596-2362; *Téléc:* 418-596-2430
st.patrice@globetrotter.net
www.ville.saint-patrice-de-beaurivage.qc.ca
Entité municipal: Municipality
Incorporation: 29 septembre 1984 *Area:* 86,18 km2
Comté ou district: Lotbinière; *Population au 2011:* 1,080
Circonscription(s) électorale(s) provinciale(s): Lotbinière
Circonscription(s) électorale(s) fédérale(s):
Lotbinière-Chutes-de-la-Chaudière
Prochaines élections: 3e novembre 2013
Lewis Camden, Maire
Frédéric Desjardins, Directrice générale

Saint-Patrice-de-Sherrington
300, rue St-Patrice
Saint-Patrice-de-Sherrington, QC J0L 2N0
Tél: 450-454-4959; *Téléc:* 450-454-5677
municipalitesherrington@intermobilex.com
Entité municipal: Parish (Paroisse)
Incorporation: 1er juillet 1855 *Area:* 91,47 km2
Comté ou district: Les Jardins-de-Napierville; *Population au 2011:* 1,971
Circonscription(s) électorale(s) provinciale(s): Huntingdon
Circonscription(s) électorale(s) fédérale(s):
Beauharnois-Salaberry
Prochaines élections: 3e novembre 2013
André Giroux, Maire
Francine Fleurent, Directrice générale

Saint-Paul
18, boul Brassard
Saint-Paul, QC J0K 3E0
Tél: 450-759-4040; *Téléc:* 450-759-6396
mairie@municipalitestpaul.qc.ca
www.municipalitestpaul.qc.ca
Entité municipal: Municipality
Incorporation: 1er juillet 1855 *Area:* 48,17 km2
Comté ou district: Joliette; *Population au 2011:* 5,122
Circonscription(s) électorale(s) provinciale(s): Joliette
Circonscription(s) électorale(s) fédérale(s): Joliette
Prochaines élections: 3e novembre 2013
Alain Bellemarre, Maire
Richard-B. Morasse, Directeur général

Saint-Paul-d'Abbotsford
926, rue Principale est
Saint-Paul-d'Abbotsford, QC J0E 1A0
Tél: 450-379-5408; *Téléc:* 450-379-9905
dg@stpauldabbotsford.qc.ca
www.saintpauldabbotsford.qc.ca
Entité municipal: Parish (Paroisse)
Incorporation: 1er juillet 1855 *Area:* 79,59 km2
Comté ou district: Rouville; *Population au 2011:* 2,870
Circonscription(s) électorale(s) provinciale(s): Iberville
Circonscription(s) électorale(s) fédérale(s): Shefford
Prochaines élections: 3e novembre 2013
Dean Thomson, Maire
Daniel-Eric St-Onge, Directeur général

Saint-Paul-de-l'Ile-aux-Noix
959, rue Principale
Saint-Paul-de-l'Ile-aux-Noix, QC J0J 1G0
Tél: 450-291-3166; *Téléc:* 450-291-5930
mairie_stpaul@netc.net
www.ile-aux-noix.qc.ca
Entité municipal: Parish (Paroisse)
Incorporation: 18 novembre 1898 *Area:* 29,47 km2
Comté ou district: Le Haut-Richelieu; *Population au 2011:* 1,877
Circonscription(s) électorale(s) provinciale(s): Huntingdon
Circonscription(s) électorale(s) fédérale(s): St-Jean
Prochaines élections: 1er novembre 2013
Marie-Lili Lenoir, Directrice générale & Sec.-Trés.
Gérard Dutil, Maire

Saint-Paul-de-la-Croix
CP 70
1A, rue du Parc
Saint-Paul-de-la-Croix, QC G0L 3Z0
Tél: 418-898-2031; *Téléc:* 418-898-2322
munstpaul@st-paul-de-la-croix.qc.ca
www.municipalite.saint-paul-de-la-croix.qc.ca
Entité municipal: Parish (Paroisse)
Incorporation: 1er janvier 1873 *Area:* 84,25 km2
Comté ou district: Rivière-du-Loup; *Population au 2011:* 367
Circonscription(s) électorale(s) provinciale(s): Rivière-du-Loup
Circonscription(s) électorale(s) fédérale(s):
Montmagny-L'Islet-Kamouraska-Rivière-du-Loup
Prochaines élections: 3e novembre 2013
Phillipe Dionne, Maire
Hélène Malenfant, Directrice générale

Saint-Paul-de-Montminy
CP 160
309, 4e av
Saint-Paul-de-Montminy, QC G0R 3Y0
Tél: 418-469-3120; *Téléc:* 418-469-3358
municipalitest-paul@globetrotter.net
www.stpauldemontminy.com
Entité municipal: Municipality
Incorporation: 1er janvier 1862 *Area:* 162,80 km2
Comté ou district: Montmagny; *Population au 2011:* 824
Circonscription(s) électorale(s) provinciale(s): Montmagny-L'Islet
Circonscription(s) électorale(s) fédérale(s):
Montmagny-L'Islet-Kamouraska-Rivière-du-Loup
Prochaines élections: 3e novembre 2013
Émile Tanguay, Maire
Claudette Aubé, Directrice générale

Saint-Paulin
CP 120
3051, rue Bergeron
Saint-Paulin, QC J0K 3G0
Tél: 819-268-2026; *Téléc:* 819-268-2890
munistpaulindg@telmilot.net
www.st-paulin.qc.ca
Entité municipal: Municipality
Incorporation: 27 février 1988 *Area:* 96,40 km2
Comté ou district: Maskinongé; *Population au 2011:* 1,534
Circonscription(s) électorale(s) provinciale(s): Maskinongé
Circonscription(s) électorale(s) fédérale(s): Berthier-Maskinongé
Prochaines élections: 3e novembre 2013
Brigitte Gagnon, Mairesse
Ghislain Lemay, Directeur général

Saint-Philémon
1531, rue Principale
Saint-Philémon, QC G0R 4A0
Tél: 418-469-2890; *Téléc:* 418-469-2726
munphile@globetrotter.net
www.saint-philemon.com
Entité municipal: Parish (Paroisse)
Incorporation: 1er janvier 1867 *Area:* 146,51 km2
Comté ou district: Bellechasse; *Population au 2011:* 742
Circonscription(s) électorale(s) provinciale(s): Bellechasse
Circonscription(s) électorale(s) fédérale(s): Lévis-Bellechasse
Prochaines élections: 3e novembre 2013
Daniel Pouliot, Maire
Diane Labrecque, Directrice générale

Saint-Philibert
403, rue Principale
Saint-Philibert, QC G0M 1X0
Tél: 418-228-8759; *Téléc:* 418-228-0432
www.st-philibert.qc.ca
Entité municipal: Municipality
Incorporation: 25 février 1921 *Area:* 57,26 km2
Comté ou district: Beauce-Sartigan; *Population au 2011:* 367
Circonscription(s) électorale(s) provinciale(s): Beauce-Sud
Circonscription(s) électorale(s) fédérale(s): Beauce
Prochaines élections: 3e novembre 2013
Marc Nasdeau, Maire
Chantale Gareau, Directrice générale
gareau.chantale@st-philibert.qc.ca3

Saint-Philippe
2225, rte Édouard-VII
Saint-Philippe, QC J0L 2K0
Tél: 450-659-7701; *Téléc:* 450-659-7702
administration@municipalite.saint-philippe.qc.ca
www.municipalite.saint-philippe.qc.ca
Entité municipal: Municipality
Incorporation: 1er juillet 1855 *Area:* 61,66 km2
Comté ou district: Roussillon; *Population au 2011:* 5,495
Circonscription(s) électorale(s) provinciale(s): La Prairie
Circonscription(s) électorale(s) fédérale(s): Brossard-La Prairie
Prochaines élections: 1er novembre 2013
Claudine Cormier, Greffière
Gaétan Brosseau, Maire

Saint-Philippe-de-Néri
CP 130
12, côte de l'Église
Saint-Philippe-de-Néri, QC G0L 4A0
Tél: 418-498-2744; *Téléc:* 418-498-2193
munic.s.phil.neri@qc.aira.com
Entité municipal: Parish (Paroisse)
Incorporation: 29 décembre 1875 *Area:* 33,08 km2
Comté ou district: Kamouraska; *Population au 2011:* 868
Circonscription(s) électorale(s) provinciale(s):
Kamouraska-Témiscouata
Circonscription(s) électorale(s) fédérale(s):
Montmagny-L'Islet-Kamouraska-Rivière-du-Loup
Prochaines élections: 3e novembre 2013
Gilles Lévesque, Maire
Pierre Leclerc, Directeur général

Saint-Pie
77, rue St-Pierre
Saint-Pie, QC J0H 1W0
Tél: 450-772-2488; *Téléc:* 450-772-2233
st-pie@villest-pie.ca
www.villest-pie.ca
Entité municipal: Town
Incorporation: 28 février 2003 *Area:* 106,47 km2
Comté ou district: Les Maskoutains; *Population au 2011:* 5,438
Circonscription(s) électorale(s) provinciale(s): Iberville
Circonscription(s) électorale(s) fédérale(s): St-Hyacinthe-Bagot
Prochaines élections: 3e novembre 2013
Note: Effective February 28, 2003, the Parish & the Village of St-Pie amalgamated to create the new City of St-Pie.
Pierre St-Onge, Maire
Denise Breton, Greffière

Saint-Pie-de-Guire
435, rue Principale
Saint-Pie-de-Guire, QC J0G 1R0
Tél: 450-784-2278; *Téléc:* 450-784-0133
stpiedeguire@bellnet.ca
www.stpiedeguire.ca
Entité municipal: Parish (Paroisse)
Incorporation: 14 juin 1866 *Area:* 52,34 km2
Comté ou district: Drummond; *Population au 2011:* 456
Circonscription(s) électorale(s) provinciale(s): Nicolet-Yamaska
Circonscription(s) électorale(s) fédérale(s): Drummond
Prochaines élections: 3e novembre 2013
Benoît Bourque, Maire
Claire Roy, Directrice générale

Saint-Pierre
485, ch du Village-de-St-Pierre nord
Joliette, QC J6E 3Z1
Tél: 450-756-2592; *Téléc:* 450-756-2735
villagestpierre@qc.aira.com
Entité municipal: Village
Incorporation: 24 avril 1922 *Area:* 10,60 km2
Comté ou district: Joliette; *Population au 2011:* 305
Circonscription(s) électorale(s) provinciale(s): Joliette
Circonscription(s) électorale(s) fédérale(s): Joliette
Prochaines élections: 3e novembre 2013
Roland Charest, Maire
Édith Gagné, Directrice générale

Saint-Pierre-Baptiste
532B, rte de l'Église
Saint-Pierre-Baptiste, QC G0P 1K0
Tél: 418-453-2286; *Téléc:* 418-453-2286
info@saintpierrebaptiste.qc.ca
www.saintpierrebaptiste.qc.ca
Entité municipal: Parish (Paroisse)
Incorporation: 1er janvier 1874 *Area:* 80,72 km2
Comté ou district: L'Érable; *Population au 2011:* 485
Circonscription(s) électorale(s) provinciale(s): Lotbinière
Circonscription(s) électorale(s) fédérale(s): Mégantic-L'Érable
Prochaines élections: 3e novembre 2013
Yvon Gingras, Maire
Annie Poirier, Directrice générale

Saint-Pierre-de-Broughton
CP 90
29, rue de la Fabrique
Saint-Pierre-de-Broughton, QC G0N 1T0
Tél: 418-424-3572; *Téléc:* 418-424-0389
muni.stpierre@ville.st-pierre-de-broughton.qc.ca
www.ville.st-pierre-de-broughton.qc.ca
Entité municipal: Municipality
Incorporation: 12 octobre 1974 *Area:* 147,460 km2
Comté ou district: Les Appalaches; *Population au 2011:* 882
Circonscription(s) électorale(s) provinciale(s): Frontenac
Circonscription(s) électorale(s) fédérale(s): Mégantic-L'Érable
Prochaines élections: 3e novembre 2013
Nicole Bourque, Mairesse
Sylvie Mercier, Directrice générale

Saint-Pierre-de-la-Rivière-du-Sud
645 - 2e av
St-Pierre-de-la-Rivière-du-Sud, QC G0R 4B0
Tél: 418-248-8277; *Téléc:* 418-248-7068
st-pierre.rivsud@globetrotter.net
www.stpierrerivieresud.net
Entité municipal: Parish (Paroisse)
Incorporation: 1er juillet 1855 *Area:* 92,28 km2
Comté ou district: Montmagny; *Population au 2011:* 920
Circonscription(s) électorale(s) provinciale(s): Montmagny-L'Islet
Circonscription(s) électorale(s) fédérale(s):
Montmagny-L'Islet-Kamouraska-Rivière-du-Loup
Prochaines élections: 3e novembre 2013
Marie Eve Proulx, Mairesse
Georges Baillargeon, Directeur général

Saint-Pierre-de-Lamy
115, rte de l'Église
Saint-Pierre-de-Lamy, QC G0L 4B0
Tél: 418-497-2447; *Téléc:* 418-497-2447
admin@saintpierredelamy.ca
Entité municipal: Municipality
Incorporation: 4 juin 1977 *Area:* 115,46 km2
Comté ou district: Témiscouata; *Population au 2011:* 112
Circonscription(s) électorale(s) provinciale(s):
Kamouraska-Témiscouata
Circonscription(s) électorale(s) fédérale(s):
Rimouski-Neigette-Témiscouata-Les Basques
Prochaines élections: 3e novembre 2013
Gaston Caron, Maire
Mireille Plourde, Directrice générale

Saint-Pierre-de-Véronne-à-Pike-River
CP 93
548, rte 202
St-Pierre-de-Véronne, QC J0J 1P0
Tél: 450-248-2120; *Téléc:* 450-248-4772
pikeriver@axion.ca
www.pikeriver.ca
Entité municipal: Municipality
Incorporation: 3 avril 1912 *Area:* 43,58 km2
Comté ou district: Brome-Missisquoi; *Population au 2011:* 525
Circonscription(s) électorale(s) provinciale(s): Brome-Missisquoi
Circonscription(s) électorale(s) fédérale(s): Brome-Missisquoi
Prochaines élections: 3e novembre 2013
Martin Bellefroid, Maire
Sonia Côté, Directrice générale

Saint-Pierre-Ile-d'Orléans
515, rte des Prêtres
Saint-Pierre-Ile-d'Orléans, QC G0A 4E0
Tél: 418-828-2855; *Téléc:* 418-828-0724
Entité municipal: Municipality
Incorporation: 1er juillet 1855 *Area:* 31,13 km2
Comté ou district: L'Ile-d'Orléans; *Population au 2011:* 1,789
Circonscription(s) électorale(s) provinciale(s): Montmorency

Circonscription(s) électorale(s) fédérale(s):
Montmorency-Charlevoix-Haute-Côte-Nord
Prochaines élections: 3e novembre 2013
Jacques Trudel, Maire
Gérard Cossette, Directeur général
gcossette@stpierreio.ca

Saint-Pierre-les-Becquets
110, rue des Loisirs
Saint-Pierre-les-Becquets, QC G0X 2Z0
Tél: 819-263-2622; *Téléc:* 819-263-0798
municipalite@st-pierre-les-becquets.qc.ca
www.st-pierre-les-becquets.qc.ca
Entité municipal: Municipality
Incorporation: 22 février 1986 *Area:* 43,00 km2
Comté ou district: Bécancour; *Population au 2011:* 1,223
Circonscription(s) électorale(s) provinciale(s): Lotbinière
Circonscription(s) électorale(s) fédérale(s):
Bas-Richelieu-Nicolet-Bécancour
Prochaines élections: 3e novembre 2013
Raymond Dion, Maire
Michèle Laquerre, Directrice générale

Saint-Placide
281, montée St-Vincent
Saint-Placide, QC J0V 2B0
Tél: 450-258-2305; *Téléc:* 450-258-3059
infosp@municipalite.st-placide.qc.ca
www.municipalite.saint-placide.qc.ca
Entité municipal: Municipality
Incorporation: 3 août 1994 *Area:* 41,95 km2
Comté ou district: Deux-Montagnes; *Population au 2011:* 1,715
Circonscription(s) électorale(s) provinciale(s): Mirabel
Circonscription(s) électorale(s) fédérale(s):
Argenteuil-Papineau-Mirabel
Prochaines élections: 3e novembre 2013
Denis Lavigne, Maire
Lise Lavigne, Directrice générale

Saint-Polycarpe
CP 380
1263, ch Élie-Auclair
Saint-Polycarpe, QC J0P 1X0
Tél: 450-265-3777; *Téléc:* 450-265-3010
mdery@munstpolycarpe.qc.ca
www.munstpolycarpe.qc.ca
Entité municipal: Municipality
Incorporation: 31 décembre 1988 *Area:* 70,80 km2
Comté ou district: Vaudreuil-Soulanges; *Population au 2011:* 1,969
Circonscription(s) électorale(s) provinciale(s): Soulanges
Circonscription(s) électorale(s) fédérale(s): Vaudreuil-Soulanges
Prochaines élections: 3e novembre 2013
Normand Ménard, Maire
Micheline Déry, Directrice générale

Saint-Prime
599, rue Principale
Saint-Prime, QC G8J 1T2
Tél: 418-251-2116; *Téléc:* 418-251-2823
rgirard@saint-prime.ca
www.saint-prime.ca
Entité municipal: Municipality
Incorporation: 29 juin 1968 *Area:* 147,43 km2
Comté ou district: Le Domaine-du-Roy; *Population au 2011:* 2,758
Circonscription(s) électorale(s) provinciale(s): Roberval
Circonscription(s) électorale(s) fédérale(s):
Roberval-Lac-St-Jean
Prochaines élections: 1er novembre 2013
Régis Girard, Sec.-Trés. & Directeur général
Bernard Généreux, Maire

Saint-Prosper
2025, 29e rue
Saint-Prosper, QC G0M 1Y0
Tél: 418-594-8135; *Téléc:* 418-594-8865
stpros@globetrotter.qc.ca
www.saint-prosper.com
Entité municipal: Municipality
Incorporation: 26 septembre 1887 *Area:* 136, 95 km2
Comté ou district: Les Etchemins; *Population au 2011:* 3,605
Circonscription(s) électorale(s) provinciale(s): Beauce-Sud
Circonscription(s) électorale(s) fédérale(s): Beauce
Prochaines élections: 3e novembre 2013
Richard Couët, Maire
Johanne Nadeau, Directrice générale

Saint-Prosper-de-Champlain
CP 68
375, rue St-Joseph
Saint-Prosper, QC G0X 3A0
Tél: 418-840-0461; *Téléc:* 418-328-4267
municipalite@st-prosper.ca
www.st-prosper.ca
Entité municipal: Parish (Paroisse)
Incorporation: 1er juillet 1855 *Area:* 92,03 km2
Comté ou district: Les Chenaux; *Population au 2011:* 505
Circonscription(s) électorale(s) provinciale(s): Champlain
Circonscription(s) électorale(s) fédérale(s):
St-Maurice-Champlain
Prochaines élections: 3e novembre 2013
Michel Grosleau, Maire
Francine Masse, Directrice générale

Saint-Raphaël
CP 1091
19, av Chanoine-Audet
Saint-Raphaël, QC G0R 4C0
Tél: 418-243-2853; *Téléc:* 418-243-2605
muraph@globetrotter.net
www.municipalite.saint-raphael.qc.ca
Entité municipal: Municipality
Incorporation: 8 décembre 1993 *Area:* 120,06 km2
Comté ou district: Bellechasse; *Population au 2011:* 2,463
Circonscription(s) électorale(s) provinciale(s): Bellechasse
Circonscription(s) électorale(s) fédérale(s): Lévis-Bellechasse
Prochaines élections: 3e novembre 2013
Gilles Breton, Maire
Paul Beaudoin, Directeur général

Saint-Raymond
375, rue St-Joseph
Saint-Raymond, QC G3L 1A1
Tél: 418-337-2202; *Téléc:* 418-337-2203
info@villesaintraymond.com
www.villesaintraymond.coma
Entité municipal: Town
Incorporation: 29 mars 1995 *Area:* 684,65 km2
Comté ou district: Portneuf; *Population au 2011:* 9,615
Circonscription(s) électorale(s) provinciale(s): Portneuf
Circonscription(s) électorale(s) fédérale(s):
Portneuf-Jacques-Cartier
Prochaines élections: 3e novembre 2013
Vacant, Maire
Chantal Plamandon, Greffière

Saint-Rémi
105, rue de la Mairie
Saint-Rémi, QC J0L 2L0
Tél: 450-454-3993; *Téléc:* 450-454-7978
administration@ville.saint-remi.qc.ca
www.ville.saint-remi.qc.ca
Entité municipal: Town
Incorporation: 20 septembre 1975 *Area:* 79,66 km2
Comté ou district: Les Jardins-de-Napierville; *Population au 2011:* 7,265
Circonscription(s) électorale(s) provinciale(s): Huntingdon
Circonscription(s) électorale(s) fédérale(s):
Beauharnois-Salaberry
Prochaines élections: 3e novembre 2013
Michel Lavoie, Maire
Diane Soucy, Greffier

Saint-Rémi-de-Tingwick
156A, rue Principale
Saint-Rémi-de-Tingwick, QC J0A 1K0
Tél: 819-359-2731; *Téléc:* 819-359-3532
info@st-remi-de-tingwick.qc.ca
Entité municipal: Parish (Paroisse)
Incorporation: 1er janvier 1882 *Area:* 72,18 km2
Comté ou district: Arthabaska; *Population au 2011:* 474
Circonscription(s) électorale(s) provinciale(s): Richmond
Circonscription(s) électorale(s) fédérale(s):
Richmond-Arthabaska
Prochaines élections: 3e novembre 2013
Estelle Luneau, Mairesse
Éva Fréchette, Directrice générale

Saint-René
778, rte Principale
Saint-René, QC G0M 1Z0
Tél: 418-382-5226; *Téléc:* 418-382-3655
muni.st.rene@globetrotter.net
Entité municipal: Parish (Paroisse)
Incorporation: 1er janvier 1945 *Area:* 61,53 km3
Comté ou district: Beauce-Sartigan; *Population au 2011:* 658
Circonscription(s) électorale(s) provinciale(s): Beauce-Sud
Circonscription(s) électorale(s) fédérale(s): Beauce
Prochaines élections: 3e novembre 2013
Jean-Guy Deblois, Maire
Michel Gilbert, Directeur général

Saint-René-de-Matane
CP 58
178, av St-René
Saint-René-de-Matane, QC G0J 3E0
Tél: 418-224-3306; *Téléc:* 418-224-3259
st-renedematane@mrcdematane.qc.ca
www.municipalite.st-rene-matane.qc.ca
Entité municipal: Municipality
Incorporation: 18 décembre 1982 *Area:* 255,58 km2
Comté ou district: Matane; *Population au 2011:* 1,089
Circonscription(s) électorale(s) provinciale(s): Matane
Circonscription(s) électorale(s) fédérale(s): Haute-Gaspésie-La Mitis-Matane-Matapédia
Prochaines élections: 3e novembre 2013
Roger Vaillancourt, Maire
Yvette Boulay, Directrice générale

Saint-Robert
CP 150
650, ch de St-Robert
Saint-Robert, QC J0G 1S0
Tél: 450-782-2844; *Téléc:* 450-782-2733
strobert@bas-richelieu.net
www.saintrobert.qc.ca
Entité municipal: Municipality
Incorporation: 17 octobre 1857 *Area:* 64,93 km2
Comté ou district: Pierre-De Saurel; *Population au 2011:* 1,794
Circonscription(s) électorale(s) provinciale(s): Richelieu
Circonscription(s) électorale(s) fédérale(s):
Bas-Richelieu-Nicolet-Bécanour
Prochaines élections: 3e novembre 2013
Gilles Salvas, Maire
Nathalie Lussier, Directrice générale

Saint-Robert-Bellarmin
10, rue Nadeau
Saint-Robert-Bellarmin, QC G0M 2E0
Tél: 418-582-3420; *Téléc:* 418-582-0052
mun-st-robert@bellarmin.ca
www.st-robertbellarmin.qc.ca
Entité municipal: Municipality
Incorporation: 1er janvier 1949 *Area:* 234,82 km2
Comté ou district: Le Granit; *Population au 2011:* 676
Circonscription(s) électorale(s) provinciale(s): Beauce-Sud
Circonscription(s) électorale(s) fédérale(s): Beauce
Prochaines élections: 3e novembre 2013
Jeannot Lachance, Maire
Suzanne Lescomb, Directrice générale

Saint-Roch-de-l'Achigan
CP 480
30, rue du Dr.-Wilfrid-Locat nord
Saint-Roch-de-l'Achigan, QC J0K 3H0
Tél: 450-588-2326; *Téléc:* 450-588-4478
mairie@saint-roch-de-lachigan.qc.ca
www.strochlachigan.com
Entité municipal: Parish (Paroisse)
Incorporation: 1er juillet 1855 *Area:* 78,83 km2
Comté ou district: Montcalm; *Population au 2011:* 4,892
Circonscription(s) électorale(s) provinciale(s): Rousseau
Circonscription(s) électorale(s) fédérale(s): Montcalm
Prochaines élections: 3e novembre 2013
Georges Locas, Maire
Philippe Riopelle, Directeur général

Saint-Roch-de-Mékinac
1212, rue Principale
Saint-Roch-de-Mékinac, QC G0X 2E0
Tél: 819-646-5635; *Téléc:* 819-646-5635
st-roch@regionmekinac.com
www.strochdemekinac.com
Entité municipal: Parish (Paroisse)
Incorporation: 2 novembre 2009 *Area:* 155,39 km2
Comté ou district: Mékinac; *Population au 2011:* 438
Circonscription(s) électorale(s) provinciale(s): Laviolette
Circonscription(s) électorale(s) fédérale(s):
St-Maurice-Champlain
Prochaines élections: 3e novembre 2013
Guy Dessureault, Maire
Robert Jourdain, Directeur général

Saint-Roch-de-Richelieu
1111, rue du Parc
Saint-Roch-de-Richelieu, QC J0L 2M0
Tél: 450-785-2755; *Téléc:* 450-785-3098
stroch@pierredesaurel.com
www.saintrochderichelieu.qc.ca
Entité municipal: Municipality
Incorporation: 4 juin 1859 *Area:* 34,86 km2

Comté ou district: Pierre-De Saurel; *Population au 2011:* 2,122
Circonscription(s) électorale(s) provinciale(s): Verchères
Circonscription(s) électorale(s) fédérale(s):
Bas-Richelieu-Nicolet-Bécancour
Prochaines élections: 3e novembre 2013
Claude Pothier, Maire
Claude Gratton, Directeur général

Saint-Roch-des-Aulnaies
379, rte de l'Église
Saint-Roch-des-Aulnaies, QC G0R 4E0
Tél: 418-354-2892; *Téléc:* 418-354-2059
munirock@globetrotter.net
www.saintrochdesaulnaies.ca
Entité municipal: Parish (Paroisse)
Incorporation: 1er juillet 1855 *Area:* 48,28 km2
Comté ou district: L'Islet; *Population au 2011:* 967
Circonscription(s) électorale(s) provinciale(s):
Kamouraska-Témiscouata
Circonscription(s) électorale(s) fédérale(s):
Montmorency-Charlevoix-Haute-Côte-Nord
Prochaines élections: 3e novembre 2013
Cécile Morin, Directrice générale
Michel Castonguay, Maire

Saint-Roch-Ouest
806, rang de la Rivière sud, RR#2
Saint-Roch-Ouest, QC J0K 3H0
Tél: 450-588-6060; *Téléc:* 450-588-0975
stroch_ouest@hotmail.com
Entité municipal: Municipality
Incorporation: 4 juin 1921 *Area:* 20,90 km2
Comté ou district: Montcalm; *Population au 2011:* 267
Circonscription(s) électorale(s) provinciale(s): Rousseau
Circonscription(s) électorale(s) fédérale(s): Montcalm
Prochaines élections: 3e novembre 2013
Claude Mercier, Maire
Sherron Kollar, Directrice générale

Saint-Romain
355, rue Principale
Saint-Romain, QC G0Y 1L0
Tél: 418-486-7374; *Téléc:* 418-486-7875
municipalite-st-romain@tellambton.net
Entité municipal: Municipality
Incorporation: 1er janvier 1858 *Area:* 112,92 km2
Comté ou district: Le Granit; *Population au 2011:* 707
Circonscription(s) électorale(s) provinciale(s):
Mégantic-Compton
Circonscription(s) électorale(s) fédérale(s): Mégantic-L'Érable
Prochaines élections: 3e novembre 2013
Jean-Luc Filion, Maire
Nicole P. Roy, Directrice générale

Saint-Rosaire
208, 6e rang
Saint-Rosaire, QC G0Z 1K0
Tél: 819-752-6178; *Téléc:* 819-752-3959
info@municipalitestrosaire.qc.ca
www.municipalitestrosaire.qc.ca
Entité municipal: Parish (Paroisse)
Incorporation: 23 mai 1896 *Area:* 109,84 km2
Comté ou district: Arthabaska; *Population au 2011:* 838
Circonscription(s) électorale(s) provinciale(s): Arthabaska
Circonscription(s) électorale(s) fédérale(s):
Richmond-Arthabaska
Prochaines élections: 3e novembre 2013
Harold Poisson, Maire
Jacques Boucher, Directeur général

Saint-Samuel
140, rue de l'Église
Saint-Samuel, QC G0Z 1G0
Tél: 819-353-1242; *Téléc:* 819-353-1499
info@saint-samuel.ca
www.saint-samuel.ca
Entité municipal: Parish (Paroisse)
Incorporation: 9 mars 1878 *Area:* 42,89 km2
Comté ou district: Arthabaska; *Population au 2011:* 743
Circonscription(s) électorale(s) provinciale(s): Richmond
Circonscription(s) électorale(s) fédérale(s):
Richmond-Arthabaska
Prochaines élections: 3e novembre 2013
René Mongrain, Maire
Suzie Constant, Directrice générale

Saint-Sauveur
1, place de la Mairie
Saint-Sauveur, QC J0R 1R6
Tél: 450-227-4633; *Téléc:* 450-227-3834
directiongenerale@ville.saint-sauveur.qc.ca
www.ville.saint-sauveur.qc.ca
Entité municipal: Town
Incorporation: 11 septembre 2002 *Area:* 47,99 km2
Comté ou district: Les Pays-d'en-Haut; *Population au 2011:* 9,881
Circonscription(s) électorale(s) provinciale(s): Bertrand
Circonscription(s) électorale(s) fédérale(s): Laurentides-Labelle
Prochaines élections: 3e novembre 2013
Note: Effective September 9, 2002, the Parish of St-Sauveur & the Village of St-Sauveur-des-Monts amalgamated to create the City of St-Sauveur.
Michel Lagacé, Maire
Normand Patrice, Greffier

Saint-Sébastien
582, rue Principale
Saint-Sébastien, QC G0Y 1M0
Tél: 819-652-2727; *Téléc:* 819-652-2584
st-sebastien@bellnet.ca
www.st-sebastien.com
Entité municipal: Municipality
Incorporation: 15 mars 1975 *Area:* 91,19 km2
Comté ou district: Le Granit; *Population au 2011:* 697
Circonscription(s) électorale(s) provinciale(s):
Mégantic-Compton
Circonscription(s) électorale(s) fédérale(s): Mégantic-L'Érable
Prochaines élections: 3e novembre 2013
Marie Douce Morin, Mairesse
Martine Rouleau, Directrice générale

Saint-Sébastien
CP 126
176, rue Dussault
Saint-Sébastien, QC J0J 2C0
Tél: 450-244-5237; *Téléc:* 450-244-6264
muniseba@netc.net
www.paroisse-saint-sebastien.ca
Entité municipal: Parish (Paroisse)
Incorporation: 17 février 1865 *Area:* 62,56 km2
Comté ou district: Le Haut-Richelieu; *Population au 2011:* 736
Circonscription(s) électorale(s) provinciale(s): Iberville
Circonscription(s) électorale(s) fédérale(s): Brome-Missisquoi
Prochaines élections: 3e novembre 2013
Michel Surprenant, Maire
Manon Donais, Directrice générale

Saint-Sévère
47, rue Principale
Saint-Sévère, QC G0X 3B0
Tél: 819-264-5656; *Téléc:* 819-264-5656
paroissestsevere@hotmail.com
Entité municipal: Parish (Paroisse)
Incorporation: 1er juillet 1855 *Area:* 31,83 km2
Comté ou district: Maskinongé; *Population au 2011:* 318
Circonscription(s) électorale(s) provinciale(s): Maskinongé
Circonscription(s) électorale(s) fédérale(s): Berthier-Maskinongé
Prochaines élections: 1er novembre 2013
Anne-Marie Sauvageau, Sec.-Trés. & Directrice générale
Yves Gélinas, Maire

Saint-Séverin
900, rue des Lacs
Saint-Séverin, QC G0N 1V0
Tél: 418-426-2423; *Téléc:* 418-426-1274
munseverin@oricom.ca
www.st-severin.qc.ca
Entité municipal: Parish (Paroisse)
Incorporation: 24 décembre 1875 *Area:* 56,22 km2
Comté ou district: Robert-Cliche; *Population au 2011:* 266
Circonscription(s) électorale(s) provinciale(s): Beauce-Nord
Circonscription(s) électorale(s) fédérale(s): Beauce
Prochaines élections: 3e novembre 2013
Daniel Perron, Maire
Paul Baker, Directeur général

Saint-Séverin
CP 120
1986, place du Centre
Saint-Séverin, QC G0X 2B0
Tél: 418-365-5844; *Téléc:* 418-365-7544
st-severin@regionmekinac.com
Entité municipal: Parish (Paroisse)
Incorporation: 11 avril 1890 *Area:* 61,97 km2
Comté ou district: Mékinac; *Population au 2011:* 860
Circonscription(s) électorale(s) provinciale(s): Laviolette
Circonscription(s) électorale(s) fédérale(s):
St-Maurice-Champlain
Prochaines élections: 3e novembre 2013
Michel Champagne, Maire
Jocelyn St-Amant, Directeur général

Saint-Siméon
CP 98
502, rue St-Laurent
Saint-Siméon, QC G0T 1X0
Tél: 418-638-2691; *Téléc:* 418-638-5145
info@saintsimeon.ca
www.saintsimeon.ca
Entité municipal: Municipality
Incorporation: 25 avril 2001 *Area:* 289,73 km2
Comté ou district: Charlevoix-Est; *Population au 2011:* 1,300
Circonscription(s) électorale(s) provinciale(s): Charlevoix
Circonscription(s) électorale(s) fédérale(s):
Montmorency-Charlevoix-Haute-Côte-Nord
Prochaines élections: 3e novembre 2013
Sylvain Tremblay, Maire
Sylvie Foster, Directrice générale

Saint-Siméon
CP 39
111, av de l'Église
Saint-Siméon, QC G0C 3A0
Tél: 418-534-2155; *Téléc:* 418-534-3830
munsseon@globetrotter.net
Entité municipal: Parish (Paroisse)
Incorporation: 29 octobre 1914 *Area:* 56,12 km2
Comté ou district: Bonaventure; *Population au 2011:* 1,179
Circonscription(s) électorale(s) provinciale(s): Bonaventure
Circonscription(s) électorale(s) fédérale(s):
Gaspésie—Îles-de-la-Madeleine
Prochaines élections: 3e novembre 2013
Jean-Guy Poirier, Maire
Jean-Pierre Gauthier, Directeur général

Saint-Simon
CP 40
30, rue de l'Église
Saint-Simon, QC G0L 4C0
Tél: 418-738-2896; *Téléc:* 418-738-2934
admin@st-simon.qc.ca
www.st-simon.qc.ca
Entité municipal: Parish (Paroisse)
Incorporation: 1er juillet 1855 *Area:* 75,62 km2
Comté ou district: Les Basques; *Population au 2011:* 438
Circonscription(s) électorale(s) provinciale(s): Rivière-du-Loup
Circonscription(s) électorale(s) fédérale(s):
Rimouski-Neigette-Témiscouata-Les Basques
Prochaines élections: 3e novembre 2013
Jérôme Rouleau, Maire
Yolande Théberge, Directrice générale

Saint-Simon
49, rue du Couvent
Saint-Simon-de-Bagot, QC J0H 1Y0
Tél: 450-798-2276; *Téléc:* 450-798-2498
st-simon@mrcmaskoutains.qc.ca
www.saint-simon.ca
Entité municipal: Parish (Paroisse)
Incorporation: 1er juillet 1855 *Area:* 68,66 km2
Comté ou district: Les Maskoutains; *Population au 2011:* 1,231
Circonscription(s) électorale(s) provinciale(s): St-Hyacinthe
Circonscription(s) électorale(s) fédérale(s): St-Hyacinthe-Bagot
Prochaines élections: 3e novembre 2013
Normand Corbeil, Maire
France Desjardins, Directrice générale

Saint-Simon-les-Mines
3338, rue Principale
Saint-Simon-les-Mines, QC G0M 1K0
Tél: 418-774-3317; *Téléc:* 418-774-3362
municipalitestsimonlesmines@sogetel.net
Entité municipal: Municipality
Incorporation: 1er juin 1950 *Area:* 44,80 km2
Comté ou district: Beauce-Sartigan; *Population au 2011:* 496
Circonscription(s) électorale(s) provinciale(s): Beauce-Sud
Circonscription(s) électorale(s) fédérale(s): Beauce
Prochaines élections: 3e novembre 2013
Martin Busque, Maire
Francine Poulin, Directrice générale

Saint-Sixte
5, rue Emery
Saint-Sixte, QC J0X 3B0
Tél: 819-983-3155; *Téléc:* 819-983-3409
Entité municipal: Municipality
Incorporation: 7 février 1893 *Area:* 83,44 km2
Comté ou district: Papineau; *Population au 2011:* 460
Circonscription(s) électorale(s) provinciale(s): Papineau
Circonscription(s) électorale(s) fédérale(s):
Argenteuil-Papineau-Mirabel
Prochaines élections: 3e novembre 2013
André Bélisle, Maire

Alain Hotte, Directeur général
alain.saintsixte@mrcpapineau.com

Saint-Stanislas
33, rue du Pont
Saint-Stanislas, QC G0X 3E0
Tél: 819-840-0703; *Téléc:* 418-328-4121
municipalite@saint-stanislas.ca
www.saint-stanislas.ca
Entité municipal: Municipality
Incorporation: 17 avril 1976 *Area:* 86,37 km2
Comté ou district: Les Chenaux; *Population au 2011:* 1,029
Circonscription(s) électorale(s) provinciale(s): Champlain
Circonscription(s) électorale(s) fédérale(s):
St-Maurice-Champlain
Prochaines élections: 3e novembre 2013
Alain Guillemette, Maire
Marc-Claude Jean, Directrice générale

Saint-Stanislas
953, rue Principale
Saint-Stanislas, QC G8L 7B4
Tél: 418-276-4476; *Téléc:* 418-276-9947
admin@st-stanislas.qc.ca
Entité municipal: Municipality
Incorporation: 24 octobre 1931 *Area:* 159,45 km2
Comté ou district: Maria-Chapdelaine; *Population au 2011:* 353
Circonscription(s) électorale(s) provinciale(s): Roberval
Circonscription(s) électorale(s) fédérale(s):
Roberval-Lac-St-Jean
Prochaines élections: 3e novembre 2013
Mario Biron, Maire
Caroline Gagnon, Directrice générale

Saint-Stanislas-de-Kostka
CP 120
221, rue Centrale
Saint-Stanislas-de-Kostka, QC J0S 1W0
Tél: 450-373-8944; *Téléc:* 450-373-8949
info@st-stanislas-de-kostka.ca
www.st-stanislas-de-kostka.ca
Entité municipal: Parish (Paroisse)
Incorporation: 1er juillet 1855 *Area:* 62,16 km2
Comté ou district: Beauharnois-Salaberry; *Population au 2011:* 1,553
Circonscription(s) électorale(s) provinciale(s): Beauharnois
Circonscription(s) électorale(s) fédérale(s):
Beauharnois-Salaberry
Prochaines élections: 3e novembre 2013
Jean-Pierre Gaboury, Maire
Louise Maheu Denis, Directrice générale

Saint-Sulpice
1089, rue Notre-Dame
Saint-Sulpice, QC J5W 1G1
Tél: 450-589-4450; *Téléc:* 450-589-9647
mun.paroissestsulpice@videotron.ca
www.municipalitesaintsulpice.com
Entité municipal: Parish (Paroisse)
Incorporation: 1er juillet 1855 *Area:* 37 km2
Comté ou district: L'Assomption; *Population au 2011:* 3,273
Circonscription(s) électorale(s) provinciale(s): L'Assomption
Circonscription(s) électorale(s) fédérale(s): Repentigny
Prochaines élections: 3e novembre 2013
Jean Gendron, Maire
Marie-Josée Masson, Directrice générale

Saint-Sylvère
837, 8e rang
Saint-Sylvère, QC G0Z 1H0
Tél: 819-285-2075; *Téléc:* 819-285-2040
mun.st.sylvere@infoteck.qc.ca
www.saint-sylvere.ca
Entité municipal: Municipality
Incorporation: 18 septembre 1976 *Area:* 85,02 km2
Comté ou district: Bécancour; *Population au 2011:* 865
Circonscription(s) électorale(s) provinciale(s): Nicolet-Yamaska
Circonscription(s) électorale(s) fédérale(s):
Bas-Richelieu-Nicolet-Bécancour
Prochaines élections: 3e novembre 2013
Claude Beaudoin, Maire
Ginette Richard, Directrice générale

Saint-Sylvestre
CP 70
423B, rue Principale
Saint-Sylvestre, QC G0S 3C0
Tél: 418-596-2384; *Téléc:* 418-596-2375
munisylvestre@altanet.ca
www.ville.saint-sylvestre.qc.ca
Entité municipal: Municipality
Incorporation: 4 décembre 1996 *Area:* 143,34 km2
Comté ou district: Lotbinière; *Population au 2011:* 1,035
Circonscription(s) électorale(s) provinciale(s): Lotbinière
Circonscription(s) électorale(s) fédérale(s):
Lotbinière-Chutes-de-la-Chaudière
Prochaines élections: 3e novembre 2013
Mario Grenier, Maire
Ginette Roger, Directrice générale

Saint-Télesphore
1425, rte 340
Saint-Télesphore, QC J0P 1Y0
Tél: 450-269-2999; *Téléc:* 450-269-2257
st-telesphore@xittel.ca
Entité municipal: Parish (Paroisse)
Incorporation: 10 avril 1877 *Area:* 59,62 km2
Comté ou district: Vaudreuil-Soulanges; *Population au 2011:* 762
Circonscription(s) électorale(s) provinciale(s): Soulanges
Circonscription(s) électorale(s) fédérale(s): Vaudreuil-Soulanges
Prochaines élections: 3e
Yvon Bériault, Maire
Nicole St-Pierre, Directrice générale

Saint-Tharcisius
CP 10
55, rue Principale
Saint-Tharcisius, QC G0J 3G0
Tél: 418-629-4727; *Téléc:* 418-629-4727
stharcisius@mrcmatapedia.qc.ca
Entité municipal: Parish (Paroisse)
Incorporation: 4 décembre 2009 *Area:* 79,61 km2
Comté ou district: La Matapédia; *Population au 2011:* 464
Circonscription(s) électorale(s) provinciale(s): Matapédia
Circonscription(s) électorale(s) fédérale(s): Haute-Gaspésie-La Mitis-Matane-Matapédia
Prochaines élections: 3e novembre 2013
Sophie Champagne, Mairesse
Joyce Kathie Collin, Directrice générale

Saint-Théodore-d-Acton
1661, rue Principale
Saint-Théodore-d-Acton, QC J0H 1Z0
Tél: 450-546-2634; *Téléc:* 450-546-2526
mun.st-theo@mrcacton.qc.ca
www.st-theodore.com
Entité municipal: Parish (Paroisse)
Incorporation: 1er janvier 1864 *Area:* 83,60 km2
Comté ou district: Acton; *Population au 2011:* 1,471
Circonscription(s) électorale(s) provinciale(s): Johnson
Circonscription(s) électorale(s) fédérale(s): St-Hyacinthe-Bagot
Prochaines élections: 3e novembre 2013
Dany Larivière, Maire
Marc Lévesque, Directrice générale

Saint-Théophile
CP 10
644, rue du Collège
Saint-Théophile, QC G0M 2A0
Tél: 418-597-3998; *Téléc:* 418-597-3015
muntheo@globetrotter.net
www.sainttheophile.qc.ca
Entité municipal: Municipality
Incorporation: 28 juin 1975 *Area:* 429,58 km2
Comté ou district: Beauce-Sartigan; *Population au 2011:* 743
Circonscription(s) électorale(s) provinciale(s): Beauce-Sud
Circonscription(s) électorale(s) fédérale(s): Beauce
Prochaines élections: 3e novembre 2013
Roland Boucher, Maire
Paula Lacoursière, Directrice générale

Saint-Thomas
1240, rte 158
Saint-Thomas, QC J0K 3L0
Tél: 450-759-3405; *Téléc:* 450-759-0059
municipalite@saintthomas.qc.ca
www.saintthomas.qc.ca
Entité municipal: Municipality
Incorporation: 1er juillet 1855 *Area:* 97,26 km2
Comté ou district: Joliette; *Population au 2011:* 3,193
Circonscription(s) électorale(s) provinciale(s): Joliette
Circonscription(s) électorale(s) fédérale(s): Joliette
Prochaines élections: 3e novembre 2013
Renè Vincent, Maire
Danielle Lambert, Directrice générale

Saint-Thomas-Didyme
9, av du Moulin
Saint-Thomas-Didyme, QC G0W 1P0
Tél: 418-274-3638; *Téléc:* 418-274-4176
www.stthomasdidyme.qc.ca
Entité municipal: Municipality
Incorporation: 11 mai 1923 *Area:* 325,36 km2
Comté ou district: Maria-Chapdelaine; *Population au 2011:* 677
Circonscription(s) électorale(s) provinciale(s): Roberval
Circonscription(s) électorale(s) fédérale(s):
Roberval-Lac-St-Jean
Prochaines élections: 3e novembre 2013
Denis Tremblay, Maire
Jean-Marc Paradis, Directeur général
jmparadis@stthomasdidyme.qc.ca

Saint-Thuribe
CP 69
385, rue Principale
Saint-Thuribe, QC G0A 4H0
Tél: 418-339-2171; *Téléc:* 418-339-3435
municipalitestthuribe@globetrotter.net
www.st-thuribe.net
Entité municipal: Parish (Paroisse)
Incorporation: 14 février 1898 *Area:* 50,81 km2
Comté ou district: Portneuf; *Population au 2011:* 288
Circonscription(s) électorale(s) provinciale(s): Portneuf
Circonscription(s) électorale(s) fédérale(s):
Portneuf-Jacques-Cartier
Prochaines élections: 3e novembre 2013
Richard Genest, Maire
Sylvie Groleau, Directrice générale

Saint-Tite
540, rue Notre-Dame
Saint-Tite, QC G0X 3H0
Tél: 418-365-5143; *Téléc:* 418-365-4020
www.villest-tite.com
Entité municipal: Town
Incorporation: 23 décembre 1998 *Area:* 91,01 km2
Comté ou district: Mékinac; *Population au 2011:* 3,880
Circonscription(s) électorale(s) provinciale(s): Laviolette
Circonscription(s) électorale(s) fédérale(s):
St-Maurice-Champlain
Prochaines élections: 3e novembre 2013
André Léveillé, Maire
Pierre Massicotte, Directeur général
pmassicotte@villest-tite.com

Saint-Tite-des-Caps
1, rue Leclerc
Saint-Tite-des-Caps, QC G0A 4J0
Tél: 418-823-2239; *Téléc:* 418-823-2527
sainttitedescaps@videotron.ca
www.sainttitedescaps.com
Entité municipal: Municipality
Incorporation: 24 décembre 1872 *Area:* 130,01 km2
Comté ou district: La Côte-de-Beaupré; *Population au 2011:* 1,506
Circonscription(s) électorale(s) provinciale(s): Charlevoix
Circonscription(s) électorale(s) fédérale(s):
Montmorency-Charlevoix-Haute-Côte-Nord
Prochaines élections: 3e novembre 2013
Pierre Dion, Maire
Marc Lachance, Directeur général

Saint-Ubalde
427B, boul Chabot
Saint-Ubalde, QC G0A 4L0
Tél: 418-277-2124; *Téléc:* 418-277-2055
info@saintubalde.com
www.st-ubalde.qc.ca
Entité municipal: Municipality
Incorporation: 3 mars 1973 *Area:* 141,28 km2
Comté ou district: Portneuf; *Population au 2011:* 1,403
Circonscription(s) électorale(s) provinciale(s): Portneuf
Circonscription(s) électorale(s) fédérale(s):
Portneuf-Jacques-Cartier
Prochaines élections: 3e novembre 2013
Pierre Saint-Germain, Maire
Serge Deraspe, Directeur général

Saint-Ulric
128, av Ulric-Tessier
Saint-Ulric, QC G0J 3H0
Tél: 418-737-4341; *Téléc:* 418-737-9242
st-ulric@mrcdematane.qc.ca
www.st-ulric.ca
Entité municipal: Municipality
Incorporation: 12 janvier 2000 *Area:* 118,68 km2
Comté ou district: Matane; *Population au 2011:* 1,642
Circonscription(s) électorale(s) provinciale(s): Matane
Circonscription(s) électorale(s) fédérale(s): Haute-Gaspésie-La Mitis-Matane-Matapédia
Prochaines élections: 3e novembre 2013
Pierre Thibodeau, Maire
Louise Coll, Directrice générale

Saint-Urbain
CP 100
917, rue St-Édouard
Saint-Urbain, QC G0A 4K0
Tél: 418-639-2467; *Téléc:* 418-639-1056
munsturb@sainturbain.qc.ca
www.sainturbain.qc.ca
Entité municipal: Parish (Paroisse)
Incorporation: 1er juilllet 1855 *Area:* 327,68 km2
Comté ou district: Charlevoix; *Population au 2011:* 1,474
Circonscription(s) électorale(s) provinciale(s): Charlevoix
Circonscription(s) électorale(s) fédérale(s):
Montmorency-Charlevoix-Haute-Côte-Nord
Prochaines élections: 3e novembre 2013
Claudette Siomard, Mairesse
Josée Desmeules, Directrice générale

Saint-Urbain-Premier
204, rue Principale
Saint-Urbain-Premier, QC J0S 1Y0
Tél: 450-427-3987; *Téléc:* 450-427-2056
dg.sainturbainpremier@videotron.ca
www.saint-urbain-premier.com
Entité municipal: Municipality
Incorporation: 1er juillet 1855 *Area:* 52,24
Comté ou district: Beauharnois-Salaberry; *Population au 2011:* 1,148
Circonscription(s) électorale(s) provinciale(s): Huntingdon
Circonscription(s) électorale(s) fédérale(s):
Beauharnois-Salaberry
Prochaines élections: 3e novembre 2013
Réjean Beaulieu, Maire
Michael Morneau, Directeur général

Saint-Valentin
790, ch de la Quatrième-Ligne
Saint-Valentin, QC J0J 2E0
Tél: 450-291-5422; *Téléc:* 450-291-5327
administration@municipalite.saint-valentin.qc.ca
Entité municipal: Parish (Paroisse)
Incorporation: 1er juillet 1855 *Area:* 40,09 km2
Comté ou district: Le Haut-Richelieu; *Population au 2011:* 470
Circonscription(s) électorale(s) provinciale(s): Huntingdon
Circonscription(s) électorale(s) fédérale(s): St-Jean
Prochaines élections: 3e novembre 2013
Pierre Chamberland, Maire
Serge Gibeau, Directeur général

Saint-Valère
2, rue du Parc
Saint-Valère, QC G0P 1M0
Tél: 819-353-3450; *Téléc:* 819-353-3459
stvalere@msvalere.qc.ca
www.msvalere.qc.ca
Entité municipal: Municipality
Incorporation: 1er janvier 1862 *Area:* 108,13 km2
Comté ou district: Arthabaska; *Population au 2011:* 1,286
Circonscription(s) électorale(s) provinciale(s): Arthabaska
Circonscription(s) électorale(s) fédérale(s):
Richmond-Arthabaska
Prochaines élections: 3e novembre 2013
Louis Hébert, Maire
Jocelyn Jutras, Directeur général

Saint-Valérien
CP 9
181, rte Centrale
Saint-Valérien-de-Rimouski, QC G0L 4E0
Tél: 418-736-5047; *Téléc:* 418-736-5922
valerien@globetrotter.net
www.municipalite.saint-valerien.qc.ca
Entité municipal: Parish (Paroisse)
Incorporation: 19 juin 1885 *Area:* 149,69 km2
Comté ou district: Rimouski-Neigette; *Population au 2011:* 893
Circonscription(s) électorale(s) provinciale(s): Rimouski
Circonscription(s) électorale(s) fédérale(s):
Rimouski-Neigette-Témiscouata-Les Basques
Prochaines élections: 3e novembre 2013
Robert Savoie, Maire
Marie-Paule Cimon, Directrice générale

Saint-Valérien-de-Milton
960, ch de Milton
Saint-Valérien-de-Milton, QC J0H 2B0
Tél: 450-549-2463; *Téléc:* 450-549-2993
administration.st-valerien@mrcmaskoutains.qc.ca
www.st-valerien-de-milton.qc.ca
Entité municipal: Township
Incorporation: 1er janvier 1864 *Area:* 106,44 km2
Comté ou district: Les Maskoutains; *Population au 2011:* 1,840
Circonscription(s) électorale(s) provinciale(s): Johnson
Circonscription(s) électorale(s) fédérale(s): St-Hyacinthe-Bagot
Prochaines élections: 3e novembre 2013
Raymonde Plamondon, Mairesse
Robert Leclerc, Directeur général

Saint-Vallier
375, montée de la Station
Saint-Vallier, QC G0R 4J0
Tél: 418-884-2559; *Téléc:* 418-884-2454
svallier@globetrotter.net
www.stvallierbellechasse.qc.ca
Entité municipal: Municipality
Incorporation: 10 mars 1993 *Area:* 42,24 km2
Comté ou district: Bellechasse; *Population au 2011:* 1,046
Circonscription(s) électorale(s) provinciale(s): Bellechasse
Circonscription(s) électorale(s) fédérale(s): Lévis-Bellechasse
Prochaines élections: 3e novembre 2013
Gilbert Vallières, Maire
Claire St-Laurent, Directrice générale

Saint-Venant-de-Paquette
5, ch du Village
Saint-Venant-de-Paquette, QC J0B 1S0
Tél: 819-658-3660; *Téléc:* 819-658-0985
stvenant@axion.ca
www.regioncoaticook.qc.ca/stvenant
Entité municipal: Municipality
Incorporation: 11 juin 1917 *Area:* 58,17 km2
Comté ou district: Coaticook; *Population au 2011:* 104
Circonscription(s) électorale(s) provinciale(s):
Mégantic-Compton
Circonscription(s) électorale(s) fédérale(s): Compton-Stanstead
Prochaines élections: 3e novembre 2013
Henri Pariseau, Maire
Manon Jacques, Directeur général

Saint-Vianney
CP 39
170, av Centrale
Saint-Vianney, QC G0J 3J0
Tél: 418-629-4082; *Téléc:* 418-629-4821
stvianney@mrcmatapedia.qc.ca
Entité municipal: Municipality
Incorporation: 27 août 1926 *Area:* 145,24 km2
Comté ou district: La Matapédia; *Population au 2011:* 477
Circonscription(s) électorale(s) provinciale(s): Matapédia
Circonscription(s) électorale(s) fédérale(s): Haute-Gaspésie-La Mitis-Matane-Matapédia
Prochaines élections: 3e novembre 2013
Georges Guénard, Maire
Roselle Caron, Directrice générale

Saint-Victor
CP 40
287, rue Marchand
Saint-Victor, QC G0M 2B0
Tél: 418-588-6854; *Téléc:* 418-588-6855
saint-vic@telvic.net
Entité municipal: Municipality
Incorporation: 31 décembre 1996 *Area:* 120,94 km2
Comté ou district: Robert-Cliche; *Population au 2011:* 2,451
Circonscription(s) électorale(s) provinciale(s): Beauce-Nord
Circonscription(s) électorale(s) fédérale(s): Beauce
Prochaines élections: 3e novembre 2013
Roland Giguère, Maire
Marc Bélanger, Directeur général

Saint-Wenceslas
1065, rue Richard
Saint-Wenceslas, QC G0Z 1J0
Tél: 819-224-7784; *Téléc:* 819-224-4036
mun.stwen@sogetel.net
www.municipalitestwenceslas.com
Entité municipal: Municipality
Incorporation: 11 octobre 1995 *Area:* 78,42 km2
Comté ou district: Nicolet-Yamaska; *Population au 2011:* 1,064
Circonscription(s) électorale(s) provinciale(s): Nicolet-Yamaska
Circonscription(s) électorale(s) fédérale(s):
Bas-Richelieu-Nicolet-Bécancour
Prochaines élections: 3e novembre 2013
Raymond Bilodeau, Maire
Carole Hélie, Directrice générale

Saint-Zacharie
735, 15e rue
Saint-Zacharie, QC G0M 2C0
Tél: 418-593-3185; *Téléc:* 418-593-3085
munzac@cablezach.com
www.st-zacharie.qc.ca
Entité municipal: Municipality
Incorporation: 18 avril 1990 *Area:* 189,70 km2
Comté ou district: Les Etchemins; *Population au 2011:* 1,751
Circonscription(s) électorale(s) provinciale(s): Beauce-Sud
Circonscription(s) électorale(s) fédérale(s): Beauce
Prochaines élections: 3e novembre 2013
Jean Paradis, Maire
Brigitte Larivière, Dirctrice générale

Saint-Zénon
6101, rue Principale
Saint-Zénon, QC J0K 3N0
Tél: 450-884-5987; *Téléc:* 450-884-5285
municipalite@st-zenon.net
www.st-zenon.org
Entité municipal: Municipality
Incorporation: 7 octobre 1895 *Area:* 488,69 km2
Comté ou district: Matawinie; *Population au 2011:* 1,115
Circonscription(s) électorale(s) provinciale(s): Berthier
Circonscription(s) électorale(s) fédérale(s): Joliette
Prochaines élections: 3e novembre 2013
Murielle Richard, Mairesse
Alain St-Vincent-Rioux, Directeur général

Saint-Zénon-du-Lac-Humqui
CP 39
156, rte 195
Lac-Humqui, QC G0J 1N0
Tél: 418-743-2177; *Téléc:* 418-743-2177
lachumqui@mrcmatapedia.qc.ca
Entité municipal: Parish (Paroisse)
Incorporation: 28 avril 1920 *Area:* 112,97 km2
Comté ou district: La Matapédia; *Population au 2011:* 366
Circonscription(s) électorale(s) provinciale(s): Matapédia
Circonscription(s) électorale(s) fédérale(s): Haute-Gaspésie-La Mitis-Matane-Matapédia
Prochaines élections: 1er novembre 2013
Maryline Pronovost, Sec.-Trés. & Directrice générale
Réginald Duguay, Maire

Saint-Zéphirin-de-Courval
CP 40
1471, rue St-Pierre
Saint-Zéphirin-de-Courval, QC J0G 1V0
Tél: 450-564-2188; *Téléc:* 450-564-2339
municipalite@saint-zephirin.ca
www.saint-zephirin.ca
Entité municipal: Parish (Paroisse)
Incorporation: 1er juillet 1855 *Area:* 71,01 km2
Comté ou district: Nicolet-Yamaska; *Population au 2011:* 737
Circonscription(s) électorale(s) provinciale(s): Nicolet-Yamaska
Circonscription(s) électorale(s) fédérale(s):
Bas-Richelieu-Nicolet-Bécancour
Prochaines élections: 3e novembre 2013
Raymond Lemaire, Maire
Hélène Chassé, Directrice générale

Saint-Zotique
1250, rue Principale
Saint-Zotique, QC J0P 1Z0
Tél: 450-267-9335; *Téléc:* 450-267-0907
dg@st-zotique.com
www.st-zotique.com
Entité municipal: Village
Incorporation: 27 mai 1967 *Area:* 24,24 km2
Comté ou district: Vaudreuil-Soulanges; *Population au 2011:* 6,773
Circonscription(s) électorale(s) provinciale(s): Soulanges
Circonscription(s) électorale(s) fédérale(s): Vaudreuil-Soulanges
Prochaines élections: 3e novembre 2013
Gaëtane Legault, Mairesse
Jean-François Messier, Directeur général

Sainte-Agathe-de-Lotbinière
CP 159
254, rue St-Pierre
Sainte-Agathe-de-Lotbinière, QC G0S 2A0
Tél: 418-599-2605; *Téléc:* 418-599-2905
administration@coopsteagathe.com
www.ste-agathelotb.qc.ca
Entité municipal: Municipality
Incorporation: 3 février 1999 *Area:* 169,50 km2
Comté ou district: Lotbinière; *Population au 2011:* 1,145
Circonscription(s) électorale(s) provinciale(s): Lotbinière
Circonscription(s) électorale(s) fédérale(s):
Lotbinière-Chutes-de-la-Chaudière
Prochaines élections: 3e novembre 2013
Michel Champagne, Maire
André Castonguay, Directeur général

Sainte-Agathe-des-Monts
50, rue St-Joseph
Sainte-Agathe-des-Monts, QC J8C 1M9
Tél: 819-326-4595; *Téléc:* 819-326-5784
info@ville.sainte-agathe-des-monts.qc.ca
www.ville.sainte-agathe-des-monts.qc.ca
Entité municipal: Town
Incorporation: 27 février 2002 *Area:* 129,03 km2
Comté ou district: Les Laurentides; *Population au 2011:* 10,115
Circonscription(s) électorale(s) provinciale(s): Bertrand
Circonscription(s) électorale(s) fédérale(s): Laurentides-Labelle
Prochaines élections: 3e novembre 2013
Denis Chalifoux, Maire
Benoît Fugère, Greffier

Sainte-Angèle-de-Mérici
CP 129
23, rue de la Fabrique
Sainte-Angèle-de-Mérici, QC G0J 2H0
Tél: 418-775-7733; *Téléc:* 418-775-5722
steangele@mitis.qc.ca
www.municipalite.sainte-angele-de-merici.qc.ca
Entité municipal: Municipality
Incorporation: 26 avril 1989 *Area:* 108,41 km2
Comté ou district: La Mitis; *Population au 2011:* 999
Circonscription(s) électorale(s) provinciale(s): Matapédia
Circonscription(s) électorale(s) fédérale(s): Haute-Gaspésie-La Mitis-Matane-Matapédia
Prochaines élections: 3e novembre 2013
Alain Carrier, Maire
Marielle Dionne, Directrice générale

Sainte-Angèle-de-Monnoir
5, ch du Vide
Sainte-Angèle-de-Monnoir, QC J0L 1P0
Tél: 450-460-7838; *Téléc:* 450-460-3853
info@sainte-angele-de-monnoir.ca
www.municipalite.sainte-angele-de-monnoir.qc.ca
Entité municipal: Parish (Paroisse)
Incorporation: 15 mars 1865 *Area:* 45,49 km2
Comté ou district: Rouville; *Population au 2011:* 1,812
Circonscription(s) électorale(s) provinciale(s): Iberville
Circonscription(s) électorale(s) fédérale(s): Shefford
Prochaines élections: 1er novembre 2013
Jacqueline Houle, Directrice générale
Michel Picotte, Maire

Sainte-Angèle-de-Prémont
2451, rue Camirand
Sainte-Angèle-de-Prémont, QC J0K 1R0
Tél: 819-268-5526; *Téléc:* 819-268-5536
adminmuni@municpremont.ca
www.municpremont.ca
Entité municipal: Municipality
Incorporation: 28 août 1917 *Area:* 38,51 km2
Comté ou district: Maskinongé; *Population au 2011:* 647
Circonscription(s) électorale(s) provinciale(s): Maskinongé
Circonscription(s) électorale(s) fédérale(s): Berthier-Maskinongé
Prochaines élections: 3e novembre 2013
Barbara Paillé, Mairesse
Jean Charland, Directeur général

Sainte-Anne-de-Beaupré
9336, av Royale
Sainte-Anne-de-Beaupré, QC G0A 3C0
Tél: 418-827-3191; *Téléc:* 418-827-8275
info@sainteannedebeaupre.com
www.sainteannedebeaupre.com
Entité municipal: Town
Incorporation: 27 janvier 1973 *Area:* 64,38 km2
Comté ou district: La Côte-de-Beaupré; *Population au 2011:* 2,854
Circonscription(s) électorale(s) provinciale(s): Charlevoix
Circonscription(s) électorale(s) fédérale(s): Montmorency-Charlevoix-Haute-Côte-Nord
Prochaines élections: 3e novembre 2013
Jean-Luc Fortin, Maire
Frédéric Drolet-Gervais, Directeur général

Sainte-Anne-de-la-Pérade
200, rue Principale
Sainte-Anne-de-la-Pérade, QC G0X 2J0
Tél: 418-325-2841; *Téléc:* 418-325-3070
municipalite@sainteannedelaperade.net
www.sainteannedelaperade.net
Entité municipal: Municipality
Incorporation: 10 mai 1989 *Area:* 107,94 km2
Comté ou district: Les Chenaux; *Population au 2011:* 2,072
Circonscription(s) électorale(s) provinciale(s): Champlain
Circonscription(s) électorale(s) fédérale(s): St-Maurice-Champlain
Prochaines élections: 3e novembre 2013
Yvon Lafond, Maire
René Roy, Directeur général

Sainte-Anne-de-la-Pocatière
395, ch des Sables est
Sainte-Anne-de-la-Pocatière, QC G0R 1Z0
Tél: 418-856-3192; *Téléc:* 418-856-9936
paroisse@ste-anne-de-la-pocatiere.com
Entité municipal: Parish (Paroisse)
Incorporation: 1er juillet 1855 *Area:* 53,68 km2
Comté ou district: Kamouraska; *Population au 2011:* 1,717
Circonscription(s) électorale(s) provinciale(s): Kamouraska-Témiscouata
Circonscription(s) électorale(s) fédérale(s): Montmagny-L'Islet-Kamouraska-Rivière-du-Loup
Prochaines élections: 3e novembre 2013
François Lagacé, Maire
Sylvie Dionne, Directrice générale

Sainte-Anne-de-la-Rochelle
145, rue l'Église
Sainte-Anne-de-la-Rochelle, QC J0E 2B0
Tél: 450-539-1654; *Téléc:* 450-539-2317
mun.steannedelarochelle@axion.ca
Entité municipal: Municipality
Incorporation: 1er juillet 1855 *Area:* 60,96 km2
Comté ou district: Le Val-St-François; *Population au 2011:* 611
Circonscription(s) électorale(s) provinciale(s): Brome-Missisquoi
Circonscription(s) électorale(s) fédérale(s): Shefford
Prochaines élections: 3e novembre 2013
J. André Bourassa Gosselin, Maire
Majella René, Directrice générale

Sainte-Anne-de-Sabrevois
CP 60
1218, rte 133
Sabrevois, QC J0J 2G0
Tél: 450-347-0066; *Téléc:* 450-347-4040
info.sabrevois@videotron.ca
Entité municipal: Parish (Paroisse)
Incorporation: 1er mars 1888 *Area:* 45,24 km2
Comté ou district: Le Haut-Richelieu; *Population au 2011:* 2,074
Circonscription(s) électorale(s) provinciale(s): Iberville
Circonscription(s) électorale(s) fédérale(s): St-Jean
Prochaines élections: 3e novembre 2013
Clément Couture, Maire
Fredy Serreyn, Directeur général

Sainte-Anne-de-Sorel
1685, ch du Chenal-du-Moine
Sainte-Anne-de-Sorel, QC J3P 5N3
Tél: 450-742-1616; *Téléc:* 450-742-1118
info@sainteannedesorel.ca
www.sainteannedesorel.ca
Entité municipal: Municipality
Incorporation: 14 mai 1877 *Area:* 36,51 km2
Comté ou district: Pierre-De Saurel; *Population au 2011:* 2,742
Circonscription(s) électorale(s) provinciale(s): Richelieu
Circonscription(s) électorale(s) fédérale(s): Bas-Richelieu-Nicolet-Bécancour
Prochaines élections: 3e novembre 2013
Pierre Lacombe, Maire
Maxime Dauplaise, Directeur général

Sainte-Anne-des-Lacs
773, ch de Ste-Anne-des-Lacs
Sainte-Anne-des-Lacs, QC J0R 1B0
Tél: 450-224-2675; *Téléc:* 450-224-8672
info@sadl.qc.ca
www.sadl.qc.ca
Entité municipal: Parish (Paroisse)
Incorporation: 28 mars 1946 *Area:* 23,45 km2
Comté ou district: Les Pays-d'en-Haut; *Population au 2011:* 3,363
Circonscription(s) électorale(s) provinciale(s): Bertrand
Circonscription(s) électorale(s) fédérale(s): Laurentides-Labelle
Prochaines élections: 3e novembre 2013
Claude Boyer, Maire
Jean-François René, Directeur général

Sainte-Anne-des-Monts
6, 1re av ouest
Sainte-Anne-des-Monts, QC G4V 1A1
Tél: 418-763-5511; *Téléc:* 418-763-3473
sadmonts@globetrotter.net
www.villesainte-anne-des-monts.qc.ca
Entité municipal: Town
Incorporation: février 2000 *Area:* 263,62 km2
Comté ou district: La Haute-Gaspésie; *Population au 2011:* 6,933
Circonscription(s) électorale(s) provinciale(s): Matane
Circonscription(s) électorale(s) fédérale(s): Haute-Gaspésie-La Mitis-Matane-Matapédia
Prochaines élections: 3e novembre 2013
Micheline Pelletier, Mairesse
Sylvie Lepage, Greffière

Sainte-Anne-du-Lac
1, rue St-François-Xavier
Sainte-Anne-du-Lac, QC J0W 1V0
Tél: 819-586-2110; *Téléc:* 819-586-2203
sainte.anne.du.lac.municipalite@tlb.sympatico.ca
www.municipalite.sainte-anne-du-lac.qc.ca
Entité municipal: Municipality
Incorporation: 30 décembre 1976 *Area:* 345,28 km2
Comté ou district: Antoine-Labelle; *Population au 2011:* 619
Circonscription(s) électorale(s) provinciale(s): Labelle
Circonscription(s) électorale(s) fédérale(s): Laurentides-Labelle
Prochaines élections: 3e novembre 2013
Aimé Lachapelle, Maire
Denise Bélec, Directrice générale

Sainte-Anne-du-Sault
539, rte Principale
Sainte-Anne-du-Sault, QC G0Z 1C0
Tél: 819-367-2210; *Téléc:* 819-367-4011
munstann@tlb.sympatico.ca
Entité municipal: Municipality
Incorporation: 21 mars 1889 *Area:* 56,09 km2
Comté ou district: Arthabaska; *Population au 2011:* 1,268
Circonscription(s) électorale(s) provinciale(s): Nicolet-Yamaska
Circonscription(s) électorale(s) fédérale(s): Richmond-Arthabaska
Prochaines élections: 3e novembre 2013
Jean-Claude Bourassa, Maire
Lyne Bertrand, Directrice générale

Sainte-Apolline-de-Patton
105, rte de l'Église
Sainte-Apolline-de-Patton, QC G0R 2P0
Tél: 418-469-3031; *Téléc:* 418-469-3051
munapoli@globetrotter.net
www.sainteapollinedepatton.ca
Entité municipal: Parish (Paroisse)
Incorporation: 14 décembre 1909 *Area:* 255,70 km2
Comté ou district: Montmagny; *Population au 2011:* 541
Circonscription(s) électorale(s) provinciale(s): Montmagny-L'Islet
Circonscription(s) électorale(s) fédérale(s): Montamagny-L'Islet-Kamouraska-Rivière-du-Loup
Prochaines élections: 3e novembre 2013
Thérèse Mercier, Mairesse
Doris Godbout, Sec.-Trés.

Sainte-Aurélie
151A, ch des Bois Francs
Sainte-Aurélie, QC G0M 1M0
Tél: 418-593-3021; *Téléc:* 418-593-3961
munsteau@sogetel.net
www.ste-aurelie.qc.ca
Entité municipal: Municipality
Incorporation: 3 avril 1909 *Area:* 78,52 km2
Comté ou district: Les Etchemins; *Population au 2011:* 910
Circonscription(s) électorale(s) provinciale(s): Beauce-Sud
Circonscription(s) électorale(s) fédérale(s): Beauce
Prochaines élections: 3e novembre 2013
Mario Pouliot, Maire
Sophie Fortin, Directrice générale

Sainte-Barbe
470, ch de l'Église
Sainte-Barbe, QC J0S 1P0
Tél: 450-371-2504; *Téléc:* 450-371-2575
info@ste-barbe.com
www.ste-barbe.com
Entité municipal: Parish (Paroisse)
Incorporation: 12 juin 1882 *Area:* 39,78 km2
Comté ou district: Le Haut-St-Laurent; *Population au 2011:* 1,403
Circonscription(s) électorale(s) provinciale(s): Huntingdon
Circonscription(s) électorale(s) fédérale(s): Beauharnois-Salaberry
Prochaines élections: 3e novembre 2013
Jean-Claude Chantigny, Maire
Chantal Girouard, Sec.-Trés.

Sainte-Béatrix
861, rue de l'Église
Sainte-Béatrix, QC J0K 1Y0
Tél: 450-883-2245; *Téléc:* 450-883-1772
administration@stebeatrix.com
www.sainte-beatrix.com
Entité municipal: Municipality
Incorporation: 11 mai 1864 *Area:* 83,52 km2
Comté ou district: Matawinie; *Population au 2011:* 1,849

Circonscription(s) électorale(s) provinciale(s): Berthier
Circonscription(s) électorale(s) fédérale(s): Joliette
Prochaines élections: 3e novembre 2013
Normand Montagne, Maire
Patricia Labby, Directrice générale

Sainte-Brigide-d'Iberville
555, rue Principale
Sainte-Brigide-d'Iberville, QC J0J 1X0
Tél: 450-293-7511; *Téléc:* 450-293-1077
ste_brigide@bellnet.ca
www.sainte-brigide.qc.ca
Entité municipal: Municipality
Incorporation: 1er juillet 1855 *Area:* 68,89 km2
Comté ou district: Le Haut-Richelieu; *Population au 2011:* 1,331
Circonscription(s) électorale(s) provinciale(s): Iberville
Circonscription(s) électorale(s) fédérale(s): St-Jean
Prochaines élections: 3e novembre 2013
Patrick Bonvouloir, Maire
Murielle Papineau, Directrice générale

Sainte-Brigitte-de-Laval
414, av Ste-Brigitte
Sainte-Brigitte-de-Laval, QC G0A 3K0
Tél: 418-825-2515; *Téléc:* 418-825-3114
mairie@sbdl.net
www.sbdl.net
Entité municipal: Municipality
Incorporation: 11 février 1875 *Area:* 111,49 km2
Comté ou district: La Jacques-Cartier; *Population au 2011:* 5,696
Circonscription(s) électorale(s) provinciale(s): Montmorency
Circonscription(s) électorale(s) fédérale(s): Portneuf-Jacques Cartier
Prochaines élections: 3e novembre 2013
Gilbert Thomassin, Maire
Gaétan Bussières, Directeur général

Sainte-Brigitte-des-Saults
CP 1051
400, rue Principale
Sainte-Brigitte-des-Saults, QC J0C 1E0
Tél: 819-336-4460; *Téléc:* 819-336-4410
muni.ste-brigitte@mrcdrummond.qc.ca
www.saintebrigittedessaults.ca
Entité municipal: Parish (Paroisse)
Incorporation: 9 mars 1878 *Area:* 69,23
Comté ou district: Drummond; *Population au 2011:* 737
Circonscription(s) électorale(s) provinciale(s): Nicolet-Yamaska
Circonscription(s) électorale(s) fédérale(s): Drummond
Prochaines élections: 3e novembre 2013
Jean-Guy Hébert, Maire
Manon Lemaire, Directrice générale

Sainte-Catherine-de-Hatley
CP 30
35, ch de North Hatley
Sainte-Catherine-de-Hatley, QC J0B 1W0
Tél: 819-843-1935; *Téléc:* 819-843-8527
munstecatherinehatley@qc.aira.com
www.sainte-catherine-de-hatley.ca
Entité municipal: Municipality
Incorporation: 28 mars 1901 *Area:* 81,43 km2
Comté ou district: Memphrémagog; *Population au 2011:* 2,464
Circonscription(s) électorale(s) provinciale(s): Orford
Circonscription(s) électorale(s) fédérale(s): Compton-Stanstead
Prochaines élections: 3e novembre 2013
Jacques Demers, Maire
Serge Caron, Directeur général

Sainte-Catherine-de-la-Jacques-Cartier
CP 250
1, rue Rouleau
Ste-Catherine-de-la-J-Cartier, QC G0A 3M0
Tél: 418-875-2758; *Téléc:* 418-875-2170
sainte-catherine-de-la-jacques-cartier@coopcscf.com
www.villescjc.com
Entité municipal: Town
Incorporation: 1er juillet 1855 *Area:* 120,61 km2
Comté ou district: La Jacques-Cartier; *Population au 2011:* 6,319
Circonscription(s) électorale(s) provinciale(s): Portneuf
Circonscription(s) électorale(s) fédérale(s): Portneuf-Jacques-Cartier
Prochaines élections: 3e novembre 2013
Jacques Marcotte, Maire
Marcel Grenier, Directeur général

Sainte-Cécile-de-Lévrard
235, rue Principale
Sainte-Cécile-de-Lévrard, QC G0X 2M0
Tél: 819-263-2104; *Téléc:* 819-263-1043
info@munstececilelvrd.ca
Entité municipal: Parish (Paroisse)
Incorporation: 11 septembre 1908 *Area:* 33,35 km2
Comté ou district: Bécancour; *Population au 2011:* 362
Circonscription(s) électorale(s) provinciale(s): Lotbinière
Circonscription(s) électorale(s) fédérale(s): Bas-Richelieu-Nicolet-Bécancour
Prochaines élections: 3me novembre 2013
Simon Brunelle, Maire
Réjean Poisson, Directeur général

Sainte-Cécile-de-Milton
CP 195
136, rue Principale
Sainte-Cécile-de-Milton, QC J0E 2C0
Tél: 450-378-1942; *Téléc:* 450-378-4621
mun@stececiledemilton.qc.ca
Entité municipal: Township
Incorporation: 1er janvier 1864 *Area:* 74,04 km2
Comté ou district: La Haute-Yamaska; *Population au 2011:* 2,128
Circonscription(s) électorale(s) provinciale(s): Johnson
Circonscription(s) électorale(s) fédérale(s): Shefford
Prochaines élections: 3e novembre 2013
Sylvain Beaudoin, Maire
Monique Fortin, Directrice générale

Sainte-Cécile-de-Whitton
4557, rue Principale
Sainte-Cécile-de-Whitton, QC G0Y 1J0
Tél: 819-583-0770; *Téléc:* 819-583-4149
muncecilewhitton@axion.ca
www.stececiledewhitton.qc.ca
Entité municipal: Municipality
Incorporation: 19 septembre 1889 *Area:* 146,59 km2
Comté ou district: Le Granit; *Population au 2011:* 892
Circonscription(s) électorale(s) provinciale(s): Mégantic-Compton
Circonscription(s) électorale(s) fédérale(s): Mégantic-L'Érable
Prochaines élections: 3e novembre 2013
Diane Turgeon, Maire
Françoise Audet, Directrice générale

Sainte-Christine
629, rue des Loisirs
Sainte-Christine, QC J0H 1H0
Tél: 819-858-2828; *Téléc:* 819-858-9911
stechristine@cooptel.qc.ca
Entité municipal: Parish (Paroisse)
Incorporation: 8 janvier 1894 *Area:* 89,40 km2
Comté ou district: Acton; *Population au 2011:* 673
Circonscription(s) électorale(s) provinciale(s): Johnson
Circonscription(s) électorale(s) fédérale(s): St-Hyacinthe-Bagot
Prochaines élections: 3e novembre 2013
Huguette St-Pierre-Beaulac, Mairesse
Caroline Lamothe, Directrice-générale

Sainte-Christine-d'Auvergne
80, rue Principale
Sainte-Christine-d'Auvergne, QC G0A 1A0
Tél: 418-329-3304; *Téléc:* 418-329-3356
ste-christine@globetrotter.net
www.ste-christine.qc.ca
Entité municipal: Municipality
Incorporation: 10 avril 1896 *Area:* 145,58 km2
Comté ou district: Portneuf; *Population au 2011:* 448
Circonscription(s) électorale(s) provinciale(s): Portneuf
Circonscription(s) électorale(s) fédérale(s): Portneuf-Jacques Cartier
Prochaines élections: 3e novembre 2013
Pierre Tourigny, Maire
Louise Quintin, Directrice générale (interim)

Sainte-Claire
135, rue Principale
Sainte-Claire, QC G0R 2V0
Tél: 418-883-3314; *Téléc:* 418-883-3845
msclaire@globetrotter.qc.ca
www.municipalite.sainte-claire.qc.ca
Entité municipal: Municipality
Incorporation: 1er octobre 1977 *Area:* 88,63 km2
Comté ou district: Bellechasse; *Population au 2011:* 3,325
Circonscription(s) électorale(s) provinciale(s): Bellechasse
Circonscription(s) électorale(s) fédérale(s): Lévis-Bellechasse
Prochaines élections: 3e novembre 2013
Fernand Fortier, Maire
Serge Gagnon, Directeur général

Sainte-Clotilde
2452, ch de l'Église
Sainte-Clotilde, QC J0L 1W0
Tél: 450-826-3129; *Téléc:* 450-826-3217
mun.steclotilde@rocler.qc.ca
Entité municipal: Parish (Paroisse)
Incorporation: 2 avril 1885 *Area:* 78,96 km2
Comté ou district: Les Jardins-de-Napierville; *Population au 2011:* 1,704
Circonscription(s) électorale(s) provinciale(s): Huntingdon
Circonscription(s) électorale(s) fédérale(s): Beauharnois-Salaberry
Prochaines élections: 3e novembre 2013
Clément Lemieux, Maire
Nicole Marcil, Directrice générale

Sainte-Clotilde-de-Beauce
307B, rue du Couvent
Sainte-Clotilde-de-Beauce, QC G0N 1C0
Tél: 418-427-2637; *Téléc:* 418-427-4303
steclotilde@hotmail.com
www.ste-clotilde.com
Entité municipal: Municipality
Incorporation: 19 novembre 1938 *Area:* 58,680 km2
Comté ou district: Les Appalaches; *Population au 2011:* 650
Circonscription(s) électorale(s) provinciale(s): Beauce-Sud
Circonscription(s) électorale(s) fédérale(s): Mégantic-L'Érable
Prochaines élections: 3e novembre 2013
Gérald Grenier, Maire
Sandy Grenier, Directrice générale

Sainte-Clotilde-de-Horton
CP 29
17, rte 122
Sainte-Clotilde-de-Horton, QC J0A 1H0
Tél: 819-336-5344; *Téléc:* 819-336-5440
info@steclotildehorton.ca
www.steclotildedehorton.ca
Entité municipal: Municipality
Incorporation: 26 mars 1997 *Area:* 118,44 km2
Comté ou district: Arthabaska; *Population au 2011:* 1,616
Circonscription(s) électorale(s) provinciale(s): Richmond
Circonscription(s) électorale(s) fédérale(s): Richmond-Arthabaska
Prochaines élections: 3e novembre 2013
Marie Désilets, Mairesse
Marlène Langlois, Directrice générale

Sainte-Croix
6310, rue Principale
Sainte-Croix, QC G0S 2H0
Tél: 418-926-3494; *Téléc:* 418-926-2570
www.ville.sainte-croix.qc.ca
Entité municipal: Municipality
Incorporation: 5 octobre 2001 *Area:* 69,64 km2
Comté ou district: Lotbinière; *Population au 2011:* 2,352
Circonscription(s) électorale(s) provinciale(s): Lotbinière
Circonscription(s) électorale(s) fédérale(s): Lotbinière-Chutes-de-la-Chaudière
Prochaines élections: 3e novembre 2013
Jacques Gauthier, Maire
Bertrand Fréchette, Directeur général
bertrand.frechette@ville.sainte-croix.qc.ca

Sainte-Edwidge-de-Clifton
1439, chemin Favreau
Sainte-Edwidge-de-Clifton, QC J0B 2R0
Tél: 819-849-7740; *Téléc:* 819-849-4212
info@ste-edwidge.ca
www.ste-edwidge.ca
Entité municipal: Township
Incorporation: 21 décembre 1895 *Area:* 99,35 km2
Comté ou district: Coaticook; *Population au 2011:* 484
Circonscription(s) électorale(s) provinciale(s): Mégantic-Compton
Circonscription(s) électorale(s) fédérale(s): Compton-Stanstead
Prochaines élections: 3e novembre 2013
Linda Ouellet, Mairesse
Réjean Fauteux, Directeur géneral

Sainte-Élisabeth
2270, rue Principale
Sainte-Élisabeth, QC J0K 2J0
Tél: 450-759-2875; *Téléc:* 450-756-4312
steelisabeth@qc.aira.com
www.ste-elisabeth.qc.ca
Entité municipal: Parish (Paroisse)
Incorporation: 1er juillet 1855 *Area:* 81,66 km2
Comté ou district: D'Autray; *Population au 2011:* 1,559
Circonscription(s) électorale(s) provinciale(s): Berthier
Circonscription(s) électorale(s) fédérale(s): Joliette
Prochaines élections: 3e novembre 2013

Mario Houle, Maire
Lorraine C. Garnelin, Directrice générale

Sainte-Élizabeth-de-Warwick
243, rue Principale
Sainte-Élizabeth-de-Warwick, QC J0A 1M0
Tél: 819-358-5162; *Téléc:* 819-358-9192
info@sainte-elizabeth-de-warwick.ca
Entité municipal: Parish (Paroisse)
Incorporation: 18 mai 1887 *Area:* 50,51 km2
Comté ou district: Arthabaska; *Population au 2011:* 374
Circonscription(s) électorale(s) provinciale(s): Richmond
Circonscription(s) électorale(s) fédérale(s):
Richmond-Arthabaska
Prochaines élections: 3e novembre 2013
Luc Le Blanc, Maire
Josée Leblond, Directrice générale

Sainte-Émélie-de-l'Énergie
241, rue Coutu
Sainte-Émélie-de-l'Énergie, QC J0K 2K0
Tél: 450-886-3823; *Téléc:* 450-886-9175
stemelie@intermonde.net
www.ste-emelie-de-lenergie.qc.ca
Entité municipal: Municipality
Incorporation: 10 juin 1884 *Area:* 170,68 km2
Comté ou district: Matawinie; *Population au 2011:* 1,644
Circonscription(s) électorale(s) provinciale(s): Berthier
Circonscription(s) électorale(s) fédérale(s): Joliette
Prochaines élections: 3e novembre 2013
Atchez Arbour, Maire
Brigitte Belleville, Directrice générale

Sainte-Eulalie
757, rue des Bouleaux
Sainte-Eulalie, QC G0Z 1E0
Tél: 819-225-4345; *Téléc:* 819-225-4078
info@municipalite.sainte-eulalie.qc.ca
www.municipalite.sainte-eulalie.qc.ca
Entité municipal: Municipality
Incorporation: 1er juillet 1864 *Area:* 90,79 km2
Comté ou district: Nicolet-Yamaska; *Population au 2011:* 871
Circonscription(s) électorale(s) provinciale(s): Nicolet-Yamaska
Circonscription(s) électorale(s) fédérale(s):
Bas-Richelieu-Nicolet-Bécancour
Prochaines élections: 3e novembre 2013
André Demers, Maire
Yvon Douville, Directeur général

Sainte-Euphémie-sur-Rivière-du-Sud
220, rue Principal est
Ste-Euphémie-sur-Rivière-du-Su, QC G0R 2Z0
Tél: 418-469-3427; *Téléc:* 418-469-3427
municipalitesteeuphemie@globetrotter.net
Entité municipal: Municipality
Incorporation: 20 juillet 1907 *Area:* 93,21 km2
Comté ou district: Montmagny; *Population au 2011:* 329
Circonscription(s) électorale(s) provinciale(s): Montmagny-L'Islet
Circonscription(s) électorale(s) fédérale(s):
Montmagny-L'Islet-Kamouraska-Rivière-du-Loup
Prochaines élections: 3e novembre 2013
Laurence Hallé, Maire
Chantal Lachance, Directrice générale

Sainte-Famille
3894, ch Royal
Sainte-Famille, QC G0A 3P0
Tél: 418-829-3572; *Téléc:* 418-829-2513
info@munstefamille.org
Entité municipal: Parish (Paroisse)
Incorporation: 1er juillet 1855 *Area:* 46,43 km2
Comté ou district: L'Ile-d'Orléans; *Population au 2011:* 851
Circonscription(s) électorale(s) provinciale(s): Montmorency
Circonscription(s) électorale(s) fédérale(s):
Montmorency-Charlevoix-Haute-Côte-Nord
Prochaines élections: 3e novembre 2013
Jean-Pierre Turcotte, Maire
Sylvie Beaulieu, Directrice générale

Sainte-Félicité
5, rte de l'Église nord
Sainte-Félicité, QC G0R 4P0
Tél: 418-359-2321; *Téléc:* 418-359-2321
mun.ste-felicite@globetrotter.net
Entité municipal: Municipality
Incorporation: 1er janvier 1950 *Area:* 95,82 km2
Comté ou district: L'Islet; *Population au 2011:* 413
Circonscription(s) électorale(s) provinciale(s): Montmagny-L'Islet
Circonscription(s) électorale(s) fédérale(s):
Montmagny-l'Islet-Kamouraska-Rivière-du-Loup
Prochaines élections: 3e novembre 2013
Georges Gagnon, Maire
Julie Bélanger, Directrice générale

Sainte-Félicité
CP 9
192, rue St-Joseph
Sainte-Félicité, QC G0J 2K0
Tél: 418-733-4628; *Téléc:* 418-733-8377
ste-felicite@mrcdematane.qc.ca
Entité municipal: Municipality
Incorporation: 10 janvier 1996 *Area:* 89,76 km2
Comté ou district: Matane; *Population au 2011:* 1,175
Circonscription(s) électorale(s) provinciale(s): Matane
Circonscription(s) électorale(s) fédérale(s): Haute-Gaspésie-La Mitis-Matane-Matapédia
Prochaines élections: 3e novembre 2013
Réginald Desrosiers, Maire
Yves Chassé, Directeur général

Sainte-Flavie
775, rte Flavie-Drapeau
Sainte-Flavie, QC G0J 2L0
Tél: 418-775-7050; *Téléc:* 418-775-5672
info@sainte-flavie.net
www.sainte-flavie.net
Entité municipal: Parish (Paroisse)
Incorporation: 1er juillet 1855 *Area:* 37,62 km2
Comté ou district: La Mitis; *Population au 2011:* 919
Circonscription(s) électorale(s) provinciale(s): Matapédia
Circonscription(s) électorale(s) fédérale(s): Haute-Gaspésie-La Mitis-Matane-Matapédia
Prochaines élections: 3e novembre 2013
Damien Ruest, Maire
Francine Roy, Directrice générale

Sainte-Florence
CP 9
29, rue des Loisirs
Sainte-Florence, QC G0J 2M0
Tél: 418-756-3491; *Téléc:* 418-756-5079
steflorence@mrcmatapedia.qc.ca
www.sainte-florence.com
Entité municipal: Municipality
Incorporation: 12 avril 1911 *Area:* 103,00 km2
Comté ou district: La Matapédia; *Population au 2011:* 414
Circonscription(s) électorale(s) provinciale(s): Matapédia
Circonscription(s) électorale(s) fédérale(s): Haute-Gaspésie-La Mitis-Matane-Matapédia
Prochaines élections: 3e novembre 2013
Réjeanne Doiron, Mairesse
Huguette Gagné, Directrice générale

Sainte-Françoise
563, 10e-et-11e rang est
Sainte-Françoise-de-Lotbinière, QC G0S 2N0
Tél: 819-287-5755; *Téléc:* 819-287-5838
municipalite@ste-francoise.com
www.visitedefermeeducative.com
Entité municipal: Municipality
Incorporation: 1er janvier 1947 *Area:* 89,12 km2
Comté ou district: Bécancour; *Population au 2011:* 479
Circonscription(s) électorale(s) provinciale(s): Lotbinière
Circonscription(s) électorale(s) fédérale(s):
Bas-Richelieu-Nicolet-Bécancour
Prochaines élections: 3e novembre 2013
Mario Lyonnais, Maire
Isabelle Dubois, Directrice générale

Sainte-Françoise
156, rue Jérémie-Beaulieu
Sainte-Françoise, QC G0L 3B0
Tél: 418-851-1502; *Téléc:* 418-851-0926
municipal@ste-francoise.qc.ca
Entité municipal: Parish (Paroisse)
Incorporation: 6 décembre 1873 *Area:* 88,54 km2
Comté ou district: Les Basques; *Population au 2011:* 399
Circonscription(s) électorale(s) provinciale(s): Rivière-du-Loup
Circonscription(s) électorale(s) fédérale(s):
Rimouski-Neigette-Témiscouata-Les Basques
Prochaines élections: 3e novembre 2013
Bernard D'Amours, Maire
Véronique Pelletier, Directrice générale

Sainte-Geneviève-de-Batiscan
30, rue St-Charles
Sainte-Geneviève-de-Batiscan, QC G0X 2R0
Tél: 418-362-2078; *Téléc:* 418-362-2111
municipalite@stegenevieve.ca
www.stegenevieve.ca
Entité municipal: Parish (Paroisse)
Incorporation: 1er juillet 1855 *Area:* 97,09 km2
Comté ou district: Les Chenaux; *Population au 2011:* 1,060
Circonscription(s) électorale(s) provinciale(s): Champlain
Circonscription(s) électorale(s) fédérale(s):
St-Maurice-Champlain
Prochaines élections: 3e novembre 2013
Christian Gendron, Maire
Line Blais, Directrice générale

Sainte-Geneviève-de-Berthier
400, rang de la Rivière-Bayonne sud
Sainte-Geneviève-de-Berthier, QC J0K 1A0
Tél: 450-836-4333; *Téléc:* 450-836-7260
munisgb@autray.net
Entité municipal: Parish (Paroisse)
Incorporation: 1er juillet 1855 *Area:* 74,67
Comté ou district: D'Autray; *Population au 2011:* 2,365
Circonscription(s) électorale(s) provinciale(s): Berthier
Circonscription(s) électorale(s) fédérale(s): Berthier-Maskinongé
Prochaines élections: 3e novembre 2013
Richard Giroux, Maire
Réjean Marsolais, Directeur général

Sainte-Germaine-Boulé
CP 5 Boulé
199, rue Roy
Sainte-Germaine-Boulé, QC J0Z 1M0
Tél: 819-787-6221; *Téléc:* 819-787-2560
stegermaine@ste-germaine.ao.ca
www.ste-germaine.ao.ca
Entité municipal: Municipality
Incorporation: 1er janvier 1954 *Area:* 108,46 km2
Comté ou district: Abitibi-Ouest; *Population au 2011:* 895
Circonscription(s) électorale(s) provinciale(s): Abitibi-Ouest
Circonscription(s) électorale(s) fédérale(s):
Abitibi-Témiscamingue
Prochaines élections: 3e novembre 2013
Jaclin Bégin, Maire
Gisèle Bisson-Lapointe, Directrice générale

Sainte-Gertrude-Manneville
391, rte 395
Sainte-Gertrude-Manneville, QC J0Y 2L0
Tél: 819-727-2244; *Téléc:* 819-727-3293
stegertman@cableamos.com
Entité municipal: Municipality
Incorporation: 1er janvier 1980 *Area:* 329,84 km2
Comté ou district: Abitibi; *Population au 2011:* 757
Circonscription(s) électorale(s) provinciale(s): Abitibi-Ouest
Circonscription(s) électorale(s) fédérale(s):
Abitibi-Témiscamingue
Prochaines élections: 3e novembre 2013
Pascal Rheault, Maire
Laurence Demers, Directrice générale

Sainte-Hedwidge
1090, rue Principale
Sainte-Hedwidge, QC G0W 2R0
Tél: 418-275-3020; *Téléc:* 418-275-4163
Entité municipal: Municipality
Incorporation: 10 mars 1909 *Area:* 469,07 km2
Comté ou district: Le Domaine-du-Roy; *Population au 2011:* 824
Circonscription(s) électorale(s) provinciale(s): Roberval
Circonscription(s) électorale(s) fédérale(s):
Roberval-Lac-St-Jean
Prochaines élections: 3e novembre 2013
Gilles Toulouse, Maire
Sylvain Privé, Directeur général
sylvain.prive@ste-hedwidge.qc.ca

Sainte-Hélène
CP 216
531, rue de l'Église sud
Sainte-Hélène, QC G0L 3J0
Tél: 418-492-6830; *Téléc:* 418-492-1854
munhel@bellnet.ca
www.sainte-helene.net
Entité municipal: Parish (Paroisse)
Incorporation: 1er juillet 1855 *Area:* 60,34 km2
Comté ou district: Kamouraska; *Population au 2011:* 911
Circonscription(s) électorale(s) provinciale(s):
Kamouraska-Témiscouata
Circonscription(s) électorale(s) fédérale(s):
Montmagny-L'Islet-Kamourask-Rivière-du-Loup
Prochaines élections: 3e novembre 2013
Marcel Guay, Maire
Maryse Oullet, Directrice générale

Sainte-Hélène-de-Bagot
379, 7e av
Sainte-Hélène-de-Bagot, QC J0H 1M0
Tél: 450-791-2455; *Téléc:* 450-791-2550
line.lupien@mrcmaskoutains.qc.ca
Entité municipal: Municipality
Incorporation: 9 juillet 1977 *Area:* 73,53 km2

Comté ou district: Les Maskoutains; *Population au 2011:* 1,637
Circonscription(s) électorale(s) provinciale(s): Johnson
Circonscription(s) électorale(s) fédérale(s): St-Hyacinthe-Bagot
Prochaines élections: 3e novembre 2013
Yves Petit, Maire
Line Lupien, Directrice générale

Sainte-Hélène-de-Mancebourg
451, rang 2e-et-3e
Mancebourg, QC J0Z 2T0
Tél: 819-333-5766; *Téléc:* 819-333-9514
mancebourg@mrcao.qc.ca
www.ste-helene.ao.ca
Entité municipal: Parish (Paroisse)
Incorporation: 10 mai 1941 *Area:* 68,29 km2
Comté ou district: Abitibi-Ouest; *Population au 2011:* 354
Circonscription(s) électorale(s) provinciale(s): Abitibi-Ouest
Circonscription(s) électorale(s) fédérale(s):
Abitibi-Témiscamingue
Prochaines élections: 3e novembre 2013
Florent Bédard, Maire
Sylvie Boutin-Bergeron, Directrice générale

Sainte-Hénédine
CP 6
111, rue Principale
Sainte-Hénédine, QC G0S 2R0
Tél: 418-935-7125; *Téléc:* 418-935-3113
munisthe@globetrotter.net
Entité municipal: Parish (Paroisse)
Incorporation: 1er juillet 1855 *Area:* 53,06
Comté ou district: La Nouvelle-Beauce; *Population au 2011:* 1,212
Circonscription(s) électorale(s) provinciale(s): Beauce-Nord
Circonscription(s) électorale(s) fédérale(s): Beauce
Prochaines élections: 3e novembre 2013
Yvon Asselin, Maire
Yvon Marcoux, Sec.-Trés.

Sainte-Irène
362, rue de la Fabrique
Sainte-Irène, QC G0J 2P0
Tél: 418-629-5705; *Téléc:* 418-629-3220
steirene@mrcmatapedia.qc.ca
Entité municipal: Parish (Paroisse)
Incorporation: 1er janvier 1953 *Area:* 134,03
Comté ou district: La Matapédia; *Population au 2011:* 341
Circonscription(s) électorale(s) provinciale(s): Matapédia
Circonscription(s) électorale(s) fédérale(s): Haute-Gaspésie-La Mitis-Matane-Matapédia
Prochaines élections: 3e novembre 2013
Alain Duchemin, Maire
Lucie Desjardins, Directrice générale

Sainte-Jeanne-d'Arc
CP 40
205, rue Principale
Sainte-Jeanne-d'Arc, QC G0J 2T0
Tél: 418-776-5660; *Téléc:* 418-776-5660
stejeanne@mitis.qc.ca
www.municipalite.sainte-jeanne-darc.qc.ca
Entité municipal: Parish (Paroisse)
Incorporation: 30 janvier 1922 *Area:* 110,82 km2
Comté ou district: La Mitis; *Population au 2011:* 313
Circonscription(s) électorale(s) provinciale(s): Matapédia
Circonscription(s) électorale(s) fédérale(s): Haute-Gaspésie-La Mitis-Matane-Matapédia
Prochaines élections: 3e novembre 2013
Maurice Chrétien, Maire
Louise Boivin, Directrice générale

Sainte-Jeanne-d'Arc
378, rue François-Bilodeau
Sainte-Jeanne-d'Arc, QC G0W 1E0
Tél: 418-276-3166; *Téléc:* 418-276-7648
jeannerm@destination.ca
Entité municipal: Village
Incorporation: 24 janvier 1970 *Area:* 270,88 km2
Comté ou district: Maria-Chapdelaine; *Population au 2011:* 1,089
Circonscription(s) électorale(s) provinciale(s): Roberval
Circonscription(s) électorale(s) fédérale(s):
Roberval-Lac-St-Jean
Prochaines élections: 1er novembre 2013
Gaston Morin, Maire
Régis Martin, Directeur général

Sainte-Julienne
1400, rte 125
Sainte-Julienne, QC J0K 2T0
Tél: 450-831-2688; *Téléc:* 450-831-4433
municipalite@sainte-julienne.com
www.sainte-julienne.com
Entité municipal: Municipality
Incorporation: 1er juillet 1855 *Area:* 102,10 km2
Comté ou district: Montcalm; *Population au 2011:* 9,331
Circonscription(s) électorale(s) provinciale(s): Rousseau
Circonscription(s) électorale(s) fédérale(s): Montcalm
Prochaines élections: 3e novembre 2013
Marcel Jetté, Maire
Diane Desjardins, Directrice générale

Sainte-Justine
167, rte 204
Sainte-Justine, QC G0R 1Y0
Tél: 418-383-5397; *Téléc:* 418-383-5398
sjustine@sogetel.net
www.stejustine.net
Entité municipal: Municipality
Incorporation: 1er janvier 1870 *Area:* 124,55 km2
Comté ou district: Les Etchemins; *Population au 2011:* 1,845
Circonscription(s) électorale(s) provinciale(s): Bellechasse
Circonscription(s) électorale(s) fédérale(s): Lévis-Bellechasse
Prochaines élections: 3e novembre 2013
Denis Beaulieu, Maire
Gilles Vézina, Directeur général

Sainte-Justine-de-Newton
CP 270
2627, rue Principale
Sainte-Justine-de-Newton, QC J0P 1T0
Tél: 450-764-3573; *Téléc:* 450-764-3180
ste-justine@rocler.qc.ca
Entité municipal: Parish (Paroisse)
Incorporation: 1er juillet 1855 *Area:* 84,14 km2
Comté ou district: Vaudreuil-Soulanges; *Population au 2011:* 973
Circonscription(s) électorale(s) provinciale(s): Soulanges
Circonscription(s) électorale(s) fédérale(s): Vaudreuil-Soulanges
Prochaines élections: 3e novembre 2013
Patricia Domingos, Mairesse
Denis Perrier, Directeur général

Sainte-Louise
CP 2130
80, rte de la Station
Sainte-Louise, QC G0R 3K0
Tél: 418-354-2509; *Téléc:* 418-354-7730
ste-louise@globetrotter.net
www.saintelouise.qc.ca
Entité municipal: Parish (Paroisse)
Incorporation: 11 décembre 1860 *Area:* 73,03 km2
Comté ou district: L'Islet; *Population au 2011:* 704
Circonscription(s) électorale(s) provinciale(s):
Kamouraska-Témiscouata
Circonscription(s) électorale(s) fédérale(s):
Montmagny-L'Islet-Kamouraska-Rivière-du-Loup
Prochaines élections: 3e novembre 2013
Denis Gagnon, Maire
Marie-Hélène Viau, Directeur générale

Sainte-Luce
1, rue Langlois
Sainte-Luce, QC G0K 1P0
Tél: 418-739-4317; *Téléc:* 418-739-4823
sainte-luce@sainteluce.ca
www.sainteluce.ca
Entité municipal: Municipality
Incorporation: 29 octobre 2001 *Area:* 74,88 km2
Comté ou district: La Mitis; *Population au 2011:* 2,851
Circonscription(s) électorale(s) provinciale(s): Matapédia
Circonscription(s) électorale(s) fédérale(s): Haute-Gaspédie-La Mitis-Matane-Matapédia
Prochaines élections: 3e novembre 2013
Gaston Gaudreault, Maire
Jean Robidoux, Directeur général

Sainte-Lucie-de-Beauregard
21, rte des Chutes
Sainte-Lucie-de-Beauregard, QC G0R 3L0
Tél: 418-223-3122; *Téléc:* 418-223-3121
ste-lucie@globetrotter.net
www.sainteluciedebeauregard.net
Entité municipal: Municipality
Incorporation: 18 novembre 1924 *Area:* 80,18 km2
Comté ou district: Montmagny; *Population au 2011:* 304
Circonscription(s) électorale(s) provinciale(s): Montagny-L'Islet
Circonscription(s) électorale(s) fédérale(s):
Montmagny-L'Islet-Kamouraska-Rivière-du-Loup
Prochaines élections: 3e novembre 2013
Louis Lachance, Maire
Bianca Deschênes, Directrice générale

Sainte-Lucie-des-Laurentides
2121, ch des Hauteurs
Sainte-Lucie-des-Laurentides, QC J0T 2J0
Tél: 819-326-3198; *Téléc:* 819-326-0592
dg@municipalite.sainte-lucie-des-laurentides.qc.ca
Entité municipal: Municipality
Incorporation: 1er janvier 1874 *Area:* 115,15 km2
Comté ou district: Les Laurentides; *Population au 2011:* 1,269
Circonscription(s) électorale(s) provinciale(s): Bertrand
Circonscription(s) électorale(s) fédérale(s): Laurentides-Labelle
Prochaines élections: 3e novembre 2013
Ghislain Schoeb, Maire
Denis Malouin, Directeur général

Sainte-Madeleine
850, rue St-Simon
Sainte-Madeleine, QC J0H 1S0
Tél: 450-795-3822; *Téléc:* 450-795-3736
administration@villestemadeleine.qc.ca
www.villestemadeleine.qc.ca
Entité municipal: Village
Incorporation: 30 décembre 1919 *Area:* 5,39 km2
Comté ou district: Les Maskoutains; *Population au 2011:* 2,356
Circonscription(s) électorale(s) provinciale(s): Verchères
Circonscription(s) électorale(s) fédérale(s): St-Hyacinthe-Bagot
Prochaines élections: 3e novembre 2013
Alain Paradis, Maire
Carole Dulude, Directrice générale

Sainte-Madeleine-de-la-Rivière-Madeleine
104, rte Principale
Madeleine-Centre, QC G0E 1P0
Tél: 418-393-2428; *Téléc:* 418-393-2869
munste-madeleine@globetrotter.net
Entité municipal: Municipality
Incorporation: 27 février 1915 *Area:* 269,35 km2
Comté ou district: La Haute-Gaspésie; *Population au 2011:* 334
Circonscription(s) électorale(s) provinciale(s): Matane
Circonscription(s) électorale(s) fédérale(s): Haute-Gaspésie-La Mitis-Matane-Matapédia
Prochaines élections: 3e novembre 2013
Joel Côté, Maire
Suzanne Roy, Directrice générale

Sainte-Marcelline-de-Kildare
500, rue Principale
Sainte-Marcelline-de-Kildare, QC J0K 2Y0
Tél: 450-883-2241; *Téléc:* 450-883-2242
info@ste-marcelline.com
www.ste-marcelline.com
Entité municipal: Municipality
Incorporation: 1er janvier 1956 *Area:* 33,66 km2
Comté ou district: Matawinie; *Population au 2011:* 1,567
Circonscription(s) électorale(s) provinciale(s): Joliette
Circonscription(s) électorale(s) fédérale(s): Joliette
Prochaines élections: 3e novembre 2013
Gaétan Morin, Maire
Catherine Haulard, Directrice générale

Sainte-Marguerite
15, rte de La Vérendrye
Sainte-Marguerite-Marie, QC G0J 2Y0
Tél: 418-756-3364; *Téléc:* 418-756-3364
stemarguerite@mrcmatapedia.qc.ca
Entité municipal: Municipality
Incorporation: 1er janvier 1957 *Area:* 83,94 km2
Comté ou district: La Matapédia; *Population au 2011:* 203
Circonscription(s) électorale(s) provinciale(s): Matapédia
Circonscription(s) électorale(s) fédérale(s): Haute-Gaspésie-La Mitis-Matane-Matapédia
Prochaines élections: 1er novembre 2013
Marlène Landry, Mairesse
Odette Corbin, Directrice générale

Sainte-Marguerite
235, rue St-Jacques
Sainte-Marguerite, QC G0S 2X0
Tél: 418-935-7103; *Téléc:* 418-935-3709
munste-marguerite@nouvellebeauce.com
Entité municipal: Parish (Paroisse)
Incorporation: 1er juillet 1855 *Area:* 82,56 km2
Comté ou district: La Nouvelle-Beauce; *Population au 2011:* 1,073
Circonscription(s) électorale(s) provinciale(s): Beauce-Nord
Circonscription(s) électorale(s) fédérale(s): Beauce
Prochaines élections: 3e novembre 2013
Adrienne Gagné, Mairesse

Nicole Chabot, Directrice générale

Sainte-Marguerite-du-Lac-Masson
414, rue de Baron-Louis-Empain
Ste-Marguerite-du-Lac-Masson, QC J0T 1L0
Tél: 450-228-2543; *Téléc:* 450-228-4008
adm@lacmasson.com
www.ste-marguerite.qc.ca
Entité municipal: Town
Incorporation: 17 octobre 2001 *Area:* 98,65 km2
Comté ou district: Les Pays-d'en-Haut; *Population au 2011:* 2,740
Circonscription(s) électorale(s) provinciale(s): Bertrand
Circonscription(s) électorale(s) fédérale(s): Laurentides-Labelle
Prochaines élections: 3e novembre 2013
Linda Fortier, Mairesse
Francine Labelle, Directrice générale

Sainte-Marie-de-Blandford
492, rte des Bosquets
Sainte-Marie-de-Blandford, QC G0X 2W0
Tél: 819-283-2127; *Téléc:* 819-283-2169
mun@saintemariedeblandford.qc.ca
Entité municipal: Municipality
Incorporation: 23 décembre 1976 *Area:* 68,29 km2
Comté ou district: Bécancour; *Population au 2011:* 466
Circonscription(s) électorale(s) provinciale(s): Lotbinière
Circonscription(s) électorale(s) fédérale(s):
Bas-Richelieu-Nicolet-Bécancour
Prochaines élections: 3e novembre 2013
Vacant, Mairesse
Galina Papantcheva, Directrice générale

Sainte-Marie-Madeleine
3541, boul Laurier
Sainte-Marie-Madeleine, QC J0H 1S0
Tél: 450-795-6272; *Téléc:* 450-795-3180
info@stemariemadeleine.qc.ca
Entité municipal: Parish (Paroisse)
Incorporation: 13 août 1879 *Area:* 49,53 km2
Comté ou district: Les Maskoutains; *Population au 2011:* 2,935
Circonscription(s) électorale(s) provinciale(s): Verchères
Circonscription(s) électorale(s) fédérale(s): St-Hyacinthe-Bagot
Prochaines élections: 3e novembre 2013
Simon Lacombe, Maire
Carole Simpson, Directrice générale

Sainte-Marie-Salomé
690, ch St-Jean
Sainte-Marie-Salomé, QC J0K 2Z0
Tél: 450-839-6212; *Téléc:* 450-839-6106
smsalome@pandore.qc.ca
Entité municipal: Parish (Paroisse)
Incorporation: 27 décembre 1888 *Area:* 34,44 km2
Comté ou district: Montcalm; *Population au 2011:* 1,164
Circonscription(s) électorale(s) provinciale(s): Joliette
Circonscription(s) électorale(s) fédérale(s): Montcalm
Prochaines élections: 3e novembre 2013
Maurice Richard, Maire
Denise Desmarais, Directrice générale

Sainte-Marthe
776, rue des Loisirs
Sainte-Marthe, QC J0P 1W0
Tél: 450-459-4284; *Téléc:* 450-459-4627
municipalite-stemarthe@sympatico.ca
www.sainte-marthe.ca
Entité municipal: Municipality
Incorporation: 27 décembre 1980 *Area:* 80,23 km2
Comté ou district: Vaudreuil-Soulanges; *Population au 2011:* 1,075
Circonscription(s) électorale(s) provinciale(s): Soulanges
Circonscription(s) électorale(s) fédérale(s): Vaudreuil-Soulanges
Prochaines élections: 3e novembre 2013
Aline Guillotte, Mairesse
Bernard Charlebois, Directeur général

Sainte-Martine
3, rue des Copains
Sainte-Martine, QC J0S 1V0
Tél: 450-427-3050; *Téléc:* 450-427-7331
saintemartine@videotron.ca
www.municipalite.sainte-martine.qc.ca
Entité municipal: Municipality
Incorporation: 8 septembre 1999 *Area:* 59,79 km2
Comté ou district: Beauharnois-Salaberry; *Population au 2011:* 4,966
Circonscription(s) électorale(s) provinciale(s): Huntingdon
Circonscription(s) électorale(s) fédérale(s):
Beauharnois-Salaberry
Prochaines élections: 3e novembre 2013
François Candau, Maire

Luc Laberge, Directeur général

Sainte-Mélanie
10, rue Louis-Charles-Panet
Sainte-Mélanie, QC J0K 3A0
Tél: 450-889-5871; *Téléc:* 450-889-4527
info@sainte-melanie.ca
www.sainte-melanie.ca
Entité municipal: Municipality
Incorporation: 1er juillet 1855 *Area:* 77,05 km2
Comté ou district: Joliette; *Population au 2011:* 2,892
Circonscription(s) électorale(s) provinciale(s): Berthier
Circonscription(s) électorale(s) fédérale(s): Joliette
Prochaines élections: 3e novembre 2013
Yves Beaulieu, Maire
Claude Gagné, Directrice générale

Sainte-Monique
101, rue Honfleur
Sainte-Monique-de-Honfleur, QC G0W 2T0
Tél: 418-347-3592; *Téléc:* 418-347-3335
ste-monique@qc.aira.com
Entité municipal: Municipality
Incorporation: 30 octobre 1930 *Area:* 155,15 km2
Comté ou district: Lac-St-Jean-Est; *Population au 2011:* 865
Circonscription(s) électorale(s) provinciale(s): Lac-St-Jean
Circonscription(s) électorale(s) fédérale(s):
Roberval-Lac-St-Jean
Prochaines élections: 3e novembre 2013
Georges Bouchard, Maire
Jean-Claude Duchesne, Directeur général

Sainte-Monique
247, rue Principale
Sainte-Monique, QC J0G 1N0
Tél: 819-289-2051; *Téléc:* 819-289-2344
municipalite@municipalitesaintemonique.com
Entité municipal: Municipality
Incorporation: 3 janvier 1996 *Area:* 58,79 km2
Comté ou district: Nicolet-Yamaska; *Population au 2011:* 548
Circonscription(s) électorale(s) provinciale(s): Nicolet-Yamaska
Circonscription(s) électorale(s) fédérale(s):
Bas-Richelieu-Nicolet-Bécancour
Prochaines élections: 3e novembre 2013
Denis Jutras, Maire
Line Camiré, Directrice générale

Sainte-Paule
191, rue de l'Église
Sainte-Paule, QC G0J 3C0
Tél: 418-737-4296; *Téléc:* 418-737-9460
ste-paule@mrcdematane.qc.ca
www.municipalite.sainte-paule.qc.ca
Entité municipal: Municipality
Incorporation: 1er janvier 1968 *Area:* 86,64 km2
Comté ou district: Matane; *Population au 2011:* 201
Circonscription(s) électorale(s) provinciale(s): Matane
Circonscription(s) électorale(s) fédérale(s): Haute-Gaspésie-La Mitis-Matane-Matapédia
Prochaines élections: 3e novembre 2013
Yvan Côté, Maire
Gilles Desjardins, Directeur général

Sainte-Perpétue
#201, 366, rue Principale sud
Sainte-Perpétue, QC G0R 3Z0
Tél: 418-359-2966; *Téléc:* 418-359-2707
munistep@globetrotter.net
www.sainteperpetue.com
Entité municipal: Municipality
Incorporation: 21 janvier 1888 *Area:* 284,51 km2
Comté ou district: L'Islet; *Population au 2011:* 1,774
Circonscription(s) électorale(s) provinciale(s): Montmagny-L'Islet
Circonscription(s) électorale(s) fédérale(s):
Montmagny-L'Islet-Kamouraska-Rivière-du-Loup;
Bas-Richelieu-Nicolet-Bécancour
Prochaines élections: 3e novembre 2013
Céline Avoine Cloutier, Mairesse
Marie-Claude Chouinard, Directrice générale

Sainte-Perpétue
2197, rang St-Joseph
Sainte-Perpétue, QC J0C 1R0
Tél: 819-336-6740; *Téléc:* 819-336-6770
municipalite@ste-perpetue.qc.ca
Entité municipal: Parish (Paroisse)
Incorporation: 9 mars 1878 *Area:* 71,14 km2
Comté ou district: Nicolet-Yamaska; *Population au 2011:* 983
Circonscription(s) électorale(s) provinciale(s): Nicolet-Yamaska
Circonscription(s) électorale(s) fédérale(s):
Bas-Richelieu-Nicolet-Bécancour
Prochaines élections: 3e novembre 2013

Line Théroux, Mairesse
Silvie Leclerc, Directrice générale

Sainte-Praxède
4795, rte 263
Sainte-Praxède, QC G0N 1E0
Tél: 418-449-2250; *Téléc:* 418-449-2251
mun.stepraxede@globetrotter.net
Entité municipal: Municipality
Incorporation: 1er janvier 1944 *Area:* 135,680 km2
Comté ou district: Les Appalaches; *Population au 2011:* 363
Circonscription(s) électorale(s) provinciale(s): Frontenac
Circonscription(s) électorale(s) fédérale(s): Mégantic-L'Érable
Prochaines élections: 3e novembre 2013
Daniel Talbot, Maire
Josée Vachon, Directrice générale

Sainte-Rita
CP 39
5, rue de l'Église ouest
Sainte-Rita, QC G0L 4G0
Tél: 418-963-2967; *Téléc:* 418-963-6539
info@municipalite.sainte-rita.qc.ca
www.municipalite.sainte-rita.qc.ca
Entité municipal: Municipality
Incorporation: 1er janvier 1948 *Area:* 142,88 km2
Comté ou district: Les Basques; *Population au 2011:* 313
Circonscription(s) électorale(s) provinciale(s): Rivière-du-Loup
Circonscription(s) électorale(s) fédérale(s):
Rimouski-Neigette-Témiscouata-Les Basques
Prochaines élections: 3e novembre 2013
Francine Ouellet, Mairesse
Marguerite D. Michaud, Directrice générale

Sainte-Rose-de-Watford
CP 39
695, rue Carrier
Sainte-Rose-de-Watford, QC G0R 4G0
Tél: 418-267-5811; *Téléc:* 418-267-5812
municipaliteste-rose@sogetel.net
www.sainterosedewatford.qc.ca
Entité municipal: Municipality
Incorporation: 17 novembre 1897 *Area:* 112,74 km2
Comté ou district: Les Etchemins; *Population au 2011:* 787
Circonscription(s) électorale(s) provinciale(s): Bellechasse
Circonscription(s) électorale(s) fédérale(s): Lévis-Bellechasse
Prochaines élections: 3e novembre 2013
Hector Provençal, Maire
Lyse Audet, Directrice générale

Sainte-Rose-du-Nord
126, rue de la Descente-des-Femmes
Sainte-Rose-du-Nord, QC G0V 1T0
Tél: 418-675-2250; *Téléc:* 418-673-2115
admin@ste-rosedunord.qc.ca
www.ste-rosedunord.qc.ca
Entité municipal: Parish (Paroisse)
Incorporation: 1er janvier 1942 *Area:* 119,03 km2
Comté ou district: Le Fjord-du-Saguenay; *Population au 2011:* 413
Circonscription(s) électorale(s) provinciale(s): Dubuc
Circonscription(s) électorale(s) fédérale(s): Chicoutimi-Le Fjord
Prochaines élections: 3e novembre 2013
Laurent Thibeault, Maire
Maryse Girard, Directrice générale

Sainte-Sabine
4, rue St-Charles
Sainte-Sabine, QC G0R 4H0
Tél: 418-383-5488; *Téléc:* 418-383-5484
munisabine@sogetel.net
Entité municipal: Parish (Paroisse)
Incorporation: 26 août 1908 *Area:* 67,28 km2
Comté ou district: Les Etchemins; *Population au 2011:* 386
Circonscription(s) électorale(s) provinciale(s): Bellechasse
Circonscription(s) électorale(s) fédérale(s): Lévis-Bellechasse
Prochaines élections: 3e novembre 2013
Denis Boutin, Maire
Réjeanne Ruel, Directrice générale

Sainte-Sabine
185, rue Principale
Sainte-Sabine, QC J0J 2B0
Tél: 450-293-7686; *Téléc:* 450-293-7604
administration@saintesabine.ca
www.saintesabine.ca
Entité municipal: Municipality
Incorporation: 19 mars 1921 *Area:* 55,42 km2
Comté ou district: Brome-Missisquoi; *Population au 2011:* 1,120
Circonscription(s) électorale(s) provinciale(s): Brome-Missisquoi
Circonscription(s) électorale(s) fédérale(s): Brome-Missisquoi
Prochaines élections: 3e novembre 2013

Laurent Phoenix, Maire
Johanne Duval, Directrice générale

Sainte-Séraphine
2660, rue du Centre-Communautaire
Sainte-Séraphine, QC J0A 1E0
Tél: 819-336-3200; *Téléc:* 819-336-3800
info@munsainteseraphine.ca
www.munsainteseraphine.ca
Entité municipal: Parish (Paroisse)
Incorporation: 7 mars 1931 *Area:* 75,73 km2
Comté ou district: Arthabaska; *Population au 2011:* 378
Circonscription(s) électorale(s) provinciale(s): Richmond
Circonscription(s) électorale(s) fédérale(s): Richmond-Arthabaska
Prochaines élections: 3e novembre 2013
Claude Lampron, Maire
Julie Paris, Directrice générale

Sainte-Sophie
2212, rue de l'Hôtel-de-Ville
Sainte-Sophie, QC J5J 1A1
Tél: 450-438-7784; *Téléc:* 450-438-1080
courrier@ste-sophie.qc.ca
www.stesophie.ca
Entité municipal: Municipality
Incorporation: 3 mai 2000 *Area:* 108,98 km2
Comté ou district: La Rivière-du-Nord; *Population au 2011:* 13,375
Circonscription(s) électorale(s) provinciale(s): Rousseau
Circonscription(s) électorale(s) fédérale(s): Rivière-du-Nord
Prochaines élections: 3e novembre 2013
Yvon Brière, Maire
Matthieu Ledoux, Directeur général

Sainte-Sophie-d'Halifax
10, rue de l'Église
Sainte-Sophie-d'Halifax, QC G0P 1L0
Tél: 819-362-2225; *Téléc:* 819-362-2225
Entité municipal: Municipality
Incorporation: 17 décembre 1997 *Area:* 91,11 km2
Comté ou district: L'Érable; *Population au 2011:* 666
Circonscription(s) électorale(s) provinciale(s): Lotbinière
Circonscription(s) électorale(s) fédérale(s): Mégantic-L'Érable
Prochaines élections: 3e novembre 2013
Marc Nadeau, Maire
Suzanne Savage, Directrice générale

Sainte-Sophie-de-Lévrard
174A, rang St-Antoine
Sainte-Sophie-de-Lévrard, QC G0X 3C0
Tél: 819-288-5804; *Téléc:* 819-288-5804
municipalite@ste-sophie-de-levrard.com
Entité municipal: Parish (Paroisse)
Incorporation: 23 avril 1875 *Area:* 82,38 km2
Comté ou district: Bécancour; *Population au 2011:* 733
Circonscription(s) électorale(s) provinciale(s): Lotbinière
Circonscription(s) électorale(s) fédérale(s): Bas-Richelieu-Nicolet-Bécancour
Prochaines élections: 3e novembre 2013
Jean-Guy Beaudet, Maire
Micheline St-Onge, Directrice générale

Sainte-Thècle
301, rue St-Jacques
Sainte-Thècle, QC G0X 3G0
Tél: 418-289-2070; *Téléc:* 418-289-3014
ste-thecle@regionmekinac.com
www.ste-thecle.qc.ca
Entité municipal: Municipality
Incorporation: 7 juin 1989 *Area:* 216,64 km2
Comté ou district: Mékinac; *Population au 2011:* 2,478
Circonscription(s) électorale(s) provinciale(s): Laviolette
Circonscription(s) électorale(s) fédérale(s): St-Maurice-Champlain
Prochaines élections: 3e novembre 2013
Alain Vallièe, Maire
Louise T.-Rompré, Sec.-Trés.

Sainte-Thérèse-de-Gaspé
CP 160
374, rte 132
Sainte-Thérèse-de-Gaspé, QC G0C 3B0
Tél: 418-385-3313; *Téléc:* 418-385-3799
muniste@globetrotter.net
Entité municipal: Municipality
Incorporation: 6 septembre 1930 *Area:* 34,36 km2
Comté ou district: Le Rocher-Percé; *Population au 2011:* 1,055
Circonscription(s) électorale(s) provinciale(s): Gaspé
Circonscription(s) électorale(s) fédérale(s): Gaspésie—Îles-de-la-Madeleine
Prochaines élections: 3e novembre 2013
Leo Lelièvre, Maire
Luc Lambert, Directeur général

Sainte-Thérèse-de-la-Gatineau
CP 155
27, ch Principal
Sainte-Thérèse-de-la-Gatineau, QC J0X 2X0
Tél: 819-449-4134; *Téléc:* 819-449-2194
info@ste-theresehq.ca
www.ste-theresehg.ca
Entité municipal: Municipality
Incorporation: 1er janvier 1946 *Area:* 67,85 km2
Comté ou district: La Vallée-de-la-Gatineau; *Population au 2011:* 526
Circonscription(s) électorale(s) provinciale(s): Gatineau
Circonscription(s) électorale(s) fédérale(s): Pontiac
Prochaines élections: 3e novembre 2013
Roch Carpentier, Maire
Mélanie Lyrette, Directrice générale

Sainte-Ursule
CP 60
215, rue Lessard
Sainte-Ursule, QC J0K 3M0
Tél: 819-228-4345; *Téléc:* 819-228-8326
dg@ste-ursule.ca
www.ste-ursule.ca
Entité municipal: Parish (Paroisse)
Incorporation: 1er juillet 1855 *Area:* 65,37 km2
Comté ou district: Maskinongé; *Population au 2011:* 1,375
Circonscription(s) électorale(s) provinciale(s): Maskinongé
Circonscription(s) électorale(s) fédérale(s): Berthier-Maskinongé
Prochaines élections: 3e novembre 2013
Réjean Carle, Maire
Diane Faucher, Directrice générale

Sainte-Victoire-de-Sorel
517, ch Ste-Victoire
Sainte-Victoire-de-Sorel, QC J0G 1T0
Tél: 450-782-3111; *Téléc:* 450-782-2687
info@saintevictoiredesorel.qc.ca
www.saintevictoiredesorel.qc.ca
Entité municipal: Parish (Paroisse)
Incorporation: 1er juillet 1855 *Area:* 74,90 km2
Comté ou district: Pierre-De Saurel; *Population au 2011:* 2,501
Circonscription(s) électorale(s) provinciale(s): Richelieu
Circonscription(s) électorale(s) fédérale(s): Bas-Richelieu-Nicolet-Bécancour
Prochaines élections: 3e novembre 2013
Solange Cournoyer, Mairesse
Michel Saint-Martin, Directeur général

Saints-Anges
CP 157
317, rue des Érables
Saints-Anges, QC G0S 3E0
Tél: 418-253-5230; *Téléc:* 418-253-5613
munsts-anges@nouvellebeauce.com
www.nouvellebeauce.com
Entité municipal: Parish (Paroisse)
Incorporation: 29 décembre 1880 *Area:* 68,61 km2
Comté ou district: La Nouvelle-Beauce; *Population au 2011:* 1,149
Circonscription(s) électorale(s) provinciale(s): Beauce-Nord
Circonscription(s) électorale(s) fédérale(s): Beauce
Prochaines élections: 3e novembre 2013
Jean-Marie Pouliot, Maire
Louise Turmel, Directrice générale

Saints-Martyrs-Canadiens
13, ch du Village
Saints-Martyrs-Canadiens, QC G0Y 1A1
Tél: 819-344-5171; *Téléc:* 819-344-2298
info@saints-martyrs-canadiens.ca
Entité municipal: Parish (Paroisse)
Incorporation: 1er janvier 1943 *Area:* 109,37 km2
Comté ou district: Arthabaska; *Population au 2011:* 227
Circonscription(s) électorale(s) provinciale(s): Richmond
Circonscription(s) électorale(s) fédérale(s): Richmond-Arthabaska
Prochaines élections: 3e novembre 2013
André Henri, Maire
Thérèse Lemay, Directrice générale

Salluit
CP 240
64, rue Aqqutituqaq
Salluit, QC J0M 1S0
Tél: 819-255-8953; *Téléc:* 819-255-8802
nvstreasurer@nvsalluit.ca
www.nvsalluit.ca
Entité municipal: Northern Village
Incorporation: 29 décembre 1979 *Area:* 14,33 km2
Comté ou district: Kativik; *Population au 2011:* 1,347
Circonscription(s) électorale(s) provinciale(s): Ungava
Circonscription(s) électorale(s) fédérale(s): Abitibi-Baie-James-Nunavik-Eeyou
Prochaines élections: 7 novembre 2012
Qalingo Angotigirk, Maire
Adamie Papigatuk, Conseiller régional

Sayabec
3, rue Keable
Sayabec, QC G0J 3K0
Tél: 418-536-5440; *Téléc:* 418-536-5572
www.municipalitesayabec.com
Entité municipal: Municipality
Incorporation: 24 décembre 1982 *Area:* 130,29 km2
Comté ou district: La Matapédia; *Population au 2011:* 1,864
Circonscription(s) électorale(s) provinciale(s): Matapédia
Circonscription(s) électorale(s) fédérale(s): Haute-Gaspésie-La Mitis-Matane-Matapédia
Prochaines élections: 3e novembre 2013
Danielle Marcoux, Mairesse
Francis Ouellet, Directeur général
francis.o@globetrotter.net

Schefferville
CP 1600
505, rue Fleming
Schefferville, QC G0G 2T0
Tél: 418-585-2471; *Téléc:* 418-585-2256
municipalite_schefferville@xplornet.ca
Entité municipal: Village
Incorporation: 1er août 1955 *Area:* 39,02 km2
Comté ou district: Caniapiscau; *Population au 2011:* 213
Circonscription(s) électorale(s) provinciale(s): Duplessis
Circonscription(s) électorale(s) fédérale(s): Manicouagan
Prochaines élections: 3e novembre 2013
Marcella Beaudoin, Maire
Marcella Beaudoin, Administratrice

Scotstown
101, ch Victoria ouest
Scotstown, QC J0B 3B0
Tél: 819-560-8433; *Téléc:* 819-560-8434
ville.scotstown@hsfqc.ca
www.scotstown-hsf.com
Entité municipal: Village
Incorporation: 24 juin 1892 *Area:* 12,40 km2
Comté ou district: Le Haut-St-François; *Population au 2011:* 547
Circonscription(s) électorale(s) provinciale(s): Mégantic-Compton
Circonscription(s) électorale(s) fédérale(s): Compton-Stanstead
Prochaines élections: 3e novembre 2013
Vacant, Maire
Nicolle Gaudreau, Directrice générale

Scott
1070, rte Kennedy
Scott, QC G0S 3G0
Tél: 418-387-2037; *Téléc:* 418-387-1837
nthibodeau@municipalitescott.com
www.municipalitescott.com
Entité municipal: Municipality
Incorporation: 29 mars 1995 *Area:* 32,91 km2
Comté ou district: La Nouvelle-Beauce; *Population au 2011:* 2,089
Circonscription(s) électorale(s) provinciale(s): Beauce-Nord
Circonscription(s) électorale(s) fédérale(s): Beauce
Prochaines élections: 3e novembre 2013
Clément Marcoux, Maire
Nicole Thibodeau, Directrice générale

Senneterre
CP 700
100, rue le Portage
Senneterre, QC J0Y 2M0
Tél: 819-737-2842; *Téléc:* 819-737-4668
info@paroissesenneterre.qc.ca
www.paroissesenneterre.qc.ca
Entité municipal: Parish (Paroisse)
Incorporation: 23 mars 1923 *Area:* 432,98 km2
Comté ou district: Vallée-de-l'Or; *Population au 2011:* 1,218
Circonscription(s) électorale(s) provinciale(s): Abitibi-Est
Circonscription(s) électorale(s) fédérale(s): Abitibi-Baie-James-Nunavik-Eeyou
Prochaines élections: 3e novembre 2013
Jacline Rouleau, Mairesse
Louise Leroux, Directrice générale

Senneterre
CP 789
551, 10e av
Senneterre, QC J0Y 2M0
Tél: 819-737-2296; *Téléc:* 819-737-4215
info@ville.senneterre.qc.ca
www.ville.senneterre.qc.ca
Entité municipal: Town
Incorporation: 13 juin 1919 *Area:* 16 524,89 km2
Comté ou district: Vallée-de-l'Or; *Population au 2011:* 2,953
Circonscription(s) électorale(s) provinciale(s): Abitibi-Est
Circonscription(s) électorale(s) fédérale(s):
Abitibi-Baie-James-Nunavik-Eeyou
Prochaines élections: 1er novembre 2013
Hélène Veillette, Greffière
Jean-Maurice Matte, Maire

Sept-Rivières
#400, 106, rue Napoléon
Sept-×les, QC G4R 3L7
Tél: 418-962-1900; *Téléc:* 418-962-3365
dg.mrc7riv@globetrotter.net
Entité municipal: Regional County Municipality
Incorporation: 18 mars 1981 *Area:* 32 153,95 km2
Population au 2011: 39,500
Note: 2 municipalités & 2 autres territoires.
Laurence Méthot-Losier, Préfet
Alain Lapierre, Directeur général

Shannon
50, rue St-Patrick
Shannon, QC G0A 4N0
Tél: 418-844-3778; *Téléc:* 418-844-2111
municipalite@shannon.ca
www.shannon.ca
Entité municipal: Municipality
Incorporation: 1er janvier 1947 *Area:* 61,79 km2
Comté ou district: La Jacques-Cartier; *Population au 2011:* 5,086
Circonscription(s) électorale(s) provinciale(s): Chauveau
Circonscription(s) électorale(s) fédérale(s):
Portneuf-Jacques-Cartier
Prochaines élections: 3e novembre 2013
Clive Kiley, Maire
Me Hugo Lépine, Directeur général

Shawville
CP 339
350, rue Main
Shawville, QC J0X 2Y0
Tél: 819-647-2979; *Téléc:* 819-647-6895
info@town.shawville.qc.ca
www.town.shawville.qc.ca
Entité municipal: Municipality
Incorporation: 1er janvier 1874 *Area:* 5,25 km2
Comté ou district: Pontiac; *Population au 2011:* 1,664
Circonscription(s) électorale(s) provinciale(s): Pontiac
Circonscription(s) électorale(s) fédérale(s): Pontiac
Prochaines élections: 3e novembre 2013
Albert Armstrong, Maire
Crystal Webb, Directrice générale

Sheenboro
59, ch de Sheenboro
Sheenboro, QC J0X 2Z0
Tél: 819-683-3862; *Téléc:* 819-683-3816
municsheenboro@hotmail.com
Entité municipal: Municipality
Incorporation: 1er janvier 1860 *Area:* 571,01 km2
Comté ou district: Pontiac; *Population au 2011:* 130
Circonscription(s) électorale(s) provinciale(s): Pontiac
Circonscription(s) électorale(s) fédérale(s): Pontiac
Prochaines élections: 3e novembre 2013
Dick Edwards, Maire
Donald Marion, Directeur général

Shefford
245, ch Picard
Shefford, QC J2M 1J2
Tél: 450-539-2258; *Téléc:* 450-539-4951
info@cantonshefford.qc.ca
www.cantonshefford.qc.ca
Entité municipal: Township
Incorporation: 1er juillet 1855 *Area:* 116,62 km2
Comté ou district: La Haute-Yamaska; *Population au 2011:* 6,711
Circonscription(s) électorale(s) provinciale(s): Shefford
Circonscription(s) électorale(s) fédérale(s): Shefford
Prochaines élections: 3e novembre 2013
Jean-Marc Desrochers, Maire
Sylvie Gougeon, Directrice générale

Shigawake
180, rte 132
Shigawake, QC G0C 3E0
Tél: 418-752-2474; *Téléc:* 418-752-7474
shigawake@navigue.com
Entité municipal: Municipality
Incorporation: 15 décembre 1924 *Area:* 77,36 km2
Comté ou district: Bonaventure; *Population au 2011:* 338
Circonscription(s) électorale(s) provinciale(s): Bonaventure
Circonscription(s) électorale(s) fédérale(s):
Gaspésie—Îles-de-la-Madeleine
Prochaines élections: 3e novembre 2013
Kenneth Duguay, Maire
Joann Ross, Directrice général

Stanbridge East
12, rue Maple
Stanbridge East, QC J0J 2H0
Tél: 450-248-3188; *Téléc:* 450-248-7744
stanbridge@axion.ca
www.stanbridgeeast.ca
Entité municipal: Municipality
Incorporation: 1er juillet 1855 *Area:* 49,05 km2
Comté ou district: Brome-Missisquoi; *Population au 2011:* 873
Circonscription(s) électorale(s) provinciale(s): Brome-Missisquoi
Circonscription(s) électorale(s) fédérale(s): Brome-Missisquoi
Prochaines élections: 3e novembre 2013
Greg Vaughan, Maire
Vera Gendreau, Directrice générale

Stanbridge Station
229, ch Principal
Stanbridge Station, QC J0J 2J0
Tél: 450-248-2125; *Téléc:* 450-248-1132
sergetherrien@bellnet.ca
Entité municipal: Municipality
Incorporation: 21 mars 1889 *Area:* 18,11 km2
Comté ou district: Brome-Missisquoi; *Population au 2011:* 276
Circonscription(s) électorale(s) provinciale(s): Brome-Missisquoi
Circonscription(s) électorale(s) fédérale(s): Brome-Missisquoi
Prochaines élections: 3e novembre 2013
Gilles Rioux, Maire
Serge Therrien, Directeur général

Stanstead
425, rue Dufferin
Stanstead, QC J0B 3E2
Tél: 819-876-7181; *Téléc:* 819-876-5560
info@stanstead.ca
www.stanstead.ca
Entité municipal: Town
Incorporation: 15 février 1995 *Area:* 21,93 km2
Comté ou district: Memphrémagog; *Population au 2011:* 2,857
Circonscription(s) électorale(s) provinciale(s): Orford
Circonscription(s) électorale(s) fédérale(s): Compton-Stanstead
Prochaines élections: 3e novembre 2013
Philippe Dutil, Maire
Edwin Johan Sullivan, Greffier

Stanstead
778, ch Sheldon
Fitch Bay, QC J1X 3W4
Tél: 819-876-2948; *Téléc:* 819-876-7007
cantonstanstead@axion.ca
Entité municipal: Township
Incorporation: 1er juillet 1855 *Area:* 113,93 km2
Comté ou district: Memphrémagog; *Population au 2011:* 1,038
Circonscription(s) électorale(s) provinciale(s): Orford
Circonscription(s) électorale(s) fédérale(s): Compton-Stanstead
Prochaines élections: 3e novembre 2013
Lionel Larochelle, Maire
Suzanne Ménard, Directrice générale

Stanstead-Est
7015, route 143
Stanstead-Est, QC J0B 3E0
Tél: 819-876-7292; *Téléc:* 819-876-7170
stansteadest@xittel.ca
Entité municipal: Municipality
Incorporation: 16 juillet 1932 *Area:* 111,70 km2
Comté ou district: Coaticook; *Population au 2011:* 603
Circonscription(s) électorale(s) provinciale(s): Orford
Circonscription(s) électorale(s) fédérale(s): Compton-Stanstead
Prochaines élections: 3e novembre 2013
Guy Lefebvre, Maire
Suzanne Boislard Côté, Directrice générale

Stoke
403, rue Principale
Stoke, QC J0B 3G0
Tél: 819-878-3790; *Téléc:* 819-878-3804
mun.stoke@videotron.ca
www.stoke.ca/Municipalite_de_Stoke/Bienvenue.html
Entité municipal: Municipality
Incorporation: 1er janvier 1864 *Area:* 239,89 km2
Comté ou district: Le Val-St-François; *Population au 2011:* 2,765
Circonscription(s) électorale(s) provinciale(s): Johnson
Circonscription(s) électorale(s) fédérale(s): Compton-Stanstead
Prochaines élections: 3e novembre 2013
Luc Cayer, Maire
Benoit Rousseau, Directrice générale

Stoneham-et-Tewkesbury
325, ch du Hibou
Stoneham-et-Tewkesbury, QC G3C 1R8
Tél: 418-848-2381; *Téléc:* 418-848-1748
mairie@villestoneham.com
www.villestoneham.com
Entité municipal: United Township (Cantons)
Incorporation: 1er juillet 1855 *Area:* 684,75 km2
Comté ou district: La Jacques-Cartier; *Population au 2011:* 7,106
Circonscription(s) électorale(s) provinciale(s): Chauveau
Circonscription(s) électorale(s) fédérale(s):
Portneuf-Jacques-Cartier
Prochaines élections: 3e novembre 2013
Robert Miller, Maire
Michel Chatigny, Directeur général

Stornoway
CP 98
507, rte 108 ouest
Stornoway, QC G0Y 1N0
Tél: 819-652-2800; *Téléc:* 819-652-2105
administration@munstornoway.gc.ca
www.munstornoway.qc.ca
Entité municipal: Municipality
Incorporation: 1er janvier 1858 *Area:* 178,32 km2
Comté ou district: Le Granit; *Population au 2011:* 559
Circonscription(s) électorale(s) provinciale(s):
Mégantic-Compton
Circonscription(s) électorale(s) fédérale(s): Mégantic-L'Érable
Prochaines élections: 3e novembre 2013
Pierre-André Gagné, Maire
Sylvie Gauthier, Directrice générale

Stratford
165, av Centrale nord
Stratford, QC G0Y 1P0
Tél: 418-443-2307; *Téléc:* 418-443-2603
mun.stratford@qc.aira.com
www.munstratford.qc.ca
Entité municipal: Township
Incorporation: 1er janvier 1874 *Area:* 125,61 km2
Comté ou district: Le Granit; *Population au 2011:* 1,062
Circonscription(s) électorale(s) provinciale(s):
Mégantic-Compton
Circonscription(s) électorale(s) fédérale(s): Mégantic-L'Érable
Prochaines élections: 3e novembre 2013
Jacques Fontaine, Maire
Manon Goulet, Directrice générale

Stukely-Sud
101, place de la Mairie
Stukely-Sud, QC J0E 2J0
Tél: 450-297-3407; *Téléc:* 450-297-3759
info@stukely-sud.com
www.stukely-sud.com
Entité municipal: Village
Incorporation: 19 septembre 1934 *Area:* 66,31 km2
Comté ou district: Memphrémagog; *Population au 2011:* 999
Circonscription(s) électorale(s) provinciale(s): Brome-Missisquoi
Circonscription(s) électorale(s) fédérale(s): Brome-Missisquoi
Prochaines élections: 3e novembre 2013
Gérald Allaire, Maire
Louisette Tremblay, Directrice générale

Sutton
11, rue Principale sud
Sutton, QC J0E 2K0
Tél: 450-538-2290; *Téléc:* 450-538-0930
p.menard@sutton.caa
www.sutton.ca
Entité municipal: Town
Incorporation: 4 juillet 2002 *Area:* 243,51 km2
Comté ou district: Brome-Missisquoi; *Population au 2011:* 3,906
Circonscription(s) électorale(s) provinciale(s): Brome-Missisquoi
Circonscription(s) électorale(s) fédérale(s): Brome-Missisquoi
Prochaines élections: 3e novembre 2013

Pierre Pelland, Maire
Jean-François D'Amour, Directrice générale

Tadoussac
162, rue des Jésuites
Tadoussac, QC G0T 2A0
Tél: 418-235-4446; *Téléc:* 418-235-4433
ville@tadoussac.com
www.tadoussac.com
Entité municipal: Village
Incorporation: 10 octobre 1899 *Area:* 74,59 km2
Comté ou district: La Haute-Côte-Nord; *Population au 2011:* 813
Circonscription(s) électorale(s) provinciale(s): René-Lévesque
Circonscription(s) électorale(s) fédérale(s):
Montmorency-Charlevoix-Haute-Côte-Nord
Prochaines élections: 3e novembre 2013
Hugues Tremblay, Maire
Marie-Claude Guérin, Directeur général

Taschereau
CP 150
52, rue Morin
Taschereau, QC J0Z 3N0
Tél: 819-796-2219; *Téléc:* 819-796-2220
taschereau@mrcao.qc.ca
www.taschereau.ao.ca
Entité municipal: Municipality
Incorporation: 27 décembre 2001 *Area:* 265,62 km2
Comté ou district: Abitibi-Ouest; *Population au 2011:* 986
Circonscription(s) électorale(s) provinciale(s): Abitibi-Ouest
Circonscription(s) électorale(s) fédérale(s):
Abitibi-Témiscamingue
Prochaines élections: 3e novembre 2013
Jean-Marie Poulin, Maire
Yves Aubut, Directeur général

Tasiujaq
CP 54
Tasiujaq, QC J0M 1T0
Tél: 819-633-9924; *Téléc:* 819-633-5026
www.nvtasiujaq.ca
Entité municipal: Northern Village
Incorporation: 2 février 1980 *Area:* 68,08 km2
Comté ou district: Kativik; *Population au 2011:* 303
Circonscription(s) électorale(s) provinciale(s): Ungava
Circonscription(s) électorale(s) fédérale(s):
Abitibi-Baie-James-Nunavik-Eeyou
Prochaines élections: 7 novembre 2012
Willie Cain, Maire
Mary Berthe, Sec.-Trés.

Témiscaming
CP 730
20, rue Humphrey
Témiscaming, QC J0Z 3R0
Tél: 819-627-3273; *Téléc:* 819-627-3019
ville.temiscaming@temiscaming.net
www.temiscaming.net
Entité municipal: Town
Incorporation: 26 mars 1988 *Area:* 861,77 km2
Comté ou district: Témiscamingue; *Population au 2011:* 2,385
Circonscription(s) électorale(s) provinciale(s):
Rouyn-Noranda-Témiscamingue
Circonscription(s) électorale(s) fédérale(s):
Abitibi-Témiscamingue
Prochaines élections: 3e novembre 2013
Philippe Barette, Maire
Maurice Paquin, Directeur général

Témiscamingue
#209, 21, rue Notre-Dame-de-Lourdes
Ville-Marie, QC J9V 1X8
Tél: 819-629-2829; *Téléc:* 819-629-3472
mrc@mrctemiscamingue.qc.ca
www.temiscamingue.net
Entité municipal: Regional County Municipality
Incorporation: 15 avril 1981 *Area:* 19 243,88 km2
Population au 2011: 16,425
Note: 20 municipalités & 2 autres territoires.
Jean-Pierre Charron, Préfet
mrc@mrctemiscamingue.qc.ca
Denis Clermont, Directeur général
denis.clermont@mrctemiscamingue.qc.ca

Témiscouata
5, rue de l'Hôtel de Ville, 2e étage
Notre-Dame-du-Lac, QC G0L 1X0
Tél: 418-899-6725; *Téléc:* 418-899-2000
admin@mrctemis.ca
www.mrctemiscouata.qc.ca
Entité municipal: Regional County Municipality
Incorporation: 1 janvier 1982 *Area:* 3 920,90 km2
Population au 2011: 20,572
Note: 20 municipalités.
Jean-Pierre Laplante, Directeur général
Serge Fortin, Préfet

Témiscouata-sur-le-Lac
79, rue Commerciale
Témiscouata-sur-le-Lac, QC G0L 1E0
Tél: 418-854-2116; *Téléc:* 418-854-0118
info@ville.cabano.qc.ca
www.ville.cabano.qc.ca
Entité municipal: Town
Incorporation: 5e mai 2010 *Area:* 227,91 km2
Comté ou district: Témiscouata; *Population au 2011:* 5,096
Circonscription(s) électorale(s) provinciale(s):
Kamouraska-Témiscouata
Note: Le 5e mai 2010, les villes de Cabano et Notre-Dame-du-Lac ont été amalgamé sous le nom de Témiscouata-sur-le-Lac.
Gilles Garon, Maire
Gilles Desrosiers, Directeur général

Terrasse-Vaudreuil
74, 7e av
Terrasse-Vaudreuil, QC J7V 3M9
Tél: 514-453-8120; *Téléc:* 514-453-1180
info@terrasse-vaudreuil.ca
www.terrasse-vaudreuil.ca
Entité municipal: Municipality
Incorporation: 1er janvier 1952 *Area:* 1,08 km2
Comté ou district: Vaudreuil-Soulanges; *Population au 2011:* 1,971
Circonscription(s) électorale(s) provinciale(s): Vaudreuil
Circonscription(s) électorale(s) fédérale(s): Vaudreuil-Soulanges
Prochaines élections: 3e novembre 2013
Manon Trudel, Mairesse
Ginette Roy, Directrice générale

Thérèse-de-Blainville
479, boul Adolphe-Chapleau
Bois-des-Filion, QC J6Z 1J9
Tél: 450-621-5546; *Téléc:* 450-621-2628
reception@mrc-tdb.org
www.mrctheresedeblainville.qc.ca
Entité municipal: Regional County Municipality
Population au 2011: 154,144
Note: 7 municipalités.
Paul Larocque, Préfet
Perrine Lapierre, Directrice générale

Thorne
775, rte 366
Ladysmith, QC J0X 2A0
Tél: 819-647-3206; *Téléc:* 819-647-2086
administration@municipalite.thorne.qc.ca
www.thornequebec.ca
Entité municipal: Municipality
Incorporation: 1er janvier 1860 *Area:* 177,33 km2
Comté ou district: Pontiac; *Population au 2011:* 292
Circonscription(s) électorale(s) provinciale(s): Pontiac
Circonscription(s) électorale(s) fédérale(s): Pontiac
Prochaines élections: 3e novembre 2013
Ross Vowles, Maire
Ginger Finan, Directrice générale

Thurso
161, rue Galipeau
Thurso, QC J0X 3B0
Tél: 819-985-2701; *Téléc:* 819-985-0134
ville.thurso@mrcpapineau.com
www.ville.thurso.qc.ca
Entité municipal: Town
Incorporation: 16 janvier 1886 *Area:* 6,77 km2
Comté ou district: Papineau; *Population au 2011:* 2,455
Circonscription(s) électorale(s) provinciale(s): Papineau
Circonscription(s) électorale(s) fédérale(s):
Argenteuil-Papineau-Mirabel
Prochaines élections: 3e novembre 2013
Maurice Boivin, Maire
Mario Boyer, Directeur général & Greffier

Tingwick
CP 150
12, rue de l'Hôtel-de-Ville
Tingwick, QC J0A 1L0
Tél: 819-359-2454; *Téléc:* 819-359-2233
c.ramsay@tingwick.ca
www.tingwick.ca
Entité municipal: Municipality
Incorporation: 12 décembre 1981 *Area:* 168,93 km2
Comté ou district: Arthabaska; *Population au 2011:* 1,395
Circonscription(s) électorale(s) provinciale(s): Richmond
Circonscription(s) électorale(s) fédérale(s):
Richmond-Arthabaska
Prochaines élections: 3e novembre 2013
Paul-Émile Simoneau, Maire
Chantale Ramsay, Directrice générale

Tourville
962, rue des Trembles
Tourville, QC G0R 4M0
Tél: 418-359-2106; *Téléc:* 418-359-3671
municipal.tourville@globetrotter.net
www.muntourville.qc.ca
Entité municipal: Municipality
Incorporation: 14 novembre 1918 *Area:* 161,51 km2
Comté ou district: L'Islet; *Population au 2011:* 633
Circonscription(s) électorale(s) provinciale(s): Montmagny-L'Islet
Circonscription(s) électorale(s) fédérale(s):
Montmagny-L'Islet-Kamouraska-Rivière-du-Loup
Prochaines élections: 3e novembre 2013
Michel Guy Anctil, Maire
Normand Blier, Directeur général

Trécesson
314, rue Sauvé
Trécesson, QC J0Y 2S0
Tél: 819-732-8524; *Téléc:* 819-732-8322
mun.trecesson@cableamos.com
www.mrcabitibi.qc.ca
Entité municipal: Township
Incorporation: 15 juillet 1918 *Area:* 198,38 km2
Comté ou district: Abitibi; *Population au 2011:* 1,138
Circonscription(s) électorale(s) provinciale(s): Abitibi-Ouest
Circonscription(s) électorale(s) fédérale(s):
Abitibi-Témiscamingue
Prochaines élections: 3e novembre 2013
Ghislain Nadeau, Maire
Joanie Lambert, Directrice générale

Très-St-Rédempteur
769, rte Principale
Très-St-Rédempteur, QC J0P 1P0
Tél: 450-451-5203; *Téléc:* 450-451-8894
dir@tressaintredemteur.ca
www.tressaintredempteur.ca
Entité municipal: Parish (Paroisse)
Incorporation: 30 décembre 1880 *Area:* 25,40 km2
Comté ou district: Vaudreuil-Soulanges; *Population au 2011:* 863
Circonscription(s) électorale(s) provinciale(s): Soulanges
Circonscription(s) électorale(s) fédérale(s): Vaudreuil-Soulanges
Prochaines élections: 3e novembre 2013
Jean Lalonde, Maire
Vacant, Directeur général

Très-St-Sacrement
CP 160
1180, rte 203
Howick, QC J0S 1G0
Tél: 450-825-0192; *Téléc:* 450-825-0193
mun-trst@videotron.ca
Entité municipal: Parish (Paroisse)
Incorporation: 2 avril 1885 *Area:* 97,30 km2
Comté ou district: Le Haut-Saint-Laurent; *Population au 2011:* 1,155
Circonscription(s) électorale(s) provinciale(s): Huntingdon
Circonscription(s) électorale(s) fédérale(s):
Beauharnois-Salaberry
Prochaines élections: 3e novembre 2013
Albert Billette, Maire
Suzanne Côté, Directrice générale

Tring-Jonction
100, av Commerciale
Tring-Jonction, QC G0N 1X0
Tél: 418-426-2497; *Téléc:* 418-426-2498
tring@bellnet.ca
www.tringjonction.qc.ca
Entité municipal: Village
Incorporation: 21 novembre 1918 *Area:* 25,71 km2
Comté ou district: Robert-Cliche; *Population au 2011:* 1,473
Circonscription(s) électorale(s) provinciale(s): Beauce-Nord
Circonscription(s) électorale(s) fédérale(s): Beauce
Prochaines élections: 3e novembre 2013
Mario Groleau, Maire
Marcel Poulin, Directeur général

Trois-Pistoles
5, rue Notre-Dame est
Trois-Pistoles, QC G0L 4K0
Tél: 418-851-1995; *Téléc:* 418-851-3567
administration@ville-trois-pistoles.ca
www.ville-trois-pistoles.ca

Entité municipal: Town
Incorporation: 9 mars 1916 *Area:* 7,74 km2
Comté ou district: Les Basques; *Population au 2011:* 3,456
Circonscription(s) électorale(s) provinciale(s): Rivière-du-Loup
Circonscription(s) électorale(s) fédérale(s):
Rimouski-Neigette-Témiscouata-Les Basques
Prochaines élections: 3e novembre 2013
Jean-Pierre Rioux, Maire
Cindy Lafrenière, Greffière

Trois-Rives
258, ch St-Joseph
Trois-Rives, QC G0X 2C0
Tél: 819-646-5686; *Téléc:* 819-646-5688
trois-rives@regionmekinac.com
www.trois-rives.com
Entité municipal: Municipality
Incorporation: 2 septembre 1972 *Area:* 675,09 km2
Comté ou district: Mékinac; *Population au 2011:* 490
Circonscription(s) électorale(s) provinciale(s): Laviolette
Circonscription(s) électorale(s) fédérale(s):
St-Maurice-Champlain
Prochaines élections: 3e novembre 2013
Lucien Mongrain, Maire
Nicole Léveillé, Directrice générale

Ulverton
151, rte 143
Ulverton, QC J0B 2B0
Tél: 819-826-5049; *Téléc:* 819-826-5181
municipalite.ulverton@bellnet.ca
Entité municipal: Municipality
Incorporation: 1er juillet 1855 *Area:* 51,28 km2
Comté ou district: Le Val-St-François; *Population au 2011:* 416
Circonscription(s) électorale(s) provinciale(s): Johnson
Circonscription(s) électorale(s) fédérale(s):
Richmond-Arthabaska
Prochaines élections: 3e novembre 2013
Vacant, Maire
Chantal Dubé, Directrice générale

Umiujaq
CP 108
Umiujaq, QC J0M 1Y0
Tél: 819-331-7000; *Téléc:* 819-331-7057
sec.treasurer@nvumiujaq.ca
www.nvumiujaq.ca
Entité municipal: Northern Village
Incorporation: 20 décembre 1986 *Area:* 25,50 km2
Comté ou district: Kativik; *Population au 2011:* 444
Circonscription(s) électorale(s) provinciale(s): Ungava
Circonscription(s) électorale(s) fédérale(s):
Abitibi-Baie-James-Nunavik-Eeyou
Prochaines élections: 7 novembre 2012
Abelie Napartuk, Maire
Sam Nuktie, Sec.-Trés.

Upton
863, rue Lanoie
Upton, QC J0H 2E0
Tél: 450-549-5611; *Téléc:* 450-549-5045
dg@upton.ca
www.upton.ca
Entité municipal: Municipality
Incorporation: 25 février 1998 *Area:* 51,02 km2
Comté ou district: Acton; *Population au 2011:* 2,075
Circonscription(s) électorale(s) provinciale(s): Johnson
Circonscription(s) électorale(s) fédérale(s): St-Hyacinthe-Bagot
Prochaines élections: 3e novembre 2013
Yves Croteau, Maire
Cynthia Bossé, Directrice générale

Val-Alain
CP 10
1245, 2e rang
Val-Alain, QC G0S 3H0
Tél: 819-744-3222; *Téléc:* 819-744-1330
municipalitevalalain@globetrotter.net
www.val-alain.com
Entité municipal: Municipality
Incorporation: 1er janvier 1950 *Area:* 103,80 km2
Comté ou district: Lotbinière; *Population au 2011:* 955
Circonscription(s) électorale(s) provinciale(s): Lotbinière
Circonscription(s) électorale(s) fédérale(s):
Lotbinière-Chutes-de-la-Chaudière
Prochaines élections: 3e novembre 2013
Rénald Grondin, Maire
France Bisson, Directrice générale

Val-Brillant
CP 220
11, rue St-Pierre ouest
Val-Brillant, QC G0J 3L0
Tél: 418-742-3212; *Téléc:* 418-742-3624
valbrillant@globetrotter.net
www.valbrillant.ca
Entité municipal: Municipality
Incorporation: 20 décembre 1986 *Area:* 80,00 km2
Comté ou district: La Matapédia; *Population au 2011:* 955
Circonscription(s) électorale(s) provinciale(s): Matapédia
Circonscription(s) électorale(s) fédérale(s): Haute-Gaspésie-La Mitis-Matane-Matapédia
Prochaines élections: 3e novembre 2013
Donald Malenfant, Maire
Lise Tremblay, Directrice générale

Val-David
2579, rue de l'Église
Val-David, QC J0T 2N0
Tél: 819-324-5678; *Téléc:* 819-322-6327
info@valdavid.com
www.valdavid.com
Entité municipal: Village
Incorporation: 10 mai 1921 *Area:* 43,17 km2
Comté ou district: Les Laurentides; *Population au 2011:* 4,450
Circonscription(s) électorale(s) provinciale(s): Bertrand
Circonscription(s) électorale(s) fédérale(s): Laurentides-Labelle
Prochaines élections: 3e novembre 2013
Nicole Davidson, Mairesse
Serge Pourreaux, Directeur général

Val-des-Bois
CP 69
595, rte 309
Val-des-Bois, QC J0X 3C0
Tél: 819-454-2280; *Téléc:* 819-454-2211
mun.valdesbois@mrcpapineau.com
www.val-des-bois.ca
Entité municipal: Municipality
Incorporation: 1er janvier 1885 *Area:* 224,34 km2
Comté ou district: Papineau; *Population au 2011:* 938
Circonscription(s) électorale(s) provinciale(s): Papineau
Circonscription(s) électorale(s) fédérale(s):
Argenteuil-Papineau-Mirabel
Prochaines élections: 3e novembre 2013
Marcel Proulx, Maire
Line Sarrazin, Directrice générale

Val-des-Lacs
349, ch de Val-des-Lacs
Val-des-Lacs, QC J0T 2P0
Tél: 819-326-5624; *Téléc:* 819-326-7065
info@municipalite.val-des-lacs.qc.ca
municipalite.val-des-lacs.qc.ca
Entité municipal: Municipality
Incorporation: 6 février 1932 *Area:* 121,82 km2
Comté ou district: Les Laurentides; *Population au 2011:* 721
Circonscription(s) électorale(s) provinciale(s): Bertrand
Circonscription(s) électorale(s) fédérale(s): Laurentides-Labelle
Prochaines élections: 1er novembre 2013
Sylvain Michaudville, Sec.-Trés. & Directeur général
Berthe Béleanger, Maire

Val-des-Monts
1, rte du Carrefour
Val-des-Monts, QC J8N 4E9
Tél: 819-457-9400; *Téléc:* 819-457-4141
administration@val-des-monts.net
www.val-des-monts.net
Entité municipal: Municipality
Incorporation: 1er janvier 1975 *Area:* 457,31 km2
Comté ou district: Les Collines-de-l'Outaouais; *Population au 2011:* 10,420
Circonscription(s) électorale(s) provinciale(s): Papineau
Circonscription(s) électorale(s) fédérale(s): Pontiac
Prochaines élections: 3e novembre 2013
Jean Lafrenière, Maire
Patricia Fillet, Directrice générale

Val-Joli
500, rte 249
Val-Joli, QC J1S 2L5
Tél: 819-845-7663; *Téléc:* 819-845-4399
val-jolidg@axion.ca
Entité municipal: Municipality
Incorporation: 1er juillet 1855 *Area:* 90,61 km2
Comté ou district: Le Val-Saint-François; *Population au 2011:* 1,501
Circonscription(s) électorale(s) provinciale(s): Johnson
Circonscription(s) électorale(s) fédérale(s):
Richmond-Arthabaska
Prochaines élections: 1er novembre 2013
Lucie Camiré, Sec.-Trés. & Directrice générale
Gilles Perron, Maire

Val-Morin
6120, rue Morin
Val-Morin, QC J0T 2R0
Tél: 819-322-5670; *Téléc:* 819-322-3923
municipalite@val-morin.ca
www.val-morin.ca
Entité municipal: Municipality
Incorporation: 27 juin 1922 *Area:* 39,00 km2
Comté ou district: Les Laurentides; *Population au 2011:* 2,772
Circonscription(s) électorale(s) provinciale(s): Bertrand
Circonscription(s) électorale(s) fédérale(s): Laurentides-Labelle
Prochaines élections: 3e novembre 2013
Jacques Brien, Maire
Pierre Delage, Directeur général

Val-Racine
CP 1
2991, ch St-Léon
Val-Racine, QC G0Y 1E0
Tél: 819-657-4790; *Téléc:* 819-657-4790
vracine@xplornet.com
www.municipalite.val-racine.qc.ca
Entité municipal: Parish (Paroisse)
Incorporation: 26 avril 1907 *Area:* 116,80 km2
Comté ou district: Le Granit; *Population au 2011:* 170
Circonscription(s) électorale(s) provinciale(s):
Mégantic-Compton
Circonscription(s) électorale(s) fédérale(s): Mégantic-L'Érable
Prochaines élections: 3e novembre 2013
Chantal Grégoire, Directrice générale
Sonia Cloutier, Mairesse

Val-St-Gilles
801, rue Principale
Val-Saint-Gilles, QC J0Z 3T0
Tél: 819-333-2158; *Téléc:* 819-333-3116
valstgilles@mrcao.qc.ca
www.valst-gilles.ao.ca
Entité municipal: Municipality
Incorporation: 1er avril 1939 *Area:* 110,54 km2
Comté ou district: Abitibi-Ouest; *Population au 2011:* 178
Circonscription(s) électorale(s) provinciale(s): Abitibi-Ouest
Circonscription(s) électorale(s) fédérale(s):
Abitibi-Témiscamingue
Prochaines élections: 3e novembre 2013
Réjean Lambert, Maire
Sylvie Lambert, Directrice générale

Valcourt
9040B, rue de la Montagne
Valcourt, QC J0E 2L0
Tél: 450-532-2688; *Téléc:* 450-532-5570
info@cantonvalcourt.qc.ca
Entité municipal: Township
Incorporation: 1er juillet 1855 *Area:* 79,64 km2
Comté ou district: Le Val-St-François; *Population au 2011:* 1,047
Circonscription(s) électorale(s) provinciale(s): Johnson
Circonscription(s) électorale(s) fédérale(s): Shefford
Prochaines élections: 1er novembre 2013
Patrice Desmarais, Maire
desmpat@cooptel.qc.ca
Sylvie Courtemanche, Directrice générale
directrice@catonvalcourt.qc.ca

Valcourt
1155, rue St-Joseph
Valcourt, QC J0E 2L0
Tél: 450-532-3313; *Téléc:* 450-532-3424
ville.valcourt@valcourt.ca
www.valcourt.ca
Entité municipal: Town
Incorporation: 19 octobre 1929 *Area:* 5,17 km2
Comté ou district: Le Val-St-François; *Population au 2011:* 2,349
Circonscription(s) électorale(s) provinciale(s): Johnson
Circonscription(s) électorale(s) fédérale(s): Shefford
Prochaines élections: 3e novembre 2013
Laurian Gagné, Maire
Manon Beauchemin, Greffière

Vallée-Jonction
259, blvd. Jean-Marie Rousseau
Vallée-Jonction, QC G0S 3J0
Tél: 418-253-5515; *Téléc:* 418-253-6731
munivj@globetrotter.net
www.valleejonction.qc.ca
Entité municipal: Municipality
Incorporation: 22 mars 1989 *Area:* 24,41 km2

Comté ou district: La Nouvelle-Beauce; *Population au 2011:* 1,940
Circonscription(s) électorale(s) provinciale(s): Beauce-Nord
Circonscription(s) électorale(s) fédérale(s): Beauce
Prochaines élections: 3e novembre 2013
Réal Bisson, Mairesse
Gervais Boily, Directeur général

Vaudreuil-Soulanges
420, av Saint-Charles
Vaudreuil-Dorion, QC J7V 2N1
Tél: 450-455-5753; *Téléc:* 450-455-0145
info@mrcvs.ca
www.mrcvs.ca
Entité municipal: Regional County Municipality
Population au 2011: 139,353
Note: 23 municipalités.
Guy-Lin Beaudoin, Directeur général
Gilles Farand, Préfet

Vaudreuil-sur-le-Lac
44, rue de l'Église
Vaudreuil-sur-le-Lac, QC J7V 8P3
Tél: 450-455-1133; *Téléc:* 450-455-8614
vsll@videotron.ca
www.vsll.ca
Entité municipal: Village
Incorporation: 29 mai 1920 *Area:* 1,73 km2
Comté ou district: Vaudreuil-Soulanges; *Population au 2011:* 1,359
Circonscription(s) électorale(s) provinciale(s): Vaudreuil
Circonscription(s) électorale(s) fédérale(s): Vaudreuil-Soulanges
Prochaines élections: 3e novembre 2013
Claude Pilon, Maire
Claudia Chebin, Directrice générale

Venise-en-Québec
CP 270
237, 16e av ouest
Venise-en-Québec, QC J0J 2K0
Tél: 450-244-5838; *Téléc:* 450-244-5550
begind@venise-en-quebec.ca
www.municipalite.venise-en-quebec.qc.ca
Entité municipal: Municipality
Incorporation: 1er janvier 1950 *Area:* 13,57 km2
Comté ou district: Le Haut-Richelieu; *Population au 2011:* 1,547
Circonscription(s) électorale(s) provinciale(s): Iberville
Circonscription(s) électorale(s) fédérale(s): Brome-Missisquoi
Prochaines élections: 3e novembre 2013
Jacques Landry, Maire
Diane Bégin, Directrice générale

Verchères
581, rte Marie-Victorin
Verchères, QC J0L 2R0
Tél: 450-583-3307; *Téléc:* 450-583-3637
mairie@ville.vercheres.qc.ca
www.ville.vercheres.qc.ca
Entité municipal: Municipality
Incorporation: 18 septembre 1971 *Area:* 7,277 km2
Comté ou district: Marguerite-D'Youville; *Population au 2011:* 5,692
Circonscription(s) électorale(s) provinciale(s): Verchères
Circonscription(s) électorale(s) fédérale(s): Verchères-Les Patriotes
Prochaines élections: 3e novembre 2013
Alexandre Bélisle, Maire
Luc Forcier, Directeur général

Ville-Marie
Édifice Gérard-Caron
21, rue St-Gabriel sud
Ville-Marie, QC J9V 1A1
Tél: 819-629-2881; *Téléc:* 819-629-3215
vvm.dgst@mrctemiscamingue.qc.ca
www.ville-marie.ca
Entité municipal: Town
Incorporation: 13 octobre 1897 *Area:* 11,94 km2
Comté ou district: Témiscamingue; *Population au 2011:* 2,595
Circonscription(s) électorale(s) provinciale(s): Rouyn-Noranda-Témiscamingue
Circonscription(s) électorale(s) fédérale(s): Abitibi-Témiscamingue
Prochaines élections: 3e novembre 2013
Bernard Flébus, Maire
Daniel Dufour, Directeur général

Villeroy
378, rue Principale
Villeroy, QC G0S 3K0
Tél: 819-385-4605; *Téléc:* 819-385-4754
info@municipalite-villeroy.ca
www.municipalite-villeroy.ca
Entité municipal: Municipality
Incorporation: 22 septembre 1924 *Area:* 100,41 km2
Comté ou district: L'Érable; *Population au 2011:* 485
Circonscription(s) électorale(s) provinciale(s): Lotbinière
Circonscription(s) électorale(s) fédérale(s): Mégantic-L'Érable
Prochaines élections: 3e novembre 2013
Michel Poisson, Maire
Angèle Germain, Directrice générale

Waltham
CP 160
69, rue de l'Hôtel-de-Ville
Waltham, QC J0X 3H0
Tél: 819-683-3027; *Téléc:* 819-683-1815
froytenuedelivres@yahoo.ca
Entité municipal: Municipality
Incorporation: 1er janvier 1859 *Area:* 451,43 km2
Comté ou district: Pontiac; *Population au 2011:* 384
Circonscription(s) électorale(s) provinciale(s): Pontiac
Circonscription(s) électorale(s) fédérale(s): Pontiac
Prochaines élections: 3e novembre 2013
Garry Marchand, Maire
Fernand Roy, Directeur-général

Warden
172, rue Principale
Warden, QC J0E 2M0
Tél: 450-539-1349; *Téléc:* 450-539-0096
info@village.warden.gc.ca
Entité municipal: Village
Incorporation: 31 mars 1916 *Area:* 5,28 km2
Comté ou district: La Haute-Yamaska; *Population au 2011:* 358
Circonscription(s) électorale(s) provinciale(s): Shefford
Circonscription(s) électorale(s) fédérale(s): Shefford
Prochaines élections: 3e novembre 2013
Philip Tétrault, Maire
Jacqueline Giroux, Directrice générale

Warwick
8, rue de l'Hôtel-de-Ville
Warwick, QC J0A 1M0
Tél: 819-358-4300; *Téléc:* 819-358-4319
ville@ville.warwick.qc.ca
www.ville.warwick.qc.ca
Entité municipal: Town
Incorporation: 15 mars 2000 *Area:* 114,01 km2
Comté ou district: Arthabaska; *Population au 2011:* 4,766
Circonscription(s) électorale(s) provinciale(s): Richmond
Circonscription(s) électorale(s) fédérale(s): Richmond-Arthabaska
Prochaines élections: 3e novembre 2013
Claude Desrochers, Maire
Lise Lemieux, Directrice générale

Waskaganish
CP 60
70, rue Waskaganish
Waskaganish, QC J0M 1R0
Tél: 819-895-8650; *Téléc:* 819-895-8901
Entité municipal: Villages Cris
Population au 2011: 2,206
Circonscription(s) électorale(s) provinciale(s): Ungava
Circonscription(s) électorale(s) fédérale(s): Abitibi-Baie-James-Nunavik-Eeyou
Steve Diamond, Maire
Susan Esau, Secrétaire-Trésorière

Waswanipi
Edifice Diom-Blacksmith
CP 8
Waswanipi, QC J0Y 3C0
Tél: 819-753-2587; *Téléc:* 819-753-2555
council@waswanipi.com
www.waswanipi.com
Entité municipal: Villages Cris
Population au 2011: 1,777
Circonscription(s) électorale(s) provinciale(s): Ungava
Circonscription(s) électorale(s) fédérale(s): Abitibi-Baie-James-Nunavik-Eeyou
Paul Gull, Maire
Samuel Gull, Directeur général

Waterloo
CP 50
417, rue de la Cour
Waterloo, QC J0E 2N0
Tél: 450-539-2282; *Téléc:* 450-539-3257
administration@ville.waterloo.gc.ca
www.ville.waterloo.qc.ca
Entité municipal: Town
Incorporation: 1er janvier 1867 *Area:* 11,52 km2
Comté ou district: La Haute-Yamaska; *Population au 2011:* 4,330
Circonscription(s) électorale(s) provinciale(s): Shefford
Circonscription(s) électorale(s) fédérale(s): Shefford
Prochaines élections: 3e novembre 2013
Pascal Russell, Maire
Luc Lafleur, Greffier

Waterville
170, rue Principale sud
Waterville, QC J0B 3H0
Tél: 819-837-2456; *Téléc:* 819-837-0786
kesmith@sympatico.ca
Entité municipal: Village
Incorporation: 1er janvier 1876 *Area:* 44,53 km2
Comté ou district: Coaticook; *Population au 2011:* 2,028
Circonscription(s) électorale(s) provinciale(s): St-François
Circonscription(s) électorale(s) fédérale(s): Compton-Stanstead
Prochaines élections: 3e novembre 2013
Gladys Bruun, Mairesse
François Fréchette, Directeur général

Weedon
525, 2e av
Weedon, QC J0B 3J0
Tél: 819-560-8550; *Téléc:* 819-560-8551
adm.weedon@hsfgc.ca
www.weedon.info
Entité municipal: Municipality
Incorporation: 9 février 2000 *Area:* 215,02 km2
Comté ou district: Le Haut-St-François; *Population au 2011:* 2,683
Circonscription(s) électorale(s) provinciale(s): Mégantic-Compton
Circonscription(s) électorale(s) fédérale(s): Compton-Stanstead
Prochaines élections: 3e novembre 2013
Jean-Claude Dumas, Maire
Émile Royer, Directeur général

Wemindji
CP 60
16, rue Beaver
Wemindji, QC J0M 1L0
Tél: 819-978-0264; *Téléc:* 819-978-0258
info@wemindji-nation.qc.ca
www.wemindji-nation.qc.ca
Entité municipal: Villages Cris
Incorporation: 28 juin 1978 *Area:* 186,22 km2
Population au 2011: 1,378
Circonscription(s) électorale(s) provinciale(s): Ungava
Circonscription(s) électorale(s) fédérale(s): Abitibi-Baie-James-Nunavik-Eeyou
Prochaines élections: 1er septembre 2012
Rodney Mark, Maire
Karen Mistacheesick, Sec.-Trés.

Wentworth
114, ch Louisa
Wentworth, QC J8H 0C7
Tél: 450-562-0701; *Téléc:* 450-562-0703
info@wentworth.ca
Entité municipal: Township
Incorporation: 1er juillet 1855 *Area:* 88,99 km2
Comté ou district: Argenteuil; *Population au 2011:* 502
Circonscription(s) électorale(s) provinciale(s): Argenteuil
Circonscription(s) électorale(s) fédérale(s): Argenteuil-Papineau-Mirabel
Prochaines élections: 1er novembre 2013
Paula Knudsen, Directrice générale
Normand Champoux, Maire

Wentworth-Nord
3488, rte Principale
Wentworth-Nord, QC J0T 1Y0
Tél: 450-226-2416; *Téléc:* 450-226-2109
info@wenworth-nord.ca
www.went-nord.ca
Entité municipal: Municipality
Incorporation: 1er janvier 1958 *Area:* 155,71 km2
Comté ou district: Les Pays-d'en-Haut; *Population au 2011:* 1,440
Circonscription(s) électorale(s) provinciale(s): Argenteuil
Circonscription(s) électorale(s) fédérale(s):

Argenteuil-Papineau-Mirabel
Prochaines élections: 3e novembre 2013
André Genest, Maire
Sophie Bélanger, Directrice générale

Westbury
168, rte 112
Westbury, QC J0B 1R0
Tél: 819-560-8450; *Téléc:* 819-560-8451
westbury@abacom.com
Entité municipal: Township
Incorporation: 16 août 1858 *Area:* 65,78 km2
Comté ou district: Le Haut-St-François; *Population au 2011:* 997
Circonscription(s) électorale(s) provinciale(s):
Mégantic-Compton
Circonscription(s) électorale(s) fédérale(s): Compton-Stanstead
Prochaines élections: 3e novembre 2013
Kenneth Coates, Maire
Adèle Madore, Directrice générale

Whapmagoostui
CP 390
Whapmagoostui, QC J0M 1G0
Tél: 819-929-3384; *Téléc:* 819-929-3203
chief@whapmagoostuifn.ca
www.whapmagoostuifn.ca
Entité municipal: Villages Cris
Incorporation: 28 juillet 1978 *Area:* 113,70 km2
Population au 2011: 874
Circonscription(s) électorale(s) provinciale(s): Ungava
Circonscription(s) électorale(s) fédérale(s):
Abitibi-Baie-James-Nunavik-Eeyou
Losty Mamianskum, Maire
Patricia-George Kawapit, Secrétaire

Wickham
893, rue Moreau
Wickham, QC J0C 1S0
Tél: 819-398-6878; *Téléc:* 819-398-7166
wickham@bellnet.ca
www.wickham.ca
Entité municipal: Municipality
Incorporation: 23 décembre 1972 *Area:* 97,72 km2
Comté ou district: Drummond; *Population au 2011:* 2,470
Circonscription(s) électorale(s) provinciale(s): Johnson
Circonscription(s) électorale(s) fédérale(s): Drummond
Prochaines élections: 3e novembre 2013
Carole Côté, Mairesse
Réal Dulmaine, Directeur général

Windsor
CP 90
22, rue St-Georges
Windsor, QC J1S 2L7
Tél: 819-845-7888; *Téléc:* 819-845-7606
info@villedewindsor.qc.ca
www.villedewindsor.qc.ca
Entité municipal: Town
Incorporation: 29 décembre 1999 *Area:* 13,78 km2
Comté ou district: Le Val-St-François; *Population au 2011:* 5,367
Circonscription(s) électorale(s) provinciale(s): Johnson
Circonscription(s) électorale(s) fédérale(s):
Richmond-Arthabaska
Prochaines élections: 3e novembre 2013
Sylvie Bureau, Mairesse
Sylvain Saint-Cyr, Directrice générale & Greffière

Wotton
CP 60
396, rue Monseigneur-L'Heureux
Wotton, QC J0A 1N0
Tél: 819-828-2112; *Téléc:* 819-828-3594
municipalite.wotton@cgocable.ca
www.wotton.ca
Entité municipal: Municipality
Incorporation: 10 mars 1993 *Area:* 142,41 km2
Comté ou district: Les Sources; *Population au 2011:* 1,453
Circonscription(s) électorale(s) provinciale(s): Richmond
Circonscription(s) électorale(s) fédérale(s):
Richmond-Arthabaska
Prochaines élections: 3e novembre 2013
Ghislain Drouin, Maire
Carole Vaillancourt, Directrice générale

Yamachiche
366, rue Ste-Anne
Yamachiche, QC G0X 3L0
Tél: 819-296-3795; *Téléc:* 819-296-3542
hoteldeville@yamachiche.ca
www.municipalite.yamachiche.qc.ca
Entité municipal: Municipality
Incorporation: 26 décembre 1987 *Area:* 106,30 km2
Comté ou district: Maskinongé; *Population au 2011:* 2,787
Circonscription(s) électorale(s) provinciale(s): Maskinongé
Circonscription(s) électorale(s) fédérale(s): Berthier-Maskinongé
Prochaines élections: 3e novembre 2013
Michel Isabelle, Maire
Linda Lafrenière, Directeur générale

Yamaska
CP 120
100, rue Guilbault
Yamaska, QC J0G 1X0
Tél: 450-789-2489; *Téléc:* 450-789-2970
yamaska@bas-richelieu.net
www.yamaska.ca
Entité municipal: Municipality
Incorporation: 19 décembre 2001 *Area:* 74,44 km2
Comté ou district: Pierre-De Saurel; *Population au 2011:* 1,644
Circonscription(s) électorale(s) provinciale(s): Richelieu;
Nicolet-Yamaska
Circonscription(s) électorale(s) fédérale(s):
Bas-Richelieu-Nicolet-Bécancour
Prochaines élections: 3e novembre 2013
Louis R. Joyal, Maire
450-789-2912
Brigitte Vachon, Directrice générale
bvachon@bas-richelieu.net

SASKATCHEWAN

Acts governing the municipal system in Saskatchewan are The Urban Municipality Act, 1984; The Rural Municipality Act, 1989; and The Northern Municipalities Act. In the province there are the following types of incorporated municipalities: Rural Municipalities, Villages, Resort Villages, Towns, and Cities, as well as Northern Towns, Northern Villages, Northern Hamlets, Northern Settlements, Resort Hamlets and Organized Hamlets. The incorporation of these municipalities is voluntary. Thus a Village that qualifies to be named a Town, can remain a Village if the population so wishes.

Rural Municipalities are divided into divisions. A Reeve is elected at large every two years. Councillors are also elected every two years but in "staggered" sequence. Rural municipal nominations are received until the third Monday in October and elections are held on the third Wednesday after the nomination period.

Villages are defined as communities with not less than 100 permanent residents and not less than 50 dwellings and/or business premises. The Village is represented by a Mayor and at least two Councillors.

Towns are defined as communities with not less that 500 permanent residents. They are represented by a Mayor and at least two Councillors.

Cities are defined as communities with not less than 5,000 residents. They are represented by a Mayor and Councillors (the number varies).

Elections for all members of council in urban municipalities occur every three years. Nominations are held in cities, towns, and villages on the second Wednesday in October and elections on the fourth Wednesday in October. In resort villages, nomination day will be the last Saturday in June and the election will be held on the fourth Saturday in July (2011, 2015, etc.).

Northern Hamlets: have a population of 50 or more and must contain 25 or more separate dwelling units or business premises. They are governed by a Mayor and two Aldermen, although they may pass a bylaw to increase the number of Aldermen to four.

Northern Villages: contain a minimum population of 100 and at least 50 dwelling units or business premises. Their council consists of a Mayor and four Councillors; although they may pass bylaws to either decrease the number of Councillors to two, or increase the number of Councillors by any even number.

Northern Towns: will have a minimum population of 500 and are governed by a Mayor and six Councillors. The council may pass a bylaw increasing or decreasing the size of council by any even number, provided the number of Councillors does not fall below two.

Election for all members of council in northern municipalities occur every three years. Council will determine the date of the election, which shall be held the second last Wednesday in September, the last Wednesday in September, or the first Wednesday in October. Nomination day is five weeks prior to the date on which the election is to be held.

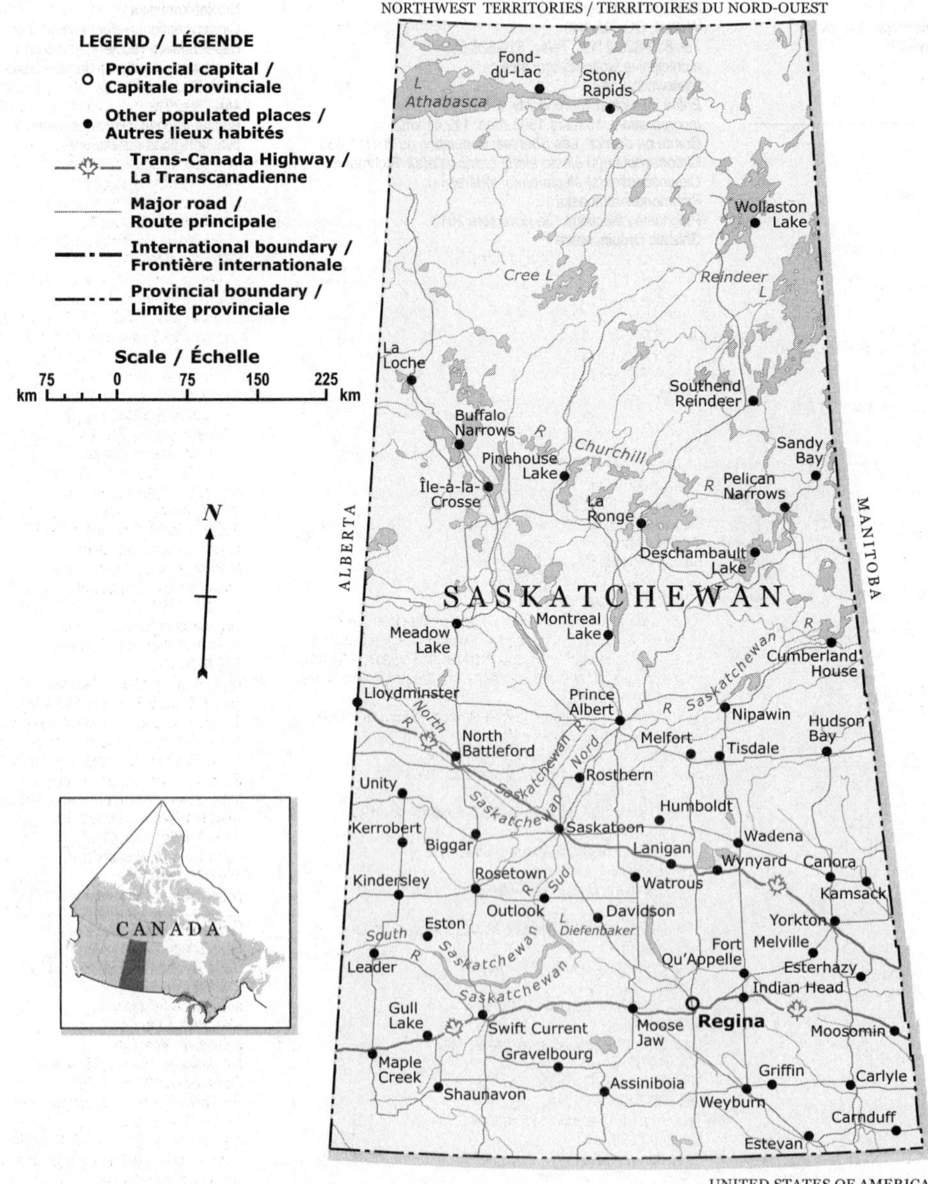

Reproduced with the permission of Natural Resources Canada, 2012

Saskatchewan

Major Municipalities in Saskatchewan

Estevan
1102 - 4 St.
Estevan, SK S4A 0W7
Tel: 306-634-1800; *Fax:* 306-634-9790
citymanager@estevan.ca
www.estevan.ca
Municipal Type: City
Incorporated: Nov. 2, 1899 *Area:* 17.56 sq km
Population in 2011: 11,054
Provincial Electoral District(s): Estevan
Federal Electoral District(s): Souris-Moose Mountain
Next Election: Oct. 24, 2012 (4 year terms)
Note: Incorporated as city on March 1, 1957.
Gary St. Onge, Mayor
mayor@estevan.ca
Lyndon Stachoski, Clerk
administration@estevan.ca
Jim Puffalt, City Manager
306-634-1803
Tim Leson, Treasurer
Rob Denys, Manager, Land Development Services
rdenys@estevan.ca
Owen Green, Manager, Public Works Services
Helen Fornwald, Manager, Leisure Services
Kevin Sutter, Manager, Water/Wastewater Treatment Services
Zeshan Halder, Engineer, Engineering Services
Ron Tocker, Fire Chief
Del Block, Police Chief

Lloydminster
City Hall
4420 - 50 Ave.
Lloydminster, SK T9V 0W2
Tel: 306-875-6184; *Fax:* 306-871-8346
info@lloydminster.ca
www.lloydminster.ca
Municipal Type: City
Incorporated: Nov. 25, 1903 *Area:* 17.34 sq km
Population in 2011: 27,804
Provincial Electoral District(s): Lloydminster
Federal Electoral District(s): Battlefords-Lloydminster
Next Election: Oct. 24, 2012 (4 year terms)
Note: Population figure represents both the Alberta & Saskatchewan populations. Incorporated as a city on Jan. 1, 1958.
Jeff Mulligan, Mayor

Moose Jaw
228 Main St. North
Moose Jaw, SK S6H 3J8
Tel: 306-694-4400; *Fax:* 306-694-4480
www.moosejaw.ca
Municipal Type: City
Incorporated: Jan. 19, 1884 *Area:* 46.82 sq km
Population in 2011: 33,274
Provincial Electoral District(s): Moose Jaw North; Moose Jaw Wakamow
Federal Electoral District(s): Palliser
Next Election: Oct. 24, 2012 (4 year terms)
Note: Incorporated as a city on Nov. 20, 1903.
Glen Hagel, Mayor
Myron Gulka-Tiechco, City Clerk

North Battleford
P.O. Box 460
1291 - 101st St.
North Battleford, SK S9A 2Y6
Tel: 306-445-1700; *Fax:* 306-445-0411
www.cityofnb.ca
Municipal Type: City
Incorporated: March 21, 1906 *Area:* 33.55 sq km
Population in 2011: 13,888
Provincial Electoral District(s): The Battlefords
Federal Electoral District(s): Battlefords-Lloydminster
Next Election: Oct. 24, 2012 (4 year terms)
Note: Proclaimed as a city on May 1, 1913.
Ian Hamilton, Mayor
ihamilton@cityofnb.ca
Debbie Wohlberg, City Clerk
dwohlberg@cityofnb.ca
Jim Toye, City Manager
jtoye@cityofnb.ca
Tim LaFreniere, City Planner
tlafreniere@citynb.ca
Stewart Schafer, Director, Public Works
Keith Anderson, Director, Parks & Recreation
kanderson@cityofnb.ca
Pat MacIsaac, Fire Chief
pmacisaac@cityofnb.ca

Prince Albert
City Hall
1084 Central Ave.
Prince Albert, SK S6V 7P3
Tel: 306-953-4884
www.citypa.ca
Municipal Type: City
Incorporated: Oct. 8, 1885 *Area:* 65.68 sq km
Population in 2011: 35,129
Provincial Electoral District(s): Prince Albert Carlton; Prince Albert Northcote
Federal Electoral District(s): Prince Albert
Next Election: Oct. 24, 2012 (4 year terms)
Note: Incorporated as a city on Oct. 8, 1904.
Jim Scarrow, Mayor
mayor@citypa.com
Cliff Skauge, Clerk
cskauge@citypa.com
Robert Cotterill, City Manager
306-953-4395
rcotterill@citypa.com
Ken Paskaruk, City Solicitor
306-953-4315
kpaskaruk@citypa.com
Jean Corneil, Director, Economic Development & Planning
306-953-4315
jcorneil@citypa.com
Chris Cvik, Director, Corporate Services
306-953-4310
ccvik@citypa.com
Joe Day, Director, Financial Services
306-953-4350
jday@citypa.com
Colin Innes, Director, Public Works
306-953-4900
cinnes@citypa.com
Greg Zeeben, Director, Community Services
306-953-4800
gzeeben@citypa.com
Les Karpluk, Fire Chief
306-953-4200
lkarpluk@citypa.com
Dale McFee, Police Chief
306-953-4222

Regina
City Hall
P.O. Box 1790
2476 Victoria Ave.
Regina, SK S4P 3C8
Tel: 306-777-7000
www.regina.ca
Municipal Type: City
Incorporated: Dec. 1, 1883 *Area:* 118.87 sq km
Population in 2011: 193,100
Provincial Electoral District(s): Regina Elphinstone-Centre; Regina Coronation Park; Regina Dewdney; Regina Douglas Park; Regina Lakeview; Regina Northeast; Regina Qu'Appelle Valley; Regina Rosemont; Regina South; Regina Walsh Acres; Regina Wascana Plains
Federal Electoral District(s): Palliser; Regina-Lumsden-Lake Centre; Regina-Qu'Appelle; Wascana
Next Election: Oct. 24, 2012 (4 year terms)
Note: Incorporated as a city on June 19, 1903.
Pat Fiacco, Mayor
Louis Browne, B.A.(Hons.), LL.B., Councillor, Ward(s): 1
306-531-5151
Jocelyn Hutchinson, Councillor, Ward(s): 2
306-584-1739
Fred Clipsham, Councillor, Ward(s): 3
306-757-8212
Michael Fougere, B.A.(Hons.), M.Sc., Councillor, Ward(s): 4
306-789-5586
John Findura, Councillor, Ward(s): 5
306-536-4250
Wade Murray, Councillor, Ward(s): 6
306-596-1035
Sharron Bryce, R.N., Councillor, Ward(s): 7
306-949-5025
Mike O'Donnell, Councillor, Ward(s): 8
306-545-7300
Terry Hincks, Councillor, Ward(s): 9
306-949-9690
Chris Szarka, Councillor, Ward(s): 10
306-551-2766
Joni Swidnicki, City Clerk
306-777-7262
Glen Davies, B.A., M.A., City Manager
Bonny Bryant, B.A., M.P.A., General Manager, Community & Protective Services
Jason Carlston, B.A., M.A., General Manager, Planning & Development
Brent Sjoberg, C.M.A., General Manager, Corporate Services
Dorian Wandzura, P.Eng., General Manager, Public Works Division
Jim Nicol, Chief of Staff, City Manager's Office
Troy Hagen, Chief, Regina Police Service
306-777-6500, Fax: 306-757-5461
rps@police.regina.sk.ca

Saskatoon
City Hall
222 - 3rd Ave. North
Saskatoon, SK S7K 0J5
Tel: 306-975-3200
www.saskatoon.ca
Municipal Type: City
Incorporated: Nov. 16, 1901 *Area:* 170.83 sq km
Population in 2011: 222,189
Provincial Electoral District(s): Saskatoon Centre; Saskatoon Eastview; Saskatoon Fairview; Saskatoon Greystone; Saskatoon Massey Place; Saskatoon Meewasin; Saskatoon Northwest; Saskatoon Nutana; Saskatoon Riversdale; Saskatoon Silver Springs; Saskatoon Southeast; Saskatoon Sutherland
Federal Electoral District(s): Blackstrap; Saskatoon-Humboldt; Saskatoon-Rosetown-Biggar; Saskatoon-Wanuskewin
Next Election: Oct. 24, 2012 (4 year terms)
Note: Incorporated as a city on May 26, 1906.
Donald J. Atchison, Mayor
306-975-3202, Fax: 306-975-3144
Darren Hill, Councillor, Ward(s): 1
darren.hill@saskatoon.ca
Pat Lorje, B.A., M.A., Councillor, Ward(s): 2
pat.lorje@saskatoon.ca
Myles Heidt, Councillor, Ward(s): 4
myles.heidt@saskatoon.ca
Randy Donauer, Councillor, Ward(s): 5
randy.donauer@saskatoon.ca
Charlie Clark, B.Ed., M.E.S., Councillor, Ward(s): 6
charlie.clark@saskatcoon.ca
Mairin Loewen, B.A., Councillor, Ward(s): 7
mairin.loewen@saskatoon.ca
Glen Penner, B.Ed., M.Ed., Councillor, Ward(s): 8
glen.penner@saskatoon.ca
Tiffany Paulsen, B.A., LL.B., Councillor, Ward(s): 9
tiffany.paulsen@saskatoon.ca
Bev Dubois, Councillor, Ward(s): 10
bev.dubois@saskatoon.ca
Janice Mann, City Clerk
306-975-3240, Fax: 306-975-2784
city.clerks@saskatoon.ca
Murray Totland, City Manager
Theresa Dust, City Solicitor
306-975-3270, Fax: 306-975-7828
city.solicitor@saskatoon.ca
Shelley Sutherland, Treasurer
306-975-3692
Brian Bentley, General Manager, Fire & Protective Services
306-975-2575, Fax: 306-975-2689
fire.protective.services@city.saskatoon.sk.ca
Marlys Bilanski, General Manager, Corporate Services
306-975-3206, Fax: 306-975-7975
Paul Gauthier, General Manager, Community Services
Mike Gutek, General Manager, Infrastructure Services
Brenda Wallace, General Manager, Utility Services
Brian Bentley, Fire Chief
Clive Weighill, Police Chief
306-975-8300
police.service@city.saskatoon.sk.ca

Swift Current
P.O. Box 340
Swift Current, SK S9H 3W1
Tel: 306-778-2777
admin@swiftcurrent.ca
www.swiftcurrent.ca
Municipal Type: City
Incorporated: Feb. 4, 1904 *Area:* 24.04 sq km
Population in 2011: 15,503
Provincial Electoral District(s): Swift Current
Federal Electoral District(s): Cypress Hills-Grasslands
Next Election: Oct. 24, 2012 (4 year terms)
Note: Incorporated as a city on Jan. 15, 1914.
Jerrod Schafer, Mayor
Lee-Ann Thibodeau, Clerk

Mac Forster, Director, Engineering
306-778-2740
eng@swiftcurrent.ca
Dean Robson, Director, Recreation & Parks
306-778-2787
Trevor Feicht, Manager, Engineering Services
306-778-2740
Andy Toth, Manager, Parks
306-778-2787
Denis Pilon, Fire Chief
306-778-2760

Weyburn
P.O. Box 370
157 - 3rd St. NE
Weyburn, SK S4H 2K6

questions@weyburn.ca
www.weyburn.ca
Municipal Type: City
Incorporated: Oct. 22, 1900 *Area:* 15.78 sq km
Population in 2011: 10,484
Provincial Electoral District(s): Weyburn-Big Muddy
Federal Electoral District(s): Souris-Moose Mountain
Next Election: Oct. 24, 2012 (4 year terms)
Note: Incorporated as a city on Sept. 1, 1913.
Debra Button, Mayor
mayor@weyburn.ca
Donette Ritcher, City Clerk
drichter@weyburn.ca
Robert Smith, City Manager
rsmith@weyburn.ca
Jon Michaud, City Assessor/Director, Finance
jmichaud@weyburn.ca
Rene Richard, Director, Engineering
rrichard@weyburn.ca
Mathew Warren, Director, Engineering
mwarren@weyburn.ca
Doug Mulhall, Manager, Community Development
dmulhall@weyburn.ca
Katelyn Struthers, Manager, Parks Services
kstruthers@weyburn.ca
Claude Morin, Superintendent, Public Works & Parks
cmorin@weyburn.ca
Kim Wilkes, Foreman, Public Works
kwilkes@weyburn.ca
Steve Debienne, Fire Chief
sdebienne@weyburn.ca
Howard Georgeson, Police Chief
hgeorgeson@weyburn.ca

Yorkton
37 - 3rd Ave. North
Yorkton, SK S3N 2W3
Tel: 306-786-1700; *Fax:* 306-786-6880
www.yorkton.ca
Municipal Type: City
Incorporated: July 11, 1894 *Area:* 24.57 sq km
Population in 2011: 15,669
Provincial Electoral District(s): Yorkton
Federal Electoral District(s): Yorkton-Melville
Next Election: Oct. 24, 2012 (4 year terms)
Note: Incorporated as a city on Feb. 1, 1928.
James Wilson, Mayor
mayor@yorkton.ca
Bonnie Schenher, City Clerk
bschenher@yorkton.ca
David Putz, City Manager
306-786-1703
dputz@yorkton.ca
Michael Buchholzer, Director, Water Works
306-828-2470
mbuchholzer@yorkton.ca
Lonnie Kaal, Director, Finance
306-786-1721
lkaal@yorkton.ca
Trent Mandzuk, Director, Public Works
306-786-1762
tmanzuk@yorkton.ca
Darcy McLeod, Director, Community Development, Parks & Recreation
306-786-1750
dmcleod@yorkton.ca
Gord Shaw, Director, Planning & Engineering
306-786-1730
gshaw@yorkton.ca
Brant Hryhorczuk, Manager, Building Services
306-786-1710
bhryhorczuk@yorkton.ca
Faisal Anwar, Officer, Economic Development
306-786-1747
fanwar@yorkton.ca
Dean Clark, Fire Chief, Fire Protective Services
306-786-1795
dclark@yorkton.ca

Other Municipalities in Saskatchewan

Abbey
P.O. Box 210
Abbey, SK S0N 0A0
Tel: 306-689-2412; *Fax:* 306-689-2901
rm229@sasktel.net
Municipal Type: Village
Incorporated: Sept. 2, 1913 *Area:* 0.77 sq km
Population in 2011: 115
Provincial Electoral District(s): Cypress Hills
Federal Electoral District(s): Cypress Hills-Grasslands
Next Election: Oct. 24, 2012 (4 year terms)
Bruce Walker, Mayor
Dianne Scriven, Administrator

Aberdeen
P.O. Box 130
207 Main St.
Aberdeen, SK S0K 0A0
Tel: 306-253-4311; *Fax:* 306-253-4201
townaberdeen@sasktel.net
www.aberdeen.ca
Municipal Type: Town
Incorporated: March 13, 1907 *Area:* 1.95 sq km
Population in 2011: 599
Provincial Electoral District(s): Humboldt
Federal Electoral District(s): Saskatoon-Humboldt
Next Election: Oct. 24, 2012 (4 year terms)
Note: Proclaimed as town on Nov. 1, 1988.
Bruce Voldeng, Mayor
Susan Thompson, Town Manager

Abernethy
P.O. Box 189
Abernethy, SK S0A 0A0
Tel: 306-333-2271; *Fax:* 306-333-2276
village@abernethy.ca
www.abernethy.ca
Municipal Type: Village
Incorporated: July 26, 1904 *Area:* 1.03 sq km
Population in 2011: 196
Provincial Electoral District(s): Last Mountain-Touchwood
Federal Electoral District(s): Regina-Qu'Appelle
Next Election: Oct. 24, 2012 (4 year terms)
Janet Englot, Mayor
themayor@sasktel.net
Sheree Emmerson, Administrator

Air Ronge
P.O. Box 100
Air Ronge, SK S0J 3G0
Tel: 306-425-2107; *Fax:* 306-425-3108
www.villageofairronge.com
Municipal Type: Northern Village
Incorporated: Oct. 1, 1983 *Area:* 6.00 sq km
Population in 2011: 1,043
Provincial Electoral District(s): Cumberland
Federal Electoral District(s): Desnethé-Missinippi-Churchill River
Next Election: Autumn 2012 (4 year terms)
Gordon Stomp, Mayor
Rachel Kunz, Administrator

Alameda
P.O. Box 36
Alameda, SK S0C 0A0
Tel: 306-489-2077; *Fax:* 306-489-4602
townofalameda@sasktel.net
www.townofalameda.ca
Municipal Type: Town
Incorporated: Dec. 29, 1898 *Area:* 2.55 sq km
Population in 2011: 342
Provincial Electoral District(s): Cannington
Federal Electoral District(s): Souris-Moose Mountain
Next Election: Oct. 24, 2012 (4 year terms)
Note: Proclaimed as town on April 15, 1907.
Allan Faber, Mayor
306-489-2047
Lynne Hewitt, Administrator

Albertville
General Delivery
Albertville, SK S0J 0A0
Tel: 306-929-2110; *Fax:* 306-929-4744
albertville@inet2000.com
Municipal Type: Village
Incorporated: Jan. 1, 1986 *Area:* 1.11 sq km
Population in 2011: 140
Provincial Electoral District(s): Saskatchewan Rivers
Federal Electoral District(s): Prince Albert
Next Election: Oct. 24, 2012 (4 year terms)
Louis Hradecki, Mayor
Valerie Fidler, Clerk

Alice Beach
P.O. Box 70
Dilke, SK S0G 1C0
Tel: 306-488-2014; *Fax:* 306-488-2047
rvab@sasktel.net
Municipal Type: Resort Village
Area: 0.71 sq km
Population in 2011: 45
Provincial Electoral District(s): Thunder Creek
Federal Electoral District(s): Regina-Lumsden-Lake Centre
Next Election: July 2016
Joan Moore, Mayor
Darlene Mann, Administrator

Alida
P.O. Box 6
Alida, SK S0C 0B0
Tel: 306-443-2228; *Fax:* 306-443-2568
villageofalida@sasktel.net
Municipal Type: Village
Incorporated: Feb. 19, 1926 *Area:* 0.35 sq km
Population in 2011: 131
Provincial Electoral District(s): Cannington
Federal Electoral District(s): Souris-Moose Mountain
Next Election: Oct. 24, 2012 (4 year terms)
James Boettcher, Mayor
Kathy Anthony, Administrator

Allan
P.O. Box 159
224 Main St.
Allan, SK S0K 0C0
Tel: 306-257-3272; *Fax:* 306-257-3337
www.allan.ca
Municipal Type: Town
Incorporated: June 9, 1910 *Area:* 1.78 sq km
Population in 2011: 648
Provincial Electoral District(s): Humboldt
Federal Electoral District(s): Blackstrap
Next Election: Oct. 24, 2012 (4 year terms)
Note: Proclaimed as town on Dec. 1, 1965.
Larry Sommerfeld, Mayor
Christine Dyck, Administrator

Alvena
P.O. Box 8
Alvena, SK S0K 0E0
Tel: 306-943-2101; *Fax:* 306-943-2155
villageofalvena@yahoo.ca
Municipal Type: Village
Incorporated: July 1, 1936 *Area:* 0.43 sq km
Population in 2011: 55
Provincial Electoral District(s): Batoche
Federal Electoral District(s): Saskatoon-Humboldt
Next Election: Oct. 24, 2012 (4 year terms)
Ernie Sawitsky, Mayor
Pamela Hilkewich, Clerk

Annaheim
P.O. Box 130
Annaheim, SK S0K 0G0
Tel: 306-598-2006; *Fax:* 306-598-2008
villageofannaheim@sasktel.net
Municipal Type: Village
Incorporated: April 1, 1977 *Area:* 0.78 sq km
Population in 2011: 219
Provincial Electoral District(s): Melfort
Federal Electoral District(s): Saskatoon-Humboldt
Next Election: Oct. 24, 2012 (4 year terms)
Donald Willenborg, Mayor
Debra Parry, Administrator

Antler
P.O. Box 83
Antler, SK S0C 0E0
Tel: 306-452-3533; *Fax:* 306-452-6114
ruttenranch@sasktel.net

Municipal Type: Village
Incorporated: March 15, 1905 *Area:* 0.72 sq km
Population in 2011: 41
Provincial Electoral District(s): Cannington
Federal Electoral District(s): Souris-Moose Mountain
Next Election: Oct. 24, 2012 (4 year terms)
James Duncan, Mayor
Bonnie Rutten, Clerk

Aquadeo
P.O. Box 501
1006 Hwy. 4
Cochin, SK S0M 0L0
Tel: 306-386-2942; *Fax:* 306-386-2544
aquadeoadmin@gmail.com
www.aquadeo.net
Municipal Type: Resort Village
Area: 0.74 sq km
Population in 2011: 84
Provincial Electoral District(s): Cut Knife-Turtleford
Federal Electoral District(s): Battlefords-Lloydminster
Next Election: July 2016
Cameron Duncan, Mayor
306-937-3018
Coleen Kitching, Acting Administrator

Arborfield
P.O. Box 280
201 Main St.
Arborfield, SK S0E 0A0
Tel: 306-769-8533; *Fax:* 306-769-8301
arborfieldrm456@sasktel.net
www.arborfieldsk.ca
Municipal Type: Town
Incorporated: June 16, 1933 *Area:* 0.88 sq km
Population in 2011: 326
Provincial Electoral District(s): Carrot River Valley
Federal Electoral District(s): Prince Albert
Next Election: Oct. 24, 2012 (4 year terms)
Note: Proclaimed as town on June 1, 1950.
Alvin Alyea, Mayor
Allan Frisky, Administrator

Archerwill
P.O. Box 130
Archerwill, SK S0E 0B0
Tel: 306-323-2161; *Fax:* 306-323-2101
villageofarcherwill@sasktel.net
www.newsaskcfdc.ca/archerwill.htm
Municipal Type: Village
Incorporated: Jan. 1, 1947 *Area:* 0.83 sq km
Population in 2011: 200
Provincial Electoral District(s): Kelvington-Wadena
Federal Electoral District(s): Yorkton-Melville
Next Election: Oct. 24, 2012 (4 year terms)
Robert Wilson, Mayor
Sheila Ottmann, Administrator

Arcola
P.O. Box 359
127 Main St.
Arcola, SK S0C 0G0
Tel: 306-455-2212; *Fax:* 306-455-2445
arcadmin@sasktel.net
Municipal Type: Town
Incorporated: April 11, 1901 *Area:* 2.59 sq km
Population in 2011: 649
Provincial Electoral District(s): Cannington
Federal Electoral District(s): Souris-Moose Mountain
Next Election: Oct. 24, 2012 (4 year terms)
Note: Proclaimed as town on Nov. 20, 1903.
Adam Manastryski, Mayor
Glenda Johnson, Administrator

Arran
P.O. Box 40
Arran, SK S0A 0B0
Tel: 306-595-4521; *Fax:* 306-595-4531
rm331@sasktel.net
Municipal Type: Village
Incorporated: Sept. 21, 1916 *Area:* 0.69 sq km
Population in 2011: 40
Provincial Electoral District(s): Canora-Pelly
Federal Electoral District(s): Yorkton-Melville
Next Election: Oct. 24, 2012 (4 year terms)
Rick Nahnybida, Mayor
Yvonne Bilsky, Administrator

Asquith
P.O. Box 160
Asquith, SK S0K 0J0
Tel: 306-329-4341; *Fax:* 306-329-4969
town.asquith@sasktel.net
townofasquith.com
Municipal Type: Town
Incorporated: Dec. 10, 1907 *Area:* 1.23 sq km
Population in 2011: 603
Provincial Electoral District(s): Biggar
Federal Electoral District(s): Saskatoon-Rosetown-Biggar
Next Election: Oct. 24, 2012 (4 year terms)
Note: Proclaimed as a town on Aug. 15, 1908.
James Madden, Mayor
Holly Cross, Administrator

Assiniboia
P.O. Box 1470
Assiniboia, SK S0H 0B0
Tel: 306-642-5553; *Fax:* 306-642-3529
townofassiniboia@sasktel.net
www.assiniboia.net
Municipal Type: Town
Incorporated: Dec. 19, 1912 *Area:* 3.78 sq km
Population in 2011: 2,418
Provincial Electoral District(s): Wood River
Federal Electoral District(s): Cypress Hills-Grasslands
Next Election: Oct. 24, 2012 (4 year terms)
Note: Proclaimed as a town on Oct. 1, 1913.
Paul Topola, Mayor
Steve Gibson, Administrator

Atwater
P.O. Box 45
Atwater, SK S0A 0C0
Tel: 306-793-2193
villageofatwater@gmail.com
Municipal Type: Village
Incorporated: Aug. 12, 1910 *Area:* 1.79 sq km
Population in 2011: 31
Provincial Electoral District(s): Melville-Saltcoats
Federal Electoral District(s): Yorkton-Melville
Next Election: Oct. 24, 2012 (4 year terms)
James Ferguson, Mayor
Sheila Shivak, Clerk

Avonlea
P.O. Box 209
Avonlea, SK S0H 0C0
Tel: 306-868-2221; *Fax:* 306-868-2221
avonlea@sasktel.net
www.avonlea.biz
Municipal Type: Village
Incorporated: Feb. 10, 1912 *Area:* 0.96 sq km
Population in 2011: 398
Provincial Electoral District(s): Indian Head-Milestone
Federal Electoral District(s): Palliser
Next Election: Oct. 24, 2012 (4 year terms)
Alex Getzlaf, Mayor
Tim Forer, Administrator

Aylesbury
201 King St.
Aylesbury, SK S0G 0B0
Tel: 306-734-5125
susy632@sasktel.net
www.craik.ca/aylesbury.html
Municipal Type: Village
Incorporated: March 31, 1910 *Area:* 1.28 sq km
Population in 2011: 10
Provincial Electoral District(s): Thunder Creek
Federal Electoral District(s): Regina-Lumsden-Lake Centre
Next Election: Oct. 24, 2012 (4 year terms)
Douglas Watt, Mayor
Jeff Murry, Village Clerk

Aylsham
P.O. Box 64
Aylsham, SK S0E 0C0
Tel: 306-862-9415
villageofaylsham@sasktel.net
Municipal Type: Village
Incorporated: Aug. 4, 1947 *Area:* 0.48 sq km
Population in 2011: 71
Provincial Electoral District(s): Carrot River Valley
Federal Electoral District(s): Prince Albert
Next Election: Oct. 24, 2012 (4 year terms)
Elizabeth F. Archer, Mayor
Dorothy E. Blue, Clerk

B-Say-Tah
P.O. Box 908
842 Broadway St.
Fort Qu'Appelle, SK S0G 1S0
Tel: 306-332-6449; *Fax:* 306-332-2923
bsaytah@sasktel.net
bsaytah.ca
Municipal Type: Resort Village
Area: 1.33 sq km
Population in 2011: 187
Provincial Electoral District(s): Indian Head-Milestone
Federal Electoral District(s): Regina-Qu'Appelle
Next Election: July 2016
Dennis Palmier, Mayor
Richelle Haanstra, Administrator

Balcarres
P.O. Box 130
209 Main St.
Balcarres, SK S0G 0C0
Tel: 306-334-2566; *Fax:* 306-334-2907
balcarrestown@sasktel.net
www.townofbalcarres.ca
Municipal Type: Town
Incorporated: Nov. 21, 1904 *Area:* 1.57 sq km
Population in 2011: 617
Provincial Electoral District(s): Last Mountain-Touchwood
Federal Electoral District(s): Regina-Qu'Appelle
Next Election: Oct. 24, 2012 (4 year terms)
Note: Proclaimed as a town on Jan. 1, 1951.
Dwight Dixon, Mayor
Bev Gelech, Administrator

Balgonie
P.O. Box 310
129 South Railway St. East
Balgonie, SK S0G 0E0
Tel: 306-771-2284; *Fax:* 306-771-2899
townofbalgonie@sasktel.net
www.townofbalgonie.ca
Municipal Type: Town
Incorporated: April 20, 1903 *Area:* 3.15 sq km
Population in 2011: 1,625
Provincial Electoral District(s): Indian Head-Milestone
Federal Electoral District(s): Regina-Qu'Appelle
Next Election: Oct. 24, 2012 (4 year terms)
Note: Proclaimed as a town on Jan. 1, 1951.
Tim Sterzer, Mayor
Val Hubbard, Administrator

Bangor
P.O. Box 35
Bangor, SK S0A 0E0
Tel: 306-728-4084
Municipal Type: Village
Incorporated: June 8, 1911 *Area:* 1.65 sq km
Population in 2011: 46
Provincial Electoral District(s): Melville-Saltcoats
Federal Electoral District(s): Yorkton-Melville
Next Election: Oct. 24, 2012 (4 year terms)
Jerome Bomberak, Mayor
Joan C. Bomberak, Clerk

Battleford
P.O. Box 40
Battleford, SK S0M 0E0
Tel: 306-937-6200; *Fax:* 306-937-2450
admin@battleford.ca
www.battleford.ca
Municipal Type: Town
Incorporated: Jan. 6, 1899 *Area:* 23.33 sq km
Population in 2011: 4,065
Provincial Electoral District(s): The Battlefords
Federal Electoral District(s): Battlefords-Lloydminster
Next Election: Oct. 24, 2012 (4 year terms)
Note: Proclaimed as a town on June 15, 1904.
Chris Odishaw, Mayor
Sheryl Ballendine, Administrator

Bear Creek
P.O. Box 69
Buffalo Narrows, SK S0M 0J0
Tel: 306-235-1726; *Fax:* 306-235-1727
Municipal Type: NS
Population in 2010: 47
Provincial Electoral District(s): Athabasca
Federal Electoral District(s): Desnethé-Missinippi-Churchill River
Next Election: Oct. 24, 2012 (4 year terms)
Dean Herman, Chair
Bruce Leier, Advisor
bruce.leier@gov.sk.ca

Beatty
P.O. Box 51
Beatty, SK S0J 0C0
Tel: 306-752-3980
fhrainville@sasktel.net
www.newsaskcfdc.ca/beatty.htm
Municipal Type: Village
Incorporated: March 31, 1921 *Area:* 0.82 sq km
Population in 2011: 63
Provincial Electoral District(s): Melfort
Federal Electoral District(s): Prince Albert
Next Election: Oct. 24, 2012 (4 year terms)
Harvey Rainville, Mayor
Linda Logan, Clerk

Beauval
P.O. Box 19
Lavoie St.
Beauval, SK S0M 0G0
Tel: 306-288-2110; *Fax:* 306-288-2348
admin.beauval@sasktel.net
Municipal Type: Northern Village
Incorporated: Oct. 1, 1983 *Area:* 6.71 sq km
Population in 2011: 756
Provincial Electoral District(s): Athabasca
Federal Electoral District(s): Desnethé-Missinippi-Churchill River
Next Election: Autumn 2012 (4 year terms)
Fred Roy, Mayor
Marie LaVallee, Administrator

Beaver Flat
P.O. Box 991
Swift Current, SK S9H 3X1
Tel: 306-582-2003; *Fax:* 306-627-3546
village.neville@sasktel.net
www.beaverflatsk.ca
Municipal Type: Resort Village
Area: 0.92 sq km
Population in 2011: 40
Provincial Electoral District(s): Thunder Creek
Federal Electoral District(s): Cypress Hills-Grasslands
Next Election: July 2016
Gerald Olson, Mayor
Linda Hornung, Clerk

Beechy
P.O. Box 153
Beechy, SK S0L 0C0
Tel: 306-859-2205; *Fax:* 306-859-2290
info@beechysask.ca; beechy@sasktel.net
www.beechysask.ca
Municipal Type: Village
Incorporated: May 11, 1925 *Area:* 1.06 sq km
Population in 2011: 239
Provincial Electoral District(s): Rosetown-Elrose
Federal Electoral District(s): Cypress Hills-Grasslands
Next Election: Oct. 24, 2012 (4 year terms)
Francis Fleuter, Mayor
Mel Hanke, Administrator

Belle Plaine
P.O. Box 63
Belle Plaine, SK S0G 0G0
Tel: 306-693-0378
Municipal Type: Village
Incorporated: Aug. 12, 1910 *Area:* 1.34 sq km
Population in 2011: 66
Provincial Electoral District(s): Thunder Creek
Federal Electoral District(s): Palliser
Next Election: Oct. 24, 2012 (4 year terms)
Donald Firomski, Mayor
Deborah Day, Clerk

Bengough
P.O. Box 188
181 Main St.
Bengough, SK S0C 0K0
Tel: 306-268-2927; *Fax:* 306-268-2988
town.bengough@sasktel.net
www.bengough.com
Municipal Type: Town
Incorporated: March 15, 1912 *Area:* 1.07 sq km
Population in 2011: 313
Provincial Electoral District(s): Weyburn-Big Muddy
Federal Electoral District(s): Souris-Moose Mountain
Next Election: Oct. 24, 2012 (4 year terms)
Note: Proclaimed as a town on April 1, 1958.
Dennis Mazenc, Mayor
Penny Nergard, Administrator

Bethune
P.O. Box 209
Bethune, SK S0G 0H0
Tel: 306-638-3188; *Fax:* 306-638-3102
villageofbethune@sasktel.net
www.villageofbethune.com
Municipal Type: Village
Incorporated: Aug. 2, 1912 *Area:* 1.04 sq km
Population in 2011: 400
Provincial Electoral District(s): Thunder Creek
Federal Electoral District(s): Regina-Lumsden-Lake Centre
Next Election: Oct. 24, 2012 (4 year terms)
Ron Gemmell, Mayor
Rodney Audette, Administrator

Bienfait
P.O. Box 220
Bienfait, SK S0C 0M0
Tel: 306-388-2969; *Fax:* 306-388-2449
bienfait@sasktel.net
Municipal Type: Town
Incorporated: April 16, 1912 *Area:* 3.09 sq km
Population in 2011: 780
Provincial Electoral District(s): Estevan
Federal Electoral District(s): Souris-Moose Mountain
Next Election: Oct. 24, 2012 (4 year terms)
Note: Proclaimed as a town on March 1, 1957.
Jamie Bonokoski, Mayor
Laurel Gilroy, Administrator

Big River
P.O. Box 220
Big River, SK S0J 0E0
Tel: 306-469-2112; *Fax:* 306-469-4856
bigriver@sasktel.net
www.bigriver.ca
Municipal Type: Town
Incorporated: Aug. 18, 1923 *Area:* 2.11 sq km
Population in 2011: 639
Provincial Electoral District(s): Saskatchewan Rivers
Federal Electoral District(s): Desnethé-Missinippi-Churchill River
Next Election: Oct. 24, 2012 (4 year terms)
Note: Proclaimed as a town on Oct. 1, 1966.
Brian Brownfield, Mayor
Gail Gear, Administrator

Big Shell
P.O. Box 428
Spiritwood, SK S0J 2M0
Tel: 306-883-2977; *Fax:* 306-883-3834
Municipal Type: Resort Village
Area: 1.02 sq km
Population in 2011: 45
Provincial Electoral District(s): Rosthern-Shellbrook
Federal Electoral District(s): Desnethé-Missinippi-Churchill River
Next Election: July 2016
Robert Boire, Mayor
Shirley Dauvin, Administrator
pdauvin@xplornet.com

Biggar
P.O. Box 489
202 - 3rd Ave. West
Biggar, SK S0K 0M0
Tel: 306-948-3317; *Fax:* 306-948-5134
townoffice@townofbiggar.com
www.townofbiggar.com
Municipal Type: Town
Incorporated: May 18, 1909 *Area:* 15.75
Population in 2011: 2,161
Provincial Electoral District(s): Biggar
Federal Electoral District(s): Saskatoon-Rosetown-Biggar
Next Election: Oct. 24, 2012 (4 year terms)
Note: Proclaimed as a town on Nov. 1, 1911.
Raymond Sadler, Mayor
Barb Barteski, Administrator

Birch Hills
P.O. Box 206
Birch Hills, SK S0J 0G0
Tel: 306-749-2232; *Fax:* 306-749-2545
birchills.town@sasktel.net
www.birchhills.ca
Municipal Type: Town
Incorporated: July 19, 1907 *Area:* 1.82 sq km
Population in 2011: 1,064
Provincial Electoral District(s): Batoche
Federal Electoral District(s): Prince Albert
Next Election: Oct. 24, 2012 (4 year terms)
Note: Proclaimed as a town on Aug. 1, 1960.
Tara Gariepy, Administrator

Bird's Point
P.O. Box 158
Stockholm, SK S0A 3Y0
Tel: 306-793-4552; *Fax:* 306-793-2017
rvbirdspoint@sasktel.net
Municipal Type: Resort Village
Area: 0.58 sq km
Population in 2011: 103
Provincial Electoral District(s): Melville-Saltcoats
Federal Electoral District(s): Yorkton-Melville
Next Election: July 2016
Robin Johnson, Mayor
Lila Sippola, Administrator

Bjorkdale
P.O. Box 27
Bjorkdale, SK S0E 0E0
Tel: 306-886-2167; *Fax:* 306-886-2181
villageofbjorkdale@live.com
www.newsaskcfdc.ca/bjorkdale.htm
Municipal Type: Village
Incorporated: April 1, 1968 *Area:* 1.39 sq km
Population in 2011: 199
Provincial Electoral District(s): Kelvington-Wadena
Federal Electoral District(s): Yorkton-Melville
Next Election: Oct. 24, 2012 (4 year terms)
James Majewski, Mayor
Katherine Clarke, Administrator

Black Point
P.O. Box 640
La Loche, SK S0M 1G0
Tel: 306-822-2727; *Fax:* 306-822-2268
Municipal Type: Northern Hamlet
Population in 2010: 47
Provincial Electoral District(s): Athabasca
Federal Electoral District(s): Desnethé-Missinippi-Churchill River
Next Election: Oct. 24, 2012 (4 year terms)
Frank Petit, Mayor
Bruce Leier, Advisor
bruce.leier@gov.sk.ca

Bladworth
P.O. Box 90
Bladworth, SK S0G 0J0
Tel: 306-567-5564; *Fax:* 306-567-4364
donna.haug@sasktel.net
Municipal Type: Village
Incorporated: July 27, 1906 *Area:* 0.84 sq km
Population in 2011: 60
Provincial Electoral District(s): Arm River-Watrous
Federal Electoral District(s): Blackstrap
Next Election: Oct. 24, 2012 (4 year terms)
Ron Bessey, Mayor
Donna Bessey, Clerk

Blaine Lake
P.O. Box 10
Blaine Lake, SK S0J 0J0
Tel: 306-497-2531; *Fax:* 306-497-2511
blainelake@sasktel.net
www.blainelake.ca
Municipal Type: Town
Incorporated: March 15, 1912 *Area:* 1.75 sq km
Population in 2011: 510
Provincial Electoral District(s): Rosthern-Shellbrook
Federal Electoral District(s): Saskatoon-Wanuskewin
Next Election: Oct. 24, 2012 (4 year terms)
Note: Proclaimed as a town on March 1, 1954.
Ernie Crowder, Mayor
Anna Brad, Administrator

Borden
P.O. Box 210
200 Shepard St.
Borden, SK S0K 0N0
Tel: 306-997-2134; *Fax:* 306-997-2201
borden@sasktel.net
www.bordensask.ca
Municipal Type: Village
Incorporated: July 19, 1907 *Area:* 0.76 sq km
Population in 2011: 245
Provincial Electoral District(s): Biggar
Federal Electoral District(s): Saskatoon-Wanuskewin
Next Election: Oct. 24, 2012 (4 year terms)
Dave Buckingham, Mayor
Sandra Long, Administrator

Brabant Lake
P.O. Box 1667
La Ronge, SK S0J 1L0
Tel: 306-758-4888; *Fax:* 306-758-4888
Other Information: Toll-Free Phone: 1-800-663-1555
Municipal Type: NS
Population in 2010: 102
Provincial Electoral District(s): Athabasca
Federal Electoral District(s): Desnethé-Missinippi-Churchill River
Next Election: Oct. 24, 2012 (4 year terms)
Solomon P. Hardlotte, Chair
Valerie Antoniuk, Advisor
306-425-4323
valerie.antoniuk@gov.sk.ca

Bracken
P.O. Box 41
Bracken, SK S0N 0G0
Tel: 306-293-2124; *Fax:* 306-293-2702
Municipal Type: Village
Incorporated: Jan. 4, 1926 *Area:* 0.60 sq km
Population in 2011: 30
Provincial Electoral District(s): Wood River
Federal Electoral District(s): Cypress Hills-Grasslands
Next Election: Oct. 24, 2012 (4 year terms)
Steve Dueck, Mayor
Ron Johnson, Administrator

Bradwell
P.O. Box 100
Bradwell, SK S0K 0P0
Tel: 306-257-4141; *Fax:* 306-257-3303
rm343@sasktel.net
Municipal Type: Village
Incorporated: July 13, 1910 *Area:* 0.42 sq km
Population in 2011: 230
Provincial Electoral District(s): Humboldt
Federal Electoral District(s): Blackstrap
Next Election: Oct. 24, 2012 (4 year terms)
Ken Hartz, Mayor
R. Doran Scott, Administrator

Bredenbury
P.O. Box 87
Bredenbury, SK S0A 0H0
Tel: 306-898-2055; *Fax:* 306-898-2103
bredenbury@sasktel.net
www.townofbredenbury.ca
Municipal Type: Town
Incorporated: May 3, 1911 *Area:* 4.80 sq km
Population in 2011: 364
Provincial Electoral District(s): Melville-Saltcoats
Federal Electoral District(s): Yorkton-Melville
Next Election: Oct. 24, 2012 (4 year terms)
Note: Proclaimed as a town on May 1, 1913.
Fred Nicholson, Mayor
Kim Varga, Administrator

Briercrest
P.O. Box 25
Briercrest, SK S0H 0K0
Tel: 306-799-2066; *Fax:* 306-799-2067
villageofbriercrest@sasktel.net
villageofbriercrest.ca
Municipal Type: Village
Incorporated: April 17, 1912 *Area:* 0.62 sq km
Population in 2011: 111
Provincial Electoral District(s): Indian Head-Milestone
Federal Electoral District(s): Palliser
Next Election: Oct. 24, 2012 (4 year terms)
Bill Duncan, Mayor
Michelle Postnikoff, Administrator

Broadview
P.O. Box 430
524 Main St.
Broadview, SK S0G 0K0
Tel: 306-696-2533; *Fax:* 306-696-3573
town.of.broadview@sasktel.net
www.broadview.ca
Municipal Type: Town
Incorporated: Dec. 29, 1898 *Area:* 2.45 sq km
Population in 2011: 574
Provincial Electoral District(s): Moosomin
Federal Electoral District(s): Souris-Moose Mountain
Next Election: Oct. 24, 2012 (4 year terms)
Note: Proclaimed as a town on May 15, 1907.
Sidney Criddle, Mayor
Mervin J. Schmidt, Administrator

Brock
P.O. Box 70
Brock, SK S0L 0H0
Tel: 306-379-2116
brockadmin@sasktel.net
Municipal Type: Village
Incorporated: July 7, 1910 *Area:* 0.74 sq km
Population in 2011: 127
Provincial Electoral District(s): Rosetown-Elrose
Federal Electoral District(s): Battlefords-Lloydminster
Next Election: Oct. 24, 2012 (4 year terms)
David Wicks, Mayor
Shannon Beheil, Administrator

Broderick
P.O. Box 29
Broderick, SK S0H 0L0
Tel: 306-867-8578
villageofbroderick@yourlink.ca
Municipal Type: Village
Incorporated: Sept. 13, 1909 *Area:* 0.91 sq km
Population in 2011: 71
Provincial Electoral District(s): Rosetown-Elrose
Federal Electoral District(s): Blackstrap
Next Election: Oct. 24, 2012 (4 year terms)
Jacob Vanderschaaf, Mayor
Sylvia Klotz, Clerk

Brownlee
P.O. Box 89
Brownlee, SK S0H 0M0
Tel: 306-759-2302
Municipal Type: Village
Incorporated: Dec. 29, 1908 *Area:* 2.42 sq km
Population in 2011: 50
Provincial Electoral District(s): Thunder Creek
Federal Electoral District(s): Regina-Lumsden-Lake Centre
Next Election: Oct. 24, 2012 (4 year terms)
Lyle Swanson, Mayor
Jackie Leggott, Clerk

Bruno
P.O. Box 370
Bruno, SK S0K 0S0
Tel: 306-369-2514; *Fax:* 306-369-2878
bruno@sasktel.net
sites.google.com/site/brunosaskatchewan
Municipal Type: Town
Incorporated: March 9, 1909 *Area:* 0.95 sq km
Population in 2011: 574
Provincial Electoral District(s): Humboldt
Federal Electoral District(s): Saskatoon-Humboldt
Next Election: Oct. 24, 2012 (4 year terms)
Note: Proclaimed as a town on Jan. 1, 1962.
Audrey Ludwig, Mayor
Kim Sopotyk, Administrator

Buchanan
P.O. Box 479
300 Central Ave.
Buchanan, SK S0A 0J0
Tel: 306-592-2144; *Fax:* 306-592-4471
buchananvillage@sasktel.net
www.buchananvillage.sasktelwebsite.net
Municipal Type: Village
Incorporated: June 11, 1907 *Area:* 1.29 sq km
Population in 2011: 225
Provincial Electoral District(s): Canora-Pelly
Federal Electoral District(s): Yorkton-Melville
Next Election: Oct. 24, 2012 (4 year terms)
Kent Zuravloff, Mayor
Nicole Monchamp, Administrator

Buena Vista
1050 Grand Ave.
Buena Vista, SK S2V 1A2
Tel: 306-729-4385; *Fax:* 306-729-4518
buenavista@sasktel.net
www.lumsden.ca/buenavista
Municipal Type: Village
Incorporated: Nov. 18, 1983 *Area:* 3.61 sq km
Population in 2011: 524
Provincial Electoral District(s): Thunder Creek
Federal Electoral District(s): Regina-Lumsden-Lake Centre
Next Election: Oct. 24, 2012 (4 year terms)
Roni Goulet, Mayor
Cindy Baumgartner, Administrator

Buffalo Narrows
P.O. Box 98
Waite St.
Buffalo Narrows, SK S0M 0J0
Tel: 306-235-4225; *Fax:* 306-235-4699
chartier.t@sasktel.net
Municipal Type: Northern Village
Incorporated: Oct. 1, 1983 *Area:* 34.10 sq km
Population in 2011: 1,153
Provincial Electoral District(s): Athabasca
Federal Electoral District(s): Churchill River/Rivière Churchill
Next Election: Autumn 2012 (4 year terms)
Bobby Woods, Mayor
Therese Chartier, Administrator

Bulyea
P.O. Box 37
Bulyea, SK S0G 0L0
Tel: 306-725-4936
info@bulyea.com
www.bulyea.com
Municipal Type: Village
Incorporated: March 9, 1909 *Area:* 1.28 sq km
Population in 2011: 102
Provincial Electoral District(s): Last Mountain-Touchwood
Federal Electoral District(s): Regina-Lumsden-Lake Centre
Next Election: Oct. 24, 2012 (4 year terms)
Darren Cameron, Mayor
Jenna Johnson, Clerk

Burstall
P.O. Box 250
428 Martin St.
Burstall, SK S0N 0H0
Tel: 306-679-2000; *Fax:* 306-679-2275
burstall@sasktel.net
www.burstall.ca
Municipal Type: Town
Incorporated: May 31, 1921 *Area:* 1.11 sq km
Population in 2011: 301
Provincial Electoral District(s): Cypress Hills
Federal Electoral District(s): Cypress Hills-Grasslands
Next Election: Oct. 24, 2012 (4 year terms)
Note: Proclaimed as a town on Nov. 1, 1976.
Ken Hook, Mayor
Lucein Stuebing, Administrator

Cabri
P.O. Box 200
Cabri, SK S0N 0J0
Tel: 306-587-2500; *Fax:* 306-587-2392
townofcabri@sasktel.net
Municipal Type: Town
Incorporated: May 13, 1912 *Area:* 1.33 sq km
Population in 2011: 399
Provincial Electoral District(s): Cypress Hills
Federal Electoral District(s): Cypress Hills-Grasslands
Next Election: Oct. 24, 2012 (4 year terms)
Note: Proclaimed as a town on April 16, 1917.
David Gossard, Mayor
Dianne Hahn, Administrator

Cadillac
P.O. Box 189
Cadillac, SK S0N 0K0
Tel: 306-785-2100; *Fax:* 306-785-2101
v.cadillac@sasktel.net
Municipal Type: Village
Incorporated: July 2, 1914 *Area:* 1.05 sq km
Population in 2011: 78
Provincial Electoral District(s): Wood River
Federal Electoral District(s): Cypress Hills-Grasslands
Next Election: Oct. 24, 2012 (4 year terms)
Holly Franklin, Mayor
Betty Moller, Clerk

Calder
P.O. Box 47
Calder, SK S0A 0K0
Tel: 306-742-2158; *Fax:* 306-742-2158
caldervillage@sasktel.net
Municipal Type: Village
Incorporated: Jan. 18, 1911 *Area:* 0.75 sq km
Population in 2011: 97
Provincial Electoral District(s): Melville-Saltcoats
Federal Electoral District(s): Yorkton-Melville
Next Election: Oct. 24, 2012 (4 year terms)
Walter Balabuk, Mayor
Kendra Busch, Administrator

Camsell Portage
c/o Ministry of Municipal Affairs
P.O. Box 5000
La Ronge, SK S0J 1L0
Tel: 306-425-4321; *Fax:* 306-425-2401
Other Information: Toll-Free Phone: 1-800-663-1555
Municipal Type: NS
Population in 2010: 37
Provincial Electoral District(s): Athabasca
Federal Electoral District(s): Desnethé-Missinippi-Churchill River
Next Election: Oct. 24, 2012 (4 year terms)
Claire B. Larocque, Chair
Shannon Cholin, Advisor
306-425-4321
shannon.cholin@gov.sk.ca

Candle Lake
P.O. Box 114
Candle Lake, SK S0J 3E0
Tel: 306-929-2236; *Fax:* 306-929-2201
rvcandlelakeoffice@sasktel.net
Municipal Type: Resort Village
Area: 63.32 sq km
Population in 2011: 765
Provincial Electoral District(s): Saskatchewan Rivers
Federal Electoral District(s): Desnethé-Missinippi-Churchill River
Next Election: July 2016
John G. Quinn, Mayor
James Burak, Administrator

Canora
P.O. Box 717
418 Main St.
Canora, SK S0A 0L0
Tel: 306-563-5773; *Fax:* 306-563-4336
admin.canora@sasktel.net
www.canora.com
Municipal Type: Town
Incorporated: April 8, 1905 *Area:* 7.31 sq km
Population in 2011: 2,219
Provincial Electoral District(s): Canora-Pelly
Federal Electoral District(s): Yorkton-Melville
Next Election: Oct. 24, 2012 (4 year terms)
Note: Proclaimed as a town on Nov. 1, 1910.
Terry Dennis, Mayor
306-563-6485
Michael Mykytyshyn, Administrator
306-563-6466

Canwood
P.O. Box 172
Canwood, SK S0J 0K0
Tel: 306-468-2016; *Fax:* 306-468-2666
canwood.town@sasktel.net
Municipal Type: Village
Incorporated: July 18, 1916 *Area:* 2.56 sq km
Population in 2011: 308
Provincial Electoral District(s): Rosthern-Shellbrook
Federal Electoral District(s): Desnethé-Missinippi-Churchill River
Next Election: Oct. 24, 2012 (4 year terms)
Gary Thall, Mayor
Lisa Quessy, Administrator

Carievale
P.O. Box 88
128 Broadway St.
Carievale, SK S0C 0P0
Tel: 306-928-2033; *Fax:* 306-928-2021
village.carievale@sasktel.net
Municipal Type: Village
Incorporated: March 14, 1903 *Area:* 0.88 sq km
Population in 2011: 236
Provincial Electoral District(s): Cannington
Federal Electoral District(s): Souris-Moose Mountain
Next Election: Oct. 24, 2012 (4 year terms)
Eric Hoefer, Mayor
Katie Steenbruggen, Administrator

Carlyle
P.O. Box 10
Carlyle, SK S0C 0R0
Tel: 306-453-2363; *Fax:* 306-453-6380
towncarlyle@sasktel.net
www.townofcarlyle.com
Municipal Type: Town
Incorporated: March 13, 1902 *Area:* 3.03 sq km
Population in 2011: 1,441
Provincial Electoral District(s): Cannington
Federal Electoral District(s): Souris-Moose Mountain
Next Election: Oct. 24, 2012 (4 year terms)
Note: Proclaimed as a town on Jan. 1, 1906.
Don Shirley, Mayor

Huguette Lutz, Chief Administrative Officer

Carmichael
P.O. Box 420
Gull Lake, SK S0N 1A0
Tel: 306-672-3501; *Fax:* 306-672-3879
rm109@sasktel.net
Municipal Type: Village
Incorporated: May 25, 1917 *Area:* 0.67 sq km
Population in 2011: 30
Provincial Electoral District(s): Cypress Hills
Federal Electoral District(s): Cypress Hills-Grasslands
Next Election: Oct. 24, 2012 (4 year terms)
Miles C. Wells, Mayor
Collette Jones, Clerk

Carnduff
P.O. Box 100
Carnduff, SK S0C 0S0
Tel: 306-482-3300; *Fax:* 306-482-3422
town.carnduff@sasktel.net
www.carnduff.ca
Municipal Type: Town
Incorporated: March 29, 1899 *Area:* 2.05 sq km
Population in 2011: 1,126
Provincial Electoral District(s): Cannington
Federal Electoral District(s): Souris-Moose Mountain
Next Election: Oct. 24, 2012 (4 year terms)
Note: Proclaimed as a town on Aug. 12, 1905.
Ross Apperley, Mayor
Annette Brown, Administrator

Caronport
P.O. Box 550
Caronport, SK S0H 0S0
Tel: 306-756-2225; *Fax:* 306-756-5007
vcoffice@sasktel.net
Municipal Type: Village
Incorporated: Jan. 1, 1988 *Area:* 1.90 sq km
Population in 2011: 1,068
Provincial Electoral District(s): Thunder Creek
Federal Electoral District(s): Palliser
Next Election: Oct. 24, 2012 (4 year terms)
Paul Blankestijn, Mayor
Brenda Thiessen, Administrator

Carrot River
P.O. Box 147
5 Main St.
Carrot River, SK S0E 0L0
Tel: 306-768-2515; *Fax:* 306-768-2930
t.carrotriver@sasktel.net
www.town.carrotriver.sk.ca
Municipal Type: Town
Incorporated: Nov. 6, 1941 *Area:* 1.46 sq km
Population in 2011: 1,000
Provincial Electoral District(s): Carrot River Valley
Federal Electoral District(s): Prince Albert
Next Election: Oct. 24, 2012 (4 year terms)
Note: Proclaimed as a town on April 1, 1948.
Robert Gagne, Mayor
Duril Touet, Administrator

Central Butte
P.O. Box 10
Central Butte, SK S0H 0T0
Tel: 306-796-2288; *Fax:* 306-796-4627
townofcentralbutte@sasktel.net
www.centralbutte.ca
Municipal Type: Town
Incorporated: April 9, 1915 *Area:* 2.24 sq km
Population in 2011: 365
Provincial Electoral District(s): Thunder Creek
Federal Electoral District(s): Cypress Hills-Grasslands
Next Election: Oct. 24, 2012 (4 year terms)
Note: Proclaimed as a town on July 1, 1967.
Alvin Klassen, Mayor
Joyce Aitken, Administrator

Ceylon
P.O. Box 188
Ceylon, SK S0C 0T0
Tel: 306-454-2202; *Fax:* 306-454-2627
rmgap39@sasktel.net
Municipal Type: Village
Incorporated: Sept. 26, 1911 *Area:* 0.75 sq km
Population in 2011: 99
Provincial Electoral District(s): Weyburn-Big Muddy
Federal Electoral District(s): Souris-Moose Mountain
Next Election: Oct. 24, 2012 (4 year terms)
Larry Harkes, Mayor
Yvonne Johnston, Administrator

Chamberlain
P.O. Box 8
Chamberlain, SK S0G 0R0
Tel: 306-638-4680; *Fax:* 306-638-3108
chamberlain@canwan.com
Municipal Type: Village
Incorporated: Jan. 31, 1911 *Area:* 0.70 sq km
Population in 2011: 88
Provincial Electoral District(s): Thunder Creek
Federal Electoral District(s): Regina-Lumsden-Lake Centre
Next Election: Oct. 24, 2012 (4 year terms)
Rita Folk, Mayor
Donna Flavel, Clerk

Chaplin
P.O. Box 210
Chaplin, SK S0H 0V0
Tel: 306-395-2221; *Fax:* 306-395-2555
village.chaplin@sasktel.net
www.chaplin.ca
Municipal Type: Village
Incorporated: Oct. 8, 1912 *Area:* 1.26 sq km
Population in 2011: 218
Provincial Electoral District(s): Thunder Creek
Federal Electoral District(s): Cypress Hills-Grasslands
Next Election: Oct. 24, 2012 (4 year terms)
Jack Doell, Mayor
Gina Hallborg, Administrator

Chitek Lake
P.O. Box 70
Chitek Lake, SK S0J 0L0
Tel: 306-984-2353; *Fax:* 306-984-1178
rvchitek@xplornet.ca
Municipal Type: Resort Village
Area: 2.54 sq km
Population in 2011: 167
Provincial Electoral District(s): Meadow Lake
Federal Electoral District(s): Desnethé-Missinippi-Churchill River
Next Election: July 2016
Albert Fee, Mayor
Cindy Larson, Clerk

Choiceland
P.O. Box 279
100 Railway Ave. East
Choiceland, SK S0J 0M0
Tel: 306-428-2070; *Fax:* 306-428-2071
choiceland.town@sasktel.net
choiceland.ca
Municipal Type: Town
Incorporated: Sept. 8, 1944 *Area:* 1.12 sq km
Population in 2011: 381
Provincial Electoral District(s): Saskatchewan Rivers
Federal Electoral District(s): Desnethé-Missinippi-Churchill River
Next Election: Oct. 24, 2012 (4 year terms)
Note: Proclaimed as a town on Jan. 1, 1979.
Robert Mardell, Mayor
Holly Toews, Administrator

Chorney Beach
P.O. Box 328
Foam Lake, SK S0A 1A0
Tel: 306-272-3359; *Fax:* 306-272-3738
rvchorneybeach@sasktel.net
Municipal Type: Resort Village
Area: 0.17 sq km
Population in 2011: 15
Provincial Electoral District(s): Kelvington-Wadena
Federal Electoral District(s): Yorkton-Melville
Next Election: July 2016
Harold Sandberg, Mayor
Gloria Leader, Clerk

Christopher Lake
P.O. Box 163
Christopher Lake, SK S0J 0N0
Tel: 306-982-4242; *Fax:* 306-982-4242
vilchr@sasktel.net
Municipal Type: Village
Incorporated: March 1, 1985 *Area:* 3.47 sq km
Population in 2011: 266
Provincial Electoral District(s): Saskatchewan Rivers
Federal Electoral District(s): Desnethé-Missinippi-Churchill River
Next Election: Oct. 24, 2012 (4 year terms)
Denis Daughton, Mayor
Jeanne Rip, Administrator

Churchbridge
P.O. Box 256
116 Vincent Ave.
Churchbridge, SK S0A 0M0
Tel: 306-896-2240; *Fax:* 306-896-2910
churchbridge@sasktel.net
www.churchbridge.com
Municipal Type: Town
Incorporated: Sept. 17, 1903 *Area:* 2.76 sq km
Population in 2011: 743
Provincial Electoral District(s): Melville-Saltcoats
Federal Electoral District(s): Yorkton-Melville
Next Election: Oct. 24, 2012 (4 year terms)
Note: Proclaimed as a town on March 1, 1964.
Jim Gallant, Mayor
Carla Kaeding, Administrator

Clavet
P.O. Box 68
Clavet, SK S0K 0Y0
Tel: 306-933-2425; *Fax:* 306-933-1995
clavetvillage@sasktel.net
Municipal Type: Village
Incorporated: Dec. 21, 1908 *Area:* 0.61 sq km
Population in 2011: 386
Provincial Electoral District(s): Humboldt
Federal Electoral District(s): Blackstrap
Next Election: Oct. 24, 2012 (4 year terms)
Blair Bentley, Mayor
Janet Patry, Administrator

Climax
P.O. Box 30
Climax, SK S0N 0N0
Tel: 306-293-2124; *Fax:* 306-293-2702
villageofclimax@sasktel.net
Municipal Type: Village
Incorporated: Dec. 11, 1923 *Area:* 1.00 sq km
Population in 2011: 182
Provincial Electoral District(s): Cypress Hills
Federal Electoral District(s): Cypress Hills-Grasslands
Next Election: Oct. 24, 2012 (4 year terms)
Nancy Kirk, Mayor
Shawna-Lee Bertram, Administrator

Cochin
P.O. Box 160
Cochin, SK S0M 0L0
Tel: 306-386-2333; *Fax:* 306-386-2305
cochinadmin@sasktel.net
www.cochin.ca
Municipal Type: Resort Village
Incorporated: 1915 *Area:* 1.35 sq km
Population in 2011: 122
Provincial Electoral District(s): Cut Knife-Turtleford
Federal Electoral District(s): Battlefords-Lloydminster
Next Election: July 2016
Alex Houk, Mayor
Donna Goertzen, Administrator

Coderre
P.O. Box 9
Coderre, SK S0H 0X0
Tel: 306-394-2070
vil.of.coderre@sasktel.net
Municipal Type: Village
Incorporated: Aug. 26, 1925 *Area:* 0.85 sq km
Population in 2011: 30
Provincial Electoral District(s): Wood River
Federal Electoral District(s): Cypress Hills-Grasslands
Next Election: Oct. 24, 2012 (4 year terms)
David Duckworth, Mayor
Barbara Arnold, Clerk

Codette
P.O. Box 100
Codette, SK S0E 0P0
Tel: 306-862-9551; *Fax:* 306-862-2432
rm487@sasktel.net
Municipal Type: Village
Incorporated: March 9, 1929 *Area:* 0.37 sq km
Population in 2011: 205
Provincial Electoral District(s): Carrot River Valley
Federal Electoral District(s): Prince Albert
Next Election: Oct. 24, 2012 (4 year terms)
Brad Reed, Mayor
Eunice Rudy, Clerk

Cole Bay
P.O. Box 80
Canoe Rd.
Cole Bay, SK S0M 0M0
Tel: 306-829-4232; *Fax:* 306-829-4312
Municipal Type: Northern Village
Incorporated: Jan. 1, 1990 *Area:* 4.95 sq km
Population in 2011: 230
Provincial Electoral District(s): Athabasca
Federal Electoral District(s): Desnethé-Missinippi-Churchill River
Next Election: Autumn 2012 (4 year terms)
Harold Aubichon, Mayor
Delphine Bouvier, Clerk

Coleville
P.O. Box 249
Coleville, SK S0L 0K0
Tel: 306-965-2281; *Fax:* 306-965-2466
rm320@sasktel.net; rmoakassist@sasktel.net
www.colevillesk.ca
Municipal Type: Village
Incorporated: July 1, 1953 *Area:* 1.27 sq km
Population in 2011: 311
Provincial Electoral District(s): Kindersley
Federal Electoral District(s): Battlefords-Lloydminster
Next Election: Oct. 24, 2012 (4 year terms)
Mike Smith, Mayor
Gillian Lund, Administrator

Colonsay
P.O. Box 190
100 Jura St.
Colonsay, SK S0K 0Z0
Tel: 306-255-2313
town.colonsay@sasktel.net
www.townofcolonsay.com
Municipal Type: Town
Incorporated: Oct. 6, 1910 *Area:* 2.46 sq km
Population in 2011: 475
Provincial Electoral District(s): Humboldt
Federal Electoral District(s): Blackstrap
Next Election: Oct. 24, 2012 (4 year terms)
Note: Proclaimed as a town on Jan. 1, 1977.
James Gray, Mayor
Deborah Prosper, Administrator

Conquest
P.O. Box 250
202 Coulthard St.
Conquest, SK S0L 0L0
Tel: 306-856-2114; *Fax:* 306-856-2114
conquest@sasktel.net
www.conquest.ca
Municipal Type: Village
Incorporated: Oct. 24, 1911 *Area:* 1 sq km
Population in 2011: 176
Provincial Electoral District(s): Rosetown-Elrose
Federal Electoral District(s): Cypress Hills-Grasslands
Next Election: Oct. 24, 2012 (4 year terms)
Colleen Reilly, Clerk

Consul
P.O. Box 185
Consul, SK S0N 0P0
Tel: 306-299-2030; *Fax:* 306-299-2031
consul@sasktel.net
Municipal Type: Village
Incorporated: June 12, 1917 *Area:* 0.65 sq km
Population in 2011: 84
Provincial Electoral District(s): Cypress Hills
Federal Electoral District(s): Cypress Hills-Grasslands
Next Election: Oct. 24, 2012 (4 year terms)
Linda Brown, Mayor
Carrie Funk, Administrator

Coronach
P.O. Box 90
Coronach, SK S0H 0Z0
Tel: 306-267-2150; *Fax:* 306-267-2296
townoffice@coronach.ca
www.coronach.ca
Municipal Type: Town
Incorporated: Feb. 3, 1928 *Area:* 2.33 sq km
Population in 2011: 711
Provincial Electoral District(s): Weyburn-Big Muddy
Federal Electoral District(s): Souris-Moose Mountain
Next Election: Oct. 24, 2012 (4 year terms)
Note: Proclaimed as a town on Jan. 1, 1977.
Alexander McBain, Mayor
Murray Setrum, Administrator

Coteau Beach
P.O. Box 195
Macrorie, SK S0L 2E0
Tel: 306-243-2037
coteaubeach@sasktel.net
www.resortvillageofcoteau.ca
Municipal Type: Resort Village
Incorporated: 1969 *Area:* 0.54 sq km
Population in 2011: 40
Provincial Electoral District(s): Rosetown-Elrose
Federal Electoral District(s): Cypress Hills-Grasslands
Next Election: July 2016
Darwin McDonald, Mayor
Lorne Arthur, Clerk

Craik
P.O. Box 60
Craik, SK S0G 0V0
Tel: 306-734-2250; *Fax:* 306-734-2688
town.craik@sasktel.net
www.craik.ca
Municipal Type: Town
Incorporated: Oct. 22, 1903 *Area:* 5.41 sq km
Population in 2011: 453
Provincial Electoral District(s): Thunder Creek
Federal Electoral District(s): Regina-Lumsden-Lake Centre
Next Election: Oct. 24, 2012 (4 year terms)
Note: Proclaimed as a town on Aug. 1, 1907.
Rick Rodgers, Mayor
Jeff Murray, Administrator

Craven
P.O. Box 30
Craven, SK S0G 0W0
Tel: 306-731-3452; *Fax:* 306-731-3162
villageofcraven@canwan.com
Municipal Type: Village
Incorporated: April 11, 1905 *Area:* 1.16 sq km
Population in 2011: 234
Provincial Electoral District(s): Last Mountain-Touchwood
Federal Electoral District(s): Regina-Lumsden-Lake Centre
Next Election: Oct. 24, 2012 (4 year terms)
Adri Vandeven, Mayor
Wendy Dunn, Administrator

Creelman
P.O. Box 177
Creelman, SK S0G 0X0
Tel: 306-433-2011; *Fax:* 306-433-2011
creelmanvillage@sasktel.net
Municipal Type: Village
Incorporated: April 6, 1906 *Area:* 1.14 sq km
Population in 2011: 115
Provincial Electoral District(s): Cannington
Federal Electoral District(s): Souris-Moose Mountain
Next Election: Oct. 24, 2012 (4 year terms)
Tyler Gerry, Mayor
Vernna Wiggins, Administrator

Creighton
123 Main St.
Creighton, SK S0P 0A0
Tel: 306-688-8253; *Fax:* 306-688-4764
townofcreighton@sasktel.net
www.townofcreighton.ca
Municipal Type: Northern Town
Incorporated: Oct. 1, 1983 *Area:* 14.39 sq km
Population in 2011: 1,498
Provincial Electoral District(s): Cumberland
Federal Electoral District(s): Desnethé-Missinippi-Churchill River
Next Election: Autumn 2012 (4 year terms)
Bruce Fidler, Mayor
Paula Muench, Administrator

Cudworth
P.O. Box 69
223 Main St.
Cudworth, SK S0K 1B0
Tel: 306-256-3492; *Fax:* 306-256-3515
town.cudworth@sasktel.net
www.townofcudworth.com
Municipal Type: Town
Incorporated: Oct. 23, 1911 *Area:* 2.21 sq km
Population in 2011: 770
Provincial Electoral District(s): Batoche
Federal Electoral District(s): Saskatoon-Humboldt
Next Election: Oct. 24, 2012 (4 year terms)
Note: Proclaimed as a town on Oct. 1, 1961.
Harold Mueller, Mayor
Yvonne Gobolos, Administrator

Cumberland House
P.O. Box 190
Cumberland St.
Cumberland House, SK S0E 0S0
Tel: 306-888-2066; *Fax:* 306-888-2103
northernvillageofchouse@sasktel.net
Municipal Type: Northern Village
Incorporated: Oct. 1, 1983 *Area:* 15.69 sq km
Population in 2011: 772
Provincial Electoral District(s): Cumberland
Federal Electoral District(s): Desnethé-Missinippi-Churchill River
Next Election: Autumn 2012 (4 year terms)
Andy McKay, Mayor
Emily Nabess, Clerk

Cupar
P.O. Box 397
Cupar, SK S0G 0Y0
Tel: 306-723-4324; *Fax:* 306-723-4644
townofcupar1@sasktel.net
www.townofcupar.com
Municipal Type: Town
Incorporated: March 21, 1906 *Area:* 0.80 sq km
Population in 2011: 579
Provincial Electoral District(s): Last Mountain-Touchwood
Federal Electoral District(s): Regina-Qu'Appelle
Next Election: Oct. 24, 2012 (4 year terms)
Note: Proclaimed as a town on Jan. 1, 1961.
Don Jeworski, Mayor
Janet Hart, Administrator

Cut Knife
P.O. Box 70
Cut Knife, SK S0M 0N0
Tel: 306-398-2363; *Fax:* 306-398-2839
rm439@sasktel.net
Municipal Type: Town
Incorporated: May 17, 1912 *Area:* 1.99 sq km
Population in 2011: 517
Provincial Electoral District(s): Cut Knife-Turtleford
Federal Electoral District(s): Battlefords-Lloydminster
Next Election: Oct. 24, 2012 (4 year terms)
Note: Proclaimed as a town on Aug. 1, 1968.
Germaine Vany, Mayor
Don McCallum, Administrator

Dafoe
P.O. Box 142
Dafoe, SK S0K 1C0
Tel: 306-554-3250
Municipal Type: Village
Incorporated: May 28, 1920 *Area:* 0.80 sq km
Population in 2011: 15
Provincial Electoral District(s): Rosetown-Elrose
Federal Electoral District(s): Regina-Qu'Appelle
Next Election: Oct. 24, 2012 (4 year terms)
Bob Pilkey, Mayor
Lana M. Bolt, Clerk

Dalmeny
P.O. Box 400
301 Railway Ave.
Dalmeny, SK S0K 1E0
Tel: 306-254-2133; *Fax:* 306-254-2142
dalmenytownoffice@sasktel.net
www.dalmeny.ca
Municipal Type: Town
Incorporated: June 17, 1912 *Area:* 2.27 sq km
Population in 2011: 1,702
Provincial Electoral District(s): Weyburn-Big Muddy
Federal Electoral District(s): Saskatoon-Wanuskewin
Next Election: Oct. 24, 2012 (4 year terms)
Note: Proclaimed as a town on April 1, 1983.
Allan Earle, Mayor
Shelley Funk, Administrator

Davidson
P.O. Box 340
Davidson, SK S0G 1A0
Tel: 306-567-2040; *Fax:* 306-567-4730
townofdavidson@sasktel.net
www.townofdavidson.com
Municipal Type: Town
Incorporated: March 7, 1904 *Area:* 4.49 sq km
Population in 2011: 1,025
Provincial Electoral District(s): Arm River-Watrous
Federal Electoral District(s): Regina-Lumsden-Lake Centre
Next Election: Oct. 24, 2012 (4 year terms)
Note: Proclaimed as a town on Nov. 15, 1906.
Mary Jane Morrison, Mayor
Gary Edom, Administrator

Debden
P.O. Box 400
Debden, SK S0J 0S0
Tel: 306-724-2040; *Fax:* 306-724-2220
vdebden@sasktel.net
www.debden.net
Municipal Type: Village
Incorporated: June 7, 1922 *Area:* 1.39 sq km
Population in 2011: 358
Provincial Electoral District(s): Saskatchewan Rivers
Federal Electoral District(s): Desnethé-Missinippi-Churchill River
Next Election: Oct. 24, 2012 (4 year terms)
Ron Reres, Mayor
Carmen Jean, Administrator

Delisle
P.O. Box 40
201 - 1st St. West
Delisle, SK S0L 0P0
Tel: 306-493-2242; *Fax:* 306-493-2263
delisle@sasktel.net
www.townofdelisle.com
Municipal Type: Town
Incorporated: Dec. 29, 1908 *Area:* 2.35 sq km
Population in 2011: 975
Provincial Electoral District(s): Biggar
Federal Electoral District(s): Saskatoon-Rosetown-Biggar
Next Election: Oct. 24, 2012 (4 year terms)
Note: Proclaimed as a town on Nov. 1, 1913.
Rita Pfoh, Mayor
306-493-2652
Mark Dubkowski, Administrator

Denare Beach
P.O. Box 70
512 - 7th Ave.
Denare Beach, SK S0P 0B0
Tel: 306-362-2054; *Fax:* 306-362-2257
denarebeach@aski.ca
www.denarebeach.net
Municipal Type: Northern Village
Incorporated: April 1, 1984 *Area:* 5.84 sq km
Population in 2011: 669
Provincial Electoral District(s): Cumberland
Federal Electoral District(s): Desnethé-Missinippi-Churchill River
Next Election: Autumn 2012 (4 year terms)
Carl Lentowicz, Mayor
Bev Wheeler, Administrator

Denholm
P.O. Box 71
Denholm, SK S0M 0R0
Tel: 306-446-0478
Municipal Type: Village
Incorporated: June 25, 1912 *Area:* 0.33 sq km
Population in 2011: 76
Provincial Electoral District(s): Biggar
Federal Electoral District(s): Battlefords-Lloydminster
Next Election: Oct. 24, 2012 (4 year terms)
Terry Welch, Mayor
Lila Yuhasz, Clerk

Denzil
P.O. Box 100
Denzil, SK S0L 0S0
Tel: 306-358-2118; *Fax:* 306-358-4828
villageofdenzil@sasktel.net
www.villageofdenzil.com
Municipal Type: Village
Incorporated: May 3, 1911 *Area:* 0.55 sq km
Population in 2011: 135
Provincial Electoral District(s): Kindersley
Federal Electoral District(s): Battlefords-Lloydminster
Next Election: Oct. 24, 2012 (4 year terms)
Murray Sieben, Mayor
Kathy Reschny, Administrator

Descharme Lake
P.O. Box 69
Buffalo Narrows, SK S0M 0J0
Tel: 306-235-1726; *Fax:* 306-235-1727
Municipal Type: NS
Population in 2010: 42
Provincial Electoral District(s): Athabasca
Federal Electoral District(s): Desnethé-Missinippi-Churchill River
Next Election: Oct. 24, 2012 (4 year terms)
John Sylvestre, Chair
Bruce Leier, Advisor
bruce.leier@gov.sk.ca

Dilke
P.O. Box 100
Dilke, SK S0G 1C0
Tel: 306-488-4866; *Fax:* 306-488-4866
dilke@canwan.com
Municipal Type: Village
Incorporated: Dec. 30, 1912 *Area:* 1.28 sq km
Population in 2011: 77
Provincial Electoral District(s): Thunder Creek
Federal Electoral District(s): Regina-Lumsden-Lake Centre
Next Election: Oct. 24, 2012 (4 year terms)
Arnold Ball, Mayor
Colleen R. Duesing, Clerk

Dinsmore
P.O. Box 278
100 Main St.
Dinsmore, SK S0L 0T0
Tel: 306-846-2220; *Fax:* 306-846-2999
dinsmore@sasktel.net
www.dinsmore.ca
Municipal Type: Village
Incorporated: Nov. 3, 1913 *Area:* 2.59 sq km
Population in 2011: 318
Provincial Electoral District(s): Rosetown-Elrose
Federal Electoral District(s): Cypress Hills-Grasslands
Next Election: Oct. 24, 2012 (4 year terms)
Janice Thomson, Mayor
j.thomson.cma@sasktel.net
Jim Main, Administrator

Disley
R.R.#1
Lumsden, SK S0G 3C0
Tel: 306-731-3355
villageofdisley@gmail.com
Municipal Type: Village
Incorporated: June 24, 1907 *Area:* 0.65 sq km
Population in 2011: 111
Provincial Electoral District(s): Thunder Creek
Federal Electoral District(s): Regina-Lumsden-Lake Centre
Next Election: Oct. 24, 2012 (4 year terms)
Gord Wilson, Mayor
Rhonda Woelk, Clerk

Dodsland
P.O. Box 400
Dodsland, SK S0L 0V0
Tel: 306-356-2106; *Fax:* 306-356-2085
rm319@sasktel.net
Municipal Type: Village
Incorporated: Aug. 23, 1913 *Area:* 2.93 sq km
Population in 2011: 212
Provincial Electoral District(s): Rosetown-Elrose
Federal Electoral District(s): Battlefords-Lloydminster
Next Election: Oct. 24, 2012 (4 year terms)
Kevin McCarthy, Mayor
Regan MacDonald, Administrator

Dore Lake
P.O. Box 608
Dore Ave.
Big River, SK S0J 0E0
Tel: 306-832-4528; *Fax:* 306-832-4525
northern.dore@sasktel.net
Municipal Type: Northern Hamlet
Incorporated: Jan. 11, 1985 *Area:* 8.03 sq km
Population in 2011: 28
Provincial Electoral District(s): Athabasca
Federal Electoral District(s): Desnethé-Missinippi-Churchill River
Next Election: Autumn 2012 (4 year terms)
Hilda McKay, Mayor
Eugenie Lafleur, Administrator

Dorintosh
P.O. Box 40
301 1st St. East
Dorintosh, SK S0M 0T0
Tel: 306-236-5166
vill.dor@sasktel.net
www.villageofdorintosh.sasktelwebsite.net
Municipal Type: Village
Incorporated: Jan. 1, 1989 *Area:* 0.88 sq km
Population in 2011: 147
Provincial Electoral District(s): Meadow Lake
Federal Electoral District(s): Desnethé-Missinippi-Churchill River
Next Election: Oct. 24, 2012 (4 year terms)
John Osborne, Mayor
Pam Dallyn, Administrator

Drake
P.O. Box 18
125 Francis St.
Drake, SK S0K 1H0
Tel: 306-363-2109; *Fax:* 306-363-2102
villageofdrake@sasktel.net
www.drake.ca
Municipal Type: Village
Incorporated: Sept. 19, 1910 *Area:* 0.72 sq km
Population in 2011: 202
Provincial Electoral District(s): Arm River-Watrous
Federal Electoral District(s): Blackstrap
Next Election: Oct. 24, 2012 (4 year terms)
Peter Nicholson, Mayor
Stuart Jantz, Administrator

Drinkwater
P.O. Box 66
Drinkwater, SK S0H 1G0
Tel: 306-693-5093; *Fax:* 306-693-4410
villageofdrinkwater@sasktel.net
Municipal Type: Village
Incorporated: June 7, 1904 *Area:* 2.64 sq km
Population in 2011: 65
Provincial Electoral District(s): Indian Head-Milestone
Federal Electoral District(s): Palliser
Next Election: Oct. 24, 2012 (4 year terms)
Ryan Briggs, Mayor
Lloyd Muma, Clerk

Dubuc
P.O. Box 126
Dubuc, SK S0A 0R0
Tel: 306-877-2172
villageofdubuc@sasktel.net
www.spreda.sk.ca/community_Dubuc.htm
Municipal Type: Village
Incorporated: May 29, 1905 *Area:* 0.63 sq km
Population in 2011: 70
Provincial Electoral District(s): Melville-Saltcoats
Federal Electoral District(s): Yorkton-Melville
Next Election: Oct. 24, 2012 (4 year terms)
Melba McAlpine, Mayor
Joan Kerr, Clerk

Duck Lake
P.O. Box 430
Duck Lake, SK S0K 1J0
Tel: 306-467-2277; *Fax:* 306-467-4434
www.ducklake.ca
Municipal Type: Town
Incorporated: Dec. 29, 1898 *Area:* 2.86 sq km
Population in 2011: 577
Provincial Electoral District(s): Batoche
Federal Electoral District(s): Saskatoon-Wanuskewin
Next Election: Oct. 24, 2012 (4 year terms)
Note: Proclaimed as a town on Nov. 1, 1911.
Denis Poirier, Mayor
Betty Fiolleau, Administrator

Duff
P.O. Box 57
Duff, SK S0A 0S0
Tel: 306-728-3570
www.spreda.sk.ca/community_Duff.htm
Municipal Type: Village
Incorporated: May 28, 1920 *Area:* 0.22 sq km
Population in 2011: 30
Provincial Electoral District(s): Last Mountain-Touchwood
Federal Electoral District(s): Yorkton-Melville
Next Election: Oct. 24, 2012 (4 year terms)
David Hollinger, Mayor
Tracey Schuman, Clerk

Dundurn
P.O. Box 185
300 Third Ave.
Dundurn, SK S0K 1K0
Tel: 306-492-2202; *Fax:* 306-492-2360
town.dundurn@sasktel.net
www.townofdundurn.ca
Municipal Type: Town
Incorporated: July 7, 1905 *Area:* 0.88 sq km
Population in 2011: 693
Provincial Electoral District(s): Arm River-Watrous
Federal Electoral District(s): Blackstrap
Next Election: Oct. 24, 2012 (4 year terms)
Note: Proclaimed as a town on Nov. 1, 1980.
Per Vinding, Mayor
Michelle Roepe, Administrator

Duval
P.O. Box 70
Duval, SK S0G 1G0
Tel: 306-725-3767; *Fax:* 306-725-4339
jeff.jones@sasktel.net
Municipal Type: Village
Incorporated: Dec. 21, 1910 *Area:* 0.75 sq km
Population in 2011: 97
Provincial Electoral District(s): Arm River-Watrous
Federal Electoral District(s): Regina-Lumsden-Lake Centre
Next Election: Oct. 24, 2012 (4 year terms)
Dale Campbell, Mayor
Jeff Jones, Clerk

Dysart
P.O. Box 70
Dysart, SK S0G 1H0
Tel: 306-432-2100; *Fax:* 306-432-2265
dysartsk@sasktel.net
www.dysartsk.com
Municipal Type: Village
Incorporated: April 6, 1909 *Area:* 1.19 sq km
Population in 2011: 218
Provincial Electoral District(s): Last Mountain-Touchwood
Federal Electoral District(s): Regina-Qu'Appelle
Next Election: Oct. 24, 2012 (4 year terms)
Brenda Macknak, Mayor
Gerry Burym, Administrator

Earl Grey
P.O. Box 100
Earl Grey, SK S0G 1J0
Tel: 306-939-2062; *Fax:* 306-939-2036
earlgreyvillage@sasktel.net
earl.sasktelwebhosting.com
Municipal Type: Village
Incorporated: July 27, 1906 *Area:* 1.31 sq km
Population in 2011: 239
Provincial Electoral District(s): Last Mountain-Touchwood
Federal Electoral District(s): Regina-Lumsden-Lake Centre
Next Election: Oct. 24, 2012 (4 year terms)
Les Scherle, Mayor
Murray Cook, Administrator

Eastend
P.O. Box 520
Eastend, SK S0N 0T0
Tel: 306-295-3322; *Fax:* 306-295-3571
eastend@sasktel.net
www.dinocountry.com
Municipal Type: Town
Incorporated: Feb. 26, 1914 *Area:* 2.71 sq km
Population in 2011: 527
Provincial Electoral District(s): Cypress Hills
Federal Electoral District(s): Cypress Hills-Grasslands
Next Election: Oct. 24, 2012 (4 year terms)
Note: Proclaimed as a town on March 15, 1920.
Scott Morvik, Mayor
Edna Laturmus, Administrator

Eatonia
P.O. Box 237
Eatonia, SK S0L 0Y0
Tel: 306-967-2251; *Fax:* 306-967-2267
eatonia@yourlink.ca
www.townofeatonia.com
Municipal Type: Town
Incorporated: Jan. 28, 1920 *Area:* 1.68 sq km
Population in 2011: 508
Provincial Electoral District(s): Kindersley
Federal Electoral District(s): Cypress Hills-Grasslands
Next Election: Oct. 24, 2012 (4 year terms)
Note: Proclaimed as a town on Jan. 1, 1954.
R.W. (Bob) Peters, Mayor
Cheryl Bailey, Administrator

Ebenezer
P.O. Box 97
Ebenezer, SK S0A 0T0
Tel: 306-783-1217; *Fax:* 306-793-1218
village.ebenezer@sasktel.net
Municipal Type: Village
Incorporated: July 1, 1948 *Area:* 0.62 sq km
Population in 2011: 175
Provincial Electoral District(s): Canora-Pelly
Federal Electoral District(s): Yorkton-Melville
Next Election: Oct. 24, 2012 (4 year terms)
Kelly Pfeifer, Mayor
Angela Filipchuk, Administrator

Echo Bay
P.O. Box 428
Spiritwood, SK S0J 2M0
Tel: 306-883-2977; *Fax:* 306-883-3834
Municipal Type: Resort Village
Area: 0.80 sq km
Population in 2011: 38
Provincial Electoral District(s): Rosthern-Shellbrook
Federal Electoral District(s): Desnethé-Missinippi-Churchill River
Next Election: July 2016
Brian McCaig, Mayor
Shirley Dauvin, Administrator
pdauvin@xplornet.com

Edam
P.O. Box 203
Edam, SK S0M 0V0
Tel: 306-397-2223; *Fax:* 306-397-2626
edamvill@sasktel.net
villageofedam.ca
Municipal Type: Village
Incorporated: Oct. 12, 1911 *Area:* 1.13 sq km
Population in 2011: 444
Provincial Electoral District(s): Cut Knife-Turtleford
Federal Electoral District(s): Battlefords-Lloydminster
Next Election: Oct. 24, 2012 (4 year terms)
Larry McDaid, Mayor
Megan Cadrain, Administrator

Edenwold
P.O. Box 130
Edenwold, SK S0G 1K0
Tel: 306-771-4121; *Fax:* 306-771-2518
office@villageofedenwold.ca
www.villageofedenwold.ca
Municipal Type: Village
Incorporated: Oct. 3, 1912 *Area:* 0.68 sq km
Population in 2011: 238
Provincial Electoral District(s): Indian Head-Milestone
Federal Electoral District(s): Regina-Qu'Appelle
Next Election: Oct. 24, 2012 (4 year terms)
Dean Josephson, Mayor
mayor@villageofedenwold.ca
Christine Galbraith, Administrator

Elbow
P.O. Box 8
Elbow, SK S0H 1J0
Tel: 306-854-2277; *Fax:* 306-854-2229
info@elbowsask.com
www.elbowsask.com
Municipal Type: Village
Incorporated: April 6, 1909 *Area:* 3.92 sq km
Population in 2011: 314
Provincial Electoral District(s): Thunder Creek
Federal Electoral District(s): Blackstrap
Next Election: Oct. 24, 2012 (4 year terms)
David Cross, Mayor
Yvonne Jess, Administrator

Elfros
P.O. Box 40
Elfros, SK S0A 0V0
Tel: 306-328-2011; *Fax:* 306-328-4490
rm307@sasktel.net
Municipal Type: Village
Incorporated: Dec. 1, 1909 *Area:* 2.52 sq km
Population in 2011: 96
Provincial Electoral District(s): Kelvington-Wadena
Federal Electoral District(s): Regina-Qu'Appelle
Next Election: Oct. 24, 2012 (4 year terms)
Karilee Zemlak, Mayor
Glenn Thompson, Administrator

Elrose
P.O. Box 458
101 Main St.
Elrose, SK S0L 0Z0
Tel: 306-378-2202; *Fax:* 306-378-2966
townofelrose@sasktel.net
www.elrose.ca
Municipal Type: Town
Incorporated: Oct. 24, 1913 *Area:* 2.76 sq km
Population in 2011: 477
Provincial Electoral District(s): Rosetown-Elrose
Federal Electoral District(s): Cypress Hills-Grasslands
Next Election: Oct. 24, 2012 (4 year terms)
Note: Proclaimed as a town on Feb. 1, 1951.
June Hintze, Mayor
Chris Hopkins, Administrator

Elstow
P.O. Box 29
Elstow, SK S0K 1M0
Tel: 306-257-3889; *Fax:* 306-257-3709
villageofelstow@gmail.com
Municipal Type: Village
Incorporated: Dec. 17, 1908 *Area:* 0.58 sq km
Population in 2011: 89
Provincial Electoral District(s): Humboldt
Federal Electoral District(s): Blackstrap
Next Election: Oct. 24, 2012 (4 year terms)
Jed Bruce, Mayor
J. Linda Barnes, Administrator

Endeavour
P.O. Box 307
Endeavour, SK S0A 0W0
Tel: 306-547-3484; *Fax:* 306-547-3484
endeavour@sasktel.net
Municipal Type: Village
Incorporated: April 29, 1953 *Area:* 0.99 sq km
Population in 2011: 94
Provincial Electoral District(s): Canora-Pelly
Federal Electoral District(s): Yorkton-Melville
Next Election: Oct. 24, 2012 (4 year terms)
Roy Sheets, Mayor
Kathleen Ambrose, Administrator

Englefeld
P.O. Box 44
135 Main St.
Englefeld, SK S0K 1N0
Tel: 306-287-3151; *Fax:* 306-287-9902
vengle@sasktel.net
www.englefeld.ca
Municipal Type: Village
Incorporated: June 13, 1916 *Area:* 0.65 sq km
Population in 2011: 247
Provincial Electoral District(s): Melfort
Federal Electoral District(s): Saskatoon-Humboldt
Next Election: Oct. 24, 2012 (4 year terms)
Darrell Athmer, Mayor
Lani Best, Administrator

Ernfold
P.O. Box 340
Morse, SK S0H 3C0
Tel: 306-629-3282; *Fax:* 306-629-3212
rm165@sasktel.net
Municipal Type: Village
Incorporated: Dec. 4, 1912 *Area:* 1.19 sq km
Population in 2011: 30
Provincial Electoral District(s): Thunder Creek
Federal Electoral District(s): Cypress Hills-Grasslands
Next Election: Oct. 24, 2012 (4 year terms)
Christine Bauck, Mayor
Mark Wilson, Administrator

Esterhazy
P.O. Box 490
600 Sumner St.
Esterhazy, SK S0A 0X0
Tel: 306-745-3942; *Fax:* 306-745-6797
town.esterhazy@sasktel.net
www.town.esterhazy.sk.ca
Municipal Type: Town
Incorporated: Dec. 3, 1903 *Area:* 4.75 sq km
Population in 2011: 2,472
Provincial Electoral District(s): Melville-Saltcoats
Federal Electoral District(s): Yorkton-Melville
Next Election: Oct. 24, 2012 (4 year terms)
Note: Proclaimed as a town on March 1, 1957.
Herb Hozjan, Mayor
Donna Rollie, Administrator

Eston
P.O. Box 757
Eston, SK S0L 1A0
Tel: 306-962-4444; *Fax:* 306-962-4224
townofeston@sasktel.net
www.eston.ca
Municipal Type: Town
Incorporated: March 28, 1916 *Area:* 2.72 sq km
Population in 2011: 1,031
Provincial Electoral District(s): Rosetown-Elrose
Federal Electoral District(s): Cypress Hills-Grasslands
Next Election: Oct. 24, 2012 (4 year terms)
Note: Proclaimed as a town on Dec. 1, 1928.
Allan Heron, Mayor
bigbird70@sasktel.net
Gary Johnson, Administrator
gjohnson.towneston@sasktel.net

Etters Beach
P.O. Box 40
Stalwart, SK S0G 4R0
Tel: 306-963-2532; *Fax:* 306-528-2080
rvettersbeach@sasktel.net
Municipal Type: Resort Village
Area: 0.12 sq km
Population in 2011: 30
Provincial Electoral District(s): Arm River-Watrous
Federal Electoral District(s): Regina-Lumsden-Lake Centre
Next Election: July 2016
Garvon Hebron, Mayor
Michele Cruise-Pratchler, Administrator

Eyebrow
P.O. Box 159
Eyebrow, SK S0H 1L0
Tel: 306-759-2167; *Fax:* 306-759-2388
eyebrowvillage@sasktel.net
villageofeyebrow.com
Municipal Type: Village
Incorporated: Jan. 8, 1909 *Area:* 2.70 sq km
Population in 2011: 139
Provincial Electoral District(s): Thunder Creek
Federal Electoral District(s): Regina-Lumsden-Lake Centre
Next Election: Oct. 24, 2012 (4 year terms)
Don Linton, Mayor
Deanne Hartell, Clerk

Fairlight
P.O. Box 55
Fairlight, SK S0G 1M0
Tel: 306-646-2006; *Fax:* 306-646-2006
admin@villageoffairlight.ca
www.villageoffairlight.ca
Municipal Type: Village
Incorporated: Oct. 5, 1909 *Area:* 2.71 sq km
Population in 2011: 40
Provincial Electoral District(s): Cannington
Federal Electoral District(s): Souris-Moose Mountain
Next Election: Oct. 24, 2012 (4 year terms)
Bary Metz, Mayor
Nadia Metz, Administrator

Fenwood
P.O. Box 66
Fenwood, SK S0A 0Y0
Tel: 306-728-2185
www.spreda.sk.ca/community_Fenwood.htm
Municipal Type: Village
Incorporated: June 30, 1909 *Area:* 1.74 sq km
Population in 2011: 40
Provincial Electoral District(s): Last Mountain-Touchwood
Federal Electoral District(s): Yorkton-Melville
Next Election: Oct. 24, 2012 (4 year terms)
Byron Dohms, Mayor
Doreen Dohms, Clerk

Fillmore
P.O. Box 185
Fillmore, SK S0G 1N0
Tel: 306-722-3330; *Fax:* 306-722-3340
v.fillmore@sasktel.net
Municipal Type: Village
Incorporated: June 10, 1905 *Area:* 1.33 sq km
Population in 2011: 255
Provincial Electoral District(s): Cannington
Federal Electoral District(s): Souris-Moose Mountain
Next Election: Oct. 24, 2012 (4 year terms)
Marvin J. Chambers, Mayor
Danielle Rice, Administrator

Findlater
P.O. Box 10
Findlater, SK S0G 1P0
Tel: 306-638-4630; *Fax:* 306-638-4630
villageoffindlater@live.ca
Municipal Type: Village
Incorporated: Sept. 27, 1911 *Area:* 1.20 sq km
Population in 2011: 50
Provincial Electoral District(s): Thunder Creek
Federal Electoral District(s): Regina-Lumsden-Lake Centre
Next Election: Oct. 24, 2012 (4 year terms)
Bob Lesperance, Mayor
Joanne Yates, Clerk

Flaxcombe
P.O. Box 136
Flaxcombe, SK S0L 1E0
Tel: 306-463-2004; *Fax:* 306-463-2004
flaxcombe@sasktel.net
Municipal Type: Village
Incorporated: June 4, 1913 *Area:* 1.49 sq km
Population in 2011: 117
Provincial Electoral District(s): Kindersley
Federal Electoral District(s): Battlefords-Lloydminster
Next Election: Oct. 24, 2012 (4 year terms)
Dolores Doolittle, Mayor
Charlotte Helfrich, Clerk

Fleming
P.O. Box 129
Fleming, SK S0G 1R0
Tel: 306-435-4244; *Fax:* 306-435-3508
thetownoffleming@sasktel.net
Municipal Type: Town
Incorporated: July 2, 1896 *Area:* 2.17 sq km
Population in 2011: 83
Provincial Electoral District(s): Moosomin
Federal Electoral District(s): Souris-Moose Mountain
Next Election: Oct. 24, 2012 (4 year terms)
Note: Proclaimed as a town on June 15, 1907.
Philip Hamm, Mayor
Helen Gurski, Administrator

Foam Lake
P.O. Box 57
Foam Lake, SK S0A 1A0
Tel: 306-272-3359; *Fax:* 306-272-3738
foamlaketown@sasktel.net
www.foamlake.com
Municipal Type: Town
Incorporated: Oct. 12, 1908 *Area:* 6.06 sq km
Population in 2011: 1,148
Provincial Electoral District(s): Kelvington-Wadena
Federal Electoral District(s): Yorkton-Melville
Next Election: Oct. 24, 2012 (4 year terms)
Note: Proclaimed as a town on March 1, 1924.
Bob Johnson, Mayor
Gloria Leader, Administrator

Forget
P.O. Box 522
Stoughton, SK S0G 4T0
Tel: 306-457-2277; *Fax:* 306-457-3149
rmtec@sasktel.net
Municipal Type: Village
Incorporated: Nov. 21, 1904 *Area:* 1.39 sq km
Population in 2011: 35
Provincial Electoral District(s): Cannington
Federal Electoral District(s): Souris-Moose Mountain
Next Election: Oct. 24, 2012 (4 year terms)
Leon Gilbertson, Mayor
Zandra Slater, Administrator

Fort Qu'Appelle
P.O. Box 309
Fort Qu'appelle, SK S0G 1S0
Tel: 306-332-5266; *Fax:* 306-332-5087
forttownoffice@sasktel.net
www.fortquappelle.com
Municipal Type: Town
Incorporated: June 25, 1898 *Area:* 5.28 sq km
Population in 2011: 2,034
Provincial Electoral District(s): Indian Head-Milestone
Federal Electoral District(s): Regina-Qu'Appelle
Next Election: Oct. 24, 2012 (4 year terms)
Note: Proclaimed as a town on Jan. 1, 1951.
Ron Osika, Mayor
Darrell Webster, Administrator

Fort San
P.O. Box 99
136 Company Ave.
Fort Qu'Appelle, SK S0G 1S0
Tel: 306-332-5979; *Fax:* 306-332-6028
rm187@sasktel.net
fort-san.ca
Municipal Type: Resort Village
Area: 2.90 sq km
Population in 2011: 187
Provincial Electoral District(s): Last Mountain-Touchwood
Federal Electoral District(s): Regina-Qu'Appelle
Next Election: July 2016
Alfred Zimmerman, Mayor
Dawn Lugrin, Clerk

Fosston
P.O. Box 160
Fosston, SK S0E 0V0
Tel: 306-322-4521; *Fax:* 306-322-4442
vilfos@sasktel.net
www.newsaskcfdc.ca/fosston.htm

Municipal Type: Village
Incorporated: Jan. 1, 1965 *Area:* 0.59 sq km
Population in 2011: 55
Provincial Electoral District(s): Kelvington-Wadena
Federal Electoral District(s): Yorkton-Melville
Next Election: Oct. 24, 2012 (4 year terms)
Ron Einarson, Mayor
Valerie Bjerland, Administrator

Fox Valley
P.O. Box 207
Fox Valley, SK S0N 0V0
Tel: 306-666-3020; *Fax:* 306-666-3020
villoffoxvalley@sasktel.net
foxvalleysask.com
Municipal Type: Village
Incorporated: Aug. 30, 1928 *Area:* 0.60 sq km
Population in 2011: 260
Provincial Electoral District(s): Cypress Hills
Federal Electoral District(s): Cypress Hills-Grasslands
Next Election: Oct. 24, 2012 (4 year terms)
Mark Hudec, Mayor
Michelle Sehn, Administrator

Francis
P.O. Box 128
Francis, SK S0G 1V0
Tel: 306-245-3624; *Fax:* 306-245-3326
town.francis@sasktel.net
Municipal Type: Town
Incorporated: Oct. 24, 1904 *Area:* 0.59 sq km
Population in 2011: 176
Provincial Electoral District(s): Indian Head-Milestone
Federal Electoral District(s): Wascana
Next Election: Oct. 24, 2012 (4 year terms)
Note: Proclaimed as a town on Sept. 24, 1906.
Richard Senger, Mayor
Ila Connery, Administrator

Frobisher
P.O. Box 235
Frobisher, SK S0C 0Y0
Tel: 306-486-2140; *Fax:* 306-486-4504
vilfrob@sdcwireless.com
Municipal Type: Village
Incorporated: July 4, 1904 *Area:* 1.35 sq km
Population in 2011: 166
Provincial Electoral District(s): Cannington
Federal Electoral District(s): Souris-Moose Mountain
Next Election: Oct. 24, 2012 (4 year terms)
Jerry Nashiem, Mayor
Bill Ringguth, Clerk

Frontier
P.O. Box 270
108 1st Ave. West
Frontier, SK S0N 0W0
Tel: 306-296-2250; *Fax:* 306-296-4586
village.frontier@sasktel.net
www.villageoffrontier.com
Municipal Type: Village
Incorporated: July 10, 1930 *Area:* 0.93 sq km
Population in 2011: 351
Provincial Electoral District(s): Cypress Hills
Federal Electoral District(s): Cypress Hills-Grasslands
Next Election: Oct. 24, 2012 (4 year terms)
Connie Korsberg, Mayor
Barb Webber, Administrator

Gainsborough
P.O. Box 120
Gainsborough, SK S0C 0Z0
Tel: 306-685-2010; *Fax:* 306-685-2161
rm.1@sasktel.net
Municipal Type: Village
Incorporated: May 25, 1894 *Area:* 0.87 sq km
Population in 2011: 291
Provincial Electoral District(s): Cannington
Federal Electoral District(s): Souris-Moose Mountain
Next Election: Oct. 24, 2012 (4 year terms)
Victor Huish, Mayor
Erin McMillen, Administrator

Garson Lake
P.O. Box 69
Buffalo Narrows, SK S0M 0J0
Tel: 306-705-8719; *Fax:* 306-235-1727
Municipal Type: NS
Population in 2010: 34
Provincial Electoral District(s): Athabasca
Federal Electoral District(s): Desnethé-Missinippi-Churchill River
Next Election: Oct. 24, 2012 (4 year terms)
Donald Laprise, Chair
Bruce Leier, Advisor
bruce.leier@gov.sk.ca

Gerald
P.O. Box 155
Gerald, SK S0A 1B0
Tel: 306-745-6786; *Fax:* 306-745-6590
vofger@sasktel.net
Municipal Type: Village
Incorporated: March 25, 1953 *Area:* 0.80 sq km
Population in 2011: 114
Provincial Electoral District(s): Melville-Saltcoats
Federal Electoral District(s): Yorkton-Melville
Next Election: Oct. 24, 2012 (4 year terms)
Rudy Lonoway, Mayor
Lila R.A. Sippola, Administrator

Gladmar
P.O. Box 54
Gladmar, SK S0C 1A0
Tel: 306-969-4952
rhoimyr@gmail.com
Municipal Type: Village
Incorporated: Feb. 15, 1968 *Area:* 0.55 sq km
Population in 2011: 58
Provincial Electoral District(s): Weyburn-Big Muddy
Federal Electoral District(s): Souris-Moose Mountain
Next Election: Oct. 24, 2012 (4 year terms)
Dale Ehrhardt, Mayor
Randy Hoimyr, Clerk

Glaslyn
P.O. Box 279
172 Main St.
Glaslyn, SK S0M 0Y0
Tel: 306-342-2144; *Fax:* 306-342-2135
villageofglaslyn@sasktel.net
glaslyn.ca
Municipal Type: Village
Incorporated: April 16, 1929 *Area:* 1.97 sq km
Population in 2011: 397
Provincial Electoral District(s): Cut Knife-Turtleford
Federal Electoral District(s): Battlefords-Lloydminster
Next Election: Oct. 24, 2012 (4 year terms)
Ken Morrison, Mayor
Jamey Kuhmayer, Clerk

Glen Ewen
P.O. Box 99
Glen Ewen, SK S0C 1C0
Tel: 306-925-2211; *Fax:* 306-925-2210
rm3@sasktel.net
www3.telus.net/public/ketchs
Municipal Type: Village
Incorporated: March 24, 1904 *Area:* 2.77 sq km
Population in 2011: 144
Provincial Electoral District(s): Cannington
Federal Electoral District(s): Souris-Moose Mountain
Next Election: Oct. 24, 2012 (4 year terms)
Glen Lewis, Mayor
Deborah Tornblam, Administrator

Glen Harbour
P.O. Box 280
212 Main St.
Nokomis, SK S0G 3R0
Tel: 306-545-5170; *Fax:* 306-528-2083
rvglenharbour@sasktel.net
www.resortvillageofglenharbour.ca
Municipal Type: Resort Village
Area: 0.35 sq km
Population in 2011: 65
Provincial Electoral District(s): Last Mountain-Touchwood
Federal Electoral District(s): Regina-Lumsden-Lake Centre
Next Election: July 2016
Ron Ulmer, Mayor
Michele Cruise-Pratchler, Administrator

Glenavon
104 Main St.
Glenavon, SK S0G 1Y0
Tel: 306-429-2110
rmchester125@sasktel.net
www.glenavonsk.ca
Municipal Type: Village
Incorporated: April 13, 1910 *Area:* 1.32 sq km
Population in 2011: 176
Provincial Electoral District(s): Moosomin
Federal Electoral District(s): Souris-Moose Mountain
Next Election: Oct. 24, 2012 (4 year terms)
Herb Schmidt, Mayor
James Hoff, Administrator

Glenside
P.O. Box 99
Glenside, SK S0H 1T0
Tel: 306-867-8932
villageofglenside@xplornet.com
Municipal Type: Village
Incorporated: March 30, 1911 *Area:* 0.77 sq km
Population in 2011: 59
Provincial Electoral District(s): Rosetown-Elrose
Federal Electoral District(s): Blackstrap
Next Election: Oct. 24, 2012 (4 year terms)
Rod Simonson, Mayor
Evelyn Swan, Administrator

Golden Prairie
P.O. Box 9
Golden Prairie, SK S0N 0Y0
Tel: 306-662-2883; *Fax:* 306-662-3954
rm141@sasktel.net
Municipal Type: Village
Incorporated: April 15, 1942 *Area:* 0.41 sq km
Population in 2011: 35
Provincial Electoral District(s): Cypress Hills
Federal Electoral District(s): Cypress Hills-Grasslands
Next Election: Oct. 24, 2012 (4 year terms)
Delmar Beck, Mayor
Quinton Jacksteit, Administrator

Goodeve
P.O. Box 160
Goodeve, SK S0A 1C0
Tel: 306-795-2272; *Fax:* 306-795-3330
www.spreda.sk.ca/community_Goodeve.htm
Municipal Type: Village
Incorporated: Aug. 18, 1910 *Area:* 2.62 sq km
Population in 2011: 45
Provincial Electoral District(s): Last Mountain-Touchwood
Federal Electoral District(s): Yorkton-Melville
Next Election: Oct. 24, 2012 (4 year terms)
Craig Sawchuk, Mayor
Diana Lee, Clerk

Goodsoil
P.O. Box 176
Goodsoil, SK S0M 1A0
Tel: 306-238-2094; *Fax:* 306-238-2098
villageofgoodsoil@sasktel.net
www.goodsoil.sasktelwebsite.net
Municipal Type: Village
Incorporated: Jan. 1, 1960 *Area:* 1.76 sq km
Population in 2011: 281
Provincial Electoral District(s): Meadow Lake
Federal Electoral District(s): Desnethé-Missinippi-Churchill River
Next Election: Oct. 24, 2012 (4 year terms)
John Purves, Mayor
Linda Brophy, Administrator

Goodwater
P.O. Box 280
Weyburn, SK S4H 2K1
Tel: 306-456-2566; *Fax:* 306-456-2440
rm37@sasktel.net
Municipal Type: Village
Incorporated: May 8, 1911 *Area:* 0.59 sq km
Population in 2011: 35
Provincial Electoral District(s): Estevan
Federal Electoral District(s): Souris-Moose Mountain
Next Election: Oct. 24, 2012 (4 year terms)
Greg Collins, Mayor
Kevin Melle, Administrator

Govan
P.O. Box 160
Govan, SK S0G 1Z0
Tel: 306-484-2011
govan@parkland.lib.sk.ca
www.govansk.com
Municipal Type: Town
Incorporated: Aug. 21, 1907 *Area:* 1.35 sq km
Population in 2011: 216
Provincial Electoral District(s): Arm River-Watrous
Federal Electoral District(s): Regina-Lumsden-Lake Centre
Next Election: Oct. 24, 2012 (4 year terms)
Note: Proclaimed as a town on Nov. 1, 1911.
Wesley Pearce, Mayor
Kelly Holbrook, Administrator

Grand Coulee
P.O. Box 72
GBS 200, RR#2
Regina, SK S4P 2Z2
Tel: 306-352-8694; *Fax:* 306-352-6659
grandcoulee.cap@sasktel.net
www.grandcoulee.ca
Municipal Type: Village
Incorporated: April 10, 1908 *Area:* 0.30 sq km
Population in 2011: 571
Provincial Electoral District(s): Regina Qu'Appelle Valley
Federal Electoral District(s): Regina-Lumsden-Lake Centre
Next Election: Oct. 24, 2012 (4 year terms)
Irvin Brunas, Mayor
Tobi Duck, Administrator

Grandview Beach
3111 Kanuka Pl.
Regina, SK S4V 2C6
Tel: 306-789-6040
grandview@sasktel.net
Municipal Type: Resort Village
Area: 0.25 sq km
Population in 2011: 25
Provincial Electoral District(s): Thunder Creek
Federal Electoral District(s): Regina-Lumsden-Lake Centre
Next Election: July 2016
Bob Stobbs, Mayor
Gail Meyer, Administrator

Gravelbourg
P.O. Box 359
Gravelbourg, SK S0H 1X0
Tel: 306-648-3301; *Fax:* 306-648-3400
gravelbourg.adm@sasktel.net; info@gravelbourg.ca
www.gravelbourg.ca
Municipal Type: Town
Incorporated: Dec. 30, 1912 *Area:* 3.23 sq km
Population in 2011: 1,116
Provincial Electoral District(s): Wood River
Federal Electoral District(s): Cypress Hills-Grasslands
Next Election: Oct. 24, 2012 (4 year terms)
Note: Proclaimed as a town on Nov. 1, 1916.
Réal Forest, Mayor
Gord Murray, Administrator

Grayson
P.O. Box 9
Railway Ave.
Grayson, SK S0A 1E0
Tel: 306-794-2011; *Fax:* 306-794-2261
villageofgrayson@sasktel.net
www.spreda.sk.ca/community_Grayson.htm
Municipal Type: Village
Incorporated: April 19, 1906 *Area:* 1.47 sq km
Population in 2011: 184
Provincial Electoral District(s): Melville-Saltcoats
Federal Electoral District(s): Yorkton-Melville
Next Election: Oct. 24, 2012 (4 year terms)
Neil Ottenbreit, Mayor
Monica Haas, Administrator

Green Lake
P.O. Box 128
110 North St.
Green Lake, SK S0M 1B0
Tel: 306-832-2131; *Fax:* 306-832-2124
green.lake@sasktel.net
www.nvgreenlake.ca
Municipal Type: Northern Village
Incorporated: Oct. 1, 1983 *Area:* 121.92 sq km
Population in 2011: 418
Provincial Electoral District(s): Athabasca
Federal Electoral District(s): Desnethé-Missinippi-Churchill River
Next Election: Autumn 2012 (4 year terms)
Fred McCallum, Mayor
Tina Rasmussen, Administrator

Greig Lake
P.O. Box 334
Elrose, SK S0M 0T0
Tel: 306-378-2351; *Fax:* 306-378-2338
jtgreiglake@sasktel.net
Municipal Type: Resort Village
Area: 0.14 sq km
Population in 2011: 23
Provincial Electoral District(s): Meadow Lake
Federal Electoral District(s): Desnethé-Missinippi-Churchill River
Next Election: July 2016
Ben Denluck, Mayor
Joan Tatomir, Administrator

Grenfell
P.O. Box 1120
Grenfell, SK S0G 2B0
Tel: 306-697-2815; *Fax:* 306-697-2484
townofgrenfell@sasktel.net
www.grenfell.ca
Municipal Type: Town
Incorporated: April 12, 1894 *Area:* 3.17 sq km
Population in 2011: 1,049
Provincial Electoral District(s): Moosomin
Federal Electoral District(s): Souris-Moose Mountain
Next Election: Oct. 24, 2012 (4 year terms)
Note: Proclaimed as a town on Nov. 1, 1911.
Marc Saleski, Mayor
Suzanne Hawkshaw, Administrator

Gull Lake
P.O. Box 150
Gull Lake, SK S0N 1A0
Tel: 306-672-3361; *Fax:* 306-672-3777
gulllaketown@sasktel.net
www.gulllakesk.ca
Municipal Type: Town
Incorporated: Jan. 12, 1909 *Area:* 2.5 sq km
Population in 2011: 989
Provincial Electoral District(s): Cypress Hills
Federal Electoral District(s): Cypress Hills-Grasslands
Next Election: Oct. 24, 2012 (4 year terms)
Note: Proclaimed as a town on Nov. 1, 1911.
Blake Campbell, Mayor
Dawnette Peterson, Administrator

Hafford
P.O. Box 220
Hafford, SK S0J 1A0
Tel: 306-549-2331; *Fax:* 306-549-2338
town.administrator@hafford.ca; hafto@littleloon.ca
www.hafford.ca
Municipal Type: Town
Incorporated: Dec. 16, 1913 *Area:* 0.80 sq km
Population in 2011: 397
Provincial Electoral District(s): Rosthern-Shellbrook
Federal Electoral District(s): Saskatoon-Wanuskewin
Next Election: Oct. 24, 2012 (4 year terms)
Note: Proclaimed as a town on Jan. 1, 1981.
Peter Kingsmill, Mayor
Valerie Fendelet, Administrator

Hague
P.O. Box 180
Hague, SK S0K 1X0
Tel: 306-225-2155; *Fax:* 306-225-4410
town.hague@sasktel.net
www.townofhague.com
Municipal Type: Town
Incorporated: Aug. 25, 1903 *Area:* 1.03 sq km
Population in 2011: 878
Provincial Electoral District(s): Martensville
Federal Electoral District(s): Saskatoon-Wanuskewin
Next Election: Oct. 24, 2012 (4 year terms)
Note: Proclaimed as a town on Nov. 1, 1991.
Patricia Wagner, Mayor
Deanna Braun, Administrator

Halbrite
P.O. Box 10
Halbrite, SK S0C 1H0
Tel: 306-458-2252; *Fax:* 306-458-2657
Municipal Type: Village
Incorporated: Feb. 26, 1904 *Area:* 1.20 sq km
Population in 2011: 108
Provincial Electoral District(s): Estevan
Federal Electoral District(s): Souris-Moose Mountain
Next Election: Oct. 24, 2012 (4 year terms)
Dwayne Carlson, Mayor
Joy M. Guider, Clerk

Hanley
P.O. Box 270
Hanley, SK S0G 2E0
Tel: 306-544-2223; *Fax:* 306-544-2261
townoffice@townofhanley.ca
www.townofhanley.ca
Municipal Type: Town
Incorporated: April 27, 1905 *Area:* 2.65 sq km
Population in 2011: 522
Provincial Electoral District(s): Arm River-Watrous
Federal Electoral District(s): Blackstrap
Next Election: Oct. 24, 2012 (4 year terms)
Note: Proclaimed as a town on Dec. 1, 1906.
Marvin Gerbrandt, Mayor
Darice Carlson, Administrator

Harris
P.O. Box 124
Harris, SK S0L 1K0
Tel: 306-656-2122; *Fax:* 306-656-2123
villageofharris@sasktel.net
Municipal Type: Village
Incorporated: Aug. 10, 1909 *Area:* 0.72 sq km
Population in 2011: 213
Provincial Electoral District(s): Rosetown-Elrose
Federal Electoral District(s): Saskatoon-Rosetown-Biggar
Next Election: Oct. 24, 2012 (4 year terms)
Ron Genest, Mayor
Rhonda Leonard, Clerk

Hawarden
P.O. Box 7
Hawarden, SK S0H 1Y0
Tel: 306-855-2020; *Fax:* 306-855-2020
villageofhawarden@yourlink.ca
Municipal Type: Village
Incorporated: July 16, 1909 *Area:* 1.24 sq km
Population in 2011: 50
Provincial Electoral District(s): Arm River-Watrous
Federal Electoral District(s): Blackstrap
Next Election: Oct. 24, 2012 (4 year terms)
Keith Carlson, Mayor
Judy Phillips, Clerk

Hazenmore
P.O. Box 36
Hazenmore, SK S0N 1C0
Tel: 306-264-3218; *Fax:* 306-264-3218
villageofkincaid@hotmail.com
Municipal Type: Village
Incorporated: Aug. 20, 1913 *Area:* 0.80 sq km
Population in 2011: 50
Provincial Electoral District(s): Wood River
Federal Electoral District(s): Cypress Hills-Grasslands
Next Election: Oct. 24, 2012 (4 year terms)
Gary Loverin, Mayor
Barbara Hunter, Administrator

Hazlet
P.O. Box 150
Hazlet, SK S0N 1E0
Tel: 306-678-2131; *Fax:* 306-678-2132
hazlet@sasktel.net
hazletsk.com
Municipal Type: Village
Incorporated: Jan. 1, 1963 *Area:* 0.55 sq km
Population in 2011: 95
Provincial Electoral District(s): Cypress Hills
Federal Electoral District(s): Cypress Hills-Grasslands
Next Election: Oct. 24, 2012 (4 year terms)
Terry Bailey, Mayor
Terry Erdelyan, Administrator

Hepburn
P.O. Box 217
311 Main St.
Hepburn, SK S0K 1Z0
Tel: 306-947-2170; *Fax:* 306-947-4202
hepburnvillage@sasktel.net
Municipal Type: Village
Incorporated: July 5, 1919 *Area:* 1.02 sq km
Population in 2011: 562
Provincial Electoral District(s): Martensville
Federal Electoral District(s): Saskatoon-Wanuskewin
Next Election: Oct. 24, 2012 (4 year terms)
Barbara Adams-Eichendorf, Mayor
Andrew Spriggs, Administrator

Herbert
P.O. Box 370
218 Dennis St.
Herbert, SK S0H 2A0
Tel: 306-784-2400; *Fax:* 306-784-2402
t.o.herbert@sasktel.net
Municipal Type: Town
Incorporated: June 11, 1907 *Area:* 3.78 sq km
Population in 2011: 759
Provincial Electoral District(s): Thunder Creek
Federal Electoral District(s): Cypress Hills-Grasslands
Next Election: Oct. 24, 2012 (4 year terms)
Note: Proclaimed as a town on Nov. 1, 1912.
Doreen Schroeder, Mayor
Reagan Funk, Administrator

Heward
P.O. Box 10
Heward, SK S0G 2G0
Tel: 306-457-2707; *Fax:* 306-457-3149
rmtec@sasktel.net
Municipal Type: Village
Incorporated: Nov. 21, 1904 *Area:* 0.99 sq km
Population in 2011: 40
Provincial Electoral District(s): Cannington
Federal Electoral District(s): Souris-Moose Mountain
Next Election: Oct. 24, 2012 (4 year terms)
Murray Sabados, Mayor
Zandra Slater, Clerk

Hodgeville
P.O. Box 307
Hodgeville, SK S0H 2B0
Tel: 306-677-2223; *Fax:* 306-677-2466
Municipal Type: Village
Incorporated: June 22, 1921 *Area:* 1.35 sq km
Population in 2011: 172
Provincial Electoral District(s): Wood River
Federal Electoral District(s): Cypress Hills-Grasslands
Next Election: Oct. 24, 2012 (4 year terms)
Paul Kerr, Mayor
Michelle Mackow, Clerk

Holdfast
P.O. Box 160
Roberts St.
Holdfast, SK S0G 2H0
Tel: 306-488-2000; *Fax:* 306-488-4609
rm.sarnia@sasktel.net
Municipal Type: Village
Incorporated: Oct. 5, 1911 *Area:* 1.29 sq km
Population in 2011: 169
Provincial Electoral District(s): Thunder Creek
Federal Electoral District(s): Regina-Lumsden-Lake Centre
Next Election: Oct. 24, 2012 (4 year terms)
Todd Thauberger, Mayor
Patti Vance, Administrator

Hubbard
P.O. Box 190
Ituna, SK S0A 1N0
Tel: 306-795-2202; *Fax:* 306-795-2202
rmofituna@sasktel.net
Municipal Type: Village
Incorporated: June 11, 1910 *Area:* 1.25 sq km
Population in 2011: 46
Provincial Electoral District(s): Last Mountain-Touchwood
Federal Electoral District(s): Regina-Qu'Appelle
Next Election: Oct. 24, 2012 (4 year terms)
Ron Rokosh, Mayor
Diane M. Olech, Administrator

Hudson Bay
P.O. Box 730
304 Main St.
Hudson Bay, SK S0E 0Y0
Tel: 306-865-2261; *Fax:* 306-865-2800
hudson.bay@sasktel.net
www.townofhudsonbay.com
Municipal Type: Town
Incorporated: Sept. 25, 1907 *Area:* 17.35 sq km
Population in 2011: 1,477
Provincial Electoral District(s): Carrot River Valley
Federal Electoral District(s): Yorkton-Melville
Next Election: Oct. 24, 2012 (4 year terms)
Note: Proclaimed as a town on Nov. 30, 1946.
Elvina Rumak, Mayor
hbmayor@sasktel.net
Richard Dolezsar, Administrator
rdolezsar@sasktel.net

Humboldt
P.O. Box 640
715 Main St.
Humboldt, SK S0K 2A0
Tel: 306-682-2525; *Fax:* 306-682-3144
www.cityofhumboldt.ca
Municipal Type: Town
Incorporated: June 30, 1905 *Area:* 11.72 sq km
Population in 2011: 5,678
Provincial Electoral District(s): Humboldt
Federal Electoral District(s): Saskatoon-Humboldt
Next Election: Oct. 24, 2012 (4 year terms)
Note: Incorporated as a city on Nov. 7, 2000.
Malcolm Eaton, Mayor
mayor.cityofhumboldt@sasktel.net
Sandra Pauli, Director
spauli.cityofhumboldt@sasktel.net

Hyas
P.O. Box 40
Hyas, SK S0A 1K0
Tel: 306-594-2817; *Fax:* 306-594-2830
hyas@sasktel.net
Municipal Type: Village
Incorporated: May 23, 1919 *Area:* 1.17 sq km
Population in 2011: 114
Provincial Electoral District(s): Canora-Pelly
Federal Electoral District(s): Yorkton-Melville
Next Election: Oct. 24, 2012 (4 year terms)
Lawrence Ostafichuk, Mayor
Denise Sorrell, Administrator

Ile à la Crosse
P.O. Box 280
Lajeunesse Ave.
Ile-a-la-Crosse, SK S0M 1C0
Tel: 306-833-2122; *Fax:* 306-833-2132
village.of.ilealacrosse@sasktel.net
www.sakitawak.ca
Municipal Type: Northern Village
Incorporated: Oct. 1, 1983 *Area:* 23.84 sq km
Population in 2011: 1,365
Provincial Electoral District(s): Athabasca
Federal Electoral District(s): Desnethé-Missinippi-Churchill River
Next Election: Autumn 2012 (4 year terms)
Duane Favel, Mayor
Dianne McCallum, Administrator

Imperial
P.O. Box 90
Imperial, SK S0G 2J0
Tel: 306-963-2220; *Fax:* 306-963-2445
town.imperial@sasktel.net
www.imperial.ca
Municipal Type: Town
Incorporated: July 4, 1911 *Area:* 1.23 sq km
Population in 2011: 349
Provincial Electoral District(s): Arm River-Watrous
Federal Electoral District(s): Regina-Lumsden-Lake Centre
Next Election: Oct. 24, 2012 (4 year terms)
Note: Proclaimed as a town on April 1, 1962.
Harvey McLane, Mayor
Sheila Newlove, Administrator

Indian Head
P.O. Box 460
Indian Head, SK S0G 2K0
Tel: 306-695-3344
office@townofindianhead.com
www.townofindianhead.com
Municipal Type: Town
Incorporated: April 19, 1902 *Area:* 3.17 sq km
Population in 2011: 1,815
Provincial Electoral District(s): Indian Head-Milestone
Federal Electoral District(s): Regina-Qu'Appelle
Next Election: Oct. 24, 2012 (4 year terms)
Allan Hubbs, Mayor
mayor@townofindianhead.com
Cam Thauberger, Administrator

Invermay
P.O. Box 234
Invermay, SK S0A 1M0
Tel: 306-593-2242; *Fax:* 306-593-2242
villageofinvermay@sasktel.net
Municipal Type: Village
Incorporated: Sept. 1, 1908 *Area:* 1.22 sq km
Population in 2011: 247
Provincial Electoral District(s): Kelvington-Wadena
Federal Electoral District(s): Yorkton-Melville
Next Election: Oct. 24, 2012 (4 year terms)
Kim C. Rioch, Mayor
Veronica L. Wolski, Clerk

Island View
Comp. 3, RR#1
Bulyea, SK S0G 0L0
Tel: 306-725-4521; *Fax:* 306-725-4863
info@resortvillageofislandview.ca
www.resortvillageofislandview.ca
Municipal Type: Resort Village
Incorporated: 1959 *Area:* 0.43 sq km
Population in 2011: 65
Provincial Electoral District(s): Last Mountain-Touchwood
Federal Electoral District(s): Regina-Lumsden-Lake Centre
Next Election: July 2016
Ray Farebrother, Mayor
Sharon Moreau, Administrator

Ituna
P.O. Box 580
Ituna, SK S0A 1N0
Tel: 306-795-2272; *Fax:* 306-795-3330
townofituna@sasktel.net
www.ituna.ca
Municipal Type: Town
Incorporated: May 30, 1910 *Area:* 1.56 sq km
Population in 2011: 711
Provincial Electoral District(s): Last Mountain-Touchwood
Federal Electoral District(s): Regina-Qu'Appelle
Next Election: Oct. 24, 2012 (4 year terms)
Note: Proclaimed as a town on Oct. 1, 1961.
Glenn Leontowich, Mayor
Angela Romanson, Administrator

Jans Bay
Maurice Ave., General Delivery
Canoe Narrows, SK S0M 0K0
Tel: 306-829-4320; *Fax:* 306-829-4424
jansbay@sasktel.net
Municipal Type: Northern Village
Incorporated: Oct. 1, 1983 *Area:* 5.94 sq km
Population in 2011: 187
Provincial Electoral District(s): Athabasca
Federal Electoral District(s): Desnethé-Missinippi-Churchill River
Next Election: Autumn 2012 (4 year terms)
Tony Maurice, Mayor
Anne Marie Couillonneur, Clerk

Jansen
P.O. Box 116
Jansen, SK S0K 2B0
Tel: 306-364-2013; *Fax:* 306-364-2088
jansen@jansen.ca
www.jansen.ca
Municipal Type: Village
Incorporated: Oct. 19, 1908 *Area:* 0.85 sq km
Population in 2011: 126
Provincial Electoral District(s): Arm River-Watrous
Federal Electoral District(s): Blackstrap
Next Election: Oct. 24, 2012 (4 year terms)
Albert Cardinal, Mayor
Joni Mack, Administrator

Kamsack
P.O. Box 729
161 Queen Elizabeth Blvd. West
Kamsack, SK S0A 1S0
Tel: 306-542-2155; *Fax:* 306-542-2975
www.kamsack.ca
Municipal Type: Town
Incorporated: March 14, 1905 *Area:* 5.85 sq km
Population in 2011: 1,825
Provincial Electoral District(s): Canora-Pelly
Federal Electoral District(s): Yorkton-Melville
Next Election: Oct. 24, 2012 (4 year terms)
Note: Proclaimed as a town on Nov. 1, 1911.
Betty Dix, Mayor
Laura Lomenda, Administrator

Kannata Valley
P.O. Box 166
Silton, SK S0G 4L0
Tel: 306-731-2447; *Fax:* 306-731-2415
office@kannatavalley.com
www.kannatavalley.com
Other Information: Toll-Free Phone: 1-877-731-2447
Municipal Type: Resort Village
Incorporated: 1966 *Area:* 0.63 sq km
Population in 2011: 101
Provincial Electoral District(s): Last Mountain-Touchwood
Federal Electoral District(s): Regina-Lumsden-Lake Centre
Next Election: July 2016
Ken MacDonald, Mayor
306-533-3936
Jack McHardy, Administrator
306-731-2447

Katepwa
P.O. Box 250
41 Elm St.
Lebret, SK S0G 2Y0
Tel: 306-332-6645; *Fax:* 306-332-5808
katepwabeach@sasktel.net
www.katepwabeach.com
Municipal Type: Resort Village
Incorporated: 1914 *Area:* 5.78 sq km
Population in 2011: 403
Provincial Electoral District(s): Last Mountain-Touchwood
Federal Electoral District(s): Regina-Qu'Appelle
Next Election: July 2016

Fred Weekley, Mayor
Glenda Hodson, Administrator

Keeler
P.O. Box 33
Keeler, SK S0H 2E0
Tel: 306-759-2302
Municipal Type: Village
Incorporated: July 5, 1910 *Area:* 1.02 sq km
Population in 2011: 0
Provincial Electoral District(s): Thunder Creek
Federal Electoral District(s): Regina-Lumsden-Lake Centre
Next Election: Oct. 24, 2012 (4 year terms)
Duncan Keeler, Mayor
Jackie Leggott, Clerk

Kelliher
P.O. Box 190
406 - 2nd Ave.
Kelliher, SK S0A 1V0
Tel: 306-675-2226; *Fax:* 306-675-2240
villageofkelliher@sasktel.net
www.kelliher.ca
Municipal Type: Village
Incorporated: April 27, 1909 *Area:* 2.81 sq km
Population in 2011: 216
Provincial Electoral District(s): Last Mountain-Touchwood
Federal Electoral District(s): Regina-Qu'Appelle
Next Election: Oct. 24, 2012 (4 year terms)
Darcy King, Mayor
Gerry Burym, Administrator

Kelvington
P.O. Box 10
201 Main St.
Kelvington, SK S0A 1W0
Tel: 306-327-4482; *Fax:* 306-327-4946
tkelv@sasktel.net
www.townofkelvington.com
Municipal Type: Town
Incorporated: Nov. 18, 1921 *Area:* 3.89 sq km
Population in 2011: 864
Provincial Electoral District(s): Kelvington-Wadena
Federal Electoral District(s): Yorkton-Melville
Next Election: Oct. 24, 2012 (4 year terms)
Note: Proclaimed as a town on May 1, 1944.
Ed Tetelowski, Mayor
Kelsey Robinson, Administrator

Kenaston
P.O. Box 129
Kenaston, SK S0G 2N0
Tel: 306-252-2211; *Fax:* 306-252-2248
kenaston@sasktel.net
www.kenaston.ca
Municipal Type: Village
Incorporated: July 18, 1910 *Area:* 1.17 sq km
Population in 2011: 285
Provincial Electoral District(s): Arm River-Watrous
Federal Electoral District(s): Blackstrap
Next Election: Oct. 24, 2012 (4 year terms)
Dan O'Handley, Mayor
Carmen Fowler, Administrator

Kendal
P.O. Box 97
115 Main St.
Kendal, SK S0G 2P0
Tel: 306-424-2722; *Fax:* 306-424-2722
villageofkendal@sasktel.net
kendalsk.com
Municipal Type: Village
Incorporated: Feb. 17, 1919 *Area:* 0.65 sq km
Population in 2011: 77
Provincial Electoral District(s): Indian Head-Milestone
Federal Electoral District(s): Wascana
Next Election: Oct. 24, 2012 (4 year terms)
Shannon Gray, Mayor
Colleen Hoffman, Administrator

Kennedy
P.O. Box 93
Kennedy, SK S0G 2R0
Tel: 306-538-2194; *Fax:* 306-538-4522
village.kennedy@sasktel.net
www.angelfire.com/ca/kennedysk
Municipal Type: Village
Incorporated: Nov. 5, 1907 *Area:* 1.60 sq km
Population in 2011: 241
Provincial Electoral District(s): Moosomin
Federal Electoral District(s): Souris-Moose Mountain
Next Election: Oct. 24, 2012 (4 year terms)
Clarence Bender, Mayor
Jane Johnson, Administrator

Kenosee Lake
P.O. Box 30
Kenosee Lake, SK S0C 2S0
Tel: 306-577-2139; *Fax:* 306-577-2261
village.kenosee@sasktel.net
Municipal Type: Village
Incorporated: Oct. 1, 1987 *Area:* 0.35 sq km
Population in 2011: 258
Provincial Electoral District(s): Cannington
Federal Electoral District(s): Souris-Moose Mountain
Next Election: Oct. 24, 2012 (4 year terms)
Lyle Basken, Mayor
Peggy Fleck, Administrator

Kerrobert
P.O. Box 558
433 Manitoba Ave.
Kerrobert, SK S0L 1R0
Tel: 306-834-2361; *Fax:* 306-834-2633
kerrobert@sasktel.net
www.kerrobertsk.com
Municipal Type: Town
Incorporated: Nov. 9, 1910 *Area:* 7.49 sq km
Population in 2011: 1,061
Provincial Electoral District(s): Kindersley
Federal Electoral District(s): Battlefords-Lloydminster
Next Election: Oct. 24, 2012 (4 year terms)
Note: Proclaimed as a town on Nov. 1, 1911.
Erhard Poggemiller, Mayor
Michele Schmidt, Administrator
kerrobert.admin@sasktel.net

Killaly
P.O. Box 69
Railway Ave.
Killaly, SK S0A 1X0
Tel: 306-748-2540
rm185@sasktel.net
www.spreda.sk.ca/community_Killaly.htm
Municipal Type: Village
Incorporated: April 28, 1909 *Area:* 2.59 sq km
Population in 2011: 74
Provincial Electoral District(s): Melville-Saltcoats
Federal Electoral District(s): Yorkton-Melville
Next Election: Oct. 24, 2012 (4 year terms)
Angie Rogalski, Mayor
Linda Hanowski, Administrator

Kincaid
P.O. Box 177
Kincaid, SK S0H 2J0
Tel: 306-264-3910; *Fax:* 306-264-3903
villageofkincaid@hotmail.com
www.villageofkincaid.ca
Municipal Type: Village
Incorporated: July 19, 1913 *Area:* 0.82 sq km
Population in 2011: 114
Provincial Electoral District(s): Wood River
Federal Electoral District(s): Cypress Hills-Grasslands
Next Election: Oct. 24, 2012 (4 year terms)
Cynthia Gross, Mayor
Barbara Hunter, Administrator

Kindersley
P.O. Box 1269
106 - 5th Ave. East
Kindersley, SK S0L 1S0
Tel: 306-463-2675; *Fax:* 306-463-4577
office@kindersley.ca
www.kindersley.ca
Municipal Type: Town
Incorporated: Jan. 10, 1910 *Area:* 12.55 sq km
Population in 2011: 4,678
Provincial Electoral District(s): Kindersley
Federal Electoral District(s): Battlefords-Lloydminster
Next Election: Oct. 24, 2012 (4 year terms)
Note: Proclaimed as a town on Nov. 1, 1910.
Wayne Foster, Mayor
waynefoster@kindersley.ca
Bernie Morton, Administrator
306-463-2675

Kinistino
P.O. Box 10
Kinistino, SK S0J 1H0
Tel: 306-864-2461; *Fax:* 306-864-2880
townofkinistino@sasktel.net
www.townofkinistino.ca
Municipal Type: Town
Incorporated: July 30, 1905 *Area:* 0.89 sq km
Population in 2011: 743
Provincial Electoral District(s): Batoche
Federal Electoral District(s): Prince Albert
Next Election: Oct. 24, 2012 (4 year terms)
Note: Proclaimed as a town on Feb. 7, 1952.
Leonard Margolis, Mayor
Rhonda Bacon, Administrator

Kinley
P.O. Box 51
Kinley, SK S0K 2E0
Tel: 306-237-4601; *Fax:* 306-237-4605
villageofkinley@sasktel.net
Municipal Type: Village
Incorporated: Jan. 7, 1909 *Area:* 1.18 sq km
Population in 2011: 45
Provincial Electoral District(s): Biggar
Federal Electoral District(s): Saskatoon-Rosetown-Biggar
Next Election: Oct. 24, 2012 (4 year terms)
Cindy Latta, Mayor
Lynne Tolley, Administrator

Kipling
P.O. Box 299
301 - 6th Ave.
Kipling, SK S0G 2S0
Tel: 306-736-2515; *Fax:* 306-736-8448
kiptown@sasktel.net; kiplingadmin@sasktel.net
www.townofkipling.ca
Municipal Type: Town
Incorporated: Sept. 13, 1909 *Area:* 2.15 sq km
Population in 2011: 1,051
Provincial Electoral District(s): Moosomin
Federal Electoral District(s): Souris-Moose Mountain
Next Election: Oct. 24, 2012 (4 year terms)
Note: Proclaimed as a town on Jan. 1, 1954.
Kelly Fish, Mayor
glokel@sasktel.net
Gail Dakue, Administrator

Kisbey
P.O. Box 249
Kisbey, SK S0C 1L0
Tel: 306-462-2212; *Fax:* 306-462-2279
vill.kisbey@sasktel.net
Municipal Type: Village
Incorporated: May 8, 1907 *Area:* 2.77 sq km
Population in 2011: 139
Provincial Electoral District(s): Cannington
Federal Electoral District(s): Souris-Moose Mountain
Next Election: Oct. 24, 2012 (4 year terms)
John Houston, Mayor
Judy Graham, Administrator

Kivimaa-Moonlight Bay
P.O. Box 120
Livelong, SK S0M 1J0
Tel: 306-845-3336; *Fax:* 306-845-3686
rvkmb@littleloon.ca
Municipal Type: Resort Village
Area: 0.55 sq km
Population in 2011: 84
Provincial Electoral District(s): Meadow Lake
Federal Electoral District(s): Battlefords-Lloydminster
Next Election: July 2016
Daryl Grant, Mayor
Jackie Helgeton, Administrator

Krydor
P.O. Box 160
Hafford, SK S0J 1A0
Tel: 306-549-2333; *Fax:* 306-549-2435
rm435@littleloon.ca
Municipal Type: Village
Incorporated: Aug. 25, 1914 *Area:* 0.82 sq km
Population in 2011: 15
Provincial Electoral District(s): Rosthern-Shellbrook
Federal Electoral District(s): Saskatoon-Wanuskewin
Next Election: Oct. 24, 2012 (4 year terms)
Stan Lucko, Mayor
Alan J. Tanchak, Clerk

Kyle
P.O. Box 520
Kyle, SK S0L 1T0
Tel: 306-375-2525; *Fax:* 306-375-2534
townofkyle@sasktel.net
www.kylesaskatchewan.ca
Municipal Type: Town
Incorporated: April 13, 1926 *Area:* 1.01 sq km

Population in 2011: 437
Provincial Electoral District(s): Rosetown-Elrose
Federal Electoral District(s): Cypress Hills-Grasslands
Next Election: Oct. 24, 2012 (4 year terms)
Note: Proclaimed as a town on Jan. 1, 1959.
Ansgar Tynning, Mayor
Audrey Blohm, Administrator

La Loche
P.O. Box 310
La Loche Ave.
La Loche, SK S0M 1G0
Tel: 306-822-2032; *Fax:* 306-822-2078
nor.vill.laloche@sasktel.net
Municipal Type: Northern Village
Incorporated: Oct. 1, 1983 *Area:* 15.59 sq km
Population in 2011: 2,611
Provincial Electoral District(s): Athabasca
Federal Electoral District(s): Desnethé-Missinippi-Churchill River
Next Election: Autumn 2012 (4 year terms)
Georgina Jolibois, Mayor
Doug Gailey, Clerk

La Ronge
P.O. Box 5680
1212 Hildebrandt Dr.
La Ronge, SK S0J 1L0
Tel: 306-425-2066; *Fax:* 306-425-3883
www.townoflaronge.ca; www.laronge.ca
Municipal Type: Northern Town
Incorporated: May 3, 1905 *Area:* 11.86 sq km
Population in 2011: 2,304
Provincial Electoral District(s): Cumberland
Federal Electoral District(s): Desnethé-Missinippi-Churchill River
Next Election: Autumn 2012 (4 year terms)
Note: Proclaimed as a northern town on Oct. 1, 1983.
Thomas Sierzycki, Mayor
laronge.mayor@sasktel.net
Davidie Zarazun, Administrator
laronge.administrator@sasktel.net

Lafleche
P.O. Box 250
35 - 2nd Ave. East
Lafleche, SK S0H 2K0
Tel: 306-472-5292; *Fax:* 306-472-3706
town.of.lafleche@sasktel.net
www.town.lafleche.sk.ca
Municipal Type: Town
Incorporated: Sept. 3, 1913 *Area:* 1.51 sq km
Population in 2011: 406
Provincial Electoral District(s): Wood River
Federal Electoral District(s): Cypress Hills-Grasslands
Next Election: Oct. 24, 2012 (4 year terms)
Note: Proclaimed as a town on June 1, 1953.
Raymond Clermont, Mayor
Lorraine McIvor, Administrator

Laird
P.O. Box 189
220A Main St.
Laird, SK S0K 2H0
Tel: 306-223-4343; *Fax:* 306-223-4349
lairdvillage@sasktel.net
www.lairdvillage.ca
Municipal Type: Village
Incorporated: May 4, 1911 *Area:* 1.29 sq km
Population in 2011: 287
Provincial Electoral District(s): Rosthern-Shellbrook
Federal Electoral District(s): Saskatoon-Wanuskewin
Next Election: Oct. 24, 2012 (4 year terms)
Doug Crowe, Mayor
Michelle Zurakowski, Administrator

Lake Alma
P.O. Box 163
Lake Alma, SK S0C 1M0
Tel: 306-447-2002
Municipal Type: Village
Incorporated: Jan. 1, 1949 *Area:* 0.47 sq km
Population in 2011: 30
Provincial Electoral District(s): Estevan
Federal Electoral District(s): Souris-Moose Mountain
Next Election: Oct. 24, 2012 (4 year terms)
Wilfred Jacobson, Mayor
Myrma Lohse, Clerk

Lake Lenore
P.O. Box 148
Lake Lenore, SK S0K 2J0
Tel: 306-368-2344; *Fax:* 306-368-2226
lakelenorevil@sasktel.net
www.newsaskcfdc.ca/lakelenore.htm
Municipal Type: Village
Incorporated: April 28, 1921 *Area:* 0.97 sq km
Population in 2011: 297
Provincial Electoral District(s): Batoche
Federal Electoral District(s): Saskatoon-Humboldt
Next Election: Oct. 24, 2012 (4 year terms)
Kerry Haeusler, Mayor
Barb Politeski, Clerk

Lampman
P.O. Box 70
215 Main St.
Lampman, SK S0C 1N0
Tel: 306-487-2462; *Fax:* 306-487-2285
browning.lampman@sasktel.net
www.lampman.sasktelwebsite.net
Municipal Type: Town
Incorporated: Aug. 16, 1910 *Area:* 2.23 sq km
Population in 2011: 713
Provincial Electoral District(s): Cannington
Federal Electoral District(s): Souris-Moose Mountain
Next Election: Oct. 24, 2012 (4 year terms)
Note: Proclaimed as a town on June 1, 1963.
Scott Greening, Mayor
Greg Wallin, Administrator

Lancer
P.O. Box 3
Lancer, SK S0N 1G0
Tel: 306-689-2925; *Fax:* 306-689-2890
Municipal Type: Village
Incorporated: Sept. 11, 1913 *Area:* 1.33 sq km
Population in 2011: 61
Provincial Electoral District(s): Cypress Hills
Federal Electoral District(s): Cypress Hills-Grasslands
Next Election: Oct. 24, 2012 (4 year terms)
Ernest Wagner, Mayor
Karen Hartman, Clerk

Landis
P.O. Box 153
Landis, SK S0K 2K0
Tel: 306-658-2155; *Fax:* 306-658-2156
villageoflandis@sasktel.net
www.landissask.ca
Municipal Type: Village
Incorporated: May 17, 1909 *Area:* 0.80 sq km
Population in 2011: 139
Provincial Electoral District(s): Biggar
Federal Electoral District(s): Battlefords-Lloydminster
Next Election: Oct. 24, 2012 (4 year terms)
Joe Sarrasin, Mayor
Sandra Beckett, Administrator

Lang
P.O. Box 97
223 Main St.
Lang, SK S0G 2W0
Tel: 306-464-2024; *Fax:* 306-464-2024
voflang@sasktel.net
www.langsk.com
Municipal Type: Village
Incorporated: July 27, 1906 *Area:* 0.64 sq km
Population in 2011: 200
Provincial Electoral District(s): Indian Head-Milestone
Federal Electoral District(s): Souris-Moose Mountain
Next Election: Oct. 24, 2012 (4 year terms)
Al Broderick, Mayor
Melissa McCloy, Administrator

Langenburg
P.O. Box 400
Langenburg, SK S0A 2A0
Tel: 306-743-2432; *Fax:* 306-743-2723
langenburgt@sasktel.net
www.town.langenburg.sk.ca
Municipal Type: Town
Incorporated: March 30, 1903 *Area:* 3.46 sq km
Population in 2011: 1,148
Provincial Electoral District(s): Melville-Saltcoats
Federal Electoral District(s): Yorkton-Melville
Next Election: Oct. 24, 2012 (4 year terms)
Note: Proclaimed as a town on Sept. 15, 1959.
Dave Schappert, Mayor
Howard McCullough, Administrator

Langham
P.O. Box 289
230 Main St. East
Langham, SK S0K 2L0
Tel: 306-283-4842; *Fax:* 306-283-4772
admin@langham.ca
www.langham.ca
Municipal Type: Town
Incorporated: June 8, 1906 *Area:* 3.98 sq km
Population in 2011: 1,290
Provincial Electoral District(s): Biggar
Federal Electoral District(s): Saskatoon-Rosetown-Biggar; Saskatoon-Wanuskewin
Next Election: Oct. 24, 2012 (4 year terms)
Note: Proclaimed as a town on Aug. 1, 1907.
Glen Thiessen, Mayor
Randy J. Sherstobitoff, Administrator

Lanigan
P.O. Box 280
Lanigan, SK S0K 2M0
Tel: 306-365-2809; *Fax:* 306-365-2960
town.lanigan@sasktel.net
www.town.lanigan.sk.ca
Municipal Type: Town
Incorporated: Aug. 21, 1907 *Area:* 8.34 sq km
Population in 2011: 1,390
Provincial Electoral District(s): Humboldt
Federal Electoral District(s): Blackstrap
Next Election: Oct. 24, 2012 (4 year terms)
Note: Proclaimed as a town on April 15, 1908.
Bernie Bishop, Mayor
Jack R. Dvernichuk, Administrator

Lashburn
P.O. Box 328
Lashburn, SK S0M 1H0
Tel: 306-285-3533; *Fax:* 306-285-3358
townoflashburn@sasktel.net
www.lashburn.ca
Municipal Type: Town
Incorporated: Dec. 8, 1906 *Area:* 3.11 sq km
Population in 2011: 967
Provincial Electoral District(s): Cut Knife-Turtleford
Federal Electoral District(s): Battlefords-Lloydminster
Next Election: Oct. 24, 2012 (4 year terms)
Note: Proclaimed as a town on March 1, 1979.
Steven Turnbull, Mayor
Vicki Seabrook, Administrator

Leader
P.O. Box 39
151 - 1st St. West
Leader, SK S0N 1H0
Tel: 306-628-3868; *Fax:* 306-628-4337
town.leader@sasktel.net
www.leader.ca
Other Information: Toll Free Phone: 1-800-424-8335
Municipal Type: Town
Incorporated: Sept. 13, 1913 *Area:* 1.70 sq km
Population in 2011: 821
Provincial Electoral District(s): Cypress Hills
Federal Electoral District(s): Cypress Hills-Grasslands
Next Election: Oct. 24, 2012 (4 year terms)
Note: Proclaimed as a town on May 1, 1947.
Craig Tondevold, Mayor
Rochelle Francis, Administrator

Leask
P.O. Box 40
15 Main St.
Leask, SK S0J 1M0
Tel: 306-466-2229; *Fax:* 306-466-2239
village.leask@sasktel.net
www.leask.ca
Municipal Type: Village
Incorporated: Sept. 3, 1912 *Area:* 0.75 sq km
Population in 2011: 413
Provincial Electoral District(s): Rosthern-Shellbrook
Federal Electoral District(s): Saskatoon-Wanuskewin
Next Election: Oct. 24, 2012 (4 year terms)
Maurice Stieb, Mayor
Brenda Lockhart, Administrator
admin.464@sasktel.net

Lebret
P.O. Box 40
Lebret, SK S0G 2Y0
Tel: 306-332-6545; *Fax:* 306-332-5338
villageoflebret@sasktel.net
Municipal Type: Village
Incorporated: Oct. 14, 1912 *Area:* 1.32 sq km

Population in 2011: 218
Provincial Electoral District(s): Last Mountain-Touchwood
Federal Electoral District(s): Regina-Qu'Appelle
Next Election: Oct. 24, 2012 (4 year terms)
Carl Olson, Mayor
Gwen Lowe, Administrator

Lemberg
P.O. Box 399
Lemberg, SK S0A 2B0
Tel: 306-335-2244; *Fax:* 306-335-2911
townoffice.lemberg@sasktel.net
www.spreda.sk.ca/community_Lemberg.htm
Municipal Type: Town
Incorporated: July 12, 1904 *Area:* 2.67 sq km
Population in 2011: 274
Provincial Electoral District(s): Last Mountain-Touchwood
Federal Electoral District(s): Yorkton-Melville
Next Election: Oct. 24, 2012 (4 year terms)
Note: Proclaimed as a town on Sept. 1, 1907.
Herbert MacDonald, Mayor
Joyce Hauck, Clerk

Leoville
P.O. Box 280
Leoville, SK S0J 1N0
Tel: 306-984-2140; *Fax:* 306-984-2337
leoville@sasktel.net
Municipal Type: Village
Incorporated: June 26, 1944 *Area:* 1.11 sq km
Population in 2011: 366
Provincial Electoral District(s): Meadow Lake
Federal Electoral District(s): Desnethé-Missinippi-Churchill River
Next Election: Oct. 24, 2012 (4 year terms)
Ron Craswell, Mayor
Mona Chalifour, Clerk

Leross
P.O. Box 68
Leross, SK S0A 2C0
Tel: 306-675-4429; *Fax:* 306-675-2097
villageofleross@sasktel.net
Municipal Type: Village
Incorporated: Dec. 1, 1909 *Area:* 1.21 sq km
Population in 2011: 37
Provincial Electoral District(s): Last Mountain-Touchwood
Federal Electoral District(s): Regina-Qu'Appelle
Next Election: Oct. 24, 2012 (4 year terms)
Francis Klyne, Mayor
Elaine Klyne, Clerk

Leroy
P.O. Box 40
Leroy, SK S0K 2P0
Tel: 306-286-3288; *Fax:* 306-286-3400
leroy@bogend.ca
www.leroy.ca
Municipal Type: Town
Incorporated: Dec. 5, 1922 *Area:* 1.06 sq km
Population in 2011: 427
Provincial Electoral District(s): Melfort
Federal Electoral District(s): Saskatoon-Humboldt
Next Election: Oct. 24, 2012 (4 year terms)
Note: Proclaimed as a town on March 1, 1963.
Morris Hartman, Mayor
Connie Porten, Administrator

Leslie Beach
P.O. Box 478
Foam Lake, SK S0A 1A0
Tel: 306-272-4579; *Fax:* 306-272-3960
thekipling@sasktel.net
Municipal Type: Resort Village
Area: 0.56 sq km
Population in 2011: 23
Provincial Electoral District(s): Kelvington-Wadena
Federal Electoral District(s): Yorkton-Melville
Next Election: July 2016
Gylan Josephson, Mayor
Brenda Kipling, Clerk

Lestock
P.O. Box 209
320 Touchwood Hills Ave.
Lestock, SK S0A 2G0
Tel: 306-274-2277; *Fax:* 306-274-2277
lestockv@sasktel.net
Municipal Type: Village
Incorporated: April 17, 1912 *Area:* 0.87 sq km
Population in 2011: 125
Provincial Electoral District(s): Last Mountain-Touchwood
Federal Electoral District(s): Regina-Qu'Appelle
Next Election: Oct. 24, 2012 (4 year terms)
Kelly Komodowski, Mayor
Frank Kasa, Administrator

Liberty
P.O. Box 59
Liberty, SK S0G 3A0
Tel: 306-963-2402; *Fax:* 306-963-2405
rm251@sasktel.net
Municipal Type: Village
Incorporated: Jan. 23, 1912 *Area:* 1.37 sq km
Population in 2011: 88
Provincial Electoral District(s): Arm River-Watrous
Federal Electoral District(s): Regina-Lumsden-Lake Centre
Next Election: Oct. 24, 2012 (4 year terms)
Terry Tannahill, Mayor
Yvonne (Bonny) Goodsman, Administrator

Limerick
P.O. Box 129
Limerick, SK S0H 2P0
Tel: 306-263-2020; *Fax:* 306-263-2013
rm73@sasktel.net
Municipal Type: Village
Incorporated: July 10, 1913 *Area:* 0.79 sq km
Population in 2011: 115
Provincial Electoral District(s): Wood River
Federal Electoral District(s): Cypress Hills-Grasslands
Next Election: Oct. 24, 2012 (4 year terms)
Robert Smith, Mayor
Tammy Franks, Administrator

Lintlaw
P.O. Box 10
Lintlaw, SK S0A 2H0
Tel: 306-325-2006; *Fax:* 306-325-2006
villageoflintlaw@sasktel.net
Municipal Type: Village
Incorporated: Dec. 14, 1921 *Area:* 1.23 sq km
Population in 2011: 162
Provincial Electoral District(s): Kelvington-Wadena
Federal Electoral District(s): Yorkton-Melville
Next Election: Oct. 24, 2012 (4 year terms)
Leonard Johnson, Mayor
Kathleen Ambrose, Administrator

Lipton
P.O. Box 219
Lipton, SK S0G 3B0
Tel: 306-336-2505; *Fax:* 306-336-2505
lipton@sasktel.net
www.villageoflipton.com
Municipal Type: Village
Incorporated: May 15, 1905 *Area:* 0.75 sq km
Population in 2011: 372
Provincial Electoral District(s): Last Mountain-Touchwood
Federal Electoral District(s): Regina-Qu'Appelle
Next Election: Oct. 24, 2012 (4 year terms)
Marvis Seel, Mayor
Marlene L. Bausmer, Administrator

Loon Lake
P.O. Box 220
Loon Lake, SK S0M 1L0
Tel: 306-837-2090; *Fax:* 306-837-4735
loonlake@sasktel.net
Municipal Type: Village
Incorporated: Jan. 1, 1950 *Area:* 0.66 sq km
Population in 2011: 314
Provincial Electoral District(s): Meadow Lake
Federal Electoral District(s): Churchill River/Rivière Churchill
Next Election: Oct. 24, 2012 (4 year terms)
Larry Heon, Mayor
Laurie Lehoux, Administrator

Loreburn
P.O. Box 177
Loreburn, SK S0H 2S0
Tel: 306-644-2097; *Fax:* 306-644-4847
villageofloreburn@yourlink.ca
Municipal Type: Village
Incorporated: May 20, 1909 *Area:* 0.62 sq km
Population in 2011: 107
Provincial Electoral District(s): Arm River-Watrous
Federal Electoral District(s): Blackstrap
Next Election: Oct. 24, 2012 (4 year terms)
Bruce Hagen, Mayor
Muriel Stronski, Clerk

Love
P.O. Box 94
Love, SK S0J 1P0
Tel: 306-276-2525
villageoflove@sasktel.net
www.villageoflove.ca
Municipal Type: Village
Incorporated: June 2, 1945 *Area:* 0.46 sq km
Population in 2011: 65
Provincial Electoral District(s): Saskatchewan Rivers
Federal Electoral District(s): Desnethé-Missinippi-Churchill River
Next Election: Oct. 24, 2012 (4 year terms)
Duane Tempel, Mayor
Valerie Rodgers, Administrator

Lucky Lake
P.O. Box 99
Lucky Lake, SK S0L 1Z0
Tel: 306-858-2234; *Fax:* 306-858-2234
rm225.vll@sasktel.net
Municipal Type: Village
Incorporated: Nov. 23, 1920 *Area:* 0.66 sq km
Population in 2011: 287
Provincial Electoral District(s): Rosetown-Elrose
Federal Electoral District(s): Cypress Hills-Grasslands
Next Election: Oct. 24, 2012 (4 year terms)
Kristopher Netzel, Mayor
D.B. (Blair) Cleaveley, Administrator

Lumsden
P.O. Box 160
300 James Street North
Lumsden, SK S0G 3C0
Tel: 306-731-2404; *Fax:* 306-731-3572
town.lumsden@sasktel.net
www.lumsden.ca
Municipal Type: Town
Incorporated: Dec. 29, 1898 *Area:* 3.82 sq km
Population in 2011: 1,631
Provincial Electoral District(s): Thunder Creek
Federal Electoral District(s): Regina-Lumsden-Lake Centre
Next Election: Oct. 24, 2012 (4 year terms)
Note: Proclaimed as a town on March 15, 1905.
Bryan Matheson, Mayor
Byron Turnbad, Administrator

Lumsden Beach
P.O. Box 704
Regina Beach, SK S0G 4C0
Tel: 306-222-0087
www.lumsdenbeach.com
Municipal Type: Resort Village
Incorporated: 1918 *Area:* 0.47 sq km
Population in 2011: 35
Provincial Electoral District(s): Thunder Creek
Federal Electoral District(s): Regina-Lumsden-Lake Centre
Next Election: July 2016
Ross Wilson, Mayor
ross.wilson@usask.ca
Myron Becker, Administrator
mvbecker@sasktel.net

Luseland
P.O. Box 130
Luseland, SK S0L 2A0
Tel: 306-372-4218; *Fax:* 306-347-4700
luseland@sasktel.net
www.townofluseland.com
Municipal Type: Town
Incorporated: Dec. 10, 1910 *Area:* 1.53 sq km
Population in 2011: 566
Provincial Electoral District(s): Kindersley
Federal Electoral District(s): Battlefords-Lloydminster
Next Election: Oct. 24, 2012 (4 year terms)
Note: Proclaimed as a town on Jan. 1, 1954.
Len Schlosser, Mayor
Karyl Richardson, Administrator

Macklin
P.O. Box 69
Macklin, SK S0L 2C0
Tel: 306-753-2256; *Fax:* 306-753-3234
town.macklin@sasktel.net
www.macklin.ca
Municipal Type: Town
Incorporated: Nov. 8, 1909 *Area:* 2.85 sq km
Population in 2011: 1,415
Provincial Electoral District(s): Kindersley
Federal Electoral District(s): Battlefords-Lloydminster
Next Election: Oct. 24, 2012 (4 year terms)
Note: Proclaimed as a town on Nov. 1, 1912.
Patrick Doetzel, Mayor

Kim G. Gartner, Administrator

MacNutt
P.O. Box 10
MacNutt, SK S0A 2K0
Tel: 306-742-4391; *Fax:* 306-742-4391
macnutt2013@hotmail.com; macnuttvillage@iewireless.ca
www.macnuttsaskatchewan.com
Municipal Type: Village
Incorporated: Feb. 22, 1913 *Area:* 0.81 sq km
Population in 2011: 65
Provincial Electoral District(s): Melville-Saltcoats
Federal Electoral District(s): Yorkton-Melville
Next Election: Oct. 24, 2012 (4 year terms)
Glen Cartwright, Mayor
Kendra Busch, Clerk

Macoun
P.O. Box 58
Macoun, SK S0C 1P0
Tel: 306-634-9352; *Fax:* 306-634-9377
macoun.sask@gmail.com
Municipal Type: Village
Incorporated: Oct. 16, 1903 *Area:* 1.68 sq km
Population in 2011: 246
Provincial Electoral District(s): Estevan
Federal Electoral District(s): Souris-Moose Mountain
Next Election: Oct. 24, 2012 (4 year terms)
Stuart Sovdi, Mayor
Carmen Dodd, Administrator

Macrorie
P.O. Box 37
Main St.
Macrorie, SK S0L 2E0
Tel: 306-243-2010; *Fax:* 306-243-2010
villageofmacrorie@sasktel.net
www.macrorie.com
Municipal Type: Village
Incorporated: Feb. 8, 1912 *Area:* 0.77 sq km
Population in 2011: 65
Provincial Electoral District(s): Rosetown-Elrose
Federal Electoral District(s): Cypress Hills-Grasslands
Next Election: Oct. 24, 2012 (4 year terms)
Cliff Kvale, Mayor
Ilona Naab, Clerk

Maidstone
P.O. Box 208
112 - 1st Ave. West
Maidstone, SK S0M 1M0
Tel: 306-893-2373; *Fax:* 306-893-4378
townofmaidstone@sasktel.net
www.townofmaidstone.com
Municipal Type: Town
Incorporated: July 19, 1907 *Area:* 4.56 sq km
Population in 2011: 1,156
Provincial Electoral District(s): Cut Knife-Turtleford
Federal Electoral District(s): Battlefords-Lloydminster
Next Election: Oct. 24, 2012 (4 year terms)
Note: Proclaimed as a town on March 1, 1955.
Connie McCulloch, Mayor
Harold Trew, Administrator

Major
P.O. Box 179
Major, SK S0L 2H0
Tel: 306-834-5493
www.major.ca
Municipal Type: Village
Incorporated: Sept. 29, 1914 *Area:* 2.78 sq km
Population in 2011: 61
Provincial Electoral District(s): Kindersley
Federal Electoral District(s): Battlefords-Lloydminster
Next Election: Oct. 24, 2012 (4 year terms)
Veryl Richelhoff, Mayor
Margaret Ostrowski, Clerk
ostrowski@yourlink.ca

Makwa
P.O. Box 159
Makwa, SK S0M 1N0
Tel: 306-236-3919; *Fax:* 306-236-3913
villageofmakwa@sasktel.net
Municipal Type: Village
Incorporated: June 1, 1965 *Area:* 0.66 sq km
Population in 2011: 97
Provincial Electoral District(s): Meadow Lake
Federal Electoral District(s): Desnethé-Missinippi-Churchill River
Next Election: Oct. 24, 2012 (4 year terms)
Maurice Jeannotte, Mayor
Raylene Barthel, Clerk

Manitou Beach
701 Lakeview Ave.
Manitou Beach, SK S0K 4T1
Tel: 306-946-2831; *Fax:* 306-946-2017
manbe@sasktel.net
www.manitoubeach.ca
Municipal Type: Resort Village
Incorporated: 1919 *Area:* 3.09 sq km
Population in 2011: 257
Provincial Electoral District(s): Arm River-Watrous
Federal Electoral District(s): Blackstrap
Next Election: July 2016
Eric Upshall, Mayor
Beverley Laird, Administrator

Mankota
P.O. Box 336
Mankota, SK S0H 2W0
Tel: 306-478-2331; *Fax:* 306-478-2525
village.mankota@sasktel.net
Municipal Type: Village
Incorporated: Feb. 3, 1941 *Area:* 1.55 sq km
Population in 2011: 211
Provincial Electoral District(s): Wood River
Federal Electoral District(s): Cypress Hills-Grasslands
Next Election: Oct. 24, 2012 (4 year terms)
Judy Smith, Mayor
Maggie Brown, Administrator

Manor
P.O. Box 295
45 Main St.
Manor, SK S0C 1R0
Tel: 306-448-2273; *Fax:* 306-448-2274
admin.manor@sasktel.net
Municipal Type: Village
Incorporated: April 15, 1902 *Area:* 2.79 sq km
Population in 2011: 322
Provincial Electoral District(s): Cannington
Federal Electoral District(s): Souris-Moose Mountain
Next Election: Oct. 24, 2012 (4 year terms)
Vickie Akins, Mayor
Joan Mills, Administrator

Maple Creek
P.O. Box 428
205 Jasper St.
Maple Creek, SK S0N 1N0
Tel: 306-662-2244; *Fax:* 306-662-4131
townofmaplecreek@sasktel.net
www.maplecreek.ca
Municipal Type: Town
Incorporated: April 28, 1896 *Area:* 4.42 sq km
Population in 2011: 2,176
Provincial Electoral District(s): Cypress Hills
Federal Electoral District(s): Cypress Hills-Grasslands
Next Election: Oct. 24, 2012 (4 year terms)
Note: Proclaimed as a town on April 30, 1903.
Barry Rudd, Mayor
mayor@maplecreek.ca
Mark D. Caswell, Administrator

Marcelin
P.O. Box 39
100 - 1st Ave. North
Marcelin, SK S0J 1R0
Tel: 306-226-2168; *Fax:* 306-226-2171
vmarcelin@sasktel.net
Municipal Type: Village
Incorporated: Sept. 25, 1911 *Area:* 1.32 sq km
Population in 2011: 158
Provincial Electoral District(s): Rosthern-Shellbrook
Federal Electoral District(s): Saskatoon-Wanuskewin
Next Election: Oct. 24, 2012 (4 year terms)
E.W. Dale Butler, Mayor
Leanne McCormick, Administrator

Marengo
P.O. Box 70
Marengo, SK S0L 2K0
Tel: 306-968-2922; *Fax:* 306-968-2278
rm292.rm322@sasktel.net
Municipal Type: Village
Incorporated: Nov. 5, 1910 *Area:* 0.87 sq km
Population in 2011: 47
Provincial Electoral District(s): Kindersley
Federal Electoral District(s): Battlefords-Lloydminster
Next Election: Oct. 24, 2012 (4 year terms)
Robert Lee, Mayor
Shelley Mohr, Administrator

Margo
P.O. Box 28
Margo, SK S0A 2M0
Tel: 306-324-2134; *Fax:* 306-324-4563
villagemargo@sasktel.net
Municipal Type: Village
Incorporated: April 24, 1911 *Area:* 0.80 sq km
Population in 2011: 100
Provincial Electoral District(s): Kelvington-Wadena
Federal Electoral District(s): Yorkton-Melville
Next Election: Oct. 24, 2012 (4 year terms)
George Dawe, Mayor
Gail Selch, Administrator

Markinch
P.O. Box 29
Markinch, SK S0G 3J0
Tel: 306-726-4355; *Fax:* 306-726-4355
vofmarkinch@canwan.com
Municipal Type: Village
Incorporated: Feb. 16, 1911 *Area:* 0.68 sq km
Population in 2011: 72
Provincial Electoral District(s): Last Mountain-Touchwood
Federal Electoral District(s): Regina-Qu'Appelle
Next Election: Oct. 24, 2012 (4 year terms)
Wendell Langford, Mayor
Rita T. Orb, Clerk

Marquis
P.O. Box 40
Marquis, SK S0H 2X0
Tel: 306-788-2022; *Fax:* 306-788-2168
rm191@sasktel.net
Municipal Type: Village
Incorporated: March 21, 1910 *Area:* 0.63 sq km
Population in 2011: 92
Provincial Electoral District(s): Thunder Creek
Federal Electoral District(s): Regina-Lumsden-Lake Centre
Next Election: Oct. 24, 2012 (4 year terms)
Ken Marcyniuk, Mayor
Ronald J. Gasper, Administrator

Marsden
P.O. Box 69
Marsden, SK S0M 1P0
Tel: 306-826-5215; *Fax:* 306-826-5512
rm442@sasktel.net
Municipal Type: Village
Incorporated: April 24, 1931 *Area:* 0.94 sq km
Population in 2011: 284
Provincial Electoral District(s): Cut Knife-Turtleford
Federal Electoral District(s): Battlefords-Lloydminster
Next Election: Oct. 24, 2012 (4 year terms)
Tracy Kurtz, Mayor
Joanne Loy, Administrator

Marshall
P.O. Box 125
Marshall, SK S0M 1R0
Tel: 306-387-6340; *Fax:* 306-387-6161
village.marshall@sasktel.net
Municipal Type: Town
Incorporated: Jan. 21, 1914 *Area:* 1.01 sq km
Population in 2011: 533
Provincial Electoral District(s): Lloydminster
Federal Electoral District(s): Battlefords-Lloydminster
Next Election: Oct. 24, 2012 (4 year terms)
Note: Proclaimed as a town on Oct. 26, 2006.
Lorne Kachur, Administrator

Martensville
P.O. Box 970
515 Centennial Dr. South
Martensville, SK S0K 2T0
Tel: 306-931-2166; *Fax:* 306-933-2468
manager@martensville.ca
www.martensville.ca
Municipal Type: Town
Incorporated: Sept. 1, 1966 *Area:* 4.78 sq km
Population in 2011: 7,716
Provincial Electoral District(s): Martensville
Federal Electoral District(s): Saskatoon-Wanuskewin
Next Election: Oct. 24, 2012 (4 year terms)
Note: Proclaimed as a town on Jan. 1, 1969.
Gordon Rutten, Mayor
rutten@martensville.caca
Lorraine Postma, Clerk

Maryfield
P.O. Box 58
Maryfield, SK S0G 3K0
Tel: 306-646-2143; *Fax:* 306-646-2193
vom.ward@sasktel.net
www.maryfieldsaskatchewan.com
Municipal Type: Village
Incorporated: Aug. 21, 1907 *Area:* 2.69 sq km
Population in 2011: 365
Provincial Electoral District(s): Cannington
Federal Electoral District(s): Souris-Moose Mountain
Next Election: Oct. 24, 2012 (4 year terms)
David Hill, Mayor
Ward Frazer, Administrator

Maymont
P.O. Box 160
Maymont, SK S0M 1T0
Tel: 306-389-2077; *Fax:* 306-389-2078
villageofmaymont@sasktel.net
Municipal Type: Village
Incorporated: June 24, 1907 *Area:* 0.66 sq km
Population in 2011: 146
Provincial Electoral District(s): Biggar
Federal Electoral District(s): Saskatoon-Wanuskewin
Next Election: Oct. 24, 2012 (4 year terms)
Denise Bernier, Mayor
Wendy Davis, Administrator

McLean
P.O. Box 56
McLean, SK S0G 3E0
Tel: 306-699-7279; *Fax:* 306-699-2347
villageofmclean@sasktel.net
www.mcleansask.com
Municipal Type: Village
Incorporated: Jan. 24, 1913 *Area:* 1.33 sq km
Population in 2011: 304
Provincial Electoral District(s): Indian Head-Milestone
Federal Electoral District(s): Regina-Qu'Appelle
Next Election: Oct. 24, 2012 (4 year terms)
Cliff Ebenal, Mayor
Nadine Jensen, Administrator

McTaggart
P.O. Box 134
McTaggart, SK S0G 3G0
Tel: 306-793-2023
Municipal Type: Village
Incorporated: Oct. 5, 1909 *Area:* 0.69 sq km
Population in 2011: 125
Provincial Electoral District(s): Weyburn-Big Muddy
Federal Electoral District(s): Souris-Moose Mountain
Next Election: Oct. 24, 2012 (4 year terms)
John Dyck, Mayor
Darlene Paquin, Administrator

Meacham
P.O. Box 9
Meacham, SK S0K 2V0
Tel: 306-376-2003; *Fax:* 306-376-2006
villageofmeacham@baudoux.ca
Municipal Type: Village
Incorporated: June 19, 1912 *Area:* 1.27 sq km
Population in 2011: 84
Provincial Electoral District(s): Humboldt
Federal Electoral District(s): Blackstrap
Next Election: Oct. 24, 2012 (4 year terms)
Perry Thiessen, Mayor
Juaneta Bendig, Clerk

Meadow Lake
120 - 1st St. East
Meadow Lake, SK S9X 1P8
Tel: 306-236-3622; *Fax:* 306-236-4299
cityhall@meadowlake.ca
www.meadowlake.ca
Municipal Type: Town
Incorporated: Aug. 24, 1931 *Area:* 7.95 sq km
Population in 2011: 5,045
Provincial Electoral District(s): Meadow Lake
Federal Electoral District(s): Desnethé-Missinippi-Churchill River
Next Election: Oct. 24, 2012 (4 year terms)
Note: Proclaimed as a town on Feb. 1, 1936.
Gary Vidal, Mayor
Cheryl Dodds, City Clerk

Meath Park
P.O. Box 255
Meath Park, SK S0J 1T0
Tel: 306-929-2112; *Fax:* 306-929-2281
villpark@sasktel.net
Municipal Type: Village
Incorporated: May 23, 1938 *Area:* 0.77 sq km
Population in 2011: 205
Provincial Electoral District(s): Saskatchewan Rivers
Federal Electoral District(s): Prince Albert
Next Election: Oct. 24, 2012 (4 year terms)
Warren Morley, Mayor
Elaine Esopenko, Administrator

Medstead
P.O. Box 148
Medstead, SK S0M 1W0
Tel: 306-342-4898; *Fax:* 306-342-2067
villageofmedstead@sasktel.net
Municipal Type: Village
Incorporated: April 23, 1931 *Area:* 0.67 sq km
Population in 2011: 120
Provincial Electoral District(s): Rosthern-Shellbrook
Federal Electoral District(s): Battlefords-Lloydminster
Next Election: Oct. 24, 2012 (4 year terms)
Trevor Short, Mayor
Christie Stafford, Administrator

Melfort
City Hall
P.O. Box 2230
202 Burrows Ave. West
Melfort, SK S0E 1A0
Tel: 306-752-5911; *Fax:* 306-752-5556
city@cityofmelfort.ca
www.cityofmelfort.ca
Municipal Type: Town
Incorporated: Nov. 4, 1903 *Area:* 14.78 sq km
Population in 2011: 5,576
Provincial Electoral District(s): Melfort
Federal Electoral District(s): Prince Albert
Next Election: Oct. 24, 2012 (4 year terms)
Note: Incorporated as a city on Sept. 2, 1980.
Doug Terry, Mayor
Heather Audette, Clerk
h.audette@cityofmelfort.ca

Melville
P.O. Box 1240
430 Main St.
Melville, SK S0A 2P0
Tel: 306-728-6840; *Fax:* 306-728-5911
cityhall@melville.ca
www.city.melville.sk.ca
Municipal Type: Town
Incorporated: Dec. 21, 1908 *Area:* 14.82 sq km
Population in 2011: 4,517
Provincial Electoral District(s): Melville-Saltcoats
Federal Electoral District(s): Yorkton-Melville
Next Election: Oct. 24, 2012 (4 year terms)
Note: Incorporated as a city on Aug. 1, 1960.
Walter Streelasky, Mayor
Michael Hotsko, City Manager
mhotsko@melville.ca

Melville Beach
P.O. Box 3250
Melville, SK S0A 2P0
Tel: 306-728-7697; *Fax:* 306-728-3180
rvmelvillebeach@gmail.com
Municipal Type: Resort Village
Area: 48.0 sq km
Population in 2011: 10
Provincial Electoral District(s): Melville-Saltcoats
Federal Electoral District(s): Yorkton-Melville
Next Election: July 2016
David Boulding, Mayor
Diane Smith, Administrator

Mendham
P.O. Box 69
Mendham, SK S0N 1P0
Tel: 306-679-2000; *Fax:* 306-679-2275
Municipal Type: Village
Incorporated: April 1, 1930 *Area:* 0.5 sq km
Population in 2011: 35
Provincial Electoral District(s): Cypress Hills
Federal Electoral District(s): Cypress Hills-Grasslands
Next Election: Oct. 24, 2012 (4 year terms)
Kevin Angerman, Mayor
Lucein Stuebing, Clerk

Meota
P.O. Box 123
Meota, SK S0M 1X0
Tel: 306-892-2277; *Fax:* 306-892-2275
vmeota@sasktel.net
Municipal Type: Village
Incorporated: July 6, 1911 *Area:* 1.55 sq km
Population in 2011: 307
Provincial Electoral District(s): Cut Knife-Turtleford
Federal Electoral District(s): Battlefords-Lloydminster
Next Election: Oct. 24, 2012 (4 year terms)
John MacDonald, Mayor
Jacquie Code, Clerk

Mervin
P.O. Box 35
Mervin, SK S0M 1Y0
Tel: 306-845-2784; *Fax:* 306-845-3563
villageofmervin@littleloon.ca
Municipal Type: Village
Incorporated: March 17, 1920 *Area:* 0.73 sq km
Population in 2011: 160
Provincial Electoral District(s): Cut Knife-Turtleford
Federal Electoral District(s): Battlefords-Lloydminster
Next Election: Oct. 24, 2012 (4 year terms)
Kenneth Knowlton, Mayor
Lora Hundt, Administrator

Metinota
P.O. Box 47
Meota, SK S0M 1X0
Tel: 306-892-2557; *Fax:* 306-892-2250
rvmetinota@sasktel.net
Municipal Type: Resort Village
Area: 170.0 sq km
Population in 2011: 89
Provincial Electoral District(s): Cut Knife-Turtleford
Federal Electoral District(s): Battlefords-Lloydminster
Next Election: July 2016
Glen Wouters, Mayor
Carmen Menssa, Administrator

Michel Village
Sylvestre Place
P.O. Box 250
Dillon, SK S0M 0S0
Tel: 306-282-4401; *Fax:* 306-282-2155
Municipal Type: Northern Hamlet
Incorporated: Nov. 1, 1983 *Area:* 3.73 sq km
Population in 2011: 66
Provincial Electoral District(s): Athabasca
Federal Electoral District(s): Desnethé-Missinippi-Churchill River
Next Election: Autumn 2012 (4 year terms)
Cliff Coombs, Mayor
Allison Janvier, Clerk

Midale
P.O. Box 128
233 Main St.
Midale, SK S0C 1S0
Tel: 306-458-2400; *Fax:* 306-458-2209
lindugan@sasktel.net
www.townofmidale.com
Municipal Type: Town
Incorporated: Aug. 10, 1907 *Area:* 1.53 sq km
Population in 2011: 562
Provincial Electoral District(s): Estevan
Federal Electoral District(s): Souris-Moose Mountain
Next Election: Oct. 24, 2012 (4 year terms)
Note: Proclaimed as a town on March 1, 1962.
Allan Hauglum, Mayor
Linda M. Dugan, Administrator

Middle Lake
P.O. Box 119
Middle Lake, SK S0K 2X0
Tel: 306-367-2149; *Fax:* 306-367-4963
middlelake@sasktel.net
Municipal Type: Village
Incorporated: Jan. 1, 1963 *Area:* 1.26 sq km
Population in 2011: 242
Provincial Electoral District(s): Batoche
Federal Electoral District(s): Saskatoon-Humboldt
Next Election: Oct. 24, 2012 (4 year terms)
Ken Herman, Mayor
Colette Hauser, Clerk

Milden
P.O. Box 70
202 Centre St.
Milden, SK S0L 2L0
Tel: 306-935-2131; *Fax:* 306-935-2020
vmilden@sasktel.net
www.villageofmilden.com
Municipal Type: Village
Incorporated: July 20, 1911 *Area:* 1.18 sq km
Population in 2011: 181

Provincial Electoral District(s): Rosetown-Elrose
Federal Electoral District(s): Cypress Hills-Grasslands
Next Election: Oct. 24, 2012 (4 year terms)
Lester Wall, Mayor
Heather Maxemniuk, Clerk

Milestone
P.O. Box 74
105 Main St.
Milestone, SK S0G 3L0
Tel: 306-436-2130; *Fax:* 306-436-2051
milcal@sasktel.net
www.milestonesk.ca
Municipal Type: Town
Incorporated: March 14, 1903 *Area:* 2.17 sq km
Population in 2011: 618
Provincial Electoral District(s): Indian Head-Milestone
Federal Electoral District(s): Souris-Moose Mountain
Next Election: Oct. 24, 2012 (4 year terms)
Note: Proclaimed as a town on Aug. 15, 1906.
Jeff Brown, Mayor
Stephen Schury, Administrator

Minton
P.O. Box 52
Minton, SK S0C 1T0
Tel: 306-969-2144; *Fax:* 306-969-2127
rmnine@sasktel.net
Municipal Type: Village
Incorporated: Jan. 1, 1951 *Area:* 0.3 sq km
Population in 2011: 60
Provincial Electoral District(s): Weyburn-Big Muddy
Federal Electoral District(s): Souris-Moose Mountain
Next Election: Oct. 24, 2012 (4 year terms)
Dennis Simpart, Mayor
Joyce Axten, Clerk

Missinipe
c/o Ministry of Municipal Affairs
P.O. Box 5000
La Ronge, SK S0J 1L0
Tel: 306-425-4323; *Fax:* 306-425-2401
Municipal Type: Northern Hamlet
Incorporated: Feb. 1, 1984 *Area:* 1.87 sq km
Population in 2011: 39
Provincial Electoral District(s): Cumberland
Federal Electoral District(s): Desnethé-Missinippe-Churchill River
Next Election: Autumn 2012 (4 year terms)
Zack Adams, Chairman
Bruce Leier, Advisor

Mistatim
P.O. Box 145
Mistatim, SK S0E 1B0
Tel: 306-889-2008; *Fax:* 306-889-4439
villageofmistatim@yourlink.ca
www.newsaskcfdc.ca/mistatim.htm
Municipal Type: Village
Incorporated: July 1, 1952 *Area:* 0.47 sq km
Population in 2011: 73
Provincial Electoral District(s): Carrot River Valley
Federal Electoral District(s): Yorkton-Melville
Next Election: Oct. 24, 2012 (4 year terms)
Gene Legare, Mayor
Ingrid Conway, Administrator

Mistusinne
P.O. Box 160
Elbow, SK S0H 1J0
Tel: 306-854-4637; *Fax:* 306-854-4668
mistusinne@sasktel.net
www.mistusinne.com
Municipal Type: Resort Village
Area: 1.49 sq km
Population in 2011: 66
Provincial Electoral District(s): Thunder Creek
Federal Electoral District(s): Cypress Hills-Grasslands
Next Election: July 2016
Lynne Saas, Mayor
Yvonne Jess, Administrator
Janice Scrimbitt, Clerk

Montmartre
P.O. Box 146
Montmartre, SK S0G 3M0
Tel: 306-424-2040; *Fax:* 306-424-2065
rm126@sasktel.net
www.montmartre-sk.com
Municipal Type: Village
Incorporated: Oct. 19, 1908 *Area:* 1.63 sq km
Population in 2011: 476

Provincial Electoral District(s): Moosomin
Federal Electoral District(s): Wascana
Next Election: Oct. 24, 2012 (4 year terms)
Robert Chittenden, Mayor
Dale Brenner, Administrator

Moosomin
P.O. Box 730
701 Main St.
Moosomin, SK S0G 3N0
Tel: 306-435-2988; *Fax:* 306-435-3343
twn.moosomin@sasktel.net
www.moosomin.com
Municipal Type: Town
Incorporated: March 20, 1889 *Area:* 5.97 sq km
Population in 2011: 2,485
Provincial Electoral District(s): Moosomin
Federal Electoral District(s): Souris-Moose Mountain
Next Election: Oct. 24, 2012 (4 year terms)
Don Bradley, Mayor
Paul Listrom, Administrator

Morse
P.O. Box 270
Morse, SK S0H 3C0
Tel: 306-629-3300; *Fax:* 306-629-3235
morse@sasktel.net
morsesask.com
Municipal Type: Town
Incorporated: March 11, 1910 *Area:* 1.45 sq km
Population in 2011: 240
Provincial Electoral District(s): Thunder Creek
Federal Electoral District(s): Cypress Hills-Grasslands
Next Election: Oct. 24, 2012 (4 year terms)
Note: Proclaimed as a town on Nov. 1, 1912.
Louis Fafard, Mayor
Gloria Weppler, Administrator

Mortlach
P.O. Box 10
Mortlach, SK S0H 3E0
Tel: 306-355-2554; *Fax:* 306-355-2557
village.mortlach@sasktel.net
www.mortlach.ca
Municipal Type: Village
Incorporated: April 19, 1906 *Area:* 2.76 sq km
Population in 2011: 289
Provincial Electoral District(s): Thunder Creek
Federal Electoral District(s): Cypress Hills-Grasslands
Next Election: Oct. 24, 2012 (4 year terms)
Gerald Forbes, Mayor
Tracey Gardner, Administrator

Mossbank
P.O. Box 370
Mossbank, SK S0H 3G0
Tel: 306-354-2294; *Fax:* 306-354-7725
townofmossbank@sasktel.net
www.mossbank.ca
Municipal Type: Town
Incorporated: Dec. 14, 1915 *Area:* 1.75 sq km
Population in 2011: 327
Provincial Electoral District(s): Wood River
Federal Electoral District(s): Palliser
Next Election: Oct. 24, 2012 (4 year terms)
Note: Proclaimed as a town on May 15, 1959.
Carl Weiss, Mayor
Cindy Kimball, Administrator

Muenster
P.O. Box 98
Muenster, SK S0K 2Y0
Tel: 306-682-2794; *Fax:* 306-682-4179
muenster@sasktel.net
Municipal Type: Village
Incorporated: Aug. 18, 1908 *Area:* 1.24 sq km
Population in 2011: 422
Provincial Electoral District(s): Humboldt
Federal Electoral District(s): Saskatoon-Humboldt
Next Election: Oct. 24, 2012 (4 year terms)
Benno Korte, Mayor
Rose M. Haeusler, Administrator

Naicam
P.O. Box 238
Naicam, SK S0K 2Z0
Tel: 306-874-2280; *Fax:* 306-874-5444
naicam.ced@sasktel.net
www.townofnaicam.ca
Municipal Type: Town
Incorporated: April 28, 1921 *Area:* 1.69 sq km
Population in 2011: 686

Provincial Electoral District(s): Melfort
Federal Electoral District(s): Saskatoon-Humboldt
Next Election: Oct. 24, 2012 (4 year terms)
Note: Proclaimed as a town on Sept. 1, 1954.
Rodger Hayward, Mayor
Lowell Prefontaine, Administrator

Neilburg
P.O. Box 280
39 Centre St.
Neilburg, SK S0M 2C0
Tel: 306-823-4321; *Fax:* 306-823-4477
neilburg@sasktel.net
Municipal Type: Village
Incorporated: Jan. 1, 1947 *Area:* 1.16 sq km
Population in 2011: 448
Provincial Electoral District(s): Cut Knife-Turtleford
Federal Electoral District(s): Battlefords-Lloydminster
Next Election: Oct. 24, 2012 (4 year terms)
Ernest Ducherer, Mayor
Janet L. Black, Administrator

Netherhill
P.O. Box 4
Netherhill, SK S0L 2M0
Tel: 306-379-2116
brockadmin@sasktel.net
Municipal Type: Village
Incorporated: April 28, 1910 *Area:* 0.73 sq km
Population in 2011: 25
Provincial Electoral District(s): Rosetown-Elrose
Federal Electoral District(s): Battlefords-Lloydminster
Next Election: Oct. 24, 2012 (4 year terms)
Winston Jones, Mayor
Shannon Beheil, Clerk

Neudorf
P.O. Box 187
Neudorf, SK S0A 2T0
Tel: 306-748-2551; *Fax:* 306-748-2647
vneudorf@sasktel.net
www.village.neudorf.sk.ca
Municipal Type: Village
Incorporated: April 25, 1905 *Area:* 2.05 sq km
Population in 2011: 272
Provincial Electoral District(s): Last Mountain-Touchwood
Federal Electoral District(s): Yorkton-Melville
Next Election: Oct. 24, 2012 (4 year terms)
Murray J. Hanowski, Mayor
Crystal Campbell, Administrator

Neville
P.O. Box 88
Neville, SK S0N 1T0
Tel: 306-627-3255; *Fax:* 306-627-3546
village.neville@sasktel.net
Municipal Type: Village
Incorporated: July 5, 1912 *Area:* 1.10 sq km
Population in 2011: 83
Provincial Electoral District(s): Wood River
Federal Electoral District(s): Cypress Hills-Grasslands
Next Election: Oct. 24, 2012 (4 year terms)
Harvey Linnen, Mayor
Linda Hornung, Clerk

Nipawin
P.O. Box 2134
210 Second Ave. East
Nipawin, SK S0E 1E0
Tel: 306-862-9866; *Fax:* 306-862-3076
townoffice@nipawin.com; info@nipawin.com
www.nipawin.com
Other Information: Toll Free Phone: 306-877-647-2946
Municipal Type: Town
Incorporated: May 7, 1925 *Area:* 8.03 sq km
Population in 2011: 4,265
Provincial Electoral District(s): Carrot River Valley
Federal Electoral District(s): Prince Albert
Next Election: Oct. 24, 2012 (4 year terms)
Note: Proclaimed as a town on May 1, 1937.
Lawrence Rospad, Mayor
Roy Tutschek, Administrator

Nokomis
P.O. Box 189
101 - 3rd Ave. West
Nokomis, SK S0G 3R0
Tel: 306-528-2010
townofnokomis@sasktel.net
nokomisweb.com
Municipal Type: Town
Incorporated: March 5, 1908 *Area:* 2.61 sq km

Population in 2011: 397
Provincial Electoral District(s): Arm River-Watrous
Federal Electoral District(s): Regina-Lumsden-Lake Centre
Next Election: Oct. 24, 2012 (4 year terms)
Note: Proclaimed as a town on Aug. 15, 1908.
Fredard Wright, Mayor
Joanne Hamilton, Administrator

Norquay
P.O. Box 327
25 Main St.
Norquay, SK S0A 2V0
Tel: 306-594-2101; *Fax:* 306-594-2347
norquay@sasktel.net
www.townofnorquay.ca
Municipal Type: Town
Incorporated: June 4, 1913 *Area:* 1.69 sq km
Population in 2011: 435
Provincial Electoral District(s): Canora-Pelly
Federal Electoral District(s): Yorkton-Melville
Next Election: Oct. 24, 2012 (4 year terms)
Note: Proclaimed as a town on March 1, 1963.
Don Tower, Mayor
Rona Seidle, Administrator

North Grove
P.O. Box 473
Moose Jaw, SK S6H 4P1
Tel: 306-694-8300; *Fax:* 306-395-2767
rvnorthgrove@shaw.ca
northgrovesk.wordpress.com
Municipal Type: Resort Village
Area: 1.03 sq km
Population in 2011: 49
Provincial Electoral District(s): Thunder Creek
Federal Electoral District(s): Regina-Lumsden-Lake Centre
Next Election: July 2016
Ron Dufresne, Mayor
Tracy Edwards, Administrator

North Portal
P.O. Box 119
North Portal, SK S0C 1W0
Tel: 306-927-5050; *Fax:* 306-927-2033
villagen@sasktel.net
Municipal Type: Village
Incorporated: Nov. 16, 1903 *Area:* 2.49 sq km
Population in 2011: 143
Provincial Electoral District(s): Estevan
Federal Electoral District(s): Souris-Moose Mountain
Next Election: Oct. 24, 2012 (4 year terms)
Murray Arnold, Mayor
Lindsay Davis, Clerk

Odessa
P.O. Box 91
Odessa, SK S0G 3S0
Tel: 306-957-2020; *Fax:* 306-957-4502
villageofodessa@sasktel.net
www.odessask.com
Municipal Type: Village
Incorporated: March 14, 1911 *Area:* 1.18 sq km
Population in 2011: 239
Provincial Electoral District(s): Indian Head-Milestone
Federal Electoral District(s): Wascana
Next Election: Oct. 24, 2012 (4 year terms)
Philip Selinger, Mayor
Sheila Leurer, Clerk

Ogema
P.O. Box 159
Ogema, SK S0C 1Y0
Tel: 306-459-2262; *Fax:* 306-459-2762
townofogema@sasktel.net
www.ogema.ca
Municipal Type: Town
Incorporated: Jan. 18, 1911 *Area:* 1.43 sq km
Population in 2011: 368
Provincial Electoral District(s): Weyburn-Big Muddy
Federal Electoral District(s): Souris-Moose Mountain
Next Election: Oct. 24, 2012 (4 year terms)
Note: Proclaimed as a town on Jan. 7, 1913.
Wayne Myren, Mayor
Peggy Tuchscherer, Administrator

Osage
P.O. Box 96
Osage, SK S0G 3T0
Tel: 306-722-3747
garry.lindakreutzer@sasktel.net
Municipal Type: Village
Incorporated: May 8, 1906 *Area:* 0.59 sq km
Population in 2011: 20
Provincial Electoral District(s): Indian Head-Milestone
Federal Electoral District(s): Souris-Moose Mountain
Next Election: Oct. 24, 2012 (4 year terms)
Garry Kreutzer, Mayor
Linda R. Kreutzer, Clerk

Osler
P.O. Box 190
228 Willow Dr.
Osler, SK S0K 3A0
Tel: 306-239-2155; *Fax:* 306-239-2194
info@townofosler.com
www.osler-sk.ca
Municipal Type: Town
Incorporated: April 9, 1904 *Area:* 0.98 sq km
Population in 2011: 1,088
Provincial Electoral District(s): Martensville
Federal Electoral District(s): Saskatoon-Wanuskewin
Next Election: Oct. 24, 2012 (4 year terms)
Note: Proclaimed as a town on Nov. 1, 1985.
Ben Buhler, Mayor
Sandra MacArthur, Chief Administrative Officer

Outlook
P.O. Box 518
Outlook, SK S0L 2N0
Tel: 306-867-8663; *Fax:* 306-867-9898
town@town.outlook.sk.ca
www.town.outlook.sk.ca
Municipal Type: Town
Incorporated: Dec. 19, 1908 *Area:* 7.83 sq km
Population in 2011: 2,204
Provincial Electoral District(s): Rosetown-Elrose
Federal Electoral District(s): Blackstrap; Cypress Hills-Grasslands
Next Election: Oct. 24, 2012 (4 year terms)
Note: Proclaimed as a town on Nov. 1, 1909.
Bob Stephenson, Mayor
Trent Michelman, Municipal Manager
michelman@town.outlook.sk.ca

Oxbow
P.O. Box 149
307 Main St.
Oxbow, SK S0C 2B0
Tel: 306-483-2300; *Fax:* 306-483-5277
oxbowtown@sasktel.net
www.oxbow.ca
Municipal Type: Town
Incorporated: March 7, 1899 *Area:* 3.1 sq km
Population in 2011: 1,285
Provincial Electoral District(s): Cannington
Federal Electoral District(s): Souris-Moose Mountain
Next Election: Oct. 24, 2012 (4 year terms)
Note: Proclaimed as a town on May 30, 1904.
Doug Pierce, Mayor
Brad Vanbeselaere, Administrator

Paddockwood
P.O. Box 188
Paddockwood, SK S0J 1Z0
Tel: 306-989-2033; *Fax:* 306-989-2033
vpaddockwood@inet2000.com
Municipal Type: Village
Incorporated: Jan. 1, 1949 *Area:* 0.65 sq km
Population in 2011: 163
Provincial Electoral District(s): Saskatchewan Rivers
Federal Electoral District(s): Prince Albert
Next Election: Oct. 24, 2012 (4 year terms)
Reg Hintz, Mayor
Diana Siurko, Clerk

Pangman
P.O. Box 189
Pangman, SK S0C 2C0
Tel: 306-442-2131; *Fax:* 306-442-2144
rm.69@sasktel.net
www.pangman.ca
Municipal Type: Village
Incorporated: May 17, 1911 *Area:* 0.73 sq km
Population in 2011: 214
Provincial Electoral District(s): Weyburn-Big Muddy
Federal Electoral District(s): Souris-Moose Mountain
Next Election: Oct. 24, 2012 (4 year terms)
Cory Henheffer, Mayor
Wayne W. Lozinsky, Administrator

Paradise Hill
P.O. Box 270
Paradise Hill, SK S0M 2G0
Tel: 306-344-2206; *Fax:* 306-344-4941
paradisehill@sasktel.net
www.paradisehill.ca
Municipal Type: Village
Incorporated: Jan. 1, 1947 *Area:* 1.99 sq km
Population in 2011: 515
Provincial Electoral District(s): Lloydminster
Federal Electoral District(s): Battlefords-Lloydminster
Next Election: Oct. 24, 2012 (4 year terms)
Larry Harland, Mayor
Marion Hougham, Clerk

Parkside
P.O. Box 48
Parkside, SK S0J 2A0
Tel: 306-747-2235; *Fax:* 306-747-3395
villageofparkside@yourlink.ca
Municipal Type: Village
Incorporated: Feb. 21, 1913 *Area:* 0.92 sq km
Population in 2011: 125
Provincial Electoral District(s): Rosthern-Shellbrook
Federal Electoral District(s): Saskatoon-Wanuskewin
Next Election: Oct. 24, 2012 (4 year terms)
David K. Moe, Mayor
Gwen Olson, Clerk

Patuanak
P.O. Box 180
Shagwenaw Dr.
Patuanak, SK S0M 2H0
Tel: 306-396-2020; *Fax:* 306-396-2092
hamofpat@sasktel.net
Municipal Type: Northern Hamlet
Incorporated: Dec. 1, 1983 *Area:* 1.34 sq km
Population in 2011: 64
Provincial Electoral District(s): Athabasca
Federal Electoral District(s): Desnethé-Missinippi-Churchill River
Next Election: Autumn 2012 (4 year terms)
Hazel Maurice, Mayor
Miranda Wolverine, Clerk

Paynton
P.O. Box 100
Paynton, SK S0M 2J0
Tel: 306-895-2023; *Fax:* 306-895-2053
village470@sasktel.net
Municipal Type: Village
Incorporated: May 2, 1907 *Area:* 0.85 sq km
Population in 2011: 151
Provincial Electoral District(s): Cut Knife-Turtleford
Federal Electoral District(s): Battlefords-Lloydminster
Next Election: Oct. 24, 2012 (4 year terms)
David Florizone, Mayor
Joan Caldwell, Administrator

Pebble Baye
P.O. Box 428
Spiritwood, SK S0J 2M0
Tel: 306-883-2977; *Fax:* 306-883-3834
www.pebblebaye.com
Municipal Type: Resort Village
Incorporated: 1983 *Area:* 0.74 sq km
Population in 2011: 33
Provincial Electoral District(s): Rosthern-Shellbrook
Federal Electoral District(s): Saskatoon-Wanuskewin
Next Election: July 2016
Steven Ward, Mayor
steveward@shaw.ca
Shirley Dauvin, Administrator
pdauvin@xplornet.com

Pelican Narrows
P.O. Box 10
Bear St.
Pelican Narrows, SK S0P 0E0
Tel: 306-632-2225; *Fax:* 306-632-2006
Municipal Type: Northern Village
Incorporated: Jan. 1, 1989 *Area:* 3.70 sq km
Population in 2011: 790
Provincial Electoral District(s): Cumberland
Federal Electoral District(s): Desnethé-Missinippi-Churchill River
Next Election: Autumn 2012 (4 year terms)
Horace Morin, Mayor
Doreen Linklater, Clerk

Pelican Pointe
P.O. Box 187
Silton, SK S0G 4L0
Tel: 306-789-9684; *Fax:* 306-761-0320
pelicanpointe-rv.sk.ca
Municipal Type: Resort Village
Area: 0.12 sq km
Population in 2011: 15
Provincial Electoral District(s): Last Mountain-Touchwood
Federal Electoral District(s): Regina-Lumsden-Lake Centre
Next Election: July 2016
Wendy Thorne, Mayor
Lynda Stack, Clerk
lstack@sasktel.net

Pelly
P.O. Box 220
Pelly, SK S0A 2Z0
Tel: 306-595-2124; *Fax:* 306-595-2050
town.pelly@sasktel.net
www.pelly.ca
Municipal Type: Village
Incorporated: May 4, 1911 *Area:* 0.96 sq km
Population in 2011: 283
Provincial Electoral District(s): Canora-Pelly
Federal Electoral District(s): Yorkton-Melville
Next Election: Oct. 24, 2012 (4 year terms)
Sharon Nelson, Mayor
Sheri Kosar, Administrator

Pennant
P.O. Box 57
Pennant, SK S0N 1X0
Tel: 306-626-3255; *Fax:* 306-626-3661
villageofpennant@sasktel.net; rm168@sasktel.net
www.villageofpennant.com
Municipal Type: Village
Incorporated: July 29, 1912 *Area:* 0.65 sq km
Population in 2011: 120
Provincial Electoral District(s): Swift Current
Federal Electoral District(s): Cypress Hills-Grasslands
Next Election: Oct. 24, 2012 (4 year terms)
Leslie Bayliss, Mayor
Brandi Prentice, Administrator

Pense
P.O. Box 125
243 Brunswick St.
Pense, SK S0G 3W0
Tel: 306-345-2332; *Fax:* 306-345-2340
pensevillage@sasktel.net
www.pense.ca
Municipal Type: Village
Incorporated: March 7, 1904 *Area:* 1.32 sq km
Population in 2011: 532
Provincial Electoral District(s): Thunder Creek
Federal Electoral District(s): Palliser
Next Election: Oct. 24, 2012 (4 year terms)
Michele LeBlanc, Mayor
mayor@pense.ca
Jennifer Lendvay, Administrator
jlendvay@pense.ca

Perdue
P.O. Box 190
Perdue, SK S0K 3C0
Tel: 306-237-4337; *Fax:* 306-237-4874
www.villageofperdue.com
Municipal Type: Village
Incorporated: July 15, 1909 *Area:* 1.10 sq km
Population in 2011: 362
Provincial Electoral District(s): Biggar
Federal Electoral District(s): Saskatoon-Rosetown-Biggar
Next Election: Oct. 24, 2012 (4 year terms)
Dave Miller, Mayor
Nancy Duns, Administrator

Pierceland
P.O. Box 39
177 Main St.
Pierceland, SK S0M 2K0
Tel: 306-839-2015; *Fax:* 306-839-2057
plandvillage@sasktel.net
Municipal Type: Village
Incorporated: Jan. 1, 1973 *Area:* 2.69 sq km
Population in 2011: 551
Provincial Electoral District(s): Lloydminster
Federal Electoral District(s): Desnethé-Missinippi-Churchill River
Next Election: Oct. 24, 2012 (4 year terms)
Jim Krushelnitzky, Mayor
Jane Eistetter, Clerk

Pilger
P.O. Box 24
Pilger, SK S0K 3G0
Tel: 306-367-4631; *Fax:* 306-367-4621
Municipal Type: Village
Incorporated: Jan. 1, 1969 *Area:* 0.52 sq km
Population in 2011: 65
Provincial Electoral District(s): Batoche
Federal Electoral District(s): Saskatoon-Humboldt
Next Election: Oct. 24, 2012 (4 year terms)
Joyce Bauer, Mayor
Gloria Struck, Clerk

Pilot Butte
P.O. Box 253
Pilot Butte, SK S0G 3Z0
Tel: 306-781-4547
townofpilotbutte@sasktel.net
www.pilotbutte.ca
Municipal Type: Town
Incorporated: Nov. 8, 1913 *Area:* 4.69 sq km
Population in 2011: 1,848
Provincial Electoral District(s): Regina Wascana Plains
Federal Electoral District(s): Regina-Qu'Appelle
Next Election: Oct. 24, 2012 (4 year terms)
Note: Proclaimed as a town on Nov. 1, 1980.
Sid Bowles, Mayor
Laurie Rudolph, Administrator

Pinehouse
P.O. Box 298
Pinehouse Ave.
Pinehouse, SK S0J 2B0
Tel: 306-884-2030; *Fax:* 306-884-2021
nvp@sasktel.net
career.kcdc.ca/comm/Pinehouse.php
Municipal Type: Northern Village
Incorporated: Oct. 1, 1983 *Area:* 6.84 sq km
Population in 2011: 978
Provincial Electoral District(s): Athabasca
Federal Electoral District(s): Desnethé-Missinippi-Churchill River
Next Election: Autumn 2012 (4 year terms)
Mike Natomagan, Mayor
Martine Smith, Clerk

Pleasantdale
P.O. Box 147
Pleasantdale, SK S0K 3H0
Tel: 306-874-5743; *Fax:* 306-874-5743
villageofpleasantdale@gmail.com
www.newsaskcfdc.ca/pleasantdale.htm
Municipal Type: Village
Incorporated: Jan. 1, 1987 *Area:* 0.56 sq km
Population in 2011: 76
Provincial Electoral District(s): Melfort
Federal Electoral District(s): Saskatoon-Humboldt
Next Election: Oct. 24, 2012 (4 year terms)
Kenneth Myhre, Mayor
Kimberley Laking, Clerk

Plenty
P.O. Box 177
Plenty, SK S0L 2R0
Tel: 306-932-2045; *Fax:* 306-932-2044
vop@sasktel.net
Municipal Type: Village
Incorporated: March 25, 1911 *Area:* 0.65 sq km
Population in 2011: 131
Provincial Electoral District(s): Rosetown-Elrose
Federal Electoral District(s): Battlefords-Lloydminster
Next Election: Oct. 24, 2012 (4 year terms)
Corey Kingwell, Mayor
Donna Lynn de Bussac, Administrator

Plunkett
P.O. Box 149
Plunkett, SK S0K 3J0
Tel: 306-944-4514; *Fax:* 306-944-4512
Municipal Type: Village
Incorporated: Dec. 28, 1921 *Area:* 0.64 sq km
Population in 2011: 75
Provincial Electoral District(s): Humboldt
Federal Electoral District(s): Blackstrap
Next Election: Oct. 24, 2012 (4 year terms)
Richard Hayes, Mayor
Helen Miller, Clerk
dhmiller@sasktel.net

Ponteix
P.O. Box 330
213 Centre St.
Ponteix, SK S0N 1Z0
Tel: 306-625-3222; *Fax:* 306-625-3204
town.ponteix@sasktel.net
www.townofponteix.com
Municipal Type: Town
Incorporated: June 24, 1914 *Area:* 1.09 sq km
Population in 2011: 605
Provincial Electoral District(s): Wood River
Federal Electoral District(s): Cypress Hills-Grasslands
Next Election: Oct. 24, 2012 (4 year terms)
Note: Proclaimed as a town on April 1, 1957.
Etiennette Binette, Mayor
Lynne Lemieux, Administrator
admin@townofponteix.com

Porcupine Plain
P.O. Box 310
151 McAllister Ave.
Porcupine Plain, SK S0E 1H0
Tel: 306-278-2262; *Fax:* 306-278-3378
porcupineplain@sasktel.net
www.porcupineplain.com
Municipal Type: Town
Incorporated: April 9, 1942 *Area:* 2.27 sq km
Population in 2011: 855
Provincial Electoral District(s): Kelvington-Wadena
Federal Electoral District(s): Yorkton-Melville
Next Election: Oct. 24, 2012 (4 year terms)
Note: Proclaimed as a town on Jan. 1, 1968.
Terry Zip, Mayor
Lousie Baht, Administrator

Preeceville
P.O. Box 560
239 Highway Ave. East
Preeceville, SK S0A 3B0
Tel: 306-547-2810; *Fax:* 306-547-3116
preeceville@sasktel.net
www.townofpreeceville.ca
Other Information: Toll Free Phone: 1-877-706-3196
Municipal Type: Town
Incorporated: Feb. 6, 1912 *Area:* 2.79 sq km
Population in 2011: 1,070
Provincial Electoral District(s): Canora-Pelly
Federal Electoral District(s): Yorkton-Melville
Next Election: Oct. 24, 2012 (4 year terms)
Note: Incorporated as a town on Nov. 30, 1946.
Garth Harris, Mayor
Lorelei Karcha, Administrator

Prelate
P.O. Box 40
Prelate, SK S0N 2B0
Tel: 306-673-2340; *Fax:* 306-673-2340
prelate@chinook.lib.sk.ca
Municipal Type: Village
Incorporated: Oct. 25, 1913 *Area:* 0.87 sq km
Population in 2011: 124
Provincial Electoral District(s): Cypress Hills
Federal Electoral District(s): Cypress Hills-Grasslands
Next Election: Oct. 24, 2012 (4 year terms)
Darrah Duchscherer, Mayor
Darlene Wagner, Clerk

Primate
P.O. Box 6
Primate, SK S0L 2S0
Tel: 306-753-3232; *Fax:* 306-753-2971
tjcl@lincsat.com
Municipal Type: Village
Incorporated: April 5, 1922 *Area:* 0.94 sq km
Population in 2011: 45
Provincial Electoral District(s): Kindersley
Federal Electoral District(s): Battlefords-Lloydminster
Next Election: Oct. 24, 2012 (4 year terms)
Daniel Allen, Mayor
Dianne Latendresse, Clerk

Prud'homme
P.O. Box 38
Prud'Homme, SK S0K 3K0
Tel: 306-654-2001; *Fax:* 306-654-2001
voprud@sasktel.net
www.prudhommevillage.com
Municipal Type: Village
Incorporated: Nov. 15, 1922 *Area:* 0.84 sq km
Population in 2011: 172
Provincial Electoral District(s): Humboldt

Federal Electoral District(s): Saskatoon-Humboldt
Next Election: Oct. 24, 2012 (4 year terms)
Preston Tkatch, Mayor
Holly Maas, Administrator

Punnichy
P.O. Box 250
Punnichy, SK S0A 3C0
Tel: 306-835-2135; *Fax:* 306-835-2401
punnichy@aski.ca
Municipal Type: Village
Incorporated: Oct. 22, 1909 *Area:* 0.68 sq km
Population in 2011: 246
Provincial Electoral District(s): Last Mountain-Touchwood
Federal Electoral District(s): Regina-Qu'Appelle
Next Election: Oct. 24, 2012 (4 year terms)
Lawrence Beyer, Mayor
Donna Colley, Administrator

Qu'Appelle
P.O. Box 60
Qu'Appelle, SK S0G 4A0
Tel: 306-699-2279; *Fax:* 306-699-2306
townquappelle@sasktel.net
www.townofquappelle.ca
Municipal Type: Town
Incorporated: Feb. 20, 1904 *Area:* 4.22 sq km
Population in 2011: 668
Provincial Electoral District(s): Indian Head-Milestone
Federal Electoral District(s): Regina-Qu'Appelle
Next Election: Oct. 24, 2012 (4 year terms)
Tom Williams, Mayor
Carol Wickenheiser, Administrator

Quill Lake
P.O. Box 9
60 Main St.
Quill Lake, SK S0A 3E0
Tel: 306-383-2592; *Fax:* 306-383-2255
quilllake@sasktel.net
www.quill-lakes.com/quilllake/village
Municipal Type: Village
Incorporated: Dec. 8, 1906 *Area:* 1.30 sq km
Population in 2011: 409
Provincial Electoral District(s): Melfort
Federal Electoral District(s): Saskatoon-Humboldt
Next Election: Oct. 24, 2012 (4 year terms)
Lyle Thibault, Mayor
Judy L. Kanak, Administrator

Quinton
P.O. Box 128
Quinton, SK S0A 3G0
Tel: 306-835-2515; *Fax:* 306-835-2515
quintonvillage@aski.ca
Municipal Type: Village
Incorporated: March 1, 1910 *Area:* 0.96 sq km
Population in 2011: 111
Provincial Electoral District(s): Arm River-Watrous
Federal Electoral District(s): Regina-Qu'Appelle
Next Election: Oct. 24, 2012 (4 year terms)
Ralph Brockman, Mayor
Lorelei Paulsen, Administrator

Rabbit Lake
P.O. Box 9
Rabbit Lake, SK S0M 2L0
Tel: 306-824-2125; *Fax:* 306-824-2150
rabbitlake@yourlink.ca
Municipal Type: Village
Incorporated: April 13, 1928 *Area:* 0.92 sq km
Population in 2011: 127
Provincial Electoral District(s): Rosthern-Shellbrook
Federal Electoral District(s): Battlefords-Lloydminster
Next Election: Oct. 24, 2012 (4 year terms)
Don Peters, Mayor
Brenda Aumack, Administrator

Radisson
P.O. Box 69
Radisson, SK S0K 3L0
Tel: 306-827-2218; *Fax:* 306-827-2218
tradisson@sasktel.net
radisson.sasktelwebhosting.com
Municipal Type: Town
Incorporated: Feb. 3, 1906 *Area:* 2.07 sq km
Population in 2011: 505
Provincial Electoral District(s): Biggar
Federal Electoral District(s): Saskatoon-Wanuskewin
Next Election: Oct. 24, 2012 (4 year terms)
Note: Proclaimed as a town on July 1, 1913.
Walter Kyliuk, Mayor
Muriel Rosser-Swift, Administrator

Radville
P.O. Box 339
Radville, SK S0C 2G0
Tel: 306-869-2477; *Fax:* 306-869-3100
town.radville@sasktel.net
www.radville.ca
Municipal Type: Town
Incorporated: Jan. 3, 1911 *Area:* 1.86 sq km
Population in 2011: 860
Provincial Electoral District(s): Estevan
Federal Electoral District(s): Souris-Moose Mountain
Next Election: Oct. 24, 2012 (4 year terms)
Note: Proclaimed as a town on May 1, 1913.
Shirley Cancade, Mayor
Shauna Bourassa, Administrator

Rama
P.O. Box 205
Rama, SK S0A 3H0
Tel: 306-593-6065; *Fax:* 306-593-2273
villagerama@yourlink.ca
Municipal Type: Village
Incorporated: Dec. 18, 1919 *Area:* 0.67 sq km
Population in 2011: 75
Provincial Electoral District(s): Kelvington-Wadena
Federal Electoral District(s): Yorkton-Melville
Next Election: Oct. 24, 2012 (4 year terms)
Darrell Dutchak, Mayor
Nicole Monchamp, Administrator

Raymore
P.O. Box 10
107 Main St.
Raymore, SK S0A 3J0
Tel: 306-746-2100; *Fax:* 306-746-4314
raymoretown@aski.ca
www.raymore.ca
Municipal Type: Town
Incorporated: Aug. 11, 1909 *Area:* 2.75 sq km
Population in 2011: 568
Provincial Electoral District(s): Arm River-Watrous
Federal Electoral District(s): Regina-Qu'Appelle
Next Election: Oct. 24, 2012 (4 year terms)
Note: Proclaimed as a town on Aug. 1, 1963.
Keith Bentz, Mayor
Gail R. Braman, Administrator

Redvers
P.O. Box 249
25 Railway Ave.
Redvers, SK S0C 2H0
Tel: 306-452-3533; *Fax:* 306-452-3701
town.of.redvers@sasktel.net
www.townofredvers.org
Municipal Type: Town
Incorporated: July 9, 1904 *Area:* 2.83 sq km
Population in 2011: 975
Provincial Electoral District(s): Cannington
Federal Electoral District(s): Souris-Moose Mountain
Next Election: Oct. 24, 2012 (4 year terms)
Note: Proclaimed as a town on July 6, 1960.
Omer Carriere, Mayor
Bonnie Rutten, Administrator

Regina Beach
P.O. Box 10
218 Centre St.
Regina Beach, SK S0G 4C0
Tel: 306-729-2202; *Fax:* 306-729-3411
townofreginabeach@sasktel.net
www.reginabeach.ca
Municipal Type: Town
Incorporated: Sept. 30, 1920 *Area:* 2.58 sq km
Population in 2011: 1,081
Provincial Electoral District(s): Thunder Creek
Federal Electoral District(s): Regina-Lumsden-Lake Centre
Next Election: Oct. 24, 2012 (4 year terms)
Note: Proclaimed as a town on Nov. 1, 1980.
George Solomon Schofield, Mayor
Christina Stanford, Administrator

Rhein
P.O. Box 40
Rhein, SK S0A 3K0
Tel: 306-273-2155; *Fax:* 306-273-2155
villageofrhein@yourlink.ca
Municipal Type: Village
Incorporated: March 10, 1913 *Area:* 1.09 sq km
Population in 2011: 158
Provincial Electoral District(s): Canora-Pelly
Federal Electoral District(s): Yorkton-Melville
Next Election: Oct. 24, 2012 (4 year terms)
Ian Bugera, Mayor
Valerie Stricker, Administrator

Richard
P.O. Box 6
Richard, SK S0M 2P0
Tel: 306-549-2331
vrichard@sasktel.net
Municipal Type: Village
Incorporated: Oct. 11, 1916 *Area:* 0.73 sq km
Population in 2011: 30
Provincial Electoral District(s): Rosthern-Shellbrook
Federal Electoral District(s): Saskatoon-Wanuskewin
Next Election: Oct. 24, 2012 (4 year terms)
Merilyn Wawryk, Mayor
Valerie Fendelet, Administrator

Richmound
P.O. Box 29
Richmound, SK S0N 2E0
Tel: 306-669-4415; *Fax:* 306-669-2044
richmound.village@sasktel.net
www.richmound.ca
Municipal Type: Village
Incorporated: May 5, 1947 *Area:* 0.47 sq km
Population in 2011: 154
Provincial Electoral District(s): Cypress Hills
Federal Electoral District(s): Cypress Hills-Grasslands
Next Election: Oct. 24, 2012 (4 year terms)
Barry Manz, Mayor
Laurie Baron, Administrator

Ridgedale
P.O. Box 27
Ridgedale, SK S0E 1L0
Tel: 306-277-2002; *Fax:* 306-277-2002
ridgedalevillage@sasktel.net
www.newsaskcfdc.ca/ridgedale.htm
Municipal Type: Village
Incorporated: Dec. 15, 1921 *Area:* 0.72 sq km
Population in 2011: 80
Provincial Electoral District(s): Carrot River Valley
Federal Electoral District(s): Prince Albert
Next Election: Oct. 24, 2012 (4 year terms)
Harvey Reimer, Mayor
Tamie Jack, Clerk

Riverhurst
P.O. Box 116
324 Teck St.
Riverhurst, SK S0H 3P0
Tel: 306-353-2220; *Fax:* 306-353-2220
villageofriverhurst@sasktel.net
www.riverhurst.ca
Municipal Type: Village
Incorporated: June 22, 1916 *Area:* 0.91 sq km
Population in 2011: 114
Provincial Electoral District(s): Thunder Creek
Federal Electoral District(s): Cypress Hills-Grasslands
Next Election: Oct. 24, 2012 (4 year terms)
Sylvia Matwe, Mayor
306-796-2006
Kyle Van Der Bosch, Administrator

Rocanville
P.O. Box 265
Rocanville, SK S0A 3L0
Tel: 306-645-2022; *Fax:* 306-645-4492
rocanville.town@sasktel.net
www.rocanville.ca
Municipal Type: Town
Incorporated: March 24, 1904 *Area:* 2.43 sq km
Population in 2011: 857
Provincial Electoral District(s): Moosomin
Federal Electoral District(s): Souris-Moose Mountain
Next Election: Oct. 24, 2012 (4 year terms)
Note: Incorporated as a town on Aug. 1, 1967.
Daryl Fingas, Mayor
Monica M. Merkosky, Administrator

Roche Percée
P.O. Box 237
Bienfait, SK S0C 0M0
Tel: 306-634-4661
Municipal Type: Village
Incorporated: Jan. 12, 1909 *Area:* 2.59 sq km
Population in 2011: 153
Provincial Electoral District(s): Estevan
Federal Electoral District(s): Souris-Moose Mountain
Next Election: Oct. 24, 2012 (4 year terms)

Reg Jahn, Mayor
Lyndon Stachoski, Administrator

Rockglen
P.O. Box 267
Rockglen, SK S0H 3R0
Tel: 306-476-2144; *Fax:* 306-476-2339
rockglen1@sasktel.net
www.rockglentourism.com
Municipal Type: Town
Incorporated: July 12, 1927 *Area:* 2.85 sq km
Population in 2011: 400
Provincial Electoral District(s): Wood River
Federal Electoral District(s): Cypress Hills-Grasslands
Next Election: Oct. 24, 2012 (4 year terms)
Note: Proclaimed as a town on Sept. 1, 1957.
Richard Prefontaine, Mayor
Sherri Spagrud, Administrator

Rose Valley
P.O. Box 460
Rose Valley, SK S0E 1M0
Tel: 306-322-2232; *Fax:* 306-322-4461
rosevalley@sasktel.net
www.townofrosevalley.com
Municipal Type: Town
Incorporated: Sept. 24, 1940 *Area:* 1.12 sq km
Population in 2011: 296
Provincial Electoral District(s): Kelvington-Wadena
Federal Electoral District(s): Yorkton-Melville
Next Election: Oct. 24, 2012 (4 year terms)
Note: Proclaimed as a town on Jan. 1, 1962.
Daniel Veilleux, Mayor
Marjorie A. Zarowny, Clerk

Rosetown
P.O. Box 398
417 Main St.
Rosetown, SK S0L 2V0
Tel: 306-882-2214; *Fax:* 306-882-3166
townofrosetown@sasktel.net
www.rosetown.ca
Municipal Type: Town
Incorporated: Aug. 24, 1909 *Area:* 10.59 sq km
Population in 2011: 2,317
Provincial Electoral District(s): Rosetown-Elrose
Federal Electoral District(s): Saskatoon-Rosetown-Biggar
Next Election: Oct. 24, 2012 (4 year terms)
Note: Proclaimed as a town on Nov. 1, 1911.
Brian Gerow, Mayor
Steven Piermantier, Administrator

Rosthern
P.O. Box 416
Rosthern, SK S0K 3R0
Tel: 306-232-4826; *Fax:* 306-232-5638
townofrosthern@sasktel.net
www.rosthern.com
Municipal Type: Town
Incorporated: Dec. 29, 1898 *Area:* 4.01 sq km
Population in 2011: 1,572
Provincial Electoral District(s): Rosthern-Shellbrook
Federal Electoral District(s): Saskatoon-Wanuskewin
Next Election: Oct. 24, 2012 (4 year terms)
Note: Proclaimed as a town on Nov. 20, 1903.
Doug Knoll, Mayor
Nicole J. Lerat, Administrator

Rouleau
P.O. Box 250
Rouleau, SK S0G 4H0
Tel: 306-776-2270; *Fax:* 306-776-2482
info@townofrouleau.com
www.townofrouleau.com
Municipal Type: Town
Incorporated: July 23, 1903 *Area:* 1.65 sq km
Population in 2011: 453
Provincial Electoral District(s): Indian Head-Milestone
Federal Electoral District(s): Palliser
Next Election: Oct. 24, 2012 (4 year terms)
Note: Proclaimed as a town on March 1, 1907.
Leroy (Pete) Westgard, Mayor
Guy Lagrandeur, Administrator

Ruddell
P.O. Box 7
Ruddell, SK S0M 2S0
Tel: 306-445-4601; *Fax:* 306-445-4611
Municipal Type: Village
Incorporated: March 18, 1914 *Area:* 0.47 sq km
Population in 2011: 20
Provincial Electoral District(s): Biggar
Federal Electoral District(s): Saskatoon-Wanuskewin
Next Election: Oct. 24, 2012 (4 year terms)
Linda Mushka, Mayor
Les Klippentein, Administrator
Klipp1951@gmail.com

Rush Lake
P.O. Box 126
Rush Lake, SK S0H 3S0
Tel: 306-784-3504; *Fax:* 306-773-0331
Municipal Type: Village
Incorporated: Oct. 16, 1911 *Area:* 0.74 sq km
Population in 2011: 65
Provincial Electoral District(s): Thunder Creek
Federal Electoral District(s): Cypress Hills-Grasslands
Next Election: Oct. 24, 2012 (4 year terms)
Stacey Beisel, Mayor
Terrie Unger, Clerk

Ruthilda
P.O. Box 90
Ruthilda, SK S0K 3S0
Tel: 306-932-4408
Municipal Type: Village
Incorporated: Feb. 3, 1921 *Area:* 0.67 sq km
Population in 2011: 10
Provincial Electoral District(s): Biggar
Federal Electoral District(s): Battlefords-Lloydminster
Next Election: Oct. 24, 2012 (4 year terms)
Jerry Gilles, Mayor
Anita Gilles, Clerk
anita@sasktel.net

St. Benedict
P.O. Box 99
St Benedict, SK S0K 3T0
Tel: 306-289-2072; *Fax:* 306-289-2077
benedictvillage@gmail.com
Municipal Type: Village
Incorporated: Jan. 1, 1964 *Area:* 0.54 sq km
Population in 2011: 82
Provincial Electoral District(s): Batoche
Federal Electoral District(s): Saskatoon-Humboldt
Next Election: Oct. 24, 2012 (4 year terms)
Edward Martin, Mayor
Helen Martinka, Clerk

St. Brieux
P.O. Box 249
300 Main St.
St Brieux, SK S0K 3V0
Tel: 306-275-2257; *Fax:* 306-275-4949
brieux@sasktel.net
Municipal Type: Town
Incorporated: Nov. 11, 1913 *Area:* 2.02 sq km
Population in 2011: 590
Provincial Electoral District(s): Batoche
Federal Electoral District(s): Saskatoon-Humboldt
Next Election: Oct. 24, 2012 (4 year terms)
Note: Proclaimed as a town on Nov. 8, 2006.
Pauline Boyer, Mayor
Kimberly Martin, Administrator

St. George's Hill
P.O. Box 160
Desjarlais St.
Dillon, SK S0M 0S0
Tel: 306-282-4408; *Fax:* 306-282-2002
sgh123@sasktel.net
Municipal Type: Northern Hamlet
Incorporated: Dec. 1, 1983 *Area:* 1.46 sq km
Population in 2011: 100
Provincial Electoral District(s): Athabasca
Federal Electoral District(s): Desnethé-Missinippi-Churchill River
Next Election: Autumn 2012 (4 year terms)
Donna Janvier, Mayor
Diana Desjarlais, Clerk

St. Gregor
P.O. Box 19
St Gregor, SK S0K 3X0
Tel: 306-366-2129; *Fax:* 306-366-2128
stgregorsk@sasktel.net
Municipal Type: Village
Incorporated: March 26, 1920 *Area:* 0.91 sq km
Population in 2011: 98
Provincial Electoral District(s): Melfort
Federal Electoral District(s): Saskatoon-Humboldt
Next Election: Oct. 24, 2012 (4 year terms)
Doug Hogemann, Mayor
Darlene Kuz, Administrator

St. Louis
P.O. Box 40
172 Riverside Dr.
St Louis, SK S0J 2C0
Tel: 306-422-8471; *Fax:* 306-422-8450
villageofstlouis@sasktel.net
www.villageofstlouis.com
Municipal Type: Village
Incorporated: May 19, 1959 *Area:* 1.08 sq km
Population in 2011: 449
Provincial Electoral District(s): Batoche
Federal Electoral District(s): Saskatoon-Humboldt
Next Election: Oct. 24, 2012 (4 year terms)
Les Rancourt, Mayor
Robin Boyer, Clerk

St. Walburg
P.O. Box 368
St Walburg, SK S0M 2T0
Tel: 306-248-3232; *Fax:* 306-248-3484
townofstwalburg@sasktel.net
www.stwalburg.com
Municipal Type: Town
Incorporated: Jan. 18, 1922 *Area:* 2.12 sq km
Population in 2011: 716
Provincial Electoral District(s): Meadow Lake
Federal Electoral District(s): Battlefords-Lloydminster
Next Election: Oct. 24, 2012 (4 year terms)
Note: Proclaimed as a town on Feb. 1, 1953.
A. V. "Tony" Leeson, Mayor
Leah Mullis, Acting Administrator

Saltcoats
P.O. Box 120
Saltcoats, SK S0A 3R0
Tel: 306-744-2212; *Fax:* 306-744-2239
saltcoats.town@sasktel.net
townofsaltcoats.ca
Municipal Type: Town
Incorporated: April 4, 1894 *Area:* 1.35 sq km
Population in 2011: 474
Provincial Electoral District(s): Melville-Saltcoats
Federal Electoral District(s): Yorkton-Melville
Next Election: Oct. 24, 2012 (4 year terms)
Note: Proclaimed as a town on Nov. 1, 1910.
Walter Farquharson, Mayor
Diane Jamieson, Administrator

Sandy Bay
P.O. Box 130
Hill St. & Sandy Bay Ave.
Sandy Bay, SK S0P 0G0
Tel: 306-754-2165; *Fax:* 306-754-2157
nvsb@sasktel.net
Municipal Type: Northern Village
Incorporated: Oct. 1, 1983 *Area:* 14.85 sq km
Population in 2011: 1,233
Provincial Electoral District(s): Cumberland
Federal Electoral District(s): Desnethé-Missinippi-Churchill River
Next Election: Autumn 2012 (4 year terms)
Daniel Bear, Mayor
Henrietta Ray, Administrator

Saskatchewan Beach
P.O. Box 220
Silton, SK S0G 4L0
Tel: 306-729-4410; *Fax:* 306-729-2017
saskbeach@sasktel.net
www.saskatchewanbeach.ca
Municipal Type: Resort Village
Area: 1.57 sq km
Population in 2011: 213
Provincial Electoral District(s): Last Mountain-Touchwood
Federal Electoral District(s): Regina-Lumsden-Lake Centre
Next Election: July 2016
Malcolm Graham, Mayor
Sharie Hall, Administrator

Sceptre
P.O. Box 128
Sceptre, SK S0N 2H0
Tel: 306-623-4244; *Fax:* 306-623-4244
sceptrevillage@xplornet.com
Municipal Type: Village
Incorporated: April 30, 1913 *Area:* 1.23 sq km
Population in 2011: 97
Provincial Electoral District(s): Cypress Hills
Federal Electoral District(s): Cypress Hills-Grasslands
Next Election: Oct. 24, 2012 (4 year terms)
Charlene King, Mayor
Sherry Egeland, Clerk

Scott
P.O. Box 96
104 Main St.
Scott, SK S0K 4A0
Tel: 306-247-2033; *Fax:* 306-247-2055
townofscott@xplornet.com
Municipal Type: Town
Incorporated: Nov. 17, 1908 *Area:* 4.39 sq km
Population in 2011: 75
Provincial Electoral District(s): Kindersley
Federal Electoral District(s): Battlefords-Lloydminster
Next Election: Oct. 24, 2012 (4 year terms)
Note: Proclaimed as a town on Nov. 1, 1910.
Eric Schell, Mayor
Stacy Hawkins, Administrator

Sedley
P.O. Box 130
Sedley, SK S0G 4K0
Tel: 306-885-2133; *Fax:* 306-885-2132
villageofsedley@sasktel.net
Municipal Type: Village
Incorporated: Aug. 3, 1907 *Area:* 1.31 sq km
Population in 2011: 337
Provincial Electoral District(s): Indian Head-Milestone
Federal Electoral District(s): Wascana
Next Election: Oct. 24, 2012 (4 year terms)
Bryan Leier, Mayor
Samantha Gillies, Clerk

Semans
P.O. Box 113
Semans, SK S0A 3S0
Tel: 306-524-2144; *Fax:* 306-524-2145
semans@aski.ca
www.semans-sask.com
Municipal Type: Village
Incorporated: Dec. 14, 1908 *Area:* 1.18 sq km
Population in 2011: 204
Provincial Electoral District(s): Arm River-Watrous
Federal Electoral District(s): Regina-Lumsden-Lake Centre
Next Election: Oct. 24, 2012 (4 year terms)
Ray Lamontagne, Mayor
Charmayne Szatkowski, Administrator

Senlac
P.O. Box 93
Senlac, SK S0L 2Y0
Tel: 306-228-4330
rm411@sasktel.net
Municipal Type: Village
Incorporated: Oct. 11, 1916 *Area:* 0.60 sq km
Population in 2011: 46
Provincial Electoral District(s): Cut Knife-Turtleford
Federal Electoral District(s): Battlefords-Lloydminster
Next Election: Oct. 24, 2012 (4 year terms)
Corinne McWalters, Mayor
Maureen Forbes, Clerk

Shackleton
P.O. Box 7
Shackleton, SK S0N 2L0
Tel: 306-587-2910; *Fax:* 306-587-2311
Municipal Type: Village
Incorporated: May 29, 1919 *Area:* 0.66 sq km
Population in 2011: 10
Provincial Electoral District(s): Cypress Hills
Federal Electoral District(s): Cypress Hills-Grasslands
Next Election: Oct. 24, 2012 (4 year terms)
Ronald J. Heron, Mayor
Marjorie A. Cator, Clerk
marjorie.cator@gmail.com

Shamrock
P.O. Box 119
Shamrock, SK S0H 3W0
Tel: 306-648-2736; *Fax:* 306-648-2798
Municipal Type: Village
Incorporated: April 30, 1924 *Area:* 0.79 sq km
Population in 2011: 20
Provincial Electoral District(s): Wood River
Federal Electoral District(s): Cypress Hills-Grasslands
Next Election: Oct. 24, 2012 (4 year terms)
Rene Fortin, Mayor
Cathy Marchessault, Clerk
rmarchessault@sasktel.net

Shaunavon
P.O. Box 820
Shaunavon, SK S0N 2M0
Tel: 306-297-2605; *Fax:* 306-297-2608
shaunavon@sasktel.net
www.shaunavon.com
Municipal Type: Town
Incorporated: Nov. 27, 1913 *Area:* 5.10 sq km
Population in 2011: 1,756
Provincial Electoral District(s): Cypress Hills
Federal Electoral District(s): Cypress Hills-Grasslands
Next Election: Oct. 24, 2012 (4 year terms)
Note: Proclaimed as a town on Nov. 1, 1914.
Sharon J. Dickie, Mayor
Jan Meyer, Administrator

Sheho
P.O. Box 130
Sheho, SK S0A 3T0
Tel: 306-849-2044
shehovillage@sasktel.net
Municipal Type: Village
Incorporated: June 30, 1905 *Area:* 1.95 sq km
Population in 2011: 130
Provincial Electoral District(s): Kelvington-Wadena
Federal Electoral District(s): Yorkton-Melville
Next Election: Oct. 24, 2012 (4 year terms)
Dennis Zoski, Mayor
Ron Sebulsky, Clerk

Shell Lake
P.O. Box 280
Shell Lake, SK S0J 2G0
Tel: 306-427-2272; *Fax:* 306-427-4800
village.sl@sasktel.net
www.rkc.ca/shell_lake/
Municipal Type: Village
Incorporated: Oct. 18, 1940 *Area:* 1.09 sq km
Population in 2011: 99
Provincial Electoral District(s): Rosthern-Shellbrook
Federal Electoral District(s): Desnethé-Missinippi-Churchill River
Next Election: Oct. 24, 2012 (4 year terms)
Anita Weiers, Mayor
Tara Bueckert, Administrator

Shellbrook
P.O. Box 40
71 Main St.
Shellbrook, SK S0J 2E0
Tel: 306-747-4900; *Fax:* 306-747-3111
shellbrook@sasktel.net
www.shellbrook.net
Municipal Type: Town
Incorporated: Nov. 18, 1909 *Area:* 2.13 sq km
Population in 2011: 1,433
Provincial Electoral District(s): Rosthern-Shellbrook
Federal Electoral District(s): Prince Albert
Next Election: Oct. 24, 2012 (4 year terms)
Note: Proclaimed as a town on April 1, 1948.
George Tomporowski, Mayor
Kelly Hoare, Administrator

Shields
P.O. Box 81
Dundurn, SK S0K 1K0
Tel: 306-492-2259; *Fax:* 306-492-2068
shields@xplornet.ca
www.shields.ca
Municipal Type: Resort Village
Area: 0.72 sq km
Population in 2011: 220
Provincial Electoral District(s): Arm River-Watrous
Federal Electoral District(s): Blackstrap
Next Election: July 2016
Eldon MacKay, Mayor
em@mackayequipment.com
Jessie Williams, Administrator

Silton
P.O. Box 1
Silton, SK S0G 4L0
Tel: 306-731-3222
villageofsilton@xplornet.ca
Municipal Type: Village
Incorporated: July 2, 1914 *Area:* 1.07 sq km
Population in 2011: 95
Provincial Electoral District(s): Last Mountain-Touchwood
Federal Electoral District(s): Regina-Lumsden-Lake Centre
Next Election: Oct. 24, 2012 (4 year terms)
Warren Wild, Mayor
Brenda Small, Clerk

Simpson
P.O. Box 10
303 George St.
Simpson, SK S0G 4M0
Tel: 306-836-2020; *Fax:* 306-836-4460
rm281@sasktel.net
www.simpsonsask.ca
Municipal Type: Village
Incorporated: July 11, 1911 *Area:* 1.41 sq km
Population in 2011: 131
Provincial Electoral District(s): Arm River-Watrous
Federal Electoral District(s): Regina-Lumsden-Lake Centre
Next Election: Oct. 24, 2012 (4 year terms)
Donald Janzen, Mayor
Darlene Mann, Administrator

Sintaluta
P.O. Box 150
Sintaluta, SK S0G 4N0
Tel: 306-727-2100; *Fax:* 306-727-2100
sintaluta@yourlink.ca
Municipal Type: Town
Incorporated: Oct. 27, 1898 *Area:* 2.70 sq km
Population in 2011: 120
Provincial Electoral District(s): Indian Head-Milestone
Federal Electoral District(s): Regina-Qu'Appelle
Next Election: Oct. 24, 2012 (4 year terms)
Note: Proclaimed as a town on June 1, 1907.
Anita Ryder, Mayor
Donna Pitre, Administrator

Sled Lake
P.O. Box 850
Big River, SK S0J 0E0
Tel: 306-832-4442; *Fax:* 306-832-2269
Municipal Type: NS
Population in 2010: 35
Provincial Electoral District(s): Athabasca
Federal Electoral District(s): Desnethé-Missinippi-Churchill River
Next Election: Oct. 24, 2012 (4 year terms)
Bruce Leier, Advisor
bruce.leier@gov.sk.ca

Smeaton
P.O. Box 70
Smeaton, SK S0J 2J0
Tel: 306-426-2044; *Fax:* 306-426-2291
smeaton@sasktel.net
www.newsaskcfdc.ca/smeaton.htm
Municipal Type: Village
Incorporated: March 7, 1944 *Area:* 1.38 sq km
Population in 2011: 181
Provincial Electoral District(s): Saskatchewan Rivers
Federal Electoral District(s): Desnethé-Missinippi-Churchill River
Next Election: Oct. 24, 2012 (4 year terms)
Joe Bernhard, Mayor
Michelle Grunerud, Administrator

Smiley
P.O. Box 90
Smiley, SK S0L 2Z0
Tel: 306-838-2020; *Fax:* 306-838-4343
rm321@sasktel.net
Municipal Type: Village
Incorporated: Nov. 26, 1913 *Area:* 0.64 sq km
Population in 2011: 60
Provincial Electoral District(s): Kindersley
Federal Electoral District(s): Battlefords-Lloydminster
Next Election: Oct. 24, 2012 (4 year terms)
William Wasylenchuk, Mayor
Charlotte Helfrich, Administrator

South Lake
#417, 310 Main St. North
Moose Jaw, SK S7H 3K1
Tel: 306-692-7399; *Fax:* 306-692-7380
contact@southlakeresort.com
www.southlakeresort.com
Municipal Type: Resort Village
Area: 1.15 sq km
Population in 2011: 48
Provincial Electoral District(s): Thunder Creek
Federal Electoral District(s): Regina-Lumsden-Lake Centre
Next Election: July 2016
Terry Rollie, Mayor
Tracy Edwards, Clerk
clerk.southlake@shaw.ca

Southend
General Delivery
Southend, SK S0J 2L0
Tel: 306-425-4323; *Fax:* 306-425-2401
Other Information: Toll-Free Phone: 1-800-663-1555
Municipal Type: Northern Hamlet
Population in 2010: 35
Provincial Electoral District(s): Cumberland
Federal Electoral District(s): Desnethé-Missinippi-Churchill River
Next Election: Oct. 24, 2012 (4 year terms)
Valerie Antoniuk, Advisor
306-425-4323
valerie.antoniuk@gov.sk.ca

Southey
P.O. Box 248
Southey, SK S0G 4P0
Tel: 306-726-2202; *Fax:* 306-726-2916
townofsouthey@sasktel.net
www.southey.ca
Municipal Type: Town
Incorporated: Nov. 9, 1907 *Area:* 1 sq km
Population in 2011: 778
Provincial Electoral District(s): Last Mountain-Touchwood
Federal Electoral District(s): Regina-Qu'Appelle
Next Election: Oct. 24, 2012 (4 year terms)
Note: Proclaimed as a town on Nov. 1, 1980.
Martin Lingelbach, Mayor
Ferne Senft, Administrator

Spalding
P.O. Box 280
Spalding, SK S0K 4C0
Tel: 306-872-2276; *Fax:* 306-872-2275
spalding.village@sasktel.net
www.newsaskcfdc.ca/spalding.htm
Municipal Type: Village
Incorporated: March 11, 1924 *Area:* 1.18 sq km
Population in 2011: 242
Provincial Electoral District(s): Melfort
Federal Electoral District(s): Saskatoon-Humboldt
Next Election: Oct. 24, 2012 (4 year terms)
Norman Foushe, Mayor
Cathy Holt, Administrator

Speers
P.O. Box 974
Speers, SK S0M 2V0
Tel: 306-246-2114; *Fax:* 306-246-2173
rm436@littleloon.ca
Municipal Type: Village
Incorporated: Dec. 24, 1915 *Area:* 0.69 sq km
Population in 2011: 65
Provincial Electoral District(s): Rosthern-Shellbrook
Federal Electoral District(s): Saskatoon-Wanuskewin
Next Election: Oct. 24, 2012 (4 year terms)
Thomas E. Nicholson, Mayor
Dean Nicholson, Clerk

Spiritwood
P.O. Box 460
Spiritwood, SK S0J 2M0
Tel: 306-883-2161; *Fax:* 306-883-3212
www.townofspiritwood.ca
Municipal Type: Town
Incorporated: Oct. 1, 1935 *Area:* 2.95 sq km
Population in 2011: 916
Provincial Electoral District(s): Rosthern-Shellbrook
Federal Electoral District(s): Desnethé-Missinippi-Churchill River
Next Election: Oct. 24, 2012 (4 year terms)
Note: Proclaimed as a town on Sept. 1, 1965.
Gary von Holwede, Mayor
Teri Scaife, Administrator

Springside
P.O. Box 414
Springside, SK S0A 3V0
Tel: 306-792-2022; *Fax:* 306-792-2210
springside.town@sasktel.net
www.townofspringside.com
Municipal Type: Town
Incorporated: Nov. 11, 1909 *Area:* 0.64 sq km
Population in 2011: 534
Provincial Electoral District(s): Canora-Pelly
Federal Electoral District(s): Yorkton-Melville
Next Election: Oct. 24, 2012 (4 year terms)
Note: Proclaimed as a town on Nov. 1, 1985.
Jack Prychak, Mayor
Joan M. Popoff, Administrator

Spy Hill
P.O. Box 69
Spy Hill, SK S0A 3W0
Tel: 306-534-2255; *Fax:* 306-534-4520
spyhillvillage@sasktel.net
vila.sasktelwebsite.net
Municipal Type: Village
Incorporated: April 22, 1910 *Area:* 1.19 sq km
Population in 2011: 204
Provincial Electoral District(s): Melville-Saltcoats
Federal Electoral District(s): Yorkton-Melville
Next Election: Oct. 24, 2012 (4 year terms)
Allan Perrin, Mayor
Susan Gawryluk, Administrator

Stanley Mission
General Delivery
Stanley Mission, SK S0J 2P0
Tel: 306-425-4323; *Fax:* 306-425-2401
Other Information: Toll-Free Phone: 1-800-663-1555
Municipal Type: NS
Population in 2010: 124
Provincial Electoral District(s): Cumberland
Federal Electoral District(s): Desnethé-Missinippi-Churchill River
Next Election: Oct. 24, 2012 (4 year terms)
Annie McLeod, Chair
306-425-4321
shannon.cholin@gov.sk.ca
Shannon Cholin, Advisor

Star City
P.O. Box 250
145 - 4th St.
Star City, SK S0E 1P0
Tel: 306-863-2282; *Fax:* 306-863-2277
town.starcity@sasktel.net
www.townofstarcity.com
Municipal Type: Town
Incorporated: April 6, 1906 *Area:* 0.7 sq km
Population in 2011: 460
Provincial Electoral District(s): Melfort
Federal Electoral District(s): Prince Albert
Next Election: Oct. 24, 2012 (4 year terms)
Note: Proclaimed as a town on Nov. 1, 1921.
Barry Petrie, Mayor
Roberta Spencer, Administrator

Stenen
P.O. Box 160
Stenen, SK S0A 3X0
Tel: 306-548-4334; *Fax:* 306-548-4334
villageofstenen@sasktel.net
Municipal Type: Village
Incorporated: Aug. 14, 1912 *Area:* 0.58 sq km
Population in 2011: 79
Provincial Electoral District(s): Canora-Pelly
Federal Electoral District(s): Yorkton-Melville
Next Election: Oct. 24, 2012 (4 year terms)
Garry Giesbrecht, Mayor
Sharon Thompson, Administrator

Stewart Valley
P.O. Box 10
210 Charles St.
Stewart Valley, SK S0N 2P0
Tel: 306-778-3611; *Fax:* 306-778-3688
vlg.stvalley@sasktel.net
www.stewartvalley.ca
Municipal Type: Village
Incorporated: Jan. 1, 1958 *Area:* 0.86 sq km
Population in 2011: 76
Provincial Electoral District(s): Swift Current
Federal Electoral District(s): Cypress Hills-Grasslands
Next Election: Oct. 24, 2012 (4 year terms)
Mike Moen, Mayor
Corie Lanceleve, Clerk

Stockholm
P.O. Box 265
Stockholm, SK S0A 3Y0
Tel: 306-793-2151; *Fax:* 306-793-4597
stockholm@sasktel.net
Municipal Type: Village
Incorporated: June 30, 1905 *Area:* 1.64 sq km
Population in 2011: 341
Provincial Electoral District(s): Melville-Saltcoats
Federal Electoral District(s): Yorkton-Melville
Next Election: Oct. 24, 2012 (4 year terms)
Fran Herperger, Mayor
Lorie Jackson, Administrator

Stony Rapids
P.O. Box 120
Johnson St.
Stony Rapids, SK S0J 2R0
Tel: 306-439-2173; *Fax:* 306-439-2098
nhstonyrap@sasktel.net
Municipal Type: Northern Hamlet
Incorporated: April 1, 1992 *Area:* 3.96 sq km
Population in 2011: 243
Provincial Electoral District(s): Athabasca
Federal Electoral District(s): Desnethé-Missinippi-Churchill River
Next Election: Autumn 2012 (4 year terms)
Sandra Hanson, Mayor
Shauna Sayazie, Clerk

Storthoaks
P.O. Box 40
Storthoaks, SK S0C 2K0
Tel: 306-449-2262; *Fax:* 306-449-2210
rm31@sasktel.net
Municipal Type: Village
Incorporated: June 5, 1940 *Area:* 0.49 sq km
Population in 2011: 93
Provincial Electoral District(s): Cannington
Federal Electoral District(s): Souris-Moose Mountain
Next Election: Oct. 24, 2012 (4 year terms)
Sydney Chicoine, Mayor
Gisele Bouchard, Administrator

Stoughton
P.O. Box 397
232 Main St.
Stoughton, SK S0G 4T0
Tel: 306-457-2413; *Fax:* 306-457-3162
stoughtontown@sasktel.net
stoughtn.sasktelwebhosting.com
Municipal Type: Town
Incorporated: Feb. 26, 1904 *Area:* 2.13 sq km
Population in 2011: 694
Provincial Electoral District(s): Cannington
Federal Electoral District(s): Souris-Moose Mountain
Next Election: Oct. 24, 2012 (4 year terms)
Note: Proclaimed as a town on June 1, 1960.
Heather Balon-Barmann, Mayor
Chris Miskolczi, Administrator

Strasbourg
P.O. Box 369
Strasbourg, SK S0G 4V0
Tel: 306-725-3707; *Fax:* 306-725-3613
strasbourg@sasktel.net
www.townofstrasbourg.ca
Municipal Type: Town
Incorporated: April 19, 1906 *Area:* 5.70 sq km
Population in 2011: 752
Provincial Electoral District(s): Last Mountain-Touchwood
Federal Electoral District(s): Regina-Lumsden-Lake Centre
Next Election: Oct. 24, 2012 (4 year terms)
Note: Proclaimed as a town on July 1, 1907.
Carol Schultz, Mayor
Barbara Griffin, Administrator

Strongfield
P.O. Box 87
Strongfield, SK S0H 3Z0
Tel: 306-857-2200
villageofstrongfield@yourlink.ca
Municipal Type: Village
Incorporated: May 3, 1912 *Area:* 0.8 sq km
Population in 2011: 40
Provincial Electoral District(s): Arm River-Watrous
Federal Electoral District(s): Blackstrap
Next Election: Oct. 24, 2012 (4 year terms)
George Bristow, Mayor
Lora-Lee McKay, Administrator

Sturgis
P.O. Box 520
209 - 1st Ave. SE
Sturgis, SK S0A 4A0
Tel: 306-548-2108; *Fax:* 306-548-2948
townofsturgis@sasktel.net
www.townofsturgis.com
Municipal Type: Town
Incorporated: Sept. 3, 1912 *Area:* 3.39 sq km
Population in 2011: 620
Provincial Electoral District(s): Canora-Pelly
Federal Electoral District(s): Yorkton-Melville
Next Election: Oct. 24, 2012 (4 year terms)
Note: Proclaimed as a town on March 1, 1951.
Don Olson, Mayor
Olivia (Bim) Bartch, Administrator

Success
P.O. Box 40
Success, SK S0N 2R0
Tel: 306-773-7934
success1@yourlink.ca
Municipal Type: Village
Incorporated: Oct. 25, 1912 *Area:* 1.38 sq km
Population in 2011: 40
Provincial Electoral District(s): Swift Current
Federal Electoral District(s): Cypress Hills-Grasslands
Next Election: Oct. 24, 2012 (4 year terms)
John Kroeker, Mayor
Donna Butler, Clerk

Sun Valley
P.O. Box 2260
Moose Jaw, SK S6H 7W6
Tel: 306-694-0055
rvsunvalley@yahoo.com
Municipal Type: Resort Village
Area: 2.33 sq km
Population in 2011: 46
Provincial Electoral District(s): Thunder Creek
Federal Electoral District(s): Regina-Lumsden-Lake Centre
Next Election: July 2016
Barry Gunther, Mayor
Kathy Mealing, Administrator

Sunset Cove
P.O. Box 2
Silton, SK S0G 4L0
Tel: 306-789-9684; *Fax:* 306-761-0320
rvsunsetcove@sasktel.net
www.rvsunsetcove.ca
Municipal Type: Resort Village
Incorporated: 1959 *Area:* 0.17 sq km
Population in 2011: 25
Provincial Electoral District(s): Last Mountain-Touchwood
Federal Electoral District(s): Regina-Lumsden-Lake Centre
Next Election: July 2016
Tom Fulcher, Mayor
thefulchers@sasktel.net
Lynda Stack, Clerk

Tantallon
P.O. Box 70
Tantallon, SK S0A 4B0
Tel: 306-643-2112; *Fax:* 306-643-2113
tantallon@sasktel.net
Municipal Type: Village
Incorporated: June 17, 1904 *Area:* 0.84 sq km
Population in 2011: 105
Provincial Electoral District(s): Melville-Saltcoats
Federal Electoral District(s): Yorkton-Melville
Next Election: Oct. 24, 2012 (4 year terms)
Jim Johnson, Mayor
Susan Gawryluk, Administrator

Tessier
P.O. Box 34
Tessier, SK S0L 3G0
Tel: 306-656-4580
Municipal Type: Village
Incorporated: Aug. 24, 1909 *Area:* 1 sq km
Population in 2011: 25
Provincial Electoral District(s): Rosetown-Elrose
Federal Electoral District(s): Saskatoon-Rosetown-Biggar
Next Election: Oct. 24, 2012 (4 year terms)
L.B. Johnson, Mayor
Barbara Shaw, Clerk

Theodore
P.O. Box 417
102 Main St.
Theodore, SK S0A 4C0
Tel: 306-647-2315; *Fax:* 306-647-2476
theodore.village@sasktel.net
www.villageoftheodore.com
Municipal Type: Village
Incorporated: July 5, 1907 *Area:* 1.73 sq km
Population in 2011: 345
Provincial Electoral District(s): Kelvington-Wadena
Federal Electoral District(s): Yorkton-Melville
Next Election: Oct. 24, 2012 (4 year terms)
Kevin Kotzer, Mayor
Lawrence Skoretz, Administrator

Thode
P.O. Box 202
Dundurn, SK S0K 1K0
Tel: 306-492-2259; *Fax:* 306-492-2068
thode@xplornet.ca
resortvillageofthode.ca
Municipal Type: Resort Village
Area: 0.73 sq km
Population in 2011: 157
Provincial Electoral District(s): Arm River-Watrous
Federal Electoral District(s): Blackstrap
Next Election: July 2016
Alan Thomarat, Mayor
Jessie Williams, Administrator

Timber Bay
General Delivery
Timber Bay, SK S0J 2T0
Tel: 306-663-5885; *Fax:* 306-663-5052
northerntimberbay@sasktel.net
Municipal Type: Northern Hamlet
Incorporated: Oct. 1, 1983 *Area:* 4.44 sq km
Population in 2011: 93
Provincial Electoral District(s): Cumberland
Federal Electoral District(s): Desnethé-Missinippi-Churchill River
Next Election: Autumn 2012 (4 year terms)
Peggy Hennie, Mayor
Sylvia LaVallee, Clerk

Tisdale
P.O. Box 1090
901 - 100 St.
Tisdale, SK S0E 1T0
Tel: 306-873-2681; *Fax:* 306-873-5700
thetownoffice@townoftisdale.com
www.townoftisdale.com
Municipal Type: Town
Incorporated: May 15, 1905 *Area:* 4.62 sq km
Population in 2011: 3,180
Provincial Electoral District(s): Carrot River Valley
Federal Electoral District(s): Prince Albert
Next Election: Oct. 24, 2012 (4 year terms)
Note: Proclaimed as a town on Nov. 1, 1920.
Roland (Rolly) Zimmer, Mayor
Brad Hvidston, Administrator

Tobin Lake
P.O. Box 1479
Nipawin, SK S0E 1E0
Tel: 306-862-2895; *Fax:* 306-862-9320
rvtobinlake@sasktel.net
www.tobinlakeresort.com
Municipal Type: Resort Village
Area: 1.81 sq km
Population in 2011: 90
Provincial Electoral District(s): Carrot River Valley
Federal Electoral District(s): Prince Albert
Next Election: July 2016
Hugh Macdonald, Mayor
Kimberly Kozak, Administrator

Togo
P.O. Box 100
Togo, SK S0A 4E0
Tel: 306-597-2114; *Fax:* 306-597-2114
villageoftogo@sasktel.net
Municipal Type: Village
Incorporated: Sept. 4, 1906 *Area:* 1.5 sq km
Population in 2011: 87
Provincial Electoral District(s): Canora-Pelly
Federal Electoral District(s): Yorkton-Melville
Next Election: Oct. 24, 2012 (4 year terms)
Loretta Erhardt, Mayor
Trudy Lockhart, Administrator

Tompkins
P.O. Box 247
5 - 2nd St.
Tompkins, SK S0N 2S0
Tel: 306-622-2020; *Fax:* 306-622-2025
villageoftompkins@sasktel.net
www.villageoftompkins.ca
Municipal Type: Village
Incorporated: June 2, 1910 *Area:* 2.65 sq km
Population in 2011: 170
Provincial Electoral District(s): Cypress Hills
Federal Electoral District(s): Cypress Hills-Grasslands
Next Election: Oct. 24, 2012 (4 year terms)
John Woodward, Mayor
Tammy Sloan, Administrator

Torquay
P.O. Box 6
Torquay, SK S0C 2L0
Tel: 306-923-2172; *Fax:* 306-923-2172
villageoftorquay@sasktel.net
Municipal Type: Village
Incorporated: Dec. 11, 1923 *Area:* 1.35 sq km
Population in 2011: 236
Provincial Electoral District(s): Estevan
Federal Electoral District(s): Souris-Moose Mountain
Next Election: Oct. 24, 2012 (4 year terms)
Michael Strachan, Mayor
Thera-Lee Deschner, Administrator

Tramping Lake
P.O. Box 157
Tramping Lake, SK S0K 4H0
Tel: 306-755-2002; *Fax:* 306-755-2022
Municipal Type: Village
Incorporated: April 10, 1917 *Area:* 1.39 sq km
Population in 2011: 55
Provincial Electoral District(s): Kindersley
Federal Electoral District(s): Battlefords-Lloydminster
Next Election: Oct. 24, 2012 (4 year terms)
Joe Fruhstuk, Mayor
Rose Simon, Clerk

Tribune
P.O. Box 61
Tribune, SK S0C 2M0
Tel: 306-456-2213; *Fax:* 306-456-2213
Municipal Type: Village
Incorporated: Feb. 18, 1914 *Area:* 1.61 sq km
Population in 2011: 25
Provincial Electoral District(s): Estevan
Federal Electoral District(s): Souris-Moose Mountain
Next Election: Oct. 24, 2012 (4 year terms)
Glenn Walkeden, Mayor
Dallas Locken, Clerk

Tugaske
P.O. Box 159
Tugaske, SK S0H 4B0
Tel: 306-759-2211; *Fax:* 306-759-2249
info@tugaske.com
www.tugaske.com
Municipal Type: Village
Incorporated: May 7, 1909 *Area:* 0.76 sq km
Population in 2011: 92
Provincial Electoral District(s): Thunder Creek
Federal Electoral District(s): Regina-Lumsden-Lake Centre
Next Election: Oct. 24, 2012 (4 year terms)
Kevin Wilson, Mayor
Daryl Dean, Administrator

Turnor Lake
P.O. Box 130
Turnor Lake, SK S0M 3E0
Tel: 306-894-2080; *Fax:* 306-894-2138
Municipal Type: Northern Hamlet
Incorporated: Oct. 1, 1984 *Area:* 4.62 sq km
Population in 2011: 0
Provincial Electoral District(s): Athabasca
Federal Electoral District(s): Desnethé-Missinippi-Churchill River
Next Election: Autumn 2012 (4 year terms)
Marius Montgrand, Mayor
Doreen Morin, Clerk
doreen9401morin@hotmail.com

Turtleford
P.O. Box 38
Turtleford, SK S0M 2Y0
Tel: 306-845-2156; *Fax:* 306-845-3320
townofturtleford@sasktel.net
Municipal Type: Town
Incorporated: Oct. 9, 1914 *Area:* 1.64 sq km
Population in 2011: 525
Provincial Electoral District(s): Cut Knife-Turtleford
Federal Electoral District(s): Battlefords-Lloydminster
Next Election: Oct. 24, 2012 (4 year terms)
Note: Proclaimed as a town on July 1, 1983.
Roland Olson, Mayor
Deanna M. Kahl Lundberg, Administrator

Tuxford
P.O. Box 28
Tuxford, SK S0H 4C0
Tel: 306-691-0785; *Fax:* 306-395-2767
vtuxford@yahoo.ca
Municipal Type: Village
Incorporated: July 19, 1907 *Area:* 0.62 sq km
Population in 2011: 91

Provincial Electoral District(s): Thunder Creek
Federal Electoral District(s): Regina-Lumsden-Lake Centre
Next Election: Oct. 24, 2012 (4 year terms)
Peter Koch, Mayor
Tracy Edwards, Clerk

Unity
P.O. Box 1030
#2, 100 First Ave. West
Unity, SK S0K 4L0
Tel: 306-228-2621; *Fax:* 306-228-4221
townofunity@sasktel.net
www.townofunity.com
Municipal Type: Town
Incorporated: May 18, 1909 *Area:* 9.77 sq km
Population in 2011: 2,389
Provincial Electoral District(s): Kindersley
Federal Electoral District(s): Battlefords-Lloydminster
Next Election: Oct. 24, 2012 (4 year terms)
Note: Proclaimed as a town on Nov. 1, 1919.
Sylvia Maljan, Mayor
Aileen Garrett, Administrator

Uranium City
c/o Ministry of Municipal Affairs
P.O. Box 5000
La Ronge, SK S0J 1L0
Tel: 306-498-3441; *Fax:* 306-498-2112
Other Information: Toll-Free Phone: 1-800-663-1555
Municipal Type: NS
Population in 2010: 201
Provincial Electoral District(s): Athabasca
Federal Electoral District(s): Desnethé-Missinippi-Churchill River
Next Election: Oct. 24, 2012 (4 year terms)
Dean Classen, Chair
Shannon Cholin, Advisor
306-425-4321
shannon.cholin@gov.sk.ca

Val Marie
P.O. Box 178
Val Marie, SK S0N 2T0
Tel: 306-298-2022; *Fax:* 306-298-2224
villageofvalmarie@sasktel.net
Municipal Type: Village
Incorporated: Sept. 13, 1926 *Area:* 0.42 sq km
Population in 2011: 98
Provincial Electoral District(s): Wood River
Federal Electoral District(s): Cypress Hills-Grasslands
Next Election: Oct. 24, 2012 (4 year terms)
Roland Facette, Mayor
Ken Hollinger, Administrator

Valparaiso
P.O. Box 473
Star City, SK S0E 1P0
Tel: 306-863-2522; *Fax:* 306-863-2255
r.m.starcity@sasktel.net
www.newsaskcfdc.ca/valparaiso.htm
Municipal Type: Village
Incorporated: July 18, 1924 *Area:* 0.69 sq km
Population in 2011: 15
Provincial Electoral District(s): Melfort
Federal Electoral District(s): Prince Albert
Next Election: Oct. 24, 2012 (4 year terms)
Margaret Emro, Mayor
Ann Campbell, Clerk

Vanguard
P.O. Box 187
Vanguard, SK S0N 2V0
Tel: 306-582-2295; *Fax:* 306-582-2296
vill.vanguard@sasktel.net
Municipal Type: Village
Incorporated: July 8, 1912 *Area:* 1.86 sq km
Population in 2011: 152
Provincial Electoral District(s): Wood River
Federal Electoral District(s): Cypress Hills-Grasslands
Next Election: Oct. 24, 2012 (4 year terms)
John Bickner, Mayor
Sandra Krushelniski, Administrator

Vanscoy
P.O. Box 480
109 Main St.
Vanscoy, SK S0L 3J0
Tel: 306-668-2008; *Fax:* 306-978-0237
vanscoy@sasktel.net
Municipal Type: Village
Incorporated: June 17, 1919 *Area:* 1.49 sq km
Population in 2011: 377
Provincial Electoral District(s): Biggar
Federal Electoral District(s): Saskatoon-Rosetown-Biggar
Next Election: Oct. 24, 2012 (4 year terms)
Jerome Robert, Mayor
Dawn Steeves, Administrator

Vibank
P.O. Box 204
101 - 2nd Ave.
Vibank, SK S0G 4Y0
Tel: 306-762-2130; *Fax:* 306-762-4722
village.of.vibank@sasktel.net
www.vibank.ca
Municipal Type: Village
Incorporated: June 23, 1911 *Area:* 0.73 sq km
Population in 2011: 374
Provincial Electoral District(s): Indian Head-Milestone
Federal Electoral District(s): Wascana
Next Election: Oct. 24, 2012 (4 year terms)
Shane Henderson, Mayor
shane.henderson@vibank.ca
Jeanette Schaeffer, Administrator

Viscount
P.O. Box 99
319 Bangor Ave.
Viscount, SK S0K 4M0
Tel: 306-944-2199; *Fax:* 306-944-2198
viscount.office@sasktel.net
www.viscount.ca
Municipal Type: Village
Incorporated: Dec. 17, 1908 *Area:* 1.18 sq km
Population in 2011: 252
Provincial Electoral District(s): Humboldt
Federal Electoral District(s): Blackstrap
Next Election: Oct. 24, 2012 (4 year terms)
Moe Kirzinger, Mayor
Valerie Schlosser, Clerk

Vonda
P.O. Box 308
204 Main St.
Vonda, SK S0K 4N0
Tel: 306-258-2035; *Fax:* 306-258-4420
vonda.to@baudoux.ca
www.townofvonda.ca
Municipal Type: Town
Incorporated: Aug. 29, 1905 *Area:* 2.86 sq km
Population in 2011: 353
Provincial Electoral District(s): Humboldt
Federal Electoral District(s): Saskatoon-Humboldt
Next Election: Oct. 24, 2012 (4 year terms)
Note: Proclaimed as a town on May 6, 1907.
Daniel Sembalerus, Mayor
Linda Denis, Clerk

Wadena
P.O. Box 730
102 Main St. North
Wadena, SK S0A 4J0
Tel: 306-338-2145; *Fax:* 306-338-3804
wadadmin@sasktel.net
www.wadena.ca
Municipal Type: Town
Incorporated: Oct. 6, 1906 *Area:* 2.91 sq km
Population in 2011: 1,306
Provincial Electoral District(s): Kelvington-Wadena
Federal Electoral District(s): Yorkton-Melville
Next Election: Oct. 24, 2012 (4 year terms)
Note: Proclaimed as a town on April 1, 1912.
Greg Linnen, Mayor
Diana Lee, Administrator

Wakaw
P.O. Box 669
121 Main St.
Wakaw, SK S0K 4P0
Tel: 306-233-4223; *Fax:* 306-233-5234
town.wakaw@sasktel.net
www.townofwakaw.com
Municipal Type: Town
Incorporated: Dec. 26, 1911 *Area:* 3.12 sq km
Population in 2011: 985
Provincial Electoral District(s): Batoche
Federal Electoral District(s): Saskatoon-Humboldt
Next Election: Oct. 24, 2012 (4 year terms)
Note: Proclaimed as a town on Aug. 1, 1953.
Ed Kidd, Mayor
Rick Kindrachuk, Administrator

Wakaw Lake
P.O. Box 58
126 - 1st St. South
Wakaw, SK S0K 4P0
Tel: 306-233-5671; *Fax:* 306-233-5672
rvwakawlake@gmail.com
www.wakawresortvillage.com
Municipal Type: Resort Village
Area: 0.59 sq km
Population in 2011: 30
Provincial Electoral District(s): Batoche
Federal Electoral District(s): Saskatoon-Humboldt
Next Election: July 2016
Maurice Rivard, Mayor
mg@baudoux.ca
Helen Thomson, Administrator

Waldeck
P.O. Box 97
Waldeck, SK S0H 4J0
Tel: 306-773-6275; *Fax:* 306-773-6275
villageofwaldeck@sasktel.net
Municipal Type: Village
Incorporated: Dec. 23, 1913 *Area:* 2 sq km
Population in 2011: 297
Provincial Electoral District(s): Thunder Creek
Federal Electoral District(s): Cypress Hills-Grasslands
Next Election: Oct. 24, 2012 (4 year terms)
Bill Martens, Mayor
Barb Cornelson, Administrator

Waldheim
P.O. Box 460
Waldheim, SK S0K 4R0
Tel: 306-945-2161; *Fax:* 306-945-2360
town.waldheim@sasktel.net
www.waldheim.ca
Municipal Type: Town
Incorporated: June 10, 1912 *Area:* 1.97 sq km
Population in 2011: 1,035
Provincial Electoral District(s): Martensville
Federal Electoral District(s): Saskatoon-Wanuskewin
Next Election: Oct. 24, 2012 (4 year terms)
Note: Proclaimed as a town on March 1, 1967.
Barbara Schultz, Mayor
D. Chris Adams, Chief Administrative Officer

Waldron
P.O. Box 87
Waldron, SK S0A 4K0
Tel: 306-728-2371
www.spreda.sk.ca/community_Waldron.htm
Municipal Type: Village
Incorporated: July 17, 1909 *Area:* 1.45 sq km
Population in 2011: 20
Provincial Electoral District(s): Melville-Saltcoats
Federal Electoral District(s): Yorkton-Melville
Next Election: Oct. 24, 2012 (4 year terms)
Raymond Kitch, Mayor
Arlene Maguire, Clerk

Wapella
P.O. Box 189
Wapella, SK S0G 4Z0
Tel: 306-532-4343; *Fax:* 306-532-4342
townofwapella@sasktel.net
www.townofwapella.com
Municipal Type: Town
Incorporated: Dec. 29, 1898 *Area:* 2.56 sq km
Population in 2011: 333
Provincial Electoral District(s): Moosomin
Federal Electoral District(s): Souris-Moose Mountain
Next Election: Oct. 24, 2012 (4 year terms)
Note: Proclaimed as a town on Nov. 20, 1903.
Gilbert Lloyd, Mayor
Charlene Neufeld, Administrator
townoffice@townofwapella.com

Warman
P.O. Box 340
107 Central St. West
Warman, SK S0K 4S0
Tel: 306-933-2133; *Fax:* 306-933-1987
town.warman@sasktel.net
www.townofwarman.ca
Municipal Type: Town
Incorporated: Aug. 3, 1906 *Area:* 5.34 sq km
Population in 2011: 7,084
Provincial Electoral District(s): Martensville
Federal Electoral District(s): Saskatoon-Wanuskewin
Next Election: Oct. 24, 2012 (4 year terms)
Note: Proclaimed as a town on July 1, 1966.

Sheryl Spence, Mayor
Ivan Gabrysh, Chief Administrative officer
ivang@warman.ca

Waseca
Douglas Place
P.O. Box 88
Waseca, SK S0M 3A0
Tel: 306-893-2211; *Fax:* 306-893-4193
villageofwaseca@sasktel.net
Municipal Type: Village
Incorporated: March 15, 1911 *Area:* 0.68 sq km
Population in 2011: 154
Provincial Electoral District(s): Cut Knife-Turtleford
Federal Electoral District(s): Battlefords-Lloydminster
Next Election: Oct. 24, 2012 (4 year terms)
Curtis Sutherland, Mayor
Sandra Sutherland, Administrator

Watrous
P.O. Box 730
Watrous, SK S0K 4T0
Tel: 306-946-3369; *Fax:* 306-946-2974
townofwatrous@sasktel.net
www.townofwatrous.com; www.watrousmanitou.com
Municipal Type: Town
Incorporated: Oct. 15, 1908 *Area:* 11.17 sq km
Population in 2011: 1,857
Provincial Electoral District(s): Arm River-Watrous
Federal Electoral District(s): Blackstrap
Next Election: Oct. 24, 2012 (4 year terms)
Note: Proclaimed as a town on Dec. 30, 1909.
Ed Collins, Mayor
Orrin Redden, Administrator

Watson
P.O. Box 276
Watson, SK S0K 4V0
Tel: 306-287-3224; *Fax:* 306-287-3442
contact@townofwatson.com
www.townofwatson.ca; www.quill-lakes.com/watson/town
Municipal Type: Town
Incorporated: Oct. 6, 1906 *Area:* 2.83 sq km
Population in 2011: 777
Provincial Electoral District(s): Melfort
Federal Electoral District(s): Saskatoon-Humboldt
Next Election: Oct. 24, 2012 (4 year terms)
Note: Proclaimed as a town on Aug. 1, 1908.
Mike Saretsky, Mayor
Cathy Coleman, Administrator

Wawota
P.O. Box 58
308 Railway Ave.
Wawota, SK S0G 5A0
Tel: 306-739-2216; *Fax:* 306-739-2216
wawota.town@sasktel.net
www.wawota.com
Municipal Type: Town
Incorporated: Dec. 10, 1907 *Area:* 1.24 sq km
Population in 2011: 560
Provincial Electoral District(s): Cannington
Federal Electoral District(s): Souris-Moose Mountain
Next Election: Oct. 24, 2012 (4 year terms)
Note: Proclaimed as a town on Feb. 1, 1975.
Norman Oliver, Mayor
Diane Smith, Administrator

Webb
P.O. Box 100
Webb, SK S0N 2X0
Tel: 306-674-2230; *Fax:* 306-674-2324
rm138@xplornet.com
Municipal Type: Village
Incorporated: June 18, 1910 *Area:* 1.41 sq km
Population in 2011: 58
Provincial Electoral District(s): Cypress Hills
Federal Electoral District(s): Cypress Hills-Grasslands
Next Election: Oct. 24, 2012 (4 year terms)
John Martens, Mayor
Raylene Packet, Administrator

Wee Too Beach
3631 Hammstrom Way East
Regina, SK S4N 7N3
Tel: 306-352-8521
weetoo@sasktel.net
www.weetoobeach.com
Municipal Type: Resort Village
Area: 0.17 sq km
Population in 2011: 35
Provincial Electoral District(s): Thunder Creek
Federal Electoral District(s): Regina-Lumsden-Lake Centre
Next Election: July 2016
Brian Benz, Mayor
Jim Ell, Administrator
306-529-2562

Weekes
P.O. Box 159
Weekes, SK S0E 1V0
Tel: 306-278-2800; *Fax:* 306-278-2395
weekes123@xplornet.ca
www.newsaskcfdc.ca/weekes.htm
Municipal Type: Village
Incorporated: Jan. 13, 1947 *Area:* 0.59 sq km
Population in 2011: 42
Provincial Electoral District(s): Kelvington-Wadena
Federal Electoral District(s): Yorkton-Melville
Next Election: Oct. 24, 2012 (4 year terms)
Kenneth Harris, Mayor
Betty Gagnon, Clerk

Weirdale
General Delivery
Albertville, SK S0J 0A0
Tel: 306-929-2625; *Fax:* 306-929-2197
weirdale@hotmail.com
Municipal Type: Village
Incorporated: April 1, 1948 *Area:* 1.36 sq km
Population in 2011: 75
Provincial Electoral District(s): Saskatchewan Rivers
Federal Electoral District(s): Prince Albert
Next Election: Oct. 24, 2012 (4 year terms)
Rolena Krawec, Mayor
Betty Glatley, Clerk

Weldon
P.O. Box 190
Weldon, SK S0J 3A0
Tel: 306-887-2070; *Fax:* 306-752-3882
weldon@sk.sympatico.ca
www.newsaskcfdc.ca/weldon.htm
Municipal Type: Village
Incorporated: Jan. 24, 1914 *Area:* 1.1 sq km
Population in 2011: 196
Provincial Electoral District(s): Batoche
Federal Electoral District(s): Prince Albert
Next Election: Oct. 24, 2012 (4 year terms)
Neil Ball, Mayor
Shelley Holmes, Administrator

Welwyn
P.O. Box 118
Welwyn, SK S0A 4L0
Tel: 306-733-2077; *Fax:* 306-733-2078
welwynvillage@hotmail.com
Municipal Type: Village
Incorporated: June 11, 1907 *Area:* 0.64 sq km
Population in 2011: 135
Provincial Electoral District(s): Moosomin
Federal Electoral District(s): Souris-Moose Mountain
Next Election: Oct. 24, 2012 (4 year terms)
Joe Santer, Mayor
Monica Pethick, Administrator

West End
P.O. Box 1765
Esterhazy, SK S0A 0X0
Tel: 306-793-4558
perch25@xplornet.com
Municipal Type: Resort Village
Area: 0.34 sq km
Population in 2011: 17
Provincial Electoral District(s): Melville-Saltcoats
Federal Electoral District(s): Yorkton-Melville
Next Election: July 2016
Iris Hanson, Mayor
Marjorie Deschambault, Administrator

Weyakwin
P.O. Box 295
Weyakwin Rd.
Weyakwin, SK S0J 1W0
Tel: 306-663-5820; *Fax:* 306-663-5112
weyakwin@sasktel.net
Municipal Type: Northern Hamlet
Incorporated: Dec. 1, 1983 *Area:* 8.2 sq km
Population in 2011: 135
Provincial Electoral District(s): Cumberland
Federal Electoral District(s): Desnethé-Missinippi-Churchill River
Next Election: Autumn 2012 (4 year terms)
Stella Brown, Mayor
Flora Kraus, Clerk

Weyburn No. 67
23 - 6 St. NE
Weyburn, SK S4H 1A7
Tel: 306-842-2314; *Fax:* 306-842-1002
rm.67@sasktel.net
Municipal Type: Municipality
Incorporated: Dec. 13, 1909 *Area:* 811.70 sq km
Population in 2011: 1,048
Next Election: Oct 2012; staggered 2 yr term
Note: URL:
www.saskbiz.ca/communityprofiles/CommunityProfile.Asp?CommunityID=1024
Carmen Sterling, Reeve
Kim McIvor, Administrator

White City
P.O. Box 220 Main
14 Ramm Ave. East
White City, SK S4L 5B1
Tel: 306-781-2355; *Fax:* 306-781-2194
townoffice@whitecity.ca
www.whitecity.ca
Municipal Type: Town
Incorporated: March 1, 1967 *Area:* 4.64 sq km
Population in 2011: 1,894
Provincial Electoral District(s): Regina Wascana Plains
Federal Electoral District(s): Regina-Qu'Appelle
Next Election: Oct. 24, 2012 (4 year terms)
Note: Proclaimed as a town on Nov. 1, 2000.
Bruce Evans, Mayor
bevans@whitecity.ca
Shauna Bzdel, Office Manager
sbzdel@whitecity.ca

White Fox
P.O. Box 38
116 Main St.
White Fox, SK S0J 3B0
Tel: 306-276-2106; *Fax:* 306-276-2131
villageofwhitefox@sasktel.net
www.whitefox.ca
Municipal Type: Village
Incorporated: July 21, 1941 *Area:* 0.85 sq km
Population in 2011: 364
Provincial Electoral District(s): Saskatchewan Rivers
Federal Electoral District(s): Desnethé-Missinippi-Churchill River
Next Election: Oct. 24, 2012 (4 year terms)
Gary Vidnes, Mayor
Kimberley Issacson, Administrator

Whitewood
P.O. Box 129
731 Lalonde St.
Whitewood, SK S0G 5C0
Tel: 306-735-2210; *Fax:* 306-735-2262
general@townofwhitewood.ca
www.townofwhitewood.ca
Municipal Type: Town
Incorporated: Dec. 31, 1892 *Area:* 3.04 sq km
Population in 2011: 950
Provincial Electoral District(s): Moosomin
Federal Electoral District(s): Souris-Moose Mountain
Next Election: Oct. 24, 2012 (4 year terms)
Malcolm Green, Mayor
Sharon Rodgers, Administrator

Wilcox
P.O. Box 130
Wilcox, SK S0G 5E0
Tel: 306-732-2030; *Fax:* 306-732-4495
rm129@sasktel.net
www.wilcox.ca
Municipal Type: Village
Incorporated: April 20, 1907 *Area:* 1.48 sq km
Population in 2011: 339
Provincial Electoral District(s): Indian Head-Milestone
Federal Electoral District(s): Palliser
Next Election: Oct. 24, 2012 (4 year terms)
Pat Vigneron, Mayor
Trish Schmidt, Village Clerk

Wilkie
P.O. Box 580
206 - 2nd Ave. West
Wilkie, SK S0K 4W0
Tel: 306-843-2692; *Fax:* 306-843-3151
contact@townofwilkie.com
www.townofwilkie.com
Municipal Type: Town
Incorporated: July 18, 1908 *Area:* 9.48 sq km
Population in 2011: 1,301
Provincial Electoral District(s): Biggar

Federal Electoral District(s): Battlefords-Lloydminster
Next Election: Oct. 24, 2012 (4 year terms)
Note: Proclaimed as a town on Nov. 1, 1910.
Kevin Glessing, Mayor
Lana Gerein, Administrator

Willow Bunch
P.O. Box 189
16 - 5th Edouard Beaupre St. East
Willow Bunch, SK S0H 4K0
Tel: 306-473-2450; *Fax:* 306-473-2773
www.willowbunch.ca
Municipal Type: Town
Incorporated: Nov. 15, 1929 *Area:* 0.84 sq km
Population in 2011: 286
Provincial Electoral District(s): Weyburn-Big Muddy
Federal Electoral District(s): Cypress Hills-Grasslands
Next Election: Oct. 24, 2012 (4 year terms)
Note: Proclaimed as a town on Oct. 1, 1960.
Renaud Bissonnette, Mayor
Margaret L. Brown, Administrator

Windthorst
P.O. Box 98
202 Angus St.
Windthorst, SK S0G 5G0
Tel: 306-224-2033; *Fax:* 306-224-4610
village.windthorst@sasktel.net
www.windthorstvillage.ca
Municipal Type: Village
Incorporated: Aug. 21, 1907 *Area:* 1.43 sq km
Population in 2011: 215
Provincial Electoral District(s): Moosomin
Federal Electoral District(s): Souris-Moose Mountain
Next Election: Oct. 24, 2012 (4 year terms)
Norm Jones, Mayor
Denise Swallow, Administrator

Wiseton
P.O. Box 160
Wiseton, SK S0L 3M0
Tel: 306-357-2022; *Fax:* 306-357-2027
villageofwiseton@sasktel.net
Municipal Type: Village
Incorporated: Sept. 23, 1913 *Area:* 0.77 sq km
Population in 2011: 88
Provincial Electoral District(s): Rosetown-Elrose
Federal Electoral District(s): Cypress Hills-Grasslands
Next Election: Oct. 24, 2012 (4 year terms)
Les Meyers, Mayor
Cheryl Joel, Administrator

Wollaston Lake
P.O. Box 189
Wollaston Lake, SK S0J 3C0
Tel: 306-633-2255; *Fax:* 306-633-2254
Municipal Type: NS
Population in 2010: 129
Provincial Electoral District(s): Cumberland
Federal Electoral District(s): Desnethé-Missinippi-Churchill River
Next Election: Oct. 24, 2012 (4 year terms)
Terri Daniels, Chair
Valerie Antoniuk, Advisor
valerie.antoniuk@gov.sk.ca

Wolseley
P.O. Box 310
Wolseley, SK S0G 5H0
Tel: 306-698-2477; *Fax:* 306-698-2953
townofwolseley@sasktel.net; administrator@wolseley.ca
www.wolseley.ca
Municipal Type: Town
Incorporated: Oct. 20, 1898 *Area:* 5.93 sq km
Population in 2011: 864
Provincial Electoral District(s): Moosomin
Federal Electoral District(s): Regina-Qu'Appelle
Next Election: Oct. 24, 2012 (4 year terms)
Dennis Fjestad, Mayor
mayor@wolseley.ca
Kimberley Palmer, Administrator

Wood Mountain
P.O. Box 89
Wood Mountain, SK S0H 4L0
Tel: 306-266-4810; *Fax:* 306-266-2020
wmtvillage@sasktel.net
www.woodmountain.ca
Municipal Type: Village
Incorporated: March 4, 1930 *Area:* 0.61 sq km
Population in 2011: 25
Provincial Electoral District(s): Wood River

Federal Electoral District(s): Cypress Hills-Grasslands
Next Election: Oct. 24, 2012 (4 year terms)
Michael Klein, Mayor
Sherry Mielke, Clerk

Wynyard
P.O. Box 220
435 Bosworth St.
Wynyard, SK S0A 4T0
Tel: 306-554-2123; *Fax:* 306-554-3224
town.office.wynyard@sasktel.net
www.townofwynyard.com
Municipal Type: Town
Incorporated: Oct. 9, 1908 *Area:* 5.29 sq km
Population in 2011: 1,767
Provincial Electoral District(s): Arm River-Watrous
Federal Electoral District(s): Regina-Qu'Appelle
Next Election: Oct. 24, 2012 (4 year terms)
Note: Proclaimed as a town on Nov. 1, 1911.
Sharon Armstrong, Mayor
Jason Chorneyko, Administrator

Yarbo
P.O. Box 96
Yarbo, SK S0A 4V0
Tel: 306-745-3532
villageofyarbo@sasktel.net
Municipal Type: Village
Incorporated: July 1, 1964 *Area:* 0.83 sq km
Population in 2011: 53
Provincial Electoral District(s): Melville-Saltcoats
Federal Electoral District(s): Yorkton-Melville
Next Election: Oct. 24, 2012 (4 year terms)
Nancy Prazma, Mayor
Harlene Swain, Clerk

Yellow Grass
P.O. Box 270
102 Coteau Ave. West
Yellow Grass, SK S0G 5J0
Tel: 306-465-2400; *Fax:* 306-465-2802
yellowgrass@signaldirect.ca
www.yellowgrass.ca
Municipal Type: Town
Incorporated: July 22, 1903 *Area:* 2.68 sq km
Population in 2011: 440
Provincial Electoral District(s): Weyburn-Big Muddy
Federal Electoral District(s): Souris-Moose Mountain
Next Election: Oct. 24, 2012 (4 year terms)
Note: Proclaimed as a town on Feb. 15, 1906.
William Wilke, Mayor
Wendy Carver, Administrator

Young
P.O. Box 359
Young, SK S0K 4Y0
Tel: 306-259-2242; *Fax:* 306-259-2247
villageoffice@young.ca
www.young.ca
Municipal Type: Village
Incorporated: June 7, 1910 *Area:* 2.51 sq km
Population in 2011: 239
Provincial Electoral District(s): Arm River-Watrous
Federal Electoral District(s): Blackstrap
Next Election: Oct. 24, 2012 (4 year terms)
Garth Sebelius, Mayor
Belinda Rowan, Administrator

Zealandia
P.O. Box 52
Zealandia, SK S0L 3N0
Tel: 306-882-4177; *Fax:* 306-882-4178
townofzealandia@yahoo.com
Municipal Type: Town
Incorporated: May 22, 1909 *Area:* 1.38 sq km
Population in 2011: 80
Provincial Electoral District(s): Rosetown-Elrose
Federal Electoral District(s): Saskatoon-Rosetown-Biggar
Next Election: Oct. 24, 2012 (4 year terms)
Note: Proclaimed as a town on Nov. 1, 1911.
Darren Haugen, Mayor
Lynn Farquharson, Clerk

Zelma
Zelma GMB #14
Allan, SK S0K 0C0
Tel: 306-257-3927; *Fax:* 306-257-4125
Municipal Type: Village
Incorporated: Aug. 10, 1910 *Area:* 0.72 sq km
Population in 2011: 35
Provincial Electoral District(s): Humboldt

Federal Electoral District(s): Blackstrap
Next Election: Oct. 24, 2012 (4 year terms)
R. Glen Crockett, Mayor
Maxine A. Fischer, Clerk

Zenon Park
P.O. Box 278
Zenon Park, SK S0E 1W0
Tel: 306-767-2233; *Fax:* 306-767-2226
vofzenon@sasktel.net
www.newsaskcfdc.ca/zenonpark.htm
Municipal Type: Village
Incorporated: July 28, 1941 *Area:* 0.56 sq km
Population in 2011: 187
Provincial Electoral District(s): Carrot River Valley
Federal Electoral District(s): Prince Albert
Next Election: Oct. 24, 2012 (4 year terms)
Cory Clapson, Mayor
Lisa LeBlanc, Administrator

Rural Municipality

Aberdeen No. 373
P.O. Box 40
Aberdeen, SK S0K 0A0
Tel: 306-253-4312; *Fax:* 306-253-4445
rm373@sasktel.net
www.rmofaberdeen.ca
Municipal Type: Rural Municipality
Incorporated: Dec. 13, 1909 *Area:* 673.43 sq km
Population in 2011: 1,016
Next Election: Oct 24, 2012 (every 2 years)
Real Hamoline, Reeve
Gary Dziadyk, Administrator

Antelope Park No. 322
P.O. Box 70
Marengo, SK S0L 2K0
Tel: 306-968-2922; *Fax:* 306-968-2278
rm292.rm322@sasktel.net
Municipal Type: Rural Municipality
Incorporated: Dec. 11, 1911 *Area:* 612.66 sq km
Population in 2011: 150
Next Election: 2013 (election every 2 years)
Gordon Dommett, Reeve
Shelley Mohr, Administrator

Antler No. 61
P.O. Box 70
Redvers, SK S0C 2H0
Tel: 306-452-3263; *Fax:* 306-452-3518
rm61@sasktel.net
Municipal Type: Rural Municipality
Incorporated: Dec. 13, 1909 *Area:* 832.23 sq km
Population in 2011: 536
Next Election: Oct 24, 2012 (every 2 years)
Ron Henderson, Reeve
Mike Wirges, Administrator

Arborfield No. 456
P.O. Box 280
Arborfield, SK S0E 0A0
Tel: 306-769-8533; *Fax:* 306-769-8301
arborfieldrm456@sasktel.net
www.arborfieldsk.ca/council.htm
Municipal Type: Rural Municipality
Incorporated: Jan. 1, 1913 *Area:* 1,416.01 sq km
Population in 2011: 453
Next Election: 2013 (election every 2 years)
Alec J. Black, Reeve
Allan Frisky, Administrator

Argyle No. 1
P.O. Box 120
Gainsborough, SK S0C 0Z0
Tel: 306-685-2010; *Fax:* 306-685-2161
rm.1@sasktel.net
saskbiz.ca/communityprofiles/communityprofile.asp?CommunityID=753
Municipal Type: Rural Municipality
Incorporated: Dec. 19, 1912 *Area:* 579.99 sq km
Population in 2011: 270
Next Election: Oct 24, 2012 (every 2 years)
Robert Meredith, Reeve
Erin McMillen, Administrator

Arlington No. 79
P.O. Box 1115
264 Centre St.
Shaunavon, SK S0N 2M0
Tel: 306-297-2108; *Fax:* 306-297-2144
rm79@sasktel.net
saskbiz.ca/communityprofiles/CommunityProfile.Asp?CommunityID=754
Municipal Type: Rural Municipality
Incorporated: Jan. 1, 1913 *Area:* 846.79 sq km
Population in 2011: 345
Next Election: Oct 24, 2012 (every 2 years)
Donald L. Lundberg, Reeve
Richard E. Goulet, Administrator

Arm River No. 252
P.O. Box 250
Davidson, SK S0G 1A0
Tel: 306-567-3103; *Fax:* 306-567-3266
rm253@sasktel.net
Municipal Type: Rural Municipality
Incorporated: Dec. 13, 1909 *Area:* 725.26 sq km
Population in 2011: 249
Next Election: 2013 (election every 2 years)
Lorne Willner, Reeve
Yvonne (Bonny) Goodsman, Administrator

Auvergne No. 76
P.O. Box 60
Ponteix, SK S0N 1Z0
Tel: 306-625-3210; *Fax:* 306-625-3681
rm76@sasktel.net
Municipal Type: Rural Municipality
Incorporated: Jan. 1, 1913 *Area:* 853.40 sq km
Population in 2011: 354
Next Election: 2013 (election every 2 years)
Allan R. Oliver, Reeve
Roxanne Empey, Administrator

Baildon No. 131
P.O. Box 1902
Moose Jaw, SK S6H 7N6
Tel: 306-693-2166; *Fax:* 306-693-2166
rm131@sasktel.net
saskbiz.ca/communityprofiles/CommunityProfile.Asp?CommunityID=757
Municipal Type: Rural Municipality
Incorporated: Dec. 9, 1912 *Area:* 846.21 sq km
Population in 2011: 594
Next Election: Oct 24, 2012 (every 2 years)
Sheldon Okerstrom, Reeve
Janna Smith, Administrator

Barrier Valley No. 397
P.O. Box 246
Archerwill, SK S0E 0B0
Tel: 306-323-2101; *Fax:* 306-323-2106
rm397@sasktel.net
saskbiz.ca/communityprofiles/CommunityProfile.Asp?CommunityID=758
Municipal Type: Rural Municipality
Incorporated: Oct. 29, 1917 *Area:* 819.99 sq km
Population in 2011: 498
Next Election: Oct 24, 2012 (every 2 years)
Quentin Ralph Hanson, Reeve
Glenda Smith, Administrator

Battle River No. 438
P.O. Box 159
Battleford, SK S0M 0E0
Tel: 306-937-2235; *Fax:* 306-937-2235
rm438@sasktel.net
saskbiz.ca/communityprofiles/CommunityProfile.Asp?CommunityID=759
Municipal Type: Rural Municipality
Incorporated: Dec. 12, 1910 *Area:* 1,061.40 sq km
Population in 2011: 1,099
Next Election: 2013 (election every 2 years)
Joseph Beckman, Reeve
Betty Johnson, Administrator

Bayne No. 371
P.O. Box 130
Bruno, SK S0K 0S0
Tel: 306-369-2511; *Fax:* 306-369-2528
rm371@sasktel.net
saskbiz.ca/communityprofiles/communityprofile.asp?CommunityID=760
Municipal Type: Rural Municipality
Incorporated: Dec. 12, 1910 *Area:* 802.93 sq km
Population in 2011: 493
Next Election: Oct 24, 2012 (every 2 years)
Gerald Picouye, Reeve
Lonnie Sowa, Administrator

Beaver River No. 622
P.O. Box 129
159 Main St.
Pierceland, SK S0M 2K0
Tel: 306-839-2060; *Fax:* 306-839-2178
rm622@sasktel.net
www.rmofbeaverriver622.ca
Municipal Type: Rural Municipality
Incorporated: Jan. 1, 1978 *Area:* 2,370.25 sq km
Population in 2011: 1,017
Next Election: 2013 (election every 2 years)
Murray Rausch, Reeve
Rita Rogers, Administrator

Bengough No. 40
P.O. Box 429
Bengough, SK S0C 0K0
Tel: 306-268-2055; *Fax:* 306-268-2054
rm40@sasktel.net
www.rm40.com
Municipal Type: Rural Municipality
Incorporated: Jan. 1, 1913 *Area:* 1,036.91 sq km
Population in 2011: 329
Next Election: 2013 (election every 2 years)
Terry Gravelle, Reeve
Lara Hazen, Administrator

Benson No. 35
P.O. Box 69
Benson, SK S0C 0L0
Tel: 306-634-9410; *Fax:* 306-634-8804
rm35@sasktel.net
saskbiz.ca/communityprofiles/CommunityProfile.Asp?CommunityID=762
Municipal Type: Rural Municipality
Incorporated: Dec. 13, 1909 *Area:* 836.39 sq km
Population in 2011: 490
Next Election: Oct 24, 2012 (every 2 years)
David Hoffort, Reeve
Laureen Keating, Administrator

Big Arm No. 251
P.O. Box 10
Stalwart, SK S0G 4R0
Tel: 306-963-2402; *Fax:* 306-963-2405
rm251@sasktel.net
saskbiz.ca/communityprofiles/communityprofile.asp?CommunityID=763
Municipal Type: Rural Municipality
Incorporated: Dec. 11, 1911 *Area:* 699.47 sq km
Population in 2011: 200
Next Election: Oct 24, 2012 (every 2 years)
Paul Remlinger, Reeve
Yvonne (Bonny) Goodsman, Administrator

Big Quill No. 308
P.O. Box 898
Wynyard, SK S0A 4T0
Tel: 306-554-2533; *Fax:* 306-554-3935
rm308@sasktel.net
Municipal Type: Rural Municipality
Incorporated: Dec. 13, 1909 *Area:* 739.86 sq km
Population in 2011: 587
Next Election: 2013 (election every 2 years)
Eugene McSymytz, Reeve
Gail Wolfe, Administrator

Big River No. 555
P.O. Box 219
Big River, SK S0J 0E0
Tel: 306-469-2323; *Fax:* 306-469-2428
rm555@sasktel.net
www.bigriver.ca/rm.html
Municipal Type: Rural Municipality
Incorporated: Oct. 1, 1977 *Area:* 2,488.22 sq km
Population in 2011: 855
Next Election: Oct 24, 2012 (every 2 years)
Doug Panter, Reeve
Donna Tymiak, Administrator

Big Stick No. 141
P.O. Box 9
Golden Prairie, SK S0N 0Y0
Tel: 306-662-2883; *Fax:* 306-662-3954
rm141@sasktel.net
Municipal Type: Rural Municipality
Incorporated: Dec. 11, 1911 *Area:* 821.40 sq km
Population in 2011: 148
Next Election: Oct 24, 2012 (every 2 years)
Edward Feil, Reeve
Quinton Jacksteit, Administrator

Biggar No. 347
P.O. Box 280
Biggar, SK S0K 0M0
Tel: 306-948-2422; *Fax:* 306-948-2250
rm347@sasktel.net
Municipal Type: Rural Municipality
Incorporated: Dec. 11, 1911 *Area:* 1,597.87 sq km
Population in 2011: 820
Next Election: Oct 24, 2012 (every 2 years)
Louise Singer, Reeve
Adrienne Urban, Administrator

Birch Hills No. 460
P.O. Box 369
Birch Hills, SK S0J 0G0
Tel: 306-749-2233; *Fax:* 306-749-2220
rm460@sasktel.net
Municipal Type: Rural Municipality
Incorporated: Dec. 11, 1911 *Area:* 554.52 sq km
Population in 2011: 663
Next Election: 2013 (election every 2 years)
Earl Mickelson, Reeve
Shiley Pratchler, Administrator

Bjorkdale No. 426
P.O. Box 10
Crooked River, SK S0E 0R0
Tel: 306-873-2470; *Fax:* 306-873-2470
rm.426.bjork@xplornet.com
saskbiz.ca/communityprofiles/CommunityProfile.Asp?CommunityID=769
Municipal Type: Rural Municipality
Incorporated: Jan. 1, 1913 *Area:* 1,458.79 sq km
Population in 2011: 900
Next Election: 2013 (election every 2 years)
Wayne Dmytriw, Reeve
Lisa Hamelin, Administrator

Blaine Lake No. 434
P.O. Box 38
Blaine Lake, SK S0J 0J0
Tel: 306-497-2282; *Fax:* 306-497-2511
rm434@sasktel.net
saskbiz.ca/communityprofiles/CommunityProfile.Asp?CommunityID=770
Municipal Type: Rural Municipality
Incorporated: Dec. 9, 1912 *Area:* 799.89 sq km
Population in 2011: 288
Next Election: 2013 (election every 2 years)
Note: Rural municipalities hold general elections every two years.
Eugene Chudskov, Reeve
Tony Obrigewitch, Administrator

Blucher No. 343
P.O. Box 100
Bradwell, SK S0K 0P0
Tel: 306-257-3344; *Fax:* 306-257-3303
rm343@sasktel.net
www.rm343.com
Municipal Type: Rural Municipality
Incorporated: Dec. 13, 1909 *Area:* 789.28 sq km
Population in 2011: 1,787
Next Election: Oct 24, 2012 (every 2 years)
Daniel Greschuk, Reeve
R. Doran Scott, Administrator

Bone Creek No. 108
P.O. Box 459
Shaunavon, SK S0N 2M0
Tel: 306-297-2570; *Fax:* 306-297-6270
rmbc@sasktel.net
Municipal Type: Rural Municipality
Incorporated: Dec. 11, 1911 *Area:* 847.16 sq km
Population in 2011: 340
Next Election: 2013 (election every 2 years)
Ben Lewans, Reeve
Lana Barle, Administrator

Bratt's Lake No. 129
P.O. Box 130
Wilcox, SK S0G 5E0
Tel: 306-732-2030; *Fax:* 306-732-4495
rm129@sasktel.net
Municipal Type: Rural Municipality
Incorporated: Jan. 1, 1913 *Area:* 844.94 sq km
Population in 2011: 350
Next Election: Oct 24, 2012 (every 2 years)
J. Barry Hamdorf, Reeve
Kevin S. Ritchie, Administrator

Britannia No. 502
P.O. Box 661
4824 - 47th St.
Lloydminster, SK S9V 0Y7
Tel: 306-825-2610; *Fax:* 306-825-8894
rm502@sasktel.net
www.rmbritannia.com
Municipal Type: Rural Municipality
Incorporated: Dec. 13, 1909 *Area:* 950.87 sq km
Population in 2011: 1,734
Next Election: 2013 (election every 2 years)
John Light, Reeve
Darcy Olson, Clerk

Brock No. 64
P.O. Box 247
Kisbey, SK S0C 1L0
Tel: 306-462-2010; *Fax:* 306-462-2016
rm64@signaldirect.ca
saskbiz.ca/communityprofiles/communityprofile.asp?CommunityID=775
Municipal Type: Rural Municipality
Incorporated: Dec. 12, 1910 *Area:* 827.53 sq km
Population in 2011: 238
Next Election: 2013 (election every 2 years)
Paul Cameron, Reeve
Michael Rattray, Administrator

Brokenshell No. 68
23 - 6th St. NE
Weyburn, SK S4H 1A7
Tel: 306-842-2314; *Fax:* 306-842-1002
rm.67@sasktel.net
saskbiz.ca/communityprofiles/CommunityProfile.Asp?CommunityID=776
Municipal Type: Rural Municipality
Incorporated: Dec. 13, 1909 *Area:* 850.01 sq km
Population in 2011: 308
Next Election: 2013 (election every 2 years)
Don Watson, Reeve
Kim McIvor, Administrator

Browning No. 34
P.O. Box 40
Lampman, SK S0C 1N0
Tel: 306-487-2444; *Fax:* 306-487-2496
browning.lampman@sasktel.net
saskbiz.ca/communityprofiles/communityprofile.asp?CommunityID=777
Municipal Type: Rural Municipality
Incorporated: Dec. 11, 1911 *Area:* 823.39 sq km
Population in 2011: 399
Next Election: 2013 (election every 2 years)
Randy Fleck, Reeve
Greg Wallin, Administrator

Buchanan No. 304
P.O. Box 10
Buchanan, SK S0A 0J0
Tel: 306-592-2055; *Fax:* 306-592-4436
rm304@sasktel.net
Municipal Type: Rural Municipality
Incorporated: Jan. 1, 1913 *Area:* 738.80 sq km
Population in 2011: 406
Next Election: 2013 (election every 2 years)
Gerald Wolkowski, Reeve
Twila Hadubiak, Administrator

Buckland No. 491
99 River St. East
Prince Albert, SK S6V 0A1
Tel: 306-763-2585; *Fax:* 306-763-6369
rm491@sasktel.net
www.rmbuckland.ca
Municipal Type: Rural Municipality
Incorporated: Dec. 11, 1911 *Area:* 791.55 sq km
Population in 2011: 3,658
Next Election: Oct 24, 2012 (every 2 years)
Larry Fladager, Reeve
reeve@rmbuckland.ca
Wendy Gowda, Administrator

Buffalo No. 409
P.O. Box 100
Wilkie, SK S0K 4W0
Tel: 306-843-2342; *Fax:* 306-843-2455
rm409@sasktel.net
saskbiz.ca/communityprofiles/communityprofile.asp?CommunityID=780
Municipal Type: Rural Municipality
Incorporated: Dec. 13, 1909 *Area:* 1,222.08 sq km
Population in 2011: 506
Next Election: Oct 24, 2012 (every 2 years)
Leslie Krochinski, Reeve
Sherry Huber, Administrator

Calder No. 241
P.O. Box 10
Wroxton, SK S0A 4S0
Tel: 306-742-4233; *Fax:* 306-742-4559
calderrm@sasktel.net
Municipal Type: Rural Municipality
Incorporated: Jan. 1, 1913 *Area:* 807.15 sq km
Population in 2011: 322
Next Election: Oct 24, 2012 (every 2 years)
Dennis Elaschuk, Reeve
Linda Napady, Administrator

Caledonia No. 99
P.O. Box 328
Milestone, SK S0G 3L0
Tel: 306-436-2050; *Fax:* 306-436-2051
milcal@sasktel.net
saskbiz.ca/communityprofiles/communityprofile.asp?CommunityID=782
Municipal Type: Rural Municipality
Incorporated: Dec. 13, 1909 *Area:* 845.68 sq km
Population in 2011: 257
Next Election: Oct 24, 2012 (every 2 years)
Richard Linton, Reeve
Stephen Schury, Administrator

Cambria No. 6
P.O. Box 210
Torquay, SK S0C 2L0
Tel: 306-923-2000; *Fax:* 306-923-2099
rm.cambria@sasktel.net
saskbiz.ca/communityprofiles/CommunityProfile.Asp?CommunityID=783
Municipal Type: Rural Municipality
Incorporated: Dec. 13, 1909 *Area:* 814.14 sq km
Population in 2011: 304
Next Election: 2013 (election every 2 years)
James Phillips, Reeve
Monica Wheeler, Administrator

Cana No. 214
P.O. Box 550
Melville, SK S0A 2P0
Tel: 306-728-5645; *Fax:* 306-728-3807
rmcana@sasktel.net
www.spreda.sk.ca/community_RM_of_Cana.htm
Municipal Type: Rural Municipality
Incorporated: Dec. 13, 1909 *Area:* 820.81 sq km
Population in 2011: 858
Next Election: 2013 (election every 2 years)
Robert Almasi, Reeve
Audrey Law, Administrator

Canaan No. 225
P.O. Box 99
Lucky Lake, SK S0L 1Z0
Tel: 306-858-2234; *Fax:* 306-858-2234
rm225.vll@sasktel.net
Municipal Type: Rural Municipality
Incorporated: Jan. 1, 1913 *Area:* 549.09 sq km
Population in 2011: 149
Next Election: Oct 24, 2012 (every 2 years)
William Sheppard, Reeve
D.B. (Blair) Cleaveley, Administrator

Canwood No. 494
P.O. Box 10
Canwood, SK S0J 0K0
Tel: 306-468-2014; *Fax:* 306-468-2666
rm494@sasktel.net
Municipal Type: Rural Municipality
Incorporated: Jan. 1, 1913 *Area:* 1,945.20 sq km
Population in 2011: 1,424
Next Election: 2013 (election every 2 years)
Jason Bischler, Reeve
Lorna Benson, Administrator

Carmichael No. 109
P.O. Box 420
Gull Lake, SK S0N 1A0
Tel: 306-672-3501; *Fax:* 306-672-3295
rm109@sasktel.net
saskbiz.ca/communityprofiles/CommunityProfile.Asp?CommunityID=787
Municipal Type: Rural Municipality
Incorporated: Dec. 9, 1912 *Area:* 846.40 sq km
Population in 2011: 440
Next Election: Oct 24, 2012 (every 2 years)
Howard Wedrick, Reeve
Collette Jones, Administrator

Caron No. 162
P.O. Box 85
Caron, SK S0H 0R0
Tel: 306-756-2353; *Fax:* 306-756-2250
rm162@sasktel.net
saskbiz.ca/communityprofiles/CommunityProfile.Asp?CommunityID=788
Municipal Type: Rural Municipality
Incorporated: Dec. 9, 1912 *Area:* 569.87 sq km
Population in 2011: 516
Next Election: 2013 (election every 2 years)
Gregory McKeown, Reeve
Sandra Thatcher, Administrator

Chaplin No. 164
P.O. Box 60
Chaplin, SK S0H 0V0
Tel: 306-395-2244; *Fax:* 306-395-2767
rm164@sasktel.net
saskbiz.ca/communityprofiles/CommunityProfile.Asp?CommunityID=789
Municipal Type: Rural Municipality
Incorporated: Jan. 1, 1913 *Area:* 802.74 sq km
Population in 2011: 147
Next Election: 2013 (election every 2 years)
Duane Doell, Reeve
Tammy Knight, Administrator

Chester No. 125
P.O. Box 180
Glenavon, SK S0G 1Y0
Tel: 306-429-2110; *Fax:* 306-429-2260
rmchester125@sasktel.net
saskbiz.ca/communityprofiles/communityprofile.asp?CommunityID=791
Municipal Type: Rural Municipality
Incorporated: Dec. 13, 1909 *Area:* 837.08 sq km
Population in 2011: 373
Next Election: Oct 24, 2012 (every 2 years)
Stan Muchowski, Reeve
James R. Hoff, Administrator

Chesterfield No. 261
P.O. Box 70
Eatonia, SK S0L 0Y0
Tel: 306-967-2222; *Fax:* 306-967-2424
rm261@sasktel.net
saskbiz.ca/communityprofiles/CommunityProfile.Asp?CommunityID=790
Municipal Type: Rural Municipality
Incorporated: Dec. 9, 1912 *Area:* 1,942.72 sq km
Population in 2011: 480
Next Election: Oct 2012; staggered 2 yr term
Dennis Hyland, Reeve
Beverly Dahl, Administrator

Churchbridge No. 211
P.O. Box 211
Churchbridge, SK S0A 0M0
Tel: 306-896-2522; *Fax:* 306-896-2743
rmchurchbridge@sasktel.net
Municipal Type: Rural Municipality
Incorporated: Jan. 1, 1913 *Area:* 958.98 sq km
Population in 2011: 673
Next Election: Oct 24, 2012 (every 2 years)
Neil Mehrer, Reeve
Brenda A. Goulden, Administrator

Clayton No. 333
P.O. Box 220
Hyas, SK S0A 1K0
Tel: 306-594-2832; *Fax:* 306-594-2944
rm333@sasktel.net
Municipal Type: Rural Municipality
Incorporated: Jan. 1, 1913 *Area:* 1,401.69 sq km
Population in 2011: 669
Next Election: Oct 24, 2012 (every 2 years)
Wayne Lazaruk, Reeve
Kelly Kim Smith, Administrator

Clinworth No. 230
P.O. Box 120
Sceptre, SK S0N 2H0
Tel: 306-623-4229; *Fax:* 306-623-4229
rm230@xplornet.com
Municipal Type: Rural Municipality
Incorporated: Dec. 9, 1912 *Area:* 1,432.75 sq km
Population in 2011: 211
Next Election: 2013 (election every 2 years)
Ken Dietz, Reeve

Sherry Egeland, Administrator

Coalfields No. 4
P.O. Box 190
Bienfait, SK S0C 0M0
Tel: 306-388-2723; *Fax:* 306-388-2330
rm.04@sasktel.net
saskbiz.ca/communityprofiles/communityprofile.asp?CommunityID=795
Municipal Type: Rural Municipality
Incorporated: Jan. 1, 1913 *Area:* 819.76 sq km
Population in 2011: 382
Next Election: 2013 (election every 2 years)
Stanley Lainton, Reeve
Valerie Pelton, Administrator

Colonsay No. 342
P.O. Box 130
100 Jura St.
Colonsay, SK S0K 0Z0
Tel: 306-255-2233; *Fax:* 306-255-2291
rm342@sasktel.net
www.townofcolonsay.ca/rural-municipality
Municipal Type: Rural Municipality
Incorporated: Dec. 13, 1909 *Area:* 549.99 sq km
Population in 2011: 240
Next Election: 2013 (election every 2 years)
Jerry Spoatyk, Reeve
Deborah Prosper, Administrator

Connaught No. 457
P.O. Box 25
Tisdale, SK S0E 1T0
Tel: 306-873-2657; *Fax:* 306-873-4442
rm457@sasktel.net
saskbiz.ca/communityprofiles/CommunityProfile.Asp?CommunityID=797
Municipal Type: Rural Municipality
Incorporated: Dec. 11, 1911 *Area:* 853.11 sq km
Population in 2011: 629
Next Election: Oct 24, 2012 (every 2 years)
Francis Chabot, Reeve
Tamie Jack, Administrator

Corman Park No. 344
111 Pinehouse Dr.
Saskatoon, SK S7K 5W1
Tel: 306-242-9303; *Fax:* 306-242-6965
rm344@rmcormanpark.ca
www.rmcormanpark.ca
Municipal Type: Rural Municipality
Incorporated: Jan. 1, 1970 *Area:* 1,978.14 sq km
Population in 2011: 8,354
Next Election: 2013 (election every 2 years)
Thomas Mel Henry, Reeve
Judy Douglas, Administrator

Cote No. 271
P.O. Box 669
Kamsack, SK S0A 1S0
Tel: 306-542-2121; *Fax:* 306-542-2428
rm271@sasktel.net
Municipal Type: Rural Municipality
Incorporated: Dec. 12, 1910 *Area:* 880.23 sq km
Population in 2011: 580
Next Election: Oct 24, 2012 (every 2 years)
Jim Tomochko, Reeve
Wendy Becenko, Administrator

Coteau No. 255
P.O. Box 30
Birsay, SK S0L 0G0
Tel: 306-573-2047; *Fax:* 306-573-2111
rm255@sasktel.net
Municipal Type: Rural Municipality
Incorporated: Dec. 12, 1910 *Area:* 899.27 sq km
Population in 2011: 420
Next Election: Oct 24, 2012 (every 2 years)
Clayton Ylioja, Reeve
Linda Van Den Bosch, Administrator

Coulee No. 136
1680 Chaplin St. East
Swift Current, SK S9H 1K8
Tel: 306-773-5420; *Fax:* 306-773-1859
rm136@sasktel.net
Municipal Type: Rural Municipality
Incorporated: Dec. 12, 1910 *Area:* 842.95 sq km
Population in 2011: 582
Next Election: 2013 (election every 2 years)
Greg Targerson, Reeve
Laurel Dyck, Administrator

Craik No. 222
P.O. Box 420
Craik, SK S0G 0V0
Tel: 306-734-2242; *Fax:* 306-734-2257
rm222@sasktel.net
www.craik.ca/rm222.html
Municipal Type: Rural Municipality
Incorporated: Dec. 9, 1912 *Area:* 883.02 sq km
Population in 2011: 299
Next Election: 2013 (election every 2 years)
Hilton Spencer, Reeve
JoAnne Yates, Administrator

Cupar No. 218
P.O. Box 400
Cupar, SK S0G 0Y0
Tel: 306-723-4726; *Fax:* 306-723-4726
rm218@sasktel.net
saskbiz.ca/communityprofiles/communityprofile.asp?CommunityID=803
Municipal Type: Rural Municipality
Incorporated: Dec. 13, 1909 *Area:* 919.01 sq km
Population in 2011: 554
Next Election: 2013 (election every 2 years)
Raymond Orb, Reeve
Loretta Young, Administrator

Cut Knife No. 439
P.O. Box 70
Cut Knife, SK S0M 0N0
Tel: 306-398-2353; *Fax:* 306-398-2839
rm439@sasktel.net
saskbiz.ca/communityprofiles/communityprofile.asp?CommunityID=804
Municipal Type: Rural Municipality
Incorporated: Dec. 13, 1909 *Area:* 651.43 sq km
Population in 2011: 359
Next Election: Oct 24, 2012 (every 2 years)
Milton Bingham, Reeve
Donald McCallum, Administrator

Cymri No. 36
P.O. Box 238
Midale, SK S0C 1S0
Tel: 306-458-2244; *Fax:* 306-458-2699
rmcymri@sasktel.net
saskbiz.ca/communityprofiles/CommunityProfile.Asp?CommunityID=805
Municipal Type: Rural Municipality
Incorporated: Dec. 13, 1909 *Area:* 832.36 sq km
Population in 2011: 524
Next Election: 2013 (election every 2 years)
Joe Vilcu, Reeve
Gwen Johnston, Administrator

Deer Forks No. 232
P.O. Box 250
Burstall, SK S0N 0H0
Tel: 306-679-2000; *Fax:* 306-679-2275
rm232@sasktel.net
Municipal Type: Rural Municipality
Incorporated: Jan. 1, 1913 *Area:* 735.49 sq km
Population in 2011: 223
Next Election: 2013 (election every 2 years)
Doug Smith, Reeve
Tim C. Lozinsky, Administrator

Douglas No. 436
P.O. Box 964
Speers, SK S0M 2V0
Tel: 306-246-2171; *Fax:* 306-246-2173
rm436@littleloon.ca
saskbiz.ca/communityprofiles/CommunityProfile.Asp?CommunityID=807
Municipal Type: Rural Municipality
Incorporated: Dec. 13, 1909 *Area:* 820.37 sq km
Population in 2011: 331
Next Election: 2013 (election every 2 years)
Nick W. Partyka, Reeve
Charles W. Linnell, Administrator

Duck Lake No. 463
P.O. Box 250
Duck Lake, SK S0K 1J0
Tel: 306-467-2011; *Fax:* 306-476-4423
rm463@sasktel.net
ducklake.ca
Municipal Type: Rural Municipality
Incorporated: Jan. 1, 1913 *Area:* 1,046.57 sq km
Population in 2011: 867
Next Election: Oct 24, 2012 (every 2 years)
Cathy Appelgren, Reeve

Marnee Gehon, Administrator

Dufferin No. 190
P.O. Box 67
Bethune, SK S0G 0H0
Tel: 306-638-3112; *Fax:* 306-638-3102
190@sasktel.net
www.villageofbethune.com/pages/dufferin.php
Municipal Type: Rural Municipality
Incorporated: Dec. 9, 1912 *Area:* 961.44 sq km
Population in 2011: 512
Next Election: 2013 (election every 2 years)
Donald McDonald, Reeve
Rodney Audette, Administrator

Dundurn No. 314
P.O. Box 159
314 - 2nd St.
Dundurn, SK S0K 1K0
Tel: 306-492-2132; *Fax:* 306-492-4758
rm314@sasktel.net
www.rmdundurn.ca
Municipal Type: Rural Municipality
Incorporated: Dec. 13, 1909 *Area:* 800.91 sq km
Population in 2011: 1,148
Next Election: 2013 (election every 2 years)
R. Fred Wilson, Reeve
Violet P. Barna, Administrator

Eagle Creek No. 376
P.O. Box 278
Asquith, SK S0K 0J0
Tel: 306-237-4424; *Fax:* 306-237-4294
rm376eaglecreek@xplornet.ca
Municipal Type: Rural Municipality
Incorporated: Dec. 13, 1909 *Area:* 833.08 sq km
Population in 2011: 580
Next Election: 2013 (election every 2 years)
M.J. Northcote, Reeve
Lloyd Cross, Administrator

Edenwold No. 158
P.O. Box 10
Balgonie, SK S0G 0E0
Tel: 306-771-2522; *Fax:* 306-771-2631
rm158@sasktel.net
www.rmedenwold.ca
Municipal Type: Rural Municipality
Incorporated: Dec. 9, 1912 *Area:* 882.67 sq km
Population in 2011: 4,167
Next Election: 2013 (election every 2 years)
Mitchell Huber, Reeve
Gail Sloan, Administrator

Elcapo No. 154
P.O. Box 668
Broadview, SK S0G 0K0
Tel: 306-696-2474; *Fax:* 306-696-3573
rm154@sasktel.net
Municipal Type: Rural Municipality
Incorporated: Dec. 12, 1910 *Area:* 846.54 sq km
Population in 2011: 481
Next Election: 2013 (election every 2 years)
Larry Parrott, Reeve
Mervin J. Schmidt, Administrator

Eldon No. 471
P.O. Box 130
212 Main St.
Maidstone, SK S0M 1M0
Tel: 306-893-2391; *Fax:* 306-893-4644
rm471@sasktel.net
www.rmeldon.ca
Municipal Type: Rural Municipality
Incorporated: Dec. 13, 1909 *Area:* 1,007.59 sq km
Population in 2011: 751
Next Election: Oct 24, 2012 (every 2 years)
Garry Taylor, Reeve
Ken E. Reiter, Administrator

Elfros No. 307
P.O. Box 40
Elfros, SK S0A 0V0
Tel: 306-328-2011; *Fax:* 306-328-4490
rm307@sasktel.net
Municipal Type: Rural Municipality
Incorporated: Dec. 13, 1909 *Area:* 696.71 sq km
Population in 2011: 432
Next Election: Oct 24, 2012 (every 2 years)
Henry Bzdel, Reeve
Glenn Thompson, Administrator

Elmsthorpe No. 100
P.O. Box 240
Avonlea, SK S0H 0C0
Tel: 306-868-2221; *Fax:* 306-868-2040
rm.100@sasktel.net
saskbiz.ca/communityprofiles/communityprofile.asp?CommunityID=816
Municipal Type: Rural Municipality
Incorporated: Dec. 12, 1910 *Area:* 843.12 sq km
Population in 2011: 210
Next Election: 2013 (election every 2 years)
Ken Miller, Reeve
Tim Forer, Administrator

Emerald No. 277
P.O. Box 160
Wishart, SK S0A 4R0
Tel: 306-576-2002; *Fax:* 306-576-2132
rm277@sasktel.net
www.rm277emerald.ca
Municipal Type: Rural Municipality
Incorporated: Dec. 12, 1910 *Area:* 854.44 sq km
Population in 2011: 447
Next Election: Oct 24, 2012 (every 2 years)
Morris Karakochuk, Reeve
Sharolyn Prisiak, Administrator

Enfield No. 194
P.O. Box 70
Central Butte, SK S0H 0T0
Tel: 306-796-2025; *Fax:* 306-796-2025
rm194@sasktel.net
Municipal Type: Rural Municipality
Incorporated: Dec. 13, 1909 *Area:* 1,014.10 sq km
Population in 2011: 270
Next Election: 2013 (election every 2 years)
Ron Kurz, Reeve
Joe Van Leuken, Administrator

Enniskillen No. 3
P.O. Box 179
307 Main St.
Oxbow, SK S0C 2B0
Tel: 306-483-2277; *Fax:* 306-483-2598
rm3@sasktel.net
www.oxbow.ca/rm-of-enniskillen
Municipal Type: Rural Municipality
Incorporated: Dec. 13, 1909 *Area:* 834.78 sq km
Population in 2011: 452
Next Election: Oct 24, 2012 (every 2 years)
Brian Northeast, Reeve
Myrna-Jean Babbings, Administrator

Enterprise No. 142
P.O. Box 150
Richmound, SK S0N 2E0
Tel: 306-669-2000; *Fax:* 306-669-2052
rm142@sasktel.net
Municipal Type: Rural Municipality
Incorporated: April 18, 1913 *Area:* 988.80 sq km
Population in 2011: 140
Next Election: 2013 (election every 2 years)
Wayne Freitag, Reeve
Rolande Davis, Administrator

Estevan No. 5
#1, 322 - 4th St.
Estevan, SK S4A 2B7
Tel: 306-634-2222; *Fax:* 306-634-2223
rm5@sasktel.net
saskbiz.ca/communityprofiles/communityprofile.asp?CommunityID=821
Municipal Type: Rural Municipality
Incorporated: Dec. 12, 1910 *Area:* 774.67 sq km
Population in 2011: 1,139
Next Election: Oct 24, 2012 (every 2 years)
Kelly Lafrentz, Reeve
Kim McIvor, Administrator

Excel No. 71
P.O. Box 100
Viceroy, SK S0H 4H0
Tel: 306-268-4555; *Fax:* 306-268-4547
rm71@sasktel.net
saskbiz.ca/communityprofiles/communityprofile.asp?CommunityID=745
Municipal Type: Rural Municipality
Incorporated: Jan. 1, 1913 *Area:* 1,122.02 sq km
Population in 2011: 427
Next Election: Oct 24, 2012 (every 2 years)
Glenn Roszell, Reeve
Mervin A. Guillemin, Administrator

Excelsior No. 166
P.O. Box 180
Rush Lake, SK S0H 3S0
Tel: 306-784-3121; *Fax:* 306-784-3479
rm166@sasktel.net
Municipal Type: Rural Municipality
Incorporated: Dec. 13, 1909 *Area:* 1,198.35 sq km
Population in 2011: 959
Next Election: 2013 (election every 2 years)
Harold Martens, Reeve
Christina Patoine, Administrator

Eye Hill No. 382
P.O. Box 69
Macklin, SK S0L 2C0
Tel: 306-753-2075; *Fax:* 306-753-2304
rm382@sasktel.net
saskbiz.ca/communityprofiles/CommunityProfile.Asp?CommunityID=823
Municipal Type: Rural Municipality
Incorporated: Dec. 12, 1910 *Area:* 797.96 sq km
Population in 2011: 614
Next Election: 2013 (election every 2 years)
Robert Brost, Reeve
Jason Pilat, Administrator

Eyebrow No. 193
P.O. Box 99
Eyebrow, SK S0H 1L0
Tel: 306-759-2101; *Fax:* 306-759-2026
rm193@sasktel.net
saskbiz.ca/communityprofiles/CommunityProfile.Asp?CommunityID=746
Municipal Type: Rural Municipality
Incorporated: Dec. 13, 1909 *Area:* 835.04 sq km
Population in 2011: 230
Next Election: Oct 24, 2012 (every 2 years)
Raymond L. Carrick, Reeve
Chris Bueckert, Administrator

Fertile Belt No. 183
P.O. Box 190
100 Ohlen St.
Stockholm, SK S0A 3Y0
Tel: 306-793-2061; *Fax:* 306-793-2063
rm183@sasktel.net
www.yellowheadreda.com/rmfertilebelt.htm
Municipal Type: Rural Municipality
Incorporated: January 1, 1913 *Area:* 1,006.68 sq km
Population in 2011: 785
Next Election: Oct 24, 2012 (every 2 years)
Arlynn Kurtz, Reeve
Lorie Jackson, Acting Administrator

Fertile Valley No. 285
P.O. Box 70
Conquest, SK S0L 0L0
Tel: 306-856-2037; *Fax:* 306-856-2211
rmfv285@yourlink.ca
Municipal Type: Rural Municipality
Incorporated: Dec. 13, 1909 *Area:* 1,016.37 sq km
Population in 2011: 511
Next Election: Oct 24, 2012 (every 2 years)
Alvin Barrington, Reeve
L. Jean Jones, Administrator

Fillmore No. 96
P.O. Box 130
Fillmore, SK S0G 1N0
Tel: 306-722-3251; *Fax:* 306-722-3775
rm96@sasktel.net
saskbiz.ca/communityprofiles/CommunityProfile.Asp?CommunityID=826
Municipal Type: Rural Municipality
Incorporated: Dec. 13, 1909 *Area:* 828.33 sq km
Population in 2011: 255
Next Election: 2013 (election every 2 years)
Robert Clay, Reeve
Vernna Wiggins, Administrator

Fish Creek No. 402
P.O. Box 160
Wakaw, SK S0K 4P0
Tel: 306-233-4412; *Fax:* 306-233-5234
rm402@sasktel.net
Municipal Type: Rural Municipality
Incorporated: Jan. 1, 1913 *Area:* 597.90 sq km
Population in 2011: 304
Next Election: 2013 (election every 2 years)
Dennis Sawitsky, Reeve
Richard Kindrachuk, Administrator

Flett's Springs No. 429
P.O. Box 160
Melfort, SK S0E 1A0
Tel: 306-752-3606; *Fax:* 306-752-3882
rm429@sasktel.net
saskbiz.ca/communityprofiles/communityprofile.asp?CommunityID=828
Municipal Type: Rural Municipality
Incorporated: Dec. 13, 1909 *Area:* 844.61 sq km
Population in 2011: 751
Next Election: Oct 24, 2012 (every 2 years)
Blaine Forsyth, Reeve
Shelley L. Holmes, Administrator

Foam Lake No. 276
P.O. Box 490
Foam Lake, SK S0A 1A0
Tel: 306-272-3334; *Fax:* 306-272-4722
rm276@sasktel.net
Municipal Type: Rural Municipality
Incorporated: Dec. 12, 1910 *Area:* 1,345.91 sq km
Population in 2011: 587
Next Election: 2013 (election every 2 years)
Chris Gislason, Reeve
Tina Douglas, Administrator

Fox Valley No. 171
P.O. Box 190
100 Centre St.
Fox Valley, SK S0N 0V0
Tel: 306-666-2055; *Fax:* 306-666-2074
rm171@sasktel.net
foxvalleysask.com/12.html
Municipal Type: Rural Municipality
Incorporated: Oct. 29, 1913 *Area:* 1,253.79 sq km
Population in 2011: 345
Next Election: Oct 24, 2012 (every 2 years)
Anthony Hoffart, Reeve
Daniel Steven Buye, Administrator

Francis No. 127
P.O. Box 36
Francis, SK S0G 1V0
Tel: 306-245-3256; *Fax:* 306-245-3203
rm127@sasktel.net
saskbiz.ca/communityprofiles/communityprofile.asp?CommunityID=831
Municipal Type: Rural Municipality
Incorporated: Dec. 13, 1909 *Area:* 1,106.80 sq km
Population in 2011: 676
Next Election: Oct 24, 2012 (every 2 years)
Clayton Schmidt, Reeve
Megan Macomber, Administrator

Frenchman Butte No. 501
P.O. Box 180
Paradise Hill, SK S0M 2G0
Tel: 306-344-2034; *Fax:* 306-344-4434
rm501@sasktel.net
www.rmfrenchmanbutte.ca
Municipal Type: Rural Municipality
Incorporated: Jan. 1, 1954 *Area:* 1,928.32 sq km
Population in 2011: 1,438
Next Election: Oct 24, 2012 (every 2 years)
B. Bonnie Mills Midgley, Reeve
Bryson Leganchuk, Administrator

Frontier No. 19
P.O. Box 30
Frontier, SK S0N 0W0
Tel: 306-296-2030; *Fax:* 306-296-2175
rm19@sasktel.net
saskbiz.ca/communityprofiles/Select_a_Community.asp?Region_ID=5
Municipal Type: Rural Municipality
Incorporated: Jan. 1, 1913 *Area:* 1,675.02 sq km
Population in 2011: 371
Next Election: Oct 24, 2012 (every 2 years)
Troy Heggestad, Reeve
Barb Webber, Administrator

Garden River No. 490
P.O. Box 70
Meath Park, SK S0J 1T0
Tel: 306-929-2020; *Fax:* 306-929-2281
rm490@sasktel.net
Municipal Type: Rural Municipality
Incorporated: Jan. 1, 1913 *Area:* 662.90 sq km
Population in 2011: 641
Next Election: 2013 (election every 2 years)
Bernard Zurkowski, Reeve
Elaine Esopenko, Administrator

Garry No. 245
P.O. Box 10
Jedburgh, SK S0A 1R0
Tel: 306-647-2450; *Fax:* 306-647-2450
rm245@yourlink.ca
Municipal Type: Rural Municipality
Incorporated: Jan. 1, 1913 *Area:* 853.59 sq km
Population in 2011: 412
Next Election: Oct 24, 2012 (every 2 years)
Garry Dubiel, Reeve
Tanis Ferguson, Administrator

Glen Bain No. 105
P.O. Box 39
Glen Bain, SK S0N 0X0
Tel: 306-264-3607; *Fax:* 306-264-3956
rm105@xplornet.com
Municipal Type: Rural Municipality
Incorporated: Dec. 11, 1911 *Area:* 843.40 sq km
Population in 2011: 205
Next Election: Oct 24, 2012 (every 2 years)
Ivan Braun, Reeve
Marilyn Scheller, Administrator

Glen McPherson No. 46
P.O. Box 277
Mankota, SK S0H 2W0
Tel: 306-478-2323; *Fax:* 306-478-2606
rm45.46@sasktel.net
Municipal Type: Rural Municipality
Incorporated: Jan. 1, 1913 *Area:* 848.29 sq km
Population in 2011: 73
Next Election: 2013 (election every 2 years)
Gordon Kruger, Reeve
Michael E. Sherven, Administrator

Glenside No. 377
P.O. Box 1084
Biggar, SK S0K 0M0
Tel: 306-948-3681; *Fax:* 306-948-3684
rm377@sasktel.net
saskbiz.ca/communityprofiles/CommunityProfile.Asp?CommunityID=838
Municipal Type: Rural Municipality
Incorporated: Dec. 13, 1909 *Area:* 905.74 sq km
Population in 2011: 267
Next Election: Oct 24, 2012 (every 2 years)
Wade Parkinson, Reeve
Cheryl Forbes, Administrator

Golden West No. 95
P.O. Box 70
Corning, SK S0G 0T0
Tel: 306-224-4456; *Fax:* 306-224-2196
goldwest@sasktel.net
saskbiz.ca/communityprofiles/communityprofile.asp?CommunityID=839
Municipal Type: Rural Municipality
Incorporated: Dec. 13, 1909 *Area:* 790.13 sq km
Population in 2011: 315
Next Election: Oct 24, 2012 (every 2 years)
J. Garth Allan, Reeve
Edward A. Mish, Administrator

Good Lake No. 274
P.O. Box 896
401 Main St.
Canora, SK S0A 0L0
Tel: 306-563-5244; *Fax:* 306-563-5005
rm274@sasktel.net
www.goodlakerm.com
Municipal Type: Rural Municipality
Incorporated: Jan. 1, 1913 *Area:* 800.06 sq km
Population in 2011: 684
Next Election: 2013 (election every 2 years)
David Popowich, Reeve
Grant Doupe, Administrator

Grandview No. 349
P.O. Box 39
Kelfield, SK S0K 2C0
Tel: 306-932-4911; *Fax:* 306-932-4923
rm349@xplornet.com
Municipal Type: Rural Municipality
Incorporated: Dec. 11, 1911 *Area:* 712.05 sq km
Population in 2011: 340
Next Election: Oct 24, 2012 (every 2 years)
Sally Germsheid, Reeve
Patti J. Turk, Administrator

Grant No. 372
P.O. Box 190
Vonda, SK S0K 4N0
Tel: 306-258-2022; *Fax:* 306-258-2011
rm372@sasktel.net
Municipal Type: Rural Municipality
Incorporated: Dec. 13, 1909 *Area:* 666.16 sq km
Population in 2011: 425
Next Election: 2013 (election every 2 years)
Julien Denis, Reeve
Brenda Skakun, Administrator

Grass Lake No. 381
P.O. Box 40
Reward, SK S0K 3N0
Tel: 306-228-2988; *Fax:* 306-228-4188
rm381@sasktel.net
Municipal Type: Rural Municipality
Incorporated: Dec. 13, 1909 *Area:* 801.29 sq km
Population in 2011: 369
Next Election: Oct 24, 2012 (every 2 years)
Scott Vetter, Reeve
Brenda M. Kasas, Administrator

Grassy Creek No. 78
P.O. Box 400
Shaunavon, SK S0N 2M0
Tel: 306-297-2520; *Fax:* 306-297-3162
rm77.78@sasktel.net
Municipal Type: Rural Municipality
Incorporated: Jan. 1, 1913 *Area:* 837.40 sq km
Population in 2011: 284
Next Election: 2013 (election every 2 years)
Kerry Kronberg, Reeve
Rhonda Bellfeuille, Administrator

Gravelbourg No. 104
P.O. Box 510
Gravelbourg, SK S0H 1X0
Tel: 306-648-2412; *Fax:* 306-648-2603
rm104@sasktel.net
saskbiz.ca/communityprofiles/CommunityProfile.Asp?CommunityID=744
Municipal Type: Rural Municipality
Incorporated: Dec. 9, 1912 *Area:* 842.08 sq km
Population in 2011: 306
Next Election: 2013 (election every 2 years)
Roland Levac, Reeve
Carolyn Bidwell, Administrator

Grayson No. 184
P.O. Box 69
Boswell St.
Grayson, SK S0A 1E0
Tel: 306-794-2044; *Fax:* 306-794-4655
grayson184@sasktel.net
Municipal Type: Rural Municipality
Incorporated: Jan. 1, 1913 *Area:* 875.22 sq km
Population in 2011: 495
Next Election: 2013 (election every 2 years)
Wilfred Schultz, Reeve
Darlene Paquin, Administrator

Great Bend No. 405
P.O. Box 150
200 Shepard St.
Borden, SK S0K 0N0
Tel: 306-997-2101; *Fax:* 306-997-2201
rm405@sasktel.net
saskbiz.ca/communityprofiles/CommunityProfile.Asp?CommunityID=846
Municipal Type: Rural Municipality
Incorporated: Dec. 12, 1910 *Area:* 830.57 sq km
Population in 2011: 499
Next Election: Oct 24, 2012 (every 2 years)
Ron Saunders, Reeve
Barry Hvidston, Administrator

Griffin No. 66
P.O. Box 70
Griffin, SK S0C 1G0
Tel: 306-842-6298; *Fax:* 306-842-6400
rm66@sasktel.net
saskbiz.ca/communityprofiles/communityprofile.asp?CommunityID=848
Municipal Type: Rural Municipality
Incorporated: Dec. 13, 1909 *Area:* 816.59 sq km
Population in 2011: 398
Next Election: 2013 (election every 2 years)
Stacey Lund, Reeve
Tawnya Moore, Administrator

Gull Lake No. 139
P.O. Box 180
Gull Lake, SK S0N 1A0
Tel: 306-672-4430; *Fax:* 306-672-3879
rm139@sasktel.net
saskbiz.ca/communityprofiles/CommunityProfile.Asp?CommunityID=849
Municipal Type: Rural Municipality
Incorporated: Jan. 1, 1913 *Area:* 836.41 sq km
Population in 2011: 201
Next Election: Oct 24, 2012 (every 2 years)
Doug Steele, Reeve
Jeanette Kerr, Administrator

Happy Valley No. 10
P.O. Box 39
Big Beaver, SK S0H 0G0
Tel: 306-267-4540; *Fax:* 306-267-4540
rm10@sasktel.net
Municipal Type: Rural Municipality
Incorporated: Jan. 1, 1913 *Area:* 812.74 sq km
Population in 2011: 148
Next Election: 2013 (election every 2 years)
David Schwab, Reeve
Vernon R. Palmer, Administrator

Happyland No. 231
P.O. Box 339
Leader, SK S0N 1H0
Tel: 306-628-3800; *Fax:* 306-628-4228
rm231@sasktel.net
Municipal Type: Rural Municipality
Incorporated: Jan. 1, 1913 *Area:* 1,259 sq km
Population in 2011: 284
Next Election: Oct 24, 2012 (every 2 years)
Timothy Geiger, Reeve
Tim C. Lozinsky, Administrator

Harris No. 316
P.O. Box 146
Harris, SK S0L 1K0
Tel: 306-656-2072; *Fax:* 306-656-2151
rm316@sasktel.net
Municipal Type: Rural Municipality
Incorporated: Dec. 12, 1910 *Area:* 805.42 sq km
Population in 2011: 224
Next Election: 2013 (election every 2 years)
Ted Gross, Reeve
Jim Angus, Administrator

Hart Butte No. 11
P.O. Box 210
Coronach, SK S0H 0Z0
Tel: 306-267-2005; *Fax:* 306-267-2391
rm11@accesscomm.ca
saskbiz.ca/communityprofiles/communityprofile.asp?CommunityID=742
Municipal Type: Rural Municipality
Incorporated: Jan. 1, 1913 *Area:* 841.98 sq km
Population in 2011: 264
Next Election: Oct 24, 2012 (every 2 years)
Donald Kirby, Reeve
Vernon R. Palmer, Administrator

Hazel Dell No. 335
P.O. Box 87
Okla, SK S0A 2X0
Tel: 306-325-4315; *Fax:* 306-352-4314
rm335@sasktel.net
Municipal Type: Rural Municipality
Incorporated: Jan. 1, 1913 *Area:* 1,394.02 sq km
Population in 2011: 511
Next Election: Oct 24, 2012 (every 2 years)
Jerry Klassen, Reeve
Miranda Serhan, Administrator

Hazelwood No. 94
P.O. Box 270
Kipling, SK S0G 2S0
Tel: 306-736-8121; *Fax:* 306-736-2496
rm94@sasktel.net
saskbiz.ca/communityprofiles/communityprofile.asp?CommunityID=854
Municipal Type: Rural Municipality
Incorporated: Jan. 1, 1913 *Area:* 780.68 sq km
Population in 2011: 246
Next Election: 2013 (election every 2 years)
Allan LaRose, Reeve
Gary Vargo, Administrator

Heart's Hill No. 352
P.O. Box 458
200 Strathcona St.
Luseland, SK S0L 2A0
Tel: 306-372-4224; *Fax:* 306-372-4770
rm352@sasktel.net
www.heartshill.ca
Municipal Type: Rural Municipality
Incorporated: Nov. 15, 1910 *Area:* 838.20 sq km
Population in 2011: 260
Next Election: 2013 (election every 2 years)
Gordon Stang, Reeve
Janet Fisher, Administrator

Hillsborough No. 132
403 Coteau St. West
Moose Jaw, SK S6H 5E1
Tel: 306-693-1329; *Fax:* 306-693-2810
rm.132@sasktel.net
Municipal Type: Rural Municipality
Incorporated: Jan. 1, 1913 *Area:* 445.25 sq km
Population in 2011: 114
Next Election: 2013 (election every 2 years)
Ernest Doyle, Reeve
Charlene Loos, Administrator

Hillsdale No. 440
P.O. Box 280
Neilburg, SK S0M 2C0
Tel: 306-823-4321; *Fax:* 306-823-4477
rm440@sasktel.net
saskbiz.ca/communityprofiles/CommunityProfile.Asp?CommunityID=857
Municipal Type: Rural Municipality
Incorporated: Jan. 1, 1913 *Area:* 1,028.75 sq km
Population in 2011: 563
Next Election: 2013 (election every 2 years)
Glenn Goodfellow, Reeve
Janet L. Black, Administrator

Hoodoo No. 401
P.O. Box 250
Cudworth, SK S0K 1B0
Tel: 306-256-3281; *Fax:* 306-256-7147
rm401@yourlink.ca
Municipal Type: Rural Municipality
Incorporated: Jan. 1, 1913 *Area:* 810.61 sq km
Population in 2011: 706
Next Election: Oct 24, 2012 (every 2 years)
Linus Hackl, Reeve
David Yorke, Administrator

Hudson Bay No. 394
P.O. Box 520
Hudson Bay, SK S0E 0Y0
Tel: 306-865-2691; *Fax:* 306-865-2857
rm394@sasktel.net
saskbiz.ca/communityprofiles/CommunityProfile.Asp?CommunityID=859
Municipal Type: Rural Municipality
Incorporated: May 1, 1977 *Area:* 12,460.90 sq km
Population in 2011: 1,122
Next Election: 2013 (election every 2 years)
Neal Hardy, Reeve
Tracy Smith, Administrator

Humboldt No. 370
P.O. Box 420
Humboldt, SK S0K 2A0
Tel: 306-682-2242; *Fax:* 306-682-3239
r.m.humboldt@sasktel.net
Municipal Type: Rural Municipality
Incorporated: Jan. 1, 1913 *Area:* 798.51 sq km
Population in 2011: 885
Next Election: 2013 (election every 2 years)
Jordan Bergermann, Reeve
Corinne Richardson, Administrator

Huron No. 223
P.O. Box 159
Tugaske, SK S0H 4B0
Tel: 306-759-2211; *Fax:* 306-759-2249
rm223@sasktel.net
www.tugaske.com/contact.shtml
Municipal Type: Rural Municipality
Incorporated: Dec. 12, 1910 *Area:* 842.11 sq km
Population in 2011: 196
Next Election: Oct 24, 2012 (every 2 years)
Corey Doerksen, Reeve
Daryl Dean, Administrator

Indian Head No. 156
P.O. Box 39
Indian Head, SK S0G 2K0
Tel: 306-695-3464; *Fax:* 306-695-3462
rm156@sasktel.net
Municipal Type: Rural Municipality
Incorporated: Aug. 6, 1884 *Area:* 759.98 sq km
Population in 2011: 380
Next Election: 2013 (election every 2 years)
Lorne Scott, Reeve
Lorelei Theaker, Administrator

Insinger No. 275
P.O. Box 179
Insinger, SK S0A 1L0
Tel: 306-647-2422; *Fax:* 306-647-2740
rm275@sasktel.net
Municipal Type: Rural Municipality
Incorporated: Jan. 1, 1913 *Area:* 849.38 sq km
Population in 2011: 325
Next Election: Oct 24, 2012 (every 2 years)
Terry Eritz, Reeve
Sonya Butuk, Administrator

Invergordon No. 430
P.O. Box 40
Crystal Springs, SK S0K 1A0
Tel: 306-749-2852; *Fax:* 306-749-2499
rm430@sasktel.net
Municipal Type: Rural Municipality
Incorporated: Dec. 11, 1911 *Area:* 853.55 sq km
Population in 2011: 651
Next Election: 2013 (election every 2 years)
Dennis Shulhan, Reeve
Trent Smith, Administrator

Invermay No. 305
P.O. Box 130
Invermay, SK S0A 1M0
Tel: 306-593-2152; *Fax:* 306-593-2152
rm.inv.305@sasktel.net
Municipal Type: Rural Municipality
Incorporated: Dec. 11, 1911 *Area:* 728.23 sq km
Population in 2011: 334
Next Election: Oct 24, 2012 (every 2 years)
Jack Prychak, Reeve
Sandra Leitch, Administrator

Ituna Bon Accord No. 246
P.O. Box 190
Ituna, SK S0A 1N0
Tel: 306-795-2202; *Fax:* 306-795-2202
rmofituna@sasktel.net
Municipal Type: Rural Municipality
Incorporated: Jan. 1, 1913 *Area:* 837.23 sq km
Population in 2011: 435
Next Election: 2013 (election every 2 years)
Terry Berezny, Reeve
Wilma Hrenyk, Administrator

Kellross No. 247
P.O. Box 10
Leross, SK S0A 2C0
Tel: 306-675-4423; *Fax:* 306-675-2097
rm247@sasktel.net
saskbiz.ca/communityprofiles/CommunityProfile.Asp?CommunityID=867
Municipal Type: Rural Municipality
Incorporated: Dec. 13, 1909 *Area:* 834.09 sq km
Population in 2011: 362
Next Election: Oct 24, 2012 (every 2 years)
John Olinik, Reeve
Edith Goddard, Administrator

Kelvington No. 366
P.O. Box 519
Kelvington, SK S0A 1W0
Tel: 306-327-4222; *Fax:* 306-327-4222
rm366@sasktel.net
saskbiz.ca/communityprofiles/CommunityProfile.Asp?CommunityID=868
Municipal Type: Rural Municipality
Incorporated: Jan. 1, 1913 *Area:* 907.37 sq km
Population in 2011: 499
Next Election: 2013 (election every 2 years)
Stanley Elmy, Reeve
Tim G. Leurer, Administrator

Key West No. 70
P.O. Box 159
Ogema, SK S0C 1Y0
Tel: 306-459-2262; *Fax:* 306-459-2762
rm.70@sasktel.net
Municipal Type: Rural Municipality
Incorporated: Dec. 12, 1910 *Area:* 825.26 sq km
Population in 2011: 287
Next Election: 2013 (election every 2 years)
Rick Dunn, Reeve
Peggy Tuchscherer, Administrator

Keys No. 303
P.O. Box 899
Canora, SK S0A 0L0
Tel: 306-563-5331; *Fax:* 306-563-6759
rm303@sasktel.net
Municipal Type: Rural Municipality
Incorporated: Jan. 1, 1913 *Area:* 661.61 sq km
Population in 2011: 417
Next Election: Oct 24, 2012 (every 2 years)
James Hallick, Reeve
Sharon Ciesielski, Administrator

Kindersley No. 290
P.O. Box 1210
Kindersley, SK S0L 1S0
Tel: 306-463-2524; *Fax:* 306-463-4197
rm290@sasktel.net
Municipal Type: Rural Municipality
Incorporated: Dec. 12, 1910 *Area:* 2,113.36 sq km
Population in 2011: 987
Next Election: 2013 (election every 2 years)
Glen Harrison, Reeve
Glenda M. Giles, Administrator

King George No. 256
P.O. Box 100
Dinsmore, SK S0L 0T0
Tel: 306-846-2022; *Fax:* 306-846-2032
rm256@sasktel.net
Municipal Type: Rural Municipality
Incorporated: Dec. 11, 1911 *Area:* 831.97 sq km
Population in 2011: 217
Next Election: 2013 (election every 2 years)
James Thorpe, Reeve
Cheryl Joel, Administrator

Kingsley No. 124
P.O. Box 239
Kipling, SK S0G 2S0
Tel: 306-736-2272; *Fax:* 306-736-2798
rm124@sasktel.net
saskbiz.ca/communityprofiles/CommunityProfile.Asp?CommunityID=873
Municipal Type: Rural Municipality
Incorporated: Dec. 12, 1910 *Area:* 844.61 sq km
Population in 2011: 421
Next Election: 2013 (election every 2 years)
Lorne Rygh, Reeve
Holly Kemp, Administrator

Kinistino No. 459
P.O. Box 310
Kinistino, SK S0J 1H0
Tel: 306-864-2474; *Fax:* 306-864-2880
rm459@sasktel.net
Municipal Type: Rural Municipality
Incorporated: Dec. 11, 1911 *Area:* 949.13 sq km
Population in 2011: 531
Next Election: Oct 24, 2012 (every 2 years)
Vance Shmyr, Reeve
Shelley Holmes, Administrator

Lac Pelletier No. 107
P.O. Box 70
Neville, SK S0N 1T0
Tel: 306-627-3226; *Fax:* 306-627-3641
rm107@sasktel.net
Municipal Type: Rural Municipality
Incorporated: Jan. 1, 1913 *Area:* 849.27 sq km
Population in 2011: 607
Next Election: Oct 24, 2012 (every 2 years)
Cornie Martens, Reeve
Rose Lawrence, Administrator

Lacadena No. 228
P.O. Box 39
Lacadena, SK S0L 1V0
Tel: 306-574-2008; *Fax:* 306-574-4753
rm228@xplornet.com
saskbiz.ca/communityprofiles/communityprofile.asp?CommunityID=876
Municipal Type: Rural Municipality
Incorporated: Dec. 12, 1910 *Area:* 1,890.08 sq km
Population in 2011: 572
Next Election: 2013 (election every 2 years)
Bradley Sander, Reeve

Wilma Moen, Administrator

Laird No. 404
P.O. Box 160
Waldheim, SK S0K 4R0
Tel: 306-945-2133; *Fax:* 306-945-4824
rmlaird@sasktel.net; info@rmoflaird.com
www.rmoflaird.com
Municipal Type: Rural Municipality
Incorporated: Dec. 12, 1910 *Area:* 729.98 sq km
Population in 2011: 1,240
Next Election: 2013 (election every 2 years)
Kenneth Petkau, Reeve
rmlaird@sasktel.net
Sandra Galambos, Administrator

Lajord No. 128
P.O. Box 36
Lajord, SK S0G 2V0
Tel: 306-781-2744; *Fax:* 306-781-1023
rm128@yourlink.ca
Municipal Type: Rural Municipality
Incorporated: Dec. 13, 1909 *Area:* 943.87 sq km
Population in 2011: 993
Next Election: 2013 (election every 2 years)
Erwin Beitel, Reeve
Rod J. Heise, Administrator

Lake Alma No. 8
P.O. Box 100
Lake Alma, SK S0C 1M0
Tel: 306-447-2022; *Fax:* 306-447-2023
rmalma@sasktel.net
saskbiz.ca/communityprofiles/communityprofile.asp?CommunityID=880
Municipal Type: Rural Municipality
Incorporated: May 5, 1913 *Area:* 822.47 sq km
Population in 2011: 250
Next Election: 2013 (election every 2 years)
Robert Thue, Reeve
Myrna Lohse, Administrator

Lake Johnston No. 102
P.O. Box 160
Mossbank, SK S0H 3G0
Tel: 306-354-2414; *Fax:* 306-354-7725
rm102.103@sasktel.net
Municipal Type: Rural Municipality
Incorporated: Dec. 9, 1912 *Area:* 567.24 sq km
Population in 2011: 160
Next Election: 2013 (election every 2 years)
Kevin Stark, Reeve
Sherry D. Green, Administrator

Lake Lenore No. 399
P.O. Box 280
St Brieux, SK S0K 3V0
Tel: 306-275-2066; *Fax:* 306-275-4667
rmll@sasktel.net
saskbiz.ca/communityprofiles/communityprofile.asp?CommunityID=883
Municipal Type: Rural Municipality
Incorporated: Jan. 1, 1913 *Area:* 724.06 sq km
Population in 2011: 536
Next Election: Oct 24, 2012 (every 2 years)
Jean Kernaleguen, Reeve
Jennifer Thompson, Administrator

Lake of the Rivers No. 72
P.O. Box 610
Assiniboia, SK S0H 0B0
Tel: 306-642-3533; *Fax:* 306-642-4382
rm72@sasktel.net
saskbiz.ca/communityprofiles/CommunityProfile.Asp?CommunityID=747
Municipal Type: Rural Municipality
Incorporated: Dec. 11, 1911 *Area:* 677.51 sq km
Population in 2011: 302
Next Election: 2013 (election every 2 years)
William Welk, Reeve
Mervin A. Guillemin, Administrator

Lakeland No. 521
P.O. Box 27
Christopher Lake, SK S0J 0N0
Tel: 306-982-2010; *Fax:* 306-982-2589
office@rmlakeland521.ca
www.rmlakeland521.ca
Municipal Type: Rural Municipality
Incorporated: Aug. 1, 1977 *Area:* 494.06 sq km
Population in 2011: 884
Next Election: Oct 24, 2012 (every 2 years)
Al Christensen, Reeve
al.christensen@yahoo.ca
Dave Dmytruk, Administrator

Lakeside No. 338
P.O. Box 9
Quill Lake, SK S0A 3E0
Tel: 306-383-2261; *Fax:* 306-383-2255
rm338@sasktel.net
saskbiz.ca/communityprofiles/communityprofile.asp?CommunityID=884
Municipal Type: Rural Municipality
Incorporated: Dec. 12, 1910 *Area:* 636.80 sq km
Population in 2011: 387
Next Election: 2013 (election every 2 years)
Arnold Boyko, Reeve
Judy Kanak, Administrator

Lakeview No. 337
P.O. Box 220
Wadena, SK S0A 4J0
Tel: 306-338-2341; *Fax:* 306-338-2595
rm337@sasktel.net
saskbiz.ca/communityprofiles/CommunityProfile.Asp?CommunityID=885
Municipal Type: Rural Municipality
Incorporated: Dec. 13, 1909 *Area:* 724.89 sq km
Population in 2011: 336
Next Election: Oct 24, 2012 (every 2 years)
Mervin Kryzanowski, Reeve
Betty Ann Bjarnason, Administrator

Langenburg No. 181
P.O. Box 489
Langenburg, SK S0A 2A0
Tel: 306-743-2341; *Fax:* 306-743-5282
rm181@sasktel.net
saskbiz.ca/communityprofiles/CommunityProfile.Asp?CommunityID=886
Municipal Type: Rural Municipality
Incorporated: Jan. 1, 1913 *Area:* 675.66 sq km
Population in 2011: 572
Next Election: Oct 24, 2012 (every 2 years)
Ken Apland, Reeve
Darwyn MacKenzie, Administrator

Last Mountain Valley No. 250
P.O. Box 160
Govan, SK S0G 1Z0
Tel: 306-484-2011; *Fax:* 306-484-2113
rm250@sasktel.net
Municipal Type: Rural Municipality
Incorporated: Dec. 13, 1909 *Area:* 871.17 sq km
Population in 2011: 267
Next Election: 2013 (election every 2 years)
Allan Magel, Reeve
Kelly Holbrook, Administrator

Laurier No. 38
P.O. Box 219
Radville, SK S0C 2G0
Tel: 306-869-2255; *Fax:* 306-869-2524
rm.38@sasktel.net
saskbiz.ca/communityprofiles/communityprofile.asp?CommunityID=888
Municipal Type: Rural Municipality
Incorporated: Dec. 13, 1909 *Area:* 840.86 sq km
Population in 2011: 321
Next Election: 2013 (election every 2 years)
Gene Gilmore, Reeve
Ursula Scott, Administrator

Lawtonia No. 135
P.O. Box 10
Hodgeville, SK S0H 2B0
Tel: 306-677-2266; *Fax:* 306-677-2446
rm135@sasktel.net
saskbiz.ca/communityprofiles/CommunityProfile.Asp?CommunityID=889
Municipal Type: Rural Municipality
Incorporated: Dec. 12, 1910 *Area:* 845.28 sq km
Population in 2011: 434
Next Election: Oct 24, 2012 (every 2 years)
Barry Leisle, Reeve
Art Thompson, Administrator

Leask No. 464
P.O. Box 190
Leask, SK S0J 1M0
Tel: 306-466-2000; *Fax:* 306-466-2091
admin.464@sasktel.net
www.leask.ca/rmoffice.html
Municipal Type: Rural Municipality
Incorporated: Dec. 9, 1912 *Area:* 1,257.36 sq km
Population in 2011: 775
Next Election: 2013 (election every 2 years)
Len Cantin, Reeve
Sheri McHanson-Budd, Administrator

Leroy No. 339
P.O. Box 100
Leroy, SK S0K 2P0
Tel: 306-286-3261; *Fax:* 306-286-3400
rm339@sasktel.net
saskbiz.ca/communityprofiles/communityprofile.asp?CommunityID=891
Municipal Type: Rural Municipality
Incorporated: Jan. 1, 1913 *Area:* 840.40 sq km
Population in 2011: 490
Next Election: Oct 24, 2012 (every 2 years)
Jerry McGrath, Reeve
Joan Fedak, Administrator

Lipton No. 217
P.O. Box 40
Lipton, SK S0G 3B0
Tel: 306-336-2244; *Fax:* 306-336-2322
rm.217@sasktel.net
Municipal Type: Rural Municipality
Incorporated: Dec. 11, 1911 *Area:* 813.69 sq km
Population in 2011: 424
Next Election: Oct 24, 2012 (every 2 years)
Corey Senft, Reeve
Nikki Czemeres, Administrator

Livingston No. 331
P.O. Box 40
Arran, SK S0A 0B0
Tel: 306-595-4521; *Fax:* 306-595-4531
rm331@sasktel.net
Municipal Type: Rural Municipality
Incorporated: Jan. 1, 1913 *Area:* 1,338.64 sq km
Population in 2011: 311
Next Election: Oct 24, 2012 (every 2 years)
Peter Jacobs, Reeve
Yvonne Bilsky, Administrator

Lomond No. 37
P.O. Box 280
Weyburn, SK S4H 2K1
Tel: 306-456-2566; *Fax:* 306-456-2440
rm37@sasktel.net
saskbiz.ca/communityprofiles/CommunityProfile.Asp?CommunityID=894
Municipal Type: Rural Municipality
Incorporated: Dec. 11, 1911 *Area:* 833.95 sq km
Population in 2011: 304
Next Election: Oct 24, 2012 (every 2 years)
John McKenzie, Reeve
Kevin Melle, Administrator

Lone Tree No. 18
P.O. Box 30
Climax, SK S0N 0N0
Tel: 306-293-2124; *Fax:* 306-293-2702
villageofclimax@sasktel.net
Municipal Type: Rural Municipality
Incorporated: Dec. 8, 1913 *Area:* 838 sq km
Population in 2011: 145
Next Election: 2013 (election every 2 years)
Shawna Bertram, Reeve
Ronald J. Johnson, Administrator

Longlaketon No. 219
P.O. Box 100
Earl Grey, SK S0G 1J0
Tel: 306-939-2144; *Fax:* 306-939-2036
rm219@sasktel.net
Municipal Type: Rural Municipality
Incorporated: Dec. 12, 1910 *Area:* 1,024.61 sq km
Population in 2011: 962
Next Election: Oct 24, 2012 (every 2 years)
Marilyn Gibson, Reeve
Murray Cook, Administrator

Loon Lake No. 561
P.O. Box 40
Loon Lake, SK S0M 1L0
Tel: 306-837-2076; *Fax:* 306-837-2282
rm561@sasktel.net
Municipal Type: Rural Municipality
Incorporated: Jan. 1, 1978 *Area:* 2,802.51 sq km
Population in 2011: 725
Next Election: Oct 24, 2012 (every 2 years)
Harvey Dimond, Reeve

Laurie Lehoux, Administrator

Loreburn No. 254
P.O. Box 40
Loreburn, SK S0H 2S0
Tel: 306-644-2022; *Fax:* 306-644-2064
rm254@sasktel.net
www.rmloreburn.ca
Municipal Type: Rural Municipality
Incorporated: Dec. 12, 1910 *Area:* 966.78 sq km
Population in 2011: 346
Next Election: 2013 (election every 2 years)
Kevin Vollmer, Reeve
mbarv@sasktel.net
Nona Stronski, Administrator

Lost River No. 313
P.O. Box 159
Allan, SK S0K 0C0
Tel: 306-257-3272; *Fax:* 306-257-3337
rm313@sasktel.net
saskbiz.ca/communityprofiles/CommunityProfile.Asp?CommunityID=899
Municipal Type: Rural Municipality
Incorporated: Dec. 11, 1911 *Area:* 549.90 sq km
Population in 2011: 209
Next Election: Oct 24, 2012 (every 2 years)
Charles E. Smith, Reeve
Christine Dyck, Administrator

Lumsden No. 189
P.O. Box 160
300 James Street North
Lumsden, SK S0G 3C0
Tel: 306-731-2404; *Fax:* 306-731-3572
rm189@sasktel.net
www.lumsden.ca
Municipal Type: Rural Municipality
Incorporated: Dec. 9, 1912 *Area:* 818.66 sq km
Population in 2011: 1,733
Next Election: Oct 24, 2012 (every 2 years)
Jim Hipkin, Reeve
Byron Tumbach, Administrator

Manitou Lake No. 442
P.O. Box 69
Marsden, SK S0M 1P0
Tel: 306-826-5215; *Fax:* 306-826-5512
rm442@sasktel.net
saskbiz.ca/communityprofiles/CommunityProfile.Asp?CommunityID=901
Municipal Type: Rural Municipality
Incorporated: Dec. 12, 1910 *Area:* 850.32 sq km
Population in 2011: 547
Next Election: 2013 (election every 2 years)
Ian Lamb, Reeve
Joanne Loy, Administrator

Mankota No. 45
P.O. Box 148
Mankota, SK S0H 2W0
Tel: 306-478-2323; *Fax:* 306-478-2606
rm45.46@sasktel.net
Municipal Type: Rural Municipality
Incorporated: Jan. 1, 1913 *Area:* 1,696.22 sq km
Population in 2011: 322
Next Election: Oct 24, 2012 (every 2 years)
Doug Williamson, Reeve
Michael E. Sherven, Administrator

Maple Bush No. 224
P.O. Box 160
Riverhurst, SK S0H 3P0
Tel: 306-353-2292; *Fax:* 306-353-2292
rm224@xplornet.com
Municipal Type: Rural Municipality
Incorporated: Dec. 13, 1909 *Area:* 811.95 sq km
Population in 2011: 167
Next Election: 2013 (election every 2 years)
Maurice Bartzen, Reeve
JoAnne Wandler, Administrator

Maple Creek No. 111
P.O. Box 188
Maple Creek, SK S0N 1N0
Tel: 306-662-2300; *Fax:* 306-662-3566
rm111@sasktel.net
Municipal Type: Rural Municipality
Incorporated: Dec. 10, 1917 *Area:* 3,242.96 sq km
Population in 2011: 1,154
Next Election: Oct 24, 2012 (every 2 years)
Greg Link, Reeve
Barbi-Rose Weisgerber, Administrator

Mariposa No. 350
P.O. Box 228
603 Atlantic Ave.
Kerrobert, SK S0L 1R0
Tel: 306-834-5037; *Fax:* 306-834-5047
rm350@sasktel.net
saskbiz.ca/communityprofiles/communityprofile.asp?CommunityID=905
Municipal Type: Rural Municipality
Incorporated: Dec. 12, 1910 *Area:* 636.73 sq km
Population in 2011: 220
Next Election: 2013 (election every 2 years)
Peter Volk, Reeve
Terry Bohn, Administrator

Marquis No. 191
P.O. Box 40
Marquis, SK S0H 2X0
Tel: 306-788-2022; *Fax:* 306-788-2168
rm191@sasktel.net
saskbiz.ca/communityprofiles/CommunityProfile.Asp?CommunityID=906
Municipal Type: Rural Municipality
Incorporated: Dec. 11, 1911 *Area:* 805.48 sq km
Population in 2011: 252
Next Election: Oct 24, 2012 (every 2 years)
Kenneth Waldenberger, Reeve
Ronald J. Gasper, Administrator

Marriott No. 317
P.O. Box 366
Rosetown, SK S0L 2V0
Tel: 306-882-4030; *Fax:* 306-882-4401
rm317@sasktel.net
Municipal Type: Rural Municipality
Incorporated: Dec. 12, 1910 *Area:* 843.29 sq km
Population in 2011: 372
Next Election: Oct 24, 2012 (every 2 years)
Colin Ahrens, Reeve
Michelle McQueen, Administrator

Martin No. 122
P.O. Box 1109
Moosomin, SK S0G 3N0
Tel: 306-532-3113; *Fax:* 306-435-4313
rm121@sasktel.net
saskbiz.ca/communityprofiles/CommunityProfile.Asp?CommunityID=908
Municipal Type: Rural Municipality
Incorporated: Jan. 1, 1913 *Area:* 556.50 sq km
Population in 2011: 333
Next Election: 2013 (election every 2 years)
David Garvey, Reeve
Elaine M. Olsen, Administrator

Maryfield No. 91
P.O. Box 70
Maryfield, SK S0G 3K0
Tel: 306-646-2033; *Fax:* 306-646-2033
rm91@sasktel.net
www.maryfieldsaskatchewan.com/map.html
Municipal Type: Rural Municipality
Incorporated: Dec. 9, 1912 *Area:* 759.63 sq km
Population in 2011: 319
Next Election: Oct 24, 2012 (every 2 years)
Bruce Lemon, Reeve
Anna Macksymchuk, Administrator

Mayfield No. 406
P.O. Box 100
Maymont, SK S0M 1T0
Tel: 306-389-2112; *Fax:* 306-389-2162
rm406@sasktel.net
saskbiz.ca/communityprofiles/communityprofile.asp?CommunityID=910
Municipal Type: Rural Municipality
Incorporated: Dec. 13, 1909 *Area:* 782.50 sq km
Population in 2011: 389
Next Election: 2013 (election every 2 years)
Ernest Voegeli, Reeve
Laurie DuBois, Administrator

McCraney No. 282
P.O. Box 129
Kenaston, SK S0G 2N0
Tel: 306-252-2240; *Fax:* 306-252-2248
rm282@sasktel.net
Municipal Type: Rural Municipality
Incorporated: Dec. 13, 1909 *Area:* 948.36 sq km
Population in 2011: 307
Next Election: 2013 (election every 2 years)
Murray Kadlec, Reeve

Mark Zdunich, Administrator

McKillop No. 220
P.O. Box 369
Strasbourg, SK S0G 4V0
Tel: 306-725-3230; *Fax:* 306-725-3613
rm220@sasktel.net
saskbiz.ca/communityprofiles/CommunityProfile.Asp?CommunityID=912
Municipal Type: Rural Municipality
Incorporated: Dec. 13, 1909 *Area:* 668.45 sq km
Population in 2011: 575
Next Election: 2013 (election every 2 years)
Murray MacPheat, Reeve
Barbara Griffin, Administrator

McLeod No. 185
P.O. Box 130
Neudorf, SK S0A 2T0
Tel: 306-748-2233; *Fax:* 306-748-2647
www.village.neudorf.sk.ca/RM%20OF%20MCLEOD.htm
Municipal Type: Rural Municipality
Incorporated: Jan. 1, 1913 *Area:* 886.6 sq km
Population in 2011: 446
Next Election: Oct 24, 2012 (every 2 years)
Wilfred G. Goebel, Reeve
Murray J. Hanowski, Administrator

Meadow Lake No. 588
P.O. Box 668
#1, 225 Centre St.
Meadow Lake, SK S9X 1L5
Tel: 306-236-5651; *Fax:* 306-236-3115
rm.588@sasktel.net
rmmeadowlake.com
Municipal Type: Rural Municipality
Incorporated: Feb. 1, 1976 *Area:* 6,303.31 sq km
Population in 2011: 2,677
Next Election: 2013 (election every 2 years)
John Lawson, Reeve
Claire Elliot, Administrator

Medstead No. 497
P.O. Box 148
Medstead, SK S0M 1W0
Tel: 306-342-4609; *Fax:* 306-342-2067
rm497@sasktel.net
saskbiz.ca/communityprofiles/communityprofile.asp?CommunityID=915
Municipal Type: Rural Municipality
Incorporated: Jan. 1, 1913 *Area:* 1,203.22 sq km
Population in 2011: 513
Next Election: Oct 24, 2012 (every 2 years)
Albert Schmirler, Reeve
Christin Egeland, Administrator

Meeting Lake No. 466
P.O. Box 26
Mayfair, SK S0M 1S0
Tel: 306-246-4228; *Fax:* 306-246-4974
rm466@sasktel.net
saskbiz.ca/communityprofiles/communityprofile.asp?CommunityID=916
Municipal Type: Rural Municipality
Incorporated: Jan. 1, 1913 *Area:* 1,066.74 sq km
Population in 2011: 376
Next Election: 2013 (election every 2 years)
Lyle Prescesky, Reeve
Janelle Lavallee, Administrator

Meota No. 468
P.O. Box 80
Meota, SK S0M 1X0
Tel: 306-892-2061; *Fax:* 306-892-2449
rm.468@sasktel.net
saskbiz.ca/communityprofiles/CommunityProfile.Asp?CommunityID=917
Municipal Type: Rural Municipality
Incorporated: Dec. 13, 1909 *Area:* 651.09 sq km
Population in 2011: 936
Next Election: 2013 (election every 2 years)
Wilbert Fennig, Reeve
Maryann Germann, Administrator

Mervin No. 499
P.O. Box 130
Turtleford, SK S0M 2Y0
Tel: 306-845-2045; *Fax:* 306-845-2950
rm499@sasktel.net
saskbiz.ca/communityprofiles/CommunityProfile.Asp?CommunityID=918
Municipal Type: Rural Municipality
Incorporated: Jan. 1, 1913 *Area:* 1,594.64 sq km

Population in 2011: 1,224
Next Election: Oct 24, 2012 (every 2 years)
Harold Kivimaa, Reeve
L. Ryan Domotor, Administrator

Milden No. 286
P.O. Box 160
113 Centre St.
Milden, SK S0L 2L0
Tel: 306-935-2181; *Fax:* 306-935-2046
rm286@sasktel.net
saskbiz.ca/communityprofiles/communityprofile.asp?CommunityID=919
Municipal Type: Rural Municipality
Incorporated: Dec. 12, 1910 *Area:* 735.31 sq km
Population in 2011: 283
Next Election: 2013 (election every 2 years)
Arnold Somerville, Reeve
Melody Nieman, Administrator

Milton No. 292
P.O. Box 70
Marengo, SK S0L 2K0
Tel: 306-968-2922; *Fax:* 306-968-2278
rm292.rm322@sasktel.net
saskbiz.ca/communityprofiles/communityprofile.asp?CommunityID=920
Municipal Type: Rural Municipality
Incorporated: Dec. 11, 1911 *Area:* 655.76 sq km
Population in 2011: 312
Next Election: 2013 (election every 2 years)
David Bond, Reeve
Shelley Mohr, Administrator

Miry Creek No. 229
P.O. Box 210
Abbey, SK S0N 0A0
Tel: 306-689-2281; *Fax:* 306-689-2901
rm229@sasktel.net
saskbiz.ca/communityprofiles/CommunityProfile.Asp?CommunityID=921
Municipal Type: Rural Municipality
Incorporated: Jan. 1, 1913 *Area:* 1,220.38 sq km
Population in 2011: 374
Next Election: Oct 24, 2012 (every 2 years)
Morgan Powell, Reeve
Jan Stern, Administrator

Monet No. 257
P.O. Box 370
Elrose, SK S0L 0Z0
Tel: 306-378-2212; *Fax:* 306-378-2212
rm257@sasktel.net
Municipal Type: Rural Municipality
Incorporated: Dec. 13, 1909 *Area:* 1,591.75 sq km
Population in 2011: 495
Next Election: Oct 24, 2012 (every 2 years)
George Myers, Reeve
Lori A. McDonald, Administrator

Montmartre No. 126
P.O. Box 120
136 Central Ave.
Montmartre, SK S0G 3M0
Tel: 306-424-2040; *Fax:* 306-424-2065
rm126@sasktel.net
www.montmartre-sk.com
Municipal Type: Rural Municipality
Incorporated: Dec. 13, 1909 *Area:* 853.91 sq km
Population in 2011: 488
Next Election: 2013 (election every 2 years)
Rodney Baumgartner, Reeve
Dale Brenner, Administrator

Montrose No. 315
P.O. Box 755
Delisle, SK S0L 0P0
Tel: 306-493-2694; *Fax:* 306-493-2694
rm315@sasktel.net
Municipal Type: Rural Municipality
Incorporated: Dec. 13, 1909 *Area:* 898.38 sq km
Population in 2011: 712
Next Election: Oct 24, 2012 (every 2 years)
Ray French, Administrator

Moose Creek No. 33
P.O. Box 10
Alameda, SK S0C 0A0
Tel: 306-489-2044; *Fax:* 306-489-2112
rm33@sasktel.net
saskbiz.ca/communityprofiles/communityprofile.asp?CommunityID=925
Municipal Type: Rural Municipality
Incorporated: Dec. 12, 1910 *Area:* 842.03 sq km
Population in 2011: 372
Next Election: Oct 24, 2012 (every 2 years)
Murray Rossow, Reeve
Sentura Freitag, Administrator

Moose Jaw No. 161
170 Fairford St. West
Moose Jaw, SK S6H 1V3
Tel: 306-692-3446; *Fax:* 306-691-0015
rm161@sasktel.net
www.moosejawrm161.ca
Municipal Type: Rural Municipality
Incorporated: Dec. 11, 1911 *Area:* 797.60 sq km
Population in 2011: 1,147
Next Election: Oct 24, 2012 (every 2 years)
Jeff Crichton, Reeve
John Eberl, Administrator

Moose Mountain No. 63
P.O. Box 445
Carlyle, SK S0C 0R0
Tel: 306-453-6175; *Fax:* 306-453-2430
rm63@sasktel.net
saskbiz.ca/communityprofiles/communityprofile.asp?CommunityID=927
Municipal Type: Rural Municipality
Incorporated: Dec. 11, 1911 *Area:* 740.91 sq km
Population in 2011: 480
Next Election: Oct 24, 2012 (every 2 years)
Note: URL:
www.creda.sk.ca/moosemountain/moose_mountain_community_profile.htm
Lyle Brown, Reeve
Ron Matsalla, Administrator

Moose Range No. 486
P.O. Box 699
Carrot River, SK S0E 0L0
Tel: 306-768-2212; *Fax:* 306-768-2211
rm486@sasktel.net
www.rmmooserange.sasktelwebsite.net
Municipal Type: Rural Municipality
Incorporated: Dec. 11, 1916 *Area:* 2,419.06 sq km
Population in 2011: 1,131
Next Election: 2013 (election every 2 years)
Ramond Mazurek, Reeve
Richard C. Colborn, Administrator

Moosomin No. 121
P.O. Box 1109
Moosomin, SK S0G 3N0
Tel: 306-435-3113; *Fax:* 306-435-4313
rm121@sasktel.net
saskbiz.ca/communityprofiles/CommunityProfile.Asp?CommunityID=929
Municipal Type: Rural Municipality
Incorporated: Jan. 1, 1913 *Area:* 566.39 sq km
Population in 2011: 504
Next Election: Oct 24, 2012 (every 2 years)
Christopher Bell, Reeve
Kendra L. Lawrence, Administrator

Morris No. 312
P.O. Box 130
121 Main St.
Young, SK S0K 4Y0
Tel: 306-259-2211; *Fax:* 306-259-2225
rm312@sasktel.net
www.young.ca/rm-morris.htm
Municipal Type: Rural Municipality
Incorporated: Dec. 13, 1909 *Area:* 847.16 sq km
Population in 2011: 316
Next Election: 2013 (election every 2 years)
Gordon Dengler, Reeve
Pamela Garner, Administrator

Morse No. 165
P.O. Box 340
Morse, SK S0H 3C0
Tel: 306-629-3282; *Fax:* 306-629-3212
rm165@sasktel.net
Municipal Type: Rural Municipality
Incorporated: Dec. 11, 1911 *Area:* 1,244.38 sq km
Population in 2011: 401
Next Election: Oct 24, 2012 (every 2 years)
Bruce Gall, Reeve
Mark Wilson, Administrator

Mount Hope No. 279
P.O. Box 190
Semans, SK S0A 3S0
Tel: 306-524-2055; *Fax:* 306-524-4526
rm279@sasktel.net
Municipal Type: Rural Municipality
Incorporated: Dec. 11, 1911 *Area:* 1,669.29 sq km
Population in 2011: 567
Next Election: Oct 24, 2012 (every 2 years)
Ernie Oblander, Reeve
Cal Shaw, Administrator

Mount Pleasant No. 2
P.O. Box 278
820 Railway Ave.
Carnduff, SK S0C 0S0
Tel: 306-482-3313; *Fax:* 306-482-5278
rm.2@sasktel.net
Municipal Type: Rural Municipality
Incorporated: Dec. 11, 1911 *Area:* 781.48 sq km
Population in 2011: 383
Next Election: 2013 (election every 2 years)
Slade Boyes, Reeve
Valerie A. Olney, Administrator

Mountain View No. 318
P.O. Box 130
Herschel, SK S0L 1L0
Tel: 306-377-2144; *Fax:* 306-377-2023
rm318@sasktel.net
Municipal Type: Rural Municipality
Incorporated: Dec. 13, 1909 *Area:* 838.67 sq km
Population in 2011: 333
Next Election: 2013 (election every 2 years)
Rodney G. Wiens, Reeve
Karen F. Martin, Administrator

Newcombe No. 260
P.O. Box 40
Glidden, SK S0L 1H0
Tel: 306-463-3338; *Fax:* 306-463-4748
rm260@yourlink.ca
saskbiz.ca/communityprofiles/communityprofile.asp?CommunityID=935
Municipal Type: Rural Municipality
Incorporated: Dec. 11, 1911 *Area:* 1,075.6 sq km
Population in 2011: 400
Next Election: 2013 (election every 2 years)
Ken McBride, Reeve
Monica Buddecke, Administrator

Nipawin No. 487
P.O. Box 250
Codette, SK S0E 0P0
Tel: 306-862-9551; *Fax:* 306-862-2432
rm487@sasktel.net
Municipal Type: Rural Municipality
Incorporated: Dec. 9, 1912 *Area:* 886.73 sq km
Population in 2011: 1,030
Next Election: Oct 24, 2012 (every 2 years)
Lyle L. Larsen, Reeve
Eunice Rudy, Administrator

North Battleford No. 437
#4, 1462 - 100th St.
North Battleford, SK S9A 0W2
Tel: 306-445-3604; *Fax:* 306-445-3694
rm437@sasktel.net
saskbiz.ca/communityprofiles/CommunityProfile.Asp?CommunityID=937
Municipal Type: Rural Municipality
Incorporated: Dec. 12, 1910 *Area:* 797.20 sq km
Population in 2011: 733
Next Election: Oct 24, 2012 (every 2 years)
Jim Rogers, Reeve
Debbie Arsenault, Administrator

North Qu'Appelle No. 187
P.O. Box 99
Fort Qu'appelle, SK S0G 1S0
Tel: 306-332-5202; *Fax:* 306-332-6028
rm187@sasktel.net
www.fortquappelle.com/rm187
Municipal Type: Rural Municipality
Incorporated: Dec. 12, 1910 *Area:* 494.98 sq km
Population in 2011: 728
Next Election: Oct 24, 2012 (every 2 years)
Betty Lou Whitley, Reeve
Dawn Lugrin, Administrator

Norton No. 69
P.O. Box 189
Pangman, SK S0C 2C0
Tel: 306-442-2131; *Fax:* 306-442-2144
rm.69@sasktel.net
www.pangman.ca/rural-municipality-of-norton-no-69-2
Municipal Type: Rural Municipality
Incorporated: Dec. 13, 1909 *Area:* 844.8 sq km
Population in 2011: 259
Next Election: Oct 24, 2012 (every 2 years)
Chuck Jacques, Reeve
Wayne Lozinsky, Administrator

Oakdale No. 320
P.O. Box 249
Coleville, SK S0L 0K0
Tel: 306-965-2281; *Fax:* 306-965-2466
rm320@sasktel.net
www.colevillesk.ca
Municipal Type: Rural Municipality
Incorporated: Dec. 13, 1909 *Area:* 806.52 sq km
Population in 2011: 258
Next Election: 2013 (election every 2 years)
Darwin Whitfield, Reeve
Gillian Lund, Administrator

Old Post No. 43
P.O. Box 70
Wood Mountain, SK S0H 4L0
Tel: 306-266-2002; *Fax:* 306-266-2020
rm43@sasktel.net
Municipal Type: Rural Municipality
Incorporated: Jan. 1, 1967 *Area:* 1,757 sq km
Population in 2011: 395
Next Election: Oct 24, 2012 (every 2 years)
Warren Spagrud, Reeve
Vickie Greffard, Clerk

Orkney No. 244
26 - 5 Ave. North
Yorkton, SK S3N 0Y8
Tel: 306-782-2333; *Fax:* 306-782-5177
orkney@sasktel.net
Municipal Type: Rural Municipality
Incorporated: Jan. 1, 1913 *Area:* 815.87 sq km
Population in 2011: 1,860
Next Election: 2013 (election every 2 years)
Barclay Westerhaug, Reeve
Donna Westerhaug, Administrator

Paddockwood No. 520
P.O. Box 187
Paddockwood, SK S0J 1Z0
Tel: 306-989-2124; *Fax:* 306-989-4625
rm520@sasktel.net
www.rmofpaddockwood.com
Municipal Type: Rural Municipality
Incorporated: Jan. 1, 1978 *Area:* 2,456.51 sq km
Population in 2011: 966
Next Election: 2013 (election every 2 years)
Leander (Lance) Fehr, Reeve
Naomi Hrischuk, Administrator

Parkdale No. 498
P.O. Box 310
Glaslyn, SK S0M 0Y0
Tel: 306-342-2015; *Fax:* 306-342-4442
rm498@sasktel.ca
saskbiz.ca/communityprofiles/CommunityProfile.Asp?CommunityID=944
Municipal Type: Rural Municipality
Incorporated: Jan. 1, 1913 *Area:* 1,388.91 sq km
Population in 2011: 631
Next Election: 2013 (election every 2 years)
Bob Gourlay, Reeve
Linda Sandwick, Administrator

Paynton No. 470
P.O. Box 10
Paynton, SK S0M 2J0
Tel: 306-895-2020; *Fax:* 306-895-4800
rm470@sasktel.net
saskbiz.ca/communityprofiles/communityprofile.asp?CommunityID=945
Municipal Type: Rural Municipality
Incorporated: Jan. 1, 1913 *Area:* 593.95 sq km
Population in 2011: 268
Next Election: 2013 (election every 2 years)
Don Ferguson, Reeve
Elaine Knowlson, Administrator

Pense No. 160
P.O. Box 190
324 Elder St.
Pense, SK S0G 3W0
Tel: 306-345-2303; *Fax:* 306-345-2583
rm160@sasktel.net
www.pense160.ca
Municipal Type: Rural Municipality
Incorporated: Jan. 1, 1913 *Area:* 841.48 sq km
Population in 2011: 471
Next Election: 2013 (election every 2 years)
Tom Lemon, Reeve
Carolynn Meadows, Administrator

Perdue No. 346
P.O. Box 208
Perdue, SK S0K 3C0
Tel: 306-237-4202; *Fax:* 306-237-4202
rm346@sasktel.net
Municipal Type: Rural Municipality
Incorporated: Dec. 13, 1909 *Area:* 826.14 sq km
Population in 2011: 463
Next Election: 2013 (election every 2 years)
Bill Peters, Reeve
Allan Kirzinger, Administrator

Piapot No. 110
P.O. Box 100
Piapot, SK S0N 1Y0
Tel: 306-558-2011; *Fax:* 306-558-2125
rm110@sasktel.net
www.rmofpiapot.ca
Municipal Type: Rural Municipality
Incorporated: Dec. 8, 1913 *Area:* 1,912.81 sq km
Population in 2011: 324
Next Election: 2013 (election every 2 years)
John Wagner, Reeve
Leah McIntosh, Administrator

Pinto Creek No. 75
P.O. Box 239
Kincaid, SK S0H 2J0
Tel: 306-264-3277; *Fax:* 306-264-3254
rm75@sasktel.net
Municipal Type: Rural Municipality
Incorporated: Jan. 1, 1913 *Area:* 845.01 sq km
Population in 2011: 239
Next Election: Oct 24, 2012 (every 2 years)
Darryl Smith, Reeve
Roxanne Empey, Administrator

Pittville No. 169
P.O. Box 150
Hazlet, SK S0N 1E0
Tel: 306-678-2131; *Fax:* 306-678-2132
rm169@sasktel.net
hazletsk.com/contact.htm
Municipal Type: Rural Municipality
Incorporated: Jan. 1, 1913 *Area:* 1,258.06 sq km
Population in 2011: 204
Next Election: Oct 24, 2012 (every 2 years)
Larry Sletten, Reeve
Terry Erdelyan, Administrator

Pleasant Valley No. 288
P.O. Box 2080
Rosetown, SK S0L 2V0
Tel: 306-882-4030; *Fax:* 306-882-4401
rm317@sasktel.net
Municipal Type: Rural Municipality
Incorporated: Dec. 11, 1911 *Area:* 830.53 sq km
Population in 2011: 345
Next Election: 2013 (election every 2 years)
Blake Jeffries, Reeve
Michelle McQueen, Administrator

Pleasantdale No. 398
P.O. Box 70
Naicam, SK S0K 2Z0
Tel: 306-874-5732; *Fax:* 306-874-2225
rm398@sasktel.net
saskbiz.ca/communityprofiles/CommunityProfile.Asp?CommunityID=951
Municipal Type: Rural Municipality
Incorporated: Dec. 11, 1911 *Area:* 757.91 sq km
Population in 2011: 611
Next Election: 2013 (election every 2 years)
Forrest Pederson, Reeve
Lowell Prefontaine, Administrator

Ponass Lake No. 367
P.O. Box 98
Rose Valley, SK S0E 1M0
Tel: 306-322-2162; *Fax:* 306-322-2168
rm367@sasktel.net
saskbiz.ca/communityprofiles/CommunityProfile.Asp?CommunityID=953
Municipal Type: Rural Municipality
Incorporated: Jan. 1, 1913 *Area:* 770.21 sq km
Population in 2011: 527
Next Election: Oct 24, 2012 (every 2 years)
Allan Nelson, Reeve
Loretta Prevost, Administrator

Poplar Valley No. 12
P.O. Box 190
Rockglen, SK S0H 3R0
Tel: 306-476-2062; *Fax:* 306-476-2175
rm12@sasktel.net
Municipal Type: Rural Municipality
Incorporated: Jan. 1, 1913 *Area:* 769.37 sq km
Population in 2011: 200
Next Election: 2013 (election every 2 years)
Nairn Nielsen, Reeve
Lynn Fisher, Administrator

Porcupine No. 395
P.O. Box 190
Porcupine Plain, SK S0E 1H0
Tel: 306-278-2368; *Fax:* 306-278-3473
rm395@sasktel.net
saskbiz.ca/communityprofiles/CommunityProfile.Asp?CommunityID=955
Municipal Type: Rural Municipality
Incorporated: Feb. 28, 1944 *Area:* 2,339.96 sq km
Population in 2011: 820
Next Election: Oct 24, 2012 (every 2 years)
Wes Black, Reeve
Nicole Smith, Administrator

Prairie Rose No. 309
P.O. Box 89
Main St.
Jansen, SK S0K 2B0
Tel: 306-364-2013; *Fax:* 306-364-2088
rm309@sasktel.net
www.jansen.ca/map.htm
Municipal Type: Rural Municipality
Incorporated: Dec. 12, 1910 *Area:* 839.08 sq km
Population in 2011: 259
Next Election: Oct 24, 2012 (every 2 years)
Bruce Elke, Reeve
306-364-2077
Joni Mack, Administrator

Prairiedale No. 321
P.O. Box 90
Smiley, SK S0L 2Z0
Tel: 306-838-2020; *Fax:* 306-838-4343
rm321@sasktel.net
saskbiz.ca/communityprofiles/CommunityProfile.Asp?CommunityID=956
Municipal Type: Rural Municipality
Incorporated: Dec. 13, 1909 *Area:* 546.74 sq km
Population in 2011: 253
Next Election: Oct 24, 2012 (every 2 years)
Tim Richelhoff, Reeve
Charlotte Helfrich, Administrator

Preeceville No. 334
P.O. Box 439
Preeceville, SK S0A 3B0
Tel: 306-547-2029; *Fax:* 306-547-2081
rm334@sasktel.net
saskbiz.ca/communityprofiles/CommunityProfile.Asp?CommunityID=958
Municipal Type: Rural Municipality
Incorporated: Jan. 1, 1913 *Area:* 1,394.80 sq km
Population in 2011: 859
Next Election: 2013 (election every 2 years)
Richard Pristie, Reeve
Lisa Peterson, Administrator

Prince Albert No. 461
99 River St. East
Prince Albert, SK S6V 0A1
Tel: 306-763-2469; *Fax:* 306-763-6369
rm461@sasktel.net
rmprincealbert.ca
Municipal Type: Rural Municipality
Incorporated: Dec. 9, 1912 *Area:* 1,019.01 sq km

Population in 2011: 3,580
Next Election: Oct 24, 2012 (every 2 years)
Norma Sheldon, Reeve
Terry-Lynn Zahara, Administrator

Progress No. 351
P.O. Box 460
Luseland, SK S0L 2A0
Tel: 306-372-4322; *Fax:* 306-372-4146
rm351@sasktel.net
saskbiz.ca/communityprofiles/communityprofile.asp?CommunityID=960
Municipal Type: Rural Municipality
Incorporated: Dec. 12, 1910 *Area:* 803.09 sq km
Population in 2011: 260
Next Election: Oct 24, 2012 (every 2 years)
Dennis Gintaut, Reeve
Janet Bosch, Administrator

Reciprocity No. 32
P.O. Box 70
Alida, SK S0C 0B0
Tel: 306-443-2212; *Fax:* 306-443-2287
rm.of.reciprocity@sasktel.net
Municipal Type: Rural Municipality
Incorporated: Dec. 11, 1911 *Area:* 733.06 sq km
Population in 2011: 386
Next Election: 2013 (election every 2 years)
Alan Arthur, Reeve
Marilyn J. Larsen, Administrator

Redberry No. 435
P.O. Box 160
Hafford, SK S0J 1A0
Tel: 306-549-2333; *Fax:* 306-549-2435
rm435@sasktel.net
saskbiz.ca/communityprofiles/CommunityProfile.Asp?CommunityID=962
Municipal Type: Rural Municipality
Incorporated: Jan. 1, 1913 *Area:* 1,015.53 sq km
Population in 2011: 372
Next Election: Oct 24, 2012 (every 2 years)
Victor Hupaelo, Reeve
Alan Tanchak, Administrator

Redburn No. 130
P.O. Box 250
Rouleau, SK S0G 4H0
Tel: 306-776-2270; *Fax:* 306-776-2482
redrou@sasktel.net
Municipal Type: Rural Municipality
Incorporated: Jan. 1, 1913 *Area:* 847.91 sq km
Population in 2011: 250
Next Election: 2013 (election every 2 years)
Ronald Hughes, Reeve
Guy Lagrandeur, Administrator

Reford No. 379
P.O. Box 100
Wilkie, SK S0K 4W0
Tel: 306-843-2342; *Fax:* 306-843-2455
rm409@sasktel.net
saskbiz.ca/communityprofiles/communityprofile.asp?CommunityID=964
Municipal Type: Rural Municipality
Incorporated: Dec. 12, 1910 *Area:* 707.06 sq km
Population in 2011: 235
Next Election: Oct 24, 2012 (every 2 years)
Charles Robert Clay, Reeve
Sherry Huber, Administrator

Reno No. 51
P.O. Box 90
Consul, SK S0N 0P0
Tel: 306-299-2133; *Fax:* 306-299-4433
rm51@sasktel.net
Municipal Type: Rural Municipality
Incorporated: Dec. 11, 1911 *Area:* 3,460.66 sq km
Population in 2011: 399
Next Election: Oct 24, 2012 (every 2 years)
Brian McMillan, Reeve
Kim Lacelle, Administrator

Riverside No. 168
P.O. Box 129
Pennant, SK S0N 1X0
Tel: 306-626-3255; *Fax:* 306-626-3661
rm168@sasktel.net
saskbiz.ca/communityprofiles/CommunityProfile.Asp?CommunityID=966
Municipal Type: Rural Municipality
Incorporated: Jan. 1, 1913 *Area:* 1,295.21 sq km

Population in 2011: 490
Next Election: 2013 (election every 2 years)
Richard Bye, Reeve
Brandi Prentice, Administrator

Rocanville No. 151
P.O. Box 298
Rocanville, SK S0A 3L0
Tel: 306-645-2055; *Fax:* 306-645-2697
rm151@sasktel.net
www.rocanville.ca/service.htm
Municipal Type: Rural Municipality
Incorporated: Dec. 9, 1912 *Area:* 758.64 sq km
Population in 2011: 533
Next Election: Oct 24, 2012 (every 2 years)
Murray D. Reid, Reeve
Sylvia Anderson, Administrator

Rodgers No. 133
P.O. Box 70
Courval, SK S0H 1A0
Tel: 306-394-4305; *Fax:* 306-394-4981
rm133@sasktel.net
saskbiz.ca/communityprofiles/CommunityProfile.Asp?CommunityID=968
Municipal Type: Rural Municipality
Incorporated: Dec. 9, 1912 *Area:* 719.80 sq km
Population in 2011: 101
Next Election: Oct 24, 2012 (every 2 years)
Lawrence Johnstone, Reeve
Kristen Hawkins Bara, Administrator

Rosedale No. 283
P.O. Box 150
107 Lincoln St.
Hanley, SK S0G 2E0
Tel: 306-544-2202; *Fax:* 306-544-2252
rm283@sasktel.net
Municipal Type: Rural Municipality
Incorporated: Dec. 13, 1909 *Area:* 921.50 sq km
Population in 2011: 515
Next Election: Oct 24, 2012 (every 2 years)
Nick Patkau, Reeve
Paulette Wolkowski, Administrator

Rosemount No. 378
P.O. Box 184
Landis, SK S0K 2K0
Tel: 306-658-2034; *Fax:* 306-658-2028
rm378@sasktel.net
saskbiz.ca/communityprofiles/communityprofile.asp?CommunityID=970
Municipal Type: Rural Municipality
Incorporated: Dec. 12, 1910 *Area:* 571.35 sq km
Population in 2011: 198
Next Election: 2013 (election every 2 years)
A. Ed Egert, Reeve
Kara Kirilenko, Administrator

Rosthern No. 403
P.O. Box 126
2022 - 6th St.
Rosthern, SK S0K 3R0
Tel: 306-232-4393; *Fax:* 306-232-5321
rm403@sasktel.net
www.rmofrosthern.ca
Municipal Type: Rural Municipality
Incorporated: Dec. 9, 1912 *Area:* 954.66 sq km
Population in 2011: 2,015
Next Election: Oct 24, 2012 (every 2 years)
Bruce K. Fehr, Reeve
Wendy Penner, Administrator

Round Hill No. 467
P.O. Box 9
Rabbit Lake, SK S0M 2L0
Tel: 306-824-2044; *Fax:* 306-824-2044
rm467@yourlink.ca
Municipal Type: Rural Municipality
Incorporated: Dec. 11, 1911 *Area:* 815.21 sq km
Population in 2011: 319
Next Election: Oct 24, 2012 (every 2 years)
William Geates, Reeve
Cindy Miller, Administrator

Round Valley No. 410
P.O. Box 538
Unity, SK S0K 4L0
Tel: 306-228-2248; *Fax:* 306-228-3483
rm410@sasktel.net
saskbiz.ca/communityprofiles/CommunityProfile.Asp?CommunityID=973

Municipal Type: Rural Municipality
Incorporated: Dec. 13, 1909 *Area:* 810.57 sq km
Population in 2011: 361
Next Election: 2013 (election every 2 years)
Francis Boskill, Reeve
Mervin Bosch, Administrator

Rudy No. 284
P.O. Box 1010
400 Saskatchewan Ave. West
Outlook, SK S0L 2N0
Tel: 306-867-9349; *Fax:* 306-867-9898
rmrudy@sasktel.net
www.rmrudy.ca
Municipal Type: Rural Municipality
Incorporated: Dec. 13, 1909 *Area:* 813.86 sq km
Population in 2011: 496
Next Election: 2013 (election every 2 years)
D. Wayne Vaxvick, Reeve
Trent Michelman, Administrator

St. Andrews No. 287
P.O. Box 488
Rosetown, SK S0L 2V0
Tel: 306-882-2314; *Fax:* 306-882-3287
rm.287@sasktel.net
Municipal Type: Rural Municipality
Incorporated: Dec. 12, 1910 *Area:* 805.30 sq km
Population in 2011: 532
Next Election: Oct 24, 2012 (every 2 years)
Garry Nisbet, Reeve
Joan Babecy, Administrator

St. Louis No. 431
P.O. Box 28
Hoey, SK S0J 1E0
Tel: 306-422-6170; *Fax:* 306-422-8520
rm431@sasktel.net
Municipal Type: Rural Municipality
Incorporated: Jan. 1, 1913 *Area:* 790.18 sq km
Population in 2011: 969
Next Election: Oct 24, 2012 (every 2 years)m
Henry Gareau, Reeve
Louise Hodgson, Administrator

St. Peter No. 369
P.O. Box 70
Annaheim, SK S0K 0G0
Tel: 306-598-2122; *Fax:* 306-598-4526
rm369@sasktel.net
Municipal Type: Rural Municipality
Incorporated: Dec. 11, 1911 *Area:* 823.22 sq km
Population in 2011: 790
Next Election: Oct 24, 2012 (every 2 years)
Danny Breker, Reeve
Brenda Nagy, Administrator

St. Philips No. 301
P.O. Box 220
Pelly, SK S0A 2Z0
Tel: 306-595-2050; *Fax:* 306-595-2050
rm301@sasktel.net
Municipal Type: Rural Municipality
Incorporated: Jan. 1, 1913 *Area:* 655.79 sq km
Population in 2011: 235
Next Election: Oct 24, 2012 (every 2 years)
Ron Sorrell, Reeve
Victoria Makohoniuk, Administrator

Saltcoats No. 213
P.O. Box 150
Saltcoats, SK S0A 3R0
Tel: 306-744-2202; *Fax:* 306-744-2455
rm.saltcoats@sasktel.net
saskbiz.ca/communityprofiles/communityprofile.asp?CommunityID=979
Municipal Type: Rural Municipality
Incorporated: Dec. 9, 1912 *Area:* 830.58 sq km
Population in 2011: 673
Next Election: Oct 24, 2012 (every 2 years)
Don Taylor, Reeve
Ronald R. Risling, Administrator

Sarnia No. 221
P.O. Box 160
Roberts St.
Holdfast, SK S0G 2H0
Tel: 306-488-2033; *Fax:* 306-488-4609
rm.sarnia@sasktel.net
Municipal Type: Rural Municipality
Incorporated: Dec. 13, 1909 *Area:* 870.11 sq km
Population in 2011: 266
Next Election: Oct 24, 2012 (every 2 years)

Brian Gottselig, Reeve
Patti Vance, Administrator

Saskatchewan Landing No. 167
P.O. Box 40
Stewart Valley, SK S0N 2P0
Tel: 306-778-2105; *Fax:* 306-778-2152
rm167@sasktel.net
Municipal Type: Rural Municipality
Incorporated: Jan. 1, 1913 *Area:* 797.52 sq km
Population in 2011: 462
Next Election: Oct 24, 2012 (every 2 years)
Darwin Johnsgaard, Reeve
Corrie Lanceleve, Administrator

Sasman No. 336
P.O. Box 130
Kuroki, SK S0A 1Y0
Tel: 306-338-2263; *Fax:* 306-338-2048
rm336@yourlink.ca
saskbiz.ca/communityprofiles/CommunityProfile.Asp?CommunityID=982
Municipal Type: Rural Municipality
Incorporated: Jan. 1, 1913 *Area:* 1,006.49 sq km
Population in 2011: 818
Next Election: 2013 (election every 2 years)
Borden Woloshyn, Reeve
Sandy Wegwitz, Administrator

Scott No. 98
P.O. Box 210
Yellow Grass, SK S0G 5J0
Tel: 306-465-2512; *Fax:* 306-465-2802
rm98@signaldirect.ca
Municipal Type: Rural Municipality
Incorporated: Dec. 13, 1909 *Area:* 850.08 sq km
Population in 2011: 176
Next Election: 2013 (election every 2 years)
Douglas Watson, Reeve
Paul P. Thiele, Administrator

Senlac No. 411
P.O. Box 130
Senlac, SK S0L 2Y0
Tel: 306-228-3339; *Fax:* 306-228-2264
rm411@sasktel.net
saskbiz.ca/communityprofiles/communityprofile.asp?CommunityID=984
Municipal Type: Rural Municipality
Incorporated: Jan. 1, 1913 *Area:* 1,026.25 sq km
Population in 2011: 195
Next Election: Oct 24, 2012 (every 2 years)
Owen Mawbey, Reeve
Pauline Herle, Administrator

Shamrock No. 134
P.O. Box 40
Shamrock, SK S0H 3W0
Tel: 306-648-3594; *Fax:* 306-648-3687
rm134@sasktel.net
www.shamrockpark.ca/html/rm134.html
Municipal Type: Rural Municipality
Incorporated: Dec. 9, 1912 *Area:* 757.52 sq km
Population in 2011: 227
Next Election: 2013 (election every 2 years)
Dwayne James, Reeve
Jody Kennedy, Administrator

Shellbrook No. 493
P.O. Box 250
Shellbrook, SK S0J 2E0
Tel: 306-747-2178; *Fax:* 306-747-4315
rm493@sasktel.net
www.shellbrook.net
Municipal Type: Rural Municipality
Incorporated: Jan. 1, 1913 *Area:* 1,237.29 sq km
Population in 2011: 1,533
Next Election: Oct 24, 2012 (every 2 years)
Robert Ernst, Reeve
Karen Beauchesne, Administrator

Sherwood No. 159
1840 Cornwall St.
Regina, SK S4P 2K2
Tel: 306-525-5237; *Fax:* 306-352-1760
admin@rmsherwood.ca
www.rmofsherwood.ca
Municipal Type: Rural Municipality
Incorporated: Dec. 11, 1911 *Area:* 719.32 sq km
Population in 2011: 929
Next Election: Oct 24, 2012 (every 2 years)
Kevin Eberle, Reeve
Rochel Kunz, Administrator

Silverwood No. 123
P.O. Box 700
Whitewood, SK S0G 5C0
Tel: 306-735-2500; *Fax:* 306-735-2524
rm123@sasktel.net
Municipal Type: Rural Municipality
Incorporated: Oct. 31, 1911 *Area:* 844.61 sq km
Population in 2011: 466
Next Election: Oct 24, 2012 (every 2 years)
William MacPherson, Reeve
Jennalee Beutler, Administrator

Sliding Hills No. 273
P.O. Box 70
Mikado, SK S0A 2R0
Tel: 306-563-5285; *Fax:* 306-563-4447
slidinghills_rm273@sasktel.net
Municipal Type: Rural Municipality
Incorporated: Jan. 1, 1913 *Area:* 853.76 sq km
Population in 2011: 520
Next Election: Oct 24, 2012 (every 2 years)
Harvey Malanowich, Reeve
Todd Steele, Administrator

Snipe Lake No. 259
P.O. Box 786
Eston, SK S0L 1A0
Tel: 306-962-3214; *Fax:* 306-962-4330
rm259admin@sasktel.net
saskbiz.ca/communityprofiles/communityprofile.asp?CommunityID=990
Municipal Type: Rural Municipality
Incorporated: Dec. 11, 1911 *Area:* 1,573.80 sq km
Population in 2011: 452
Next Election: Oct 24, 2012 (every 2 years)
T. A. (Ted) Koester, Reeve
Debbie Shaw, Administrator

Souris Valley No. 7
P.O. Box 40
Oungre, SK S0C 1Z0
Tel: 306-456-2676; *Fax:* 306-456-2480
rm07@eclipsewireless.ca
Municipal Type: Rural Municipality
Incorporated: Dec. 13, 1909 *Area:* 817.52 sq km
Population in 2011: 240
Next Election: Oct 24, 2012 (every 2 years)
Dallas Pederson, Reeve

South Qu'Appelle No. 157
P.O. Box 66
Qu'Appelle, SK S0G 4A0
Tel: 306-699-2257; *Fax:* 306-699-2856
rm157@sasktel.net
www.rm157.ca
Municipal Type: Rural Municipality
Incorporated: Aug. 6, 1884 *Area:* 889.73 sq km
Population in 2011: 1,271
Next Election: Oct 24, 2012 (every 2 years)
Ken MacPherson, Reeve
Darlene Tyson, Administrator

Spalding No. 368
P.O. Box 10
Spalding, SK S0K 4C0
Tel: 306-872-2166; *Fax:* 306-872-2275
bob368@sasktel.net
saskbiz.ca/communityprofiles/CommunityProfile.Asp?CommunityID=993
Municipal Type: Rural Municipality
Incorporated: Dec. 11, 1911 *Area:* 811.47 sq km
Population in 2011: 447
Next Election: 2013 (election every 2 years)
Eugene Eggerman, Reeve
Cathy Holt, Administrator

Spiritwood No. 496
P.O. Box 340
Spiritwood, SK S0J 2M0
Tel: 306-883-2034; *Fax:* 306-883-2557
rm496@sasktel.net
saskbiz.ca/communityprofiles/communityprofile.asp?CommunityID=994
Municipal Type: Rural Municipality
Incorporated: Dec. 9, 1929 *Area:* 2,410.62 sq km
Population in 2011: 1,382
Next Election: 2013 (election every 2 years)
Grant Cadieu, Reeve
Gloria Teer, Administrator

Spy Hill No. 152
P.O. Box 129
Spy Hill, SK S0A 3W0
Tel: 306-534-2022; *Fax:* 306-534-2230
rm152@sasktel.net
Municipal Type: Rural Municipality
Incorporated: Dec. 11, 1911 *Area:* 679.28 sq km
Population in 2011: 366
Next Election: 2013 (election every 2 years)
Bernard Mikolas, Reeve
Carey Nicholauson, Administrator

Stanley No. 215
P.O. Box 70
238 - 3rd Ave. West
Melville, SK S0A 2P0
Tel: 306-728-2818; *Fax:* 306-728-2818
rm.ofstanley@sasktel.net
Municipal Type: Rural Municipality
Incorporated: Jan. 1, 1913 *Area:* 855.40 sq km
Population in 2011: 516
Next Election: Oct 24, 2012 (every 2 years)
Kenneth Petlock, Reeve
Marie Steiner, Administrator

Star City No. 428
P.O. Box 370
Star City, SK S0E 1P0
Tel: 306-863-2522; *Fax:* 306-863-2255
r.m.starcity@sasktel.ca
saskbiz.ca/communityprofiles/CommunityProfile.Asp?CommunityID=997
Municipal Type: Rural Municipality
Incorporated: Jan. 1, 1913 *Area:* 824.85 sq km
Population in 2011: 911
Next Election: 2013 (election every 2 years)
Kenneth Naber, Reeve
Levina Cronk, Administrator

Stonehenge No. 73
P.O. Box 129
Limerick, SK S0H 2P0
Tel: 306-263-2020; *Fax:* 306-263-2013
rm73@sasktel.net
www.rmstonehenge.ca
Municipal Type: Rural Municipality
Incorporated: Dec. 11, 1911 *Area:* 985.74 sq km
Population in 2011: 403
Next Election: Oct 24, 2012 (every 2 years)
Larry Lethbridge, Reeve
Tammy A. Franks, Administrator

Storthoaks No. 31
P.O. Box 40
Storthoaks, SK S0C 2K0
Tel: 306-449-2262; *Fax:* 306-449-2210
rm31@sasktel.net
Municipal Type: Rural Municipality
Incorporated: Dec. 11, 1911 *Area:* 582.57 sq km
Population in 2011: 304
Next Election: Oct 24, 2012 (every 2 years)
James E. Lorette, Reeve
Elissa Henrion, Administrator

Surprise Valley No. 9
P.O. Box 52
Minton, SK S0C 1T0
Tel: 306-969-2144; *Fax:* 306-969-2127
rmnine@sasktel.net
Municipal Type: Rural Municipality
Incorporated: Jan. 1, 1913 *Area:* 813.38 sq km
Population in 2011: 193
Next Election: Oct 24, 2012 (every 2 years)
Note: URL:
www.saskbiz.ca/communityprofiles/CommunityProfile.Asp?CommunityID=1000
Herb Axten, Reeve
Joyce Axten, Administrator

Sutton No. 103
P.O. Box 100
Mossbank, SK S0H 3G0
Tel: 306-354-2414; *Fax:* 306-354-7725
rm102.103@sasktel.net
Municipal Type: Rural Municipality
Incorporated: Dec. 11, 1911 *Area:* 822.40 sq km
Population in 2011: 240
Next Election: Oct 24, 2012 (every 2 years)
Richard Nagel, Reeve
Sherry D. Green, Administrator

Swift Current No. 137
2024 South Service Rd. West
Swift Current, SK S9H 5J5
Tel: 306-773-7314; *Fax:* 306-773-9538
rmsc137@sasktel.net
Municipal Type: Rural Municipality
Incorporated: Dec. 12, 1910 *Area:* 1,107.7 sq km
Population in 2011: 2,032
Next Election: Oct 24, 2012 (every 2 years)
Robert Neufeld, Reeve
Linda Boser, Administrator

Tecumseh No. 65
P.O. Box 300
Stoughton, SK S0G 4T0
Tel: 306-457-2277; *Fax:* 306-457-3149
rmtec@sasktel.net
Municipal Type: Rural Municipality
Incorporated: Dec. 13, 1909 *Area:* 826.11 sq km
Population in 2011: 270
Next Election: Oct 24, 2012 (every 2 years)
Zandra Slater, Reeve
Kathy Rasmussen, Administrator

Terrell No. 101
P.O. Box 60
Spring Valley, SK S0H 3X0
Tel: 306-475-2803; *Fax:* 306-475-2805
street101@sasktel.net
Municipal Type: Rural Municipality
Incorporated: Jan. 1, 1913 *Area:* 864.06 sq km
Population in 2011: 224
Next Election: Oct 24, 2012 (every 2 years)
Darrell Howe, Reeve
Kimberly Sippola, Administrator

The Gap No. 39
P.O. Box 188
Ceylon, SK S0C 0T0
Tel: 306-454-2202; *Fax:* 306-454-2627
rmgap39@sasktel.net
Municipal Type: Rural Municipality
Incorporated: Dec. 12, 1903 *Area:* 830.92 sq km
Population in 2011: 230
Next Election: Oct 24, 2012 (every 2 years)
Keith Kaufmann, Reeve
Yvonne Johnston, Administrator

Three Lakes No. 400
P.O. Box 100
Middle Lake, SK S0K 2X0
Tel: 306-367-2172; *Fax:* 306-367-2011
rm400@sasktel.net
Municipal Type: Rural Municipality
Incorporated: Jan. 1, 1913 *Area:* 772.49 sq km
Population in 2011: 620
Next Election: 2013 (election every 2 years)
Allen Baumann, Reeve
Tim Schmidt, Administrator

Tisdale No. 427
P.O. Box 128
Tisdale, SK S0E 1T0
Tel: 306-873-2334; *Fax:* 306-873-4442
rm427@sasktel.net
Municipal Type: Rural Municipality
Incorporated: Dec. 9, 1912 *Area:* 849.24 sq km
Population in 2011: 916
Next Election: Oct 24, 2012 (every 2 years)
Robert C. Jackson, Reeve
Fern Lucas, Administrator

Torch River No. 488
P.O. Box 40
White Fox, SK S0J 3B0
Tel: 306-276-2066; *Fax:* 306-276-2099
rm488@sasktel.net
Municipal Type: Rural Municipality
Incorporated: Jan. 1, 1950 *Area:* 5,179 sq km
Population in 2011: 1,468
Next Election: 2013 (election every 2 years)
Note: URL:
www.saskbiz.ca/communityprofiles/CommunityProfile.Asp?CommunityID=1008
Dennis Scott, Reeve
Nathalie Hipkins, Administrator

Touchwood No. 248
P.O. Box 160
Punnichy, SK S0A 3C0
Tel: 306-835-2110; *Fax:* 306-835-2100
rm248@aski.ca
Municipal Type: Rural Municipality
Incorporated: Dec. 12, 1910 *Area:* 706.72 sq km
Population in 2011: 267
Next Election: 2013 (election every 2 years)
Ernest Matai, Reeve
Lorelei Paulsen, Administrator

Tramping Lake No. 380
P.O. Box 129
104 Main St.
Scott, SK S0K 4A0
Tel: 306-247-2033; *Fax:* 306-247-2055
rmtrampinglake@xplornet.com
Municipal Type: Rural Municipality
Incorporated: Dec. 12, 1910 *Area:* 615.56 sq km
Population in 2011: 410
Next Election: 2013 (election every 2 years)
Peter Volk, Reeve
Stacy Hawkins, Administrator

Tullymet No. 216
P.O. Box 190
Balcarres, SK S0G 0C0
Tel: 306-334-2366; *Fax:* 306-334-2930
rm216@sasktel.net
www.townofbalcarres.ca
Municipal Type: Rural Municipality
Incorporated: Jan. 1, 1913 *Area:* 562.99 sq km
Population in 2011: 220
Next Election: 2013 (election every 2 years)
Larry Jankoski, Reeve
Sheila Keisig, Administrator

Turtle River No. 469
P.O. Box 128
Edam, SK S0M 0V0
Tel: 306-397-2311; *Fax:* 306-397-2346
rm469@sasktel.net
Municipal Type: Rural Municipality
Incorporated: Dec. 9, 1912 *Area:* 664.49 sq km
Population in 2011: 360
Next Election: Oct 24, 2012 (every 2 years)
Louis McCaffrey, Reeve
Nicole Collins, Administrator

Usborne No. 310
P.O. Box 310
Lanigan, SK S0K 2M0
Tel: 306-365-2924; *Fax:* 306-365-2129
rm310@sasktel.net
Municipal Type: Rural Municipality
Incorporated: Dec. 13, 1909 *Area:* 810.38 sq km
Population in 2011: 547
Next Election: 2013 (election every 2 years)
Don Bowman, Reeve
Keith Schulze, Administrator

Val Marie No. 17
P.O. Box 59
Val Marie, SK S0N 2T0
Tel: 306-298-2009; *Fax:* 306-298-2224
rm17@sasktel.net
Municipal Type: Rural Municipality
Incorporated: Jan. 1, 1969 *Area:* 3,105.26 sq km
Population in 2011: 405
Next Election: Oct 24, 2012 (every 2 years)
Mike Waldner, Reeve
Cathy Legault, Administrator

Vanscoy No. 345
P.O. Box 187
Vanscoy, SK S0L 3J0
Tel: 306-668-2060; *Fax:* 306-668-1338
rm345@sasktel.net
rmvanscoy.ca
Municipal Type: Rural Municipality
Incorporated: Dec. 13, 1909 *Area:* 866.68 sq km
Population in 2011: 2,714
Next Election: Oct 24, 2012 (every 2 years)
Floyd Chapple, Reeve
Shawn Antosh, Administrator

Victory No. 226
P.O. Box 100
Beechy, SK S0L 0C0
Tel: 306-859-2270; *Fax:* 306-859-2271
rm.226@yourlink.ca
Municipal Type: Rural Municipality
Incorporated: Dec. 8, 1919 *Area:* 1,375.44 sq km
Population in 2011: 443
Next Election: 2013 (election every 2 years)
Wes Jansen, Reeve
Diane Watt, Administrator

Viscount No. 341
P.O. Box 100
215 Bangor Ave.
Viscount, SK S0K 4M0
Tel: 306-944-2044; *Fax:* 306-944-2016
patrm341@sasktel.net
Municipal Type: Rural Municipality
Incorporated: Dec. 13, 1909 *Area:* 831.23 sq km
Population in 2011: 371
Next Election: Oct 24, 2012 (every 2 years)
Russell Deneiko, Reeve
Patrick T. Clavelle, Administrator

Wallace No. 243
26 - 5 Ave. North
Yorkton, SK S3N 0Y8
Tel: 306-782-2455; *Fax:* 306-782-5177
wallace@sasktel.net
Municipal Type: Rural Municipality
Incorporated: Dec. 11, 1911 *Area:* 832.01 sq km
Population in 2011: 879
Next Election: Oct 24, 2012 (every 2 years)
Garry Liebrecht, Reeve
Kim Waddell, Administrator

Walpole No. 92
P.O. Box 117
Wawota, SK S0G 5A0
Tel: 306-739-2545; *Fax:* 306-739-2777
rm92@sasktel.net
Municipal Type: Rural Municipality
Incorporated: Dec. 12, 1910 *Area:* 844.66 sq km
Population in 2011: 338
Next Election: 2013 (election every 2 years)
Hugh Smyth, Reeve
Rhonda M. Hall, Administrator

Waverley No. 44
P.O. Box 70
Glentworth, SK S0H 1V0
Tel: 306-266-4920; *Fax:* 306-266-2077
rm44@yourlink.ca
Municipal Type: Rural Municipality
Incorporated: Feb. 1, 1913 *Area:* 1,429.30 sq km
Population in 2011: 359
Next Election: 2013 (election every 2 years)
Lloyd Anderson, Reeve
Deidre Nelson, Administrator

Wawken No. 93
P.O. Box 90
Wawota, SK S0G 5A0
Tel: 306-739-2332; *Fax:* 306-739-2222
rm93@sasktel.net
Municipal Type: Rural Municipality
Incorporated: Jan. 1, 1913 *Area:* 766.53 sq km
Population in 2011: 559
Next Election: Oct 24, 2012 (every 2 years)
Hector Lamontagne, Reeve
Debbie Saville, Administrator

Webb No. 138
P.O. Box 100
Webb, SK S0N 2X0
Tel: 306-674-2230; *Fax:* 306-674-2324
rm138@xplornet.com
Municipal Type: Rural Municipality
Incorporated: Dec. 13, 1909 *Area:* 1,098.78 sq km
Population in 2011: 533
Next Election: 2013 (election every 2 years)
Dennis Fiddler, Reeve
Raylene Packet, Administrator

Wellington No. 97
P.O. Box 1390
Weyburn, SK S4H 3J9
Tel: 306-842-5606; *Fax:* 306-842-5601
rm97@sasktel.net
Municipal Type: Rural Municipality
Incorporated: Dec. 13, 1909 *Area:* 838.68 sq km
Population in 2011: 356
Next Election: Oct 24, 2012 (every 2 years)
Bernie Kot, Reeve
Lloyd Muma, Administrator

Wheatlands No. 163
P.O. Box 129
Mortlach, SK S0H 3E0
Tel: 306-355-2233; *Fax:* 306-355-2351
rm163@sasktel.net
Municipal Type: Rural Municipality
Incorporated: Dec. 13, 1909 *Area:* 827.4 sq km

Population in 2011: 149
Next Election: Oct 24, 2012 (every 2 years)
Gary Stirling, Reeve
Julie Gerbrandt, Administrator

Whiska Creek No. 106
P.O. Box 10
Vanguard, SK S0N 2V0
Tel: 306-582-2133; *Fax:* 306-582-4950
rm106@sasktel.net
Municipal Type: Rural Municipality
Incorporated: Jan. 1, 1913 *Area:* 851.89 sq km
Population in 2011: 499
Next Election: 2013 (election every 2 years)
Keith Carleton, Reeve
Teresa Richards, Administrator

White Valley No. 49
P.O. Box 520
Eastend, SK S0N 0T0
Tel: 306-295-3553; *Fax:* 306-295-3571
rm49@sasktel.net
Municipal Type: Rural Municipality
Incorporated: Jan. 1, 1913 *Area:* 2,026.88 sq km
Population in 2011: 478
Next Election: Oct 24, 2012 (every 2 years)
Note: URL:
www.saskbiz.ca/communityprofiles/CommunityProfile.Asp?CommunityID=1027
James Leroy, Reeve
Edna Laturnus, Administrator

Willner No. 253
P.O. Box 250
Davidson, SK S0G 1A0
Tel: 306-567-3103; *Fax:* 306-567-3266
rm253@sasktel.net
Municipal Type: Rural Municipality
Incorporated: Jan. 1, 1913 *Area:* 834.97 sq km
Population in 2011: 245
Next Election: Oct 24, 2012 (every 2 years)
Len Palmer, Reeve
Yvonne (Bonny) Goodsman, Administrator

Willow Bunch No. 42
P.O. Box 220
16 Edouard Beaupré St.
Willow Bunch, SK S0H 4K0
Tel: 306-473-2302; *Fax:* 306-473-2312
www.willowbunch.ca/wb/rm
Municipal Type: Rural Municipality
Incorporated: Nov. 21, 1912 *Area:* 1,047.8 sq km
Population in 2011: 361
Next Election: 2013 (election every 2 years)
David Kirby, Reeve
Margaret L. Brown, Administrator

Willow Creek No. 458
P.O. Box 5
Brooksby, SK S0E 0H0
Tel: 306-863-4143; *Fax:* 306-863-2366
rm458@staffcomm.com
Municipal Type: Rural Municipality
Incorporated: Dec. 9, 1912 *Area:* 845.18 sq km
Population in 2011: 693
Next Election: 2013 (election every 2 years)
Note: URL:
www.saskbiz.ca/communityprofiles/CommunityProfile.Asp?CommunityID=1030
John Deck, Reeve
Vicki Baptist, Administrator

Willowdale No. 153
P.O. Box 58
Whitewood, SK S0G 5C0
Tel: 306-735-2344; *Fax:* 306-735-4495
rm153@sasktel.net
Municipal Type: Rural Municipality
Incorporated: Jan. 1, 1913 *Area:* 605.06 sq km
Population in 2011: 297
Next Election: Oct 24, 2012 (every 2 years)
Kenneth Aldous, Reeve
Robert Lang, Administrator

Wilton No. 472
P.O. Box 40
Marshall, SK S0M 1R0
Tel: 306-387-6244; *Fax:* 306-387-6598
rm472@sasktel.net
Municipal Type: Rural Municipality
Incorporated: Dec. 13, 1909 *Area:* 1,042.72 sq km
Population in 2011: 1,494
Next Election: 2013 (election every 2 years)
Glen Dow, Reeve
Darren Elder, Administrator

Winslow No. 319
P.O. Box 310
Dodsland, SK S0L 0V0
Tel: 306-356-2106; *Fax:* 306-356-2085
rm319@sasktel.net
Municipal Type: Rural Municipality
Incorporated: Dec. 13, 1909 *Area:* 798.07 sq km
Population in 2011: 324
Next Election: Oct 24, 2012 (every 2 years)
Martin McGrath, Reeve
Regan MacDonald, Administrator

Wise Creek No. 77
P.O. Box 400
Shaunavon, SK S0N 2M0
Tel: 306-297-2520; *Fax:* 306-297-3162
rm77.78@sasktel.net
Municipal Type: Rural Municipality
Incorporated: Jan. 1, 1913 *Area:* 843.85 sq km
Population in 2011: 157
Next Election: Oct 24, 2012 (every 2 years)
Frank Dunham, Reeve
Rhonda Bellefeuille, Administrator

Wolseley No. 155
P.O. Box 370
Wolseley, SK S0G 5H0
Tel: 306-698-2522; *Fax:* 306-698-2664
rm155@sasktel.net
Municipal Type: Rural Municipality
Incorporated: Dec. 13, 1909 *Area:* 774.26 sq km
Population in 2011: 405
Next Election: Oct 24, 2012 (every 2 years)
Edward Dureault, Reeve
Rose Zimmer, Administrator

Wolverine No. 340
P.O. Box 28
Burr, SK S0K 0T0
Tel: 306-682-3640; *Fax:* 306-682-3640
rm340@sasktel.net
Municipal Type: Rural Municipality
Incorporated: Dec. 13, 1909 *Area:* 834.78 sq km
Population in 2011: 464
Next Election: 2013 (election every 2 years)
Bryan Gibney, Reeve
Sandi Dunne, Administrator

Wood Creek No. 281
P.O. Box 10
303 George St.
Simpson, SK S0G 4M0
Tel: 306-836-2020; *Fax:* 306-836-4460
rm281@sasktel.net
Municipal Type: Rural Municipality
Incorporated: Dec. 13, 1909 *Area:* 832.34 sq km
Population in 2011: 205
Next Election: Oct 24, 2012 (every 2 years)
John McArthur, Reeve
Darlene Mann, Administrator

Wood River No. 74
P.O. Box 250
35 - 2nd Ave. East
Lafleche, SK S0H 2K0
Tel: 306-472-5235; *Fax:* 306-472-3706
rm74@sasktel.net
Municipal Type: Rural Municipality
Incorporated: Dec. 9, 1912 *Area:* 838.45 sq km
Population in 2011: 324
Next Election: 2013 (election every 2 years)
Duane Filson, Reeve
Deirdre Nelson, Administrator

Wreford No. 280
P.O. Box 99
Nokomis, SK S0G 3R0
Tel: 306-528-2202; *Fax:* 306-528-4411
rm280@sasktel.net
Municipal Type: Rural Municipality
Incorporated: Dec. 12, 1910 *Area:* 798.55 sq km
Population in 2011: 150
Next Election: 2013 (election every 2 years)
Dean Hobman, Reeve
Melanie Rich, Administrator

YUKON TERRITORY

LEGISLATION: Municipal Act, Municipal Finance and Community Grants Act, Assessment and Taxation Act.

Requirements for municipal incorporation in the Yukon are based on population: town 300–2,500, city over 2,500. Any community may become a Local Advisory Area, an advisory body to the minister, as a first step in local governance. A community may also incorporate as a Rural Government with limited powers, as a developmental step in becoming a full municipality. The Yukon Municipal Act does not include provisions for unorganized settlements or First Nation communities.

Municipal elections are held every three years and polling day is the third Thursday of October in each election year. Mayors and councillors are elected for a three-year period (2009, 2012, etc.).

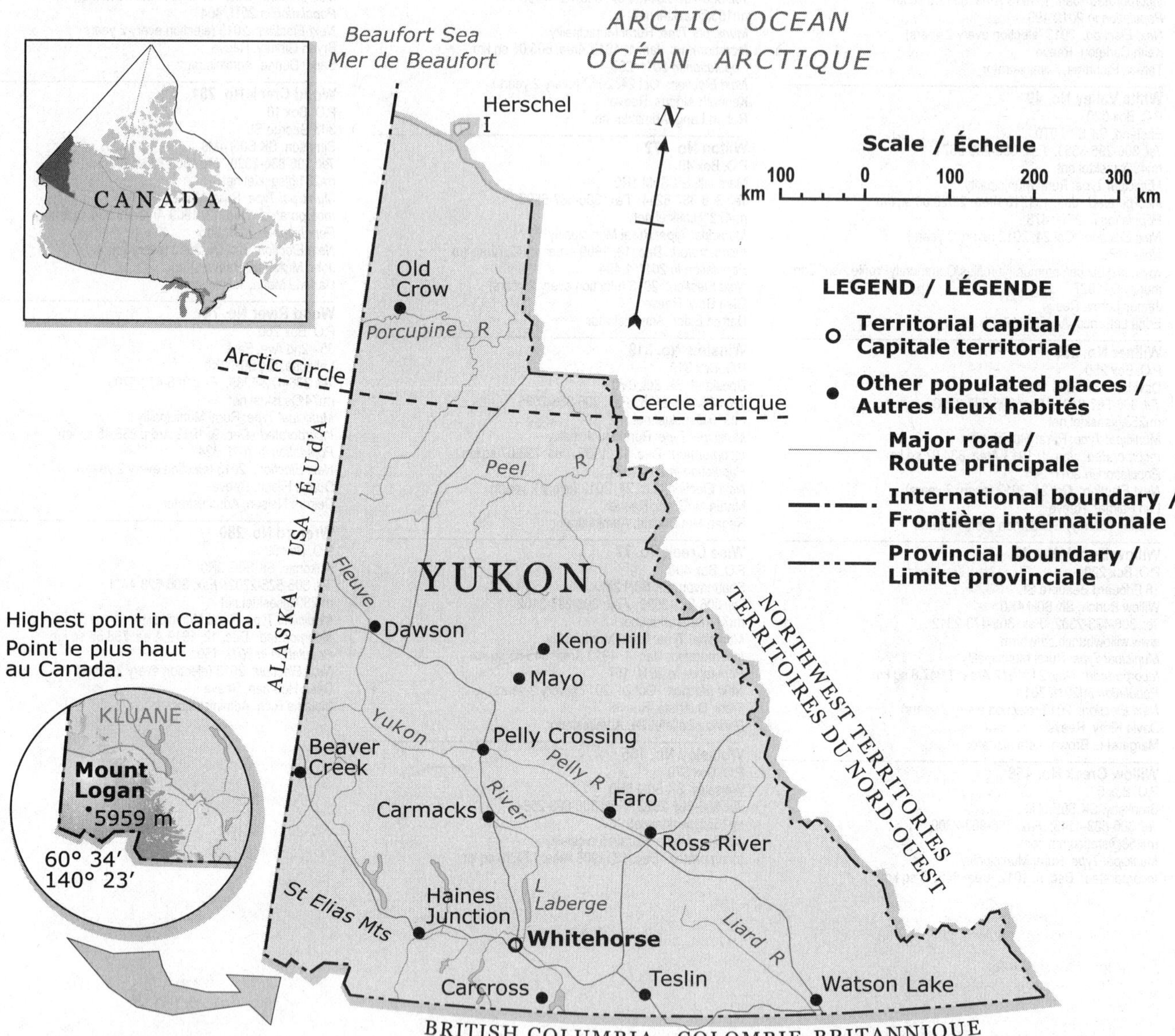

Reproduced with the permission of Natural Resources Canada, 2012

www.atlas.gc.ca

Yukon Territory

Major Municipalities in Yukon Territory

Whitehorse
2121 Second Ave.
Whitehorse, YT Y1A 1C2
Tel: 867-667-6401; *Fax:* 867-668-8384
council.services@whitehorse.ca, www.city.whitehorse.yk.ca
Municipal Type: City
Incorporated: June 1, 1950 *Area:* 416.43 sq km
Population in 2011: 23,276
Provincial Electoral District(s): Whitehorse Centre; Whitehorse West; Copperbelt North; Copperbelt South; McIntyre-Takhini; Mountainview; Porter Creek Centre; Porter Creek North; Porter Creek South; Riverdale North; Riverdale South
Federal Electoral District(s): Yukon
Next Election: Oct. 18, 2012 (3 year terms)
Bev Buckway, Mayor
867-668-8626
bev.buckway@whitehorse.ca
Dave Austin, Councillor
dave.austin@whitehorse.ca
Doug Graham, Councillor
doug.graham@whitehorse.ca
Betty Irwin, Councillor
betty.irwin@whitehorse.ca
Ranj Pillai, Councillor
ranj.pillai@whitehorse.ca
Florence Roberts, Councillor
florence.roberts@whitehorse.ca
Dave Stockdale, Councillor
dave.stockdale@whitehorse.ca
Dennis Shewfelt, City Manager
867-668-8650, Fax: 867-668-8639
dennis.shewfelt@whitehorse.ca
Brian Crist, Director, Operations
867-668-8301, Fax: 867-668-8386
brian.crist@whitehorse.ca
Robert Fendrick, Director, Administrative Services
867-668-8612, Fax: 867-668-8384
robert.fendrick@whitehorse.ca
Mike Gau, Manager, Planning & Development Services
867-668-8333, Fax: 867-668-8395
planning.services@whitehorse.ca
Dave Muir, Manager, Transit
867-668-8391
dave.muir@whitehorse.ca
Terry O'Toole, Manager, Public Works
867-668-8351
terry.o'toole@whitehorse.ca
David Pruden, Manager, Bylaw Services
867-334-1082
david.pruden@whitehorse.ca
Linda Rapp, Manager, Parks & Recreation
867-668-8325, Fax: 867-668-8675
parks.recreation@whitehorse.ca
Clive Sparks, Fire Chief
867-668-8383
clive.sparks@whitehorse.ca
Mike Stevely, Manager, Information Systems
867-334-2100
mike.stevely@whitehorse.ca
Wayne Tuck, Manager, Engineering & Environmental Services
867-668-8306
wayne.tuck@whitehorse.ca
George White, Manager, Maintenance & Safety Services
867-668-8345
george.white@whitehorse.ca
Pippa McNeil, Co-Coordinator, Environmental Services
867-668-8312
environment@whitehorse.ca
Sabine Schweiger, Co-Coordinator, Environmental Services
867-668-8312
environment@whitehorse.ca
Sheila Dodd, Supervisor, Economic Development & Tourism
867-668-8660
sheila.dodd@whitehorse.ca
Ray Osborne, Supervisor, Utility Stations
867-668-8669
ray.osborne@whitehorse.ca

Other Municipalities in Yukon Territory

Carmacks
P.O. Box 113
Carmacks, YT Y0B 1C0
Tel: 867-863-6271; *Fax:* 867-863-6606
carmacks@northwestel.net, www.carmacks.ca
Municipal Type: Village
Incorporated: Nov. 1, 1984 *Area:* 36.90 sq km
Population in 2011: 503
Provincial Electoral District(s): Mayo-Tatchun
Federal Electoral District(s): Yukon
Next Election: Oct. 18, 2012 (3 year terms)
Elaine Wyatt, Mayor
867-863-6211
vocmayor@northwestel.net
Cory Bellmore, Chief Administrative Officer
voccao@northwestel.net

Dawson City
P.O. Box 308
1336 Front St.
Dawson City, YT Y0B 1G0
Tel: 867-993-7400; *Fax:* 867-993-7434
cityofdawson@cityofdawson.ca
www.cityofdawson.ca/municipalinfo
Municipal Type: Town
Incorporated: Jan. 9, 1902 *Area:* 32.45 sq km
Population in 2011: 1,319
Provincial Electoral District(s): Klondike
Federal Electoral District(s): Yukon
Next Election: Oct. 18, 2012 (3 year terms)
Peter Jenkins, Mayor
mayor@cityofdawson.ca
Jeff Renaud, Chief Administrative Officer
cao@cityofdawson.ca

Deep Creek
Whitehorse, YT
Tel: 867-667-6966
Other Information: Yukon Land Planning Office Phone: 867-456-3827
Municipal Type: Local Advisory Area
Incorporated: 2001 *Area:* 1.39 sq km
Population in 2011: 20
Provincial Electoral District(s): Lake LaBerge
Federal Electoral District(s): Yukon
Vacant, Chair

Faro
P.O. Box 580
200 Campbell St.
Faro, YT Y0B 1K0
Tel: 867-994-2728; *Fax:* 867-994-3154
www.faroyukon.ca
Municipal Type: Town
Incorporated: June 13, 1969 *Area:* 203.57 sq km
Population in 2011: 344
Provincial Electoral District(s): Pelly-Nisutlin
Federal Electoral District(s): Yukon
Next Election: Oct. 18, 2012 (3 year terms)
Heather Campbell, Mayor
Ken Hodgins, Chief Administrative Officer
cao-faro@faroyukon.ca

Haines Junction
P.O. Box 5339
Haines Junction, YT Y0B 1L0
Tel: 867-634-7100; *Fax:* 867-634-2008
www.hainesjunctionyukon.com
Municipal Type: Village
Incorporated: Oct. 1, 1984 *Area:* 34.08 sq km
Population in 2011: 593
Provincial Electoral District(s): Kluane
Federal Electoral District(s): Yukon
Next Election: Oct. 18, 2012 (3 year terms)
George Nassiopoulos, Mayor
mayor06-vhj@yknet.ca
Michael Riseborough, Chief Administrative Officer
vhj@yknet.yk.ca

Ibex Valley
P.O. Box 20624
Whitehorse, YT Y1A 7A2
Tel: 867-667-7844; *Fax:* 867-393-1966
Municipal Type: Local Advisory Area
Area: 209.06 sq km
Population in 2011: 346
Provincial Electoral District(s): Kluane-Lake LaBerge
Federal Electoral District(s): Yukon
Trish Macpherson, Chair & Councillor

Marsh Lake
P.O. Box 1325
Marsh Lake, YT Y0B 1Y2
Tel: 867-660-5347
marshlakelac@mail.com, www.angelfire.com/yt2/marshlakelac
Municipal Type: Local Advisory Area
Population in 2011: 619
Provincial Electoral District(s): Mount Lorne-Southern Lakes
Federal Electoral District(s): Yukon
Malcolm Taggart, Chair & Councillor, Ward(s): 3. Old Constabulary
mtaggart@northwestel.net

Mayo
P.O. Box 160
Mayo, YT Y0B 1M0
Tel: 867-996-2317; *Fax:* 867-996-2907
mayo@northwestel.net, www.yukonweb.com/community/mayo
Municipal Type: Village
Incorporated: June 1, 1984 *Area:* 0.87 sq km
Population in 2011: 226
Provincial Electoral District(s): Mayo/Tatchun
Federal Electoral District(s): Yukon
Next Election: Oct. 18, 2012 (3 year terms)
Scott Bolton, Mayor
Margrit Wozniak, Chief Administrative Officer

Mount Lorne
P.O. Box 10009
Whitehorse, YT Y1A 7A1
Tel: 867-667-7083; *Fax:* 867-667-7083
mtlorne@northwestel.net, www.mountlorne.yk.net
Municipal Type: Local Advisory Area
Area: 160.15 sq km
Population in 2011: 408
Provincial Electoral District(s): Mount Lorne-Southern Lakes
Federal Electoral District(s): Yukon
Peter Percival, Chair & Councillor, Ward(s): Cowley Lake
867-668-6817

South Klondike
P.O. Box 4
Carcross, YT Y0B 1B0
Tel: 867-821-3461
Municipal Type: Local Advisory Area
Incorporated: Aug. 15, 2006 *Area:* 15.96 sq km
Population in 2011: 289
Provincial Electoral District(s): Mount Lorne-Southern Lakes
Federal Electoral District(s): Yukon
Daniel Kemble, Chair & Councillor, Ward(s): 3

Tagish
P.O. Box 92
Tagish, YT Y0B 1T0
Tel: 867-399-4002; *Fax:* 867-399-3006
tagishclub@northwestel.net; tac@northwestel.net
Municipal Type: Local Advisory Area
Incorporated: 2005 *Area:* 43.38 sq km
Population in 2011: 391
Provincial Electoral District(s): Mount Lorne-Southern Lakes
Federal Electoral District(s): Yukon
Paul Dabbs, Chair

Teslin
P.O. Box 32
Teslin, YT Y0A 1B0
Tel: 867-390-2530; *Fax:* 867-390-2104
vteslin@northwestel.net, www.teslin.ca
Municipal Type: Village
Incorporated: Aug. 1, 1984 *Area:* 2.22 sq km
Population in 2011: 122
Provincial Electoral District(s): Pelly-Nisutlin
Federal Electoral District(s): Yukon
Next Election: Oct. 18, 2012 (3 year terms)
Clara Jules, Mayor
Frank Thomas, Chief Administrative Officer
frank.thomas@northwestel.net

Watson Lake
P.O. Box 590
Watson Lake, YT Y0A 1C0
Tel: 867-536-8000; *Fax:* 867-536-7522
twl@northwestel.net, www.watsonlake.ca
Municipal Type: Town
Incorporated: April 1, 1984 *Area:* 5.16 sq km
Population in 2011: 802
Provincial Electoral District(s): Watson Lake
Federal Electoral District(s): Yukon
Next Election: Oct. 18, 2012 (3 year terms)
Richard Durocher, Mayor
Stephen Conway, Chief Administrative Officer

SECTION 9
GOVERNMENT/JUDICIAL

Following the federal listings, this section is arranged by province. Within each province, listings are by type of court, then by city.

Federal

Supreme Court of Canada
301 Wellington St., Ottawa, ON K1A 0J1
Tel: 613-995-4330; *Fax:* 613-996-3063
Toll-Free: 888-551-1185
reception@scc-csc.gc.ca; media@scc-csc.gc.ca
www.scc-csc.gc.ca
Other information: TTY: 613-944-7895; Registry, E-mail: registry-greffe@scc-csc.gc.ca; Court Library, E-mail: library-bibliotheque@scc-csc.gc.ca; Tours, E-mail: tour-visite@scc-csc.gc.ca

In 1875, the Supreme Court of Canada was created by an Act of Parliament. The Court is a general court of appeal, which consists of nine judges. The Governor in Council appoints the judges, who remain in the position until the age of 75. There is a Chief Justice of Canada, plus eight puisne judges. A Registrar is also appointed by the Governor in Council. The Registrar is responsible for all the administrative work in the Court, & answers directly to the Chief Justice. There are approximately 200 employees of the Supreme Court. The Supreme Court sits in Ottawa where, each year, three sessions are held. Approximately 80 appeals are heard by the Court every year. The hearings are open to the public. Cases for review come from the provincial & territorial appellate courts & the Federal Court of Appeal, in criminal, civil, constitutional & administrative law matters. Decisions of the Supreme Court of Canada may be unanimous, or a majority may decide.

Chief Justice of Canada: The Rt. Hon. Madam Chief Justice Beverley McLachlin, 613-992-6940, Fax: 613-952-3092
Puisne Judges (The Honourable Mr. / Madam Justice)
Louis LeBel
Morris J. Fish
Rosalie Silberman Abella
Marshall Rothstein
Thomas Albert Cromwell
Andromache Karakatsanis
Michael J. Moldaver
To be appointed
Administration:
Registrar: Roger Bilodeau, 613-996-9277, Fax: 613-996-9138
Deputy Registrar: Mary Sue McFadyen, 613-996-7521, Fax: 613-941-5817
Director General: Corporate Services Sector, Lynn Potter, 613-996-0429, Fax: 613-947-2860
Director: Library & Information Management Branch, Rosalie Fox, 613-996-9971, Fax: 613-991-0258
Director: Finance & Administrative Branch, Cathy Gaudet, 613-992-1765, Fax: 613-947-2860
Director: Information Management & Technology, Catherine Laforce, 613-947-0682, Fax: 613-991-0258
Director: Human Resources, Library, Anne-Marie Larivière, 613-995-4224, Fax: 613-996-7266

Federal Court of Appeal
Cour d'appel fédérale
Courts Administration Service, Ottawa, ON K1A 0H9
Tel: 613-995-5063;
Media Enquiries: media-fca@fca-caf.gc.ca
www.fca-caf.gc.ca
Other information: TTY: 613-995-4640

The Federal Court of Appeal was established by Parliament in accordance with provision of section 101 of the Constitution Act, 1867. The Court is a bilingual tribunal, which sits & hears cases anywhere in Canada. Both common law & civil law are administered by the Federal Court of Appeal. Decisions of the Federal Court of Appeal impact all Canadians. Responsibilities of the Court include enforcing rights & obligations between Canadians & the federal government, & interpreting & implementing Canada's international obligations.

Chief Justice of the Federal Court of Appeal: The Hon. Pierre Blais, 613-995-5106
Judges (The Hon. Mr. / Madam Justice):
Gilles Létourneau(Supernumerary)
Marc Noël
Marc Nadon
John Maxwell Evans
Karen Sharlow
J.D. Denis Pelletier
Eleanor R. Dawson
Johanne Trudel
David W. Stratas
Robert M. Mainville
Johanne Gauthier
Administration:
Judicial Administrator: Suzelle Bazinet, 613-995-5117, Fax: 613-952-6439

Court Martial Appeal Court of Canada
Cour d'Appel de la Cour Martiale
Thomas D'Arcy McGee Building, 90 Sparks St., Ottawa, ON K1A 0H9
Tel: 613-996-6795;
Media enquiries: media-fca@fca-caf.gc.ca
www.cmac-cacm.ca
Other information: TTY: 613-947-0407

The Court Martial Appeal Court of Canada was established by the Parliament of Canada, pursuant to its authority under section 101 of the Constitution Act,1867. The Court administers the National Defence Act & the Criminal Code. The Court Martial Appeal Court of Canada hears appeals from military courts. Military courts, known as courts martial, try members of the Canadian Forces, as well as civilians accompanying military personnel abroad, for crimes & offences against the Code of Service Discipline. The Code of Service Discipline is found in Part III & Part VII of the National Defence Act. Military personnel are subjected to military law, except when the offence has little to do with their military role. Offences, such as murder & manslaughter, are tried in civilian courts. There is a right of appeal to the Supreme Court of Canada from the Court Martial Appeal Court of Canada on questions of law.

Chief Justice: The Hon. Mr. Justice Edmond P. Blanchard, 613-995-7886
Designated Judges (The Hon. Mr. / Madam Justice):
Yvon Pinard
Joanne B. Veit(Supernumerary Judge)
Gilles Létourneau
Marc Noël
Sandra J. Simpson
Marc Nadon
Danièle Tremblay-Lamer
Karen M. Weiler
Eugene Glen Ewaschuk
Douglas R. Campbell
Pierre Blais
John Maxwell Evans
François Lemieux
Karen Sharlow
Ross Goodwin
Elizabeth A. Bennett
John A. O'Keefe
J.D. Denis Pelletier
Eleanor R. Dawson
Dolores M. Hansen
Elizabeth Heneghan
Michel Beaudry
Luc Martineau
Simon Noël
Judith A. Snider
Johanne Gauthier
James O'Reilly
James Russell
J. David Watt
A. Donald K. MacKenzie
Joseph T. Robertson
Deborah J. McCawley
Sean J. Harrington
Richard G. Mosley
Michel M.J. Shore
Michael L. Phelan
Anne L. Mactavish
Yves de Montigny
Roger T. Hughes
Robert L. Barnes
Johanne Trudel
Leonard S. Mandamin
Russel W. Zinn
Alexandre Deschênes
J. Douglas Cunningham
Guy Cournoyer
Douglas N. Abra
Richard Boivin
David Near
Robert Mainvile
Jamie W.S. Saunders
Administration:
Chief Administrator of the Court: Daniel Gosselin, 613-996-4778
Deputy Chief Administrator: Murielle Brazeau, 613-943-3458
Judicial Administrator: Dorothée Paquin, 613-995-7886
Contact: Media, Chantelle Bowers, 613-995-5063, Fax: 613-941-9454
media-fca@fca-caf.gc.ca

Tax Court of Canada
200 Kent St., Ottawa, ON K1A 0M1
Tel: 613-992-0901; *Fax:* 613-957-9034
Toll-Free: 800-927-5499
www.tcc-cci.gc.ca
Other information: TTY: 613-943-0946

In 1983, the Tax Court of Canada was established, pursuant to the Tax Court of Canada Act. The Court operates independently of the Canada Revenue Agency & other departments of the Government of Canada. Many of the appeals to the Tax Court of Canada are related to income tax, the goods & services tax, & employment insurance. References are also heard from the Canada Revenue Agency to provide interpretations of the legislation within its jurisdiction.

Chief Justice: The Honourable Mr. Justice Gerald J. Rip, 613-992-1994
Associate Chief Justice: The Honourable Mr. Justice Eugene P. Rossiter, 613-992-2159
Judges in order of seniority (The Honourable Mr./Madam Justice):
Theodore E. Margeson(Supernumerary Judge)
Pierre Archambault
Cameron Hugh McArthur(Supernumerary Judge)
Lucie Lamarre
Alain Tardif(Supernumerary Judge)
Eric A. Bowie(Supernumerary Judge)
Joe E. Hershfield
Diane Campbell
Campbell J. Miller
François M. Angers
Leslie M. Little
Brent Paris
Judith Woods
Georgette Anne Sheridan
Paul Bédard
Réal Favreau
Wyman W. Webb
Gaston Jorré
Patrick J. Boyle
Valerie Miller
Robert James Hogan
Steven K. D'Arcy
Frank J. Pizzitelli
Johanne D'Auray
Administration:
Registrar of the Court: Roula Eatrides, 613-944-7758
roula.eatrides@cas-satj.gc.ca

Federal Court
Cour fédérale
Courts Administration Service, 90 Sparks St., Ottawa, ON K1A 0H9
Tel: 613-992-4238; *Fax:* 613-952-3653
Toll-Free: 800-663-2096
Media Enquiries: media-fct@fct-cf.gc.ca
www.fct-cf.gc.ca
Other information: TTY: 613-995-4640

The Federal Court is a trial court. The jurisdiction of the Federal Court is conferred by the Federal Courts Act, as well as close to one hundred other applicable federal statutes. Its broad federal jurisdiction includes the following: Crown litigation, access to information, admiralty & maritime disputes, citizenship, communications, customs, immigration & refugee matters, intellectual property rights, labour relations, national security, parole & penitentiary proceedings, tax, transportation & aeronautics, war veterans & limited criminal jurisdiction. The Court conducts hearings & renders decisions in disputes anywhere in Canada.

Chief Justice of the Federal Court: The Hon. Mr. Justice Paul S. Crampton, 613-996-5901
Judges (The Hon. Mr. / Madam Justice):
Yvon Pinard(Supernumerary)
Sandra J. Simpson
Danièle Tremblay-Lamer(Supernumerary)
Douglas R. Campbell
François Lemieux(Supernumerary)
John A. O'Keefe
Elizabeth Heneghan
Dolores Hansen
Edmond P. Blanchard
Michel Beaudry(Supernumerary)
Luc Martineau
Simon Noël
Judith A. Snider
James Russell
James W. O'Reilly
Sean J. Harrington
Richard Mosley
Michel M.J. Shore
Michael L. Phelan
Anne L. Mactavish
Yves de Montigny
Roger T. Hughes
Robert L. Barnes
Leonard S. Mandamin
Russel W. Zinn
David G. Near
Richard Boivin

Marie-Josée Bédard
André F. Scott
Donald J. Rennie
Mary J.L. Gleeson
Jocelyne Gagné
Catherine M. Kane
Prothonotaries:
Richard Morneau, 514-496-7840
Roza Aronovitch, 613-947-3356
Roger Lafrenière, 604-666-7435
Mireille Tabib, 613-947-2453
Martha Milczynski, 416-954-9006
Kevin R. Aalto, 416-954-9009
Administration:
Registrar of the Federal Court: Manon Pitre
Judicial Administrator: Giovanna Calamo, 613-995-1285

Courts Administration Service
Service administratif des tribunaux judiciaires

434 Queen St., Ottawa, ON K1A 0H9

Tel: 613-943-4355;
Media Enquiries: reception@cas-satj.gc.ca
www.cas-satj.gc.ca
Other information: TTY: 613-995-4640

In 2003, the Courts Administration Service was established by the Courts Administration Service Act, S.C. 2002, c. 8. The Courts Administration Service provides administrative services to the following courts of law: the Federal Court, the Federal Court of Appeal, the Tax Court of Canada, & the Court Martial Appeal Court of Canada. Examples of the duties of the Courts Administration Service are as follows: providing support services, such as library services, to judges, prothonotaries, & staff; maintaining courts records; providing facilities & security for judges, prothonotaries, & staff; & informing litigants on rules of practice & procedures.

Administration:
Chief Administrator: Daniel Gosselin, 613-996-4778
Deputy Chief Administrator, Judicial & Registry Services: Murielle Brazeau, 613-943-3458
Deputy Chief Administrator, Corporate Services: Francine Côté, 613-996-1611
Executive Director, Project Management: Gerry R. Montpetit, 613-992-9104
Director General: Information Management & Information Technology, Eric Cloutier, 613-992-9393
Director General: Administrative, Facilities, & Security Services, Eric R. Delage, 613-944-6614, Fax: 613-943-7948
Director General, Human Resources: Nathalie Dunn, 613-995-4453
Director General, Finance & Contracting Services: Paul Waksberg, 613-992-1745, Fax: 613-941-4915
Director, Corporate Secretariat: R. Monet, 613-943-4782
Director, Library Services: Jean Weerasinghe, 613-995-1382
Manager, Communications: Isabelle Rodier, 613-943-4355
isabelle.rodier@cas-satj.gc.ca

Registry of the Courts Administration Service
Principal Office, Ottawa, ON K1A 0H9

Local Offices:

Calgary
Canadian Occidental Tower, 635 - Eighth Ave. SW, Calgary, AB T2P 3M3
; *Fax:* 403-292-5329
Other information: TTY: 403-292-5879; After hours duty officer can be contacted at 403-292-5920
Director: Nancy Gagné, 403-292-5417

Charlottetown
Sir Louis Henry Davies Law Courts, 42 Water St., P.O. Box 2000, Charlottetown, PE C1A 8B9

Edmonton
Tower 1, Scotia Place, #530, 10060 Jasper Ave., P.O. Box 51, Edmonton, AB T5J 3R8
;
Other information: Duty Officers (for matters of an urgent nature which arise after regular business hours), Phone: 780-495-4651
Director: Kathy Dobransky, 780-495-2216

Fredericton
Westmorland Place, #100, 82 Westmorland St., Fredericton, NB E3B 3L3
; *Fax:* 506-452-3584
Other information: TTY: 506-452-3036; Duty Officers (for matters of an urgent nature which arise after regular business hours), Phone: 506-452-3016
Director: Willa Doyle, 506-452-3016
Registry Officer: Michel Morneault, 506-452-3016

Halifax
#1720, 1801 Hollis St., 17th Fl., Halifax, NS B3J 3N4
; *Fax:* 902-426-5514
Other information: TTY: 902-426-9776; Duty Officers (for matters of an urgent nature which arise after regular business hours), Phone: 902-229-3719
Director: Elizabeth Caverly, 902-426-3282
Registry Officer: Michael Kowalchuk, 902-426-3282

Montréal
Registry of the Federal Courts, 30, rue McGill, Montréal, QC H2Y 3Z7
; *Fax:* 514-283-6004
Other information: TTY: 514-283-3017; Duty Officers (for matters of an urgent nature which arise after regular business hours), Phone: 514-346-7884

Québec
Palais de Justice, #500A, 300, boul Jean Lesage, Québec, QC G1K 8K6
; *Fax:* 418-648-4051
Other information: TDD: 418-648-4644; Duty Officers (for matters of an urgent nature which arise after regular business hours), Phone: 418-648-4920
Director: Claire Drolet, 418-648-7778

Regina
Court House, 2425 Victoria Ave., Regina, SK S4P 3V7
Executive Director: Lana Krogan, 306-787-0991
Registry Officer: Margaret Pelletier, 306-787-5421

Toronto
Registry of the Federal Courts, #200, 180 Queen St. West, Toronto, ON M5V 3L6
;
Other information: TTY: 416-954-4245; Duty Officers (for matters of an urgent nature which arise after regular business hours), Phone: 416-677-1054

Saint John
Provincial Building, #413, 110 Charlotte St., 4th Fl., Saint John, NB E2L 2J4
Registry Officer: Edward Joas, 506-636-4990

St. John's
The Court House, Duckworth St., P.O. Box 937, St. John's, NL A1C 5M3
Deputy District Administrator: Darlene Wells, 709-772-2811
Registry Officer: Daphne Lewis, 709-772-2884

Saskatoon
The Court House, 520 Spadina Cres. East, Saskatoon, SK S7K 2H6
District Administrator: Dennis Berezowsky, 306-933-5139

Vancouver
The Pacific Centre, 701 West Georgia St., P.O. Box 10065, Vancouver, BC V7Y 1B6
; *Fax:* 604-666-8181
Other information: TTY: 604-666-9228; Duty Officers (for matters of an urgent nature which arise after regular business hours), Phone: 604-512-4471
Regional Director General: Western, Sam Thuraisamy

Whitehorse
Andrew A. Phillipsen Law Centre, 2134 Second Ave., P.O. Box 2703, Whitehorse, YT Y1A 2C6
; *Toll-Free:* 800-665-3329
District Administrator: Shauna Curtin, 867-667-5441
Registry Officer: Sue Bergren, 867-667-5441

Winnipeg
363 Broadway St., 4th Fl., Winnipeg, MB R3C 3N9
; *Fax:* 204-983-7636
Other information: TTY: 204-984-4440; Duty Officers (for matters of an urgent nature which arise after regular business hours), Phone: 204-983-2509
Director: Jennifer MacGillivray, 204-983-7610
Registry Officer: Robert M'vondo, 204-983-2509
Registry Officer: Renée Taillefer, 204-983-2509

Yellowknife
Court House, 4905 - 49th St., P.O. Box 1320, Yellowknife, NT X1A 2L9
District Administrator: Robin Anne Mould, 867-873-2044
Registry Officer: Bernice Dillman, 867-873-2044

Alberta

Alberta Court of Appeal

Law Courts, 1A Sir Winston Churchill Sq., Edmonton, AB T5J 0R2

Tel: 780-422-2416; *Fax:* 780-422-4127
www.albertacourts.ab.ca/ca

The Alberta Court of Appeal hears appeals from the following courts: the Provincial Court; the Court of Queen's Bench; & administrative tribunals. The Court of Appeal also provides opinions on questions referred from the Lieutenant Governor under the Judicature Act. Court of Appeal justices are appointed by the federal government. Sittings are held in Edmonton & Calgary.

Chief Justice of Alberta: The Honourable Catherine A. Fraser
Justices of the Court of Appeal (The Hon. Mr. / Madam Justice):
Jean E. Côté
Ellen I. Picard
Ronald L. Berger
Peter T. Costigan
Keith G. Ritter
Jack Watson
Frans F. Slatter
Myra B. Bielby
Administration:
Registrar: Sue Stushnoff, 780-422-7710, Fax: 780-427-5507
sue.stushnoff@gov.ab.ca
Deputy Registrar: Danielle Umrysh, 780-422-7714, Fax: 780-422-4127
danielle.umrysh@gov.ab.ca
Office Manager: Julie Ulmer, 780-422-4223, Fax: 780-422-4127
julie.ulmer@gov.ab.ca

Courts:

Calgary: Court of Appeal
TransCanada Pipelines Tower, #2600, 450 - 1st St. SW, Calgary, AB T2P 5H1
Tel: 403-297-2206; *Fax:* 403-297-5294
www.albertacourts.ab.ca/ca
Justices of the Court of Appeal (The Hon. Mr. / Madam Justice):
Carole M. Conrad
Constance D. Hunt
Marina S. Paperny
Constance D. O'Brien
Peter W.L. Martin
Patricia A. Rowbotham
J.D. Bruce McDonald
Administration:
Deputy Registrar: Ileen Moore, 403-297-3949, Fax: 403-297-5294
ileen.moore@gov.ab.ca
Director, Operations: D. Beaton, 403-297-6077, Fax: 403-297-7528

Alberta Court of Queen's Bench

Calgary Courts Centre, #705N, 601 - 5th St. SW, Calgary, AB T2P 5P7

Tel: 403-297-7538; *Fax:* 403-297-8617
www.albertacourts.ab.ca

In Alberta, the Court of Queen's Bench is the Superior Trial Court. The Court hears trials in both civil & criminal matters, as well as appeals from decisions of the Provincial Court. The Chief Justice & other Justices are also judges of Surrogate Matters. Sittings of the Court of Queen's Bench are held in various areas throughout Alberta.

Chief Justice: The Honourable Neil C. Wittmann
Associate Chief Justice: The Honourable J.D. Rooke
Justices (The Honourable Mr. / Madam Justice):
Allen B. Sulatycky
Bonnie L. Rawlins
T.F. McMahon
Suzanne M. Bensler
Lloyd David Wilkins(Supernumerary Judge)
C. Adele Kent
Peter J. McIntyre
Carolyn S. Phillips
Peter Macdonnell Clark
Sal Joseph LoVecchio
William P. Sullivan
Colleen Lynn Kenny
Gerard C. Hawco
C. Scott Brooker
Barbara E.C. Romaine
Rosemary E. Nation
Aexander G. Park
Bryan E. Mahoney
Elizabeth A. Hughes
Marshsa C. Erb
Karen M. Horner
Sheilah L. Martin
Alan D. Macleod
K.M. Eidsvik
E.C. Wilson
J. Strekaf
K.D. Yamauchi
R.G. Stevens
P.R. Jeffrey
S.L. Hunt McDonald
J.T. McCarthy
W.A. Tilleman

R.J. Hall
G.H. Poelman
B.L. Veldhuis
C.M. Jones
B.A. Millar
Administration:
Kathleen McAusland(Senior Manager)

Courts:

Drumheller: Court of Queen's Bench
Court House, 511 - 3 Ave. West, P.O. Box 759, Drumheller, AB T0J 0Y0
Tel: 403-820-7300; *Fax:* 403-823-6073
www.albertacourts.ab.ca
Manager: Janice McGuckin, 403-820-7300, Fax: 403-823-6073
janice.mcguckin@gov.ab.ca

Edmonton: Court of Queen's Bench
Law Courts, 1A Sir Winston Churchill Sq., Edmonton, AB T5J 0R2
Tel: 780-422-2492; *Fax:* 780-422-9742
www.albertacourts.ab.ca
Justices (The Honourable Mr. / Madam Justice):
M.D. Gates
Joanne B. Veit
Lawrie J. Smith
Donald Lee
Mary T. Moreau
Richard P. Marceau
R. Paul Belzil
Mel A. Binder
Sterling M. Sanderman
Doreen A. Sulyma
Brian R. Burrows
Gerald A. Verville
L. Darlene Acton
Terrance D. Clackson
Andrea B. Moen
S.J. Greckol
Eric F. Macklin
Vital O. Ouellette
Donna C. Read
Stephen D. Hillier
Juliana E. Topolniski
Adam W. Germain
June M. Ross
John J. Gill
Dennis R.G. Thomas
R.A. Graesser
D.L. Shelley
K.G. Nielsen
M.G. Crighton
D.J. Manderscheid
Beverley A. Browne
J.H. Goss
P.B. Michalyshyn
Senior Manager: Maria Lavorato, 780-422-2492, Fax: 780-427-0629
maria.lavorato@gov.ab.ca
Manager: Diane Royan, 780-422-2492, Fax: 780-427-0629
diane.royan@gov.ab.ca
Manager: Susan Logan, 780-422-9475, Fax: 780-427-0629
susan.logan@gov.ab.ca

Fort McMurray: Court of Queen's Bench
Court House, 9700 Franklin Ave., Fort McMurray, AB T9H 4W3
Tel: 780-743-7136; *Fax:* 780-743-7135
www.albertacourts.ab.ca
Manager: M. Campbell

Grande Prairie: Court of Queen's Bench
Court House, 10260 - 99 St., Grande Prairie, AB T8V 2H4
Tel: 780-538-5340; *Fax:* 780-538-5493
www.albertacourts.ab.ca
Manager: Rogena Hunt, 780-538-5340, Fax: 780-538-5493
rogena.hunt@gov.ab.ca
Senior Judicial Clerk: Michelle Wilmott, 780-538-5340, Fax: 780-538-5493
michelle.wilmott@gov.ab.ca

High Level: Court of Queen's Bench
Court House, 10106 - 100 Ave., P.O. Box 1560, High Level, AB T0H 1Z0
Tel: 780-926-3715; *Fax:* 780-926-4068
www.albertacourts.ab.ca
Criminal sittings are held as required.
Manager: S. Rendle

Hinton: Court of Queen's Bench
Court House, 237 Jasper St. West, P.O. Box 6450, Hinton, AB T7V 1X7
Tel: 780-865-8280; *Fax:* 780-865-8253
www.albertacourts.ab.ca
Administration
Manager: K. Hanington

Lethbridge: Court of Queen's Bench
Court House, 320 - 4 St. South, Lethbridge, AB T1J 1Z8
Tel: 403-381-5196; *Fax:* 403-381-5128
www.albertacourts.ab.ca
Justices (The Honourable Mr. / Madam Justice):
J.H. Langston
D.K. Miller
R.A. Jerke
Administration:
Gwen Chadsey(Manager)

Medicine Hat: Court of Queen's Bench
Law Courts, 460 First St. SE, Medicine Hat, AB T1A 0A8
Tel: 403-529-8710; *Fax:* 403-529-8607
www.albertacourts.ab.ca
Manager: W. Garner, 403-529-8710, Fax: 403-529-8607

Peace River: Court of Queen's Bench
Court House, 9905 - 97 Ave., P.O. Box 900-34, Peace River, AB T8S 1T4
Tel: 780-624-6256; *Fax:* 780-624-7101
www.albertacourts.ab.ca
Manager: Pam Testawich, 780-624-6256, Fax: 780-624-7101
pam.testawich@gov.ab.ca

Red Deer: Court of Queen's Bench
Court House, 4909 - 48 Ave., Red Deer, AB T4N 3T5
Tel: 403-340-5220; *Fax:* 403-340-7984
www.albertacourts.ab.ca
K.L. Sisson
Monica R. Bast
Administration:
Sandra Mitchell(Senior Manager)
T. Kintzel(Manager)

St. Paul: Court of Queen's Bench
Court House, 4704 - 50 St., P.O. Box 1900, St Paul, AB T0A 3A0
Tel: 780-645-6324; *Fax:* 780-645-6273
www.albertacourts.ab.ca
Manager: Wanda Whelan, 780-645-6324, Fax: 780-645-6273
wanda.whelan@gov.ab.ca

Wetaskiwin: Court of Queen's Bench
Law Courts, 4605 - 51 St., Wetaskiwin, AB T9A 1K7
Tel: 780-361-1258; *Fax:* 780-361-1319
www.albertacourts.ab.ca
Manager: Edwina Segboer, 780-361-1204, Fax: 780-361-1338
edwina.segboer@gov.ab.ca

Alberta Provincial Court

Law Courts, 1A Sir Winston Churchill Sq., Edmonton, AB T5J 0R2
Tel: 780-427-8713; *Fax:* 780-422-9736
www.albertacourts.ab.ca
The Provincial Court of Alberta serves as the point of entry to the justice system in the following areas of law: civil matters (Small Claims Court), related to damages & debt & pretrial conferences; criminal law; family law, such as Parenting & Contact Orders; traffic offences, under federal statutes, provincial statutes, & municipal bylaws; & Criminal Code offences committed by youth from ages 12 to 17. Circuit point courts are situated throughout the province.
A.G. Vickery(Chief Judge)
A.H. Lefever(Deputy Chief Judge)
J.K. Wheatley(Assistant Chief Judge (Family & Youth))

Courts:

Calgary - Civil, Criminal, Family, Regional, Traffic, & Youth
Calgary Courts Centre, 601 - 5th St. SW, Calgary, AB T2P 5P7
Tel: 403-297-3122; *Fax:* 403-297-2932
www.albertacourts.ab.ca
A.G. Vickery(Chief Judge)
R.J. Wilkins(Assistant Chief Judge)
Administration:
Senior Manager: Basem Hage, 403-297-3681, Fax: 403-592-4896
basem.hage@gov.ab.ca

Calgary - Civil
Calgary Courts Centre, #606S, 601 - 5th St. SW, Calgary, AB T2P 5P7
Tel: 403-297-7217; *Fax:* 403-297-7374
www.albertacourts.ab.ca
L.D. Young(Assistant Chief Judge)
L.L. Burt
N.R. Hess
D.B. Higa
M.A. McCorquodale
Administrator: Marilyn Clisdell, 403-297-7217, Fax: 403-297-7374
marilyn.clisdell@gov.ab.ca

Calgary - Criminal
Calgary Courts Centre, #402S, 601 5th St. SW, Calgary, AB T2P 5P7
Tel: 403-297-3122; *Fax:* 403-297-3179
www.albertacourts.ab.ca
A.G. Vickery(Chief Judge)
R.J. Wilkins(Assistant Chief Judge (Calgary & Calgary Region))
Administration:
A/Manager: C. Robitaille, 403-297-3122, Fax: 403-297-2932

Calgary - Family
Calgary Courts Centre, #704N, 601 - 5th St. SW, Calgary, AB T2P 5P7
Tel: 403-297-3471; *Fax:* 403-297-3461
www.albertacourts.ab.ca
Judges:
V.T. Tousignant(Assistant Chief Judge)
G.J. Burrell
E.R.R. Carruthers
L.T.L. Cook-Stanhope
K.J. Jordan
T. LaRochelle
S.E. Lipton
L.K. McLellan
R.J. O'Gorman
S. Prowse O'Ferrall
J.R. Shaw
Administration:
Manager: Lisa Lindquist, 403-297-3926, Fax: 403-297-3461
lisa.lindquist@gov.ab.ca

Calgary - Regional
Calgary Courts Centre, #607S, 601 - 5th St. SW, Calgary, AB T2P 5P7
Tel: 403-297-3010; *Fax:* 403-297-3237
www.albertacourts.ab.ca
Circuit point courts are located in the following places: Airdrie (#113, 104 - 1 Ave. NW), Canmore (#101, 800 Railway Ave.), Cochrane (213 - 1 St., West), Didsbury (1611 - 15 Ave.), Okotoks (98 McRae St.), & Tsuu T'ina Nation (9911 Chula Blvd., Sarcee).
Judges:
R.J. Wilkins(Assistant Chief Judge, Calgary & Calgary Regional)
P.B. Barley
E.J. Creighton
G.J. Gaschler
L.R. Grieve
P.M. McIlhargey
J. Shriar
Administration:
Manager: L. Blair-Kaye, 403-297-3010, Fax: 403-297-3237

Calgary - Traffic
Calgary Courts Centre, #203S, 601 - 5th St. SW, Calgary, AB T2P 5P7
Tel: 403-297-2283; *Fax:* 403-297-2220
www.albertacourts.ab.ca
Traffic Commissioner: M.A. Brown
Traffic Commissioner: J.K. Conley
Traffic Commissioner: D.C. Elliott
Traffic Commissioner: J.G. Szekeres
Manager: M. Siller, 403-297-2283, Fax: 403-297-2220

Calgary - Youth
Calgary Courts Centre, #201N, 601 - 5th St. SW, Calgary, AB T2P 5P7
Tel: 403-297-3473; *Fax:* 403-297-4892
www.albertacourts.ab.ca
Judges:
V.T. Tousignant(Assistant Chief Judge)
G.J. Burrell
E.R.R. Carruthers
L.T.L. Cook-Stanhope
K.J. Jordan
T. LaRochelle
S.E. Lipton
L.K. McLellan
R.J. O'Gorman
S. Prowse O'Ferrall
J.R. Shaw
Manager: Lisa Lindquist, 403-297-3926, Fax: 403-297-3461
lisa.lindquist@gov.ab.ca

Camrose
Court House, 5210 - 49 Ave., Camrose, AB T4V 3Y2
Tel: 780-679-1240; *Fax:* 780-679-1253
www.albertacourts.ab.ca
A circuit point court is located in Killam (4903 - 50 St.).
Judges:
W.A. Andreassen
Administration:
Manager: Debbie Tkachuk, 780-679-1240, Fax: 780-679-1253
debbie.tkachuk@gov.ab.ca

Drumheller
Court House, 511 - 3 Ave. West, P.O. Box 759, Drumheller, AB T0J 0Y0
Tel: 403-820-7300; *Fax:* 403-823-6073
www.albertacourts.ab.ca
Circuit point courts are situated in the following places: Hanna (401 Centre St.), Siksika Nation (Junction of Highways 901 & 547), & Strathmore (226 - 2 Ave.).
Administration:
Manager: Janice McGuckin, 403-820-7300, Fax: 403-823-6073
janice.mcguckin@gov.ab.ca

Edmonton - Civil, Criminal, Family & Youth, & Traffic
Law Courts, 1A Sir Winston Churchill Sq., Edmonton, AB T5J 0R2
Tel: 780-427-8713; *Fax:* 780-422-9736
www.albertacourts.ab.ca
A.G. Vickery(Chief Judge)
A.H. Lefever(Deputy Chief Judge)
J.M. Filice(Assistant Chief Judge (Family & Youth))
J.K. Wheatley(Assistant Chief Judge (Edmonton Region))
L.D. Young(Assistant Chief Judge (Civil))
Senior Manager: Brenda Haynes, 780-427-8713, Fax: 780-422-9736
brenda.haynes@gov.ab.ca

Edmonton - Civil
Law Courts, 1A Sir Winston Churchill Sq., Edmonton, AB T5J 0R2
Tel: 780-422-2508; *Fax:* 780-427-4348
www.albertacourts.ab.ca
Judges:
L.D. Young(Assistant Chief Judge)
K. Haymour
G.W. Sharek
J.L. Skitsko
Administration:
A/Administrator: L. Malcolm, 780-422-2508, Fax: 780-427-4348

Edmonton - Criminal
Law Courts, 1A Sir Winston Churchill Sq., Edmonton, AB T5J 0R2
Tel: 780-427-7868; *Fax:* 780-422-9736
www.albertacourts.ab.ca
A.G. Vickery(Chief Judge)
A.H. Lefever(Deputy Chief Judge)
J.K. Wheatley(Assistant Chief Judge)
C.D. Gardner(Assistant Chief Judge (Edmonton Region))
Administration:
Manager: Kerri McPhee, 780-427-7869, Fax: 780-422-9736
kerri.mcphee@gov.ab.ca

Edmonton - Family & Youth
Law Courts, 1A Sir Winston Churchill Sq., Edmonton, AB T5J 0R2
Tel: 780-427-2743; *Fax:* 780-427-5797
www.albertacourts.ab.ca
J.M. Filice(Assistant Chief Judge)
W.S. Andrew
M.J. Burch
D. Dalton
J.G. Easton
J.D. Franklin
G.B.N. Ho
J.C. Koshman
P.E. Kvill
S.C. Miller
M.J. Savaryn
Manager: Barbara Petryk, 780-427-2743, Fax: 780-427-5797
barb.petryk@gov.ab.ca
Administrator: Donna Blauel, 780-427-2743, Fax: 780-427-5797
donna.blauel@gov.ab.ca

Edmonton - Traffic & Civil
Law Courts, 1A Sir Winston Churchill Sq., Edmonton, AB T5J 0R2
Tel: 780-427-4724; *Fax:* 780-427-5791
www.albertacourts.ab.ca
Traffic Commissioner: D.R. Ackroyd
Traffic Commissioner: I. Yaverbaum
Manager: L. Hawryluk

Fort McMurray
Court House, 9700 Franklin Ave., Fort McMurray, AB T9H 4W3
Tel: 780-743-7195; *Fax:* 780-743-7395
www.albertacourts.ab.ca
A circuit point court is located in Fort Chipewyan (Multi-Plex, Flett St.).
S.A. Cleary
J.R. Jacques
Manager: Michelle Campbell, 780-743-7195, Fax: 780-743-7395
michelle.l.campbell@gov.ab.ca

Fort Saskatchewan
Court House, 10504 - 100 Ave., Fort Saskatchewan, AB T8L 3S9
Tel: 780-998-1200; *Fax:* 780-998-7222
www.albertacourts.ab.ca
A circuit point court is located in Boyle (5006 - 3 St.).
D.G. Rae
Manager: Bonnie Matvichuk, 780-998-1200, Fax: 780-998-7222
bonnie.matvichuk@gov.ab.ca

Grande Prairie
Court House, 10260 - 99 St., Grande Prairie, AB T8V 2H4
Tel: 780-538-5340; *Fax:* 780-538-5493
www.albertacourts.ab.ca
Circuit point courts are located in the following places: Fox Creek (100 - 4 Ave.) & Valleyview (5102 - 50 Ave.).
M.B. Golden
B.R. Hougestol
J.A. Watson
Manager: Rogena Hunt, 780-538-5360, Fax: 780-538-5454
rogena.hunt@gov.ab.ca

High Level
Court House, 10106 - 100 Ave., P.O. Box 1560, High Level, AB T0H 1Z0
Tel: 780-926-3715; *Fax:* 780-926-4068
www.albertacourts.ab.ca
Circuit point courts are located in the following places: Assumption (Court House, Chateh) & Fort Vermilion (4607 River Rd.).
A/Manager: S. Shumik, 780-926-3715, Fax: 780-926-4068

High Prairie
Court House, 4911 - 53 Ave., P.O. Box 1470, High Prairie, AB T0G 1E0
Tel: 780-523-6600; *Fax:* 780-523-6643
www.albertacourts.ab.ca
Circuit point courts are located in the following places: Red Earth Creek (122 Forestry Rd.), Slave Lake (101 - 3 St., SW), & Wabasca-Desmarais (867 Stony Point Rd.).
T.R. Goodson
Manager: Mae Fjeld, 780-523-6600, Fax: 780-523-6643
mae.fjeld@gov.ab.ca

Hinton
Court House, 237 Jasper St. West, P.O. Box 6450, Hinton, AB T7V 1X7
Tel: 780-865-8280; *Fax:* 780-865-8253
www.albertacourts.ab.ca
Circuit point courts are located in the following places: Edson (111 - 54 St.), Grande Cache (Provincial Building, Hoppe Ave.), & Jasper (629 Patricia St.).
J.P. Higgerty
D.C. Norheim
Manager: Karen Hanington, 780-865-8280, Fax: 780-865-8253
karen.hanington@gov.ab.ca

Leduc
Court House, 4612 - 50 St., Leduc, AB T9E 6L1
Tel: 780-986-6911; *Fax:* 780-986-0345
www.albertacourts.ab.ca
Circuit point courts are located in the following places: Breton (4911 - 50 Ave.) & Drayton Valley (5136 - 51 Ave.).
M.M. White
Manager: Marilea McMullen, 780-986-6911, Fax: 780-986-0345
marilea.mcmullen@gov.ab.ca

Lethbridge
Court House, 320 - 4th St. South, Lethbridge, AB T1J 1Z8
Tel: 403-381-5223; *Fax:* 403-381-5763
www.albertacourts.ab.ca
Circuit point courts are located in the following places: Cardston (576 Main St.), Pincher Creek (782 Main St.), & Taber (5126 - 49 Ave.).
J.N. LeGrandeur(Assistant Chief Judge, Southern Region)
G.R. DeBow
T.G. Hironaka
G.S. Maxwell
S.L. Oishi
E.W. Peterson
P.G. Pharo
D.G. Redman
Administrator: M. McCulloch, 403-381-5525, Fax: 403-381-5763
maria.mcculloch@gov.ab.ca

Medicine Hat
Law Courts, 460 - First St. SE, Medicine Hat, AB T1A 0A8
Tel: 403-529-8644; *Fax:* 403-529-8606
www.albertacourts.ab.ca
E.D. Brooks
F.C. Fisher
D.J. Greaves
G.K. Krinke
Manager: W. Garner, 403-529-8644, Fax: 403-529-8606

Peace River
Court House, 9905 - 97 Ave., P.O. Box 900-34, Peace River, AB T8S 1T4
Tel: 780-624-6256; *Fax:* 780-624-7101
www.albertacourts.ab.ca
Circuit point courts are located in the following places: Fairview (10209 - 109 St.) & Falher (028 Main St., SE).
E.J. Simpson(Assistant Chief Judge, Northern Region)
J.R. McIntosh
G.W. Paul
C.K.W. Thietke
Administrator: Pam Testawich, 780-624-6256, Fax: 780-624-6175
pam.testawich@gov.ab.ca

Red Deer
Court House, 4909 - 48 Ave., Red Deer, AB T4N 3T5
Tel: 403-340-5250; *Fax:* 403-340-7985
www.albertacourts.ab.ca
Circuit point courts are located in the following places: Coronation (4909 Royal St.), Rimbey (5025 - 55 St.), Rocky Mountain House (4919 - 51 St.), & Stettler (4705 - 49 Ave.).
W.A. Skinner(Assistant Chief Judge, Central Region)
G.E. Deck
J.D. Holmes
J.A. Hunter
J.B. Mitchell
D.J. Plosz
E.D. Riemer
Senior Manager: Sandra Mitchell, 403-340-5250, Fax: 403-340-7985
sandra.mitchell@gov.ab.ca
Manager: K. Saunders, 403-340-5250, Fax: 403-340-7985

St Albert
Court House, 3 St. Anne St., St Albert, AB T8N 2E8
Tel: 780-458-7300; *Fax:* 780-460-2963
www.albertacourts.ab.ca
Circuit point courts are located in the following places: Athabasca (4903 - 50 St.), Barrhead (6203 - 49 St.), Morinville (10008 - 107 St.), & Westlock (10003 - 100 St.).
B.H. Fraser
B.R. Garriock
N.A.F. Mackie
Manager: Joanne McNeilly, 780-458-7300, Fax: 780-460-2963
joanne.mcneilly@gov.ab.ca

St Paul
Court House, 4704 - 50 St., P.O. Box 1900, St Paul, AB T0A 3A0
Tel: 780-645-6324; *Fax:* 780-645-6273
www.albertacourts.ab.ca
Circuit point courts are located in the following places: Bonnyville (4902 - 50 Ave.) & Lac La Biche (9503 Beaver Hill Rd.).
D.E. Demetrick
K.D. Williams
Manager: Wanda Whelan, 780-645-6324, Fax: 780-645-6273
wanda.whelan@gov.ab.ca

Sherwood Park
Court House, 190 Chippewa Rd., Sherwood Park, AB T8A 4H5
Tel: 780-464-0114; *Fax:* 780-449-1490
www.albertacourts.ab.ca
J. Maher
Manager: B. Longley, 780-464-0114, Fax: 780-449-1490

Stony Plain
Court House, 4711 - 44 Ave., Stony Plain, AB T7Z 1N5
Tel: 780-963-6205; *Fax:* 780-963-6402
www.albertacourts.ab.ca
Circuit point courts are located in the following places: Evansburg (4921 - 50 St.), Glenevis (Administration Office, Alexis Reserve), Mayerthorpe (5013 - 50 St.), & Whitecourt (5020 - 52 Ave.).
P. Ayotte
K.E. Tjosvold
Manager: Brenda Majeau, 780-968-6205, Fax: 780-963-6402
brenda.majeau@gov.ab.ca

Vermilion
Provincial Building, 4701 - 52nd St., P.O. Box 30, Vermilion, AB T9X 1J9
Tel: 780-853-8130; *Fax:* 780-853-8200
www.albertacourts.ab.ca
Circuit point courts are located in the following places: Lloydminster (5124 - 50 St.), Vegreville (4809 - 50 St.), & Wainwright (738 - 2 Ave.).
P.T. Johnston
Administrator: Ruth Westman, 780-853-8130, Fax: 780-853-8200
ruth.westman@gov.ab.ca

Wetaskiwin
Law Courts, 4605 - 51 St., Wetaskiwin, AB T9A 1K7
Tel: 780-361-1204; *Fax:* 780-361-1338
www.albertacourts.ab.ca
A circuit point court is located in Ponoka (5110 - 49 Ave.).
B.D. Rosborough
Manager: Edwina Segboer, 780-361-1204, Fax: 780-361-1338
edwina.segboer@gov.ab.ca

British Columbia

British Columbia Court of Appeal
The Law Courts, #400, 800 Hornby St., Vancouver, BC V6Z 2C5
Tel: 604-660-2468; *Fax:* 604-660-1951
www.courts.gov.bc.ca/Court_of_Appeal
The Court of Appeal is the highest court in the province. It hears appeals from the Supreme Court, & from the Provincial Court on some criminal matters. It also hears reviews and appeals from some administrative boards and tribunals.
Chief Justice: The Hon. Lance S.G. Finch
Justices of Appeal (The Hon. Mr./Madam Justice):
E.A. Bennett
E.C. Chiasson
I.T. Donald
S.D. Frankel
N.J. Garson
H.M. Groberman
J.E. Hall
David C. Harris
C.E. Hinkson
P.A. Kirkpatrick
R.E. Levine
R.T.A. Low
P.D. Lowry
A.W. MacKenzie
K.E. Neilson
M.V. Newbury
J.E. Prowse
C.A. Ryan
M. Saunders
D.M. Smith
K.J. Smith
D.F. Tysoe
Administration:
Registrar: Jennifer Jordan, 604-660-2729
Administration:
Deputy Registrar: Maria Littlejohn

British Columbia Supreme Court
The Law Courts, 800 Smithe St., Vancouver, BC V6Z 2E1
Tel: 604-660-2800; *Fax:* 604-660-1723
www.courts.gov.bc.ca/supreme_court
The Supreme Court is a trial court of original jurisdiction for all civil & criminal matters arising in B.C., save & except matters expressly excluded by statute. It hears most appeals from the Provincial Court.
Chief Justice: The Hon. Robert J. Bauman
Assoc. Chief Justice: The Hon. Austin F. Cullen
Judges (The Hon. Mr./Madam Justice):
Patrice Abrioux
E.J. Adair
Kenneth N. Affleck
W.G. Baker
S.K. Ballance
G.T.W. Bowden
B. Brown
C.J. Bruce
G.D. Burnyeat
B. Butler
B.I. Cohen
F.W. Cole
V.R. Curtis
D.J. Dardi
B.M. Davies
G. Dickson
J.R. Dillon
W. Ehrcke
L.A. Fenlon
B. Fisher
Gregory J. Fitch
S.C. Fitzpatrick
L.B. Gerow
R.B.T. Goepel
J.C. Grauer
V. Gray
B.M. Greyell
S.A. Griffin
J.M. Gropper
J.R. Groves
H.J. Holmes
M.A. Humphries
S.F. Kelleher
D. Kloegman
P.D. Leask
L.A. Loo
M.A. Mainsonville
D.M. Masuhara
E.M. Myers
P.J. Pearlman
S.R. Romilly
C.J. Ross
L.D. Russell
J.E.D. Savage
Terence A. Schultes
R.J. Sewell
J.S. Sigurdson
A.H. Silverman
H.A. Slade
W.B. Smart
N.H. Smith
S.S. Stromberg-Stein
P.G. Voith
Paul W. Walker
Jeanne E. Watchuk
Gordon C. Weatherill
C.A. Wedge
P.M. Willcock
R.S.K. Wong

Courts:

Campbell River
500 - 13 Ave., Campbell River, BC V9W 6P1
Tel: 250-286-7510; *Fax:* 250-286-7512
Registry (County): Vancouver Island
District Manager: Michael Hammell
michael.hammell@gov.bc.ca

Chilliwack
Court House, 46085 Yale Rd., Chilliwack, BC V2P 2L8
Tel: 604-795-8350; *Fax:* 604-795-8393
Registry (County): Westminster
W. Grist
B. Joyce
District Manager: Marian Moore, 604-795-8300, Fax: 604-795-8345

Courtenay
Court House, #100, 420 Cumberland Rd., Courtenay, BC V9N 2C4
Tel: 250-334-1115; *Fax:* 250-334-1191
Registry (County): Vancouver Island
District Manager: R. Krayenhoff
rolph.krayenhoff@gov.bc.ca

Cranbrook
Court House, 102 - 11 Ave. South, Cranbrook, BC V1C 2P3
Tel: 250-426-1234; *Fax:* 250-426-1352
Registry (County): Kootenay
T. Melnick
Deputy District Registrar: Debbie Schroeter
debbie.schroeter@gov.bc.ca

Duncan
Court House, 238 Government St., Duncan, BC V9L 1A5
Tel: 250-746-1227; *Fax:* 250-746-1244
Registry (County): Vancouver Island
District Manager: Joanne Power
joanne.power@gov.bc.ca

Fort Nelson
4604 Sunset Dr., P.O. Box 1000, Fort Nelson, BC V0C 1R0
Tel: 250-774-5999; *Fax:* 250-774-6904
Registry (County): Cariboo
Court Administrator: Linda Brekelmans
linda.brekelmans@gov.bc.ca

Fort St. John
Court House, 10600 - 100 St., Fort St John, BC V1J 4L6
Tel: 250-787-3231; *Fax:* 250-787-3518
Registry (County): Cariboo
Deputy Registrar: Gloria Carew
gloria.carew@gov.bc.ca

Golden
837 Park Dr., P.O. Box 1500, Golden, BC V0A 1H0
Tel: 250-344-7581; *Fax:* 250-344-7715
Registry (County): Kootenay
Court Administrator: Lori-Ann Roseberry
loriann.roseberry@gov.bc.ca

Kamloops
Court House, #223 - 455 Columbia St., Kamloops, BC V2C 6K4
Tel: 250-828-4344; *Fax:* 250-828-4332
Registry (County): Yale
R. Blair
S.D. Dley
H. Hyslop
I.C. Meiklem
R. Powers
Manager, Scheduling: David McCoy, 250-828-4021, Fax: 250-828-4080
sc.scheduling_ka@courts.gov.bc.ca

Kelowna
Court House, 1355 Water St., Kelowna, BC V1Y 9R3
Tel: 250-470-6900; *Fax:* 250-470-6939
Registry (County): Yale
G. Barrow
A. Beames
T. Brooke
P. Rogers
Manager, Scheduling: Barb Turik
sc.scheduling_ok@courts.gov.bc.ca

Nanaimo
Court House, 35 Front St., Nanaimo, BC V9R 5J1
Tel: 250-741-3805; *Fax:* 250-741-3809
Registry (County): Vancouver Island
D.A. Halfyard
B.D. MacKenzie
J. Power
S. Shabbits
Senior Manager: Tanya Hingley, 250-741-3812, Fax: 250-741-3809
tanya.hingley@gov.bc.ca

Nelson
Court House, 320 Ward St., Nelson, BC V1L 1S6
Tel: 250-354-6165; *Fax:* 250-354-6133
Registry (County): Kootenay
T. McEwan
District Manager: Wendy Schwab, 250-354-6165, Fax: 250-354-6539
wendy.schwab@gov.bc.ca

New Westminster
Court House, Begbie Sq., 651 Carnarvon St., New Westminster, BC V3M 1C9
Tel: 604-660-8551; *Fax:* 604-660-2072
Registry (County): Vancouver
E. Arnold-Bailey
L. Bernard
N. Brown
R. Crawford
J.S. Harvey
I.B. Josephson
K.M. Ker
R. McKinnon
A. Saunders
T. Schultes
J. Truscott
F. Verhoeven
J. Williams
L.P. Williamson
Administrator: Laura Mayes, 604-660-8557, Fax: 604-660-2047
laura.mayes@gov.bc.ca

Penticton
Court House, #116, 100 Main St., Penticton, BC V2A 5A5
Tel: 250-492-1231; *Fax:* 250-492-1378
Toll-Free: 888-526-8555
Registry (County): Yale
District Manager: Sylvia Judge
sylvia.judge@gov.bc.ca

Port Alberni
2999 - 4 Ave., Port Alberni, BC V9Y 8A5
Tel: 250-720-2424; *Fax:* 250-720-2426
Toll-Free: 877-741-3820
Registry (County): Vancouver Island
District Manager: Lowell Boran
lowell.boran@gov.bc.ca

Powell River
#103, 6953 Alberni St., Powell River, BC V8A 2B8
Tel: 604-485-3630; *Fax:* 604-485-3637
Toll-Free: 877-741-3820
Registry (County): Vancouver Island
District Manager: Bryna Ary
bryna.ary@gov.bc.ca

Prince George
Court House
J.O. Wilson Sq., 250 George St., Prince George, BC V2L 5S2
Tel: 250-614-2700; *Fax:* 250-614-2737
Registry (County): Cariboo
W. Parrett
Senior District Manager: Patty Walker, 250-614-2700, Fax: 250-614-2737
patricia.walker@gov.bc.ca

Prince Rupert
Court House, 100 Market Pl., Prince Rupert, BC V8J 1B8
Tel: 250-624-7525; *Fax:* 250-624-7538
Registry (County): Prince Rupert
R.D. Punnett
Manager, Scheduling: Crystal Foerster, 250-624-7474, Fax: 250-624-7538
sc.scheduling_pr@courts.gov.bc.ca

Quesnel
Court House, #305, 350 Barlow Ave., Quesnel, BC V2J 2C1
Tel: 250-992-4256; *Fax:* 250-992-4171
Registry (County): Cariboo
District Manager: Einar Gunnarson
einar.gunnarson@gov.bc.ca

Rossland
Court House, 2288 Columbia Ave., P.O. Box 639, Rossland, BC V0G 1Y0
Tel: 250-362-7368; *Fax:* 250-362-9632
Registry (County): Kootenay
District Manager: Trudy Williams
trudy.williams@gov.bc.ca

Salmon Arm
Court House, #550, 2nd Ave. NE, Salmon Arm, BC V1E 4S4
Tel: 250-832-1610; *Fax:* 250-832-1749
Registry (County): Yale
Manager, Scheduling: David McCoy
sc.scheduling_ka@courts.gov.bc.ca

Smithers
3793 Alfred St., P.O. Box 5000, Smithers, BC V0J 2N0
Tel: 250-847-7376; *Fax:* 250-847-7710
Registry (County): Prince Rupert
District Manager: J. Caird
janet.caird@gov.bc.ca

Terrace
Court House, 3408 Kalum St., Terrace, BC V8G 2N6
Tel: 250-638-2111; *Fax:* 250-638-2123
Registry (County): Prince Rupert
District Manager: Laura Pistell
laura.pistell@gov.bc.ca

Vernon
Court House, 3001 - 27th St., Vernon, BC V1T 4W5
Tel: 250-549-5422; *Fax:* 205-549-5621
Registry (County): Yale
District Manager: Sheree Marshall, 250-549-5420
sheree.marshall@gov.bc.ca

Victoria
Court House, #2, 850 Burdett Ave., Victoria, BC V8W 1B4
Tel: 250-356-1478; *Fax:* 250-356-6279
Registry (County): Vancouver Island
K. Bracken
J. Dorgan
R. Johnston
M.D. Macaulay
R.W. Metzger
D. Wilson
R. Wilson
Senior District Manager: Charlene Kornaga, 250-356-1461
charlene.kornaga@gov.bc.ca

Williams Lake
Court House, 540 Borland St., Williams Lake, BC V2G 1R8
Tel: 250-398-4301; *Fax:* 250-398-4459
Registry (County): Cariboo
Deputy Registrar: Rhonda Hykawy, 250-398-4308, Fax: 250-398-4459

British Columbia Provincial Court

Pacific Centre, #602, 700 West Georgia St., P.O. Box 10287, Vancouver, BC V7Y 1E8
Tel: 604-660-2864; *Fax:* 604-660-1108
info@provincialcourt.bc.ca
www.provincialcourt.bc.ca

The Provincial Court is a statutory, trial court. It hears cases in criminal, family, youth, small claims & traffic matters.

Chief Judge: The Hon. T. Crabtree
Assoc. Chief Judge: The Hon. Gurmail Gill
Assoc. Chief Judge: The Hon. Nancy Phillips
Assoc. Chief Judge: The Hon. M. Brecknell
Judges (The Hon.):
R. Low
Administration:
G. Hayes(Administrative Judicial Justice)
P. Schwartz(Administrative Judicial Justice)
D. North(Judicial Case Manager)

Courts:

Abbotsford
32203 South Fraser Way, Abbotsford, BC V2T 1W6
Tel: 604-855-3200; *Fax:* 604-855-3232
R.B. Caryer
D. Gardner
B.G. Hoy
C.G. Maltby
R.R. Romano
J. Rounthwaite
K.D. Skilnick
Judicial Case Manager: Healther Holt

Campbell River
500 - 13 Ave., Campbell River, BC V9W 6P1
Tel: 250-286-7650; *Fax:* 250-286-7512
B. Saunderson
Judicial Case Manager: Christine M. Ballman

Chilliwack
46085 Yale Rd., Chilliwack, BC V2P 2L8
Tel: 604-795-8350; *Fax:* 604-795-8345
T.J. Crabtree
R. MacKay
W.A. Young
Judicial Case Manager: Andrea Schulz

Courtenay
#100, 420 Cumberland Rd., Courtenay, BC V9N 2C4
Tel: 250-334-1115; *Fax:* 250-334-1191
P. Doherty
Judicial Case Manager: Christine M. Ballman

Cranbrook
#147, 102 - 11 Ave. South, Cranbrook, BC V1C 2P3
Tel: 250-426-1234; *Fax:* 250-426-1352
W.G. Sheard
R.J. Webb
Judicial Case Manager: Megan Jensen

Dawson Creek
#205, 1201 - 103 Ave., Dawson Creek, BC V1G 4J2
Tel: 250-784-2278; *Fax:* 250-784-2339
R.R. Blaskovits
Judicial Case manager: Faye Campbell

Duncan
238 Government St., Duncan, BC V9L 1A5
Tel: 250-746-1219; *Fax:* 250-746-1244
J. Wood
Judicial Case Manager: Shannon L. Cole

Fort St. John
10600 - 100 St., Fort St John, BC V1J 4L6
Tel: 250-787-3231; *Fax:* 250-787-3518
R.S. Bowry
B.A. Daley
Judicial Case Manager: Faye Campbell

Golden
837 Park Dr., P.O. Box 1500, Golden, BC V0A 1H0
Tel: 250-344-7581; *Fax:* 250-344-7715

Kamloops
#223, 455 Columbia St., Kamloops, BC V2C 6K4
Tel: 250-828-4344; *Fax:* 250-828-4332
C.D. Cleaveley
D. Dley
S. Frame(Admin. Judge)
S.R. Harrison
H. Rohrmoser
J.E. Hughes
Judicial Case Manager: Sheila D. Paul

Kelowna
#1, 1355 Water St., Kelowna, BC V1Y 9R3
Tel: 250-470-6900; *Fax:* 250-470-6939
E.M. Burdett
J.P. Cartwright
B.J. Chapman
P.V. Hogan
W.W. Klinger
R.R. Smith
J.J. Threlfall(Acting Chief Judge)
A. Wallace
Judicial Case Manager: Kathy Bullach

Mackenzie
64 Centennial Dr., P.O. Box 2050, Mackenzie, BC V0J 2C0
Tel: 250-997-3377; *Fax:* 250-997-5617

Masset
1666 Orr St., P.O. Box 230, Masset, BC V0T 1M0
Tel: 250-626-5512; *Fax:* 250-626-5491

Nakusp
415 Broadway St., P.O. Box 328, Nakusp, BC V0G 1R0
Tel: 250-265-4253; *Fax:* 250-265-4413

Nanaimo
Court House, 35 Front St., Nanaimo, BC V9R 5J1
Tel: 250-741-3805; *Fax:* 250-741-3809
J.D. Cowling
T.A. Dohm(Admin. Judge)
R.A. Gould
E.L. Iverson
J.I.D. Joe
B.R. Klaver
John Dodd
Judicial Case Manager: Veronica Mitchell

Nelson
320 Ward St., Nelson, BC V1L 1S6
Tel: 250-354-6165; *Fax:* 250-354-6539
L.J. Mrozinski
Judicial Case Manager: Sandra Hadikin

New Westminster
Law Courts, Begbie Sq., New Westminster, BC V3M 1C9
Tel: 604-660-8522; *Fax:* 604-660-8977
T. Alexander
G.P. Angelomatis
D.M.B. Steinberg
C.M. Proctor
Judicial Case Manager: Lila MacDonald

North Vancouver
200 East 23 St., North Vancouver, BC V7L 4R4
Tel: 604-981-0200; *Fax:* 604-981-0234
J. Auxier
C.C. Baird Ellan
J. Challenger
J. Gedye
D.E. Moss
W.J. Rodgers(Admin. Judge)
Phillip Lim
Judicial Case Manager: Suzanne McLarty

Penticton
100 Main St., Penticton, BC V2A 5A5
Tel: 250-492-1231; *Fax:* 250-492-1378
G.G. Sinclair
Judicial Case Manager: Mar Warwick

Port Alberni
2999 - 4 Ave., Port Alberni, BC V9Y 8A5
Tel: 250-720-2424; *Fax:* 250-720-2426
J.E. Saunders

Port Coquitlam
2620 Mary Hill Rd., #A, Port Coquitlam, BC V3C 3B2
Tel: 604-927-2100; *Fax:* 604-927-2222
M.R. Buller-Bennett
P.L.J. de Couto
S. Dossa
A. Dyer
D.D. Pothecary
D.A. St. Pierre
A.J. Spence
D. Stone
Judicial Case Manager: Marylynn deKeruzec

Port Hardy
9300 Trustee Rd., P.O. Box 279, Port Hardy, BC V0N 2P0
Tel: 604-949-6122; *Fax:* 604-949-9283

Powell River
#103, 6953 Alberni St., Powell River, BC V8A 2B8
Tel: 604-485-3630; *Fax:* 604-485-3637

Prince George
J.O. Wilson Square, 250 George St., Prince George, BC V2L 5S2
Tel: 250-614-2700; *Fax:* 250-614-2717
M.J. Brecknell
B.L. Dollis
M.A. Gray
D. O'Byrne(Admin. Judge)
R.S. Tindale
R.E. Walker
D.H. Weatherly
C.D. Jolly
Judicial Case Manager: Debra Pillipow

Prince Rupert
#200, 100 Market Pl., Prince Rupert, BC V8J 1B8
Tel: 250-624-7525; *Fax:* 250-627-7538
A.K. Krantz
H.J. Seidemann III(Admin. Judge)
Judicial Case Manager: Crystal M. Foerster

Quesnel
#115, 350 Barlow Ave., Quesnel, BC V2J 2C2
Tel: 250-992-4256; *Fax:* 250-992-4171
R.D. Morgan
Judicial Case Manager: Sherry Jasper

Richmond
7577 Elmridge Way, Richmond, BC V6X 4J2
Tel: 604-660-6900; *Fax:* 604-660-1797
R.D. Fratkin

J.E. McKinnon
P.R. Meyers
M. Rae
E.D. Schmidt
P.L. Dodwell
Judicial Case Manager: Candace Goodrich

Rossland
Court House, 2288 Columbia Ave., P.O. Box 639, Rossland, BC V0G 1Y0
Tel: 250-362-7368; *Fax:* 250-362-9632
D.L. Sperry

Salmon Arm
#550, 2nd Ave. NE, P.O. Box 100 Main, Salmon Arm, BC V1E 4S4
Tel: 250-832-1610; *Fax:* 250-832-1749
E.F. de Walle

Sechelt
5480 Shorncliffe Ave., Sechelt, BC V0N 3A0
Tel: 604-740-8929; *Fax:* 604-740-8924
A. Rounthwaite

Smithers
3793 Alfred St., P.O. Box 5000, Smithers, BC V0J 2N0
Tel: 250-847-7376; *Fax:* 250-847-7710
C. Birnie
J.R. Milne
Judicial Case Manager: Sharon Portsch

Surrey
14340 - 57 Ave., Surrey, BC V3X 1B2
Tel: 604-572-2200; *Fax:* 604-572-2280
K.W. Ball
M.C. Borowicz
J.G. Cohen
P.M. Dohm
H. Field
G. Gill(Assoc. Chief Judge)
E. Gordon
P. Gulbransen(Admin. Judge)
R.P. Harris
M.B. Hicks
P.A. Hyde
J.F. Lenaghan
J.R. Lytwyn
W.G. MacDonald
S.K. MacGregor
R.D. Miller
R. Raven
A. Rounthwaite
W.F. Stewart
K. Walker
J.O. Wingham
Judicial Case Manager: Doreen J. Hodge
Judicial Case Manager: Judith Jenvey
Judicial Case Manager: Sandra Thorne
Judicial Case Manager: Bianca L. West

Terrace
3408 Kalum St., Terrace, BC V8G 2N6
Tel: 250-638-2111; *Fax:* 250-638-2123
Judicial Case Manager: Lyne Leonardes

Valemount
38 Dogwood St., Valemount, BC V0E 2Z0
Tel: 250-566-4652; *Fax:* 250-566-9732

Vancouver
Robson Sq., 800 Hornby St., P.O. Box 21, Vancouver, BC V6Z 2C5
Tel: 604-660-8989; *Fax:* 604-660-8950
B.K. Davis
H.K. Dhillon
A. Ehrcke
E.A. Ferbey
R.M. Gallagher
D.R. Pendleton
N.N. Phillips(Assoc. Chief Judge)
V. Romilly
A.R. Tweedale
J.F. Werier
W.F.W. Yee
J. Arntsen
M. Kobiljski
Z. Makhdoom
Judicial Case Manager: Barbara Brown
Judicial Case Manager: Clare Mayhew
Judicial Case Manager: Judith Norton

Vancouver - Criminal Division
222 Main St., Vancouver, BC V6A 2S8
Tel: 604-660-4200; *Fax:* 604-775-1134
C.L. Bagnall
B.E. Bastin
G.T.W. Bowden
E. Burgess
R.P. Chen
J. Galati
M.F. Giardini
J.E. Godfrey
T.J. Gove
F.E. Howard
W.J. Kitchen
R.R. Low(Admin. Judge)
M.O. MacLean
T.D. McGee
M. McMillan
J.F. Palmer
G.M. Rideout
D. Senniw
D.I. Smyth
C.E. Warren
J.E. Watchuk
H. Weitzel
Judicial Case Manager: Kelly Butler
Judicial Case Manager: Laura Caporale
Judicial Case Manager: Johnny Ceraldi
Judicial Case Manager: Teresa L. Hill
Judicial Case Manager: Catherine J. Johnstone
Judicial Case Manager: Jovanka Mihic
Judicial Case Manager: Lori Stokes

Vernon
3001 - 27 St., Vernon, BC V1T 4W5
Tel: 250-549-5422; *Fax:* 250-549-5621
D.A. Betton(Admin. Judge)
M.G. Takahashi
Judicial Case Manager: D.C. Krenz

Victoria
#2, 850 Burdett Ave., Victoria, BC V8W 1B4
Tel: 250-356-1478; *Fax:* 250-356-6279
E.C. Blake
A.F. Brooks
L.F.E. Chaperon
L.J.M. Harvey
R.A. Higinbotham
J.M. Hubbard
J.N. Kay
B.D. MacKenzie
B.M. Neal
E.J. Quantz(Admin. Judge)
L.W. Smith
S.E. Wishart
G.E. Madrick
Judicial Case Manager: A. Bruce
Judicial Case Manager: Deborah Henry
Judicial Case Manager: Yvonne Locke

Victoria - Western Communities
1756 Island Hwy., Victoria, BC V9B 1H8
Tel: 250-391-2888; *Fax:* 250-391-2877
A.J. Palmer
Judicial Case Manager: Shannon Cole

Williams Lake
540 Borland St., Williams Lake, BC V2G 1R8
Tel: 250-398-4310; *Fax:* 250-398-4459
E.L. Bayliff
R. Walters
Judicial Case Manager: Sherry Jasper

Manitoba

Manitoba Court of Appeal
Law Courts Bldg., #100E, 408 York Ave., Winnipeg, MB R3C 0P9
Tel: 204-945-2647; *Fax:* 204-948-2072
www.manitobacourts.mb.ca

The Court is the senior & final court in the province & has appellate jurisdiction in all civil & criminal cases adjudicated by the Court of Queen's Bench & indictable offences adjudicated by the Provincial Court. The Court hears, in limited circumstances & as mandated by statute, appeals from professional bodies & some government boards & tribunals.

Chief Justice: The Hon. Mr. Richard J. Scott
Justices of Appeal (The Hon. Mr./Madam Justice):
Martin H. Freedman
Barbara M. Hamilton
Richard J.F. Chartier
Alan D. MacInnes
Michael A. Monnin
Freda M. Steel
Holly C. Beard

Manitoba Court of Queen's Bench
Law Courts Bldg., 408 York Ave., Winnipeg, MB R3C 0P9
Tel: 204-945-0344; *Fax:* 204-948-2369
www.manitobacourts.mb.ca

The highest trial court for the province, The Court of Queen's Bench is a court of original jurisdiction & hears all civil & criminal cases arising in Manitoba, except matters expressly excluded by statute. The Court is comprised of the General Division, and the Family Division; it also has appellate jurisdiction & hears appeals from decisions of the Provincial Court in less serious criminal & quasi-criminal matters, decisions of the Hearing Officers in small claims matters, & decisions made by Masters of the court.

Chief Justice: The Hon. Mr. Glenn D. Joyal
Assoc. Chief Justice: General Division, The Hon. Mr. William J. Burnett
Assoc. Chief Justice: Family Division, The Hon. Madam A. Lori Douglas
Judges, General Division (The Hon. Mr./Madam Justice):
Robert Carr(Supernumerary)
A.R. Clearwater(Supernumerary)
Shawn D. Greenberg
Kenneth R. Hanssen(Supernumerary)
Morris Kaufman(Supernumerary)
Brenda L. Keyser
Deborah J. McCawley
Rodney H. Mykle
Perry Schulman(Supernumerary)
Karen I. Simonsen
C. Murray Sinclair
Lori T. Spivak
Colleen Suche
Laurie P. Allen
Frank Aquila
Douglas N. Abra
Robert A. Dewar
Robyn M. Diamond
Robert B. Doyle
A. Catherine Everett
Marilyn E. Goldberg
William Johnston
Donald M. Little
Joan G. McKelvey
Joan A. MacPhail
Chris W. Martin
John A. Menzies
Gerald W. Mercier
Brian Midwinter
Jeffrey J. Oliphant(Supernumerary)
Marianne Rivoalen
Richard A. Saull
Kris Stefanson(Supernumerary)
Michael A. Thomson
Douglas D. Yard
Donald P. Bryk
Robert G. Cummings
Gerald L. Chartier
Diana M. Cameron
Shane I. Perlmutter
Herbert Rempel

Courts:

Brandon
Court of Queen's Bench, 1104 Princess Ave., P.O. Box 68, Brandon, MB R7A 0P9
Tel: 204-726-6240; *Fax:* 204-726-6547
R. Mykle
J.A. Menzies
Master/Registrar in Bankruptcy: Errick G. Harrison

Dauphin
Court of Queen's Bench, 114 River Ave. West, Dauphin, MB R7N 0J7
Tel: 204-622-2087; *Fax:* 204-622-2099
D. Bryk

Portage la Prairie
Court of Queen's Bench, 20 3rd St. SE, Portage la Prairie, MB R1N 1M9
Tel: 204-239-3383; *Fax:* 204-239-3402

The Pas
Court of Queen's Bench, 300 - 3rd St. East, P.O. Box 1259, The Pas, MB R9A 1L2
Tel: 204-627-8420; *Fax:* 204-623-6528

Thompson
Court of Queen's Bench, 59 Elizabeth Dr., P.O. Box 34, Thompson, MB R8N 1X4
Tel: 204-677-6757; *Fax:* 204-677-6686

Manitoba Provincial Court
Law Courts Bldg., 408 York Ave., Main Fl., Winnipeg, MB R3C 0P9
Tel: 204-945-3454; *Fax:* 204-945-7130
www.manitobacourts.mb.ca
The Provincial Court has jurisdiction in youth & select family & criminal matters, including summary conviction offences.
Chief Judge: The Hon. Kenneth Champagne
Assoc. Chief Judge: The Hon. Murray Thompson
Assoc. Chief Judge: The Hon. Janice leMaistre
Assoc. Chief Judge: Michel L.J. Chartier
Judges (His/Her Hon.):
Herbert Lawrence Allen
Catherine Carlson
Sandra L. Chapman
Brian G. Colli
John Combs
Brian M. Corrin
Kathlyn Mary A. Curtis
Judith A. Elliott
Robin A. Finlayson
Marvin F. Garfinkel
Wanda M. Garreck
John P. Guy
Christine Harapiak
Mary Kate Harvie
Robert M. Heinrichs
Shauna Hewitt-Michta
Sidney B. Lerner
Theodore J. Lismer
Tracey M. Lord
Lee Ann M. Martin
Jean McBride
Malcolm W. McDonald
Kelly Moar
Timothy Preston
Heather R. Pullan
Doreen Redhead
Fred H. Sandhu
Dale C. Schille
Donald R. Slough
Marva J. Smith
Lynn A. Stannard
Brent D. Stewart
Krystyna D. Tarwid
Patti-Anne L. Umpherville
Raymond E. Wyant
R.L. (Rocky) Pollack
Carena Roller
Cynthia A. Devine
Timothy J.P. Killeen

Courts:
Brandon
Provincial Court, 1104 Princess Ave., Brandon, MB R7A 0P9
J. Combs
B.D. Giesbrecht
K. Tarwid
Sheriff: M. Drosdoski, 204-726-6552

Dauphin
Provincial Court, 114 River Ave. West, Dauphin, MB R7N 0J7
R.W. Thompson
C. Harapiak
Sheriff: D. Werbiski, 204-622-2088

Portage la Prairie
Provincial Court, 25 Tupper St., Portage la Prairie, MB R1N 3K1
R.G. Cummings
Sheriff: R. Sim, 204-239-3379

The Pas
300 - 3 St. East, The Pas, MB R9A 1L2
Roger Grégoire
B.D. Stewart
Sheriff: R.A. Gray, 204-627-8431

Thompson
Provincial Court, 59 Elizabeth Dr., Thompson, MB R8N 1X4
B.G. Colli
M. Thompson
Sheriff: Dale Manning, 204-677-6764

New Brunswick

New Brunswick Court of Appeal
Justice Bldg., #202, 427 Queen St., P.O. Box 6000, Fredericton, NB E3B 5H1
Tel: 506-453-2452; *Fax:* 506-453-7921
www.gnb.ca/cour
The Court of Appeal has appellate jurisdiction in civil & criminal matters.
Chief Justice: The Hon. Mr. J. Ernest Drapeau
Justices of Appeal (The Hon. Mr./Madam Justice):
Alexandre Deschênes(Supernumerary)
Margaret E.L. Larlee(Supernumerary)
J.C. Marc Richard
Joseph T. Robertson
Wallace S. Turnbull(Supernumerary)
B. Richard Bell
Kathleen A. Quigg
Bradley V. Green

New Brunswick Court of Queen's Bench
Justice Bldg., 427 Queen St., P.O. Box 6000, Fredericton, NB E3B 5H1
Tel: 506-453-2015; *Fax:* 506-444-5675
www.gnb.ca/cour
The Court of Queen's Bench is a court of original jurisdiction, having jurisdiction in all civil & criminal matters arising in New Brunswick, except those expressly excluded by statute. The Court is comprised of two divisions: Trial & Family.
Moncton: **Chief Justice:** The Hon. David D. Smith, 506-856-2300, Fax: 506-856-2751
Administration:
Registrar: Bankruptcy/Divorce & Matrimonial Causes, Michael J. Bray, 506-453-2452
Deputy Registrar: Bankruptcy, Elizabeth Nicholas, 506-453-2452

Courts:
Bathurst
Court House, 254 St. Patrick St., P.O. Box 5001, Bathurst, NB E2A 3Z9
Tel: 506-547-2151; *Fax:* 506-547-2966
G.W. Boisvert
Réginald Léger
J.R. McIntyre
Regional Manager: R.G. Boudreau
Clerk (Trial Division) & Administrator (Family Division): Donald Arseneau
Sheriff/Coroner: Edgar Aubé

Campbellton
Court House, 157 Water St., P.O. Box 5001, Campbellton, NB E3N 3H5
Tel: 506-789-2368; *Fax:* 506-789-2062
Raymond J. Guerette
Gladys J. Young
Clerk (Trial Division) & Administrator (Family Division): Johanne Martin
Sheriff/Coroner: Walter Thompson

Edmundston
121 Church St., P.O. Box 5001, Edmundston, NB E3V 3L3
Tel: 506-753-2025; *Fax:* 506-737-4419
Thomas E. Cyr
Lucie Lavigne
Clerk, Administrator (Family Division) & Regional Manager: Jean-François Cyr
Clerk, Administrator (Family Division) & Regional Manager: Sylvie Dumont
Sheriff/Coroner: Paul Ringuette

Fredericton
Court House, 427 Queen St., P.O. Box 6000, Fredericton, NB E3B 5H1
Tel: 506-453-2015;
Other information: Fax: 506/453-7921 (Family); 506/444-4392 (Trial)
Myrna Athey
Paulette Garnett
D.H. Russell
Regional Manager: Dominique Laundry
Sheriff/Coroner: Keith Ball
Clerk (Trial Division) & Administrator (Family Division): Jean-Marie Goguen
Clerk (Trial Division) & Administrator (Family Division): Joy Toole

Moncton
770 Main St., P.O. Box 5001, Moncton, NB E1C 8R3
Tel: 506-856-2305; *Fax:* 506-856-2951
Colette M. d'Entremont
B.M. Robichaud
P.S. Creaghan
J. Alfred Landry
Guy A. Richard
George S. Rideout
Roger Savoie
Jacques A. Sirois
C.J. David D. Smith
Regional Director, Court Services: David Léger
Clerk (Trial Division) & Administrator (Family Division): Anne Richard
Sheriff/Coroner: Rhéal LeBlanc

Miramichi
Court House, 599 King George Hwy., Miramichi, NB E1V 1N6
Tel: 506-627-4021; *Fax:* 506-627-4134
Thomas Riordon
Stephen J. McNally
Administrator: Cynthia Goulette
Clerk: Matthew Cripps
Sheriff/Coroner:Vacant

Saint John
110 Charlotte St., P.O. Box 5001, Saint John, NB E2L 4Y9
Tel: 506-658-2400; *Fax:* 506-658-3070
Anne D. Wooder
Robert L. Tuck
P.S. Glennie
William T. Grant
Robert J. Higgins
H.H. McLellan
J.W. Turnbull
Regional Manager: Tom Bishop
Clerk (Trial Division) & Administrator (Family Division): Sharon LeBlanc
Clerk (Trial Division) & Administrator (Family Division): George S. Thériault
Sheriff/Coroner: Joan Collins

Woodstock
Court House, 689 Main St., P.O. Box 5001, Woodstock, NB E7M 5C6
Tel: 506-325-4414; *Fax:* 506-325-4447
Judy L. Clendening
Deputy Clerk (Trial Division) & Deputy Administrator (Fam: Andrea Hull
Sheriff/Coroner: Tim Wiebe

New Brunswick Provincial Court
Justice Bldg., #105, 427 Queen St., P.O. Box 6000, Fredericton, NB E3B 5H1
Tel: 506-453-2120;
www.gnb.ca/cour
The Provincial Court has jurisdiction in select criminal matters as well as youth matters.
Chief Judge: His Hon. R. Leslie Jackson
Assoc. Chief Judge: The Hon. Pierre W. Arseneault

Courts:
Carleton County
689 Main St., P.O. Box 5001, Woodstock, NB E7M 5C6
Tel: 506-325-4415; *Fax:* 506-325-3906
R. Leslie Jackson(Chief Judge)

Charlotte County
41 King St., P.O. Box 5001, St Stephen, NB E3L 2C1
Tel: 506-466-7507; *Fax:* 506-466-7508
David C. Walker

Gloucester County (Bathurst)
#223, 254 St. Patrick St., P.O. Box 5001, Bathurst, NB E2A 3Z9
Tel: 506-547-2155; *Fax:* 506-547-7448
Frederic Arsenault(Supernumerary)

Gloucester County (Tracadie-Sheila)
Place Tracadie, 3514 Main St., 1st Fl., Tracadie, NB E1X 1C9
Tel: 506-394-3700; *Fax:* 506-394-3696
Donald J. LeBlanc

Kent County
#1, 9358 Main St., P.O. Box 5001, Richibucto, NB E4W 5R5
Tel: 506-523-7611; *Fax:* 506-526-7155
Joseph C. Michaud(Supernumerary)

Kings County
#2, 648 Main St., Hampton, NB E5N 6C8
Tel: 506-832-6015; *Fax:* 506-832-6079
Henrik G. Tonning

Madawaska County
Carrefour Assomption, #235, 121 rue de l'Église, P.O. Box 5001, Edmundston, NB E3V 3L3
Tél: 506-735-2026; *Téléc:* 506-735-2396
George S. Pérusse(Surnuméraire)

Northumberland County
673 King George Hwy., Miramichi, NB E1V 1N6
Tel: 506-627-4018
Denis T. Lordon
John C. Friel

Restigouche County
#202, 157 Water St., P.O. Box 5001, Campbellton, NB E3N 3H5
Tel: 506-789-2337; *Fax:* 506-789-2186
Pierre F. Dubé
Steven M. Hutchinson

Saint John County
15 Market Square, 3rd Fl., P.O. Box 5001, Saint John, NB E2L 1E8
Tel: 506-658-2568
Alfred H. Brien
Anne M. Jeffries
William J. McCarroll
James G. McNamee(Supernumerary)
W. Andrew LeMesurier

Sunbury-Queens Counties
P.O. Box 94, Oromocto, NB E2V 2G4
Tel: 506-347-4020; *Fax:* 506-357-4032
The courthouse is located at 23 Route 102 Highway, River Road, in Burton, NB.
Patricia L. Cumming

Victoria County
426 Broadway, P.O. Box 5001, Grand Falls, NB E3Z 1G1
Tel: 506-473-7700; *Fax:* 506-473-7379
Jacques Desjardins(Supernumerary)

Westmorland County
Assumption Place, 770 Main St., P.O. Box 5001, Moncton, NB E1C 8R3
Tel: 506-856-2301; *Fax:* 506-856-3226
Pierre W. Arseneault(Assoc. Chief Judge)
Jolène Richard
Anne Dugas-Horsman
Irwin E. Lampert
Michael McKee(Supernumerary)
J. Camille Vautour

York County
Justice Bldg., #105, 427 Queen St., P.O. Box 6000, Fredericton, NB E3B 5H1
Tel: 506-453-2120
Judges (His/Her Hon.):
Mary Jane Richards
Julian Dickson

New Brunswick Probate Court
Justice Bldg., 423 Queen St., P.O. Box 6000, Fredericton, NB E3B 5H1
Tel: 506-453-2015;
www.gnb.ca/cour
The Probate Court has jurisdiction in estate matters. Clerks of the Court of Queen's Bench are, ex officio, Clerks of Probate Court. Court locations throughout New Brunswick; contact: Clerk of Probate, Court Services Office (Queen's Bench).

Newfoundland & Labrador

Supreme Court of Newfoundland & Labrador: Judicial Centres
Courthouse, 309 Duckworth St., P.O. Box 937, St. John's, NL A1C 5M3
Tel: 709-729-1137; *Fax:* 709-729-6623
inquiries@supreme.court.nl.ca
www.court.nl.ca/supreme/general
The Supreme Court also has jurisdiction in Bankruptcy.
Senior Deputy Registrar: Bankruptcy, Darlene Wells
darlenewells@gov.nl.ca

Courts:
Corner Brook
Courthouse, 82 Mt. Bernard Ave., P.O. Box 2006, Corner Brook, NL A2H 6J8
Tel: 709-637-2485; *Fax:* 709-637-2569
W.H.N. Goodridge
Alan (Tex) Seaborn
Deputy Registrar: Sandra Oxford, 709-637-2224, Fax: 709-637-2569

Gander
Law Court Bldg., 98 Airport Blvd., P.O. Box 2222, Gander, NL A1V 2N9
Tel: 709-256-1115; *Fax:* 709-256-1120
R.P. Whalen
Asst. Deputy Registrar: Lynetta Payne, 709-256-1115, Fax: 709-256-1120

Grand Bank
T. Alex Hickman Courthouse, P.O. Box 910, Grand Bank, NL A0E 1W0
Tel: 709-832-1720; *Fax:* 709-832-2755
Maureen Dunn
G.A. Handrigan
Asst. Deputy Registrar: Wilson Crowley, 709-832-1720, Fax: 709-832-2755

Grand Falls - Windsor
The Law Courts, 55 Cromer Ave., Grand Falls, NL A2A 1W9
Tel: 709-292-4260; *Fax:* 709-292-4224
A. Schwartz(Supernumerary)
K.J. Goulding
Asst. Deputy Registrar: Edward Lannon, 709-292-4260, Fax: 709-292-4224

Happy Valley - Goose Bay
Courthouse, 214 Hamilton River Rd., P.O. Box 1139 B, Happy Valley-Goose Bay, NL A0P 1E0
Tel: 709-896-7892; *Fax:* 709-896-9212
R.P. Stack
Asst. Deputy Registrar: Paula Parsons, 709-896-7891, Fax: 709-896-9212

Supreme Court of Newfoundland & Labrador: Court of Appeal
287 Duckworth St., P.O. Box 937, St. John's, NL A1C 5M3
Tel: 709-729-0066; *Fax:* 709-729-7909
courtofappealinquiries@supreme.court.nl.ca
www.court.nl.ca/supreme/appeal
The Court of Appeal has appellate jurisdiction in criminal & civil matters from decisions of the lower courts & designated administrative boards & tribunals.
Chief Justice: The Hon. J.D. Green
Justices of Appeal (The Hon. Mr./Madam Justice):
L. Barry
M.F. Harrington
L.R. Hoegg
K.J. Mercer
M. Rowe
C.K. Wells
G. Welsh
C.W. White

Supreme Court of Newfoundland & Labrador: Trial Division
Court House, 309 Duckworth St., P.O. Box 937, St. John's, NL A1C 5M3
Tel: 709-729-1137; *Fax:* 709-729-6623
www.court.nl.ca/supreme/general
The Trial Division is a court of original jurisdiction having jurisdiction in all civil & criminal matters arising in Newfoundland, except those excluded by statute. With the exception of the judicial area of St. John's, the Trial Division's original jurisdiction extends to particular family matters. The Registrar,and staff in the Estates Division of the Supreme Court, carrys out public guardian, guardian ad litem and public trustree functions.
Chief Justice: The Hon. David B. Orsborn
Judges (The Hon.):
J.S. Adams
G.D. Butler
W.G. Dymond
A.E. Faour
R.A. Fowler
D.E. Fry
R.M. Hall
R.J. Halley
R.D. LeBlanc
Deborah J. Paquette(Q.C.)
D.L. Russell(Supernumerary)
C.R. Thompson
Angela Whitehead

Supreme Court of Newfoundland & Labrador: United Family Court
21 King's Bridge Rd., St. John's, NL A1C 3K4
Tel: 709-637-2250; *Fax:* 709-637-8036
FamilyInquiries@supreme.court.nl.ca
www.court.nl.ca/supreme/family
Judicial matters regarding families are shared/divided between the Supreme & Provincial Courts along geographical boundaries. The United Family Court, a division of the Supreme Court, has exclusive jurisdiction for all family matters on the Avalon Peninsula (including Bell Is.). In the "expanded service area" of the United Family Court (from Holyrood to Port Blandford & Bonavista Peninsula), however, there is concurrent jurisdiction.
Gillian D. Butler
Judges (The Hon.):
J.D. Cook
Mary E. Noonan
S.B. O'Regan(Supernumerary)
David A. Peddle

Provincial Court of Newfoundland & Labrador
Atlantic Place, 215 Water St., P.O. Box 68, St. John's, NL A1C 6C9
Tel: 709-729-1004; *Fax:* 709-729-2161
inquiries@provincial.court.nl.ca
www.court.nl.ca/provincial
The Provincial Court has jurisdiction in select criminal & family (outside the judicial area of St. John's) matters as well as small claims & youth matters.
Chief Judge: The Hon. D. Mark Pike
Assoc. Chief Judge: The Hon. Robert B. Hyslop
Judges (The Hon.):
G.O. Brown
C.J. Flynn
G. Harding
D. Orr
D. Power
L. Skanes
R. Smith
L. Spracklin
J. Woodrow
Administration:
Director: Court Services, Pamela Ryder-Lahey
plahey@provincial.court.nl

Courts:
Clarenville
47 Marine Dr., Clarenville, NL A5A 1M5
Tel: 709-466-2635; *Fax:* 709-466-3147
P.J. Kennedy

Corner Brook
84 Mt. Bernard Ave., P.O. Box 2006, Corner Brook, NL A2H 6J8
Tel: 709-637-2323; *Fax:* 709-637-2656
C. Allen-Westby
W. Gorman
K. Howe

Gander
98 Airport Rd., P.O. Box 2222, Gander, NL A1V 2N9
Tel: 709-256-1100; *Fax:* 709-256-1097
M. Madden
B. Short

Happy Valley-Goose Bay
P.O. Box 3014 B, Happy Valley-Goose Bay, NL A0P 1E0
Tel: 709-896-7870; *Fax:* 709-896-8767
W. English
J. Joy

Grand Bank
Grand Bank-Fortune Hwy., P.O. Box 339, Grand Bank, NL A0E 1W0
Tel: 709-832-1450; *Fax:* 709-832-1758
H. Porter

Grand Falls
Law Courts Bldg., Grand Falls, NL A2A 1W9
Tel: 709-292-4212; *Fax:* 709-292-4388
T. Chalker
R.J. Whiffen

Harbour Grace
Harvey St., P.O. Box 519, Harbour Grace, NL A0A 2M0
Tel: 709-596-6141; *Fax:* 709-596-4304
www.hrgrace.ca/court.html
J. Brazil

Stephenville
35 Alabama Dr., Stephenville, NL A2N 3K9
Tel: 709-643-2966; *Fax:* 709-643-4022
J. Jenkins

Wabush
Whiteway Dr., P.O. Box 1060, Wabush, NL A0R 1B0
Tel: 709-282-6617; *Fax:* 709-282-6905
W.A. Trahey

Northwest Territories

Northwest Territories Court of Appeal
Court House, P.O. Box 550, Yellowknife, NT X1A 2N4
Tel: 867-873-7643; *Fax:* 867-873-0291
www.nwtcourts.ca/Courts
The Court of Appeal has appellate jurisdiction in criminal & civil matters from the Supreme Court & Territorial Court.
Chief Justice: The Hon. C.A. Fraser
Justices of Appeal (The Hon. Mr./Madam Justice):
Ronald L. Berger
M.B. Bielby
L.A.M. Charbonneau
C.M. Conrad
J.E. Côté
S. Cooper
Peter T. Costigan
Adelle Fruman
L.F. Gower
C. Hunt
E.D. Johnson
Robert G. Kilpatrick
P.W.L. Martin
J.D.B. McDonald
E.A. McFadyen
C.D. O'Brien
B.K. O'Ferrall
M.S. Paperny

E. Picard
K.G. Ritter
P.A. Rowbotham
Virginia A. Schuler
K. Shaner
N.A. Sharkey
F.F. Slatter
S.H. Smallwood
Ronald S. Veale
J. Watson
Neil C. Wittmann
Administration:
Registrar: Anne Mould

Northwest Territories Supreme Court
P.O. Box 550, Yellowknife, NT X1A 2N4
Tel: 867-873-7643; *Fax:* 867-873-0291
www.nwtcourts.ca/Courts/sc.htm
The Supreme Court is a court of original jurisdiction & has jurisdiction in all civil & criminal matters arising in the Northwest Territories, except those expressly excluded by statute.
The Hon. V.A. Schuler
Judges (The Hon. Mr./Madam Justice):
L.A. Charbonneau
K. Shaner
S. Smallwood
Administration:
Director: Court Services, Anne Mould

Northwest Territorial Court
P.O. Box 550, Yellowknife, NT X1A 2N4
Tel: 867-873-7643; *Fax:* 867-873-0291
www.nwtcourts.ca/Courts/tc.htm
The Territorial Court has jurisdiction in small claims, youth, family & select criminal matters.
Chief Judge: The Hon. Robert D. Gorin
Judges (His/Her Hon.):
Bernadette E. Schmaltz
Christine Gagnon
Garth Malakoe
Administration:
Director: Court Services, Anne Mould

Northwest Territories: Justice of the Peace Court
P.O. Box 550, Yellowknife, NT X1A 2N4
Tel: 867-920-8020; *Fax:* 867-873-0203
www.nwtcourts.ca/Courts/jp.htm
The Justices of the Peace have jurisdiction in summary conviction matters arising out of territorial statute, municipal by-law & select criminal matters.

Nova Scotia

Nova Scotia Court of Appeal
The Law Courts Bldg., 1815 Upper Water St., Halifax, NS B3J 1S7
Tel: 902-424-4900; *Fax:* 902-424-0524
www.courts.ns.ca/Appeals/index_ca.htm
Other information: twitter.com/CourtsNS_NSCA
The Nova Scotia Court of Appeal is the province's highest court and has appellate jurisdiction in civil & criminal matters. It sits only in Halifax and hears appeals from both the Supreme and Provincial Courts.
Chief Justice: The Hon. Michael MacDonald
Justices of Appeal (The Hon. Justice):
Duncan R. Beveridge
Peter M.S. Bryson
David P.S. Farrar
Joel E. Fichaud
M. Jill Hamilton
Linda L. Oland
Jamie W.S. Saunders
Administration:
Registrar: Court of Appeal, Annette M. Boucher, 902-424-6187
boucheam@gov.ns.ca

Nova Scotia Supreme Court
The Law Courts Bldg., 1815 Upper Water St., Halifax, NS B3J 1S7
Tel: 902-424-4900; *Fax:* 902-424-0524
www.courts.ns.ca/supreme/index_sc.htm
The Supreme Court is the highest trial court in the province with jurisdiction in all civil & criminal matters, except those expressly excluded by statute. It hears appeals on Provincial Court, Small Claims Court and Residential Tenancies Board matters.
Chief Justice: The Hon. Joseph P. Kennedy, 902-424-6939, Fax: 902-424-0536
Assoc. Chief Justice: The Hon. Deborah K. Smith
Judges (The Hon. Mr./Madam Justice):
A.P. Boudreau(Supernumerary)
F.A. Cacchione(Supernumerary)
K. Coady
C.R. Coughlan
P.J. Duncan
S.M. Hood
A.J. LeBlanc
A.D. MacAdam(Supernumerary)
G.G. McDougall
G. Moir
J.D. Murphy
A.W.D. Pickup
M.H. Robertson
P. Rosinski
Robert Wright
Associate Chief Justice: L.I. O'Neil
Judges, Family Division (The Hon. Mr./Madam Justice):
Carole A. Beaton
Judges, Family Division (The Hon. Mr./Madam Justice):
D.C. Campbell
L.J. Dellapinna
Robert Ferguson(Supernumerary)
D. Gass
E. Jollimore
M.C. Legere-Sers
M. Lynch
B.A. MacDonald
R.J. Williams
Administration:
Registrar in Bankruptcy: Richard W. Cregan, 902-424-6908

Courts:

Amherst
16 Church St., 3 Fl., Amherst, NS B4H 3A6
Tel: 902-667-2256; *Fax:* 902-667-5498
J.E. Scanlon

Annapolis Royal
Justice Centre, 377 St. George St., Annapolis Royal, NS B0S 1A0
Tel: 902-532-5462; *Fax:* 902-532-7225
C.E. Haliburton(Supernumerary)

Antigonish
Justice Centre, 11 James St., Antigonish, NS B2G 1R6
Tel: 902-863-7394; *Fax:* 902-863-7479
D.L. MacLellan(Supernumerary)
N.M. Scaravelli

Bridgewater
Court House, 141 High St., Bridgewater, NS B4V 1W2
Tel: 902-543-4679; *Fax:* 902-543-0678
M. Stewart

Digby
Justice Centre, 119 Queen St., Digby, NS B0V 1A0
Tel: 902-245-7134; *Fax:* 902-245-6722
C.E. Haliburton(Supernumerary)
P.L. Muise

Kentville
Justice Centre, 87 Cornwallis St., Kentville, NS B4N 2E5
Tel: 902-679-6070; *Fax:* 902-679-6178
G.M. Warner

Pictou/New Glasgow
Court House, 69 Water St., P.O. Box 1750, Pictou, NS B0K 1H0
Tel: 902-485-6373; *Fax:* 902-485-6737
D.L. MacLellan(Supernumerary)
N.M. Scaravelli

Port Hawkesbury
#201, 15 Kennedy St., Port Hawkesbury, NS B9A 2Y1
Tel: 902-625-4218; *Fax:* 902-625-4084

Sydney
Justice Centre, #6, 136 Charlotte St., Sydney, NS B1P 1C3
Tel: 902-563-3550; *Fax:* 902-563-2224
C.A. Bourgeois
F.C. Edwards(Supernumerary)
S.J. MacDonald
P.J. Murray
T.M. Forgeron
K. Haley
M.C. MacLellan
D.W. Wilson

Truro
Justice Centre, 1 church St., Truro, NS B2N 3Z5
Tel: 902-893-3953; *Fax:* 902-893-6114
J.E. Scanlan

Yarmouth
Justice Centre, 164 Main St., Yarmouth, NS B5A 1C2
Tel: 902-742-0500; *Fax:* 902-742-0678
P.L. Muise

Nova Scotia: Probate Court
Law Courts Bldg, 1815 Upper Water St., Halifax, NS B3J 1S7
Tel: 902-424-7422; *Fax:* 902-424-0524
The Probate Court has jurisdiction in respect of estate matters.

Courts:

Amherst
Justice Centre, 16 Church St., 3rd Fl., Amherst, NS B4H 3A6
Tel: 902-667-2256; *Fax:* 902-667-1108
Registrar: Anne Marie LeBlanc

Annapolis Royal
Justice Centre, 377 St. George St., P.O. Box 129, Annapolis Royal, NS B0S 1A0
Tel: 902-532-5462; *Fax:* 902-532-7225
Registrar: Sandra Gennette

Antigonish
Justice Centre, 11 James St., Antigonish, NS B2G 1R6
Tel: 902-863-7396; *Fax:* 902-863-7479
Registrar: Lorna Chisholm

Bridgewater
Justice Centre, 141 High St., Bridgewater, NS B4V 1W2
Tel: 902-543-0816; *Fax:* 902-543-0678
Registrar: Claire Feener

Digby
Court House, Queen St., P.O. Box 1089, Digby, NS B0V 1A0
Tel: 902-245-7134; *Fax:* 902-245-6722
Registrar: Sandra Gennette

Halifax
Law Courts Bldg., 1815 Upper Water St., Halifax, NS B3J 1S7
Tel: 902-424-7422; *Fax:* 902-424-0524
Registrar: Sharron Atton

Kentville
Justice Centre, 87 Cornwallis St., Kentville, NS B4N 2E5
Tel: 902-679-5540; *Fax:* 902-679-6178
Registrar: Susan Campbell-Baltzer

Pictou/New Glasgow
69 Water St., P.O. Box 1750, Pictou, NS B0K 1H0
Tel: 902-485-4351; *Fax:* 902-485-6737
Registrar: Laura Lannon

Port Hawkesbury
Justice Centre, #201, 15 Kennedy St., Port Hawkesbury, NS B9A 2Y1
Tel: 902-625-4269; *Fax:* 902-625-4084
Registrar: Karen Gillies

Sydney
Justice Centre, #6, 136 Charlotte St., Sydney, NS B1P 1C3
Tel: 902-563-3545; *Fax:* 902-563-5701
Registrar: Shauna Wilson

Truro
Justice Centre, 1 Church St., Truro, NS B2N 3Z5
Tel: 902-893-5870; *Fax:* 902-893-6114
Registrar: Anne Marie LeBlanc

Yarmouth
Justice Centre, 164 Main St., Yarmouth, NS B5A 1C2
Tel: 902-742-5469; *Fax:* 902-742-0678
Registrar: Ruth Hulbert

Nova Scotia Provincial Court
5250 Spring Garden Rd., Halifax, NS B3J 1E7
Tel: 902-424-8718; *Fax:* 902-424-0551
www.courts.ns.ca/provincial/index_pc.htm
The Provincial Court has jurisdiction over almost all indictable charges under provincial & federal statutes and regulations. When judges are not available, presiding Justices of the Peace deal with release or detention of those arrested.
Chief Judge: The Hon. Patrick H. Curran
Judges (The Hon.):
B.J. Beach
J.S. Campbell
M.C. Chisholm
A.S. Derrick
W.B. Digby
T. Gabriel
M.B. Sherar
C.H.F. Williams

Courts:

Amherst
16 church St., 3rd Fl., Amherst, NS B4H 3A6
Tel: 902-667-2256; *Fax:* 902-667-1108
C.A. Beaton

Annapolis Royal
Justice Centre, 377 St. George St., Annapolis Royal, NS B0S 1A0
Tel: 902-245-4567

Antigonish
11 James St., Antigonish, NS B2G 1R6
Tel: 902-863-3676; *Fax:* 902-863-7479
J.D. Embree

Bridgewater
Justice Centre, 141 High St., Bridgewater, NS B4V 1W2
Tel: 902-543-4679; *Fax:* 902-543-0678
J.H. Burrill
A. Crawford

Dartmouth
#200, 277 Pleasant St., Dartmouth, NS B2Y 3S2
Tel: 902-424-2390; *Fax:* 902-424-0677
F.I. Buchan
R.B. Gibson
F.P. Hoskins
W. MacDonald
A. Murphy
T.K. Tax
P.S. Williams

Digby
119 Queen St., P.O. Box 1089, Digby, NS B0V 1A0
Tel: 902-245-4567; *Fax:* 902-245-6722
J. Batiot

Kentville
Justice Centre, 87 Cornwallis St., Kentville, NS B4N 2E5
Tel: 902-679-6070; *Fax:* 902-679-6190
C. MacDonald
M.L. Melvin
A.T. Tufts

New Glasgow
Justice Centre, 115 MacLean St., New Glasgow, NS B2H 4M5
Tel: 902-755-5106; *Fax:* 902-755-7181

Port Hawkesbury
Justice Centre, #201, 15 Kennedy St., Port Hawkesbury, NS B9A 2Y1
Tel: 902-625-2605; *Fax:* 902-625-4084
L. Halfpenny-MacQuarrie

Sydney
Harbour Place, #6, 136 Charlotte St., Sydney, NS B1P 1C3
Tel: 902-563-3510; *Fax:* 902-563-3421
A.P. Ross
D.J. Ryan
J.M. Whalen
B.D. Williston

Truro
Justice Centre, 540 Prince St., Truro, NS B2N 1G1
Tel: 902-893-5840; *Fax:* 902-893-6261
J.G. MacDougall
R.J. MacKinnon

Yarmouth
Justice Centre, 164 Main St., Yarmouth, NS B5A 1C2
Tel: 902-742-0500; *Fax:* 902-742-0678
R.M.J. Prince

Nova Scotia: Family Court
NS
The Family Court has jurisdiction in family matters & also functions as a Youth Court for cases involving youths aged 12 to 15 years.
Chief Judge: His Hon. Patrick H. Curran
Jamie S. Campbell
Marc C. Chisholm
Anne S. Derrick
William Digby
Timothy Gabriel
Administration:
Director: Court Services, Judith McPhee, 902-424-4632, Fax: 902-424-7596
mcpheeja@gov.ns.ca

Courts:
Amherst
Justice Centre, 16 Church St., 3rd Fl., Amherst, NS B4H 3A6
Tel: 902-667-2256; *Fax:* 902-667-1108
C.A. Beaton
J.M. Dewolfe
Senior Officer: Patrick Dornan

Antigonish
Justice Centre, 11 James St., Antigonish, NS B2G 1R6
Tel: 902-863-7312; *Fax:* 902-863-7479
James C. Wilson

Bridgewater
Justice Centre, 141 High St., Bridgewater, NS B4V 1W2
Tel: 902-543-4679; *Fax:* 902-543-0678
J.H. Burrill
W. Dyer

Kentville
136 Exhibition St., Kentville, NS B4N 4E5
Tel: 902-679-6075; *Fax:* 902-679-6081
R. Levy
M.L. Melvin

Truro
542 Prince St., Truro, NS B2N 1G1
Tel: 902-893-5840; *Fax:* 902-893-6261
D.R. Hubley
J.G. MacDonald
R.J. MacKinnon
Officer: Keith Mumford

Yarmouth
Justice Centre, 164 Main St., Yarmouth, NS B5A 1C2
Tel: 902-742-0550; *Fax:* 902-742-0678
J.D. Comeau
Officer: Bob LeBlanc

Nova Scotia Justice Centres
NS

Amherst
16 Church St., 3rd Fl., Amherst, NS B4H 3A6
Tel: 902-667-2256; *Fax:* 902-667-1108
Court Administrator: Lynn Sorensen

Antigonish
11 James St., Antigonish, NS B2G 1R6
Tel: 902-863-3676; *Fax:* 902-863-7479
Court Administrator: Janice Gillis-MacLean

Bridgewater
141 High St., Bridgewater, NS B4V 1W2
Tel: 902-543-4679; *Fax:* 902-543-0678
Court Administrator: Paul Fay

Digby/Annapolis
119 Queen St., P.O. Box 1089, Digby, NS B0V 1A0
Tel: 902-245-4567; *Fax:* 902-245-6722
Court Administrator: Alan Hamilton

Halifax
1815 Upper Water St., Halifax, NS B3J 1S7
Tel: 902-424-6900; *Fax:* 902-424-0524
Prothonotary: Annette Boucher
Court Administrator: Court of Appeal/Supreme Court, Wayne Stewart
Court Administrator: Supreme Court, Family Div., John Campbell
Court Administrator: Provincial Court, Peter James

Kentville
87 Cornwallis St., Kentville, NS B4N 2E5
Tel: 902-679-6070; *Fax:* 902-679-6178
Court Administrator: Laurie Wanamaker

Pictou/New Glasgow
115 MacLean St., 1st Fl., New Glasgow, NS B2H 4M5
Tel: 902-755-7364; *Fax:* 902-755-7783
Court Administrator: Jim Hahnen

Port Hawkesbury
#201, 15 Kennedy St., Port Hawkesbury, NS B9A 2Y1
Tel: 902-625-4793; *Fax:* 902-625-4084
Acting Court Administrator: Janice Gillis-MacLean

Sydney
Harbour Place, #6, 136 Charlotte St., Sydney, NS B1P 1C3
Tel: 902-563-3510; *Fax:* 902-563-3421
Court Administrator: Pam Kachafanas

Truro
540 Prince St., Truro, NS B2N 1G1
Tel: 902-893-5840; *Fax:* 902-893-6261
Court Administrator: Lynn Sorensen

Yarmouth
Court House, 164 Main St., Yarmouth, NS B5A 1C2
Tel: 902-742-0500; *Fax:* 902-742-0678
Court Administrator: Alan Hamilton

Nunavut

Nunavut Court of Justice
#224, Arnakallak Bldg., P.O. Box 297, Iqaluit, NU X0A 0H0
Tel: 867-975-6100; *Fax:* 867-975-6168
Toll-Free: 866-286-0546
www.nucj.ca
A unified court that serves both federal and territorial claims, with one location in Iqaluit and one that travels to various communities throughout the territory.
Senior Judge: The Hon. Robert Kilpatrick
Justices (The Hon. Mr./Madam Justice):
Susan Cooper
Earl Johnson
Andrew Mahar
Neil Sharkey
Bonnie M. Tulloch

Nunavut Court of Justice
#224, Arnakallak Bldg., P.O. Box 297, Iqaluit, NU X0A 0H0
Tel: 867-975-6120; *Fax:* 867-975-6169
www.nunavutcourtofjustice.ca
Deputy Judges appointed as required.
Resident Judges (The Hon. Mr./Madam Justice):
Beverley A. Browne(Sr. Judge)
Earl D. Johnson
Robert G. Kilpatrick

Ontario

Court of Appeal for Ontario
Osgoode Hall, 130 Queen St. West, Toronto, ON M5H 2N5
Tel: 416-327-5020; *Fax:* 416-327-5032
www.ontariocourts.on.ca/coa/en/index.htm
The Court of Appeal is the final court of appeal for Ontario. Appeals from the Court of Appeal may be pursued in the Supreme Court of Canada.
Chief Justice: The Hon. Mr. Warren K. Winkler
Assoc. Chief Justice: The Hon. Mr. Dennis R. O'Connor
Justices (The Hon. Mr./Madam Justice):
Robert P. Armstrong
Robert A. Blair
Eleanore A. Cronk
David H. Doherty
Edward W. Ducharme
Gloria J. Epstein
Kathryn N. Feldman
Eileen E. Gillese
Stephen T. Goudge
Alexandra Hoy
Russell G. Juriansz
Harry S. LaForme
Susan E. Lang
John I. Laskin
Jean L. MacFarland
James MacPherson
Sarah E. Pepall
Marc Rosenberg
Paul S. Rouleau
Robert J. Sharpe
Janet M. Simmons
Michael H Tulloch
David Watt
Karen M. Weiler
Administration:
Senior Legal Officer: John Kromkamp, 416-327-5276
Registrar & Manager: Court Operations, Huguette Thomson
Deputy Registrar & Manager of Court Operations: Sandra Theroulde
Deputy Registrar & Manager of Judicial Support: Daniel Marentic

Ontario Superior Court of Justice
Osgoode Hall, 130 Queen St. West, Toronto, ON M5H 2N5
; *Fax:* 416-327-6209
www.ontariocourts.on.ca/scj/en/index.htm
In addition to its regular trial court functions, the Superior Court of Justice has two branches: the Divisional Court which generally hears appeals from a final order of a Judge of the Superior Court involving disputes of up to $25,000, & the Small Claims Court which generally hears cases involving claims up to $10,000. The Governor General appoints the Judges to all but the Ontario Court of Justice.
Chief Justice: The Hon. Heather F. Smith, 416-327-5000
Assoc. Chief Justice: The Hon. J. Douglas Cunningham, 416-327-5000

Central East Region
50 Eagle St. West, 4th Fl., Newmarket, ON L3Y 6B1
Tel: 905-853-4800; *Fax:* 905-853-4849
Regional Senior Justice: Michael Brown
Justices (The Hon. Mr./Madam Justice):
R.C. Boswell
J.C. Corkery
G.P. DiTomaso
M.P. Eberhard
M.L. Edwards
J.E. Ferguson
M.K. Fuerst
C.A. Gilmore
B. Glass
F. Graham
D.S. Gunsolus

M.J. Hatton
S.E. Healey
P.H. Howden
Jayne E. Hughes
A.P. Ingram
R.P. Kaufman
M.L. Lack
P. Lauwers
B.G. MacDougall
J.R. MacKinnon
P.Z. Magda
John R. McCarthy
John P.L. McDermot
H.A. McGee
J.R. McIsaac
Michael K. McKelvey
E.B. Minden
G.M. Mulligan
A. Mullins
C.S. Nelson
H.K. O'Connell
L. Olah
E. Quinlan
S. Rogers
A.R. Rowsell
D. Salmers
M.A.C. Scott
J.B. Shaughnessy
A. Sosna
A.J. Stong
D.R. Timms
R.A. Wildman
T.M. Wood

Central South Region
45 Main St. East, Hamilton, ON L8N 2B7
Tel: 905-645-5262; *Fax:* 905-645-5261
Regional Senior Justice: James R.H. Turnbull
Harrison S. Arrell
David A. Broad
C.E. Brown
Grant A. Campbell
K.A. Carpenter-Gunn
J.J. Cavarzan
Deborah L. Chappel
David S. Crane
P.J. Flynn
C. Stephen Glithero
D.J. Gordon
P.B. Hambly
J.R. Henderson
J.C. Kent
C. Lafrenière
Richard A. Lococo
T.R. Lofchik
W.L. MacPherson
T. Maddalena
B.H. Matheson
Randolph Mazza
M.J. McLaren
J.A. Milanetti
D. Parayeski
A. Pazaratz
J.W. Quinn
J.A. Ramsay
Robert B. Reid
R.D. Reilly
J.W. Scott
James W. Sloan
D.M. Steinberg
D.J. Taliano
Gerald E. Taylor
C.A. Tucker
L.M. Walters
A.C.R. Whitten

Central West Region
#100, 7755 Hurontario St., Brampton, ON L6W 4T1
Tel: 905-456-4700
Regional Senior Justice: Francine E. Van Melle
D.F. Baltman
J.R. Bellegham
T.A. Bielby
K.D. Coats
Clayton Conlan
P.A. Daley
F. Dawson
Meredith Donohue
T.M. Dunn
S.B. Durno
Dale F. Fitzpatrick
J.M. Fragomeni
D.K. Gray

C.N. Herold
S.C. Hill
C.W. Hourigan
K.A. Langdon
G.D. Lemon
A.D.K. MacKenzie
G.M. Miller
N.M. Mossip
C. Murray
T.P. O'Connor
D. Price
L. Ricchetti
S.S. Seppi
L.L. Snowie
J.R. Sproat
R.M. Thompson
K.M. van Rensburg
B.J. Wein

East Region
161 Elgin St., Ottawa, ON K2P 2K1
Tel: 613-239-1560
Regional Senior Justice: Charles T. Hackland
Brian W. Abrams
C.D. Aitken
P.B. Annis
R.N. Beaudoin
D.M. Belch
J.A. Blishen
R.G. Byers
M.Z. Charbonneau
M.S. James
John M. Johnston
P.B. Kane
S.J. Kershman
J. Lafrance-Cardinal
P.F. Lalonde
R. Leroy
H.S. Levenson Polowin
M.T. Linhares de Sousa
V.J. MacKinnon
H.K. MacLeod-Beliveau
R.L. Maranger
C. McKinnon
H.R. McLean
J.A. McMunagle
J. McNamara
M. Métivier
Timothy Minnema
J.A. Parfett
K.D. Pedlar
R. Pelletier
M. Quigley
L.D. Ratushny
T.D. Ray
C. Robertson
G.T. Roccamo
A.J. Roy
D.J.A. Rutherford
R.F. Scott
A.D. Sheffield
R.J. Smith
Wolfram Tausendfreund
Gary W. Trammer
A.C. Trousdale
Bonnie Warkentin

Metropolitan Toronto
361 University Ave., Toronto, ON M5G 1Y1
Tel: 416-327-5990; *Fax:* 416-327-6056
Regional Senior Justice: The Hon. Edward F. Then
B.A. Allen
T.L. Archibald
D. Aston
N.L. Backhouse
E.P. Belobaba
M. Benotto
Carole J. Brown
D.M. Brown
C.L. Campbell
Kenneth L. Campbell
S. Chapnik
R.A. Clark
M. Code
B.A. Conway
David L. Corbett
K.B. Corrick
B.L. Croll
P.A. Cumming
G. Czutrin
M.R. Dambrot
T. Ducharme
T. Dunnet

E.G. Ewaschuk
M.D. Forestell
E.E. Frank
A.M. Gans
N.E. Garton
Robert F. Goldstein
S.R. Goodman
S.E. Greer
P.A. Grossi
Glenn A. Hainey
A.L. Harvison Young
T.P. Herman
S. Himel
C. Horkins
P.G. Jarvis
J.E. Kelly
F.P. Kiteley
G.R. Klowak
Emile R. Kruzick
J. Lax
T.R. Lederer
S.N. Lederman
W. Low
E.M. Macdonald
J.A.B. Macdonald
I.A. MacDonnell
F.N. Marrocco
P.T. Matlow
J.D. McCombs
Thomas J. McEwen
J.B. McMahon
F.E. McWatt
R.E. Mesbur
A.M. Molloy
J.P. Moore
G.B. Morawetz
Edward W. Morgan
F.J.C. Newbould
I.V.B. Nordheimer
A.J. O'Marra
Brian P. O'Marra
V. Paisley
G.I. Pardu
L.A. Pattillo
M.A. Penny
P.M. Perell
C. Perkins
A. Pollack
R.W.M. Pitt
L.B. Roberts
H.E. Sachs
M.A. Sanderson
H.J.W. Siegel
G.F. Speigel
C.M. Speyer
N.J. Spies
Suzanne M. Stevenson
E.M. Stewart
D.G. Stinson
G.R. Strathy
K. Swinton
J.A. Thornburn
W.B. Trafford
G.T. Trotter
Kevin W. Whitaker
J.C. Wilkins
D.A. Wilson
J. Wilson

Northeast Region
155 Elm St. West, Sudbury, ON P3C 1T9
Tel: 705-564-7600
Regional Senior Justice: Louise L. Gauthier
R.R.D. Cornell
R.G. Del Frate
M. Gregory Ellies
E.E. Gareau
R.D. Gordon
P.C. Hennessy
N.M.J. Karam
E.J. Koke
C.A.M. Macdonald
I.S. McMillan
D.J. Nadeau
J.S. O'Neill
J.S. Poupore
R.A. Riopelle
P.U. Rivard
G.T. Valin
W.L. Whalen
J.A.S. Wilcox

Northwest Region
277 Camelot St., Thunder Bay, ON P7A 4B3
Tel: 807-343-2710

Regional Senior Justice: Helen M. Pierce
J. dePencier Wright
F. Bruce Fitzpatrick
J.S. Fregeau
J.F. McCartney
T.A. Platana
D.C. Shaw
G.P. Smith
E.W. Stach

Southwest Region
80 Dundas St. East, London, ON N6A 6A2
Tel: 519-660-3000; *Fax:* 519-660-3087

Regional Senior Justice: Thomas A. Heeney
Christopher Bondy
A.W. Bryant
G.A. Campbell
S.K. Campbell
Thomas J. Carey
John Desotti
J.M.W. Donohue
R.C. Gates
Andrew J. Goodman
K.A. Gorman
A. Duncan Grace
Paul J. Henderson
R.J. Haines
T.A. Heeney
Peter B. Hockin
Ian F. Leach
Denise M Korpan
L. Leitch
M. Marshman
D.R. McDermid
Victor Mitrow
J.N. Morissette
M.J. Nolan
T.L.J. Patterson
R.M. Pomerance
J.G. Quinn
H.A. Rady
S. Rogin
W. Tausendfreund
L.C. Templeton
B.G. Thomas
H. Vogelsang

Ontario Court of Justice

#2300, 1 Queen St. West, P.O. Box 91, Toronto, ON M5C 2W5
Tel: 416-327-5660; *Fax:* 416-326-4787
www.ontariocourts.on.ca/ocj/en/index.htm

The Ontario Court of Justice generally performs functions assigned to it by Acts such as the *Criminal Code* the *Provincial Offences Act* the *Family Law Act* the *Children's Law Reform Act* & the *Child & Family Services Act* & is a youth court. The Lieutenant Governor in Council, on the recommendation of the Attorney General, appoints the justices.

Chief Justice: The Hon. Annemarie E. Bonkalo
Assoc. Chief Justice: The Hon. Peter D. Griffiths
Assoc. Chief Justice: The Hon. John A. Payne

Central East Region
440 Kent St. West, Lindsay, ON K9V 6K2
Tel: 705-324-1400

Regional Senior Justice: Gregory Regis
S.C. Armstrong
G.W. Beatty
R.W. Beninger
P.L. Bellefontaine
M. Block
R. Blouin
P.N. Bourque
Lisa Cameron
L.E. Chester
H.I. Chisvin
J.C. Crawford
N.A. Dawson
J.A. De Filippis
P. De Freitas
M.T.E. Devlin
J.A. Douglas
J.D. Evans
W.A. Gorewich
R. Graydon
D.J. Halikowski
M. Harpur
C.R. Harris
A. Hourigan
Cynthia Johnston
J.F. Kenkel
G.D. Krelove
S.C. MacLean
R.P. Main
Enno J. Meijers
R.A. Minard
J.R. Morgan
R.J. Richards
E. Rosenberg
D.M. Stone
Peter Tetley
G. Wakefield
P.C. West
T.C. Whetung
J.B. Wilson
P.J. Wright

Central West Region
#518B, 45 Main St. East, Hamilton, ON L8N 2B7
Tel: 905-645-5333; *Fax:* 905-645-5375

Regional Senior Justice: The Hon. Kathryn L. Hawke
P.H.M. Agro
I.W. André
H.K. Atwood
J.C. Baldock
L.M. Baldwin
J.C. Blacklock
L. Botham
Joseph W. Bovard
S.D. Brown
F.M. Campling
S.R. Clark
T. Colvin
D.S. Cooper
S. Coroza
I. Cowan
T.A. Culver
P.R. Currie
B. Duncan
P.W. Dunn
G.B. Edward
F.L. Forsyth
G.S. Gage
Robert Gee
D. Harris
R. Jennis
N.S. Kastner
J.J. Keaney
R. Kelly
J. Kerrigan Brownridge
M.F. Khoorshed
R.J. LeDressay
J. Maresca
E. Martin
D.B. Maund
K.L. McLeod
J. Nadel
C.A. Nelson
Sheilagh O'Connor
M. Pawagi
B.E. Pugsley
E. Ready
R.H.K. Schwarzl
Kevin Sherwood
B.R. Shilton
M. Speyer
J.D. Takach
L.P. Thibideau
D.T. Vyse
A. Watson
P.H. Wilkie
B.E. Zabel
R. Zisman
M. Ziolak

East Region
161 Elgin St., 2nd Fl., Ottawa, ON K2P 2K1
Tel: 613-239-1153

Regional Senior Justice: The Hon. Lise Maisonneuve
P.R. Adams
A. Alder
C.D. Anderson
Judith C. Beaman
Jonathan Brunet
E. Deluzio
C.S. Dorval
H.L. Fraser
Franco Giamberardino
G. Griffin
S.J. Hunter
C.A. Kehoe
R. Lajoie
Jean Legault
B.W. Lennox
Allan G. Letourneau
Jacqueline Loignon
W. Malcolm
B.E. MacPhee
S.A.J. March
J.D. Nadelle
D.M. Nicholas
David Paciocco
H.E. Perkins-McVey
S.G. Radley-Walters
G. Renaud
R.G. Selkirk
J.D. Wake
J.N. Wilson
J.P. Wright

Northeast Region
#201, 159 Cedar St., Sudbury, ON P3E 6A5
Tel: 705-564-7600

Regional Senior Justice: The Hon. Annemarie E. Bonkalo
E.K. Bignell
P.J. Boucher
A. Buttazzoni
R.E.W. Carr
L. Duchesneau-McLachlan
W.F. Fitzgerald
G.N. Glaude
N. Gregson
A.L. Guay
Richard A. Humphrey
J.D. Keast
L. Klein
J. Kukurin
R.W. Lalande
M.P. Lambert
J. Lebel
G.R. Maille
M. McLeod
Alain H. Perron
M. Rocheleau
G.P. Rodgers
L. Serré
R.P. Villeneuve

Northwest Region
1805 East Arthur St., 1st Fl., Thunder Bay, ON P7E 5N7
Tel: 807-625-1600; *Fax:* 807-625-0062

Regional Senior Justice: The Hon. Marc L.G.H. Bode
D.P. Baig
P.T. Bishop
J. Elder
D. Di Giuseppe
D.G. Fraser
J.R. Hoshizaki
J.L. Pelletier
F. Valente

Toronto
Old City Hall, #156, 60 Queen St. West, Toronto, ON M5H 2M4
Tel: 416-327-5893

Regional Senior Justice: The Hon. Faith M. Finnestad
Sandra Bacchus
K.N. Barnes
F. Bhabha
Robert G. Bigelow
M. Bloomenfeld
Ronald D. Boivin
H. Borenstein
C. Brewer
B.A. Brown
Harvey P. Brownstone
L.M. Budzinski
K.J. Caldwell
B. Cavion
A.P. Chapin
T.P. Cleary
S.F. Clements
M.L. Cohen
D.P. Cole
C. Curtis
A. Di Zio
S.G. Dobney
Philip Anthony Downes
D. Fairgrieve
Lucia Favret
L.T. Feldman
P. French
M. Green
M.B. Greene
J.M. Grossman
D.G. Hackett

Aston Joseph Hall
P.A.J. Harris
M.L. Hogan
W.B. Horkins
P. Hryn
Carolyn J. Jones
P. Jones
H.L. Katarynych
R. Khawly
B. Knazan
N.L. Kozloff
A.T. Lacavera
G.S. Lapkin(Senior Judge)
E.N. Libman
S.B. Linden
T.R. Lipson
S.E. Marin
Heather Adair McArthur
S. Merenda
C. Mocha
J.C. Moore
E.B. Murray
S.S. Nakatsuru
P.E. Newton
F.C. O'Donnell
D.I. Oleskiw
M. Omatsu
E.F. Ormston
R.J. Otter
D.A.W. Paulseth
L.C. Pringle
S. Ray
P.H. Reinhardt
J.M. Ritchie
P. Robertson
R. Rutherford
R. Schneider
B.M. Scully
S.R. Shamai
S.B. Sherr
G. Sparrow
R.J. Spence
J. Sutherland
P.M. Taylor
A. Tuck-Jackson
C.H. Vaillancourt
G. Waldman
B. Weagant
F.M. Weinper
W.R. Wolski
M. Wong
K.. Wright
B.J. Young
M.A. Zuker

West Region
80 Dundas St. East, 1st Fl., #D, London, ON N6A 6A4
Tel: 519-660-3090; *Fax:* 519-660-3098
Regional Senior Justice: The Hon. Kathleen E. McGowan
J. Elliott Allen
D.J. Austin
S.S. Bondy
G.J. Brophy
G.A. Campbell
D.G. Carr
J. Caspers
L.C. Dean
G.F. DeMarco
N. Douglas
M. Epstein
S.J. Fuerth
Jonathon C. George
L. Glenn
P.A. Hardman
Steven P. Harrison
G.F. Hearn
G.M. Hornblower
M. Hoffman
R.G.E. Hunter
P.R.W. Isaacs
P.J.S. Kowalyshyn
Jeanine Elisabeth LeRoy
J.T. Lynch
A.E.E. McFadyen
A. Thomas McKay
K.L. McKerlie
M.A. McSorley
J. Morneau
S.M. Nicklas
M. O'Dea
D.W. Phillips
G.A. Pockele
W.G. Rabley
M. Rawlins
M.L.D. Roberts
L.J. Rogers
R.W. Rogerson
E.M. Schnall
J.S. Skowronski
B. Tobin
C.R. Westman
M.F. Woolcott

Court Services Division
McMurtry-Scott Bldg., #204, 720 Bay St., Toronto, ON M7A 2S9
Tel: 416-326-4263; *Fax:* 416-326-2652
www.attorneygeneral.jus.gov.on.ca/english/courts
Court Services Division manages the court offices in communities across Ontario: scheduling court cases, maintaining records & files, collecting fines & fees, enforcing civil orders, and providing information to the public. It also provides administration support to judicial offices in the Superior Court of Justice & the Ontario Court of Justice: providing clerks, court reporters, registrars and interpreters for court proceedings.

Regional Court: Central East
#210, 1091 Gorham St., Newmarket, ON L3Y 8X7
Tel: 905-836-5621; *Fax:* 905-836-5620
Areas served include: Barrie, Bracebridge, Huntsville, Lindsay, Kawartha Lakes, Muskoka, Newmarket, Orillia, Peterborough, Whitby, York Region. Total court locations: 24.
Acting Director: Court Operations, Sarina Kashak Regional Court: Central West
John Sopinka Courthouse, #518B, 45 Main St. East, Hamilton, ON L8N 2B7
Tel: 905-645-5333; *Fax:* 905-645-5375
Areas served include: Brampton, Brantford, Burlington, Hamilton, Niagara Region, Oakville, Orangeville, St. Catharines, Welland. Total court locations: 15.
Director: Court Operations, Joanne Spriet Regional Court: East
#100, Preston St., Ottawa, ON K1S 1N4
Tel: 613-239-1551; *Fax:* 613-239-1273
Areas served include: Bancroft, Belleville, Brockville, Cornwall, Kingston, Ottawa, Pembroke, Perth. Total court locations: 29.
Director: Court Operations, Thomas Fagan Regional Court: North East
#501, 159 Cedar St., Sudbury, ON P3E 6A5
Tel: 705-564-7675; *Fax:* 705-564-7664
Areas served include: Kapuskasing, Kirkland Lake, Moosonee, North Bay, Parry Sound, Sault Ste. Marie, Sturgeon Falls, Sudbury, Timmins. Court services are regularly provided in French, Ojibway & Cree. Total court locations: 35.
Director: Court Operations, Paul Langlois Regional Court: North West
277 Camelot St., Thunder Bay, ON P7A 4B3
Tel: 807-343-2747; *Fax:* 807-345-6383
Areas served include: Dryden, Fort Severn, Kenora, Nipigon, Rainy River, Thunder. There are significant Aboriginal populations in this region and court services are regularly provided in Ojibway and Oji-Cree. Many locations are fly-in. Total court locations: 42.
Director: Court Operations, Robert Gordon Regional Court: Toronto
#1601, 720 Bay St., Toronto, ON M5G 1Z6
Tel: 416-326-4249; *Fax:* 416-326-2073
Areas served: Greater Toronto Area. Total court locations: 11.
Acting Director: Court Operations, Lou Bartucci Regional Court: West
80 Dundas St., #D, London, ON N6A 6A4
Tel: 519-660-3090; *Fax:* 519-660-3098
Areas served include: Cambridge, Chatham, Fergus, Guelph, Kitchener, London, Owen Sound, Sarnia, Waterloo, Windsor. Total court locations: 24.
Director: Court Operations, Len Griffiths

Prince Edward Island

Prince Edward Island Supreme Court: Trial Division
Sir Louis Henry Davies Law Courts Bldg., 42 Water St., P.O. Box 2000, Charlottetown, PE C1A 7N8
The Supreme Court is a Court of original jurisdiction & has jurisdiction in all civil (including family, estate & small claims) & criminal matters arising in Prince Edward Island.
Chief Justice: The Hon. Madam Jacqueline Matheson
Justices (The Hon. Mr./Madam Justice):
Gordon Campbell
Wayne Cheverie
John K. Mitchell
Benjamin Taylor
Administration:
Registrar: Charles Thompson, 902-368-6669
Deputy Registrar: Estates Section, Gloria Panting
Deputy Registrar: General Section, Janet O'Brien
Deputy Registrar: Small Claims Section, Roxanne Smith
Deputy Registrar: Family Section, Sandra Mitchell
Court Services Manager: Judy Turpin, 902-368-6005

Prince Edward Island Supreme Court
Sir Louis Henry Davies Law Courts, 42 Water St., P.O. Box 2000, Charlottetown, PE C1A 7N8
Tel: 902-368-6000; *Fax:* 902-368-0266
Chief Justice: The Hon. Jacqueline R. Matheson

Prince Edward Island Supreme Court: Court of Appeal
Sir Louis Henry Davies Law Courts, 42 Water St., P.O. Box 2000, Charlottetown, PE C1A 7N8
The Court of Appeal has appellate jurisdiction in criminal & civil matters.
Chief Justice: The Hon. Mr. David H. Jenkins
John McQuaid
Michele M. Murphy
Deputy Registrar: Appeal Division, Gloria Panting

Prince Edward Island Provincial Court
Kelly Bldg., 3 Harbourside Access Rd., Charlottetown, PE C1A 8R4
Tel: 902-368-6000
The Provincial Court has jurisdiction in select criminal matters as well as youth matters.
Chief Judge: The Hon. John R. Douglas, 902-368-6011, Fax: 902-368-6743

Courts:
Queens & Kings Counties: Provincial Court
Law Courts Bldg., P.O. Box 2290, Charlottetown, PE C1A 8C1
Jeffrey Lantz
Nancy K. Orr

Prince County: Provincial Court
Law Courts Bldg., P.O. Box 2020, Summerside, PE C1N 4M1

Prince Edward Island: Judicial Officers
PE

Courts:
Kings County
Court House, Kent St., P.O. Box 89, Georgetown, PE C0A 1L0
Tel: 902-652-2924; *Fax:* 902-652-2701
georgetown@pei.sympatico.ca
www.georgetown.ca/courthouse.html
Deputy Registrar: Shirley Clory, 902-652-8990

Queens County
Law Courts, P.O. Box 2000, Charlottetown, PE C1A 7N8
Chief Sheriff: Frank Driscoll, 902-368-6055
Prothonotary: Charles P. Thompson
Court Services Manager: Tanya Tynski, 902-368-6005

Prince County
Court House, P.O. Box 2020, Summerside, PE C1N 4M1
Sheriff: Ron Dowling, 902-888-8191

Québec

Cour Supérieure du Québec
Québec Superior Court
300, boul Jean-Lesage, Québec, QC G1K 8K6
Tél: 418-649-3400; *Téléc:* 418-528-0932
www.tribunaux.qc.ca/c-superieure/index-cs.html
Affaires civiles et commerciales dont l'enjeu est de 70 000$ ou plus; litiges en matières administratives et familiale, faillite, procès devant jury en matière pénale, et appels en matière de poursuites sommaires
Juge en chef: L'hon. François Rolland
Juge en chef associé: L'hon. Robert Pidgeon
Juge en chef adjoint: L'hon. André Wery

Abitibi—Rouyn-Noranda—Témiscamingue
QC
Robert Dufresne
Jocelyn Geoffroy
Laurent Guertin
Ivan St-Julien(Juge surnuméraire)
Jacques Viens(Juge surnuméraire)

Alma
QC
Gratien Duchesne

Arthabaska
QC
Jules Allard(Juge surnuméraire)

Baie-Comeau—Mingan
QC
Paul Corriveau

Bonaventure
QC
Jean-Roch Landry

Chicoutimi
QC
Jacques Babin
Roger Banford(Juge surnuméraire)
Martin Dallaire
Carl Lachance
Jean-Claude Larouche(Juge surnuméraire)

Granby
Paul-Marcel Bellavance
Suzanne Mireault

Hull—Pontiac—Labelle
QC
Martin Bédard
Pierre Dallaire
Dominique Goulet
Pierre Isabelle
Louis-Philippe Landry(Juge surnuméraire)
Jean-Pierre Plouffe(Juge surnuméraire)
Suzanne Tessier

Laval
QC
Michel Déziel
Jacques R. Fournier
Pierre Journet(Juges surnuméraire)

Longueuil
QC
Jean-Jude Chabot
Carole Julien
Gilles Mercure
Réjean F. Paul(Juge surnuméraire)

Montréal
QC
Christiane Alary
Louisa Arcand
Claude Auclair
Roger E. Baker(Juge surnuméraire)
Guylène Beaugé
Pierre Béliveau
Nicole Bénard(Juge surnuméraire)
Marc-André Blanchard
Jean-Guy Boilard(Juge surnuméraire)
Sylviane W. Borenstein(Juge surnuméraire)
Sophie Bourque
James L. Brunton
Jean-François Buffoni
Pepita G. Capriolo
Michel A. Caron
Kirkland Casgrain
Robert Castiglio
Martin Castonguay
Claude Champagne
Paul G. Chaput(Juge surnuméraire)
France Charbonneau
Jean-Pierre Chrétien
Carol Cohen
Chantal Corriveau
Guy Cournoyer
Suzanne Courteau
Marie-France Courville
Louis Crête(Juge surnuméraire)
Louis-Paul Cullen
Claude Dallaire
Marc David
Wilbrod Claude Décarie
Jean-François de Grandpré
Michel Delorme
André Denis(Juge surnuméraire)
Sylvie Devito
Marc De Wever
Kevin Downs(Juge surnuméraire)
Gérard Dugré
Benoît Emery
Lucie Fournier
William Fraiberg
Pierre-C. Gagnon
Clément Gascon
Marie Gaudreau
Jacques Gauthier
Nicole M. Gibeau
Danielle Grenier(Juge surnuméraire)
Jean Guibault(Juge surnuméraire)
Carole Hallée
Gilles Hébert(Juge surnuméraire)
Pierre Jasmin(Juge surnuméraire)
Marie-Christine Laberge
Louis Lacoursière
Jean-Yves Lalonde
Julien Lanctôt
Hélène Langlois
Claude Larouche(Juge surnuméraire)
Hélène Le Bel(Juge surnuméraire)
Luc Lefebvre
Louise Lemelin
Johanne Mainville(Juge surnuméraire)
Catherine Mandeville
Diane Marcelin(Juge surnuméraire)
Geneviève Marcotte
J. Fraser Martin(Juge surnuméraire)
Israel Mass(Juge surnuméraire)
Chantal Masse
Lise Matteau
Paul Mayer
Danièle Mayrand
Michèle Monast
Richard Mongeau
Robert Mongeon
Richard Nadeau
Francine Nantel
Pierre Nollet
Daniel W. Payette
Mark G. Peacock
Micheline Perrault
Eva Petras
Claudette Picard
Sophie Picard
Ginette Piché(Juge surnuméraire)
Yves Poirier
Hélène Poulin
André Prévost
Steve J. Reimnitz
Danielle Richer
Brian J. Riordan
Jeannine M. Rousseau(Juge surnuméraire)
André Roy
Claudine Roy
Manon Savard
Jean-Pierre Sénécal
Joel Avery Silcoff
Marie St-Pierre
Pierre Tessier(Juge surnuméraire)
Daniel H. Tingley(Juge surnuméraire)
Anne-Marie Trahan
Clément Trudel(Juge surnuméraire)
Danielle Turcotte
Martin Vauclair
Jocelyn Verrier
André Vincent
Richard Wagner
Dionysia Zerbisias(Juge surnuméraire)
Jerry Zigman(Juge surnuméraire)

Rimouski
QC
Gilles Blanchet
Claude-Henri Gendreau

Sherbrooke
QC
Pierre Boily(Juge surnuméraire)
Martin Bureau
Léo Daigle
Gaétan Dumas
Line Samoisette
Yves Tardif
François Tôth

St-Maurice
QC
Raymond W. Pronovost

Trois-Rivières
850, rue Hart, Trois-Rivières, QC G9A 1T9
Tél: 819-372-4153;
www.justice.gouv.qc.ca; www.tribunaux.qc.ca/c-superieure
Alain Bolduc
Ivan Godin
Guy Lebrun(Juge surnuméraire)
Robert Legris(Juge surnuméraire)
Michel Richard
Marc St-Pierre

Cour du Québec
Court of Québec
300, boul Jean-Lesage, Québec, QC G1K 8K6
Tél: 418-649-3400; *Téléc:* 418-528-0932
www.tribunaux.qc.ca/c-quebec/

Composée d'au plus 290 juges dont la juge en chef, le juge en chef associé, 4 juges en chef adjoints, et 18 juges coordonnateurs et coordonnateurs adjoints; matières civile, criminelle et pénale; matière de jeunesse; matière administrative ou en appel dans les cas prévus par la loi; cour d'archives.

Juge en chef: L'honorable Élizabeth Corte
Juge en chef associé: L'honorable Mario Tremblay
Juge en chef adjointe: Chambre criminelle et pénale, L'honorable Danielle Côté
Juge en chef adjoint: Chambre de la jeunesse, L'honorable Claude C. Boulanger
Juge en chef adjoint: Cours municipales, L'honorable André Perreault
Juge en chef adjoint: Chambre civile, L'honorable Pierre E. Audet
Daniel Bédard(Juge coordonnateur)
Jean-Paul Decoste(Juge coordonnateur)
Alain Désy(Juge coordonnateur)
Micheline Laliberté(Juge coordonnatrice)
Lynne Landry(Juge coordonnatrice)
Denis Saulnier(Juge coordonnateur)
Charles G. Grenier(Juge coordonnateur)
Jean-Pierre Archambault(Juge coordonnateur adjoint)
Pierre E. Labelle(Juge coordonnateur adjoint)
Marc Bisson(Juge coordonnateur adjoint)
Pierre E. Labelle(Juge coordonnateur adjoint)
Chantale Pelletier(Juge coordonnatrice adjointe)
Lucie Rondeau(Juge coordonnatrice adjointe)
Ann-Marie Jones(Juge coordonnatrice adjointe)
Anne Bélanger(Directrice déléguée à l'administration)
Juges (Les honorables):
Michel Auger
Andrée Bergeron
Lina Bond
Hélène Bouillon
Christian Boulet
Peter Bradley
André-J. Brochet
Gilles Charest
Pierre Coderre
René de la Sablonnière
Louis Dionne
Colette Duford
Jean-Pierre Dumais
Pierre A. Gagnon
Paule Gaumond
Marie-Claude Gilbert
François Godbout
Line Gosselin
Anne Laberge
Judith Landry
Dominique Langis
Daniel Lavoie
Jean-Louis Lemay
Bernard Lemieux
Alain Morand
André Plante
Pierre-L. Rousseau
Carol St-Cyr
Claude Tremblay
Jacques Tremblay
Alain Turgeon
Suzanne Villeneuve
Réna Émond(Juge de paix magistrat)
Sylvie Marcotte(Juge de paix magistrat)
Nicole Martin(Juge de paix magistrat)

Abitibi-Témiscamingue - Amos
Claude P. Bigué
Lucille Chabot
Jean-Pierre Gervais

Abitibi-Témiscamingue - Rouyn-Noranda
Marc E. Grimard
Richard Laflamme
Nancy McKenna
Marie-Claude Bélanger(Juge de paix magistrat)

Abitibi-Témiscamingue - Val d'Or
Daniel Bédard(Juge coordonnateur)
Denyse Leduc
Renée Lemoine

Est du Québec - Baie-Comeau
François Boisjoli
Michel Dionne

Est du Québec - Matane
VACANTE

Est du Québec - New-Carlisle
Jean Bécu
Robert Lévesque
Luc Marchildon(Juge de paix magistrat)

Est du Québec - Percé
Embert Whittom

Est du Québec - Rimouski
Richard Côté
Jean-Paul Decoste(Juge coordonnateur)
James Rondeau
Lucie Morissette(Juge de paix magistrat)

Est du Québec - Rivière-du-Loup
Martin Gagnon
Luce Kennedy
Guy Ringuet
Julie Dionne(Juge de paix magistrat)

Est du Québec - Sept-Iles
Nathalie Aubry
Gabriel de Pokomandy(Coordonnateur)
Michel Parent
Louise Gallant(Juge de paix magistrat)

Estrie - Drummondville
Gilles Lafrenière
Marie-Josée Ménard

Estrie - Granby
Pierre Bachand
Serge Champoux
Johanne Denis
François Marchand
Monique Perron(Juge de paix magistrat)

Estrie - Sherbrooke
Michel Beauchemin
Conrad Chapdelaine
Danielle Côté
Alain Désy
Michel DuBois
Paul Dunnigan
Michel Durand
Hélène Fabi
Lise Gagnon
Patrick Théroux(Juge coordonnateur)
Sylvie Desmeules(Juge de paix magistrat)

Laval—Lanaudière—Laurentides - Joliette
Normand Bonin
François Landry
Richard Landry
Denis Le Reste
Maurice Parent
Jean Roy
Marc Vanasse
Danielle Michaud(Juge de paix magistrat)

Laval—Lanaudière—Laurentides - Laval
Jean-Pierre Archambault
Lise Gaboury
Françoise Garneau-Fournier
Dominique Larochelle
Marie-Suzanne Lauzon
Julie Messier
Micheline Sasseville
Gaby Dumas(Juge de paix magistrat)

Laval—Lanaudière—Laurentides - Saint-Jérôme
Pierre E. Audet(Juge coordonnateur adjoint)
François Beaudoin
Jean R. Beaulieu
Valmont Beaulieu
Omer Boudreau
Paul Chevalier(Juge coordonnateur)
Antoine Cloutier
Monique Fradette
Jean-Claude Gagnon
Diane Girard
Normand Lafond
Marie Lapointe
Jean La Rue
Ginette Maillet
Georges Massol
Claude Melançon
Carol Richer
Jean Sirois
Michèle Toupin
Nathalie DuPerron Roy(Juge de paix magistrat)
Jean-Georges Laliberté(Juge de paix magistrat)

Mauricie—Bois-Francs - Shawinigan
Richard Poudrier

Mauricie—Bois-Francs - Trois-Rivières
Yvan Cousineau
Jacques Lacoursière
Guy Lambert
Nicole Mallette
Daniel Perreault
Jacques Rioux
Dominique Slater
Guylaine Tremblay
Alain Trudel
Jacques Trudel
Pierre Verrette(Juge de paix magistrat)

Mauricie—Bois-Francs - Victoriaville
Pierre Labbé(Juge coordonnateur)
Gaétan Ratté(Juge de paix magistrat)

Montérégie - Longueuil
Mireille Allaire
Pierre Bélisle
Marc Bisson(Juge coordonnateur adjoint)
Virgile Buffoni
Mario Gervais
Jean Gravel
Anne-Marie Jacques
Micheline Laliberté(Juge coordonnatrice)
Claude Laporte
Louise Leduc
Richard Marleau
Nancy Moreau
Denys Noël
Ellen Paré
Robert Proulx
Claude Provost
Jean-Pierre Saintonge
Chantal Sirois
Marie-Josée Hénault(Juge de paix magistrat)
Marc Renaud(Juge de paix magistrat)

Montérégie - Saint-Hyacinthe
Guy Fortier
Yves Morier
Viviane Primeau
Robert Lanctôt(Juge de paix magistrat)

Montérégie - Saint-Jean-sur-Richelieu
Michel Bédard
Éric Simard

Montérégie - Salaberry-de-Valleyfield
Linda Despots
Marie-Chantal Doucet
Gilbert Lanthier
Michel Mercier
Claude Montpetit
Odette Perron
Marie-Andrée Villeneuve
Patricia Compagnone(Juge de paix magistrat)

Montérégie - Sorel-Tracy
VACANTE

Montréal
Juges (Les honorables):
Normand Amyot(Juge coordonnateur adjoint)
Denis Asselin
Armando Aznar
Normand Bastien
Lucille Beauchemin
Michel Bellehumeur
Serge Boisvert
Louise Bourdeau
François Bousquet
Jean-Pierre Boyer
Jean-Paul Braun
Alain Breault
Carole Brosseau
Gilles Cadieux
David L. Cameron
Brigitte Charron
Louise Comeau
Suzanne Coupal
Sylvain Coutlée
Antonio De Michele
Taya Di Pietro
Daniel Dortélus
Sylvie Durand
Jean-B. Falardeau
Gilles Garneau
Lucie Godin
Brigitte Gouin
Louis Grégoire
Yves Hamel
Suzanne Handman
Patrick Healy
Martin Hébert
Patrice Hurtubise
Michel Jasmin
Ann-Marie Jones
Jean-F. Keable
Pierre E. Labelle
Céline Lacerte-Lamontagne
Gilson Lachance
Sylvie Lachapelle
Claude Lamoureux
Gilles Lareau
Denis Lavergne
Daniel Lavery
Marie Michelle Lavigne
Claude Leblond
Guy Lecompte
Michèle Lefebvre
Louis A. Legault
Gérald Locas
Robert Marchi
Eliana Marengo
Salvatore Mascia
Rolande Matte
Claude Millette
Hélène V. Morin
Jacques A. Nadeau
Gilles L. Ouellet
Manon Ouimet
Jacques Paquet
Claude Parent(Juge coordonnateur adjoint (criminelle/pénale))
Michèle Pauzé(Présidente)
Michel A. Pinsonnault(Président)
Louise Provost(Présidente)
Diane Quenneville
André Renaud
Isabelle Rheault
Henri Richard
Robert Sansfaçon
Denis Saulnier(Juge coordonnateur adjoint (jeunesse))
Mark Shamie
Christian M. Tremblay
Suzanne Vadboncoeur
Ruth Veillet(Juge coordonnatrice)
Julie Veilleux
Louise Villemure
Lori Renée Weitzman
Juanita Westmoreland-Traoré
Dominique Wilhelmy
Gaétan Zonato

Outaouais - Gatineau
Gatien Fournier
Nicole Gibeault
Jean-François Gosselin
Lynne Landry(Juge coordonnatrice)
Réal R. Lapointe
Serge Laurin
Rosemarie Millar
Michel Séguin
Louise Turpin
Christine Auger(Juge de paix magistrat)
Georges Benoît(Juge de paix magistrat)

Québec—Chaudière-Appalaches - Montmagny
Jogues Lavoie

Québec—Chaudière-Appalaches - Saint-Joseph-de-Beauce
Hubert Couture
Yannick Couture(Juge de paix magistrat)

Saguenay—Lac-Saint-Jean - Alma
Maurice Abud(Juge coordonnateur)

Saguenay—Lac-Saint-Jean - Saguenay (Chicoutimi)
Jean-Paul Aubin
Paul Casgrain
Richard P. Daoust
Pierre Lortie
Micheline Paradis
Johanne Roy
Pierre Simard
Doris Thibault
Réjean Bédard(Juge de paix magistrat)

Saguenay—Lac-Saint-Jean - Roberval
Rosaire Larouche
Michel Boissonneault(Juge de paix magistrat)

Québec: Les Palais de justice et Points de service de justice
Courts & Judicial Service Centres

QC Alma
725, rue Harvey ouest, Alma, QC G8B 1P5
Tél: 418-668-3334; *Téléc:* 418-662-3697

Amos
891, rue 3e ouest, Amos, QC J9T 2T4
Tél: 819-444-5063; *Téléc:* 819-444-5204

Baie Comeau
71, av Mance, Baie-Comeau, QC G4Z 1N2
Tél: 418-296-5534; *Téléc:* 418-294-8717
Ligne sans frais: 866-854-4075 Campbell's Bay
30, rue John, Campbell's Bay, QC J0X 1K0
Tél: 819-648-5222; *Téléc:* 819-648-5931

Chicoutimi

227, rue Racine est, 1er étage, Chicoutimi, QC G7H 7B4
Tél: 418-696-9926; *Téléc:* 418-698-3558
Cowansville
920, rue Principale, Cowansville, QC J2K 0E3
Tél: 450-263-3520; *Téléc:* 450-266-1415
Drummondville
1680, boul St-Joseph, Drummondville, QC J2C 2G3
Tél: 819-478-2513; *Téléc:* 819-475-8459
Granby
Édifice Roger-Paré, #1.32, 77, rue Principale, Granby, QC J2G 9B3
Tél: 450-776-7110; *Téléc:* 450-776-4080
Hâvre-Aubert
#102, 405, ch d'En-Haut, Hâvre-Aubert, QC G4T 9A7
Tél: 418-937-2201; *Téléc:* 418-937-9038
Hull
17, rue Laurier, Gatineau, QC J8X 4C1
Tél: 819-776-8100; *Téléc:* 819-772-3347
Joliette
200, rue Saint-Marc, Joliette, QC J6E 8C2
Tél: 450-753-4807; *Téléc:* 450-752-1733
Lac-Mégantic
#316, 5527, rue Frontenac, Lac-Mégantic, QC G6B 1H6
Tél: 819-583-1268; *Téléc:* 819-583-0703
La Malbaie
30, ch de la Vallée, La Malbaie, QC G5A 1A3
Tél: 418-665-3991; *Téléc:* 418-665-1125
La Tuque
290, rue Saint-Joseph, P.O. Box 6, La Tuque, QC G9X 3Z8
Tél: 819-523-9533; *Téléc:* 819-523-3603
Laval
2800, boul Saint-Martin ouest, Laval, QC H7T 2S9
Tél: 450-686-5015; *Téléc:* 450-686-5005
Longueuil
1111, boul Jacques-Cartier est, Longueuil, QC J4M 2J6
Tél: 450-646-4010; *Téléc:* 450-928-7982
Maniwaki
266, rue Notre-Dame, 1er étage, Maniwaki, QC J9E 2J8
Tél: 819-449-3222; *Téléc:* 819-449-6085
Mont-Laurier
645, rue de la Madone, Mont-Laurier, QC J9L 1T1
Tél: 819-623-9666; *Téléc:* 819-623-6859
Montmagny
25, rue du Palais de Justice, Montmagny, QC G5V 1P6
Tél: 418-248-0909; *Téléc:* 418-248-2437
Montréal
1, rue Notre-Dame est, Montréal, QC H2Y 1B6
Tél: 514-393-2721; *Téléc:* 514-873-4760
New Carlisle
87, rue Gérard-D.-Lévesque, New Carlisle, QC G0C 1Z0
Tél: 418-752-3376; *Téléc:* 418-752-6979
Percé
124, rte 132, P.O. Box 188, Percé, QC G0C 2L0
Tél: 418-782-2055; *Téléc:* 418-782-2906
Québec
300, boul Jean-Lesage, Québec, QC G1K 8K6
Tél: 418-649-3400; *Téléc:* 418-528-0932
Rimouski
183, av de la Cathédrale, Rimouski, QC G5L 5J1
Tél: 418-727-3852; *Téléc:* 418-727-3635
Rivière-du-Loup
33, rue de la Cour, Rivière-du-Loup, QC G5R 1J1
Tél: 418-862-3579; *Téléc:* 418-867-8794
Ligne sans frais: 800-463-8009 Roberval
750, boul St-Joseph, Roberval, QC G8H 2L5
Tél: 418-275-3666; *Téléc:* 418-275-6169
Rouyn-Noranda
2, av du Palais, Rouyn-Noranda, QC J9X 2N9
Tél: 819-763-3058; *Téléc:* 819-763-3389
Saint-Hyacinthe
1550, rue Dessaulles, Saint-Hyacinthe, QC J2S 2S8
Tél: 450-778-6559; *Téléc:* 450-778-6557
Saint-Jean-sur-Richelieu
109, rue Saint-Charles, Saint-Jean-sur-Richelieu, QC J3B 2C2
Tél: 450-347-1392; *Téléc:* 450-346-8437
Saint-Jérôme
25, rue de Martigny ouest, Saint-Jérôme, QC J7Y 4Z1
Tél: 514-431-4406; *Téléc:* 514-569-3143
Saint-Joseph-de-Beauce
795, av du Palais, Saint-Joseph-de-Beauce, QC G0S 2V0
Tél: 418-397-7187; *Téléc:* 418-397-7968
Salaberry-de-Valleyfield
180, rue Salaberry ouest, Salaberry-de-Valleyfield, QC J6T 2J2
Tél: 450-370-4006; *Téléc:* 450-370-3022
Sept-Iles
425, boul Laure, Sept-Iles, QC G4R 1X6
Tél: 418-962-3044; *Téléc:* 418-964-8714
Ligne sans frais: 866-405-7951 Shawinigan
212, 6e rue, Shawinigan, QC G9N 8B6
Tél: 819-536-2571; *Téléc:* 819-536-2992
Sherbrooke
375, rue King ouest, Sherbrooke, QC J1H 6B9
Tél: 819-822-6910; *Téléc:* 819-820-3134
Sorel-Tracy
46, rue Charlotte, Sorel-Tracy, QC J3P 6N5
Tél: 450-742-2786; *Téléc:* 450-746-7394
Thetford Mines
#1.23, 693, rue St-Alphonse ouest, Thetford Mines, QC G6G 3X3
Tél: 418-338-2118; *Téléc:* 418-335-7756
Trois-Rivières
850, rue Hart, Trois-Rivières, QC G9A 1T9
;
Other information: Fax civile: 819/371-6096; Fax criminel: 819/371-6111 Victoriaville
800, boul Bois-Francs sud, Victoriaville, QC G6P 5W5
Tél: 819-357-2054; *Téléc:* 819-357-5517
Ville-Marie
8, rue Saint-Gabriel nord, Ville-Marie, QC J9V 1Z9
Tél: 819-629-6473; *Téléc:* 819-622-6367

Points de service:

Amqui
29, boul Saint-Benoît ouest, Amqui, QC G5J 2E4
Tél: 418-629-4488; *Téléc:* 418-629-6450

Carleton
17, rue Lacroix, Carleton, QC G0C 1J0
Tél: 418-364-3442; *Téléc:* 418-364-7036

Dolbeau-Mistassini
1420, boul Walberg, 1er étage, Dolbeau-Mistassini, QC G8L 1H4
Tel: 418-276-0683; *Fax:* 418-276-6110

Forestville
Édifice Renato, 24, rte 138 ouest, P.O. Box 400, Forestville, QC G0T 1E0
Tél: 418-587-4471; *Téléc:* 418-587-6639
Ligne sans frais: 866-854-4075

Gaspé
11, rue de la Cathédrale, Gaspé, QC G4X 2V9
Tél: 418-368-5756; *Téléc:* 416-360-8030

Jonquière
Édifice Marguerite-Belley, 3950, boul Harvey, RC, Jonquière, QC G7X 8L6
Tel: 418-695-7991; *Fax:* 418-698-3558

Lachute
#216, 505, rue Béthany, Lachute, QC J8H 4A6
Tél: 450-562-3711; *Téléc:* 450-569-7645

Magog
Hôtel de Ville, #127, 7, rue Principale est, Magog, QC J1X 1Y4
Tél: 819-843-7323; *Téléc:* 819-843-4533

Matane
382, av Saint-Jérôme, Matane, QC G4W 3B3
Tél: 418-562-2497; *Téléc:* 418-560-8746

Mont-Joli
40, rue de l'Hôtel-de-Ville, Mont-Joli, QC G5H 1W8
Tél: 418-775-8811; *Téléc:* 418-775-7517

Sainte-Agathe-des-Monts
85, rue Saint-Vincent, Sainte-Agathe-des-Monts, QC J8C 2A8
Tél: 819-326-6462; *Téléc:* 819-569-7645

Sainte-Anne-des-Monts
10-B, boul Sainte-Anne ouest, Sainte-Anne-des-Monts, QC G4V 1P3
Tél: 418-763-2791; *Téléc:* 418-763-3107

Cour d'Appel du Québec
Québec Court of Appeal

Édifice Ernest-Cormier, 100, rue Notre-Dame Est, Montréal, QC H2Y 4B6
Tél: 514-393-2022;
courdappelqc@justice.gouv.qc.ca
www.tribunaux.qc.ca/c-appel/index.html

Le plus haut tribunal du Québec; la cour est la gardienne de l'intégrité du droit civil de la province; en matière civile, la cour entend les appels des jugements finals de la Cour supérieure et de la Cour du Québec lorsque la valeur de l'objet du litige en appel est à 50 000$ ou plus; outrage, adoption, évaluation psychiatrique, garde en établissement, faillite et divorce.

Juge en chef: L'hon. Nicole Duval Hesler
Juges (Les honorables):
Marie-France Bich
Jean Bouchard
Jacques Chamberland(Juge surnuméraire)
Pierre J. Dalphond
François Doyon
Jacques Dufresne
Julie Dutil
André Forget(Juge surnuméraire)
Guy Gagnon
Jacques R. Fournier
Clément Gascon
Paul-Arthur Gendreau(Juge surnuméraire)
Lorne Giroux
Allan Ross Hilton
Nicholas Kasirer
Jacques A. Léger
Benoît Morin(Juge surnuméraire)
Yves-Marie Morissette
François Pelletier
Louis Rochette
André Rochon
Marie St-Pierre
France Thibault
Paul Vézina(Juge surnuméraire)
Richard Wagner

Montréal
Édifice Ernest-Cormier, #2.22, 100, rue Notre-Dame est, Montréal, QC H2Y 4B6
Tél: 514-393-2022; *Téléc:* 514-864-7270
Coordonnatrice juridique: Lysanne P. Legault

Québec
Palais de justice de Québec, #4.27, 300, boul Jean-Lesage, Québec, QC G1K 8K6
Tél: 418-649-3401; *Téléc:* 418-646-6961
Coordonnatrice juridique: Claire Roberge

Cours municipales du Québec
Québec Municipal Courts

Édifice Louis-Philippe-Pigeon, 1200, route de l'Église, 6e étage, Québec, QC G1V 4M1
Tél: 418-643-5140; *Ligne sans frais:* 866-536-5140
informations@justice.gouv.qc.ca
www.justice.gouv.qc.ca

Les cours municipales ont une compétence limitée en matière civile, notamment dans le domaine des réclamations de taxes; en matière pénale en ce qui concerne les infractions aux règlements municipaux et les infractions aux lois québécoises; et pour entendre et juger les infractions visées par la partie XXVII du Code criminel.

Juge responsable: Charles G. Grenier

Courts:

Lévis
5333, rue de la Symphonie, Charny, QC G6X 3B6
Tél: 418-832-4695;
www.ville.levis.qc.ca
Jacques Ouellet

Bedford
1, rue Principale, Bedford, QC J0J 1A0
Tél: 450-248-7742; *Téléc:* 450-248-3220
www.paquette.qc.ca
Alain Boisvert

Bellechasse MRC
100, Monseigneur Bilodeau, P.O. Box 130, St-Lazare-de-Bellechasse, QC G0R 3J0
Tél: 418-883-3347;
www.paquette.qc.ca
Claude Fortin

Beloeil
777, rue Laurier, Beloeil, QC J3G 4S9
Tél: 450-467-2835; *Téléc:* 450-464-5445
cour-mun@ville.beloeil.qc.ca
www.paquette.qc.ca
Luc Alarie

Mascouche
3034, Ste-Marie, Mascouche, QC J7K 1P1
Tél: 450-474-4133;
www.paquette.qc.ca
Claude Lemire

Blainville
Hôtel de ville, 1000, ch du Plan-Bouchard, Blainville, QC J7C 3S9
Tél: 450-434-5224; *Téléc:* 450-434-8285
www.ville.blainville.qc.ca, www.paquette.qc.ca
Guy Saulnier

Longueuil
100, Place Charles-Lemoyne, Longueuil, QC J4K 2T4
Tél: 450-463-7006; *Téléc:* 450-646-8897
www.longueuil.ca
Richard Alary
Guy Houle
Bruno Themens

Ste-Marie
270, av Marguerite Bourgeos, P.O. Box 1750, Sainte-Marie, QC G6E 3C7
Tél: 418-387-2301; *Téléc:* 418-387-2454
www.paquette.qc.ca
Paul Routhier

Boisbriand
940, boul de la Grande-Allée, Boisbriand, QC J7G 2J7
Tél: 450-435-1954; *Téléc:* 450-435-6398
service.cour.municipale@ville.boisbriand.qc.ca
www.paquette.qc.ca
André Hotte

L'Islet MRC
364, rue Verreault, Saint-Jean-Port-Joli, QC G0R 3G0
Tél: 418-598-3076; *Téléc:* 418-598-6880
www.paquette.qc.ca
Jacques Ouellet

Loretteville
305, rue Racine, Loretteville, QC G2B 1E7
Tél: 418-842-1921;
www.paquette.qc.ca
Louis-M. Vachon
Claude Fournier
Jean-Pierre Gignac
Paulin Cloutier

Louiseville
105, av St-Laurent ouest, Louiseville, QC J5V 1J6
Tél: 819-228-9437
Jocelyn Crête

Magog
7, rue Principale E., Magog, QC J1X 1Y4
Tél: 819-843-6501; *Téléc:* 819-843-3599
www.paquette.qc.ca
Pierre Geoffroy

St-Rédempteur
85, rue 19e, St-Rédempteur, QC G6K 1C3
Tél: 418-836-4400;
www.paquette.qc.ca; www.barreau.qc.ca
Commune St-Nicholas, St-Rédempteur, Bernières et St-Étienne de Lauzon.
Jacques Ouellet
Louis-Marie Vachon

Marieville
682, rue St-Charles, Marieville, QC J3M 1P9
Tél: 450-460-4444;
www.paquette.qc.ca
Louis-B. Grignon

Mirabel
14 026, boul du Curé-Labelle, Mirabel, QC J7J 1A1
Tél: 450-435-6408;
www.paquette.qc.ca
Michel Paquin

Mistassini
173, St-Michel, P.O. Box 219, Mistissini, QC G0W 2C0
Michel J. Lapointe
Jacquelin Légaré

St-Pierre
69, av 5e, Saint-Pierre, QC H8R 1P1
Tél: 514-364-5153;
www.paquette.qc.ca
Pierre G. Bouchard

Montmagny
134, rue St-Jean-Baptiste est, Montmagny, QC G5V 1K6
Tél: 418-248-3361;
www.paquette.qc.ca
Louis-Marie Vachon

Candiac
100, boul Montcalm N., Candiac, QC J5R 3L8
Tél: 450-444-6060; *Téléc:* 450-444-0789
www.paquette.qc.ca
Jean-Pierre Dépelteau

St-Raymond
375, rue St-Joseph, Saint-Raymond, QC G3L 1A1
Tél: 418-337-2202; *Téléc:* 418-337-2203
www.paquette.qc.ca
Jean-R. Côté

Chambly
1, Place de la Mairie, Chambly, QC J3L 4X1
Tél: 450-658-8788; *Téléc:* 450-658-4214
www.paquette.qc.ca
Gilles R. Pelletier

St-Rémi
105, Perras, Saint-Rémi, QC J0L 2L0
Tél: 450-454-3994; *Téléc:* 450-454-6898
www.paquette.qc.ca
Pascal Pillarella

Charlesbourg
160, rue 76e est, Charlesbourg, QC G1H 7H5
Tél: 418-641-6179; *Téléc:* 418-641-6594
Jean-Pierre Gignac

Charny
5333, rue de la Symphonie, Charny, QC G6X 3B6
Raymond Lavoie

Ste-Thérèse
6, rue de l'Église, P.O. Box 100, Sainte-Thérèse, QC J7E 4H7
Tél: 450-434-1440; *Téléc:* 450-434-1499
www.paquette.qc.ca
Guy Saulnier

Châteauguay
#101, 265, boul d'Anjou, Châteauguay, QC J6J 5J9
Tél: 450-698-3245; *Téléc:* 450-698-3259
courmun@ville.chateauguay.qc.ca
www.ville.chateauguay.qc.ca
La cour a le mandat de veiller à l'application des lois et des règlements municipaux, provinciaux et fédéraux pour Châteauguay, Mercier, Léry et Beauharnois.
Paul Lemieux

Chibougamau
650, 3e rue, Chibougamau, QC G8P 1P1
Tél: 418-748-3132; *Téléc:* 418-748-6562
www.paquette.qc.ca
Frédérique Lalancette

St-Tite
540, rue Notre-Dame, Saint-Tite, QC G0X 3H0
Tél: 418-365-5143
Claude Trudel

Saguenay
201, rue Racine est, P.O. Box 129, Chicoutimi, QC G7H 5B8
Tél: 418-698-3161;
www.paquette.qc.ca

Salaberry-de-Valleyfield
61, Sainte-Cécile, Salaberry-de-Valleyfield, QC J6T 1L8
Tél: 450-370-4305; *Téléc:* 450-370-4868
www.paquette.qc.ca
Paul Lemieux

Montréal-Est
11 370, rue Notre-Dame est, Montréal, QC H1B 2W6
Tél: 514-645-7431;
www.paquette.qc.ca
Florent Bisson
Jean Hébert

Montréal-Nord
11 211 av. Hébert, Montréal-Nord, QC H1H 3X5
Tél: 514-328-4079;
www.paquette.qc.ca
Jacques Lamontagne
Robert Diamond

Montréal-Ouest
50, av Westminster S., Montréal, QC H4X 1Y7
Tél: 514-481-8125
Frank Schlesinger

Mont-Royal
20, av Roosevelt, Mount-Royal, QC H3R 1Z4
Tél: 514-734-2907
Pierre-G. Bouchard
Jacques Laurier

Mont-Saint-Hilaire
Hôtel de Ville, 100, rue du Centre-Civique, Mont-Saint-Hilaire, QC J3H 3M8
Tél: 450-467-2854;
courmunicipale@villemsh.ca
www.ville.mont-saint-hilaire.qc.ca

Nicolet
180, Mgr. Panet, Nicolet, QC J3T 1S6
Tél: 819-293-6901; *Téléc:* 819-293-6767
www.paquette.qc.ca
Jacques Desaulniers

Outremont
1433. ave. Van Horne, Outremont, QC H2V 1K9
Tél: 514-495-6250;
www.paquette.qc.ca
Pierre-J. Raîche
Georges-E. Laurin

Pierrefonds
13 665, boul Pierrefonds, Pierrefonds, QC H9H 2Z4
Tél: 514-624-1124;
www.paquette.qc.ca
Philippe Clément
Pierre Mondor

Pincourt
919, ch Duhamel, Pincourt, QC J7V 4G8
Robert La Haye

Plessisville
1700, rue St-Calixte, Plessisville, QC G6L 1R3
Tél: 819-362-3284;
www.paquette.qc.ca
Jules Bellavance

Pointe-Claire
401, boul. Saint-Jean, Pointe-Claire, QC H9R 3J2
Tél: 514-630-1205;
www.paquette.qc.ca
Pierre Mondor
Philippe Clément

Princeville
50, St-Jacques ouest, Princeville, QC G6L 4Y5
Tél: 819-364-5179; *Téléc:* 819-364-5198
www.paquette.qc.ca
Claude Caron

Repentigny
435, boul d'Iberville, Repentigny, QC J6A 2B6
Tél: 450-654-2358;
www.paquette.qc.ca
Gilles Thouin

Rimouski
205, av de la Cathédrale, P.O. Box 710, Rimouski, QC G5L 7C7
Tél: 418-724-3181; *Téléc:* 418-724-9795
greffe@ville.rimouski.qc.ca
www.paquette.qc.ca
Jean Blouin

Roberval
851, boul Saint-Joseph, Roberval, QC G8H 2L6
Tél: 418-275-0202; *Téléc:* 418-275-5031
www.paquette.qc.ca
Jacquelin Légaré

Rosemère
100, rue Charbonneau, Rosemère, QC J7A 3W1
Tél: 450-621-3500; *Téléc:* 450-472-3607
www.paquette.qc.ca
Robert Diamond

Roxboro
13 Centre Commercial, Roxboro, QC H8Y 2N9
Tél: 514-684-0555;
www.paquette.qc.ca
Ronald J. Montcalm
Philippe Clément

Ste-Adèle
1381, boul Sainte-Adele, Sainte-Adèle, QC J8B 1A3
Tél: 450-229-2921; *Téléc:* 450-229-4179
www.paquette.qc.ca
Jacques Laverdure

Ste-Agathe-des-Monts
50, rue St-Joseph, Sainte-Agathe-des-Monts, QC J8C 1M9
Tél: 819-326-4595; *Téléc:* 819-326-6331
www.paquette.qc.ca
J.H. Denis Gagnon

Ste-Anne-de-Bellevue
109, Ste-Anne, P.O. Box 40, Sainte-Anne-de-Bellevue, QC H9X 1M2
Tél: 514-457-5500;
www.paquette.qc.ca
Pascal Pillarella
Jacques Ghanimé

St-Bruno-de-Montarville
1585, boul Montarville, St-Bruno-de-Montarville, QC J3V 3T8
Tél: 450-441-8303;
www.paquette.qc.ca
Guy Houle
Marc Gravel

St-Césaire
1111, St-Paul, Saint-Césaire, QC J0L 1T0
Tél: 450-469-3108; *Téléc:* 450-469-5275
www.paquette.qc.ca
Michel Brun

St-Constant
147, rue St-Pierre, P.O. Box 130, Saint-Constant, QC J5A 2G2
Tél: 450-638-2010; *Téléc:* 450-632-0788
www.paquette.qc.ca
Jacques Laurier

St-Eustache
168, Dorion, Saint-Eustache, QC J7R 2G2
Tél: 450-472-4440
Guy Saulnier

St-Félicien
1058, boul. Sacré-Coeur, P.O. Box 7000, Saint-Félicien, QC G8K 2R5
Tél: 418-679-0251; *Téléc:* 418-679-1449
www.paquette.qc.ca
Frédérique Lalancette

Sainte-Foy
1130, rte de l'Église, Sainte-Foy, QC G1V 4X6
Tél: 418-641-6179; *Téléc:* 418-641-6539
www.ville.quebec.qc.ca

St-Georges
11 700, boul. LaCroix, St-Georges, QC G5Y 1L3
Tél: 418-228-5555; *Téléc:* 418-226-2282
www.paquette.qc.ca
Gabriel Garneau

St-Hubert
4800, Leckie, Saint-Hubert, QC J3Z 1H4
Tél: 450-445-7862;
www.paquette.qc.ca
Jean Herbert
Claude Céré

Saint-Hyacinthe
700, de l'Hôtel-de-Ville, Saint-Hyacinthe, QC J2S 5B2
Tél: 450-778-8319; *Téléc:* 450-778-8628
cour-municipale@ville.st-hyacinthe.qc.ca
www.paquette.qc.ca
Gilles Charpentier

St-Jean-Chrysostome
959, rue de l'Hotel de Ville, St-Jean-Chrysostome-de-Lév, QC G6Z 2N8
Tél: 418-839-9417;
www.paquette.qc.ca
Claude Fortin
Jean-Pierre Gignac

Saint-Jean-sur-Richelieu
188, Jacques-Cartier N., P.O. Box 1025, Saint-Jean-sur-Richelieu, QC J3B 7B2
Tél: 450-357-2087; *Téléc:* 450-357-2750
cour.municipale@ville.saint-jean-sur-richelieu.qc.ca
www.paquette.qc.ca
Pierre-Armand Tremblay

St-Jérôme MRC
280, Labelle, Saint-Jérome, QC J7Z 5L1
Tél: 450-436-1511; *Téléc:* 450-436-4506
Jacques Laverdure

St-Lambert
55, Argyle, Saint-Lambert, QC J4P 2H3
Tél: 450-923-6555;
www.paquette.qc.ca
Marc Gravel
Guy Houle

Saint-Laurent
1405, de l'Église, Saint-Laurent, QC H4L 2H4
Tél: 514-855-6060;
www.paquette.qc.ca
Pierre G. Bouchard
Lison Asseraf

St-Léonard-de-Port-Maurice
8400, boul Lacordaire, St-Léonard, QC H1R 3B1
Tél: 514-328-8447;
www.paquette.qc.ca
Robert LaHaye
Richard Chassé

St-Luc
347, boul St-Luc, Saint-Luc, QC J2W 2A2
Tél: 450-359-2444;
www.paquette.qc.ca
Denis Boudrias
Pascal Pillarella

Acton Vale
1025, rue Boulay, P.O. Box 640, Acton Vale, QC J0H 1A0
Tél: 450-546-2704;
www.paquette.qc.ca
Louis-B. Grignon

Alma
140, rue St-Joseph S., Alma, QC G8B 3R1
Tél: 418-669-5020; *Téléc:* 418-669-5019
www.paquette.qc.ca
Jean-M. Morency

Asbestos
#201, 185, rue du Roi, Asbestos, QC J1T 1S4
Tél: 819-879-6971; *Téléc:* 819-879-4102
www.paquette.qc.ca
Pierre G. Geoffroy

Barkmère
RR#1, P.O. Box 11, Argenteuil, QC J0T 1A0

Coaticook
14, rue Adams, #14, Coaticook, QC J1A 1K3
Tél: 819-849-2721; *Téléc:* 819-849-4883
www.paquette.qc.ca
Pierre A. Cloutier

Cowansville
220, Place Municipale, Cowansville, QC J2K 1T4
Tél: 450-263-5434; *Téléc:* 450-263-4332
www.paquette.qc.ca
Pierre Raiche

Delson
50, Ste-Thérèse, Delson, QC J0L 1G0
Jacques Laurier

Deux-Montagnes
#101, 400, boul Deux-Montagnes, Deux-Montagnes, QC J7R 5C2
Tél: 450-473-8688; *Téléc:* 450-473-0094
www.paquette.qc.ca
Jacques Lamontagne

Dolbeau-Mistassini
1100, boul Walberg, Dolbeau-Mistassini, QC J7R 5C2
Tél: 450-473-8688;
www.paquette.qc.ca
Jacquelin Légaré

Donnacona
138, av Pleau, P.O. Box 609, Donnacona, QC G01 1T0
Tél: 418-285-3163; *Téléc:* 418-285-0020
www.paquette.qc.ca
Claude Fournier

Dorion
190, St-Charles, P.O. Box 70, Dorion, QC J7V 5V8
Manon Bourbonnais

Dorval
530, boul Bouchard, Dorval, QC H9S 1B2
Tél: 514-633-4146;
www.paquette.qc.ca
Georges É. Laurin
Jean-Pierre Dépelteau

Drummondville
415, rue Lindsay, P.O. Box 398, Drummondville, QC J2B 6W3
Tél: 819-478-6556; *Téléc:* 819-478-0920
courmunicipale@ville.drummondville.qc.ca
www.paquette.qc.ca
Michel Houle

Haut-St-François MRC
146, Angus Nord, East Angus, QC J0B 1R0
Tél: 819-832-2868; *Téléc:* 819-832-2868
Pierre-A. Cloutier

Farnham
477, de l'Hôtel-de-Ville, Farnham, QC J2N 2H3
Tél: 450-293-3178; *Téléc:* 450-260-1376
www.paquette.qc.ca
Claude Hamann

Gatineau
La Mairie- 280, boul. Maloney E., Gatineau, QC J8P 1C6
Tél: 819-243-2345; *Téléc:* 819-595-4289
www.paquette.qc.ca
François Gravel
Yves Daoust

Granby
125, Simonds S., Granby, QC J2J 1P7
Tél: 450-776-8340; *Téléc:* 450-776-8342
www.paquette.qc.ca
Pierre G. Geoffroy

Grand'Mère
333, av 5e, P.O. Box 350, Grand-Mère, QC G9T 5L1
Tél: 819-538-1614;
www.paquette.qc.ca
Jean-Marc Champagne
Jocelyn Crête

Greenfield Park
156, boul Churchill, Greenfield Park, QC J4V 2M3
Tél: 450-446-8108;
www.paquette.qc.ca
Jean-Guy Clément
Denis Boudrias

Hampstead
5569, ch. De la Reine-Marie, Hampstead, QC H3X 1W5
Tél: 514-369-8200;
www.paquette.qc.ca
Lison Asseraf
Pierre Mondor

Hudson
rue Principale, Hudson, QC J0P 1H0
Robert La Haye

Iberville
855, 1ère, Iberville, QC J2X 3C7
Tél: 450-357-2744;
www.paquette.qc.ca
Pierre-Armand Tremblay
Denis Boudrias

Ile-Perrot
110, boul Perrot, Ile-Perrot, QC J7V 3G1
Jacques Laverdure

Joliette
245, Papineau, Joliette, QC J6E 2K8
Tél: 450-753-8123;
www.paquette.qc.ca
Other information: Email: cour.municipale@ville.joliette.qc.ca
Louis Laporte

Jonquière
2201, rue de Montfort, P.O. Box 278, Jonquière, QC G7X 4P6
Tél: 418-546-2238;
www.paquette.qc.ca
Jean-Jacques Turcotte
Alain Côté

La-Baie
422, rue Victoria, La Baie, QC G7B 3M4
Tél: 418-697-5000;
www.paquette.qc.ca
Alain Côté
Jean-Jacques Turcotte

Lachine
1800, boul St-Joseph, Lachine, QC H8S 2N4
Tél: 514-634-3471;
www.paquette.qc.ca
Sophie Beauchemin
Manon Bourbonnais

Lachute
380, rue Principale, Lachute, QC J8H 1Y2
Tél: 450-562-3781; *Téléc:* 450-562-1431
www.paquette.qc.ca
Guy Saulnier

Lac Mégantic
#201, 5527, rue Frontenac, Lac-Mégantic, QC G6B 1H6
Tél: 819-583-2815; *Téléc:* 819-583-2841
cour.municipale@ville.lac-megantic.qc.ca
www.ville.lac-megantic.qc.ca; www.paquette.qc.ca
Gabriel Garneau

La Pocatière
412, 9e rue, P.O. Box 668, La Pocatière, QC G0R 1Z0
Tél: 418-856-3394; *Téléc:* 418-856-5465
www.paquette.qc.ca
Jacques Ouellet

La Prairie
170, boul. Taschereau, #400, La Prairie, QC J5R 5H6
Tél: 450-444-0540;
www.paquette.qc.ca
Claude Céré

Lasalle
55, av Dupras, Lasalle, QC H8R 4A8
Tél: 514-367-6270;
www.paquette.qc.ca
Denis Laberge

L'Assomption
399, rue Dorval, L'Assomption, QC J5W 1A1
Tél: 450-589-5671; *Téléc:* 450-589-4512
courmunicipale@ville.lassomption.qc.ca
www.ville.lassomption.qc.ca; www.paquette.qc.ca
Gilles Thouin

La Tuque
558, rue Commerciale, La Tuque, QC G9X 3A9
Tél: 819-523-2052; *Téléc:* 819-523-4536
www.paquette.qc.ca
Claude Trudel

Senneville
35, ch. Senneville, Senneville, QC H9X 1B8
Tél: 514-457-6020;
www.paquette.qc.ca
Pierre Mondor
Philippe Clément

Sept-Iles
546, av Dequen, Sept-Iles, QC G4R 2R4
Tél: 418-964-3249; *Téléc:* 418-964-3259
www.paquette.qc.ca
Guy Pettigrew

Shawinigan MRC
550, de l'Hôtel de Ville, P.O. Box 400, Shawinigan, QC G9N 6V3
Tél: 819-536-7216; *Téléc:* 819-536-2797
Claude Trudel

Shawinigan
1550, rue 118e, P.O. Box 400, Shawinigan, QC G9P 3V3
Tél: 819-536-7216;
www.paquette.qc.ca
Claude Trudel
Jocelyn Crête

Sherbrooke
191, rue Palais, P.O. Box 1614, Sherbrooke, QC J1H 5M4
Tél: 819-821-5600; *Téléc:* 819-821-5599
www.paquette.qc.ca
Roland Lamoureux

Sillery
1445, av Maguire, Sillery, QC G1T 2W9
Tél: 418-684-2134;
www.paquette.qc.ca
René Paquet
Jean-Pierre Gignac

Sorel-Tracy
3025, boul de Tracy, Sorel-Tracy, QC J3R 1C2
Tél: 450-742-7775; *Téléc:* 450-742-2420
www.agcmq.qc.ca
Jacques Guertin

Terrebonne
Édifice Louis Lepage, 754, rue Saint-Pierre, Terrebonne, QC J6W 1E4
Tél: 450-471-4192;
www.paquette.qc.ca
Michel Paquin

Thetford-Mines
144, rue Notre-Dame ouest, P.O. Box 489, Thetford Mines, QC G6G 5T3
Tél: 418-335-2981; *Téléc:* 418-335-7089
www.paquette.qc.ca
Gilles Ouellet

Trois-Rivières
1401, Royale, 2 étage, P.O. Box 969, Trois-Rivières, QC G9A 5K2
Tél: 819-372-4628; *Téléc:* 819-379-7551
www.paquette.qc.ca
Jocelyn Crête

Trois-Rivières-Ouest
500, Côte du Richelieu, Trois-Rivières, QC G9A 2Z1
Tél: 819-375-7731;
www.paquette.qc.ca
Jocelyn Crête
Claude Trudel

Val-Bélair
1105, av de l'Église N., Val-Bélair, QC G3K 1X5
Tél: 418-842-7184;
www.paquette.qc.ca
Jean-Pierre Gignac
Claude Fortin

Val-d'Or
855, 2e Ave., P.O. Box 400, Val-d'Or, QC J9P 4P4
Tél: 819-824-9613; *Téléc:* 819-825-6650
courmunicipale@ville.valdor.
www.paquette.qc.ca
Jacques Barbès

Verdun
#104, 4555, av Verdun, Verdun, QC H4G 1M4
Tél: 514-765-7060;
www.paquette.qc.ca
Jacques Ghanimé
Pascal Pillarella

Victoriaville
1, Notre-Dame O., P.O. Box 370, Victoriaville, QC G6P 6T2
Tél: 819-758-4338; *Téléc:* 819-758-9292
www.paquette.qc.ca
Michel Houle

Waterloo
417, rue de la Cour, #210, P.O. Box 430, Waterloo, QC J0E 2N0
Tél: 450-539-2422; *Téléc:* 450-539-3257
www.paquette.qc.ca
Michel Brun

Westmount
21, rue Stanton, Westmount, QC H3Y 3B1
Tél: 514-989-5260;
www.paquette.qc.ca
Keith A. Ham
Ronald Montcalm

Matawinie MRC
3184, 1e av, P.O. Box 1239, Rawdon, QC J0K 1S0
Tél: 450-834-5441;
cour@mrcmatawinie.qc.ca
www.paquette.qc.ca
Michel Lalande

Montcalm
1530, rue Albert, P.O. Box 308, Sainte-Julienne, QC J0K 2T0
Tél: 450-831-2182;
www.paquette.qc.ca
Marguerite M. Brochu

Baie-Comeau
1000, rue de Mingan, Baie-Comeau, QC G5C 3C3
Tel: 418-589-1518; *Fax:* 418-589-1556
www.paquette.qc.ca
Micheline Fournier

D'Autray MRC
118, Notre-Dame, Le Gardeur, QC J5Z 3C3
; *Téléc:* 450-585-7035
Marguerite M. Brochu

Haut-Saint Laurent MRC
23, Laurier, 6e étage, Hull, QC J8X 4C8
Tel: 819-595-7272;
www.paquette.qc.ca
Vacant

Val-St-François MRC
#101, 3, Greenlay S., Sainte-Grégoire-de-Greenlay, QC J1S 2J1
Tel: 819-845-2016; *Fax:* 819-845-3209
www.paquette.qc.ca
Pierre G. Geoffroy

Vaudreuil-Soulanges MRC
190, Saint-Charles, Vaudreuil-Dorion, QC J7V 2L3
Tel: 450-455-9480; *Fax:* 450-373-7967
www.paquette.qc.ca
Manon Bourbonnais

Colline-de-L'Outaouais
216, ch Haute-Chelsea, Chelsea, QC J9B 1J4
Tel: 819-827-0516; *Fax:* 819-827-5712
lst-pierre@mrcdescollines.co
www.paquette.qc.ca
Slobodan Delev

Lotbinière MRC
#4, 372, rue St-Joseph, P.O. Box 40, Laurier-Station, QC G0S 1N0
Tél: 418-728-2787; *Téléc:* 418-728-2501
www.paquette.qc.ca
Paulin Cloutier

Côte-de-Beaupré MRC
3, rue de la Seigneurie, Château-Richer, QC G0A 1N0
Tél: 418-824-3444; *Téléc:* 418-824-3917
M. Jacques Ouellet

Montréal
#101, 775, rue Gosford, Montréal, QC H2Y 3B9
Tél: 514-872-2534; *Téléc:* 514-872-8271
cour-municipale@ville.montreal.qc.ca
www.ville.montreal.qc.ca; www.paquette.qc.ca
Morton S. Minc(Juge-président)
Nathalie Haccoun
Richard Starck

Québec
285, rue de la Maréchausée, Québec, QC G1K 8W5
Tél: 418-691-6340; *Téléc:* 418-641-6512
greffecourmunicipale@ville.quebec.qc.ca
www.ville.quebec.qc.ca
Paulin Cloutier(Juge-président)

Laval
55, boul des Laurentides, Laval, QC H7G 2T1
Tél: 450-662-4466; *Téléc:* 450-662-8501
www.paquette.qc.ca
Bernard Caron
Jean H. Charbonneau
Yves Fournier

Saskatchewan

Saskatchewan: Court of Appeal
Court House, 2425 Victoria Ave., Regina, SK S4P 3W6
Tel: 306-787-5382;
CARegistrar@sasklawcourts.ca
www.sasklawcourts.ca

The Court of Appeal has appellate jurisdiction with respect to any judgement, order or decree made by the Court of Queen's Bench & any matter granted to it by statute.

Chief Justice of Saskatchewan: The Hon. John Klebuc
Justices of Appeal (The Hon. Mr./Madam Justice):
S.J. Cameron(Supernumerary)
W.J. Vancise(Supernumerary)
M.A. Gerwing(Supernumerary)
R.G. Richards
R.K. Ottenbreit
G.A. Smith(Supernumerary)
J.G. Lane(Supernumerary)
G.R. Jackson
N.W. Caldwell
M.J. Herauf
Administration:
Registrar: Melanie Baldwin

Saskatchewan Court of Queen's Bench
2425 Victoria Ave., Regina, SK S4P 4W6
Tel: 306-787-5371; *Fax:* 306-787-1307
www.sasklawcourts.ca

The Court of Queen's Bench is a court of original jurisdiction having jurisdiction in civil & criminal matters arising in Saskatchewan, except those matters expressly excluded by statute.

Chief Justice: The Hon. M.D. Popescul
Justices (The Hon. Mr./Madam Justice):
D.P. Ball
B.A. Barrington-Foote(Supernumerary)
C.L. Dawson
W.F. Gerein(Supernumerary)
E.J. Gunn
G.M. Kraus
F.J. Kovach
D.E.W. McIntyre
I.D. McLellan(Supernumerary)
J.E. McMurtry
N.S. Sandomirsky
E.A. Scheibel(Supernumerary)
P.A. Whitmore
D.L. Wilson
T.C. Zarzeczny
Administration:
Local Registrar: Bev McDonald
Sheriff: J. Rhinelander

Courts:
Battleford
Court House, 291 - 23 St. West, P.O. Box 340, Battleford, SK S0M 0E0
Tel: 306-446-7670; *Fax:* 306-446-7737
Administration:
Sheriff, Local Registrar: Linda Popp

Estevan
Court House, 1016 - 4 St., Estevan, SK S4A 0W5
Tel: 306-637-4530; *Fax:* 306-637-4536
G.A. Chicoine
Deputy Sheriff & Local Registrar: Peggy Boxrud
Sheriff & Local Registrar: Patricia Buttner

Humboldt
Court House, 805 - 8 Ave., P.O. Box 490, Humboldt, SK S0K 2A0
Tel: 306-682-6730; *Fax:* 306-682-3536
Sheriff & Local Registrar: Eleanor Neigel
Deputy Sheriff & Deputy Local Registrar: Elaine Lange

Melfort
Court House, 409 Main St., P.O. Box 850, Melfort, SK S0E 1A0
Tel: 306-752-6265; *Fax:* 306-752-6264
Deputy Sheriff & Deputy Local Registrar: D. Willenborg

Moose Jaw
Court House, 64 Ominica St. West, Moose Jaw, SK S6H 1W9
Tel: 306-694-3602; *Fax:* 306-694-3056

L.B. MacDonald

Prince Albert
Court House, Prince Albert, SK S6V 4W7
Tel: 306-953-3200; *Fax:* 306-953-3210
R.D. Maher
A.R. Rothery
Sheriff & Local Registrar: Maria Lynn Freeland

Saskatoon
520 Spadina Cres. East, Saskatoon, SK S7K 2H6
Tel: 306-933-5137; *Fax:* 306-975-4818
G.N. Allbright
G.W. Baynton(Supernumerary)
G.M. Currie
M.L. Dovell
P. Foley
N.G. Gabrielson
I. Goldenberg(Supernumerary)
P. Hrabinsky(Supernumerary)
J. Klebuc
J.D. Koch
R.C. Mills
G.A. Smith
D.H. Wright(Supernumerary)
Local Registrar: D. Berezowsky
Sheriff: G. Laing

Swift Current
Court House, 121 Lorne St. West, Swift Current, SK S9H 0J4
Tel: 306-778-8400; *Fax:* 306-778-8581
D.B. Konkin
Sheriff & Local Registrar: R. Peterson

Weyburn
Court House, 301 Prairie Ave., Weyburn, SK S4H 0L4
Tel: 306-848-2359; *Fax:* 306-848-2540
Sheriff & Local Registrar: Patricia Buttner

Wynyard
Court House, 410 Ave. C East, P.O. Box 369, Wynyard, SK S0A 4T0
Tel: 306-554-2561; *Fax:* 306-554-3405
Administration:
Deputy Sheriff/Local Registrar & Court Clerk: Stan Urbanoski

Yorkton
Court House, 29 Darlington St. East, Yorkton, SK S3N 0C2
Tel: 306-786-1515; *Fax:* 306-786-1521
J.L.G. Pritchard
Sheriff, Court Clerk & Local Registrar: S. Urbanoski

Saskatoon Family Law Division
224 - 4 Ave. South, 9th Fl., Saskatoon, SK S7K 5M5
Tel: 306-933-5174; *Fax:* 306-933-5703
Justices (The Hon. Mr./Madam Justice):
J.A. Ryan-Froslie
R.S. Smith
Y.G.K. Wilkinson
M.R. Wright
Administration:
Local Registrar: Dennis Berezowsky
Deputy Local Registrar: Kathy Brower

Saskatchewan Provincial Court
1815 Smith St., Regina, SK S4P 2N5
Tel: 306-787-5250; *Fax:* 306-787-7037
www.sasklawcourts.ca
The Provincial Court has jurisdiction in both civil (including small claims & family) & select criminal (including young offender) matters.
Chief Judge: The Hon. C.A. Snell

Courts:
Estevan
Court House, 1016 - 4th St., Estevan, SK S4A 0W5
Tel: 306-637-4528; *Fax:* 306-637-4536
J. Benison

La Ronge
1320 La Ronge Ave., P.O. Box 5000, La Ronge, SK S0J 1L0
Tel: 306-425-4505; *Fax:* 306-425-4269
Sid Robinson
W.K. Tucker

Lloydminster
4815 - 50 St., Lloydminster, SK S9V 0M8
Tel: 306-825-6420; *Fax:* 306-825-6497
K.J. Young

Meadow Lake
#3, 212 - 1 St. East, Meadow Lake, SK S9X 1T7
Tel: 306-236-7575; *Fax:* 306-236-7598
J. Nightingale
E. Kalenith

Melfort
107 Crawford Ave. East, P.O. Box 6500, Melfort, SK S0E 1A0
Tel: 306-752-6230; *Fax:* 306-752-6126
L. Dyck
B. Morgan

Moose Jaw
#211, 110 Ominica St. West, Moose Jaw, SK S6H 6V2
Tel: 306-694-3612; *Fax:* 306-694-3043
D. Kovatch
D. Orr

North Battleford
3 Railway Ave. East, North Battleford, SK S9A 2P9
Tel: 306-446-7400; *Fax:* 306-446-7432
D. Kaiser
V.H. Meekma
D. O'Hanlon

Prince Albert
188 -11th St. West, P.O. Box 3003, Prince Albert, SK S6V 6G1
Tel: 306-953-2640; *Fax:* 306-953-2819
T.B. Bekolay
Stephen Carter
T.W. Ferris
H.W. Goliath
G.M. Morin
H.R.E. Weisgerber

Regina
1815 Smith St., Regina, SK S4P 3V7
Tel: 306-787-5250; *Fax:* 306-787-7037
K.E. Bellerose
D. Bogdasavich
A. Crugnole-Reid
D.E. Fenwick
L. Halliday
B.D. Henning
D. Morris
L.J. Smith
L.C.A. Snell
C. Toth

Saskatoon
220 - 19 St. East, Saskatoon, SK S7K 2H6
Tel: 306-933-5250; *Fax:* 306-933-7043
R.G. Bell
B.P. Carey
B.L. Huculak
R.D. Jackson
M.D. Irwin
P. Kolenick
D.A. Lavoie
G.T. Seniuk
B. Singer
M.E. Turpel-Lafond
S.P. Whelan
T.W. White

Swift Current
Court House, 121 Lorne St. West, Swift Current, SK S9H 0J4
Tel: 306-778-8390; *Fax:* 306-778-8581
L.A. Matsulla

Wynyard
Court House, 410 Ave. C East, P.O. Box 1449, Wynyard, SK S0A 4T0
Tel: 306-554-2155; *Fax:* 306-554-3405
D. Ebert

Yorkton
Court House, 120 Smith St. East, Yorkton, SK S3N 3V3
Tel: 306-786-1400; *Fax:* 306-786-1422
K.A. Andrychuck
R. Green
P.R. Koskie

Yukon Territory

Yukon Territory: Court of Appeal
Court Registry, 2134 Second Ave. (Ground Fl.), Whitehorse, YT Y1A 5H6
Tel: 867-667-3429; *Fax:* 867-393-6212
Toll-Free: 800-661-0408
courtservices@gov.yk.ca
www.yukoncourts.ca/courts/appeal.htm
The Court of Appeal has appellate jurisdiction in all civil & criminal matters from decisions by the Territorial Court & Supreme Court.
Justices of Appeal (The Hon. Mr./Madam Justice):
Lance S.G. Finch
Elizabeth A. Bennett
Edward C. Chiasson
I.T. Donald
S. David Frankel
Nicole J. Garson
Harvey M. Groberman
J. Hall
David C. Harris
Christopher E. Hinkson
Pamela A. Kirkpatrick
R.E. Levine
R.T.A. Low
P.D. Lowry
K. Mackenzie
Kathryn E. Neilson
M. Newbury
J. Prowse
C.A. Ryan
M.E. Saunders
Daphne M. Smith
K.J. Smith
David Franklin Tysoe
Administration:
Registrar: Jennifer L. Jordan

Yukon Territory: Supreme Court
Court Services J-3, 2134 Second Ave., P.O. Box 2703, Whitehorse, YT Y1A 2C6
Tel: 867-667-5937; *Fax:* 867-393-6212
Toll-Free: 800-661-0408
courtservices@gov.yk.ca
www.yukoncourts.ca/courts/supreme.html
The Supreme Court is a superior court of record having original jurisdiction in all civil & criminal matters arising in the Yukon, unless excluded by statute.
Judges (The Hon. Mr./Madam Justice):
Leigh F. Gower
Ronald S. Veale
Ex-Officio Judges (The Hon. Mr./Madam Justice):
Beverly A. Brown
Earl Johnson
Robert G. Kilpatrick
Virginia A. Schuler
John Z. Vertes
Deputy Judges (The Hon. Mr./Madam Justice):
Marion Allan
Mary Lou Benotto
C. Scott Brooker
Beverley Browne
Louise Charbonneau
Carole M. Conrad
Donald Cooper
Susan Cooper
Wallace M. Darichuk
Barry Davies
Todd Ducharme
Marsha Erb
René P. Foisy
Geoffrey Gaul
Adam Germain
John Gill
Ross Goodwin
Stephen Goudge
Harvey Groberman
Joel Groves
R.J. Haines
Thomas Heeney
Chris Hinkson
Mary Humphries
Earl Johnson
Stephen Kelleher
Colleen Kenny
Adele Kent
Brenda Keyser
Robert Kilpatrick
Arthur M. Lutz
Richard P. Marceau
Ernest A. Marshall
Sheilah Martin
D.J. Martinson
Peter McIntyre
John Menzies
Andrea Moen
Mary Moreau
Rosemary Nation
Dennis O'Connor
Vital Ouellette
Edward Richard
Jacelyn Ryan-Froslie
Virginia Schuler
Neil Sharkey
Erwin Stach
Sunni Stromberg-Stein
John Vertes

David Watt
Alan Whitten
Randall Wong
Administration:
Registrar: Sharon Kerr, 867-667-3429, Fax: 867-393-6212
Sheriff: Navhreet Jijhar

Yukon Territory: Territorial Court

Court Services J-3, 2134 Second Ave., P.O. Box 2703, Whitehorse, YT Y1A 2C6
Tel: 867-667-5438; *Fax:* 867-393-6400
Toll-Free: 800-661-0408
courtservices@gov.yk.ca
www.yukoncourts.ca/courts/territorial.html

The Territorial Court has jurisdiction in family, youth & select criminal matters.

Chief Judge: The Hon. Michael Cozens
Judges (The Hon. Mr./Madam Justice):
Karen Ruddy
John Faulkner
Peter Ayotte
Gerald J. Barnable
Cunliffe Barnett
Michael S. Block
René Foisy
Christine V. Harapiak
Murray J. Hinds
Mike Hubbard
Heino Lilles
Deborah Livingstone
Donald S. Luther
C.Gail Maltby
Nancy K. Orr
Jacques R. Roy
E. Dennis Schmidt
Richard W. Thompson
Raymond E. Wyant
Administration:
Senior Court Clerk: Sharon Kerr
Territorial Court Clerk: Tara Boland
Territorial Court Clerk: Dawson City, Susan Coulson
Territorial Court Clerk: Lucretia Flemming
Territorial Court Clerk: Watson Lake, Stella Hearty
Territorial Court Clerk: Dorothy Irwin
Territorial Court Clerk: Karin Keeley-Eriksson
Territorial Court Clerk: Sharon Kerr
Territorial Court Clerk: Arlene Ogden

SECTION 10
HOSPITALS & HEALTH CARE FACILITIES

Listings in this section are arranged by province, and then by city. Each provincial section includes the following six categories.

Government Department

Regional Health Authorities

Hospitals

Community Health Centres

Long Term/Retirement Care

Mental Health Facilities

Alberta

Government Departments in Charge

ALBERTA: Alberta Health & Wellness
PO Box 1360 Stn. Main, 10025 Jasper Ave., 22nd Fl., Edmonton, AB T5J 2N3
Tel: 780-427-7164 *Fax:* 780-427-1171
TTY: 780-427-9999
health.ahinform.gov.ab.ca
www.health.alberta.ca

Note: Alberta Health is the ministry that sets policy, legislation and standards for the health system in Alberta. The ministry allocates health funding and administers provincial programs such as the Alberta Health Care Insurance Plan and provides expertise on communicable disease control.
Hon. Fred Horne, Minister of Health
Dr. James Talbot, Chief Medical Officer of Health

Regional Health Authorities

***Edmonton:* Alberta Health Services (AHS)**
Seventh Street Plaza, 14th Fl., North Tower, 10030 - 107 St. NW, Edmonton, AB T5J 3E4
Tel: 780-342-2000 *Fax:* 780-342-2060
Toll-Free: 1-888-342-2471
AHS.Corp@albertahealthservices.ca
www.albertahealthservices.ca
Info Line: 1-888-408-5465
Social Media: www.facebook.com/applemagca; twitter.com/ahs_behealthy; twitter.com/ahs_media; www.youtube.com/ahschannel

Year Founded: 2009
Number of Employees: 90000
Note: Provincial governance board, overseeing hospitals, other health facilities, & ground ambulance service in Alberta. Includes 99 acute care hospitals, 5 stand-alone psychiatric facilities, 8118 acute care beds, 21683 continuing care beds/spaces, plus equality partnership in 40 primary care networks.
Dr. Chris Eagle, President; CEO
Catherine Roozen, Chair

Hospitals

Hospitals - General

***Athabasca:* Athabasca Healthcare Centre**
Affiliated with: Alberta Health Services
3100 - 48 Ave., Athabasca, AB T9S 1M9
Tel: 780-675-6000 *Fax:* 780-675-7050
www9.albertahealthservices.ca
Number of Beds: 26 acute care beds; 1 palliative care bed; 23 continuing care beds
Note: Hospital Specialties: Emergency services; Diagnostic imaging; Laboratory services; Acute care; Obstetrics; Pediatrics; Continuing care; Rehabilitation; Recreation services; Palliative care
Mary Proskie, Manager, Healthcare Centre
Dr. Brian Oldale, Chief, Medical Staff

***Banff:* Banff Mineral Springs Hospital**
Covenant Health
Affiliated with: Alberta Health Services
PO Box 1050, 305 Lynx St., Banff, AB T1L 1H7
Tel: 403-762-2222 *Fax:* 403-762-4193
info@banffmineralspringshospital.ca
www.banffmineralspringshospital.ca
Year Founded: 1930
Note: Hospital Specialties: Emergency services; Surgery; Acute care; Maternal & child care; Physiotherapy; Occupational therapy; Recreation therapy; Music therapy; Mental health services; P.A.R.T.Y. program, to Prevent Alcohol & Risk-Related Trauma in Youth; Continuing care; Outpatient clinics; Palliative care
Cindy Mulherin, Executive Director

***Barrhead:* Barrhead Healthcare Centre**
Affiliated with: Alberta Health Services
4815 - 51 Ave., Barrhead, AB T7N 1M1
Tel: 780-674-2221 *Fax:* 780-674-3541
www.albertahealthservices.ca
Number of Beds: 34 beds
Note: Hospital specialties: Emergency services; Diagnostic imaging; Laboratory Services; Obstetrics; Community cancer centre; Rehabilitation services; Social work; Diet counselling; Education programs; Outpatient clinics; Palliative care
Heather Thompson, Manager, Healthcare Centre
Dr. Elizabeth Thompson, Chief, Medical Staff

***Bassano:* Bassano Health Centre**
Affiliated with: Alberta Health Services
608 - 5 Ave., Bassano, AB T0J 0B0
Tel: 403-641-6100 *Fax:* 403-641-2157
www.albertahealthservices.ca
Year Founded: 1914
Number of Beds: 3 acute care beds; 7 continuting care beds; 1 palliative care bed
Note: Hospital Specialties: Emergency services; Diagnostic imaging; Acute care; Physiotherapy; Occupational therapy; Physiotherapy; Mental health services; Nutrition services; Social work; Continuing care; Respite care; Palliative care

***Beaverlodge:* Beaverlodge Municipal Hospital**
Affiliated with: Alberta Health Services
PO Box 480, 422 - 10A St., Beaverlodge, AB T0H 0C0
Tel: 780-354-2136 *Fax:* 780-354-8355
www.albertahealthservices.ca
Number of Beds: 18 acute care beds
Note: Hospital Specialties: Emergency services; Radiology; Medical laboratory; Acute care; Obstetrics; Physiotherapy; Occupational therapy; Palliative care

***Black Diamond:* Oilfields General Hospital**
Affiliated with: Alberta Health Services
717 Government Rd., Black Diamond, AB T0L 0H0
Tel: 403-933-2222 *Fax:* 403-933-2031
www.albertahealthservices.ca
Note: Specialties: Adult Aboriginal mental health services (403-933-3800); Healthy Moms, Health Babies Program (403-933-6505); Laboratory services (403-933-6502); Occupational therapy (403-933-3800); Physical therapy; Pulmonary medicine; Speech language pathology (403-933-6505)

***Black Diamond:* Oilfields General Hospital**
PO Box 1, 717 Government Rd., Black Diamond, AB T0L 0H0
Tel: 403-933-2222 *Fax:* 403-933-2031
Murray Kobe, Administrator

***Blairmore:* Crowsnest Pass Health Centre**
Affiliated with: Alberta Health Services
2001 - 107th St., Blairmore, AB T0K 0E0
Tel: 403-562-5011 *Fax:* 403-562-8992
Note: Specialties: Emergency services (403-562-2831); Diagnostic imaging services; Laboratory services; Surgery; Obstetrics; Neonatal intensive care nursery; Pediatrics; Critical care services; Acute care; Rehabilitation services, including occupational therapy & therapeutic recreation; Southern Alberta Renal Program (403-564-4661); Continuing care; Palliative care

***Bonnyville:* Bonnyville Healthcare Centre**
Affiliated with: Alberta Health Services
5001 Lakeshore Dr., Bonnyville, AB T9N 2J7
Tel: 780-826-3311 *Fax:* 780-826-6526
www.albertahealthservices.ca
Year Founded: 1986
Number of Beds: 24 acute care beds; 30 continuing care beds; 9 day care beds
Note: Hospital Specialties: Emergency services; Regional laboratory services (780-826-3311 ext. 265); Diagnostic imaging; Pathology; Surgery; Acute care; Community Cancer Centre (780-826-3311, ext. 227); Cardiac stress testing(780-826-3311, ext. 255); Obstetrics; Rehabilitation; Medical accupunture; Occupational therapy (780-826-8266); Respiratory therapy (780-826-3311, ext. 304); Continuing care (780-826-3311, Ext 272); Palliative care (780-826-3311, ext. 286); Number of Employees: 281

***Bow Island:* Bow Island Health Centre**
Affiliated with: Alberta Health Services
938 Centre St., Bow Island, AB T0K 0G0
Tel: 403-545-3200 *Fax:* 403-545-2281
www.albertahealthservices.ca
Number of Beds: 10 acute care beds; 20 continuing care beds
Note: Hospital Specialties: Emergency services; Diagnostic imaging & laboratory services (403-545-3209); Acute care; Maternal child services; Physiotherapy (403-545-3207); Occupational therapy (403-529-8851); Continuing care; Respite Services (403-545-3208)

***Boyle:* Boyle Healthcare Centre**
Affiliated with: Alberta Health Services
PO Box 330, 5004 Lakeview Rd., Boyle, AB T0A 0M0
Tel: 780-689-3731 *Fax:* 780-689-3951
www.albertahealthservices.ca
Year Founded: 1966
Number of Beds: 19 acute care beds; 1 palliative care bed
Note: Hospital Specialties: Emergency services; Diagnostic imaging; Laboratory services; Acute care services; Nutrition services (780-675-2231); Community health; Social work; Palliative care
Carol Ulliac, Manager, Healthcare Centre
Dr. Marthinius Doman, Chief, Medical Staff

***Brooks:* Brooks Health Centre**
Affiliated with: Alberta Health Services
440 - 3rd St. East, Brooks, AB T1R 1B3
Tel: 403-501-3232 *Fax:* 403-362-6039
Number of Beds: 40 acute care beds; 75 long term care beds
Note: Hospital Specialties: Emergency services; Ambulatory care; Acute care; Obstetrics; Pediatrics (403-501-3211); Physiotherapy; Occupational therapy; Recreational therapy; Living Healthy Program / Cardiac rehabilitation (403-793-6659); Diabetes education; Community health; Social work (403-501-3266); Continuing care (403-501-3227); Palliative care

***Calgary:* Alberta Children's Hospital**
Affiliated with: Alberta Health Services
Former Name: Alberta Crippled Children's Hospital; Junior Red Cross Hospital
West Campus, University of Calgary, 2888 Shaganappi Trail NW, Calgary, AB T3B 6A8
Tel: 403-955-7211
TTY: 1-866-408-54
943.Link@calgaryhealthregion.ca
www.calgaryhealthregion.ca/ACH
Year Founded: 1922
Note: Hospital Specialties: Pediatrics (birth to age 18); Emergency services (403-955-7070); Sugery; Complex Pain Service (403-955-7430); Diagnostic imaging (403-955-7656); Burn treatment (403-955-7853); Eating disorder program - day treatment (403-943-1500); Therapeutic arts; Child health information (Family & Community Resource Centre)

***Calgary:* Foothills Medical Centre**
Affiliated with: Alberta Health Services
1403 - 29 St. NW, Calgary, AB T2N 2T9
Tel: 403-944-1110
www.albertahealthservices.ca
Note: Hospital Specialties: Emergency services (403-944-1405); Trauma services (403-944-4339); Diagnostic imaging; Acute care; Gynecology (403-944-1301); Newborn care (403-944-1352); Cardiology (403-944-1381); Gastrointestinal services (403-944-4711); Hematology (403-944-1157); Adult neuropsychology service (403-944-1340); Neurology (403-944-1312); Psychiatry (403-944-1321); Renal services (403-944-1137); Movement Disorders Program (403-944-4364); Occupational therapy (403-944-1432); Respiratory services (403-944-1319); Social work (403-944-1560); Addiction services (403-943-1500)

***Calgary:* Peter Lougheed Centre**
Affiliated with: Alberta Health Services
3500 - 26 Ave. NE, Calgary, AB T1Y 6J4
Tel: 403-943-4555 *Fax:* 403-943-4878
Number of Beds: 513 beds

***Calgary:* Rockyview General Hospital**
Affiliated with: Alberta Health Services
7007 - 14 St. SW, Calgary, AB T2V 1P9
Tel: 403-943-3000 *Fax:* 403-943-3434
www.albertahealthservices.ca
Number of Beds: 566 beds
Note: Services include: emergency, acute care, addiction network, CT imaging, cardiac intensive care/coronary care units, colorectal surgery, cystoscopy, diagnostic imaging, electroencephalography, endoscopy, geriatric assessment and rehabilitation, obstetrics/gynecology outpatient.
Dr. Stephen Duckett, President/CEO, AHS
Nancy Guebert, Vice-President
Teresa Davidson, Site Director

***Camrose:* St. Mary's Hospital**
Affiliated with: Alberta Health Services
4607 - 53 St., Camrose, AB T4V 1Y5
Tel: 780-679-6100 *Fax:* 780-679-6196
www.stmaryscamrose.com
Year Founded: 1924
Number of Beds: 76 beds
Note: An acute care facility with services including emergency, cardiology, diabetic education, diagnostic imaging (CT scans, fluoroscopy, radiology, mammography, ultrasound), community cancer clinic, women's health, pediatrics, palliative care, respiratory therapy, occupational therapy, mental health, urology. The facility operates under the governance of Covenant Health, a Catholic provider of healthcare.
R. Patrick Dumelie, President/CEO, Covenant Health
Rosa Rudelich, Vice-President/CFO, Covenant Health
Fran Ross, Vice-President, Communications, Covenant Health

***Canmore:* Canmore General Hospital**
Affiliated with: Alberta Health Services
1100 Hospital Pl., Canmore, AB T1W 1N2
Tel: 403-678-5536 *Fax:* 403-678-9874
www.albertahealthservices.ca

Note: Hospital Specialties: Emergency services; Diagnostic imaging (403-678-7216); Laboratory services; Surgical services; Obstetrics; Newborn care; Acute care; Cardiology; Audiology; Chemotherapy treatments; Wound centre; Occupational therapy; Physical therapy; Recreation therapy; Speech language pathology; Mental health; Aboriginal hospital Liaison; Diabetes prevention; Adult day support program (403-678-7200); Respite care; Long term care; Palliative care

***Castor:* Our Lady of the Rosary Hospital**
Affiliated with: Alberta Health Services
PO Box 329, 5402 - 47 St., Castor, AB T0C 0X0
Tel: 403-882-3434 *Fax:* 403-882-2751
Number of Beds: 5 acute care, 20 continuing care beds, 2 respite
Marilyn Weber, Executive Director
Barry Straub, Maintenance

***Claresholm:* Claresholm General Hospital**
Affiliated with: Alberta Health Services
221 - 43 Ave., Claresholm, AB T0L 0T0
Tel: 403-682-3750
www.albertahealthservices.ca

Note: Hospital Specialties: Emergency services (403-682-3700); Diagnostic imaging (403-682-3725); Cardiology electrocardiogram services; Acute care; Occupational therapy (403-625-8640); Physiotherapy (403-625-8617); Recreation therapy (403-625-8613); Mental health services; Respite care; Palliative care

***Cold Lake:* Cold Lake Healthcare Centre**
Affiliated with: Alberta Health Services
314 - 25 St., Cold Lake, AB T9M 1G6
Tel: 780-639-3322 *Fax:* 780-639-2255
www.albertahealthservices.ca
Number of Beds: 31 continuing care beds; 24 acute care beds; 2 palliative care beds
Note: Hospital Specialties: Emergency services; Diagnostic imaging services; Laboratory services; Surgical services; Acute care; Ambulatory care; Obstetrics; Pediatrics; Eating disorder services (780-998-5225); Rehabilitation services, including physiotherapy, occupational therapy, recreation therapy, & respiratory therapy; Continuing care (780-639-6515); Dementia care; Respite services; Palliative care
James Murray, Manager, Cold Lake Healthcare Centre
Dr. Siegfried Heydenrych, Chief, Medical Staff

***Consort:* Consort Hospital & Care Centre**
Affiliated with: Alberta Health Services
5402 - 52 Ave., Consort, AB T0C 1B0
Tel: 403-577-3555 *Fax:* 403-577-3950
www.albertahealthservices.ca

Note: Hospital Specialties: Emergency services; Diagnostic imaging; Laboratory services; Acute care; Occupational therapy; Physiotherapy; Recreation therapy; Continuing care; Palliative care

***Coronation:* Coronation Hospital & Care Centre**
Affiliated with: Alberta Health Services
5000 Municipal Rd., Coronation, AB T0C 1C0
Tel: 403-577-3803 *Fax:* 403-578-3474
www.albertahealthservices.ca

Note: Hospital Specialties: Emergency services (403-578-3200); Diagnostic imaging (403-578-3804); Laboratory services (403-578-3804, ext. 308); Acute care; Nutrition services (403-309-6199); Diabetes education (403-314-5780); Occupational therapy; Physical therapy; Recreation therapy; Speech language pathology (403-343-4822); Continuing care (403-343-4822); Supportive living; Seniors Mental Health Program; Palliative care (403-578-3680)

***Daysland:* Daysland Health Centre**
Affiliated with: Alberta Health Services
5920 - 51st Ave., Daysland, AB T0B 1A0
Tel: 780-374-3746 *Fax:* 780-374-2111
www.albertahealthservices.ca
Number of Beds: 16 acute care beds; 10 rehabilitation beds
Note: Hospital Specialties: Emergency services; Laboratory services; Surgery; Acute care; Obstetrics; Rehabilitation services, including occupational therapy, physiotherapy, & respiratory therapy; Pediatric speech language services; Social work; Respite care; Palliative care
Mariann Wolbeck, Health Centre Coordinator
mariann.wolbeck@albertahealthservice

***Devon:* Devon General Hospital**
Affiliated with: Alberta Health Services
101 Erie St. South, Devon, AB T9G 1A6
Tel: 780-342-7000
www.albertahealthservices.ca
Number of Beds: 9 acute care beds; 10 continuing care beds; 2 respite beds
Note: Hospital Specialties: Emergency services; Laboratory services; Radiology services (780-342-7075); Acute care; Rehabilitation services; Mental health therapy (780-963-6151); Public health (780-342-7069); Tuberculosis testing & immunization (780-342-7069); Diabetes education; Nutrition information; Social work (780-987-8200); Adult day program; Home care (780-342-7020); Continuing care

***Didsbury:* Didsbury District Health Services**
Affiliated with: Alberta Health Services
1210 - 20th Ave., Didsbury, AB T0M 0W0
Tel: 403-335-9393 *Fax:* 403-335-4816
www.albertahealthservices.ca

Note: Hospital Specialties: Emergency services; Laboratory services (403-335-7224;); Diagnostic imaging; Acute care; Rehabilitation, including occupational therapy & physiotherapy; Speech language pathology (403-335-7623); Clinical nutrition services (403-335-9437); Public health services; Respite care; Long term care; Palliative care

***Drayton Valley:* Drayton Valley Hospital & Care Centre**
Affiliated with: Alberta Health Services
4550 Madsen Ave., Drayton Valley, AB T7A 1N8
Tel: 780-542-5321 *Fax:* 780-621-4966
www.albertahealthservices.ca
Number of Beds: 34 acute care beds; 50 long term care beds
Note: Hospital Specialties: Emergency services; Diagnostic imaging (780-621-4945); Laboratory services (780-542-5321); Acute care; Obstetrics (780-542-5321); Northern Alberta Renal Program (780-542-2010); Occupational therapy, physiotherapy, & recreation therapy (780-542-4415); Asthma education (780-621-4866); Diabetes education(403-314-5780); Nutrition services (403-309-6199); Long-term care; Palliative care (780-621-4917)

***Drumheller:* Drumheller Health Centre**
Affiliated with: Alberta Health Services
351 - 9 St. NW, Drumheller, AB T0J 0Y1
Tel: 403-823-6500 *Fax:* 403-823-5076
www.albertahealthservices.ca

Note: Hospital Specialties: Emergency services; Diagnostic imaging; Acute care; Obstetrics; Cardiac Rehabilitation Program (403-820-7201); Chemotherapy treatments (403-820-7985); Occupational therapy, physical therapy, & recreation therapy; Mental health services (403-820-7863); Nutrition Services (403-309-6199); Public health (403-820-6004); Diabetes education (403-314-5780); Asthma education (403-820-7264); Continuing care (403-820-7245); Respite care (403-820-6020); Home care (403-820-6004); Palliative care (403-820-7241)

***Edmonton:* Grey Nuns Community Hospital**
Affiliated with: Alberta Health Services
Former Name: Grey Nuns Community Hospital & Health Centre
1100 Youville Dr. West, Edmonton, AB T6L 5X8
Tel: 780-735-7000
www.capitalhealth.ca
Number of Beds: 267 beds

***Edmonton:* Misericordia Community Hospital**
Affiliated with: Alberta Health Services
Former Name: Misericordia Community Hospital & Health Centre
16940 - 87 Ave., Edmonton, AB T5R 4H5
Tel: 780-735-2611 *Fax:* 780-930-5774
www.capitalhealth.ca
Number of Beds: 259 beds

***Edmonton:* Royal Alexandra Hospital**
Affiliated with: Alberta Health Services
10240 Kingsway Ave., Edmonton, AB T5H 3V9
Tel: 780-735-4111
www.albertahealthservices.ca

Number of Beds: 678 beds
Note: Emergency, acute care of the elderly, adolescent pregnancy clinic, otolaryngology, angiography, child & adolescent psychiatry, colonoscopy, diabetic foot clinic, diagnostic imaging, electroencephalography, gastroscopy, radiology, intensive care unit, liver clinic, mental health clinic, ophthalmology, prenatal nutrition counselling, plastics surgery, recto/colo Clinic, rehabilitation services, rheumatology, sexual assault response team, ultrasound, urology. Located in this hospital is the Lois Hole Hospital for Women.
Dr. Stephen Duckett, President/CEO, AHS
Joanna Pawlyshyn, Vice-President
Lois Stefaniuk, Site Director

***Edmonton:* University of Alberta Hospital & Stollery Children's Hospital**
Affiliated with: Alberta Health Services
8440 - 112 St. NW, Edmonton, AB T6G 2B7
Tel: 780-735-7000
www.albertahealthservices.ca
Number of Beds: 687 beds
Note: A clinical, research and teaching facility, its specialized services include cardiac sciences, neurosciences, surgery, medicine, renal, critical and trauma care, burn unit. Other areas of focus include amyotrophic lateral sclerosis, anaesthesiology, angiography, audiology, bronchoscopy, cardiology, cardiovascular intensive care unit, CT scans, continence, dental clinic, E. Garner King Critical Care Unit, ECG/Holter monitoring, ENT, ears nose & throat surgery, eating disorders, echocardiography, endoscopy, fluoroscopy, gastroenterology and hepatology, general surgery, geriatric assessment, hemodialysis, hepatitis, laboratory, MRI, medical microbiology, multiple sclerosis, neurosurgery, nuclear medicine, nutrition counselling, occupational therapy, orthopaedic surgery, palliative care, pediatric chronic pain, physical therapy, plastic surgery, psychiatry, pulmonary medicine, radiology, respiratory therapy, rheumatology, sexual assault response, social work, speech language pathology, spine assessment, spiritual care, stress, stroke, surgery, pediatric sleep disturbance, teleStroke, transplantation, tuberculosis, ultrasound, urology. Also located within the facility are the Mazankowski Alberta Heart Institute and the Stollery Children's Hospital, specializing in pediatric cardiac surgery and organ transplantation.
Dr. Stephen Duckett, President/CEO, AHS
Dr. David Megren, CMO/Executive Vice-President, AHS
Glenda Coleman-Miller, Site Vice-President
Amelda Foster, Site Director

***Edson:* Edson Healthcare Centre**
Affiliated with: Alberta Health Services
4716 - 5th Ave., Edson, AB T7E 1S8
Tel: 780-723-3331 *Fax:* 780-723-7787
www.albertahealthservices.ca

Note: Hospital Specialties: Emergency services; Diagnostic imaging; Laboratory services (780-712-6840); Surgical services & recovery; Acute care; Ambulatory care; Obstetrics; Pediatrics; Rehabilitation services; Social work (780-712-6862, ext. 324); Respite care; Continuing care (780-723-2229); Palliative care

***Elk Point:* Elk Point Healthcare Centre**
Affiliated with: Alberta Health Services
5310 - 50th Ave., Elk Point, AB T0A 1A0
Tel: 780-724-3847 *Fax:* 780-724-3085
www.albertahealthservices.ca
Number of Beds: 30 continuing care beds; 11 acute care beds; 1 palliative care bed
Note: Hospital Specialties: Diagnostic imaging; Laboratory services; Acute care; Ambulatory care; Obstetrics; Rehabilitation services, including physical therapy & recreation therapy; Community health services; Social work (780-645-3396); Continuing care; Respite care; Palliative care
Paulette Levasseur, Manager, Healthcare Centre
Dr. D. Ramful, Medical Director

***Fairview:* Fairview Health Complex**
Affiliated with: Alberta Health Services
10628 - 110 St., Fairview, AB T0H 1L0
Tel: 780-835-6100
www.albertahealthservices.ca
Number of Beds: 25 beds
Note: Hospital Specialties: Emergency services; Intensive care unit; Acute care; Obstetrics; Pediatrics; Rehabilitation services, including occupational therapy, physiotherapy, & therapeutic recreation; Mental health services (780-835-6149); Cardiac education (780-835-6117); Prenatal education & counselling (780-835-4951); Healthy Families Program (780-835-6139); Diabetes Prevention & Wellness Program (780-835-6117); Environmental Public Health Program (780-835-4951); Social work (780-835-6112); Nutrition services; Continuing care (780-835-6180); Palliative care (780-835-4951)

***Fort McMurray:* Northern Lights Regional Health Centre**
Affiliated with: Alberta Health Services
7 Hospital St., Fort McMurray, AB T9H 1P2
Tel: 780-791-6161 *Fax:* 780-791-6029
Number of Beds: 94 beds

Patricia L. Eelton, CEO

***Fort Saskatchewan:* Fort Saskatchewan Health Centre**
Affiliated with: Alberta Health Services
9430 - 95 St., Fort Saskatchewan, AB T8L 1R8
Tel: 780-998-2256
www.albertahealthservices.ca
Number of Beds: 32 beds
Note: Specialties: Emergency services; Surgical services; Acute care; Obstetrics; Respiratory therapy; COPD Rehabilitation Program (780 992-5801); Neurological physical therapy services (780-992-5824); Occupational therapy; Nutritional counselling (780-992-5812); Social work

***Fort Vermilion:* St. Theresa General Hospital**
Affiliated with: Alberta Health Services
4506 - 46 Ave., Fort Vermilion, AB T0H 1N0
Tel: 780-927-3761 *Fax:* 780-927-4271
Number of Beds: 10 long-term care, 21 acute care beds
Note: Services include emergency, blood collection, clinical nutrition, continuing care, diagnostic imaging, interpretive services, lab, maternity, mental health, occupational therapy, palliative care, pediatrics, physical therapy, school dental services, spiritual care.
Dr. Stephen Duckett, President/CEO, AHS
Dr. David Megren, Executive Vice-President/CMO, AHS
Kerry Williamson, Senior Media Relations Advisor, AHS
780-407-2602

***Fox Creek:* Fox Creek Health Care Centre**
Affiliated with: Alberta Health Services
600 - 3rd St., Fox Creek, AB T0H 1P0
Tel: 780-622-3545
www.albertahealthservices.ca
Number of Beds: 4 acute care beds
Note: Specialties: Emergency services; Laboratory services; Acute care; Prenatal classes & Healthy Beginnings Program (780-622-3730); Pediatrics; Cardiac & diabetes education (780-524-7027); Home care & palliative care (780-622-3730)

***Grande Cache:* Grande Cache Community Health Complex**
Affiliated with: Alberta Health Services
PO Box 629, 10200 Shand Ave., Grande Cache, AB T0E 0Y0
Tel: 780-827-3701 *Fax:* 780-827-2859
tracy.peddy@pchr.ca
Number of Beds: 12 acute care, 4 continuing care beds
Tracy Peddy, Director, Health Services

***Grande Prairie:* Queen Elizabeth II Hospital**
Affiliated with: Alberta Health Services
10409 - 98 St., Grande Prairie, AB T8V 2E8
Tel: 780-538-7100 *Fax:* 780-538-1500
Number of Beds: 48 med, 10 NICU, 22 Obs/Gen, 14 Ped, 26 psy, 8 rehab, 40 sur
Diane Calvert, Chief Operating Officer

***Grimshaw:* Grimshaw/Berwyn & District Community Health Centre**
Affiliated with: Alberta Health Services
PO Box 648, 5612 Wilcox Rd., Grimshaw, AB T0H 1W0
Tel: 780-332-6500 *Fax:* 780-618-4522
Number of Beds: 4 beds, 10 continuing care beds
Carmen Johnson, Chairperson

***Hanna:* Hanna Health Centre**
Affiliated with: Alberta Health Services
PO Box 730, 904 Centre St. North, Hanna, AB T0J 1P0
Tel: 403-854-3331 *Fax:* 403-854-3253
Number of Beds: 18 acute care, 49 continuing care beds, 12 assisted living beds
Ken Hansenen, Site Leader

***Hardisty:* Hardisty Health Centre**
Affiliated with: Alberta Health Services
PO Box 269, 4531 - 47 Ave., Hardisty, AB T0B 1V0
Tel: 780-888-3742 *Fax:* 780-888-2427
Number of Beds: 5 acute care, 15 continuing care beds
Evelyn Scott, Health Centre Coordinator

***High Level:* Ranchlands Village Mall**
Affiliated with: Alberta Health Services
Former Name: High Level General Hospital; Northwest Health Centre
1829 Ranchlands Blvd. NW, High Level, AB T0H 1Z0
Tel: 403-943-9700 *Fax:* 403-943-9735
Number of Beds: 30 beds
Patricia Pelton, CEO

***High Prairie:* High Prairie Health Complex**
Affiliated with: Alberta Health Services
4620 - 53 Ave, High Prairie, AB T0G 1E0
Tel: 780-523-6440 *Fax:* 780-523-6642
Number of Beds: 25 acute care, 35 long-term care, continuing care 35
Kate Butler, Director, Health Services

***High River:* High River General Hospital**
Affiliated with: Alberta Health Services
560 - 9 Ave. SW, High River, AB T1V 1B3
Tel: 403-652-2200 *Fax:* 403-652-0199
www.calgaryhealthregion.ca
Number of Beds: 103 beds
Rosemary Burness, Community Health Services Leader
Gesina Allan, Purchasing Manager
Geraldine Polanchek, Director, Finance & Support Services

***Hinton:* Hinton Healthcare Centre**
Affiliated with: Alberta Health Services
1280 Switzer Dr., Hinton, AB T7V 1V2
Tel: 780-865-3333 *Fax:* 780-865-1099
Number of Beds: 21 beds
Lisa McConnell, Health Centre Manager
Doug Johnson, Supervisor, Environmental Services

***Innisfail:* Innisfail Health Centre**
Affiliated with: Alberta Health Services
5023 - 42 St., Innisfail, AB T4G 1A9
Tel: 403-227-7800 *Fax:* 403-227-7801
Number of Beds: 102 beds
Cindy Mulherin, Site Leader

***Jasper:* Seton Jasper Healthcare Centre**
Affiliated with: Alberta Health Services
PO Box 310, 518 Robson St., Jasper, AB T0E 1E0
Tel: 780-852-3344 *Fax:* 780-852-3413
www9.albertahealthservices.ca/Default.aspx?cid=156&lang=1
Number of Beds: 11 beds; 10 for acute care and 1 for palliative care
Note: Emergency, acute care services, diagnostic imaging, eating disorder services, mental health services, occupational therapy, palliative care, physiotherapy, social work
Dr. Stephen Duckett, President; CEO, AHS
Lorna Chisholm, Site Manager
Dr. Mark Addison, Chief, Medical Staff

***Killam:* Killam Healthcare Centre**
Affiliated with: Alberta Health Services
PO Box 40, 5203 - 49 Ave., Killam, AB T0B 2L0
Tel: 780-385-3741 *Fax:* 780-385-3904
www.ech.ab.ca
Number of Beds: 5 acute care, 45 continuing care beds, 4 other
Geri Clark, Chief Executive Director

***Lac La Biche:* William J. Cadzow Health Centre**
Affiliated with: Alberta Health Services
PO Box 507, 9200 - 95 St., Lac La Biche, AB T0A 2C0
Tel: 780-623-4404 *Fax:* 780-623-5904
Number of Beds: 23 acute care, 41 long-term care beds

***Lac La Biche:* William J. Cadzow Lac La Biche Healthcare Centre**
Affiliated with: Alberta Health Services
Former Name: Lac La Biche Health Care Centre
PO Box 507, 9110 - 93 St., Lac La Biche, AB T0A 2C0
Tel: 780-623-4404 *Fax:* 780-623-5904
Number of Beds: 65 beds

***Lamont:* Lamont Health Care Centre**
Affiliated with: Alberta Health Services
5216 - 53 St., Lamont, AB T0B 2R0
Tel: 780-895-2211 *Fax:* 780-895-7305
www.ech.ab.ca
Number of Beds: 14 acute, 105 continuing care beds
Harold James, Executive Director

***Leduc:* Leduc Community Hospital**
Affiliated with: Alberta Health Services
Former Name: Leduc Community Hospital & Health Centre
4210 - 48 St., Leduc, AB T9E 5Z3
Tel: 780-986-7711
www.capitalhealth.ca
Number of Beds: 54 beds

***Lethbridge:* Lethbridge Regional Hospital**
Affiliated with: Alberta Health Services
960 - 19 St. South, Lethbridge, AB T1J 1W5
Tel: 403-382-6111 *Fax:* 403-388-6011
Number of Beds: 236 acute care, 41 mental health
Cheryl Dick, CEO

***Magrath:* Magrath Hospital**
Affiliated with: Alberta Health Services
PO Box 550, 37E - 2 Ave. North, Magrath, AB T0K 1J0
Tel: 403-758-3331 *Fax:* 403-758-3332
Number of Beds: 3 acute care beds, 21 auxiliary beds
Pam Whitnack, CEO
Grace Navratil, Housekeeping Supervisor

***Manning:* Manning Community Health Centre**
Affiliated with: Alberta Health Services
Bag 1260, 600 - 2 St. NE, Manning, AB T0H 2M0
Tel: 780-836-3391 *Fax:* 780-836-7352
Number of Beds: 11 acute care, 16 long-term care beds
Jo Kelemen, Director, Health Services

***Mayerthorpe:* Mayerthorpe Healthcare Centre**
Affiliated with: Alberta Health Services
PO Box 30, 4417 - 45 St., Mayerthorpe, AB T0E 1N0
Tel: 780-786-2261 *Fax:* 780-786-2023
Number of Beds: 25 acute care, 30 long-term care beds
Karen Kyle, Facility Supervisor
Gwen Hunt, Purchasing Agent

***McLennan:* McLennan Sacred Heart Community Health Centre**
Affiliated with: Alberta Health Services
Bag 2000, McLennan, AB T0H 2L0
Tel: 780-324-3730 *Fax:* 780-324-4206
barbara.mader@pchr.ca
www.pchr.ca
Number of Beds: 20 acute care, 45 long-term care beds
Note: community health centre; nursing home
Barbara Mader, Director, Health Services

***Medicine Hat:* Medicine Hat Regional Hospital**
Affiliated with: Alberta Health Services
666 - 5 St. SW, Medicine Hat, AB T1A 4H6
Tel: 403-529-8000 *Fax:* 403-529-8998
www.palliserhealth.ca
Number of Beds: 177 beds
L. Iwasiw, Senior Vice-President
G. Lukasiewich, Director, Physical Plant/Maintenance

***Milk River:* Milk River Health Centre**
Affiliated with: Alberta Health Services
Former Name: Milk River Hospital
PO Box 90, 517 Centre Ave. East, Milk River, AB T0K 1M0
Tel: 403-647-3500
Number of Beds: 21 auxiliary beds, 3 community support beds, 1 respite
Brad Moser, Head, Housekeeping

***Mundare:* Mary Immaculate Hospital**
Affiliated with: Alberta Health Services
PO Box 349, Mundare, AB T0B 3H0
Tel: 780-764-3730 *Fax:* 780-764-3039
www.ech.ab.ca
Number of Beds: 30 continuing care
Note: auxiliary/clinic (out patient)
Rhonda McCarty, Executive Director

***New Westminster:* Royal Columbian Hospital**
Affiliated with: Fraser Health Authority
330 East Columbia St., New Westminster, AB V3L 3W7
Tel: 604-520-4253
feedback@fraserhealth.ca
www.fraserhealth.ca/find_us/locations/our_locations?site_id=178
9
Year Founded: 1862
Number of Beds: 352 acute care beds
Note: Emergency , acute care services, care for the elderly, angiography, antepartum care services, bone densitometry, cardiac services, diabetes education, bronchoscopy services, ultrasound, fluoroscopy, respiratory unit, radiography, surgery unit, hand clinic, haemodialysis, psychiatry, intensive care unit, intrapartum care, magnetic resonance imaging, mammography, oncology, neonatal intensive care, neurological services, orthopaedic surgery, paediatrics, pantomography, family counselling, physiotherapy, plastic surgery, respiratory therapy, social work services, ultrasound, vascular and thoracic surgery
Dr. Nigel Murray, President/CEO, FHA
Dr. Andrew Webb, Vice-President, FHA, Medicine
Brian Woods, CFO, FHA
Gillian Harwood, Executive Director, FHA
Miriam Stewart, Director, Health Services

***Olds:* Olds Hospital & Care Centre**
Affiliated with: Alberta Health Services
3901 - 57 Ave., Olds, AB T4H 1T4
Tel: 403-556-3381 *Fax:* 403-556-2199
Number of Beds: 81 beds
Colleen Simon, Site Leader

Oyen: **Big Country Hospital**
Affiliated with: Alberta Health Services
312 - 3 Ave. East, Oyen, AB T0J 2J0
Tel: 403-664-3651 *Fax:* 403-502-8649
Number of Beds: 10 acute care, 30 continuing care beds
Lynne Baisley, Director, Health Services Northern Area
Wayne Trembley, Supervisor, Physical Plant

Peace River: **Peace River Community Health Centre**
Affiliated with: Alberta Health Services
Bag 400, 10101 - 68 St., Peace River, AB T8S 1T6
Tel: 780-624-7500 *Fax:* 780-618-3472
www.pchr.ca
Number of Beds: 30 acute care, 40 long-term care beds
Note: long-term care facility, nursing home, outpatient services, treatment centre, community health centre, home care office
Sandra Herritt, Director, Health Services

Picture Butte: **Piyami Place**
Affiliated with: Alberta Health Services
Former Name: Picture Butte Hospital
301 Cowan Ave., Picture Butte, AB T0K 1V0
Tel: 403-732-4811 *Fax:* 403-388-6011
Number of Beds: 15 suites
Pam Whitnack, CEO

Pincher Creek: **Pincher Creek Health Centre**
Affiliated with: Alberta Health Services
Former Name: Pincher Creek Hospital
1222 Bev McLachlin Dr., Pincher Creek, AB T0K 1W0
Tel: 403-627-1234 *Fax:* 403-627-5275
www.chr.ab.ca
Number of Beds: 16 acute care beds, 3 auxiliary beds
Pam Whitnack, CEO
Brian Meaney, Acting Maintenance Supervisor

Ponoka: **Ponoka Hospital & Healthcare Centre**
Affiliated with: Alberta Health Services
5800 - 57 Ave., Ponoka, AB T4J 1P1
Tel: 403-783-3341 *Fax:* 403-783-6907
Number of Beds: 75 beds
Sue MacKenzie, Site Leader
Hardy Kohlman, Director, Physical Plant

Provost: **Provost Health Centre**
Affiliated with: Alberta Health Services
PO Box 270, 5002 - 54 Ave., Provost, AB T0B 3S0
Tel: 780-753-2291 *Fax:* 780-608-8850
www.ech.ab.ca
Number of Beds: 15 acute care, 37 continuing care beds, 10 alternative housing
Lana Clark, Health Services Coordinator

Raymond: **Raymond Hospital**
Affiliated with: Alberta Health Services
PO Box 599, 150 North 4th St. E, Raymond, AB T0K 2S0
Tel: 403-752-4561 *Fax:* 403-627-5275
www.albertahealthservices.ca
Number of Beds: 12 acute care, 35 auxiliary beds
Note: Emergency, obstetrics, and palliative care, diagnostic imaging, rehabilitation
Dr. Stephen Duckett, President; CEO, AHS
Dr. David Megran, Executive Vice-President, CMO, AHS

Red Deer: **Red Deer Regional Hospital Centre**
Affiliated with: Alberta Health Services
3942 - 50A Ave., Red Deer, AB T4N 4E7
Tel: 403-343-4422 *Fax:* 403-341-8632
www.albertahealthservices.ca
Number of Beds: 365 beds
Note: Emergency, dialysis clinic, cancer clinic and a pediatric and special care nursery
Dr. Stephen Duckett, President/CEO, AHS
Dr. David Megran, Executive Vice-President, CMO, AHS

Redwater: **Redwater Health Centre**
Affiliated with: Alberta Health Services
4812 - 58 St., Redwater, AB T0A 2W0
Tel: 780-942-3932 *Fax:* 780-942-2373
www.albertahealthservices.ca
Number of Beds: 13 beds
Note: 24-hour emergency services, palliative care, lab services, respiratory services, radiology, nutritional counselling, and a visiting optometrist office
David S. Diamond, Chief Operating Officer, AHS

Slave Lake: **Slave Lake Healthcare Centre**
Affiliated with: Alberta Health Services
309 - 6 St. NE, Slave Lake, AB T0G 2A2
Tel: 780-805-3500 *Fax:* 780-805-3574
www.albertahealthservices.ca
Number of Beds: 43 beds (24 acute care beds including 2 labor and delivery beds, 1 palliative care bed, 2 special care beds, plus 20 continuing care beds)
Note: Emergency, acute care, continuing care, pharmacy, renal dialysis, rehabilitation, obstetrics, occupational therapy, pediatrics, respiratory therapy, social work, ultrasound and X-Ray
Dr. Stephen Duckett, President/CEO, AHS
Steve Marcotte, Healthcare Centre Manager
Dr. Paul Caffaro, Chief, Medical Staff

Smoky Lake: **Smoky Lake - George McDougall Memorial Healthcare Centre**
Affiliated with: Alberta Health Services
PO Box 340, 4212 - 55 Ave., Smoky Lake, AB T0A 3C0
Tel: 780-656-3034 *Fax:* 780-656-5010
www.albertahealthservices.ca
Number of Beds: 12 acute care beds, including 1 palliative care bed; 23 continuing care beds
Note: Hospital Specialties: Emergency services; Diagnostic imaging; Laboratory services; Ambulatory services; Acute care; Rehabilitation; Occupational therapy; Physical therapy services; Respiratory therapy; Therapeutic recreation; Community health services; Nutrition services; Social work; Continuing care; Palliative care
David Ponich, Manager, Healthcare Centre
Dr. Anton Raubenheimer, Chief, Medical Staff

Spirit River: **Central Peace Health Complex**
Affiliated with: Alberta Health Services
5010 - 45th Ave., Spirit River, AB T0H 3G0
Tel: 780-864-3993
www.albertahealthservices.ca
Number of Beds: 10 acute care beds; 16 continuing care beds
Note: Hospital Specialties: Emergency care; Laboratory services; Acute care; Newborn hearing screening program; Pediatrics; Rehabilitation; Physical therapy; Nutrition counselling (780-864-3063); Continuing care; Palliative care

St Albert: **Sturgeon Community Hospital**
Affiliated with: Alberta Health Services
Former Name: Sturgeon Community Hospital & Health Centre
201 Boudreau Rd., St Albert, AB T8N 6C4
Tel: 780-418-8200 *Fax:* 780-460-6262
www.albertahealthservices.ca/facilities.asp?pid=facility&rid=1000932
Number of Beds: 167 beds
Note: A comprehensive health facility with services including emergency, cardiac rehabilitation, diagnostic imaging (CT scans, radiology, fluoroscopy), geriatric evaluation, intensive care unit, mental health emergency, nutrition counselling, obstetrical outpatient clinic, physical therapy/occupational therapy, prenatal program, sexual assault response team, spiritual care, surgery.
Dr. Stephen Duckett, President/CEO, AHS
Linda Cargill, Executive Director, Community & Rural Hospitals, AHS

St. Paul: **St. Therese/St. Paul Healthcare Centre**
Affiliated with: Alberta Health Services
4713 - 48 Ave., St. Paul, AB T0A 3A3
Tel: 780-645-3331 *Fax:* 780-645-1702
www9.albertahealthservices.ca/Default.aspx?cid=162&lang=1
Number of Beds: 80 beds (30 acute care beds, including 3 special care beds, 2 palliative care beds; there is also a 30-bed continuing care facility and a 20-bed psych
Note: Services include emergency, diagnostic imaging (ultrasound, x-ray), eating disorder services, obstetrics, pharmacy, rehabilitation, renal dialysis, and laboratory.
Dr. Stephen Duckett, President/CEO, AHS
Bev Belland, Site Manager
Dr. Albert Harmse, Chief of Medical Staff

Stettler: **Stettler Hospital & Care Centre**
Affiliated with: Alberta Health Services
5912 - 47 Ave., Stettler, AB T0C 2L0
Tel: 403-742-7400 *Fax:* 403-742-1244
www.albertahealthservices.ca
Number of Beds: 150 beds (with 50 acute care, 40 long-term care, 2 respite beds)
Note: Services include emergency, continuing care, diabetes education, diagnostic imaging, enterostomal therapy, homecare, mental health, obstetrics, occupational therapy (for acute & continuing care), palliative care, pharmacy, physical therapy, respiratory therapy, sleep program, speech language pathology
Dr. Stephen Duckett, President/CEO, AHS
Donna Stelmachovich, Vice-President, Seniors Health, AHS
Diane Ecklund, Site Program Supervisor

Stony Plain: **WestView Health Centre**
Affiliated with: Alberta Health Services
4405 South Park Dr., Stony Plain, AB T7Z 2M7
Tel: 780-968-3600 *Fax:* 780-963-7612
Number of Beds: 68 beds
Joy Myskiw, Area Team Leader

Strathmore: **Strathmore District Health Services**
Affiliated with: Alberta Health Services
200 Brent Blvd., Strathmore, AB T1P 1J9
Tel: 403-934-4204 *Fax:* 403-934-3948
www.albertahealthservices.ca
Number of Beds: 25 acute care, 23 long-term care beds
Note: An acute care hospital with services including cardiology, nutrition services, continuing care, diabetes education, diagnostic imaging, fluoroscopy, Holter monitoring, home care, laboratory, medical genetics, occupational therapy, palliative care, pharmacy, physical therapy, psychiatric assessment, respiratory services, respite care, speech language pathology
Dr. Stephen Duckett, President/CEO, AHS
Donna Stelmachovich, Vice-President, Seniors Health, AHS
Dr. Jim Silvius, Senior Medical Director, AHS

Sundre: **Sundre Hospital & Care Centre**
Affiliated with: Alberta Health Services
709 - 1 St. NE, Sundre, AB T0M 1X0
Tel: 403-638-3033 *Fax:* 403-638-4971
www.albertahealthservices.ca
Number of Beds: 13 acute care, 15 continuing care beds
Note: A facility offering long-term and acute care with services including emergency, clinical nutrition, continuing care counseling, diabetes education, diagnostic imaging, enterostomal therapy, laboratory, obstetrics, occupational therapy, palliative care, pharmacy, physical therapy, speech language pathology.
Dr. Stephen Duckett, President/CEO, AHS
Linda Cargill, Executive Director, Community & Rural Hospitals, AHS
Bonny Jones, Site Coordinator

Swan Hills: **Swan Hills Healthcare Centre**
Affiliated with: Alberta Health Services
PO Box 266, 29 Freeman Dr., Swan Hills, AB T0G 2C0
Tel: 780-333-7000 *Fax:* 780-333-7009
www9.albertahealthservices.ca/Default.aspx?cid=163&lang=1
Year Founded: 1985
Number of Beds: 4 acute care beds
Note: A community centre with services including emergency, general medicine, laboratory, nutrition services pharmacy, radiology.
Dr. Stephen Duckett, President/CEO, AHS
Patricia Baker, Site Manager
Dr. J. Hankinson, Site Medical Director

Taber: **Taber Health Centre**
Affiliated with: Alberta Health Services
Former Name: Taber Hospital
4326 - 50 Ave., Taber, AB T0K 2G0
Tel: 403-223-7211 *Fax:* 403-388-6011
www.albertahealthservices.ca
Number of Beds: 19 acute care, 15 auxiliary, 55 nursing home beds
Note: This acute and continuing care facility has services including emergency, diagnostic imaging, home care, laboratory, neonatal intensive care, occupational therapy, pediatrics, therapeutic recreation.
Dr. Stephen Duckett, CEO, AHS
Bruce Conway, Senior Media Relations Advisor, South, AHS
403-943-1212

Tofield: **Tofield Health Centre**
Affiliated with: Alberta Health Services
PO Box 1200, 5543 - 44 St., Tofield, AB T0B 4J0
Tel: 780-662-3263 *Fax:* 780-662-3835
www.albertahealthservices.ca
Number of Beds: 16 acute care, 50 continuing care beds
Note: Services include emergency, acute care, communicable disease control, continuing care, home care, laboratory, occupational therapy, palliative care, physiotherapy, prenatal education, radiology, respiratory therapy, respite care, speech language services, surgery
Dr. Stephen Duckett, President/CEO, AHS
Dr. Dave Megren, Executive Vice-President/CMO, AHS
Roman Cooney, Senior Vice-President, Communications, AHS
Betty Kolewaski, Site Administrator

Two Hills: **Two Hills Health Centre**
Affiliated with: Alberta Health Services
PO Box 458, 4401 - 53 Ave., Two Hills, AB T0B 4K0
Tel: 780-657-3344 *Fax:* 780-657-2508
www.albertahealthservices.ca
Year Founded: 1986
Number of Beds: 75 beds (6 acute care, 60 continuing care, 9 stroke rehabilitation beds)
Note: A multi-level care complex with services including emergency, acute care, communicable disease control, genetics, mental health clinics, nutrition, continuing care, diabetes education, home care, laboratory, occupational therapy, adult

community rehab program, oral health, palliative care, pharmacy, prenatal education, radiology, respiratory therapy, respite care, social work, stroke & geriatric empowerment unit
Dr. Stephen Duckett, President/CEO, AHS
Cheryl Knight, Executive Director, Continuing Care, Integrated Services Rural, AHS
Kathy Miskew, Interm Site Coordinator

***Valleyview:* Valleyview Health Complex**
Affiliated with: Alberta Health Services
4802 Highway St., Valleyview, AB T0H 3N0
Tel: 780-524-3356 *Fax:* 780-524-4462
Number of Beds: 15 acute care, 17 long-term care beds
Tracy Brown, Site Manager
Debbie Stewart, Chairman

***Vegreville:* St. Joseph's General Hospital**
Affiliated with: Alberta Health Services
5241 - 43 St., Vegreville, AB T9C 1R5
Tel: 780-632-2811 *Fax:* 780-603-4401
www.albertahealthservices.ca
Number of Beds: 35 beds; 6 station dialysis unit
Note: An acute care facility offering services in emergency, medicine, laboratory, diagnostic imaging (x-ray, ultrasound), dialysis, diabetic education, occupational therapy, respiratory therapy, surgery and day support
Dr. Stephen Duckett, President/CEO, AHS
Dr. David Megren, Executive Vice-President/CMO, AHS
Kerry Williamson, Senior Media Relations Advisor, North Region, AHS
780-407-2602

***Vermilion:* Vermilion Health Centre**
Affiliated with: Alberta Health Services
5720 - 50 Ave., Vermilion, AB T9X 1K7
Tel: 780-853-5305 *Fax:* 780-853-4786
www.ech.ab.ca
Number of Beds: 25 acute care, 48 continuing care beds
Debora Okrainetz, Health Centre Coordinator

***Viking:* Viking Health Centre**
Affiliated with: Alberta Health Services
PO Box 60, 5110 - 57 Ave., Viking, AB T0B 4N0
Tel: 780-336-4786 *Fax:* 780-336-4983
www.ech.ab.ca
Number of Beds: 16 acute care beds
Note: Community health care services; acute & continuing care facilities
Kathryn Miskew, Health Centre Coordinator

***Vulcan:* Vulcan Community Health Centre**
Affiliated with: Alberta Health Services
610 Elizabeth St. South, Vulcan, AB T0L 2B0
Tel: 403-485-3333 *Fax:* 403-485-2336
Number of Beds: 8 acute care, 15 long-term care beds
Patty Greene, Executive Leader

***Wabasca:* Wabasca/Desmarais Healthcare Centre**
Affiliated with: Alberta Health Services
Former Name: Wabasca/Desmarais General Hospital
PO Box 450, Wabasca, AB T0G 2K0
Tel: 780-891-3007 *Fax:* 780-891-3784
trisslin@aspenrha.ab.ca
www.aspenrha.ab.ca
Number of Beds: 10 beds
Kirk Richardson

***Wainwright:* Wainwright Health Centre**
Affiliated with: Alberta Health Services
530 - 6 Ave., Wainwright, AB T9W 1R6
Tel: 780-842-3324 *Fax:* 780-842-4290
www.ech.ab.ca
Number of Beds: 25 acute care, 69 continuing care beds
Cheryl Huxley, Health Centre Coordinator

***Westlock:* Westlock Healthcare Centre**
Affiliated with: Alberta Health Services
#103, 10030 - 106 St., Westlock, AB T7P 2G4
Tel: 780-349-3301 *Fax:* 780-349-6973
Number of Beds: 45 beds
Joyce Nadeau, Site Supervisor
Richard Baker, Director of Plant Operations

***Wetaskiwin:* Wetaskiwin Hospital & Health Centre**
Affiliated with: Alberta Health Services
Former Name: Crossroads Hospital & Health Centre - Wetaskiwin
6910 - 47 St., Wetaskiwin, AB T9A 3N3
Tel: 780-361-7100 *Fax:* 780-361-4107
www.dthr.ab.ca
Number of Beds: 76 acute care, 79 long-term care beds
Bruce Finkel, Site Leader

***Whitecourt:* Whitecourt Healthcare Centre**
Affiliated with: Alberta Health Services
20 Sunset Blvd., Whitecourt, AB T7S 1M8
Tel: 780-778-2285 *Fax:* 780-778-5161
Number of Beds: 24 beds
Marj Stockwell, Facility Supervisor

Auxiliary Hospitals

***Breton:* Breton Health Centre**
Affiliated with: Alberta Health Services
4919 - 49th Ave., Breton, AB T0C 0P0
Tel: 780-696-4701 *Fax:* 780-696-4747
www.albertahealthservices.ca
Year Founded: 1994
Number of Beds: 23 long term care beds
Note: Hospital Specialties: Laboratory services (780-696-3731); Occupational therapy; Physical therapy; Recreational therapy; Speech language pathology; Clinical nutrition services (403-309-6199); Continuing care (780-696-3731); Home care; Palliative care (780-696-4713)

***Cardston:* Cardston Health Centre**
Affiliated with: Alberta Health Services
PO Box 1440, 144 - 2nd St. West, Cardston, AB T0K 0K0
Tel: 403-653-5234
www.albertahealthservices.ca
Note: Hospital Specialties: Emergency services; Diagnostic imaging (403-653-4399); Surgery; Obstetrics: Acute care; Rehabilitation; Therapeutic Recreation (403-653-5253); Speech language pathology; Continuing care (403-653-5262); Palliative care
Cindy Baker, Manager, Cardston Acute Care
403-653-4411, CBaker@chr.ab.ca

***Carmangay:* Little Bow Continuing Care Centre**
316 Armstrong St., Carmangay, AB T0L 0N0
Tel: 403-643-3511 *Fax:* 403-643-4222
Number of Beds: 20 beds
Pete Sherstabetoff, Supervisor, Plant Maintenance

***Claresholm:* Willow Creek Continuing Care Centre**
Affiliated with: Alberta Health Services
4221 - 8 St., Claresholm, AB T0L 0T0
Tel: 403-625-3361 *Fax:* 403-625-3822
Number of Beds: 100 beds
Pat Manderville, Health Services Leader
Pat Manderville, Community Care Leader

***Lacombe:* Lacombe Community Health Centre**
Affiliated with: Alberta Health Services
5010 - 51 St., Lacombe, AB T4L 1W2
Tel: 403-782-3218 *Fax:* 403-782-2866
Kerry Bales, Community Care Home Care Manager

***Lethbridge:* St. Michael's Health Centre**
Affiliated with: Alberta Health Services
1400 - 9 Ave. South, Lethbridge, AB T1J 4V5
Tel: 403-382-6400 *Fax:* 403-382-6433
Year Founded: 1929
Number of Beds: 202 beds (148 continuing care, 36 rehabilitation, 18 palliative)
Note: A long-term care (continuing care) facility focusing on assisted living, palliative care, post-acute rehabilitative program, Bridges program (care for the elderly in their own home). It operates under the governance of Covenant Health, a Catholic healthcare provider.
R. Patrick Dumelie, President/CEO, Covenant Health
Al Pierog, Vice-President, Seniors Health, Covenant Health
Fran Ross, Vice-President, Communications, Covenant Health

***Trochu:* St. Mary's Health Care Centre**
Affiliated with: Alberta Health Services
PO Box 100, 451 de Chauney Ave., Trochu, AB T0M 2C0
Tel: 403-442-3955 *Fax:* 403-341-8632
Number of Beds: 28 beds
Kathryn Kane-Upton, CEO

***Westlock:* Westlock Long Term Care Centre**
Affiliated with: Alberta Health Services
9732 - 100 Ave., Westlock, AB T7P 2G3
Tel: 780-349-3306 *Fax:* 780-349-5647
Number of Beds: 103 beds
Susan Gokiert, Coninuing Care Centre Manager
Brian Hyndman, Supervisor, Plant Maintenance

Community Health Centres

Community Health Care Centres

***Airdrie:* Airdrie Regional Health Centre**
Affiliated with: Alberta Health Services
604 Main St. South, Airdrie, AB T4B 1C9
Tel: 403-912-8400 *Fax:* 403-948-6284
www.calgaryhealthregion.ca

***Athabasca:* Athabasca Community Health Services**
Affiliated with: Alberta Health Services
3401 - 48 Ave., Athabasca, AB T9S 1M7
Tel: 780-675-2231 *Fax:* 780-675-3111
Rosalie Stobee, Supervisor

***Banff:* Banff Community Health Centre**
Affiliated with: Alberta Health Services
PO Box 1266, 301 Lynx St., Banff, AB T1L 1B3
Tel: 403-762-2990 *Fax:* 403-762-5570
Dr. Judith MacDonald, Designated Physician

***Barrhead:* Barrhead Community Health Services**
Affiliated with: Alberta Health Services
6203 - 49 Ave., Barrhead, AB T7N 1A1
Tel: 780-674-3408 *Fax:* 780-674-3941
Toll-Free: 780-674-3408
Lorraine Lindberg, CHS Supervisor

***Bashaw:* Bashaw**
Affiliated with: Alberta Health Services
5308, 53 St., Bashaw, AB T0B 0H0
Tel: 780-372-3731 *Fax:* 780-372-4050
www.ech.ab.ca
Lee Fredeen-Kohlert, Contact

***Bashaw:* Hospital Bashaw**
Affiliated with: Alberta Health Services
PO Box 449, 4909 - 50 St., Bashaw, AB T0B 0H0
Tel: 780-372-3731 *Fax:* 780-372-4050
www.ech.ab.ca
Number of Beds: 25 beds, 4 program beds
Evelyn Kraft, Interim Health Centre Coordinator

***Beaumont:* Beaumont Public Health Authority**
Affiliated with: Alberta Health Services
4918 - 50 Ave., Beaumont, AB T4X 1J9
Tel: 780-929-4822 *Fax:* 780-929-4828
www.capitalhealth.ca

***Beaverlodge:* Beaverlodge Public Health Centre**
Affiliated with: Alberta Health Services
PO Box 120, 412 - 10A St., Beaverlodge, AB T0H 0C0
Tel: 780-354-2647 *Fax:* 780-354-1550
Janet Wallace, Director, Health Services

***Black Diamond:* Black Diamond Health Unit**
Affiliated with: Alberta Health Services
PO Box 1, 717 Government Rd. S, Black Diamond, AB T0L 0H0
Tel: 403-933-8505 *Fax:* 403-933-2031

***Blairmore:* Community Health - Crowsnest Pass**
Affiliated with: Alberta Health Services
2001 - 107 St., Blairmore, AB T0K 0E0
Tel: 403-388-6009 *Fax:* 403-388-6011

***Bonnyville:* Bonnyville Community Health Services**
Affiliated with: Alberta Health Services
4904 - 50 Ave., Bonnyville, AB T9N 2G4
Tel: 780-826-3381 *Fax:* 780-826-6470
Joan Panteluk, Community Health Services Supervisor

***Bow Island:* Bow Island Public Health/Home Care**
Affiliated with: Alberta Health Services
PO Box 949, Bow Island, AB T0K 0G0
Tel: 403-525-2296 *Fax:* 403-525-6357
www.palliserhealth.org

***Boyle:* Boyle Community Health Services**
Affiliated with: Alberta Health Services
5004 Lakeview Rd., Boyle, AB T0A 0M0
Tel: 780-689-2677 *Fax:* 780-689-2835
Note: home care office

***Brooks:* Brooks Home Care**
Affiliated with: Alberta Health Services
#11 - 311 Ninth St. SE, Brooks, AB T1A 8E3
Tel: 403-362-7766 *Fax:* 403-362-7778

***Calgary:* 8th & 8th Health Centre**
Affiliated with: Alberta Health Services
912 - 8 Ave. SW, Calgary, AB T2P 1H9
Tel: 403-781-1200 *Fax:* 403-205-4979

***Calgary:* Bowness Community Health Centre**
Affiliated with: Alberta Health Services
6328 - 35 Ave. NW, Calgary, AB T3B 1S4
Tel: 403-288-7744 *Fax:* 403-288-3223

***Calgary:* East Community Health Centre**
Affiliated with: Alberta Health Services
112 - 28 St. SE, Calgary, AB T2A 5J9
Tel: 403-248-8868 *Fax:* 403-273-3219

***Calgary:* Forest Lawn District Office**
Affiliated with: Alberta Health Services
3810 - 17 Ave. SE, Calgary, AB T1X 1E1
Tel: 403-944-7300 *Fax:* 403-248-0429
Lisa Oake, Secretary

***Calgary:* Millican-Odgen Community Health Centre**
Affiliated with: Alberta Health Services
2880 Glenmore Trail SE, Calgary, AB T2C 2E6
Tel: 403-944-7225
Lorraine Dunn, Manager

***Calgary:* North Hill Community Health Centre**
Affiliated with: Alberta Health Services
1920 - 14 Ave. NW, Calgary, AB T2N 1M5
Tel: 403-282-1612 *Fax:* 403-282-0039

***Calgary:* Northwest Health Centre**
Affiliated with: Alberta Health Services
#109, 1829 Ranchlands Blvd. NW, Calgary, AB T3G 2A7
Tel: 403-943-9700 *Fax:* 403-943-9735

***Calgary:* Shaganappi Complex**
Affiliated with: Alberta Health Services
3415 - 8th Ave. SW, Calgary, AB T3C 0E8
Tel: 403-944-7373 *Fax:* 403-246-0326
Note: Immunization services are provided.

***Calgary:* South Calgary Health Centre**
Affiliated with: Alberta Health Services
31 Sunpark Plaza SE, Calgary, AB T2X 3W5
Tel: 403-943-9300
Note: The health centre is open from 8:00am to 10:00pm, each day of the year. The following services are provided: urgent care (403-943-9300); health information (403-943-9469); nutrition classes (403-943-2584); immunization (403-943-9500); diagnostic imaging (403-873-2336); laboratory services (403-777-5121); parent drop-in (403-943-9500); pediatric asthama services (403-943-9139); pulmonary rehabilitation (403-943-9433); speech language pathology (403-943-9484); & mental health services (403-943-1500).

***Calgary:* Thornhill District Office**
Affiliated with: Alberta Health Services
6617 Centre St. NW, Calgary, AB T2K 4Y5
Tel: 403-274-4515 *Fax:* 403-944-2224

***Calgary:* Village Square Community Health Centre**
Affiliated with: Alberta Health Services
2623 - 56 St. NE, Calgary, AB T1Y 6E7
Tel: 403-944-7000 *Fax:* 403-285-6304

***Calling Lake:* Calling Lake Community Health Services**
Affiliated with: Alberta Health Services
Highway 813, Calling Lake, AB T0G 0G0
Tel: 780-331-3760 *Fax:* 780-331-2200

***Camrose:* Camrose Public Health, Home Care, Rehab**
Affiliated with: Alberta Health Services
4615 - 56 St., Camrose, AB T4V 4M5
Tel: 780-679-2900 *Fax:* 780-679-2929
www.ech.ab.ca
Monica O'Gorman

***Canmore:* Canmore Public Health Office**
Affiliated with: Alberta Health Services
Provincial Building, #104, 800 Railway Ave., Canmore, AB T1W 1P1
Tel: 403-678-5656 *Fax:* 403-678-5068
Note: Public health programs

***Cardston:* Cardston Community & Wellness Site**
Affiliated with: Alberta Health Services
Provincial Bldg., PO Box 1590, 576 Main St., Cardston, AB T0K 0K0
Tel: 403-388-6099 *Fax:* 403-388-6011
Note: community health centre & home care office
Pam Whitnack, CEO

***Claresholm:* Claresholm Public Health & Community Care**
Affiliated with: Alberta Health Services
PO Box 1391, 5221 - 2nd St. West, Claresholm, AB T0L 0T0
Tel: 403-625-4061 *Fax:* 403-625-4062
Pat Manderville, Facility Coordinator

***Coaldale:* Coaldale Community Health**
Affiliated with: Alberta Health Services
PO Box 1000, 2012 - 18 St., Coaldale, AB T1M 1M8
Tel: 403-345-6507 *Fax:* 403-345-2043
Number of Beds: 40 continuing care, 4 community care beds
Bob Parker, Environmental Services

***Coaldale:* Community Health - Coaldale**
Affiliated with: Alberta Health Services
2012 - 18 St., Coaldale, AB T1M 1M8
Tel: 403-345-3000 *Fax:* 403-345-2043
Toll-Free: 866-345-8800
www.albertahealthservices.ca

***Cochrane:* Cochrane Community Health Centre**
Affiliated with: Alberta Health Services
60 Grande Blvd., Cochrane, AB T4C 0S4
Tel: 403-851-8000 *Fax:* 403-932-7219
Note: Home care public health programs

***Cold Lake:* Cold Lake Community Health Services**
Affiliated with: Alberta Health Services
4720 - 55 St., Cold Lake, AB T9M 1V9
Tel: 780-594-4404 *Fax:* 780-594-2404
Anne Tucker, Supervisor

***Cold Lake:* Elizabeth Settlement Community Health Services**
Affiliated with: Alberta Health Services
4720 - 55 St., Cold Lake, AB T9M 1V8
Tel: 780-594-3383
Anne Tucker, Supervisor

***Consort:* Consort Community Health Centre**
Affiliated with: Alberta Health Services
5410 - 52 Ave., Consort, AB T0C 1B0
Tel: 403-577-3770 *Fax:* 403-577-2235
www.albertahealthservices.ca
Note: Specialties: Public health promotion & services, including nutrition services & postnatal follow-up; Education programs, including diabetes & car seat education; Immunization clinics; Alberta Aids to Daily Living Program; Home care; Respite care; Continuing care counselling & placement coordination

***Coronation:* Coronation Community Health Centre**
Affiliated with: Alberta Health Services
4909 Royal St., Coronation, AB T0C 1C0
Tel: 403-578-3200 *Fax:* 403-578-2702
Note: Coronation Community Health Centre provides the following services: health promotion (403-578-3200); immunization (403-578-3200); oral health program (403-578-3200); prenatal education (403-578-3200); breastfeeding support services (403-578-3200); child safety seat program (403-578-3200); speech language pathology (403-578-3200); & continuing care counselling (403-578-3200).

***Drayton Valley:* Drayton Valley Community Health Centre**
Affiliated with: Alberta Health Services
4110 - 50 Ave., Drayton Valley, AB T7A 0B3
Tel: 780-542-4415 *Fax:* 780-621-4998
www.dthr.ab.ca

***Drumheller:* Drumheller Health Unit**
Affiliated with: Alberta Health Services
601 - 7 St. East, Drumheller, AB T0J 0Y5
Tel: 403-823-3341 *Fax:* 403-823-6657

***Eckville:* Eckville Community Health Centre**
Affiliated with: Alberta Health Services
PO Box 150, 5120 - 51 Ave., Eckville, AB T0M 0X0
Tel: 403-746-2201 *Fax:* 403-341-8632
Number of Beds: 20 beds
Kevin McEntee, Administrator
Ken Kissick, Maintenance

***Edmonton:* Bonnie Doon Public Health Centre**
Affiliated with: Alberta Health Services
8314 - 88 Ave. NW, Edmonton, AB T6C 1L1
Tel: 780-413-5670 *Fax:* 780-466-3110
www.capitalhealth.ca

***Edmonton:* Capital Health Home Care**
Affiliated with: Alberta Health Services
10216 - 124th St., Edmonton, AB T5N 4A3
Tel: 780-408-5465 *Fax:* 780-488-3401
www.capitalhealth.ca
Linda Killick, Director

***Edmonton:* Castle Downs Public Health Centre**
Affiliated with: Alberta Health Services
214-10807 Castle Downs Rd. NW, Edmonton, AB T5X 3N7
Tel: 780-413-5787 *Fax:* 780-413-9746
www.capitalhealth.ca

***Edmonton:* Eastwood Public Health Centre**
Affiliated with: Alberta Health Services
7919 - 118 Ave. NW, Edmonton, AB T5B 0R5
Tel: 780-413-5645 *Fax:* 780-474-5760
www.capitalhealth.ca

***Edmonton:* Mill Woods Public Health Centre**
Affiliated with: Alberta Health Services
7525 - 38 Ave. NW, Edmonton, AB T6K 3X9
Tel: 780-413-5685 *Fax:* 780-461-2504
www.capitalhealth.ca
Marianne Stewart, Sr. Operating Officer

***Edmonton:* North Central Public Health Centre**
Affiliated with: Alberta Health Services
25-9204 - 144th Ave. NW, Edmonton, AB T5E 6A3
Tel: 780-413-5600 *Fax:* 780-457-5638
www.capitalhealth.ca

***Edmonton:* Northeast Community Health Centre**
Affiliated with: Alberta Health Services
14007 - 50 St., Edmonton, AB T5A 5E4
Tel: 780-472-5000 *Fax:* 780-472-5188
Toll-Free: 866-408-5465
www.capitalhealth.ca

***Edmonton:* Twin Brooks Public Health Centre**
Affiliated with: Alberta Health Services
201-1110 - 113 St. NW, Edmonton, AB T6J 7J4
Tel: 780-413-5630 *Fax:* 780-437-6270
www.capitalhealth.ca

***Edmonton:* West Jasper Place Public Health Centre**
Affiliated with: Alberta Health Services
9720 - 182 St. NW, Edmonton, AB T5T 3T9
Tel: 780-413-5700 *Fax:* 780-484-9516
www.capitalhealth.ca

***Edmonton:* Woodcroft Public Health Centre**
Affiliated with: Alberta Health Services
13221 - 115 Ave. NW, Edmonton, AB T5M 4B7
Tel: 780-413-5720 *Fax:* 780-451-5886
www.capitalhealth.ca

***Edson:* Edson Community Health Services**
Affiliated with: Alberta Health Services
5028 - 3 Ave., Edson, AB T7E 1X4
Tel: 780-723-4421 *Fax:* 780-852-3413
Margaret Fern, CHS Supervisor

***Elk Point:* Elk Point Community Health Services**
Affiliated with: Alberta Health Services
5310 - 50 Ave., Elk Point, AB T0A 1A0
Tel: 780-724-3532 *Fax:* 780-943-2575
Joan Panteluk, Community Health Services Supervisor

***Elnora:* Elnora Community Health Centre**
Affiliated with: Alberta Health Services
PO Box 659, 425 - 8 Ave., Elnora, AB T0M 0Y0
Tel: 403-773-3636 *Fax:* 403-341-8632

***Evansburg:* Evansburg Health Centre**
Affiliated with: Alberta Health Services
5225 - 50 St., Evansburg, AB T0E 0T0
Tel: 780-727-2288 *Fax:* 780-727-2809
www.capitalhealth.ca

***Fishing Lake:* Fishing Lake Community Health Services**
Affiliated with: Alberta Health Services
c/o Elk Point Community Health Services, 5310 - 50 Avenue, Bag 3, Fishing Lake, AB T0A 1A0
Tel: 780-943-2202 *Fax:* 780-943-2575

Joan Panteluk, Community Health Services Supervisor

***Fort MacLeod:* Fort Macleod Community Health**
Affiliated with: Alberta Health Services
Fort Macleod Health Centre, PO Box 820, 744 - 26 St. South, Fort MacLeod, AB T0L 0Z0
Tel: 403-553-5351 *Fax:* 403-553-4567
www.albertahealthservices.ca

Note: Specialties: Community mental health services (403-553-5340); Home care services (403-553-5300); Prenatal education & immunization program (403-553-5351)

***Fort MacLeod:* Fort Macleod Health Centre**
Affiliated with: Alberta Health Services
744 - 26 St. South, Fort MacLeod, AB T0L 0Z0
Tel: 403-553-5311
www.albertahealthservices.ca

Note: Specialties: Emergency services (403-553-4487); Diagnostic imaging services (403-553-4487); Laboratory services (403-553-4487); Occupational therapy; Services to persons with developmental disabilities; Southern Alberta Renal Program (403-553-3690)

***Fort Saskatchewan:* Fort Saskatchewan Health Unit**
Affiliated with: Alberta Health Services
10420 - 98th Ave., Fort Saskatchewan, AB T8L 2N6
Tel: 780-998-3366
www.albertahealthservices.ca

Note: Specialties: Audiology service (780-992-5801); Mental health services (780-342-2388); Health for Two Program (780-342-2366); Immunization services (780-342-2366)

***Fox Creek:* Aspen Health Services**
PO Box 430, Fox Creek, AB T0H 1P0
Tel: 780-622-3730 *Fax:* 780-622-4169

***Gibbons:* Gibbons Health Unit**
Affiliated with: Alberta Health Services
4720 50 Ave., Gibbons, AB T0A 1N0
Tel: 780-923-3700 *Fax:* 780-923-2373
www.capitalhealth.ca

***Gift Lake:* Public Health Centre**
Affiliated with: Alberta Health Services
PO Box 60, Gift Lake, AB T0G 1B0
Tel: 780-767-2101 *Fax:* 780-767-2095
Kate Butler, Director, Health Services

***Glendon:* Glendon Community Health Clinic**
Affiliated with: Alberta Health Services
PO Box 570, Glendon, AB T0A 1P0
Tel: 780-635-3861 *Fax:* 780-635-4213
Joan Panteluk, Home Care Services Manager

***Grande Cache:* Public Health Centre/Mistahia Health Unit**
Affiliated with: Alberta Health Services
1001 Hoppe Ave., Grande Cache, AB T0E 0Y0
Tel: 780-827-3504 *Fax:* 780-827-2728
Tracy Peddy, Director, Health Services

***Grande Prairie:* College & Community Health Centre**
Affiliated with: Alberta Health Services
10620 - 104 Ave., Grande Prairie, AB T8V 8J8
Tel: 780-518-7500 *Fax:* 780-538-4400
Dr. Peter Lindsay

***Grande Prairie:* Public Health Centre**
Affiliated with: Alberta Health Services
10320 - 99 St., Grande Prairie, AB T8V 6J4
Tel: 780-513-7500 *Fax:* 780-532-1550

***Grande Prairie:* Public Health Centre**
Affiliated with: Alberta Health Services
10121 - 97 Ave., Grande Prairie, AB T8V 0N5
Tel: 780-532-4447 *Fax:* 780-864-4187

***Hanna:* Hanna Health Unit**
Affiliated with: Alberta Health Services
Former Name: Hanna Health Unit
PO Box 730, 904 Centre St. North, Hanna, AB T0J 1P0
Tel: 403-854-3331 *Fax:* 403-854-3233

***High Level:* Health Care Centre**
PO Box 2000, 10207 - 103 St., High Level, AB T0H 1Z0
Tel: 780-926-7000 *Fax:* 780-926-7001

***High Level:* Paddle Prairie Health Centre**
Affiliated with: Alberta Health Services
PO Box 46, High Level, AB T0H 2W0
Tel: 780-981-2188 *Fax:* 780-981-2190
www.capitalhealth.ca

***High Prairie:* Community Health Services**
PO Bag 1, High Prairie, AB T0G 1E0
Tel: 780-523-6450 *Fax:* 780-523-6458

***High River:* High River Public Health Centre**
Affiliated with: Alberta Health Services
PO Box 5638, 310 Macleod Trail, High River, AB T1V 1M7
Tel: 403-652-5450 *Fax:* 403-652-5455

***Hobbema:* Hobbema Community Health Clinic**
Affiliated with: Carewest Health Authority
PO Box 189, Hobbema, AB T0C 1N0
Tel: 780-585-2020 *Fax:* 780-585-3965
Helen Littlechild, Nurse in Charge

***Hughenden:* Hughenden Public Health: Home Care**
Affiliated with: Alberta Health Services
PO Box 25, 33 Mackenzie Ave., Hughenden, AB T0B 2E0
Tel: 780-753-6180 *Fax:* 780-753-2064
www.ech.ab.ca
Lana Clark

***Jasper:* Jasper Community Health Services**
Affiliated with: Alberta Health Services
529 Turret St., Jasper, AB T0E 1E0
Tel: 780-852-4759 *Fax:* 780-852-3413
Joan Connors, Supervisor

***Kinuso:* Kinuso Public Health Centre**
Affiliated with: Alberta Health Services
PO Box 208, Kinuso, AB T0G 1K0
Tel: 780-775-3501 *Fax:* 780-775-3944
Kate Butler, Director, Health Services

***Kitscoty:* Kitscoty Public Health**
Affiliated with: Alberta Health Services
PO Box 508, 4922 - 59 Ave., Kitscoty, AB T0B 2P0
Tel: 780-846-2824 *Fax:* 780-846-2731
www.ech.ab.ca

Note: community health & home care office
Randey Ferster

***La Crete:* La Crete Health Centre**
Affiliated with: Alberta Health Services
PO Box 295, 10601 - 100th Ave., La Crete, AB T0H 1H0
Tel: 780-928-3242 *Fax:* 780-928-3080

***Lac La Biche:* Buffalo Lake Settlement Health Unit**
Affiliated with: Alberta Health Services
c/o Lac La Biche Health Unit, PO Box 869, 9503 Beaverhill Rd., Lac La Biche, AB T0A 2C0
Tel: 780-689-4471 *Fax:* 780-689-2615
Tracy Smith, Supervisor

***Lac La Biche:* Community Health Services**
Affiliated with: Alberta Health Services
PO Box 297, 9503 Beaver Hill Rd., Lac La Biche, AB T0A 2C0
Tel: 780-623-4471 *Fax:* 780-623-4212
Tracy Smith, Supervisor

***Lac La Biche:* Kikino Settlement Community Health Services**
Affiliated with: Alberta Health Services
c/o Lac La Biche Health Unit, PO Box 869, 9503 Beaverhill Rd., Lac La Biche, AB T0A 2C0
Tel: 780-623-7797 *Fax:* 780-623-4212
Tracy Smith, Supervisor

***Lacombe:* Lacombe Hospital & Care Centre**
Affiliated with: Alberta Health Services
5430 - 47 Ave., Lacombe, AB T4L 1G8
Tel: 403-782-3336 *Fax:* 403-782-2818
Number of Beds: 101 beds
M. Stotz, Site Leader
Rob Grodaes, Plant Maintenance Director

***Lamont:* Lamont Public Health, Home Care**
Affiliated with: Alberta Health Services
Bag 10, 5216 - 53 St., Lamont, AB T0B 2R0
Tel: 780-895-2211 *Fax:* 780-895-2200
www.ech.ab.ca
Janet Kiist, Contact

***Leduc:* Leduc Public Health Centre**
Affiliated with: Alberta Health Services
4219 - 50 St., Leduc, AB T9E 8C9
Tel: 780-980-4644 *Fax:* 780-980-4666
www.capitalhealth.ca

***Lethbridge:* Community Health**
Affiliated with: Alberta Health Services
960 19 St. South, Lethbridge, AB T1J 0C6
Tel: 403-388-6009 *Fax:* 403-388-6011
Pam Whitnack, CEO

***Lethbridge:* Lethbridge Community Health - Lethbridge Centre Tower**
Affiliated with: Alberta Health Services
400 - 4th Ave. South, Lethbridge, AB T1J 4E1
Tel: 403-388-6009 *Fax:* 403-388-6011
Pam Whitnack, CEO

***Lethbridge:* Lethbridge Community Health Site/Health Unit**
Affiliated with: Alberta Health Services
806 - 2 Ave. South, Lethbridge, AB T1J 4L5
Tel: 403-388-6666 *Fax:* 403-627-5275
Pam Whitnack, CEO
Brian Dalshary, Coordinator, Environmental Services

***Magrath:* Magrath Community & Wellness Site**
Affiliated with: Alberta Health Services
PO Box 126, 135 West Civic Ave., Magrath, AB T0K 1J0
Tel: 403-388-6009 *Fax:* 403-388-6011
Pam Whitnack, CEO

***Manning:* Peace Country Health Unit**
Affiliated with: Alberta Health Services
PO Box 1260, 118 - 2 Ave., Manning, AB T0H 2M0
Tel: 780-836-3391 *Fax:* 780-836-2860

***Mannville:* Mannville Home Care, Public Health/Rehab**
Affiliated with: Alberta Health Services
PO Box 1000, 5007 - 46 St., Mannville, AB T0B 2W0
Tel: 780-763-3989 *Fax:* 780-736-3678
www.ech.ab.ca
Gladys Burrows
780-632-3331

***Mayerthorpe:* Mayerthorpe Community Health Services**
Affiliated with: Alberta Health Services
4417 - 45 St., Mayerthorpe, AB T0E 1N0
Tel: 780-786-4198 *Fax:* 780-786-2023
Doug Kemp, Supervisor

***McLennan:* Peace Country Health Unit - McLennan**
Affiliated with: Alberta Health Services
c/o Sacred Heart Community Health Centre, 350 - 3 Ave., McLennan, AB T0H 2L0
Tel: 780-324-3750 *Fax:* 780-324-4256

***Medicine Hat:* Medicine Hat Community Health Services**
Affiliated with: Alberta Health Services
2948 Dunmore Rd. SE, Medicine Hat, AB T1A 8E3
Tel: 403-502-8200 *Fax:* 403-528-2250

***Milk River:* Milk River/Warner Community & Wellness Site**
Affiliated with: Alberta Health Services
PO Box 90, 517 Centre Ave., Milk River, AB T0K 1M0
Tel: 403-647-3500 *Fax:* 403-627-5275

***Morinville:* Morinville Public Health Centre**
Affiliated with: Alberta Health Services
Former Name: Morinville Health Services
10008 - 107 St., Morinville, AB T8R 1L3
Tel: 780-939-3388 *Fax:* 780-939-7126
www.capitalhealth.ca

***Myrnam:* Myrnam Home Care**
Affiliated with: Alberta Health Services
PO Box 220, 4802 - 49 Ave., Myrnam, AB T0B 3K0
Tel: 780-366-3891 *Fax:* 780-366-3919
www.ech.ab.ca
Judy Flessau, Contact
780/632-3331

***Okotoks:* Okotoks Health & Wellness Centre**
Affiliated with: Alberta Health Services
11 Cimarron Common, Okotoks, AB T1S 2E9
Tel: 403-995-2600
Peer Mikelsen, Public Health Inspector

***Olds:* Olds Community Health Centre**
Affiliated with: Alberta Health Services
#103, 5030 - 50th St., Olds, AB T4H 1S1
Tel: 403-556-8441 *Fax:* 403-556-6842
Denise McBain, Vice-President, Community Health Services

***Onoway:* Onoway Community Health Servics**
Affiliated with: Alberta Health Services
PO Box 1047, 4919 Lac Ste Anne Trail, Onoway, AB T0E 1V0
Tel: 780-967-4440 *Fax:* 780-967-2547
Doug Kemp, Supervisor

***Oyen:* Oyen Community Health Services**
Affiliated with: Alberta Health Services
c/o Big Country Hospital, PO Box 296, 315 - 3 St. East, Oyen, AB T0J 2J0
Tel: 403-664-3651 *Fax:* 403-664-2934

***Peerless Lake:* Peerless Lake Community Health Services**
Affiliated with: Alberta Health Services
PO Box 90, Peerless Lake, AB T0G 2W0
Tel: 780-869-3930 *Fax:* 780-869-2053
Cindy Harmata, Supervisor

***Picture Butte:* Community Health**
Affiliated with: Alberta Health Services
301 Cowan Ave., Picture Butte, AB T0K 1V0
Tel: 403-732-4762 *Fax:* 403-627-5275

***Pincher Creek:* Community Health**
Affiliated with: Alberta Health Services
1222 Bev McLachlin Dr., Pincher Creek, AB T0K 1W0
Tel: 403-388-6009 *Fax:* 403-388-6011
Pam Whitnack, CEO

***Ponoka:* Ponoka Community Health Centre**
Affiliated with: Alberta Health Services
5900 Hwy. 2A, Ponoka, AB T4J 1P6
Tel: 403-783-4491 *Fax:* 403-341-8632
Denise McBain, Vice-President, Community Health Services

***Provost:* Provost Public Health, Home Care**
Affiliated with: Alberta Health Services
5419 - 44 St., Provost, AB T0B 3S0
Tel: 780-753-6180 *Fax:* 780-753-2064
www.ech.ab.ca
Lana Clark

***Rainbow Lake:* Rainbow Lake Health Centre**
Affiliated with: Alberta Health Services
PO Box 177, Rainbow Lake, AB T0H 2Y0
Tel: 780-956-3646 *Fax:* 780-926-3338
www.nlhr.ca

***Raymond:* Community Health**
Affiliated with: Alberta Health Services
PO Box 251, 200N - 2nd St. West, Raymond, AB T0K 2S0
Tel: 403-752-3303 *Fax:* 403-752-4655
Pam Whitnack, CEO

***Red Deer:* Red Deer 49th Street Community Health Centre**
Affiliated with: Alberta Health Services
4755 - 49th St., Red Deer, AB T4N 1T6
Tel: 403-314-5225
www.albertahealthservices.ca
Note: Specialties: Public health; Diabetes education (403-314-5780); Audiology (403-314-5225); Pediatric rehabilitation (403-314 5240); Speech language pathology (403-314-5250); Hanen parent program (403-314-5250)

***Red Deer:* Red Deer Community Health Centre**
Affiliated with: Alberta Health Services
2845 Bremner Ave., Red Deer, AB T4R 1S2
Tel: 403-341-2100 *Fax:* 403-341-8632
John Vogelzans, President/CEO

***Red Earth Creek:* Red Earth Creek Community Health Services**
Affiliated with: Alberta Health Services
PO Box 109, Red Earth Creek, AB T0G 1X0
Tel: 780-649-2242 *Fax:* 780-649-2029
Cindy Harmata

***Redwater:* Redwater Health Care Centre**
Affiliated with: Alberta Health Services
4812 - 58 St., Redwater, AB T0A 2W0
Tel: 780-942-3801 *Fax:* 780-942-2024
www.capitalhealth.ca

***Rimbey:* Rimbey Community Health Centre**
Affiliated with: Alberta Health Services
4709 - 51 Ave., Rimbey, AB T0C 2J0
Tel: 403-843-2288 *Fax:* 403-843-3050
Denise McBain, Administrator

***Rocky Mountain House:* Rocky Mountain House Community Health Centre**
Affiliated with: Alberta Health Services
5016 - 52 Ave., Rocky Mountain House, AB T0M 1T0
Tel: 403-845-3030 *Fax:* 403-845-4975
Number of Beds: 30 continuing care beds

***Sedgewick:* Sedgewick Public Health, Home Care, Rehab**
Affiliated with: Alberta Health Services
PO Box 12, 4822 - 50 St., Sedgewick, AB T0B 4C0
Tel: 780-384-3652 *Fax:* 780-608-8850
www.ech.ab.ca
Marlene Adam

***Sherwood Park:* Health First Strathcona Primary Care Centre**
Affiliated with: Alberta Health Services
140 - 80 Chippewa Rd., Sherwood Park, AB T0B 4C0
Tel: 780-449-5380 *Fax:* 780-942-2373
www.capitalhealth.ca

***Sherwood Park:* Strathcona County Health Centre**
Affiliated with: Alberta Health Services
2 Brower Dr., Sherwood Park, AB T8H 1V4
Tel: 780-342-4600

***Slave Lake:* Slave Lake Community Health Services**
Affiliated with: Alberta Health Services
309 - 6 St. NE, Slave Lake, AB T0G 2A4
Tel: 780-849-3947 *Fax:* 780-805-3550
Cindy Harmata, Community Health Services Supervisor

***Smoky Lake:* Smoky Lake Community Health Services**
Affiliated with: Alberta Health Services
4212 - 55 Ave., Smoky Lake, AB T0A 3C0
Tel: 780-656-3595 *Fax:* 780-943-2575
Gloria Strachan, Supervisor

***Spirit River:* Public Health Centre**
Affiliated with: Alberta Health Services
Former Name: Mistahia Health Unit - Spirit River
PO Box 187, Spirit River, AB T0H 3G0
Tel: 780-864-3063 *Fax:* 780-864-4187
Karen Osborne, Director, Health Services

***St Albert:* St. Albert Public Health Centre**
Affiliated with: Alberta Health Services
23 Sir Winston Churchill Ave., St Albert, AB T8N 2S7
Tel: 780-459-6671 *Fax:* 780-460-7062
www.capitalhealth.ca

***St Paul:* St Paul Community Health Services**
Affiliated with: Alberta Health Services
5610 - 50 Ave., St Paul, AB T0A 3A1
Tel: 780-645-3396 *Fax:* 780-943-2575
Leanne Betts, Community Health Services Supervisor

***Stettler:* Stettler Community Health Center**
Affiliated with: Alberta Health Services
5911 - 50 Ave. SS 2, Stettler, AB T0C 2L0
Tel: 403-742-3326 *Fax:* 403-641-8632
www.dthr.ab.ca
Jenn Currie, Director of Public Health

***Sundre:* Sundre Community Health Centre**
Affiliated with: Alberta Health Services
212 - 6 Ave. NE, Sundre, AB T0M 1X0
Tel: 403-638-4063 *Fax:* 403-341-8632
Note: health unit
Dr. Rudy Zimmer

***Swan Hills:* Swan Hills Community Health Services**
Affiliated with: Alberta Health Services
29 Freeman Dr., Swan Hills, AB T0G 2C0
Tel: 780-333-7077 *Fax:* 780-891-3784
Lorraine Lindberg, Supervisor

***Sylvan Lake:* Sylvan Lake Community Health Centre**
Affiliated with: Alberta Health Services
4602 - 49 Ave, Sylvan Lake, AB T4S 1M7
Tel: 403-887-2241
www.albertahealthservices.ca
Note: Specialties: Public health services; Health promotion; Car seat education program; Child & adolescent services; Speech language pathology; Mental health services; Continuing care counselling; Environmental public health program; Breast health program; Prenatal education program; Communicable disease control; Home care; Physiotherapy; Immunization clinics; Tobacco reduction program; Respite care
Lori Sparrow, Coordinator

***Taber:* Community Health**
Affiliated with: Alberta Health Services
5009 - 56th St., Taber, AB T1G 1M8
Tel: 403-223-4403 *Fax:* 403-627-5275
Pam Whitnack, CEO

***Thorhild:* Thorhild Community Health Services**
Affiliated with: Alberta Health Services
302 - 2 Ave., Thorhild, AB T0A 3J0
Tel: 780-398-3879 *Fax:* 780-398-2671
Gloria Strachan, Supervisor

***Thorsby:* Thorsby Public Health Centre**
Affiliated with: Alberta Health Services
4825 Hankin St., Thorsby, AB T0C 2P0
Tel: 780-789-4800 *Fax:* 780-789-4811
www.capitalhealth.ca

***Two Hills:* Two Hills Public Health, Home Care, Rehab**
Affiliated with: Alberta Health Services
c/o Two Hills Health Centre, PO Box 458, 4401 - 53 Ave., Two Hills, AB T0B 4K0
Tel: 780-657-3361 *Fax:* 780-608-8850
www.ech.ab.ca
Judy Flessau, Contact
780/632-3331,

***Valleyview:* Valleyview Public Health Centre**
Affiliated with: Alberta Health Services
Former Name: Mistahia Health Unit, Valleyview; Valleyview District Home Care Office
5112 - 50 Ave., Valleyview, AB T0H 3N0
Tel: 780-524-3338 *Fax:* 780-524-3153
Tracy Brown, Director, Health Services

***Vauxhall:* Vauxhall Community Care**
Affiliated with: Alberta Health Services
408 - 1 Ave., Vauxhall, AB T0K 2K0
Tel: 403-388-6009 *Fax:* 403-388-6011
Note: home care office, public health office
Pam Whitnack, CEO

***Vegreville:* Vegreville Public Health, Home Care, Rehab**
Affiliated with: Alberta Health Services
5318 - 50 St., Vegreville, AB T9C 1R1
Tel: 780-632-3331 *Fax:* 780-632-4334
www.ech.ab.ca
Bonnie Litwin, Contact

***Vermilion:* Vermilion Public Health, Home Care, Rehab**
Affiliated with: Alberta Health Services
4701 - 52nd St., Vermilion, AB T9X 1J9
Tel: 780-853-5270 *Fax:* 780-853-7362
www.ech.ab.ca
Note: community health & home care office
Gladys Burrows

***Viking:* Viking Home Care/Public Health/Rehab Office**
Affiliated with: Alberta Health Services
5110 - 57 Ave., Viking, AB T0B 4N0
Tel: 780-336-4782 *Fax:* 780-608-8850
www.ech.ab.ca
Hilda Tucker

***Vilna:* Vilna Community Health Services**
Affiliated with: Alberta Health Services
Former Name: Our Lady's Health Centre
5103 Dr. Frobb Ave., Vilna, AB T0A 3L0
Tel: 780-636-3533 *Fax:* 780-943-2575

***Vulcan:* Vulcan Health Unit**
Affiliated with: Alberta Health Services
Vulcan Community Health Centre, PO Box 214, 610 Elizabeth St., Vulcan, AB T0L 2B0
Tel: 403-485-2285 *Fax:* 403-485-2336
Wendy Shearer, Health Services Access Coordinator

Wabasca: **Wabasca/Desmarais Community Health Services**
Affiliated with: Alberta Health Services
PO Box 9, Wabasca, AB T0G 2K0
Tel: 780-891-3931 *Fax:* 780-891-3011
Brenda Jenkins, Supervisor

Wainwright: **Wainwright Public Health, Home Care**
Affiliated with: Alberta Health Services
Public Health #22, 810 - 14 Ave., Wainwright, AB T9W 1R2
Tel: 780-842-4077 *Fax:* 780-842-3151
www.ech.ab.ca
Randey Ferster

Westlock: **Westlock Community Health Services**
Affiliated with: Alberta Health Services
10024 - 107 St., Westlock, AB T7P 1H7
Tel: 780-349-3316 *Fax:* 780-349-5725
Rick Saint, Community Health Services Supervisor

Wetaskiwin: **Wetaskiwin Community Health Centre**
Affiliated with: Alberta Health Services
5610 - 40 Ave., Wetaskiwin, AB T9A 3E4
Tel: 780-361-4333 *Fax:* 780-361-8554
Malcolm Maxwell, CEO
Lucy Beck, Coordinator, Environmental Services

Whitecourt: **Whitecourt Community Health Services**
Affiliated with: Alberta Health Services
20 Sunset Blvd., Whitecourt, AB T7S 1M8
Tel: 780-778-5555 *Fax:* 780-778-3852

Willingdon: **Willingdon Home Care**
Affiliated with: Alberta Health Services
Former Name: Mary Immaculate Hospital
5303 - 49 St., Willingdon, AB T0B 4R0
Tel: 780-367-2928 *Fax:* 780-367-2379
www.ech.ab.ca
Judy Flessau, Manager, Health Services

Winfield: **Winfield Community Health Centre**
Affiliated with: Alberta Health Services
Former Name: Crossroads Health Unit - Winfield
PO Box 114, Winfield, AB T0C 2X0
Tel: 780-682-4757 *Fax:* 780-682-4750

Nursing Stations

Chateh: **Assumption Nursing Station**
PO Box 90, Chateh, AB T0H 0S0
Tel: 780-321-3971 *Fax:* 780-321-3820
Number of Beds: 1 bed
Joanne Smith, Nurse in Charge

Fort Chipewyan: **Fort Chipewyan Nursing Station**
PO Box 350, Fort Chipewyan, AB T0P 1B0
Tel: 780-697-3650 *Fax:* 780-697-3565

Rocky Mountain House: **Rocky Mountain House**
Big Horn Health Station, PO Box 1617, Rocky Mountain House, AB T4T 1A1
Tel: 403-845-3660 *Fax:* 403-845-3011

Trout Lake: **Trout Lake Health Station**
Affiliated with: Alberta Health Services
General Delivery, Trout Lake, AB T0G 2N0
Tel: 780-869-3922 *Fax:* 780-869-2054
www.albertahealthservices.ca
Note: Specialties: Public health services; Community care nursing; Health education; Environmental health services; Healthy Beginnings, a support program for families with new infants; Immunization; Nutrition services; Social work; Rehabilitation services

Worsley: **Worsley Community Health Centre**
Affiliated with: Alberta Health Services
General Delivery, Worsley, AB T0H 3W0
Tel: 780-685-3752 *Fax:* 780-685-2007
Rose Mary McDonald, Nurse

Special Treatment Centres

Calgary: **Carewest Dr. Vernon Fanning Extended Care Centre**
Affiliated with: Alberta Health Services
722 - 16 Ave. NE, Calgary, AB T2E 6V7
Tel: 403-230-6900 *Fax:* 403-230-6902
www.albertahealthservices.ca
Number of Beds: 294 beds
Mark Ewan, Director

Calgary: **Tom Baker Cancer Centre (TBCC)**
Affiliated with: Alberta Health Services
1331 - 29 St. NW, Calgary, AB T2N 4N2
Tel: 403-521-3723 *Fax:* 403-521-3245
Toll-Free: 866-238-3735
support@albertabreast.com (Alberta Breast Cancer Program)
www.albertahealthservices.ca
Note: Specialties: Medical oncology; Surgery (E-mail, Alberta Radiosurgery Centre: arcinfo@cancerboard.ab.ca); Radiation oncology; Radiology; Chemotherapy treatments; Psychosocial resources; Pathology; Genetics; Research
Dr. George Browman, Director

Calgary: **Women's Health Resources (WHR)**
Affiliated with: Alberta Health Services
Former Name: Grace Women's Health Centre
Foothills Medical Centre, 1403 - 29 St. NW, Calgary, AB T2N 2T9
Tel: 403-944-2270
www.albertahealthservices.ca
Patricia DeWitt, Manager

Camrose: **Rosehaven Care Center (The Bethany Group)**
Affiliated with: Alberta Health Services
4612 - 53 St., Camrose, AB T4V 1Y5
Tel: 780-679-2000 *Fax:* 780-679-2001
www.thebethanygroup.ca
Number of Beds: 100 beds
Note: Faith-based organization that operates a wide range of homes and services for older, disabled and vulnerable people in the Central Alberta area, serving over 1000 residents through over 600 staff members.
Marilyn Wood, Administrator

Edmonton: **Cross Cancer Institute**
Affiliated with: Alberta Health Services
11560 University Ave. NW, Edmonton, AB T6G 1Z2
Tel: 780-432-8771 *Fax:* 780-432-8411
www.albertahealthservices.ca
Number of Beds: 46 beds
Note: cancer treatment
Dr. Carol Cass

Edmonton: **Glenrose Rehabilitation Hospital**
Affiliated with: Alberta Health Services
10230 - 111 Ave., Edmonton, AB T5G 0B7
Tel: 780-735-7999 *Fax:* 780-735-7976
ihender@cha.ab.ca
www.cha.ab.ca/glenrose
Number of Beds: 240 beds
Note: rehabilitation centre

Edmonton: **McConnell Place North**
9113 - 144 Ave., Edmonton, AB T5E 6K2
Tel: 780-496-2575 *Fax:* 780-472-6699
Year Founded: 1995
Number of Beds: 36 beds
Note: Specialty: Residential care for persons with Alzheimer disease; Reminiscence therapy
Nat Mitchell, Manager

Edmonton: **Woman's Health Options**
Former Name: Morgentaler Clinic of Edmonton
12409 - 109A Ave., Edmonton, AB T5M 4A7
Tel: 780-484-1124 *Fax:* 780-489-3379
info@whol.ca
www.womanshealthoptions.com
Note: abortion clinic
Kim Cholewa, Manager

Grande Prairie: **Grande Prairie Cancer Centre**
Affiliated with: Alberta Health Services
Queen Elizabeth II Hospital, 10409 - 98 St., Grande Prairie, AB T8V 2E8
Tel: 780-538-7588 *Fax:* 780-532-9120
Note: cancer treatment; outpatient facility

Lethbridge: **Children's C.A.R.E.**
Affiliated with: Alberta Health Services
801 1 Ave. South, Lethbridge, AB T1J 1L6
Tel: 403-388-6666 *Fax:* 403-328-5934
Note: children's assessment, rehabilitation & education centre
Pam Whitnack, CEO

Lethbridge: **Jack Ady Cancer Centre**
Affiliated with: Alberta Health Services
Former Name: Alberta Health Services
#2H209, 960 - 19th St. South, Lethbridge, AB T1J 1W5
Tel: 403-329-0633 *Fax:* 403-320-0508
Note: cancer treatment
Dr. David R. Holland, Medical Director

Medicine Hat: **Medicine Hat Cancer Clinic**
Affiliated with: Alberta Health Services
Medicine Hat Regional Hospital, 666 - 5th St. SW, Medicine Hat, AB T1A 4H6
Tel: 403-529-8817
Year Founded: 1989
Number of Beds: 4 treatment beds + 10 treatment chairs
Note: Specialties: Colposcopy screening; Diagnostic imaging; Chemotherapy; Pain management; Counselling; Palliative treatment
Dr. Josh Foley, Director

Peace River: **Peace River Community Cancer Centre**
PO Box Bag 400, 10101, 68 St., Peace River, AB T8S 1T6
Tel: 780-624-7500 *Fax:* 780-624-7593
jillwood@cancerboard.ab.ca
Number of Beds: 3 treatment chairs
Note: cancer treatment

Red Deer: **Central Alberta Cancer Centre**
Affiliated with: Alberta Health Services
3942 - 50A Ave., Red Deer, AB T4N 4E7
Tel: 403-343-4526 *Fax:* 403-346-1160
Note: cancer treatment outpatient facility
Dr. Neil Graham, Director

Nursing Homes

Athabasca: **Athabasca Extendicare**
Affiliated with: Alberta Health Services
PO Box 119, 4517 - 53 St., Athabasca, AB T9S 1K4
Tel: 780-675-2291 *Fax:* 780-675-3833
Number of Beds: 50 beds
Note: Private; affiliated with Regional Health Authority
Joan Cody, Administrator

Barrhead: **Barrhead Continuing Care Centre**
Affiliated with: Alberta Health Services
Former Name: Keir Care Centre
5336 - 59 Ave., Barrhead, AB T7N 1L2
Tel: 780-674-4506 *Fax:* 780-674-3003
Number of Beds: 115 beds
Note: auxiliary
Susan Oleskiw, Site Supervisor

Blairmore: **York Creek Lodge**
Affiliated with: Alberta Health Services
1810 - 112 St., Blairmore, AB T0K 0J0
Tel: 403-562-2102 *Fax:* 403-562-2106
Number of Beds: 20 beds

Bonnyville: **Extendicare - Bonnyville**
Affiliated with: Alberta Health Services
4602 - 47 Ave., Bonnyville, AB T9N 2E8
Tel: 780-826-3341 *Fax:* 780-826-4890
www.extendicare.com
Number of Beds: 50 beds
Steve Krim, Administrator

Calgary: **Beverly Centre - Glenmore**
Affiliated with: Alberta Health Services
1729 - 90 Ave. SW, Calgary, AB T2V 4S1
Tel: 403-253-8806 *Fax:* 403-212-3532
Number of Beds: 200 beds

Calgary: **Bow View Manor**
Affiliated with: Alberta Health Services
4628 Montgomery Blvd. NW, Calgary, AB T3B 0K7
Tel: 403-288-4446 *Fax:* 403-288-8522
Number of Beds: 193 beds
Norma J. Jackson, Administrator

Calgary: **Bow-Crest Health Centre**
Affiliated with: Alberta Health Services
5927 Bowness Rd. NW, Calgary, AB T3B 0C7
Tel: 403-288-2373 *Fax:* 403-288-2403
www.albertahealthservices.ca
Number of Beds: 150 beds
Michael Harris, Administrator

Calgary: Carewest George Boyack
Affiliated with: Alberta Health Services
1203 Centre Ave. NE, Calgary, AB T2E 0A5
Tel: 403-267-2750 *Fax:* 403-267-2757
www.carewest.org
Number of Beds: 221 beds
Marg Marlin, Administrator

Calgary: Clifton Manor
Affiliated with: Alberta Health Services
4726 - 8 Ave. SE, Calgary, AB T2A 0A8
Tel: 403-272-9831 *Fax:* 403-248-5788
lkellner@fgcc.ab.ca
www.straffordfoundation.org/clifton
Number of Beds: 246 beds
Jack A. King, Administrator

Calgary: Extendicare - Cedars Villa
Affiliated with: Alberta Health Services
3330 - 8 Ave. SW, Calgary, AB T3C 0E7
Tel: 403-249-8915 *Fax:* 403-246-7561
Number of Beds: 248 beds
Lori Young, Administrator

Calgary: Extendicare - Hillcrest
Affiliated with: Alberta Health Services
1512 - 8 Ave. NW, Calgary, AB T2N 1C1
Tel: 403-289-0236 *Fax:* 403-289-2350
Number of Beds: 112 beds
Pierre Poirier, Administrator

Calgary: Father Lacombe Nursing Home
Affiliated with: Alberta Health Services
332 - 146 Ave. SE, Calgary, AB T2X 2A3
Tel: 403-256-4641 *Fax:* 403-254-6297
Number of Beds: 110 beds
Note: adult day support program offered M-F, 15 clients/day
Bill Ruckdashel, Site Pastoral Care Coordinator

Calgary: Glamorgan Care Centre
Affiliated with: Alberta Health Services
105 Galbraith Dr. S, Calgary, AB T3E 4Z5
Tel: 403-242-5911 *Fax:* 403-242-7613
Number of Beds: 52 beds
Joel Bond, Administrator

Calgary: Intercare/Brentwood Care Centre
Affiliated with: Alberta Health Services
2727 - 16 Ave. NW, Calgary, AB T2N 3Y6
Tel: 403-289-2576 *Fax:* 403-282-7027
Number of Beds: 120 beds
Michela Smith, Director, Care

Calgary: Intercare/Chinook Care Centre
Affiliated with: Alberta Health Services
1261 Glenmore Trail SW, Calgary, AB T2V 4Y8
Tel: 403-252-0141 *Fax:* 403-253-0292
Number of Beds: 149 beds
Lorraine Nygard, Director, Care

Calgary: Intercare/Southwood Care Centre
Affiliated with: Alberta Health Services
211 Heritage Dr. SE, Calgary, AB T2H 1M9
Tel: 403-252-1194 *Fax:* 403-253-0393
Number of Beds: 177 beds
Oriel Morrison, Regional Director

Calgary: Mayfair Nursing Home
Affiliated with: Alberta Health Services
211 Heritage Dr. SW, Calgary, AB T2H 1M9
Tel: 403-252-1194 *Fax:* 403-253-0393
Number of Beds: 142 beds
Joel Bond, Administrator

Calgary: Mount Royal Care Centre
Affiliated with: Alberta Health Services
1813 - 9 St. SW, Calgary, AB T2T 3C2
Tel: 403-244-8994 *Fax:* 403-244-5939
Number of Beds: 107 beds
Colin McMillan, Administrator

Camrose: Bethany Long Term Care Centre
Affiliated with: Alberta Health Services
4501 - 47 St., Camrose, AB T4V 1H9
Tel: 780-679-1000 *Fax:* 780-679-1020
www.ech.ab.ca
Number of Beds: 130 beds; 78 supportive housing
B. Olsen, Manager, Health Support Services

Cardston: Chinook Lodge
Affiliated with: Alberta Health Services
451 - 3rd St. West, Cardston, AB T0K 0K0
Tel: 403-653-4324 *Fax:* 403-653-1506
Number of Beds: 20 beds

Cardston: Grandview Nursing Home
Affiliated with: Alberta Health Services
PO Box 1440, 990 Main St., Cardston, AB T0K 0K0
Tel: 403-653-4054 *Fax:* 403-627-5275
Number of Beds: 40 nursing home beds
Pam Whitnack, CEO
Ron Schow, Director, Physical Plant

Coaldale: Sunny South Lodge
Affiliated with: Alberta Health Services
Green Acres Foundation Housing for Seniors, 1122 - 20 Ave., Coaldale, AB T1M 1L4
Tel: 403-345-5955
Number of Beds: 20 beds

Edmonton: Good Samaritan Millwoods Centre
Mill Woods Centre, 101 Youville Dr. East NW, Edmonton, AB T6L 7A4
Tel: 780-413-3501 *Fax:* 780-963-9808
Number of Beds: 60 beds

Fort MacLeod: Extendicare - Fort Macleod
Affiliated with: Alberta Health Services
654 - 29 St., Fort MacLeod, AB T0L 0Z0
Tel: 403-553-3955 *Fax:* 403-553-2812
www.extendicare.com
Number of Beds: 50 beds
Greg Guyn, Administrator

Grande Prairie: Grande Prairie Care Centre
Affiliated with: Alberta Health Services
10039 - 98 St., Grande Prairie, AB T8V 2E7
Tel: 780-532-3525 *Fax:* 780-532-6504
Number of Beds: 60 beds
Dorothy Brown, Administrator; Director, Nursing

High Prairie: J.B. Wood Extended Care Unit
Affiliated with: Alberta Health Services
Bag 1, High Prairie, AB T0G 1E0
Tel: 780-523-6470 *Fax:* 780-523-6642
Number of Beds: 35 beds
Ron Benson, CEO

Lethbridge: Columbia House - Enhanced
Affiliated with: Alberta Health Services
785 Columbia Blvd. West, Lethbridge, AB T1K 4T8
Number of Beds: 50 beds

Lethbridge: Edith Cavell Care Centre
Affiliated with: Alberta Health Services
1255 - 5 Ave. South, Lethbridge, AB T1J 0V6
Tel: 403-328-6631 *Fax:* 403-627-5275
Number of Beds: 120 beds
Marian Teierle, Administrator

Lethbridge: Extendicare - Lethbridge
Affiliated with: Alberta Health Services
1821 - 13 St. North, Lethbridge, AB T1H 2V4
Tel: 403-328-6664 *Fax:* 403-328-9294
Number of Beds: 120 beds
Joyce Adachi, Administrator

Lethbridge: Golden Acres Lodge
Affiliated with: Alberta Health Services
1615 - 13 St. North, Lethbridge, AB T1H 2V2
Tel: 403-328-5111 *Fax:* 403-327-8909
Number of Beds: 45 beds

Lethbridge: Good Sam's - Park Meadow
Affiliated with: Alberta Health Services
1511 - 15th Ave. North, Lethbridge, AB T1H 1W2
Tel: 403-328-9404 *Fax:* 403-328-8208
Number of Beds: 40 nursing home, 44 DAL, 1 community support beds

Lethbridge: Good Sam's - West Highlands
Affiliated with: Alberta Health Services
2867 Gary Dr. West, Lethbridge, AB T1J 5A3
Tel: 403-380-6275 *Fax:* 403-380-6732
Number of Beds: 10 nursing home, 60 DAL, 30 enhanced beds

Linden: Linden Nursing Home
Affiliated with: Alberta Health Services
PO Box 220, Linden, AB T0M 1J0
Tel: 403-546-3966 *Fax:* 403-546-4061
www.dthr.ab.ca
Number of Beds: 37 beds
Roland Toews, Administrator
Leonard Toeurs, Director, Physical Plant

Mayerthorpe: Mayerthorpe Extendicare
Affiliated with: Alberta Health Services
4706 - 54 St., Mayerthorpe, AB T0E 1N0
Tel: 780-786-2211 *Fax:* 780-786-4710
Number of Beds: 50 beds
Note: private, affiliated with Regional Health Authority
Michael Belanger, Administrator

Picture Butte: Piyami Lodge
Affiliated with: Green Acres Foundation
301 Rogers Ave., Picture Butte, AB T0K 1V0
Tel: 403-732-4811 *Fax:* 403-732-4580
www.greenacres.ab.ca/residence/piyami-lodge
Number of Beds: 32 rooms
Note: Independent living & enhanced care options
Linda McFalls, Manager

Pincher Creek: Good Sam's - Vista Villa
Affiliated with: Alberta Health Services
1240 Ken Thornton Blvd., Pincher Creek, AB T0K 1W0
Tel: 403-627-1900 *Fax:* 403-627-3939
Number of Beds: 10 nursing home, 40 DAL, 5 community support beds

Ponoka: Northcott Care Centre
Affiliated with: Alberta Health Services
4209 - 48 Ave., Ponoka, AB T4J 1P4
Tel: 403-783-4764 *Fax:* 403-341-8632
Number of Beds: 72 beds
Arthur Ulveland, Managing Director

Red Deer: Red Deer Nursing Home
Affiliated with: Alberta Health Services
Bag 5030, 4736 - 30 St., Red Deer, AB T4N 5H8
Tel: 403-343-4458 *Fax:* 403-341-4988
Number of Beds: 117 beds
Chris Hume, Clinical Manager

Spruce Grove: Good Samaritan Spruce Grove Care Centre
5600 - 50 St., Spruce Grove, AB T7X 3Y8
Tel: 780-962-3415 *Fax:* 780-962-3416
www.gss.org
Number of Beds: 30 beds
Alice Sears, Director, Operations

St Paul: Extendicare - St. Paul
Affiliated with: Alberta Health Services
4614 - 47 Ave., St Paul, AB T0A 3A0
Tel: 780-645-3375 *Fax:* 780-645-4290
Number of Beds: 75 beds
Steve Krim, Administrator

Stony Plain: Good Samaitan George Henning Place
4808 - 57 Ave., Stony Plain, AB T7Z 2J9
Tel: 780-963-3403 *Fax:* 780-963-9808
www.gss.org
Number of Beds: 30 beds
Alice Sears, Director, Operations

Taber: Clearview Lodge - Enhanced
Affiliated with: Alberta Health Services
4730 - 50th Ave., Taber, AB T1G 1N6
Tel: 780-963-3403 *Fax:* 780-963-9808
Number of Beds: 20 beds

Viking: Extendicare - Vicking
Affiliated with: Alberta Health Services
PO Box 430, 5020 - 57 Ave., Viking, AB T0B 4N0
Tel: 780-336-4790 *Fax:* 780-336-4004
www.ech.ab.ca
Number of Beds: 60 beds
Brant Poirier, Administrator

Long Term/Retirement Care

Long Term Care Facilities

Airdrie: Bethany Airdrie
Affiliated with: Alberta Health Services
1736 - 1st Ave. NW, Airdrie, AB T4B 2C4
Tel: 403-948-6022 *Fax:* 403-912-0958
info@bethanycare.com
www.bethanycare.com
Number of Beds: 124 beds
Heath Miller, Administrator

Bentley: Bentley Care Centre
Affiliated with: Alberta Health Services
4834 - 52 Ave., Bentley, AB T0C 0J0
Tel: 403-748-4115 *Fax:* 403-748-2727
www.albertahealthservices.ca

Note: Specialties: Continuing Care services; Physiotherapy; Occupational therapy; Recreational therapy; Palliative care

***Blackie:* Nanton Mountain View Estates**
PO Box 50, Blackie, AB T0L 0J0
Tel: 403-684-3805

Note: private support home

***Bon Accord:* Oak Hills Boys Ranch**
PO Box 97, Bon Accord, AB T0A 0K0
Tel: 403-921-2121 *Fax:* 403-921-2379
www.oakhillboysranch.ca

Number of Beds: 30 beds
Note: group home
Anton Smith, Executive Director

***Calgary:* Bethany Calgary**
Affiliated with: Alberta Health Services
916 - 18A St. NW, Calgary, AB T2N 1C6
Tel: 403-284-6000 *Fax:* 403-284-6085
info@bethanycare.com
www.bethanycare.com

Number of Beds: 476 beds
Note: respite care
Ian West, Administrator

***Calgary:* Bethany Harvest Hills**
Affiliated with: Alberta Health Services
19 Harvest Gold Manor NE, Calgary, AB T3K 4Y1
Tel: 403-226-8200 *Fax:* 403-226-7265
info@bethanycare.com
www.bethanycare.com

Number of Beds: 60 long-term care beds
Note: provides a familiar home environment for residents in middle to late stages of Alzheimer disease & related dementias
Shelagh Slater, Administrator

***Calgary:* Bow Park Court**
Affiliated with: Alberta Health Services
200 - 200 Scenic Bow Pl. NW, Calgary, AB T3L 1S5
Tel: 403-297-6539 *Fax:* 403-287-4651

Number of Beds: 24 beds
D. Grant, Manager

***Calgary:* Carewest - Cross Bow**
Affiliated with: Alberta Health Services
1011 Centre Ave. NE, Calgary, AB T2E 0A3
Tel: 403-267-2950 *Fax:* 403-267-2995

Number of Beds: 98 beds
Note: continuing care

***Calgary:* Carewest - Glenmore Park**
Affiliated with: Alberta Health Services
6909 - 14 St. SW, Calgary, AB T2V 1P8
Tel: 403-258-7650 *Fax:* 403-258-7676

Number of Beds: 147 beds
Note: continuing care

***Calgary:* Carewest - Royal Park**
Affiliated with: Alberta Health Services
4222 Sarcee Rd. SW, Calgary, AB T3E 7J8
Tel: 403-240-7475 *Fax:* 403-240-7476

Number of Beds: 50 beds

***Calgary:* Margaret House Residential Treatment Centre**
Affiliated with: Alberta Health Services
404 - 94 Ave. SE, Calgary, AB T2J 0E8
Tel: 403-253-2291 *Fax:* 403-253-6974
www.autism.ca

Number of Beds: 20 beds
Note: group home
Dave Mikkelsen, Executive Director

***Calgary:* Salvation Army Agape Hospice**
Affiliated with: Alberta Health Services
1302 - 8 Ave. NW, Calgary, AB T2N 1B8
Tel: 403-282-6588 *Fax:* 403-284-1778
ab.salvationarmy.ca/calgary/health.html

Number of Beds: 18 beds
Note: Hospice for terminally ill
David Luginbuhl, Executive Director

***Camrose:* Bethany Group**
Affiliated with: Alberta Health Services
4612 - 53 St., Camrose, AB T4V 1Y6
Tel: 780-679-2000 *Fax:* 780-679-2001
www.thebethanygrp.ca

Number of Beds: 288 beds
Marilyn Wood, Director Health Services

***Cochrane:* Bethany Cochrane**
Affiliated with: Alberta Health Services
302 Quigley Dr., Cochrane, AB T4C 1X9
Tel: 403-932-6422 *Fax:* 403-932-4617
info@bethanycare.com
www.bethanycare.com

Number of Beds: 78 long-term care, 50 residential care beds
Note: adult day support program; residential care
Barb Fredrich, Administrator

***Edmonton:* Allen Gray Continuing Care Centre**
Affiliated with: Alberta Health Services
5005 - 28 Ave. NW, Edmonton, AB T6L 7G1
Tel: 780-469-2371 *Fax:* 780-465-2073
www.capitalhealth.ca

***Edmonton:* L'Arche Association of Edmonton**
Affiliated with: Alberta Health Services
7708 - 83 St., Edmonton, AB T6C 2Y8
Tel: 780-465-0618 *Fax:* 780-465-8091
edmoffice@larcheedmonton.org
www.larcheedmonton.org

Number of Beds: 24 beds
Note: group home
Grant Kaminski, Executive Director

***Edmonton:* CapitalCare Dickinsfield**
Affiliated with: Alberta Health Services
14225 - 94 St. NW, Edmonton, AB T5E 6C6
Tel: 780-496-3300 *Fax:* 780-476-4585
www.albertahealthservices.ca; www.capitalcare.net

Year Founded: 1979
Number of Beds: 275
Note: Specialties: Continuing care; Secure units for residents with dementia; Supportive & comfort units fo residents in middle to later stages of dementia; Care for young adults who are disabled; Young adult day support program
Betty Thompson, Administrator

***Edmonton:* CapitalCare Grandview**
Affiliated with: Alberta Health Services
6215 - 124 St. NW, Edmonton, AB T6H 3V1
Tel: 780-496-7100 *Fax:* 780-496-7150
www.albertahealthservices.ca; www.capitalcare.net

Year Founded: 1973
Number of Beds: 149 beds
Note: Specialties: Continuing care for persons with dementia & who are chronically disabled; Secure unit for residents wtih dementia who are at risk of leaving the building; Supportive & comfort units for residents in middle to later stages of dementia; Orthopedic sub-acute program

***Edmonton:* CapitalCare Lynnwood**
Affiliated with: Alberta Health Services
8740 - 165 St., Edmonton, AB T5R 2R8
Tel: 780-496-2500 *Fax:* 780-484-8089
www.albertahealthservices.ca; www.capitalcare.net

Year Founded: 1966
Number of Beds: 296 beds
Note: Specialties: Continuing care; Behavioural assessment & stabilization uit; Secure unit for residents with dementia; Supportive & comfore care units for rsidents in middle to later stages of dementia; Mental health services
Iris Neumann, Administrator
Ralph Anderson, Manager, Maintenance

***Edmonton:* CapitalCare Norwood**
Affiliated with: Alberta Health Services
10410 - 111 Ave., Edmonton, AB T5G 3A2
Tel: 780-496-3200 *Fax:* 780-474-9806
www.albertahealthservices.ca; www.capitalcare.net

Year Founded: 1963
Number of Beds: 235 beds
Note: Specialties: Continuing care; Brian injury unit; Chronic ventilator unit; Medical sub-acute program; Transition program; Palliative care

***Edmonton:* Devonshire Care Centre**
Affiliated with: Alberta Health Services
1808 - 142 St., Edmonton, AB T6R 3H2
Tel: 780-665-8050 *Fax:* 780-665-8051
www.capitalhealth.ca

***Edmonton;* Edmonton Chinatown Care Centre**
Affiliated with: Alberta Health Services
9539 - 102A Ave. NW, Edmonton, AB T5H 0G2
Tel: 780-429-0888
www.capitalhealth.ca

***Edmonton:* Edmonton General Continuing Care Centre**
Affiliated with: Alberta Health Services
11111 Jasper Ave., Edmonton, AB T5K 0L4
Tel: 780-482-8111
www.caritas.ab.ca

***Edmonton:* Eric Cormack Centre**
9835 - 112 St., Edmonton, AB T5K 2E7
Tel: 403-427-2764 *Fax:* 403-422-2815
paulette.killam@gov.ab.ca

Number of Beds: 80 beds
Note: institution
Paulette Killam, Executive Director

***Edmonton:* Extendicare - Holyrood**
Affiliated with: Alberta Health Services
8008 - 95 Ave., Edmonton, AB T6C 2T1
Tel: 780-469-1307 *Fax:* 780-469-5196
www.capitalhealth.ca

Note: continuing care centre

***Edmonton:* Extendicare - Somerset**
Affiliated with: Alberta Health Services
13210 - 114 St., Edmonton, AB T5E 5E2
Tel: 780-454-8616 *Fax:* 780-447-5906
www.capitalhealth.ca

***Edmonton:* Good Samaritan Dr. Gerald Zetter Centre**
Affiliated with: Alberta Health Services
9649 - 71 Ave., Edmonton, AB T6E 5J2
Tel: 780-431-3621 *Fax:* 780-431-3699
goodsaminfo@gss.org
www.gss.org

***Edmonton:* Good Samaritan Mount Pleasant Care Centre**
Affiliated with: Alberta Health Services
10530 - 56 Ave. NW, Edmonton, AB T6H 0X7
Tel: 780-431-3600 *Fax:* 780-431-3949
goodsaminfo@gss.org
www.gss.org

***Edmonton:* Good Samaritan Southgate Care Centre**
Affiliated with: Alberta Health Services
4225 - 107 St. NW, Edmonton, AB T6J 2P1
Tel: 780-431-3600 *Fax:* 780-431-3898
goodsaminfo@gss.org
www.gss.org

***Edmonton:* Hardisty Nursing Home**
Affiliated with: Alberta Health Services
6420 - 101 Ave. NW, Edmonton, AB T6A 0H5
Tel: 780-466-9267 *Fax:* 780-450-9457
www.capitalhealth.ca

***Edmonton:* Kensington Village**
Affiliated with: Alberta Health Services
12603 - 135 Ave., Edmonton, AB T5L 5B1
Tel: 780-447-3840 *Fax:* 780-482-6532
www.capitalhealth.ca

***Edmonton:* Kipnes Centre for Veterans**
Affiliated with: Alberta Health Services
4470 McCrae Ave., Edmonton, AB T5E 6M8
Tel: 780-442-5700 *Fax:* 780-442-5711
www.capitalhealth.ca

***Edmonton:* McConnell Place West**
Affiliated with: Alberta Health Services
8720 - 165 St., Edmonton, AB T5R 5Y8
Tel: 780-413-4770 *Fax:* 780-413-4773
www.capitalhealth.ca

Number of Beds: 36 beds
Gwenne Tweddle, Manager

***Edmonton:* Miller Crossing Continuing Care Services**
Affiliated with: Alberta Health Services
145251 - 50 St., Edmonton, AB T5E 6M8
Tel: 780-478-9212 *Fax:* 780-478-2894
www.capitalhealth.ca

***Edmonton:* Millwoods Shepherd's Care Centre**
Affiliated with: Alberta Health Services
6620 - 28th Ave. NW, Edmonton, AB T6K 2R1
Tel: 780-463-9810 *Fax:* 780-462-1643
www.capitalhealth.ca

***Edmonton:* Rosecrest Home**
Affiliated with: Alberta Health Services
10205 - 134 Ave., Edmonton, AB T5E 1J2
Tel: 403-427-0927 *Fax:* 403-427-4408
www.capitalhealth.ca
Number of Beds: 22 beds
Note: institution
MaryAnn Sinclair, Executive Director

***Edmonton:* St. Joseph's Auxiliary Hospital**
Affiliated with: Alberta Health Services
10707 - 29 Ave. NW, Edmonton, AB T6J 6W1
Tel: 780-430-9110 *Fax:* 780-430-9777
www.stjosephs.ab.ca

***Edmonton:* St. Michael's Long Term Care Centre**
Affiliated with: Alberta Health Services
7404 - 139 Ave. NW, Edmonton, AB T5C 3H7
Tel: 780-473-5621 *Fax:* 780-472-4506
smeccs@smhg.ca
www.smhg.ca
Number of Beds: 153 beds
Stan C. Fisher, President; CEO

***Edmonton:* Salvation Army Sunset Lodge**
Affiliated with: Alberta Health Services
11034 - 124 St., Edmonton, AB T5X 6C4
Tel: 780-454-5484 *Fax:* 780-455-7196
www.capitalhealth.ca
Number of Beds: 108 beds
Note: intermediate care
Maj. Blake Mooney, Executive Director

***Edmonton:* South Terrace Continuing Care Centre**
Affiliated with: Alberta Health Services
5905 - 112 St. NW, Edmonton, AB T6H 3J4
Tel: 780-434-1451 *Fax:* 780-436-4300
www.capitalhealth.ca
Number of Beds: 134 beds
C.W. Dillane, President/CEO

***Edmonton:* South Terrace Continuing Care Centre**
5905 - 112 St. NW, Edmonton, AB T6H 3J4
Tel: 780-434-1451 *Fax:* 780-436-4300
southterrace@reveraliving.com
www.reveraliving.com

***Edmonton:* Venta Nursing Home**
Affiliated with: Alberta Health Services
Former Name: Venta Nursing Home
13525 - 102 St. NW, Edmonton, AB T5E 4K3
Tel: 780-476-6633 *Fax:* 780-476-6943
www.capitalhealth.ca

***Edmonton:* Victoria: Salvation Army Sunset Lodge**
Affiliated with: Vancouver Island Health Authority
952 Arm Street, Edmonton, AB V9A 4G7
Tel: 250-385-3422 *Fax:* 250-385-3183
Number of Beds: 41 beds
Note: seniors' lodge with residential mental health program
Blake Mooney, Executive Director

***Evansburg:* Good Samaritan Pembina Village**
Affiliated with: Alberta Health Services
5225 - 50 St., Evansburg, AB T0E 0T0
Tel: 780-727-4441 *Fax:* 780-727-2410
www.capitalhealth.ca

***Fort Saskatchewan:* Rivercrest Care Centre**
Affiliated with: Alberta Health Services
Former Name: Rivercrest Lodge Nursing Home
10104 - 101 Ave., Fort Saskatchewan, AB T8L 2A5
Tel: 780-998-2425 *Fax:* 780-992-9432
www.capitalhealth.ca
Eleanor Low, Administrator

***Grande Prairie:* Mackenzie Place Continuing Care**
Affiliated with: Alberta Health Services
10409 - 98 St., Grande Prairie, AB T8V 2E8
Tel: 780-538-7100 *Fax:* 780-538-1500
www.capitalhealth.ca
Number of Beds: 128 beds
Shana Hammy-Bugarin, Director, Continuing Care

***Hythe:* Hythe Continuing Care Centre**
Affiliated with: Alberta Health Services
PO Box 100, Hythe, AB T0H 2C0
Tel: 780-356-3818 *Fax:* 780-356-3633
Number of Beds: 29 long-term care beds
Note: continuing care centre
Donna Turner, Director, Health Services

***Islay:* Islay Care Centre**
Affiliated with: Alberta Health Services
PO Box 55, Islay, AB T0B 2J0
Tel: 780-744-3795 *Fax:* 780-608-8850
www.ech.ab.ca
Number of Beds: 12 continuing care beds, 8 assisted living
Audrey Cusack, Health Centre Coordinator

***Leduc:* Extendicare - Leduc**
Affiliated with: Alberta Health Services
PO Box 280, 4309 - 50 St., Leduc, AB T9E 6K6
Tel: 780-986-2245 *Fax:* 780-986-0669
www.capitalhealth.ca

***Leduc:* Salem Manor Nursing Home**
Affiliated with: Alberta Health Services
4419 - 46 St., Leduc, AB T9E 6L2
Tel: 780-986-8654 *Fax:* 780-986-4130
www.capitalhealth.ca
Bernie Pankonin, Administrator

***Lethbridge:* Sifton Family & Youth Services**
528 Stafford Dr. North, Lethbridge, AB T1H 2B2
Tel: 403-381-5411 *Fax:* 403-382-4565
Number of Beds: 12 beds
Note: group home
Ross Wakelen, Director

***Mannville:* Mannville Care Centre**
Affiliated with: Alberta Health Services
5007 - 46 St., Mannville, AB T0B 2W0
Tel: 780-763-3621 *Fax:* 780-608-8850
www.ech.ab.ca
Number of Beds: 23 beds
Debora Okrainetz, Nursing Manager

***Medicine Hat:* Dr. Dan McCharles Extended Care Centre**
Affiliated with: Alberta Health Services
666 - 5 St. SW, Medicine Hat, AB T1A 4H6
Tel: 403-529-7000 *Fax:* 403-529-8950
Number of Beds: 42 beds
Barb Cameron, Manager, Extended/Home Care

***Medicine Hat:* Riverview**
603 Prospect Dr. SW, Medicine Hat, AB T1A 4C2
Tel: 403-527-5531 *Fax:* 403-527-5175
riverview@reveraliving.com
www.reveraliving.com
Goldie Boyd, Administrator
Audrey Powers, Care Coordinator

***Morinville:* Aspen House**
9706 - 100 Ave., Morinville, AB T8R 1T2
Tel: 780-939-7482 *Fax:* 780-939-6144
Number of Beds: 40 beds; 4 respite beds
Note: assisted living
Grace Regnier, Site Manager

***Radway:* Radway Continuing Care Centre**
Affiliated with: Alberta Health Services
PO Box 70, 5002 - 52 St., Radway, AB T0A 2V0
Tel: 780-736-3740 *Fax:* 780-736-2353
Number of Beds: 20 permanent, 4 waiting beds
Gloria Strachan

***Red Deer:* Valley Park Manor**
Affiliated with: Alberta Health Services
5505 - 60 Ave., Red Deer, AB T4N 4W2
Tel: 403-343-4722 *Fax:* 403-341-5938
Number of Beds: 100 beds
Note: elderly, medically frail
Candace Spurell, Vice-President

***Red Deer:* West Park Lodge**
Affiliated with: Alberta Health Services
5715 - 41 St. Crescent, Red Deer, AB T4N 1B3
Tel: 403-343-7471 *Fax:* 403-343-3424
info@westparklodge.com
www.westparklodge.com
Number of Beds: 37 beds
Note: senior's lodge; assisted living
Evelyne Gaudet, Administrator

***Sherwood Park:* CapitalCare Strathcona**
Affiliated with: Alberta Health Services
12 Brower Dr., Sherwood Park, AB T8H 1V3
Tel: 780-467-3366 *Fax:* 780-467-4095
www.albertahealthservices.ca; www.capitalcare.net
Year Founded: 1994
Number of Beds: 75 beds
Note: Specialties: Continuing care; Secure dementia unit; Eden Alternative philosophy of care; Recreational programs; Occupational therapy; Respite program; Adult community day support program

***Sherwood Park:* Sherwood Park Care Center**
Affiliated with: Alberta Health Services
2020 Brentwood Blvd., Sherwood Park, AB T8A 0X1
Tel: 780-467-2281 *Fax:* 780-449-1529
admin@advhealth.org

***Smoky Lake:* Smoky Lake Continuing Care Centre**
Affiliated with: Alberta Health Services
47607 - 52 Ave., Smoky Lake, AB T0A 3C0
Tel: 780-656-3818 *Fax:* 780-656-3010
Number of Beds: 32 beds
David Ponich, Continuing Care Centre Supervisor

***St Albert:* Youville Home**
Affiliated with: Alberta Health Services
9 St Vital Ave., St Albert, AB T8N 1K1
Tel: 780-460-6900 *Fax:* 780-459-4139

***Standoff:* Kainai Continuing Care Centre**
PO Box 380, Standoff, AB T0L 1Y0
Tel: 403-737-3652 *Fax:* 403-737-3487
counserv@telusplanet.net
Number of Beds: 50 beds
Note: Blood Tribe Dept. of Health
Cecilia Black Water, Director, Health Services

***Stony Plain:* Good Samaritan Care Centre**
Affiliated with: Alberta Health Services
5600 - 50 St., Stony Plain, AB T7Z 1P8
Tel: 780-963-2261 *Fax:* 780-963-5156
goodsaminfo@gss.org
www.gss.org
Bob Taillefer, Coordinator, Environmental Services

***Vegreville:* Heritage Home**
Affiliated with: Alberta Health Services
4570 Maple St., Vegreville, AB T9C 1X2
Tel: 780-603-0853 *Fax:* 780-603-0867
www.ech.ab.ca
Wanda White, Site Manager

***Vegreville:* Vegreville Care Centre**
Affiliated with: Alberta Health Services
5225 - 43 St., Vegreville, AB T9C 1S1
Tel: 780-632-2871 *Fax:* 780-632-6680
www.ech.ab.ca
Number of Beds: 87 beds
Peggy Standen, Coordinator, Health Care

***Youngstown:* Youngstown House**
PO Box 9, Youngstown, AB T0J 3P0
Tel: 403-779-3920 *Fax:* 403-779-3946
Number of Beds: 50 beds
Note: group home
Dianne Bradley, Manager

Nursing Homes

***Calgary:* Carewest Sarcee**
Affiliated with: Alberta Health Services
3504 - 29th St. SW, Calgary, AB T3E 2L3
Tel: 403-686-8100 *Fax:* 403-686-8104
www.carewest.ca; www.albertahealthservices.ca
Note: Specialties: Comprehensive community care for seniors; Short stay rehabilitation; Long term care; Alzheimer's & dementia services; Palliative care at Sarcee Hospice, which has 15 hospice rooms

***Galahad:* Galahad Care Centre**
Affiliated with: Alberta Health Services
PO Box 88, 1 Main St., Galahad, AB T0B 1R0
Tel: 780-583-3788 *Fax:* 780-583-2105
Note: Specialties: Continuing care; Respite care; Palliative care

Retirement Residences

***Calgary:* Carewest Colonel Belcher Veterans' Care Centre & Seniors' Care Residence**
Affiliated with: Alberta Health Services
1939 Veterans Way NW, Calgary, AB T3B 5Y8
Tel: 403-944-7800
www.carewest.ca; www.albertahealthservices.ca
Year Founded: 2003
Number of Beds: 175 residents in seniors' residence, most of whom are veterans
Note: Specialties: Continuing care services; Care centre offering areas for persons with Alzheimer's disease & other dementias; Day support program for seniors (403-944-7852)

Mental Health Facilities

Mental Health Hospitals/Facilities

Airdrie: **Airdrie Mental Health Clinic**
Affiliated with: Alberta Health Services
112 - 1 Ave. NW, Airdrie, AB T4B 2B3
Tel: 403-948-3878 *Fax:* 403-948-7926
maureen.gilberg@calgaryhealthregion.ca

Athabasca: **Athabasca Mental Health Clinic**
Affiliated with: Alberta Health Services
3401 - 48 Ave., Athabasca, AB T9S 1M7
Tel: 780-675-5404 *Fax:* 780-675-3994

Banff: **Banff Mental Health Clinic**
Affiliated with: Banff Community Health Centre
301 Lynx St., Banff, AB T1L 1B3
Tel: 403-762-4451 *Fax:* 403-762-5570

Note: Outpatient clinic

Barrhead: **Barrhead Mental Health Clinic**
Affiliated with: Alberta Health Services
PO Box 4054, 6203 - 49 St., Barrhead, AB T7N 1A1
Tel: 780-674-8243 *Fax:* 780-674-8352
Lorraine Lindberg

Black Diamond: **Black Diamond Mental Health Clinic**

Oilfields General Hospital, PO Box 1, 717 Government Road, Black Diamond, AB T0L 0H0
Tel: 403-933-3800 *Fax:* 403-933-4353
Toll-Free: 1-877-652-4700

Bonnyville: **Bonnyville Mental Health Clinic**
Affiliated with: Alberta Health Services
PO Box 6917, 5201 - 44 St., Bonnyville, AB T9N 2H4
Tel: 780-826-2404 *Fax:* 780-826-6114
Joan Panteluk

Bow Island: **Bow Island Mental Health Clinic**
Affiliated with: Alberta Health Services
802 - 6 St., Bow Island, AB T0K 0G0
Tel: 403-545-5120 *Fax:* 403-545-6357

Brooks: **Brooks Community Mental Health Services**
Affiliated with: Alberta Health Services
Bag 300, Brooks, AB T1R 1C5
Tel: 403-793-6655 *Fax:* 403-795-6656

Calgary: **Central Calgary Mental Health Clinic**
Affiliated with: Alberta Health Services
1000 - 8 Ave. SW, Calgary, AB T2P 3M7
Tel: 403-297-7311 *Fax:* 403-297-5354

Calgary: **Northwest Calgary Mental Health Clinic**
Affiliated with: Alberta Health Services
#280, 1620 - 29th St. NW, Calgary, AB T2N 4L7
Tel: 403-297-7345 *Fax:* 403-297-4543

Calgary: **Wood's Homes (Alberta) Mental Health & Child Welfare Services**
Affiliated with: Alberta Health Services
9400 - 48 Ave. NW, Calgary, AB T3B 2B2
Tel: 403-247-6751 *Fax:* 403-268-0878
jane.matheson@woodshomes.ca
www.woodshomes.ca
Number of Beds: 110 beds
Dr. Jane Matheson, CEO

Calgary: **Wood's Homes Child & Adolescent Mental Health Services**
Affiliated with: Alberta Health Services
805 - 37 St. NW, Calgary, AB T2N 4N8
Tel: 403-270-4102 *Fax:* 403-286-0878
askus@woodshomes.ca
www.woodshomes.ca
Number of Beds: 150 beds
Note: day treatment, educational, outreach services; longterm care: permanent care (child welfare services) residential; treatment centre for adolescents & families; services for street youth, educational/day treatment services, caregiver services
Dr. Jane Matheson, CEO

Camrose: **Mental Health Centre**
Affiliated with: Alberta Health Services
4911 - 49 St., Camrose, AB T4V 1J9
Tel: 780-679-1764 *Fax:* 780-608-8850
www.ech.ab.ca
Brenda Nelson
780/679-1765

Canmore: **Mental Health Clinic**
Affiliated with: Alberta Health Services
Provincial Building, 3rd Floor, 302 - 800 Railway Ave., Canmore, AB T1W 1P1
Tel: 403-678-4696 *Fax:* 403-678-1951
www.ech.ab.ca

Cardston: **Cardston Mental Health Clinic**
Affiliated with: Alberta Health Services
Provincial Building, PO Box 1590, 576 Main St., Cardston, AB T0K 0K0
Tel: 403-653-5115 *Fax:* 403-653-2926

Chestermere: **Chestermere Lake Mental Health Clinic**
Affiliated with: Alberta Health Services
#250, 124 East Chestermere Dr., Chestermere, AB T1X 1M1
Tel: 403-207-8770 *Fax:* 403-944-2224

Claresholm: **Claresholm Centre for Mental Health & Addictions**
Affiliated with: Alberta Health Services
PO Box 490, 139 - 43 Ave. West, Claresholm, AB T0L 0T0
Tel: 403-682-3500 *Fax:* 403-625-8506
claresholmcentre@albertahealthservices.ca
claresholmcentre.com
Year Founded: 1933
Number of Beds: 120 beds
Darrell Coates, Site Manager
Barb Gordon, Care Manager

Cochrane: **Cochrane Addiction & Mental Health Clinic**
Affiliated with: Alberta Health Services
60 Grande Blvd., Cochrane, AB T4C 0S4
Tel: 403-932-3455 *Fax:* 403-932-2971

Cold Lake: **Cold Lake Mental Health Clinic**
Affiliated with: Alberta Health Services
#208, 314 - 25th St., Cold Lake, AB T9M 1G6
Tel: 780-639-4922 *Fax:* 780-639-4990
Anne Tucker

Didsbury: **Didsbury Mental Health Clinic**
Affiliated with: Alberta Health Services
1210 - 20 Ave., Didsbury, AB T0M 0W0
Tel: 403-335-7285 *Fax:* 403-335-7227

Drayton Valley: **Drayton Valley Mental Health Clinic**
Affiliated with: Alberta Health Services
PO Box 7276, 5136 - 51 Ave., Drayton Valley, AB T7A 1S5
Tel: 780-542-3140 *Fax:* 780-542-4461
www.dthr.ab.ca

Edmonton: **Alberta Hospital Edmonton**
Affiliated with: Alberta Health Services
PO Box 307, 17480 Fort Rd., Edmonton, AB T5J 2J7
Tel: 780-472-5555 *Fax:* 780-472-5508
www.capitalhealth.ca
Year Founded: 1923
Number of Beds: 410 beds
Note: Provides assessment, diagnosis, treatment, education & consultation. Conducts research. Programs include: Adult Psychiatry, Geriatric Psychiatry, & the Northern Alberta Forensic Psychiatry Program.

Edmonton: **Edmonton Mental Health Clinic**
Affiliated with: Alberta Health Services
9942 - 108th St., Edmonton, AB T5K 2J5
Tel: 780-342-7700 *Fax:* 780-427-0424
www.albertahealthservices.ca

Edson: **Edson Mental Health Centre**
Affiliated with: Alberta Health Services
Provincial Bldg., #100, 111 - 54 St., Edson, AB T7E 1T2
Tel: 780-723-8294 *Fax:* 780-723-8297
Margaret Fern

Fort McMurray: **Fort McMurray Mental Health Services**
Affiliated with: Alberta Health Services
7 Hospital St., Fort McMurray, AB T9H 1P2
Tel: 780-791-6194 *Fax:* 780-791-6219

Gibbons: **Gibbons Mental Health Clinic**
5018 - 50 St., Gibbons, AB T0A 1N0
Tel: 780-923-3700 *Fax:* 780-923-3939

Grande Cache: **Grande Cache Mental Health Clinic**
702 Pine Plaza, Grande Cache, AB T0E 0Y0
Tel: 780-827-4998 *Fax:* 780-827-4787
Note: community clinic

Grande Prairie: **Grande Prairie Mental Health Clinic**
#600, 10014 - 99th St., Grande Prairie, AB T8V 3N4
Tel: 780-538-5160 *Fax:* 780-538-6279

Hanna: **Hanna Mental Health Clinic**
Affiliated with: Alberta Health Services
904 Centre St. North, Hanna, AB T0J 1P0
Tel: 403-854-5276 *Fax:* 403-854-5280

Hardisty: **Hardisty Mental Health Clinic**
Affiliated with: Alberta Health Services
PO Box 269, 4531 - 47 St., Hardisty, AB T0B 1V0
Tel: 780-888-8306 *Fax:* 780-888-2427
carol.roberts@ech.ab.ca
www.ech.ab.ca
Brenda Nelson
780/679-1765

High Level: **High Level Mental Health Clinic**
Affiliated with: Alberta Health Services
PO Box 400, High Level, AB T0H 1Z0
Tel: 780-926-3791 *Fax:* 780-926-2944
www.capitalhealth.ca

High Prairie: **High Prairie Mental Health Clinic**
Affiliated with: Alberta Health Services
High Prairie Health Complex, PO Box 1, 4444 - 53 Ave., High Prairie, AB T0G 1E0
Tel: 780-926-3791 *Fax:* 780-767-6491
www.capitalhealth.ca

High River: **High River Mental Health Clinic**
PO Box 5309, 310 Macleod Trail, 2nd Floor, High River, AB T1V 1M5
Tel: 403-652-8340 *Fax:* 403-652-1456

Hinton: **Hinton Mental Health Clinic**
Affiliated with: Alberta Health Services
Former Name: Hinton Mental Health Centre
1280A Switzer Dr., Hinton, AB T7V 1T5
Tel: 780-865-8247 *Fax:* 780-865-8327
Louise Maurik

Innisfail: **Innisfail Mental Health Clinic**
Affiliated with: Alberta Health Services
5023 - 42 St., Innisfail, AB T4G 1A9
Tel: 403-227-4601 *Fax:* 403-227-5683

Jasper: **Jasper Mental Health Clinc**
Affiliated with: Alberta Health Services
PO Box 310, 518 Robson St., Jasper, AB T0E 1E0
Tel: 780-852-6616 *Fax:* 780-852-3413
Joan Connors

Killam: **Killam Mental Health Club**
Affiliated with: Alberta Health Services
4811 - 49 Ave., Killam, AB T0B 2L0
Tel: 780-385-7160 *Fax:* 780-608-8850
www.ech.ab.ca
Brenda Nelson
780-679-1765

La Crete: **La Crete Mental Health Club**
Affiliated with: Alberta Health Services
Unit 2, 10001 - 100 Av., La Crete, AB T0H 2H0
Tel: 780-928-4215 *Fax:* 780-928-4237
www.nlhr.ca

Lac La Biche: **Lac La Biche Mental Health Clinic**
Affiliated with: Alberta Health Services
9503 Beaver Hill Rd., Lac La Biche, AB T0A 2C0
Tel: 780-623-5230 *Fax:* 780-623-5232
Tracy Smith

Leduc: **Leduc Mental Health Clinic**
Affiliated with: Alberta Health Services
4210 - 48 St., Leduc, AB T9E 5Z3
Tel: 780-986-2660 *Fax:* 780-986-9292
www.capitalhealth.ca

Lethbridge: **Lethbridge Mental Health Clinic**
200 - 5 Ave. South, Lethbridge, AB T1K 4L1
Tel: 403-381-5260 *Fax:* 403-382-4518
mhc-leth@amhb.ab.ca
Diane Conley, Administrator

Mayerthorpe: **Mayerthorpe Mental Health Clinic**
Affiliated with: Alberta Health Services
PO Box 30, 4417 - 45 St., Mayerthorpe, AB T0E 1N0
Tel: 780-786-2279 *Fax:* 780-786-2023
Doug Kemp

Medicine Hat: **Medicine Hat Mental Health Clinic**
#4, 181 Carry Dr. SE, Medicine Hat, AB T1B 3T2
Tel: 403-529-3500 *Fax:* 403-529-3562

Morinville: **Morinville Mental Health Clinic**
Affiliated with: Alberta Health Services
10008 - 107 St., Morinville, AB T8R 1L3
Tel: 780-939-3388 *Fax:* 780-939-1216
www.capitalhealth.ca

Olds: **Olds Mental Health Centre**
Affiliated with: Alberta Health Services
Olds Provincial Bldg., 5025 - 50th St., Olds, AB T4H 1R9
Tel: 403-556-4204
www.albertahealthservices.ca

Note: Specialties: Mental health services; Crisis response; Counselling; Telemental health psychiatric consultation service

Onoway: **Onoway Mental Health Clinic**
Affiliated with: Alberta Health Services
PO Box 1047, 5115 Lac Ste Anne Trail, Onoway, AB T0E 1V0
Tel: 780-967-9117 *Fax:* 780-967-2547
Doug Kemp

Oyen: **Oyen Mental Health Clinic**
Affiliated with: Alberta Health Services
312 - 3 Ave. E, Oyen, AB T0J 2J0
Tel: 403-664-3651 *Fax:* 403-664-2934

Peace River: **Peace River Mental Health Clinic**
Affiliated with: Alberta Health Services
10015 - 98 St., 3rd Floor, Peace River, AB T8S 1T4
Tel: 780-624-6151 *Fax:* 780-624-6565
Brenda Nelson

Pincher Creek: **Pincher Creek Mental Health Clinic**
PO Box 1052, 696 Kerrle Street, Pincher Creek, AB T0K 1W0
Tel: 403-627-1121 *Fax:* 403-627-1145
mhc-pinchercreek@amhb.ab.ca

Ponoka: **Ponoka Mental Health Clinic**
Affiliated with: Alberta Health Services
#223, 5110 - 49th Ave., Ponoka, AB T4J 1R6
Tel: 403-783-7903 *Fax:* 403-783-7926
dorothy.ranta@amhb.ab.ca

Provost: **Provost Mental Health Centre**
Affiliated with: Alberta Health Services
5419 - 44 St., Provost, AB T0B 3S0
Tel: 780-753-2575 *Fax:* 780-753-8096
www.ech.ab.ca
Brenda Nelson
780/679-1765

Raymond: **Raymond Care Centre**
Affiliated with: Alberta Health Services
PO Box 260, Raymond, AB T0K 2S0
Tel: 403-752-3316 *Fax:* 403-752-4147
Number of Beds: 30 beds
Note: geriatric psychiatric facility (longterm & rehab)

Raymond: **Raymond Mental Health Clinic**
Affiliated with: Alberta Health Services
150N - 4 St. East, Raymond, AB T0K 2S0
Tel: 403-752-7960 *Fax:* 403-627-5275

Red Deer: **Red Deer Mental Health Centre**
Affiliated with: Alberta Health Services
4755 - 49 St., Red Deer, AB T4N 1T6
Tel: 403-340-5466 *Fax:* 403-340-4874
Di Uosburgh, Executive Director

Rimbey: **Rimbey Mental Health Centre**
Affiliated with: Alberta Health Services
PO Box 471, 5025 - 55 St., Rimbey, AB T0C 2J0
Tel: 403-843-2406 *Fax:* 403-843-2337

Sherwood Park: **Sherwood Park Mental Health Clinic**
Capital Health Region
2 Brower Dr., Sherwood Park, AB T8A 3Y1
Tel: 780-449-5380 *Fax:* 780-464-3705
mhcsherwoodpark@cha.ab.ca
www.capitalhealth.ca
Anita Murphy, Manager

Slave Lake: **Slave Lake Mental Health Clinic**
Affiliated with: Alberta Health Services
309 - 6 St., Slave Lake, AB T0G 2A2
Tel: 780-805-3502 *Fax:* 780-805-3550
Cindy Harmata

Smoky Lake: **Smoky Lake Mental Health Clinic**
Affiliated with: Alberta Health Services
4212 - 55 Ave., Smoky Lake, AB T0A 3C0
Tel: 780-656-3034 *Fax:* 780-656-5010
Gloria Strachan

St Albert: **St. Albert Mental Health Clinic**
Affiliated with: Alberta Health Services
Sir Winston Churchill Ave., St Albert, AB T8N 3A4
Tel: 780-459-2820 *Fax:* 780-460-7152
www.capitalhealth.ca

St Paul: **St. Paul Mental Health Clinic**
Affiliated with: Alberta Health Services
4713 - 48 Ave., St Paul, AB T0A 3A4
Tel: 780-645-1850 *Fax:* 780-645-2788
Leanne Betts

Stettler: **Stettler Mental Health Clinic**
Affiliated with: Alberta Health Services
PO Box 600, 4835 - 50 Ave. SS, Stettler, AB T0C 2L0
Tel: 403-742-7591 *Fax:* 403-742-7916

Stony Plain: **Stony Plain Addiction & Mental Health Clinic**
Affiliated with: WestView Health Centre
Former Name: Stony Plain Mental Health Clinic
Westview Health Centre, 4405 South Park Dr., Stony Plain, AB T7Z 2M7
Tel: 780-963-6151 *Fax:* 780-963-7186

Strathmore: **Strathmore Mental Health Clinic**
Former Name: Strathmore Mental Health Centre
Hilton Plaza, PO Box 2002, 209 - 3 St., Strathmore, AB T1P 1K2
Tel: 403-934-5174 *Fax:* 403-934-2685

Swan Hills: **Swan Hills Mental Health Clinic**
Affiliated with: Alberta Health Services
PO Box 261, 29 Freeman Dr., Swan Hills, AB T0G 2C0
Tel: 780-333-4241 *Fax:* 780-333-7009
Lorraine Lindberg

Sylvan Lake: **Sylvan Lake Mental Health Centre**
Affiliated with: Alberta Health Services
4602 - 49 Ave., Sylvan Lake, AB T4S 1M7
Tel: 403-887-2241 *Fax:* 403-887-2641

Taber: **Taber Mental Health Clinic**
5011 - 49 Ave., Taber, AB T1G 1V9
Tel: 403-223-7932 *Fax:* 403-223-7902

Three Hills: **Three Hills Mental Health Centre**
Affiliated with: Alberta Health Services
PO Box 1717, 160 - 3 Ave. South, Three Hills, AB T0M 2A0
Tel: 403-443-8532 *Fax:* 403-443-8541

Tofield: **Tofield Mental Health Clinic & Children's Resource Centre**
Affiliated with: Alberta Health Services
5024 - 51 Ave., Tofield, AB T0B 4J0
Tel: 780-662-7061 *Fax:* 780-662-3854
www.albertahealthservices.ca
Brenda Nelson

Valleyview: **Valleyview Mental Health Clinic**
Affiliated with: Alberta Health Services
PO Box 358, 4802 Highway St., Valleyview, AB T0H 3N0
Tel: 780-524-7050

Vegreville: **Vegreville Mental Health Clinic**
Affiliated with: Alberta Health Services
5318 - 50 Ave., Vegreville, AB T9C 1R1
Tel: 780-632-2714 *Fax:* 780-632-4954
Brenda Nelson
780/679-1765

Vegreville: **Vegreville Mental Health Clinic**
Affiliated with: Alberta Health Services
PO Box 90, 5318 - 50 St., Vegreville, AB T9C 1R1
Tel: 780-632-2714 *Fax:* 780-632-4954
www.ech.ab.ca

Note: 24-hour crisis line: 780-632-7070
Brenda Nelson

Vermilion: **Vermilion Mental Health Clinic**
Affiliated with: Alberta Health Services
Provincial Building, PO Box 14, 4701 - 52 St., Vermilion, AB T9X 1J9
Tel: 780-853-8168 *Fax:* 780-853-8279
www.ech.ab.ca

Brenda Nelson
780/679-1765

Wainwright: **Wainwright Mental Health Clinic**
Affiliated with: Alberta Health Services
PO Box 20, 810 - 14 Ave., Wainwright, AB T9W 1R2
Tel: 780-842-7522 *Fax:* 780-842-7520
www.ech.ab.ca
Brenda Nelson

Wetaskiwin: **Wetaskiwin Mental Health Clinic**
Affiliated with: Alberta Health Services
5201 - 50 Ave., Wetaskiwin, AB T9A 0S7
Tel: 780-361-1245 *Fax:* 780-361-1387
mhc-wetaskiwin@amhb.ab.ca

Special Care Homes

Lloydminster: **Dr. Cooke Extended Care Centre**
Affiliated with: Prairie North Health Region
3915 - 56 Ave., Lloydminster, AB T9V 0Z7
Tel: 780-871-7900 *Fax:* 780-875-3505
Number of Beds: 105 beds
Joan Zimmer, Director, Continuing Care

British Columbia

Government Departments in Charge

BRITISH COLUMBIA: British Columbia Ministry of Health Services
1515 Blanshard St., 6th Fl., Victoria, BC V8W 3C8
Tel: 250-952-1297 *Fax:* 250-952-1052
hlth.health@gov.bc.ca
www.gov.bc.ca/health
Hon. Michael de Jong, Minister of Health
250-953-3547, hlth.minister@gov.bc.ca

Regional Health Authorities

Kelowna: **Interior Health Authority**
Corporate Office, 220-1815 Kirschner Rd., Kelowna, BC V1Y 4N7
Tel: 250-862-4200 *Fax:* 250-862-4201
www.interiorhealth.ca
Social Media: www.facebook.com/InteriorHealth; twitter.com/Interior_Health; www.youtube.com/user/InteriorHealthAuth; www.linkedin.com/company/interior-health-authority

Note: Facilities: 20 community health centres; 16 community hospitals; 4 service area hospitals; 2 tertiary referral hospitals. Area Served: Thompson Cariboo Shuswap Health Service Area; Okanagan Health Service Area; Kootenay Boundary Health Service Area; East Kootenay Health Service Area
Dr. Robert Halpenny, President; Chief Executive Officer
Norman Embree, Board Chair
Dr. Keith Hutchison, Chair, Health Authority Medical Advisory Committee
Donna Lommer, Chief Financial Officer; Vice-President, Residential Services
Dr. Jeremy Etherington, Vice-President, Medicine / Quality
Joanne Konnert, Vice-President, Tertiary Services
Martin McMahon, Vice-President, Planning / Strategic Services
Andrew Neuner, Vice-President, Community Integration
Brenda Rebman, Vice-President, People / Clinical Services
Cathy Renkas, Vice-President, Communications / Public Affairs
Allan Sinclair, Vice-President, Acute Services

Prince George: **Northern Health Authority**
Former Name: Northern Interior Health Board
#600, 299 Victoria St., Prince George, BC V2L 5B8
Tel: 250-565-2649 *Fax:* 250-565-2640
Toll-Free: 866-565-2999
hello@northernhealth.ca
www.northernhealth.ca
Social Media: www.facebook.com/NorthernHealth; twitter.com/northern_health; www.youtube.com/northernhealthbc; www.linkedin.com/company/northern-health-authority
Population Served: 300000*Number of Employees:* 7000
Note: Services administered through 3 service delivery areas: Northwest, Northeast, Northern Interior. Over two dozen hospitals, 14 long-term care facilities, many public health units, and many offices providing specialized care.
Cathy Ulrich, CEO

Surrey: **Fraser Health Authority**
Central City Tower, #400, 102nd Ave., Surrey, BC V3T 0H1
Tel: 604-587-4600 *Fax:* 604-587-4666
Toll-Free: 1-877-935-5669
feedback@fraserhealth.ca
www.fraserhealth.ca
Social Media: twitter.com/Fraserhealth

Number of Beds: 12 acute care hospitals; 7760 residental care beds; mental health care, public health, home and community care
Area Served: Burnaby to White Rock to Hope in British Columbia*Population Served:* 1600000*Number of Employees:* 23000
Dr. Nigel Murray, President; Chief Executive Officer
David Mitchell, Board Chair
Martin Pochurko, Chief Financial Officer
Philip Barker, Vice-President, Information Management
Geoffrey Crampton, Vice-President, People & Organization Development
Peter Goldthorpe, Vice-President, Capital Projects, Real Estate, & Facilities
Brian Woods, Vice-President, Corporate Services Integration
Marc Pelletier, Vice-President, Clinical Operations & Clinical Support
Dr. Andrew Webb, Vice-President, Medicine
David Plug, Chief Communications Officer

***Vancouver:* Provincial Health Services Authority (PHSA)**
700 - 1380 Burrard St., Vancouver, BC V6Z 2H3
Tel: 604-675-7400 *Fax:* 604-708-2700
www.phsa.ca

Note: PHSA operates provincial agencies including BC Children's Hospital, BC Transplant, and BC Cancer Agency. It is also responsible for specialized provincial health services like chest surgery and trauma services.
Lynda Cranston, President/CEO
Wynne Powell, Board Chair

***Vancouver:* Vancouver Coastal Health**
Vancouver Coastal Health Corporate Office, 601 West Broadway, 11th Fl., Vancouver, BC V5Z 4C2
Tel: 604-736-2033 *Fax:* 604-736-7601
Toll-Free: 1-866-884-0888
feedback@vch.ca
www.vch.ca
Social Media: twitter.com/vchhealthcare; www.flickr.com/photos/vancouvercoastalhealth
Population Served: 1000000*Number of Employees:* 13000
Note: Area Served: Vancouver; Richmond; the North Shore; Coast Garibaldi; Sea-to-Sky; Sunshine Coast; Powell River; Bella Bella; Bella Coola
Kip Woodward, Board Chair
Dr. David N. Ostrow, President; Chief Executive Officer
Mary Ackenhusen, Chief Operating Officer
Duncan Campbell, Chief Financial Officer; Vice-President, Systems Development; Performance
Dr. Patricia Daly, Chief Medical Health Officer; Vice-President, Public Health
Susan Wannamaker, Chief Nursing Officer; Executive Lead, Professional Practice
Clay Adams, Vice-President, Communications & Public Affairs
Dr. Jeff Coleman, Vice-President, Regional Programs & Service Integration
Dr. Patrick O'Connor, Vice-President, Medicine, Quality, & Safety

***Victoria:* Vancouver Island Health Authority**
Former Name: Capital Health Region
1952 Bay St., Victoria, BC V8R 1J8
Tel: 250-370-8699 *Fax:* 250-370-8750
Toll-Free: 877-370-8699
info@viha.ca
www.viha.ca
Social Media: www.facebook.com/135150073228437; twitter.com/vanislandhealth
Number of Beds: 1307 acute care; 4593 residential, VIHA & contracted beds
Area Served: Vancouver Island and the islands of the George Strait*Population Served:* 765000
Howard Waldner, President; CEO

Hospitals

Hospitals - General

***Alert Bay:* Cormorant Island Health Centre**
Affiliated with: Vancouver Island Health Authority
PO Box 223, 49 School Rd., Alert Bay, BC V0N 1A0
Tel: 250-974-5585 *Fax:* 250-974-5422
info@viha.ca
www.viha.ca

Number of Beds: 10 multi-purpose beds
Note: Hospital Specialties: Emergency services; Acute care; Medical imaging; General laboratory services (250-974-5585, ext. 3); Adult mental health & addiction services; Care to adults with developmental or physical disabilities; Public health services; Rural health services (250-755-6281)
Dr. Richard Stanwick, Chief Medical Health Officer, Vancouver Island Health Authority

***Ashcroft:* Ashcroft & District General Hospital**
Affiliated with: Interior Health Authority
700 Ash-Cache Creek Hwy., Ashcroft, BC V0K 1A0
Tel: 250-453-2211 *Fax:* 250-453-9685
www.interiorhealth.ca

Year Founded: 1970
Number of Beds: 24 beds

***Bella Bella:* R.W. Large Memorial Hospital**
Affiliated with: Vancouver Coastal Health Authority
88 Waglisla St., Bella Bella, BC V0T 1Z0
Tel: 250-957-2314 *Fax:* 250-957-2612
feedback@vch.ca
www.vch.ca/EN/find_locations/find_locations/?&site_id=2136
Number of Beds: 16 beds
Note: Provincial hospital offering ltc/acute care, pharmacy, diagnostic imaging services, telehealth services
Dr. David N. Ostrow, President; CEO, VCH

***Bella Coola:* Bella Coola General Hospital (BCGH)**
Affiliated with: Vancouver Coastal Health
PO Box 434, 1025 Elcho St., Bella Coola, BC V0T 1C0
Tel: 250-799-5311 *Fax:* 250-799-5635
feedback@vch.ca
www.vch.ca
Number of Beds: 10 acute care beds; 5 extended care beds
Note: Hospital Specialties: Emergency services; Walk-in clinic; Laboratory services; Acute care; Long term care; Mental health services; Public health; Physiotherapy; Home support
Michel Bazille, Administrator, Health Services
250-799-5308, ext. 2
Lorinda Andersen, Director, Patient Care
250-799-5311, ext. 2, lorinda.andersen@vch.ca

***Burnaby:* Burnaby Hospital**
Affiliated with: Fraser Health Authority
3935 Kincaid St., Burnaby, BC V5G 2X6
Tel: 604-412-6131 *Fax:* 604-412-6190
www.fraserhealth.ca
Number of Beds: 309 acute care beds
Note: Hospital Specialties: Emergency services; Diagnostic testing; General surgery; Perinatal services; Neonatal intensive care; Oncology; Mental health services; Critical care; Palliative care
Arden Krystal, Executive Director

***Campbell River:* Campbell River & District Regional Hospital**
Affiliated with: Vancouver Island Health Authority
Also Known As: Campbell River General Hospital
375 - 2nd Ave., Campbell River, BC V9W 3V1
Tel: 250-850-2141 *Fax:* 250-286-9675
www.viha.ca

Note: Hospital Specialties: Emergency care; Surgical services: Intensive care; Cardiac care; Laboratory services; Acute care; Rehabilitation services (250-286-7045); Aboriginal health; Diabetes education (250-850-2607); Nutrition services (250-286-7013)
Dr. Richard Crow, Executive Vice-President; Chief Medical Officer, Vancouver Island Health Authority
Sandy Murphy, Nurse, Aboriginal Health
250-850-2602, sandy.murphy@viha.ca

***Chetwynd:* Chetwynd Hospital & Health Centre**
Affiliated with: Northern Health Authority
PO Box 507, 5500 Hospital Rd., Chetwynd, BC V0C 1J0
Tel: 250-788-2236 *Fax:* 250-788-7247
hello@northernhealth.ca
www2.northernhealth.ca

Note: Hospital Specialty: Acute care
Betty McCracken Morris, Chief Operating Officer, Northeast Health Service Delivery Area

***Chilliwack:* Chilliwack General Hospital**
Affiliated with: Fraser Health Authority
45600 Menholm Rd., Chilliwack, BC V2P 1P7
Tel: 604-795-4141 *Fax:* 604-795-4110
feedback@fraserhealth.ca
www.fraserhealth.ca

Note: Hospital Specialties: Emergency services; Laboratory services; Ambulatory care; Rehabilitation services
Dr. Andrew Webb, Vice-President, Medicine, Fraser Health

***Clearwater:* Dr. Helmcken Memorial Hospital (DHM)**
Affiliated with: Interior Health Authority
640 Park Dr., RR#1, Clearwater, BC V0E 1N0
Tel: 250-674-2244 *Fax:* 250-674-2477
www.interiorhealth.ca
Number of Beds: 6 beds
Note: Hospital Specialties: Community hospital level 1 services; Emergency services; Acute care; Physiotherapy; Recreation therapy; Dietician services; Public health; Environmental health protection services; Home care nursing
Nicole Lacroix, Coordinator, Recreation Therapy
Nicole.Lacroix@interiorhealth.ca

***Comox:* St. Joseph's General Hospital**
Affiliated with: Vancouver Island Health Authority
2137 Comox Ave., Comox, BC V9M 1P2
Tel: 250-339-2242 *Fax:* 250-339-1432
www.sjghcomox.ca

Year Founded: 1913
Number of Beds: 235 beds (110 in acute care and 125 in complex care)
Note: A comprehensive health facility with services in emergency, colposcopy, dermatology, diabetes, diagnostic imaging (mammography, radiology, ultrasound), extended care, general surgery, gastroenterology, internal medicine, maternity, obstetrics/gynaecology, oncology, ophthalmology, orthopaedics, paediatrics, palliative care, pathology, psychiatry and urology
Michael Pontus, President/CEO
250-339-1409,
Dr. Stefan Schovanek, President, Medical Staff

***Cranbrook:* East Kootenay Regional Hospital (EKRH)**
Affiliated with: Interior Health Authority
13 - 24th Ave. North, Cranbrook, BC V1C 3H9
Tel: 250-426-5281 *Fax:* 250-426-5285
Toll-Free: 866-288-8082
www.interiorhealth.ca

Note: Hospital Specialties: Emergency services; Laboratory services; Diagnostic imaging; General surgery; Intensive care unit; Obstetrics; Pediatrics; Oncology (250-417-6228); Ophthalmology; Orthopedics; Urology; Otolaryncology; Rehabilitation services; Psychiatry
Dr. Jeremy Etherington, Vice-President, Medicine / Quality, Interior Health
Allan Sinclair, Vice-President, Acute Services, Interior Health
Kate Fox, Coordinator, Volunteers, East Kootenay Regional Hospital
250-417-2746, katefox@shaw.ca

***Creston:* Creston Valley Hospital (CVH)**
Affiliated with: Interior Health Authority
PO Box 3000, 312 - 15th Ave. North, Creston, BC V0B 1G0
Tel: 250-428-2286 *Fax:* 250-428-4860
www.interiorhealth.ca
Number of Beds: 16 beds
Note: Hospital Specialties: Emergency services; Trauma care; Diagnostic imaging; Laboratory services; Acute care; Ambulatory care; Obstetrics; Pediatrics; Rehabilitation services, including occupational therapy & physiotherapy; Mental health services; Diabetes education; Dietitian services; Outpatient renal dialysis unit; Chronic disease management; Adult day care; Number of Employees: 150
Cindy Kozak-Campbell, Interior Health Authority Health Services Administrator, Creston
Dr. Atma Persad, Chief of Staff
Deryn Collier, Coordinator, Recruitment

***Dawson Creek:* Dawson Creek & District Hospital**
Affiliated with: Northern Health Authority
11100 - 13th St., Dawson Creek, BC V1G 3W8
Tel: 250-782-8501 *Fax:* 250-783-7301
Number of Beds: 62 acute care beds
Note: Hospital Specialties: Emergency services (250-784-7393); Diagnostic imaging; Laboratory services; General surgery; Intensive care unit; Acute care; Maternity services; Rehabilitation services, including physiotherapy, occupational, & respiratory therapy; Adult psychiatry inpatient unit (250-784-7369); Diabetes education. Serves Chetwynd, Tumbler Ridge, Pouce Coupe, Ft. St. John, Ft. Nelson, and parts of North Western Alberta.

***Delta:* Delta Hospital**
Affiliated with: Fraser Health Authority
5800 Mountain View Blvd., Delta, BC V4K 3V6
Tel: 604-946-1121 *Fax:* 604-538-3320
feedback@fraserhealth.ca
www.fraserhealth.ca

Note: Hospital Specialties: Emergency services; General surgery; Ambulatory care; Cardiac services; Occupational therapy; Physiotherapy; Respiratory therapy; Speech language

pathology services; Diabetes education; Asthma education; Nutrition counselling; Social work; Palliative care
Arden Krystal, Vice-President, Clinical Operations, Fraser Health

Dr. Andrew Webb, Vice-President, Medicine, Fraser Health
Andrew.Webb@fraserhealth.ca

Duncan: Cowichan District Hospital (CDH)
Affiliated with: Vancouver Island Health Authority
3045 Gibbins Rd., Duncan, BC V9L 1E5
Tel: 250-737-2030 *Fax:* 250-715-1212
www.viha.ca
Number of Beds: 95 beds
Note: Hospital Specialties: Emergency services; Laboratory services; Medical imaging: Intensive care unit; Acute care; Maternity; Rehabilitation services; Adult mental health & addiction services; Breast Health Hereditary Cancer Program; Hemodialysis; Occupational therapy & physiotherapy (250-709-3000); Nutrition services (250-370-8111); Respiratory ambulatory service; Palliative care
Dr. Richard Crow, Chief Medical Officer; Executive Vice-President, Vancouver Island Health Authority
Catherine Mackay, Chief Operating Officer; Executive Vice President, Vancouver Island Health Authority
Gerry Giles, Chair, Cowichan Valley Regional Hospital District
Jim Potts, Manager, CDH Pharmacy

Fernie: Elk Valley Hospital
Affiliated with: Interior Health Authority
PO Box 670, 1501 - 5th Ave., Fernie, BC V0B 1M0
Tel: 250-423-4453 *Fax:* 250-423-3732
www.interiorhealth.ca
Number of Beds: 20 beds
Note: Hospital Specialties: Emergency services; Diagnostic imaging; Laboratory services; Ambulatory care; Acute care; Obstetrics; Pediatrics; Occupational therapy; Physiotherapy; Mental health services; Dietitian services; Pain management education; Public health; Home support services. Number of Employees: 100

Fort Nelson: Fort Nelson Hospital
Affiliated with: Northern Health Authority
PO Box 60, 5315 Liard Street, Fort Nelson, BC V0C 1R0
Tel: 250-774-8100 *Fax:* 250-774-8110
hello@northernhealth.ca
www2.northernhealth.ca
Note: Hospital Specialties: Emergency care; Intensive care; Medical imaging; Addictions counselling services (250-565-2649); Adult day centre (250-565-7451); Diabetes education (250-774-6916)
Betty McCracken Morris, Chief Operating Officer, Northern Health, Northeast Health Service Delivery

Fort St James: Stuart Lake Hospital
Affiliated with: Northern Health Authority
PO Box 1060, 600 Stuart Dr. East, Fort St James, BC V0J 1P0
Tel: 250-996-8201 *Fax:* 250-996-8777
hello@northernhealth.ca
www2.northernhealth.ca/Contact_Us/Northern_Interior/FraserLakeandVanderhoofcontacts.asp
Number of Beds: 12 beds (6 acute care, 6 long-term care beds)
Note: Services include emergency, laboratory and x-ray facilities.
Cathy Ulrich, CEO, NHA
250-565-2649
Michael McMillan, COO, Northern Interior, NHA
Bruna Schnepf., Director, Patient Care
250-567-2211

Fort St John: Fort St. John Hospital & Health Centre
Affiliated with: Northern Health Authority
9636 - 100th Ave., Fort St John, BC V1J 1Y3
Tel: 250-262-5200 *Fax:* 250-262-5294
www2.northernhealth.ca
Number of Beds: 44 beds
Note: Hospital Specialties: Diagnostics; Surgery; Intensive care; Acute care; Maternity services; Rehabilitation; Hemo dialysis; Palliative care
Betty McCracken Morris, Chief Operating Officer, Northern Health, Northeast Health Service Delivery

Fort St John: Fort St John Hospital & Peace Villa
Affiliated with: Northern Health Authority
8407 - 112 Ave., Fort St John, BC V1J 0J5
Tel: 250-262-5200
Number of Beds: 55 acute care beds; 123 residental care beds
Note: Hospital and long-term care facility is expected to open in the fall of 2012.
Maureen Haley, Communications Officer
250-565-7336

Golden: Golden & District General Hospital
Affiliated with: Interior Health Authority
835 - 9th St. North RR 2, Golden, BC V0A 1H2
Tel: 250-344-5271 *Fax:* 250-344-2511
Number of Beds: 8 beds
Tish Smith

Grand Forks: Boundary Hospital
Affiliated with: Interior Health Authority
7649 - 22nd St., Grand Forks, BC V0H 1H2
Tel: 250-443-2100 *Fax:* 250-442-8331
www.interiorhealth.ca
Number of Beds: 12 acute care beds
Note: Hospital specialties: Emergency services; Laboratory services; Radiology; Acute care; Chemotherapy; Renal dialysis; Ambulatory care
Louise Fitzgerald, Social Worker
250-443-2162, Louise.Fitzgerald@interiorhealth.ca

Hazelton: Wrinch Memorial Hospital
Affiliated with: Northern Health Authority
#999, 2510 Highway 62, Hazelton, BC V0J 1Y0
Tel: 250-842-5339 *Fax:* 250-842-5685

Hope: Fraser Canyon Hospital
Affiliated with: Fraser Health Authority
1275 - 7th Ave., Hope, BC V0X 1L4
Tel: 604-869-5656 *Fax:* 604-860-7732
feedback@fraserhealth.ca
www.fraserhealth.ca

Note: Hospital Specialties: Emergency services; Diagnostic laboratory services (604-860-7702); Acute care; Social work; Nutrition counselling; Palliative care (604-860-7713)

Invermere: Invermere & District Hospital
Affiliated with: Interior Health Authority
850 - 10th Ave., Invermere, BC V0A 1K0
Tel: 250-342-9201 *Fax:* 250-342-6303
Number of Beds: 8 acute care, 35 residential beds
Colleen Wagner, Contact
250-342-9201 ext. 24

Kamloops: Royal Inland Hospital
Affiliated with: Interior Health Authority
311 Columbia St., Kamloops, BC V2C 2T1
Tel: 250-374-5111 *Fax:* 250-314-2333
Toll-Free: 877-288-5688
patient.concerns@interiorhealth.ca
www.interiorhealth.ca/health-services.aspx?id=284
Number of Beds: 226 beds
Note: Tertiary acute care hospital; angiography/interventional radiology, bone density, CT scan, mammography, MRI, nuclear medicine, ultrasound, X-Ray
Dr. Robert Halpenny, President/CEO, IHA
Donna Lommer, CFO, IHA, Medical Services

Kelowna: Kelowna General Hospital
Affiliated with: Interior Health Authority
2268 Pandosy St., Kelowna, BC V1Y 1T2
Tel: 250-862-4000 *Fax:* 250-862-4201
www.interiorhealth.ca
Number of Beds: 329 beds
Rick Riley, COO
Dave Macintosh, Director, Purchasing Services

Kitimat: Kitimat General Hospital & Health Centre
Affiliated with: Northern Health Authority
920 Lahakas Blvd. South, Kitimat, BC V8C 2S3
Tel: 250-632-2121 *Fax:* 250-632-8726
Number of Beds: 54 beds

Ladysmith: Ladysmith & District General Hospital
Affiliated with: Vancouver Island Health Authority
1111 - 4 Ave., Ladysmith, BC V0R 2E0
Tel: 250-739-5777 *Fax:* 250-245-3238
Number of Beds: 42 beds
Chuck Rowe, CEO

Langley: Langley Memorial Hospital
Affiliated with: Fraser Health Authority
Former Name: Langley Health Services
22051 Fraser Hwy., Langley, BC V3A 4H4
Tel: 604-534-4121 *Fax:* 604-534-8283
Number of Beds: 166 acute care beds, 230 residential care beds
Leanne Heppill, Executive Director
Harry Berglund, Director of Purchasing

Lillooet: Lillooet District Hospital & Community Health Programs
Affiliated with: Interior Health Authority
951 Murray St., Lillooet, BC V0K 1V0
Tel: 250-256-4233 *Fax:* 250-256-1336

Number of Beds: 6 beds
Jennifer Thur

MacKenzie: MacKenzie & District Hospital
Affiliated with: Northern Health Authority
45 Centennial Dr., MacKenzie, BC V0J 2C0
Tel: 250-997-3263 *Fax:* 250-997-3940
Number of Beds: 5 beds
Raelene Shea, Exec. Dir.

Maple Ridge: Ridge Meadows Hospital
Affiliated with: Fraser Health Authority
Former Name: Ridge Meadows Hospice Society
PO Box 5000, 11666 Laity St., Maple Ridge, BC V2X 7G5
Tel: 604-463-4111 *Fax:* 604-463-1888
feedback@fraserhealth.ca
fraserhealth.ca/find_us/locations/our_locations?site_id=1787
Number of Beds: 104 acute care, 150 residential care beds, 20-bed psychiatric care unit
Dr. Nigel Murray, President/CEO, FHA
Dr. Greg Kotylak, Head, Surgery
Valerie Spurrell, Director, Acute Care

McBride: McBride & District Hospital
Affiliated with: Northern Health Authority
1126, 5th Ave., McBride, BC V0J 2E0
Tel: 250-569-2251 *Fax:* 250-569-3369
Number of Beds: 16 beds
Vic Chicoine, Administrator

Merritt: Nicola Valley General Hospital
Affiliated with: Interior Health Authority
3451 Voght St., Merritt, BC V1K 1C6
Tel: 250-378-3271 *Fax:* 250-378-3287
Number of Beds: 8 beds
Doug Sage

Mission: Mission Memorial Hospital
Affiliated with: Fraser Health Authority
7324 Hurd St., Mission, BC V2V 3H5
Tel: 604-826-6261 *Fax:* 604-826-9513
Number of Beds: 20 acute care, 75 residential care beds
Vivian Giglio, Executive Director, Health Services

Nakusp: Arrow Lakes Hospital
Affiliated with: Interior Health Authority
97 East 1st Ave., Nakusp, BC V0G 1R0
Tel: 250-265-3622 *Fax:* 250-265-4435
www.interiorhealth.ca
Number of Beds: 6 acute inpatient beds; 14 residential beds (Minto House residential unit)
Note: Hospital Specialties: Emergency services; Acute care; Public health; Physiotherapy; Occupational therapy; Home care; Mental health services; Palliative care Number of Employees: 50

Nanaimo: Nanaimo Regional General Hospital
Affiliated with: Vancouver Island Health Authority
1200 Dufferin Cres., Nanaimo, BC V9S 2B7
Tel: 250-754-2141 *Fax:* 250-755-7633
Number of Beds: 329 beds
Allison Cutler, Executive Director, Medicine, Chronic Disease Management/Primary Health

Nelson: Kootenay Lake Hospital
Affiliated with: Interior Health Authority
3 View St., Nelson, BC V1L 2V1
Tel: 250-352-3111 *Fax:* 250-354-2320
Toll-Free: 866-352-3111
www.interiorhealth.ca
Number of Beds: 30 beds
Dorothy Wayling, Site Director

New Denver: Slocan Community Health Centre
Affiliated with: Interior Health Authority
401 Galena Ave., New Denver, BC V0G 1S0
Tel: 250-358-7911 *Fax:* 250-358-7117
www.interiorhealth.ca/health-services.aspx?id=350&terms=slocan
Number of Beds: 30 beds
Note: Primary, long-term care faciltiy with services including emergency, mental health services, occupational therapy, physiotherapy, podiatry, respiratory therapy, X-ray & ECG
Dr. Robert Halpenny, CEO, IHA
Ann Weir, Health Centre Manager
Fax: 250-358-7801, ann.weir@interiorhealth.ca

North Vancouver: Lions Gate Hospital
Affiliated with: Vancouver Coastal Health Authority
231 - 15 St. East, North Vancouver, BC V7L 2L7
Tel: 604-988-3131 *Fax:* 604-984-5838
www.vch.ca
Number of Beds: 268 beds

Ellen Pekeles, COO

***Oliver:* South Okanagan General Hospital**
Affiliated with: Interior Health Authority
7139 - 362nd Ave., Oliver, BC V0H 1T0
Tel: 250-498-5000 *Fax:* 250-498-5004
www.interiorhealth.ca/health-services.aspx?id=11846
Number of Beds: 18 beds
Note: A level 1, community hospital with services including emergency, radiology, acute care, outpatient ambulatory care
Dr. Robert Halpenny, President/CEO, IHA
Allan Sinclair, Vice-President, Acute Services, IHA
Mary Doughtery, Patient Care Quality Officer, South Okanagan
250-862-4300, mary.dougherty@interiorhealth.ca

***Penticton:* Penticton Regional Hospital**
Affiliated with: Interior Health Authority
550B Carmi Ave., Penticton, BC V2A 3G6
Tel: 250-492-4000 *Fax:* 250-492-9068
Number of Beds: 148 beds
Lorraine Ferguson

***Port Alberni:* West Coast General Hospital**
Affiliated with: Vancouver Island Health Authority
3949 Port Alberni Hwy., Port Alberni, BC V9Y 7L1
Tel: 250-723-2135 *Fax:* 250-723-8805
Number of Beds: 43 acute care, 32 extended care beds
Jim Latham, Director, Physical Plant

***Port Alice:* Port Alice Hospital**
Affiliated with: Vancouver Island Health Authority
1090 Marine Dr., Port Alice, BC V0N 2N0
Tel: 250-284-3555 *Fax:* 250-284-6163
Number of Beds: 3 beds
Jean Wheeler, Manager

***Port Hardy:* Port Hardy Hospital**
Affiliated with: Vancouver Island Health Authority
9120 Granville, Port Hardy, BC V0N 2P0
Tel: 250-949-6161 *Fax:* 250-949-7000
Number of Beds: 17 beds
Ron Benson, CEO

***Port McNeill:* Port McNeill & District Hospital**
Affiliated with: Vancouver Island Health Authority
2750 Kingcome Place, Port McNeill, BC V0N 2R0
Tel: 250-956-4461 *Fax:* 250-956-4823
Number of Beds: 10 beds

***Port Moody:* Eagle Ridge Hospital (ERH)**
Affiliated with: Fraser Health Authority
475 Guildford Way, Port Moody, BC V3H 3W9
Tel: 604-461-2022 *Fax:* 604-461-9972
feedback@fraserhealth.ca
www.fraserhealth.ca
Year Founded: 1984
Note: Hospital Specialties: Emergency services; General surgery unit; Acute care; Ambulatory care; Cardiac care; Medical oncology unit; Rehabilitation services, including physiotherapy & occupational therapy; Respiratory therapy; Diabetes education; Asthma education; Nutrition counselling; Palliative care
Arden Krystal, Vice-President, Clinical Operations
Dr. Andrew Webb, Vice-President, Medicine, Fraser Health

***Powell River:* Powell River General Hospital**
Affiliated with: Vancouver Coastal Health Authority
5000 Joyce Ave., Powell River, BC V8A 5R3
Tel: 604-485-3211 *Fax:* 604-485-3245
Number of Beds: 33 beds
Jerry Causier, Manager, Acute Services

***Prince George:* Prince George Regional Hospital**
Affiliated with: Northern Health Authority
1475 Edmonton St., Prince George, BC V2M 1S2
Tel: 250-565-2000 *Fax:* 250-565-2343
Number of Beds: 338 beds
Ginger Brown, Executive Director
Adrian Van Peenen, Director, Physical Plant

***Prince Rupert:* Prince Rupert Regional Hospital**
Affiliated with: Northern Health Authority
1305 Summit Ave., Prince Rupert, BC V8J 2A6
Tel: 250-624-2171 *Fax:* 250-624-2195
Number of Beds: 71 beds

***Princeton:* Princeton General Hospital**
Affiliated with: Interior Health Authority
98 Ridgewood Ave., Princeton, BC V0X 1W0
Tel: 250-295-3233
Number of Beds: 6 acute care beds
Marilyn Harkness, Administrator
Alex Smith, Head, Plant Maintenance

***Queen Charlotte:* Queen Charlotte Islands General Hospital**
Affiliated with: Northern Health Authority
PO Box 9, 3203 - 3rd Ave., Queen Charlotte, BC V0T 1S0
Tel: 250-559-4300 *Fax:* 250-559-4312
Number of Beds: 21 beds
George Cheyne, CEO

***Quesnel:* GR Baker Memorial Hospital**
Affiliated with: Northern Health Authority
543 Front St., Quesnel, BC V2J 2K7
Tel: 250-985-5600 *Fax:* 250-992-5652
www2.northernhealth.ca
Year Founded: 1955
Number of Beds: 38 beds
Note: Hospital Specialties: Emergency services; Intensive care; Crisis stabilization; Acute care; Maternity services; Occupational therapy; Physiotherapy
Michael McMillan, Chief Operating Officer, Northern Health

***Revelstoke:* Queen Victoria Hospital & Health Centre**
Affiliated with: Interior Health Authority
1200 Newlands Rd., Revelstoke, BC V0E 2S0
Tel: 250-837-2131 *Fax:* 250-837-4788
www.interiorhealth.ca
Number of Beds: 38 beds
Dorothy Schiller
Andrew Neuner
Ron Hawkins, Maintenance Supervisor

***Richmond:* Richmond Hospital**
Affiliated with: Vancouver Coastal Health Authority
Former Name: The Richmond Hospital
7000 Westminster Hwy., Richmond, BC V6X 1A2
Tel: 604-278-9711 *Fax:* 604-244-5191
feedback@vch.ca
www.vch.ca/find_locations/find_locations/?&site_id=135
Number of Beds: 175 beds
Note: Emergency, ambulatory care, diagnostics, intensive care and coronary care, maternity, psychiatry and surgery
Dr. David N. Ostrow, President/CEO, VCH
Duncan Adams, Vice-President, Communications & Public Affairs, VCH

***Saanichton:* Saanich Peninsula Hospital**
Affiliated with: Vancouver Island Health Authority
2166 Mount Newton Cross Rd., Saanichton, BC V8M 2B2
Tel: 250-544-7676 *Fax:* 250-652-7521
www.viha.ca/finding_care/facilities/saanich_peninsula_hospital.htm
Number of Beds: 48 acute beds, 144 extended care beds
Note: Emergency, breast surgical oncology, imaging - bone mineral densitometry, CT scan; 10-bed palliative care unit; acute & extended care
Howard Waldner, President; CEO, VIHA
William Boomer, Vice-President; CFO, VIHA
Catherine Mackay, Executive Vice-President; COO, VIHA

***Salmon Arm:* Shuswap Lake General Hospital**
Affiliated with: Interior Health Authority
601 - 10th St. NE, Salmon Arm, BC V1E 4N6
Tel: 250-833-3600 *Fax:* 250-833-3611
Toll-Free: 877-299-1599
lab.interiorhealth.ca/site_gi.aspx?id=32
Number of Beds: 40 beds
Note: Emergency, acute care beds, diagnostic imaging, radiology, obstetrical care
Dr. Robert Halpenny, CEO, IHA
Dr. Warren Bell, President, Medical Staff

***Salt Spring Island:* The Lady Minto Gulf Islands Hospital**
Affiliated with: Vancouver Island Health Authority
Former Name: Lady Minto Hospital
135 Crofton Rd., Salt Spring Island, BC V8K 1T1
Tel: 250-538-4800 *Fax:* 250-538-4870
www.viha.ca/finding_care/facilities/lady_minto_gulf_islands_hospital.htm
Number of Beds: 50 beds (19 acute care, 31 extended care beds)
Note: Services include emergency, laboratory, diagnostic imaging (fluoroscope, ultrasound, x-rays), breast oncology, surgery
Howard Waldner, President/CEO, VIHA
250-370-8692
Bill Boomer, Vice-President/CFO, VIHA
250-370-8602
Shannon Marshall, Communications Officer, VIHA
250-370-8270, shannon.marshall@viha.ca
Bill Relph, Site Manager

***Sechelt:* St. Mary's Hospital**
Affiliated with: Vancouver Coastal Health Authority
5544 Sunshine Coast Highway, Sechelt, BC V0N 3A0
Tel: 604-885-2224 *Fax:* 604-885-8628
feedback@vch.ca
www.vch.ca/EN/find_locations/find_locations/?&site_id=152
Number of Beds: 31 beds
Note: Services include emergency, tomography, fluoroscopy, mammography, renal program (dialysis units), ultrasound, laboratory, radiology, youth clinic.
Dr. David N. Ostrow, President/CEO, VCHA
Duncan Campbell, CFO/Vice-President, Systems Devlopment, VCHA
Trudi Beutel, Public Affairs Officer, VCHA
trudi.beutel@vch.ca

***Smithers:* Bulkley Valley District Hospital**
Affiliated with: Northern Health Authority
PO Box 370, 3950 - 8th Ave., Smithers, BC V0J 2N0
Tel: 250-847-2611 *Fax:* 250-847-2446
Number of Beds: 25 beds
Area Served: Communities from Houston in the east to Hazelton in the west.
Note: Hospital Specialties: Emergency services; Medical imaging; Acute care; Maternity services; Long term care; Palliative care

***Sparwood:* Sparwood General Hospital & Health Care Centre**
Affiliated with: Interior Health Authority
PO Box 9, 570 Pine Ave., Sparwood, BC V0B 2G0
Tel: 250-425-6212 *Fax:* 250-425-2313
www.interiorhealth.ca/health-services.aspx?id=352
Note: A primary health care centre with services including emergency, medical clinic, on-site lab & x-ray, dialysis, wellness centre focusing on diabetic, cardiac and respiratory education, as well as nutrition counselling and pain management counselling
Dr. Robert Halpenny, President/CEO, IHA
Dr. Jeremy Etherington, Vice-President, Medicine/Quality, IHA
Donna Lommer, CFO/Vice-President, Residential Services, IHA

***Squamish:* Squamish General Hospital**
Affiliated with: Vancouver Coastal Health Authority
38140 Behrner Dr., Squamish, BC V0N 3G0
Tel: 604-892-5211 *Fax:* 604-892-9417
feedback@vch.ca
www.vch.ca/EN/find_locations/find_locations/?&site_id=150
Number of Beds: 21 beds
Note: Services include emergency, general medicine and surgery, obstetrics, palliative care, physiotherapy, pharmacy, diagnostic imaging, laboratory, ambulatory care, chemotherapy, fluoroscopy, diabetic day clinic, residential care
Dr. David N. Ostrow, President/CEO, VCHA
Duncan Campbell, CFO/Vice-President, Systems Development, VCHA
Tina Hua, Manager, Acute Services, VCHA

***Stewart:* Stewart Health Centre**
Affiliated with: Northern Health Authority
PO Box 8, 904 Brightwell St., Stewart, BC V0T 1W0
Tel: 250-636-2221 *Fax:* 250-636-2715
www2.northernhealth.ca/Contact_Us/Northwest/Stewartcontacts.asp
Number of Beds: 3 beds
Note: Services include acute care, home support, physicians, counseling services, pharmacy, visiting specialists, mammography, ambulance services.
Cathy Ulrich, CEO, NHA
Shawn Terlson, CFO, NHA
Marina Ellinson, COO, Northwest, NHA
Dr. Ronald Chapman, Chief Medical Health Officer, NHA
Dr. Suzanne Johnston, Chief Nursing Officer, NHA

***Summerland:* Summerland Memorial Health Centre**
Affiliated with: Interior Health Authority
Former Name: Summerland General Hospital
Also Known As: Summerland Health Centre
PO Box 869, 12815 Atkinson Rd., Summerland, BC V0H 1Z0
Tel: 250-404-8000 *Fax:* 250-404-8005
www.interiorhealth.ca/health-services.aspx?id=268
Year Founded: 1967
Number of Beds: 50 beds
Note: A community health and residential care facility with services including surgery (cataract, ear, nose & throat, and dental), occupational therapy, physical therapy, laboratory services, x-ray, home support, social work, diabetes education, long-term case management.
Dr. Robert Halpenny, President/CEO, IHA

Cathy Renkas, Vice-President, Communications/Public Affairs, IHA
Bob Heise, Community Health Services Administrator

Surrey: Matsqui-Sumas-Abbotsford General Hospital
Affiliated with: Fraser Health Authority
10334, 152A Street, Surrey, BC V3R 7P8
Tel: 604-587-4600 *Fax:* 604-587-4666
Number of Beds: 202 beds
Vivian Giglio, Executive Director
Ed Towndow, Supervisor, Building Services/Environmental Dept.
Jeri Lynch, Purchasing Agent

Surrey: Surrey Memorial Hospital
Affiliated with: Fraser Health Authority
13750 - 96 Ave., Surrey, BC V3V 1Z2
Tel: 604-581-2211 *Fax:* 604-588-3320
feedback@fraserhealth.ca
fraserhealth.ca/find_us/locations/our_locations?site_id=1792
Number of Beds: 450 acute care, 186 residential care beds
Note: A comprehensive health centre with services including emergency, adolescent psychiatry, angiography, antepartum care, asthma education, diagnostic imaging (CT scans, bone densitometry, fluoroscopy, mammography, MRI, radiology, ultrasound), cardiology, outpatient speech language pathology, dental surgery, drug and alcohol resource team, hospice palliative care, intensive care , neonatal intensive care, ophthalmology, otolaryngology, paediatric oncology, pharmacy, plastic surgery, postpartum care, psychiatry, respiratory therapy, STI/HIV clinic, sexual assault, sleep lab, social work, speech language pathology, spiritual care, urological surgery, vascular and thoracic surgery, youth wellness centre.
Dr. Nigel Murray, President/CEO, FHA
Dr. Andrew Webb, Vice-President, Medicine, FHA
Loretta Solomon, Site Executive Director
Loretta.Solomon@fraserhealth.ca
Dr. Urbain Ip, Site Medical Director

Terrace: Mills Memorial Hospital
Affiliated with: Northern Health Authority
4720 Haugland Ave., Terrace, BC V8G 2W7
Tel: 250-635-2211 *Fax:* 250-635-7639
Number of Beds: 52 beds
Cholly Boland, Health Services Administrator

Tofino: Tofino General Hospital
Affiliated with: Vancouver Island Health Authority
PO Box 190, 261 Neill St., Tofino, BC V0R 2Z0
Tel: 250-725-3212 *Fax:* 250-725-3150
info@viha.ca
www.viha.ca/finding_care/facilities/tofino_general_hospital.htm
Year Founded: 1954
Number of Beds: 10 beds
Note: Services include emergency, echocardiography, laboratory, mental health, physiotherapy, radiology
Howard Waldner, President/CEO, VIHA
250-370-8692
Brian Jackson, Director, Rural Health Services, VIHA
Kathryn Kilpatrick, Site Manager
Monica E. MacDonald, Site Administrative Assistant
250-725.3204, monica.macdonald@viha.ca

Trail: Kootenay Boundary Regional Hospital
Affiliated with: Interior Health Authority
Former Name: Trail Regional Hospital
1200 Hospital Bench, Trail, BC V1R 4M1
Tel: 250-368-3311 *Fax:* 250-364-3422
Toll-Free: 866-368-2314
info@kbrh.ca
www.kbrh.ca
Number of Beds: 75 beds
Lynn Johnstone

Vancouver: Holy Family Hospital
Affiliated with: Vancouver Coastal Health Authority
7801 Argyle St., Vancouver, BC V5P 3L6
Tel: 604-321-2661 *Fax:* 604-321-6886
www.providencehealthcare.org
Number of Beds: 218 beds
Note: Rehabilitation
Dianne Doyle, President; CEO

Vancouver: Mount Saint Joseph Hospital
Affiliated with: Vancouver Coastal Health Authority
3080 Prince Edward St., Vancouver, BC V5T 3N4
Tel: 604-874-1141 *Fax:* 604-877-8125
www.providencehealthcare.org
Number of Beds: 208 beds
Dianne Doyle, President; CEO

Vancouver: St. Paul's Hospital
Affiliated with: Vancouver Coastal Health Authority
1081 Burrard St., Vancouver, BC V6Z 1Y6
Tel: 604-682-2344 *Fax:* 604-684-6532
Number of Beds: 520 acute care beds
Dianne Doyle, President; CEO

Vancouver: UBC Hospital
Affiliated with: Vancouver Coastal Health Authority
Also Known As: UBC Health Sciences Centre Hospital
2211 Westbrook Mall, Vancouver, BC V6T 2B5
Tel: 604-822-7121 *Fax:* 604-822-7268
feedback@vch.ca
www.vch.ca/EN/find_locations/find_locations/?&site_id=164
Year Founded: 1968
Number of Beds: 191 beds
Note: Divided into 3 buildings, the Detwiller Pavilion is known for its psychiatric unit, the Purdy Pavilion offers functional stress injury clinic, MRI, movement disorder clinic, residential care, while the Koerner Pavilion offers acute neurology, Alzheimer clinic, angiography, bladder care, brain research, breast reconstruction, CT scans, fluoroscopy, Huntington disease clinic, laboratory, multiple sclerosis clinic, nuclear medicine, nutrition counselling, radiology, sleep disorders program, speech language pathology, spirometry, surgical clinic, ultrasound, urgent care centre.
Dr. David N. Ostrow, President/CEO, VCHA
Anne Sutherland Boal, COO, Vancouver Acute, VCHA
Dr. Susan Stromberg, Medical Director, Urgent Care Centre, UBC
Tiffany Akins, Regional Communications Leader, VCHA
604-319-7530

Vancouver: Vancouver General Hospital
Affiliated with: Vancouver Coastal Health Authority
855 West 12th Avenue, Vancouver, BC V5Z 1M9
Tel: 604-875-4111 *Fax:* 604-875-4035
www.vanhosp.bc.ca
Number of Beds: 583 beds
Susan Wannamaker, Senior Operating Officer
C. Roach, Manager, Physical Plant
Maggie Sinclair, Waste Management, Physical Plant

Vanderhoof: St. John Hospital
Affiliated with: Northern Health Authority
3255 Hospital Rd., Vanderhoof, BC V0J 3A0
Tel: 250-567-2211 *Fax:* 250-567-9713
hello@northernhealth.ca
www.northernhealth.ca
Year Founded: 1941
Number of Beds: 24 acute care
Note: Services include emergency, labor & delivery, diagnostic imaging (X-ray, ultrasound), orthopedic surgery, general surgeries, physiotherapy, visiting specialists
Cathy Ulrich, CEO, NHA
Michael McMillan, COO, Northern Interior Region, NHA

Vernon: Vernon Jubilee Hospital
Affiliated with: Interior Health Authority
2101 - 32 St. South, Vernon, BC V1T 5L2
Tel: 250-558-1200 *Fax:* 250-545-0369
Number of Beds: 123 beds
Peter Dutoit
R. Lediet, Manager, Physical Plant

Victoria: Glengarry Extended Care Hospital
Affiliated with: Vancouver Island Health Authority
1780 Fairfield Rd., Victoria, BC V8S 1G7
Tel: 250-595-4321 *Fax:* 250-370-5727
Number of Beds: 212 beds
Carrie Peter, Coordinator, Volunteer Resources

Victoria: Mount Tolmie Extended Care Hospital
Affiliated with: Vancouver Island Health Authority
3690 Richmond Rd., Victoria, BC V8P 4R6
Tel: 250-370-5626 *Fax:* 250-370-5755
Number of Beds: 75 beds
Note: extended care hospital

Victoria: Priory Hospital
Affiliated with: Vancouver Island Health Authority
567 Goldstream Ave., Victoria, BC V9B 2W4
Tel: 250-370-5626 *Fax:* 250-370-5779
Number of Beds: 75 beds
Note: extended care hospital

Victoria: Queen Alexandra Centre for Children's Health
Affiliated with: Vancouver Island Health Authority
2400 Arbutus Rd., Victoria, BC V8N 1V7
Tel: 250-519-5390 *Fax:* 250-721-6837
Number of Beds: 20 beds
Note: acute & extended care

Victoria: Royal Jubilee Hospital
Affiliated with: Vancouver Island Health Authority
1952 Bay St., Victoria, BC V8R 1J8
Tel: 250-370-8000 *Fax:* 250-370-8804
info@viha.ca
www.viha.ca/finding_care/facilities/royal_jubilee_hospital.htm
Number of Beds: 425 beds
Note: Acute care, cystic fibrosis clinic, rehabilitation services, breast physiotherapy, breast surgical oncology. Located in Memorial Pavilion.
Howard Waldner, President/CEO, VIHA
Catherine Mackay, Executive Vice-President/COO, VIHA
Shannon Marshall, Media Contact, Communications, VIHA
250-370-8270

Victoria: Victoria General Hospital
Affiliated with: Vancouver Island Health Authority
1 Hospital Way, Victoria, BC V8Z 6R5
Tel: 250-727-4212 *Fax:* 250-727-4106
Number of Beds: 349 including 50 paeds
Note: acute care

White Rock: Peace Arch Hospital
Affiliated with: Fraser Health Authority
15521 Russell Ave., White Rock, BC V4B 2R4
Tel: 604-531-5512 *Fax:* 604-531-0726
www.peacearchhospital.com
Number of Beds: 475 acute care, 300 residential care beds
Jackie Smith, Executive Director

Williams Lake: Cariboo Memorial Hospital
Affiliated with: Interior Health Authority
517 North 6th Ave., Williams Lake, BC V2G 2G8
Tel: 250-392-4411 *Fax:* 250-392-2157
www.interiorhealth.ca
Note: Hospital Specialties: Emergency services: Diagnostic imaging; Laboratory services (250-392-8215); Ambulatory care; Acute care; Obstetrics
Deb Runge, Site Manager
Deborah.Runge@interiorhealth.ca

Federal Hospitals

Abbotsford: Pacific Institution / Regional Treatment Centre
Correctional Services Canada, Dept. of the Solicitor General
Former Name: Regional Health Centre (Pacific)
Also Known As: Pacific Institution
PO Box 3000, 33344 King Rd., Abbotsford, BC V2S 4P4
Tel: 604-870-7700 *Fax:* 604-870-7746
www.csc-scc.gc.ca/text/facilit/institutprofiles/pacific-eng.shtml
Year Founded: 1972
Number of Beds: 122 beds
Note: Psychiatric care unit, health centre, rehabilitation unit, regional reception/assessment centre and intensive program unit; a mens' facility
Dr. Zender Katz, Executive Director

Private Hospitals

Abbotsford: Menno Hospital
Affiliated with: Fraser Health Authority
32945 Marshall Rd., Abbotsford, BC V2S 1K1
Tel: 604-859-7631 *Fax:* 604-859-6931
www.mennoplace.ca
Number of Beds: 150 beds
Robert V. Turnbull, Chief Operating Officer
Chris Dean, Director, Environmental Services

Burnaby: Willingdon Park Hospital
Affiliated with: Fraser Health Authority
Former Name: Willingdon Private Hospital
4435 Grange St., Burnaby, BC V5H 1P4
Tel: 604-433-2455 *Fax:* 604-433-5804
Number of Beds: 95 beds
Arnold Bennewith, Administrator
Joy Lee, Superintendent

Coquitlam: Como Lake Private Hospital & Nursing Home
657 Gatensbury St., Coquitlam, BC V3J 5G9
Tel: 604-939-9277 *Fax:* 604-939-6518
Number of Beds: 95 beds
Note: Specialties: Complex health care & personal assistance in a residential setting; Adult day program

Coquitlam: Lakeshore Care Centre
Affiliated with: Fraser Health Authority
657 Gatensbury St., Coquitlam, BC V3J 5G9
Tel: 604-939-9277 Fax: 604-939-6518
Number of Beds: 95 beds
Lynn Aarvold, Administrator

Kelowna: Still Waters Private Hospital
1450 Sutherland Ave., Kelowna, BC V1Y 5Y5
Tel: 250-860-2216 Fax: 250-860-3655
Number of Beds: 79 beds
Note: A long-term care home for seniors and the disabled. Rooms are rented and geared to income. Licensed care included. Other services include 24-hr. emergency response, laundry, housekeeping. There is a fulltime resident manager.
David Kornell, Executive Director

Langley: Simpson Manor
Affiliated with: Fraser Health Authority
Former Name: Simpsons Private Hospital
PO Box 40, 8838 Glover Rd., Langley, BC V1M 2R4
Tel: 604-888-0711 Fax: 604-888-1218
inquiries@simpsonmanor.ca
www.simpsonmanor.ca
Note: Long-term care for seniors, permanent and semi-premament residency; adult day program, 9-5 pm weekdays; a 2-storey facility with 42 resident rooms per floor, mostly single occupancy, and 18 double rooms
Debbie Eglsaer, Director, Resident Care
Director@SimpsonManor.ca
Ingo Riesen, Administrator
604-888-4699, Administrator@SimpsonManor.ca

Maple Ridge: Holyrood Manor
Affiliated with: Fraser Health Authority
22710 Holyrood Ave., Maple Ridge, BC V2X 3E6
Tel: 604-467-8831 Fax: 604-467-8262
holyrood@reveraliving.com
Number of Beds: 123 beds
Ann MacMillan, Administrator

North Vancouver: North Shore Private Hospital & Lynn Valley Care Centre
1070 Lynn Valley Rd., North Vancouver, BC V7J 1Z8
Tel: 604-988-4181 Fax: 604-988-0814
lesliecymet@nsph.ca
www.lynnvalleycare.com
Number of Beds: 142 beds
Dr. Mehdi Sherkat, Administrator

Vancouver: Amherst Private Hospital & Nursing Home
375 West 59th Ave., Vancouver, BC V5X 1X3
Tel: 604-321-6777 Fax: 604-322-0123
Year Founded: 1964
Number of Beds: 74 beds
Note: Hospital Specialties: Complex care

Vancouver: Point Grey Private Hospital
2423 Cornwall Ave., Vancouver, BC V6K 1B9
Tel: 604-733-7133 Fax: 604-733-8298
pghosp@telus.net
Number of Beds: 52 beds
Maureen McIntosh, Administrator

Victoria: Wayside House Christian Science Care Facility
Affiliated with: Vancouver Island Health Authority
550 Foul Bay Rd., Victoria, BC V8S 4H1
Tel: 250-598-4521 Fax: 250-598-4547
inquiries@waysidehousevictoria.org
Number of Beds: 9 beds
Susan Waterman, Administrator

Auxiliary Hospitals

100 Mile House: 100 Mile District General Hospital
Affiliated with: Interior Health Authority
South Cariboo Health Centre, PO Box 399, 555 Cedar Ave. South, 100 Mile House, BC V0K 2E0
Tel: 250-395-7600 Fax: 250-395-7578
www.interiorhealth.ca
Note: Hospital Specialties: Maternity; Diagnostic imaging; Physiotherapy; MMental health; Public health; Diabetic education; Adult day service; Home support
Gayle Dunsmuir, Contact, Hospice
gayle.hospice@shawbiz.ca
Wendy Reilly, Contact, Residential Care
Wendy.Reilly@interiorhealth.ca

Vancouver: BC Children's Hospital
Affiliated with: Provincial Health Services Authority
Former Name: Crippled Children's Hospital; Children's Hospital
4480 Oak St., Vancouver, BC V6H 3N1
Tel: 604-875-2000 Toll-Free: 888-300-3088
comm@cw.bc.ca
www.bcchildrens.ca
Year Founded: 1928
Note: Hospital Specialties: Emergency services; Ambulatory care; Pediatric surgery; Specialized pediatric health services; Intensive & trauma care; Specialized programs for children with congenital or acquired heart disease; Onclogy; Kidney transplants; Bone marrow transplants; Cochlear implant service; Medical genetics program; Mental health services for children & youth; Assessment & diagnosis for children with complex developmental behavioural conditions; Healthy Buddies, a child-centred health promotion program; Centre for Healthy Weights; Safe Start, an injury prevention program; Research; Child health information (Family Resource Library)
Larry Gold, President

Vancouver: BC Women's Hospital & Health Centre
Affiliated with: Provincial Health Services Authority
4500 Oak St., Vancouver, BC V6H 3N1
Tel: 604-875-2424 Toll-Free: 1-888-300-3088
comm@cw.bc.ca (Communications)
www.bcwomens.ca
Note: Hospital Specialties: Health care for women, newborn, & families; Gynecological & reproductive health services; Sexual assault service; HIV care of women & children; Birth control & abortion support & counselling; Substance dependency; Psychology; Social work; Aboriginal Health Program; Osteoporosis
Dr. Jan Christilaw, President

Victoria: Aberdeen Hospital
Affiliated with: Vancouver Island Health Authority
1450 Hillside Ave., Victoria, BC V8T 2B7
Tel: 250-370-5626 Fax: 250-370-5612
www.viha.ca
Note: Hospital Specialty: Extended care for the elderly & young adults with neurological challenges
Helene Driscoll, Coordinator, Therapy / Seniors Health

Community Health Care Centres

Parksville: Oceanside Health Centre
Affiliated with: Vancouver Island Health Authority
Albemi Hwy., Parksville, BC V9P 1M9
Note: The center is expected to open in 2013. The Centre will be able to care for approximately 75% of patients who might typically visit an Emergency Department and not need to be admitted.

Community Health Centres

Community Health Care Centres

Alexis Creek: Alexis Creek Health Centre
Affiliated with: Interior Health Authority
2591 Morton St., Alexis Creek, BC V0L 1A0
Tel: 250-394-4313 Fax: 250-964-5179

Armstrong: Pleasant Valley Health Centre
Affiliated with: Interior Health Authority
3800 Patten Dr., Armstrong, BC V0E 1B2
Tel: 250-546-4720 Fax: 250-546-9821
Number of Beds: 40 beds
Peter DuToit

Barriere: Barriere & District Health Centre
Affiliated with: Interior Health Authority
PO Box 659, 537 Barriere Town Rd., Barriere, BC V0E 1M0
Tel: 250-672-9731 Fax: 250-672-5144
Linda Basran

Castlegar: Castlegar & District Community Health Centre
Affiliated with: Interior Health Authority
709 - 10th St., Castlegar, BC V1N 2H7
Tel: 250-365-7711 Fax: 250-365-1236
www.interiorhealth.ca
Note: Specialties: Ambulatory care; Family medicine; Laboratory services

Chase: Chase Health Centre
Affiliated with: Interior Health Authority
825 Thompson Ave., Chase, BC V0E 1M0
Tel: 250-679-3312 Fax: 250-679-5329
Bonnie Lee

Chemainus: Chemainus Health Authority
Affiliated with: Vancouver Island Health Authority
PO Box 499, 9909 Esplanade St., Chemainus, BC V0R 1K0
Tel: 250-246-3291 Fax: 250-246-3844
Number of Beds: 75 beds
Note: diagnostic & treatment centre, multilevel care facility
Joan Roberts, Director

Cumberland: Cumberland Health Care Centre
Affiliated with: Vancouver Island Health Authority
PO Box 400, 2696 Windermere Ave., Cumberland, BC V0R 1S0
Tel: 250-336-8531 Fax: 250-336-2100
Number of Beds: 75 beds
Don Brown, CEO

Elkford: Elkford Health Centre
Affiliated with: Interior Health Authority
PO Box 640, 212 Alpine Way, Elkford, BC V0B 1H0
Tel: 250-865-2247 Fax: 250-865-2797
Number of Beds: 4 beds
Wendy Timmerman, Site Manager

Fort Smith: Fort Smith Public Health Unit
Affiliated with: Fort Smith Health & Social Services Authority
PO Box 1080, Fort Smith, BC Z0E 0P0
Tel: 867-872-6203 Fax: 867-872-6260

Fraser Lake: Fraser Lake Community Health Centre
Affiliated with: Northern Health Authority
130 Chowsunket St., Fraser Lake, BC V0J 1S0
Tel: 250-699-7742 Fax: 250-699-6987
Kay Scott, CEO

Gold River: Gold River Health Clinic
Affiliated with: Vancouver Island Health Authority
601 Trumpeter Dr., Gold River, BC V0P 1G0
Tel: 250-283-2626 Fax: 250-283-7561
Enid O'Hara, Area Director of Rural Services, Campbell River/Nootka/Comac Valley

Hudson's Hope: Hudson's Hope Gething Diagnostic & Treatment Centre
Affiliated with: Northern Health Authority
PO Box 599, 10309 Kyllo St., Hudson's Hope, BC V0C 1V0
Tel: 250-783-9991 Fax: 250-783-9125
Number of Beds: 2 emergency beds
Andrew Neuner, CEO
Susan Mochoruk, Nurse Manager

Kaslo: Victorian Community Health Centre of Kaslo
Affiliated with: Interior Health Authority
Former Name: Victoria Hospital of Kaslo
673 A Ave., Kaslo, BC V0G 1M0
Tel: 250-353-2291 Fax: 250-353-2738
Number of Beds: 20 beds
Christie Heuston, Site Director

Logan Lake: Logan Lake Primary Health Care Organization
Affiliated with: Interior Health Authority
Former Name: Logan Lake Health Centre
5 Beryl Ave., Logan Lake, BC V0K 1W0
Tel: 250-523-9414 Fax: 250-523-6869
Number of Beds: 4 beds
Marsha Wilson, Care Coordinator

Lytton: St. Bartholomew's Health & Healing Centre
Affiliated with: Interior Health Authority
PO Box 1089, Lytton, BC V0K 1Z0
Tel: 250-455-2221 Fax: 250-455-6621
Jennifer Thur, Manager, Health Services

Pemberton: Pemberton Health Centre
Affiliated with: Vancouver Coastal Health Authority
Former Name: Pemberton Diagnostic & Treatment Centre
PO Box 8, 1403 Portage Rd., Pemberton, BC V0N 2L0
Tel: 604-894-6939 Fax: 604-894-6918
Number of Beds: 5 beds
Dr. Rebecca Lindley, President, Med Staff

Sparwood: **Sparwood General Healthcare Centre**
Affiliated with: Interior Health Authority
PO Box 9, 570 Pine Ave., Sparwood, BC V0B 2G0
Tel: 250-425-6212 *Fax:* 250-425-2313
wendy.timmerman@interiorhealth.ca

Number of Beds: 12 beds
Wendy Timmerman, Site Manager

Tahsis: **Tahsis Health Centre**
Affiliated with: Vancouver Island Health Authority
PO Box 399, 1085 Maquinna Dr., Tahsis, BC V0P 1X0
Tel: 250-934-6322 *Fax:* 250-934-6404
Enid O'Hara, Area Director of Rural Health Services, Campbell River/Nootka/Comoc Valley

Tatla Lake: **West Chilcotin Health Centre**
Affiliated with: Interior Health Authority
Tatla Lake Nursing Station, 16452 Chilcotin Highway 20, Tatla Lake, BC V0L 1V0
Tel: 250-476-1114 *Fax:* 250-476-1266

Tumbler Ridge: **Tumbler Ridge Health Care Centre**
Affiliated with: Northern Health Authority
PO Box 80, 220 Front St., Tumbler Ridge, BC V0C 2W0
Tel: 250-242-5271 *Fax:* 250-242-3889
Number of Beds: 2 holding beds
Note: diagnostic & treatment centre
Beth Kidd, COO

Valemount: **Valemount Health Centre**
Affiliated with: Northern Health Authority
PO Box 697, 1445 - 5 Ave., Valemount, BC V0E 2Z0
Tel: 250-566-9138 *Fax:* 250-566-4319

Note: outpatient health centre
Marilyn Harkness, Administrator
Vic Chicoine, Executive Director

Nursing Stations

Alexis Creek: **Red Cross Outpost Nursing Station**
PO Box 39, 2591 Morton Rd., Alexis Creek, BC V0L 1A0
Tel: 250-394-4313 *Fax:* 250-394-5179
Number of Beds: 1 beds
Note: Red Cross Outpost Nursing Stations correspondence should be sent to Manager of Outpost Hospital Program, Canadian Red Cross Society, 4750 Oak St., 3rd Fl., Vancouver BC V6H 2N9
Pat Kermeen, Manager

Anahim Lake: **Anahim Lake Nursing Station**
Affiliated with: Interior Health Authority
Hudson Rd., Anahim Lake, BC V0L 1C0
Tel: 250-742-3305 *Fax:* 250-742-3336
anahim_lake_nursing_station@hc-sc.gc.ca

Atlin: **Atlin Health Centre**
Affiliated with: Northern Health Authority
Former Name: Red Cross Outpost Hospital
PO Box 330, 3rd St., Atlin, BC V0W 1A0
Tel: 250-651-7677 *Fax:* 250-651-7687
www.northernhealth.ca

Number of Beds: 1 treatment stretcher
Note: Public health; 24-hour emergency care; 2 nurse outpost setting

Bamfield: **Red Cross Outpost Nursing Station**
Affiliated with: Vancouver Island Health Authority
353 Bamfield Rd., Bamfield, BC V0R 1B0
Tel: 250-728-3312 *Fax:* 250-728-3054
Number of Beds: 3 beds
Pat Kermeen, Manager, Outpost Hospital Program

Blue River: **Red Cross Outpost Hospital**
PO Box 18, 858 Main St., Blue River, BC V0E 1J0
Tel: 250-673-8311 *Fax:* 250-673-2380

Pat Kermeen, Manager, Outpost Hospital Program

Edgewood: **Red Cross Outpost Nursing Station**
322 Monashee Ave., Edgewood, BC V0G 1J0
Tel: 250-269-7313 *Fax:* 250-269-7520
Pat Kermeen, Manager, Outpost Hospital Program

Hartley Bay: **Hartley Bay Nursing Station**
341 Wee Xaa Avenue, Hartley Bay, BC V0V 1A0
Tel: 250-841-2556 *Fax:* 250-841-2554
hbnshd@citytel.net

Number of Beds: 1 bed
Angela Clifton, Health Director

Iskut: **Iskut Nursing Station**
Affiliated with: Northern Health Authority
PO Box 9, Iskut, BC V0J 1K0
Tel: 250-234-3511 *Fax:* 250-234-3512
Toll-Free: 866-660-6607
feddie.louie@ivhs.ca
www.ivhs.ca

Freddie Carlick, Health Director

Kincolith: **Kincolith Nursing Station**
General Delivery, Kincolith, BC V0V 1B0
Tel: 250-326-4258

Kitkatla: **Kitkatla Nursing Station**
General Delivery, Kitkatla, BC V0V 1C0
Tel: 250-848-2254 *Fax:* 250-848-2263
kitkatla_nursing_station@hc-sc.gc.ca

Klemtu: **Klemtu Nursing Station**
General Delivery, Klemtu, BC V0T 1L0
Tel: 250-839-1221 *Fax:* 250-839-1184
alma_wert@hc-sc.gc.ca

Kyuquot: **Red Cross Outpost Nursing Station**
100 Okime Island, Kyuquot, BC V0P 1J0
Tel: 250-332-5289 *Fax:* 250-332-5215
Pat Kermeen, Manager, Outpost Hospital Program

Takla Landing: **Takla Landing Nursing Station**
General Delivery, Takla Landing, BC V0J 2T0
Tel: 250-564-9334 *Fax:* 250-564-9334

Telegraph Creek: **Telegraph Creek Nursing Station**
PO Box 112, Telegraph Creek, BC V0J 2W0
Tel: 250-235-3211 *Fax:* 250-235-3213

Special Treatment Centres

Burnaby: **Burnaby Family Court Centre - Outpatient Clinic**
3405 Willingdon Ave., Burnaby, BC V5G 3H4
Tel: 604-660-5870 *Fax:* 604-660-1109
Number of Beds: 9 beds
Fred Bannon, Director

Houston: **Houston Health Centre**
Affiliated with: Northern Health Authority
3150 - 14 St., Houston, BC V0J 1Z0
Tel: 250-845-2294 *Fax:* 250-845-2005
Number of Beds: 2 holding beds
Hanna White, Administrator

Kamloops: **Phoenix Centre**
922 - 3 Ave., Kamloops, BC V2C 6W5
Tel: 250-374-4634 *Fax:* 250-374-4621
ksad@phoenixcentre.org
www.phoenixcentre.org

Number of Beds: 20 beds
Note: detox centre

Vancouver: **Arthritis Society**
Affiliated with: Vancouver Coastal Health Authority
895 - 10 Ave. West, Vancouver, BC V5Z 1L7
Tel: 604-879-7511 *Fax:* 604-871-4500
Melanie Crombie, Executive Director

Vancouver: **British Columbia Cancer Agency**
Affiliated with: Provincial Health Services Authority
600 - 10 Ave. West, Vancouver, BC V5Z 4E6
Tel: 604-877-6000 *Fax:* 604-872-4596
www.bccancer.bc.ca

Note: cancer treatment
Simon B. Sutcliffe, President
Mohan Bains, Supervisor, Biomedical Waste
Tom Bennett, Supervisor, Waste Management

Vancouver: **Elizabeth Bagshaw Women's Clinic**
Affiliated with: Vancouver Coastal Health Authority
200 - 1177 West Broadway, Vancouver, BC V6H 1G3
Tel: 604-736-7878 *Fax:* 604-736-8081
Toll-Free: 877-736-7171
www.elizabethbagshawclinic.ca

Note: abortion clinic
Cheryl Davies, Administrator

Vancouver: **Everywoman's Health Centre Abortion Control Clinic**
Affiliated with: Vancouver Coastal Health Authority
210 - 2525 Commercial Dr., Vancouver, BC V5A 4C1
Tel: 604-322-6692 *Fax:* 604-322-6632
www.everywomanshealthcentre.ca

Number of Beds: 6 recovery room, 2 procedure room beds
Note: abortion clinic
J. Foley, Executive Director

Vancouver: **G.F. Strong Centre**
Affiliated with: Vancouver Coastal Health Authority
4255 Laurel St., Vancouver, BC V5Z 2G9
Tel: 604-734-1313 *Fax:* 604-737-6359
www.gfstrong.com

Number of Beds: 92 beds
Note: rehabilitation treatment centre
Patti Flaherty, Senior Operation Officer

Vancouver: **Sunny Hill Health Centre for Children**
Affiliated with: Provincial Health Services Authority
3644 Slocan St., Vancouver, BC V5M 3E8
Tel: 604-453-8300 *Fax:* 604-453-8301
Number of Beds: 18 beds
Note: Provincial rehabilitation & assessment centre for children with disabilities

Victoria: **British Columbia Cancer Agency**
Affiliated with: Vancouver Coastal Health Authority
2410 Lee Ave., Victoria, BC V8R 6V5
Tel: 250-519-5500 *Fax:* 250-519-2012
Toll-Free: 800-670-3322
www.bccancer.bc.ca

Note: comprehensive cancer centre
B. Weinerman, Vice-President

Whistler: **Diagnostic & Treatment Centre**
Affiliated with: Vancouver Coastal Health Authority
Former Name: Whistler Diagnostic & Treatment Centre
4380 Lorimer Rd., Whistler, BC V0N 1B4
Tel: 604-932-4911 *Fax:* 604-932-4992
Number of Beds: 13 beds
Tina Hua, Manager, Acute Services

Nursing Homes

Abbotsford: **Menno Home**
Affiliated with: Fraser Health Authority
32910 Brundige Ave., Abbotsford, BC V2S 1N2
Tel: 604-853-2411 *Fax:* 604-859-0751
Number of Beds: 196 beds
Arthur J. Enns, Administrator

Abbotsford: **Sunrise Special Care Facility**
2411 Railway St., Abbotsford, BC V2S 2E3
Tel: 604-853-3078
Number of Beds: 8 beds
Mona McMillan, Head Nursing

Burnaby: **St. Michael's Centre**
Affiliated with: Fraser Health Authority
7451 Sussex Ave., Burnaby, BC V5J 5C2
Tel: 604-412-2154 *Fax:* 604-434-6469
mribchester@stmichaels.bc.ca
www.saintmichaelscentre.org

Number of Beds: 128 extended care, 16 hospice beds
Helene Elias, Acting Executive Director
Severino Tolfo, Director, Environmental Services

Chilliwack: **Eden Care Centre**
Affiliated with: Fraser Health Authority
Former Name: Eden Rest Home
9100 Charles St., Chilliwack, BC V2P 5K6
Tel: 604-792-8166 *Fax:* 604-792-1111
edencare@telus.net

Number of Beds: 89 beds
Elaine Price, Administrator

Coquitlam: **Burquitlam Lions Care Centre**
Affiliated with: Fraser Health Authority
560 Sydney Ave., Coquitlam, BC V3K 6A4
Tel: 604-939-6485 *Fax:* 604-939-4728
ddines@burquitlamlionscare.com
www.burquitlamlionscare.com

Number of Beds: 76 beds
Renee Danylczuk, Administrator

Duncan: **Cowichan Lodge**
Affiliated with: Vancouver Island Health Authority
3045 Gibbins Rd., Duncan, BC V9L 1E5
Tel: 250-748-3331 *Fax:* 250-748-3032
www.viha.ca

Number of Beds: 85 beds
Laurie Chisholm

Gibsons: **Kiwanis Village Care Home**
841 Kiwanis Way, Gibsons, BC V0N 1V9
Tel: 604-886-8132 *Fax:* 604-886-8483

Number of Beds: 37 beds
Dennis Regnier, Site Manager

***Kamloops:* Extendicare - Pine Grove Lodge**
Affiliated with: Interior Health Authority
313 McGowan Ave., Kamloops, BC V2B 2N8
Tel: 250-376-5701 *Fax:* 250-376-5770
cnh-pinegrove@extendicare.com
www.motimahal.ca

Number of Beds: 75 beds
Robert S. Moffitt, Administrator

***Kamloops:* Kamloops Personal Care Home Ltd. - Garden Manor**
63 Nicola St. West, Kamloops, BC V2C 1J5
Tel: 250-374-7612 *Fax:* 250-374-7605

Number of Beds: 24 beds
John H. Stewart, Administrator

***Kamloops:* Overlander Extended Care Hospital**
Affiliated with: Interior Health Authority
953 Southill St., Kamloops, BC V2B 7Z9
Tel: 250-554-2323 *Fax:* 250-554-5557
Number of Beds: 189 beds

***Kelowna:* Gordon House**
3091 Walnut Rd., Kelowna, BC V1W 3V2
Tel: 250-763-5290 *Fax:* 250-763-5207

Number of Beds: 8 beds
Valerie Bosch, Administrator

***Langley:* Murrayville Manor Ltd.**
21616 - 46 Ave., Langley, BC V3A 3J4
Tel: 604-530-9033 *Fax:* 604-530-9023

Number of Beds: 39 beds
Wayne Mills, Administrator

***Nanaimo:* Columbian Centre Society**
2356 Rosstown Rd., Nanaimo, BC V9T 3R7
Tel: 250-758-8711 *Fax:* 250-751-1128

Number of Beds: 10 beds
Tom Grauman, Administrator

***Nelson:* Mount St. Francis Hospital**
Affiliated with: Interior Health Authority
1300 Gordon Rd., Nelson, BC V1L 3M5
Tel: 250-352-3531 *Fax:* 250-352-6942

Number of Beds: 79 beds
Cydney Higgins

***Parksville:* Trillium Lodge**
Affiliated with: Vancouver Island Health Authority
PO Box 940, 401 Moilliet St., Parksville, BC V9P 2G9
Tel: 250-248-8353 *Fax:* 250-248-8388
Number of Beds: 106 beds
Gillian Forsyth, Director, Care

***Pouce Coupe:* Pouce Coupe Care Home**
Affiliated with: Northern Helath Authority
PO Box 98, 5216 - 50 Ave., Pouce Coupe, BC V0C 2C0
Tel: 250-786-6116 *Fax:* 250-786-0197
Number of Beds: 55 beds
Dave Price, Resident Care Manager

***Salmon Arm:* Bastion Place**
700 - 11 St. NE, Salmon Arm, BC V1E2S5
Tel: 250-833-3616 *Fax:* 250-833-3605
Number of Beds: 101 beds
Brenda Veerman

***Sidney:* Rest Haven Lodge**
2281 Mills Rd., Sidney, BC V8L 2C3
Tel: 250-656-0717 *Fax:* 250-656-4745
Number of Beds: 75 beds
Bernard Skoretz, Administrator

***Surrey:* Argyll Lodge**
14590 - 106A Ave., Surrey, BC V3R 1T4
Tel: 604-581-4174 *Fax:* 604-582-6348
Number of Beds: 25 beds
Baljit Kandola, Administrator

***Surrey:* Cherington Place**
Affiliated with: Fraser Health Authority
13453 - 111A Ave., Surrey, BC V3R 2C5
Tel: 604-581-2885 *Fax:* 604-582-9028
cherington@telus.net
seniorshome.com
Number of Beds: 75 beds
Annamae Clarke, Administrator

***Surrey:* K & C Care Ltd.**
1504 - 160 St., Surrey, BC V4A 4N9
Tel: 604-531-7900 *Fax:* 604-531-2338

Number of Beds: 10 beds
Kwan-Ying Jen, President

***Terrace:* Terraceview Lodge**
Affiliated with: Northern Health Authority
4103 North Sparks South, Terrace, BC V8G 5G9
Tel: 250-638-0223 *Fax:* 250-635-9775

Number of Beds: 75 beds
Doris Mitchell, Administrator

***Vancouver:* Ananda**
1249 - 8 Ave. East, Vancouver, BC V5T 1V3
Tel: 604-872-7134 *Fax:* 604-872-8420

Number of Beds: 20 beds
Darrell Burnham, Executive Director

***Vancouver:* Britannia Lodge**
1090 Victoria Dr., Vancouver, BC V5L 4G2
Tel: 604-255-3711 *Fax:* 604-255-3712
britannia.lodge@shaw.ca

Number of Beds: 45 beds
A. Filsoof, Administrator

***Vancouver:* Louis Brier Home & Hospital**
Affiliated with: Vancouver Coastal Health Authority
1055 West 41st Ave., Vancouver, BC V6M 1W9
Tel: 604-261-9376 *Fax:* 604-266-8712

Number of Beds: 93 beds
Peter Kafka, CEO
Patrick Chan, Director, Administration

***Vancouver:* St. Jude's Anglican Home**
Affiliated with: Vancouver Coastal Health Authority
810 - 27 Ave. East, Vancouver, BC V5Z 2G7
Tel: 604-874-3200 *Fax:* 604-874-3459
info@stjudes.bc.ca
www.stjudes.ca

Number of Beds: 55 beds
Chris Norman, Administrator

***Vernon:* Sunshine Lodge**
9604 Shamanski Dr., Vernon, BC V1B 2L7
Tel: 250-542-9350

Number of Beds: 18 beds
C. Baziw, Administrator

***Vernon:* Twin Cedars Rest Home**
3201 - 37 Ave., Vernon, BC V1T 2Y4
Tel: 250-542-4983 *Fax:* 250-542-4924

Number of Beds: 29 beds
Charlene Fair, Administrator

***Victoria:* Glenwarren Lodge**
Affiliated with: Vancouver Island Health Authority
1230 Balmoral Rd., Victoria, BC V8T 1B3
Tel: 250-383-2323 *Fax:* 250-383-6359

Number of Beds: 131 beds
Note: intermediate & extended care
Norman Carelius, Administrator

***West Vancouver:* Capilano Care Centre**
Affiliated with: Vancouver Coastal Health Authority
525 Clyde Ave., West Vancouver, BC V7T 1C4
Tel: 604-926-6856 *Fax:* 604-926-9169
Number of Beds: 215 beds
Ann MacMillan, Administrator

***West Vancouver:* West Vancouver Care Centre**
Affiliated with: Vancouver Coastal Health Authority
1675 - 27 St., West Vancouver, BC V7V 4K9
Tel: 604-925-1247 *Fax:* 604-925-3507
Number of Beds: 75 beds
Courtenay Woodworth, Administrator

***White Rock:* Buena Vista Rest Home**
15109 Buena Vista Ave., White Rock, BC V4B 1Y2
Tel: 604-536-6752

Number of Beds: 12 beds
Elaine Lasoto, Administrator

Long Term/Retirement Care

Long Term Care Facilities

***100 Mile House:* Mill Site Lodge**
76 Horse Lake Road, 100 Mile House, BC V0K 2E0
Tel: 250-395-3366 *Fax:* 250-395-7692
Number of Beds: 26 beds
Allison Ruault, Director, Health Services

***Abbotsford:* Bevan Lodge**
Affiliated with: Fraser Health Authority
33386 Bevan Ave., Abbotsford, BC V2S 5G6
Tel: 604-850-5416 *Fax:* 604-850-5418

Number of Beds: 15 beds
Hendrik Van Ryk, Administrator

***Abbotsford:* M.S.A. Manor Society**
Affiliated with: Fraser Health Authority
2510 Gladwin Rd., Abbotsford, BC V2T 3N9
Tel: 604-853-5831 *Fax:* 604-853-1647
Number of Beds: 34 beds
Dennis Magnusson, Administrator

***Abbotsford:* Maplewood House**
Affiliated with: Fraser Health Authority
1919 Jackson St., Abbotsford, BC V2S 2Z8
Tel: 604-853-5585 *Fax:* 604-853-4224
Number of Beds: 76 beds
Dennis Magnusson, Director

***Abbotsford:* Sherwood Crescent Manor Ltd.**
Affiliated with: Fraser Health Authority
32073 Sherwood Cres., Abbotsford, BC V2T 1C1
Tel: 604-853-7854 *Fax:* 604-853-9910
sherwoodcrescentmanor@telus.net
Number of Beds: 41 permanent, 10 transitional care, 3 respite beds
Note: intermediate/residential care
Marilyn Smart, Director, Care

***Abbotsford:* Tabor Home**
Affiliated with: Fraser Health Authority
31944 Sunrise Cres., Abbotsford, BC V2T 1N5
Tel: 604-859-8715 *Fax:* 604-859-6695
Number of Beds: 121 beds
Jack Pauls, Administrator

***Abbotsford:* Valhaven Rest Home**
Affiliated with: Fraser Health Authority
4212 Balmoral St., Abbotsford, BC V4X 1Y5
Tel: 604-856-2812 *Fax:* 604-856-3243
Number of Beds: 22 beds
Barb Schmidt

***Agassiz:* Glenwood Care Centre**
Affiliated with: Fraser Health Authority
1458 Glenwood Dr., Agassiz, BC V0M 1A2
Tel: 604-796-9202 *Fax:* 604-796-9186
www.fraserhealth.ca

Note: Glenwood Care Centre provide residential care & day programs for the elderly.

***Aldergrove:* Jackman Manor**
Affiliated with: Fraser Health Authority
27447 - 28 Ave., Aldergrove, BC V4W 3L9
Tel: 604-856-4161 *Fax:* 604-856-2562
Number of Beds: 87 beds
Sheila Bridger, Administrator

***Aldergrove:* La Rosa de Matsqui**
28711 Huntington Rd., Aldergrove, BC V0X 1A0
Tel: 604-856-1555 *Fax:* 604-856-3252
Number of Beds: 15 beds
Carlos Arthur, Manager

***Armstrong:* Pioneer Square Willodale Guest Home**
2865 Willowdale Dr., Armstrong, BC V0E 1B1
Tel: 250-546-3396 *Fax:* 250-546-9033
Number of Beds: 20 beds
Kevin Svoboda, Administrator

***Burnaby:* L'Arche Greater Vancouver**
7401 Sussex Ave., Burnaby, BC V5J 3V6
Tel: 604-435-9544 *Fax:* 604-434-1933
office@larchevancouver.org
www.larchevancouver.org
Social Media: larchevancouver.wordpress.com
Year Founded: 1974
Number of Beds: 125 beds
Note: services for developmentally disabled adults
Denise Haskett, Executive Director & Community Leader

***Burnaby:* Carlton Gardens**
Affiliated with: Fraser Health Authority
4125 Canada Way, Burnaby, BC V5G 1G9
Tel: 604-438-8224 *Fax:* 604-438-6571
Number of Beds: 152 beds
Gwen Gordon, General Manager

***Burnaby:* Dania Home Society**
Affiliated with: Fraser Health Authority
4279 Norland Ave., Burnaby, BC V5G 3Z6
Tel: 604-299-2414 *Fax:* 604-299-7775
margaretd@dania.bc.ca

Number of Beds: 67 beds

Margaret Douglas-Matthews, Administrator

Burnaby: Fair Haven United Church Homes
Affiliated with: Fraser Health Authority
7557 Sussex Ave., Burnaby, BC V5J 3V6
Tel: 604-435-0525 Fax: 604-435-7031
mharrison@fairhaven.bc.ca
Number of Beds: 100 beds
Maureen Harrison, Administrator

Burnaby: Fellburn Care Centre
Affiliated with: Fraser Health Authority
6050 Hastings St. East, Burnaby, BC V5B 1R6
Tel: 604-412-6510 Fax: 604-299-1015
Number of Beds: 110 beds
Note: extended care facility
Carol Wheeler, Administrator

Burnaby: Finnish Manor
Affiliated with: Fraser Health Authority
3460 Kalyk Ave., Burnaby, BC V5G 3B2
Tel: 604-434-2666 Fax: 604-439-7448
Number of Beds: 60 beds
Sinikka Seppanen, Administrator

Burnaby: George Derby Centre
Affiliated with: Fraser Health Authority
7550 Cumberland St., Burnaby, BC V3N 3X5
Tel: 604-521-2676 Fax: 604-521-0220
www.georgederbycentre.ca
Number of Beds: 300 beds
Janice Mitchell, Executive Director

Burnaby: Harmony Court Centre
Affiliated with: Fraser Health Authority
Former Name: Canada Way Care Centre & Lodge
7195 Canada Way, Burnaby, BC V5E 3R7
Tel: 604-527-3300 Fax: 604-526-0203
www.harmonycourtcarecentre.ca
Number of Beds: 55 beds
Note: Intermediate care facility
Dr. Kabir Jivraj, Managing Director

Burnaby: New Vista Society
Affiliated with: Fraser Health Authority
Former Name: New Vista Care Home
7550 Rosewood St., Burnaby, BC V5E 3Z3
Tel: 604-527-6000 Fax: 604-527-6001
suzannej@newvista.bc.ca
www.newvista.bc.ca
Number of Beds: 236 beds
Number of Employees: 25
Note: The Society operates a complex care home and provides housing for low-income families and seniors.
Carol Finnie, CEO
carolf@newvista.bc.ca

Burnaby: Normanna Rest Home
Affiliated with: Fraser Health Authority
7725 - 4 St., Burnaby, BC V3N 5B6
Tel: 604-522-5812 Fax: 604-522-5803
Number of Beds: 100 beds
Note: multi level care
Margaret Douglas-Matthews, Administrator

Burns Lake: Pines Care Home
Affiliated with: Northern Health Authority
PO Box 479, 800 Center St., Burns Lake, BC V0J 1E0
Tel: 250-692-7752 Fax: 250-692-7462
Number of Beds: 30 beds
Note: multi-level care

Campbell River: Yucalta Lodge
Affiliated with: Vancouver Island Health Authority
555 - 2 Ave., Campbell River, BC V9W 3V1
Tel: 250-286-1051 Fax: 250-850-0328
Number of Beds: 100 beds
Note: multi-level care
Linda Harley, Manager, Residential services

Castlegar: Castleview Care Centre
Affiliated with: Interior Health Authority
2300 - 14 Ave., Castlegar, BC V1N 4A6
Tel: 250-365-7277 Fax: 250-365-3291
Number of Beds: 61 beds
Kimberly Hunter, Administrator

Castlegar: Talarico Place
Affiliated with: Interior Health Authority
709 - 10 St., Castlegar, BC V1N 1A1
Tel: 250-365-7221 Fax: 250-304-1238
Number of Beds: 60 beds
Meg Milner

Chilliwack: McIntosh Lodge
Affiliated with: Fraser Health Authority
44586 McIntosh Dr., Chilliwack, BC V2P 7W8
Tel: 604-795-2500 Fax: 604-795-5693
Number of Beds: 25 beds
Lynda Marlett, Administrator

Chilliwack: Valleyhaven Guest Home
Affiliated with: Fraser Health Authority
45450 Menholm Rd., Chilliwack, BC V2P 1M2
Tel: 604-792-0037 Fax: 604-792-6766
Number of Beds: 52 beds
Gillian McCunnie, Director of Care

Chilliwack: Waverly of Chilliwack
Affiliated with: Fraser Health Authority
8445 Young Rd. South, Chilliwack, BC V2P 4P2
Tel: 604-792-6340 Fax: 604-792-5611
Number of Beds: 15 beds
Debbie Davidson, Administrator

Coquitlam: Cartier House
Affiliated with: Fraser Health Authority
1419 Cartier Ave., Coquitlam, BC V3K 2C6
Tel: 604-939-4654 Fax: 604-939-6442
Number of Beds: 78 beds
Linda Clary, Administrator

Coquitlam: Foyer Maillard
Affiliated with: Fraser Health Authority
1010 Alderson Ave., Coquitlam, BC V3K 1W1
Tel: 604-937-5578 Fax: 604-937-7133
services@foyermaillard.com
Number of Beds: 45 beds
Doris Brisebois, Administrator

Courtenay: Glacier View Lodge
2450 Back Rd., Courtenay, BC V9N 9G8
Tel: 250-338-1451 Fax: 250-338-1115
www.glacierviewlodge.ca
Number of Beds: 100 beds
Michael Pontus, President/CEO

Courtenay: Laurel Lodge
280 - 2nd St., Courtenay, BC V9N 1B7
Tel: 250-334-3083 Fax: 250-338-2253
Number of Beds: 27 beds
Note: seniors' support home
David Reghr, Administrator

Cranbrook: F.W. Green Memorial Home
1700 - 4th St. South, Cranbrook, BC V1C 6E1
Tel: 250-426-3710 Fax: 250-426-3622
Number of Beds: 86 beds
Allan Sinclair

Cranbrook: Rocky Mountain Lodge
20 - 23rd Ave. South, Cranbrook, BC V1C 5V1
Tel: 250-489-3361 Fax: 250-489-3545
Number of Beds: 63 beds
Allan Sinclair

Creston: Pioneer Villa
Affiliated with: Interior Health Authority
1909 Ash St., RR#5, Creston, BC V0B 1G5
Tel: 250-428-7188 Fax: 250-428-5192
Number of Beds: 31 beds
Cheryl Comin, Manager

Creston: Swan Valley Lodge
Affiliated with: Interior Health Authority
818 Vancouver St., Creston, BC V0B 1G0
Tel: 250-428-2283 Fax: 250-428-9318
Number of Beds: 90 beds, including 6 respite and 23-bed dementia unit
Note: Residential care
Cindy Kozak-Campbell

Dawson Creek: Rotary Manor
Affiliated with: Northern Health Authority
1121 - 90 Ave., Dawson Creek, BC V1G 5A3
Tel: 250-719-3480 Fax: 250-719-3781
Number of Beds: 44 beds
Elaine Washington, Residential Program Manager

Delta: Delta Lodge
4501 Arthur Dr., Delta, BC V4K 2X3
Tel: 604-946-6221 Fax: 604-946-6542
Number of Beds: 21 beds
Jesus Supnet, Administrator

Delta: Delta View Habilitation Centre
9341 Burns Dr., Delta, BC V4K 3N3
Tel: 604-596-8842 Fax: 604-596-8858
jdevji@deltaview.ca
www.deltaview.ca
Number of Beds: 80 beds
Note: cares for peoples with Alzheimer's disease; specializing in caring for people with difficult behaviour
Jane Devji, Manager

Delta: Heritage Home
Affiliated with: Fraser Health Authority
5681 Ladner Trunk Rd., Delta, BC V4K 1X3
Tel: 604-946-4013 Fax: 604-946-4034
Number of Beds: 29 beds
Jasmine Barredo, Director of Care

Delta: Kinsmen Care Home
Affiliated with: Fraser Health Authority
5410 - 10 Ave., Delta, BC V4M 3X8
Tel: 604-943-0155 Fax: 604-943-0947
kinsmen.vcn.bc.ca
Number of Beds: 101 beds
Gerald Arksey, Chairman

Delta: Northcrest Care Centre
Affiliated with: Fraser Health Authority
6771 - 120th St., Delta, BC V4E 2A7
Tel: 604-597-7878 Fax: 604-597-7805
general@northcrestcare.ca
Number of Beds: 106 beds
Sue Emmons, Executive Director

Delta: West Shore Laylum
Affiliated with: Fraser Health Authority
4900 Central Ave., Delta, BC V4K 2G7
Tel: 604-946-2822 Fax: 604-946-2217
Number of Beds: 55 beds
Kris Coonfer, Administrator

Duncan: Cairnsmore Place
Affiliated with: Vancouver Island Health Authority
250 Cairnsmore St., Duncan, BC V9L 4H2
Tel: 250-709-3080 Fax: 250-746-0351
Number of Beds: 100 beds

Enderby: Parkview Place
Affiliated with: Interior Health Authority
PO Box 129, Granville St., Enderby, BC V0E 1V0
Tel: 250-546-6131 Fax: 250-546-9943
Number of Beds: 31 beds
Peter DuToit

Fort Langley: Simpson Private Hospital
Affiliated with: Fraser Health Authority
PO Box 40, 8838 Glover Rd., Fort Langley, BC V1M 2R4
Tel: 604-888-0711 Fax: 604-888-1218
Number of Beds: 55 beds
Note: intermediate & extended care
Ingo Riesen, Controller

Fort St John: North Peace Care Centre
Affiliated with: Northern Health Authority
9907 - 110 Ave., Fort St John, BC V1J 2S9
Tel: 250-785-8941 Fax: 250-785-2296
www.northernhealth.ca
Number of Beds: 95 beds
Note: Complex care special care unit
Larry Tokarchuk, COO
Bob Smalley, Director, Plant Services

Golden: Durand Manor
8th Ave. & 9th St., Golden, BC V0A 1H0
Tel: 250-344-5271 Fax: 250-344-2511
Number of Beds: 27 beds
Note: group home for the elderly mainly who are no longer able to live in the community

Grand Forks: Boundary Lodge Assisted Living
7130 - 9th St., Grand Forks, BC V0H 1H4
Tel: 250-443-0006 Fax: 250-443-0015
Number of Beds: 18 assisted living units

Grand Forks: Hardy View Lodge
Affiliated with: Interior Health Authority
2320 - 78 Ave., Grand Forks, BC V0H 1H0
Tel: 250-443-2080 Fax: 250-442-3663
Number of Beds: 35 beds
Trish Hallstrom, Director of Care

Invermere: Columbia House
850 - 10th St., Invermere, BC V0A 1K0
Tel: 250-342-2329 Fax: 250-342-2319
Number of Beds: 20 beds

Rose Bard

Kamloops: Liberty Manor
470 Hilltop Ave., Kamloops, BC V2B 2S3
Tel: 250-376-3788

Note: group home
Claire Ann Brodie, Executive Director, Continuing Care Services

Kamloops: Panderosa Lodge
425 Columbia St., Kamloops, BC V2C 2T4
Tel: 250-374-5671 *Fax:* 250-374-8873
Number of Beds: 157 beds
Claire Ann Brodie, Director

Kelowna: Avonlea House
Avonlea Care Centre Limited
Affiliated with: Interior Health Authority
1658 Blondeaux Cres., Kelowna, BC V1Y 4J7
Tel: 250-762-4378 *Fax:* 250-762-0167
avonleahouse@avonleacare.com
www.avonleacare.com

Number of Beds: 14 beds
Note: specialized care home for severely brain-injured
Dr. Abbas Moledina, Managing Director/Administrator
Lunda Asselstine, Director of Care/Manager

Kelowna: David Lloyd Jones Home
934 Bernard Ave., Kelowna, BC V1Y 6P8
Tel: 250-762-2706 *Fax:* 250-762-5961
Number of Beds: 64 beds
Rick Riley

Kelowna: May Bennett Home
Affiliated with: Interior Health Authority
965 West Highway 33, Kelowna, BC V1X 1Y8
Tel: 250-763-6277 *Fax:* 250-763-6262
Number of Beds: 24 beds
Nancy Kilpatrick, Director

Kelowna: Parkside Residence Ltd.
Affiliated with: Interior Health Authority
265 Gray Rd., Kelowna, BC V1X 1W8
Tel: 250-765-8482 *Fax:* 250-765-8213
Number of Beds: 23 beds
Alena Merhaut, Administrator

Kelowna: Sutherland Hills Rest Home
Affiliated with: Interior Health Authority
3081 Hall Rd., Kelowna, BC V1W 2R5
Tel: 250-860-2380 *Fax:* 250-860-2399
tlcalhoun@shawcable.com
Number of Beds: 100 beds
Wendy Calhoun, Facility Director

Kelowna: Three Links Manor
Affiliated with: Interior Health Authority
1449 Kelglen Cres., Kelowna, BC V1Y 8P4
Tel: 250-763-2585 *Fax:* 250-763-6773
Number of Beds: 81 beds
Rick Riley

Kelowna: Windsor Manor Care Centre
Affiliated with: Interior Health Authority
355 Terai Ct., Kelowna, BC V1X 5X6
Tel: 250-979-6000 *Fax:* 250-979-6002
Number of Beds: 149 beds
Bev Powell, Administrator

Kimberley: Kimberley Special Care Home
Affiliated with: Interior Health Authority
386 - 2nd Ave., Kimberley, BC V1A 2Z8
Tel: 250-427-4807 *Fax:* 250-427-5377
Number of Beds: 51 beds, 15 mental health
Allan Sinclair, Site Manager

Ladysmith: Four All Seasons Retirement Lodge
Affiliated with: Vancouver Island Health Authority
3464 Yellowpoint Rd., Ladysmith, BC V0R 1E6
Tel: 250-245-4237 *Fax:* 250-245-7757
4allseasons@telus.net
Number of Beds: 22 beds
Gerard B. Huard, Administrator

Langley: Highland Lodge
Affiliated with: Fraser Health Authority
20619 Eastleigh Cres., Langley, BC V3A 4C3
Tel: 604-534-7186 *Fax:* 604-534-7139
feedback@fraserhealth.ca
Number of Beds: 60 beds
Dave Stott, Director, Care

Langley: Langley Gardens
Affiliated with: Fraser Health Authority
8888 - 202nd St., Langley, BC V1M 4A7
Tel: 604-881-8122 *Fax:* 604-881-8199
www.cpac-care.com

Number of Beds: 73 beds
Lisa Kachur, General Manager

Langley: Langley Lodge
Affiliated with: Fraser Health Authority
5451 - 204th St., Langley, BC V3A 5M9
Tel: 604-530-2305 *Fax:* 604-532-4205
www.langleylodge.org

Number of Beds: 153 beds
Note: seniors
Debra Haupman, Executive Director

Lillooet: Mountain View Lodge
Affiliated with: Interior Health Authority
844 Main Street, Lillooet, BC V0K 1V0
Tel: 250-455-2221 *Fax:* 250-455-6621
Number of Beds: 22 beds
Jennifer Thur

Maple Ridge: Golden Ears Retirement Centre
Affiliated with: Fraser Health Authority
12155 Edge St., Maple Ridge, BC V2X 6G7
Tel: 604-467-5511 *Fax:* 604-467-0510
Number of Beds: 52 beds
Doreen Fleming, Administrator

Mission: Grand Street Lodge
Affiliated with: Fraser Health Authority
7755 Grand St., Mission, BC V2V 3T6
Tel: 604-826-6646 *Fax:* 604-820-8550
Number of Beds: 23 beds
Annamae Clark, Administrator

Mission: Pleasant View Care Home
Affiliated with: Fraser Health Authority
7530 Hurd St., Mission, BC V2V 3H9
Tel: 604-826-2154 *Fax:* 604-826-8672
www.pvhs.ca

Number of Beds: 76 beds
Judith E. Ray, Administrator

Nakusp: Halcyon Community Home
PO Box 910, 83 - 8th Ave., Nakusp, BC V0G 1R0
Tel: 250-265-3692 *Fax:* 250-265-4141
Number of Beds: 14 beds
Note: Intermediate care
Deborah Austin

Nanaimo: Kiwanis Village Lodge
Affiliated with: Vancouver Island Health Authority
1221 Kiwanis Crescent, Nanaimo, BC V9S 5Y1
Tel: 250-753-6471 *Fax:* 250-740-2816
Number of Beds: 102 beds
Virginia Ostrand, Administrator

Nanaimo: Malaspina Gardens Inc.
Affiliated with: Vancouver Island Health Authority
388 Machleary St., Nanaimo, BC V9R 2G9
Tel: 250-754-7711 *Fax:* 250-754-2175
Number of Beds: 133 beds
Diane DeRepentigny, General Manager

Nanaimo: Travellers Lodge
Affiliated with: Vancouver Island Health Authority
1298 Nelson St., Nanaimo, BC V9S 2K5
Tel: 250-758-4676 *Fax:* 250-758-4698
ot@nantralodge.bc.ca

Number of Beds: 93 beds
Sandra Rummy, Administrator/Director

Nelson: Nelson Jubilee Manor
Affiliated with: Interior Health Authority
500 Beasley St., Nelson, BC V1L 6G9
Tel: 250-352-7011 *Fax:* 250-352-7044
Number of Beds: 39 beds
Kim Irving

New Westminster: Blue Spruce Cottage
Affiliated with: Fraser Health Authority
509 St. George St., New Westminster, BC V3L 1L1
Tel: 604-521-4316 *Fax:* 604-521-6600
Number of Beds: 15 beds
Betty Dewitte, Manager

New Westminster: Buchanan Lodge
Affiliated with: Fraser Health Authority
409 Blair Ave., New Westminster, BC V3L 4A4
Tel: 604-522-7033 *Fax:* 604-522-3689
Number of Beds: 112 beds
Penny Lang, Administrator

New Westminster: Kiwanis Intermediate Care Centre
Affiliated with: Fraser Health Authority
35 Clute St., New Westminster, BC V3L 1Z5
Tel: 604-525-6471 *Fax:* 604-525-8522
sbrowne@kiwaniscarecentre.com
Number of Beds: 74 beds, 2 respite beds
Note: intermediate care
Shirley Brown, Administrator

New Westminster: Queen's Park Care Centre
Affiliated with: Fraser Health Authority
260 Sherbrooke St., New Westminster, BC V3L 5E8
Tel: 604-520-0911 *Fax:* 604-517-8651
Number of Beds: 219 beds
Note: extended care facility
Carol Wheeler, Director

New Westminster: Royal City Manor
77 Jamieson Ct., New Westminster, BC V3L 5P8
Tel: 604-522-6699 *Fax:* 604-522-1022
royalcitymanor@reveraliving.com
www.reveraliving.com
Kevin Perry, Administrator

New Westminster: Salvation Army Buchanan Lodge
Affiliated with: Fraser Health Authority
409 Blair Ave., New Westminster, BC V3L 4A4
Tel: 604-522-7033 *Fax:* 604-522-3689
Number of Beds: 112 beds
Capt. Penny Lang

North Vancouver: Cedarview Lodge
Affiliated with: Vancouver Coastal Health Authority
1200 Cedar Village Close, North Vancouver, BC V7J 3P3
Tel: 604-904-6400 *Fax:* 604-904-6411
Number of Beds: 90 beds, 30 assisted living units
Note: intermediate care
Lynne Pentland, Manager

North Vancouver: Evergreen House
Affiliated with: Vancouver Coastal Health Authority
231 - 15 St. East, North Vancouver, BC V7L 2L7
Tel: 604-988-3131 *Fax:* 604-984-5838
Number of Beds: 293 beds
Rizwan Damji, Director of Seniors

North Vancouver: H & H Total Care Services
Affiliated with: Vancouver Coastal Health Authority
4530 Meadowbank Close, North Vancouver, BC V7K 2L2
Tel: 604-987-7569 *Fax:* 604-597-8032

Note: specializing in Huntington & brain injury care
Hank Van Ryk, Manager

North Vancouver: N.S. Kiwanis Care Centre
Affiliated with: Vancouver Coastal Health Authority
2444 Burr Pl., North Vancouver, BC V7H 3A5
Tel: 604-924-8300 *Fax:* 604-924-8325
Number of Beds: 192 beds
Carol Mothersill, Admin.
Cathy Baxter, Clinical Manager

North Vancouver: United Lodge
Affiliated with: Vancouver Coastal Health Authority
116 West 23rd St., North Vancouver, BC V7M 2A9
Tel: 604-987-5010 *Fax:* 604-987-9378
Number of Beds: 22 beds
Abraham Calaguian, Administrator

Oliver: Sunnybank Retirement Centre
36657 - 79th St., Oliver, BC V0H 1T0
Tel: 250-498-4951 *Fax:* 250-498-2287
Number of Beds: 51 beds
Janice Little, Care Coordinator

Osoyoos: Country Squire Retirement Villa
9707 - 87th St., RR#2, Osoyoos, BC V0H 1V0
Tel: 250-495-6568 *Fax:* 250-495-7466
Number of Beds: 31 beds
G. Munro, Administrator

Osoyoos: Sagebrush Lodge
Affiliated with: Vancouver Island Health Authority
4816 - 89 St., Osoyoos, BC V0H 1V1
Tel: 250-495-2666 *Fax:* 250-495-2605
Number of Beds: 52 beds
Lorraine Ferguson

***Parksville:* Arrowsmith Lodge**
Affiliated with: Vancouver Island Health Authority
266 Moilliet St., Parksville, BC V9P 1M9
Tel: 250-248-4331 *Fax:* 250-248-4813
Number of Beds: 58 beds
Pam Swanson, Administrator

***Parksville:* Halliday House of BC**
Affiliated with: Vancouver Island Health Authority
188 McCarter St., Parksville, BC V9P 1A1
Tel: 250-248-2835 *Fax:* 250-248-2403
Number of Beds: 20 beds
Louise Hughes, Manager

***Penticton:* Haven Hill Retirement Centre**
Affiliated with: Interior Health Authority
415 Haven Hill Rd., Penticton, BC V2A 4E9
Tel: 250-492-2600 *Fax:* 250-492-2498
info@havenhill.ca
www.havenhill.ca
Number of Beds: 83 beds
Brian Wyatt, Administrator

***Penticton:* Penticton & District Retirement Centre**
Affiliated with: Interior Health Authority
439 Winnipeg St., Penticton, BC V2A 6P5
Tel: 250-770-7400 *Fax:* 250-492-1091
Number of Beds: 101 beds
Betty Ashton, Care Unit Coordinator

***Port Alberni:* Echo Village**
Affiliated with: Vancouver Island Health Authority
4200 - 10th Ave., Port Alberni, BC V9Y 4X3
Tel: 250-724-1090 *Fax:* 250-724-2115
Number of Beds: 65 beds
Barbara A. Stevenson, Administrator

***Port Alberni:* Fir Park Village**
Affiliated with: Vancouver Island Health Authority
4411 Wallace St., Port Alberni, BC V9Y 7Y5
Tel: 250-724-6541 *Fax:* 250-724-6543
bstevenson@acccs.ca
Number of Beds: 62 beds
Barb Stevenson, Executive Director

***Port Alberni:* Tsawaayuus-Rainbow Gardens**
Affiliated with: Vancouver Island Health Authority
6151 Russell Pl., Port Alberni, BC V9Y 7W3
Tel: 250-724-5655 *Fax:* 250-724-5666
Number of Beds: 30 beds
Lillian Thomas, Administrator

***Port Coquitlam:* Hawthorne Care Centre**
Affiliated with: Fraser Health Authority
2111 Hawthorne Ave., Port Coquitlam, BC V3C 1W3
Tel: 604-941-4051 *Fax:* 604-941-5829
Number of Beds: 125 beds
Lenore Pickering, Administrator

***Port Coquitlam:* Melissa Park Lodge**
Affiliated with: Fraser Health Authority
2175 Mary Hill Rd., Port Coquitlam, BC V3C 3A2
Tel: 604-942-4325 *Fax:* 604-526-2984
Number of Beds: 20 beds
Ronald Wong, Manager

***Pouce Coupe:* Peace River Haven**
Affiliated with: Northern Health Authority
PO Box 188, 5213 - 50th Ave., Pouce Coupe, BC V0C 2C0
Tel: 250-786-6100 *Fax:* 250-786-6107
Number of Beds: 60 beds
Note: intermediate level
Elaine Washington, Resident Care Manager

***Prince George:* AiMHi - Prince George Association for Community Living**
500 Victoria St., 3rd Fl., Prince George, BC V2L 2J9
Tel: 250-564-6408
aimhi@aimhi.ca
www.aimhi.ca
Number of Beds: 47 beds
Note: non-profit, supports individuals with developmental disabilities & children with special needs
Carol Burbee, Contact

***Prince George:* Alward Place**
Affiliated with: Northern Health Authority
2121 - 6th Ave., Prince George, BC V2M 1L9
Tel: 250-565-7493
Number of Beds: 120 apartments

***Prince George:* Simon Fraser Lodge**
2410 Laurier Cres., Prince George, BC V2M 2B3
Tel: 250-563-3413 *Fax:* 250-563-7209
Number of Beds: 131 beds
Kathy Giene, Administrator

***Prince Rupert:* Acropolis Manor**
Affiliated with: Northern Health Authority
1325 Summit Ave., Prince Rupert, BC V8J 4C1
Tel: 250-622-6400 *Fax:* 250-627-1490
Year Founded: 2009
Number of Beds: 61 beds
Karen Inkpen, Clinical Coordinator

***Princeton:* Ridgewood Lodge**
98 Ridgewood Dr., Princeton, BC V0X 1W0
Tel: 250-295-5551 *Fax:* 250-295-4081
Number of Beds: 37 beds
Marilyn Harkness, Administrator

***Qualicum Beach:* Arranglen Lodge**
Affiliated with: Vancouver Island Health Authority
2300 Fowler Rd., Qualicum Beach, BC V9K 2A5
Tel: 250-752-9277 *Fax:* 250-752-5525
Number of Beds: 85 beds
Diane Derepentigny, Administrator

***Qualicum Beach:* Eagle Park Health Care Facility**
Affiliated with: Vancouver Island Health Authority
777 Jones St., Qualicum Beach, BC V9K 2L1
Tel: 250-752-7075 *Fax:* 250-752-8316
Number of Beds: 10 beds
Jill Forsythe, Director, Residential Care

***Quesnel:* Dunrovin Park Lodge**
Affiliated with: Northern Health Authority
351 Murphy St., Quesnel, BC V2J 3S3
Tel: 250-992-5263 *Fax:* 250-992-5277
Number of Beds: 75 beds
Val Waymark, Program Manager, Home & Community Care

***Revelstoke:* Shuswap Lake General Hospital**
Affiliated with: Interior Health Authority
601 - 10th St. NE, Revelstoke, BC V1E 4N6
Tel: 250-833-3600 *Fax:* 250-833-3611
Number of Beds: 21 beds
Dorothy Schiller

***Richmond:* Courtyard Gardens**
Affiliated with: Vancouver Coastal Health Authority
7051 Moffatt Rd., Richmond, BC V6Y 3W2
Tel: 604-273-1225 *Fax:* 604-273-9253
mkg.mgr.cyg@diversicare.ca
courtyardgardens.ca
Number of Beds: 31 intermediate care beds, 107 assisted living apts, 1 respi
Note: 107 suites of assisted living
Maggie Keatley, General Manager

***Richmond:* Fraserview Intermediate Care Lodge Co. Ltd.**
Affiliated with: Vancouver Coastal Health Authority
9580 Williams Rd., Richmond, BC V7A 1H2
Tel: 604-274-3510 *Fax:* 604-275-0996
Number of Beds: 105 beds
A.M. Baron, Administrator

***Richmond:* Pinegrove Place**
Affiliated with: Vancouver Coastal Health Authority
11331 Mellis Dr., Richmond, BC V6X 1L8
Tel: 604-278-1296 *Fax:* 604-273-0050
Number of Beds: 75 beds
Gordon Milner, Administrator

***Richmond:* Richmond Lions Manor**
Affiliated with: Vancouver Coastal Health Authority
11771 Fentiman Pl., Richmond, BC V7E 3M4
Tel: 604-274-6311 *Fax:* 604-274-2543
Number of Beds: 132 beds
S. Garrison, Medical Coordinator

***Richmond:* Rosewood Manor**
Affiliated with: Vancouver Coastal Health Authority
6260 Blundell Rd., Richmond, BC V7C 5C4
Tel: 604-271-3590 *Fax:* 604-271-3551
Number of Beds: 120 beds
Note: intermediate & complex care
Deborah Goegan, Administrator

***Salt Spring Island:* Greenwoods**
Affiliated with: Vancouver Island Health Authority
133 Blain Rd., Salt Spring Island, BC V8K 1Z9
Tel: 250-537-5561 *Fax:* 250-537-1124
Number of Beds: 50 beds
Andrew Brown, Administrator

***Sechelt:* Shorncliffe Intermediate Care**
Affiliated with: Vancouver Coastal Health
Former Name: Shorncliffe
5847 Medusa St., Sechelt, BC V0N 3A0
Tel: 604-885-5126 *Fax:* 604-885-5140
Number of Beds: 60 beds
Dennis Regnier, Coordinator

***Shawnigan Lake:* Acacia Ty Mawr Lodge**
2655 Shawnigan Lake Rd. East, Shawnigan Lake, BC V0R 2W0
Tel: 250-743-2124 *Fax:* 250-743-2130
Number of Beds: 35 beds
J. Neil Stuart, Administrator

***Sidney:* Sidney Intermediate Care Home Ltd.**
9888 - 5th St., Sidney, BC V8L 2X3
Tel: 250-656-0121 *Fax:* 250-656-0189
Number of Beds: 52 beds
Susan Irvine, Administrator

***Smithers:* Buckley Lodge**
Affiliated with: Northern Health Authority
3668 - 11th Ave., Smithers, BC V0J 2N0
Tel: 250-847-4443 *Fax:* 250-847-3895
Number of Beds: 73 beds
Heather Hodson, Administrator

***South Surrey:* Peace Portal Lodge**
Affiliated with: Fraser Health Authority
15441 - 16th Ave., South Surrey, BC V4A 8T8
Tel: 604-535-2273 *Fax:* 604-535-3051
adevos@retirementconcepts.com
www.retirementconcepts.com
Number of Beds: 27 beds
Susan Wilson, Administrator

***Squamish:* Hilltop House**
Affiliated with: Vancouver Coastal Health Authority
38146 Behrner Dr., Squamish, BC V8B 0J3
Tel: 604-892-9337 *Fax:* 604-892-6091
Number of Beds: 10 beds for dementia care, 31 intermediate care, 20 extended
Note: long term care
Marian Biln

***Summerland:* Kelly Care Centre**
12801 Kelly Ave., Summerland, BC V0H 1Z0
Tel: 250-494-7911 *Fax:* 250-494-4027
Number of Beds: 79 beds
Lorraine Ferguson

***Surrey:* Amenida Seniors' Community**
Affiliated with: Fraser Health Authority
Former Name: Newton Regency Care Home
13855 - 68 Ave., Surrey, BC V3W 2G9
Tel: 604-597-9333 *Fax:* 604-597-8032
homecareliving.ca
Year Founded: 2010
Number of Beds: 136 beds
Note: Independent, assisted living
Teena Love, General Manager
604-597-9333 ext 126, teena.love@homecareliving.ca
Sandra Prance, Administrative Coordinator
604-597-9333 ext 126, sandra.prance@homecareliving.ca

***Surrey:* Bear Creek Lodge**
Affiliated with: Fraser Health Authority
13646 - 94A Ave., Surrey, BC V3V 1N1
Tel: 604-581-4028 *Fax:* 604-581-8523
Number of Beds: 115 beds
Hendrik Van Ryk, COO

***Surrey:* Centennial Park Lodge**
Affiliated with: Fraser Health Authority
11861 - 99 Ave., Surrey, BC V3V 2M3
Tel: 604-584-6811 *Fax:* 604-581-4768
kahmon@telus.net
Number of Beds: 26 beds
Kevin Ahmon, Administrator

***Surrey:* Crescent Gardens**
Affiliated with: Fraser Health Authority
1222 King George Hwy., Surrey, BC V4A 9W6
Tel: 604-541-8861 *Fax:* 604-541-8871
crescentgardens@chartwellreit.ca
www.chartwellreit.ca
Number of Beds: 53 beds
Ann Varona, Director of Care

***Surrey:* Evergreen Cottages**
Affiliated with: Fraser Health Authority
15660 - 84th Ave., Surrey, BC V3A 2N5
Tel: 604-597-7906 *Fax:* 604-597-9025
www.evergreen-cottages.com
Number of Beds: 33 beds
Marion Butte, Administrator

***Surrey:* Fleetwood Place**
Affiliated with: Fraser Health Authority
16011 - 83rd Ave., Surrey, BC V3S 8M2
Tel: 604-590-6860 *Fax:* 604-590-6861
messages@fleetwoodplace.ca
Number of Beds: 75 beds
Kevin Ahmon, Administrator

***Surrey:* Guildford Seniors Village**
Affiliated with: Fraser Health Authority
14584 - 104A Ave., Surrey, BC V3R 1R3
Tel: 604-582-0808 *Fax:* 604-582-7011
Number of Beds: 60 beds
Leslie Karmazinuk, Administrator

***Surrey:* Hilton Villa Care Centre**
Affiliated with: Fraser Health Authority
13525 Hilton Rd., Surrey, BC V3R 5J3
Tel: 604-588-3424 *Fax:* 604-588-3433
Number of Beds: 124 beds
Al Jina, Administrator

***Surrey:* Kinsmen Place Lodge**
Affiliated with: Fraser Health Authority
13333 Old Yale Rd., Surrey, BC V3T 5A2
Tel: 604-588-0445 *Fax:* 604-588-7211
www.kinsmenplace.org
Number of Beds: 143 beds
Note: intermediate care
Karen Holt, Director, Resident Care

***Surrey:* Morgan Place**
Affiliated with: Fraser Health Authority
3288 - 156A St., Surrey, BC V3S 9T1
Tel: 604-535-7328 *Fax:* 604-535-7386
www.morganplace.ca
Number of Beds: 122 beds
Betty Ahmon, Administrator

***Surrey:* Zion Park Manor**
Affiliated with: Fraser Health Authority
5939 - 180th St., Surrey, BC V3S 4L2
Tel: 604-576-2891 *Fax:* 604-576-8046
Number of Beds: 142 beds
Thomas Crump, Administrator

***Trail:* Columbia View Lodge**
Affiliated with: Interior Health Authority
2920 Laburnum Dr., Trail, BC V1R 4N2
Tel: 250-364-1271 *Fax:* 250-364-0911
Number of Beds: 77 beds
Note: complex care facility
Norma Mildenberger, Director, Residential Care

***Trail:* Kiro Manor**
Affiliated with: Interior Health Authority
1500 Columbia Ave., Trail, BC V1R 1J9
Tel: 250-364-1214 *Fax:* 250-364-1261
Number of Beds: 9 beds
Norman Mildenberger

***Trail:* Poplar Ridge Pavillion**
Affiliated with: Interior Health Authority
1200 Hospital Bench, Trail, BC V1R 4M1
Tel: 250-368-3311 *Fax:* 250-364-3422
Number of Beds: 50 beds
Frank Marino, Health Service Administrator

***Vancouver:* Adanac Park Lodge**
Affiliated with: Vancouver Coastal Health Authority
851 Boundary Rd., Vancouver, BC V5K 4T2
Tel: 604-299-7567 *Fax:* 604-299-7424
Number of Beds: 72 beds
Dan Levitt, Executive Director

***Vancouver:* Amica at Arbutus Manor**
Affiliated with: Vancouver Coastal Health Authority
2125 Eddington Dr., Vancouver, BC V6L 3A9
Tel: 604-736-8936 *Fax:* 604-731-8933
Number of Beds: 125 beds
Holly Goldsmith, Facilities Manager

***Vancouver:* Arbutus Care Centre**
Affiliated with: Vancouver Coastal Health Authority
4505 Valley Dr., Vancouver, BC V6L 2L1
Tel: 604-261-4292 *Fax:* 604-261-7849
arbutus@reveraliving.com
www.reveraliving.com
Number of Beds: 161 beds
Note: Specialty: Complex residential care; Nursing care; Foot care; Social work; Recreational therapy; Music therapy

***Vancouver:* Balfour House**
Affiliated with: Vancouver Coastal Health Authority
1490 Balfour St., Vancouver, BC V6H 1Y1
Tel: 604-733-0222 *Fax:* 604-714-1386
Number of Beds: 18 beds
D. Morton, Administrator

***Vancouver:* Blenheim Lodge**
Affiliated with: Vancouver Coastal Health Authority
3263 Blenheim St., Vancouver, BC V6L 2X7
Tel: 604-732-8717 *Fax:* 604-732-7316
Number of Beds: 109 beds
Derek Morton, Administrator

***Vancouver:* Braddan Private Hospital**
Affiliated with: Vancouver Coastal Health Authority
2450 - 2nd Ave., Vancouver, BC V6K 1J6
Tel: 604-731-2127 *Fax:* 604-731-0283
mcintosh@axion.net
Number of Beds: 51 beds
Maureen McIntosh, Administrator

***Vancouver:* Broadway Pentecostal Lodge**
Affiliated with: Vancouver Coastal Health Authority
1377 Lamey's Mill Rd., Vancouver, BC V6H 3S9
Tel: 604-733-1441 *Fax:* 604-731-1484
Number of Beds: 114 beds
Jeanette Thompson, Administrator

***Vancouver:* Chalmers Lodge Personal Care Home**
Affiliated with: Vancouver Coastal Health Authority
1450 - 12th Ave. West, Vancouver, BC V6H 1M9
Tel: 604-731-3178 *Fax:* 604-731-3140
info@chalmerslodge.ca
www.chalmerslodge.ca
Year Founded: 1970
Number of Beds: 115 units
Note: Personal care home
K.P.S. Aujlay, CEO

***Vancouver:* City Centre Care Society - Central City Lodge**
Affiliated with: Vancouver Coastal Health Authority
415 West Pender St., Vancouver, BC V6B 1V2
Tel: 604-681-9111 *Fax:* 604-681-5546
Number of Beds: 122 beds
Note: multilevel care; supportive housing - addictions recovery
Catherine Adair, Executive Director

***Vancouver:* City Centre Care Society - Cooper Place**
Affiliated with: Vancouver Coastal Health Authority
306 Cordova St. East, Vancouver, BC V6A 1L5
Tel: 604-684-2545 *Fax:* 604-684-2575
Number of Beds: 72 beds
Antonia Reynolds, Manager, Assisted Living

***Vancouver:* Columbus Residence**
Affiliated with: Vancouver Coastal Health Authority
704 West 69th Ave., Vancouver, BC V6P 2W3
Tel: 604-321-4405 *Fax:* 604-321-4543
Number of Beds: 76 beds
Peter Horsfield, Executive Director

***Vancouver:* Crofton Manor**
Affiliated with: Vancouver Coastal Health Authority
2803 - 41 Ave. West, Vancouver, BC V6N 4B4
Tel: 604-263-0921 *Fax:* 604-263-7719
www.reveraliving.com/crofton
Number of Beds: 194 suites
Carol Omstead, General Manager

***Vancouver:* Dogwood Lodge**
Affiliated with: Vancouver Coastal Health Authority
500 West 57th Ave., Vancouver, BC V6P 6E8
Tel: 604-324-6882 *Fax:* 604-324-7226
Number of Beds: 113 beds
Susan Fong, Administrator

***Vancouver:* Fair Haven United Church Home**
Affiliated with: Vancouver Coastal Health Authority
2720 East 48th St., Vancouver, BC V5S 1G7
Tel: 604-433-2939 *Fax:* 604-433-4547
cmothersill@fairhaven.bc.ca
Number of Beds: 69 beds
Carol Mothersill, CEO

***Vancouver:* False Creek Residence**
Affiliated with: Vancouver Coastal Health Authority
1167 Forge Walk, Vancouver, BC V6H 3R1
Tel: 604-731-0401 *Fax:* 604-731-9546
info@rils.ca
www.rils.ca
Number of Beds: 24 beds
Kathleen Mason, Executive Director

***Vancouver:* German-Canadian Care Home**
Affiliated with: Vancouver Coastal Health Authority
2010 Harrison Dr., Vancouver, BC V5P 2P6
Tel: 604-713-6500 *Fax:* 604-713-6548
Number of Beds: 144 beds
Donna Dougan, CEO

***Vancouver:* Haro Park Centre**
Affiliated with: Vancouver Coastal Health Authority
1233 Haro St., Vancouver, BC V6E 3Y5
Tel: 604-687-5584 *Fax:* 604-687-0645
info@haropark.org
www.haropark.org
Number of Beds: 190 suites
Shayne Ramsay, Chief Executive Officer

***Vancouver:* Icelandic Care Home**
Affiliated with: Vancouver Coastal Health Authority
2020 Harrison Dr., Vancouver, BC V5P 2P6
Tel: 604-321-3812 *Fax:* 604-321-3863
Number of Beds: 64 beds
Marlene Wynes, Administrator

***Vancouver:* Kopernik Lodge**
Kopernik Nicolaus Foundation
Affiliated with: Vancouver Coastal Health Authority
3150 Rosemont Dr., Vancouver, BC V5S 2C9
Tel: 604-438-2474 *Fax:* 604-438-5344
admin@kopernik-lodge.bc.ca
www.kopernik-foundation.org
Number of Beds: 87 beds
Note: intermediate care facility
Diana Ollmann, Administrator/CEO

***Vancouver:* L & T Rehabilitation Services Ltd.**
Affiliated with: Vancouver Coastal Health Authority
3103 Kings Way, Vancouver, BC V5R 5J9
Tel: 604-439-7545 *Fax:* 604-439-1326
Number of Beds: 19 beds
Joan Grimsrud, Administrator

***Vancouver:* Lakeview Care Centre**
3490 Porter St., Vancouver, BC V5N 4H2
Tel: 604-874-2803 *Fax:* 604-874-7744
Number of Beds: 165 beds
Pat May, Administrator

***Vancouver:* Little Mountain Place**
Affiliated with: Vancouver Coastal Health Authority
330 East 36th Ave., Vancouver, BC V5W 3Z4
Tel: 604-325-2298 *Fax:* 604-325-3655
www.littlemountaincare.ca
Number of Beds: 117 beds
Dan Levitt, Executive Director

***Vancouver:* Renfrew Care Centre**
Affiliated with: Vancouver Coastal Health Authority
1880 Renfrew St., Vancouver, BC V5M 3H9
Tel: 604-255-7723 *Fax:* 604-255-2045
Number of Beds: 88 beds
Loraine Coffin, Administrator

***Vancouver:* Royal Arch Masonic Home**
Affiliated with: Vancouver Coastal Health Authority
7850 Champlain Cres., Vancouver, BC V5S 4C7
Tel: 604-437-7343 *Fax:* 604-437-7373
Number of Beds: 151 beds
Gregory Runzer, Administrator

***Vancouver:* Royal Ascot Care Centre**
Affiliated with: Vancouver Coastal Health Authority
2455 Broadway East, Vancouver, BC V5M 1Y7
Tel: 604-254-5559 *Fax:* 604-254-5523
Number of Beds: 82 beds
Cheryl Scarlett, Administrator

***Vancouver:* St. Bernard House**
Affiliated with: Vancouver Coastal Health Authority
547 - 12th Ave. East, Vancouver, BC V5T 2H6
Tel: 604-874-8657 *Fax:* 604-984-7933
Number of Beds: 12 beds
David A. Russell, Administrator

Vancouver: St. Vincent's Hospital
Affiliated with: Vancouver Coastal Health Authority
4650 Oak St., Vancouver, BC V6H 4J4
Tel: 604-877-3220 *Fax:* 604-877-3215
Number of Beds: 150 beds
Note: extended care facility
Carl Roy, President; CEO

Vancouver: St. Vincent's Hospital Langara
Affiliated with: Vancouver Coastal Health Authority
255 - 62nd Ave. West, Vancouver, BC V5X 4V4
Tel: 604-325-4116 *Fax:* 604-877-3081
www.providencehealthcare.org
Number of Beds: 221 beds
Note: long-term care facility
Carl Roy, President; CEO

Vancouver: Salvation Army Southview Terrace
Affiliated with: Vancouver Coastal Health Authority
3131 East 58th Ave., Vancouver, BC V5S 4V2
Tel: 604-438-3367 *Fax:* 604-438-0262
Note: personal care facility

Vancouver: South Granville Park Lodge
Affiliated with: Vancouver Coastal Health Authority
1645 West 14th Ave., Vancouver, BC V6J 2J4
Tel: 604-732-8633 *Fax:* 604-732-9833
sgplodge@telus.net
www.sgplodge.com
Number of Beds: 120 beds
Zdenka Votrubova, Director, Nursing

Vancouver: Three Links Care Centre
Affiliated with: Vancouver Coastal Health Authority
2934 East 22nd Ave., Vancouver, BC V5M 2Y4
Tel: 604-434-7211 *Fax:* 604-438-7563
info@threelinks.com
www.threelinks.com
Number of Beds: 90 beds
Note: complex care facility
Tom Novak, CEO

Vancouver: Villa Cathay Care Home
Affiliated with: Vancouver Coastal Health Authority
970 Union St., Vancouver, BC V6A 3V1
Tel: 604-254-5621 *Fax:* 604-254-5230
www.villacathay.ca
Number of Beds: 188 beds
Hudson Chong, COO

Vancouver: Windermere Care Centre
Affiliated with: Vancouver Coastal Health Authority
900 West 12th Ave., Vancouver, BC V5Z 1N3
Tel: 604-736-8676 *Fax:* 604-736-8682
infor@windermerecare.ca
www.windermerecare.ca
Number of Beds: 196 beds
Note: complex care
Ross Sugimoto, Administrator

Vancouver: Yaletown House Society
Affiliated with: Vancouver Coastal Health Authority
1099 Cambie St., Vancouver, BC V6B 5A8
Tel: 604-689-0022 *Fax:* 604-662-7954
Number of Beds: 130 beds
Carol Crichton, Executive Director

Vancouver: Youville Residence
Affiliated with: Vancouver Coastal Health Authority
4950 Heather, Vancouver, BC V5Z 3L9
Tel: 604-261-9371 *Fax:* 604-261-9047
www.providencehealthcare.org
Number of Beds: 84 beds
Note: intermediate care facility with Alzheimer ward
Carl Roy, President; CEO

Vanderhoof: Omineca Lodge
Affiliated with: Northern Health Authority
Bag 5000, 242 Louvain St., Vanderhoof, BC V0J 3A0
Tel: 250-567-2216 *Fax:* 250-567-2677
Number of Beds: 36 beds
Note: intermediate care
Ray Scott, Administrator, Health Services

Vernon: Bethany House
Affiliated with: Interior Health Authority
3904 - 27 St., Vernon, BC V1T 4X7
Tel: 250-545-2060 *Fax:* 250-545-4060
Number of Beds: 37 beds
Kevin Svoboda, Facilities Manager

Vernon: Birch Lodge
Affiliated with: Interior Health Authority
7446 Hwy. 6, Vernon, BC V1B 3H4
Tel: 250-545-6849
Number of Beds: 29 beds
T. Huber, Facilities Manager

Vernon: Gateby Intermediate Care Facility
Affiliated with: Interior Health Authority
3000 Gateby Pl., Vernon, BC V1T 8V8
Tel: 250-545-4456 *Fax:* 250-545-4439
Number of Beds: 75 beds
Peter DuToit

Vernon: Noric House Extended Care
Affiliated with: Interior Health Authority
1400 Mission Rd., Vernon, BC V1T 9C3
Tel: 250-545-9167 *Fax:* 250-545-4980
mary.napier@interiorhealth.ca
Number of Beds: 85 beds
Peter DuToit

Victoria: Beacon Hill Villa
635 Superior St., Victoria, BC V8V 1V1
Tel: 250-383-5447 *Fax:* 250-361-4395
Number of Beds: 80 beds
May Sauder, Administrator

Victoria: Beckley Farm Lodge
Affiliated with: Vancouver Island Health Authority
530 Simcoe St., Victoria, BC V8V 1V1
Tel: 250-381-4421 *Fax:* 250-381-0112
Number of Beds: 70 beds
Note: complex care & adult day centre
Jan Robertson, Administrator

Victoria: Central Care Home
Affiliated with: Vancouver Island Health Authority
844 Johnston St., Victoria, BC V8W 1N3
Tel: 250-384-1313 *Fax:* 250-384-9760
torr@baptisthousing.org
Number of Beds: 147 beds
Note: intermediate care
Tim Orr, Administrator

Victoria: Chinatown Care Centre
555 Herald St., Victoria, BC V8W 1S5
Tel: 250-381-4322 *Fax:* 250-920-0318
Number of Beds: 31 beds
May Sauder, Executive Director

Victoria: Craigdarroch Care Home
Affiliated with: Vancouver Island Health Authority
1048 Craigdarroch Rd., Victoria, BC V8W 1N3
Tel: 250-595-3813 *Fax:* 250-595-3836
Number of Beds: 18 beds
J.O. Scott, Administrator

Victoria: Hart Home Seniors Residence
Affiliated with: Vancouver Island Health Authority
1961 Fairfield Rd., Victoria, BC V8S 1H5
Tel: 250-598-3542 *Fax:* 250-598-2594
harthouse@shaw.ca
Number of Beds: 20 beds
Note: intermediate care home
Melanie Sundquist, Manager

Victoria: James Bay Lodge
Affiliated with: Vancouver Island Health Authority
336 Simcoe St., Victoria, BC V8V 1L2
Tel: 250-388-6457 *Fax:* 250-381-2969
Number of Beds: 208 beds
Note: intermediate care
Stan Dubas, Administrator

Victoria: The Kensington Retirement Living
3965 Shelbourne St., Victoria, BC V8N 6J4
Tel: 250-477-1232 *Fax:* 250-472-1271
Number of Beds: 116 suites
Alaine Reimer, General Manager

Victoria: Kiwanis Pavilion
Affiliated with: Vancouver Island Health Authority
Former Name: Oak Bay Kiwanis Pavilion
3034 Cedar Hill Rd., Victoria, BC V8T 3J3
Tel: 250-598-2022 *Fax:* 250-598-0023
www.obkp.org
Number of Beds: 117 beds
Note: multi level care facility
William B. Cuthill, Administrator

Victoria: Lodge at Broadmead
Affiliated with: Vancouver Island Health Authority
4579 Chatterton Way, Victoria, BC V8X 4Y7
Tel: 250-658-0311 *Fax:* 250-658-0948
www.tvcs.ca
Number of Beds: 229 beds
Evelyn Stewart, Executive Director

Victoria: Luther Court
Affiliated with: Vancouver Island Health Authority
1525 Cedar Hill Cross Rd., Victoria, BC V8P 5M1
Tel: 250-477-7241 *Fax:* 250-477-5740
jsolomon@luthercourtsociety.org
Number of Beds: 66 beds
Joanne Solomonson, CEO

Victoria: Mount Edwards Court Care Home
Affiliated with: Vancouver Island Health Authority
1002 Vancouver St., Victoria, BC V8V 3V8
Tel: 250-385-2241 *Fax:* 250-385-4842
torr@baptisthousing.org
Number of Beds: 83 beds
Tim Orr, Administrator

Victoria: Mount St. Mary Hospital
Affiliated with: Vancouver Island Health Authority
861 Fairfield Rd., Victoria, BC V8V 5A9
Tel: 250-480-3100 *Fax:* 250-480-3110
www.mtstmary.victoria.bc.ca
Number of Beds: 200 beds
Note: extended care
Colleen Black, CEO
Doug Moffatt, Physical Plant

Victoria: Oak Bay Lodge
Affiliated with: Vancouver Island Health Authority
2251 Cadboro Bay Rd., Victoria, BC V8R 5H3
Tel: 250-370-6600 *Fax:* 250-370-6601
Number of Beds: 245 beds
Heather Cook
Heather.cook@gov.bc.ca

Victoria: Rose Manor
Affiliated with: Vancouver Island Health Authority
857 Rupert Terrace, Victoria, BC V8V 3E5
Tel: 250-383-0414 *Fax:* 250-360-2039
www.rosemanor.ca
Number of Beds: 128 beds
James Baird, Administrator

Victoria: Sandringham Hospital
Affiliated with: Vancouver Island Health Authority
1650 Fort St., Victoria, BC V8R 1H9
Tel: 250-595-2313 *Fax:* 250-595-4137
Number of Beds: 85 beds
Stan Dubas, Administrator

West Vancouver: Capilano Care Centre
Affiliated with: Vancouver Island Health Authority
525 Clyde Ave., West Vancouver, BC V7T 1C4
Tel: 604-926-6856 *Fax:* 604-926-0245
Number of Beds: 217 beds
Donna Moroz, Administrator

West Vancouver: Hollyburn House
Affiliated with: Vancouver Coastal Health Authority
2095 Marine Dr., West Vancouver, BC V7V 4V5
Tel: 604-922-7616 *Fax:* 604-922-9163
Number of Beds: 102 suites
June Messmer, General Manager

West Vancouver: Inglewood Care Centre
Affiliated with: Vancouver Coastal Health Authority
725 Inglewood Ave., West Vancouver, BC V7T 1X5
Tel: 604-922-9394 *Fax:* 604-922-2709
Number of Beds: 231 beds
Note: multi-level care
Nick Whittle, Administrator

Westbank: Brookhaven Extended Care Centre
Affiliated with: Interior Health Authority
1775 Shannon Lake Rd., Westbank, BC V4T 2N7
Tel: 250-862-4040 *Fax:* 250-862-4048
dolorese.rudnicki@interiorhealth.ca
www.interiorhealth.ca
Number of Beds: 168 beds
Dolorese Rudnicki, Primary Contact

Westbank: Pine Acres Home
Affiliated with: Interior Health Authority
1902 Pheasant Lane, Westbank, BC V4T 2H4
Tel: 250-768-7676 *Fax:* 250-768-3234

Number of Beds: 40 community beds, 23 private care beds
Note: Complex care
JoAnn Derrickson, Administrator

Westbank: Westside Care Centre
Affiliated with: Interior Health Authority
3324 Old Okanagan Hwy., Westbank, BC V4T 1N3
Tel: 250-768-0488 *Fax:* 250-768-4777
Number of Beds: 98 beds
Elizabeth Harris, Managing Director

White Rock: Bel Air Rest Home
Affiliated with: Fraser Health Authority
14824 North Bluff Rd., White Rock, BC V4B 3E2
Tel: 604-536-1224 *Fax:* 604-536-1267
Number of Beds: 31 beds
Karen Armitage, Director

White Rock: Evergreen Baptist Home
Affiliated with: Fraser Health Authority
1550 Oxford St., White Rock, BC V4B 3R5
Tel: 604-536-3344 *Fax:* 604-541-3803
www.evergreen-home.com
Number of Beds: 157 beds
Linda Ingham, Administrator

White Rock: Ocean View Care Home
Affiliated with: Fraser Health Authority
15628 Buena Vista Ave., White Rock, BC V4B 1Z4
Tel: 604-531-2273 *Fax:* 604-531-8782
Number of Beds: 71 beds
Note: Specialty: Residential care for seniors; Secure unit for persons with dementia
Pat Mulcahy, Administrator

Williams Lake: Jubilee Care Home
Affiliated with: Interior Health Authority
196 - 2nd Ave. North, Williams Lake, BC V2G 1Z6
Tel: 250-398-7736 *Fax:* 250-398-7736
Number of Beds: 7 beds
Note: Mental health group home
Doris Foote, Administrator

Winfield: Lake Country Lodge
10163 Konschuh Rd., Winfield, BC V4V 2M2
Tel: 250-766-3007 *Fax:* 250-766-3178
admin@lakecountrylodge.ca
www.lakecountrylodge.ca
Number of Beds: 34 beds
Cathy Redden, Facilities Manager

Nursing Homes

Coquitlam: Belvedere Care Centre
Affiliated with: Fraser Health Authority
Also Known As: Belvedere Care Centre & Residences at Belvedere
739 Alderson Ave., Coquitlam, BC V3K 7B3
Tel: 604-939-5991 *Fax:* 604-939-5910
belvederecare@telus.net
www.belvederecare.com
Number of Beds: 148 complex care beds at care centre; 114 units for seniors at assisted living centre, including a secure unit for 11 residents
Note: Specialties: Complex care for seniors; Assisted living for residents with mild cognitive impairment; Wellness programs; Diabetes management; Therapy; Rehabilitation; Dementia care; Chronic care; Palliative care
Berton B. Evertt, Chair; Chief Executive Officer
Annamae Clarke, Vice-President
Andrew Butler, Manager, Strategic Planning
Jennifer Cuvelier, Manager, Administration Services
Aileen Mellors-Luyt, Manager, Support Services
Karen Slutsken, Manager, Resident Relations
Fay Woodward, Manager, Resident Services
Dr. Azim Ladhani, Medical Coordinator
Linda Tod, Coordinator, Quality Improvement
Greg Graham, Controller
Gayle Vanags, Registered Dietitian

Coquitlam: Dufferin Care Centre
Retirement Concepts
1131 Dufferin St., Coquitlam, BC V3B 7X5
Tel: 604-552-1166 *Fax:* 604-552-3116
www.retirementconcepts.com
Number of Beds: 153 beds
Note: Specialties: Continuing care; Nursing care; Physiotherapy; Recreation therapy; Music therapy
Pat Kittler, General Manager
pkittler@retirementconcepts.com
Shannon Johnson, Director, Care
Elaine Drysdale, Coordinator, Administration
edrysdale@retirementconcepts.com

Doris Robinson, Coordinator, Marketing
604-375-9193, drobinson@retirementconcepts.com

Merritt: Coquihalla Gillis House
Affiliated with: Interior Health Authority
1699 Tutill Crt., Merritt, BC V1K 1B8
Tel: 250-378-3271

Vancouver: George Pearson Centre (GPC)
Affiliated with: Vancouver Coastal Health Authority
700 West 57th Ave., Vancouver, BC V6P 1S1
Tel: 604-321-3231 *Fax:* 604-321-7833
feedback@vch.ca
www.vch.ca
Year Founded: 1952
Number of Beds: 120 beds; 1 respite bed
Note: Specialties: Residential & complex medical care for adults with severe disabilities, such as cerebral palsy, multiple sclerosis, & spinal cord & traumatic brain injury; Special care units for ventilator dependent residents & persons with tracheostomies; Occupational therapy, physical therapy, pool therapy, music therapy, & respiratory therapy; Speech language pathology; Social work

Retirement Residences

Burnaby: CPAC (Carlton Gardens) Inc.
4125 Canada Way, Burnaby, BC V5G 1G9
Tel: 604-438-8224 *Fax:* 604-438-6571
Note: Specialty: Care for the elderly

Coquitlam: Parkwood Manor
1142 Dufferin St., Coquitlam, BC V3B 6V4
Tel: 604-941-7651 *Fax:* 604-941-4223
parkwoodmanor@lrc.ca
www.reveraliving.com
Number of Beds: 139 suites
Note: Independent living, convalescent & respite options
Wilma Mitchell, General Manager

Surrey: Whitecliff
15501 - 16th Ave., Surrey, BC V4A 9M5
Tel: 604-538-7227 *Fax:* 604-538-4919
www.reveraliving.com
Number of Beds: 133 suites; 18 beds
Note: Independent living, convalescent & respite options
Sherry Fossum, General Manager

Victoria: Parkwood Court
3000 Shelbourne St., Victoria, BC V8R 4M8
Tel: 250-598-1575 *Fax:* 250-598-7372
parkwoodcourt@lrc.ca
www.reveraliving.com
Number of Beds: 83 suites
Note: Assisted living, respite & convalescent options
Jan Bard, General Manager

Victoria: Parkwood Place
3051 Shelbourne St., Victoria, BC V8R 6T2
Tel: 250-598-1565 *Fax:* 250-598-8222
parkwoodplace@lrc.ca
www.reveraliving.com
Linda Bartel, Director, Marketing

Personal Care Homes

Langley: Evergreen Timbers
Affiliated with: Fraser Health Authority
5464 - 203 St., Langley, BC V3A 0A4
Tel: 604-530-7171 *Fax:* 604-530-7104
www.fraserhealth.ca
Number of Beds: 58 units
Note: Evergreen Timbers is an assisted living residence that is owned & operated by the Langley Lions Senior Citizens Housing Society.

Mental Health Hospitals/Facilities

Terrace: Birchwood Place
Affiliated with: Northern Health Authority
3183 Kofoed Dr., Terrace, BC V8G 3P8
Tel: 250-635-2171 *Fax:* 250-635-7057

Mental Health Facilities

Mental Health Hospitals/Facilities

Burnaby: Craigend Rest Home
5488 Patterson Ave., Burnaby, BC V5H 2M5
Tel: 604-433-8600
Number of Beds: 10 beds
Gardenia Sayo, Manager

Kamloops: Forensic Psychiatric Services Commission (B.C.)
Kamloops Clinic
#5, 1315 Summit Dr., Kamloops, BC V2C 5R9
Tel: 250-377-2660 *Fax:* 250-371-3894
www.bcmhas.ca/ForensicService/ForensicRegionalServices.htm
Rose Dumont, Coordinator

Kamloops: Kamloops Youth Forensic Psychiatric Services
#8, 1315 Summit Dr., Kamloops, BC V2C 5R9
Tel: 250-828-4940 *Fax:* 250-828-4946
Note: for young offenders directed by court/probation to assessment/treatment
Judie Hogg, Regional Office Manager
250/861-7601

Kelowna: White Heather Manor
3728 Casorso Rd., Kelowna, BC V1W 4M8
Tel: 250-763-6554 *Fax:* 250-763-6754
Number of Beds: 24 beds

Maple Ridge: Trejan Lodge Ltd.
25402 Johnson Ave., Maple Ridge, BC V4R 1G3
Tel: 604-467-3377 *Fax:* 604-467-0705
Note: Specialty: Long-term care
Mary Blume, Care Manager

Mission: Waddell's Haven Guest Home
12459 Dewdney Trunk Rd., Mission, BC V2V 5X4
Tel: 604-826-7420
Number of Beds: 30 beds
Betty Baird, Manager

Nanaimo: Forensic Psychiatric Services Commission (B.C.)
Regional
Former Name: Nanaimo Adult Forensic Psychiatric Community Services
#101, 190 Wallace St., Nanaimo, BC V9R 5B1
Tel: 250-739-5000 *Fax:* 250-739-5001
www.bcmhas.ca/ForensicService/ForensicRegionalServices.htm
L Barr, Office Manager

Nanaimo: Nanaimo Youth Forensic Psychiatric Services
#101, 190 Wallace St., Nanaimo, BC V9R 5B1
Tel: 250-741-5733 *Fax:* 250-741-5740
Note: youth forensic psychiatric outpatient clinic
André Picard, Coordinator

Port Coquitlam: Forensic Psychiatric Services Commission (B.C.)
Forensic Psychiatric Hospital
70 Colony Farm Rd., Port Coquitlam, BC V3C 5X9
Tel: 604-524-7700 *Fax:* 604-524-7905
www.bcmhas.ca/ForensicService/ForensicHospital/default.htm
Number of Beds: 190 beds
Note: State-of-the-art facility which provides specialized clinical services & comprehensive rehabilitative & vocational programs.
Leslie Arnold, President, Mental Health

Port Coquitlam: Riverview Hospital
500 Lougheed Hwy., Port Coquitlam, BC V3C 4J2
Tel: 604-524-7000 *Fax:* 604-524-7016
www.bcmhs.bc.ca
Number of Beds: 256 beds
Note: psychiatric teaching hospital
Leslie Arnold, President, Mental Health

Prince George: Forensic Psychiatric Services Commission (B.C.)
Prince George Clinic
1594 - 7 Ave., 2nd Fl., Prince George, BC V2L 3P4
Tel: 250-561-8060 *Fax:* 250-561-8075
www.bcmhas.ca/ForensicService/ForensicRegionalServices.htm
Julia Thompson, Acting Regional Director

Richmond: Westminster House
Affiliated with: Vancouver Coastal Health Authority
11675 Bird Rd., Richmond, BC V6X 1N7
Tel: 604-270-9510 *Fax:* 604-270-3539
Number of Beds: 10 beds
André Chevrier, Director

Victoria: Pacific Operational Trauma & Stress Support Centre (OTSSC)
Canadian Forces Health Services
PO Box 17000 Stn. Forces, Victoria, BC V9A 7N2
Tel: 250-363-4411
Year Founded: 1999
Note: Specialties: Assistance to serving members of the Canadian Forces & their families, who are dealing with psychological, emotional, spiritual, & social problems stemming from military operations, especially deployments abroad; Psychiatry; Psychology; Social work; Community health nursing; Educational programs; Chaplain services

Victoria: Victoria Youth Forensic Psychiatric Services
1515 Quadra St., Victoria, BC V8V 3P3
Tel: 250-387-1465 *Fax:* 250-387-3217
www.mcf.gov.bc.ca/yfps/index.htm
Gregg Badger, Regional Manager

Manitoba

Government Departments in Charge

MANITOBA: Manitoba Health
Regional Affairs Division
300 Carlton St., Winnipeg, MB R3B 3M9
Tel: 204-786-7301 *Fax:* 204-775-3412
www.gov.mb.ca/health/index.html
Donna Forbes, Asst. Deputy Minister, Regional Affairs

Regional Health Authorities

Brandon: Western Regional Health Authority
150A - 7th St., Brandon, MB R7A 7M2
Tel: 204-571-8400 *Toll-Free:* 1-855-260-8250
RHAmergers@gov.mb.ca
www.westernmbrha.ca

Note: Western RHA is an amaigamation of Brandon Regional Health Authority, Assiniboine Regional Health Authority and Parkland Regional Health Aauthority. Services include: public health, home care, long term care, mental health services, comprehensive health services (cancer care, cardiac, birthing & neonatal, rehabilitation, surgery).
Penny Gilson, CEO
Margaret MacDonald, Board Chair

Churchill: Churchill Regional Health Authority
Affiliated with: Winnipeg Regional Health Authority
PO Box 2500, 162 Laverendrye St., Churchill, MB R0B 0E0
Tel: 204-675-8881 *Fax:* 204-675-2243
www.churchillrha.com
Derry Martens, CEO
204-675-8325, dmartens@churchillrha.mb.ca

Flin Flon: Northern Regional Health Authority
Former Name: Nor-Man Regional Health Authority Inc. & Burntwood Regional Health Authority
84 Church St., Flin Flon, MB R8A 1L8
Tel: 204-687-1300 *Fax:* 204-687-6405
www.norman-rha.mb.ca; www.brha.mb.ca

Note: Northern Regional Health Authority is an amaigamation of NOR-MAN Regional Health Authority and Burntwood REgional Health Authority.
Helga Bryant, CEO
Doug Lauvstad, Board Chair

La Broquerie: Southern Regional Health Authority
Former Name: South Eastman Health/Santé Sud-Est Inc., Regional Health Authority Central Manitoba
PO Box 470, La Broquerie, MB R0A 0W0
Tel: 204-424-5880 *Fax:* 204-424-5888
Toll-Free: 866-716-5633
www.sehealth.mb.ca; www.rha-central.mb.ca

Note: Southern RHA is an amaigamation of South Eastman Regional Health Authority and Regional Health Authority Central Manitoba.
Kathy McPhail, CEO
Denise Harder, Board Chair

Pinawa: Interlake-Eastern Regional Health Authority
Former Name: Interlake Regional Health Authority, North Eastman Regional Health Authority
PO Box 339, Pinawa, MB R0E 1L0
Tel: 204-753-2012 *Toll-Free:* 1-877-753-2012
neha@neha.mb.ca
neha.mb.ca

Note: Interlake-Eastern RHA is an amaigamation of Interlake Regional Health Authority and North Eastman Regional Health Authority.
John Stinson, CEO
Diane Kelly, Board Chair

Winnipeg: Winnipeg Regional Health Authority
650 Main St., 4th Fl., Winnipeg, MB R3B 1E2
Tel: 204-926-7000 *Fax:* 204-926-7007
info@wrha.mb.ca
www.wrha.mb.ca
Social Media: www.facebook.com/winnipeghealthregion; twitter.com/wpghealthregion; www.youtube.com/user/WinnipegHealthRegion

Arlene Wilgosh, President; CEO
Dr. John Wade, Board Chair

Hospitals

Hospitals - General

Altona: Altona Community Memorial Health Centre/Eastview Place
Affiliated with: Southern Regional Health Authority
PO Box 660, 240 - 5 Ave. NE, Altona, MB R0G 0B0
Tel: 204-324-6411 *Fax:* 204-324-8482
Number of Beds: 22 acute care, 65 long-term care beds
Edith Calder, Facility Contact
e.calder@ahc.rha-central.mb.ca

Arborg: Arborg & District Health Centre
Affiliated with: Interlake-Eastern Regional Health Authority
PO Box 10, Arborg, MB R0C 0A0
Tel: 204-376-5247 *Fax:* 204-376-5669
www.irha.mb.ca
Number of Beds: 16 beds + 40 long term care beds in an attached personal care home
Note: Specialties: Diagnostic services

Ashern: Lakeshore General Hospital
Affiliated with: Interlake-Eastern Regional Health Authority
PO Box 110, Ashern, MB R0C 0E0
Tel: 204-768-2461 *Fax:* 204-768-2337
Number of Beds: 15 beds
Jan O'Flanagan, District Director

Beausejour: Beausejour District Hospital
Affiliated with: Interlake-Eastern Regional Health Authority
PO Box 1178, Beausejour, MB R0E 0C0
Tel: 204-268-1076 *Fax:* 204-268-1207
www.neha.mb.ca
Number of Beds: 30 acute care beds
Note: Hospital Specialties: Imaging; Physiotherapy; Occupational therapy; Number of Employees: 86
Glennda Gould, Manager, Care Team

Boissevain: Boissevain Health Centre
Affiliated with: Western Regional Health Authority
PO Box 899, 305 Mill Rd., Boissevain, MB R0K 0E0
Tel: 204-534-2451 *Fax:* 204-534-6487
dgraham@arha.ca (Area Manager)
www.assiniboine-rha.ca
Number of Beds: 20 beds
Note: Specialties: Emergency services; Diagnostic services; Acute care; Mental health services; Public health services; Home care; Respite care

Brandon: Brandon Regional Health Centre
Affiliated with: Western Regional Health Authority
150 McTavish Ave. East, Brandon, MB R7A 2B3
Tel: 204-578-4219 *Fax:* 204-578-4969
www.brandonrha.mb.ca
Number of Beds: 336 beds
Note: A regional referral acute care hospital & teaching facility. Services include in- & out-patient care, rehabilitation, diagnositics, & clinics.
Kathy McPhail, Vice-President, Acute Care & Diagnostic Services
K. Martinook, Director, Physical Plant

Carman: Carman Memorial Hospital
Affiliated with: Southern Regional Health Authority
PO Box 610, 350 - 4 St., SW, Carman, MB R0G 0J0
Tel: 204-745-2021 *Fax:* 204-745-2756
www.rha-central.mb.ca
Number of Beds: 25 beds
Note: Hospital Specialties: Surgerey; Acute care; Obstetrics Physiotherapy; Diabetes education; Dietitian service; Palliative care; Number of Employees: 190 at Carman Hospital & the nearby Boyne Lodge personal care home
Mary Heard, Director, Health Services - Carman
m.heard@rha-central.mb.ca

Crystal City: Rock Lake Hospital/Rock Lake Health District
Affiliated with: Southern Regional Health Authority
PO Box 130, 135 Machray Ave., Crystal City, MB R0K 0N0
Tel: 204-873-2132 *Fax:* 204-873-2185
pking@rlh.rha-central.mb.ca
Number of Beds: 16 acute care beds
Pam King, Facility Contact

Dauphin: Dauphin Regional Health Centre (DRHC)
Affiliated with: Western Regional Health Authority
625 - 3rd St. SW, Dauphin, MB R7N 1R7
Tel: 204-638-3010 *Toll-Free:* 1-800-259-7541
Number of Beds: 90 beds
Note: Hospital Specialties: Emergency medical services; Computed Tomography (CT) services; Ultrasound service; Surgical services; Acute care; Obstetrics; Chemotherapy; Hemodialysis; 10 bed acute care psychiatric unit; Manitoba Telehealth site
Kevin McKnight, Chief Executive Officer, Parkland Regional Health Authority
Blaine Kraushaar, Coordinator, Community Relations
204-622-6237, Fax: 204-622-6232, bkraushaar@prha.mb.ca

Deloraine: Deloraine Health Centre
Affiliated with: Western Regional Health Authority
PO Box 447, Deloraine, MB R0M 0M0
Tel: 204-747-2745 *Fax:* 204-747-2160
www.assiniboine-rha.ca

Note: Hospital Specialties: Emergency medical services; Diagnostic services (204-747-2431); Deloraine Community Cancer Program (204-747-1836); Acute care; Mental health services; Public health services; Home care
D. Graham, Area Manager
dgraham@arha.ca

Eriksdale: E.M. Crowe Memorial Hospital
Affiliated with: Interlake-Eastern Regional Health Authority
PO Box 130, 1st St. NE, Eriksdale, MB R0C 0W0
Tel: 204-739-2611 *Fax:* 204-739-2065

Note: Hospital Specialties: Emergency services; X-ray services; Doppler ultrasound carotid artery scans
Jan O'Flanagan, Director, North West District, Interlake Regional Health Auth
Kevin O'Donovan, Manager, Public Relations, Interlake Regional Health Authori

Flin Flon: Flin Flon General Hospital Inc.
Affiliated with: Northern Regional Health Authority
PO Box 340, Flin Flon, MB R8A 1N2
Tel: 204-687-7591 *Fax:* 204-687-8494
www.norman-rha.mb.ca
Number of Beds: 44 acute care beds
Note: Hospital Specialty: Acute care
Lois Moberly, Executive Director, Clinical Services
204-687-9610

Gillam: Gillam Hospital Incorporated
Affiliated with: Northern Regional Health Authority
PO Box 2000, 15 Gillam Dr., Gillam, MB R0B 0L0
Tel: 204-652-2600 *Fax:* 204-652-2536
Number of Beds: 10 beds, including 3 long term beds
Note: Hospital Specialties: Emergency services; Laboratory services; Acute care; Public health; Long term care

Gimli: Gimli Community Health Centre (GCHC)
Affiliated with: Interlake-Eastern Regional Health Authority
Johnson Memorial Hospital, PO Box 250, 120 - 6th Ave., Gimli, MB R0C 1B0
Tel: 204-642-5116 *Fax:* 204-642-5860
info@irha.mb.ca
www.irha.mb.ca

Year Founded: 2004
Number of Beds: 14 acute beds; 4 special care beds; 2 palliative care beds
Note: Specialties: Diagnostic services (204-642-4519); Laboratory services; Acute care; Chemotherapy program (204-642-4520); Physiotherapy; Occupational therapy; Community health (204-642-6051); Adult day program; Palliative care
Dr. Cary Chapnick, Vice-President, Medical Services, Interlake Regional Health Authori
204-642-4524, cchapnick@irha.mb.ca
Lorne Charbonneau, Vice-President, Health Services, Interlake Regional Health Authorit
204-467-4749, lcharbonneau@irha.mb.ca

***Gladstone:* Seven Regions Health Centre**
Affiliated with: Southern Regional Health Authority
PO Box 1000, 24 Mill St., Gladstone, MB R0J 0T0
Tel: 204-385-2968 *Fax:* 204-385-3053
Number of Beds: 14 acute care beds
Dorothy Doell, Facility Contact
d.doell@srhc.rha-central.mb.ca

***Grandview:* Grandview District Hospital**
Affiliated with: Western Regional Health Authority
PO Box 339, 644 Mill St., Grandview, MB R0L 0Y0
Tel: 204-546-2425 *Fax:* 204-546-3269
Number of Beds: 18 beds
John Kelly, COO

***Hodgson:* Percy E. Moore Hospital**
Affiliated with: Interlake-Eastern Regional Health Authority
PO Box 190, Hodgson, MB R0C 1N0
Tel: 204-372-8444 *Fax:* 204-372-6991
Year Founded: 1973
Number of Beds: 16 beds; 4 bassinets
Area Served: RM of Fisher, Peguis, Fisher River, & KinonjeoshtegonPopulation Served: 10,000
Note: The hospital is operated by First Nations & Inuit Health of Health Canada.

***Lynn Lake:* Lynn Lake District Hospital**
Affiliated with: Northern Regional Health Authority
PO Box 2030, 640 Camp St., Lynn Lake, MB R0B 0W0
Tel: 204-356-2474 *Fax:* 204-356-8023
dtitterson@brha.mb.ca
www.thompson.ca/dbs/brha
Number of Beds: 11 general beds, 6 long term care beds, 2 chronic beds
Note: Specialties: Public health services; Mental health services; Medical clinic; Long-term care. Number of employees: 22

***McCreary:* McCreary/Alonsa Health Centre**
Affiliated with: Western Regional Health Authority
PO Box 250, 613 PTH 50, McCreary, MB R0J 1B0
Tel: 204-835-2482 *Fax:* 204-835-2713
Number of Beds: 13 beds
Note: Blood draining services, EKG, palliative care, Telehealth
Charlie Sitwell, Administrator

***Melita:* Melita Health Centre**
Affiliated with: Assiniboine Regional Health Authority
PO Box 459, Melita, MB R0M 1L0
Tel: 204-522-3403 *Fax:* 204-522-3161
koberlin@arha.ca
www.assiniboine-rha.ca
Number of Beds: 11 beds

***Morris:* Morris General Hospital**
Affiliated with: Southern Regional Health Authority
PO Box 519, 215 Railroad Ave. East, Morris, MB R0G 1K0
Tel: 204-746-2301 *Fax:* 204-746-2197
www.rha-central.mb.ca
Number of Beds: 23 acute care beds
Brad Street, Facility Contact
b.street@mgh.rha-central.mb.ca

***Norway House:* Norway House Hospital**
General Delivery, Norway House, MB R0B 1B0
Tel: 204-359-6731 *Fax:* 204-359-6599
www.nhhsinc.ca
Year Founded: 1925
Leonard York, Administrator

***Pinawa:* Pinawa Hospital**
Affiliated with: Interlake-Eastern Regional Health Authority
PO Box 220, 30 Vanier Dr., Pinawa, MB R0E 1L0
Tel: 204-753-2334
Year Founded: 1964
Number of Beds: 17 beds
Note: Specialties: Acute care; Community cancer care program; Physiotherapy; Occupational therapy; Palliative care
May Fast, Care Team Manager

***Pine Falls:* Pine Falls Health Complex**
Affiliated with: Interlake-Eastern Regional Health Authority
PO Box 2000, 37 Maple St., Pine Falls, MB R0E 1M0
Tel: 204-367-4441
www.neha.mb.ca
Number of Beds: 23 inpatient beds + 20 personal care home beds
Note: Specialties: Health & social services; Primary medical care combined with traditional aboriginal approaches to health care; Hemodialysis; Physiotherapy; Occupational therapy; Mental health services; Palliative care
Brenda Neufeld, Director of Acute Care

***Portage la Prairie:* Portage District General Hospital**
Affiliated with: Southern Regional Health Authority
524 - 5 St. SE, Portage la Prairie, MB R1N 3A8
Tel: 204 239-2211 *Fax:* 204-239-1941
Number of Beds: 89 acute care beds
Note: 660 staff
Pat Nodrick, Director, Health Services
p.nodrick@pdgh.rha-central.mb.ca

***Russell:* Russell District Health Centre**
Affiliated with: Western Regional Health Authority
Bag Service 2, Russell, MB R0J 1W0
Tel: 204-773-2125 *Fax:* 204-773-2142
Number of Beds: 32 acute care beds; 40 PCH
Barb Kostesky, Community Health Director

***Selkirk:* Selkirk & District General Hospital**
Affiliated with: Interlake-Eastern Regional Health Authority
PO Box 5000, 100 Easton Dr., Selkirk, MB R1A 2M2
Tel: 204-482-5800 *Fax:* 204-785-9113
www.irha.mb.ca/programs.htm
Year Founded: 1907
Number of Beds: 49 beds
Note: Emergency & outpatient services, acute care, surgery, obstetrics, physiotherapy, diagnostic imaging, chemotherapy, dialysis, palliative care, mental health services
Kevin Beresford, CEO, IRHA
204-467-4742, kberesford@irha.mb.ca
Dianne Mestdagh, Director, South East District, IRHA
204-785-7430, dmestdagh@irha.mb.ca
Edie Telenko, Executive Assistant, Selkirk
204-785-7424, etelenko@irha.mb.ca

***Shoal Lake:* Shoal Lake - Strathclair Health Centre**
Affiliated with: Western Regional Health Authority
PO Box 490, Shoal Lake, MB R0J 1Z0
Tel: 204-759-2336 *Fax:* 204-759-2230
assiniboinerha@arha.ca
www.assiniboine-rha.ca/index.php/health_sites/view?id=36
Number of Beds: 40 personal care home beds
Note: Emergency, acute care, diagnostic services, mental Health Services, home care services, regional palliative care program, regional occupational & physiotherapy services
Roseanne Yaremchuk, Area Manager
ryaremchuk@arha.ca

***St Claude:* St. Claude Health District**
Affiliated with: Southern Regional Health Authority
PO Box 400, 33 Roy St., St Claude, MB R0G 1Z0
Tel: 204-379-2585 *Fax:* 204-379-2655
Number of Beds: 10 beds; 18 long-term care beds
Mona Spencer, Facility Contact

***Ste Anne:* Hôpital Ste Anne Hospital**
Affiliated with: Southern Regional Health Authority
52 St Gerard St., Ste Anne, MB R5H 1C4
Tel: 204-422-8837 *Fax:* 204-422-9929
info@fondshopitalsteanne.ca
www.fondshopitalsteanne.ca
Number of Beds: 21 beds
Carole Lavack, Facility Manager

***Ste Rose du Lac:* Ste Rose General Hospital**
Affiliated with: Western Regional Health Authority
PO Box 60, 480 - 3rd Ave. East, Ste Rose du Lac, MB R0L 1S0
Tel: 204-447-2131 *Fax:* 204-629-3460
Number of Beds: 26 beds
Note: Specialty: Diagnostic services
Glen Kozak, Executive Director

***Steinbach:* Bethesda Hospital / Bethesda Place Complex**
Affiliated with: Southern Regional Health Authority
316 Henry St., Steinbach, MB R5G 0P9
Tel: 204-326-6411
www.sehealth.mb.ca
Number of Beds: 64 acute care beds; 20 rehabilitation beds
Note: Specialties: Emergency services; Diagnostic services; Laboratory services; Acute care; Cardiac care; Cancer care; Obstetrics; Physiotherapy; Occupational therapy; Speech-language pathology services; Social work; Personal care at Bethesda Place; Palliative care; Number of Employees: 471
Patti Fries, Manager, Facility
204-346-5168,
Don Fast, Clinical Manager, Medicine, ER, & CancerCare
Debbie Harms, Clinical Manager, Surgery, Obstetrics, Rehabilitation, & Therapy
Ginette Morgan, Clinical Manager, Long Term Care (Bethesda Place)
Wally Driedger, Manager, Physical Plant
Marie Lacey, Manager, Nutrition & Food Services
Pam Beaudoin, Coordinator, Recreation
Ruth Campbell, Coordinator, Human Resources

***Swan Lake:* Lorne Memorial Hospital**
Affiliated with: Southern Regional Health Authority
9 - 2nd St. North, Swan Lake, MB R0G 2S0
Tel: 204-836-2132 *Fax:* 204-836-2044
Number of Beds: 18 acute care beds
Note: Hospital Specialties: Imaging health unit; Advanced palliative care program. Number of Employees: 60
Kristal McKitrick-Bazin, Facility Contact
k.mckitrick-bazin@lmh.rha-central.mb

***Swan River:* Swan Valley Health Centre**
Affiliated with: Western Regional Health Authority
PO Box 448, 1011 Main St., Swan River, MB R0L 1Z0
Tel: 204-734-3441 *Fax:* 204-629-3484
Year Founded: 2005
Number of Beds: 52 acute-care beds
Note: Services include acute care, ambulatory care, audiology, chemotherapy, diabetes education, diagnostics, dialysis, emergency service, mental health, physiotherapy, occupational therapy, speech language pathology, surgery.
Allan Bradley, CEO, PRHA
Blaine Kraushaar, Coordinator, Community Relations, PRHA
204-622-6237, Fax: 204-622-6232, bkraushaar@prha.mb.ca
Neoma Stiegler, Clinical Services Manager
204-734-6664, nstiegler@prha.mb.ca

***Teulon:* Teulon Hunter Memorial Hospital**
Affiliated with: Interlake-Eastern Regional Health Authority
PO Box 89, 3rd Ave. SE, Teulon, MB R0C 3B0
Tel: 204-886-2433 *Fax:* 204-886-2653
info@irha.mb.ca
www.irha.mb.ca
Number of Beds: 20 beds
Note: Services include emergency, ambulatory care, acute care, diagnostic imaging, laboratory, pharmacy, surgery, physiotherapy, dietary services, occupational therapy, opthamology.
Kevin Beresford, CEO, IRHA
204-467-4742, kberesford@irha.mb.ca
Shannon Montgomery, South West District Director, IRHA
smontgomery@irha.mb.ca
Kevin O'Donovan, Public Relations Manager, IRHA
204-467-4747, kodonovan@irha.mb.ca
Dr. Abdalla Rizk, Site Chief of Staff

***The Pas:* The Pas Health Complex Inc.**
Affiliated with: Northern Regional Health Authority
Former Name: St. Anthony's General Hospital
PO Box 240, 67 - 1st St. West, The Pas, MB R9A 1K4
Tel: 204-623-6431 *Fax:* 204-623-9263
Year Founded: 1969
Number of Beds: 118 beds
Note: Specialties: Acute care; Ambulatory clinic program; Dialysis; Physiotherapy; Occupational therapy; Social services; Chronic care; Long-term care
Drew Lockhart, CEO

***Thompson:* Thompson General Hospital**
Affiliated with: Northern Regional Health Authority
871 Thompson Dr. South, Thompson, MB R8N 0C8
Tel: 204-677-2381 *Fax:* 204-778-1413
brha@brha.mb.ca
www.brha.mb.ca
Number of Beds: 74 beds
Note: A community facility with services including emergency, aboriginal interpretive services, cancer care, diagnostics, dialysis, obstetrics, palliative care, psychiatric acute care unit, rehabilitation, respiratory therapy, spiritual care, surgery
Gloria King, CEO, BRHA
204-677-5399, gking@brha.mb.ca
Dr. Hussam Azzam, Vice-President, Medical Services, BRHA
204-677-5376, hazzam@brha.mb.ca
Dr. Hisham Tassi, Site Head, Medical Services
204-677-5314, htassi@brha.mb.ca

***Winkler:* Boundary Trails Health Centre**
Affiliated with: Southern Regional Health Authority
PO Box 2000 Stn. Main, Winkler, MB R6W 1H8
Tel: 204-331-8800 *Fax:* 204-331-8801
www.rha-central.mb.ca
Number of Beds: 40 medical beds; 25 rehabilitation beds; 18 surgical services beds; 7 obstetrics / birthing beds; 4 intensive

care unit beds
Note: Hospital specialties: Emergency services; Diagnostics, Laboratory services; Surgery; Intensive care; Acute care; Chemotherapy; Dialysis; Physiotherapy; Occupational therapy; Audiology; Mental health services; Public health; Home care
Number of Employees: 450
Linda Buhr, Director, Health Services
l.buhr@rha-central.mb.ca
Kristy Radke, Director, Support Services
k.radke@rha-central.mb.ca

***Winnipeg:* Concordia Hospital**
Affiliated with: Winnipeg Regional Health Authority
1095 Concordia Ave., Winnipeg, MB R2K 3S8
Tel: 204-667-1560 *Fax:* 204-667-1049
www.concordiahospital.mb.ca
Note: Hospital Specialties: Emergency services; Diagnostic imaging; Laboratory services (204-661-7174); Surgery (a major centre for hip and knee replacements); Intensive care; A.M.I. (Acute Myocardial Infarct) Program; Occupational therapy (204-661-7216); Physiotherapy (204-661-7354); Respiratory therapy (204-661-7346); Oncology haematology service; Social work (204-661-7185); Cardiac Teaching Program (nurse home visit); Lifeline personal response & support services
Henry Tessman, President; Chief Operating Officer

***Winnipeg:* Health Sciences Centre**
Affiliated with: Winnipeg Regional Health Authority
820 Sherbrook St., Winnipeg, MB R3A 1R9
Tel: 204-774-6511 *Fax:* 204-787-3912
www.hsc.mb.ca
Number of Beds: 850 beds
Note: teaching hospital
Adam Topp, COO
Dana Erickson, Vice-President; CAO
Dr. Perry Gray, Vice-President; Chief Medical Officer

***Winnipeg:* Riverview Health Centre**
Affiliated with: Winnipeg Regional Health Authority
1 Morley Ave. East, Winnipeg, MB R3L 2P4
Tel: 204-478-6203 *Fax:* 204-478-6212
rhcinfo@rhc.mb.ca
www.riverviewhealthcentre.com
Number of Beds: 388 beds
Note: Long-term care, catering to the needs of the elderly and rehabilitation patients
Norman R. Kasian, President/CEO
Sheldon Mindell, Development Officer
smindell@rhc.mb.ca

***Winnipeg:* St. Boniface General Hospital**
Affiliated with: Winnipeg Regional Health Authority
409 Taché Ave., Winnipeg, MB R2H 2A6
Tel: 204-233-8563 *Fax:* 204-231-0640
sbghweb@sbgh.mb.ca
www.sbgh.mb.ca
Year Founded: 1871
Number of Beds: 524 beds
Note: Catholic tertiary care facility & teaching hospital affiliated with the University of Manitoba & dedicated to the values of care of the Sisters of Charity of Montreal (Grey Nuns). Emergency services, family medicine, mental health, geriatrics & rehabilitation, surgery, women's health, paediatrics. Number of staff, including support & healthcare staff: 4,000+
Dr. Michel Tétreault, President/CEO

***Winnipeg:* The Salvation Army Grace General Hospital**
Affiliated with: Winnipeg Regional Health Authority
300 Booth Dr., Winnipeg, MB R3J 3M7
Tel: 204-837-0111
pr@ggh.mb.ca
www.gracehospital.ca
Year Founded: 1904
Number of Beds: 270 beds
Note: Specialties: Emergency & critical care programs; Surgery program; Mental health services; Hospice care
Maj. John McFarlane, President; CEO
204-837-0143
Scott Wichenko, Director, Materials Management
Art Isaak, Director, Housekeeping

***Winnipeg:* Seven Oaks General Hospital**
Affiliated with: Winnipeg Regional Health Authority
2300 McPhillips St., Winnipeg, MB R2V 3M3
Tel: 204-632-7133 *Fax:* 204-697-2106
www.sogh.ca
Social Media: www.facebook.com/SevenOaksGeneralHospital; twitter.com/sevenoakswpg
Year Founded: 1981
Number of Beds: 298 beds
Note: Comprehensive health services, including emergency, surgery, rehabilitation/geriatric/mental health services, intensive care, dialysis, pulmonary rehabilitation program, hearing centre, dental services
Carrie Solmundson, President; COO
Dr. Ricardo Lobato de Faria, Chief Medical Officer
Tim Walker, Board Chair

***Winnipeg:* Victoria General Hospital**
Affiliated with: Winnipeg Regional Health Authority
2340 Pembina Hwy., Winnipeg, MB R3T 2E8
Tel: 204-269-3570 *Fax:* 204-261-0223
info@vgh.mb.ca
www.vgh.mb.ca
Number of Beds: 231 beds
Note: Comprehensive health care. Number of staff: 1,200
Ray J. Racette, President; CEO

***Winnipegosis:* Winnipegosis Health Centre**
Affiliated with: Western Regional Health Authority
Former Name: Winnipegosis General Hospital
PO Box 280, 230 Bridge St., Winnipegosis, MB R0L 2G0
Tel: 204-656-4881 *Fax:* 204-629-3489
Number of Beds: 15 acute care beds
Glen Kozak, COO

Community Health Centres

Community Health Care Centres

***Baldur:* Baldur Health Centre/Baldur Health District**
Affiliated with: Western Regional Health Authority
PO Box 128, Baldur, MB R0K 0B0
Tel: 204-535-2373 *Fax:* 204-535-2116
www.assiniboine-rha.ca
Number of Beds: 14 beds
Bev Towler

***Benito:* Benito Primary Health Centre**
Affiliated with: Western Regional Health Authority
PO Box 490, 200 - 1st St. East, Benito, MB R0L 0C0
Tel: 204-539-2815 *Fax:* 204-539-2482
www.prha.mb.ca
Note: Specialties: Community health; Mental health services

***Birtle:* Birtle Health Centre**
Affiliated with: Western Regional Health Authority
PO Box 2000, Birtle, MB R0M 0C0
Tel: 204-842-3317 *Fax:* 204-842-3375
www.assiniboine-rha.ca
Number of Beds: 14 acute care, 20 long-term care beds
Roseanne Yaremchuk, Area Manager

***Brandon:* 7th Street Health Access Centre**
Affiliated with: Western Regional Health Authority
20 - 7th St., Brandon, MB R7A 6M8
Tel: 204-578-4800 *Fax:* 204-578-4950
www.brandonrha.mb.ca
Note: Community Health Nurse; Adult Community Mental Health Worker; Community Social Worker; Addictions Services; Housing Resource Worker; Cultural Facilitators; Supports to Services in Group Living; Supports to Seniors living at Home; Mental Health Peer Support Educator; Community Volunteer Income Tax Program; YWCA Family Violence Outreach Program.
Vicky Legassie, Program Manager

***Carberry:* Carberry Plains District Health Centre**
Affiliated with: Western Regional Health Authority
Bag Service #1, 1st Ave., Carberry, MB R0K 0H0
Tel: 204-834-2144 *Fax:* 204-834-3333
Number of Beds: 10 acute care, 36 PCH beds
Deb Obach, Director

***Cartwright:* Davidson Memorial Health Centre**
Affiliated with: Western Regional Health Authority
Former Name: Cartwright & District Hospital
PO Box 118, Cartwright, MB R0K 0L0
Tel: 204-529-2483 *Fax:* 204-529-2562
www.assiniboine-rha.ca
Number of Beds: 10 beds
Bev Towler

***Churchill:* Churchill Health Centre**
Affiliated with: Winnipeg Regional Health Authority
General Delivery, Churchill, MB R0B 0E0
Tel: 204-675-8318 *Fax:* 204-675-2243
www.churchillrha.com
Note: Specialties: Primary care; Public health services
Derry Martens, Chief Executive Officer, Churchill Regional Health Authority Inc.

***Emerson:* Emerson Hospital/Personal Care Home**
Affiliated with: Southern Regional Health Authority
Former Name: Emerson Hospital/Personal Care Home
PO Box 428, 26 Main St., Emerson, MB R0A 0L0
Tel: 204-373-2109 *Fax:* 204-373-2748
Number of Beds: 4 acute care, 20 long-term care beds
Paul Enns, Director of Health Services
penns@rha-central.mb.ca

***Erickson:* Erickson Health Centre**
Affiliated with: Western Regional Health Authority
PO Box 250, Erickson, MB R0J 0P0
Tel: 204-636-7777 *Fax:* 204-636-2471
www.assiniboine-rha.ca
Number of Beds: 9 acute care, 16 PCH beds
Judith McDowell, Community Health Director

***Glenboro:* Glenboro Health District Hospital**
Affiliated with: Western Regional Health Authority
PO Box 310, Glenboro, MB R0K 0X0
Tel: 204-827-2438 *Fax:* 204-827-2199
www.assiniboine-rha.ca
Number of Beds: 20 personal care beds
Note: acute care, personal home care
Marilyn McGregor, Manager

***Hamiota:* Hamiota District Health Centre**
Affiliated with: Western Regional Health Authority
177 Birch Ave., Hamiota, MB R0M 0T0
Tel: 204-764-2412 *Fax:* 204-764-2049
www.assiniboine-rha.ca
Number of Beds: 30 personal care home beds
Greg Paddock, Area Manager

***Hartney:* Hartney Medical Nursing Unit**
Affiliated with: Western Regional Health Authority
PO Box 28, Hartney, MB R0M 0X0
Tel: 204-858-2054 *Fax:* 204-858-2303
Number of Beds: 9 beds
Shirley Kloon, Manager

***Killarney:* Tri-Lake Health Centre**
Affiliated with: Assiniboine Regional Health Authority
PO Box 5000, Killarney, MB R0K 1G0
Tel: 204-523-4661 *Fax:* 204-523-8948
dobach@arha.ca
www.assiniboine-rha.ca

***Lac du Bonnet:* Lac du Bonnet District Health Centre**
Affiliated with: Interlake-Eastern Regional Health Authority
PO Box 1030, Lac du Bonnet, MB R0E 1A0
Tel: 204-345-1219 *Fax:* 204-268-8609
Mary Power, Home Care Manager

***Leaf Rapids:* Leaf Rapids Health Centre**
Affiliated with: Northern Regional Health Authority
PO Box 370, Leaf Rapids, MB R0B 1W0
Tel: 204-473-2441 *Fax:* 204-473-8273
cvieira@brha.mb.ca
Number of Beds: 8 beds
Bernette Alexander, Manager, Leaf Rapids Health Program

***MacGregor:* MacGregor Health Centre**
Affiliated with: Southern Regional Health Authority
PO Box 250, 87 Grafton St. South, MacGregor, MB R0H 0R0
Tel: 204-685-2850 *Fax:* 204-685-2529
Number of Beds: 6 beds
Note: Specialties: Respite care; convalescent care; Palliative services; Number of Employees: 52
Sharon Stewart, Facility Contact

***Manitou:* Pembina-Manitou Health Centre**
Affiliated with: Southern Regional Health Authority
PO Box 129, 232 Carrie St., Manitou, MB R0G 1G0
Tel: 204-242-2744 *Fax:* 204-242-3062
Number of Beds: 8 acute care, 18 long-term care beds
Linda Pearce, Facility Contact

***Minnedosa:* Minnedosa Health Centre**
Affiliated with: Western Regional Health Authority
PO Box 960, Minnedosa, MB R0J 1E0
Tel: 204-867-2701 *Fax:* 204-867-2239
Number of Beds: 27 acute care
Judith McDowell

***Neepawa:* Neepawa District Memorial Hospital**
Affiliated with: Western Regional Health Authority
PO Box 1240, Neepawa, MB R0J 1H0
Tel: 204-476-2394 *Fax:* 204-476-5007
Number of Beds: 38 beds

K.D. Braden, Community Health Director

***Notre Dame de Lourdes:* Notre Dame Medical Nursing Inc.**
Affiliated with: Southern Regional Health Authority
PO Box 190, Notre Dame de Lourdes, MB R0G 1M0
Tel: 204-248-2112 *Fax:* 204-248-2499

Note: Specialty: Acute care
Cheryl Harrison, Facility Contact
c.harrison@fnd.rha-central.mb.ca

***Rivers:* Riverdale Health Centre/Riverdale Health Services District**
Affiliated with: Western Regional Health Authority
PO Box 428, 512 Quebec St., Rivers, MB R0K 1X0
Tel: 204-328-5321 *Fax:* 204-328-7130
Number of Beds: 14 acute care, 20 PCH beds, 12 Elderly Persons Housing units
Greg Paddock, Community Health Director

***Roblin:* Roblin Health Centre**
Affiliated with: Western Regional Health Authority
PO Box 940, 15 Hospital St., Roblin, MB R0L 1P0
Tel: 204-937-2142 *Fax:* 204-629-3453
Number of Beds: 25 bed hospital, 60 bed personal care home
Number of Employees: 125
Note: Emergency & diagnostic services, podiatry, speech therapy, physiotherapy, dietician.
Cheryl Jerome, COO

***Rossburn:* Rossburn District Health Centre**
Affiliated with: Western Regional Health Authority
PO Box 40, Rossburn, MB R0J 1V0
Tel: 204-859-2413 *Fax:* 204-859-2526
Number of Beds: 10 acute care, 20 long-term care beds
Barb Kostesky, Area Manager

***Shoal Lake:* Shoal Lake-Strathclair Health Centre**
Affiliated with: Western Regional Health Authority
PO Box 490, Shoal Lake, MB R0J 1Z0
Tel: 204-759-2336 *Fax:* 204-759-2480
ryaremchuk@arha.ca
www.assiniboine-rha.ca
Number of Beds: 12 acute care, 40 long-term care beds

***Snow Lake:* Snow Lake Health Centre**
Affiliated with: Northern Regional Health Authority
PO Box 453, Snow Lake, MB R0B 1M0
Tel: 204-358-2287 *Fax:* 204-358-7310
Number of Beds: 6 beds
Mae de Graff, Site Administrator

***Souris:* Souris Health District**
Affiliated with: Deloraine Health Centre
PO Box 10, Souris, MB R0K 2C0
Tel: 204-483-2121 *Fax:* 204-483-2310
Number of Beds: 30 beds
Shirley Kloon, Manager

***St Pierre Jolys:* Centre Medico-Social De Salaberry District Health Centre**
Affiliated with: Southern Regional Health Authority
454 Prefontaine Ave., St Pierre Jolys, MB R0A 1V0
Tel: 204-433-7611 *Fax:* 204-433-7455
Number of Beds: 14 hospital beds, 22 personal care home beds
Note: acute care & emergency with personal care home

***Stonewall:* Stonewall & District Health Centre**
Affiliated with: Interlake-Eastern Regional Health Authority
589 - 3rd Ave. South, Stonewall, MB R0C 2Z0
Tel: 204-467-5514
Number of Beds: 15 beds
Note: Specialties: Clinic services; Community health services; Emergency outpatient services
Keith Bytheway, District Services

***Thompson:* Burntwood Community Health Resource Centre**
Affiliated with: Northern Regional Health Authority
50 Selkirk Avenue, Thompson, MB R8N 0M7
Tel: 204-677-1777 *Fax:* 204-677-1755
smacdonald@brha.mb.ca
Shane MacDonald, Manager
204-677-1796, smacdonald@brha.mb.ca

***Treherne:* Tiger Hills Health District**
Affiliated with: Western Regional Health Authority
PO Box 130, Treherne, MB R0G 2V0
Tel: 204-723-2133 *Fax:* 204-723-2869
Number of Beds: 13 acute beds; 20 pch
Deb Obach, Area Manager

***Virden:* Virdin Health Centre**
Affiliated with: Western Regional Health Authority
PO Box 400, Virden, MB R0M 2C0
Tel: 204-748-1230 *Fax:* 204-748-2053
mcarson@arha.ca
Number of Beds: 25 acute; 100 long-term care
Meegan Carson, Manager

***Vita:* Vita & District Health Centre Inc.**
Affiliated with: Southern Regional Health Authority
217 First Ave. West, Vita, MB R0A 2K0
Tel: 204-425-7763 *Fax:* 204-425-3545
Number of Beds: 10 acute care, 44 long-term care beds
Note: with personal care home
Shawny Elyk Prevost, Facility Manager

***Wawanesa:* Wawanesa & District Memorial Health Centre**
Affiliated with: Western Regional Health Authority
PO Box 309, Wawanesa, MB R0K 2G0
Tel: 204-824-2335 *Fax:* 204-824-2148
Number of Beds: 6 acute beds; 20 pch
Deb Obach, Manager

***Whitemouth:* Whitemouth District Health Centre**
Affiliated with: Interlake-Eastern Regional Health Authority
PO Box 160, Whitemouth, MB R0E 2G0
Tel: 204-348-7191 *Fax:* 204-348-7911
www.neha.mb.ca
Number of Beds: 24 beds, 1 palliative, 1 respite
Heather Frederick, Care Team Manager

***Winnipeg:* Aboriginal Health & Wellness Centre**
Affiliated with: Winnipeg Regional Health Authority
#214-215, 181 Higgins Ave., Winnipeg, MB R3B 3G1
Tel: 204-925-3700 *Fax:* 204-925-3709
www.abcentre.org
Darlene Hall, Executive Director

***Winnipeg:* Centre de santé Saint-Boniface**
#D-1048, 409, av Taché, Winnipeg, MB R2H 2A6
Tel: 204-235-3910 *Fax:* 204-237-9057
access@centredesante.mb.ca
www.centredesante.mb.ca
Note: community health care office
Micheline St-Hilaire, Acting Executive Director

***Winnipeg:* Health Action Centre - Health Sciences Centre**
Affiliated with: Winnipeg Regional Health Authority
425 Elgin Ave., Winnipeg, MB R3A 1P2
Tel: 204-940-1626 *Fax:* 204-942-7828
Note: community health care centre

***Winnipeg:* Hope Centre Health Care Inc.**
Affiliated with: Winnipeg Regional Health Authority
1644 Dublin Ave., Winnipeg, MB R3H 0X5
Tel: 204-982-4673 *Fax:* 204-953-3510
admin@hopecentreinc.org
www.hopecentreinc.org
Jeannette DeLong, Executive Director
jdelong@hopecentreinc.org

***Winnipeg:* Klinic Community Health Centre**
Affiliated with: Winnipeg Regional Health Authority
870 Portage Ave., Winnipeg, MB R3G 0P1
Tel: 204-784-4090 *Fax:* 204-772-7998
klinic@klinic.mb.ca
www.klinic.mb.ca
Note: community health centre & mental health facility
Lori Johnson, Executive Director

***Winnipeg:* MFL Occupational Health Centre, Inc.**
Affiliated with: Winnipeg Regional Health Authority
#102, 275 Broadway, Winnipeg, MB R3C 4M6
Tel: 204-949-0811 *Fax:* 204-956-0848
Toll-Free: 888-843-1229 (i
mflohc@mflohc.mb.ca
www.mflohc.mb.ca
Year Founded: 1983
Note: Specialties: Occupational health (health issues related to work experiences); Improvement of workplace health & safety conditions & elimination of hazards
Carol Loveridge, Executive Director

***Winnipeg:* Misericordia Health Centre**
Affiliated with: Winnipeg Regional Health Authority
99 Cornish Ave., Winnipeg, MB R3C 1A2
Tel: 204-774-6581 *Fax:* 204-783-6052
info@misericordia.mb.ca
www.misericordia.mb.ca
Number of Beds: 250
Note: nursing home, outpatient services
Rosie Jacuzzi, President; CEO

***Winnipeg:* Mount Carmel Clinic**
Affiliated with: Winnipeg Regional Health Authority
886 Main St., Winnipeg, MB R2W 5L4
Tel: 204-582-2311 *Fax:* 204-582-1341
www.mountcarmel.ca
Brenda Slobozian, Executive Director

***Winnipeg:* Nine Circles Community Health Centre**
Affiliated with: Winnipeg Regional Health Authority
705 Broadway, Winnipeg, MB R3G 0X2
Tel: 204-940-6000 *Fax:* 204-940-6003
Toll-Free: 888-305-8647
ninecircles@ninecircles.ca
www.ninecircles.ca
Social Media: www.facebook.com/NineCirclesCommunityHealthCentre; twitter.com/ninecircleschc
Note: Non-profit centre specializing in STI/HIV prevention and care services
John C. Stinson, Executive Director

***Winnipeg:* Nor'west Cooperative Health & Social Service Centre Inc.**
Affiliated with: Winnipeg Regional Health Authority
#103, 61 Tyndall Ave., Winnipeg, MB R2X 2T4
Tel: 204-633-5955 *Fax:* 204-633-4666
Nancy Henrichs, Executive Director

***Winnipeg:* Women's Health Clinic Inc.**
Affiliated with: Winnipeg Regional Health Authority
419 Graham Ave., Unit A, Winnipeg, MB R3C 0M3
Tel: 204-947-1517 *Fax:* 204-943-3844
Toll-Free: 866-947-1517
TTY: 204-956-0385
www.womenshealthclinic.org
Year Founded: 1981
Jennifer Howard, Executive Director
Carolyn Clarke, Nurse Practioner

***Winnipeg:* Youville Centre - Community Health Resource Centre**
33 Marion St., Winnipeg, MB R2H 0S8
Tel: 204-233-0262 *Fax:* 204-233-1520
www.youville.ca
Sylvia Oosterveen, Executive Director

Nursing Stations

***Bloodvein:* Bloodvein Nursing Station**
General Delivery, Bloodvein, MB R0C 0J0
Tel: 204-395-2161 *Fax:* 204-395-2087

***Brochet:* Brochet Nursing Station**
General Delivery, Brochet, MB R0B 0B0
Tel: 204-323-2120 *Fax:* 204-323-2650

***Cross Lake:* Cross Lake Nursing Station**
General Delivery, Cross Lake, MB R0B 0J0
Tel: 204-676-2011 *Fax:* 204-676-3179

***Easterville:* Easterville Nursing Station**
PO Box 122, Easterville, MB R0C 0V0
Tel: 204-329-2212 *Fax:* 204-329-2337
Ethel McKay, Community Health Representative

***God's Narrows:* God's Lake Narrows Nursing Station**
4321, God's Narrows, MB R0B 0M0
Tel: 204-335-2557

***Gods River:* God's River Health Station**
General Delivery, Gods River, MB R0B 0N0
Tel: 204-366-2355 *Fax:* 204-366-2474

***Grand Rapids:* Grand Rapids Nursing Station**
PO Box 53, Grand Rapids, MB R0C 1E0
Tel: 204-639-2215 *Fax:* 204-639-2448

***Ilford:* Ilford Nursing Station**
General Delivery, Ilford, MB R0B 0S0
Tel: 204-288-4348 *Fax:* 204-288-4360

***Island Lake:* Garden Hill Nursing Station**
General Delivery, Island Lake, MB R0B 0T0
Tel: 204-456-2343 *Fax:* 204-456-2866

***Lac Brochet:* Lac Brochet Nursing Station**
General Delivery, Lac Brochet, MB R0B 2E0
Tel: 204-337-2161 *Fax:* 204-337-2143

***Little Grand Rapids:* Little Grand Rapids Nursing Station**
General Delivery, Little Grand Rapids, MB R0B 0V0
Tel: 204-397-2115 *Fax:* 204-397-2016

Note: Number of Employees: 1 community health worker

***Little Grand Rapids:* Pauingassi Nursing Station**
PO Box 32, Little Grand Rapids, MB R0B 2G0
Tel: 204-397-2395 *Fax:* 204-397-2104

***Moose Lake:* Moose Lake Nursing Station**
General Delivery, Moose Lake, MB R0B 0Y0
Tel: 204-678-2252 *Fax:* 204-678-2343

***Negginan:* Poplar River Nursing Station**
General Delivery, Negginan, MB R0B 0Z0
Tel: 204-244-2102 *Fax:* 204-244-2001

***Oxford House:* Oxford House Nursing Station**
Affiliated with: Northern Regional Health Authority
General Delivery, Oxford House, MB R0B 1C0
Tel: 204-538-2347 *Fax:* 204-538-2445

Note: Specialties: Acute care; Public health programs. Number of Employees: 5 nurses + an administrative clerk + a maintenance person
Helen Weenusk, Secretary

***Pikwitonei:* Pikwitonei Health Centre**
Affiliated with: Northern Regional Health Authority
General Delivery, Pikwitonei, MB R0B 1E0
Tel: 204-288-4348 *Fax:* 204-458-2468
www.thompson.ca/dbs/brha
Marion Ellis, Director

***Pukatawagan:* Pukatawagan Nursing Station**
Also Known As: Nikawiy Nursing Station
General Delivery, Pukatawagan, MB R0B 1G0
Tel: 204-553-2271 *Fax:* 204-553-2402

Note: Serving the Mathias Colomb Cree Nation

***Red Sucker Lake:* Red Sucker Lake Nursing Station**
General Delivery, Red Sucker Lake, MB R0B 1H0
Tel: 204-469-5351 *Fax:* 204-469-5769

Note: Number of staff: 2 nurses, visiting physician, dentist, optometrist, pediatrician, & psychologist

***Shamattawa:* Shamattawa Nursing Station**
General Delivery, Shamattawa, MB R0B 1K0
Tel: 204-565-2370 *Fax:* 204-565-2519

***South Indian Lake:* South Indian Lake Nursing Station**
138730, South Indian Lake, MB R0B 1N0
Tel: 204-374-2013 *Fax:* 204-374-2039
Micheline Morine, Contact
613-946-5534

***Split Lake:* Split Lake Nursing Station**
General Delivery, Split Lake, MB R0B 1P0
Tel: 204-342-2033 *Fax:* 204-342-2319

***St Theresa Point:* St Theresa Point Nursing Station**
PO Box 410, St Theresa Point, MB R0B 1J0
Tel: 204-462-2264 *Fax:* 204-462-2642
Richard Hopper, Clerk

***Thicket Portage:* Thicket Portage Health Centre**
PO Box 39, Thicket Portage, MB R0B 0L0
Tel: 204-286-3254 *Fax:* 204-286-3216
www.thompson.ca/dbs/brha
Marion Ellis, Director

***Wabowden:* Wabowden Health Centre**
PO Box 160, General Delivery, Wabowden, MB R0B 1S0
Tel: 204-689-2600 *Fax:* 204-689-2180
Marion Ellis, Director

***Wasagamack Bay:* Wasagamack Nursing Station**
General Delivery, Wasagamack Bay, MB R0B 1Z0
Tel: 204-457-2024 *Fax:* 204-457-2348

***York Landing:* York Landing Nursing Station**
General Delivery, York Landing, MB R0B 2B0
Tel: 204-341-2325 *Fax:* 204-341-2179

Special Treatment Centres

***Brandon:* Westman Crisis Centre**
Affiliated with: Western Regional Health Authority
Town Centre, B13 - 800 Rosser Avenue, Brandon, MB R7A 6N5
Tel: 204-725-4411 *Toll-Free:* 888-379-7699
Number of Beds: 8 beds
Allison Done, Program Manager

***Reston:* Reston District Health Centre**
Affiliated with: Western Regional Health Authority
PO Box 250, Reston, MB R0M 1X0
Tel: 204-877-3925 *Fax:* 204-877-3998
Number of Beds: 13 beds
Meegan Carson

***Winnipeg:* CancerCare Manitoba**
Affiliated with: Winnipeg Regional Health Authority
675 McDermot Ave., Winnipeg, MB R3E 0V9
Tel: 204-787-2197 *Fax:* 204-787-1184
Toll-Free: 866-561-1026
www.cancercare.mb.ca

Note: cancer treatment, ambulatory care only
Dr. Dhali Dhaliwal, President; CEO
204-787-2241
Vivian Painter, Director of Nursing
204-787-4155

***Winnipeg:* Jane's Clinic**
883 Corydon Ave., Winnipeg, MB R3M 0W7
Tel: 204-477-1887 *Fax:* 204-447-1888

Note: abortion clinic

***Winnipeg:* New Directions for Children, Youth, Adults & Families**
Former Name: Children's Home of Winnipeg
#400, 491 Portage Ave., Winnipeg, MB R3B 2E4
Tel: 204-786-7051 *Fax:* 204-774-6468
TTY: 204-774-8541
www.newdirections.mb.ca

Note: 19 programs: residential, day & family support services
Dr. Elizabeth Adkins, Executive Director

***Winnipeg:* Reh-Fit Centre**
Former Name: Manitoba Cardiac Institute
1390 Taylor Ave., Winnipeg, MB R3M 3V8
Tel: 204-488-8023 *Fax:* 204-488-4819
reh-fit@reh-fit.com
www.reh-fit.com
Social Media: www.facebook.com/RehFit; twitter.com/RehFit
Year Founded: 1979
Note: Rehabilitation centre
Albert Krahn, Chair
Sue Boreskie, CEO
204-488-5850, sue.boreskie@reh-fit.com
Patrick Harrington, Director, Finance & Operations
204-488-5858, patrick.harrington@reh-fit.com
Janet Cranston, Director, Support Services
204-488-5855, janet.cranston@reh-fit.com
Dean Luchik, Director, Health & Fitness
204-488-5856, dean.luchik@reh-fit.com

Long Term/Retirement Care

Long Term Care Facilities

***Arborg:* Riverdale Place Homes Inc.**
PO Box 968, Arborg, MB R0C 0A0
Tel: 204-376-2940 *Fax:* 204-376-5051
riverdale@mts.net
Number of Beds: 19 beds
Note: Provides residential services to adults with intellectual disabilities.
K. Finnson, Executive Director

***St-Malo:* Chalet Malouin**
PO Box 1010, 14 St. Hilaire St., St-Malo, MB R0A 1T0
Tel: 204-347-5753 *Fax:* 204-347-5107
chaletmalouin@mts.net
Number of Beds: 47 independent living apartments; 38 assisted living / supportive housing suites
Note: Chalet Malouin is a bilingual housing complex for seniors.
Louise Maynard, Administrator

***Swan River:* Association for Community Living - Swan River**
PO Box 1282, Swan River, MB R0L 1Z0
Tel: 204-734-9114 *Fax:* 204-734-3704
Number of Beds: 17 beds
G. Mitchell, Services Coordinator

***Winnipeg:* L'Arche Winnipeg Inc.**
118 Regent Ave. East., Winnipeg, MB R2C 0C1
Tel: 204-237-0300 *Fax:* 204-237-0316
office@larchewinnipeg.org
www.larchewinnipeg.org
Number of Beds: 28 beds
Note: group homes for persons with a developmental disability
Dennis Butcher, Executive Director

***Winnipeg:* Deer Lodge Centre**
Affiliated with: Winnipeg Regional Health Authority
2109 Portage Ave., Winnipeg, MB R3J 0L3
Tel: 204-837-1301
info@deerlodge.mb.ca
(www.deerlodge.mb.ca
Number of Beds: 487 beds, including 155 personal care beds for veterans
Note: Specialties: Rehabilitation services, including physiotherapy, occupational therapy, respiratory therapy, & therapeutic recreation services; Speech-language pathology; Services for ALS patients; Peritoneal dialysis; Operational Stress Injuries Clinic; Movement Disorders Clinic; Audiological services; Assistive technology products & services; Outreach programs in geriatric mental health; Social work; Day hospital & adult day care for cognitively impaired clients; Long term care; Geriatric research
Réal Cloutier, Chief Operating Officer; Winnipeg Regional Health, Long Term Care
204-831-2110, rcloutier@deerlodge.mb.ca
Ed Courcelles, Chief Financial Officer,
ecourcelles@deerlodge.mb.ca
204-831-2116
Jo-Ann LaPointe-McKenzie, Chief Nursing Officer
204-831-2529, JlapointeMcKenzie@deerlodge.mb.ca
Dr. David Strang, Chief Medical Officer
204-831-2920, dstrang@deerlodge.mb.ca
Janet Clark, Director, Allied Health Services
204-831-2570, jeclark@deerlodge.mb.ca
Cheryl LeBlue, Director, Human Resources
204-831-2103, cleblue@deerlodge.mb.ca
Sylvia Ptashnik, Director, Resident Services
204-831-2108, sptashnik@deerlodge.mb.ca

***Winnipeg:* Parkview Place**
440 Edmonton St., Winnipeg, MB R3B 2M4
Tel: 204-942-5291 *Fax:* 204-947-1969
parkviewplace@reveraliving.com
www.reveraliving.com
Number of Beds: 277 beds
Donald M. Solar, Administrator
Noel Gray, Director of Nursing

***Winnipeg:* Poseidon Care Centre**
70 Poseidon Bay, Winnipeg, MB R3M 3E5
Tel: 204-452-6204 *Fax:* 204-474-2173
poseidon@reveraliving.com
www.reveraliving.com
Number of Beds: 218 beds
Marg Fisher, Administrator

***Winnipeg:* St. Amant Inc.**
Affiliated with: Winnipeg Regional Health Authority
440 River Rd., Winnipeg, MB R2M 3Z9
Tel: 204-256-4301 *Fax:* 204-257-4349
inquiries@stamant.mb.ca
www.stamant.mb.ca
Number of Beds: 216 beds
Note: Developmental disability resource centre
Dr. Carl Stephens, President; CEO

***Winnipeg:* The Wellington**
3161 Grant Ave., Winnipeg, MB R3R 3R1
Tel: 204-831-0788 *Fax:* 204-896-0576
thewellington@lrc.ca
www.reveraliving.com
Number of Beds: 117 suites
Note: Independent living
Warren Stephenson, Executive Director

Retirement Residences

***Winnipeg:* Metropolitan Kiwanis Courts**
2300 Ness Ave., Winnipeg, MB R3J 1A2
Tel: 204-885-7700 *Fax:* 204-831-1022
shunter@kiwaniscourts.ca

Year Founded: 2000
Note: Specialties: Assisted living
Heather Ritchie, Exec. Dir.

Personal Care Homes

Arborg: **Arborg Pioneer Health**
Affiliated with: Interlake-Eastern Regional Health Authority
Former Name: Pioneer Health Services Inc
PO Box 10, Arborg, MB R0C 0A0
Tel: 204-376-5226 *Fax:* 204-376-5669
Number of Beds: 40 beds
Ruby Tretiak, District Director
C. Cherepak, Head Nurse

Ashern: **Ashern Personal Care Home**
Affiliated with: Interlake-Eastern Regional Health Authority
PO Box 110, Ashern, MB R0C 0E0
Tel: 204-768-2461 *Fax:* 204-768-2337
Number of Beds: 20 beds
Jan O'Flanagan, District Director

Baldur: **Baldur Manor Inc.**
Affiliated with: Western Regional Health Authority
PO Box 128, Baldur, MB R0K 0B0
Tel: 204-535-2456 *Fax:* 204-535-2116
Number of Beds: 20 beds
Bev Towler

Beausejour: **East-Gate Lodge**
Affiliated with: Interlake-Eastern Regional Health Authority
PO Box 1690, 646 James Ave., Beausejour, MB R0E 0C0
Tel: 204-268-1029 *Fax:* 204-268-3525
Number of Beds: 80 beds
Mary Ann Austman, Care Team Manager

Benito: **Benito Health Centre Personal Care Home**
Affiliated with: Parkland Regional Health Authority
PO Box 490, Benito, MB R0L 0C0
Tel: 204-539-2815 *Fax:* 204-539-2482
Number of Beds: 20 beds

Birtle: **Birtle Personal Care Home**
PO Box 10, Birtle, MB R0M 0C0
Tel: 204-842-3323 *Fax:* 204-842-3375
Number of Beds: 20 beds
Gerry Berry, Director

Boissevain: **Evergreen Place**
Affiliated with: Western Regional Health Authority
PO Box 899, Boissevain, MB R0K 0E0
Tel: 204-534-2451 *Fax:* 204-534-6487
Number of Beds: 20 beds
Marilyn McGregor, Area Manager

Boissevain: **Westview Lodge**
Affiliated with: Western Regional Health Authority
200 Student Street, Boissevain, MB R0K OE0
Tel: 204-534-2455 *Fax:* 204-534-6633
Number of Beds: 42 beds

Brandon: **Dinsdale Personal Care Home**
Affiliated with: Western Regional Health Authority
510 - 6th St., Brandon, MB R7A 3N9
Tel: 204-727-3636 *Fax:* 204-727-2103
Number of Beds: 60 beds
Maj. Wilson Perrin, Administrator

Brandon: **Fairview Home**
Affiliated with: Western Regional Health Authority
1351 - 13th St., Brandon, MB R7A 4S5
Tel: 204-728-6696 *Fax:* 204-727-7616
Number of Beds: 248 beds
Trudy Curtis, Coordinator, Resident Services

Brandon: **Hillcrest Place**
Affiliated with: Western Regional Health Authority
930 - 26th St., Brandon, MB R7B 2B8
Tel: 204-728-6690 *Fax:* 204-726-0089
Number of Beds: 100 beds
Kathy Traill, Administrator

Brandon: **Rideau Park Personal Care Home**
Affiliated with: Western Regional Health Authority
525 Victoria Ave. East, Brandon, MB R7A 6S9
Tel: 204-727-1734 *Fax:* 204-726-6690
www.brandonrha.mb.ca
Number of Beds: 98 beds
Cheryl Bourdeau d'Hui, Coordinator, Resident Services

Carberry: **Carberry Personal Care Home**
220 First Ave., Carberry, MB R0K 0H0
Tel: 204-834-2076 *Fax:* 204-834-3333
www.townofcarberry.ca/PCHome.htm
Number of Beds: 36 beds

Carman: **Boyne Lodge Personal Care Home**
Affiliated with: Southern Regional Health Authority
120 - 4th Ave. SW, Carman, MB R0G 0J0
Tel: 204-745-6715 *Fax:* 204-745-6152
Number of Beds: 70 long-term care beds
Janet Wigley, Facility Contact
j.wigley@bvl.rha-central.mb.ca

Dauphin: **Dauphin Personal Care Home Inc.**
Affiliated with: Western Regional Health Authority
625 Third St. SW, Dauphin, MB R7N 1R7
Tel: 204-638-3010 *Fax:* 204-638-2199
Number of Beds: 90 beds
Melodie Powell, Site Manager

Dauphin: **St. Paul's Home**
Affiliated with: Western Regional Health Authority
703 Jackson St., Dauphin, MB R7N 2N2
Tel: 204-638-3129 *Fax:* 204-638-9294
Number of Beds: 70 beds
G. Karpinka, Administrator

Deloraine: **Bren-Del-Win Lodge**
Affiliated with: Western Regional Health Authority
103 Kellet St. South, Deloraine, MB R0M 0M0
Tel: 204-747-2119 *Fax:* 204-747-2160
Number of Beds: 30 beds
Miriam Nichol, Community Health Manager

Elkhorn: **Elkwood Manor Personal Care Home**
Affiliated with: Western Regional Health Authority
PO Box 70, Elkhorn, MB R0M 0N0
Tel: 204-845-2575 *Fax:* 204-845-2371
www.assiniboine-rha.ca
Number of Beds: 24 beds
Meegan Carson, Manager

Emerson: **Emerson Personal Care Home**
PO Box 428, 26 Main St., Emerson, MB R0A 0L0
Tel: 204-373-2109 *Fax:* 204-373-2748
Number of Beds: 20 beds
Paulette Goossen, Nurse Manager

Erickson: **Erickson Personal Care Home**
60 Queen E Rd., Erickson, MB R0J 0P0
Tel: 204-636-7777
Number of Beds: 16 beds

Eriksdale: **Eriksdale Personal Care Home**
Affiliated with: Interlake-Eastern Regional Health Authority
PO Box 130, 40 Railway Ave., Eriksdale, MB R0C 0W0
Tel: 204-739-2611 *Fax:* 204-739-2065
Number of Beds: 20 beds
Patty Johnson, District Director
Helen Melville, Director of Nursing

Fisher Branch: **Fisher Personal Care Home**
Affiliated with: Interlake-Eastern Regional Health Authority
PO Box 119, 7 Chalet Dr., Fisher Branch, MB R0C 0Z0
Tel: 204-372-8703 *Fax:* 204-372-8710
Number of Beds: 30 beds

Flin Flon: **Flin Flon Personal Care Corporation (PCH)**
Affiliated with: Northern Regional Health Authority
PO Box 340, Flin Flon, MB R8A 1N2
Tel: 204-687-9630 *Fax:* 204-687-8494
mrha@normanrha.mb.ca
www.norman-rha.mb.ca
Number of Beds: 30 beds

Flin Flon: **Northern Lights Manor**
Affiliated with: Northern Regional Health Authority
PO Box 14, 274 Bracken St., Flin Flon, MB R8A 1P4
Tel: 204-687-7325 *Fax:* 204-687-8494
Number of Beds: 36 beds
Note: Personal care home
Shauna Cupples, Unit Manager

Gilbert Plains: **Gilbert Plains Health Centre**
Affiliated with: Western Regional Health Authority
PO Box 368, 100 Cutforth St. North, Gilbert Plains, MB R0L 0X0
Tel: 204-638-2118 *Fax:* 204-548-2516
Number of Beds: 30 beds
Joan Gryba, Site Manager

Gimli: **Betel Home Foundation**
Affiliated with: Interlake-Eastern Regional Health Authority
PO Box 10, Gimli, MB R0C 1B0
Tel: 204-642-5004 *Fax:* 204-642-7243
www.betelhomefoundation.ca
Number of Beds: 80 beds
Brenna Raemer, Executive Director

Gladstone: **Third Crossing Manor**
Affiliated with: Southern Regional Health Authority
PO Box 1000, 24 Mill St., Gladstone, MB R0J 0T0
Tel: 204-385-2474 *Fax:* 204-385-2163
www.rha-central.mb.ca
Year Founded: 1974
Number of Beds: 50 residential capacity
Shirley Guenther, Facility Contact
s.guenther@tcm.rha-central.mb.ca

Glenboro: **Glenboro Personal Care Home Inc.**
Affiliated with: Western Regional Health Authority
PO Box 310, Glenboro, MB R0K 0X0
Tel: 204-827-5304 *Fax:* 204-827-2199
drea@arha.ca
Number of Beds: 20 beds
Marilyn McGregor

Grandview: **Grandview Personal Care Home Inc.**
Affiliated with: Western Regional Health Authority
PO Box 130, 308 Jackson St., Grandview, MB R0L 0Y0
Tel: 204-546-2769 *Fax:* 204-546-2207
Number of Beds: 39 beds
John Kelly, COO

Grunthal: **Menno Home for the Aged**
Affiliated with: Southern Regional Health Authority
235 Park St., Grunthal, MB R0A 0R0
Tel: 204-434-6496
www.sehealth.mb.ca
Year Founded: 1960
Number of Beds: 40 beds
Ken Knaggs, Administrator

Hamiota: **Hamiota Personal Care Home**
177 Birch Ave., Hamiota, MB R0M 0T0
Tel: 204-764-2011 *Fax:* 204-764-2049
www.hamiota.com/health_centre.html
Number of Beds: 30 beds
Marlene Andrew, Area Manager

Killarney: **Tri Lake Health Centre**
Affiliated with: Western Regional Health Authority
Former Name: Bayside Personal Care Home Inc.
PO Box 400, Killarney, MB R0K 1G0
Tel: 204-523-4661 *Fax:* 204-523-8948
Number of Beds: 60 beds
L. Blixhavn, Head Nurse

Lac du Bonnet: **Lac du Bonnet Personal Care Home**
Affiliated with: Interlake-Eastern Regional Health Authority
PO Box 1030, 75 McIntosh Ave., Lac du Bonnet, MB R0E 1A0
Tel: 204-345-8675 *Fax:* 204-345-9245
Number of Beds: 30 beds
Merle Fischer, Care Team Manager

Lundar: **Lundar Personal Care Home**
Affiliated with: Interlake-Eastern Regional Health Authority
97 - 1st St. South, Lundar, MB R0C 1Y0
Tel: 204-762-5663
Number of Beds: 20 beds
Patty Johnson, District Director
Patty Johnson, Director of Nursing

MacGregor: **MacGregor Personal Care Home**
Affiliated with: Southern Regional Health Authority
PO Box 250, 87 Grafton St. South, MacGregor, MB R0H 0R0
Tel: 204-685-2850 *Fax:* 204-685-2529
Number of Beds: 20 beds
Garry Mattin, Executive Director

McCreary: **McCreary/Alonsa Personal Care Home Inc.**
Affiliated with: Western Regional Health Authority
PO Box 250, McCreary, MB R0J 1B0
Tel: 204-835-2482 *Fax:* 204-835-2713
Number of Beds: 20 beds
Charlie Sitwell, Administrator

Melita: **Melita & Area Personal Care Home**
Affiliated with: Western Regional Health Authority
147 Summit St., Melita, MB R0M 1L0
Tel: 204-522-3403
Number of Beds: 20 beds
Note: Specialties: Long-term care; Respite care
Georgina Henuset

Morden: **Tabor Home Inc.**
Affiliated with: Southern Regional Health Authority
230 - 9th St. South, Morden, MB R6M 1Y3
Tel: 204-822-4848 *Fax:* 204-822-5289
info@taborhome.ca
www.taborhome.ca
Year Founded: 1951
Number of Beds: 60 residential capacity
Note: Specialties: Nursing services for persons who require long-term care; Activity program; Social work; Alternative needs area, for residents who experience difficulties in the areas of thought, memory, & perception; Adult day program
Sherry Hildebrand, Facility Director
s.hildebrand@taborhome.ca

Morris: **Red River Valley Lodge Inc.**
Affiliated with: Southern Regional Health Authority
PO Box 507, 136 Ottawa St. West, Morris, MB R0G 1K0
Tel: 204-746-2394 *Fax:* 204-746-2123
Number of Beds: 40 long-term care beds
Clara Wiebe, Facility Contact
c.wiebe@rrvl.rha-central.mb.ca

Nelson House: **Nisichawaysihk Personal Care Home**
PO Box 460, Nelson House, MB R0B 1A0
Tel: 204-484-2350 *Fax:* 204-484-2011
Number of Beds: 24 beds

Norway House: **Pinaow Wachi Inc. Personal Care Home**
PO Box 98, Norway House, MB R0B 1B0
Tel: 204-359-6606 *Fax:* 204-359-6949
Number of Beds: 26 beds
B. Rowden, Administrator

Notre Dame de Lourdes: **Foyer Notre Dame Inc.**
Affiliated with: Southern Regional Health Authority
PO Box 130, 283 Notre Dame Ave. West, Notre Dame de Lourdes, MB R0G 1M0
Tel: 204-248-2092 *Fax:* 204-248-2499
Number of Beds: 60 long-term care beds

Oakbank: **Kin Place**
Affiliated with: Interlake-Eastern Regional Health Authority
PO Box 28, Oakbank, MB R0E 1J0
Tel: 204-444-6128 *Fax:* 204-444-7868
Number of Beds: 40 beds
Liz Hogue, Care Team Manager

Pilot Mound: **Prairie View Lodge**
Affiliated with: Southern Regional Health Authority
#26, 424 Broadway Ave. West, Pilot Mound, MB R0G 1P0
Tel: 204-825-2717 *Fax:* 204-825-2267
Number of Beds: 30 long-term care beds (24 EPH units)
Ginger Collins, CEO, Director of Health
v.collins@rha-central.mb.ca

Pilot Mound: **Rock Lake Personal Care Home Inc.**
Affiliated with: Southern Regional Health Authority
#27, 115 Brown St. South, Pilot Mound, MB R0G 1P0
Tel: 204-825-2246 *Fax:* 204-825-2267
vcollins@rha-central.mb.ca
www.rocklakehealthdistrict.ca
Number of Beds: 24 long-term care beds
Ginger Collins, CEO

Pine Falls: **Sunnywood Personal Care Home**
Affiliated with: Interlake-Eastern Regional Health Authority
PO Box 2000, Spruce St., Pine Falls, MB R0E 1M0
Tel: 204-367-8201
www.neha.mb.ca
Number of Beds: 20 beds
Note: Specialties: Nursing care; Recreation services; Occupational therapy; Physiotherapy; Podiatry; Mental health services; Respite care
Lorraine Dent-Prychun, Director of Long Term Care

Portage la Prairie: **Douglas Campbell Lodge**
Affiliated with: Southern Regional Health Authority
150 - 9 St. SE, Portage la Prairie, MB R1N 3T6
Tel: 204-239-6006 *Fax:* 204-239-0055
www.rha-central.mb.ca
Number of Beds: 60 long-term care beds
Colleen Fletcher, Facility Contact
c.fletcher@dcl.rha-central.mb.ca

Portage la Prairie: **Lions Prairie Manor**
Affiliated with: Southern Regional Health Authority
24 - 9th St. SE, Portage la Prairie, MB R1N 3V4
Tel: 204-857-7864 *Fax:* 204-857-8207
Number of Beds: 150 beds
Cathy Asham, Facility Contact

Roblin: **Crocus Court Personal Care Home**
PO Box 940, 15 Hospital St., Roblin, MB R0L 1P0
Tel: 204-937-2149 *Fax:* 204-937-8892
Number of Beds: 60 beds

Rossburn: **Rossburn Personal Care Home Inc.**
PO Box 40, Rossburn, MB R0J 1V0
Tel: 204-859-2413 *Fax:* 204-859-2526
Number of Beds: 20 beds

Russell: **Russell & District Personal Care Home Inc.**
Affiliated with: Western Regional Health Authority
PO Box 400, Russell, MB R0J 1W0
Tel: 204-773-3117 *Fax:* 204-773-2232
Number of Beds: 40 beds
Barb Kostesky, Area Manager

Sandy Lake: **Sandy Lake Medical Nursing Home Inc.**
Affiliated with: Western Regional Health Authority
PO Box 7, Sandy Lake, MB R0J 1X0
Tel: 204-585-2107 *Fax:* 204-585-5352
gkowaluk@arha.ca
Number of Beds: 36 beds
Barb Kostesky, Area Manager

Selkirk: **Betel Personal Care Home, Selkirk**
Affiliated with: Interlake-Eastern Regional Health Authority
212 Manchester Ave., Selkirk, MB R1A 0B6
Tel: 204-482-4471 *Fax:* 204-482-4651
www.betelhomefoundation.ca/selkirk.html
Number of Beds: 92 beds
Brenna Raemer, Administrator
B. Armstrong, Plant Manager

Selkirk: **Red River Place**
Affiliated with: Interlake-Eastern Regional Health Authority
133 Manchester Ave., Selkirk, MB R1A 0B5
Tel: 204-482-3036 *Fax:* 204-482-9499
mgd_redriverplace@extendicare.com
www.ltcam.mb.ca
Number of Beds: 104 beds
Note: Personal care facility, member of the Long Term Care Association of Manitoba
M.S. Fages, Executive Director
J. Chennell, Director of Nursing

Selkirk: **Tudor House Personal Care Home**
Affiliated with: Interlake-Eastern Regional Health Authority
800 Manitoba Ave., Selkirk, MB R3C 2C9
Tel: 204-482-6601 *Fax:* 204-482-4369
tudor@geriatricare.ca
www.geriatricare.ca/tudorhouse
Year Founded: 1971
Number of Beds: 76 beds
Note: Specialties: Care for seniors, physically & mentally handicapped adults, & persons with dementia; Hospice-type care for the dying
Ashley Martyniw, CEO/Administrator

Souris: **Souris District Personal Care Home**
Affiliated with: Western Regional Health Authority
PO Box 10, Souris, MB R0L 2C0
Tel: 204-483-2121 *Fax:* 204-483-2310
gpaddock@arha.ca
Number of Beds: 43 beds
Marilyn McGregor

St Adolphe: **St. Adolphe Personal Care Home**
Affiliated with: Southern Regional Health Authority
PO Box 40, St Adolphe, MB R5A 1A1
Tel: 204-883-2181 *Fax:* 204-883-2394
stadolphepch@mts.net
Number of Beds: 42 beds
Robert Brosseau, Administrator

St Pierre Jolys: **Repos Jolys**
Affiliated with: Southern Regional Health Authority
PO Box 320, St Pierre Jolys, MB R0A 1V0
Tel: 204-433-7611 *Fax:* 204-433-7455
Year Founded: 1995
Number of Beds: 22 beds
Note: this personal care home is justaposed to Centre Medico-Spcial De Salaberry District Health Centre
Elaine McPherson, Facility Manager

Ste Anne: **Villa Youville Inc.**
Affiliated with: Southern Regional Health Authority
208 Central Ave., Ste Anne, MB R0A 1R0
Tel: 204-422-5624 *Fax:* 204-422-5842
Number of Beds: 66 beds
Claude Lachance, Executive Director
Noel Deslauriers, Coordinator, Environmental Services

Ste Rose du Lac: **Dr. Gendreau Memorial Personal Care Home Inc.**
Affiliated with: Western Regional Health Authority
PO Box 420, Ste Rose du Lac, MB R0L 1S0
Tel: 204-447-2019 *Fax:* 204-447-2267
Number of Beds: 65 beds
Glen Kozak, Administrator

Steinbach: **Rest Haven Care Services**
Affiliated with: Southern Regional Health Authority
185 Woodhaven Ave., Steinbach, MB R5G 1K7
Tel: 204-326-2206 *Fax:* 204-326-3521
Number of Beds: 60 long-term care beds
Note: Owned and operated by seven area Evangelical Mennonite Conference churches
Marlin J. Roth, CEO

Stonewall: **Rosewood Lodge**
Affiliated with: Interlake-Eastern Regional Health Authority
436 - 1 Ave. North, Stonewall, MB R0C 2Z0
Tel: 204-467-5257 *Fax:* 204-467-4763
knattrass@irha.mb.ca
www.irha.mb.ca
Number of Beds: 50 beds
Note: Personal care home
Keith Bytheway, South West District Director

Swan River: **Swan River Valley Lodge (1991) Inc.**
Affiliated with: Western Regional Health Authority
1013 Main St., Swan River, MB R0L 1Z0
Tel: 204-734-3441 *Fax:* 204-734-9081
www.svhf.mb.ca
Number of Beds: 70 beds
Note: Number of staff: 7 Registered Nurses, 41 other staff
Mary Ellen Parsons, Clinical Services Manager
204-734-3441, mparsons@prha.mb.ca

Swan River: **Swan River Valley Personal Care Home Inc.**
Affiliated with: Western Regional Health Authority
334 - 8 Ave. South, Swan River, MB R0L 1Z0
Tel: 204-734-4521 *Fax:* 204-734-9965
www.svhf.mb.ca
Number of Beds: 60 beds
Note: Personal care home. Number of staff: 8 Registered Nurses, 31 Nurses' Aides, 5 other staff
Michelle Vandepoele, Nurse Manager
mvandepoele@prha.mb.ca

Teulon: **Goodwin Lodge**
Affiliated with: Interlake-Eastern Regional Health Authority
PO Box 89, 3rd Ave. SE, Teulon, MB R0C 3B0
Tel: 204-886-2433 *Fax:* 204-886-2653
Number of Beds: 20 beds
Keith Bytheway, District Director

The Pas: **St. Paul's Personal Care Home**
Former Name: St. Paul's Residence
PO Box 240, The Pas, MB R9A 1K4
Tel: 204-623-9226
Number of Beds: 60 beds
Shauna Cupples, Regional Manager

Thompson: **Cambridge Residence**
PO Box 81, 65 McGill, Thompson, MB R8N 1M9
Tel: 204-778-7582
Number of Beds: 8 beds
Johanna Fudge, Manager

Treherne: **Tiger Hills Manor Inc.**
Affiliated with: Western Regional Health Authority
PO Box 130, Treherne, MB R0G 2V0
Tel: 204-723-2023
www.assiniboine-rha.ca
Number of Beds: 22 beds
Note: Specialties: Long-term care
Deb Obach

Virden: Sherwood Nursing Home
Affiliated with: Western Regional Health Authority
223 Hargrave St. East, Virden, MB R0M 2C0
Tel: 204-748-1546
www.assiniboine-rha.ca
Number of Beds: 50 beds
Note: Specialties: Long-term personal care; Respite care
Meegan Carson, Area Manager

Virden: West Man Nursing Home Inc.
Affiliated with: Western Regional Health Authority
PO Box 1630, 427 Frame St. E, Virden, MB R0M 2C0
Tel: 204-748-1230 *Fax:* 204-748-3432
ghenuset@arha.ca
Number of Beds: 50 beds
Meegan Carson

Wawanesa: Wawanesa Personal Care Home Inc.
Affiliated with: Western Regional Health Authority
PO Box 309, Wawanesa, MB R0K 2G0
Tel: 204-824-2335 *Fax:* 204-824-2148
Number of Beds: 20 beds
Deb Obach, Area Manager

Whitemouth: Whitemouth District Health Centre Personal Care Home
Affiliated with: Interlake-Eastern Regional Health Authority
PO Box 160, Whitemouth, MB R0E 2G0
Tel: 204-348-7191 *Fax:* 204-348-7911
Number of Beds: 24 PCH beds
Heather Frederick, Care Team Manager

Winkler: Salem Home Inc.
Affiliated with: Southern Regional Health Authority
165 - 15 St., Winkler, MB R6W 1T8
Tel: 204-325-4316 *Fax:* 204-325-5442
salem@salemhome.net
www.salemhome.net
Number of Beds: 145 long-term care beds
Note: Personal care home owned and operated by 14 Mennonite churches
Sherry Janzen, Facility Contact
s.janzen@salemhome.net

Winnipeg: Beacon Hill Lodge
Affiliated with: Winnipeg Regional Health Authority
190 Fort St., Winnipeg, MB R3C 1C9
Tel: 204-942-7541 *Fax:* 204-944-0136
Number of Beds: 175 beds
Shelley Gurvey, Administrator

Winnipeg: Bethania Mennonite Personal Care Home Inc.
Affiliated with: Winnipeg Regional Health Authority
1045 Concordia Ave., Winnipeg, MB R2K 3S7
Tel: 204-667-0795 *Fax:* 204-667-7078
Number of Beds: 148 beds
Anita Kampen, Executive Director

Winnipeg: Calvary Place Personal Care Home
Affiliated with: Winnipeg Regional Health Authority
1325 Erin St., Winnipeg, MB R3E 3R6
Tel: 204-943-4424 *Fax:* 204-783-7524
Number of Beds: 100 beds
Dale Berry

Winnipeg: Charleswood Care Centre
Affiliated with: Winnipeg Regional Health Authority
5501 Roblin Blvd., Winnipeg, MB R3R 0G8
Tel: 204-888-3363 *Fax:* 204-896-4763
Number of Beds: 155 beds

Winnipeg: Concordia Place Personal Care Home
1000 Molson St., Winnipeg, MB R2K 4L5
Tel: 204-661-7372 *Fax:* 204-661-7297
Number of Beds: 140 beds
Les Janzen, COO

Winnipeg: Convalescent Home of Winnipeg
Affiliated with: Winnipeg Regional Health Authority
276 Hugo St. North, Winnipeg, MB R3M 2N6
Tel: 204-453-4663 *Fax:* 204-453-7149
www.wrha.mb.ca
Number of Beds: 84 residents
Note: Specialty: Long-term care
A.L. (Tony) Fraser, Executive Director
Rhonda Crane, Director of Nursing

Winnipeg: Deaf Centre Manitoba
#101, 285 Pembina Hwy., Winnipeg, MB R3L 2E1
Tel: 204-284-0802 *Fax:* 204-284-9373
Number of Beds: 57 beds
Doug Momotiuk, Exec. Dir.

Winnipeg: Donwood Manor Personal Care Home
Affiliated with: Winnipeg Regional Health Authority
171 Donwood Dr., Winnipeg, MB R2G 0V9
Tel: 204-668-4410 *Fax:* 204-663-5429
jheinrichs@donwoodmanor.org
www.donwoodmanor.org
Number of Beds: 121 beds
James Heinrichs, Executive Director

Winnipeg: Extendicare - Oakview Place
Affiliated with: Winnipeg Regional Health Authority
2395 Ness Ave., Winnipeg, MB R3J 1A5
Tel: 204-888-3005 *Fax:* 204-831-8101
cnh_oakviewplace@extendicare.com
www.extendicarecanada.com
Number of Beds: 245 beds
Note: Specialties: Nursing & supportive care; Rehabilitation & rehabilitative services; Optometry services; Dental services; Social & therapeutic programs; Adult day program; Care for persons with Alzheimer's disease and related dementias; Palliative care
Terry Vanbocquestal, Administrator
Carol Rowley, Director of Care

Winnipeg: Extendicare - Tuxedo Villa
Affiliated with: Winnipeg Regional Health Authority
2060 Corydon Ave., Winnipeg, MB R3P 0N3
Tel: 204-889-2650 *Fax:* 204-896-0258
cnh_tuxedovilla@extendicare.com
www.extendicarecanada.com
Number of Beds: 213 beds
Note: Specialties: Professional nursing & supportive care; Rehabilitation services; Care for persons with Alzheimer's disease & related dementias; Optometry services; Social & therapeutic programs
Ronald Parent, Administrator

Winnipeg: Fort Garry Care Centre Ltd.
Affiliated with: Winnipeg Regional Health Authority
Pembina Campus, 1776 Pembina Hwy., Winnipeg, MB R3T 2G2
Tel: 204-269-6939 *Fax:* 204-275-2192
Number of Beds: 64 beds
Gerald Kalef, Executive Director
Germain Sicotte, Maintenance Manager

Winnipeg: Foyer Valade Inc.
Affiliated with: Winnipeg Regional Health Authority
450 River Rd., Winnipeg, MB R2M 5M4
Tel: 204-254-3332 *Fax:* 204-254-0329
Number of Beds: 115 beds
Francis LaBossière, Executive Director
C. Dupuis, Environmental Services

Winnipeg: Fred Douglas Society Inc.
Affiliated with: Winnipeg Regional Health Authority
Former Name: Fred Douglas Lodge
1275 Burrows Ave., Winnipeg, MB R2X 0B8
Tel: 204-586-8541 *Fax:* 204-586-5510
admin@fdl.mb.ca
www.freddouglassociety.com
Number of Beds: 136 beds
Theresa Jachnycky, Chief Executive Officer
Marilyn Allan, Director of Resident Care

Winnipeg: Golden Door Geriatric Centre
Affiliated with: Winnipeg Regional Health Authority
1679 Pembina Hwy., Winnipeg, MB R3T 2G6
Tel: 204-269-6308 *Fax:* 204-269-5626
info@goldendoor.ca
www.goldendoor.ca
Number of Beds: 78 beds
Lorrie LeBlanc, Administrator
Mary P. Entwistle, Director, Nursing

Winnipeg: Golden Links Lodge
Affiliated with: Winnipeg Regional Health Authority
PO Box 248, 2280 St. Mary's Rd., Winnipeg, MB R2M 4A5
Tel: 204-257-9947 *Fax:* 204-257-2405
info@goldenlinks.mb.ca
www.goldenlinks.mb.ca
Number of Beds: 88 beds
Dorene Rosmus, Administrator

Winnipeg: Golden West Centennial Lodge
Affiliated with: Winnipeg Regional Health Authority
811 School Rd., Winnipeg, MB R2Y 0S8
Tel: 204-888-3311 *Fax:* 204-831-0544
swright@goldenwest.ca
goldenwest.ca
Number of Beds: 116 beds
Capt. William Preston, Executive Director
Terry Desautels, RN, MN, Director of Care
tdesautels@goldenwest.ca

Winnipeg: Heritage Lodge Personal Care Home
Former Name: Heritage Lodge Personal Care Home Inc
3555 Portage Ave., Winnipeg, MB R3K 0X2
Tel: 204-888-7940 *Fax:* 204-832-6544
heritagelodge@reveraliving.com
www.retirementresidencesreit.com/homes/82/
Number of Beds: 86 beds
Kim Hykawy, Administrator
Mary Baranski, Assistant Director of Nursing
Len Falco, Maintenance Supervisor

Winnipeg: Holy Family Nursing Home
165 Aberdeen Ave., Winnipeg, MB R2W 1T9
Tel: 204-589-7381 *Fax:* 204-589-8605
Number of Beds: 276 beds
Jean Piche, Executive Director
Mike Ostryniuk, Plant Supt.

Winnipeg: Kildonan Personal Care Centre Inc.
1970 Henderson Hwy., Winnipeg, MB R2G 1P2
Tel: 204-334-4633 *Fax:* 204-334-4632
kildonan@reveraliving.com
Number of Beds: 120 beds
Edward Bird, Administrator

Winnipeg: Lions Personal Care Centre
Affiliated with: Winnipeg Regional Health Authority
320 Sherbrook St., Winnipeg, MB R3B 2W6
Tel: 204-784-1240 *Fax:* 204-784-2723
Number of Beds: 116 rooms
Helmut Epp, CEO

Winnipeg: Luther Home
Affiliated with: Winnipeg Regional Health Authority
1081 Andrews St., Winnipeg, MB R2V 2G9
Tel: 204-338-4641 *Fax:* 204-338-4643
info@lutherhome.mb.ca
www.lutherhome.com
Year Founded: 1969
Number of Beds: 80 personal care home beds, including a respite bed
Note: Specialties: Physio, occupational, massage, & music therapy; Foot care
Ray Koop, Director of Care

Winnipeg: Maples Personal Care Home
Affiliated with: Winnipeg Regional Health Authority
500 Mandalay Dr., Winnipeg, MB R2P 1V4
Tel: 204-632-8570 *Fax:* 204-697-0249
Number of Beds: 200 beds
Linda Norton, Administrator
Nancy Coey, Director, Nursing

Winnipeg: Meadowood Manor
Affiliated with: Winnipeg Regional Health Authority
577 St. Anne's Rd., Winnipeg, MB R2M 5B2
Tel: 204-257-2394
info@meadowood.ca
www.meadowood.ca
Number of Beds: 88 beds
Note: Specialties: Long-term care; Rehabilitation services; Foot care services; Social work; Recreation programs; Respite care; Palliative care
Charles Kunze, Administrator
E. Verplaetse, Director of Resident Services

Winnipeg: Middlechurch Home of Winnipeg Inc.
Affiliated with: Winnipeg Regional Health Authority
280 Balderstone Ave., Winnipeg, MB R4A 4A6
Tel: 204-339-1947 *Fax:* 204-338-3498
www.middlechurchhome.mb.ca
Year Founded: 1884
Number of Beds: 197 beds
Note: Specialties: Care of older people; Activity centre; Physiotherapy; Occupational therapy; Pet therapy; Adult day program; Respite care. Number of employees: 320
Heather Temple, Executive Director

Winnipeg: Park Manor Personal Care Home Inc.
Affiliated with: Winnipeg Regional Health Authority
301 Redonda St., Winnipeg, MB R2C 1L7
Tel: 204-222-3251 *Fax:* 204-222-3237
www.parkmanor.ca
Number of Beds: 44 private rooms + 20 semi-private rooms + 4 four-bed rooms
Note: Specialties: Therapeutic recreation; Education sessions for residents & families; Adult day program; Palliative care
Charles L. Toop, Executive Director

Robert Ivany, Director, Nursing
B. Gmiterek, Maintenance Director

Winnipeg: Pembina Place Mennonite Personal Care Home
Affiliated with: Winnipeg Regional Health Authority
285 Pembina Hwy., Winnipeg, MB R3L 2E1
Tel: 204-284-0802 Fax: 204-474-0073
Number of Beds: 57 beds

Winnipeg: River East Personal Care Home Ltd.
Affiliated with: Winnipeg Regional Health Authority
1375 Molson St., Winnipeg, MB R2K 4K8
Tel: 204-668-7460 Fax: 204-668-7459
Number of Beds: 120 beds
Virginia Zazula, Administrator

Winnipeg: St. Joseph's Residence Inc.
Affiliated with: Winnipeg Regional Health Authority
1149 Leila Ave., Winnipeg, MB R2P 1S6
Tel: 204-697-8031 Fax: 204-697-8075
jmcfarlane@stjosephsresidence.mb.ca
Number of Beds: 100 beds
Note: Personal care home
Marianna Muzyka, Executive Director
Luba Sirdar, Director, Nursing Services
Ben Korving, Director, Direct Services

Winnipeg: St. Norbert Personal Care Home
Affiliated with: Winnipeg Regional Health Authority
50 St Pierre St., Winnipeg, MB R3V 1J6
Tel: 204-269-4538 Fax: 204-269-6374
Number of Beds: 91 beds
Robert Brousseau, Administrator
Shirley Beaulieu, Director, Nursing

Winnipeg: The Saul & Claribel Simkin Centre
The Sharon Home Inc.
Affiliated with: Winnipeg Regional Health Authority
Also Known As: The Simkin Centre
1 Falconridge Dr., Winnipeg, MB R3Y 1V9
Tel: 204-586-9781 Fax: 204-589-9760
Year Founded: 2002
Number of Beds: 200 beds
Note: Specialties: Care for elders of Jewish community; Therapeutic recreation; Walking track for residents recovering from hip surgery or a stroke; Tracking program for resident safety; Adult day program

Winnipeg: Vista Park Lodge
Affiliated with: Winnipeg Regional Health Authority
144 Novavista Dr., Winnipeg, MB R2N 1P8
Tel: 204-257-6688 Fax: 204-257-0446
Year Founded: 1981
Number of Beds: 100 beds
Betty Jane Jones, Administrator; Director, Nursing

Winnipeg: West Park Manor
Affiliated with: Winnipeg Regional Health Authority
3199 Grant Ave., Winnipeg, MB R3R 1X2
Tel: 204-889-3330 Fax: 204-832-9555
Number of Beds: 150 beds
K.D. Reimche, Administrator
M. Gutierrez, A/Director of Nursing

Winnipegosis: Winnipegosis-Mossey River Personal Care Home
Affiliated with: Western Regional Health Authority
PO Box 280, 230 Bridge St., Winnipegosis, MB R0L 2G0
Tel: 204-656-4481 Fax: 204-656-4402
Number of Beds: 20 beds
Glen Kozak, COO

Mental Health Facilities

Mental Health Hospitals/Facilities

Altona: Altona & District Association for the Mentally Handicapped Inc.
PO Box 330, 122 - 10th Ave. NW, Altona, MB R0G 0B0
Tel: 204-324-5401
otc@mts.net
Number of Beds: 5 beds
Anne Klassen, General Manager

Brandon: Centre for Adult Psychiatry
Affiliated with: Western Regional Health Authority
AP1, 150 McTavish Ave. East, Brandon, MB R7A 2B3
Tel: 204-578-4555 Fax: 204-578-4940
cap@brandonrha.mb.ca
www.brandonrha.mb.ca
Number of Beds: 25 beds
Lynda Stiles, Program Manager

Brandon: Centre for Geriatric Psychiatry
Affiliated with: Western Regional Health Authority
Assiniboine Centre, 150 McTavish Ave. East, Brandon, MB R7A 2B3
Tel: 204-578-5460 Fax: 204-578-4948
Number of Beds: 22
Wendy Dryburgh, Program Manager

Brandon: Child & Adolescent Treatment Centre
Affiliated with: Western Regional Health Authority
1240 - 10 St., Brandon, MB R7A 7L6
Tel: 204-727-3445 Fax: 204-727-3451
www.brandonrha.mb.ca
Number of Beds: 10 beds

Brandon: Community Mental Health Services
The Town Centre, #B13, 800 Rosser Ave., Brandon, MB R7A 6N5
Tel: 204-578-2400 Fax: 204-578-2822
mhpc@brandonrha.mb.ca
Sharon Young, Manager
youngs@brandonrha.mb.ca

Portage la Prairie: Manitoba Developmental Centre
PO Box 1190, 3rd St. NE, Portage la Prairie, MB R1N 3C6
Tel: 204-856-4200 Fax: 204-856-4258
Toll-Free: 800/473-4603
csd@gov.mb.ca
Number of Beds: 375 beds
Note: developmental centre for residents with intellectual disabilities
Donna Bjore, CEO

Selkirk: Selkirk Mental Health Centre
Affiliated with: Interlake-Eastern Regional Health Authority
PO Box 9600, 825 Manitoba Ave., Selkirk, MB R1A 2B5
Tel: 204-482-3810 Fax: 204-785-8936
Toll-Free: 800-881-3073
smhc@gov.mb.ca
www.gov.mb.ca/health/smhc/index.html
Number of Beds: 252 beds
Note: Long-term mental health inpatient care & rehabilitation
D. Bellehumeur, CEO

Winkler: Eden Health Care Services
Affiliated with: Southern Regional Health Authority
PO Box 129, 309 Main St., Winkler, MB R6W 4A4
Tel: 204-325-5355 Fax: 204-325-8742
ehcs@edenhealthcare.ca
www.edenhealth.mb.ca
Number of Beds: 40 beds
Eckhard Goerz, Facility Contact

Winkler: Eden Mental Health Centre
Affiliated with: Southern Regional Health Authority
1500 Pembina Ave., Winkler, MB R6W 1T4
Tel: 204-325-4325 Fax: 204-325-8429
edenment@edenhealth.mb.ca
www.edenhealth.mb.ca
Number of Beds: 30 beds
Les Zacharias, Administrator
les.zacharias@edenhealth.mb.ca

Winnipeg: Manitoba Adolescent Treatment Centre Inc.
Affiliated with: Winnipeg Regional Health Authority
120 Tecumseh St., Winnipeg, MB R3E 2A9
Tel: 204-477-6391 Fax: 204-783-8948
info@matc.ca
www.matc.ca
Number of Beds: 25 beds
Note: Mental health services for children, youth, and families
Dr. Keith Hildahl, CEO

New Brunswick

Government Departments in Charge

NEW BRUNSWICK: Dept. of Health Communications
Affiliated with: Horizon Health Network
Former Name: Dept. of Health & Community Services
HSBC Place, PO Box 5100, Fredericton, NB E3B 5G8
Tel: 506-457-4800 Fax: 506-453-5243
HealthInfo@gnb.ca; InfoSante@gnb.ca
www.gnb.ca/0051/index-e.asp
Jennifer Graham, Communications Officer
506-444-3506, Fax: 506-444-4697, Jennifer.Graham@gnb.ca

Regional Health Authorities

Bathurst: Vitalité Health Network
Former Name: Restigouche Health Authority/Régie de la santé du Restigouche
#600, 275 Main St., Bathurst, NB E2A 1A9
Tel: 506-544-2133 Fax: 506-544-2145
Toll-Free: 1-888-472-2220
info@rrsa.ca
www.santevitalitehealth.ca
Year Founded: 2008
Number of Beds: 1,197 beds
Population Served: 250000Number of Employees: 7600
Note: The Vitalité Health Network amalgamates Regional Health Authority 4, the Restigouche Health Authority, the Acadie-Bathurst Health Authority, and the Beauséjour Health Authority. The network is comprised of 11 hospitals, 6 community health centres, and a centre for psychiatric care.
Andrée Robichaud, President/CEO
Aldéa Landry, President of the Board of Directors

Miramichi: Horizon Health Network
Affiliated with: Horizon Health Network
Former Name: Regional Health Authority B
155 Pleasant St., Miramichi, NB E1V 1Y3
Tel: 506-623-5500 Fax: 506-623-5533
Horizon@horizonnb.ca
www.horizonnb.ca
Year Founded: 2008
Number of Beds: 1,675 beds
Area Served: Provinces of New Brunswick, PEI, and northern Nova ScotiaNumber of Employees: 13000
Note: Along with the Vitalité Health Network, the Horizon Health Network amalgamates the 8 former regional health authorities in New Brunswick. Horizon Health Network servies the Moncton, Saint John, Fredericton and Miramichi areas, as well as communities in Nova Scotia and Prince Edward Island; 924 physicians; 5,000 nurses; 25 nurse practitioners; 2,175 health care professionals; 4,800 support staff; 3,500 volunteers.
Donald J. Peters, President/CEO

Hospitals

Hospitals - General

Bath: Northern Carleton Hospital
Affiliated with: Vitalité Health Network
82 Hospital St., Bath, NB E7J 1B9
Tel: 506-278-2400 Fax: 506-278-2449
Number of Beds: 17 beds
Denise Gray, Facilities Manager
Peter Byron, Manager, Housekeeping

Bathurst: Hôpital régional Chaleur
Affiliée à: Vitalité Health Network
Ancien nom: Centre hospitalier régional
1750, Sunset Drive, Bathurst, NB E2A 4L7
Tél: 506-544-3000 Téléc: 506-544-2440
Ligne sans frais: 888-695-9222
www.santeacadie-bathursthealth.ca
Nombre de lits: 215 beds
Stéphane Legacy, Administrateur d'établissement

Blacks Harbour: Fundy Health Centre
Affiliated with: Horizon Health Network
34 Hospital St., Blacks Harbour, NB E5H 1K2
Tel: 506-456-4200 Fax: 506-456-4222
Note: Specialties: Primary care; Rehabilitation services

Campbellton: Campbellton Regional Hospital
Affiliated with: Vitalité Health Network
PO Box 880, 189 Lily Lake Rd., Campbellton, NB E3N 3H3
Tel: 506-789-5000 Fax: 506-789-5025
www.santerestigouchehealth.com; www.santevitalitehealth.ca
Year Founded: 1991
Number of Beds: 166 beds/lits
Note: The hospital is part of the Vitalité Health Network, one of 2 regional health authorities formed in 2008 to amalgamate the provincial health authority structure in New Brunswick; 900 employees; 17 family physicians; 200 nurses; 27 specialists; 35 health care professionals; emergency and ambulatory care; obstetrics and gynecology; pediatrics; psychiatry; geriatric medicine; rehabilitation; orthopedics; palliative care.
Ruth Lyons, Facility Director

Edmundston: Hôpital régional d'Edmundston
Affiliée à: Vitalité Health Network
275, boul Hébert, Edmundston, NB E3V 4E4
Tél: 506-739-2200 Téléc: 506-739-2231
Nombre de lits: 169 lits
Dr. Édouard Hendriks, Administrateur d'établissement

***Fredericton:* Dr. Everett Chalmers Regional Hospital**
Affiliated with: Horizon Health Network
PO Box 9000, 700 Priestman St., Fredericton, NB E3B 5N5
Tel: 506-452-5400 *Fax:* 506-452-5670
www.rhab-rrsb.ca
Year Founded: 1976
Number of Beds: 314 beds
Note: Hospital Specialties: Emergency services; Diagnostic services; Surgery; Intensive care; Primary care; Obstetrics; Neonatology; Pediatrics; Reconstructive & restorative medicine; Cardiac care; Rheumatology; Oncology; Dermatology; Gastroenterology; Neurology; Dialysis; Psychiatry; Geriatric care. Number of Employees: 2,000+ nurses, health care professionals, & support staff; 58 family physicians; 88 specialists
Dr. Ward Murdock, Chief of Staff, Fredericton, Horizon Health Network
Dr. Peter Feero, Chief of Surgery, Fredericton, Horizon Health Network
Dr. David Addleman, Chief of Psychiatry, Fredericton, Horizon Health Network

***Grand Manan:* Grand Manan Hospital Ltd.**
Affiliated with: Horizon Health Network
196 Rte. 776, Grand Manan, NB E5G 1A3
Tel: 506-662-4060 *Fax:* 506-662-4050
Number of Beds: 8 beds
Karen Thomas, Facility Manager

***Grand-Sault:* Hôpital général de Grand-Sault inc.**
Affiliée à: Vitalité Health Network
CP 7061, 625, boul Evérard H. Daigle, Grand-Sault, NB E3Z 2R9
Tél: 506-473-7555
Nombre de lits: 20 lits
Solange Bossé, Directrice d'établissement

***Harvey Station:* Harvey Community Hospital Ltd.**
Affiliated with: Horizon Health Network
2019 Rte. 3, Harvey Station, NB E6K 3E9
Tel: 506-366-6400 *Fax:* 506-366-6403
Shirley Moffatt, Nurse Manager

***Lamèque:* Hôpital de Lamèque/Centre de santé communautaire de Lamèque**
Affiliée à: Vitalité Health Network
29, rue de l'Hôpital, Lamèque, NB E8T 1C5
Tél: 506-344-2261 *Téléc:* 506-344-3403
Nombre de lits: 12 lits
Dina Chiasson, Directrice d'établissement

***Miramichi:* Miramichi Regional Hospital**
Affiliée à: Horizon Health Network
500 Water St., Miramichi, NB E1V 3G5
Tél: 506-623-3000 *Téléc:* 506-623-3465
Nombre de lits: 161 lits
Gary Foley, Acting President/CEP

***Moncton:* Hôpital régional Dr.-Georges-L.-Dumont**
Affiliée à: Horizon Health Network
330, av Université, Moncton, NB E1C 2Z3
Tél: 506-862-4000 *Téléc:* 506-862-4256
www.beausejour-nb.ca
Nombre de lits: 362 lits
Dr. Louis-Marie Simard, Président et Directeur général par intérim
Blondine Arseneau, Conseillère en environnement

***Moncton:* The Moncton Hospital**
Affiliated with: Horizon Health Network
135 MacBeath Ave., Moncton, NB E1C 6Z8
Tel: 506-857-5520 *Fax:* 506-857-5545
generalinquiries@serha.ca
www.serha.ca
Number of Beds: 381 beds
Note: Comprehensive health care, including trauma care, intensive care units for cardiac care, neonatal care, medical/surgical care; child & adolescent psychiatric unit; burn unit; ambulance service
Donald J. Peters, President/CEO

***Oromocto:* Oromocto Public Hospital**
Affiliated with: Horizon Health Network
103 Winnebago St., Oromocto, NB E2V 1C6
Tel: 506-357-4700 *Fax:* 506-357-4735
www.rivervalleyhealth.nb.ca
Number of Beds: 45 beds
Note: Specialties: Day surgery; Breast cancer screening centre; Close observation unit; William R. Duffie Unit, a healthy aging & restorative program. Number of employees: 15 family physicians + 1 radiologist + visiting surgeons + nurses, & professional & support staff
Darlene Cogswell, Facility Coordinator

John Swanwick, Lab Manager

***Plaster Rock:* Tobique Valley Hospital Inc.**
Affiliated with: Horizon Health Network
120 Main St., Plaster Rock, NB E7G 2E5
Tel: 506-356-6600
www.rivervalleyhealth.nb.ca
Year Founded: 1957
Note: Specialties: Nursing care service; Physiotherapy
Susan Kukurski, Facility Coordinator
Ron Lewis, Plant Manager

***Sackville:* Sackville Memorial Hospital**
Affiliated with: Horizon Health Network
8 Main St., Sackville, NB E4L 4A3
Tel: 506-364-4100 *Fax:* 506-536-1983
generalinquiries@serha.ca
www.serha.ca/sackville_hospital
Number of Beds: 21 beds
France Gauthier, Acting Manager

***Saint John:* Saint John Regional Hospital**
Affiliated with: Horizon Health Network
PO Box 2100, Tucker Park Rd., Saint John, NB E2L 4L2
Tel: 506-648-6000 *Fax:* 506-648-6364
Number of Beds: 524 beds
Note: Teaching hospital affiliated with Dalhousie University, New Brunswick Community College, University of New Brunswick and Memorial University in St. John's Newfoundland
Dora Nicinski, President/CEO

***Saint John:* Saint John Regional Hospital - Ridgewood Veterans Wing**
Affiliated with: Horizon Health Network
PO Box 2100, 422 Bay St., Saint John, NB E2L 4L2
Tel: 506-635-2420 *Fax:* 506-635-2425
www.ahsc.health.nb.ca/AboutUs/OurFacilities/facvets.shtml
Year Founded: 1976
Number of Beds: 80 beds
Note: A facility for veterans who require long-term care; maintains a close relationship with Veteran Affairs Canada and the Royal Canadian Legion.
Maxine Walsh, Regional Manager, Veterans Care, AHSC
506-635-2150, walma@reg2.health.nb.ca
Michael Park, Regional Manager, Long Term Mental Health Services, AHSC
parmi@reg2.health.nb.ca

***Saint John:* St. Joseph's Hospital**
Affiliated with: Horizon Health Network
130 Bayard Dr., Saint John, NB E2L 3L6
Tel: 506-632-5555 *Fax:* 506-632-5551
Number of Beds: 62 beds
Daryl Steeves, Facility Manager

***Saint-Quentin:* Hôtel-Dieu de St-Quentin**
Affiliée à: Vitalité Health Network
21, rue Canada, Saint-Quentin, NB E8A 2P6
Tél: 506-235-2300 *Téléc:* 506-235-7201
nicole-d.labrie@rrs4.ca
Nombre de lits: 6 lits
Nicole Labrie, Directrice d'établissement
Monette Dupéré, Chef de service à l'entretien ménager

***St Stephen:* Charlotte County Hospital**
Affiliated with: Horizon Health Network
4 Garden St., St Stephen, NB E3L 2L9
Tel: 506-465-4444
Number of Beds: 44 beds
Note: Specialties: Ambulatory care; Diagnostic services; Rehabilitative services; Restorative health; Physiotherapy; Speech-language pathology; Respiratory therapy; Occupational therapy; Adult & youth addiction counselling; Diabetic education; Oncology outreach services; Sexual health clinic; Cardiac risk clinic; Healthy lung clinic; Palliative care
Yvonne Bartlette, Facility Manager

***Ste-Anne-de-Kent:* Hôpital Stella Maris de Kent**
Affiliée à: Vitalité Health Network
7714, rte 134, Ste-Anne-de-Kent, NB E4S 1H5
Tél: 506-743-7800 *Téléc:* 506-743-7813
www.beausejour-nb.ca
Nombre de lits: 20 lits
Lise Guerrette-Daigle, Directeur d'établissement
Gloria Melanson, Chef, Entretien mén.

***Sussex:* Sussex Health Centre**
Affiliated with: Horizon Health Network
75 Leonard Dr., Sussex, NB E4E 2P7
Tel: 506-432-3100
www.ahsc.health.nb.ca

Number of Beds: 25 beds
Note: Specialties: Acute care; Family medicine; Dialysis; IV therapy day hospital; Rehabilitative services; Palliative care
Elspeth Stanley, Facility Adminstrator

***Tracadie-Sheila:* Hôpital de Tracadie-Sheila**
Affiliée à: Vitalité Health Network
400, rue des Hospitalières, Tracadie-Sheila, NB E1X 1G5
Tél: 506-394-3000 *Téléc:* 506-394-3034
Nombre de lits: 20 lits
Odette Robichaud, Directrice d'établissement
A. Saulnier, Directeur, Installations matériels

Community Health Centres

Community Health Care Centres

***Baie-Sainte-Anne:* Baie-Ste-Anne Health Centre**
Affiliated with: Horizon Health Network
13, rue de l'Église, Baie-Sainte-Anne, NB E9A 1A9
Tel: 506-228-2004 *Fax:* 506-228-2008
www.rha7.ca
Note: Patients may access the services of a physician who works 3 days per week, & a full time nurse on site; monthly public health & diabetic clinics; weekly lab.
Monica Lloyd, Contact

***Bathurst:* NB Extra Mural Program Bathurst Unit**
Affiliated with: Vitalité Health Network
1750 Sunset Dr., Bathurst, NB E2Z 4L7
Tel: 506-455-3030
Norma McGraw, Manager

***Belledune:* Centre de santé de Jacquet River Health Centre**
Affiliated with: Vitalité Health Network
41 Mack St., Belledune, NB E8G 2R3
Tel: 506-237-3222 *Fax:* 506-237-3224
www.santerestigouchehealth.com
Lynn DeGroot, Administratrice d'établissement

***Blackville:* Blackville Health Centre**
Affiliated with: Horizon Health Network
2 Shaffer Lane, Blackville, NB E9B 1P4
Tel: 506-843-2910 *Fax:* 506-843-2911
www.rha7.ca
Ann Dickison, Contact

***Boiestown:* Upper Miramichi Health Services Centre - Boiestown**
Affiliated with: Horizon Health Network
#2, 6154, rte 8, Boiestown, NB E6A 1M4
Tel: 506-369-2700 *Fax:* 506-369-2702
Lori Amos, Nurse Manager

***Campobello:* NB Extra Mural Program St Stephen Unit - Campobello Office**
Affiliated with: Horizon Health Network
640, rte 774, Welshpool, Campobello, NB E5E 1A5
Tel: 506-752-4110 *Fax:* 506-752-4106
Sue Ness, Manager

***Caraquet:* Hôpital de l'Enfant-Jésus (RHSJT)**
Affiliée à: Vitalité Health Network
Ancien nom: Hôpital de l'Enfant-Jésus-RHSJT
1, boul St-Pierre, Caraquet, NB E1W 1B6
Tél: 506-726-2100 *Téléc:* 506-726-2226
www.caremapnb.ca
Dina Chiasson, Directrice d'établissement
Guy Gallien, Chef de service, Installations matériels

***Caraquet:* Programme extra mural du NB Unite de la Penisule Acadienne - Bureau de Caraquet**
Affiliated with: Vitalité Health Network
442, blvd. Saint-Pierre ouest, Caraquet, NB E1W 1A3
Tel: 506-726-2800 *Fax:* 506-726-2808
Norma McGraw, Manager

***Chipman:* Chipman Health Centre**
Affiliated with: Horizon Health Network
9 Civic Ct., Chipman, NB E4A 2H8
Tel: 506-339-7650 *Fax:* 506-339-7652
horizonnb.ca
Roddy Barton, Nurse Manager

***Dalhousie:* Centre de santé communautaire St. Joseph**
Affiliated with: Vitalité Health Network
#1, 280, rue Victoria, Dalhousie, NB E8C 2R6
Tel: 506-684-7000 *Fax:* 506-684-4751
www.santerestigouchehealth.com; www.santevitalitehealth.ca

Note: Le Réseau de santé Vitalité regroupe les huit anciennes régies régionales dans la province. Le Centre a pour mission d'améliorer l'accès aux soins de santé primaires, et l'état de santé des collectivités; promotion de la santé, prévention des maladies et blessures, et traitement des maladies chroniques; services diagnostiques; soins ambulatoires.
Lynn Kelly deGroot, Directrice d'établissement

***Dalhousie:* NB Extra Mural Program Restigouche Unit**
Affiliated with: Vitalité Health Network
#2, 280 Victoria St., Dalhousie, NB E8C 2R6
Tel: 506-684-7060 *Fax:* 506-684-7334
Claire Dennie, Manager

***Deer Island:* Deer Island Health Centre**
Affiliated with: Horizon Health Network
999 Rte. 772, Deer Island, NB E5V 1P2
Tel: 506-747-4150 *Fax:* 506-747-4151
Susan Ness, Facility Manager

***Dieppe:* Programme extra mural du NB Blanche Bourgeois Unit**
Affiliated with: Vitalité Health Network
30, rue Englehart, Unité B, Dieppe, NB E1A 8H3
Tel: 506-862-4400 *Fax:* 506-862-4415
Rino Lang, Manager

***Doaktown:* Central Miramichi Community Health Centre (CMCHC)**
Affiliated with: Horizon Health Network
Former Name: Upper Miramichi Health Services Centre - Doaktown
11 Prospect St., Doaktown, NB E9C 1C8
Tel: 506-365-6100 *Fax:* 506-365-6104
Lorri Amos, Nurse Manager

***Edmundston:* Programme extra mural du NB Unite d'Edmundston**
Affiliated with: Vitalité Health Network
275, boul Hebert, 4e étage, Edmundston, NB E3V 4N4
Tel: 506-739-2160 *Fax:* 506-739-2163
Carlene Pelletier, Manager

***Fredericton:* NB Extra Mural Program Fredericton Unit**
Affiliated with: Horizon Health Network
PO Box 9000, 700 Priestman St., Fredericton, NB E3B 5N5
Tel: 506-452-5800 *Fax:* 506-452-5858
Christine DeJong, Manager

***Fredericton:* NB Extra Mural Program Sussex Unit**
Affiliated with: Horizon Health Network
Health Services Complex, #4, 20 Kennedy Dr., Fredericton, NB E4E 2P1
Tel: 506-432-3280 *Fax:* 506-432-3250
Sue Ness, Manager

***Fredericton:* NB Extra Mural Program Fredericton Unit - Boiestown Office**
Affiliated with: Horizon Health Network
c/o Fredericton Unit, PO Box 9000, 700 Priestman St., Fredericton, NB E3B 5N5
Tel: 506-369-2711 *Fax:* 506-369-2722
Christine DeJong, Manager

***Fredericton Junction:* Fredericton Junction Health Centre**
Affiliated with: Horizon Health Network
233 Sunbury Dr., Fredericton Junction, NB E3L 1S1
Tel: 506-368-6501 *Fax:* 506-368-6502
Ruth Richardson, Nurse Manager

***Grand Manan:* NB Extra Mural Program Eastern Charlotte Unit - Grand Manan**
Affiliated with: Horizon Health Network
Grand Manan Hospital, 196 Rte. 776, Grand Manan, NB E5G 1A3
Tel: 506-662-4055 *Fax:* 506-662-4054
Sue Ness, Manager

***Grand-Sault:* Programme extra mural du NB Unite de Grand-Sault**
Affiliée à: Vitalité Health Network
CP 7812, 532, ch Madawaska, Grand-Sault, NB E3Z 3E8
Tél: 506-473-7492 *Téléc:* 506-473-7476
Carlene Pelletier, Manager

***Kedgwick:* Programme extra mural du NB Unite de Grand-Sault - Kedgwick Office**
CP 1002, Kedgwick, NB E8B 1Z7
Tél: 506-284-3444 *Téléc:* 506-284-3446
Carlene Pelletier, Manager

***Lamèque:* Programme extra mural du NB Unte de la Peninsule Acadienne - Bureau de Lameque**
Affiliated with: Vitalité Health Network
29, rue l'hopital Lemeque, Lamèque, NB E8T 1C5
Tel: 506-344-3000 *Fax:* 506-344-3001
Norma McGraw, Manager

***McAdam:* MacLean Memorial Hospital**
Affiliated with: Vitalité Health Network
PO Box 311, 15 Saunders Rd., McAdam, NB E6J 1K9
Tel: 506-784-6300 *Fax:* 506-784-6306
Shirley Moffat, Nurse Manager

***Minto:* Queens North Community Health Centre**
Affiliated with: Horizon Health Network
PO Box 1004, 1100 Pleasant Dr., Minto, NB E4B 3Y6
Tel: 506-327-7800 *Fax:* 506-327-7850
Sandra Parker, Nurse Manager
Kivon Snihur, Supervisor, Housekeeping

***Miramichi:* NB Extra Mural Program Miramichi Unit**
Affiliated with: Horizon Health Network
500 Water St., Miramichi, NB E1V 3G5
Tel: 506-623-6350 *Fax:* 506-623-6370
Joanne Sonier, Manager

***Miramichi:* NB Extra Mural Program Miramichi Unit - Blackville Office**
Affiliated with: Horizon Health Network
500 Water St., Miramichi, NB E1V 3G5
Tel: 506-623-6312 *Fax:* 506-623-6370
Joanne Sonier, Manager

***Miramichi:* NB Extra Mural Program Miramichi Unit - Neguac Office**
Affiliated with: Horizon Health Network
500 Water St., Miramichi, NB E1V 3G5
Tel: 506-623-6311 *Fax:* 506-623-6370
Joanne Sonier, Manager

***Moncton:* NB Extra Mural Program Driscoll Unit**
Affiliated with: Horizon Health Network
#107, 1600 Main St., Moncton, NB E1E 1G5
Tel: 506-867-6500 *Fax:* 506-867-6509
generalinquiries@serha.ca
www.serha.ca/extra_mural

Note: Home healthcare program for eligible residents
Fonda Kazi, Vice President, Community Health

***Nackawic:* Nackawic Community Health Centre**
Affiliated with: Horizon Health Network
Nackawic Shopping Centre, Upper Floor, #201, 135 Otis Dr., Nackawic, NB E6G 1H1
Tel: 506-575-6600 *Fax:* 506-575-6603
Shirley Moffatt, Nurse Manager

***Néguac:* Neguac Health Centre**
Affiliated with: Horizon Health Network
38 Otho St., Néguac, NB E9C 4H3
Tel: 506-776-3876 *Fax:* 506-776-3877
Anna Stymiest, Contact

***Oromocto:* NB Extra Mural Program Oromocto Unit**
Affiliated with: Horizon Health Network
275A Restigouche Rd., Oromocto, NB E2V 2H1
Tel: 506-357-4900 *Fax:* 506-357-4904
Christine DeJong, Manager

***Oromocto:* NB Extra Mural Program Oromocto Unit - Minto Office**
Affiliated with: Horizon Health Network
c/o NB Extra Mural Program, 275A Restigouche Rd., Oromocto, NB E2V 2H1
Tel: 506-327-4900 *Fax:* 506-327-4904
Christine DeJong, Manager

***Paquetville:* Centre de santé de Paquetville**
Affiliée à: Vitalité Health Network
1096, du Parc, Paquetville, NB E8R 1J4
Tél: 506-764-2424 *Téléc:* 506-764-2425
www.paquetville.com

***Perth-Andover:* NB Extra Mural Program Woodstock Unit - Perth-Andover Sub Unit**
Affiliated with: Horizon Health Network
#2, 500 East Riverside Dr., Perth-Andover, NB E7H 1Z1
Tel: 506-273-7222 *Fax:* 506-273-7220
Christine DeJong, Manager

***Petitcodiac:* Petitcodiac Health Centre**
Affiliated with: Horizon Health Network
25 Railway Ave., Petitcodiac, NB E4Z 6H4
Tel: 506-756-3400 *Fax:* 506-756-3406
generalinquiries@serha.ca
www.serha.ca/petitcodiac

Note: Number of staff: 3 physicians, 1 dentist. Foot care & diabetes clinics by appointment, drop-in services, visiting dietician
Heather Steeves, Nurse Manager

***Pointe-Verte:* Centre de santé de Chaleur Health Centre**
Affiliée à: Vitalité Health Network
Ancien nom: Centre de santé Pointe Verte
382, rue Principale, Pointe-Verte, NB E8J 2X6
Tél: 506-542-2434 *Téléc:* 506-783-8623

***Quispamsis:* NB Extra Mural Program Kennebecasis Valley Unit**
Affiliated with: Horizon Health Network
PO Box 21025, 175 Old Hampton Hwy., Quispamsis, NB E2E 4Z4
Tel: 506-848-4600 *Fax:* 506-848-4620
Sue Ness, Manager

***Rexton:* Health Services Centre Rexton**
Affiliated with: Horizon Health Network
82 Main St., Rexton, NB E4W 5N4
Tel: 506-523-7940 *Fax:* 506-523-7949
generalinquiries@serha.ca
www.serha.ca

Year Founded: 1974
Note: Drop-in services, clinics, immunization, nutrition & diabetes education
Lucille Cormier, Nurse Manager

***Riverside-Albert:* Albert County Health & Wellness Centre**
Affiliated with: Horizon Health Network
8 Forestdale Rd., Riverside-Albert, NB E4H 3Y7
Tel: 506-882-3100 *Fax:* 506-882-3101
generalinquiries@serha.ca
www.serha.ca/albert_county

Year Founded: 1961
Note: Multidisciplinary, primary health care services
Marlene Hueston, Nurse Manager

***Rogersville:* Rogersville Health Centre**
Affiliated with: Horizon Health Network
9, rue des Ormes, Rogersville, NB E4Y 1S6
Tel: 506-775-2030 *Fax:* 506-775-2025
Glorine Caissie, Contact

***Sackville:* NB Extra Mural Program Tantramar Unit**
Affiliated with: Horizon Health Network
8 Main St., Sackville, NB E4L 4A3
Tel: 506-364-4400 *Fax:* 506-364-4405
generalinquiries@serha.ca
www.serha.ca/extra_mural

Year Founded: 1979
Note: Home healthcare program for eligible residents
Fonda Kazi, Vice President, Community Health

***Saint John:* Hospice Greater Saint John**
Affiliated with: Horizon Health Network
Former Name: Hospice Saint John & Sussex
385 Dufferin Row, Saint John, NB E2M 2J9
Tel: 506-632-5593 *Fax:* 506-632-5592
info@hospicesj.ca
www.hospicesj.ca

Note: Number of employees: 4
Sandy Johnson, Executive Director

***Saint John:* NB Extra Mural Program Saint John Unit**
Affiliated with: Horizon Health Network
West End Office Park, 1490 Manawagonish Rd., Saint John, NB E2M 3Y4
Tel: 506-649-2626 *Fax:* 506-649-2540
Note: in-home support
Sue Ness, Manager

***Saint John:* St. Joseph's Community Health Centre**
Affiliated with: Horizon Health Network
116 Coburg St., Saint John, NB E2L 3K1
Tel: 506-632-5537 *Fax:* 506-632-5539
www.sjfn.nb.ca
Dawn Marie Buck, Contact

***Saint John:* Senior Watch Inc.**
Affiliated with: Horizon Health Network
33 Hanover St., Saint John, NB E2L 3G1
Tel: 506-634-8906 *Fax:* 506-633-2992
senior@seniorwatch.com
www.seniorwatch.com
Note: New Brunswick-based firm specializing in developing and managing new programs for Seniors
Jean E. Porter Mowatt, President/CEO

***Sainte-Anne-de-Madawaska:* Centre de santé Ste-Anne**
Affiliated with: Vitalité Health Network
1, rue de la Clinique, Sainte-Anne-de-Madawaska, NB E7E 1B9
Tel: 506-445-6200 *Fax:* 506-445-6201
Dr. Édouard Hendriks, Administrateur d'établissement (par intérim)

***Shediac:* Centre médical régional de Shédiac**
Affiliated with: Vitalité Health Network
PO Box 1477, 419, rue Main, Shediac, NB E4P 2B8
Tel: 506-533-2700 *Fax:* 506-533-2710
Lise Guerrette-Daigle, Administrateur d'établissement

***Shediac:* Programme extra mural du NB Shediac Unit**
Affiliated with: Vitalité Health Network
423 Main St., Shediac, NB E4P 2B6
Tel: 506-533-2800
Rino Lang, Manager

***St George:* NB Extra Mural Program Eastern Charlotte Unit**
Affiliated with: Horizon Health Network
#401, 124 Main St., St George, NB E5C 3S3
Tel: 506-755-4660 *Fax:* 506-755-4665
Sue Ness, Manager

***St Stephen:* NB Extra Mural Program St Stephen Unit**
Affiliated with: Horizon Health Network
#100, 73 Milltown Blvd., St Stephen, NB E3L 1G5
Tel: 506-465-4520 *Fax:* 506-465-4523
Sue Ness, Manager

***Stanley:* Stanley Health Services Centre**
Affiliated with: Horizon Health Network
PO Box 340, Stanley, NB E6B 2K5
Tel: 506-367-7730 *Fax:* 506-367-7738
Charlene Merrill, Nurse Manager
Penny Higgs, Director, Nursing
Ronald Hay, Maintenance Supervisor

***Ste-Anne de Kent:* Programme extra mural du NB Kent Unit**
Affiliée à: Vitalité Health Network
7717, route 134, Livraison Générale, Ste-Anne de Kent, NB E4S 1H5
Tél: 506-743-2000
Rino Lang, Manager

***Tracadie Sheila:* Progrmme extra mural du NB Unite de la Peninsule Acadienne - Bureau de Tracadie**
Affiliated with: Vitalité Health Network
Centre hospitalier de Tracadie, PO Box 3180 Stn. Bureau-Chef, 3512-2, rue Principale, Tracadie Sheila, NB E1X 1G5
Tel: 506-394-4100 *Fax:* 506-394-4117
Norma McGraw, Manager

***Woodstock:* NB Extra Mural Program Woodstock Unit**
Affiliated with: Horizon Health Network
Nurses' Residence, #310, 787 Main St., Woodstock, NB E7M 2E9
Tel: 506-325-6838 *Fax:* 506-325-6862
Christine DeJong, Manager

Special Treatment Centres

***Edmundston:* Services de toxicomanie**
Affiliée à: Vitalité Health Network
62, rue Queen, Edmundston, NB E3V 1A1
Tél: 506-735-2092 *Téléc:* 506-835-2700
www.rrs4-rha4.nb.ca
Nombre de lits: 10 lits
Note: Service de désintoxification interne
Carmen Bouchard
Carmen.Bouchard@chr4.health.nb.ca

***Fredericton:* Addiction Services**
Affiliated with: Horizon Health Network
c/o Victoria Health Centre, 65 Brunswick St., Fredericton, NB E3B 1G5
Tel: 506-452-5558 *Fax:* 506-452-5533
Gordon Skead, Regional Director

***Fredericton:* Fredericton Site of The Morgentaler Clinic**
The Morgentaler Clinic
Affiliated with: Horizon Health Network
554 Brunswick St., Fredericton, NB E3B 1H5
Tel: 506-451-9060 *Fax:* 506-451-9062
nbclinic@nb.aibn.com
www.morgentalernb.ca
Note: Specialties: Abortion care services; Abortion aftercare

***Fredericton:* Stan Cassidy Centre for Rehabilitation**
Affiliated with: Horizon Health Network
180 Woodbridge St., Fredericton, NB E3B 4R3
Tel: 506-452-5225 *Fax:* 506-452-5190
Number of Beds: 20 beds
Dr. Ron Harris, Administrative Director
Calvin Gesner, Maintenance Director

***Moncton:* Addiction Services**
Affiliated with: Horizon Health Network
125 Mapleton Rd., Moncton, NB E1C 9G8
Tel: 506-856-2333 *Fax:* 506-856-6057
generalinquiries@serha.ca
www.serha.ca/addiction_services
Number of Beds: 20 beds
Note: Detoxification unit, methadone maintenance treatment program, addiction prevention & education, counseling, assessments
Michelina Mancuso, Regional Manager

***Petit-Rocher:* Services Résidentiels Nepisiguit Inc.**
#312, 702, rue Principale, Petit-Rocher, NB E8J 1V1
Tél: 506-542-2404 *Téléc:* 506-542-2406
srninc@nb.aibn.com
www.gnb.ca
Nombre de lits: 22 lits
Note: Service résidentiel à toutes les personnes ayant des handicaps de la région Nepisiguit
Luc DeRoche, Directeur général

***Saint John:* Workers' Rehabilitation Centre**
Affiliated with: Horizon Health Network
PO Box 160, 1 Portland St., Saint John, NB E2L 3X9
Tel: 506-738-8411 *Fax:* 506-738-3470
www.whscc.nb.ca
Note: occupational rehabilitation
Dr. R. Brian Connell, Vice-President, Compensation & Rehabilitation

***Saint John West:* Ridgewood Addiction Services**
Affiliated with: Horizon Health Network
PO Box 3566 Stn. B, 416 Bay St., Saint John West, NB E2M 4Y1
Tel: 506-674-4300 *Fax:* 506-658-3774
www.ahsc.health.nb.ca
Number of Beds: 90 beds
Note: Comprehensive addiction treatment programs, detoxification, outpatient & short term residential services, addiction prevention & education, community reintegration
Bonnie Lambert, Executive Director
lambo@reg2.health.nb.ca

Nursing Homes

***Bath:* River View Manor Inc.**
Affiliated with: Vitalité Health Network
96 Hospital St., Bath, NB E7J 1B9
Tel: 506-278-6030 *Fax:* 506-278-5962
www.riverviewmanor.ca
Year Founded: 1981
Number of Beds: 40 beds
Note: Nursing home
Kay Simonds, Administrator
Randy Giberson, Supervisor, Plant Maintenance

***Bathurst:* Le Foyer Notre-Dame de Lourdes Inc.**
Affiliée à: Vitalité Health Network
2055, Vallée-Lourdes, Bathurst, NB E2A 4P8
Tél: 506-549-5085 *Téléc:* 506-548-5052
dg.fndl@nb.aibn.com
Nombre de lits: 100 lits
Claire Savoie, Directeur général
506-549-5071 ext.202, dg.fndl@nb.aibn.com

***Bathurst:* Robert L. Knowles Veterans Unit, Villa Chaleur**
795, rue Champlain, Bathurst, NB E2A 4M8
Tel: 506-549-5582 *Fax:* 506-545-6424
Number of Beds: 13 beds
Lucie Fournier, Administrator

***Blacks Harbour:* Fundy Nursing Home**
34 Hospital St., Blacks Harbour, NB E5H 1C2
Tel: 506-456-4218 *Fax:* 506-456-4259
Number of Beds: 26 beds
Debbie Harris, Administrator

***Boiestown:* Central New Brunswick Nursing Home Inc.**
Affiliated with: Vitalité Health Network
3458 Rte. 625, Boiestown, NB E6A 1C8
Tel: 506-369-7262 *Fax:* 506-369-2331
Number of Beds: 30 beds
Manley Black, Administrator

***Bouctouche:* Manoir Saint-Jean Baptiste**
Affiliée à: Vitalité Health Network
5, av Richard, Bouctouche, NB E4S 3T2
Tél: 506-743-7344 *Téléc:* 506-743-7343
Nombre de lits: 50 lits
Robert Allain, Administrateur
506/743-7346
Edmond Babineau, Chef, Installations matériels

***Campbellton:* Campbellton Nursing Home Inc.**
Affiliated with: Vitalité Health Network
PO Box 850, 101 Dover St., Campbellton, NB E3N 3K6
Tel: 506-789-7350 *Fax:* 506-789-7360
Number of Beds: 100 beds
Ken Murray, Executive Director
506/789-7351
Randy Johnson, Supervisor, Plant Maintenance

***Caraquet:* Villa Beauséjour Inc.**
Affiliée à: Vitalité Health Network
CP 5608, 253, boul St-Pierre ouest, Caraquet, NB E1W 1B7
Tél: 506-726-2744 *Téléc:* 506-726-2745
Nombre de lits: 62 lits
Roger Landry, Directeur général
506/726-2741
Annette Chiasson, Director, Nursing
Dennis Power, Maintenance Supervisor

***Dalhousie:* Dalhousie Nursing Home Inc.**
Affiliated with: Vitalité Health Network
#1, 296 Victoria St., Dalhousie, NB E8C 2R8
Tel: 506-684-7800 *Fax:* 506-684-7832
Number of Beds: 105 beds
Diane Léger, Administrator
506/684-7805
Maurice Savoie, Director, Physical Plant

***Edmundston:* Villa des Jardins Inc.**
Affiliée à: Vitalité Health Network
50, rue Queen, Edmundston, NB E3V 3N4
Tél: 506-735-2112 *Téléc:* 506-735-2462
Nombre de lits: 30 lits
Carole Ouellette, Administrateur
506/735-2115

***Fredericton:* Pine Grove**
Affiliated with: Horizon Health Network
521 Woodstock Rd., Fredericton, NB E3B 2J2
Tel: 506-444-3400 *Fax:* 506-444-3407
Pam Bowen, Administrator

Fredericton: York Care Centre
Affiliated with: Horizon Health Network
Former Name: York Manor Inc.
100 Sunset Dr., Fredericton, NB E3A 1A3
Tel: 506-444-3880 *Fax:* 506-444-3544
info@yorkmanor.nb.ca
www.yorkmanor.nb.ca
Number of Beds: 198 beds
Ken McGeorge, Administrator

Fredericton Junction: White Rapids Manor Inc.
Affiliated with: Horizon Health Network
233 Sunbury Dr., Fredericton Junction, NB E5L 1S1
Tel: 613-368-6508 *Fax:* 613-368-6512
brees@whiterapidsmanor.nb.ca
Number of Beds: 36 beds
Kathy Jenkins, Administrator

Gagetown: Orchard View Long Term Care Facility
Affiliated with: Vitalité Health Network
Former Name: Gagetown Nursing Home Ltd.
2230 Rte 102, Gagetown, NB E5M 1A1
Tel: 506-488-3544 *Fax:* 506-488-3551
bdaniels@ochardviewltc.ca
www.orchardviewcare.ca
Year Founded: 1972
Number of Beds: 40 beds
Betty Daniels, Administrator
506/488-3586
Charlotte Hiscock, Director of Care

Grand Falls: Grand Falls Manor Inc.
Affiliée à: Vitalité Health Network
433, rue Evangeline, Grand Falls, NB E3Z 1G5
Tél: 506-473-7726 *Téléc:* 506-473-7849
Nombre de lits: 69 lits
Maurice Richard, Administrateur
506/473-7726
Gaetan Theriult, Director, Physical Plant

Grand Manan: Grand Manan Nursing Home Inc.
Affiliated with: Horizon Health Network
266, Rte. 776, Grand Manan, NB E5G 1A5
Tel: 506-662-7111 *Fax:* 506-662-7117
Number of Beds: 30 beds
Joanne Ingalls, Administrator
506-662-7111

Hampton: Dr. V.A. Snow Centre Inc.
54 Demille Ct., Hampton, NB E5N 5S7
Tel: 506-832-6210 *Fax:* 506-832-7674
info@snownursing.com
snownursing.com
Number of Beds: 50 beds
Terry MacNeill, Administrator
506/832-6214
Bill Bettle, Maintenance Supervisor

Hartland: Central Carleton Nursing Home Inc.
139 Rockland Rd., Hartland, NB E7P 1E9
Tel: 506-375-3033 *Fax:* 506-375-3035
Number of Beds: 30 beds
Gwen Cullins-Jones, Administrator

Inkerman: Résidences Inkerman Inc.
1171, ch Pallot, Inkerman, NB E8P 1C2
Tél: 506-336-3909 *Téléc:* 506-336-3912
Nombre de lits: 30 lits
Michel Haché, Directeur genéral
Paul Doucet, Coordinateur, Services environnementaux

Lamèque: Les Résidences Lucien Saindon Inc.
26, rue de l-H"pital, Lamèque, NB E8T 1C3
Tél: 506-344-3232 *Téléc:* 506-344-3240
Nombre de lits: 54 lits
Gaëtan Haché, Directeur général
506/344-3245

Memramcook: Foyer St. Thomas de la Vallée de Memramcook Inc.
100, rue Notre-Dame, Memramcook, NB E3K 3W3
Tél: 506-758-2110 *Téléc:* 506-758-9489
pierrela@nb.aibn.com
Nombre de lits: 30 lits
Pierre Landry, Directeur général
Alexandre Gaudet, Directrice, Installations matériels

Mill Cove: Mill Cove Nursing Home Inc.
5647 Rte 105, Mill Cove, NB E4C 3A5
Tel: 506-488-3033 *Fax:* 506-488-3037
mcceo@millcovenh.com
www.millcovenh.com
Note: Specialties: Nursing care for persons with special needs; Podiatry; Psychology; Rehabilitation; Snoezelen rooms
G. Paul Mills, Administrator
506/488-3033, ext. 2

Minto: W.G. Bishop Nursing Home
1100 Pleasant Dr., Minto, NB E4B 3Y6
Tel: 506-327-7853 *Fax:* 506-327-7812
www.wgbishopnursinghome.org
Number of Beds: 30 beds
Kathy Donaldson, Administrator
506/327-7809

Miramichi: Miramichi Senior Citizens Home Inc.
Affiliated with: Horizon Health Network
1400 Water St., Miramichi, NB E1N 1A4
Tel: 506-778-6810 *Fax:* 506-778-6860
msch@nb.aibn.com
www.miramichiseniorshome.com
Number of Beds: 81 beds
Margaret Manderson, Administrator
Macrena Jardine, Director, Plant Maintenance

Miramichi: Mount Saint Joseph Nursing Home
Affiliated with: Horizon Health Network
PO Box 1002, 51 Lobban Ave., Miramichi, NB E1N 3W4
Tel: 506-778-6550 *Fax:* 506-778-0193
Number of Beds: 133 beds
Robert B. Stewart, Executive Director
506/778-6555
Jan Flieger, Director, Support Services

Moncton: Kenneth E. Spencer Memorial Home Inc.
Affiliated with: Horizon Health Network
35 Atlantic Baptist Ave., Moncton, NB E1E 4N3
Tel: 506-858-7870 *Fax:* 506-858-9674
info@abschi.com
Number of Beds: 200 beds
Barbara Cook, Administrator
Byron Cole, Director of Support Services

Moncton: Villa du Repos Inc.
Affiliée à: Horizon Health Network
474, promenade Elmwood, Moncton, NB E1A 2X3
Tél: 506-857-3560 *Téléc:* 506-859-1619
Nombre de lits: 126 lits
Paul Williams, Directeur général
Louis Audet, Directeur, Installations matériels

Paquetville: Manoir Édith B. Pinet Inc.
1189, rue des Fondateurs, Paquetville, NB E8R 1A9
Tél: 506-764-2444 *Téléc:* 506-764-2451
Nombre de lits: 30 lits
Léonard Légère, Administrateur
506/764-2445
Guy Thériault, Directeur, Installations phys.

Perth-Andover: Victoria Glen Manor Inc.
30 Beech Glen Rd., Perth-Andover, NB E7H 1J9
Tel: 506-273-4885 *Fax:* 506-273-4975
office@vgm.ca
www.vgm.ca
Number of Beds: 65 beds
Note: Long-term care home
Eric Haddad, Administrator
506/273-4824

Port Elgin: Westford Nursing Home
57 West Main St., Port Elgin, NB E4M 1L7
Tel: 506-538-2307 *Fax:* 506-538-7293
admwnh@nb.aibn.com
www.westfordnursinghome.com
Year Founded: 1986
Number of Beds: 30 beds
Note: Home for seniors and physically and mentally challenged adults
Judith White, Executive Director
Ian Hurley, Manager, Environmental Support Services

Rexton: Rexton Lions Nursing Home Inc.
84 Main St., Rexton, NB E4W 2B3
Tel: 506-523-7720 *Fax:* 506-523-7703
rex_general@nb.aibn.com
Number of Beds: 30 beds
Dianne Robichaud, Administrator
506/523-7778

Riverview: The Salvation Army Lakeview Manor
50 Suffolk St., Riverview, NB E1B 4K6
Tel: 506-387-2012 *Fax:* 506-387-7200
www.maritime.salvationarmy.ca
Number of Beds: 50 beds
Note: Specialties: Geriatric care; Care for persons with dementia
Maj. Shirley King, Executive Director

Rogersville: Foyer Assomption
CP 296, 62, rue Assomption, Rogersville, NB E4Y 1S5
Tél: 506-775-2040 *Téléc:* 506-775-2053
Nombre de lits: 50 lits
Anne Cormier, Directrice générale
506/775-2043
Ronald Poirier, Chef, Installations matériels

Saint John: Carleton-Kirk Lodge
Affiliated with: Horizon Health Network
2 Carleton Kirk Pl., Saint John, NB E2M 5B8
Tel: 506-635-7040 *Fax:* 506-635-7038
Number of Beds: 70 beds
Tim Stevens, Executive Director

Saint John: Church of St. John & St. Stephen Home Inc.
Affiliated with: Horizon Health Network
130 University Ave., Saint John, NB E2K 4K3
Tel: 506-634-6001 *Fax:* 506-634-6126
Note: Specialty: Long-term care
Darlene Cannell, Administrator

Saint John: Kennebec Manor Inc.
Affiliated with: Horizon Health Network
475 Woodward Ave., Saint John, NB E2K 4N1
Tel: 506-632-9628 *Fax:* 506-658-9376
Number of Beds: 70 beds
Judith Ann Lane, Administrator
506/658-0591

Saint John: Loch Lomond Villa, Inc.
Affiliated with: Horizon Health Network
185 Loch Lomond Rd., Saint John, NB E2J 3S3
Tel: 506-643-7175 *Fax:* 506-643-7198
bwilkins@lochlomondvilla.nb.ca (Executive Assistant)
www.lochlomondvilla.com
Year Founded: 1973
Number of Beds: 196 beds
Note: Specialties: Specialized units for Alzheimers & Psychogeriatric needs
Cindy Donovan, Administrator
506/643-7130,
Valerie O'Leary, Director, Nursing
Paul Mills, Director, Operations

Saint John: Rocmaura Inc.
Affiliated with: Horizon Health Network
10 Park St., Saint John, NB E2K 4P1
Tel: 506-643-7050 *Fax:* 506-643-7053
reception@rocmaura.com
www.rocmaura.com
Year Founded: 1972
Number of Beds: 150 beds
Note: Christian nursing home; affiliated with the Sisters of Charity of the Immaculate Conception (SCIC)
Sr. Susan Quinn, Administrator
506/643-7060
Harry Seele, Maintenance Supervisor

Saint John: Turnbull Nursing Home Inc.
Affiliated with: Horizon Health Network
Former Name: Turnbull Home
231 Britain St., Saint John, NB E2L 0A4
Tel: 506-643-7200 *Fax:* 506-648-9786
turnbulloffice@nb.aibn.com
Number of Beds: 50 beds
Note: Specialty: Long-term care
Elizabeth Crouchman, Administrator
506/643-7211
Brian Worden, Director, Physical Plant

Saint-Antoine: Foyer Saint-Antoine
7, av de l'Église, Saint-Antoine, NB E4V 1L6
Tél: 506-525-4040 *Téléc:* 506-525-4090
www3.nbnet.nb.ca/fsa
Nombre de lits: 30 lits
Gilles C. Ouellette, Administrateur
Gérard-Eugene Richard, Chef, Installations matériels

Saint-Basile: Foyer Saint-Joseph de Saint-Basile Inc.
475, rue Principale, Saint-Basile, NB E7C 1J2
Tél: 506-263-3462 *Téléc:* 506-263-3467
Nombre de lits: 126 lits
Louisette Landry-Bouchard, Directrice générale
506/263-3465

Roger Lévesque, Directeur, Installations matériels

Saint-Léonard: Foyer Notre-Dame de Saint-Léonard Inc.
604, rue Principale, Saint-Léonard, NB E7E 2H5
Tél: 506-423-3151 Téléc: 506-423-3152
Nombre de lits: 45 lits
Denis J. Michaud, Administrateur
506/423-3150

Saint-Louis-de-Kent: Villa Maria Inc.
19, rue du College, Saint-Louis-de-Kent, NB E4X 1C2
Tél: 506-876-3488 Téléc: 506-876-3466
Nombre de lits: 73 lits
Jean Paul Mazerolle, Administrateur
Sylvio Gigou, Directeur, Installations matériels

Saint-Quentin: Résidence Mgr. Melanson Inc.
11, rue Levesque, Saint-Quentin, NB E8A 1T1
Tél: 506-235-6030 Téléc: 506-235-6075
Nombre de lits: 42 lits
Susie Roy, Directrice générale
Rejeanne Chouinere, Superviseur
Claude Paquet, Chef, Installations

Shediac: Villa Providence Shédiac Inc.
403, rue Main, Shediac, NB E4P 2B9
Tél: 506-532-4484 Téléc: 506-532-5909
roger.hebert@vp-vr.ca
Nombre de lits: 190 lits
Roger T. Hébert, Directeur général
Regin LeBlanc, Chef, Entretien ménager

Shippagan: Les Résidences Mgr. Chiasson Inc.
128, rue Mgr Chiasson, Shippagan, NB E8S 1X7
Tél: 506-336-3266 Téléc: 506-336-3099
Nombre de lits: 100 lits
Octave Haché, Directeur général

St Andrews: Passamaquoddy Lodge Inc.
230 Sophia St., St Andrews, NB E5B 2C2
Tel: 506-529-5240 Fax: 506-529-5258
lezlie.leblanc@nb.aibn.com
www.passamaquoddylodge.ca
Number of Beds: 60 beds
Note: Nursing home
Catherine Smith, Administrator
506/529-5242
F. Meredith, Supervisor, Plant Maintenance

St Stephen: Lincourt Manor Inc.
PO Box 116, 1 Chipman St., St Stephen, NB E3L 2W9
Tel: 506-466-7855 Fax: 506-466-7853
Note: Specialty: Long term care
Jane Lyons, Administrator
Ron Hall, Maintenance Supervisor

St Stephen: Maria F. Ganong Seniors Residence
Former Name: Maria F. Ganong Old Folks Home
Also Known As: Lonicera Hall
28 Union St., St Stephen, NB E3L 1T1
Tel: 506-466-1471
lonicerahall@nb.aibn.com
www.lonicerahall.com
Number of Beds: 19 rooms
Pat Steves, Administrator

Stanley: Nashwaak Villa Inc.
PO Box 340, 32 Lime Kiln Rd., Stanley, NB E6B 2K5
Tel: 506-367-7731 Fax: 506-367-7745
Number of Beds: 30 beds
Bonnie MacNeil, Administrator
506/367-7734

Sussex: Kiwanis Nursing Home Inc.
11 Bryant Dr., Sussex, NB E4E 2P3
Tel: 506-432-3118 Fax: 506-432-3104
knhi@nb.aibn.com
Number of Beds: 70 beds
Keri Marr, CA, Administrator
Ralph Mayfield, Director, Plant Maintenance

Tabusintac: Tabusintac Nursing Home
10 Old Manse Rd., Tabusintac, NB E9H 1G4
Tel: 506-779-4100 Fax: 506-779-8149
Betty Blake, Administrator

Tracadie-Sheila: Villa Saint-Joseph Inc.
3400, rue Albert, Tracadie-Sheila, NB E1X 1C8
Tél: 506-394-4800 Téléc: 506-394-4826
Nombre de lits: 64 lits
Paul Arseneau, Directeur général
506/394-4820

Welshpool: Campobello Lodge
Affiliated with: Horizon Health Network
640 Rte. 774, #2, Welshpool, NB ESE 1A5
Tel: 506-752-7101 Fax: 506-752-7105
Number of Beds: 30 beds
Sherry Johnston, Administrator
506/752-7030
Raye Brown, Maintenance Supervisor

Long Term/Retirement Care

Special Treatment Centres

Campbellton: Notre-Dame House Inc.
PO Box 158, Campbellton, NB E3N 3G4
Tel: 506-789-0390 Fax: 506-753-3718
maisonnotredame@nb.aibn.com
Note: Maison Notre-Dame is a shelter for women who have experienced violence or abuse.
Stefanie Savoie, Executive Director

Long Term Care Facilities

Acadieville: Villa Acadie Ltée
4057, rte. 480, Acadieville, NB E4Y 1Z3
Tél: 506-775-6088
Nombre de lits: 13 lits
Bernice Doiron, Proprietor

Baker Brook: Résidence Notre Dame
CP 38, 3741, rue Principale, Baker Brook, NB E7A 2A5
Tél: 506-258-3322
Nombre de lits: 18 lits
Roland Bouchard, Directeur général

Fredericton: Women's Institute Home
681 Union St., Fredericton, NB E3A 3N8
Tel: 506-454-0798 Fax: 506-451-8949
nbwi@nb.aibn.com
www.nbwi.ca
Number of Beds: 21 beds
Marion Briand, Supervisor

Miramichi: Howard Henderson House Inc.
Affiliated with: Horizon Health Network
225 Wellington St., Miramichi, NB E1N 1N1
Tel: 506-773-6522
Note: Residential care is provided for adults who are mentally or physically challenged.
Cathy McDonald, Director

Moncton: Alternative Residences Alternatives (ARA)
Affiliated with: Horizon Health Network
100 Botsford St., Moncton, NB E1C 4W9
Tel: 506-854-7229 Fax: 506-853-6051
altres@rogers.com
Note: Alternative Residences provides supervision & support to persons with a mental illness. Services include assistance with medication intake, the development of social & personal skills, dietary guidance, assistance with budgets, & searches for housing.
Alternative Residences' subidized shared housing complexes accommodate 28, with minimal staff support. The organization's affordable community apartments house 16 clients.
Chantal Ricker, General Manager & Human Resources Officer
Susan McLure, Accounting Officer
Marc Babin, House Coordinator, Crisis Intervention Centre
Luc Bellefleur, House Coordinator, Halls Street
Nancy MacKinnon, House Coordinator, Transition House
Jay Poirier, House Coordinator, Church Street
Catherine Reeder, House Coordinator, Cameron Street

Moncton: Birchmount Lodge
Affiliated with: Horizon Health Network
144 Birchmount Dr., Moncton, NB E1C 8E7
Tel: 506-384-7573 Fax: 506-384-8143
Number of Beds: 32 beds
Donald Vossburgh, Administrator

Moncton: Moncton Community Residences
Affiliated with: Horizon Health Network
357 Collishaw St., Moncton, NB E1C 9R2
Tel: 506-858-0550 Fax: 506-858-0271
mcri3@nb.aibn.com
Number of Beds: 30 beds
Jerry Kirkpatrick, General Manager

Moncton: Moncton Community Residences Inc.
Affiliated with: Horizon Health Network
Former Name: Reade House
357 Collishaw St., Moncton, NB E1C 9R2
Tel: 506-858-0550 Fax: 506-858-0271
mcri@nb.aibn.com
www.monctoncommunityresidences.com
Number of Beds: 5 beds
Note: Provides residential services to people with developmental challenges, ranging from group homes to assistance with independent living
Jerry Kirkpatrick, Administrator

Moncton: Moncton Community Residences Inc.
Affiliated with: Horizon Health Network
Former Name: West Lane House
357 Collishaw St., Moncton, NB E1C 9R2
Tel: 506-858-0550 Fax: 506-858-0271
mcri3@nb.aibn.com
Number of Beds: 8 beds
Note: Provides residential services to developmentally challenged adults
Jerry Kirkpatrick, Administrator

Moncton: Moncton Community Residences, Inc.
Affiliated with: Horizon Health Network
Former Name: Norwood House
357 Collishaw St., Moncton, NB E1C 9R2
Tel: 506-858-0550 Fax: 506-858-0271
mcri3@nb.aibn.com
Number of Beds: 6 beds
Note: Provides residential services to people with developmental challenges
Jerry Kirkpatrick, Administrator

Pennfield: Collingwood Home
249 Black Harbour Rd., Rte. 176, Pennfield, NB E5H 2M1
Tel: 506-456-3533
Number of Beds: 20 beds
Dan Drost, Administrator

Riverview: Grass Home
Former Name: N-Joy Homes Ltd.
774 Coverdale Rd., Riverview, NB E1B 3L5
Tel: 506-386-1740 Fax: 506-386-7040
Number of Beds: 24 beds
John Grass, Proprietor/Administrator

Robertville: La Villa Sormany Inc.
1735, ch. Ste Thérèse, Rte. 322, Robertville, NB E8K 2T6
Tél: 506-542-2731 Téléc: 506-542-2733
Nombre de lits: 40 lits
Lucie Marteau, Directrice générale

Sackville: Drew Nursing Home
165 Main St., Sackville, NB E4L 4S2
Tel: 506-364-4900 Fax: 506-364-4921
office@drewnursinghome.ca
www.drewnursinghome.ca
Number of Beds: 130 beds
Note: senior apartments
Linda Leroux, Administrator
506/364-4822
Ray Letcher, Director, Environmental Services

Saint John: New Direction Inc.
Affiliated with: Horizon Health Network
PO Box 549, Saint John, NB E2L 3Z8
Tel: 506-643-6207 Fax: 506-643-6209
newdir3@nb.aibn.com
Number of Beds: 43 beds
Note: Provides housing and support services to persons suffering from mental illness
Gayle Capson, Executive Director

Saint John: Westport Residential Facility
Affiliated with: Horizon Health Network
427 Prince St., Saint John, NB E2M 1R2
Tel: 506-674-2069 Fax: 506-832-0808
Number of Beds: 18 beds
Beverly Rideout, Administrator

Sainte-Anne-de-Madawaska: Foyer Mont St-Joseph
8, rue St-Joseph, Sainte-Anne-de-Madawaska, NB E7E 1L1
Tél: 506-445-2755
Nombre de lits: 16 lits

Tabusintac: Foyer Prime Breau
14 Covedell Rd., Tabusintac, NB E9H 1E6
Tél: 506-779-4445
Nombre de lits: 4 lits
Roséanna Breau, Propriétrice

Mental Health Facilities

Mental Health Hospitals/Facilities

Campbellton: **Centre Hospitalier Restigouche**
Affiliée à: Vitalité Health Network
CP 10, 63, ch Gallant, Campbellton, NB E3N 3G2
Tél: 506-789-7000 *Téléc:* 506-789-7065
www.santerestigouchehealth.com
Nombre de lits: 150 lits

Saint John: **Centracare Saint John Inc.**
Affiliated with: Horizon Health Network
PO Box 3220 Stn. B, 414 Bay St., Saint John, NB E2M 4H7
Tel: 506-649-2550 *Fax:* 506-649-2520
Number of Beds: 50 beds
Ed Harriet, Contact
506-649-2712

Shippagan: **Pavillon St-Jérôme Inc.**
150, 17e rue, Shippagan, NB E8S 1G4
Tél: 506-336-8609 *Téléc:* 506-336-8652
Nombre de lits: 12 lits
Note: résidence pour adultes handicapés intellectuels
Louise Pichette, Directrice

Special Care Homes

Campbellton: **Duguay's Special Care Home**
20 Dover St., Campbellton, NB E3N 1P3
Tel: 506-789-1208
Number of Beds: 9 units
Note: Duguay's is a licensed special care home in New Brunswick.
Susan Duguay, Administrator

Harvey Station: **Swanhaven Adult Residential Facility**
1915, Rte. 3, Harvey Station, NB E6K 3K1
Tel: 506-366-2950 *Fax:* 506-366-1010
Number of Beds: 25 units
Note: Specialty: Long-term care
Frances P. Ward, Owner

Moncton: **Ritchie V Manor II**
Affiliated with: Horizon Health Network
2031 Mountain Rd., Moncton, NB E1G 1B1
Tel: 506-384-7658
Number of Beds: 20 beds
Debbie Teakles, Proprietor

Moncton: **Smith Special Care Home Ltd.**
Affiliated with: Horizon Health Network
56 Dorchester St., Moncton, NB E1E 3A7
Tel: 506-383-2826 *Fax:* 506-383-2826
Number of Beds: 10 beds
Connie Whitman

Ratters Corner: **Wilson Special Care Home**
510 Drury's Cove Rd., Ratters Corner, NB E4E 3L4
Tel: 506-433-5532
Number of Beds: 5 beds
Sharon Wilson, Proprietor

Saint John: **Champlain House**
Affiliated with: Horizon Health Network
18 Hayes Ave., Saint John, NB E2M 5K3
Tel: 506-672-4651
Year Founded: 1983
Number of Beds: 5 beds
Barbara McMullin, Administrator
barb.mcmullin@rogers.com

Saint John: **Forest Hills Special Care Home**
Affiliated with: Horizon Health Network
Former Name: Burnside Special Care Home
30 Mountain Rd., Saint John, NB E2J 2W8
Tel: 506-633-0743
Number of Beds: 10 beds
Janet Hebert, Proprietor

Saint John: **Seale Special Care Home**
Affiliated with: Horizon Health Network
295 Millidge Ave., Saint John, NB E2K 2M9
Tel: 506-693-3719
Number of Beds: 5 beds
Verna Seale, Proprietor

Titusville: **Yvonne's Special Care Home**
1773 Rte. 860, Titusville, NB E5N 3W2
Tel: 506-832-7186
Number of Beds: 18 units
Note: Yvonne's is a special care home for the elderly.
Yvonne Clark, Proprietor

Newfoundland & Labrador

Government Departments in Charge

NEWFOUNDLAND & LABRADOR: Newfoundland & Labrador Department of Health & Community Services
1st Floor West Block, Confederation Bldg., PO Box 8700, St. John's, NL A1B 4J6
Tel: 709-729-4984 *Fax:* 709-729-5824
healthinfo@gov.nl.ca
www.gov.nl.ca/health
Hon. Susan Sullivan, Minister
709-729-3124, SusanSullivan@gov.nl.ca

Regional Health Authorities

Corner Brook: **Western Health**
Former Name: Western Regional Integrated Health Authority
PO Box 2005, 1 Brookfield Ave., Western Memorial Hosp, Corner Brook, NL A2H 6C7
Tel: 709-637-5245 *Fax:* 709-637-5159
www.westernhealth.nl.ca
Number of Beds: 226 acute care, 441 long-term care
Population Served: 79460*Number of Employees:* 3100
Note: 26 office sites, community based medical services from 26 medical clinic sites (including traveling clinic sites), and eight health facilities. The health facilities include two hospitals: Sir Thomas Roddick Hospital in Stephenville and Western Memorial Regional Hospital in Corner Brook; four health centres: Dr. Charles L. LeGrow Health Centre in Port aux Basques, Bonne Bay Health Centre in Norris Point, Calder Health Centre in Burgeo and Rufus Guinchard Health Centre in Port Saunders; and two long term care centres: Corner Brook Long Term Care Centre in Corner Brook and Bay St. George Long Term Care Centre in Stephenville Crossing. Within its facilities, Western Health operates 276 acute care beds, and 464 long term care beds, as well as 40 enhanced assisted living beds for individuals with mild to moderate dementia.
Dr. Susan Gillam, President/CEO

Grand Falls-Windsor: **Central Health**
Regional Office, 21 Carmelite Rd., Grand Falls-Windsor, NL A2A 1Y4
Tel: 709-292-1289
www.centralhealth.nl.ca
Number of Beds: 519 long term care beds; 269 acute care beds; 32 residential units; 28 bassinets
Population Served: 94000*Number of Employees:* 3179
Karen McGrath, Chief Executive Officer
7092922138, karen.mcgrath@centralhealth.nl.ca
Sherry Freake, Chief Operating Officer, Gander
7092565531, sherry.freake@centralhealth.nl.ca
Sean Tulk, Chief Operating Officer, Grand Falls-Windsor
7092922454, sean.tulk@centralhealth.nl.ca
Trudy Stuckless, Chief Nursing Officer; Vice-President, Professional Standards
7092922151, trudy.stuckless@centralhealth.nl.ca
Rosemarie Goodyear, Senior Vice-President, Quality, Planning, & Priorities
7096516328, rosemarie.goodyear@centralhealth.nl.
Heather Brown, Vice-President, Rural Health
7092922151, heather.brown@centralhealth.nl.ca
Terry Ings, Vice-President, Human Resources
7092565531, terry.ings@centralhealth.nl.ca
John Kattenbusch, Vice-President, Finance & Corporate Services
7092565401, john.kattenbusch@centralhealth.nl.ca
Dr. Michael Zuckerman, Vice-President, Medical Services
7092922151, michael.zuckerman@centralhealth.nl.c
Stephanie Power, Director, Communications
7092565532, stephanie.power@centralhealth.nl.ca

Happy Valley-Goose Bay: **Labrador-Grenfell Regional Health Authority**
Former Name: Labrador-Grenfell Health
PO Box 7000 Stn. C, Labrador Health Centre, Happy Valley-Goose Bay, NL A0P 1C0
Tel: 709-897-2267 *Fax:* 709-896-4032
www.lghealth.ca
Year Founded: 2005
Area Served: North of Bartlett's Harbour on the Northern Peninsula, Labrador*Population Served:* 37000*Number of Employees:* 1660
Eric Power, Acting CEO & Vice President, Finance & Corporate Services
Dr. Michael Jong, Vice-President, Medical Services
Norma Forsey, Vice President, Quality Management
Ozette Simpson, Chief Operating Officer/Vice President, Long Term Care
Julie Nicholas, Vice President & COO, Acute Care
Della Connell, Vice President & COO, Community & Aboriginal Affairs
Barbara Blake, Vice President, People & Information

St. John's: **Eastern Health Integrated Health Authority**
Also Known As: Eastern Health
Health Sciences Centre, Prince Philip Dr., St. John's, NL A1B 3V6
Tel: 709-777-1399 *Toll-Free:* 1-877-444-1399
zelda.burt@easternhealth.ca
www.easternhealth.ca
Info Line: 1-888-709-2929
Number of Beds: 1,696 long term care beds; 987 acute care beds; 9 observation beds
Area Served: Avalon, Burin and Bonavista Peninsulas*Population Served:* 290000*Number of Employees:* 13000
Note: Facilities: 80+ hospitals, health care centres, long-term care facilities, & community care sites. Number of Employees: 12,000+ health care & support services professionals. Area Covered: Region of Newfoundland & Labrador east of Port Blandford, including Port Blandford, the Avalon, Burin, & Bonavista Peninsulas, & Bell Island (111 incorporated municipalities, 69 local service districts, & 66 unincorporated municipal units)
Vickie Kaminski, President; Chief Executive Officer
709-777-1301, ceo@easternhealth.ca
Michael J. O'Keefe, Chair
Norma Baker, Chief Operating Officer, Adult Acute Care (St. John's)
Beverley Clarke, Chief Operating Officer, Community, Children & Women, & Mental Health
Pat Coish-Snow, Chief Operating Officer, Peninsulas
Alice Kennedy, Chief Operating Officer, Long Term Care (St. John's) & Community Living
Fay Matthews, Chief Operating Officer, Rural Avalon Child Youth & Family Services
George Butt, Vice-President, Corporate Services
Stephen Dodge, Vice-President, People & Information Services
Dr. Oscar Howell, Vice-President, Medical Services & Diagnostics
Wayne Miller, Vice-President, Planning, Quality, & Research

Hospitals

Hospitals - General

Burin: **Burin Peninsula Health Care Centre**
Affiliated with: Eastern Regional Integrated Health Authority
PO Box 340, Burin, NL A0E 1E0
Tel: 709-891-1040 *Fax:* 709-891-3375
www.easternhealth.ca
Number of Beds: 42 beds
Note: Hospital Specialties: Diagnostic imaging; Laboratory services; General surgery; Acute care; Gynecology; Obstetrics; Pediatrics; Psychiatry; Speech pathology, Physiotherapy, Occupational therapy; Respiratory therapy; Palliative care
Kim Green, Manager, Acute Care
709-891-3490, Fax: 709-891-3375, kim.green@easternhealth.ca

Clarenville: **Dr. G.B. Cross Memorial Hospital**
Affiliated with: Eastern Regional Integrated Health Authority
67 Manitoba Dr., Clarenville, NL A5A 1K3
Tel: 709-466-3411
www.easternhealth.ca
Note: Hospital Specialties: Surgery; Intensive care; Obstetrics; Respiratory therapy; Physiotherapy; Dietitian services; Palliative care
Dr. Oscar Howell, Vice-President, Medical Services & Diagnostics, Eastern Health

Corner Brook: **Western Memorial Regional Hospital**
Affiliated with: Western Health
PO Box 2005, Corner Brook, NL A2H 6J7
Tel: 709-637-5000 *Fax:* 709-637-5410
Number of Beds: 192 acute care beds
M. Wasmeier

Fogo: **Fogo Island Health Centre**
Affiliated with: Central Regional Integrated Health Authority
PO Box 9, Fogo, NL A0G 2B0
Tel: 709-266-2221
www.centralhealth.nl.ca
Year Founded: 1953
Note: Hospital Specialties: Primary care; Public health

Karen McGrath, Chief Executive Officer, Central Regional Health Authority

Gander: James Paton Memorial Hospital
Affiliated with: Central Regional Integrated Health Authority
125 TransCanada Hwy., Gander, NL A1V 1P7
Tel: 709-256-2500 *Fax:* 709-256-7800
Number of Beds: 92 acute care beds
J. Horwood

Grand Falls-Windsor: Central Newfoundland Regional Health Centre
Affiliated with: Central Regional Integrated Health Authority
50 Union St., Grand Falls-Windsor, NL A2A 2E1
Tel: 709-292-2500 *Fax:* 709-292-2249
Note: Hospital Specialties: Emergency services; Radiology; Surgical care; Ambulatory care services; Maternal / newborn unit; Cardiology; Neurology; Otolaryngology; Rehabilitation services; Physiotherapy; Occupational therapy; Pharmacy services
Kelly Adams, Chief Operating Officer
kelly.adams@centralhealth.nl.ca

Happy Valley-Goose Bay: Labrador Health Centre
Affiliated with: Labrador-Grenfell Regional Integrated Health Authority
Former Name: Melville Hospital
PO Box 7000 Stn. C, Happy Valley-Goose Bay, NL A0P 1C0
Tel: 709-897-2000 *Fax:* 709-896-4032
Number of Beds: 25 beds
Note: Full diagnostic services; Rehabilitation
E. Harding
Ed Sharpe, Supervisor, Plant Maintenance

Labrador City: Captain William Jackman Memorial Hospital (CWJ)
Affiliated with: Labrador-Grenfell Regional Integrated Health Authority
410 Booth Ave., Labrador City, NL A2V 2K1
Tel: 709-944-2632
www.lghealth.ca
Year Founded: 1965
Number of Beds: 14 acute care beds; 6 long term care beds
Note: Hospital Specialties: Emergency services; Diagnostic imaging; Intensive care; Acute care; Obstetrics; Physiotherapy; Occupational therapy; Speech therapy; Respiratory therapy; Health education; Respite care; Long term care; Palliative care

St. Anthony: Charles S. Curtis Memorial Hospital
Affiliated with: Labrador-Grenfell Regional Integrated Health Authority
Also Known As: Curtis Hospital
178-200 West St., St. Anthony, NL A0K 4S0
Tel: 709-454-3333
www.lghealth.ca
Number of Beds: 50 hospital beds; 48 long term care beds at the John M. Gray Centre, which is adjoined to Charles S. Curtis Memorial Hospital
Note: Hospital Specialties: General surgery; Radiology; Pathology; Obstetrics; Gynecology; Genetics research; Pediatrics; Ophthalmology; Chemotherapy services; Orthopedics; Urology; Psychiatry; Rehabilitation services, including occupational therapy & physiotherapy; Acute care; Diabetes education; Social work
Michael Jong, Vice-President, Medical Services, Labrador-Grenfell Health

St. John's: Dr. Leonard A. Miller Centre
Former Name: Quidi Vidi Hospital
Also Known As: The Miller Centre
100 Forest Rd., St. John's, NL A1A 1E5
Tel: 709-777-6555
Year Founded: 1851
Note: Specialty: Continuing care; Rehabilitation; Residential care for veterans of Newfoundland & Labrador; Centre for Nursing Studies

St. John's: The General Hospital/Health Sciences Centre
Affiliated with: Eastern Regional Integrated Health Authority
300 Prince Phillip Dr., St. John's, NL A1B 3V6
Tel: 709-777-6300 *Fax:* 709-777-6770
www.easternhealth.ca/OurServices.aspx?d=2&id=118&p=75
Number of Beds: 344 acute care beds
Note: A tertiary acute care facility & teaching hospital affiliated with Memorial University Schools of Medicine, Nursing, & Pharmacy.
Vickie Kaminski, President/CEO, ERIHA
709-777-1301, ceo@easternhealth.ca
Deborah Collins, Manager, Media Relations, ERIHA
709-777-1339, deborah.collins@easternhealth.ca

St. John's: Janeway Children's Health and Rehabilitation Centre
Affiliated with: Eastern Regional Integrated Health Authority
300 Prince Philip Dr., St. John's, NL A1B 3V6
Tel: 709-777-6300 *Fax:* 709-777-4446
www.easternhealth.ca
Number of Beds: 83 beds
Note: teaching hospital
Carol Chafe, Program Director
Keith Collins, Environmental Services Manager
709/778-4222

St. John's: St. Clare's Mercy Hospital
Affiliated with: Eastern Regional Integrated Health Authority
154 LeMarchant Rd., St. John's, NL A1C 5B8
Tel: 709-777-1317 *Fax:* 709-777-5470
Year Founded: 1922
Number of Beds: 216 acute care beds
Note: tertiary hospital
Ernie Power, Director, Plant Maintenance
L. Jones, CEO

Stephenville: Sir Thomas Roddick Hospital
Affiliated with: Western Health
142 Minnesota Dr., Stephenville, NL A2N 1H0
Tel: 709-643-5111 *Fax:* 709-643-2700
westernhealth.nl.ca/index.php/locations/hospitals/sir-thomas-roddick-hospital
Year Founded: 2003
Number of Beds: 44 acute care beds
Note: A comprehensive care facility, with services including emergency, surgery, obstetrics, gynecaelogy, renal care
Karen Alexander, Site Manager
Dr. Alan McComiskey, Chief of Staff

Community Health Centres

Community Health Care Centres

Badgers Quay: Brookfield/Bonnews Health Care Centre
Affiliated with: Central Regional Integrated Health Authority
PO Box 209, Badgers Quay, NL A0G 1B0
Tel: 709-536-2405 *Fax:* 709-536-3334
www.cehcib.nf.ca
Year Founded: 1944
Number of Beds: 12 beds
Kevin Green, Facility Manager
Winston Perry, Director, Maintenance Services

Baie Verte: Baie Verte Peninsula Health Centre
Affiliated with: Central Regional Integrated Health Authority
Baie Verte, NL A0K 1B0
Tel: 709-532-4281 *Fax:* 709-532-4939
Number of Beds: 26 acute care beds, 18 long-term care beds, 1 respite bed
Joyce Barker, Facility Director

Bell Island: Dr. Walter Templeman Community Health Centre
Affiliated with: Eastern Regional Integrated Health Authority
PO Box 580, Wabana, Bell Island, NL A0A 4H0
Tel: 709-488-2821 *Fax:* 709-488-2600
Number of Beds: 20 Beds
T. O'Brien
Jerry Butler, Director, Plant Maintenance

Bonavista: Bonavista Peninsula Health Centre
Affiliated with: Eastern Regional Integrated Health Authority
Former Name: Bonavista Community Health Centre
PO Box 1, Bonavista, NL A0C 1B0
Tel: 709-468-7881 *Fax:* 709-468-7223
Pauline Pardy, Director, Patient/Resident Care

Burgeo: Calder Health Care Centre
Affiliated with: Western Health
PO Box 190, Burgeo, NL A0M 1A0
Tel: 709-886-3350 *Fax:* 709-886-3382
westernhealth.nl.ca
Number of Beds: 3 acute care, 18 continuing care beds
Laurie Porter, Director of Nursing/Site Coordinator

Churchill Falls: Churchill Falls Community Health Centre
Affiliated with: Labrador-Grenfell Regional Integrated Health Authority
General Delivery, Churchill Falls, NL A0R 1A0
Tel: 709-925-3381 *Fax:* 709-925-3246
www.lghealth.ca
Joan Paul Kent, Nurse in Charge

Flowers Cove: Strait of Belle Isle Health Centre
Affiliated with: Labrador-Grenfell Regional Integrated Health Authority
General Delivery, Flowers Cove, NL A0K 2N0
Tel: 709-456-2401
www.lghealth.ca
Number of Beds: 3 beds
Note: Specialties: Ambulatory care; Family medicine; Public health services; Pre-natal classes; Post-natal visiting; Preschool & baby assessments; Dental services; Rehabilitation services; Home care
Judy Applin Poole

Grand Bank: Grand Bank Community Health Centre
Affiliated with: Eastern Regional Integrated Health Authority
PO Box 310, Grand Bank, NL A0E 1W0
Tel: 709-832-2500 *Fax:* 709-832-1164
Joan Penney, Director, Patient/Resident Care
Cyril Parsons, Utility Supervisor

Harbour Breton: Connaigre Peninsula Health Centre
Affiliated with: Central Regional Integrated Health Authority
Former Name: Harbour Breton Health Centre
PO Box 70, Harbour Breton, NL A0H 1P0
Tel: 709-885-2359 *Fax:* 709-885-2358
www.cwhc.nl.ca/cp.htm
Number of Beds: 20 beds: 6 acute, 12 continuing , 1 palliative, 1 respite
Sharon Skinner, Facility Director

Norris Point: Bonne Bay Health Centre
Affiliated with: Western Health
PO Box 70, Norris Point, NL A0K 3V0
Tel: 709-458-2211 *Fax:* 709-458-2074
Number of Beds: 8 acute care, 14 continuing care beds

Northwest River: NorthWest River Clinic
Affiliated with: Labrador-Grenfell Regional Integrated Health Authority
General Delivery, Northwest River, NL A0P 1M0
Tel: 709-497-8351 *Fax:* 709-497-8521

Old Perlican: Dr. A.A. Wilkinson Memorial Health Centre
Affiliated with: Eastern Regional Integrated Health Authority
PO Box 70, Old Perlican, NL A0A 3G0
Tel: 709-587-2200 *Fax:* 709-587-2275
Number of Beds: 4 beds
M. Oliver

Port Saunders: Rufus Guinchard Health Care Centre
Affiliated with: Western Health
PO Box 40, Port Saunders, NL A0K 4H0
Tel: 709-861-3533 *Fax:* 709-861-3772
Number of Beds: 1 palliative care, 6 acute care, 22 continuing care beds
Paulette Lavers, Director of Nursing/Site Coordinator

Port aux Basques: Dr. Charles L. LeGrow Health Centre
Affiliated with: Western Health
PO Box 250, Port aux Basques, NL A0M 1C0
Tel: 709-695-2175 *Fax:* 709-695-3118
westernhealth.nl.ca
Number of Beds: 14 acute care, 30 continuing care beds
S. Savoury, Director of Nursing/Site Coordinator

Springdale: Green Bay Community Health Centre
Affiliated with: Central Regional Integrated Health Authority
PO Box 280, Springdale, NL A0J 1T0
Tel: 709-673-3911 *Fax:* 709-673-3186
Number of Beds: 8 beds; 1 special care, 2 convalescent, 1 palliative
Rose Saunders, Facility Director

Twillingate: **Notre Dame Bay Memorial Health Centre**
Affiliated with: Central Regional Integrated Health Authority
General Delivery, Twillingate, NL A0G 4M0
Tel: 709-884-2131 *Fax:* 709-884-2586
Number of Beds: 31 long-term care beds + 18 acute care beds
Note: Specialties: Outpatient services; Social work; Physiotherapy; Recreation therapy; Dietetics; Diabetes education; Health promotion & protection; Respite care, for children with special needs
Katherine Walters, Director, Health Services
B. Hamlyn, Supervisor, Plant Maintenance

Whitbourne: **Dr. W. H. Newhook Community Health Centre**
Affiliated with: Eastern Regional Integrated Health Authority
General Delivery, Whitbourne, NL A0B 3K0
Tel: 709-759-2300 *Fax:* 709-759-2387
L. English

Nursing Stations

Black Tickle: **Black Tickle Nursing Station**
Affiliated with: Labrador-Grenfell Regional Integrated Health Authority
General Delivery, Black Tickle, NL A0K 1N0
Tel: 709-471-8872 *Fax:* 709-471-8893

Cartwright: **Cartwright Community Clinic**
Affiliated with: Labrador-Grenfell Regional Integrated Health Authority
General Delivery, Cartwright, NL A0K 1V0
Tel: 709-938-7285

Charlottetown: **Charlottetown Community Clinic**
Affiliated with: Labrador-Grenfell Regional Integrated Health Authority
Former Name: Charlottetown Nursing Station
General Delivery, Charlottetown, NL A0K 5Y0
Tel: 709-949-0259
Number of Beds: 3 beds

Forteau: **Labrador South Health Centre**
Affiliated with: Labrador-Grenfell Regional Integrated Health Authority
Forteau, NL A0K 2P0
Tel: 709-931-2450 *Fax:* 709-931-2000
Number of Beds: 15 long-term care beds; 5 in-patient beds
Cornelia Linstead

Hopedale: **Hopedale Nursing Station**
Affiliated with: Labrador-Grenfell Regional Integrated Health Authority
General Delivery, Hopedale, NL A0P 1G0
Tel: 709-933-3857 *Fax:* 709-933-3744
Number of Beds: 3 beds

Makkovik: **Makkovik Nursing Station & Community Service**
Affiliated with: Labrador-Grenfell Regional Integrated Health Authority
General Delivery, Makkovik, NL A0P 1J0
Tel: 709-923-2229 *Fax:* 709-923-2428
Note: Specialties: Pharmaceutical services; Social work. Number of Employees: 2 nurses + 1 part time physician

Mary's Harbour: **Mary's Harbour Community Clinic**
Affiliated with: Labrador-Grenfell Regional Integrated Health Authority
Mary's Harbour, NL A0K 3P0
Tel: 709-921-6228 *Fax:* 709-921-6975
Number of Beds: 1 holding bed + 1 crib
Note: Number of Employees: 3 nurses + 1 social worker + 1 personal care attendant + 1 maintenance person

Nain: **Nain Nursing Station**
Affiliated with: Labrador-Grenfell Regional Integrated Health Authority
General Delivery, Nain, NL A0P 1L0
Tel: 709-922-2912 *Fax:* 709-922-2103

Natuashish: **Natuashish Nursing Station**
Affiliated with: Labrador-Grenfell Regional Integrated Health Authority
Former Name: Davis Inlet Nursing Station
General Delivery, Natuashish, NL A0P 1A0
Tel: 709-478-8842 *Fax:* 709-478-8817

Port Hope Simpson: **Port Hope Simpson Community Clinic**
Affiliated with: Labrador-Grenfell Health
General Delivery, Port Hope Simpson, NL A0K 4E0
Tel: 709-960-0271 *Fax:* 709-960-0392
www.lghealth.ca
Year Founded: 1975
Note: Specialties: Emergency room, basic trauma, cardiac monitoring & resuscitation, dental suite. Number of staff: 9

Postville: **Postville Community Clinic**
Affiliated with: Labrador-Grenfell Health
General Delivery, Postville, NL A0P 1N0
Tel: 709-479-9851 *Fax:* 709-479-9715
www.lghealth.ca
Number of Beds: 1 bed, 1 crib
Note: Number of staff: 3

Rigolet: **Rigolet Nursing Station**
Affiliated with: Labrador-Grenfell Regional Integrated Health Authority
General Delivery, Rigolet, NL A0P 1P0
Tel: 709-947-3386 *Fax:* 709-947-3401
Note: Number of staff: 2 Registered Nurses; visiting physician, dentist & specialists

Roddickton: **White Bay Central Health Centre**
Affiliated with: Labrador-Grenfell Regional Integrated Health Authority
General Delivery, Roddickton, NL A0K 4P0
Tel: 709-457-2215
Number of Beds: 5 beds

St Lewis: **St. Lewis Nursing Station**
Affiliated with: Labrador-Grenfell Regional Integrated Health Authority
General Delivery, St Lewis, NL A0K 4W0
Tel: 709-939-2230 *Fax:* 709-939-2342

Special Treatment Centres

St. John's: **Dr. H. Bliss Murphy Cancer Centre**
Newfoundland Cancer Treatment & Research Foundatio, 300 Prince Philip Dr., St. John's, NL A1B 3V6
Tel: 709-777-6480 *Fax:* 709-753-0927
www.nctrf.nf.ca
Bertha Paulse, CEO

St. John's: **St. John's Site of The Morgentaler Clinic**
The Morgentaler Clinic
#408, 59 Hamlyn Rd. Plaza, St. John's, NL A1E 5X7
Tel: 709-754-3572 *Fax:* 709-754-6626
Toll-Free: 800-755-2044
sjmc@nf.aibn.com
Year Founded: 1990
Note: Specialties: Abortion services; Counselling

Nursing Homes

Botwood: **Dr. Hugh Twomey Health Care Centre**
Affiliated with: Central Regional Integrated Health Authority
PO Box 250, Botwood, NL A0H 1E0
Tel: 709-257-2874 *Fax:* 709-257-4613
Number of Beds: 77 long-term care, 2 respite, 1 palliative care beds
Brenda Kelly, Facility Director

Buchans: **A.M. Guy Memorial Health Centre**
Affiliated with: Central Regional Integrated Health Authority
PO Box 10, Buchans, NL A0H 1G0
Tel: 709-672-3326 *Fax:* 709-672-3390
Number of Beds: 22 beds: 18 long-term, 2 acute care, 1 holding, 1 palliative
Roslyn Lane, Facility Director

Carbonear: **Harbour Lodge Nursing Home**
Affiliated with: Eastern Regional Integrated Health Authority
86 Highroad South, Carbonear, NL A1Y 1A4
Tel: 709-945-5400
www.easternhealth.ca/OurServices.aspx?d=2&id=142&p=76
Number of Beds: 127 beds
Debbie Farrell, Facility Manager
Harry Meados, Director, Environmental Services

Carbonear: **Inter Faith Citizens Home**
Affiliated with: Eastern Regional Integrated Health Authority
41 Water St., Carbonear, NL A1Y 1B1
Tel: 709-945-5300 *Fax:* 709-945-5323
Number of Beds: 53 beds
Deborah Farrell, Facility Manager

Clarke's Beach: **Pentecostal Senior Citizen's Home**
Affiliated with: Eastern Regional Integrated Health Authority
PO Box 130, Clarke's Beach, NL A0A 1W0
Tel: 709-786-2993
www.easternhealth.ca
Number of Beds: 75 beds
Note: Specialties: Nursing care for persons who require Level I, II, & III type care; Social work; Physiotherapy; Occupational therapy; Podiatry; Hearing & vision care
Beverley Bellefleur, Facility Manager

Corner Brook: **Inter Faith Home for Senior Citizens**
Affiliated with: Western Health
1 Elizabeth St., Corner Brook, NL A2H 5L8
Tel: 709-639-9247 *Fax:* 709-639-1126
Number of Beds: 103 long-term care beds
P. Griffin, Director of Nursing/Site Coordinator

Corner Brook: **J.I. O'Connell Centre**
Affiliated with: Western Health
PO Box 2005, 1 Hospital Hill, Corner Brook, NL A2H 6J7
Tel: 709-637-5000 *Fax:* 709-634-3047
Number of Beds: 104 beds

Gander: **Lakeside Homes**
Affiliated with: Central Regional Integrated Health Authority
95 Airport Blvd., Gander, NL A1V 2L7
Tel: 709-256-8850 *Fax:* 709-256-4259
www.cehcib.nf.ca/web/lakeside.htm
Number of Beds: 102 beds; 1 respite
Marlyce Greene, Facility Manager
Sam Butt, Maintenance Supervisor

Gander Bay South: **Riverview Retirement Home Ltd.**
Also Known As: Gander Bay Retirement Home
Gander Bay South, NL A0G 2H0
Tel: 709-676-2773
Number of Beds: 40 beds
Shaun Lane

Grand Bank: **Blue Crest Inter Faith Home**
Affiliated with: Eastern Regional Integrated Health Authority
PO Box 160, Grand Bank, NL A0E 1W0
Tel: 709-832-1660 *Fax:* 709-832-2103
Number of Beds: 70 long-term care beds
Joan Penney, Director, Patient/Resident Care
Cyril Parsons, Maintenance Manager

Grand Falls-Windsor: **Carmelite House**
Affiliated with: Central Regional Integrated Health Authority
21 Carmelite Rd., Grand Falls-Windsor, NL A2A 1Y4
Tel: 709-292-2528 *Fax:* 709-292-2593
Number of Beds: 60 longterm care beds
Michelle Hatt, Facility Director
mhatt@cwhc.nl.ca

Happy Valley-Goose Bay: **Harry L. Paddon Memorial Home**
Affiliated with: Labrador-Grenfell Regional Integrated Health Authority
PO Box 766 Stn. B, Happy Valley-Goose Bay, NL A0P 1E0
Tel: 709-896-3615 *Fax:* 709-896-5241
Number of Beds: 48 beds
K. White
Ronald Lyall, Supervisor, Maintenance

Lewisporte: **North Haven Manor Senior Citizens' Home**
Affiliated with: Central Regional Integrated Health Authority
PO Box 880, 21 Centennial Dr., Lewisporte, NL A0G 3A0
Tel: 709-535-6767 *Fax:* 709-535-8383
Number of Beds: 62 long-term care, 1 palliative, 2 respite beds
Debbie Colbourne, Facility Director

Mount Pearl: **Masonic Park Nursing Home**
Affiliated with: Eastern Regional Integrated Health Authority
Former Name: Masonic Park Senior Citizen's Home
#4000, Bldg. 15, Masonic Park, Mount Carson Ave., Mount Pearl, NL A1N 3K6
Tel: 709-368-6081
www.masonicpark.ca; www.easternhealth.ca
Year Founded: 1982
Number of Beds: 40 long term beds + 200 self-contained cottage

& apt. units
Note: Specialties: Long-term care for seniors
Rolanda Ryan, Resident Care Manager

Springdale: Valley Vista Senior Citizens' Home
Affiliated with: Central Regional Integrated Health Authority
PO Box 130, Springdale, NL A0J 1T0
Tel: 709-673-3936 *Fax:* 709-673-2832
Number of Beds: 75 long-term care beds, 3 respite
Rose Saunders, Facility Director

St Anthony: John M. Gray Centre
Affiliated with: Labrador-Grenfell Regional Integrated Health Authority
Former Name: St. Anthony Interfaith Home
PO Box 69, St Anthony, NL A0K 4S0
Tel: 709-454-0371 *Fax:* 709-454-4134
Year Founded: 1998
Number of Beds: 48 long-term care beds
Dr. Michael Jong, Vice President Medical Affairs
Boyd Rowe, Chief Executive Officer

St. John's: Agnes Pratt Home
Affiliated with: Eastern Regional Integrated Health Authority
239 Topsail Rd., St. John's, NL A1E 2B4
Tel: 709-579-0185 *Fax:* 709-739-5457
www.easternhealth.ca/AboutEH.aspx?d=2&id=150&p=76
Number of Beds: 128 long-term care beds
Linda Colllingwood, Administrator

St. John's: Hoyles-Escasoni Complex
Affiliated with: Eastern Regional Integrated Health Authority
10 Escasoni Pl., St. John's, NL A1A 3R6
Tel: 709-753-7590 *Fax:* 709-753-9620
Number of Beds: 377 beds
Annette Clarke, Manager, Resident Care

St. John's: Saint Luke's Home
Affiliated with: Eastern Regional Integrated Health Authority
24 Road Deluxe, St. John's, NL A1E 5Z3
Tel: 709-579-0052 *Fax:* 709-579-7317
Number of Beds: 126 beds
Note: Nursing homel also owns and operates 54 independent living cottages and the 76-unit Bishop John Meaden Manor Complex
Barbara Ivany, Administrator

St. John's: St. Patrick's Mercy Home
Affiliated with: Eastern Regional Integrated Health Authority
146 Elizabeth Ave., St. John's, NL A1B 1S5
Tel: 709-726-2687 *Fax:* 709-726-0722
Number of Beds: 214 beds
Note: Long-term care facility affiliated with the Roman Catholic Diocese of St. John's
Sr. Phyllis Corbett, Administrator

Stephenville Crossing: Bay St. George Long Term Care Centre
Affiliated with: Western Health
Former Name: Bay St. George Senior Citizens Home
PO Box 250, Stephenville Crossing, NL A0N 2C0
Tel: 709-646-5800 *Fax:* 709-646-2375
Number of Beds: 114 beds
Anne Doyle, Nursing

Long Term/Retirement Care

Long Term Care Facilities

Bonavista: Golden Heights Manor
Affiliated with: Eastern Regional Integrated Health Authority
Postal Service #1, Bonavista, NL A0C 1B0
Tel: 709-468-2043 *Fax:* 709-468-1549
Number of Beds: 64 beds
Pauline Pardy

Placentia: Placentia Health Centre
Affiliated with: Eastern Regional Integrated Health Authority
PO Box 480, Placentia, NL A0B 2Y0
Tel: 709-227-2061 *Fax:* 709-227-5476
www.easternhealth.ca
Number of Beds: 10 acute care, 75 long term care beds
Note: Acute care, long term care (Lions Manor Nursing Home), on an in-patient & out-patient basis
Diane Reid, Facility Manager
W. Whittle, Director, Environmental Services

St Brides: Bay View Manor
General Delivery, St Brides, NL A0B 2Z0
Tel: 709-337-2569
Number of Beds: 10 beds
Note: personal care home
Jerome Quinlan
Beverly Russell

St Lawrence: U.S. Memorial Community Health Centre
Affiliated with: Eastern Regional Integrated Health Authority
PO Box 398, 1 Memorial Dr., St Lawrence, NL A0E 2V0
Tel: 709-873-2330 *Fax:* 709-873-2390
Number of Beds: 40 beds
Note: Long term & protective care units, ambulatory care clinic, nutritional services, pharmacy, visiting specialty clinics
Jocelyn Dunphy, Co-ordinator, Patient/Resident Care

Personal Care Homes

Arnolds Cove: Hilltop Manor
PO Box 280, 96 Spencers Cove Rd., Arnolds Cove, NL A1A 4Y6
Tel: 709-463-5000 *Fax:* 709-463-1005
hollismetcalge@hotmail.com
Number of Beds: 32 beds
Trey Metcalfe

Baie Verte: Baie Verte Manor Ltd.
PO Box 561, 20 High St., Baie Verte, NL A0K 1B0
Tel: 709-532-4615 *Fax:* 709-532-4643
Number of Beds: 30 beds
Donna Rideout, Owner/Administrator

Baie Verte: H. Pardy Manor
PO Box 1, Baie Verte, NL A0K 1B0
Tel: 709-532-4603 *Fax:* 709-329-3281
Number of Beds: 22 beds
Kim Sacrey, Manager

Bay Bulls: Walsh's Personal Care Home
PO Box 42, Rte. 10, Bay Bulls, NL A0A 1C0
Tel: 709-334-2619
Number of Beds: 10 beds
Delores Walsh, Proprietor

Bell Island: Island Manor
PO Box 728, Bell Island, NL A0A 4H0
Tel: 709-488-2966
Number of Beds: 10 beds
Jocelyn Russell

Bishop's Cove: Smith's Personal Care Home
PO Box 86, RR#1, Bishop's Cove, NL A0A 3X0
Tel: 709-589-2189
Number of Beds: 4 beds
Mildred Naomi Smith

Bishops Falls: Exploits Manor
PO Box 850, 2 Helen Tulk Dr., Bishops Falls, NL A0H 1C0
Tel: 709-258-5555
Number of Beds: 30 beds
Alex Faulkner

Cape Anguille: Hilliard's Personal Care Home
PO Box 18, Cape Anguille, NL A0N 1H0
Tel: 709-955-2339
Number of Beds: 14 beds
Minnie Hilliard, Owner/Administrator

Carmanville: Carmanville Manor
PO Box 42, Carmanville, NL A0G 1N0
Tel: 709-534-2244 *Fax:* 709-534-2244
Number of Beds: 21 beds
Jeanne Clarke

Catalina: Seaside Lodge
PO Box 182, Catalina, NL A0C 1J0
Tel: 709-469-3160 *Fax:* 709-469-3161
Number of Beds: 50 beds
Note: Personal care home
Shirley Barney

Catalina: Shirley's Haven
PO Box 29, Catalina, NL A0C 1J0
Tel: 709-469-3160 *Fax:* 709-469-3161
Social Media: facebook.com/pages/Shirleys-Haven-Personal-Care-Home/7799 4615307
Number of Beds: 50 beds
Shirley Barney

Clarenville: Clarenville Rest Home
PO Box 951, 13 Legion Rd., Clarenville, NL A0E 1J0
Tel: 709-466-2447
patrickmolloy@nf.aibn.com
clarenvilleretirementcentre.ca
Number of Beds: 30 beds
Michelle Holloway, Proprietor/Administrator

Clarkes Beach: Brigus Personal Care Home
PO Box 515, Clarkes Beach, NL A0A 1W0
Tel: 709-786-9693 *Fax:* 709-786-4757
Number of Beds: 9 beds
Denise Smith, Co-owner
Keith Smith, Co-owner

Conception Bay South: Greenslade's Personal Care Home
Former Name: Greenslade Special Care Home
12 Wettlaufer Rd., Conception Bay South, NL A1X 7P6
Tel: 709-834-3047 *Fax:* 709-834-3087
Number of Beds: 14 beds
Wayne Greenslade

Corner Brook: Brake's Personal Care Home
292 Curling St., Corner Brook, NL A2H 3J7
Tel: 709-785-5092
Number of Beds: 6 beds
Vera Brake
Vivian Brake

Corner Brook: Mountain View Estates
161 Premier Dr., Corner Brook, NL A2H 7M6
Tel: 709-637-7960 *Fax:* 709-634-0235
www.mountainviewestates.ca
Number of Beds: 84 beds
Note: Nursing home
Byron Brake

Corner Brook: Mountain View House
PO Box 3850, RR#2, Corner Brook, NL A2H 6B9
Tel: 709-783-2019
Number of Beds: 30 beds
Note: Nursing home
Byron Brake

Corner Brook: Xavier House Inc.
19 Mount Bernard Ave., Corner Brook, NL A2H 6K7
Tel: 709-634-2787
Number of Beds: 20 beds
Sr. Rosalie Carey, Administrator

Deer Lake: Deer Lake Manor
#119, 123 Nicholsville Rd., Deer Lake, NL A8A 1W6
Tel: 709-635-2868
Number of Beds: 31 Beds
Dwight Ball, Contact

Embree: Parson's Retirement Home
PO Box 82, Embree, NL A0G 2A0
Tel: 709-535-6094
Number of Beds: 16 beds
Robert Parsons

Flowers Cove: Ivey Durley Place
Former Name: Straits-St Barbe Chronic Care
PO Box 157, Flowers Cove, NL A0K 2N0
Tel: 709-456-9104
Number of Beds: 20 beds
Judy Way, Contact
709-456-2022
Dennis Coates, Contact
704/456-2022

Fogo: Riverhead Manor
PO Box 375, Fogo, NL A0G 2B0
Tel: 709-266-2336
Number of Beds: 17 beds
Luther Piercey

Gander: Nightingale Manor
11 Hadfield St., Gander, NL A1V 2V6
Tel: 709-256-3711
Number of Beds: 60 beds
Lawrence Guy

Glovertown: Baywatch Manor
PO Box 120, Glovertown, NL A0G 2M0
Tel: 709-533-2600
baywatchmanor@nf.aibn.com
www.baywatchmanor.ca
Number of Beds: 38 beds
Denise Button

Glovertown: Oram's Birchview Manor
PO Box 10, Glovertown, NL A0G 2L0
Tel: 709-266-2336
Number of Beds: 50 beds
Note: Specialty: Personal care
Paul Oram

Goulds: Kelly's Personal Care Home
Former Name: Kelly Boarding Home
478 Main Road, Goulds, NL A1S 1G3
Tel: 709-745-5343
Number of Beds: 19 beds
Linda Spurrell, Proprietor
709/745-5343

Goulds: Lawlor's Personal Care Home
PO Box 419, Goulds, NL A1S 1G5
Tel: 709-745-1956
Number of Beds: 14 beds
Albert Lawlor

Goulds: Maloney's Personal Care Home
PO Box 568, Barton's Rd., Goulds, NL A1S 1G3
Tel: 709-745-4986
Number of Beds: 10 beds
Note: Nursing Home
Mary Maloney, Contact

Grand Falls-Windsor: Golden Years Estate
348 Grenfell Heights, Grand Falls-Windsor, NL A2H 2R8
Tel: 709-489-7263 Fax: 709-489-7306
zettalane@tgyestate.com
www.thegoldenyearsestate.com
Number of Beds: 67 beds
Zetta Lane, Owner

Grand Falls-Windsor: Islandside Manor
PO Box 814, Grand Falls-Windsor, NL A2A 2P7
Tel: 709-483-2121
Number of Beds: 24 beds
Max Arnold

Grand Falls-Windsor: Twin Town Manor
15 King St., Grand Falls-Windsor, NL A1B 1J6
Tel: 709-489-0988 Fax: 709-489-1880
Number of Beds: 96 beds
Guy Bailey, Contact

Happy Valley-Goose Bay: Pine Lodge Personal Care Home
PO Box 264 Stn. C, 3 Spruce Ave., Happy Valley-Goose Bay, NL A0P 1C0
Tel: 709-896-5512 Fax: 709-896-5465
Note: Specialties: Personal care for seniors & person with an intellectual disability
Diane Oliver-Scales

Hickmans Harbour: Blundons' Personal Care Home
PO Box 90, Hickmans Harbour, NL A0C 1P0
Tel: 709-466-2189
Number of Beds: 20 beds
Effie Blundon, Proprietor

Holyrood: Kennedy's Riverside Boarding Home Ltd.
Former Name: Kennedy's Riverside Manor Limited
PO Box 114, Holyrood, NL A0A 2R0
Tel: 709-229-6886
Number of Beds: 33 beds
Geneviève Kennedy

Holyrood: Tobin's Guest Home Inc.
PO Box 95, Holyrood, NL A0A 2R0
Tel: 709-229-7464
Number of Beds: 30 beds
Betty Tobin
Walter Tobin

Holyrood: Woodford's Golden Care
PO Box 158, Con Bay Hwy., Holyrood, NL A0A 2R0
Tel: 709-229-3343
Number of Beds: 10 beds
Josephine Woodford

Holyrood: Woodford's Golden Care Home
PO Box 158, Holyrood, NL A0A 2R0
Tel: 709-229-3343
Number of Beds: 10 beds
Josephine Woodford, Contact

Kelligrews: Gully Pond Manor
39 Gully Pond Rd., Kelligrews, NL A1X 6Z2
Tel: 709-834-8083
Number of Beds: 20 beds
Ruby Hennessey

Kilbride: Hennessey's Personal Care Home
222 Old Bay Bulls Rd., Kilbride, NL A1G 1E1
Tel: 709-368-5558 Fax: 709-368-4910
Number of Beds: 16 beds
Catherine Hennessey, Proprietor

Lark Harbour: Guardian Angel Seniors Home
PO Box 91, Lark Harbour, NL A0L 1L0
Tel: 709-681-2288
Number of Beds: 20 beds
Brian Park

Lewisporte: Pleasantville Manor
PO Box 207, Lewisporte, NL A0G 3A0
Tel: 709-535-0941 Fax: 709-535-0943
Number of Beds: 60 beds
Rhonda Simms, Owner, Operator

Long Pond: Allison's Manor
PO Box 14099, 332 Ancorage Rd., Long Pond, NL A0A 2Y0
Tel: 709-834-8541 Fax: 709-834-6336
Number of Beds: 42 beds
Sharon Stone, Administrator

Mary's Harbour: Harbourview Manor
PO Box 153, Mary's Harbour, NL A0K 3P0
Tel: 709-921-6440
Number of Beds: 20 beds
Elaine Rumbolt

Mount Carmel: Silverdale Manor
PO Box 86, Mount Carmel, NL A0B 2M0
Tel: 709-521-2377
Number of Beds: 25 beds
Angela DeCaria

Mount Pearl: Pearl House
163 Park Ave., Mount Pearl, NL A1N 1K6
Tel: 709-368-3850
Number of Beds: 44 beds
Lawrence Guy

Musgrave Harbour: Hillcrest Manor
PO Box 100, Musgrave Harbour, NL A0G 3J0
Tel: 709-655-2777
Number of Beds: 30 beds
Lawrence Guy

Musgravetown: Greenwood Rest Home Ltd.
PO Box 9, Bunyan's Cove Rd., Musgravetown, NL A0C 1Z0
Tel: 709-467-5243
Number of Beds: 20 beds
Wilfred Greening

New Harbour: Honeysuckle Estates Inc.
PO Box 46, New Harbour, NL A0B 2P0
Tel: 709-582-3604
Number of Beds: 14 beds
Joan Hillier

New Harbour: Jackson's Country Manor
New Harbour Barrens, New Harbour, NL A0B 2P0
Tel: 709-588-2382
Number of Beds: 39 Beds
Wallace Jackson, Contact
709/582-2888

Norris Point: Crockers Retirement Home
PO Box 1, Norris Point, NL A0K 3V0
Tel: 709-458-2429
Number of Beds: 20 beds
Gerald Crocker

Paradise: Shady Rest Lodge
PO Box 3034, Paradise, NL A1L 3W2
Tel: 709-895-6786
Number of Beds: 21 beds
Cavell Murphy, Contact

Pollards Point: Main River Manor Ltd.
Former Name: Golden Crest Haven
General Delivery, Pollards Point, NL A0K 4B0
Tel: 709-482-2334
Number of Beds: 20 beds
Dale Gillingham, Contact

Port aux Basques: Mountain Hope Manor
PO Box 957, Port aux Basques, NL A0M 1C0
Tel: 709-695-3458 Fax: 709-695-3751
Number of Beds: 32 beds
Ida Lawrence

Porterville: Bayside Manor
PO Box 134, RR#1, Porterville, NL A0G 3A0
Tel: 709-654-3171 Fax: 709-654-2176
Number of Beds: 50 beds
Ron Sheppard, Proprietor

Roddickton: Roddickton House
Former Name: Claudelle Manor
PO Box 40, Roddickton, NL A0K 4P0
Tel: 709-457-2166 Fax: 709-457-2079
Number of Beds: 22 beds
Note: Nursing home
Chris Decker

Shearstown: Maple Lodge
PO Box 10, Shearstown, NL A0A 3V0
Tel: 709-786-7051
Number of Beds: 16 beds
Note: Nursing home
William Tetford, Proprietor

St Albans: K.M. Homes Limited
8 Meadow Pl, St Albans, NL A0H 2E0
Tel: 709-538-3162
www.centralhealth.nl.ca/k-m-homes-ltd
Number of Beds: 30 beds
Shirley Ingram

St Lawrence: Mount Margaret Manor
PO Box 278, St Lawrence, NL A0E 2V0
Tel: 709-873-3199
Number of Beds: 31 beds
Mildred Marsden

St Marys: Lewis' Personal Care Home, Inc.
PO Box 219, St Marys, NL A0B 3B0
Tel: 709-525-2244
Number of Beds: 20 beds
Carolann Lewis, Proprietor

St Marys: Neville's Special Care Home
General Delivery, St Marys, NL A0B 3B0
Tel: 709-525-2098
Number of Beds: 21 beds
Paul Neville

St. John's: Katherine House
90 Lemarchant Rd., St. John's, NL A1E 1P1
Tel: 709-754-3864
Number of Beds: 10 beds
Barry Oliver
709/754-3864
Linda Ebsary, Proprietor
709/754-3864

St. John's: Margaret's Manor
57 Bonaventure Ave., St. John's, NL A1C 3Z3
Tel: 709-722-4040
Number of Beds: 40 beds
Note: Nursing home
William Clarke

St. John's: North Pond Home
34 Virginia Place, St. John's, NL A1A 3G6
Tel: 709-437-1415 Fax: 709-726-8187
Number of Beds: 35 beds
Maxine Isaacs
Barry Isaacs

Stephenville: Silverwood Manor
42 Kippens Rd., Stephenville, NL A2N 1A7
Tel: 709-643-6550
westernhealth.nl.ca
Number of Beds: 30 beds
Judy Gallant

Trepassey: Ocean View Rest Home
PO Box 5, Trepassey, NL A0A 4B0
Tel: 709-438-2227
Number of Beds: 19 beds
Anne Pennell, Contact
Jerome Devereaux, Contact

Twillingate: Sunset Manor
PO Box 638, Twillingate, NL A0G 4M0
Tel: 709-884-5301
Number of Beds: 23 beds
Note: Rest home
Margaret Woods

Wesleyville: Otterbury Manor
PO Box 42, 428 Main St., Wesleyville, NL A0G 4R0
Tel: 709-536-3383
Number of Beds: 30 beds

Elsie Carter

White Bay: Hamlyn Manor Inc.
PO Box 59, Seal Cove, White Bay, NL A0K 5E0
Tel: 709-531-2085
Number of Beds: 17 beds
Calvin Hamlyn

Witless Bay: Alderwood Estates
Former Name: Dunn's Personal Care Home
PO Box 10, Witless Bay, NL A0A 4K0
Tel: 709-334-2183 Fax: 709-334-2058
www.alderwoodestates.ca
Number of Beds: 52 beds
Debbie Dunne

Mental Health Facilities

Mental Health Hospitals/Facilities

St. John's: Waterford Hospital
Affiliated with: Eastern Regional Integrated Health Authority
Waterford Bridge Rd., St. John's, NL A1E 4J8
Tel: 709-777-3300 Fax: 709-777-3993
www.easternhealth.ca
Number of Beds: 80 acute care, 104 continuing care beds
Note: Mental Health Program, acute & outpatient care; dialysis services, blood collection, x-ray clinics
Beverley Clarke, COO, Community & Children & Mental Health
Louise Jones, Interim President/CEO, Eastern Health

Northwest Territories

Government Departments in Charge

NORTHWEST TERRITORIES: Dept. of Health & Social Services
PO Box 1320, Centre Square Tower, Yellowknife, NT X1A 2L9
Tel: 867-920-6173 Fax: 867-873-0266
Toll-Free: 800-661-0830
www.hlthss.gov.nt.ca
Tom Beaulieu, Minister of Health & Social Services, Executive
867-669-2399
Nick Saturnino, Director, Health Services Administration
867-777-7400,

Regional Health Authorities

Behchoko: Tlicho Community Services Agency
PO Box 5, Behchoko, NT X0E 0Y0
Tel: 867-392-3000 Fax: 867-392-3001
tcsa@tlicho.net
www.tlicho.ca
Note: A person can contact a member of the primary community care team in their home community and receive access to healthcare services in their own community, in the region and, as necessary, outside the NWT.
Alfonz Nitsiza, Board Chair

Fort Simpson: Dehcho Health & Social Services Authority (DHSSA)
Former Name: Deh Cho Health & Social Services Board
PO Box 246, Fort Simpson, NT X0E 0N0
Tel: 867-695-3815 Fax: 867-695-2920
health_beat@gov.nt.ca
www.dhssa.ca
Year Founded: 1997
Population Served: 3409
Note: Area Served: Fort Liard; Fort Providence; Fort Simpson; Hay River Reserve; Jean Marie River; Kakisa; Nahanni Butte; Trout Lake; Wrigley, Dehcho Region, NWT.
Allan J. Landry, Chair
Kathy Tsetso, Chief Executive Officer
KATHY_TSETSO@gov.nt.ca
David Humphrey, Director, Finance & Administration
Fax: 867-695-2054
Minnie Letcher, Director, Community Programs
MINNIE_LETCHER@gov.nt.ca
Claude Gingras, Manager, Social Services
Cindy MacDonald, Manager, Health Services
CINDY_MACDONALD@gov.nt.ca
Tracy Humphrey, Coordinator, Risk Management & Planning
TRACY_HUMPHREY@gov.nt.ca
Rene Lamothe, Coordinator, Traditional Healing
RENE_LAMOTHE@gov.nt.ca

Fort Smith: Fort Smith Health & Social Services Authority
PO Box 1080, Fort Smith, NT X0E 0P0
Tel: 867-872-6200 Fax: 867-872-6275
Population Served: 2466
Note: Facilities: Fort Smith Health & Social Services Centre; Northern Lights Special Care Home; Polar Crescent Group Home; Sutherland House; Tapwe House; Trailcross Treatment Centre; Fort Smith Wellness Centre. Area Covered: Southern Northwest Territories, including the Town of Fort Smith, Salt River First Nations, & Métis Nation Local 50
Robert Tordiff, Chief Executive Officer
867-872-6201, Fax: 867-872-6291,
ROBERT_TORDIFF@gov.nt.ca
Natalie Campbell, Director, Quality Assurance & Risk Management
867-872-6237, NATALIE_CAMPBELL@gov.nt.ca
Julie Lys, Director, Patient Services
867-872-6217, JULIE_LYS@gov.nt.ca
Phyllis Mawdsley, Director, Community Services
867-872-6300, PHYLLIS_MAWDSLEY@gov.nt.ca
Suzanne Sihikal, Director, Northern Lights Special Care Home
867-872-6296, SUZANNE_SIHIKAL@gov.nt.ca
Katerina Tsaknaki, Director, Finance
867-872-6235, KATERINA_TSAKNAKI@gov.nt.ca
Linda McDevitt, Officer, Human Resources
867-872-6507, LINDA_MCDEVITT@gov.nt.ca

Hay River: Hay River Health & Social Services Authority (HRHSSA)
3 Gaetz Dr., Hay River, NT X0E 0R8
Tel: 867-874-7115 Fax: 867-874-7109
www.hrhssa.org
Area Served: Southern shore of Great Slave Lake, NWT, Enterprise & Hay RiverPopulation Served: 3832
Note: Facilities: Hay River Emergency Group Home; Hay River Public Health Unit; Hay River Social Services Office; H.H. Williams Memorial Hospital (29 acute / extended care beds); Hay River Medical Clinic; Woodland Manor (15 long term care beds); Hay River Reserve Health Station; Hay River Reserve Social Services; Enterprise Social Services.
Sue Cullen, Chief Executive Officer
867-874-7110, SUE_CULLEN@gov.nt.ca
George Blandford, Director, Finance & Administration
867-874-7119, GEORGE_BLANDFORD@gov.nt.ca
Joletta Larocque, Director, Community & Continuing Care
867-874-7117, JOLETTA_LAROCQUE@gov.nt.ca
Corina Guy, Director, Clinical & Dianostic Services
867-874-7162, hrhssa_clientrelations@gov.nt.ca
Sheryl Courtoreille, Coordinator, Quality Improvment
867-874-7168, SHERYL_COURTOREILLE@gov.nt.ca

Inuvik: Beaufort-Delta Health & Social Services Authority (BDHSSA)
Former Name: Inuvik Regional Health & Social Services Authority
PO Box Bag 2, 285 Mackenzie Rd., Inuvik, NT X0E 0T0
Tel: 867-777-8000 Fax: 867-777-8062
bdhssa.nt.ca
Year Founded: 1988
Number of Beds: 51 beds
Population Served: 9500Number of Employees: 300
Note: Serves the communities of Aklavik, Fort McPherson, Inuvik, Paulatuk, Sachs Harbour, Tsiigehtchic, Tuktoyaktuk, & Ulukhaktok. Services provided through the Inuvik Regional Hospital & community clinics, & include continuing care, health promotion, counselling, social programs, nutrition, telehealth, rehabilitation & diabetes education.
Deborah Tynes, CEO
deborah_tynes@gov.nt.ca

Norman Wells: Sahtu Health & Social Services Authority
PO Box 340, Norman Wells, NT X0E 0V0
Tel: 867-587-3438 Fax: 867-587-3436
Toll-Free: 1-800-661-0830
www.shssa.org
Year Founded: 2005
Area Served: Communities along the Mackenzie ValleyPopulation Served: 2700
Patricia Kyle, CEO

Yellowknife: Stanton Territorial Health Authority
Former Name: Stanton Regional Health Board
PO Box 10, 550 Byrne Rd., Yellowknife, NT X1A 2N1
Tel: 867-669-4111 Fax: 867-669-4128
www.sthb.org
Kay Lewis, CEO

Yellowknife: Yellowknife Health & Social Services Authority
Former Name: Yellowknife Health & Social Services Board
PO Box 608, 4702 Franklin Ave., Yellowknife, NT X1A 2N5
Tel: 867-873-7276 Fax: 867-873-0289
yhssa@gov.nt.ca
www.yhssa.org
Area Served: Dettah, Fort Resolution, Lutsel K'e, NDilo and YellowknifePopulation Served: 19000
Note: Community health & social services board
Les Harrison, CEO

Hospitals

Hospitals - General

Hay River: H.H. Williams Memorial Hospital
Affiliated with: Hay River Health & Social Service Authority
3 Gaetz Dr., Hay River, NT X0E 0R8
Tel: 867-874-7100 Fax: 867-874-7118
Number of Beds: 23 acute, 8 extended care beds
Note: long-term care facility
Paul Vieira, CEO

Inuvik: Inuvik Regional Hospital
Affiliated with: Beaufort-Delta Health & Social Services Authority
Bag 2, Inuvik, NT X0E 0T0
Tel: 867-777-8000 Fax: 867-777-8054
bdhssa.nt.ca
Number of Beds: 51 beds
Note: Location: 285 Mackenzie Rd., Inuvik. Provides emergency services, surgery, obstetrics, acute care, long term care, pharmacy, diagnostic imaging & lab, physician clinics, visiting specialists, & referral.

Community Health Centres

Community Health Care Centres

Aklavik: Susie Husky Health & Social Services Centre
Affiliated with: Beaufort-Delta Health & Social Services Authority
Former Name: Susie Husky Health Centre
PO Box 114, Aklavik, NT X0E 0A0
Tel: 867-978-2516 Fax: 867-978-2160
www.bdhssa.nt.ca
Note: Specialties: Clinics, such as chronic disease & well child, woman, & man clinics; School health program; Health promotion; Dental therapy; Home care; Immunization programs; Rehabilitative services; Child protection; Child & family services; Palliative care. Number of Employees: 1 nurse in charge + 3 community health nurses + 2 community social service workers; 1 dental therapist + 1 community health representative + 1 home support worker + 1 clerk + 1 caretaker

Behchoko: Behchoko Health Centre
Affiliated with: Tlicho Community Services Agency
Former Name: Rae Health Centre
Bag 5, Behchoko, NT X0E 0Y0
Tel: 867-392-6351 Fax: 867-392-6612

Deline: Deline Health Centre
Affiliated with: Sahtu Health & Social Services Authority
PO Box 199, General Delivery, Deline, NT X0E 0G0
Tel: 867-589-3111 Fax: 867-589-5570

Fort Good Hope: Fort Good Hope Health Centre
Affiliated with: Sahtu Health & Social Services Authority
PO Box 9, Fort Good Hope, NT X0E 0H0
Tel: 867-598-2211 Fax: 867-598-2605

Fort Liard: Fort Liard Health Centre
Affiliated with: Dehcho Health & Social Services Authority
General Delivery, Fort Liard, NT X0G 0A0
Tel: 867-770-4301 Fax: 867-770-3235
cao@fortliard.com

Fort McPherson: William Firth Health Centre
Affiliated with: Beaufort-Delta Health & Social Services Authority
PO Box 56, Fort McPherson, NT X0E 0J0
Tel: 867-952-2586 Fax: 867-952-2620

Fort Providence: **Fort Providence Health Centre**
Affiliated with: Dehcho Health & Social Services Authority
PO Box 229, Fort Providence, NT X0E 0L0
Tel: 867-699-4511 *Fax:* 867-699-3226

Fort Simpson: **Fort Simpson Health Centre**
Affiliated with: Dehcho Health & Social Services Authority
PO Box 246, Fort Simpson, NT X0E 0N0
Tel: 867-695-7000 *Fax:* 867-695-2920
www.dhssa.ca

Fort Smith: **Fort Smith Health Centre**
Affiliated with: Fort Smith Health & Social Services Authority
c/o Fort Smith Health & Social Services, PO Box 1080, Fort Smith, NT X0E 0P0
Tel: 867-872-6203 *Fax:* 867-872-6275
Number of Beds: 25 beds

Gameti: **Gamèti Health Centre**
Affiliated with: Tlicho Community Services Agency
Former Name: Gameti/Rae Lakes Outpatient Centre
General Delivery, Gameti, NT X0E 1R0
Tel: 867-997-3141 *Fax:* 867-997-3045

Hay River: **Hay River Public Health Unit**
Affiliated with: Hay River Health & Social Service Authority
3 Gaetz Dr., Hay River, NT X0E 0R8
Tel: 867-874-7201 *Fax:* 867-874-7211
www.hrhssa.org

Inuvik: **Inuvik Public Health Unit**
Affiliated with: Beaufort-Delta Health & Social Services Authority
Bag 2, Inuvik, NT X0E 0T0
Tel: 867-777-7246 *Fax:* 867-777-3255

Inuvik: **Inuvik Public Health Unit**
Affiliated with: Beaufort-Delta Health & Social Services Authority
Bag 2, Inuvik, NT X0E 0T0
Tel: 867-777-7246 *Fax:* 867-777-3255
Barb Lennie, Nurse-in-Charge

Jean Marie River: **Jean Marie River Health Cabin**
Affiliated with: Dehcho Health & Social Services Authority
General Delivery, Jean Marie River, NT X0E 0N0
Tel: 867-809-2900 *Fax:* 867-809-2902

Lutselk'e: **Lutselk'e Health Centre**
Affiliated with: Yellowknife Health & Social Services Authority
PO Box 56, Lutselk'e, NT X0E 1A0
Tel: 867-370-3111 *Fax:* 867-370-3022
Note: Specialties: Public health programs; Counselling & crisis intervention & referrals

Nahanni Butte: **Nahanni Butte Medical Health Clinic**
Affiliated with: Dehcho Health & Social Services Authority
General Delivery, Nahanni Butte, NT X0E 0N0
Tel: 867-602-2203 *Fax:* 867-602-2021

Norman Wells: **Norman Wells Health Centre**
Affiliated with: Sahtu Health & Social Services Authority
PO Box 8, Norman Wells, NT X0E 0V0
Tel: 867-587-2250 *Fax:* 867-587-2934

Paulatuk: **Paulatuk Health Centre**
Affiliated with: Beaufort-Delta Health & Social Services Authority
PO Box 114, General Delivery, Paulatuk, NT X0E 1N0
Tel: 867-580-3231 *Fax:* 867-580-3300
Number of Beds: 1 bed

Sachs Harbour: **Sachs Harbour Health Centre**
Affiliated with: Beaufort-Delta Health & Social Services Authority
PO Box 14, Sachs Harbour, NT X0E 0Z0
Tel: 867-690-4181 *Fax:* 867-690-3802

Tuktoyaktuk: **Rosie Ovayouk Health Centre**
Affiliated with: Beaufort-Delta Health & Social Services Authority
Bag 1000, Tuktoyaktuk, NT X0E 1C0
Tel: 867-977-2321 *Fax:* 867-977-2535

Tulita: **Tulita Health Centre**
Affiliated with: Sahtu Health & Social Services Authority
PO Box 145, Tulita, NT X0E 0K0
Tel: 867-588-4251 *Fax:* 867-588-3000
www.shssa.org
Note: Specialties: Primary care; Health promotion & prevention. Number of Employees: 3 nurses + 2 prevention & health promotion workers + 1 community social service worker + 1 mental health & addictions worker + 1 home support worker + support staff

Ulukhaktok: **Emegak Health Centre**
Affiliated with: Beaufort-Delta Health & Social Services Authority
PO Box 160, Ulukhaktok, NT X0E 0S0
Tel: 867-396-3111 *Fax:* 867-396-3221

Ulukhaktok: **Ulukhaktok Community Wellness Centre**
Affiliated with: Beaufort-Delta Health & Social Services Authority
c/o Emegak Health & Social Services Centre, PO Box 160, Ulukhaktok, NT X0E 0S0
Tel: 867-396-4688 *Fax:* 867-396-2934
Note: Specialties: Assessments; Crisis intervention; Therapeutic counselling; Education & awareness. Number of Employees: 1 mental health & addictions counsellor + 1 community wellness worker

Wekweti: **Wekweètì Health Centre**
Affiliated with: Tlicho Community Services Agency
General Delivery, Wekweti, NT X0E 1W0
Tel: 867-713-2904 *Fax:* 867-713-2904

Wha Ti: **Whati Health Centre**
Affiliated with: Tlicho Community Services Agency
Former Name: Wha Ti Outpatient Health Centre
General Delivery, Wha Ti, NT X0E 1P0
Tel: 867-573-3261 *Fax:* 867-573-3701

Wrigley: **Wrigley Health Centre**
Affiliated with: Dehcho Health & Social Services Authority
PO Box 58, General Delivery, Wrigley, NT X0E 1E0
Tel: 867-581-3441 *Fax:* 867-581-3200

Yellowknife: **Yellowknife Public Health Centre**
Affiliated with: Yellowknife Health & Social Services Authority
PO Box 608, Yellowknife, NT X1A 2N5
Tel: 867-920-6570 *Fax:* 867-873-0158

Nursing Stations

Colville Lake: **Colville Lake Health Station**
Affiliated with: Sahtu Health & Social Services Authority
PO Box 50, Colville Lake, NT X0E 1L0
Tel: 867-709-2409 *Fax:* 867-709-2504

Fort Resolution: **Fort Resolution Health Centre**
Affiliated with: Yellowknife Health & Social Services Authority
General Delivery, Fort Resolution, NT X0E 0M0
Tel: 867-394-4511 *Fax:* 867-394-3117

Trout Lake: **Trout Lake Health Station**
Affiliated with: Dehcho Health & Social Services Authority
Trout Lake Health Cabin, PO Box 39, Trout Lake, NT X0E 1Z0
Tel: 867-206-2838 *Fax:* 867-206-2024
Versa Vendron

Tsiigehtchic: **Tsiigehtchic Health & Social Services Centre**
Affiliated with: Beaufort-Delta Health & Social Services Authority
General Delivery, Tsiigehtchic, NT X0E 0B0
Tel: 867-953-3361 *Fax:* 867-777-8049

Special Treatment Centres

Fort Liard: **Fort Liard Mental Health & Addictions Program**
Affiliated with: Dehcho Health & Social Services Authority
General Delivery, Fort Liard, NT X0G 0A0
Tel: 867-770-4770 *Fax:* 867-770-4813

Fort Simpson: **Fort Simpson Mental Health & Addictions Program**
Affiliated with: Dehcho Health & Social Services Authority
PO Box 246, Fort Simpson, NT X0E 0N0
Tel: 867-695-3815 *Fax:* 867-695-2920
Elsie Gresl, Coordinator

Hay River: **Hay River Reserve Wellness Centre**
Affiliated with: Dehcho Health & Social Services Authority
#3 Gaetz Dr., Hay River, NT X0E 0R8
Tel: 867-874-2838 *Fax:* 867-874-6305
www.hrhssa.org
Anne Firth-Jones, Community Wellness Worker

Nursing Homes

Fort Smith: **Northern Lights Special Care Home**
Affiliated with: Fort Smith Health & Social Services Authority
PO Box 1319, Fort Smith, NT X0E 0P0
Tel: 867-872-5403 *Fax:* 867-872-5404
Number of Beds: 21 beds
Suzanne Sihikal, Administrator

Yellowknife: **The Cottage Corner**
Affiliated with: Yellowknife Health & Social Services Authority
Former Name: Aven Manor
Also Known As: Aven Cottage
#1, 5710 - 50th Ave., Yellowknife, NT X1A 1E9
Tel: 867-920-2443 *Fax:* 867-873-9915
Number of Beds: 29 beds
Greg Debogorski, Executive Director

Long Term/Retirement Care

Long Term Care Facilities

Fort Simpson: **Fort Simpson Long Term Care Home**
Affiliated with: Dehcho Health & Social Services Authority
PO Box 246, Fort Simpson, NT X0E 0N0
Tel: 867-695-7080 *Fax:* 867-695-7083

Fort Simpson: **Stanley Isaiah Support of Living Home**
Affiliated with: Dehcho Health & Social Services Authority
PO Box 240, Fort Simpson, NT X0E 0N0
Tel: 867-695-2365 *Fax:* 867-695-2364
Note: independent living adult

Hay River: **Woodland Manor**
Affiliated with: Hay River Health & Social Service Authority
52 Woodland Dr., Hay River, NT X0E 0R8
Tel: 867-874-7226 *Fax:* 867-874-7234
www.hlthss.gov.nt.ca
Number of Beds: 15 beds
Janet Leask, Coordinator, Residential Care

Inuvik: **Billy Moore Home**
Affiliated with: Beaufort-Delta Health & Social Services Authority
PO Box 1078, Inuvik, NT X0E 0T0
Tel: 867-777-3204 *Fax:* 867-777-2472

Inuvik: **Charlotte Vehus Home**
Affiliated with: Beaufort-Delta Health & Social Services Authority
PO Box 1800, Inuvik, NT X0E 0T0
Tel: 867-777-4780 *Fax:* 867-777-4687

Mental Health Facilities

Mental Health Hospitals/Facilities

Yellowknife: **Yellowknife Mental Health Clinic**
Affiliated with: Yellowknife Health & Social Services Authority
PO Box 10, Yellowknife, NT X1A 2N5
Tel: 867-873-7042 *Fax:* 867-873-0487
Corliss McCloskey, Manager, Psychiatric Services

Nova Scotia

Government Departments in Charge

NOVA SCOTIA: Nova Scotia Department of Health & Wellness
Joseph Howe Bldg., PO Box 488, 1690 Hollis St., Halifax, NS B3J 2R8
Tel: 902-424-3377 *Fax:* 902-424-0559
Toll-Free: 800-387-6665
TTY: 800-670-8888
health.minister@gov.ns.ca
novascotia.ca/dhw
Hon. David Wilson, Minister
902-864-0396, dave@davidawilsonmla.ca

Regional Health Authorities

***Amherst:* Cumberland Health Authority**
PO Box CHA, 34 Prince Arthur St., Amherst, NS B4H 3B3
Tel: 902-661-1090 *Fax:* 902-667-1125
ann.keddy@cha.nshealth.ca
www.cha.nshealth.ca
Year Founded: 2001
Area Served: Cumberland County*Population Served:* 33000*Number of Employees:* 800
Note: The District's services range from acute to long-term care and include public health, addiction and mental health programs. Has five health care facilities and several community-based sites.
Bruce Saunders, Chair
H. Bruce Quigley, Chief Executive Officer,
bruce.quigley@cha.nshealth.ca
Darla MacPherson, Vice-President, Community Health
Darla.MacPherson@cha.nshealth.ca
Rakesh Minocha, Vice-President, Operations
rakesh.minocha@cha.nshealth.ca
Cheryl Northcott, Vice-President, Patient Care Services
cheryl.northcott@cha.nshealth.ca
Ann Keddy, Director, Public Relations
902-661-1090, ann.keddy@cha.nshealth.ca

***Antigonish:* Guysborough Antigonish Strait Health Authority (GASHA)**
25 Bay St., Antigonish, NS B2G 2G5
Tel: 902-867-4500 *Fax:* 902-863-1176
Toll-Free: 1-800-565-2511
Donalda.Macgillivary@gasha.nshealth.ca
www.gasha.nshealth.ca
Year Founded: 2001
Area Served: Counties of Guysborough, Antigonish, Richmond & south Inverness*Population Served:* 44515*Number of Employees:* 1000
Note: Facilities: St. Martha's Regional Hospital; Strait Richmond Hospital, Evanston, Richmond County; Guysborough Memorial Hospital; St. Mary's Memorial Hospital; Eastern Memorial Hospital, Canso.
Liz Millett, Interim CEO & Vice President, Patient Care
902-867-4500 ex 4266, Liz.Millett@gasha.nshealth.ca
David Samson, Chair
Dr. Jeremy Hillyard, District Chief of Staff
902-867-4500 ex 4266, Jeremy.Hillyard@gasha.nshealth.ca
Madonna MacDonald, Vice-President, Community Health
902-867-4500, ext.., Madonna.Macdonald@gasha.nshealth.ca
Heather MacKay, Director, Public Relations
902-867-4500, ext. 4, Fax: 902-867-1059,
Heather.MacKay@gasha.nshealth.ca
David MacKenzie, Vice-President, Operations
902-867-4500, ext. 4, David.mackenzie@gasha.nshealth.ca

***Bridgewater:* South Shore District Health Authority**
90 Glen Allan Dr., Bridgewater, NS B4V 3S6
Tel: 902-527-2266 *Fax:* 902-527-5269
thawkesworth@ssdha.nshealth.ca
www.ssdha.nshealth.ca
Year Founded: 2001
Area Served: Lunenburg and Queens Counties*Population Served:* 60000*Number of Employees:* 1100
Note: South Shore Regional Hospital (Bridgewater), Fishermen's Memorial Hospital (Lunenburg), & Queens General Hospital (Liverpool). Community-based programs for addiction services, palliative care, public health, mental health
Kevin McNamara, CEO
Roxanne Smith, Chair

***Halifax:* Capital Health District**
#2142, 1796 Summer St., Halifax, NS B3H 3A7
Tel: 902-473-2700
EXJW@cdha.nshealth.ca
www.cdha.nshealth.ca
Social Media: www.facebook.com/CapitalHealth; twitter.com/capital_health
Population Served: 400000*Number of Employees:* 12000
Chris Power, President; Chief Executive Officer
902-473-2240
Gaynor Watson-Creed, Medical Officer of Health
902-481-5800
Catherine Gaulton, General Counsel; Vice-President, Performance Excellence
902-473-2626
Paula Bond, Vice-President, People-Centred Care, Acute Care
902-473-7084
Ray LeBlanc, Vice President, Innovation & Learning, Medicine
902-473-7310
Kathy MacNeil, Vice-President, People
902-473-7995
Amanda Whitewood, Vice-President & COO, Sustainability
902-473-3317
John McCarthy, Officer, Board Development
902-473-1143, Fax: 902-473-3368,
John.McCarthy@cdha.nshealth.ca
Anne Bereziuk, Patient Representative
902-473-2133, anne.bereziuk@cdha.nshealth.ca

***Kentville:* Annapolis Valley Health (AVH)**
15 Chipman Dr., Kentville, NS B4N 3V7
Tel: 902-678-7381 *Toll-Free:* 1-800-886-9757
pr@avdha.nshealth.ca
www.avdha.nshealth.ca
Population Served: 84000
Janet Knox, President; Chief Executive Officer
902-538-3431, Fax: 902-538-7609, ceo@avdha.nshealth.ca
David B. Logie, Board Chair
902-538-3431, Fax: 902-538-7609, lbobbitt@avdha.nshealth.ca (Linda Bo
Dr. Lynne Harrigan, Vice-President, Medicine
902-538-3424, Fax: 902-538-3432
Tamara Gilley, Director, Public Relations
902-538-3468, Fax: 902-678-9553, tgilley@avdha.nshealth.ca

***New Glasgow:* Pictou County District Health Authority**
c/o Aberdeen Hospital, 835 East River Rd., New Glasgow, NS B2H 3S6
Tel: 902-752-7600 *Fax:* 902-752-6231
www.pcha.nshealth.ca
Eileen MacIsaac, Public Relations
902-752-7600 ext1124, eileen.macisaac@pcha.nshealth.ca

***Sydney:* Cape Breton District Health Authority**
1482 George St, Sydney, NS B1P 1P3
Tel: 902-567-8000 *Fax:* 902-563-2717
www.cbdha.nshealth.ca
Social Media: www.facebook.com/300633586615252
Number of Beds: 484 acute care beds; 206 veteran & continuing care beds
Population Served: 130000*Number of Employees:* 3500
Note: The Cape Breton District Health Authority provides acute care, continuing care, programs and services through its hospitals, clinics and continuing care facilities within Cape Breton County, Northern and Central Inverness County and Victoria County.
Dianne Calvert Simms, Chief Executive Officer
902-567-7802
Yvon LeBlanc, Chair
Dr. M.A. Naqvi, Chief of Staff; Medical Director
902-567-7806
Evelyn Schaller, Chief Nursing Officer; Vice-President, Patient Services
902-567-7814
Jim Merkley, Vice-President, Operations
902-842-2842
Mary Lou O'Neil, Vice-President, Clinical Services
902-563-2711
Lindsay Peach, Vice-President, Community Health
902-794-5449
Greg Boone, Director, Public Affairs
902-567-7791

***Truro:* Colchester East Hants Health Authority (CEHHA)**
207 Willow St., Truro, NS B2N 5A1
Tel: 902-893-5554 *Fax:* 902-893-0040
Toll-Free: 1-800-460-2110
humanresources-cehha@cehha.nshealth.ca
www.cehha.nshealth.ca
Year Founded: 2001
Area Served: Colchester County and the Municipality of East Hants*Population Served:* 73000
Note: Facilities: Colchester Regional Hospital, Truro, NS; Lillian Fraser Memorial Hospital, Tatamagouche, NS; East Hants Resource Centre, Elmsdale, NS.
John K. MacDonald, Chair
Peter MacKinnon, Chief Executive Officer
peter.mackinnon@cehha.nshealth.ca
Dr. Martin Dzierzanowski, Head, Surgery
Krista Wood, Director, Public Relations
902-893-5554 ex 2409, Fax: 902-893-0040,
krista.wood@cehha.nshealth.ca

***Yarmouth:* South West Health**
Former Name: Western Regional Health Board
60 Vancouver St., Yarmouth, NS B4A 2P5
Tel: 902-742-3541 *Fax:* 902-742-0369
www.swndha.nshealth.ca
Number of Beds: 536 beds
Population Served: 62000*Number of Employees:* 1312
Note: Includes Yarmouth Regional Hospital, Harbourside Lodge, Veteran's Place and Dalhousie University School of Nursing, Yarmouth Site.
Blaise MacNeil, President & CEO
Gerald Pottier, Chair
Cathy Blades, Vice President, Clinical Care
Anthony Muise, Vice President, Operations
Tanya Nixon, Vice President, Community Health
Dr. Edwin Janke, Chief of Medical Staff
Mark Muise, Director, Finance
Anna Babin, Director, Human Resources
Fraser Mooney, Coordinator, Communications

Hospitals

Hospitals - General

***Amherst:* Cumberland Regional Health Care Centre (CRHCC)**
Affiliated with: Cumberland Health Authority #5
19428 Hwy. #2, RR#6, Amherst, NS B4H 1N6
Tel: 902-667-3361 *Fax:* 902-667-6306
www.cha.nshealth.ca
Year Founded: 2002
Note: Hospital Specialties: Level 2 emergency services; Diagnostic imaging; Laboratory services; Surgery; Intensive care unit; Maternal / child unit (902-667-5400, ext. 6144); Acute care; Ambulatory care; Physiotherapy; Occupational therapy; Respiratory therapy; Diabetes education; Social work (902-667-5400, ext. 6219); Palliative care (902-667-5400, ext. 6373)
Dr. David Gass, Chief of Staff, Cumberland Health Authority
david.gass@cha.nshealth.ca
Cheryl Northcott, Vice-President, Patient Care Services, Cumberland Health Authority
cheryl.northcott@cha.nshealth.ca
Ann Keddy, Director, Public Relations, Cumberland Health Authority
902-661-1090, ann.keddy@cha.nshealth.ca

***Antigonish:* St. Martha's Regional Hospital**
Affiliated with: Guysborough Antigonish Strait Health Authority #7
25 Bay St., Antigonish, NS B2G 2G5
Tel: 902-863-2830 *Fax:* 902-867-1059
www.erhb.ns.ca/Facilities/St_Marthas/default.htm
Number of Beds: 80 beds
Note: regional hospital
Liz Millett, Vice President, Patient Care
David MacKenzie, Vice President, Operations

***Baddeck:* Victoria County Memorial Hospital**
Affiliated with: Cape Breton District Health Authority #8
PO Box 220, 30 Old Margaree Rd., Baddeck, NS B0E 1B0
Tel: 902-295-2112 *Fax:* 902-295-3432
www.cbdha.nshealth.ca
Number of Beds: 12 beds
Diane Grant, Administrator

***Bridgewater:* South Shore Regional Hospital**
Affiliated with: South Shore District Health Authority #1
Former Name: Health Services Association of the South Shore
90 Glen Allan Dr., Bridgewater, NS B4V 3S6
Tel: 902-543-4603 *Fax:* 902-543-4719
www.ssdha.nshealth.ca/ssrh.htm
Number of Beds: 80 beds
Note: A primary and secondary care hospital and designated district trauma centre, services include emergency & ambulatory care, diagnostic imaging (radiography/fluoroscopy, ultrasound, mammography, CT scanning, nuclear medicine), intensive care, surgery, EKG, gastroenterology, mental health services, obstetrics, opthamology, pediatrics, cardiac care, respiratory therapy, rheumatology, rehabilitation, palliative, pharmacy, walk-in clinic

Alice Leverman, CEO, SSDHA
aleverman@ssdha.nshealth.ca
Dr. Peter Vaughan, Medical Director, SSDHA
Theresa Hawkesworth, Communications Officer, SSDHA
902-527-2266, thawkesworth@ssdha.nshealth.ca

Canso: Eastern Memorial Hospital
Affiliated with: Guysborough Antigonish Strait Health Authority #7
PO Box 10, 1746 Union St., Canso, NS B0H 1H0
Tel: 902-366-2794 *Fax:* 902-366-2740
www.gasha.nshealth.ca
Year Founded: 1948
Number of Beds: 6 beds
Note: Hospital Specialties: Emergency services; Diagnostic imaging; Physiotherapy; Psychology services; Social services; Nutritional counselling; Diabetes education; Outreach nursing; Palliative care
Rose Richardson, Manager, Eastern Memorial Hospital Facility
Rose.Richardson@gasha.nshealth.ca

Cheticamp: Sacred Heart Community Health Centre
Affiliated with: Cape Breton District Health Authority #8
Former Name: Sacred Heart Hospital
PO Box 129, 15102 Cabot Trail, Cheticamp, NS B0E 1H0
Tel: 902-224-1500 *Fax:* 902-224-2903
www.cbdha.nshealth.ca
Number of Beds: 10 beds
Note: Emergency & outpatient services, lab, physiotherapy, nutrition counseling, foot & eye clinics, diagnostic imaging, palliative care
John Malcom, CEO, CBDHA
Mary Lou O'Neil, Vice-President, Clinical Services, CBDHA
Dr. M. A. Naqvi, Medical Director; Chief of Staff, CBDHA

Cleveland: Strait Richmond Hospital
Affiliated with: Guysborough Antigonish Strait Health Authority #7
138 Hospital Rd., RR#1, Cleveland, NS B0E 1J0
Tel: 902-625-3100 *Fax:* 902-625-3804
www.gasha.nshealth.ca
Year Founded: 1980
Number of Beds: 20 beds
Note: Specialties: Inpatient unit for addiction services; Mental health services; Social work services; Physiotherapy; Occupational therapy; Physicians clinics, such as pediatrics & orthopedics; Ambulatory care clinics, such as a living with stroke program, a well men's clinic, & a well women's clinic
Andrea Boyd-White, Facility Manager
Andy Parland, Director, Maintenance; Chief Engineer

Dartmouth: Dartmouth General Hospital (DGH)
Affiliated with: Capital District Health Authority #9
325 Pleasant St., Dartmouth, NS B2Y 4G8
Tel: 902-465-8300
www.cdha.nshealth.ca
Note: Hospital Specialties: Emergency services (902-465-8333); Diagnostic services; Laboratory services; Surgery; Critical care; Gynaecology; Urology; Orthopedics; Ophthalmology; Ear, nose, & throat; Renal dialysis; Nutrition counselling; Osteoporosis Multidisciplinary Education Program
Gaynor Watson-Creed, Medical Officer of Health, Capital Health
902-481-5800
Laura Brine, Patient Representative
902-460-4544, Fax: 902-465-2729,
laura.brine@cdha.nshealth.ca
Natalie Morris, Contact, Dartmouth Osteoporosis Multidisciplinary Education
902-860-3719, morrisn@cdha.nshealth.ca
Marlene Regan, Contact, DGH Nutrition Counselling Department
902-465-8514

Digby: Digby General Hospital
Affiliated with: Southwest Health
75 Warwick St., Digby, NS B0V 1A0
Tel: 902-245-2501 *Fax:* 902-245-5517
www.swndha.nshealth.ca
Note: Hospital Specialties: Emergency services (902-245-1303); Diagnostic imaging (1-877-742-2571); Laboratory services (902-245-2502, ext. 3213); Primary care; Ambulatory care; Cardiac & respiratory services (902-245-2502, ext. 3264); Restorative care (902-245-2502, ext. 3337); Physiotherapy & occupational therapy (902-245-2502, ext. 3257); Recreation therapy (902-245-2502, ext. 3280); Mental health services (902-245-4709); Diabetes education (902-245-2502, ext. 3274); Nutrition counselling (902-245-2502, ext. 3341); Public health (902-245-2557); Hearing & Speech Centre (902-245-2502, ext. 3265); Palliative care (902-245-2502, ext. 3335)
Hubert d'Entremont, Manager, Digby General Hospital Site
902)-245-2502, ext., Fax: 902-245-2803,
hubertdentremont@swndha.nshealth.ca

Guysborough: Guysborough Memorial Hospital
Affiliated with: Guysborough Antigonish Strait Health Authority #7
PO Box 170, Guysborough, NS B0H 1N0
Tel: 902-533-3702 *Fax:* 902-533-4066
Number of Beds: 10 beds
Elaine MacMaster, Facility Manager
emacmaster@gasha.nshealth.ca
Tom DeLorey, Supervisor, Plant Maintenance

Halifax: IWK Health Centre
PO Box 9700, 5850/5980 University Ave., Halifax, NS B3K 6R8
Tel: 902-470-8888
feedback@iwk.nshealth.ca
www.iwk.nshealth.ca
Social Media: www.facebook.com/iwkhealthcentre; twitter.com/iwkhealthcentre; www.youtube.com/iwkhealthcentre
Number of Beds: 324 beds
Number of Employees: 3200
Note: The IWK Health Centre provides care to women, children, youth and families in the Maritime provinces and beyond. In addition to providing highly specialized (tertiary) care, the IWK also provides primary care services.
Anne McGuire, President/CEO
Anne Cogdon, Executive Director

Halifax: Queen Elizabeth II Health Sciences Centre
Affiliated with: Capital District Health Authority #9
1796 Summer St., Halifax, NS B3H 2A7
Tel: 902-473-2700 *Fax:* 902-473-4183
capitalnews@cdha.nshealth.ca
www.cdha.nshealth.ca
Number of Beds: 983 beds
Note: The largest teaching hospital in Atlantic Canada, the QEII provides general & specialized medical care, including mental health programs, cancer care, long-term care, geriatric assessment & restorative care
Karen MacRury-Sweet, Health Services Director, Nursing, Cardiac, Thoracic & Emergency Care

Inverness: Inverness Consolidated Memorial Hospital
Affiliated with: Cape Breton District Health Authority #8
Former Name: Inverness Consolidated Hospital
PO Box 610, 39 James St., Inverness, NS B0E 1N0
Tel: 902-258-2100 *Fax:* 902-258-3025
Number of Beds: 48 beds
Note: Acute & continuing care
Claire MacQuarrie, Facilities Manager
Sandy Gillis, Head, Plant Services

Kentville: Valley Regional Hospital
Affiliated with: Annapolis Valley District Health Authority #3
150 Exhibition St., Kentville, NS B4N 5E3
Tel: 902-678-7381 *Fax:* 902-679-1904
Year Founded: 1992
Note: Medicine, surgery, obstetrics, pediatrics, intensive care, emergency services, psychiatry, addictions. Number of staff: 700 staff, 100 physicians
Janet Knox, President/CEO, Annapolis Valley Health

Liverpool: Queens General Hospital
Affiliated with: South Shore District Health Authority #1
PO Box 370, 175 School St., Liverpool, NS B0T 1K0
Tel: 902-354-3436 *Fax:* 902-354-4614
Number of Beds: 22 beds
Anne Kelley, Site Manager

Lunenburg: Fishermen's Memorial Hospital
Affiliated with: South Shore District Health Authority #1
PO Box 1180, 14 High St., Lunenburg, NS B0J 2C0
Tel: 902-634-8801
www.ssdha.nshealth.ca
Number of Beds: 23 beds for veterans' care; 10 addiction services beds; 12 restorative care beds; 12 alternate level of care beds; 6 acute care beds; 2 observation be
Note: Hospital Specialties: Laboratory services; Diagnostic imaging; Acute care; Ambulatory care; Addiction services; Rehabilitation services; Restorative care; Respiratory therapy; Asthma Care Centre; Palliative care
Dr. Peter Vaughan, Medical Director, South Shore Health
902-527-5271, Fax: 902-527-5269
Phil Langford, Vice-President, Operations, South Shore Health
902-634-7308, Fax: 902-634-3668,
plangford@ssdha.nshealth.ca

Middle Musquodoboit: Musquodoboit Valley Memorial Hospital
Affiliated with: Capital District Health Authority #9
492 Archibald Brook Rd., Middle Musquodoboit, NS B0N 1X0
Tel: 902-384-2220 *Fax:* 902-384-3310
Number of Beds: 8 beds
Sheila Martin, Director, Health Services

Middleton: Soldiers Memorial Hospital
Affiliated with: Annapolis Valley District Health Authority #3
PO Box 730, Middleton, NS B0S 1P0
Tel: 902-825-3411 *Fax:* 902-825-0599
www.avdha.nshealth.ca/smh
Number of Beds: 62 beds (25 medical/surgical beds, 25 long term care beds, 12 beds for transitional patients)
Note: Services include emergency, acute care, addictions care, enterostomal therapy, surgery, diagnostic imaging, occupational & physiotherapy, nutrition services, diabetes education, speech language pathology services
Janet Knox, President/CEO, AVH
902-538-3431, ceo@avdha.nshealth.ca
Tamara Gilley, Public Relations Director, AVH
902-538-3468, Fax: 902-678-9553, tgilley@avdha.nshealth.ca
Joanne Wentzell, Site Manager

Musquodoboit Harbour: Twin Oaks Memorial Hospital
Affiliated with: Capital District Health Authority #9
7702 - 7 Hwy., Musquodoboit Harbour, NS B0J 2L0
Tel: 902-889-4110 *Fax:* 902-889-4144
www.cdha.nshealth.ca/default.aspx?page=SubPage¢erContent.Id.0=9233&category.Categories.1=22
Year Founded: 1976
Number of Beds: 14 beds
Note: Services include emergency, acute care, addiction services, diabetic and foot clinics, diagnostic imaging, hearing and speech clinic, Home Care Nova Scotia, laboratory, nutrition counseling, occupational therapy, outpatient services, palliative & respite care, physiotherapy, social services; Twin Oaks/Birches Continuting Care Centre. A helipad is located at the back of the hospital.
Chris Power, President/CEO, CDHA
Sheila Martin, Director, Health Services
902-889-2200, sheila.martin@cdha.nshealth.ca
Marilyn Cipak, Manager, Health Services
902-889-4106, Fax: 902-889-4140,
marilyn.cipak@cdha.nshealth.ca

Neils Harbour: Buchanan Memorial Community Health Centre
Affiliated with: Cape Breton District Health Authority #8
32610 Cabot Trail, Neils Harbour, NS B0C 1N0
Tel: 902-336-2200 *Fax:* 902-336-2399
www.cbdha.nshealth.ca
Note: Specialty: Acute care

North Sydney: Northside General Hospital
Affiliated with: Cape Breton District Health Authority #8
PO Box 399, 520 Purves St., North Sydney, NS B2A 3M4
Tel: 506-794-8521 *Fax:* 506-794-3355
Number of Beds: 21 beds
Note: Emergency & ambulatory care, diagnostic imaging, lab, day surgery, diabetic education, respiratory therapy, mental health clinic; Taigh Solas, a 21-bed continuing care facility, comprises the 3rd floor of the hospital
Sharon Sheppard, Director, Continuing Care

Pictou: Sutherland Harris Memorial Hospital
Affiliated with: Pictou County District Health Authority #6
PO Box 1059, 222 Haliburton Rd., Pictou, NS B0K 1H0
Tel: 902-485-4324 *Fax:* 902-485-8835
www.pcha.nshealth.ca/sutherlandharris/aboutus/default.htm
Year Founded: 1928
Number of Beds: 20 long-term beds for veterans, 12 restorative care beds
Note: A community facility with services incuding the Northumberland Veterans Unit, Restorative Care Unit, geriatric consultation, occupational therapy, palliative care, physiotherapy, social work, speech language therapy, special clinics (for dermatology, diabetes education, podiatry, vascularity, women's health).

Patrick Lee, CEO, PCHA
pat.lee@pcha.nshealth.ca
Dr. Nicole Boutilier, Interim Vice-President, Medical Affairs, PCHA
nicole.boutilier@pcha.nshealth.ca
Eileen MacIsaac, Public Relations Officer, PCHA
902-752-7600, eileen.macisaac@pcha.nshealth.ca

Sheet Harbour: Eastern Shore Memorial Hospital
Affiliated with: Capital District Health Authority #9
22737 Hwy. #7, Sheet Harbour, NS B0J 3B0
Tel: 902-885-2554 *Fax:* 902-885-3200
www.cdha.nshealth.ca
Year Founded: 1976
Number of Beds: 16 beds
Note: Hospital Specialties: Emergency services; Diagnostic imaging; Laboratory services; Ambulatory care; Acute care; Physiotherapy; Occupational therapy; Social services; Diabetes education (902-885-3606); Respite care; Palliative care
Harold Taylor, Manager, Health Services
902-885-3616, harold.taylor@cdha.nshealth.ca
Natasha Sharpe, Facility Secretary
902-885-3678, Fax: 902-885-3200, natasha.sharpe@cdha.nshealth.ca

Shelburne: Roseway Hospital
Affiliated with: Southwest Nova District Health Authority #2
PO Box 610, 1606 Sandy Point Rd., Shelburne, NS B0T 1W0
Tel: 902-875-3011 *Fax:* 902-875-1580
www.swndha.nshealth.ca/pages/roseway.htm
Number of Beds: 26 beds
Note: Emergency, diagnostic services, rehabilitation services, nutrition counseling, mental health & addiction services, speech therapy, continuing care, VON, visiting specialists
Jodi Ybarra, Site Manager, Administration
jybarra@swndha.nshealth.ca
Debbie Sutherland, Nurse Manager, Nursing
dsutherland@swndha.nshealth.ca

Sherbrooke: St. Mary's Memorial Hospital
Affiliated with: Guysborough Antigonish Strait Health Authority #7
PO Box 299, 91 Hospital Rd., Sherbrooke, NS B0J 3C0
Tel: 902-522-2882 *Fax:* 902-522-2556
Number of Beds: 6 beds
Teresa MacInnis, Facility Manager

Sydney: Cape Breton Regional Hospital
Affiliated with: Cape Breton District Health Authority #8
1482 George St., Sydney, NS B1P 1P3
Tel: 902-567-8000
www.cbdha.nshealth.ca
Year Founded: 1995
Note: Hospital Specialties: Emergency services; Diagnostic imaging; Laboratory services; Ambulatory care; Surgery; Intensive care; Acute care; Obstetrics; Oncology; Renal dialysis; Physical therapy; Occupational therapy; Speech therapy; Respiratory therapy; Diabetes education; Social work; Mental health; Mi'kmaq liaison; Geriatrics; Palliative care

Tatamagouche: Lillian Fraser Memorial Hospital
Affiliated with: Colchester East Hants Health Authority #4
PO Box 40, 110 Blair Ave., Tatamagouche, NS B0K 1V0
Tel: 902-657-2382 *Fax:* 902-657-3745
www.cehha.nshealth.ca/Lillian Fraser/index.cfm
Number of Beds: 10 beds
Bain Brown, Maintenance Supervisor

Truro: Colchester Regional Hospital
Affiliated with: Colchester East Hants Health Authority #4
207 Willow St., Truro, NS B2N 5A1
Tel: 902-893-4321 *Fax:* 902-893-5559
Toll-Free: 1-800-460-2110
humanresources-cehha@cehha.nshealth.ca (Human Resources, Colchester)
www.cehha.nshealth.ca
Number of Beds: 126 beds
Note: Hospital Specialties: Emergency services; Diagnostic imaging; Laboratory services; Acute care; Maternal / child services; Coronary care; Hearing & speech centre; Ophthalmology, Occupational therapy; Physiotherapy; Wound management; Asthma care centre; Diabetes centre; Social work; Veterans' unit; Palliative care
Krista Wood, Director, Public Relations
902-893-5554, ext. 2, krista.wood@cehha.nshealth.ca

Windsor: Hants Community Hospital
Affiliated with: Capital District Health Authority #9
89 Payzant Dr., Windsor, NS B0N 2T0
Tel: 902-792-2000 *Fax:* 902-798-6002
www.cdha.nshealth.ca
Number of Beds: 34 acute care beds
Sherri Parker, Director, Health Services
sherri.parker@cdha.nshealth.ca

Yarmouth: Yarmouth Regional Hospital
Affiliated with: Southwest Nova District Health Authority #2
60 Vancouver St., Yarmouth, NS B5A 2P5
Tel: 902-742-3541 *Fax:* 902-742-0369
Number of Beds: 139 beds
Blaise MacNeil, President; CEO
John Sullivan, Director, Physical Plant
Chris Newell, Director, Environmental Services

Community Health Centres

Community Health Care Centres

Annapolis Royal: Annapolis Community Health Centre
Affiliated with: Annapolis Valley District Health Authority #3
PO Box 426, 821 St. George St., Annapolis Royal, NS B0S 1A0
Tel: 902-532-2381 *Fax:* 902-532-2113
duggan.achc@avdha.nshealth.ca
www.avdha.nshealth.ca/achc/

Berwick: Western Kings Memorial Health Centre
Affiliated with: Annapolis Valley District Health Authority #3
PO Box 490, 121 Orchard St., Berwick, NS B0P 1E0
Tel: 902-538-3111 *Fax:* 902-538-9590
www.avdha.nshealth.ca
Note: Outpatient department, lab, diagnostic imaging, physiotherapy, nutritional counseling, dialysis, mental health clinic, VON Adult Day Care
Cheryl Grosvold, Site Manager

Dartmouth: Regional Residential Services Society (RRSS)
#LKD1, 202 Brownlow Ave., Dartmouth, NS B3B 1T5
Tel: 902-465-4022 *Fax:* 902-465-3124
beverley.wicks@rrss.ns.ca
www.rrss.ns.ca
Number of Beds: 185 beds
Note: Developmental residences & group homes, supported apartments, short & long term respite services, personal support planning, counseling, assessment. Number of staff: 400+
Carol Ann Brennan, Executive Director
carolann.brennan@rrss.ns.ca

Lower Sackville: Cobequid Community Health Centre
Affiliated with: Capital District Health Authority #9
70 Memory Lane, Lower Sackville, NS B4C 2J3
Tel: 902-869-6100 *Fax:* 902-865-4816
Margaret Merlin, Health Facility Manager

Parrsboro: South Cumberland Community Care Centre
Affiliated with: Cumberland Health Authority #5
PO Box 489, 50 Jenks Ave., Parrsboro, NS B0M 1S0
Tel: 902-254-2540 *Fax:* 902-254-2504
Number of Beds: 14 beds
Connie Ellis, Site Manager

Pugwash: North Cumberland Memorial Hospital
Affiliated with: Cumberland Health Authority #5
PO Box 242, 260 Church St., Pugwash, NS B0K 1L0
Tel: 902-243-2521 *Fax:* 902-243-2941
Number of Beds: 4 beds
Beryl MacLean, Site Manager

Springhill: All Saints Springhill Hospital
Affiliated with: Cumberland Health Authority #5
Former Name: All Saint's Hospital
PO Box 700, 10 Princess St., Springhill, NS B0M 1X0
Tel: 902-597-3773 *Fax:* 902-597-3440
Number of Beds: 20 beds
Note: Beds are provided for restorative care, transitional care, & palliative care. There is also a 10-bed inpatient addictions treatment program.
Beryl MacLean, Site Manager

Sydney: Public Health Services
Affiliated with: Guysborough Antigonish Strait Health Authority #7
235 Townsend St., Sydney, NS B1P 5E7
Tel: 902-563-2400 *Fax:* 902-563-0508
Eileen Woodford

Wolfville: Eastern Kings Memorial Community Health Centre
Affiliated with: Annapolis Valley District Health Authority #3
Former Name: Eastern Kings Community Health Centre
PO Box 1180, Wolfville, NS B0P 1X0
Tel: 902-542-2266 *Fax:* 902-542-4619
www.go.ednet.ns.ca/~healthque/
Marg Blakeney, Site Manager

Special Treatment Centres

Halifax: IWK Mental Health Program
Former Name: Atlantic Child Guidance Center
#1001, 6080 Young St., Halifax, NS B3K 5L2
Tel: 902-464-4110 *Fax:* 902-464-3008
www.iwk.nshealth.ca
Wayne Hollett, Interim Executive Director

Halifax: Nova Scotia Hearing & Speech Centres
Provincial Centre, Park Lane Terraces, PO Box 120, #401, 5657 Spring Garden Rd., Halifax, NS B3J 3R4
Tel: 902-492-8289 *Fax:* 902-423-0532
info@nshsc.nshealth.ca
www.nshsc.ns.ca
Note: Specialties: Speech-language pathology services; Audiology services Augmentative communication program; Cochlear implant program; Industrial & community audiology; Newborn hearing screening program
Anne Mason-Browne, Vice-President, Speech

Waterville: Kings Regional Rehabilitation Centre
PO Box 128, 1349 County Home Rd., Waterville, NS B0P 1V0
Tel: 902-538-3103 *Fax:* 902-538-7022
krrc.nsnet.org
Number of Beds: 199 beds
Note: residential rehab
Betty E. Mattson, Administrator

Yarmouth: Addiction Services
District Health Authorities 1, 2, & 3
Former Name: Western Drug Dependency Program
c/o Yarmouth Regional Hospital, 60 Vancouver St., Yarmouth, NS B5A 2P5
Tel: 902-742-2406 *Fax:* 902-742-0684
addictions-yrh@swndha.nshealth.ca
Hubert Devine, Regional Program Manager

Nursing Homes

Annapolis Royal: Annapolis Royal Nursing Home
9745, St. George St., RR#2, Annapolis Royal, NS B0S 1A0
Tel: 902-532-2240 *Fax:* 902-532-7151
lindab@macleodgroup.ca
annapolisroyalnursinghome.ca
Number of Beds: 51 beds; 2 respite
Linda R. Bailey, Administrator

Annapolis Royal: Northhills Nursing Home Ltd.
PO Box 220, 5038 Granville Rd., Annapolis Royal, NS B0S 1A0
Tel: 902-532-5555 *Fax:* 902-532-7449
Number of Beds: 50 beds
Note: adult residential centre
Leonard S. Tedds, Administrator

Arichat: St. Anne Community & Nursing Care Centre
Affiliated with: Guysborough Antigonish Strait Health Authority #7
2313 Main St., PO Box Drawer 30, Arichat, NS B0E 1A0
Tel: 902-226-2826 *Fax:* 902-226-1529
eric.burke@sacentre.nshealth.ca
Number of Beds: 24 beds
Eric Burke, Administrator

Beaverbank: Scotia Nursing Homes Ltd.
Affiliated with: Capital District Health Authority #9
Former Name: Scotia Nursing Homes Ltd.
125 Knowles Cres., Beaverbank, NS B4G 1E7
Tel: 902-865-6364 *Fax:* 902-865-3582
julie.frail@rosecrest.ca
www.scotianursinghomes.ca
Number of Beds: 49 beds + 1 respite

Patricia Bland, Administrator

Berwick: Grand View Manor
110A Commercial St., Berwick, NS B0P 1E0
Tel: 902-538-3118 Fax: 902-538-3998
admin@grandviewmanor.org
www.grandviewmanor.org
Number of Beds: 142 beds
Graham E. Hardy, Administrator

Bridgetown: Mountain Lea Lodge
170 Church St., RR#1, Bridgetown, NS B0S 1C0
Tel: 902-665-4489 Fax: 902-665-2900
Number of Beds: 106 beds + 1 respite
Larry Marsters, Administrator

Bridgewater: Hillside Pines
77 Exhibition Dr., Bridgewater, NS B4V 3K6
Tel: 902-543-1525 Fax: 902-543-8083
Number of Beds: 50 beds
Sheila MacKinnon, Administrator

Caledonia: North Queens Nursing Home
9565 Highway #8, Caledonia, NS B0T 1B0
Tel: 902-682-2553 Fax: 902-682-2602
www.nqnh.ca
Number of Beds: 42 beds + 2 respite
Note: adult residential centre
Norma Lenco, Administrator

Canso: Canso Seaside Manor
PO Box 70, 1748 Union St., Canso, NS B0H 1H0
Tel: 902-366-3030 Fax: 902-366-2154
djbennett.csm@ns.aliantzinc.ca
Number of Beds: 15 beds
Darren Bennett, Administrator

Dartmouth: Oakwood Terrace
Affiliated with: Capital District Health Authority #9
10 Mount Hope Ave., Dartmouth, NS B2Y 4K1
Tel: 902-469-3702 Fax: 902-469-3824
www.oakwoodterrace.ns.ca
Year Founded: 1982
Number of Beds: 111 beds
Note: Specialties: Physiotherapy; Adult Day Program; Medical services; Palliative care
Leonard Tedds, Administrator
Pat Nightingale, Nurse Manager
Gary Comeau, Coordinator, Recreation Therapy & Volunteer Services

Dartmouth: Woodside Manor
351 Pleasant St., Dartmouth, NS B2Y 3S4
Tel: 902-463-5845
Number of Beds: 29 beds
Cathy Prothro, Site Manager

Digby: Tideview Terrace
Affiliated with: Southwest Nova District Health Authority #2
PO Box 1120, 51 West St., Digby, NS B0V 1A0
Tel: 902-245-4718 Fax: 902-245-6674
Number of Beds: 89 beds
Note: Specialties: Long-term care (level II); Dementia care; Adult day programs; Respite care; Palliative care
Lynda Casey, Administrator

Eastern Passage: Ocean View Manor
Affiliated with: Capital District Health Authority #9
PO Box 130, 1909 Caldwell Rd., Eastern Passage, NS B3G 1M4
Tel: 902-465-6020 Fax: 902-465-4929
admin@ovm.ca
www.ovm.ca
Year Founded: 1967
Number of Beds: 176 residents
Note: Specialties: Physiotherapy; Occupational therapy; Recreation therapy; Social work; Respite care; Palliative care
Dion Mouland, Administrator

Glace Bay: Victoria Haven Nursing Home
PO Box 219, 5 Third St., Glace Bay, NS B1A 5V2
Tel: 902-849-4127 Fax: 902-849-8826
www.victoriahaven.ca
Number of Beds: 50 beds, 4 respite
Marie McPhee, Administrator

Glenwood: Nakile Home for Special Care
Affiliated with: Southwest Nova District Health Authority #2
Former Name: Nakile Home for the Aged
35 Nakile Dr., RR#1, Glenwood, NS B0W 1W0
Tel: 902-643-2707 Fax: 902-643-2862
bertha@nakile.ns.ca
www.nakilehome.ca
Number of Beds: 35 beds + 1 respite
Bertha Brannen, Administrator

Halifax: Glades Lodge
Affiliated with: Capital District Health Authority #9
25 Alton Dr., Halifax, NS B3N 1M1
Tel: 902-477-1777 Fax: 902-477-8174
glades.lodge@gemhealth.com
Number of Beds: 123 beds + 1 respite
Tara Deveau, Administrator
902-477-1777, ext102, tara.deveau@gemhealth.com

Halifax: Maplestone Enhanced Care
Affiliated with: Capital District Health Authority #9
245 Main Ave., Halifax, NS B3M 1B7
Tel: 902-443-1971 Fax: 902-443-9037
Number of Beds: 87 beds
Note: Nursing home
Renee Donovan-Grey, Administrator
Debbie Thompson, Environmental Services

Halifax: Melville Lodge Long Term Care Center
50 Shoreham Lane, Halifax, NS B3P 2R3
Tel: 902-479-1030 Fax: 902-477-1663
www.gemhealth.com
Year Founded: 1984
Number of Beds: 122 beds
Bernice Clake-Dibblee, Administrator

Halifax: Northwoodcare Inc.
Affiliated with: Capital District Health Authority #9
2615 Northwood Terrace, Halifax, NS B3K 3S5
Tel: 902-454-8311 Fax: 902-455-6408
information@nwood.ns.ca
www.nwood.ns.ca
Number of Beds: 406 beds
Note: Adult residental centre
Lloyd O. Brown, Administrator

Halifax: Parkstone Enhanced Care
Affiliated with: Capital District Health Authority #9
156 Parkland Dr., Halifax, NS B3S 1N9
Tel: 902-446-7275 Fax: 902-446-4044
dryan@shannex.com
Number of Beds: 185 beds, 5 respite beds
Note: Nursing home
Carol Ann Gallant, Administrator

Halifax: Saint Vincent's Nursing Home
Affiliated with: Capital District Health Authority #9
Former Name: Saint Vincent Guest Home
2080 Windsor St., Halifax, NS B3K 5B2
Tel: 902-429-0550 Fax: 902-492-3703
info@svnh.ca
www.svnh.ca
Number of Beds: 149 beds
Note: Nursing home affiliated with the Roman Catholic Archdiocese of Halifax
Kristin Schmitz, Administrator

Kentville: Evergreen Home for Special Care
655 Park St., Kentville, NS B4N 3V7
Tel: 902-678-7355 Fax: 902-678-5292
evergreen@evergreenhome.ns.ca
evergreenhome.ns.ca
Number of Beds: 97 beds; 20 children's beds; 2 respite beds
Note: adult residential centre
Fred Houghton, Administrator

Liverpool: Queens Manor
PO Box 1283, 20 Hollands Dr., Liverpool, NS B0T 1K0
Tel: 902-354-3451 Fax: 902-354-5383
www.queensmanor.ca
Number of Beds: 60 beds + 1 respite
Norma Lenco, Administrator

Lockeport: Surf Lodge Nursing Home
Affiliated with: Southwest Nova District Health Authority #2
PO Box 160, 73 Howe St., Lockeport, NS B0T 1L0
Tel: 902-656-2014
www.surflodge.ca
Note: Specialties: Long-term care; Massage therapy; Activity program; Physiotherapy

Margaret Coates, Administrator

Lunenburg: Harbour View Haven
PO Box 1480, 25 Blockhouse Hill Rd., Lunenburg, NS B0J 2C0
Tel: 902-634-8836 Fax: 902-634-8792
www.hvh.ca
Number of Beds: 129 beds + 1 respite
Barry Granter, Administrator

Mahone Bay: Mahone Nursing Home
PO Box 320, 640 Main St., Mahone Bay, NS B0J 2E0
Tel: 902-624-8341 Fax: 902-624-6338
www.mahonenursinghome.com
Year Founded: 1965
Note: Specialties: Long-term care Physiotherapy & occupational therapy; Palliative care
Anne Kennedy, Administrator

Meteghan: Villa Acadienne
Affiliée à: Southwest Nova District Health Authority #2
CP 248, 8403 Hwy. 1, Meteghan, NS B0W 2J0
Tél: 902-645-2065 Téléc: 902-645-3899
www.villaacadienne.com
Nombre de lits: 84 beds + 2 respite
Lucille Maillet, Administrator

Middle Musquodoboit: Musquodoboit Valley Home for Special Care (Braeside)
Affiliated with: Capital District Health Authority #9
126 Higginsville Rd., Middle Musquodoboit, NS B0N 1X0
Tel: 902-384-3007 Fax: 902-384-3310
Number of Beds: 28 beds + 1 respite
Diana Graham-Lentz, Site Manager

Musquodoboit Harbour: The Birches Nursing Home
Affiliated with: Capital District Health Authority #9
#7702, 7 Hwy. RR#2, Musquodoboit Harbour, NS B0J 2L0
Tel: 902-889-3474
Number of Beds: 42 residents
Note: Specialties: Long-term care for older adults; Community outreach adult day programs
Sheila Martin, Manager, Health Care Facility

New Germany: Rosedale Home for Special Care
Former Name: Rosedale Home
Trunk 10, #4927, RR#2, New Germany, NS B0R 1E0
Tel: 902-644-2008 Fax: 902-644-3260
Year Founded: 1984
Number of Beds: 29 beds
Maureen Wade, Administrator

New Glasgow: Glen Haven Manor
Affiliated with: Pictou County District Health Authority #6
739 East River Rd., New Glasgow, NS B2H 5E9
Tel: 902-752-2588 Fax: 902-752-0053
info@glenhavenmanor.ca
glenhavenmanor.atlanticwebfitters.net
Number of Beds: 202 beds
Note: adult residential centre
Lisa M. Smith, Administrator

New Waterford: Maple Hill Manor
Affiliated with: Cape Breton District Health Authority #8
700 King St., New Waterford, NS B1H 3Z5
Tel: 902-862-6495 Fax: 902-862-9294
maplehillmanor1@ns.sympatico.ca
www.maplehillmanor.ca
Number of Beds: 50 beds
Note: Long term & secured care
Cathy MacPhee, Administrator

North Sydney: Northside Community Guest Home
Affiliated with: Cape Breton District Health Authority #8
11 Queen St., North Sydney, NS B2A 1A2
Tel: 902-794-4733 Fax: 902-794-9021
www.northsideguesthome.com
Number of Beds: 105 beds
Joanne MacNeil, Administrator

Pictou: Maritime Odd Fellows Home
Affiliated with: Pictou County District Health Authority #6
PO Box 850, 143 Haliburton Rd., Pictou, NS B0K 1H0
Tel: 902-485-5492 Fax: 902-485-6868
Number of Beds: 47 beds
Note: Specialty: Long-term care; Therapeutic recreation
Janet Johnston, Administrator

***Sheet Harbour:* Duncan MacMillan Nursing Home**
Affiliated with: Capital District Health Authority #9
Former Name: Duncan MacMillan Home for the Aged
PO Box 68, 22639 7 Hwy., Sheet Harbour, NS B0J 3B0
Tel: 902-885-2545 *Fax:* 902-885-3289
Number of Beds: 25 beds + 1 respite
Sheila Martin, Health Care Facility Manager

***Shelburne:* Roseway Manor Inc.**
Affiliated with: Southwest Nova District Health Authority #2
PO Box 518, 1604 Lake Rd., Sandy Point, Shelburne, NS B0T 1W0
Tel: 902-875-4707 *Fax:* 902-875-4105
admin@rosewaymanor.ca
Number of Beds: 65 beds + 1 respite
Jerry Fraser, Administrator

***Sherbrooke:* High-Crest Sherbrooke Home for Special Care**
Affiliated with: Guysborough Antigonish Strait Health Authority #7
PO Box 284, 53 Court St., Sherbrooke, NS B0J 3C0
Tel: 902-522-2147 *Fax:* 902-522-2628
high-crestsherbrooke@high-crest.com
www.high-crest.com/highcresther.html
Number of Beds: 39 beds
Marion Carroll, Administrator

***Stellarton:* Valley View Villa**
Affiliated with: Pictou County District Health Authority #6
6125 Trafalgar Rd., RR#1, Stellarton, NS B0K 1S0
Tel: 902-755-5780 *Fax:* 902-755-3104
emaceachern@vvvilla.ca
www.valleyviewvilla.com
Year Founded: 1978
Number of Beds: 109 beds + 4 respite
Note: Home for special care
Norman Ferguson, Administrator

***Sydney:* Breton Bay Nursing Home**
70 St. Anthony Dr., Sydney, NS B1S 2R5
Tel: 902-539-4560 *Fax:* 902-567-6234
Number of Beds: 264 beds
Ellen Stoddard, Administrator

***Sydney:* Cove Guest Home**
Affiliated with: Cape Breton District Health Authority #8
320 Alexander St., Sydney, NS B1S 2G1
Tel: 902-539-5267 *Fax:* 902-539-7565
www.coveguesthome.com
Year Founded: 1944
Archie MacKeigan, CEO

***Sydney:* Harbourstone Enhanced Care**
Affiliated with: Cape Breton District Health Authority #8
84 Kenwood Dr., Sydney, NS B1S 3V7
Tel: 902-539-4560 *Fax:* 902-567-6234
www.shannex.com/enhanced_care/harbourstone.html
Year Founded: 2002
Number of Beds: 268 beds + 4 respite
Ellen Stoddard, Administrator

***Sydney:* New Dawn Guest Home**
50 Military Rd., Sydney, NS B1N 3K6
Tel: 902-539-2221 *Fax:* 902-564-8309
Number of Beds: 30 beds + 1 respite
Note: Residential care facility
Janet Gillis-Hussey, Administrator

***Sydney:* R.C. MacGillivray Guest Home Society**
Affiliated with: Cape Breton District Health Authority #8
25 Xavier Dr., Sydney, NS B1S 2R9
Tel: 902-539-6110 *Fax:* 902-567-0437
Number of Beds: 78 beds, 2 respite, 1 adult protection
John W. Coffey, Administrator

***Sydney Mines:* Miner's Memorial Manor**
Affiliated with: Cape Breton District Health Authority #8
15 Lorne St., Sydney Mines, NS B1V 3B9
Tel: 902-736-1992 *Fax:* 902-736-0667
Number of Beds: 35 beds + 2 respite
Harry Blinkhorn, Administrator

***Tatamagouche:* Willow Lodge**
Affiliated with: Colchester East Hants Health Authority #4
PO Box 249, 100 Blair Ave., Tatamagouche, NS B0X 1V0
Tel: 902-657-3101 *Fax:* 902-657-3859
douglas.cunningham@willowlodge.ca
Number of Beds: 51 beds
Douglas Cunningham, Administrator

***Truro:* Cedarstone Enhanced Care**
Affiliated with: Colchester East Hants Health Authority #4
378 Young St., Truro, NS B2N 7H2
Tel: 902-895-2891 *Fax:* 902-893-2361
cedarstoneinfo@shannex.com
shannex.com/cedarstone_enhanced_care.html
Number of Beds: 124 beds + 2 respite
Population Served: 126

***Truro:* The Mira Long Term Care Center**
426 Young St., Truro, NS B2N 7B1
Tel: 902-895-8715 *Fax:* 902-897-1903
themira@gemhealth.com
www.gemhealth.com
Year Founded: 1999
Number of Beds: 90 beds
Note: Specialty: Long-term care for seniors; Medication administration; Peritoneal dialysis unit; Seniors' dental clinic; Palliative care
Lynn Smith, Administrator

***Windsor:* Haliburton Place**
Affiliated with: Capital District Health Authority #9
89 Payzant Dr., Windsor, NS B0N 2T0
Tel: 902-792-2026 *Fax:* 902-798-6002
Number of Beds: 30 beds + 2 respite
Theresa Fillatre, Healthcare Facility Manager

***Windsor:* Hants County Residence for Senior Citizens**
Affiliated with: Capital District Health Authority #9
Former Name: Dykeland Lodge
Also Known As: Dykeland Lodge
124 Cottage St., Windsor, NS B0N 2T0
Tel: 902-798-8346 *Fax:* 902-798-8312
info@dykelandlodge.ca
www.dykelandlodge.ca
Year Founded: 1974
Number of Beds: 111 beds
Emily Samson, Administrator

***Windsor:* Windsor Elms United Church Senior Citizens' Home**
Affiliated with: Capital District Health Authority #9
590 King St., Windsor, NS B0N 2T0
Tel: 902-798-2251 *Fax:* 902-798-0914
Number of Beds: 107 beds + 1 respite
Sherry Keen, Administrator

***Windsor:* Windsor House**
PO Box 938, 16 Wentworth St., Windsor, NS B0N 2T0
Tel: 902-798-2115
Number of Beds: 16 beds
Gordon Armsworthy, Proprietor

***Wolfville:* Wolfville Nursing Home**
601 Main St., Comp. C5, Site 11, RR#2, Wolfville, NS B0P 1X0
Tel: 902-542-2429 *Fax:* 902-542-4048
Number of Beds: 66 beds + 1 respite bed
Paul MacDonald, Administrator

***Yarmouth:* Harbourside Lodge**
60 Vancouver St., Yarmouth, NS B5A 2P5
Tel: 902-742-3328 *Fax:* 902-742-1427
Number of Beds: 32 beds
Sandra M. Boudreau, Executive Director

***Yarmouth:* Villa Saint Joseph-du-Lac**
Affiliated with: Southwest Nova District Health Authority #2
PO Box 810, Yarmouth, NS B5A 4A5
Tel: 902-742-7128 *Fax:* 902-742-4230
rickatkinson@villasaintjoseph.com
www.villasaintjoseph.com
Number of Beds: 79 beds
Barry Granter, Administrator

***Yarmouth:* Villa St-Joseph-du-Lac**
Affiliée à: Southwest Nova District Health Authority #2
CP 810, RR#1, Yarmouth, NS B5A 4A5
Tél: 902-742-7128 *Téléc:* 902-742-4230
rickatkinson@villasaintjoseph.com
www.villasaintjoseph.com
Nombre de lits: 79 lits
Barry Granter, Administrator

Long Term/Retirement Care

Long Term Care Facilities

***Advocate Harbor:* Bayview Memorial Health Centre**
Affiliated with: Cumberland Health Authority #5
Advocate Harbor, NS B0M 1A0
Tel: 902-392-2859 *Fax:* 902-392-2625
www.cha.nshealth.ca
Number of Beds: 12 beds
Note: also community health services

***Advocate Harbour:* Chignecto Manor Co-op Ltd.**
24 Bayview Manor Rd., Advocate Harbour, NS B0M 1A0
Tel: 902-392-2028
Shirley Morris, Administrator

***Antigonish:* L'Arche Antigonish**
4 West St., Antigonish, NS B2G 1R8
Tel: 902-863-5000 *Fax:* 902-863-8224
info@larcheantigonish.org
www.larcheantigonish.org
Year Founded: 1979
Note: The Antigonish community is home to 13 people with developmental disabilities. Programs also include day programs & summer camps that offer learning experiences & foster cooperation.

***Antigonish:* Highland Crest Home**
Affiliated with: Guysborough Antigonish Strait Health Authority #7
44 Hillcrest St., Antigonish, NS B2G 1Z3
Tel: 902-863-3855 *Fax:* 902-863-1833
mbeaver@high-crest.com
www.high-crest.com/highlandcresthome.html
Number of Beds: 40 beds
Note: residential care facility
Mary Beaver, Administrator

***Barrington:* Bayside Home Adult Residential Centre**
PO Box 238, 96 Bayside Dr., Barrington, NS B0W 1E0
Tel: 902-637-2098 *Fax:* 902-637-3151
www.baysidehome.ca
Number of Beds: 20 beds
Note: adult residential centre
Paula Hatfield, Administrator
phatfield@sundha.nshealth.ca

***Bridgetown:* Annapolis County Adult Residential Centre**
PO Box 548, Bridgetown, NS B0S 1C0
Tel: 902-665-4566 *Fax:* 902-665-5265
www.nsnet.org
Number of Beds: 34 beds
Note: adult residential centre
Patricia A. MacDougall, Administrator

***Bridgetown:* Grace Haven Enterprises Ltd.**
9791 Hwy 1, Bridgetown, NS B0S 1C0
Tel: 902-665-4224 *Fax:* 902-825-1400
Number of Beds: 20 beds
Note: residential care facility
Donna Hatt, Administrator

***Bridgetown:* Saunders Rest Home**
PO Box 114, 9 Freeman St., Bridgetown, NS B0S 1C0
Tel: 902-665-4331 *Fax:* 902-665-4768
Number of Beds: 8 beds
Shaun Saunders, Administrator

***Bridgewater:* La Have Manor Corp. Adult Residential Centre**
PO Box 270, Bridgewater, NS B4V 2W9
Tel: 902-543-7851 *Fax:* 902-543-8332
info@lahavemanor.ca
www.lahavemanor.ca
Number of Beds: 97 beds
Note: adult residential centre
Thomas Wright, Executive Director

***Bridgewater:* LaHave Manor Corp. Group Home**
58 Alexandra Ave., Bridgewater, NS B4V 1H1
Tel: 902-543-7712 *Fax:* 902-543-1816
info@lahavemanor.ca
www.lahavemanor.ca
Number of Beds: 9 beds
Note: group home for mentally challenged adults
Lorelei Mason, House Coordinator

***Chester:* Bonny Lea Farm**
PO Box 560, 5 Collicutt Rd., Chester, NS B0J 1J0
Tel: 902-275-5622 *Fax:* 902-275-2567
www.bonnyleafarm.ca
Number of Beds: 35 beds
Note: adult residential centre; small option units & apartments
David Outhouse, Managing Director
davidouthouse@sswap.ca

***Dartmouth:* Harbour Glen Manor Ltd.**
229 Pleasant St., Dartmouth, NS B2Y 3R5
Tel: 902-465-5770
Number of Beds: 18 beds
Note: residential care facility
Raymond MacDonald

***Dartmouth:* Hilltop Villa**
Affiliated with: Capital District Health Authority #9
200 Main St., Dartmouth, NS B2X 1S3
Tel: 902-435-6186 *Fax:* 902-435-9354
Number of Beds: 24 beds
Jin Young Jung, Administrator
Yoo Kyung Jung, Administrator

***Enfield:* Corridor Community Options Society**
Former Name: Lantz Residential Programs
21 Convent Rd., Enfield, NS B2T 1C9
Tel: 902-883-9404 *Fax:* 902-883-1251
Number of Beds: 14 beds
Note: Group home/small options home; vocational training/social enterprise; runs the Lantz Residential Programs & Corridor Community Options for Adults
Robin C. Strickland, Executive Director
ccosdirector@gmail.com
Ross Young, Manager, Corridor Community Options for Adults
ccoa.manager@gmail.com

***Glace Bay:* Terrace Manor**
208 South St., Glace Bay, NS B1A 1W1
Tel: 902-849-2849 *Fax:* 902-842-0359
John MacAulay, Administrator

***Greenfield:* Hillsview Acres**
PO Box 4, 14 Middlefield Rd., RR#1, Greenfield, NS B0T 1E0
Tel: 902-685-2966 *Fax:* 902-685-2446
Number of Beds: 28 beds + 1 respite
Raymond Fiske, Administrator

***Halifax:* Basinview Drive Developmental Residence**
3838 Basinview Dr., Halifax, NS B3K 5A2
Tel: 902-455-7421
Number of Beds: 8 beds
Ruth McIver, Supervisor

***Halifax:* Haven Manor**
6411 Cobourg Rd., Halifax, NS B3H 2A6
Tel: 902-421-1167 *Fax:* 902-421-1168
Number of Beds: 17 beds
Hilda Stevens, Administrator

***Halifax:* Homes for Independent Living**
2505 Oxford St., Halifax, NS B3L 2T5
Tel: 902-422-9591 *Fax:* 902-425-3151
hil@hfx.eastlink.ca
www.nsnet.org/hil/
Year Founded: 1980
Number of Beds: 6 group home beds, with 1 respite bed
Note: Specialty: Programs & accommodation for young adults with physical disabilities; Community outreach programs
JoAnne Abraham, Supervisor

***Halifax:* Lynden Rest Home**
1019 Lucknow St., Halifax, NS B3H 2T2
Tel: 902-420-0697 *Fax:* 902-492-3936

***Halifax:* Melville Gardens Residential & Level 2 Nursing Care Facility**
11 Ramsgate Lane, Halifax, NS B3P 2S9
Tel: 902-477-3135 *Fax:* 902-477-2718
www.gemhealth.com
Year Founded: 1991
Paul Hussain, Administrator
Syed Hussain, GEM Management Group, Owner

***Halifax:* Point Pleasant Lodge**
1121 South Park St., Halifax, NS B3H 2W6
Tel: 902-421-1599 *Fax:* 902-429-9722
guestservices@pointpleasantlodge.com
www.pointpleasantlodge.com
Number of Beds: 104 guest rooms
Note: A specialty hotel, with guest rooms for people directly or indirectly associated with medical attention in the Halifax area
Robert S. Manuel, CEO

***Halifax:* Robert Allen Drive Development Residence**
31 Robert Allen Dr., Halifax, NS B3M 3G9
Tel: 902-443-6804
Number of Beds: 7 beds
Note: developmental residence
Angela Fraser, Supervisor

***Halifax:* Vernon St. Group Home**
1648 Vernon St., Halifax, NS B3H 3N1
Tel: 902-422-6742
Number of Beds: 7 beds
Note: group home

***Howie Center:* My Cape Breton Home for Seniors**
Affiliated with: Cape Breton District Health Authority #8
PO Box 856, 171 Curry St., Howie Center, NS B1P 6J1
Tel: 902-564-4461 *Fax:* 902-564-4247
Number of Beds: 7 beds
Sherry MacNeil, Owner/Operator

***Kentville:* Wedgewood House**
19 Leverett Ave., Kentville, NS B4N 2K5
Tel: 902-678-1242 *Fax:* 902-679-2808
Number of Beds: 15 beds
Note: Residential care facility
Ingrid Althouse, Administrator

***Lower West Pubnico:* Pont du Marais Home Ltd.**
Affiliated with: Southwest Nova District Health Authority #2
PO Box 236, Lower West Pubnico, NS B0W 2C0
Tel: 902-762-3099 *Fax:* 902-762-2072
Number of Beds: 23 beds + 2 respite
Note: Residential care facility
Charlene LeBlanc, Administrator

***Margaree Valley:* Brookside Residential Care Facility**
PO Box 83, Margaree Valley, NS B0E 2C0
Tel: 902-248-2181 *Fax:* 902-248-2056
brook@ns.sympatico.ca
Number of Beds: 11 beds; 2 respite beds
Note: residential care facility
Lorraine Robertson, Owner

***Meteghan:* Au Logis Meteghan Ltd.**
Affiliated with: Southwest Nova District Health Authority #2
PO Box 128, 8405 Hwy. 1, Meteghan, NS B0W 2J0
Tel: 902-645-3594 *Fax:* 902-645-3594
Number of Beds: 20 beds, 2 respite
Note: residential care
Joanne Deveau, Administrator

***Meteghan:* Cottage Celeste**
Affiliated with: Southwest Nova District Health Authority #2
PO Box 314, 8064 Hwy. 1, Meteghan, NS B0W 2J0
Tel: 902-645-2248
foyerceleste@bellaliant.net
Number of Beds: 19 beds
Kathy MacDonald, Administrator

***Middle Musquodoboit:* Musquodoboit Valley Home for Special Care - Braeside**
126 Higginsville Rd., Middle Musquodoboit, NS B0N 1X0
Tel: 902-384-3007 *Fax:* 902-384-3310
Number of Beds: 28 beds
Diana Graham-Lentz, Site Manager

***New Glasgow:* High-Crest Home New Glasgow**
Affiliated with: Pictou County District Health Authority #6
Former Name: Sunset Haven Home
253 Forbes St., New Glasgow, NS B2G 4P5
Tel: 902-752-3461 *Fax:* 902-752-2672
mgammon@high-crest.com
www.high-crest.com
Number of Beds: 36 beds
Note: Specialties: Medication monitoring; Recreational program
Rosalie Parsons, Administrator

***New Glasgow:* Highland Community Residential Services**
224 Temperance St., New Glasgow, NS B2H 3B4
Tel: 902-752-1755 *Fax:* 902-752-4256
info@hcrsweb.ca
hcrsweb.ca
Year Founded: 1977
Number of Beds: 70 beds
Note: residential care facility
Jack MacIssac, Director

***Oxford:* Four Seasons Manor**
PO Box 134, Oxford, NS B0M 1P0
Tel: 902-447-2819
Number of Beds: 24 beds
Note: residential care facility
Herbert Hochhold, Administrator

***Oxford:* Shady Rest Ltd.**
237 Water St., Oxford, NS B0M 1P0
Tel: 902-447-2786
Note: residential care facility

***Pugwash:* Residential & Rehabilitation Services Inc.**
PO Box 130, Pugwash, NS B0K 1L0
Tel: 902-243-2571 *Fax:* 902-243-3222
Note: Specialties: Residential care & support services for persons who are mentally challenged & disabled; Day programs; Life & vocational skills programs; Social development programs; Advocacy services
Ronald Langille, CEO

***Saulnierville:* La Maison au Coucher du Soleil Ltd.**
RR#1, Saulnierville, NS B0W 2Z0
Tél: 902-769-2270 *Téléc:* 902-769-3850
Fondée en: 1974
Nombre de lits: 32 lits
Personnel: 20
Note: residential care facility
Nicole Amirault, Administrator

***Shelburne:* Mary's Abide-A-While Home Ltd.**
Affiliated with: Southwest Nova District Health Authority #2
PO Box 609, 188 Water St., Shelburne, NS B0T 1W0
Tel: 902-875-4384 *Fax:* 902-875-4384
Number of Beds: 16 beds
Mary Davis, Administrator

***South Berwick:* New Visions Home for Seniors**
PO Box 566, 4507 Hwy. 1, South Berwick, NS B0P 1E0
Tel: 902-538-9579 *Fax:* 902-538-0390
newvision2@ns.sympatico.ca
www.newvision2.ca
Year Founded: 1993
Number of Beds: 25 beds + 1 respite
Helen B. Walsh, Administrator

***Stellarton:* Riverview Home Corp.**
6105 Trafalgar Rd., RR#1, Stellarton, NS B0K 1S0
Tel: 902-755-4884 *Fax:* 902-755-3207
riverview@eastlink.ca
Number of Beds: 106 beds + 3 community homes & supervised depts.
Note: Residential care facility for mentally and/or physically challenged adults, group homes, & developmental residence.
Number of staff: 150
Nancy Clarke, CEO

***Stewiacke:* Elmwood Manor Limited**
PO Box 189, 98 Riverside Ave., Stewiacke, NS B0N 2J0
Number of Beds: 14 beds
Note: residential care facility
Germaine M. Roberts, Administrator

***Sydney:* Cape Breton Community Housing Association**
PO Box 1292, 50 Dorchester St., 2nd Fl., Sydney, NS B1P 6K3
Tel: 902-539-0025 *Fax:* 902-562-5476
communityhousing@cbcha.ca
www.cbcha.ca
Year Founded: 1977
Note: The organization helps clients develop skills so they may live independently in the community. Information sessions are held on a regular basis.

***Sydney:* Mayfair Guest Home**
37 George St., Sydney, NS B1P 1H4
Tel: 902-539-5611
Rosemary Ingraham-MacEache, Proprietor/Administrator

Sydney: Resi-Care (Cape Breton) Association
146 Vulcan Ave., Sydney, NS B1P 5W5
Tel: 902-539-0935 *Fax:* 902-562-0717
Number of Beds: 60 beds
Note: group home
Michael Walsh, Executive Director

Sydney River: Braemore Home
PO Box 515, Sydney River, NS B1P 6H4
Tel: 902-539-7640 *Fax:* 902-539-5340
admin@braemorehome.ns.ca
www.braemorehome.ns.ca
Number of Beds: 124 beds
Note: adult residential & rehabilitation
Debra MacPherson, Administrator

Tatamagouche: Maplewood Manor
Affiliated with: Colchester East Hants Health Authority #4
150 Blair Ave., Tatamagouche, NS B0K 1V0
Tel: 902-657-2876 *Fax:* 902-657-1022
maplewood.manor@ns.aliantzinc.ca
Social Media: www.linkedin.com/in/jeffersonwilliams
Number of Beds: 6 beds
Jeff Williams, Owner & Administrator

Truro: Karlaine Place Ltd.
Affiliated with: Colchester East Hants Health Authority #4
PO Box 691, 104 Pictou Rd., Truro, NS B2N 5E5
Tel: 902-895-5111 *Fax:* 902-893-1513
Number of Beds: 8 beds
Note: residential care facility
Robert Barnhill, Administrator

Truro: Townsview Estates
Affiliated with: Colchester East Hants Health Authority #4
PO Box 1825, 310 Abenaki Rd., Truro, NS B2N 5Z5
Tel: 902-895-9559 *Fax:* 902-893-8094
sheila_peck@hotmail.com
Number of Beds: 85 beds
Note: Residential care facility
Sheila Peck, Administrator

Truro: Westside Villa
Affiliated with: Colchester East Hants Health Authority #4
421 Prince St., Truro, NS B2N 1E6
Tel: 902-893-8463 *Fax:* 902-893-8107
Number of Beds: 26 beds
E. Louise Boyle, Administrator

Windsor: Kendall Lane Housing Society
PO Box 556, Windsor, NS B0N 2T0
Tel: 902-798-4375 *Fax:* 902-798-4378
vpghinc@gmail.com
www.vpgh.ca/klhs.html
Year Founded: 1993
Number of Beds: 6 beds
Note: small option home
Dorothy Blakely, Manager

Windsor: Kings Meadows Residence
RR#1, Windsor, NS B0N 2T0
Tel: 902-798-4657
www.nsnet.org/meadow
Number of Beds: 10 beds
Barbara Campbell, Administrator

Windsor: Victoria Park Guest House
Affiliated with: Capital District Health Authority #9
PO Box 556, 350 King St., Windsor, NS B0N 2T0
Tel: 902-798-4375 *Fax:* 902-798-4378
vpghinc@@gmail.com
www.vpgh.ca
Year Founded: 1989
Number of Beds: 15 beds
Note: Adult residential care facility
Dorothy Blakely, Administrator
Tom Blakely, Administrator

Wolfville: Wolfville Elms Residential Care Facility
705 Main St., Wolfville, NS B4P 2N4
Tel: 902-542-2420 *Fax:* 902-542-1048
wnh.home@ns.sympatico.ca
Number of Beds: 26 beds + 2 respite
Paul MacDonald, Administrator

Yarmouth: Sunset Terrace
8 James St., Yarmouth, NS B5A 2V1
Tel: 902-742-3322
Janet Doucette, Administration

Nursing Homes

Antigonish: R.K. MacDonald Nursing Home
Affiliated with: Guysborough Antigonish Strait Health Authority #7
64 Pleasant St., Antigonish, NS B2G 1W7
Tel: 902-863-2578 *Fax:* 902-863-4437
lcrocker@rkmacdonald.ca
www.gov.ns.ca/health/
Number of Beds: 108 beds + 1 respite
Lorna Crocker, Administrator

Cheticamp: Foyer Père Fiset
Affiliée à: Cape Breton District Health Authority #8
CP 219, 15092 Cabot Trail, Cheticamp, NS B0E 1H0
Tél: 902-224-2087 *Téléc:* 902-224-1188
www.cbdha.nshealth.ca
Nombre de lits: 60 lits

Glace Bay: Seaview Manor
Affiliated with: Cape Breton District Health Authority #8
275 South St., Glace Bay, NS B1A 1W6
Tel: 902-849-7300 *Fax:* 902-849-7401
cathypower@seaside.ns.ca
www.seaviewmanor.ca
Number of Beds: 101 beds, 2 respite
Catherine Power, Administrator

Glace Bay: Taigh Na Mara
Affiliated with: Cape Breton District Health Authority #8
974 Main St., Glace Bay, NS B1A 4L8
Tel: 902-842-3900 *Fax:* 902-842-3926
Number of Beds: 67 beds
Note: Continuing care for residents & veterans
Sharon Sheppard, Administrator

Inverness: Aite Curam
Affiliated with: Cape Breton District Health Authority #8
PO Box 610, 39 James St., Inverness, NS B0E 1N0
Tel: 902-258-1914 *Fax:* 902-258-3025
www.cbdha.nshealth.ca/HL_AiteCuram.htm
Number of Beds: 11 beds
Note: Part of Inverness Consolidated Memorial Hospital
Clare MacQuarrie, Facility Manager

New Waterford: Waterford Heights
Affiliated with: Cape Breton District Health Authority #8
c/o New Waterford Consolidated Hospital, 716 King St., New Waterford, NS B1H 3Z5
Tel: 902-862-6411 *Fax:* 902-862-8277
Number of Beds: 24 beds
Sharon Sheppard, Administrator

Pictou: Shiretown Nursing Home
Affiliated with: Pictou County District Health Authority #6
PO Box 250, 270 Haliburton Rd., Pictou, NS B0K 1H0
Tel: 902-485-4341 *Fax:* 902-485-9203
bonniel@shiretown.ca
www.shiretown.ca
Number of Beds: 89 beds
Note: Nursing & residential care
Bonnie Linkletter, Administrator
Tammy MacKenzie, Director of Care

Port Hawkesbury: Port Hawkesbury Nursing Home
Affiliated with: Guysborough Antigonish Strait Health Authority #7
2 MacQuarrie Dr. Extension, Port Hawkesbury, NS B9A 3A2
Tel: 902-625-1460 *Fax:* 902-625-3232
www.porthawkesburynursinghome.ca
Number of Beds: 50 beds + 4 respite
Note: Adult residential centre
Leona Wilneff, Administrator

St Peters: Richmond Villa
Affiliated with: Guysborough Antigonish Strait Health Authority #7
PO Box 250, 9361 Pepperell St., St Peters, NS B0E 3B0
Tel: 902-535-3030 *Fax:* 902-535-2256
richmondvilla@ns.sympatico.ca
www.richmondvilla.ca
Number of Beds: 59 nursing home beds, 8 resident care beds
Note: Nursing & residential care centre
Margaret Morrison, Administrator
Heather MacQueen, Director of Care

Mental Health Facilities

Mental Health Hospitals/Facilities

Dartmouth: East Coast Forensic Psychiatric Hospital
Affiliated with: Capital District Health Authority #9
88 Gloria McClusky Ave., Dartmouth, NS B3B 2B8
Tel: 902-460-7300 *Fax:* 902-460-7337
Number of Beds: 30 rehabilitation beds; 24 mentally ill offender beds
Louise Bradley, Director, Forensic Services

Dartmouth: Nova Scotia Hospital
Affiliated with: Capital District Health Authority #9
PO Box 1004, 300 Pleasant St., Dartmouth, NS B2Y 3Z9
Tel: 902-464-3111 *Fax:* 902-464-6032
shelley.peterson@cdha.nshealth.ca (Volunteer services)
www.cdha.nshealth.ca
Note: Specialties: Mental health programs
Linda Judge, Director, Capital District Mental Health Programs

Halifax: Metro Community Housing Association
Tower 1, #215, 7001 Mumford Rd., Halifax, NS B3L 4N9
Tel: 902-453-6444 *Fax:* 902-453-1188
info@mcha.ns.ca
www.mcha.ns.ca
Number of Beds: 86 residential capacity & 79 supported apartments
Note: Specialties: Support & residential services to persons who have experienced mental health difficulties
Cathy Crouse, Executive Director

Special Care Homes

Glace Bay: Jones Manor
Affiliated with: Cape Breton District Health Authority #8
1 Minto St., Glace Bay, NS B1Z 5B2
Tel: 902-849-1605
Number of Beds: 7 beds
Calvin Jones, Administrator

Kingston: Tibbetts Home Wilmot
PO Box 519, 15074 Hwy. #1, Kingston, NS B0P 1R0
Tel: 902-765-6614 *Fax:* 902-765-3807
tibbco2001@yahoo.com
Number of Beds: 25 beds
Wanda Tibbetts, Administrator

Nunavut

Government Departments in Charge

NUNAVUT: Dept. of Health & Social Services
PO Box 1000 Stn. 1000, 1107 Sivummut Bldg., 3rd Fl., Iqaluit, NU X0A 0H0
Tel: 867-975-5766 *Fax:* 867-975-5705
health@gov.nu.ca
www.hss.gov.nu.ca
Hon. Keith Peterson, Minister
kpeterson@gov.nu.ca
Dr. Geraldine Osbourne, Chief Medical Officer of Health
gosborne@gov.nu.ca

Hospitals

Hospitals - General

Dryden: Dryden Regional Health Centre (DRHC)
PO Box 3003, 58 Goodall St., Dryden, NU P8N 2Z6
Tel: 807-223-8200 *Fax:* 807-223-2370
TTY: 807-223-8295
www.dh.dryden.on.ca
Number of Beds: 31 acute care beds; 10 chronic / rehabilitation care beds
Note: Hospital Specialties: Emergency services; Diagnostic imaging (807-223-8253); Acute care; Obstetrics; Critical care; Mental health & addiction services (807-223-6678); Occupational therapy (807-223-8214); Physiotherapy (807-223-8259); Sexual assault & domestic violence services (807-223-7427); Diabetes education (807-223-8208); Counselling; Chronic care
Dr. Karen Mazurski, Chief of Staff
Dr. Mark Dahmer, Chief, Emergency
Dr. Steven Viherjoki, Chief, Inpatient Services
Siobain Moore, Administrative Director, Workplace Culture & Organizational Health
807-223-8829, smoore@dh.dryden.on.ca

Iqaluit: Baffin Regional Hospital
PO Box 200, Iqaluit, NU X0A 0H0
Tel: 867-979-7300 *Fax:* 867-979-7347

Number of Beds: 25 inpatient beds; 19 acute care adult beds; 6 pediatric beds; 8 newborn bassinets
Note: Hospital Specialties: Emergency & outpatient department; X-ray department; Laboratory; Acute care; Pediatrics

***Iqaluit:* Qikiqtani General Hospital**
PO Box 1000 Stn. 1040, Iqaluit, NU X0A 0H0
Tel: 867-975-8600
Number of Beds: 35 beds
Note: Birthing rooms, surgery, diagnostic imaging & lab, state-of-the-art community health care
Katherine Walters, Director

Community Health Centres

Community Health Care Centres

***Arctic Bay:* Arctic Bay Health Centre**
PO Box 60, Arctic Bay, NU X0A 0A0
Tel: 867-439-8816 *Fax:* 867-439-8315
Gail Redpath, Nurse Manager

***Arviat:* Arviat Health Centre**
General Delivery, Arviat, NU X0C 0E0
Tel: 867-857-2816 *Fax:* 867-857-2980
Sandy Ranahan, Nurse Manager

***Baker Lake:* Baker Lake Health Centre**
PO Box 120, Baker Lake, NU X0C 0A0
Tel: 867-793-2816 *Fax:* 867-793-2812
Donna Brown, Nurse Manager

***Cambridge Bay:* Cambridge Bay Health Centre**
PO Box 83, Cambridge Bay, NU X0E 0C0
Tel: 867-983-2531 *Fax:* 867-983-2262
www.cambridgebay.ca/services/health.htm
Number of Beds: 2 beds

***Cape Dorset:* Cape Dorset Health Centre**
PO Box 180, Cape Dorset, NU X0A 0C0
Tel: 867-897-8820 *Fax:* 867-897-8914

***Chesterfield Inlet:* Chesterfield Inlet Health Centre**
PO Box 9, Chesterfield Inlet, NU X0C 0B0
Tel: 867-898-9968 *Fax:* 867-898-9122

***Clyde River:* Clyde River Health Centre**
PO Box 40, Clyde River, NU X0A 0E0
Tel: 867-924-6377 *Fax:* 867-924-6244

***Coral Harbour:* Coral Harbour Health Centre**
PO Box 120, Coral Harbour, NU X0C 0C0
Tel: 867-925-9916 *Fax:* 867-925-8380

***Gjoa Haven:* Gjoa Haven Haputtit Health Centre**
General Delivery, Gjoa Haven, NU X0E 1J0
Tel: 867-360-7441 *Fax:* 867-360-6110

***Grise Fjord:* Grise Fjord Health Centre**
PO Box 81, Grise Fjord, NU X0A 0J0
Tel: 867-980-9923 *Fax:* 867-980-9067

***Hall Beach:* Hall Beach Health Centre**
General Delivery, Hall Beach, NU X0A 0K0
Tel: 867-928-8827 *Fax:* 867-928-8847

***Igloolik:* Igloolik Health Centre**
PO Box 240, Igloolik, NU X0A 0L0
Tel: 867-934-8837 *Fax:* 867-934-8901

***Iqaluit:* Iqaluit Public Health Clinic**
PO Box 200, Iqaluit, NU X0A 0H0
Tel: 867-979-5306 *Fax:* 867-979-4830

***Kimmirut:* Kimmirut Health Centre**
PO Box 30, Kimmirut, NU X0A 0N0
Tel: 867-939-2217 *Fax:* 867-939-2068

***Kugaaruk:* St. Theresa Kugaaruk Health Centre**
General Delivery, Kugaaruk, NU X0E 1K0
Tel: 867-769-6441 *Fax:* 867-769-6059

***Kugluktuk:* Kugluktuk Health Centre**
General Delivery, Kugluktuk, NU X0E 0E0
Tel: 867-982-4531 *Fax:* 867-982-3115

***Pangnirtung:* Pangnirtung Health Centre**
PO Box 454, Pangnirtung, NU X0A 0R0
Tel: 867-473-8977 *Fax:* 867-473-8519
www.pangnirtung.ca/home
Note: Specialty: General health care by registered nurses; Individual counseling & referral; Massage therapy; Workshops for stress relief

***Pond Inlet:* Pond Inlet Health Centre**
PO Box 216, Pond Inlet, NU X0A 0S0
Tel: 867-899-8840 *Fax:* 867-899-8997
Year Founded: 2004
Population Served: 1290
Note: Comprehensive health care. Number of employees: 20
Di Schulze, Supervisor, Health & Community Programs

***Qikiqtarjuaq:* Qikiqtarjuaq Health Centre**
PO Box 911, Qikiqtarjuaq, NU X0A 0B0
Tel: 867-927-8916 *Fax:* 867-927-8217

***Rankin Inlet:* Rankin Inlet Health Centre**
Bag 008, Rankin Inlet, NU X0C 0G0
Tel: 867-645-2816 *Fax:* 867-645-2688

***Repulse Bay:* Repulse Bay Health Centre**
General Delivery, Repulse Bay, NU X0C 0H0
Tel: 867-462-9916 *Fax:* 867-462-4212
Number of Beds: 2 beds
Population Served: 612

***Resolute:* Resolute Health Centre**
PO Box 180, Resolute, NU X0A 0V0
Tel: 867-252-3844 *Fax:* 867-252-3601

***Sanikiluaq:* Sanikiluaq Health Centre**
PO Box 145, Sanikiluaq, NU X0A 0W0
Tel: 867-266-8965 *Fax:* 867-266-8802
http://webmail.gov.nu.ca
Note: Provides general health care, counseling & referral. Services in Inuktitut & English
Joanne Watson, Nurse in Charge

***Taloyoak:* Taloyoak Judy Hill Memorial Health Centre**
General Delivery, Taloyoak, NU X0E 1B0
Tel: 867-561-5111 *Fax:* 867-561-6906
Number of Employees: 5

***Whale Cove:* Whale Cove Health Centre**
PO Box 3, Whale Cove, NU X0A 0K0
Tel: 867-896-9916 *Fax:* 867-896-9115

Nursing Stations

***Broughton Island:* Qikiqtarjuaq Health Centre**
PO Box 911, Broughton Island, NU X0A 0B0
Tel: 867-927-8916 *Fax:* 867-927-8217
Christine Kellett, Nursing Supervisor

Long Term/Retirement Care

Long Term Care Facilities

***Arviat:* Andy Aulatjut Elders' Centre**
PO Box 147, Arviat, NU X0C 0E0
Tel: 867-857-2667 *Fax:* 867-857-2668

***Chesterfield Inlet:* St. Therese Home**
PO Box 1, Chesterfield Inlet, NU X0C 0B0
Tel: 867-898-9917 *Fax:* 867-898-9080
Note: Homecare facility

***Iqaluit:* Iqaluit Elders' Facility**
Pairijait Tigumivik Society, PO Box 640, Iqaluit, NU X0A 0H0
Tel: 867-979-7408 *Fax:* 867-979-8864

Mental Health Facilities

Mental Health Hospitals/Facilities

***Iqaluit:* Akausisarvik Mental Health Facilty**
Baffin Hospital, PO Box 1000 Stn. 1048, Iqaluit, NU X0A 0H0
Tel: 867-979-7379
Number of Beds: 13 beds
Katherine Walters, Director, Hospital Services

Ontario

Government Departments in Charge

ONTARIO: Ministry of Health & Long-Term Care
Hepburn Block, Queen's Park, 80 Grosvenor St., 10th Fl., Toronto, ON M7A 1S2
Tel: 416-327-4327 *Fax:* 416-314-8721
Toll-Free: 800-268-1153
www.health.gov.on.ca
Social Media: www.facebook.com/217753654940869; twitter.com/ONThealth; www.youtube.com/user/ontariomohltc
Deb Matthews, Minister

Regional Health Authorities

***Ajax:* Central East Local Health Integration Network**
Harwood Plaza, #204A, 314 Harwood Ave. South, Ajax, ON L1S 2J1
Tel: 905-427-5497 *Fax:* 905-427-9659
Toll-Free: 1-866-804-5446
centraleast@lhins.on.ca
www.centraleastlhin.on.ca
Social Media: twitter.com/CentralEastLHIN
Area Served: From Victoria Park to Algonquin Park*Population Served:* 1400000
Deborah Hammons, Chief Executive Officer
Wayne Gladstone, Chair
Paul Barker, Senior Director, System Finance & Performance Management
James Meloche, Senior Director, System Design & Implementation

***Arnprior:* Arnprior Regional Health**
350 John St. North, Arnprior, ON K7S 2P6
Tel: 613-623-3166
www.arnpriorregionalhealth.ca
Note: Acute, long-term and other healthcare services
Eric Hanna, President/CEO

***Belleville:* South East Local Health Integration Network**
71 Adam St., Belleville, ON K8N 5K3
Tel: 613-967-0196 *Fax:* 613-967-1341
Toll-Free: 866-831-5446
southeast@lhins.on.ca
www.southeastlhin.on.ca
Social Media: www.facebook.com/227389740864
Population Served: 10000
Note: The South East region extends from Brighton on the west to Prescott and Cardinal on the east, north to Perth and Smith Falls, and back to Bancroft. Includes 8 hospitals, 1 Cancer Centre, 36 long-term care homes, Community Care Access Centres, 2 Children's Treatment Centres, 4 Community Health Centres, 16 Community Mental Health Services, 14 Community Support Services, and 8 Substance Abuse Programs.
Paul Huras, CEO
paul.huras@lhins.on.ca
Wynn Turner, Acting Chair
wynn.turner@lhins.on.ca

***Brampton:* Central West Local Health Integration Network**
#300, 8 Nelson St. West, Brampton, ON L6X 4J2
Tel: 905-455-1281 *Fax:* 905-455-0427
Toll-Free: 1-866-370-5446
centralwest@lhins.on.ca
www.centralwestlhin.on.ca
Area Served: From northern Dufferin County to northern Peel Region*Population Served:* 800144
Note: 53 health service providers in central west Ontario including a community care access centre, 2 community health centres, 13 community support services, 2 hospitals (four sites), 23 long-term care homes, and 8 mental health and addiction agencies.
Brock Hovey, Interim Chief Executive Officer
brock.hovey@lhins.on.ca
Joe McReynolds, Chair
David Colgan, Senior Director, Health System Integration
david.colgan@lhins.on.ca
Priya Ramsingh, Director, Communications & Community Engagement
priya.ramsingh@lhins.on.ca
Elizabeth Salvaterra, Director, ER/ALC & Decision Support
elizabeth.salvaterra@lhins.on.ca
Neil McIntosh, Director, Performance & Accountability
neil.mcintosh@lhins.on.ca
Tellis George, Director, Funding & Allocation
tellis.george@lhins.on.ca

***Chatham:* Erie St. Clair Local Health Integration Network**
180 Riverview Dr., Chatham, ON N7M 5Z8
Tel: 519-351-5677 *Fax:* 519-351-9672
Toll-Free: 1-866-231-5446
eriestclairlhin@lhins.on.ca
www.eriestclairlhin.on.ca
Social Media: www.facebook.com/111002926463; twitter.com/ESCLHIN; www.youtube.com/user/esclhin?feature=mhee
Area Served: Counties of Chatham-Kent, Sarnia/Lambton and Windsor/Essex*Population Served:* 649000

Gary Switzer, Chief Executive Officer
gary.switzer@lhins.on.ca
Dave Cook, Chair
Ralph Ganter, Senior Director, Health System Design & Implementation
ralph.ganter@lhins.on.ca
Pete Crvenkovski, Director, Performance Quality & Knowledge Management
pete.crvenkovski@lhins.on.ca
Ron Shepard, Director, Communications & Community Engagement
ron.sheppard@lhins.on.ca
Matthew Little, Director, Corporate Services/Controller
matthew.little@lhins.on.ca
Ruth Augi, Corporate Coordinator
ruth.augi@lhins.on.ca

Grimsby: Hamilton Niagara Haldimand Brant Local Health Integration Network (HNHB LHI)/RLISS de Hamilton Niagara Haldimand Brant
264 Main St. East, Grimsby, ON L3M 1P8
Tel: 905-945-4930 *Fax:* 905-945-1992
Toll-Free: 1-866-363-5446
hamiltonniagarahaldimandbrant@lhins.on.ca
www.hnhblhin.on.ca
Area Served: Brant, Burlington, Haldimand, Hamilton, Niagara, Norfolk*Number of Employees:* 34
Note: Facilities: 87 long term care homes; 10 hospitals (23 hospital sites); 7 community health centres (10 sites); 1 community care access centre. Programs: 80 community support services; 45 community mental health & addictions programs.
Donna Cripps, Chief Executive Officer
donna.cripps@lhins.on.ca
Michael Shea, Chair
Philip Christoff, Director, Quality & Risk Management
philip.christoff@lhins.on.ca
Steve Isaak, Director, Health System Transformation
steven.isaak@lhins.on.ca
Patricia Ciccarelli, Director, Finance
patricia.ciccarelli@lhins.on.ca
Jennifer Everson, Physician Lead, Clinical Health Transformation
jennifer.everson@lhins.on.ca
Trish Nelson, Director, Communications & Corporate Services
trish.nelson@lhins.on.ca
Rosalind Tarrant, Director, Access to Care
rosalind.tarrant@lhins.on.ca

Kitchener: Waterloo Wellington Local Health Integration Network
East Bldg., #220, 50 Sportsworld Crossing Rd., Kitchener, ON N2P 0A4
Tel: 519-650-4472 *Fax:* 519-650-3155
Toll-Free: 866-306-5446
waterloowellington@lhins.on.ca
www.waterloowellingtonlhin.on.ca
Social Media: www.facebook.com/pages/Waterloo-Wellington-LHIN/1419574922543419; twitter.com/WW_LHIN
Area Served: Waterloo, Kitchener, Cambridge and Guelph.
Note: Not-for-profit organization that works to plan, integrate, and fund local health services
Bruce Lauckner, CEO
bruce.lauckner@lhins.on.ca
Joan Fisk, Chair

London: South West Local Health Integration Network
#700, 201 Queens Ave., London, ON N6A 1J1
Tel: 519-672-0445 *Toll-Free:* 866-294-5446
southwest@lhins.on.ca
www.southwestlhin.on.ca
Social Media: www.facebook.com/SouthWestLHIN; twitter.com/SouthWestLHIN; www.youtube.com/user/SouthWestLHIN/videos; linkedin.com/company/south-west-local-health-integration-network
Area Served: Area from Lake Erie to the Bruce Peninsula*Population Served:* 1000000
Note: The South West Local Health Integration Network (LHIN) is a crown agency responsible for the planning, integration and funding of nearly 200 health service providers including hospitals, long-term care homes, mental health and addictions agencies, community support services, community health centres, and the South West Community Care Access Centre.
Michael Barrett, CEO
Jeff Low, Chair
Mark Brintnell, Senior Director, Performance, Contract & Accountability
Kelly Gillis, Senior Director, Planning, Integration & Community Engagement

Lisa Johnson, Manager, Corporate Services
Glenn Lanteigne, Chief Information Officer

Markham: Central Local Health Integration Network
#210, 140 Allstate Pkwy., Markham, ON L3R 5Y8
Tel: 905-948-1872 *Fax:* 905-948-8011
Toll-Free: 1-866-392-5446
Central@lhins.on.ca
www.centrallhin.on.ca
Population Served: 1800000
Kim Baker, Chief Executive Officer
John M. Langs, Chair
Karin Dschankilic, Senior Director, Performance, Contracts, & Allocations
Nancy Lum-Wilson, Director, Health System Planning & Design
Jeff Kwan, Director, Performance, Contract, Allocation & eHealth

Annette Marcuzzi, Director, Strategic Alignment
Sue Turcotte, Director, Finance & Risk Management
Sandra Upeslacis, Manager, Communications

North Bay: North East Local Health Integration Network
555 Oak St. East, 3rd Fl., North Bay, ON P1B 8E3
Tel: 705-840-2872 *Fax:* 705-840-0142
Toll-Free: 866-906-5446
northeast@lhins.on.ca
www.nelhin.on.ca
Social Media: www.facebook.com/NorthEastLHIN?v=info&ref=ts; twitter.com/NorthEastLHIN
Population Served: 550000
Note: The North East LHIN brings 186 of the region's health care partners together - hospitals, community support services, mental health and addictions, community health centres, long-term care homes, and the Community Care Access Centre.
Louise Paquette, CEO
louise.paquette@lhins.on.ca
Wallace Wiwchar, Acting Chair

Oakville: Mississauga Halton Local Health Integration Network (MH LHIN)
#500, 700 Dorval Dr., Oakville, ON L6K 3V3
Tel: 905-337-7131 *Fax:* 905-337-8330
Toll-Free: 866-371-5446
mississaugahalton@lhins.on.ca
www.mississaugahaltonlhin.on.ca
Population Served: 1100000
Note: Includes the south-west portion of the City of Toronto, the south part of Peel Region, and all of Halton Region except for Burlington, which is part of the Hamilton Niagara Haldimand Brant LHIN.
Bill MacLeod, CEO
Graeme Goebelle, Chair
Narendra Shah, Chief Operating Officer
Andrew Hussain, Regional CIO & eHealth Lead

Orillia: North Simcoe Muskoka Local Health Integration Network
#127-130, 210 Memorial Ave., Orillia, ON L3V 7V1
Tel: 705-326-7750 *Fax:* 705-326-1392
Toll-Free: 866-903-5446
northsimcoemuskoka@lhins.on.ca
www.nsmlhin.on.ca
Social Media: twitter.com/NSMLHIN
Population Served: 453710*Number of Employees:* 30
Note: Encompasses the District of Muskoka, most of the County of Simcoe and a portion of Grey County. North Simcoe Muskoka is home to four First Nations. 77 individual health service provider organizations.
Bernie Blais, CEO
bernie.blais@lhins.on.ca
Robert Morton, Chair

Ottawa: Champlain Local Health Integration Network
#204, 1900 City Park Dr., Ottawa, ON K1J 1A3
Tel: 613-747-6784 *Fax:* 613-747-6519
Toll-Free: 1-866-902-5446
champlain@lhins.on.ca
www.champlainlhin.on.ca; www.rlisschamplain.on.ca
Social Media: facebook.com/pages/Champlain-LHIN-RLISS-de-Champlain/287875554109; www.youtube.com/user/ChamplainLHIN/videos
Year Founded: 2005
Population Served: 1147000
Note: Facilities: 100+ community support services, including mental health & addictions agencies; 61 long-term care homes; 21 hospitals; 7 community health centres plus satellites, 1 community care access centre. Area Served: Renfrew County; City of Ottawa; Prescott & Russell; Stormont; Dundas & Glengarry; North Grenville; four parts of North Lanark

Chantale LeClerc, Chief Executive Officer
chantale.leclerc@lhins.on.ca
Dr. Wilbert Keon, Board Chair
wilbert.keon@lhins.on.ca
Glenn Alexander, Chief Information Officer
Glenn.Alexander@lhins.on.ca
Suzanne Dionne, Senior Director, Performance, Contract, & Allocation
Nicole Lafrenière, Senior Director, Health System Integration
Elaine Medline, Director, Communications

Thunder Bay: North West Local Health Integration Network
#201, 975 Alloy Dr., Thunder Bay, ON P7B 5Z8
Tel: 807-684-9425 *Fax:* 807-684-9533
Toll-Free: 866-907-5446
northwest@lhins.on.ca.
www.northwestlhin.on.ca
Year Founded: 2005
Note: The North West LHIN is responsible for planning, integrating and funding many local health services, including hospitals, the Community Care Access Centre, community health centres, long-term care homes, community support service agencies and community mental health and addiction services. The North West LHIN extends from just west of White River to the Manitoba border and from Hudson Bay in the north down to the United States border.
Laura Kokocinski, CEO
Joy Warkentin, Chair

Toronto: Toronto Central Local Health Integration Network (LHIN)
#201, 425 Bloor St. East, Toronto, ON M4W 3R4
Tel: 416-921-7453 *Fax:* 416-921-0117
Toll-Free: 866-383-5446
torontocentral@lhins.on.ca
www.torontocentrallhin.on.ca
Population Served: 1150000
Note: 174 health service providers including hospitals, the Toronto Central Community Care Access Centre, community support services, Community Health Centres, mental health and addictions agencies and long-term care homes are funded through the TC LHIN.
Camille Orridge, CEO
Angela Ferrante, Chair
Dr. Howard Ovens, Lead, Emergency
Dr. Niall Ferguson, Lead, Critical Care
Janine Hopkins, Senior Director, Community Engagement & Corporate Affairs
William B. Manson, Senior Director, Performance Management
Vania Sakelaris, Senior Director, Health System Integration & Design and Development
Raj Krishnapillai, Senior Director, Finance & Corporate & Shared Services (CFO)
Rachel Solomon, Senior Director, Performance Measurement & Information Management

Hospitals - General

Chapleau: Chapleau Health Services (SSCHS)/Services de sante de Chapleau
6 Broomhead Rd., Chapleau, ON P0M 1K0
Tel: 705-864-1520 *Fax:* 705-864-0449
chapleauhr@sschs.ca
www.sschs.ca
Number of Beds: 14 acute care beds at Chapleau General Hospital; 19 long term care beds, 4 chronic care beds, & 2 respite beds at the Bignucolo Residence
Note: Specialties: Emergency services; Acute care; Occupational therapy; Rehabilitation services; Adult mental health services; Counselling; Services for the for the developmentally disabled; Diabetes education; Community services, such as Meals on Wheels, home support services, & Lifeline; Operation of a nursing station in Foleyet; Long term care; Chronic care; Respite care
Gail Bignucolo, Chief Executive Officer
705-864-3050
Robin Greer, Manager, Diabetes Education
rgreer@sschs.ca

Hospitals

Hospitals - General

Ajax: Rouge Valley Ajax & Pickering Affiliated with: Rouge Valley Health System
580 Harwood Ave. South, Ajax, ON L1S 2J4
Tel: 905-683-2320 *Fax:* 905-683-2618
www.rougevalley.ca
Number of Beds: 130 beds
Note: Emergency, cancer care, cardiac care, continuing care & rehabilitation, diagnostic imaging, maternal, paediatrics, surgery

Rik Ganderton, President/CEO, RVHS
boardofdirectors@rougevalley.ca
David Brazeau, Director, RVHS, Public Affairs & Community Relations
647-294-8885, dbrazeau@rougevalley.ca

Alexandria: Glengarry Memorial Hospital
20260 County Road 43, Alexandria, ON K0C 1A0
Tel: 613-525-2222 *Fax:* 613-525-4515
www.hgmh.on.ca

Number of Beds: 37 beds
Linda Morrow, CEO

Alliston: Stevenson Memorial Hospital (SMH)
PO Box 4000, 200 Fletcher Cres., Alliston, ON L9R 1W7
Tel: 705-435-6281 *Fax:* 705-434-5138
information@smhosp.on.ca
www.smhosp.on.ca

Number of Beds: 36 beds
Note: Specialties: Acute care; Day surgery; Diagnostic imaging; Ambulatory care clinics; Obstetrics / Gynaecology
Edward Takacs, President/CEO

Almonte: Almonte General Hospital (AGH)
75 Spring St., Almonte, ON K0A 1A0
Tel: 613-256-2500 *Fax:* 613-256-8549
tmclelland@agh-fvm.com
www.almontegeneral.com

Note: Hospital Specialties: Emergency services; Diagnostic services; Acute care; Physiotherapy
Ray K. Timmons, Executive Director
613-256-2514, rtimmons@agh-fvm.com
Donna Leafloor, Assistant Executive Director, Patient & Resident Services
dleafloor@agh-fvm.com
Randy Shaw, Assistant Executive Director, Support Services
rshaw@agh-fvm.com
Jamie Welsford, Assistant Executive Director, Finance & Information Technology
jwelsford@agh-fvm.com
Rena L. Bowen, Director, Special Services
rbowen@agh-fvm.com
Michael Doyle, Director, Human Resources
mdoyle@agh-fvm.com
Beth Lepack, Director, Medical Records
blepack@agh-fvm.com
Nina Mukerjee, Director, Physiotherapy
nmukerjee@agh-fvm.com
Pam Murphy, Director, Long-Term Care
pmurphy@agh-fvm.com

Arnprior: Arnprior & District Memorial Hospital
Affiliated with: Arnprior Regional Health
350 John St. North, Arnprior, ON K7S 2P6
Tel: 613-623-3166 *Fax:* 613-623-4844
lab@arnpriorhospital.com
www.arnpriorhospital.com

Note: Hospital Specialties: Emergency services; Diagnostic imaging; Acute care; Ontario Breast Screening Program; Diabetes clinic; Physiotherapy; Speech therapy; Urotherapy; Palliative care
Eric Hanna, Chief Executive Officer
eric.hanna@arnpriorhospital.com
Leah Levesque, Director, Patient & Resident Services
Michelle Lewis, Director, Human Resources
michelle.lewis@arnpriorhospital.com
Tim Sonnenburg, Director, Finance & Support Services
tim.sonnenburg@arnpriorhospital.com
Wendy Knechtel, Manager, Public Relations & Fundraising
wknechtel@arnpriorhospital.com
Cindy O'Greysik, Manager, Health Records
cindy.ogreysik@arnpriorhospital.com
Karen Graham, Supervisor, Food Services
karen.graham@arnpriorhospital.com

Atikokan: Atikokan General Hospital
120 Dorothy St., Atikokan, ON P0T 1C0
Tel: 807-597-4215 *Fax:* 807-597-4305
www.aghospital.on.ca

Number of Beds: 41 beds
Note: Hospital services: Emergency services; Diagnostic services; Acute care; Cardiac care; Rehabilitation services; Counselling & addictions program; Diabetic counselling; Complex continuing care; Long-term care; Number of Employees: 100
Robert G. Wilson, Chief Executive Officer
robert.wilson@aghospital.on.ca
Kim Cross, Assistant Executive Director, Finance
kim.cross@aghospital.on.ca
Wayne Smith, Assistant Executive Director, Patient Care Services
wayne.smith@aghospital.on.ca
Marie Cornell, Manager, Lab
marie.cornell@aghospital.on.ca
Bridget Davidson, Manager, Health Records & Privacy
bridget.davidson@aghospital.on.ca
Donna Mallard, Nurse, Diabetic Health
donna.mallard@aghospital.on.ca

Attawapiskat: James Bay General Hospital
General Delivery, Attawapiskat, ON P0L 1A0
Tel: 705-997-2150 *Fax:* 705-997-2121
hr@jbgh.org
www.jbgh.org

Number of Beds: 16 beds
Cecile Rose, Wing Director

Bancroft: Quinte Health Care North Hastings
Quinte Health Care
Former Name: North Hastings District Hospital
PO Box 157, 1-H Manor Lane, Bancroft, ON K0L 1C0
Tel: 613-332-2825 *Fax:* 613-332-3847
www.qhc.on.ca/Default.aspx?cid=275&lang=1

Number of Beds: 6 beds
Note: Primary healthcare facility; acute care/emergency; dialysis unit
Pat Tresierra, Interim Site Administrator

Barrie: Royal Victoria Regional Health Centre (RVH)
Former Name: Royal Victoria Hospital
201 Georgian Dr., Barrie, ON L4M 6M2
Tel: 705-728-9802 *Fax:* 705-726-0822
TTY: 705-739-5618
webmaster@rvh.on.ca
www.rvh.on.ca

Year Founded: 1897
Number of Beds: 299 beds
Area Served: Simcoe County and the districts of Muskoka and Parry Sound*Number of Employees:* 2162
Note: Comprehensive services, including emergency, cardiology, intensive care unit, renal services, chronic disease management, imaging (CT scans, MRIs, mammograms, BMDs, ultrasound, angiography); specializing in cancer care, surgical services, critical care, mental health rehabilitation services, as well as women and children's programs; 280 physicians, staff of 2,300.
Janice Skot, President; CEO
SkotJ@rvh.on.ca
Brian Edmunds, COO
edmondsb@rvh.on.ca
Hilary Rodriques, Vice-President Finance; CFO
rodriguesh@rvh.on.ca
Sandy McFarlane, Vice-President; Chief Nursing Executive, Patient Programs

Barry's Bay: St. Francis Memorial Hospital
PO Box 129, 7 St. Francis Memorial Dr., Barry's Bay, ON K0J 1B0
Tel: 613-756-3044 *Fax:* 613-756-0106
www.sfmhosp.com

Year Founded: 1960
Number of Beds: 27 beds (13 continuing care beds, 14 active care beds)
Note: A comprehensive care facility with services including emergency, complex continuing care, physiotherapy, dialysis, diagnostic imaging (ultrasound, mammography, bone densitometry), holter monitor, respirology, diabetic clinic, foot care clinic, general surgery, ear, nose & throat, mental health, orthotist. Private, semi-private and ward rooms are available.
Randy Penney, CEO
Jeremy Stevenson, COO
Joanne Pecarskie, Executive Assistant
pecarskiej@sfmhosp.com
Darlene Sernoskie, Director, Operations
Joan Kuiack, Director, Patient Care Services

Belleville: Quinte Health Care Belleville General
Quinte Health Care
265 Dundas St. East, Belleville, ON K8N 5A9
Tel: 613-969-7400 *Fax:* 613-968-8234
www.qhc.on.ca/Default.aspx?cid=273&lang=1

Year Founded: 1886
Number of Beds: 192 beds
Note: Emergency, cardiology, children's treatment centre, intensive care, obstetrics, oncology, outpatient clinics, orthopaedics, psychiatry/mental health services, rehabilitation, radiology, surgical services, District Stroke Centre
Mary Clare Egberts, President; CEO, Quinte Health Care
Dr. Mohamed Gaber, Chief of Staff

Blind River: Blind River District Health Centre (BRDHC)/Pavillion Santé du District de Blind River
Former Name: Robb Hospital; St. Joseph's General Hospital
525 Causley St., Blind River, ON P0R 1B0
Tel: 705-356-2265 *Fax:* 705-356-1220
webinfo@brdhc.on.ca
www.brdhc.on.ca

Year Founded: 1928
Number of Beds: 16 acute care beds
Note: Hospital Specialties: Emergency services; Acute care; Diagnostic imaging; Medical laboratory services; Long term care; Health promotion; Physiotherapy; Diabetes education; Dietician services; Social work; Palliative care
Gaston Lavigne, Chief Executive Officer
705-356-2265, ext. 2, glavigne@brdhc.on.ca
Dr. Chris Barnes, Chief of Staff
705-356-1666, cstjules@brdhc.on.ca
Mary Ellen Luukkonen, Chief Nursing Officer; Director, Clinical Services
705-356-2265, ext. 2, mluukkonen@brdhc.on.ca
Jennifer Stanton Smith, Chief Financial Officer
705-356-2265, ext. 2, jsmith@brdhc.on.ca
Dan Lewis, Director, Environmental Services
705-356-2265, ext., dlewis@brdhc.on.ca

Bowmanville: Lakeridge Health Corporation
Bowmanville Site
47 Liberty St. South, Bowmanville, ON L1C 2N4
Tel: 905-623-3331 *Fax:* 905-623-0681
www.lakeridgehealth.on.ca

Number of Beds: 686 beds
C. Kooy, COO

Bracebridge: Muskoka Algonquin Healthcare - South Muskoka Memorial Hospital Site
Affiliated with: Muskoka Algonquin Healthcare
Also Known As: South Muskoka Memorial Hospital
75 Ann St., Bracebridge, ON P1L 2E4
Tel: 705-645-4400 *Fax:* 705-645-4594
info@mahc.ca
www.mahc.ca/Content.cfm?C=6169&SC=1&SCM=0&MI=4181&L1M=4150

Number of Beds: 75 beds
Note: Services include emergency, intensive care unit, surgery, endoscopy/gastroenterology, urology, ophthamology, oncology, obstetrics, antenatal, paediatrics, diabetes centre, social work, occupational therapy, speech/language therapy, pathology, complex continuing care, laboratory services, diagnostic imaging (radiography, tomography, ultrasound, bone densitometry, mammography), cardio-respiratory services, pharmacy
Barry Monaghan, CEO, MAHC
barry.monaghan@mahc.ca
Dr. David Mathies, Chief of Staff, MAHC
liz.parrott@mahc.ca
Bev McFarlane, Chief Nursing Officer, MAHC
bev.mcfarlane@mahc.ca

Brampton: William Osler Health Centre - Brampton Civic Hospital Campus
2100 Bovaird Dr. East, Brampton, ON L6R 3J7
Tel: 905-494-2120
www.williamoslerhc.on.ca

Year Founded: 2007
Number of Beds: 479
Note: Comprehensive health care. The William Osler Health Centre is comprised of the Brampton Civic Hospital, Etobicoke General, & the Peel Memorial Hospital (currently in re-development)
Ken White, Supervisor

Brantford: Brantford General Hospital Site
Brant Community Healthcare System
200 Terrace Hill St., Brantford, ON N3R 1G9
Tel: 519-752-7871
www.bchsys.org

Year Founded: 1885
Number of Beds: 300+ beds
Note: Hospital Specialties: Emergency medicine; Acute care; Critical care; Surgery; Ambulatory care; Obstetrics; Paediatrics; Brant Community Cancer Clinic; S.C. Johnson Dialysis Clinic; Mental health; Gynaecology; Number of Employees: 1,282 (175 physicians & 26 members of the Department of Dentistry)
James Hornell, President; Chief Executive Officer, Brant Community Healthcare System
519-751-5500
Lina Rinaldi, Vice-President, Patient Services
519-751-5544. ext. 2,
Charmaine Roye, Chief, Medical Staff
519-751-5544, ext. 2
David Cameron, Director, Medical Affairs
519-751-5544, ext. 2

Patricia Debrusk, Director, Surgical & Ambulatory Services
519-751-5544, ext. 2
Diane Draper, Director, Critical Care, Maternal / Child Care, Dialysis, Med
519-751-5544, ext. 4
Don Manning, Director, Diagnostic Services
519-751-5544, ext. 2
Heather Riddell, Director, Emergency Services & Urgent Care
519-751-5544, ext. 2
Terry Dalimonte, Manager, Dialysis, Diabetic Education, & Paediatrics
519-751-5544, ext. 4
Robert Davidson, Manager, Human Resources
519-751-5544, ext. 2
Jill Randall, Manager, Critical Care
519-751-5544, ext. 2

Brockville: Brockville General Hospital (BGH)
75 Charles St., Brockville, ON K6V 1S8
Tel: 613-345-5649 *Fax:* 613-345-8336
www.bgh-on.ca
Year Founded: 1889
Number of Beds: 141 beds
Note: Hospital Specialties: Emergency services; Diagnostic services; Laboratory services; Acute care; Child development program; Rehabilitation services, including physiotherapy, occupational therapy, & speech therapy; Respiratory therapy; Stroke prevention clinic; Ontario breast screening clinic; Pain clinic; Complex continuing care; Palliative care
Hugh Bates, Chair
chair.of.the.board@bgh-on.ca
Ray Marshall, President; Chief Executive Officer
marra@bgh-on.ca
Dr. Robert Beveridge, Chief, Medical Staff
bevro@bgh-on.ca
Heather Crawford, Chief Nursing Executive; Vice-President, Clinical Services
Maggie Wheeler, Officer, Communications
613-345-5649, ext. 1

Burk's Falls: Burk's Falls & District Health Centre
Affiliated with: Muskoka Algonquin Healthcare
Former Name: Almaguin Health Centre
PO Box 520, 150 Huston St., Burk's Falls, ON P0A 1C0
Tel: 705-382-2900 *Fax:* 705-382-2257
Toll-Free: 1-800-661-2900
info@mahc.ca
www.mahc.ca
Number of Beds: 7 sub-acute care beds
Note: Specialties: Physiotherapy; Nutritional counselling; Palliative care
Barry Monaghan, Chief Executive Officer, Muskoka Algonquin Healthcare
705-789-0022, ext. 2, barry.monaghan@mahc.ca

Burlington: Joseph Brant Memorial Hospital
1230 North Shore Blvd., Burlington, ON L7R 4C4
Tel: 905-632-3730 *Fax:* 905-336-6480
corporatecommunications@jbmh.com
www.jbmh.com
Number of Beds: 285 beds
Don Scott, President/CEO

Cambridge: Cambridge Memorial Hospital
Former Name: South Waterloo Memorial Hospital
700 Coronation Blvd., Cambridge, ON N1R 3G2
Tel: 519-621-2330 *Fax:* 519-740-4938
TTY: 519-621-9180
information@cmh.org; patientrelations@cmh.org (Patient relations)
www.cmh.org
Year Founded: 1953
Note: Hospital Specialties: Emergency services; Surgical services; Women's & Children's Services; Cardio Respiratory Unit; Oncology; Rehabilitation; Palliative care; Number of Employees: 1,200 (283 medical staff)
Patrick Gaskin, Chief Executive Officer
519-621-2330, ext. 2
Dr. Michael Lawrie, Chief, Staff
519-621-2330, ext. 2
Katrina Power, Chief Finance Officer
519-621-2330, ext. 2
Susan Gregoroff, Chief Nursing Executive; Vice-President, Clinical Programs
519-621-2330, ext. 2
Ann Bartlett, Director, Patient Services
519-621-2330, ext. 3
Karen Anderson Keith, Program Manager, Mental Health
519-621-2330, ext. 3
Charles Bauman, Program Manager, Palliative Care, Rehabilitation, & Oncology
519-621-2330, ext. 5, Fax: 519-740-4950
Alan Clay, Program Manager, Public Affairs & Communications
519-621-2330, ext. 2
Susan Harris-Howe, Program Manager, Emergency
519-621-2330, ext. 2
Scott Hutchings, Program Manager, ICU & Medicine
519-621-2330, ext. 5
Ruth McKinley, Program Manager, Diagnostic Imaging
519-621-2330, ext. 2
Deb Snider, Program Manager, Women's & Children's Health

Campbellford: Campbellford Memorial Hospital (CMH)
146 Oliver Rd., Campbellford, ON K0L 1L0
Tel: 705-653-1140 *Fax:* 705-653-4371
CEO-EA@cmh.ca
www.cmh.ca
Number of Beds: 34 beds
Note: Hospital Specialties: Emergency services; Radiology (705-653-1140, ext. 2125); Laboratory services; Ambulatory care (705-653-1140, ext. 2100); Acute care; Occupational therapy (705-653-1140, ext. 2111); Ontario Breast Screening Program (705-653-3104); Nutrition clinic (705-653-1140, ext. 2132)
Derek Nice, Chair
Brad Hilker, President, CEO, CFO
bhilker@cmh.ca
Jan Raine, Chief Nursing Officer
jraine@cmh.ca

Carleton Place: Carleton Place & District Memorial Hospital
211 Lake Ave. East, Carleton Place, ON K7C 1J4
Tel: 613-257-2200 *Fax:* 613-257-3026
info@carletonplacehosp.com
www.carletonplacehospital.ca
Note: Hospital Specialties: Diagnostic imaging (613-253-3804); Laboratory services (613-257-2200, ext. 152); Physiotherapy (613-253-3822); Speech & language (613-253-3823)
Dr. Dewar Burnett, Chair
Dr. Martin White, Chief, Staff
Dr. Roger Drake, President, Medical Staff
Toni Surko, Secretary to the Board
613-253-3825, tsurko@carletonplacehosp.com

Chatham: Chatham-Kent Health Alliance (CKHA)
PO Box 2030, 80 Grand Ave. West, Chatham, ON N7M 5L9
Tel: 519-352-6400
howarewedoing@ckha.on.ca
www.ckha.on.ca
Year Founded: 1998
Number of Beds: 300 beds
Note: Hospital Specialties: Emergency services; District Stroke Centre; Sexual Assault Treatment Centre; Diagnostic imaging; Ontario Breast Screening Program; Surgery; Orthopedics; Women & children's health care services; Asthma Care Centre; Rehabilitation services, including physiotherapy & occupational therapy; Mental health services, including an Early Psychosis Intervention Program for youth; Dialysis; Post coronary classes; Diabetes education; Nutritional counselling; Complex continuing care; Number of Employees: 1,300
Colin Patey, President; Chief Executive Officer, cpatey@ckha.on.ca
Anthony DiCaita, Chief Financial Officer; Vice-President
adicaita@ckha.on.ca
Shona Elliott, Chief Human Resource Officer; Vice-President
selliott@ckha.on.ca
Crystal Houze, Chief Nursing Executive
chouze@ckha.on.ca
Dr. Gary Tithecott, Chief of Staff
chiefofstaff@ckha.on.ca
Kim Bossy, Director, Communications & Public Affairs
kbossy@ckha.on.ca

Chesley: South Bruce Grey Health Centre - Chesley Site
Affiliated with: Chesley & District Memorial Hospital
39 - 2nd St. SE, Chesley, ON N0G 1L0
Tel: 519-363-2340 *Fax:* 519-363-9871
www.sbghc.on.ca
Year Founded: 1944
Number of Beds: 15 beds
Note: A rural health centre with services including emergency, internal medicine, nutrition services, diagnostic imaging (ultrasound, ECG, radiography), lab, physiotherapy, spirometry, healthy heart program, prenatal and postnatal care
Paul L. Davies, President/CEO, SBGHC
pdavies@sbghc.on.ca
Rhonda Ridgeway, Site Manager/Director, Patient Care
rridgeway@sbghc.on.ca

Clinton: Clinton Public Hospital
Affiliated with: Huron Perth Healthcare Alliance
98 Shipley St., Clinton, ON N0M 1L0
Tel: 519-482-3440 *Fax:* 519-482-5960
administration@hpha.ca; humanresources@hpha.ca
www.hpha.ca
Number of Beds: 17 acute care beds
Note: Hospital Specialties: Emergency services; Ambulatory care; Acute care; Physiotherapy; Diabetes education
Dr. Maarten Bokhout, Chief, Clinton Public Hospital Site
Bonnie Royal, Administrator, Clinton Public Hospital Site
bonnie.royal@hpha.ca
Greg Stewart, Chair, Local Advisory Committee

Cobourg: Northumberland Hills Hospital
Former Name: Northumberland Health Care Corp.
1000 DePalma Dr., Cobourg, ON K9A 5W6
Tel: 905-372-6811 *Fax:* 905-372-4243
info@nhh.ca
www.nhh.ca
Number of Beds: 80 acute care, 39 complex care, 18 rehabilitation beds
Note: community hospital
Joan Ross, CEO

Cochrane: The Lady Minto Hospital
PO Box 4000, 241 - 8 St., Cochrane, ON P0L 1C0
Tel: 705-272-7200 *Fax:* 705-272-5486
micsgroup.com/Site_Published/Micsgroup/minto_about.aspx
Year Founded: 1915
Number of Beds: 66 beds (20 acute, 8 complex continuing care, 2 OBS, 2 paediatrics, 1 special care and 33 long-term care beds)
Note: An acute general facility with services including emergency, complex continuing care, out-patient, ambulatory care, obstetrics, paediatrics, surgery, and long-term care services. The Villa Minto chronic care wing houses a long-term care unit.
Dan O'Mara, CEO, MICs Group of Health Services
dan.omara@micsgroup.com
Dr. Rita Affleck, Chief of Staff
Dr. Lawrence McPherrin, President, Medical Staff

Cornwall: Cornwall Community Hospital - McConnell Avenue Site
840 McConnell Ave., Cornwall, ON K6H 5S5
Tel: 613-938-4240 *Fax:* 613-930-4502
communications@cornwallhospital.ca
www.cornwallhospital.ca
Note: Hospital Specialties: Emergency services; Diagnostic imaging; Surgery; Cardio-respiratory therapy; Critical care; Maternal Child Program; Rehabilitation services, including occupational therapy, physiotherapy, social work, & speech-language pathology; Neurology; Orthopaedics; Ambulatory care; Geriatric services; Palliative care
Fernand Hamelin, Chair
Jeanette Despatie, Chief Executive Officer
Dr. Ashley Cook, Chief of Staff
Julie Lampron, Director, Diagnostic Imaging Department
julie.lampron@cornwallhospital.ca

Cornwall: Cornwall Community Hospital - Second Street Site
510 Second St. East, Cornwall, ON K6H 1Z6
Tel: 613-932-3300
www.cornwallhospital.ca
Note: Hospital Specialties: Assault & Sexual Abuse Program (Phone: 613-932-3300, ext. 4202; Toll-Free Phone: 1-866-263-1560; TTY: 613-936-4643; E-mail: asap@cornwallhospital.ca); Psychiatric care (613-932-3300, ext. 4204); Outpatient Mental Health Program (613-932-3300, ext. 4278); Withdrawal management services (613-938-8506)
Fernand Hamelin, Chair
Jeanette Despatie, Chief Executive Officer

Deep River: Deep River & District Hospital (DRDH)
117 Banting Dr., Deep River, ON K0J 1P0
Tel: 613-584-3333 *Fax:* 613-584-4920
Toll-Free: 1-866-571-8168
www.drdh.org
Year Founded: 1974
Note: Hospital Specialties: Emergency department (613-584-1266 ext. 166); Laboratory services (613-584-1266, ext 120); Diagnostic imaging (613-584-1266, ext 160); Cardiac care services; Physiotherapy; Nutritional counselling; Long term care
Paul Fehrenbach, Chair
Larry Schruder, Chief Executive Officer
Stacey Mortson, Chief Financial Officer
Dr. Elizabeth Noulty, Chief of Staff
Lianne Wheeler, Chief Nursing Officer

Allison Felix, Director, Rehabilitation Services
Terry Corbett, Manager, Laboratory / DI
Garry Hartlin, Manager, IT
Cara McGuire, Manager, Medical Records, Reception, & Admitting
Sean Patterson, Manager, Support Services
Ralph Roloff, Certified Orthotist
613-582-7219
Ericia Van Drunen, Contact, Clinical Nutrition
613-584-1266, ext. 1

Dunnville: Haldimand War Memorial Hospital
206 John St., Dunnville, ON N1A 2P7
Tel: 905-774-7431 *Fax:* 905-774-6776
kanger@hwmh.ca
www.hwmh.ca

Number of Beds: 34 beds
David Montgomery, CEO

Durham: South Bruce Grey Health Centre - Durham Site
Affiliated with: Durham Memorial Hospital
PO Box 638, 320 College St., Durham, ON N0G 1R0
Tel: 519-369-2340 *Fax:* 519-369-6180
www.sbghc.on.ca

Year Founded: 1946
Number of Beds: 19 beds
Note: A rural health centre with services incuding emergency, audiology, cardiorespiratory care, bone densitometry, dermatology, ear/nose/throat, hearing aid testing, urology, nutrition services, diagnostic imaging (ultrasound, ECG, radiography), lab, physiotherapy, healthy heart program, prenatal and postnatal care
Paul L. Davies, President/CEO, SBGHC
pdavies@sbghc.on.ca
Maureen Rydall, Site Manager/Director, Patient Care
mrydall@sbghc.on.ca

Elliot Lake: St. Joseph's General Hospital
70 Spine Rd., Elliot Lake, ON P5A 1X2
Tel: 705-848-7181 *Fax:* 705-848-4414
www.sjgh.ca

Year Founded: 1958
Number of Beds: 57 beds, plus 12 day-surgery beds
Note: Services include emergency, bone density, cardiology, chemotherapy, chiropody, clinical nutrition, diabetes education, ears, nose, & throat, electrocardiogram, endoscopy, gastroenterology, gerontology, intensive care, mental health, nephrology, obstetrics, ophthamology, orthopedics, paediatrics, palliative care, pastoral care, physiotherapy, radiology, renal dialysis (as a satellite of Sudbury Regional Hospital), speech therapy, social work, surgery, urology, ultrasound. The hospital corporation also manages St. Joseph's Manor long term care facility, & the Oaks Substance Abuse Treatment Centre.
Michael Hukezalie, CEO
mhukezalie@sjgh.ca

Englehart: Englehart & District Hospital Inc.
PO Box 69, 61 Fifth St., Englehart, ON P0J 1H0
Tel: 705-544-2301 *Fax:* 705-544-5222
dmitchell@edhospital.on.ca
www.edhospital.on.ca

Note: Hospital Specialties: Emergency services; Diagnostic imaging; Laboratory services; Physiotherapy; Occupational therapy; Respiratory therapy; Chronic care (14 chronic care beds)
Mary Lynn Kirkey, Chair
Lois Kozak, Chief Executive Officer
Dr. A. Vera, Chief of Staff

Espanola: Espanola General Hospital (EGH)/Hôpital Général d' Espanola
825 McKinnon Dr., Espanola, ON P5E 1R4
Tel: 705-869-1420 *Fax:* 705-869-2608
info@esphosp.on.ca
www.esphosp.on.ca

Year Founded: 1949
Note: Hospital Specialties: Primary care; Therapeutic care; Preventive services; Diabetes education; Social work services; Assisted living; Long term care
Gisele Guenard, Chief Executive Officer
Catherine Gray, Director, Care

Exeter: South Huron Hospital Association
24 Huron St. West, Exeter, ON N0M 1S2
Tel: 519-235-2700 *Fax:* 519-235-3405
shha.administration@shha.on.ca
www.shha.on.ca

Year Founded: 1953
Number of Beds: 19 beds (11 acute, 4 rehab, 4 chronic care)
Note: Serving the municipalities of South Huron and Bluewater, services include emergency care, acute, in-patient services, diagnostic imaging (x-ray, ultrasound, bone mineral density, ECG, Holter monitors, pulmonary testing), physiotherapy, speech/language therapy, complex continuing care, and a range of out-patient clinics.
Debra Hunt, CEO/Chief Nursing Executive

Fergus: Groves Memorial Community Hospital
235 Union St. East, Fergus, ON N1M 1W3
Tel: 519-843-2010 *Fax:* 519-843-5331
info@gmch.fergus.net
www.gmch.ca

Number of Beds: 42 beds
Jerome Quenneville, President; CEO

Fort Albany: James Bay General Hospital
Fort Albany Wing
General Delivery, Fort Albany, ON P0L 1H0
Tel: 705-278-3330 *Fax:* 705-278-1121
www.jbgh.org

Number of Beds: 17 beds
Andrew Poonae, Wing Dir.
Alexandra Sutherland, Administrator

Fort Erie: Douglas Memorial Hospital Site (NHS)
Niagara Health System / Système de santé de Niagara
230 Bertie St., Fort Erie, ON L2A 1Z2
Tel: 905-378-4647 *Fax:* 905-871-7765
www.niagarahealth.on.ca

Year Founded: 1931
Number of Beds: 46 beds
Note: Hospital Specialties: Urgent Care Centre; Acute care; Outpatient programs, including a methadone clinic & a satellite Ontario Breast Screening Program; Complex continuing care
Debbie Sevenpifer, President; Chief Executive Officer, Niagara Health System
Frank Demizio, Vice-President, Patient Services, Douglas Memorial Hospital
Christine Clark, Chief Communications Officer, Niagara Health System
Bala Kathiresan, Chief Operating Officer, Niagara Health System

Angela Zangari, Chief Financial Officer, Niagara Health System

Fort Frances: Riverside Health Care Facilities Inc.
110 Victoria Ave., Fort Frances, ON P9A 2B7
Tel: 807-274-3266 *Fax:* 807-274-2898
www.riversidehealthcare.ca

Year Founded: 1989
Number of Beds: 55 beds (Fort Frances), 15 beds (Emo), 24 beds (Rainy River)
Note: Operates the La Verendrye General Hospital (Fort Frances- acute care, continuing care, obstetrics & surgery); the Emo Health Centre (Emo- acute care, urgent care, long tern care, diagnostic imaging, physiotherapy, dental clinic); & Rainy River Health Centre (Rainy River- acute care, long term care, diagnostic imaging, dental clinic)
Wayne Woods, President/CEO

Georgetown: Halton Healthcare Services Corp. - Georgetown Hospital
Former Name: Georgetown & District Memorial Hospital
1 Princess Anne Dr., Georgetown, ON L7G 2B8
Tel: 905-873-0111 *Fax:* 905-873-9653
www.haltonhealthcare.com

Year Founded: 1961
Number of Beds: 33 acute care beds, 20 continuing care beds
Note: Number of staff: 346, 20 family physicians, 14 specialists
Cindy McDonell, COO

Geraldton: Geraldton District Hospital
500 Hogarth Ave., Geraldton, ON P0T 1M0
Tel: 807-854-1862 *Fax:* 807-854-1568
www.tbrhsc.net

Year Founded: 1963
Number of Beds: 23 acute care beds; 26 long term care beds
Note: Hospital Specialties: Emergency services; Diagnostic imaging; Laboratory services; Acute care; Physiotherapy; Occupational therapy; Social work; Diabetes education; Long term care
Kurt Pristanski, Chief Executive Officer
kpristanski@geraldtondh.com
Dr. R. Laine, Chief of Staff

Goderich: Alexandra Marine & General Hospital (AMGH)
120 Napier St., Goderich, ON N7A 1W5
Tel: 519-524-8689 *Fax:* 519-524-5579
stephanie.page@amgh.on.ca
www.amgh.on.ca

Number of Beds: 54 acute, long-term, & psychiatric care beds
Note: Hospital Specialties: Emergency services; Ambulatory care; Psychiatry; Diagnostic imaging; Physiotherapy; Occupational therapy; Speech & language pathology; Diabetes education; Social work; Number of employees: 250
William R. Thibert, President; Chief Executive Officer
william.thibert@amgh.on.ca
Dr. Patrick Conlon, Chief of Staff
Dr. Mike Dawson, President, Medical Staff

Grimsby: West Lincoln Memorial Hospital
169 Main St. East, Grimsby, ON L3M 1P3
Tel: 905-945-2253 *Fax:* 905-945-0504
comments@wlmh.on.ca
www.wlmh.on.ca

Number of Beds: 60 beds
Note: Number of staff: 385, 15 medical staff
David Bird, CEO

Guelph: Guelph General Hospital
115 Delhi St., Guelph, ON N1E 4J4
Tel: 519-822-5350 *Fax:* 519-822-2170
info@gghorg.ca
www.gghorg.ca

Number of Beds: 165 beds; 11 critical care, 55 surgery, 22 obstetrics
Note: Total employees: 1200, 224 physicians
Richard Ernst, President; CEO

Guelph: St. Joseph's Health Centre
100 Westmount Road, Guelph, ON N1H 5H8
Tel: 519-824-6000 *Fax:* 519-763-0264
www.sjhh.guelph.on.ca

Year Founded: 1861
Number of Beds: 235 beds (144 long-term care beds and 91 specialty beds)
Note: Residential long-term & respite care, complex continuing care, rehabilitation, community outreach, nutrition & food services, outpatient clinics, palliative care, recreation therapy, speech/language pathology services, social worker
Marianne Walker, President/CEO
president@sjhcg.ca

Hagersville: West Haldimand General Hospital
75 Parkview Rd., Hagersville, ON N0A 1H0
Tel: 905-768-3311 *Fax:* 905-768-1820
webmaster@whgh.ca
www.whgh.ca

Year Founded: 1964
Number of Beds: 33 beds
Note: Acute & complex continuing care, surgery, diagnostic imaging, senior support services
Paul Mailloux, CEO

Haliburton: Haliburton Site of Haliburton Highlands Health Service (HHHS)
Haliburton Highlands Health Service
PO Box 115, 7199 Gellert Rd., Haliburton, ON K0M 1S0
Tel: 705-457-1392 *Fax:* 705-457-2398
info@hhhs.on.ca; physio@hhhs.on.ca (Physiotherapy)
www.hhhs.on.ca

Year Founded: 2000
Number of Beds: 13 acute care beds + 1 maternity bed
Note: Specialties: Acute care; Physiotherapy
Keith Sansford, Pres./CEO

Hamilton: Hamilton Health Sciences
Chedoke Hospital
PO Box 2000 Stn. A, Sanitorium Road, MPO, Hamilton, ON L8N 3Z5
Tel: 905-521-2100 *Fax:* 905-521-7959
www.hamiltonhealthsciences.ca

Number of Beds: 129 beds
Murray T. Martin, President/CEO

Hamilton: Hamilton Health Sciences Corp.
Hamilton General Hospital
Former Name: Hamilton Health Sciences Corp, Hamilton General Division
237 Barton St. East, Hamilton, ON L8L 2X2
Tel: 905-521-2100 *Fax:* 905-527-1941

Year Founded: 1848
Number of Beds: 304 beds
Note: Hospital Specialty: Cardiac & Vascular; Neurosciences & Trauma; Population Health Institute.

Hamilton: Hamilton Health Sciences Corp.
Juravinski Hospital
711 Concession St., Hamilton, ON L8V 1C3
Tel: 905-527-4322 *Fax:* 905-575-2662

Year Founded: 1917
Number of Beds: 228
Note: Hospital Specialty: Oncology; Orthopedics; Rehabilitation; Palliative Care; Nuclear medecine; Infectious diseases; Diagnostic imaging; General surgery

***Hamilton:* St. Joseph's Healthcare**
50 Charlton Ave. East, Hamilton, ON L8N 4A6
Tel: 905-522-1155 *Fax:* 905-521-6066
www.stjosham.on.ca
Number of Beds: 600 acute care
Dr. Kevin Smith, President/CEO

***Hamilton:* St. Peter's Hospital**
88 Maplewood Ave., Hamilton, ON L8M 1W9
Tel: 905-777-3837 *Fax:* 905-549-7003
info@stpetes.ca
www.hhsc.ca/body.cfm?id=1575
Year Founded: 1890
Number of Beds: 250 beds
Note: A complex, continuing care hospital, with speciality programs in behavioural health, palliative care, rehabilitation, and community services. The facility operates under the umbrella of Hamilton Health Sciences.
Murray T. Martin, President/CEO, HHS
Murray Glendining, Executive Vice-President, Corporate Affairs, HHS
Donna Cripps, President, St. Peter's Hospital
Dr. Richard Seeley, Chief of Staff, St. Peter's Hospital

***Hanover:* Hanover & District Hospital**
90 - 7 Ave., Hanover, ON N4N 1N1
Tel: 519-364-2340 *Fax:* 519-364-6602
www.hanoverhospital.on.ca
Number of Beds: 80 beds; 36 acute care, 2 obstetrics, 2 palliative
Katrina Wilson, President; CEO

***Hawkesbury:* Hôpital Général de Hawkesbury & District General Hospital**
1111 Ghislain St., Hawkesbury, ON K6A 3J7
Tel: 613-632-1111 *Fax:* 613-636-6183
www.hawkesburyhospital.com
Year Founded: 1984
Number of Beds: 69 beds
Luc Séguin, Vice-President, Administration

***Hearst:* Hôpital Nôtre-Dame Hospital**
1405 Edward St., Bag 8000, Hearst, ON P0L 1N0
Tél: 705-362-4291 *Téléc:* 705-372-2923
www.ndh.on.ca
Nombre de lits: 44 lits
France Dallaire, CEO

***Hornepayne:* Hornepayne Community Hospital**
PO Box 190, 278 Front St., Hornepayne, ON P0M 1Z0
Tel: 807-868-2442 *Fax:* 807-868-2697
www.hornepayne.com/Hospital/hospital.htm
Number of Beds: 20 beds; 12 Long-term care, 8 Acute care
Lisa Verrino, CEO
Lisa.Verrino@hornepaynehospital.ca

***Huntsville:* Huntsville District Memorial Hospital Affiliated with: Muskoka Algonquin Healthcare**
100 Frank Miller Dr., Huntsville, ON P1H 1H7
Tel: 705-789-2311 *Fax:* 705-789-0557
info@mahc.ca
www.mahc.ca
Number of Beds: 76 beds, 6 special care beds
Barry Monaghan, CEO

***Ingersoll:* Alexandra Hospital**
29 Noxon St., Ingersoll, ON N5C 3V6
Tel: 519-485-1700 *Fax:* 519-485-9606
feedback@ah.tvh.ca; Robin.Schultz@ah.tvh.ca
www.alexandrahospital.on.ca
Year Founded: 1909
Number of Beds: 35 acute care beds
Note: Hospital Specialties: Emergency services; Diagnostic & laboratory services; Outpatient rehabilitation; Number of Employees: 168
Tom McHugh, Chief Executive Officer
519-485-1732, tom.mchugh@ah.tvh.ca
Jill Matsuo, President, Medical Staff
Martha Bancroft, Contact, Human Resources
519-485-9603, Martha.Bancroft@ah.tvh.ca

***Iroquois Falls:* Anson General Hospital**
58 Anson Dr., Iroquois Falls, ON P0K 1E0
Tel: 705-258-3911 *Fax:* 705-258-3221
Number of Beds: 21 active care beds; 15 chronic care beds; 4 palliative or long-term rehabilitation care beds
Note: Hospital Specialties: Emergency services; Chronic care; Diabetes education; Palliative care; Snoezelen room

***Kapuskasing:* Sensenbrenner Hospital**
101 Progress Cres., Kapuskasing, ON P5N 3H5
Tel: 705-337-6111 *Fax:* 705-337-4021
info@sensenbrennerhospital.on.ca
www.senhosp.ca
Number of Beds: 30 active care
Allan Yarush, CEO

***Kemptville:* Kemptville District Hospital**
PO Box 2007, 2675 Concession Rd., Kemptville, ON K0G 1J0
Tel: 613-258-6133
www.kdh.on.ca
Number of Beds: 23 acute care beds
Colin Goodfellow, Chief Executive Officer
613-258-6133 ext.132, Fax: 613-258-7853,

***Kenora:* Lake of the Woods District Hospital**
21 Sylvan St. West, Kenora, ON P9N 3W7
Tel: 807-468-9861 *Fax:* 807-468-3939
admin@lwdh.on.ca
www.lwdh.on.ca
Number of Beds: 104 beds
Mark Balcaen, CEO

***Kincardine:* South Bruce Grey Health Centre - Kincardine Site**
Kincardine & District General Hospital
43 Queen St., Kincardine, ON N2Z 1G6
Tel: 519-396-3331 *Fax:* 519-396-3699
www.sbghc.on.ca
Year Founded: 1908
Number of Beds: 36 beds
Note: A rural health centre with services including emergency, cardiorespiratory care, dental services, bone densitometry, gynecology, internal medicine, pediatrics, respirology, rheumatology, surgery, urology, nutrition services, diagnostic imaging (ultrasound, ECG, radiography), lab, physiotherapy, pharmacy, healthy heart program, prenatal and postnatal care
Paul L. Davies, President/CEO, SBGHC
pdavies@sbgh.on.ca
Kate Kincaid, Site Manager/Director, Patient Care
kkincaid@sbghc.on.ca

***Kingston:* Kingston General Hospital**
76 Stuart St., Kingston, ON K7L 2V7
Tel: 613-548-3232 *Fax:* 613-548-6042
web@kgh.kari.net
www.kgh.kari.net
Year Founded: 1838
Number of Beds: 456 beds
Note: Teaching hospital; Research hospital; Total employees: 3,737; Medical Staff: 546
Janet Davidson, President/CEO
Dr. Paul Belliveau, President, Medical Staff

***Kingston:* The Religious Hospitaliers of Saint-Joseph of the Hotel Dieu of Kingston**
166 Brock St., Kingston, ON K7L 5G2
Tel: 613-544-3310 *Fax:* 613-544-9897
holdenc@hdh.kari.net
www.hoteldieu.com
Year Founded: 1845
Note: An ambulatory care teaching facility with services including emergency, audiology, breast assessment, detoxification centre, diabetes education, ophthalmology, pastoral care, pediatrics, psychiatry, sexual assault/domestic violence program, day surgery, urgent care and mental health programs. It is affiliated with Queen's University and is partnered with Kingston's university hospitals.
Dr. David Pichora, CEO
Steve Miller, CFO
Sandi Cox, Chief, Patient Care
Elizabeth Bardon, Chief, Public Relations & Community Engagement

***Kirkland Lake:* Kirkland & District Hospital**
145 Government Rd. East, Kirkland Lake, ON P2N 3P4
Tel: 705-567-5251 *Fax:* 705-568-2115
www.kdhospital.com
Number of Beds: 62 beds
Hal Fjeldsted, CEO
hfjelsted@kdhospital.com
Dr. Mark Spiller, Chief of Staff
aallison@kdhospital.com
Louis Gravel, Manager, Information Systems
lgravel@kdhospital.com

***Kitchener:* Grand River Hospital Corp. Kitchener-Waterloo Health Centre**
PO Box 9056, 835 King St. West, Kitchener, ON N2G 1G3
Tel: 519-749-4300 *Fax:* 519-749-4208
info@grhosp.on.ca
www.grandriverhospital.on.ca
Number of Beds: 495 beds (including Freeport Health Centre site)
Note: Hospital Specialty: acute, complex continuing & cancer care
Malcolm Maxwell, President/CEO
malcolm.maxwell@grhosp.on.ca

***Kitchener:* Grand River Hospital Corp. Freeport Health Centre**
PO Box 9056, 3570 King St. East, Kitchener, ON N2A 2W1
Tel: 519-749-4300 *Fax:* 519-894-8349
www.grandriverhospital.on.ca
Number of Beds: 139 continuing care, 32 short-term rehab beds
Note: Complex continuing care, chronic care, rehabilitation & restoration
Malcolm Maxwell, President/CEO
malcolm.maxwell@grhosp.on.ca

***Kitchener:* St. Mary's General Hospital**
911 Queen's Blvd., Kitchener, ON N2M 1B2
Tel: 519-744-3311 *Fax:* 519-749-6426
info@smgh.ca
www.smgh.ca
Number of Beds: 191 acute care beds
Note: Catholic hospital, home to the Regional Cardiac Care Centre
Bruce M. Antonello, President/CEO

***Leamington:* Leamington District Memorial Hospital**
194 Talbot St. West, Leamington, ON N8H 1N9
Tel: 519-322-2501 *Fax:* 519-322-1677
www.leamingtonhospital.com
Number of Beds: 81 beds
Note: complex continuing care & rehab
J. Stenger, CEO

***Lindsay:* Ross Memorial Hospital**
10 Angeline St. North, Lindsay, ON K9V 4M8
Tel: 705-324-6111 *Fax:* 705-328-2817
Toll-Free: 800-510-7365
www.rmh.org
Year Founded: 1902
Number of Beds: 175 beds: 36 continuing care; 16 rehabilitation; 10 palliative; 8 intensive care; 40 adult beds; 36 adult surgical beds
Note: Emergency, mental health services, complex continuing care, rehabilitation, palliative care, surgery, women's health, pediatrics, physiotherapy, diagnostic imaging, cardiac & diabetes care, outpatient pain clinic
Brian Payne, President/CEO
Varouj Eskedjian, Vice-President, Diagnostics & Support

***Lions Head:* Lion's Head Hospital Grey Bruce Health Services**
22 Moore St., Lions Head, ON N0H 1W0
Tel: 519-793-3424
www.gbhs.on.ca/lionshead.php
Number of Beds: 6 inpatient beds
Note: Specialties: Acute care; Preschool speech therapy; Diabetes education; Physiotherapy Palliative care. Number of employees: 25
Sue McCutcheon, Site Director

***Listowel:* Listowel Memorial Hospital Affiliated with: Listowel & Wingham Hospitals Alliance**
255 Elizabeth St. East, Listowel, ON N4W 2P5
Tel: 519-291-3120 *Fax:* 519-291-5440
www.lwha.ca
Year Founded: 1919
Number of Beds: 51 beds
Note: Acute & complex continuing care. Number of staff: 10 physicians
Liz Phelan, CEO (Interim)
liz.phelan@lwha.ca

***Little Current:* Manitoulin Health Centre**
PO Box 640, 11-13 Meredith St. West, Little Current, ON P0P 1K0
Tel: 705-368-2300 *Fax:* 705-368-3566
www.mhc.on.ca
Number of Beds: 16 beds
James D. Van Camp, CEO

London: Children's Hospital Site
London Health Sciences Centre
Former Name: Children's Hospital of Western Ontario
800 Commissioners Rd. East, London, ON N6A 5W9
Tel: 519-685-8484
www.lhsc.on.ca
Info Line: 519-685-8380

Note: Hospital Specialties: Specialized paediatric inpatient & outpatient services; Paediatric critical care unit; Child & adolescent mental health care program; Acute paediatric rehabilitation services; Gastroenterology, transplant, hepatology, & nutrition; Medical genetics; Respiratory therapy; Asthma clinic; Cystic fibrosis; Hematology & oncology

London: Parkwood Hospital
Affiliated with: St. Joseph's Health Care, London
801 Commissioners Rd. East, London, ON N6C 5J1
Tel: 519-685-4000 *Fax:* 519-685-4052
Communications.Department@sjhc.london.on.ca
www.sjhc.london.on.ca

Number of Beds: 530 beds

London: St. Joseph's Health Care, London
268 Grosvenor St., London, ON N6A 4V2
Tel: 519-646-6000 *Fax:* 519-646-6006
www.sjhc.london.on.ca

Number of Beds: 1,660 beds
Note: Includes St. Joseph's Hospital; Mount Hope Centre for Long Term Care; Parkwood Hospital (chronic, longterm & veterans facility); Lawson Health Research Institute; Regional Mental Health Care, London & Regional Mental Health Care, St Thomas
Cliff Nordal, President/CEO

London: St. Joseph's Hospital
Affiliated with: St. Joseph's Health Care, London
PO Box 5777, 268 Grosvenor St., London, ON N6A 4V2
Tel: 519-646-6000

Number of Beds: 177 beds

London: South Street Hospital Site
London Health Sciences Centre
375 South St., London, ON N6A 4G5
Tel: 519-685-8500
www.lhsc.on.ca
Info Line: 519-685-8380

Note: Hospital Specialties: Adult mental health care program
Cliff Nordal, President; CEO

London: University Hospital Site
London Health Sciences Centre
339 Windermere Rd., London, ON N6A 5A5
Tel: 519-685-8500
motslhsc@lhsc.on.ca (general transplant inquiries)
www.lhsc.on.ca
Info Line: 519-685-8380

Note: Hospital Specialties: Emergency services; Medical-surgical intensive care; Cardiac surgery; Regional Stroke Centre for the Southwestern Ontario Region; London Health Sciences Centre cochlear implant program; Orthopaedics program; London Multiple Sclerosis Clinic; Multi-organ transplant program
Tony Dagnone, President/CEO

London: Victoria Hospital Site
London Health Sciences Centre
PO Box 5010, 800 Commissioners Rd. East, London, ON N6A 5W9
Tel: 519-685-8500
leanne.siebenmorgen@lhsc.on.ca (Trauma program)
www.lhsc.on.ca
Info Line: 519-685-8380

Year Founded: 1995
Note: Hospital Specialties: Emergency services; Critical Care Trauma Center; Bleeding disorders program; Maternal newborn care; Prostate cancer centre; Trauma progam
Dr. Tony Dagnone, President/CEO

Manitouwadge: Manitouwadge General Hospital
1 Health Care Lane, Manitouwadge, ON P0T 2C0
Tel: 807-826-3251 *Fax:* 807-826-4216
infoserv@mh.on.ca
www.mh.on.ca

Number of Beds: 18 beds
Judith C. Harris, CEO

Marathon: Wilson Memorial General Hospital
26 Peninsula Rd., PO Bag W, Marathon, ON P0T 2E0
Tel: 807-229-1740 *Fax:* 807-229-1721
www.wmgh.net

Year Founded: 1971
Number of Beds: 25 beds
Note: Number of staff: 7 physicians
Paul Paradis, CEO

Markdale: Markdale Hospital
Grey Bruce Health Services
Also Known As: Centre Grey Hospital
PO Box 406, 55 Isla St., Markdale, ON N0C 1H0
Tel: 519-986-3040
www.gbhs.on.ca/markdale.php

Number of Beds: 18 inpatient beds
Note: Specialties: Day surgery service; Acute care; Physiotherapy services; Diabetes education; Palliative care
Pat Campbell, President; CEO

Markham: Markham-Stouffville Hospital (MSH)
PO Box 1800, 381 Church St., Markham, ON L3P 7P3
Tel: 905-472-7000
TTY: 905-472-7585
myhospital@msh.on.ca
www.msh.on.ca
Info Line: 905-472-7100

Year Founded: 1990
Note: Specialties: Emergency medicine; Surgical care; Child, adolescent, & adult mental health services; Genetics counselling; Obstetrical assessment; The Childbirth Centre; Paediatrics; Occupational therapy & Physiotherapy; Geriatrics; Sleep disorders; Speech language pathology; Palliative care. Number of Employees: 275 physicians + 1,700 staff
Janet M. Beed, President/CEO

Matheson: Bingham Memorial Hospital
PO Box 70, 507 - 8th Ave., Matheson, ON P0K 1N0
Tel: 705-273-2424 *Fax:* 705-273-1617

Year Founded: 1955
Number of Beds: 11 acute care beds; 6 chronic care beds
Note: Hospital Specialties: Emergency services; Laboratory services; Radiology services; Acute care; Chemotherapy; Physiotherapy; Respiratory therapy; Dietician services; Diabetes education; Chronic care; Palliative care; Number of Employees: 72 (Bingham Memorial Hospital & adjoined Rosedale Centre)
Daniel O'Mara, Chief Executive Officer
705-273-2424, ext. 2, micsceo@puc.net
Sharon Hill, Coordinator, Human Resources
705-273-2424, ext. 3
Beverley Magee, Coordinator, Diabetes Program
Beverley.magee@micsgroup.com

Mattawa: Mattawa Hospital
PO Box 70, 217 Turcotte Park Rd., Mattawa, ON P0H 1V0
Tel: 705-744-5511 *Fax:* 705-744-6020
admin@mattawahospital.ca
www.mhsmattawa.on.ca

Year Founded: 1878
Number of Beds: 19 beds
Note: Specialties: Primary care; Acute care; Ambulatory programs; Diabetic resource centre; Adult & children's mental health services; Paediatric, urology, psychiatry, & women's clinic; Physiotherapy services; Palliative care
Edward Darby, CEO

Meaford: Meaford Hospital
Grey Bruce Health Services
229 Nelson St. West, Meaford, ON N4L 1A3
Tel: 519-538-1311
www.gbhs.on.ca/meaford.php

Number of Beds: 20 inpatient beds
Note: Specialties: Diagnostic support; Laboratory services; Inpatient primary care; Ambulatory care services; Diabetes education; Physiotherapy; Palliative care. Number of Employees: 116
Carol Gouett, Site Director

Midland: Huronia District Hospital
PO Box 760, 1112 St. Andrews Dr., Midland, ON L4R 4P4
Tel: 705-526-1300 *Fax:* 705-526-2007
www.nsha.on.ca

Number of Beds: 72 acute care beds, 8 ICU beds
Carol Lambie, Interim CEO

Milton: Halton Healthcare Services Corp. - Milton District Hospital
30 Derry Rd. East, Milton, ON L9T 2X5
Tel: 905-878-2383 *Fax:* 905-878-7047

Number of Beds: 43 acute care beds, 25 complex continuing care beds
Note: Number of staff: 385, 29 physicians, 30 specialists
Allan Halls, COO

Mindemoya: Manitoulin Health Centre
Mindemoya Medical Clinic
PO Box 156, Mindemoya, ON P0P 1S0
Tel: 705-377-5371 *Fax:* 705-377-5372

Number of Beds: 14 beds
Dan Charette, Pat. Care Coord.

Minden: Minden Site of Haliburton Highlands Health Services (HHHS)
Haliburton Highlands Health Service
PO Box PO Box 30, 6 McPherson St, Minden, ON K0M 2K0
Tel: 705-286-2140 *Fax:* 705-286-6384
info@hhhs.on.ca; physio@hhhs.on.ca (Physiotherapy)
www.hhhs.on.ca

Note: Specialties: Physiotherapy; Diabetes education
Keith Sansford, Executive Director

Mississauga: The Credit Valley Hospital
2200 Eglinton Ave. West, Mississauga, ON L5M 2N1
Tel: 905-813-2200 *Fax:* 905-813-4444
Toll-Free: 1-877-292-4284
cvhpr@cvh.on.ca
www.cvh.on.ca

Year Founded: 1985
Number of Beds: 471 beds
Note: A comprehensive health care facility with services including emergency, Addictions and Concurrent Disorders Centre, ambulatory care, asthma education, cancer care, cardiopulmonary, complex continuing care, critical care, diabetes care centre, diagnostic imaging, eating disorders program, endoscopy, genetics, geriatric assessment, laboratory, maternal child services, mental health, music therapy, occupational therapy, paediatrics, physiotherapy, psychology, renal program, social work, spiritual care, surgery.
Michelle DiEmanuele, President/CEO
905-813-1100, mdiemanuele@cvh.on.ca
Dr. Matt Gysler, Chief, Medical Staff
mgysler@cvh.on.ca
Wendy Johnson, Chief, Communications & Public Affairs
905-813-2617, wjohnson@cvh.on.ca

Mississauga: Trillium Health Centre - Mississauga Site
Former Name: Queensway General Hospital
100 Queensway West, Mississauga, ON L5B 1B8
Tel: 905-848-7100 *Fax:* 905-848-7140
publicrelations@thc.on.ca
www.trilliumhealthcentre.org

Number of Beds: 748 beds (for acute, rehabilitation and chronic care)
Note: Inpatient services include emergency care centre, birthing centre, critical care, intensive care, neurosurgery, stroke & cardiac care, sexual assault & domestic violence services, women's & children's health (Colonel Harland Sanders Family Care Centre)
Janet M. Davidson, President /CEO
May Chang, CFO/Vice-President, Corporate Services
Dr. Gopal Bhatnagar, Chief of Staff
Larry Roberts, Media Relations Consultant
905-848-7580, lroberts@thc.on.ca

Moose Factory: Weeneebayko Area Health Authority/Weeneebayko General Hospital
PO Box 664, 19 Hospital Dr., Moose Factory, ON P0L 1W0
Tel: 705-658-4544 *Fax:* 705-658-4917
www.weeneebaykohealth.ca

Number of Beds: 58 beds
Note: WAHA offers emergency room and operating room services along with In-Patient and Out-Patient services.
Bernie D. Schmidt, CEO

Mount Forest: North Wellington Health Care
Louise Marshall Hospital Site
630 Dublin St., Mount Forest, ON N0G 2L3
Tel: 519-323-2210 *Fax:* 519-323-3741
www.nwhealthcare.ca

Number of Beds: 19 beds
Pierre Noel, CEO

Napanee: Lennox & Addington County General Hospital
PO Box 300, 8 Richmond Park Dr., Napanee, ON K7R 2Z4
Tel: 613-354-3301 *Fax:* 613-354-7157
web.lacgh.napanee.on.ca

Number of Beds: 33 beds; 25 active care; 8 chronic care
Note: Number of employees: 200
Wayne Coveyduck, Executive Director
Dr. Tom Touzel, Chief of Staff

New Liskeard: Temiskaming Hospital
421 Shepherdson Rd., New Liskeard, ON P0J 1P0
Tel: 705-647-8121 *Fax:* 705-647-5800
www.temiskaming-hospital.com

Year Founded: 1980
Number of Beds: 59 beds (40 acute, 11 chronic, 5 obstetric & 3 special care unit beds)
Note: This community facility offers services including emergency, cardiac rehabilitation, diagnostic imaging (CT scans), laboratory, nutrition services, occupational therapy, pastoral care, pharmacy, physiotherapy, respiratory therapy, speech language pathology and Telestroke Program. Visiting specialists conduct services in neurology, nephrology, obstetrics and gynecology, orthotics, rehab/physical medicine, psychiatry, ophthalmology and pediatrics.
Bruce Cunningham, CEO
Lenord Alfred, Director, Support Services
Sylvie Lavictoire, Director, Clinical Services
Dr. Raymond Rahn, President, Medical Staff
Dr. Céline Léger-Nolet, Hospital Stroke Leader
705-647-1088

Newbury: Four Counties Health Services Site (FCHS)
Middlesex Hospital Alliance
1824 Concession Dr., RR#3, Newbury, ON N0L 1Z0
Tel: 519-693-7111
www.mhalliance.on.ca

Note: Specialties: Emergency care; Diagnostic services; Physiotherapy (519-693-7111, ext. 2441); Diabetes Education Centre (519-693-7111, ext. 2489); Adult Day Centre
Michael A. Mazza, Chief Executive Officer, Middlesex Hospital Alliance
Dr. Jon Dreyer, Chief of Staff, Four Counties Health Services Site

Newmarket: Southlake Regional Health Centre
Former Name: York County Hospital
596 Davis Dr., Newmarket, ON L3Y 2P9
Tel: 905-895-4521 *Fax:* 905-830-5972
communications@southlakeregional.org
www.southlakeregional.org

Year Founded: 1922
Number of Beds: 375 beds
Note: Comprehensive health care services including emergency, cancer care, cardiac care centre, arthritis care, birthing unit, diabetes education, diagnostic imaging (bone densitometry, CT scan, MRI, mammography, nuclear medicine, ultrasound, x-ray), eating disorders, mental health programs, neonatal intensive care unit, obstetrics, pediatrics & perinatal care, palliative care, respiratory therapy, thoracic surgery
Daniel P. Carriere, President/CEO
Terry Kuula, CFO/Vice-President, Finance
Paul Clarry, Vice-President, Facilities & Paramedical Services
Dr. Nancy Merrow, Chief of Staff

Niagara Falls: Greater Niagara General Site of Niagara Health System (NHS)
Niagara Health System / Système de santé de Niagara
5546 Portage Rd., Niagara Falls, ON L2E 6X2
Tel: 905-378-4647 *Fax:* 905-358-8435
www.niagarahealth.on.ca

Year Founded: 1907
Number of Beds: 180+ beds
Note: Hospital Specialties: Emergency services; Intensive care; Ambulatory care; Acute care; Maternal / child care services; Women's Health Centre, including the Ontario Breast Screening Program; Mental health services; Geriatric assessment; Regional Stroke Program; Complex continuing care
Debbie Sevenpifer, President; Chief Executive Officer, Niagara Health System
Frank Demizio, Vice-President, Patient Services, Greater Niagara General Site
Su Bolibruck, Director, Clinical Programs (Chronic Kidney Disease, Cardiolo
905-378-4647, ext. 3
Heather Scott, Director, Clinical Programs (Mental Health)
905-378-4647, ext. 5

Niagara on the Lake: Niagara-on-the-Lake Site of Niagara Health System (NHS)
Niagara Health System / Système de santé de Niagara
176 Wellington St., Niagara on the Lake, ON L0S 1J0
Tel: 905-378-4647 *Fax:* 905-468-7690
www.niagarahealth.on.ca

Year Founded: 1921
Number of Beds: 22 beds
Note: Hospital Specialties: Acute care; Walk-in clinic; Complex continuing care
Debbie Sevenpifer, President; Chief Executive Officer, Niagara Health System
Linda Boich, Vice-President, Patient Services, Niagara-on-the-Lake Hospital Site
Dr. Joanna Hope, Chief of Staff, Niagara Health System

Nipigon: Nipigon District Memorial Hospital
PO Box 37, 125 Hogan Rd., Nipigon, ON P0T 2J0
Tel: 807-887-3026 *Fax:* 807-887-2800
lenders@ndmh.ca
www.ndmh.ca

Number of Beds: 37 beds
Lori Marshall, Site Administrator

North Bay: North Bay General Hospital
PO Box 2500, 750 Scollard St., North Bay, ON P1B 5A4
Tel: 705-474-8600 *Fax:* 705-495-7956
mhurst@nbgh.on.ca
www.nbgh.on.ca

Number of Beds: 204 beds
Mark Hurst, Pres./CEO

North Bay: North Bay General Hospital McLaren Site
PO Box 2500, 720 McLaren St., North Bay, ON P1B 3L9
Tel: 705-474-8600 *Toll-Free:* 888-602-2222
www.nbgh.on.ca

Denis Labelle, Executive Director

Oakville: Halton Healthcare Services Corp. - Oakville-Trafalgar Memorial Hospital
327 Reynolds St., Oakville, ON L6J 3L7
Tel: 905-845-2571 *Fax:* 905-338-4636

Number of Beds: 262 acute care beds, 39 rehab beds, 21 continuing care beds
Note: Full service acute care hospital. Number of staff: 2,056, 96 physicians, 101 specialists
Dale Clement, COO

Orangeville: Headwaters Orangeville
100 Rolling Hills Dr., Orangeville, ON L9W 4X9
Tel: 519-941-2410 *Fax:* 519-942-0483
www.headwatershealth.ca

Number of Beds: 108 beds
Cholly Boland, President; CEO

Orillia: Orillia Soldiers' Memorial Hospital (OSMH)
170 Colborne St. West, Orillia, ON L3V 2Z3
Tel: 705-325-2201
administration@osmh.on.ca; tadyni@osmh.on.ca (Community relations)
www.osmh.on.ca

Number of Beds: 230 inpatient beds
Note: Specialties: Paediatric & neonatal services; Regional diagnostic imaging centre of excellence; Surgical services; Critical care; Dialysis; Oncology; Chronic disease management; Complex continuing care; Diabetes education; Sexual & domestic violence services; Mental health services; Outpatient clinics. Number of Employees: 300 physicians + 1,200 staff + 400+ volunteers
Glen H. Penwarden, Executive Director

Oshawa: Lakeridge Health Corporation Oshawa Site
1 Hospital Ct., Oshawa, ON L1G 2B9
Tel: 905-576-8711 *Fax:* 905-721-4735
www.lakeridgehealth.on.ca

Number of Beds: 437 beds
J. Dusek, COO

Ottawa: Children's Hospital of Eastern Ontario (CHEO)
401 Smyth Rd., Ottawa, ON K1H 8L1
Tel: 613-737-7600
kouri@cheo.on.ca (Patient Representative Office)
www.cheo.on.ca

Year Founded: 1974
Number of Beds: 112 pediatric, oncology, adolescent medicine, & surgery beds; 25 psychiatry beds; 20 neonatal intensive care unit beds; 10 intensive care unit beds
Note: Hospital Specialties: Pediatric health for children & youth aged 0 to 18 years; Emergency services; Surgery; Ontario Newborn Screening Program; Neonatal intensive care; Genetics; Oncology; Dialysis; Cardiology; Neurology; Provincial Centre of Excellence for Child & Youth Mental Health; Number of Employees: 1,500 administrative, service, & allied health staff; 630 nursing staff; 183 physicians
Michel Bilodeau, President; Chief Executive Officer
Dr. Carrol Pitters, Chief of Staff
Jerry Bisson, Chief Financial Officer; Senior Vice-President
Pat Elliott-Miller, Chief Nursing Executive; Vice-President, Patient Services
Tyson Roffey, Chief Information Officer
Ginette Champagne, Vice-President, Human Resources
Dr. Martin H. Osmond, Vice-President, Research
Susan Richardson, Vice-President, Professional Services
Ann Fuller, Director, Public Relations

Ottawa: Hôpital Montfort
713, ch Montréal, Ottawa, ON K1K 0T2
Tél: 613-746-4621 *Téléc:* 613-748-4947
Ligne sans frais: 800-276-0161
montfort@montfort.on.ca
www.hopitalmontfort.com

Nombre de lits: 208 lits
Gérald Savoie, Président/Directeur général

Ottawa: The Ottawa Hospital Civic Campus
1053 Carling Ave., Ottawa, ON K1Y 4E9
Tel: 613-722-7000
webmaster@ottawahospital.on.ca
www.ottawahospital.on.ca

Number of Beds: 1,066 beds across the system
Note: Comprehensive, patient-focussed care; University of Ottawa Heart Institute. Number of staff total TOH: 11,566 staff, 1,150 physicians
Dr. Jack Kitts, President/CEO
Dr. Jeffrey Turnbull, Chief of Staff

Ottawa: The Ottawa Hospital General Campus
501 Smyth Rd., Ottawa, ON K1H 8L6
Tel: 613-722-7000 *Fax:* 613-737-8470
www.ottawahospital.on.ca

Number of Beds: 1,066 beds across the system
Note: Comprehensive, patient-focussed care, including the University of Ottawa Eye Institute. Number of staff total TOH: 11,566 staff, 1,150 physicians
Dr. Jack Kitts, President/CEO
Dr. Jeffrey Turnbull, Chief of Staff

Ottawa: The Ottawa Hospital Riverside Campus
1967 Riverside Dr., Ottawa, ON K1H 7W9
Tel: 613-722-7000 *Fax:* 613-738-8526

Number of Beds: 1,066 beds across the system
Note: Comprehensive, patient-focussed care, including Eye Care Centre, & the Shirley E. Greenberg Women's Health Centre. Number of staff total TOH: 11,566 staff, 1,150 physicians

Dr. Jack Kitts, President/CEO
Dr. Jeffrey Turnbull, Chief of Staff

Ottawa: Queensway Carleton Hospital
3045 Baseline Rd., Ottawa, ON K2H 8P4
Tel: 613-721-2000 *Fax:* 613-721-4770
communications@qch.on.ca
www.qch.on.ca

Number of Beds: 264 beds
Note: Diagnostic imaging, emergency services, family medicine, geriatrics, lab, rehabilitation, obstetrics & gynaecology, paediatrics, psychiatry, surgery. Number of staff: 1,798, 234 physicians, 3 midwives.
Tom Schonberg, President/CEO
Dr. Andrew Falconer, Chief of Staff

Owen Sound: Grey Bruce Health Services
1800 - 8 St. East, Owen Sound, ON N4K 6M9
Tel: 519-376-2121
web@gbhs.on.ca
www.gbhs.on.ca

Pat Campbell, President; CEO

Owen Sound: Owen Sound Hospital Grey Bruce Health Services
PO Box 1800, 1800 - 8th St. East, Owen Sound, ON N4K 6M9
Tel: 519-376-2121
library@gbhs.on.ca
www.gbhs.on.ca/owensound.php

Note: Specialties: Community addiction treatment services; Community mental health services; Community outreach; Critical care services; Grey Bruce District Stroke Centre; Grey Bruce Huron paramedic base hospital program; Ontario breast screening program; Preschool speech & language service; Sleep lab; Sexual assault & partner abuse care; Surgical services; Nuclear medicine; Psychogeriatric unit; Palliative care. Number of Employees: 60 specialists + 21 family physicians + 1,129 nurses, therapists, technologists, & support staff

Palmerston: North Wellington Health Care Corporation
Palmerston & District Hospital Site
500 Whites Rd., Palmerston, ON N0G 2P0
Tel: 519-343-2030 *Fax:* 519-343-3821
www.nwhealthcare.ca

Number of Beds: 19 beds
Jerome Quenneville, President/CEO
519-323-3333 ext2258, Fax: 519-323-2955,
jquenneville@nwhealthcare.ca

Paris: Willett Hospital Site
Brant Community Healthcare System (BCHS)
Also Known As: The Willett
238 Grand River St. North, Paris, ON N3L 2N7
Tel: 519-442-2251
www.bchsys.org

Year Founded: 1922
Number of Beds: A total of 350 beds are part of The Brant Community Healthcare System, which consists of The Willett Hospital in Paris, Ontario & the Brantford Genera
Note: Hospital Specialties: Urgent care; Diagnostic imaging; Recreational therapy; Physiotherapy; Occupational therapy; Counselling services; Community health, including health & wellness education
James Hornell, President; Chief Executive Officer, Brant Community Healthcare System
519-751-5500
Andrew McRobert, Director, Health & Addiction Services, & Pastoral Care
519-751-5544, ext. 2
Heather Riddell, Director, Emergency Services / Urgent Care
519-751-5544, ext. 2
Jill Berridge, Manager, Rehabilitation Services
519-751-5544, ext. 2
Karen Kuzmich, Manager, Wellness & Healthcare Integration
519-442-4000, ext. 6
Nancy Wheeler, Manager, Imaging
519-751-5547

Pembroke: Pembroke Regional Hospital
Former Name: Pembroke General Hospital
705 MacKay St., Pembroke, ON K8A 1G8
Tel: 613-732-2811 *Fax:* 613-732-9986
pr@pemreghos.org
www.pemgenhos.org

Number of Beds: 165 beds
Pierre Noel, President/CEO

Penetanguishene: Penetanguishene General Hospital
25 Jeffery St., Penetanguishene, ON L9M 1K6
Tel: 705-549-7431 *Fax:* 705-549-4031
www.nsha.on.ca

Number of Beds: 51 beds
Note: Hospital, regional rehab. & complex continuing care, dialysis
Doris Shirriff, Executive Director
Robert Robitaille, Director, Environmental Services

Perth: Perth & Smiths Falls District Hospital
Perth Site
Also Known As: Great War Memorial Site
33 Drummond St. West, Perth, ON K7H 2K1
Tel: 613-267-1500 *Fax:* 613-264-0365
webinquiry@psfdh.on.ca
www.psfdh.on.ca

Note: Specialties: Acute care; Health promotion programs; Ambulatory care; Rehabilitation services; Chronic care; Palliative care

Peterborough: Peterborough Regional Health Centre (PRHC)
1 Hospital Dr., Peterborough, ON K9J 7C6
Tel: 705-743-2121 *Fax:* 705-876-5120
TTY: 705-876-5141
info@prhc.on.ca
www.prhc.on.ca

Number of Beds: 494 beds
Note: Specialties: Acute care; Emergency services; Diagnostic imaging; Surgical services; Regional renal program; Mental health services; Maternal child services. Number of Employees: 2,000 staff; 350 physicians with privileges; 600 volunteers
Wendy Fucile, Interim President/CEO

Petrolia: Charlotte Eleanor Englehart Hospital (CEEH)
Bluewater Health
Former Name: Charlotte Eleanor Englehart Hospital
450 Blanche St., Petrolia, ON N0N 1R0
Tel: 519-882-4325 *Fax:* 519-882-3711
www.bluewaterhealth.ca

Year Founded: 1911
Number of Beds: 23 acute care beds; 18 continuing care beds
Note: Hospital Specialties: Emergency services; Acute care; Ambulatory care; Continuing care services
Sue Denomy, President; Chief Executive Officer, Bluewater Health
519-464-4400, ext. 4, Fax: 519-336-8780,
sdenomy@bluewaterhealth.ca

Picton: Quinte Health Care Prince Edward County Memorial
Quinte Health Care
403 Main St. East, Picton, ON K0K 2T0
Tel: 613-476-1008 *Fax:* 613-476-8600
www.qhc.on.ca/Default.aspx?cid=276&lang=1

Year Founded: 1959
Number of Beds: 24 beds
Note: Emergency services, obstetrics, physiotherapy, outpatient clinics, radiology, pharmacy
Mary Clare Egberts, President; CEO, Quinte Health Care

Port Colborne: Port Colborne Site of Niagara Health System (NHS)
Niagara Health System / Système de santé de Niagara
260 Sugarloaf St., Port Colborne, ON L3K 2N7
Tel: 905-378-4647 *Fax:* 905-834-0404
www.niagarahealth.on.ca

Year Founded: 1951
Number of Beds: 46 beds inpatient beds for complex continuing care; 35 beds at the New Port Centre for addiction recovery
Note: Hospital Specialties: Urgent Care Centre; Ontario Breast Screening Program; Eating Disorders Clinic; Addiction recovery, including a methadone clinic; Complex continuing care
Debbie Sevenpifer, President; Chief Executive Officer, Niagara Health System
Bala Kathiresan, Chief Operating Officer, Niagara Health System

Sue Matthews, Chief Nursing Executive; Vice-President, Patient Services, Port Colborne Site
Norma Medulun, Director, Clinical Program (Addiction Recovery)
905-378-4647, ext. 6

Port Perry: Lakeridge Health Corporation
Port Perry Site
451 Paxton St., Port Perry, ON L9L 1A8
Tel: 905-985-7321 *Fax:* 905-985-5829
www.lakeridgehealth.on.ca

Number of Beds: 24 beds
Carol Anderson, Site Leader

Rainy River: Rainy River Health Centre
Affiliated with: Riverside Health Care Facilities Inc.
114 - 4th St., Rainy River, ON P0W 1L0
Tel: 807-852-3232 *Fax:* 807-852-3565
riverside@rhcf.on.ca
www.riversidehealthcare.ca

Number of Beds: 24 beds
Note: Emergency, diagnostic imaging, acute and long term care facility
Tammie McNally, Nurse Manager

Red Lake: Red Lake Margaret Cochenour Memorial Hospital
Also Known As: Red Lake Hospital
PO Box 5005, 51 Hwy. 105, Red Lake, ON P0V 2M0
Tel: 807-727-2066 *Fax:* 807-727-2923
info@redlakehospital.ca
www.redlakehospital.ca

Year Founded: 1973
Number of Beds: 14 acute care beds, 4 long term care beds
Note: Emergency services, lab, radiology & ultrasound, rehabilitation, sugery, endoscopy, nutritional services, chemotherapy, telehealth.
Janice Mullin, Chief Executive Officer

Renfrew: Renfrew Victoria Hospital
499 Raglan St. North, Renfrew, ON K7V 1P6
Tel: 613-432-4851 *Fax:* 613-432-8649
www.renfrewhosp.com

Year Founded: 1897
Number of Beds: 101 beds
Note: Birthing room & obstetrical care, pediatrics, chronic care, geriatric care, surgery, physiotherapy , palliative care, nephrology, urology, cardiac care, dialysis services, satellite oncology service, diagnostic imaging & ultrasound, dermatology, ophthalmology
Randy Penney, President/CEO
Julia Boudreau, Vice-President, Corporate Services

Richmond Hill: York Central Hospital
10 Trench St., Richmond Hill, ON L4C 4Z3
Tel: 905-883-1212 *Fax:* 905-883-2455
www.yorkcentral.on.ca

Number of Beds: 427 beds, 116 long-term care beds
Note: Total staff: 1732 Employees
William M. Leacy, President/CEO

Sarnia: Bluewater Health
Former Name: Charlotte Eleanor Englehart Hospital; Sarnia General Hospital; St. Joseph's Health
Norman Site, 89 Norman St., Sarnia, ON N7T 6S3
Tel: 519-464-4400 *Fax:* 519-336-8780
www.bluewaterhealth.ca

Year Founded: 2002
Number of Beds: 211 acute care beds; 88 complex continuing care beds
Note: Hospital Specialties: Emergency medicine; Laboratory services; Surgery; Acute care; Obstetrics; Pediatrics; Rehabilitation; Mental health services; Dialysis; Diabetes education; Nutrition services; Sexual & Domestic Assault Treatment Centre; Complex continuing care; Palliative care; Number of Employees: 2,070
Sue Denomy, President; Chief Executive Officer
519-464-4470, ext. 4, Fax: 519-336-8780,
sdenomy@bluewaterhealth.ca
Stephen Anema, Chief Financial Officer
519-464-4400, ext. 4, Fax: 519-346-4600,
sanema@bluewaterhealth.ca
Kim Bossy, Chief, Communications & Public Affairs
519-464-4400, ext. 4, Fax: 519-346-4600,
kbossy@bluewaterhealth.ca
Michael Lapaine, Chief Operating Officer; Vice-President, Operations
519-464-4400, ext. 4, Fax: 519-336-8780,
mlapaine@bluewaterhealth.ca
Dr. Martin Lees, Chief, Professional Staff & Quality / Risk Management
519-464-4400, ext. 4, Fax: 519-464-4501,
mlees@bluewaterhealth.ca
Barb O'Neil, Chief, Nursing & Interprofessional Practice
519-464-4400, ext. 4, Fax: 519-346-4600,
boneil@bluewaterhealth.ca

Sault Ste Marie: Sault Area Hospital
969 Queen St. East, Sault Ste Marie, ON P6A 2C4
Tel: 705-759-3434 *Fax:* 705-759-3640
publicaffairs@sah.on.ca
www.sah.on.ca

Number of Beds: 289 beds
Note: Acute care hospital with over 1900 employees, 400 volunteers, and 125 physicians on staff.
Ron Gagnon, Interim President; CEO

Seaforth: Huron-Perth Healthcare Alliance
Seaforth Community Hospital
PO Box 99, 24 Centennial Dr., Seaforth, ON N0K 1W0
Tel: 519-527-1650 *Fax:* 519-527-8414
www.hpha.ca

Number of Beds: 34 beds
Andrew Williams, CEO
andrew.williams@hpha.ca

Seaforth: Seaforth Community Hospital
Affiliated with: Huron Perth Healthcare Alliance
PO Box 99, 24 Centennial Dr., Seaforth, ON N0K 1W0
Tel: 519-527-1650 *Fax:* 519-527-8414
administration@hpha.ca
www.hpha.ca/default.aspx?cid=48&lang=1

Year Founded: 1965
Number of Beds: 18 beds
Note: Emergency & ambulatory care, cardiorespiratory, diagnostic imaging, lab, physiotherapy, occupational therapy, chemotherapy, nutrition, diabetes education, dialysis, women's care & pediatrics, general surgery, intensive care & telemetry units, mental health services, dentistry. Heliport & Seaforth Medical Clinic
Andrew Williams, CEO, HPHA
519-272-8202, andrew.williams@hpha.ca
Ken Haworth, Vice-President; CFO, Operations, HPHA
519-272-8210, ken.haworth@hpha.ca
Bonnie Royal, Site Administrator; Program Director, Seaforth
519-527-3000, bonnie.royal@hpha.ca

Simcoe: Norfolk General Hospital
365 West St., Simcoe, ON N3Y 1T7
Tel: 519-426-0130 *Fax:* 519-429-6998
www.ngh.on.ca

Number of Beds: 121 beds
Kelly Isfan, CEO

Sioux Lookout: Sioux Lookout Meno Ya Win Health Centre
PO Box 909, 1 Meno Ya Win Way, Sioux Lookout, ON P8T 1B4
Tel: 807-737-3000 *Fax:* 807-737-5127
info@slmhc.on.ca
www.slmhc.on.ca
Number of Beds: 41 beds; 5 chronic care beds
Note: Primary health care services including a broad range of basic and some specialist hospital services, specialized community based programs and services responding to population health needs (withdrawal management, suicide, TB, etc.), long term care and integrated traditional and modern medicine. Serves Nishnawbe-Aski communities north of Sioux Lookout, the Treaty # 3 community of Lac Seul First Nation, as well as to residents of Pickle Lake and Savant Lake.
Dave Murray, President & CEO
Doug Moynihan, Vice-President, Corporate Services
Barb Linkewich, Vice President, Health Services

Smiths Falls: Smiths Falls Site of Perth & Smiths Falls District Hospital
Perth & Smiths Falls District Hospital
60 Cornelia St. West, Smiths Falls, ON K7A 2H9
Tel: 613-283-2330 *Fax:* 613-283-8990
webinquiry@psfdh.on.ca
www.psfdh.on.ca
Note: Specialties: Acute care; Ambulatory care; Dialysis unit; Cataract surgery; Diabetes counselling; Children's mental health services; Sexual assault & domestic violence program; Vascular protection clinic; Chronic care; Palliative care. Number of Employees: 560
Todd Stepanuik, President/CEO

Smooth Rock Falls: Hôpital de Smooth Rock Falls Hospital
PO Box 219, 107 Kelly Road, Smooth Rock Falls, ON P0L 2B0
Tel: 705-338-2781 *Fax:* 705-338-4410
info@srfhosp.ca
www.srfhosp.ca
Number of Beds: 14 acute care beds, 23 long term care beds
Note: Primary care, including the North Cochrane Detoxification Centre. Number of staff: 85 staff, 1 FT & 3 PT physicians
Fabien L. Hébert, CEO

Southampton: Southampton Hospital
Grey Bruce Health Services
340 High St., Southampton, ON N0H 2L0
Tel: 519-797-3230
www.gbhs.on.ca/southampton.php
Number of Beds: 16 inpatient beds
Note: Specialties: Day surgery services; Outpatient services, such as a women's health clinic; Home & community support services, such as the Day Away Program; Diabetes education; Physiotherapy; Palliative care. Number of employees: 105
Carolyn Zacharuk, Site Director

St Catharines: Ontario Street Site of Niagara Health System
Niagara Health System / Système de santé de Niagara
Former Name: Hotel Dieu Hospital
155 Ontario St., St Catharines, ON L2R 5K3
Tel: 905-378-4647 *Fax:* 905-682-5533
www.niagarahealth.on.ca
Year Founded: 1948
Number of Beds: 43 beds for addiction management
Note: Hospital Specialties: Urgent Care Centre; Dialysis Program, including peritoneal dialysis, hemodialysis, & a pre-renal clinic; Addiction management services, including counselling, detoxification, & post-addiction services
Debbie Sevenpifer, President; Chief Executive Officer, Niagara Health System
Anne Atkinson, Vice-President, Patient Services, Ontario Street Site
Norma Medulun, Director, Clinical Program (Addiction Recovery)
905-378-4647, ext. 6

St Catharines: St. Catharines General Site of Niagara Health System (NHS)
Niagara Health System / Système de santé de Niagara
142 Queenston St., St Catharines, ON L2R 2Z7
Tel: 905-378-4647 *Fax:* 905-684-1468
www.niagarahealth.on.ca
Year Founded: 1865
Number of Beds: 200+ beds
Note: Hospital Specialties: Emergency services; Surgery; Acute care; Ambulatory care; Maternal & child services; Oncology; Ontario Breast Screening Program; Sexual Assault / Domestic Violence Treatment Centre; Mental health services; Critical care; Palliative care
Debbie Sevenpifer, President; Chief Executive Officer, Niagara Health System
Anne Atkinson, Vice-President, Patient Services, St. Catharines General Site
Terry McMahon, Vice-President, Human Resources, Niagara Health System
Dr. Joanna Hope, Chief of Staff, Niagara Health System
Bala Kathiresan, Chief Operating Officer, Niagara Health System

Donna Rothwell, Chief Nursing; Professional Practice Officer, Maternal; Child Care
Angela Zangari, Chief Financial Officer, Niagara Health System
Patricia Morka, Director, Clinical Program (Emergency & Critical Care)
905-378-4647, ext. 3
Heather Scott, Director, Clinical Program (Mental Health)
905-378-4647, ext. 5
Patty Welychka, Director, Clinical Program (Surgical Services)
905-378-4647, ext. 3

St Marys: St. Marys Memorial Hospital
Affiliated with: Huron Perth Healthcare Alliance
PO Box 940, 267 Queen St. West, St Marys, ON N4X 1B6
Tel: 519-284-1332 *Fax:* 519-284-8324
smmh.administration@hphp.org
www.hpha.ca
Year Founded: 1950
Number of Beds: 21 beds
Note: Primary care services include emergency, cardiac care, gynecology & pediatrics, rehabilitation, diagnostic imaging, orthopedic care
Andrew Williams, CEO, HPHA
519-272-8202, andrew.williams@hpha.ca.
Dr. Laurel Moore, Chief Of Staff, HPHA
519-272-8210, dr.laurel.moore@hpha.ca
Shirley Veenendaal, Site Administrator
shirley.veenendaal@hpha.ca

St Thomas: St. Thomas Elgin General Hospital
189 Elm St., St Thomas, ON N5R 5C4
Tel: 519-631-2020 *Fax:* 519-631-1825
TTY: 519-6317789
publicrelations@stegh.on.ca
www.stegh.on.ca
Year Founded: 1954
Number of Beds: 166 beds
Number of Employees: 800
Note: A comprehensive health care facility with services including emergency, rehabiltation, complex Care, social work, diagnostic imaging, laboratory, pharmacy, surgery, diabetes education, cardiac intensive care, maternal care unit.
Paul Collins, President /CEO
pcollins@stegh.on.ca
Malcolm Hopkins, Vice-President, Corporate Services
mhopkins@stegh.on.ca
Dr. Nancy Whitmore, Vice-President & Chief of Staff, Medical Affairs
nwhitmor@stegh.on.ca
Sharon Cattrysse, Interim Chief Nursing Officer

Stratford: Stratford General Hospital
Affiliated with: Huron Perth Healthcare Alliance
46 General Hospital Dr., Stratford, ON N5A 2Y6
Tel: 519-271-2120 *Fax:* 519-271-7137
administration@hpha.ca
www.hpha.ca/default.aspx?cid=49&lang=1
Year Founded: 1896
Number of Beds: 153 beds (110 acute care beds, 25 chronic care beds, 15 rehab beds, 3 neonatal intensive care beds)
Note: A comprehensive care facility with services including emergency & ambulatory care, diagnostic imaging (CT scans, x-ray, ultrasound, mammography), obstetrics, gynecology, pediatrics, psychiatry, ophthalmology, complex continuing care, palliative care, rehabilitation, maternity, satellite dialysis unit, speech language pathology, surgery.
Andrew Williams, CEO, HPHA
519-272-8202, andrew.williams@hpha.ca
Dr. Laurel Moore, Chief of Staff, HPHA
519-272-8210, dr.laurel.moore@hpha.ca

Strathroy: Strathroy Middlesex General Hospital
Affiliated with: Middlesex Hospital Alliance
395 Carrie St., Strathroy, ON N7G 3J4
Tel: 519-245-5295 *Fax:* 519-245-0366
www.mhalliance.on.ca
Year Founded: 1914
Number of Beds: 77 beds (of which 60 are acute care beds)
Note: A full-service, community hospital with comprehensive outpatient services, primary & secondary care. Services include emergency & trauma care, cataract surgery, diagnostic imaging (bone mineral density, CT scans, x-rays, mammography, ultrasound), intensive care/coronary care unit, obstetrics, urology, orthopedics, gynecology, otolaryngology, ophthalmology and some operative dental.
Michael A. Mazza, CEO, MHA
Dr. Marc Raymond, President, Medical Staff
Dr. Paul Ferner, Chief of Staff

Sturgeon Falls: The West Nipissing General Hospital
725 Coursol Rd., Sturgeon Falls, ON P2B 2Y6
Tel: 705-753-3110 *Fax:* 705-753-0210
marthe.levac@wngh.ca
www.wngh.ca
Year Founded: 1977
Number of Beds: 56 beds
Note: Number of staff: 9 physicians, 1 nurse practitioner
Yves Campeau, Executive Director

Sudbury: Sudbury Regional Hospital - Laurentian Site (HRSRH-LS)/H"pital régional de Sudbury - Emplacement Laurentien
41 Ramsey Lake Rd., Sudbury, ON P3E 5J1
Tel: 705-523-7100 *Fax:* 705-523-7112
Toll-Free: 1-866-469-0822
communications@hrsrh.on.ca
www.hrsrh.on.ca
Number of Beds: 530 acute care beds
Note: Complex continuing care, assistive communication clinic, chiropody clinic, eating disorders clinic, HIV/AIDS clinic, intensive rehabilitation, physiotherapy, occupational therapy
Vickie Kaminski, President/CEO

Sudbury: Sudbury Regional Hospital - Memorial Site
865 Regent St. South, Sudbury, ON P3E 3Y9
Tel: 705-523-7100 *Toll-Free:* 1-866-469-0822
communications@hrsrh.on.ca
www.hrsrh.on.ca
Number of Beds: 189 beds
Vickie Kaminski, CEO
Chris McKibbon, Chief of Staff

Sudbury: Sudbury Regional Hospital - St. Joseph's Health Centre
700 Paris St., Sudbury, ON P3B 3B5
Tel: 705-523-7100
communications@hrsrh.on.ca
www.hrsrh.on.ca
Jo-Anne Palkovits, CEO

Terrace Bay: The McCausland Hospital
20B Cartier Rd., Terrace Bay, ON P0T 2W0
Tel: 807-825-3273 *Fax:* 807-825-9623
admin@mccauslandhospital.com
www.mccauslandhospital.com
Year Founded: 1980
Number of Beds: 45 beds (23 community beds, 22 long-term beds)
Note: Services include emergency, cancer care, diabetes program, diagnostic imaging (ECG, Holter monitors, radiology, ultrasound), laboratory, obstetrics & gynecology, physiotherapy, seniors drop-in program, surgery.
Paul Paradis, CEO
ceo@mccauslandhospital.com
Dr. David Hurst, Chief of Staff

Thunder Bay: Hogarth-Westmount Hospital
300 Lillie St., Thunder Bay, ON P7C 4Y7
Tel: 807-625-1110 *Fax:* 807-623-4520
Number of Beds: 228 beds
Barry Brown, Executive Director
Richard Roberts, Director, Physical Plant

Thunder Bay: St. Joseph's Care Group
Former Name: St. Joseph's Care Group
PO Box 3251, 35 North Algoma St., Thunder Bay, ON P7B 5G7
Tel: 807-343-2431 *Fax:* 807-345-4994
www.sjcg.net
Number of Beds: 224 beds
Carl White, President
Jack Tallon, Director, Materials Management

Thunder Bay: Thunder Bay Regional Health Sciences Centre
980 Oliver Rd., Thunder Bay, ON P7B 6V4
Tel: 807-684-6000
tbrhsc@tbh.net
www.tbrhsc.com

Year Founded: 2004
Number of Beds: 375 acute care beds (28 beds for anesthetic recovery, 40 beds for day surgery recovery)
Note: A comprehensive, multi-disciplinary, acute care facility with services incuding emergency, ambulatory care, asthma education, cardiology, critical care unit, dentistry, diagnostic imaging (breast MRI, CT scans, radiology), dietitians, forensics, Holter monitoring, Hospice Northwest, ICU, laboratory, maternity, oncology (brachytherapy), paediatrics, renal program, respiratory therapy, surgery, trauma rooms. The TBRHSC amalgamates the former Port Arthur & McKellar sites of the Thunder Bay Regional Hospital.
Andrée Robichaud, President/CEO
Lori Marshall, Vice-President, Medicine, Cardiology, Mental Health and Maternal/Ch
Dr. Blair Schoales, Chief of Staff
Don Edwards, Director, Communications
807-684-6010

Tillsonburg: Tillsonburg District Memorial Hospital
PO Box 3100, 167 Rolph St., Tillsonburg, ON N4G 3Y9
Tel: 519-842-3611 *Fax:* 519-688-1031
mail@tdmh.on.ca
www.tillsonburghospital.on.ca
Number of Beds: 79 beds
Note: Services include emergency, ambulatory care, Community Care Access Centre, complex continuing care, diagnostic imaging (ultrasound, nuclear medicine, mammography, x-ray, fluoroscopy), diabetes education, dialysis, dietitian, geriatric rehab therapy program, intensive coronary care, interpreter services, mental health, palliative care, pastoral care, pharmacy, physiotherapy, surgery.
Tom McHugh, President/CEO
Dr. Gerry Rowland, President, Medical Staff
Frank Deutsch, Senior Executive Leader/CFO
Julie Ellery, Senior Executive Leader, Patient Services

Timmins: Timmins & District Hospital
700 Ross Ave. East, Timmins, ON P4N 8P2
Tel: 705-267-2131 *Fax:* 705-267-6311
evainio@tadh.com
www.tadh.com
Number of Beds: 159 beds
Note: Level C referral hospital, providing services in English & French; mental health services; medical, surgical, obstetrics & pediatrics, intensive care; complex continuing care & interim long term care
Esko Vainio, President/CEO

Toronto: The Hospital for Sick Children
Also Known As: SickKids
555 University Ave., Toronto, ON M5G 1X8
Tel: 416-813-1500
inquiry.patientrep@sickkids.ca; hr.recruiter@sickkids.ca
www.sickkids.ca
Info Line: 416-813-6621
Note: Specialties: Paediatric academic health sciences; Paediatric emergency medicine; Trauma; Developmental paediatrics; Fetal cardiac program, cardiac transplants, cardiovascular surgery, & cardiac critical care; Neonatology; Clinical & metabolic genetics; Cleft lip & palate; Neurology & neurosurgery; Cochlear implants; Haematology / Oncology; Communication disorders; Infectious diseases; Immunology & allergy; Gastroenterology, hepatology, & nutrition; Orthotics & medical devices; Rehabilitation; Child & youth counselling; Program for international patients (cindy.fiore@sickkids.ca)
Mary Jo Haddad, Pres./CEO
Scott Menzies, Director, Environmental & Central Services
Valerie O'Grady, Waste Management Coordinator

Toronto: Humber River Regional Hospital Church St. Site
200 Church St., Toronto, ON M9N 1N8
Tel: 416-249-8111 *Fax:* 416-243-4547
www.hrrh.on.ca
Reuben Devlin, President; CEO
Dr. Jack Barkin, Chief of Staff

Toronto: Humber River Regional Hospital Keele St. Site
2175 Keele St., Toronto, ON M6M 3Z4
Tel: 416-249-8111
www.hrrh.on.ca

Toronto: Humber River Regional Hospital Finch Ave. Site
2111 Finch Ave. West, Toronto, ON M3N 1N1
Tel: 416-744-2500 *Fax:* 416-747-3882
administration@hrrh.on.ca
www.hrrh.on.ca
Number of Beds: 610 beds
Reuben Devlin, President/CEO
Barbara Collins, COO; Vice-President, Planning; Support Services
Scott Jarrett, Vice-President, Patient Programs
Richard Kelly, Vice-President, Human Resources & Support Services
Peter Wegener, Vice-President, Finance & Information Systems

Toronto: Humber River Regional Hospital - Keele St. Site
2175 Keele St., Toronto, ON M6M 3Z4
Tel: 416-651-6111 *Fax:* 416-658-2192
www.hrrh.on.ca

Toronto: Mount Sinai Hospital
#334, 600 University Ave., Toronto, ON M5G 1X5
Tel: 416-596-4200 *Fax:* 416-586-8555
patientrelationsunit@mtsinai.on.ca
www.mountsinai.on.ca
Number of Beds: 472 beds
Note: Teaching and research Hospital; Home to five Centres of Excellence
Joseph Mapa, Pres./CEO

Toronto: North York General Hospital - Branson Site
555 Finch Ave. West, Toronto, ON M2R 1N5
Tel: 416-633-9420 *Fax:* 416-635-2537
www.nygh.on.ca
Number of Beds: 205 beds
Note: Urgent & ambulatory care, Ontario Breast Screening Program site, pediatric speech & language services, diagnostic imaging, geriatric medicine & psychiatry, Gale & Graham Wright Prostrate Centre
Bonnie Adamson, President/CEO

Toronto: North York General Hospital - General Site
4001 Leslie St., Toronto, ON M2K 1E1
Tel: 416-756-6000 *Fax:* 416-756-6384
www.nygh.on.ca
Number of Beds: 400 beds
Note: Community teaching hospital affiliated with the University of Toronto. Comprehensive health care services including full service emergency unit
Bonnie Adamson, President/CEO

Toronto: Rouge Valley Centenary
Affiliated with: Rouge Valley Health System
2867 Ellesmere Rd., Toronto, ON M1E 4B9
Tel: 416-284-8131 *Fax:* 416-281-7323
www.rougevalley.ca
Year Founded: 1967
Number of Beds: 285 beds
Note: Emergency, cardiac care, mental health, paediatrics.
Rik Ganderton, President/CEO, RVHS
boardofdirectors@rougevalley.ca
David Brazeau, Director, RVHS, Public Affairs & Community Relations
647-294-8885, dbrazeau@rougevalley.ca

Toronto: St. Joseph's Health Centre
30 The Queensway, Toronto, ON M6R 1B5
Tel: 416-530-6000 *Fax:* 416-530-6346
www.stjoe.on.ca
Year Founded: 1921
Number of Beds: 376 beds
Note: Services include emergency & critical care, women/children/family health, seniors' care, surgery, oncology, diagnostic imaging, rehabilitation. This teaching hospital was founded by the Sisters of St. Joseph.
Carolyn Baker, President/CEO
Dale McGregor, Executive Vice-President/CFO
Dr. Tom Harmantas, Chief of Staff

Toronto: St. Michael's Hospital
1 Queen Wing, 30 Bond St., Toronto, ON M5B 1W8
Tel: 416-360-4000 *Fax:* 416-360-7304
www.stmichaelshospital.com
Number of Beds: 527 inpatient
Note: Catholic hospital with a focus on teaching and research affiliated with the University of Toronto
Jeffrey Lozon, President; CEO
William Rosenitsch, Director, Material Management

Toronto: The Salvation Army Toronto Grace Health Centre
Also Known As: Toronto Grace Hospital
650 Church St., Toronto, ON M4Y 2G5
Tel: 416-925-2251 *Fax:* 416-925-3211
www.torontograce.org
Year Founded: 1905
Number of Beds: 119 beds
Note: A patient-centred, palliative and complex continuing care facility focusing on holistic and respite care for patients, families and friends through inpatient and community outreach programs.
Marilyn Rook, President/CEO
Monica Codjoe, Vice-President, Patient Services
Dr. David Van Der Hout, Medical Director
Alexis Dishaw, Director, Communications, Community Engagement & Strategic
Beth D'Angelo, Manager, Patient Care
edangelo@torontograce.org
John P. Murray, Spokesperson, Public Relations & Development
416-998-0117, John_Murray@can.salvationarmy.org

Toronto: The Scarborough Hospital - Birchmount Campus
Former Name: The Scarborough Hospital - Grace Campus
3030 Birchmount Rd., Toronto, ON M1W 3W3
Tel: 416-495-2400 *Fax:* 416-431-8204
info@tsh.to
www.tsh.to
Number of Beds: 650 beds total
Note: A health facility with emphasis on emergency outpatient psychiatric concerns, notably its Regional Crisis Program, an emergency response team to acute psychiatric crises. Total staff: 3,700
Dr. John Wright, President/CEO
Dr. Steven Jackson, Chief of Medical Staff
Ester Lipnicki, Executive Director, Patient Services & Quality Care
Dave Bourne, Manager, Corporate Communications
dbourne@tsh.to
Sara Kirkup, Manager, Regional Crisis Program
416-495-2891, Fax: 416-495-2880, skirkup@tsh.to

Toronto: The Scarborough Hospital - General Campus
3050 Lawrence Ave. East, Toronto, ON M1P 2V5
Tel: 416-438-2911 *Fax:* 416-431-8204
info@tsh.to
www.tsh.to
Social Media: www.facebook.com/ScarboroughHospital; twitter.com/ScarboroughHosp; www.flickr.com/photos/tshphotos; tshtoptips.wordpress.com; www.linkedin.com/company/the-scarborough-hospital
Year Founded: 552
Number of Beds: 556 beds (medical 266, surgical 134, paediatric 14, ICU/CCU 32, obstetric 44, mental health 50, rehab 16 beds)
Number of Employees: 3300
Note: A comprehensive community facility with services including emergency, cardio-respiratory & critical care, specialized geriatrics, family medicine & community services, maternal/newborn & child care, mental health, nephrology & dialysis, oncology, surgery, sexual assault care & domestic violence program, orthopedics & rehabilitation.
Dr. John Wright, President/CEO
Dr. David Rose, Interim Chief of Staff
Dr. Robert Ting, President, Medical Staff Association
Rhonda Seidman-Carlson, Vice President & Chief Nursing Executive, Interprofessional Practice
Paul Torre, Chair, TSH Foundation
Stephen Smith, Chair

Toronto: Sunnybrook Health Sciences Centre
2075 Bayview Ave., Toronto, ON M4N 3M5
Tel: 416-480-6100
questions@sunnybrook.ca
www.sunnybrook.ca
Year Founded: 1948
Number of Beds: 1,212 beds
Note: A comprehensive health facility with a focus on cancer care (Odette Cancer Centre), cardiac care (Schulich Heart Centre), musculoskeletal care (Holland Musculoskeletal Program), brain science program (stroke, dementias, mood disorders), women's health, infertility, perinatal care, pediatrics, emergency services, trauma & critical care, veterans' care & residence, research & education. Number of staff: 10,000
Dr. Barry A. McLellan, President/CEO
Dr. Michael Julius, Vice-President, Research
Dr. Wendy Levinson, Physician-in-Chief
Dr. Gordon Rubenfeld, Chief, Trauma, Emergency and Critical Care

Toronto: Sunnybrook Health Sciences Centre - Perinatal & Gynaecology Unit
New Women's College Hospital, 76 Grenville St., Toronto, ON M5S 1B2
Tel: 416-323-6400 *Fax:* 416-323-7314
www.sunnybrook.ca
Note: The facility focuses on perinatal care (labour, delivery, newborn care), gynaecological conditions, mature women's

health, infertility, cancers with an aim to high quality, individualized care. On site are a pregnancy & birth unit, high risk unit, NICU, HPV Vaccine Clinic.
Dr. Barry A. McLellan, President/CEO

Toronto: Toronto East General Hospital
825 Coxwell Ave., Toronto, ON M4C 3E7
Tel: 416-461-8272 *Fax:* 416-469-6106
ptrep@tegh.on.ca (Patients); community@tegh.on.ca (Community)
www.tegh.on.ca
Year Founded: 1929
Note: Specialties: Ambulatory & community services; Emergency; Diagnostic imaging; Laboratory medicine; Surgery; Maternal & newborn care; Diabetes education community network; Mental health services; Complex continuing care & rehabilitation; Progressive weaning centre
Robert Devitt, President; CEO
Joanne Holgate, Director, Environmental Services
416-469-6471

Toronto: Trillium Health Centre - West Toronto Site
150 Sherway Dr., Toronto, ON M9C 1A5
Tel: 416-259-6671 *Fax:* 416-253-2500
publicrelations@thc.on.ca
www.trilliumhealthcentre.org
Note: An ambulatory care facility with services including urgent care centre (8:00 a.m.-10:00 p.m. only, daily), day surgery, diabetes management centre, cardiac wellness & rehabilitation, Kingsway Financial Spine Centre, The Betty Wallace Women's Health Centre (focusing on osteoporosis and breast disease). There is no emergency centre here; it is located at branch in Mississauga.
Janet M. Davidson, President /CEO
Ruby Brown, Executive Vice-President/COO
Dr. Gopal Bhatnagar, Chief of Staff
Larry Roberts, Media Relations Consultant
905-848-7580, lroberts@thc.on.ca

Toronto: University Health Network
Former Name: The Toronto Hospital
190 Elizabeth St., Toronto, ON M5G 2C4
Tel: 416-340-3388 *Fax:* 416-340-4896
patientrelations@uhn.ca
www.uhn.ca
Number of Beds: 1,093 beds (total, all sites)
Note: Comprised of Princess Margaret Hospital, Toronto General Hospital, & Toronto Western Hospital, UHN is a comprehensive health care, research & teaching facility with fields of focus including cancer care, cardiac care, musculoskeletal health & arthritis, neuroscience, ophthalmology, surgical & critical care, transplantation. The network is affiliated with the University of Toronto, Faculty of Medicine.
Dr. Robert S. Bell, President /CEO
416-340-3300
Kevin Empey, Executive Vice President, Clinical Support & Corporate Services
Dr. Mary Ferguson Paré, Chief Nurse Executive; Vice-President, Professional Affairs
Gillian Howard, Vice-President, Public Affairs & Communications
416-340-4838, gillian.howard@uhn.ca

Toronto: University Health Network - Toronto General Hospital
200 Elizabeth St., Toronto, ON M5G 2C4
Tel: 416-340-4800 *Fax:* 416-340-5054
uhn.info@uhn.on.ca
www.uhn.ca/applications/TGH/iNews/default.aspx
Year Founded: 1829
Number of Beds: 471 beds
Note: A comprehensive, health care and teaching facility, its specialties include cardiac care (Peter Munk Cardiac Centre), transplantation, kidney diseases & care, tropical disease, eating disorders, nephrology, psychiatry, HIV/AIDS care, telemedicine. It is home to the MaRS Discovery District, a not-for-profit research corporation with funding from both private and public sectors.
Dr. Robert Bell, President/CEO, UHN
416-340-3300
Dr. Charlie Chan, Vice-President, Medical Affairs, UHN
Marnie Escaf, Site Lead/Vice-President, UHN
Gillian Howard, Vice-President, Public Affairs & Communications, UHN
416-340-4838, gillian.howard@uhn.on.ca

Toronto: University Health Network - Toronto Western Hospital
399 Bathurst St., Toronto, ON M5T 2S8
Tel: 416-603-5800
uhn.info@uhn.on.ca
www.uhn.ca/applications/TWH/iNews/default.aspx
Year Founded: 1905
Number of Beds: 256 beds
Note: The facility focuses on neural/sensory science research & treatment, musculoskeletal health. Other fields of specialty include acupuncture for addictions, Asian Initiative in Mental Health program, asthma care, cardiac/pulmonary wellness centre, chronic pain, dermatology, diabetes education, epilepsy, geriatrics, memory, neuro-ophthalmology, neuro-otology, neurosurgery, occupational lung disease, outpatient physiotherapy, peritoneal dialysis, plastic surgery, Portuguese mental health & addictions, psychiatry, renal clinic, sleep, spinal cord, Tourette's syndrome, tuberculosis, urology.
Dr. Robert Bell, President/CEO, UHN
416-340-3300
Dr. Charlie Chan, Vice-President, Medical Affairs, UHN
Kathy Sabo, Site Lead/Vice-President
kathy.sabo@uhn.on.ca
Gillian Howard, Vice-President, Public Affairs & Communications, UHN
416-340-4838, gillian.howard@uhn.on.ca

Toronto: William Osler Health Centre - Etobicoke General Hospital Campus
101 Humber College Blvd., Toronto, ON M9V 1R8
Tel: 416-747-2120
Number of Beds: 250 beds
Note: Comprehensive health care services. The William Osler Health Centre is comprised of the Etobicoke General Hospital, Brampton Civic Hospital, & the Peel Memorial Hospital (in re-development)
Dawne Barbiei, Site Executive; Chief Nursing Officer

Trenton: Quinte Health Care Trenton Memorial Quinte Health Care
242 King St., Trenton, ON K8V 5S6
Tel: 613-392-2540 *Fax:* 613-392-3749
www.qhc.on.ca/Default.aspx?cid=274&lang=1
Year Founded: 1951
Number of Beds: 33 beds
Note: Emergency services, intensive care, outpatient clinics, lab, pharmacy, radiology, surgical service, psychiatry
Wendy Parker, Site Administrator
Ext. 5376

Uxbridge: Uxbridge Site of Markham-Stouffville Hospital
Markham-Stouffville Hospital
Former Name: Uxbridge Cottage Hospital
PO Box 5003, 4 Campbell Dr., Uxbridge, ON L9P 1S4
Tel: 905-852-9771
myhospital@msh.on.ca
www.msh.on.ca
Info Line: 905-852-9771
Year Founded: 1959
Number of Beds: 20 beds
Note: Specialties: Diagnostic services; Rhabilitation services, such as physiotherapy & diabetes education
Lorne Zen, Actg. COO

Walkerton: South Bruce Grey Health Centre - Walkerton Site
Walkerton Hospital
PO Box 1300, 21 McGivern St. W., Walkerton, ON N0G 2V0
Tel: 519-881-1220 *Fax:* 519-881-0452
www.sbghc.on.ca
Year Founded: 1900
Number of Beds: 38 beds
Note: A rural health centre with services including emergency, cardio-respiratory care, dental care, ear/nose/throat, family birthing centre, internal medicine, pediatrics, surgery, urology, nutrition services, diagnostic imaging, lab, physiotherapy, healthy heart program
Paul L. Davies, President/CEO, SBGHC
pdavies@sbghc.on.ca
Jill Machan, Site Manager/Director, Patient Care
jmachan@sbghc.on.ca

Wawa: Lady Dunn Health Centre
PO Box 179, 17 Government Rd., Wawa, ON P0S 1K0
Tel: 705-856-2335 *Fax:* 705-856-7533
Toll-Free: 866-832-3321
www.ldhc.com
Number of Beds: 26 beds
Sally Garland, CEO
Gary Trudeau, Chair, Environmental Committee
Holly Morrison-Smith, Manager, Environmental Services

Whitby: Lakeridge Health Corporation Whitby Site
300 Gordon St., Whitby, ON L1N 5T2
Tel: 905-668-6831 *Fax:* 905-665-2406
www.lakeridgehealth.on.ca
Number of Beds: 74 beds
Carol Anderson, Site Lead

Wiarton: Wiarton Hospital
Grey Bruce Health Services
369 Mary St., Wiarton, ON N0H 2T0
Tel: 519-534-1260 *Fax:* 519-534-4450
www.gbhs.on.ca/wiarton.php
Number of Beds: 18 inpatient beds
Note: Specialties: Acute care; Dental surgery; Diabetes education; Physiotherapy; Mental health & addictions programs; Palliative care. Number of employees: 107
Pat Campbell, Pres./CEO

Winchester: Winchester District Memorial Hospital
566 Louise St., Winchester, ON K0C 2K0
Tel: 613-774-2422 *Fax:* 613-774-0453
www.wdmh.on.ca
Number of Beds: 70 beds
Note: Teaching hospital with emergency care, general surgery, cardiac & respiratory care, diabetes care, obstetrics & pediatrics, rehabilitation, palliative care, chemotherapy, diagnostic imaging
Trudy Reid, President/CEO
treid@wdmh.on.ca

Windsor: Hôtel Dieu Grace Hospital
1030 Ouellette Ave., Windsor, ON N9A 1E1
Tel: 519-973-4444 *Fax:* 519-973-0803
www.hdgh.org
Number of Beds: 305 beds
John Coughlin, Pres./CEO
Patricia Somers, Vice President of Operations

Windsor: The Windsor Regional Hospital - Metropolitan Campus
1995 Lens Ave., Windsor, ON N8W 1L9
Tel: 519-254-5577 *Fax:* 519-254-2317
www.wrh.on.ca
Year Founded: 1928
Number of Beds: 669 beds (total of all WRH sites)
Note: An acute care facility with services including emergency, ambulatory care, intensive care, Breast Health Centre, cardiac & critical care, diagnostic imaging (nuclear medicine/MRI), endoscopy, family birthing centre, Oncology Inpatient Program, paediatrics, regional cancer services, surgery
David Musyj, President/CEO
Dr. Gary Ing, Medical Chief of Staff
Karen McCullough, Vice-President/Chief Nursing Executive, Acute Care Services
Ron Foster, Vice-President, Public Affairs, Communication and Philanthropy
fosterr@wrh.on.ca

Windsor: The Windsor Regional Hospital - Western Campus
1453 Prince Rd., Windsor, ON N9C 3Z4
Tel: 519-254-5577 *Fax:* 519-254-2317
www.wrh.on.ca
Year Founded: 1910
Number of Beds: 669 beds (total of all WRH sites)
Note: Services include inter-disciplinary rehabilitation, complex continuing care, long term care, specialized mental health services, audiology, speech language pathology, acquired brain injury treatment, geriatric assessment & consultation program, physiotherapy, occupational therapy and chiropody. The Malden Park Continuing Care Centre is also located at this campus.
David Musyj, President/CEO
Dr. Gary Ing, Medical Chief of Staff
Sharon Pillon, Vice-President, Complex Continuing Care/Rehabilitation
Ron Foster, Vice-President, Public Affairs, Communications and Philanthropy
fosterr@wrh.on.ca

Wingham: Wingham & District Hospital
Affiliated with: Listowel & Wingham Hospitals Alliance
270 Carling Terrace, Wingham, ON N0G 2W0
Tel: 519-357-3210 *Fax:* 519-357-3522
www.lwha.ca
Number of Beds: 50 beds
Note: Acute care facility, emergency services, surgery, obstetrics & pediatrics, rehabilitation, specialist clinics; affiliated with the London Regional Cancer Centre; air ambulance service; medical clinic. Number of staff: 6 physicians, resident surgeon, 2 anesthetists
Margret Comack, CEO
margret.comack@lwha.ca

Woodstock: Woodstock General Hospital
270 Riddell St., Woodstock, ON N4S 6N4
Tel: 519-421-4211 *Fax:* 519-537-5142
www.wgh.on.ca

Number of Beds: 120 beds
Natasa Veljovic, President/CEO

Federal Hospitals

Ottawa: Canadian Forces Health Care Centre Ottawa

713 Montreal Rd., Ottawa, ON K1K 0T2
Tel: 945-1140; 61 *Fax:* 613-991-1543
www.forces.gc.ca/health-sante

Note: Hospital Specialties: Primary health care services to the military community in the National Capital Region (613-945-1502); Laboratory services; Surgery; Cardio Pulmonary Unit; Operational Trauma & Stress Support Centre (613-945-1060); Mental health (613-945-1060); Addiction counselling (613-945-1060); Ophthalmology (613-945-1550); Physiotherapy (613-945-1585); Preventive medicine (613-945-1604); Public health
LCol Gisele Fontaine, Commanding Officer
LCol Michel P. Deilgat, NCR Surgeon
CPO2 Mario Richard, Clinic Sergeant-Major
Cdr. Nathalie Tremblay, Officer, Patient Relations
Fax: 613-945-1836

Private Hospitals

Penetanguishene: Hôpital Privé Beechwood Private Hospital

58 Church St., Penetanguishene, ON L9M 1B3
Tel: 705-549-7473 *Fax:* 705-549-7194
bph@bellnet.ca

Number of Beds: 20 beds
Larry Bellisle, CEO

Thornhill: Shouldice Hospital Ltd.

PO Box 370, 7750 Bayview Ave., Thornhill, ON L3T 4A3
Tel: 905-889-1125 *Fax:* 905-889-4216
Toll-Free: 800-291-7750
postoffice@shouldice.com
www.shouldice.com

Year Founded: 1945
Number of Beds: 89 beds
Note: Specializes in hernia repair; walk-in clinic
Dr. Cassim Degani, Chief Surgeon

Toronto: Don Mills Surgical Unit Inc. (DMSU) Centric Health Group

#208, 20 Wynford Dr., Toronto, ON M3C 1J4
Tel: 416-441-2111 *Fax:* 416-441-2114
Toll-Free: 1-888-857-6069
info@dmsu.com
www.dmsu.com

Number of Beds: 20 in-patient beds
Note: Hospital Specialties: Opthamology; Orthopedic surgery; Plastic & reconstructive surgery; Number of Employees: 16 surgeons; 10 anesthesiologists
Dr. Robert G. Gordon, Superintendent

Toronto: St. Joseph's Infirmary Former Name: St. Joseph's Morrow Park Infirmary & Private Hospital

3377 Bayview Ave., Toronto, ON M2M 2S4
Tel: 416-222-1101 *Fax:* 416-222-0186

Number of Beds: 57 beds
Catherine McDonough, Administrator
Diane Hibrant, Nursing Administrator

Woodbridge: Cosmetic Surgery Hospital (CSH)

The Manor, 4650 Hwy. 7, Woodbridge, ON L4L 1S7
Tel: 905-851-7701 *Fax:* 905-856-4406
info@cosmeticsurgeryhospital.com
www.cosmeticsurgeryhospital.com

Year Founded: 1970
Note: Hospital Specialties: Plastic & cosmetic surgery; Clinical obesity
Dr. Lloyd N. Carlsen, Director
Dr. Paul Braude, Medical Director, Ageless

Woodstock: Woodstock Private Hospital

369 Huron St., Woodstock, ON N4S 7A5
Tel: 519-537-8162 *Fax:* 519-537-7204
wph@gtn.net

Number of Beds: 16 beds
Note: Chronic care hospital
Irma C. Vander Zwaag, Administrator
Marg Atkinson, Head, Housekeeping

Auxiliary Hospitals

Toronto: Baycrest Hospital Baycrest Geriatric Health Care System

3560 Bathurst St., Toronto, ON M6A 2E1
Tel: 416-785-2500 *Fax:* 416-785-2378
webmaster@baycrest.org
www.baycrest.org

Year Founded: 1986
Number of Beds: 300 hospital beds
Note: Hospital Specialties: Acute geriatric care; Rehabilitation; Psychiatry; Behavioural neurology; Complex continuing care for the elderly; Palliative care
William Reichman, President; Chief Executive Officer
David Conn, Vice-President, Education
Laurie Harrison, Chief Financial Officer; Vice-President, Corporate Services
Paul Katz, Chief of Staff; Vice-President, Medical Services
Joni Kent, Vice-President, Human Resources & Organizationa Effectiveness
Karima Velji, Chief Nursing Executive; Vice-President, Clinical; Residential Programs
Nancy Webb, Vice-President, Public Affairs & Stakeholders Relations

Welland: Welland Hospital Site (NHS) Niagara Health System / Système de santé de Niagara

Third St., Welland, ON L3B 4W6
Tel: 905-378-4647 *Fax:* 905-732-3268
www.niagarahealth.on.ca

Year Founded: 1908
Number of Beds: 160 beds
Note: Hospital Specialties: Emergency service; Intensive care; Acute care; Ambulatory care; Maternal & child care services; Ontario Breast Screening Program; Dialysis; Nephrology; Mental health services; Complex continuing care
Debbie Sevenpifer, President; Chief Executive Officer, Niagara Health System
Christine Clark, Chief Communications Officer, Niagara Health System
Sue Matthews, Chief Nursing Executive; Vice-President, Patient Services, Welland Hospital Site
Su Bolibruck, Director, Clinical Programs (Chronic Kidney Disease, Cardiolo
905-378-4647, ext. 3
Patricia Morka, Director, Clinical Programs (Emergency & Critical Care)
905-378-4647, ext. 3
Debbie Smith, Director, Clinical Programs (Primary Care Services)
905-378-4647, ext. 5

Community Health Centres

Community Health Care Centres

Ajax: The Youth Centre Former Name: Barbara Black Centre for Youth Resources

#5, 360 Bayly St. West, Ajax, ON L1S 1P1
Tel: 905-428-1212 *Fax:* 905-428-9151
www.theyouthcentre.ca
Social Media:
www.facebook.com/pages/The-Youth-Centre/10821991386

Susan Bland, Executive Director

Barrie: Barrie Community Health Centre

56 Bayfield St., Barrie, ON L4M 3A5
Tel: 705-734-9690 *Fax:* 705-734-0239
bchc@csolve.net
www.bchc.ca

Note: Community-focused health promotion, illness prevention, & primary care services. Services provided by physicians, registered nurses, social workers, physiotherapists, & dietitians. North Innisfil office located at: 902 Lockhart Rd., 705-431-9245.
Carla Palmer, Executive Director

Barrie: CCAC North Simcoe Muskoka

#100, 15 Sperling Dr., Barrie, ON L4M 6K9
Tel: 705-721-8010 *Fax:* 705-792-6294
Toll-Free: 888-721-2222 ex
www.ccac-ont.ca

Note: With offices in Barrie & Huntsville, provides health & personal support services for individuals living independently at home or making the transition to alternative care settings; information & referral, advocacy.
Al Scarth, Board Chair

Belleville: CCAC South East - Belleville Branch Office

Bayview Mall, 470 Dundas St. East, Belleville, ON K8N 1G1
Tel: 613-966-3530 *Fax:* 613-966-0996
Toll-Free: 1-800-668-0901
www.ccac-ont.ca

John Hill, Board Chair

Brampton: CCAC Central West

199 County Court Blvd., 3rd Fl., Brampton, ON L6W 4P3
Tel: 905-796-0040 *Fax:* 905-796-5620
Toll-Free: 1-800-733-1177
www.ccac-ont.ca

David Lehtovaara, Board Chair

Brantford: CCAC Hamilton Niagara Haldimand Brant - Brant Branch Office

274 Colborne St., Brantford, ON N3T 2H5
Tel: 519-759-7752 *Fax:* 519-759-7130
Toll-Free: 1-866-759-7752
www.ccac-ont.ca

Note: Head office for the region
Melody Miles, Executive Director

Burlington: CCAC Hamilton Niagara Haldimand Brant - Burlington Branch Office

440 Elizabeth St., 4th Fl., Burlington, ON L7R 2M1
Tel: 905-639-5228 *Fax:* 905-639-5320
Toll-Free: 1-800-810-0000
www.ccac-ont.ca

Melody Miles, Executive Director

Cambridge: Langs Farm Village Association

1145 Concession Rd., Cambridge, ON N3H 4L5
Tel: 519-653-1470 *Fax:* 519-653-6277
info@langs.org

William Davidson, Executive Director
519-653-1470 ext 236, billd@langs.org
Kerry-Lynn Wilkie, Director Programs, Partnerships, & Evaluation
519-653-1470 ext 234, kerrylynnw@langs.org

Chatham: CCAC Erie St. Clair

PO Box 306, 712 Richmond St., Chatham, ON N7M 5K4
Tel: 519-436-2222 *Toll-Free:* 888-447-4468
www.ccac-ont.ca

Note: Head Office located at the Chatham-Kent branch, with other branch offices located in Sarnia & Windsor. Provides access to in-home health & personal support services to help individuals live independently at home, & assists with the transition to long term care when living at home is no longer possible
Rose Scott, Board Chair

Cornwall: CCAC North East Cornwall Branch Office

709 Cotton Mill St., Cornwall, ON K6H 7K7
Tel: 613-936-1171 *Fax:* 800-274-6955
Toll-Free: 800-267-0852
information@champlain.ccac-ont.ca
www.ccac-ont.ca

David Marshall, Executive Director

Cornwall: Centre de santé communautaire de l'Estrie

#6, 841, rue Sydney, Cornwall, ON K6H 3J7
Tél: 613-937-2683 *Téléc:* 613-937-2698
info@cscestrie.on.ca
www.cscestrie.on.ca
Média social:
www.facebook.com/pages/CSCE/179209222111118;
twitter.com/CSCE

Marc Bisson

Emo: Emo Health Centre Affiliated with: Riverside Health Care Facilities Inc.

PO Box 390, 260 Front St., Emo, ON P0W 1E0
Tel: 807-482-2881 *Fax:* 807-482-2493
www.riversidehealthcare.ca

Number of Beds: 12 long-term, 3 acute care beds
Wayne Woods

Forest: North Lambton Community Health Centre Affiliated with: Erie St. Clair Local Health Integration Network

PO Box 1120, 3 - 59 King St. West, Forest, ON N0N 1J0
Tel: 519-786-4545 *Fax:* 519-786-6318
nlinfo@nlchc.com
www.nlchc.com
Social Media: www.facebook.com/NorthLambtonCHC

Mac Redmond, Executive Director

Grand Bend: Grand Bend Area Community Health Centre
PO Box 1269, 29 Gill Rd., Grand Bend, ON N0M 1T0
Tel: 519-238-2362 *Fax:* 519-238-6478
www.gbachc.ca

Dr. Glenn Bartlett, Executive Director

Guelph: Waterloo Wellington CCAC - Guelph Branch
Also Known As: WWCCAC
#201, 450 Speedvale Ave. West, Guelph, ON N1H 7G7
Tel: 519-823-2550 *Fax:* 519-823-8682
Toll-Free: 888-883-3313
information@ww.ccac-ont.ca
www.ww.ccac-ont.ca

Note: Long-term care placement services; information & referral to other community services; in-home health services; school health support services; access to long-term care facilities; access to adult day programs; mental health & palliative care services

Hamilton: CCAC Hamilton Niagara Haldimand Brant - Hamilton Branch Office
310 Limeridge Rd. West, Hamilton, ON L9C 2V2
Tel: 905-523-8600 *Fax:* 905-528-1883
Toll-Free: 1-800-450-8002
www.ccac-ont.ca

Melody Miles, Executive Director

Hamilton: Centre de santé communautaire Hamilton/Niagara
460, rue Main est, 2e étage, Hamilton, ON L8N 1K4
Tél: 905-528-0163 *Téléc:* 905-528-9196
cschn@cschn.ca
www.centredesantecommunautaire.com

Robert Bisson, Directeur général

Hamilton: Hamilton Urban Core Community Health Centre
71 Rebecca St., Hamilton, ON L8R 1B6
Tel: 905-522-3233 *Fax:* 905-522-3433
dbrooks@hucchc.com
www.hucchc.com

Denise Brooks, Executive Director
dbrooks@hucchc.com

Hamilton: North Hamilton Community Health Centre
554 John St. North, Hamilton, ON L8L 4S1
Tel: 905-523-6611 *Fax:* 905-523-5173
www.northhamiltonchc.org

Year Founded: 1987
Note: Offers a variety of services and programs, including programs for men and women living with HIV/AIDS and programs for new immigrants/refugees
Beth Beader, Executive Director

Huntsville: Muskoka-East Parry Sound CCAC
100 Frank Miller Dr., Huntsville, ON P1H 1H7
Tel: 705-789-6451 *Fax:* 705-789-1982
www.mahc.ca

Vaughn Adamson, Executive Director

Ignace: Mary Berglund Community Health Centre (MBCHC)
PO Box 450, Ignace, ON P0T 1T0
Tel: 807-934-6719 *Fax:* 807-934-6552
mbchced@bellnet.ca
www.maryberglundchc.com

Note: Specialties: Primary care; Public health nursing; Physiotherapy; Chronic disease follow-up; Health promotion; Men's & women's wellness clinics; Blood sugar & blood pressure screening programs; Chiropractic services; Massage therapy
Lillian Napierala, Executive Director

Kenora: CCAC North West - Kenora Branch Office
21 Wolsley St., 2nd Fl., Kenora, ON P9N 3W7
Tel: 807-467-4757 *Fax:* 807-468-1437
Toll-Free: 1-877-661-6621
www.ccac-ont.ca

Tuija Puiras, Executive Director
tuija.puiras@nw.ccac-ont.ca

Kingston: CCAC South East - Kingston Head Office
#300, 1471 John Counter Blvd., Kingston, ON K7M 8S8
Tel: 613-544-8200 *Fax:* 613-544-3888
www.ccac-ont.ca

John Hill, Board Chair

Kingston: North Kingston Community Health Centre
400 Elliot Ave., Kingston, ON K7K 6M9
Tel: 613-542-2949 *Fax:* 613-542-3872
info@nkchc.kchc.ca
www.kchc.ca/nkchc

Hersh Sehdev, Executive Director

Kirkland Lake: CCAC North East Kirkland Lake Branch Office
53 Government Rd. West, Kirkland Lake, ON P2N 2E5
Tel: 705-567-2222 *Fax:* 705-567-9407
Toll-Free: 888-602-2222
www.ccac-ont.ca

Denis Labelle, Executive Director
denis.labelle@timisk.ccac-ont.ca

Kitchener: CCAC Waterloo Wellington
800 King St. West, Kitchener, ON N2G 1E8
Tel: 519-748-2222 *Fax:* 519-883-5555
Toll-Free: 1-888-883-3313
information@ww.ccac-ont.ca
www.ccac-ont.ca

Note: Head office for the region
Helene Ireton, Executive Assistant

Kitchener: Kitchener Downtown Community Health Centre
59 Frederick St., Kitchener, ON N2H 2L3
Tel: 519-745-4404 *Fax:* 519-745-3709
mail@kdchc.org
www.kdchc.org

Sheila Braidek, Executive Director

Lanark: North Lanark County Community Health Centre
207 Robertson Dr., Lanark, ON K0G 1K0
Tel: 613-259-2182 *Fax:* 613-259-5235
Toll-Free: 866-762-0496
lmahon@lanarkcounty.ca
northlanarkchc.on.ca

Wanda MacDonald

Lindsay: CCAC Central East - Lindsay Branch Office
370 Kent St. W, Lindsay, ON K9V 6G8
Tel: 705-324-9165 *Fax:* 705-324-0884
Toll-Free: 1-800-347-0285
www.cacc-ont.ca

William N. Botshka, Board Chair

London: CCAC London & Eastern Middlesex
356 Oxford St. West, London, ON N6H 1T3
Tel: 519-473-2222 *Fax:* 519-472-4045
Toll-Free: 1-800-811-5146
info-london@sw.ccac-ont.ca
www.ccac-ont.ca

Note: Head office for the South West CCAC & regional office for London & E. Middlesex
Sandra Coleman, Executive Director, South West CCAC

London: London InterCommunity Health Centre
659 Dundas St. East, London, ON N5W 2Z1
Tel: 519-660-0874 *Fax:* 519-642-1532
mail@lihc.on.ca (General); orders@lihc.on.ca (Resources)
www.lihc.on.ca

Year Founded: 1989
Note: Specialties: Inclusive & equitable health & social services to persons who experience barriers to care; Mental health care; Diabetes program; Options clinic HIV anonymous testing; Health & youth outreach services. Number of employees: 70
Michelle Hurtubise

Longlac: NorWest Community Health Centre - Longlac Site
PO Box 910, 99 Skinner Ave., Longlac, ON P0T 1T0
Tel: 807-876-2271 *Fax:* 807-876-2473
www.norwestchc.org/longlac.htm

Merrickville: Merrickville District Community Health Centre
PO Box 550, 354 Read St., Merrickville, ON K0G 1N0
Tel: 613-269-3400 *Fax:* 613-269-4958
info@mdchc.on.ca
www.mdchc.on.ca

Note: Specialties: Social work; Dietitian services; Health education; Individual & family counselling; Case management, such as asthma; Foot care services; Flu clinics; Immunizations
Peter McKenna, Executive Director

Mount Brydges: Southwest Middlesex Health Centre
22262 Mill Rd., RR#5, Mount Brydges, ON N0L 1W0
Tel: 519-264-2800 *Fax:* 519-264-2742
www.smhc.net

Year Founded: 1974
Area Served: Mount Brydges & the surrounding area
Note: Appointments are necessary.
Gary Wood, Centre Administrator

New Liskeard: Centre de santé communautaire du Témiskaming
CP 38, 83, av Whitewood, New Liskeard, ON P0J 1P0
Tél: 705-647-5775 *Téléc:* 705-647-6011
Jocelyne Maxwell, Directrice générale

Newmarket: CCAC Central - Newmarket Head Office
Former Name: Etobicoke & York CCAC
#1, 1100 Gorham St., Newmarket, ON L3Y 8Y8
Tel: 905-895-1240
info@central.ccac-ont.ca
www.ccac-ont.ca

Vikram Gulati, Board Chair

North Bay: Near North CCAC
1164 Devonshire Ave., North Bay, ON P1B 6X5
Tel: 705-476-2222 *Fax:* 705-476-6719
Toll-Free: 888-533-2222
www.nearnorth.ccac-ont.ca

Lloy Schindeler, Executive Director

Oshawa: Oshawa Community Health Centre
Dr. Bryce A. Brown Wellness Centre, 115 Grassmere Ave., Oshawa, ON L1H 3X7
Tel: 905-723-0036 *Fax:* 905-432-3902
info@ochc.ca; help@ochc.ca (Volunteering & support
www.ochc.ca

Note: Specialties: Child development; Youth recreation; Women's wellness; Health promotion; Fmaily community outreach; Education services, such as the diabetes education program; Counselling; Parenting groups; Regular check-ups; Rehabilitation
Lee Kierstead, Executive Director

Ottawa: Bruyère Continuing Care
Former Name: Sisters of Charity of Ottawa Health Service, Élisabeth Bruyère Pavilion
43 Bruyère St., Ottawa, ON K1N 5C8
Tel: 613-562-0050 *Fax:* 613-562-6367
communications@bruyere.org
www.bruyere.org

Year Founded: 1993
Number of Beds: 757 beds
Note: hospital with complex continuing care, rehabilitation, palliative care & long term care services; includes Elisabeth-Bruyere Health Centre, Saint-Vincent Hospital, Résidence Saint-Louis & Villa Marguerite
Jean Bartkowiak, President; CEO

Ottawa: Carlington Community & Health Services
900 Merivale Rd., Ottawa, ON K1Z 5Z8
Tel: 613-722-4000 *Fax:* 613-761-1805
TTY: 613-761-2161
info@carlington.ochc.org
www.carlington.ochc.org

Michael Birmingham, Executive Director

Ottawa: CCAC Champlain
#100, 4200 Labelle St., Ottawa, ON K1J 1J8
Tel: 613-745-5525 *Fax:* 613-745-6984
Toll-Free: 1-800-538-0520
information@champlain.ccac-on.ca
www.ccac-ont.ca

Note: Health & personal support services for individuals living independently at home or recuperating from a hospital stay; advocacy for seniors; support for caregivers & families; assistance with transition to new care settings; information & referral. Serving communities of Renfrew County, Ottawa, & the Eastern Counties
Lynn Graham, Board Chair

Ottawa: Centretown Community Health Centre
420 Cooper St., Ottawa, ON K2P 2N6
Tel: 613-233-4443 *Fax:* 613-233-3987
info@centretownchc.org
www.centretownchc.org
Social Media:
www.facebook.com/CentretownCHC.CSCduCentreville;
twitter.com/centretownchc

Ottawa: Ottawa Community Care Access Centre (CCAC)/Centre d'accès aux soins communautaires
#100, 4200 Labelle St., Ottawa, ON K1J 1J8
Tel: 613-745-5525 *Fax:* 613-745-6984
Toll-Free: 800-538-0520
TTY: 613-745-0049
information@champlain.ccac-ont.ca
www.ccac-ont.ca

Note: Specialties: Home care; Coordination of community care; Information about long-term care options
Sandra Golding, Executive Director

Ottawa: Pinecrest-Queensway Health & Community Services (PQCHC)
1365 Richmond Rd., 2nd Fl., Ottawa, ON K2B 6R7
Tel: 613-820-4922 *Fax:* 613-820-2006
general@pqhcs.com
www.pqchc.com
Wanda MacDonald, Executive Director

Ottawa: Sandy Hill Community Health Centre
211 Nelson St., Ottawa, ON K1N 1C7
Tel: 613-789-1500 *Fax:* 613-789-7962
info@sandyhillchc.on.ca
www.sandyhillchc.on.ca

Note: Provides a variety of Health and Social Services in the Eastern Ottawa region
Karen Patzer, Executive Director

Ottawa: Somerset West Community Health Centre
55 Eccles St., Ottawa, ON K1R 6S3
Tel: 613-238-8210 *Fax:* 613-238-7595
info@swchc.on.ca
www.swchc.on.ca
Jack McCarthy, Executive Director

Ottawa: South-East Ottawa Centre for a Healthy Community
#600, 1355 Bank St., Ottawa, ON K1H 8K7
Tel: 613-737-5115 *Fax:* 613-739-8199
office@seochc.on.ca
www.seochc.on.ca

Owen Sound: CCAC North Bruce & Grey Counties
255 - 18th St. West, Owen Sound, ON N4K 6Y1
Tel: 519-371-2112 *Fax:* 519-371-5612
Toll-Free: 1-888-371-2112
www.ccac-ont.ca
Sandra Coleman, Executive Director, South West CCAC

Parry Sound: West Parry Sound Health Centre
6 Albert St., Parry Sound, ON P2A 3A4
Tél: 705-746-9321
www.wpshc.com
Fondée en: 1897
Nombre de lits: 49 beds
Note: Acute & complex continuing care, rehabilitation, on-site Lakeland Long Term Care Facility (90 beds), Community Care Access Centre, emergency services, surgery, diagnostic imaging, chemotherapy, sleep disorder clinic, lab, telehealth, Base Hospital Program & nursing stations in Britt, Pointe au Baril, Rosseau, Whitestone, Argyle & Moosedeer, specialist clinics
Norm Maciver, CEO

Peterborough: CCAC Central East - Peterborough Branch Office
#202, 700 Clonsilla Ave., Peterborough, ON K9J 5Y3
Tel: 705-743-2212 *Fax:* 705-743-9559
Toll-Free: 1-888-235-7222
www.ccac-ont.ca
William N. Botshka, Board Chair

Portland: Country Roads Community Health Centre
PO Box 58, 4319 Cove Rd., Portland, ON K0G 1V0
Tel: 613-272-3302 *Fax:* 613-272-3463
Toll-Free: 888-998-9927
info@crchc.on.ca
Sandra Chant, Executive Director

Richmond Hill: CCAC Central - Richmond Hill Site
Former Name: York Region CCAC
#400, 9050 Yonge St., Richmond Hill, ON L4C 9S6
Tel: 905-763-9928
info@central.ccac-ont.ca
www.ccac-ont.ca
Vikram Gulati, Board Chair

Sault Ste Marie: Algoma Community Care Access Centre
390 Bay St. 2nd Fl., Sault Ste Marie, ON P6A 1X2
Tel: 705-949-1650 *Fax:* 705-949-1663
Toll-Free: 800-668-7705
marjo.keranen@algoma.ccac-ont.ca
www.ccac-ont.ca
Jim Dalgliesh, Executive Director

Sault Ste Marie: Group Health Centre Sault Ste. Marie
240 McNabb St., Sault Ste Marie, ON P6B 1Y5
Tel: 705-759-1234 *Fax:* 705-759-7469
Toll-Free: 800-461-2407
inquiries@ghc.on.ca
www.ghc.on.ca

Note: GHC is a progressive, multidisciplinary, consumer-sponsored health care facility, built by private funds donated by local union members. A partnership of the Sault Ste. Marie & District Group Health Association & the Algoma District Medical Group. Number of staff: 300+
Tom Bonell, Chairman, Group Health Association

Seaforth: CCAC Huron County
PO Box 580, 32 Centennial Dr., Seaforth, ON N0K 1W0
Tel: 519-527-0000 *Fax:* 519-527-1255
Toll-Free: 1-800-267-0535
www.ccac-ont.ca
Sandra Coleman, Executive Director, South West CCAC

Simcoe: CCAC Hamilton Niagara Haldimand Brant - Haldimand-Norfolk Branch Office
76 Victoria St., Simcoe, ON N3Y 1L5
Tel: 519-426-7400 *Fax:* 519-426-4384
Toll-Free: 1-800-265-8068
www.ccac-ont.ca
Melody Miles, Executive Director

Smiths Falls: CCAC South East - Smith Falls Branch Office
#1, 52 Abbott St. North, Smiths Falls, ON K7A 1W3
Tel: 613-283-8012 *Fax:* 613-283-0308
Toll-Free: 1-800-267-6041
www.ccac-ont.ca
John Hill, Board Chair

St Catharines: CCAC Hamilton Niagara Haldimand Brant - Niagara Branch Office
149 Hartzel Rd., St Catharines, ON L2P 1N6
Tel: 905-684-9441 *Fax:* 905-684-8463
Toll-Free: 1-800-263-5480
www.ccac-ont.ca
Melody Miles, Executive Director

St Jacobs: Woolwich Community Health Centre
10 Parkside Dr., St Jacobs, ON N0B 2N0
Tel: 519-664-3794 *Fax:* 519-664-2182
genmail@wchc.on.ca
www.wchc.on.ca
Denise Squire, Executive Director

St Thomas: CCAC Elgin County
294 Talbot St., St Thomas, ON N5P 4E3
Tel: 519-631-9907 *Fax:* 519-631-2236
Toll-Free: 1-800-563-3098
info-stthomas@sw.ccac-ont.ca
www.ccac-ont.ca
Sandra Coleman, Executive Director, South West CCAC

Stratford: CCAC Perth County
Former Name: Perth County Community Care Access Centre
65 Lorne Ave. East, Stratford, ON N5A 6S4
Tel: 519-273-2222 *Fax:* 519-273-2139
Toll-Free: 1-800-269-3683
www.ccac-ont.ca
Sandra Coleman, Executive Director, South West CCAC

Sudbury: Centre de santé communautaire de Sudbury
19, rue de Frood, Sudbury, ON P3C 4Y9
Tél: 705-670-2274 *Téléc:* 705-670-2277
www.santesudbury.ca
Yves Doyon, Président

Sudbury: Manitoulin-Sudbury CCAC
1760 Regent St. South, Sudbury, ON P3E 3Z8
Tel: 705-522-3461 *Fax:* 705-522-8018
Toll-Free: 800-461-2919
info@ms.ccac-ont.ca
www.ms.ccac-ont.ca
Nancy Mongeon, Executive Director

Thunder Bay: NorWest Community Health Centre - Thunder Bay Site
525 Simpson St., Thunder Bay, ON P7C 3J6
Tel: 807-622-8235 *Fax:* 807-622-7637
kbinette@norwestchc.org
www.norwestchc.org/thunder_bay.htm
Wendy Talbot, Executive Director

Timmins: Cochrane District CCAC
Also Known As: Timmins Branch Office
#101, 330 Second Ave., Timmins, ON P4N 8A4
Tel: 705-267-7766 *Fax:* 705-267-7795
Toll-Free: 888-668-2222
www.ccac-ont.ca
Richard Joly, CEO

Timmins: Misiway Milopemahtesewin Community Health Centre
130 Wilson Ave., Timmins, ON P4N 2S9
Tel: 705-264-2200 *Fax:* 705-264-2243
misiwayoa@vianet.ca
www.misiway.ca
Cah-Ling Lew, Executive Director

Tobermory: Tobermory Clinic
Grey Bruce Health Services
7275 Hwy. 6, Tobermory, ON NOH 270
Tel: 519-793-3445
www.gbhs.on.ca/tobermory.php

Note: Specialties: Family health; Community care; Minor day surgery; Mental health counselling. Number of Employees: 4 physicians + 1 nurse practitioner + 1 social worker + several clinic nurses

Toronto: Access Alliance Multicultural Community Health Centre
#500, 340 College St., Toronto, ON M5T 3A9
Tel: 416-324-8677 *Fax:* 416-324-9074
mail@accessalliance.ca
www.accessalliance.ca

Note: Provides community health services to refugees & immigrants
Axelle Janczur, Executive Director

Toronto: Anishnawbe Health Toronto
225 Queen St. East, Toronto, ON M5A 1S4
Tel: 416-360-0486 *Fax:* 416-365-1083
www.aht.ca
Year Founded: 1984
Note: An accredited community health centre, utilizing traditional healing approaches. A range of services is available, including fetal alcohol spectrum disorder services, diabetic care, HIV testing, mental health services & psychiatry, counselling, naturopathy, chiropody, women's services, massage therapy, & dental services. Other centres located at: 179 Gerrard St. E., 416-920-2605; and 22 Vaughan Rd., 416-657-0379. Mental Health Crisis Management Service: 416-891-8606.
Joe Hester, Executive Director

Toronto: Anne Johnston Health Station
2398 Yonge St., Toronto, ON M4P 2H4
Tel: 416-486-8666 *Fax:* 416-486-8660
TTY: 416-486-6759
info@ajhs.ca
www.ajhs.ca

Toronto: Bernard Betel Centre for Creative Living
1003 Steeles Ave. West, Toronto, ON M2R 3T6
Tel: 416-225-2112 *Fax:* 416-225-2097
reception@betelcentre.org
www.betelcentre.org

Note: provide education, recreation, arts, fitness and health services
Adam Silver, Acting Executive Director
416-225-2112 ext 135, adams@betelcentre.org

Toronto: Black Creek Community Health Centre
#5, 2202 Jane St., Toronto, ON M3M 1A4
Tel: 416-249-8000 *Fax:* 416-249-4594
www.bcchc.com
Cary Milner, Executive Director

Toronto: CCAC Central - Sheppard Site
#700, 45 Sheppard Ave. East, Toronto, ON M2N 5W9
Tel: 416-222-2241
info@central.ccac-ont.ca
www.ccac-ont.ca
Vikram Gulati, Board Chair

***Toronto:* CCAC Central East - Scarborough Branch Office**
1940 Eglinton Ave. East, 3rd Fl., Toronto, ON M1L 4R1
Tel: 416-750-2444 *Fax:* 416-750-4117
Toll-Free: 1-866-779-1931
www.ccac-ont.ca
William N. Botshka, Board Chair

***Toronto:* CCAC Toronto Central**
#305, 250 Dundas St. West, Toronto, ON M5T 2Z5
Tel: 416-506-9888 *Fax:* 416-506-0374
Toll-Free: 1-866-243-0061
toronto_ccac@toronto.ccac-ont.ca
www.ccac-ont.ca
Judith Hayward, Board Chair

***Toronto:* CCAC Toronto Central - Leaside Park Drive Site-East York**
Former Name: East York Access Centre
#1, 1 Leaside Park Dr., Toronto, ON M4H 1R1
Tel: 416-423-3559 *Fax:* 416-423-9800
toronto_ccac@toronto.ccac-ont.ca
www.ccac-ont.ca
Judith Hayward, Executive Director

***Toronto:* Central Toronto Community Health Centres Queen West Community Health Centre**
168 Bathurst St., Toronto, ON M5V 2R4
Tel: 416-703-8482 *Fax:* 416-703-8479
www.ctchc.com
Note: Medical services (with specialized services for the homeless), psychiatric & mental health services, individual & group counselling, harm reduction program (safer sex, safer drug use, Hepatitis C & HIV prevention), needle exchange, diabetes education program, chiropody, perinatal nursing, dental clinic.
Hal DeLair, Executive Director

***Toronto:* Central Toronto Community Health Centres Shout Clinic**
467 Jarvis St., Toronto, ON M4Y 2G8
Tel: 416-927-8553 *Fax:* 416-927-9365
info@ctchc.com
www.ctchc.com
Year Founded: 1992
Note: Walk-in medical clinic providing comprehensive health care services to homeless & street involved youth, 16-24 years of age.
Hal DeLair, Executive Director

***Toronto:* Centre francophone de Toronto**
Ancien nom: Centre médico-social communautaire
22, rue College, Toronto, ON M5G 1K3
Tél: 416-922-2672 *Téléc:* 416-922-6624
www.centrefranco.org
Lisa Marie Baudry, Directrice générale

***Toronto:* Davenport Perth Neighbourhood Centre (DPNCHC)**
1900 Davenport Rd., Toronto, ON M6N 1B7
Tel: 416-658-6812 *Fax:* 416-656-1264
info@dpnchc.ca
dpnchc.ca
Keith McNair, Executive Director

***Toronto:* East End Community Health Centre**
343 Coxwell Ave., Toronto, ON M4L 3B5
Tel: 416-778-5858 *Fax:* 416-778-5855
Joyce Kalsen, Executive Director

***Toronto:* Family Health Centre**
Toronto East General Hospital
840 Coxwell Ave., Toronto, ON M4C 5T2
Tel: 416-469-6464 *Fax:* 416-469-6164
ptrep@tegh.on.ca (Patients); community@tegh.on.ca (Community)
www.tegh.on.ca
Year Founded: 2002
Note: Specialties: Low-risk obstetrics; Psychotherapy; Telephone health advisory service

***Toronto:* Flemingdon Health Centre**
10 Gateway Blvd., Toronto, ON M3C 3A1
Tel: 416-429-4991 *Fax:* 416-422-3573
fhcinfo@fhc-chc.com
www.fhc-chc.com
Peter Yue, Executive Director

***Toronto:* Four Villages Community Health Centre**
1700 Bloor St. West, Toronto, ON M6P 4C3
Tel: 416-604-0640 *Fax:* 416-604-3367
www.4villageschc.ca
Almerinda Rebelo, Executive Director

***Toronto:* Lawrence Heights Community Health Centre**
12 Flemington Rd., Toronto, ON M6A 2N4
Tel: 416-787-2862 *Fax:* 416-787-3761
Andrea Cohen, Executive Director

***Toronto:* Parkdale Community Health Centre**
1229 Queen St. West, Toronto, ON M6K 1L2
Tel: 416-537-2455 *Fax:* 416-537-5133
Note: Specialties: Service in several languages; Primary care; Educational programs, such as pre- and post-natal classes; Support groups; Counselling; Mental health support; HIV testing
Simone Hammond, Executive Director

***Toronto:* Regent Park Community Health Centre**
465 Dundas St. East, Toronto, ON M5A 2B2
Tel: 416-364-2261 *Fax:* 416-364-0822
rpchc@regentparkchc.org
www.regentparkchc.org
Year Founded: 1973
Note: Emphasis on an integrated approach: health promotion, disease prevention, social services. A community-founded & operated facility, with a focus on comprehensive, accessible care. Services in English, Cantonese, Mandarin, Vietnames, Somali & Spanish. The Pathways to Education Program for youth at risk, created & first implemented in Regent Park, has been adopted by communities across Canada
Carolyn Acker, Executive Director

***Toronto:* Scarborough Centre for Healthy Communities**
Former Name: West Hill Community Services
2660 Eglinton Ave. East, Toronto, ON M1K 2S3
Tel: 416-284-5931 *Fax:* 416-724-5205
www.schcontario.ca
Year Founded: 1977
Number of Employees: 130
Note: 38 distinct and integrated services across 9 sites. They provide medical assistance through their clinics, are involved in a youth program and have other social support programs including a food bank.
Jeanie Joaquin, CEO
416-847-4093

***Toronto:* South Riverdale Community Health Centre**
955 Queen St. East, Toronto, ON M4M 3P3
Tel: 416-461-1925 *Fax:* 416-461-3578
www.srchc.ca
Lynne Raskin, Executive Director

***Toronto:* Stonegate Community Health Centre**
150 Berry Rd., Toronto, ON M8Y 1W3
Tel: 416-231-7070 *Fax:* 416-231-2663
info@stonegatechc.org
www.stonegatechc.org
Note: Specialties: Asthma care program research; Pre & post natal programs; Early years care programs; Women's programs; Seniors' programs; Housing support & case management
Lucia Furgivele, Executive Director

***Toronto:* Women's Health in Women's Hands**
#500, 2 Carlton St., Toronto, ON M5B 1J3
Tel: 416-593-7655 *Fax:* 416-593-5867
TTY: 416-593-5835
info@whiwh.com
www.whiwh.com
Notisha Massaquoi, Executive Director

***Tweed:* Gateway Community Health Centre**
PO Box 99, 41 McClellan St., Tweed, ON K0K 3J0
Tel: 613-478-1211 *Fax:* 613-478-6692
info@gatewaychc.org
www.gatewaychc.org
Jeanne Goodhand, Executive Director

***West Lorne:* West Elgin Community Health Centre**
PO Box 761, 168 Main St., West Lorne, ON N0L 2P0
Tel: 519-768-1715 *Fax:* 519-768-2548
info@wechc.on.ca
www.wechc.on.ca
Note: Provides health services and community programs to residents of the western Elgin area

***Whitby:* CCAC Central East - Whitby Head Office**
Former Name: Durham Access to Care
Whitby Corporate Centre, 209 Dundas St. East, 5th Fl., Whitby, ON L1N 7H8
Tel: 905-430-3308 *Fax:* 905-430-3297
Toll-Free: 1-800-263-3877
www.ccac-ont.ca
William N. Botshka, Board Chair

***Windsor:* CCAC Erie St. Clair**
Windsor Branch
5415 Tecumseh Rd. East, 2nd Fl., Windsor, ON N8T 1C5
Tel: 519-258-8211 *Fax:* 519-258-6288
Toll-Free: 888-447-4468
ccac.reception@we.ccac-ont.ca
www.we.ccac-ont.ca
Mary Wilson, Executive Director

***Windsor:* Sandwich Community Health Centre**
PO Box 7391, 749 Felix Ave., Windsor, ON N9C 4E9
Tel: 519-258-6002 *Fax:* 519-528-3693
mailbox@sandwichchc.org
www.sandwichchc.org
Year Founded: 1982

***Windsor:* Teen Health Centre**
Head Office, 1585 Ouellette Ave., Windsor, ON N8X 1K5
Tel: 519-253-8481 *Fax:* 519-253-4362
www.teenhealthcentre.com
Note: Specialties: Counselling; Primary care; Special Additions, a prenatal program; Diabetes In Action, a community based diabetes program; Street Health Homeless Initiative Program, a program to serve homeless or at-risk persons in Windsor & Essex County
Sheila Gordon, Executive Director

***Woodstock:* CCAC Oxford County**
1147 Dundas St., Woodstock, ON N4S 8W3
Tel: 519-539-1284 *Fax:* 519-539-0065
Toll-Free: 1-800-561-5490
info-woodstock@sw.ccac-ont.ca
www.ccac-ont.ca
Sandra Coleman, Executive Director, South West CCAC

Special Treatment Centres

***Barrie:* Royal Victoria Hospital of Barrie Community Care Centre for Substance Abuse**
70 Wellington St. West, Barrie, ON L4N 1K4
Tel: 705-728-4226 *Fax:* 705-728-7308
www.rvh.on.ca
Number of Beds: 17 beds
Note: Intoxification management, withdrawal management, assessments, family education, discharge planning
Jack Vandenberg, Director

***Brantford:* Lansdowne Children's Centre**
39 Mount Pleasant St., Brantford, ON N3T 1S7
Tel: 519-753-3153 *Fax:* 519-753-5927
info@lansdownecc.com
www.lansdownecentre.ca
Martin McIntyre, Director

***Cambridge:* Cambridge Site of KidsAbility - Centre for Child Development**
KidsAbility - Centre for Child Development
Former Name: Rotary Children's Centre
c/o Chaplin Family YMCA, 250 Hespeler Rd., Cambridge, ON N1R 3H3
Tel: 519-621-7580 *Fax:* 519-621-4651
www.kidsability.ca
Year Founded: 1957
Note: Specialty: Services for children & young adults with physical, developmental, & communication disabilities

***Chatham:* Children's Treatment Centre of Chatham-Kent**
Former Name: Prism Centre for Audiology & Children's Rehabilitation
355 Lark St., Chatham, ON N7L 5B2
Tel: 519-354-0520 *Fax:* 519-354-7355
Toll-Free: 877-352-0089
dlitwinmakey@childrenstreatment-ck.com
www.childrenstreatment-ck.com
Donna Litwin-Makey, Executive Director
519-354-0520 ext.228

Cornwall: **Cornwall Withdrawal Management Services**
Cornwall Community Hospital
35 Second St. East, Cornwall, ON K6H 1Z6
Tel: 613-938-8506 *Fax:* 613-938-2867
www.cornwallhospital.ca/en/WithdrawalManagement
Number of Beds: 16 beds
Note: Cornwall's Withdrawal Management Services hosts AA & NA meetings & group therapy for men & women sixteen years of age & over. Strategies & information are provided to prevent substance misuse. The organization is bilingual.

Fergus: **Fergus Site of KidsAbility - Centre for Child Development**
KidsAbility - Centre for Child Development
Former Name: Rotary Children's Centre
160 St. David St. South, Fergus, ON N1M 2L3
Tel: 519-787-2612 *Fax:* 519-843-7597
www.kidsability.ca
Year Founded: 1957
Note: Specialty: Services for children & young adults with physical, developmental, & communication disabilities

Guelph: **Guelph Site of KidsAbility - Centre for Child Development**
KidsAbility - Centre for Child Development
Former Name: Rotary Children's Centre
c/o West End Community Centre, 21 Imperial Rd. South, Guelph, ON N1K 1X3
Tel: 519-780-0186 *Fax:* 519-780-0470
www.kidsability.ca
Year Founded: 1957
Note: Specialty: Services for children & young adults with physical, developmental, & communication disabilities

Hamilton: **Hamilton Regional Cancer Centre**
699 Concession St., Hamilton, ON L8V 5C2
Tel: 905-387-9495 *Fax:* 905-575-6323
www.hrcc.on.ca
Dr. George Browman, CEO

Kingston: **Cancer Centre of Southeastern Ontario**
25 King St. West, Kingston, ON K7L 5P9
Tel: 613-544-2630 *Fax:* 613-544-9708
Toll-Free: 800-567-5722
www.krcc.on.ca

Kingston: **Child Development Centre (CDC)/Le Centre de développement de l'enfant**
Hotel Dieu Hospital
c/o Hotel Dieu Hospital, 166 Brock St., Kingston, ON K7L 5G2
Tel: 613-544-3400 *Fax:* 613-545-3557
www.kingstoncdc.ca
Area Served: Kingston & the surrounding area
Note: Most services at the Child Development Centre require physician referral. The Infant Develpment Program accepts children directly from parents.

Kingston: **Kingston Detoxification Centre**
Hotel Dieu Hospital
240 Brock St., Kingston, ON K7L 5G2
Tel: 613-549-6461
www.hoteldieu.com
Note: The Detoxification Centre provides counselling, self-help groups, & referral to community services

Kitchener: **Waterloo Regional Withdrawal Management Centre**
52 Glasgow St., Kitchener, ON N2G 1N6
Tel: 519-749-4300 *Fax:* 519-749-4328
Number of Beds: 21 beds

London: **London Regional Cancer Program**
London Health Sciences Centre
PO Box 5165, 790 Commissioners Rd. East, London, ON N6A 4L6
Tel: 519-685-8600
LRCPEducation@lhsc.on.ca (Patient education)
www.lhsc.on.ca
Note: Specialties: Inpatient & outpatient cancer care; Radiation therapy; Chemotherapy; Syooirt services, such as social work & diet & nutrition counselling
Dr. Michael Sherar, Vice-President

London: **Thames Valley Children's Centre**
779 Baseline Rd. East, London, ON N6C 5Y6
Tel: 519-685-8680 *Fax:* 519-685-8689
tvcc@tvcc.on.ca; innovations@tvcc.on.ca (Innovative products/books)
www.tvcc.on.ca
Year Founded: 1949
Note: Specialties: Rehabilitation services for children with physical disabilities, developmental delays, & communication disorders; Assessment & diagnosis services; Autism intervention program; Intensive behavioural intervention; Physiotherapy; Occupational therapy; Research; School support program.
Number of Employees: 350+ + 500 volunteers + 55 students
John A. LaPorta, Exec. Director/CEO

Mississauga: **Erinoak Kids**
2277 South Millway, Mississauga, ON L5L 2M5
Tel: 905-820-7111 *Fax:* 905-820-1333
Note: Outpatient services only
Diana Thomson, Executive Director

Oshawa: **Grandview Children's Centre**
Former Name: Grandview Rehabilitation & Treatment Centre of Durham Region
600 Townline Rd. South, Oshawa, ON L1H 7K6
Tel: 905-728-1673 *Fax:* 905-728-2961
Toll-Free: 800-304-6180
www.grtc.ca
Vicky Earle, Executive Director

Ottawa: **The Ottawa Children's Treatment Centre (OCTC)/Le Centre de traitement pour enfants d'Ottawa**
395 Smyth Rd., Ottawa, ON K1H 8L2
Tel: 613-737-0871 *Fax:* 613-523-5167
Toll-Free: 800-565-4839
www.octc.ca
Note: From several locations in Ottawa & area, The Centre provides specialized care for children with multiple physical, developmental & behavioural needs. Services in English & French
Kathleen Stokely, Executive Director

Ottawa: **Ottawa Regional Cancer Centre**
General Campus, 501 Smyth Rd., Ottawa, ON K1H 1C4
Tel: 613-737-7700
patientlibrary@ottawahospital.on.ca
www.ottawahospital.on.ca/sc/cancer/index-e.asp
Note: Specialties: Screening; Early Detection; Diagnosis; Treatment; Supportive Care; Palliative Care; Research
Dr. William K. Evans, CEO

Ottawa: **Ottawa Site of The Morgentaler Clinic**
The Morgentaler Clinic
65 Bank St., Ottawa, ON K1P 5N2
Tel: 613-567-8300 *Fax:* 613-567-9128
info@yenott.com
www.morgentaler.ca
Note: Specialty: Abortion services; Counselling

Ottawa: **Rehabilitation Centre (TRC)**
The Ottawa Hospital
505 Smyth Rd., Ottawa, ON K1H 8M2
Tel: 613-737-7350
TTY: 613-526-1132
patientrelations@ottawahospital.on.ca
www.ottawahospital.on.ca
Note: Specialties: Rehabilitation of persons with a disabling physical illness or injury; Prosthetics & orthotics; Physiotherapy; Occupational therapy; Respiratory therapy; Speech-language pathology; Psychological services; Vocational rehabilitation counselling; Social work; Research
Cathy Danbrook, CEO

Peterborough: **Five Counties Children's Centre**
872 Dutton Rd., Peterborough, ON K9H 7G1
Tel: 705-748-2221 *Fax:* 705-748-3526
Toll-Free: 888-779-9916
www.fivecounties.on.ca
Note: Children with special needs 0-19 years of age
Diane Pick, CEO

Sarnia: **Pathways Health Centre for Children**
1240 Murphy Rd., Sarnia, ON N7S 2Y6
Tel: 519-542-3471 *Fax:* 519-542-4115
info@pathwayscentre.org
www.pathwayscentre.org
Note: Children's treatment centre
Jenny Greensmith, Executive Director

Sault Ste Marie: **Children's Rehabiliation Centre - Algoma**
74 Johnson Ave., Sault Ste Marie, ON P6C 2V5
Tel: 705-759-1131 *Fax:* 705-759-0783
Toll-Free: 800-268-1079
info@crcalgoma.ca
www.crcalgoma.ca
Note: Outpatient health services centre
Donna Morrison, Executive Director

Sault Ste Marie: **Sault Ste. Marie Detoxification Unit**
911 Queen St. East, Sault Ste Marie, ON P6A 2B6
Tel: 705-942-1872 *Fax:* 705-759-6369
Number of Beds: 15 beds
Note: detox centre
Raimo Viitala, Manager

St Agatha: **kidsLINK (NDSA)**
PO Box 190, 1855 Notre Dame Dr., St Agatha, ON N0B 2L0
Tel: 519-746-5437 *Fax:* 519-746-3055
Number of Beds: 26 beds
Note: Children's mental health residential & day treatment services; outpatient services, respite, prevention & early intervention for children & families
Sonia Pouyat, CEO

St Catharines: **Hôtel Dieu Shaver Health & Rehabilitation Centre**
Affiliated with: Hamilton Niagara Haldimand Brant Local Health Integration Network
Former Name: H"tel-Dieu Health Sciences Hospital - Niagara
541 Glenridge Ave., St Catharines, ON L2T 4C2
Tel: 905-685-1381 *Fax:* 905-687-3232
info@hoteldieushaver.org
www.hoteldieushaver.org
Number of Beds: 124 beds
Note: Complex Continuing Care & Rehabilitation
Jane Rufrano, CEO

St Catharines: **Niagara Peninsula Children's Centre**
567 Glenridge Ave., St Catharines, ON L2T 4C2
Tel: 905-688-3550 *Fax:* 905-688-1055
Toll-Free: 800-896-5496
info@npcc.on.ca
www.npcc.on.ca
Note: Children's rehabilitation centre
John TeBrake, Executive Director

St Catharines: **Niagara Regional Men's Withdrawal Management Service**
Affiliated with: Niagara Health System
10 Adams St., St Catharines, ON L2R 2V8
Tel: 905-682-7211
Number of Beds: 18 beds
Note: The withdrawal management service offers crisis intervention, assessments, counselling, self-help groups, & treatment referrals for inpatients & outpatients.

St Catharines: **St Catharines Detoxification (Women's) Unit**
6 Adams St., St Catharines, ON L2R 2V8
Tel: 905-687-9721 *Fax:* 905-687-9768
Number of Beds: 14 beds
Norma Medulun, Director

Sudbury: **Children's Treatment Centre**
c/o Laurentian Hospital, 1204 St Jerome St., Sudbury, ON P3A 2V9
Tel: 705-523-7337 *Fax:* 705-560-4273
Note: outpatient, community-based rehabilitation centre
Sally Spence, Coordinator
Pat Tessier, Environmental Services

Sudbury: **Women's Withdrawal Management Service**
336 Pine St., Sudbury, ON P3C 1X8
Tel: 705-671-7167 *Fax:* 705-675-5730
Number of Beds: 13 beds
Note: non-medical withdrawal management service
Amanda Conrad, Principal

Thunder Bay: **George Jeffrey Children's Treatment Centre**
200 Brock St. East, Thunder Bay, ON P7E 0A2
Tel: 807-623-4381 *Fax:* 807-623-6626
Toll-Free: 888-818-7330
www.georgejeffrey.com
Note: special needs children

Eiji Tsubouchi, CEO

Timmins: Cochrane Temiskaming Children's Treatment Centre
733 Ross Ave. East, Timmins, ON P4N 8S8
Tel: 705-264-4700 *Fax:* 705-268-3585
Toll-Free: 800-575-3210

Year Founded: 1980
Area Served: Districts of Cochrane and Temiskaming*Number of Employees:* 30
Note: Services include consultation, assessment, treatment and education.
Mary MacKay, Executive Director

Toronto: Bloorview Kids Rehab Bloorview Site
Former Name: Bloorview Children's Hospital
150 Kilgour Road, Toronto, ON M4G 1R8
Tel: 416-425-6220 *Fax:* 416-425-6591
Toll-Free: 1-800-363-2440
info@bloorview.ca
www.bloorview.ca

Number of Beds: 75
Note: pediatric rehabilitation & continuing care complex
Valerie McMurty, President/CEO

Toronto: Bob Rumball Centre for the Deaf
2395 Bayview Ave., Toronto, ON M2L 1A2
Tel: 416-449-9651 *Fax:* 416-449-8881
TTY: 416-449-2728
www.bobrumball.org

Number of Beds: 56 beds
Note: long-term care facility for the deaf
Rev. Bob Rumball, Executive Director
Robert Ray, Director, Physical Plant

Toronto: Bridgepoint Hospital
Former Name: The Riverdale Hospital
14 St. Matthews Rd., Toronto, ON M4M 2B5
Tel: 416-461-8252 *Fax:* 416-461-5696
info@bridgepointhealth.ca
www.bridgepointhealth.ca

Number of Beds: 547 beds
Note: chronic care & rehabilitation hospital
Marian Walsh, President/CEO
Bill Grant, Director, Engineering
416/461-2190
Joseph Mancuso, Director, Environmental Services & Facilities Planning
Robert Carman, Chair

Toronto: Cabbagetown Women's Clinic
302 Gerrard St. East, Toronto, ON M5A 2G7
Tel: 416-323-0642 *Fax:* 416-323-3099
Toll-Free: 800-399-1592
www.cabbagetownwomensclinic.com

Year Founded: 1989
Note: Licensed as and Independent Health facility funded by the Ontario Min. of Health & Long Term Care, the clinic provides medical services to women seeking a legal & safe abortion.

Toronto: Casey House Hospice
9 Huntley St., Toronto, ON M4Y 2K8
Tel: 416-962-7600 *Fax:* 416-962-5147
info@caseyhouse.on.ca
www.caseyhouse.com

Number of Beds: 13 beds; 120 home care clients
Note: hospice; home care office
Catherine Adam, Interim CEO
Dr. Ann Stewart, MD MSc CCFP, Medical Director
416-962-7660 ext 280

Toronto: Centre for Addiction & Mental Health ARF Site
Former Name: Addiction Research Foundation
33 Russell St., Toronto, ON M5S 2S1
Tel: 416-595-6000 *Fax:* 416-595-9997
Toll-Free: 800-463-6273
webmaster@camh.net
www.camh.net

Number of Beds: 614 beds
Note: drug rehabilitation centre
Dr. Paul Garfinkel, President; CEO

Toronto: Centre for Addiction & Mental Health (Corporate Office)
33 Russell St., Toronto, ON M5S 2S1
Tel: 416-535-8501
webmaster@camh.net
www.camh.ca

Number of Beds: 614 beds
Note: addiction treatment
Dr. Catherine Zahn, President/CEO

Toronto: Choice in Health Clinic
#301, 1678 Bloor St. West, Toronto, ON M4X 1W3
Tel: 416-975-9300 *Fax:* 416-975-0314
Toll-Free: 866-565-9300
www.choiceinhealth.ca

Note: abortion clinic
Michelle Joseph, Executive Director

Toronto: Eye Bank of Canada Ontario Division
c/o Dept. of Ophthalmology, University of Toronto, 1929 Spadina Cres., Toronto, ON M5S 2J5
Tel: 416-978-7355 *Fax:* 416-978-1522
eye.bank@utoronto.ca
www.eyebank.utoronto.ca

Dr. David Rootman, Medical Director
Dr. William Dixon, Medical Co-director

Toronto: Marvelle Koffler Breast Centre
J. & W. Lebovic Health Complex, Mount Sinai Hospit, 600 University Ave., 12th Fl., Toronto, ON M5G 1X5
Tel: 416-586-8799
www.mountsinai.on.ca/care/mkbc

Year Founded: 1995
Note: Specialties: Outpatient facility for breast health & disease; Mammography / Breast imaging; Pathology; Surgery; Psychiatry; Nutrition; Boutique addressing the needs of women who have experienced breast cancer; Palliative medicine
Dr. P. Goodwin, Director

Toronto: The Morgentaler Clinic
727 Hillsdale Ave. East, Toronto, ON M4S 1V4
Tel: 416-932-0446 *Fax:* 416-932-0837
Toll-Free: 800-556-6835
mclinic@passport.ca
www.morgentaler.ca

Note: Specialties: Abortion services; Counselling; Contraceptive education; Testing for sexually transmitted infections
Dr. Henry Morgentaler, Director

Toronto: Runnymede Healthcare Centre
625 Runnymede Rd., Toronto, ON M6P 3A3
Tel: 416-762-7316 *Fax:* 416-762-3836
www.runnymedehc.ca

Year Founded: 1945
Note: Specialties: Complex continuing care for persons with long-term disorders, such as neurological disorders; Occupational therapy; Physiotherapy; Speech-language pathology; Social work
Normand A. Allaire, President; CEO

Toronto: St. John's Rehabilitation Hospital
285 Cummer Ave., Toronto, ON M2M 2G1
Tel: 416-226-6780 *Fax:* 416-226-6265
info@stjohnsrehab.com
www.stjohnsrehab.com

Number of Beds: 160 beds
Note: Ontario's only hospital dedicated to specialized rehabilitation services & care: burn injuries, organ transplant rehabilitation, cancer, cardiovascular surgery, strokes & other neurological conditions, traumatic injuries & complex medical conditions. Teaching site for the University of Toronto & a leading research facility. A multicultural & multifaith environment dedicated to the values of care of the Sisters of St. John the Divine
Malcolm Moffat, President; CEO
Joyce Bailey, Board Chair

Toronto: St. Michael's Hospital Detoxification Centre

314 Adelaide St. East, Toronto, ON M5A 1N1
Tel: 416-864-5078 *Fax:* 416-864-5146
Number of Beds: 22 beds
Note: detoxification hospital
John Rutledge, Director

Toronto: Sunnybrook Health Sciences Centre - Holland Orthopaedic & Arthritic Centre
43 Wellesley St. East, Toronto, ON M4Y 1H1
Tel: 416-967-8500 *Fax:* 416-967-8521
www.sunnybrook.ca

Note: Care for complex injuries of the musculoskeletal system, with a focus on traumatic injury management, joint reconstruction & replacement, surgery, sports & activity-related injury management, rehabilitation, rheumatology. The Clinic has a second location at the main Sunnybrook site, 2075 Bayview Ave., Toronto
Dr. Barry A. McLellan, President/CEO

Toronto: Sunnybrook Health Sciences Centre - The Odette Cancer Centre
2075 Bayview Ave., Toronto, ON M4N 3M5
Tel: 416-480-5000 *Fax:* 416-217-1338
www.sunnybrook.ca

Note: Comprehensive cancer care, multidisciplinary, evidence-based approach; research, education & community outreach
Dr. Barry A. McLellan, President/CEO

Toronto: Toronto Rehabilitation Institute
Also Known As: Toronto Rehab
550 University Ave., Toronto, ON M5G 2A2
Tel: 416-597-3422 *Fax:* 416-597-1977
communications@torontorehab.on.ca
www.torontorehab.com

Number of Beds: 541 beds
Note: Rehabilitation & complex continuing care; includes Hillcrest Centre; Lakeside Long-Term Care Centre; Lyndhurst Centre; E.W. Bickle Centre; Rumsey Centre, & University Centre

Mark Rochon, President/CEO

Toronto: Toronto Western Hospital - Addiction Outpatient/Aftercare Clinic
399 Bathurst St., Toronto, ON M5T 2S8
Tel: 416-603-5735

Note: Assessment & referral, individual & group therapy, counseling, psychiatric consultation, education. Services in English, French, Portuguese, Polish

Toronto: University Health Network - Princess Margaret Hospital
610 University Ave., Toronto, ON M5G 2M9
Tel: 416-946-2000
uhn.info@uhn.on.ca
www.uhn.ca/PMH/

Year Founded: 1952
Number of Beds: 130 inpatient beds
Note: A teaching hospital of the University of Toronto, PMH is a global leader in the fight against cancer & one of the top cancer treatment & research centres in the world. Specialties include: surgical oncology, chemotherapy, psychosocial oncology, radiation therapy, bone marrow transplantation, radiation oncology, hematology, & medical imaging. The Ontario Cancer Institute comprises the research wing of the hospital. Staff: 139+ oncologists, 400 RN's, 1,178 support staff
Sarah Downey, Executive Director; Site Lead

Toronto: West End Creche Child & Family Clinic
197 Euclid Ave., Toronto, ON M6J 2J8
Tel: 416-868-1827 *Fax:* 416-868-1827
Tony Diniz, Executive Director

Toronto: West Park Healthcare Centre
Former Name: West Park Hospital
82 Buttonwood Ave., Toronto, ON M6M 2J5
Tel: 416-243-3600 *Fax:* 416-243-8947
feedback@westpark.org
www.westpark.org

Number of Beds: 477 beds
Note: rehabilitation & chronic care facility
Anne-Marie Malek, President/CEO
Mike Bonnah, Director, Facilities & Materials Management

Toronto: Withdrawal Management Centre Toronto East General Hospital
985 Danforth Ave., Toronto, ON M4J 1M1
Tel: 416-461-2010 *Fax:* 416-461-1164
ptrep@tegh.on.ca (Patients); community@tegh.on.ca (Community)
www.tegh.on.ca

Number of Beds: 22 beds
Note: Specialties: Crisis intervention for adult males; Physical care for males in acute states of intoxication; Withdrawal from alcohol & other addictive substances; Addictions assessments; Counselling; Rehabilitation services; Education on substance abuse to family members
D. Smith, Manager

Waterloo: KidsAbility - Centre for Child Development
Former Name: Rotary Children's Centre
500 Hallmark Dr., Waterloo, ON N2K 3P5
Tel: 519-886-8886 *Fax:* 519-886-7292
Toll-Free: 888.372.2259
www.kidsability.ca

Year Founded: 1957
Note: Specialties: Services for children & young adults with physical, developmental, & communication disabilities; Autism intervention; Occupational therapy; Physiotherapy;

Speech-language therapy; Augmentative communication; Therapeutic recreation; Social work. Number of Employees: 200 + 300 volunteers
Stephen Swatridge, Executive Director

Windsor: The John McGivney Children's Centre
Former Name: Children's Rehabilitation Centre of Essex County
3945 Matchette Rd., Windsor, ON N9C 4C2
Tel: 519-252-7281 *Fax:* 519-252-5873
info@jmccentre.ca
www.jmccentre.ca
Social Media: www.facebook.com/243715438993933
Carolyn Tavolieri, President

Windsor: Windsor Withdrawal Management Residential Service
Windsor Regional Hospital
1453 Prince Rd., Windsor, ON N9C 3Z4
Tel: 519-257-5225 *Fax:* 519-253-1752
www.wrh.on.ca
Number of Beds: 20 beds
Area Served: Counties of Essex, Kent, & Lambton, Ontario
Note: The agency assists men & women who are 16 years of age or older to access treatment for addiction. The service is funded by the Ministry of Health & Long-term Care.
Bill Marcotte, Service Director, Addiction Services
bill_marcotte@wrh.on.ca

Nursing Homes

Ailsa Craig: Craigholme Nursing Home
221 Main St. East, RR#1, Ailsa Craig, ON N0M 1A0
Tel: 519-293-3215 *Fax:* 519-293-3941
www.craigwielgardens.on.ca
Number of Beds: 83 beds

Alexandria: Community Nursing Home
PO Box 300, 92 Centre St., Alexandria, ON K0C 1A0
Tel: 613-525-2022 *Fax:* 613-525-2023
www.cnhalexandria.ca
Number of Beds: 70 beds
Terry A. Dubé
tdube@clmi.ca

Almonte: Almonte Country Haven
333 Country St., Almonte, ON K0A 1A0
Tel: 613-256-3095 *Fax:* 613-256-3096
www.omniway.com/ourhomes/almonte.htm
Number of Beds: 82 beds
Marilyn Colton, Administrator
mcolton@omniway.ca

Almonte: Fairview Manor
PO Box 1360, 75 Spring St., Almonte, ON K0A 1A0
Tel: 613-256-3113 *Fax:* 613-256-5780
tmclelland@agh-fvm.com
www.almontegeneral.com
Number of Beds: 100 beds
Mary Wilson Trider, President, CEO
613-256-2514 ext2220
Linda Chaplin, Administrator

Aurora: Willows Estate
13837 Yonge St., Aurora, ON L4G 3G8
Tel: 905-727-0128 *Fax:* 905-841-0454
www.omni-way.com
Number of Beds: 84 beds
Note: Specialties: Long-term care; Care for persons with Alzheimer's disease & dementia; Life enrichment program
Alison Duva, Office Manager
aduva@omniway.ca
Linda Burr, Administrator
lburr@omniway.ca

Aylmer: Chateau Gardens Nursing Home
465 Talbot St. West, Aylmer, ON N5H 1K8
Tel: 519-773-3423 *Fax:* 519-765-2573
www.chartwellreit.ca
Number of Beds: 59 beds
Mary Vergeer, Administrator

Aylmer: Terrace Lodge
475 Talbot St. East, 49462 Talbot Line, Aylmer, ON N5H 3A5
Tel: 519-773-9205 *Fax:* 519-765-2627
www.elginhomes.ca
Number of Beds: 100 beds
Note: Specialties: Long-term care; Secure unit; Physiotherapy; Activity program; Adult day program, including a specialized program for Alzheimer's patients; Respite care; Palliative care
Rhonda Duffy, Administrator
519-756-2627 ext 222, rduffy@elgin-county.on.ca

Bancroft: Hastings Centennial Manor
PO Box 758, 1 Manor Lane, Bancroft, ON K0L 1C0
Tel: 613-332-2070 *Fax:* 613-332-2837
www.hastingscounty.com
Number of Beds: 110 beds
Claudette Dignard-Remillard, Director
Kathy Plunkett, Site Manager

Barrie: Coleman Care Centre
140 Cundles Rd. West, RR#2, Barrie, ON L4M 4S4
Tel: 705-726-8691 *Fax:* 705-726-5085
colemancare@rogers.com
Number of Beds: 112 beds
Pam Wiebe, Administrator
pam.wiebe@schlegelvillages.com
Rita Dunn, Director Nursing Care
rita.dunn@schlegelvillages.com

Barrie: Grove Park Home for Senior Citizens
234 Cook St., Barrie, ON L4M 4H5
Tel: 705-726-1003 *Fax:* 705-726-1076
business.office@groveparkhome.on.ca
www.groveparkhome.on.ca
Number of Beds: 143 beds

Barrie: Leisureworld Caregiving Centre - Barrie
130 Owen St., Barrie, ON L4M 3H7
Tel: 705-726-8621 *Fax:* 705-726-0821
michelle.tosh@leisureworld.ca
www.leisureworld.ca/barrie.html
Number of Beds: 57 beds
Mary LaChapelle, Administrator

Barrys Bay: Valley Manor Nursing Home
PO Box 880, 88 Mintha St., Barrys Bay, ON K0J 1B0
Tel: 613-756-2643 *Fax:* 613-756-7601
www.valleymanor.org
Number of Beds: 90 beds
Note: Adult Day Program
Ron Coulas, Director, Physical Plant
Linda Shulist, Administrator

Beamsville: Albright Manor
5050 Hillside Dr., Beamsville, ON L0R 1B2
Tel: 905-563-8252 *Fax:* 905-563-5223
info@albrightcentre.ca
Number of Beds: 231 beds
John E. Buma, CEO
Margery Digiando, Admissions Coordinator
905-563-8252 ext 127

Beeton: Simcoe Manor Home for the Aged
PO Box 100, 5988 8th Line, Beeton, ON L0G 1A0
Tel: 905-729-2267 *Fax:* 905-729-4350
Number of Beds: 126 beds
Earl Gray, Supervisor

Belleville: Bellmont Long-Term Care Facility
Former Name: Montgomery Lodge Nursing Home.
250 Bridge St. West, Belleville, ON K8P 5N3
Tel: 613-968-4434 *Fax:* 613-968-5443
belmont@cogeco.net
Number of Beds: 128 beds
Denise Mackey, Administrator/Primary Executive
dmackey.belmont@cogeco.net

Belleville: Belmont Long Term Care Facility
250 Bridge St. West, Belleville, ON K8P 1B6
Tel: 613-968-4434 *Fax:* 613-968-3207
Number of Beds: 60 beds
Denise Mackey, Administrator
dmackey.belmont@cogeco.net

Belleville: Hastings Manor
PO Box 458, 476 Dundas St. West, Belleville, ON K8N 5B2
Tel: 613-968-6467 *Fax:* 613-967-0128
info@hastingsmanorfoundation.ca
www.hastingsmanorfoundation.ca
Year Founded: 1908
Number of Beds: 253 beds

Belleville: Westgate Lodge
37 Wilkie St., Belleville, ON K8P 4E4
Tel: 613-966-1323 *Fax:* 613-966-5126
admin@westgatelodge.ca
www.crownridgehealth.ca/westgate-lodge
Number of Beds: 88 beds

Bobcaygeon: Pinecrest Nursing Home
3418 County Rd. 36, RR#2, Bobcaygeon, ON K0M 1A0
Tel: 705-738-2366 *Fax:* 705-738-9414
Number of Beds: 65 beds
Note: Specialties: Activation program
Teresa Driver, Administrator

Bolton: King Nursing Home
49 Sterne St., Bolton, ON L7E 5T1
Tel: 905-857-4117 *Fax:* 905-857-5181
Year Founded: 1966
Number of Beds: 86 beds
Janice L. King, Administrator
janice.king@kingnursinghome.com

Bolton: Vera M. Davis Community Care Centre
80 Allan Dr., Bolton, ON L7E 1P7
Tel: 905-857-0975 *Fax:* 905-857-7872
Number of Beds: 64 beds
Wendy Beattie, Administrator

Bradford: Specialty Care Bradford Valley
Former Name: Bradford Place Nursing Home
2656 6th Line, RR#1, Bradford, ON L3Z 2A4
Tel: 905-952-2270 *Fax:* 905-775-0263
suggestions@specialty-care.com
www.specialty-care.com
Number of Beds: 150 beds
Luanne Campeau, Administrator
luanne.campeau@specialty-care.com

Brampton: Extendicare - Brampton
7891 McLaughlin Rd., Brampton, ON L6Y 5H8
Tel: 905-459-4904 *Fax:* 905-459-5625
cnh_brampton@extendicare.com
www.extendicarecanada.com/brampton/
Number of Beds: 150 beds

Brampton: Leisureworld Caregiving Centre - Brampton Meadows
215 Sunny Meadows Blvd., Brampton, ON L6R 3B5
Tel: 905-458-7604
adm.bm@leisureworld.ca
www.leisureworld.ca/brampton_meadows.html
Number of Beds: 160 beds
Angie Heinze, Administrator

Brampton: Leisureworld Caregiving Centre - Brampton Woods
9257 Goreway Dr., Brampton, ON L6T 3Y7
Tel: 905-799-7502
susan.wendt@leisureworld.ca
www.leisureworld.ca/brampton_woods.html
Number of Beds: 160 beds
Susan Wendt, Administrator

Brampton: Peel Manor
525 Main St. North, Brampton, ON L6X 1N9
Tel: 905-453-4140 *Fax:* 905-453-9140
Number of Beds: 177 beds
Note: Long-term care centre
Jim Egan, Administrator

Brantford: Hardy Terrace Long Term Care
612 Mount Pleasant Rd., RR#2, Brantford, ON N3T 5L5
Tel: 519-484-2431 *Fax:* 519-484-2590
Number of Beds: 69 beds
Lloyd Smith, Administrator

Brantford: Leisureworld Caregiving Centre - Brantford
389 West St., Brantford, ON N3R 3V9
Tel: 519-759-4666 *Fax:* 519-759-0200
adm.brantford@leisureworld.ca
www.leisureworld.ca/brantford.html
Number of Beds: 120 permanent, 2 short stay beds
Christy Whiddet, Director of Care
Shelley Desgagne, Administrator
adm.brantford@leisureworld.ca

Brockville: St. Lawrence Lodge
PO Box 1130, 1803 Prescott Rd. East, Brockville, ON K6V 5W2
Tel: 613-345-0255 *Fax:* 613-345-1029
info@stll.org
www.stll.org
Number of Beds: 240 beds
Note: Long-term care home
Tom Harrington, Aministraor
tharrington@stll.org

Brockville: Sherwood Park Manor
1814 County Rd. 2 East, Brockville, ON K6V 5T1
Tel: 613-342-5531 *Fax:* 613-342-3767
Number of Beds: 107 beds
Shawn Souder, Administrator
J. Vanderwal, Director, Physical Plant

Brunner: Country Meadows Retirement & Living Centre
Ana St., Lot 16, Brunner, ON N0K 1C0
Tel: 519-595-8903 *Fax:* 519-595-8272
brunner@perth.net
Number of Beds: 43 beds
Charlotte Heibein, Administrator

Brussels: Huronlea Home for the Aged
820 Turnberry St. South, Brussels, ON N0G 1H0
Tel: 519-887-9267 *Fax:* 519-482-5263
Number of Beds: 64 beds; 2 respite beds
Barb Springhall, Administrator

Burlington: Cama Woodlands Nursing Home
159 Panin Rd., Burlington, ON L7P 5A6
Tel: 905-681-6441 *Fax:* 905-681-2678
a.lawlor@bellnet.ca
www.camawoodlands.com
Number of Beds: 64 beds

Burlington: Maple Villa Long Term Care Centre
441 Maple Ave., Burlington, ON L7S 1L8
Tel: 905-639-2264 *Fax:* 905-639-3034
maplevilla@maplevilla.ca
www.maplevilla.ca
Number of Beds: 93 beds

Cambridge: Fairview Mennonite Home
515 Langs Dr., Cambridge, ON N3H 5E4
Tel: 519-653-5719 *Fax:* 519-650-1242
Number of Beds: 84 beds
Earl Gerber, Director, Maintenance
T. Kennel, Exec. Dir.

Cambridge: Golden Years Nursing Home
PO Box 3277, 704 Eagle St. North, Cambridge, ON N3H 4T3
Tel: 519-653-5493 *Fax:* 519-650-1495
nancy@goldenyearscambridge.com
www.goldenyearscambridge.com
Number of Beds: 88 beds
Nancy Kauffman-Lambert, Administrator

Campbellford: Burnbrae Gardens
320 6th Line East, Campbellford, ON K0L 1L0
Tel: 705-653-4100 *Fax:* 705-653-2598
www.omniway.ca
Number of Beds: 43 beds
Rosie Coppens, Office Manager
rcoppens@omniway.com
Rosie Coppens, Office Manager

Cannifton: E.J. McQuigge Lodge
PO Box 68, 38 Black Diamond Rd., Cannifton, ON K0K 1K0
Tel: 613-966-7717 *Fax:* 613-966-7646
www.mcquiggelodge.com
Number of Beds: 56 beds
Anita Garland, Administrator
agarland@mcquiggelodge.com

Cannington: Bon-Air Nursing Home
PO Box 400, 131 Laidlaw St. South, Cannington, ON L0E 1E0
Tel: 705-432-2385 *Fax:* 705-432-3331
www.chartwellreit.ca
Number of Beds: 55 units
Lynne Disik, Administrator

Chapleau: Bignucolo Residence
PO Box 757, 6 Broomhead Rd., Chapleau, ON P0M 1K0
Tel: 705-864-1520 *Fax:* 705-864-0449
Year Founded: 1998
Number of Beds: 25 beds
Note: Specialties: Long-term care; Chronic care; Respite care; Pet therapy

Chatham: St. Andrews Residence
99 Park St., Chatham, ON N7M 3R5
Tel: 519-354-8103 *Fax:* 519-351-2407
info@standrewsresidence.com
www.standrewsresidence.com
Number of Beds: 95 beds
W.L. Alexander, Administrator/CEO

Chesley: Elgin Abbey Nursing & Retirement Home
PO Box 7, 380 First Ave. North, Chesley, ON N0G 1L0
Tel: 519-363-3195 *Fax:* 519-363-0375
elginabbey@xplornet.ca
Number of Beds: 41 beds; 27 long-term-care, 14 retirement home
Tracee Givens, Administrator

Clinton: Huronview Home for the Aged
77722A London Rd. Hwy 4 S, RR#5, Clinton, ON N0M 1L0
Tel: 519-482-3451 *Fax:* 519-482-5263
www.huroncounty.ca/homesaged
Number of Beds: 119 beds
Barb Springall, Administrator

Cobourg: Extendicare - Cobourg
130 Densmore Rd., Cobourg, ON K9A 5W2
Tel: 905-372-0377 *Fax:* 905-372-0477
cnh_cobourg@extendicare.com
www.extendicarecanada.com
Number of Beds: 69 beds

Collingwood: Collingwood Nursing Home Limited
250 Campbell St., Collingwood, ON L9Y 4J9
Tel: 705-445-3991 *Fax:* 705-445-5060
cnh@collingwoodnursinghome.com
www.collingwoodnursinghome.com
Number of Beds: 60 beds
Peter Zober, President, Owner
peter@collingwoodnursinghome.com

Corbeil: Nipissing Manor Nursing Care Centre
1202 Hwy. 94, RR#1, Corbeil, ON P0H 1K0
Tel: 705-752-1100 *Fax:* 705-752-2570
nipissingmanor@bellnet.ca
Number of Beds: 143 beds
Wentworth E. Graham, Administrator

Cornwall: Glen-Stor-Dun Lodge
1900 Montréal Rd., Cornwall, ON K6H 7L1
Tel: 613-933-3384 *Fax:* 613-933-7214
www.cornwall.ca
Number of Beds: 132 beds
Norm Quenneville, Administrator
Donna Derouchie, Administrator

Cornwall: Parisien Manor
439 Second St. East, Cornwall, ON K6H 1Z2
Tel: 613-933-2592 *Fax:* 613-933-3839
www.parisienmanor.ca
Year Founded: 1982
Note: Specialties: Long-term care; Activation programs; Counselling; Social services; Dental services; Music therapy; Physiotherapy; Occupational therapy; Foot care
Terry Dube, Administrator

Cornwall: St. Joseph's Villa (Cornwall)
14 York St., Cornwall, ON K6J 5T2
Tel: 613-933-6040 *Fax:* 613-933-9429
executiveoffices@stjosephscentre.ca
www.stjosephscentre.ca
Number of Beds: 150 beds
Bonnie Ruest, Executive Director
Allan Greg, Director, Physical Plant

Cornwall Island: Tsi ion kwa nonh so:te
Former Name: Akwesasne Adult Care Facility
RR#3, Cornwall Island, ON K6H 5R7
Tel: 613-932-1409 *Fax:* 613-932-8845
Number of Beds: 30 beds
Note: Specialties: Geriatric residential health care; Water therapy; Palliative care
Bonnie Cole, Administrator

Creemore: Creedan Valley Nursing Home
PO Box 309, 143 Mary St., Creemore, ON L0M 1G0
Tel: 705-466-3437 *Fax:* 705-466-3063
Number of Beds: 96 beds

Creemore: Leisureworld Caregiving Centre - Creedan Valley
143 Mary St., Creemore, ON L0M 1G0
Tel: 705-466-3437
adm.creedan@leisureworld.ca
www.leisureworld.ca/creedan.html
Number of Beds: 95 beds
Paula Rentner, Administrator

Deep River: North Renfrew Long-Term Care Centre
PO Box 1988, 47 Ridge Rd., Deep River, ON K0J 1P0
Tel: 613-584-1900 *Fax:* 613-584-9183
nrltcsin@magma.ca
www.magma.ca/~nrltcsin
Number of Beds: 20 long-term care; 9 supportive care; 1 respite
Ann Aikens, Administrator

Delhi: Delhi Long Term Care Centre
750 Gibraltar St., Delhi, ON N4B 3B3
Tel: 519-582-3400 *Fax:* 519-582-0300
krusz@peoplecare.on.ca
Year Founded: 1972
Number of Beds: 60 beds
Deborah Beckman, Executive Director
Subryan Bangaru, Assistant Director Resident Care

Elmira: Leisureworld Caregiving Centre - Elmira
120 Barnswallow Dr., Elmira, ON N3B 2Y9
Tel: 519-669-5777
angie.heinz@leisureworld.ca
www.leisureworld.ca/elmira.html
Number of Beds: 92 permanent, 2 short stay beds
Cathy Holland, Administrator

Englehart: Northview Nursing Home
PO Box 1139, 77 River Rd., Englehart, ON P0J 1H0
Tel: 705-544-8191 *Fax:* 705-544-8255
northview@ntl.sympatico.ca
Number of Beds: 48 beds
Tracey Gemmill, Administrator/DOC
tgemmill@conmedhealth.com
A. Saunders, Director, Physical Plant

Espanola: Espanola Nursing Home
825 McKinnon Dr., Espanola, ON P5E 1R4
Tel: 705-869-1420 *Fax:* 705-869-1420
Number of Beds: 30 beds
Paul L. Davies, Administrator
Diane Mokohonuk, Environmental Manager

Essex: Iler Lodge
Former Name: Essex Health Care Centre
111 Iler Ave., Essex, ON N8M 1T6
Tel: 519-776-9482
www.reveraliving.com
Number of Beds: 104 beds
Cheryl Labute, Administrator

Etobicoke: Highbourne Lifecare Centre
420 The East Mall, Etobicoke, ON M9B 3Z9
Tel: 416-621-8000 *Fax:* 416-621-8003
Number of Beds: 250 beds
Evelyn McDonald, Administrator

Fergus: Wellington County Terrace Home for the Aged
474 Wellington Rd., Fergus, ON N1M 0A1
Tel: 519-846-5359
Number of Beds: 176 beds
Peter M. Barnes, Administrator
R. Granger, Purchasing Director
Don Giles, Director, Housekeeping

Forest: North Lambton Rest Home
PO Box 640, 39 Morris St., Forest, ON N0N 1J0
Tel: 519-786-2151 *Fax:* 519-786-2156
Number of Beds: 87 beds
Jeffrey J. Harvey, Manager

Fort Erie: Crescent Park Lodge
4 Hagey Ave., Fort Erie, ON L2A 5M5
Tel: 905-871-8330 *Fax:* 905-991-1456
Number of Beds: 68 beds
Lisa Hussman, Director of Nursing
Rose Turner, Administrator

Gananoque: Carveth Care Centre
375 James St., Gananoque, ON K7G 2Z1
Tel: 613-382-4752 *Fax:* 613-382-8514
brettgibson@gibsonfamilyhealthcare.ca
www.gibsonfamilyhealthcare.com
Number of Beds: 94 beds
Brett Gibson, Administrator
613-382-4752 ext.102
Ray Gentile, Supervisor, Plant Maintenance

Georgetown: Bennett Health Care Centre
1 Princess Anne Dr., Georgetown, ON L7G 2B8
Tel: 905-873-0115 *Fax:* 905-873-1403
info@bennetthealthcarecentre.ca
www.bennetthealthcarecentre.ca
Number of Beds: 66 beds
Mark Ewer, Administrator

Gloucester: Extendicare - Laurier Manor
1715 Montréal Rd., Gloucester, ON K1J 6N4
Tel: 613-741-5122 *Fax:* 613-741-8432
cnh_lauriermanor@extendicare.com
Number of Beds: 240 beds

Goderich: Maitland Manor
290 South St., Goderich, ON N7A 4G6
Tel: 519-524-7324 *Fax:* 519-524-8739
adunn@extendicare.com
Number of Beds: 91 beds
Note: Specialties: Long-term care; Restorative care programs;

Foot care; Specialized skin & wound care program; Physiotherapy; Music therapy; Respite care
Angie Dunn, Administrator

Gravenhurst: Leisureworld Caregiving Centre - Muskoka
200 Kelly Dr., Gravenhurst, ON P1P 1P3
Tel: 705-687-3444 *Fax:* 705-687-9094
admin.muskoka@leisureworld.ca
www.leisureworld.ca/muskoka.html
Year Founded: 1999
Number of Beds: 180 long-term care, 2 short term beds, 28 retirement suites
Denise Ward, Administrator
adm.muskoka@leisureworld.ca
Holly Farrell, Director of Care

Grimsby: Kilean Lodge
83 Main St. East, Grimsby, ON L3M 1N6
Tel: 905-945-9243 *Fax:* 905-945-1126
Kilean@reveraliving.com
www.reveraliving.com
Number of Beds: 50 beds
Robin Mackie, Executive Director
905-945-9243 ext2102

Grimsby: Shalom Manor
12 Bartlett Ave., Grimsby, ON L3M 4N5
Tel: 905-945-9631 *Fax:* 905-945-1211
info@shalommanor.ca
www.shalommanor.ca
Year Founded: 1966
Number of Beds: 144 beds
Note: Home for the aged affiliated with the Christian Reformed Church
Peet Konnie, CEO
Rita Fluit, Director, Nursing
Yettie Termorshuizen, Director, Environmental Services

Guelph: Eden House Nursing Home
Affiliated with: Waterloo Wellington Local Health Integration Network
5016 Wellington Rd. 29, Guelph, ON N1H 6H8
Tel: 519-856-4622 *Fax:* 519-856-1274
admin@edenhousecarehome.ca
www.edenhousecarehome.ca
Number of Beds: 58 nursing home, 21 retirement home

Guelph: Lapointe-Fisher Nursing Home
271 Metcalfe St., Guelph, ON N1E 4Y8
Tel: 519-821-9030 *Fax:* 519-821-6021
guelph@lapointefisher.ca
www.lapointefisher.ca
Number of Beds: 92 beds
Tom Hudson, Administrator
Reg Carreor, Environmental Services Supervisor

Haileybury: Extendicare - Tri-Town
PO Box 999, 143 Bruce St., Haileybury, ON P0J 1K0
Tel: 705-672-2151 *Fax:* 705-672-5348
cnh_tritown@extendicare.com
www.extendicarecanada.com
Number of Beds: 60 beds
Ghislaine Julien, Administrator

Haliburton: Extendicare - Haliburton
PO Box 780, 167 Park St., Haliburton, ON K0M 1S0
Tel: 705-457-1722 *Fax:* 705-457-3914
cnh_haliburton@extendicare.com
www.extendicarecanada.com/haliburton
Number of Beds: 60 beds
Jane Rosenberg, Administrator
Doug Holmes, Maintenance Supervisor

Halton Hills: Extendicare - Halton Hills
9 Lindsay Court, Halton Hills, ON L7G 6G9
Tel: 905-702-8760 *Fax:* 905-702-7430
cnh_haltonhills@extendicare.com
www.extendicarecanada.com/georgetown
Number of Beds: 130 beds

Hamilton: Arbour Creek Long Term Care Centre
2717 King St. East, Hamilton, ON L8G 1J3
Tel: 905-573-4900 *Fax:* 905-573-4340
thomashealthcare.com
Number of Beds: 128 beds
Shirley Thomas Weir
sthomasweir@thomashealthcare.com

Hamilton: Extendicare - Hamilton
90 Chedmac Dr., Hamilton, ON L9C 7S6
Tel: 905-318-4472 *Fax:* 905-318-1162
cnh_hamilton@extendicare.com
www.extendicarecanada.com/hamilton/
Number of Beds: 160 beds

Hamilton: Hamilton Continuing Care
125 Wentworth St. South, Hamilton, ON L8N 2Z1
Tel: 905-527-1482 *Fax:* 905-527-0679
lprestonorchard@thecaringnetwork.ca
www.hamiltonltc.com
Number of Beds: 64 beds
Lorraine Preston-Orchard, Administrator

Hamilton: Macassa Lodge
701 Upper Sherman Ave., Hamilton, ON L8V 3M7
Tel: 905-546-2800 *Fax:* 905-546-4989
saphsweb@hamilton.ca
www.hamilton.ca/phcs/macassa
Number of Beds: 270 beds
Note: Specialties: Long term care; Adult day program; Social work
Mark Ewer, Administrator

Hamilton: Parkview Nursing Centre
545 King St. West, Hamilton, ON L8P 1C1
Tel: 905-525-5903 *Fax:* 905-525-8717
www.parkviewnursingcentre.com
Number of Beds: 126 beds
Andrea Pohl, Administrator
Tom Sachade, Manager, Maintenance/Plysical Plant

Hamilton: Victoria Nursing Home
176 Victoria Ave. North, Hamilton, ON L8L 5G1
Tel: 905-527-9111 *Fax:* 905-526-1871
www.victoriagardens.ca
Number of Beds: 76 beds
Ranka Stipancic, Administrator

Hanover: Hanover Care Centre
700 - 19 Ave., Hanover, ON N4N 3S6
Tel: 519-364-3700 *Fax:* 519-364-7194
hcc@bmts.com
Number of Beds: 41 beds
Dennis Laver, Director, Physical Plant
Bill Garcia, Administrator

Hearst: Foyer des Pionniers
PO Box 1538, 1317 Edward St., Hearst, ON P0L 1N0
Tel: 705-372-2978 *Fax:* 705-372-2996
Number of Beds: 61 beds
Joëlle Lacroix, Director of Care, Administrator
jlacroix@hearst.ca
Jeanne Comeau, Activity Director

Ingersoll: Leisureworld Caregiving Centre - Oxford
263 Wonham St. South, Ingersoll, ON N5C 3P6
Tel: 519-485-3920
adm.oxford@leisureworld.ca
www.leisureworld.ca
Year Founded: 1975
Number of Beds: 80 long-term care beds
Note: Specialties: Restorative care; Physiotherapy program; Pet therapy; Palliative care
Carolee Milliner, Administrator
Ted Cripps, Environmental Services Supervisor

Iroquois Falls: South Centennial Manor
240 Fyfe St., Iroquois Falls, ON P0K 1E0
Tel: 705-258-3836 *Fax:* 705-258-3694
Number of Beds: 68 beds
Dan O'Mara, CEO
Richard Hadley, Director, Physical Plant

Kapuskasing: Extendicare - Kapuskasing
PO Box 460, 45 Ontario St., Kapuskasing, ON P5N 2Y5
Tel: 705-335-8337 *Fax:* 705-337-6051
cnh_kapuskasing@extendicare.com
www.extendicarecanada.com/kapuskasing/
Number of Beds: 60 beds
Jacynthe Ouellette, Administrator

Kapuskasing: North Centennial Manor
2 Kimberley Dr., Kapuskasing, ON P5N 1L5
Tel: 705-335-6125 *Fax:* 705-337-1091
Number of Beds: 71 beds
Note: non-profit charitable home for the aged
Gil M. Dionne, Administrator
Jean-Claude Lauzon, Supervisor, Plant Maintenance

Kemptville: Bayfield Manor Nursing & Retirement Home
PO Box 300, 100 Elvira St., Kemptville, ON K0G 1J0
Tel: 613-258-7484 *Fax:* 613-258-3838
bayfield@bayfieldmanor.on.ca
www.bayfieldmanor.on.ca
Number of Beds: 66 bed nursing home + 46 suite retirement home
Michael J. Hall, Administrator

Kenora: Birchwood Terrace Central Park Lodge
PO Box 2630, 237 Lakeview Drive, R.R. #1, Kenora, ON P9N 3X8
Tel: 807-468-9532 *Fax:* 807-468-4060
birchwoodterrace@reveraliving.com
Number of Beds: 94 beds
Soili Helppi, Executive Director
soili.helppi@reveraliving.com

Kenora: Pinecrest Home for the Aged
1220 Valley Dr., Kenora, ON P9N 2W7
Tel: 807-468-3165 *Fax:* 807-468-6346
Kevin L. Queen, Administrator

King City: King City Lodge Nursing Home
146 Fog Rd., King City, ON L7B 1A3
Tel: 905-833-5037 *Fax:* 905-833-5925
www.kingcitylodge.com
Number of Beds: 36 beds
Kelly Graham, Administrator; Director, Nursing

Kingston: Extendicare - Kingston
309 Queen Mary Rd., Kingston, ON K7M 6P4
Tel: 613-549-5010 *Fax:* 613-549-7347
cnh_kingston@extendicare.com
www.extendicarecanada.com/kingston/
Number of Beds: 150 beds
Marilyn C. Benn, Administrator

Kingston: Rideaucrest Home
175 Rideau St., Kingston, ON K7K 3H6
Tel: 613-530-2818 *Fax:* 613-531-9107
Number of Beds: 170 beds
Note: municipal home for the aged
John D. Smith, Administrator

Kirkland Lake: Extendicare - Kirkland Lake
PO Box 3900, 155 Government Rd. East, Kirkland Lake, ON P2N 3P4
Tel: 705-567-3268 *Fax:* 705-567-4638
cnh_kirklandlake@extendicare.com
www.extendicarecanada.com/kirklandlake/
Number of Beds: 100 beds
Susan Enouy, Administrator

Kirkland Lake: Teck Pioneer Residence
145A Government Rd. East, Kirkland Lake, ON P2N 3P4
Tel: 705-567-3264
www.teckpioneerresidence.com
Year Founded: 1965
Note: Specialties: Nursing services for long-term care residents; Dementia care; Activity program; Restorative care
Nancy Allick, Administrator
Donna LeGros, Director, Nursing
Phil Sullivan, Environmental Services Supervisor

Kitchener: A.R. Goudie Eventide Home (Salvation Army)
369 Frederick St., Kitchener, ON N2H 2P1
Tel: 519-744-5182 *Fax:* 519-744-3887
info@argoudieeventide.ca
www.argoudieeventide.ca
Number of Beds: 80 beds
Gary Butt, Executive Director
gbutt@argoudieeventide.ca
Anabela Henriques, Manager, Resident Care Services
ahenriques@argoudieeventide.ca
Alison Westman, Manager, Dietary & Environmental Services
awestman@argoudieeventide.ca

Kitchener: Forest Heights Long Term Care Centre
60 Westheights Dr., Kitchener, ON N2N 2A8
Tel: 519-576-3320 *Fax:* 519-745-3227
generalforestheights@reveraliving.com
www.reveraliving.com
Number of Beds: 240 beds
Patti Fetter, Executive Director

Kitchener: Trinity Village Care Centre (TVCC)
2727 Kingsway Dr., Kitchener, ON N2C 1A7
Tel: 519-893-6320 *Fax:* 519-893-3432
www.trinityvillage.com
Number of Beds: 150 residential capacity
Note: Specialties: Eden Alternative Philosophy of Care; Long-term care; Therapeutic services; Recreation programming; Palliative care
Debby Riepert, Administrator
Elizabeth Barnes, Supervisor, Environmental Health

***Kitchener:* Village of Winston Park**
695 Blockline Rd., Kitchener, ON N2E 3K1
Tel: 519-576-2430 *Fax:* 519-576-8990
barb.sutcliffe@schlegelvillages.com
www.winstonpark.net
Number of Beds: 271 beds
Michael Schmidt, Administrator

***Lakefield:* Extendicare - Lakefield**
19 Fraser St., Lakefield, ON K0L 2H0
Tel: 705-652-7112 *Fax:* 705-652-7733
cnh_lakefield@extendicare.com
www.extendicarecanada.com/lakefield/
Number of Beds: 100 beds

***Leamington:* Leamington Nursing Home**
24 Franklin Rd., Leamington, ON N8H 4B7
Tel: 519-326-3289 *Fax:* 519-326-0102
Number of Beds: 120 beds
Roxanne Belli, Administrator

***Leamington:* Leamington United Mennonite Home**
35 Pickwick Dr., Leamington, ON N8H 2P2
Tel: 519-326-6109 *Fax:* 519-326-3595
Number of Beds: 82 beds
Linda Tiessen, Administrator

***Leamington:* Sun Parlor Home for Senior Citizens**
175 Talbot St. East, Leamington, ON N8H 1L9
Tel: 519-326-5731 *Fax:* 519-326-8952
www.countyofessex.on.ca/countyservices/sunparlor_home.asp
Year Founded: 1900
Number of Beds: 206 beds
Note: Specialties: Long-term care; Mental health services; Physiotherapy; Restorative care programs; Speech therapy; Occupational therapy; Audiology screening; Life enrichment services
Bill MacDonald, Administrator

***Lindsay:* Extendicare - Kawartha Lakes**
125 Colborne St. East, Lindsay, ON K9V 4R3
Tel: 705-878-5392 *Fax:* 705-878-7910
cnh_kawarthalakes@extendicare.com
www.extendicarecanada.com/lindsaykawartha/
Number of Beds: 64 beds

***Lions Head:* Golden Dawn Nursing Home**
PO Box 129, 80 Main St., Lions Head, ON N0H 1W0
Tel: 519-793-3433 *Fax:* 519-793-4503
office@goldendawn.ca
Number of Beds: 45 beds
Kevin Jones, Administrator
Deborah Shaw, R.N., Director of Residence Care

***Little Current:* Manitoulin Centennial Manor**
PO Box 460, 70 Robinson St. West, Little Current, ON P0P 1K0
Tel: 705-368-2710 *Fax:* 705-368-2694
Number of Beds: 60 beds
Cathy Deacon, Administrator; Director, Residential Services

***London:* Chelsey Park (Oxford) Nursing Home**
310 Oxford St. West, London, ON N6H 4N6
Tel: 519-432-1855 *Fax:* 519-679-7324
www.chelseypark.com
Number of Beds: 243 beds
Note: retirement community
Sandra Gormandy, General Manager
519-432-1845 ext.234, gm.cprc@diversicare.ca

***London:* Extendicare - London**
860 Waterloo St., London, ON N6A 3W6
Tel: 519-433-6658 *Fax:* 519-642-1711
cnh_london@extendicare.com
www.extendicarecanada.com/london/index.aspx
Number of Beds: 170 beds
Charles Marczinski, Administrator
John Plachta, Supervisor, Maintenance

***London:* McCormick Home**
2022 Kains Rd., London, ON N6K 0A8
Tel: 519-432-2648 *Fax:* 519-645-6982
www.mccormickhome.on.ca
Number of Beds: 160 beds
Note: Specialties: Long-term care; Ddementia care; Alzheimer outreach services day program; Social work
Michael P. Boucher, Executive Director
Roy Langille, Director, Physical Operations

***Long Sault:* Woodland Villa**
30 Mille Roches Rd., Long Sault, ON K0C 1P0
Tel: 613-534-2276 *Fax:* 613-534-8559
mrasenberg@omniway.ca
www.omni-way.com/ourhomes/woodland.htm
Number of Beds: 112 beds
Michael Rasenberg, Administrator

***Markdale:* Grey Gables Home for the Aged**
Former Name: Grey Owen Lodge
PO Box 380, 206 Toronto St. South, Markdale, ON N0C 1H0
Tel: 519-986-3010 *Fax:* 519-986-4644
jennifer.cornell@grey.ca
Number of Beds: 66 beds
Shirley Person, Administrator

***Markham:* Markhaven, Home for Seniors**
54 Parkway Ave., Markham, ON L3P 2G4
Tel: 905-294-2233 *Fax:* 905-294-6521
markhaven@markhaven.ca
www.markhaven.ca
Note: Specialties: Medical care; Nursing care; Physiotherapy; Special needs activities. Number of Employees: 149
Don Jennings, Maintenance Supervisor
Noreen Kallai, Executive Director

***Maryhill:* Twin Oaks of Maryhill Inc.**
1360 Maryhill Rd., Maryhill, ON N0B 2B0
Tel: 519-648-2117
www.twinoaksmaryhill.com
Number of Beds: 31 beds
Note: Specialties: Secured area
Ralph Link, Administrator

***Mattawa:* Algonquin Nursing Home**
PO Box 270, 231 Tenth St., Mattawa, ON P0H 1V0
Tel: 705-744-2202 *Fax:* 705-744-2787
Toll-Free: 800-579-4284
vala@anh.ca
www.anh.ca
Number of Beds: 72 beds
Leonard Simpson, Maintenance
Zena Monestime, Administrator

***Meaford:* Meaford Long Term Care Centre**
135 William St., Meaford, ON N4L 1T4
Tel: 519-538-1010 *Fax:* 519-538-5699
businessoffice@meafordlongtermcare.com
www.meafordlongtermcare.com
Number of Beds: 77 beds
Note: Specialties; Restorative care program; Psychogeriatric outreach; Life enrichment programs; Services of a wound care specialist; Services of a pain specialist; Palliative care
Doris Bilitz, Administrator
Randy Turner, Environmental Services

***Merrickville:* Hilltop Manor**
1005 St Lawrence St., Merrickville, ON K0G 1N0
Tel: 613-269-4707 *Fax:* 613-269-3534
elizabeth@hilltopmanor.ca
www.hilltopmanor.ca
Number of Beds: 89 beds

***Merrickville:* Hilltop Manor Nursing Home Ltd.**
PO Box 430, 1005 St. Lawrence St., Merrickville, ON K0G 1N0
Tel: 613-269-4707 *Fax:* 613-269-3534
elizabeth@hilltopmanor.ca
www.hilltopmanor.ca
Number of Beds: 60 beds

***Metcalfe:* Township of Osgoode Care Centre**
7650 Snake Island Rd., Metcalfe, ON K0A 2P0
Tel: 613-821-1034 *Fax:* 613-821-0070
lnorris@osgoodecare.com
www.osgoodecare.ca
Number of Beds: 100 beds
Note: Specialties: Long-term nursing care; Organized leisure activities
Lori Norris, Administrator
Martha Wheeler, Director, Care

***Milverton:* Knollcrest Lodge**
50 William St., Milverton, ON N0K 1M0
Tel: 519-595-8121 *Fax:* 519-595-8199
srae@knollcrestlodge.com
www.knollcrestlodge.com
Social Media: www.facebook.com/knollcrest.lodge
Number of Beds: 77 beds
Susan Rae, Administrator

***Minden:* Hyland Crest Senior Citizens' Home**
PO Box 30, 6 McPherson St., Minden, ON K0M 2K0
Tel: 705-286-2140 *Fax:* 705-286-6384
mvieira@hhhs.on.ca
www.hhhs.ca
Number of Beds: 62 beds
Foster Loucks, Administrator
Peter Fearrey, Director, Facilities & Projects
pfearrey@hhhs.on.ca

***Mississauga:* Carmel Heights Seniors' Residence**
Former Name: Carmel Heights Home for the Aged
1720 Sherwood Forest Circle, Mississauga, ON L5K 1R1
Tel: 905-822-5298
carmelheights@rogers.com
www.carmelheights.ca
Number of Beds: 48 beds
Note: home for the aged residential care
Sr. M. Veronica, Administrator

***Mississauga:* Chelsey Park (Streetsville) Nursing Home**
1742 Bristol Rd. West, Mississauga, ON L5M 1X9
Tel: 905-826-3045 *Fax:* 905-826-9978
Number of Beds: 118 beds
Susan Bock, Administrator
susan.bock@leisureworld.ca
Barbara Ashenhurst, Director of Care
barb.ashenhurst@leisureworld.ca

***Mississauga:* Chelsey Park Nursing Home**
2250 Hurontario St., Mississauga, ON L5B 1M8
Tel: 905-270-0411 *Fax:* 905-270-1749
Number of Beds: 237 beds
Dr. Alice Grzesiak, Administrator

***Mississauga:* Extendicare - Mississauga**
855 John Watt Blvd., Mississauga, ON L5W 1G2
Tel: 905-696-0719 *Fax:* 905-696-8875
cnh_mississauga@extendicare.com
www.extendicarecanada.com/mississauga
Number of Beds: 140 beds

***Mississauga:* Mississauga Lifecare Centre**
55 The Queensway West, Mississauga, ON L5B 1B5
Tel: 905-270-0170 *Fax:* 905-270-8465
Number of Beds: 26 respite; 166 long-term care
Ina Reynolds, Administrator
Bill Cody, Director, Maintenance

***Mississauga:* Mississauga Long Term Care Facility**
Former Name: Mississauga Nursing Home Inc.
26 Peter St. North, Mississauga, ON L5H 2G7
Tel: 905-278-2213
www.mltcfacility.com
Number of Beds: 55 beds
Novak Bajin, Administrator

***Mississauga:* Sheridan Villa**
2460 Truscott Dr., Mississauga, ON L5J 3Z8
Tel: 905-791-8668 *Fax:* 905-823-7971
www.peelregion.ca/ltc/sheridan
Number of Beds: 236 beds
Inga Mazuryk, Administrator

***Mississauga:* Tyndall Nursing Home Ltd.**
1060 Eglinton Ave. East, Mississauga, ON L4W 1K3
Tel: 905-624-1511 *Fax:* 905-629-9346
info@tyndallnursinghome.com
tyndallnursinghome.com
Number of Beds: 151 residents
Note: Specialties: Long-term care; Restorative feeding program
B.D. Jolly, Administrator
Alisea Vernon, Health; Safety Committee

***Mitchell:* Mitchell Nursing Home Ltd.**
Affiliated with: Ritz Lutheran Villa
184 Napier St., Mitchell, ON N0K 1N0
Tel: 519-348-8861 *Fax:* 519-348-4214
Year Founded: 1969
Number of Beds: 48 beds
Cathy Wight, Administrator

***New Hamburg:* Nithview Home & Seniors Village**
200-218 Boullee St., New Hamburg, ON N0B 2G0
Tel: 519-662-2280 *Fax:* 519-662-1090
Year Founded: 1972
Number of Beds: 96 beds
Note: Mennonite nursing home
Brent Martin, Administrator

***Newcastle:* Fosterbrooke Long Term Care Facility**
330 King St. West, Newcastle, ON L1B 1G9
Tel: 905-987-4703 *Fax:* 905-987-3621
www.reveraliving.com/fosterbrooke
Number of Beds: 88 beds

***Newmarket:* Central Care Corporation - Mackenzie Place**
52 George St., Newmarket, ON L3Y 4V3
Tel: 905-853-3242 *Fax:* 905-895-5139
www.reveraliving.com/mackenzieplace
Number of Beds: 93 beds

***Newmarket:* Eagle Terrace**
329 Eagle St., Newmarket, ON L3Y 1K3
Tel: 905-895-5187 *Fax:* 905-895-2645
EagleTerrace@reveraliving.com
www.reveraliving.com
Number of Beds: 70 beds
Diane T. Brunelle-Marleau, Executive Director
905-895-5187 ext 302, diane.brunelle-marleau@reveraliving.
Elizabeth Laur, Director

***Newmarket:* Eagle Terrace**
329 Eagle St., Newmarket, ON L3Y 1K3
Tel: 905-895-5187 *Fax:* 905-895-2645
eagleterrace@reveraliving.com
retirementresidencesreit.com/homes/07/
Number of Beds: 70 beds
Michael Griffin, Administrator

***Newmarket:* Maple Health Centre - York Region Long-Term Care & Seniors Branch**
194 Eagle St., Newmarket, ON L3Y 1J6
Tel: 905-895-3628 *Fax:* 905-895-5843
Number of Beds: 100 beds
Lynn Parsons, Assistant Administrator; Director, Care

***Newmarket:* Newmarket Health Centre-York Region Long-Term Care & Seniors Branch**
194 Eagle St., Newmarket, ON L3Y 1J6
Tel: 905-895-3628 *Fax:* 905-895-5843
Number of Beds: 132 beds
Marlene Parsons, Assistant Administrator; Director, Care

***Niagara Falls:* Oakwood Park Lodge**
6747 Oakwood Dr., Niagara Falls, ON L2E 7E3
Tel: 905-356-8732 *Fax:* 905-356-2122
oakwoodparklodge@cogeco.net
www.conmedhealth.com
Year Founded: 1975
Number of Beds: 153 beds
Paul Taylor, Administrator

***Niagara Falls:* The Salvation Army Honorable Ray & Helen Lawson Eventide Home**
5050 Jepson St., Niagara Falls, ON L2E 1K5
Tel: 905-356-1221 *Fax:* 905-356-9609
info@niagaraeventide.ca
www.niagaraeventide.ca
Note: Specialties: Long-term care for senior; Activity program
Maj. Grace Herber, Administrator
Harold Barwes, Head, Maintenance

***Niagara Falls:* Valley Park Lodge**
6400 Valley Way, Niagara Falls, ON L2E 7E3
Tel: 905-358-3277 *Fax:* 905-358-3012
Number of Beds: 65 beds
Jennifer Kennedy, Administrator
Ron Jones, Maintenance Supervisor

***North Bay:* Leisureworld Caregiving Centre - North Bay**
401 William St., North Bay, ON P1A 1X5
Tel: 705-476-2602 *Fax:* 705-476-1624
ruth.gauthier@leisureworld.ca
www.leisureworld.ca/northbay.html
Number of Beds: 147 suites, 1 short stay bed; 6 convalescent care
Ruth Gauthier, Administrator
Carol Passmore, Director, Nursing

***North York:* Thompson House**
1 Overland Dr., North York, ON M3C 2C3
Tel: 416-447-7244 *Fax:* 416-447-6364
info@betterlivinghealth.org
www.betterlivinghealth.org
Number of Beds: 136 beds
Note: Specialties: Long-term care; Nursing care; Physiotherapy; Rehabilitative services; Recreation program; Restorative care; Social work; Palliative care
Bernita Borgh, Vice-President, Residential Services

***Northbrook:* Pine Meadow Nursing Home**
PO Box 100, 124 Lloyd St., Northbrook, ON K0H 2G0
Tel: 613-336-9120 *Fax:* 613-336-9144
Year Founded: 1993
Number of Beds: 60 beds
Note: Specialties: Residential nursing care for seniors
Kim Harvey, Administrator

***Norwich:* Norvilla Nursing Home**
11 Elgin St. East, Norwich, ON N0J 1P0
Tel: 519-863-2717 *Fax:* 519-863-3955
Number of Beds: 40 beds

***Ohsweken:* Iroquois Lodge**
PO Box 309, 1755 Chiefswood Rd, Ohsweken, ON N0A 1M0
Tel: 519-445-2224 *Fax:* 519-445-4180
iroquoislodge@on.aibn.com
Number of Beds: 50 beds
Wanda Green, Administrator
Patti Powless, Nursing Supervisor

***Orillia:* Oak Terrace**
291 Mississauga St. West, Orillia, ON L3V 3B9
Tel: 705-325-2289 *Fax:* 705-325-7178
oakterrace@reveraliving.com
Note: Specialties: Foot care; Physiotherapy programs; Restorative care programs; Dental services; Music therapy; Pet therapy
Marianne Williams, Administrator

***Oshawa:* Extendicare - Oshawa**
82 Park Rd. North, Oshawa, ON L1J 4L1
Tel: 905-579-0011 *Fax:* 905-579-1733
cnh_oshawa@extendicare.com
www.extendicarecanada.com/oshawa/index.aspx
Number of Beds: 175 beds

***Ottawa:* Extendicare - Medex**
1865 Baseline Rd., Ottawa, ON K2C 3K6
Tel: 613-225-5650 *Fax:* 613-225-0960
cnh_medex@extendicare.com
www.extendicarecanada.com/ottawamedex
Number of Beds: 193 beds

***Ottawa:* Extendicare - New Orchard Lodge**
99 New Orchard Ave., Ottawa, ON K2B 5E6
Tel: 613-820-2110 *Fax:* 613-820-6380
cnh_neworchardlodge@extendicare.com
www.extendicarecanada.com/ottawaneworchard
Number of Beds: 111 beds

***Ottawa:* Extendicare - Starwood**
114 Starwood Rd., Ottawa, ON K2G 3N5
Tel: 613-224-3960 *Fax:* 613-224-9309
cnh_starwood@extendicare.com
www.extendicarecanada.com/nepean
Number of Beds: 192 beds

***Ottawa:* Extendicare - West End Villa**
2179 Elmira Dr., Ottawa, ON K2C 3S1
Tel: 613-829-3501 *Fax:* 613-829-3504
cnh_westendvilla@extendicare.com
www.extendicarecanada.com/ottawawestendvilla
Number of Beds: 240 beds
Note: nursing home

***Ottawa:* Glebe Centre Inc.**
Former Name: Bronson Place
950 Bank St., Ottawa, ON K1S 5G6
Tel: 613-238-2727 *Fax:* 613-238-4759
info@glebecentre.ca
www.glebecentre.ca
Janice Bridgewater, Senior Centre Director
jbridgewater@glebecentre.ca

***Ottawa:* Island Lodge**
1 Porter's Island, Ottawa, ON K1N 5M2
Tel: 613-789-5100 *Fax:* 613-789-3704
Number of Beds: 165 beds
Diane Officer, Executive Director
Ray Duffy, Environmental Services

***Ottawa:* Perley & Rideau Veterans' Health Centre**
1750 Russell Rd., Ottawa, ON K1G 5Z6
Tel: 613-526-7170 *Fax:* 613-526-7172
www.prvhc.com
Year Founded: 1995
Number of Beds: 450 residential capacity
Note: Specialties: Geriatric care; Recreation services; Dementia programming; Respite care for people in the mid-stages of dementia; Convalescent care
Greg Fougère, Executive Director
Bob Paré, Manager, Plant Services
Kerry Kelly, Manager, Housekeeping Linen Svs. & Materials Management

***Ottawa:* Villa Marconi**
1026 Baseline Rd., Ottawa, ON K2C 0A6
Tel: 613-727-6201 *Fax:* 613-727-9352
villamarconi@villamarconi.com
www.villamarconi.com
Number of Beds: 125 beds
Walter Cibischino, President

***Owen Sound:* Lee Manor**
875 - 6 St. East, Owen Sound, ON N4K 5W5
Tel: 519-376-4420 *Fax:* 519-371-5406
www.greycounty.on.ca
Number of Beds: 150 beds
Note: Municipal home for aged
Marjorie McNeil, Administrator

***Parkhill:* Chateau Gardens Parkhill**
250 Tain St., Parkhill, ON N0M 2K0
Tel: 519-294-6342 *Fax:* 519-294-0107
www.chartwellreit.ca
Number of Beds: 59 beds

***Parry Sound:* Belvedere Heights**
21 Belvedere Ave., Parry Sound, ON P2A 2A2
Tel: 705-746-5871 *Fax:* 705-774-7300
bh@zeuter.com
www.belvedereheights.com
Number of Beds: 101 beds
Bev Preuss, CEO

***Pembroke:* Miramichi Lodge**
725 Pembrooke St. W, Pembroke, ON K8A 8S9
Tel: 613-735-0175 *Fax:* 613-735-8061
Number of Beds: 166 beds
Shelley Sheedy, Administrator

***Perth:* Lanark Lodge**
115 Christie Lake Rd., Perth, ON K7H 3C6
Tel: 613-267-4225 *Fax:* 613-264-2668
lanarklodge@county.lanark.on.ca
Number of Beds: 163 beds
Whynn Turner, Administrator

***Perth:* Perth Community Care Centre**
101 Christie Lake Rd., RR#4, Perth, ON K7H 3C6
Tel: 613-267-2506 *Fax:* 613-267-7060
adm.perth@diversicare.ca
www.diversicare.ca
Number of Beds: 121 residential capacity
Note: Specialties: Long-term care; Activity program; Restorative care program; Physiotherapy
Joyce Firlotte, Administrator

***Peterborough:* Extendicare - Peterborough**
80 Alexander Ave., Peterborough, ON K9J 6B4
Tel: 705-743-7552 *Fax:* 705-742-9664
cnh_peterborough@extendicare.com
extendicarepeterborough.com
Number of Beds: 172 beds

***Peterborough:* St. Joseph's at Fleming**
Former Name: Marycrest Home of the Aged; Anson House
659 Brealey Dr., Peterborough, ON K9K 2R8
Tel: 705-743-4744 *Fax:* 705-743-7532
www.stjosephsatfleming.com
Year Founded: 2004
Debra Cooper Burger, Administrator

***Petrolia:* Fiddick's Nursing Home**
PO Box 340, 437 First Ave., Petrolia, ON N0N 1R0
Tel: 519-882-0370 *Fax:* 519-882-0375
www.fiddicksnursinghome.com
Number of Beds: 128 beds
Michael Fiddick, Administrator
Todd Fiddick, Supervisor, Plant Maintenance

***Picton:* H.J. MacFarland Memorial Home**
603 Hwy 49, RR#2, Picton, ON K0K 2T0
Tel: 613-476-2138 *Fax:* 613-476-6952
hjm.info@pecounty.on.ca
Number of Beds: 84 beds
Ellen Gervais, Administrator
egervais@pecounty.on.ca

***Picton:* Kentwood Park**
PO Box 1298, 2 Ontario St., Picton, ON K0K 2T0
Tel: 613-476-5671 *Fax:* 613-476-3986
www.omni-way.com/ourhomes/kentwood.htm
Number of Beds: 48 beds
Tina Cole, Administrator/Nursing Administrative Services Manager
tcole@omniway.ca

***Picton:* Picton Manor Nursing Home**
9 Hill St. West, Picton, ON K0K 2T0
Tel: 613-476-6140 *Fax:* 613-476-5240
www.pictonmanor.com
Number of Beds: 78 beds
Note: Specialties: Nursing care; Restorative care; Activity program; Life enrichment progran; Palliative care
Norma Bongard, Administrator

***Picton:* West Lake Terrace**
PO Box 2229, R.R. #1, 1673 County Rd. #12, Picton, ON K0K 2T0
Tel: 613-393-2055 *Fax:* 613-393-2057
Number of Beds: 47 beds
Mary Lynn Lester, Administrator

***Plantagenet:* Pinecrest Nursing Home Ltd.**
PO Box 250, 101 Parent St., RR#1, Plantagenet, ON K0B 1L0
Tel: 613-673-4835 *Fax:* 613-673-2675
Note: Specialties: Long-term care; Activity program
Marcel Parent, Administrator

***Port Dover:* Dover Cliffs Long Term Care Centre, Port Dover**
Former Name: Versa-Care Centre, Port Dover
PO Box 430, 501 St. George St., Port Dover, ON N0A 1N0
Tel: 519-583-1422 *Fax:* 519-583-3197
paulinel.robinson@reveraliving.com
Number of Beds: 70 beds
Pauline Lyne, Executive Director
Shelly Desgagne, Office Manager
shellydesgagne@cplodges.com

***Port Hope:* Community Nursing Home**
20 Hope St. South, Port Hope, ON L1A 2M8
Tel: 905-885-6367 *Fax:* 905-885-6368
www.cnhporthope.ca
Number of Beds: 97 beds
Nancy Jordan, Administrator
njordan@clmi.ca

***Port Hope:* Extendicare - Port Hope**
360 Croft St., Port Hope, ON L1A 4K8
Tel: 905-885-1266 *Fax:* 905-885-5328
cnh_porthope@extendicare.com
www.extendicarecanada.com/porthope
Number of Beds: 128 beds

***Port Perry:* Community Nursing Home**
PO Box 660, 15941 Simcoe St. North, Port Perry, ON L9L 1A6
Tel: 905-985-3205 *Fax:* 905-985-3721
www.cnhportperry.ca
Number of Beds: 107 beds
Rosemary Mifsud, Administrator
rmifsud@clmi.ca
Jennifer Castaneda, Director of Care
jcastaneda@clmi.ca

***Powassan:* Eastholme Home for the Aged**
PO Box 400, 62 Big Bend Ave., Powassan, ON P0H 1Z0
Tel: 705-724-2005 *Fax:* 705-724-5429
easthome@onlink.net
www.eastholme.ca
Number of Beds: 104 beds
Steven Piekarski, Administrator

***Prescott:* Wellington House**
PO Box 401, 990 Edward St. North, Prescott, ON K0E 1T0
Tel: 613-925-2834 *Fax:* 613-925-5425
Number of Beds: 60 beds
Note: Long-term care facility
Bernadette Timco, Administrator
Diana Gaudet, Supervisor, Environmental Services

***Puslinch:* Morriston Park Nursing Home Inc.**
7363 Calfass Rd., RR#2, Puslinch, ON N0B 2J0
Tel: 519-822-9179 *Fax:* 519-822-4459
Number of Beds: 28 beds
Alfred Urfey, Administrator

***Red Lake:* Northwood Lodge**
PO Box 420, Hwy 105, Red Lake, ON P0V 2M0
Tel: 807-727-2323 *Fax:* 807-727-3546
northwood.lodge@kenoradistricthomes.ca
Number of Beds: 32 beds
Note: home for the aged
Doris Coghill, Administrator

***Renfrew:* Bonnechere Manor**
470 Albert St., Renfrew, ON K7V 4L5
Tel: 613-432-4873 *Fax:* 613-432-7138
Year Founded: 1958
Number of Beds: 177 beds
Shayne Hoelke, Admintstrator

***Renfrew:* Groves Park Lodge Long Term Care Facility**
Former Name: Groves Park Lodge Nursing Home
470 Raglan St. North, Renfrew, ON K7V 1P5
Tel: 613-432-5823 *Fax:* 613-432-5287
carrol.haywood@gemhealth.com
www.gemhealth.com/gem_health_care_group_groves_park.html
Number of Beds: 75 beds
Carrol Haywood, Administrator

***Richmond Hill:* Leisureworld Caregiving Centre - Richmond Hill**
170 Red Maple Rd., Richmond Hill, ON L4B 4T8
Tel: 905-731-2273
jodi.macisaac@leisureworld.ca
www.leisureworld.ca/richmondhill.html
Number of Beds: 160 beds
Jodi MacIsaac, Administrator

***Richmond Hill:* Mariann Home**
9915 Yonge St., Richmond Hill, ON L4C 1V1
Tel: 905-884-9276 *Fax:* 905-884-1800
bernard.boreland@mariannhome.com
Number of Beds: 64 beds
Note: Specialties: Peritoneal dialysis; Care for seniors with cognitive or psychiatric impairment; Palliative care. Number of employees: 80
Sr. Mary William Verhoeven, Administrator

***Rockland:* St. Joseph Nursing Home**
1615 Laurier St., Rockland, ON K4K 1C8
Tel: 613-446-5126 *Fax:* 613-446-1516
Number of Beds: 64 beds
Ginette Whittingham, Administrator

***Sarnia:* Vision Nursing Home**
229 Wellington St., Sarnia, ON N7T 1G9
Tel: 519-336-6551 *Fax:* 519-336-5878
recept@vision74.com
vision74.webs.com
Number of Beds: 108 permanent beds, 2 respite
Note: Christian-based nursing home
Bernard Bax, Administrator
Neil Whittle, Supervisor, Maintenance

***Sault Ste Marie:* Extendicare - Tendercare**
770 Great Northern Rd., Sault Ste Marie, ON P6A 5K7
Tel: 705-949-3611 *Fax:* 705-945-6303
cnh_tendercare@extendicare.com
www.extendicarecanada.com/saultsaintmarietendercare
Number of Beds: 120 beds

***Sault Ste Marie:* Extendicare - Van Daele**
39 Van Daele St., Sault Ste Marie, ON P6B 4V3
Tel: 705-949-7934 *Fax:* 705-945-0968
cnh_vandaele@extendicare.com
www.extendicarecanada.com/saultsaintmarievandaele
Number of Beds: 150 beds

***Sault Ste Marie:* F.J. Davey Home**
733 Third Line East, Sault Ste Marie, ON P6A 5K7
Tel: 705-942-2204 *Fax:* 705-942-2234
www.fjdaveyhome.org
Number of Beds: 184 beds
Peter J. MacLean, Administrator
705-945-2204 ext 217, pmaclean@fjdaveyhome.org

***Sault Ste Marie:* Mauno Kaihla Koti**
723 North St., Sault Ste Marie, ON P6B 6G8
Tel: 705-945-9987 *Fax:* 705-945-1217
adminsec@theofra.org
Number of Beds: 63 beds
Helina McGrath, Director, Care Services

***Scarborough:* Kennedy Lodge Nursing Home**
1400 Kennedy Rd., Scarborough, ON M1P 4V6
Tel: 416-752-8282 *Fax:* 416-752-0645
kennedylodge@reveraliving.com
Number of Beds: 289 beds
Note: long term care facility
Donna Michaels, Administrator

***Schumacher:* Extendicare - Timmins**
Affiliated with: North East Local Health Integration Network
PO Box 817, 15 Hollinger Lane, Schumacher, ON P0N 1G0
Tel: 705-360-1913 *Fax:* 705-268-3975
cnh_timmins@extendicare.com
www.extendicarecanada.com/schumacher
Number of Beds: 121 beds
Claude Roy, Administrator

***Selby:* Village Green Long Term Care Facility**
PO Box 94, Selby, ON K0K 2Z0
Tel: 613-388-2693 *Fax:* 613-388-2694
Number of Beds: 66 beds
Linda Pierce, Administrator

***Simcoe:* Cedarwood Village**
500 Queensway West, Simcoe, ON N3Y 4R4
Tel: 519-426-8305 *Fax:* 519-426-2511
Number of Beds: 91 beds

***Simcoe:* Norfolk Hospital Nursing Home (NHNH)**
365 West St., Simcoe, ON N3Y 1T7
Tel: 519-426-0130 *Fax:* 519-429-6988
residents@ngh.on.ca (Residents' e-mail)
www.ngh.on.ca
Year Founded: 1975
Number of Beds: 80 beds
Note: Specialties: Long-term nursing care; Activation program; Wound care; Physiotherapy; Occupational therapy; Speech Therapy; Restorative care; Pet therapy; Social work; Psychogeriatics; Palliative care
William C. Lewis, Executive Director
J.J. Knott, Director, Physical Plant

***Sioux Lookout:* William A. (Bill) George Extended Care Facility**
75 Fifth Ave., Sioux Lookout, ON P8T 1K9
Tel: 807-737-1364 *Fax:* 807-737-2449
Number of Beds: 20 beds

***Smiths Falls:* Broadview Nursing Centre**
210 Brockville St., Smiths Falls, ON K7A 3Z4
Tel: 613-283-1845 *Fax:* 613-283-7073
bnc@on.aibn.com
Number of Beds: 75 beds
Sandra Sheridan, Director of Care

***St Catharines:* Extendicare - St. Catharines**
283 Pelham Rd., St Catharines, ON L2S 1X7
Tel: 905-688-3311 *Fax:* 905-688-5774
cnh_stcatharines@extendicare.com
www.extendicarecanada.com/saintcatherines
Number of Beds: 152 beds

***St Catharines:* Heidehof Home for the Aged**
600 Lake St., St Catharines, ON L2N 4J4
Tel: 905-935-3344 *Fax:* 905-935-0081
www.heidehof.com
Number of Beds: 106 beds
Elena Caddis, Administrator
ecaddis@heidehof.com
Erika Ledwez, Manager, Resident & Community Relations
eledwez@heidehof.com

***St Catharines:* Tabor Manor**
1 Tabor Dr., St Catharines, ON L2N 1V9
Tel: 905-934-2548
office@tabormanor.net
www.tabormanor.net/site
Number of Beds: 82 residential capacity
Note: Specialties: Accommodation & nursing care to senior citizens, especially those of the Mennonite constituency in Niagara; Activity program; Foot care
Ben Wohlgemut, Administrator
Tony Carrière, Director, Physical Plant

***St Catharines:* West Park Health Centre**
103 Pelham Rd., St Catharines, ON L2S 1S9
Tel: 905-688-1031 *Fax:* 905-688-9646
Number of Beds: 93 beds
Natalie Foster, Administrator

***St Jacobs:* Derbecker's Heritage House Ltd.**
54 Eby St., St Jacobs, ON N0B 2N0
Tel: 519-664-2921 *Fax:* 519-664-2380
Number of Beds: 72 beds
Pamela Derbecker, Administrator

***Stoney Creek:* Pine Villa Nursing Home**
490 Hwy. #8, Stoney Creek, ON L8G 1G6
Tel: 905-662-5033
info.pinevilla@thomashealthcare.com
www.thomashealthcare.com

Year Founded: 1967
Number of Beds: 38 beds
Note: Specialties: Nursing care; Enhanced restorative care program; Physiotherapy; Foot care; Massage therapy; Activity program
Conrad Thomas, Administrator

Stouffville: Green Gables Manor Inc.
9th Line Rd., RR#2, Stouffville, ON L4A 7X3
Tel: 905-640-1310 *Fax:* 905-640-2231
Number of Beds: 69 beds
Gerald Harquail, President

Stouffville: Parkview Home for the Aged
123 Weldon Rd., Stouffville, ON L4A 0G8
Tel: 905-640-1911 *Fax:* 905-640-4051
admin@parkviewhome.ca
www.parkviewhome.ca
Number of Beds: 109 beds
Note: Long-term care facility
Wallace Kribs, Home Administrator
Michael MacDonald, Director, Environmental Services

Stratford: Hillside Manor
5066 Perth East Line 34, RR#5, Stratford, ON N5A 6S6
Tel: 519-393-5132 *Fax:* 519-393-5130
hillsidemanor@reveraliving.com
www.reveraliving.com/homes/19/
Number of Beds: 90 beds
Sylvie Ledermueller, Administrator
Mary Anne Weller, Director of Care

Stratford: PeopleCare Stratford
198 Mornington St., Stratford, ON N5A 5G3
Tel: 519-271-4440 *Fax:* 519-271-4446
www.peoplecare.ca
Year Founded: 1980
Number of Beds: 60 residents
Note: Specialties: Long-term care; Activity program; Restorative care
Patricia Kelly, Administrator

Stratford: Spruce Lodge Senior Citizens Residence
643 West Gore St., Stratford, ON N5A 1L4
Tel: 519-271-4090 *Fax:* 519-271-5862
Number of Beds: 128 beds

Strathroy: Strathmere Lodge
PO Box 5000, 599 Albert St., Strathroy, ON N7G 3J3
Tel: 519-245-2520 *Fax:* 519-245-5711
www.county.middlesex.on.ca/strathmerelodge
Year Founded: 1880
Note: Specialties: Special care area for Alzheimer residents; Respite care & short stays
Larry Hills, Administrator
Terry Meservia, Supervisor, Maintenance

Sturgeon Falls: Au Château Home for the Aged
100 Michaud St., PO Bag 110, Sturgeon Falls, ON P2B 2Z4
Tel: 705-753-1550 *Fax:* 705-753-3135
Number of Beds: 162 beds
Wayne M. Foisey, Administrator
Simone Brazeau, Coordinator, Environmental Services

Sudbury: Extendicare - Falconbridge
281 Falconbridge Rd., Sudbury, ON P3A 5K4
Tel: 705-566-7980 *Fax:* 705-566-2997
cnh_falconbridge@extendicare.com
www.extendicarecanada.com/sudburyfalconbridge/
Number of Beds: 234 beds
James Foreman, Administrator
J. Kovacs, Director, Physical Plant

Sudbury: Extendicare - York
333 York St., Sudbury, ON P3E 5J3
Tel: 705-674-4221 *Fax:* 705-674-4281
cnh_york@extendicare.com
www.extendicarecanada.com/sudburyyork
Number of Beds: 288 beds

Tavistock: Bonnie Brae Health Care Centre
PO Box 489, 55 Woodstock St. North, Tavistock, ON N0B 2R0
Tel: 519-655-2420 *Fax:* 519-655-3432
paula.thomson@bonniebrae.ca
www.reveraliving.com/homes/51
Number of Beds: 80 beds
Joyce Penney, Administrator
joycepenney@reveraliving.com

Tecumseh: Banwell Gardens
3000 Banwell Rd., Tecumseh, ON N8N 2M4
Tel: 519-735-3204 *Fax:* 519-735-1836
www.reveraliving.com/banwell
Number of Beds: 142 beds

Tecumseh: Brouillette Manor
11900 Brouillette Ct., Tecumseh, ON N8N 4X8
Tel: 519-735-9810 *Fax:* 519-735-8569
Number of Beds: 60 beds
Nancy Comiskey, Administrator

Tecumseh: Extendicare - Tecumseh
2475 St. Alphonse St., Tecumseh, ON N8N 2X2
Tel: 519-739-2998 *Fax:* 519-739-2815
cnh_tecumseh@extendicare.com
www.extendicarecanada.com/tecumseh
Number of Beds: 128 beds

Thessalon: Algoma Manor
135 Dawson St., Thessalon, ON P0R 1L0
Tel: 705-842-2840 *Fax:* 705-842-2650
bharten@adhfa.org
www.adsab.on.ca/algomamanor/index.htm
Number of Beds: 106 beds
Peter MacLean, Administrator
Mark Heller, Coordinator, Environmental Services

Thornbury: Errinrung Residence
Former Name: Errinrung Nursing & Retirement Home
PO Box 69, 67 Bruce St., Thornbury, ON N0H 2P0
Tel: 519-599-2737 *Fax:* 519-599-3410
Number of Beds: 74 beds
Note: Total Employees: 38 f-t; 30 p-t
Yvonne Taylor, Director of Retirement Home
Deb Hughson, Director of Care

Thunder Bay: Bethammi Nursing Home, St. Joseph's Heritage
63 Carrie St., Thunder Bay, ON P7A 4J2
Tel: 807-768-4400 *Fax:* 807-768-8820
Number of Beds: 110 beds
Carl White, President
Victor Carlson, Director, Environmental Services

Thunder Bay: Dawson Court Home for the Aged
523 North Algoma St., Thunder Bay, ON P7A 5C2
Tel: 807-684-2926 *Fax:* 807-345-8854
Number of Beds: 150 beds
Michael Kennedy, Administrator
mkennedy@thunderbay.ca

Thunder Bay: Grandview Lodge/Thunder Bay
200 Lillie St. North, Thunder Bay, ON P7C 5Y2
Tel: 807-625-2923 *Fax:* 807-623-4075
Number of Beds: 150 beds
Wendy Kirkpatrick

Thunder Bay: Pioneer Ridge
750 Tungsten St., Thunder Bay, ON P7B 6R1
Tel: 807-684-3910 *Fax:* 807-684-3916
www.thunderbay.ca
Number of Beds: 150 beds
Note: Specialties: Long-term nursing care for older persons; Restorative care; Rehabilitation; Units for persons with cognitive challenges, Alzheimer's disease, & other dementias; Secure therapeutic parks; Life enrichment program
Joyce Greene, Administrator

Tillsonburg: Maple Manor Nursing Home
73 Bidwell St., Tillsonburg, ON N4G 3T8
Tel: 519-842-3563 *Fax:* 519-842-3038
Number of Beds: 102 beds
George Kaniuk, Administrator

Timmins: Golden Manor Home for the Aged
481 Melrose Blvd., Timmins, ON P4N 5H3
Tel: 705-360-2664 *Fax:* 705-360-2683
golden_manor@timmins.ca
Number of Beds: 174 beds
Heather Bozzer, Administrator
Claude Bruneau, Supervisor, Maintenance

Toronto: Barton Place Long Term Care Facility
914 Bathurst St., Toronto, ON M5R 3G5
Tel: 416-533-9473 *Fax:* 416-538-2685
Number of Beds: 130 beds

Toronto: Bendale Acres
2920 Lawrence Ave. East, Toronto, ON M1P 2T8
Tel: 416-397-7000 *Fax:* 416-397-7067
Number of Beds: 302 beds
Nicole McGouran
416-397-7000, nmcgour@toronto.ca
Richard Doberstein, Supervisor, Maintenance
Russ Persons, Manager, Building Services

Toronto: Casa Verde Health Centre
3595 Keele St., Toronto, ON M3J 1M7
Tel: 416-633-3431 *Fax:* 416-633-6736
www.diversicare.ca
Number of Beds: 252 beds

Toronto: Castleview Wychwood Towers
351 Christie St., Toronto, ON M6G 3C3
Tel: 416-392-5700 *Fax:* 416-392-4157
Number of Beds: 490 beds

Toronto: Cheltenham Nursing Home
5935 Bathurst St., Toronto, ON M2R 1Y8
Tel: 416-223-4050 *Fax:* 416-223-4159
admin.cheltenham@leisureworld.ca
www.leisureworld.ca/cheltenham.html
Number of Beds: 170 beds
Andrea McLister, Administrator

Toronto: Christie Gardens
600 Melita Cres., Toronto, ON M6G 3Z4
Tel: 416-530-1330 *Fax:* 416-530-1686
www.christiegardens.org
Social Media: www.facebook.com/ChristieGardens
Number of Beds: 88 beds

Toronto: Craiglee Nursing Home
102 Craiglee Dr., Toronto, ON M1N 2M7
Tel: 416-264-2000 *Fax:* 416-267-8176
Number of Beds: 94 beds

Toronto: Cummer Lodge Home for the Aged
205 Cummer Ave., Toronto, ON M2M 2E8
Tel: 416-392-9500 *Fax:* 416-392-9499
Number of Beds: 391 beds
Leah Walters, Administrator
George Abiad, Manager, Building Services

Toronto: Drs. Paul & John Rekai Centre
Also Known As: Rekai Centre
345 Sherbourne St., Toronto, ON M5A 2S3
Tel: 416-964-1599 *Fax:* 416-969-3907
Number of Beds: 129 beds
Linda Joyal, Director of Resident Programs

Toronto: Ehatare Nursing Home
40 Old Kingston Rd., Toronto, ON M1E 3J5
Tel: 416-284-0828 *Fax:* 416-284-5595
ehatare@on.aibn.com
Number of Beds: 32 beds
Ruth McFarlane, Administrator
Enno Pflug, Director, Physical Plant

Toronto: Extendicare - Bayview
550 Cummer Ave., Toronto, ON M2K 2M2
Tel: 416-226-1331 *Fax:* 416-226-2745
cnh_bayview@extendicare.com
www.extendicarecanada.com/willowdale/
Number of Beds: 203 beds
Susan Schendel, Administrator

Toronto: Extendicare - Guildwood
60 Guildwood Pkwy., Toronto, ON M1E 1N9
Tel: 416-266-7711 *Fax:* 416-269-5123
cnh_guildwood@extendicare.com
www.extendicarecanada.com/westhill/
Number of Beds: 169 beds
Dwayne Wyrwas, Administrator

Toronto: Extendicare - Rouge Valley
551 Conlins Rd., Toronto, ON M1B 5S1
Tel: 416-282-6768 *Fax:* 416-282-6766
cnh_rougevalley@extendicare.com
www.extendicarecanada.com/torontorougevalley
Number of Beds: 192 beds

Toronto: Extendicare Scarborough
3830 Lawrence Ave. East, Toronto, ON M1G 1R6
Tel: 416-439-1243 *Fax:* 416-439-4818
cnh_scarborough@extendicare.com
www.extendicarecanada.com/scarborough/index.aspx
Specialties: Nursing care for seniors; Care for persons with Alzheimer's or other dementias; Physiotherapy; Optometry services; Social & therapeutic programs

Toronto: Fairview Nursing Home
14 Cross St., Toronto, ON M6J 1S8
Tel: 416-534-8829 *Fax:* 416-538-1658
info@fairviewnursinghome.com
ww.fairviewnursinghome.com
Number of Beds: 108 beds

Toronto: Fudger House
439 Sherbourne St., Toronto, ON M4X 1K6
Tel: 416-392-5252 *Fax:* 416-392-4174
Number of Beds: 249 beds

Toronto: Garden Court Nursing Home
1 Sand Beach Rd., Toronto, ON M8V 2W2
Tel: 416-259-6172 *Fax:* 416-259-7925
Number of Beds: 45 beds
Deana Bennett, Administrator
deanab@sympatico.ca
Pat Collins, Supervisor, Plant Maintenance

Toronto: Hellenic Care for Seniors
33 Winona Dr., Toronto, ON M6G 3Z7
Tel: 416-654-3904 *Fax:* 416-654-1080
hcare@hellenichome.org
www.hellenichome.org
Number of Beds: 81 beds
Dorothy Godbold, Administrator

Toronto: Heritage Nursing Home
1195 Queen St. East, Toronto, ON M4M 1L6
Tel: 416-461-8185 *Fax:* 416-461-5472
administrator@heritagenursinghome.com
www.heritagenursinghome.com
Number of Beds: 201 beds
Note: Specialties: Long-term nursing care; Supervision & security for residents with Alzheimer's Disease or dementia; Restorative care, including physiotherapy; Activation & recreation program; Chinese programs
Melba Graham, Administrator

Toronto: Ivan Franko Ukrainian Home (Etobicoke)
767 Royal York Rd., Toronto, ON M8Y 2T3
Tel: 416-239-7364
Number of Beds: 85 beds
Maria Kiebalo, Administrator

Toronto: Kipling Acres
2233 Kipling Ave., Toronto, ON M9W 4L3
Tel: 416-392-2300
Year Founded: 1959
Number of Beds: 337 beds
Gina Filice, Administrator
gfilice@toronto.ca

Toronto: Lakeshore Lodge
3197 Lakeshore Blvd. West, Toronto, ON M8V 3X5
Tel: 416-392-9400 *Fax:* 416-392-9401
www.toronto.ca/homesfortheaged/lakeshore.htm
Number of Beds: 150 beds
Robert Price, Administrator
rprice@toronto.ca

Toronto: Leisureworld Caregiving Centre - Ellesmere
1000 Ellesmere Rd., Toronto, ON M1P 5G2
Tel: 416-291-0222
adm.ellesmere@leisureworld.ca
www.leisureworld.ca/ellesmere.html
Number of Beds: 224 beds
Michael Aikins, Administrator

Toronto: Leisureworld Caregiving Centre - Etobicoke
70 Humberline Dr., Toronto, ON M9W 7H3
Tel: 416-213-7300
lora.palmer@leisureworld.ca
www.leisureworld.ca/etobicoke.html
Number of Beds: 160 beds
Lora Palmer, Administrator
Caterina Ierino, Director of Care

Toronto: Leisureworld Caregiving Centre - Lawrence
2005 Lawrence Ave. West, Toronto, ON M9N 3V4
Tel: 416-243-8879
adm.lawrence@leisureworld.ca
www.leisureworld.ca/lawrence.html
Year Founded: 2002
Number of Beds: 224 beds; 2 respite
Gary Bowers, Administrator
Amo Nandlall, Director of Care

Toronto: Leisureworld Caregiving Centre - Norfinch
22 Norfinch Dr., Toronto, ON M3N 1X1
Tel: 416-623-1120 *Fax:* 416-623-1121
anne.deelstramcnara@leisureworld.ca
www.leisureworld.ca/norfinch.html
Year Founded: 2003
Number of Beds: 160 beds
Anne Deelstra McNamara, Administrator
Jane Pristach, Director of Nursing

Toronto: Leisureworld Caregiving Centre - O'Connor
1800 O'Connor Dr., Toronto, ON M4A 1W7
Tel: 416-285-2000
jeanette.sanichar@leisureworld.ca
www.leisureworld.ca/oc_gate.html
Year Founded: 2001
Number of Beds: 318 beds
Jeanette Sanichar, Administrator
Stacey Gamble, Assistant Director of Nursing

Toronto: Leisureworld Caregiving Centre - Rockcliffe
Former Name: Rockcliffe Long Term Care Facility
3015 Lawrence Ave. East, Toronto, ON M1P 2V7
Tel: 416-264-3201 *Fax:* 416-264-2914
adm.rockcliffe@leisureworld.ca
www.leisureworld.ca/rockcliffe.html
Year Founded: 1972
Number of Beds: 204 beds
Andrea E. Boswell, Administrator
Nelson Urbe, Maintenance Technician

Toronto: Leisureworld Caregiving Centre - St. George
225 St. George St., Toronto, ON M5R 2M2
Tel: 416-967-3985 *Fax:* 416-967-3951
jane.noble@leisureworld.ca
www.leisureworld.ca/stgeorge.html
Number of Beds: 238 beds
Barbara Beecroft, Director of Nursing
Jane Noble, Administrator

Toronto: Leisureworld Caregiving Centre - Scarborough
130 Midland Ave., Toronto, ON M1N 4B2
Tel: 416-264-2301 *Fax:* 416-264-3704
terry.teare@leisureworld.ca
www.leisureworld.ca/scarborough.html
Number of Beds: 299 long-term care, 53 retirement beds
Note: Retirement beds in adjoining Midland Gardens
Terry Teare, Administrator
Kathy Metcalfe, Director of Care

Toronto: Lincoln Place Nursing Home
429 Walmer Rd., Toronto, ON M5P 2X9
Tel: 416-967-6949 *Fax:* 416-928-1965
Number of Beds: 248 beds

Toronto: Mon Sheong Home for the Aged
36 D'Arcy St., Toronto, ON M5T 1J7
Tel: 416-977-3762 *Fax:* 416-977-3231
msf@monsheong.org
www.monsheong.org
Number of Beds: 105 beds
Ricky Kwan, Administrator
Joseph Wong, Supervisor, Housekeeping/Maintenance

Toronto: North Park Nursing Home
450 Rustic Rd., Toronto, ON M6L 1W9
Tel: 416-247-0531 *Fax:* 416-247-6159
northparknursinghome@rogers.com
Number of Beds: 75 beds
Alayne Twaddle, Director, Residential Care

Toronto: Norwood Nursing Home Ltd.
122 Tyndall Ave., Toronto, ON M6K 2E2
Tel: 416-535-3011
administration@norwoodcare.ca
Year Founded: 1957
Number of Beds: 60 beds
Note: Specialties: Long-term care; Rehabilitative care; Palliative care room
Dr. Horst Sebald, Administrator

Toronto: True Davidson Acres
200 Dawes Rd., Toronto, ON M4C 5M8
Tel: 416-397-0400
Year Founded: 1973
Note: Specialties: Nursing care; Rehabilitation; Recreation program; Music & art therapy
Sylvia Moreland, Administrator

Toronto: Ukrainian Canadian Care Centre
60 Richview Rd., Toronto, ON M9A 5E4
Tel: 416-243-7653 *Fax:* 416-243-7452
www.stdemetrius.ca
Number of Beds: 152 beds
Note: Specialties: Long-term care; Therapeutic recreation; Social work
Sandy Lomaszewycz, Executive Director
Natalie Popowich, Coordinator, Environmental Services

Toronto: Wesburn Manor
400 The West Mall, Toronto, ON M9C 5S1
Tel: 416-394-3600 *Fax:* 416-394-3606
Number of Beds: 192 beds
Elaine Russell, Administrator

Toronto: The Wexford Residence Inc.
1860 Lawrence Ave. East, Toronto, ON M1R 5B1
Tel: 416-752-8877 *Fax:* 416-752-8414
Toll-Free: 1-877-807-0810
information@thewexford.org
www.thewexford.org
Year Founded: 1978
Number of Beds: 166 long-term care residents
Note: Specialties: Long-term care & apartment accommodation for seniors; Secure units for persons with cognitive impairments; Physiotherapy; Podiatry; Life enrichment therapy
Nicholas J. Manherz, Executive Director
Alan Pitts, Coordinator, Environmental Services

Toronto: Yee Hong Centre for Geriatric Care
2311 McNicoll Ave., Toronto, ON M1V 5L3
Tel: 416-321-6333 *Fax:* 416-321-6313
centre@yeehong.com
www.yeehong.com
Number of Beds: 250 beds
Florence Wong, CEO

Toronto: Yorkview Lifecare Centre
2045 Finch Ave. West, Toronto, ON M3N 1M9
Tel: 416-745-0811 *Fax:* 416-745-0568
Number of Beds: 276 beds
Marce Fulford, Administrator

Trenton: Trent Valley Lodge
195 Bay St., Trenton, ON K8V 1H9
Tel: 613-392-9235 *Fax:* 613-392-0688
tvl@bellnet.ca
Year Founded: 1970
Number of Beds: 70 beds
Note: Specialties: Restorative care; Activation services; Long-term stroke care
Bill Weaver, Administrator

Trout Creek: Lady Isabelle Nursing Home
PO Box 10, 102 Corkery St., Trout Creek, ON P0H 2L0
Tel: 705-723-5232 *Fax:* 705-723-5794
main@ladyisabelle.ca
www.ladyisabelle.ca
Number of Beds: 66 beds
Sadie Newman, Administrator
George Newman, Manager, Physical Plant/Material Management

Unionville: Bethany Lodge
23 Second St., Unionville, ON L3R 2C2
Tel: 905-477-3838 *Fax:* 905-477-2888
www.bethanylodge.org
Number of Beds: 128 beds
Basil Tambakis, Administrator

Vineland: United Mennonite Home (UMH)
Former Name: United Mennonite Home for the Aged
4024 Twenty-Third St., Vineland, ON L0R 2C0
Tel: 905-562-7385 *Fax:* 905-562-3711
thehome@umh.ca
www.umh.ca
Year Founded: 1955
Number of Beds: 128 beds
Note: Specialties: Activity program; Physiotherapy; Pet therapy
Art Sieb, Administrator

Virgil: Heritage Place
1743 Four Mile Creek Rd., Virgil, ON L0S 1T0
Tel: 905-468-1111
Number of Beds: 36 beds
Tim Siemens, CEO

Walkerton: Brucelea Haven
PO Box 1600, 41 McGivern St. West, Walkerton, ON N0G 2V0
Tel: 519-881-1570 *Fax:* 519-881-0231
emacewen@brucecounty.on.ca
www.brucecounty.on.ca/bruceleahaven.php

Year Founded: 1898
Number of Beds: 144 beds
Elanor McEwen, Administrator
Lesley Borth, Director of Care

Wardsville: Babcock Community Care Centre
Former Name: Babcock Nursing Home
196 Wellington St., Wardsville, ON N0L 2N0
Tel: 519-693-4415 *Fax:* 519-693-4876
admin@babcockonline.com
www.babcockonline.com
Social Media:
www.facebook.com/BabcockCommunityCareCentre
Number of Beds: 60 beds
Area Served: Elgin, Kent, Lambton, Middlesex
J.C. Babcock, Administrator/Owner

Warkworth: Community Nursing Home
PO Box 68, 97 Mill St., Warkworth, ON K0K 3K0
Tel: 705-924-2311 *Fax:* 705-924-1711
cnhwarakworth@communitylifecare.on.ca
www.cnhwarkworth.ca
Number of Beds: 60 beds
Lisa Allanson, Administrator
lallanson@clmi.ca
Linda Black, Environmental Contact

Waterdown: Alexander Place
329 Parkside Dr., Waterdown, ON L0K 2H0
Tel: 905-689-2662
alexanderplace@jarlette.com
www.hamiltonltc.org/facilities/alexander.htm
Number of Beds: 128 beds

Waterloo: Parkwood Mennonite Home Inc.
726 New Hampshire St., Waterloo, ON N2K 4M1
Tel: 519-885-4810 *Fax:* 519-885-6720
info@parkwoodmennonitehome.com
www.fairviewmennonitehomes.com/parkwood
Number of Beds: 96 beds
Gloria Dirks, Administrator
John McCutchen, Manager, Environmental Services

Welland: Foyer Richelieu Welland Inc.
655, av Tanguay, Welland, ON L3B 6A1
Tél: 905-734-1400 *Téléc:* 905-734-1386
www.foyerrichelieu.com
Fondée en: 1989
Nombre de lits: 61 beds
Sean Keays, Directeur général

Welland: Woodlands of Sunset
Affiliated with: Hamilton Niagara Haldimand Brant Local Health Integration Network
920 Pelham St., Welland, ON L3C 1Y5
Tel: 905-892-3845 *Fax:* 905-892-5882
www.niagararegion.ca/living/seniors/woodlands_of_sunset.aspx
Number of Beds: 120 beds
Tom Hunter, Administrator
G. Meek, Manager, Purchasing

Whitby: Fairview Lodge
PO Box 300, 632 Dundas St. West, Whitby, ON L1N 5S3
Tel: 905-668-5851 *Fax:* 905-668-8934
Number of Beds: 198 beds
Laura MacDermaid, Administrator

Wiarton: Gateway Haven
PO Box 10, 671 Frank St., Wiarton, ON N0H 2T0
Tel: 519-534-1113 *Fax:* 519-534-4733
bcgwh@brucecounty.on.ca
Number of Beds: 100 beds
Eleanor MacEwen, Administrator
emacewen@brucecounty.on.ca
Dianne Kiss, Director of Care, dkiss@brucecounty.on.ca

Wikwemikong: Wikwemikong Nursing Home
281 Wikwemikong Way, Wikwemikong, ON P0P 2J0
Tel: 705-859-3107 *Fax:* 705-859-2245
Number of Beds: 60 beds

Winchester: Dundas Manor Nursing Home
PO Box 970, 533 Clarence St., Winchester, ON K0C 2K0
Tel: 613-774-2293 *Fax:* 613-774-4015
ross.alguire@dundasmanor.ca
Number of Beds: 98 beds
Note: seniors home
Cholly Boland, Administrator
cboland@dundasmanor.ca
Daniel Dorey, Maintenance Supervisor

Windsor: Chateau Park Nursing Home
2990B Riverside Dr. West, Windsor, ON N9C 1A2
Tel: 519-254-4341 *Fax:* 519-254-7931
Number of Beds: 59 beds
Annemarie White, Administrator
awhite@meritascare.ca

Windsor: Extendicare - Southwood Lakes
1255 North Talbot Rd., Windsor, ON N9G 3A4
Tel: 519-945-7249 *Fax:* 519-945-7816
cnh_southwoodlakes@extendicare.com
www.extendicarecanada.com/windsor
Number of Beds: 150 beds

Windsor: Malden Park Continuing Care Centre
1453 Prince Rd., Windsor, ON N9C 3Z4
Tel: 519-257-5451 *Fax:* 519-257-5444
TTY: 519-257-5106
Number of Beds: 145 beds
Note: Long-term Care Facility
Al Grundner, Administrator

Windsor: Villa Maria Home for the Aged
2856 Riverside Dr. West, Windsor, ON N9C 1A2
Tel: 519-254-3763 *Fax:* 519-254-7657
Number of Beds: 120 beds
Note: home for the aged
Ken Deane, President/CEO

Woodbridge: Pine Grove Lodge
8403 Islington Ave. West, Woodbridge, ON L4L 1X3
Tel: 905-850-3605
pinegrovelodge@chartwellreit.ca
www.chartwellreit.ca
Year Founded: 1959
Number of Beds: 40 suites
Note: Specialties; Long-term care; Medication administration; Wellness monitoring; Cultural & activity program, catering to Italian & Canadian cultures; Recreation therapy; Occupational therapy; Physiotherapy; Podiatry; Respite care

Woodslee: Country Village Health Care Centre
County Rd. 8, RR#2, Woodslee, ON N0R 1V0
Tel: 519-839-4812 *Fax:* 519-839-4813
Number of Beds: 104 beds
Mary Butler, Executive Director
519-839-4812, mary.butler@countryvillage.ca
Doug Ferguson, Manager, Maintenance

Zurich: Blue Water Rest Home
37792 Zurich-Hensall Road, RR 3, Zurich, ON N0M 2T0
Tel: 519-236-4373 *Fax:* 519-236-7685
bwrh.info@bluewaterresthome.com
Number of Beds: 65 beds
Martha Craig, Administrator

Special Care Homes

Hamilton: Good Shepherd Centre
PO Box 1003, 135 Mary St., Hamilton, ON L8N 3R1
Tel: 905-528-9109 *Fax:* 905-546-1743
Year Founded: 1972
Number of Beds: 60 beds
Carmen Salcicciolі, Director

Long Term/Retirement Care

Long Term Care Facilities

Alliston: Good Samaritan Nursing Home
481 Victoria St. East, Alliston, ON L9R 1J8
Tel: 705-435-5722 *Fax:* 705-435-0235
gsnh@csolve.net
Number of Beds: 64 beds

Amherstburg: Richmond Terrace
89 Rankin Ave., Amherstburg, ON N9V 1E7
Tel: 519-736-5571 *Fax:* 519-736-2995
www.richmondterrace.ca
Number of Beds: 115 beds
Laura Scott, Administrator
lscott@richmondterrace.ca

Ancaster: The Willowgrove Long Term Care Residence
Affiliated with: Chartwell Seniors Housing REIT
1217 Old Mohawk Rd., Ancaster, ON L9K 1P6
Tel: 905-304-6781
www.chartwellreit.ca
Number of Beds: 168 units
Stephen Suske, CEO, Chartwell Seniors Housing REIT

Aurora: Aurora Resthaven
32 Mill St., Aurora, ON L4G 2R9
Tel: 905-727-1939 *Fax:* 905-727-6299
www.chartwellreit.ca
Number of Beds: 176 beds

Aurora: Blue Hills Child & Family Service
402 Bloomington Rd. West, Aurora, ON L4G 3G8
Tel: 905-773-4323 *Fax:* 905-773-8133
Toll-Free: 1-866-536-4323
gendeliv@bluehillschildandfamily.ca
www.bluehillschildandfamily.ca
Number of Beds: 9 beds
Note: children's mental health centre; special care home; outpatient services; family therapy
Sylvia Pivko, Executive Director
spivko@bluehillschildandfamily.ca

Aylmer: Chateau Gardens Aylmer
465 Talbot St. West, Aylmer, ON N5H 1K8
Tel: 519-773-3423 *Fax:* 519-765-2573
www.chateaugardens.com
Number of Beds: 60 beds

Barrie: Heritage Place
20 Brooks St., Barrie, ON L4N 7X2
Tel: 705-728-2389 *Fax:* 705-728-6049
www.ioof.com/?page_id=13
Doreen M. Saunders, CEO
dsaunders@ioof.com

Barrie: I.O.O.F. Senior Citizen Homes Inc.
Heritage Place, 10 Brooks St., Barrie, ON L4N 5L3
Tel: 705-728-2389 *Fax:* 705-728-6024
www.ioof.com
Number of Beds: 155 beds long-term care; 80 units supportive housing; 20 uni
Note: long-term care & seniors housing
Doreen M. Saunders, CEO
dsaunders@ioof.com
Deirdre Britton, Director of Resident Care
dbritton@ioof.com

Barrie: Victoria Village Manor
78 Ross St., Barrie, ON L4N 1G3
Tel: 705-728-3456 *Fax:* 705-728-4057
www.victoriavillage.ca
Number of Beds: 128 long-term care beds, 57 life-lease housing units

Beaverton: Lakeview Manor
133 Main St. West, Beaverton, ON L0K 1A0
Tel: 705-426-7388 *Fax:* 705-426-4218
Number of Beds: 149 beds
Note: home for the aged
John Rankin, Acting Administrator
Barb Surge, Director of Care

Belleville: Welcome to Community Living Belleville & Area
Former Name: Plainfield Community Homes; Plainfield Children's Home
91 Millennium Pkwy., Belleville, ON K8N 4Z5
Tel: 613-969-7407 *Fax:* 613-969-7775
www.plainfield.org
Social Media:
www.facebook.com/communitylivingbellevilleandarea
Year Founded: 1951
Note: Community Living Belleville & Area works toward the full inclusion in community life of persons with intellectual disabilities.
John B. Klassen, Executive Director
Stephen Ollerenshaw, Director, Finance
Katherine Potts, Director, Human Resources
Christine Semark, Director, Services
Jim Burgess, Manager, Buildings & Property
Sharon Wright, Manager, Community Development & Volunteer Services

Blind River: Golden Birches Terrace
525 Causley St., Blind River, ON P0R 1B0
Tel: 705-356-2265 *Fax:* 705-356-1220
webinfo@brdhc.on.ca
www.brdhc.on.ca
Number of Beds: 42 beds
Gaston Lavigne, CEO

Bracebridge: The Pines Long Term Care Home
Also Known As: The Pines
98 Pine St., Bracebridge, ON P1L 1N5
Tel: 705-645-4488 *Fax:* 705-645-6857
mlodge@muskoka.on.ca
Year Founded: 1961
Number of Beds: 160 beds
Note: Long term care residence
Henriette Koning, Administrator
705-645-4488 ext 403, hkoning@muskoka.on.ca
Charmaine Kaye, Director of Care

***Bradford:* Specialty Care Bradford Valley**
2656 Line 6, Bradford, ON L3Z 3H5
Tel: 905-952-2270 *Fax:* 905-775-0263
olivia.schmitz@specialty-care.com
www.specialty-care.com
Olivia Schmitz, Administrator

***Brampton:* Leisureworld Caregiving Centre - Tullamore**
133 Kennedy Rd. South, Brampton, ON L6W 3G3
Tel: 905-459-2324
adm.tullamore@leisureworld.ca
www.leisureworld.ca
Year Founded: 1965
Number of Beds: 159 beds
Note: Specialties: Long-term care; Restorative care; Occupational therapy; Physiotherapy; Care for persons with Alzheimer's disease; Respite care; Pet therapy; Palliative care
Wendy Shelley, Administrator

***Brampton:* Rosedale Retirement Residence**
12 William St., Brampton, ON L6V 1L2
Tel: 905-454-3788 *Fax:* 905-846-0447
Number of Beds: 12 beds
Rose Hamilton, Administrator

***Brampton:* Specialty Care Woodhall Park**
10260 Kennedy Rd. North, Brampton, ON L6T 3S1
Tel: 905-495-4695 *Fax:* 905-495-4693
david.wilson@specialty-care.com
www.specialty-care.com
Number of Beds: 147 beds
David Wilson, Administrator

***Brantford:* Brantwood Residential Development Centre**
Former Name: Brant Sanatorium
Also Known As: Brantwood Centre
25 Bell Lane, Brantford, ON N3T 1E1
Tel: 519-753-2658 *Fax:* 519-753-5639
info@brantwood.ca
www.brantwood.ca
Year Founded: 1913
Note: Brantwood provides services to persons who live in twelve group homes located in the city of Brantford & Brant County. A community day program is available for individuals who live in the community.
Dianne Belliveau, Executive Director
Ellen Brocklebank, Director, Support Services
Candace Clark, Director, Support Services
Jo-Anne Link, Director, Operations
Louise Rodgers, Director, Quality Assurance
Steve Wood, Director, Finance
Cindy Chatzis, Nurse Manager
Murray Haire, Manager, Facilities
Loraine Verplanke, Manager, Administration & Human Resources

***Brantford:* John Noble Home**
97 Mount Pleasant St., Brantford, ON N3T 1T5
Tel: 519-756-2920 *Fax:* 519-754-1521
info@jnh.ca
www.jnh.ca
Number of Beds: 156 beds
Eleanor Maslin, Administrator

***Brantford:* St. Joseph's Lifecare Centre**
Former Name: St. Joseph's Hospital
99 Wayne Gretzky Pkwy., Brantford, ON N3S 6T6
Tel: 519-751-7096 *Fax:* 519-753-7996
www.sjlc.ca
Romeo Cercone, Administrator

***Brighton:* Maplewood**
PO Box 249, 12 Maplewood Ave., Brighton, ON K0K 1H0
Tel: 613-475-2442 *Fax:* 613-475-4445
www.omniway.ca
Number of Beds: 49 beds
Note: Long-term care residence
Carolyn Adams, Office Manager
cadams@omniway.ca
Nancy McNairn, Administrator
nmcnairn@omniway.ca

***Burlington:* Billings Court Manor**
3700 Billings Court, Burlington, ON L7N 3N6
Tel: 905-333-4006 *Fax:* 905-333-4416
Toll-Free: 888-274-6445
Number of Beds: 160 units
Ann Chartier, Administrator

***Burlington:* Participation House - Hamilton & District**
1022 Waterdown Rd., Burlington, ON L7T 1N3
Tel: 905-527-7949 *Fax:* 905-333-8711
info@participationhouse.hamilton.on.ca
www.participationhouse.hamilton.on.ca
Number of Beds: 39 beds
Note: Provides services designed to enhance the quality of life of adults with disabilities
Cindy Kinnon, Executive Director

***Chatham:* Copper Terrace Long Term Care Facility**
91 Tecumseh Rd., Chatham, ON N7M 1B3
Tel: 519-354-5442 *Fax:* 519-354-0362
www.copperterrace.ca
Number of Beds: 151 beds
Kathy Morningstar, Administrator
kmorningstar@ckha.on.ca

***Chatham:* Meadow Park Care Centre - Chatham**
110 Sandys St., Chatham, ON N7L 4X3
Tel: 519-351-1330 *Fax:* 519-351-7933
www.jarlette.com
Number of Beds: 97 beds
Anne Marie Rumble, Administrator
amrumble@jarlette.com
Joanne Wytinck, Director of Care
jwytinck@jarlette.com

***Chatham:* Riverview Gardens**
Former Name: Thamesview Lodge
519 King St. West, Chatham, ON N7M 1G8
Tel: 519-352-4823 *Fax:* 519-352-2891
CKseniors@chatham-kent.ca
www.chatham-kent.ca
Number of Beds: 320 beds

***Chatsworth:* Country Lane Long Term Care Centre**
RR#3, Chatsworth, ON N0H 1G0
Tel: 519-794-2244 *Fax:* 519-794-2597
mkennedy-mcgregor@extindicare.com
www.reveraliving.com
Number of Beds: 34 beds
Lynn Jamieson, Administrator

***Chesley:* Parkview Manor**
98 - 3rd St. SE, Chesley, ON N0G 1L0
Tel: 519-363-2416 *Fax:* 519-363-2171
cwoods2@extendicare.com
www.extendicare.com
Number of Beds: 34 beds
Carole Woods, Administrator
cwoods2@extendicare.com

***Clarence Creek:* Centre d'accueil Roger-Séguin**
435 Lemay St., Clarence Creek, ON K0A 1N0
Tel: 613-488-2053 *Fax:* 613-488-2274
www.centrerogerseguin.org
Number of Beds: 115 beds
Note: charitable
Charles Lefebvre, Administrator

***Cobourg:* Golden Plough Lodge**
983 Burnham St., Cobourg, ON K9A 5J6
Tel: 905-372-8759 *Fax:* 905-372-8525
www.northumberlandcounty.ca
Number of Beds: 162 beds
Marion Morton, Receptionist
905-372-8759 ext3268, mortonm@northumberlandcounty.ca

***Cochrane:* Villa Minto**
PO Box 280, 241 - 8 St., Cochrane, ON P0L 1C0
Tel: 705-272-7200 *Fax:* 705-272-4155
Number of Beds: 33 beds
Note: Villa Minto is an independent LTC facility housed in the chronic care wing of The Lady Minto Hospital
Dan O'Mara, Administrator

***Cornwall:* Sandfield Place**
Also Known As: 458422 Ontario Limited
220 Emma St., Cornwall, ON K6J 5V8
Tel: 613-933-6972 *Fax:* 613-938-2261
sandfield@bellnet.ca
www.sandfieldplace.ca
Number of Beds: 53 long term care beds, 34 retirement beds
Note: Long term care & retirement living
Bill Kinnear, Administrator
bill.kinnear@bellnet.ca

***Delaware:* Middlesex Terrace**
2094 Gideon Dr., R.R.#1, Delaware, ON N0L 1E0
Tel: 519-652-3483 *Fax:* 519-652-6915
www.middlesexterrace.ca
Number of Beds: 105 beds
Tanya Pol, Administrator
tpol@middlesexterrace.ca
Jan Shkilynk, RN, Director of Nursing
jshkilnyk@middlesexterrace.ca

***Dundas:* St. Joseph's Villa (Dundas)**
Affiliated with: Hamilton Niagara Haldimand Brant Local Health Integration Network
56 Governor's Rd., Dundas, ON L9H 5G7
Tel: 905-627-3541 *Fax:* 905-628-0825
www.sjv.on.ca
Number of Beds: 378 beds
Shawn Gadsby, President

***Dundas:* Wentworth Lodge**
41 South St. West, Dundas, ON L9H 4C4
Tel: 905-546-2618 *Fax:* 905-546-2854
wentworthlodge@hamilton.ca
www.hamilton.ca/phcs/wentworth
Number of Beds: 160 beds
Note: home for the aged
Lynda Secord, Administrator

***Dunnville:* Grandview Lodge**
657 Lock St. West, Dunnville, ON N1A 1V9
Tel: 905-774-7547 *Fax:* 905-774-1440
www.haldimandcounty.on.ca
Number of Beds: 128 beds
Joanne Jackson, Administrator
905-774-7547 ext 224, jjackson@haldimandcounty.on.ca
Kim Mauro, Director of Nursing
905-774-7547 ext 234, kmauro@haldimandcounty.on.ca

***Durham:* Rockwood Terrace**
PO Box 660, 575 Sadler St. East, Durham, ON N0G 1R0
Tel: 519-369-6035 *Fax:* 519-369-6736
www.greycounty.ca
Number of Beds: 100 beds
Note: Long term care
Karen Kraus, Administrator
kkraus@greycounty.ca

***Elmira:* Chateau Gardens (Elmira) Nursing Home**
11 Herbert St., Elmira, ON N3B 2B8
Tel: 519-669-2921 *Fax:* 519-669-3027
Number of Beds: 48 beds

***Elmvale:* Sara-Vista Long Term Care Facility**
27 Simcoe St., Elmvale, ON L0L 1P0
Tel: 705-322-2182
www.reveraliving.com
Number of Beds: 60 beds
Karen Jones, Administrator

***Etobicoke:* Westside Long-Term Care**
Former Name: Central Park Lodge West Side
1145 Albion Rd., Etobicoke, ON M9V 4J7
Tel: 416-745-4800 *Fax:* 416-745-0445
vaishali.thorat@reveraliving.com
www.reveraliving.com/westside
Number of Beds: 218 beds
Area Served: Etobicoke North; Greater Toronto Area; Peel Region
Vaishali Thorat, Resident Services Coordinator
416-745-4800 ext 238

***Fort Erie:* Gilmore Lodge**
50 Gilmore Rd., Fort Erie, ON L2A 2M1
Tel: 905-871-6160 *Fax:* 905-871-0435
Number of Beds: 79 beds
Bev Goodman, Administrator

***Fort Erie:* Maple Park Lodge**
6 Hagey Ave., Fort Erie, ON L2A 5M5
Tel: 905-994-0224 *Fax:* 905-994-8628
Number of Beds: 96 units
Note: Nursing home

***Fort Frances:* Rainycrest Home for the Aged**
550 Osborne St., Fort Frances, ON P9A 3T2
Tel: 807-274-3266 *Fax:* 807-274-7368
E.Bodnar@rhcf.on.ca
Number of Beds: 147 beds
Note: home for the aged
Jill Colquhoun, Administrator
Allan Johnstone, Coordinator, Environmental Services

***Glenburnie:* Fairmount Home for the Aged**
2069 Battersea Rd., RR#1, Glenburnie, ON K0H 1S0
Tel: 613-546-4264 *Fax:* 613-546-0489
jshillington@frontenaccounty.ca
www.frontenaccounty.ca/?q=fairmount_home

Number of Beds: 128 beds
Note: home for the aged
Julie Shillington, Administrator

Gore Bay: Manitoulin Lodge
3 Main St., Gore Bay, ON P0P 1H0
Tel: 705-282-2007 *Fax:* 705-282-3422
www.jarlette.com
Number of Beds: 61 beds
Lorna Fogg, Administrator
lfogg@jarlette.com

Grimsby: Deer Park Villa
150 Central Ave., Grimsby, ON L3M 4Z3
Tel: 905-945-4164
www.niagararegion.ca
Number of Beds: 39 beds
Kim Eros, Administrator/Director of Resident Care
kim.eros@regional.niagara.on.ca

Guelph: The Elliott Community
170 Metcalfe St., Guelph, ON N1E 4Y3
Tel: 519-822-0491 *Fax:* 519-822-5658
info@elliottcommunity.org
www.elliottcommunity.org
Number of Beds: 270 beds
Note: Retirement suites & long term care
Trevor Lee, CEO

Haileybury: Temiskaming Lodge
100 Bruce St., Haileybury, ON P0J 1K0
Tel: 705-672-2123 *Fax:* 705-672-5734
www.jarlette.com
Number of Beds: 82 beds
Francine Gosselin, Administrator
fgosselin@jarlette.com

Hamilton: Baywoods Place
Affiliated with: Revera Inc.
330 Main St. East, Hamilton, ON L8N 3T9
Tel: 905-523-7134
www.reveraliving.com/baywoods
Note: Programs provided at Baywoods Place include the following: rehabilitation, recreation, music therapy, skin & wound care, Snoezelen multi-sensory therapy, pet therapy, & safety programs.

Hamilton: Grace Villa LTCH
45 Lockton Cres., Hamilton, ON L8V 4V5
Tel: 905-387-4812 *Fax:* 905-387-4814
whall@gracevilla.ca
www.gracevilla.ca
Number of Beds: 184 beds
Wendy Hall, Administrator

Hamilton: Idlewyld Manor
449 Sanatorium Rd., Hamilton, ON L9C 2A7
Tel: 905-574-2000 *Fax:* 905-574-0482
office@idlewyldmanor.com
www.idlewyldmanor.com
Number of Beds: 101 beds
Maureen Goodram, Executive Director

Hamilton: St. Elizabeth Villa
391 Rymal Rd. West, Hamilton, ON L9B 1V2
Tel: 905-388-9691 *Fax:* 905-388-9953
stelizabeth.villa@bellnet.ca
www.stelizabethhomesociety.org
Note: assisted living
Sr. Maria Szucs, Administrator

Hamilton: St. Peter's Residence at Chedoke
125 Redfern Ave., Hamilton, ON L9C 7W9
Tel: 905-777-3837 *Fax:* 905-383-1099
reception@stpeterscc.ca
www.stpetes.ca
Number of Beds: 210 beds
Donna Cripps, President/CEO

Hamilton: Shalom Village
70 Macklin St. North, Hamilton, ON L8S 3S1
Tel: 905-529-1613 *Fax:* 905-529-7542
info@shalomvillage.on.ca
www.shalomvillage.on.ca
Number of Beds: 60 beds
Note: Long term care & assisted living, day program; kosher meals provided; Jewish & ecumenical services. Shalom Village Too with 64 beds & 30 apartments is located adjacent
Jeanette O'Leary, Chief Executive Coach

Hamilton: Townsview Lifecare Centre
39 Mary St., Hamilton, ON L8R 3L8
Tel: 905-523-6427 *Fax:* 905-528-0610
eyi_townsview_complex@extendicare.com
www.hamiltonltc.org
Number of Beds: 219 beds
Andrew Adamyk, Administrator
aadamyk@extendicare.com

Hamilton: The Wellington
1430 Upper Wellington St., Hamilton, ON L9A 5H3
Tel: 905-385-2111 *Fax:* 905-385-2110
www.thewellington.ca
Number of Beds: 102 long term care beds, 80 retirement beds
Note: Long term care & retirement community
Tanya Macdonald, Administrator
Doretta Skidmore, Contact, Residence Information
dskidmore@thewellington.ca

Huntsville: Muskoka Landing
65 Rogers Cove Dr., Huntsville, ON P1H 2L9
Tel: 705-788-7713 *Fax:* 705-788-1424
www.jarlette.com
Number of Beds: 94 long-term care beds
Bill Thurlow, Administrator
bthurlow@jarlette.com

Jacksons Point: Cedar Lane Lodge
PO Box 384, 895 Lake Dr., Jacksons Point, ON L0E 1L0
Tel: 905-722-8928 *Fax:* 905-722-8928
Note: Housing is provided for adults who require support for daily living.
Jeff Smith, Administrator

Jasper: Rosebridge Manor
131 Roses Bridge Rd., RR#2, Jasper, ON K0G 1G0
Tel: 613-283-5471 *Fax:* 613-283-9012
www.omniway.com
Number of Beds: 78 beds
Dorothy Broeders-Morin, Administrator
dmorin@omniway.ca
Gary Foster, Director, Housekeeping/Physical Plant

Kincardine: Trillium Court Seniors Community
550 Phillip Pl., Kincardine, ON N2Z 3A6
Tel: 519-396-4400 *Fax:* 519-366-9092
trillium@reveraliving.com
www.reveraliving.com
Number of Beds: 40 beds + 60 retirement suites
Note: Independent & assisted living, retirement lodge, long-term care, respite & convalescent options
Pam Campbell, Administrator
M. Furnvale, Supervisor, Environmental Services

Kingston: Providence Manor
275 Sydenham St., Kingston, ON K7K 1G7
Tel: 613-549-4164 *Fax:* 613-549-7472
nowlans@providencecare.ca
www.pccchealth.org
Number of Beds: 243 beds
Note: Long-term care
Shelagh Nowlan, Site Administrator

Kingston: St. Mary's of the Lake Hospital
340 Union St., Kingston, ON K7L 5A2
Tel: 613-544-5220 *Fax:* 613-544-8558
bonuttim@providencecare.ca
www.pccchealth.org
Number of Beds: 144 beds
Note: Acute care, complex continuing care, geriatric medicine, rehabilitation, palliative care, respite care
Michele Bonutti, Site Administrator/CFO

Kingston: Specialty Care Trillium Centre
800 Edgar St., Kingston, ON K7M 8S4
Tel: 613-547-0040 *Fax:* 613-547-3734
info@specialty-care.com
www.specialty-care.com
Number of Beds: 234 units
Note: Comprehensive long-term care services. Trillium Ridge Retirement Community located adjacent
Jennifer Powley, Administrator

Kitchener: Lanark Heights Long-Term Care
46 Lanark Cres., Kitchener, ON N2N 2Z8
Tel: 519-743-4200 *Fax:* 519-743-4225
info@lanarkcare.com
www.lanarkcare.com
Number of Beds: 107 units

Kitchener: Sunnyside Home
247 Franklin St. North, Kitchener, ON N2A 1Y5
Tel: 519-893-8482 *Fax:* 519-893-4450
www.region.waterloo.on.ca
Number of Beds: 251 residential capacity
Note: Specialty: Long-term care
Gail Carlin, Administrator
Wendy Reid, Chair, Health & Safety Committee
Reg Weber, Supervisor, Maintenance

Kitchener: Westmount Long Term Care Residence
200 David Bergey Dr., Kitchener, ON N2E 3Y4
chartwellreit.ca/locations/westmount-ltc-residence/index.php
Number of Beds: 160 suites
Note: Westmount Long Term Care Residence for seniors offers services to help maintain independence & wellness.

Kitchener: The Westmount Long Term Care Residence
Affiliated with: Chartwell Seniors Housing REIT
200 David Bergey Dr., Kitchener, ON N2E 3Y4
Tel: 519-570-2115 *Fax:* 519-579-9770
www.chartwellreit.ca
Number of Beds: 160 units
Stephen Suske, CEO, Chartwell Seniors Housing REIT

Komoka: Country Terrace Long Term Care Home
Affiliated with: South West Local Health Integration Network
Former Name: Country Terrace Nursing Home
10072 Oxbow Dr., RR#3, Komoka, ON N0L 1R0
Tel: 519-657-2955 *Fax:* 519-657-8516
kdann@omniway.ca
www.omniway.ca/ourhomes_details.php?id=20
Number of Beds: 120 beds
Chen Armitage, Administrator

L'Orignal: Résidence Champlain
Affiliated with: Chartwell Seniors Housing REIT
428 Front Rd. West, L'Orignal, ON K0B 1K0
Tel: 613-675-4617
champlain@chartwellreit.ca
www.chartwellreit.ca
Number of Beds: 60 beds
Stephen Suske, CEO, Chartwell Seniors Housing REIT

Lancaster: Chateau Gardens (Lancaster)
PO Box 429, 105 Military Rd. North, Lancaster, ON K0C 1N0
Tel: 613-347-3016 *Fax:* 613-347-1680
www.chartwellreit.ca
Number of Beds: 60 beds

Limoges: Résidence Limoges
131-133 Ottawa St., Limoges, ON K0A 2M0
Tél: 613-443-5303 *Téléc:* 613-443-1943
Nombre de lits: 25 lits
François Grégoire, Administrateur

Limoges: St. Viateur Nursing Home
1003 Limoges Rd. South, Limoges, ON K0A 2M0
Tel: 613-443-5751 *Fax:* 613-443-5950
Number of Beds: 64 beds
Richard R. Marleau, Administrator

Lindsay: Frost Manor
225 Mary St. West, Lindsay, ON K9V 5K3
Tel: 705-324-8333 *Fax:* 705-878-5840
www.omniway.com
Number of Beds: 62 beds
Connie Daly, Administrator
cdaly@omniway.ca

London: Anago Resources Inc.
371 Princess Ave., London, ON N6B 2A7
Tel: 519-435-1099 *Fax:* 519-435-0062
info@anago.on.ca
www.anago.on.ca
Number of Beds: 63 beds
Note: young offenders; developmental handicap group home; child & family intervention treatment
Mandy L. Bennett, Executive Director

London: Chateau Gardens London
2000 Blackwater Rd., London, ON N5X 4K6
Tel: 519-434-2727
Number of Beds: 95 beds

London: Chelsey Park Retirement Community
310 Oxford St. West, London, ON N6H 4N6
Tel: 519-432-1855 *Fax:* 516-432-7548
www.chelseypark.com
Number of Beds: 247 beds

Diane Pope, Customer Relations Manager
519-432-1845 ext.235, info.cprc@diversicare.ca

London: Dearness Services
710 Southdale Rd., London, ON N6E 1R8
Tel: 519-661-0400 *Fax:* 519-661-0446

Number of Beds: 348 beds
L. Hignett, Administrator

London: Longworth Long Term Care
590 Longworth Rd., London, ON N6K 4X9
Tel: 519-472-6424 *Fax:* 519-472-8852
info@longworthcare.com
www.longworthcare.com

Number of Beds: 160 beds
Note: Specialties: Long term care; Restorative care program; Massage therapy; Physiotherapy; Family & personal counseling services

London: Meadow Park Care Centre & Retirement Lodge - London
1210 Southdale Rd. East, London, ON N6E 1B4
Tel: 519-686-0484 *Fax:* 519-686-9932
www.jarlette.com

Note: Long term care facility & retirement lodge
Terri Daly, Administrator, Care Centre
tdaly@jarlette.com
Michelle Gatt, General Manager, Retirement Lodge
mgatt@jarlette.com

London: St. Joseph's Health Care, London
21 Grosvenor St., London, ON N6A 1Y1
Tel: 519-646-6000 *Fax:* 519-646-6054
Communications.Department@sjhc.london.on.ca
www.sjhc.london.on.ca

Number of Beds: 390 beds
Jane Boudreau-Bailey, Director

Markham: The Woodhaven Long Term Care Residence
Affiliated with: Chartwell Seniors Housing REIT
380 Church St., Markham, ON L6B 1E1
Tel: 905-472-3320
www.chartwellreit.ca

Number of Beds: 192 units
Stephen Suske, CEO, Chartwell Seniors Housing REIT

Maxville: Maxville Manor
80 Mechanic St. West, Maxville, ON K0C 1T0
Tel: 613-527-2170 *Fax:* 613-527-3103
www.maxvillemanor.ca

Year Founded: 1968
Number of Beds: 120 beds + 2 respite beds
Note: Specialties: Long-term care services; Therapy services; The Seniors' Centre, providing outreach services to persons in the community with physical disabilities & special needs; Adult day program; Seniors' clinics, such as hearing, optometry, & foot care. Number of Employees: 130
R.E.C. Munro, Executive Director
Sally Bennett, Director, Nursing
Neil McCormick, Director, Environmental Services

Midland: Hillcrest Village Care Centre
Former Name: St. Andrew's Centennial Manor
255 Russell St., Midland, ON L4R 5L6
Tel: 705-526-3781 *Fax:* 705-526-5656
information@hvcc.ca
www.hvcc.ca

Number of Beds: 100 beds
Walter Ens, Administrator

Milton: Allendale
185 Ontario St. South, Milton, ON L9T 2M4
Tel: 905-878-4141 *Fax:* 905-878-8797
Toll-Free: 866-442-5866
johnstoi@halton.ca
www.halton.ca/scs/seniors/ltc/allendale.htm

Number of Beds: 300 beds
Ingrid Johnston, Administrator

Milton: Mount Nemo Christian Nursing Home
4486 Guelph Line, RR#2, Milton, ON L9T 2X6
Tel: 905-335-3636 *Fax:* 905-335-3699
mountnemonursinghome@cogeco.net
www.mountnemochristiannh.on.ca

Number of Beds: 60 beds
Note: long term care home

Mississauga: Cawthra Gardens
590 Lolita Gardens, Mississauga, ON L5A 4N8
Tel: 905-306-9984
www.delcare.com

Number of Beds: 192 beds

Mississauga: Chelsey Park Mississauga Long-Term Care Facility
2250 Hurontario St., Mississauga, ON L5B 1M8
Tel: 905-270-0411

Number of Beds: 237 beds

Mississauga: Chelsey Park Streetsville Long-Term Care Facility
1742 Bristol Rd. West, Mississauga, ON L5M 1X9
Tel: 905-826-3045

Mississauga: Heritage House Retirement Home
73 King St. West, Mississauga, ON L5B 1H1
Tel: 905-279-4800 *Fax:* 905-615-8141
theheritagehouse@rogers.com
www.heritagehouseonline.com

Note: Specialties: Physiotherapy; Occupational therapy; Specialized rehabilitative care; Recovery from surgery; Cardiac care program; Orthopedic care; Acitvity program; Respite or short stays
Janice MacInnis, Administrator
Angus MacInnis, Administrator

Mississauga: Specialty Care Mississauga Road
4350 Mississauga Rd., Mississauga, ON L5M 7C8
Tel: 905-812-1175 *Fax:* 905-812-1173
gayle.stuart@specialty-care.com
www.specialty-care.com

Number of Beds: 160 beds
Gayle Stuart, Administrator

Mississauga: Villa Forum
175 Forum Dr., Mississauga, ON L4Z 4E5
Tel: 905-501-1443 *Fax:* 905-501-0094

Number of Beds: 160 units
Note: Long-term care facility

Mississauga: The Wenleigh Long Term Care Residence
Affiliated with: Chartwell Seniors Housing REIT
2065 Leanne Blvd., Mississauga, ON L5K 2L6
Tel: 905-822-4663
www.chartwellreit.ca

Number of Beds: 161 units
Stephen Suske, CEO, Chartwell Seniors Housing REIT

Mitchell: Ritz Lutheran Villa
Rd. 164 - 4118A, RR#5, Mitchell, ON N0K 1N0
Tel: 519-348-8612 *Fax:* 519-348-4420
info@ritzlutheranvilla.com
www.ritzlutheranvilla.com

Number of Beds: 83 beds
Note: charitable home for the aged, retirement community with rental apartments & life lease town homes
Brent E. Nafziger, Administrator
Randy Satchell, Building Services Supervisor

Napanee: The John M. Parrott Centre
Former Name: Lenadco Home
309 Bridge St. West, Napanee, ON K7R 2G4
Tel: 613-354-3306 *Fax:* 613-354-7387
bsmith@lennox-addington.on.ca
www.lennox-addington.on.ca

Number of Beds: 168 beds
Note: Long term care
Brian Smith, Director

Nepean: Carleton Lodge
55 Lodge Rd., Nepean, ON K2C 3H1
Tel: 613-825-3763 *Fax:* 613-825-0245
ottawa.ca

Number of Beds: 160 beds

Newmarket: Southlake Residential Care Village
640 Grace St., Newmarket, ON L3Y 2L1
Tel: 905-895-7661 *Fax:* 905-895-9806
www.southlakeregional.org/southlakeresidentialcarevillage.html
Year Founded: 2004
Number of Beds: 192 beds
Note: Number of staff: 200
Terry Collins, Executive Director
tcollins@extendicare.com

Niagara Falls: Bella Senior Care Residence
8720 Willoughby Dr., Niagara Falls, ON L2G 7X3
Tel: 905-295-2727
info@bellaseniorcare.com
www.bellaseniorcare.com

Number of Beds: 160 units

Niagara on the Lake: Chateau Gardens - Niagara
PO Box 985, 120 Wellington St., Niagara on the Lake, ON L0S 1J0
Tel: 905-468-2111 *Fax:* 905-468-4463
www.chartwellreit.ca

Number of Beds: 124 beds

Niagara on the Lake: Upper Canada Lodge
272 Wellington St., Niagara on the Lake, ON L0S 1J0
Tel: 905-468-4208 *Fax:* 905-468-0520
uppercanada@niagararegion.ca

Year Founded: 1988
Number of Beds: 80 beds
Colleen Johnson, Administrator
Dave Shedden, Supervisor, Maintenance

North Bay: Cassellholme
400 Olive St., North Bay, ON P1B 6J4
Tel: 705-474-4250 *Fax:* 705-474-6129
www.cassellholme.on.ca

Number of Beds: 240 beds
Note: home for the aged
Brenda Loubert, CEO
705-474-4250 ext 300, loubertb@cassellholme.on.ca

Oakville: The Waterford Long Term Care Residence
Affiliated with: Chartwell Seniors Housing REIT
2140 Baronwood Dr., Oakville, ON L6M 4V6

Year Founded: 2003
Number of Beds: 168 units
Stephen Suske, CEO, Chartwell Seniors Housing REIT

Oakville: Wyndham Manor
291 Reynolds St., Oakville, ON L6J 3L5
Tel: 905-849-7766

Number of Beds: 128 beds

Orillia: The Leacock Care Centre
25 Museum Dr., Orillia, ON L3V 7T9
Tel: 705-325-9181 *Fax:* 705-325-5179
www.jarlette.com

Number of Beds: 145 long-term care beds
Marilyn Hauser, Administrator
mhauser@jarlette.com

Orleans: Kingsway Arms at St. Joseph Manor
1510 St. Joseph Blvd., Orleans, ON K1C 7L1
Tel: 613-830-4000 *Fax:* 613-830-7607
manoirstjoseph@on.aibn.com
www.kingswayarms.com/stjoseph.php

Number of Beds: 80 beds
Jeannine Zacconi, Director of Care

Orleans: Madonna Long Term Care Facility
1541 St. Joseph Blvd., Orleans, ON K1C 1S9
Tel: 613-824-2040
www.chartwellreit.ca

Note: Specialties: Restorative care; Palliative care

Orleans: Résidence Saint-Louis
879, ch Hiawatha Park, Orleans, ON K1C 2Z6
Tél: 613-824-1720 *Téléc:* 613-824-8064

Nombre de lits: 198 lits
Note: Établissement francophone de soins de longue durée
Jean Bartkowiak, President-directeur général, Service de santé SCO Health Service

Oshawa: Hillsdale Estates
590 Oshawa Blvd. North, Oshawa, ON L1G 5T9
Tel: 905-579-1777 *Fax:* 905-579-3911

Year Founded: 2003
Number of Beds: 435 beds
Len Cserhati, Administrator
Linda Doherty, Director, Resident Care

Oshawa: Thorntonview
186 Thornton Rd. South, Oshawa, ON L1J 5Y2
Tel: 905-576-5181 *Fax:* 905-576-0078
thorntonview@reveraliving.com
www.reveraliving.com

Number of Beds: 154 beds
Note: Long-term care, palliative care, services for physically challenged adults
Arlene Inkster, Administrator

Oshawa: The Wynfield Long Term Care Residence
451 Woodmount Dr., Oshawa, ON L1G 8E3
Tel: 905-571-0065 *Fax:* 905-579-4902
www.chartwellreit.ca

Number of Beds: 172 beds
Katherine Jackson, Administrator
Stephen Suske, CEO, Chartwell Seniors Housing REIT

Ottawa: Carlingview Manor
2330 Carling Ave., Ottawa, ON K2B 7H1
Tel: 613-820-9328 *Fax:* 613-820-9774
www.reveraliving.com/carlingview
Number of Beds: 320 beds
Lori Norris, Administrator

Ottawa: Hillel Lodge
Also Known As: The Bess & Moe Greenberg Family Hillel Lodge
10 Nadolny Sachs Private, Ottawa, ON K2A 4G7
Tel: 613-728-3900 *Fax:* 613-728-6550
Number of Beds: 100 beds
Stephen Schneiderman, Executive Director

Ottawa: Hillel Lodge (The Bess & Moe Greenberg Family)
10 Nadolny Sachs Pvt., Ottawa, ON K2A 4G7
Tel: 613-728-3900 *Fax:* 613-728-6550
sss@hillel-ltc.com
www.hillel-ltc.com
Number of Beds: 100 beds
Note: Charitable home for the aged
Stephen Schneiderman, Executive Director

Ottawa: Manoir Wymering Manor
845 Kirkwood Ave., Ottawa, ON K1Z 5Y1
Tel: 613-722-8811 *Fax:* 613-722-0795
manoirwymeringmanor@gmail.com
Year Founded: 1974
Note: Wymering Manor is a member of the Ontario Homes for Special Needs Association.
Linda Lafrance, Administrator
Laura Kelly, Director

Ottawa: St. Patrick's Home of Ottawa Inc.
2865 Riverside Dr., Ottawa, ON K1V 8N5
Tel: 613-731-4660 *Fax:* 613-731-4056
lindachaplin@stpats.ca
www.stpats.ca
Number of Beds: 202 beds
Note: home for the aged
Sr. Mona Martin, Executive Director

Ottawa: The Salvation Army Ottawa Booth Centre
Former Name: Metropole & Salvage Depot
171 George St., Ottawa, ON K1N 5W5
Tel: 613-241-1573 *Fax:* 613-241-2818
www.ottawaboothcentre.org
Year Founded: 1908
Note: Specialties: Anchorage Program, an addiction treatment program; Street outreach
Carson Durdle, Executive Director

Owen Sound: Versa-Care Summit Place
850 - 4th St. East, Owen Sound, ON N4K 6A3
Tel: 519-376-3212 *Fax:* 519-371-0923
summitplace@reveraliving.com
www.reveraliving.com
Number of Beds: 159 beds
Renate Cowan, Executive Director
renate.cowan@reveraliving.com

Palmerston: Royal Terrace
600 Whites Rd., Palmerston, ON N0G 2P0
Tel: 519-343-2611 *Fax:* 519-343-2860
royalter@wightman.ca
www.royalterracepalmerston.ca
Number of Beds: 121 beds
Note: Long-term & residential care
Kash Ramchandani, Administrator

Paris: Park Lane Terrace
295 Grand River St. North, Paris, ON N3L 2N9
Tel: 519-442-2753 *Fax:* 519-442-6176
www.parklaneterrace.ca
Number of Beds: 132 beds
Debora Saville, Administrator
dsaville@parklaneterrace.ca

Parry Sound: Lakeland Long Term Care Facility
6 Albert St., Parry Sound, ON P2A 3A4
Tel: 705-746-9667 *Toll-Free:* 1-866-959-9005
lfabiano@lakelandltc.com
www.lakelandltc.com
Note: Located within the West Parry Sound Health Centre complex
Norman Maciver, CEO

Pembroke: Marianhill
600 Cecelia St., Pembroke, ON K8A 7Z3
Tel: 613-735-6838 *Fax:* 613-732-3934
www.marianhill.ca
Number of Beds: 200 beds
Note: Catholic long-term and chronic care facility
Terry McBurney, Executive Director

Penetanguishene: Georgian Manor
7 Harriett St., Penetanguishene, ON L9M 1K8
Tel: 705-549-3166 *Fax:* 705-549-6062
www.georgianvillage.ca
Number of Beds: 107 beds
Note: home for the aged

Penetanguishene: Ruth Haarer Home for Special Care
Former Name: Ruth Haarer Residence
PO Box 1067, 2 Water St., Penetanguishene, ON L9M 1V6
Tel: 705-549-7296
Number of Beds: 18 beds
Ruth Haarer, Administrator

Peterborough: Fairhaven Home
881 Dutton Rd., Peterborough, ON K9H 7S4
Tel: 705-743-0881 *Fax:* 705-743-6292
info@fairhavenltc.com
fairhavenltc.com
Year Founded: 1960
Number of Beds: 253 beds
Note: home for the aged
Alex Clarke, President

Peterborough: Riverview Manor
1155 Water St., Peterborough, ON K9H 3P8
Tel: 705-748-6706 *Fax:* 705-748-5407
magreco@omniway.ca
www.omni-way.com
Number of Beds: 124 beds
Sue Matwey, Administrator

Peterborough: Springdale Country Manor
2698 Clifford Line, Peterborough, ON K9J 6X6
Tel: 705-742-8811 *Fax:* 705-742-8812
www.omni-way.com/ourhomes/springdale.htm
Number of Beds: 65 beds
Maureen Imamovic, Administrator
mimamovic@omniway.ca

Petrolia: Lambton Meadowview Villa
3958 Petrolia Line, RR#4, Petrolia, ON N0N 1R0
Tel: 519-882-1470 *Fax:* 519-882-1633
Toll-Free: 800-565-3890
Number of Beds: 123 beds, 2 short stay beds
Note: home for the aged
Jeff Harvey, Resident Manager
519-882-1470 ext5009, jeff.harvey@county-lambton.on.ca

Port Colborne: Northland Manor
Northland Pointe, 2 Fielder Ave., Port Colborne, ON L3K 6G4
Tel: 905-835-9335 *Fax:* 905-835-6518
northland@niagararegion.ca
Number of Beds: 150 beds
Note: Long-term care facility
Maureen Shantz, Administrator

Port Stanley: Extendicare - Port Stanley
4551 East Rd., Port Stanley, ON N5L 1J6
Tel: 519-782-3339 *Fax:* 519-782-4756
cnh_portstanley@extendicare.com
www.extendicarecanada.com/portstanley
Number of Beds: 60 beds

Ridgetown: The Village on the Ridge
Former Name: The Village Retirement Residence
9 Myrtle St., Ridgetown, ON N0P 2C0
Tel: 519-674-5427 *Fax:* 519-674-2422
village-residence@reveraliving.com
Number of Beds: 40 beds in nursing home; 70 beds in retirement home
Donna Kingelin

Rockland: St. Joseph Long-Term Care Facility
1615 Laurier St., Rockland, ON K4K 1C8
Tel: 613-446-5126
Number of Beds: 64 units

Sarnia: Sumac Lodge
1464 Blackwell Rd., Sarnia, ON N7S 5M4
Tel: 519-542-3421 *Fax:* 519-542-3604
sumaclodge@reveraliving.com
www.reveraliving.com
Number of Beds: 100 beds
Ann Currie, Executive Director
ann.currie@reveraliving.com

Sarnia: Twin Lakes Terrace
Affiliated with: Steeves & Rozema Group
1310 Murphy Rd., Sarnia, ON N7S 6K5
Tel: 519-542-2939 *Fax:* 519-542-0879
kim_vandam@srgroup.ca
www.srgroup.ca
Number of Beds: 56 beds; 60 long-term care beds
Note: Independent & assisted living, convalescent & respite options
Kim Van Dam, Managing Director

Sarsfield: Sarsfield Colonial Home
PO Box 130, 2861 Colonial Rd., Sarsfield, ON K0A 3E0
Tel: 613-835-2977 *Fax:* 613-835-2982
Number of Beds: 46 beds
Chantal Crispin, Administrator
chantalcrispin@rogers.com

Shelburne: Dufferin Oaks Home for the Aged
151 Centre St., Shelburne, ON L0N 1S4
Tel: 519-925-2140 *Fax:* 519-925-5067
www.dufferincounty.on.ca
Number of Beds: 160 beds
Note: non-profit municipal long-term care facility

Simcoe: Norview Lodge
PO Box 604, 44 Rob Blake Way, Simcoe, ON N3Y 4L8
Tel: 519-426-0902 *Fax:* 519-426-9867
www.norfolkcounty.on.ca
Number of Beds: 179 beds
Note: home for the aged
Kim Jenereaux, Administrator
Brian Koncir, Supervisor, Maintenance

St Catharines: Henley House Limited
20 Earnest St., St Catharines, ON L2N 7T2
Tel: 905-937-9703
www.chartwellreit.ca
Number of Beds: 160 beds
Note: Specialties: Long-term nursing & personal care; Therapeutic programs; Physiotherapy; Restorative care; Palliative care

St Catharines: Linhaven
403 Ontario St., St Catharines, ON L2N 1L5
Tel: 905-934-3364 *Fax:* 905-934-6975
Number of Beds: 248 beds
Note: Specialties: Long term care; Alzheimer's disease, memory loss, & related dementias; Respite services; Adult day service
Dan Oettinger, Administrator

St Catharines: Niagara Ina Grafton Gage Home
413 Linwell Rd., St Catharines, ON L2M 7Y2
Tel: 905-935-6822 *Fax:* 905-935-6847
poneill@niggv.on.ca
www.niggv.on.ca
Number of Beds: 40 beds
Note: supportive housing for seniors
Patrick O'Neill, CEO

St Thomas: Kettle Creek Residence
58 St. George St., St Thomas, ON N5P 2L1
Tel: 519-633-7647 *Fax:* 519-633-9312
Helmut Beh, Owner

St Thomas: Valleyview Home for the Aged
350 Burwell Rd., St Thomas, ON N5P 0A3
Tel: 519-631-1030 *Fax:* 519-631-3462
mccarroll@valleyview.st-thomas.on.ca
Number of Beds: 136 beds
Note: home for the aged
Michael Carroll, Administrator

St. Thomas: Elgin Manor Home for the Aged
39232 Fingal Line, St. Thomas, ON N5P 3S5
Tel: 519-631-0620 *Fax:* 519-631-2307
www.elginhomes.ca
Number of Beds: 90 beds
Pat Vendevenne, Director, Homes & Senior Services
pvandevenne@elgin-county.on.ca

Stittsville: Specialty Care Granite Ridge
5501 Abbott St., Stittsville, ON K2S 2C5
Tel: 613-836-0331 *Fax:* 613-241-1986
norm.slatter@specialty-care.com
www.specialty-care.com
Number of Beds: 224 beds
Norm Slatter, Administrator

Stoney Creek: Clarion Nursing Home
337 Hwy. 8, Stoney Creek, ON L8G 1E7
Tel: 905-664-2281 *Fax:* 905-664-2966
info@clarionnursinghome.on.ca
www.clarionnursinghome.on.ca

Number of Beds: 100 beds

Stoney Creek: Heritage Green Nursing Home
353 Isaac Brock Dr., Stoney Creek, ON L8J 2J3
Tel: 905-573-7177 *Fax:* 905-573-7151
info@hgseniorcare.com
www.hamiltonltc.org/facilities/heritage.htm
Number of Beds: 167 beds
Rosemary Okimi, Administrator
Reg Charles, Manager, Maintenance

Stoney Creek: Stoney Creek Lifecare Centre
199 Glover Rd., Stoney Creek, ON L8E 5J2
Tel: 905-643-1795
eyi_stoneycreek_lc@extendicare.com
www.hamiltonltc.org
Number of Beds: 45 beds
Stephanie Zajczenko-Opdam, Administrator
sopdam@extendicare.com

Stouffville: Specialty Care Bloomington Cove
13621 Ninth Line, Stouffville, ON L4A 7X3
Tel: 905-640-1310 *Fax:* 905-640-0995
bernard.boreland@specialty-care.com
www.specialty-care.com
Number of Beds: 112 beds
Bernard Boreland, Administrator

Stratford: L'Arche Stratford
PO Box 522 Stn. Main Street, Stratford, ON N5A 6T7
Tel: 519-271-9751 *Fax:* 519-271-1861
info@larche.stratford.on.ca
www.larche.ca/en/communities/stratford/
Number of Beds: 24 beds

Stratford: Greenwood Court
90 Greenwood Dr., Stratford, ON N5A 7W5
Tel: 519-273-4662 *Fax:* 519-273-1458
Number of Beds: 45 beds
Fred Zehr, Administrator

Thunder Bay: OPTIONS Northwest Personal Support Services
95 Cumberland St. North, Thunder Bay, ON P7A 4M1
Tel: 807-344-4994 *Fax:* 807-346-5811
www.optionsnorthwest.com
Year Founded: 1965
Note: Specialty: Personal & residential support for persons with developmental challenges, physical disabilities, chronic behaviour problems, & mental health challenges; Counselling; Support groups
Bernard Travis, Executive Director

Thunder Bay: Roseview Manor
Former Name: Central Park Lodge
99 Shuniah St., Thunder Bay, ON P7A 2Z2
Tel: 807-344-6929 *Fax:* 807-344-7132
roseviewmanor@reveraliving.com
www.reveraliving.com
Number of Beds: 157 beds
Gail Gallant, Executive Director

Tilbury: Tilbury Manor Long-Term Care Home
PO Box 160, 16 Fort St., Tilbury, ON N0P 2L0
Tel: 519-682-0243 *Fax:* 519-682-2358
adm.tilbury@diversicare.ca
www.diversicare.ca
Number of Beds: 75 beds
Jennifer Middleton, Administrator

Toronto: Baycrest Centre for Geriatric Care
3560 Bathurst St., Toronto, ON M6A 2E1
Tel: 416-785-2500 *Fax:* 416-785-2464
www.baycrest.org
Number of Beds: 300 beds
Note: group home

Toronto: Cheltenham Long-Term Care Facility
5935 Bathurst St., Toronto, ON M2R 1Y8
Tel: 416-223-4050
adm.cheltenham@leisureworld.ca
www.leisureworld.ca/cheltenham.html
Number of Beds: 170 beds

Toronto: Copernicus Lodge
66 Roncesvalles Ave., Toronto, ON M6R 3A7
Tel: 416-536-7122 *Fax:* 416-536-8242
www.copernicuslodge.com
Number of Beds: 108 beds
Note: home for the aged
Tracy Kamino, CEO

Toronto: Dom Lipa Nursing Home & Seniors Centre
52 Neilson Dr., Toronto, ON M9C 1V7
Tel: 416-621-3820 *Fax:* 416-621-9773
info@domlipa.ca
www.domlipa.ca
Number of Beds: 66 nursing home, 30 retirement beds
Theresa MacDermid, Administrator
t.macdermid@domlipa.ca

Toronto: The Gibson Long Term Care Centre
Affiliated with: Chartwell Seniors Housing REIT
Former Name: Extendicare - North York
1925 Steeles Ave. East, Toronto, ON M2H 2H3
Tel: 416-493-4666 *Fax:* 416-493-4886
gibsonltc@chartwellreit.ca
www.chartwellreit.ca
Number of Beds: 202 beds
Stephen Suske, CEO, Chartwell Seniors Housing REIT

Toronto: Ina Grafton Gage Home (Toronto)
2 O'Connor Dr., Toronto, ON M4K 2K1
Tel: 416-422-4890 *Fax:* 416-422-1613
info@iggh.org
www.iggh.org
Number of Beds: 110 beds
Gordon Blowes, Administrator
Hernando Zorilla, Director, Physical Plant

Toronto: Kingsway Arms at McCowan
2881 Eglinton Ave. East, Toronto, ON M4G 2K3
Tel: 416-266-4445 *Fax:* 416-264-8377
mccowan.kams@rogers.com
www.kingswayarms.com/mccowan.php
Gina Cook, Executive Director
Tim Valyear, Director, Marketing
marketingoffice.kams@rogers.com

Toronto: Lakeside Long-Term Care Centre
150 Dunn Ave., Toronto, ON M6K 2R6
Tel: 416-533-2828
www.torontorehab.com/patient/longterm/index.htm
Number of Beds: 128 Beds

Toronto: Maynard Nursing Home
28 Halton St., Toronto, ON M6J 1R3
Tel: 416-533-5198 *Fax:* 416-533-3531
www.maynardnursinghome.com
Year Founded: 1961
Number of Beds: 77 beds
Note: Specialties: Service to residents of Portuguese origin; Recreational & social activities
Rosemary Mifsud, Administrator

Toronto: Nisbet Lodge
740 Pape Ave., Toronto, ON M4K 3S7
Tel: 416-469-1105 *Fax:* 416-469-2996
info@nisbetlodge.com
www.nisbetlodge.com
Number of Beds: 103 beds
Note: Christian long-term care home
Glen Moorhouse, Executive Director

Toronto: North York General Hospital - Seniors' Health Centre
2 Buchan Ct., Toronto, ON M2J 5A3
Tel: 416-756-0066 *Fax:* 416-495-9738
www.nygh.on.ca
Number of Beds: 192 beds
Note: Long term care facility, ambulatory geriatric services
Bonnie Adamson, CEO

Toronto: The O'Neill Centre
33 Christie St., Toronto, ON M6G 3B1
Tel: 416-536-1116 *Fax:* 416-536-6941
cfiore@oneillcentre.ca
www.oneillcentre.ca
Number of Beds: 172 beds
Note: Resident care & retirement living
Cathy Fiore, Administrator

Toronto: Oakdale Child & Family Service Ltd.
291 Chisholm Ave., Toronto, ON M4C 4W5
Tel: 416-699-5600 *Fax:* 416-699-6547
tor-oakdale@bellnet.ca
www.oakdaleservices.com
Note: Specialties: Long & short term care for children with special needs; Teaching independence in life skills, social & community awareness, & appropriate communication methods
Lisa Bache, Administrator

Toronto: Providence Healthcare
Former Name: Providence Centre Home for the Aged, Chronic Care & Rehabilitation Hospital
3276 St. Clair Ave. East, Toronto, ON M1L 1W1
Tel: 416-285-3666 *Fax:* 416-285-3758
info@providence.on.ca
www.providence.on.ca
Number of Beds: 288 long-term care, 347 hospital beds
Note: Comprised of Providence Hospital, the Cardinal Ambrozic Houses of Providence, & Providence Community Centre; long-term care, rehabilitation & complex continuing care, community clinics, Alzheimer Day Program, caregiver support services, Tamil Caregiver Project. Focus is on the mission & values of the founding Sisters of St. Joseph
Neil McEvoy, President/CEO
Josie Walsh, Vice President, Programs; Chief Nurse Executive
Dr. Peter Nord, Vice President, Medical Affairs; Chief of Staff

Toronto: La Salle Manor
61 Fairfax Cres., Toronto, ON M1L 1Z7
Tel: 416-752-3932 *Fax:* 416-752-4047
lasallemanor@rogers.com
Note: The manor is a private retirement home for De La Salle Brothers & Sisters of Service.
Br. Francis McCrea, Director

Toronto: Shepherd Lodge
3760 Sheppard Ave. East, Toronto, ON M1T 3K9
Tel: 416-609-5700 *Fax:* 416-609-8329
info@shepherdvillage.org
www.shepherdvillage.org
Year Founded: 1961
Number of Beds: 252 beds

Toronto: Suomi-Koti Toronto
Also Known As: Toronto Finnish Cdn Srs Centre & Nursing Home
795 Eglinton Ave. East, Toronto, ON M4G 4E4
Tel: 416-425-4134 *Fax:* 416-425-6319
seniorscentre@suomikoti.ca
www.suomikoti.ca
Number of Beds: 88 apartment units, 34 nursing beds
Juha Mynttinen, Administrator
Leila Carnegie, Director of Care

Toronto: Villa Colombo Homes for the Aged Inc.
40 Playfair Ave., Toronto, ON M6B 2P9
Tel: 416-789-2113 *Fax:* 416-789-5435
general@villacolombo.on.ca
www.villacharities.com
Number of Beds: 391 beds
Pat Stoddart, Administrator
Mac Brett, Director, Housekeeping/Maintenance

Toronto: West Park Long-Term Care Centre
82 Buttonwood Ave., Toronto, ON M6M 2J5
Tel: 416-243-3600 *Fax:* 416-243-8947
feedback@westpark.org
www.westpark.org
Note: Rehabilitation, complex continuing care, and long-term care facility

Toronto: The Westbury Long Term Care Centre
495 The West Mall, Toronto, ON M9C 5S3
Tel: 416-622-7094
www.chartwellreit.ca
Note: Specialties: Nursing & personal care; Restorative care; Social, recreational, & physical activity programs; Specialized neighbourhood for persons with dementia; Palliative care

Trenton: Crown Ridge Place Nursing Home
106 Crown St., Trenton, ON K8V 6R3
Tel: 613-392-1289 *Fax:* 613-392-6360
gfreeman@crownridgehealth.ca
Number of Beds: 84 beds
Greg Freeman, Administrator

Unionville: Union Villa
Unionville Home Society, 4300 Hwy. #7 East, Unionville, ON L3R 1L8
Tel: 905-477-2839
customerservice@uhs.on.ca
www.uhs.on.ca/uhs_unionvilla.php
Year Founded: 1970
Number of Beds: 160 residential capacity
Note: Specialties: Long-term nursing care; Activation program; Therapeutic mental & physical stimulation; Respite care; Day guest program
Graham Constantine, President/CEO

Val Caron: Elizabeth Centre
2100 Main St., Val Caron, ON P3N 1S7
Tel: 705-897-7695 *Fax:* 705-897-0181
www.jarlette.com
Number of Beds: 128 beds
Shelly Murphy, Administrator
smurphy@jarlette.com

Vanier: Centre d'accueil Champlain
275 Perrier Ave., Vanier, ON K1L 5C6
Tel: 613-746-3543 *Fax:* 613-746-5572
Year Founded: 1969
Number of Beds: 160 beds
Note: home for the aged
Pierre Arsenault, Administrator

Wallaceburg: Fairfield Park
1934 Dufferin Ave., Wallaceburg, ON N8A 4M2
Tel: 519-627-1663 *Fax:* 519-627-9920
www.fairfieldpark.ca
Number of Beds: 99 beds
Tracey Maxim, Administrator
Shona Outridge, Director of Operations

Watford: Watford Quality Care Centre
PO Box 400, 344 Victoria St., Watford, ON N0M 2S0
Tel: 519-876-2928 *Fax:* 519-876-3930
www.watfordqualitycare.ca
Number of Beds: 62 beds
Lynne-Anne Gallaway, Administrator
lgallaway@watfordqualitycare.ca

West Hill: Leisureworld Caregiving Centre - Altamont
92 Island Rd., West Hill, ON M1C 2P5
Tel: 416-284-4781 *Fax:* 416-284-3634
adm.altamont@leisureworld.ca
www.leisureworld.ca/Altamont.html
Year Founded: 1968
Number of Beds: 159 beds

Willowdale: Carefree Lodge
306 Finch Ave. East, Willowdale, ON M2N 4S5
Tel: 416-397-1500 *Fax:* 416-397-1501
ltc-cfl@toronto.ca
www.ccac-ont.ca
Number of Beds: 127 beds
Note: home for the aged
Debbie Araujo, Administrator

Windsor: Huron Lodge
1881 Cabana Rd. West, Windsor, ON N9G 1C7
Tel: 519-253-6060 *Fax:* 519-977-8027
www.citywindsor.ca/000278.asp
Number of Beds: 256 beds
Note: Number of Employees: 160
Lucie B. Lombardo, Administrator
Linda Larsh, Manager, Environmental Services

Windsor: Regency Park Nursing Home
567 Victoria Ave., Windsor, ON N9A 4N1
Tel: 519-254-1141 *Fax:* 519-254-3759
Number of Beds: 72 beds
Annemarie White, Administrator

Woodbridge: Kristus Darzs Latvian Home
11290 Pine Valley Dr., Woodbridge, ON L4L 1A6
Tel: 905-832-3300 *Fax:* 905-832-2029
kristusdarzs@kdlatvianhome.com
www.kdlatvianhome.com
Number of Beds: 100 beds
Jolanta Linde, Director of Operations

Woodstock: Woodingford Lodge
300 Juliana Dr., Woodstock, ON N4V 0A1
Tel: 519-421-5556 *Fax:* 519-533-0781
www.county.oxford.on.ca
Number of Beds: 228 beds
Beth Martin, Administrator

Nursing Homes

Ajax: Ballycliffe Lodge Ltd.
70 Station Rd., Ajax, ON L1S 1R9
Tel: 905-683-7321 *Fax:* 905-427-5846
ballycliffelodge@chartwellreit.ca
www.chartwellreit.ca
Number of Beds: 100 beds; 65 retirement lodge beds
W. Brent Binions, President, CEO

Amherstview: Helen Henderson Care Centre
343 Amherst Dr., Amherstview, ON K7N 1X3
Tel: 613-384-4585 *Fax:* 613-384-9407
www.gibsonfamilyhealthcare.com
Number of Beds: 70 retirement home beds; 102 nursing home beds
Larry Gibson, Administrator
613-384-4585 ext222, lisagibson@gibsonfamilyhealthcare.co

Arnprior: The Grove Arnprior & District Nursing Home
Affiliated with: Arnprior Regional Health
275 Ida St. North, Arnprior, ON K7S 3M7
Tel: 613-623-6547 *Fax:* 613-623-4554
eric.hanna@arnpriorhospital.com
www.arnpriorhospital.com
Number of Beds: 60 beds

Arthur: Caressant Care Nursing and Retirement Homes Limited
Caressant Care Arthur
PO Box 700, 215 Eliza St., Arthur, ON N0G 1A0
Tel: 519-848-3795 *Fax:* 519-848-2273
www.caressantcare.com
Number of Beds: 80 beds
James Lavelle, President

Blenheim: Blenheim Community Village
PO Box 220, 10 Mary Ave., Blenheim, ON N0P 1A0
Tel: 519-676-8119 *Fax:* 519-676-0610
www.reveraliving.com/blenheim
Number of Beds: 101 beds
Note: nursing home & retirement lodge

Bobcaygeon: Specialty Care Case Manor
Former Name: Case Manor Nursing Home
28 Boyd St., Bobcaygeon, ON K0M 1A0
Tel: 705-738-2374 *Fax:* 705-738-3821
www.specialty-care.com
Number of Beds: 96 beds
John Rankin, Administrator
john.rankin@specialty-care.com

Bourget: Caressant Care Nursing and Retirement Homes Limited
Caressant Care Bourget
PO Box 99, 2279 Laval St., Bourget, ON K0A 1E0
Tel: 613-487-2331 *Fax:* 613-487-3464
www.caressantcare.com
Number of Beds: 50 beds

Bowmanville: Marnwood Life Care Centre
26 Elgin St., Bowmanville, ON L1C 3C8
Tel: 905-623-5731 *Fax:* 905-623-4497
Number of Beds: 60 beds
Note: Specialties: Social work; Physiotherapy

Bowmanville: Strathaven Life Care Centre
264 King St. East, Bowmanville, ON L1C 1P9
Tel: 905-623-2553 *Fax:* 905-623-1374
Number of Beds: 199 beds

Brampton: Holland Christian Homes Inc.
Former Name: Faith Manor Nursing Home
7900 McLaughlin Rd. South, Brampton, ON L6V 3N2
Tel: 905-459-3333 *Fax:* 905-459-8667
www.hch.ca
Number of Beds: 120 beds
Note: Dutch Heritage
John Kalverda, Executive Director
johnka@hch.ca
Peter Dykstra, Administrator, Grace Manor
petedy@hch.ca

Brantford: Versa-Care Centre - Brantford
425 Park Rd. North, Brantford, ON N3R 7G5
Tel: 519-759-1040 *Fax:* 519-759-5343
www.reveraliving.com
Number of Beds: 167 beds

Burlington: The Brant Centre Long Term Care Residence
Affiliated with: Chartwell Seniors Housing REIT
1230 Northshore Blvd. East, Burlington, ON L7S 1C5
Tel: 905-639-2848
www.chartwellreit.ca
Year Founded: 2003
Number of Beds: 175 beds
Adam Banks, Administrator
Barbara Murphy, Director of Care
Stephen Suske, CEO, Chartwell Seniors Housing REIT

Cambridge: Caressant Care Nursing and Retirement Homes Limited
Cambridge Country Manor
3680 Speedsville Rd., Cambridge, ON N3H 4R6
Tel: 519-650-0100 *Fax:* 519-650-1697
Number of Beds: 79 beds
Brenda Nadeau, Administrator

Cambridge: Riverbend Place Retirement Community
650 Coronation Blvd., Cambridge, ON N1R 7S6
Tel: 519-740-3820 *Fax:* 519-740-0961
www.reveraliving.com
Number of Beds: 146 beds
Note: Assisted living & independent living programs; short term, respite & convalescent options; community includes nursing home, retirement lodge, apartments
Margaret Dykeman, Administrator

Cambridge: Saint Luke's Place
1624 Franklin Blvd., Cambridge, ON N3C 3P4
Tel: 519-658-5183 *Fax:* 519-658-2991
www.saintlukesplace.ca
Number of Beds: 150 beds
Note: home for the aged; provides long term care, retirement home & apartments
Rita Soluk, Administrator

Carleton Place: Stoneridge Manor
256 High St., Carleton Place, ON K7C 1X1
Tel: 613-257-4355 *Fax:* 613-253-2190
www.reveraliving.com/stoneridge
Number of Beds: 60 beds
Michelle Ferguson, Administrator
michelle.ferguson@reveraliving.com

Cobden: Caressant Care Nursing and Retirement Homes Limited
Caressant Care Cobden
12 Wren Dr., Cobden, ON K0J 1K0
Tel: 613-646-2109
www.caressantcare.com
Year Founded: 2000
Number of Beds: 60 beds
Linda Tracey, Administrator

Cobourg: Streamway Villa Nursing Home
19 James St. West, Cobourg, ON K9A 2J8
Tel: 905-372-0163 *Fax:* 905-372-0581
www.omniway.ca
Number of Beds: 59 beds
Kylie Szczebonski, Administrator, Director of Care
kszczebonski@omniway.ca

Collingwood: Bay Haven Senior Care Community
Former Name: Bay Haven Nursing Home Inc.
499 Hume St., Collingwood, ON L9Y 4H8
Tel: 705-445-6501 *Fax:* 705-445-6506
info@bayhaven.com
www.bayhaven.com
Number of Beds: 60 beds
Karen Milligan, Administrator

Collingwood: Sunset Manor Home & Village
49 Raglan St., Collingwood, ON L9Y 4X1
Tel: 705-445-4499 *Fax:* 705-445-9742
Year Founded: 1968
Number of Beds: 148 beds
Note: Sunset Manor Home for the Aged is a municipal, Long-Term Care facility.
Tolleen Parkin, Administrator
tolleen.parkin@simcoe.ca
Katy Harrison, Director, Resident Care
kim.byberg@simcoe.ca

Cornwall: Heartwood - Cornwall
201 - 11 St. East, Cornwall, ON K6H 2Y6
Tel: 613-933-7420
www.reveraliving.com
Number of Beds: 118 beds
Donna Derouchie, Administrator

Courtland: Caressant Care Nursing and Retirement Homes Limited
Caressant Care Courtland
Former Name: Sacred Heart Villa
PO Box 279, 4850 County Rd. 59, Courtland, ON N0J 1E0
Tel: 519-688-0710 *Fax:* 519-688-0052
Number of Beds: 54 beds
Linda Hare, Administrator
Gilbert Dooms, Supervisor, Maintenance

Embrun: St. Jacques Nursing Home
PO Box 870, 915 Notre Dame St., Embrun, ON K0A 1W0
Tel: 613-443-3442 *Fax:* 613-443-1716
info@stjacques.ca
www.stjacques.ca
Number of Beds: 60 beds

Ginette Beaudin, Administrator
gbeaudin@stjacques.ca

Exeter: Exeter Villa Nursing & Retirement Home
Affiliated with: ATK Care Inc.
155 John St. East, Exeter, ON N0M 1S1
Tel: 519-235-1581 *Fax:* 519-235-3219
exevilla@cabletv.on.ca
www.atkcareinc.ca/exeterservices
Number of Beds: 57 nursing care beds, 66 retirement beds
Nancy Tweddle, Administrator

Fergus: Caressant Care Nursing and Retirement Homes Limited
Caressant Care Fergus
450 Queen St. East, Fergus, ON N1M 2Y7
Tel: 519-843-2400
www.caressantcare.com
Year Founded: 1986
Number of Beds: 87 beds
Shannon Brinkman, Administrator
Marion Douglas, Director, Nursing

Fordwich: Fordwich Village Nursing Home
Affiliated with: ATK Care Inc.
3063 Adelaide St., Fordwich, ON N0G 1V0
Tel: 519-335-3168 *Fax:* 519-335-3825
fordwichadmin@tnt21.com
www.atkcareinc.ca/fordwich.htm
Number of Beds: 33 beds
Note: Long term care facility
Susan Jaunzemis, Administrator, Director of Care

Hagersville: Norcliffe LifeCare Centre
85 Main St. North, Hagersville, ON N0A 1H0
Tel: 905-768-1641 *Fax:* 905-768-1685
Number of Beds: 60 units
Note: Retirement home
Myrna Marran, Contact

Hamilton: Baywoods Place
Former Name: Versa-Care Centre - Hamilton
330 Main St. East, Hamilton, ON L8N 3T9
Tel: 905-523-7134
www.reveraliving.com/baywoods
Number of Beds: 128 beds
Walter Sguazzin, Administrator

Hamilton: St. Olga's Lifecare Centre
570 King St. West, Hamilton, ON L8P 1C2
Tel: 905-522-8572 *Fax:* 905-522-1553
eyi_st.olgas_LC@extendicare.com
www.hamiltonltc.org/facilities/st_olgas.htm
Number of Beds: 93 beds
Judy Peck, Administrator
jpeck@extendicare.com

Harriston: Caressant Care Nursing and Retirement Homes Limited
Caressant Care Harriston
PO Box 520, 24 Louise St., Harriston, ON N0G 1Z0
Tel: 519-338-3700 *Fax:* 519-338-2744
www.caressantcare.com
Number of Beds: 89 beds
Note: Long term care facility, with secure unit for residents with dementia, & adjacent retirement home.
Mary-Therese Haid, Administrator
Eleanor MacEwen, Infection Control

Hawkesbury: Résidence Prescott et Russell
1020, boul Cartier, Hawkesbury, ON K6A 1W7
Tél: 613-632-2755 *Téléc:* 613-632-4056
www.prescott-russell.on.ca
Nombre de lits: 146 lits
Note: Maison de soins de longue durée. Employés: 171
Louise Lalonde, Administratrice
François Martineau, Directeur des soins infirmiers
Danielle Duval, Coordonnatrice, Admissions; Services financiers

Hensall: Queensway Nursing & Retirement Home
PO Box 369, 100 Queen St. East, Hensall, ON N0M 1X0
Tel: 519-262-2830 *Fax:* 519-262-3403
queensway.admin@tcc.on.ca
Number of Beds: 60 beds nursing home & 57 beds retirement home
Note: retirement home
Kathy Holdsworth, Administrator

Huntsville: Fairvern Nursing Home Inc.
Affiliated with: Muskoka Algonquin Healthcare
14 Mill St., Huntsville, ON P1H 2A4
Tel: 705-789-4476 *Fax:* 705-789-1371
fairvernmail@mahc.ca
www.mahc.ca; www.fairvernnursinghome.ca
Number of Beds: 76 beds
Barry Lockhart, CEO
Christopher Thomas, Chair

Keswick: Specialty Care Cedarvale Lodge
121 Morton Dr., Keswick, ON L4P 2M5
Tel: 905-476-2656 *Fax:* 905-476-5689
www.specialty-care.com
Number of Beds: 100 beds
Note: Nursing home with 40-bed retirement home attached
Donna Taylor, Administrator
donna.taylor@specialty-care.com

Kitchener: Forest Heights Long Term Care Centre
60 Westheights Dr., Kitchener, ON N2N 2A8
Tel: 519-576-3320 *Fax:* 519-745-3227
generalforestheights@reveraliving.com
www.reveraliving.com
Number of Beds: 240 beds
Patti Fetter, Executive Director

Listowel: Caressant Care Nursing and Retirement Homes Limited
Caressant Care Listowel
710 Reserve Ave., Listowel, ON N4W 2L1
Tel: 519-291-1041 *Fax:* 519-291-5420
www.caressantcare.com
Number of Beds: 52 beds
Lara Martinez, Administrator

London: Versa-Care Elmwood Place
Former Name: Elmwood Place
46 Elmwood Pl. West, London, ON N6J 1J2
Tel: 519-433-7259 *Fax:* 519-660-0158
elmwoodpl@reveraliving.com
www.reveraliving.com/homes/lo/
Number of Beds: 97 beds
Lorell Jones, Administrator

Marmora: Caressant Care Nursing and Retirement Homes Limited
Caressant Care Marmora
58 Bursthall St., Marmora, ON K0K 2M0
Tel: 613-472-3130 *Fax:* 613-472-5388
www.caressantcare.com
Number of Beds: 84 beds
Linda Merkley, Administrator

Matheson: Rosedale Centre
507 - 8th Ave., Matheson, ON P0K 1N0
Year Founded: 1989
Number of Beds: 20 beds
Note: Specialty: Long term nursing & supportive care; Foot care; Therapy; Number of Employees: 72 (Bingham Memorial Hospital & adjoined Rosedale Centre)
Daniel O'Mara, Chief Executive Officer
705-273-2424, ext. 2, micsceo@puc.net

Mount Forest: Saugeen Valley Nursing Centre Ltd.
465 Dublin St., Mount Forest, ON N0G 2L3
Tel: 519-323-2140 *Fax:* 519-323-3540
svnc@wightman.ca
Number of Beds: 87 beds
Note: Nursing & respite care
Andrea Parsons, Administrator

Norwood: Pleasant Meadow Manor
Affiliated with: OMNI
99 Alma St., Norwood, ON K0L 2V0
Tel: 705-639-5308 *Fax:* 705-639-5309
www.omni-way.com/ourhomes/pleasant.htm
Number of Beds: 61 beds
Note: Long term care
Fraser Wilson, CEO
Sandra Brow, Administrator; Director of Care

Orangeville: Avalon Care Centre & Retirement Lodge
355 Broadway Ave., Orangeville, ON L9W 3Y3
Tel: 519-941-3351 *Fax:* 519-941-9532
www.jarlette.com
Number of Beds: 137 long term care beds, 77 retirement lodge beds
Note: Long term care centre & retirement residence
Chan Sooklal, Administrator, Care Centre
csooklal@jarlette.com
Debbie Rydall, General Manager, Retirement Lodge
drydall@jarlette.com

Orillia: Trillium Manor Home for the Aged
12 Grace Ave., Orillia, ON L3V 2K2
Tel: 705-325-1504 *Fax:* 705-325-7661
Year Founded: 1969
Number of Beds: 122 beds
Janice McQuaig, Site Administrator
Jane Sinclair, General Manager, Health & Cultural Services

Ottawa: La Villa Marguerite
75 Bruyere St., Ottawa, ON K1N 5C8
Tel: 613-562-4262 *Fax:* 613-562-4223
www.scohs.on.ca
Number of Beds: 71 beds
Note: Long-term care
Jean Bartkowiak, President/CEO, Service de santé SCO Health Service

Owen Sound: Versa-Care Georgian Heights
1115 - 10 St. East, Owen Sound, ON N4K 6B1
Tel: 519-371-1441 *Fax:* 519-371-1092
www.reveraliving.com
Number of Beds: 40 beds
Joanne Porter, Administrator

Owen Sound: Versa-Care Maple View
1029 - 4th Ave. West, Owen Sound, ON N4K 4W1
Tel: 519-376-2522 *Fax:* 519-376-3110
mapleview@reveraliving.com
www.reveraliving.com
Number of Beds: 29 beds
Andrea Hodgkins, Acting Administrator

Paris: Telfer Place Retirement Residence
245 Grand River St. North, Paris, ON N3L 3V8
Tel: 519-442-4411 *Fax:* 519-442-6724
telferplaceretirementresidence@reveraliving.com
www.reveraliving.com
Number of Beds: 45 beds
Note: Independent living program; retirement lodge, apartments; long-term care; convalescent & respite options
Kathy Le Gresley, Administrator
Henry Filetstra, Supervisor, Maintenance

Picton: Versa-Care Hallowell House
PO Box 800, 13628 Loyalist Pkwy., Picton, ON K0K 2T0
Tel: 613-476-4444 *Fax:* 613-476-1566
leanne.weir@reveraliving.com
www.reveraliving.com
Number of Beds: 97 beds
Area Served: Prince Edward County, South East
Leanne Weir, Executive Director

Port Hope: Regency Manor Retirement & Nursing Home
66 Dorset St. East, Port Hope, ON L1A 1E3
Tel: 905-885-4558 *Fax:* 905-885-7386
regency.admin@bellnet.ca
Number of Beds: 101 beds
Jo Harris, General Manager

Sarnia: Trillium Villa
1221 Michigan Ave., Sarnia, ON N7S 3Y3
Tel: 519-542-5529 *Fax:* 519-542-5953
john_scotland@srgroup.ca
www.ltc.snr.on.ca
Year Founded: 1970
Number of Beds: 152 beds
Joyce Haneca, Administrator

Sault Ste Marie: Great Northern Retirement Home
760 Great Northern Rd., Sault Ste Marie, ON P6A 5K7
Tel: 705-945-9405 *Fax:* 705-945-6303
Number of Beds: 120 retirement, 34 interim nursing home beds
Nadia Longo, Administrator

Seaforth: Seaforth Manor Nursing Home
100 James St., Seaforth, ON N0K 1W0
Tel: 519-527-0030 *Fax:* 519-527-2862
seaforth.admin@tcc.on.ca
Number of Beds: 118 beds
Note: Nursing & retirement home
Catherine Schalk, Administrator

Shelburne: Shelburne Residence
200 Robert St., Shelburne, ON L0N 1S1
Tel: 519-925-3746 *Fax:* 519-925-1476
shelburne.admin@bellnet.ca
Number of Beds: 60 nursing beds, 28 retirement rooms
Note: Combined nursing home & retirement facility
Mike Dickin, Administrator

St Catharines: Tufford Nursing Home
312 Queenston St., St Catharines, ON L2P 2X4
Tel: 905-682-0503
www.hamptontufford.com
Year Founded: 1960
Number of Beds: 64 residential capacity
Note: Specialties: Long-term nursing care; Social work; Physiotherapy; Podiatry; Activation program; Palliative care

St Catharines: Versa-Care Centre - St. Catharines
168 Scott St., St Catharines, ON L2N 1H2
Tel: 905-934-3321 *Fax:* 905-934-9011
vcstcatharines@reveraliving.com
www.reveraliving.com
Number of Beds: 200 beds
Sandra A. Fredericks, Administrator

St Marys: Kingsway Lodge
310 Queen St. East, RR #6, St Marys, ON N4X 1C8
Tel: 519-284-2921 *Fax:* 519-284-4468
info@kingswaylodge.com
www.kingswaylodge.com
Number of Beds: 89 beds, 52 units
Scott A. Mackay, Administrator
smackay@on.aibn.com

St Marys: Wildwood Care Centre Inc.
PO Box 2200, 100 Ann St., St Marys, ON N4X 1A1
Tel: 519-284-3628 *Fax:* 519-284-0575
nursinghomeliving@wildwoodcarecentre.co
www.wildwoodcarecentre.com
Social Media:
www.facebook.com/pages/Wildwood-Care-Centre-Inc/26105994 0770; twitter.com/WildwoodCC
Number of Beds: 82 beds

St Thomas: Caressant Care Nursing and Retirement Homes Limited
Caressant Care St. Thomas - Mary Bucke St. Facility
4 Mary Bucke St., St Thomas, ON N5R 5J6
Tel: 519-633-3164 *Fax:* 519-631-8362
www.caressantcare.com
Number of Beds: 60 beds
Ann Starswell, Administrator

St. Thomas: Caressant Care Nursing and Retirement Homes Limited
Caressant Care St. Thomas - Bonnie Place Facility
15 Bonnie Pl., St. Thomas, ON N5R 5T8
Tel: 519-633-6493 *Fax:* 519-633-9329
www.caressantcare.com
Number of Beds: 182 beds
Note: Long term care facility, with secure unit for residents with dementia.
Vicki Martinez, Administrator

Stayner: Stayner Nursing Home
PO Box 350, 244 Main St. East, Stayner, ON L0M 1S0
Tel: 705-428-3614 *Fax:* 705-428-0537
Number of Beds: 49 beds
Lorraine Baker, Administrator

Stirling: Stirling Manor Nursing Home
PO Box 220, 218 Edward St., Stirling, ON K0K 3E0
Tel: 613-395-2596 *Fax:* 613-395-0930
www.stirling-rawdon.com
Number of Beds: 75 beds
Judith Norlock, Administrator
judy_manor@hotmail.com
Linda Phillips, Acting Director, Nursing
Cheryl Campbell, Office Manager

Strathroy: Sprucedale Care Centre Inc.
96 Kittridge Ave. East, Strathroy, ON N7G 2A8
Tel: 519-245-2808 *Fax:* 519-245-1767
Number of Beds: 62 beds
Darren Micallef, Administrator
darren@sprucedale.ca

Sutton: River Glen Haven Nursing Home
Affiliated with: ATK Care Inc.
160 High St., Sutton, ON L0E 1R0
Tel: 905-722-3631 *Fax:* 905-722-8638
rghadmin@bellnet.ca
www.atkcareinc.ca/suttonservices.htm
Number of Beds: 109 beds
Note: Long term & secured care
Karen Ryan, Administrator

Tavistock: Caressant Care Nursing and Retirement Homes Limited
The Maples Home for Seniors
94 William St., Tavistock, ON N0B 2R0
Tel: 519-655-2344 *Fax:* 519-655-2162
Number of Beds: 43 beds
Lois Riehl, Administrator

Thunder Bay: Pinewood Court
2625 East Walsh St., Thunder Bay, ON P7E 2E5
Tel: 807-577-1127
pinewoodcourt@reveraliving.com
www.reveraliving.com
Number of Beds: 75 beds
Note: Long term care
Cheryl Grant, Administrator
Ron Campbell, Director, Environmental Services

Thunder Bay: Versa-Care Centre - Thunder Bay
135 South Vickers St., Thunder Bay, ON P7E 1J2
Tel: 807-623-9511 *Fax:* 807-623-6992
vcthunderbay@reveraliving.com
www.reveraliving.com
Number of Beds: 161 beds
Joanne Lent, Executive Director

Toronto: Apotex Centre, Jewish Home for the Aged & The Louis & Leah Posluns Centre for Stroke & Cognition
3560 Bathurst St., Toronto, ON M6A 2E1
Tel: 416-785-2500 *Fax:* 416-785-2437
www.baycrest.org
Number of Beds: 472 beds
Note: Care is offered to adults 65 years of age & older within the context of orthodox Jewish traditions.

Toronto: St. Clair O'Connor Community Nursing Home
2701 St. Clair Ave. East, Toronto, ON M4B 3M3
Tel: 416-757-8757 *Fax:* 416-751-7315
Number of Beds: 25 beds
Susan Gallant, Administrator
s.gallant@scoc.ca

Toronto: Seven Oaks
9 Neilson Rd., Toronto, ON M1E 5E1
Tel: 416-392-3500 *Fax:* 416-392-3579
www.toronto.ca/ltc/sevenoaks.htm/
Year Founded: 1989
Number of Beds: 249 beds
Note: Services for long term care, including adult day programs, services to the Armenian & Tamil communities, & an on-site child care centre
Karen Wallace, Administrator

Toronto: Tendercare Living Centre
1020 McNicoll Ave., Toronto, ON M1W 2J6
Tel: 416-499-2020 *Fax:* 416-499-3379
peggyli@tendercare.ca
www.tendercare.ca
Number of Beds: 254 beds
Note: Nursing home & retirement community
Francis Martis, Administrator

Toronto: Tony Stacey Centre for Veterans Care
59 Lawson Rd., Toronto, ON M1C 2J1
Tel: 416-284-9235 *Fax:* 416-284-7169
info@tonystaceycentre.ca
www.tonystaceycentre.ca
Year Founded: 1977
Number of Beds: 100 beds
Jennifer Lange, Director, Development and Publi Relations
jlaing@tonystaceycentre.ca
Neala A. Taylor, Board Chair

Toronto: Versa-Care Centre - Rexdale
95 Humber College Blvd., Toronto, ON M9V 5B5
Tel: 416-746-7466 *Fax:* 416-740-5812
Number of Beds: 158 beds
Andrew Shinder, Administrator
Glen Elliott, Director, Physical Plant

Toronto: White Eagle Residence
Affiliated with: Chartwell Seniors Housing REIT
138 Dowling Ave., Toronto, ON M6K 3A6
Tel: 416-533-7935 *Fax:* 416-533-5154
www.chartwellreit.ca
Number of Beds: 56 beds
Stephen Suske, CEO, Chartwell Seniors Housing REIT

Uxbridge: ReachView Village
Former Name: Versa-Care Centre, Uxbridge
130 Reach St., Uxbridge, ON L9P 1L3
Tel: 905-852-5281 *Fax:* 905-852-0117
reachviewvillage@reveraliving.com
www.reveraliving.com
Number of Beds: 100 beds

Waterloo: Pinehaven Nursing Home & Retirement Residence
229 Lexington Rd., Waterloo, ON N2K 2E1
Tel: 519-885-0255 *Fax:* 519-885-4216
jross@thecaringnetwork.ca
www.pinehaven.ca
Number of Beds: 85 beds
Note: Specialty: long term care
Joanne Ross, Administrator

Whitby: Sunnycrest Nursing Home
1635 Dundas St. East, Whitby, ON L1N 2K9
Tel: 905-576-0111 *Fax:* 905-576-4712
info@sunnycrest.ca
www.sunnycrest.ca
Number of Beds: 136 beds
Jane Smith, Administrator
jsmith@sunnycrest.ca

Windsor: Riverside Place
3181 Meadowbrook Lane, Windsor, ON N8T 0A4
Tel: 519-974-0148 *Fax:* 519-974-7305
riversideplace@reveraliving.com
www.reveraliving.com

Windsor: Versa-Care Windsor Place
350 Dougall Ave., Windsor, ON N9A 4P4
Tel: 519-256-7868 *Fax:* 519-256-1991
vcwindsorplace@reveraliving.com
www.reveraliving
Number of Beds: 244 beds
Bonnie Spry, Administrator

Woodbridge: Pine Grove Lodge Retirement Resident
Former Name: Devonshire Pine Grove Inc.
8403 Islington Ave. North, Woodbridge, ON L4L 1X3
Tel: 905-850-3605
www.chartwellreit.ca
Number of Beds: 100 nursing home beds & 40 retirement residence suites

Woodstock: Caressant Care Nursing and Retirement Homes Limited
Caressant Care Woodstock
81 Fyfe Ave., Woodstock, ON N4S 8Y3
Tel: 519-539-6461 *Fax:* 519-539-7467
www.caressantcare.com
Number of Beds: 240 beds
Judy Peck, Administrator

Retirement Residences

Amherstburg: Victoria Street Manor
184 Victoria St. South, Amherstburg, ON N9V 2K5
Tel: 519-736-2525 *Fax:* 519-736-8587
www.countyofessex.on.ca
Number of Beds: 14 beds
Note: Specialties: Residential care for seniors; Medication administration
Della Dyck, Manager

Amherstview: Briargate Retirement Living Centre
4567 Bath Rd., Amherstview, ON K7N 1A8
Tel: 613-384-9333 *Fax:* 613-384-4443
briargate@reveraliving.com
Number of Beds: 95 beds
Leanne Weir, Executive Director

Ancaster: Carrington Place Retirement Home
75 Dunham Dr., Ancaster, ON L9G 1X7
Tel: 905-648-0343
www.carringtonplaceretirement.ca
Note: Services include respite care for seniors, physiotherapy, an exercise program, & social activities.
Lois Aguas, Administrator
loisaguas.carringtonplace@gmail.com
Lynn Gledhill, Director, Activity
Paula Kamula, Director, Community Resources

Ancaster: Highgate Retirement Residence
325 Fiddlers Green Rd., Ancaster, ON L9G 1W9
Tel: 905-648-8399 *Fax:* 905-648-3350
Number of Beds: 40 beds
Clare Aiken, Administrator

***Arnprior:* Arnprior Villa Retirement Residence**
15 Arthur St., Arnprior, ON K7S 1A1
Tel: 613-623-0414 *Fax:* 613-623-0947
arnprior@reveraliving.com
www.reveraliving.com
Number of Beds: 81 beds
Becky Hollingsworth, Executive Director

***Aurora:* Aurora Retirement Centre**
145 Murray Dr., Aurora, ON L4G 2C7
Tel: 905-841-2777 *Fax:* 905-841-1562
auroraretirement@chartwellreit.ca
www.chartwellreit.ca/home_locations/aurora_ret.htm
Number of Beds: 58 units
Avril Davies, Administrator

***Aurora:* Park Place Manor**
15055 Yonge St., Aurora, ON L4G 6T4
Tel: 905-727-2952 *Fax:* 905-727-5435
parkplacemanor@chartwellreit.ca
www.chartwellreit.ca
Number of Beds: 93 suites
Note: Specialties: Recreational activities; Wellness monitoring; Foot care; Respite, trial, seasonal, & convalescent stay
John Jeffs, Administrator

***Barrie:* Barrie Manor Retirement Residence**
340 Blake St., Barrie, ON L4M 1L3
Tel: 705-722-3611 *Fax:* 705-722-4530
www.barriemanor.ca
Social Media: www.facebook.com/barriemanor
Note: Services include nursing care, senior's day away program, overnight post-op, respite care, physiotherapy, massage therapy, foot care, & recreation.

***Barrie:* Mulcaster Mews**
130 Mulcaster St., Barrie, ON L4M 3M9
Tel: 705-725-9119 *Fax:* 705-725-8848
maggierae@look.ca
www.mulcastermews.webs.com
Number of Beds: 52 beds
Maggie Rae, Administrator

***Barrie:* Roberta Place Long-Term Care**
503 Essa Rd., Barrie, ON L4N 9E4
Tel: 705-733-3232 *Fax:* 705-733-2592
www.jarlette.com/robertaplace_ltc.html
Number of Beds: 139 long term care beds
Carolyn McLeod, Administrator
cmcleod@jarlette.com

***Barrie:* Roberta Place Retirement Lodge**
489 Essa Rd., Barrie, ON L4N 9E4
Tel: 705-728-2900 *Fax:* 705-728-8535
www.jarlette.com/roberta_rh.html
Number of Beds: 138 bed retirement lodge
Pam Story, General Manager, Retirement Lodge
pstory@jarlette.com

***Barrie:* Simcoe Terrace Retirement Community**
Affiliated with: Specialty Care Retirement Communities
44 Donald St., Barrie, ON L4N 1E3
Tel: 705-722-5750 *Fax:* 705-722-7041
info@simcoeterrace.com
www.simcoeterrace.com
Note: Simcoe Terrace offers nursing services, physiotherapy, rest & recuperation stays, leisure activities, & spa services.

***Barrie:* Woods Park Care Centre**
110 Lillian Cres., Barrie, ON L4N 5H7
Tel: 705-739-6881 *Fax:* 705-739-0638
www.woodspark.on.ca
Number of Beds: 67 units
Note: nursing home/retirement home
Cathy Cotton, Administrator
ccotton@woodspark.on.ca

***Beachburg:* Country Haven Retirement Home**
1387 Beachburg Rd., RR#1, Beachburg, ON K0J 1C0
Tel: 613-582-7021 *Fax:* 613-582-7075
chrh@nrtco.net
www.countryhavenretirementhome.com
Number of Beds: 75 beds
Anil Verma, M.A., M.B.A., General Manager

***Belleville:* Bayview Retirement Home**
435 Dundas St. West, Belleville, ON K8P 1B6
Tel: 613-966-6268 *Fax:* 613-966-6675
www.chartwellreit.ca
Number of Beds: 60 beds
Patricia Tooze, Administrator

***Belleville:* The Richmond Retirement Residence**
175 North Front St., Belleville, ON K8P 4Y8
Tel: 613-966-4407
www.richmondretirement.ca
Note: Specialties: Medication management; Wellness program; Social & therapeutic programs; Respite stays
Andrea E. McLister, Administrator

***Bracebridge:* Bracebridge Villa Retirement Lodge**
690 Hwy. 118 West, Bracebridge, ON P1L 1W8
Tel: 705-645-6364 *Fax:* 705-645-1684
info@bracebridgevilla.ca
www.bracebridgevilla.ca
Number of Beds: 82 units
Corrine Hall, Manager

***Bracebridge:* James Street Place**
148 James St., Bracebridge, ON P1L 1S7
Tel: 705-645-1431 *Fax:* 705-645-5415
jamesstreet@chartwellreit.ca
www.chartwellreit.ca/home_locations/james_street.htm
Number of Beds: 73 suites
Rosalid Taylor, Administrator

***Brampton:* Woodhall Park Retirement Village**
10250 Kennedy Rd., RR#4, Brampton, ON L6T 3S1
Tel: 905-846-1441
postmaster@woodhallpark.ca
www.woodhallpark.ca
Number of Beds: 80 suites
Andrew Post, Administrator

***Brantford:* Amber Lea Place**
Affiliated with: Mundi Holdings Ltd.
384 St. Paul Ave., Brantford, ON N3R 4N4
Tel: 519-754-0000 *Fax:* 519-759-1401
info@amberleaplace.com
www.amberleaplace.com
Number of Beds: 50 beds
Dev Mundi, Administrator

***Brantford:* Charlotte Villa Retirement Residence**
120 Darling St., Brantford, ON N3T 5W6
Tel: 519-759-5250 *Fax:* 519-759-8403
charlotte@reveraliving.com
www.reveraliving.com
Number of Beds: 80 beds
Note: Independent & assisted living, secured living for dementia care
Carol Sterkenburg, Administrator/Care Coordinator

***Brantford:* Tranquility Place**
PO Box 3000, 436 Powerline Rd., Brantford, ON N3T 6G5
Tel: 519-759-2222
www.allegroresidences.ca
Year Founded: 1988
Note: Specialties: Physiotherapy; Foot care clinic; Physical activities
Paul Rade, General Manager

***Brighton:* Applefest Lodge**
PO Box 850, 120 Elizabeth St., Brighton, ON K0K 1H0
Tel: 613-475-3510 *Fax:* 613-475-3431
Number of Beds: 50 beds
Marilyn McLeod, Manager
interest@applefestlodge.com

***Brockville:* Bridlewood Manor**
1026 Bridlewood Dr., Brockville, ON K6V 7J8
Tel: 613-345-2477 *Fax:* 613-345-4188
www.reveraliving.com/bridlewood
Number of Beds: 67 units
Dennis Daoust, Executive Director

***Brockville:* Rosedale Retirement Centre**
Affiliated with: Chartwell Seniors Housing REIT
1813 County Rd. 2E, RR#1, Brockville, ON K6V 5T1
Tel: 613-342-0200 *Fax:* 613-342-8729
rosedale@chartwellreit.ca
www.chartwellreit.ca
Number of Beds: 69 suites
Stephen Suske, CEO, Chartwell Seniors Housing REIT

***Burlington:* Appleby Place**
500 Appleby Line, Burlington, ON L7L 5Z6
Tel: 905-333-1611 *Fax:* 905-333-0596
applebyplace@lrc.ca
www.reveraliving.com/homes/8001/
Number of Beds: 90 units
Mary Turnbull, General Manager

***Burlington:* Bethany Residence**
2387 Industrial St., Burlington, ON L7P 3A1
Tel: 905-335-3463 *Fax:* 905-335-1202
info@bethanyresidence.ca
www.bethanyresidence.ca
Number of Beds: 121 beds
Sheri Levy-Abraham, Manager

***Burlington:* Brantwood Lifecare Centre**
802 Hager Ave., Burlington, ON L7S 1X2
Tel: 905-637-3481 *Fax:* 905-637-7514
Number of Beds: 178 beds

***Burlington:* Christopher Terrace Retirement Home**
3131 New St., Burlington, ON L7N 3P8
Tel: 905-632-5072 *Fax:* 905-632-5074
www.residencesallegro.com
Number of Beds: 80 beds
Laurie Johnston, Manager

***Burlington:* Lakeshore Place Retirement Residence**
5314 Lakeshore Rd., Burlington, ON L7L 6L8
Tel: 905-333-0009 *Fax:* 905-333-3103
info@caregard.ca
www.lakeshoreplace.ca/lakeshore.htm
Number of Beds: 156 beds (residential care, assisted & daily living)
Note: assisted living retirement residence
Nancy Fischer, Administrator

***Burlington:* Park Avenue Manor**
924 Park Ave. West, Burlington, ON L7T 1N7
Tel: 905-333-3323
parkavenuegm@cogeco.net
www.chartwellreit.ca
Number of Beds: 69 suites
Note: Specialties: Recreational activities; Medication administration; Wellness monitoring; Respite care; Convalescent, seasonal, & trial stays
Carrie T. Campbell, General Manager

***Cambridge:* Avonlea Place**
611 Dunbar Rd., Cambridge, ON N3H 2T4
Tel: 519-650-1102 *Fax:* 519-650-3382
avonleaplace@rogers.com
Number of Beds: 32 beds
Jason Rumph

***Cambridge:* Queen's Square Terrace**
Affiliated with: Chartwell Seniors Housing REIT
10 Melville St. North, Cambridge, ON N1S 1H5
Tel: 519-621-2777 *Fax:* 519-622-1299
www.chartwellreit.ca
Number of Beds: 80 suites
Stephen Suske, CEO, Chartwell Seniors Housing REIT

***Carleton Place:* Carleton Place Manor**
6 Arthur St., Carleton Place, ON K7C 4S4
Tel: 613-253-7360 *Fax:* 613-253-5048
Number of Beds: 115 rooms
Corrie Berryman, Executive Director

***Chatham:* Maple City Retirement Residence**
97 McFarlane Ave., Chatham, ON N7L 4V6
Tel: 519-354-7111 *Fax:* 519-351-5780
adm.maplecity@diversicare.ca
www.diversicare.ca
Number of Beds: 75 beds
Hilda Michielsen, Administrator

***Chatham:* Residence on The Thames**
Affiliated with: Steeves & Rozema Group
850 Grand Ave. West, Chatham, ON N7L 5H5
Tel: 519-351-7220 *Fax:* 519-436-0360
crystal_houle@srgroup.ca
www.srgroup.ca
Number of Beds: 75 beds
Note: Independent living
Liddy Krieger, Executive Director
Crystal Houle, Office Manager

***Codrington:* Golden Pond House Retirement Residence**
387 Goodrich Rd., Codrington, ON K0K 1R0
Tel: 613-475-4846 *Fax:* 613-475-4961
gandrmgt@sympatico.ca
www.goldenpondretirement.ca
Number of Beds: 28 beds
Joan Dorland, Administrator

***Cornwall:* Chateau Cornwall**
41 Amelia St., Cornwall, ON K6H 7E5
Tel: 613-937-4700 *Fax:* 613-932-6407
www.chartwellreit.ca

Number of Beds: 105 suites
Denis Carr, Manager

Delhi: Delrose Retirement Residence
725 Gibraltar St., Delhi, ON N4B 3C7
Tel: 519-582-4072 *Fax:* 519-582-0005
Bonnie Guthrie, Administrator
bonnieguthrie@nor-del.com

Dresden: Park Street Place Retirement Residence
650 Park St., Dresden, ON N0P 1M0
Tel: 519-683-4474 *Fax:* 519-683-4555
www.diversicare.ca
Year Founded: 1987
Note: Specialties: Foot care; Physiotherapy; Medication management; Recreational activities; Respite & convalescent stays
Hilda Michielsen, Administrator

Dundas: The Georgian Retirement Residence
Affiliated with: Chartwell Seniors Housing REIT
255 Governor's Rd., Dundas, ON L9H 3K4
Tel: 905-627-8444 *Fax:* 905-627-9820
www.chartwellreit.ca
Number of Beds: 60 suites
Stephen Suske, CEO, Chartwell Seniors Housing REIT

Elliot Lake: Huron Lodge
100 Manitoba Rd., Elliot Lake, ON P5A 3T1
Tel: 705-848-2019 *Fax:* 705-848-1306
www.huronlodge.ca
Note: Huron Lodge is a residence for 36 older adults. Respite service is available.
Gilbert A. Contant, Chief Executive Officer
gil@huronlodge.ca

Fort Erie: Garrison Place Retirement Residence
373 Garrison Rd., Fort Erie, ON L2A 1N1
Tel: 905-871-6410 *Fax:* 905-871-5422
garrisonplace@reveraliving.com
www.reveraliving.com
Number of Beds: 80 beds
Note: Secured living for dementia care residents; respite & convalescent options
Judy Gibson, Manager

Georgetown: Mountainview Residence
222 Mountainview Rd. North, Georgetown, ON L7G 3R2
Tel: 905-877-1800 *Fax:* 905-873-9083
info@mountainviewresidence.com
www.mountainviewresidence.com
Number of Beds: 82 suites
Christopher Summer, Manager

Gloucester: Blackburn Lodge Seniors Residence
2412 Cléroux Cres., Gloucester, ON K1W 1A3
Tel: 613-837-7467 *Fax:* 613-837-0250
info@blackburnlodge.com
www.blackburnlodge.com
Note: Health services are provided, as well as personal services & activities.
David Porter, BA, BComm, CA, Executive Director & President
porterd@blackburnlodge.com
Sanjee Mendis, Director, Care
smendis@blackburnlodge.com
Shawna Melanson, Manager, Dining Room
smelanson@blackburnlodge.com
Katie St-Cyr, Activity Coordinator
kstcyr@blackburnlodge.com

Gloucester: Camilla Gardens Retirement Residence
1119 Bathgate Dr., Gloucester, ON K1J 9N4
Tel: 613-747-7000 *Fax:* 613-747-1804
camillagardens@bellnet.ca
www.camillaresidence.yp.ca
Note: Camilla Gardens accommodates 54 residents. Nursing supervision & assistance with person needs are available. Camilla Gardens also offers short term convalescent, respite, or trial stays.
Lyne Bellefeuille, Administrator

Gloucester: Elmsmere Retirement Residence
889 Elmsmere St., Gloucester, ON K1J 8G4
Tel: 613-745-2409 *Fax:* 613-745-4955
elmsmereplace@reveraliving.com
Number of Beds: 57 units
Pierre Lefebvre, Manager

Gloucester: Ogilvie Villa
1345 Ogilvie Rd., Gloucester, ON K1J 7P5
Tel: 613-742-6524 *Fax:* 613-742-7380
ogilvie@reveraliving.com
www.reveraliving.com
Year Founded: 1995
Number of Beds: 64 residential capacity
Note: Specialties: Recreation program; Short term stays
Bob Lemay, Manager

Goderich: Goderich Place Retirement Residence
30 Balvina Dr. East, Goderich, ON N7A 4L5
Tel: 519-524-4243
dcgoderichplace@hurontel.on.ca
www.goderichplace.com
Note: Goderich Place is a residence for seniors that offers bachelor, one, & two bedroom suites.
Barb Sproul, General Manager

Goderich: Maple Grove Lodge
45 Nelson St. East, Goderich, ON N7A 1R7
Tel: 519-524-8610
Number of Beds: 25 beds
Note: Nursing home

Gravenhurst: Gravenhurst Manor
300 Muskoka Rd. North, Gravenhurst, ON P1P 1N8
Tel: 705-687-3356 *Fax:* 705-687-5685
www.chartwellreit.ca/home_locations/gravenhurst.htm
Number of Beds: 50 suites
Gay Pengilly, Administrator

Grimsby: Maplecrest Village Retirement Residence
85 Main St. East, Grimsby, ON L3M 1N6
Tel: 905-945-7044 *Fax:* 905-945-6187
maplecrest@reveraliving.com
Number of Beds: 80 beds
Leanne Dabbs, Administrator

Guelph: College Place Retirement Residence
Former Name: Meadowcroft Place Retirement Centre
166 College Ave. West, Guelph, ON N1G 1S4
Tel: 519-822-0090 *Fax:* 519-822-2310
www.reveraliving.com
Number of Beds: 57 residential capacity
Note: Specialties: Assisted living program; Podiatry services; Recreation program; Short term stays
Alice Johnstone, Executive Director

Guelph: Norfolk Manor
128 Norfolk St., Guelph, ON N1H 4J8
Tel: 519-837-1100 *Fax:* 519-836-4003
david@norfolkmanor.ca
www.norfolkmanor.ca
Number of Beds: 67 beds
David Ing, Manager

Guelph: Stone Lodge Retirement Residence
165 Cole Rd., Guelph, ON N1G 4N9
Tel: 519-767-0880 *Fax:* 519-767-1690
stonelodge@reveraliving.com
www.reveraliving.com
Number of Beds: 130 units
Note: Independent & assisted living; convalescent & respite options
E. Lyn Fisher, Administrator

Guelph: Village of Riverside Glen
60 Woodlawn Rd. East, Guelph, ON N1H 8M8
Tel: 519-822-5272 *Fax:* 519-822-5520
www.oakwoodretirement.com/riverside.html
Number of Beds: 196 beds
Michell Vermeeren, Manager

Hamilton: Atrium Villa
467 Main St. East, Hamilton, ON L8M 1K1
Tel: 905-521-4442 *Fax:* 905-521-8247
www.chartwellreit.ca/home_locations/atrium_villa.htm
Number of Beds: 67 units
Margaret Coulter, Manager

Hamilton: Proctor Manor Retirement Home
Former Name: Proctor Manor Nursing Home
81 Proctor Blvd., Hamilton, ON L8M 2M5
Tel: 905-545-2427 *Fax:* 905-547-7195
Number of Beds: 23 beds
Joyce Carey, Manager

Hamilton: Stinson Manor
112 Stinson St., Hamilton, ON L8N 1S5
Tel: 905-521-9112 *Fax:* 905-521-9106

Hamilton: Townsview Retirement Residence
52 Catherine St. North, Hamilton, ON L8R 1J1
Tel: 905-527-1200
www.ourhomeyourhomecanada.ca
Number of Beds: 57 residential capacity
Note: Specialties: Personal nursing care; Catheter care; Colostomy care; Diabetes care; Oxygen care; Wellness program; Medication administration; Activity program
Derrick Bernardo, Administrator

Hanover: The Village Seniors Community
101 Tenth St., Hanover, ON N4N 1M9
Tel: 519-364-4320 *Fax:* 519-364-6953
thevillageseniors'community@reveraliving.com
www.reveraliving.com
Number of Beds: 70 long-term, 95 retirement beds, 100 seniors' apartments
Karen Kraus, Administrator

Harrow: Harrowood Seniors Community
Former Name: Harrowood Rest Home
1 Pollard Dr., Harrow, ON N0R 1G0
Tel: 519-738-2286 *Fax:* 519-738-2700
harrowoodseniorscommunity@bellnet.ca
www.harrowood.ca
Number of Beds: 105 beds
Note: seniors community
Carol Chisholm, Administrator

Hawkesbury: Place Mont Roc
100 Industrial Blvd., Hawkesbury, ON K6A 3M8
Tel: 613-632-2900
Number of Beds: 95 beds
Heather Sheffield, Administrator

Huntsville: Rogers Cove Retirement Residence
Affiliated with: Chartwell Seniors Housing REIT
4 Coveside Dr., Huntsville, ON P1H 2J9
Tel: 705-789-1600 *Fax:* 705-789-8781
rogerscove@chartwellreit.ca
www.chartwellreit.ca
Number of Beds: 55 suites
Stephen Suske, CEO, Chartwell Seniors Housing REIT

Ingersoll: Oxford Manor Retirement Home
276 Oxford St., Ingersoll, ON N5G 2W1
Tel: 519-485-0350 *Fax:* 519-485-7254
oxfordmanor@chartwellreit.ca
www.chartwellreit.ca
Number of Beds: 46 units
Note: Specialties: Activity program; Medication administration; Wellness monitoring; Respite care; Trial stays
Diance Nant, Administrator

Kanata: Chartwell House Kanata
20 Shirley's Brook Dr., Kanata, ON K2K 2W8
Tel: 613-591-8939 *Fax:* 613-591-1933
Number of Beds: 81 beds
Johanne Laframboise, General Manager
jlaframboise@chartwellreit.ca
Lisa Giles, Community Relations Manager
lgiles@chartwellreit.ca

Kanata: Fairfield Manor Retirement Home
17 Lombardo Dr., Kanata, ON K2L 4E8
Tel: 613-592-5772 *Fax:* 613-592-8928
info@fairfieldmanor.ca
www.fairfieldmanor.ca
Number of Beds: 46 beds
Kate Gray, Administrator

Kanata: Kanata Retirement Residence
145 Castlefrank Rd. South, Kanata, ON K2L 3X9
Tel: 613-831-3333 *Fax:* 613-831-0153
kanataplace@reveraliving.com
Number of Beds: 66 units
Robyn Bosik, Executive Director

Kanata: Walden Retirement Residence
27 Weaver Cres., Kanata, ON K2K 2Z8
Tel: 613-591-3991 *Fax:* 613-591-9647
Number of Beds: 93 beds
Heidi Eichenberger, General Manager

Kincardine: Malcolm Place
PO Box 100, 255 Durham St., Kincardine, ON N2Z 2Y6
Tel: 519-396-5800 *Fax:* 519-396-5236
info@malcolmplace.ca
www.malcolmplace.ca
Number of Beds: 41 beds
Note: Retirement Residence
Dorinda Bowers, Administrator

Kingston: The Rosewood
833 Sutton Mills Ct., Kingston, ON K7P 2N9
Tel: 613-384-7131 Fax: 613-634-3247
debbie.helferty@specialty-care.com
www.speciality-care.com
Number of Beds: 70 units
Note: Independent living
Debbie Helferty, General Manager

Kingston: St. Lawrence Place
181 Ontario St., Kingston, ON K7L 5M1
Tel: 613-544-5900 Fax: 613-544-9971
st.lawrence@reveraliving.com
www.reveraliving.com
Number of Beds: 71 units
Margaret Bennett, Executive Director

Kingston: Trillium Ridge Retirement Community
800 Edgar St., Kingston, ON K7M 8S4
Tel: 613-547-0040 Fax: 613-547-3734
taimi.post@specialty-care.com
www.specialty-care.com
Note: Independent living. Specialty Care Trillium Centre long-term care residence located adjacent
Taimi Post, Director, Marketing & Resident Services

Kingsville: Kings Manor Residence
54 Spruce St. North, Kingsville, ON N9Y 3J1
Tel: 519-733-8376
augustinevillas@yahoo.ca
www.kingsmanorresidence.com
Number of Beds: 9 beds
Marie Mayhew, Manager
foreverhome1@ymail.com

Kitchener: Bankside Terrace
71 Bankside Dr., Kitchener, ON N2N 3L1
Tel: 519-749-9999 Fax: 519-749-1947
www.chartwellreit.ca/home_locations/bankside_terrace.htm
Number of Beds: 86 units
Brad Lawrence, Manager

Kitchener: Conestoga Lodge Retirement Residence
55 Hugo Cres., Kitchener, ON N2M 5J1
Tel: 519-576-2140 Fax: 519-576-1790
sbarkshire@thecaringnetwork.ca
www.conestogalodge.com
Number of Beds: 88 beds
Betty Cushing, Manager

Kitchener: Fergus Place Retirement Residence
Former Name: Meadowcroft Place
164 Fergus Ave., Kitchener, ON N2A 2H2
Tel: 519-894-9600 Fax: 519-894-3383
fergus@reveraliving.com
www.reveraliving.com
Number of Beds: 76 residential capacity
Note: Specialty: Short term stays
Jane Hagelberg, Administrator

Kitchener: Lafontaine Terrace
169 Borden Ave. North, Kitchener, ON N2H 3J5
Tel: 519-576-2800 Fax: 519-742-4242
lafontaine@on.aibn.com
Jeff Edwards, Administrator

Kitchener: Lanark Place Retirement Residence
44 Lanark Cres., Kitchener, ON N2N 2Z8
Tel: 519-743-0121 Fax: 519-743-8901
info@lanarkcare.com
www.lanarkcare.com
Number of Beds: 107 units
Nancy Douglas, Manager

Kitchener: Victoria Place Retirement Residence
290 Queen St. South, Kitchener, ON N2G 1W3
Tel: 519-576-1300 Fax: 519-744-7097
victoriaplace@reveraliving.com
www.reveraliving.com
Number of Beds: 73 beds
Note: Independent & assisted living
Deb Gemmell, Executive Director

Leamington: Erie Glen Manor Retirement Residence
119 Robson Rd., Leamington, ON N8H 3V4
Tel: 519-322-2384 Fax: 519-322-1411
Number of Beds: 81 beds
Shelley Gould, Administrator

Leamington: Leamington Lodge Residential Care Centre Ltd.
PO Box 353, 24 Russell St., Leamington, ON N8H 3W3
Tel: 519-326-3591 Fax: 519-326-8787
Number of Beds: 40 beds
Jane Lee, Administrator

London: Ashwood Manor Ltd.
79 David St., London, ON N6P 1B4
Tel: 519-652-9006 Fax: 519-652-2592
info@ashwoodmanor.com
www.ashwoodmanor.com
Number of Beds: 72 units
Kathleen Hobden, Administrator

London: Central Park Lodge - London
279 Horton St., London, ON N6B 1L3
Tel: 519-434-4544 Fax: 519-673-4971
cplondon@reveraliving.com
www.reveraliving.com
Number of Beds: 87 units
Note: Assisted living
Susan O'Neill, Administrator

London: Horizon Place Retirement Residence
Former Name: Meadowcroft Place
760 Horizon Dr., London, ON N6H 5G3
Tel: 519-641-6330 Fax: 519-641-0570
horizon@reveraliving.com
www.reveraliving.com
Number of Beds: 84 residential capacity
Note: Specialties: Assisted living program; Recreation therapy; Podiatry; Short term stays
Marilyn Weekley, Manager

London: Kensington Village
1340 Huron St., London, ON N5V 3R3
Tel: 519-455-3910 Fax: 519-455-1570
sbrooks@kensingtonvillage.org
www.kensingtonvillage.org
Year Founded: 1984
Number of Beds: 139 suites
Peter Schlegel, Administrator
519-455-3910 ext.290, pschlegel@kensingtonvillage.org
Wendy Harrison, Director, Retirement Care
519-455-3910 ext.248, wharrison@kensingtonvillage.org

London: Longworth Retirement Residence
600 Longworth Rd., London, ON N6K 4X9
Tel: 519-472-1115 Fax: 519-472-1134
info@longworthcare.com
www.longworthcare.com
Number of Beds: 126 suites
Note: Specialty: Retirement / assisted living; Physiotherapy; Massage therapy; Reiki; Reflexology

London: Waverley Mansion Retirement Residence
10 Grand Ave., London, ON N5C 1K9
Tel: 519-667-1381 Fax: 519-667-9601
gm.waverley@diversicare.ca
www.diversicare.ca
Year Founded: 1987
Number of Beds: 65 beds
Note: Specialties: Supported care services for older adults; Medication administration & supervision; Physiotherapy; Foot care; Recreational program; Respite care; Convalescent stays
Suzi McArthur, Administrator

Midland: King Place Retirement Residence
750 King St., Midland, ON L4R 4K5
Tel: 705-526-0514 Fax: 705-526-8769
kingplace@reveraliving.com
www.reveraliving.com
Number of Beds: 80 beds
Note: Independent & assisted living; secured living for dementia care residents; respite & convalescent options
Sharon Penrose, Manager

Midland: The Villa Care Centre & Retirement Lodge
689 Yonge St., Midland, ON L4R 2E1
Tel: 705-526-4238 Fax: 705-526-5080
www.jarlette.com
Number of Beds: 158 beds
Edith Robitaille, Administrator
erobitaille@jarlette.com
Tanya Wilfling, General Manager
twilfling@jarlette.com
Michelle Lloyd, Customer Service Coordinator
mlloyd@jarlette.com

Mississauga: Beechwood Place
1500 Rathburn Rd. East, Mississauga, ON L4W 4L7
Tel: 905-238-0800 Fax: 905-238-4926
beechwoodplace@lrc.ca
Number of Beds: 137 suites
Deborah Rushton, Executive Director
Julie Shuster, Director of Marketing

Mississauga: Bough Beeches Place Retirement Residence
Former Name: Meadowcroft Place
1130 Bough Beeches Blvd., Mississauga, ON L4W 4G3
Tel: 905-625-2022 Fax: 905-238-3052
boughbeeches@reveraliving.com
www.reveraliving.com
Year Founded: 1984
Number of Beds: 109 residential capacity
Note: Specialties: Assisted living program; Secured living program, for persons with dementia & Alzheimers disease; Short term stays; Fitness program; Podiatry services
Karen Douglas, Administrator

Mississauga: Erin Mills Lodge
2132 Dundas St. West, Mississauga, ON L5K 2K7
Tel: 905-823-6700 Fax: 905-823-2410
care@sifton.com
www.sifton.com
Number of Beds: 141 retirement units, 86 long-term care beds
Mary Whalen, Administrator

Mississauga: King Gardens Retirement Residence
85 King St. East, Mississauga, ON L5A 4G6
Tel: 905-566-4545 Fax: 905-566-0327
kinggardens@reveraliving.com
www.reveraliving.com/homes/226
Number of Beds: 147 beds
Agnes Kupny, Executive Director

Morrisburg: Chartwell Senior Housing
Former Name: Hartford Retirement Centre
3 Fifth St. West, Morrisburg, ON K0C 1X0
Tel: 613-543-3984 Fax: 613-543-4262
hartford@chartwellreit.ca
www.chartwellreit.ca
Number of Beds: 101 suites
Kimberly Hodkinson, General Manager
khodkinson@chartwellreit.ca
Tracy Jones, Marketing Manager
tjones@chartwellreit.ca

Mount Forest: Birmingham Lodge
356A Birmingham St. East, Mount Forest, ON N0G 2L2
Tel: 519-323-4019 Fax: 519-323-3005
www.diversicare.ca
Number of Beds: 95 units
Ilonka van Willigen, Administrator

Napanee: The Riverine Independent & Retirement Living
328 Dundas St. West, Napanee, ON K7R 4B5
Tel: 613-354-8188 Fax: 613-354-8186
Toll-Free: 866-387-2217
Number of Beds: 42 beds
Note: Specialties: Medication administration; Social & recreational program
Greg Freeman, Manager

Nepean: Riverpark Place Retirement Residence
1 Corkstown Rd., Nepean, ON K2H 1B6
Tel: 613-828-8882 Fax: 613-828-8908
info@caregard.ca
www.riverparkplace.ca
Number of Beds: 173 beds (residential care, assisted & daily living)
Cathy Arthurs-Hall, Administrator

Nepean: Stillwater Creek Retirement Community
18 Robertson Rd., Nepean, ON K2H 1C6
Tel: 613-828-7575 Fax: 613-828-7524
info@caregard.ca
www.stillwatercreek.ca
Year Founded: 2001
Number of Beds: 204 units
Note: Specialties: Independent living; Assisted living; Recreation programs
Mike Traub, Administrator

Newmarket: Alexander Muir Retirement Residence
197 Prospect St., Newmarket, ON L3Y 3T7
Tel: 905-836-8399 Fax: 905-836-9322
www.residencesallegro.com/en/
Social Media: www.facebook.com/146878375366800
Number of Beds: 96 units
Michael Ayers, General Manager

Niagara Falls: Cavendish Manor Retirement Residence
5781 Dunn St., Niagara Falls, ON L2G 2N9
Tel: 905-354-2733 Fax: 905-354-4164
www.cavendishmanor.com
Number of Beds: 69 units

Janice Amos, Manager

Niagara Falls: Chippawa Place
4118 Main St., Niagara Falls, ON L2G 6C2
Tel: 905-295-6744 *Fax:* 905-295-6306
Toll-Free: 877-702-8135
chippawaplace@hotmail.com
Year Founded: 1994
Number of Beds: 26 beds
Mark Budic, Administrator
Susan Budic, Administrator

Niagara Falls: Lundy Manor Retirement Residence
7860 Lundy's Lane, Niagara Falls, ON L2H 1H1
Tel: 905-356-1511 *Fax:* 905-356-1736
lundy@reveraliving.com
www.reveraliving.com
Number of Beds: 95 capacity
Note: Specialties: Assisted living program; Short term stays; Podiatry services
Art Derbernardi, Manager

Niagara Falls: Willoughby Manor
Affiliated with: Chartwell Seniors Housing REIT
3584 Bridgewater St., Niagara Falls, ON L2G 6H1
Tel: 905-295-6288 *Fax:* 905-295-4767
willoughbymanor@chartwellreit.ca
www.chartwellreit.ca
Number of Beds: 52 suites
Note: Retirement residence, with convalescent, respite & seasonal stay options
Stephen Suske, CEO, Chartwell Seniors Housing REIT

North Bay: Barclay House Retirement Residence
Affiliated with: Chartwell Seniors Housing REIT
600 Chippewa St. West, North Bay, ON P1B 9E7
Tel: 705-476-6585 *Fax:* 705-476-6542
www.chartwellreit.ca
Number of Beds: 64 suites
Stephen Suske, CEO, Chartwell Seniors Housing REIT

Norwood: Maple View Retirement Centre
90 Victoria St., RR#2, Norwood, ON K0L 2V0
Tel: 705-639-5374 *Fax:* 705-639-1793
Number of Beds: 60 beds
Kim Ward, Administrator

Oakville: Churchill Place
345 Church St., Oakville, ON L6J 7G4
Tel: 905-338-3311 *Fax:* 905-338-7117
churchillplace@lrc.ca
www.reveraliving.com
Number of Beds: 69 suites
Note: Independent living, convalescent & respite options
Carole Huppenthal, General Manager

Oakville: The Kensington
25 Lakeshore Rd. West, Oakville, ON L6K 3X8
Tel: 905-844-4000 *Fax:* 905-842-9229
thekensingtonon@lrc.ca
www.reveraliving.com
Number of Beds: 120 suites
Note: Independent living
Judy Martin, General Manager

Oakville: Oakville Senior Citizens Residence
#2220, 2222 Lakeshore Rd. West, Oakville, ON L6L 5G5
Tel: 905-827-4139 *Fax:* 905-827-8047
oscr@oakvilleseniors.com
www.oakvilleseniors.com
Number of Beds: 164 apartment tower units + 172 residential tower rooms

Oakville: Trafalgar Lodge Retirement Residence
299 Randall St., Oakville, ON L6J 6B4
Tel: 905-842-8408 *Fax:* 905-842-8410
trafalgar@reveraliving.com
www.reveraliving.com
Number of Beds: 75 units
Note: Independent & assisted living; convalescent & respite options
Eileen Brajovic, Executive Director

Orangeville: Lord Dufferin Centre
32 First St., Orangeville, ON L9W 2E1
Tel: 519-941-8433 *Fax:* 519-941-2615
www.lorddufferincentre.ca
Number of Beds: 78 private suites
Note: Specialties: Physiotherapy; Foot care
Donna Holwell, Manager

Orillia: Atrium Retirement Residence
230 Coldwater Rd. West, Orillia, ON L3V 3M2
Tel: 705-325-7300 *Fax:* 705-325-9078
atrium@chartwellreit.ca
chartwellreit.ca/home_locations/atrium.htm
Number of Beds: 50 units
Miriam Leduc, Manager

Orillia: Birchmere Retirement Residence
234 Bay St., Orillia, ON L3V 3W8
Tel: 705-326-8520 *Fax:* 705-326-5273
birchmere@on.aibn.com
Number of Beds: 77 beds
Jackie Payne, Administrator

Orillia: Champlain Manor
65 Fittons Rd. West, Orillia, ON L3V 3V2
Tel: 705-326-8597 *Fax:* 705-326-9831
champlainmanor@on.aibn.com
www.retireorillia.com
Number of Beds: 65 beds
Jackie Payne, Administrator

Orillia: Spencer House
835 West Ridge Blvd., Orillia, ON L3V 8B3
Tel: 705-326-6609
admin.orillia@leisureworld.ca
www.leisureworld.ca
Number of Beds: 120 long-term care; 58 retirement beds
Lorne Simon, President, Chairman

Oshawa: Cedarcroft Place (Oshawa)
649 King St. East, Oshawa, ON L1H 8P9
Tel: 905-723-9490
www.reveraliving.com/cedarcroft
Number of Beds: 102 units
Marjorie Beattie, Administrator

Ottawa: Amica at Bearbrook Court
2645 Innes Rd., Ottawa, ON K1B 3J7
Tel: 613-837-8720 *Fax:* 613-837-8107
bearbrook@amica.ca
www.amica.ca/bearbrook/
Number of Beds: 122 suites
Luke Goulette, General Manager

Ottawa: Billings Lodge
1180 Bélanger Ave., Ottawa, ON K1H 8A2
Tel: 613-737-7877
www.billingslodge.ca
Number of Beds: 100 beds
Alain Brunet, Administrator

Ottawa: Colonel By Retirement Residence
43 Aylmer St., Ottawa, ON K1S 4R5
Tel: 613-730-2002
www.reveraliving.com/colonelby
Number of Beds: 135 units

Ottawa: The Edinburgh Retirement Residence
10 Vaughan St., Ottawa, ON K1M 2H6
Tel: 613-747-2233 *Fax:* 613-747-6741
edinburgh@reveraliving.com
www.reveraliving.com
Number of Beds: 66 beds
Note: Independent & assisted living programs
Mary Albota, Administrator

Ottawa: Hunt Club Manor
1351 Hunt Club Rd., Ottawa, ON K1V 1A6
Tel: 613-733-4776 *Fax:* 613-733-0496
www.retirementresidences.com/homes/8018/
Number of Beds: 78 beds
Tracy Fowers, General Manager

Ottawa: Manoir Gallien
162 Murray St., Ottawa, ON K1N 5M8
Tel: 613-241-1331 *Fax:* 613-241-2693
info@manoirgalleon.com
Number of Beds: 75 units
Note: Senior's residence
Sandra Sullivan, Administrator

Ottawa: New Edinburgh Square
420 Mackay St., Ottawa, ON K1M 2C4
Tel: 613-744-0901 *Fax:* 613-742-3039
newedinburghsquare@chartwellreit.ca
www.chartwellreit.ca
Number of Beds: 111 suites
Jacqueline Brown, General Manager

Ottawa: Parklane Residence
1095 Merivale Rd., Ottawa, ON K1Z 6A9
Tel: 613-725-1064 *Fax:* 613-728-3533
Number of Beds: 107 beds
Note: Retirement residence
Claude Desforges, Manager

Ottawa: Presland Residence
198 Presland Rd., Ottawa, ON K1K 2B8
Tel: 613-745-0089 *Fax:* 613-745-6060
Mario Grégoire, Administrator
613-745-0089 ext 221

Ottawa: Rideau Place On-The-River
Affiliated with: Chartwell Seniors Housing REIT
550 Wilbrod St., Ottawa, ON K1N 9M3
Tel: 613-234-6003 *Fax:* 613-234-9498
rideauplace@chartwellreit.ca
www.chartwellreit.ca; www.rideauplace.com
Number of Beds: 98 suites
Note: Retirement residence; short-term respite & convalescent care
Stephen Suske, CEO, Chartwell Seniors Housing REIT
Brian Kimberley, Marketing Manager

Ottawa: Rothwell Heights Retirement Residence
1735 Montréal Rd., Ottawa, ON K1J 6N4
Tel: 613-744-2322
Number of Beds: 114 units
Anita Hurtubise, Administrator

Ottawa: Sandy Hill Retirement Residence
353 Friel St., Ottawa, ON K1N 7W7
Tel: 613-234-3838 *Fax:* 613-234-5472
sandyhill@reveraliving.com
www.reveraliving.com
Number of Beds: 71 beds
Note: Independent & assisting living programs; respite, convalescent options
Mélanie Lefebvre, Executive Director

Ottawa: Sterling Place Retirement Residence
2716 Richmond Rd., Ottawa, ON K2B 8M3
Tel: 613-829-6527 *Fax:* 613-829-6201
sterling@reveraliving.com
www.reveraliving.com
Number of Beds: 116 beds
Note: Independent & assisted living programs; dementia care; respite & convalescent options
Rosemary Rowley, Manager

Ottawa: Stittsville Retirement Community
1354 Stittsville Main St., Ottawa, ON K2S 1V4
Tel: 613-836-2216 *Fax:* 613-836-1903
www.reveraliving.com
Number of Beds: 75 beds
Note: Independent living
Pat Leishman, Manager

Ottawa: Thorncliffe Place Retirement Home
1 Thorncliffe Pl., Ottawa, ON K2H 9N9
Tel: 613-596-3853 *Fax:* 613-596-6225
info@thorncliffeplace.com
www.thorncliffeplace.com
Year Founded: 1989
Number of Beds: 81 suites
Note: Specialties: Activity program; Supervision of medications; Memory support; Elderobics; Convalescent stays
Don Francis, Administrator

Ottawa: Watford House Residence
75 Powell Ave., Ottawa, ON K1S 1Z9
Tel: 613-230-7423 *Fax:* 613-230-9194
Number of Beds: 22 beds
Anatoli Brouchkov, Administrator

Ottawa: The Westwood
Former Name: Central Park Lodges - Ottawa 1
2374 Carling Ave., Ottawa, ON K2B 7G5
Tel: 613-820-7333
Year Founded: 1961
Number of Beds: 135 units
Note: Independent & assisted living, respite & convalescent options. Central Park Lodge Ottawa 2 located at 2370 Carling Ave.
Ray Hould, General Manager

Ottawa: Windsor Park Manor Retirement Living
990 Hunt Club Rd., Ottawa, ON K1V 8S8
Tel: 613-249-0722 *Fax:* 613-249-0575
info@windsorparkmanor.ca
www.windsorparkmanor.ca
Note: Convalescence, respite, & short term stays are available.
Diane Thauvette-Chénier, Co-Owner & General Manager

***Owen Sound:* Central Place**
855 - 3 Ave. East, Owen Sound, ON N4K 2K6
Tel: 519-371-1968 *Fax:* 519-371-5357
info@cpretirement.ca
www.cpretirement.ca
Year Founded: 1998
Number of Beds: 90 beds
John Landen, President

***Owen Sound:* Hannah Walker Place**
832 - 2 Ave. West, Owen Sound, ON N4K 4M5
Tel: 519-371-1664 *Fax:* 519-371-5286
Number of Beds: 57 beds
Linda Crigger, Administrator
linda@owensoundretirement.com

***Owen Sound:* John Joseph Place**
854 - 2 Ave. West, Owen Sound, ON N4K 4M5
Tel: 519-371-3240 *Fax:* 519-371-6441
Number of Beds: 44 beds
Linda Crigger, Facility Manager

***Pakenham:* Country View Lodge**
4676 Darks Side Rd., Pakenham, ON K0A 2X0
Tel: 613-624-5714 *Fax:* 613-624-5715
info@countryviewlodge.ca
www.countryviewlodge.ca
Number of Beds: 34 beds
Note: retirement home with assisted living/nursing service
Subhash Chadha, Operating Manager
613-866-7142

***Paris:* Penmarvian Retirement Home**
185 Grand River St. North, Paris, ON N3L 2N2
Tel: 519-442-7140 *Fax:* 519-442-7156
info@penmarvian.com
www.penmarvian.com
Year Founded: 1980
Number of Beds: 38 beds
Note: Specialties: Nursing care; Activity program
Maria Toncic, Administrator

***Perth:* Rideau Ferry Country Home**
1333, Rideau Ferry Rd., RR#5, Perth, ON K7H 3C7
Tel: 613-267-6213 *Fax:* 613-267-6261
Number of Beds: 45 units
Note: Offers both retirement residences and assisted daily living services
Mary Ross, Administrator

***Peterborough:* Empress Gardens Retirement Residence**
131 Charlotte St., Peterborough, ON K9J 2T6
Tel: 705-876-1314 *Fax:* 705-876-1908
www.empressgardens.ca
Number of Beds: 88 beds
Joanne Stone, Executive Director

***Peterborough:* Peterborough Manor**
1039 Water St., Peterborough, ON K9H 3P5
Tel: 705-748-5343 *Fax:* 705-876-4741
peterboroughmanor@chartwellreit.ca
www.chartwellreit.ca
Number of Beds: 101 suites
Note: Specialties: Medication administration; Wellness monitoring; Assistance to persons with oxygen, catheters, & ostomies; Activity program; Podiatry; Respite care; Convalescent stays
Martha Creally, Administrator

***Peterborough:* Princess Gardens Retirement Residence**
100 Charlotte St., Peterborough, ON L9J 7L4
Tel: 705-750-1234 *Fax:* 705-750-0711
Toll-Free: 1-866-741-6036
www.princessgardens.ca
Number of Beds: 132 beds
Note: Independent retirement amenities; assisted living/enriched care options; respite & convalescent care
Juris Taurins, Manager

***Pickering:* Community Nursing Home**
1955 Valley Farm Rd., Pickering, ON L1V 1X6
Tel: 905-831-2522 *Fax:* 905-420-5030
mlacroxi@clmi.ca
www.cnhpickering.ca
Number of Beds: 233 long-term care beds, 61 retirement suites
Metzie Lacroxi, RN, BHA, Administrator
mlacroxi@clmi.ca

***Port Hope:* The Tower of Port Hope Retirement Residence**
Affiliated with: Chartwell Seniors Housing REIT
164 Peter St., Port Hope, ON L1A 1C6
Tel: 905-885-7261 *Fax:* 905-885-1519
towerofporthope@chartwellreit.ca
www.chartwellreit.ca
Number of Beds: 44 suites
Stephen Suske, CEO, Chartwell Seniors Housing REIT
Julie Inglis, Administrator

***Port Perry:* West Shore Village**
293 Perry St., Port Perry, ON L9L 1S6
Tel: 905-985-8660 *Fax:* 905-985-1881
Toll-Free: 1-800-248-0848
info@westshorevillage.ca
www.westshorevillage.ca
Number of Beds: 71 suites
Note: Specialties: Supported living for seniors; Foot care; Reflexology; Massage therapy; Recreational program; Respite care
Karen Arbuckle, Manager

***Renfrew:* Quail Creek Retirement Centre**
450 Albert St., Renfrew, ON K7V 4K4
Tel: 613-432-9502 *Fax:* 613-432-9533
quailcreek@chartwellreit.ca
www.chartwellreit.ca
Number of Beds: 58 beds
Bev Powell, Administrator

***Richmond:* Richmond Lodge Ltd.**
PO Box 1030, 6197 Perth St., Richmond, ON K0A 2Z0
Tel: 613-838-5016 *Fax:* 613-838-5017
Number of Beds: 42 beds
Note: Retirement residence
Claudette Richel, Administrator

***Richmond Hill:* Brookside/Hilltop Retirement Residence**
980 Elgin Mills Rd. East, Richmond Hill, ON L4S 1M4
Tel: 905-884-9248 *Fax:* 905-884-9745
brooksideplace@reveraliving.com
www.retirementresidences.com/homes/208
Number of Beds: 140 units
Sandra Fernandez, Executive Director

***Rockland:* Résidence Jardins Bellerive**
2950 Laurier St., Rockland, ON K4K 1T3
Tel: 613-446-7122 *Fax:* 613-446-7343
Number of Beds: 80 Units
Youri Brouchkov, Administrator

***Rockland:* Résidence Simon Inc.**
845, rue St-Jean, Rockland, ON K4K 1K5
Tél: 613-446-7023 *Téléc:* 613-446-4867
Nombre de lits: 46 lits
Albert Bourdeau, Propriétaire

***Sarnia:* Marshall Gowland Manor**
749 Devine St., Sarnia, ON N7T 1X3
Tel: 519-336-3720 *Fax:* 519-336-3734
www.lambtononline.com
Year Founded: 2004
Number of Beds: 126 beds
Note: Specialties: Long-term care; Day programs
Jackie Miller, Resident Manager

***Sarnia:* Residence on The St. Clair**
Affiliated with: Steeves & Rozema Group
170 Front St. South, Sarnia, ON N7T 2M5
Tel: 519-336-1455 *Fax:* 519-336-8966
cathy_mcintosh@srgroup.ca
www.srgroup.ca
Number of Beds: 73 beds
Note: Independent living, convalescent & respite options
Cathy McIntosh, Managing Director

***Sarnia:* Rosewood Manor**
Affiliated with: Steeves & Rozema Group
711 Indian Rd. North, Sarnia, ON N7T 7Z5
Tel: 519-332-8877 *Fax:* 519-332-5047
heather_taylor@srgroup.ca
www.srgroup.ca
Number of Beds: 55 beds
Note: Independent & assisted living
Heather Taylor, Executive Director

***Sault Ste Marie:* Pathways Retirement Residence**
Former Name: Pathways Seniors Residence
375 Trunk Rd., Sault Ste Marie, ON P6A 6T5
Tel: 705-759-1079 *Fax:* 705-759-1211
info@pathwaysret.com
www.pathwaysret.com
Number of Beds: 133 beds
Elaine Robertson, Administrator

***Seaforth:* Maplewood Manor**
PO Box 488, 13 Church St., Seaforth, ON N0K 1W0
Tel: 519-527-1440
Note: The manor has 32 rooms in a former school building.

***Simcoe:* Heritage Lodge**
182 Norfolk St. South, Simcoe, ON N3Y 2W4
Tel: 519-428-0930 *Fax:* 519-428-9103
Annemarie Barker, Administrator

***Smiths Falls:* Willowdale Retirement Centre**
Affiliated with: Chartwell Seniors Housing REIT
9 Armstrong Dr., Smiths Falls, ON K7A 5H7
Tel: 613-283-0691 *Fax:* 613-283-0350
willowdale@chartwellreit.ca
www.chartwellreit.ca
Number of Beds: 59 suites
Stephen Suske, CEO, Chartwell Seniors Housing REIT

***St Catharines:* The Loyalist Retirement Residence**
190 King St., St Catharines, ON L2R 3J7
Tel: 905-641-4422 *Fax:* 905-641-4989
Toll-Free: 800-337-9137
info@loyalist-retirement.com
www.loyalist-retirement.com
Number of Beds: 118 residential capacity
Note: Specialties: Assisted living; Nursing supervision; Medication administration; Podiatry services; Recreation & fitness program; Respite care; Convalescent stays
Lydia Tarasiuk, Administrator

***St Catharines:* Mount Carmel Home**
78 Yates St., St Catharines, ON L2R 5R9
Tel: 905-685-9155
Year Founded: 1920
Number of Beds: 69 beds
Note: seniors residence
M. Anne, Administrator

***St Catharines:* Tufford Manor Retirement Home**
312 Queenston Rd., St Catharines, ON L2P 2X4
Tel: 905-682-0411 *Fax:* 905-682-2770
help@hamptontufford.com
www.hamptontufford.com
Number of Beds: 53
Note: Offers long & short-term stays; on-site physiotherapy; medication administration; & maintenance, laundry, & housekeeping
Karen Balayewich, Manager
karenbalayewichrpn@hotmail.com
Greg Latanik, Administrator, Facility

***St Thomas:* Metcalfe Gardens Retirement Residence**
45 Metcalfe St., St Thomas, ON N5R 5Y1
Tel: 519-631-9393 *Fax:* 519-631-2563
www.diversicare.ca
Year Founded: 1988
Number of Beds: 97 suites
Note: Specialties: Foot care; Physiotherapy; Recreation programs; Respite care
Deborah Geerlinks, Administrator

***St. Joachim:* St. Joachim Manor**
2718 County Rd. 42, St. Joachim, ON N0R 1S0
Tel: 519-728-1215 *Fax:* 519-728-0113
Number of Beds: 23 beds
Zlatko Horvat, Owner
Nada Horvat, Owner

***Stoney Creek:* Stoney Creek Retirement Residence**
199 Glover Rd., Stoney Creek, ON L8E 5J2
Tel: 905-643-1795 *Fax:* 905-643-1085
Year Founded: 1994
Number of Beds: 39 units
Note: Specialties: Activity program; Catheter care; Colostomy care; Oxygen care; Diabetes care; Medication administration; Wellness program
Genny Lourenco, Retirement Manager

***Stratford:* Anne Hathaway Residence**
Former Name: The Griffin Residence
480 Downie St., Stratford, ON N5A 7Y5
Tel: 519-275-2125 *Fax:* 519-275-2126
www.chartwellreit.ca
Number of Beds: 68 beds
Dianne Roth, Administrator

***Stratford:* Cedarcroft Place Retirement Residence**
Affiliated with: All Seniors Care Living Centres
260 Church St., Stratford, ON N5A 2R6
Tel: 519-275-0030 *Fax:* 519-273-0373
www.allseniorscare.com/en/residences/on/cedarcroft-place
Number of Beds: 100 beds
Note: Covalescent & respite care are available.
Dan Vito, Director
danvito@allseniorscare.com

***Sudbury:* Westmount Retirement Residence**
Affiliated with: Chartwell Seniors Housing REIT
599 William Ave., Sudbury, ON P3A 5W3
Tel: 705-566-6221 *Fax:* 705-566-0808
www.chartwellreit.ca
Number of Beds: 84 suites
Stephen Suske, CEO, Chartwell Seniors Housing REIT

***Temiskaming Shores:* Northdale Manor**
PO Box 370, 142-130 Lakeshore Rd., Temiskaming Shores, ON P0J 1P0
Tel: 705-647-6541 *Fax:* 705-647-8284
nordale@ntl.sympatico.ca
www.northdalemanor.ca
Number of Beds: 70 suites
Note: Retirement home
Jan Edwards, Administrator

***Thornhill:* Glynnwood Retirement Living**
Affiliated with: Revera Inc.
7700 Bayview Ave., Thornhill, ON L3T 5W1
Tel: 905-881-9475 *Toll-Free:* 1-877-929-9222
www.reveraliving.com/glynnwood
Note: Customized care plans are available.
Paul Mitchell, Administrator

***Thorold:* Cobblestone Gardens Retirement Residence**
Affiliated with: Mundi Holdings Ltd.
Former Name: Chestnut Court
10 Ormond St. North, Thorold, ON L2V 1Y7
Tel: 905-227-5550 *Fax:* 905-227-5575
info@cobblestonegardens.ca
www.cobblestonegardens.ca
Year Founded: 1984
Note: Nursing assessments & care plans are available.
Elizabeth Dumoulin, Administrator
Jeannie Redekop, Director, Care

***Tilbury:* Hudson Manor**
PO Box 1150, 36 Lawson St., Tilbury, ON N0P 2L0
Tel: 519-682-3366 *Fax:* 519-682-0688
Number of Beds: 50 beds
Debbie Ouellette, Administrator

***Tillsonburg:* Tillsonburg Retirement Centre**
Affiliated with: Chartwell Seniors Housing REIT
183 Rolph St., Tillsonburg, ON N4G 3Y9
Tel: 519-688-0347 *Fax:* 519-688-2471
tillsonburgretirement@chartwellreit.ca
www.chartwellreit.ca
Number of Beds: 51 suites
Stephen Suske, CEO, Chartwell Seniors Housing REIT

***Timmins:* Chateau Georgian Retirement Residence**
455 Cedar St. North, Timmins, ON P4N 8K4
Tel: 705-267-7935
www.chartwellreit.ca
Number of Beds: 63 suites
Note: Specialties: Wellness monitoring; Physical therapy; Recreation therapy; Podiatry; Respite care; Convalescent stays
Lynn Budd, Manager

***Toronto:* The Annex Retirement Residence**
123 Spadina Rd., Toronto, ON M5R 2T1
Tel: 416-961-6446 *Fax:* 416-961-3299
theannex@reveraliving.com
www.reveraliving.com
Number of Beds: 102 beds
Note: Independent & assisted living, secured living for dementia care
Maria Silva, General Manager

***Toronto:* The Balmoral Club**
155 Balmoral Ave., Toronto, ON M4V 1J5
Tel: 416-927-0055 *Fax:* 416-927-0925
balmoralclub@amica.ca
www.amica.ca
Number of Beds: 66 beds
Monica Byrne, Administrator

***Toronto:* Baycrest Centre for Geriatric Care Terraces of Baycrest**
55 Ameer Ave., Toronto, ON M6A 2Z1
Tel: 416-785-2500 *Fax:* 416-785-2496
mjacobson@baycrest.org
www.baycrest.org
Info Line: 416-785-2379
Social Media: www.facebook.com/baycrestcentre; twitter.com/baycrest
Number of Beds: 199 Apartments
Note: supportive living
Sheila Smyth, Director

***Toronto:* Baycrest Centre for Geriatric Care**
3560 Bathurst St., Toronto, ON M6A 2E1
Tel: 416-785-2500 *Fax:* 416-785-2464
kconnelly@baycrest.org
www.baycrest.org
Social Media: www.facebook.com/baycrestcentre; twitter.com/baycrest; www.youtube.com/thebaycrestchannel
Number of Beds: 300 beds
Stephen W. Herbert, President/CEO

***Toronto:* Beach Arms Retirement Residence**
505 Kingston Rd., Toronto, ON M4L 1V5
Tel: 416-698-0414 *Fax:* 416-698-9839
info@beacharms.com
www.beacharms.com
Number of Beds: 80 beds
Susan Turner, Administrator

***Toronto:* Belmont House**
55 Belmont St., Toronto, ON M5R 1R1
Tel: 416-964-9231 *Fax:* 416-964-1448
information@belmonthouse.com
www.belmonthouse.com
Number of Beds: 55 apartments, 26 retirement suites; 140 long-term care beds
Note: Total employees: 28
Maria Elias, Chief Executive Officer
melias@belmonthouse.com

***Toronto:* Centennial Park Place Retirement Residence**
Former Name: Meadowcroft Place Retirement Residence
25 Centennial Park Rd., Toronto, ON M9C 5H1
Tel: 416-621-2139 *Fax:* 416-621-9801
centennial@reveraliving.com
www.reveraliving.com
Number of Beds: 48 residential capacity
Note: Specialty: Podiatry services; Fitness program
Naida McKechnie, Manager

***Toronto:* Central Park Lodges - Queens Drive 1**
265 Queens Dr., Toronto, ON M6L 3C6
Tel: 416-241-1113 *Fax:* 416-241-1801
queensdr2@reveraliving.com
www.reveraliving.com
Number of Beds: 113 beds
Note: Independent & assisted living, respite & convalescent options. Central Park Lodge Queens Drive 2 located at 303 Queens Drive
Brenda MacCallum, General Manager

***Toronto:* Central Park Lodges - Queens Drive 2**
303 Queens Dr., Toronto, ON M6L 3C1
Tel: 416-241-1113 *Fax:* 416-241-1801
queensdr2@reveraliving.com
www.reveraliving.com
Number of Beds: 156 units
Note: Independent & assisted living. Central Park Lodge Queens Drive 1 located at 265 Queens Drive
L. Kabot, Administrator

***Toronto:* Don Mills Seniors' Apartments**
1055-1057 Don Mills Rd., Toronto, ON M3C 1W9
Tel: 416-445-7555 *Fax:* 416-445-0417
donmillsseniorsapts@lrc.ca
www.reveraliving.com/homes/8005/
Number of Beds: 143 suites
Erik Smith, General Manager

***Toronto:* Donway Place**
8 The Donway East, Toronto, ON M3C 3R7
Tel: 416-445-7555 *Fax:* 416-445-0417
www.reveraliving.com/homes/8006/
Number of Beds: 245 suites
Erik Smith, Administrator

***Toronto:* Eden Manor**
251 St George St., Toronto, ON M5R 2M2
Tel: 416-515-1136 *Fax:* 416-515-1137
edenmanor@bellnet.ca
www.edenmanor.ca
Number of Beds: 25 beds
W. Boggs, Administrator

***Toronto:* Fellowship Towers**
877 Yonge St., Toronto, ON M4W 3M2
Tel: 416-923-8887 *Fax:* 416-923-1343
inquiries@fellowshiptowers.com
www.fellowshiptowers.com
Number of Beds: 284 beds
Marilyn Burton, Administrator
mburton@fellowshiptowers.com

***Toronto:* Forest Hill Place**
645 Castlefield Ave., Toronto, ON M5N 3A5
Tel: 416-785-1511 *Fax:* 416-785-6228
www.reveraliving.com/foresthill
Number of Beds: 125 suites

***Toronto:* Glebe Manor Retirement Residence**
17 Glebe Rd. West, Toronto, ON M5P 1C8
Tel: 416-485-1150 *Fax:* 416-485-6378
J.T. Whitebread, Administrator

***Toronto:* Grenadier Retirement Residence**
2100 Bloor St. West, Toronto, ON M6S 1M7
Tel: 416-769-2885 *Fax:* 416-769-7238
www.thegrenadier.com
Note: Specialties: Physiotherapy; Wellness program; Activity program; Medication administration; Short-term stays
Dwight Mountney, Administrator

***Toronto:* Harold & Grace Baker Centre**
1 Northwestern Ave., Toronto, ON M6M 2J7
Tel: 416-654-2889 *Fax:* 416-654-0217
bakercentre@reveraliving.com
www.reveraliving.com
Number of Beds: 233 beds
Milena Sujer, Administrator
Owen Shaw, Manager, Environmental Services

***Toronto:* Hazelton Place**
111 Avenue Rd., Toronto, ON M5R 3J8
Tel: 416-928-0111 *Fax:* 416-928-0118
www.hazeltonplace.ca
Number of Beds: 130 units
Lillian Russell, General Manager

***Toronto:* Lansing Retirement Residence**
10 Senlac Rd., Toronto, ON M2N 6P8
Tel: 416-250-7029 *Fax:* 416-250-7853
Number of Beds: 110 beds
Jill Estioko, Manager

***Toronto:* Leaside Retirement Residence**
10 William Morgan Dr., Toronto, ON M4H 1E7
Tel: 416-425-3722 *Fax:* 416-425-3946
leaside@reveraliving.com
www.reveraliving.com
Number of Beds: 211 beds
Note: Secured living for dementia care
P. Lemdal, General Manager

***Toronto:* Livingston Lodge Retirement Residence**
65 Livingston Rd., Toronto, ON M1E 1L1
Tel: 416-264-4348 *Fax:* 416-264-4340
www.residencesallegro.com
Number of Beds: 103 capacity
Note: Specialities: Physiotherapy; Foot care
Janet Iwaszozenko, Executive Director

***Toronto:* McNicoll Manor**
1020 McNicoll Ave., Toronto, ON M1W 2J6
Tel: 416-499-3313 *Fax:* 416-499-3379
www.tendercare.ca
Note: Specialties: Physiotherapy
Maureen McAlaster, Coordinator

***Toronto:* New Horizons Tower**
1140 Bloor St. West, Toronto, ON M6H 4E6
Tel: 416-536-6111 *Fax:* 416-536-6748
welcome@newhorizonstower.com
www.newhorizonstower.com
Number of Beds: 197 beds
Note: Christian nursing home
Ian C. Logan, Administrator

***Toronto:* Pine Villa Retirement Residence**
1035 Eglinton Ave. West, Toronto, ON M6C 2C8
Tel: 416-787-5626 *Fax:* 416-787-3441
pinevilla@reveraliving.com
www.reveraliving.com
Number of Beds: 71 units
Note: Specialties: Medication administration; Assistance for residents who require oxygen, catheters, & ostomies; Physiotherapy; Podiatry; Recreation therapy
Sharon Rosenblum, Executive Director

***Toronto:* Rayoak Place Retirement Residence**
Also Known As: Meadowcroft Place
1340 York Mills Rd., Toronto, ON M3A 3R1
Tel: 416-391-0633 *Fax:* 416-391-3320
rayoakplace@reveraliving.com
www.reveraliving.com
Number of Beds: 66 beds
Note: Independent & assisted living
Linda Mullins, Manager

***Toronto:* Shepherd Terrace Retirement Suites**
3758 Sheppard Ave. East, Toronto, ON M1T 3K9
Tel: 416-609-5700 *Fax:* 416-293-6229
www.shepherdvillage.org
Number of Beds: 144 units, including 112 assisted living suites
Brock Hall, Administrator

***Toronto:* Terrace Gardens Retirement Residence**
3705 Bathurst St., Toronto, ON M6A 2E8
Tel: 416-789-7670 *Fax:* 416-789-3372
terrace@reveraliving.com
www.reveraliving.com
Note: Jewish retirement residence; independent & assisted living, secured living for dementia care, convalescent & respite options; COR supervised, mashgiach on site

***Trenton:* The Carrington, A Retirement Residence**
114 Whites Rd., RR#2, Trenton, ON K8V 5P5
Tel: 613-392-1615 *Fax:* 613-392-3879
Toll-Free: 1-877-392-1615
www.thecarringtonretirement.com
Number of Beds: 37 units
Note: The Carrington is an approved member of the Ontario Retirement Communities Association. Services include the availability of nuses & health care aides, assistance with daily living activities & outside agency services, plus social, cultural, & recreational programming.

***Utterson:* Rowanwood Retirement Residence**
81 Rowanwood Rd., Utterson, ON P0B 1M0
Tel: 705-789-6424 *Fax:* 705-789-1821
Number of Beds: 86 beds
Gail Sargeant, Manager

***Vankleek Hill:* Heritage Lodge Retirement Residence**
Former Name: Vankleek Residence
48 Wall St., Vankleek Hill, ON K0B 1R0
Tel: 613-678-2690 *Fax:* 613-678-6760
vankleek@reveraliving.com
Number of Beds: 72 beds
Sandra McCormick, Executive Director

***Varry's Bay:* Water Tower Lodge**
9 Stafford St., Varry's Bay, ON K0J 1B0
Tel: 613-756-9086
watertowerlodge@nrtco.net
www.watertowerlodge.com
Number of Beds: 44 units

***Vineland:* The Orchards Retirement Residence**
Heritage Village, 3421 Frederick Ave., Vineland, ON L0R 2C0
Tel: 905-562-7357 *Fax:* 905-562-3051
Toll-Free: 800-263-4957
www.residencesallegro.com
Year Founded: 1999
Note: Specialties: Medication management; Personal care assistance; Activities program; Physiotherapy; Respite & convalescence care
Bonnie Magwood, Administrator

***Walkerton:* Maple Court Villa**
5 Fourth St., Walkerton, ON N0G 2V0
Tel: 519-881-2233 *Fax:* 519-881-0336
maplecourt@chartwellreit.ca
Number of Beds: 47 Suites
Note: Nursing home
JoAnn Todd, Administrator

***Waterloo:* Luther Village on the Park**
Luthewood
139 Father David Bauer Dr., Waterloo, ON N2L 6L1
Tel: 519-747-4413
www.luthervillage.org
Note: Specialties: Assisted living

***Waterloo:* Terrace on the Square**
Affiliated with: Chartwell Seniors Housing REIT
100 Caroline St. South, Waterloo, ON N2L 1X5
Tel: 519-749-2888 *Fax:* 519-749-1674
terraceonthesquare@chartwellreit.ca
www.chartwellreit.ca
Number of Beds: 88 suites
Stephen Suske, CEO, Chartwell Seniors Housing REIT

***Windsor:* Central Park Lodge - Windsor**
3387 Riverside Dr. East, Windsor, ON N8Y 1A8
Tel: 519-948-5293 *Fax:* 519-948-7513
windsor@reveraliving.com
www.reveraliving.com
Number of Beds: 141 units
Note: Independent & assisted living, secured living for dementia care, respite & convalescent options
Jean Piccinato, General Manager
Marc St. Pierre, Manager, Physical Plant

***Windsor:* Devonshire Seniors' Residence**
901 Riverside Dr. West, Windsor, ON N9A 7J6
Tel: 519-252-2273 *Fax:* 519-252-2324
Toll-Free: 877-521-5686
www.orca-homes.com
Number of Beds: 259 beds
Sharon Woodward, General Manager

***Wingham:* Braemar Retirement Centre**
719 Josephine St. North, Wingham, ON N0G 2W0
Tel: 519-357-3430 *Fax:* 519-357-2303
Toll-Free: 1-888-817-5828
info@braemar-rc.com
www.braemar-rc.com
Number of Beds: 25 beds
Archie Macgowan, Administrator
519-357-3430 ext.224, macgowana@hurontel.on.ca
M.C. MacGowan, President/CEO
519-357-3430 ext.235, mcmacgowan@braemar-rc.com

Mental Health Hospitals/Facilities

***Lindsay:* Chimo Youth & Family Services**
227 Kent St. West, Lindsay, ON K9V 2Z1
Tel: 705-324-3300 *Fax:* 705-324-3304
Toll-Free: 1-888-454-6275
Note: Chimo Youth & Family Services is accredited under Children's Mental Health Ontario. Programs include clinical & crisis care, group meetings, day treatment, & residential & respite care.

Mental Health Facilities

Mental Health Hospitals/Facilities

***Aurora:* Southdown Institute**
1335 St. John's Rd. East, Aurora, ON L4G 3G8
Tel: 905-727-4214 *Fax:* 905-727-4214
administration@southdown.on.ca;
assessment@southdown.on.ca
www.southdown.on.ca
Number of Beds: 44 beds
Note: Specialties: Residential & outpatient psychological treatment to clergy & religious; Psychodynamic group therapy; Individual & group addiction counselling; 12-step groups; Specialized group treatment for persons who have violated sexual boundaries; Art therapy; Health education
Dr. Raymond Dlugos, CEO

***Brockville:* Brockville Mental Health Centre**
Former Name: Brockville Psychiatric Hospital
PO Box 1050, 1804 Hwy. 2 East, Brockville, ON K6V 5W7
Tel: 613-345-1461 *Fax:* 613-342-6194
www.rohcg.on.ca
Number of Beds: 200 beds
George Weber, President/CEO

***Fergus:* Fergus Community Mental Health Clinic**
Trellis Mental Health & Developmental Services
234 St. Patrick St. East, Upper Level, Fergus, ON N1M 1M6
Tel: 519-843-6191 *Fax:* 519-843-7608
Toll-Free: 1-800-265-7723
www.trellis.on.ca
Note: Services include mental health assessments, medication monitoring, individual & group therapy, & education.
Fred Wagner, Executive Director
519-821-2060

***Guelph:* Homewood Health Centre**
150 Delhi St., Guelph, ON N1E 6K9
Tel: 519-824-1010 *Fax:* 519-824-8751
www.homewood.org/healthcentre/main.php
Year Founded: 1883
Number of Beds: 312 beds
Note: Number of Employees: 650; Specialty: Behavioural, addiction & psychiatric services
W. Sheppard, Director, Environmental Services
Dr. Edgardo L. Pérez, CEO; Chief of Staff

***Hamilton:* St. Joseph's Centre for Mountain Health Services**
PO Box 585, 100 - 5 St. West, Hamilton, ON L8N 3K7
Tel: 905-388-2511 *Fax:* 905-575-6038
www.stjosham.on.ca
Number of Beds: 165 beds
Darlene Barnes, Vice-President
Al Manente, Director, Plant Services
Zenek J. Dybka, Assistant, Hospital Services

***Kingston:* Ongwanada Hospital**
191 Portsmouth Ave., Kingston, ON K7M 8A6
Tel: 613-548-4417 *Fax:* 613-548-8135
www.ongwanada.com
Year Founded: 1948
Number of Beds: 227 beds
Note: Specialties: Support for persons with developmental disabilities; Day support; Medical services; Vocational & life skills training; Occupational therapy; Physiotherapy; Hydrotherapy; Snoezelen Room; Community behavioural services; Respite care; Research. Number of employees: 494
Robert W. Seaby, Executive Director

***Kingston:* Providence Care - Mental Health Services**
Former Name: Kingston Psychiatric Hospital
PO Box 603, 752 King St., Kingston, ON K7L 4X3
Tel: 613-546-1101 *Fax:* 613-548-5588
prowsea@providencecare.ca
www.pccchealth.org
Number of Beds: 198 beds
Note: Adult Treatment & Rehabilitation, Geriatric Psychiatry, Forensic Psychiatry
Allen Prowse, Vice President, Mental Health; Administrator

***London:* Child & Parent Resource Institute (CPRI)**
600 Sanatorium Rd., London, ON N6H 3W7
Tel: 519-858-2774 *Fax:* 519-858-3913
Toll-Free: 877-494-2774
Gillian.Kriter@ontario.ca
Number of Beds: 75 beds
Anne Stark, Administrator

***London:* Regional Mental Healthcare, London**
Affiliated with: St. Joseph's Health Care, London
PO Box 5532 Stn. B, 850 Highbury Ave., London, ON N6A 4H1
Tel: 519-455-5110 *Fax:* 519-455-9986
Communications.Department@sjhc.london.on.ca
www.sjhc.london.on.ca
Number of Beds: 385 beds

***North Bay:* Northeast Mental Health Centre**
Former Name: North Bay Psychiatric Hospital
PO Box 3010, 4700 Hwy. 11 North, North Bay, ON P1B 8L1
Tel: 705-474-1200 *Fax:* 705-472-1694
www.nemhc.on.ca
W. Duguette, Chief Engineer/Maintenance Supervisor

***Oakville:* Central West Specialized Developmental Services**
Former Name: Oaklands Regional Centre
53 Bond St., Oakville, ON L6K 1L8
Tel: 905-844-7864 *Fax:* 905-844-3545
sbadali@cwsds.ca
Year Founded: 2006
Note: Specialties: Care & support to persons with multiple developmental disabilities; Basic life skill development; Psychiatry; Behaviour therapy; Occupational therapy; Speech therapy; Respite care
Jim Preston, Director

Ottawa: Royal Ottawa Health Care Group
1145 Carling Ave., Ottawa, ON K1Z 7K4
Tel: 613-722-6521 *Fax:* 613-722-4577
www.rohcg.on.ca
Number of Beds: 199 beds (Royal Ottawa Hospital)
Bruce Swan, CEO
Jerry Rogers, Director, Environmental Services

Penetanguishene: Penetanguishene Mental Health Centre
500 Church St., Penetanguishene, ON L9M 1G3
Tel: 705-549-3181 *Fax:* 705-549-1549
www.mhcva.on.ca
W. Gregoire, Manager, Plant Services

St Thomas: Regional Mental Health Care, St. Thomas
Affiliated with: St. Joseph's Health Care, London
PO Box 2004, 467 Sunset Dr., St Thomas, ON N5P 3V9
Tel: 519-631-8510 *Fax:* 519-633-0852
Communications.Department@sjhc.london.on.ca
www.sjhc.london.on.ca
Number of Beds: 145 beds

Sudbury: Northeast Mental Health Centre Sudbury Campus
680 Kirkwood Dr., Sudbury, ON P3E 1X3
Tel: 705-675-9193 *Fax:* 705-675-6817
dchateauvert@nemhc.on.ca
www.nemhc.on.ca
Number of Beds: 12 children's beds
Robert Cunningham, CEO

Sudbury: Sudbury Regional Hospital - Kirkwood Site
680 Kirkwood Dr., Sudbury, ON P3E 1X3
Tel: 705-675-9193 *Toll-Free:* 1-866-469-0822
communications@hrsrh.on.ca
www.hrsrh.on.ca
Note: Acute inpatient psychiatry services
Vickie Kaminiski, CEO
Chris McKibbon, Chief of Staff

Thunder Bay: Lakehead Psychiatric Hospital
PO Box 2930, 580 Algoma St. North, Thunder Bay, ON P7B 5G4
Tel: 807-343-4300 *Fax:* 807-343-4387
Toll-Free: 800-209-9034
www.sjcg.net/services/mentalhealth/lph/
Dawn Eccles, Coordinator, Environmental Services

Toronto: Bellwood Health Services Inc.
1020 McNicoll Ave., Toronto, ON M1W 2J6
Tel: 416-495-0926 *Fax:* 416-495-7943
Toll-Free: 800-387-6198
info@bellwood.ca
www.bellwood.ca
Note: Specialties: Treatment & education for persons who struggle with addictions, such as alcohol & drugs, eating disorders, post traumatic stress disorder, problem gambling, & problematic sexual behaviour; Assessment; Withdrawal management services; Residential treatment program for persons with alcohol addiction; 12-step education & support groups; Life skills coaching; Stress management; Group therapy; Nutritional education & counselling
M. Linda Bell, Chief Executive Officer
Laura Bhoi, President
Janet Lansche, Vice-President, Finance & Administration
Susan McGrail, Director, Clinical Services
Dr. Mark Weiss, Medical Director
Mani Alcaide, Manager, Nursing
Michael Hartmann, Manager, Continuing Care & Volunteer Services
Penny Lawson, Manager, Family Services & Special Programs

Toronto: Community Outreach Services (COS) Toronto East General Hospital
#203, 177 Danforth Ave., Toronto, ON M4K 1N2
Tel: 416-461-2000 *Fax:* 416-461-2222
ptrep@tegh.on.ca (Patients); community@tegh.on.ca (Community)
www.tegh.on.ca
Note: Specialties: Community based mental health services; Counselling to adults; Supported housing; Psychiatric treatment; Psycho-social rehabilitation; Family support program; Community & school outreach program

Toronto: Thistletown Regional Centre for Children & Adolescents
51 Panorama Ct., Toronto, ON M9V 4L8
Tel: 416-326-0600 *Fax:* 416-326-9078
Note: Specialties: Counselling for children & youth up to 19 years of age; Family assessment & therapy; Treatment & education for youth with autism & developmental disorders; Sexual abuse treatment & family education; Home support; Outpatient services
Dr. Gail Gonda, Administrator

Toronto: Youthdale Treatment Centres
227 Victoria St., Toronto, ON M5B 1T8
Tel: 416-368-4896
www.youthdale.ca
Note: Youthdale provides mental health services to approximately 5,000 children & their families each year. A crisis service line is available (416-363-9990). The non-profit, charitiable community agency also offers clinical services that include psychiatric crisis response, residential treatment, & outpatient consultation.

Whitby: Whitby Mental Health Centre
700 Gordon St., Whitby, ON L1N 5S9
Tel: 905-668-5881 *Fax:* 905-430-4032
Toll-Free: 1-800-341-6323
communications@wmhc.ca
www.whitbymentalhealthcentre.ca
Note: Specialized, tertiary mental health care on an inpatien/outpatient basis. Residences in Stouffville, Oshawa; community service sites in Newmarket, Georgina, Maple, Uxbridge, Port Perry, Bowmanville, Lindsay & Whitby. Number of staff: 1,200
Glenna Raymond, President/CEO

Special Care Homes

Aurora: Kerry's Place Autism Services
#190, 34 Berczy St., Aurora, ON L4G 1W9
Tel: 905-841-6611 *Fax:* 905-841-1461
www.kerrysplace.com
Year Founded: 1974
Note: autistic adults home
Dr. Glenn Rampton, Executive Director
grampton@kerrysplace.org

Belleville: Cheshire Homes (Hastings - Prince Edward) Inc.
41 Pinnacle St. South, Belleville, ON K8N 3A1
Tel: 613-966-2941 *Fax:* 613-966-2461
receptionist@cheshirehpe.ca
www.cheshirehpe.ca
Year Founded: 1973
Note: Cheshire Homes offers support housing & an outreach program to physically disabled adults.

Brantford: Participation House Brantford
PO Box 2048, 10 Bell Lane, Brantford, ON N3T 5W5
Tel: 519-756-1430 *Fax:* 519-756-0795
www.participationhousebrantford.org
Number of Beds: 30 beds
Note: Non-for-profit organization serving the needs of adults with physical disabilities
Steve Leighfield, Executive Director

Cochrane: Cochrane Community Living
PO Box 2330, 18 2nd Ave., Cochrane, ON P0L 1C0
Tel: 705-272-5365 *Fax:* 705-272-4983
iccl@puc.net
Number of Beds: 12 beds in 3 facilities
Mac Hiltz, Interim Executive Director

Collingwood: Canford House
695 St. Marie St., Collingwood, ON L9Y 3L4
Tel: 705-445-5203 *Fax:* 705-445-7357
Number of Beds: 32 beds
Wayne Canning, Administrator

Cornwall: Open Hands Residential Services
109B York St., Cornwall, ON K6J 3Y9
Tel: 613-933-0012 *Fax:* 613-932-5134
www.ocapdd.on.ca
Note: The non-profit agency offers both residential & daytime community support services to persons with development disabilities. Open Hands is operated by the Ottawa Carleton Association for Persons with Developmental Disabilities (OCAPDD).
David A. Ferguson, Executive Director
dferguson@ocapdd.on.ca

Dryden: Patricia Gardens Care Home
#100, 35 Van Horne Ave., Dryden, ON P8N 3B4
Tel: 807-223-5278

Gravenhurst: Val-Glo Home for Special Care
Doe Lake Rd., RR#3, Gravenhurst, ON P1P 1R3
Tel: 705-687-6285
Number of Beds: 14 beds
Dianne Rivers, Administrator

Hamilton: Lynwood Hall Child & Family Centre
526 Upper Paradise Rd., Hamilton, ON L9C 5E3
Tel: 905-389-1361 *Fax:* 905-389-8765
www.lynwoodhall.com
Note: Specialties: Mental health services, including day treatment, home-based services, & residential services
Alex Thomson, Executive Director

Hanmer: Kingsley Residential Home
PO Box 118, 36 Oscar St., Hanmer, ON P3P 1X6
Tel: 705-969-5538
Number of Beds: 6 beds
Jeannine Kingsley, Proprietor

Hanover: HARC Inc.
521 - 11th Ave., Hanover, ON N4N 2J3
Tel: 519-364-6100 *Fax:* 519-364-7488
Number of Beds: 15 beds
Charlie Caudle, Executive Director

Holland Landing: Cedar Lane Residential Home
19704 Holland Landing Rd., Holland Landing, ON L9N 1M8
Tel: 905-836-4272 *Fax:* 905-836-8277
Cathy Dowling, Contact

Keswick: Pipe & Slipper Home
2926 Old Homestead Rd., Keswick, ON L4P 3E9
Tel: 905-476-3601 *Fax:* 905-476-8386
Note: Residential care is provided for adults. Referral is necessary.
Joe Pollard, Contact

Kilworthy: Trentview House
1647 Kilworthy Rd., RR#1, Kilworthy, ON P0E 1G0
Tel: 705-689-5685 *Fax:* 705-689-5844
trentviewhouse@encode.com
Year Founded: 1979
Number of Beds: 25 beds
Note: Specialties: Services for adults with mental health disabilities

Kitchener: Sunbeam Lodge
389 Pinnacle Dr., Kitchener, ON N2G 3W5
Tel: 519-896-6718
teena@sunbeamlodge.com
www.sunbeamlodge.com
Number of Beds: 22 beds
Note: Specialties: Lont-term residential care & treatment for children with special needs; Day program; Physiotherapy treatment; Kinesiology; Communications programs; Independent living skills program. Number of Employees: 9 Registered Nurses & Registered Practical Nurses + 2 Kinessiologists + 1 Program Coordinator + 21 Child Care Attendants + 1 Dietician + 2 Housekeepers + 1 Executive Secretary
John Vos, Administrator
Shabnam Vos, Administrator

Kitchener: Sunbeam Residential Development Centre
2749 Kingsway Dr., Kitchener, ON N2C 1A7
Tel: 519-893-6200 *Fax:* 519-893-9034
postmaster@sunbeamcentre.com
www.sunbeamcentre.com
Year Founded: 1956
Note: Specialties: Care for individuals with diverse & complex developmental challenges; Long-term & short-term support; Activation; Sensory stimulation
Dr. Shaune Lawton, Executive Director

Lucan: Crest Support Services
13570 Elginfield Rd., RR#1, Lucan, ON N0M 2J0
Tel: 519-227-6766 *Fax:* 519-227-6768
www.crestsupportservices.ca
Note: Specialties: Services for adults with mental health or developmental disabilities; Accommodation services; Operation of three small businesses to provide training & employment opportunities
David Ragobar, Executive Director
david@thecrestcentre.com

***Markham:* Participation House**
9 Butternut Lane, Markham, ON L3P 3M1
Tel: 905-294-0944 *Fax:* 905-294-7834
postmaster@participationhouse.net
www.participationhouse.net
Number of Beds: 52 beds
Note: Provides services designed to enhance the qualify of life of people with disabilities
Sharon M. Lawlor, Executive Director

***Nepean:* Total Communication Environment (TCE)**
#5, 203 Colonnade Rd. South, Nepean, ON K2E 7K3
Tel: 613-228-0999 *Fax:* 613-228-1402
TTY: 613-228-8669
tceadmin@tceottawa.org; tcehr@tceottawa.org (Human Resources)
www.tceottawa.org
Year Founded: 1979
Note: Specialties: Services for adults with multiple disabilities & special communication needs; Respite care; Day services; Outreach to long-term care homes
Karen Anderson, Executive Director

***Newmarket:* Brigitta's Residential Home Inc.**
128 Arden Ave., Newmarket, ON L3Y 4H6
Tel: 905-895-5890
Number of Beds: 22 beds
Brigitta Miller, Administrator

***Newmarket:* Brookside Lodge**
542 Wellington St., Newmarket, ON L3Y 2C6
Tel: 905-853-7342
Number of Beds: 29 beds
Dave Sedore, Proprietor

***Newmarket:* Brown's Residential Home**
399 Queen St., Newmarket, ON L3Y 2G9
Tel: 905-898-1955
Note: Supportive residential care is provided for adults.
Lori Robbins, Contact

***Newmarket:* Heritage Lodge**
508 College St., Newmarket, ON L3Y 1C6
Tel: 905-853-1587
Number of Beds: 22 beds
Note: Heritage Lodge is a home for special care to assist persons with a mental health disability.

***Newmarket:* Lakeview Place Home for Special Care**
#223, 16715-12 Yonge St., Newmarket, ON L3X 1X4
Tel: 905-898-1015 *Fax:* 905-898-6414
tshsyr@allstream.net
Number of Beds: 19 beds
Monica Auerbach, Executive Director

***Newmarket:* Parkview Manor**
683 Gorham St., Newmarket, ON L3Y 1L5
Tel: 905-895-9064 *Fax:* 905-895-9064
cwoods2@extendicare.com
Number of Beds: 23 beds
Note: Home for special care
John Gaspar, Director

***North Bay:* North Bay & District Association for Community Living**
161 Main St. East, North Bay, ON P1B 1A9
Tel: 705-476-3288 *Fax:* 705-476-4788
www.nbdacl.org
Number of Beds: 35 beds
Rheal Thorn, Executive Director

***Orangeville:* Dufferin Association for Community Living**
065371 County Rd. 3, Orangeville, ON L9W 2Y9
Tel: 519-941-8971 *Fax:* 519-941-9121
info@communitylivingdufferin.ca
www.communitylivingdufferin.ca
Social Media: www.facebook.com/communitylivingdufferin; twitter.com/cldufferin; www.youtube.com/user/CLDufferin/videos
Note: Dufferin Association for Community Living assists children & adults with developmental disabilities.
Residential services include supported independent living, the operation of group homes & a home for adults with Prader Willi Syndrome, a family home program, a transitional living co-operative, & respite care. The association's group homes provide accommodations for 56 adults with developmental disabilities.
Sheryl Chandler, Executive Director
sheryl@communitylivingdufferin.ca
Diane Slater, Director, Adult Services
diane@communitylivingdufferin.ca
Ann Somerville, Director, Business & Finance
ann@communitylivingdufferin.ca
Karen Bowen, Manager, Preschool Resource Program
karen@communitylivingdufferin.ca
Nadene Buck, Manager, Residential
nadene@communitylivingdufferin.ca
Joyce Cook, Manager, Options
joyce@communitylivingdufferin.ca
Teresa Donaldson, Manager, Systems
teresa@communitylivingdufferin.ca
Darlene Morrow, Manager, Residential
darlene@communitylivingdufferin.ca
Lindsay Pendleton, Manager, Residential
lindsay@communitylivingdufferin.ca
Catherine Ryan, Manager, Residential
cryan@communitylivingdufferin.ca
Denyse Small, Manager, Employment Services
denyse@communitylivingdufferin.ca

***Ottawa:* Roberts/Smart Centre**
1199 Carling Ave., Ottawa, ON K1Z 8N8
Tel: 613-728-1946 *Fax:* 613-728-4986
Toll-Free: 800-279-9941
info@rsc-crs.com
www.robertssmartcentre.com
Number of Beds: 47 beds
Cameron Macleod, Executive Director

***Owen Sound:* Kent Residential Home**
Former Name: Tucker's Residential Home
1065 - 9 Ave. West, Owen Sound, ON N4K 5R8
Tel: 519-371-5029 *Fax:* 519-371-3237
Number of Beds: 18 beds
Note: residential home for people with mental illness
Yvonne Kent

***Oxford Mills:* Old Mill Guest Home**
PO Box 218, 12 Bridge St., Oxford Mills, ON K0G 1S0
Tel: 613-258-3366 *Fax:* 613-258-3130
Number of Beds: 22 beds
Note: Specialties: Residential services for post-psychiatric patients; Social programs

***Peterborough:* Community Living Peterborough**
223 Aylmer St., Peterborough, ON K9J 3K3
Tel: 705-743-2411 *Fax:* 705-743-3722
www.communitylivingpeterborough.ca
Social Media: www.facebook.com/group.php?gid=133788739991973; www.youtube.com/user/CommunityLivingPtbo
Note: The following services are provided: supported housing for adults over the age of 21; family support; community access; & employment options.
Jack Gillan, Chief Executive Officer
Joanne Duquette, Director, Business & Administration
Barb Hiland, Director, Operations
Cindy Hobbins, Manager, Community Development, Communications, & Quality Enhancement
Pat McNamara, Manager, Transitional Aged Youth, Supported Housing
Edna O'Toole, Manager, Community Access

***Peterborough:* Kinark Child & Family Services**
Corporate Office, #200, 500 Hood Rd., Peterborough, ON K9H 7L7
Tel: 905-474-9595 *Fax:* 905-474-1448
Toll-Free: 1-888-454-6275
info@kinark.on.ca
www.kinark.on.ca
Social Media: www.facebook.com/kinark; twitter.com/mykinark
Note: Services include crisis services, therapeutic family programs, child care, day treatment, residential treatment, adventure-based programming, autism services, & youth justice services.
Peter Moore, Executive Director

***Petrolia:* Lambton County Developmental Services**
Former Name: Lambton County Association for Mentally Handicapped
PO Box 1210, 339 Centre St., Petrolia, ON N0N 1R0
Tel: 519-882-0933 *Fax:* 519-882-3386
administration@lcds.on.ca
www.lcds.on.ca
Number of Beds: 68 beds
Note: Provides services to persons with intellectual disabilities
Don Seymour, Executive Director

***Powassan:* Eide's Residential Home**
495 Main St., Powassan, ON P0H 1Z0
Tel: 705-724-2748

***Saint-Pascal-Baylon:* St. Pascal Residential Home**
2454 du Lac Rd., RR#1, Saint-Pascal-Baylon, ON K0A 3N0
Tel: 613-488-2626

***St Catharines:* Montebello Place**
Former Name: Horvath Residence
1 Montebello Pl., St Catharines, ON L2R 6B5
Tel: 905-984-6506 *Fax:* 905-984-6504
Year Founded: 1973
Number of Beds: 15 beds
Sharon Okum, Co-Owner
David Okum, Co-Owner

***St Thomas:* Tara Hall Residential Care Home**
38 Chester St., St Thomas, ON N5R 1V2
Tel: 519-631-4937 *Fax:* 519-631-1526
tarahall@rogers.com
Year Founded: 1988
Number of Beds: 36 beds
Note: Specialties: Assisted living for adults with an intellectual disability, brain injury, or mental illness
James Akey, Manager

***Thunder Bay:* Marcinowsky Residential Home**
601 Alice Ave., RR#14, Thunder Bay, ON P7G 1X1
Tel: 807-767-6199
Number of Beds: 10 beds
Stephanie Marcinowsky, Administrator/Owner

***Toronto:* Community Head Injury Resource Services (CHIRS)**
Former Name: Ashby House
62 Finch Ave. West, Toronto, ON M2N 7G1
Tel: 416-240-8000 *Fax:* 416-240-1149
Chirs@chirs.com
www.chirs.com
Year Founded: 1978
Note: A range of residential services are offered for persons living with the effects of acquired brain injury. Community Head Injury Resource Services serves the Greater Toronto Area.

***Toronto:* Griffin Centre**
24 Silverview Dr., Toronto, ON M2M 2B3
Tel: 416-222-1153 *Fax:* 416-222-1321
contact@griffin-centre.org
www.griffin-centre.org
Number of Beds: 10 beds
Laurie Dart, Executive Director

***Toronto:* Hincks-Dellcrest Treatment Centre**
440 Jarvis St., Toronto, ON M4Y 2H4
Tel: 416-924-1164 *Fax:* 416-924-8208
info@hincksdellcrest.org
www.hincksdellcrest.org
Note: Children's mental health
John Spekkens, Executive Director

***Toronto:* Salvation Army Broadview Village**
1132 Broadview Ave., Toronto, ON M4K 2S5
Tel: 416-425-1052 *Fax:* 416-425-6579
Number of Beds: 61 beds
Note: Facility for adults with developmental disabilities
Capt. Glenda Davis, Director

***Vars:* Pine Rest Residence**
PO Box 109, 5876 Bearbrook Rd., Vars, ON K0A 3H0
Tel: 613-835-2849 *Fax:* 613-835-9335
Number of Beds: 33 residential capacity
Note: Specialties: Residential care for persons with developmental disabilities, psychiatric disabilities, or those who suffer from alcoholism; Medication supervision; Respite care
Raymond Meloche, Administrator

***Vars:* Résidence Ste-Marie**
PO Box 73, 5855, ch Buckland, Vars, ON K0H 3H0
Tel: 613-835-2525
Number of Beds: 40 lits
Note: Spécialisée à la prestation des soins aux personnes atteintes de maladie mentale grave; soins infirmiers, activités hebdomadaires
Gaétan Brisson, Propriétaire
Suzanne Brisson, Propriétaire

***Vineland:* Amber Lodge**
4024 Martin Rd., RR#1, Vineland, ON L0R 2C0
Tel: 905-562-7272 *Fax:* 905-892-9700
William Ram, Administrator/Owner

***Vineland:* Bethesda Home for the Mentally Handicapped Inc.**
PO Box 1000, Vineland, ON L0R 2C0
Tel: 905-562-4184 *Fax:* 905-562-4621
Number of Beds: 42 beds

Donald Boese, Executive Director

Waterloo: Children's Mental Health Services Lutherwood
285 Benjamin Rd., Waterloo, ON N2J 3Z4
Tel: 519-884-1470 *Fax:* 519-886-8479
www.lutherwood.ca
Number of Beds: 6 beds (Bridgelands program); 10 beds (Woodlands program)
Note: Specialties: Day treatment program; Residential treatment program; Group & individual skills training; Individual & family counselling; Home support; Community integration; Crisis support

Waterloo: Lutherwood
Administrative Office, 139 Father David Bauer Dr., Waterloo, ON N2L 6L1
Tel: 519-884-7755 *Fax:* 519-884-9071
admin@lutherwood.ca
www.lutherwood.ca
Note: Specialties: Mental health services for children & families, including assessment, a youth shelter, housing support services, residential treatment, family crisis & prevention counselling, a community services program, & school-based interventions; Senior services, including independent & supported living resources
John Colangeli, CEO

Waterloo: Underhill Residential Home
127 Erb St. West, Waterloo, ON N2L 1T7
Tel: 519-884-7160 *Fax:* 519-884-5936
Note: Specialties: Residential & personal care services for seniors & persons with mental health concerns

Prince Edward Island

Government Departments in Charge

PRINCE EDWARD ISLAND: Department of Community Services, Seniors & Labour
Jones Bldg., PO Box 2000, 11 Kent St., 2nd Fl., Charlottetown, PE C1A 7N8
Tel: 902-620-3777 *Fax:* 902-368-4740
Toll-Free: 1-866-594-3777
www.gov.pe.ca/sss
Note: The Department of Community Services and Seniors contributes to the well-being of individuals, families and communities by working collaboratively to promote the development of healthy, self-reliant individuals as well as supporting and protecting vulnerable members in the Island community.
Hon. Valerie Docherty, Minister, Community Services, Seniors & Labour
Carol Anne Duffy, Deputy Minister
Rona Smith, Director, Child & Family Services
902-368-5396, Fax: 902-368-4258, ronasmith@gov.pe.ca
W. Lorne Clow, Director, Housing, Seniors & Corporate Support
902-368-6109, Fax: 902-894-0242, wlclow@gov.pe.ca
Bob D. Creed, Director, Social Programs
902-368-6446, Fax: 902-620-3553, bdcreed@gov.pe.ca
Michelle Harris-Genge, Director, Interministerial Women's Secretariat
mdharris-genge@gov.pe.ca

PRINCE EDWARD ISLAND: Department of Health & Wellness
PO Box 2000, 105 Rochford St., 4th Fl. North, Charlottetown, PE C1A 7N8
Tel: 902-368-6414 *Fax:* 902-368-4121
www.gov.pe.ca/health
Note: This group is responsible for providing overall management direction to the department and for overseeing long-term strategic planning.
Hon. Doug W. Currie, Minister, Health & Wellness
902-368-5250, Fax: 902-368-4121, dwcurrie@gov.pe.ca
Dr. Michael Mayne, Deputy Minister
902-368-5290, Fax: 902-368-4121, mbmayne@gov.pe.ca
Keith Dewar, CEO, Health PEI
902-368-4935, Fax: 902-368-4974, kdewar@gov.pe.ca

Regional Health Authorities

Charlottetown: Health PEI
PO Box 2000, Charlottetown, PE C1A 7N8
Tel: 902-368-6130 *Fax:* 902-368-6136
healthinput@gov.pe.ca
www.healthpei.ca
Social Media: twitter.com/health_pei
Year Founded: 2010
Note: Health PEI is responsible for the operation and delivery of publicly funded health services in Prince Edward Island.
Leo Steven, Board Chair
Keith Dewar, CEO

Hospitals

Hospitals - General

Alberton: Western Hospital Corporation
Affiliated with: Health PEI
PO Box 10, Alberton, PE C0B 1B0
Tel: 902-853-8650 *Fax:* 902-853-8651
Number of Beds: 25 beds
Marlene Bolger, Administrator

Charlottetown: Queen Elizabeth Hospital Inc. (QEH)
Affiliated with: Health PEI
PO Box 6600, 60 Riverside Dr., Charlottetown, PE C1A 8T5
Tel: 902-894-2111 *Fax:* 902-894-2416
TTY: 902-894-2204
www.healthpei.ca/qeh
Year Founded: 1982
Number of Beds: 274 beds
Note: Acute care hospital, with burn care services, coronary care, psychiatry, physiotherapy, occupational therapy, orthpedic & specialized gynecological surgery, eye surgery, plastic surgery, neonatal intensive care, cancer care, diagnostic imaging
Rick Adams, Executive Director
Kelley Rayner, Director, Hospital Services

Montague: King's County Memorial Hospital
Affiliated with: Health PEI
409 McIntyre Ave., Montague, PE C0A 1R0
Tel: 902-838-0777 *Fax:* 902-838-0770
njfallis@ihis.org
Number of Beds: 30 beds
Jean Fallis, Administrator
njfallis@ihis.org

O'Leary: Community Hospital O'Leary
Affiliated with: Health PEI
PO Box 160, 14 MacKinnon Dr., O'Leary, PE C0B 1V0
Tel: 902-859-8700 *Fax:* 902-859-8774
Year Founded: 1957
Number of Beds: 13 acute care beds + 24 long-term care beds + 1 respite bed
Note: Specialties: Acute care; Immunization program; Lifeline emergency response system; Long-term care (Phone: 902-859-8750, Fax: 902-859-8756); Respite care
Phil Jost, CEO

Souris: Souris Hospital
Affiliated with: Health PEI
PO Box 640, 17 Knights Ave., Souris, PE C0A 2B0
Tel: 902-687-7150 *Fax:* 902-687-7175
www.healthpei.ca/index.php3?number=1020338&lang=E
Number of Beds: 17 beds
Note: Acute care rural facility
Betty Fraser, CEO, KHR
Terry Campbell, Site Administrator

Summerside: Prince County Hospital
Affiliated with: Health PEI
PO Box 3000, 65 Roy Boates Ave., Summerside, PE C1N 2A9
Tel: 902-432-2500 *Fax:* 902-438-4511
gmmartin@ihis.org
www.pchcare.com
Number of Beds: 102 beds
Note: Specialties: Emergency, surgery, internal medicine, obstetrics, pediatrics, psychiatry, radiology, rehabilitation, oncology
Arlene Gallant-Bernard, Executive Director

Tyne Valley: Stewart Memorial Hospital
Affiliated with: Health PEI
PO Box 10, Tyne Valley, PE C0B 2C0
Tel: 902-831-7900 *Fax:* 902-831-7901
Number of Beds: 23 beds
Note: Specialties: Acute care; Long-term care, Respite care; Palliative care
Aleah MacLennan, Nursing Coordinator

Community Health Centres

Community Health Care Centres

Charlottetown: Home Care Support
Affiliated with: Health PEI
PO Box 2000, 115 Murchison Lane., Charlottetown, PE C1A 7N5
Tel: 902-368-4790 *Fax:* 902-368-4858
Nora McCabe

Montague: Home Care Support
Affiliated with: Health PEI
PO Box 820, Montague, PE C0A 1R0
Tel: 902-838-0950 *Fax:* 902-838-0774
Sandy MacLean, Home Care Nursing Supervisor

O'Leary: Home Care Support
Affiliated with: Health PEI
PO Box 160, O'Leary, PE C0B 1V0
Tel: 902-859-8730 *Fax:* 902-859-8701
Sonia Wallace, Contact
smwallace@ihis.org

Special Treatment Centres

Charlottetown: Euston Street Group Home
Affiliated with: Health PEI
190 Euston St., Charlottetown, PE C1A 1W8
Tel: 902-566-2964
Note: Respite care is available for adolescents who are in the care of the Director of Child Welfare.

Charlottetown: Maple Street Group Home
Affiliated with: Health PEI
14 Vail Dr., Charlottetown, PE C1A 2L5
Tel: 902-368-1699
Number of Beds: 12 beds; one 72-hour emergency care bed
Note: adolescent group home
Donnie Campbell, Manager

Charlottetown: Provincial Addictions Treatment Facility
PO Box 2000, Charlottetown, PE C1A 7N8
Tel: 902-368-4120 *Fax:* 902-368-6229
Toll-Free: 1-888-299-8399
www.gov.pe.ca/hirc
Number of Beds: 41 beds
Note: To provide safe, medically supervised detoxification
Jim Good, Family Counselor

Charlottetown: Provincial Adolescent Group Home
PO Box 2000, 185 Beach Grove Rd., Charlottetown, PE C1E 1Z7
Tel: 902-368-6420 *Fax:* 902-368-6428
mamacmillan@ihis.org
Number of Beds: 9 beds; 1 emergency 72-hour bed
Note: adolescent residential treatment
John MacMillan, Manager, Adolescent Services

Nursing Homes

Alberton: Maplewood Manor
Affiliated with: Health PEI
PO Box 400, 400 Church St., Alberton, PE C0B 1B0
Tel: 902-853-8610 *Fax:* 902-853-8616
Number of Beds: 47 beds
Note: government-run
Phil Jost, CEO

Charlottetown: Beach Grove Home
Affiliated with: Health PEI
200 Beach Grove Rd., Charlottetown, PE C1E 1L3
Tel: 902-368-6750 *Fax:* 902-368-6764
Number of Beds: 131 beds
Cecil Villard, Director

Charlottetown: Garden Home
Affiliated with: Health PEI
310 North River Rd., Charlottetown, PE C1A 3M4
Tel: 902-892-4131 *Fax:* 902-892-7326
admin@peiseniorshomes.com
Number of Beds: 112 beds
Note: private
Phyllis Johnson, General Manager, Director of Care
generalmanager@peiseniorshomes.com

Charlottetown: Lennox Nursing Home
Affiliated with: Health PEI
140 Water St., Charlottetown, PE C1A 1A7
Tel: 902-894-4968 *Fax:* 902-368-2004
Number of Beds: 25 beds
Note: private

Tamara Casford, Administrator

***Charlottetown:* MacMillan Lodge Ltd.**
Affiliated with: Health PEI
PO Box 1861, 230 Richmond St., Charlottetown, PE C1A 1J5
Tel: 902-894-7173 *Fax:* 902-894-3818
Year Founded: 1999
Claudette MacMillan, Owner/Operator

***Charlottetown:* Park West Lodge**
Affiliated with: Health PEI
22 Richmond St., Charlottetown, PE C1A 1H4
Tel: 902-566-2260 *Fax:* 902-894-7818
Kevin Gauthier

***Charlottetown:* PEI Atlantic Baptist Homes Inc.**
Affiliated with: Health PEI
16 Centennial Dr., Charlottetown, PE C1A 5C5
Tel: 902-566-5975 *Fax:* 902-368-3760
Number of Beds: 101 beds
Note: Specialty: Long-term care by an interdisciplinary team
Enid Dollar, Administrator

***Charlottetown:* The Prince Edward Home**
Affiliated with: Health PEI
5 Brighton Rd., Charlottetown, PE C1A 8T6
Tel: 902-368-5946 *Fax:* 902-368-5646
www.healthpei.ca/pehome
Number of Beds: 128 beds (2 respite beds, 1 transition bed, 79 long term care beds, 27 under 60 beds, 8 palliative care beds and 11 restorative/convalescent care beds
Note: Palliative care, convalescent, respite care; long-term care; day program for seniors; meals-on-wheels program
Don Gorveatt, Director

***Montague:* Riverview Manor**
Affiliated with: Health PEI
PO Box 820, 14 Rosedale Rd., Montague, PE C0A 1R0
Tel: 902-838-0772 *Fax:* 902-838-5294
www.healthpei.ca/riverviewmanor
Number of Beds: 49 beds
Note: Long-term & palliative care
Judy Fraser, Administrator

***Souris:* Colville Manor**
Affiliated with: Health PEI
PO Box 640, 20 MacPhee Ave., Souris, PE C0A 2B0
Tel: 902-687-7090 *Fax:* 902-687-7103
www.healthpei.ca/colvillemanor
Number of Beds: 52 beds; 4 households, each with 13 residents in this facility

***Summerside:* Summerset Manor**
Affiliated with: Health PEI
205 Lefurgey Ave., Summerside, PE C1N 2L9
Tel: 902-888-8310 *Fax:* 902-888-8338
Number of Beds: 82 beds
Note: Specialties: Long-term care; Operation of the Chapman Centre, a day program that provides therapeutic services to seniors who live in their own home; Physiotherapy; Occupational therapy; Foot care; Respite care
Faye Feener, Manager

***Summerside:* Wedgewood Manor**
Affiliated with: Health PEI
310 Brophy St., Summerside, PE C1N 5N4
Tel: 902-888-8340 *Fax:* 902-888-8369
Faye Feener, Manager

Long Term/Retirement Care

Long Term Care Facilities

***Alberton:* Rev. W.J. Phillips Residence**
Affiliated with: Health PEI
Alberton, PE C0B 1B0
Tel: 902-853-3109 *Fax:* 902-853-2485
www.phillipsresidence.com
Number of Beds: 14 beds; 14 independent living units
Note: community care & beds
Garth MacKinnon

***Belfast:* Dr. John Gillis Memorial Lodge**
Affiliated with: Health PEI
Eldon Belfast PO, Belfast, PE C0A 1A0
Tel: 902-659-2337 *Fax:* 902-659-2865
douglas@gillislodge.com
Number of Beds: 62 beds
Douglas MacKenzie

***Charlottetown:* Andrews of Charlottetown**
Affiliated with: Health PEI
73 Malpeque Rd., Charlottetown, PE C1A 7J9
Tel: 902-368-2790 *Fax:* 902-894-3464
info@andrewsofpei.com
andrewsofpei.com/andrews_of_charlottetown.php
Number of Beds: 72 beds
Note: community care beds

***Charlottetown:* Champion Lodge**
Affiliated with: Health PEI
48 Green St., Charlottetown, PE C1A 2E8
Tel: 902-894-8968 *Fax:* 902-894-3878
Number of Beds: 8 beds
Colleen MacDonald

***Charlottetown:* Charlotte Residence**
Affiliated with: Health PEI
39 All Souls Lane, Charlottetown, PE C1A 1P9
Tel: 902-894-8134
Number of Beds: 26 beds
Joyce Pickles, Administrator

***Charlottetown:* Corrigan Lodge**
Affiliated with: Health PEI
8 Ellis Rd., Charlottetown, PE C1A 8N4
Tel: 902-894-5858
Number of Beds: 16 beds
Note: community care beds

***Charlottetown:* Langille House**
Affiliated with: Health PEI
214 Kent St., Charlottetown, PE C1A 1P2
Tel: 902-628-8228 *Fax:* 902-628-6656
Number of Beds: 33 beds
Note: community care beds
Shirley Keenan

***Charlottetown:* McQuaid Lodge**
Affiliated with: Health PEI
36 Kent St., Charlottetown, PE C1A 1M8
Tel: 902-892-0791
Gerard Arsenault

***Charlottetown:* Old Rose Lodge**
Affiliated with: Health PEI
319 Queen St., Charlottetown, PE C1A 4C4
Tel: 902-368-8313
Helen Roberts

***Charlottetown:* Stamper Residence**
Affiliated with: Health PEI
29 Fitzroy St., Charlottetown, PE C1A 1R2
Tel: 902-894-3815
Number of Beds: 20 beds
Joyce Pickles, Administrator

***Charlottetown:* Tenderwood Lodge Inc.**
Affiliated with: Health PEI
15 Hawthorne Ave., Charlottetown, PE C1A 5X8
Tel: 902-566-5174

***Crapaud:* South Shore Villa**
Affiliated with: Health PEI
PO Box 111, 159 Sherwwod Forest Dr., Crapaud, PE C0A 1J0
Tel: 902-658-2228 *Fax:* 902-658-2576
Number of Beds: 52 beds
Note: Parent ID changed only, 08/10 — Not a complete update
Lynn Dawson

***Georgetown:* Carroll's Lodge**
Affiliated with: Health PEI
PO Box 133, 110 Gordon St., Georgetown, PE C0A 1L0
Tel: 902-652-2369
Number of Beds: 7 beds
Barb Carroll

***Hunter River:* Rosewood Residence**
Affiliated with: Health PEI
PO Box 97, 4260 Hopedale Rd., Route 13, Hunter River, PE C0A 1N0
Tel: 902-964-2436 *Fax:* 902-964-2436
info@rosewoodresidence.ca
www.rosewoodresidence.ca
Number of Beds: 41 beds
Note: community care beds
Lori E. Weeks, Director

***Kensington:* MacEwen Mews Seniors Residence**
Affiliated with: Health PEI
RR#6, Kensington, PE C0B 1M0
Tel: 902-836-4678

***Lower Montague:* Shady Rest Convalescent Home**
Affiliated with: Health PEI
RR#2, Lower Montague, PE C0A 1R0
Tel: 902-838-4298 *Fax:* 902-838-4298
Number of Beds: 37 beds
Note: community care beds
Jackie MacKay, Owner/Operator

***Miscouche:* Miscouche Villa**
Affiliated with: Health PEIs
PO Box 40, 20 Lady Slipper Dr., Miscouche, PE C0B 1T0
Tel: 902-436-1946 *Fax:* 902-436-3215
Number of Beds: 35 beds
Note: community care beds
Barbara Perry, Manager

***Montague:* MacKinnon Pines Community Care Facility**
Affiliated with: Health PEI
PO Box 298, 505 Campbellton St., Montague, PE C0A 1R0
Tel: 902-838-2656 *Fax:* 902-838-3542

***Montague:* Queens Gardens**
Affiliated with: Health PEI
394 Queens Rd., Montague, PE C0A 1R0
Tel: 902-838-8440
Number of Beds: 7 beds

***New Glasgow:* River View Home**
Affiliated with: Health PEI
RR#2, New Glasgow, PE C0A 1N0
Tel: 902-964-2795 *Fax:* 902-621-0453
Number of Beds: 20 beds
Note: community care beds for seniors & the mentally challenged
Kathy Dutton, Proprietor
Martin Dutton

***O'Leary:* Lady Slipper Villa**
Affiliated with: Health PEI
PO Box 40, 490 Main St., O'Leary, PE C0B 1V0
Tel: 902-859-3544 *Fax:* 902-859-3255
Number of Beds: 47 beds
Note: community care beds
Karen Cook, Administrator

***Souris:* Bayview Lodge**
Affiliated with: Health PEI
22 Washington St., Souris, PE C0A 2B0
Tel: 902-687-3122 *Fax:* 902-687-3512
Number of Beds: 32 beds
Note: community care beds
Gerard Arsenault

***Summerside:* Andrews of Summerside**
Affiliated with: Health PEI
317 Pope Rd., Summerside, PE C1N 6G4
Tel: 902-436-0859 *Fax:* 902-436-1565
info@andrewsofpei.com
www.andrewsofpei.com/andrews_of_summerside.php
Number of Beds: 58 beds
Note: community care facility
Erroll Andrews, Administrator

***Summerside:* MacDonald's Community Care Home Inc.**
Affiliated with: Health PEI
197 Cambridge St., Summerside, PE C1N 1N1
Tel: 902-436-7359

***Tignish:* Tignish Seniors Home Care Cooperative Limited**
Affiliated with: Health PEI
116 MacLeod Lane, Tignish, PE C0B 2B0
Tel: 902-882-4663
Year Founded: 2002
Note: Specialty: Assisted living
Leslie VanHee, Administrator

***Tyne Valley:* Murphy's Country Lodge**
Affiliated with: Health PEI
Tyne Valley, PE C0B 2C0
Tel: 902-831-2213 *Fax:* 902-831-2309
Number of Beds: 11 beds
Note: community care beds
Earlene Murphy

Personal Care Homes

***Charlottetown:* Corrigan Lodge / Corrigan Home Inc.**
Affiliated with: Health PEI
22 Hemlock Ct., Charlottetown, PE C1A 8E3
Tel: 902-894-9686 *Fax:* 902-894-3686

Number of Beds: 28 beds
Note: The licensed community care facility is privately owned & operated.

Charlottetown: Elm Crest Lodge
Affiliated with: Health PEI
267 Richmond St., Charlottetown, PE C1A 1J7
Tel: 902-566-5996

Note: Elm Crest Lodge is a privately owned community care facility, licensed in Prince Edward Island.

Kensington: Clinton View Lodge
Affiliated with: Health PEI
PO Box 8, RR#6, Kensington, PE C0B 1M0
Tel: 902-866-2276 *Fax:* 902-886-2073

Note: The community care facility is privately owned. It is located at 30 Clinton View Court in Clinton.

Wellington: La Coopérative Le Chez-Nous Ltée
Affiliated with: Health PEI
PO Box 88, 64 Sunset Dr., Wellington, PE C0B 2E0
Tel: 902-854-3426 *Fax:* 902-854-3055
cheznous@pei.aibn.com
Year Founded: 1993
Number of Beds: 37 beds
Area Served: Évangéline region
Note: The community care facility is privately owned & operated. French is spoken at the housing complex.
Edgar Arsenault, Director

Mental Health Facilities

Mental Health Hospitals/Facilities

Charlottetown: Hillsborough Hospital & Special Care Centre
Affiliated with: Health PEI
PO Box 1929, 115 Murchison Lane, Charlottetown, PE C1A 7N5
Tel: 902-368-5400 *Fax:* 902-368-5467
www.gov.pe.ca/health
Number of Beds: 75 beds
Note: Specialties: Psychiatry; Medical services for persons with acute or long-term mental illnesses or mental handicaps, & psychogeriatric patients; Day services for former patients; Assessment; Behavioural management
Cecil Villard, Administrator
Don Hughes, Director, Environmental Services

Charlottetown: Sherwood Home
Affiliated with: Health PEI
75 Murchison Lane, Charlottetown, PE C1N 7N5
Tel: 902-368-4141 *Fax:* 902-368-4931
Number of Beds: 16 beds (3 respite, 13 long-term care)
Note: Sherwood Home is a provincial residential service for persons with physical and/or developmental disabilities. The home offers residential, respite and day program services.
Andrew MacDougal, Administrator

Québec

Département gouvernemental responsable

QUÉBEC: Ministère de la Santé et des services sociaux
1075, ch Ste-Foy, Québec, QC G1S 2M1
Tél: 418-266-8900 *Téléc:* 418-644-4574
Ligne sans frais: 800-707-3380
info@msss.gouv.qc.ca
www.msss.gouv.qc.ca

Agences de la santé et de services sociaux

Baie-Comeau: Agence de la santé et des services sociaux de la Côte-Nord
691, rue Jalbert, Baie-Comeau, QC G5C 2A1
Tél: 418-589-9845 *Téléc:* 418-589-8574
www.agencesante09.gouv.qc.ca

Note: Centres de santé et de services sociaux (CSSS): CSSS de la Haute-Côte-Nord; CSSS de la Minganie; CSSS de Port-Cartier; CSSS de Manicouagan; CSSS Sept-Iles; CSSS de la Basse-Côte-Nord; CSSS de l'Hématite
Réginald Caron, Président, Conseil d'administration
Gaétan Garon, Président-directeur général
Martin Bouchard, Commissaire régional aux plaintes, et à la qualité des services

Chicoutimi: Agence de la santé et des services sociaux du Saguenay-Lac-Saint-Jean
930, rue Jacques-Cartier est, Chicoutimi, QC G7H 7K9
Tél: 418-545-4980 *Téléc:* 418-545-8791
Ligne sans frais: 1-800-370-4980
info@santesaglac.gouv.qc.ca
www.santesaglac.gouv.qc.ca
Média social: www.facebook.com/SanteSagLac
Population desservi: 270 063
Note: Centres de santé et de services sociaux (CSSS): CSSS Maria-Chapdelaine; CSSS Cléophas-Claveau; CSSS de Jonquière; CSSS de Lac-Saint-Jean-Est; CSSS Domaine-du-Roy; CSSS de Chicoutimi
Bruno Dahl, Président, Conseil d'administration
Martine Couture, Présidente-directrice générale, Agence
martine.couture@ssss.gouv.qc.ca
Jean-François Saint-Gelais, Coordonnateur des communications

Gaspé: Agence de la santé et des services sociaux de la Gaspésie-Iles-de-la-Madeleine
144, boul Gaspé, Gaspé, QC G4X 1A9
Tél: 418-368-2349 *Téléc:* 418-368-4942
agence11@ssss.gouv.qc.ca
www.agencesssgim.ca
Média social:
www.facebook.com/group.php?gid=176786372354584

Note: Centres de santé et de services sociaux (CSSS): CSSS de La Haute-Gaspésie; CSSS du Rocher-Percé; CSSS des Iles; CSSS de la Baie-des-Chaleurs; CSSS de La Côte-de-Gaspé
Jean-Marie LeBrasseur, Président, Conseil d'administration
Anne Joncas Côté, Commissaire aux plaintes et à la qualité des services

Gatineau: Agence de la santé et des services sociaux de l'Outaouais
104, rue Lois, Gatineau, QC J8Y 3R7
Tél: 819-776-7660 *Téléc:* 819-771-8632
www.rrsss07.gouv.qc.ca

Note: Centres de santé et de services sociaux (CSSS): CSS du Pontiac; CSSS de la Vallée-de-la-Gatineau; CSSS des Collines; CSSS de Gatineau; CSSS de Papineau
Dr. Guy Morissette, Président-directeur général de l'Agence
819-776-7660
Hélène Dupont, Directrice de santé publique
819-776-7660, Fax: 819-777-0271
Marie-France Bégis, Chef du service des communications
819-776-7650

Joliette: Agence de la santé et des services sociaux de Lanaudière
245, rue du Curé-Majeau, Joliette, QC J6E 8S8
Tél: 450-759-1157 *Téléc:* 450-759-0023
Ligne sans frais: 1-800-668-9229
agencelanaudiere@ssss.gouv.qc.ca
www.agencelanaudiere.qc.ca

Note: Centres de santé et de services sociaux (CSSS): CSSS du Sud de Lanaudière; CSSS du Nord de Lanaudière
Paul-Yvon de Billy, Président, Conseil d'administration
Lucie Leduc, Présidente-directrice générale
Fax: 450-759-1781, Lucie.Leduc@ssss.gouv.qc.ca
Jean-Jacques Lamarche, Commissaire régional aux plaintes, et à la qualité des services
Fax: 450-759-1781
Jean-Claude Berlinguet, Directeur des affaires médicales et universitaires
Fax: 450-759-0023
Gynette Caillé, Directrice des ressources financières
Fax: 450-759-0023
Yves Paul Dugal, Directeur des ressources matérielles et techniques
Fax: 450-753-5633, Yves-Paul.Dugal@ssss.gouv.qc.ca
Claire Pagé, Directrice des services sociaux
Fax: 450-753-5633, Claire.Pagé@ssss.gouv.qc.ca
Doris Prince, Directrice des communications, et des realations publiques
Fax: 450-759-1781, Doris.Prince@ssss.gouv.qc.ca
Daniel Sirois, Directeur régionalisé des ressources informationnelles
Fax: 450-759-0023, Daniel.Sirois@ssss.gouv.qc.ca
Jean-Pierre Trépanier, Directeur de santé publique
Fax: 450-759-5149

Laval: Agence de la santé et des services sociaux de Laval
Tour A, 800, boul Chomedey, Laval, QC H7N 3Y4
Tél: 450-978-2000 *Téléc:* 450-978-2100
communications.agencelaval@ssss.gouv.qc.ca
www.ssssIaval.gouv.qc.ca

Note: Centres de santé et de services sociaux (CSSS): CSSS de Laval
Luc Villiard, Président, Conseil d'administration
Claude Desjardins, Président-directeur général
Denis Blanchard, Directeur des affaires réseau
Dre Nicole Damestoy, Directrice de santé publique
Yves St-Onge, Directeur des affaires administratives
Dr. Martin Archambault, Chef du département régional de médecine générale
Julie Desjardins, Directrice associée des affaires médicales, et santé physique

Longueuil: Agence de la santé et des services sociaux de la Montérégie
1255, rue Beauregard, Longueuil, QC J4K 2M3
Tél: 450-928-6777 *Téléc:* 450-679-6443
www.santemonteregie.qc.ca/agence

Note: Centres de santé et de services sociaux (CSSS): CSSS Pierre-Boucher; CSSS Haut-Richelieu-Rouville; CSSS Champlain - Charles-Le Moyne; CSSS Pierre-De Saurel; CSSS du Suroît; CSSS Jardins-Roussillon; CSSS la Pommeraie; CSSS Richelieu-Yamaska; CSSS de Vaudreuil-Soulanges; CSSS du Haut-Saint-Laurent; CSSS de la Haute-Yamaska
Nicole Mongeon, Présidente, Conseil d'administration
Richard Deschamps, Président-directeur général, et secrétaire, conseil d'administration

Montréal: Agence de la santé et des services sociaux de Montréal
3725, rue St-Denis, Montréal, QC H2X 3L9
Tél: 514-286-6500 *Téléc:* 514-286-5669
www.agence.santemontreal.qc.ca

Note: Centres de santé et de services sociaux (CSSS): CSSS de l'Ouest-de-l'Ile; CSSS de Dorval-Lachine-LaSalle; CSSS du Sud-Ouest-Verdun; CSSS Cavendish; CSSS de la Montagne; CSSS de Bordeaux-Cartierville-Saint-Laurent; CSSS d'Ahuntsic et Montréal-Nord; CSSS du Coeur-de-l'Ile; CSSS Jeanne-Mance; CSSS de Saint-Léonard et Saint-Michel; CSSS Lucille-Teasdale; CSSS de la Pointe-de-l'Ile
Dr Victor C. Goldbloom, Président, Conseil d'administration
Yvon Lamarre, Vice-président, Conseil d'administration
Danielle McCann, Présidente-directrice générale, de l'Agence; Secrétaire, Conseil d'administration
François Charbonneau, Président, du comité de planification et d'évaluation
Pierre Dupuis, Président, du comité de vérification
Monika Throner, Présidente, du comité de vigilance et de la qualité

Québec: Agence de la santé et des services sociaux de la Capitale-Nationale
555, boul Wilfrid-Hamel est, Québec, QC G1M 3X7
Tél: 418-525-1500 *Ligne sans frais:* 1-888-299-1495
www.rrsss03.gouv.qc.ca
Info Line: 418-525-1495
Région desservi: Les territoires de Charlevoix et de Portneuf (69 municipalités)*Population desservi:* 669 316
Note: Centres de santé et de services sociaux (CSSS): CSSS de Portneuf; CSSS de la Vieille-Capitale; CSSS de Québec-Nord; CSSS de Charlevoix
Yves Blouin, Président, Conseil d'administration
Guy Thibodeau, Secrétaire, Conseil d'administration
Pascale St-Pierre, Responsable, Services des communications
418-525-1452,

Rimouski: Agence de la santé et des services sociaux du Bas-St-Laurent
#115, 288, rue Pierre-Saindon, Rimouski, QC G5L 9A8
Tél: 418-724-5231 *Téléc:* 418-723-1597
www.agencesssbsl.gouv.qc.ca

Population desservi: 201 326
Note: Centres de santé et de services sociaux (CSSS): CSSS des Basques; CSSS de Kamouraska; CSSS de la Mitis; CSSS de Témiscouata; CSSS de la Matapédia; CSSS de Matane; CSSS de Rimouski-Neigette; CSSS de Rivière-du-Loup.
Le Territoire desservi: 8 territoires de MRC du Bas-Saint-Laurent (114 municipalités)
Jean-Paul Morin, Président, Conseil d'administration
Jean-Maurice Lechasseur, Vice-président, Conseil d'administration
Isabelle Malo, Secrétaire, Conseil d'administration

Rouyn-Noranda: Agence de la santé et des services sociaux de l'Abitibi-Témiscamingue
1, 9e rue, Rouyn-Noranda, QC J9X 2A9
Tél: 819-764-3264 *Téléc:* 819-797-1947
www.sante-abitibi-temiscamingue.gouv.qc.ca
Région desservi: La région de l'Abitibi-Témiscamingue (65 municipalités)*Population desservi:* 145 835

Note: Centres de santé et de services sociaux (CSSS): CSSS des Aurores-Boréales; CSSS les Eskers de l'Abitibi; CSSS de Rouyn-Noranda; CSSS de la Vallée-de-l'Or; CSSS du Témiscamingue
Suzanne Huard, Présidente, Conseil d'administration de l'Agence
Jacques Boissonneault, Président-directeur général et secrétaire du conseil
Daniel Arsenault, Directeur des ressources informationnelles
Marie-Lyne Blier, Directrice des ressources financières et matérielles
Réal Lacombe, Directeur de santé publique
Roland Lord, Directeure des services de santé
Normand Mongeau, Directeur du personnel réseau et de l'agence
Dr. Jean-Guy Ricard, Directeur médical régional traumatologie
Denise Stewart, Directrice des activités stratégiques

Saint-Jérôme: Agence de la santé et des services sociaux des Laurentides
#210, 1000, rue Labelle, Saint-Jérôme, QC J7Z 5N6
Tél: 450-436-8622 *Téléc:* 450-432-8712
infosantelaurentides@ssss.gouv.qc.ca
www.santelaurentides.qc.ca

Population desservi: 552 349
Note: Centres de santé et de services sociaux (CSSS): CSSS des Pays-d'en-Haut; CSSS de Thérèse-De Blainville; CSSS des Sommets; CSSS d'Antoine-Labelle; CSSS du Lac-des-Deux-Montagnes; CSSS de Saint-Jérôme; CSSS d'Argenteuil
Jean Poitras, Président, Conseil d'administration
Marc Fortin, Président-directeur générale
450-432-8707
Luc Bergeron, Directeur des ressources humaines
450-432-8714
Julie Boucher, Directrice régionale de la santé physique
450-432-8726
Martin Delage, Directeur des ressources immobilières, et informationnelles
450-432-8727
Dr. Éric Goyer, Directeur de santé publique
450-432-8731
Chantal Huguerot, Directrice des ressources financières
450-432-8715

Sainte-Marie: Agence de la santé et des services sociaux de Chaudière-Appalaches
363, rte Cameron, Sainte-Marie, QC G6E 3E2
Tél: 418-386-3363 *Téléc:* 418-386-3361
reception.rr12@ssss.gouv.qc.ca
www.agencesss12.gouv.qc.ca

Note: Centres de santé et de services sociaux (CSSS): CSSS des Etchemins; CSSS de la région de Thetford; CSSS de Montmagny-L'Islet; CSSS Alphonse-Desjardins; CSSS de Beauce
Duane Benoît, Présidente-directrice générale de l'agence

Sherbrooke: Agence de la santé et des services sociaux de l'Estrie
Complexe Saint-Vincent-de-Paul, #300, 300, rue King est, Sherbrooke, QC J1G 1B1
Tél: 819 829-3400 *Téléc:* 819 569-8894
information.agence05@ssss.gouv.qc.ca
www.santeestrie.qc.ca
Région desservi: Municipalités & territoires de l'Estrie
Note: Centres de santé et de services sociaux (CSSS): CSSS du Haut-Saint-François; CSSS des Sources; CSSS du Val-Saint-François; CSSS de la MRC-de-Coaticook; CSSS de Memphrémagog; CSSS du Granit; CSSS Institut Universitaire de gériatrie de Sherbrooke
Denis Paré, Président, Conseil d'administration
Lynda B. Provencher, Vice-présidente, Conseil d'administration
Johanne Turgeon, Secrétaire, Conseil d'administration

Trois-Rivières: Agence de la santé et des services sociaux de la Mauricie et du Centre-du-Québec
550, rue Bonaventure, Trois-Rivières, QC G9A 2B5
Tél: 819-693-3636 *Téléc:* 819-373-1627
www.agencesss04.qc.ca

Personnel: 15000
Note: Centres de santé et de services sociaux (CSSS): CSSS du Haut-Saint-Maurice; CSSS de Maskinongé; CSSS de la Vallée-de-la-Batiscan; CSSS d'Arthabaska-et-de-L'Érable; CSSS de Trois-Rivières; CSSS Drummond; CSSS de l'Énergie; CSSS de Bécancour - Nicolet-Yamaska
Gérald Lapierre, Président, Conseil d'administration
Éric Chevalier, Vice-président, Conseil d'administration
Jean-Denis Allaire, Président-directeur général de l'Agence

Centres de santé et de services sociaux

Alma: CSSS de Lac-Saint-Jean-Est
Affiliée à: Agence de la santé et des services sociaux du Saguenay-Saint-Jean
CP 1300, 300, boul Champlain sud, Alma, QC G8B 3N8
Tél: 418-669-2000
www.santealma.qc.ca

Note: Les Installations (Services de CH, CHSLD, et CLSC): Hôpital d'Alma; CLSC Secteur-Centre (Alma); CLSC Secteur-Nord (L'Ascension-de-Notre-Seigneur); CLSC Secteur-Sud (Métabetchouan-Lac-à-la-Croix); Centre d'hébergement Isidore-Gauthier; Centre d'hébergement Métabetchouan-Lac-à-la-Croix; Centre d'hébergement Le normandie
Jean McNicoll, Président, Conseil d'administration
Camil Dion, Directeur général et secrétaire
camil.dion@ssss.gouv.qc.ca
Pierre Bouchard, Directeur des ressources financières, matérielles et informationnelles
Danny Côté, Directeur des ressources humaines
Caroline Guay, Directrice des soins infirmerses, et du réseau de services soutien à l'autonomie
Marie-Karlynn Laflamme, Directrice des communications et de la performance
Josée Lalancette, Directrice des programmes de santé publique, et des services généraux
Daniel Olivier, Directeur du programme santé physique, et des services hospitaliers
Annie Poirier, Directrice des réseaux de services santé mentale, et jeunesse/enfance/famille
Guy Verreault, Directeur des services professionnels

Amos: CSSS Les Eskers de l'Abitibi (CSSSEA)
Affiliée à: Agence de la santé et des services sociaux de l'Abitibi-Témiscamingue
622, 4e rue ouest, Amos, QC J9T 2S2
Tél: 819-732-3341
www.csssea.ca

Population desservi: 24 500
Note: Les Installations (Services de CH, CHSLD, et CLSC): Hôpital Hôtel-Dieu d'Amos (819-732-3341); Centre d'hébergement Harricana (819-732-6521); CLSC Les Eskers (Amos, Barraute, Berry, Guyenne, La Corne, La Motte, Landrienne, Launay, Preissac, Rochebaucourt, Saint-Dominique-du-Rosaire, Saint-Félix-de-Dalquier, Saint-Marc-de-Figuery, Saint-Mathieu-d'Harricana, Sainte-Gertrude-Manneville, Trécesson - secteur La Ferme, Trécesson - secteur Villemontel).
Le Territoire desservi: 17 municipalités, deux territoires non organisés (TNO) et la communauté algonquine de Pikogan, MRC d'Abitibi
Jean McGuire, Président, Conseil d'administration
Michel Michaud, Directeur général
michel_michaud@ssss.gouv.qc.ca

Amqui: CSSS de la Matapédia
Affiliée à: Agence de la santé et des services sociaux du Bas-St-Laurent
135, rue de l'Hôpital, Amqui, QC G5J 2K5
Tél: 418-629-2211
www.csssmatapedia.qc.ca

Personnel: 502
Note: Services à la population: Services hospitaliers et urgence; Services diagnostiques; Services de réadaptation; Services ambulatoires; Services de pastorale; Services offerts en CLSC; Services de soutien à domicile; Services d'hébergement de longue durée; Services gériatriques
Jeanne-D'Arc Voyer, Présidente, Conseil d'administration
Alain Paquet, Directeur général
Pierre d'Anjou, Directeur des ressources financières, matérielles et informationnelles
Dre Claire Jean, Directrice des services professionnels
Annie Leclerc, Directrice des ressources humaines
Bertin Lévesque, Directeur des soins infirmiers
Michel Simard, Directeur des programmes et des activités cliniques

Asbestos: CSSS des Sources
Affiliée à: Agence de la santé et des services sociaux de l'Estrie
Centre administratif, 475, 3e av, Asbestos, QC J1T 1X6
Tél: 819-879-7151 *Téléc:* 819-879-0075
www.dessources.santeestrie.qc.ca

Fondée en: 1997
Population desservi: 15 000
Note: Les Installations (Services de CH, CHSLD, et CLSC): Hôpital, CLSC, et Centre d'hébergement d'Asbestos.
Municipalités: Asbestos; Danville; Saint-Adrien; Saint-Camille; Saint-Georges-de-Windsor; Saint-Joseph-de-Ham-Sud; Wotton
Michel Drouin, Président, Conseil d'administration

Mario Morand, Directeur général
mmorand.dessources@ssss.gouv.qc.ca

Baie-Comeau: CSSS de Manicouagan (CSSSM)
Affiliée à: Agence de la santé et des services sociaux de la Côte-Nord
635, boul Joliet, Baie-Comeau, QC G5C 1P1
Tél: 418-589-3701 *Téléc:* 418-589-9654
Ligne sans frais: 1-877-484-3701
09.csssm.opinions@ssss.gouv.qc.ca
www.csssmanicouagan.qc.ca
Nombre de lits: 115 lits d'hébergement; 106 lits d'hospitalisation de courte durée
Région desservi: MRC de la Haute-Côte-Nord et de Manicouagan*Population desservi:* 44 264*Personnel:* 900
Note: Les Installations (Services de CH, CHSLD, et CLSC): Hôpital Le Royer (418-589-3701); Centre d'hébergement Boisvert (418-296-2501); Centre d'hébergement N.-A.-Labrie (418-589-2425); CLSC Corinne-Vallée-Therrien (418-939-2226); CLSC Marie-Leblanc-Côté (418-567-2274); CLSC Lionel-Charest (418-296-2572)
Jean-Marc Cliche, Président, Conseil d'administration
Daniel Côté, Directeur général
Dan_Cote@ssss.gouv.qc.ca
Marie-France Brunelle, Directrice des services financiers, informatiques et techniques
Josée Desgagnés, Directrice de programmes, services généraux et santé physique
Roger Dubé, Directeur des services professionnels
Suzie Malouin, Directrice, personnes en perte d'autonomie
Jacqueline St-Pierre, Directrice de la qualité; Directrice, des soins infirmiers
Anne Trmblay, Directrice, parents, enfants, familles et jeunes en difficulté

Beauceville: CSSS de Beauce (CSSSB)
Affiliée à: Agence de la santé et des services sociaux de Chaudière-Appalaches
253, rte 108, Beauceville, QC G5X 2Z3
Tél: 418-774-3304 *Téléc:* 418-227-1175
Ligne sans frais: 1-866-271-0971
csssbeauce@ssss.gouv.qc.ca
www.csssbeauce.qc.ca
Région desservi: MRC Beauce-Sartigan; MRC Robert-Cliche
Note: Les Installations (Services de CH, CHSLD, et CLSC): Hôpital de Saint-Georges (418-228-2031); CLSC de Saint-Joseph-de-Beauce (418-397-5722); CLSC de Beauceville (418-774-5722); CLSC de La Guadeloupe (418-459-3441); CLSC de Saint-Georges (418-228-2244); CLSC de Saint-Gédéon-de-Beauce (418-582-3355); Centre d'hébergement de Beauceville (418-774-3304); Centre d'hébergement de Saint-Georges, secteur est (418-228-2021); Centre d'hébergement de Saint-Georges, secteur ouest (418-228-2081)
Brigitte Busque, Présidente, Conseil d'administration
Huguette Giroux, Directrice générale et secrétaire

Brossard: CSSS Champlain - Charles-Le Moyne (CSSSCCLM)
CP 100, 5811, boul Taschereau, Brossard, QC J4Z 1A5
Tél: 450-445-4452
www.santemonteregie.qc.ca/champlain
Nombre de lits: 473 lits d'hospitalisation et 195 en hébergement
Population desservi: 220 000*Personnel:* 4 700
Note: Les Installations (Services de CH, CHSLD, et CLSC): Hôpital Charles-Le Moyne (450-466-5000); Centre d'hébergement Champlain (450-672-3320); Centre d'hébergement Henriette-Céré (450-672-3320); CLSC Saint-Hubert (450-443-7400); CLSC Samuel-de-Champlain (450-445-4452); Centre Saint-Lambert (450-672-3320); Centre de recherche appliquée (450-466-5433); Centre de recherche clinique (450-466-5024); Centre de prêt d'équipements Panama (450-462-5193); Centre externe de néphrologie Greenfield Park (450-466-5000, poste 3645); Centre externe de néphrologie Saint-Lambert (450-466-5000, poste 3646); Clinique externe de pédopsychiatrie (450-466-5000, poste 2414); Hôpital de jour pour adolescents (450-466-5000, poste 2008); Clinique externe de psychiatrie pour adultes (450-466-5620); Clinique externe de psychiatrie pour adultes (450-466-5453); Centre de jour, Clinique Labonté (450-466-5455); Maison Brodeur (450-448-4763); Suivi intensif dans la communauté (450-466-5605); Groupe de médecine familiale de l'Unité de médecine familiale Charles-Le Moyne (450-466-5630).
Le Territoire desservi: Arrondissements de Greenfield Park, du Vieux-Longueuil et de Saint-Hubert
Marc Duclos, Président, Conseil d'administration
Michel Gervais, Directeur général
michel.gervais@rrsss16.gouv.qc.ca

Candiac: CSSS Jardins-Roussillon
Affiliée à: Agence de la santé et des services sociaux de la Montérégie
90, boul Marie-Victorin, Candiac, QC J5R 1C1
Tél: 450-659-7661
www.santemonteregie.qc.ca/jardins-roussillon
Population desservi: 189 000
Note: Les Installations (Services de CH, CHSLD, et CLSC): Hôpital Anna-Laberge (450-699-2425); Centre d'hébergement de Châteauguay (450-692-8231); Centre d'hébergement de La Prairie (450-659-9148); Centre d'hébergement de Saint-Rémi (450-454-4694); Centre de services Lauzon (450-699-7901); CLSC Châteauguay (450-699-3333); CLSC Jardin-du-Québec, Napierville (450-245-3336); CLSC Jardin-du-Québec, Saint-Rémi (450-454-4671); CLSC Kateri (450-659-7661); Centre d'hébergement Champlain Châteauguay (450-632-4451, poste 313); Centre d'hébergement Champlain Jean-Louis-Lapierre (450-632-4451, poste 313); Centre hospitalier Kateri Memorial (450-638-3930).
Le Territoire desservi: Candiac, Châteauguay, Delson, Hemmingford Canton et Village, La Prairie, Léry, Mercier, Napierville, Saint-Bernard-de-Lacolle, Saint-Constant, Saint-Cyprien de Napierville, Sainte-Catherine, Sainte-Clotilde, Saint-Édouard, Sainte-Martine, Saint-Isidore, Saint-Jacques-le-Mineur, Saint-Mathieu, Saint-Michel, Saint-Patrice-de-Sherrington, Saint-Philippe, Saint-Rémi, Saint-Urbain-Premier
Sylvie Gaudreau, Présidente, Conseil d'administration
Paul Moreau, Directeur général
paul.moreau@rrsss16.gouv.qc.ca

Cap-aux-Meules: CSSS des Iles (Iles-de-la-Madeleine)
Affiliée à: Agence de la santé et des services sociaux de la Gaspésie-Iles-de-la-Madeleine
430 ch Principal, Cap-aux-Meules, QC G4T 1R9
Tél: 418-986-2121
www.csssdesiles.qc.ca
Média social: www.facebook.com/group.php?gid=151244821567542
Note: Les Installations (Services de CH, CHSLD, et CLSC): Hôpital de l'Archipel (418-986-2121); Centre d'hébergement Villa Plaisance (418-986-2121); CLSC de Bassin (418-937-2572); CLSC de Cap-aux-Meules (418-986-2572); CLSC de l'Ile d'Entrée (418-986-4299); CLSC de l'Est (418-985-2572); Centre de réadaptation en DI-TED (418-986-3590)
Gaston Bourque, Président, Conseil d'administration
Marie Gibeault, Directrice générale
Philippe Simon Laplante, Directeur des ressources humaines
ps.laplante.archipel@ssss.gouv.qc.ca
Céline Lafrance, Conseillère en communication

Chandler: CSSS du Rocher-Percé
Affiliée à: Agence de la santé et des services sociaux de la Gaspésie-Iles-de-la-Madeleine
CP 3300, 451, rue Monseigneur Ross est, Chandler, QC G0C 1K0
Tél: 418-689-2261
www.csssrocherperce.com
Note: Les Installations (Services de CH, CHSLD, et CLSC): Hôpital de Chandler (418-689-2261); Centre d'hébergement Villa-Pabos (418-689-6621); CLSC Chandler (418-689-2572); CLSC Percé (418-782-2572); CLSC Gascons (418-396-2572)
Philippe Berger, Président, Conseil d'administration
Chantal Duguay, Directrice générale

Chicoutimi: CSSS de Chicoutimi
Affiliée à: Agence de la santé et des services sociaux du Saguenay-Saint-Jean
CP 5006, 305, St Vallier, Chicoutimi, QC G7H 5H6
Tél: 418-541-1000
www.csss-chicoutimi.qc.ca
Personnel: 3 300
Note: Les Installations (Services de CH, CHSLD, et CLSC): Hôpital de Chicoutimi (418-541-1000); Centre d'hébergement Beaumanoir (418-698-3900); Centre d'hébergement Mgr-Victor-Tremblay (418-698-3907); Centre d'hébergement de la Colline (418-549-5474); CLSC de Chicoutimi (418-543-2221); CLSC Maintien à domicile (418-693-3924). Médecins: 300
Richard Bergeron, Président, Conseil d'administration
Gilles Gagnon, Directeur général
418-541-1099, Gilles.gagnon@ssss.gouv.qc.ca

Coaticook: CSSS de la MRC de Coaticook
Affiliée à: Agence de la santé et des services sociaux de l'Estrie
138, rue Jeanne-Mance, Coaticook, QC J1A 1W3
Tél: 819-849-9102 *Téléc:* 819-849-6735
www.cssscoaticook.ca
Région desservi: MRC de Coaticook (12 municipalités)*Population desservi:* 18 770*Personnel:* 300
Note: Les Installations (Services de CH, CHSLD, et CLSC): Centre hospitalier de Coaticook (819-849-9102); CLSC (1 point de service); 1 centre d'hébergement en soins de longue durée (92 lits); Clinique médicale GMF des Frontières (819-849-4808)
Gérard Ruest, Président, Conseil d'administration
Donald Massicotte, Directeur général

Cowansville: CSSS la Pommeraie
Affiliée à: Agence de la santé et des services sociaux de la Montérégie
950, rue Principale, Cowansville, QC J2K 1K3
Tél: 450-266-4342
www.santemonteregie.qc.ca/lapommeraie
Fondée en: 2004
Note: Les Installations (Services de CH, CHSLD, et CLSC): Hôpital Brome-Missisquoi-Perkins (450-266-4342, option 5); Centre d'accueil de Cowansville (450-266-4342, option 3); CHSLD de Bedford (450-248-4304); Foyer Sutton (450-538-3332); Les Foyers Farnham (450-293-3167); CLSC de Bedford (450-248-4321 poste 0); CLSC de Cowansville (450-266-4342, option 4); CLSC de Farnham (450-293-3622); CLSC de Sutton (450-266-4342, option 4); CLSC de VIlle de Lac-Brome (450-242-2001); Service de soutien à domicile (450-266-4342, option 2).
Le Territoire desservi: La MRC de Brome-Missisquoi en plus des municipalités de Sainte-Brigide-d'Iberville et de l'Ange-Gardien
Roger Fournier, Administrateur provisoire
roger.fournier@rrsss16.gouv.qc.ca
Bruno Petrucci, Directeur général
bruno.petrucci@rrsss16.gouv.qc.ca

Dolbeau-Mistassini: CSSS Maria-Chapdelaine
Affiliée à: Agence de la santé et des services sociaux du Saguenay-Lac-Saint-Jean
L'Hôpital, 2000, boul Sacré-Coeur, Dolbeau-Mistassini, QC G8L 2R5
Tél: 418-276-1234
www.csssmariachapdelaine.com
Nombre de lits: 120 lits de longue durée; 48 lits de courte durée; 8 lits de réadaptation; 51 lits de ressources intermédiaires; 55 unités de logement
Population desservi: 28 285*Personnel:* 740
Note: Les Installations (Services de CH, CHSLD, et CLSC): L'Hôpital, Dolbeau-Mistassini; L'Oasis, Dolbeau-Mistassini; Les Jardins du Monastère, Dolbeau-Mistassini; Centre de Normandin, Normandin
André Perron, Président, Conseil d'administration
Normand Brassard, Directeur général
normand.brassard.cmc@ssss.gouv.qc.ca

Donnacona: CSSS de Portneuf
Affiliée à: Agence de la santé et des services sociaux de la Capitale-Nationale
CP 370, 250, boul Gaudreau, Donnacona, QC G3M 1L7
Tél: 418-285-3025 *Téléc:* 418-285-3508
www.csssdeportneuf.qc.ca
Nombre de lits: 14 lits de santé physique; 347 lits d'hébergement permanent; 3 lits d'hébergement temporaire
Personnel: 931
Note: Les Installations (Services de CH, CHSLD, et CLSC): Hôpital régional de Portneuf (418-337-4611); Centre d'hébergement Donnacona (418-285-3025); Centre d'hébergement Pont-Rouge (418-873-4661); Centre d'hébergement Saint-Casimir (418-339-2861); Centre d'hébergement Saint-Marc-des-Carrières (418-268-3511); Centre d'hébergement Saint-Raymond (418-337-4661); CLSC Donnacona (418-285-2626); CLSC Pont-Rouge (418-873-6062); CLSC Rivière-à-Pierre (418-323-2253); CLSC Saint-Marc-des-Carrières (418-268-3571); CLSC Saint-Raymond (418-337-4611); CLSC Saint-Ubalde (418-277-2256). Médecins: 45
Philippe Leboeuf, Président, Conseil d'administration
Chantale Simard, Directrice générale et secrétaire
chantale_simard@ssss.gouv.qc.ca

Drummondville: CSSS Drummond
Affiliée à: Agence de la santé et des services sociaux de la Mauricie et du Centre-du-Québec
Centre administratif, Hôpital Sainte-Croix, 570, rue Hériot, Drummondville, QC J2B 1C1
Tél: 819-478-6464
csssdrummond@ssss.gouv.qc.ca
www.csssdrummond.qc.ca
Note: Les Installations (Services de CH, CHSLD, et CLSC): Hôpital Sainte-Croix (819-478-6464); Centre d'hébergement Frederick-George-Heriot (819-477-0544); Centre d'hébergement L'Accueil Bon-Conseil (819-336-2122); Centre d'hébergement Marguerite-D'Youville (819-478-6464); Clinique de radiologie Drummond (819-477-5747); CLSC Drummond (819-474-2572); Point de service Wickham (819-474-2572); Point de service Notre-Dame-du-Bon-Conseil (819-474-2572); Point de service Saint-Guillaume (819-474-2572); Point de service Victoriaville - santé au travail des Bois-Francs (819-758-6488); Point de service Drummondville - santé au travail (819-474-8428)
Gérald Lapierre, Président, Conseil d'administration
Michel Doyon, Directeur général
819-478-6401, michel_doyon@ssss.gouv.qc.ca

Fermont: CSSS de l'Hématite
Affiliée à: Agence de la santé et des services sociaux de la Côte-Nord
CP 550, 1, rue Aquilon, Fermont, QC G0G 1J0
Tél: 418-287-5461
rh.hematite@ssss.gouv.qc.ca (ressources humaines)
Michel Baron, Président, Conseil d'administration
Normand Ducharme, Directeur général
Normand_Ducharme@ssss.gouv.qc.ca

Gaspé: CSSS de La Côte-de-Gaspé
215, boul de York ouest, Gaspé, QC G4X 2W2
Tél: 418-368-3301
www.cssscotedegaspe.ca
Population desservi: 18 952
Note: Les Installations (Services de CH, CHSLD, et CLSC): Hôpital Hotel-Dieu de Gaspé (418-368-3301); Centre d'hébergement Mgr-Ross (418-368-3301); CLSC de Barachois (418-645-2572); CLSC de Gaspé (418-368-2572); CLSC de Grande-Vallée (418-393-2572); CLSC de Murdochville (418-784-2572); CLSC de Rivière-au-Renard (418-269-2572); Unité de médecine familiale (418-368-6663)
Yvan Landry, Président, Conseil d'administration
Lise Pouliot, Directrice générale
lise.pouliot.chgaspe@ssss.gouv.qc.ca
Nicole Bilodeau, Directrice, Personnes en perte d'autonomie
Sylvain Bouchard, Directeur des services communautaires et psychosociaux
L. Castilloux, Directrice des services ambulatoires, et de la santé mentale
Dr. Antoine Groulx, Directeur des services professionnels, et des affaires médicales
Daniel Martin, Directeur des resources financières, et informationnelles
Gérald O'Connor, Directeur des ressources humaines, et du développement organisationnel
Marie-France Ouellet, Directrice des soins infirmiers, et de la santé physique
Gaétan Vézina, Directeur des services techniques et hôteliers

Gatineau: CSSS de Gatineau
Affiliée à: Agence de la santé et de services sociaux de l'Outaouais
777, boul de la Gappe, Gatineau, QC J8T 8R2
Tél: 819-966-6560 *Téléc:* 819-966-6565
www.csssgatineau.qc.ca
Média social: twitter.com/csssgatineau
Note: Les Installations (Services de CH, CHSLD, et CLSC): Hôpital de Gatineau (819-966-6100); Hôpital de Hull (819-966-6200); Hôpital de jour gériatrique (819-664-2060); Hôpital Pierre-Janet (819-771-7761); Centre d'hébergement - Foyer du Bonheur (819-966-6410); Centre d'hébergement - La Pietà (819-966-6420); Centre d'hébergement - Bon séjour (819-966-6450); Centre d'hébergement - Renaissance (819-966-6440); CLSC de Gatineau - boul de la Gappe (819-966-6550); CLSC de Gatineau - av Gatineau (819-966-6550); CLSC de Gatineau - rue Saint-Rédempteur (819-966-6510); CLSC de Gatineau - boul du Mont-Bleu (819-966-6530); CLSC de Gatineau - boul Saint-Raymond (819-966-6525); CLSC de Gatineau - rue LeGuerrier (819-966-6540); CLSC de Gatineau - Maison Bruyère (819-966-6540); CLSC de Gatineau - boul Alexandre-Taché (819-966-6580); Unité de médecine familiale (819-966-6380); Maison de naissance de l'Outaouais (819-966-6585); Pavillon Marcel D'amour (819-776-8093); Résidence de Hull (819-770-2992); Équipe de réadaptation (819-772-9777, poste 7221); Résidence Corbeil (819-777-2042); Résidence de Gatineau (819-568-3349)
Bruno Bonneville, Président, Conseil d'administration
Denis Beaudoin, Directeur général
denis_beaudoin@ssss.gouv.qc.ca
Denis Marleaun, Directeur général adjoint

Gatineau: CSSS de Papineau
Affiliée à: Agence de la santé et de services sociaux de l'Outaouais
578, rue MacLaren est, Gatineau, QC J8L 2W1
Tél: 819-986-9917
csss_papineau@ssss.gouv.qc.ca
www.cssspapineau.qc.ca
Note: Les Installations (Services de CH, CHSLD, et CLSC):

Hôpital de Papineau (819-986-3341); Centre d'hébergement Vallée-de-la-Lièvre (819-986-4115); CLSC et Centre d'hébergement Petite-Nation (819-983-7341); CLSC Vallée-de-la-Lièvre (rue Maclaren est, Gatineau; av Buckingham, Gatineau; Val-des-Bois)
Lucie Lalonde, Présidente, Conseil d'administration
Gilles Clavel, Directeur général
Gilles.Clavel@ssss.gouv.qc.ca

***Granby:* CSSS de la Haute Yamaska (CSSSHY)**
Affiliée à: Agence de la santé et des services sociaux de la Montérégie
Centre administratif, 205, boul Leclerc ouest, Granby, QC J2G 1T7
Tél: 450-375-8000
communication.cssshy@rrsss16.gouv.qc.ca
www.santemonteregie.qc.ca/granby-region

Fondée en: 2004
Nombre de lits: 303 lits de longue durée; 150 lits de courte durée
Personnel: 2 000
Note: Les Installations (Services de CH, CHSLD, et CLSC): Hôpital de Granby (450-375-8000); Centre d'hébergement de Waterloo (450-539-5512, poste 500); Centre d'hébergement Leclerc (450-375-8000, poste 0); Centre d'hébergement Marie-Berthe-Couture (450-375-8003, poste 2662); Centre d'hébergement Villa Bonheur (450-776-5222, poste 300); Centre d'hébergement Vittie & Desjardins (450-776-5222, poste 422); CLSC de la rue Principale / Santé au travail (450-776-6116); CLSC Notre-Dame (450-375-1442); Centre Providence (450-375-8000); CLSC de Waterloo (450-539-3340); CLSC St-Joseph (450-375-1442); CLSC Yvan-Duquette (450-375-1442).
Médecins: 72 médecins omnipraticiens et 52 spécialistes.
Le Territoire desservi: Bromont; Granby; Roxton Pond; Saint-Alphonse; Saint-Joachim-de-Shefford; Sainte-Cécile-de-Milton; Saint-Paul d'Abbotsford; Shefford; Warden; Waterloo
Jean-Marc Savoie, Président, Conseil d'administration
Yves Fortin, Directeur général
yves.fortin@rrsss16.gouv.qc.ca

***Havre-Saint-Pierre:* CSSS de la Minganie (CSSSM)**
Affiliée à: Agence de la santé et des services sociaux de la Côte-Nord
1035, promenade des Anciens, Havre-Saint-Pierre, QC G0G 1P0
Tél: 418-538-2212 *Téléc:* 418-538-3038
www.csssminganie.com

Nombre de lits: 13 lits (CH); 41 lits (CHSLD); 19 lits (Foyer - CHSLD)
Personnel: 235
Note: Points de service: Rivière-au-Tonnerre (418 465-2146); Rivière Saint-Jean (418-949-2865); Longue-Pointe-de-Mingan (418-949-2402); Baie-Johan-Beetz (418-539-0169); Aguanish (418-533-2301); Natashquan (418-726-3387); Foyer (418-538-2212, poste 365); Port-Menier (418-535-0176)
Carold Boies, Président, Conseil d'administration
Danièle Limoges, Directrice générale
daniele_limoges@ssss.gouv.qc.ca
Daniel Bouillon, Directeur des services administratifs
Sylvie Méthot, Directrice, des services aux personnes en perte d'autonomie
Dre Mimi Samson, Directrice des services professionnels
Mireille Vigneault, Directrice de la santé physique, des services généraux, et direction des soins infirmiers
Lucie Cormier, Chef de l'administration des programmes
Lysanne Cormier, Chef de l'unité et de réadaptation
Marie-Hélène Drapeau, Chef du service social
Denis Tremblay, Chef des installations matérielles, et des services techniques

***Jonquière:* CSSS de Jonquière**
Affiliée à: Agence de la santé et des services sociaux du Saguenay-Lac-Saint-Jean
Centre administratif et hospitalier, CP 1200, 2230, rue de l'Hôpital, Jonquière, QC G7X 7X2
Tél: 418-695-7700
csssjonquiere@ssss.gouv.qc.ca
www.csssjonquiere.qc.ca

Note: Les Installations (Services de CH, CHSLD, et CLSC): Centre administratif et hospitalier; CLSC Jonquière (St-Ambroise); Centre de réadaptation en déficience physique; Centre de réadaptation en dépendance; Centre d'hébergement Des Chênes; Centre d'hébergement Georges-Hébert; Centre d'hébergement Ste-Marie; Centre d'hébergement des Années d'Or
Hélène Deschênes, Présidente, Conseil d'administration
Régis Harvey, Directeur général
Regis.Harvey.jonq@ssss.gouv.qc.ca

***La Baie:* CSSS Cléophas-Claveau**
Affiliée à: Agence de la santé et des services sociaux du Saguenay-Lac-Saint-Jean
Centre hospitalier, CP 38, 1000, rue Docteur-Desgagné, La Baie, QC G7B 3P9
Tél: 418-544-3381
www.cssscleophasclaveau.qc.ca

Note: Les Installations (Services de CH, CHSLD, et CLSC): Centre hospitalier; Centre d'hébergement Bagotville; Centre d'hébergement St-Joseph; CLSC de La Baie; CLSC L'Anse-Saint-Jean
Michel Truchon, Président, Conseil d'administration
Martine Nepton, Directrice générale
martine.nepton@ssss.gouv.qc.ca

***La Malbaie:* CSSS de Charlevoix**
Affiliée à: Agence de la santé et des services sociaux de la Capitale-Nationale
535, boul de Comporté, La Malbaie, QC G5A 1S8
Tél: 418-435-5150
www.cssscharlevoix.qc.ca

Note: Les Installations (Services de CH, CHSLD, et CLSC): Hôpital de Baie-Saint-Paul (418-435-5150); Hôpital de La Malbaie (418-665-1700); Centre d'hébergement Pierre-Dupré (418-435-5562); Centre d'hébergement de Clermont (418-665-1712); Centre d'hébergement Bellerive (418-665-1727); Centre d'hébergement de Saint-Siméon (418-638-2414); CLSC de Baie-Saint-Paul (418-435-5475); CLSC de l'Isle-aux-Coudres (418-438-2788); CLSC de La Malbaie (418-665-6413); CLSC de Saint-Siméon (418 638-2369); CLSC de Baie-Sainte-Catherine (418-237-4272); CRDI Beausoleil (418-439-5976); CRDI de La Malbaie (418-665-7662); CRDI de Saint-Hilarion (418-457-4098); CRDI de Saint-Placide (418-435-2980); CRDI de Saint-Siméon (418-638-2861); CRDI de Saint-Urbain (418-639-2428); CRDI Saindon (418-439-1645)
Diane Truchon-Mailloux, Présidente, Conseil d'administration
Guy Thibodeau, Directeur général
guy_thibodeau@ssss.gouv.qc.ca

***La Sarre:* CSSS des Aurores-Boréales (CSSSAB)**
Affiliée à: Agence de la santé et des services sociaux de l'Abitibi-Témiscamingue
CP 6000, 679, 2e rue est, La Sarre, QC J9Z 2X7
Tél: 819-333-2311
www.csssab.qc.ca

Population desservi: 21 308
Note: Les Installations (Services de CH, CHSLD, et CLSC): Centre de soins de courte durée (Centre hospitalier et siège social, 819-333-2311); Centre d'hébergement de soins de longue durée de Macamic (819-782-4661); Centre d'hébergement de soins de longue durée de La Sarre (819-333-5525); Centre d'hébergement de soins de longue durée de Palmarolle (819-787-2612); CLSC (Beaucanton, Duparquet, Dupuy, Gallichan, La Sarre, Macamic, Normétal, Palmarolle, Taschereau)
Huguette Théberge, Présidente, Conseil d'administration
Paul Fortin, Directeur général
paul_fortin@ssss.gouv.qc.ca
Maggy Vallières, Adjointe à la direction générale

***La Tuque:* CSSS du Haut-Saint-Maurice (CSSSHSM)**
Affiliée à: Agence de la santé et des services sociaux de la Mauricie et du Centre-du-Québec
885, boul Ducharme, La Tuque, QC G9X 3C1
Tél: 819-523-4581 *Téléc:* 819-523-7992
www.cssshsm.qc.ca

Note: Le Territoire desservi: Les régions du Centre-du-Québec, de Lanaudière, des Laurentides, de l'Abitibi-Témiscamingue, de la Baie-James, de Québec et du Saguenay-Lac Saint-Jean
Jacques Fraser, Président, Conseil d'administration
Rémy Beaudoin, Directeur général
remy_beaudoin@ssss.gouv.qc.ca
Claude Bouchard, Directeur des services professionnels
Sandra Burquel, Directrice des programmes-services, Enfance-Jeunesse-Famille et santé publique
Joan Dugas, Directrice des services administratifs
Danielle Noël, Directrice des programmes-services, santé physique et santé mentale et dépendances
Sylvie Girard, Directrice générale adjointe
Marjolaine St-Pierre, Commissaire locale aux plaintes, et à la qualité des services

***Lac-Etchemin:* CSSS des Etchemins**
Affiliée à: Agence de la santé et des services sociaux de Chaudière-Appalaches
Centre administratif, 331, rue du Sanatorium, Lac-Etchemin, QC G0R 1S0
Tél: 418-625-3101
csssetchemins@ssss.gouv.qc.ca
www.csssetchemins.qc.ca

Région desservi: MRC des Etchemins (13 municipalités)*Population desservi:* 17 250
Note: Les Installations (Services de CH, CHSLD, et CLSC): Centre d'hébergement de Saint-Prosper (418-594-8159); CLSC de Saint-Prosper (418-594-8282); L'Équinoxe (pour la clientèle en santé mentale); L'Intemporel (pour la clientèle en santé mentale); Duplex (pour la clientèle adulte ayant des troubles cognitifs); RAC à Sainte-Justine (pour la clientèle en santé mentale); Résidence Le Tremplin (pour la clientèle en déficience physique); L'Intermédiaire (pour la clientèle en santé mentale); L'Atelier du Lac (pour l'intégration socioprofessionnelle)
Pascale Goudreau, Présidente, Conseil d'administration
Lucie Laflamme, Directrice générale
lucielaflamme@ssss.gouv.qc.ca

***Lac-Mégantic:* CSSS du Granit**
Affiliée à: Agence de la santé et des services sociaux de l'Estrie
3569, rue Laval, Lac-Mégantic, QC G6B 1A5
Tél: 819-583-0330 *Téléc:* 819-583-5239
Ligne sans frais: 1-800-827-2572
info.granit@ssss.gouv.qc.ca
www.csssgranit.qc.ca

Note: Les Installations (Services de CH, CHSLD, et CLSC): CHSLD - Centre de jour (Point de service Lac-Mégantic); CLSC-CHSLD - Centre de jour (Point de service Lambton); CLSC (Point de chute Saint-Ludger); CLSC (Point de chute Notre-Dame des Bois)
Suzanne Boulanger, Présidente, Conseil d'administration
Pierre Latulippe, Directeur général
platulippe.granit@ssss.gouv.qc.ca

***Lachine:* CSSS de Dorval-Lachine-LaSalle (CSSS DLL)**
Affiliée à: Agence de la santé et des services sociaux de Montréal
1900, rue Notre-Dame, Lachine, QC H8S 2G2
Tél: 514-362-8000
www.csssdll.qc.ca

Population desservi: 131 911
Note: Les Installations (Services de CH, CHSLD, et CLSC): Hôpital de LaSalle / Longue durée de l'hôpital de LaSalle (514-362-8000); CLSC de LaSalle (514-364-2572); CLSC de Dorval-Lachine (514-639-0650); Centre d'hébergement de Dorval (514-631-9094); Centre d'hébergement de Lachine (514-634-7161); Centre d'hébergement de LaSalle (514-364-6700); Centre d'hébergement Nazaire-Piché (514-637-2326).
Le Territoire desservi: Les arrondissements montréalais de LaSalle et Lachine; La municipalité de Dorval
Gertrude Pellerin, Présidente, Conseil d'administration
Yves Masse, Directeur général
Yves.Masse.dll@ssss.gouv.qc.ca

***Lachute:* CSSS d'Argenteuil**
Affiliée à: Agence de la santé et des services sociaux des Laurentides
145, av de la Providence, Lachute, QC J8H 4C7
Tél: 450-562-3761 *Téléc:* 450-566-3316
www.csssargenteuil.qc.ca

Fondée en: 2003
Région desservi: MRC d'Argenteuil*Population desservi:* 30 000
Note: Les Installations: Bureau de Grenville (819-242-0778); Équipe jeunesse (450-562-9608)
Johanne Dumouchel, Présidente, Conseil d'administration
Raymond Roberge, Directeur général
Carole Deschambault, Secrétaire
Jacques M. Hébert, Trésorier

***Laval:* CSSS de Laval**
Affiliée à: Agence de la santé et de services sociaux de Laval
1515, boul Chomedey, Laval, QC H7V 3Y7
Tél: 450-975-5598
www.cssslaval.qc.ca
Média social: www.facebook.com/cssslaval; twitter.com/cssslaval

Fondée en: 2004
Nombre de lits: 751 lits d'hébergement longue durée; 512 lits d'hospitalisation courte durée
Population desservi: 407 193*Personnel:* 6 379
Note: Les Installations (Services de CH, CHSLD, et CLSC): Hôpital de la Cité-de-la-Santé, avec centre de prélèvements,

UMF et CICL (450-668-1010); Centre ambulatoire (450-978-8300); Centre d'hébergement Fernand-Larocque (450-661-5440); Centre d'hébergement Idola-Saint-Jean (450-668-6750); Centre d'hébergement de La Pinière (450-661-3305); Centre d'hébergement Rose-de-Lima (450-622-6996); Centre d'hébergement de Sainte-Dorothée (450-689-0933); Centre intégré de services de première ligne de l'ouest de l'Ile (450-627-2530); CLSC du Marigot (450-668-1803); CLSC des Mille-Iles (450-661-2572, 450 972-6808); CLSC du Ruisseau-Papineau (450-687-5690); CLSC de Sainte-Rose (450-622-5110)
Gaston Joly, Président, Conseil d'administration
Luc Lepage, Directeur général
luc_lepage_csssl@ssss.gouv.qc.ca
Dre Nicole Damestoy, Directrice de la prévention-promotion
Lucie Gagnon, Directrice des soins infirmiers
Dr Alain Goudreau, Directrice des services professionnels et hospitaliers, et des affaires médicales
Martin Lavertu, Directeur des ressources techniques
Benoît Tétreault, Directeur des services multidisciplinaires
Jo Ann Veilette, Directrice des ressources financières

Les Escoumins: CSSS de la Haute-Côte-Nord (CSSSHCN)
Affiliée à: Agence de la santé et des services sociaux de la Côte-Nord
Centre administratif, CP 1000, 4, rue de l'Hôpital, Les Escoumins, QC G0T 1K0
Tél: 418-233-2931
www.cssshcn.gouv.qc.ca
Population desservi: 13,000*Personnel:* 300
Note: Les Installations (Services de CH, CHSLD, et CLSC): Pavillon Les Escoumins(418-233-2931); Pavillon Forestville (418-587-2865); Pavillon Bergeronnes (418-232-6224); Point de service Sacré-Coeur (418-236-4637)
Denis Asselin, Président
Daniel Côté, Directeur général et secrétaire
dan_cote@ssss.gouv.qc.ca

Lévis: CSSS Alphonse-Desjardins
Affiliée à: Agence de la santé et des services sociaux de Chaudière-Appalaches
Centre administratif, 143, rue Wolfe, Lévis, QC G5X 3Z1
www.csssalphonsedesjardins.ca
Fondée en: 2011
Région desservi: Lévis; Bellechasse; Lotbinière; Nouvelle-Beauce
Note: Le Centre de santé et de services sociaux Alphonse-Desjardins a été créé suite à la fusion du Centre de santé det de services sociaux du Grand Littoral et du CHAU Hôtel-Dieu.
Julie Suzanne Doyon, Présidente, Conseil d'administration
Raymond Coulombe, Directeur général
Raymond_coulombe@ssss.gouv.qc.ca

Longueuil: CSSS Pierre-Boucher
Affiliée à: Agence de la santé et des services sociaux de la Montérégie
1333, boul Jacques-Cartier est, Longueuil, QC J4M 2A5
Tél: 450-468-8848
www.santemonteregie.qc.ca/cssspierreboucher
Population desservi: 246 000
Note: Les Installations (Services de CH, CHSLD, et CLSC): Hôpital Pierre-Boucher (450-468-8111); Centre d'hébergement de Contrecoeur (450-468-8410); Centre d'hébergement de Lajemmerais (450-463-2995); Centre d'hébergement de Mgr-Coderre (450-448-3111); Centre d'hébergement du Chevalier-De Lévis (450-670-5110); Centre d'hébergement du Manoir-Trinité (450-674-4948); Centre d'hébergement Jeanne-Crevier (450-641-0590); Centre d'hébergement René-Lévesque (450-651-2210); CLSC de Longueuil-Ouest (450-651-9830); CLSC des Seigneuries de Boucherville (450-655-3630; CLSC des Seigneuries de Contrecoeur (450-468-8413; CLSC des Seigneuries de Saint-Amable (450-468-5250); CLSC des Seigneuries de Sainte-Julie (450-468-3670); CLSC des Seigneuries de Varennes (450-677-2917); CLSC des Seigneuries de Verchères (450-448-3700); CLSC Simonne-Monet-Chartrand (450-463-2850); Centre d'accueil Saint-Laurent inc. (450-670-5480).
Le Territoire desservi: Arrondissement du Vieux-Longueuil, Boucherville, Calixa-Lavallée, Contrecoeur, Saint-Amable, Sainte-Julie, Varennes et Verchères
Luc Genest, Président, Conseil d'administration
Caroline Barbir, Directrice générale
cbarbir@csssspb.gouv.qc.ca
Philippe Benoît, Directeur des ressources humaines, et du développement organisationnel
Guy Bergeron, Directeur administratif des services professionnels
Éric Champagne, Directeur des ressources financières
Nathalie Chauvin, Directrice des services techniques
France Descôteaux, Directrice des communications, et des relations publiques
Sylvie Desmarais, Directrice de la gestion des risques, de l'assurance qualité et de la performance
Dr. Michel Laurence, Directeur médical et des services professionnels
Dr. François Raymond, Directeur médical à la qualité à la gestion des risques, et à la sécurité des patients
Nicolas Raymond, Directeur des ressources informationnelles

Louiseville: CSSS de Maskinongé (CSSSM)
Affiliée à: Agence de la santé et des services sociaux de la Mauricie et du Centre-du-Québec
41, boul Comtois, Louiseville, QC J5V 2H8
Tél: 819-228-2731
www.csssm.qc.ca
Personnel: 500
Note: Les Installations: Centre Comtois, Louiseville; Centre de services Avellin-Dalcourt, Louiseville; Point de service Saint-Paulin; Point de service Saint-Alexis-des-Monts; Le GMF Saint-Laurent
Jacques Lafrenière, Président, Conseil d'administration
Jocelyn Milot, Directeur général
France Castilloux, Directrice intérimaire des soins infirmiers, et des programmes services
Dr. Guy Croisetière, Directeur des services professionnels
Guy Houde, Directeur des ressources financières, techniques et informationnelles
Benoit LaRue, Directeur des ressources humaines, et du développement des compétences
Josée Mercier, Directrice de la santé publique et qualité
Monique Lupien, Commissaire locale aux plaintes, et à la qualité des services

Lourdes-de-Blanc-Sablon: CSSS de la Basse-Côte-Nord (CSSSBCN)
Affiliée à: Agence de la santé et des services sociaux de la Côte-Nord
CP 130, 1070, boul Docteur-Camille-Marcoux, Lourdes-de-Blanc-Sablon, QC G0G 1W0
Tél: 418-461-2144 *Téléc:* 418-461-2583
www.csssbcn.gouv.qc.ca
Nombre de lits: 22 lits de courte durée (hospitalisation); 14 lits (Pavillon D.G. Hodd, Harrington Harbour); 15 lits (Unité Antoinette-Malouin, Blanc-Sablon)
Population desservi: 5 500*Personnel:* 250
Note: Les Installations: Point de service de Rivière-St-Paul (418-379-2244); Point de service de St-Augustin (418-947-2321); Point de service de La Tabatière (418-773-2232); Point de service de La Tabatière (418-773-2232); Point de service de Mutton Bay (418-773-2212); Point de service de Tête-à-la-Baleine (418-242-2112); Point de service de Harrington Harbour (418-795-3353); Pavillon D.G. Hodd (418 795-3353); Point de service de Chevery (418 787-2277); Point de service de Kégaska (418-726-3382)
Gaétan Garon, Administrateur provisoire, Conseil d'administration
Martin Beaumont, Directeur général

Magog: CSSS de Memphrémagog
Affiliée à: Agence de la santé et des services sociaux de l'Estrie
50, rue Saint-Patrice est, Magog, QC J1X 3X3
Tél: 819-843-2572 *Ligne sans frais:* 1-800-268-2572
www.csssm.santeestrie.qc.ca
Note: Les Installations (Services de CH, CHSLD, et CLSC): Hôpital de Memphrémagog; Point de service de Mansonville (450-292-3376); Point de service de Stanstead (819-876-7521)
Jacques Juby, Président, Conseil d'administration
Monique Corbeil, Directrice générale
819-843-3381, mcorbeil.mm@ssss.gouv.qc.ca

Maniwaki: CSSS de la Vallée-de-la-Gatineau (CSSSVG)
Affiliée à: Agence de la santé et de services sociaux de l'Outaouais
309, boul Desjardins, Maniwaki, QC J9E 2E7
Tél: 819-449-2300 *Téléc:* 819-449-7330
www.csssvg.qc.ca
Population desservi: 20 000
Note: Les Installations (Services de CH, CHSLD, et CLSC): L'hôpital de Maniwaki; Le Foyer Père Guinard de Maniwaki; Le Foyer d'accueil de Gracefield; Les CLSC de Low, Gracefield, et Maniwaki
Jacques Cyr, Président, Conseil d'administration
Sylvie Martin, Directrice générale
Sylvie_Martin@ssss.gouv.qc.ca
Stéphane Lalonde, Directeur général adjoint
stephane_lalonde@ssss.gouv.qc.ca
Henri Bertrand, Directeur des affaires médicales
henri_bertrand@ssss.gouv.qc.ca
Josée Laroche, Directrice programme santé physique / DSI
josee_laroche@ssss.gouv.qc.ca
Manon Moreau, Directrice des ressources financières et techniques
manon_moreau@ssss.gouv.qc.ca
Michael O'Leary, Directeur, programme personnes âgées en perte d'autonomie
michaelo'leary@ssss.gouv.qc.ca
Diane Marenger, Commissaire local aux plaintes et à la qualité
diane_marenger@ssss.gouv.qc.ca

Mansfield-et-Pontefract: CSSS du Pontiac
Affiliée à: Agence de la santé et des services sociaux de l'Outaouais
CP 430, 160, ch de la Chute, Mansfield-et-Pontefract, QC J0X 1V0
Tél: 819-683-3000 *Téléc:* 819-683-3682
Ligne sans frais: 1-800-567-9625
info@santepontiac.qc.ca
www.santepontiac.qc.ca
Média social:
www.facebook.com/pages/CSSS-du-Pontiac/213024748134?ref=nf
Note: Les Installations (Services de CH, CHSLD, et CLSC): Centre Hospitalier du Pontiac; Pavillon Centre d'accueil Pontiac; Pavillon Manoir Sacré Cour; CLSC Bryson; CLSC Chapeau; CLSC de Mansfield-et-Pontefract, Fort-Coulonge; CLSC Otter-Lake; CLSC Quyon; CLSC Rapides-des-Joachims
Jean-Guy Patenaude, Président, Conseil d'administration
Richard Grimard, Directeur général
richard_grimard@ssss.gouv.qc.ca
Lucille Bélair, Présidente, Conseil des infirmières et infirmiers
Dr. Freydoun Homayounfar, Président, Conseil des médecins, dentistes et pharmaciens
Georges Robitaille, Président, Conseil multidisciplinaire

Maria: CSSS de la Baie-des-Chaleurs (CSSSBC)
Affiliée à: Agence de la santé et des services sociaux de la Gaspésie-Iles-de-la-Madeleine
Centre administratif, 419, boul Perron, Maria, QC G0C 1Y0
Tél: 418-759-3443 *Téléc:* 418-759-5063
csssbc@csssbc.qc.ca
www.csssbc.qc.ca
Fondée en: 2004
Région desservi: MRC d'Avignon; MRC de Bonaventure*Population desservi:* 32 591*Personnel:* 1 100
Note: Les Installations (Services de CH, CHSLD, et CLSC): Hôpital de Maria (418-759-3443); Centre d'hébergement de Maria (418-759-3458); Centre d'hébergement de Matapédia (418-865-2221); Centre d'hébergement de New Carlisle (418-752-3386); CLSC Malauze de Matapédia (418-865-2221); CLSC de Pointe-à-la-Croix (418-788-5454); CLSC de Saint-Omer (418-364-7064); CLSC de Caplan (418-388-2572); CLSC de Paspébiac (418-752-2572); Unité de médecine familiale Baie-des-Chaleurs (418-759-1336, poste 2811).
Médecins: 67
Gérald Arsenault, Président, Conseil d'administration
Jean-Philippe Legault, Directeur général et secrétaire
Michael Bond, Directeur, ressources humaines
Line Débigaré, Directrice des ressources financières, et de la performance
Dr. François Dumas, Directeur, services professionnels et soutien clinique
Charles Guérette, Directeur de programmes santé publique, santé mentale, famille-enfance-jeunesse, serv. psychosociaux
Martin Pelletier, Directeur des services techniques, et ressources informationnelles
Francis Picarou, Directeur du programme santé physique, et des soins infirmiers

Matane: CSSS de Matane
Affiliée à: Agence de la santé et des services sociaux du Bas-Saint-Laurent
Centre Administratif, Hôpital de Matane, 333, rue Thibault, Matane, QC G4W 2W5
Tél: 418-562-3135 *Téléc:* 418-562-9374
www.csssmatane.com
Note: Les Installations (Services de CH, CHSLD, et CLSC): Hôpital de Matane (45 lits); Centre d'hébergement de Matane (106 lits); CLSC de Matane (Les Méchins, Baie-des-Sables)
Louis Pelletier, Président, Conseil d'administration
Nicole Morin, Directrice générale

Mont-Joli: CSSS de La Mitis
Affiliée à: Agence de la santé et des services sociaux du Bas-Saint-Laurent
800, av du Sanatorium, Mont-Joli, QC G5H 3L6
Tél: 418-775-7261
cmssc_dg@centremitissien.net (direction générale)
www.centremitissien.net
Raymond Martel, Président, Conseil d'administration
Manon Dufresne, Directrice générale et secrétaire

Mont-Laurier: CSSS d'Antoine-Labelle (CSSSAL)
Affiliée à: Agence de la santé et des services sociaux des Laurentides
515, boul Albiny-Paquette, Mont-Laurier, QC J9L 1K8
Tél: 819-623-1228
www.csssal.org
Média social:
www.facebook.com/group.php?gid=182385008476466
Fondée en: 2004
Nombre de lits: 404 lits
Région desservi: MRC d'Antoine-Labelle_Personnel:_ 1 500
Note: Les Installations (Services de CH, CHSLD, et CLSC): Hôpital de Mont-Laurier (819-623-1234); Centre d'Hébergement Sainte-Anne (819-623-5940); CLSC Notre-Dame-du-Laus (819-767-2488); Services à la communauté de Mont-Laurier (819-623-1228); Centre de services de Rivière-Rouge (819-275-2118)
Gaétan Chartrand, Président, Conseil d'administration
Jean-Pierre Urbain, Directeur général
Jean-Pierre.Urbain@ssss.gouv.qc.ca
Mario Bisson, Directeur des ressources financières
bisson.mario@ssss.gouv.qc.ca
Jacques Fréchette, Directeur du programme santé mentale
jacques.frechette@ssss.gouv.qc.ca
Pierre Gfeller, Directeur des services professionnels et hospitaliers
pierregfeller@ssss.gouv.qc.ca
Mario Houle, Directeur des ressources informationnelles, et services techniques
mario.houle.al@ssss.gouv.qc.ca
François Leduc, Directeur des ressources humaines
francois.leduc@ssss.gouv.qc.ca
Benoît Major, Directeur, programme perte d'autonomie liée au vieillissement
benoit.major@ssss.gouv.qc.ca
Michèle Mayer, Directrice de la qualité des services
michele.mayer@ssss.gouv.qc.ca
Nathalie Maurais, Directrice des soins infirmiers
nathalie.maurais@ssss.gouv.qc.ca
Michelle Meilleur, Directrice du programme services à la communauté
michelle_meilleur@ssss.gouv.qc.ca
Pierre Roy, Directeur du programme santé physique
pierre.roy2@ssss.gouv.qc.ca

Montmagny: CSSS de Montmagny-L'Islet
Affiliée à: Agence de la santé et des services sociaux de Chaudière-Appalaches
350, boul Taché ouest, Montmagny, QC G5V 3R8
Tél: 418-249-2511
www.csssml.qc.ca
Nombre de lits: 251 lits (longue durée); 71 lits (courte durée)
Population desservi: 41 496_Personnel:_ 1 400
Note: Les Installations (Services de CH, CHSLD, et CLSC): Hôpital de Montmagny (418-248-0630); Maisons d'hébergement Sainte-Perpétue (418-359-2247); Maisons d'hébergement de Saint-Eugène (418-247-3927); Centre d'hébergement de Cap-Saint-Ignace (418-246-5644); Centre d'hébergement de Saint-Fabien-de-Panet (418-249-4054); Centre d'hébergement de Saint-Jean Port-Joli (418-598-3355); Centre d'hébergement de Montmagny (418-248-1572); CLSC de Saint-Jean Port-Joli (418-598-3355); CLSC de Saint-Pamphile (418-356-3393); CLSC de Saint-Fabien-de-Panet (418-249-2572); CLSC de Montmagny (418-248-2572); CLSC de L'Isle-aux-Grues (418-248-4651); Édifice Wingen (418-248-0639); Service santé au travail Chaudière-Appalaches (Montmagny, Saint-Georges, Saint-Jean-Chrysostome, Thetford Mines)
Josée Caron, Présidente, Conseil d'administration
Daniel Paré, Directeur général
Daniel.Pare.csssml@ssss.gouv.qc.ca
Ginette Bernier, Directrice de la qualité des services, et des soins infirmiers
Josée Chouinard, Directrice du programme, perte d'autonomie liée au vieillissent
Martin Cloutier, Directeur des services administratifs
Guylaine Fortin, Directrice des services dans la communauté
France Nicole, Directrice du programme de santé physique
Annie Tremblay, MD, Directrice des services professionnels

Montréal: CSSS Cavendish
Affiliée à: Agence de la santé et des services sociaux de Montréal
Centre administratif, 5425, av Bessborough, Montréal, QC H4V 2S7
Tél: 514-484-7878
emplois.cvd@ssss.gouv.qc.ca (ressources humaines)
www.cssscavendish.qc.ca
Population desservi: 119 840_Personnel:_ 1 265
Note: Les Installations (Services de CH, CHSLD, et CLSC): Hôpital Richardson (514-484-7878); CLSC René-Cassin (514-484-7878); CLSC de Notre-Dame-de-Grâce - Montréal-Ouest (514-484-7878); Centre d'hébergement Henri-Bradet (514-484-7878); Centre d'hébergement St-Andrew (514-932-3630); Centre d'hébergement Father-Dowd (514-932-3630); Centre d'hébergement St-Margaret (514-932-3630)
Alan Maislin, Président, Conseil d'administration
Francine Dupuis, Directrice générale
514-483-1380, francine.dupuis.cvd@ssss.gouv.qc.ca

Montréal: CSSS d'Ahuntsic et Montréal-Nord (CSSSAM-N)
Affiliée à: Agence de la santé et des services sociaux de Montréal
1725, boul Gouin est, Montréal, QC H2C 3H6
Tél: 514-384-2028
www.csssamn.ca
Population desservi: 170 000
Note: Les Installations (Services de CH, CHSLD, et CLSC): Hôpital Fleury; Centre d'hébergement de Louvain; Centre d'hébergement Laurendeau; Centre d'hébergement Légaré; Centre d'hébergement Paul-Lizotte; CLSC d'Ahuntsic; CLSC de Montréal-Nord
Denis Rousseau, Président, Conseil d'administration
Diane Daigle, Directrice générale
diane.daigle.csssamn@ssss.gouv.qc.ca

Montréal: CSSS de Bordeaux-Cartierville-Saint Laurent
Affiliée à: Agence de la santé et des services sociaux de Montréal
555, boul Gouin ouest, Montréal, QC H3L 1K5
Tél: 514-331-3025
info_bcstl@ssss.gouv.qc.ca
www.csssbcstl.qc.ca
Note: Les Installations (Services de CH, CHSLD, et CLSC): Centre d'hébergement Notre-Dame-de-la-Merci (514-331-3020); Centre d'hébergement Saint-Joseph-de-la-Providence (514-334-3120); Centre d'hébergement de Saint-Laurent (514-744-4981); Centre d'hébergement de Cartierville (514-337-7300); Pavillon des Bâtisseurs (514-334-4817); CLSC de Bordeaux-Cartierville (514-331-2572); CLSC de Saint-Laurent (514-748-6381); Centre Notre-Dame-des-Anges (514-331-0076); Résidence Tournesol (514-333-6930); Pavillon Grenet (Résidence Notre-Dame des Anges)
Geneviève Hotte, Présidente, Conseil d'administration
Daniel Corbeil, Directeur général
d.corbeil@ssss.gouv.qc.ca

Montréal: CSSS de l'Ouest-de-l'Ile
Affiliée à: Agence de la santé et des services sociaux de Montréal
160, av Stillview, Montréal, QC H9R 2Y2
Tél: 514-630-2225 _Téléc:_ 514-630-2371
communications.csss@ssss.gouv.qc.ca
www.csssouestdelile.qc.ca
Note: Les Installations (Services de CH, CHSLD, et CLSC): Hôpital général du Lakeshore (514-630-2225); CLSC de Pierrefonds (514-626-2572); CLSC du Lac-Saint-Louis (514-697-4110); Centre d'hébergement Denis-Benjamin-Viger (514-620-6310).
Le Territoire desservi: Les arrondissments de de Pierrefonds-Roxboro et de L'Ile-Bizard-Sainte-Geneviève; Les villes de Baie d'Urfé, Beaconsfield, Dollard-des-Ormeaux, Kirkland, Pointe-Claire, Sainte-Anne-de-Bellevue, et Senneville
Richard Legault, Président, Conseil d'administration
Suzanne Turmel, Directrice générale
sturmel@ssss.gouv.qc.ca

Montréal: CSSS de la Montagne
Affiliée à: Agence de la santé et des services sociaux de Montréal
#314, 5700, ch de la Côte-des-Neiges, Montréal, QC H3T 2A8
Tél: 514-731-1386
www.csssdelamontagne.qc.ca
Note: Les Installations (Services de CH, CHSLD, et CLSC): CLSC de Côte-des-Neiges, Montréal (514-731-8531); CLSC de Côte-des-Neiges, Point de service Outremont; CLSC Métro (514-934-0354); CLSC de Parc-Extension (514-273-9591); Maison de naissance Côte-des-Neiges (514-736-2323); Programme régional d'accueil et d'intégration des demandeurs d'asile (PRAIDA).
Le Territoire desservi: Le quartier Côte-des-Neiges de l'arrondissement Côte-des-Neiges / Notre-Dame-de-Grâce; L'arrondissement Outremont; Le quartier Parc-Extension de l'arrondissement Villeray-Saint-Michel-Parc-Extension; Le district Peter-McGill de l'arrondissement Ville-Marie; Une partie de l'arrondissement Plateau Mont-Royal; Les villes de Mont-Royal et Westmount
Denis Sirois, Président, Conseil d'administration
Marc Sougavinski, Directeur général
Marc.Sougavinski.cdn@ssss.gouv.qc.ca

Montréal: CSSS de la Pointe-de-l'Ile
Affiliée à: Agence de la santé et des services sociaux de Montréal
9503, rue Sherbrooke est, Montréal, QC H1L 6P2
Tél: 514-356-2572
www.cssspointe.ca
Population desservi: 191 980
Note: Les Installations (Services de CH, CHSLD, et CLSC): Centre d'hébergement Biermans (514-351-9891); Centre d'hébergement François-Séguenot (514-642-4050); Centre d'hébergement Judith-Jasmin (514-354-5990); Centre d'hébergement Pierre-Joseph-Triest (514-353-1227); CLSC de Mercier-Est-Anjou (514-356-2572); CLSC de Pointe-aux-Trembles-Montréal-Est (514-642-4050); CLSC de Rivière-des-Prairies (514-494-4924); Manoir Claudette Barré (514-351-0200); Ressource intermédiaire Claudette Barré (514-351-0200); Ressource intermédiaire Limoges (514-852-3898)
Cécile Légaré, Présidente, Conseil d'administration
Andre Gagnière, Directeur général
andre.gagniere.pdi@ssss.gouv.qc.ca

Montréal: CSSS de Saint-Léonard et Saint-Michel
Affiliée à: Agence de la santé et des services sociaux de Montréal
Centre administratif, 3130, rue Jarry est, Montréal, QC H1Z 4N8
Tél: 514-593-7400
communication.slsm@ssss.gouv.qc.ca
www.csss-stleonardstmichel.qc.ca
Région desservi: La partie centre-est de l'île de Montréal, QC
Note: Les Installations (Services de CH, CHSLD, et CLSC): Centre d'hébergement des Quatre-Temps (514-722-3000); Centre d'hébergement des Quatre-Saisons (514-722-3000); Centre d'hébergement de Saint-Michel (514-722-3000); CLSC de Saint-Léonard (514-722-3000); CLSC de Saint-Michel (514-722-3000)
Mario Discepola, Président, Conseil d'administration
Suzanne Hébert, Directrice générale
514-722-3000, suzanne.hebert.stmi@ssss.gouv.qc.ca
Suzanne Boivin, Directrice ressources humaines
Aline Bourgon, Directrice des soins infimiers et de la qualité
Francine Corbin, Directrice des services financiers, techniques, et informationnels
Mario Gagnon, Directeur famille-enfance-jeunesse, et santé publique
Dr. Christian Lauriston, Directeur des services professionnels
Catherine Leblanc, Directrice, des services aux personnes en perte d'autonomie
Michel Levesque, Directeur de l'hébergement

Montréal: CSSS du Coeur-de-l'Ile
Affiliée à: Agence de la santé et des services sociaux de Montréal
1385, rue Jean-Talon est, Montréal, QC H2E 1S6
Tél: 514-495-6754
www.cssscoeurdelile.ca
Région desservi: Les quartiers de Villeray et de La Petite-Patrie, QC
Note: Les Installations (Services de CH, CHSLD, et CLSC): Hôpital Jean-Talon (514-495-6767); Centre d'hébergement Auclair (514-272-3011); Centre d'hébergement Paul-Gouin (514-273-3681); CLSC de La Petite-Patrie (514-273-4508); CLSC de Villeray (514-376-4141); Clinique externe de psychiatrie (514-729-3036); Pavillon Dorion (514-495-6767)
Jean-Paul Cadieux, Président, Conseil d'administration
Sonia Bélanger, Directrice générale et secrétaire
sonia.belanger.cdi@ssss.gouv.qc.ca
Nicole Clouâtre, Directrice générale adjointe
Manon Charpentier, Directrice, des services aux personnes en perte d'autonomie
Roger Chénard, Directeur des services techniques
Dr. Georges Dadour, Directeur des services professionnels
Josée Filion, Directrice des services de santé physique
Mario Jarquin, Directeur des services aux clientèles spécifiques
Julie Lapointe, Directrice des services généraux

Suzanne Lavallée, Directrice de la qualité, et de la planification stratégique
Claudette Lessard, Directrice des ressources financières, et des technologies de l'information
Rolande Marquès, Directrice des ressources humaines, et du développement organisationnel
Liza O'Doherty, Directrice des soins infirmiers
Paul C. Veilleux, Directeur des services multidisciplinaires, et de la santé publique

Montréal: CSSS du Sud-Ouest-Verdun
Affiliée à: Agence de la santé et des services sociaux de Montréal
Centre administratif et direction générale, 6161, rue Laurendeau, Montréal, QC H4E 3X6
Tél: 514-762-2777
www.sov.qc.ca
Nombre de lits: 209 lits d'hospitalisation en courte durée; 1280 lits d'hébergement de longue durée
Région desservi: la partie sud-ouest de l'île de Montréal*Population desservi:* 139 655*Personnel:* 3 810
Note: Les Installations (Services de CH, CHSLD, et CLSC): Hôpital de Verdun (514-362-1000); CLSC de Saint-Henri (514-933-7541); CLSC de Verdun (514-766-0546); CLSC de Ville-Émard-Côte-Saint-Paul (514-766-0546); Centre d'hébergement Champlain (514-766-8513); Centre d'hébergement de Saint-Henri (514-931-0851); Centre d'hébergement des Seigneurs (514-935-4681); Centre d'hébergement du Manoir-de-Verdun (514-769-8801); Centre d'hébergement Louis-Riel (514-931-2263); Centre d'hébergement Réal-Morel (514-761-5874); Centre d'hébergement Yvon-Brunet (514-765-8000)
Lorraine Duchesne-Noiseux, Présidente, Conseil d'administration
Danielle McCann, Directrice générale
514-766-0546, danielle.mccann@ssss.gouv.qc.ca

Montréal: CSSS Jeanne-Mance
Affiliée à: Agence de la santé et des services sociaux de Montréal
4625, av de Lorimier, Montréal, QC H2H 2B4
Tél: 514-842-7180 *Téléc:* 514-380-5152
www.csssjeannemance.ca
Population desservi: 138 490
Note: Les Installations (Services de CH, CHSLD, et CLSC): Centre d'hébergement Armand-Lavergne; Centre d'hébergement Bruchési; Centre d'hébergement du Centre-Ville-de-Montréal; Centre d'hébergement du Manoir-de-l'Age-d'Or; Centre d'hébergement Émilie-Gamelin; Centre d'hébergement Ernest-Routhier; Centre d'hébergement Jean-De La Lande; CLSC des Faubourgs - Parthenais (514-527-2361); CLSC des Faubourgs - Sanguinet (514-527-2361); CLSC des Faubourgs - Visitation (514-527-2361); CLSC du Plateau-Mont-Royal (514-521-7663); CLSC Saint-Louis-du-Parc (514-286-9657). Le Territoire desservi: Les quartiers de voisinage Saint-Louis, Mile End, Plateau-Est, et Plateau-Ouest, situés dans l'arrondissement Plateau-Mont-Royal; Sainte-Marie, Saint-Jacques, Faubourg Saint-Laurent, et Vieux-Montréal, situés dans l'arrondissement Ville-Marie
Ron Rayside, Président, Conseil d'administration
Sylvie Simard, Directrice générale et secrétaire
514-525-1900, sylvie.simard@ssss.gouv.qc.ca

Montréal: CSSS Lucille-Teasdale
Affiliée à: Agence de la santé et des services sociaux de Montréal
3095, rue Sherbrooke est, Montréal, QC H1W 1B2
Tél: 514-523-1173
www.cssslucilleteasdale.qc.ca
Région desservi: Les quartiers Hochelaga-Maisonneuve, Mercier-Ouest, et Rosemont
Note: Les Installations (Services de CH, CHSLD, et CLSC): Centre d'hébergement Éloria-Lepage (514-252-1710); Centre d'hébergement Jeanne-Le Ber (514-251-6000); Centre d'hébergement J.-Henri-Charbonneau (514-523-1173); Centre d'hébergement de la Maison-Neuve (514-527-2161); Centre d'hébergement Marie-Rollet (514-729-5281); Centre d'hébergement Robert-Cliche (514-374-8660); Centre d'hébergement Rousselot (514-254-9421); CLSC de Hochelaga-Maisonneuve (514-253-2181); CLSC Olivier-Guimond (514-255-2365); CLSC de Rosemont (514-524-3541); Centre de crise de l'entremise (Un service public d'intervention de crise psychosociale pour l'Est de Montréal, 514-351-9592)
Lise Tremblay, Présidente, Conseil d'administration
Daniel Corbeil, Directeur général,
Daniel.Corbeil.lteas@ssss.gouv.qc.ca
Danièle Bourque, Directrice des ressources humaines
Monique Chicoyne, Directrice de la performance, de la qualité de l'information
Guylaine Gendron, Directrice des ressources techniques
Dr. Hong Huy Duong, Directeur des services professionnels
France Mailhot, Directrice, des services aux personnes en perte d'autonomie
Marguerite Paiement, Directrice des services de première ligne, et santé publique
Lina Vachon, Directrice des soins infirmiers, des risques et de la qualité

Nicolet: CSSS de Bécancour - Nicolet-Yamaska (CSSSBNY)
Affiliée à: Agence de la santé et des services sociaux de la Mauricie et du Centre-du-Québec
Centre administratif, Centre Christ-Roi, 675, rue St-Jean-Baptiste, Nicolet, QC J3T 1S4
Tél: 819-293-2071 *Téléc:* 819-293-6160
Ligne sans frais: 1-800-263-2572
www.csssbny.qc.ca
Note: Les Installations (Services de CH, CHSLD, et CLSC): Centre Christ-Roi (819-293-2071); Centre Filles de la Sagesse (819-293-8337); Centre Fortierville (819-287-4442); Centre d'hébergement Deschaillons (819-292-2262); Centre d'hébergement Fortierville (819-287-4686); Centre d'hébergement Lucien-Shooner (450-568-2712); Centre d'hébergement Romain-Becquet (819-263-2245); Centre d'hébergement Saint-Célestin (819-229-3617); Point de service Gentilly (819-298-2144); Point de service Saint-Grégoire (819-233-2719); Point de service Saint-Léonard-d'Aston (819-399-3666)
Hervé Dionne, Président, Conseil d'administration
Danielle Gamelin, Directrice générale
Danielle_Gamelin@ssss.gouv.qc.ca
Claudette Boutin, Directrice des services à la communauté, et multidisciplinaires
Marie-Claude Brunelle, Directrice des soins infirmiers
Francine Courchesne, Directrice de la santé physique, et des services diagnostiques
Yves Forcier, Directeur des ressources humaines
Evelyne Pagé, Directrice, des services aux personnes en perte d'autonomie
Guylaine Provencher, Directrice des services financiers, techniques et informationnels
Dominique Tardif, Directeur des services professionnels

Notre-Dame-du-Lac: CSSS de Témiscouata
Affiliée à: Agence de la santé et des services sociaux du Bas-St-Laurent
58, rue de l'Église, Notre-Dame-du-Lac, QC G0L 1X0
Tél: 418-899-6751
www.cssstemiscouata.com
Note: Les Installations (Services de CH, CHSLD, et CLSC): Hôpital de Notre-Dame-du-Lac; CLSC de Cabano; CLSC de Dégelis; CLSC de Lac-des-Aigles; CLSC de Pohénégamook; Clinique médicale de Squatec; Centre d'hébergement Squatec; Centre d'hébergement St-Louis; Centre d'hébergement Rivière-Bleue; La Maison du Lac; La Villa Saint-Louis; Résidence Dégelico; Les Habitations Jules Edouard; R.I. Véronique Lavoie; Le Manoir de l'Érable Argenté
Guy Raymond, Président, Conseil d'administration
Thérèse Viel, Directrice générale
Richard Déry, Directeur des services professionnels et hospitaliers
Gaston Madore, Directeur des services financiers, techniques, informationnels
Josée Soucy, Directrice des ressources humaines

Ormstown: CSSS du Haut-Saint-Laurent (CSSSHSL)
Affiliée à: Agence de la santé et des services sociaux de la Montérégie
28, rue Gale, Ormstown, QC J0S 1K0
Tél: 450-829-2321
dotation_cssshsl@rrsss16.gouv.qc.ca (ressources humaines)
www.santemonteregie.qc.ca/haut-saint-laurent
Nombre de lits: 125 lits (longue durée); 49 lits (courte durée); 9 lits (hébergement temporaire)
Population desservi: 25 200*Personnel:* 500
Note: Les Installations (Services de CH, CHSLD, et CLSC): Hôpital Barrie Memorial (450-829-2321); Centre d'hébergement d'Ormstown (450-829-2321); Centre d'hébergement du comté de Huntingdon (450-829-2321); CLSC Huntingdon (450-829-2321); Point de service du CLSC Huntingdon (450-829-2321).
Le Territoire desservi: La MRC du Haut Saint-Laurent (Dundee, Elgin, Franklin, Godmanchester, Havelock, Hinchinbrooke, Howick, Huntingdon, Ormstown, Saint-Anicet, Saint-Chrysostome, Sainte-Barbe, Très-Saint-Sacrement)
Milton Reddick, Président, Conseil d'administration
Sophie Doucet, Directrice général
Sophie.doucet@rrsss16.gouv.qc.ca
Pierre Dubois, Conseiller aux communications, et aux relations avec la communauté
pierre_dubois@rrsss16.gouv.qc.ca

Port-Cartier: CSSS de Port-Cartier
Affiliée à: Agence de la santé et des services sociaux de la Côte-Nord
3, rue de Shelter Bay, Port-Cartier, QC G5B 2W9
Tél: 418-766-2572 *Téléc:* 418-766-5229
info.portcartier@ssss.gouv.qc.ca
www.csssportcartier.ca
Population desservi: 8 000*Personnel:* 160
Clermont Tremblay, Président, Conseil d'administration
Daniel Camiré, Directeur général
Daniel_Camire@ssss.gouv.qc.ca
Sylvie Dugas, Directrice des services communautaires
Francine Girard, Directrice des soins et milieu de vie
Nadine Lapierre, Directrice réseau des ressources humaines, et développement organisationnel
Nathalie Minville, Directrice réseau des finances

Québec: CSSS de la Vieille-Capitale
Affiliée à: Agence de la santé et des services sociaux de la Capitale-Nationale
1, av du Sacré-Coeur, Québec, QC G1N 2W1
Tél: 418-529-4777
www.csssvc.qc.ca
Fondée en: 2004
Population desservi: 290 000*Personnel:* 3 500
Note: Les Installations (Services de CH, CHSLD, et CLSC): CLSC de Cap-Rouge-Saint-Augustin; CLSC de la Basse-Ville; CLSC de la Haute-Ville; CLSC de la Haute-Ville, édifice Courchesne; CLSC de Limoilou; CLSC de L'Ancienne-Lorette; CLSC de Sainte-Foy-Sillery; CLSC de Sainte-Foy-Sillery, Pavillon Marguerite-D'Youville; CLSC des Rivières; Centre d'hébergement Christ-Roi; Centre d'hébergement de Limoilou; Centre d'hébergement Hôpital général de Québec; Centre d'hébergement Le Faubourg; Centre d'hébergement Louis-Hébert; Centre d'hébergement Notre-Dame-de-Lourdes; Centre d'hébergement Sacré-Cour; Centre d'hébergement Saint-Antoine; Unité de médecine familiale de la Haute-Ville; Unité de médecine familiale Laurier; Unité de médecine familiale Laval; Unité de médecine familiale Saint-François d'Assise
Jean-Marie Bélanger, Président, Conseil d'administration
Hugues Matte, Directeur général
hugues.matte@csssvc.qc.ca
Pierre Fortin, Directeur général adjoint, des affaires administratives et de la qualité
Dr. Alain-Philippe Lemieux, Directeur général adjoint des affaires universitaires, et cliniques, et des services professionnels
Marie-Claude Alain, Directrice de la santé mentale, de l'enfance et de la jeunesse
Céline Allard, Directrice du soutien à domicile
Robert Gagné, Directeur de l'hébergement
Agnès Gaudreault, Directrice des soins infirmiers
France Goudreault, DDirectrice des ressources humaines
Marlène Imbeault, Directrice des services de santé généraux
Dr. Bernard Jean, Directeur de l'enseignement médical; directeur adjoint, services professionnels
Jean Lapointe, Directeur des services techniques, des ressources, et du développement durable

Québec: CSSS Québec-Nord
Affiliée à: Agence de la santé et des services sociaux de la Capitale-Nationale
Centre administratif, 2915, av du Bourg-Royal, 4e étage, Québec, QC G1C 3S2
Tél: 418-661-5666
www.csssqn.qc.ca
Fondée en: 2004
Personnel: 3,000
Note: Les Installations (Services de CH, CHSLD, et CLSC): Hôpital Ste-Anne-de-Beaupré; Hôpital Chauveau; Centre d'hébergement du Fargy; Centre d'hébergement Saint-Augustin; Centre d'hébergement Yvonne-Sylvain; Centre d'hébergement Roy-Rousseau; Centre d'hébergement Charlesbourg; Centre d'hébergement Alphonse-Bonenfant; Centre d'hébergement Loretteville; CLSC de la Jacques-Cartier (Loretteville, Sainte-Catherine-de-la-Jacques-Cartier); CLSC La Source Sud; CLSC La Source Nord; CLSC La Source La Maisonnée; CLSC Orléans (Beauport, Ile d'Orléans, Beaupré, Maizerets, Montmorency); Unité de médicine familiale
Claude Vanasse, Président, Conseil d'administration
Lucie Lacroix, Directrice générale
418-780-0738, lucie.Lacroix@ssss.gouv.qc.ca

Rimouski: CSSS de Rimouski-Neigette
Affiliée à: Agence de la santé et des services sociaux du Bas-St-Laurent
Hôpital régional - Rimouski, 150, av Rouleau, Rimouski, QC G5L 5T1
Tél: 418-724-3000 *Téléc:* 418-724-8632
www.chrr.qc.ca
Média social: www.facebook.com/pages/CSSS-de-Rimouski-Neigette/185128391529883; twitter.com/CSSS_Rimouski_N

Personnel: 2 200
Note: Les Installations (Services de CH, CHSLD, et CLSC): L'Hôpital régional - Rimouski; Le CLSC - Rimouski (Saint-Fabien, Saint-Marcellin, Saint-Narcisse); Le Centre d'hébergement - Rimouski
Martin Boucher, Président, Conseil d'administration
Michel Beaulieu, Directeur général
418-723-7851

***Rivière-du-Loup:* CSSS de Rivière-du-Loup**
Affiliée à: Agence de la santé et des services sociaux du Bas-St-Laurent
Le Centre hospitalier régional de Grand-Portage, 75, rue St-Henri, Rivière-du-Loup, QC G5R 2A4
Tél: 418-868-1010
www.csssrivieredulоup.qc.ca

Note: Les Installations (Services de CH, CHSLD, et CLSC): Centre hospitalier régional de Grand-Portage ((CHRGP); Centre d'hébergement Saint-Joseph; Centre d'hébergement Saint-Antonin; Centre d'hébergement St-Cyprien; CLSC Rivière et Marées; L'Estran Centre de réadaptation en alcoolisme et toxicomanie du Bas-Saint-Laurent
Doris Laliberté-Kirouac, Présidente, Conseil d'administration
Daniel Lévesque, Directeur général et secrétaire

***Roberval:* CSSS Domaine-du-Roy**
Affiliée à: Agence de la santé et des services sociaux du Saguenay-Lac-Saint-Jean
Édifice Hôtel-Dieu de Roberval, 450, rue Brassard, Roberval, QC G8H 1B9
Tél: 418-275-0110 *Téléc:* 418-275-6202
www.csssdomaineduroy.com

Note: Les Installations (Services de CH, CHSLD, et CLSC): Hôtel-Dieu de Roberval; Centre d'hébergement Roberval; Centre d'hébergement Saint-Félicien; CLSC Saint-Félicien; CLSC Roberval; Mission de Centre de réadaptation en alcoolisme et autres toxicomanies (CRAT); Centre de réadaptation pour alcooliques et autres toxicomanes Saint-Antoine
France Guay, Présidente, Conseil d'administration
Jacques Dubois, Directeur général
jacques.dubois@ssss.gouv.qc.ca
Édith Simard, Directrice générale adjointe; Directrice, Communications
Marika Bordes, Directrice des programmes, Famille-Enfance-Jeunesse, et Santé mentale et dépendances
Dre Suzanne Gagné, Directrice des services professionnels
Valérie Gagnon, Directrice des ressources humaines, et du développement organisationnel
Jean-Claude Lavoie, Directeur des ressources financières, informationnelles et techniques
Julie Lavoie, Directrice des programmes santé physique, services généraux et diagnostiques
Line Marois, Directrice des programmes, Perte d'autonomie liée, au vieillissement et déficiences

***Rouyn-Noranda:* CSSS de Rouyn-Noranda (CSSSRN)**
Affiliée à: Agence de la santé et des services sociaux de l'Abitibi-Témiscamingue
4, 9e rue, Rouyn-Noranda, QC J9X 2B2
Tél: 819-764-5858
www.csssrn.qc.ca
Fondée en: 2004
Population desservi: 39 615*Personnel:* 1 200
Note: Les Installations (Services de CH, CHSLD, et CLSC): Hôpital, Rouyn-Noranda (819-764-5131); Centre d'hébergement, Rouyn-Noranda (819-762-0908); CLSC, Rouyn-Noranda (819-762-8144) (Beaudry-Cloutier, Cadillac, Cléricy-Mont-Brun, Montbeillard-Rollet, Destor)
Luc Blanchette, Président, Conseil d'administration
Huguette Lemay, Directrice générale
huguette_lemay@ssss.gouv.qc.ca

***Saint-Charles-Borromée:* CSSS du Nord de Lanaudière**
Affiliée à: Agence de la santé et des services sociaux de Lanaudière
#5D18, 1000, boul Sainte-Anne, Saint-Charles-Borromée, QC J6E 6J2
Tél: 450-759-8222
www.cssnl.qc.ca
Région desservi: MRC de D'Autray, de Joliette, de Matawinie, et de Montcalm*Population desservi:* 200 000*Personnel:* 4 300
Note: Les Installations (Services de CH, CHSLD, et CLSC): Centre hospitalier régional De Lanaudière; Centre d'hébergement Alphonse-Rondeau; Centre d'hébergement Desy; Centre d'hébergement Sainte-Élisabeth; Centre d'hébergement Parphilia-Ferland; Centre d'hébergement Saint-Eusèbe; Centre d'hébergement du Piedmont; Centre d'hébergement Saint-Donat; Centre d'hébergement Brassard; Centre d'hébergement Saint-Antoine de Padoue; Centre d'hébergement Saint-Jacques; Centre d'hébergement Saint-Liguori; CLSC de Berthier; CLSC de Lavaltrie; CLSC de Saint-Gabriel; CLSC de Joliette; CLSC de Chertsey; CLSC de Saint-Jean-de-Matha; CLSC de Saint-Donat; CLSC de Saint-Michel-des-Saints; CLSC de Saint-Esprit; Centre de réadaptation en dépendances Le Tremplin de Saint-Charles-Borromée; Centre de réadaptation en dépendances Le Tremplin de Repentigny; Centre de réadaptation en dépendances Le Tremplin de Terrebonne; Services externes psychiatriques intégrés pour adultes de Rawdon; Services psychiatriques pour enfants et adolescents; Unité de médecine familiale du Nord de Lanaudière.
Nombre de médecins, dentistes, et de pharmaciens: 350
Nadine Boire, Présidente, Conseil d'administration
Marie Beauchamp, Directrice générale
Marie.Beauchamp@ssss.gouv.qc.ca
Anne-Marie Blanchard, Directrice administrative des programmes santé mentale, famille-enfance-jeunesse, déficience intellectuelle
Hélène Boisvert, Directrice administrative des programmes, perte d'autonomie liée au vieillissement
Hélène Brien, Directrice administrative des programmes, services généraux, santé publique
Pascale Gagné, Directrice des ressources financières, et approvisionnements
Robin Gagnon, Directeur administratif, des programmes de santé physique
Dre Line Duchesne, Directrice des services professionnels, et des affaires médicales
Martin Labrie, Directeur de la prestation sécuritaire des soins, et services et des soins infirmiers
Dre Élise Martel, Directrice de l'enseignement médical
Olivier Malo, Directeur des ressources humaines
Jean-Claude Préville, Directeur des services techniques et hôteliers
Jean-Yves Tremblay, Directeur des services multidisciplinaires
Pierre Tremblay, Directeur des ressources informationnelles

***Saint-Eustache:* CSSS du Lac-des-Deux-Montagnes**
Affiliée à: Agence de la santé et des services sociaux des Laurentides
Direction générale, 520, boul Arthur-Sauvé, Saint-Eustache, QC J7R 5B1
Tél: 450-473-6811 *Téléc:* 450-473-6966
Ligne sans frais: 1-888-234-3837
www.moncsss.com
Média social:
www.facebook.com/group.php?gid=142242479159314;
twitter.com/CSSS2Montagnes

Fondée en: 2004
Personnel: 2 550
Note: Les Installations (Services de CH, CHSLD, et CLSC): Hôpital de Saint-Eustache (450-473-6811); Centre d'hébergement de Saint-Eustache (450-472-0013); Centre d'hébergement de Saint-Benoît (450-258-2481); CLSC Jean-Olivier-Chénier (450-491-1233); CLSC Mirabel (450-475-7938); Clinique externe de psychiatrie (450-473-1533
Antonio Lavigne, Président, Conseil d'administration
Roch Martel, Directeur général
roch.martel.hse@ssss.gouv.qc.ca

***Saint-Hyacinthe:* CSSS Richelieu-Yamaska**
Affiliée à: Agence de la santé et des services sociaux de la Montérégie
2750, boul Laframboise, Saint-Hyacinthe, QC J2S 4Y8
Tél: 450-771-3333
www.santemonteregie.qc.ca/richelieu-yamaska
Population desservi: 200 000*Personnel:* 3 572
Note: Les Installations (Services de CH, CHSLD, et CLSC): Hôpital Honoré-Mercier (450-771-3333); Centre d'hébergement Andrée-Perrault (450-771-4536); Centre d'hébergement de la MRC-d'Acton (450-546-3234); Centre d'hébergement de l'Hôtel-Dieu-de-Saint-Hyacinthe (450-771-3333); Centre d'hébergement de Montarville (450-461-2650); Centre d'hébergement Marguerite-Adam (450-467-1631); CLSC de la MRC-d'Acton (450-546-2572); CLSC des Maskoutains (450-778-2572); CLSC des Maskoutains - Point de service Aux Quatre-vents (450-778-2572); CLSC des Maskoutains - Point de service Centre-ville (450-778-2572); CLSC des Patriotes (450-536-2572); CLSC des Patriotes - Point de service Saint-Bruno (450-461-1012); Accueil du Rivage inc. (450-787-3436); Centre d'hébergement Champlain des Pommetiers (450-464-7666); Unité de médecine familiale Richelieu-Yamaska, Saint-Hyacinthe (450-771-3333).
Nombre de médecins, dentistes, et de pharmaciens: 203.
Le Territoire desservi: La MRC de la Vallée-du-Richelieu, la MRC des Maskoutains et la MRC d'Acton (37 municipalités)
Jean Lemonde, Président, Conseil d'administration
Réjeanne Boudreau, Directrice générale
Richard Bois, Directeur des ressources informationnelles, et des technologies biomédicales
Suzanne Boivin, Directrice du programme santé physique
Claude Dallaire, Directeur des communications et des relations publiques
Maryse Hébert, Directrice des programmes de santé mentale, famille-enfance-jeunesse
Normand Kingsley, Directeur des affaires médicales
Lise Langlois, Directrice des services ambulatoires, et de première ligne
Vicky Lavoie, Directrice des ressources humaines
France Leblond, Directrice des services d'hôtellerie, et de nutrition clinique
Marie-Christine Paradis, Directrice des ressources financières
Yolaine Rioux, Directrice des programmes de santé publique, des soins infirmiers
Chantal Savard, Directrice du programme hébergement-milieu de vie
Hélène St-Jacques, Directrice des ressources techniques

***Saint-Jean-sur-Richelieu:* CSSS Haut-Richelieu-Rouville**
Affiliée à: Agence de la santé et des services sociaux de la Montérégie
978, boul du Séminaire nord, Saint-Jean-sur-Richelieu, QC J3A 1E5
Tél: 450-358-2572
www.santemonteregie.qc.ca/haut-richelieu-rouville
Fondée en: 2004
Population desservi: 181 000*Personnel:* 3 500
Note: Les Installations (Services de CH, CHSLD, et CLSC): Hôpital du Haut-Richelieu, Saint-Jean-sur-Richelieu (450-359-5000); Centre d'hébergement Champagnat, Saint-Jean-sur-Richelieu (450-347-3769); Centre d'hébergement Georges-Phaneuf, Saint-Jean-sur-Richelieu (450-346-1133); Centre d'hébergement Gertrude-Lafrance, Saint-Jean-sur-Richelieu (450-359-5555); Centre d'hébergement Sainte-Croix, Marieville (450-460-4475); Centre d'hébergement Saint-Joseph, Chambly (450-658-6271); Centre d'hébergement Val-Joli, Saint-Césaire (450-469-3194); CLSC de Henryville (450-299-2828); CLSC de la Vallée-des-Forts, Saint-Jean-sur-Richelieu (450-358-2572); CLSC de Saint-Césaire (450-469-0269); CLSC du Richelieu (450-658-7561); Manoir Soleil, Chambly (450-658-4441); Clinique jeunesse 12-21 ans, Saint-Jean-sur-Richelieu (450-358-2572); Clinique jeunesse du Bassin de Chambly 12-24 ans, Chambly (450-658-2016); Point de chute de Lacolle (450-299-2828); Services de consultation externe - psychiatrie, réadaptation pédiatrique, clinique d'évaluation TED (450-346-2222).
Médecins: 300.
Le Territoire desservi: MRC de Rouville, MRC du Haut-Richelieu et MRC de la Vallée-du-Richelieu (21 municipalités)
Robert Blanchard, Président, Conseil d'administration
Christine Lessard, Directrice générale
christine.lessard@rrsss16.gouv.qc.ca

***Saint-Pascal:* CSSS de Kamouraska**
Affiliée à: Agence de la santé et des services sociaux du Bas-Saint-Laurent
575, rue Martin, Saint-Pascal, QC G0L 3Y0
Tél: 418-856-7000 *Téléc:* 418-492-1793
Personnel: 619
Note: Les Installations (Services de CH, CHSLD, et CLSC): Hôpital Notre-Dame-de-Fatima (49 lits); Centre d'hébergement D'Anjou, Saint-Pacôme (53 lits); Centre d'hébergement Thérèse-Martin, Rivière-Ouelle (46 lits); Centre d'hébergement Villa Maria, Saint-Alexandre (52 lits); CLSC, Saint-Pascal; CLSC, La Pocatière; CLSC, Saint-André
Jean Desjardins, Président, Conseil d'administration
Gilles Tremblay, Directeur général

***Saint-Tite:* CSSS de la Vallée-de-la-Batiscan**
Affiliée à: Agence de la santé et des services sociaux de la Mauricie et du Centre-du-Québec
Centre administratif, CP 430, 750, rue du Couvent, Saint-Tite, QC G0X 3H0
Tél: 418-365-7555 *Téléc:* 418-365-6009

Note: Les Installations (Services de CH, CHSLD, et CLSC): Centre d'hébergement et CLSC de Saint-Narcisse; Centre d'hébergement et CLSC de Sainte-Thècle; Centre d'hébergement et CLSC de Sainte-Anne-de-la-Pérade; Centre d'hébergement et CLSC Mgr Paquin; CLSC Sainte-Geneviève-de-Batiscan
Gilles Maurais, Président, Conseil d'administration
Alain Corriveau, Directeur général

***Sainte-Adèle:* CSSS des Pays-d'en-Haut (CSSSPDH)**
Affiliée à: Agence de la santé et des services sociaux des Laurentides
707, boul de Sainte-Adèle, Sainte-Adèle, QC J8B 2N1
Tél: 450-229-6601 *Téléc:* 450-229-8513
Ligne sans frais: 1-800-363-2520
www.cssspdh.net
Région desservi: MRC des Pays-d'en-Haut (10 municipalités)
Note: Les Installations (Services de CH, CHSLD, et CLSC): Centre d'hébergement des Hauteurs (450-229-6601); Point de service de Saint-Sauveur, famille, enfance, jeunesse (450-227-3447); Point de service de Piedmont (450-227-1571); Établissement de détention de Saint-Jérôme
Louise Caron-Gareau, Présidente, Conseil d'administration
Sylvie Laganière, Directrice générale
sylvie_laganière@ssss.gouv.qc.ca
Christine De Sève, Directrice des ressources humaines, et du service de la paie
Steve Desjardins, Directeur de la qualité des soins et services, et des ressources informationnelles
Maryse Janelle, Directrice programmes, perte d'autonomie liée au vieillissement
Lucie Lalande, Directrice enfance-jeunesse-famille, adultes, santé publique, santé mentales, dépendances
Marie-Paule Mongeau, Directrice des ressources financières et matérielles
Dr. Chantal Valois, Directrice des services professionnels

***Sainte-Agathe-des-Monts:* CSSS des Sommets**
Affiliée à: Agence de la santé et des services sociaux des Laurentides
Pavillon administratif Jacques-Duquette, 234, rue Saint-Vincent, Sainte-Agathe-des-Monts, QC J8C 2B8
Tél: 819-324-4007
recrutement.sommets@ssss.gouv.qc.ca (ressources humaines)
www.csss-sommets.com
Média social: www.csss-sommets.com/fr/71/Videos.html
Nombre de lits: 217 lits de longue durée; 104 lits de courte durée
Région desservi: MRC des Laurentides et des environs*Personnel:* 1 500
Note: Les Installations (Services de CH, CHSLD, et CLSC): Hôpital Laurentien (819-324-4000); Pavillon Philippe-Lapointe (819-324-4000); Centre d'hébergement de Mont-Tremblant (819-425-2793); Centre d'hébergement de Labelle (819-686-2372); CLSC de Sainte-Agathe-des-Monts (819-326-3111); CLSC de Mont-Tremblant (819-425-3771); CLSC de Labelle (819-686-2117)
Jacques Morin, Président, Conseil d'administration
Yves Lachapelle, Directeur général
Alain Paquette, Directeur des communications, et des relations avec la communauté
819-324-4088

***Sainte-Thérèse:* CSSS de Thérèse-De Blainville**
Affiliée à: Agence de la santé et des services sociaux des Laurentides
55, rue Saint-Joseph, Sainte-Thérèse, QC J7E 4Y5
Tél: 450-430-4553
www.csssthereseDeblainville.qc.ca
Nombre de lits: 344 lits (hébergement et soins de longue durée); 20 lits (réadaptation fonctionnelle intensive); 13 lits (hébergement temporaire)
Région desservi: MRC de Thérèse-De Blainville (7 municipalités)*Population desservi:* 155 000
Note: Les Installations (Services de CH, CHSLD, et CLSC): Centre d'hébergement Drapeau-Deschambault, Sainte-Thérèse; Centre d'hébergement Hubert-Maisonneuve, Rosemère; Centre de prélèvement, Sainte-Thérèse; Services médicaux, Sainte-Thérèse; Un point de chute, Sainte-Anne.
Médecins: 28
Robert Dean, Président, Conseil d'administration
Diane Filiatrault, Directrice générale et secrétaire

***Salaberry-de-Valleyfield:* CSSS du Suroît**
Affiliée à: Agence de la santé et des services sociaux de la Montérégie
150, rue Saint-Thomas, Salaberry-de-Valleyfield, QC J6T 6C1
Tél: 450-371-9920 *Ligne sans frais:* 1-800-694-9920
www.cssssuroit.qc.ca
Région desservi: Salaberry-de-Valleyfield; Beauharnois; Vaudreuil-Dorion
Note: Les Installations (Services de CH, CHSLD, et CLSC): Hôpital du Suroît (450-371-9920); Centre d'hébergement Cécile-Godin (450-429-6403); Centre d'hébergement Docteur-Aimé-Leduc (450-373-4818); CLSC de Beauharnois (450-429-6455); CLSC de Salaberry-de-Valleyfield (450-371-0143); Centre de jour pour adultes, Salaberry-de-Valleyfield (450-373-7321); Clinique externe pour adultes, Salaberry-de-Valleyfield (450-373-6252); Clinique externe pour jeunes, Salaberry-de-Valleyfield (450-373-5705); Clinique externe pour adultes, Vaudreuil-Dorion (450-455-7967); Clinique externe pour jeunes, Vaudreuil-Dorion (450-455-3356)
Nicole Marleau, Présidente, Conseil d'administration
François Rabeau, Directeur général
francois.rabeau@rrsss16.gouv.qc.ca
Danielle Dubois, Directrice générale adjointe
Lyne Daoust, Directrice réseau santé physique
Dre Line Duchesne, Directrice des affaires médicales
Michel Feugeas, Directeur des ressources informationnelles
Claudette Giguère, Directrice réseau personne en perte d'autonomie
Chantal Leduc, Directrice réseau santé mentale
Ginette Pariseault, Directrice réseau famille, services généraux, développement des communautés
Sophie Pouliot, Directrice des ressources humaines
Louise Roussel, Directrice des soins infirmiers
Daniel Sauvé, Directeur des ressources techniques
Daniel Trudeau, Directeur des ressources financières

***Sept-Iles:* CSSS de Sept-Iles (CSSSSI)**
Affiliée à: Agence de la santé et des services sociaux de la Côte-Nord
45, rue Père Divet, Sept-Iles, QC G4R 3N7
Tél: 418-962-9761 *Téléc:* 418-962-2701
www.cssssi.qc.ca
Région desservi: Sept-Iles; Port-Cartier; Minganie; Basse-Côte-Nord; Hématite*Population desservi:* 52 157*Personnel:* 950+
René Cummings, Président
Martin Beaumont, Directeur général

***Shawinigan:* CSSS de l'Énergie**
Affiliée à: Agence de la santé et des services sociaux de la Mauricie et du Centre-du-Québec
Centre administratif, 1705, av Georges, Shawinigan, QC G9N 2N1
Tél: 819-536-7500
info@cssse.qc.ca
www.etrehumain.ca
Note: Les Installations (Services de CH, CHSLD, et CLSC): Hôpital du Centre-de-la-Mauricie (819-536-7500); Centre d'hébergement Joseph-Garceau (819-537-5173); Centre d'hébergement Laflèche (819-533-2500); Centre d'hébergement Saint-Maurice (819-536-0071); CLSC du Centre-de-la-Mauricie (819-539-8371); CIC de Shawinigan (819-537-6647); Centre régional de santé mentale (819-536-7500)
Pierrette Jacob, Présidente, Conseil d'administration
Martine Rioux, Directrice générale
819-536-7501

***Sherbrooke:* CSSS Institut universitaire de gériatrie de Sherbrooke (CSSS IUG)**
Affiliée à: Agence de la santé et des services sociaux de l'Estrie
1036, rue Belvédère sud, Sherbrooke, QC J1H 4C4
Tél: 819-821-1150
www.csss-iugs.ca
Personnel: 2 735
Note: Les Installations (Services de CH, CHSLD, et CLSC): CLSC Sherbrooke (5 points de service); Centre d'hébergement St-Vincent; Centre d'hébergement St-Joseph; Hôpital et centre d'hébergement Argyll; Hôpital et centre d'hébergement D'Youville; Centre de maternité de l'Estrie.
Médecins et médecins spécialistes: 100
Carol Fillion, Directeur général
cfillion.csss-iugs@ssss.gouv.qc.ca
Diane Gingras, Présidente, Conseil d'administration

***Sorel-Tracy:* CSSS Pierre-De Saurel**
Affiliée à: Agence de la santé et des services sociaux de la Montérégie
400, av Hôtel-Dieu, Sorel-Tracy, QC J3P 1N5
Tél: 450-746-6062
www.santemonteregie.qc.ca/sorel-tracy
Fondée en: 2004
Population desservi: 50 910*Personnel:* 1 500
Note: Les Installations (Services de CH, CHSLD, et CLSC): Hôtel-Dieu de Sorel (450-746-6000); Centre d'hébergement Élisabeth-Lafrance (450-746-5555); Centre d'hébergement de Tracy (450-743-4924); Centre d'hébergement J.-Arsène-Parenteau (450-742-5936); CLSC Gaston-Bélanger (450-746-4545); Résidence Sorel-Tracy inc. (450-742-9428); Centre de jour, Sorel-Tracy (450-743-5569); Hôpital de jour, Sorel-Tracy (450-743-5569).
Le Territoire desservi: Massueville; Saint-Gérard-de-Majella; Saint-Roch-de-Richelieu; Saint-Aimé; Saint-Joseph-de-Sorel; Sorel-Tracy; Saint-David; Sainte-Anne-de-Sorel; Saint-Ours; Yamaska; Sainte-Victoire-de-Sorel; Saint-Robert
Lucie Rouillard-Pépin, Présidente, Conseil d'administration
Lise Chagnon, Directrice générale
lise.chagnon@rrsss16.gouv.qc.ca
Dr. Gérald Désaulniers, Directeur des services professionnels
Daniel Vincent, Responsable des communications
daniel.vincent@rrsss16.gouv.qc.ca

***St-Jérôme:* CSSS de Saint-Jérôme**
Affiliée à: Agence de la santé et des services sociaux des Laurentides
290, rue Montigny, St-Jérôme, QC J7Z 5T3
Tél: 450-432-2777 *Ligne sans frais:* 1-866-963-2777
www.cdsj.org
Nombre de lits: 405 lits de courte durée dont 85 en psychiatrie; 305 lits répartis en trois centres d'hébergement
Personnel: 3 200
Note: Les Installations (Services de CH, CHSLD, et CLSC): Hôpital régional de Saint-Jérôme (450-432-2777); Centre d'hébergement Youville (450-432-2777, poste 26761); Centre d'hébergement L'Auberge (450-432-2777, poste 23621); Centre d'hébergement Lucien-G.-Rolland (450-432-2777, poste 23221); CLSC de Saint-Jérôme, famille, enfance, jeunesse, services à la collectivité (450-432-2777, poste 25000); CLSC de Saint-Jérôme, soutien à domicile (450-432-2777, poste 26221); CLSC de Saint-Jérôme, santé mentale et services psychosociaux (450-432-2777, poste 26500); Clinique de développement (450-432-2777, poste 23600); Maison de naissance du Boisé (450-432-2777, poste 23660); Centre de prélèvements (450-432-2777, poste 22197).
Médecins: 350
Gaétam Ruel, Président, Conseil d'administration
François Therrien, Directeur général
Francois.Therrien@cdsj.org

***Ste-Anne-des-Monts:* CSSS de La Haute-Gaspésie**
Affiliée à: Agence de la santé et des services sociaux de la Gaspésie-Iles-de-la-Madeleine
Centre administratif, 50, rue du Belvédère, Ste-Anne-des-Monts, QC G4V 1X4
Tél: 418-763-2261
www.cssshautegaspesie.qc.ca
Personnel: 450
Note: Les Installations (Services de CH, CHSLD, et CLSC): Centre hospitalier (418-763-2261); CHSLD de Cap-Chat (418) 786-5523); CLSC de Sainte-Anne-des-Monts (418-763-7771); CLSC de Cap-Chat (418-786-5594); CLSC de Marsoui (418-288-5511); CLSC de Mont-Louis (418-797-2744); Centre de réadaptation (418-763-5000)
Diane Lever, Présidente, Conseil d'administration
Hélène Laprise, Directrice générale
Corinne Bouchard, Directrice des ressources financières, matérielles et informationnelles
Marie-Josée Chrétien, Directrice des soins infirmiers
Jean Faucon, Directeur du programme dépendance
jean.faucon.cssshg@ssss.gouv.qc.ca
Pierre Francoeur, Directeur des ressources humaines, et du développement organisationnel
Louise Landry, Directrice de la santé physique, et du soutien thérapeutique
louise.landry.cssshg@ssss.gouv.qc.ca
Marie-Sylvie Lapointe, Directrice des programmes sociaux, communautaires et santé mentale
Marjorie Pigeon, Directrice de la qualité, de la performance, et du projet clinique

***Terrebonne:* CSSS du Sud de Lanaudière**
Affiliée à: Agence de la santé et des services sociaux de Lanaudière
Centre administratif, 911, montée des Pionniers, Terrebonne, QC J6V 2H2
Tél: 450-654-7525 *Téléc:* 450-470-2640
Ligne sans frais: 1-888-654-7525
www.csss.sudlanaudiere.ca
Note: Les Installations (Services de CH, CHSLD, et CLSC): Hôpital Pierre-Le Gardeur; CLSC Lamater; CLSC Meilleur; Centres d'hébergement; Centre de jour L'Escale; Hôpital de jour de psychiatrie de la MRC Les Moulins; Hôpital de jour de psychiatrie de la MRC de L'Assomption; Clinique externe de psychiatrie de Charlemagne; SIME (Suivi Intensif dans le Milieu en Équipe); Clinique externe de psychiatrie de L'Assomption
Doris Gagné, Présidente, Conseil d'administration
Bernard Fortin, Directeur général
Bernard.Fortin@cssssl.ca
Audrey Bouchard, Directrice des soins infirmiers
Michel Cimon, Directeur des services professionnels, et affaires médicales
Richard Dépelteau, Directeur des ressources matérielles, et des services techniques
Louis Deschamps, Directeur des programmes et services de santé physique
Manon Desjardins, Directrice des programmes, et services de soutien à l'autonomie
Annie Du Mont, Directrice des ressources humaines

Ghislaine Gauthier, Directrice des programmes, et services de santé mentale adulte
Gilles Gougeon, Directeur des services financiers
Julie Vaillancourt, Directrice des programmes, et services enfance-jeunesse-famille

Thetford Mines: CSSS de la région de Thetford (CSSSRT)
Affiliée à: Agence de la santé et des services sociaux de Chaudière-Appalaches
Centre administratif, 1717, rue Notre-Dame est, Thetford Mines, QC G6G 2V4
Tél: 418-338-7755
csssrt@ssss.gouv.qc.ca
www.centresantethetford.ca
Fondée en: 2004
Nombre de lits: 330 lits (hébergement); 96 lits (soins de courte durée)
Région desservi: MRC des Appalaches (19 municipalités)*Population desservi:* 43 390*Personnel:* 1 383
Note: Les Installations (Services de CH, CHSLD, et CLSC): Hôpital de Thetford Mines (418-338-7777); Centre d'hébergement Denis-Marcotte (418-338-4556); Centre d'hébergement Saint-Alexandre (418-338-7777); Centre d'hébergement Marc-André-Jacques (418-427-2068); Centre d'hébergement Lac-Noir (418-423-7508); Centre d'hébergement René-Lavoie (418-449-2020); CLSC de Thetford Mines (418-338-3511); CLSC de Disraeli (418-449-3513); CLSC de East Broughton (418-427-2015); CLSC d'Adstock (418-422-2024).
Nombre de médecins et de pharmaciens: 68
Aline Visser Rahal, Présidente, Conseil d'administration
Martin Lord, Directeur général
martin.lord@ssss.gouv.qc.ca

Trois-Pistoles: CSSS des Basques
Affiliée à: Agence de la santé et des services sociaux du Bas-St-Laurent
550, rue Notre-Dame est, Trois-Pistoles, QC G0L 4K0
Tél: 418-851-1111
Recrutement@csssbasques.qc.ca (ressources humaines)
www.csssbasques.qc.ca
Roberto Dionne, Président, Conseil d'administration
Line Moisan, Directrice générale et secrétaire
Johanne Carignan, Commissaire locale aux plaintes, et à la qualité de l'établissement

Trois-Rivières: CSSS de Trois-Rivières
Affiliée à: Agence de la santé et des services sociaux de la Mauricie et du Centre-du-Québec
731, rue Sainte-Julie, Trois-Rivières, QC G9A 1Y1
Tél: 819-370-2214
www.cssstr.qc.ca
Note: Les Installations (Services de CH, CHSLD, et CLSC): Centre hospitalier affilié universitaire régional (819-697-3333); Centre Cloutier-du Rivage (819-370-2100); Centre St-Joseph (819-370-2100); Centre d'hébergement Cooke (819-370-2100); Centre d'hébergement Louis-Denoncourt (819-376-2566); Centre d'hébergement Roland-Leclerc (819-370-2100); Centre de services Les Forges (819-379-5650); Centre Ste-Geneviève (819-370-2200, poste 46101); Centre de l'Horloge (819-370-2100); Centre Arc-en-Ciel (pédopsychiatrie, 819-374-6291); Centre de prêt d'équipement (819-370-2100)
Charles Walker, Président, Conseil d'administration
Lucie Letendre, Directrice générale
lucie_letendre@ssss.gouv.qc.ca
Louise Lavigueur, Responsable de l'accès à l'information

Val-d'Or: CSSS de la Vallée-de-l'Or (CSSSVO)
Affiliée à: Agence de la santé et des services sociaux de l'Abitibi-Témiscamingue
725, 6e rue, Val-d'Or, QC J9P 3Y1
Tél: 819-825-6711
www.csssvo.qc.ca
Média social: www.facebook.com/group.php?gid=189290301107018
Fondée en: 2004
Nombre de lits: 88 lits (CH); 175 lits (CHSLD)
Population desservi: 43 000
Note: Les Installations (Services de CH, CHSLD, et CLSC): Hôpital de Val-d'Or (819-825-5858); Hôpital psychiatrique de Malartic (819-825-5858); Centre d'hébergement de Val-d'Or (819-825-5858); Centre d'hébergement Saint-Martin de Malartic (819-825-5858); CLSC de Val-d'Or (819-825-5858); CLSC de Senneterre (819-825-5858); CLSC de Malartic (819-825-5858); Unité de médecine familiale de la Vallée-de-l'Or (819-825-5858, poste 3549); Clinique externe de psychiatrie (819-825-5858)
Michel Langevin, Président, Conseil d'administration
Jérôme Lamont, Directeur général
jerome.lamont@ssss.gouv.qc.ca

Vaudreuil-Dorion: CSSS de Vaudreuil-Soulanges
Affiliée à: Agence de la santé et des services sociaux de la Montérégie
490, boul Harwood, Vaudreuil-Dorion, QC J7V 7H4
Tél: 450-455-6171
www.santemonteregie.qc.ca/vaudreuil-soulanges
Fondée en: 2004
Population desservi: 140 000
Note: Les Installations (Services de CH, CHSLD, et CLSC): Centre d'hébergement de Coteau-du-Lac (450-763-5951); Centre d'hébergement de Rigaud (450-451-5329); Centre d'hébergement de Vaudreuil (450-455-6177); Centre d'hébergement Laurent-Bergevin (514-453-5860); LSC de Vaudreuil-Soulanges, Rigaud (450-451-6609); CLSC de Vaudreuil-Soulanges, Saint-Polycarpe (450-265-3771); CLSC Vaudreuil-Soulanges, Vaudreuil-Dorion (450-455-6171); Le Manoir Harwood (450-424-6458)
Gilbert Beaulieu, Président, Conseil d'administration
Michel Lapointe, Directeur général
michel.lapointe@rrsss16.gouv.qc.ca
Nelson Boulianne, Directeur des ressources humaines, informationnelles, et développement organisationnel
Gaétan Drolet, Directeur des services professionnels
Normand Gaudet, Directeur des programmes perte d'autonomie
Lina Lauzier, Directrice qualité, gestion des risques, soins infirmers et supervision clinique
Gaëtan Martin, Directeur des ressources financières et matérielles
Dominique Pilon, Directeur des services généraux et spécifiques

Victoriaville: CSSS d'Arthabaska-et-de-l'Érable
Affiliée à: Agence de la santé et des services sociaux de la Mauricie et du Centre-du-Québec
Centre administratif, 5, rue des Hospitalières, Victoriaville, QC G6P 6N2
Tél: 819-357-6001
www.csssae.qc.ca
Note: Les Installations (Services de CH, CHSLD, et CLSC): Hôtel-Dieu d'Arthabaska; CLSC Suzor-Coté; CLSC des Bois-Francs; CLSC de l'Érable; CLSC Saint-Louis; Centre d'hébergement du Chêne; Centre d'hébergement du Roseau; Centre d'hébergement des Étoiles-d'Or; Centre d'hébergement du Sacré-Coeur; Centre d'hébergement des Quatre-Vents; Centre d'hébergement des Bois-Francs; Centre d'hébergement de Saint-Eusèbe; Centre d'hébergement du Tilleul
Marcel Dubois, Président, Conseil d'administration
Claude Charland, Directeur général
Claude.Charland@ssss.gouv.qc.ca
Jean-François Bussières, Directeur des programmes famille, santé publique, et santé mentale
Sylvain Chartier, Directeur des ressources humaines
Johan Deloffre, Directeur des ressources informationnelles, et de la performance et direction
Raymond Dufour, Directeur des services techniques et d'alimentation
Hélène Hinse, Directrice des soins infirmiers
Philippe Rancourt, Directeur du programme personnes en perte d'autonomie
Stéphane Sénéchal, Directeur des services financiers
Josée Simoneau, Directrice du programme santé physique
Dr. Christian Vinette, Directeur des services professionnels, et des affaires médicales

Ville-Marie: CSSS du Témiscamingue (CSSST)
Affiliée à: Agence de la santé et des services sociaux de l'Abitibi-Témiscamingue
Ancien nom: CSSS du Lac-Témiscamingue; CSSS de Témiscaming-et-de-Kipawa
Services administratifs, 22, rue Notre-Dame nord, Ville-Marie, QC J9V 1W8
Tél: 819-622-2773 *Téléc:* 819-629-3257
www.cssst.ca
Fondée en: 2011
Population desservi: 17 000*Personnel:* 600
Note: Les Installations (Services de CH, CHSLD, et CLSC): Pavillon Sainte-Famille (CH et CLSC); Pavillon Témiscaming-Kipawa (CH, CLSC, et CHSLD); Pavillon Duhamel (CHSLD). Points de services: Angliers; Laforce; Latulipe; Moffet; Nédélec; Notre-Dame-du-Nord; Rémigny
Raymond Gagnon, Président
Jacynthe Bérubé, Directrice générale
jacynthe_berube@ssss.gouv.qc.ca

Wakefield: CSSS des Collines
Affiliée à: Agence de la santé et de services sociaux de l'Outaouais
CP 160 Stn. Wakefield, 101, ch Burnside, Wakefield, QC J0X 3G0
Tél: 819-459-3080
www.santedescollines.qc.ca
Personnel: 275
Note: Les Installations (Services de CH, CHSLD, et CLSC): L'Hôpital Mémorial de Wakefield; Le Centre d'hébergement La Pêche; Le CLSC des Collines (Cantley, Chelsea, Masham, Val-des-Monts).
Les Municipalités: Cantley; Chelsea; La Pêche; Val-des-Monts (excluant le secteur Poltimore)
Jean-Paul Racine, Président, Conseil d'administration
André Désilets, Directeur général
AndreDesilets@ssss.gouv.qc.ca

Weedon: CSSS du Haut-Saint-François
Affiliée à: Agence de la santé et des services sociaux de l'Estrie
460, 2e av, Weedon, QC J0B 3J0
Tél: 819-877-3434 *Téléc:* 819-877-3714
www.cssshsf.com
Nombre de lits: 108 lits (2 centres d'hébergement en soins de longue durée)
Région desservi: MRC du Haut-Saint-François (14 municipalités)*Population desservi:* 22 157
Note: Les Installations (Services de CH, CHSLD, et CLSC): Centre d'hébergement d'East Angus (819-832-2487); Centre d'hébergement de Weedon (819-877-2500); CLSC de Weedon (819-877-3434); CLSC de Cookshire (819-875-3373); CLSC de La Patrie (819-888-2811); CLSC d'East Angus (819-832-4961)
Michel Rouleau, Président, Conseil d'administration
Mario Morand, Directeur général
Anne Simard, Directrice générale adjointe; Directrice de la qualité
asimard.hsf@ssss.gouv.qc.ca
Renée Audet, Directrice des ressources humaines
Nathalie Bois, Directrice des services administratifs et techniques
Luce Cardinal, Directrice des programmes spécifiques, généraux et santé publique
Luc Langlois, Directeur, Perte d'autonomie liée au vieillissement
Joanne Roy, Directrice des soins infirmiers et de la santé physique, responsable des services accueil-réception-archives

Windsor: CSSS du Val-Saint-François
Affiliée à: Agence de la santé et des services sociaux de l'Estrie
Centre administratif, 79, rue Allen, Windsor, QC J1S 2P8
Tél: 819-542-2777 *Téléc:* 819-845-5521
recrutement.vsf@ssss.gouv.qc.ca (services administratifs)
www.vsf.santeestrie.qc.ca
Note: Les Installations (Services de CH, CHSLD, et CLSC): CLSC - Urgence mineure de Windsor; CLSC de Richmond; CLSC de Valcourt; Centre d'hébergement de Windsor; Centre d'hébergement de Richmond; Centre d'hébergement de Valcourt
Pascal Collin, Président, Conseil d'administration
Pierre Lalande, Directeur général
819-845-2792, plalande.vsf@ssss.gouv.qc.ca

Hôpitaux

Centres hospitaliers

Amos: Hôpital Hôtel-Dieu d'Amos
Affiliée à: Centre de santé et de services sociaux les Eskers de l'Abitibi
622, 4e rue ouest, Amos, QC J9T 2S2
Tél: 819-732-3341 *Téléc:* 819-732-7054
www.sante-abitibi-temiscamingue.gouv.qc.ca
Nombre de lits: 96 lits
Note: Services diagnostiques; urgence et traumatologie; othopédie; rhumatologie; ophtalmologie; chirurgie plastique/reconstructive/maxillo-faciale; gynécologie; obstétrique; gériatrie; physiotherapie; réadaptation cardio-respiratoire.
Michel Michaud, Directeur général, CSSS Les Eskers de l'Abitibi
michel_michaud@ssss.gouv.qc.ca

Baie-Saint-Paul: Hôpital de Baie-Saint-Paul
Affiliée à: Centre de santé et de services sociaux de Charlevoix
74, rue Ambroise-Fafard, Baie-Saint-Paul, QC G3Z 2J6
Tél: 418-435-5150
www.cssscharlevoix.qc.ca
Nombre de lits: 40 lits hospitaliers; 56 lits de soins de longue durée
Note: Services: anesthésie, chirurgie, gériatrie, psychiatrie, radiologie, ophtalmologie, urologie; soins généraux et spécialisés; urgence.
Micheline Tremblay, Directrice générale, CSSS de Charlevoix
micheline.tremblay@ssss.gouv.qc.ca

***Beaupré:* Hôpital Sainte-Anne-de-Beaupré**
Affiliée à: Centre de santé et de services sociaux de Québec-Nord
11000, rue des Montagnards, Beaupré, QC G0A 1E0
Tél: 418-827-3738
www.csssqn.qc.ca
Nombre de lits: 172 lits
Note: Services infirmiers, médicaux, et psychosociaux.
Lucie Lacroix, Directrice générale, CSSS de Québec-Nord

***Chandler:* Hôpital de Chandler**
Affiliée à: Centre de santé et de services sociaux du Rocher-Percé
CP 3300, 451, rue Mgr Ross est, Chandler, QC G0C 1K0
Tél: 418-689-2261 *Téléc:* 418-689-5945
Nombre de lits: 113 lits
Note: Soins hospitaliers; soins de longue durée; a fusionné avec le CLSC-CHSLD Pabok en 2004.
Chantal Duguay, Directrice générale

***Châteauguay:* Hôpital Anna-Laberge**
Affiliée à: Centre de santé et de services sociaux Jardins-Roussillon
200, boul Brisebois, Châteauguay, QC J6K 4W8
Tél: 450-699-2425 *Ligne sans frais:* 800-700-0621
Nombre de lits: 226 lits hospitaliers
Paul Moreau, Directeur général, CSSS Jardins-Roussillon

***Chibougamau:* Centre régional de santé et services sociaux Baie-James**
Affiliée à: Centre régional de la santé et des services sociaux de la Baie-James
312, 3e rue, Chibougamau, QC G8P 1N5
Tél: 418-748-3575 *Téléc:* 418-748-6391
Ligne sans frais: 866-748-2676
rh.crsssbj@ssss.gouv.qc.ca
www.crsssbaiejames.gouv.qc.ca
Média social: www.facebook.com/CRSSSBJ
Nombre de lits: 32
Diane Laboissonnière, Directrice générale

***Côte Saint-Luc:* Hôpital Mont-Sinai**
5690, boul Cavendish, Côte Saint-Luc, QC H4W 1S7
Tél: 514-369-2222 *Téléc:* 514-369-2225
lschembre.sinai@ssss.gouv.qc.ca
www.sinaimontreal.ca
Nombre de lits: 57 lits
Michel Amar, Directeur général

***Donnacona:* Centre hospitalier Portneuf**
Affiliée à: Centre de santé et de services sociaux de Portneuf
250, boul Gaudreau, Donnacona, QC G3M 1L7
Tél: 418-285-3025 *Téléc:* 418-285-3656
csssdeportneuf.qc.ca
Nombre de lits: 369 lits
Lucie Gagnon, Directrice générale
Philippe Leboeuf, Président du conseil d'administration

***Drummondville:* Hôpital Sainte-Croix**
Affiliée à: Centre de santé et de services sociaux Drummond
570, rue Heriot, Drummondville, QC J2B 1C1
Tél: 819-478-6464
csssdrummond@ssss.gouv.qc.ca
www.csssdrummond.qc.ca
Nombre de lits: 191 lits
Note: Anatomopathologie, chirurgie générale, gynécologie-obstétrique, pédiatrie, médecine familiale/interne/nucléaire, ophtalmologie, orthopédie, psychiatrie, radiologie, urologie.
Nagui Habashi, Directeur général, CSSS Drummond

***Gaspé:* Hôpital Hôtel-Dieu**
215, boul de York ouest, Gaspé, QC G4X 2W2
Tél: 418-368-3301 *Téléc:* 418-368-7150
www.cssscotedegaspe.ca
Nombre de lits: 56 lits hospitaliers
Jean-Pierre Tremblay, Directeur général

***Gatineau:* Hôpital de Gatineau**
Affiliée à: Centre de santé et de services sociaux de Gatineau
909, boul de La Vérendrye, Gatineau, QC J8P 7H2
Tél: 819-966-6100
www.csssgatineau.qc.ca
Nombre de lits: 243 lits
André O. Rodier, Directeur général, CSSS de Gatineau
819-966-6560
Dr. André Moreau, Directeur, Services professionels/Affaires médicales
819-966-6104
Gilles Coulombe, Directeur, Soins infirmiers/Pratiques professionnelles
819-966-6540

***Gatineau:* Hôpital de Hull**
Affiliée à: Centre de santé et de services sociaux de Gatineau
116, boul Lionel-Émond, Gatineau, QC J8Y 1W7
Tél: 819-966-6200 *Téléc:* 819-966-6306
www.csssgatineau.qc.ca
Nombre de lits: 265 lits
André O. Rodier, Directeur général, CSSS de Gatineau
819-966-6560

***Gatineau:* Hôpital de Papineau**
Affiliée à: Centre de santé et de services sociaux de Papineau
155, rue Maclaren est, Gatineau, QC J8L 0C2
Tél: 819-986-3341 *Téléc:* 819-986-4000
csss_papineau@ssss.gouv.qc.ca
www.cssspapineau.qc.ca
Nombre de lits: 63 lits hospitaliers; 55 lits soins longue durée
Gilles Clavel, Directeur général (par intérim), CSSS de Papineau

***Greenfield Park:* Hôpital Charles LeMoyne**
Affiliée à: Centre de santé et de services sociaux Champlain - Charles-Le Moyne
3120, boul Taschereau, Greenfield Park, QC J4V 2H1
Tél: 450-466-5000 *Téléc:* 450-466-8887
www.santemonteregie.qc.ca/hclm
Nombre de lits: 571 lits
Note: L'Hôpital est le centre hospitalier régional et universitaire de la Montérégie; affilié à l'Université de Sherbrooke; soins et services de court durée en santé physique, santé mentale, réadaptation; recherche; enseignement universitaire.
Yvan Gendron, Directeur général
Dr. Alphonse Montminy, Directeur, Services professionnels et hospitaliers
Ginette Brunelle, Directrice, Soins infirmiers

***Kahnawake:* Conseil des Mohawks de Kahnawake**
CP 720, Kahnawake, QC J0L 1B0
Tél: 450-638-3930 *Téléc:* 450-638-4634
www.kahnawake.com
Nombre de lits: 10 lits hospitaliers, 33 lits longue durée
Suzanne Horn, Directrice générale

***La Malbaie:* Hôpital de La Malbaie**
Affiliée à: Centre de santé et de services sociaux de Charlevoix
CP 340, 303, rue St-Étienne, La Malbaie, QC G5A 1T1
Tél: 418-665-1700
www.cssscharlevoix.qc.ca
Nombre de lits: 56 lits hospitaliers
Micheline Tremblay, Directrice générale, CSSS de Charlevoix
micheline.tremblay@ssss.gouv.qc.ca

***LaSalle:* Hôpital de LaSalle**
Affiliée à: Centre de santé et de services sociaux de Dorval-Lachine-LaSalle
8585, Terrasse Champlain, LaSalle, QC H8P 1C1
Tél: 514-362-8000
www.santemontreal.qc.ca
Nombre de lits: 110 lits hospitaliers, 123 lits longue durée

***Laval:* Hôpital de la Cité-de-la-Santé**
Affiliée à: Centre de santé et de services sociaux de Laval
1755, boul René-Laennec, Laval, QC H7M 3L9
Tél: 450-668-1010
Nombre de lits: 414 lits hospitaliers; 38 lits de psychiatrie
Luc Lepage, Directeur général, CSSS de Laval
Alain Goudreau, Directeur, Services professionnels et hospitaliers/Affaires mé

***Laval:* Jewish Rehabilitation Hospital**
3205, Place Alton-Goldbloom, Laval, QC H7V 1R2
Tél: 450-688-9550 *Téléc:* 450-688-3673
www.hjr-jrh.qc.ca
Fondée en: 1962
Nombre de lits: 120
André Ibghy, Executive Director
450/688-9550 ext.201, Fax: 450/688-4401, aibghy_hjr@ssss.gouv.qc.ca

***Laval:* Santé Courville inc.**
5200, 80e rue, Laval, QC H7R 5T6
Tél: 450-627-7990 *Téléc:* 450-627-7993
Nombre de lits: 120 lits
Christine Durocher, Directrice générale

***Lévis:* Hôtel-Dieu de Lévis**
143, rue Wolfe, Lévis, QC G6V 3Z1
Tél: 418-835-7121 *Téléc:* 418-835-7143
info@hdl.qc.ca
www.hdl.qc.ca
Nombre de lits: 343 lits
Hervé Moysan, Directeur général
Robert Amyot, Directeur, Services techniques
Diana Lancup, Responsable des services sanitaires et lingerie

***Longueuil:* Hôpital Pierre-Boucher**
Affiliée à: Centre de santé et de services sociaux Pierre-Boucher
1333, boul Jacques-Cartier est, Longueuil, QC J4M 2A5
Tél: 450-468-8111
Nombre de lits: 340 lits
Note: Urgence; soins intensifs; soins palliatifs; services médicaux; chirurgie; psychiatrie.
Caroline Barbir, Directrice générale, CSSS Pierre-Boucher

***Maria:* Hôpital de Maria**
Affiliée à: Centre de santé et de services sociaux de la Baie-des-Chaleurs
419, boul Perron, Maria, QC G0C 1Y0
Tél: 418-759-3443 *Téléc:* 418-759-5063
Nombre de lits: 77 lits
Note: Unité de médecine familiale Baie-des-Chaleurs: 418-759-1336, poste 2811.
Bernard Nadeau, Directeur général, CSSS de la Baie-des-Chaleurs

***Mont-Laurier:* Hôpital de Mont-Laurier**
Affiliée à: Centre de santé et de services sociaux d'Antoine-Labelle
2561, ch de la Lièvre sud, Mont-Laurier, QC J9L 3G3
Tél: 819-623-1234 *Téléc:* 819-440-4376
Nombre de lits: 62 lits
Jean-Pierre Urbain, Directeur général, CSSS d'Antoine-Labelle

***Montmagny:* Hôpital de Montmagny**
Affiliée à: Centre de santé et de services sociaux de Montmagny-L'Islet
350, boul Taché ouest, Montmagny, QC G5V 3R8
Tél: 418-248-0630 *Téléc:* 418-248-6838
Spécialités: Oncologie; Radiologie; Psychiatrie; Physiothérapie; Ergothérapie; Inhalothérapie
Note: Répartition des lits: 40 lits de médecine-chirurgie; 12 lits de santé mentale; 10 lits de soins de longue durée; 10 civières à l'urgence; 10 civières en chirurgie d'un jour; 5 lits d'obstétrique; 5 lits de pédiatrie; 5 lits d'évaluation réadaptation en gériatrie; 4 lits de soins intensifs

***Montréal:* Centre hospitalier de l'Université de Montréal**
3840, rue St-Urbain, Montréal, QC H2W 1T8
Tél: 514-890-8000 *Téléc:* 514-412-7224
Nombre de lits: 1217 lits hospitaliers, 170 lits longue durée
Denis R. Roy, Directeur général

***Montréal:* Centre hospitalier de St. Mary**
3830, av Lacombe, Montréal, QC H3T 1M5
Tél: 514-345-3511 *Téléc:* 514-345-3836
www.smhc.qc.ca
Nombre de lits: 251 lits hospitaliers, 65 lits longue durée
Arvind K. Joshi, Directeur général

***Montréal:* Centre hospitalier Jacques-Viger**
1051, rue St-Hubert, Montréal, QC H2L 3Y5
Tél: 514-842-7181
Nombre de lits: 447 lits

***Montréal:* Centre hospitalier Richardson / Centre Henri Bradet**
Affiliée à: Centre de santé et de services sociaux Cavendish
5425, rue Bessborough, Montréal, QC H4V 2S7
Tél: 514-483-1380 *Téléc:* 514-483-4596
Nombre de lits: 42 lits hospitaliers, 125 lits longue durée
Karen Kennedy, Personne ressource
514-484-7878 ext2126, karen.kennedy.cvd@ssss.gouv.qc.ca

***Montréal:* Centre universitaire de santé McGill - Hôpital neurologique de Montréal**
3801, University, Montréal, QC H3A 2B4
Tél: 514-934-1934 *Téléc:* 514-398-3338
www.muhc.mcgill.ca
Nombre de lits: 1,193 lits, 173 lits longue durée
Arthur T. Porter, Directeur général
Jean Pierre Bertrand, Directeur, Services techniques
Stephen Black, Manager, Environmental Services

***Montréal:* Hôpital Catherine Booth de l'Armée du Salut**
4375, av Montclair, Montréal, QC H4B 2J5
Tél: 514-481-0431 *Téléc:* 514-481-0029
Nombre de lits: 84 lits
Note: réadaptation
Edith Verstege, Directrice générale (intérim)

***Montréal:* Hôpital de réadaptation Lindsay**
6363, ch Hudson, Montréal, QC H3S 1M9
Tél: 514-737-3661 *Téléc:* 514-737-0592
cloe.rodrigue.irglm@ssss.gouv.qc.ca
www.hopital-lindsay.qc.ca
Nombre de lits: 155 lits
Note: hôpital spécialisé de courte-durée
Réjean Plante, Directeur général

***Montréal:* Hôpital du Sacré-Coeur de Montréal**
5400, boul Gouin ouest, Montréal, QC H4J 1C5
Tél: 514-338-2222 *Téléc:* 514-338-2384
www.hscm.ca
Nombre de lits: 554 lits hospitaliers
Note: outpatient services & trauma centre
Michel Larivière, Directeur général
Julien Ricard, Chef de service de la salubrité
514/338-2214

***Montréal:* Hôpital Fleury**
Affiliée à: Centre de santé et de services sociaux d'Ahuntsic et Montréal-Nord
2180 rue Fleury est, Montréal, QC H2B 1K3
www.csssamn.ca
Nombre de lits: 174 lits
Région desservi: Le territoire d'Ahuntsic et de Montréal-Nord, QC
Spécialités: Prélèvements; Urgence psychiatrique

***Montréal:* Hôpital général de Montréal**
1650, av Cedar, Montréal, QC H3G 1A4
Tél: 514-934-1934 *Téléc:* 514-934-8200
www.muhc.ca
Nombre de lits: 417 beds
Arthur T. Porter, Directeur général

***Montréal:* Hôpital général juif Sir Mortimer B. Davis**
3755, ch C"te Ste-Catherine, Montréal, QC H3T 1E2
Tél: 514-340-8222 *Téléc:* 514-340-7510
Nombre de lits: 571 lits hospitaliers, 100 lits longue durée
Henri Elbaz, Directeur général
Jacques Benzaquen, Directeur, Services techniques

***Montréal:* Hôpital Maisonneuve-Rosemont**
5415, boul de l'Assomption, Montréal, QC H1T 2M4
Tél: 514-252-3400 *Téléc:* 514-252-3408
www.maisonneuve-rosemont.org
Nombre de lits: 617 lits hospitaliers, 183 lits longue durée
Carole Deschambeault, Directrice générale

***Montréal:* Hôpital Santa Cabrini**
5655, rue St-Zotique est, Montréal, QC H1T 1P7
Tél: 514-252-6000 *Téléc:* 514-252-6453
www.santacabrini.qc.ca
Nombre de lits: 141 lits hospitaliers
Irène Giannetti, Directrice générale

***Montréal:* Hopital Shriners pour enfants (Quebec) inc.**
1529, av Cedar, Montréal, QC H3G 1A6
Tél: 514-842-4464 *Téléc:* 514-842-7553
Nombre de lits: 40 lits
Maureen Brennan, Directrice générale

***Montréal:* Institut de cardiologie de Montréal**
5000, rue Bélanger est, Montréal, QC H1T 1C8
Tél: 514-376-3330 *Téléc:* 514-593-2540
www.icm-mhi.org
Nombre de lits: 153 lits
Robert Busilacchi, Directeur général

***Montréal:* Institut Philippe Pinel de Montréal**
10905, boul Henri-Bourassa est, Montréal, QC H1C 1H1
Tél: 514-648-8461 *Téléc:* 514-494-4406
www.pinel.qc.ca/
Nombre de lits: 295 lits
Paul-André Lafleur, Directeur général
Paul-Emile Trudeau, Directeur, Services techniques

***Montréal:* Institut universitaire de gériatrie de Montréal (IUGM)**
Pavillon Côte-des-Neiges, 4565, ch Queen-Mary, Montréal, QC H3W 1W5
Tél: 514-340-2800 *Téléc:* 514-340-2802
communication.iugm@ssss.gouv.qc.ca
www.iugm.qc.ca
Louis-Alexandre Rail, Président, Conseil d'administration
Louise Ann Maziack, Vice-présidente
Marie-France Simard, Directrice générale & Secrétaire

***Ormstown:* Hôpital Barrie Memorial**
Affiliée à: Centre de santé et de services sociaux du Haut-Saint-Laurent
Centre de santé et de services sociaux du Haut-Sai, CP 200, 28, rue Gale, Ormstown, QC J0S 1K0
Tél: 450-829-2321 *Téléc:* 450-829-3582
Nombre de lits: 49 lits hospitaliers
Francine Lortie, Directrice générale
francine.lotrie@rrsss16.gouv.qc.ca

***Pointe-Claire:* Hôpital général du Lakeshore**
Affiliée à: Centre de santé et de services sociaux de l'Ouest-de-l'Ile
160, ch Stillview, Pointe-Claire, QC H9R 2Y2
Tél: 514-630-2225 *Téléc:* 514-630-3302
Nombre de lits: 227 lits hospitaliers, 30 lits longue durée
Luc Lepage, Directeur général

***Québec:* Centre hospitalier affilié universitaire de Québec**
1401, 18e rue, Québec, QC G1J 1Z4
Tél: 418-649-0252 *Téléc:* 418-649-5557
www.cha.quebec.qc.ca
Nombre de lits: 668 lits
Marie Girard, Directeur général

***Québec:* Centre hospitalier universitaire de Québec (CHUQ)**
11, C"te du Palais, Québec, QC G1R 2J6
Tél: 418-525-4444 *Téléc:* 418-691-5205
www.chuq.qc.ca
Nombre de lits: 187 lits hospitaliers; 946 lits (courte durée et pouponnière); 100 lits (hébergement et soins de longue durée); 54 lits (néonatalogie)
René Rouleau, Directeur général

***Québec:* Hôpital Jeffery Hale**
1250, ch Ste-Foy, Québec, QC G1S 2M6
Tél: 418-683-4471 *Téléc:* 418-683-8980
dg.jhale@sympatico.ca
www.jefferyhale.org
Nombre de lits: 12 lits hospitaliers, 100 lits longue durée
Louis Hanrahan, Directeur général
Réné Corriveau, Coordonnateur, services techniques

***Rimouski:* Hôpital régional de Rimouski**
Affiliée à: Centre de santé et de services sociaux de Rimouski-Neigette
150, av Rouleau, Rimouski, QC G5L 5T1
Tél: 418-723-7851 *Téléc:* 418-724-8632
courrierweb.crsssr@ssss.gouv.qc.ca
www.chrr.qc.ca
Nombre de lits: 255 lits
Raymond Coulombe, Directeur général, CSSS de Rimouski-Neigette

***Rivière-Rouge:* Centre de services de Rivière-Rouge**
Affiliée à: Centre de santé et de services sociaux d'Antoine-Labelle
1525, rue L'Annonciation nord, Rivière-Rouge, QC J0T 1T0
Tél: 819-275-2118 *Téléc:* 819-275-2464
Jean-Pierre Urbain, Directeur général, CSSS d'Antoine-Labelle

***Roberval:* Hôtel-Dieu de Roberval / Centre d'hébergement Roberval**
Affiliée à: Centre de santé et de services sociaux Domaine-du-Roy
450, rue Brassard, Roberval, QC G8H 1B9
Tél: 418-275-0110 *Téléc:* 418-275-6202
hdr@ssss.gouv.qc.ca
www.cmdp-roberval.com
Nombre de lits: 135 lits hospitaliers; 100 lits de soins de longue durée
Note: L'hôpital offre service d'urgence, médecine générale/interne/nucléaire, ophtalmologie, obstétrique, orthopédie, pédiatrie, chirurgie, psychiatrie, urologie, réadaptation physique.
Jacques Dubois, Directeur général, CSSS Domaine-du-Roy

***Saint-Hyacinthe:* Hôpital Honoré-Mercier**
Affiliée à: Centre de santé et de services sociaux Richelieu-Yamaska
2750, boul Laframboise, Saint-Hyacinthe, QC J2S 4Y8
Tél: 450-771-3333 *Téléc:* 450-771-3748
info@lesommetavotreportee.qc.ca
www.lesommetavotreportee.qc.ca;
www.santemonteregie.qc.ca/richelieu-yamaska
Nombre de lits: 273 lits
Note: Centre mère-enfant-famille; Pédiatrie; Soins intensifs; Chirurgie.
Daniel Castonguay, Directeur général, CSSS Richelieu-Yamaska
Dr. Diane Poirier, Directrice, Affaires médicales
Carmen Messier, Directrice, Soins infirmiers/Pratiques professionnelles

***Saint-Jean-sur-Richelieu:* Hôpital du Haut-Richelieu**
Affiliée à: Centre de santé et de services sociaux Haut-Richelieu-Rouville
978, boul du Séminaire nord, Saint-Jean-sur-Richelieu, QC J3A 1B7
Tél: 450-359-5000 *Téléc:* 450-359-5251
Nombre de lits: 307 lits
Note: L'Hôpital, et le centre administratif du CSSS Haut-Richelieu-Rouville.
Christine Lessard, Directrice générale, CSSS Haut-Richelieu-Rouville
Dr. Krystyna Pecko, Directrice générale adjointe/Directrice des affaires mé

***Sainte-Anne-de-Bellevue:* Hôpital Sainte-Anne**
Le ministère des affaires des anciens combattants, 305, boul des Anciens-Combattants, Sainte-Anne-de-Bellevue, QC H9X 1Y9
Tél: 514-457-3440 *Ligne sans frais:* 800-361-9287
information@vac-acc.gc.ca
www.vac-acc.gc.ca
Nombre de lits: 590 lits
Rachel Corneille-Gravel, Directrice générale

***Shawinigan-Sud:* Hôpital du Centre-de-la Mauricie**
Affiliée à: Centre de santé et de services sociaux de l'Énergie
50, 119e rue, Shawinigan-Sud, QC G9P 5K1
Tél: 819-536-7500
Nombre de lits: 178 lits hospitaliers, 45 lits longue durée

***Shawville:* Centre hospitalier du Pontiac**
Affiliée à: Centre de santé et de services sociaux du Pontiac
200, rue Argue, Shawville, QC J0X 2Y0
Tél: 819-647-2211 *Téléc:* 819-647-2409
www.santepontiac.qc.ca
Nombre de lits: 71 lits
Richard Grimard, Directeur général
Jacques Boissonneault, Chef de service, Biologie médicale

***Sherbrooke:* Centre hospitalier universitaire de Sherbrooke**
555, rue Murray, Sherbrooke, QC J1G 2K8
Tél: 819-346-1110 *Téléc:* 819-822-6789
www.chus.qc.ca
Média social: www.facebook.com/CHUSherbrooke; twitter.com/CHUSherbrooke
Nombre de lits: 682 lits
Patricia Gauthier, Directrice générale

***Terrebonne:* Hôpital Pierre-Le Gardeur**
Affiliée à: Centre de santé et de services sociaux du Sud de Lanaudière
911, montée des Pionniers, Terrebonne, QC J6V 2H2
Tél: 450-654-7525
www.chpierrelegardeur.ca
Nombre de lits: 273 lits

***Trois-Pistoles:* Centre hospitalier Trois-Pistoles**
550, rue Notre-Dame est, Trois-Pistoles, QC G0L 4K0
Tél: 418-851-1111 *Téléc:* 418-851-2934
www.agencesssbsl.gouv.qc.ca
Nombre de lits: 60 lits
Line Moisan, Directrice générale, CSSS des Basques

***Trois-Rivières:* Centre St-Joseph**
Affiliée à: Centre de santé et de services sociaux de Trois-Rivières
731, rue Sainte-Julie, Trois-Rivières, QC G9A 1Y1
Tél: 819-370-2100
www.cssstr.qc.ca
Nombre de lits: 198 lits hospitaliers; 100 lits de soins de longue durée
Note: Centre St-Joseph: services hospitaliers; Résidence La Providence: hébergement 819-370-2200, poste 43104.

Jacques Longval, Directeur général, CSSS de Trois-Rivières

***Verdun:* Hôpital Douglas**
6875, boul Lasalle, Verdun, QC H4H 1R3
Tél: 514-761-6131 *Téléc:* 514-761-4816
dredea@douglas.mcgill.ca
www.douglas.qc.ca
Nombre de lits: 210 lits hospitaliers, 192 lits longue durée
Note: mental hospital affiliated with McGill University; also community services, outpatient services, housing, social rehabilitation, specialized services (eating disorders, alcoholism & drug abuse, schizophrenia, aging, dementia & Alzheimer dementia)
Jacques Hendlisz, Directeur général

***Verdun:* Pavillon Manoir**
Ancien nom: CHSLD Champlain - Manoir de Verdun
5500, boul Lasalle, Verdun, QC H4H 1N9
Tél: 514-769-8801
Nombre de lits: 220 lits

***Victoriaville:* Hôtel-Dieu d'Arthabaska**
Affiliée à: Centre de santé et de services sociaux d'Arthabaska-et-de-L'Érable
5, rue des Hospitalières, Victoriaville, QC G6P 6N2
Tél: 819-357-2030 *Téléc:* 819-357-7406
www.csssae.qc.ca
Nombre de lits: 199 lits
Marcel Dubois, Président, Conseil d'administration, CSSS d'Arthabaska-et-de-l

Hôpitaux privés

***Kahnawake:* Kateri Memorial Hospital Centre**
Affiliated with: Centre de santé et de services sociaux Jardins-Roussillon
Also Known As: Tehsakotitsén:tha
PO Box 10, Kahnawake, QC J0L 1B0
Tel: 450-638-3930 *Fax:* 450-638-4634
admin@kmhc.ca
www.kmhc.ca; www.santemonteregie.qc.ca/jardins-roussillon
Number of Beds: 43 beds/lits
Note: Family medicine, home care, community health, infection prevention and control, nutrition services, occupational therapy, physiotherapy, speech therapy, social services.
Susan Horne, Executive Director

***Montréal:* Brassard Plasticien**
Ancien nom: Centre métropolitain de Chirurgie Plastique Inc.
995, rue de Salaberry, Montréal, QC H3L 1L2
Tél: 514-288-2097 *Téléc:* 514-288-3547
information@drbrassard.com
www.drbrassard.com
Nombre de lits: 17 lits
Pierre Brassard, Directeur général

***Montréal:* Hôpital Marie-Clarac**
3530, boul Gouin est, Montréal, QC H1H 1B7
Tél: 514-321-8800 *Téléc:* 514-321-9626
ressourceshumaines.macl@ssss.gouv.qc.ca
www.hopitalmarie-clarac.qc.ca
Nombre de lits: 204 lits
Sr. Pierre-Anne Mandato, Directrice générale

***Montréal:* Hôpital Shriners pour enfants (Québec) inc.**
1529, av Cedar, Montréal, QC H3G 1A6
Tél: 514-842-4464 *Téléc:* 514-842-7553
Nombre de lits: 40 lits
Maureen Brennan, Directrice générale
John Krisa, Superviseur, Installations matériels

***Sillery:* La Maison Michel Sarrazin**
2101, ch St-Louis, Sillery, QC G1T 2P5
Tél: 418-688-0878 *Téléc:* 418-681-8636
info@michel-sarrazin.ca
www.michel-sarrazin.ca
Nombre de lits: 15 lits
Michel L'Heureux, Directeur général

Centres locaux des services communautaires (CLSC)

***Aupaluk:* Dispensaire d'Aupaluk**
Aupaluk, QC J0M 1X0
Tél: 819-491-9090 *Téléc:* 819-491-7020
clsc.aupaluk@ssss.gouv.qc.ca
Nombre de lits: 1 lit
Madge Pomerleau, Directrice générale

***Barachois:* CLSC de Barachois**
Affiliée à: Centre de santé et de services sociaux de La Côte-de-Gaspé
1070, rte 132, Barachois, QC G0C 1A0
Tél: 418-645-2572 *Téléc:* 418-645-2106
Note: CSSS Côte-de-Gaspé.

***Bassin:* CLSC de Bassin**
Affiliée à: Centre de santé et de services sociaux des Iles
CP 57, 702, ch du Bassin, Bassin, QC G4T 0C8
Tél: 418-937-2572 *Téléc:* 418-937-5381

***Bedford:* CLSC de Bedford**
Affiliée à: Centre de santé et de services sociaux la Pommeraie
CP 1140, 34, rue St-Joseph, Bedford, QC J0J 1A0
Tél: 450-248-4321 *Téléc:* 450-248-7435
www.santemonteregie.qc.ca/lapommeraie
Nombre de lits: 45 lits

***Beloeil:* CLSC des Patriotes**
Affiliée à: Centre de santé et de services sociaux Richelieu-Yamaska
300, rue Serge-Pepin, Beloeil, QC J3G 0B8
Tél: 450-536-2572 *Téléc:* 450-536-6367
communication.csssry@rrsss16.gouv.qc.ca
www.santemonteregie.qc.ca/richelieu-yamaska
Fondée en: 1985
Région desservi: MRC de la Vallée-du-Richelieu
Spécialités: Cliniques de vaccination; Clinique du diabète; Programmes en périnatalité; Services à domicile aux personnes en perte d'autonomie

***Boucherville:* CLSC des Seigneuries de Boucherville**
Affiliée à: Centre de santé et de services sociaux Pierre-Boucher
160, boul De Montarville, Boucherville, QC J4B 6S2
Tél: 450-655-3630 *Téléc:* 450-655-8530
www.santemonteregie.qc.ca/cssspierreboucher
Caroline Barbir, Directrice générale, CSSS Pierre-Boucher

***Candiac:* CLSC Kateri**
Affiliée à: Centre de santé et de services sociaux Jardins-Roussillon
90, boul Marie-Victorin, Candiac, QC J5R 1C1
Tél: 450-659-7661 *Téléc:* 450-444-6260
Nombre de lits: 340 lits
Paul Moreau, Directeur général, CSSS Jardins-Roussillon

***Cantley:* CLSC Cantley**
850, Montée de la Source, Cantley, QC J8V 3H4
Tel: 819-459-1112 *Fax:* 819-827-5818
Toll-Free: 877-459-1112
www.santedescollines.qc.ca
Pierre Rochon, Directeur général, CSSS des Collines

***Cap-Chat:* CLSC de Cap-Chat**
Affiliée à: Centre de santé et de services sociaux de La Haute-Gaspésie
49, rue Notre-Dame, Cap-Chat, QC G0E 1E0
Tél: 418-786-5594 *Téléc:* 418-786-2638
www.agencesssgim.ca; www.ccsshautegaspesie.qc.ca
Robert Deschênes, Directeur général

***Cap-aux-Meules:* CLSC de Cap-aux-Meules**
Affiliée à: Centre de santé et de services sociaux des Iles
420, ch Principal, Cap-aux-Meules, QC G4T 1S1
Tél: 418-986-2572 *Téléc:* 418-986-4911

***Caplan:* CLSC de Caplan**
Affiliée à: Centre de santé et de services sociaux de la Baie-des-Chaleurs
96, rte 132, Caplan, QC G0C 1H0
Tél: 418-388-2572 *Téléc:* 418-388-2645
Bernard Nadeau, Directeur général, CSSS de la Baie-des-Chaleurs

***Châteauguay:* CLSC Châteauguay**
Affiliée à: Centre de santé et de services sociaux Jardins-Roussillon
101, rue Lauzon, Châteauguay, QC J6K 1C7
Tél: 450-699-3333 *Téléc:* 450-691-6202
Paul Moreau, Directeur général, CSSS Jardins-Roussillon

***Chertsey:* CLSC de Chertsey**
Affiliée à: Centre de santé et de services sociaux du Nord de Lanaudière
485, rue Dupuis, Chertsey, QC J0K 3K0
Tél: 450-882-2488

***Côte Saint-Luc:* CLSC René-Cassin**
Affiliée à: Centre de santé et de services sociaux Cavendish
#600, 5800, boul Cavendish, Côte Saint-Luc, QC H4W 2T5
Tél: 514-484-7878 *Téléc:* 514-485-2978
www.cssscavendish.qc.ca
Spécialités: Services médicaux; Services psychosociaux; Centre d'éducation pour la santé; Clinique enfance - jeunesse; Services de nutrition; Vaccination

***Drummondville:* CLSC Drummond**
Affiliée à: Centre de santé et de services sociaux Drummond
350, rue Saint-Jean, Drummondville, QC J2B 5L4
Tél: 819-474-2572
csssdrummond@ssss.gouv.qc.ca
www.csssdrummond.qc.ca
Note: Santé au travail: 819-474-8428
Nagui Habashi, Directeur général, CSSS Drummond

***Forestville:* Pavillon Forestville**
Affiliée à: Centre de santé et de services sociaux de la Haute-Côte-Nord
CP 790, 2, 7e rue, Forestville, QC G0T 1E0
Tél: 418-587-2212 *Téléc:* 418-587-2865
www.cssshcn.gouv.qc.ca
Nombre de lits: 20 lits
Micheline Anctil, Directrice générale

***Gascons:* CLSC Gascons**
Affiliée à: Centre de santé et de services sociaux du Rocher-Percé
CP 28, 63, rte 132, Gascons, QC G0C 1P0
Tél: 418-396-2572 *Téléc:* 418-396-2367
Note: CSSS du Rocher-Percé.

***Gaspé:* CLSC de Gaspé**
Affiliée à: Centre de santé et de services sociaux de La Côte-de-Gaspé
CP 6397, 205, boul de York ouest, 2e étage, Gaspé, QC G4X 2R8
Tél: 418-368-2572 *Téléc:* 418-368-1532
Note: CSSS Côte-de-Gaspé.

***Gatineau:* CLSC de Gatineau - Point de service de la Gappe**
Affiliée à: Centre de santé et de services sociaux de Gatineau
777, boul de la Gappe, Gatineau, QC J8T 8R2
Tél: 819-966-6550 *Téléc:* 819-966-6552
www.csssgatineau.qc.ca
Note: Services généraux santé; soins infirmiers et ambulatoires; consulation médicale pour les clientèles vulnérables.
André O. Rodier, Directeur général, CSSS de Gatineau
Micheline Malette, Directrice, Services généraux/Santé publique 819-966-6510

***Gatineau:* CLSC de Gatineau - Point de service Gatineau**
Affiliée à: Centre de santé et de services sociaux de Gatineau
80, av Gatineau, Gatineau, QC J8T 4J3
Tél: 819-966-6550 *Téléc:* 819-966-6572
www.csssgatineau.qc.ca
Note: Centre local de services communautaires.
André O. Rodier, Directeur général, CSSS de Gatineau

***Gatineau:* CLSC de Gatineau - Point de service LeGuerrier**
Affiliée à: Centre de santé et de services sociaux de Gatineau
425, rue LeGuerrier, Gatineau, QC J9H 6N8
Tél: 819-966-6540 *Téléc:* 819-966-6541
www.csssdegatineau.qc.ca
André O. Rodier, Directeur général, CSSS de Gatineau 819-966-6560
Micheline Malette, Directrice, Services généraux/Santé publique

***Gatineau:* CLSC Vallée-de-la-Lièvre**
Affiliée à: Centre de santé et de services sociaux de Papineau
578, rue Maclaren est, Gatineau, QC J8L 2W1
Tél: 819-986-3359 *Téléc:* 819-986-5671
csss_papineau@ssss.gouv.qc.ca
www.cssspapineau.qc.ca

Gilles Clavel, Directeur général (par intérim), CSSS de Papineau

***Grande-Entrée:* CLSC d'Old Harry**
CP 2, site 5, rte 199, Grande-Entrée, QC G4T 7B3
Tél: 418-985-2572 *Téléc:* 418-985-2862
www.agencesssgim.ca; www.csssdesiles.qc.ca
Germain Chevarie, Directeur général

***Grande-Vallée:* CLSC de Grand-Vallée**
71, rue St-François-Xavier est, Grande-Vallée, QC G0E 1K0
Tél: 418-393-2572 *Téléc:* 418-393-2952

Note: CSSS Côte-de-Gaspé.

***Grosse-Ile:* CLSC de l'Est**
Affiliée à: Centre de santé et de services sociaux des Iles
773, ch Principal, Grosse-Ile, QC G4T 6B5
Tél: 418-985-2572 *Téléc:* 418-985-2862

***Huntingdon:* CLSC Huntingdon**
Affiliée à: Centre de santé et de services sociaux du Haut-Saint-Laurent
10, rue King, Huntingdon, QC J0S 1H0
Tél: 450-829-2321 *Téléc:* 450-264-6801
pierre_dubois@rrsss16.gouv.qc.ca
www.santemonteregie.qc.ca/haut-saint-laurent

Spécialités: Services médicaux; Santé mentale adulte et jeunesse; Santé publique; Clinique de vaccination; Soutien à domicile

***Ile d'Entrée:* CLSC de l'Ile d'Entrée**
Affiliée à: Centre de santé et de services sociaux des Iles
Ile d'Entrée, QC G4T 1Z1
Tél: 418-986-4299 *Téléc:* 418-986-4094

***Joliette:* CLSC de Joliette**
Affiliée à: Centre de santé et de services sociaux du Nord de Lanaudière
380, boul Base-de-Roc, Joliette, QC J6E 9J6
Tél: 450-755-2111 *Téléc:* 450-755-4896
www.santelanaudiere.qc.ca

Spécialités: Clinique santé; Centre d'enseignement sur l'asthme; Clinique d'enseignement sur le diabète; Services de santé mentale; Cessation tabagique

***Jonquière:* CLSC de Jonquière**
Affiliée à: Centre de santé et de services sociaux de Jonquière
CP 580, 3667, boul Harvey, Jonquière, QC G7X 3A9
Tél: 418-695-2572

***Kawawachikamach:* CLSC Naskapi**
CP 5154, 9 Naskapi Rd., Kawawachikamach, QC G0G 2Z0
Tél: 418-585-2897 *Téléc:* 418-585-3126
Région desservi: La communauté autochtone de Kawawachikamach*Population desservi:* 600
Luc Guènette, Directeur général (intérim)

***Kipawa:* Health Centre of Eagle Village**
3 Omiga St., Kipawa, QC J0Z 2H0
Tél: 819-627-9060 *Téléc:* 819-627-1885
david.mclaren@evfn.ca
www.evfn.ca/HealthCentre.html
David McLaren, Health Director
davidm@eaglevillagefirstnation.ca

***Kuujjuaq:* Centre de santé Tulattavik de l'Ungava**
Affiliée à: Régie régionale de la santé et des services sociaux du Nunavik
CP 149, Kuujjuaq, QC J0M 1C0
Tél: 819-964-2905 *Téléc:* 819-964-6353
information_rrsss17@ssss.gouv.qc.ca
www.rrsss17.gouv.qc.ca; www.ungava.info
Nombre de lits: 15 lits hospitaliers; 10 lits de soins de longue durée
Note: Urgence; soins médicaux; soins infirmiers; maternité; radiologie; pharmacie; électrocardiographie; laboratoire; physiothérapie.
Madge Pomerleau, Directrice générale
madge.pomerleau@ssss.gouv.qc.ca

***La Malbaie:* CLSC de La Malbaie**
535, boul de Comporté, La Malbaie, QC G5A 1S8
Tél: 418-665-6413
www.cssscharlevoix.qc.ca
Micheline Tremblay, Directrice générale, CSSS de Charlevoix
micheline.tremblay@ssss.gouv.qc.ca

***LaSalle:* CLSC de LaSalle**
Affiliée à: Centre de santé et de services sociaux de Dorval-Lachine-LaSalle
8550, boul Newman, LaSalle, QC H8N 1Y5
Tél: 514-364-2572 *Téléc:* 514-364-6365
www.santemontreal.qc.ca
Jean-Paul Bouchard, Directeur général

***Lachine:* CLSC de Dorval-Lachine**
Affiliée à: Centre de santé et de services sociaux de Dorval-Lachine-LaSalle
1900, rue Notre-Dame, Lachine, QC H8S 2G2
Tél: 514-639-0650 *Téléc:* 514-639-0666
www.santemontreal.qc.ca

Note: Services de santé; services sociaux curatifs et préventifs.
Paul Perreault, Directeur général

***Laval:* CLSC des Mille-Iles**
Affiliée à: Centre de santé et de services sociaux de Laval
4731, boul Levesque est, Laval, QC H7C 1M9
Tél: 450-661-2572 *Téléc:* 450-661-6177

Note: Les autres points de service CLSC: Marigot (2 sites), Mille-Iles (304, boul Cartier ouest), Ruisseau-Papineau (2 sites), et Sainte-Rose.
Luc Lepage, Directeur général, CSSS de Laval

***Longueuil:* CLSC de Longueuil-Ouest**
Affiliée à: Centre de santé et de services sociaux Pierre-Boucher
201, boul Curé-Poirier, Longueuil, QC J4J 2G4
Tél: 450-651-9830 *Téléc:* 450-651-4606
www.santemonteregie.qc.ca/cssspierreboucher
Caroline Barbir, Directrice générale, CSSS Pierre-Boucher

***Longueuil:* CLSC Simonne-Monet-Chartrand**
Affiliée à: Centre de santé et de services sociaux Pierre-Boucher
1303, boul Jacques-Cartier est, Longueuil, QC J4M 2Y8
Tél: 450-463-2850 *Téléc:* 450-646-7552
www.santemonteregie.qc.ca/cssspierreboucher
Caroline Barbir, Directrice générale, CSSS Pierre-Boucher

***Low:* CLSC de Low**
Affiliée à: Centre de santé et de services sociaux de la Vallée-de-la-Gatineau
CP 130, 334, rte 105, Low, QC J0X 2C0
Tél: 819-422-3548 *Téléc:* 819-422-3568

***Marsoui:* CLSC de Marsoui**
Affiliée à: Centre de santé et de services sociaux de La Haute-Gaspésie
CP 154, 1, rue du Quai, Marsoui, QC G0E 1S0
Tél: 418-288-5511 *Téléc:* 418-288-2572
www.agencesssgim.ca; www.cssshautegaspesie.qc.ca

***Matapédia:* CLSC Malauze de Matapédia**
Affiliée à: Centre de santé et de services sociaux de la Baie-des-Chaleurs
14, rue Perron est, Matapédia, QC G0J 1V0
Tél: 418-865-2221 *Téléc:* 418-865-2317

Note: Services sociaux; programme petite enfance; clinique de vaccination et dépistage; programme de santé mentale; services aux personnes handicapées; soutien à domicile; service dentaire. Le centre d'hébergement est situé au deuxième étage du CLSC.
Bernard Nadeau, Directeur général, CSSS de la Baie-des-Chaleurs

***Métabetchouan-Lac-a-la-Cr:* CLSC Secteur-Sud**
Affiliée à: Centre de santé et de services sociaux de Lac-Saint-Jean-Est
1895, rte 169, Métabetchouan-Lac-a-la-Cr, QC G8G 1B4
Tél: 418-349-2861 *Téléc:* 418-349-8774
Nombre de lits: 168 lits

***Mont-Louis:* CLSC de Mont-Louis**
Affiliée à: Centre de santé et de services sociaux de La Haute-Gaspésie
CP 100, 19, 1er av ouest, Mont-Louis, QC G0E 1T0
Tél: 418-797-2744 *Téléc:* 418-797-5173
www.agencesssgim.ca; www.cssshautegaspesie.qc.ca

***Montréal:* Clinique communautaire de Pointe St-Charles**
500, av Ash, Montréal, QC H3K 2R4
Tél: 514-937-9251 *Téléc:* 514-937-3492
ccpsc.qc.ca
Pascal Lebrun, Président

***Montréal:* CLSC d'Ahuntsic**
Affiliée à: Centre de santé et de services sociaux d'Ahuntsic et Montréal-Nord
1165, boul Henri-Bourassa est, Montréal, QC H2C 3K2
Tél: 514-381-4221
www.csssamn.ca

Spécialités: Prélèvements; Services sociaux courants; Réadaptation; Information sur les vaccins

***Montréal:* CLSC de Bordeaux-Cartierville**
Affiliée à: Centre de santé et de services sociaux de Bordeaux-Cartierville-Saint-Laurent
11822, av du Bois-de-Boulogne, Montréal, QC H3M 2X6
Tél: 514-331-2572 *Téléc:* 514-331-5827
www.santemontreal.qc.ca

***Montréal:* CLSC de Côte-des-Neiges**
Affiliée à: Centre de santé et de services sociaux de la Montagne
5700, ch de la C"te-des-Neiges, Montréal, QC H3T 2A8
Tél: 514-731-8531 *Téléc:* 514-731-9600
www.santemontreal.qc.ca; www.clsccote-des-neiges.qc.ca
Marc Sougavinski, Directeur général

***Montréal:* CLSC de Hochelaga-Maisonneuve**
Affiliée à: Centre de santé et de services sociaux Lucille-Teasdale
4201, rue Ontario est, Montréal, QC H1V 1K2
Tél: 514-253-2181 *Téléc:* 514-253-1239
www.cssslucilleteasdale.qc.ca

Spécialités: Les services de santé; Les services sociaux

***Montréal:* CLSC de La Petite Patrie**
Affiliée à: Centre de santé et de services sociaux du Coeur-de-l'Ile
6520, rue de Saint-Vallier, Montréal, QC H2S 2P7
Tél: 514-273-4508
www.cssscoeurdelile.ca

Spécialités: Service de santé; Services sociaux; Services de psychogériatrie; Services d'aide à domicile; Réadaptation; Services d'information

***Montréal:* CLSC de Mercier-Est — Anjou**
Affiliée à: Centre de santé et de services sociaux de la Pointe-de-l'Ile
9503, rue Sherbooke est, Montréal, QC H1L 6P2
Tél: 514-356-2572
www.cssspointe.ca

Note: Les Services: Sevices de prélèvement; Services pour les futurs parents, nourrissons, enfant âgés de moins de 5 ans et leurs parents; Clinique des jeunes (jeunes âgés de 12 à 18 ans); Santé mentale; Radiologie

***Montréal:* CLSC de Montréal-Nord**
Affiliée à: Centre de santé et de services sociaux d'Ahuntsic et Montréal-Nord
11441, boul Lacordaire, Montréal, QC H1G 4J9
Tél: 514-384-2000
www.csssamn.ca

Spécialités: Clinique des adultes; Clinique des jeunes; Informations et counselling; Clinique d'avortement; Pose de dispositifs intra-utérins (DIU)

***Montréal:* CLSC de Parc Extension**
Affiliée à: Centre de santé et de services sociaux de la Montagne
7085, rue Hutchison, Montréal, QC H3N 1Y9
Tél: 514-273-9591 *Téléc:* 514-273-8954
www.csssdelamontagne.qc.ca

Spécialités: Soins infirmiers et médicaux; Services psychosociaux; Réadaptation; Aide domestique; Assistance personnelle

***Montréal:* CLSC de Rivière-des-Prairies**
Affiliée à: Centre de santé et de services sociaux de la Pointe-de-l'Ile
8655, boul Perras, Montréal, QC H1E 4M7
Tél: 514-494-4924

Spécialités: Les services de santé; Les services sociaux

***Montréal:* CLSC de Rosemont**
Affiliée à: Centre de santé et de services sociaux Lucille-Teasdale
Centre administratif, 2909, rue Rachel est, Montréal, QC H1W 0A9
Tél: 514-524-3541
www.cssslucilleteasdale.qc.ca

Spécialités: Services de santé; Services psychosociaux; Services sociaux scolaires; Services de maintien à domicile; Service de santé dentaire

***Montréal:* CLSC de Saint-Henri**
Affiliée à: Centre de santé et de services sociaux du Sud-Ouest-Verdun
3833, rue Notre-Dame ouest, Montréal, QC H4C 1P8
Tél: 514-933-7541
www.sov.qc.ca

***Montréal:* CLSC de Saint-Michel**
Affiliée à: Centre de santé et de services sociaux de Saint-Léonard et Saint-Michel
3355, rue Jarry est, Montréal, QC H1Z 2E5
Tél: 514-722-3000
www.csss-stleonardstmichel.qc.ca

Spécialités: Clinique médicale; Prélèvements; Vaccination (514-374-8223); Soutien à domicile

***Montréal:* CLSC de Villeray**
Affiliée à: Centre de santé et de services sociaux du Coeur-de-l'Ile
1425, rue Jarry est, Montréal, QC H2E 1A7
Tél: 514-376-4141 *Téléc:* 514-722-3758
dotation.cdi@ssss.gouv.qc.ca (l'information sur les emplois)
www.csssscoeurdelile.ca

Fondée en: 1985
Spécialités: Promotion de la santé; Intervention psychosociale; Services thérapeutiques; Vaccination des enfants; Support à l'allaitement; Soutien à domicile

***Montréal:* CLSC des Faubourgs - Visitation**
Affiliée à: Centre de santé et de services sociaux Jeanne-Mance
1705, rue de la Visitation, Montréal, QC H2L 3C3
Tél: 514-527-2361 *Téléc:* 514-598-7754
www.csssjeannemance.ca

Ron Rayside, Président du Conseil d'administration, CSSS Jeanne-Mance
Sylvie Simard, Directrice générale intérimaire, CSSS Jeanne-Mance

***Montréal:* CLSC du Plateau Mont-Royal**
Affiliée à: Centre de santé et de services sociaux Jeanne-Mance
4625, av de Lorimier, Montréal, QC H2H 2B4
Tél: 514-521-7663
www.csssjeannemance.ca

Spécialités: Services psychosociaux; Services médicaux courants; Service en nutrition; Service d'échange de seringues pour personnes toxicomanes; Réadaptation

***Montréal:* CLSC du Plateau-Mont-Royal**
4625, av de Lorimier, Montréal, QC H2H 2B4
Tél: 514-521-7663

***Montréal:* CLSC Métro**
Affiliée à: Centre de santé et de services sociaux de la Montagne
1801, boul de Maisonneuve ouest, Montréal, QC H3H 1J9
Tél: 514-934-0354 *Téléc:* 514-934-6155
www.csssdelamontagne.qc.ca

Spécialités: Clinique médicale; Services sociaux; Programmes de santé pour les écoles et les garderies; Thérapie familiale et de couple

***Montréal:* CLSC Notre-Dame-de-Grâce - Montréal-Ouest**
Affiliée à: Centre de santé et de services sociaux Cavendish
2525, boul Cavendish, Montréal, QC H4B 2Y4
Tél: 514-484-7878 *Téléc:* 514-485-6406
www.cssscavendish.qc.ca

Note: Les Services: Centre de prélèvements; Clinique d'hypertension artérielle du CSSS Cavendish (514-484-7878, poste 3098); Maladie pulmonaire obstructive chronique (514-484-7878); Centre d'abandon du tabagisme (514 484-7878, poste 3068); Clinique de la santé des femmes (514-484-7878, poste 3067)

***Montréal:* CLSC Olivier-Guimond**
Affiliée à: Centre de santé et de services sociaux Lucille-Teasdale
5810, rue Sherbrooke est, Montréal, QC H1N 1B2
Tél: 514-255-2365 *Téléc:* 514-255-1443
www.cssslucilleteasdale.qc.ca

Spécialités: Maladies infectieuses; Santé mentale; Violence conjugale et familiale; Santé dentaire; Nutrition; Réadaptation

***Montréal:* CLSC Pointe-aux-Trembles - Montréal-Est**
Affiliée à: Centre de santé et de services sociaux de la Pointe-de-l'Ile
13926, rue Notre-Dame est, Montréal, QC H1A 1T5
Tél: 514-642-4050
www.cssspointe.ca

Spécialités: Services sociaux; Réadaptation; Aide domestique; Vaccination

***Montréal:* CLSC Saint-Louis-du-Parc**
Affiliée à: Centre de santé et de services sociaux Jeanne-Mance
#100, 15, av du Mont-Royal ouest, Montréal, QC H2T 2R9
Tél: 514-286-9657 *Téléc:* 514-286-9706
www.csssjeannemance.ca

Ron Rayside, Président du Conseil d'administration, CSSS Jeanne-Mance
Sylvie Simard, Directrice générale intérimaire, CSSS Jeanne-Mance

***Montréal:* Santé au travail**
#430, 75, rue de Port-Royal, Montréal, QC H3L 3T1
Tél: 514-858-2460 *Téléc:* 514-858-6568

***Murdochville:* CLSC de Murdochville**
Affiliée à: Centre de santé et de services sociaux de La Côte-de-Gaspé
600, rue Dr William-May, Murdochville, QC G0E 1W0
Tél: 418-784-2572 *Téléc:* 418-784-3629

Note: CSSS Côte-de-Gaspé.

***New Carlisle:* Centre de santé Le Rivage**
CP 208, 96, rte 132, New Carlisle, QC G0C 1H0
Tél: 418-388-2572 *Téléc:* 418-388-2645

***Paspébiac:* CLSC de Paspébiac**
Affiliée à: Centre de santé et de services sociaux de la Baie-des-Chaleurs
273, boul Gérard-D.-Lévesque ouest, Paspébiac, QC G0C 2K0
Tél: 418-752-2572 *Téléc:* 418-752-6734

Bernard Nadeau, Directeur général, CSSS de la Baie-des-Chaleurs

***Percé:* CLSC de Percé**
Affiliée à: Centre de santé et de services sociaux du Rocher-Percé
CP 269, 98, rte 132, Percé, QC G0C 2L0
Tél: 418-782-2572 *Téléc:* 418-782-5501

Note: CSSS du Rocher-Percé.

***Plessisville:* CLSC-CHSLD de l'Érable**
1331, rue Saint-Calixte, Plessisville, QC G6L 1P4
Tél: 819-362-6301 *Téléc:* 819-362-6300
www.csssae.qc.ca

Nombre de lits: 40 lits de soins de longue durée
Note: CLSC de l'Érable, et l'Unité de soins longue durée de l'Érable.
Marcel Dubois, Président, Conseil d'administration, CSSS d'Arthabaska-et-de-l

***Pohénégamook:* CLSC de Pohénégamook**
Affiliée à: Centre de santé et de services sociaux de Témiscouata
1922, rue St-Vallier, Pohénégamook, QC G0L 2T0
Tél: 418-859-2450 *Téléc:* 418-859-1285
www.cssstemiscouata.com

Camil Dion, Directeur général, CSSS de Témiscouata

***Pointe-Claire:* CLSC du Lac-Saint-Louis**
Affiliée à: Centre de santé et de services sociaux de l'Ouest-de-l'Ile
180, av Cartier, Pointe-Claire, QC H9S 4S1
Tél: 514-697-4110
www.csssouestdelile.qc.ca

Note: Les Services: Santé sexuelle (514-697-4110, poste 1313); Suivis post-natals (514-697-4110, poste 1346); Soutien à l'allaitement (514-697-4110, poste 1346); Suivi diététique (514-697-4110, poste 1346); Vaccination (514-697-4110); Suivis intensifs et continus pour la clientèle vulnérable (514-697-4110, poste 1346); Clinique des jeunes (514-697-4110, poste 1313); Services psychosociaux (514-697-4110, poste 1334); Santé dentaire (514-697-4110)

***Pointe-à-la-Croix:* CLSC de Pointe-à-la-Croix**
Affiliée à: Centre de santé et de services sociaux de la Baie-des-Chaleurs
48, boul Interprovincial, Pointe-à-la-Croix, QC G0C 1L0
Tél: 418-788-5454 *Téléc:* 418-788-2510

Bernard Nadeau, Directeur général, CSSS de la Baie-des-Chaleurs

***Puvirnituq:* Centre de santé Inuulitsivik**
Affiliated with: Régie régionale de la santé et des services sociaux du Nunavik
ch Baie d'Hudson, Puvirnituq, QC J0M 1P0
Tél: 819-988-2957 *Fax:* 819-988-2796
inuulitsivik@ssss.gouv.qc.ca
www.inuulitsivik.ca

Number of Beds: 17 lits hospitaliers; 8 lits de soins de longue durée
Note: Soins médicaux, soins dentaires; sages-femmes; services en santé mentale; télemedicine; laboratoire; points de service: Akulivik, Inukjuak, Ivujivik, Kuujjuarapik, Puvirnituq, Salluit et Umiujuaq.
Jane Beaudoin, Directrice générale

***Quaqtaq:* Dispensaire de Quaqtaq**
General Delivery, Quaqtaq, QC J0M 1J0
Tél: 819-492-9090

Région desservi: Nunavik (région sociosanitaire)
Spécialités: Services intégrés de dépistage et de prévention des infections transmissibles sexuellement et par le sang (SIDEP)

***Québec:* CLSC de la Haute-Ville**
Affiliée à: Centre de santé et de services sociaux de la Vieille-Capitale
55, ch Ste-Foy, Québec, QC G1R 1S9
Tél: 418-641-2572
www.csssvc.qc.ca

Note: Services: Consultations médicales (418-682-75940); Consultations psychosociales (418-641-2572); Clinique jeunesse (418-682-7594); Contraception orale d'urgence (418-682-7594); Cours prénataux (418-641-2572); Vaccination (418-682-7594); Soutien à domicile (418-651-3888)

***Québec:* CLSC de la Jacques-Cartier (Loretteville)**
Affiliée à: Centre de santé et de services sociaux de Québec-Nord
11999A, rue de l'Hôpital, Québec, QC G2A 2T7
Tél: 418-843-2572 *Téléc:* 418-843-7569
www.csssqn.qc.ca

Spécialités: Clinique prénatale (418-661-7195); Soutien à domicile; Services infirmiers

***Richelieu:* CLSC du Richelieu**
Affiliée à: Centre de santé et de services sociaux Haut-Richelieu-Rouville
300, ch de Marieville, Richelieu, QC J3L 3V8
Tél: 450-658-7561 *Téléc:* 450 658-4390
www.santemonteregie.qc.ca/haut-richelieu-rouville

Spécialités: Rencontres prénatales; Clinique de la petite enfance (450-658-7561, poste 4164)

***Richmond:* CLSC de Richmond**
Affiliée à: Centre de santé et de services sociaux du Val-Saint-François
110, rue Barlow, Richmond, QC J0B 2H0
Tél: 819-542-2777 *Téléc:* 819-826-3867
vsf.santeestrie.qc.ca

Pierre Lalande, Directeur général, CSSS du Val-Saint-François

***Rimouski:* CLSC Rimouski**
Affiliée à: Centre de santé et de services sociaux de Rimouski-Neigette
165, rue des Gouverneurs, Rimouski, QC G5L 7R2
Tél: 418-724-7204 *Téléc:* 418-724-5494
courrierweb.crsssr@ssss.gouv.qc.ca
www.chrr.qc.ca

Note: 3 autres points de service: Saint-Fabien, Saint-Marcellin, et Saint-Narcisse
Raymond Coulombe, Directeur général, CSSS de Rimouski-Neigette

Rivière-au-Renard: **CLSC de Rivière-au-Renard**
Affiliée à: Centre de santé et de services sociaux de La Côte-de-Gaspé
154, boul Renard est, Rivière-au-Renard, QC G4X 5R5
Tél: 418-269-2572 *Téléc:* 418-269-5294
Nombre de lits: 3 lits
Note: CSSS Côte-de-Gaspé.
Jean-Pierre Tremblay, Directeur général

Rivière-du-Loup: **CLSC de Rivière-du-Loup**
22, rue Saint-Laurent, Rivière-du-Loup, QC G5R 4W5
Tél: 418-867-2642 *Téléc:* 418-867-4713
www.csssriviereduloup.qc.ca
Raymond April, Directeur général, CSSS Rivière-du-Loup

Rouyn-Noranda: **CLSC de Rouyn-Noranda**
Affiliée à: Centre de santé et de services sociaux de Rouyn-Noranda
3, 9e rue, Rouyn-Noranda, QC J9X 2A9
Tél: 819-764-5131 *Téléc:* 819-764-2948
www.sante-abitibi-temiscamingue.gouv.qc.ca; www.csssrn.qc.ca
Note: Point de service CLSC, et consultations externes CHSGS.
Huguette Lemay, Directrice générale, CSSS de Rouyn-Noranda

Saint-Félicien: **Centre local de services communautaires des Prés-Bleus**
Édifice Bon-Conseil
CP 10, 1209, boul Sacre-Coeur, Saint-Félicien, QC G8K 2P8
Tél: 418-679-5270 *Téléc:* 418-679-1748
Jean-Guy Lamothe, Directeur général (par intérim)

Saint-Hubert: **CLSC Saint-Hubert**
Affiliée à: Centre de santé et de services sociaux Champlain - Charles-Le Moyne
6800, boul Cousineau, Saint-Hubert, QC J3Y 8Z4
Tél: 450-443-7400
www.santemonteregie.qc.ca/champlain
Région desservi: L'arrondissement Saint-Hubert de la Ville de Longueuil
Spécialités: Rencontres prénatales (450-443-7400, option 6); Consultations psychosociales (450-443-7400, poste 7318)
Suzanne Beauchamp, Directrice générale

Saint-Jean-sur-Richelieu: **CLSC de la Vallée-des-Forts**
Affiliée à: Centre de santé et de services sociaux Haut-Richelieu-Rouville
978, boul du Séminaire nord, Saint-Jean-sur-Richelieu, QC J3A 1E5
Tél: 450-358-2572 *Téléc:* 450-349-0724
Christine Lessard, Directrice générale, CSSS Haut-Richelieu-Rouville

Saint-Léonard: **CLSC de Saint-Léonard**
Affiliée à: Centre de santé et de services sociaux de Saint-Léonard et Saint-Michel
5540, rue Jarry est, Saint-Léonard, QC H1P 1T9
Tél: 514-328-3460
csss-stleonardstmichel.qc.ca
Suzanne Hébert, Directrice générale, CSSS de Saint-Léonard et Saint-Michel

Saint-Ludger: **CLSC Saint-Ludger**
Affiliée à: Centre de santé et de services sociaux du Granit
210-A, rue La Salle, Saint-Ludger, QC G0M 1W0
Tél: 819-548-0330 *Téléc:* 819-548-5553
www.csssgranit.qc.ca
Pierre Latulippe, Directeur général, CSSS du Granit

Saint-Omer: **CLSC de Saint-Omer**
Affiliée à: Centre de santé et de services sociaux de la Baie-des-Chaleurs
107, rte 132 ouest, Saint-Omer, QC G0C 2Z0
Tél: 418-364-7064 *Téléc:* 418-364-7119
Bernard Nadeau, Directeur général, CSSS de la Baie-des-Chaleurs

Saint-Paulin: **CLSC de St-Paulin**
Affiliée à: Centre de santé de et de services sociaux de Maskinongé
2841, rue Laflèche, Saint-Paulin, QC J0K 3G0
Tél: 819-268-2572
www.csssm.qc.ca
Spécialités: Services infirmiers courants; Vaccination

Saint-Rémi: **CLSC Jardin-du-Québec**
Affiliée à: Centre de santé et de services sociaux Jardins-Roussillon
2, rue Sainte-Famille, Saint-Rémi, QC J0L 2L0
Tél: 450-454-4671 *Téléc:* 450-454-4538
Paul Moreau, Directeur général, CSSS Jardins-Roussillon

Sherbrooke: **CLSC de Sherbrooke - Point de service 50 rue Camirand**
Affiliée à: CSSS Institut universitaire de gériatrie de Sherbrooke
50, rue Camirand, Sherbrooke, QC J1H 4J5
Tél: 819-780-2222
www.csss-iugs.ca
Note: Autres points de service: 95, rue Camirand; 356, rue King ouest; 1200, rue King est; et 8, rue Speid.
Carol Fillion, Directeur général, CSSS-Institut universitaire de gériatrie de Sherbro

Sorel-Tracy: **CLSC Gaston-Bélanger**
Affiliée à: Centre de santé et de services sociaux Pierre-De Saurel
Également connu sous le nom de: CLSC du Havre
30, rue Ferland, Sorel-Tracy, QC J3P 3C7
Tél: 514-743-5569 *Téléc:* 514-743-1803
Nombre de lits: 18 lits
Jacques Blais, Directeur général
Jeanine Larosée, Chef, Entretient sanitaire

Sorel-Tracy: **Hôpital Richelieu / CLSC du Havre**
30, rue Ferland, Sorel-Tracy, QC J3P 3C7
Tél: 450-743-5569 *Téléc:* 450-743-1803
Ginette Rhealt, Manager

Ste-Anne-des-Monts: **CLSC de Sainte-Anne-des-Monts**
Affiliée à: Centre de santé et de services sociaux de La Haute-Gaspésie
52, rue Belvédère, Ste-Anne-des-Monts, QC G4V 1X4
Tél: 418-763-7771 *Téléc:* 418-763-7176
www.agencesssgim.ca; www.cssshautegaspesie.qc.ca

Ste-Catherine-de-la-J-Car: **CLSC de la Jacques-Cartier (Sainte-Catherine-de-la-Jacques-Cartier)**
Affiliée à: Centre de santé et de services sociaux de Québec-Nord
4570, rte de Fossambault, Ste-Catherine-de-la-J-Car, QC G3N 2T6
Tél: 418-843-2572 *Téléc:* 418-843-7569
www.csssqn.qc.ca
Spécialités: Soutien à domicile; Services infirmiers

Ste-Cécile-de-Masham: **CLSC des Collines**
Affiliée à: Centre de santé et de services sociaux des Collines
9, ch Passe-Partout, Ste-Cécile-de-Masham, QC J0X 2W0
Tél: 819-456-1112 *Téléc:* 819-456-4531
Ligne sans frais: 877-459-1112
www.santedescollines.qc.ca
Nombre de lits: Centre d'hébergement La Pêche: 32 lits.
Note: Y compris le Centre d'hébergement La Pêche et le CLSC Masham.
Pierre Rochon, Directeur général, CSSS des Collines
Jean-Paul Racine, Président, Conseil d'administration

Terrebonne: **CLSC Lamater**
Affiliée à: Centre de sante et des services sociaux du Sud de Lanaudière
2099, boul des Seigneurs, Terrebonne, QC J6X 4A7
Tél: 450-471-2881 *Téléc:* 450-964-4007
www.csss.sudlanaudiere.ca
Spécialités: Clinique médicale; Services sociaux scolaires; Service en santé mentale; Services dentaires préventifs; Clinique des jeunes; Vaccination

Trois-Rivières: **Centre de service Les Forges**
Affiliée à: Centre de santé et de services sociaux de Trois-Rivières
CP 1298, 500, rue St-Georges, Trois-Rivières, QC G9A 5L2
Tél: 819-379-5650
www.cssstr.qc.ca
Spécialités: Soutien à domicile

Victoriaville: **CLSC Suzor-Côté**
Affiliée à: Centre de santé et de services sociaux d'Arthabaska-et-de-L'Érable
100, rue de l'Ermitage, Victoriaville, QC G6P 9N2
Tél: 819-758-7281
www.csssae.qc.ca
Marcel Dubois, Président, Conseil d'administration, CSSS d'Arthabaska-et-de-l

Centres de traitments spécialisés (comprend: cliniques d'avortement, cliniques de soins aux cancéreux, centres de réadaptation professionnelle, centres de traitement)

Amos: **Centre Normand**
621, rue Harricana, Amos, QC J9T 2P9
Tél: 819-732-8241 *Téléc:* 819-727-2210
www.sante-abitibi-temiscamingue.gouv.qc.ca; www.centrenormand.org
Nombre de lits: 10 lits
Note: Offre des services de réadaptation aux personnes qui présentent une dépendance - à l'alcool, drogues illicites, médicaments, jeu; services de support psychosocial.
Pierre Michel Guay, Directeur général
pierremichel_guay@ssss.gouv.qc.ca

Amos: **CRDI Abitibi-Témiscamingue Clair-Foyer**
841, 3e rue ouest, Amos, QC J9T 2T4
Tél: 819-732-6511 *Téléc:* 819-732-0922
www.sante-abitibi-temiscamingue.gouv.qc.ca
Nombre de lits: 31 lits
Note: Centre de réadaptation (déficience intellectuelle); services de support.
Denis Plourde, Directeur général
danplo@ssss.gouv.qc.ca

Baie-Comeau: **Centre de protection et de réadaptation de la Côte-Nord**
835, boul Joliet, Baie-Comeau, QC G5C 1P5
Tél: 418-589-9927 *Téléc:* 418-589-4304
cprcn_dg@ssss.gouv.qc.ca
www.cprcn.qc.ca
Note: et centre jeunesse
Claude Montigny, Directeur général

Baie-Comeau: **Centre de protection et de réadaptation de la Côte-Nord**
836, boul Joliet, Baie-Comeau, QC G5C 1P5
Tél: 418-589-9927 *Téléc:* 418-589-4304
cprcn_dg@ssss.gouv.qc.ca
www.cprcn.qc.ca
Nombre de lits: 225 lits
Claude Montigny, Directeur général

Beauceville: **Centre de réadaptation en dépendance de Chaudière-Appalaches**
Ancien nom: Centre de réadaptation en alcoolisme et toxicomanie de Chaudière-Appalaches
253, rte 108, Beauceville, QC G5X 2Z3
Tél: 418-774-3329 *Téléc:* 418-774-4423
www.acrdq.qc.ca
Nombre de lits: 14 lits
Huguette Giroux, Directrice générale

Bonaventure: **Centre de réadaptation de la Gaspésie - Point de service MRC de Bonaventure**
CP 667, 238, av Port-Royal, Bonaventure, QC G0C 1E0
Tél: 418-534-4243 *Téléc:* 418-534-2411
www.agencesssgim.ca
Note: Déficiences physiques et intellectuelles.

Bonaventure: **Centre jeunesse Gaspésie/Les Iles - Point de service Unité La Balise**
CP 308, 193, av Port Royal, Bonaventure, QC G0C 1E0
Tél: 418-534-3283 *Téléc:* 418-534-4024
www.agencesssgim.ca
Nombre de lits: 12 lits
Note: Pour mésadaptées socio-affectifs.

Bonaventure: **Centre jeunesse Gaspésie/Les Iles - Point de service Succursale Bonaventure-Avignon**
CP 308, 106, av Port-Royal, Bonaventure, QC G0C 1E0
Tél: 418-534-2272 *Téléc:* 418-534-4278
www.agencesssgim.ca

Cap-aux-Meules: **Centre jeunesse Gaspésie/Les Iles - Point de service Succursale des Iles**
CP 268, 539-2, ch Principal, Cap-aux-Meules, QC G4T 1E7
Tél: 418-986-2230 *Téléc:* 418-986-5445
www.agencesssgim.ca

***Carleton:* Centre de réadaptation de la Gaspésie - Point de service MRC d'Avignon - Carleton**
CP 26, 314, boul Perron ouest, Carleton, QC G0C 1J0
Tél: 418-364-6037 *Téléc:* 418-364-7040
www.agencesssgim.ca
Note: Déficience intellectuelle.

***Chandler:* Centre de réadaptation de la Gaspésie - Point de service MRC du Rocher-Percé**
CP 2168, 328, boul René-Lévesque ouest, Chandler, QC G0C 1K0
Tél: 418-689-4286 *Téléc:* 418-689-7155
www.agencesssgim.ca
Note: Déficiences physiques et intellectuelles.

***Chandler:* Centre jeunesse Gaspésie/Les Iles - Point de service Succursale Rocher-Percé**
CP 280, 105, rue Commerciale ouest, Chandler, QC G0C 1K0
Tél: 418-689-2286 *Téléc:* 418-689-4643
www.agencesssgim.ca

***Chicoutimi:* Le Centre jeunesse du Saguenay — Lac-Saint-Jean**
1109, av Bégin, Chicoutimi, QC G7H 4P1
Tél: 418-549-4853 *Téléc:* 418 693-0765
www.cjsaglac.ca
Maurice Gagnon, Président, Conseil d'administration
Marc Thibeault, Directeur général
Richard Chamberland, Commissaire aux plaintes et à la qualité des services
plaintes@cjsaglac.ca
Danielle Tremblay, Directrice de la protection de la jeunesse
Brigitte Savaria, Agente d'information

***Dixville:* Centre d'accueil Dixville inc. CRDITED Estrie**
301, rue Saint-Alexandre, Dixville, QC J0B 1P0
Tél: 819-849-4831 *Téléc:* 819-849-6673
info.crditedestrie@ssss.gouv.qc.ca
www.crditedestrie.qc.ca
Fondée en: 1958
Note: Le centre de réadaptation en déficience intellectuelle et troubles envahissants du développement Estre (CRDITED Estrie) est composé de deux établissements du réseau de la santé et des services sociaux du Québec, soit le Centre d'accueil Dixville inc. et le Centre Notre-Dame de l'Enfant (Sherbrooke) inc.
Gaétan Duford, Président, Conseil d'administration
Danielle Lareau, Directrice générale, et secrétaire, conseil d'administration
Jean-Luc Gosselin, Commissaire aux plaintes et à la qualité des services

***Fatima:* Centre de réadaptation de la Gaspésie - Point de service MRC des Iles-de-la-Madeleine**
CP 549, 695, ch des Caps, Fatima, QC G4T 2S9
Tél: 418-986-4870 *Téléc:* 418-986-2623
www.agencesssgim.ca
Note: Déficience physique.

***Gaspé:* Centre de réadaptation de la Gaspésie - Point de service MRC de La Côte-de-Gaspé**
CP 6320, 150, rue Mgr Ross, aile 550, Gaspé, QC G4X 2R8
Tél: 418-368-2306 *Téléc:* 418-368-7761
www.agencesssgim.ca
Note: Déficiences physiques et intellectuelles.

***Gaspé:* Centre jeunesse Gaspésie/Les Iles**
#100, 205, boul de York ouest, Gaspé, QC G4X 2V7
Tél: 418-368-1803 *Téléc:* 418-368-5478
www.agencesssgim.ca
Nombre de lits: 55 lits

***Gaspé:* Centre jeunesse Gaspésie/Les Iles - Point de service Unité La Vigie**
418, montée Wakeham, Gaspé, QC G4X 2V7
Tél: 418-368-1803 *Téléc:* 418-368-8744
www.agencesssgim.ca
Nombre de lits: 14 places
Note: Centre de réadaptation.

***Gaspé:* Centre jeunesse Gaspésie/Les Iles - Point de service Unité La Rade**
#100, 205, boul de York ouest, Gaspé, QC G4X 2V7
Tél: 418-368-1803 *Téléc:* 418-368-6303
www.agencesssgim.ca

***Gaspé:* Centre jeunesse Gaspésie/Les Iles - Point de service Succursale Côte-de-Gaspé**
#100, 205, boul de York ouest, Gaspé, QC G4X 2V7
Tél: 418-368-3381 *Téléc:* 418-368-5101
www.agencesssgim.ca

***Gatineau:* Centre Jellinek**
Ancien nom: Pavillon Jelinek
25, rue Saint-François, Gatineau, QC J9A 1B1
Tél: 819-776-5584 *Téléc:* 819-776-0255
Ligne sans frais: 866-776-5585
jellinek@jellinek.org
www.jellinek.org
Nombre de lits: 33 places
Note: centre de réadaptation des drogues, de l'alcool ou du jeu
Raymond Rochon, Directeur général

***Gatineau:* Les Centres jeunesse de l'Outaouais**
105, boul Sacré-Coeur, Gatineau, QC J8X 1C5
Tél: 819-771-6631
cjoutaouais.qc.ca
Nombre de lits: 149 lits
Note: centre jeunesse, protection
Luc Cadieux, Directeur général
Luc.Cadieux@ssss.gouv.qc.ca

***Gatineau:* Pavillon du Parc inc.**
768, boul St-Joseph, Gatineau, QC J8Y 4B8
Tél: 819-684-1022 *Téléc:* 819-684-1023
info@pavillonduparc.qc.ca
www.pavillonduparc.qc.ca
Nombre de lits: 92 lits
Note: centre de réadaptation
Thierry Boyer, Directeur général

***Joliette:* Centre de réadaptation La Myriade**
339, boul Base-de-Roc, Joliette, QC J6E 5P3
Tél: 450-753-9600 *Téléc:* 450-753-1930
Ligne sans frais: 450-753-9622
www.crlamyriade.qc.ca
Nombre de lits: 38 lits
Robert Lasalle, Directeur général

***Joliette:* Les Centres jeunesse de Lanaudière (CJL)**
260, rue Lavaltrie sud, Joliette, QC J6E 5X7
Tél: 450-756-4555 *Téléc:* 450-756-0814
Ligne sans frais: 1-800-229-1152
www.centresjeunessedelanaudiere.qc.ca
Jacques Perreault, Président, Conseil d'administration
Richard Provost, Vice-président
Christian Gagné, Directeur général & Secrétaire

***Kuujjuaq:* Centre de santé Tulattavik de l'Ungava**
CP 149, Kuujjuaq, Kuujjuaq, QC J0M 1C0
Tél: 514-735-7645 *Téléc:* 514-735-7641
recrutement@ungava.info
www.ungava.info
Nombre de lits: 23 lits

***Lachine:* Centre de réadaptation de l'Ouest de Montréal (CROM/WMR)/West Montreal Readaptation Centre**
8000, rue Notre-Dame, Lachine, QC H8R 1H2
Tél: 514-363-3025 *Téléc:* 514-364-0608
infocrom@ssss.gouv.qc.ca
www.crom-wmrc.ca
Média social: www.facebook.com/CROM.WMRC
Région desservi: CSSS de l'Ouest de l'Ile; CSSS Cavendish; CSSS de la Montagne
Spécialités: Services spécialisés pour des adultes et enfants présentant une déficience intellectuelle ou un trouble du spectre autistique
Gary Whittaker, Président
Jacques Nolin, Vice-président
Ron Creary, Secrétaire et Directeur général

***Laval:* Centre Jeunesse de Laval**
308, boul Cartier ouest, Laval, QC H7N 2J2
Tél: 450-975-4150
www.centrejeunessedelaval.ca
Guy Villeneuve, Président, Conseil d'administration
Jean-Guy Blanchet, Premier vice-président, Conseil d'administration
Danièle Dulude, Secrétaire, Conseil d'administration
Yvon Shedleur, Trésorier, Conseil d'administration
Carole Du Sault, Responsable, services des communications

***Laval:* CRDI Normand-Laramée**
304, boul Cartier ouest, Laval, QC H7N 2J2
Tél: 450-972-2099
crdinl@ssss.gouv.qc.ca
www.crdinl.qc.ca
Note: Le CRDI Normand-Laramée est membre actif du Consortium national de recherche sur l'intégration sociale.
Claude Belley, Directeur général
France Duquette, Responsable, service conseil aux communications
Fax: 450-972-2020
Michèle Girard, Responsable, direction des services à la clientèle
Fax: 450-972-2041
Isabelle Portelance, Responsable, coordination des services enfance-famille
450-972-2041

***Lévis:* Centre de réadaptation en déficience intellectuelle de Chaudière-Appalaches**
55, rue du Mont-Marie, Lévis, QC G6V 0B8
Tél: 418-833-3218 *Téléc:* 418-833-9849
Ligne sans frais: 866-333-3218
crdi@chaudiere.appalaches@ssss.gouv.qc.ca
www.crditedca.com
Nombre de lits: 674 lits
Dominique Paquette, Directeur général

***Lévis:* Les Centres jeunesse Chaudière-Appalaches**
#300, 100, rue Monseigneur-Bourget, Lévis, QC G6V 2Y9
Tél: 418-837-9331 *Téléc:* 418-838-8860
www.cj12.qc.ca
Nombre de lits: 146 lits
Note: Services de la protection de la jeunesse; service aux jeunes contrevenants; service d'adoption; services de réadaptation. Installations: Lévis, Saint-Romuald, Montmagny, Sainte-Marie, Saint-Joseph, Saint-Georges & Thetford Mines.
Pierre Morin, Directeur général

***Longueuil:* Centre de réadaptation en déficience intellectuelle Montérégie-est (CRDITED)**
1255, rue Beauregard, Longueuil, QC J4K 2M3
Tél: 450-679-6511 *Téléc:* 450-928-3315
16_crdime_information@ssss.gouv.qc.ca
www.crdime.qc.ca
Média social: www.facebook.com/CRDITEDME
Nombre de lits: 1157 lits
Johanne Gauthier, Directrice générale

***Longueuil:* Centre jeunesse de la Montérégie (CJM)**
575, rue Adoncour, Longueuil, QC J4G 2M6
Tél: 450-928-5125 *Téléc:* 450-679-3731
Ligne sans frais: 1-800-641-1315
www.centrejeunessemonteregie.qc.ca
Marc Rodier, Président
Camil Picard, Directeur général & Secrétaire
Lucie Savaria-Pellegrin, Trésorière

***Montréal:* Association montréalaise pour les aveugles**
7000, rue Sherbrooke ouest, Montréal, QC H4B 1R3
Tél: 514-489-8201 *Téléc:* 514-489-3477
Nombre de lits: 8 lits
Note: centre de réadaptation (déficience visuelle) et CHSLD

***Montréal:* Atelier le Fil d'Ariane inc.**
#100, 4837, rue Boyer, Montréal, QC H2J 3E6
Tél: 514-842-5592 *Téléc:* 514-842-8343
atelier.bureau.ariane@ssss.gouv.qc.ca
www.atelierlefildariane.org
Nombre de lits: 20 places
Note: Un atelier de travail pour des adultes ayant des limitations fonctionnelles sur le plan intellectuel; l'atelier favorise l'intégration sociale & communautaire & l'autonomie personnelle & professionnelle des artisans.
Lisette Claveau, Directrice générale

***Montréal:* Centre d'accueil le programme de Portage inc.**
Également connu sous le nom de: Portage
885, square Richmond, Montréal, QC H3J 1V8
Tél: 514-939-0202
info@portage.ca
www.portage.ca
Média social: www.facebook.com/PortageCanada?ref=ts; twitter.com/PortageCanada
Fondée en: 1970
Note: Portage operates drug addiction treatment centres in the Québec cities of Montréal, Québec, Beaconsfield, Prévost, & Saint-Malachie. Centres in Atlantic Canada, Ontario, & British Columbia assist adolescents.
Peter Howlett, President
Peter Vamos, Executive Director, The Portage Program for Drug Dependencies
Seychelle Harding, Director, Communications
sharding@portage.ca

***Montréal:* Centre de réadaptation Constance-Lethbridge**
7005, boul de Maisonneuve ouest, Montréal, QC H4B 1T3
Tél: 514-487-1770 *Ligne sans frais:* 866-487-1891
www.constance-lethbridge.qc.ca
Note: déficience motrice

***Montréal:* Centre de réadaptation en déficience intellectuelle et en troubles envahissants du développement (CRDITED)**
#110, 75, rue de Port-Royal est, Montréal, QC H3L 3T1
Tél: 514-387-1234 *Téléc:* 514-387-8715
www.crditedmtl.ca
Fondée en: 2011
Joseph-Charles Giguère, Président, Conseil d'administration
Louis-Marie Marsan, Directeur général, et secrétaire, conseil d'administration

***Montréal:* Centre Dollard-Cormier**
950, rue de Louvain est, Montréal, QC H2M 2E8
Tél: 514-385-3490 *Téléc:* 514-385-2462
cqdt.cdc@ssss.gouv.qc.ca
www.centredollardcormier.qc.ca
Nombre de lits: 55 lits
Madeleine Roy, Directrice générale

***Montréal:* Centre hospitalier universitaire Sainte-Justine**
3175, ch de la C"te Sainte-Catherine, Montréal, QC H3T 1C5
Tél: 514-345-4931 *Téléc:* 514-345-4808
www.chu-sainte-justine.org
Média social: www.facebook.com/ChuSteJustine; twitter.com/ChuSteJustine
Nombre de lits: 55 lits
Khiem Dao, Directeur général

***Montréal:* Centre jeunesse de Montréal - Institut universitaire**
4675, rue Bélanger, Montréal, QC H1T 1C2
Tél: 514-593-3979
courrier@cjm-iu.qc.ca
www.centrejeunessedemontreal.qc.ca
Média social: www.facebook.com/cjmiu.fanpage; www.youtube.com/user/centrejeunessemtl
Nombre de lits: 826 admissions
Note: services psychosociaux et de réadaptation
Jean-Marc Potvin, Directeur général

***Montréal:* Centre Miriam**
8160, ch Royden, Montréal, QC H4P 2T2
Tél: 514-345-0210 *Téléc:* 514-345-8965
mircea.bruj.miriam@ssss.gouv.qc.ca
www.centremiriam.ca
Fondée en: 1960
Note: Miriam Home supports persons with intellectual disabilities.
Dr. Abraham Fuks, M.D., President, Board of Directors
Daniel Amar, Executive Director

***Montréal:* La Corporation du centre de réadaptation Lucie-Bruneau**
2275, av Laurier est, Montréal, QC H2H 2N8
Tél: 514-527-4527 *Téléc:* 514-527-0979
info@luciebruneau.qc.ca
Nombre de lits: 50 lits
Note: centre de réadaptation (déficience motrice)
Pierre Paul Milette, Directeur général

***Montréal:* Hôpital de réadaptation Villa Medica**
225, rue Sherbrooke est, Montréal, QC H2X 1C9
Tél: 514-288-8201
rh@villamedica.ca
www.villamedica.ca
Nombre de lits: 150 lits
Note: centre hospitalier de réadaptation
Michel Duchesne, Directeur général

***Montréal:* L'institut de réadaptation de Montréal**
6300, av Darlington, Montréal, QC H3S 2J4
Tél: 514-340-2085 *Téléc:* 514-340-2091
www.irm.qc.ca
Nombre de lits: 102 lits
Note: centre de réadaptation
Jacques R. Nolet, Directeur général

***Montréal:* Institut Raymond-Dewar**
3600, rue Berri, Montréal, QC H2L 4G9
Tél: 514-284-2581 *Téléc:* 514-284-5086
ird@raymond-dewar.gouv.qc.ca
www.raymond-dewar.qc.ca
Note: centre de réadaptation (déficience auditive et de la parole et du language)
Pierre-Paul Lachapelle, Directeur général

***Montréal:* Maison Elisabeth**
2131, av de Marlowe, Montréal, QC H4A 3L4
Tél: 514-482-2488 *Téléc:* 514-482-9467
questions@maisonelizabethhouse.com
www.maisonelizabethhouse.com
Nombre de lits: 18 lits
Linda Schachtler, Directrice générale

***Montréal:* Montréal Site of the Morgentaler Clinic The Morgentaler Clinic**
#710, 30, boul St Joseph est, Montréal, QC H2T 1G9
Tel: 514-844-4844 *Fax:* 514-844-7883
Toll-Free: 888-401-4844
cliniquem@bellnet.ca
www.morgentalermontreal.ca
Year Founded: 1968
Note: Specialties: Pregnancy termination services; Post-abortion service

***Puvirnituq:* Centre de santé Inuulitsivik**
ch Baie d'Hudson, Puvirnituq, QC J0M 1P0
Tél: 819-988-2957 *Téléc:* 819-988-2796
inuulitsivik@ssss.gouv.qc.ca
www.inuulitsivik.ca
Nombre de lits: 8

***Québec:* Centre de réadaptation en déficience intellectuelle de Québec (CRDIQ)**
7843, rue des Santolines, Québec, QC G1G 0G4
Tél: 418-683-2511 *Téléc:* 418-683-9735
infocrdiq@ssss.gouv.qc.ca
www.crdiq.qc.ca
Fondée en: 2001
Nombre de lits: 530 lits
Catherine Chagnon, Direction général

***Québec:* Centre de réadaptation Ubald-Villeneuve**
2525, ch de la Canardière, Québec, QC G1J 2G3
Tél: 418-663-5008 *Téléc:* 418-663-6575
communication@cruv.qc.ca
www.cruv.qc.ca
Andrée Deschênes, Directrice générale

***Québec:* Institut de réadaptation en déficience physique de Québec**
525, boul Wilfrid Hamel, Québec, QC G1M 2S8
Tél: 418-529-9141 *Téléc:* 418-529-7318
communications@irdpq.qc.ca
www.irdpq.qc.ca
Nombre de lits: 165 lits
Note: centre de réadaptation (déficience physique)
Richard Brousseau, Directeur général

***Restigouche:* Centre jeunesse Gaspésie/Les Iles - Point de service Unité Gignu**
CP 193, 4, ch Pacific, Restigouche, QC G0C 2R0
Tél: 418-788-5605 *Téléc:* 418-788-2751
www.agencesssgim.ca

***Rimouski:* Centre de réadaptation en déficience intellectuelle du Bas St-Laurent (CRDIBSL) Ancien nom: Centre de réadaptation intellectuelle du Bas St-Laurent**
274, rue Potvin, Rimouski, QC G5L 7P5
Tél: 418-723-4425 *Téléc:* 418-722-6113
info.crditedbsl@sss.gouv.qc.ca
www.crdibsl.qc.ca
Nombre de lits: 348 lits
Guylaine Côté, Directrice générale

***Rimouski:* Centre jeunesse du Bas-St-Laurent**
CP 3500, 287, rue Pierre-Saindon, 3e étage, Rimouski, QC G5L 8V5
Tél: 418-723-1255 *Téléc:* 418-722-0620
www.agencesssbsl.gouv.qc.ca
Nombre de lits: 73 lits
Marie-Sylvie Bêche, Directrice générale

***Roberval:* Centre de réadaptation en déficience intellectuelle du Saguenay-Lac-Saint-Jean**
835, rue Roland, Roberval, QC G8H 3J5
Tél: 418-275-1360 *Téléc:* 418-275-6595
www.crdited02.qc.ca
Nombre de lits: 617 lits
Note: Centre de réadaptation pour personnes présentant une déficience intellectuelle
Johanne Houde, Directrice générale

***Rouyn-Noranda:* Centre de réadaptation La Maison**
CP 1055, 100, ch Docteur-Lemay, Rouyn-Noranda, QC J9X 5C8
Tél: 819-762-6592 *Téléc:* 819-762-2049
www.sante-abitibi-temiscamingue.gouv.qc.ca; www.crlm.qc.ca
Nombre de lits: 55 lits
Note: Centre de réadaptation (déficience physique, troubles envahissants du développement).
Line St-Amour, Directrice générale
Line_St-Amour@ssss.gouv.qc.ca

***Saint-Jean-sur-Richelieu:* Les services de réadaptation du Sud-Ouest et du Renfort**
#105, 315, rue MacDonald, Saint-Jean-sur-Richelieu, QC J3B 8J3
Tél: 450-348-6121 *Téléc:* 450-348-8440
www.srsor.qc.ca
Nombre de lits: 581 lits
Gilles Bertrand, Directeur général

***Saint-Jérôme:* Centre du Florès**
#252, 500, boul des Laurentides, Saint-Jérôme, QC J7Z 4M2
Tél: 450-569-2970 *Téléc:* 450-569-2961
Ligne sans frais: 877-569-2970
centreduflores@ssss.gouv.qc.ca
www.centreduflores.com
Fondée en: 1995
Nombre de lits: 0
Note: centre de réadaptation
Lyse Beaudet, Direction générale

***Saint-Jérôme:* Centre jeunesse des Laurentides**
#241, 500, boul des Laurentides, Saint-Jérôme, QC J7Z 4M2
Tél: 450-436-7607 *Téléc:* 450-436-4811
Ligne sans frais: 866-492-3263
www.cjlaurentides.qc.ca
Nombre de lits: 160 lits
France Trépanier, Direction général

***Saint-Jérome:* Pavillon Ste-Marie inc.**
45, rue du Pavillon, Saint-Jérome, QC J7Y 3R6
Tél: 450-438-3583 *Téléc:* 450-438-7481
Nombre de lits: 100 lits
Francyne Jolicoeur, Directrice générale

***Saint-Philippe:* Pavillon Foster**
CP 119, 6, rue Foucreault, Saint-Philippe, QC J0L 2K0
Tél: 450-659-8911 *Téléc:* 450-659-7173
www.pavillonfoster.org
Nombre de lits: 20 lits
Note: alcohol/drug rehabilitation
John Topp, Directeur général

***Saint-Romuald:* Centre de réadaptation en déficience physique Chaudière-Appalaches**
2055, boul de la Rive-Sud, Saint-Romuald, QC G6W 2S5
Tél: 418-834-5888 *Téléc:* 418-834-0018
www.rrss12.gouv.qc.ca
Nombre de lits: 48 lits
Note: Programmes: Déficience auditive, Déficience du langage, Déficience motrice (enfant, adulte), Clinique de sclérose en plaques, Programme d'évaluation & de réadaptation en conduite automobile, Neurotraumatisme, Dépistage du traumatisme craniocérébral léger, Programme intensif de gestion autonome de la douleur, et Programme de suppléance à la communication. Points de service: Beauce-Etchemin (Beauceville), Montmagny-L'Islet (Montmagny), l'Amiante (Thetford Mines), et Littoral (Charny).

***Sept-Iles:* Bande indienne des montagnes de Sept-Iles/Maliotenam**
1089, rue Dequen, Sept-Iles, QC G4R 4L9
Tél: 418-962-0222 *Téléc:* 418-968-0935
Nombre de lits: 29 lits

***Sherbrooke:* Centre de réadaptation Estrie (CRE)**
#200, 300, rue King est, Sherbrooke, QC J1G 1B1
Tél: 819-346-8411 *Téléc:* 819-346-4580
www.centredereadaptationestrie.org
Média social: www.facebook.com/centredereadaptationestrie
Spécialités: Réadaptation fonctionnelle intensive; Ressources résidentielles et d'hébergement
Nicole Marchand, Directrice générale
nmarchand.cre@ssss.gouv.qc.ca
Violaine Dublis, Agente administrative

***Sherbrooke:* Centre Jean-Patrice Chaisson/Maison St-Georges**
1930, rue King ouest, Sherbrooke, QC J1J 2E2
Tél: 819-821-2500 *Téléc:* 819-563-8322

Nombre de lits: 45 lits
Note: centre de réadaptation des drogues
Denis Bougie, Directeur général

Sherbrooke: Centre jeunesse de l'Estrie
594, boul Queen Victoria, Sherbrooke, QC J1H 3R7
Tél: 819-564-7100 *Téléc:* 819-564-7109
Ligne sans frais: 1-800-567-3495

Sherbrooke: Centre Notre-Dame de l'Enfant (Sherbrooke) inc. (CNDE)
CRDITED Estrie
1621, rue Prospect, Sherbrooke, QC J1J 1K4
Tél: 819-346-8471 *Téléc:* 819-346-8473
info.crditedestrie@ssss.gouv.qc.ca
www.crditedestrie.qc.ca
Fondée en: 1965
Note: Le centre de réadaptation en déficience intellectuelle et troubles envahissants du développement Estre (CRDITED Estrie) est composé de deux établissements du réseau de la santé et des services sociaux du Québec, soit le Centre Notre-Dame de l'Enfant (Sherbrooke) inc. et le Centre d'accueil Dixville inc.

Sherbrooke: Villa Marie-Claire inc.
470, rue Victoria, Sherbrooke, QC J1H 3J2
Tél: 819-563-1622 *Téléc:* 819-563-6990
Nombre de lits: 15 lits
Louisette Breton, Directrice générale

Ste-Anne-des-Monts: Centre de réadaptation de la Gaspésie
CP 370, 230, rte du Parc, Ste-Anne-des-Monts, QC G4V 2C4
Tél: 418-763-3325 *Téléc:* 418-763-5631
Nombre de lits: 131 lits
Jacques Tremblay, Directeur général

Ste-Anne-des-Monts: Centre de réadaptation de la Gaspésie - Point de service MRC de la Haute-Gaspésie
230, rte du Parc, Ste-Anne-des-Monts, QC G4V 2C4
Tél: 418-763-3325 *Téléc:* 418-763-5631
www.agencesssgim.ca
Note: Déficiences physiques et intellectuelles.

Ste-Anne-des-Monts: Centre de réadaptation L'Escale
Affiliée à: Centre de santé et de services sociaux de La Haute-Gaspésie
52, rue Belvedere, Ste-Anne-des-Monts, QC G4V 1X4
Tél: 418-763-5000 *Téléc:* 418-763-9024
Note: Pour personnes toxicomanes. Le Centre relocalisera en 2010. Les nouvelles installations seront adjacentes à l'Hôpital des Monts.

Ste-Anne-des-Monts: Centre jeunesse Gaspésie/Les Iles - Point de service Succursale Haute-Gaspésie
#EB-132, 230, rte du Parc, Ste-Anne-des-Monts, QC G4V 2C4
Tél: 418-763-2251 *Téléc:* 418-763-2538
www.agencesssgim.ca

Trois-Rivières: Centre de réadaptation Interval
1775, rue Nicolas-Perrot, Trois-Rivières, QC G9A 1C5
Tél: 819-378-4083 *Téléc:* 819-693-0237
www.centreinterval.qc.ca
Nombre de lits: 40 lits
Note: centre de réadaptation (déficience motrice)
Serge Lemieux, Directeur général

Trois-Rivières: Centre jeunesse de la Mauricie et Centre-du-Québec
Centre administratif, 1455, boul du Carmel, Trois-Rivières, QC G8Z 3R7
Tél: 819-378-5481
communications_cjmcq@ssss.gouv.qc.ca
www.cjmcq.qc.ca
Robert Nolin, Président, Conseil d'administration
Serge Bisaillon, Directeur général
Gérald Milot, Vice-président, Conseil d'administration
Jean-Pierre Vézina, Secrétaire, Conseil d'administration

Trois-Rivières: CRDITED de la Mauricie et du Centre-du-Québec
3255, rue Foucher, Trois-Rivières, QC G8Z 1M6
Tél: 819-379-6868 *Téléc:* 819-379-5155
Ligne sans frais: 1-888-379-7732
crditedmcqiu_recrutement@ssss.gouv.qc.ca (ressources humaines)
www.crditedmcq.qc.ca
Média social: www.facebook.com/crditedmcq.iu; twitter.com/crditedmcqiu
Région desservi: La région sociosanitaire de la Mauricie et du Centre-du-Québec
Note: Le Centre de réadaptation en déficience intellectuelle et en troubles envahissants du développement de la Mauricie et du Centre-du-Québec (CRDITED MCQ) est affilié à l'Université du Québec à Trois-Rivières (UQTR).
Sylvie Dupras, Directrice générale

Trois-Rivières: Domremy Mauricie-Centre-du-Québec
440, rue des Forges, Trois-Rivières, QC G9A 2H5
Tél: 819-374-4744 *Téléc:* 819-374-4502
DomremyMCQ@ssss.gouv.qc.ca
www.domremymcq.ca
Nombre de lits: 30 lits
Note: centre de réadaptation des drogues
Pierre Bourassa, Directeur général

Val-d'Or: Centre jeunesse de l'Abitibi-Témiscamingue
700, boul Forest, Val-d'Or, QC J9P 2L3
Tél: 819-825-0002 *Téléc:* 819-825-5132
www.cjat.qc.ca
Fondée en: 1996
Nombre de lits: 57 lits
Personnel: 450
Catherine Langlois, Direction générale
cathlang@ssss.gouv.qc.ca

Verdun: Teen Haven
4360, boul Lasalle, Verdun, QC H4G 2A8
Tel: 514-769-5050 *Fax:* 514-769-3510
teenhaven@b2b2c.ca
Number of Beds: 15 lits
Robert Johnson, Managing Director

Wemotaci: Conseil de la Nation Atikamekw
Wemotaci, QC G0X 3R0
Tél: 418-523-6153 *Téléc:* 418-676-8965
Nombre de lits: 9
Clément St-Cyr, Directeur général

Westmount: Centre de jeunesse Mont Saint-Patrick Inc.
6, Weredale Park, Westmount, QC H3Z 1Y6
Tél: 514-747-1936
Nombre de lits: 9 lits
Note: centre de réadaptation (déficience visuelle)

Westmount: Les Centres de jeunesse Shawbridge
5 Weredale Park, Westmount, QC H3Z 1Y5
Tél: 514-989-1885
Nombre de lits: 138 lits
Note: centre de réadaptation (déficience motrice)
Michael Udy, Directeur général

Westmount: Les centres de la jeunesse et de la famille Batshaw
Ancien nom: Les centres de la jeunesse et de la famille Saint-Georges
5, Weredale Park, Westmount, QC H3Z 1Y5
Tél: 514-989-1885
www.batshaw.qc.ca
Nombre de lits: 243 lits
Note: centre de réadaptation (déficience motrice) + déficience sensorielle
Margaret Douek, Directeur général

Centres d'hébergement et des soins de longue durée (CHSLD)

Acton Vale: Centre d'hébergement de la MRC-d'Acton
Affiliée à: Centre de santé et de services sociaux Richelieu-Yamaska
1268, rue Ricard, Acton Vale, QC J0H 1A0
Tél: 450-546-3234 *Téléc:* 450-546-4811
info@lesommetavotreportee.qc.ca
Nombre de lits: 81 lits
Daniel Castonguay, Directeur général, CSSS Richelieu-Yamaska
Réjeanne Boudreau, Directrice du Programme hébergement-milieu de vie, CSSS Richelieu-Yamaska

Akwesasne: Conseil Mohawk d'Akwesasne
CP 40, Akwesasne, QC H0M 1A0
Tél: 613-575-2507
Nombre de lits: 30 lits
Patti Jocko-Adia Conieti, Directrice générale

Amos: Centre d'hébergement Harricana
Affiliée à: Centre de santé et de services sociaux les Eskers de l'Abitibi
612, 5e av ouest, Amos, QC J9T 4L3
Tél: 819-732-6521 *Téléc:* 819-732-7526
www.csssea.ca
Nombre de lits: 103 lits de longue durée
Spécialités: Les unités de psychogériatrie (34 lits)

Anjou: CHSLD Le Royer
7351, rue Jean-Desprez, Anjou, QC H1K 5A6
Tél: 514-493-9397 *Téléc:* 514-493-9103
Nombre de lits: 96 lits
Guy Joly, Directeur général

Baie-Saint-Paul: Centre d'hébergement Pierre-Dupré
Affiliée à: Centre de santé et de services sociaux de Charlevoix
CP 1779, 10, rue Boivin, Baie-Saint-Paul, QC G3Z 1B0
Tél: 418-435-5562 *Téléc:* 418-435-4049
Nombre de lits: 60 lits
Robert Vallières, Directeur général

Beaconsfield: Manoir Beaconsfield
34, av Woodland, Beaconsfield, QC H9W 4V9
Tél: 514-694-2000 *Téléc:* 514-694-5000
Nombre de lits: 23 lits
Annie Maffre, Directrice générale

Beauharnois: Centre d'accueil le Vaisseau d'Or
55, rue Saint-André, Beauharnois, QC J6N 3G7
Tél: 450-429-6403 *Téléc:* 450-429-6602
Nombre de lits: 88 lits
Lise Bélisle-Bélanger, Directrice générale

Beauport: Centre d'hébergement du Fargy
Affiliée à: Centre de santé et de services sociaux de Québec-Nord
700, boul des Chutes, Beauport, QC G1E 2B7
Tél: 418-663-9934
Nombre de lits: 60 lits, 4 lits d'hébergement temporaires

Beauport: Centre d'hébergement Saint-Augustin
Affiliée à: Centre de santé et de services sociaux de Québec-Nord
2135, rue Terrasse-Cadieux, Beauport, QC G1C 1Z2
Tél: 418-667-3910
www.csssqn.qc.ca
Nombre de lits: 34 lits de gériatrie

Beloeil: Centre d'hébergement Champlain-Beloeil
221, rue Brunelle, Beloeil, QC J3G 2M9
Tél: 514-467-3356
Nombre de lits: 53 lits

Beloeil: Centre d'hébergement Marguerite-Adam
425, rue Hubert, Beloeil, QC J3G 2T1
Tél: 450-467-1631 *Téléc:* 450-467-4210
info@lesommetavotreportee.qc.ca
www.lesommetavotreportee.qc.ca;
www.santemonteregie.qc.ca/richelieu-yamaska
Nombre de lits: 70 lits
Daniel Castonguay, Directeur général, CSSS Richelieu-Yamaska
Réjeanne Boudreau, Directrice du Programme hébergement-milieu de vie, CSSS Richelieu-Yamaska

Berthierville: CHSLD Le Château inc.
1231, rue Dr Olivier-M.-Gendron, Berthierville, QC J0K 1A0
Tél: 450-836-6241 *Téléc:* 450-836-4013
Nombre de lits: 64 lits
Guy Ducharme, Directeur général

Boucherville: Centre d'hébergement Jeanne-Crevier
Affiliée à: Centre de santé et de services sociaux Pierre-Boucher
151, rue De Muy, Boucherville, QC J4B 4W7
Tél: 450-641-0595 *Téléc:* 450-641-3082
www.santemonteregie.qc.ca/cssspierreboucher
Nombre de lits: 93 lits
Caroline Barbir, Directrice générale, CSSS Pierre-Boucher

Brossard: Centre d'accueil Marcelle Ferron inc.
8600, boul Marie Victorin, Brossard, QC J4X 1A1
Tél: 450-923-1430 *Téléc:* 450-923-1805
info@chsldmarcelleferron.com
Nombre de lits: 175 lits
Zefferino Guiducci, Directeur général

***Brossard:* CHSLD Vigi Brossard**
Affiliée à: Vigi Santé Ltée
5955, boul Grande-Allée, Brossard, QC J4Z 3G4
Tél: 450-656-8500 *Téléc:* 450-656-8586
www.vigisante.com
Nombre de lits: 66 lits
Note: Agence/région administrative: Agence de la santé et des services sociaux de Montérégie.

***Cap-aux-Meules:* Centre d'hébergement Villa Plaisance**
Affiliée à: Centre de santé et de services sociaux des Iles
596, ch Principal, Cap-aux-Meules, QC G4T 1G1
Nombre de lits: 50 lits
Note: CSSS des Iles.
Germain Chevarie, Directeur général

***Chambly:* Manoir Soleil inc.**
Affiliée à: Centre de santé et de services sociaux Haut-Richelieu-Rouville
125, rue Daigneault, Chambly, QC J3L 1G7
Tél: 450-658-4441 *Téléc:* 450-658-6521
Nombre de lits: 68 lits
Nancy Gaudet, Directrice générale

***Chandler:* Centre d'hébergement Villa-Pabos**
Affiliée à: Centre de santé et de services sociaux du Rocher-Percé
75, rue des Cèdres, Chandler, QC G0C 1K0
Tél: 418-689-6621 *Téléc:* 418-689-4860
Note: CSSS du Rocher-Percé.

***Chandler:* CLSC-CHSLD Pabok**
CP 1090, 633, av Daignault, Chandler, QC G0C 1K0
Tél: 418-689-2572 *Téléc:* 418-689-4707
www.agencesssgim.ca
Nombre de lits: 62 lits
Note: A fusionné avec le Centre hospitalier de Chandler en 2004.
Chantal Duguay, Directrice générale

***Charlesbourg:* Centre d'hébergement de Charlesbourg**
Affiliée à: Centre de santé et de services sociaux de Québec-Nord
7150, boul Cloutier, Charlesbourg, QC G1H 5V5
Tél: 418-628-0456 *Téléc:* 418-622-8676
Nombre de lits: 64 lits
Note: Hébergement permanent, centre de jour

***Châteauguay:* Centre d'hébergement Champlain Châteauguay**
Affiliée à: Centre de santé et de services sociaux Jardins-Roussillon
210, rue Salaberry sud, Châteauguay, QC J6K 3M9
Tél: 450-632-4451 *Téléc:* 450-699-1696
www.santemonteregie.qc.ca/jardins-roussillon
Nombre de lits: 96 lits
Paul Moreau, Directeur général, CSSS Jardins-Roussillon

***Chicoutimi:* Centre d'hébergement Mgr-Victor-Tremblay**
Affiliée à: Centre de santé et de services sociaux de Chicoutimi
1236, rue D'Angoulême, Chicoutimi, QC G7H 6P9
Tél: 418-698-3911
Nombre de lits: 50 lits

***Chicoutimi:* CHSLD de Chicoutimi**
904, rue Jacques-Cartier est, Chicoutimi, QC G7H 2A9
Tél: 418-698-3900 *Téléc:* 418-543-6285
Nombre de lits: 104 lits
Benoît Duplessis, Directeur général

***Clermont:* Foyer de Clermont inc.**
CP 520, 6, rue du Foyer, Clermont, QC G4A 1G8
Tél: 418-439-4684 *Téléc:* 418-439-4062
Nombre de lits: 42 lits

***Cleveland:* Foyer Wales**
506, rte 243, Cleveland, QC J0B 2H0
Tél: 819-826-3266 *Téléc:* 819-826-2549
info@waleshome.ca
waleshome.ca
Nombre de lits: 222 lits
Simms Stuart, Directeur général

***Contrecoeur:* CLSC des Seigneuries de Contrecoeur / Centre d'hébergement De Contrecoeur**
Affiliée à: Centre de santé et de services sociaux Pierre-Boucher
4700, rte Marie-Victorin, Contrecoeur, QC J0L 1C0
Tél: 450-587-5025 *Téléc:* 450-587-8411
uppercanada@niagararegion.ca
Nombre de lits: 52 lits
Note: Centre d'hébergement, et le point de service CLSC des Seigneuries de Contrecoeur (450-652-2917).
Caroline Barbir, Directrice générale, CSSS Pierre-Boucher

***Côte Saint-Luc:* Centre d'hébergement Waldorf inc.**
7400, ch de la C"te-Saint-Luc, Côte Saint-Luc, QC H4W 3J4
Tél: 514-369-1000 *Téléc:* 514-489-3968
lewaldorf@reveraliving.com
www.reveraliving.com
Nombre de lits: 20 lits
Aileen Rabinovitch, Directrice générale

***Côte Saint-Luc:* Les résidences montréalaises de l'église unie pour personnes agées**
5790, av Parkhaven, Côte Saint-Luc, QC H4W 1Y1
Tél: 514-482-0590 *Téléc:* 514-482-2643
Nombre de lits: 216 beds
Annette Rudy, Dir. gen.

***Coteau-du-Lac:* Pavillon Laura Ferguson**
CP 909, 60, ch du Fleuve, Coteau-du-Lac, QC J0P 1B0
Tél: 514-267-3379
Nombre de lits: 15 places
Paul-Henri Boutin, Directeur général

***Cowansville:* Résidence Manoir Beaumont (1988) Inc.**
430, rue Beaumont, Cowansville, QC J2K 1W1
Tél: 514-263-6235 *Téléc:* 514-263-8598
Nombre de lits: 36 lits
Note: Hébergement et soins de longue durée
Monique Fréchette, Directrice générale

***Deux-Montagnes:* CHSLD Vigi Deux-Montagnes inc.**
580, 20e av, Deux-Montagnes, QC J7R 7E9
Tél: 450-473-5111 *Téléc:* 450-491-4686
www.vigisante.com
Nombre de lits: 76 lits
Note: Agence/région administrative: Agence de la santé et des services sociaux des Laurentides.
Robert Fournier, Directeur général

***Disraéli:* Centre d'hébergement René-Lavoie**
Affiliée à: Centre de santé et de services sociaux de la région de Thetford
CP 698, 260, av Champlain, Disraéli, QC G0N 1E0
Tél: 418-449-2020 *Téléc:* 418-449-4006
csssrt@ssss.gouv.qc.ca
www.centresantethetford.ca/sante-quebec/
Nombre de lits: 47 lits

***Dolbeau:* Pavillon Maison du Bel Age**
2020, rue Provencher, Dolbeau, QC G8L 3E6
Tél: 418-276-1866 *Téléc:* 418-276-1866
Nombre de lits: 53 places
Note: Maison d'hébergement pour personnes agées autonomes
Gisèle Laroche, Directrice générale

***Dollard-des-Ormeaux:* Vigi Santé Ltée**
197, rue Thornhill, Dollard-des-Ormeaux, QC H9B 3H8
Tél: 514-684-0930 *Téléc:* 514-684-0179
www.vigisante.com
Nombre de lits: 1,500 lits
Note: Propriétaire et administrateur de 15 centres d'hébergement, présente dans plusieurs régions du Québec. Le siège du CHSLD Vigi Dollard-des-Ormeaux, avec 160 lits.
Vincenzo Simonetta, Directeur général

***Dorval:* Centre d'hébergement Chartwell inc.**
2400, ch Herron, Dorval, QC H9S 5W3
Tél: 514-396-6565
www.chartwellreit.ca
Nombre de lits: 325 lits
Claudette Cloutier, Directrice générale

***Drummondville:* Centre d'hébergement Frederick-George-Heriot**
Affiliée à: Centre de santé et de services sociaux Drummond
75, rue St-Georges, Drummondville, QC J2C 4G6
Tél: 819-477-0544
csssdrummond@ssss.gouv.qc.ca
www.csssdrummond.qc.ca
Nombre de lits: 354 lits
Nagui Habashi, Directeur général, CSSS Drummond
Lyse Garant, Directrice du Programme, Personnes en perte d'autonomie

***Farnham:* Les Foyers Farnham**
Affiliée à: Centre de santé et de services sociaux la Pommeraie
800, rue Saint-Paul nord, Farnham, QC J2N 2K6
Tél: 450-293-3167 *Téléc:* 450-293-7878
Nombre de lits: 61 lits

***Gaspé:* Centre d'hébergement Mgr-Ross**
Affiliée à: Centre de santé et de services sociaux de La Côte-de-Gaspé
150, rue Mgr Ross, Gaspé, QC G4X 2S7
Tél: 418-368-3301 *Téléc:* 418-368-6730
Nombre de lits: 129 lits
Note: CSSS Côte-de-Gaspé.

***Gatineau:* Centre d'hébergement - Bon Séjour**
Affiliée à: Centre de santé et de services sociaux de Gatineau
134, rue Jean-René Monette, Gatineau, QC J8P 7C3
Tél: 819-966-6450 *Téléc:* 819-966-6453
www.csssgatineau.qc.ca
Nombre de lits: 100 lits
Nancy Bergeron, Directrice adjointe en hébergement, Soutien à l'autonomie
819-966-6440

***Gatineau:* Centre d'hébergement - Foyer du Bonheur**
Affiliée à: Centre de santé et de services sociaux de Gatineau
125, boul Lionel-Émond, Gatineau, QC J8Y 5S8
Tél: 819-966-6410 *Téléc:* 819-966-6414
www.csssgatineau.qc.ca; www.santeoutaouais.qc.ca
Nombre de lits: 263 lits
Nancy Bergeron, Directrice adjointe en hébergement, Soutien à l'autonomie
819-966-6440

***Gatineau:* Centre d'hébergement - La Pietà**
Affiliée à: Centre de santé et de services sociaux de Gatineau
273, rue Laurier, Gatineau, QC J8X 3W8
Tél: 819-966-6420 *Téléc:* 819-966-6421
www.csssgatineau.qc.ca; www.santeoutaouais.qc.ca
Nombre de lits: 158 lits
Nancy Bergeron, Directrice adjointe en hébergement, Soutien à l'autonomie
819-966-6440

***Gracefield:* Le Foyer d'accueil de Gracefield**
Affiliée à: Centre de santé et de services sociaux de la Vallée-de-la-Gatineau
CP 317, 1, rue du Foyer, Gracefield, QC J0X 1W0
Tél: 819-463-2100 *Téléc:* 819-463-4721
Nombre de lits: 31 lits
Bruno Larivière, Coordonateur, Hébergement

***Granby:* Centre d'hébergement Villa Bonheur**
Affiliée à: Centre de santé et de services sociaux de la Haute-Yamaska
71, rue Court, Granby, QC J2G 4Y7
Tél: 450-776-5222 *Téléc:* 450-372-7617
Nombre de lits: 108 lits

***Grand-Mère:* CHSLD du Centre Mauricie**
1650, 6e av, Grand-Mère, QC G9T 2K4
Tél: 819-533-2500 *Téléc:* 819-538-7640
Nombre de lits: 150 lits; 36 places en pavillon d'hébergement
Guy D'Anjou, Directeur général

***Huntingdon:* Centre d'hébergement du comté de Huntingdon**
Affiliée à: Centre de santé et de services sociaux du Haut-Saint-Laurent
198, rue Châteauguay, Huntingdon, QC J0S 1H0
Tél: 450-829-2321 *Téléc:* 450-264-4923
www.santemonteregie.qc.ca/haut-saint-laurent
Nombre de lits: 60 lits

***Ile-Bizard:* Centre d'hébergement Denis-Benjamin Viger**
Affiliée à: Centre de santé et de services sociaux de l'Ouest-de-l'Ile
3292, rue Cherrier, Ile-Bizard, QC H9C 1E4
Tél: 514-620-6310 *Téléc:* 514-620-6553
www.csssouestdelile.qc.ca
Nombre de lits: 125 lits

Ile-Perrot: Centre d'hébergement Laurent-Bergevin
Affiliée à: Centre de santé et de services sociaux de Vaudreuil-Soulanges
Également connu sous le nom de: Centre d'accueil Laurent-Bergevin
200, boul Perrot, Ile-Perrot, QC J7V 7M7
Tél: 514-453-5860 Téléc: 514-453-8939
Nombre de lits: 82 lits

Irlande: Pavillon Morisset-Huppé Inc.
Ancien nom: Ressource Intermédiare
CP 2060, 290, rte 165, Irlande, QC G6H 2N7
Tél: 418-428-3568 Téléc: 418-420-3021
Fondée en: 1980
Nombre de lits: 9 places
Note: Hébergement pour adultes en déficience intellectuells et handicapés physiques.
Lucie Morisset-Huppé, Directrice générale
morisset28@hotmail.com

Joliette: Centre d'hébergement de Saint-Eusèbe
Affiliée à: Centre de santé et de services sociaux du Nord de Lanaudière
585, boul Manseau, Joliette, QC J6E 3E5
Tél: 450-759-8222 Téléc: 450-759-1579
www.msss.gouv.qc.ca
Nombre de lits: 159 lits
Jean-Claude Berlinguet, Directeur général

Jonquière: Centre d'hébergement Georges-Hébert
Affiliée à: Centre de santé et de services sociaux de Jonquière
2841, rue Faraday, Jonquière, QC G7S 5C8
Tél: 418-695-7727 Téléc: 418-695-7737
wpp01.msss.gouv.gc.ca
Nombre de lits: 75 lits

Jonquière: Centre d'hébergement Sainte-Marie
Affiliée à: Centre de santé et de services sociaux de Jonquière
2184, rue Perrier, Jonquière, QC G7X 9C9
Tél: 418-695-7800 Téléc: 418-695-7738
Nombre de lits: 66 lits
Note: Hébergement permanent et temporaire

Jonquière: Pavillon Arvida
Affiliée à: an
CP 1200, 1841, rue Deschênes, Jonquière, QC G7S 4K6
Tél: 418-548-8231 Téléc: 418-548-6875
Nombre de lits: 60 lits

La Baie: Foyer de Bagotville
562, rue Victoria, La Baie, QC G7B 3M6
Tél: 418-544-2853 Téléc: 418-544-6407
Nombre de lits: 33 lits

La Baie: Foyer St-Joseph de La Baie inc.
1893, rue Alexis-Simard, La Baie, QC G7B 2K9
Tél: 418-544-2673 Téléc: 418-544-8936
Nombre de lits: 48 lits

La Guadeloupe: Pavillon Notre-Dame
CP 490, 437, 15e rue ouest, La Guadeloupe, QC G0M 1G0
Tél: 418-459-3476 Téléc: 418-459-6428
Nombre de lits: 50 lits
Richard Busque, Directeur général

La Sarre: CHSLD de La Sarre
Affiliée à: Centre de santé et de services sociaux des Aurores-Boréales
22, 1ère av est, La Sarre, QC J9Z 1C4
Tél: 819-333-5525 Téléc: 819-333-5527
www.csssab.qc.ca
Nombre de lits: 25 chambres privées
Spécialités: Les services d'hébergement; Physiothéapie; Ergothérapie; Le service psychosocial

LaSalle: Centre d'hébergement de LaSalle
Affiliée à: Centre de santé et de services sociaux de Dorval-Lachine-LaSalle
8686, rue Centrale, LaSalle, QC H8P 3N4
Tél: 514-364-6700
www.santemontreal.qc.ca
Nombre de lits: 202 lits
Léonard Vincent, Directeur général

LaSalle: Hôpital Ste-Thérèse inc.
9307, boul LaSalle, LaSalle, QC H8R 2M7
Tél: 514-366-3556 Téléc: 514-367-3718
Nombre de lits: 47 lits

Labelle: Centre d'hébergement de Labelle
Affiliée à: Centre de santé et de services sociaux des Sommets
CP 38, 50, rue de l'Église, Labelle, QC J0T 1H0
Tél: 819-686-2372 Téléc: 819-686-1950
Nombre de lits: 46 lits
Jacques Morin, Président, Conseil d'administration, CSSS des Sommets

Lac-Bouchette: Centre d'hébergement de Lac-Bouchette inc.
Édifice Foyer de Lac-Bouchette, CP 39, 99, rte de l'Ermitage, Lac-Bouchette, QC G0W 1V0
Tél: 418-348-6313 Téléc: 418-348-6342
Nombre de lits: 14 lits
Jacques Dubois, Directeur général, CSSS Domaine-du-Roy

Lac-Mégantic: CHSLD / Centre de jour Lac-Mégantic
Affiliée à: Centre de santé et de services sociaux du Granit
3675, rue du Foyer, Lac-Mégantic, QC G6B 2K2
Tél: 819-583-0330 Téléc: 819-583-0900
Nombre de lits: 46 lits
Pierre Latulippe, Directeur général, CSSS du Granit

Lac-au-Saumon: Centre d'hébergement Marie-Anne Ouellet
6, rue Turbide, Lac-au-Saumon, QC G0J 1M0
Tél: 418-778-5816 Téléc: 418-778-3391
www.csssmatapedia.qc.ca
Nombre de lits: 96 lits
Alain Paquet, Directeur général, CSSS de La Matapédia

Lachine: Centre d'hébergemen Nazaire-Piché
Affiliée à: Centre de santé et de services sociaux de Dorval-Lachine-LaSalle
150, 15e av, Lachine, QC H8S 3L9
Tél: 514-637-1780
www.santemontreal.qc.ca
Nombre de lits: 100 lits
Marie-Hélène Girard, Directrice générale

Lachine: Centre d'hébergement de Lachine
650, place d'Accueil, Lachine, QC H8S 3Z5
Tél: 514-634-7161
www.santemontreal.qc.ca
Nombre de lits: 217 lits

Lambton: CLSC / CHSLD de Lambton
Affiliée à: Centre de santé et de services sociaux du Granit
310-A, rue Principale, Lambton, QC G0M 1H0
Tél: 418-486-7441 Téléc: 418-486-2172
www.csssgrant.qc.ca
Nombre de lits: 32 lits
Note: Le point de service Lambton regroupe un centre local de services communautaire (CLSC), un centre d'hébergement, et un centre de jour.
Pierre Latulippe, Directeur général, CSSS du Granit

Lanoraie: Centre d'hébergement Alphonse-Rondeau
Affiliée à: Centre de santé et de services sociaux du Nord de Lanaudière
419, rue Faust, Lanoraie, QC J0K 1E0
Tél: 450-887-2343
www.csssnl.qc.ca
Nombre de lits: 75 places d'hébergement permanent

Laval: Centre d'hébergement de la Rive Prodimax inc.
4605, boul Sainte-Rose, Laval, QC H7R 5S9
Tél: 450-627-5599 Téléc: 450-627-5107
www.sssslaval.gouv.qc.ca
Nombre de lits: 79 lits
Note: Centre privé non-conventioné.
Jacques Le Guern, Directeur général

Laval: Centre d'hébergement de la Villa-des-Tilleuls inc.
5590, boul des Laurentides, Laval, QC H7K 2K2
Tél: 450-628-0322 Téléc: 450-622-3674
msss.gouv.qc.ca; www,sssslaval.gouv.qc.ca
Nombre de lits: 68 lits
Note: Centre privé non-conventioné.
Réginald Ratle, Directeur général

Laval: Centre d'hébergement de Sainte-Dorothée
Affiliée à: Centre de santé et de services sociaux de Laval
350, boul Samson ouest, Laval, QC H7X 1J4
Tél: 514-689-0933 Téléc: 514-689-3147
Nombre de lits: 277 lits
Note: Les autres centres d'hébergement: Fernand-Larocque, Idola-Saint-Jean, La Pinière, et Rose-de-Lima.
Luc Lepage, Directeur général, CSSS de Laval

Laval: Centre d'hébergement l'Eden de Laval inc
8528, boul Lévesque est, Laval, QC H7A 1W6
Tél: 450-665-6283
msss.qc.ca; www.sssslaval.gouv.qc.ca
Nombre de lits: 43 lits
Note: Centre privé non-conventioné.
Alain Fafard, Directeur général

Laval: Centre d'hébergement St-François inc.
4105, Montée Masson, Laval, QC H7B 1B6
Tél: 450-666-6541 Téléc: 450-666-1601
Nombre de lits: 53 lits
Marie-Christine Moulin, Directrice générale

Laval: CHSLD Saint-Jude inc.
4410, boul St-Martin ouest, Laval, QC H7T 1C3
Tél: 450-687-7714 Téléc: 450-682-0330
Nombre de lits: 204 lits
Daniel Leclair, Directeur général

Laval: Manoir St-Patrice inc.
3615, boul Perron, Laval, QC H7V 1P4
Tél: 450-681-1621 Téléc: 450-681-6120
Nombre de lits: 132 lits
Ann Carey, Directrice générale

Laval: La Résidence du Bonheur
5855, rue Boulard, Laval, QC H7B 1A3
Tél: 450-666-1567 Téléc: 450-666-6387
info@residencedubonheur.com
www.residencedubonheur.com; www.sssslaval.gouv.qc.ca
Nombre de lits: 50 lits
Note: Centre privé non-conventionné.
John Pakis, Directeur général
john.pakis@residencedubonheur.com

Laval: Résidence Riviera inc.
2999, boul Notre-Dame, Laval, QC H7V 4C4
Tél: 450-682-0111 Téléc: 450-682-0154
www.chsldresidenceriviera.com
Nombre de lits: 128 lits
Jean Nadon, Directeur général
Michel Samson, Directeur, Services techniques

Lévis: CLSC-CHSLD de la MRC Desjardins
15, rue de l'Arsenal, Lévis, QC G6V 4P6
Tél: 418-835-3400 Téléc: 418-835-1978
Nombre de lits: 95 lits
Renée Lachance-Auger, Directrice générale

Lévis: Pavillon Bellevue inc.
99, rue Monseigneur-Bourget, Lévis, QC G6V 9V2
Tél: 418-833-3490 Téléc: 418-833-6874
Nombre de lits: 50 lits
Claude Talbot, Directeur général

Lévis: Villa Mon Domaine inc.
109, av Mont-Marie, Lévis, QC G6V 8B4
Tél: 418-837-6408 Téléc: 418-837-2626
Nombre de lits: 57 lits
Jean-Noël Begin, Directeur général

Longueuil: Centre d'accueil St-Laurent inc.
Affiliée à: Centre de santé et de services sociaux Pierre-Boucher
480, rue LeMoyne ouest, Longueuil, QC J4H 1X1
Tél: 450-670-5480 Téléc: 450-670-9874
Nombre de lits: 32 lits
Note: CHSLD privé non conventionné
Caroline Barbir, Directrice générale, CSSS Pierre-Boucher

Longueuil: Centre d'hébergement de Mgr-Coderre
Affiliée à: Centre de santé et de services sociaux Pierre-Boucher
2761, rue Beauvais, Longueuil, QC J4M 2A4
Tél: 450-448-3607 Téléc: 450-448-4322
www.santemonteregie.qc.ca/cssspierreboucher
Nombre de lits: 154 lits
Caroline Barbir, Directrice générale, CSSS Pierre-Boucher

Longueuil: Centre d'hébergement du Chevalier-De Lévis
Affiliée à: Centre de santé et de services sociaux Pierre-Boucher
40, rue Lévis, Longueuil, QC J4H 1S5
Tél: 450-670-5391 Téléc: 450-670-7292
www.santemonteregie.qc.ca/cssspierreboucher
Nombre de lits: 142 lits
Caroline Barbir, Directrice générale, CSSS Pierre-Boucher

Longueuil: **Centre d'hébergement du Manoir-Trinité**
Affiliée à: Centre de santé et de services sociaux Pierre-Boucher
1275, boul Jacques-Cartier est, Longueuil, QC
Tél: 450-674-4948 *Téléc:* 450-674-8571
www.santemonteregie.qc.ca/cssspierreboucher
Nombre de lits: 115 personnes âgées en soins de longue durée (3 chambres adaptées pour résidents obèses)
Spécialités: Un centre de jour offrant des services à des adultes en perte d'autonomie demeurant à domicile; Services de réadaptation

Longueuil: **Centre d'hébergement René-Lévesque**
Affiliée à: Centre de santé et de services sociaux Pierre-Boucher
1901, rue Claude, Longueuil, QC J4G 1Y5
Tél: 450-651-4609 *Téléc:* 450-670-7731
www.santemonteregie.qc.ca/cssspierreboucher
Nombre de lits: 224 lits
Caroline Barbir, Directrice générale, CSSS Pierre-Boucher

Loretteville: **Foyer de Loretteville inc.**
165, rue Lessard, Loretteville, QC G2B 2V9
Tél: 418-842-9191 *Téléc:* 418-842-4472
Nombre de lits: 74 lits

Lyster: **Centre d'hébergement des Quatre-Vents**
2180, rue Bécancour, Lyster, QC G0S 1V0
Tél: 819-389-5923 *Téléc:* 819-389-5969
Nombre de lits: 26 lits
Marcel Dubois, Président, Conseil d'administration, CSSS d'Arthabaska-et-de-l

Magog: **Gestion SGH Inc.**
Ancien nom: Résidence Ste-Marguerite Marie
64, rue St-Pierre, Magog, QC J1X 3A2
Tél: 819-843-0202 *Téléc:* 819-843-9518
Nombre de lits: 27 lits
Carine Thuin, Directeur général

Malartic: **Centre d'hébergement Saint-Martin de Malartic**
Affiliée à: Centre de santé et de services sociaux de la Vallée-de-l'Or
CP 639, 701, rue de la Paix, Malartic, QC J0Y 1Z0
Tél: 819-757-3663 *Téléc:* 819-757-3309
www.sante-abitibi-temiscamingue.gouv.qc.ca; www.csssvo.qc.ca
Nombre de lits: 57 lits
Note: Centre d'hébergement/centre de jour.
Jérôme Lamont, Directeur général, CSSS de la Vallée-de-l'Or
Marie Cloutier, Directrice, Programme personnes en perte d'autonomie

Maria: **Centre d'hébergement de Maria**
Affiliée à: Centre de santé et de services sociaux de la Baie-des-Chaleurs
491, boul Perron, Maria, QC G0C 1Y0
Tél: 418-759-3458 *Téléc:* 418-759-5103
Nombre de lits: 91 lits
Bernard Nadeau, Directeur général, CSSS de la Baie-des-Chaleurs

Marieville: **Centre d'hébergement Sainte-Croix**
Affiliée à: Centre de santé et de services sociaux Haut-Richelieu-Rouville
300, rue Docteur-Poulin, Marieville, QC J3M 1L7
Tél: 450-460-4475 *Téléc:* 450-460-4104
Nombre de lits: 128 lits
Lucie Tétreault, Directrice, Personnes en perte d'autonomie liée au vieillisemen

Matane: **Centre d'hébergement de Matane**
Affiliée à: Centre de santé et de services sociaux de Matane
150, av Saint-Jér"me, Matane, QC G4W 3A2
Tél: 418-562-4154 *Téléc:* 418-562-9281
www.agencesssbsl.gouv.qc.ca
Nombre de lits: 106 lits
Nicole Morin, Directrice générale, CSSS de Matane

Matapédia: **Centre d'hébergement de Matapédia**
Affiliée à: Centre de santé et de services sociaux de la Baie-des-Chaleurs
14, boul Perron est, Matapédia, QC G0J 1V0
Tél: 418-865-2221 *Téléc:* 418-865-2317
www.csssbc.qc.ca
Spécialités: Services d'hébergement; Réadaptation

Mont-Joli: **CHSLD de La Mitis**
800, av du Sanatorium, Mont-Joli, QC G5H 3L6
Tél: 418-775-7261 *Téléc:* 418-775-1241
www.centremitissien.net
Nombre de lits: 175 lits
Isabelle Malo, Directrice générale, CSSS de La Mitis
cmssc_dg@centremitissien.net

Mont-Laurier: **Centre d'Hébergement Sainte-Anne**
Affiliée à: Centre de santé et de services sociaux d'Antoine-Labelle
411, rue de la Madone, Mont-Laurier, QC J9L 1S1
Tél: 819-623-5940 *Téléc:* 819-623-7347
www.csssal.org
Nombre de lits: 128 lits
Jean-Pierre Urbaine, Directeur général, CSSS d'Antoine-Labelle
Jean-Pierre St-Louis, Coordonnateur des unités de vie, CHSA

Mont-Royal: **CHSLD Vigi Mont-Royal**
Affiliée à: Vigi Santé Ltée
275, av Brittany, Mont-Royal, QC H3P 3C2
Tél: 514-739-5593 *Téléc:* 514-733-7973
www.vigisante.com
Nombre de lits: 273 lits
Note: Agence/région administrative: Agence de la santé et des services sociaux de Montréal.
Vincent Simonetta, Directeur général

Montmagny: **CLSC et Centre d'hébergement de Montmagny**
Affiliée à: Centre de santé et de services sociaux de Montmagny-L'Islet
168, rue Saint-Joseph, Montmagny, QC G5V 1H8
Tél: 418-248-1572 *Téléc:* 418-248-3374
www.csssml.qc.ca
Nombre de lits: 65 lits
Région desservi: Le territoire de Montmagny-L'Islet

Montréal: **Centre d'hébergement Rousselot**
Affiliée à: Centre de santé et de services sociaux Lucille-Teasdale
5655, rue Sherbrooke est, Montréal, QC H1N 1A4
Tél: 514-254-9421 *Téléc:* 514-254-3967
Nombre de lits: 157 lits
Robert Boucher, Directeur général

Montréal: **Les Cèdres - Le Centre d'accueil pour personnes âgées**
#200, 1275, Côte-Vertu, Montréal, QC H4L 4V2
Tél: 514-389-1023 *Téléc:* 514-389-0581
info@centrelescedres.ca
www.centrelescedres.ca
Rose Khoury, BSc.N, M.A., Directrice générale
Fadia El Khoury, BSc.Inf., MSc, Directrice des services àla clientèle
Susan Kouri, B.Com., Coordinatrice des services communautaires
Susan.Kouri.BCSTL@ssss.gouv.qc.ca

Montréal: **Centre d'accueil Father Dowd**
6565, ch Hudson, Montréal, QC H3S 2T7
Tél: 514-341-1007 *Téléc:* 514-341-8988
www.chssn.org
Nombre de lits: 134 lits
Carole McDonough, Directrice générale

Montréal: **Centre d'accueil Heritage Inc.**
5716, ch de la C"te-Saint-Antoine, Montréal, QC H4A 1R9
Tél: 514-484-2645
Nombre de lits: 16 lits
Ron Marolia, Directeur général

Montréal: **Centre d'accueil St-Margaret**
50, av Hillside, Montréal, QC H3Z 1V9
Tél: 514-932-3630 *Téléc:* 514-932-4379

Montréal: **Centre d'hébergement Armand-Lavergne**
Affiliée à: Centre de santé et de services sociaux Jeanne-Mance
3500, rue Chapleau, Montréal, QC H2K 4N3
Tél: 514-527-8921
www.csssjeannemance.ca; www.santemontreal.qc.ca
Nombre de lits: 182 lits
Note: Centre de jour; centre d'hébergement permanent.
Ron Rayside, Président du Conseil d'administration, CSSS Jeanne-Mance
Sylvie Simard, Directrice générale intérimaire, CSSS Jeanne-Mance

Montréal: **Centre d'hébergement Biermans**
Affiliée à: Centre de santé et de services sociaux de la Pointe-de-l'Ile
7905, rue Sherbrooke est, Montréal, QC H1L 1A4
Tél: 514-351-9891

Montréal: **Centre d'hébergement de Cartierville**
Affiliée à: Centre de santé et de services sociaux de Bordeaux-Cartierville-Saint-Laurent
12235, rue Grenet, Montréal, QC H4J 2N9
Tél: 514-337-7300 *Téléc:* 514-337-4188
Nombre de lits: 285 lits
Eveline Lyrette, Directrice générale

Montréal: **Centre d'hébergement de Louvain**
Affiliée à: Centre de santé et de services sociaux d'Ahuntsic et Montréal-Nord
9600, rue St-Denis, Montréal, QC H2M 1P2
Tél: 514-381-7256 *Téléc:* 514-381-6486
Nombre de lits: 155 lits
Richard Jean, Directeur général

Montréal: **Centre d'hébergement de Saint-Michel**
Affiliée à: Centre de santé et de services sociaux de Saint-Léonard et Saint-Michel
3130, rue Jarry est, Montréal, QC H1Z 4N8
Tél: 514-722-3000
csss-stleonardstmichel.qc.ca
Nombre de lits: 192 lits
Note: Centre administratif du CSSS, et centre d'hébergement.
Suzanne Hébert, Directrice générale, CSSS de Saint-Léonard et Saint-Michel
Johanne Maître, Directrice de l'hébergement, CSSS de Saint-Léonard et Saint-Michel

Montréal: **Centre d'hébergement des Quatre-Temps**
Affiliée à: Centre de santé et de services sociaux de Saint-Léonard et Saint-Michel
7400, boul Saint-Michel, Montréal, QC H2A 2Z8
Tél: 514-270-9271 *Téléc:* 514-270-6779
csss-stleonardstmichel.qc.ca
Nombre de lits: 192 lits
Suzanne Hébert, Directrice générale, CSSS de Saint-Léonard et Saint-Michel
Johanne Maître, Directrice de l'hébergement, CSSS de Saint-Léonard et Saint-Michel

Montréal: **Centre d'hébergement du Centre-Ville-de-Montréal**
Affiliée à: Centre de santé et de services sociaux Jeanne-Mance
66, boul René-Lévesque est, Montréal, QC H2X 1N3
Tél: 514-861-9331 *Téléc:* 514-861-8385
Nombre de lits: 196 lits
Ron Rayside, Président du Conseil d'administration, CSSS Jeanne-Mance
Sylvie Simard, Directrice générale intérimaire, CSSS Jeanne-Mance

Montréal: **Centre d'hébergement du Manoir-de-l'Age-d'Or**
Affiliée à: Centre de santé et de services sociaux Jeanne-Mance
3430, rue Jeanne-Mance, Montréal, QC H2X 2J9
Tél: 514-842-1147 *Téléc:* 514-842-1146
www.csssjeannemance.ca
Nombre de lits: 189 lits
Ron Rayside, Président du Conseil d'administration, CSSS Jeanne-Mance
Sylvie Simard, Directrice générale intérimaire, CSSS Jeanne-Mance

Montréal: **Centre d'hébergement Émilie-Gamelin**
Affiliée à: Centre de santé et de services sociaux Jeanne-Mance
1440, rue Dufresne, Montréal, QC H2K 3J3
Tél: 514-527-8921 *Téléc:* 514-527-3587
www.csssjeannemance.ca
Nombre de lits: 184 lits
Ron Rayside, Président du Conseil d'administration, CSSS Jeanne-Mance
Sylvie Simard, Directrice générale intérimaire, CSSS Jeanne-Mance

Montréal: **Centre d'hébergement Légaré**
Affiliée à: Centre de santé et de services sociaux d'Ahuntsic et Montréal-Nord
1615, av Émile-Journault, Montréal, QC H2M 2G3
Tél: 514-384-5490
www.santemontreal.qc.ca
Nombre de lits: 105 lits
Daniel Corbeil, Directeur général

Montréal: Centre d'hébergement Louis Riel
Affiliée à: Centre de santé et de services sociaux du Sud-Ouest-Verdun
2120, rue Augustin-Cantin, Montréal, QC H3K 3G3
Tél: 514-931-2263 *Téléc:* 514-931-2299
Nombre de lits: 100 lits
Germain Harvey, Directeur général

Montréal: Centre d'hebergement Marie-Rollet
5003, rue Saint-Zotique est, Montréal, QC H1T 1N6
Tél: 514-729-5281 *Téléc:* 514-593-5568
Nombre de lits: 110 lits
Note: Hébergement et soins de longue durée
Renée Pettigrew, Directrice

Montréal: Centre d'hébergement Marie-Rollet
Affiliée à: Centre de santé et de services sociaux Lucille-Teasdale
7445, rue Hochelaga, Montréal, QC H1N 3V2
Tél: 514-251-6000
Nombre de lits: 351 lits

Montréal: Centre d'hébergement Paul-Gouin
Affiliée à: Centre de santé et de services sociaux du Coeur-de-l'Ile
5900, rue St-Vallier, Montréal, QC H2S 2P3
Tél: 514-273-3681 *Téléc:* 514-273-7645
Nombre de lits: 100 lits

Montréal: Centre d'hébergement St-Andrew
Affiliée à: Centre de santé et de services sociaux Cavendish
50 av Hillside, Montréal, QC H3Z 1V9
Tél: 514-932-3630 *Téléc:* 514-932-4379
Nombre de lits: 300 lits
Carole McDonough, Directeur général

Montréal: Centre d'hébergement Yvon-Brunet
Affiliée à: Centre de santé et de services sociaux du Sud-Ouest-Verdun
6250, av Newman, Montréal, QC H4E 4K4
Tél: 514-765-8000 *Téléc:* 514-765-8064
Fondée en: 1982
Nombre de lits: 185 lits
Daniel Chartrand, Directeur du programme hébergement
Danielle McCann, Directrice générale
danielle.mccann@ssss.gouv.qc.ca

Montréal: Centre de soins prolongés Grace Dart
5155, rue Ste-Catherine est, Montréal, QC H1V 2A5
Tél: 514-255-2833 *Téléc:* 514-255-6275
Nombre de lits: 381 lits
Léon Gilbert, Directeur général (intérim)

Montréal: Centre Le Cardinal inc.
12900, rue Notre-Dame est, Montréal, QC H1A 1R9
Tél: 514-645-2766 *Téléc:* 514-640-6267
Nombre de lits: 204 lits
Léonard Chevarie, Directeur général

Montréal: CHSLD Bourget inc.
11570, rue Notre-Dame est, Montréal, QC H1B 2X4
Tél: 514-645-1673 *Téléc:* 514-645-1673
Nombre de lits: 112 lits
Note: Un établissement privé.
Diane Girard, Directrice générale

Montréal: Les CHSLD de mon quartier
Ancien nom: gentre-hospitalier -Centre d'accueil Gouin-Rosemont; CHSLD Jeanne-Leber
7445, rue Hochelaga, Montréal, QC H1N 3V2
Tél: 514-251-6011 *Téléc:* 514-251-9826
Nombre de lits: 351 lits
France Mailhot, Directrice générale

Montréal: CHSLD Jean XXIII inc.
6900, 15e av, Montréal, QC H1X 2V9
Tél: 514-725-2190 *Téléc:* 514-728-5901
Nombre de lits: 24 lits
Marie-Claire Lamontagne, Directrice générale

Montréal: CHSLD juif de Montréal
5725, av Victoria, Montréal, QC H3W 3H6
Tél: 514-738-4500 *Téléc:* 514-738-2611
www.chsldjuif.ca
Nombre de lits: 160 beds
Barbara Gold, Dir. gén. (intérim)

Montréal: CHSLD Manoir Fleury inc.
2145, rue Fleury est, Montréal, QC H2B 1J8
Tél: 514-388-1553 *Téléc:* 514-388-4161
Nombre de lits: 25 lits
Rose Renzo, Directrice générale

Montréal: CHSLD Marie-Claret inc.
Affiliée à: Vigi Santé Ltée
3345, boul Henri-Bourassa est, Montréal, QC H1H 1H6
Tél: 514-322-4380 *Téléc:* 514-326-8811
www.vigisante.com
Nombre de lits: 78 lits
Note: Agence/région administrative: Agence de la santé et des services sociaux de Montréal.
Jean-Guy Laplante, Directeur général

Montréal: CHSLD Providence Notre-Dame-de-Lourdes
1870, boul Pie-IX, Montréal, QC H1V 2C6
Tél: 514-527-4595 *Téléc:* 514-527-4475
Nombre de lits: 162 lits
Robert St-Pierre, Directeur général

Montréal: Groupe Champlain inc.
Affiliée à: Groupe Santé Sedna inc.
7150, rue Marie-Victorin, Montréal, QC H1G 2J5
Tél: 514-324-2044 *Téléc:* 514-324-5900
www.groupechamplain.qc.ca
Fondée en: 1966
Nombre de lits: 1443 lits
Note: 15 établissements

Montréal: L'Hôpital Chinois de Montréal (1963)
189, av Viger est, Montréal, QC H2X 3Y9
Tél: 514-871-0961 *Téléc:* 514-871-0966
montrealchinesehospital.ca
Nombre de lits: 128 lits
Anthony Shao, Directeur général

Montréal: Institut Canadien-Polonais du Bien-Etre inc.
5655, rue Bélanger, Montréal, QC H1T 1G2
Tél: 514-259-2551 *Téléc:* 514-259-9948
Nombre de lits: 126 lits
Anna Brychcy, Directrice générale

Montréal: Petites Soeurs des Pauvres - Ma Maison St-Joseph
5605, rue Beaubien est, Montréal, QC H1T 1X4
Tél: 514-254-4991 *Téléc:* 514-257-1742
Nombre de lits: 80 lits
Sr. Cécile de L'Enfant-Jésus, Directrice générale

Montréal: Résidence Berthiaume-du Tremblay
1635, boul Gouin est, Montréal, QC H2C 1C2
Tél: 514-381-1841 *Téléc:* 514-381-1090
www.berthiaume-du-tremblay.com
Nombre de lits: 246 lits
Nicole Ouellet, Directrice générale
nicole_ouellet@sss.gouv.qc.ca

Montréal: La Résidence Fulford
1221, rue Guy, Montréal, QC H3H 2K8
Tél: 514-935-5933 *Téléc:* 514-933-3773
fulford@fulfordresidence.com
www.fulfordresidence.com
Nombre de lits: 6 lits
Note: residence for women
Rt. Rev. Barry Clarke, Président

Montréal: Résidence Rive Soleil inc.
15150, rue Notre-Dame est, Montréal, QC H1A 1W6
Tél: 514-642-5509 *Téléc:* 514-642-8320
Nombre de lits: 50 lits
Christiane Chaussé, Directrice générale

Montréal: Résidence Sainte-Claire inc.
8950, rue Sainte-Claire est, Montréal, QC H1L 1Z1
Tél: 514-351-3877 *Téléc:* 514-352-5956
Nombre de lits: 38 lits
Yvan Daniel, Directeur général

Montréal: Résidence St-Jacques
8712, rue St-Hubert, Montréal, QC H2M 1Y5
Tél: 514-389-5800 *Téléc:* 514-389-8399
Fondée en: 1989
Nombre de lits: 25 lits
Paulette Théodore, Directrice générale

Montréal: Résidences Mance-Décary (CHSLD)
1800, rue St-Jacques, Montréal, QC H3J 2R5
Tél: 514-935-4681 *Téléc:* 514-935-6189
Nombre de lits: 580 lits
André Paquette, Directeur général

Montréal-Nord: CHSLD Gouin inc.
Affiliée à: Groupe Champlain inc.
4445, boul Henri-Bourassa est, Montréal-Nord, QC H1H 5M4
Tél: 514-327-6209 *Téléc:* 514-327-9912
www.groupechamplain.qc.ca
Nombre de lits: 93 lits
Note: Agence/région administrative: Agence de la santé et des services sociaux de Montréal.

Montréal-Nord: Résidence Angelica inc.
3435, boul Gouin est, Montréal-Nord, QC H1H 1B1
Tél: 514-324-6110 *Téléc:* 514-324-9332
Nombre de lits: 400 lits
Sr. Anne-Marie Marolo, Directrice générale

Montréal-Nord: Villa Belle Rive inc.
5320, boul Gouin est, Montréal-Nord, QC H1G 1B4
Tél: 514-321-1367
Nombre de lits: 27 lits
Louis-René Lanctôt, Directeur général

New Carlisle: Centre d'hébergement de New Carlisle
Affiliée à: Centre de santé et de services sociaux de la Baie-des-Chaleurs
108, rue Principale, New Carlisle, QC G0C 1Z0
Tél: 418-752-3386 *Téléc:* 418-752-6483
Nombre de lits: 75 lits
Bernard Nadeau, Directeur général, CSSS de la Baie-des-Chaleurs

Normandin: Centre de Normandin
Affiliée à: Centre de santé et de services sociaux Maria-Chapdelaine
1205, rue St-Cyrille, Normandin, QC G8M 4K1
Tél: 418-274-1234 *Téléc:* 418-274-6970
www,csssmariachapdelaine.com
Nombre de lits: 35 lits de soins de longue durée
Note: Centre d'hébergement; point de service CLSC; centre de jour.
Normand Brassard, Directeur général, CSSS Maria Chapdelaine

North Hatley: Connaught Home
Massawippi Chrisntian Retirement Homes
77 Main St., North Hatley, QC J0B 2C0
Tél: 819-842-2164 *Téléc:* 819-842-2667
info@mcrh.ca
www.mcrh.ca
Nombre de lits: 41 lits
Sandra Klinck, RN
819-842-2164 ext23
Donna Barker
819-842-2164 ext21

North Hatley: La Maison Blanche de North Hatley inc.
CP 298, 977, rue Massawippi, North Hatley, QC J0B 2C0
Tél: 819-842-2478 *Téléc:* 819-842-2470
Nombre de lits: 60 lits
Serge Croteau, Directeur général

Notre-Dame-du-Bon-Conseil: Centre d'hébergement L'Accueil Bon-Conseil
Affiliée à: Centre de santé et de services sociaux Drummond
91, rue Saint-Thomas, Notre-Dame-du-Bon-Conseil, QC J0C 1A0
Tél: 819-336-2122
csssdrummond@ssss.gouv.qc.ca
www.csssdrummond.qc.ca
Nombre de lits: 52 lits
Note: Centre d'hébergement; le point de service CLSC: 819-474-2572.
Nagui Habashi, Directeur général, CSSS Drummond

Notre-Dame-du-Nord: CHSLD des premières nations du Timiskaming
20, av Algonquin, Notre-Dame-du-Nord, QC J0Z 3B0
Tél: 819-723-2225 *Téléc:* 819-723-2112
www.sante-abitibi-temiscamingue.gouv.qc.ca; wpp01.msss.gouv.qc.ca
Nombre de lits: 20 lits
Note: Établissement privé non conventionné
Estelle St-Cyr Perreault, Directrice générale

Oka: Manoir Oka inc.
CP 567, 2083, ch Oka, Oka, QC J0N 1E0
Ligne sans frais: 800-251-9902
manoiroka@videotron.ca
manoiroka.com
Nombre de lits: 34 lits
Robert Fournier, Directeur général

***Ormstown:* Centre d'hébergement d'Ormstown**
Affiliée à: Centre de santé et de services sociaux du Haut-Saint-Laurent
65, rue Hector, Ormstown, QC J0S 1K0
Tél: 450-829-2321 *Téléc:* 450-829-3110
www.santemonteregie.qc.ca/haut-saint-laurent
Fondée en: 1978
Nombre de lits: 74 lits

***Palmarolle:* CHSLD de Palmarolle**
Affiliée à: Centre de santé et de services sociaux des Aurores-Boréales
136, rue Principale, Palmarolle, QC J0Z 3C0
Tél: 819-787-2612 *Téléc:* 819-787-3293
www.csssab.qc.ca
Nombre de lits: 22 chambres privées
Spécialités: Les services d'hébergement; Physiothérapie; Ergothéapie; Optométrie

***Pierrefonds:* Manoir Pierrefonds inc. - 9130-9377QC.inc.**
18465, boul Gouin ouest, Pierrefonds, QC H9K 1A6
Tél: 514-626-6651 *Téléc:* 514-626-6415
Nombre de lits: 183 unités
Lorraine Lincourt, Directrice générale

***Pierreville:* Centre d'hébergement Lucien Shooner**
Affiliée à: Centre de santé et de services sociaux de Bécancour - Nicolet-Yamaska
CP 220, 50, rue Lt-Gouv.-Paul-Comtois, Pierreville, QC J0G 1J0
Tél: 450-568-2712 *Téléc:* 450-568-3658
Nombre de lits: 38 lits
Marcel Nolet, Directeur général

***Plessisville:* Centre d'hébergement des Bois-Francs**
Affiliée à: Centre de santé et de services sociaux d'Arthabaska-et-de-L'Érable
1450, av Trudelle, Plessisville, QC G6L 3K4
Tél: 819-362-3558 *Téléc:* 819-362-9266
Nombre de lits: 40 lits
Michel Lauzon, Directeur général

***Pointe-Claire:* CHSLD Bayview inc.**
Également connu sous le nom de: Centre Bayview
27, ch Lakeshore, Pointe-Claire, QC H9S 4H1
Tél: 514-695-9384 *Téléc:* 514-695-5723
www.chsldbayview.com
Nombre de lits: 128 lits
Note: Un établissement privé de soins de longue durée.
George Guillon, Directeur général

***Princeville:* Centre d'hébergement de Saint-Eusèbe**
Également connu sous le nom de: Foyer St-Eusèbe
CP 610, 435, rue Saint-Jacques, Princeville, QC G6L 5C5
Tél: 819-364-2355 *Téléc:* 819-364-7824
www.csssae.qc.ca
Nombre de lits: 26 lits
Marcel Dubois, Président, Conseil d'administration, CSSS d'Arthabaska-et-de-l

***Québec:* Centre d'accueil Nazareth inc.**
715, rue des Glacis, Québec, QC G1R 3P8
Tél: 418-694-0492 *Téléc:* 418-694-9452
Nombre de lits: 75 lits
Louise Gaudreault, Directrice générale

***Québec:* Centre d'hébergement Louis-Hebert**
Affiliée à: Centre de santé et de services sociaux de la Vieille-Capitale
1550, rue Pointe-aux-Lièvres nord, Québec, QC G1L 4M8
Tél: 418-529-5511 *Téléc:* 418-524-1143
Nombre de lits: 52 lits
Richard Rousseau, Directeur général par intérim

***Québec:* Centre d'hébergement Saint-Antoine**
Affiliée à: Centre de santé et de services sociaux de la Vieille-Capitale
1451, boul Père-Lelièvre, Québec, QC G1M 1N8
Tél: 418-683-2516 *Téléc:* 418-683-4031
www.csssvc.qc.ca
Nombre de lits: 284 lits
Note: Hébergement et soins de longue durée

***Québec:* Centre d'hébergement St-Jean-Eudes (CHSJE)**
6000, 3e av ouest, Québec, QC G1H 7J5
Tél: 418-627-1124 *Téléc:* 418-627-4995
www.chsje.qc.ca
Nombre de lits: 150 lits
Note: Le Centre d'hébergement St-Jean-Eudes est un établissement privé conventionné

Clémence Boucher, Directrice générale
clemence_boucher @ssss.gouv.qc.ca
Nicolas Labrèche, Directeur général-adjoint
nicolas.labreche@ssss.gouv.qc.ca
Louise Godin, Commissaire locale aux plaintes, et à la qualité des services
418-563-2917

***Québec:* Centre hospitalier Nôtre-Dame du Chemin inc.**
510, ch Ste-Foy, Québec, QC G1S 2J5
Tél: 418-681-7882 *Téléc:* 418-681-5387
Nombre de lits: 50 lits
Antoine Pichette, Directeur général

***Québec:* CLSC de la Basse-Ville**
Affiliée à: Centre de santé et de services sociaux de la Vieille-Capitale
260, boul Langelier, Québec, QC G1K 5N1
Tél: 418-529-0931 *Téléc:* 418-521-5801
msss.gouv.qc.ca
André Métivier, Directeur général

***Québec:* La Corporation Notre-Dame de Bon-Secours**
990, rue Gérard-Morisset, Québec, QC G1S 1X6
Tél: 418-681-4637
Nombre de lits: 20 lits
Michel Bilodrau, Directeur général

***Québec:* Foyer Ste-Marie-des-Anges Résidence**
2390, boul Masson, Québec, QC G1P 1J4
Tél: 418-871-5365
www.cmafhaiti.org/foyer.htm
Nombre de lits: 14 chambres
Note: Pour personnes retraitées autonomes et en perte d'autonomie
Gisèle Boivin, Directrice générale

***Québec:* Hôpital Ste-Monique inc.**
4805, boul Wilfrid Hamel, Québec, QC G1P 2J7
Tél: 418-871-8701 *Téléc:* 418-871-0105
Nombre de lits: 58 lits
Andrée Begin, Directrice générale
Edith Tassé, Directrice, Soins infirmiers et du personnel

***Rawdon:* CHSLD Heather I**
Également connu sous le nom de: Manoir Heather/Heather Lodge
3931, ch Lakeshore, Rawdon, QC J0K 1S0
Tél: 450-834-3070 *Téléc:* 450-834-5805
info@manoirheather.com
www.manoirheather.com
Nombre de lits: 76 lits
Note: CHSLD Heather II: 3462, 3e av, Rawdon, QC J0K 1S0, 450-834-2512.
Paul Arbec, Directeur général

***Rawdon:* Monsieur Rémy Landry**
Affiliée à: Agences de développement de réseaux locaux de services de santé et de services sociaux
Ancien nom: Centre d'Accueil Bouleaux Argentés
3567, rue Church, Rawdon, QC J0K 1S0
Tél: 450-834-2794 *Téléc:* 450-834-8286
Nombre de lits: 16 lits
Rémy Landry, Directeur général

***Richmond:* Centre d'hébergement de Richmond**
Affiliée à: Centre de santé et de services sociaux du Val-Saint-François
980, rue McGauran, Richmond, QC J0B 2H0
Tél: 819-542-2777 *Téléc:* 819-826-5724
vsf.santeestrie.qc.ca
Nombre de lits: 54 lits
Pierre Lalande, Directeur général, CSSS du Val-Saint-François

***Richmond:* Wales Home**
506, rte 243 nord, Richmond, QC J0B 2H0
Tél: 819-826-3266 *Téléc:* 819-826-2549
www.waleshome.ca
Nombre de lits: 190 lits
Stuart Simms, Directeur général

***Rimouski:* Centre d'hébergement de Rimouski**
Affiliée à: Centre de santé et de services sociaux de Rimouski-Neigette
645, boul Saint-Germain ouest, Rimouski, QC G5L 3S2
Tél: 418-724-4111 *Téléc:* 418-724-0604
courrierweb.crsssr@ssss.gouv.qc.ca
www.chrr.qc.ca
Nombre de lits: 246 lits

Raymond Coulombe, Directeur général, CSSS de Rimouski-Neigette

***Rimouski:* Foyer Ste-Bernadette inc.**
280, av Belzile, Rimouski, QC G5L 8K7
Tél: 418-723-0040 *Téléc:* 418-723-0615
Nombre de lits: 24 lits
Claude Talbot, Directeur général

***Rimouski:* Manoir de Caroline inc.**
280, rue Belzile, Rimouski, QC G5L 8K7
Tél: 418-723-0611 *Téléc:* 418-723-0615
Nombre de lits: 85 lits

***Rivière-Bleue:* Centre d'hébergement Rivière-Bleue**
Affiliée à: Centre de santé et de services sociaux de Témiscouata
45, rue du Foyer sud, Rivière-Bleue, QC G0L 2B0
Tél: 418-893-5511 *Téléc:* 418-893-7151
www.cssstemiscouata.com
Nombre de lits: 44 lits
Monique Dumas, Directrice, Services des personnes en perte d'autonomie, CSSS d

***Rivière-Ouelle:* Centre Thérèse-Martin**
Affiliée à: Centre de santé et de services sociaux de Kamouraska
100, ch de la Petite-Anse, Rivière-Ouelle, QC G0L 2C0
Tél: 418-856-7000 *Téléc:* 418-856-4381
www.agencesssbsl.gouv.qc.ca
Michel Beaulieu, Directeur général, CSSS de Kamouraska

***Rivière-du-Loup:* Centre d'hébergement Saint-Joseph**
28, rue Joly, Rivière-du-Loup, QC G5R 3H2
Tél: 418-862-6385 *Téléc:* 418-862-1986
www.csssriviereduloup.qc.ca
Nombre de lits: 145 lits
Raymond April, Directeur général, CSSS de Rivière-du-Loup

***Rouyn-Noranda:* Centre d'hébergement de Rouyn-Noranda**
Affiliée à: Centre de santé et de services sociaux de Rouyn-Noranda
512, av Richard, Rouyn-Noranda, QC J9X 4M1
Tél: 819-762-0908 *Téléc:* 819-764-5036
www.sante-abitibi-temiscamingue.gouv.qc.ca; www.csssrn.qc.ca
Nombre de lits: 157 lits
Note: Centre d'hébergement, centre de jour, hôpital de jour.
Huguette Lemay, Directrice générale, CSSS de Rouyn-Noranda
Annie Audet, Directrice, Programme des personnes en perte d'autonomie

***Saint-Alexandre-de-Kamour:* Centre Villa Maria**
Affiliée à: Centre de santé et de services sociaux de Kamouraska
404, av du Foyer, Saint-Alexandre-de-Kamour, QC G0L 2G0
Tél: 418-856-7000 *Téléc:* 418-495-2829
Michel Beaulieu, Directeur général, CSSS de Kamouraska

***Saint-André-Avellin:* CLSC et Centre d'hébergement Petite-Nation**
Affiliée à: Centre de santé et de services sociaux de Papineau
14, rue Saint-André, Saint-André-Avellin, QC J0V 1W0
Tél: 819-983-7341 *Téléc:* 819-983-7812
www.cssspapineau.qc.ca
Gilles Clavel, Directeur général (par intérim), CSSS de Papineau

***Saint-Antoine-sur-Richeli:* Accueil du Rivage inc.**
Affiliée à: Centre de santé et de services sociaux Richelieu-Yamaska
1008, ch du Rivage, Saint-Antoine-sur-Richeli, QC J0L 1R0
Tél: 450-787-3436 *Téléc:* 450-787-1156
communication.csssry@rrsss16.gouv.qc.ca
www.santemonteregie.qc.ca
Nombre de lits: 36 lits
Jean Bergeron, Directeur général

***Saint-Antonin:* Centre d'hébergement de Saint-Antonin**
Affiliée à: Centre de santé et de services sociaux de Rivière-du-Loup
CP 430, 286, rue Principale, Saint-Antonin, QC G0L 2J0
Tél: 418-862-7993 *Téléc:* 418-862-5278
www.csssriviereduloup.qc.ca
Nombre de lits: 42 lits
Raymond April, Directeur général, CSSS de Rivière-du-Loup

***Saint-Augustin-de-Desmaur:* Jardins du Haut Saint-Laurent (1992) inc.**
4770, rue Saint-Felix, Saint-Augustin-de-Desmaur, QC G3A 1B1
Tél: 418-872-4936 *Téléc:* 418-872-4245
info@jardins-hsl.com
www.jardins-hsl.com
Nombre de lits: 140 lits

***Saint-Bernard-de-Lacolle:* Florence Groulx inc.**
7, rue Saint-Louis RR#2, Saint-Bernard-de-Lacolle, QC J0J 1V0
Tél: 450-246-3879 *Téléc:* 450-246-4111
Nombre de lits: 50 lits
Daniel Gaudette, Directeur général

***Saint-Bruno-de-Montarvill:* Centre d'hébergement de Montarville**
Affiliée à: Centre de santé et de services sociaux Richelieu-Yamaska
265, boul Seigneurial ouest, Saint-Bruno-de-Montarvill, QC J3V 2H4
Tél: 450-461-2650 *Téléc:* 450-461-2968
info@lesommetavotreportee.qc.ca
www.lesommetavotreportee.qc.ca;
www.santemonteregie.qc.ca/richelieu-yamaska
Nombre de lits: 155 lits
Daniel Castonguay, Directeur général, CSSS Richelieu-Yamaska
Réjeanne Boudreau, Directrice du Programme hébergement-milieu de vie, CSSS Richelieu-Yamaska

***Saint-Casimir:* Centre d'hébergement Saint-Casimir**
Affiliée à: Centre de santé et de services sociaux de Portneuf
CP 10, 605, rue Fleury, Saint-Casimir, QC G0A 3L0
Tél: 418-339-2861 *Téléc:* 418-339-2875
Nombre de lits: 64 lits
Fernand Morasse, Directeur général

***Saint-Célestin:* Centre d'hébergement Saint-Célestin**
Affiliée à: Centre de santé et de services sociaux de Bécancour - Nicolet-Yamaska
CP 90, 475, rue Houde, Saint-Célestin, QC J0C 1G0
Tél: 819-229-3617 *Téléc:* 819-229-1165
Nombre de lits: 52 lits
Marcel Nolet, Directeur général

***Saint-Constant:* Centre d'hébergement Jean-Louis-Lapierre**
Affiliée à: Centre de santé et de services sociaux Jardins-Roussillon
199, rue St-Pierre, Saint-Constant, QC J5A 2N8
Tél: 450-632-4451 *Téléc:* 450-632-2004
www.santemonteregie.qc.ca/jardins-roussillon
Nombre de lits: 76 lits
Paul Moreau, Directeur général, CSSS Jardins-Roussillon

***Saint-Cyprien:* Centre d'hébergement de Saint-Cyprien**
Affiliée à: Centre de santé et de services sociaux de Rivière-du-Loup
101-C, rue Collin, Saint-Cyprien, QC G0L 2P0
Tél: 418-963-2272
www.csssriviereduloup.qc.ca
Nombre de lits: 20 lits
Raymond April, Directeur général, CSSS de Rivière-du-Loup

***Saint-Eustache:* Centre d'hébergement de Saint-Eustache**
Affiliée à: Centre de santé et de services sociaux du Lac-des-Deux-Montagnes
CP 850, 55, rue Chenier, Saint-Eustache, QC J7R 4Y8
Tél: 450-472-0013 *Téléc:* 450-472-3104
Nombre de lits: 194 lits

***Saint-Eustache:* Société en commandite centre d'accueil l'Ermitage**
112, 25e av, Saint-Eustache, QC J7P 2V2
Tél: 450-473-5961 *Téléc:* 450-491-1847
Nombre de lits: 78 lits
Kevin Shemie, Directeur général

***Saint-Félicien:* Centre d'hébergement de Saint-Félicien**
Affiliée à: Centre de santé et de services sociaux Domaine-du-Roy
Édifice Foyer de la Paix, 1229, boul Sacré-Coeur, Saint-Félicien, QC G8K 1A5
Tél: 418-679-1585 *Téléc:* 418-679-2376
hdr@ssss.gouv.qc.ca
www.cmdp-roberval.com
Nombre de lits: 46 lits
Note: Hébergement permanent et temporaire; centre de jour.
Jacques Dubois, Directeur général, CSSS Domaine-du-Roy

***Saint-Gabriel-de-Brandon:* Centre d'hébergement Desy**
Affiliée à: Centre de santé et de services sociaux du Nord de Lanaudière
CP 840, 90, rue Maskinonge, Saint-Gabriel-de-Brandon, QC J0K 2N0
Tél: 450-835-4712 *Téléc:* 450-835-7606
Nombre de lits: 54 lits
Jacques Morin, Comptable

***Saint-Georges:* Centre hospitalier de l'Assomption**
16750, boul Lacroix, Saint-Georges, QC G5Y 2G4
Tél: 416-228-2041

***Saint-Georges-de-Beauce:* CHSLD L'Assomption**
Affiliée à: Groupe Champlain inc.
16750, boul Lacroix, Saint-Georges-de-Beauce, QC G5Y 2G4
Tél: 418-228-2041 *Téléc:* 418-228-9366
www.groupechamplain.qc.ca
Nombre de lits: 96 lits
Note: Agence/région administrative: Agence de la santé et des services sociaux de Lanaudière.

***Saint-Hubert:* Centre d'hébergement Henriette Céré**
Affiliée à: Centre de santé et de services sociaux Champlain - Charles-Le Moyne
6435, ch de Chambly, Saint-Hubert, QC J3Y 3R6
Tél: 450-672-3320

***Saint-Hubert:* Pavillon St-Hubert**
3823, rue Grand Boulevard, Saint-Hubert, QC J4T 2M3
Tél: 450-445-3598 *Téléc:* 450-462-3767

***Saint-Hyacinthe:* Centre d'hébergement Andrée-Perrault**
Affiliée à: Centre de santé et de services sociaux Richelieu-Yamaska
1955, av Pratte, Saint-Hyacinthe, QC J2S 7W5
Tél: 514-771-4536 *Téléc:* 450-771-5499
info@lesommetavotreportee.qc.ca
www.lesommetavotreportee.qc.ca;
www.santemonteregie.qc.ca/richelieu-yamaska
Nombre de lits: 70 lits
Daniel Castonguay, Directeur général, CSSS Richelieu-Yamaska
Réjeanne Boudreau, Directrice du Programme hébergement-milieu de vie, CSSS Richelieu-Yamaska

***Saint-Hyacinthe:* CHSLD Résidence Bourg-Joli inc.**
2915, boul Laframboise, Saint-Hyacinthe, QC J2S 4Z3
Tél: 450-773-4197 *Téléc:* 450-773-6545
Nombre de lits: 24 lits
Marc Breton, Directeur général

***Saint-Jean-sur-Richelieu:* Centre d'hébergement Georges-Phaneuf**
Affiliée à: Centre de santé et de services sociaux Haut-Richelieu-Rouville
230, rue Jacques-Cartier nord, Saint-Jean-sur-Richelieu, QC J3B 6T4
Tél: 450-346-1133 *Téléc:* 450-346-2199
www.santemonteregie.qc.ca/haut-richelieu-rouville
Nombre de lits: 124 lits
Lucie Tétreault, Directrice, Personnes en perte d'autonomie liée au vieillissme

***Saint-Jean-sur-Richelieu:* Centre d'hébergement Gertrude-Lafrance**
Affiliée à: Centre de santé et de services sociaux Haut-Richelieu-Rouville
150, boul Saint-Luc, Saint-Jean-sur-Richelieu, QC J3A 1G2
Tél: 450-349-5555 *Téléc:* 450-348-7693
www.santemonteregie.qc.ca/haut-richelieu-rouville
Nombre de lits: 174 lits
Lucie Tétreault, Directrice, Personnes en perte d'autonomie liée au vieillissme

***Saint-Jérome:* Centre d'hébergement L'Auberge**
Affiliée à: Centre de santé et de services sociaux de Saint-Jérôme
66, rue Danis, Saint-Jérome, QC J7Y 2R3
Tél: 514-436-3131
Nombre de lits: 92 lits

***Saint-Jérome:* CHSLD de la Rivière du Nord**
531, rue Laviolette, Saint-Jérome, QC J7Y 2T8
Tél: 450-436-3061 *Téléc:* 450-436-8328
Nombre de lits: 305 lits
Note: Centres d'hébergement: Youville, l'Auberge, et Lucien G. Rolland.
Jean-Pierre Perreault, Directeur général

***Saint-Lambert:* CHSLD de la MRC de Champlain**
831, av Notre-Dame, Saint-Lambert, QC J4R 1S1
Tél: 450-672-3320 *Téléc:* 450-672-3370
andree.ouellette@rrsss16.gouv.qc.ca
Nombre de lits: 313 lits
Gisèle Lacoste, Directrice générale
Real Guilbert, Directeur, Services techniques

***Saint-Lambert:* Résidence du Parc**
33, av Argyle, Saint-Lambert, QC J4P 3P5
Tél: 450-878-3081 *Téléc:* 450-465-4369
residenceduparc@reveraliving.com
www.reveraliving.com
Nombre de lits: 105 lits
Denyse Saey, Directrice générale

***Saint-Laurent:* Les Cèdres - Centre d'accueil pour personnes âgées**
#200, 1275, boul de la C"te-Vertu, Saint-Laurent, QC H4L 4V2
Tél: 514-389-1023 *Téléc:* 514-389-0581
info@cedarshome.ca
www.centrelescedres.ca
Nombre de lits: 25 lits
Rose Khoury, Directrice générale

***Saint-Laurent:* Centre d'hébergement de Saint-Laurent**
Affiliée à: Centre de santé et de services sociaux de Bordeaux-Cartierville-Saint-Laurent
1055, av Ste-Croix, Saint-Laurent, QC H4L 3Z2
Tél: 514-744-4981 *Téléc:* 514-744-0895
Nombre de lits: 154 lits

***Saint-Liguori:* Centre d'hébergement Saint-Liguori**
Affiliée à: Centre de santé et de services sociaux du Nord de Lanaudière
771, rue Principale, Saint-Liguori, QC J0K 2X0
Tél: 450-753-7062 *Téléc:* 450-753-3208
Nombre de lits: 48 lits
Paul-Yvon de Billy, Directeur général

***Saint-Louis-du-Ha!-Ha!:* Centre d'hébergement St-Louis**
Affiliée à: Centre de santé et de services sociaux de Témiscouata
25, rue Saint-Philippe, Saint-Louis-du-Ha!-Ha!, QC G0L 3S0
Tél: 418-854-2631 *Téléc:* 418-854-0430
www.cssstemiscouata.com
Nombre de lits: 43 lits
Monique Dumas, Directrice, Services des personnes en perte d'autonomie, CSSS d

***Saint-Michel-de-Bellechas:* CHSLD Vigi Notre-Dame de Lourdes**
CP 10, 80, rue Principale, Saint-Michel-de-Bellechas, QC G0R 3S0
Tél: 418-884-2811 *Téléc:* 418-884-3714
www.vigisante.com
Nombre de lits: 40 lits
Note: Agence/région administrative: Agence de la santé et des services sociaux de Chaudière-Appalaches.
Vincent Simonetta, Directeur général
Michelle Harvey, Directeur adjointe, Services techniques

***Saint-Michel-des-Saints:* Centre d'hébergement Brassard**
Affiliée à: Centre de santé et de services sociaux du Nord de Lanaudière
CP 309, 390, rue Brassard, Saint-Michel-des-Saints, QC J0K 3B0
Tél: 514-833-6331 *Téléc:* 514-833-6093
Nombre de lits: 35 lits
Jean-Jacques Lamarche, Directeur général par intérim

***Saint-Michel-du-Squatec:* CHSLD de Squatec**
Affiliée à: Centre de santé et de services sociaux de Témiscouata
Ancien nom: Domaine du Sommet
10, rue Saint-André, Saint-Michel-du-Squatec, QC G0L 4H0
Tél: 418-855-2442 *Téléc:* 418-855-2357
www.cssstemiscouata.com
Nombre de lits: 24 lits
Monique Dumas, Directrice, Services des personnes en perte d'autonomie, CSSS d

Saint-Pacôme: **Centre d'hébergement D'Anjou**
Affiliée à: Centre de santé et de services sociaux de Kamouraska
127, rue Galarneau, Saint-Pacôme, QC G0L 3X0
Tél: 418-856-7000
www.agencesssbsl.gouv.qc.ca
Nombre de lits: 53 lits d'hébergement permanents
Mireille Drapeau, Coordonnatrice

Saint-Pierre-de-l'Ile-d'O: **Centre d'hébergement Alphonse-Bonenfant**
Affiliée à: Centre de santé et de services sociaux de Québec-Nord
1199, ch Royal, Saint-Pierre-de-l'Ile-d'O, QC G0A 4E0
Tél: 418-828-9114
www.csssqn.qc.ca
Nombre de lits: 50 lits
Aline Prémont, Directeur général

Saint-Pierre-les-Becquets: **Centre d'hébergement Romain-Becquet**
Affiliée à: Centre de santé et de services sociaux de Bécancour - Nicolet-Yamaska
255, rte Marie-Victorin, Saint-Pierre-les-Becquets, QC G0X 2Z0
Tél: 819-263-2245 *Téléc:* 819-263-2636
Nombre de lits: 35 lits
Note: Hébergement permanent et temporaire
Jacqueline Côté, Chef, Administration

Saint-Raymond: **Centre hébergement Saint-Raymond**
Affiliée à: Centre de santé et de services sociaux de Portneuf
324, rue Saint-Joseph, Saint-Raymond, QC G3L 1J7
Tél: 418-337-4611 *Téléc:* 418-337-4662
www.csssdeportneuf.qc.ca
Nombre de lits: 63 lits d'hébergement permanent; 1 lit d'hébergement temporaire

Saint-Rémi: **Centre d'hébergement de Saint-Rémi**
Affiliée à: Centre de santé et de services sociaux Jardins-Roussillon
CP 820, 110, rue du Collège, Saint-Rémi, QC J0L 2L0
Tél: 450-454-4694 *Téléc:* 450-454-3614
Nombre de lits: 58 lits
Paul Moreau, Directeur général, CSSS Jardins-Roussillon

Saint-Romuald: **CHSLD Chanoine-Audet inc.**
Affiliée à: Groupe Champlain inc.
2155, ch du Sault, Saint-Romuald, QC G6W 2K7
Tél: 418-834-5322 *Téléc:* 418-834-5754
www.groupechamplain.qc.ca
Nombre de lits: 96 lits
Note: Agence/région administrative: Agence de la santé et des services sociaux de Chaudière-Appalaches.

Saint-Siméon: **CLSC-CHSLD de Saint-Siméon**
Affiliée à: Centre de santé et de services sociaux de Charlevoix
CP 7, 371, rue Saint-Laurent, Saint-Siméon, QC G0T 1X0
Tél: 418-638-2414
www.cssscharlevoix.qc.ca
Nombre de lits: 18 lits
Note: Centre local de services communautaires (418-638-2369); centre d'hébergement et centre de jour.
Micheline Tremblay, Directrice générale, CSSS de Charlevoix
micheline.tremblay@ssss.gouv.qc.ca

Saint-Timothée: **La Maison des Aîne(e)s**
1, rue des Aînes, Saint-Timothée, QC J6S 6M8
Tél: 450-377-3925 *Téléc:* 450-377-3490
Nombre de lits: 38 lits
Denis Charland, Directeur général

Saint-Tite: **Centre d'hébergement et CLSC Mgr Paquin**
Affiliée à: Centre de santé et de services sociaux de la Vallée-de-la-Batiscan
CP 400, 580, rue du Couvent, Saint-Tite, QC G0X 3H0
Tél: 418-365-5107 *Téléc:* 418-365-7914
www.csssvalleebatiscan.qc.ca
Nombre de lits: 55 lits

Sainte-Anne-de-la-Pérade: **Centre multiservice Foyer de la Pérade**
CP 217, 60, rue de la Fabrique, Sainte-Anne-de-la-Pérade, QC G0X 2J0
Tél: 418-325-2313 *Téléc:* 418-325-3233
Nombre de lits: 42 lits
Gilles Cossette, Directeur général

Sainte-Cécile: **Pavillon Ste-Cécile**
4581, rue Principale, Sainte-Cécile, QC G0Y 1J0
Tél: 819-583-0400 *Téléc:* 819-583-0983
Nombre de lits: 15 lits

Sainte-Foy: **Résidence Paul Triquet**
Également connu sous le nom de: La Maison Paul-Triquet
789, rue de Belmont, Sainte-Foy, QC G1V 4V2
Tél: 418-657-6890 *Téléc:* 418-657-6894
maisonpaultriquet@mail.cuhq.qc.ca
www.chuq.qc.ca/maisonpaultriquet
Fondée en: 1987
Nombre de lits: 64 lits
Note: Centre d'hébergement de soins de longue durée pour anciens combattants
René Rouleau, Directeur général

Sainte-Sophie: **Centre d'hébergement Jaclo Inc.**
CP 129, 2319, rue Sainte-Marie, Sainte-Sophie, QC J0R 1S0
Tél: 450-436-5627 *Téléc:* 450-436-6663
Nombre de lits: 31 lits
Claude Brière, Directeur général
Jacqueline Brière, Président

Sainte-Thérèse: **Centre d'hébergement Drapeau-Deschambault**
Affiliée à: Centre de santé et de services sociaux de Thérèse-De Blainville
100, rue du Chanoine Lionel-Groulx, Sainte-Thérèse, QC J7E 5E1
Tél: 450-437-4267 *Téléc:* 450-437-0788
www.cssstheresedeblainville.qc.ca
Nombre de lits: 223 lits
André Poirier, Directeur général, CSSS de Thérèse-De Blainville

Sainte-Thérèse: **CHSLD Boise Ste-Thérèse Inc.**
179, Place Fabien-Drapeau, Sainte-Thérèse, QC J7E 5W6
Tél: 450-430-6767 *Téléc:* 450-430-6965
Nombre de lits: 41 CHSLD privé; 60 autonomes
Stephanie Drolet, Directrice générale

Saint-Éphrem-de-Beauce: **Résidence St-Éphrem inc.**
CP 310, 1, rue Plante, Saint-Éphrem-de-Beauce, QC G0M 1R0
Tél: 418-484-2121 *Téléc:* 418-484-2144
restep@telstep.net
Nombre de lits: 40 lits

Salaberry-de-Valleyfield: **Les Centres du Haut St-Laurent (CHSLD) Valleyfield**
80, rue de Marche, Salaberry-de-Valleyfield, QC J6T 1P5
Tél: 450-373-4818 *Téléc:* 450-373-0325
chsl@rocler.qc.ca
Nombre de lits: 177 lits
Claude Chayer, Directeur général

Shawinigan: **CHSLD Vigi Les Chutes**
Affiliée à: Vigi Santé Ltée
5000, av Albert-Tessier, Shawinigan, QC G9N 8P9
Tél: 819-539-5408 *Téléc:* 819-539-5400
www.vigisante.com
Nombre de lits: 64 lits
Note: Agence/région administrative: Agence de la santé et des services sociaux de la Mauricie.

Shawville: **Pavillon Centre d'accueil Pontiac**
Affiliée à: Centre de santé et de services sociaux du Pontiac
CP 2001, 290, rue Marion, Shawville, QC J0X 2Y0
Tél: 819-647-5755 *Téléc:* 819-647-2453
Nombre de lits: 50 lits
Joan Brown, Manager

Sherbrooke: **Centre d'hébergement St-Joseph**
Affiliée à: CSSS Institut universitaire de gériatrie de Sherbrooke
611, boul Queen-Victoria nord, Sherbrooke, QC J1H 3R6
Tél: 819-780-2222
www,csss-iugs.ca
Nombre de lits: 144 lits
Carol Fillion, Directeur général, CSSS-Institut universitaire de gériatrie de Sherbro

Sherbrooke: **CHSLD Vigi Shermont inc.**
Affiliée à: Vigi Santé Ltée
3220, 12e av nord, Sherbrooke, QC J1H 5H3
Tél: 819-820-8900 *Téléc:* 819-820-8902
www.vigisante.com
Nombre de lits: 52 lits
Note: Agence/région administrative: Agence de la santé et des services sociaux de l'Estrie.
Jean Sevigny, Directeur général

Sherbrooke: **Les Dominicaines des saints anges gardiens**
Ancien nom: Mont St-Dominique
361, rue Moore, Sherbrooke, QC J1H 1C1
Tél: 819-346-5512 *Téléc:* 819-563-5023
Nombre de lits: 50 lits
Nevenka Skrindar, Directrice générale

Sillery: **Pavillon Saint-Dominique**
1045, boul René-Lévesque ouest, Sillery, QC G1S 1V3
Tél: 418-681-3561 *Téléc:* 418-687-9196
info@domaine-saint-dominique.com
www.domaine-saint-dominique.com
Nombre de lits: 152 lits

Sillery: **Saint Brigid's Home Inc.**
1645, ch Saint-Louis, Sillery, QC G1S 4M3
Tél: 418-681-4687 *Téléc:* 418-527-6862
www.jefferyhale.org
Nombre de lits: 162 lits
Louis Hanrahan, Directeur général

Sorel-Tracy: **Centre d'hébergement de Tracy**
Affiliée à: Centre de santé et de services sociaux Pierre-De Saurel
4025, rue Frontenac, Sorel-Tracy, QC J3R 4G8
Tél: 450-742-9427 *Téléc:* 450-742-9668
Nombre de lits: 64 lits

Sorel-Tracy: **Centre d'hébergement J.-Arsène-Parenteau**
Affiliée à: Centre de santé et de services sociaux Pierre-De Saurel
Également connu sous le nom de: Foyer Richelieu
40, rue de Ramezay, Sorel-Tracy, QC J3P 3Y7
Tél: 514-742-5936 *Téléc:* 514-742-1613
Nombre de lits: 60 lits
Jacques Blais, Directeur général

Sorel-Tracy: **CHSLD du Bas-Richelieu**
151, rue George, Sorel-Tracy, QC J3P 1C8
Tél: 450-746-5555 *Téléc:* 450-746-4897
www.soreltracyregion.net
Nombre de lits: 261 lits
René Legault, Directeur général (intérim)

St-Charles-de-Bellechasse: **Résidence Charles Couillard Inc.**
20, av St-Georges, St-Charles-de-Bellechasse, QC G0R 2T0
Tél: 418-887-6455 *Téléc:* 418-887-1316
Nombre de lits: 35 lits
Gerard Dion, Directeur général

St-Jean-de-Dieu: **Villa Dubé**
Affiliée à: Centre de santé et de services sociaux des Basques
20, rue de la Villa, St-Jean-de-Dieu, QC G0L 3M0
Tél: 418-963-2713
www.agencesssbsl.gouv.qc.ca
Spécialités: Centre d'hébergement et de soins longue durée
Nathalie Dumont, Gestonnaire

St-Jovite: **CLSC-CHSLD des Trois Vallées - Résidence St-Jovite**
CP 910, 925, rue Ouimet, St-Jovite, QC J0T 2H0
Tél: 819-425-2793 *Téléc:* 819-425-8857
Nombre de lits: 69 lits
Christine Lessard, Directrice générale

Ste-Marguerite-du-Lac-Mas: **Manoir de la Pointe Bleue (1978)**
428, rue du Baron-Louis-Empain, Ste-Marguerite-du-Lac-Mas, QC J0T 1L0
Tél: 450-228-2503 *Téléc:* 450-228-3312
Nombre de lits: 91 lits
Jacqueline Gagnon, Directrice générale

Sutton: **Foyer Sutton**
Affiliée à: Centre de santé et de services sociaux la Pommeraie
50, rue Western, Sutton, QC J0E 2K0
Tél: 514-538-3332 *Téléc:* 514-538-0514
Nombre de lits: 71 places
Spécialités: Centre d'hébergement

Terrebonne: **CHSLD de La Côte Boisée inc.**
4300, rue d'Angora, Terrebonne, QC J6X 4P1
Tél: 450-471-5877 *Téléc:* 450-471-7511
Nombre de lits: 140 lits
Gerald Asselin, Directeur général

***Thetford Mines:* Résidence La Rosée d'Or**
736, boul Ouellet ouest, Thetford Mines, QC G6G 4X5
Tél: 418-335-7681 *Téléc:* 418-338-3774
Nombre de lits: 9 lits
Laurent Chartier

***Trois-Rivières:* Centre d'hébergement Cooke**
Affiliée à: Centre de santé et de services sociaux de Trois-Rivières
3450, rue Ste-Marguerite, Trois-Rivières, QC G8Z 1X3
Tél: 819-375-7713
www.cssstr.qc.ca
Nombre de lits: 190 lits
Jacques Longval, Directeur général, CSSS de Trois-Rivières

***Trois-Rivières:* Centre d'hébergement Louis-Denoncourt**
Affiliée à: Centre de santé et de services sociaux de Trois-Rivières
435, rue Saint-Roch, Trois-Rivières, QC G9A 2L9
Tél: 819-376-2566 *Téléc:* 819-376-5620
www.cssstr.qc.ca
Nombre de lits: 75 lits
Note: Hébergement permanent
Jacques Longval, Directeur général, CSSS de Trois-Rivières

***Trois-Rivières:* Résidence Joseph-Denys**
1274, rue Laviolette, Trois-Rivières, QC G9A 1W4
Tél: 819-378-4837 *Téléc:* 819-374-6697
www.cssstr.qc.ca
Nombre de lits: 119 lits
Note: Hébergement permanent et temporaire.
Jacques Longval, Directeur général, CSSS de Trois-Rivières

***Upton:* Domaine du Bel Age**
CP 89, 906, rue Lanoie, Upton, QC J0H 2E0
Tél: 514-549-4404
Nombre de lits: 9 lits
Jacqueline Gosslin, Directrice générale

***Vanier:* Centre Christ-Roi**
Affiliée à: Centre de santé et de services sociaux de Bécancour - Nicolet-Yamaska
300, boul Wilfrid-Hamel, Vanier, QC G1M 2R9
Tél: 418-682-1711 *Téléc:* 418-682-1770
Nombre de lits: 142 lits
Note: Hébergement permanent/soins de longue durée, hôpital de jour, hébergement temporaire, consultations externes
Gaétan Garon, Directeur général
Lucien Jobin, Directeur, Services techniques
Francine Smith, Chef du service d'entretien sanitaire

***Varennes:* Centre d'hébergement de Lajemmerais**
Affiliée à: Centre de santé et de services sociaux Pierre-Boucher
60, rue D'Youville, Varennes, QC J3X 1R1
Tél: 450-463-2995 *Téléc:* 450-468-8329
www.santemonteregie.qc.ca/cssspierreboucher
Fondée en: 1971
Nombre de lits: 120 personnes en soins de longue durée dans trois unités de vie
Spécialités: Un centre de jour pour la clientèle en perte d'autonomie vivant à domicile; Une unité prothétique; éadaptation
Bertin Riverin, Directeur général

***Vaudreuil-Dorion:* 2863-9839 Québec inc.**
170, rue Boileau, Vaudreuil-Dorion, QC J7V 8A3
Tél: 450-424-6458
Nombre de lits: 51 lits
Denis Charland, Directeur général

***Verdun:* Centre d'hébergement Réal Morel**
Affiliée à: Centre de santé et de services sociaux du Sud-Ouest-Verdun
3500, rue Wellington, Verdun, QC H4G 1T3
Tél: 514-761-5874 *Téléc:* 514-761-7264
www.sov.qc.ca
Nombre de lits: 148 lits

***Victoriaville:* Centre d'hébergement du Chêne**
Affiliée à: Centre de santé et de services sociaux d'Arthabaska-et-de-L'Érable
61, rue de l'Ermitage, Victoriaville, QC G6P 6X4
Tél: 819-758-7511 *Téléc:* 819-758-2398
www.csssae.qc.ca
Nombre de lits: 122 lits
Note: Les autres centres d'hébergement: Quatre-Vents, Saint-Eusèbe, Sacré-Coeur, Étoiles-d'Or, et Roseau.
Marcel Dubois, Président, Conseil d'administration, CSSS d'Arthabaska-et-de-l

***Victoriaville:* Centre d'hébergement du Roseau**
Affiliée à: Centre de santé et de services sociaux d'Arthabaska-et-de-l'Érable
Ancien nom: La Résidence le Roseau
45, rue de l'Ermitage, Victoriaville, QC G6P 6X4
Tél: 819-758-7511
www.csssae.qc.ca
Phillippe Rancourt, Directeur du programme Personnes en pete d'autonomie

***Waterloo:* Centre gériatrique Courville**
CP 580, 5305, av Courville, Waterloo, QC J0E 2N0
Tél: 450-539-1821 *Téléc:* 450-539-1937
Nombre de lits: 52 lits
Kenneth Courville, Président
kenneth.courville@santecourville.com
Christine Durocher, Directrice générale
christine.durocher@santecourville.com

***Waterville:* Foyer de Waterville**
265, rue Compton est, Waterville, QC J0B 3H0
Tél: 819-837-2454 *Téléc:* 819-837-2916
Nombre de lits: 20 lits
Edith Nadeau, Responsable
418-661-8484

***Weedon:* Centre d'hébergement de Weedon**
Affiliée à: Centre de santé et de services sociaux du Haut-Saint-François
Également connu sous le nom de: CHSLD de Weedon
245, rue Saint-Janvier, Weedon, QC J0B 3J0
Tél: 819-877-2500 *Téléc:* 819-877-3089
www.cssshsf.com.qc.ca

***Westmount:* Chateau Westmount inc.**
4860, boul de Maisonneuve ouest, Westmount, QC H3Z 3G2
Tél: 514-369-3000 *Téléc:* 514-369-0014
zara.pilian@chateauwestmount.ca
www.chateauwestmount.ca
Nombre de lits: 112 lits
Nancy Fournier, Ressources humaines
nancy.fournier@chateauwestmount.ca

Centres d'accueil et d'hébergement

***Buckingham:* Centre d'accueil de Buckingham**
111, rue Lucerne, Buckingham, QC J8L 2M4
Tél: 819-986-1043 *Téléc:* 819-986-9602
Nombre de lits: 79 lits
Jacques Prud'Homme, Directeur général

***Côte Saint-Luc:* Centre hospitalier gériatrique Maimonides**
5795, av Caldwell, Côte Saint-Luc, QC H4W 1W3
Tél: 514-483-2121 *Téléc:* 514-483-1086
www.donaldbermanmaimonides.net
Nombre de lits: 387 lits
Lucie Tremblay, Director of Nursing & Clinical Services
514-483-2121 ext 2290

***Gatineau:* Résidence Ste-Marie**
156, boul Lorrain, Gatineau, QC J8P 2G2
Tél: 819-663-5736 *Téléc:* 819-643-1358
Nombre de lits: 23 lits
Palmyra Séguin, Directrice générale

***Grandes-Bergeronnes:* Pavillon Bergeronnes**
Affiliée à: Centre de santé et de services sociaux de la Haute-Côte-Nord
CP 68, 450, rue de la Mer, Grandes-Bergeronnes, QC G0T 1G0
Tél: 418-232-6224 *Téléc:* 418-232-6771
Nombre de lits: 32 lits
Micheline Anctil, Directeur général

***Ham-Nord:* Foyer Saints-Anges de Ham-Nord inc.**
CP 269, 493, rue Principale, Ham-Nord, QC G0P 1A0
Tél: 819-344-2940 *Téléc:* 819-344-2584
Nombre de lits: 38 lits
Alain Lavertu, Directeur général

***Iberville:* Pavillon Iberville Enr.**
135, 8e av, Iberville, QC J2X 1K8
Tél: 514-346-9292
Nombre de lits: 15 lits
Rachèle Dorval, Propriétaire

***La Doré:* Ressource intermédiaire de La Doré**
Également connu sous le nom de: Résidence La Doré
CP 190, 4921, rue des Peupliers, La Doré, QC G0W 2J0
Tél: 418-256-3851 *Téléc:* 418-256-3608
hdr@ssss.gouv.qc.ca
www.cmdp-roberval.com
Nombre de lits: 21 lits
Guy Dufour, Directeur général

***Montréal:* Centre d'hebergement Judith Jasmin**
Affiliée à: Centre de santé et de services sociaux de la Pointe-de-l'Ile
8850, rue Bisaillon, Montréal, QC H1K 4N2
Tél: 514-354-5990 *Téléc:* 514-354-4916
Nombre de lits: 75 lits

***Montréal:* Donald Berman Maimonides Geriatric Centre**
5795, av Caldwell, Montréal, QC H4W 1W3
Tél: 514-483-2121 *Téléc:* 514-483-1086
www.donaldbermanmaimonides.net
Média social: www.facebook.com/MaimonidesGeriatricCentre?ref=ts; twitter.com/MaimonidesGC; www.youtube.com/user/MaimonidesGeriatric
Note: The Donald Berman Maimonides Geriatric Centre is a McGill University Teaching Centre. The centre assists Montréal's Jewish seniors who are not able to live alone.
Ron Waxman, Board President
Barbra Gold, Executive Director
Lucie Tremblay, Director, Nursing & Clinical Services

***Montréal:* Résidence Pie IX**
4090, rue Martial, Montréal, QC H1H 1X4
Tél: 514-327-2333 *Téléc:* 514-327-3276
Nombre de lits: 42 lits
Note: Centre de réadaptation
Serge Beauchamp, Directeur général

***Montréal-Nord:* Pavillon de la Détente 1993 Enr.**
6880, boul Gouin est, Montréal-Nord, QC H1G 6L8
Tél: 514-321-5107 *Téléc:* 514-328-8987
Nombre de lits: 55 lits
Irène Sirois, Administratrice

***Pierrefonds:* Manoir Ile de l'Ouest**
17725, boul Pierrefonds, Pierrefonds, QC H9J 3L1
Tél: 514-620-9850
Nombre de lits: 63 lits
Heather Karakas, Directrice générale

***Roberval:* Résidence des Érables**
992, boul Saint-Joseph, Roberval, QC G8H 2L9
Tél: 418-275-4376
Nombre de lits: 23 lits
Note: déficience intellectuelle

***Saint-Benoît-Labre:* Pavillon Baillargeon inc.**
357, rte 271, Saint-Benoît-Labre, QC G0M 1P0
Tél: 418-228-9141 *Téléc:* 418-226-3772
Nombre de lits: 35 places

***Saint-Eustache:* Domaine des Trois Pignons**
112, 25e av, Saint-Eustache, QC J7P 2V2
Tél: 450-473-5961 *Téléc:* 450-491-1847
Nombre de lits: 92 lits

***Saint-Fabien:* Pavillon St-Fabien**
CP 520, 142, 1re rue, Saint-Fabien, QC G0L 2Z0
Tél: 418-869-2709
Nombre de lits: 27 lits
Sylvain Paquet, Directeur général

***Saint-Zacharie:* Résidence l'Eden**
668, 12e av, Saint-Zacharie, QC G0M 2C0
Tél: 418-593-5200 *Téléc:* 418-593-5200
Fondée en: 1964
Nombre de lits: 30 lits

***Sainte-Geneviève:* Château sur le Lac**
16289, boul Gouin ouest, Sainte-Geneviève, QC H9H 1E2
Tél: 514-620-9794 *Téléc:* 514-696-3196
info@chateausurlelac.com
chateausurlelac.com
Nombre de lits: 50 lits
B.S. Kachra, Directeur général

***Verdun:* Manoir des Floralies Verdun**
1050, rue Gordon, Verdun, QC H4G 2S2
Tél: 514-766-2858
Nombre de lits: 103 lits

Louise Fontaine, Directrice générale

***Baie-d'Urfé:* Maxwell Residence**
678, rue Surrey, Baie-d'Urfé, QC H9X 3S1
Tel: 514-457-3111 *Fax:* 514-457-7909
www.maxwellresidence.com

Note: Specialties: Fitness center & health programs
R.W. Maxwell, Administrator

***Laval:* Les Loggias et Villa Val des Arbres Chartwell Seniors Housing REIT**
3245, boul St-Martin est, Laval, QC H7E 4T6
Tel: 450-661-0911 *Fax:* 450-661-9820
www.chartwellreit.ca; www.villavaldesarbres.com

Note: Centre privé non-conventionné; 163 unités, 48 appartements, 115 chambres.
Denis Lagueux, Président, Chartwell-Québec

Hôpitaux psychiatriques et assistance communautaire

***Beauport:* L'Institut universitaire en santé mentale de Québec**
Ancien nom: Centre hospitalier Robert Giffard
2601, ch. de la Canardière, Beauport, QC G1J 2G3
Tél: 418-663-5000 *Téléc:* 418-663-9774
www.institutsmq.qc.ca

Nombre de lits: 503 lits
Michel Gervais, Directeur général

***Fatima:* Centre de réadaptation en DI-TED**
Affiliée à: Centre de santé et de services sociaux des Iles
695, ch des Caps, Fatima, QC G4T 2S9
Tél: 418-986-3590 *Téléc:* 418-986-5778

***Gatineau:* Hôpital Pierre-Janet**
Affiliée à: Centre de santé et de services sociaux de Gatineau
20, rue Pharand, Gatineau, QC J9A 1K7
Tél: 819-771-7761 *Téléc:* 819-771-2908
www.chpj.ca

Nombre de lits: 87 lits
Pierre Gagnon, Directeur général
Michel Thivierge, Chef, Services techniques
819/776-8096

***Malartic:* Hôpital psychiatrique de Malartic**
Affiliée à: Centre de santé et de services sociaux de la Vallée-de-l'Or
CP 800, 1141, rue Royale, Malartic, QC J0Y 1Z0
Tél: 819-757-4342 *Téléc:* 819-757-4330
www.sante-abitibi-temiscamingue-gouv.qc.ca; www.csssvo.qc.ca

Nombre de lits: 34 lits
Note: Services de santé mentale et psychiatrie; soins aigus; soins de longue durée.
Jérôme Lamont, Directeur général, CSSS de la Vallée-de-l'Or
Alain Beaucage, Directeur, Programme santé mentale/psychiatrie

***Montréal:* Hôpital Louis-H. Lafontaine**
7401, rue Hochelaga, Montréal, QC H1N 3M5
Tél: 514-251-4000
www.hlhl.qc.ca

Nombre de lits: 606 lits

***Montréal:* Hôpital Rivière-des-Prairies**
7070, boul Perras, Montréal, QC H1E 1A4
Tél: 514-323-7260 *Téléc:* 514-323-8622
www.hrdp.qc.ca

Nombre de lits: 125 lits
Michel Lapointe, Directeur général

***Québec:* Centre de réadaptation en santé mentale Également connu sous le nom de: La Maisonnée**
855, boul Louis XIV, Québec, QC G1H 1A6
Tél: 418-628-0662 *Téléc:* 418-628-5440
Nombre de lits: 11 places (centre de réadaptation; 6 places (résidences communautaires)
Région desservi: Région de la Capitale-Nationale

Saskatchewan

Government Departments in Charge

SASKATCHEWAN: Saskatchewan Health
T.C. Douglas Building, 3475 Albert St., Regina, SK S4S 6X6
Tel: 306-787-0146 *Fax:* 306-787-8310
Toll-Free: 1-800-667-7766
info@health.gov.sk.ca
www.health.gov.sk.ca

Note: Establishes policy & standards, provides funding, supports regional health authorities, & ensures the provision of essential health services. Branches: acute & emergency services, communications, community care branch, Deputy Minister's Office, drug plan & extended benefits, financial services, Health Information Solutions Centre, health registration & vital statistics, human resources, medical services, policy & planning branch, population health, primary health services, regional accountability, regional policy, Saskatchewan Disease Control Laboratory, & workforce planning.
Hon. Don McMorris, Minister

Regional Health Authorities

***Black Lake:* Athabasca Health Authority**
PO Box 124, Black Lake, SK S0J 0H0
Tel: 306-439-2200 *Fax:* 306-439-2211
vrobillard@athabascahealth.ca
www.athabascahealth.ca

Note: Provides health care services to the First Nations communities of Black Lake, & Fond du Lac; Stony Rapids; Uranium City; & Camsell Portage.
Vince Robillard, CEO
Caroline Isadore, Board Chair

***Buffalo Narrows:* Keewatin Yatthé Regional Health Authority (KYRHA)**
Metis Society Bldg., PO Box 40, Pederson Ave., Buffalo Narrows, SK S0M 0J0
Tel: 306-235-2220 *Fax:* 306-235-2229
Toll-Free: 866-274-8506
richard.petit@kyrha.sk.ca
www.kyrha.ca

Number of Beds: 58 beds
Richard Petit, CEO
Tina Rasmussen, Chair

***La Ronge:* Mamawetan Churchill River Health Region**
PO Box 6000, La Ronge, SK S0J 1L0
Tel: 306-425-2422 *Fax:* 306-425-5513
information@mcrrha.sk.ca
www.mcrrha.sk.ca

Year Founded: 2002
Area Served: North eastern part of Saskatchewan*Population Served:* 22000*Number of Employees:* 300
Andrew McLetchie, CEO
Ron Woytowich, Chair

***Moose Jaw:* Five Hills Health Region**
455 Fairford St. East, Moose Jaw, SK S6H 1H3
Tel: 306-694-0296 *Fax:* 306-694-0282
Toll-Free: 1-888-425-1111
inquiries@fhhr.ca
www.fhhr.ca
Area Served: South-central Saskatchewan*Population Served:* 54000*Number of Employees:* 1200
Note: Five Hills Health Region is home to 14 health facilities, including acute care, long term care and wellness centres.
Cheryl Craig, Chief Executive Officer
Betty Collicott, Chair

***North Battleford:* Prairie North Health Region**
1092 - 107 St., North Battleford, SK S9A 1Z1
Tel: 306-446-6606 *Fax:* 306-446-4114
www.pnrha.ca
Area Served: Northwest part of central Saskatchewan
David Fan, CEO
Bonnie O'Grady, Chair

***Prince Albert:* Prince Albert Parkland Health Region**
1521 - *th Ave. West, Prince Albert, SK S6V 5K1
Tel: 306-765-6400 *Fax:* 306-763-6401
Toll-Free: 800-922-1834
kholmgren@paphr.sk.ca
www.paphr.sk.ca
Area Served: North central Saskatchewan*Population Served:* 80000
Cecile Hunt, CEO
Gord Dobrowolsky, Chair

***Regina:* Regina Qu'Appelle Health Region**
2180 - 23 Ave., Regina, SK S4S 0A5
Tel: 306-766-5100 *Fax:* 306-766-5414
Toll-Free: 888-354-8111
publicaffairs@rqhealth.ca
www.rqhealth.ca

Number of Beds: 1,504 beds
Population Served: 245000
Dwight Nelson, President; CEO
Lloyd Boutilier, Chair

***Rosetown:* Heartland Regional Health Authority**
PO Box 2110, 100 Hwy. #4 South, Rosetown, SK S0L 2V0
Tel: 306-882-4111 *Fax:* 306-882-1389
heartland@hrha.sk.ca
www.hrha.sk.ca
Number of Beds: 499 long term care beds; 67 acute care; 50 other
Area Served: West-central Saskatchewan*Population Served:* 44051
Note: Facilities in 16 communities, including a district hospital in Kindersley. Services include primary & acute health care, emergency services, telehealth, public health, dental health, counselling, addictions services, occupation therapy, speech & language therapy, nutrition.
Gregory Cummings, CEO/President
Richard Anderson, Board Chair

***Saskatoon:* Saskatoon Health Region**
c/o Saskatoon City Hospital, 701 Queen St., Saskatoon, SK S7K 0M7
Tel: 306-655-7500
general.inquiries@saskatoonhealthregion.ca
www.saskatoonhealthregion.ca
Info Line: 1-877-800-0002
Social Media: www.facebook.com/SaskatoonHealthRegion; twitter.com/SaskatoonHealth; www.youtube.com/user/SaskatoonHealthReg
Population Served: 300,000
Note: The health region serves over 100 regional municipalities, cities, towns, villages, & First Nation communities in Saskatchewan. Facilities include hospitals, community health centres, long term care homes, home care services, public health offices, primary health centres, & the Kinsment Children's Centre.
Maura Davies, President & Chief Executive Officer
Dr. Corya Neufdorf, Chief Medical Health Officer
Bonnie Blakley, Vice-President, People & Partnerships
Sandra Blevins, Vice-President, Integrated Health Services
Dr. Alan Casson, Vice-President, Integrated Health Services
Dr. Martha E. Horsburgh, Vice-President, Research & Innovation

Nilesh Kavia, Vice-President, Finance & Corporate Services
Petrina McGrath, Vice-President, Quality & Interprofessional Practice
Dr. George Pylypchuk, Vice-President, Practitioner Staff Affairs

***Swift Current:* Cypress Health Region**
429 - 4th Ave. NE, Swift Current, SK S9H 2J9
Tel: 306-778-5100 *Fax:* 306-773-9513
Toll-Free: 1-888-461-7443
info@cypressrha.ca
www.cypresshealth.ca
Area Served: Western Saskatchewan*Population Served:* 44000*Number of Employees:* 1650
Note: Facilities: 20 hospitals, long term care facilities, & health centres.
Tyler Bragg, Chair
Dr. Ivo Radevski, Senior Medical Officer
Beth Adashynski, Executive Director, Quality & Privacy
Larry Allsen, Executive Director, Finance
Bryce Martin, Executive Director, Communications
Brenda Schwan, Executive Director, Human Resources
Beth Vachon, Executive Director, Community Health Services
Kim Kruse, Director, Executive & Board Support

***Tisdale:* Kelsey Trail Regional Health Authority**
PO Box 1780, 901 - 108 Ave. Wet, Tisdale, SK S0E 1T0
Tel: 306-873-6600 *Fax:* 306-873-6605
tthompson@kthr.sk.ca
www.kelseytrailhealth.ca
Social Media: www.facebook.com/pages/Kelsey-Trail-Health-Region/123342694465; twitter.com/kelseytrail; www.linkedin.com/company/kelsey-trail-health-region
Number of Beds: 61 beds
Glen Kozak, CEO
Rennie Harper, Chair

Weyburn: **Sun Country Health Region**
PO Box 2003, Weyburn, SK S4H 2Z9
Tel: 306-842-8339 *Fax:* 306-842-8738
info@schr.sk.ca
www.suncountry.sk.ca
Number of Beds: 461 beds
Area Served: Southeast portion of Saskatchewan*Population Served:* 56529
Note: There are 28 facilities and 34 public health programs.
Marga Cugnet, CEO
Marilyn Charlton, Chair

Yorkton: **Sunrise Regional Health Authority**
270 Bradbrooke Dr., Yorkton, SK S3N 2K6
Tel: 306-786-0100 *Fax:* 306-786-0122
www.sunrisehealthregion.sk.ca
Number of Beds: 561 beds
Population Served: 58000*Number of Employees:* 2700
Note: Sunrise Health Region stretches from the Qu'Appelle Valley to the northern boreal forest, and from the parklands of the Manitoba border into the Saskatchewan prairie farmlands.
Suann Laurent, CEO
Greg Kobylka, Chair

Hospitals

Hospitals - General

Arcola: **Arcola Health Centre**
Affiliated with: Sun Country Regional Health Authority
PO Box 419, 607 Prairie Ave., Arcola, SK S0C 0G0
Tel: 306-455-2771 *Fax:* 306-455-2397
www.suncountry.sk.ca
Note: Hospital Specialties: Emergency; Inpatient services

Assiniboia: **Assiniboia Union Hospital**
Affiliated with: Five Hills Regional Health Authority
501 - 6 Ave., Assiniboia, SK S0H 0B0
Tel: 306-642-3351
www.fhhr.ca
Number of Beds: 12 acute care beds; 4 respite / palliative care beds
Note: Hospital specialties: Emergency service; Acute care; Laboratory service; Respite care; Palliative care

Balcarres: **Balcarres Integrated Care Centre (BICC)**
Affiliated with: Regina Qu'Appelle Health Region
PO Box 340, 100 South Elgin St., Balcarres, SK S0G 0C0
Tel: 306-334-2634 *Fax:* 306-334-2674
www.rqhealth.ca
Year Founded: 1999
Number of Beds: 9 acute care beds; 42 long term beds; 2 respite beds
Note: Hospital Specialties: Emergency services; Acute care; Physiotherapy; Diabetes education; Mental health & drug & alcohol counselling; Respite services; Day care services; Home care nursing; Long term care Number of Employees: 90
Lorraine Mazerall, Facility Manager
lorraine.mazerall@rqhealth.ca
Elaine Stefanick, Coordinator, Care

Big River: **Big River Health Centre**
Affiliated with: Prince Albert Parkland Regional Health Authority
PO Box 100, 220 - 1st Ave. North, Big River, SK S0J 0E0
Tel: 306-469-2220
www.paphr.sk.ca
Number of Beds: 9 acute care beds; 28 long term care beds; 2 respite care beds; 1 palliative care bed
Note: Specialties: Emergency services; Acute care; Laboratory services; Public health services; Physiotherapy; Occupational therapy; Long term care; Home care; Respite care; Palliative care

Biggar: **Biggar Hospital**
Affiliated with: Heartland Regional Health Authority
PO Box 130, 501 - 1 Ave. West, Biggar, SK S0K 0M0
Tel: 306-948-3323 *Fax:* 306-948-2011
Number of Beds: 13 acute care beds, 2 other
Note: Acute care.
Marian Fritz, Facility Manager

Broadview: **Broadview Hospital**
Affiliated with: Regina Qu'Appelle Health Region
PO Box 100, 901 Nina St., Broadview, SK S0G 0K0
Tel: 306-696-2441 *Fax:* 306-696-2611
www.rqhealth.ca
Number of Beds: 16 acute care beds
Note: Hospital Specialties: Emergency services; Diagnostic services; Ambulatory care; Native liaison work; Respite care; Palliative care

Jacqui Fawcett-Kennett, Manager
jacqui.fawcett-kennett@rqhealth.ca

Canora: **Canora Hospital**
Affiliated with: Sunrise Regional Health Authority
PO Box 749, 1219 Main St., Canora, SK S0A 0L0
Tel: 306-563-5621 *Fax:* 306-563-5571
Year Founded: 1968
Number of Beds: 16 acute care beds; 10 long term care beds; 2 respite beds
Note: Hospital Specialties: Emergency services; Laboratory services; Radiology; Acute care; Occupational therapy; Respite care; Long term care
Karen Kraynick, Administrator

Central Butte: **Central Butte Regency Hospital**
Affiliated with: Five Hills Regional Health Authority
PO Box 40, Central Butte, SK S0H 0T0
Tel: 306-796-2190
inquiries@fhhr.ca
www.fhhr.ca
Number of Beds: 5 acute care beds; 22 residents at special care home
Note: Hospital Specialties: Acute care; Special care home

Davidson: **Davidson & District Health Centre**
Affiliated with: Heartland Regional Health Authority
PO Box 758, 900 Government Rd., Davidson, SK S0G 1A0
Tel: 306-567-2801 *Fax:* 306-567-2073
www.townofdavidson.com/services/healthservices.php
Number of Beds: 40 long term care beds, 2 acute care, 6 other
Number of Employees: 70
Note: Acute care, long term care.
Cathy Hinther, Care Team Manager

Esterhazy: **St. Anthony's Hospital**
Affiliated with: Sunrise Regional Health Authority
PO Box 280, 216 Ancona St., Esterhazy, SK S0A 0X0
Tel: 306-745-3973 *Fax:* 306-745-3245
Year Founded: 1940
Number of Beds: 22 acute care beds
Note: Emergency & outpatient services, visiting primary care services & dietition, x-ray
Joe Kirwan, CEO, SRHA
306-786-0103, Fax: 306-786-0122
Sharon Tropin, Director, Communication, SRHA
306- 786-0144
Carol Unchulenko, Facility Administrator
carol.unchulenko@shr.sk.ca

Estevan: **St. Joseph's Hospital**
Affiliated with: Sun Country Regional Health Authority
PO Box 5000, 1174 Nicholson Rd., Estevan, SK S4A 2V6
Tel: 306-637-2400 *Fax:* 306-637-2490
Number of Beds: 93 beds
Darwin Giem, Executive Director
Emile Wilvers, Maintenance Manager
306-634-0418

Fort Qu'Appelle: **All Nations Healing Hospital (ANHH)**
Affiliated with: Regina Qu'Appelle Health Region
PO Box 300, 450 - 8th St., Fort Qu'Appelle, SK S0G 1S0
Tel: 306-332-5611 *Fax:* 306-332-5033
gboehme@fhqtc.com (Director of ANHH & Health Services)
www.fortquappelle.com/anhh.html
Number of Beds: 13 acute care beds + 1 palliative care bed
Note: Hospital Specialties: First Nations health services; Acute care; Emergency services; Women's health (306-332-2673); Mental health; Diabetes education; Nutrition education; Number of Employees: 100
Lorna Breitkreuz, Director, Client Services
306-332-2440, lbreitkreuz@fhqtc.com

Gravelbourg: **St. Joseph's Hospital/Foyer d'Youville**
Affiliated with: Five Hills Regional Health Authority
PO Box 50, 216 Bettez St., Gravelbourg, SK S0H 1X0
Tel: 306-648-3185 *Fax:* 306-648-3440
janice.michaud@fhhr.ca
www.stjosephshospital-gravelbourg.com
Number of Beds: 9 hospital beds, 50 nursing home beds

Hafford: **Hafford Hospital & Special Care Centre**
Affiliated with: Prince Albert Parkland Regional Health Authority
PO Box 130, 213 South Ave. East, Hafford, SK S0J 1A0
Tel: 306-549-4266 *Fax:* 306-549-4660
Number of Beds: 18 beds
Linda E. Fendelet, Director of Care

Herbert: **Herbert Morse Hospital**
Affiliated with: Cypress Regional Health Authority
PO Box 220, 303 Brownlee St., Herbert, SK S0H 2A0
Tel: 306-784-2202 *Fax:* 306-784-3452

Hudson Bay: **Hudson Bay Health Care Facility**
Affiliated with: Kelsey Trail Regional Health Authority
PO Box 940, 614 Prince St., Hudson Bay, SK S0E 0Y0
Tel: 306-865-2219 *Fax:* 306-865-2429
Number of Beds: 15 beds
Note: integrated facility with acute, long-term care & respite & daycare
Sharon Wood, Director, Health Services

Humboldt: **Humboldt District Hospital**
Affiliated with: Saskatoon Health Region
Former Name: St. Elizabeth's Hospital
PO Box 10, 1210 - 9 St. North, Humboldt, SK S0K 2A0
Tel: 306-682-2603 *Fax:* 306-682-4046
www.saskatoonhealthregion.ca/your_health/ch_humbolt.htm
Number of Beds: 42 beds
Rick Schindel, Executive Director

Ile-a-la-Crosse: **St. Joseph's Hospital**
Affiliated with: Keewatin Yatthé Regional Health Authority
PO Bag 500, Ile-a-la-Crosse, SK S0M 1C0
Tel: 306-833-2016 *Fax:* 306-833-2556
Number of Beds: 31 beds, including 12 longterm care beds
Lorraine Roy, Administrator

Indian Head: **Indian Head Union Hospital**
Affiliated with: Regina Qu'Appelle Health Region
PO Box 340, 300 Hospital St., Indian Head, SK S0G 2K0
Tel: 306-695-2272 *Fax:* 306-695-2525
Number of Beds: 15 beds
Peter Fell, Supervisor, Plant Maintenance
Karen Earnshaw, Manager

Kamsack: **Kamsack Hospital/Kamsack Nursing Home**
Affiliated with: Sunrise Regional Health Authority
PO Box 429, 341 Stewart St., Kamsack, SK S0A 1S0
Tel: 306-542-2635 *Fax:* 306-542-4360
Number of Beds: 20 acute care, 77 long-term care, 2 respite beds
Chris Meyer, Hospital Administrator

Kelvington: **Kelvington Hospital**
Affiliated with: Kelsey Trail Regional Health Authority
PO Box 70, 512 - 1 Ave. South, Kelvington, SK S0A 1W0
Tel: 306-327-4711 *Fax:* 306-327-5115
Number of Beds: 18 beds
Denise Geck, Director, Health Services

Kerrobert: **Kerrobert Integrated Health Care Facility**
Affiliated with: Heartland Health Region
PO Box 320, 635 Alberta Ave., Kerrobert, SK S0L 1R0
Tel: 306-834-2646 *Fax:* 306-834-1007
Number of Beds: 26 long term care beds, 24 acute/program/long term care
Note: Long term care facility + health centre.
Fenton Yeo, Facility Manager
B. Roszell, Supervisor, Physical Plant

Kindersley: **Kindersley Integrated Health Care Facility**
Affiliated with: Heartland Regional Health Authority
1003 - 1 St. West, Kindersley, SK S0L 1S2
Tel: 306-463-2611 *Fax:* 306-463-4550
Number of Beds: 21 acute care beds, 5 other; 80 long term care beds
Note: Long term care; acute care.
Wanda Desrosiers, Facility Manager
Harvey Penner, Chief Engineer

Kipling: **Kipling Memorial Health Centre**
Affiliated with: Sun Country Health Region
PO Box 420, 803 - 1 St., Kipling, SK S0G 2S0
Tel: 306-736-2552 *Fax:* 306-736-8407
Number of Beds: 14 beds
Colleen Easton, Manager, Health Services
A. Gall, Supervisor, Physical Plant

La Loche: **La Loche Health Centre**
Affiliated with: Keewatin Yatthé Regional Health Authority
Bag 1, La Loche, SK S0M 1G0
Tel: 306-822-6333 *Fax:* 306-822-2112
Toll-Free: 888-688-7072

Number of Beds: 27 beds
Mary Bradstreet-Metali, Director, Primary Care

Lanigan: Lanigan Hospital
Affiliated with: Saskatoon Health Region
PO Box 609, 306 Downing Dr., Lanigan, SK S0K 2M0
Tel: 306-365-1400 *Fax:* 306-365-3354
www.saskatoonhealthregion.ca/your_health/ch_lanigan.htm
Number of Beds: 10 beds
Janet Lees, Manager

Leader: Leader Hospital
Affiliated with: Cypress Regional Health Authority
423 Main St. East, Leader, SK S0N 1H0
Tel: 306-628-3845 *Fax:* 306-628-3320
www.cypresshealth.ca/leader.htm
Number of Beds: 24

Lestock: St. Joseph's Integrated Care Centre
Affiliated with: Regina Qu'Appelle Health Region
PO Box 280, 505 Westmoor St., Lestock, SK S0A 2G0
Tel: 306-274-2215 *Fax:* 306-274-2045
Number of Beds: 16 beds
F. Ricci, Manager, Plant Maintenance
Kate Beattie, Manager

Lloydminster: Lloydminster Hospital
Affiliated with: Prairie North Health Region
3820 - 43 Ave., Lloydminster, SK S9V 1Y5
Tel: 306-820-6000 *Fax:* 306-825-6516
Number of Beds: 58 acute care beds
Note: Hospital Specialties: Cancer treatment & Care-Alberta Community Cancer Centres; Hemodialysis - Northern Alberta Renal Program; Surgical services & recovery; Obstetrics; Paediatrics; Special care unit. Number of Employees: 664
Lois Sonnega, Director, Acute Care

Loon Lake: Loon Lake Hospital & Special Care Home
Affiliated with: Prairie North Health Region
PO Box 69, 510 - 2nd Ave., Loon Lake, SK S0M 1L0
Tel: 306-837-2114 *Fax:* 306-837-2268
Neal Sylvestre, Director, Rural Health Facilities

Maidstone: Maidstone Health Complex
Affiliated with: Prairie North Health Region
PO Box 160, 214 - 5th Ave. East, Maidstone, SK S0M 1M0
Tel: 306-893-2622 *Fax:* 306-893-2922
Number of Beds: 11 acute beds + 24 long-term care beds + 2 respite beds
Note: Specialties: Community health services, including home care & counselling; Acute care; Long-term care wing; Respite care; Palliative care
Emily Hardy, Facility Manager

Maple Creek: Maple Creek Hospital
Affiliated with: Cypress Regional Health Authority
PO Box 1330, Hwy. 21 South, Maple Creek, SK S0N 1N0
Tel: 306-662-2611 *Fax:* 306-662-3210
www.cypresshealth.ca/maplecreek.htm
Number of Beds: 20

Meadow Lake: Northwest Health Facility
Affiliated with: Prairie North Health Region
Also Known As: Meadow Lake Hospital
#2, 711 Centre St., Meadow Lake, SK S9X 1E6
Tel: 306-236-1500 *Fax:* 306-236-3244

Note: Specialty: Acute care; Diagnostic imaging
Debbie Carey, Director, Acute Care Services

Melfort: Melfort Hospital
Affiliated with: Kelsey Trail Regional Health Authority
PO Box 1480, 510 Broadway Ave., Melfort, SK S0E 1A0
Tel: 306-752-8700 *Fax:* 306-752-8711
www.kelseytrailhealth.ca

Note: Specialties: Acute care; General Surgery; Radiology services; Chemotherapy; Mental health & addiction services; Diabetes & Heart Health Centre; Palliative care
Judy Blair, Director, Health Services

Melville: St. Peter's Hospital
Affiliated with: Sunrise Regional Health Authority
PO Box 1810, 200 Heritage Dr., Melville, SK S0A 2P0
Tel: 306-728-5407 *Fax:* 306-728-4870
Year Founded: 1942
Number of Beds: 30 acute care beds
Note: Emergency services, obstetrics, general surgery, outpatient services, physiotherapy, social work, Lifeline Response Centre, chemotherapy outreach program, pharmacy
Joe Kirwan, CEO, SRHA
306-786-0103, Fax: 306-786-0122
Sharon Tropin, Director, Communications, SRHA
306- 786-0144
Kim Bucsis, Site Manager
Fax: 306-728-1859, kim.bucsis@shr.sk.ca

Moose Jaw: Moose Jaw Union Hospital
Affiliated with: Five Hills Regional Health Authority
455 Fairford St. East, Moose Jaw, SK S6H 1H3
Tel: 306-694-0200 *Fax:* 306-694-5596
Number of Beds: 120 beds
Dan Florizone, CEO
John Borody, President; CEO

Moosomin: Southeast Integrated Care Centre - Moosomin
Affiliated with: Regina Qu'Appelle Health Region
Former Name: Moosomin Union Hospital
PO Box 1, 320 Gertie St., Moosomin, SK S0G 3N0
Tel: 306-435-3303 *Fax:* 306-435-3211
Number of Beds: 27 in-patient; 58 long-term
Dan Ireland, Supervisor, Physical Plant
Sharon Ann Wood, Manager

Nipawin: Nipawin Hospital
Affiliated with: Kelsey Trail Regional Health Authority
PO Box 389, 800 - 6 St. East, Nipawin, SK S0E 1E0
Tel: 306-862-4643 *Fax:* 306-862-9310
Number of Beds: 36 beds
Marg Currie, Director, Health Services

North Battleford: Battlefords Union Hospital
Affiliated with: Prairie North Health Region
1092 - 107 St., North Battleford, SK S9A 1Z1
Tel: 306-446-6600 *Fax:* 306-446-6561
www.pnrha.ca
Number of Beds: 200 beds
Note: Hospital specialties: Emergency services; Acute care; Day patient clinic
Shelly Horsman, Nurse Manager
Shelly.Horsman@pnrha.ca
Sharon Jaindl, Health Information Services
Sharon.Jaindl@pnrha.ca
Pam Nyholt, Supervisor, Laboratory
Pam.Nyholt@pnrha.ca

Outlook: Outlook & District Health Centre
Affiliated with: Heartland Regional Health Authority
PO Box 369, 500 Semple St., Outlook, SK S0L 2N0
Tel: 306-867-8676 *Fax:* 306-867-9449
Year Founded: 2008
Number of Beds: 11 acute care beds + 45 continuing care beds
Note: Specialties: Acute care; Diagnostic services; Therapies; Community health; Public health inspections; Mental health services; Home care; Long-term care; Respite care; Adult day care; Palliative care

Porcupine Plain: Porcupine Carragana Hospital
Affiliated with: Kelsey Trail Regional Health Authority
PO Box 70, Windsor Ave., Porcupine Plain, SK S0E 1H0
Tel: 306-278-2211 *Fax:* 306-278-3088
Number of Beds: 13 beds
Christine Pohl, Director, Health Services
Keith Butler, Supervisor, Physical Plant

Preeceville: Preeceville & District Health Centre
Affiliated with: Sunrise Regional Health Authority
Former Name: Preeceville Hospital; Preeceville & District Integrated Health Care Facility
PO Box 469, 712 - 7 St. NE, Preeceville, SK S0A 3B0
Tel: 306-547-2102 *Fax:* 306-547-2223
Number of Beds: 10 acute care, 38 long-term care beds
Note: Doctors' medical clinic, acute & long-term care
G. Jolson, Director, Physical Plant
Joanne Bodnar, Nurse Administrator

Prince Albert: Victoria Hospital
Affiliated with: Prince Albert Parkland Regional Health Authority
1200 - 24 St. West, Prince Albert, SK S6V 5T4
Tel: 306-764-1551 *Fax:* 306-763-5322
Number of Beds: 147 beds
Tom Graham, Director, Housekeeping
John Piggott, Director, Operations

Redvers: Redvers Health Centre
Affiliated with: Sun Country Regional Health Authority
PO Box 30, 18 Eichhorst St., Redvers, SK S0C 2H0
Tel: 306-452-3553 *Fax:* 306-452-3556
Number of Beds: 12 beds
Myrna Petersen, Manager, Health Services
Joe Chicione, Maintenance

Regina: Pasqua Hospital
Affiliated with: Regina Qu'Appelle Health Region
4101 Dewdney Ave., Regina, SK S4T 1A5
Tel: 306-766-2222 *Fax:* 306-766-2745
Number of Beds: 179 beds
Dwight Nelson, President; CEO
Darrell Tunstead, Director, Property Management Services
306-766-2314

Regina: Regina General Hospital
Affiliated with: Regina Qu'Appelle Health Region
1440 - 14 Ave., Regina, SK S4P 0W5
Tel: 306-766-4444 *Fax:* 306-766-4723
Number of Beds: 404 beds
Note: Offers full-range acute care services; home to the Wasakaw Pisim Native Health Centre, Sleep Disorders Centre, and 50-bed mental health facility
Dwight Nelson, President; CEO
Darrell Tunstead, Director, Property Management Services
306-766-2314

Rosetown: Rosetown & District Health Centre
Affiliated with: Heartland Health Region
PO Box 850, Hwy. 4 North, Rosetown, SK S0L 2V0
Tel: 306-882-2672 *Fax:* 306-882-3335
Year Founded: 1964
Number of Beds: 22 beds
Gail Adamowski, Facility Manager

Rosthern: Rosthern Hospital
Affiliated with: Saskatoon Health Region
PO Box 309, 2016 - 2 St., Rosthern, SK S0K 3R0
Tel: 306-232-4811 *Fax:* 306-232-4887
Year Founded: 1950
Number of Beds: 30 beds
Note: Acute care facility with six physicians on-staff, plus 60 employees
Henry Zacharias, Supervisor
Robert Hogel, Administrator

Saskatoon: Royal University Hospital
Affiliated with: Saskatoon Health Region
103 Hospital Dr., Saskatoon, SK S7N 0W8
Tel: 306-655-1000 *Fax:* 306-655-1037
Year Founded: 1955
Number of Beds: 377 beds
Jim Fergusson, President
Dr. Clarence Clotter, MHO; General Manager, Public Health Services
306-655-4338, Fax: 306-655-4414

Saskatoon: St. Paul's Hospital
Affiliated with: Saskatoon Health Region
1702 - 20 St. West, Saskatoon, SK S7M 0Z9
Tel: 306-655-5800 *Fax:* 306-655-5555
www.stpaulshospital.org
Number of Beds: 213 beds
Brenda FizGerald, CEO
Jerri Taman, Manager, Housekeeping
David Loveridge, Manager, Powerhouse

Saskatoon: Saskatoon City Hospital
Affiliated with: Saskatoon Health Region
701 Queen St., Saskatoon, SK S7K 0M7
Tel: 306-655-8000 *Fax:* 306-655-8269
Year Founded: 1909
Number of Beds: 280 beds
John Malcolm, President
Richard Rodda, Vice-President, Support Services & Operations

Shellbrook: Shellbrook & District Hospital
Affiliated with: Prince Albert Parkland Regional Health Authority
PO Box 70, 211 - 2nd Ave. W, Shellbrook, SK S0J 2E0
Tel: 306-747-2603 *Fax:* 306-747-3004
Number of Beds: 20 beds
Mansford Kennedy, Supervisor, Physical Plant
Clifford E. Skange, Administrator

Spiritwood: Spiritwood & District Health Complex
Affiliated with: Prince Albert Parkland Regional Health Authority
PO Box 159, 400 - 1 St. East, Spiritwood, SK S0J 2M0
Tel: 306-883-2133 *Fax:* 306-883-4446
Toll-Free: 800-887-6251
Number of Beds: 36 beds
Cecile Hunt, CEO, PAPRHA
306-765-6405, Fax: 306-765-6401
Carroll Joyes, Director, Long Term Care, PAPRHA

Doug Dahl, Communication Officer, PAPRHA
306-765-6409

Swift Current: Cypress Regional Hospital
Affiliated with: Cypress Regional Health Authority
Former Name: Swift Current Regional Hospital
2004 Saskatchewan Dr., Swift Current, SK S9H 5M8
Tel: 306-778-9400 *Fax:* 306-773-9431
www.cypressrha.ca/facilities_sc_page.htm
Year Founded: 1951
Note: Services include intensive care, long-term care, palliative care, inpatient and outpatient surgery, renal dialysis, pediatric care, CT scans, obstetrics/gynecology, midwifery and general medical care.
Beth Vachon, interim CEO, CRHA
Bryce Martin, Executive Director, Communications, CRHA

Tisdale: Tisdale Hospital
Affiliated with: Kelsey Trail Regional Health Authority
PO Box 1630, 2010 - 110th Ave. West, Tisdale, SK S0E 1T0
Tel: 306-873-2621 *Fax:* 306-873-5994
www.kelseytrailhealth.ca
Note: Specialties: Acute care; Diabetes & Heart Health Centre; Hemodialysis satellite unit; Mental health & addiction services; Home care; Palliative care
Anne Haley-Callaghan, Manager, Community Health

Unity: Unity & District Health Centre
Former Name: Unity Hospital
PO Box 741, Hwy. 14 North, Unity, SK S0K 4L0
Tel: 306-228-2666 *Fax:* 306-228-2292
Year Founded: 2001
Note: Specialties: Acute care; Diagnostic services; Maternity services; Community health services; Public health nursing; Mental health services; Counselling; Physiotherapy; Occupational therapy; Home care; Long-term care; Respite care; Palliative care
Kim Halter, Facility Manager
Randy Scherr, Supervisor, Plant Maintenance

Uranium City: Uranium City Health Centre
Affiliated with: Athabasca Health Authority
PO Box 360, Baska Rd., Uranium City, SK S0J 2W0
Tel: 306-498-2412 *Fax:* 306-498-2577

Wadena: Wadena Hospital
Affiliated with: Saskatoon Health Region
PO Box 10, 533 - 5 St. NE, Wadena, SK S0A 4J0
Tel: 306-338-2515 *Fax:* 306-338-2720
Year Founded: 1989
Number of Beds: 18 beds
Note: Provides acute, respite, and long-term care
Dayle Maryniak, Site Manager

Wakaw: Wakaw Health Centre
Affiliated with: Saskatoon Regional Health Authority
Former Name: Wakaw Hospital
PO Box 309, 301 - 1 St. North, Wakaw, SK S0K 4P0
Tel: 306-233-4611 *Fax:* 306-233-5990
saskatoonhealthregion.ca
Note: Health centre, X-ray, Home care, Community services, Municipal medical clinic
Corinne Slobodian, Contact

Watrous: Watrous Hospital
Affiliated with: Saskatoon Health Region
PO Box 130, 702 - 4 St. East, Watrous, SK S0K 4T0
Tel: 306-946-1200 *Fax:* 306-946-2369
Number of Beds: 14 beds
J. Reichert, Supervisor, Physical Plant
Wendy Crouch, Manager

Wawota: Wawota Memorial Health Centre
Affiliated with: Sun Country Regional Health Authority
PO Box 60, 609 Choo Foo Cres., Wawota, SK S0G 5A0
Tel: 306-739-2244 *Fax:* 306-739-2479
Number of Beds: 6 beds
Laurel Charles, Manager, Health Services

Weyburn: Weyburn General Hospital
Affiliated with: Sun Country Regional Health Authority
PO Box 2003, 201 - 1 Ave. NE, Weyburn, SK S4H 2Z9
Tel: 306-842-8400 *Fax:* 306-842-0737
www.suncountry.sk.ca
Number of Beds: 50 beds
Lee Spencer, CEO
Gene Schmidt, Director, Materials Management
Don Rose, Director, Physical Plant

Wolseley: Wolseley Memorial Union Hospital
Affiliated with: Regina Qu'Appelle Health Region
PO Box 458, 801 Ouimet St., Wolseley, SK S0G 5H0
Tel: 306-698-2213 *Fax:* 306-698-2988
www.rqhealth.ca
Number of Beds: 15 beds
Jeanette Switzer, Facilities Manager

Wynyard: Wynyard Integrated Facility
Affiliated with: Saskatoon Health Region
PO Box 670, 300 - 1st St. West, Wynyard, SK S0A 4T0
Tel: 306-554-6126 *Fax:* 306-554-2765
www.saskatoonhealthregion.ca
Number of Beds: 58 beds
J. Skilinick, Supervisor, Physical Plant
Lara Prystai, Manager, Client Services

Yorkton: Yorkton Regional Health Centre
Affiliated with: Sunrise Regional Health Authority
270 Bradbrooke Dr., Yorkton, SK S3N 2K6
Tel: 306-782-2401 *Fax:* 306-786-6295
Number of Beds: 87 beds; 6 ICU; 12 Pediatrics; 15 maternity; 21 surgery
Donna Milbrandt, Director, Client Services

Federal Hospitals

Saskatoon: Regional Psychiatric Centre (Prairies)
c/o Correctional Service Canada, 2520 Central Ave., Saskatoon, SK S7K 3X5
Tel: 306-975-5400 *Fax:* 306-975-6024
Number of Beds: 210 beds
Peter Guenter, Executive Director

Community Health Centres

Community Health Care Centres

Arborfield: Arborfield & District Health Care Centre
Affiliated with: Kelsey Trail Regional Health Authority
PO Box 160, 5 Ave., Arborfield, SK S0E 0A0
Tel: 306-769-8757 *Fax:* 306-769-8759
www.kelseytrailhealth.ca
Number of Beds: 36 beds
Sharon Frisky, Director, Health Services

Beauval: Beauval Health Centre
Affiliated with: Keewatin Yatthé Regional Health Authority
PO Box 68, Beauval, SK S0M 0G0
Tel: 306-288-4800 *Fax:* 306-288-2225
Robin Wallace, Nurse, Primary Care

Beechy: Beechy Health Centre
Affiliated with: Heartland Regional Health Authority
PO Box 68, 226 1st Ave. North, Beechy, SK S0L 0C0
Tel: 306-859-2118 *Fax:* 306-859-2206
www.beechysask.ca/healthcare.htm
Note: Primary health care, lab/radiology services, visiting community health services: public health, counselling, occupational health, nutrition.
Cathy Ringrose, Contact

Birch Hills: Birch Hills Medical Centre
Affiliated with: Prince Albert Parkland Regional Health Authority
PO Box 578, 7 Wilson St., Birch Hills, SK S0J 0G0
Tel: 306-749-3331 *Fax:* 306-749-2440
www.birchhills.ca/health.html
Karl Humeniuk, CEO

Black Lake: Athabasca Health Facility
Affiliated with: Athabasca Health Authority
PO Box 124, Black Lake, SK S0J 0H0
Tel: 306-439-2200 *Fax:* 306-439-2210
Year Founded: 2003
Number of Beds: 14 beds
Note: Located on the Chicken Indian Reserve. Services include acute care, birthing services, long term care, emergency & ambulatory care, public health, mental health, addictions therapy, traditional healing, radiology & lab services.

Borden: Borden Primary Health Centre
Affiliated with: Saskatoon Health Region
Former Name: Borden Community Health Centre
PO Box 90, Borden, SK S0K 0N0
Tel: 306-997-2110 *Fax:* 306-997-2114
www.saskatoonhealthregion.ca
Monica Kohlhammer, Administrator

Buffalo Narrows: Buffalo Narrows Health Centre
Affiliated with: Keewatin Yatthé Regional Health Authority
PO Box 40, Buffalo Narrows, SK S0M 0J0
Tel: 306-235-5800 *Fax:* 306-235-4500
Kate Cote, Nurse, Primary Care

Cabri: Prairie Health Care Centre
Affiliated with: Cypress Regional Health Authority
PO Box 79, 517 - 1 St. North, Cabri, SK S0N 0J0
Tel: 306-587-2623 *Fax:* 306-587-2751
www.cypresshealth.ca/cabri.htm
Number of Beds: 22 beds
Dean Scott, Supervisor, Maintenance

Carrot River: Carrot River Health Centre
Affiliated with: Kelsey Trail Regional Health Authority
PO Box 10, 4101 - 1 Ave. West, Carrot River, SK S0E 0L0
Tel: 306-768-2725 *Fax:* 306-768-3233
www.town.carrotriver.sk.ca/healthcare.htm
Number of Beds: 38 beds
Bessie Lefebvre, Director, Health Services

Climax: Border Health Centre
Affiliated with: Cypress Regional Health Authority
PO Box 60, 301 - 1 St. West, Climax, SK S0N 0N0
Tel: 306-293-2222 *Fax:* 306-293-2860
www.cypresshealth.ca/climax
Number of Beds: 4 beds

Coronach: Coronach Health Centre
Affiliated with: Sun Country Health Region
PO Box 150, 240 South Ave. East, Coronach, SK S0H 0Z0
Tel: 306-267-2022 *Fax:* 306-267-2324
Number of Beds: 15 beds
Judy Ludtke, Manager, Community Health Services
306-267-2123

Craik: Craik & District Health Centre
Affiliated with: Five Hills Regional Health Authority
PO Box 208, 620 Mary St., Craik, SK S0G 0V0
Tel: 306-734-2288 *Fax:* 306-734-2248
www.fhhr.ca
Number of Beds: 15 long-term care beds; 3 respite/palliative beds

Creighton: Creighton Health Centre
Affiliated with: Mamawetan Churchill River Health Region
PO Box 219, 298 - 1st St. East, Creighton, SK S0P 0A0
Tel: 306-688-8620 *Fax:* 306-688-8629
www.mcrrha.sk.ca

Cumberland House: Cumberland House Health Centre
Affiliated with: Kelsey Trail Regional Health Authority
PO Box 8, 2nd Ave., Cumberland House, SK S0E 0S0
Tel: 306-888-2244 *Fax:* 306-884-2269

Cupar: Cupar Health Centre
Affiliated with: Regina Qu'Appelle Health Region
PO Box 100, Cupar, SK S0G 0Y0
Tel: 306-723-4300 *Fax:* 306-723-4416
www.rqhealth.ca
Betty Smith, Acting Manager

Cut Knife: Cut Knife Health Complex
Affiliated with: Prairie North Health Region
PO Box 220, 102 Dion Ave., Cut Knife, SK S0M 0N0
Tel: 306-398-4718 *Fax:* 306-398-2206
www.pnrha.ca
Number of Beds: 28 long-term care beds; 2 respite beds; 1 palliative care bed; 2 observation beds
Note: attached Special Care Home
Louise Blais, Facility Manager

Delisle: Delisle Community Health & Social Centre
Affiliated with: Saskatoon Health Region
305 First St. West, Delisle, SK S0L 0P0
Tel: 306-493-2810 *Fax:* 306-493-2812

Dinsmore: Dinsmore Health Care Centre
Affiliated with: Heartland Regional Health Authority
PO Box 219, 207 - 1st St. East, Dinsmore, SK S0L 0T0
Tel: 306-846-2222 *Fax:* 306-846-2225
Number of Beds: 18 long term care beds, 4 other
Population Served: 375
Note: Long term care; visiting care services include physiotherapy, occupational therapy, mental health consultation, nutrition, child health.
Anne Rankin, Facility Manager

Jim Cheyne, Supervisor, Plant Maintenance

Dodsland: Dodsland Clinic
Former Name: Dodsland Health Centre
4 Ave., Dodsland, SK S0L 0V0
Tel: 306-356-2104
Note: community-owned clinic

Eastend: Eastend Wolf Willow Health Centre
Affiliated with: Cypress Regional Health Authority
PO Box 490, 555 Redcoat Dr., Eastend, SK S0N 0T0
Tel: 306-295-3534 *Fax:* 306-295-3223
Number of Beds: 28 beds

Eatonia: Eatonia Health Centre
Affiliated with: Heartland Regional Health Authority
205 - 2nd Ave. West, Eatonia, SK S0L 0Y0
Tel: 306-967-2591 *Fax:* 306-967-2373
www.townofeatonia.com/services/healthcare.html
Note: Physician services; wellness program; lab/radiology; home care services; emergency services; occupational therapy; pharmacy deliveries.
Faye Hofer, Facility Manager

Edam: Lady Minto Health Care Center
Affiliated with: Prairie North Health Region
PO Box 330, Edam, SK S0M 0V0
Tel: 306-397-2222 *Fax:* 306-397-2225
caroll.s@pnrha.ca
Number of Beds: 2 convalescent, 3 respite, 1 palliative, 14 long-term care beds
Note: integrated facility
Caroll Spence, Facility Manager

Elrose: Elrose Health Centre
Affiliated with: Heartland Regional Health Authority
PO Box 100, 505 Main St., Elrose, SK S0L 0Z0
Tel: 306-378-2882 *Fax:* 306-378-2812
Number of Beds: 30 long term care beds, 3 other
Note: Long term care; respite/palliative & convalescent.
Wendy Smith, Care Team Manager

Eston: Eston Health Centre
Affiliated with: Heartland Regional Health Authority
PO Box 667, 800 Main St., Eston, SK S0L 1A0
Tel: 306-962-3667 *Fax:* 306-962-3900
Number of Beds: 32 long term care beds, 4 other
Ruth Miller, Facility Manager, Care
R. Hartsook, Supervisor, Plant Maintenance

Fillmore: Fillmore Union Health Centre
Affiliated with: Sun Country Health Region
Former Name: Fillmore Health Centre
PO Box 246, 100 Main St., Fillmore, SK S0G 1N0
Tel: 306-722-3315 *Fax:* 306-722-3877
Number of Beds: 25 beds
Reg Fisher, Manager, Physical Plant Maintenance
Linda Wilson, Director, Community Services

Foam Lake: Foam Lake Health Centre
Affiliated with: Sunrise Regional Health Authority
PO Box 190, 715 Saskatchewan Ave. East, Foam Lake, SK S0A 1A0
Tel: 306-272-3325 *Fax:* 306-272-4449
Brianna Arneson, Manager, Health Services

Gainsborough: Gainsborough & Area Health Centre
Affiliated with: Sun Country Health Region
PO Box 420, 312 Stephens St., Gainsborough, SK S0G 1S0
Tel: 306-685-2277 *Fax:* 306-685-4636
Number of Beds: 19 beds
R. Spencer, Supervisor, Physical Plant
Laurie Cole, Administrator

Goodsoil: L. Gervais Memorial Health Centre
Affiliated with: Prairie North Health Region
PO Box 100, Main St., Goodsoil, SK S0M 1A0
Tel: 306-238-2100 *Fax:* 306-238-4449
Number of Beds: 12 long-term care beds; 2 respite beds; 4 convalescent/palliative beds
Note: health centre with a nursing home & attached special care home
Louise Roth, Facility Manager

Grenfell: Grenfell Health Centre
Affiliated with: Regina Qu'Appelle Health Region
PO Box 243, 721 Stella St., Grenfell, SK S0G 2B0
Tel: 306-697-2853 *Fax:* 306-697-3459
www.rqhealth.ca
Diana Lerner, Manager

Gull Lake: Gull Lake Special Care Centre
Affiliated with: Cypress Regional Health Authority
PO Box 539, 751 Grey St., Gull Lake, SK S0N 1A0
Tel: 306-672-4700 *Fax:* 306-672-4133
www.cypresshealth.ca/gulllake.htm
Number of Beds: 37 beds

Hodgeville: Hodgeville Health Centre
Affiliated with: Cypress Regional Health Authority
PO Box 232, 105 Main St., Hodgeville, SK S0H 2B0
Tel: 306-677-2292 *Fax:* 306-677-2584

Imperial: Long Lake Valley Integrated Facility
Affiliated with: Regina Qu'Appelle Health Region
PO Box 180, Imperial, SK S0G 2J0
Tel: 306-963-2210 *Fax:* 306-963-2518
publicaffairs@rqhealth.ca (Regina Qu'Appelle Health Region)
Year Founded: 1992
Number of Beds: 15 long term care beds; 3 respite or palliative beds
Note: Specialties: Short-term & long-term care; Respite & day care services; Well baby clinics; Foot Care clinics; Outreach programs; Education programs
Wanda Gustafson, Administrator

Invermay: Invermay Health Centre/Gateway Lodge
Affiliated with: Sunrise Regional Health Authority
PO Box 160, 303 - 4 Ave. North, Invermay, SK S0A 1M0
Tel: 306-593-2133 *Fax:* 306-593-4566
Number of Beds: 26 beds
Oney Pollock, Manager, Health Services

Ituna: Ituna Pioneer Health Care Centre
Affiliated with: Sunrise Regional Health Authority
PO Box 130, 320 - 5 Ave. East, Ituna, SK S0A 1N0
Tel: 306-795-2471 *Fax:* 306-795-3592
Number of Beds: 38 beds
Shelley Cherney, Administrator, Health Services

Kincaid: Kincaid Health Centre
Affiliated with: Five Hills Regional Health Authority
PO Box 179, Municipal Rd., Kincaid, SK S0H 2J0
Tel: 306-264-3233 *Fax:* 306-264-3878
Pat Williamson, Sec.-Treas.

Kinistino: Kinistino Health Centre
Affiliated with: Prince Albert Parkland Regional Health Authority
111 Meyers Ave., Kinistino, SK S0J 1H0
Tel: 306-864-2292
Number of Beds: 10 beds

Kyle: Kyle & District Health Centre
Affiliated with: Heartland Health Region
PO Box 70, 208 - 3 Ave. East, Kyle, SK S0L 1T0
Tel: 306-375-2251 *Fax:* 306-375-2422
Number of Beds: 19 beds
Wendy Gunderson, Facility Manager

La Ronge: La Ronge Health Centre
Affiliated with: Mamawetan Churchill River Health Region
PO Box 6000, 227 Backlund St., La Ronge, SK S0J 1L0
Tel: 306-425-2422
www.mcrrha.sk.ca
Number of Beds: 18 acute, 14 longterm, 8 detox, 8 pediatric, 2 respite
Kathy Chisholm, CEO

Lafleche: LaFleche & District Health Centre
Affiliated with: Five Hills Regional Health Authority
PO Box 159, 315 Main St., Lafleche, SK S0H 2K0
Tel: 306-472-5230 *Fax:* 306-472-5405
www.fhhr.ca/Lafleche.htm
Number of Beds: 16 beds

Lampman: Lampman Community Health Centre
Affiliated with: Sun Country Health Region
PO Box 100, 309 - 2 Ave. East, Lampman, SK S0C 1N0
Tel: 306-487-2561 *Fax:* 306-487-3103
www.suncountry.sk.ca
Number of Beds: 22 beds
Cyndee Hoium, Contact
G. Neumier, Manager, Plant Maintenance

Langenburg: Langenburg Health Care Complex
Affiliated with: Sunrise Regional Health Authority
PO Box 370, 200 Heritage Dr., Langenburg, SK S0A 2A0
Tel: 306-743-2661 *Fax:* 306-743-5025
Number of Beds: 48 beds

Leoville: Evergreen Health Centre
Affiliated with: Prince Albert Parkland Regional Health Authority
PO Box 160, 238 - 2nd St., Leoville, SK S0J 1N0
Tel: 306-984-2136 *Fax:* 306-984-2046
www.princealbertparklandhealth.com
Number of Beds: 17 beds
Note: Nursing home
Terri Kirushelniski, Director of Care

Leroy: Leroy Community Health & Social Centre
Affiliated with: Saskatoon Health Region
PO Box 7, 211 - 1 Ave. NE, Leroy, SK S0K 2P0
Tel: 306-286-3347 *Fax:* 306-286-3888

Lloydminster: Lloydminster & District Co-operative Health Services Ltd.
PO Box 530, Lloydminster, SK S9V 0Y6
Tel: 306-825-4427

Lucky Lake: Lucky Lake Health Centre
Affiliated with: Heartland Health Region
First Ave., Lucky Lake, SK S0L 1Z0
Tel: 306-858-2133 *Fax:* 306-858-2312
Bruce Iverarity, Maintenance
Betty Ann Trumbley, Facility Manager

Macklin: St. Joseph's Health Centre
Affiliated with: Heartland Health Region
PO Box 190, Hwy. 31 North, Macklin, SK S0L 2C0
Tel: 306-753-2115 *Fax:* 306-753-2181
Number of Beds: 3 acute care; 23 long term care
Fenton Yeo, Executive Director

Maryfield: Maryfield Health Centre
Affiliated with: Sun Country Regional Health Authority
PO Box 164, 233 Main St., Maryfield, SK S0G 3K0
Tel: 306-646-2133 *Fax:* 306-646-2088

Midale: Mainprize Manor & Health Centre
Affiliated with: Sun Country Health Region
PO Box 239, 206 South St., Midale, SK S0C 1S0
Tel: 306-458-2300 *Fax:* 306-458-2764
Note: Specialties: Doctor clinics; Outpatient service; Day respite care; Long-term care
Bernadette Wright, Director, Community Services

Montmartre: Montmartre Health Centre
Affiliated with: Regina Qu'Appelle Health Region
PO Box 206, 237 - 2 Ave. East, Montmartre, SK S0G 3M0
Tel: 306-424-2222 *Fax:* 306-424-2227
Number of Beds: 16 beds
Marg Hayes, Facility Manager

Mossbank: Mossbank Wellness Centre
Affiliated with: Five Hills Regional Health Authority
Former Name: Mossbank Health Centre
General Delivery, Mossbank, SK S0H 3G0
Tel: 306-354-2300 *Fax:* 306-354-2819

Neilburg: Manitou Health Centre
Affiliated with: Prairie North Health Region
PO Box 190, 105 - 2nd Ave. W, Neilburg, SK S0M 2C0
Tel: 306-823-4262 *Fax:* 306-823-4590
Louise Blais, Coordinator, Health Services

Neudorf: Neudorf Health & Social Centre
420 Main St., Neudorf, SK S0A 2T0
Tel: 306-748-2566 *Fax:* 306-748-2868
Note: Senior centre

Nokomis: Nokomis Health Centre (Puffer Special Care Home Corp.).
Affiliated with: Saskatoon Health Region
PO Box 98, 103 - 2 Ave. East, Nokomis, SK S0G 3R0
Tel: 306-528-2114 *Fax:* 306-528-4655
Number of Beds: 17 beds
Wendy Renwick, Manager, Client Services

Oxbow: Galloway Health Centre
Affiliated with: Sun Country Health Region
PO Box 268, 917 Tupper St., Oxbow, SK S0C 2B0
Tel: 306-483-2956 *Fax:* 306-483-5178
info@schr.sk.ca
www.suncountry.sk.ca
Number of Beds: 14 beds
Bill Cannon, Community Coordinator

***Pangman:* Pangman Health Centre**
Affiliated with: Sun Country Regional Health Authority
PO Box 90, 211 Keeler St., Pangman, SK S0C 2C0
Tel: 306-442-2044 *Fax:* 306-442-4227
www.suncountry.sk.ca
Note: Specialties: Rehabilitation services; Public health inspection; Mental health services; Diabetes program; Ambulance services; Home care; Palliative care
Pat Kessler, Community Health Services Manager

***Paradise Hill:* Paradise Hill Health Centre**
Affiliated with: Prairie North Health Region
PO Box 179, 1st Ave., Paradise Hill, SK S0M 2G0
Tel: 306-344-2255 *Fax:* 306-344-2277
www.pnrha.ca
Neal Sylvestre, Director, Rural Facilities

***Pinehouse:* Pinehouse Health Centre**
Affiliated with: Mamawetan Churchill River Health Region
PO Box 70, Pinehouse, SK S0J 2B0
Tel: 306-884-5670 *Fax:* 306-884-5689
www.mcrrha.sk.ca
Note: Specialties: Public health; Health education; Primary care; Addiction services; Mental health services; Home care services

***Ponteix:* Ponteix Health Centre**
Affiliated with: Cypress Health Region
PO Box 600, 428 - 2 Ave., Ponteix, SK S0N 1Z0
Tel: 306-625-3382 *Fax:* 306-625-3764
Toll-Free: 1-877-800-0002
www.cypresshealth.ca/ponteix.htm/
Note: Specialties: Radiology, Laboratory Services, Home Care, Nutrition, Mental Health, Baby Clinic, Public Health, Foyer St. Joseph Nursing Home, Ambulance Service

***Prince Albert:* Prince Albert Co-Operative Health Centre**
Affiliated with: Prince Albert Parkland Regional Health Authority
110 - 8th St. East, Prince Albert, SK S6V 0V7
Tel: 306-763-6464 *Fax:* 306-763-2101
www.coophealth.com
Year Founded: 1962
Frank Regel, Board Chair
f.d.regel@sasktel.net
Renee Danylczuk, Executive Director
Brenda Brake, Director, Support Programs & Services
Trina Ferguson, Director, Medical Support Services
Cheryl Tkachuk, Manager, Finance

***Quill Lake:* Quill Lake Community Health & Social Centre**
Affiliated with: Saskatoon Health Region
PO Box 126, 50 Main St., Quill Lake, SK S0A 3E0
Tel: 306-383-2266 *Fax:* 306-383-2290

***Radville:* Radville Marian Health Centre**
Affiliated with: Sun Country Health Region
217 Warren St., Radville, SK S0C 2G0
Tel: 306-869-2224 *Fax:* 306-869-2653
Number of Beds: 51 beds
Robert Shaw, Administrator

***Raymore:* Raymore Community Health & Social Centre**
Affiliated with: Regina Qu'Appelle Health Region
PO Box 134, 806 - 2 Ave., Raymore, SK S0A 3J0
Tel: 306-746-2231 *Fax:* 306-746-4639
Year Founded: 1981
Andrea Sebastian, Contact

***Regina:* Al Ritchie Health Action Centre**
Affiliated with: Regina Qu'Appelle Health Region
325 Victoria Ave., Regina, SK S4N 0P5
Tel: 306-766-7660 *Fax:* 306-766-7409
www.rqhealth.ca
Note: Provides GED exam support services, skills registry, job search support, prenatal nutrition advice, community computer, Dad's Group, family crafts, quit smoking program, seniors' potluck lunch, community kitchen, foot care, primary care nurse (by appt), food bank referrals, video lending library.
D. Lemon, Supervisor

***Regina:* Four Directions Community Health Centre**
Affiliated with: Regina Qu'Appelle Health Region
3510 - 5 Ave., Regina, SK S4T 0M2
Tel: 306-766-7540 *Fax:* 306-766-7534

***Rockglen:* Grasslands Health Centre**
Affiliated with: Five Hills Regional Health Authority
PO Box 219, 1006 Hwy. 2, Rockglen, SK S0H 3R0
Tel: 306-476-2030 *Fax:* 306-476-2534
Number of Beds: 17 beds

***Rose Valley:* Rose Valley Health Centre**
Affiliated with: Kelsey Trail Regional Health Authority
PO Box 310, 119 McCallum St., Rose Valley, SK S0E 1M0
Tel: 306-322-2115 *Fax:* 306-322-2037
Judy Moen, Community Health Manager

***Sandy Bay:* Sandy Bay Health Centre**
Affiliated with: Mamawetan Churchill River Health Region
PO Box 39, Sandy Bay, SK S0P 0G0
Tel: 306-754-5400 *Fax:* 306-754-5429
Note: Provides Primary Care, Public Health, Health Education, Telehealth, and Home Care services

***Saskatoon:* Community Health Services (Saskatoon) Association Ltd. (CHSA)**
Affiliated with: Saskatoon Health Region
455 Second Ave. North, Saskatoon, SK S7K 2C2
Tel: 306-652-0300 *Fax:* 306-664-4120
Year Founded: 1962
Note: Health services are offered at the Downtown Clinic & the Westside Clinic.
Anne Doucette, President, Board of Directors
Tim Archer, Executive Director, Saskatoon Community Clinic

***Smeaton:* Smeaton & District Health Centre**
Affiliated with: Kelsey Trail Regional Health Authority
PO Box 158, 2nd Ave. West, Smeaton, SK S0J 2J0
Tel: 306-426-2051 *Fax:* 306-426-2299
www.kelseytrailhealth.ca
Margo Marshall, Community Coordinator

***Southey:* Southey Health Action Centre**
Affiliated with: Regina Qu'Appelle Health Region
PO Box 519, 280 Burns Ave., Southey, SK S0G 4P0
Tel: 306-726-2239 *Fax:* 306-726-4472
www.rqhealth.ca
Year Founded: 1995

***Spalding:* Spalding Community Health Centre**
Affiliated with: Saskatoon Health Region
PO Box 220, 133 Centre St., Spalding, SK S0K 4C0
Tel: 306-872-2011 *Fax:* 306-872-2186
Jan Berger, Manager

***St Walburg:* St Walburg Health Complex**
Affiliated with: Prairie North Health Region
PO Box 339, 410 3rd Ave. West, St Walburg, SK S0M 2T0
Tel: 306-248-6719 *Fax:* 306-248-3413
www.pnrha.ca
Number of Beds: 31 beds
Note: attached special care home
Chris Thiele, Facility Manager

***Strasbourg:* Strasbourg & District Health Centre**
Affiliated with: Saskatoon Health Region
303 Edward St., Strasbourg, SK S0G 4V0
Tel: 306-725-3220 *Fax:* 306-725-4060
www.townofstrasbourg.ca
Year Founded: 1974
Note: Specialties: Physiotherapy; Counselling; Public health services
Tracy Hastings, Manager

***Turtleford:* Riverside Health Complex**
Affiliated with: Prairie North Health Region
PO Box 10, 1 St. South, Hwy. 303, Turtleford, SK S0M 2Y0
Tel: 306-845-2195 *Fax:* 306-845-2772
www.pnrha.ca
Number of Beds: 31 beds
Note: Attached special care home
Neal Sylvestre, Director, Rural Health Facilities

***Vanguard:* Vanguard Health Care Centre**
Affiliated with: Cypress Regional Health Authority
PO Box 190, Division St., Vanguard, SK S0N 2V0
Tel: 306-582-2044 *Fax:* 306-582-4833
Note: Weekly clinic, nurse practitioner on staff, lab & x-ray services twice a week, visiting health professionals
Dr. Suresh Kassett, Family Physician

***Weyakwin:* Weyakwin Health Centre**
Affiliated with: Mamawetan Churchill River Health Region
General Delivery, Weyakwin, SK S0J 1W0
Tel: 306-663-6100 *Fax:* 306-663-6165
www.mcrrha.sk.ca

***Whitewood:* Whitewood Community Health Centre**
Affiliated with: Regina Qu'Appelle Health Region
PO Box 669, 921 Gambetta St., Whitewood, SK S0G 5C0
Tel: 306-735-2688 *Fax:* 306-735-2512
www.rqhealth.ca
Specialties: Outpatient / ambulatory care services
Note: Services: Public health (306-735-2929); Parenting Plus (306-697-4048); Mental health services for children (306-697-4021); Mental health services for adults (306-697-4023); Nutrition services (306-697-4037); Home care services (306-696-2500)

***Wilkie:* Wilkie & District Health Centre/Poplar Courts**
Affiliated with: Heartland Regional Health Authority
PO Box 459, 304 - 7 Ave. East, Wilkie, SK S0K 4W0
Tel: 306-843-2644 *Fax:* 306-843-3222
Number of Beds: 4 acute care, 37 long-term care beds
Carrien Glassford, Care Team Manager

***Willow Bunch:* Willow Bunch Wellness Centre**
Affiliated with: Five Hills Regional Health Authority
PO Box 6, 17 - 3 St. East, Willow Bunch, SK S0H 4K0
Tel: 306-473-2310 *Fax:* 306-473-2677

***Wynyard:* Wynyard & District Community Health Centre**
Affiliated with: Saskatoon Health Region
PO Box 1539, 210 Ave. B East, Wynyard, SK S0A 4T0
Tel: 306-554-3363

Nursing Stations

***Stony Rapids:* Black Lake Nursing Station**
General Delivery, Stony Rapids, SK S0J 2R0
Tel: 306-284-2124 *Fax:* 306-264-2090

Special Treatment Centres

***Melville:* Saul Cohen Family Resource Centre**
Affiliated with: Sunrise Regional Health Authority
PO Box 164, 200 Heritage Dr., Melville, SK S0A 2P0
Tel: 306-728-7320 *Fax:* 306-728-4925
Note: Outpatient counseling & support individuals & families affected by addictions
Sherry Shumay

***North Battleford:* Saskatchewan Hospital**
Affiliated with: Prairie North Health Region
PO Box 39, North Battleford, SK S9A 2X8
Tel: 306-446-6800 *Fax:* 306-445-5392
Number of Beds: 156 beds
Note: psychiatric rehabilitation hospital
Linda Shynkaruk, Director

***Regina:* Wascana Rehabilitation Centre**
Affiliated with: Regina Qu'Appelle Health Region
2180 - 23 Ave., Regina, SK S4S 0A5
Tel: 306-766-5100 *Fax:* 306-766-5244
Number of Beds: 307 inpatient
Note: rehabilitation centre, long term care centre
Dwight Nelson, President; CEO

Long Term Care Facilities

***Cudworth:* Cudworth Nursing Home/Health Centre**
Affiliated with: Saskatoon Health Region
PO Box 190, 607 - 4 Ave., Cudworth, SK S0K 1B0
Tel: 306-256-3423 *Fax:* 306-256-3343
Number of Beds: 32 beds
Rose Normand, Site Manager

Nursing Homes

***Assiniboia:* Assiniboia Pioneer Lodge**
Affiliated with: Five Hills Regional Health Authority
PO Box 1120, 800 - 1 St. West, Assiniboia, SK S0H 0B0
Tel: 306-642-3311 *Fax:* 306-642-3099
Number of Beds: 128 beds
Jim Larson, Administrator

***Assiniboia:* Ross Payant Centennial Home**
Affiliated with: Five Hills Regional Health Authority
Former Name: Ross Payant Centennial Home
PO Box 1120, 300 Jubilee Place, Assiniboia, SK S0H 0B0
Tel: 306-642-3330 *Fax:* 306-642-3243

Number of Beds: 38 beds

***Big River:* Lakewood Lodge**
PO Box 760, Big River, SK S0J 0E0
Tel: 306-469-2333 *Fax:* 306-469-2193
Number of Beds: 29 beds
Helen Donald, Director, Care

***Birch Hills:* Birchview Nursing Home**
Affiliated with: Prince Albert Parkland Regional Health Authority
PO Box 578, 7 Wilson St., Birch Hills, SK S0J 0G0
Tel: 306-749-2288
Number of Beds: 30 beds
Note: Respite care is available.

***Broadview:* Broadview & District Centennial Lodge Inc.**
Affiliated with: Regina Qu'Appelle Health Region
PO Box 670, 310 Calgary St., Broadview, SK S0G 0K0
Tel: 306-696-2458 *Fax:* 306-696-2577
Number of Beds: 35 beds
Note: The facility offers an Adult Day Support Program.
Linda Zinkhan, Manager

***Canwood:* Whispering Pine Place Inc.**
Affiliated with: Prince Albert Parkland Regional Health Authority
PO Box 418, 300 - 1st Ave., Canwood, SK S0J 0K0
Tel: 306-468-2900 *Fax:* 306-468-2199
Number of Beds: 30 beds
Population Served: 1720
Brenda Person, Administrator

***Carlyle:* Moose Mountain Lodge**
Affiliated with: Sun Country Health Region
PO Box 729, 6 St. West, Carlyle, SK S0C 0R0
Tel: 306-453-2434 *Fax:* 306-453-2726
Number of Beds: 52 beds
Joanne Hollingshead, Manager
Harold Smith, Maintenance

***Carnduff:* Sunset Haven**
Affiliated with: Sun Country Health Region
PO Box 250, 415 Spencer St., Carnduff, SK S0C 0S0
Tel: 306-482-3424 *Fax:* 306-482-5233
www.suncountry.sk.ca
Note: Specialties: Long-term care; Home care; Palliative care
Cathy Stephenson, Sec.-Treas.
Shirley Wright, Director of Care

***Cupar:* Cupar & District Nursing Home Inc.**
Affiliated with: Regina Qu'Appelle Health Region
PO Box 310, 213 Mills St., Cupar, SK S0G 0Y0
Tel: 306-723-4666 *Fax:* 306-723-4248
Number of Beds: 48 beds
Betty Smith, Interim Administrator

***Duck Lake:* Duck Lake & District Nursing Home Inc. Goodwill Manor**
Affiliated with: Saskatoon Health Region
PO Box 370, 501 Victoria Ave., Duck Lake, SK S0K 1J0
Tel: 306-467-4440 *Fax:* 306-467-2220
Number of Beds: 30 beds
Jean-Marie Allard, Facility Coordinator

***Estevan:* Estevan Regional Nursing Home**
Affiliated with: Sun Country Health Region
PO Box 5000, 1921 Wallock Rd., Estevan, SK S4A 2B5
Tel: 306-634-2689 *Fax:* 306-634-7906
Number of Beds: 76 beds
Christine Stephany, Contact

***Eston:* Jubilee Lodge Inc.**
Affiliated with: Heartland Health Region
PO Box 667, 800 Main St., Eston, SK S0L 1A0
Tel: 306-962-3667 *Fax:* 306-962-3900
ruth.miller@hrha.sk.ca
Number of Beds: 37 beds
Ruth Miller, Administrator
W. Turner, Director, Physical Plant

***Foam Lake:* Foam Lake Jubilee Home**
Affiliated with: Sunrise Regional Health Authority
PO Box 460, 421 Alberta Ave. East, Foam Lake, SK S0A 1A0
Tel: 306-272-4141 *Fax:* 306-272-4973
Number of Beds: 52 beds
Arlene Scratton, Manager, Health Services

***Grenfell:* Grenfell & District Pioneer Home**
Affiliated with: Regina Qu'Appelle Health Region
PO Box 760, 710 Regina Ave., Grenfell, SK S0G 2B0
Tel: 306-697-2842 *Fax:* 306-697-2280
Number of Beds: 34 beds
Diana Lerner, Manager
Rick Gerhardt, Maintenance

***Indian Head:* Golden Prairie Home**
Affiliated with: Regina Qu'Appelle Health Region
PO Box 250, 916 Eden St., Indian Head, SK S0G 2K0
Tel: 306-695-3636 *Fax:* 306-695-2698
Number of Beds: 38 beds
Population Served: 1800
Karen Earnshaw, Manager

***Kelvington:* Kelvindell Lodge**
Affiliated with: Kelsey Trail Regional Health Authority
PO Box 280, 701 - 6 Ave. West, Kelvington, SK S0A 1W0
Tel: 306-327-5151 *Fax:* 306-327-4504
Number of Beds: 46 beds
Shelley Rutherford, Asst. Manager, Community Health
Kevin O'Neil, Maintenance

***Kindersley:* Heritage Manor**
Affiliated with: Heartland Health Region
1003 - 1st St. West, Kindersley, SK S0L 1S2
Tel: 306-463-2611 *Fax:* 306-465-4550
Number of Beds: 80 beds
Wanda Desrosiers, Facility Manager
Peter Whiteman, Director, Physical Plant

***Kinistino:* Jubilee Lodge**
Affiliated with: Prince Albert Parkland Regional Health Authority
PO Box 370, 410 Myers Ave., Kinistino, SK S0J 1H0
Tel: 306-864-2851 *Fax:* 306-864-3220
Number of Beds: 30 beds
Number of Employees: 50
Carol Pryznyk, Administrator

***Kipling:* Willowdale Lodge**
Affiliated with: Sun Country Health Region
PO Box 537, 128 - 4 St. South, Kipling, SK S0G 2S0
Tel: 306-736-2218 *Fax:* 306-736-2986
www.suncountry.sk.ca
Note: Respite care is available.
Kelly Beattie, Contact
Linus Blacstock, Maintenance

***Langham:* Langham Senior Citizens Home**
Affiliated with: Saskatoon Health Region
PO Box 287, Main St., Langham, SK S0K 2L0
Tel: 306-283-4210 *Fax:* 306-283-4212
www.saskatoonhealthregion.ca
Year Founded: 1971
Specialties: Restorative & supportive care
Note: Langham Senior Citizens Home has 28 residents who live in long term care & transitional living care.

***Leader:* Western Senior Citizens Home**
Affiliated with: Cypress Regional Health Authority
PO Box 69, 400 - 1 St. West, Leader, SK S0N 1H0
Tel: 306-628-3565 *Fax:* 306-628-3733
Number of Beds: 36 beds
Note: Level 3 & 4

***Lumsden:* Lumsden & District Heritage Home Inc.**
Affiliated with: Regina Qu'Appelle Health Region
PO Box 479, 10 Aspen Bay, Lumsden, SK S0G 3C0
Tel: 306-731-2247 *Fax:* 306731-3307
heritagehome@rqhealth.ca
Number of Beds: 30 long-term care beds
Note: Specialties: Assisted living services for seniors; Adult day support program
Wilf Frey, Maintenance
Shirley Wright, Executive Director

***Maple Creek:* Cypress Lodge Nursing Home**
Affiliated with: Cypress Health Region
PO Box 1330, 510 Hwy. 21 South, Maple Creek, SK S0N 1N0
Tel: 306-662-2671
www.cypresshealth.ca
Number of Beds: 48 beds
Specialties: Long term care services; Exercise maintenance programs
Note: Respite care is available.

***Melfort:* Nirvana Pioneer Villa**
PO Box 1480, Melfort, SK S0E 1A0
Tel: 306-752-8827 *Fax:* 306-752-8822
Sandy Weseen, Coordinator, Care

***Melfort:* Parkland Place**
Affiliated with: Kelsey Trail Regional Health Authority
Former Name: Parkland Care Centre
PO Box 2260, 402 Bemister Ave. East, Melfort, SK S0E 1A0
Tel: 306-752-1777 *Fax:* 306-752-1776
www.kelseytrailhealth.ca
Number of Beds: 103 long-term care beds; 2 respite beds
Note: Specialty: Acquired brain injury program
Melanie Woods, Coordinator, Care

***Melville:* St. Paul Lutheran Home**
Affiliated with: Sunrise Regional Health Authority
PO Box 1390, 100 Heritage Dr., Melville, SK S0A 2P0
Tel: 306-728-7340 *Fax:* 306-728-5471
Number of Beds: 144 beds
Note: Long-term care facility affiliated with the Evangelical Lutheran Church in Canada
Gord Wyatt, Director, Long-term Care

***Moose Jaw:* Extendicare Moose Jaw**
1151 Coteau St. West, Moose Jaw, SK S6H 5G5
Tel: 306-693-5191 *Fax:* 306-692-1770
cnh_moosejaw@extendicare.com
www.extendicarecanada.com/moosejaw/index.aspx
Number of Beds: 127 beds
Specialties: Nursing & supportive care; Rehabilitation services; Therapeutic & social programs

***Moose Jaw:* Providence Place**
Affiliated with: Five Hills Regional Health Authority
100 - 2nd Ave. NE, Moose Jaw, SK S6H 1B8
Tel: 306-694-8081 *Fax:* 306-694-8804
www.provplace.ca
Number of Beds: 188 beds
Note: Geriatric long-term care, assessment & rehabilitation
Raymond E. Mullire

***Nipawin:* Pineview Lodge**
Affiliated with: Kelsey Trail Regional Health Authority
PO Box 2105, 400 - 6th Ave. East, Nipawin, SK S0E 1E0
Tel: 306-862-9828 *Fax:* 306-862-2400
www.kelseytrailhealth.ca
Number of Beds: 96 beds
Note: Specialties: Long-term care; Dementia care unit; Day care services; Respite care

***North Battleford:* River Heights Lodge**
Affiliated with: Prairie North Health Region
2001 - 99 St., North Battleford, SK S9A 0S3
Tel: 306-446-6950 *Fax:* 306-445-6032
Number of Beds: 106 beds
Note: Special care home
Kelly Day, Facility Manager

***Ponteix:* Foyer St-Joseph Nursing Home**
Affiliated with: Cypress Regional Health Authority
PO Box 310, 428 - 2 Ave., Ponteix, SK S0N 1Z0
Tel: 306-625-3366 *Fax:* 306-625-3918
Number of Beds: 30 beds
Larry Piché, Director, Physical Plant

***Porcupine Plain:* Red Deer Nursing Home**
Affiliated with: Kelsey Trail Regional Health Authority
PO Box 70, 330 Oak St., Porcupine Plain, SK S0E 1H0
Tel: 306-278-2469 *Fax:* 306-278-3088
Number of Beds: 36 long-term care beds; 2 respite beds
Chris Pohl, Community Health Manager

***Preeceville:* Preeceville Lions Housing Corp. Ltd.**
Affiliated with: Sunrise Regional Health Authority
PO Box 348, 26 - 3 Ave. NW, Preeceville, SK S0A 3B0
Tel: 306-547-3112 *Fax:* 306-547-3215
Number of Beds: 28 beds; 1 respite
N. Babiuk, Physical Plant
Joanne Bodnar, Manager, Health Services

***Redvers:* Redvers Centennial Haven**
Affiliated with: Sun Country Health Region
PO Box 399, 18 Eichhorst St., Redvers, SK S0C 2H0
Tel: 306-452-3331 *Fax:* 306-452-3556
Number of Beds: 24 beds
Myrna Peterson, Manager, Health Services

***Regina:* Extendicare - Elmview**
Affiliated with: Regina Qu'Appelle Health Region
4125 Rae St., Regina, SK S4S 3A5
Tel: 306-586-1787 *Fax:* 306-585-0255
Number of Beds: 50 beds

Cathy Hauck, Administrator

Regina: Extendicare - Parkside
Affiliated with: Regina Qu'Appelle Health Region
4540 Rae St., Regina, SK S4S 3B4
Tel: 306-586-0220 *Fax:* 306-585-0622
www.extendicare.com
Number of Beds: 228 beds
Lloyd Wood, Maintenance Supervisor
Dona Jones, Administrator

Regina: Extendicare - Sunset
Affiliated with: Regina Qu'Appelle Health Region
260 Sunset Dr., Regina, SK S4S 2S3
Tel: 306-586-3355 *Fax:* 306-584-8082
cnh_sunset@extendicare.com
Number of Beds: 152 beds
Sandra Callan, Administrator

Regina: Qu'Appelle House
Affiliated with: Regina Qu'Appelle Health Region
1425 College Ave., Regina, SK S4P 1B4
Tel: 306-522-0335 *Fax:* 306-522-4800
Number of Beds: 34 beds
Diane Serban, Executive Director

Regina: Regina Lutheran Home
Affiliated with: Regina Qu'Appelle Health Region
1925 - 5 Ave. North, Regina, SK S4R 7W1
Tel: 306-543-4055 *Fax:* 306-543-4094
Number of Beds: 91 beds
Note: Nursing home
Glenn Knapp, Director, Maintenance
Allan Hoffman, Executive Director

Regina: Regina Pioneer Village Ltd.
Affiliated with: Regina Qu'Appelle Health Region
430 Pioneer Dr., Regina, SK S4T 6L8
Tel: 306-757-5646 *Fax:* 306-757-5001
Number of Beds: 390 beds
Arnold Evancio, Manager, Maintenance
Dick Chinn, CEO

Regina: Santa Maria Senior Citizens Home
Affiliated with: Regina Qu'Appelle Health Region
4215 Regina Ave., Regina, SK S4S 0J5
Tel: 306-766-7100 *Fax:* 306-766-7115
Number of Beds: 147 beds
Bill Wilson, Manager, Maintenance
Beverly Olineck, Administrator

Rosetown: Wheatbelt Centennial Lodge Inc.
Affiliated with: Heartland Regional Health Authority
PO Box 250, 301 Centennial Dr., Rosetown, SK S0L 2V0
Tel: 306-882-2672 *Fax:* 306-882-3335
Number of Beds: 28 beds
B. Madden, Director, Physical Plant
Gail Adamowski, Facility Manager

Rosthern: Mennonite Nursing Home Inc.
Affiliated with: Saskatoon Health Region
PO Box 370, Hwy. 11 South, Rosthern, SK S0K 3R0
Tel: 306-232-4861 *Fax:* 306-232-5611
www.saskatoonhealthregion.ca
Year Founded: 1963
Note: Specialties: Long-term care; Adult Day Program
Joan Lemauviel, CEO

Saltcoats: Lakeside Manor Care Home Inc.
Affiliated with: Sunrise Regional Health Authority
PO Box 340, 101 Crescent Lake Rd., Saltcoats, SK S0A 3R0
Tel: 306-744-2353 *Fax:* 306-744-2414
Number of Beds: 28 beds, 2 respite
Shirley Pachal, Facility Manager

Saskatoon: Jubilee Residences
Affiliated with: Saskatoon Health Region
2202 McEown Ave., Saskatoon, SK S7L 3L6
Tel: 306-382-2626 *Fax:* 306-382-2633
www.jubileeresidences.ca
Year Founded: 1955
Specialties: Nursing & personal care; Physical & occupational therapy
Note: Long term care is provided to 200 older adults at Stensrud & Porteous Lodges. Independent living suites are available for approximately 300 older adults at the Cosmopolitan, Eamer, & Mount Royal facilities.
R.J. Cowan, Board Chair
Yvonne Morgan, Chief Executive Officer
Annette Claffey, Vice-President, Quality Care
Erin Yohnke, Vice-President, Corporate Services
Karen Chaskavich, Director, Care Team, Porteous Lodge
Valerie Hnatuk, Director, Care Team, Stensrud Lodge
Andre Moss, Director, Staff Development & Therapies, Porteous Lodge
Ron Neufield, Director, Housing & Facilities
Vince Salamon, Director, Quality Improvement, Stensrud Lodge
Katherine Soule Blaser, Director, Human Resources

Saskatoon: Oliver Lodge Special Care Home
Affiliated with: Saskatoon Health Region
1405 Faulkner Cres., Saskatoon, SK S7L 3R5
Tel: 306-382-4111 *Fax:* 306-382-9822
Year Founded: 1949
Number of Beds: 139 beds
Note: Specialties: Specialized services for persons with dementia; Day program for seniors; Respite care
Morley Mitchell, Administrator

Saskatoon: Parkridge Centre
Affiliated with: Saskatoon Health Region
110 Gropper Cres., Saskatoon, SK S7M 5N9
Tel: 306-655-3800 *Fax:* 306-655-3801
www.parkridgequalityoflife.com
Number of Beds: 217 beds
Karen Knelsen, Resident Care Services
Dale Gagnon, Manager, Plant Operation

Saskatoon: St. Ann's Senior Citizens Village Corp.
Affiliated with: Saskatoon Health Region
2910 Louise St., Saskatoon, SK S7J 3L8
Tel: 306-374-8900 *Fax:* 306-477-2623
Number of Beds: 80 beds
Note: Affiliated with the Catholic Health Ministry of Saskatchewan
R.A. Sveinbjornson, Administrator

Saskatoon: St. Joseph's Home
Affiliated with: Saskatoon Health Region
33 Valens Dr., Saskatoon, SK S7L 3S2
Tel: 306-382-6306 *Fax:* 306-384-0140
Number of Beds: 85 beds
Sr. Theodosia , Administrator

Saskatoon: Saskatoon Convalescent Home
Affiliated with: Saskatoon Health Region
101 - 31 St. West, Saskatoon, SK S7L 0P6
Tel: 306-244-7155 *Fax:* 306-244-2066
www.saskatoonconvalescenthome.com
Number of Beds: 59 beds
Patricia Jarvis, Administrator

Saskatoon: Sherbrooke Community Centre
Affiliated with: Saskatoon Health Region
401 Acadia Dr., Saskatoon, SK S7H 2E7
Tel: 306-655-3600 *Fax:* 306-655-3727
www.sherbrookecommunitycentre.ca
Number of Beds: 270 beds
Note: Long-term care home. Also provides a Community Day Program for 100 local residents
Bruce Pyett, Director, Maintenance
Suellen Beatty, CEO

Saskatoon: Sunnyside Adventist Care Centre
Affiliated with: Saskatoon Health Region
Former Name: Sunnyside Nursing Home
2200 St. Henry Ave., Saskatoon, SK S7M 0P5
Tel: 306-653-1267 *Fax:* 306-653-7223
admin@sunnysidecare.ca
www.sunnysidecare.ca
Year Founded: 1964
Note: Specialties: Nursing care; Physiotherapy; Activity program; Palliative care
Collin Akre, Administrator

Spiritwood: Idylwild Lodge
PO Box 159, Spiritwood, SK S0J 2M0
Tel: 306-883-2267 *Fax:* 306-883-3121
Number of Beds: 35 beds
Carroll Joyes, Director, Care
Louis Willick, Director, Maintenance

Stoughton: Newhope Pioneer Lodge Inc.
Affiliated with: Sun Country Health Region
PO Box 38, 123 Government Rd. North, Stoughton, SK S0G 4T0
Tel: 306-457-2552 *Fax:* 306-457-3732
Number of Beds: 30 beds
Linda Wilson, Director, Community Services

Swift Current: Palliser Regional Care Centre
Affiliated with: Cypress Regional Health Authority
440 Central Ave. South, Swift Current, SK S9H 3G6
Tel: 306-778-5160
www.cypresshealth.ca
Number of Beds: 94 beds

Swift Current: Prairie Pioneers Lodge
Affiliated with: Cypress Regional Health Authority
302 Central Ave. South, Swift Current, SK S9H 3G3
Tel: 306-778-5192 *Fax:* 306-773-1635
Number of Beds: 41 beds

Swift Current: Swift Current Care Centre (SCCC)
Affiliated with: Cypress Regional Health Authority
700 Aberdeen St. SE, Swift Current, SK S9H 3E3
Tel: 306-773-9371 *Fax:* 306-773-1353
www.cypresshealth.ca
Number of Beds: 63 beds
Note: Specialties: Nursing care from Registered Nurses, Registered Psychiatric Nurses, & Licensed Practical Nurses; Social work; Activity program; Respite care program

Tisdale: Newmarket Manor
Affiliated with: Kelsey Trail Regional Health Authority
PO Box 2620, 2001 Newmarket Dr., Tisdale, SK S0E 1T0
Tel: 306-873-5828 *Fax:* 306-873-4822
Number of Beds: 40 beds
Ann Boxall, Director, Care

Tisdale: Sasko Park Lodge
Affiliated with: Kelsey Trail Regional Health Authority
PO Box 1330, 806 - 97 Ave., Tisdale, SK S0E 1T0
Tel: 306-873-4585 *Fax:* 306-873-2404
Number of Beds: 33 beds, 15 suites
Ann Boxall, Director, Care

Turtleford: Riverside Health Complex Integrated Facility
Former Name: Turtle River Nusing Home
PO Box 10, 1st St. S, Turtleford, SK S0M 2Y0
Tel: 306-845-2195 *Fax:* 306-845-2772
Number of Beds: 27 beds
Patrick Blais, Coordinator, Health Services

Waldheim: Menno Homes of Saskatchewan Inc.
PO Box 130, Waldheim, SK S0K 4R0
Tel: 306-945-2070 *Fax:* 306-945-4641
menno.homes@sasktel.net
Year Founded: 1963
Number of Beds: 105 residential capacity
Note: Number of Employees: 105
Marlin J. Roth, Executive Director

Watrous: Manitou Lodge
Affiliated with: Saskatoon Health Region
PO Box 130, 404 - 1 St., Watrous, SK S0K 4T0
Tel: 306-946-3718 *Fax:* 306-946-2296
Number of Beds: 35 beds
Debbie Okrainetz, Manager, Client Services

Wawota: Deer View Lodge
Affiliated with: Sun Country Health Region
PO Box 240, 201 Wilfred St., Wawota, SK S0G 5A0
Tel: 306-739-2400
Number of Beds: 30 beds
Note: Area Served: Regional Municipality of Walpole; Regional Municipality of Wawken; Regional Municipality of Maryfield; Wawota; Maryfield; Fairlight; half the villages of Kennedy & Kenosee, & half the Regional Municipality of Moose Mountain

Wolseley: Lakeside Home
Affiliated with: Regina Qu'Appelle Health Region
PO Box 10, 710 Quimet St., Wolseley, SK S0G 5H0
Tel: 306-698-2573 *Fax:* 306-698-2975
www.rqhealth.ca
Number of Beds: 80 beds
Area Served: Wolseley, SK
Specialties: Long term care
Note: Lakeside Home is linked to Wolseley Memorial Hospital.

Yorkton: Yorkton & District Nursing Home Corporation
Affiliated with: Sunrise Regional Health Authority
200 Bradbrooke Dr., Yorkton, SK S3N 2K5
Tel: 306-786-0801 *Fax:* 306-786-0808
Number of Beds: 243 beds
Lynn Wrishko, Manager, Health Services
Brenda Walsh, Manager, Health Services

Long Term/Retirement Care

Long Term Care Facilities

***Lanigan:* Central Parkland Lodge**
Affiliated with: Saskatoon Health Region
PO Box 459, Lanigan, SK S0K 2M0
Tel: 306-365-1420 *Fax:* 306-365-2053
www.saskatoonhealthregion.ca
Number of Beds: 35 beds
Specialties: Long term health care for senior citizens

***Lloydminster:* Jubilee Home**
Affiliated with: Prairie North Health Region
3902 - 45 Ave., Lloydminster, SK S9V 1Z2
Tel: 306-820-5950 *Fax:* 306-825-9869
Note: Respite care is available.
Lori Anderson, Facility Manager
Lori.Anderson@pnrha.ca

***Middle Lake:* Bethany Pioneer Village Inc.**
Affiliated with: Saskatoon Health Region
PO Box 8, Middle Lake, SK S0K 2X0
Tel: 306-367-2033 *Fax:* 306-367-2155
bethanyv@sasktel.net
www.bethanypioneervillage.com
Year Founded: 1956
Specialties: Care for seniors & others with similar needs
Note: Bethany Pioneer Village provides independent living suites, assisted living, & special care. The facitility is recognized by Lutheran Church Canada as a service organization.
Ray Brockman, Chair
Alice Kirsch, Secretary
Carl Grundmann, Treasurer

***Wadena:* Pleasant View Care Home**
Affiliated with: Saskatoon Health Region
PO Box 10, 533 - 5 St. NE, Wadena, SK S0A 4J0
Tel: 306-338-2412 *Fax:* 306-338-2074
www.saskatoonhealthregion.ca
Dayle Maryniak, Manager

Nursing Homes

***Moose Jaw:* Pioneer Housing Lodge & Village**
Affiliated with: Five Hills Regional Health Authority
1000 Albert St., Moose Jaw, SK S6H 2Y2
Tel: 306-693-4616

Personal Care Homes

***Avonlea:* Coteau Range Manor**
Affiliated with: Five Hills Regional Health Authority
PO Box 60, 210 New Warren Pl., Avonlea, SK S0H 0C0
Tel: 306-868-2033
Number of Beds: 30 beds
Note: Respite care is available at the personal care home.

***Bangor:* Morris Lodge Society Inc.**
PO Box 54, Lots 4-12, Block 6, Main St., Bangor, SK S0A 0E0
Tel: 306-728-5322 *Fax:* 306-728-2048
Number of Beds: 20 beds

***Beechy:* Beechy Community Care Home**
205 Railway Ave., Beechy, SK S0L 0C0
Tel: 306-859-4470 *Fax:* 306-859-4470
bcch@sasktel.net
Note: Personal care is provided to ten elderly residents.
Noel Taylor, Contact

***Codette:* Serenity Lane**
Affiliated with: Kelsey Trail Regional Health Authority
PO Box 152, Codette, SK S0E 0P0
Tel: 306-862-2579
Number of Beds: 10 beds
Debbie Karlee

***Eatonia:* Eatonia Oasis Living Inc.**
Former Name: Eatonia Personal Care Home
PO Box 217, 205, 2nd Ave. W, Eatonia, SK S0L 0Y0
Tel: 306-967-2447 *Fax:* 306-967-2373
eatoniaoasisliving.com
Number of Beds: 23 beds
Lorraine Bews, Chairperson

***Estevan:* Creighton Lodge**
1028 Hillcrest Dr., Estevan, SK S4A 1Y7
Tel: 306-634-4154

***Herbert:* Herbert Heritage Manor**
Former Name: Herbert Senior Citizens Home
PO Box 10, Herbert, SK S0H 2A0
Tel: 306-784-3167 *Fax:* 306-784-3564
Year Founded: 1962
Number of Beds: 40 beds
Note: Personal care home level 1 & 2
Brian D. Penner, Administrator

***Kamsack:* Eaglestone Lodge Personal Care Home Inc.**
PO Box 1330, Kamsack, SK S0A 1S0
Tel: 306-542-2620 *Fax:* 306-542-4342
Number of Beds: 42 beds
Joyce Maclean, Chairman of the Board, Care

***Moose Jaw:* Capilano Court**
Affiliated with: Five Hills Regional Health Authority
1236 - 3rd Ave. NW, Moose Jaw, SK S6H 3V3
Tel: 306-693-4518

***Moose Jaw:* Chez Nous Senior Citizens Home**
Affiliated with: Five Hills Regional Health Authority
1101 Grafton Ave., Moose Jaw, SK S6H 3S4
Tel: 306-693-4371
chez.nous@sasktel.net
www.cheznoushome.ca

***Moose Jaw:* Oxford Place Inc.**
Affiliated with: Five Hills Regional Health Authority
1007 Main St. North, Moose Jaw, SK S6H 0X1
Tel: 306-692-2837 *Fax:* 306-692-3837
oxfordplace@sasktel.net

***Moose Jaw:* Valley View Centre**
PO Box 1300, Moose Jaw, SK S6H 4R2
Tel: 306-694-3000 *Fax:* 306-694-3003
Number of Beds: 348 beds
Terry Hardy, Director

***Oxbow:* Bow Valley Villa Corp.**
319 Wylie Ave., Oxbow, SK S0C 2B0
Tel: 306-483-2744 *Fax:* 306-483-2915

***Pangman:* Deep South Personal Care Home**
Affiliated with: Sun Country Regional Health Authority
PO Box 150, 211 Keeler St., Pangman, SK S0C 2C0
Tel: 306-442-2043 *Fax:* 306-442-4261
Note: Deep South Care Home is a private personal care home for 22 residents.
Lisa Still, Home Administrator

***Ponteix:* Rolling Hills Villa Ltd.**
PO Box 148, 332 - 2 St. West, Ponteix, SK S0N 1Z0
Tel: 306-625-3511

***Prince Albert:* Nelson Care Home Ltd.**
Affiliated with: Prince Albert Parkland Regional Health Authority
1336 - 7th St. East, Prince Albert, SK S6V 0V1
Tel: 306-922-9506

***Rosthern:* Rosthern Mennonite Home for the Aged**
PO Box 790, 510 - 4 Ave., Rosthern, SK S0K 3R0
Tel: 306-232-4822
Number of Beds: 20 beds
Jacob Loewen, Chair

***Saskatoon:* Arbor Villa Care Home Inc.**
Affiliated with: Saskatoon Health Region
201 Lewis Cres., Saskatoon, SK S7L 7H5
Tel: 306-384-1419
Number of Beds: 7 single bedrooms; 1 double bedroom
Note: The personal care home offers respite care.
Agnes Lopez, Operator

***Saskatoon:* Ashton Care Home Inc.**
Affiliated with: Saskatoon Health Region
438 Ave. Y North, Saskatoon, SK S7L 3L2
Tel: 306-382-8975
Number of Beds: 7 single bedrooms; 2 double bedrooms
Note: Respite care is available.
Emyou Mekonnen, Contact

***Saskatoon:* Balicanta Personal Care Home**
Affiliated with: Saskatoon Health Region
Also Known As: Balicanta Holdings Ltd.
510 Spencer Cres., Saskatoon, SK S7K 7T4
Tel: 306-934-5903 *Fax:* 306-934-5903
Number of Beds: 6 single bedrooms; 3 double bedrooms
Note: Personal care is provided for twelve residents. Respite care is available.
I. Balicanta, Contact

***Saskatoon:* Bergman's Private Home Care**
Affiliated with: Saskatoon Health Region
333 LaRonge Rd., Saskatoon, SK S7K 4S1
Tel: 306-934-2031 *Fax:* 306-934-2031

***Saskatoon:* Betty Sandulak Personal Care Home**
Affiliated with: Saskatoon Health Region
122 Adilman Dr., Saskatoon, SK S7K 7S5
Tel: 306-931-7859
Number of Beds: 10 beds
Note: Respite care is available.

***Saskatoon:* Fairhaven Care Home Inc.**
Affiliated with: Saskatoon Health Region
139 Olmstead Rd., Saskatoon, SK S7M 4L9
Tel: 306-974-1156
Number of Beds: 6 single rooms; 3 double rooms
Note: Respite care is available.

***Saskatoon:* M & M Private Care Home**
Affiliated with: Saskatoon Health Region
518/520 Russell Rd., Saskatoon, SK S7K 6L6
Tel: 306-242-6501 *Fax:* 306-934-8027
Number of Beds: 12 beds
Note: Specialties: Diabetic care; Respite care
Marionela Cabello

***Saskatoon:* Marg's Care Home Ltd.**
Affiliated with: Saskatoon Health Region
310 Adilman Dr., Saskatoon, SK S7K 7K5
Tel: 306-975-1189

***Shellbrook:* T.L.C. Personal Care Home**
308 - 3rd Ave. East, Shellbrook, SK S0J 2E0
Tel: 306-747-3123
Year Founded: 1997

***Speers:* Oasis Personal Care Home**
Affiliated with: Prince Albert Parkland Regional Health Authority
PO Box 26, Speers, SK S0M 2V0
Tel: 306-246-2067 *Fax:* 306-246-2028
info@oasiscarehome.ca
www.oasiscarehome.ca
Year Founded: 1993
Delbert Miller, Co-Owner; Operator
Sheila Miller, Co-Owner; Operator

***St Louis:* Regnier Personal Care Home Inc.**
457 River Rd., St Louis, SK S0J 2C0
Tel: 306-422-8223
Lynn Regnier

***Theodore:* Theodore Health Centre**
Affiliated with: Sunrise Regional Health Authority
PO Box 70, 615 Anderson Ave., Theodore, SK S0A 4C0
Tel: 306-647-2115 *Fax:* 306-647-2238
Number of Beds: 20 beds
Note: Specialties: Long-term care; Nursing services; Phlebotomy service; Respite care; Palliative care
Donna Gawryliuk, Head Nurse

***Watson:* Quill Plains Centennial Lodge/Watson Health Complex**
Affiliated with: Saskatoon Health Region
PO Box 220, 402 - 2 St. NE, Watson, SK S0K 4V0
Tel: 306-287-3791 *Fax:* 306-287-3386
Number of Beds: 54 beds

***Weyburn:* Crocus Plains Villa Ltd.**
Affiliated with: Sun Country Regional Health Authority
1135 Park Ave., Weyburn, SK S4H 0K6
Tel: 306-842-0616 *Fax:* 306-842-2361
www.crocusplainsvilla.com
Note: Care planning is provided by a multidisciplinary team. Crocus Plains Villa features a secured area for persons with a cognitive impairment. The personal care home also offers respite care.
Nick Turanich, President
nickturanich@sasktel.net

***Weyburn:* Parkway Lodge Personal Care Home**
Affiliated with: Sun Country Regional Health Authority
420 - 8 Ave. SE, Weyburn, SK S4H 3N2
Tel: 306-842-7868

***Weyburn:* Tatagwa View**
Affiliated with: Sun Country Regional Health Authority
Former Name: Souris Valley Extended Care Centre
PO Box 2003, 808 Souris Valley Rd., Weyburn, SK S4H 2Z9
Tel: 306-842-8398 *Fax:* 306-842-8341
www.suncountry.sk.ca
Year Founded: 2005
Number of Beds: 123 beds
Note: Specialties: Long-term care; Mental health services (10 beds); Acquired brain injury services; Diabetes program; Rehabilitation services; Day care centre; Palliative care
Marnell Cornish, Administrator

Special Care Homes

***Fort Qu'appelle:* Echo Lodge Special Care Home**
Affiliated with: Regina Qu'Appelle Health Region
PO Box 1790, 560 Broadway St. West, Fort Qu'appelle, SK S0G 1S0
Tel: 306-332-4300 *Fax:* 306-332-5708
Note: Echo Lodge has 50 residents. Adult day care & respite care are available.

***Prince Albert:* Herb Bassett Home**
Affiliated with: Prince Albert Parkland Regional Health Authority
PO Box 3000, 1220 - 25 St. West, Prince Albert, SK S6V 5T4
Tel: 306-765-6000
Number of Beds: 144 beds (2 repite care beds)
Note: Herb Basset Home hosts an adult day program.

***Saskatoon:* Luther Seniors' Centre**
LutherCare Communities
1800 Alexandra Ave., Saskatoon, SK S7K 3C7
Tel: 306-664-0366 *Fax:* 306-664-0395
lsc@luthercare.com
www.luthercare.com
Year Founded: 1985
Note: Specialties: Day program for adults with irreversible dementia; Social services; Nursing; Personal care; Sensory stimulation

***Saskatoon:* Luther Special Care Home**
LutherCare Communities
1212 Osler St., Saskatoon, SK S7N 0T9
Tel: 306-664-0300
luthercare@shaw.ca
www.luthercare.com
Year Founded: 1955
Number of Beds: 129 beds, including 49 special needs beds & 2 respite beds
Note: Specialties: Secure special needs unit for residents with cognitive impairment; Nursing care; Physio, occupational, & recreational therapy; Community day program for seniors at risk; Respite care

***Saskatoon:* LutherCare Communities**
Affiliated with: Saskatoon Health Region
Former Name: Lutheran Sunset Home
Main Corporate Office, 1212 Osler St., Saskatoon, SK S7N 0T9
Tel: 306-664-0300 *Fax:* 306-664-0311
luthercare@shaw.ca
www.luthercare.com
Year Founded: 1955
Note: Specialties: Group living for young adults; Community day programs for adults; Home support; Intermediate care; Seniors' housing; Long-term nursing care
Bernard McCallion, CEO

***Strasbourg:* Last Mountain Pioneer Home**
Affiliated with: Saskatoon Health Region
PO Box 459, Strasbourg, SK S0G 4V0
Tel: 306-725-3342
www.saskatoonhealthregion.ca
Connie Fuessel, Manager

Mental Health Facilities

Special Care Homes

***Arborfield:* Arborfield Special Care Lodge**
Affiliated with: Kelsey Trail Regional Health Authority
PO Box 160, 509 - 5th Ave., Arborfield, SK S0E 0A0
Tel: 306-769-8757 *Fax:* 306-769-8759
ww.kelseytrailhealth.ca
Number of Beds: 36 beds
Sharon Frisky, Community Coordinator

***Battleford:* Battlefords District Care Centre**
Affiliated with: Prairie North Health Region
PO Box 69, 1308 Winnipeg St., Battleford, SK S0M 0E0
Tel: 306-446-6900 *Fax:* 306-937-2258
Number of Beds: 124 beds

***Canora:* Canora Gateway Lodge**
Affiliated with: Sunrise Regional Health Authority
PO Box 1387, 212 Centre Ave. East, Canora, SK S0A 0L0
Tel: 306-563-5685 *Fax:* 306-563-5711
Number of Beds: 77 long-term beds; 1 respite
Oney Pollock, Manager, Health Services

***Carrot River:* Pasquia Special Care Home**
Affiliated with: Kelsey Trail Regional Health Authority
PO Box 250, 4101 - 1 Ave West, Carrot River, SK S0E 0L0
Tel: 306-862-2725 *Fax:* 306-768-3233
Number of Beds: 35 long-term care beds
Andrew Will

***Dalmeny:* Spruce Manor Special Care Home**
Affiliated with: Saskatoon Health Region
PO Box 190, 701 First St., Dalmeny, SK S0K 1E0
Tel: 306-254-2162 *Fax:* 306-254-2175
sprucemanor.mennonite.net
Year Founded: 1950
Number of Beds: 36 beds
Tom Nicholls, Administrator
Jonathan Redekop, Maintenance

***Esterhazy:* Centennial Special Care Home**
Affiliated with: Sunrise Regional Health Authority
PO Box 310, 300 James St., Esterhazy, SK S0A 0X0
Tel: 306-745-6444 *Fax:* 306-745-2741
Number of Beds: 59 beds
Doreen Strong, Manager, Health Services

***Herbert:* Herbert Nursing Home Inc.**
Affiliated with: Cypress Regional Health Authority
PO Box 520, 405 Herbert Ave., Herbert, SK S0H 2A0
Tel: 306-784-2466 *Fax:* 306-784-2449
herbert@sk.sympatico.ca
Year Founded: 1951
Number of Beds: 53 beds
Gordon Milton, Administrator
Lyle Zacharias, Director, Plant Maintenance

***Humboldt:* St. Mary's Villa**
Affiliated with: Saskatoon Health Region
PO Box 1360, 1109 - 13 St. North, Humboldt, SK S0K 2A0
Tel: 306-682-2628 *Fax:* 306-682-3211
Number of Beds: 101 beds
Jan Berger, Site Manager

***Langenberg:* Centennial Special Care Home**
Affiliated with: Sunrise Regional Health Authority
PO Box 370, 407 2nd St. South, Langenberg, SK S0A 2A0
Tel: 306-743-2232 *Fax:* 306-743-5025
Number of Beds: 47 beds

***Langenburg:* Centennial Special Care Home**
PO Box 370, 407, 2 St. South, Langenburg, SK S0A 2A0
Tel: 306-743-2232 *Fax:* 306-743-5025
Number of Beds: 44 long-term care beds; 2 respite beds; 1 palliative care bed

***Mankota:* Prairie View Health Centre**
Affiliated with: Cypress Regional Health Authority
PO Box 390, 241 - 1 Ave., Mankota, SK S0H 2W0
Tel: 306-628-3565 *Fax:* 306-628-3733
Number of Beds: 20 beds

***Meadow Lake:* Northland Pioneers Lodge Inc.**
Affiliated with: Prairie North Health Region
515 - 3 St. West, Meadow Lake, SK S9X 1L1
Tel: 306-236-1500 *Fax:* 306-236-3244
Number of Beds: 55 beds
Shelley Wasyliw, Facility Manager

***Moosomin:* Eastern Saskatchewan Pioneer Lodge**
Affiliated with: Regina Qu'Appelle Health Region
506 Windover Ave., Bag 3, Moosomin, SK S0G 3N0
Tel: 306-435-2326 *Fax:* 306-435-3335
Number of Beds: 58 beds

***Nipawin:* Nipawin District Nursing Home**
Affiliated with: Kelsey Trail Regional Health Authority
PO Box 2105, 400 - 6th Ave. East, Nipawin, SK S0E 1E0
Tel: 306-862-9828 *Fax:* 306-862-2400
Number of Beds: 96 beds

***North Battleford:* Villa Pascal**
Affiliated with: Prairie North Health Region
Also Known As: Société Joseph Breton Inc.
1301 - 113 St., North Battleford, SK S9A 3K1
Tel: 306-445-8465 *Fax:* 306-445-5117
Number of Beds: 40 beds
Thérèse Michaud, Administrator

***Prince Albert:* Mont St. Joseph Home Inc.**
Affiliated with: Prince Albert Parkland Regional Health Authority
777 - 28 St. East, Prince Albert, SK S6V 8C2
Tel: 306-953-4500 *Fax:* 306-953-4550
Number of Beds: 120 beds
Note: Special care home
Brian Martin, Executive Director

***Raymore:* Silver Heights Special Care Home**
Affiliated with: Regina Qu'Appelle Health Region
PO Box 549, 402 McLean St., Raymore, SK S0A 3J0
Tel: 306-746-5744 *Fax:* 306-746-5747
Number of Beds: 30 beds
Population Served: 600
Kate Beattie, Facility Manager

***Regina:* Salvation Army William Booth Special Care Home**
Affiliated with: Regina Qu'Appelle Health Region
50 Angus Rd., Regina, SK S4R 8P6
Tel: 306-543-0655 *Fax:* 306-543-1292
Number of Beds: 83 beds
Capt. Graham Brown, Executive Director

***Saskatoon:* Circle Drive Special Care Home Inc.**
Affiliated with: Saskatoon Health Region
PO Box 60020, 3055 Preston Ave. South, Saskatoon, SK S7T 1C3
Tel: 306-955-4800 *Fax:* 306-955-2376
circlecare@saskatoonhealthregion.ca
circledrivespecialcarehome.ca
Number of Beds: 50 beds
Diane Martin, Director of Care
Clint Kinchen, Administrator
Trevor Hanna, Board Chair

***Saskatoon:* Extendicare - Preston**
Affiliated with: Saskatoon Health Region
2225 Preston Ave., Saskatoon, SK S7J 2E7
Tel: 306-374-2242 *Fax:* 306-373-2203
cnh_preston@extendicare.com
www.extendicarecanada.com/saskatoon/index.aspx
Number of Beds: 82 beds
Patricia Amos, Administrator

***Saskatoon:* Senior Sisters of Sion Residence**
Affiliated with: Saskatoon Health Region
333 Acadia Dr., Saskatoon, SK S7H 3V5
Tel: 306-374-9566 *Fax:* 306-374-6648
kaymac@sasktel.net
Number of Beds: 27 beds
Sr. Katherine MacDonald, Director

***Saskatoon:* Ursuline Sisters of St Angela's Convent (St Angela's)**
Affiliated with: Saskatoon Health Region
1212 College Dr., Saskatoon, SK S7N 0W4
Tel: 306-242-5566 *Fax:* 306-975-7046
Number of Beds: 5 beds

***Warman:* Warman Mennonite Special Care Home**
Affiliated with: Saskatoon Health Region
PO Box 100, 201 - 3 Ave. North, Warman, SK S0K 4S0
Tel: 306-933-2011 *Fax:* 306-933-2782
Number of Beds: 31 beds
John Friesen, Administrator

***Weyburn:* Weyburn Special Care Home**
Affiliated with: Sun Country Health Region
PO Box 2003, 704 - 5th St. NE, Weyburn, SK S4H 2Z9
Tel: 306-842-4455 *Fax:* 306-842-1433
www.suncountry.sk.ca
Note: Respite care is available.

Yukon Territory

Government Departments in Charge

YUKON TERRITORY: Health & Social Services
PO Box 2703, Whitehorse, YT Y1A 2C6
Tel: 867-667-5770 *Fax:* 867-667-3096
Toll-Free: 1-800-661-0408
hss@gov.yk.ca
www.hss.gov.yk.ca
Social Media: www.facebook.com/yukonhss; twitter.com/HSSYukon; www.youtube.com/user/hssyukongovernment

Hon. Doug Graham, Minister
doug.graham@gov.yk.ca
Stuart J. Whitley, Deputy Minister

Hospitals

Hospitals - General

***Watson Lake:* Watson Lake Hospital**
PO Box 500, Watson Lake, YT Y0A 1C0
Tel: 867-536-4444 *Fax:* 867-536-7302
Number of Beds: 10 beds
Note: Number of staff: 1 nurse-in-charge, 7 additional nurses
Sue Rudd, Nurse in Charge

***Whitehorse:* Whitehorse General Hospital (WGH)**
5 Hospital Rd., Whitehorse, YT Y1A 3H7
Tel: 867-393-8700 *Fax:* 867-393-8771
www.whitehorsehospital.ca
Year Founded: 1902
Number of Beds: 49 in-patient beds; 10 surgical day care beds; 10 bassinets for newborns
Number of Employees: 350+
Specialties: Medical imaging services; Laboratory services; Diabetes Education Centre; Nutrition services; First Nations health programs; Therapy services

Community Health Centres

Community Health Care Centres

***Beaver Creek:* Beaver Creek Health Centre**
General Delivery, Beaver Creek, YT Y0B 1A0
Tel: 867-862-4444 *Fax:* 867-862-7909

***Carmacks:* Carmacks Health Centre**
PO Box 230, Carmacks, YT Y0B 1C0
Tel: 867-863-4444 *Fax:* 867-863-6612
carmacks.nic@gov.yk.ca
Number of Beds: 2 beds
Jocelyn Rhode, Acting Nurse Practitioner in Charge

***Dawson:* Dawson City Health Centre**
PO Box 10, Dawson, YT Y0B 1G0
Tel: 867-993-4444 *Fax:* 867-993-5811

***Destruction Bay:* Destruction Bay Health Centre**
General Delivery, Destruction Bay, YT Y0B 1H0
Tel: 867-841-4444 *Fax:* 867-841-5274

***Faro:* Faro Health Centre**
PO Box 99, Faro, YT Y0B 1K0
Tel: 867-994-4444 *Fax:* 867-994-3457

***Haines Junction:* Haines Junction Health Centre**
PO Box 5334, Haines Junction, YT Y0B 1L0
Tel: 867-634-4444 *Fax:* 867-634-2733

***Mayo:* Mayo Nursing Station**
PO Box 98, Mayo, YT Y0B 1M0
Tel: 867-996-4444 *Fax:* 867-996-2018
hc.mayo@gov.yk.ca
Note: Specialties: Public health services; Health promotion services; Home care services. Number of Employees: 1 doctor + 3 community nurse practitioners

***Old Crow:* Old Crow Health Centre**
General Delivery, Old Crow, YT Y0B 1N0
Tel: 867-996-4444 *Fax:* 867-966-3614
www.oldcrow.ca/nursing
Year Founded: 1960
Note: Specialties: Nursing care; Health promotion; Home & community care

***Pelly Crossing:* Pelly Crossing Health Centre**
General Delivery, Pelly Crossing, YT Y0B 1P0
Tel: 867-537-4444 *Fax:* 867-537-3611
hc.pelly-crossing@gov.yk.ca

***Ross River:* Ross River Health Centre**
General Delivery, Ross River, YT Y0B 1S0
Tel: 867-969-4444 *Fax:* 867-969-2014

***Teslin:* Teslin Health Centre**
General Delivery, Teslin, YT Y0A 1B0
Tel: 867-390-4444
Note: Specialties: Public health services; Health promotion; Clinical care by community nurses; Home care

***Watson Lake:* Watson Lake Health Centre**
PO Box 500, Watson Lake, YT Y0A 1C0
Tel: 867-536-7483 *Fax:* 867-536-7011
Sue Rudd

Long Term/Retirement Care

Long Term Care Facilities

***Dawson City:* McDonald Lodge for Seniors**
PO Box 310, 636 - 5th Ave., Dawson City, YT Y0B 1G0
Tel: 867-993-5345 *Fax:* 867-993-5849
Toll-Free: 1-800-661-0408
Number of Beds: 11 residential beds, including 2 respite beds
Note: 0pecialties: Residential care for seniors & physically challenged persons who require moderate assistance; Recreational & therapeutic activities; Respite care; Home support services; Palliative care
Adeline Griffin-Viney, Manager

***Whitehorse:* Copper Ridge Place**
60 Lazulite Dr., Whitehorse, YT Y1A 6S9
Tel: 867-393-7500 *Fax:* 867-393-7510
bev.oyler@gov.yk.ca
www.hss.gov.yk.ca/copperridgeplace.php
Number of Beds: 96 beds

***Whitehorse:* Norman D. Macaulay Lodge**
2 Klondike Rd., Whitehorse, YT Y1A 3L5
Tel: 867-667-5955 *Fax:* 867-393-6237
Number of Beds: 44 beds

SECTION 11
LAW FIRMS

Major Law Firms

Aird & Berlis LLP
Former Name: Aird, Zimmerman & Berlis
#1800, Brookfield Place, CP 754, 181 Bay St., Toronto, ON M5J 2T9 Canada
Tel: 416-863-1500; *Fax:* 416-863-1515

www.airdberlis.com
www.facebook.com/pages/Aird-Berlis/116517495028459,
twitter.com/AirdBerlis,
www.linkedin.com/company/aird-&-berlis-llp
Profile: 1 Offices, 130 Lawyers, Founded in: 1919
Legal services in the areas of Banking Law, Corporate & Commercial Law, Corporate Finance, Insolvency & Restructuring, Litigation, Real Estate Law, and Tax Law
Senior and Managing Partners:
Jack Bernstein, Senior Partner
416-865-7766
jbernstein@airdberlis.com
Leo F. Longo, Senior Partner
416-865-7778
llongo@airdberlis.com

Bennett Jones LLP - Calgary
#4500, Bankers Hall East Tower, 855 - 2nd St. SW, Calgary, AB T2P 4K7
Tel: 403-298-3100; *Fax:* 403-265-7219

www.bennettjones.ca
twitter.com/BennettJonesLaw
Profile: 6 Offices, 351 Lawyers, Founded in: 1922
Senior and Managing Partners:
Perry Spitznagel, Vice-Chair & Managing Partner

Blaney McMurtry LLP
#1500, 2 Queen St. East, Toronto, ON M5C 3G5
Tel: 416-593-1221; *Fax:* 416-593-5437

info@blaney.com
www.blaney.com
Profile: 1 Offices, 125 Lawyers, Founded in: 1954
Senior and Managing Partners:
Michael J. Penman, Senior Partner
416-593-3966
D. Barry Prentice, Senior Partner
416-593-3953
Crawford W. Spratt, Senior Partner
416-593-3965
cspratt@blaney.com

Borden Ladner Gervais LLP - Calgary
Centennial Place, East Tower
#1900, 520 - 3rd Ave. SW, Calgary, AB T2P 0R3
Tel: 403-232-9500; *Fax:* 403-266-1395

info@blg.com
www.blg.com
Profile: 6 Offices, 750 Lawyers
The firm provides legal services in the following areas: Energy; Forestry & Mining; Municipal; Oil & Gas; Environmental
Senior and Managing Partners:
D. George Kelly
403-232-9508
gkelly@blg.com
James W. Surbey, Senior Partner
403-232-9537
jsurbey@blg.com
David C. Whelan, Managing Partner
403-232-9555
dwhelan@blg.com

Burnet, Duckworth & Palmer LLP
Also Known AS: BD&P
#2400, 525 - 8th Ave. SW, Calgary, AB T2P 1G1
Tel: 403-260-0100; *Fax:* 403-260-0332

counsel@bdplaw.com
www.bdplaw.com
Profile: 1 Offices, 135 Lawyers, Founded in: 1915
Corporate; Commercial; Taxation; Real Estate; Securities
Senior and Managing Partners:
Harry S. Campbell, Q.C., Senior Partner; Vice-Chair
403-260-0281
hsc@bdplaw

Cain Lamarre Casgrain Wells - Val-d'Or
#202, 855, 3e av, Val-d'Or, QC J9P 1T2
Tél: 819-825-4153; *Téléc:* 819-825-9769

info@clcw.ca
www.clcw.qc.ca
Profile: 16 Offices, 160 Lawyers, Founded in: 1999

Cassels Brock & Blackwell LLP
#2100, Scotia Plaza, 40 King St. West, Toronto, ON M5H 3C2

Tel: 416-869-5300; *Fax:* 416-360-8877

www.casselsbrock.com
Profile: 1 Offices, 200 Lawyers, Founded in: 1888
Full-service law firm, with an emphasis on tax and business law, both domestic and international
Senior and Managing Partners:
David R. Peterson, P.C., Q.C., Senior Partner
416-869-5451
dpeterson@casselsbrock.com

Davies Ward Phillips & Vineberg LLP
Former Name: Davies Ward & Beck
1 First Canadian Place, 44th Fl., Toronto, ON M5X 1B1
Tel: 416-863-0900; *Fax:* 416-863-0871

www.dwpv.com
twitter.com/_Davies_
Profile: 3 Offices, 240 Lawyers, Founded in: 1961
Business transactions & business operations including acquisitions, divestitures, financing, securities, real estate & land development
Senior and Managing Partners:
William M. Ainley, Senior Partner
416-863-5509
wainley@dwpv.com
Robert T. Bauer, Senior Partner
416-863-5552
rbauer@dwpv.com
Carol Hansell, Senior Partner
416-863-5592
chansell@dwpv.com
D. Shawn McReynolds, Managing Partner
416-863-5538
smcreynolds@dwpv.com
Kevin J. Thomson, Senior Partner
416-863-5590
kthomson@dwpv.com

Davis LLP - Vancouver
Former Name: Davis & Company LLP
#2800, Park Place, 666 Burrard St., Vancouver, BC V6C 2Z7
Tel: 604-687-9444; *Fax:* 604-687-1612

www.davis.ca
Profile: 8 Offices, 240 Lawyers, Founded in: 1892
As a full-service law firm, Davis LLP provides a comprehensive range of legal services to clients around the world, through offices across Canada & in Japan. The firm has 88 partners worldwide, & 134 other lawyers around the world. Business can be conducted in English, French, Japanese, Spanish, Mandarin, Cantonese, Korean, German, Italian, Dutch, Estonian, & Polish. Established in Vancouver in 1892, the firm has more than 220 lawyers working in integrated practice groups that focus on client service & specialization. Davis strives to help clients achieve their business objectives & resolve business problems quickly & effectively. The firm is strong in all the traditional areas of legal practice. Across the firm, lawyers continuously cultivate commercial & government relationships to both facilitate the conduct of business & to identify new business opportunities for clients. Davis & its lawyers are recognized as leaders in numerous domestic & international ratings publications.
Senior and Managing Partners:
D. Ross Clark, Q.C., Senior Partner
604-643-2911
drclark@davis.ca
Kathryn I. Denhoff, Senior Partner
604-643-2995
kdenhoff@davis.ca
Timothy G. Duholke, FCA, Senior Tax Advisor
604-643-6400
tduholke@davis.ca
W. Ross Ellison, Q.C., Senior Partner
604-643-2918
rellison@davis.ca
Brian F. Hiebert, Managing Partner
604-643-2917
bhiebert@davis.ca
Stuart B. Morrow, Senior Partner
604-643-2948
sbmorrow@davis.ca
Linda I. Parsons, Q.C., Senior Partner
604-643-6445
lparsons@davis.ca
Dale G. Sanderson, Q.C., Senior Partner
604-643-6330
dsanderson@davis.ca

Fasken Martineau - Toronto
Former Name: Fasken Martineau DuMoulin LLP
#2400, Bay Adelaide Centre, P.O. Box 20, 333 Bay St., Toronto, ON M5H 2T6
Tel: 416-366-8381; *Fax:* 416-364-7813
Toll-Free: 800-268-8424
toronto@fasken.com
www.fasken.com
www.facebook.com/group.php?gid=154446131283771,
twitter.com/faskenmartineau,
www.linkedin.com/company/fasken-martineau-dumoulin
Profile: 9 Offices, 675 Lawyers, Founded in: 1863
Fasken Marineau provides legal services to the full array of participants in the financial services industry; our clients include leading Canadian & foreign banks, life & property & casualty insurance companies, loan & trust companies, cooperatives & credit unions, finance companies, insurance agents & brokers & other financial services providers; we pride ourselves on knowing each client's business & the current issues & trends affecting them; we work closely with our clients across the breadth of their transactional investment & other activities & in their relations with Canadian regulators; our group regularly provides advice regarding mergers & acquisitions, financings, restructurings, the establishment of financial services businesses, the development & distribution of financial services products & all manner of regulatory issues with both federal & provincial regulators
Senior and Managing Partners:
John A. Campion, Senior Partner
416-865-4357
jcampion@fasken.com
David N. Corbett, Managing Partner, Firm
416-868-3504
dcorbett@fasken.com
Martin K. Denyes, Managing Partner, Ontario
416-868-3489
mdenyes@fasken.com
Stephen Erlichman, Senior Partner
416-865-4552
serlichman@fasken.com
Jeff Kaufman, Senior Partner
416-868-3417
jkaufman@fasken.com
Samuel R. Rickett, Senior Partner
416-868-3436
srickett@fasken.com

Fraser Milner Casgrain LLP - Toronto
#400, Toronto-Dominion Centre, 77 King St. West, Toronto, ON M5K 0A1
Tel: 416-863-4421; *Fax:* 416-863-4592

www.fmc-law.com
twitter.com/FMC_LAW
Profile: 6 Offices, 500 Lawyers, Founded in: 1839
The firm provides legal services in the following areas: Business Immigration; Competition/Antitrust/Foreign Investment Review; Corporate & Commercial Law; Corporate Governance; Employment & Labour Law; Financial Services; Franchising; Insolvency & Restructuring; Intellectual Property Law; International Trade Law; Mergers & Acquisitions; Pensions & Benefits Law; Private Equity & Venture Capital; Public-Private Partnerships; Real Estate Law; Corporate Finance & Securities; Tax Law; and Wealth Management
Senior and Managing Partners:
Ronald A. Goldenberg, SeniorPartner
416-863-4724
ronald.goldenberg@fmc-law.com
Thomas J. Hunter, Senior Partner
416-863-4555
tom.hunter@fmc-law.com
Michael N. (Mike) Kaplan, Managing Partner
416-863-4421
mike.kaplan@fmc-law.com

Goodmans LLP
Former Name: Goodman Phillips & Vineberg
#3400, Bay Adelaide Centre, 333 Bay St., Toronto, ON M5H 2S7
Tel: 416-979-2211; *Fax:* 416-979-1234

info@goodmans.ca
www.goodmans.ca
Profile: 2 Offices, 200 Lawyers, Founded in: 1917
Goodmans is a leading Canadian law firm, well-recognized across Canada & internationally for its excellence & market leadership in large-scale corporate transactions. Goodmans is a full-service business law firm that offers clients a wide range of services & expertise in all of the major business law areas, including: Broadcasting, Telecommunications & New Media; Commercial Real Estate; Corporate & Commercial Law; Corporate Restructuring; Corporate Finance & Securities;

Litigation; Mergers & Acquisitions; Municipal, Planning & Property Tax Law; Pensions; Trusts & Estates & Tax. With over 200 lawyers, Goodmans provides a complete spectrum of legal advice & representation to domestic & foreign business clients ranging from emerging technology companies to financial institutions & conglomerates
Senior and Managing Partners:

Gowling Lafleur Henderson LLP - Toronto
Also Known AS: Gowlings
#1600, 1 First Canadian Place, 100 King St. West, Toronto, ON M5X 1G5
Tel: 416-862-7525; *Fax:* 416-862-7661
www.gowlings.com
Profile: 11 Offices, 750 Lawyers, Founded in: 1887
With over 750 professionals in offices across Canada, & in London & Moscow, Gowlings offers comprehensive legal services & solutions in all areas of business & corporate law to key industries. In addition, the firm's practice groups are skilled & experienced in the areas of intellectual property law, advocacy, international trade law, technology law, administrative law, and government affairs. Named one of The Best Employers in Canada for 2011
Senior and Managing Partners:
Eric Gross, Senior Partner
416-862-5409
eric.gross@gowlings.com
Peter J. Lukasiewicz, Managing Partner
416-862-4328
peter.lukasiewicz@gowlings.com
Stephen A. Pike, ManagingPartner
416-369-7349
stephen.pike@gowlings.com
Robin D. Walker, Q.C., Senior Partner
416-862-4401
robin.walker@gowlings.com
Lilly A. Wong, Senior Partner
416-369-4630
lilly.wong@gowlings.com

Heenan Blaikie S.E.N.C.R.L/SRL - Montréal
#2500, 1250, boul René-Lévesque ouest, Montréal, QC H3B 4Y1
Tel: 514-846-1212; *Fax:* 514-846-3427
www.heenanblaikie.com
Profile: 11 Offices, 550 Lawyers, Founded in: 1973
Heenan Blaikie LLP business law practitioners provide a full range of services to some of Canada's largest corporations & financial institutions, as well as to many smaller, growth-oriented companies in all types of transactions & corporate governance issues: mergers & acquisitions, international & domestic joint ventures, reorganizations, regulatory matters, venture capital investment, financing arrangements with commercial & private lenders, directors' & officers' liabilities, trademark & copyright matters; software licensing & outsourcing contracts
Senior and Managing Partners:
Roy L. Heenan, Q.C., Founding Partner
514-846-2264
rheenan@heenan.ca
Donald J. Johnston, Founding Partner
514-846-2280
djohnston@heenan.ca

Lavery, de Billy - Montréal
#4000, 1, Place Ville-Marie, Montréal, QC H3B 4M4
Tel: 514-871-1522; *Fax:* 514-871-8977
info@lavery.qc.ca
www.laverydebilly.com
Profile: 3 Offices, 175 Lawyers, Founded in: 1913
Senior and Managing Partners:

Macleod Dixon LLP
#3700, Canterra Tower, 400 Third Ave. SW, Calgary, AB T2P 4H2
Tel: 403-267-8222; *Fax:* 403-264-5973
danielle.gill@macleoddixon.com
www.macleoddixon.com
Profile: 7 Offices, 300 Lawyers, Founded in: 1912
Senior and Managing Partners:

MacPherson Leslie & Tyerman LLP - Regina
Also Known AS: MLT
#1500, Hill Centre I, 1874 Scarth St., Regina, SK S4P 4E9
Tel: 306-347-8000; *Fax:* 306-352-5250
www.mlt.com
Profile: 4 Offices, 115 Lawyers, Founded in: 1920
Client-centered & business-oriented law firm; experience extends from the more traditional practice areas of business law (such as corporate finance, mergers & acquisitions, tax, insolvency, commercial litigation) to other rapidly developing areas
Senior and Managing Partners:

McCarthy Tétrault LLP - Toronto
#5300, Toronto-Dominion Bank Tower, Box 48, Toronto, ON M5K 1E6
Tel: 416-362-1812; *Fax:* 416-868-0673
Toll-Free: 877-244-7711
info@mccarthy.ca; tschier@mccarthy.ca (Media contact)
www.mccarthy.ca
Profile: 6 Offices, 616 Lawyers, Founded in: 1855
One of our largest practice areas is in corporate finance, where we represent public issuers & underwriters in corporate finance matters involving the preparation of prospectuses & other offering documents for public & private offerings; we have extensive experience in dealing with mergers & acquisitions & corporate reorganizations; our practice has involved us in many significant takeovers, as well as the development & implementation of defensive strategies in hostile bid situations to improve shareholder values
Senior and Managing Partners:
James M. Farley, Q.C., Senior Counsel
416-601-7840
jfarley@mccarthy.ca

McMillan LLP - Toronto
Former Name: McMillan Binch LLP/Mendelsohn GP; McMillan Binch Mendelsohn
#4400, Brookfield Place, 181 Bay St., Toronto, ON M5J 2T3
Tel: 416-865-7000; *Fax:* 416-865-7048
Toll-Free: 888-622-4624
info@mcmillan.ca
www.mcmillan.ca
Profile: 5 Offices, 395 Lawyers, Founded in: 1903
Senior and Managing Partners:
Graham W.S. Scott, Q.C., Senior Partner
416-865-7247
graham.scott@mcmillan.ca
Michael P. Whitcombe, Senior Partner
416-865-7126
michael.whitcombe@mcmillan.ca

Miller Thomson LLP - Toronto
#5800, Scotia Plaza, P.O. Box 1011, 40 King St. West, Toronto, ON M5H 3S1
Tel: 416-595-8500; *Fax:* 416-595-8695
Toll-Free: 888-762-5559
toronto@millerthomson.com
www.millerthomson.com
twitter.com/millerthomson,
www.linkedin.com/company/Miller-Thomson-LLP
Profile: 11 Offices, 470 Lawyers, Founded in: 1957
Bankruptcy; Corporate Commercial; E-Commerce; Estates/Pensions; Financial Services; Franchising; Insolvency & Insurance; Mergers & Acquisitions; Securities; Tax Law
Senior and Managing Partners:
Barbara R.C. Doherty, Senior Partner
416-595-8621
bdoherty@millerthomson.com
Clifford Goldlist, Senior Partner
416-601-4117
cgoldlist@millerthomson.com

Norton Rose OR LLP - Montréal
Former Name: Ogilvy Renault LLP/S.E.N.C.R.L., s.r.l. - Montréal
#2500, 1 Place Ville Marie, Montréal, QC H3B 1R1
Tél: 514-847-4747; *Téléc:* 514-286-5474
montreal@nortonrose.com
www.nortonrose.com
Profile: 5 Offices, 450 Lawyers, Founded in: 1879
Asset-based Lending; Banking & Financial Products; Corporate & Commercial Law; Insolvency & Restructuring; Mergers & Acquisitions; Projects & Project Finance; Securities; Tax
Senior and Managing Partners:
R. Luc Beaulieu, Senior Partner
514-847-4428
luc.beaulieu@nortonrose.com
Marc S. Benoît, Senior Partner
514-847-6049
marc.benoit@nortonrose.com
Lise Bergeron, Senior Partner
514-847-4506
lise.bergeron@nortonrose.com
Jean G. Bertrand, Managing Partner
514-847-4401
jean.bertrand@nortonrose.com
Pierre Bienvenu, Senior Partner
514-847-4452
pierre.bienvenu@nortonrose.com
Danièle Boutet, Senior Partner
514-847-4527
daniele.boutet@nortonrose.com
Claude Brunet, Senior Partner
514-847-4726
claude.brunet@nortonrose.com
Michel G. Carle, Senior Partner
514-847-4501
michel.carle@nortonrose.com
Mario M. Caron, Senior Partner
514-847-4525
mario.caron@nortonrose.com
Christine A. Carron, Senior Partner
514-847-4404
christine.carron@nortonrose.com
Jules Charette, Senior Partner
514-847-4450
jules.charette@nortonrose.com
Robert P. Charlton, Senior Partner
514-847-4459
robert.charlton@nortonrose.com
John A. Coleman, Managing Partner
514-847-4503
john.coleman@nortonrose.com
David R. Collier, Senior Partner
514-847-4539
david.collier@nortonrose.com
Jean-Pierre Colpron, Senior Partner
514-847-4880
jean-pierre.colpron@nortonrose.com
Marc Duquette, Senior Partner
514-847-4508
marc.duquette@nortonrose.com
François Fontaine, Senior Partner
514-847-4413
francois.fontaine@nortonrose.com
L. Yves Fortier, C.C., Q.C., Senior Partner
514-847-4740
yves.fortier@nortonrose.com
William Hesler, Q.C., Senior Partner
514-847-4510
william.hesler@nortonrose.com
Pierre Hébert, Senior Partner
514-847-4474
pierre.hebert@nortonrose.com
Olivier F. Kott, Senior Partner
514-847-4445
olivier.kott@nortonrose.com
Louise Laplante, Senior Partner
514-847-4433
louise.laplante@nortonrose.com
Hélène Lefebvre, Senior Partner
514-847-4457
helene.lefebvre@nortonrose.com
Francis R. Legault, Senior Partner
514-847-4495
francis.legault@nortonrose.com
Brian Mulroney, P.C., C.C., LL.D., Senior Partner
514-847-4779
brian.mulroney@nortonrose.com
Kevin P. Murphy, Senior Partner
514-847-4293
kevin.murphy@nortonrose.com
Jean Piette, Senior Partner
514-847-4584
jean.piette@nortonrose.com
Pierre Pronovost, Senior Partner
514-847-4485
pierre.pronovost@nortonrose.com
Martin Rochette, Senior Partner
514-847-4430
martin.rochette@nortonrose.com
Michel G. Sylvestre, Senior Partner
514-847-4460
michel.sylvestre@nortonrose.com
Gilles Touchette, Senior Partner
514-847-4532
gilles.touchette@nortonrose.com

Osler, Hoskin & Harcourt LLP - Toronto
Also Known AS: Osler
#6100, P.O. Box 50, One First Canadian Place, Toronto, ON M5X 1B8
Tel: 416-362-2111; *Fax:* 416-862-6666
counsel@osler.com
www.osler.com
Profile: 5 Offices, 500 Lawyers,
Advises many of Canada's corporate leaders as well as U.S. &

international parties with extensive interests in Canada; third-party research confirms the firm's preeminent position in the marketplace; with over 500 lawyers based in Toronto, Montréal, Ottawa, Calgary & New York, our critical mass of experience with the largest domestic & cross-border business combinations enables us to exercise acknowledged strengths in mergers & acquisitions, tax, competition & litigation, & leverage our specialty expertise in fields like commercial property & infrastructure projects, IP & IT, among many others
Senior and Managing Partners:
Terrence R. Burgoyne, Senior Partner
416-862-6601
tburgoyne@osler.com
Judith E. Harris, Senior Partner
416-862-4609
jharris@osler.com
Andrew H. Kingissepp, Senior Partner
416-862-6507
akingissepp@osler.com
Harvey Kirsh, Senior Partner
416-862-6844
hkirsh@osler.com
Dale R. Ponder, Managing Partner
416-862-6500
dponder@osler.com

Stewart McKelvey - Halifax
Former Name: Stewart McKelvey Stirling Scales
#900, Purdy's Wharf Tower One, P.O. Box 997, Stn. Central, 1959 Upper Water St., Halifax, NS B3J 2X2
Tel: 902-420-3200; *Fax:* 902-420-1417
halifax@stewartmckelvey.com
www.stewartmckelvey.com
Profile: 6 Offices, 220 Lawyers, Founded in: 1867
Senior and Managing Partners:

Torys LLP
Former Name: Tory Tory DesLauriers & Binnington
#3000, Toronto-Dominion Centre, P.O. Box 270, 79 Wellington St. West, Toronto, ON M5K 1N2
Tel: 416-865-0040; *Fax:* 416-865-7380
www.torys.com
twitter.com/torysllp, www.linkedin.com/company/torys-llp
Profile: 3 Offices, 276 Lawyers, Founded in: 1941
Torys LLP is an international business law firm with offices in Toronto, New York and Calgary. Torys is known for its seamless cross-border services in a range of areas, including mergers and acquisitions; corporate and capital markets; litigation and dispute resolution; restructuring and insolvency; taxation; competition and antitrust; environmental, health and safety; debt finance and lending; project development and finance; managed assets; private equity and venture capital; financial institutions; pension and employment; intellectual property; technology, media and telecom; life sciences; real estate; infrastructure and energy; climate change and emissions trading; and personal client services.

Provincial Law Firms

Alberta

***Airdrie*: Warnock & Rathgeber - *2**
Also Known As: Warnock Rathgeber & Company
Former Name: Warnock, Rathgeber & Hassett
225 First Ave. NW, Airdrie, AB T4B 2M8
Tel: 403-948-0009; *Fax:* 403-948-6740
office@wrlawyers.ca
www.wrlawyers.ca

***Banff*: Karras Rathbone - *2**
P.O. Box 899, Stn. Main, 205 Bear St., Banff, AB T1L 1A9
Tel: 403-762-2770; *Fax:* 403-762-5961
karalaw@telus.net

***Barrhead*: Driessen Law Office - *1**
P.O. Box 4220, Stn. Main, 5017 - 50 Ave., Barrhead, AB T7N 1A2
Tel: 780-674-2276; *Fax:* 780-674-4592
solutions@driessenlaw.ca

***Blairmore*: Valerie J. Danielson Law Office - *1**
P.O. Box 1620, 13143 - 20th Ave., Blairmore, AB T0K 0E0
Tel: 403-562-2132; *Fax:* 403-562-2700
valeriejdanielson@shaw.ca

***Bonnyville*: Allan Wayne Fraser, Professional Corporation - *1**
CP 6710, Stn. Main, 4816 - 50 Ave., Bonnyville, AB T9N 2H2
Tel: 780-826-3355; *Fax:* 780-826-6132
awfraser@telusplanet.net

***Bonnyville*: Wood & Wiebe - *2**
#101, CP 8060, Stn. Main, 4811 - 50 Ave., Bonnyville, AB T9N 2J3
Tel: 780-826-5767; *Fax:* 780-826-4654
woodwieb@telusplanet.net

***Brooks*: Bell Law Office - *1**
CP 670, Stn. Main, Brooks, AB T1R 1B6
Tel: 403-362-3447; *Fax:* 403-362-4379
dhb@telus.net

***Brooks*: Susan E. Robertson - *1**
411B Third Ave. West, Brooks, AB T1R 0B2
Tel: 403-362-4064; *Fax:* 403-362-4024

***Calgary*: Laurie Allen & Associates, Barristers, Solicitors, Mediators - *5**
#800, 355 - 4 Ave. SW, Calgary, AB T2P 0J1
Tel: 403-266-5556; *Fax:* 403-266-5427
mail@laurieallen.com
www.laurieallen.com

***Calgary*: Robert J.E. Allen Law Office - *1**
#206, 4600 Crowchild Trail NW, Calgary, AB T3A 2L6
Tel: 403-216-5522; *Fax:* 403-216-5524
admin@calgarylawyer.net

***Calgary*: Anderson Law Firm - *1**
14 Strathridge Grove SW, Calgary, AB T3H 4M1
Tel: 403-253-4597; *Fax:* 403-253-4599
latitude@telus.net

***Calgary*: Linda A. Anderson - *1**
#16, 2439 - 54 Ave. SW, Calgary, AB T3E 1M4
Tel: 403-243-6400; *Fax:* 403-243-0126
linda@lindaandersonlaw.com

***Calgary*: Arkell Damen Hoffman, Barristers, Solicitors, & Notaries - *3**
Former Name: Arkell, Damen
109 - 14 Ave. SE, Calgary, AB T2G 1C6
Tel: 403-531-4151; *Fax:* 403-531-4153
info@adh-law.com

***Calgary*: Theodore L. Babie - *1**
615 - 36 St. NE, Calgary, AB T2A 4W3
Tel: 403-273-3673; *Fax:* 403-273-0931

***Calgary*: Deborah L. Barron - *1**
#303, Mayfair Place, 6707 Elbow Drive SW, Calgary, AB T2V 0E5
Tel: 403-238-0000; *Fax:* 403-238-2255
dbarron@deborahbarronlaw.com
www.deborahbarronlaw.com

***Calgary*: Batting, Der, Barristers & Solicitors - *1**
#2410, 645 - 7 Ave. SW, Calgary, AB T2P 4G8
Tel: 403-263-4949; *Fax:* 403-261-8977
rbatting@telus.net; debhaigh@telus.net
www.rbattinglaw.com

***Calgary*: Alan V.M. Beattie, Q.C. - *1**
3621 - 1A St. SW, Calgary, AB T2S 1R4
Tel: 403-245-5255; *Fax:* 403-228-0254
beattiea@shaw.ca

***Calgary*: Gary E. Bilyk Professional Corporation - *1**
#602, 706 - 7 Ave. SW, Calgary, AB T2P 0Z1
Tel: 403-266-2810; *Fax:* 403-264-1151
gebilyklawyer@shaw.ca

***Calgary*: Blumell & Hartney - *2**
#203, 2411 - 4 St. NW, Calgary, AB T2M 2Z8
Tel: 403-282-4544; *Fax:* 403-284-4535
b.blumell@shawbiz.ca; m.hartney@shaw.ca

***Calgary*: Michael J. Bondar, Professional Corporation - *1**
#1840, 801 - 6 Ave. SW, Calgary, AB T2P 3W2
Tel: 403-266-5511; *Fax:* 403-237-6620
mjbondar@shaw.ca

***Calgary*: Borden Ladner Gervais LLP - Calgary - *111**
Also Known As: BLG Calgary
Centennial Place, East Tower, #1900, 520 - 3rd Ave. SW, Calgary, AB T2P 0R3
Tel: 403-232-9500; *Fax:* 403-266-1395
info@blg.com
www.blg.com

***Calgary*: Bruni & Company - *2**
707 - 15th Ave. SW, Calgary, AB T2R 0R8
Tel: 403-266-5664; *Fax:* 403-262-6343
brunicorp@shaw.ca

***Calgary*: Lisa M. Burgis - *1**
#2410, 645 - 7 Ave. SW, Calgary, AB T2P 4G8
Tel: 403-213-2999; *Fax:* 403-261-8977
lburgis@telus.net

***Calgary*: Burstall Winger LLP - *26**
#1600, Dome Tower, 333 - 7th Ave. SW, Calgary, AB T2P 2Z1
Tel: 403-264-1915; *Fax:* 403-266-6016
info@burstall.com
www.burstall.com

***Calgary*: Butlin Oke Roberts & Nobles - *5**
Former Name: Butlin Oke Roberts Nobles Braun; Butlin Oke Roberts & Nobles; Butlin Oke & Roberts
#100, 1501 - 1 St. SW, Calgary, AB T2R 0W1
Tel: 403-543-7750; *Fax:* 403-543-7759

***Calgary*: Richard Cairns, Q.C. - *1**
#210, The Burns Bldg., 237 - 8 Ave. SE, Calgary, AB T2G 5C3
Tel: 403-205-3155; *Fax:* 403-546-0034
counsel@echambers.ca
www.echambers.ca

***Calgary*: Calgary Legal Guidance**
#100, 840 - 7th Ave. SW, Calgary, AB T2P 3G2
Tel: 403-234-9266; *Fax:* 403-234-9299
clg@clg.ab.ca
www.clg.ab.ca

***Calgary*: Cameron Horne Law Office LLP, Barristers & Solicitors - *2**
Former Name: A.B. Cameron
#820, 10201 Southport Rd. SW, Calgary, AB T2W 4X9
Tel: 403-531-2700; *Fax:* 403-531-2707
sandy@cameronhorne.ca; geoff@cameronhorne.ca
www.cameronhorne.ca

***Calgary*: Campbell O'Hara - *6**
Former Name: Campbell Taylor O'Hara
#1160, 1122 - 4th St. SW, Calgary, AB T2R 1M1
Tel: 403-294-0030; *Fax:* 403-229-2977

***Calgary*: Caron & Partners LLP, Barristers & Solicitors - *16**
#2100, Scotia Centre, 700 - 2 St. SW, 21st Fl., Calgary, AB T2P 2W1
Tel: 403-262-3000; *Fax:* 403-237-0111
legalservices@caronpartners.com
www.caronpartners.com

***Calgary*: Carscallen Leitch LLP - *29**
Former Name: Carscallen Lockwood LLP
#1500, 407 - 2 St. SW, Calgary, AB T2P 2Y3
Tel: 403-262-3775; *Fax:* 403-262-2952
info@cllawyers.com
www.cllawyers.com

***Calgary*: Castle & Associates, Barristers & Solicitors - *7**
#302, 221 - 10th Ave. SE, Calgary, AB T2G 0V9
Tel: 403-265-3403; *Fax:* 403-269-3217
mailbox@castleandassociates.ca
www.castleandassociates.ca

***Calgary*: Checkland & Company - *4**
#1100, 444 - 5th Ave. SW, Calgary, AB T2P 2T8
Tel: 403-233-9101; *Fax:* 403-233-9135

***Calgary*: Clark & Associates - *2**
Also Known As: Brian N. Clark Professional Corporation
#203, 136 - 17 Ave. NE, Calgary, AB T2E 1L6
Tel: 403-520-2011; *Fax:* 403-230-3509
bclark@clarkandassociates.ca
www.clarkandassociates.ca

***Calgary*: Clark Dymond McCaffery O'Brien-Kelly - *3**
Former Name: Clark Dymond McCaffery
#300, 1122 - 4 St. SW, Calgary, AB T2R 1M1
Tel: 403-265-7070; *Fax:* 403-232-6750
lawcdmg@telusplanet.net

***Calgary*: James K. Conley - *1**
#210, The Burns Bldg., 237 - 8th Ave. SE, Calgary, AB T2G 5C3
Tel: 403-290-0994; *Fax:* 403-265-7680
jkconley@telus.net

***Calgary*: Timothy J. Corcoran - *1**
#701, 4656 Westwinds Dr. NE, Calgary, AB T3J 3Z5
Tel: 403-263-6000; *Fax:* 403-280-7666
alberta@lawyer.com

* *indicates number of lawyers*

***Calgary*: Cornerstone Law Group LLP - *2**
Former Name: Keeler Law Firm; Milne & Company
#420, 10655 Southport Rd. SW, Calgary, AB T2W 4Y1
Tel: 403-296-1700; *Fax:* 403-258-0020
tom@cornerstonelaw.ca; jordan@cornerstonelaw.ca
www.cornerstonelaw.ca

***Calgary*: Craig Law LLP - *3**
Former Name: Mullen Craig
3408 - 114 Ave. SE, Calgary, AB T2Z 3V6
Tel: 403-297-0130; *Fax:* 403-297-0133

***Calgary*: Cuming & Gillespie - *2**
Former Name: McNally Cuming Raymaker; McNally Cuming
#1130, 396 - 11th Ave. SW, Calgary, AB T2R 0C5
Tel: 403-571-0555; *Fax:* 403-232-8818
Toll-Free: 800-682-2480
james@cglaw.ca
www.cglaw.ca

***Calgary*: D'Souza & Associates - *3**
Former Name: D'Souza Smith Wallace
#202, 811 Manning Rd. NE, Calgary, AB T2E 7L4
Tel: 403-531-9520; *Fax:* 403-272-6586

***Calgary*: Daniel J. Aberle Professional Corporation - *1**
Former Name: Stirling, Aberle & Row
#305, 602 - 11 Ave. SW, Calgary, AB T2R 1J8
Tel: 403-229-1129; *Fax:* 403-245-9660

***Calgary*: Gary A. Daniels - *1**
#200, 209 - 19 St. NW, Calgary, AB T2N 2H9
Tel: 403-297-0800; *Fax:* 403-283-7000
garyadaniels@shaw.ca

***Calgary*: Dartnell & Lutz - *2**
Former Name: Dartnell, Wenngatz & Lutz
#840, 840 - 6 Ave. SW, Calgary, AB T2P 3E5
Tel: 403-264-8484; *Fax:* 403-263-9110
dartnell-lutz@shaw.ca

***Calgary*: Davison Worden Mather LLP - *6**
#1710, 540 - 5 Ave. SW, Calgary, AB T2P 0M2
Tel: 403-262-7745; *Fax:* 403-262-7011
www.dwmlaw.ca

***Calgary*: Dawe Law Office - *3**
#200, 1409 Edmonton Trail NE, Calgary, AB T2E 3K8
Tel: 403-277-3100; *Fax:* 403-230-5855
info@dawelawoffice.com

***Calgary*: Demiantschuk, Lequier, Burke & Hoffinger - *10**
Also Known As: DLBH LLP Barristers & Solicitors
#1200, 1015 - 4th St. SW, Calgary, AB T2R 1J4
Tel: 403-252-9937; *Fax:* 403-263-8529
assistance@legalsolutions.ca
www.legalsolutions.ca

***Calgary*: Balfour Q.H. Der, Q.C. - *1**
#2410, 645 - 7 Ave. SW, Calgary, AB T2P 4G8
Tel: 403-234-8824; *Fax:* 403-261-8977
bqhder@telus.net

***Calgary*: Dixon Law Firm - *2**
#1020, Canadian Centre, 833 - 4 Ave. SW, Calgary, AB T2P 3T5
Tel: 403-297-9480; *Fax:* 403-266-1487

***Calgary*: Docken & Company - *3**
#900, 800 - 6th Ave. SW, Calgary, AB T2P 3G3
Tel: 403-269-3612; *Fax:* 403-269-8246
info@docken.com
www.docken.com

***Calgary*: Dunphy Best Blocksom LLP, Barristers & Solicitors - *20**
#2100, 777 - 8th Ave. SW, Calgary, AB T2P 3R5
Tel: 403-265-7777; *Fax:* 403-269-8911
info@dbblaw.com
www.dbblaw.com

***Calgary*: Edy, Dalton - *6**
#800, 1015 - 4 St. SW, Calgary, AB T2R 1J4
Tel: 403-263-3200; *Fax:* 403-263-3202
reception@edydalton.com; sjdalton@edydalton.com
www.edydalton.com

***Calgary*: Ellert Law - *2**
#510, 706 - 7 Ave. SW, Calgary, AB T2P 0Z1
Tel: 403-269-3315; *Fax:* 403-269-3329
dale.ellert@ellertlaw.com

***Calgary*: P. Robert Enns - *1**
#222, 1100 - 8 Ave. SW, Calgary, AB T2P 3T9
Tel: 403-262-6588; *Fax:* 403-262-6590
prenns@shaw.ca

***Calgary*: Everard Kubitz & Mueller - *3**
Former Name: Everard & Kubitz
#308, 2116 - 27 Ave. NE, Calgary, AB T2E 7A6
Tel: 403-250-7100; *Fax:* 403-291-5473
lawyers@ekmlawyers.com

***Calgary*: Faber Bickman Leon - *7**
Former Name: Faber Gurevitch Bickman
#350, 603 - 7 Ave. SW, Calgary, AB T2P 2T5
Tel: 403-263-1540; *Fax:* 403-269-2653
lfaber@fbllaw.ca; dbickman@fbllaw.ca; lleon@fbllaw.ca
www.fbllaw.ca

***Calgary*: Fagan & Chow - *2**
#375, 926 - 5th Ave. SW, Calgary, AB T2P 0N7
Tel: 403-517-1777; *Fax:* 403-517-1776
davidg_chow@yahoo.ca
www.patrickfagan.com

***Calgary*: Felesky Flynn LLP - *33**
#5000, Suncor Energy, 150 - 6th Ave. SW, Calgary, AB T2P 3Y7
Tel: 403-260-3300; *Fax:* 403-263-9649
felesky@felesky.com
www.felesky.com

***Calgary*: P.L. Fiess - *1**
#312, 602 - 11 Ave. SW, Calgary, AB T2R 1J8
Tel: 403-266-0033; *Fax:* 403-261-4958
phillfeiss@hotmail.com

***Calgary*: Fleishman-Hillard Canada Inc. - *1**
#1410, 540 - 5th St. SW, Calgary, AB T2P 0M2
Tel: 403-266-4710;
www.fleishman.ca

***Calgary*: Fleming LLP, Barristers & Solicitors - *10**
Former Name: Fleming, Kambeitz LLP
#900, 926 - 5th Ave. SW, Calgary, AB T2P 0N7
Tel: 403-266-5550; *Fax:* 403-265-6910
Toll-Free: 877-566-5550
www.flemingllp.com

***Calgary*: Fric, Lowenstein & Co. LLP - *4**
#310, 2891 Sunridge Way, Calgary, AB T1Y 7K7
Tel: 403-291-2594; *Fax:* 403-291-2668
friclow@telusplanet.net

***Calgary*: Gaetano & Associates - *1**
327 Kincora Heights NW, Calgary, AB T3R 1N3
Tel: 403-730-3474; *Fax:* 403-730-3471
jdgaetano@shaw.ca

***Calgary*: German Fong Albus, Barristers & Solicitors - *3**
#418, Hewlett Packard Bldg., 715 - 5 Ave. SW, Calgary, AB T2P 2X6
Tel: 403-263-7880; *Fax:* 403-237-7075
mjfong@gfal-law.com; sfalbus@gfal-law.com
www.gfal-law.com

***Calgary*: Global Public Affairs Inc.**
#460, 800 - 6th Ave. SW, Calgary, AB T2P 3G3
Tel: 403-264-3800; *Fax:* 403-264-3808
kanderson@globalpublic.com
www.globalpublicaffairs.ca

***Calgary*: The Law Firm of W. Donald Goodfellow, Q.C. - *3**
#715, 999 - 8th St. SW, Calgary, AB T2R 1J5
Tel: 403-228-7102; *Fax:* 403-228-7199
wdonald@goodfellowqc.com; pbiggar@goodfellowqc.com
www.goodfellowqc.com

***Calgary*: Gorman, Gorman, Burns & Watson - *2**
#500, 1135 - 17 Ave. SW, Calgary, AB T2T 0B6
Tel: 403-244-5515; *Fax:* 403-244-5605

***Calgary*: David M. Gottlieb, Law Office - *1**
#8, 5602 - 4 St. NW, Calgary, AB T2K 1B2
Tel: 403-275-4881; *Fax:* 403-274-0367
gottlieb.david@telusplanet.net

***Calgary*: A.F.W. Grenon - *1**
#200, 1210 - 11th Ave. SW, Calgary, AB T3C 0M4
Tel: 403-571-4450; *Fax:* 403-571-4444

***Calgary*: Hadley & Davis - *2**
#311, 1711 - 4 St. SW, Calgary, AB T2S 1V8
Tel: 403-264-1234; *Fax:* 403-264-0999
info@hadleydavis.com
www.hadleydavis.com

***Calgary*: Bryan F. Hagel - *1**
#23, 2451 Dieppe Ave. SW, Calgary, AB T3E 7K1
Tel: 403-243-8360; *Fax:* 403-287-3008
bryanfhagel@yahoo.ca

***Calgary*: Hansen & Company - *2**
538 - 9 Ave. SE, Calgary, AB T2G 0S1
Tel: 403-261-6890; *Fax:* 403-263-1632
Toll-Free: 800-523-6162
info@hansen-company.com
www.hansen-company.com

***Calgary*: Larry S. Heald - *1**
#300, 840 - 6 Ave. SW, Calgary, AB T2P 3E5
Tel: 403-266-2131; *Fax:* 403-261-6862
heald@shaw.ca

***Calgary*: Stephen Graham Heinz - *1**
#2900, 350 - 7 Ave. SW, Calgary, AB T2P 3N9
Tel: 403-262-4462; *Fax:* 403-265-4496
stephen.heinz@3web.net

***Calgary*: Hill & Knowlton Strategies Canada**
Also Known As: Hill & Knowlton Calgary
#300, Watermark Tower, 530 - 8th Ave. SW, Calgary, AB T2P 3S8
Tel: 403-299-9380; *Fax:* 403-299-9389
www.hkstrategies.ca/calgary-public-relations

***Calgary*: Michael M. Jamison - *1**
2503 - 22 St. SW, Calgary, AB T2T 5G3
Tel: 403-217-1250; *Fax:* 403-287-1968
mmjlaw2@shaw.ca

***Calgary*: Jensen Shawa Solomon Duguid Hawkes LLP - *20**
Former Name: May Jensen Shawa Solomon LLP
#800, Lancaster Bldg., 304 - 8 Ave. SW, Calgary, AB T2P 1C2
Tel: 403-571-1520; *Fax:* 403-571-1528
inquiries@jssbarristers.ca
www.jssbarristers.ca

***Calgary*: Jivraj Knight & Pritchett, Barristers & Solicitors - *3**
Also Known As: JKP Barristers & Solicitors
#1000, 444 - 5 Ave. SW, Calgary, AB T2P 2T8
Tel: 403-261-0017; *Fax:* 403-266-6030
mailbox@jkp-law.com; knight@JKP-Law.com;
jivraj@JKP-Law.com
www.jkp-law.com

***Calgary*: Kelly & Kelly - *4**
#220, 3505 - 32nd St. NE, Calgary, AB T1Y 5Y9
Tel: 403-266-6296; *Fax:* 403-264-2954
kellykp@telusplanet.net; tjolliff@telusplanet.net

***Calgary*: Robert D. Kerr - *1**
#300, 840 - 6 Ave. SW, Calgary, AB T2P 3E5
Tel: 403-265-1331; *Fax:* 403-265-1332
bkerr@shaw.ca

***Calgary*: Jack A. King, Q.C. - *1**
10 Forest Grove Pl. SE, Calgary, AB T2A 7G6
Tel: 403-235-4600

***Calgary*: George R. Klatt - *1**
#400, Centre 70, 7015 Macleod Trail SW, Calgary, AB T2H 2K6
Tel: 403-255-3033; *Fax:* 403-255-0403

***Calgary*: Kuefler & Company - *3**
#012, 601 - 10th Ave. SW, Calgary, AB T2R 0B2
Tel: 403-237-0123; *Fax:* 403-237-0128
quinn.kuefler@kueflerlaw.com

***Calgary*: Laird, Armstrong, Barristers & Solicitors - *4**
#870, 234 - 5149 Country Hills Blvd. NW, Calgary, AB T3A 5K8
Tel: 403-233-0050; *Fax:* 403-266-1238
inquiries@lairdarmstrong.com
www.lairdarmstrong.com

** indicates number of lawyers*

Calgary: **Catherine G. Langlois - *1**
#2410, 645 - 7 Ave. SW, Calgary, AB T2P 4G8
Tel: 403-531-9300; *Fax:* 403-261-8977
civillaw@telus.net

Calgary: **Lauzon Law Office - *1**
#218, 5403 Crowchild Trail NW, Calgary, AB T3B 4Z1
Tel: 403-288-7601; *Fax:* 403-288-3689

Calgary: **Laven & Company, Legal Counsel - *3**
#900, McFarlane Tower, 700 - 4th Ave. SW, Calgary, AB T2P 3J4
Tel: 403-263-2444; *Fax:* 403-265-1792
www.lavenco.com

Calgary: **Lee & Kong - *2**
#330, 1324 - 17 Ave. SW, Calgary, AB T2T 5S8
Tel: 403-233-9432; *Fax:* 403-237-9614
leekong@canada.com

Calgary: **Corinna Lee - *1**
509 - 20th Ave. SW, Calgary, AB T2S 0E7
Tel: 403-228-2238; *Fax:* 403-228-5550

Calgary: **Lehan, Menzies, Walters & Abdi - *6**
9937 Fairmount Dr. SE, Calgary, AB T2J 0S2
Tel: 403-261-4010; *Fax:* 403-261-4040

Calgary: **Lenhardt Law Office - *1**
#301, 888 - 7 Ave. SW, Calgary, AB T2P 3J3
Tel: 403-237-6970; *Fax:* 403-237-6974

Calgary: **Lirenman, Peterson - *3**
#300, Notre Dame Place, 255 - 17 Ave. SW, Calgary, AB T2S 2T8
Tel: 403-245-0111; *Fax:* 403-245-0115

Calgary: **Lord Russell - *6**
410 - 6th St. SW, Calgary, AB T2P 1X2
Tel: 403-262-7722; *Fax:* 403-262-5991
simonl@telus.net; vicruss@telus.net

Calgary: **Low, Glenn & Card - *6**
#120, 3636 - 23 St. NE, Calgary, AB T2E 8Z5
Tel: 403-291-2532; *Fax:* 403-291-2534
lawyer@lgc-law.com

Calgary: **Machida Mack Shewchuk Meagher LLP - *6**
#1300, 707 - 7th Ave. SW, Calgary, AB T2P 3H6
Tel: 403-221-8333; *Fax:* 403-221-8339
nmachida@mmsmlawyers.com

Calgary: **Birjinder P.S. Mangat**
#217, 3825 - 34 St. NE, Calgary, AB T1Y 6Z8
Tel: 403-735-6088; *Fax:* 403-735-6089
bmangat@cadvision.com

Calgary: **Masuch, Albert LLP - *9**
Former Name: Masuch, Albert & Neale LLP
#209, 10836 - 24 St. SE, Calgary, AB T2Z 4C9
Tel: 403-543-1100; *Fax:* 403-543-1111
www.manlaw.com

Calgary: **McCaffery Mudry Pritchard LLP, Barristers & Solicitors - *7**
Former Name: McCaffery Goss Mudry LLP
#2200, 736 - 6 Ave. SW, Calgary, AB T2P 3T7
Tel: 403-260-1400; *Fax:* 403-260-1444
postmaster@mccafferylaw.ca
www.mccafferylaw.ca

Calgary: **McConnell MacInnes - *7**
Former Name: McConnell, MacInnes, Graham
1245 - 70 Ave. SE, Calgary, AB T2H 2X8
Tel: 403-278-7001; *Fax:* 403-271-2826
kfm@mcmaclaw.com; jrm@mcmaclaw.com

Calgary: **McGown Johnson - *4**
#120, 7260 - 12th St. SE, Calgary, AB T2H 2S5
Tel: 403-255-5114; *Fax:* 403-258-3840

Calgary: **McKenna Law Office - *1**
1505 - 5 St. SW, Calgary, AB T2R 1P2
Tel: 403-716-2092; *Fax:* 403-234-7911
paul@mckennalegal.com

Calgary: **McKinnon Carstairs - *2**
#525, First Alberta Place, 777 - 8 Ave. SW, Calgary, AB T2P 3R5
Tel: 403-261-8822; *Fax:* 403-261-4892
rlmckinnon@mckinnoncarstairs.com

Calgary: **McLeod & Company LLP - *37**
14505 Bannister Rd. SE, 3rd Fl., Calgary, AB T2X 3J3
Tel: 403-278-9411; *Fax:* 403-271-1769
pnbreen@mcleod-law.com; tmcarswell@mcleod-law.com
www.mcleod-law.com

Calgary: **McManus & Hubler - *2**
63 Rockcliff Landing NW, Calgary, AB T3G 5Z5
Tel: 403-208-6099; *Fax:* 403-208-6018
Toll-Free: 877-423-6054
sean@mcmanus-hubler.ca
www.mcmanus-hubler.ca

Calgary: **Anne E. McTavish - *1**
7410E - 5th St. SE, Calgary, AB T2H 2L9
Tel: 403-252-4965; *Fax:* 403-253-7743
anne.mctavish@telusplanet.net

Calgary: **Miles, Davison LLP - *24**
Former Name: Miles, Davison, McCarthy; McNiven Kelly
#1600, Bow Valley Square II, 205 - 5th Ave. SW, Calgary, AB T2P 2V7
Tel: 403-298-0333; *Fax:* 403-263-6840
thefirm@milesdavison.com
www.milesdavison.com

Calgary: **Millar Smith & Associates, Barristers, Solicitors, Notaries - *1**
#300, 1130 Kensington Rd. NW, Calgary, AB T2N 3P3
Tel: 403-283-1925; *Fax:* 403-270-8033
millar.associates@shaw.ca
www.wes-law.com

Calgary: **Milne, Davis & Young - *2**
#850, 933 - 17th Ave. SW, Calgary, AB T2T 5R6
Tel: 403-229-3000; *Fax:* 403-229-3282
milnedavisyoung@shaw.ca

Calgary: **MNP LLP**
715 5th Ave. S.W., 7th Fl., Calgary, AB T2P 2X6
Tel: 403-444-0150;
www.mnp.ca

Calgary: **Moore Wittman Phillips - *6**
#850, 1015 - 4 St. SW, Calgary, AB T2R 1J4
Tel: 403-269-8500; *Fax:* 403-269-8515
mwp@nucleus.com

Calgary: **Maureen Morgan - *1**
#206, P.O. Box 73001, Stn. RPO Woodbine, 2525 Woodview Dr. SW, Calgary, AB T2W 6E4
Tel: 403-233-2215; *Fax:* 403-264-1328
maureenmorgan96@hotmail.com

Calgary: **Richard W. Muenz - *1**
#2410, 645 - 7 Ave. SW, Calgary, AB T2P 4G8
Tel: 403-543-6666; *Fax:* 403-261-8977
rwmuenz@telus.net

Calgary: **Munro & Wood, Barristers & Solicitors - *2**
#500, 2424 - 4 St. SW, Calgary, AB T2S 2T4
Tel: 403-299-9285; *Fax:* 403-228-1389
katewood@telus.net
www.munrowood.ca

Calgary: **Murray & Company - *1**
#104, 2003 - 14 St. NW, Calgary, AB T2M 3N4
Tel: 403-297-9850; *Fax:* 403-297-9855
murraywg@shaw.ca

Calgary: **North Hill Law Office - *1**
P.O. Box 32053, Stn. RPO Bankview, 2619 - 14 St. SW, Calgary, AB T2T 5X6
Tel: 403-282-1515; *Fax:* 403-220-1575
oldmanncuba@hotmail.com

Calgary: **O'Brien, Devlin, Markey & Macleod, Barristers & Solicitors - *3**
#1310, Watermark Tower, 530 - 8th Ave. SW, Calgary, AB T2P 3S8
Tel: 403-265-5616; *Fax:* 403-264-8146
nobrien@obriendevlin.com; bdevlin@obriendevlin.com
www.obriendevlin.com

Calgary: **Olson Lemons LLP, Barristers & Solicitors - *6**
744 - 4 Ave. SW, 10th Fl., Calgary, AB T2P 3T4
Tel: 403-974-3400; *Fax:* 403-974-3427
hr@olsonlemons.com (Human Resources)
www.olsonlemons.com

Calgary: **Ouellette, Rice - *2**
Former Name: Clayton A. Rice
#425, 630 - 6 Ave. SW, Calgary, AB T2P 0S8
Tel: 403-263-3855; *Fax:* 403-265-5855
oullette-rice@telusplanet.net

Calgary: **Parlee McLaws LLP - *82**
#3400, Suncor Energy Centre, 150 - 6th Ave. SW, Calgary, AB T2P 3Y7
Tel: 403-294-7000; *Fax:* 403-265-8263
lawyers@parlee.com
www.parlee.com

Calgary: **Peterson, Shields, & Galbraith - *6**
Former Name: Peterson, Shields, Milen, Mullen & Galbraith
#204, 755 Lake Bonavista Dr. SE, Calgary, AB T2J 0N3
Tel: 403-271-9710; *Fax:* 403-271-3942
info@petersonshields.com; rmp@petersonshields.com

Calgary: **Phipps Law Office - *1**
#303, 8180 MacLeod Trail SE, Calgary, AB T2H 2B8
Tel: 403-531-0182; *Fax:* 403-531-0180

Calgary: **Pittman MacIsaac & Roy - *4**
#2600, West Tower, Sun Life Plaza, 144 - 4th Ave. SW, Calgary, AB T2P 3N4
Tel: 403-237-6566; *Fax:* 403-237-6594
www.pmrlaw.ca

Calgary: **Pomerance & Company - *3**
#1430, 1122 - 4th St. SW, Calgary, AB T2R 1M1
Tel: 403-278-5840; *Fax:* 403-271-6929
Toll-Free: 866-278-5840
pomeranc@telus.net
www.pomerancelaw.ca

Calgary: **Lawrence S. Portigal - *1**
6638 Bow Cres. NW, Calgary, AB T3B 2B9
Tel: 403-286-6380; *Fax:* 403-286-6821
lportig@yahoo.com

Calgary: **PricewaterhouseCoopers LLP - *3**
#3100, Petro-Canada Centre, 111 - 5th Ave. SW, Calgary, AB T2P 0M9
Tel: 403-509-7500; *Fax:* 403-781-1825
www.pwc.com/ca

Calgary: **ProVenture Law LLP - *4**
#2, Mount Royal Village, 880 - 16th Ave. SW, Calgary, AB T2R 1J9
Tel: 403-294-5710; *Fax:* 403-262-4860
www.proventurelaw.com

Calgary: **Purdy & Purdy - *2**
#801, 1015 - 4th St. SW, Calgary, AB T2R 1J4
Tel: 403-777-4850; *Fax:* 403-777-4855

Calgary: **Radke & Associates - *2**
#205, 5917 - 1A St. SW, Calgary, AB T2H 0G4
Tel: 403-252-4466; *Fax:* 403-258-0695
radkelaw@telus.net; lisakerwin@radkeandassociates.com
www.radkeandassociates.com

Calgary: **Rae & Company, Barristers, Solicitors, Notaries Public - *3**
#2910, 715 - 5 Ave. SW, Calgary, AB T2P 2X6
Tel: 403-264-8389; *Fax:* 403-264-8399
mfandrick@raeandcompany.com;
jmlemieux@raeandcompany.com
www.raeandcompany.com

Calgary: **Reich Nichol - *2**
Former Name: Reich Underwood
#226, 4935 - 40 Ave. NW, Calgary, AB T3A 2N1
Tel: 403-288-6500; *Fax:* 403-288-6510
jimreich@telusplanet.net; blake.nichol@telus.net

Calgary: **Riccio Law - *2**
#100, 4103B Centre St. North, Calgary, AB T2E 2Y6
Tel: 403-289-3131; *Fax:* 403-289-2396
ariccio@shaw.ca; jsymonds@shawcable.com
www.nvo.com/riccio

Calgary: **Rogers & Company, Barristers & Solicitors**
#200, 815 - 10 Ave. SW, Calgary, AB T2R 0B4
Tel: 403-263-6805; *Fax:* 403-263-6800

Calgary: **Ross, Hepner - *4**
921 - 18 Ave. SW, Calgary, AB T2T 0H2
Tel: 403-244-6800; *Fax:* 403-265-2455
rosslk@shaw.ca; hepnera@telusplanet.net

** indicates number of lawyers*

***Calgary*: A. Charles Ruff - *1**
#202, 1409 Edmonton Trail NE, Calgary, AB T2E 3K8
Tel: 403-230-0999; *Fax:* 403-230-0991
chasruff@shaw.ca

***Calgary*: Salmon & Company - *2**
#1100, 707 - 7 Ave. SW, Calgary, AB T2P 3H6
Tel: 403-231-2705; *Fax:* 403-705-1214
david@salmonco.ca

***Calgary*: Schwartzberg Law Office - *1**
3923 - 17 Ave. SW, Calgary, AB T3E 0C3
Tel: 403-232-1302; *Fax:* 403-249-6655
schwartzberglaw@shawcable.com

***Calgary*: Scott Venturo LLP - *22**
#203, Eau Claire Market, 200 Barclay Parade SW, Calgary, AB T2P 4R5
Tel: 403-261-9043; *Fax:* 403-265-4632
Toll-Free: 877-505-5651
www.scottventuro.com

***Calgary*: Sefcik & Company - *1**
Former Name: Douglas M. Sefcik
#212, 20 Sunpark Plaza SE, Calgary, AB T2X 3T2
Tel: 403-258-1124; *Fax:* 403-640-1220

***Calgary*: William J. Shachnowich - *1**
1700 Varsity Estates Dr. NW, Calgary, AB T3B 2W9
Tel: 403-269-1313; *Fax:* 403-210-0106
shachnow@telus.net

***Calgary*: Shea Nerland Calnan LLP - *16**
#2800, 715 - 5th Ave. SW, Calgary, AB T2P 2X6
Tel: 403-299-9600; *Fax:* 403-299-9601
snc@snclaw.com
www.snclaw.com

***Calgary*: Shennette Leuschner McKay - *7**
#710, 909 - 11th Ave. SW, Calgary, AB T2R 1L7
Tel: 403-269-8282; *Fax:* 403-269-8295
louise@slmfamilylaw.ca; hlmckay@slmfamilylaw.ca

***Calgary*: Smith & Smith - *2**
#503, 1300 - 8 St. SW, Calgary, AB T2R 1B2
Tel: 403-229-1727; *Fax:* 403-229-1730

***Calgary*: Smith Law Office - *1**
348 - 14 St. NW, Calgary, AB T2N 1Z7
Tel: 403-283-8018; *Fax:* 403-270-3065
j.smith@smithlawoffice.ca

***Calgary*: Smith Mack Lamarsh - *3**
#450, United Place, 808 - 4 Ave. SW, Calgary, AB T2P 3E8
Tel: 403-234-7779; *Fax:* 403-263-7897
cmsmith@telusplanet.net; slamarsh@telusplanet.net

***Calgary*: W. Murray Smith - *1**
348 - 14 St. NW, Calgary, AB T2N 1Z7
Tel: 403-283-8018; *Fax:* 403-270-3065

***Calgary*: Sparrow Law Office - *1**
#10, 628 - 12 Ave. SW, Calgary, AB T2R 0H6
Tel: 403-234-9722; *Fax:* 403-237-8748
sparrow@nucleus.com

***Calgary*: Spier Harben - *11**
#1400, Iveagh House, 707 - 7th St. SW, Calgary, AB T2P 3H6
Tel: 403-263-5130; *Fax:* 403-264-9600
asattin@spierharben.com

***Calgary*: Stephens Holman Devraj - *2**
Former Name: Stephens & Holman
412 - 16th Ave. NE, Calgary, AB T2E 1K2
Tel: 403-265-6400; *Fax:* 403-262-9294
rishmad@shdlawyers.ca
www.shdlawyers.ca

***Calgary*: Stewart & McCullough - *4**
#307, 1228 Kensington Rd. NW, Calgary, AB T2N 3P7
Tel: 403-270-2641; *Fax:* 403-670-7025
martin.meronek@shaw.ca

***Calgary*: Peter A. Stone - *1**
Former Name: Paterson Foster
1923 - 5th St. SW, Calgary, AB T2S 2B2
Tel: 403-283-8460; *Fax:* 403-283-8461
pstone@telusplanet.net

***Calgary*: Stones Carbert Waite Wells LLP - *14**
Former Name: Stones Carbert Waite LLP
#2000, Encor Place, 645 - 7th Ave. SW, Calgary, AB T2P 4G8
Tel: 403-263-5656; *Fax:* 403-263-5553
info@scwlawyers.com
www.scwlawyers.com

***Calgary*: Story Law Office - *1**
#240, 3015 - 12 St. NE, Calgary, AB T2E 7J2
Tel: 403-250-1918; *Fax:* 403-250-3287

***Calgary*: Sugimoto & Company - *5**
#204, 2635 - 37 Ave. NE, Calgary, AB T1Y 5Z6
Tel: 403-291-4650; *Fax:* 403-291-4099
sugimoto@sugimotolaw.com

***Calgary*: Nancy A. Swanby - *1**
#700, One Executive Place, 1816 Crowchild Trail NW, Calgary, AB T2M 3Y7
Tel: 403-520-5455; *Fax:* 403-220-1389
nancy@swanby.com

***Calgary*: Szabo & Company, Barristers & Solicitors**
#400, 1111 - 11th Ave. SW, Calgary, AB T2R 0G5
Tel: 403-229-1111; *Fax:* 403-245-0569
Toll-Free: 866-229-0717
info@szaboco.com
www.szaboco.com

***Calgary*: Michael J. Tadman - *1**
#10, 628 - 12 Ave. SW, Calgary, AB T2R 0H6
Tel: 403-234-9722; *Fax:* 403-237-8748
tadman@nucleus.com

***Calgary*: M.S. Takada - *1**
#200, 604 - 1 St. SW, Calgary, AB T2P 1M7
Tel: 403-234-9477; *Fax:* 403-261-1839

***Calgary*: Taylor Conway - *2**
Former Name: Taylor, Zinkhofer & Conway
#440, 7220 Fisher St. SE, Calgary, AB T2H 2H8
Tel: 403-259-4028; *Fax:* 403-640-0103

***Calgary*: Thackray Burgess - *34**
#1900, 736 - 6 Ave. SW, Calgary, AB T2P 3T7
Tel: 403-531-4700; *Fax:* 403-531-4720

***Calgary*: Thompson, Ball & McMahon - *2**
Former Name: Thompson, Ball & Associates
#534, 11012 Macleod Trail SE, Calgary, AB T2J 6A5
Tel: 403-271-5050; *Fax:* 403-271-5298
thompsonball@telus.net; jpmcm@telus.net

***Calgary*: Thornborough, Smeltz - *4**
Former Name: Thornborough, Smeltz, Gillis & Mebs
#630, Southcentre Executive Tower, 11012 Macleod Trail SE, Calgary, AB T2J 6A5
Tel: 403-271-3221; *Fax:* 403-271-6684
tammy@thornsmeltz.com

***Calgary*: TingleMerrett LLP, Barristers & Solicitors - *12**
#1250, Standard Life Bldg., 639 - 5th Ave. SW, Calgary, AB T2P 0M9
Tel: 403-571-8000; *Fax:* 403-571-8008
cmerrett@tinglemerrett.com; dallison@tinglemerrett.com
www.tinglemerrett.com

***Calgary*: Richard T. Tumanon - *1**
#301, 5555 Falsbridge Dr. NE, Calgary, AB T3J 3E8
Tel: 403-262-3841; *Fax:* 403-269-7173

***Calgary*: Van Harten Foster Iovinellis - *6**
#1206, 734 - 7 Ave. SW, Calgary, AB T2P 3P8
Tel: 403-269-3655; *Fax:* 403-237-5109
hmvh@shaw.ca; vofi@shaw.ca; roadlawyers@shaw.ca

***Calgary*: Vickers & Associates - *3**
#600, 805 - 10th Ave. SW, Calgary, AB T2R 0B4
Tel: 403-269-9400; *Fax:* 403-266-2447
hvickers@vickerassoc.com; dhendrix@vickersassoc.com

***Calgary*: Vinci, Phillips - *2**
1509 - 26 Ave. SW, Calgary, AB T2T 1C4
Tel: 403-265-4323; *Fax:* 403-262-8087

***Calgary*: Walsh Wilkins Creighton LLP - *18**
#2800, 801 - 6 Ave. SW, Calgary, AB T2P 4A3
Tel: 403-267-8400; *Fax:* 403-264-9400
mail@wwclawyers.com
www.wwclawyers.com

***Calgary*: Samuel D.C. Wan - *1**
191 Edgepark Way NW, Calgary, AB T3A 4T2
Tel: 403-973-0678

***Calgary*: Peter M. Ward - *1**
#300, 400 - 5th Ave. SW, Calgary, AB T2P 0L6
Tel: 403-263-1158; *Fax:* 403-264-9218

***Calgary*: Warren Tettensor Amantea LLP - *12**
1413 - 2nd St. SW, Calgary, AB T2R 0W7
Tel: 403-228-7007; *Fax:* 403-244-1948
info@warren.ab.ca
www.warren.ab.ca

***Calgary*: Peggy A. Wedderburn - *1**
#16, 2439 - 54th Ave. SW, Calgary, AB T3E 1M4
Tel: 403-242-8081; *Fax:* 403-246-2055
pwedderburn@shaw.ca

***Calgary*: West End Legal Centre - *1**
1705 - 10th Ave. SW, Calgary, AB T3C 0K1
Tel: 403-249-5297; *Fax:* 403-249-5001
welc@telusplanet.net

***Calgary*: White & Company - *2**
#204, 3716 - 61 Ave. SE, Calgary, AB T2C 1Z4
Tel: 403-236-2110; *Fax:* 403-279-4842

***Calgary*: Wilson Laycraft - *10**
#1601, 333 - 11th Ave. SW, Calgary, AB T2R 1L9
Tel: 403-290-1601; *Fax:* 403-290-0828
reception@wilcraft.com
www.wilcraft.com

***Calgary*: Dawn M. Wilson - *1**
44 Bow Village Cres. NW, Calgary, AB T3B 4X2
Tel: 403-247-9090; *Fax:* 403-247-9090

***Calgary*: Wise Walden Barkauskas - *5**
Former Name: Foster, Wise & Walden
#600, 700 - 4 Ave. SW, Calgary, AB T2P 3J4
Tel: 403-263-6601; *Fax:* 403-269-6785
jdwise@divorceinc.com; mewalden@divorceinc.com
www.wisedivorce.com; www.divorceinc.com

***Calgary*: Stephen R. Wojcik - *1**
604 - 1 St. SW, 2nd Fl., Calgary, AB T2P 1M7
Tel: 403-547-4415; *Fax:* 403-208-0717
wojicks@shaw.ca

***Calgary*: Wolch, Hursh, deWit & Watts - *4**
Former Name: Wolch, Ogle, Wilson, Hursh & deWit
#1500, 633 - 6 Ave. SW, Calgary, AB T2P 2Y5
Tel: 403-265-6500; *Fax:* 403-263-1111
hersh@wolch.com; lhursh@shawcable.com;
wtdewit@shawcable.com

***Calgary*: Wolfman & Company - *2**
#700, 640 - 8th Ave. SW, Calgary, AB T2P 1G7
Tel: 403-263-6710; *Fax:* 403-266-1896
info@wolfmanlaw.com

***Calgary*: David I. Wolfman - *1**
Former Name: Wolfman Ryder Barristers & Solicitors
328 Pumphill Gardens SW, Calgary, AB T2V 4M7
Tel: 403-266-4433; *Fax:* 403-266-4433
thewolfmans@telus.net

***Calgary*: Yanko & Popovic Law Firm - *2**
Former Name: Yanko & Company
#302, 325 - 25 St. SE, Calgary, AB T2A 7H8
Tel: 403-262-0262; *Fax:* 403-204-0284

***Calgary*: Youth Criminal Defence Office - *9**
#600, 444 - 5 Ave. SW, Calgary, AB T2P 2T8
Tel: 403-297-4400; *Fax:* 403-297-4201
sfellger@ycdo.ca

***Calgary*: Zenith Hookenson LLP**
#218, Mayfair Place, 6707 Elbow Dr. SW, Calgary, AB T2V 0E4
Tel: 403-259-5041; *Fax:* 403-258-0719

***Calgary*: Jeffrey C. Zhang - *1**
#512, 206 - 7 Ave. SW, Calgary, AB T2P 0W7
Tel: 403-465-5632; *Fax:* 403-265-1645

***Calgary*: Zinner & Sara - *2**
#145, 1935 - 32 Ave. NE, Calgary, AB T2E 7C8
Tel: 403-262-7363; *Fax:* 403-233-0392

***Camrose*: Andreassen Borth, Barristers, Solicitors, Notaries, Mediators - *4**
Former Name: Andreassen Olson Borth
#200, 4870 - 51 St., Camrose, AB T4V 1S1
Tel: 780-672-3181; *Fax:* 780-672-0682
aob@telusplanet.net
www.andreassenolsonborth.com

** indicates number of lawyers*

Camrose: Farnham West Stolee LLP - *3
Former Name: Farnham, Ziebart
5016 - 52 St., Camrose, AB T4V 1V7
Tel: 780-679-0444; *Fax:* 780-679-0958
camlaw@telusplanet.net

Camrose: Fielding & Company LLP - *4
#100, 4918 - 51 St., Camrose, AB T4V 1S3
Tel: 780-672-8851; *Fax:* 780-672-4707
lawyers@camroselaw.com
www.camroselaw.com

Camrose: Knaut, Johnson - *2
4925 - 51 St., Camrose, AB T4V 1S4
Tel: 780-672-5561; *Fax:* 780-672-5565

Canmore: Canmore Legal Services - *1
Also Known As: Schneider Law Office
909A Railway Ave., Canmore, AB T1W 1P3
Tel: 403-678-9818; *Fax:* 403-609-2333
johnschneider@shaw.ca

Canmore: Tannis J. Naylor - *1
826B - 10th St., Canmore, AB T1W 2A7
Tel: 403-678-5777; *Fax:* 403-678-5679
t_naylor@telus.net

Canmore: Peter Perren - *1
726 - 10 St., Canmore, AB T1W 2A6
Tel: 403-678-6988; *Fax:* 403-678-5952
pperren@telusplanet.net

Canmore: Rencz & Docking - *2
#225, 1001 - 6th Ave., Canmore, AB T1W 3L8
Tel: 403-678-5823; *Fax:* 403-678-4890
www.canmorelawyer.com

Carstairs: Stiles & Naqi - *2
Former Name: Stiles Law Office
P.O. Box 790, 209 - 10th Ave. South, Carstairs, AB T0M 0N0
Tel: 403-337-3357; *Fax:* 403-337-3359

Chestermere: Karl H.H. Trobst - *1
368 West Chestermere Dr., Chestermere, AB T1X 1B3
Tel: 403-272-1056;
karltrobst@hotmail.com

Coaldale: Leonard D. Fast - *1
P.O. Box 1360, Stn. Main, 1709 - 20 Ave., Coaldale, AB T1M 1N2
Tel: 403-345-4415; *Fax:* 403-345-2719
lfastlaw@telusplanet.net

Coaldale: Lammi Law - *1
P.O. Box 1329, Stn. Main, 1910 - 18 St., Coaldale, AB T1M 1N1
Tel: 403-345-3922; *Fax:* 403-345-2172
lammilaw@telusplanet.net

Cochrane: Fercho & Associates - *1
#14, 205 - 1 St. East, Cochrane, AB T4C 1X6
Tel: 403-932-4477; *Fax:* 403-932-4084
rfercho@lawyers.com

Cochrane: Franchi - Rothecker Law Office - *1
Former Name: Rothecker Law Office
629 - 2 St. West, Cochrane, AB T4C 1Z7
Tel: 403-932-3843; *Fax:* 403-932-3108
reception@rotheckerlaw.ca

Cochrane: Mabbott & Company, Barristers & Solicitors - *4
#5, 201 Grand Blvd., Cochrane, AB T4C 2G4
Tel: 403-932-3066; *Fax:* 403-932-3076
reception@mabbott.ca
www.mabbott.ca

Cold Lake: Todd & Drake LLP - *4
Former Name: Todd, Drake, Williams, Findlater LLP
P.O. Box 908, 4807 - 51 St., Cold Lake, AB T9M 1P2
Tel: 780-594-7151; *Fax:* 780-594-7155
Toll-Free: 877-594-7151
rmtodd@tdlaw.ca; ldrake@tdlaw.ca
www.tdlaw.cawww.facebook.com/pages/Todd-Drake-LLP/16833
9593224163, www.twitter.com/toddrakellp

Coronation: E. Roger Spady - *1
P.O. Box 328, 5015 Victoria Ave., Coronation, AB T0C 1C0
Tel: 403-578-3131; *Fax:* 403-578-2660

Daysland: Patricia E. Spencer - *1
P.O. Box 372, 5037 - 46 St., Daysland, AB T0B 1A0
Tel: 780-374-2199; *Fax:* 780-374-2259
spinner7@telus.net

Didsbury: Brian M. Forestell - *1
P.O. Box 625, 1701 - 20th Ave., Didsbury, AB T0M 0W0
Tel: 403-335-8491; *Fax:* 403-335-8589
briandid@telusplanet.net

Didsbury: Roy D. Shellnutt - *1
P.O. Box 898, 2021 - 19th Ave., Didsbury, AB T0M 0W0
Tel: 403-335-2145; *Fax:* 403-335-3185
shellnutlaw@hotmail.com

Drumheller: Ross, Todd & Company - *3
P.O. Box 970, 98 - 3 Ave. West, Drumheller, AB T0J 0Y0
Tel: 403-823-5186; *Fax:* 403-823-6407
reception@drumhellerlaw.com;
sharon.clark@drumhellerlaw.com

Drumheller: Schumacher, Gough & Company - *2
Former Name: Schumacher, Gough & Pedersen
P.O. Box 2800, 196 - 3rd Ave. West, Drumheller, AB T0J 0Y0
Tel: 403-823-2424; *Fax:* 403-823-6984
Toll-Free: 866-923-2424
sgp_law@telus.net; sgp_harry@telus.net

Edmonton: Abbey Hunter Davison - *4
Former Name: Abbey Hunter Davison Spencer
9636 - 102A Ave., Edmonton, AB T5H 0G5
Tel: 780-421-8585; *Fax:* 780-425-0472
dhabbey@shaw.ca

Edmonton: David R. Abbey - *1
#780, TransAlta Place, 10150 - 100 St. NW, Edmonton, AB T5J 0P6
Tel: 780-423-2793; *Fax:* 780-423-2750
dabbey@telus.net

Edmonton: Abells Regan - *2
Former Name: Elizabeth M. Regan
#950, Canadian Western Bank Place, 10303 Jasper Ave. NW, Edmonton, AB T5J 3N6
Tel: 780-442-4420; *Fax:* 780-424-9370
rsabells@abellsregan.com; emregan@abellsregan.com

Edmonton: Ackroyd LLP Barristers & Solicitors - *17
#1500, First Edmonton Place, 10665 Jasper Ave., Edmonton, AB T5J 3S9
Tel: 780-423-8905; *Fax:* 780-423-8946
aprd@ackroydlaw.com
www.ackroydlaw.com

Edmonton: Jack N. Agrios, Q.C., LL.B, O.C. - *1
#1325, Manulife Place, 10180 - 101 St., Edmonton, AB T5J 3S4
Tel: 780-696-6915; *Fax:* 780-969-6901
jack@jackagrios.com

Edmonton: Andrew, March & Oake - *9
#300, 10020 - 101A Ave. NW, Edmonton, AB T5J 3G2
Tel: 780-429-3391; *Fax:* 780-424-8483

Edmonton: Ares Law - *1
LeMarchand Tower, 11507 - 100 Ave., Edmonton, AB T5K 2R2
Tel: 780-488-1951; *Fax:* 780-482-6048

Edmonton: Attia, Reeves, Tensfeldt, Snow - *9
Former Name: Attia, Reeves
#200, 10525 Jasper Ave. NW, Edmonton, AB T5J 1Z4
Tel: 780-424-3334; *Fax:* 780-424-4252

Edmonton: Baker Purdon Caskenette - *2
Former Name: Baker & Purdon
10263 - 178 St., Edmonton, AB T5S 1M3
Tel: 780-489-5566; *Fax:* 780-486-7735
bpurdon@planet.eon.net

Edmonton: Barry Elgert Peddie - *3
Former Name: Barry, Elgert, Kraus & Peddie
10432 Jasper Ave. NW, Edmonton, AB T5J 1Z3
Tel: 780-429-3005; *Fax:* 780-425-8931
kpeddie@beplaw.ca

Edmonton: Dennis E. Bayrak - *1
#800, 10310 Jasper Ave. NW, Edmonton, AB T5J 2W4
Tel: 780-426-4884; *Fax:* 780-425-9358
bayrak@telus.net

Edmonton: Beresh Cunningham Aloneissi O'Neill Hurley - *10
Former Name: Beresh DePoe Cunningham
#300, MacLean Block, Box 300, 10110 - 107 St., Edmonton, AB T5J 1J4
Tel: 780-421-4766; *Fax:* 780-429-0346
Toll-Free: 877-277-4766
bdc@bdc.ca

Edmonton: Helmut Berndt - *1
Former Name: Berndt & Associates
#1780, 10020 - 101A Ave. NW, Edmonton, AB T5J 3G2
Tel: 780-439-6643; *Fax:* 780-439-6696

Edmonton: Bhalla Law Offices - *1
9360 - 34 Ave., Edmonton, AB T6E 5X8
Tel: 780-450-6155; *Fax:* 780-490-0116
rajiv@bhallalawoffice.com

Edmonton: Biamonte Cairo & Shortreed LLP - *13
#1600, 10025 - 102A Ave., Edmonton, AB T5J 2Z2
Tel: 780-425-5800; *Fax:* 780-426-1600
Toll-Free: 888-425-2620
biamonte@biamonte.com

Edmonton: Bishop & McKenzie LLP - *29
#2500, 10104 - 103 Ave., Edmonton, AB T5J 1V3
Tel: 780-426-5550; *Fax:* 780-426-1305
edmonton@bishopmckenzie.com
www.bishopmckenzie.com

Edmonton: Bitner & Associates Law Offices - *1
6932 Roper Rd. NW, Edmonton, AB T6B 3H9
Tel: 780-461-6633; *Fax:* 780-461-9239
www.bitnerlaw.com

Edmonton: Kerry A. Bjarnason - *1
#600, 9707 - 110 St., Edmonton, AB T5K 2L9
Tel: 780-433-4547; *Fax:* 780-482-6613
kbjarnason@telusplanet.net

Edmonton: Bosecke & Song LLP - *3
#306, 9945 - 50th St., Edmonton, AB T6A 0L4
Tel: 780-469-0494; *Fax:* 780-469-4181
firm@edmontonlaw.ca
www.edmontonlaw.ca

Edmonton: Braithwaite Boyle - *5
Braithwaite Boyle Bldg., 11816 - 124 St. NW, Edmonton, AB T5L 0M3
Tel: 780-451-9191; *Fax:* 780-451-9198
Toll-Free: 800-661-4902
ken.braithwaite@accidentinjurylawyer.com
www.accidentinjurylawyer.com

Edmonton: Braul McEvoy & Gee - *3
#2170, Sun Life Place, 10123 - 99 St., Edmonton, AB T5J 3H1
Tel: 780-423-2481; *Fax:* 780-423-2474
lawyers@braullaw.ab.ca

Edmonton: Broda & Company - *1
13723 - 93 St., Edmonton, AB T5E 5V6
Tel: 780-456-9330; *Fax:* 780-456-9339

Edmonton: Brosseau & Associates - *2
#1955, Commerce Place, 10155 - 102 St. NW, Edmonton, AB T5J 4G8
Tel: 780-426-4000; *Fax:* 780-424-4616

Edmonton: Brownlee LLP - *59
Former Name: Brownlee Fryett
#2200, Commerce Place, 10155 - 102 St., Edmonton, AB T5J 4G8
Tel: 780-497-4800; *Fax:* 780-424-3254
e-mail@brownleelaw.com
www.brownleelaw.com

Edmonton: Bryan & Company LLP - *38
#2600, Manulife Place, Box 2600, 10180 - 101 St., Edmonton, AB T5J 3Y2
Tel: 780-423-5730; *Fax:* 780-428-6324
Toll-Free: 800-357-9265
info@bryanco.com; djcorrigan@bryanco.com (Advocacy)
www.bryanco.com

Edmonton: Cameron & Cameron - *3
#390, 10187 - 104 St., Edmonton, AB T5J 0Z9
Tel: 780-423-5300; *Fax:* 780-423-5333
cnclaw@telusplanet.net

Edmonton: Campbell & Company - *5
#100, 4208 - 97 St. NW, Edmonton, AB T6E 5Z9
Tel: 780-434-6565; *Fax:* 780-434-1692

** indicates number of lawyers*

Edmonton: Campbell & Van Doesburg - *2
#300, 10230 - 142 St., Edmonton, AB T5N 3Y6
Tel: 780-451-2661; *Fax:* 780-452-1051
charles@campbellvandoesburg.com

Edmonton: A.F. Campbell - *1
#2410, Oxford Tower, 10235 - 101 St. NW, Edmonton, AB T5J 3G1
Tel: 780-428-8882; *Fax:* 780-421-0818
pgl31416@telusplanet.ca

Edmonton: J.K.J. Campbell
#208, Whitemud Business Park, 4245 - 97 St. NW, Edmonton, AB T6E 5Y7
Tel: 780-434-8777; *Fax:* 780-436-6357
johncam@telusplanet.net

Edmonton: Canadian Corporate Consultants Ltd. - *1
#1202, 10109 - 106 St., Edmonton, AB T5J 3L7
Tel: 780-429-4488; *Fax:* 780-425-3575
cancorpavi@compusmart.ab.ca
www.cancorp.com

Edmonton: Carr & Company - *3
#1296, 10665 Jasper Ave., Edmonton, AB T5J 3S9
Tel: 780-425-5959; *Fax:* 780-423-4728
mail@carrlaw.com
www.carrlaw.com

Edmonton: Chadi & Company - *7
#1901, 10060 Jasper Ave. NW, Edmonton, AB T5J 3R8
Tel: 780-429-2300; *Fax:* 780-441-9876

Edmonton: Chamberlain Hutchison - *3
#155, 10403 - 122 St. NW, Edmonton, AB T5N 4C1
Tel: 780-423-3661; *Fax:* 780-426-1293
ajclaw@telus.net

Edmonton: Chatwin Cox & Michalyshyn - *6
#1000, 10060 Jasper Ave. NW, Edmonton, AB T5J 3R8
Tel: 780-421-7667; *Fax:* 780-424-7231
lawyers@chatwin.ab.ca

Edmonton: Chomicki Baril Mah LLP - *19
#1201, TD Tower, 10088 - 102 Ave., Edmonton, AB T5J 4K2
Tel: 780-423-3441; *Fax:* 780-420-1763
office_admin@cbmllp.com
www.cbmllp.com

Edmonton: Chopra, Chopra & Chopra - *1
#517, 12111 - 51 St., Edmonton, AB T6H 6A3
Tel: 780-429-4961; *Fax:* 780-426-3512
manichopra.msn@attcanada.net

Edmonton: Michael H. Clancy - *1
9844 - 106 St. NW, Edmonton, AB T5K 1B8
Tel: 780-424-9014; *Fax:* 780-424-9023
Toll-Free: 800-647-7723

Edmonton: Cleall Barristers Solicitors - *12
Former Name: Cleall Pahl
#2500, Commerce Place, 10155 - 102nd St., Edmonton, AB T5J 4G8
Tel: 780-425-2500; *Fax:* 780-425-1222
main@cleall.ca
www.cleall.ca

Edmonton: Cochard Johnson - *2
Former Name: Cochard Gordon
#607, Royal Bank Bldg., 10117 Jasper Ave., Edmonton, AB T5J 1W8
Tel: 780-429-9929; *Fax:* 780-429-9981

Edmonton: Coley, Hennessy & Cassis - *3
#212, 3132 Parsons Rd., Edmonton, AB T6N 1L6
Tel: 780-468-2551; *Fax:* 780-466-8006
chc@connect.ab.ca

Edmonton: Combe & Kent - *2
#800, 10310 Jasper Ave. NW, Edmonton, AB T5J 2W4
Tel: 780-425-4666; *Fax:* 780-425-9358

Edmonton: Coulter & Power - *2
#2200, Metropolitan Pl., 10303 Jasper Ave., Edmonton, AB T5J 3N6
Tel: 780-413-2300; *Fax:* 780-420-0049

Edmonton: C.D. Cousineau - *1
#215, 11098 - 156 St. SW, Edmonton, AB T5P 4M8
Tel: 780-455-0485; *Fax:* 780-447-5853

Edmonton: Cox Trofimuk Campbell - *4
#2400, 10303 Jasper Ave., Edmonton, AB T5J 3T8
Tel: 780-422-6242; *Fax:* 780-428-1137

Edmonton: Ted R. Croll - *1
#1300, 10665 Jasper Ave., Edmonton, AB T5J 3S9
Tel: 780-420-9903; *Fax:* 780-424-3631
trcroll@shaw.ca

Edmonton: Cummings Andrews Mackay LLP - *8
#500, 10150 - 100 St. NW, Edmonton, AB T5J 0P6
Tel: 780-428-8222; *Fax:* 780-426-2670
Toll-Free: 800-565-5745
cam@cummings.ab.ca
www.cummings.ab.ca

Edmonton: Brock I. Dagenais - *1
#1405, TD Tower, 10088 - 102 Ave., Edmonton, AB T5J 2Z1
Tel: 780-424-8519; *Fax:* 780-425-0931
brock.dagenais@gmail.com

Edmonton: Davidson Gregory Danyliuk - *3
110 Place, 10008 - 110 St., Edmonton, AB T5K 1J6
Tel: 780-482-5496; *Fax:* 780-482-1930
Toll-Free: 866-887-8868
crimlaw@telusplanet.net

Edmonton: Dawson, Stevens, Duckett & Shaigec - *10
Former Name: Anderson, Dawson, Knisely, Stevens & Shaigec
#300, Anderson Dawson Bldg., 9924 - 106 St., Edmonton, AB T5K 1C4
Tel: 780-424-9058; *Fax:* 780-425-0172
Toll-Free: 800-661-3176
www.dsscrimlaw.com

Edmonton: de Villars Jones - *5
#300, Noble Bldg., 8540 - 109 St., Edmonton, AB T6G 1E6
Tel: 780-433-9000; *Fax:* 780-433-9780
adev@sagecounsel.com

Edmonton: Dean Duckett Carlson - *9
#700, 10104 - 103 Ave. NW, Edmonton, AB T5J 0H8
Tel: 780-423-3366; *Fax:* 780-423-0505
office@deanduckett.com
www.deanduckett.com

Edmonton: Gary A. Dlin - *1
7904 Gateway Blvd., Edmonton, AB T6E 6C3
Tel: 780-438-4972; *Fax:* 780-435-1037

Edmonton: Doherty Schuldhaus - *2
#219, 6203 - 28 Ave., Edmonton, AB T6L 6K3
Tel: 780-450-1106; *Fax:* 780-461-8612

Edmonton: Duncan & Craig LLP, Lawyers & Mediators - *46
#2800, Scotia Place, 10060 Jasper Ave., Edmonton, AB T5J 3V9
Tel: 780-428-6036; *Fax:* 780-428-9683
Toll-Free: 800-782-9409
edmonton@dcllp.com
www.dcllp.com

Edmonton: Durocher Simpson - *6
Old Strathcona Law Office, 7904 Gateway Blvd., Edmonton, AB T6E 6C3
Tel: 780-420-6850; *Fax:* 780-425-9185
mail@dursim.com
www.dursim.com

Edmonton: E.L. Eccleston - *1
235 North Town Mall, Edmonton, AB T5E 6C1
Tel: 780-478-6635; *Fax:* 780-476-8587
eccl@telusplanet.net

Edmonton: David C. Elliott - *1
9724 - 101A St. NW, Edmonton, AB T5K 2R6
Tel: 780-425-7337; *Fax:* 780-425-5710
words@davidelliott.ca

Edmonton: Embury & McFayden - *1
#602, Centre 104, 5241 Calgary Trail NW, Edmonton, AB T6H 5G8
Tel: 780-439-7302; *Fax:* 780-433-6510
emburymc@telus.net

Edmonton: Emery Jamieson LLP - *26
#1700, Oxford Tower, 10235 - 101st St., Edmonton, AB T5J 3G1
Tel: 780-426-5220; *Fax:* 780-420-6277
Toll-Free: 866-212-5220
general@emeryjamieson.com
www.emeryjamieson.com

Edmonton: Environmental Law Centre (ELC) - *4
#800, 10025 - 106 St., Edmonton, AB T5J 1G4
Tel: 780-424-5099; *Fax:* 780-424-5133
Toll-Free: 800-661-4238
elc@elc.ab.ca
www.elc.ab.ca

Edmonton: Ewasiuk & Associates - *1
#311, 8925 - 51 Ave. SE, Edmonton, AB T6E 5J3
Tel: 780-465-1155; *Fax:* 780-465-2507
ealaw@telusplanet.net

Edmonton: Feehan Law Office - *2
Former Name: Mark E. Feehan
#1740, Sun Life Place, 10123 - 99 St., Edmonton, AB T5J 3H1
Tel: 780-424-6425; *Fax:* 780-424-6477

Edmonton: Field Law - Edmonton - *59
Former Name: Field LLP
#2000, Oxford Tower, 10235 - 101st St., Edmonton, AB T5J 3G1
Tel: 780-423-3003; *Fax:* 780-428-9329
Toll-Free: 800-222-6479
wbrown@fieldlaw.com; lturner@fieldlaw.com
www.fieldlaw.com

Edmonton: Fix & Smith - *2
10277 - 97 St. NW, Edmonton, AB T5J 0L9
Tel: 780-424-2245; *Fax:* 780-423-0425

Edmonton: Fleming & Gubbins - *2
9636 - 102A ave. NW, Edmonton, AB T5H 0G5
Tel: 780-424-9505; *Fax:* 780-425-0472

Edmonton: Frieser Robinson MacKay - *6
Freiser Robinson MacKay Building, 10410 - 81 Ave., Edmonton, AB T6E 1X5
Tel: 780-429-1717; *Fax:* 780-421-8335
Toll-Free: 877-302-1717
inquiries@frmlaw.com
www.frmlaw.com

Edmonton: Galbraith Empson - *2
#1750, 10123 - 99 St., Edmonton, AB T5J 3H1
Tel: 780-424-9558; *Fax:* 780-424-5852
galson@shaw.ca

Edmonton: Galbraith Law - *1
17318 - 106 Ave., Edmonton, AB T5S 1H9
Tel: 780-483-6111; *Fax:* 780-483-6411
Toll-Free: 866-483-6111
stan@galbraith.ab.ca
www.galbraith.ab.ca

Edmonton: Richard Gariepy - *1
Former Name: Gariepy & Lloyd
10039 - 117 St., Edmonton, AB T5K 1W7
Tel: 780-482-7370; *Fax:* 780-482-2553

Edmonton: Gawlinski & Parkatti, Barristers & Solicitors - *2
Former Name: Gawlinski Parkatti Verhaeghe
#Sun Life Pl., #990, 10123 - 99th St., Edmonton, AB T5J 3H1
Tel: 780-428-6645; *Fax:* 780-428-6649
sjgawlinski@gp-law.ca; dtparkatti@gp-law.ca
www.gp-law.ca

Edmonton: Blair M. Geiger - *1
7904 Gateway Blvd. NW, Edmonton, AB T6E 6C3
Tel: 780-438-4972; *Fax:* 780-436-7771
bgeiger@telusplanet.net

Edmonton: Dale Gibson Consulting Barrister - *1
11018 - 125 St. NW, Edmonton, AB T5M 0M1
Tel: 780-452-9530; *Fax:* 780-453-5872
giblaw@telusplanet.net

Edmonton: R.D. Gillespie - *1
#300, 10209 - 97 St., Edmonton, AB T5J 0L6
Tel: 780-424-3255; *Fax:* 780-429-2615
robert.gillespie@interbaun.com

Edmonton: Gledhill Larocque - *5
#300, 10209 - 97 St., Edmonton, AB T5J 0L6
Tel: 780-425-3511; *Fax:* 780-426-5919

Edmonton: Goldford Law Office - *2
#200, 10735 - 107th St., Edmonton, AB T5H 0W6
Tel: 780-482-1000; *Fax:* 780-482-0963
hgoldford@goldfordlaw.com

** indicates number of lawyers*

Edmonton: **Gunn Prithipaul & Hatch - *5**
Former Name: Gunn & Prithipaul
#100, 9924 - 106th St. NW, Edmonton, AB T5K 1C4
Tel: 780-488-4460; *Fax:* 780-488-4783
info@gplegal.ca
www.gplegal.ca

Edmonton: **Hajduk Gibbs LLP, Barristers & Solicitors - *4**
#202, Platinum Place Bldg., 10120 - 118 St. NW, 2nd Fl., Edmonton, AB T5K 1Y4
Tel: 780-428-4258; *Fax:* 780-425-9439
Toll-Free: 800-749-9989
info@hajdukandgibbs.com
www.hajdukandgibbs.com

Edmonton: **Hall & Van Campenhout - *2**
12026 - 102 Ave. NW, Edmonton, AB T5K 0R9
Tel: 780-482-5732; *Fax:* 780-482-5736

Edmonton: **Hansma Bristow & Finlay LLP, Barristers, Solicitors & Notaries Public - *7**
13815 - 127 St. NW, 2nd Fl., Edmonton, AB T6V 1A8
Tel: 780-456-3661; *Fax:* 780-457-9381
info@hblaw.ca; hansma@hblaw.ca; r.finlay@hblaw.ca

Edmonton: **Hardman Law Office - *1**
18067 - 107 Ave., Edmonton, AB T5S 1K3
Tel: 780-484-2041; *Fax:* 780-484-8950
hardman@compusmart.ab.ca

Edmonton: **R. Allan Harris Professional Corp. - *1**
#1090, The Phipps-McKinnon Bldg., 10020 - 101A Ave., Edmonton, AB T5J 3G2
Tel: 780-421-1641; *Fax:* 780-421-1936

Edmonton: **Haymour Kalil - *1**
#2031, Scotia Place 2, 10060 Jasper Ave. NW, Edmonton, AB T5J 3R8
Tel: 780-425-5700; *Fax:* 780-429-4573
haymour@telusplanet.net

Edmonton: **Christopher R. Head - *1**
#2400, 10303 Jasper Ave., Edmonton, AB T5J 3T8
Tel: 780-422-6242; *Fax:* 780-428-1137
Toll-Free: 877-797-6242
chead@danet.com

Edmonton: **H.J.D. Henderson - *1**
10938 - 124 St., Edmonton, AB T5M 0H5
Tel: 780-451-2769; *Fax:* 780-451-3534
hamish.henderson@telus.net

Edmonton: **Hendrickson Gower Massing & Olivieri LLP - *8**
#2250, Scotia 1, 10060 Jasper Ave., Edmonton, AB T5J 3R8
Tel: 780-421-8816; *Fax:* 780-424-5864
Toll-Free: 800-421-8816
www.hgmolaw.com

Edmonton: **Henning Byrne - *7**
Former Name: Henning Byrne Whitmore & McKall
#1450, Standard Life Centre, 10405 Jasper Ave. NW, Edmonton, AB T5J 3N4
Tel: 780-421-1707; *Fax:* 780-425-9438
Toll-Free: 888-702-1707
general@henningbyrne.com
www.henningbyrne.com

Edmonton: **Heritage Law Offices - *5**
#108, 284 - 109 St., Edmonton, AB T6J 6B7
Tel: 780-436-0011; *Fax:* 780-436-7000

Edmonton: **B.J. Herring - *1**
10402 - 155 St., Edmonton, AB T5P 2M3
Tel: 780-469-2609

Edmonton: **Leroy N. Hiller - *1**
#1720, Sun Life Place, 10123 - 99th St., Edmonton, AB T5J 3H1
Tel: 780-424-6660; *Fax:* 780-426-2980
lnhiller@telusplanet.net

Edmonton: **John Hinton - *1**
5508 - 141 St. NW, Edmonton, AB T6H 4A2
Tel: 780-434-4710; *Fax:* 780-437-4281

Edmonton: **Hladun & Company - *4**
#300, 10711 - 102 St., Edmonton, AB T5H 2T8
Tel: 780-423-1888; *Fax:* 780-424-0934
inquiries@hladun.com

Edmonton: **Terry E. Hofmann - *1**
P.O. Box 51070, Stn. Highlands, 6525 - 118 Ave., Edmonton, AB T5W 5G5
Tel: 780-448-3885; *Fax:* 780-448-5840

Edmonton: **Douglas B. Holman - *1**
#700, 10150 - 100 St. NW, Edmonton, AB T5J 0P6
Tel: 780-429-3644; *Fax:* 780-429-3685

Edmonton: **William K. Horwitz - *1**
#140, 17010 - 103 Ave., Edmonton, AB T5S 1K7
Tel: 780-486-3100; *Fax:* 780-489-9671

Edmonton: **Stanley V.T. Hum - *1**
#1003, 10010 - 106 St. SW, Edmonton, AB T5J 3L8
Tel: 780-453-8988; *Fax:* 780-424-7379
stan_hum@hotmail.com

Edmonton: **Hustwick Payne - *9**
#600, Capital Pl., 9707 - 110 St. NW, Edmonton, AB T5K 2L9
Tel: 780-482-6555; *Fax:* 780-482-6613
reception@hplegal.com
www.hplegal.ca

Edmonton: **Implementation & Advisory Group Ltd. - *2**
#1400, Baker Centre, 10025 - 106 St., Edmonton, AB T5J 1G4
Tel: 780-482-5577; *Fax:* 780-482-5939

Edmonton: **Jiwaji Law Office - *2**
Former Name: Jiwaji, Moosa Y; Stothert-Kennedy & Jiwaji
#204, 2603 Hewes Way NW, Edmonton, AB T6L 6W6
Tel: 780-448-0467; *Fax:* 780-448-3962
moosaj@telus.net

Edmonton: **John Stadnyk Law Office, Barristers & Solicitors - *1**
Former Name: Kobewka Stadnyk
#300, 14925 - 111 Ave., Edmonton, AB T0A 0M0
Tel: 780-414-0222; *Fax:* 780-414-0002
Toll-Free: 877-414-0222
www.stadnyklaw.com
john@stadnyklaw.com

Edmonton: **Jomha, Skrobot LLP - *3**
#2260, 10123 - 99th St. NW, Edmonton, AB T5J 3H1
Tel: 780-424-0688; *Fax:* 780-424-0695
jomhalaw@telusplanet.net

Edmonton: **Kennedy Agrios - *5**
#1325, 10180 - 101 St. NW, Edmonton, AB T5J 3S4
Tel: 780-969-6900; *Fax:* 780-969-6901

Edmonton: **Kirwin LLP - *7**
Former Name: Kirwin & Kirwin
#200, 10339 - 124 St. NW, Edmonton, AB T5N 3W1
Tel: 780-448-7401; *Fax:* 780-453-3281
mail@kirwinllp.com

Edmonton: **Robert A. Kiss - *1**
Former Name: Kiss & Davidson
17393 - 108 Ave, Edmonton, AB T5S 1G2
Tel: 780-447-7205; *Fax:* 780-481-6258

Edmonton: **Kolthammer, Batchelor & Laidlaw LLP - *4**
#208, 11062 - 156 St. NW, Edmonton, AB T5P 4M8
Tel: 780-489-5003; *Fax:* 780-486-2107
kolthamm@telusplanet.net

Edmonton: **I. Samuel Kravinchuk - *1**
#800, 10310 Jasper Ave. NW, Edmonton, AB T5J 2W4
Tel: 780-426-4884; *Fax:* 780-425-9359

Edmonton: **Katherine A. Kubica - *1**
1910 Sun Life Place, 10123 - 99 St., Edmonton, AB T5J 3H1
Tel: 780-425-8000; *Fax:* 780-425-8488

Edmonton: **Kuckertz Law Office - *2**
#202, 8003 - 102 St., Edmonton, AB T6E 4A2
Tel: 780-432-9308; *Fax:* 780-439-9950
h.kuckertz@kuckertzlaw.com

Edmonton: **Kulasa Campbell - *3**
#100, 10703 - 181 St. NW, Edmonton, AB T5S 1N3
Tel: 780-484-0665; *Fax:* 780-486-7282
tkulasa@connect.ab.ca

Edmonton: **Larbalestier Stewart - *2**
#2400, 10303 Jasper Ave., Edmonton, AB T5J 3T8
Tel: 780-422-6242; *Fax:* 780-428-1137
Toll-Free: 877-797-6242
lastlaw@larbalestierstewart.com

Edmonton: **Laurier Law Office - *3**
8623 - 149 St., Edmonton, AB T5R 1B3
Tel: 780-486-0207; *Fax:* 780-483-0848

Edmonton: **Keith M. Leslie - *1**
1612 - 89 St. NW, Edmonton, AB T6K 2A9
Tel: 780-463-4019; *Fax:* 780-468-2976
kleslie@agt.net

Edmonton: **Linton Law Office - *1**
Former Name: Kathleen S.V. Linton
#200, 10426 - 81 Ave. NW, Edmonton, AB T6E 1X5
Tel: 780-415-5540; *Fax:* 780-415-5541
kathy.linton@lintonlawoffice.com

Edmonton: **Philip G. Lister Professional Corporation - *1**
Former Name: Lister & Associate
#2410, Oxford Tower, 10235 - 101 St., Edmonton, AB T5J 3G1
Tel: 780-422-6114; *Fax:* 780-421-0818
phil@listerlaw.com

Edmonton: **Julie C. Lloyd - *1**
#950, 10303 Jasper Ave. NW, Edmonton, AB T5J 3N6
Tel: 780-442-4417; *Fax:* 780-424-9370
jclloyd@telusplanet.net

Edmonton: **Peter T.K. Loong - *1**
10704 - 108 St., 2nd Fl., Edmonton, AB T5H 3A3
Tel: 780-424-3200; *Fax:* 780-424-2369
peterloonglaw@telusplanet.net

Edmonton: **Lyons Albert & Cook - *2**
#306, 10328 - 81 Ave. NW, Edmonton, AB T6E 1X2
Tel: 780-437-0743; *Fax:* 780-438-6695
laclaw@telusplanet.net

Edmonton: **Reginald S. MacDonald - *1**
#301, 10171 Saskatchewan Dr. NW, Edmonton, AB T6E 4R5
Tel: 780-439-7000; *Fax:* 780-439-7248

Edmonton: **J.D. MacEachern - *1**
#910, CN Tower, 10004 - 104 Ave. NW, Edmonton, AB T5J 0K1
Tel: 780-428-1079; *Fax:* 780-429-6121
maceac@shaw.ca

Edmonton: **Mah & Company - *2**
#1013, TD Tower, 10088 - 102 Ave., Edmonton, AB T5J 2Z1
Tel: 780-428-3888; *Fax:* 780-425-8383

Edmonton: **Malhotra & Company - *1**
#315, 10909 Jasper Ave., Edmonton, AB T5J 3L9
Tel: 780-423-5792; *Fax:* 780-426-0081

Edmonton: **James W. Mandick Professional Corporation - *1**
#1850, 10123 - 99 St. NW, Edmonton, AB T5J 3H1
Tel: 780-423-3311; *Fax:* 780-423-3321
jmandick@wmlaw.ca

Edmonton: **M.B. Marcovitch - *1**
#1300, 10665 Jasper Ave. NW, Edmonton, AB T5J 3S9
Tel: 780-453-4390; *Fax:* 780-424-3631

Edmonton: **Matheson & Company LLP - *6**
10410 - 81 Ave., Edmonton, AB T6E 1X5
Tel: 780-433-5881; *Fax:* 780-432-9453
general@mathesonlaw.com

Edmonton: **McGee Richard - *3**
#1155, Weber Centre, 5555 Calgary Trail NW, Edmonton, AB T6H 5P9
Tel: 780-437-2240; *Fax:* 780-438-5788
trichard@mcgeerichard.com
www.mcgeerichard.com

Edmonton: **McKay-Carey & Company - *1**
#1900, 10123 - 99 St. NW, Edmonton, AB T5J 3H1
Tel: 780-424-0222; *Fax:* 780-421-0834

Edmonton: **McKee & Company - *2**
#281, 11717 - 42 St. NW, Edmonton, AB T5W 4V8
Tel: 780-471-1100; *Fax:* 780-471-1150
mckee.co@shaw.ca

** indicates number of lawyers*

Edmonton: **Mckenzie House Law Group - *2**
Former Name: G.D. Honey
#8603, 104 St. NW, Edmonton, AB T6E 4G6
Tel: 780-424-3558; *Fax:* 780-424-5515

Edmonton: **McLennan Ross LLP - Edmonton - *46**
Former Name: Wallbridge & Cairns
#600, West Chambers, 12220 Stony Plain Rd., Edmonton, AB T5N 3Y4
Tel: 780-482-9200; *Fax:* 780-482-9100
Toll-Free: 800-567-9200
info@mross.com
www.mross.com

Edmonton: **McMenemy & Tilleard. - *2**
Former Name: Michael J. Tilleard
#700, 10150 - 100 St. NW, Edmonton, AB T5J 0P6
Tel: 780-429-3644; *Fax:* 780-429-3685

Edmonton: **R. McPhail - *1**
#150, 12225 - 105 Ave., Edmonton, AB T5N 0Y3
Tel: 780-482-5947; *Fax:* 780-482-2429

Edmonton: **McPike Johnston Barristers & Solicitors - *2**
11914 - 129 Ave., Edmonton, AB T5E 0N3
Tel: 780-455-6678; *Fax:* 780-453-1093
mcpike@4lawyer.ca

Edmonton: **Ingrid E. Meier - *1**
9718 - 92 St., Edmonton, AB T6C 3S4
Tel: 780-436-5954; *Fax:* 780-401-3204
lawyer@meier.ca

Edmonton: **Ron J. Meleshko - *1**
15412 - 55 St. NW, Edmonton, AB T5Y 2S4
Tel: 780-414-0298

Edmonton: **Melnyk & Co. - *3**
#200, 9939 Jasper Ave., Edmonton, AB T5J 2W8
Tel: 780-428-8900; *Fax:* 780-429-8889
melnykco@telusplanet.net

Edmonton: **Joseph J. Michaels - *1**
#1985 Sun Life Place, 10123 - 99 St. NW, Edmonton, AB T5J 3H1
Tel: 780-424-0354

Edmonton: **Miller Boileau Family Law Group - *3**
11835 - 102nd Ave. NW, Edmonton, AB T5K 0R6
Tel: 780-482-2888; *Fax:* 780-482-4600
mail@millerboileau.com
www.millerboileau.com

Edmonton: **Mintz & Chow - *6**
#400, 10357 - 109 St. NW, Edmonton, AB T5J 1N3
Tel: 780-425-2041; *Fax:* 780-425-2195
mincho@telusplanet.net

Edmonton: **W. Robert Mitchell - *1**
#405, 10408 - 124 St., Edmonton, AB T5N 1R5
Tel: 780-482-5791; *Fax:* 780-488-0965

Edmonton: **Murray, Chilibeck & Horne - *3**
10605 - 172nd St. NW, Edmonton, AB T5S 1P1
Tel: 780-484-2323; *Fax:* 780-486-4289

Edmonton: **Alann J. Nazarevich - *1**
9803 - 31 Ave., Edmonton, AB T6N 1C5
Tel: 780-430-0363; *Fax:* 780-430-0984

Edmonton: **Neuman Thompson - *6**
#200, 12220 Stony Plain Rd. NW, Edmonton, AB T5N 3Y4
Tel: 780-482-7645; *Fax:* 780-488-0026

Edmonton: **Kenneth Ng - *1**
3234 Parsons Rd.W, Edmonton, AB T6N 1M2
Tel: 780-988-9188; *Fax:* 780-496-9717

Edmonton: **Nicholl & Akers - *7**
#200, 10187 - 104 St. NW, Edmonton, AB T5J 0Z9
Tel: 780-429-2771; *Fax:* 780-425-1665

Edmonton: **Nickerson Roberts Holinski & Mercer - *9**
Former Name: Nickerson, Roberts
#100, 7712 - 104 St., Edmonton, AB T6E 4C5
Tel: 780-428-0041; *Fax:* 780-425-0272
reception@nrhmlaw.com
www.nrhmlaw.com

Edmonton: **Gregory O'Laughlin - *1**
#300, 10209 - 97 St. NW, Edmonton, AB T5J 0L6
Tel: 780-424-9059; *Fax:* 780-429-2615

Edmonton: **Ronald J. Obirek - *1**
#240, 6005 - 103 St. NW, Edmonton, AB T6H 2H3
Tel: 780-496-9046; *Fax:* 780-436-9669
rjobirek@telusplanet.net

Edmonton: **Ogilvie LLP - *26**
#1400, 10303 Jasper Ave., Edmonton, AB T5J 3N6
Tel: 780-421-1818; *Fax:* 780-429-4453
info@ogilvielaw.com
www.ogilvielaw.com

Edmonton: **Kelly R. Palmer - *1**
#1800, 10250 - 101 St. NW, Edmonton, AB T5J 3P4
Tel: 780-448-9275; *Fax:* 780-423-0163

Edmonton: **Phillip G. Parker - *1**
10704 - 108 St., 2nd Fl., Edmonton, AB T5H 3A3
Tel: 780-424-3200; *Fax:* 780-424-2369

Edmonton: **Patrick & Patrick - *1**
#800, 10310 Jasper Ave. NW, Edmonton, AB T5J 2W4
Tel: 780-426-4884; *Fax:* 780-425-9358

Edmonton: **Patrick Dolphin Professional Corporation - *1**
Former Name: Edney, Hattersley & Dolphin
10621 - 124 St. NW, Edmonton, AB T5N 1S5
Tel: 780-423-4081; *Fax:* 780-425-5247

Edmonton: **Penonzek Murray - *2**
Former Name: Kenneth W. Penonzek Professional Corp
#147, 10403 - 122 St. NW, Edmonton, AB T5N 4C1
Tel: 780-482-1199; *Fax:* 780-482-1883
k.penonzek@shawbiz.ca

Edmonton: **Patrick J. Phelan - *1**
#1550, Sun Life Pl., 10123 - 99 St., Edmonton, AB T5J 3H1
Tel: 780-424-7730; *Fax:* 780-428-4484
patrick.phelan@telus.net

Edmonton: **Roy A. Philion - *1**
#880, 10020 - 101 Ave. NW, Edmonton, AB T5J 3G2
Tel: 780-423-2977; *Fax:* 780-424-8098

Edmonton: **Ronald W. Poitras - *1**
#300, 10209 - 97 St., Edmonton, AB T5J 0L6
Tel: 780-424-3270; *Fax:* 780-429-2615

Edmonton: **Polack, Meindersma, Liddell - *3**
#300, High Park Corner, 14925 - 111 Ave., Edmonton, AB T5M 2P6
Tel: 780-486-0926; *Fax:* 780-444-1393

Edmonton: **Pringle & Associates - *7**
#300, Transalta Place, 10150 - 100 St. NW, Edmonton, AB T5J 0P6
Tel: 780-424-8866; *Fax:* 780-426-1470
www.pringleandassociates.com

Edmonton: **Prismatic Group Inc. - *1**
#205, 3132 Parsons Rd., Edmonton, AB T6N 1L6
Tel: 780-495-0200; *Fax:* 780-439-2369
www.prismatic.ca

Edmonton: **Pundit & Chotalia - *2**
#1506, Edmonton City Centre, 10025 - 102A Ave., Edmonton, AB T5J 2Z2
Tel: 780-421-0861; *Fax:* 780-425-6048
shirish@chotalia.com

Edmonton: **Rand Kiss Turner - *3**
Former Name: Frohlich Rand Kiss
#1600, 10020 - 101A Ave. NW, Edmonton, AB T5J 3G2
Tel: 780-423-1984; *Fax:* 780-423-1969

Edmonton: **M. Naeem Rauf**
#300, 10209 - 97 St., Edmonton, AB T5J 0L6
Tel: 780-453-4399; *Fax:* 780-429-2615

Edmonton: **Peter E. Recto - *1**
6423 - 154th Avenue, Edmonton, AB T5Y 2N7
Tel: 780-423-1283; *Fax:* 780-473-8324
recto2001@hotmail.com

Edmonton: **H.M. Reich - *1**
#1550, Sun Life Place, 10123 - 99 St., Edmonton, AB T5J 3H1
Tel: 780-424-7732; *Fax:* 780-428-4484
reichlaw@telus.net

Edmonton: **Reynolds, Mirth, Richards & Farmer LLP - *36**
#3200, Manulife Place, 10180 - 101 St., Edmonton, AB T5J 3W8
Tel: 780-425-9510; *Fax:* 780-429-3044
Toll-Free: 800-661-7673
mail@rmrf.com
www.rmrf.com

Edmonton: **Richard D. Rennick Professional Corporation - *1**
Former Name: Rennick & Di Pinto
#2200, 10123 - 99 St. NW, Edmonton, AB T5J 3H1
Tel: 780-426-5510; *Fax:* 780-420-1645
lawfirm@rennicklaw.ca

Edmonton: **Richards Hunter - *4**
Former Name: Worton Hunter & Callaghan, and Richard Wood Toogood
#1270, 5555 Calgary Trail NW, Edmonton, AB T6H 5P9
Tel: 780-436-8554; *Fax:* 780-436-8566
main@wortonhunter.com

Edmonton: **Ritchie Mill Law Office - *5**
#102, 10171 Saskatchewan Dr. NW, Edmonton, AB T6E 4R5
Tel: 780-431-1444; *Fax:* 780-431-1499
Toll-Free: 888-333-8818
office@rmlo.com

Edmonton: **James A. Robertson - *1**
#300, Wentworth, 10209 - 97 St. NW, Edmonton, AB T5J 0L6
Tel: 780-423-1680; *Fax:* 780-421-7304
jamesrob@shaw.ca

Edmonton: **Terry J. Romaniuk - *1**
9743 - 89 Ave. NW, Edmonton, AB T6E 2S1
Tel: 780-433-8127;

Edmonton: **David W. Ross - *1**
8623 - 149 St., Edmonton, AB T5R 1B3
Tel: 780-425-1965; *Fax:* 780-483-0848
dwross@bigfoot.com

Edmonton: **James D. Ross - *1**
#1003, Highfield Place, 10010 - 106 St., Edmonton, AB T5J 3L8
Tel: 780-482-3144; *Fax:* 780-424-7379

Edmonton: **Samy F. Salloum - *1**
1341 Carter Crest Rd., Edmonton, AB T6R 2L6
Tel: 780-426-7777; *Fax:* 780-426-7778

Edmonton: **Savaryn & Savaryn - *1**
P.O. Box 45083, Stn. Landsdowne, Edmonton, AB T6H 5Y1
Tel: 780-422-7548;
savaryn@telusplanet.net

Edmonton: **Savich Law Office - *1**
#200, 10350 - 172 St., Edmonton, AB T5S 1G9
Tel: 780-486-7300; *Fax:* 780-489-0682
don@savichlaw.ca
www.savichlaw.ca

Edmonton: **B.M. Schloss - *1**
#800, Sun Life Place, 10123 - 99 St. NW, Edmonton, AB T5J 3H1
Tel: 780-448-9300; *Fax:* 780-489-9982
bschloss@schloss.ca

Edmonton: **Schwab, Schwab & Schwab - *3**
Former Name: Schwab, Rowe & Parsons
9908 - 106 St., Edmonton, AB T5K 1C4
Tel: 780-426-6715; *Fax:* 780-426-2301
schwab@telusplanet.net

Edmonton: **D.L. Schwartz - *1**
#324, 10909 Jasper Ave. NW, Edmonton, AB T5J 3L9
Tel: 780-424-0259; *Fax:* 780-424-0299
thebigkahuna@interbaun.com

Edmonton: **Sharek Logan & van Leenen LLP - *8**
Also Known As: Sharek & Company
Former Name: Sharek Logan Collingwood van Leenen LLP
#701, Tower 2, Scotia Place, 10060 Jasper Ave. NW, Edmonton, AB T5J 3R8
Tel: 780-413-3100; *Fax:* 780-413-3152
www.sharekco.com

Edmonton: **G.P. Shewchuk - *1**
#310, 8944 - 182 St. NW, Edmonton, AB T5T 2E3
Tel: 780-481-1299; *Fax:* 780-481-1674

** indicates number of lawyers*

***Edmonton*: William Shim**
#2000B, Sun Life Place, 10123 - 99 St. NW, Edmonton, AB T5J 3H1
Tel: 780-423-8060; *Fax:* 780-425-4201

***Edmonton*: Shores Belzil Jardine - *9**
#1800, 10250 - 101 St. NW, Edmonton, AB T5J 3P4
Tel: 780-448-9275; *Fax:* 780-423-0163
louis@shoresbelzil.com
www.shoresbelzil.com

***Edmonton*: Shtabsky & Tussman LLP - *7**
#1400, 10025 - 102A Ave., Edmonton, AB T5J 2Z2
Tel: 780-429-4671; *Fax:* 780-424-3580
st400@stlaw.com
www.stlaw.com

***Edmonton*: W.J. Shymko - *1**
#200, 10105 - 108 Ave., Edmonton, AB T5H 1A7
Tel: 780-425-6414; *Fax:* 780-425-6416

***Edmonton*: Simons & Stephens - *2**
#710, 10055 - 106 St. NW, Edmonton, AB T5J 2Y2
Tel: 780-482-1536; *Fax:* 780-488-1914
nsimons@telus.net

***Edmonton*: Larry A. Sitko - *1**
#201, 12907 - 97 St. NW, Edmonton, AB T5E 4C2
Tel: 780-476-7686; *Fax:* 780-476-7688

***Edmonton*: Snyder & Associates LLP - *11**
#2500, 10123 - 99 St., Edmonton, AB T5J 3H1
Tel: 780-426-4133; *Fax:* 780-424-1588
Toll-Free: 877-426-4148
www.snyder.ca

***Edmonton*: Stewart Law Offices - *2**
11724 - 103 Ave. NW, Edmonton, AB T5K 0S7
Tel: 780-482-3800; *Fax:* 780-482-5600
stwlaw@telusplanet.net

***Edmonton*: Stillman LLP - *6**
#300, 10335 - 172 St., Edmonton, AB T5S 1K9
Tel: 780-484-4445; *Fax:* 780-484-4184
Toll-Free: 888-258-2529
lawyers@stillmanllp.com

***Edmonton*: Strategic Results Consulting Inc. - *1**
13652 Ravine Dr., Edmonton, AB T5N 3L9
Tel: 780-994-9184;
www.strategicresultsconsulting.com

***Edmonton*: André A. Szaszkiewicz - *1**
#202, 1289 - 91 St., Edmonton, AB T6X 1H1
Tel: 780-452-2000; *Fax:* 780-455-7229
andresz@telusplanet.net

***Edmonton*: Tarrabain & Company - *9**
Former Name: Tarrabain O'Byrne & Co
#2150, Tower One, Scotia Place, 10060 Jasper Ave., Edmonton, AB T5J 3R8
Tel: 780-429-1010; *Fax:* 780-429-0101
lawyers@tarrabain.com
www.tarrabain.com

***Edmonton*: Christopher G. Taskey - *1**
8603 - 104th St. NW, Edmonton, AB T6E 4G6
Tel: 780-424-3558; *Fax:* 780-423-5515
ctaskey@shawbiz.ca

***Edmonton*: Taylor & Jewell - *2**
#215, Millbourner Mall, 38 Ave. NW, Edmonton, AB T6K 3L6
Tel: 780-450-5761; *Fax:* 780-468-4524

***Edmonton*: R.I. Tennant - *1**
#712, 10010 - 106 St., Edmonton, AB T5J 3L8
Tel: 780-425-2289

***Edmonton*: Sylvia O. Tensfeldt - *1**
#200, 10525 Jasper Ave. NW, Edmonton, AB T5J 1Z4
Tel: 780-424-3334; *Fax:* 780-424-4252

***Edmonton*: Thom Law Office - *1**
8506 - 104 St., Edmonton, AB T6E 4G4
Tel: 780-434-5870; *Fax:* 780-436-8420
len@thomlaw.com
www.thomlaw.com

***Edmonton*: Tkachuk & Patterson - *2**
#1260, First Edmonton Place, 10665 Jasper Ave. NW, Edmonton, AB T5J 3S9
Tel: 780-428-1593; *Fax:* 780-426-6679
tkalaw@alberta.com

***Edmonton*: George Turcin - *1**
15819 Stony Plain Rd., Edmonton, AB T5P 3Z7
Tel: 780-452-3208; *Fax:* 780-447-5410

***Edmonton*: Helen S. Tymoczko - *1**
#106, 10108 - 125 St., Edmonton, AB T5N 4B6
Tel: 780-472-1758; *Fax:* 780-476-4085

***Edmonton*: M. Brent Tyson - *1**
#300, 10209 - 97th St. NW, Edmonton, AB T5J 0L6
Tel: 780-488-3333; *Fax:* 780-429-2615
brent@tysonlaw.ca
www.tysonlaw.ca

***Edmonton*: Venkatraman Purewal & Pillay - *4**
Former Name: Venkatraman & Purewal
#303, 9811 - 34 Ave., Edmonton, AB T6E 5X9
Tel: 780-436-7060; *Fax:* 780-436-7064
lawyers@vplaw.ca

***Edmonton*: Wachowich & Company - *4**
#555, 10310 Jasper Ave. NW, Edmonton, AB T5J 2W4
Tel: 780-429-0555; *Fax:* 780-425-4795
mail@wachowich.com
www.wachowich.com

***Edmonton*: Welsh & Company - *1**
#888, 4445 Calgary Trail South, Edmonton, AB T6H 5R7
Tel: 780-438-3500; *Fax:* 780-438-3129

***Edmonton*: Uwe Welz - *1**
7904 - 103 St., Edmonton, AB T6E 6C3
Tel: 780-432-7711; *Fax:* 780-439-1177
uwpc@telusplanet.net

***Edmonton*: Westwood Consultants - *1**
#1206, 5328 Calgary Trial South, Edmonton, AB T6H 4J8
Tel: 780-437-7990;
coultier.denise@ic.gc.ca

***Edmonton*: Wheatley Sadownik - *4**
#2000, 10123 - 99 St., Edmonton, AB T5J 3H1
Tel: 780-423-6671; *Fax:* 780-420-6327
mail@wheatleysadownik.com
www.wheatleysadownik.com

***Edmonton*: Willis Bokenfohr Thorsrud - *3**
Former Name: Willis & Bokenfohr
#410, ATB Place, 9888 Jasper Ave., Edmonton, AB T5J 5C6
Tel: 780-452-2764; *Fax:* 780-452-3247

***Edmonton*: Witten LLP, Barristers & Solicitors - *42**
#2500, Canadian Western Bank Place, 10303 Jasper Ave., Edmonton, AB T5J 3N6
Tel: 780-428-0501; *Fax:* 780-429-2559
lawyers@wittenlaw.com
www.wittenlaw.com

***Edmonton*: Collin Wong - *1**
10704 - 108 St., 2nd Fl., Edmonton, AB T5H 3A3
Tel: 780-488-7003; *Fax:* 780-488-1593
cwongpf@compusmart.ab.ca

***Edmonton*: Peter S. Wong - *1**
#204, Kingsdale Professional Centre, 9644 - 54 Ave., Edmonton, AB T6E 5V1
Tel: 780-430-1070; *Fax:* 780-430-1773
pwong@sequiter.com

***Edmonton*: Wood Law Office - *2**
#304, 10209 - 97 St. NW, Edmonton, AB T5J 0L6
Tel: 780-482-3291; *Fax:* 780-452-1821
laurieiwood@gmail.com

***Edmonton*: Hu Eliot Young Law Office - *1**
8520 - 104 St. NW, Edmonton, AB T6E 4G4
Tel: 780-425-8400; *Fax:* 780-424-3777
heyoung@telusplanet.net

***Edmonton*: Ronald J. Young - *1**
#204, 10265 - 107 St., Edmonton, AB T5J 5G2
Tel: 780-424-3311; *Fax:* 780-425-9609

***Edmonton*: A.R. Zariwny - *1**
#200, 10351 - 82 Ave. NW, Edmonton, AB T6E 1Z9
Tel: 780-433-5999; *Fax:* 780-439-6456
zlo@oanet.com

***Edson*: Robert W. Anderson - *1**
P.O. Box 6748, 202B - 50 St., Edson, AB T7E 1V1
Tel: 780-723-3245; *Fax:* 780-723-5443
rwandlaw@telus.net

***Edson*: Dennis C. Calvert - *1**
P.O. Box 6658, Stn. Main, 107 - 50 St., Edson, AB T7E 1V1
Tel: 780-723-6047; *Fax:* 780-723-3602

** indicates number of lawyers*

***Fairview*: H.A. Byers - *1**
P.O. Box 2200, Fairview, AB T0H 1L0
Tel: 780-835-4100; *Fax:* 780-835-4171

***Fort MacLeod*: Vallance & Co. - *1**
P.O. Box 757, 249 Main St., Fort MacLeod, AB T0L 0Z0
Tel: 403-553-4484; *Fax:* 403-553-3444
Toll-Free: 866-553-4484
vallance@shockwave.com

***Fort McMurray*: Campbell & Cooper - *4**
Former Name: Campbell, Germain, Cooper & Jean
#212, 9714 Main St., Fort McMurray, AB T9H 1T6
Tel: 780-791-7787; *Fax:* 780-791-0750
laywers@mcmurraylaw.com

***Fort McMurray*: Gorsalitz Law Office - *1**
9912 Manning Ave., Fort McMurray, AB T9H 2B9
Tel: 780-791-4115; *Fax:* 780-743-0040

***Fort McMurray*: Samuel N. Mason - *1**
#104, 10012 Franklin Ave., Fort McMurray, AB T9H 2K6
Tel: 780-743-5002; *Fax:* 780-743-4150

***Fort McMurray*: Wolff Taitinger - *2**
10019R Franklin Ave., Fort McMurray, AB T9H 2K7
Tel: 780-790-9040; *Fax:* 780-743-1813
main@wolftaitlaw.com

***Fort Saskatchewan*: Fotty & Torok-Both - *4**
10509 - 100 Ave., Fort Saskatchewan, AB T8L 1Z5
Tel: 780-998-4841; *Fax:* 780-998-4821

***Fort Saskatchewan*: Jenkins & Jenkins - *2**
#200, 9906 - 102 St., Fort Saskatchewan, AB T8L 2C3
Tel: 780-998-4200; *Fax:* 780-998-4370
cjenkins@jenkins-law.com

***Grande Cache*: Harry Arnesen - *1**
P.O. Box 385, 2502 Pine Plaza, Grande Cache, AB T0E 0Y0
Tel: 780-827-2458; *Fax:* 780-827-3734

***Grande Prairie*: Dobko & Wheaton - *4**
10022 - 102 Ave., Grande Prairie, AB T8V 0Z7
Tel: 780-539-6200; *Fax:* 780-532-9052
Toll-Free: 866-539-6200
www.dwlaw.ca

***Grande Prairie*: Gurevitch Headon & Associates - *3**
Former Name: Burgess & Gurevitch
9931 - 106 Ave., Grande Prairie, AB T8V 1J4
Tel: 780-539-3710; *Fax:* 780-532-2788
Toll-Free: 866-720-3710
gplaw@telus.net
www.grandeprairielaw.ca

***Grande Prairie*: Howey Law Office - *1**
201 Professional Bldg., 9905 - 101 Ave., Grande Prairie, AB T8V 0X7
Tel: 780-539-0690; *Fax:* 780-539-3813

***Grande Prairie*: Kay, McVey, Smith & Carlstrom LLP - *11**
#600, Windsor Ct., 9835 - 101st Ave., Grande Prairie, AB T8V 5V4
Tel: 780-532-7771; *Fax:* 780-532-1158
Toll-Free: 888-531-7771
ksms@kayship.com
www.kayship.com

***Grande Prairie*: Lewis & Chrenek - *5**
#108, 9824 - 97 Ave., Grande Prairie, AB T8V 7K2
Tel: 780-539-6800; *Fax:* 780-539-7975
lewchr@telusplanet.net

***Grande Prairie*: Robert S. Pollick Professional Corporation, Barristers & Solicito - *1**
#200, 10006 - 101 Ave., Grande Prairie, AB T8V 0Y1
Tel: 780-538-8290; *Fax:* 780-538-4515
enniski@telusplanet.net

***Grande Prairie*: Walisser Shavers LLP - *2**
#202, 10027 - 101 Ave., Grande Prairie, AB T8V 0X9
Tel: 780-532-0315; *Fax:* 780-532-3369
loganw@telusplanet.net

***Hanna*: Ross, Todd & Company - *3**
P.O. Box 1330, 124 - 2 Ave. West, Hanna, AB T0J 1P0
Tel: 403-854-4431; *Fax:* 403-854-2561
reception@drumhellerlaw.com

***High Prairie*: Harry J. Jong - *2**
P.O. Box 1379, High Prairie, AB T0G 1E0
Tel: 780-523-4554; *Fax:* 780-523-5550
hjlaw@cablecomet.com

High River: A. George Dearing Professional Corp. - *1
#103, 14 - 2 Ave. SE, High River, AB T1V 2B8
Tel: 403-652-2771; Fax: 403-652-2699
info@ageorgedearing.ca
www.ageorgedearing.ca

Hinton: Johnson McClelland Murdoch - *4
213 Pembina Ave., Hinton, AB T7V 2B3
Tel: 780-865-2222; Fax: 780-865-8857
lawyer@jmmlaw.ca

Hinton: Woods & Robson - *2
110 Brewster Dr., Hinton, AB T7V 1B4
Tel: 780-865-3086; Fax: 780-865-7149
woodsrob@telusplanet.net

Hobbema: J. Wilton Littlechild, Q.C. - *1
P.O. Box 370, Hobbema, AB T0C 1N0
Tel: 780-585-3038; Fax: 780-585-2025
jwlittle@incentre.net

Innisfail: Tulloch Law Office - *1
P.O. Box 6099, 5030 - 50 St., Innisfail, AB T4G 1S7
Tel: 403-227-5591; Fax: 403-227-1230
carolyntulloch@telus.net

Lac La Biche: John W. Kozina - *1
Also Known As: Kozina Law Office
Former Name: Kozina & Gregory
P.O. Box 1439, 10130 Alberta Ave., Lac La Biche, AB T0A 2C0
Tel: 780-623-4818; Fax: 780-623-2933

Lac La Biche: Thomas R. Maccagno
P.O. Box 1270, 10120 - 101 Ave., Lac La Biche, AB T0A 2C0
Tel: 780-623-4177; Fax: 780-623-2266

Leduc: James K. Arends - *1
#206, 5904A - 50 St., Leduc, AB T9E 6J5
Tel: 780-986-1443; Fax: 780-980-5385
jarends@shaw.ca

Leduc: Elgert & Company - *1
5206 - 50 St., Leduc, AB T9E 6Z6
Tel: 780-986-3487; Fax: 780-986-2040
herbelgert@shaw.ca

Leduc: Jackie, Handerek & Forester, Barristers & Solicitors - *6
4710 - 50th St., Leduc, AB T9E 6W2
Tel: 780-986-5081; Fax: 780-986-8807
jhf@leduclawyers.ab.ca
www.leduclawyers.ab.ca

Leduc: E. Kahlke - *1
5102 - 50 Ave., Leduc, AB T9E 6V4
Tel: 780-986-8427; Fax: 780-986-3108

Leduc: Zalapski & Pahl - *4
#1, 5304 - 50 St., Leduc, AB T9E 6Z6
Tel: 780-986-8428; Fax: 780-986-2552

Lethbridge: Douglas N. Alger - *1
#203, 434 - 7 St. South, Lethbridge, AB T1J 2G7
Tel: 403-380-6005; Fax: 403-380-6088
alger@algerlaw.com
www.algerlaw.com

Lethbridge: Claudia R. Connolly - *3
#202, 506 - 4 Ave. South, Lethbridge, AB T1J 0N5
Tel: 403-329-8188; Fax: 403-328-7079

Lethbridge: Davidson & Williams LLP - *11
P.O. Box 518, 501 - 4 St. South, Lethbridge, AB T1J 4X2
Tel: 403-328-1766; Fax: 403-320-5434
lethbridge@davidsonandwilliams.com
www.davidsonandwilliams.com

Lethbridge: Frank de Walle - *1
323 - 7 St. South, Lethbridge, AB T1J 2G4
Tel: 403-328-8800; Fax: 403-328-8502
dewalle@telusplanet.net

Lethbridge: Dimnik & Company - *4
334 - 12 St. South, Lethbridge, AB T1J 2R1
Tel: 403-320-9800; Fax: 403-320-9124
info@lethbridgelawyers.com
www.lethbridgelawyers.com

Lethbridge: Dodic Toone Maclean - *4
416B Stafford Dr. South, Lethbridge, AB T1J 2L2
Tel: 403-329-1330; Fax: 403-329-1311

Lethbridge: Huckvale Wilde Harvie MacLennan LLP - *7
P.O. Box 1028, 410 - 6th St. South, Lethbridge, AB T1J 4A2
Tel: 403-328-8856; Fax: 403-380-4050
mad@huckvale.ca

Lethbridge: R.F. Llewellyn - *1
#202, 1921 Mayor Magrath Dr. South, Lethbridge, AB T1K 2R8
Tel: 403-329-0222; Fax: 403-329-8489

Lethbridge: MacLachlan McNab Hembroff - *6
1003 - 4th Ave. South, Lethbridge, AB T1J 0P7
Tel: 403-381-4966; Fax: 403-329-9300
mmh@mmhlawyers.com
www.mmhlawyers.com

Lethbridge: William F. Malcolm Professional Corporation - *1
Former Name: Townsend, Malcolm, Kenwood & Company
406 Stafford Dr. South, Lethbridge, AB T1J 2L2
Tel: 403-329-0001; Fax: 403-329-0868

Lethbridge: Millar & Keith LLP - *2
Former Name: Millar, Thiessen & Keith
200 - 3rd St. South, Lethbridge, AB T1J 1Y7
Tel: 403-327-5716; Fax: 403-329-4063
mtklaw@telusplanet.net

Lethbridge: Milne Pritchard Law Office - *2
#807, 400 - 4 Ave. South, Lethbridge, AB T1J 4E1
Tel: 403-329-1133; Fax: 403-329-0395
www.milnepritchard.com

Lethbridge: Harold N. Moodie - *1
P.O. Box 9, Stn. Main, 212 - 5 St. South, 2nd Fl., Lethbridge, AB T1J 3Y3
Tel: 403-328-0005; Fax: 403-329-0945

Lethbridge: Peterson & Purvis LLP - *8
P.O. Box 1165, 537 - 7th St. South, Lethbridge, AB T1J 4A4
Tel: 403-328-9667; Fax: 403-320-1393
p-plaw@telusplanet.net

Lethbridge: Pollock & Company - *3
Former Name: Fletcher, Norton & Pollock
#200, 434 - 7th St. South, Lethbridge, AB T1J 4K1
Tel: 403-329-6900; Fax: 403-327-9790
Toll-Free: 800-262-4857
dlplaw@lawpollock.com
www.lawpollock.com

Lethbridge: Rhonda Ruston, Q.C. - *1
501 - 4 St. South, Lethbridge, AB T1J 4K2
Tel: 403-328-4483; Fax: 403-206-7435
rkruston@telusplanet.net

Lethbridge: Shapiro & Company - *1
#200, 427 - 5 St. South., Lethbridge, AB T1J 2B6
Tel: 403-328-9300; Fax: 403-328-9307
shapco@telusplanet.net

Lethbridge: Stringam Denecky LLP Law Office - *15
314 - 3 St. South, Lethbridge, AB T1Y 1J9
Tel: 403-328-5577; Fax: 403-327-1141
results@stringam.ca; sdenecky@stringam.ca
www.stringam.cawww.facebook.com/stringamdenecky,
www.linkedin.com/company/stringam-denecky-llp

Lloydminster: Kindrachuk Dobson - *1
Former Name: Kindrachuk Law Office
Stafford Building, 5014 - 48 St., 2nd fl., Lloydminster, AB T9V 0H8
Tel: 780-875-6600; Fax: 780-875-6601
info@kindrachukdobson.com

Lloydminster: Kirzinger, Wells - *2
#203, 5101 - 48 St., Lloydminster, AB T9V 0H9
Tel: 780-875-8400; Fax: 780-875-8499

Lloydminster: Knight Law Office - *1
4912 - 50th Ave., Lloydminster, AB S9V 1K5
Tel: 780-875-9555; Fax: 780-875-9557
bknight@silvercrest.ca

Lloydminster: Lonsdale Law Office - *1
P.O. Box 1248, 5117 - 48 St., Lloydminster, AB S9V 1G1
Tel: 780-875-5185; Fax: 780-875-6547
lonsdalelaw@lgl.cc
www.lgl.cc

Medicine Hat: Biddell Law Office - *3
735 - 2 St. SE, Medicine Hat, AB T1A 0E2
Tel: 403-527-7737; Fax: 403-528-8907
kbiddell@monarch.net

Medicine Hat: Gordon, Smith & Company - *3
P.O. Box 490, 378 - 1 St. SE, Medicine Hat, AB T1A 7G2
Tel: 403-527-5506; Fax: 403-527-0577
gsco@shockware.com

Medicine Hat: William L. Haynes - *1
#108, 1235 Southview Dr. SE, Medicine Hat, AB T1B 4K3
Tel: 403-528-8883; Fax: 403-526-7698
bill@hayneslaw.net

Medicine Hat: Hill & Hill - *2
#6, 3151 Dunmore Rd. SE, Medicine Hat, AB T1B 2H2
Tel: 403-527-1544; Fax: 403-526-2551

Medicine Hat: Leis, Wiese & Company - *3
#1, 1364 Southview Dr. SE, Medicine Hat, AB T1B 4E7
Tel: 403-527-7766; Fax: 403-527-7788

Medicine Hat: MacLean Wiedemann - *3
525 - 2 St. SE, Medicine Hat, AB T1A 0C5
Tel: 403-527-3343; Fax: 403-526-0473

Medicine Hat: Niblock & Company - *6
P.O. Box 609, Stn. Main, 420 Macleaod Trail SE, Medicine Hat, AB T1A 7G5
Tel: 403-526-2806; Fax: 403-526-2356

Medicine Hat: Pritchard & Company LLP - *7
#204, P.O. Box 100, 430 - 6th Ave. SE, Medicine Hat, AB T1A 7E8
Tel: 403-527-4411; Fax: 403-527-9806
lawyers@pritchardandcompany.com
www.pritchardandcompany.com

Medicine Hat: D.G. Schindel - *1
#1, 3295 Dunmore Rd. SE, Medicine Hat, AB T1B 3R2
Tel: 403-529-5548; Fax: 403-529-2694
daryl@millerlaw.ca

Medicine Hat: Sihvon Carter Fisher & Berger LLP - *8
499 - 1st St. SE, Medicine Hat, AB T1A 0A7
Tel: 403-526-2600; Fax: 403-526-3217
scfb@scfb.ca
www.scfb.ca

Nanton: Laurie M. Gordon - *1
P.O. Box 586, 2213 - 20th St., Nanton, AB T0L 1R0
Tel: 403-646-6111; Fax: 403-646-6112
lmgordon@telusplanet.net

Nanton: Robert G. Roddie, Q.C. - *1
P.O. Box 100, 2113 - 20 St., Nanton, AB T0L 1R0
Tel: 403-646-2211; Fax: 403-646-3159
rodmclaw@telusplanet.net

Okotoks: Diane Luttmer Professional Corporation - *1
Former Name: Diane Dolsen
P.O. Box 267, Okotoks, AB T1S 1A5
Tel: 403-938-8296; Fax: 403-938-8286
dluttmer@platinum.ca

Okotoks: Charles A. Dixon - *1
P.O. Box 1169, 51 Riverside Gate, Okotoks, AB T1S 1B2
Tel: 403-938-8131; Fax: 403-938-6365

Okotoks: Edward D. Simper - *1
P.O. Box 1117, Stn. Main, 84 Elizabeth St., Okotoks, AB T1S 1B2
Tel: 403-938-2101; Fax: 403-938-6020
simpered@fclc.com

Okotoks: SJE Consulting Ltd. - *1
51 Ranch Rd., Okotoks, AB T1S 1W9
Tel: 877-753-2678; Fax: 877-753-2679
inquiries@sjeconsulting.com
www.sjeconsulting.com

Olds: R. Brent Carlyle
P.O. Box 3755, 4911 - 51 Ave., Olds, AB T4H 1P5
Tel: 403-556-7762; Fax: 403-556-8859
brentc@reveal.ca

Olds: Alvin F. Ganser - *1
P.O. Box 4040, 4834 - 50 St., Olds, AB T4H 1P7
Tel: 403-556-8481; Fax: 403-556-3830

** indicates number of lawyers*

Olds: **Martinson & Harder - *3**
#1, 5401 - 49 Ave., Olds, AB T4H 1G3
Tel: 403-556-8955; *Fax:* 403-556-8895
contact@martinsonharder.com

Parksville: **Evans & Company - *1**
P.O. Box 40, Stn. Main, 182 Memorial Ave., Parksville, AB V2P 2G3
Tel: 250-248-5748; *Fax:* 250-248-5758
evansandco@telus.net

Peace River: **Mathieu Hryniuk LLP - *7**
P.O. Box 6210, 10012 - 101 St., Peace River, AB T8S 1S2
Tel: 780-624-2565; *Fax:* 780-624-5766
Toll-Free: 800-661-1962
mh@mhllp.ca
mhllp.ca

Peace River: **Thietke, Murphy & Harcourt - *5**
Former Name: Simpson, Thietke & Associates
P.O. Box 6778, 9910 - 97 Ave., Peace River, AB T8S 1S5
Tel: 780-624-1122; *Fax:* 780-624-4443
Toll-Free: 800-353-6270

Pincher Creek: **Jasman & Evans - *1**
P.O. Box 2530, 985 East Ave., Pincher Creek, AB T0K 1W0
Tel: 403-627-2877; *Fax:* 403-627-4495
jasman_evans@shaw.ca

Ponoka: **Noble & Kidd - *1**
P.O. Box 4278, 5024 - 51 Ave., Ponoka, AB T4J 1R7
Tel: 403-783-3325; *Fax:* 403-783-5080
noblekid@telus.net

Ponoka: **Richard D. Wyrozub - *1**
P.O. Box 4338, Stn. Main, Ponoka, AB T4J 1R7
Tel: 403-783-5521; *Fax:* 403-783-2012

Priddis: **Rath & Company - *7**
RR#1, Box 44, Site 8, Priddis, AB T0L 1W0
Tel: 403-931-4047; *Fax:* 403-931-4048
rathco@telus.net

Red Deer: **Brian Adair - *1**
#207, 4909 - 48 St., Red Deer, AB T4N 1S8
Tel: 403-342-1777; *Fax:* 403-341-4775

Red Deer: **Susan K. Allison - *1**
4919 - 48 St., 2nd Floor, Red Deer, AB T4N 1S8
Tel: 403-340-3136; *Fax:* 403-343-7016

Red Deer: **Duhamel Manning Feehan Warrender Glass LLP - *13**
5233 - 49 Ave., Red Deer, AB T4N 6G5
Tel: 403-343-0812; *Fax:* 403-340-3545
altalaw@reddeeraltalaw.com
www.reddeeraltalaw.com

Red Deer: **Dunkle McBeath - *2**
5004 - 48 Ave., Red Deer, AB T4N 3T6
Tel: 403-347-5522; *Fax:* 403-347-5632
dkm_law@telusplanet.net

Red Deer: **Flanagan Sully - *2**
Former Name: Flanagan, Sully, Surkan
#202, 4825 - 47 St., Red Deer, AB T4N 1R3
Tel: 403-342-7715; *Fax:* 403-347-5955
fslaw@telusplanet.net

Red Deer: **C.E. Forgues - *1**
7891 - 50 Ave., Red Deer, AB T4P 2S4
Tel: 403-342-7044; *Fax:* 403-342-7055

Red Deer: **Gerig Hamilton Neeland - *5**
#501, 4901 - 48 St., Red Deer, AB T4N 6M4
Tel: 403-343-2444; *Fax:* 403-343-6522
info@ghnh.net

Red Deer: **Donald A. Gross - *1**
#274, 4919 - 59 St., Red Deer, AB T4N 6C9
Tel: 403-343-3715; *Fax:* 403-343-7435

Red Deer: **Johnston Ming Manning LLP - *13**
Royal Bank Bldg., 4943 - 50th St., 3rd & 4th Fl., Red Deer, AB T4N 1Y1
Tel: 403-346-5591; *Fax:* 403-346-5599
info@jmmlawrd.ca
www.johnstonmingmanning.com

Red Deer: **Lee & Short - *4**
4801 - 49 St., Red Deer, AB T4N 1T8
Tel: 403-343-1212; *Fax:* 403-341-3066
galbrecht@leeshort.com

Red Deer: **Brian S. MacNairn - *1**
#201, 5008 Ross St., Red Deer, AB T4N 1Y3
Tel: 403-347-2700; *Fax:* 403-346-5825
macnairn@telusplanet.net

Red Deer: **P.E.B. MacSween - *1**
4824 - 51 St., Red Deer, AB T4N 2A5
Tel: 403-342-5595; *Fax:* 403-342-7519

Red Deer: **Peter C. McElhaney - *1**
#201, 4702 - 49th Ave., Red Deer, AB T4N 6L5
Tel: 403-346-2026; *Fax:* 403-309-1969

Red Deer: **Gerald W. Neufeld - *1**
#209, 4815 Gaetz Ave., Red Deer, AB T4N 4A5
Tel: 403-343-2202; *Fax:* 403-343-2203
gneufeld@telusplanet.net

Red Deer: **Patrick A. Penny - *1**
#290, 4819C - 48 Ave., Red Deer, AB T4N 3T2
Tel: 403-342-9595; *Fax:* 403-346-9778

Red Deer: **Schnell Hardy Jones LLP - *8**
Former Name: Schnell, MacSween & Hardy
#504, 4909 - 49th St., Red Deer, AB T4N 1V1
Tel: 403-342-7400; *Fax:* 403-340-0520
Toll-Free: 800-342-7405
lawyers@schnell-law.com
www.schnell-law.com

Red Deer: **Sisson Warren Sinclair - *9**
#600, First Red Deer Place, 4911 - 51 St., Red Deer, AB T4N 6V4
Tel: 403-343-3320; *Fax:* 403-343-6069
email@swslawyers.com

Red Deer: **William D. Weiswasser - *1**
#104, 4808 Ross St., Red Deer, AB T4N 1X5
Tel: 403-343-0317; *Fax:* 403-343-0318
mediate@agt.net

Redwater: **D.L. McCallum - *1**
P.O. Box 396, Redwater, AB T0A 2W0
Tel: 780-942-3040; *Fax:* 780-942-2003
Toll-Free: 800-390-2257

Rimbey: **David R. Pfau - *1**
P.O. Box 1009, 5001 - 50th Ave., Rimbey, AB T0C 2J0
Tel: 403-843-2296; *Fax:* 403-843-2344

Rocky Mountain House: **Peter Crossley Law Office - *1**
P.O. Box 1108, 4616 - 47 Ave., Rocky Mountain House, AB T4T 1A8
Tel: 403-845-2828; *Fax:* 403-845-4630

Rocky Mountain House: **Dunsford & Scott - *3**
P.O. Box 370, 5135 - 48 Ave., Rocky Mountain House, AB T4T 1A3
Tel: 403-845-7112; *Fax:* 403-845-4670
reception@dunsfordandscott.com

Rocky Mountain House: **Woollard Hopkins & Company - *2**
5133 - 49 St., Rocky Mountain House, AB T4T 1B8
Tel: 403-845-2545; *Fax:* 403-845-2285
wooll@woollardhopkins.com

Sherwood Park: **Stanley H. King - *1**
77 Chippewa Rd., Sherwood Park, AB T8A 6J7
Tel: 780-910-7475; *Fax:* 780-416-4891
stan@westana.com

Sherwood Park: **Wayne LeDrew - *1**
#16, 140 Athabascan Ave., Sherwood Park, AB T8A 4E3
Tel: 780-467-3014; *Fax:* 780-464-8504
wledrew@telusplanet.net

Sherwood Park: **Nigro & Company - *1**
282 Kaska Rd., Sherwood Park, AB T8A 4G7
Tel: 780-467-9559; *Fax:* 780-467-0720

Sherwood Park: **Thomas E. Spratlin - *1**
Former Name: Spratlin Tonnellier
#14B, 363 Sioux Rd., Sherwood Park, AB T8A 4W7
Tel: 780-464-5404; *Fax:* 780-417-1759
spratlin@telus.net

Slave Lake: **Allan G. McMillan - *1**
#2, 221 - 3 Ave. NW, Slave Lake, AB T0G 2A1
Tel: 780-849-2227; *Fax:* 780-849-2143
mcmillan@telusplanet.net

Slave Lake: **Twinn Barristers & Solicitors - *1**
Former Name: Catherine M. Twinn
P.O. Box 1460, 810 Caribou Trail NE, Slave Lake, AB T0G 2A0
Tel: 780-849-4319; *Fax:* 780-805-3274
ctwinn@twinnlaw.com

Spruce Grove: **Ayers & Company - *2**
#210, P.O. Box 4372, Stn. Main, 215 McLeod Ave., Spruce Grove, AB T7X 3B5
Tel: 780-962-9500; *Fax:* 780-962-9535

Spruce Grove: **N.L.A. (Loretta) Edlund - *1**
#35, 54023 SH 779, Spruce Grove, AB T7X 3V5
Tel: 780-968-1668; *Fax:* 780-968-1667
nlaedlund@gmail.com

Spruce Grove: **Randall C. Heil - *1**
#201, Cumbria Centre, 93 McLeod Ave., Spruce Grove, AB T7X 2Z9
Tel: 780-962-9700; *Fax:* 780-962-9329
rheil@telus.net

Spruce Grove: **Robert A. Joly - *1**
#4, 20 McLeod Ave., Spruce Grove, AB T7X 3Y1
Tel: 780-962-4447; *Fax:* 780-962-3638
bbjoly@shaw.ca

Spruce Grove: **Robinson & Company - *2**
P.O. Box 4113, 16 Westgrove Dr., Spruce Grove, AB T7X 3B3
Tel: 780-962-0660; *Fax:* 780-962-0622
brbnsn@telusplanet.net

St Albert: **Goldsman, Ritzen, Shadlyn - *5**
Former Name: Goldsman & Ritzen
#609, Grandin Park Tower, 22 Sir Winston Churchill Ave., St Albert, AB T8N 1B4
Tel: 780-458-0500; *Fax:* 780-459-2472

St Albert: **K. June Koska Professional Corporation - *1**
40 Berrymore Dr., St Albert, AB T8N 6B8
Tel: 780-460-1721; *Fax:* 780-460-1334

St Albert: **Vaughn H. Myers - *1**
#201, Mission Hill Plaza, 398 St. Albert Rd., St Albert, AB T8N 5J9
Tel: 780-460-2505; *Fax:* 780-459-5088

St Albert: **Oddleifson & Kaup - *2**
#118, 7 St. Anne St., St Albert, AB T8N 2X4
Tel: 780-459-2220; *Fax:* 780-459-0621

St Albert: **Quantz Law Group - *3**
Former Name: Stonhouse & Downie
#220, 8 Perron St., St Albert, AB T8N 1E4
Tel: 780-458-7690; *Fax:* 780-458-5510
info@quantzlaw.com
www.quantzlaw.com

St Albert: **Thomas A. Rowand Professional Corp. - *1**
#208, Summit Centre, 200 Boudreau Rd., St Albert, AB T8N 6B9
Tel: 780-458-9440; *Fax:* 780-458-9442
trowand@telusplanet.net

St Albert: **Wallace Law Office - *1**
#3, 30 Rayborn Cres., St Albert, AB T8N 5B7
Tel: 780-458-7717; *Fax:* 780-460-1818
kdwl@telusplanet.net

St Albert: **Weary & Company - *2**
#400, 30 Green Grove Dr., St Albert, AB T8N 5H6
Tel: 780-459-5596; *Fax:* 780-459-6572

St Albert: **William Glabb Law Office - *1**
Former Name: William P. Glabb
#601, Grandin Park Tower, 22 Sir Winston Churchill Ave., St Albert, AB T8N 1B4
Tel: 780-459-2200; *Fax:* 780-459-2281
wmglabblawoffice@shaw.ca
www.williamglabblawoffice.com

St Paul: **Lamoureux & Lawrence - *4**
4713 - 50th St., St Paul, AB T0A 3A4
Tel: 780-645-5202; *Fax:* 780-645-6507
law@stpaul-law.ca

Stony Plain: **Birdsell Grant LLP - *8**
Former Name: Birdsell Grant Gardner Morck
#102, 5300 - 50 St., Stony Plain, AB T7Z 1T8
Tel: 780-963-8181; *Fax:* 780-963-9618
info@birdsell.ca

** indicates number of lawyers*

Stony Plain: M.P. Stone - *1
#300, P.O. Box 56, Stn. Main, RR#3, Stony Plain, AB T7Z 1X3

Strathmore: Getz & Associates - *2
P.O. Box 2370, 225A Wheatland Trail, Strathmore, AB T1P 1K3
Tel: 403-934-2500; *Fax:* 403-934-2794
johng@getzlaw.ca

Strathmore: R.E.J. Jarvis - *2
#110, 304 - 3 Ave., Strathmore, AB T1P 1Z1
Tel: 403-934-5000; *Fax:* 403-934-4853
rejarvis@shaw.ca

Sylvan Lake: Brian C. Flanagan - *1
#203, 5043 - 50A St., Sylvan Lake, AB T4S 1R1
Tel: 403-887-5441; *Fax:* 403-887-3010
burflan@telusplanet.net

Sylvan Lake: Deborah M. Hanly - *1
P.O. Box 9113, Stn. Main, 20 Woodland Cres., Sylvan Lake, AB T4S 1S6
Tel: 403-887-4410; *Fax:* 403-887-4416
Toll-Free: 877-887-7789
tax-law@shaw.ca

Sylvan Lake: Vanden Brink Law Office - *1
Former Name: Vanden Brink & Madden
P.O. Box 9613, Stn. Main, Sylvan Lake, AB T4S 1S8
Tel: 403-885-2222; *Fax:* 403-885-2226
benbrink@direcway.com

Taber: Baldry Sugden, LLP - *3
5401 - 50 Ave., Taber, AB T1G 1V2
Tel: 403-223-3585; *Fax:* 403-223-1732
balsug@telusplanet.net

Three Hills: Norman L. Tainsh Prof. Corp. - *1
P.O. Box 1234, 205 Main St., Three Hills, AB T0M 2A0
Tel: 403-443-2200; *Fax:* 403-443-2025
Toll-Free: 888-939-2200
ntainsh@tainsh.ca

Turner Valley: Beverly A.B. Broadhurst - *1
#2, P.O. Box 501, 101 Sunset Blvd. SW, Turner Valley, AB T0L 2A0
Tel: 403-933-3255; *Fax:* 403-933-4104

Vermilion: Reynolds & Flemke - *2
#11, 5125 - 50 Ave., Vermilion, AB T9X 1A8
Tel: 780-853-5339; *Fax:* 780-853-4200

Vermilion: Wheat Law Office - *2
5042 - 49 Ave., Vermilion, AB T9X 1B7
Tel: 780-853-4707; *Fax:* 780-853-4499
wheatlaw@telusplanet.net

Wainwright: Peter Van Winssen - *1
1013 - 5 Ave., Wainwright, AB T9W 1L6
Tel: 780-842-5140; *Fax:* 780-842-3830

Westlock: Tims & Company - *2
#2, P.O. Box 490, 9831 - 107th St., Westlock, AB T7P 1R9
Tel: 780-349-5366; *Fax:* 780-349-6510

Wetaskiwin: Deckert Allen Cymbaluk Genest - *4
#301, P.O. Box 6060, 5201 - 51st Ave., Wetaskiwin, AB T9A 2E8
Tel: 780-352-3301; *Fax:* 780-352-5976

Wetaskiwin: McDonald Street Law Office - *1
4408 - 51 St., Wetaskiwin, AB T9A 1K5
Tel: 780-352-0369; *Fax:* 780-352-0393

Wetaskiwin: Schumacher & Associates - *4
5118 - 50 Ave., Wetaskiwin, AB T9A 0S6
Tel: 780-352-6691; *Fax:* 780-352-0599
schumacher@incentre.net

Whitecourt: McConnell Law Office - *1
P.O. Box 1795, Stn. Main, 5115 Highway St., Whitecourt, AB T7S 1P5
Tel: 780-778-4945; *Fax:* 780-778-3851

British Columbia

100 Mile House: Centennial Law Corporation - *3
P.O. Box 819, 100 Mile House, BC V0K 2E0
Tel: 250-395-3881; *Fax:* 250-395-2644
centenniallaw@bcinternet.net

100 Mile House: George J. Wool - *1
5741 Simon Lake Rd., 100 Mile House, BC V0K 2E1
Tel: 250-791-9295; *Fax:* 250-791-9228
gwool@bcinternet.net

Abbotsford: Joshua M. Bach - *1
#506, 2700 McCallum Rd., Abbotsford, BC V2S 6X9
Tel: 800-506-6304

Abbotsford: Kenneth R. Beatch - *1
2459 Pauline St., Abbotsford, BC V2S 3S1
Tel: 604-853-9555; *Fax:* 604-859-3361
ken@drugdefence.com
www.drugdefence.com

Abbotsford: Bronson, Jones & Company - *5
Former Name: Bronson & Company
#300, 2890 Garden St., Abbotsford, BC V2T 4W7
Tel: 604-852-5100; *Fax:* 604-850-2164

Abbotsford: Fast Welwood & Wiens - *4
#305, 2692 Clearbrook Rd., Abbotsford, BC V2T 2Y8
Tel: 604-850-6640; *Fax:* 604-857-1833
info@faswel.com

Abbotsford: Larry W. Goddard - *1
#105, 2955 Gladwin Rd., Abbotsford, BC V2T 5T4
Tel: 604-853-3535; *Fax:* 604-853-9033

Abbotsford: Linley Welwood LLP - *7
Former Name: Linley, Duignan & Company; Welwood Wiens Warkentin
#305, 2692 Clearbrook Rd., Abbotsford, BC V2T 2Y8
Tel: 604-850-6640; *Fax:* 604-850-6616
www.linleywelwood.com

Abbotsford: Marcotte Law Office - *1
#1, 33775 Essendene Ave., Abbotsford, BC V2S 2H1
Tel: 604-855-6688; *Fax:* 604-855-6515

Abbotsford: Palmer Gillen - *2
#1, 33775 Essendene Ave., Abbotsford, BC V2S 2H1
Tel: 604-859-3887; *Fax:* 604-859-3883
www.abbotsfordlawyers.com

Abbotsford: Robertson, Downe & Mullally - *20
Also Known As: RDM Lawyers
33695 South Fraser Way, Abbotsford, BC V2S 2C1
Tel: 604-853-0774; *Fax:* 604-852-3829
Toll-Free: 888-853-0774
info@rdmlawyers
www.rdmlawyers.com

Abbotsford: Lloyd H. Wilson - *1
2644 Montrose Ave., Abbotsford, BC V2S 3T6
Tel: 604-853-3355; *Fax:* 604-853-2644
lloydhwilson_company@hotmail.com

Armstrong: Blakely & Co. - *1
#201, P.O. Box 357, 2595 Pleasant Valley Blvd., Armstrong, BC V0E 1B0
Tel: 250-546-3188; *Fax:* 250-546-2677
blakely@junction.net

Armstrong: Culos & Company - *1
Former Name: Clarke & Company
P.O. Box 70, 2553 Pleasant Valley Blvd., Armstrong, BC V0E 1B0
Tel: 250-546-2448; *Fax:* 250-546-2621
robculos@telus.net

Brentwood Bay: Sandra E. Jenko - *1
#112, 7088 West Saanich, Brentwood Bay, BC V8M 1P9
Tel: 250-652-5151

Burnaby: Baily McLean, Barristers & Solicitors - *2
Former Name: Greenbank Murdoch & Company; Baily, McLean, Greenbank & Murdoch
#900, Metrotower II, 4720 Kingsway, Burnaby, BC V5H 4M2
Tel: 604-437-6611; *Fax:* 604-437-3065
info@bmgm.com
www.bmgm.com

Burnaby: Bergen Legal Services - *1
5816 Sherban Ct., Burnaby, BC V5B 4P2
Tel: 604-291-9291; *Fax:* 604-291-9335

Burnaby: W.E. Bergmann - *1
4550 East Hastings St., Burnaby, BC V5C 2K4
Tel: 604-298-8211; *Fax:* 604-298-8216

Burnaby: Cobbett & Cotton - *7
4259 East Hastings St., Burnaby, BC V5C 2J5
Tel: 604-299-6251; *Fax:* 604-299-6627
mail@cobett-cotton.com

Burnaby: Edwards, Edwards & Edwards - *3
#510, 5021 Kingsway, Burnaby, BC V5H 4A5
Tel: 604-433-2445; *Fax:* 604-433-8209

Burnaby: James K. Fitzsimmons - *1
#200, 6960 Royal Oak Ave., Burnaby, BC V5J 4J2
Tel: 604-298-8939; *Fax:* 604-298-8956

Burnaby: Robert A. Foran - *1
#275, c/o UMA Group Ltd., 3001 Wayburne Dr., Burnaby, BC V5G 4W3
Tel: 604-631-6232; *Fax:* 604-685-1035
bob.foran@uma.aecom.com
www.umagroup.com

Burnaby: James K. Fraser Law Corporation - *1
#200, 4603 Kingsway, Burnaby, BC V5H 4M4
Tel: 604-433-0010; *Fax:* 604-435-0269
jkf@jkf.ca

Burnaby: Hawthorne, Piggott & Company - *7
#208, 1899 Willingdon Ave., Burnaby, BC V5C 5T1
Tel: 604-299-8371; *Fax:* 604-299-1523
lawyers@hawthornelaw.com

Burnaby: Hwang & Company - *3
#333, 4501 North Rd., Burnaby, BC V3N 4R7
Tel: 604-421-3669; *Fax:* 604-421-6339
mh@korcanlaw.com

Burnaby: O'Neill, Rozenberg - *2
#201, 4547 Hastings St., Burnaby, BC V5C 2K3
Tel: 604-294-8311; *Fax:* 604-294-5278
Toll-Free: 800-354-1888

Burnaby: Pihl & Company - *1
#205, 5481 Kingsway, Burnaby, BC V5H 2G1
Tel: 604-437-8837; *Fax:* 604-437-3529

Burnaby: Russell Kuhl & Co. - *2
#220, 4411 Hastings St., Burnaby, BC V5C 2K1
Tel: 604-298-1038; *Fax:* 604-298-1037
russellradio@telus.net; mail@jeffkuhl.com

Burnaby: Sellens & Associates - *3
#330, 9940 Lougheed Hwy., Burnaby, BC V3J 1N3
Tel: 604-421-0716; *Fax:* 604-421-7692

Burnaby: Starr & Company - *2
#205, 5481 Kingsway, Burnaby, BC V5H 2G1
Tel: 604-435-5588; *Fax:* 604-435-5588
gbstarr@telus.net

Burnaby: Warren, Eder - *2
#216, 3989 Henning Dr., Burnaby, BC V5C 6P8
Tel: 604-687-0134; *Fax:* 604-687-5176
Toll-Free: 800-461-3455
warren&eder@shawbiz.ca

Burnaby: Maureen J. Wesley - *1
4270 McGill St., Burnaby, BC V5C 1M9
Tel: 604-298-6555; *Fax:* 604-298-6540

Burnaby: Patricia Yaremovich - *1
#105, 6540 East Hastings St., Burnaby, BC V5B 4Z5
Tel: 604-320-0688; *Fax:* 604-320-0007
pyaremovich@shaw.ca

Campbell River: Graham & Frame - *2
#301, 1100 Island Hwy., Campbell River, BC V9W 8C6
Tel: 250-286-6691; *Fax:* 250-286-1191
fisherrk@telus.net

Campbell River: Claire I. Moglove - *1
#201, 909 Island Hwy., Campbell River, BC V9W 2C2
Tel: 250-286-9946; *Fax:* 250-286-0052
cmaglove@island.net

Campbell River: Shook, Wickham, Bishop & Field - *9
Former Name: McVea, Shook, Wickham & Bishop
906 Island Hwy., Campbell River, BC V9W 2C3
Tel: 250-287-8355; *Fax:* 250-287-8112
info@crlawyers.ca
www.crlawyers.ca

Campbell River: Karen D. Stevan - *1
475 Evergreen Rd., Campbell River, BC V9W 3R6
Tel: 250-286-3308; *Fax:* 250-286-3387
kdstevan@yahoo.ca

** indicates number of lawyers*

Campbell River: **Tees Kiddle Spencer - *4**
#200, 1260 Shoppers Row, Campbell River, BC V9W 2C8
Tel: 250-287-7755; *Fax:* 250-287-3999
Toll-Free: 800-224-7755
tks@tkslaw.com
www.tkslaw.com

Castlegar: **Polonicoff & Perehudoff - *2**
1115 - 3 St., Castlegar, BC V1N 2A1
Tel: 250-365-3343; *Fax:* 250-365-6307
polper@netidea.com

Castlegar: **Wyllie & Co. - *1**
1418 Columbia Ave., Castlegar, BC V1N 3K3
Tel: 250-365-8451; *Fax:* 250-365-3488
wyllielaw@telus.net
www.macisaacgroup.com

Chemainus: **Mary Lynn Bancroft - *1**
Box 168, 9834 Croft St., Chemainus, BC V0R 1K0
Tel: 250-246-4771; *Fax:* 250-246-2547
mbancroft@shaw.ca

Chilliwack: **Kaye Thome Toews & Hansford - *7**
Former Name: Kaye, Toews & Caldwell
CP 372, 9202 Young Rd., Chilliwack, BC V2P 6J4
Tel: 604-792-1977; *Fax:* 604-792-7077
Toll-Free: 888-792-1977
ktc@ktclawoffice.com
www.ktthlawyers.com

Clearbrook: **Kuzminski Neufeld Rebane, Valley Law Group - *3**
Former Name: Kuzminski & Haraldsen
#201, 2890 Garden St., Clearbrook, BC V2T 4W7
Tel: 604-853-5401; *Fax:* 604-853-8358

Clearwater: **John Kurta - *1**
P.O. Box 5171, 32 East Old North Thompson Hwy., Clearwater, BC V0E 1N0
Tel: 250-674-2126; *Fax:* 250-674-3493

Comox: **Schaffrick & Sutton - *2**
1984 Comox Ave., Comox, BC V9M 3M7
Tel: 250-339-3363; *Fax:* 250-339-3315
Toll-Free: 877-778-8866

Coquitlam: **David Boulding - *1**
#206, 2922 Glen Dr., Coquitlam, BC V3B 2P7
Tel: 604-945-2043; *Fax:* 604-945-2063
dmboulding@shaw.ca

Coquitlam: **Drysdale Bacon McStravick - *7**
Former Name: Feller Bacon McStravick
#211, 1015 Austin Ave., Coquitlam, BC V3K 3N9
Tel: 604-939-8321; *Fax:* 604-939-7584
inquiries@dbmlaw.ca
www.dbmlaw.ca

Coquitlam: **Spagnuolo & Company Real Estate Lawyers - *10**
#300, 906 Roderick Ave., Coquitlam, BC V3K 1R1
Tel: 604-527-4242; *Fax:* 604-527-8976
Toll-Free: 888-873-2829
info@bcrealestatelawyers.com
www.bcrealestatelawyers.com

Coquitlam: **Spraggs & Company - *1**
#202, 1030 Westwood St., Coquitlam, BC V3C 4E4
Tel: 604-464-3333

Coquitlam: **Taylor Bardal - *3**
#220, 1024 Ridgeway Ave., Coquitlam, BC V3J 1S5
Tel: 604-931-3477; *Fax:* 604-931-1277

Coquitlam: **Judy Wong - *1**
#205, 3030 Lincoln Ave., Coquitlam, BC V3B 6B4
Tel: 604-945-6982; *Fax:* 604-945-6819

Coquitlam: **Zipp & Company - *2**
820 Henderson Ave., Coquitlam, BC V3K 1P2
Tel: 604-936-7743

Courtenay: **James E. Dow - *1**
#7, 625 Cliffe Ave., Courtenay, BC V9N 2J6
Tel: 250-338-7701; *Fax:* 250-338-6641
jamesdow@shaw.ca

Courtenay: **Ives Burger, Barristers & Solicitors - *3**
Former Name: Gibson Kelly & Ives
505 - 5 St., Courtenay, BC V9N 1K2
Tel: 250-334-2416; *Fax:* 250-334-3198
info@ivesburgerlaw.com
www.ivesburgerlaw.com

Courtenay: **C.H.L. Morris - *1**
949 Fitzgerald Ave., Courtenay, BC V9N 2R6
Tel: 250-338-5311; *Fax:* 250-338-1818
crispinmorris@shaw.ca

Courtenay: **Roy William Pouss - *1**
243 - 4th St., Courtenay, BC V9N 1G7
Tel: 250-334-3188; *Fax:* 250-334-3174

Courtenay: **Swift Datoo Law Corporation - *8**
#201, 467 Cumberland Rd., Courtenay, BC V9N 2C5
Tel: 250-334-4461; *Fax:* 250-334-2335
Toll-Free: 877-334-4461
lawyers@swiftdatoo.com
www.swiftdatoo.com

Cranbrook: **Patrick J. Dearden - *1**
#201, 129 - 10th Ave. South, Cranbrook, BC V1C 2N1
Tel: 250-426-7431; *Fax:* 250-426-3746

Cranbrook: **Kelle M. Maag Law Corporation - *1**
20 - 11th Ave. South, Cranbrook, BC V1C 2P1
Tel: 250-426-5508; *Fax:* 250-426-1904

Cranbrook: **Murielle A. Matthews - *1**
801B Baker St., Cranbrook, BC V1C 1A3
Tel: 250-426-0601; *Fax:* 250-426-0642

Cranbrook: **Miles, Daroux, Zimmer & Sheard - *4**
45 - 8th Ave. South, Cranbrook, BC V1C 2K4
Tel: 250-489-3350; *Fax:* 250-489-2235
s.daroux@shaw.ca

Cranbrook: **Rella & Paolini - *2**
#6, 10 Ave. South, 2nd Fl., Cranbrook, BC V1C 2M8
Tel: 250-426-8981; *Fax:* 250-426-8987
Toll-Free: 866-426-8981
rellaco@shaw.ca

Cranbrook: **Robertson & Co. - *1**
#200, 135 - 10 Ave. South, Cranbrook, BC V1C 2N1
Tel: 250-489-4346; *Fax:* 250-489-1899
robertson@cranbrooklaw.com
www.cranbrooklaw.com

Cranbrook: **Steidl, Kambeitz - *2**
#201, 907 Baker St., Cranbrook, BC V1C 1A4
Tel: 250-426-7211; *Fax:* 250-426-6100
sk@steidlco.com

Cranbrook: **Darrel C. Symington - *1**
123 - 12th Ave. South, Cranbrook, BC V1C 2S2
Tel: 250-489-2800; *Fax:* 250-489-1173
dsymington@cyberllink.ca

Dawson Creek: **Higson Apps - *3**
Former Name: Plenert Higson
#201, 1136 - 103 Ave., Dawson Creek, BC V1G 2G7
Tel: 250-782-9134; *Fax:* 250-782-9135
Toll-Free: 888-782-9134
rapps@plenerthigson.com

Dawson Creek: **Mitchell Schuller - *3**
#2, 933 - 103 Ave., Dawson Creek, BC V1G 2G4
Tel: 250-782-8155; *Fax:* 250-782-4525
mitchellschuller@shawcable.com

Delta: **James M. Antifay Law Corporation - *1**
#212, 7313 - 120 St., Delta, BC V4C 6P5
Tel: 604-572-8333; *Fax:* 604-572-6744
jantifay@allstream.net
www.antifayjamesm.supersites.ca

Delta: **James Broad - *1**
9337 - 120 St., Delta, BC V4C 6R8
Tel: 604-585-3422; *Fax:* 604-585-3613

Delta: **Buckley Hogan - *3**
Former Name: Buckley & Buckley
9453 - 120 St., Delta, BC V4C 6S2
Tel: 604-588-0431; *Fax:* 604-588-0062
lawyers@buckho.com

Delta: **Delta Legal Office - *1**
#211, 7313 - 120 St., Delta, BC V4C 6P5
Tel: 604-599-1188; *Fax:* 604-599-1975
iggibson@deltalegal.com

Delta: **Danielle D. Deschamps-Carlson - *3**
#201, 5155 Trunk Rd., Delta, BC V4K 1W4
Tel: 604-940-8182; *Fax:* 604-940-9892
info@severidelawgroup.com

Delta: **Lehal & Company - *1**
#200, 6905 - 120th St., Delta, BC V4E 2A8
Tel: 604-596-1321; *Fax:* 604-596-1320

Delta: **Leung, Arthur-Leung - *1**
5110 Ladner Trunk Rd., Delta, BC V4K 1W3
Tel: 604-940-8888; *Fax:* 604-946-6628

Delta: **David C. McPhillips - *1**
4924 - 2A Ave., Delta, BC V4M 3V1
Tel: 604-943-6750; *Fax:* 604-943-6350

Delta: **Stasiuk & Rose - *2**
#203, 1205 - 56 St., Delta, BC V4L 2A6
Tel: 604-943-8272; *Fax:* 604-943-8416
r.stasiuk@stasiuk-rose.com

Delta: **TNT Lawyers - *3**
7929 - 120 St., Delta, BC V4C 6P6
Tel: 604-502-5615; *Fax:* 604-591-8722
Toll-Free: 800-750-5122
info@icbcinjurylawyers.ca
www.icbcinjurylawyers.ca

Delta: **Dell C. Valair - *1**
10 - 5900 Ferry Rd., Delta, BC V4K 5C3
Tel: 604-940-3318; *Fax:* 604-940-3324
dell@lightspeed.ca

Delta (Tsawwassen): **Millichamp & Company - *1**
#210, 1530 - 56 St., Delta (Tsawwassen), BC V4L 2A8
Tel: 604-943-7401; *Fax:* 604-943-7402
millichamplawco@gmail.com

Duncan: **Donald S. Allan - *1**
#204, 225 Canada Ave., Duncan, BC V9L 1T6
Tel: 250-748-2340; *Fax:* 250-748-2343
d.s.allan@shaw.ca

Duncan: **Coleman Fraser Parcells - *4**
Former Name: Coleman Parceus Fraser Whittome
#202, 58 Station St., Duncan, BC V9L 1M4
Tel: 250-748-1013; *Fax:* 250-743-8318
Toll-Free: 888-748-1013

Duncan: **Desjardins & Arndt - *2**
Former Name: Molnar, Desjardins & Arndt
466 TransCanada Highway, Duncan, BC V9L 3R6
Tel: 250-748-5253; *Fax:* 250-746-1511
vincedesjardins@shaw.ca

Duncan: **Robert W. Nelford - *1**
3250 Hillwood Rd., Duncan, BC V9L 5K6
Tel: 250-746-8555; *Fax:* 250-748-1957
robertn@com-net.com

Duncan: **Orchard & Company - *5**
321 St. Julian St., Duncan, BC V9L 3S5
Tel: 250-746-5899; *Fax:* 250-746-7182
admin@orchardandco.ca
www.orchardandco.ca

Duncan: **Ridgway & Company - *5**
#200, 44 Queens Rd., Duncan, BC V9L 2W4
Tel: 250-746-7121; *Fax:* 250-746-4070
info@ridgco.com
www.ridgco.com

Duncan: **Taylor Granitto - *4**
466 Trans Canada Hwy., Duncan, BC V9L 3R6
Tel: 250-748-4444; *Fax:* 250-748-5920
Toll-Free: 800-665-5414
dtaylor@taylor-co.com
www.taylor-co.com

Duncan: **J.B. Whittaker - *1**
Stn. Main, 7334 Waltons Mountain Rd., RR#1, Duncan, BC V9L 5W8
Tel: 250-748-6674

Fernie: **R.W. Bentley - *1**
P.O. Box 2038, Fernie, BC V0B 1M0
Tel: 250-423-9241; *Fax:* 250-423-6440
bentleylaw@elkvalley.net

Fort St John: **Earmme & Associates - *3**
Former Name: Daley & Earmme
10740 - 101st Ave., Fort St John, BC V1J 2B4
Tel: 250-785-6961; *Fax:* 250-785-6967

Fort St John: **Rodney J. Strandberg Law Corp. - *1**
#320, 9900 - 100 Ave., Fort St John, BC V1J 5S7
Tel: 250-787-7760; *Fax:* 250-787-7752
strandberglaw@telus.net

Garibaldi Highlands: **Brian N. Hughes - *1**
#201, P.O. Box 557, 1364 Pemberton Ave., Garibaldi Highlands, BC V0N 1T0
Tel: 604-892-5114; *Fax:* 604-892-0114

* *indicates number of lawyers*

Gibsons: **Peter J. Holden - *1**
995 Grandview Rd., RR#10, Gibsons, BC V0N 1V3
Tel: 604-630-3913; *Fax:* 604-630-3914

Gibsons: **J. Wayne Rowe - *1**
758 School Rd., Gibsons, BC V0N 1V0
Tel: 604-886-2029; *Fax:* 604-886-9191

Gibsons: **Leanne L. Turnbull - *1**
523 Central Ave., RR#1, Gibsons, BC V0N 1V1
Tel: 604-886-7666; *Fax:* 604-886-7636
leeturnbull@dccnet.com

Hope: **Kennedy, Jensen - *2**
CP 1719, 400 Park St., Hope, BC V0X 1L0
Tel: 604-869-9981; *Fax:* 604-869-7640
www.kennedyjensen.com

Hornby Island: **Sally Campbell - *1**
4505 Roburn Rd., Hornby Island, BC V0R 1Z0
Tel: 250-335-2272; *Fax:* 250-335-0895
scampbel@island.net
www.island.net/~scampbell

Hornby Island: **Sue M. Kelly - *1**
P.O. Box 14, Stn. Anderson, Hornby Island, BC V0R 1Z0
Tel: 250-335-0735; *Fax:* 250-335-0732
smkelly@telus.net

Invermere: **Kluge, Boyd - *2**
P.O. Box 2647, 906 - 8 Ave., Invermere, BC V0A 1K0
Tel: 250-342-4447; *Fax:* 250-342-3298
barnim@telus.net

Kamloops: **Bilkey, Quinn - *7**
#301, 186 Victoria St., Kamloops, BC V2C 5R3
Tel: 250-374-6661; *Fax:* 250-828-2836
info@bilkeyquinn.com
www.bilkeyquinn.com

Kamloops: **George Coutlee & Co. - *1**
1270 Salish Rd., Kamloops, BC V2H 1K1
Tel: 250-372-9922; *Fax:* 250-372-1114

Kamloops: **Cundari & Company Law Corporation - *4**
#810, 175 - 2 Ave., Kamloops, BC V2C 5W1
Tel: 250-372-3368; *Fax:* 250-372-5554
cundari@cundarilaw.com
www.cundarilaw.com

Kamloops: **Fulton & Company LLP, Lawyers & Trade-Mark Agents - *26**
#300, 350 Lansdowne St., Kamloops, BC V2C 1Y1
Tel: 250-372-5542; *Fax:* 250-851-2300
law@fultonco.com
www.fultonco.com

Kamloops: **Gibraltar Law Group - *3**
#102, 418 St. Paul St., Kamloops, BC V2C 2J6
Tel: 250-374-3737; *Fax:* 250-374-0035
Toll-Free: 877-374-3737
mail@gibraltarlawgroup.com
www.gibraltarlawgroup.com

Kamloops: **Gillespie Renkema Barnett Broadway LLP - *1**
#200, 121 St. Paul St., Kamloops, BC V2C 3K8
Tel: 250-374-4463; *Fax:* 250-374-5250

Kamloops: **HMZ Law - *5**
Former Name: Horne Marr Zak
#600, 175 Second Ave., Kamloops, BC V2C 5W1
Tel: 250-372-1221; *Fax:* 250-372-8339
Toll-Free: 800-558-1933
hmz@hmzlaw.com
www.hmzlaw.com

Kamloops: **Jensen Carroll Watt - *7**
#300, Old Firehall #1, 125 - 4 Ave., Kamloops, BC V2C 3N3
Tel: 250-372-8811; *Fax:* 250-828-6697
Toll-Free: 800-949-3362
jmc@jmc.bc.ca

Kamloops: **Kahle & Co. Law Corporation - *1**
243A Seymour St., Kamloops, BC V2C 2E7
Tel: 250-828-8666; *Fax:* 250-828-0048
Toll-Free: 888-529-1937
kahleco@telus.net
www.kahleco.com

Kamloops: **Mary MacGregor Law Corporation - *1**
975 Victoria St., Kamloops, BC V2C 2C1
Tel: 250-828-0282; *Fax:* 250-828-0287
mary.macgregor@mmlc.ca
www.marymacgregor.ca

Kamloops: **Mair Jensen Blair Lawyers LLP - *15**
#700, 275 Lansdowne St., Kamloops, BC V2C 6H6
Tel: 250-374-3161; *Fax:* 250-374-6992
info@mjblaw.com
www.mjblaw.com

Kamloops: **David A. McMillan - *1**
#401, 286 St. Paul St., Kamloops, BC V2C 6G4
Tel: 250-828-0702; *Fax:* 250-828-0703
dmlawoff@telus.net

Kamloops: **Morelli Chertkow LLP, Lawyers - *11**
#300, 180 Seymour St., Kamloops, BC V2C 2E3
Tel: 250-374-3344; *Fax:* 250-374-1144
Toll-Free: 888-374-3350
info@morellichertkow.com
www.morellichertkow.com

Kamloops: **Craig Nixon Law Corp. - *1**
#880, 175 - 2nd Ave., Kamloops, BC V2C 5W1
Tel: 250-374-1555; *Fax:* 250-374-9992
onlc@direct.ca

Kamloops: **Oien, Church - *2**
#212, 220 - 4th Ave., Kamloops, BC V2C 3N6
Tel: 250-851-8323; *Fax:* 250-851-8373
Toll-Free: 888-857-8323
oienchurch@telus.net

Kamloops: **Stanford & Company - *1**
#212, 220 - 4th Ave., Kamloops, BC V2C 3N5
Tel: 250-851-8582; *Fax:* 250-851-8583
michelle_stanford@telus.net

Kamloops: **Taylor Epp & Dolder - *3**
#300, 153 Seymour St., Kamloops, BC V2C 2C8
Tel: 250-374-3456; *Fax:* 250-828-6808
taylor_epp_dolder@telus.net

Kamloops: **Wozniak & Walker - *2**
533 Nicola St., Kamloops, BC V2C 2P9
Tel: 250-374-6226; *Fax:* 250-374-4485

Kaslo: **T.R. Humphries - *1**
P.O. Box 636, Kaslo, BC V0G 1M0
Tel: 250-353-2292; *Fax:* 250-353-7430
Trhlaw@telus.net

Kelowna: **Beairsto Sabey - *3**
#201, 401 Glenmore Rd., Kelowna, BC V1V 1Z6
Tel: 250-762-6111; *Fax:* 250-762-6480
Toll-Free: 866-268-6383
lawyers@sabeyrule.ca

Kelowna: **Benson Law LLP**
270 Hwy. 33 West, Kelowna, BC V1X 1X7
Tel: 250-491-0206; *Fax:* 250-491-0266
www.bensoncolaw.ca

Kelowna: **Burgess & Company - *2**
#202, 3528 Scott Rd., Kelowna, BC V1W 3H6
Tel: 250-861-5533; *Fax:* 250-861-4442
dblaw@shawcable.com

Kelowna: **Christiansen, Drummond - *2**
Former Name: Christiansen, Newcombe
#207, 389 Queensway Ave., Kelowna, BC V1Y 8E6
Tel: 250-862-2332; *Fax:* 250-862-2353
cnklaw@telus.net

Kelowna: **Doak Shirreff LLP - *14**
#200, Chancery Place, 537 Leon Ave., Kelowna, BC V1Y 2A9
Tel: 250-763-4323; *Fax:* 250-763-4780
Toll-Free: 800-661-4959
thefirm@doakshirreff.com
www.doakshirreff.com

Kelowna: **Fraser Murray Huck - *3**
#200, 1449 St Paul St., Kelowna, BC V1Y 7S5
Tel: 250-868-8306; *Fax:* 250-868-8301
cfraser@frasermurraylaw.com

Kelowna: **Glazier Polley - *4**
Former Name: Wageman Glazier & Polley
1674 Bertram St., 2nd Fl., Kelowna, BC V1Y 9G4
Tel: 250-763-3343; *Fax:* 250-763-9524

Kelowna: **Gordon & Company - *2**
#102, 1433 St. Paul St., Kelowna, BC V1Y 2E4
Tel: 250-860-9997; *Fax:* 250-860-9937
gordonco@uniserve.com

Kelowna: **Laura J. Gosset - *1**
#214, 440 Cascia Dr., Kelowna, BC V1W 4Y4
Tel: 250-764-8434; *Fax:* 250-764-1817
lauragosset@shaw.ca

Kelowna: **Wade D. Jenson - *1**
#200, 369 Queensway Ave., Kelowna, BC V1Y 8E6
Tel: 250-868-2239; *Fax:* 250-861-5079

Kelowna: **Martin Johnson Law Corporation - *2**
Also Known As: The Heritage Law Group
830 Bernard Ave., Kelowna, BC V1Y 6P5
Tel: 250-868-2848; *Fax:* 250-868-3080
Toll-Free: 877-868-2848
office@heritagelawgroup.com
www.heritagelawgroup.com

Kelowna: **Roberta L. Jordan - *1**
#16, 4524 Eldorado Ct., Kelowna, BC V1W 1G3
Tel: 250-764-0888; *Fax:* 250-764-0680

Kelowna: **Robert O. Levin - *2**
#607, 1708 Dolphin Ave., Kelowna, BC V1Y 9S4
Tel: 250-868-2101; *Fax:* 250-868-2414
robert@rlevin.com

Kelowna: **M. Gail Miller - *1**
#904, 1708 Dolphin Ave., Kelowna, BC V1Y 9S4
Tel: 250-763-6767; *Fax:* 250-763-0980

Kelowna: **Petraroia Langford Rush LLP - *5**
Former Name: Petraroia, Langford, Edwards & Rush
#800, 1708 Dolphin Ave., Kelowna, BC V1Y 9S4
Tel: 250-861-5332; *Fax:* 250-861-8772
info@plrllp.comm
www.plerlaw.com

Kelowna: **Pihl & Associates Law Corporation - *6**
#300, 1465 Ellis St., Kelowna, BC V1Y 2A3
Tel: 250-762-5434; *Fax:* 250-762-5450
lawyers@pihl.bc.ca
www.okanaganlawyers.com

Kelowna: **Porter Ramsay LLP - *9**
#200, 1465 Ellis St., Kelowna, BC V1Y 2A3
Tel: 250-763-7646; *Fax:* 250-762-9960
Toll-Free: 888-933-4411
lawyers@porterramsay.com
www.porterramsay.com

Kelowna: **Pushor Mitchell LLP, Lawyers & Trade-Mark Agents - *31**
1665 Ellis St., 3rd Fl., Kelowna, BC V1Y 2B3
Tel: 250-762-2108; *Fax:* 250-762-9115
Toll-Free: 800-558-1155
lawyers@pushormitchell.com
www.pushormitchell.com

Kelowna: **Schlosser & Co. - *1**
3017 Tutt St., Kelowna, BC V1Y 2H4
Tel: 250-763-1393

Kelowna: **Daniel E. Spelliscy - *1**
715 Sutherland Ave., Kelowna, BC V1Y 5X4
Tel: 250-862-9586; *Fax:* 250-862-2677
dspelliscy@yahoo.com

Kelowna: **Thomas Butler LLP - *4**
#700, 1708 Dolphin Ave., Kelowna, BC V1Y 9S4
Tel: 250-763-0200; *Fax:* 250-762-8848
www.thomasbutlerllp.com

Kelowna: **Tinker, Churchill, Wallis - *3**
Former Name: Tinker, Churchill, Rule
1573 Ellis St., Kelowna, BC V1Y 2A7
Tel: 250-763-7333; *Fax:* 250-763-5507
reception@tinkerchurchill.com
www.bevchurchillfamilylawyer.com

Kelowna: **Douglas W. Welder - *1**
#200, 586 Leon Ave., Kelowna, BC V1Y 6J6
Tel: 250-868-8228; *Fax:* 250-868-8232
welder@okanagan.net

Kelowna: **Marc R.B. Whittemore - *1**
830 Bernard Ave., Kelowna, BC V1V 6P5
Tel: 250-868-2202; *Fax:* 250-868-2270
marc@whittemorelawcorporation.com

** indicates number of lawyers*

***Kelowna*: Robert J. Wotherspoon - *1**
2730 Cordova Way, Kelowna, BC V1Z 2N3
Tel: 250-769-5342

***Kimberley*: Walford & Associates Law Corp. - *1**
290 Wallinger Ave., Kimberley, BC V1A 1Z1
Tel: 250-427-0111; *Fax:* 250-427-0555
Toll-Free: 866-427-0111
randall@resortlaw.com
www.resortlaw.com

***Kitimat*: Wozney & Company - *2**
366 City Centre, Kitimat, BC V8C 1T6
Tel: 250-632-7151; *Fax:* 250-632-7100
rwozney@telus.net

***Ladysmith*: Robson, O'Connor - *2**
P.O. Box 1890, 22 High St., Ladysmith, BC V9G 1B4
Tel: 250-245-7141; *Fax:* 250-245-2921
Toll-Free: 800-641-1311
robcon@shawcable.com

***Langley*: Bryenton, Rosberg & Company - *4**
#300, 20689 Fraser Hwy., Langley, BC V3A 4G4
Tel: 604-530-7135; *Fax:* 604-530-7118
bryros@telus.net

***Langley*: Campbell, Burton & McMullan LLP - *11**
#200, 4769 - 222 St., Langley, BC V2Z 3C1
Tel: 604-533-3821; *Fax:* 604-533-5521
info@cbmlawyers.com
www.cbmlawyers.com

***Langley*: Darnell & Company Lawyers - *2**
#202, 6351 - 197 St., Langley, BC V2Y 1X8
Tel: 604-532-9119; *Fax:* 604-532-9127
www.langleylaw.ca

***Langley*: Fleming, Olson & Taneda - *3**
4038 - 200B St., Langley, BC V3A 1N9
Tel: 604-533-3411; *Fax:* 604-533-8749
fotlawyers@aol.com

***Langley*: Carl D. Holm - *1**
#102, 20475 Douglas Cres., Langley, BC V3A 4B6
Tel: 604-533-1401; *Fax:* 604-533-2024

***Langley*: Jarvis McGee - *4**
Former Name: Jarvis Burns McGee
#130, 5769 - 201A St., Langley, BC V3A 8H9
Tel: 604-530-8319; *Fax:* 604-530-8319
www.icbccases.com or www.jarvismcgee.com

***Langley*: J. Michael Le Dressay & Associates - *2**
20570 - 56th Ave., Langley, BC V3A 3Z1
Tel: 604-530-2191; *Fax:* 604-530-6282
jmledressay@stargate.ca

***Langley*: MacDonald, Boyle & Jeffery - *1**
20450 Fraser Hwy., Langley, BC V3A 4G2
Tel: 604-530-3141; *Fax:* 604-530-9573

***Langley*: Peter Minten Personal Law Corporation - *1**
Former Name: Cherrington Easingwood Kearl
20570 - 56 Ave., Langley, BC V3A 3Z1
Tel: 604-530-2191; *Fax:* 604-530-6282
pminten@stargate.ca

***Langley*: Waterstone Law Group LLP - *9**
#304, 20338 - 65th Ave., Langley, BC V2Y 2X3
Tel: 604-533-2300; *Fax:* 604-533-2387
Toll-Free: 800-880-1667
info@waterstonelaw.com
www.waterstonelaw.com

***Lantzville*: Kristin Rongve - *1**
Former Name: Loy & Rongve
7180 Lantzville Rd., Lantzville, BC V0R 2H0
Tel: 250-390-3157; *Fax:* 250-390-4857

***Lillooet*: R. Kendel Kaser - *1**
P.O. Box 1449, 416 Main St., Lillooet, BC V0K 1V0
Tel: 250-256-7519; *Fax:* 250-256-7554

***Madeira Park*: Michael C. Crowe - *1**
P.O. Box 310, 12874 Madeira Park Rd., Madeira Park, BC V0N 2H0
Tel: 604-883-9875; *Fax:* 604-883-9873
m_crowe@sunshine.net

***Maple Ridge*: Vernon & Thompson Law Group - *4**
22311 - 119 Ave., Maple Ridge, BC V2X 2Z2
Tel: 604-463-6281; *Fax:* 604-463-7497
law@vernon-thompson.com

***Matsqui Village*: John Andrew Miner - *1**
CP 219, 34033 Lougheed Hwy., Matsqui Village, BC V2V 5X8
Tel: 604-826-3930; *Fax:* 604-826-4172

***Mill Bay*: Hicks & Co. - *2**
#24, Mill Bay Shopping Centre, P.O. Box 83, 2720 Mill Bay Rd., Mill Bay, BC V0R 2P0
Tel: 250-743-3756; *Fax:* 250-743-3756

***Mission*: Jarrett & Company - *1**
9701 Dewdney Trunk Rd., Mission, BC V2V 7G5
Tel: 604-826-5582

***Mission*: MacDonald Klassen Law Office - *1**
Former Name: Marianne Walters Law Corp
#2, 7331 James St., Mission, BC V2V 3V5
Tel: 604-820-1059; *Fax:* 604-820-1080
Toll-Free: 866-820-1059
macdonald_klassen_law@telus.net

***Mission*: Taylor, Tait, Ruley & Company - *6**
33066 First Ave., Mission, BC V2V 1G3
Tel: 604-826-1266; *Fax:* 604-826-4288
info@taylortait.com
www.taylortait.com

***Nanaimo*: David C. Brown - *1**
#106, 360 Selby St., Nanaimo, BC V9R 2R5
Tel: 250-741-8201; *Fax:* 250-741-8202
david-brown@shaw.ca

***Nanaimo*: Carlson & Company - *3**
669 Terminal Ave. North, Nanaimo, BC V9S 4K1
Tel: 250-753-7582; *Fax:* 250-753-7583
lawyers@carlson-law.com

***Nanaimo*: Fabris McIver Hornquist & Radcliffe - *4**
Former Name: Fabris McIver Hornquist
CP 778, 40 Cavan St., Nanaimo, BC V9R 5M2
Tel: 250-753-6661; *Fax:* 250-753-6648

***Nanaimo*: Hamilton Waterman Kaine - *2**
70 Prideaux St., Nanaimo, BC V9R 2M5
Tel: 250-755-1783; *Fax:* 250-755-1780
debra@hwklaw.ca

***Nanaimo*: Heath & Company - *7**
#200, 1808 Bowen Rd., Nanaimo, BC V9S 5W4
Tel: 250-753-2202; *Fax:* 250-753-3949
Toll-Free: 866-753-2202
consult@nanaimolaw.com
www.nanaimolaw.com

***Nanaimo*: A. Peter Hertzberg - *1**
#206, 75 Front St., Nanaimo, BC V9R 5H9
Tel: 250-753-1891; *Fax:* 250-753-1892
Toll-Free: 866-753-1891
hertzberglaw@telus.net

***Nanaimo*: Hobbs Hargrave - *2**
301 Franklyn St., Nanaimo, BC V9R 2X5
Tel: 250-753-3477; *Fax:* 250-753-7927
bhobbs@hobbslaw.com
www.hobbslaw.com

***Nanaimo*: Johnston Franklin - *4**
Former Name: Johnston, Lewis & Franklin
#210, 3260 Norwell Dr., Nanaimo, BC V9T 1X5
Tel: 250-756-3823; *Fax:* 250-756-6188
Toll-Free: 888-343-0782
lawyers@johnstonfranklin.ca
www.johnstonfranklin.ca

***Nanaimo*: Gary R. Korpan - *1**
3598 Hammond Bay Rd., Nanaimo, BC V9T 1E9
Tel: 250-758-9445; *Fax:* 250-754-8263
gkorpan@island.net

***Nanaimo*: Manning & Kirkhope - *2**
430 Wentworth St., Nanaimo, BC V9R 3E1
Tel: 250-753-6766; *Fax:* 250-753-0080
Toll-Free: 877-753-6766
office@mannkirk.com
www.mannkirk.com

***Nanaimo*: Merrill, Long & Co. - *2**
201 Milton St., Nanaimo, BC V9R 2K5
Tel: 250-754-4441; *Fax:* 250-754-4286
ranlaw@telus.net
www.merrilllong.com

***Nanaimo*: Mont & Walker Law Corporation - *4**
Former Name: Allin Anderson Mont & Walker Law Corp
201 Selby St., Nanaimo, BC V9R 2R2
Tel: 250-753-6435; *Fax:* 250-753-5285
mont@islandlaw.ca
www.islandlaw.ca

***Nanaimo*: Petley-Jones & Co. Law Corp. - *1**
5732 Hammond Bay Rd., Nanaimo, BC V9T 5N2
Tel: 250-758-7370; *Fax:* 250-758-8703
info@petley-jones.net
www.petley-jones.net

***Nanaimo*: Ramsay Lampman Rhodes - *16**
Former Name: Ramsay Thompson Lampman
111 Wallace St., Nanaimo, BC V9R 5B2
Tel: 250-754-3321; *Fax:* 250-754-1148
Toll-Free: 800-263-3321
info@rlr-law.com
www.rlr-law.com

***Nanaimo*: Robert N. Stacey Law Corp. - *1**
Former Name: Old City Quarter Law Office
#10, 321 Wesley St., Nanaimo, BC V9R 2T5
Tel: 250-753-0844; *Fax:* 250-753-0877
rnstacey@telus.net
www.bcdivorceonline.com

***Nanaimo*: Elisabeth Strain**
#103, 360 Selby St., Nanaimo, BC V9R 2R5
Tel: 250-753-0860; *Fax:* 250-753-0861
elisabeth@strain.ca
www.strain.ca

***Nanaimo*: Victor Svacek - *1**
#206, 75 Front St., Nanaimo, BC V9R 5H9
Tel: 250-753-1891; *Fax:* 250-753-1892
Toll-Free: 866-753-1891
svaceklaw@telus.net

***Nanaimo*: Vining, Senini - *6**
P.O. Box 190, Stn. Main, 30 Front St., Nanaimo, BC V9R 5K9
Tel: 250-754-1234; *Fax:* 250-754-8080

***Nanaimo*: Eric L. Williams - *1**
55 Front St., Nanaimo, BC V9R 5H9
Tel: 250-741-1100; *Fax:* 250-741-1094
Toll-Free: 888-959-1100
eric.williams@telus.net

***Nanaimo*: C.D. Wilson & Associates - *1**
630 Terminal Ave. N., Nanaimo, BC V9S 4K2
Tel: 250-741-1400; *Fax:* 250-741-1441
nanaimo@cdwilson.bc.ca

***Nelson*: Susan Kurtz - *1**
407 Nelson Ave., Nelson, BC V1L 2N1
Tel: 250-354-1881; *Fax:* 250-354-1808

***Nelson*: Nasmyth, Morrow & Bogusz - *2**
#105, 465 Ward St., Nelson, BC V1L 1S7
Tel: 250-352-3171; *Fax:* 250-352-1777
nmgb@telus.net

***Nelson*: Stacey, Trillo & Company - *2**
#1, 405 Baker St., Nelson, BC V1L 4H7
Tel: 250-352-3125; *Fax:* 250-352-3145
greg@stacey-trillo.com
www.stacey-trillo.com

***Nelson*: Terry Napora Law Office - *1**
Former Name: Napora Underwood & Co.
608 Baker St., Nelson, BC V1L 4J4
Tel: 250-352-3321; *Fax:* 250-354-4547
Toll-Free: 800-579-5338
tnapora@napwood.ca

***Nelson*: Susan E. Wallach - *1**
#4, 577 Baker St., Nelson, BC V1L 4J1
Tel: 250-352-6124; *Fax:* 250-352-3460

***New Westminster*: Gordon J. Bondoreff - *1**
#202, 713 Columbia St., New Westminster, BC V3M 1B2
Tel: 604-526-4491; *Fax:* 604-526-5979
gbondoreff@telus.net

***New Westminster*: Dickey, Browning, Ray, Soga, Dunne - *5**
Former Name: Dickey, Browning, McShane, Dunne
#203, 668 Carnarvon St., New Westminster, BC V3M 5Y6
Tel: 604-526-4525; *Fax:* 604-526-8595
info@triallawyers.ca
www.triallawyers.ca

** indicates number of lawyers*

***New Westminster*: Raymond E. Drabik Law Corp. - *1**
#217, 713 Columbia St., New Westminster, BC V3M 1B2
Tel: 604-526-4875; *Fax:* 604-526-4879
red_law@telus.net

***New Westminster*: Goodwin & Mark - *6**
#217, 713 Columbia St., New Westminster, BC V3M 1B2
Tel: 604-522-9884; *Fax:* 604-526-8044
gm@goodmark.ca
www.goodmark.ca

***New Westminster*: Angela S. Kerslake - *1**
131 - 8th St., New Westminster, BC V3M 3P6
Tel: 604-520-6276; *Fax:* 604-520-5765

***New Westminster*: Kinman Mulholland - *2**
Former Name: Kinman Amlani Mulholland
#400, 628 Sixth Ave., New Westminster, BC V3M 6Z1
Tel: 604-526-1805; *Fax:* 604-526-8056
info@kamlawyers.com
www.kamlawyers.com

***New Westminster*: Scarborough, Herman, Harvey & Bluekens - *4**
900 Quayside Dr., 10th Fl., New Westminster, BC V3M 6G1
Tel: 604-521-2223; *Fax:* 604-521-7772
sbluekens@shh.bc.ca

***North Saanich*: Barbara J. Yates - *1**
430 Wain Rd., North Saanich, BC V8L 5P9
Tel: 250-656-0979; *Fax:* 250-656-4333

***North Vancouver*: Ardagh Hunter - *2**
#300, 1401 Lonsdale Ave., North Vancouver, BC V7M 2H9
Tel: 604-986-4366; *Fax:* 604-986-9286
account@ahtlaw.com

***North Vancouver*: Begin & Company - *1**
#302, 140 West 15th St., North Vancouver, BC V7M 1R6
Tel: 604-987-5297; *Fax:* 604-980-6322
beginandco@shaw.ca

***North Vancouver*: Trevors R. Bjurman - *1**
#205, 1433 Lonsdale Ave., North Vancouver, BC V7M 2H9
Tel: 604-983-3728; *Fax:* 604-983-0148
bjurman@smartt.com

***North Vancouver*: Oren E. Breitman - *1**
1503 Dovercourt Rd., North Vancouver, BC V7K 1K6
Tel: 604-218-9480; *Fax:* 604-984-0502
orenb@shaw.ca

***North Vancouver*: Forrest, Gray, Lewis & Gillett - *1**
#201, 145 - 15th St. East, North Vancouver, BC V7L 2P7
Tel: 604-988-5244; *Fax:* 604-988-0093
fglg@dowco.com

***North Vancouver*: Charlotte C. Gregory - *1**
205 St. Patrick's Ave., North Vancouver, BC V7L 3N3
Tel: 604-983-2886; *Fax:* 604-983-2886
cgregory@istar.ca

***North Vancouver*: M. Hollander - *1**
#320, 145 West 17 St., North Vancouver, BC V7M 1V5
Tel: 604-986-4354; *Fax:* 604-986-9183
marjon@intergate.ca

***North Vancouver*: Jabour, Sudeyko - *1**
#603, 145 East 13th St., North Vancouver, BC V7L 2L4
Tel: 604-986-8600; *Fax:* 604-986-4872
Toll-Free: 877-860-7575
dsudeyko@telus.net
www.jaboursudeyko.com

***North Vancouver*: Robert W. Johnson - *1**
#300, 1401 Lonsdale Ave., North Vancouver, BC V7M 2H9
Tel: 604-984-0305; *Fax:* 604-984-0304
robert.johnson@ahtlaw.com

***North Vancouver*: E.B. Kroon - *1**
#100, 132 East 14 St., North Vancouver, BC V7L 2N3
Tel: 604-980-7021; *Fax:* 604-980-7426

***North Vancouver*: Lakes & Whyte LLP - *6**
Former Name: Lakes, Straith & Whyte LLP
#200, 879 Marine Dr., North Vancouver, BC V7P 1R7
Tel: 604-984-3646; *Fax:* 604-984-8573
Toll-Free: 800-488-7788
info@lakeswhyte.com
www.lakeswhyte.com

***North Vancouver*: Lee T. Lau Law Corp. - *1**
365 Lynn Ave., North Vancouver, BC V7J 2C4
Tel: 604-988-5222; *Fax:* 604-988-5356
lau@leelau.net
www.leelau.net

***North Vancouver*: Lynn Valley Law - *1**
#40, 1199 Lynn Valley Rd., North Vancouver, BC V7J 3H2
Tel: 604-985-8000; *Fax:* 604-985-5999
admin@lynnlaw.ca
www.lynnlaw.ca

***North Vancouver*: North Shore Law LLP - *15**
Former Name: Bradbrooke Crawford Green
171 West Esplanade, 6th Floor, North Vancouver, BC V7M 3J9
Tel: 604-980-8571; *Fax:* 604-980-4019
Toll-Free: 877-980-8571
inquiries@northshorelaw.com
www.northshorelaw.com

***North Vancouver*: Ron Perrick Law Corp. - *2**
#480, 145 West 17 St., North Vancouver, BC V7M 1V5
Tel: 604-984-9521; *Fax:* 604-984-9104

***North Vancouver*: Poyner Baxter LLP - *3**
#408, 145 Chadwick Ct., North Vancouver, BC V7M 3K1
Tel: 604-988-6321; *Fax:* 604-988-3632
info@poynerbaxter.com
www.poynerbaxter.com

***North Vancouver*: Ratcliff & Company LLP - *27**
#500, East Tower, 221 West Esplanade, North Vancouver, BC V7M 3J3
Tel: 604-988-5201; *Fax:* 604-988-1452
admin@ratcliff.com
www.ratcliff.com

***North Vancouver*: Robert C. Reid - *1**
#233, 1433 Lonsdale Ave., North Vancouver, BC V7M 2H9
Tel: 604-984-4357; *Fax:* 604-984-4326
robertcreid@hotmail.com

***North Vancouver*: D.A. Roper - *1**
334 West 15th St., North Vancouver, BC V7M 1S5
Tel: 604-986-0488; *Fax:* 604-984-3463
roperlaw@shawbiz.ca

***North Vancouver*: Thomas Immigration Law Group - *2**
Former Name: David L. Thomas Law Corporation
1885 Marine Dr., North Vancouver, BC V7P 1V5
Tel: 604-988-0795; *Fax:* 604-988-0718
office@executive-visa.com
www.executive-visa.com

***Oliver*: Gordon & Young - *3**
P.O. Box 1800, 36011 - 97th St., Oliver, BC V0H 1T0
Tel: 250-498-4941; *Fax:* 250-498-4100

***Osoyoos*: Gordon & Company - *2**
#202, 8309 Main St., Osoyoos, BC V0H 1V0
Tel: 250-495-6508; *Fax:* 250-495-6404
gordonco@telus.net
www.sunnyosoyoos.com/webpages/gordon_company.htm

***Parksville*: Davis & Avis - *2**
#201, CP 1600, 156 Morison Ave., Parksville, BC V9P 2H5
Tel: 250-248-5731; *Fax:* 250-248-5730
law@davis-avis.com
www.davis-avis.com

***Parksville*: John A. Hossack & Company - *1**
CP 1486, 311 McKinnon St., Parksville, BC V9P 2H4
Tel: 250-248-9241; *Fax:* 250-248-8375
john@hossack-law.com
www.hossack-law.com

***Parksville*: Patricia E. Lebedovich - *1**
P.O. Box 214, Parksville, BC V9P 2G4
Toll-Free: 866-711-3084
lebedovich@shaw.ca

***Peachland*: John E. Humphries Law Corporation - *1**
5848B Beach Ave., Peachland, BC V0H 1X7
Tel: 250-767-2221; *Fax:* 250-767-3477
johnehumphrieslaw@hotmail.com

***Penticton*: Boyle & Company - *10**
#3201, 100 Front St., Penticton, BC V2A 1H1
Tel: 250-492-6100; *Fax:* 250-492-4877
Toll-Free: 800-665-8244
www.boyleco.bc.ca

***Penticton*: Gilchrist & Company - *4**
#101, 123 Martin St., Penticton, BC V2A 7X6
Tel: 250-492-3033; *Fax:* 250-492-6162
info@gilchristlaw.com
www.gilchristlaw.com

***Penticton*: Kathryn J. Ginther - *1**
#301, 301 Main St., Penticton, BC V2A 5B7
Tel: 250-487-4355; *Fax:* 250-487-4356
kjg@kgintherlaw.com

***Penticton*: Halbauer & Company - *1**
Former Name: Halbauer & McAndrews
#104, 2504 Skana Lake Road, Penticton, BC V2A 6G1
Tel: 250-492-7225; *Fax:* 250-492-7395
www.pentictonlawyers.com

***Penticton*: Thomas A. Kampman - *1**
409 Ellis St., Penticton, BC V2A 4M1
Tel: 250-493-6786; *Fax:* 250-493-3964
tom@kampmanoliverkeene.com

***Penticton*: Zaseybida, Bonga - *2**
#101, 100 Nanaimo Ave. East, Penticton, BC V2A 1M4
Tel: 250-492-2244; *Fax:* 250-492-0090
zaseybida-bonga@telus.net

***Pitt Meadows*: Becker & Company Law Offices - *1**
#230, 19150 Lougheed Hwy., Pitt Meadows, BC V3Y 2H6
Tel: 604-465-9993; *Fax:* 604-465-0066
info@becker-company.com
www.becker-company.com

***Port Alberni*: Badovinac, Scoffield & Mosley - *3**
3290 - 3 Ave., Port Alberni, BC V9Y 4E1
Tel: 250-724-1275; *Fax:* 250-724-7200
bsm@albernilaw.com
www.albernilaw.com

***Port Alberni*: Beckingham & Co. - *2**
5029 Argyle St., Port Alberni, BC V9Y 1V5
Tel: 250-724-0111; *Fax:* 250-724-4422
beck@port.island.net

***Port Coquitlam*: John K. Bledsoe - *1**
2239B McAllister Ave., Port Coquitlam, BC V3C 2A9
Tel: 604-941-6162; *Fax:* 604-941-4369

***Port Coquitlam*: Darychuk Deane-Cloutier - *2**
Former Name: Macleod Thorson Darychuk
#310, 2755 Lougheed Hwy., Port Coquitlam, BC V3B 5Y9
Tel: 604-464-2644; *Fax:* 604-464-2533

***Port Coquitlam*: David Greenbank - *1**
Former Name: Greenbank Murdoch & Company
#2300, 2850 Shaughnessy St., Port Coquitlam, BC V3C 6K5
Tel: 604-941-6215; *Fax:* 604-941-6207
dgreenbank@dgreenbank.com
dgreenbank.com

***Port Coquitlam*: Payne & Associates - *1**
#105, 1465 Salisbury Ave., Port Coquitlam, BC V3B 6J3
Tel: 604-944-4115; *Fax:* 604-944-4120

***Port Coquitlam*: Larry W. Pippard - *1**
#2, 3397 Hastings St., Port Coquitlam, BC V3B 4M8
Tel: 604-464-5615;
larrywpippard@shaw.ca

***Port Coquitlam*: Henry Sarava - *1**
#2300, 2850 Shaughnessy St., Port Coquitlam, BC V3C 6K5
Tel: 604-944-2114; *Fax:* 604-552-7709
henrysarava@hotmail.com
www.lawyers.com/saravacriminaldefence

***Port Coquitlam*: Smyth & Co. - *4**
#330, 2755 Lougheed Hwy., Port Coquitlam, BC V3B 5Y9
Tel: 604-942-6560; *Fax:* 604-942-1347

***Port Hardy*: Nowosad & Company - *1**
CP 1289, 8700 Market St., Port Hardy, BC V0N 2P0
Tel: 250-949-6031; *Fax:* 250-949-2633
info@macisaacgroup.com
www.macisaacgroup.com

***Port Moody*: Burke Tomchenko Morrison - *5**
Former Name: Burke Tomchenko & Fraser
#301, 2502 St. Johns St., Port Moody, BC V3H 2B4
Tel: 604-937-1166; *Fax:* 604-937-5577
firm@btmlawyers.com
www.btmlawyers.com

* *indicates number of lawyers*

***Port Moody*: Morrison Voss - *2**
2225 Clarke St., Port Moody, BC V3H 1Y6
Tel: 604-937-4757; *Fax:* 604-937-4714
Toll-Free: 866-944-8888
jsvoss@morrisonvoss.com

***Powell River*: Garling Ostensen - *1**
4581 Marine Ave., Powell River, BC V8A 2K7
Tel: 604-485-2818; *Fax:* 604-485-7161
garost@powellriverlawyers.com

***Powell River*: James Garrett-Rempel - *1**
4766 Michigan Ave., Powell River, BC V8A 2S9
Tel: 604-485-9898; *Fax:* 604-485-9850
jgrlaw@shaw.ca
www.garrett-rempel.com

***Powell River*: F. Gregory Reif - *1**
#201, 4801 Joyce Ave., Powell River, BC V8A 3B7
Tel: 604-485-2056; *Fax:* 604-485-2196
gregreif@telus.net

***Powell River*: Whyard Villani - *3**
4448A Marine Ave., Powell River, BC V8A 2K2
Tel: 604-485-6188; *Fax:* 604-485-6923
info@whyardvillani.com
www.whyardvillani.com

***Prince George*: Coller Levine, Barristers & Solicitors - *2**
Former Name: Bill A. Coller.
1140 - 3rd Ave., Prince George, BC V2L 3E5
Tel: 250-960-2169; *Fax:* 250-960-2196
coller@collerlevine.ca
www.collerlevine.ca

***Prince George*: John A. Davis - *1**
#1, 1515 - 2 Ave., Prince George, BC V2L 3B8
Tel: 250-564-5544; *Fax:* 250-562-9427
jdlaw@shawcable.com

***Prince George*: Dick Byl Law Corporation - *8**
#900, 550 Victoria St., Prince George, BC V2L 2K1
Tel: 250-564-3400; *Fax:* 250-564-7873
Toll-Free: 800-835-0088
dbyl@dbylaw.com
www.dbylaw.com

***Prince George*: Fatt & Elson, Barristers & Solicitors - *2**
#503, 1488 - 4th Ave., Prince George, BC V2L 4Y2
Tel: 250-564-1334; *Fax:* 250-564-4266
Toll-Free: 888-564-1334
lawyers@fattandelson.com

***Prince George*: Fletcher Repstock - *5**
440 Brunswick St., Prince George, BC V2L 2B6
Tel: 250-564-1313; *Fax:* 250-563-4362
Toll-Free: 877-690-1110
repstock@netbistro.com

***Prince George*: Richard C. Gibbs - *1**
1134 - 3rd Ave., Prince George, BC V2L 3E5
Tel: 250-564-6460; *Fax:* 250-562-0671
rcgibbs@telus.net

***Prince George*: Heather Sadler Jenkins LLP - *16**
#700, Royal Bank Bldg., P.O. Box 4500, 550 Victoria St., Prince George, BC V2L 2K1
Tel: 250-565-8000; *Fax:* 250-565-8001
Toll-Free: 866-565-8777
hsj@hsjlawyers.com
www.hsjlawyers.com

***Prince George*: Hope Heinrich, Barristers & Solicitors - *9**
1598 - 6th Ave., Prince George, BC V2L 5G7
Tel: 250-563-0681; *Fax:* 250-562-3761
Toll-Free: 800-663-8230

***Prince George*: Richard B. Krehbiel - *1**
6932 View Pl., Prince George, BC V2K 4C6
Tel: 250-962-5843; *Fax:* 250-962-5842
rkrehbie@pgweb.com

***Prince George*: Leverman & Company - *1**
Courtyard Lane, 1057 - 3rd Ave., Prince George, BC V2L 3E3
Tel: 250-564-1212; *Fax:* 250-756-1588

***Prince George*: Ronald W. Madill - *1**
1033 - 3rd Ave., Prince George, BC V2L 3E3
Tel: 250-562-5000; *Fax:* 250-562-5105

***Prince George*: J.A. Mooney - *1**
1033 - 3rd Ave., Prince George, BC V2L 3B3
Tel: 250-562-3324; *Fax:* 250-562-9444
jim@jamesmooney.com

***Prince George*: Traxler Haines - *6**
Former Name: Ramsay Nosè Traxler Haines
#614, 1488 - 4 Ave., Prince George, BC V2L 4Y2
Tel: 250-563-7741; *Fax:* 250-563-2953

***Prince George*: Tyo Law Corp. - *1**
#304, 1488 - 4 Ave., Prince George, BC V2L 4Y2
Tel: 250-564-9757; *Fax:* 250-564-9734
Toll-Free: 877-365-4093
tyolaw@shaw.ca

***Prince George*: Weatherly & Brown - *2**
925 Vancouver St., Prince George, BC V2L 2P6
Tel: 250-563-8110; *Fax:* 250-563-1466

***Prince George*: Wilbur & Company - *1**
1057 - 3rd Ave., Prince George, BC V2L 3E3
Tel: 250-564-1444; *Fax:* 250-563-2842
dwilbur@shaw.ca

***Prince George*: Wilson King LLP - *10**
Former Name: Wilson, King & Company
#1000, 299 Victoria St., Prince George, BC V2L 5B8
Tel: 250-960-3200; *Fax:* 250-562-7777
Toll-Free: 800-365-4566
www.wilsonking.com

***Prince Rupert*: Marina C-K Kan - *1**
P.O. Box 722, Prince Rupert, BC V8J 3S1
Tel: 250-624-6060; *Fax:* 250-624-6451

***Prince Rupert*: Narbonne Law Office - *1**
P.O. Box 256, Prince Rupert, BC V8J 3P6
Tel: 250-624-4899; *Fax:* 250-624-3046
www.narbonnelawoffice.com

***Prince Rupert*: Irene G. Peters Law Corp. - *2**
Former Name: Peters & O'Byrne
#304, 1488 - 14 Ave., Prince Rupert, BC V2L 4Y2
Tel: 250-627-7771; *Fax:* 250-624-2191

***Prince Rupert*: Punnett & Johnston - *2**
#7, 222 - 3rd Ave. West, Prince Rupert, BC V8J 1L1
Tel: 250-624-2106; *Fax:* 250-627-8805
pj@citytel.net

***Prince Rupert*: Silversides, Merrick & McLean - *4**
Former Name: Silversides, Seidemann & Kucher
P.O. Box 188, 217 - 3rd Ave. West, Prince Rupert, BC V8J 3P7
Tel: 250-624-2116; *Fax:* 250-627-7786
reception@silverco.ca

***Qualicum Beach*: Marshall & Lamperson - *2**
CP 879, 710 Memorial Ave., Qualicum Beach, BC V9K 1T2
Tel: 250-752-5615; *Fax:* 250-752-2055
doug@qualicumlaw.ca

***Qualicum Beach*: Rodway & Perry - *2**
#1, CP 138, 699 Beach Rd., Qualicum Beach, BC V9K 1S7
Tel: 250-752-9526; *Fax:* 250-752-9521
rodwayandperry@shaw.ca
www.macisaacgroup.com

***Qualicum Beach*: Walker & Wilson, Barristers & Solicitors - *2**
#2, 707 Primrose St., Qualicum Beach, BC V9K 2K1
Tel: 250-752-6951; *Fax:* 250-752-6022
kwalker@qblaw.ca
www.qblaw.ca

***Quesnel*: John B. Schmitz - *1**
633 Clark St., Quesnel, BC V2J 1L3
Tel: 250-992-6793; *Fax:* 250-992-6795

***Revelstoke*: Bernard C. Lavallée - *1**
Former Name: Lavallée, Rackel
P.O. Box 244, 109 Connaught Ave., Revelstoke, BC V0E 2S0
Tel: 250-837-5168; *Fax:* 250-837-5178
bcl59lawyer@rctvonline.net

***Revelstoke*: Robert A. Lundberg Law Corporation - *1**
119 Campbell Ave., Revelstoke, BC V0E 2S0
Tel: 250-837-5196; *Fax:* 250-837-4746
robertlundberg@rctvonline.net

***Richmond*: Ash, O'Donnell, Hibbert - *4**
#1, 11575 Bridgeport Rd., Richmond, BC V6X 1T5
Tel: 604-273-9111; *Fax:* 604-273-1117
aohlaw2007@gmail.com
www.ashodonnellhibbert.ca

***Richmond*: David G. Baker, Barrister - *1**
#210, 7340 Westminster Hwy., Richmond, BC V6X 1A1
Tel: 604-244-7587; *Fax:* 604-303-6922
davegbaker@yahoo.ca
www.davidgbaker.ca

***Richmond*: Berger & Company - *2**
#130, 8400 Granville Ave., Richmond, BC V6Y 1P6
Tel: 604-273-9959; *Fax:* 604-273-9910
eberger@telus.net
www.berger-and-company.com

***Richmond*: David W. Blinkhorn - *1**
#230, 7360 Westminster Hwy., Richmond, BC V6X 1A1
Tel: 604-244-7880; *Fax:* 604-244-9611

***Richmond*: V.N. Carvalho - *1**
13811 Gilbert Rd., Richmond, BC V7E 2H8
Tel: 604-274-5636; *Fax:* 604- -
vncarvalho@shaw.ca

***Richmond*: S.R. Chamberlain, Barrister & Solicitor - *2**
Former Name: S.R. Chamberlain, Q.C
#1, 7100 River Rd., Richmond, BC V6X 1X5
Tel: 604-244-0646; *Fax:* 604-244-0617
mail@src-law.com

***Richmond*: Robert J. Charlton - *1**
Also Known As: Robert J. Charlton Personal Law Corporation
#816, 6081 No. 3 Rd., Richmond, BC V6Y 2B2
Tel: 604-214-7818; *Fax:* 604-214-7819
rjc@rjcharlton.com
www.rjcharlton.com

***Richmond*: Chouinard & Company - *2**
#816, 6081 No. 3 Rd., Richmond, BC V6Y 2B2
Tel: 604-214-7818; *Fax:* 604-214-7819
Toll-Free: 877-685-8999
ray@chouinardlaw.com
www.chouinardlaw.com

***Richmond*: Cohen, Buchan, Edwards - *9**
#208, 4940 No. 3 Rd., Richmond, BC V6X 3A5
Tel: 604-273-6411; *Fax:* 604-273-4512
gary@cbelaw.com
www.cbelaw.com

***Richmond*: John C. Fairburn**
#305, 5811 Cooney Rd., Richmond, BC V6X 3M1
Tel: 604-279-8283; *Fax:* 604-279-8243
fairburnlaw@execcentre.com

***Richmond*: Fast & Company, Barristers & Solicitors - *2**
#5080, 8171 Ackroyd Rd., Richmond, BC V6X 3K1
Tel: 604-273-6424; *Fax:* 604-273-2290
mlfast@fastandco.ca
www.fastandco.ca

***Richmond*: Forbes & Boyle - *3**
#215, 8171 Cook Rd., Richmond, BC V6Y 3T8
Tel: 604-273-7575; *Fax:* 604-273-8475
info@forbesboyle.ca

***Richmond*: Douglas B. Graves - *1**
#317, 8055 Anderson Rd., Richmond, BC V6Y 1S2
Tel: 604-276-0069

***Richmond*: Henderson Livingston Stewart LLP - *4**
Old Steveston Courthouse, 12011 - 3rd Ave., Richmond, BC V7E 3K1
Tel: 604-241-2855; *Fax:* 604-241-2866
office@hlslawyers.com
www.steveston.bc.ca

***Richmond*: Bernard Hoodekoff - *1**
#206, 5811 Cooney Rd., Richmond, BC V6X 3M1
Tel: 604-278-8451; *Fax:* 604-278-8453

***Richmond*: Humphry Paterson - *2**
#205, 8171 Park Rd., Richmond, BC V6Y 1S9
Tel: 604-278-3031; *Fax:* 604-278-3021
humpat@telus.net

** indicates number of lawyers*

Richmond: INC Business Lawyers - *2
Former Name: Moir & Moir
#1201, 11871 Horseshoe Way, Richmond, BC V7A 5H5
Tel: 604-272-6960; *Fax:* 604-272-6959
Toll-Free: 888-272-7771
info@incorporate.ca
www.incorporate.ca

Richmond: Jang Cheung Lee Chu Law Corporation - *7
Former Name: Jang, Cheung, Lee
#700, London Plaza, 5951 No. 3 Rd., Richmond, BC V6X 2E3
Tel: 604-276-8300; *Fax:* 604-276-8309
office@jclclawcorp.com
www.jclclawcorp.com

Richmond: Kahn Zack Ehrlich Lithwick - *10
#270, 10711 Cambie Rd., Richmond, BC V6X 3G5
Tel: 604-270-9571; *Fax:* 604-270-8282
Toll-Free: 888-529-6368
general@kzellaw.com
www.kzellaw.com

Richmond: Nancy L. Kinsman, Barrister & Solicitor - *1
#315, 8171 Cook Rd., Richmond, BC V6Y 3T8
Tel: 604-273-4664; *Fax:* 604-273-7442
nkinsman@familylawbc.ca
www.familylawbc.ca

Richmond: Kenneth B. Krag - *1
#228, 8055 Anderson Rd., Richmond, BC V6Y 1S2
Tel: 604-270-8702; *Fax:* 604-270-6708

Richmond: Theodore Kuchta - *1
8480 Rosebank Cres., Richmond, BC V7A 2K6
Tel: 604-274-4513; *Fax:* 604-276-2800
tedkuch@aol.com

Richmond: Susan Label - *1
#250, 11590 Cambie Rd., Richmond, BC V6X 3Z5
Tel: 604-273-6448; *Fax:* 604-273-6998
www.susanlabel.com

Richmond: Morley A. Levitt - *1
#120, 11181 Voyageur Way, Richmond, BC V6X 3N9
Tel: 604-270-9611; *Fax:* 604-270-4588
info@protectmyestate.ca
www.protectmyestate.ca

Richmond: Lim & Company - *5
#320, 7480 Westminster Hwy., Richmond, BC V6X 1A1
Tel: 604-303-0788; *Fax:* 604-303-0789
info@lim-and-company-law.com
www.lim-and-company-lawyers.com

Richmond: V. Brent Louie, Personal Law Corporation - *1
#203, 2680 Shell Rd., Richmond, BC V6X 4C9
Tel: 604-270-8708; *Fax:* 604-270-8735
vblouie@shaw.ca

Richmond: Peter Li & Company - *2
Former Name: Peter S.K. Li
#110, 4400 Hazelbridge Way, Richmond, BC V6X 3R8
Tel: 604-273-6308; *Fax:* 604-273-6393
peterliandco@yahoo.com

Richmond: Phillips Paul - *2
#215, 4800 No. 3 Rd., Richmond, BC V6X 3A6
Tel: 604-273-5297; *Fax:* 604-273-1643
philpaul@direct.ca

Richmond: Rees-Thomas & Company - *3
#5080, 8171 Ackroyd Rd., Richmond, BC V6X 3K1
Tel: 604-279-9300; *Fax:* 604-273-2290
info@reesthomas.com

Richmond: Scardina & Co. - *1
#215, 4800 No. 3 Rd., Richmond, BC V6X 3A6
Tel: 604-273-5558; *Fax:* 604-273-5550

Richmond: Spry Hawkins Micner - *1
#440, VanCity Tower, 5900 No. 3 Rd., Richmond, BC V6X 3P7
Tel: 604-233-7001; *Fax:* 604-233-7017
annette@willpowerlaw.com
www.willpowerlaw.com

Richmond: Bruce A. Thompson Law Corp. - *1
#215, Churchill Centre, 2nd Fl., 8171 Cook Rd., Richmond, BC V6Y 3T8
Tel: 604-270-7773; *Fax:* 604-273-8475

Richmond: Wong & Tsang - *4
#310, 8120 Granville Ave., Richmond, BC V6Y 1P3
Tel: 604-279-9023; *Fax:* 604-279-9025

Richmond: Mary E.B. Wood - *1
#724, 6081 - No. 3 Rd., Richmond, BC V6Y 2B2
Tel: 604-273-5547; *Fax:* 604-273-3044
mebwood@telus.net
www.marywoodlawyer.com

Roberts Creek: Lynn Chapman - *1
1947 Crystal Cr., Roberts Creek, BC V0N 2W1
Tel: 604-885-0356; *Fax:* 604-885-0358
lchapman@dccnet.com

Saanichton: C.J. Kip Wilson - *1
#6, 7855 East Saanich Rd., Saanichton, BC V8M 2B4
Tel: 250-544-0727; *Fax:* 250-544-0728
kipwilson@home.com

Salmon Arm: Brooke, Jackson, Downs - *4
Centennial Building, CP 67, 51 - 3rd St. NE, Salmon Arm, BC V1E 4N2
Tel: 250-832-9311; *Fax:* 250-832-3801
bjdlaw@sunwave.net
www.bjdlaw.com

Salmon Arm: Derek McManus Law Corporation - *1
CP 57, 450 Lakeshore Dr. NE, Salmon Arm, BC V1E 4N2
Tel: 250-833-4720; *Fax:* 250-832-4787
corp@salmonarmlaw.com
www.salmonarmlaw.com

Salmon Arm: Seale Law Corp. - *1
CP 3248, 450 Lakeshore Dr. NE, Salmon Arm, BC V1E 4S1
Tel: 250-832-9301; *Fax:* 250-832-9300

Salmon Arm: Sivertz Kiehlbauch - *3
Former Name: Sivertz, Kiehlbauch & Zachernuk
#320, P.O. Box 190, 351 Hudson Ave. NE, Salmon Arm, BC V1E 4N3
Tel: 250-832-8031; *Fax:* 250-832-6177

Salmon Arm: Verdurmen & Company - *1
Former Name: Verdurmen & Lee
CP 826, 450 Lakeshore Dr. NE, Salmon Arm, BC V1E 4N9
Tel: 250-833-0914; *Fax:* 250-833-0924
vlex@telus.net
www.macisaacgroup.com

Salt Spring Island: Fisher, Murphy & Woodward - *1
Former Name: Ian H. Clement Law Corporation
#1, 105 Rainbow Rd., Salt Spring Island, BC V8K 2V5
Tel: 250-537-5505; *Fax:* 250-537-5099
www.saltspringlawfirm.comwww.facebook.com/pages/Fisher-Murphy-Woodward-Lawyers/253823191300084

Salt Spring Island: J. Anthony McEwen - *1
1860 Fulford-Ganges Rd., Salt Spring Island, BC V8K 2A5
Tel: 250-653-4979; *Fax:* 250-653-9212

Salt Spring Island: James Pasuta - *1
P.O. Box 414, Stn. Ganges, 560 Fulford-Ganges Rd., Salt Spring Island, BC V8K 2W1
Tel: 250-537-9995; *Fax:* 250-537-9975

Sechelt: William C. Prowse - *1
6866 Island View Rd., Sechelt, BC V0N 3A8
Tel: 604-740-0303; *Fax:* 604-740-0306
transmed@telus.net

Sechelt: Robinson & Co. Law Office - *1
P.O. Box 920, Sechelt, BC V0N 3A0
Tel: 604-885-7541; *Fax:* 604-885-7561
robco@telus.net

Sidney: Alice E. Finall - *1
2412B Beacon Ave., 2nd Fl., Sidney, BC V8L 1X4
Tel: 250-656-6668; *Fax:* 250-656-9366
final@telus.net

Sidney: Henley & Walden - *4
#201, 2377 Bevan Ave., Sidney, BC V8L 4M9
Tel: 250-656-7231; *Fax:* 250-656-0937
Toll-Free: 800-656-7231
inquiries@henleywalden.com
www.henleywalden.com

Sidney: McKimm & Lott - *7
9830 - 4th St., Sidney, BC V8L 2Z3
Tel: 250-656-3961; *Fax:* 250-655-3329
reception@mclott.com
www.mclott.com

Smithers: Perry & Company - *4
CP 790, 1081 Main St., Smithers, BC V0J 2N0
Tel: 250-847-4341; *Fax:* 250-847-5634
www.perryco.ca

Smithers: G. Ronald Toews, Q.C. - *1
P.O. Box 970, 3835 - 10th Ave., Smithers, BC V0J 2N0
Tel: 250-847-2187; *Fax:* 250-847-2183
grt@buckley.net

Sooke: Hallgren & Faulkner - *2
P.O. Box 939, 104-6739 West Coast Rd., Sooke, BC V9Z 1H9
Tel: 250-642-5271; *Fax:* 250-642-6006
Toll-Free: 800-358-5271
info@hallgrenfaulkner.ca

Squamish: Race & Company - *6
#201, CP 1850, 1365 Pemberton Ave., Squamish, BC V0N 3G0
Tel: 604-892-5254; *Fax:* 604-892-5461
d.race@racesq.com
www.raceandcompany.com

Summerland: Bell, Jacoe & Company, Barristers & Solicitors - *2
P.O. Box 520, 13211 Victoria Rd. North, Summerland, BC V0H 1Z0
Tel: 250-494-6621; *Fax:* 250-494-8055
Toll-Free: 800-663-0392
belljacoe@shaw.ca
www.bell-jacoe.com

Surrey: Alan J. Benson - *1
#106, 15585 - 24 Ave., Surrey, BC V4A 2J4
Tel: 604-538-4911; *Fax:* 604-538-5754

Surrey: Roger S. Bhatti - *1
#203, 8556 - 120th St., Surrey, BC V3W 3N5
Tel: 604-590-1177; *Fax:* 604-596-8800
rblaw@intergate.ca

Surrey: Spencer A. Bowers - *1
8893 - 160 St., Surrey, BC V4N 2X8
Tel: 604-951-9224; *Fax:* 604-951-9224
sabowers@axionet.com

Surrey: Brawn, Karras & Sanderson - *3
#340, 5620 - 152nd St., Surrey, BC V3A 3K2
Tel: 604-588-5344; *Fax:* 604-588-2331
infodesk@bkslaw.com
www.bkslaw.com

Surrey: Caissie & Company - *1
#205, 15127 - 100 Ave., Surrey, BC V3R 0N9
Tel: 604-586-7200; *Fax:* 604-583-5870
info@calaw.bc.ca
www.calaw.bc.ca

Surrey: James L. Davidson & Company - *3
#403, P.O. Box 271, 16033 - 108 Ave., Surrey, BC V4N 1P2
Tel: 604-951-2990; *Fax:* 604-951-2991
jld@look.ca

Surrey: Paul E. Del Rossi - *1
#1012, 7445 - 132nd St., Surrey, BC V3W 1J8
Tel: 604-590-5600; *Fax:* 604-590-5626
Toll-Free: 866-990-5600
pdelrossi@sternandalbert.com

Surrey: G. Egolf - *1
14135 - 60 Ave., Surrey, BC V3X 2N2
Tel: 604-594-4166

Surrey: Fritz Shirreff & Vickers - *4
Former Name: Fritz Lail Shirreff & Vickers
#201, 15127 - 100th Ave., Surrey, BC V3R 0N9
Tel: 604-582-5157; *Fax:* 604-582-5167
info@fsvlawyers.com
www.fsvlawyers.com

Surrey: Greig, Wilson & Rasmussen LLP - *5
Former Name: Greig, Wilson & Brajovic
#300, Guildford Landmark Bldg., 15127 - 100th Ave., Surrey, BC V3R 0N9
Tel: 604-583-7917; *Fax:* 604-583-7139
info@gwrlawyers.com
www.gwrlawyers.com

Surrey: Guildford Law Group - *3
#200, 10330 - 152 St., Surrey, BC V3R 4G8
Tel: 604-585-1196; *Fax:* 604-585-3293
www.guildfordlaw.com

** indicates number of lawyers*

***Surrey*: Hamilton Duncan Armstrong & Stewart Law Corporation - North Surrey - *20**
#1450, Station Tower Gateway, 13401 - 108th Ave., Surrey, BC V3T 5T3
Tel: 604-581-4677; *Fax:* 604-581-5947
info@hdas.com
www.hdas.com

***Surrey*: Hamilton Duncan Armstrong & Stewart Law Corporation - South Surrey - *19**
#210, Rodeo Square, 5620 - 152nd St., Surrey, BC V3S 3K2
Tel: 604-575-8088; *Fax:* 604-575-8118
info@hdas.com
www.hdas.com

***Surrey*: Sharen Janeson - *1**
#456, 15355 - 24 Ave., Surrey, BC V4A 2H9
Tel: 604-536-6884; *Fax:* 604-618-9500
sjaneson@shaw.ca

***Surrey*: Kaminsky & Company - *4**
#220, 7525 King George Blvd., Surrey, BC V3W 5A8
Tel: 604-591-7877; *Fax:* 604-591-1978
inbox@kaminskyco.com
www.kaminskyco.com

***Surrey*: Kane, Shannon & Weiler - *21**
#220, 7565 - 132nd St., Surrey, BC V3W 1K5
Tel: 604-591-7321; *Fax:* 604-591-7149
info@ksw.bc.ca
www.ksw.bc.ca

***Surrey*: Kereluk & Company - *1**
#125, 15225 - 104 Ave., Surrey, BC V3R 6Y8
Tel: 604-589-3278; *Fax:* 604-589-8473
mail@kereluklaw.com
www.kereluklaw.com

***Surrey*: James R. Kitsul - *1**
19395 Langley Bypass, Surrey, BC V3S 6K1
Tel: 604-539-2610; *Fax:* 604-534-3811
kitsul@supersave.ca

***Surrey*: William D. MacLeod Law Corp. - *1**
#205A, York Business Centre, 12830 - 80 Ave., Surrey, BC V3W 3A8
Tel: 604-572-7200; *Fax:* 604-572-7213

***Surrey*: MacMillan, Tucker, & Mackay - *3**
5690 - 176A St., Surrey, BC V3S 4H1
Tel: 604-574-7431; *Fax:* 604-574-3021

***Surrey*: Maier & Co. - *1**
#310, 10524 King George Hwy., Surrey, BC V3S 2X2
Tel: 604-582-5951; *Fax:* 604-588-0779
maier@telus.net

***Surrey*: Manthorpe Law Offices - *1**
#102, 15399 - 102A Ave., Surrey, BC V3R 7K1
Tel: 604-582-7743; *Fax:* 604-582-7753

***Surrey*: A.L. McAndrew - *1**
#240, 13711 - 72 Ave., Surrey, BC V3W 2P2
Tel: 604-591-2288; *Fax:* 604-591-7366

***Surrey*: Cameron C. McLeod - *1**
#310, 10524 King George Hwy, Surrey, BC V3T 2X2
Tel: 604-583-6318; *Fax:* 604-588-0779
mcleodlaw@dccnet.com

***Surrey*: McQuarrie Hunter LLP - *26**
#200, 13889 - 104th Ave., Surrey, BC V3T 1W8
Tel: 604-581-0461; *Fax:* 604-581-7110
www.mcquarrie.com

***Surrey*: Allan D. McRae - *1**
#309, 1656 Martin Dr., Surrey, BC V4A 6E7
Tel: 604-538-1511

***Surrey*: Murchison Thomson & Clarke LLP - *23**
#101, Surrey Central Business Park, 7565 - 132 St., Surrey, BC V3W 1K5
Tel: 604-590-8855; *Fax:* 604-590-2000
info@murchisonthomson.com
www.murchisonthomson.com

***Surrey*: Nyack & Persad - *2**
#201, 9380 - 120 St., Surrey, BC V3V 4B9
Tel: 604-588-9933; *Fax:* 604-588-2731
nyackpersad@hotmail.com

***Surrey*: Michael G. Parent, Law Corporation - *1**
#203, 15225 - 104 Ave., Surrey, BC V3R 6Y8
Tel: 604-589-6437; *Fax:* 604-589-7238

***Surrey*: Peterson Stark Scott - *11**
#300, 10355 - 136A Street, Surrey, BC V3T 5R3
Tel: 604-588-9321; *Fax:* 604-589-5391
Toll-Free: 800-555-3288
sry@psslaw.ca
www.psslaw.ca

***Surrey*: Donald F. Porter - *1**
#203, 8318 - 120 St., Surrey, BC V3W 3N4
Tel: 604-594-5155; *Fax:* 604-594-1304
dfporter@allstream.net

***Surrey*: Richards & Richards - *3**
10325 - 150 St., Surrey, BC V3R 4B1
Tel: 604-588-6844; *Fax:* 604-588-8800
richard.george@richardslaw.com

***Surrey*: E.R. Swedahl - *1**
#11, 15243 - 91 Ave., Surrey, BC V3R 8P8
Tel: 604-581-3232; *Fax:* 604-589-3741

***Surrey*: Taylor, Bjorge & Company - *2**
#205, 1676 Martin Dr., Surrey, BC V4A 6E7
Tel: 604-536-1117; *Fax:* 604-536-0445

***Surrey*: Gordon G. Walters - *1**
12321 Beecher St., Surrey, BC V4A 3A7
Tel: 604-596-3300; *Fax:* 604-535-7350

***Surrey*: P. Barry Whaites - *1**
Former Name: Whaites & King
#200, 5746 - 176A St., Surrey, BC V3S 4H2
Tel: 604-574-0770; *Fax:* 604-574-0107

***Terrace*: Crampton Personal Law Corporation - *2**
4623 Park Ave., Terrace, BC V8G 1V5
Tel: 250-635-6330; *Fax:* 250-635-4795
Toll-Free: 800-667-0080
Gordon_Crampton@telus.net; bryan_crampton@telus.net

***Terrace*: Talstra & Company - *3**
#101, 3219 Eby St., Terrace, BC V8G 4R3
Tel: 250-638-1137; *Fax:* 250-638-1306
Toll-Free: 877-998-4222

***Terrace*: Warner Bandstra Brown - *5**
#200, 4630 Lazelle Ave., Terrace, BC V8G 1S6
Tel: 250-635-2622; *Fax:* 250-635-4998

***Trail*: Ghilarducci & Cromarty - *2**
1309 Bay Ave., Trail, BC V1R 4A7
Tel: 250-368-6455; *Fax:* 250-368-6107

***Trail*: McEwan Harrison & Co. - *5**
1432 Bay Ave., Trail, BC V1R 4B1
Tel: 250-368-8211; *Fax:* 250-368-9401
www.mcewanharrison.com

***Trail*: Westcott Simpkin & Co. - *1**
1402 Bay Ave., Trail, BC V1R 4B1
Tel: 250-358-9171; *Fax:* 250-368-3369
westcottlaw@shawbiz.ca

***Ucluelet*: James P. Roth - *1**
CP 909, 1566 Peninsula Rd., Ucluelet, BC V0R 3A0
Tel: 250-726-4307; *Fax:* 250-726-2180
info@macisaacgroup.com
www.macisaacgroup.com

***Vancouver*: Aaron, Gordon & Daykin - *6**
Former Name: Aaron, MacGregor, Gordon & Daykin
#600, 815 Hornby St., Vancouver, BC V6Z 2E6
Tel: 604-689-7571; *Fax:* 604-685-8563
reception@agdlaw.ca
www.agdlaw.ca

***Vancouver*: Access Law Group - *7**
#1700, 1185 Georgia St. West, Vancouver, BC V6E 4E6
Tel: 604-689-8000; *Fax:* 604-689-8835
reception@accesslaw.ca
www.accesslaw.ca

***Vancouver*: Jack A. Adelaar - *1**
#1702, 808 Nelson St., Vancouver, BC V6Z 2H2
Tel: 604-687-8840; *Fax:* 604-687-8370
jadelaar@telus.net

***Vancouver*: Adrian & Company - *2**
5660 Yew St., Vancouver, BC V6M 3Y3
Tel: 604-266-7811; *Fax:* 604-266-5869

***Vancouver*: Alexander Holburn Beaudin & Lang, LLP - *75**
#2700, P.O. Box 10057, 700 West Georgia St., Vancouver, BC V7Y 1B8
Tel: 604-484-1700; *Fax:* 604-484-9700
Toll-Free: 877-688-1351
info@ahbl.ca
www.ahbl.ca

***Vancouver*: William J. Alexander Law Corporation - *1**
#167, 1917 - 4th Ave. West, Vancouver, BC V6J 1M7
Tel: 604-831-3743; *Fax:* 604-831-6273

***Vancouver*: Allan & Lougheed - *2**
1622 - 7th Ave. West, 2nd Fl., Vancouver, BC V6J 1S5
Tel: 604-733-2411; *Fax:* 604-736-6225
aandllaw@telus.net

***Vancouver*: Altridge & Company - *1**
#741, 1489 Marine Dr., Vancouver, BC V7T 1B8
Tel: 604-688-3557; *Fax:* 604-688-0535
pga@altridge.com
www.altridge.com

***Vancouver*: Alvin Hui Law Corp. - *1**
1606 Hornby St., Vancouver, BC V6Z 2T4
Tel: 604-732-3898; *Fax:* 604-739-2821
ahlc@telus.net

***Vancouver*: Paul Andersen - *2**
1662 - 8th Ave. West, Vancouver, BC V6J 4R8
Tel: 604-734-8411; *Fax:* 604-734-8511
andersen_paul@telus.net

***Vancouver*: Brian W. Anderson Law Corporation - *1**
835 Granville St., 2nd Fl., Vancouver, BC V6Z 1K7
Tel: 604-684-5367

***Vancouver*: Jane Anderson - *1**
#1782, 808 Nelson St., Vancouver, BC V6Z 2H2
Tel: 604-488-1162; *Fax:* 604-488-0666
janeanderso@telus.net

***Vancouver*: Anfield Sujir Kennedy & Durno - *6**
#1600, Pacific Centre, P.O. Box 10068, 609 Granville St., Vancouver, BC V7Y 1C3
Tel: 604-669-1322; *Fax:* 604-669-3877
mailbox@askdlaw.com

***Vancouver*: Armstrong Simpson - *4**
Former Name: Armstrong & Company
#2080, 777 Hornby St., Vancouver, BC V6Z 1S4
Tel: 604-683-7361; *Fax:* 604-662-3231

***Vancouver*: Aydin Bird - *4**
Former Name: Aydin & Co
#530, North Office Tower, 650 - 41 Ave. West, Vancouver, BC V5Z 2M9
Tel: 604-266-5828; *Fax:* 604-266-3929
aydin@aydinco.com
www.aydinco.com

***Vancouver*: Baker & Baker - *3**
808 Nelson St., 17th Fl., Vancouver, BC V6Z 2H2
Tel: 604-642-0107; *Fax:* 604-681-3504
info@bakerbaker.ca
www.bakerbaker.ca

***Vancouver*: Barbeau, Evans, Goldstein - *4**
#280, 666 Burrard St., Vancouver, BC V6C 2X8
Tel: 604-688-4900; *Fax:* 604-688-0649
info@beg-law.com
www.beg-law.com

***Vancouver*: Gail Barnes - *1**
149 Main St., Vancouver, BC V6A 2S5
Tel: 604-684-1124; *Fax:* 604-684-1122
egray@sprint.ca

***Vancouver*: Barrigar Intellectual Property Law - *5**
#202, 543 Seymour St., Vancouver, BC V6C 1X8
Tel: 604-689-9255; *Fax:* 604-689-9265
email@barrigar.com
www.barrigar.com

***Vancouver*: Basham Thompson & Liu - *7**
#2550, Granville Sq., 200 Granville St., Vancouver, BC V6C 1S4
Tel: 604-601-3863; *Fax:* 604-681-8632

** indicates number of lawyers*

Vancouver: **Beach Avenue Barristers, A Law Corporation - *3**
Former Name: Epstein Wood
#150, 1008 Beach Avenue, Vancouver, BC V6E 1T7
Tel: 604-629-0429; *Fax:* 604-689-4451

Vancouver: **Beck, Robinson & Company - *4**
#700, 686 West Broadway, Vancouver, BC V5Z 1G1
Tel: 604-874-0204; *Fax:* 604-874-0820
lawyers@beckrobinson.com
www.beckrobinson.com

Vancouver: **P.J. Beirne**
157 Alexander St., 3rd Fl., Vancouver, BC V6A 1B8
Tel: 604-683-4311; *Fax:* 604-683-4317

Vancouver: **David R. Bellamy - *1**
#101, 1012 Beach Ave., Vancouver, BC V6E 1T7
Tel: 604-662-8900; *Fax:* 604-662-8902
dbellamy@bellamy.bc.ca

Vancouver: **Robert W. Bellows - *1**
#620, 1385 West 8 Ave., Vancouver, BC V6H 3V9
Tel: 604-736-5500; *Fax:* 604-736-5522
rbellows@telus.net

Vancouver: **Bennett, Parkes - *2**
#460, 2609 Granville St., Vancouver, BC V6H 3H3
Tel: 604-734-6838; *Fax:* 604-738-6789

Vancouver: **Bernard & Partners - *15**
#1500, 570 Granville St., Vancouver, BC V6C 3P1
Tel: 604-681-1700; *Fax:* 604-681-1788
tuytel@bernardpartners.com
www.bernardpartners.com

Vancouver: **Shoni Lee Bernard - *1**
5052 Victoria Dr., Vancouver, BC V5P 3T8
Tel: 604-473-9330; *Fax:* 604-323-0093

Vancouver: **Beruschi & Company - *2**
#501, 905 West Pender St., Vancouver, BC V6C 1L6
Tel: 604-669-3116; *Fax:* 604-669-5886
admin@beruschi.com

Vancouver: **Raymond J. Bianchin - *1**
#410, 2609 Granville St., Vancouver, BC V6H 3H3
Tel: 604-683-8111; *Fax:* 604-685-0194

Vancouver: **Birnie & Company - *2**
#2433, Three Bentall Centre, P.O. Box 49116, Stn. Bentall, 595 Burrard St., Vancouver, BC V7X 1G4
Tel: 604-688-4511; *Fax:* 604-688-0511
dbirnie@birnieco.com

Vancouver: **Pamela S. Boles - *1**
#210, 970 Burrard St., Vancouver, BC V6Z 2R4
Tel: 604-688-5001; *Fax:* 604-685-5006

Vancouver: **Bolton & Muldoon - *4**
#360, 1122 Mainland St., Vancouver, BC V6B 5L1
Tel: 604-687-7078; *Fax:* 604-687-3022

Vancouver: **Boughton Law Corporation - *50**
Also Known As: Boughton
Former Name: Boughton Peterson Yang Anderson
#700, P.O. Box 49290, 595 Burrard St., Vancouver, BC V7X 1S8
Tel: 604-687-6789; *Fax:* 604-683-5317
lawyers@boughton.ca
www.boughton.ca

Vancouver: **Joyce W. Bradley - *1**
P.O. Box 45565, Stn. Westside, Vancouver, BC V6S 2N5
Tel: 604-732-3886; *Fax:* 604-732-3781
jwbmediate@telus.net

Vancouver: **W. Anita Braha - *1**
P.O. Box 65986, Stn. F, Vancouver, BC V5N 5L4
Tel: 604-251-2526; *Fax:* 604-251-2606

Vancouver: **H.K. Brown - *1**
#1504, 100 West Pender St., 15th Fl., Vancouver, BC V6B 1R8
Tel: 604-684-1021; *Fax:* 604-688-6243
henrykbrownlawcorporation@telus.net

Vancouver: **Peter W. Brown Law Corp. - *2**
2081 - 37 Ave. West, Vancouver, BC V6M 1N7
Tel: 604-261-0300; *Fax:* 604-261-0312
peterwbrown@owblawcorp.com

Vancouver: **J.G. Buchanan - *1**
#788, 601 West Broadway, Vancouver, BC V5Z 4C2
Tel: 604-876-0343; *Fax:* 604-876-9035

Vancouver: **Bull, Housser & Tupper LLP - *100**
#3000, Royal Centre, P.O. Box 11130, 1055 West Georgia St., Vancouver, BC V6E 3R3
Tel: 604-687-6575; *Fax:* 604-641-4949
Toll-Free: 888-687-6575
mailbox@bht.com
www.bht.com

Vancouver: **Susan P. Burak, Lawyer, Mediator & Collaborative Lawyer - *1**
1622 - 7th Ave West, 2nd Fl., Vancouver, BC V6J 1S5
Tel: 604-733-2411; *Fax:* 604-736-6225
ajzburak@shaw.ca

Vancouver: **Burke & Jones - *2**
687 - 20th Ave. East, Vancouver, BC V5V 1M9
Tel: 604-879-6365; *Fax:* 604-879-6367
acb@burkeandjones.com

Vancouver: **Burns, Fitzpatrick, Rogers & Schwartz - *8**
#1400, 510 Burrard St., Vancouver, BC V6C 3A8
Tel: 604-685-0121; *Fax:* 604-685-2104
bfrs@bfrs.ca
www.bfrs.ca

Vancouver: **Burrard Communications Inc. - *1**
#200, 409 Granville St., Vancouver, BC V6C 1T2
Tel: 604-619-1980; *Fax:* 604-689-0477
info@theburrardgroup.com

Vancouver: **Bradley M. Caldwell - *1**
#401, 815 Hornby St., Vancouver, BC V6Z 2E6
Tel: 604-689-8894; *Fax:* 604-689-5739

Vancouver: **Cawkell Brodie Glaister LLP - *4**
Former Name: Cawkell, Brodie
#1260, 1188 Georgia St. West, Vancouver, BC V6E 4A2
Tel: 604-684-3323; *Fax:* 604-684-3350
info@cawkell.org
www.cawkell.com

Vancouver: **Chalke & Company - *1**
708-1155 W. Pender St., Vancouver, BC V6E 2P4
Tel: 604-980-4855; *Fax:* 604-980-6469

Vancouver: **Chan Yue & Lee - *1**
#212, 475 Main St., Vancouver, BC V6A 2T7
Tel: 604-687-4576; *Fax:* 604-683-3258
canyua@intergate.ca

Vancouver: **Chen & Leung - *9**
#728, North Tower, Oakridge Centre, 650 - 41st Ave. West, Vancouver, BC V5Z 2M9
Tel: 604-264-8331; *Fax:* 604-264-8387
info@cllawyers.ca
www.cllawyers.ca

Vancouver: **Chow & Company - *1**
378 Smithe St., Vancouver, BC V6B 1T7
Tel: 604-669-0268; *Fax:* 604-669-9863
n-chow@telus.net

Vancouver: **Gregory T. Chu - *1**
#650, 1188 West Georgia St., Vancouver, BC V6E 4A2
Tel: 604-628-5005; *Fax:* 604-987-9939
gtchu@telus.net

Vancouver: **Clark Wilson LLP - *80**
#800, 885 Georgia St. West, Vancouver, BC V6C 3H1
Tel: 604-687-5700; *Fax:* 604-687-6314
agb@cwilson.com
www.cwilson.com

Vancouver: **Cobb St. Pierre - *6**
#308, 425 Carrall St., Vancouver, BC V6B 6E3
Tel: 604-602-9770; *Fax:* 604-684-9690
info@acquit.ca

Vancouver: **Cochran Bradshaw - *3**
439 Helmcken St., Vancouver, BC V6B 2E6
Tel: 604-681-9200; *Fax:* 604-681-8339
cochranlaw@telus.net

Vancouver: **Morley E. Cofman Law Corporation - *1**
#1500, 701 West Georgia St., Vancouver, BC V7Y 1C6
Tel: 604-696-6674; *Fax:* 604-801-5911
mcofman@shaw.ca

Vancouver: **Leonard M. Cohen - *1**
#570, 999 West Broadway, Vancouver, BC V5Z 1K5
Tel: 604-731-8118

Vancouver: **Brian Coleman Q.C. - *1**
#380, 425 Carrall St., Vancouver, BC V6B 6E3
Tel: 604-683-5821; *Fax:* 604-683-9354
coleman@telus.net

Vancouver: **Guy J. Collette - *1**
#605, 1080 Howe St., Vancouver, BC V6Z 2T1
Tel: 604-662-7777; *Fax:* 604-669-4053
guy@collettelaw.com
www.collettelaw.com

Vancouver: **Collins & Cullen - *2**
#750, 999 West Broadway, Vancouver, BC V5Z 1K5
Tel: 604-730-2678; *Fax:* 604-730-2628

Vancouver: **James Comparelli - *2**
#704, 510 West Hastings St., Vancouver, BC V6B 1L8
Tel: 604-683-6888; *Fax:* 604-683-4497
james@comparelli.com
www.comparelli.com

Vancouver: **Carla Courtenay Law Office - *1**
#501, 815 Hornby St., Vancouver, BC V6Z 2E6
Tel: 604-682-2200; *Fax:* 604-682-2246
lilias@cclaw.bc.ca
www.cclaw.bc.ca

Vancouver: **Coutts Weiler & Pulver - *8**
Former Name: Schiller, Coutts, Weiler & Gibson
#1485, P.O. Box 253, 555 Burrard St., Vancouver, BC V7X 1M9
Tel: 604-682-1866; *Fax:* 604-682-6947
info@cwplaw.ca
www.cwplaw.ca

Vancouver: **Raffaele Crescenzo - *1**
#206, 1651 Commercial Dr., Vancouver, BC V5L 3Y3
Tel: 604-255-9030; *Fax:* 604-255-9075

Vancouver: **F.S. Crestani - *1**
5052 Victoria Dr., Vancouver, BC V5P 3T8
Tel: 604-251-1168; *Fax:* 604-253-7726

Vancouver: **Kenneth Cristall - *1**
#610, P.O. Box 12110, 808 Nelson St., Vancouver, BC V6Z 2H2
Tel: 604-654-2250; *Fax:* 604-682-8879

Vancouver: **Harry Crosby - *1**
5052 Victoria Dr., Vancouver, BC V5P 3T8
Tel: 604-321-6922; *Fax:* 604-323-0093

Vancouver: **Crossin Coristine Woodall - *5**
#660, 220 Cambie St., Vancouver, BC V6B 2M9
Tel: 604-689-3242; *Fax:* 604-689-3292

Vancouver: **Cruickshank Huinink Zukerman - *3**
#250, 1122 Mainland St., Vancouver, BC V6B 5L1
Tel: 604-688-3933; *Fax:* 604-681-6677

Vancouver: **Cummings Law Corporation - *1**
#320, 650 West 41st Ave., Vancouver, BC V5Z 2M9
Tel: 604-264-7038; *Fax:* 604-264-7039
info@cummingslawcorp.com

Vancouver: **Barbara J. Curran**
#407, 825 Granville St., Vancouver, BC V6Z 1K9
Tel: 604-689-4501; *Fax:* 604-689-5572
bjcurran@telus.net

Vancouver: **Cuttler & Company**
CP 12184, Stn. Nelson Square, #1811, 808 Nelson St., Vancouver, BC V6Z 2H2
Tel: 604-673-4225; *Fax:* 604-633-1838

Vancouver: **D. Brad Henry Law Corporation - *1**
Former Name: Epstein Wood
#1900, 1177 West Hastings Street, Vancouver, BC V6E 2K3
Tel: 604-718-6892; *Fax:* 604-718-6873

Vancouver: **Aspha J. Dada & Co. - *2**
2479 Kingsway, Vancouver, BC V5R 5G8
Tel: 604-433-3300; *Fax:* 604-436-3937
info-ajd@telus.net

Vancouver: **Dallas & Company - *2**
852 Seymour St., Vancouver, BC V6B 3L6
Tel: 604-681-6171; *Fax:* 604-683-1000
dallas&co@telus.net

** indicates number of lawyers*

***Vancouver*: A. Kenneth Dangerfield - *1**
#1000, P.O. Box 49290, Stn. Bentall, 595 Burrard St., Vancouver, BC V7X 1S8
Tel: 604-687-6789; *Fax:* 604-683-5317
kdangerfield@boughton.ca

***Vancouver*: Greg Delbigio**
#1720, 355 Burrard St., Vancouver, BC V6C 2G8
Tel: 604-687-9831; *Fax:* 604-687-7089
greg_delbigio@telus.net

***Vancouver*: A.J. DeMeulemeester - *1**
#202, 119 Pender St. West, Vancouver, BC V6B 1S5
Tel: 604-685-6610; *Fax:* 604-682-5687

***Vancouver*: Derpak, White & Company - *3**
#901, 1788 Broadway West, Vancouver, BC V6J 1Y1
Tel: 604-736-9791; *Fax:* 604-736-7197
derpakwhite@telus.net

***Vancouver*: Directis Consulting Group Ltd. - *1**
#720, 999 Broadway West, Vancouver, BC V5Z 1K5
Tel: 604-730-2668;
sue@directis.ca

***Vancouver*: J.W. Dobbin - *1**
123 Main St., Vancouver, BC V6A 2S5
Tel: 604-669-6045; *Fax:* 604-669-6041
jwd@jwdobbin.com

***Vancouver*: David H. Doig & Associates - *2**
#1450, 1188 Georgia St. West, Vancouver, BC V6E 4A2
Tel: 604-687-8874; *Fax:* 604-687-8134
ddoig@daviddoig.com

***Vancouver*: Dolden Wallace Folick LLP - *17**
888 Dunsmuir St., 10th Fl., Vancouver, BC V6C 3K4
Tel: 604-689-3222; *Fax:* 604-689-3777
info@dolden.com
www.dolden.com

***Vancouver*: Donaldson Jetté - *4**
#490, 1090 Hornby St., Vancouver, BC V6B 2W9
Tel: 604-681-5232; *Fax:* 604-681-1331
hrusso@donaldsonjette.ca

***Vancouver*: Donna L. Kydd Law Corporation - *1**
#250, 1501 West Broadway, Vancouver, BC V6J 4Z6
Tel: 604-732-5031; *Fax:* 604-732-5071
dlkydd@kyddlaw.ca; sthomas@kyddlaw.ca
www.kyddlaw.ca

***Vancouver*: Donovan & Company - *9**
73 Water St., 6th Fl., Vancouver, BC V6B 1A1
Tel: 604-688-4272; *Fax:* 604-688-4282
allan_donovan@aboriginal-law.com
www.aboriginal-law.com

***Vancouver*: Emil M. Doricic - *1**
195 Alexander St., 2nd Fl., Vancouver, BC V6A 1B8
Tel: 604-688-8338; *Fax:* 604-688-8356

***Vancouver*: Le Dressay & Company - *1**
#103, 1525 - 8th Ave. West, Vancouver, BC V6J 1T5
Tel: 604-739-0017; *Fax:* 604-739-0041
dan@ledressay.com

***Vancouver*: DuMoulin Boskovich LLP - *16**
#1800, Manulife Place, Box 52, 1095 West Pender St., Vancouver, BC V6E 2M6
Tel: 604-669-5500; *Fax:* 604-688-8491
Toll-Free: 800-288-9893
info@dubo.com
www.dubo.comwww.linkedin.com/company/2293070?trk=tyah

***Vancouver*: Dunnaway, Jackson & Associates - *2**
Former Name: Dunnaway, Jackson & Hamilton
#1205, 808 Nelson St., Vancouver, BC V6Z 2H2
Tel: 604-682-0007; *Fax:* 604-682-8711

***Vancouver*: Edwards, Kenny & Bray LLP - *27**
#1900, The Grosvenor Bldg., 1040 West Georgia St., Vancouver, BC V6E 4H3
Tel: 604-689-1811; *Fax:* 604-689-5177
inquiry@ekb.com
www.ekb.com

***Vancouver*: Ellis, Nauss & Jones - *2**
#600, 1665 West Broadway, Vancouver, BC V6J 1X1
Tel: 604-731-9276; *Fax:* 604-734-0206

***Vancouver*: Ellis, Roadburg - *2**
#200, 853 Richards St., Vancouver, BC V6B 3B4
Tel: 604-669-7131; *Fax:* 604-669-7684

***Vancouver*: Embarkation Law Group - *6**
#600, P.O. Box 26, 609 West Hastings St., 6th Fl., Vancouver, BC V6B 4W4
Tel: 604-662-7404; *Fax:* 604-662-7466
Toll-Free: 888-662-7404
info@elgcanada.com
www.elgcanada.com

***Vancouver*: Dick W. Eng Law Corp. - *1**
#701, 601 Broadway West, Vancouver, BC V5Z 4C2
Tel: 604-877-0880; *Fax:* 604-877-0330
dick.eng@telus.net

***Vancouver*: Robert J. Falconer, Q.C. - *1**
#400, 409 Granville St., Vancouver, BC V6C 1T2
Tel: 604-683-5674; *Fax:* 604-682-8417
robert.falconer@axion.net

***Vancouver*: Fan & Co. - *3**
#601, 609 Gore Ave., Vancouver, BC V6A 2Z8
Tel: 604-683-0471; *Fax:* 604-683-8748
hfan@telus.net

***Vancouver*: Farris, Vaughan, Wills & Murphy LLP - *87**
700 West Georgia St., 25th Floor, Vancouver, BC V7Y 1B3
Tel: 604-684-9151; *Fax:* 604-661-9349
info@farris.com
www.farris.com

***Vancouver*: Fayers & Company - *2**
#380, 5740 Cambie St., Vancouver, BC V5Z 3A6
Tel: 604-325-1246; *Fax:* 604-325-1261

***Vancouver*: Larry C. Flader - *1**
4244 Doncaster Way, Vancouver, BC V6S 2L6
Tel: 604-224-7225

***Vancouver*: Robert S. Fleming - *1**
#107, 5605 Hampton Pl., Vancouver, BC V6T 2H2
Tel: 604-682-1659; *Fax:* 604-633-1838
rsfleming@telus.net

***Vancouver*: Constance C. Fogal - *1**
3570 Hull St., Vancouver, BC V5N 4R9
Tel: 604-872-2128

***Vancouver*: Fraser & Company - *9**
#1200, 999 Hastings St. West, Vancouver, BC V6C 2W2
Tel: 604-669-5244; *Fax:* 604-669-5791
securities@fraserlaw.com

***Vancouver*: Gordon J. Fretwell Law Corp. - *1**
#1780, 400 Burrard St., Vancouver, BC V6C 3A6
Tel: 604-689-1280; *Fax:* 604-689-1288
law@fretwell.ca
www.fretwell.ca

***Vancouver*: Friesen & Epp - *4**
5660 Yew St., Vancouver, BC V6M 3Y3
Tel: 604-264-8386; *Fax:* 604-264-8815
erwinepp@stargate.ca

***Vancouver*: Ganapathi & Company - *2**
#302, 1224 Hamilton St., Vancouver, BC V6B 2S8
Tel: 604-689-9222; *Fax:* 604-689-4888
Toll-Free: 866-689-9222
nathan@ganapathico.com; info@ganapathico.com
www.ganapathico.com

***Vancouver*: Alnoor R.S. Gangji - *1**
#788, 601 West Broadway, Vancouver, BC V5Z 4C2
Tel: 604-708-3783; *Fax:* 604-876-9035
aglawyer@dowco.com

***Vancouver*: Donald R. Gardner - *1**
#402, 195 Alexander St., Vancouver, BC V6A 1N8
Tel: 604-687-1766; *Fax:* 604-687-0181
barristerfromsmu@hotmail.com

***Vancouver*: Robert G. Gateman - *1**
#202, 1112 Brougton St., Vancouver, BC V6G 2A8
Tel: 604-687-4911;
gateman@interchange.bc.ca

***Vancouver*: Gayle D. Gavin - *1**
4168 - 11th Ave., Vancouver, BC V6R 2L6
Tel: 604-222-2827

***Vancouver*: Getz Prince Wells LLP - *8**
#1810, 1111 West Georgia St., Vancouver, BC V6E 4M3
Tel: 604-685-6367; *Fax:* 604-685-9798
admin@getzpw.com
www.getzpw.com

***Vancouver*: Gibbons Fowler Nathanson - *6**
#440, The Marine Building, 355 Burrard St., Vancouver, BC V6C 2G8
Tel: 604-684-0778; *Fax:* 604-684-0799
reception@gibbonsfowler.com
www.gibbonsfowler.com

***Vancouver*: Kenneth Glasner Q.C. Law Corp. - *1**
#1414, P.O. Box 12158, 808 Nelson St., Vancouver, BC V6Z 2H2
Tel: 604-683-4181; *Fax:* 604-683-0226
glasnerqc@telus.net

***Vancouver*: Global Trade Resources - *1**
#609, 1009 Expo Blvd., Vancouver, BC V6Z 2V9
Tel: 604-306-7475; *Fax:* 604-682-7477
irehmanji@novuscom.net

***Vancouver*: Goldman Zimmer Bray - *3**
Former Name: Goldman Lakhani Zimmer Bray
#950, 1111 Melville St., Vancouver, BC V6E 3V6
Tel: 604-682-6181; *Fax:* 604-683-5723
ngoldman@goldmath.com

***Vancouver*: C.H.J. Gordon - *1**
#115, 2025 - 1st Ave. West, Vancouver, BC V6J 1H1
Tel: 604-730-8838

***Vancouver*: P.D. Gornall - *1**
#1820, 355 Burrard St., Vancouver, BC V6C 2G8
Tel: 604-681-7932; *Fax:* 604-775-8555
pdg@telus.net

***Vancouver*: GR Strategies Inc. - *1**
#602, 134 Abbott St., Vancouver, BC V6B 2K4
Tel: 604-685-6303;
cg@grstrategies.com

***Vancouver*: Granger & Co. - *2**
#1400, 777 Hornby St., Vancouver, BC V6Z 1S4
Tel: 604-685-1900; *Fax:* 604-685-2034

***Vancouver*: Murray H. Grant - *1**
#2020, P.O. Box 11547, 650 West Georgia St., Vancouver, BC V6B 4N7
Tel: 604-683-9621; *Fax:* 604-683-5084

***Vancouver*: Granville Law Group - *2**
Former Name: Vertlieb Anderson
#200, 835 Granville St., Vancouver, BC V6Z 1K7
Tel: 604-669-6580; *Fax:* 604-688-7291

***Vancouver*: Grossman & Stanley, Business Lawyers - *4**
#800, Box 55, 1090 West Georgia St., Vancouver, BC V6E 3V7
Tel: 604-683-7454; *Fax:* 604-683-8602
info@grossmanstanley.com
www.grossmanstanley.com

***Vancouver*: Gudmundseth Mickelson LLP - *6**
#2525, 1075 West Georgia St., Vancouver, BC V6E 3C9
Tel: 604-685-6272; *Fax:* 604-685-8434
info@lawgm.com

***Vancouver*: W.F. Guinn - *1**
671G Market Hill, Vancouver, BC V5Z 4B5
Tel: 604-872-6658; *Fax:* 604-876-3304

***Vancouver*: Guy & Company - *1**
#100, 190 Alexander St., Vancouver, BC V6A 1B5
Tel: 604-681-6164; *Fax:* 604-681-7420
guy_and_company@telus.net

***Vancouver*: Hara & Company - *2**
#301, 460 Nanaimo St., Vancouver, BC V5L 4W3
Tel: 604-255-4800; *Fax:* 604-255-8111
haraco@telus.net

***Vancouver*: Harper Grey LLP - *53**
Former Name: Harper Grey Easton
#3200, Vancouver Centre, 650 West Georgia St., Vancouver, BC V6B 4P7
Tel: 604-687-0411; *Fax:* 604-669-9385
info@harpergrey.com
www.harpergrey.com

***Vancouver*: Harris & Brun - *6**
555 West Georgia St., Vancouver, BC V6B 1Z5
Tel: 604-683-2466; *Fax:* 604-683-4541

** indicates number of lawyers*

***Vancouver*: Harris & Company LLP - *33**
Bentall 5, 550 Burrard St., 14th Floor, Vancouver, BC V6C 2B5
Tel: 604-684-6633; *Fax:* 604-684-6632
info@harrisco.com
www.harrisco.com

***Vancouver*: Heddema & Partners LLP - *4**
#2800, P.O. Box 49279, Stn. Bentall Centre, 1055 Dunsmuir St., Vancouver, BC V7X 1P4
Tel: 604-669-4416; *Fax:* 604-681-4184
lawyers@heddemalaw.ca

***Vancouver*: John E. Helsing - *1**
#347, 1275 West 6th Ave., Vancouver, BC V6H 1A6
Tel: 604-739-7731; *Fax:* 604-738-7134

***Vancouver*: Hemsworth, Schmidt - *2**
#430, 580 Hornby St., Vancouver, BC V6C 3B6
Tel: 604-687-4456; *Fax:* 604-687-0586

***Vancouver*: Hobbs Giroday - *3**
#908, 938 Howe St., Vancouver, BC V6Z 1N9
Tel: 604-669-6609; *Fax:* 604-669-6612
www.hobbsgiroday.com

***Vancouver*: Hogan & Company - *1**
#900, 850 Hastings St. West, Vancouver, BC V6C 1E1
Tel: 604-687-8806; *Fax:* 604-687-7089

***Vancouver*: Holmes & Company - *2**
Former Name: Holmes & Greenslade
#1880, 1066 Hastings St. West, Vancouver, BC V6E 3X1
Tel: 604-688-7861; *Fax:* 604-688-0426
sdh@holmescompany.com
www.holmescompany.comwww.linkedin.com/company/holmes-a nd-company

***Vancouver*: Holmes & King - *4**
#1300, 1111 Georgia St. West, Vancouver, BC V6E 4M3
Tel: 604-681-1310; *Fax:* 604-681-1307
lawyers@mhklaw.com

***Vancouver*: Hoogbruin & Company - *1**
#650, 1188 West Georgia St., Vancouver, BC V6E 4A2
Tel: 604-609-3783; *Fax:* 604-682-8348

***Vancouver*: Hordo & Bennett - *8**
Former Name: McAlpine & Hordo
#1801, Nelson Sq., P.O. Box 12146, 808 Nelson St., Vancouver, BC V6Z 2H2
Tel: 604-682-5250; *Fax:* 604-682-7872
general@hrb.bc.ca

***Vancouver*: Peter J. Hull - *1**
869 West 20 Ave., Vancouver, BC V5Z 1Y3
Tel: 604-874-0200

***Vancouver*: Wayne Hum & Co. - *1**
#1608, 1166 Alberni St., Vancouver, BC V6E 3Z3
Tel: 604-687-6806; *Fax:* 604-687-6809

***Vancouver*: Forrest C. Hume - *1**
#700, 1080 Howe St., Vancouver, BC V6Z 2T1
Tel: 604-488-1499; *Fax:* 604-488-1489
fchume@humelawcorp.com

***Vancouver*: Hunter Litigation Chambers - *19**
Former Name: Hunter Voith
#2100, 1040 West Georgia St., Vancouver, BC V6E 4H1
Tel: 604-891-2400; *Fax:* 604-647-4554
www.litigationchambers.com

***Vancouver*: F.M. Irvine - *1**
4447, West 5th Ave., Vancouver, BC V6R 1S4
Tel: 604-224-5125; *Fax:* 604-224-5128
sirvine@interchange.ubc.ca

***Vancouver*: Alex Irwin Law Corp. - *1**
Also Known As: Irwin, White & Jennings
#2620, Royal Centre, 1055 West Georgia St., Vancouver, BC V6E 3R5
Tel: 604-664-3720; *Fax:* 604-689-2806
alex@iwjlaw.com
www.iwjlaw.com

***Vancouver*: Vahan A. Ishkanian - *1**
#1100, 1200 - 73rd Ave. West, Vancouver, BC V6P 6G5
Tel: 604-267-3033; *Fax:* 604-264-6133
vishkanian@pepito.ca

***Vancouver*: Bridget M. Jacob - *1**
#1500, 701 West Georgia St., Vancouver, BC V7Y 1C6
Tel: 604-738-1080; *Fax:* 604-738-1088
Toll-Free: 888-738-1082
bmjacob@telus.net

***Vancouver*: Donald Jang - *1**
#701, 601 West Broadway, Vancouver, BC V5Z 4C2
Tel: 604-877-0880; *Fax:* 604-877-0330

***Vancouver*: Jeffery & Calder - *4**
#601, 815 Hornby St., Vancouver, BC V6Z 2E6
Tel: 604-669-5534; *Fax:* 604-669-7563
contact@jefferycalder.com
www.jefferycalder.com

***Vancouver*: Jenkins Marzban Logan LLP - *17**
#900, Nelson Square, 808 Nelson St., Vancouver, BC V6Z 2H2
Tel: 604-681-6564; *Fax:* 604-681-0766
info@jml.ca
www.jml.ca

***Vancouver*: J. Douglas Jevning - *1**
#1503, 100 West Pender St., Vancouver, BC V6B 1R8
Tel: 604-688-7414; *Fax:* 604-688-6243
doug_jevning@telus.net

***Vancouver*: Josephson Angus Barristers - *3**
Former Name: Josephson & Company
#906, Cathedral Place, 925 West Georgia St., Vancouver, BC V6C 3L2
Tel: 604-684-9887; *Fax:* 604-684-3221
contacts@jabarristers.ca
www.jabarristers.ca

***Vancouver*: Steven B. Jung - *1**
#701, 601 West Broadway, Vancouver, BC V5Z 4C2
Tel: 604-877-2684; *Fax:* 604-877-0330
stevenjung@telus.net

***Vancouver*: R.N. Jussa - *1**
#204, 4676 Main St., Vancouver, BC V5V 3R7
Tel: 604-872-8191; *Fax:* 604-872-8217

***Vancouver*: Michael A. Kale Law Office - *1**
#1301, 808 Nelson St., Vancouver, BC V6Z 2H2
Tel: 604-685-8877; *Fax:* 604-685-3259
mkale@stevenskale.com

***Vancouver*: Kaplan & Waddell - *3**
#102, 2590 Granville St., Vancouver, BC V6H 3H1
Tel: 604-736-8021; *Fax:* 604-736-3845

***Vancouver*: Katz & Company - *1**
#1018, Nelson Square, P.O. Box 12135, 808 Nelson St., Vancouver, BC V6Z 2H2
Tel: 604-669-6226; *Fax:* 604-669-6752

***Vancouver*: Peter M. Kendall - *1**
#850, 475 West Georgia St., Vancouver, BC V6B 4M9
Tel: 604-685-3512; *Fax:* 604-681-9142

***Vancouver*: C. Robert Kennedy - *1**
#206, 190 Alexander St., Vancouver, BC V6A 1B5
Tel: 604-684-3927; *Fax:* 604-684-3228

***Vancouver*: Kerfoot & Company - *4**
#300, 5687 Yew St., Vancouver, BC V6M 3Y2
Tel: 604-263-2565; *Fax:* 604-263-2737
bbk@kerfootandco.com
www.kerfootandco.com

***Vancouver*: Khanna & Co. - *1**
#1540, 1100 Melville St., Vancouver, BC V6E 4A6
Tel: 604-605-5500; *Fax:* 604-689-5596

***Vancouver*: Killam Cordell Murray - *4**
#2000, 401 Georgia St. West, Vancouver, BC V6B 5A1
Tel: 604-622-5252; *Fax:* 604-622-5244
sgc@killamcordel.com

***Vancouver*: William N. King - *1**
#400, United Kingdom Bldg., 409 Granville St., Vancouver, BC V6C 1T2
Tel: 604-682-1245; *Fax:* 604-682-8417
janice.s@shaw.ca

***Vancouver*: Klein, Lyons - *9**
#1100, 1333 Broadway West, Vancouver, BC V6H 4C1
Tel: 604-874-7171; *Fax:* 604-874-7180
info@kleinlyons.com
www.kleinlyons.com

***Vancouver*: KM Technical Services - *1**
#PH 21, 2175 - 3 Ave. West, Vancouver, BC V6K 1L2
Tel: 250-247-9577;
konrad.mauch@shaw.ca

***Vancouver*: Koffman Kalef LLP - *22**
885 West Georgia St., 19th Fl., Vancouver, BC V6C 3H4
Tel: 604-891-3688; *Fax:* 604-891-3788
info@kkbl.com
www.kkbl.com

***Vancouver*: Dimitri A. Kontou - *1**
#1550, 355 Burrard St., Vancouver, BC V6G 2C8
Tel: 604-662-7244; *Fax:* 604-687-3097
dkontou@telus.net

***Vancouver*: Gordon Kopelow - *1**
#302, 1110 Hamilton St., Vancouver, BC V6B 2S2
Tel: 604-684-0096; *Fax:* 604-684-0048
gjkopelow@telus.net

***Vancouver*: Kornfeld & Company - *2**
#310, 698 Seymour St., Vancouver, BC V6B 3K6
Tel: 604-689-3838; *Fax:* 604-689-0526

***Vancouver*: Kornfeld Mackoff Silber LLP - *16**
#1100, Bentall Centre, CP 11, 505 Burrard St., Vancouver, BC V7X 1M5
Tel: 604-331-8300; *Fax:* 604-683-0570
Toll-Free: 866-331-8999
spertschi@kmslawyers.com
www.kmslawyers.com

***Vancouver*: Ron Y. Kornfeld - *1**
1622 7th Ave. West, 2nd Fl., Vancouver, BC V6J 1S5
Tel: 604-733-2448; *Fax:* 604-736-5131
rykornfeld@telus.net

***Vancouver*: Yoke Lam - *1**
#328, 88 East Pender St., Vancouver, BC V6A 1T1
Tel: 604-689-1123; *Fax:* 604-689-2003

***Vancouver*: Lando & Company - *6**
#2010, Royal Centre, P.O. Box 11140, 1055 Georgia St. West, Vancouver, BC V6E 3P3
Tel: 604-682-6821; *Fax:* 604-662-8293
info@lando.ca
www.lando.ca

***Vancouver*: Georgialee A. Lee & Associates - *4**
#1201, P.O. Box 12163, 808 Nelson St., Vancouver, BC V6Z 2H2
Tel: 604-669-2030; *Fax:* 604-669-2038

***Vancouver*: Stan N. Lanyon - *1**
#650, 475 Georgia St. West, Vancouver, BC V6B 4M9
Tel: 604-608-6108; *Fax:* 604-683-3846
stan.lanyon@arboffices.com

***Vancouver*: Laughton & Company - *2**
#1090, 1090 Georgia St. West, Vancouver, BC V6E 3V7
Tel: 604-683-6665; *Fax:* 604-683-6622

***Vancouver*: Law Office of David J. MacFarlane, Barrister & Solicitor**
Former Name: Macfarlane, Pearkes
#490, 99 West Broadway, Vancouver, BC V5Z 1K5
Tel: 604-732-7481; *Fax:* 604-732-3205
macper@telus.net

***Vancouver*: Lawson Lundell LLP - Vancouver - *100**
#1600, Cathedral Place, 925 West Georgia St., Vancouver, BC V6C 3L2
Tel: 604-685-3456; *Fax:* 604-669-1620
genmail@lawsonlundell.com
www.lawsonlundell.com

***Vancouver*: Laxton & Company - *3**
1285 West Pender St., 10th Fl., Vancouver, BC V6E 4B1
Tel: 604-682-3871; *Fax:* 604-682-3704

***Vancouver*: Valmon J. LeBlanc - *1**
#1400, 1125 Howe St., Vancouver, BC V6Z 2K8
Tel: 604-687-0909; *Fax:* 604-688-0933

***Vancouver*: Lecovin & Company - *2**
#560, P.O. Box 193, 1125 Howe St., Vancouver, BC V6Z 2K8
Tel: 604-687-1721; *Fax:* 604-687-1799
lecovin@intergate.ca

***Vancouver*: Lee & Company - *2**
#203, 856 Homer St., Vancouver, BC V6B 2W5
Tel: 604-687-1212; *Fax:* 604-669-6868

** indicates number of lawyers*

***Vancouver*: Jack L. Lee - *1**
127 East Pender St., 3rd Fl., Vancouver, BC V6A 1T6
Tel: 604-683-7241; *Fax:* 604-683-3279

***Vancouver*: Judith C. Lee - *1**
Sun Tower, 100 West Pender St., 10th Fl., Vancouver, BC V6B 1R8
Tel: 604-688-7972; *Fax:* 604-683-3886
judithlee@shaw.ca

***Vancouver*: Lesperance Mendes - *7**
#410, 900 Howe St., Vancouver, BC V6Z 2M4
Tel: 604-685-3567; *Fax:* 604-685-7505
kmw@lmlaw.ca
www.lmlaw.ca

***Vancouver*: Lew & Lee - *3**
#108, 329 Main St., Vancouver, BC V6A 2S9
Tel: 604-685-8331; *Fax:* 604-685-8334

***Vancouver*: Chuck Lew - *1**
#1010, 207 Hastings St. West, Vancouver, BC V6B 1H7
Tel: 604-688-3601; *Fax:* 604-688-7866
lewlaw@uniserve.com

***Vancouver*: H.H. Lew & Company - *1**
22 - 10th Ave. West, Vancouver, BC V5Y 1R6
Tel: 604-879-3151; *Fax:* 604-879-3707
hhlew@shaw.ca

***Vancouver*: Lex Pacifica Law Corporation - *1**
Former Name: John H. Shevchuk, Law Corporation
#1000, 543 Granville St., Vancouver, BC V6C 1X8
Tel: 604-689-1024; *Fax:* 604-689-1028
johnshevchuk@lexpacifica.com

***Vancouver*: Rhona M. Lichtenwald - *1**
#620, 1385 West 8 Ave., Vancouver, BC V6H 3V9
Tel: 604-739-4655; *Fax:* 604-739-9976
rhona@collaborativelawyer.ca
www.collaborativelawyer.ca

***Vancouver*: Carey Linde Personal Law Corporation - *2**
Also Known As: Divorce for Men
#605, 1080 Howe St., Vancouver, BC V6Z 2T1
Tel: 604-684-7794; *Fax:* 604-682-1243
lawyer@divorce-for-men.com
www.divorce-for-men.com

***Vancouver*: Lindsay Kenney LLP - Vancouver - *55**
Also Known As: LK Law
#1800, 401 West Georgia St., Vancouver, BC V6B 5A1
Tel: 604-687-1323; *Fax:* 604-687-2347
Toll-Free: 866-687-1323
info@lklaw.ca
www.lklaw.ca

***Vancouver*: Lipetz & Company - *1**
#202, 2902 West Broadway, Vancouver, BC V6K 2G8
Tel: 604-733-5611; *Fax:* 604-738-5611

***Vancouver*: Keith A. Lo - *2**
#338, 237 Keefer St., Vancouver, BC V6A 1X6
Tel: 604-687-4315; *Fax:* 604-681-2289

***Vancouver*: Logan & Company**
#1500, 1030 Georgia St. West, Vancouver, BC V6E 2Y3
Tel: 604-682-8521; *Fax:* 604-682-8753

***Vancouver*: Loh & Company - *4**
#708, North Tower, 650 - 41st Ave. West, Vancouver, BC V5Z 2M9
Tel: 604-261-1234; *Fax:* 604-261-1222
general@lohandco.com

***Vancouver*: R.H. Long & Co. - *1**
865 - 46th Ave. West, Vancouver, BC V5Z 2R4
Tel: 604-876-0492; *Fax:* 604-876-3219
rhlong@shaw.ca

***Vancouver*: Tim Louis & Company - *1**
#208, 175 East Broadway, Vancouver, BC V5T 1W2
Tel: 604-732-7678; *Fax:* 604-732-7579
timlouis@timlouislaw.com
www.timlouislaw.com

***Vancouver*: Lowe & Company - *6**
#900, 777 West Broadway, Vancouver, BC V5Z 4J7
Tel: 604-875-9338; *Fax:* 604-875-1325
info@canadavisalaw.com
www.canadavisalaw.com

***Vancouver*: Phillip R. Lundrie - *2**
#3, 2597 Hastings St. East, 2nd Fl., Vancouver, BC V5K 1Z2
Tel: 604-257-3588; *Fax:* 604-257-3511
plundrie@aol.com

***Vancouver*: Lyons Hamilton - *4**
#404, 815 Hornby St., Vancouver, BC V6Z 2E6
Tel: 604-684-6718; *Fax:* 604-684-2501
lyonsco@mdi.ca

***Vancouver*: Macaulay McColl LLP - *9**
#1575, P.O. Box 11635, 650 West Georgia St., Vancouver, BC V6B 4N9
Tel: 604-687-9811; *Fax:* 604-687-8716
Toll-Free: 800-233-4405
lawyers@macaulay.com
www.macaulay.com

***Vancouver*: Macdonald Fahey**
Former Name: Epstein Wood
#1900, 1177 West Hastings Street, Vancouver, BC V6E 2K3
Tel: 604-718-6869; *Fax:* 604-629-2175

***Vancouver*: MacKenzie Fujisawa LLP - *20**
#1600, 1095 West Pender St., Vancouver, BC V6E 2M6
Tel: 604-689-3281; *Fax:* 604-685-6494
lawyers@maclaw.bc.ca
www.mackenziefujisawa.com

***Vancouver*: MacKinlay Woodson Diebel - *2**
#1170, 1040 West Georgia St., Vancouver, BC V6E 4H1
Tel: 604-669-1511; *Fax:* 604-669-1566
corp@woodsonlaw.bc.ca

***Vancouver*: M. Diane MacKinnon - *1**
#728, 650 - 41st Ave. West, Vancouver, BC V5Z 2M9
Tel: 604-263-7891; *Fax:* 604-263-5781
mdmac@telus.net

***Vancouver*: MacLean Family Law Group - *4**
Former Name: MacLean Nicol
#3103, 1077 Cordova St. West, Vancouver, BC V6C 2C6
Tel: 604-602-9000; *Fax:* 604-682-0556
info@bcfamilylaw.ca

***Vancouver*: MacLeod & Company - *2**
#1900, 777 Hornby St., Vancouver, BC V6Z 1S4
Tel: 604-687-6731; *Fax:* 604-682-2534
bmacleod@macleodlaw.com
www.macleodlaw.com

***Vancouver*: Morag M.J. MacLeod - *1**
#800, 555 West Georgia St., Vancouver, BC V6B 1Z6
Tel: 604-430-8444; *Fax:* 604-430-1164
celtlaw@telus.net

***Vancouver*: Maitland & Company - *5**
#700, 625 Howe St., Vancouver, BC V6C 2T6
Tel: 604-681-7474; *Fax:* 604-681-3896
Toll-Free: 877-681-7474
maitco@maitland.com
www.maitland.com/Newindex

***Vancouver*: Mark R. Epstein Law Corporation - *2**
Former Name: Epstein Wood
#1900, 1177 West Hastings Street, Vancouver, BC V6E 2K3
Tel: 604-685-4321; *Fax:* 604-685-7901

***Vancouver*: Maxwell Bulmer Hopman - *4**
900 Helmcken St., Vancouver, BC V6Z 1B3
Tel: 604-669-4912; *Fax:* 604-662-3975

***Vancouver*: Joanne S. McClusky - *1**
#810, 675 Hastings St. West, Vancouver, BC V6B 1N2
Tel: 604-689-4010; *Fax:* 604-684-2349
jmcclusky@telus.net

***Vancouver*: McCrea & Associates - *4**
#102, 1012 Beach Ave., Vancouver, BC V6E 1T7
Tel: 604-662-8200; *Fax:* 604-662-8225
lawyers@mccrealaw.ca
www.mccrealaw.ca

***Vancouver*: McCullough O'Connor Irwin LLP - *14**
#2610, Oceanic Plaza, 1066 West Hastings St., Vancouver, BC V6E 3X1
Tel: 604-687-7077; *Fax:* 604-687-7099
moimail@moisolicitors.com
www.moisolicitors.com

***Vancouver*: Ruth E. McIntyre - *1**
#1520, 355 Burrard St., Vancouver, BC V6C 2G8
Tel: 604-688-5185; *Fax:* 604-688-5186
www.rmcintyre.com

***Vancouver*: McKenzie & Company - *2**
891 Helmcken St., Vancouver, BC V6Z 1B1
Tel: 604-687-7811; *Fax:* 604-685-4358

***Vancouver*: McLachlan Brown Anderson - *9**
938 Howe St., 10th Fl., Vancouver, BC V6Z 1N9
Tel: 604-331-6000; *Fax:* 604-331-6008

***Vancouver*: Bruce E. McLeod - *1**
#1120, 1040 West Georgia St., Vancouver, BC V6E 4H1
Tel: 604-682-3133; *Fax:* 604-682-3161
bmcleod1@telus.net

***Vancouver*: McNeney & McNeney - *5**
#300, 195 Alexander St., Vancouver, BC V6A 1N8
Tel: 604-867-1766; *Fax:* 604-687-0181
Toll-Free: 800-535-6565
bikerlaw@kwik.net

***Vancouver*: Richard A. McPhee - *1**
#1025, 1185 West Georgia St., Vancouver, BC V6E 4E6
Tel: 604-682-0926; *Fax:* 604-688-8615
vml@pro.net

***Vancouver*: Megan Ellis & Company - *2**
Former Name: Stowe Ellis
#700, 555 Georgia St. West, Vancouver, BC V6B 1Z6
Tel: 604-683-7144; *Fax:* 604-683-0207

***Vancouver*: Brian E. Mickelson - *1**
100 West Pender St., 2nd Fl., Vancouver, BC V6B 1R8
Tel: 604-688-8588; *Fax:* 604-681-0652

***Vancouver*: John L. Mickelson - *2**
#302, 1110 Hamilton St., Vancouver, BC V6B 2S2
Tel: 604-684-0040; *Fax:* 604-684-0048
dajones@telus.net

***Vancouver*: Michael Mines - *1**
#1550, 355 Burrard St., Vancouver, BC V6C 2G8
Tel: 604-688-1460; *Fax:* 604-687-3097

***Vancouver*: MMK Consulting Inc. - *1**
#480, 1140 West Pender St., Vancouver, BC V6E 4G1
Tel: 604-484-4620; *Fax:* 604-738-2801
info@mmkconsulting.com
www.mmkconsulting.com

***Vancouver*: Morris & Co. - *2**
#460, 850 West Hastings St., Vancouver, BC V6C 1E1
Tel: 604-685-5175; *Fax:* 604-669-2744

***Vancouver*: Don Morrison - *2**
#1109, 207 West Hastings St., Vancouver, BC V6B 1H7
Tel: 604-685-7097; *Fax:* 604-662-7511
don.morrison@telus.net
www.donmorrisonlaw.com

***Vancouver*: Mortimer & Rose - *2**
#920, 777 Hornby St., Vancouver, BC V6Z 1S4
Tel: 604-669-0440; *Fax:* 604-669-0228

***Vancouver*: Murdy & McAllister - *7**
#1155, Two Bentall Centre, P.O. Box 49059, Stn. Bentall, 555 Burrard St., Vancouver, BC V7X 1C4
Tel: 604-689-5263; *Fax:* 604-689-9029

***Vancouver*: Murphy, McComb, Witten - *2**
#208, 2800 - 1st Ave. East, Vancouver, BC V5M 4N9
Tel: 604-255-9018; *Fax:* 604-255-8588
info@mmw.bc.ca

***Vancouver*: Murray Jamieson - *6**
#200, 1152 Mainland St., Vancouver, BC V6B 4X2
Tel: 604-688-0777; *Fax:* 604-688-9700
www.murrayjamieson.com

***Vancouver*: James B. Myers Law Corporation**
#740, 475 West Georgia St., Vancouver, BC V6B 4M9
Tel: 604-682-2670; *Fax:* 604-682-2348

***Vancouver*: Myers, Waddell, McMurdo & Karp - *10**
Former Name: Myers, Johnson, Ross & Foster
195 Alexander St., 5th Fl., Vancouver, BC V6A 1B8
Tel: 604-688-8331; *Fax:* 604-688-8350
Toll-Free: 888-244-9995
lm@myersco.ca
www.myersco.ca or www.vancouverdefencelawyer.com

***Vancouver*: Nathanson, Schachter & Thompson LLP - *8**
#750, 900 Howe St., Vancouver, BC V6Z 2M4
Tel: 604-662-8840; *Fax:* 604-684-1598
info@nst.bc.ca
www.nst.bc.ca

** indicates number of lawyers*

Vancouver: **Nelson & Vanderkruyk - *3**
#440, 355 Burrard St., Vancouver, BC V6C 2G8
Tel: 604-684-1311; *Fax:* 604-684-6402
nelsonvanderkruyk@nvlaw.ca

Vancouver: **B.J. Nelson - *1**
#103, 1012 Beach Ave., Vancouver, BC V6E 1T7
Tel: 604-685-7317; *Fax:* 604-682-3965

Vancouver: **Ng Ariss Fong - *3**
Former Name: Ng & Ariss
#219, P.O. Box 160, 900 Howe St., Vancouver, BC V6Z 2M4
Tel: 604-331-1155; *Fax:* 604-677-5410
general@ngariss.com
www.ngariss.com

Vancouver: **Kimball R. Nichols - *1**
1591 Bowser Ave., Vancouver, BC V7P 2Y4
Tel: 604-682-0541; *Fax:* 604-924-5541

Vancouver: **K.F. Nordlinger, Q.C. & Associates - *4**
#109, 1008 Beach Ave., Vancouver, BC V6E 1T7
Tel: 604-689-5134; *Fax:* 604-689-5323
katherine@nordlinger.net

Vancouver: **Northwest Law Group - *6**
Former Name: O'Neill & Company
#1880, 1055 West Georgia St., Vancouver, BC V6E 3P3
Tel: 604-687-5792; *Fax:* 604-687-6650

Vancouver: **Norton Stewart Business Lawyers - *5**
#1600, P.O. Box 11104, 1055 West Georgia St., Vancouver, BC V6E 3P3
Tel: 604-687-0555; *Fax:* 604-689-1248

Vancouver: **Oland & Company - *2**
#2020, Vancouver Centre, P.O. Box 11547, 650 West Georgia St., Vancouver, BC V6B 4N7
Tel: 604-683-9621; *Fax:* 604-669-4556
shiplaw@aboland.com

Vancouver: **Glen Orris Q.C. Law Corporation - *1**
#500, 815 Hornby St., Vancouver, BC V6Z 2E6
Tel: 604-669-6711; *Fax:* 604-669-5180
glen@orrislawcorp.com

Vancouver: **Osten & Osten - *1**
#356, P.O. Box 11113, 5740 Cambie St., Vancouver, BC V6E 3A6
Tel: 604-683-9104; *Fax:* 604-688-0034

Vancouver: **Owen Bird Law Corporation - *33**
#2900, Three Bentall Centre, CP 49130, 595 Burrard St., Vancouver, BC V7X 1J5
Tel: 604-688-0401; *Fax:* 604-688-2827
inquiries@owenbird.com
www.owenbird.com

Vancouver: **Oyen Wiggs Green & Mutala LLP, Intellectual Property Lawyers - *16**
#480, The Station, 601 West Cordova St., Vancouver, BC V6B 1G1
Tel: 604-669-3432; *Fax:* 604-681-4081
Toll-Free: 866-475-2922
mail@patentable.com
www.patentable.com

Vancouver: **Paine Edmonds LLP - *15**
#1100, 510 Burrard St., Vancouver, BC V6C 3A8
Tel: 604-683-1211; *Fax:* 604-681-5084
Toll-Free: 800-669-8599
law@paine-edmonds.com
www.paine-edmonds.com

Vancouver: **Palkowski & Company Law Corp. - *3**
#703, 938 Howe St., Vancouver, BC V6Z 1N9
Tel: 604-331-4422; *Fax:* 604-331-4466
rjlegal@palkowski.com
www.palkowski.com

Vancouver: **Pape Salter Teillet - *3**
#460, 220 Cambie St., Vancouver, BC V6B 2M9
Tel: 604-681-3002; *Fax:* 604-681-3050
admin@pstlaw.ca

Vancouver: **Al Paquette - *1**
#5, 8431 Granville St., Vancouver, BC V6P 4Z9
Tel: 604-261-3211; *Fax:* 604-261-5382

Vancouver: **Peck & Company - *1**
#610, 744 Hastings St. West, Vancouver, BC V6C 1A5
Tel: 604-669-0208; *Fax:* 604-669-0616

Vancouver: **D.B. Phelps - *1**
#1200, 805 Broadway West, Vancouver, BC V5Z 1K1
Tel: 604-736-3722; *Fax:* 604-736-3725

Vancouver: **Pierce Law Group - *1**
#850, 475 Georgia St. West, Vancouver, BC V6B 4M9
Tel: 604-681-4434; *Fax:* 604-681-9142
contact@bcdisabilitylaw.com

Vancouver: **Vincent E. Pigeon - *1**
#410, 688 Hastings St. West, Vancouver, BC V6B 1P1
Tel: 604-684-2889; *Fax:* 604-685-2900
vpigeon@telus.net
www.vincentpigeonlawter.com

Vancouver: **Sarah B. Pollard - *1**
#400, 1681 Chestnut St., Vancouver, BC V6J 4M6
Tel: 604-732-5667; *Fax:* 604-732-1262
lawoffice@sprint.ca

Vancouver: **Susan L. Polsky Shamash - *1**
#150, 4600 Jacombs Rd., Vancouver, BC V6V 3B1
Tel: 604-664-7800; *Fax:* 604-664-7898
Toll-Free: 800-663-2782

Vancouver: **Lianne Potter Law Corporation - *1**
#218, 470 Granville St., Vancouver, BC V6C 1V5
Tel: 604-688-0042; *Fax:* 604-688-0062
lpotter@lwp-lawcorp.com

Vancouver: **Poulsen & Co. - *4**
#1800, 999 West Hastings St., Vancouver, BC V6C 2W2
Tel: 604-681-0123; *Fax:* 604-683-1375
pchapman@poulsenlaw.com
www.poulsenlaw.com

Vancouver: **Quinlan Abrioux - *14**
Also Known As: QA Law
#1510, TD Tower, P.O. Box 10031, Stn. Pacific Centre, 700 West Georgia St., Vancouver, BC V7Y 1A1
Tel: 604-687-3711; *Fax:* 604-687-3741
www.qalaw.com

Vancouver: **Quorum Business Lawyers - *7**
#1450, 1075 West Georgia St., Vancouver, BC V6E 3C9
Tel: 604-682-0701; *Fax:* 604-682-7359
www.quorumlaw.com

Vancouver: **Radelet & Company - *2**
#1330, 1075 Georgia St. West, Vancouver, BC V6E 3C9
Tel: 604-689-0878; *Fax:* 604-689-1386
james@radelet.com

Vancouver: **Richard Raibmon - *1**
#1535, Nelson Sq., P.O. Box 12134, 808 Nelson St., Vancouver, BC V6Z 2H2
Tel: 604-688-8551; *Fax:* 604-687-1799
rlrlaw@uniserve.com

Vancouver: **Rankin, Bond - *2**
#200, 157 Alexander St., Vancouver, BC V6A 1B8
Tel: 604-682-3621; *Fax:* 604-682-3919

Vancouver: **Rao, McKercher & Company - *2**
#908, 510 Burrard St., Vancouver, BC V6C 3A8
Tel: 604-664-7474; *Fax:* 604-664-7477

Vancouver: **Gayle M. Raphanel - *1**
#501, 815 Hornby St., Vancouver, BC V6Z 2E6
Tel: 604-682-2200; *Fax:* 604-682-2246
gmr@dowco.com

Vancouver: **Richards Buell Sutton LLP - *37**
#700, 401 West Georgia St., Vancouver, BC V6B 5A1
Tel: 604-682-3664; *Fax:* 604-688-3830
info@rbs.ca
www.rbs.ca

Vancouver: **Ritchie Sandford - *2**
#1300, 355 Burrard St., Vancouver, BC V6C 2G8
Tel: 604-684-0778; *Fax:* 604-684-0799

Vancouver: **Roberts & Stahl - *5**
#500, 220 Cambie St., Vancouver, BC V6B 2M9
Tel: 604-684-6377; *Fax:* 604-684-6387
cbarthe@robertsstahl.com
www.robertsstahl.com

Vancouver: **Daniel J. Rogers - *1**
Also Known As: RLO
#1210, 1140 Pender St. West, Vancouver, BC V6E 4G1
Tel: 604-681-5600; *Fax:* 604-681-1475
dan@shorttco.com

Vancouver: **Roper Greyell LLP, Employment & Labour Lawyers - *24**
Former Name: Greyell MacPhail
#800, Park Place, 666 Burrard St., Vancouver, BC V6C 3P3
Tel: 604-806-0922; *Fax:* 604-806-0933
info@ropergreyell.com
www.greyell.com

Vancouver: **Rosenberg & Rosenberg - *3**
671D Market Hill, Vancouver, BC V5Z 4B5
Tel: 604-879-4505; *Fax:* 604-879-4934
rosenberg_law@telus.net

Vancouver: **Rosenbloom & Aldridge - *3**
#440, 355 Burrard St., Vancouver, BC V6C 2G8
Tel: 604-605-5555; *Fax:* 604-684-6402
rosenbloom_aldridge@telus.net

Vancouver: **J.H. Rosner - *1**
#770, 475 Georgia St. West, Vancouver, BC V6B 4M9
Tel: 604-687-6638; *Fax:* 604-682-2481
roslaw@telus.net

Vancouver: **R.D. Ross Q.C. - *1**
4741 West 2 Ave., Vancouver, BC V6T 1C1
Tel: 604-228-9701; *Fax:* 604-228-9055

Vancouver: **Howard Rubin Law Corp. - *1**
405E - 4 St., Vancouver, BC V7L 1J4
Tel: 604-984-2030; *Fax:* 604-988-0068
howard@howard-rubin.com

Vancouver: **Morrie Sacks Law Corporation - *1**
#207, 1525 - 8th Ave. West, Vancouver, BC V6T 1T5
Tel: 604-685-7629; *Fax:* 604-685-7630
morrie@collaborativedivorce.ca
www.nocourtdivorce.ca

Vancouver: **Salley Bowes Harwardt Law Corp. - *4**
#1750, 1185 Georgia St. West, Vancouver, BC V6E 4E6
Tel: 604-688-0788; *Fax:* 604-688-0778
info@sbh.bc.ca
www.sbh.bc.ca

Vancouver: **Gary M. Salloum - *1**
286 - 21st Ave. West, Vancouver, BC V5Y 2E5

Vancouver: **Gregory L. Samuels - *1**
#585, 1385 - 8th Ave., Vancouver, BC V6H 3V9
Tel: 604-742-4242; *Fax:* 604-742-4243
gls@borderlaw.com

Vancouver: **Charles A. Sandberg - *1**
#108, 2786 - 16 Ave. West, Vancouver, BC V6K 4M1
Tel: 604-734-7768; *Fax:* 604-733-1229

Vancouver: **Michael D. Sanders - *1**
811 Drake St., Vancouver, BC V6Z 1C1
Tel: 604-669-5005; *Fax:* 604-669-1334

Vancouver: **Sangra, Moller - *6**
#1000, Cathedral Place, 925 Georgia St. West, Vancouver, BC V6C 3L2
Tel: 604-662-8808; *Fax:* 604-669-8803
info@sangramoller.com
www.sangramoller.com

Vancouver: **Catherine A. Sas - *1**
#501, 134 Abbott St., Vancouver, BC V6B 2K4
Tel: 604-689-5444; *Fax:* 604-689-5666
Toll-Free: 888-689-5445
casas@axionet.com
www.canadian-visa-lawyer.com

Vancouver: **P.N. Scarisbrick - *1**
234 Abbott St., Vancouver, BC V6B 2K8
Tel: 604-688-0495; *Fax:* 604-688-0201

Vancouver: **Scarlett Manson Angus - *4**
#1200, 777 Hornby St., Vancouver, BC V6Z 1S4
Tel: 604-684-4777; *Fax:* 604-684-7773
lawfirm@smalaw.com

Vancouver: **Antya Schrack - *1**
#116, 970 Burrard St., Vancouver, BC V6Z 2R4
Tel: 604-682-2078; *Fax:* 604-682-6697
schrack@telus.net
www.immigrate-to-canada.ca

Vancouver: **Schroeder & Company - *3**
#1119, 808 Nelson St., Vancouver, BC V6Z 2H2
Tel: 604-688-6737; *Fax:* 604-688-0271
fschroeder@schroeder.bc.ca

** indicates number of lawyers*

***Vancouver*: Schuman Daltrop Basran & Robin - *4**
900 Helmcken St., Vancouver, BC V6Z 1B3
Tel: 604-669-4912; *Fax:* 604-669-4911

***Vancouver*: David A. Schwartz - *1**
#600, 890 West Pender St., Vancouver, BC V6C 1J9
Tel: 604-687-0811; *Fax:* 604-687-1327
Toll-Free: 855-687-0811
schwartzdav@gmail.com
www.davidschwartzsecuritieslaw.com

***Vancouver*: A.P. Serka, Q.C. - *1**
#788, 601 West Broadway, Vancouver, BC V5Z 4C2
Tel: 604-876-8761; *Fax:* 604-876-9035

***Vancouver*: Shandro Dixon Edgson - *6**
#400, 999 Hastings St. West, Vancouver, BC V6C 2W2
Tel: 604-689-0400; *Fax:* 604-685-2009
law@sdelawyers.com

***Vancouver*: Shapiro Hankinson & Knutson**
Two Bental Centre, #700, 555 Burrard St., Vancouver, BC V7X 1M8
Tel: 604-684-0727; *Fax:* 604-684-7094

***Vancouver*: Murray H. Shapiro - *1**
694 West 19th Ave., Vancouver, BC V5Z 1X1
Tel: 604-879-6777; *Fax:* 604-879-6728

***Vancouver*: Shapray, Cramer & Associates - *4**
#670, World Trade Centre, 999 Canada Pl., Vancouver, BC V6C 3E1
Tel: 604-681-0900; *Fax:* 604-681-0920

***Vancouver*: S.S. Shelton - *1**
3469 Commercial St., Vancouver, BC V5N 4E8
Tel: 604-251-2144; *Fax:* 604-251-2781

***Vancouver*: George Shimizu - *1**
#718, P.O. Box 50959, 808 Nelson St., Vancouver, BC V6Z 2H2
Tel: 604-685-4467; *Fax:* 604-685-4408
geoshimizu@telus.net

***Vancouver*: Silbernagel & Company - *2**
#700, 595 Howe St., Vancouver, BC V6C 2T5
Tel: 604-687-9621; *Fax:* 604-687-5960
stephen@silbernagellaw.com

***Vancouver*: Simon Wener - *2**
#620, 1385 - 8 Ave. West, Vancouver, BC V6H 3V9
Tel: 604-736-5500; *Fax:* 604-736-5522
info@simonwener.com
www.simonwener.com

***Vancouver*: Singleton Urquhart LLP - *35**
#1200, 925 Georgia St. West, Vancouver, BC V6C 3L2
Tel: 604-682-7474; *Fax:* 604-682-1283
su@singleton.com
www.singleton.com

***Vancouver*: Sisett & Co. - *2**
Also Known As: Ian Sisett Law Corporation
#603, 601 West Broadway, Vancouver, BC V5Z 4C2
Tel: 604-879-8811; *Fax:* 604-879-7346
Toll-Free: 800-446-5879
sisett@sisettlaw.com
www.sisettlaw.com

***Vancouver*: Skorah Doyle - *2**
#2100, 200 Granville St., Vancouver, BC V6C 1S4
Tel: 604-602-8501; *Fax:* 604-608-1660

***Vancouver*: Smart & Williams - *3**
#1190, 840 Howe St., Vancouver, BC V6Z 2L2
Tel: 604-687-6278; *Fax:* 604-687-6298
vlang@smartwilliams.com

***Vancouver*: Smith & Hughes - *2**
#102, 4088 Cambie St., Vancouver, BC V5Z 2X8
Tel: 604-683-4176; *Fax:* 604-683-2621
rhughes@smithhughes.com
www.smith-hughes.com

***Vancouver*: South Fraser Law Group - *4**
Former Name: Unterman & Associates
#200, 6330 Fraser St., Vancouver, BC V5W 3A4
Tel: 604-321-3232; *Fax:* 604-325-0093
lawyers@southfraserlaw.com
www.southfraserlaw.com

***Vancouver*: Michael P.S. Spearing - *1**
#501, 1949 Beach Ave., Vancouver, BC V6G 1Z2
Tel: 604-681-0699;
michaelspearing@telus.net

***Vancouver*: Specht & Pryer - *4**
Oceanic Plaza, 1066 West Hastings St., 20th Fl., Vancouver, BC V6E 3X2
Tel: 604-736-0883; *Fax:* 604-736-0118
staff@spechtandpryer.com

***Vancouver*: Spring Brammall - *1**
2774 Granville St., Vancouver, BC V6H 3J3
Tel: 604-732-3881; *Fax:* 604-732-3883

***Vancouver*: Stamp of Approval - *1**
5914 Elm St., Vancouver, BC V6N 1A9
Tel: 604-266-0020;
stampofapproval@telus.net

***Vancouver*: Stephens & Holman - *6**
#500, 1200 - 33 St. West, Vancouver, BC V6P 6Z6
Tel: 604-730-4100; *Fax:* 604-736-2867
simon.holman@stephenandhelman.com
www.stephensandholman.com

***Vancouver*: John S. Stowe - *1**
#301, 134 Abbott St., Vancouver, BC V6B 2K4
Tel: 604-684-1665; *Fax:* 604-687-3097
john_stowe@bc.sympatico.ca

***Vancouver*: Sugden, McFee & Roos - *9**
#700, The Landing, 375 Water St., Vancouver, BC V6B 5N3
Tel: 604-687-7700; *Fax:* 604-687-5596
www.smrlaw.ca

***Vancouver*: Sutherland & Company - *1**
Former Name: Sutherland Johnston
#1620, 401 Georgia St. West, Vancouver, BC V6B 5A1
Tel: 604-688-0047; *Fax:* 604-688-8880

***Vancouver*: David F. Sutherland & Associates - *1**
1710 Dunbar St., Vancouver, BC V6R 3L8
Tel: 604-737-8711; *Fax:* 604-737-8655
dfs@dfsutherland.com

***Vancouver*: Tao & Company - *2**
#860, 999 West Broadway, Vancouver, BC V5Z 1K5
Tel: 604-730-8219; *Fax:* 604-730-2553

***Vancouver*: Taylor & Blair - *2**
#270, 1385 - 8th Ave. West, Vancouver, BC V6H 3V9
Tel: 604-737-6900; *Fax:* 604-737-6901

***Vancouver*: Taylor & Company - *2**
Former Name: Taylor Wray
#218, 470 Granville St., Vancouver, BC V6C 1V5
Tel: 604-662-8373; *Fax:* 604-662-8321
wtaylor@twlaw.ca

***Vancouver*: Taylor Jordan Chafetz - *8**
#1010, 777 Hornby St., Vancouver, BC V6Z 1S4
Tel: 604-683-2223; *Fax:* 604-683-2798
tsaumure@tjclaw.com
www.tjclaw.com

***Vancouver*: Colin Taylor Law Corporation**
#502, 888 Bute St., Vancouver, BC V6E 1Y5
Tel: 604-798-8775; *Fax:* 604-608-6117
colintaylor@telus.net

***Vancouver*: G.J. Te Hennepe - *1**
#203, 4545 West 10th Ave., Vancouver, BC V6R 4N2
Tel: 604-228-1433; *Fax:* 604-228-9822
tehennepe@telus.net

***Vancouver*: Isaac Thau - *1**
#101, 1012 Beach Ave., Vancouver, BC V6E 1T7
Tel: 604-685-4220; *Fax:* 604-685-0400
Ithau@orbitinc.net

***Vancouver*: Eric P. Thiessen - *1**
#702, 756 Great Northern Way, Vancouver, BC V5T 1E4
Tel: 604-876-6220; *Fax:* 604-876-6253

***Vancouver*: Thomas, Rondeau - *7**
#300, 576 Seymour St., Vancouver, BC V6b 3K1
Tel: 604-688-6775; *Fax:* 604-688-6995
cthomas@thomasrondeau.com
www.thomasrondeau.com

***Vancouver*: Thompson & Elliott - *4**
1285 West Broadway, 8th Fl., Vancouver, BC V6H 3X8
Tel: 604-731-1161; *Fax:* 604-731-6527

***Vancouver*: Bonnie L. Thorpe - *1**
6909 Cambie St., Vancouver, BC V6P 3H1
Tel: 604-325-0020; *Fax:* 604-325-0020

***Vancouver*: Timothy J. Vondette Law Corporation - *1**
#506, 1128 Hornby St., Vancouver, BC V6Z 2L4
Tel: 604-669-6990; *Fax:* 604-669-6944
tvondette@aol.com

***Vancouver*: Anthony G.V. Tobin - *1**
#816, 938 Howe St., Vancouver, BC V6Z 1N9
Tel: 604-331-1591; *Fax:* 604-688-8120
agvtobin@endisputes.com
www.endisputes.com

***Vancouver*: Toews & Company - *2**
#1488, 777 Hornby St., Vancouver, BC V6Z 1S4
Tel: 604-601-5365; *Fax:* 604-681-3019
info@toewsco.net

***Vancouver*: Tupper, Jonsson & Yeadon - *6**
#1710, 1177 Hastings St. West, Vancouver, BC V6E 2L3
Tel: 604-683-9262; *Fax:* 604-681-0139
tupjon@globalserve.net

***Vancouver*: La Van & Company - *3**
#704, 1478 West Hastings St., Vancouver, BC V6G 3J6
Tel: 604-669-1411; *Fax:* 604-669-9080
jack@lavanco.com

***Vancouver*: Winfred A. van der Sande - *1**
2774 Granville St., Vancouver, BC V6H 3J3
Tel: 604-739-7989; *Fax:* 604-732-3883

***Vancouver*: C.J. Van Twest - *1**
#405, 1160 Burrard St., Vancouver, BC V6Z 2E8
Tel: 604-683-8874; *Fax:* 604-683-8841
twest@interchange.ubc.ca

***Vancouver*: Varty & Company - *2**
#900, 555 Burrard St., Vancouver, BC V7X 1M8
Tel: 604-684-5356; *Fax:* 604-443-5001
www.vartylaw.ca

***Vancouver*: Vector Corporate Finance Lawyers - *3**
Former Name: Scott, Bissett
#1040, 999 West Hastings St., Vancouver, BC V6C 2W2
Tel: 604-683-1102; *Fax:* 604-683-2643
www.vectorlaw.com

***Vancouver*: Vermette & Co. - *2**
#230, P.O. Box 40, 200 Granville St., Vancouver, BC V6C 1S4
Tel: 604-331-0381; *Fax:* 604-331-0382
ip@vermetteco.com
www.vermetteco.com

***Vancouver*: Von Dehn & Company - *3**
#700, 595 Howe St., Vancouver, BC V6C 2T5
Tel: 604-688-4541; *Fax:* 604-687-5960
vondehnco@telus.net

***Vancouver*: T. Wing Wai - *1**
#205, 475 Main St., Vancouver, BC V6A 2T7
Tel: 604-688-2291; *Fax:* 604-688-8983

***Vancouver*: Walker & Company - *1**
#1500, 1030 West Georgia St., Vancouver, BC V6E 2Y3
Tel: 604-682-1147; *Fax:* 604-681-7705
agwalker@telus.net

***Vancouver*: Gregory A. Wasko - *1**
1306 Bidwell St., #D, Vancouver, BC V6G 2L1
Tel: 604-662-3038

***Vancouver*: Watson Goepel Maledy LLP - *36**
#1700, 1075 West Georgia St., Vancouver, BC V6E 3C9
Tel: 604-688-1301; *Fax:* 604-688-8193
wgm@wgmlaw.com
www.wgmlaw.com

***Vancouver*: Elizabeth E. Watson - *1**
#4412, 349 Georgia St. West, Vancouver, BC V6B 3Z8
Tel: 604-877-1412; *Fax:* 604-877-0134
ewatson@telus.net

***Vancouver*: Richard H. Watts Law Corporation - *1**
1776 - 29th Av. West, Vancouver, BC V6J 2Z5
Tel: 604-682-2671; *Fax:* 604-648-8142

***Vancouver*: Webster Hudson & Akerly LLP - *14**
#510, 1040 West Georgia St., Vancouver, BC V6E 4H1
Tel: 604-682-3488; *Fax:* 604-682-3438
www.wha.bc.ca

** indicates number of lawyers*

Vancouver: **Western Policy Consultants Inc. (WPC Inc.) - *1**
#1450, Toronto Dominion Bank Tower, P.O. Box 10015, 700 West Georgia St., Vancouver, BC V7Y 1A1
Tel: 604-684-2228; *Fax:* 604-683-6345
info@westernpolicy.com

Vancouver: **K.S. Westlake - *1**
#1720, 355 Burrard St., Vancouver, BC V6C 2G8
Tel: 604-687-9831; *Fax:* 604-687-7089
kenwestlake@telus.net

Vancouver: **Westpoint Law Group - *1**
Former Name: Epstein Wood
#1900, 1177 West Hastings Street, Vancouver, BC V6E 2K3
Tel: 604-718-6886; *Fax:* 604-629-1882

Vancouver: **Wilcox & Company Law Corporation - *3**
Former Name: Dale W. Wilcox Law Corporation
#1910, 777 Hornby St., Vancouver, BC V6Z 1S4
Tel: 604-687-1374; *Fax:* 604-687-2731
dwilcox@wilcoxlawcorp.com

Vancouver: **Ron J. Wilinofsky - *1**
#202, 1275 - 6th Ave. West, Vancouver, BC V6H 1A6
Tel: 604-736-6818; *Fax:* 604-688-5032

Vancouver: **Williamson Giesen Murray - *2**
Former Name: Williamson Giesen
#200, 1290 Homer St., Vancouver, BC V6B 2Y5
Tel: 604-681-1004; *Fax:* 604-684-1199
www.wgmlaw.ca

Vancouver: **P.J. Wilson - *1**
#400, 744 West Hastings St., Vancouver, BC V6C 1A5
Tel: 604-684-4751; *Fax:* 604-684-8319

Vancouver: **Andrew J. Winstanley - *1**
#410, 688 Hastings St. West, Vancouver, BC V6B 1P1
Tel: 604-682-2939; *Fax:* 604-682-2241
ajwinstanley@teleus.net

Vancouver: **Stephen K. Winter Law Corp. - *1**
Former Name: Stephen K. Winters
#910, 808 Hastings St. West, Vancouver, BC V6C 2X4
Tel: 604-682-3733; *Fax:* 604-688-5590
swinters@uniserve.com

Vancouver: **David J. Wizinsky - *1**
#450, 800 Pender St. West, Vancouver, BC V6C 2V6
Tel: 604-805-6114; *Fax:* 604-689-5528
wiz@uniserve.com

Vancouver: **George Wong & Company - *1**
155 East Pender St., Vancouver, BC V6A 1T6
Tel: 604-687-6166; *Fax:* 604-687-8002
gwco@telus.net

Vancouver: **P.L. Wong - *1**
#407, 1541 West Broadway, Vancouver, BC V6J 1W7
Tel: 604-731-5301; *Fax:* 604-731-1266

Vancouver: **W.G. Wong - *1**
145 Keefer St., 2nd Fl., Vancouver, BC V6A 1X3
Tel: 604-685-9361; *Fax:* 604-684-1299
wwong@radiant.net

Vancouver: **Robert Wood & Company - *2**
Former Name: Dawson, Wood & Company
#100, 2501 Spruce St., Vancouver, BC V6N 2P8
Tel: 604-731-1200; *Fax:* 604-266-0119
rwood@dawsonwood.com

Vancouver: **A.K. Wooster - *1**
#570, 999 West Broadway, Vancouver, BC V5Z 1K5
Tel: 604-684-1204; *Fax:* 604-684-1206
akwoods@aol.com

Vancouver: **D.W.H. Yerxa - *1**
#1200, 805 West Broadway, Vancouver, BC V5Z 1K1
Tel: 604-873-5225

Vancouver: **Young & Noble - *1**
#1119, 808 Nelson St., Vancouver, BC V6Z 2H2
Tel: 604-669-9755; *Fax:* 604-921-4817
john.noble@youngnoble.com

Vancouver: **Young, Anderson - *19**
#1616, Nelson Square, CP 12147, 808 Nelson St., Vancouver, BC V6Z 2H2
Tel: 604-689-7400; *Fax:* 604-689-3444
Toll-Free: 800-665-3540
reception@younganderson.ca
www.younganderson.ca

Vancouver: **David L. Youngson - *1**
#10, 1656 - 11th Ave. West, Vancouver, BC V6J 2B9
Tel: 604-266-6588; *Fax:* 604-266-6393
saluspopuli@shaw.ca

Vancouver: **Xiao Zheng - *1**
#450, 1040 West Georgia St., Vancouver, BC V6E 4H1
Tel: 604-608-0387; *Fax:* 604-608-0385
zheng@axionet.com

Vancouver: **Deborah Lynn Zutter - *1**
609 West Hastings, 6th Fl., Vancouver, BC V6B 4W4
Tel: 604-219-2259; *Fax:* 604-662-7466
dzutter@telus.net
www.debzutter.com

Vanderhoof: **Steven F. Peleshok - *1**
P.O. Box 1128, 2608 Burrard Ave., Vanderhoof, BC V0J 3A0
Tel: 250-567-9277; *Fax:* 250-567-2657

Vernon: **Allan Francis Pringle LLP - *6**
3009B - 28 St., Vernon, BC V1T 4Z7
Tel: 250-542-1177; *Fax:* 250-542-1105
office@afp-law.ca
www.afp-law.ca

Vernon: **Cancade Crosby - *2**
2608 - 48 Ave., Vernon, BC V1T 8K8
Tel: 250-549-1999; *Fax:* 250-558-3910
Toll-Free: 877-646-1999
cancadelaw@hotmail.com

Vernon: **Danyliu & Company - *1**
9055 Binns Rd., Vernon, BC V1B 3B7
Tel: 250-549-3111; *Fax:* 250-549-4135
Toll-Free: 888-549-3186
danyliu@shaw.ca

Vernon: **Kenneth R. Fiddes - *1**
#2, 2908 - 31 Ave., Vernon, BC V1T 2G4
Tel: 250-542-5391; *Fax:* 250-542-4199
fiddes@shaw.ca

Vernon: **Alan M. Gaudette - *1**
#9, 11341 Kidston Rd., Vernon, BC V1B 1Z4
Tel: 250-545-3132; *Fax:* 250-545-1617
amgaudette@shaw.ca

Vernon: **Kern & Company Law Corp. - *1**
#3, 2908 - 32 St., Vernon, BC V1T 5M1
Tel: 250-549-2184; *Fax:* 250-549-2207
kernlaw@junction.net

Vernon: **Kidston & Company - *4**
#200, 3005 - 30th St., Vernon, BC V1T 2M1
Tel: 250-545-0711; *Fax:* 250-545-4776
tmm@kidston.ca
www.kidston.ca

Vernon: **John S. Maguire Barrister & Solicitor - *1**
Former Name: Sigalet, Maguire & Cole
3018 - 29 St., Vernon, BC V1T 5A7
Tel: 250-545-6054; *Fax:* 250-545-7227
jsmag@sigmag.com

Vernon: **Nixon Wenger - *19**
3201 - 30 Ave., 4th Fl., Vernon, BC V1T 2C6
Tel: 250-542-5353; *Fax:* 250-542-7273
Toll-Free: 800-243-5353
nw@nixonwenger.com
www.nixonwenger.com

Vernon: **Robert Moffat Law Corp. - *1**
2912 - 29th St., Vernon, BC V1T 5A6
Tel: 250-542-1312; *Fax:* 250-542-2788
Toll-Free: 800-371-0181
moffatvernon@shawcable.com

Vernon: **Steiner & Company - *1**
3107A - 31 Ave., Vernon, BC V1T 2G9
Tel: 250-545-1371; *Fax:* 250-542-5630
Toll-Free: 800-661-2600

Victoria: **Acheson Whitley - *5**
Former Name: Acheson & Co
535 Yates St., 4th Fl., Victoria, BC V8W 2Z6
Tel: 250-384-6262; *Fax:* 250-384-5353
Toll-Free: 877-275-8766
info@achesonwhitley.com
www.achesonwhitley.com

Victoria: **Robert D. Adair - *1**
#201, 4430 Chatterton Way, Victoria, BC V8X 5J2
Tel: 250-479-9367; *Fax:* 250-479-8316
adair@adairlaw.ca

Victoria: **Anniko, Hunter - *2**
#201, 300 Gorge Rd. West, Victoria, BC V9A 1M8
Tel: 250-385-1233; *Fax:* 250-385-4078
ah@annikohunter-law.com

Victoria: **Jacqueline Beltgens - *1**
3929 Woodhaven Terrace, Victoria, BC V8N 1S7
Tel: 250-385-3909;
jbeltgens@pinc.com

Victoria: **Berge, Hart & Cassels - *3**
Former Name: Berge, Sasges & Hart
1207 Quadra St., Victoria, BC V8W 2K8
Tel: 250-388-9477; *Fax:* 250-388-9470
admin@bergehart.ca

Victoria: **Christopher Brennan - *1**
1027 Pandora Ave., Victoria, BC V8V 3P6
Tel: 250-388-9024; *Fax:* 250-388-9060
chrisbrennan@shaw.ca

Victoria: **Cardinal Law - *7**
736 Broughton St., Victoria, BC V8W 1E1
Tel: 250-386-8707; *Fax:* 250-386-3265
Toll-Free: 800-459-9499
info@cardlaw.com
www.cardlaw.com

Victoria: **Carr Buchan & Co. - *5**
520 Comerford St., Victoria, BC V9A 6K8
Tel: 250-388-7571; *Fax:* 250-388-7327
Toll-Free: 888-313-7571
carrbuchan@esquimaltlaw.com; fhughes@esquimaltlaw.com

Victoria: **Clapp & Company - *1**
4599 Chatterton Way, Victoria, BC V8X 4Y7
Tel: 250-479-1422; *Fax:* 250-479-1667

Victoria: **Clay & Company. Lawyers & Mediators - *6**
837 Burdett Ave., Main Fl., Victoria, BC V8W 1B3
Tel: 250-386-2261; *Fax:* 250-389-1336
Toll-Free: 877-688-9634
lawyers@clay.bc.ca
www.clay.bc.ca

Victoria: **Gary E. Coad Law Corp. - *1**
#8, 2727 Quadra St., Victoria, BC V8T 4E5
Tel: 250-388-9003; *Fax:* 250-388-3577
coad@islandnet.com

Victoria: **Considine & Company, Barristers & Solicitors - *1**
30 Dallas Rd., Victoria, BC V8V 0A2
Tel: 250-381-7788; *Fax:* 250-381-1042
www.considinelaw.com

Victoria: **Cook Roberts LLP - *20**
1175 Douglas St., 7th Fl., Victoria, BC V8W 2E1
Tel: 250-385-1411; *Fax:* 250-413-3300
lawmark@cookroberts.bc.ca
www.cookroberts.bc.ca

Victoria: **Cox, Taylor - *9**
Burnes House, 26 Bastion Sq., 3rd Fl., Victoria, BC V8W 1H9
Tel: 250-388-4457; *Fax:* 250-382-4236
mailbox@coxtaylor.bc.ca

Victoria: **Crease Harman & Company - *14**
#800, 1070 Douglas St., Victoria, BC V8W 2S8
Tel: 250-388-5421; *Fax:* 250-388-4294
creaseharman@creaseharman.com
www.creaseharman.com

Victoria: **Dinning Hunter Lambert & Jackson - Victoria Head Office - *15**
Former Name: Dinning Crawford; Dinning Hunter
1202 Fort St., Victoria, BC V8V 3L2
Tel: 250-381-2151; *Fax:* 250-386-2123
Toll-Free: 800-246-5457
info@dinninghunter.com
www.dinninghunter.com

Victoria: **Jeremy S.G. Donaldson - *1**
2555 Sinclair Rd., Victoria, BC V8N 1B8
Tel: 250-721-5759; *Fax:* 250-721-5475

Victoria: **Easdon & Company - *1**
#500, 645 Fort St., Victoria, BC V8W 1G2
Tel: 250-386-3544; *Fax:* 250-380-7299
easdonlaw@pacificcoast.net

Victoria: **Michael W. Egan - *1**
#104C, 3550 Saanich Rd., Victoria, BC V8X 1X2
Tel: 250-382-3426; *Fax:* 250-382-3427

** indicates number of lawyers*

***Victoria*: Frank A.V. Falzon Law Corporation - *1**
#200, 3561 Shelbourne St., Victoria, BC V8P 4G8
Tel: 250-384-3995; *Fax:* 250-384-4924
favf@islandnet.com

***Victoria*: P.S. Finnegan - *1**
#6, 1140 Fort St., Victoria, BC V8V 3K8
Tel: 250-384-4252; *Fax:* 250-384-4252
psfinnegan@shaw.ca

***Victoria*: Firestone & Tyhurst - *2**
#301, 919 Fort St., Victoria, BC V8V 3K3
Tel: 250-386-1112; *Fax:* 250-386-1124

***Victoria*: Joseph Gereluk Law Office - *1**
#401, 1011 Fort St., Victoria, BC V8V 3K5
Tel: 250-380-1423; *Fax:* 250-380-0920

***Victoria*: Larry P. Gilbert - *1**
479 Sturdee St., Victoria, BC V9A 6R2
Tel: 250-478-8881; *Fax:* 250-478-8801

***Victoria*: Peter Golden - *1**
#218, 852 Fort St., Victoria, BC V8W 1H8
Tel: 250-361-3131; *Fax:* 250-361-9161

***Victoria*: Goult & Company - *1**
2185 Theatre Lane, Victoria, BC V8R 6T1
Tel: 250-595-1621; *Fax:* 250-595-5888
goultco@shaw.ca

***Victoria*: Green & Helme - *4**
Former Name: Green & Claus
1161 Fort St., Victoria, BC V8V 3K9
Tel: 250-361-9600; *Fax:* 250-361-9181
greenandhelme@greenclaus.com

***Victoria*: Lenore B. Harlton - *1**
#105, 230 Menzie St., Victoria, BC V8V 2G7
Tel: 250-382-5161; *Fax:* 250-382-5160

***Victoria*: Hatter, Thompson, Shumka & McDonagh - *4**
#201, 919 Fort St., Victoria, BC V8V 3K3
Tel: 250-388-4931; *Fax:* 250-386-8088
Toll-Free: 800-667-0705

***Victoria*: James I. Heller - *1**
#7, 547 Herald St., Victoria, BC V8W 1S5
Tel: 250-360-1040; *Fax:* 250-188-8824
jimheller@shaw.ca

***Victoria*: Holmes & Isherwood - *1**
1190 Fort St., Victoria, BC V8V 3K8
Tel: 250-383-7157; *Fax:* 250-383-1535

***Victoria*: Horne Coupar - *8**
Royal Trust Building, 612 View St., 3rd Fl., Victoria, BC V8W 1J5
Tel: 250-388-6631; *Fax:* 250-388-5974
Toll-Free: 866-467-2490
answers@hc-law.com
www.hc-law.com

***Victoria*: Raymond T. Horne - *1**
#46, 530 Marsett Pl., Victoria, BC V8Z 7J2
Tel: 250-658-6756;
rhorne@istar.ca

***Victoria*: Hutchison Oss-Cech Marlatt, Barristers & Solicitors - *5**
Former Name: The Seigel Law Group
#1, 505 Fisgard St., Victoria, BC V8W 1R3
Tel: 250-360-2500;
info@hom-law.com
www.hom-law.com

***Victoria*: Jawl & Bundon - *8**
1007 Fort St., 4th Fl., Victoria, BC V8V 3K5
Tel: 250-385-5787; *Fax:* 250-385-4364
info@jawlandbundon.com

***Victoria*: W.S. Johnson Law Corp. - *1**
Former Name: W.S. Johnson
#309, 895 Fort St., Victoria, BC V8W 1H7
Tel: 250-382-2404; *Fax:* 250-382-2426

***Victoria*: Jones Emery Hargreaves Swan - *12**
#1212, 1175 Douglas St., Victoria, BC V8W 2E1
Tel: 250-382-7222; *Fax:* 250-382-5436
lawyers@jonesemery.com

***Victoria*: Alice Shun Yee Lo - *1**
#401, 1011 Fort St., Victoria, BC V8V 3K5
Tel: 250-380-1423; *Fax:* 250-380-0920
alicelo@telus.net

***Victoria*: Susan J. Loney Law Office - *1**
1006 Russell St., Victoria, BC V9A 3X9
Tel: 250-384-1804; *Fax:* 250-384-1805
loneylaw@shaw.ca

***Victoria*: Lovett Westmacott - *2**
Former Name: Lovett Westmacott & Clancy
#417, 645 Fort St., Victoria, BC V8W 1G2
Tel: 250-480-7481; *Fax:* 250-480-7455
admin@lwpubliclaw.ca

***Victoria*: MacIsaac & Company - *6**
CP 933, 1117 Wharf St., 3rd Fl., Victoria, BC V8W 1T7
Tel: 250-381-5353; *Fax:* 250-380-7272
Toll-Free: 800-663-6299
info@macisaacgroup.com
www.macisaacgroup.com

***Victoria*: MacIsaac & MacIsaac - *4**
2227 Sooke Rd., Victoria, BC V9B 1W8
Tel: 250-478-1131; *Fax:* 250-478-3106
mac@macisaaclaw.ca

***Victoria*: MacMinn & Company - *5**
846 Broughton St., Victoria, BC V8W 1E4
Tel: 250-381-6444; *Fax:* 250-381-7857

***Victoria*: Maguire & Company - *1**
1727 Jefferson Ave., Victoria, BC V8N 2B3
Tel: 250-370-0300; *Fax:* 250-370-0302
magco@telus.net

***Victoria*: David A. Main - *1**
#330, 702 Fort St., Victoria, BC V8W 1H2
Tel: 250-383-4541; *Fax:* 250-382-5160

***Victoria*: Marshall Allen & Massey - *4**
Former Name: Brooks & Marshall
1519 Amelia St., Victoria, BC V8W 2K1
Tel: 250-920-0144; *Fax:* 250-920-0177

***Victoria*: McConnan, Bion, O'Connor & Peterson - *14**
#420, 880 Douglas St., Victoria, BC V8W 2B7
Tel: 250-385-1383; *Fax:* 250-385-2841
Toll-Free: 888-385-1383
info@mcbop.com
www.mcbop.com

***Victoria*: McCullough Parsons Blazina - *10**
#200, 1011 Fort St., Victoria, BC V8V 3K5
Tel: 250-480-1529; *Fax:* 250-480-4910
Toll-Free: 800-360-6488
info@mpblawyers.com
mpblawyers.com

***Victoria*: McMicken & Bennett - *2**
303 - 1111 Blanshard St., Victoria, BC V8W 2H7
Tel: 250-385-9555; *Fax:* 250-385-9841
lawyer@mcmickenbennett.bc.ca

***Victoria*: Milton, Johnson - *2**
#204, 947 Fort St., Victoria, BC V8V 3K3
Tel: 250-385-5523; *Fax:* 250-385-7420

***Victoria*: Robert Moore-Stewart - *1**
#616, 620 View St., Victoria, BC V8W 1J6
Tel: 250-380-1887; *Fax:* 250-380-9134
rmoorest@telus.net

***Victoria*: Jane B. Morley - *1**
Former Name: Morley & Ross
#417, 645 Fort St., Victoria, BC V8W 1G2
Tel: 250-480-7487; *Fax:* 250-480-7488
jbmorley@mrlaw.ca

***Victoria*: Catherine Morris - *1**
Lampion Pacific Law Corporation, Victoria, BC
www.lampion.bc.ca

***Victoria*: David Mulroney & Company - *6**
#701, 1803 Douglas St., Victoria, BC V8T 5C3
Tel: 250-389-6022; *Fax:* 250-389-6033

***Victoria*: Neighbourhood Law Centre - *1**
Former Name: Amicus Law Centre
207 Menzies St., Victoria, BC V8V 2G6
Tel: 250-383-5012; *Fax:* 250-385-1174
amicus@islandnet.com
www.islandnet.com/~amicus

***Victoria*: John M. Orr Law Office - *1**
#102, 2358 The Esplanade, Victoria, BC V8P 3K7
Tel: 250-595-8675; *Fax:* 250-595-7421
orrlaw@shaw.ca

***Victoria*: Pearlman Lindholm - *14**
#201, 19 Dallas Rd., Victoria, BC V8V 5A6
Tel: 250-388-4433; *Fax:* 250-388-5856
nphilpott@pearlmanlindholm.com
www.pearlmanlindholm.com

***Victoria*: Purves, Hickford - *3**
Former Name: Purves, Hickford, Horne & Curry
#203, 1028 Fort St., Victoria, BC V8V 3K4
Tel: 250-361-1645; *Fax:* 250-386-6609
ph_h@shaw.ca

***Victoria*: Quadra Legal Centre - *3**
#101, 2750 Quadra St., Victoria, BC V8T 4E8
Tel: 250-380-1566; *Fax:* 250-380-3090

***Victoria*: Randall & Company - *3**
#103, 1006 Fort St., Victoria, BC V8V 3K4
Tel: 250-382-9282; *Fax:* 250-382-0366
randall@randallco.com

***Victoria*: Nichola Reid & Company - *2**
#214, 284 Helmcken Rd., Victoria, BC V9B 1T2
Tel: 250-744-1844; *Fax:* 250-744-1890

***Victoria*: Marlene Russo - *1**
#110, 1175 Cook St., Victoria, BC V8V 4A1
Tel: 250-380-0076; *Fax:* 250-380-0092
marlene_russo@telus.net

***Victoria*: Salmond, Ashurst - *3**
1620 Cedar Hill Cross Rd., Victoria, BC V8P 2P6
Tel: 250-477-4143; *Fax:* 250-477-4451
derekgsalmon@ashurst.com

***Victoria*: Sihota & Starkey - *1**
1248 Esquimalt Rd., Victoria, BC V9A 3N8
Tel: 250-381-5111; *Fax:* 250-381-3947
crisstarkey@pacificcoast.net

***Victoria*: Skillings & Company - *1**
#B, 777 Blanshard St., Victoria, BC V8W 2G9
Tel: 250-388-5136; *Fax:* 250-388-5195
skillco@shawcable.com

***Victoria*: Smith Hutchison Law Corporation - *2**
#202, 1640 Oak Bay Ave., Victoria, BC V8W 1E5
Tel: 250-388-6666; *Fax:* 250-389-0400
mhutchqc@bclawfirm.com
www.bclawfirm.com

***Victoria*: Stevenson, Doell & Company - *4**
999 Fort St., Victoria, BC V8V 3K3
Tel: 250-388-7881; *Fax:* 250-388-7324

***Victoria*: Stevenson, Luchies & Legh - *6**
#300, 848 Courtney St., Victoria, BC V8W 1C4
Tel: 250-381-4040; *Fax:* 250-414-5180
Toll-Free: 888-381-8555
lawyers@sll.ca
www.sll.ca

***Victoria*: Straith & Company - *3**
#704, 880 Douglas St., Victoria, BC V8W 2B7
Tel: 250-386-1434; *Fax:* 250-386-1421
Toll-Free: 877-636-1434
inquiries@straithlaw.ca

***Victoria*: Christine A. Stretton - *1**
#204, 947 Fort St., Victoria, BC V8V 3K3
Tel: 250-388-5333; *Fax:* 250-382-8644
castretton@pacificcoast.net

***Victoria*: Diane E. Tourell - *1**
#520, 645 Fort St., Victoria, BC V8W 1G2
Tel: 250-384-1443; *Fax:* 250-360-1778
detourell@qswireless.com

***Victoria*: Dalmar F. Tracy - *1**
#206, 1005 Cook St., Victoria, BC V8V 3Z6
Tel: 250-384-5331; *Fax:* 250-384-5206

** indicates number of lawyers*

***Victoria*: Jill K. Turner - *1**
#101, 4475 Viewmount Ave., Victoria, BC V8Z 6L8
Tel: 250-360-0983; *Fax:* 250-658-1949
jill@turnelegal.com

***Victoria*: Turnham Woodland, Barristers & Solicitors - *4**
1002 Wharf St., Victoria, BC V8W 1T4
Tel: 250-385-1122; *Fax:* 250-385-6522
hturnham@turnwood.bc.ca
www.turnhamwoodland.ca

***Victoria*: Aaltje van Grootheest - *1**
4054 Knibbs Green, Victoria, BC V8Z 6Y7
Tel: 250-479-4692; *Fax:* 250-479-5162
avglaw@telus.net

***Victoria*: Velletta & Company - *7**
Former Name: Gordon & Velletta
#302, 852 Fort St., Victoria, BC V8W 1H8
Tel: 250-383-9104; *Fax:* 250-383-1922
Toll-Free: 866-383-9104
mail@victorialaw.bc.ca
www.victorialaw.bc.ca

***Victoria*: Waddell Raponi Lawyers - *5**
1002 Wharf St., Victoria, BC V8W 1T4
Tel: 250-385-4311; *Fax:* 250-385-2012
www.waddellraponi.com

***Victoria*: Peter I. Waldmann - *1**
1982 Forrester St., Victoria, BC V8R 3H1
Tel: 250-381-3113; *Fax:* 250-381-3122
Toll-Free: 877-381-3113
waldmann@shaw.ca

***Victoria*: Wilson Marshall - *5**
#200, 911 Yates St., Victoria, BC V8V 4X3
Tel: 250-385-8741; *Fax:* 250-385-0433
Toll-Free: 877-385-8741
reception@wilsonmarshall.com

***Victoria*: Wong & Doerksen - *2**
1618 Government St., Victoria, BC V8W 1Z3
Tel: 250-381-7799; *Fax:* 250-386-7799
kdoerksen@wongdoerksen.com

***Victoria*: Woodward & Company - *14**
844 Courtney St., 2nd Fl., Victoria, BC V8W 1C4
Tel: 250-383-2356; *Fax:* 250-380-6560
reception@woodwardandcompany.com
www.woodwardandcompany.com

***Victoria*: Wendy K. Zimmerman - *1**
1006 Russell St., Victoria, BC V9A 3K9
Tel: 250-384-1804; *Fax:* 250-384-1805
Toll-Free: 800-313-9581
wendy@vicwestlaw.ca
www.vicwestlaw.ca

***West Vancouver*: Alan Stewart Andree, Esq. - *1**
#21, 285 - 17th St., West Vancouver, BC V7V 3S6
Tel: 604-922-6999; *Fax:* 604-922-6912
stewart@alansr.com

***West Vancouver*: Brister, Yeager Law Corporation - *2**
#202, 1555 Marine Dr., West Vancouver, BC V7V 1N9
Tel: 604-921-1295; *Fax:* 604-921-1297
ryeager@dimissal.ca
www.dismissal.ca

***West Vancouver*: Christopher B. Chu - *1**
#200, 100 Park Royal South, West Vancouver, BC V7T 1A2
Tel: 604-925-5898; *Fax:* 604-648-8361
cbchu@mail.com

***West Vancouver*: David T. Forsyth - *1**
#1110, 100 Park Royal South, West Vancouver, BC V7T 1A2
Tel: 604-925-0045; *Fax:* 604-926-7782
dforsyth33@shaw.ca

***West Vancouver*: Wm. Randall Fowle - *3**
#1003, 100 Park Royal South, West Vancouver, BC V7T 1A2
Tel: 604-922-6310; *Fax:* 604-922-6302
Toll-Free: 800-663-8996
fowle@axion.net

***West Vancouver*: G.C. Geraghty - *1**
#200, 100 Park Royal South, West Vancouver, BC V7T 1A2
Tel: 604-921-9221; *Fax:* 604-921-9125
geraghty@gglawcorp.com
www.gglawcorp.com

***West Vancouver*: Goluboff & Mazzei, Barristers & Solicitors - *3**
#201, 585 - 16th St., West Vancouver, BC V7V 3R8
Tel: 604-925-6900; *Fax:* 604-926-7817
rgoluboff@goluboffmazzei.com
www.goluboffmazzei.com

***West Vancouver*: James C. Hutchinson - *1**
#200, 100 Park Royal, West Vancouver, BC V7T 1A2
Tel: 604-926-2876; *Fax:* 604-926-2836

***West Vancouver*: Ketchum Communications Ltd. - *1**
3230 Mathers Ave., West Vancouver, BC V7T 2W6
Tel: 604-922-5204; *Fax:* 604-922-9774

***West Vancouver*: Myrle L. Lawrence, Law Corporation - *1**
#203, 815 Main St., West Vancouver, BC V7T 2Z3
Tel: 604-925-9260; *Fax:* 604-925-9261
mlawrence@veritaslaw.ca

***West Vancouver*: McCrea & Company - *1**
#101, 2221 Folkestone Way, West Vancouver, BC V7S 2Y6
Tel: 604-926-4524; *Fax:* 604-926-0222

***West Vancouver*: McLean Armstrong - *6**
#300, 1497 Marine Dr., West Vancouver, BC V7T 1B8
Tel: 604-925-0672; *Fax:* 604-925-8984
info@mcleanarmstrong.com
www.mcleanarmstrong.com

***West Vancouver*: E. Michael McMahon - *1**
#204, 2408 Haywood Ave., West Vancouver, BC V7V 1Y1
Tel: 604-926-1076; *Fax:* 604-926-1023
www.taxlitigate.com

***West Vancouver*: John Moonen & Associates Ltd. - *1**
6475 Fox St., West Vancouver, BC V7W 2C3
Tel: 604-921-6433; *Fax:* 604-921-6433
johnmoonen@telus.net

***West Vancouver*: Ryan & Associates - *1**
1220 Esquimalt Ave., West Vancouver, BC V7T 1K3
Tel: 604-341-8121;

***West Vancouver*: David H. Stoller - *1**
#801, 100 Park Royal S., West Vancouver, BC V7T 1A2
Tel: 604-922-4702; *Fax:* 604-922-0374
stoller@fireplug.net

***West Vancouver*: Ann Marie Sweeney - *1**
#104, 1590 Bellevue Ave., West Vancouver, BC V7V 1A7
Tel: 604-922-0131; *Fax:* 604-922-0171

***Westbank*: Bassett & Company - *5**
#260, 2300 Carrington Rd., Westbank, BC V4T 2N6
Tel: 250-768-5152; *Fax:* 250-768-3003
info@okanaganlaw.com
www.okanaganlaw.com

***Whistler*: Mountain Law Corporation - *1**
Former Name: Shrimpton & Company
#200, 1410 Alpha Lake Rd., Whistler, BC V0N 1B1
Tel: 604-938-4947; *Fax:* 604-938-0471
shrimpco@direct.ca
www.mountainlaw.com

***Whistler*: Ian D. Reith - *1**
#14, 4227 Village Stroll, RR#4, Whistler, BC V0N 1B4
Tel: 604-932-6501; *Fax:* 604-932-5615

***Whistler*: Taylor & Company Law Corporation - *1**
Black Tusk Village, 60 Rock Ridge, Whistler, BC V0N 1B1
Tel: 604-938-4840

***Whistler*: Whistler Law Offices - *1**
Former Name: Davies & McLean
#209, 4368 Main St., Whistler, BC V0N 1B1
Tel: 604-938-1763; *Fax:* 604-938-1764
Toll-Free: 877-938-1763
www.whistlerlawoffices.com

***White Rock*: Cleveland & Doan - *3**
1321 Johnston Rd., White Rock, BC V4B 3Z3
Tel: 604-536-5002; *Fax:* 604-536-7002
lawyers@cleveland-doan.com
www.cleveland-doan.com

***White Rock*: E.G. Mark - *1**
15252 Thrift Ave., White Rock, BC V4B 2L2
Tel: 604-542-0202; *Fax:* 604-542-0203

***White Rock*: Medland & Company - *1**
14582 - 18th Ave., White Rock, BC V4A 5V5
Tel: 604-230-8476; *Fax:* 604-535-4145
medlandco@shaw.ca

***White Rock*: Joseph M. Prodor - *1**
15260 Thrift Ave., White Rock, BC V4B 2L1
Tel: 604-536-4676; *Toll-Free:* 877-577-6367
jprodor@axionet.com

***Williams Lake*: Alan P. Czepil - *1**
#202, 366 Yorston St., Williams Lake, BC V2G 4J5
Tel: 250-398-7001; *Fax:* 250-398-5651
czepl@telus.net

***Williams Lake*: Vanderburgh & Company - *3**
#5, 123 Borland St., Williams Lake, BC V2G 1R1
Tel: 250-392-7161; *Fax:* 250-392-7060
aev@cariboolaw.com
www.cariboolaw.com

***Winlaw*: Kenyon McGee - *1**
P.O. Box 11, 5612 Hwy. 6, Winlaw, BC V0G 2J0
Tel: 250-226-7615; *Fax:* 250-226-7818
kmlaw@netidea.com

Manitoba

***Beausejour*: Bellan Wasylin & Associates - *5**
P.O. Box 520, 527 Park Ave., Beausejour, MB R0E 0C0
Tel: 204-268-2000; *Fax:* 204-268-3519

***Beausejour*: Middleton & Middleton - *1**
P.O. Box 1150, 527 Park Ave., Beausejour, MB R0E 0C0
Tel: 204-268-4566; *Fax:* 204-268-4572
Toll-Free: 866-222-3259
wcmiddle@mb.sympatico.ca

***Brandon*: Burgess Law Office - *1**
724 - 18th St., Brandon, MB R7A 5B5
Tel: 204-725-7070; *Fax:* 204-727-5995
burgesslaw@mts.net

***Brandon*: Henry N. Carroll Q.C. - *3**
1331 Princess Ave., Brandon, MB R7A 0R4
Tel: 204-727-2266; *Fax:* 204-727-0548

***Brandon*: Terri E. Deller Law Office - *1**
801 Princess Ave., Brandon, MB R7A 0P5
Tel: 204-726-0128;
dellerlaw@westman.wave.ca

***Brandon*: Donald Legal Services - *2**
#6, 940 Princess Ave., Brandon, MB R7A 0P6
Tel: 204-729-4900; *Fax:* 204-728-4477
ld@donaldlegal.com; rlonstrup@donaldlegal.com

***Brandon*: Hunt, Miller & Co. LLP - *7**
Former Name: Hunt, Miller & Combs
148 - 8 St., Brandon, MB R7A 3X1
Tel: 204-727-8491; *Fax:* 204-727-4350
hmc@westman.wave.ca

***Brandon*: Paterson Patterson Wyman & Abel**
#1, Carriage House, 1040 Princess Ave., Brandon, MB R7A 0P8
Tel: 204-727-2424; *Fax:* 204-728-4670
patersons@mts.net
www.patersons.ca

***Brandon*: James W. Potter - *1**
1202 Princess Ave., Brandon, MB R7A 0R3
Tel: 204-727-6431; *Fax:* 204-727-2818

***Brandon*: Roy, Johnston & Company - *8**
363 - 10 St., Brandon, MB R7A 4E9
Tel: 204-727-0761; *Fax:* 204-726-1339
royjohnstonco@westman.wave.ca

***Carman*: Brown & Associates - *2**
P.O. Box 1240, 71 Main St. South, Carman, MB R0G 0J0
Tel: 204-745-2028; *Fax:* 204-745-3513
lawyers@brownlawoffice.org
www.brownlawoffice.org

***Carman*: Lee & Lee - *2**
5 Centre Ave. West, Carman, MB R0G 0J0
Tel: 204-745-6751; *Fax:* 204-745-3481

***Dauphin*: Dawson Law Office - *1**
34 - 1 Ave. NW, Dauphin, MB R7N 1G7
Tel: 204-638-4101; *Fax:* 204-638-8541

** indicates number of lawyers*

***Dauphin*: Hawkins & Sanderson - *1**
20 - 2nd Ave. NW, Dauphin, MB R7N 1H2
Tel: 204-638-4121; *Fax:* 204-638-5942

***Dauphin*: Irwin Law Office - *2**
122 Main St. North, Dauphin, MB R7N 1C2
Tel: 204-638-9249; *Fax:* 204-638-3647
irwinlaw@mts.net

***Dauphin*: Johnston & Company - *7**
P.O. Box 551, 18 - 3 Ave. NW, Dauphin, MB R7N 2V4
Tel: 204-638-3211; *Fax:* 204-638-9646
irwinlaw@mts.net

***Dauphin*: Johnston & Company - *5**
P.O. Box 551, 18 - 3rd Ave. NW, Dauphin, MB R7N 2V4
Tel: 204-638-3211; *Fax:* 204-638-9646
jandco@mb.sympatico.ca

***Dauphin*: Parkland Community Law Centre - *4**
31 - 3rd Ave. NE, Dauphin, MB R7N 0Y5
Tel: 204-622-7000; *Fax:* 204-622-7029
Toll-Free: 800-810-6977

***Deloraine*: Sheldon Lanchbery - *1**
P.O. Box 489, Deloraine, MB R0M 0M0
Tel: 204-747-2082; *Fax:* 204-747-2180
slanchbery@escape.ca

***Erickson*: Platt Law Office - *1**
Erickson Professional Centre, P.O. Box 70, 36 Main St., Erickson, MB R0J 1P0
Tel: 204-636-7838; *Fax:* 204-636-7861
ajp@plattlegal.ca
www.plattlegal.ca

***Flin Flon*: Ginnell, Bauman, Watt - *2**
P.O. Box 697, 47 Main St., Flin Flon, MB R8A 1N5
Tel: 204-687-3431; *Fax:* 204-687-5219

***Brandon*: Meighen, Haddad & Company - *15**
P.O. Box 22105, 110 - 11 St., Brandon, MB R7A 6Y9
Tel: 204-727-8461; *Fax:* 204-726-1948
mail@mhlaw.ca
www.mhlaw.ca

***Hamiota*: Meighen, Haddad & Company**
General Delivery, Hamiota, MB R0M 0T0
Tel: 204-764-2710; *Fax:* 204-764-2727
reception@mhlaw.ca

***Killarney*: Val Duke Barrister & Solicitor - *1**
P.O. Box 99, Killarney, MB R0K 1G0
Tel: 204-523-4464; *Fax:* 204-523-5676
valdukelawoffice@mts.net

***Manitou*: Selby Law Office - *2**
P.O. Box 279, 351 Main St., Manitou, MB R0G 1G0
Tel: 204-242-2801; *Fax:* 204-242-2723
selbylaw@mts.net

***Minnedosa*: Sims & Company - *2**
P.O. Box 460, 76 Main St. South, Minnedosa, MB R0J 1E0
Tel: 204-867-2717; *Fax:* 204-867-2434
minnedosa@simsco.mb.ca
www.simsco.mb.ca

***Morden*: Hoeschen & Sloane**
326 Stephen St., Morden, MB R6M 1T5
Tel: 204-822-4463; *Fax:* 204-822-6416
hslaw@mts.net

***Neepawa*: Taylor Law Office - *2**
P.O. Box 309, 269 Hamilton St, Neepawa, MB R0J 1H0
Tel: 204-476-2336; *Fax:* 204-476-5783
taylaw@mymts.net

***Portage la Prairie*: Greenberg & Greenberg - *2**
P.O. Box 157, 231 Saskatchewan Ave. East, Portage la Prairie, MB R1N 3B2
Tel: 204-857-6878; *Fax:* 204-857-3011
greenlaw@mts.net

***Portage la Prairie*: Miller Pressey Selinger - *1**
P.O. Box 368, 103 Saskatchewan Ave. East, Portage la Prairie, MB R1N 3B7
Tel: 204-857-3436; *Fax:* 204-857-9238
mpslaw@mts.net

***Roblin*: Marcel J.J.R. Gregoire - *1**
P.O. Box 1630, 158 Main St., Roblin, MB R0L 1P0
Tel: 204-937-2117; *Fax:* 204-937-4576
mgreg@mb.sympatico.ca

***Russell*: Mason D. Jardine - *1**
P.O. Box 1270, 346 Main St., Russell, MB R0J 1W0
Tel: 204-773-2165; *Fax:* 204-773-2920
mjardine@escape.ca

***Selkirk*: W. Douglas Kitchen - *1**
1202 River Rd., Selkirk, MB R1A 2E1
Tel: 204-482-8929

***Selkirk*: Kohaykewych & Associates - *1**
413 Main St., Selkirk, MB R1A 1V2
Tel: 204-482-7925; *Fax:* 204-482-7099
kohaykewych@mts.net

***Selkirk*: David L. Moore & Assoc. - *2**
407 Main St., Selkirk, MB R1A 1T9
Tel: 204-482-3921; *Fax:* 204-482-5564
Toll-Free: 877-482-3921
d.moore.law@mts.net

***Souris*: Forrest & Forrest - *1**
P.O. Box 276, 4 Crescent Ave., Souris, MB R0K 2C0
Tel: 204-483-2171; *Fax:* 204-483-3389
fforrest@mts.net

***Steinbach*: Loewen Henderson Banman Legault LLP - *4**
Former Name: Loewen Henderson Banman; Plett Goossen & Associates
#200, 250 Main St., Steinbach, MB R5G 1Y8
Tel: 204-326-6454; *Fax:* 204-326-6917

***Steinbach*: Smith Neufeld Jodoin - *14**
P.O. Box 1267, Steinbach, MB R5G 1M9
Tel: 204-326-3442; *Fax:* 204-326-2154
lawyers@snj.mb.ca
www.snj.mb.ca

***Stonewall*: Grantham Law Offices - *1**
Westside Plaza, P.O. Box 1400, #1, 333 Main St., Stonewall, MB R0C 2Z0
Tel: 204-467-5527; *Fax:* 204-467-5550

***Swan River*: Burnside & Company - *2**
P.O. Box 340, 509 Main St. East, Swan River, MB R0L 1Z0
Tel: 204-734-3485; *Fax:* 204-734-2872
ggb@burnsideferris.com

***Swan River*: Palsson Law Office - *2**
P.O. Box 1238, 114 - 5th Ave. North, Swan River, MB R0L 1Z0
Tel: 204-734-4528; *Fax:* 204-734-5085

***Teulon*: Steven R. Shinnie - *1**
P.O. Box 149, 34 Main St., Teulon, MB R0C 3B0
Tel: 204-886-3959; *Fax:* 204-886-3962

***The Pas*: Bjornsson & Wight Law Office - *2**
#3, P.O. Box 1769, 314 Edwards Ave., The Pas, MB R9A 1L5
Tel: 204-627-1200; *Fax:* 204-627-1210
dblwlaw@mailme.ca

***The Pas*: Mirwaldt & Gray - *3**
P.O. Box 2280, 272 - 2nd St. West, The Pas, MB R9A 1M1
Tel: 204-623-7845; *Fax:* 204-623-5353
mirwgray@mail.mts.net

***The Pas*: Watkins Law Office - *1**
P.O. Box 1349, Stn. Main, 114 - 3rd St., The Pas, MB R9A 1L3
Tel: 204-623-6472; *Fax:* 204-623-6486

***Thompson*: Mayer, Dearman & Pellizzaro - *3**
7 Selkirk Ave., Thompson, MB R8N 0M4
Tel: 204-677-2393; *Fax:* 204-778-8125

***Thompson*: McDonald, Huberdeau - *3**
Former Name: McDonald, Thompson, Huberdeau
Westwood Mall, 436 Thompson Dr. North, Thompson, MB R8N 0C6
Tel: 204-677-2366; *Fax:* 204-677-3249

***Thompson*: Ronald J. Nadeau Law Office - *1**
76 Severn Cres., Thompson, MB R8N 1M6
Tel: 204-677-4807; *Fax:* 204-778-6559

***Virden*: McNeill Harasymchuk McConnell - *3**
P.O. Box 520, 243 Raglan St. S, Virden, MB R0M 2C0
Tel: 204-748-1220; *Fax:* 204-748-3007

***Winkler*: Hoeschen & Stewart**
#6, 720 Norquay Dr., Winkler, MB R6W 4A6
Tel: 204-325-4233; *Fax:* 204-325-9889
hslaw@mts.net

***Winnipeg*: 6327435 Canada Ltd - *1**
#203, 897 Corydon Ave., Winnipeg, MB R3M 0W7
Tel: 204-453-1965; *Fax:* 204-475-5247

***Winnipeg*: Abrams George Tweed Wawrykow - *4**
Former Name: Abrams & Tweed
#4, 549 Regent Ave. West, Winnipeg, MB R2C 1R9
Tel: 204-949-3080; *Fax:* 204-949-3089
btweed@atwlaw.ca

***Winnipeg*: Agrawal Law Office - *1**
Former Name: Ram Kishore Agrawal
#B, 83 Sherbrook St., Winnipeg, MB R3C 2B2
Tel: 204-779-7265; *Fax:* 204-779-6334

***Winnipeg*: Aikins, MacAulay & Thorvaldson LLP - *90**
#30th Floor, 360 Main St., Winnipeg, MB R3C 4G1
Tel: 204-957-0050; *Fax:* 204-957-0840
amt@aikins.com
www.aikins.com

***Winnipeg*: Alexander Law Office - *1**
387 Broadway Ave., Winnipeg, MB R3C 0V5
Tel: 204-943-1677; *Fax:* 204-949-9232
dalaw_101@hotmail.com

***Winnipeg*: Antymniuk & Antymniuk - *3**
#11, 1500 Dakota St., Winnipeg, MB R2N 3Y7
Tel: 204-254-3511; *Fax:* 204-257-5139

***Winnipeg*: Scott Armstrong Law Office - *1**
64 Silver Springs Bay, Winnipeg, MB R2K 4L4
Tel: 204-663-8772; *Fax:* 204-663-8432
armstrong.scott@usa.net

***Winnipeg*: Asper Foundation - *1**
#1504, 201 Portage Ave., Winnipeg, MB R3B 3K6
Tel: 204-989-5538; *Fax:* 204-989-5536
www.asperfoundation.com

***Winnipeg*: Assiniboia Law Group - *1**
Former Name: Barber Law Office
3651 Roblin Blvd., Winnipeg, MB R3R 0E2
Tel: 204-949-3240; *Fax:* 204-949-3249
jbarber@shawbiz.ca

***Winnipeg*: Bernstein & Hirsch - *3**
#508, 283 Portage Ave., Winnipeg, MB R3B 2B5
Tel: 204-942-0706; *Fax:* 204-957-1345

***Winnipeg*: Booth, Dennehy LLP - *15**
387 Broadway Ave., Winnipeg, MB R3C 0V5
Tel: 204-957-1717; *Fax:* 204-943-6199
general@dek-law.com

***Winnipeg*: Broadway Law Group - *6**
#300, 326 Broadway Ave., Winnipeg, MB R3C 0S5
Tel: 204-984-9420; *Fax:* 204-947-2757

***Winnipeg*: Brodsky & Company - *3**
#1212, 363 Broadway Ave., Winnipeg, MB R3C 3N9
Tel: 204-940-4433; *Fax:* 204-940-4435

***Winnipeg*: Bradley J. Brooks - *1**
P.O. Box 27009, 360 Main St., Winnipeg, MB R3C 4T3
Tel: 204-992-4700; *Fax:* 204-992-2462
Toll-Free: 888-259-4700
bbrooks@cite-on-site.ca

***Winnipeg*: Bueti, Baumstark - *2**
Former Name: Bueti, Baumstark, Kunzman
#206, 897 Corydon Ave., Winnipeg, MB R3M 0W7
Tel: 204-475-3570; *Fax:* 204-453-0136

***Winnipeg*: Campbell Marr - *13**
10 Donald St., Winnipeg, MB R3C 1L5
Tel: 204-942-3311; *Fax:* 204-943-7997
dimarr@campbellmarr.com
www.campbellmarr.com

***Winnipeg*: Michael Capozzi - *1**
45 Wharton Blvd., Winnipeg, MB R2Y 0S9
Tel: 204-832-4807; *Fax:* 204-895-2336

***Winnipeg*: Cassidy Ramsay - *7**
385 St. Mary Ave., 2nd Fl., Winnipeg, MB R3C 0N1
Tel: 204-943-7454; *Fax:* 204-943-9563
kwan@cassidyramsay.com

***Winnipeg*: Champagne Law Office - *1**
390 Provencher Blvd., Unit F, Winnipeg, MB R2H 0H1
Tel: 204-956-1199; *Fax:* 204-956-5333

** indicates number of lawyers*

***Winnipeg*: Chapman Goddard Kagan - *8**
1864 Portage Ave., Winnipeg, MB R3J 0H2
Tel: 204-888-7973; *Fax:* 204-832-3461
Toll-Free: 800-665-6119
info@cgklaw.ca
www.cgklaw.ca

***Winnipeg*: Jack M. Chapman & Associates - *1**
#246, 2026 Corydon Ave., #162, Winnipeg, MB R3P 0N5
Tel: 204-942-9994; *Fax:* 204-885-7420
ve4ae@aol.com

***Winnipeg*: Cherniack Smith - *7**
#200, 100 Osborne St., Winnipeg, MB R3L 1Y5
Tel: 204-452-4000; *Fax:* 204-477-1856

***Winnipeg*: S. Cohan - *1**
#607, 386 Broadway, Winnipeg, MB R3C 3R6
Tel: 204-944-1413; *Fax:* 204-943-5102

***Winnipeg*: Phillip F.B. Cramer Law Office - *1**
390 York St., Winnipeg, MB R3C 0P3
Tel: 204-987-0070; *Fax:* 204-987-0076
pfcramer@mts.net

***Winnipeg*: D'Arcy & Deacon LLP - *34**
330 St. Mary Ave., 12th Fl., Winnipeg, MB R3C 4E1
Tel: 204-942-2271; *Fax:* 204-943-4242
inquiries@darcydeacon.com
www.darcydeacon.com

***Winnipeg*: Deeley, Fabbri, Sellen - *15**
#903, 386 Broadway, Winnipeg, MB R3C 3R6
Tel: 204-949-1710; *Fax:* 204-956-4457
info@dfslaw.ca
www.dfslaw.ca

***Winnipeg*: Dowhan & Dowhan - *2**
61 Albert St., Winnipeg, MB R3B 1G3
Tel: 204-942-4235; *Fax:* 204-956-4560

***Winnipeg*: Duboff Edwards Haight & Schachter - *10**
#1900, 155 Carlton St., Winnipeg, MB R3C 3H8
Tel: 204-942-3361; *Fax:* 204-942-3362
duboff@dehslaw.com

***Winnipeg*: Edmond & Associates - *4**
#204, 1120 Grant Ave., Winnipeg, MB R3M 2A6
Tel: 204-452-5314; *Fax:* 204-452-5989
gedmond@edmond.ca

***Winnipeg*: Einarson & Einarson - *3**
#1105, 444 St. Mary Ave., Winnipeg, MB R3C 3T1
Tel: 204-942-2419

***Winnipeg*: Fredrick D. & Associates Inc. - *1**
#830, 167 Lombard Ave., Winnipeg, MB R3C 0B3
Tel: 204-453-8065; *Fax:* 204-475-2067
fmantey@fdanda.com

***Winnipeg*: David Friesen Q.C. & Associates - *1**
#711, 213 Notre Dame Ave., Winnipeg, MB R3B 1N3
Tel: 204-942-2171

***Winnipeg*: Richard S. Fulham - *1**
1900 Portage Ave., Winnipeg, MB R3J 0H9
Tel: 204-957-1413; *Fax:* 204-957-1858

***Winnipeg*: Funk & Strell - *2**
#1400, 1 Lombard Pl., Winnipeg, MB R3B 0X3
Tel: 204-957-5600; *Fax:* 204-949-1043
funk@mts.net

***Winnipeg*: Zachary I. Garber - *1**
385 St. Mary Ave., 2nd Fl., Winnipeg, MB R3C 0N1
Tel: 204-943-7454; *Fax:* 204-943-9563

***Winnipeg*: J. David George & Associates - *2**
108 Regent Ave. East, Winnipeg, MB R2C 0C1
Tel: 204-982-7503; *Fax:* 204-222-4761
david-dg@shaw.ca

***Winnipeg*: Martin D. Glazer - *1**
#506, 294 Portage Ave., Winnipeg, MB R3C 0B9
Tel: 204-942-6560; *Fax:* 204-942-2696
mglazlaw@mts.net

***Winnipeg*: Martin Gutnik - *1**
#307, 1661 Portage Ave., Winnipeg, MB R3J 3T7
Tel: 204-786-8924; *Fax:* 204-786-8525
martin@gutnik.com
www.gutnik.com

***Winnipeg*: Habing Law - *3**
2643 Portage Ave., Winnipeg, MB R3J 0P9
Tel: 204-832-8322; *Fax:* 204-832-3906
ron@habinglaw.com

***Winnipeg*: Hogue, ALain J. Law Office - *1**
194 Provencher Blvd., Winnipeg, MB R2H 0G3
Tél: 204-237-9600; *Téléc:* 204-233-2689

***Winnipeg*: Hook & Smith - *4**
#201, 3111 Portage Ave., Winnipeg, MB R3K 0W4
Tel: 204-885-4520; *Fax:* 204-837-9846
general@hookandsmith.com

***Winnipeg*: Inkster Christie Hughes LLP, Barristers & Solicitors - *13**
Former Name: Inkster, Christie, Hughes, Mackay
#700, 444 St. Mary Ave., Winnipeg, MB R3C 3T1
Tel: 204-947-6801;
info@inksterchristie.ca
www.inksterchristie.ca

***Winnipeg*: Frederick Innis - *1**
8 Ruskin Row, Winnipeg, MB R3M 2R6
Tel: 204-231-9600;
innis@shaw.ca

***Winnipeg*: Marion Ironquil Meadmore - *1**
1187 Fleet Ave., Winnipeg, MB R3M 1K9
Tel: 204-947-1509

***Winnipeg*: Karasevich Windsor Jenion Hedley LLP - *4**
#440, 5 Donald St. South, Winnipeg, MB R3L 2T4
Tel: 204-477-0285; *Fax:* 204-453-8876
jgk@escape.ca

***Winnipeg*: D.R. Knight Law Office - *5**
#202, 900 Harrow St. East, Winnipeg, MB R3M 3Y7
Tel: 204-948-0400; *Fax:* 204-948-0401
don.knight@knightlaw.ca

***Winnipeg*: Krawchuk & Company - *2**
#2250, 360 Main St., Winnipeg, MB R3C 3Z3
Tel: 204-943-4561; *Fax:* 204-947-5724
krawchukandco@mts.net

***Winnipeg*: Frank Lawrence - *1**
#202, 1382 Henderson Hwy., Winnipeg, MB R2G 1M8
Tel: 204-338-9705

***Winnipeg*: Victoria E. Lehman Law Offices - *1**
412 Wardlaw Ave., Winnipeg, MB R3L 0L7
Tel: 204-453-6416; *Fax:* 204-477-1379

***Winnipeg*: Levene, Tadman, Gutkin, Golub LLP - *16**
#700, 330 St. Mary Ave., Winnipeg, MB R3C 3Z5
Tel: 204-957-0520; *Fax:* 204-957-1696
www.lt.mb.ca

***Winnipeg*: Liffman Soronow - *2**
#210, 400 St. Mary Ave., Winnipeg, MB R3C 4K5
Tel: 204-925-6070; *Fax:* 204-944-0513
hal@escape.ca

***Winnipeg*: Loewen & Martens, Barristers & Solicitors - *5**
Former Name: Loewen, Martens & Rempel
1101 Henderson Hwy., Winnipeg, MB R2G 1L4
Tel: 204-338-9364; *Fax:* 204-338-8379
lmlaw@shawbiz.ca

***Winnipeg*: MacInnes, Burbidge - *2**
#500, 177 Lombard Ave., Winnipeg, MB R3B 0W5
Tel: 204-942-5256; *Fax:* 204-942-5259

***Winnipeg*: Hilary C. Maxim - *1**
212B Regent Ave. West, Winnipeg, MB R2C 1R2
Tel: 204-224-2600; *Fax:* 204-222-2824

***Winnipeg*: McDonald Law Office - *1**
258 Tache Ave., Winnipeg, MB R2H 1Z9
Tel: 204-927-3900; *Fax:* 204-927-3909
Toll-Free: 800-393-1110
info@mcdonaldlaw.ca
www.mcdonaldlaw.ca

***Winnipeg*: McJannet Rich - *5**
#1710, Newport Centre, 330 Portage Ave., Winnipeg, MB R3C 0C4
Tel: 204-957-0951; *Fax:* 204-989-0688

***Winnipeg*: McRoberts Law Office LLP - *13**
#200, Madison Square, 1630 Ness Ave., Winnipeg, MB R3J 3X1
Tel: 204-944-7907; *Fax:* 204-772-1684
consult@mcrobertslawoffice.com
www.mcrobertslawoffice.com

***Winnipeg*: Michaels & Stern - *2**
#300, 326 Broadway Ave., Winnipeg, MB R3C 0S5
Tel: 204-989-5500; *Fax:* 204-989-5508
michaelsandstern@mts.net

***Winnipeg*: Peter J. Moss - *5**
1002 Pembina Hwy., Winnipeg, MB R3T 1Z5
Tel: 204-284-3221; *Fax:* 204-284-7960
mosslaw@shaw.ca

***Winnipeg*: Murray & Kovnats - *2**
#100, 1600 Ness Ave., Winnipeg, MB R3J 3W7
Tel: 204-957-1700; *Fax:* 204-942-2325
brmk1@aol.com

***Winnipeg*: Mutchmor, Violago, Overall, Grimes - *3**
390 York Ave., Winnipeg, MB R3C 0P3
Tel: 204-989-1300; *Fax:* 204-989-1301

***Winnipeg*: Myers Weinberg LLP - *25**
#724, Cargill Bldg., 240 Graham Ave., Winnipeg, MB R3C 0J7
Tel: 204-942-0501; *Fax:* 204-956-0625
info@myersfirm.com

***Winnipeg*: Stanley S. Nozick - *1**
Former Name: Nozick, Sinder & Associates
#605, 386 Broadway, Winnipeg, MB R3C 3R6
Tel: 204-944-8227; *Fax:* 204-944-9246
snozick@escape.ca

***Winnipeg*: Orle, Davidson, Giesbrecht, Bargen - *10**
280 Stradbrook Ave., Winnipeg, MB R3L 0J6
Tel: 204-989-2760; *Fax:* 204-989-2774
general@odgb.mb.ca
www.odgb.mb.ca

***Winnipeg*: Murray S. Palay - *1**
#703, 161 Portage Ave. East, Winnipeg, MB R3B 0Y4
Tel: 204-944-2491; *Fax:* 204-944-8046
mpalay@quadasset.com

***Winnipeg*: Pam Smith & Company - *4**
#1210, 363 Broadway, Winnipeg, MB R3C 3N9
Tel: 204-982-4414; *Fax:* 204-943-2573
smsmgmt@mts.net

***Winnipeg*: Parashin Law Office - *1**
404 McGregor St., Winnipeg, MB R2W 4X5
Tel: 204-582-3558

***Winnipeg*: Perlov Stewart LLP - *5**
#610, One Lombard Place, Winnipeg, MB R3B 3G5
Tel: 204-944-9295; *Fax:* 204-956-4270
www.pslfirm.ca

***Winnipeg*: Phillips, Aiello - *10**
668 Corydon Ave., Winnipeg, MB R3M 0X7
Tel: 204-949-7700; *Fax:* 204-452-0922
Toll-Free: 866-949-7701
phillipsaiello@phillipsaiello.ca

***Winnipeg*: Pitblado LLP - *57**
#2500, Commodity Exchange Tower, 360 Main St., Winnipeg, MB R3C 4H6
Tel: 204-956-0560; *Fax:* 204-957-0227
firm@pitblado.com
www.pitblado.com

***Winnipeg*: Pollock & Company - *5**
#1120, 363 Broadway, Winnipeg, MB R3C 3N9
Tel: 204-956-0450; *Fax:* 204-947-0109
mail@pollockandcompany.com

***Winnipeg*: Gordon C. Pollock - *1**
#1401, 180 Tuxedo Ave., Winnipeg, MB R3P 2A6
Tel: 204-489-4945; *Fax:* 204-489-5071
gpollock7@shaw.ca

***Winnipeg*: Posner & Trachtenberg - *2**
#710, 491 Portage Ave., Winnipeg, MB R3B 2E4
Tel: 204-940-9602; *Fax:* 204-944-8878

***Winnipeg*: Jay C. Prober - *1**
#208, 387 Broadway Ave., Winnipeg, MB R3C 0V5
Tel: 204-957-1205; *Fax:* 204-943-6199

** indicates number of lawyers*

***Winnipeg*: Pullan Kammerloch Frohlinger - *10**
Former Name: Pullan Guld Kammerloch
#300, 240 Kennedy St., Winnipeg, MB R3C 1T1
Tel: 204-956-0490; *Fax:* 204-947-3747
firm@pkf-law.com
www.pkflawyers.com

***Winnipeg*: Radchuk & Company - *1**
10 Salvia Bay, Winnipeg, MB R2V 2L8
Tel: 204-338-8880; *Fax:* 204-334-5241

***Winnipeg*: Arlene S. Ratuski - *1**
#201, 1215 Henderson Hwy., Winnipeg, MB R2G 1L8
Tel: 204-334-4994; *Fax:* 204-339-6449

***Winnipeg*: Edward Rice - *1**
#301, 63 Albert St., Winnipeg, MB R3B 1G4
Tel: 204-944-1905; *Fax:* 204-947-5895
ricelaw@mts.net

***Winnipeg*: Russell Ridd - *1**
405 Broadway, 6th Fl., Winnipeg, MB R3C 3L6
Tel: 204-945-2871; *Fax:* 204-945-1260
rridd@gov.mb.ca

***Winnipeg*: Robertson Shypit Soble Wood - *5**
#202, 1555 St. Mary's Rd., Winnipeg, MB R2M 5L9
Tel: 204-257-6061; *Fax:* 204-254-7183

***Winnipeg*: James F.C. Rose - *1**
582 Bruce Ave., Winnipeg, MB R3J 0W5
Tel: 204-889-3885; *Fax:* 204-889-3885
Toll-Free: 800-414-8091
jamesrose@shaw.ca
www.members.shaw.ca/jamesrose/baddebt.htm

***Winnipeg*: Rosenbaum & Company - *4**
#201, 2211 McPhillips St., Winnipeg, MB R2V 3M5
Tel: 204-338-4663; *Fax:* 204-338-4667

***Winnipeg*: Sheldon Rosenstock - *1**
848 Waterloo St., Winnipeg, MB R3N 0T6
Tel: 204-488-4121; *Fax:* 204-488-1869
rosensto@shaw.ca
www.rosenstockimmigration.com

***Winnipeg*: Rutledge Law Office - *2**
Former Name: Rutledge & Dyker
#310, 3025 Portage Ave., Winnipeg, MB R3K 2E2
Tel: 204-987-7575; *Fax:* 204-837-3638
rutlaw@mts.net

***Winnipeg*: Mario J. Santos - *1**
#206, 819 Sargent Ave., Winnipeg, MB R3E 0B9
Tel: 204-783-0554; *Fax:* 204-772-4231

***Winnipeg*: Shewchuk & Associates - *2**
2645 Portage Ave., Winnipeg, MB R3J 0P9
Tel: 204-889-4595

***Winnipeg*: Sinclair & Associates - *2**
#231, 1120 Grant Ave., Winnipeg, MB R3M 2A6
Tel: 204-474-2468; *Fax:* 204-474-2535
sgilchrist@sinclairassociates.ca

***Winnipeg*: Slusky & Slusky - *1**
#1028, 363 Broadway, Winnipeg, MB R3C 3N9
Tel: 204-943-5455; *Fax:* 204-942-4301

***Winnipeg*: Soronow Law Office**
Former Name: Liffman Soronow
#210, 400 St. Mary Ave., Winnipeg, MB R3C 4K5
Tel: 204-925-6074; *Fax:* 204-944-0513
sgs@mts.net

***Winnipeg*: J.S. Sukhan - *1**
1158 Clarence Ave., Winnipeg, MB R3T 1S9
Tel: 204-284-0728

***Winnipeg*: Tacium, Vincent, Orlikow - *1**
#200, 99A Scurfield Blvd., Winnipeg, MB R3Y 1G4
Tel: 204-989-8767; *Fax:* 204-989-8765
resolveconflict@mb.aibn.com

***Winnipeg*: Tapper Cuddy LLP - *23**
Former Name: Scufield Tupper Cuddy
#1000, 330 St. Mary Ave., Winnipeg, MB R3C 3Z5
Tel: 204-944-8777; *Fax:* 204-947-2593
tc@tcwpg.com
www.tcwpg.com

***Winnipeg*: Taylor McCaffrey LLP - *62**
400 St. Mary Ave., 9th Fl., Winnipeg, MB R3C 4K5
Tel: 204-949-1312; *Fax:* 204-957-0945
www.tmlawyers.com

***Winnipeg*: Tepley Law Office - *1**
#401, 460 Main St., Winnipeg, MB R3B 1B6
Tel: 204-942-7218

***Winnipeg*: Teskey Legal & ADR Services - *1**
1905 One Evergreen Pl., Winnipeg, MB R3L 0E9
Tel: 204-943-8395; *Fax:* 204-943-1288
teskey@mb.sympatico.ca

***Winnipeg*: Thompson Dorfman Sweatman LLP - *68**
#2200, CanWest Global Place, 201 Portage Ave., Winnipeg, MB R3B 3L3
Tel: 204-957-1930; *Fax:* 204-934-0570
tds@tdslaw.com
www.tdslaw.com

***Winnipeg*: John F. Thullner - *1**
#102, 2200 McPhillips St., Winnipeg, MB R2V 3P4
Tel: 204-694-0161

***Winnipeg*: Tupper & Adams - *8**
200 Portage Ave., 4th Fl., Winnipeg, MB R3C 3X2
Tel: 204-942-0161; *Fax:* 204-943-2385
general@tupper-adams.mb.ca
www.tupper-adams.mb.ca

***Winnipeg*: W.R. Van Walleghem - *1**
#206, 1120 Grant Ave., Winnipeg, MB R3M 2A6
Tel: 204-477-0210; *Fax:* 204-452-9746

***Winnipeg*: Walsh & Company - *3**
426 Portage Ave., Winnipeg, MB R3C 0C9
Tel: 204-947-2282; *Fax:* 204-943-0211
paulwalsh@walshandco.com

***Winnipeg*: Warkentin & Calver - *1**
3651 Roblin Blvd., Winnipeg, MB R3R 0E2
Tel: 204-949-3230; *Fax:* 204-949-3249
pcalver@warkcal.ca
www.warkcal.ca

***Winnipeg*: E. Waskiw - *1**
441 Perth Ave., Winnipeg, MB R2V 0T9
Tel: 204-334-7372

***Winnipeg*: Arthur M. Werier - *1**
905 Corydon Ave., Winnipeg, MB R3M 0W8
Tel: 204-475-7923

***Winnipeg*: Wilder Wilder & Langtry - *8**
#1500, Richardson Bldg., 1 Lombard Pl., Winnipeg, MB R3B 0X3
Tel: 204-947-1456; *Fax:* 204-957-1368
Toll-Free: 888-470-0847
admin@wilderwilder.com
www.wilderwilder.com

***Winnipeg*: Zaifman Associates - *4**
191 Lombard Ave., 5th Fl., Winnipeg, MB R3B 0X1
Tel: 204-944-8888; *Fax:* 204-956-2909
zaifman@zaifmanlaw.com
www.pureimmigration.com

***Winnipeg*: Saheel, Zaman Law Corporation - *4**
#1130, 363 Broadway, Winnipeg, MB R3C 3N9
Tel: 204-943-9922; *Fax:* 204-975-1802
szaman@szamanlaw.com

***Winnipeg*: Daria Zyla - *1**
1230 Hector Bay West, Winnipeg, MB R3M 3R9
Tel: 204-452-5626; *Fax:* 204-475-7979

New Brunswick

***Atholville*: Roger G. Gauvin - *1**
65 Fairview St., Atholville, NB E3N 4N3
Tel: 506-753-4545; *Fax:* 506-753-2006

***Bathurst*: Chiasson & Roy - *3**
#203, Stn. Main, 216 Main St., Bathurst, NB E2A 3Z2
Tel: 506-548-3375; *Fax:* 506-548-4264

***Bathurst*: John Douglas Hazen - *1**
132 Main St., Bathurst, NB E2A 1A4
Tel: 506-545-9220; *Fax:* 506-545-9224

***Bathurst*: Robichaud, Theriault, Riordon, Arseneault - *5**
Former Name: Robichaud, Williamson, Theriault & Johnstone
#300, Keystone Place, P.O. Box 506, 270 Douglas Ave., Bathurst, NB E2A 3Z4
Tel: 506-548-8822; *Fax:* 506-548-5297

***Bouctouche*: Yvon J.G. LeBlanc - *2**
25, boul Irving, Bouctouche, NB E4S 3J5
Tel: 506-743-2427; *Fax:* 506-743-8314
lebbell@nbnet.nb.ca

***Bouctouche*: Mark Robere - *1**
#2, 6, rue Station, Bouctouche, NB E4S 3X1
Tel: 506-743-2262; *Fax:* 506-743-9014
roberem@nbnet.nb.ca

***Campbellton*: J.Yvon Arseneau C.P. Inc. - *3**
Former Name: Arseneau & Associés
P.O. Box 520, Stn. Main, 112 Roseberry St., Campbellton, NB E3N 3G9
Tel: 506-753-3000; *Fax:* 506-753-2393
jyarseneau@nb.aibn.com

***Campbellton*: Terrance H. Delaney, Q.C. - *2**
#206, P.O. Box 490, 123 Water St., Campbellton, NB E3N 3G9
Tel: 506-753-7618; *Fax:* 506-759-7315
terra1@nb.sympatico.ca

***Caraquet*: Alie A. LeBouthillier - *1**
CP 5661, 295, boul St-Pierre ouest, Caraquet, NB E1W 1B7
Tél: 506-727-3484; *Téléc:* 506-727-3484
alie@nb.aira.com

***Chipman*: Nicholas D. DiCarlo**
P.O. Box 489, Stn. Main, 131 Main St., Chipman, NB E4A 3N6
Tel: 506-339-6688; *Fax:* 506-339-5598
ndicarlo@nbaibn.com

***Chipman*: Sharon R. Lockwood - *1**
28 Northrup Dr., Chipman, NB E4A 2P7
Tel: 506-339-6632; *Fax:* 506-339-5130
sharon.lockwood@nb.aibn.com

***Dalhousie*: Dubé & Associate - *2**
P.O. Box 1900, 390 William St., Dalhousie, NB E0K 1B0
Tel: 506-684-5661; *Fax:* 506-684-5011

***Dieppe*: Martin J. Aubin - *1**
250 Acadie Ave., Dieppe, NB E1A 1G5
Tel: 506-856-6083; *Fax:* 506-853-0110

***Dieppe*: Thompson & Thompson - *2**
379 Champlain St., Dieppe, NB E1A 1P2
Tel: 506-859-7794; *Fax:* 506-859-1297

***Edmundston*: Roger D. Poitras - *1**
87, ch Canada, Edmundston, NB E3V 1V6
Tél: 506-739-7335; *Téléc:* 506-735-4139

***Fredericton*: Cleveland J. Allaby - *1**
#200, 480 Queen St., Fredericton, NB E3B 1B6
Tel: 506-459-9737; *Fax:* 506-452-8962
allabycj@nbnet.nb.ca

***Fredericton*: Atkinson & Atkinson - *1**
P.O. Box 700, 108 Queen St., Fredericton, NB E3B 5B4
Tel: 506-451-7777; *Fax:* 506-451-1029
fealaw@nb.aibn.com

***Fredericton*: Carol H.Y. Boxill - *1**
P.O. Box 1321, Stn. A, 57 Carleton St., Fredericton, NB E3B 5E3
Tel: 506-454-5108; *Fax:* 506-450-3880
aa623@fan.nb.ca

***Fredericton*: Le Cabinet Bertrand Law - *1**
Former Name: Bertrand & Bertrand
#402, 850 Prospect St., Fredericton, NB E3B 9M5
Tel: 506-450-3325; *Fax:* 506-450-6333
bertran2@nbnet.nb.ca

***Fredericton*: B.H. Campbell - *1**
P.O. Box 295, Stn. A, 334 Saint John St., Fredericton, NB E3B 4B6
Tel: 506-458-8140; *Fax:* 506-450-6186
bhclaw@nb.aibn.com

***Fredericton*: Leycester D. D'Arcy - *1**
P.O. Box 93, Stn. A, Fredericton, NB E3B 4Y2
Tel: 506-454-2552

***Fredericton*: Dean & McMath - *2**
406 Regent St., Fredericton, NB E3B 3X7
Tel: 506-458-8555; *Fax:* 506-444-0920
dwmcmath@deanmcmath.ca

***Fredericton*: Eddy & Downs - *2**
#210, P.O. Box 1205, Stn. A, 65 Regent St., Fredericton, NB E3B 5C8
Tel: 506-443-9700; *Fax:* 506-443-9710

** indicates number of lawyers*

Fredericton: Gaffney & Burke - *2
466 Bowlen St., Fredericton, NB E3A 2T4
Tel: 506-458-8124; *Fax:* 506-458-2652
gaffneyburke@nb.aibn.com

Fredericton: Gordon F. Gregory Law Office - *1
#2, 110 Queen St., Fredericton, NB E3B 1A5
Tel: 506-458-8060; *Fax:* 506-459-8288

Fredericton: Hughes, Yeamans, Campbell - *2
P.O. Box 295, 551 Charlotte St., Fredericton, NB E3B 4Y9
Tel: 506-458-8140; *Fax:* 506-450-6186

Fredericton: Kenny & Murray - *5
P.O. Box 1572, Stn. A, 228 Brunswick St., Fredericton, NB E3B 5G2
Tel: 506-458-1108; *Fax:* 506-458-2645
kenny@nbnet.nb.ca

Fredericton: Matthews McCrea Elliott - *7
Former Name: Matthews Teriault
197 Main St., Fredericton, NB E3A 1E1
Tel: 506-458-5959; *Fax:* 506-460-5934
office@matthewsmccreaelliott.com
www.matthewsmccreaelliott.com

Fredericton: Charles S. McAllister - *1
68 London Ct., Fredericton, NB E3B 6K9
Tel: 506-454-6852

Fredericton: Daniel W. McCormack - *1
P.O. Box 1356, Stn. A, 259 Brunswick St., Fredericton, NB E3B 5S3
Tel: 506-459-3331; *Fax:* 506-457-6332

Fredericton: McNally & Smart - *2
P.O. Box 3152, Stn. LCD 1, 819 Union St., Fredericton, NB E3A 5G9
Tel: 506-472-4872; *Fax:* 506-472-9844

Fredericton: Mockler Peters Oley Rouse - *7
Former Name: Mockler, Peters, Oley, Rouse & Williams
P.O. Box 547, Stn. A., 839 Aberdeen St., Fredericton, NB E3B 5A6
Tel: 506-444-6589; *Fax:* 506-444-6550
www.mpor.ca

Fredericton: J. Shawn O'Toole - *1
#201, 346 Queen St., Fredericton, NB E3B 1B2
Tel: 506-458-8833; *Fax:* 506-454-1999

Fredericton: Mark C. Paul-Elias - *1
#5, Pepper Creek Plaza, 336, Rte. 10, Richibucto Rd., Fredericton, NB E3A 7E1
Tel: 506-458-1880; *Fax:* 506-458-9868
peppercreek@brunnet.net

Fredericton: Pink Larkin - *4
Former Name: Pink Breen Larkin
#210, 1133 Regent St., Fredericton, NB E3B 3Z2
Tel: 506-458-1989; *Fax:* 506-458-1127
www.pinklarkin.com

Fredericton: Gerald R. Pugh - *1
57 Carleton St., 4th Fl., Fredericton, NB E3B 3T2
Tel: 506-450-2666; *Fax:* 506-457-4295
drwp@nb.aibn.com

Fredericton: Yerxa, Stephenson - *3
#208, P.O. Box 175, Stn. A, 403 Regent St., Fredericton, NB E3B 4Y9
Tel: 506-459-1450; *Fax:* 506-459-2301
lawoffice@yerstep.com
www.yerstep.com

Grand Falls: Duffie, DesChênes - *2
Box 7336, 346 Chapel St., Grand Falls, NB E3Z 2M4
Tel: 506-473-2221; *Fax:* 506-473-3253
peduffie@nbnet.nb.ca

Grand Falls: Godbout, Ouellette - *2
698 E.H. Daigle Blvd., Grand Falls, NB E3Z 2S1
Tel: 506-473-6272; *Fax:* 506-473-6065
godouel@nbnet.nb.ca

Grand Falls: Gilles A. Pichette, Q.C. - *1
P.O. Box 7128, 257 Broadway, Grand Falls, NB E3Z 2K1
Tel: 506-473-4776; *Fax:* 506-473-6493
gillespichette@nb.aibn.com

Grand Falls: Peter Seheult - *1
#7248, 275 Sheriff St., Grand Falls, NB E3Z 3A1
Tel: 506-473-2164; *Fax:* 506-473-5543
seheult@nbnet.nb.ca

Hampton: Veniot Law Office - *1
Former Name: Veniot Loughery Levine
71 Randall Dr., Hampton, NB E5N 6A4
Tel: 506-832-3418; *Fax:* 506-832-3755

Lamèque: Roger A. Noël - *2
CP 2038, Stn. Main, 5120E, rte 113, Lamèque, NB E8T 3N4
Tél: 506-344-2217; *Téléc:* 506-344-5380
info@eteudelegalenoel.com

Memramcook: Jacques Gauthier - *1
835, rue Principale, Memramcook, NB E4K 2R9
Tél: 506-758-9002; *Téléc:* 506-758-2400
acadian22@hotmail.com

Minto: Mario DiCarlo - *1
255 Main St., Minto, NB E4B 3R8
Tel: 506-327-3777; *Fax:* 506-327-6080
mariodicarlo@bellaliant.net

Minto: Sheila R. Thorne - *1
24 Queen St., Minto, NB E4B 3P2
Tel: 506-327-6120

Miramichi: Rosemary Losier - *1
P.O. Box 112, Stn. Main, 173 Wellington St., Miramichi, NB E1N 3A5
Tel: 506-773-6817

Miramichi: Maynes, Mahoney & Tremblay - *4
P.O. Box 518, 1723 Water St., Miramichi, NB E1N 3A8
Tel: 506-778-8336; *Fax:* 506-778-2103

Moncton: Michel C. Arsenault - *1
1255 Main St., Moncton, NB E1C 1H9
Tel: 506-857-8008; *Fax:* 506-857-8885
mcalaw@nb.aibn.com

Moncton: Bingham Robinson McLennan Ehrhardt & Teed - *18
Former Name: Bingham MacAulay Ehrhardt Teed
#300, Heritage Court, 95 Foundry St., Moncton, NB E1C 5H7
Tel: 506-857-8856; *Fax:* 506-857-2017

Moncton: Robert N. Charman - *1
170 Highfield St., Moncton, NB E1C 5P2
Tel: 506-854-8656; *Fax:* 506-854-8684
rcharman@nbnet.nb.ca

Moncton: Corporate Communications Limited - *1
844 Main St., Moncton, NB E1C 1G2
Tel: 506-855-1771; *Fax:* 506-859-1691
mrobichaud@cclgroup.ca

Moncton: Delehanty Rinzler Druckham - *3
Former Name: Tedford Delehanty Rinzler
#101, P.O. Box 1083, 720 Main St., Moncton, NB E1C 8P6
Tel: 506-857-3030; *Fax:* 506-857-0085
www.drdlaw.ca

Moncton: Forbes Roth Basque - *7
P.O. Box 480, Moncton, NB E1C 8L9
Tel: 506-857-4880; *Fax:* 506-857-0151

Moncton: Fowler & Fowler - *2
69 Waterloo St., Moncton, NB E1C 0E1
Tel: 506-857-8811; *Fax:* 506-857-9297

Moncton: John D. Hughes
P.O. Box 29072, 98 Bonaccord St., Moncton, NB E1G 4R3
Tel: 506-382-9072

Moncton: LeBlanc Boucher Rodger Bourque - *3
740 Main St., Moncton, NB E1C 1E6
Tel: 506-858-0110; *Fax:* 506-858-9497
lbrb@nbnet.nb.ca

Moncton: LeBlanc Boudreau Maillet - *6
Former Name: LeBlanc Boudreau Desjardins Maillet
#200, 735 Main St., Moncton, NB E1C 1E5
Tel: 506-858-5666; *Fax:* 506-858-5570
leblord@nbnet.nb.ca

Moncton: LeBlanc, Martin, Sweet & Cormier - *5
Former Name: Cantini, LeBlanc, Martin, Sweet & Cormier
P.O. Box 1285, 51 Highfield St., Moncton, NB E1C 8P9
Tel: 506-859-1212; *Fax:* 506-859-7309

Moncton: Susan D. LeBlanc - *1
76 Albert St., Moncton, NB E1C 1B1
Tel: 506-859-4402; *Fax:* 506-859-9195

Moncton: Letcher & Murray - *3
76 Albert St., Moncton, NB E1C 1B1
Tel: 506-857-2070; *Fax:* 506-859-9195

Moncton: Lise Lorrain - *1
P.O. Box 25117, RPO Mountain Rd., Moncton, NB E1C 9M9
Tel: 506-855-6084; *Fax:* 506-389-3867
llorrain@nbnet.nb.ca

Moncton: Maxwell - Matheson - *2
Former Name: Wendell J. Maxwell
Assumption Place, 770 Main St., 10th Fl., Moncton, NB E1C 1E7
Tel: 506-857-8470; *Fax:* 506-857-4031

Moncton: Mitchell Law Office - *1
Former Name: MacPherson Mitchell
89 Church St., Moncton, NB E1C 4Z4
Tel: 506-853-1105; *Fax:* 506-853-9348

Moncton: Murphy Collette Murphy - *7
250 Lutz St., Moncton, NB E1C 5G3
Tel: 506-856-8560; *Fax:* 506-856-8579
manager@murco.nb.ca
www.murco.nb.ca

Moncton: Murphy, Murphy & Mollins - *3
89 Church St., Moncton, NB E1C 4Z4
Tel: 506-857-9120; *Fax:* 506-857-9129
mmmlaw@nb.aibn.com

Moncton: Alan D. Schelew - *1
#100, P.O. Box 182, 803 Main St., Moncton, NB E1C 8K9
Tel: 506-857-2272; *Fax:* 506-857-2276
schelew@nb.aibn.com
www.monctonlawyer.com

Oromocto: Blair W. McKay - *1
#3, 291 Restigouche Rd., Oromocto, NB E2V 2H2
Tel: 506-446-3000; *Fax:* 506-446-9010

Perth-Andover: Mark C. Johnson - *1
Former Name: Crocco, Hunter, Purvis, Johnson
P.O. Box 3066, 1143 West Riverside Dr., Perth-Andover, NB E7H 5G5
Tel: 506-273-6818; *Fax:* 506-273-6590
mjlaw@nb.aibn.com

Perth-Andover: Stewart C. Paul, Law Office - *1
P.O. Box 2981, Stn. Main, Perth-Andover, NB E7H 5M2
Tel: 506-273-4445; *Fax:* 506-273-4491

Petit-Rocher: Robert M. Boudreau - *1
561 rue Principale, Petit-Rocher, NB E8J 1J4
Tél: 506-783-4246; *Téléc:* 506-783-2354
rboudro@nbnet.nb.ca

Richibucto: Joseph Robichaud
#1, 9406 Main St., Richibucto, NB E4W 4E1
Tel: 506-523-4442; *Fax:* 506-523-4819

Riverview: McAllister & Grew - *3
704A Coverdale Rd., Riverview, NB E1B 3L1
Tel: 506-853-3040; *Fax:* 506-859-9588
hgrew@nbnet.nb.ca

Riverview: Wilbur & Wilbur - *2
706B Coverdale Rd., Riverview, NB E1B 3L1
Tel: 506-387-7715; *Fax:* 506-387-5875
swilbur@wilburandwilbur.com
www.wilburandwilbur.com

Sackville: Meldrum Law - *2
7 Bridge St., Sackville, NB E4L 3N6
Tel: 506-536-3870; *Fax:* 506-536-2131
Toll-Free: 866-792-1416
meldrumk@nbnet.nb.ca

Sackville: Ove B. Samuelsen - *1
1 Squire St., Sackville, NB E4L 4K8
Tel: 506-536-0511; *Fax:* 506-536-1169
ovesam@nbnet.nb.ca

Saint John: Michael D. Bamford
#420, 40 Charlotte St., Saint John, NB E2L 2H6
Tel: 506-634-8130; *Fax:* 506-633-0389

Saint John: Barry Spalding - Saint John Office - *20
Former Name: Barry Spalding Richard
#710, Mercantine Centre, P.O. Box 6010, Stn. A, 55 Union Street, Saint John, NB E2L 4R5
Tel: 506-633-4226; *Fax:* 506-633-4206
Toll-Free: 888-743-4226
info@barryspalding.com
www.barryspalding.com

** indicates number of lawyers*

Saint John: **Boyle, Dennis - *1**
345 Lancaster Ave. West, Saint John, NB E2M 2L3
Tel: 506-634-7575; *Fax:* 506-634-8237

Saint John: **Clark Drummie - *22**
P.O. Box 6850, 40 Wellington Row, Saint John, NB E2L 4S3
Tel: 506-633-3800; *Fax:* 506-633-3811
cd@clarkdrummie.ca
www.clarkdrummie.ca

Saint John: **Correia & Collins - *3**
1 Market Sq., Stn. A, Saint John, NB E2L 4S4
Tel: 506-648-1700; *Fax:* 506-648-1701
www.correiaandcollins.com

Saint John: **Allen G. Doyle Law Office - *1**
45 Canterbury St., Saint John, NB E2L 2C6
Tel: 506-633-4198; *Fax:* 506-633-1645
a.g.doyle@nb.aibn.com

Saint John: **Lynda D. Farrell - *4**
City Hall, P.O. Box 1971, Stn. Main, 15 Market Sq., 8th Fl., Saint John, NB E2L 4L1
Tel: 506-658-2860; *Fax:* 506-658-2802

Saint John: **Gilbert McGloan Gillis - *15**
P.O. Box 7174, 22 King St., Saint John, NB E2L 1G3
Tel: 506-634-3600; *Fax:* 506-634-3612
Toll-Free: 888-246-4529
gmg@gmglaw.com
www.gmglaw.com

Saint John: **Gorman Nason - *10**
P.O. Box 7286, Stn. A, 121 Germain St., Saint John, NB E2L 4S6
Tel: 506-634-8600; *Fax:* 506-634-8685
info@GormanNason.com
www.gormannason.com

Saint John: **John M. Henderson - *1**
#410, 40 Charlotte St., Saint John, NB E2L 2H6
Tel: 506-652-5502; *Fax:* 506-634-1795
jmhlaw@nbnet.nb.ca

Saint John: **Frank J. Hogan - *1**
491 Bay St. West, Saint John, NB E2M 7L3
Tel: 506-635-1462; *Fax:* 506-672-4545
hoganfj@nbnet.nb.ca

Saint John: **Mary Ann G. Holland - *1**
P.O. Box 7041, Stn. Brunswick, 120 Prince William St., Saint John, NB E2L 4S4
Tel: 506-652-3774; *Fax:* 506-633-0581
lawyer@nbnet.nb.ca

Saint John: **W. Rodney Macdonald - *1**
108 Prince William St., Saint John, NB E2L 2B3
Tel: 506-632-8999; *Fax:* 506-634-1532

Saint John: **A. Wilber MacLeod Q.C. - *1**
108 Prince William St., Saint John, NB E2L 2B3
Tel: 506-632-8999

Saint John: **Elizabeth T. McLeod, QC - *1**
#5C, Brunswick Sq., P.O. Box 20045, 28 King St., Saint John, NB E2L 5B2
Tel: 506-632-4048; *Fax:* 506-652-6594

Saint John: **Mosher Chedore**
#300, 33 Charlotte St., 3rd Fl., Saint John, NB E2L 2H3
Tel: 506-634-1600; *Fax:* 506-634-0740
lawfirm@nb.sympatico.ca

Saint John: **Richard A. Northrup - *1**
#420, 40 Charlotte St., Saint John, NB E2L 2H6
Tel: 506-634-8134; *Fax:* 506-693-3473
nbrick@nb.aibn.com

Saint John: **Riley, John G. - *1**
#410, 40 Charlotte St., Saint John, NB E2L 2H6
Tel: 506-634-1188; *Fax:* 506-634-1795
jgrileylaw@nb.aibn.com

Saint John: **Sherwood & Flanagan - *2**
10 Peel St., Saint John, NB E2L 3G9
Tel: 506-634-0001; *Fax:* 506-634-0456
mary-eileen@sherwoodandflanagan.com

Saint John: **Teed & Teed, Barristers & Solicitors - *1**
P.O. Box 6639, Stn. A, 127 Prince William St., Saint John, NB E2L 4S1
Tel: 506-634-7320; *Fax:* 506-634-7423
info@teedandteed.com
www.teedandteed.com

Saint John: **Whelly & Kelly - *4**
122 Carleton St., Saint John, NB E2L 2Z7
Tel: 506-634-1193; *Fax:* 506-693-9040
partner@nb.aibn.com

Saint John: **Patrick R. Wilbur - *1**
#410, P.O. Box 6601, Stn. Brunswick, 40 Charlotte St., Saint John, NB E2L 4S1
Tel: 506-632-6001; *Fax:* 506-633-6031
prwilburlaw@nb.aibn.com

Saint John: **Theodore E. Wilson - *1**
10 Prince Edward St., Saint John, NB E2L 4M5
Tel: 506-633-8788; *Fax:* 506-632-2023

Shediac: **Michel C. Leger - *2**
CP 1900, 5, rue Mill, Shediac, NB E4P 2H8
Tél: 506-532-0100; *Téléc:* 506-532-6332
mike0100@nbnet.nb.ca

Shippagan: **Godin, Lizotte, Robichaud, Guignard - *4**
246, boul J.D.Gauthier, Shippagan, NB E8S 1P9
Tél: 506-336-0400; *Téléc:* 506-336-0409
glrg@nbnet.nb.ca

Shippagan: **Theriault, Larocque, Boudreau - *3**
Former Name: Theriault, Larocque & Associés
P.O. Box 160, 283 J.D. Gauthier Blvd., Shippagan, NB E8S 1N6
Tel: 506-336-4726; *Fax:* 506-336-1159
tla@nbnet.nb.ca

St Andrews: **David A. Bartlett - *1**
Former Name: Larsen & Bartlett
239 Water St., St Andrews, NB E5B 1B3
Tel: 506-529-9000; *Fax:* 506-529-9003
bartllaw@nb.aibn.com

St George: **Peter A. Johnston Law Office - *2**
4 Main St., St George, NB E5C 3J1
Tel: 506-755-3376; *Fax:* 506-755-8044
larjon@nbnet.nb.ca

St. Stephen: **Ronald W. Sutherland - *1**
71 King St., St. Stephen, NB E3L 2C4
Tel: 506-466-5330; *Fax:* 506-466-3692

Sussex: **D. James Garrish - *1**
#1, 480 Main St., Sussex, NB E4S 2S4
Tel: 506-433-4234; *Fax:* 506-432-1814
gersmi@nbnet.nb.ca

Sussex: **Palmer & Palmer - *2**
17 Queen St., Sussex, NB E4E 2A4
Tel: 506-433-2168; *Fax:* 506-433-4740

Sussex: **Purnell & Fulton - *1**
30 Church Ave., Sussex, NB E4E 1Y7
Tel: 506-433-4215; *Fax:* 506-433-4216
lawyers@nbnet.nb.ca

Tracadie-Sheila: **Doiron, Lebouthillier, Boudreau, Allain - *4**
CP 3010, Stn. Bureau, 3674, rue Principale, Tracadie-Sheila, NB E1X 1G5
Tél: 506-395-0044; *Téléc:* 506-395-0050
dllb@nbnet.nb.ca

Woodstock: **McCue Brewer Dickinson - *3**
179 Broadway St., Woodstock, NB E7M 1B7
Tel: 506-325-2835; *Fax:* 506-328-6248
mblaw@nbnet.nb.ca

Woodstock: **Stephen L. Wilson - *1**
Former Name: Wilson & Kinney
#1, 733 Main St., Woodstock, NB E7M 2E6
Tel: 506-325-1100; *Fax:* 506-328-4873
stepwil@nbnet.nb.ca

Newfoundland & Labrador

Bay Roberts: **Moores, Andrews, Collins - *3**
P.O. Box 806, Bay Roberts, NL A0A 1G0
Tel: 709-786-7114; *Fax:* 709-786-6952
mac@mac-law.ca

Bay Roberts: **Morrow & Morrow - *2**
P.O. Box 870, 344 Conception Bay Hwy., Bay Roberts, NL A0A 1G0
Tel: 709-786-9207; *Fax:* 709-786-9507
morrow@nf.aibn.com

Carbonear: **J. William Finn - *1**
66 Powell Dr., Carbonear, NL A1Y 1A5
Tel: 709-596-5143; *Fax:* 709-596-3208

Channel-Port-aux-Basques: **Marks & Parsons - *4**
#3, P.O. Box 640, 9 Barhaven Dr., Channel-Port-aux-Basques, NL A0M 1C0
Tel: 709-695-7341; *Fax:* 709-695-3944
b.marks@mplaw.com

Clarenville: **Hughes & Brannan Law Offices - *2**
357 Memorial Dr., Clarenville, NL A5A 1R8
Tel: 709-466-3106; *Fax:* 709-466-3107
hughes.brannan@nfld.net

Conception Bay South: **Robert R. Regular - *2**
#110, Villa Nova Plaza, 120 Conception Bay Hwy., Conception Bay South, NL A1W 3A6
Tel: 709-834-2132; *Fax:* 709-834-3025
rregular@robertregularlaw.com

Corner Brook: **Monaghan, Murphy & Watton - *4**
Mercantile Trust Bldg., Box 815, Stn. Main, 17 West St., Corner Brook, NL A2H 6H9
Tel: 709-634-3231; *Fax:* 709-634-8889
contacts@monmar.nf.net

Corner Brook: **Poole Althouse, Barristers & Solicitors - *10**
Former Name: Poole, Althouse, Thompson & Thomas
Western Trust Bldg., P.O. Box 812, 49 - 51 Park St., Corner Brook, NL A2H 6H7
Tel: 709-634-3136; *Fax:* 709-634-8247
Toll-Free: 877-634-3136
info@pa-law.ca
www.poolealthouse.ca

Corner Brook: **Watton, Graham, Law Office - *1**
Noton Bldg., P.O. Box 188, 133 Riverside Dr., Corner Brook, NL A2H 6C7
Tel: 709-639-7490; *Fax:* 709-634-7229
watton@nf.aibn.com

Gander: **Easton Hillier Lawrence Preston - *8**
Former Name: Easton Facey Hillier Lawrence
Polaris Bldg., 61 Elizabeth Dr., Gander, NL A1V 1G4
Tel: 709-256-4006; *Fax:* 709-651-2850
Toll-Free: 800-256-4006
info@ganderlawyers.com
www.ganderlawyers.com

Labrador City: **Miller & Hearn - *2**
P.O. Box 129, Stn. Main, Labrador City, NL A2V 2K3
Tel: 709-944-3666; *Fax:* 709-944-5494
miller&hearn@crrstv.net

Mount Pearl: **Budden, Morris - *5**
184 Park Ave., Mount Pearl, NL A1N 1K8
Tel: 709-747-0077; *Fax:* 709-747-0104
lawyers@buddenmorris.com
www.buddenmorris.com

Paradise: **Aylward, Chislett & Whitten - *3**
#200, 1655 Topsail Road, Paradise, NL A1L 1V1
Tel: 709-722-6000; *Fax:* 709-726-1225
contact@acwlaw.ca
www.acwlaw.ca

Paradise: **Susan L. Fisher - *1**
15 Deborah Lynn Hts., Paradise, NL A1L 3E6
Tel: 709-773-1806; *Fax:* 709-773-1807
susanfisher@nl.rogers.com

Springdale: **Shawn C.A. Colbourne Law Office - *1**
P.O. Box 69, 8 Juniper Rd., Springdale, NL A0J 1T0
Tel: 709-673-3693; *Fax:* 709-673-3991
colbourne.5@nf.sympatico.ca

St. John's: **Benson Myles - *21**
#900, Atlantic Place, P.O. Box 1538, 215 Water St., St. John's, NL A1C 5N8
Tel: 709-579-2081; *Fax:* 709-579-2647
info@bensonmyles.com
www.bensonmyles.com

St. John's: **Browne, Fitzgerald, Morgan, Avis - *6**
Terrace on the Square, Level II, P.O. Box 23135, RPO Churchill Sq., St. John's, NL A1B 4J9
Tel: 709-724-3800; *Fax:* 709-754-3800

St. John's: **Bruce & Company - *1**
11 Church Hill, St. John's, NL A1C 3Z7
Tel: 709-738-0006; *Fax:* 709-738-0375
bruceco@nf.sympatico.ca

** indicates number of lawyers*

St. John's: Cox & Palmer - St. John's - *43
Former Name: Patterson Palmer; Cox Hanson O'Reilly Matheson
#1000, Scotia Centre, 235 Water St., St. John's, NL A1C 1B6
Tel: 709-738-7800; Fax: 709-738-7999
stjohns@coxandpalmer.com
www.coxandpalmer.com

St. John's: Crosbie, Ches Barristers - *5
169 Water St., St. John's, NL A1C 1B1
Tel: 709-579-4000; Fax: 709-579-9671
Toll-Free: 888-579-3262
ccb@chescrosbie.nf.net

St. John's: Michael W. Dodd & Associates - *2
#301, P.O. Box 578, Stn. C, 291 Water St., St. John's, NL A1C 5K8
Tel: 709-754-4098; Fax: 709-754-3223
mdodd@mdoddlaw.com

St. John's: Duffy & Associates
#102, 95 Bonaventure Ave., St. John's, NL A1B 2X5
Tel: 709-757-8285; Fax: 709-757-8284

St. John's: Christopher English - *1
3 Pine Bud Pl., St. John's, NL A1B 1N1
Tel: 709-754-4855; Fax: 709-737-2164
cenglish@mun.ca

St. John's: Fraize Law Offices - *2
P.O. Box 5217, St. John's, NL A1C 5W1
Tel: 709-726-7978; Fax: 709-726-8201
tfraize@fraizelawoffices.nf.net

St. John's: French, Noseworthy & Associates - *5
Former Name: French, Dunne & Associates
#122, Elizabeth Towers, 100 Elizabeth Ave., St. John's, NL A1B 1S1
Tel: 709-754-1800; Fax: 709-754-2701
jbfrench@nf.aibn.com

St. John's: L. Power Consulting Inc. - *1
59 Hayward Ave., St. John's, NL A1C 3W6
Tel: 709-682-3543; Fax: 709-726-4849
leopower@nf.sympatico.ca

St. John's: Lewis, Day - *2
#A, 84 Airport Rd., 1st Fl., St. John's, NL A1A 4Y3
Tel: 709-753-2545; Fax: 709-753-2266
Toll-Free: 877-553-2545
kellyhall@lewisday.ca, admin@lewisday.ca
www.lewisday.com

St. John's: Lewis, Sinnott, Shortall, Hurley - *4
#300, TD Place, P.O. Box 884, Stn. C, 140 Water St., St. John's, NL A1C 5L7
Tel: 709-753-7810; Fax: 709-738-2965
lssh@nf.aibn.com

St. John's: Martin Whalen Hennebury Stamp - *11
P.O. Box 5910, 15 Church Hill, St. John's, NL A1C 5X4
Tel: 709-754-1400; Fax: 709-754-0915
info@mwhslaw.com
www.mwhslaw.com

St. John's: John W. McGrath - *2
18 Argyle St., St. John's, NL A1A 1V3
Tel: 709-726-5250; Fax: 709-738-0614
jwmcgrath@nf.aibn.com

St. John's: Noonan, Oakley - *2
P.O. Box 5303, St. John's, NL A1C 5W1
Tel: 709-726-9598; Fax: 709-726-9614
joakley@nfld.net

St. John's: Earle O'Dea - *15
P.O. Box 5955, 323 Duckworth St., St. John's, NL A1C 5X4
Tel: 709-726-3524; Fax: 709-726-9600
odeaearle@odeaearle.nf.ca
www.odeaearle.nf.ca

St. John's: Ottenheimer Baker - *19
Former Name: White, Ottenheimer & Baker
Baine Johnson Centre, P.O. Box 5457, 10 Fort William Pl., St. John's, NL A1C 5W4
Tel: 709-722-7584; Fax: 709-722-9210
info@ottenheimerbaker.com
www.ottenheimerbaker.com

St. John's: Ottenheimer Boone - *2
8 Albany St., St. John's, NL A1E 3C5
Tel: 709-579-8890; Fax: 709-579-1647

St. John's: Roebothan, McKay & Marshall - *13
Former Name: Williams, Roebothan, McKay & Marshall
P.O. Box 5236, 209 Duckworth St., St. John's, NL A1C 5W1
Tel: 709-753-5805; Fax: 709-753-5221
Toll-Free: 800-563-5563
wrmm@wrmm.nf.net

St. John's: Keith Rose
18 Argyle St., St. John's, NL A1A 1V3
Tel: 709-738-2190; Fax: 709-738-0614

St. John's: Graham A. Wells - *1
P.O. Box 26111, Stn. LeMarchant, 10 Freshwater Rd., St. John's, NL A1C 5T9
Tel: 709-739-7768; Fax: 709-739-4434

Stephenville: Fred R. Stagg, Barrister & Solicitor - *1
28 Main St., Stephenville, NL A2N 2Z4
Tel: 709-643-5651; Fax: 709-643-5369
fstagg@frs-law.com

Northwest Territories

Hay River: MacDonald & Associates - *3
#5, 6 Courtoreille St., Hay River, NT X0E 1G2
Tel: 867-874-6727; Fax: 867-874-6828
dmacdonald@nt.sympatico.ca

Hay River: Stephen M. Shabala - *1
Former Name: Stephen Simpson
#205, 31 Capital Dr., Hay River, NT X0E 1G2
Tel: 867-874-3365; Fax: 867-874-6955

Yellowknife: Denroche & Associates - *3
P.O. Box 2910, Stn. Main, 5107 - 53rd. St., Yellowknife, NT X1A 2R2
Tel: 867-920-4151; Fax: 867-920-4252
reception@denrochelaw.ca
www.denrochelaw.ca

Yellowknife: Peter C. Fuglsang & Associates - *1
P.O. Box 2459, Stn. Main, 4912 - 49 St., Yellowknife, NT X1A 2P8
Tel: 867-920-4344; Fax: 867-873-3386

Yellowknife: Keenan Bengts Law Office - *2
P.O. Box 262, 5018 - 47th St., Yellowknife, NT X1A 2N2
Tel: 867-873-8631; Fax: 867-920-2511
kbengtslaw@theedge.ca

Yellowknife: Marshall & Company - *1
P.O. Box 1236, Stn. Main, 5125 - 48 St., Yellowknife, NT X1A 2N9
Tel: 867-873-4969; Fax: 867-873-6567
mmarshall@marshall.yk.com
www.marshall.yk.com

Yellowknife: Peterson, Stang & Malakoe - *7
P.O. Box 939, 4902 - 49 St., Yellowknife, NT X1A 2N7
Tel: 867-669-8450; Fax: 867-873-6543
lawyers@norlaw.nt.ca
www.norlaw.nt.ca

Yellowknife: Phillips & Wright - *2
#1008, 4920 - 52nd St., Yellowknife, NT X1A 3T1
Tel: 867-873-3335; Fax: 867-873-2773

Yellowknife: Wallbridge & Associates - *3
P.O. Box 383, 5016 - 47th St., Yellowknife, NT X1A 2N3
Tel: 867-920-4000; Fax: 867-920-7389
garth@wallbridgelaw.net

Nova Scotia

Amherst: Beaton, Blaikie, Nurse & Farrell - *3
P.O. Box 295, Amherst, NS B4H 3Z2
Tel: 902-667-0515; Fax: 902-667-6161
bblaw@ns.sympatico.ca

Amherst: Fairbanks Law Office - *1
P.O. Box 103, Amherst, NS B4H 3Y6
Tel: 902-667-7579; Fax: 902-667-0644
william.fairbanks@ns.aliantzinc.ca
www.fairbankslawoffice.com

Amherst: Hicks, LeMoine - *3
P.O. Box 279, 15 Princess St., Amherst, NS B4H 3Z2
Tel: 902-667-7214; Fax: 902-667-5886
info@hickslemoine.ca
www.hickslemoine.ca

Amherst: Jerry Langille, Inc. - *1
P.O. Box 548, 55 Church St., Amherst, NS B4H 4A1
Tel: 902-667-3856; Fax: 902-667-0104
jerry@jllaw.com

Annapolis Royal: Armstrong & Armstrong - *1
P.O. Box 575, Annapolis Royal, NS B0S 1A0
Tel: 902-532-2155; Fax: 902-532-7211
armstrong@ns.aliantzinc.ca

Annapolis Royal: Patricia L. Reardon - *1
P.O. Box 366, 234 St. George St., Annapolis Royal, NS B0S 1A0
Tel: 902-532-7904; Fax: 902-532-7775
preardon@auracom.com

Antigonish: Daniel J. MacIsaac - *1
P.O. Box 1478, Stn. Main, 30 Church St., Antigonish, NS B2G 2L7
Tel: 902-863-5398; Fax: 902-863-9440

Antigonish: MacPherson MacNeil Macdonald - *2
188 Main St., Antigonish, NS B2G 2B9
Tel: 902-863-2925; Fax: 902-863-2925
mthree@eastlink.com

Antigonish: William F. Meehan, Q.C. - *1
P.O. Box 1803, Stn. Main, 195 Main St., Antigonish, NS B2G 2M5
Tel: 902-863-3136; Fax: 902-863-6270
wmeehan@hotmail.com

Arichat: Ivo R. Winter - *1
P.O. Box 180, 14 Bay St., Arichat, NS B0E 1A0
Tel: 902-226-3711; Fax: 902-226-1837
ivowinter@ns.sympatico.ca

Baddeck: Daniel T.L. Chiasson - *1
P.O. Box 567, 137 Upper Twinning St., Baddeck, NS B0E 1B0
Tel: 902-295-1245; Fax: 902-295-2610
dan.baddeck@ns.sympatico.ca

Barrington: G. David Eldridge - *1
P.O. Box 157, 2459 Hwy. 3, Barrington, NS B0W 1E0
Tel: 902-637-2878; Fax: 902-637-2025
eldridgeqc@eastlink.ca

Bedford: Cameron Rhindress - *1
Former Name: Rusk & McCay
1394 Bedford Hwy., Bedford, NS B4A 1E2
Tel: 902-835-7444; Fax: 902-835-3819
crhindross@accesscable.net

Bedford: David J. Cook - *2
#216, 1496 Bedford Hwy., Bedford, NS B4A 1E5
Tel: 902-835-8355; Fax: 902-835-1301
tchambers@accesswave.ca

Bedford: Gillis Associates, Barristers & Solicitors - *2
Former Name: Gillis & Walden
#310, Sun Tower, 1550 Bedford Hwy., Bedford, NS B4A 1E6
Tel: 902-835-6174; Fax: 902-835-1486
Toll-Free: 866-277-3863
admin@gillisassociates.ca
www.gillisassociates.ca

Bedford: Kent & Barrett - *2
#404, 1550 Bedford Hwy., Bedford, NS B4A 1E6
Tel: 902-835-1011; Fax: 902-835-4565

Bedford: Melnick, Doll, Condran - *3
#302, 1160 Bedford Hwy., Bedford, NS B4A 1C1
Tel: 902-835-2300; Fax: 902-835-2303
melnick.doll.condran@ns.sympatico.ca

Bedford: Pressé Mason, Barristers & Solicitors - *4
1254 Bedford Hwy., Bedford, NS B4A 1C6
Tel: 902-832-1175; Fax: 902-832-1856
Toll-Free: 800-630-2254
lawyers@pressemason.ns.ca
www.pressemasonlaw.ca

Berwick: Astek Legal Services - *1
3799 Welsford St., Berwick, NS B0P 1E0
Tel: 902-538-3916; Fax: 902-538-3632
astek1@ns.sympatico.ca

Berwick: Stewart & Turner - *2
P.O. Box 208, 196 Cottage St., Berwick, NS B0P 1E0
Tel: 902-538-3123; Fax: 902-538-7933

* indicates number of lawyers

Berwick: Waterbury Newton - *2
P.O. Box 475, 188 Commercial St., Berwick, NS B0P 1E0
Tel: 902-538-3168; _Fax:_ 902-538-8680
reception@wnns.ca
www.nslawyers.com

Bridgewater: Conrad & Feindel - *3
70 Dufferin St., Bridgewater, NS B4V 2G3
Tel: 902-543-4655; _Fax:_ 902-543-6853
conradfeindel@eastlink.ca

Bridgewater: J. Patrick Morris - *1
344 King St., Bridgewater, NS B4V 1A9
Tel: 902-543-6661; _Fax:_ 902-543-6639
morris@eastlink.ca

Bridgewater: Power, Dempsey, Cooper & Leefe - *5
84 Dufferin St., Bridgewater, NS B4V 2G3
Tel: 902-543-7815; _Fax:_ 902-543-3196
pdclaw@ns.sympatico.ca

Bridgewater: The Law Offices of Timothy A. Reid - *1
176 Aberdeen Rd., Bridgewater, NS B4V 2S9
Tel: 902-543-1303; _Fax:_ 902-543-3243
tareid@ns.sympatico.ca

Bridgewater: Romneylaw Inc. - *2
Former Name: Romney & Romney
P.O. Box 368, 136 Aberdeen Rd., Bridgewater, NS B4V 2W9
Tel: 902-543-4444; _Fax:_ 902-543-0232
romneylaw1@eastlink.ca

Bridgewater: Taylor & Silver - *2
82 Aberdeen Rd., Bridgewater, NS B4V 2S6
Tel: 902-543-0068; _Fax:_ 902-543-7243

Canning: Cornwallis Legal Services - *1
P.O. Box 69, 765 Canard St., Lower Canard, Canning, NS B0P 1H0
Tel: 902-582-3372; _Fax:_ 902-582-3201

Chester: Cassidy Nearing Berryman
27 Pleasant St., Chester, NS B0J 1J0
Tel: 902-275-3032; _Fax:_ 902-423-2485
cassidy@cnb.ca

Chester: Welland & Associates - *1
P.O. Box 504, Chester, NS B0J 1J0
Tel: 902-275-4792; _Fax:_ 902-275-4414
welland@ns.sympatico.ca

Cheticamp: Réjean Aucoin - *1
P.O. Box 328, Cheticamp, NS B0E 1H0
Tel: 902-224-1450; _Fax:_ 902-224-2224
rejean.aucoin@ns.sympatico.ca

Cheticamp: C&E Management Consulting - *1
P.O. Box 972, Cheticamp, NS B0E 1H0
Tel: 902-224-1662;
chester.muise@ns.sympatico.ca

Cheticamp: Carmel A. Lavigne - *1
P.O. Box 579, 15595 Cabot Trail, Cheticamp, NS B0E 1H0
Tel: 902-224-2551; _Fax:_ 902-224-2555
clavigne@ns.sympatico.ca

Dartmouth: Bailey & Associates - *6
#800, 46 Portland St., Dartmouth, NS B2Y 1H4
Tel: 902-465-4888; _Fax:_ 902-465-4844
appointments@baileylawyers.com
www.baileylawyers.com

Dartmouth: Boyne Clarke - *39
#700, Belmont House, P.O. Box 876, 33 Alderney Dr., Dartmouth, NS B2Y 3Z5
Tel: 902-469-9500; _Fax:_ 902-463-7500
Toll-Free: 800-207-6589
info@boyneclarke.ns.ca
www.boyneclarke.ns.ca

Dartmouth: Burton Ronald W. Lawyers - *1
169 Main St., Dartmouth, NS B2X 1S1
Tel: 902-434-4492; _Fax:_ 902-434-5485
burtonl@ns.sympatico.ca

Dartmouth: Casey Rodgers Chisholm Penny - *6
#203, 175 Main St., Dartmouth, NS B2X 1S1
Tel: 902-434-6181; _Fax:_ 902-434-7737
www.crcplaw.com

Dartmouth: Corporate Strategic Consulting - *1
60 Bellbrook Cres., Dartmouth, NS B2W 6S2
Tel: 902-434-3998; _Fax:_ 902-434-8933
richie.mann@ns.sympatico.ca

Dartmouth: David A. Grant - *1
63 Tacoma Dr., Dartmouth, NS B2W 3E7
Tel: 902-463-6300; _Fax:_ 902-435-7910
davidgrant@ns.sympatico.ca

Dartmouth: Heritage House Law Office - *5
92 Ochterloney St., Dartmouth, NS B2Y 1C5
Tel: 902-465-6669; _Fax:_ 902-466-4412
helenf@heritagelaw.ca; cheryla@heritgelaw.ca

Dartmouth: Landry McGillivray, Barristers, Solicitors, Notaries - *10
#300, Quaker Landing, P.O. Box 1200, Stn. Main, 33 Ochterloney St., Dartmouth, NS B2Y 4B8
Tel: 902-463-8800; _Fax:_ 902-463-0590
slg@landrymcgillivray.ns.ca
www.landrymcgillivray.ca

Dartmouth: Langille & Associates - *1
#201, P.O. Box 767, 56 Portland St., Dartmouth, NS B2Y 3Z3
Tel: 902-463-5200; _Fax:_ 902-465-5200
ken.langille@ns.aliantzinc.ca

Dartmouth: Owen & Morrison - *3
#604, Queen Sq., 45 Alderney Dr., Dartmouth, NS B2Y 2N6
Tel: 902-463-8100; _Fax:_ 902-465-2581

Dartmouth: Lester Pyne - *1
194 Caledonia Rd., Dartmouth, NS B2X 1L4
Tel: 902-434-6167; _Fax:_ 902-434-5448

Dartmouth: RAMentor - *1
6 Wyndholme Ave., Dartmouth, NS B2Y 1T3
Tel: 902-464-9628; _Fax:_ 902-461-1350
rmackay1@ns.sympatico.ca

Dartmouth: Sealy Cornish - *4
#200, Box 300, 56 Portland St., Dartmouth, NS B2Y 1H2
Tel: 902-466-2500; _Fax:_ 902-463-0500
sealycornish@scolaw.ns.ca

Dartmouth: Weldon McInnis - *7
118 Ochterloney St., Dartmouth, NS B2Y 1C7
Tel: 902-469-2421; _Fax:_ 902-463-4452
Toll-Free: 800-757-2421
office@weldonmcinnis.ca
www.weldonmcinnis.ca

Dartmouth: Wolfson, Schelew, Zatzman - *3
#500, Bank of Commerce Bldg., P.O. Box 2308, 73 Tacoma Dr., Dartmouth, NS B2W 3Y4
Tel: 902-435-7000; _Fax:_ 902-435-4085
Toll-Free: 888-990-5263
wszlaw@wsz.ns.ca
www.atyp.com/wsz

Digby: Brian E. McConnell - *1
P.O. Box 1239, 3 Birch St., Digby, NS B0V 1A0
Tel: 902-245-5856; _Fax:_ 902-245-6800
bmcconnell@ns.aliantzinc.ca

Digby: James L. Outhouse Q.C. - *1
P.O. Box 1567, 78 Water St., Digby, NS B0V 1A0
Tel: 902-245-2551; _Fax:_ 902-245-6622
jamesouthouse@ns.aliantzinc.ca

Elmsdale: Quigley's Law Office - *1
P.O. Box 653, 214 Hwy. 214, Elmsdale, NS B2S 1J7
Tel: 902-883-2757; _Fax:_ 902-883-4401
kquigleylaw@aol.com

Enfield: Blackburn English - *3
287 Hwy. 2, Enfield, NS B2T 1C9
Tel: 902-883-2264; _Fax:_ 902-883-8744
blackburn.english@ns.sympatico.ca

Fall River: Miller Campbell & Associates
3301 Hwy. 2, Unit A, Fall River, NS B2T 1J2
Tel: 902-860-0030; _Fax:_ 902-865-8262
pbmiller@millercampbell.com

Glace Bay: Crosby, Burke & Macrury
P.O. Box 86, Stn. Main, 38 Union St., Glace Bay, NS B1A 5V1
Tel: 902-849-3971; _Fax:_ 902-849-7009

Glace Bay: McIntyre, Gillis & O'Leary - *2
P.O. Box 187, Stn. Main, 65 Minto St., Glace Bay, NS B1A 5V2
Tel: 902-849-6507; _Fax:_ 902-849-0555
gblaw@auracom.com

Glace Bay: David H. Raniseth - *1
P.O. Box 249, 34 McKeen St., Glace Bay, NS B1A 5B9
Tel: 902-849-0960; _Fax:_ 902-849-6512

Greenwood: David A. Proudfoot Barrister & Solicitor - *1
Former Name: AndersonSinclair
P.O. Box 100, 811 Central Ave., Greenwood, NS B0P 1N0
Tel: 902-765-3301; _Fax:_ 902-765-6493
amplaw2@ns.sympatico.ca

Guysborough: Campbell & MacKeen - *2
P.O. Box 200, 146 Main St., Guysborough, NS B0H 1N0
Tel: 902-533-2644; _Fax:_ 902-533-3526

Halifax: Frederick Angus - *1
#935, 5991 Spring Garden Rd., Halifax, NS B3H 1Y6
Tel: 902-420-9595; _Fax:_ 902-423-8040
fred.angus@ns.sympatico.ca

Halifax: Richard G. Arab - *1
7147 Abbott Dr., Halifax, NS B3J 1L1
Tel: 902-420-9355; _Fax:_ 902-444-3441
rarab@hfx.eastlink.ca

Halifax: Ashworth Dennis - *4
#200, P.O. Box 307, 5162 Duke St., Halifax, NS B3J 2N7
Tel: 902-429-8590; _Fax:_ 902-423-2968
bmtlaw@bmtlaw.ns.ca

Halifax: Auld Allen - *2
1452 Dresden Row, Halifax, NS B3J 3T5
Tel: 902-492-3633; _Fax:_ 902-492-3655
auld@auldallen.ns.ca
www.auldallen.ns.ca

Halifax: Barss, Hare & Turner - *1
#137, Roy Bldg., Stn. Central, 1657 Barrington St., Halifax, NS B3J 2A1
Tel: 902-423-1249

Halifax: Beaton Derrick - *2
1345 Hollis St., Halifax, NS B3J 1T8
Tel: 902-474-7482; _Fax:_ 902-474-8115

Halifax: Beveridge, MacPherson & Duncan - *3
Former Name: Beveridge, Lambert & Duncan
P.O. Box 547, Stn. Central, 1684 Barrington St., 4th Fl., Halifax, NS B3J 2R7
Tel: 902-423-9143; _Fax:_ 902-422-7837

Halifax: Marven C. Block, Q.C. - *1
#305, Coburg Pl., 6389 Coburg Rd., Halifax, NS B3H 2A5
Tel: 902-425-5077; _Fax:_ 902-429-5198
lomar@istar.ca

Halifax: Blois, Nickerson & Bryson - *17
#500, P.O. Box 2147, 1568 Hollis St., Halifax, NS B3J 3B7
Tel: 902-425-6000; _Fax:_ 902-429-7347
info@bloisnickerson.com
www.bloisnickerson.com

Halifax: Burchell Hayman Parish - *23
#1800, 1801 Hollis St., Halifax, NS B3J 3N4
Tel: 902-423-6361; _Fax:_ 902-420-9326
firm@burchells.ca
www.burchells.ca

Halifax: Evangeline Cain-Grant - *1
6156 Quinpool Rd., Halifax, NS B3L 1A3
Tel: 902-422-3500; _Fax:_ 902-422-9660

Halifax: Cantini Law Group
#1301, 2000 Barrington St., Halifax, NS B3J 3K1
Tel: 902-420-9577; _Fax:_ 902-423-0887

Halifax: CFN Consultants - *1
#300, TD Centre, 1791 Barrington St., Halifax, NS B3J 3K9
Tel: 902-491-4279; _Fax:_ 902-429-5237
www.cfnconsultants.com

Halifax: Christie Cuffari Law Office - *1
Former Name: Clare Christie's Law Office
#310, 1657 Barrington St., Halifax, NS B3J 2A1
Tel: 902-422-2297; _Fax:_ 902-422-2162
cclo@ca.inter.net

Halifax: The Law Office of Peter Claman, Q.C. - *1
#1503, P.O. Box 68, 1959 Upper Water St., Halifax, NS B3J 2L4
Tel: 902-492-4000; _Fax:_ 902-492-4001

Halifax: Coady Filliter - *7
#208, 880 Spring Garden Rd., Halifax, NS B3H 1Y1
Tel: 902-429-6264; _Fax:_ 902-423-3044
wroy@coadyfilliter.com

* indicates number of lawyers

***Halifax*: Cooper & McDonald - *6**
Old Auction House, 1669 Granville St., Halifax, NS B3J 1X2
Tel: 902-429-2191; *Fax:* 902-425-3217

***Halifax*: Corporate Communications Limited - *2**
2695 Dutch Village Rd., Halifax, NS B3L 4V2
Tel: 902-421-1777; *Fax:* 902-453-5221

***Halifax*: Corporated Communications Limited - *1**
#400, 7051 Bayers Rd., Halifax, NS B3L 4V2
Tel: 902-722-3150; *Fax:* 902-453-5221

***Halifax*: Cragg & Weir - *3**
6452 Quinpool Rd., Halifax, NS B3L 1A8
Tel: 902-422-1776; *Fax:* 902-429-0016
bob.cragg@ns.sympatico.ca

***Halifax*: Crowe Dillon Robinson - *8**
#2000, 7075 Bayers Rd., Halifax, NS B3L 2C1
Tel: 902-453-1732; *Fax:* 902-454-9948

***Halifax*: Gilles J. Deveau - *1**
P.O. Box 163, Stn. Central, Halifax, NS B3J 2M4
Tel: 902-454-8105; *Fax:* 902-454-4551
gilles.deveau@ns.sympatico.ca

***Halifax*: Kevin P. Downie, Barrister & Solicitor - *1**
#1402, P.O. Box 580, Stn. M, 5121 Sackville St., Halifax, NS B3J 2R7
Tel: 902-425-7233; *Fax:* 902-425-2252
kpdownie@ns.aliantzinc.ca

***Halifax*: Sally B. Faught - *1**
#1307, 2000 Barrington St., Halifax, NS B3J 3K1
Tel: 902-423-8200; *Fax:* 902-423-3100
sbf.gdl@ns.sympatico.ca

***Halifax*: Michael F. Feindel - *1**
Nolan Davis Bldg., P.O. Box 22162, Stn. Bayers, 7020 Mumford Rd., Halifax, NS B3L 4T7
Tel: 902-455-7730; *Fax:* 902-455-7739

***Halifax*: Garson, Knox & MacDonald - *3**
1741 Brunswick St., Halifax, NS B3J 3X8
Tel: 902-425-0222; *Fax:* 902-423-4690

***Halifax*: Gilbert L. Gaudet - *1**
6156 Quinpool Rd., Halifax, NS B3L 1A3
Tel: 902-422-1243

***Halifax*: Simon L. Gaum, Q.C. - *1**
#206, Tower One, Halifax Shopping Centre, 7001 Mumford Rd., Halifax, NS B3L 4N9
Tel: 902-423-6391; *Fax:* 902-455-0974

***Halifax*: Gavras McClure - *2**
Former Name: Pavey Gavras Associates
#300, Vogue Bldg., 1649 Barrington St., Halifax, NS B3J 1Z9
Tel: 902-423-5711; *Fax:* 902-431-9444
jgavras@hfx.eastlink.ca

***Halifax*: Goldberg Thompson - *8**
#400, Sentry Place, 1559 Brunswick St., Halifax, NS B3J 2G1
Tel: 902-421-1161; *Fax:* 902-425-0266
inquiries@uncommonlaw.com
www.goldbergthompson.com

***Halifax*: Harvey Hebert & Manthorne - *5**
Former Name: Harvey & Hebert Affiliated Law Practices
#501, 1819 Granville St., Halifax, NS B3J 1X8
Tel: 902-492-0614; *Fax:* 902-492-0634
Toll-Free: 877-492-0614
general@harveyhebert.com

***Halifax*: Beatrice A. Havlovic - *1**
1459 Brenton St., Halifax, NS B3J 3S7
Tel: 902-423-8100; *Fax:* 902-423-6011
bhavlovic@linguanet.ca

***Halifax*: Haynes Group of Lawyers, Inc. - *4**
Also Known As: Haynes LAW
#200, 1718 Argyle St., Halifax, NS B3J 3N6
Tel: 902-422-8400; *Fax:* 902-422-4465
Toll-Free: 888-880-7774
info@hayneslaw.ca
www.hayneslaw.ca

***Halifax*: Walter E. Hopkins - *1**
#105, 276 Bedford Hwy., Halifax, NS B3M 2K6
Tel: 902-445-2984; *Fax:* 902-445-4333

***Halifax*: Glen E. Jefferson - *1**
40 Gateway Rd., Halifax, NS B3M 1M9
Tel: 902-443-2039; *Fax:* 902-443-6721

***Halifax*: MacDonald Elliott Legal Services - *2**
#343, 7071 Bayers Rd., Halifax, NS B3L 2C2
Tel: 902-454-9827; *Fax:* 902-454-7630
macdonaldlegal@hfx.eastlink.ca

***Halifax*: MacDonald Law Office, Paton & Paton - *1**
12 Robert Allen Dr., Halifax, NS B3M 3G8
Tel: 902-457-5111; *Fax:* 902-457-5113
act@istar.com

***Halifax*: Kenneth A. MacInnis & Associates - *3**
#340, 1801 Hollis St., Halifax, NS B3J 3N4
Tel: 902-421-1817; *Fax:* 902-423-8504

***Halifax*: McGinty McCleave - *3**
#705, Park Lane, Box 227, 5657 Spring Garden Rd., Halifax, NS B3J 3R4
Tel: 902-422-5881; *Fax:* 902-422-5882
mcginty.mccleave@ns.aliantzinc.ca

***Halifax*: Medjuck & Medjuck - *2**
#700, Summit Place, P.O. Box 1074, 1601 Lower Water St., Halifax, NS B3J 2X1
Tel: 902-429-4061; *Fax:* 902-422-7639
medjuck@ns.sympatico.ca

***Halifax*: Merrick Jamieson Sterns Washington & Mahody - *7**
#503, 5475 Spring Garden Rd., Halifax, NS B3J 3T2
Tel: 902-429-3123; *Fax:* 902-429-3522

***Halifax*: Metcalf & Company - *6**
Benjamin Wier House, 1459 Hollis St., Halifax, NS B3J 1V1
Tel: 902-420-1990; *Fax:* 902-429-1171
metcalf&company@metcalf.ns.ca
www.metcalf.ns.ca

***Halifax*: Moore & Associates - *4**
P.O. Box 1537, Stn. Central, 1475 Hollis St., Halifax, NS B3J 2Y3
Tel: 902-420-1066; *Fax:* 902-420-1938
mcm.ma@ns.sympatico.ca

***Halifax*: Morris & Bureau - *3**
#307, 6080 Young St., Halifax, NS B3K 5L2
Tel: 902-454-8070; *Fax:* 902-454-7070

***Halifax*: Andrew Munro - *1**
Former Name: Slone & Munro
#501, 5162 Duke St., Halifax, NS B3J 1N7
Tel: 902-492-3310; *Fax:* 902-492-0013
amunro@eastlink.ca

***Halifax*: John P. Nisbet - *1**
142 Main Ave., Halifax, NS B3M 1B2
Tel: 902-445-3736

***Halifax*: Noseworthy, Di Costanzo, Diab - *3**
Former Name: Thomson, Noseworthy, Di Costanzo
6470 Chebucto Rd., Halifax, NS B3L 1L4
Tel: 902-444-4747; *Fax:* 902-444-4301

***Halifax*: Clyde A. Paul & Associates - *4**
349 Herring Cove Rd., Halifax, NS B3R 1V9
Tel: 902-477-2518; *Fax:* 902-479-1482
capaul@ns.sympatico.ca

***Halifax*: Pink, Joel E. Q.C., & Associates, Barristers & Solicitors - *3**
#300, 1583 Hollis St., Halifax, NS B3H 2P8
Tel: 902-492-0550; *Fax:* 902-492-0570
www.criminaldefence.com

***Halifax*: Quackenbush, Thomson & Robbins - *5**
2571 Windsor St., Halifax, NS B3K 5C4
Tel: 902-492-1655; *Fax:* 902-492-1697
qtr@qtrlaw.com

***Halifax*: Ritch Durnford, Lawyers - *16**
Former Name: Huestis Ritch
#1200, CIBC Bldg., 1809 Barrington St., Halifax, NS B3J 3K8
Tel: 902-429-3400; *Fax:* 902-422-4713
info@ritchdurnford.com; library@ritchdurnford.com
www.ritchdurnford.com

***Halifax*: Joseph S. Roza - *1**
#210, 6021 Young St., Halifax, NS B3K 2A1
Tel: 902-425-5111; *Fax:* 902-425-5112
j.roza@ns.sympatico.ca
www.josephroza.com

***Halifax*: Scaravelli & Associates - *5**
#2030, 1801 Hollis St., Halifax, NS B3J 3N4
Tel: 902-429-4104; *Fax:* 902-423-4009
Toll-Free: 877-429-4104

***Halifax*: Singleton & Associates - *2**
Former Name: Singleton Morrison
2579 Windsor St., Halifax, NS B3K 5C4
Tel: 902-492-7000; *Fax:* 902-492-4309
tsingleton@singleton.ns.ca

***Halifax*: Stockton, Maxwell & Elliott - *3**
6309 Chebucto Rd., Halifax, NS B3L 1K9
Tel: 902-422-6055; *Fax:* 902-429-7655

***Halifax*: Wagner & Associates - *5**
1869 Upper Water St., Halifax, NS B3J 1S9
Tel: 902-425-7330; *Fax:* 902-422-1233
Toll-Free: 800-465-8794
seriousinjury@wagnerlaw.ca
www.wagnerandassociates.com

***Halifax*: Walker's Law Office Inc. - *1**
Former Name: Walker & Associates
6221 Jubilee Rd., Halifax, NS B3H 2G3
Tel: 902-425-5297; *Fax:* 902-425-5095
catherinewalker@eastlink.ca

***Halifax*: Walker, Dunlop - *6**
PO Box 36057, RPO Spring Garden, Halifax, NS B3J 3J1
Tel: 902-423-8121; *Fax:* 902-429-0621
walker.dunlop@ns.sympatico.ca

***Halifax*: Wickwire Holm - *22**
Former Name: Merrick Holm
#2100, P.O. Box 1054, 1801 Hollis St., Halifax, NS B3J 2X6
Tel: 902-429-4111; *Fax:* 902-429-8215
Toll-Free: 866-429-4111
wh@wickwireholm.com
www.wickwireholm.com

***Halifax*: Warren K. Zimmer - *1**
#200, P.O. Box 786, 5162 Duke St., Halifax, NS B3J 2V2
Tel: 902-429-7787; *Fax:* 902-429-7788
wkzimmer@istar.ca

***Halifax*: Diane K. Zwicker - *1**
1561 Vernon St., Halifax, NS B3H 3M8
Tel: 902-425-2193;
dzwicker@sprint.ca

***Kentville*: Forse, Nathanson - *2**
P.O. Box 655, 325 Main St., Kentville, NS B4N 3X7
Tel: 902-678-1616; *Fax:* 902-678-1615
Toll-Free: 800-667-3879

***Kentville*: Donald C. Fraser - *1**
P.O. Box 668, Stn. Main, 35R Webster St., Kentville, NS B4N 3X9
Tel: 902-678-4006; *Fax:* 902-678-2999
fraser.law@ns.aliantzinc.ca

***Kentville*: Manning & Associates - *1**
27 Cornwallis St., Kentville, NS B4N 2E2
Tel: 902-679-1600; *Fax:* 902-679-5122
chris.manning@manningassociates.ca

***Kentville*: Muttarts Law Firm - *7**
Also Known As: Muttart Tufts Dewolfe & Coyle
P.O. Box 515, 20 Cornwallis St., Kentville, NS B4N 3X3
Tel: 902-678-2157; *Fax:* 902-678-9455
mtdc_law@mtdc.ns.ca
www.mtdc.ns.ca

***Kentville*: Tayllor MacLellan Cochrane - *1**
Also Known As: TMC Law
50 Cornwallis St., Kentville, NS B4N 2E4
Tel: 902-678-6156; *Fax:* 902-678-6010
Toll-Free: 888-486-2529
lawfirm@tmclaw.com
www.tmclaw.com

***Lake Echo*: Randy Price Consulting Ltd. - *1**
1 Country Lake Dr., Lake Echo, NS B3E 1E4
Tel: 902-446-0857; *Fax:* 902-446-0857

***Liverpool*: Allen C. Fownes - *1**
#188, P.O. Box 1739, 190 Main St., Liverpool, NS B0T 1K0
Tel: 902-354-2744; *Fax:* 902-354-2746
acfownes@novascotialaw.com
www.novascotialaw.com

***Liverpool*: Tutty & DiPersio - *2**
#167, P.O. Box 760, 171 Main St., Liverpool, NS B0T 1K0
Tel: 902-354-5756; *Fax:* 902-354-7395

** indicates number of lawyers*

***Lower Sackville*: David F. Farwell - *1**
Former Name: Farwell & Hines
#206, Vogue Optical Plaza, 405 Sackville Dr., Lower Sackville, NS B4C 2R9
Tel: 902-865-5537; *Fax:* 902-865-4354
davidfarwell@ns.sympatico.ca

***Lower Sackville*: Robert W. Newman & Associates - *1**
85 Sackville Cross Rd., Lower Sackville, NS B4C 2M2
Tel: 902-864-2722; *Fax:* 902-864-3164
robert.newman@ns.sympatico.ca

***Lower Sackville*: Richardson's Law Office - *2**
#100A, 800 Sackville Dr., Lower Sackville, NS B4E 1R8
Tel: 902-864-2300; *Fax:* 902-864-4410
Toll-Free: 877-304-2300
richardson@novalawyer.com
www.novalawyer.com

***Lunenburg*: Burke & Macdonald - *2**
P.O. Box 549, 28 King St., Lunenburg, NS B0J 2C0
Tel: 902-634-8354; *Fax:* 902-634-4226

***Martock*: Foxcreek Consulting Services - *1**
383 Windsor Backroad, RR#1, Martock, NS B0N 2T0
Tel: 902-497-1691;
foxcreek@ns.sympatico.ca

***Middleton*: Cole Sawler - *2**
P.O. Box 400, 264 Main St., Middleton, NS B0S 1P0
Tel: 902-825-6288; *Fax:* 902-825-4340
officemanager@colesawlerlaw.ca
www.colesawlerlaw.ca

***Middleton*: C. Hanson Dowell Q.C. - *1**
Former Name: Hanson T. Dowell Q.C.
P.O. Box 910, 250 Main St., Middleton, NS B0S 1P0
Tel: 902-825-3059; *Fax:* 902-825-3154
lawdow@ns.sympatico.ca

***Middleton*: Durland, Gillis & Schumacher, Associates - *2**
Former Name: Durland Gillis Parker & Richter
P.O. Box 700, 74 Commercial St., Middleton, NS B0S 1P0
Tel: 902-825-3415; *Fax:* 902-825-2522

***Musquodoboit Harbour*: Eastern Shore Law Centre - *1**
P.O. Box 357, 1653 Ostrea Lake Rd., Musquodoboit Harbour, NS B0J 2L0
Tel: 902-889-3796; *Fax:* 902-889-3735
easternshorelaw@aol.com
www.easternshorelaw.com

***New Glasgow*: R.A. Balmanoukian - *1**
137 McColl St., New Glasgow, NS B2H 4Z6
Tel: 902-755-3393; *Fax:* 902-755-6373
blackacre@north.nsis.com

***New Glasgow*: Goodman MacDonald & Patterson - *3**
P.O. Box 697, Stn. Main, 47 Riverside Dr., New Glasgow, NS B2H 5G2
Tel: 902-752-5090; *Fax:* 902-755-3545

***New Glasgow*: MacIntosh, MacDonnell & MacDonald - *10**
#260, Aberdeen Business Centre, P.O. Box 368, Stn. Main, 610 East River Rd., 2nd Fl., New Glasgow, NS B2H 5E5
Tel: 902-752-8441; *Fax:* 902-752-7810
Toll-Free: 888-752-8441
office@macmacmac.ns.ca

***New Waterford*: Charles Broderick - *1**
P.O. Box 151, 3316 Plummer Ave., New Waterford, NS B1H 4K4
Tel: 902-862-6471; *Fax:* 902-862-9513
cblaw@istar.ca

***New Waterford*: M. Sweeney Hinchey - *1**
3383 Plummer Ave., New Waterford, NS B1H 1Z1
Tel: 902-862-2368; *Fax:* 902-862-9581
hinchems@yahoo.com

***North Sydney*: M. Mora B. Maclennan - *1**
33 Archibald Ave., North Sydney, NS B2A 2W6
Tel: 902-794-2060; *Fax:* 902-794-3558

***North Sydney*: Michael A. Tobin - *1**
P.O. Box 1925, Stn. Main, 254 Commercial St., North Sydney, NS B2A 3S9
Tel: 902-794-8803; *Fax:* 902-794-9869
miketobinlaw@syd.eastlink.ca

***Pictou*: MacLean & MacDonald - *2**
P.O. Box 730, 90 Coleraine St., Pictou, NS B0K 1H0
Tel: 902-485-4347; *Fax:* 902-485-8887
law@macleanmacdonald.com

***Pictou*: Scanlan Graham Scanlan - *2**
P.O. Box 1720, 94 Water St., Pictou, NS B0K 1H0
Tel: 902-485-4313; *Fax:* 902-485-5083
sgslaw@ns.sympatico.ca

***Port Hawkesbury*: Pickup & MacDowell - *2**
#2, 308 Philpott St., Port Hawkesbury, NS B9A 2B8
Tel: 902-625-2500; *Fax:* 902-625-0500
pkpmd@auracom.com

***Port Hood*: Francis X. Moloney - *1**
P.O. Box 122, 351 Main St., Port Hood, NS B0E 2W0
Tel: 902-787-3113; *Fax:* 902-787-3105

***Pubnico*: d'Entremont & Boudreau - *2**
P.O. Box 118, Pubnico, NS B0W 2W0
Tel: 902-762-3119; *Fax:* 902-762-3124
rjboudreau@klis.com

***Shelburne*: Celia J. Melanson, Barristor & Solicitor, Inc. - *1**
P.O. Box 562, 171 Water St., Shelburne, NS B0T 1W0
Tel: 902-875-4188; *Fax:* 902-875-1316
celia.melanson@ns.sympatico.ca
www.celiamelanson.com

***Shelburne*: Donald R. Miller - *1**
6767 Shore Rd. RR#3, Shelburne, NS B0T 1W0
Tel: 902-637-2527; *Fax:* 902-637-2165

***Shelburne*: Johanne L. Tournier - *1**
Shelburne Industrial Park, Site 3, Comp. 4, RR#2, Shelburne, NS B0T 1W0
Tel: 902-875-4753; *Fax:* 902-875-3783
jasmith77@juno.com

***Sherbrooke*: Robin W. Archibald - *1**
P.O. Box 176, Sherbrooke, NS B0J 3C0
Tel: 902-522-2067; *Fax:* 902-522-2299
robinlaw@auracom.com

***Shubenacadie*: Carruthers & MacDonell Law Office Inc. - *3**
Chubenacadie Professional Centre, P.O. Box 280, #204, 5 Mill Village Rd., Shubenacadie, NS B0N 2H0
Tel: 902-758-2591; *Fax:* 902-758-4022

***Stellarton*: Hector J. MacIsaac - *1**
P.O. Box 849, 253 Foord St., Stellarton, NS B0K 1S0
Tel: 902-752-5143; *Fax:* 902-928-1299

***Stellarton*: R.E. O'Blenis - *1**
P.O. Box 1500, 179 Foord St., Stellarton, NS B0K 1S0
Tel: 902-752-1575

***Stellarton*: Skoke & Company**
P.O. Box 850, Foord St., Stellarton, NS B0K 1S0
Tel: 902-755-5711; *Fax:* 902-752-6561

***Sydney*: Anderson, Nathanson - *1**
P.O. Box 79, Stn. Pier Post., 797 Victoria Rd., Sydney, NS B1N 3B1
Tel: 902-849-5110; *Fax:* 902-849-6110
andnat@andersonnathanson.com

***Sydney*: Cusack Law Office - *1**
205 Charlotte St., Sydney, NS B1P 1C4
Tel: 902-564-8396; *Fax:* 902-564-0030
cusacklaw@ns.sympatico.ca

***Sydney*: Vincent A. Gillis - *1**
P.O. Box 847, Stn. A, 321 Townsend St., Sydney, NS B1P 6J1
Tel: 902-562-3222; *Fax:* 902-539-4199
vagillislaw@ns.sympatico.ca

***Sydney*: Khattar & Khattar - *6**
P.O. Box 387, 378 Charlotte St., Sydney, NS B1P 6H2
Tel: 902-539-9696; *Fax:* 902-562-7147
Toll-Free: 888-542-8827
elaine@khattar.ca

***Sydney*: John G. Khattar - *1**
P.O. Box 1626, 463 Prince St., Sydney, NS B1P 5L6
Tel: 902-564-6611; *Fax:* 902-564-8805
jkhatter@syd.eastlink.ca

***Sydney*: Lorway MacEachern - *4**
112 Charlotte St., Sydney, NS B1P 1B9
Tel: 902-539-4447; *Fax:* 902-564-9844
northlaw@cbnet.ns.ca

***Sydney*: MacDonald & MacLennan - *1**
P.O. Box 1148, 275 Charlotte St., Sydney, NS B1P 6J7
Tel: 902-564-4429; *Fax:* 902-539-2303

***Sydney*: H.F. MacIntyre & Associates - *2**
P.O. Box 788, Stn. A, 245 Charlotte St., Sydney, NS B1P 6J1
Tel: 902-562-4224; *Fax:* 902-562-0606
macintyre.assoc@ns.sympatico.ca

***Sydney*: Hugh R. McLeod - *1**
P.O. Box 306, 275 Charlotte St., Sydney, NS B1P 6H2
Tel: 902-539-2261; *Fax:* 902-539-3386
hugh.mcleod@ns.sympatico.ca

***Sydney*: John W. Morgan - *1**
29 Riverdale Dr., Sydney, NS B1R 1P2
Tel: 902-539-2800; *Fax:* 902-563-5585
jwmorgan@cbrm.ns.ca

***Sydney*: Ralph W. Ripley Barrister & Solicitor Inc. - *1**
#202, P.O. Box 7, 295 Charlotte St., Sydney, NS B1P 6G9
Tel: 902-564-4446; *Fax:* 902-539-7765
rripley@ns.aliantzinc.ca

***Sydney*: M. Joseph Rizzetto - *1**
#206, 275 Charlotte St., 2nd Fl., Sydney, NS B1P 1C6
Tel: 902-562-6262; *Fax:* 902-539-3567
info@rizzetto.ns.ca

***Sydney*: Rudderham Chernin Law Office Inc. - *2**
500 George St., Sydney, NS B1P 1K6
Tel: 902-567-0250; *Fax:* 902-567-0252
info@rclaw.ns.ca

***Truro*: Archibald Lederman - *2**
P.O. Box 1100, Stn. Main, 43 Walker St., Truro, NS B2N 5G9
Tel: 902-895-0524; *Fax:* 902-893-7608
plederman@archibaldlederman.ca

***Truro*: Burchell, MacDougall - *18**
P.O. Box 1128, 710 Prince St., Truro, NS B2N 5H1
Tel: 902-895-1561; *Fax:* 902-895-7709
Toll-Free: 800-565-1200
truro@burchellmacdougall.com
www.burchellmacdougall.com

***Truro*: David F. Curtis Q.C. - *1**
#202, P.O. Box 458, 640 Prince St., Truro, NS B2N 1G4
Tel: 902-895-0528; *Fax:* 902-893-1158
dcurtislaw@ns.aliantzinc.ca

***Truro*: Melinda J. MacLean, Q.C. - *1**
P.O. Box 126, Stn. Main, 188 Queen St., Truro, NS B2N 5B6
Tel: 902-895-2866; *Fax:* 902-893-1455

***Truro*: McLellan, Richards & Bégin - *2**
P.O. Box 1064, 779 Prince St., Truro, NS B2N 5G9
Tel: 902-895-4417; *Fax:* 902-897-9890
Toll-Free: 866-600-0011
www.truro-law.com

***Truro*: Gerard P. Scanlan - *1**
P.O. Box 1228, Stn. Main, 640 Prince St., Truro, NS B2N 5N2
Tel: 902-895-9249; *Fax:* 902-893-3078
scanpayn@tru.eastlink.ca

***Truro*: Yuill Chisholm Killawee - *2**
541 Prince St., Truro, NS B2N 1E8
Tel: 902-893-0243; *Fax:* 902-897-0282

***Upper Tantallon*: Smith-Camp & Associates - *1**
#203, 5209 St. Margaret's Bay Rd., Upper Tantallon, NS B3Z 1E3
Tel: 902-826-2193; *Fax:* 902-826-1043
smithcamplaw@hotmail.com

***Waverley*: David Chown Consulting - *1**
P.O. Box 5095, Waverley, NS B2R 1S2
Tel: 902-860-1104; *Fax:* 902-860-2655

***Westville*: S. Charles Facey, Q.C. - *1**
P.O. Box 610, 1912 Drummond Rd., Westville, NS B0K 2A0
Tel: 902-396-4191; *Fax:* 902-396-3606
charles.facey@ns.sympatico.ca

** indicates number of lawyers*

***Windsor*: Adams & Company - *2**
P.O. Box 2379, 189 Gerrish St., Windsor, NS B0N 2T0
Tel: 902-798-8384; *Fax:* 902-798-0432
hadams.adamsco@ns.sympatico.ca

***Windsor*: How Lawrence White Bowes - *3**
P.O. Box 3177, 98 Gerrish St., Windsor, NS B0N 2T0
Tel: 902-798-5997; *Fax:* 902-798-8925
jjwhite@scotialaw.com; dbowes@scotialaw.com
www.scotialaw.com

***Windsor*: Nelson Law - *2**
Former Name: Nelson Gardiner
P.O. Box 2018, 258 King St., Windsor, NS B0N 2T0
Tel: 902-798-5797; *Fax:* 902-798-2332
nelson.law@ns.sympatico.ca

***Windsor*: John D. Romans - *1**
P.O. Box 1024, 140 King St., Windsor, NS B0N 2T0
Tel: 902-798-8311

***Wolfville*: Kimball Brogan Law Office - *4**
121 Front St., Wolfville, NS B4P 1A6
Tel: 902-542-5757; *Fax:* 902-542-5759
Toll-Free: 800-294-7851
info@kimballbrogan.ca
www.kimballbrogan.ca

***Wolfville*: Dianne E. Thompson-Sheppard, Q.C. - *1**
80 Kent Ave., Wolfville, NS B4P 1V1
Tel: 902-542-2388; *Fax:* 902-542-0794
paddles@ns.sympatico.ca

***Yarmouth*: R.K. Murray Judge - *1**
28 Ellis Ave., Yarmouth, NS B5A 2X2
Tel: 902-742-0383; *Fax:* 902-742-2300

Nunavut

***Iqaluit*: Chandler & Cooper - *2**
P.O. Box 2021, Iqaluit, NU X0A 0H0
Tel: 867-979-3505; *Fax:* 867-979-3506
norhtlaw@nunanet.com

***Iqaluit*: McIsaac, Penner - *3**
Maliiganik Tukisiiniakvik Society, P.O. Box 29, Iqaluit, NU X0A 0H0
Tel: 867-979-5377; *Fax:* 867-979-4346

Ontario

***Ajax*: William E. Foden - *2**
572 Kingston Rd. West, Ajax, ON L1T 3A2
Tel: 905-428-8200; *Fax:* 905-428-8666
foden@on.aibn.com

***Ajax*: Glover & Associates, Barristers, Solicitors, Notaries**
Former Name: Glover, Darryl T.G
562 Kingston Rd. West, Ajax, ON L1T 3A2
Tel: 905-619-3700; *Fax:* 905-619-0022
info@gloverlaw.ca
www.gloverlaw.ca

***Ajax*: Greening & Bucknam - *1**
#202, 50 Commercial Ave., Ajax, ON L1S 2H5
Tel: 905-683-7037; *Fax:* 905-683-7627
bucknam@rogers.com

***Ajax*: Graham F. Pinos, Q.C. - *1**
31 Leah Cres., Ajax, ON L1T 3J2
Tel: 416-428-6838; *Fax:* 416-428-0212
graham.pinos@rogers.com

***Ajax*: Reilly D'Heureux Lanzi LLP - *4**
Pickering Village, 555 Kingston Rd. West, 2nd Fl., Ajax, ON L1S 6M1
Tel: 905-427-4077; *Fax:* 905-427-4042
mpreilly@reillylegal.com
www.reillylegal.com

***Ajax*: Singh, Tucciarone - *2**
#206, 158 Harwood Ave. South, Ajax, ON L1S 2H6
Tel: 905-683-1042; *Fax:* 905-683-7794
Toll-Free: 800-801-4602
singh-tucciarone@on.aibn.com

***Ajax*: Juanita Wislesky - *1**
#202, 15 Harwood Rd. Ave. South, Ajax, ON L1S 2B9
Tel: 905-686-1686;
juanita_wislesky@yahoo.ca

***Ajax*: George D. Wright - *1**
543 Kingston Rd. West, Ajax, ON L1S 6M1
Tel: 905-427-7200; *Fax:* 905-427-2999

***Alexandria*: Jean-Marc Lefebvre, Q.C. - *2**
P.O. Box 519, 32 Main St. North, Alexandria, ON K0C 1A0
Tel: 613-525-1358; *Fax:* 613-525-3411
lefebvre@bellnet.ca

***Alexandria*: Nelligan O'Brien Payne - *46**
139 Main St. South, Alexandria, ON K0C 1A0
Tel: 613-525-2396; *Fax:* 613-525-2752
Toll-Free: 888-565-9912
info@nelligan.ca
www.nelligan.ca

***Allenford*: Richard R. Evans - *1**
P.O. Box 14, 7771 Hwy. 21, Allenford, ON N0H 1A0
Tel: 519-934-2875; *Fax:* 519-934-1460
rrevans@bmts.com

***Alliston*: John W. Clarke - *1**
#3, P.O. Box 408, Stn. Main, 103 Victoria St. West, Alliston, ON L9R 1V6
Tel: 705-435-4301; *Fax:* 705-435-3407

***Alliston*: Mary L. Galbraith - *1**
Former Name: Darling, Smith, McLean
22 Church St. South, Alliston, ON L9R 1V9
Tel: 705-435-4324; *Fax:* 705-435-2628

***Alliston*: Gilmore & Gilmore - *2**
P.O. Box 250, 458 Victoria St. East, Alliston, ON L9R 1V5
Tel: 705-435-4339; *Fax:* 705-435-6520
Toll-Free: 877-855-3425
info@gilmoreandgilmore.com
www.gilmoreandgilmore.com

***Alliston*: James W. Smith - *1**
P.O. Box 730, Stn. Main, 8 Victoria St. East, Alliston, ON L9R 1V9
Tel: 705-435-0160; *Fax:* 705-435-5049
jsmithl@bellnet.ca

***Almonte*: L.G. William Chapman - *1**
P.O. Box 362, 77 Little Bridge St., Almonte, ON K0A 1A0
Tel: 613-256-3072; *Fax:* 613-256-5164
lgwilliamchapman@bellnet.ca
www.lgwilliamchapman.com

***Almonte*: Elizabeth A. Swarbrick - *4**
#107, P.O. Box 639, 83 Little Bridge St., Almonte, ON K0A 1A0
Tel: 613-256-9811; *Fax:* 613-256-9814
elizabeth@familyfocusedlaw.com
www.familyfocusedlaw.com

***Almonte*: Evelyn Wheeler - *1**
P.O. Box 1540, 38 Mill St., Almonte, ON K0A 1A0
Tel: 613-256-4148; *Fax:* 613-256-4708
www.evelynwheeler.com

***Amherstburg*: Baker Busch - *2**
41 Sandwich St. South, Amherstburg, ON N9V 1Z5
Tel: 519-736-2154; *Fax:* 519-736-2466

***Amherstburg*: Robert D. McKerrow - *1**
57 Richmond St., Amherstburg, ON N9V 1G1
Tel: 519-736-8555; *Fax:* 519-736-1413
rkrow@bellnet.ca

***Amherstview*: William E.M. Vince - *1**
6 Speers Blvd., #G, Amherstview, ON K7N 1Z6
Tel: 613-389-6727; *Fax:* 613-389-6256
wvince@cogeco.ca

***Ancaster*: G. Kevin Eggleton - *1**
#110, 911 Golf Links Rd., Ancaster, ON L9K 1H9
Tel: 905-304-5297; *Fax:* 905-304-7711

***Ancaster*: Randy L. Levinson - *1**
58 Cumming Ct., Ancaster, ON L9G 1V3
Tel: 905-648-7239; *Fax:* 905-648-4437
randy@randylevinson.com
www.randylevinson.com

***Ancaster*: Wynne, Dingwall & Pringle - *3**
Former Name: Wynne & Dingwall
Stn. Ancaster, 231 Wilson St. East, #B, Ancaster, ON L9G 2B8
Tel: 905-648-1851; *Fax:* 905-648-1715
www.ancasterlaw.com

***Angus*: Gordon R. MacKenzie Professional Corporation - *1**
Former Name: MacKenzie, Greenfield
P.O. Box 600, Unit A, 189 Mill St., Angus, ON L0M 1B2
Tel: 705-424-1331; *Fax:* 705-424-6441
gmackenzie@on.aibn.com
www.yourlocallawyer.com

***Arnprior*: M. Martha Coady - *1**
32 John St. North, Arnprior, ON K7S 2N2
Tel: 613-623-7327; *Fax:* 613-623-8506

***Arnprior*: Pamela R. LeMay - *1**
64 McGonigal St. West, Arnprior, ON K7S 1M1
Tel: 613-623-7705; *Fax:* 613-623-2189
plemay@lemaylaw.ca

***Arnprior*: C.P. Merla - *1**
#4, 75 Elgin St. West, Arnprior, ON K7S 3T9
Tel: 613-623-6593; *Fax:* 613-623-8947

***Aurora*: Gordon F. Allan - *1**
12 St. John's Sideroad East, Aurora, ON L4G 3G8
Tel: 905-895-3425; *Fax:* 905-726-3098

***Aurora*: Boland Howe Barristers LLP - *5**
130 Industrial Pkwy. North, Aurora, ON L4G 4C3
Tel: 905-841-5717; *Fax:* 905-841-7128
info@bolandhowe.com
www.bolandhowe.com

***Aurora*: Di Cecco, Jones - *2**
#205, 15171 Yonge St., Aurora, ON L4G 1M1
Tel: 905-751-1517; *Fax:* 905-751-1518
dicecco.jones@diceccojones.com

***Aurora*: Laurion Law Office - *1**
41 Wellington St. East, Aurora, ON L4G 1H6
Tel: 905-841-2222; *Fax:* 905-841-3388
jlaurion@laurionlaw.com

***Aurora*: Barry W. Switzer - *1**
P.O. Box 246, 15187 Yonge St., Aurora, ON L4G 1L8
Tel: 905-727-9488; *Fax:* 905-841-8647

***Aurora*: Thomas McPherson & Associates - *2**
Former Name: McPherson, Thomas & Associates
P.O. Box 338, 15220 Yonge St., Aurora, ON L4G 3H4
Tel: 905-727-3151; *Fax:* 905-841-2164
mcpherson@auroralaw.net
www.mcphersonassoc.yp.ca

***Aylmer*: Doyle & Prendergast - *2**
10 Sydenham St. East, Aylmer, ON N5H 1L2
Tel: 519-773-3105; *Fax:* 519-765-1728

***Aylmer*: Gloin, Hall & Shields - *4**
139 Talbot St. East, Aylmer, ON N5H 1H3
Tel: 519-773-9221; *Fax:* 519-765-1885
ghsaylaw@amtelecom.net

***Bancroft*: Glenna M. Ireland - *1**
P.O. Box 1361, 11 Fairway Blvd., Bancroft, ON K0L 1C0
Tel: 613-332-0406; *Fax:* 613-332-0609

***Bancroft*: L.C. Plater - *1**
P.O. Box 1150, 129 Hastings St. North, Bancroft, ON K0L 1C0
Tel: 613-332-1605; *Fax:* 613-332-2619

***Bancroft*: Robert C. Henderson & Associates - *2**
P.O. Box 225, 51 Hastings St. North, Bancroft, ON K0L 1C0
Tel: 613-332-0500; *Fax:* 613-332-5733
rchenderson@bellnet.ca

***Barrie*: Nancy Lee Allison - *1**
P.O. Box 308, 285 Grove Street East, Barrie, ON L4M 2R2
Tel: 705-737-5702; *Fax:* 705-737-1614
nlalliso@csolve.net

***Barrie*: John G. Alousis - *1**
76 Mulcaster St., Barrie, ON L4M 3M4
Tel: 705-735-0065; *Fax:* 705-735-0277
john@alousislaw.com
www.alousislaw.com

***Barrie*: Peter D. Archibald - *1**
P.O. Box 907, 59 Collier St., Barrie, ON L4M 4Y6
Tel: 705-726-4511; *Fax:* 705-726-0613
pda@bconnex.net

** indicates number of lawyers*

***Barrie*: Brian Bond**
25 Poyntz St., Barrie, ON L4M 3N8
Tel: 705-734-1550; *Fax:* 705-734-0306
bwb@bondlaw.ca

***Barrie*: Susan Joyce Brenner - *1**
130 Collier St., Barrie, ON L4M 1H3
Tel: 705-734-1801; *Fax:* 705-734-2324

***Barrie*: Thomas Bryson - *1**
11 Sophia St. West, Barrie, ON L4N 1H9
Tel: 705-728-2232; *Fax:* 705-728-7525
tbrysonlaw@bellnet.ca

***Barrie*: Burgar, Rowe - *18**
P.O. Box 758, 90 Mulcaster St., Barrie, ON L4M 4Y5
Tel: 705-721-3377; *Fax:* 705-721-4025
burgarrowe@burgarrowe.com
www.burgarrowe.com

***Barrie*: Peter C. Card - *1**
111 Toronto St., Barrie, ON L4N 1V1
Tel: 705-739-9111; *Fax:* 705-739-8111

***Barrie*: Carroll Heyd Chown - *5**
#20, P.O. Box 548, 556 Bryne Dr., Barrie, ON L4M 4T7
Tel: 705-722-4400; *Fax:* 705-722-0704
admin@chcbarristers.com

***Barrie*: Cowan & Carter - *1**
P.O. Box 722, 107 Collier St., Barrie, ON L4M 4Y5
Tel: 705-728-4521; *Fax:* 705-728-8744

***Barrie*: Craig Boswell McDermot - *4**
158 Dunlop St. East, Barrie, ON L4M 1B1
Tel: 705-734-2911; *Fax:* 705-734-2047

***Barrie*: Cugelman & Eisen - *2**
#201, 28 Owen St., Barrie, ON L4M 3G7
Tel: 705-721-1888; *Fax:* 705-721-7755
cugelman@cugelmaneisen.com
www.cugelmaneisen.com

***Barrie*: Alfred W.J. Dick - *1**
80 Worsley St., Barrie, ON L4M 1L8
Tel: 705-728-9006; *Fax:* 705-728-9876

***Barrie*: Julianne Ecclestone - *1**
80 Worsley St., Barrie, ON L4M 1L8
Tel: 705-725-8050; *Fax:* 705-722-0189

***Barrie*: Brian G. Galbraith - *4**
Former Name: Brian G. Galbraith
124 Dunlop St. West, Barrie, ON L4N 1B1
Tel: 705-727-4242; *Fax:* 705-727-4240
Brian@GalbraithFamilyLaw.com
www.galbraithfamilylaw.com

***Barrie*: Klaus N. Jacoby - *1**
P.O. Box 350, 34 Clapperton St., Barrie, ON L4M 4T5
Tel: 705-726-0238; *Fax:* 705-726-9197
jaco@jacobylaw.ca

***Barrie*: Mark A. Kelly - *1**
43 Worsley St., Barrie, ON L4M 1L7
Tel: 705-739-6955; *Fax:* 705-739-6956
markkelly@bellnet.ca

***Barrie*: Peter Lamprey - *1**
78 Worsley St., Barrie, ON L4M 1L8
Tel: 705-722-1114; *Fax:* 705-720-1155
peter@plamprey.com
www.plamprey.com

***Barrie*: Christine D. Lunn - *1**
118 Collier St., Barrie, ON L4M 1H4
Tel: 705-739-0929; *Fax:* 705-725-7977

***Barrie*: McLellan Associates - The Law Store - *1**
510 Bayfield St., Barrie, ON L4M 4S5
Tel: 705-726-7765; *Fax:* 705-726-8071

***Barrie*: J. Marvin Menzies - *1**
#104, P.O. Box 1175, Stn. Main, 89 Dunlop St. East, Barrie, ON L4M 5E2
Tel: 705-722-5432; *Fax:* 705-722-0218
marvinmenzies@on.aibn.com

***Barrie*: R. John Mitchell - *1**
P.O. Box 1, 40 Clapperton St., Barrie, ON L4M 4S9
Tel: 705-726-8855; *Fax:* 705-721-0782

***Barrie*: Murray/Ralston - *3**
119 Collier St., Barrie, ON L4M 1H5
Tel: 705-737-3229; *Fax:* 705-737-5380
admin@murraytalston.com
www.murrayralston.com

***Barrie*: Gerald E. Norman - *1**
P.O. Box 732, 99 Bayfield St., Barrie, ON L4M 4Y5
Tel: 705-726-2772; *Fax:* 705-734-1942
geraldnorman@normanlawoffice.ca
www.normanlawoffice.ca

***Barrie*: Oatley, Vigmond, Personal Injury Lawyers LLP - *14**
151 Ferris Lane, Barrie, ON L4M 6C1
Tel: 705-726-9021; *Fax:* 705-726-2132
Toll-Free: 888-662-2481
info@oatleyvigmond.com
www.oatleyvigmond.com

***Barrie*: Owen, Harris-Lowe - *4**
Former Name: Owen, Dickey
P.O. Box 848, 26 Owen St., Barrie, ON L4M 4Y6
Tel: 705-726-1181; *Fax:* 705-726-1463
odlaw@owendickey.com
www.owendickey.com

***Barrie*: Michael E. Reed - *1**
105 Collier St., Barrie, ON L4M 1H2
Tel: 705-726-4300; *Fax:* 705-725-7910
michael@michaelreedlaw.com
www.michaelreedlaw.com

***Barrie*: Catherine A. Rogers - *1**
78 Mulcaster St., Barrie, ON L4M 3M4
Tel: 705-734-2800; *Fax:* 705-734-2807

***Barrie*: Charles F. Ruttan - *1**
23 Owen St., Barrie, ON L4M 3G8
Tel: 705-737-0688; *Fax:* 705-722-4749
chuckruttan@ruttanlaw.ca

***Barrie*: Mark Scharf - *1**
103 Collier St., Barrie, ON L4M 1H2
Tel: 705-728-0555; *Fax:* 705-722-3741

***Barrie*: Dennis Tascona Barrister & Solicitor - *1**
130 Collier St, Barrie, ON L4M 1H4
Tel: 705-734-1801; *Fax:* 705-734-2324
dennistascona@bellnet.ca

***Barrie*: Joseph N. Tascona - *1**
84 Worsley St., Barrie, ON L4M 1L8
Tel: 705-725-1769; *Fax:* 705-725-1772

***Barrie*: Eric C. Taves - *1**
P.O. Box 295, 86 Worsley St., Barrie, ON L4M 4T2
Tel: 705-728-4770; *Fax:* 705-728-7642
etaves@etaves-law.com
www.etaves-law.com

***Barrie*: George W. Taylor, Q.C. - *1**
46 Kempenfelt Dr., Barrie, ON L4M 1B9
Tel: 705-728-8352

***Beamsville*: M.G. Vandeyar - *1**
#7, Lincoln Kingsway Plaza, P.O. Box 489, 5041 King St., Beamsville, ON L0R 1B0
Tel: 905-563-8818; *Fax:* 905-563-7750

***Beaverton*: Woodcock & Tomlinson - *1**
P.O. Box 512, 402 Simcoe St., Beaverton, ON L0K 1A0
Tel: 705-426-7317; *Fax:* 705-426-5740

***Belle River*: J.L. Deziel - *1**
P.O. Box 909, 531 Notre Dame, Belle River, ON N0R 1A0
Tel: 519-728-2000; *Fax:* 519-728-4599
Toll-Free: 800-501-3494
jldeziel@cogeco.net

***Belleville*: Wendy J. Elliott - *1**
187B North Front St., Belleville, ON K8P 3C1
Tel: 613-966-0394; *Fax:* 613-966-1307
wjelliott@hotmail.com

***Belleville*: Graydon & Hurley - *2**
112 Front St., Belleville, ON K8N 2Y7
Tel: 613-966-4614; *Fax:* 613-966-6182

***Belleville*: Edward J. Kafka - *3**
P.O. Box 243, 309 Front St., Belleville, ON K8N 5A2
Tel: 613-968-3416; *Fax:* 613-968-3417
elkafka.barr@bellnet.ca

***Belleville*: Richard R. Ketcheson - *1**
#200, 199 Front St., Belleville, ON K8N 5H5
Tel: 613-966-1123; *Fax:* 613-966-0478

***Belleville*: O'Flynn Weese LLP - *10**
Former Name: O'Flynn, Weese & Tausendfreund LLP
65 Bridge St. East, Belleville, ON K8N 1L8
Tel: 613-966-5222; *Fax:* 613-966-7991
info@owtlaw.com
www.owtlaw.com

***Belleville*: Procter Professional Corporation - *4**
Former Name: Procter, Cameron
#204, P.O. Box 700, 365 Front St. North, Belleville, ON K8N 5B3
Tel: 613-962-2584; *Fax:* 613-962-0968
wprocter@procterlaw.ca

***Belleville*: Reynolds O'Brien LLP - *8**
P.O. Box 1327, 183 Front St., Belleville, ON K8N 5J1
Tel: 613-966-3031; *Fax:* 613-966-2390
mail@reynoldsobrien.com
www.reynoldsobrien.com

***Belleville*: Peter A. Robertson - *1**
#101, 3 Applewood Dr., Belleville, ON K8P 4E3
Tel: 613-969-9611; *Fax:* 613-969-9775
Toll-Free: 800-561-6385
probertson@cogeco.net
www.cdncounsel.com

***Belleville*: C. Roderick Rolston - *1**
#202, 175 Front St., Belleville, ON K8N 2Y9
Tel: 613-962-9154; *Fax:* 613-962-8109
Toll-Free: 800-361-4437
rrolston@reach.net

***Belleville*: Templeman Menninga LLP - *24**
#200, P.O. Box 234, 205 Dundas St. East, Belleville, ON K8N 5A2
Tel: 613-966-2620; *Fax:* 613-966-2866
info@tmlegal.com
www.tmlegal.ca

***Belleville*: Berend Van Huizen - *1**
210 Church St., Belleville, ON K8N 3C3
Tel: 613-962-8645; *Fax:* 613-962-7689
berend@berendvanhuizenlaw.com
www.berendvanhuizenlaw.com

***Blenheim*: Kerr & Wood - *1**
P.O. Box 1150, 15 George St., Blenheim, ON N0P 1A0
Tel: 519-676-5465; *Fax:* 519-676-3918
kerrwood@ciaccess.com

***Blyth*: John C. Myers - *1**
P.O. Box 280, 439 Queen St. North, Blyth, ON N0M 1H0
Tel: 519-523-9148; *Fax:* 519-523-9148

***Bobcaygeon*: Robert J. Walker - *1**
P.O. Box 243, 4 King St. West, Bobcaygeon, ON K0M 1A0
Tel: 705-738-3588; *Fax:* 705-738-4252

***Bolton*: Jean P. Carberry - *1**
34 Queen St., Bolton, ON L4E 1B3
Tel: 905-857-2332; *Fax:* 905-857-2367
jpclaw@jpclaw.ca

***Bolton*: W. Ross Milliken - *1**
P.O. Box 225, 49 Queen St. North, Bolton, ON L7E 5T2
Tel: 905-857-2835; *Fax:* 905-857-0097
ross.milliken@boltonlaw.ca
www.rossmilliken.com

***Bolton*: Neiman, Callegari - *2**
#H3, 18 King St. East, Bolton, ON L7E 1E8
Tel: 905-857-0095; *Fax:* 905-857-0488
info@neimancallegari.ca
www.neimancallegari.ca

***Bolton*: Mark E. Penfold - *2**
P.O. Box 225, 49 Queen St. North, Bolton, ON L7E 5T2
Tel: 905-857-2835; *Fax:* 905-857-0091
Toll-Free: 800-954-4054
mark.penfold@boltonlaw.ca

***Bowmanville*: William Brown - *1**
P.O. Box 1, 71 Mearns Court, Bowmanville, ON L1C 4N4
Tel: 905-623-3305; *Fax:* 905-623-3287

** indicates number of lawyers*

***Bowmanville*: Mervyn B. Kelly - *1**
42 Prince St., Bowmanville, ON L1C 1G6
Tel: 905-623-4444;
merv@claringtonlawyers.com
www.claringtonlawyers.com

***Bracebridge*: Ronald G. Burk - *1**
32 Wharf Rd., Bracebridge, ON P1L 2A7
Tel: 705-645-3007; *Fax:* 705-645-3998
rgburklaw@on.aibn.com

***Bracebridge*: Brian G. Jacques - *1**
#103, P.O. Box 1227, 145 Ontario Street, Bracebridge, ON P1L 2A7
Tel: 705-645-8743; *Fax:* 705-645-8895
brianjacqueslaw@bellnet.ca

***Bracebridge*: Lee, Roche & Kelly - *4**
P.O. Box 990, 6 Dominion St., Bracebridge, ON P1L 1V2
Tel: 705-645-2286; *Fax:* 705-645-5541
Toll-Free: 866-331-1100
nickroche@lrklaw.ca

***Bracebridge*: Penelope A. Lithgow - *1**
58B Ontario St., Bracebridge, ON P1L 2A6
Tel: 705-645-8118

***Bracebridge*: Brian E. Slocum - *1**
63 Quebec St., Bracebridge, ON P1L 2A4
Tel: 705-645-2900; *Fax:* 705-645-2549
slocum@slocumlaw.com

***Bracebridge*: Judith L. Stephenson - *1**
58 Ontario St., Bracebridge, ON P1L 2A6
Tel: 705-645-5251; *Fax:* 705-645-9193

***Bracebridge*: Sugg, Fitton & Taylor LLP - *2**
5 Chancery Lane 1, Bracebridge, ON P1L 2E3
Tel: 705-645-5211; *Fax:* 705-645-8021
chancerylane@cogeco.net

***Bracebridge*: Bruce McLeod Thompson - *1**
3 Dominion Street, Bracebridge, ON P1L 2E6
Tel: 705-646-1000; *Fax:* 705-646-9510
Toll-Free: 800-661-8080

***Bracebridge*: Peter N. Ward - *1**
P.O. Box 10009, Stn. Main, 47 Quebec St., Bracebridge, ON P1L 1W6
Tel: 705-645-1338

***Bracebridge*: Wyjad Fleming Associates - *2**
Former Name: Pinckard Wyjad Associates
P.O. Box 177, 39 Dominion St., Bracebridge, ON P1L 1T6
Tel: 705-645-8787; *Fax:* 705-645-3390
bracebridge@wylaw.ca
www.wylaw.ca

***Bradford*: Evans & Evans - *2**
P.O. Box 190, 21 Holland St. West, Bradford, ON L3Z 2A8
Tel: 905-775-3381; *Fax:* 905-775-8835
law@evansevans.ca

***Bradford*: Gaska & Ballantyne-Gaska - *2**
P.O. Box 1677, Stn. Main, 60 Barrie St., Bradford, ON L3Z 2B9
Tel: 905-775-0015; *Fax:* 905-775-7772
ballantyne.gaska@rogers.com

***Bradford*: E. Pauline Taylor - *1**
76 Holland St. West, Bradford, ON L3Z 2B6
Tel: 905-775-9606; *Fax:* 905-775-0692

***Brampton*: Linda B. Alexander - *1**
#201, 197 County Court Blvd., Brampton, ON L6W 4P6
Tel: 905-450-7757; *Fax:* 905-455-9190
email@lindaalexander.com
lindaalexander.com

***Brampton*: Bowyer, Greenslade, Webster, Allison LLP, Barristers, Solicitors - *3**
#600, 24 Queen St. East, Brampton, ON L6V 1A3
Tel: 905-451-1300; *Fax:* 905-451-4451

***Brampton*: Edmond O'Donoghue Brown - *1**
#100, 205 County Court Blvd., Brampton, ON L6W 4R6
Tel: 905-454-4141; *Fax:* 905-454-4463
edbrown@bellnet.ca

***Brampton*: Connon & Iacobelli - *2**
#403, 201 County Court Blvd., Brampton, ON L6W 4L2
Tel: 905-454-3070; *Fax:* 905-454-2964
connon-iacobelli@on.aibn.com

***Brampton*: D.R. Cook & Company - *3**
Former Name: Dennis R. Cook
#1, 20 Regan Rd., Brampton, ON L7A 1C3
Tel: 905-840-7650; *Fax:* 905-840-7749

***Brampton*: Dale, Streiman & Kurz - *6**
480 Main St. North, Brampton, ON L6V 1P8
Tel: 905-455-7300; *Fax:* 905-455-5848
Toll-Free: 866-219-8109
mail@dsklaw.com
www.dsklaw.com

***Brampton*: Dalzell & Waite - *2**
Former Name: Dalzell, Inglis, Waite
#19, 1 Bartley Bull Pkwy., Brampton, ON L6W 3T7
Tel: 905-454-2288; *Fax:* 905-454-2297

***Brampton*: Davis Webb LLP - *7**
Former Name: Davis Webb Schulze & Moon LLP
#800, 24 Queen St. East, Brampton, ON L6V 1A3
Tel: 905-451-6714; *Fax:* 905-454-1876
info@daviswebb.ca
www.daviswebb.com

***Brampton*: Fader Furlan Moss LLP - *7**
#200, 134 Queen St. East, Brampton, ON L6V 1B2
Tel: 905-459-6160; *Fax:* 905-459-4606
Toll-Free: 877-468-8494
www.faderfurlanmoss.com

***Brampton*: Folites Legal Professional Coporation - *2**
Former Name: Ron E. Folkes
#1, 14 Nelson St. West, Brampton, ON L6X 1B7
Tel: 905-457-2118; *Fax:* 905-457-3707
ronefolkes@folkeslaw.ca
www.folkeslaw.com

***Brampton*: Pina Grella - *1**
#101, 8501 Mississauga Rd., Brampton, ON L6Y 5G8
Tel: 905-453-6000; *Fax:* 905-453-6016
pina@grellalaw.com

***Brampton*: Hillier & Hillier - *1**
165 Main St. North, Brampton, ON L6X 1N1
Tel: 905-453-8636; *Fax:* 905-453-6267
ava@avahillier.ca

***Brampton*: Stephen A. Holmes - *1**
180 Queen St. West, Brampton, ON L6X 1A8
Tel: 905-796-3030; *Fax:* 905-796-2157
sholmes@on.aibn.com
www.stephenholmeslawoffice.com

***Brampton*: Hope & Henderson Law Office - *2**
Former Name: Henderson Law Office
253 Main St. North, Brampton, ON L6X 1N3
Tel: 905-451-7700; *Fax:* 905-451-6620
henlaw@sympatico.ca

***Brampton*: John H. Kalina - *1**
#304, 197 County Court Blvd., Brampton, ON L6W 4P6
Tel: 905-456-8055; *Fax:* 905-487-9613
Toll-Free: 866-503-7354
hjkalina@lawyer4u.ca
www.lawyer4u.ca

***Brampton*: Kania Lawyers - *7**
223 Main St. North, Brampton, ON L6X 1N2
Tel: 905-451-3222; *Fax:* 905-451-1267
Toll-Free: 877-485-2642
www.kanialawyers.com

***Brampton*: Lawrence, Lawrence, Stevenson - *14**
43 Queen St. West, Brampton, ON L6Y 1L9
Tel: 905-451-3040; *Fax:* 905-451-5058
lls@lawrences.com
www.lawrences.com

***Brampton*: D.R. Lent - *1**
38 Queen St. West, Brampton, ON L6X 1A1
Tel: 905-457-4215; *Fax:* 905-457-6454

***Brampton*: R.J. Linton - *1**
21 John St., Brampton, ON L6W 1Z1
Tel: 905-453-3145; *Fax:* 905-454-2270

***Brampton*: D.F. Logan Law Office - *1**
#201, 45 Bramalea Rd., Brampton, ON L6T 2W4
Tel: 905-791-0375; *Fax:* 905-791-6549

***Brampton*: Alison R. Mackay - *1**
#400, 201 County Court Blvd., Brampton, ON L6W 4L2
Tel: 905-455-6000; *Fax:* 905-456-1209
mackaya@rogers.com
www.alisonmackay.yp.ca

***Brampton*: Holmes A. Matheson - *1**
#301, 134 Queen St. East, Brampton, ON L6V 1B2
Tel: 905-451-6504; *Fax:* 905-451-0288
hamatheson@on.aibn.com

***Brampton*: McCabe, Filkin & Garvie - *5**
Former Name: James A. Garvie
#320, Plaza II, 350 Rutherford Rd. South, Brampton, ON L6W 4P7
Tel: 905-452-7400; *Fax:* 905-452-6444
mfa@mccabefilkin.com

***Brampton*: McClelland Law, A Professional Corporation, Lawyers - *2**
Former Name: McLelland & Novak
202 Main St. North, Brampton, ON L6V 1P1
Tel: 905-793-3026; *Fax:* 905-793-2446
info@mcclellandlaw.com
www.mcclellandlaw.com

***Brampton*: W. John McCulligh - *1**
#301, 197 County Court Blvd., Brampton, ON L6W 4P6
Tel: 905-459-1545; *Fax:* 905-459-2826
wmcculligh@bellnet.ca

***Brampton*: Kotak Nainesh - *1**
#405, City South Plaza, 7700 Hurontario St., Brampton, ON L6Y 4M3
Tel: 905-459-6464; *Fax:* 905-459-0550

***Brampton*: North Peel & Dufferin Community Legal Services - *4**
#601, 24 Queen St. East, Brampton, ON L6V 1A3
Tel: 905-455-0160; *Fax:* 905-455-0832
Toll-Free: 866-455-0160

***Brampton*: Laszlo Pandy - *1**
26 Bramsteele Rd., Brampton, ON L6W 1B3
Tel: 905-457-0977; *Fax:* 905-457-8108

***Brampton*: Prouse, Dash & Crouch - *11**
50 Queen St. West, Brampton, ON L6X 4H3
Tel: 905-451-6610; *Fax:* 905-451-1549
Toll-Free: 877-217-4732
pdc@pdclawyers.ca
www.prousedash.ca

***Brampton*: Richardson, Schnall & Sanderson - *1**
#402, 134 Queen St. East, Brampton, ON L6V 1B2
Tel: 905-451-1593; *Fax:* 905-451-3132

***Brampton*: Simmons, Da Silva & Sinton - *11**
#200, 201 County Court Blvd., Brampton, ON L6W 4L2
Tel: 905-457-1660; *Fax:* 905-457-5641
www.sdslawfirm.com

***Brampton*: Mark E. Skursky - *1**
#101, 2 Fisherman Dr., Brampton, ON L7A 1B5
Tel: 905-840-0001; *Fax:* 905-840-0002
skurskylawoffice@on.aibn.com

***Brampton*: George Paul Smith - *1**
280 Main St. North, Brampton, ON L6V 1P6
Tel: 905-457-9791; *Fax:* 905-457-9798
gpsmith@pathcom.com
www.peelbarristers.com

***Brampton*: Victor E. Szumlanski - *1**
9610 McLaughlin Rd. North, Brampton, ON L6X 0B8
Tel: 905-456-1673; *Fax:* 905-456-1201

***Brampton*: Alan Wainwright - *1**
#102, 197 County Court Blvd., Brampton, ON L6W 4P6
Tel: 905-453-9520; *Fax:* 905-450-7842
awainwright@bellnet.ca
www.peelbarristers.com/wainwright

***Brampton*: Cynthia K. Waite - *3**
Former Name: Waite and Associates
#102, 197 County Court Blvd., Brampton, ON L6W 4P6
Tel: 905-450-3800; *Fax:* 905-450-8376
cyndy@wjfamilylaw.com

***Brampton*: Michael J. Walsh - *1**
280 Main St. North, Brampton, ON L6V 1P6
Tel: 905-453-4105; *Fax:* 905-457-3075
walaw@on.aibn.com

** indicates number of lawyers*

***Brampton*: J.T. Wiley - *1**
#100, 205 County Court Blvd., Brampton, ON L6W 4R6
Tel: 905-454-5600; *Fax:* 905-454-4463

***Brantford*: Douglas C. Ainsworth - *1**
Stn. Main, 120B Market St., Brantford, ON N3T 3A1
Tel: 519-756-4220; *Fax:* 519-756-3462

***Brantford*: Boddy, Ryerson - *6**
#101, P.O. Box 1265, 172 Dalhousie St., Brantford, ON N3T 5T3
Tel: 519-753-8417; *Fax:* 519-753-7421

***Brantford*: Donald C. Calder - *1**
40 Nelson St., Brantford, ON N3T 2M8
Tel: 519-759-1910; *Fax:* 519-759-2881

***Brantford*: S. Frost - *1**
101 Wellington St., Brantford, ON N3T 2M1
Tel: 519-753-4113

***Brantford*: Guiler Law Office - *1**
36 King St., Brantford, ON N3T 3C5
Tel: 519-751-4517; *Fax:* 519-751-4725
guilerlaw@kwic.com

***Brantford*: Sandra J. Harris - *1**
#202, 50 King St., Brantford, ON N3T 3C7
Tel: 519-756-0350; *Fax:* 519-756-6611
sjharrison@on.aibn.com

***Brantford*: Hospodar, Davies & Goold - *3**
120 Market St., Brantford, ON N3T 3A1
Tel: 519-759-0082; *Fax:* 519-759-8490

***Brantford*: M. John Jakub - *1**
45 Peel St., Brantford, ON N3S 5L7
Tel: 519-754-0495; *Fax:* 519-754-1882
johnjakub@rogers.com

***Brantford*: Lefebvre & Lefebvre LLP - *7**
P.O. Box 488, 75 Chatham St., Brantford, ON N3T 5N9
Tel: 519-756-3350; *Fax:* 519-756-4727
info@lefebvrelawyers.ca
www.lefebvrelawyers.ca

***Brantford*: Miller, Miller & Maltby - *2**
11 Nelson St., Brantford, ON N3T 2M6
Tel: 519-753-4118; *Fax:* 519-753-2596

***Brantford*: Reeves & Buck LLP - *3**
#B101, 325 West St., Brantford, ON N3R 3V6
Tel: 519-759-0900; *Fax:* 519-759-7702
firm@reevesbuck.ca
www.reevesbuck.ca

***Brantford*: Carmelo N. Runco - *1**
107 Wellington St, Brantford, ON N3T 2M1
Tel: 519-754-0405

***Brantford*: Newton Staats - *3**
P.O. Box 1417, 188 Mohawk St., Brantford, ON N3S 2X2
Tel: 519-756-5217; *Fax:* 519-756-4783
staatsnewton@on.aibn.com

***Brantford*: Trepanier Verity - *6**
P.O. Box 144, Stn. Main, 63 Charlotte St., Brantford, ON N3T 2W6
Tel: 519-756-8700; *Fax:* 519-756-5454
info@trepanierverity.com

***Brantford*: Underwood, Ion & Johnson LLP - *2**
Former Name: Underwood & Ion
P.O. Box 1536, 442 Grey St., Unit B, Brantford, ON N3T 5V6
Tel: 519-759-0920; *Fax:* 519-759-2122
dennis@uijlaw.com

***Brantford*: Paul Vandervet - *1**
P.O. Box 1495, 107 Wellington St., Brantford, ON N3T 5V6
Tel: 519-759-4240; *Fax:* 519-759-4863
vandervet@bellnet.ca

***Brantford*: Wayne P. Vipond - *1**
#103, 49 Henderson Ave., Brantford, ON N3R 4V8
Tel: 519-751-0240; *Fax:* 519-751-0251
wvipond@bellnet.ca

***Brantford*: Waterous, Holden, Amey, Hitchon LLP - *19**
P.O. Box 1510, 20 Wellington St., Brantford, ON N3T 5V6
Tel: 519-759-6220; *Fax:* 519-759-8360
law@waterousholden.com
www.waterousholden.com

***Brantford*: Michael R. White - *1**
#103, North Brantford Professional Centre, 525 Park Rd. North, Brantford, ON N3R 7K8
Tel: 519-752-9004; *Fax:* 519-752-0449

***Brantford*: Wyatt, Purcell, Stillman & Karkkainen - *3**
P.O. Box 1115, Stn. Main, 442 Grey St., Brantford, ON N3S 7N3
Tel: 519-756-5800; *Fax:* 519-756-3861
wyattpurcell@wyatturcell.com

***Brigden*: W.E. Tennyson - *1**
P.O. Box 232, 3015 Brigden Rd., Brigden, ON N0N 1B0
Tel: 519-864-1189; *Fax:* 519-864-1966
tennysonlaw@bellnet.ca

***Brighton*: Ben A. Ring - *1**
P.O. Box 1600, 13 Young St., Brighton, ON K0K 1H0
Tel: 613-475-3444; *Fax:* 613-475-3447

***Brighton*: Thompson Law Office - *1**
67 Main St., Brighton, ON K0K 1H0
Tel: 613-475-1175; *Fax:* 613-475-4012
thomsonlaw@bellnet.ca

***Brighton*: Weaver & Curtis - *2**
P.O. Box 1660, 25 Main St., Brighton, ON K0K 1H0
Tel: 613-475-4645; *Fax:* 613-475-4646

***Brockville*: Barr & O'Brien - *2**
#206, 9 Broad St., Brockville, ON K6V 6Z4
Tel: 613-498-0800; *Fax:* 613-498-0001
Toll-Free: 800-673-3429
www.barrobrien.com

***Brockville*: Michael P. Bird - *1**
#304, 9 Broad St., Brockville, ON K6V 6Z4
Tel: 613-342-1183; *Fax:* 613-342-0887
mpbird@ripnet.com

***Brockville*: Fitzpatrick & Culic - *1**
21 Pine St., Brockville, ON K6V 1E9
Tel: 613-342-6693; *Fax:* 613-342-8449
culiclaw@ripnet.com

***Brockville*: R.W. Flood - *1**
13 Hartley St., Brockville, ON K6V 3N2
Tel: 613-345-0087; *Fax:* 613-342-5294

***Brockville*: Fraser & Bickerton - *1**
#100, P.O. Box 692, 36 Broad St., Brockville, ON K6V 5V8
Tel: 613-345-3377; *Fax:* 613-345-3372
www.fraserbickerton.ca

***Brockville*: David A. Hain - *1**
P.O. Box 757, 58 King St. East, Brockville, ON K6V 5W1
Tel: 613-342-5577; *Fax:* 613-342-1773
david@hainlaw.com
www.hainlaw.com

***Brockville*: Hammond Osborne - *2**
#207, 9 Broad St., Brockville, ON K6V 6Z4
Tel: 613-498-0944; *Fax:* 613-498-0946
Toll-Free: 877-498-0944
rob@hammondosborne.ca
www.hammondosborne.ca

***Brockville*: Henderson Johnston Fournier - *2**
Equity Bldg., 61 King St. East, Brockville, ON K6V 5V4
Tel: 613-345-5613; *Fax:* 613-345-6473
info@hendersonjohnstonfournier.com
www.hendersonjohnstonfournier.com

***Brockville*: John M. Johnston - *1**
P.O. Box 81, 2 Court House Ave., Brockville, ON K6V 4T1
Tel: 613-345-5335; *Fax:* 613-345-4496
jjohnsto@ripnet.com

***Brockville*: John H. Macintosh, Q.C. - *1**
P.O. Box 451, 2 Court House Ave., Brockville, ON K6V 5V6
Tel: 613-345-5653; *Fax:* 613-345-6022
jmacintosh@ripnet.com

***Brockville*: Michael J. O'Shaughnessy - *1**
P.O. Box 2121, Stn. Main, 21 Court House Ave., Brockville, ON K6V 6N5
Tel: 613-342-4491; *Fax:* 613-342-6405
mike@courthouse.ca
www.michaeloshaugnessy.ca

***Brockville*: Harry R. Preston - *1**
#201, P.O. Box 1814, Stn. Main, 68 King St. West, Brockville, ON K6V 3P9
Tel: 613-342-1866; *Fax:* 613-342-1634
preslaw@bellnet.ca

***Brockville*: Wilson Evely - *1**
P.O. Box 1, 3 Court Terrace, Brockville, ON K6V 4T4
Tel: 613-345-1907; *Fax:* 613-345-4604
wilson-evely@bellnet.ca

***Brooklin*: Mason Bennett Johncox - *3**
79 Baldwin St., Brooklin, ON L1M 1A4
Tel: 905-620-4499; *Fax:* 905-620-7738
inquiries@whitbylawyers.com
www.whitbylawyers.com

***Bruce Mines*: Peterson & Peterson**
P.O. Box 100, 76 Taylor St., Bruce Mines, ON P0R 1C0
Tel: 705-785-3491; *Fax:* 705-785-3768
la~ryd.peterson@sympatico.ca

***Burlington*: Cleaver Crawford LLP - *2**
2019 Caroline St., Burlington, ON L7R 1L1
Tel: 905-634-5581; *Fax:* 905-634-1563
eldon.hunt@cleavercrawford.ca

***Burlington*: Dunlop & Associates - *3**
3556 Commerce Ct., Burlington, ON L7N 3L7
Tel: 905-681-3311; *Fax:* 905-681-3565
info@dunloplaw.com
www.dunloplaw.com

***Burlington*: Feltmate Delibato Heagle LLP - *14**
#200, 3600 Billings Ct., Burlington, ON L7N 3N6
Tel: 905-639-8881; *Fax:* 905-639-8017
www.fdhlawyers.com

***Burlington*: Forbes Law Office - *1**
Former Name: Forbes, Conant, Barristers & Solicitors
#2, 3455 Harvester Rd., Burlington, ON L7N 3P2
Tel: 905-333-1622; *Fax:* 905-333-1624
robf@forbeslaw.ca

***Burlington*: Green Germann - *3**
P.O. Box 400, 411 Guelph Line, Burlington, ON L7R 3Y3
Tel: 905-639-1222; *Fax:* 905-632-6977
info@greengermann.ca
www.greengermann.ca

***Burlington*: Haber & Associates, Lawyers - *5**
3370 South Service Rd., 2nd Fl., Burlington, ON L7N 3M6
Tel: 905-639-8894; *Fax:* 905-639-0459
sharon@haber-lawyer.com
www.haber-lawyer.com

***Burlington*: Catherine A. Haber - *1**
3370 South Service Rd., 2nd Fl., Burlington, ON L7N 3M6
Tel: 905-333-4421; *Fax:* 905-333-0575
cahaber@allstream.net
www.haberlaw.goldbook.ca

***Burlington*: Hastings, Charlebois - *2**
3513 Mainway Dr., Burlington, ON L7M 1A9
Tel: 905-332-1888; *Fax:* 905-332-0021
mail@hclawyers.ca

***Burlington*: John Hicks Law Office - *1**
#7, 541 Brant St., Burlington, ON L7R 2G6
Tel: 905-681-3131; *Fax:* 905-333-6688
john.hicks@bellnet.ca

***Burlington*: Hofbauer Associates - *3**
#205, 1455 Lakeshore Rd. North, Burlington, ON L7S 2J1
Tel: 905-634-0040; *Fax:* 905-349-0809
info@capatents.com
www.capatents.com

***Burlington*: Richard R. Kosterski - *1**
394 Guelph Line, Burlington, ON L7R 3L4
Tel: 905-637-8249; *Fax:* 905-637-6015
richard@kosterskilaw.ca

***Burlington*: Martin & Hillyer Associates - *8**
Former Name: Lakeshore Law Chambers
2122 Old Lakeshore Rd., Burlington, ON L7R 1A3
Tel: 905-637-5641; *Fax:* 905-637-5404
info@lakeshorelaw.com
www.martinandhillyer.com

***Burlington*: Muir & Unmat - *2**
Former Name: Douglas W. Muir Q.C.
468 Elizabeth St., Burlington, ON L7R 2M2
Tel: 905-634-8030; *Fax:* 905-333-4613

***Burlington*: J. Douglas Redfearn - *1**
#220, 3385 Harvester Rd., Burlington, ON L7N 3N2
Tel: 905-333-5322; *Fax:* 905-333-9835
redfearn@familylawassociates.ca
www.familylawassociates.ca

** indicates number of lawyers*

***Burlington*: Robert J. Redhead Ltd. - *1**
616 Holly Hill Cres., Burlington, ON L7L 3Z7
Tel: 905-631-7573; *Fax:* 905-631-6708
info@redheadlimited.com
www.redheadlimited.com

***Burlington*: Simpson & Rich - *1**
#12, 460 Brant St., Burlington, ON L7R 4B6
Tel: 905-681-1521; *Fax:* 905-333-5075
gdrlaw@worldchat.com

***Burlington*: SimpsonWigle LAW LLP - *27**
Former Name: Simpson, Wigle LLP
#501, Sims Square Bldg., 390 Brant St., Burlington, ON L7R 4J4
Tel: 905-639-1052; *Fax:* 905-333-3960
Toll-Free: 800-434-4414
info@simpsonwigle.com
www.simpsonwigle.com

***Burlington*: Thomas R. Sutherland Q.C. - *1**
3310 South Service Road, Burlington, ON L7N 3M6
Tel: 905-634-5521; *Fax:* 905-631-7914

***Burlington*: Harold Kim Taylor - *1**
3380 South Service Road, Burlington, ON L7N 3J5
Tel: 905-681-6400; *Fax:* 905-681-6510

***Burlington*: Thatcher & Wands - *2**
1457 Ontario St., Burlington, ON L7S 1G6
Tel: 905-681-0444; *Fax:* 905-681-2937
office@thatcherandwands.com
www.thatcherandwands.com

***Burlington*: Elizabeth A. Urban - *1**
3365 Harvester Rd., Main Level, Burlington, ON L7N 3N2
Tel: 905-333-6640; *Fax:* 905-681-6510

***Burlington*: Wright Law Office - *1**
452 Locust Street, Burlington, ON L7S 1V1
Tel: 905-633-7738;
thompsonlaw@bellnet.ca

***Caledon East*: George W. Jenney - *1**
15891 Airport Rd., Caledon East, ON L7C 1J3
Tel: 905-584-9300; *Fax:* 905-584-9233

***Caledonia*: Arrell Law LLP - *3**
Former Name: Arrell, Brown, Osier, Murray & Rosewell
2 Caithness St. West, Caledonia, ON N3W 2J2
Tel: 905-765-5414; *Fax:* 905-765-5144
www.arrellplacelaw.com

***Caledonia*: Benedict & Ferguson - *2**
322 Argyle St. South, Caledonia, ON N3W 1K8
Tel: 905-765-4004; *Fax:* 905-765-3001

***Caledonia*: L.S. Humenik - *1**
P.O. Box 2112, 19 Argyle St. North, Caledonia, ON N3W 1B6
Tel: 905-765-3162; *Fax:* 905-765-4313
larman@mountaincable.net

***Callander*: George D. Olah - *1**
492 Main Street, Callander, ON P0H 1H0
Tel: 705-752-1323; *Fax:* 705-752-1283
georgeolah@bellnet.ca

***Cambridge*: Brownell & Reier - *2**
Former Name: Bond & Brownell
32 Grand Ave. South, Cambridge, ON N2S 2L6
Tel: 519-623-2311; *Fax:* 519-623-6957
info@brownellandreier.ca
www.brownellandreier.ca

***Cambridge*: Copp & Cosman - *2**
#409, Cambridge Place, P.O. Box 1729, Stn. Galt, 73 Water St. North, Cambridge, ON N1R 7G8
Tel: 519-623-4799; *Fax:* 519-623-7154
cosman@coppcosman.com

***Cambridge*: Teresa L. Fairborn - *1**
135 Argyle St. South, Cambridge, ON N3H 1P8
Tel: 519-653-1460; *Fax:* 519-653-4169
teresa@fairbornllb.com

***Cambridge*: Gary E.J. Hauser - *1**
1666 King St. East, Cambridge, ON N3H 3R7
Tel: 519-653-1521; *Fax:* 519-650-1466
ghauser@golden.net

***Cambridge*: George R. Ingram - *1**
#206, P.O. Box 1447, 99 Main St., Cambridge, ON N1R 1W1
Tel: 519-621-9000; *Fax:* 519-621-9009
gringram@sentex.net

***Cambridge*: Rein Kao - *1**
24 Queens Square, Cambridge, ON N1S 1H6
Tel: 519-624-8722; *Toll-Free:* 888-559-2726

***Cambridge*: David A. Kinder - *1**
546 Grand Ridge Dr., Cambridge, ON N1S 4Y9
Tel: 519-740-6676; *Fax:* 519-623-8545
kinder@sympatico.ca

***Cambridge*: William Korz, Q.C. - *1**
Former Name: Korz & Associates
927 King Street, Cambridge, ON N3H 5M3
Tel: 519-653-7174; *Fax:* 519-653-5222
wmkorz@execulink.com

***Cambridge*: George E. Loker - *1**
P.O. Box 1723, Stn. Galt, 108 Myers Rd., Cambridge, ON N1R 2Z8
Tel: 519-621-4300; *Fax:* 519-621-4300
eloker@golden.net

***Cambridge*: Paul M. Mann Professional Corp. - *1**
25 George St. South, Cambridge, ON N1S 2N3
Tel: 519-623-0700; *Fax:* 519-622-4091
info@paulmann.ca
www.paulmann.ca

***Cambridge*: McDonald Ross - *2**
9 Brant Rd. South, Cambridge, ON N1S 2W4
Tel: 519-622-0499; *Fax:* 519-740-6368
jwm@mcdonaldross.com

***Cambridge*: Jane A. McKenzie - *1**
Netus Business Centre, 19 Thorne St., Cambridge, ON N2H 4W1
Tel: 519-745-7614; *Fax:* 519-745-9778
jane.mckenzie@execulink.com
www.cambridgefamilylaw.com

***Cambridge*: McSevney Law Offices - *2**
Former Name: Onorato Law Offices
708 Duke St., Cambridge, ON N3H 3T6
Tel: 519-653-3217; *Fax:* 519-653-3702
www.mcsevneylaw.com

***Cambridge*: Pavey, Law & Witteveen LLP - *5**
Former Name: Pavey, Law & Wannop LLP
P.O. Box 1707, Stn. Galt, 19 Cambridge St., Cambridge, ON N1R 3R8
Tel: 519-621-7260; *Fax:* 519-621-1304
info@paveylaw.com
www.paveylaw.com

***Cambridge*: Pettitt, Schwarz - *2**
#403, 73 Water St. North, Cambridge, ON N1R 7L6
Tel: 519-621-2450; *Fax:* 519-621-5750
bob@pettittschwarz.com
www.pettittschwarz.com

***Cambridge*: Linda L. Ratcliffe - *1**
927 King St. East, Cambridge, ON N3H 3P4
Tel: 519-650-0763; *Fax:* 519-653-5222

***Cambridge*: Henry R. Shields - *1**
2 Water St. North, Cambridge, ON N1R 3B1
Tel: 519-622-2150; *Fax:* 519-623-0997
henryshields@on.aibn.com

***Cambridge*: J. Craig Wilson - *1**
P.O. Box 1297, 2 Water St. North, Cambridge, ON N1R 3B1
Tel: 519-622-0192

***Cambridge*: W.C. Wraight - *1**
P.O. Box 22103, 15 Main St., Cambridge, ON N1R 8E3
Tel: 519-623-3330; *Fax:* 519-621-0136

***Campbellford*: Paul D.H. Burgess - *1**
P.O. Box 1540, 64 Front St. North, Campbellford, ON K0L 1L0
Tel: 705-653-5555; *Fax:* 705-653-5557
burgess-law@heydon.com

***Campbellville*: Robert B. Burgess, Q.C. - *1**
P.O. Box 86, 8220 MacArthur Dr., Campbellville, ON L0P 1B0
Tel: 905-854-2790; *Fax:* 905-854-1968
rbburgess@sympatico.ca

***Campbellville*: justenvironment - *1**
15 Timber Run Crt., Campbellville, ON L0P 1B0
Tel: 905-659-4732; *Fax:* 905-659-4733
mrudolph@justenvironment.com
www.justenvironment.com

***Carleton Place*: Kenneth J. Bennett - *1**
32 Beckwith Street, Carleton Place, ON K7C 2T2
Tel: 613-257-1655; *Fax:* 613-257-8837

***Carleton Place*: P.D. Courtice - *1**
P.O. Box 29, 164 Bridge St., Carleton Place, ON K7C 2V7
Tel: 613-257-5001; *Fax:* 613-257-8797
pdclaw@on.aibn.com

***Carleton Place*: N. Alan Jones - *1**
92 Bridge St., Carleton Place, ON K7C 2V3
Tel: 613-257-3811; *Fax:* 613-253-0479
ajones@bellnet.ca

***Carp*: Nutrisphere - *1**
118 Grey Fox Dr., Carp, ON K0A 1L0
Tel: 613-256-4091; *Fax:* 613-256-4091
helyn.mac@sympatico.ca

***Casselman*: Benoit & Benoit - *1**
#661, CP 650, 661, rue Principale, Casselman, ON K0A 1M0
Tél: 613-764-3694; *Téléc:* 613-764-3198
cbrisson@bellnet.ca

***Casselman*: Mireille C. LaViolette - *1**
CP 179, 719, rue Principale, Casselman, ON K0A 1M0
Tél: 613-764-3747; *Téléc:* 613-764-1000
info@mireillelaviolette.com
www.mireillelaviolette.com

***Chapleau*: Weaver, Simmons LLP - *27**
Civic Centre, P.O. Box 329, Pine St., Chapleau, ON P0M 1K0
Tel: 705-864-1505;
thefirm@weaversimmons.com
www.weaversimmons.com

***Chatham*: James E.S. Allin - *1**
186 Wellington Street West, Chatham, ON N7M 2G6
Tel: 519-352-6540; *Fax:* 519-352-9097
jallin@ciaccess.com

***Chatham*: Benoit, Van Raay, Spisani, Fuerth & Quaglia - *5**
P.O. Box 1087, Stn. Main, 124 Thames St., Chatham, ON N7L 2Y8
Tel: 519-352-8580; *Fax:* 519-352-4114

***Chatham*: Mark M. MacKew - *1**
237 Wellington St. West, Chatham, ON N7M 1J9
Tel: 519-354-0407; *Fax:* 519-354-3250
mark@mackewlaw.com
www.mackewlaw.com

***Chatham*: Stanley G. Mayes - *1**
16 Victoria Ave., Chatham, ON N7L 2Z6
Tel: 519-436-1040; *Fax:* 519-436-2442
mail@mayeslawfirm.ca
www.mayeslawfirm.ca

***Chatham*: Gudrun Mueller-Wilm - *1**
P.O. Box 554, Stn. C, 6 Harvey St., Chatham, ON N7M 1L6
Tel: 519-358-1822; *Fax:* 519-358-7406

***Chatham*: F. Vaughn Pugh - *1**
190 Wellington St. West, Chatham, ON N7M 1J6
Tel: 519-354-4360;
fvpugh@on.aibn.com

***Chatham*: John B. Trinca - *1**
P.O. Box 428, 75 Thames St., Chatham, ON N7L 1S4
Tel: 519-352-7750; *Fax:* 519-352-4159
jtrinca@mnsi.net

***Chatham*: Paul D. Watson - *1**
P.O. Box 661, 213 King St., 2nd Fl., Chatham, ON N7M 1E6
Tel: 519-351-7721; *Fax:* 519-351-7726
pdwoffice@cogeco.net

***Chelmsford*: Gerard E. Guimond**
P.O. Box 2225, 3527 Errington Ave. North, Chelmsford, ON P0M 1L0
Tel: 705-855-4511; *Fax:* 705-855-5631

***Chesley*: McClelland Law Office - *1**
159 - 1st Ave. South, Chesley, ON N0G 1L0
Tel: 519-363-3293; *Fax:* 519-363-2315

***Chesley*: Ross C. McLean - *2**
P.O. Box 118, 27 1st Ave. South, Chesley, ON N0G 1L0
Tel: 519-363-3190; *Fax:* 519-363-2213
rossmclean@bmts.com

** indicates number of lawyers*

***Chesterville*: Cass, Grenkie - *4**
P.O. Box 700, 13 Ralph St., Chesterville, ON K0C 1H0
Tel: 613-448-2735; *Fax:* 613-448-1395
cassgrenkie@gglrlaw.ca

***Clinton*: Philip B. Cornish - *1**
35 Ontario St., Clinton, ON N0M 1L0
Tel: 519-482-1434; *Fax:* 519-482-1481

***Clinton*: D. Gerald Hiltz - *1**
P.O. Box 1087, 52 Huron St., Clinton, ON N0M 1L0
Tel: 519-482-3414; *Fax:* 519-482-7525

***Coboconk*: Tyler P. Higgins**
P.O. Box 219, 6654 Hwy. 35, Coboconk, ON K0M 1K0
Tel: 705-454-2625;

***Cobourg*: John D. Carroll - *1**
P.O. Box 475, 35 King St. East, Cobourg, ON K9A 1K6
Tel: 905-372-5424; *Fax:* 905-372-1943
shazam@eagle.ca

***Cobourg*: Rodger F. Cooper - *1**
#102, 253 Division St., Cobourg, ON K9A 3P9
Tel: 905-372-8728; *Fax:* 905-372-0720
Toll-Free: 888-251-1945
cooper@eagle.ca

***Cobourg*: Ember Leigh Hamilton - *1**
161 Sutherland Crescent, Cobourg, ON K9A 5L6
Tel: 905-373-0589; *Fax:* 905-373-0928
ember@eagle.com

***Cobourg*: Hustler & Kay - *2**
301 Division St., Cobourg, ON K9A 3R2
Tel: 905-372-1991; *Fax:* 905-372-1995
gkay@on.aibn.com

***Cobourg*: Irvine & Irvine - *1**
24 Covert St., Cobourg, ON K9A 2L6
Tel: 905-372-5449; *Fax:* 905-372-1707
rirvine@eagle.ca

***Cobourg*: SMM Law Professional Corp. - *3**
Former Name: Stewart, Mitchell & Macklin.
#205, The Fleming Bldg., 1005 Elgin St., Cobourg, ON K9A 5J4
Tel: 905-372-3395; *Fax:* 905-372-1695
smmlaw@smmlaw.com
www.smmlaw.com

***Cobourg*: Anne Marie Steger - *1**
P.O. Box 9, 256 George St., Cobourg, ON K9A 3L6
Tel: 905-372-2217; *Fax:* 905-372-1783
anne.marie@bellnet.ca

***Cobourg*: William J. Taggart - *1**
35 King St. East, Cobourg, ON K9A 1K6
Tel: 905-372-8700; *Fax:* 905-372-1943

***Colborne*: J.A. Carter - *1**
P.O. Box 699, 26 King St. East, Colborne, ON K9A 1K7
Tel: 905-355-3322; *Fax:* 905-355-3104
Toll-Free: 877-399-3322
jcarter@bellnet.ca

***Collingwood*: Baulke Augaitis Stahr LLP - *4**
Former Name: Baulke & Augaitis LLP
P.O. Box 100, 150 Hurontario St., Collingwood, ON L9Y 3Z4
Tel: 705-445-4930; *Fax:* 705-445-1871
Toll-Free: 866-230-9993
info@collingwoodlaw.com
www.collingwoodlaw.com

***Collingwood*: Besse, Merrifield & Cowan LLP - *3**
47 Hurontario St., Collingwood, ON L9Y 2L7
Tel: 705-446-2000; *Fax:* 705-446-1044
Toll-Free: 888-879-3052
besse@blclawoffices.com
www.bmclawoffices.com

***Collingwood*: Christie/Cummings - *3**
325 Hume St., Collingwood, ON L9Y 1W4
Tel: 705-444-3650; *Fax:* 705-444-0024
maccummings@christiecummings.com

***Collingwood*: Compenso Consulting Inc - *1**
Former Name: 2053891 Ontario Limited
#3, 115 Hurontario Street, Collingwood, ON L9Y 2L9
Tel: 705-445-8540; *Fax:* 705-445-2681
info@compenso.ca
www.compenso.ca

***Collingwood*: Brian Greasley - *1**
P.O. Box 490, 33 Ste. Marie St., Collingwood, ON L9Y 3J9
Tel: 705-429-5199; *Fax:* 705-445-2269

***Collingwood*: Larry E. Lant - *1**
P.O. Box 248, Stn. Main, 217 Minnesota St., Collingwood, ON L9Y 3S4
Tel: 705-445-2886; *Fax:* 705-444-5837
lantlaw@on.aibn.com

***Collingwood*: Neathery & Mumford - *2**
#4, 450 Hume St., Collingwood, ON L9Y 1W6
Tel: 705-444-6051; *Fax:* 705-444-0969

***Concord*: Bisceglia & Associates - *4**
#200, 7941 Jane St., Concord, ON L4K 4L6
Tel: 905-695-5200; *Fax:* 905-695-5201
www.lawtoronto.com

***Concord*: Talal Chehab**
#208, 3100 Steeles Ave. West, Concord, ON L4K 3R1
Tel: 905-738-2463; *Fax:* 905-738-4901

***Concord*: John G. Chris - *1**
8700 Dufferin St., Concord, ON L4K 4S6
Tel: 416-661-5989; *Fax:* 905-669-0444
postmaster@jgc-law.com
www.jgc-law.com

***Concord*: D'Ambrosio Law Office - *1**
#300, 3100 Steeles Ave. West, Concord, ON L4K 3R1
Tel: 905-761-7400; *Fax:* 905-738-4901
romeo36@colosseum.com

***Concord*: John De Matteis - *1**
#300, 3100 Steeles Ave. West, Concord, ON L4K 3R1
Tel: 905-738-4900; *Fax:* 905-738-4901

***Concord*: Patrick Di Monte - *1**
#211, 3100 Steeles Ave. West, Concord, ON L4K 3R1
Tel: 905-738-2101; *Fax:* 905-738-1168
patdimonte@on.aibn.com

***Concord*: Louis M. Fried - *1**
#212, 2180 Steeles Ave. West, Concord, ON L4K 2Z5
Tel: 905-738-0180; *Fax:* 905-738-6203
Toll-Free: 866-306-3286
louismfried@on.aibn.com

***Concord*: Thomas F. Kowal - *1**
#300, 3100 Steeles Ave. West, Concord, ON L4K 3R1
Tel: 905-738-5755; *Fax:* 905-738-4901
tkowal@allstream.net

***Concord*: Okell & Weisman - *2**
#407, 1600 Steeles Ave. West, Concord, ON L4K 4M2
Tel: 905-761-8711; *Fax:* 905-761-8633

***Concord*: Norman S. Panzica - *1**
A, 9100 Jane St., Concord, ON L4K 4L8
Tel: 905-738-1078; *Fax:* 905-738-0528
npanzica@rogers.com
www.normanpanzica.com

***Concord*: Piersanti & Company - *5**
#10, 445 Edgeley Blvd., Concord, ON L4K 4G1
Tel: 905-738-2176; *Fax:* 905-738-5182
piersanti@look.com

***Concord*: Alan G. Silverstein - *2**
#318, 1600 Steeles Ave. West, Concord, ON L4K 4M2
Tel: 905-761-1600; *Fax:* 905-761-0948
alan.silverstein@rogers.com

***Cornwall*: Adams, Sherwood, Swabey & Follon - *4**
305 - 2 St. East, Cornwall, ON K6H 1Y8
Tel: 613-938-3330; *Fax:* 613-938-7885
adams@adamssherwood.ca
www.adamssherwoof.ca

***Cornwall*: Bergeron Filion - *2**
103 Sydney St., Cornwall, ON K6H 3H1
Tel: 613-932-2911; *Fax:* 613-932-2356
bobbergeron@pppoe.ca

***Cornwall*: Tilton T. Donihee - *1**
132 2nd Street East, Cornwall, ON K6H 1Y4
Tel: 613-933-0792; *Fax:* 613-938-7632
tdoniee@gta.igs.net

***Cornwall*: Giovanniello, Bellefeuille - *2**
340 - 2nd St. East, Cornwall, ON K6H 1Y9
Tel: 613-938-0294; *Fax:* 613-932-2374
law@gblawfirm.ca
www.gblawfirm.ca

***Cornwall*: Guindon, MacLean & Castle - *3**
50 - 2 St. East, Cornwall, ON K6H 1Y3
Tel: 613-933-3931; *Fax:* 613-933-6123
info@g-m-c.on.ca

***Cornwall*: Law Office of Diane M. Lahaie - *1**
28 - 7 St. West, Cornwall, ON K6J 2X9
Tel: 613-936-8833; *Fax:* 613-936-6717

***Cornwall*: Anne Marie Levesque - *1**
110 Sydney St., Cornwall, ON K6H 3H2
Tel: 613-932-7654; *Fax:* 613-938-1692
amlevesque@sympatico.ca

***Cornwall*: Ian D. Paul - *1**
5 Third St. East, Cornwall, ON K2H 2L6
Tel: 613-933-9455; *Fax:* 613-933-7566
ipaul@on.aibn.com

***Cornwall*: D. Randolph Ross - *1**
120 Sydney St., Cornwall, ON K6H 3H2
Tel: 613-932-2044; *Fax:* 613-937-0993
drross@mail2.glen-net.ca

***Cornwall*: Donald J. White - *1**
700 Montreal Rd., Cornwall, ON K6H 1C4
Tel: 613-933-6443; *Fax:* 613-933-6453
nwhite10@cogeco.ca

***Cornwall*: Wilson, Poirier, Byrne - *2**
132 - 2nd St. West, Cornwall, ON K6J 1G5
Tel: 613-938-2224; *Fax:* 613-938-8005
apoirier@bellnet.ca; tombyrne@bellnet.ca

***Deep River*: Thomas E. Roche - *1**
Former Name: Roche & Dakin
P.O. Box 1240, 27 Champlain St., Deep River, ON K0J 1P0
Tel: 613-584-3392; *Fax:* 613-584-4922
rochdaki@bellnet.ca

***Delhi*: John R. Hanselman - *1**
138 Eagle St., Delhi, ON N4B 1S5
Tel: 519-582-0770; *Fax:* 519-582-1876

***Dresden*: Timothy D. Mathany - *1**
P.O. Box 568, 347 St. George St. South, Dresden, ON N0P 1M0
Tel: 519-683-6219; *Fax:* 519-683-6548

***Dryden*: Beamish MacKinnon - *5**
P.O. Box 86, 100 Claybanks Rd., Dryden, ON P8N 2Y7
Tel: 807-223-7478; *Fax:* 807-223-6402
beamishmackinnon@beamacklaw.ca

***Dryden*: McAuley & Partners - *4**
P.O. Box 159, 4 Whyte Ave., Dryden, ON P8N 2Y8
Tel: 807-223-2254; *Fax:* 807-223-3794
www.mcauleylaw.com

***Dryden*: Vermeer & Van Walleghem - *2**
P.O. Box 938, Stn. Main, 65 King St., 2nd Fl., Dryden, ON P8N 2Z5
Tel: 807-223-3311; *Fax:* 807-223-4133
lawweb@vermeerlaw.com
www.vermeerlaw.com

***Dundalk*: John L. Ferris - *1**
360 Main St. East, Dundalk, ON N0C 1B0
Tel: 519-923-2031; *Fax:* 519-923-5131

***Dundas*: David S. Lesperance - *1**
#202, 84 King St. West, Dundas, ON L9H 1T9
Tel: 905-627-3037; *Fax:* 905-627-9868
dsl@globalrelocate.com
www.globalrelocate.com

***Dunnville*: G. Donald Chambers - *1**
110 Lock St. East, Dunnville, ON N1A 1J7
Tel: 905-744-7485; *Fax:* 905-774-7486

***Dunrobin*: Goodfellow Agricola Consultants Inc. - *1**
2005 - 6th Line Rd. RR#1, Dunrobin, ON K0A 1T0
Tel: 613-832-0865;
randal@goodfellowagricola.com
www.goodfellowagricola.com

***Dutton*: Martin Joldersma - *1**
P.O. Box 279, 159 Main Street, Dutton, ON N0L 1J0
Tel: 519-762-2882; *Fax:* 519-762-2880
martinjoldersma@on.aibn.com

** indicates number of lawyers*

Elliot Lake: Kearns Law Office - *1
15 Manitoba Rd., Elliot Lake, ON P5A 2A6
Tel: 705-848-3601; *Fax:* 705-848-8416
Toll-Free: 800-268-7733
kearn1@bellnet.ca

Elmira: Cynthia M. Rudavsky - *1
9 Church St. West, Elmira, ON N3B 1M2
Tel: 519-669-2200; *Fax:* 519-669-4349
rudavsky@sentex.net

Elmira: Woods, Clemens & Fletcher Professional Corporation - *4
Former Name: Woods & Clemens
P.O. Box 216, 9 Memorial Ave., Elmira, ON N3B 2R1
Tel: 519-669-5101; *Fax:* 519-669-5618
lawoffice@woodsclemens.ca

Elora: J.E. Morris - *1
149 Geddes Street, Elora, ON N0B 1S0
Tel: 519-846-5366; *Fax:* 519-846-8170
john@johnmorrislaw.ca

Elora: Gregory A. Oakes - *1
155 Geddes St., Elora, ON N0B 1S0
Tel: 519-846-5555; *Fax:* 519-846-5554

Embrun: Campbell & Sabourin LLP/SRL - *2
#1, 165 Bay St., Embrun, ON K0A 1W1
Tel: 613-443-5683; *Fax:* 613-443-3285
info@campbellaw.on.ca
www.campbellaw.on.ca

Embrun: Jean G. Martel - *1
800, rue Notre Dame, Embrun, ON K0A 1W1
Tel: 613-443-3267; *Fax:* 613-443-3857
martelj@rogers.com

Essex: Hickey, Bryne - *2
14 Centre St., Essex, ON N8M 1N9
Tel: 519-776-7349; *Fax:* 519-776-8161
byrnelaw@bellnet.ca

Etobicoke: John H. Bailey - *1
#901, 701 Evans Ave., Etobicoke, ON M9C 1A3
Tel: 416-622-2725; *Fax:* 416-622-8952
jhblaw@aol.com

Etobicoke: Birks, Langdon & Elliott - *2
#329, 4195 Dundas St. West, Etobicoke, ON M8X 1Y4
Tel: 416-239-3431; *Fax:* 416-239-8259

Etobicoke: Christie & Associates - *4
750 Scarlett Road, Etobicoke, ON M9P 2V1
Tel: 416-249-8300; *Fax:* 416-249-1480

Etobicoke: P.G. Derry - *1
1 Eva Road, Etobicoke, ON M9C 4Z5
Tel: 416-868-6483; *Fax:* 416-364-1697

Exeter: Little Masson & Reid - *2
71 Main St. North, Exeter, ON N0M 1S0
Tel: 519-235-0670; *Fax:* 519-235-1603

Exeter: Raymond & McLean - *1
P.O. Box 100, 387 Main St. South, Exeter, ON N0M 1S0
Tel: 519-235-2234; *Fax:* 519-235-2671
raymclea@quadro.net

Fenelon Falls: David J. Gowanlock - *1
P.O. Box 607, 16 May St., Fenelon Falls, ON K0M 1N0
Tel: 705-887-2582; *Fax:* 705-887-1871

Fenelon Falls: John D. Walden
57 Lindsay St., Fenelon Falls, ON K0M 1N0
Tel: 705-887-2941

Fergus: Leigh G. Fishleigh - *1
169 St. Andrew St. West, Fergus, ON N1M 1N6
Tel: 519-843-7100; *Fax:* 519-843-3038
leigh.fishleigh@bellnet.ca

Fergus: Grant & Acheson - *4
P.O. Box 128, 265 Bridge St., Fergus, ON N1M 2W7
Tel: 519-843-1960; *Fax:* 519-843-6888
www.grant-acheson.com

Fonthill: Jill Anthony - *4
P.O. Box 743, 10 Hwy. 20 East, Fonthill, ON L0S 1E0
Tel: 905-892-2621; *Fax:* 905-892-1022
janthony@jillanthony.com
www.jillanthony.com

Fort Erie: Hagan & McDowell - *2
P.O. Box 68, 29 Jarvis St., Fort Erie, ON L2A 5M6
Tel: 905-871-4440; *Fax:* 905-871-9266
rmcdowell@computan.com

Fort Erie: D.J. Jacobi - *1
P.O. Box 1028, 1321 Garrison Rd., Fort Erie, ON L2A 1P3
Tel: 905-871-4244

Fort Frances: Clare Allan Brunetta - *1
P.O. Box 656, 420 Victoria Ave., Fort Frances, ON P9A 3M9
Tel: 807-274-9809; *Fax:* 807-274-8760
cbrunetta@nwonet.net

Fort Frances: Lawrence A. Eustace - *1
510 Portage Ave., Fort Frances, ON P9A 2A3
Tel: 807-274-3247; *Fax:* 807-274-6447
larry@eustace-law.com

Fort Frances: J. Rod McLeod - *1
Site 206 - 10, 1455 Idylwild Drive, Fort Frances, ON P9A 3M6
Tel: 807-274-2832; *Fax:* 807-274-7968
rod@mcleodlawoffice.com

Fort Frances: Lawrence G. Phillips - *1
237 Church St., Fort Frances, ON P9A 1C7
Tel: 807-274-8525; *Fax:* 807-274-5758
phillaw19@hotmail.com

Fort Frances: Donald A. Taylor - *1
504 Armit Ave., Fort Frances, ON P9A 2H7
Tel: 807-274-7811; *Fax:* 807-274-8485
dalaw@shaw.ca

Gananoque: Michael R. Eyolfson - *1
#5, 140 Garden St., Gananoque, ON K7G 1H9
Tel: 613-382-7772; *Fax:* 613-382-3030
elfson@sprint.ca

Gananoque: Steacy & Delaney - *1
Stn. Main, 110 Stone St., Gananoque, ON K7G 2A1
Tel: 613-382-2137; *Fax:* 613-382-7794
l.stacey@ganlaw.com
www.gananoque.com/steacyanddelaney

Georgetown: Clinton D. Banbury - *1
#2, 211 Guelph St., Georgetown, ON L7G 5B5
Tel: 905-877-5252; *Fax:* 905-877-4100
cbanbury@banburylaw.com

Georgetown: Jeffrey L. Eason - *1
P.O. Box 159, Stn. Main, 116 Guelph St., Georgetown, ON L7G 4T1
Tel: 905-877-6961; *Fax:* 905-877-9725
jeffreyleason@bellnet.ca

Georgetown: Helson Kogon Ashbee Schaljo & Associates LLP - *5
132 Mill St., Georgetown, ON L7G 2C6
Tel: 905-877-5206; *Fax:* 905-877-3948
helsonkogon.general@cogeco.net

Georgetown: W. Glen How & Associates
P.O. Box 40, Georgetown, ON L7G 4T1
Tel: 905-873-4545; *Fax:* 905-873-4522
wghow@wghow.ca

Georgetown: R.T. Howitt, Q.C. - *1
#301, 83 Mill St., Georgetown, ON M9C 1X6
Tel: 905-877-5139; *Fax:* 905-877-1155

Georgetown: William H. Manderson - *1
#1004, 83 Mill Street, Georgetown, ON L7G 5E9
Tel: 905-873-0121;
billmanderson@on.aibn.com

Georgetown: R. Paul Millman - *1
116 Guelph St., Georgetown, ON L7G 4A3
Tel: 905-873-9481; *Fax:* 905-873-9483
rpmlaw@on.aibn.com

Georgetown: Sopinka & Kort - *2
145 Mill St., Georgetown, ON L7G 2C2
Tel: 905-877-0196; *Fax:* 905-877-0604
wsopinka@sopinka-kort.com

Glencoe: Gary R. Merritt - *1
P.O. Box 309, 213 Main St., Glencoe, ON N0L 1M0
Tel: 519-287-3432; *Fax:* 519-287-2498
merritt@bellnet.ca

Gloucester: John Lutes Consulting Inc. - *1
1135 St. Germain Cr., Gloucester, ON K1C 2L7
Tel: 613-830-0203; *Fax:* 613-830-0250

Gloucester: MacQuarrie Whyte Killoran - *3
#208, 1980 Ogilvie Rd., Gloucester, ON K1J 9L3
Tel: 613-748-1600; *Fax:* 613-748-0800
info@mwklaw.ca
www.ottawaorleanslawyers.com; www.mwklaw.ca

Goderich: Mary E. Cull - *1
50 East St., Goderich, ON N7A 1N3
Tel: 519-524-1115; *Fax:* 519-524-1116

Goderich: Donnelly & Murphy - *7
18 Court House Square, Goderich, ON N7A 3Y7
Tel: 519-524-2154; *Fax:* 519-524-8550
admin@dmlaw.on.ca

Goderich: Timothy G. Macdonald - *1
1 Nelson St. East, Goderich, ON N7A 1R7
Tel: 519-524-1120; *Fax:* 519-524-2576

Goderich: Norman B. Pickell - *1
58 South Street, Goderich, ON N7A 3L5
Tel: 519-524-8335; *Fax:* 519-524-1530
pickell@normanpickell.com
www.normanpickell.com

Goderich: Troyan & Fincher - *2
44 North St., Goderich, ON N7A 2T4
Tel: 519-524-2115; *Fax:* 519-524-4481
troyanfincher@cabletv.on.ca

Gore Bay: Terence E. Land, Barrister & Solicitor - *1
Former Name: Armstrong & Land
P.O. Box 90, 4 Eleanor St., Gore Bay, ON P0P 1H0
Tel: 705-282-2710; *Fax:* 705-282-2205

Gore Bay: James E. Weppler - *1
P.O. Box 222, 65 Meredith St., Gore Bay, ON P0P 1H0
Tel: 705-282-3354; *Fax:* 705-282-3211

Grand Bend: Michael G. Forrester - *1
General Delivery, 82 Ontario St. South, Grand Bend, ON N0M 1T0
Tel: 519-238-5297; *Fax:* 519-238-5234

Gravenhurst: Stuart & Cruickshank - *2
P.O. Box 1270, 195 Church St., Gravenhurst, ON P1P 1V4
Tel: 705-687-3441; *Fax:* 705-687-5405
s.c@bellnet.ca

Gravenhurst: Lyle A. Sullivan - *1
225 Muskoka Rd. South, Gravenhurst, ON P1P 1H6
Tel: 705-687-2219; *Fax:* 705-687-7951
lyleasullivan@bellnet.ca

Grimsby: Donald C. Loney - *1
Former Name: Sinclair, Murakami, Loney & Van Velzen
55 Main St. East, Grimsby, ON L3M 1R3
Tel: 905-945-9271; *Fax:* 905-945-3066
Toll-Free: 800-363-5073
sml@on.aibn.com

Grimsby: George Krusell - *1
260 Main St. East, Grimsby, ON L3M 1P8
Tel: 905-945-2300; *Fax:* 905-945-8529

Grimsby: Lovett & Cunningham - *2
P.O. Box 100, 66 Main St. East, Grimsby, ON L3M 4G1
Tel: 905-945-2269; *Fax:* 905-945-6652

Grimsby: Palios & Associates - *1
#1, 11 Ontario, Grimsby, ON L3M 3G8
Tel: 905-945-6007; *Fax:* 905-945-6670
npalios@palioslaw.com

Guelph: AlanCo Inc. - *1
#42, 1550 Gordon St., Guelph, ON N1L 1C7
Tel: 519-546-3960;
frank.johansen@alanco.ca

Guelph: Lynn Archbold - *1
27 Cork St., Guelph, ON N1H 2W9
Tel: 519-763-4748; *Fax:* 519-763-4207
lynnarchbold@bellnet.ca

Guelph: Dason Law Office - *1
Former Name: Hugh Guthrie Q.C. Professional Corporation
367 Woolwich St., Guelph, ON N1H 3W4
Tel: 519-824-2020; *Fax:* 519-824-2023

Guelph: Charles R. Davidson
172 Woolwich St., Guelph, ON N1H 3V5
Tel: 519-767-6637; *Fax:* 519-826-5212
charles@crdavidson.ca

** indicates number of lawyers*

***Guelph*: Guy D.E. Farb - *1**
22 Paisley St., Guelph, ON N1H 2N6
Tel: 519-763-6644; *Fax:* 519-763-8091
lawguy@execulink.comwww.linkedin.com/pub/guy-farb/18/559/986

***Guelph*: Siobhan Ann Hanley - *1**
98 Surrey St. East, Guelph, ON N1H 3P9
Tel: 519-824-2586; *Fax:* 519-824-6661
shanley@bellnet.ca

***Guelph*: INAC Services Limited - *1**
232 Dublin St. North, Guelph, ON N1H 4P3
Tel: 519-766-1395; *Fax:* 519-766-1348
dreynolds@inacservices.com
www.inacservices.com

***Guelph*: Jackman & Rowles - *2**
P.O. Box 37, Stn. Main, 17 Cork St. West, Guelph, ON N1H 2W9
Tel: 519-824-4883; *Fax:* 519-821-2910
mmjr@on.aibn.com

***Guelph*: Philip B. Langlotz - *1**
35C Spring St., Guelph, ON N1E 1Z9
Tel: 519-837-3609;
langlotz@golden.net

***Guelph*: Maiocco & DiGravio - *2**
230 Speedvale Ave. West, Guelph, ON N1H 1C4
Tel: 519-836-2710; *Fax:* 519-836-7312

***Guelph*: McElderry, Morris - *5**
P.O. Box 875, 84 Woolwich St., Guelph, ON N1H 3T9
Tel: 519-822-8150; *Fax:* 519-822-1921

***Guelph*: Bryna D. McLeod - *1**
221 Woolwich St., Guelph, ON N1H 3V4
Tel: 519-767-2141; *Fax:* 519-763-2204
www.brynamcleod.com

***Guelph*: Charles Milne & Company Inc. - *1**
68 Bridle Path, RR#3, Guelph, ON N1H 6H9
Tel: 519-767-9062; *Fax:* 519-767-9428
charles@sgci.com

***Guelph*: Moon Heath LLP - *3**
P.O. Box 180, Stn. Main, 164 Norfolk St., Guelph, ON N1H 6J9
Tel: 519-824-2540; *Fax:* 519-763-6785
info@moonheath.com
www.moonheath.com

***Guelph*: Nicholson & Doney - *3**
P.O. Box 1505, 137 Norfolk St., Guelph, ON N1H 6N9
Tel: 519-837-3000; *Fax:* 519-837-1758
Toll-Free: 888-839-1898
ron@nicholsondoney.ca
www.nicholsondoney.ca

***Guelph*: Judith C. Sidlofsky Stoffman - *1**
#226, 2 Quebec St., Guelph, ON N1H 2T3
Tel: 519-822-8226; *Fax:* 519-822-8227

***Guelph*: SmithValeriote Law Firm LLP - *21**
#100, P.O. Box 1240, Stn. Main, 105 Silvercreek Pkwy. North, Guelph, ON N1H 6N6
Tel: 519-837-2100; *Fax:* 519-837-1617
info@smithvaleriote.com
www.smithvaleriote.com

***Guelph*: Sorbara, Schumacher, McCann LLP - *18**
Former Name: Flynn & Sorbara
457 Woolwish Street, Guelph, ON N1H 3X6
Tel: 519-836-1510; *Fax:* 519-836-9215
firm@sorbaralaw.com
www.sorbaralaw.com

***Guelph*: Vorvis, Anderson, Gray, Armstrong LLP - *4**
353 Elizabeth Street, Guelph, ON N1H 2X9
Tel: 519-824-7400; *Fax:* 519-824-7521
vaga@vaga.ca
www.vaga.ca

***Hagersville*: James R. Baxter - *1**
P.O. Box 490, 19 King St. West, Hagersville, ON N0A 1H0
Tel: 905-768-3363; *Fax:* 905-768-1550
jrbaxter@mountaincable.net

***Haileybury*: Byck Law Office - *1**
Former Name: Smith, Wowk
439 Ferguson Ave., Haileybury, ON P0J 1K0
Tel: 705-672-2600; *Fax:* 705-672-2779
temlaw@nt.net
www.temlaw.com

***Haliburton*: R.G. Selbie - *1**
P.O. Box 186, Haliburton, ON K0M 1S0
Tel: 705-457-2435; *Fax:* 705-457-3074

***Halton Hills*: Steven C. Foster - *2**
#201, 232 Guelph St., Halton Hills, ON L7G 4B1
Tel: 905-873-0204; *Fax:* 905-873-4962
sfoster@arnold-foster.com

***Hamilton*: John S. Abrams - *1**
#300, 69 John St. South, Hamilton, ON L8N 2B9
Tel: 905-522-3600; *Fax:* 905-529-1570
jabrams@bellnet.ca

***Hamilton*: Agro, Zaffiro - *19**
P.O. Box 2069, Stn. LCD 1, 1 James St. South, Hamilton, ON L8N 3G6
Tel: 905-527-6877; *Fax:* 905-527-6843
mail@agrozaffiro.com
www.agrozaffiro.com

***Hamilton*: Deborah Lee Barfknecht - *1**
#601, 25 Main St. West, Hamilton, ON L8P 1H1
Tel: 905-521-1898; *Fax:* 905-521-0486

***Hamilton*: R.B. Barrs - *1**
#204, 640 Upper James St., Hamilton, ON L9C 2Z2
Tel: 905-387-9212; *Fax:* 905-387-6109

***Hamilton*: Bartolini, Berlingieri , Barrafato; Fortino LLP - *5**
#101, 154 Main St. East, Hamilton, ON L8N 1G9
Tel: 905-577-6833; *Fax:* 905-577-6839
lawfirm@bbb-lawyers.on.ca

***Hamilton*: John A. Bland - *1**
#801, Union Gas Bldg., 20 Hughson St. South, Hamilton, ON L8N 2A1
Tel: 905-524-3533; *Fax:* 905-524-5142

***Hamilton*: Peter Borkovich - *1**
Former Name: Borkovich Ingrassia Macaluso
46 Jackson St. East, Hamilton, ON L8N 1L1
Tel: 905-527-0990; *Fax:* 905-521-1976

***Hamilton*: Brock Howard Bedford - *1**
166 John St. South, Hamilton, ON L8N 2C4
Tel: 905-527-3867; *Fax:* 905-527-3860

***Hamilton*: Burns, Vasan & Associates - *6**
Former Name: Burns, Vasan, Limberis, Vitulli LLP
#305, 21 King St. West, Hamilton, ON L8P 4W9
Tel: 905-522-1381; *Fax:* 905-522-0855
douglasburns@bvlvlaw.ca

***Hamilton*: Camporese & Associates - *2**
#805, Commerce Place, 1 King St. West, Hamilton, ON L8P 1A4
Tel: 905-522-7068; *Fax:* 905-522-5734

***Hamilton*: K.K. Channan - *1**
947 Main St. East, Hamilton, ON L8M 1M9
Tel: 905-544-9411; *Fax:* 905-544-6155
kkchannan@sympatico.ca
www.kkchannan.yp.ca

***Hamilton*: Gary Chertkoff, Q.C. - *1**
#412, 20 Jackson St. West, Hamilton, ON L8P 1L2
Tel: 905-522-2439; *Fax:* 905-522-9198

***Hamilton*: Child, Chaimovitz - *2**
#250, 100 Main St. East, Hamilton, ON L8N 3W4
Tel: 905-526-7030; *Fax:* 905-526-0682
info@childchaimovitz.ca

***Hamilton*: Michael P. Clarke - *1**
#1400, 25 Main St. West, Hamilton, ON L8P 1H1
Tel: 905-527-4399; *Fax:* 905-521-0210
michaelpclarke@bellnet.ca

***Hamilton*: Clyde Halford - *1**
336 Sanatorium Rd., Hamilton, ON L9C 2A4
Tel: 905-388-0973; *Fax:* 905-388-2797

***Hamilton*: Confente, Garcea - *2**
#340, 69 John St. South, Hamilton, ON L8N 2B9
Tel: 905-529-9999; *Fax:* 905-529-1160

***Hamilton*: Connor, Connor, Guyer & Araiche - *2**
#210, 1104 Fennell Ave. East, Hamilton, ON L8T 1R9
Tel: 905-385-3229; *Fax:* 905-385-6182
ccga@mountaincable.net

***Hamilton*: Earl R. Cranfield Q.C. - *1**
#608, 20 Hughson St. South, Hamilton, ON L8N 2A1
Tel: 905-528-0089; *Fax:* 905-528-7692
ecranfield@nas.net

***Hamilton*: Janis P. Criger - *1**
#700, 25 Main St. West, Hamilton, ON L8P 1H1
Tel: 905-525-4639; *Fax:* 905-525-2103
jpcriger@crigerlaw.com
www.craiglaw.ca

***Hamilton*: Cummins Seto - *3**
65 Walnut St. South, Hamilton, ON L8N 2L2
Tel: 905-528-5150; *Fax:* 905-528-1150
www.cumminsseto.com

***Hamilton*: Stephen F. De Wetter - *1**
#1215, 25 Main St. West, Hamilton, ON L8P 1H1
Tel: 905-521-8878; *Fax:* 905-577-0229
dewetterlaw@gmail.com

***Hamilton*: DiCenzo & Associates - *2**
#41, 1070 Stone Church Rd. East, Hamilton, ON L8W 3K8
Tel: 905-574-3300; *Fax:* 905-574-1766
adicenzo@weblaw.ca

***Hamilton*: Dudzic, Barristers & Solicitors - *2**
#1014, P.O. Box 988, Stn. LCD1, 105 Main St. East, Hamilton, ON L8N 3R1
Tel: 905-528-4251; *Fax:* 905-528-5325
dudziclaw@dudziclaw.com

***Hamilton*: Duxbury Law Professional Corporation Barristers & Solicitors - *2**
Former Name: Duxbury, Brian
#1500, 1 King St. West, Hamilton, ON L8P 1A4
Tel: 905-570-1242; *Fax:* 905-570-1955
brian@duxburylaw.ca

***Hamilton*: Paul H. Ennis, Q.C - *1**
#502, 105 Main St. East, Hamilton, ON L8N 1G6
Tel: 905-525-9335; *Fax:* 905-525-9988

***Hamilton*: Evans Sweeny Bordin LLP, Lawyers & Advocates - *7**
Former Name: Evans-Lawyers/Advocates
#1201, 1 King St. West, Hamilton, ON L8P 1A4
Tel: 905-523-5666; *Fax:* 905-523-8098
jfe@esblawyers.com
www.esblawyers.com

***Hamilton*: Evans, Philp - *23**
P.O. Box 930, Stn. A, Hamilton, ON L8N 3P9
Tel: 905-525-1200; *Fax:* 905-525-7897
info@evansphilp.com
www.evansphilp.com

***Hamilton*: Foreman Rosenblatt & Lewis - *3**
425 York Blvd., Hamilton, ON L8R 3M3
Tel: 905-525-3570; *Fax:* 905-523-0363
ylcinfo@yorklawcentre.com

***Hamilton*: Frankel Law Offices - *1**
#1001, 105 Main St. East, Hamilton, ON L8N 1G6
Tel: 905-522-3972; *Fax:* 905-528-2767
stephan@frankelaw.ca
www.frankelaw.ca

***Hamilton*: Genesee & Clarke - *3**
#2225, 25 Main St. West, Hamilton, ON L8P 1H1
Tel: 905-527-6666; *Fax:* 905-522-7085
frank@geneseeclarke.com

***Hamilton*: Gerald Swaye & Associates Professional Corporation - *7**
Also Known As: Swaye, Gerald A., Q.C., C.S.
#901, 105 Main St. East, Hamilton, ON L8N 1G6
Tel: 905-524-2861; *Fax:* 905-524-2313
gswaye@swaye.ca
www.swaye.ca

***Hamilton*: Robbie D. Gordon - *1**
P.O. Box 490, 488 Ferguson Ave., Hamilton, ON L8L 4Z5
Tel: 705-672-3338; *Fax:* 705-672-2451

** indicates number of lawyers*

***Hamilton*: Guyatt, Grasznbeek & Millikin - *1**
Also Known As: Collaborative Family Law
Former Name: Guyatt & Millikin
#401, 20 Jackson St. West, Hamilton, ON L8P 1L2
Tel: 905-528-8369; *Fax:* 905-528-8066
keith.millikin@bellnet.ca

***Hamilton*: Harper, Jaskot - *5**
#200, 1 James St. South, Hamilton, ON L8P 4R5
Tel: 905-522-3517; *Fax:* 905-522-3555
Toll-Free: 800-522-3517
www.jaskotfamilylaw.ca

***Hamilton*: Harvey Katz & Associates, Barristers, Solicitors, & Notaries Public - *3**
14 Hess St. South, Hamilton, ON L8P 3M8
Tel: 905-523-1442; *Fax:* 905-525-3817
harvey@hjklaw.on.ca
www.hjklaw.on.ca

***Hamilton*: Michael E. Hinchey - *1**
203 MacNab St. South, Hamilton, ON L8P 3C8
Tel: 905-525-1630; *Fax:* 905-527-3686

***Hamilton*: Inch Hammond Professional Corporation - *10**
Former Name: Inch, Easterbrook & Shaker
#1500, 1 King St. West, Hamilton, ON L8P 4X8
Tel: 905-525-4481; *Fax:* 905-525-0031
ies@inchlaw.com

***Hamilton*: Brian J. Inglis - *1**
#803, 20 Hughson St. South, Hamilton, ON L8N 2A1
Tel: 905-527-6727; *Fax:* 905-527-6310
inglislaw@interlynx.net

***Hamilton*: Jaskula, Sherk - *2**
#915, 25 Main St., Hamilton, ON L8P 1H1
Tel: 905-577-1040; *Fax:* 905-577-7775
csherk@jaskulasherk.com

***Hamilton*: George E. Johnson - *1**
19 Augusta St., Hamilton, ON L8N 1P6
Tel: 905-523-7333; *Fax:* 905-523-1311

***Hamilton*: Kathryn A. Junger - *1**
19 Augusta St., Hamilton, ON L8N 1P6
Tel: 905-523-7333; *Fax:* 905-523-1311

***Hamilton*: H.E. Katz - *1**
15 Bold St., Hamilton, ON L8P 1T3
Tel: 905-522-0040; *Fax:* 905-522-2981
call@howardkatzlaw.com

***Hamilton*: Michael W. Kelly - *1**
#101, 154 Main St. East, Hamilton, ON L8N 1G9
Tel: 905-546-1920; *Fax:* 905-546-8471
mikelly@bellnet.ca

***Hamilton*: Mary Elizabeth Kneeland Barrister & Solicitor - *1**
131 John St. South, Ground Level, Hamilton, ON L8N 2C3
Tel: 905-572-7737; *Fax:* 905-529-8819
an261@hwcn.org

***Hamilton*: John O. Krawchenko - *1**
175 Hunter Street East, Hamilton, ON L8N 4E7
Tel: 905-546-0525; *Fax:* 905-546-0596

***Hamilton*: Landeg, Spitale - *2**
#806, 20 Hughson St. South, Hamilton, ON L8N 2A1
Tel: 905-529-7462; *Fax:* 905-528-6787

***Hamilton*: Lazier Hickey Langs O'Neal - *10**
25 Main St. West, 15th Fl., Hamilton, ON L8P 1H1
Tel: 905-525-3652; *Fax:* 905-525-6278
lawfirm@lazierhickey.com
www.lazierhickey.com

***Hamilton*: Lees & Lees - *1**
#2225, 25 Main St. West, Hamilton, ON L8P 1H1
Tel: 905-523-7830; *Fax:* 905-523-4677
leeslaw@leesandlees.ca

***Hamilton*: W.J.I. Malcolm - *1**
#709, 20 Hughson St. South, Hamilton, ON L8N 2A1
Tel: 905-528-4291; *Fax:* 905-528-4292

***Hamilton*: McArthur, Vereschagin & Brown LLP - *4**
195 James St. South, Hamilton, ON L8P 3A8
Tel: 905-527-6900; *Fax:* 905-527-5177
sam@labourlaw.com

***Hamilton*: Anthony E. McCusker - *2**
#101, 200 Aberdeen Avenue, Hamilton, ON L8P 2P9
Tel: 905-523-0593; *Fax:* 905-522-0988
Toll-Free: 877-523-3909
mccusker@on.aibn.com

***Hamilton*: McHugh Mowat Whitmore Ionico MacPherson LLP - *6**
337 Queenston Rd., Hamilton, ON L8K 1H7
Tel: 905-549-4676; *Fax:* 905-549-5819
www.mmwimlawfirm.ca

***Hamilton*: McLelland & Dean - *1**
1 King St. West, 7th Fl., Hamilton, ON L8P 1A4
Tel: 905-546-0393; *Fax:* 905-527-6286

***Hamilton*: McQuesten Legal & Community Services - *3**
1440 Main St. East, Hamilton, ON L8K 6M3
Tel: 905-545-0442; *Fax:* 905-545-2645

***Hamilton*: Millar, Alexander - *2**
#830, 120 King St. West, Hamilton, ON L8P 4V2
Tel: 905-528-1186

***Hamilton*: Milligan Gresko Brown Vitulli Limberis LLP, Barristers & Solicitors - *4**
#1060, 120 King St. West, Hamilton, ON L8P 4V2
Tel: 905-522-7700; *Fax:* 905-528-6543
gjg@mgblawyers.ca
www.mgbvllaw.com

***Hamilton*: E.Y. Morwick - *1**
97 John St. South, Hamilton, ON L8N 2C2
Tel: 905-529-2343; *Fax:* 905-528-0070

***Hamilton*: Nolan Law Offices - *3**
1 King St. West, 7th Fl., Hamilton, ON L8P 1A4
Tel: 905-522-9261; *Fax:* 905-525-5836
info@nolanlaw.ca
www.nolalnaw.ca

***Hamilton*: J.Z. Olenski - *1**
#200, 845 Upper James St., Hamilton, ON L9C 3A3
Tel: 905-387-3922; *Fax:* 905-387-0291
johnlenski@netscape.net

***Hamilton*: George J. Parker - *1**
142 James St. South, Lower Level, Hamilton, ON L8P 3A2
Tel: 905-523-5636; *Fax:* 905-523-4910

***Hamilton*: A. Pazaratz - *1**
117 Hunter St. East, Hamilton, ON L8N 1M5
Tel: 905-523-5850; *Fax:* 905-528-0722

***Hamilton*: Michael S. Puskas - *1**
46 Jackson St. East, Hamilton, ON L8N 1L1
Tel: 905-527-4495; *Fax:* 905-527-4496
michael.puskas@bellnet.ca

***Hamilton*: Daniel P. Randazzo - *1**
44 Hughson St. South, Hamilton, ON L8N 2A7
Tel: 905-777-1773; *Fax:* 905-777-1774
randazzo@netinc.ca

***Hamilton*: Geoffrey M. Read - *1**
172 Main St. East, Hamilton, ON L8N 1G9
Tel: 905-684-3187; *Fax:* 905-522-6677

***Hamilton*: Robinson, McCallum, McKerracher, Graham - *1**
#300, 69 John St. South, Hamilton, ON L8N 2B9
Tel: 905-528-1435; *Fax:* 905-529-1570
m.graham@on.aibn.com

***Hamilton*: Rory J. Cornale - *1**
#301, 4 Hughson St. South, Hamilton, ON L8N 3Z1
Tel: 905-521-9989; *Fax:* 905-525-7737
rory.cornale@derubeis-chetcuti.com

***Hamilton*: Ross & McBride - *30**
P.O. Box 907, Stn. LCD1, 1 King St. West, Hamilton, ON L8N 3P6
Tel: 905-526-9800; *Fax:* 905-526-0732
www.rossmcbride.com

***Hamilton*: Ross & McBride LLP - *37**
Former Name: Martin, Martin, Evans, Husband
Commerce Place, P.O. Box 907, 1 King Street West, 10th Fl., Hamilton, ON L8N 3P6
Tel: 905-526-9800; *Fax:* 905-526-0732
contact@rossmcbride.com
www.rossmcbride.com

***Hamilton*: Michael N. Rubenstein - *1**
#200, 242 James St. South, Hamilton, ON L8P 3B3
Tel: 905-525-9636; *Fax:* 905-521-0690
smerz@primus.ca

***Hamilton*: L.I. Sapiano - *1**
#1500, 105 Main St. East, Hamilton, ON L8N 1G6
Tel: 905-523-1665; *Fax:* 905-523-4436
lsapiano@gta.igs.net

***Hamilton*: Scarfone Hawkins LLP - *19**
P.O. Box 926, Stn. Depot 1, 1 James St. South, 14th Fl., Hamilton, ON L8N 3P9
Tel: 905-523-1333; *Fax:* 905-523-5878
info@shlaw.ca
www.scarfonehawkinsllp.com

***Hamilton*: Monica U.M. Scholz - *1**
184 Jackson St. East, Hamilton, ON L8N 1L4
Tel: 905-577-6070; *Fax:* 905-577-6051

***Hamilton*: Schreiber & Smurlick - *1**
1219 Main St. East, Hamilton, ON L8K 1A5
Tel: 905-545-1107

***Hamilton*: Simpson & Watson - *3**
950 King St. West, Hamilton, ON L8S 1K8
Tel: 905-527-1174; *Fax:* 905-577-0661
davidsimpson@simpsonwatson.com
www.simpsonwatson.com

***Hamilton*: Smith & Smith - *1**
1416 King St. East, Hamilton, ON L8M 1H8
Tel: 905-544-6034

***Hamilton*: F.P. Sondola - *1**
#205, 124 James St. South, Hamilton, ON L8P 2Z4
Tel: 905-523-1970; *Fax:* 905-523-1971

***Hamilton*: Shelley M. Stanzlik - *1**
120 Jackson St. East, Hamilton, ON L8N 1L3
Tel: 905-777-1155; *Fax:* 905-777-1142
rgee@icom.ca

***Hamilton*: Jay Warren State - *1**
P.O. Box 907, Stn. LCD 1, 1 King St. West, Hamilton, ON L8N 3P6
Tel: 905-572-5818; *Fax:* 905-526-0732
jstate@rossmcbride.com

***Hamilton*: J.J. Steadman - *1**
124 MacNab St. South, Hamilton, ON L8P 3C3
Tel: 905-529-6400; *Fax:* 905-521-1924

***Hamilton*: Sullivan, Festeryga, Lawlor & Arrell - *17**
1 James St. South, 11th Fl., Hamilton, ON L8P 4R5
Tel: 905-528-7963; *Fax:* 905-577-0077
general@sullivanfesteryga.com
www.sullivanfesteryga.com

***Hamilton*: Szpiech, Ellis, Skibinski, Shipton - *4**
414 Main St. East, Hamilton, ON L8N 1J9
Tel: 905-524-2454; *Fax:* 905-523-1733
sess@on.aibn.com

***Hamilton*: Edward Tharen - *1**
1243 Barton St. East, Hamilton, ON L8H 2V8
Tel: 905-547-1618; *Fax:* 905-549-5654

***Hamilton*: Thoman Soule LLP, Lawyers - *6**
Former Name: Thoman, Soule, Gage LLP
P.O. Box 187, Stn. LCD 1, 46 Jackson St. East, Hamilton, ON L8N 3C5
Tel: 905-529-8195; *Fax:* 905-529-7906
info@thomansoule.com
www.thomansoule.com

***Hamilton*: Tkach & Tokiwa - *1**
#71, Mountain Plaza Mall, 651 Upper James St., Hamilton, ON L9C 5R8
Tel: 905-383-3545; *Fax:* 905-574-3020
tkachlaw@mountaincable.net

***Hamilton*: Turkstra Mazza Associates - *6**
Former Name: Turkstra Mazza Shinehoft Mihailovich Associates
15 Bold St., Hamilton, ON L8P 1T3
Tel: 905-529-3476; *Fax:* 905-529-3663

***Hamilton*: Jennifer M. Vandenberg - *1**
172 Main St. East, Hamilton, ON L8N 1G9
Tel: 905-572-6611; *Fax:* 905-572-9440
jvandenberg@cogeco.ca

** indicates number of lawyers*

***Hamilton*: Wasserman & Associates - *1**
Former Name: Robert G. Wasserman
#6, 105 Main St. East, Hamilton, ON L8N 1G6
Tel: 905-522-4242; *Fax:* 905-521-0052

***Hamilton*: Gary Leonard Waxman - *1**
#234, 845 Upper James St., Hamilton, ON L9C 3A3
Tel: 905-388-0585; *Fax:* 905-575-1613
waxman@mountaincable.net

***Hamilton*: Weisz, Rocchi & Scholes - *6**
#200, Effort Trust Bldg., 242 Main St. East, Hamilton, ON L8N 1H5
Tel: 905-523-1842; *Fax:* 905-523-4011
info@wrs.on.ca
www.wrs.on.ca

***Hamilton*: Nicholas R. White - *1**
120 Jackson St. East, Hamilton, ON L8N 1L3
Tel: 905-521-8901; *Fax:* 905-521-9564
nwhite@netaccess.on.ca

***Hamilton*: Yachetti, Lanza & Restivo - *6**
#100, 154 Main St. East, Hamilton, ON L8N 1G9
Tel: 905-528-7534; *Fax:* 905-528-5275
info@ylrlawyers.com
www.ylrlawyers.com

***Hanover*: Kenneth P. Duffy - *1**
414 - 10 St., Hanover, ON N4N 1P6
Tel: 519-364-1440; *Fax:* 519-364-6023
kduffy@wightman.ca

***Hanover*: Robert W. Garcia Professional Corporation - *2**
P.O. Box 37, Hanover, ON N4N 3C3
Tel: 519-364-3643; *Fax:* 519-364-6594
rgarcia@garcia-law.com

***Hanover*: Halpin & McMeeken, Barristers & Solicitors - *1**
478 Tenth St., Hanover, ON N4N 1R4
Tel: 519-364-5505; *Fax:* 519-364-0165
kevin@hanoverlaw.ca
www.hanoverlaw.ca

***Harrow*: Golden & Golden - *1**
P.O. Box 279, 13 King St. West, Harrow, ON N0R 1G0
Tel: 519-738-4111; *Fax:* 519-738-3470

***Harrow*: Karl G. Melinz - *1**
P.O. Box 880, 41A Centre St. West, Harrow, ON N0R 1G0
Tel: 519-738-2232; *Fax:* 519-738-9080
kgmelinz@mmsi.net

***Hawkesbury*: Gerald E. Langlois & Associates - *2**
Former Name: Langlois/Gauthier
471 McGill St., Hawkesbury, ON K6A 1R1
Tel: 613-632-8600; *Fax:* 613-632-5274
langlois@hawk.igs.net

***Hawkesbury*: Julien & Cormier Professional Corporation - *2**
132 Race St., Hawkesbury, ON K6A 1V2
Tel: 613-632-0148; *Fax:* 613-632-1810

***Hawkesbury*: Lachapelle Law Office - *1**
444 McGill St., Hawkesbury, ON K6A 1R2
Tel: 613-632-7032; *Fax:* 613-632-5472
lachapellelawoffice@bellnet.ca

***Hawkesbury*: Pilon Professional Corporation - *1**
Former Name: Smith Lacombe Marcotte
280 Main St. West, Hawkesbury, ON K6A 2H7
Tel: 613-632-0103; *Fax:* 613-632-2800
pilons@bellnet.ca

***Hawkesbury*: Woods Parisien - *2**
#200, 115 Main St. East, Hawkesbury, ON K6A 1A1
Tel: 613-632-8557; *Fax:* 613-632-8559
parisien@on.aibn.com

***Hillsburgh*: Robert P. Harper - *1**
P.O. Box 10, 115 Main St., Hillsburgh, ON N0B 1Z0
Tel: 519-855-4961; *Fax:* 519-855-4029
robertharper@bellnet.ca

***Huntsville*: James S. Anderson**
#5, 133 Hwy. 60, Huntsville, ON P1H 1C2
Tel: 705-789-8823; *Fax:* 705-789-1272
jamesanderson@sympatico.ca

***Huntsville*: A.B. Cochran - *1**
#5, 133 Hwy. 60, Huntsville, ON P1H 1C2
Tel: 705-789-5538; *Fax:* 705-789-1272
acochran@vianet.ca

***Huntsville*: G.A. Smith - *1**
Also Known As: Glen A. Smith
#1, 3 Fairy Ave., Huntsville, ON P1H 1G7
Tel: 705-789-8829; *Fax:* 705-789-2984
glensmith@bellnet.ca

***Ingersoll*: Nesbitt Coulter LLP - *1**
183 Thames St. South, Ingersoll, ON N5C 2T6
Tel: 519-485-5651; *Fax:* 519-485-6582
mborndahl@nesbittlaw.com

***Innisfil*: D. Anne Cheney - *1**
P.O. Box 7074, 1984 Wilkinson St., Innisfil, ON L9S 1A8
Tel: 705-734-9644; *Fax:* 705-734-0333

***Innisfil*: Patrick A. Duco - *1**
2093 Lilac Dr., #B, Innisfil, ON L9S 1Z1
Tel: 705-436-1020; *Fax:* 705-436-1027

***Innisfil*: Gibson & Adams LLP - *4**
8000 Yonge St., Innisfil, ON L9S 1L5
Tel: 705-436-1701; *Fax:* 705-436-1710
ganda@gibsonandadams.ca

***Iroquois Falls*: J. Kenneth Alexander - *1**
P.O. Box 290, Stn. A, 283 Main St., Iroquois Falls, ON P0K 1G0
Tel: 705-232-4309; *Fax:* 705-232-5274

***Iroquois Falls*: Susan T. McGrath - *1**
P.O. Box 700, Iroquois Falls, ON P0K 1G0
Tel: 705-232-4055; *Fax:* 705-232-6301
mcgrath@nt.net

***Jarvis*: W.E. Kelly - *1**
P.O. Box 430, 32 Main St. North, Jarvis, ON N0A 1J0
Tel: 519-587-4561; *Fax:* 519-587-5052

***Kanata*: Alan Pratt Law Office - *2**
Former Name: Pratt, Alan
#201, 105 Schneider Rd., Kanata, ON K2K 1Y3
Tel: 613-254-5415; *Fax:* 613-254-9859

***Kanata*: LaBarge Weinstein - *16**
#800, 515 Legget Dr., Kanata, ON K2K 3G4
Tel: 613-599-9600; *Fax:* 613-599-0018
info@lwlaw.com
www.lwlaw.com

***Kanata*: PwM Consulting - *1**
#344, 300 Earl Grey Dr., Kanata, ON K2T 1C1
Tel: 613-839-1555; *Fax:* 613-839-2555
peterm@pwmconsulting.com

***Kanata*: J. Jacques Robert**
486 Hazeldean Rd., Kanata, ON K2L 1V4
Tel: 613-860-1377; *Fax:* 613-837-7664

***Kapuskasing*: Bourgeault Brunelle Dumais Boucher - *4**
P.O. Box 446, 7 Cain Ave., Kapuskasing, ON P5N 1S8
Tel: 705-335-6121; *Fax:* 705-335-8127

***Kapuskasing*: J.M. Michel Majerovich - *1**
28 Kolb Ave., Kapuskasing, ON P5N 1G1
Tel: 705-335-5051; *Fax:* 705-337-5051

***Kapuskasing*: Perras Mongenais - *2**
Former Name: Perras et Associés
10B Circle St., Kapuskasing, ON P5N 1T3
Tel: 705-335-3939; *Fax:* 705-335-3960

***Kapuskasing*: Guy A. Wainwright - *1**
19 Cain Ave., Kapuskasing, ON P5N 1T2
Tel: 705-335-8501; *Fax:* 705-337-1474
gwainrt@ntl.sympatico.ca

***Kenora*: Carten Law Office - *2**
#201, P.O. Box 2050, Stn. Main, 344 Second St. South, Kenora, ON P9N 3X8
Tel: 807-468-3036; *Fax:* 807-468-7576
cartenlaw@gokenora.com

***Kenora*: David James Elliott - *1**
Stone House, 225 Main St. South, Kenora, ON P9N 1T3
Tel: 807-468-3355; *Fax:* 807-468-7858

***Kenora*: Gibson & Wexler - *2**
P.O. Box 2450, 111 Main St. South, Kenora, ON P9N 3X8
Tel: 807-468-3061; *Fax:* 807-468-7940

***Kenora*: Hook, Seller & Lundin - *4**
#204, Bannister Centre, 301 - 1 Ave. South, Kenora, ON P9N 1W2
Tel: 807-468-9831; *Fax:* 807-468-8384
jthook@hsllawyers.com
www.hsllawyers.com

***Kenora*: Barbara E. Minshall - *1**
105 Main St., Kenora, ON P9N 1T1
Tel: 807-468-3038; *Fax:* 807-468-8122
bminshall@voyageur.ca

***Kenora*: Shewchuk, MacDonell, Ormiston, Richardt & Fregeau LLP - *6**
P.O. Box 1970, 214 Main St. South, Kenora, ON P9N 1T2
Tel: 807-468-9828; *Fax:* 807-468-5504
www.kenoralaw.com

***Keswick*: Iain T. Donnell - *1**
183 Simcoe Ave., Keswick, ON L4P 2H6
Tel: 905-476-9100; *Fax:* 905-476-2027

***Keswick*: R.E. Pollock - *1**
#300, 449 The Queensway South, Keswick, ON L4P 2C9
Tel: 905-476-0021; *Fax:* 905-476-0134

***Kincardine*: Marshall & Mahood - *2**
Former Name: Mahood & Darcy
313 Lambton St., Kincardine, ON N2Z 2Y8
Tel: 519-396-8144; *Fax:* 519-396-9446
marshall.mahood@tn2.com

***Kincardine*: William S. Mathers - *1**
226 Queen St., Kincardine, ON N2Z 2S5
Tel: 519-396-4147; *Fax:* 519-396-1872
wwmlawyer@bmts.com

***Kingston*: Wm. J.F. Bishop - *2**
P.O. Box 1403, 338 Montreal St., Kingston, ON K7L 5C6
Tel: 613-544-0644; *Fax:* 613-544-2197
bill.bishop@on.aibn.com

***Kingston*: Black, Lloyd, Caron - *2**
P.O. Box 247, 249 Brock St., Kingston, ON K7L 4V8
Tel: 613-546-3286; *Fax:* 613-549-1193
blcm@adan.kingston.net

***Kingston*: Caldwell & Moore - *2**
260 Barrie St., Kingston, ON K7L 3K7
Tel: 613-545-1860; *Fax:* 613-545-1862
caldwell-moore@cogeco.ca

***Kingston*: Jack W. Chong - *1**
Former Name: Chong & O'Neill
P.O. Box 1382, Stn. Main, 273 King St. East, Kingston, ON K7L 5C6
Tel: 613-549-1225; *Fax:* 613-549-3882

***Kingston*: Robert K. Cooper - *1**
11 Carruthers St., Kingston, ON K7L 1L9
Tel: 613-544-3634

***Kingston*: Cunningham, Swan, Carty, Little & Bonham LLP - *24**
#201, City Place II, 1473 John Counter Blvd., Kingston, ON K7M 8Z6
Tel: 613-544-0211; *Fax:* 613-542-9814
info@cswan.com
www.cswan.com

***Kingston*: Ecclestone & Ecclestone LLP - *2**
Former Name: C.E. John Ecclestone
1046 Gardiners Rd., Kingston, ON K7P 1R7
Tel: 613-384-0735; *Fax:* 613-384-0731
email@ecclaw.net
www.ecclaw.net

***Kingston*: Elizabeth I Ollson - *1**
1770 Bath Rd., Kingston, ON K7M 4Y2
Tel: 613-384-8122; *Fax:* 613-384-7056
eollson@kos.net

***Kingston*: John R. Gale - *1**
238 Wellington St., 1st Fl., Kingston, ON K7K 2Y8
Tel: 613-546-4283; *Fax:* 613-546-9861
info@galeforlaw.ca
www.galeforlaw.ca

***Kingston*: Wayne C. Gay & Associate - *2**
P.O. Box 370, Stn. Main, 275 Ontario St., Kingston, ON K7L 4W2
Tel: 613-549-4300; *Fax:* 613-549-6948
waynegay@waynegay.com

** indicates number of lawyers*

Kingston: **Good & Elliott Hawkins LLP - *3**
Former Name: Good & Elliott
P.O. Box 1253, Stn. Main, 153 Brock St., Kingston, ON K7L 4Y8
Tel: 613-544-1330; *Fax:* 613-547-4538

Kingston: **Wayne R.J. Headrick - *1**
1770 Bath Rd., Kingston, ON K7M 4Y2
Tel: 613-384-4403; *Fax:* 613-384-7056
wheadrik@kos.net

Kingston: **Hickey & Hickey - *2**
P.O. Box 110, 93 Clarence St., Kingston, ON K7L 4V6
Tel: 613-548-3191; *Fax:* 613-548-8195
hickeym@on.aibn.com

Kingston: **Mary Ann Higgs - *1**
#206, P.O. Box 700, 275 Ontario St., Kingston, ON K7L 4X1
Tel: 613-548-7399; *Fax:* 613-548-1862
maryannhiggs@on.aibn.com

Kingston: **Jack Soule Consulting - *1**
60 Riverside Dr., Kingston, ON K7L 4V1
Tel: 613-541-0013; *Fax:* 613-541-0112
jack@soule.ca

Kingston: **Jacob Macpherson Menard - *2**
#102, 780 Midpark Dr., Kingston, ON K7M 7P6
Tel: 613-389-1999; *Fax:* 613-384-8777
macpherson@kingston-lawyers.ca

Kingston: **R. Wayne Keeler - *1**
11 Drayton Ave., Kingston, ON K7K 4X5
Tel: 613-531-4600; *Fax:* 613-547-4577
keelerw@kos.net

Kingston: **Wayne T. King - *1**
#203, P.O. Box 221, 303 Bagot St., Kingston, ON K7L 4V8
Tel: 613-547-6481; *Fax:* 613-547-9025
wayne.tking@bellnet.ca

Kingston: **R. Graham Lord - *1**
1770 Bath Rd., Kingston, ON K7M 4Y2
Tel: 613-384-4403; *Fax:* 613-384-7056
rglord@kingston.net

Kingston: **J. Bruce MacNaughton - *1**
P.O. Box 1621, 45 Johnson St., Kingston, ON K7L 5C8
Tel: 613-546-9990; *Fax:* 613-546-6176
bruce@macnaughton.law.com

Kingston: **Mary-Jo Maur - *1**
#1, 151 Wellington St., Kingston, ON K7L 3E1
Tel: 613-530-2665; *Fax:* 613-530-2241
mary-jo.maur@bellnet.ca

Kingston: **M.A. McCue - *1**
#201A, 837 Princess St., Kingston, ON K7L 1G8
Tel: 613-542-3700; *Fax:* 613-542-5700
mamccue@kingston.net

Kingston: **G.Y. McDiarmid - *1**
P.O. Box 1010, Stn. Main, 3 Rideau St., Kingston, ON K7L 4X8
Tel: 613-546-3274; *Fax:* 613-546-1493
gmcdiarmid@on.aibn.com

Kingston: **Morley Law Office - *1**
211 Division St., Kingston, ON K7K 3Z2
Tel: 613-542-2192; *Fax:* 613-542-2393
info@lesmorley.com
www.lesmorley.com

Kingston: **Fergus J. (Chip) O'Connor - *1**
P.O. Box 1959, 104 Johnson St., Kingston, ON K7L 5J7
Tel: 613-546-5581; *Fax:* 613-546-5540
oconnor@kos.net

Kingston: **Philip M. Osanic - *1**
817 Blackburn Mews, Kingston, ON K7P 2N6
Tel: 613-634-4440; *Fax:* 613-634-4443

Kingston: **J. Yvonne Pelley - *1**
817 Blackburn Mews, Kingston, ON K7P 2N6
Tel: 613-634-4440; *Fax:* 613-634-4443
jypelley@on.aibn.com

Kingston: **Racioppo Zuber Coetzee Dionne LLP**
#201, 574 Princess St., Kingston, ON K7L 1C9
Tel: 613-544-1482; *Fax:* 613-546-3633

Kingston: **Jennifer L. Sims - *1**
#201, 303 Bagot St., Kingston, ON K7K 5W7
Tel: 613-530-2230; *Fax:* 613-530-2231

Kingston: **Douglas M. Slack - *1**
#1, 817 Blackburn Mews, Kingston, ON K7P 2N6
Tel: 613-384-7260; *Fax:* 613-384-7262
dm.slack@utoronto.ca

Kingston: **Britton C. Smith - *1**
P.O. Box 1376, Stn. Main, 74 Johnson St., Kingston, ON K7L 5C6
Tel: 613-547-3798; *Fax:* 613-547-6814

Kingston: **Letitia M. Steele - *1**
P.O. Box 29013, Stn. Portsmouth, Kingston, ON K7M 8W6
Tel: 613-542-1795; *Fax:* 613-542-2471

Kingston: **Tepper Law Office - *1**
P.O. Box 1265, Stn. Main, 461 Princess St., Kingston, ON K7L 4Y8
Tel: 613-546-1169; *Fax:* 613-546-6992
gtepper@kingston.net

Kingston: **A.F. Thomson - *1**
232 Brock St., Kingston, ON K7L 1S4
Tel: 613-549-5111; *Fax:* 613-549-4074
thomson@kingston.net

Kingston: **Thomas W. Troughton - *1**
#103, P.O. Box 668, Stn. Main, 780 Midpark Dr., Kingston, ON K7L 4X1
Tel: 613-634-0302; *Fax:* 613-384-8777
troughton@frontenaclaw.on.ca

Kingston: **Trousdale & Trousdale - *2**
#200, 184 Wellington St., Kingston, ON K7L 3E4
Tel: 613-546-2231; *Fax:* 613-546-9001

Kingston: **Willoughby MacLeod Warkentin LLP - *2**
Former Name: Willoughby, MacLeod
734 Arlington Park Place, Kingston, ON K7M 8H9
Tel: 613-384-5678; *Fax:* 613-384-6025
info@macleodlaw.net

Kingsville: **Dunnion & Dunmore - *1**
59 Main St. East, Kingsville, ON N9Y 1A1
Tel: 519-733-6573; *Fax:* 519-733-3172
pdunmore@cogeco.net

Kirkland Lake: **Judith L. Munn - *1**
P.O. Box 970, 11 Station Rd. South, Kirkland Lake, ON P2N 3L2
Tel: 705-567-9224; *Fax:* 705-567-9227
judmunn@ntl.aibn.com

Kirkland Lake: **G. Shorrock - *1**
P.O. Box 490, Kirkland Lake, ON P2N 3J5
Tel: 705-567-5213; *Fax:* 705-567-3987
shorlaw@ntl.sympatico.ca

Kitchener: **Derek K. Babcock - *1**
28 Weber St. West, Kitchener, ON N2H 3Z2
Tel: 519-742-3570; *Fax:* 519-576-7451
dbabcock@on.aibn.com

Kitchener: **Thomas L. Brock - *1**
17 Irvin St., Kitchener, ON N2H 1K6
Tel: 519-742-1270; *Fax:* 519-742-6973

Kitchener: **Chris Lawyers - *1**
194 Weber St. East, Kitchener, ON N2H 1E4
Tel: 519-570-4400; *Fax:* 519-570-4242
Toll-Free: 888-570-9697
contactus@chrislawyers.com
www.chrislawyers.com

Kitchener: **J. Mark Coffey - *1**
#705, Corporation Square, 30 Duke St. West, Kitchener, ON N2H 3W5
Tel: 519-742-5100; *Fax:* 519-742-5229

Kitchener: **H.J. Cox - *1**
#610, 50 Queen St. North, Kitchener, ON N2H 6P4
Tel: 519-744-6551; *Fax:* 519-744-9885
hjcox@golden.net

Kitchener: **N.A. Crawford - *1**
1444 King St. East, Kitchener, ON N2G 2N7
Tel: 519-743-3615; *Fax:* 519-743-2212

Kitchener: **Dietrich Law Office - *2**
Former Name: G.B. Dietrich
141 Duke St. East, Kitchener, ON N2H 1A6
Tel: 519-749-0770; *Fax:* 519-749-0288
george.deitrich@sympatico.ca

Kitchener: **Farhood, Boehler & Associates - *2**
#510, 101 Frederick St., Kitchener, ON N2H 6R2
Tel: 519-744-9949; *Fax:* 519-744-7974

** indicates number of lawyers*

Kitchener: **Timothy C. Flannery - *1**
82 Weber St. East, Kitchener, ON N2H 1C7
Tel: 519-578-8017; *Fax:* 519-578-8327
flannery@golden.net

Kitchener: **George C. Amos - *1**
276 Frederick St., Kitchener, ON N2H 2N4
Tel: 519-576-8480; *Fax:* 519-579-3042
george@amoslaw.ca

Kitchener: **Giffen LLP - *12**
Former Name: Giffen Lee LLP
#500, Commerce House, P.O. Box 2396, 50 Queen St. North, Kitchener, ON N2H 6M3
Tel: 519-578-4150; *Fax:* 519-578-8740
Toll-Free: 866-688-4150
info@giffenlawyers.com
www.giffenlawyers.com

Kitchener: **R. Haalboom, Q.C. - *1**
7 Duke St. West, Kitchener, ON N2H 6N7
Tel: 519-579-2920; *Fax:* 519-576-0471
richard@haalboom.ca

Kitchener: **R.J. Hare - *1**
741 King St. West, Kitchener, ON N2G 1E3
Tel: 519-576-6710

Kitchener: **Richard H.F. Herold - *1**
53 Roy St., Kitchener, ON N2H 4B4
Tel: 519-749-0555; *Fax:* 519-741-9041

Kitchener: **Hertzberger & Associates, Barristers & Solicitors - *2**
Former Name: Hertzberger, Olsen & Associates
Penthouse, Corporation Square, 30 Duke St. West, Kitchener, ON N2H 3W5
Tel: 519-570-1944; *Fax:* 519-570-0989
reception@hertzbergerlaw.com
www.hertzbergerlaw.com

Kitchener: **J.T. Jansen - *1**
46 Brembel St., Kitchener, ON N2B 3T8
Tel: 519-741-1911; *Fax:* 519-741-5945
timjansen@bellnet.ca

Kitchener: **Kay Professional Corporation - *4**
Former Name: Kay, Bogdon
177 Victoria St. North, Kitchener, ON N2H 5C5
Tel: 519-579-1220; *Fax:* 519-743-8063
law@kaylaw.ca
www.kaylaw.ca

Kitchener: **Kelly & Co. - *3**
#903, 50 Queen St. North, Kitchener, ON N2H 6P4
Tel: 519-579-3360; *Fax:* 519-579-2556
bkelly@kellylaw.com
www.kellylaw.com

Kitchener: **Kokila D. Khanna**
#900, 50 Queen St. North, Kitchener, ON N2H 6P4
Tel: 516-571-1542; *Fax:* 516-571-0945

Kitchener: **Sheldon Kosky - *1**
71 Weber St. East, Kitchener, ON N2H 1C6
Tel: 519-578-1480; *Fax:* 519-579-2537

Kitchener: **Stephanie A. Krug - *1**
17 Irvin St., Kitchener, ON N2H 1K6
Tel: 519-743-1603; *Fax:* 519-742-6973
stephaniekrug@aol.com

Kitchener: **R.G.R. Lawrence, Q.C. - *1**
18 Irvin St., Kitchener, ON N2H 1K8
Tel: 519-742-4443; *Fax:* 519-578-4201

Kitchener: **Ludwig, Lichtenheldt & Eby - *3**
P.O. Box 1463, Stn. C, 97 Frederick St., Kitchener, ON N2G 4H6
Tel: 519-579-3000; *Fax:* 519-579-5660

Kitchener: **Madorin, Snyder LLP - *16**
P.O. Box 1234, Stn. C, 55 King St. West, Kitchener, ON N2G 4G9
Tel: 519-744-4491; *Fax:* 519-741-8060
reception@kw-law.com
www.kw-law.com

Kitchener: **Richard Marchak - *1**
#9, 300 Victoria St. North, Kitchener, ON N2H 6R9
Tel: 519-570-3635; *Fax:* 519-570-0104

Kitchener: Tracy L.M. Miller - *1
#203, 7 Duke St. West, Kitchener, ON N2H 6N7
Tel: 519-745-1912; *Fax:* 519-745-1987

Kitchener: Mollison, McCormick - *6
P.O. Box 2307, Stn. B, 71 Weber St. East, Kitchener, ON N2H 6L2
Tel: 519-579-1040; *Fax:* 519-579-2537
mmollison@mollisonlaw.com

Kitchener: Morrison Reist - *2
279 Queen St. South, Kitchener, ON N2G 1W4
Tel: 519-576-5351; *Fax:* 519-576-5411
Toll-Free: 800-354-5723
law@morrisonreist.com
www.morrisonreist.com

Kitchener: Morscher & Morscher - *1
85 Margaret Ave. North, Kitchener, ON N2J 3R2
Tel: 519-749-8100; *Fax:* 519-749-8141

Kitchener: Jacqueline Mulvey - *1
293 Frederick St., Kitchener, ON N2H 2N6
Tel: 519-744-3704; *Fax:* 519-744-3662
jmulvey@golden.net

Kitchener: Mark T. Nowak - *1
370 Frederick St., Kitchener, ON N2H 2P3
Tel: 519-746-8340; *Fax:* 519-746-8144
marknowak@bellnet.ca

Kitchener: John E. Opolko - *1
372 Queen St. South, Kitchener, ON N2G 1W7
Tel: 519-743-2670; *Fax:* 519-743-2670

Kitchener: Wayne G. Rabley - *1
234 Frederick St., Kitchener, ON N2H 2M8
Tel: 519-570-1010; *Fax:* 519-570-4458

Kitchener: B.H. Ritter - *1
17 Irvin St., Kitchener, ON N2H 1K6
Tel: 519-744-1169; *Fax:* 519-742-6973
britter1@aol.com

Kitchener: Roetsch & Schaffer - *2
284 Frederick St., Kitchener, ON N2H 2N4
Tel: 519-576-5310; *Fax:* 519-576-2797

Kitchener: John D. E. Shannon - *1
30 Spetz St., Kitchener, ON N2H 1K1
Tel: 519-743-3654; *Fax:* 519-578-9521
jdeslaw@bellnet.ca

Kitchener: Sloane & Pinchen - *2
#301, 824 King St. North, Kitchener, ON N2G 1G1
Tel: 519-578-3094; *Fax:* 519-578-3682
craig@sloanepinchen.com; david@sloanepinchen.com

Kitchener: Smith, Hunt, Buck - *2
P.O. Box 2008, Stn. C, Kitchener, ON N2H 6L1
Tel: 519-579-3400; *Fax:* 519-741-9041
office@smithhuntbuck.com

Kitchener: Smyth, Hobson - *1
#206, 7 Duke St. West, Kitchener, ON N2H 6N7
Tel: 519-578-9400; *Fax:* 519-578-7482

Kitchener: Carolyn R. Thomas & Associate - *1
#900, 50 Queen St. North, Kitchener, ON N2H 6P4
Tel: 519-576-4459; *Fax:* 519-576-9349
carolyn@carolynrthomas.ca
www.carolynrthomas.ca

Kitchener: Teresa Tummillo-Goy - *1
228 Frederick St., Kitchener, ON N2H 2M8
Tel: 519-888-9440; *Fax:* 519-888-9750
teresa@ttglaw.ca

Kitchener: Voll & Santos - *2
30 Spetz St., Kitchener, ON N2H 1K1
Tel: 519-578-3400; *Fax:* 519-578-9521

Kitchener: Walters Gubler - *2
#604, 30 Duke St. West, Kitchener, ON N2H 3W5
Tel: 519-578-8010; *Fax:* 519-578-9395
inquiries@wglaw.org

Kitchener: Wildeboer Dellelce LLP - *2
Former Name: Wildeboer Rand Thomson Apps & Dellelce LLP
#401, 72 Victoria St. South, Kitchener, ON N2G 4Y9
Tel: 519-741-8708; *Fax:* 519-741-9576
www.wildlaw.ca

Kitchener: Colleen J. Winn - *1
604 Charles St. East, Kitchener, ON N2G 2R5
Tel: 519-743-3981; *Fax:* 519-743-3647

Kitchener: Stephen C. Woodworth - *1
#9, 300 Victoria St. North, Kitchener, ON N2H 6R9
Tel: 519-570-0033; *Fax:* 519-570-0104

Kitchener: W.R. Zalman - *1
#102, 684 Belmont Ave. West, Kitchener, ON N2M 1N6
Tel: 519-579-6170; *Fax:* 519-579-6171

Kleinburg: Black & Associates - *3
#1, 10472 Islington Ave., Kleinburg, ON L0J 1C0
Tel: 905-939-8050; *Fax:* 905-939-8025
blackm@bellnet.ca
www.blackandassociates.ca

L'Orignal: Rodrigue Landriault - *1
P.O. Box 315, L'Orignal, ON K0B 1K0
Tel: 613-675-4526; *Fax:* 613-235-7442

L'Orignal: Tolhurst & Miller - *4
1030 King St., L'Orignal, ON K0B 1K0
Tel: 613-675-4512; *Fax:* 613-675-1103
Toll-Free: 866-752-8277
www.tolhurstandmiller.on.ca

Lakefield: Baker & Cole - *2
Former Name: T.E. Cole
8 Bridge St., Lakefield, ON K0L 2H0
Tel: 705-652-8161; *Fax:* 705-652-7088
thomas.cole@nexicom.net

Lakefield: G.A. Booth - *1
P.O. Box 116, 34 Bridge St., Lakefield, ON K0L 2H0
Tel: 705-652-3378; *Fax:* 705-652-6823
gary@boothlawoffice.org

Lancaster: Paul D. Syrduk - *1
P.O. Box 9, 10 Oak St., Lancaster, ON K0C 1N0
Tel: 613-347-2423; *Fax:* 613-347-7118
syruduk@glen-net.ca

Leamington: Owen Spettigue Professional Corporation - *1
P.O. Box 327, 57 Talbot St. East, Leamington, ON N8H 3W3
Tel: 519-326-2687; *Fax:* 519-326-1344
cowenspettiguelaw@bellnet.ca

Leamington: Reid, Collins, Ricci, Enns & Rollier - *5
60 Talbot St. West, Leamington, ON N8H 1M4
Tel: 519-326-3237; *Fax:* 519-326-8139
rrcre@mnsi.net

Lefaivre: Hydroplane Services Mergus Inc. - *1
2575 Conc. 2, Lefaivre, ON K0B 1J0
Tel: 613-676-2510

Lindsay: Brent Walmsley - *1
#220, Kent Place Mall, 189 Kent St. West, Lindsay, ON K9V 5G6
Tel: 705-878-8131; *Fax:* 705-878-4642

Lindsay: Cornell, Mortlock & Sillberg - *1
P.O. Box 536, Stn. Main, 272 Kent St. West, Lindsay, ON K9V 4S5
Tel: 705-324-4312; *Fax:* 705-324-7525

Lindsay: J.W. Evans - *1
P.O. Box 427, Stn. Main, 219 Kent St. West, Lindsay, ON K9V 4S5
Tel: 705-324-3207; *Fax:* 705-328-1128

Lindsay: Evans, Whitford, Nagel Associates - *3
18 York St. South, Lindsay, ON K9V 3A2
Tel: 705-328-2727; *Fax:* 705-328-2770

Lindsay: Frost, Frost & Gorwill - *1
#217, 189 Kent St. West, Lindsay, ON K9V 5G6
Tel: 705-324-2193; *Fax:* 705-324-9879

Lindsay: Carol E. Jamieson - *1
18 Cambridge St. North, Lindsay, ON K9V 4C3
Tel: 705-878-8864; *Fax:* 705-878-1813
caroljamieson@cogeco.ca

Lindsay: Timothy W. Johnston - *1
#218, The Kent Place Mall, 189 Kent St. West, Lindsay, ON K9V 5G6
Tel: 705-328-2393; *Fax:* 705-328-2428

Lindsay: J. Scott McLeod - *1
#7, 1 William St. South, Lindsay, ON K9V 3A3
Tel: 705-324-6711; *Fax:* 705-324-5723

Lindsay: Scott & Scott - *1
#219, P.O. Box 660, 189 Kent St. West, Lindsay, ON K9V 4S5
Tel: 705-324-5181; *Fax:* 705-324-8077

Lindsay: Leonard S. Siegel - *1
P.O. Box 997, 11 Adelaide St. North, Lindsay, ON K9V 5N4
Tel: 705-878-7990; *Fax:* 705-878-7992
lsiegel@kawarthalaw.ca

Listowel: Pratt & Pratt - *1
P.O. Box 10, 280 Inkerman St. West, Listowel, ON N4W 3H2
Tel: 519-291-3612; *Fax:* 519-291-3613
dwpratt@prattlawoffice.ca

London: Ambrogio & Ambrogio - *2
#611, 200 Queens Ave., London, ON N6A 1J3
Tel: 519-438-7219; *Fax:* 519-438-5919

London: Anissimoff Professional Corporation - *3
#201, Richmond North Office Centre, 235 North Centre Rd., London, ON N5X 4E7
Tel: 519-673-5591; *Fax:* 519-673-6784
serge@anissimoff.on.ca

London: Karl Arvai Professional Corp. - *4
Former Name: Karl Arvai
#1508, 140 Fullarton St., London, ON N6A 5P2
Tel: 519-672-0911; *Fax:* 519-642-1272
k.arvai@karlarvai.com

London: Daniel S.J. Bangarth - *1
#209, 1069 Wellington Rd. South, London, ON N6E 2H6
Tel: 519-472-2340; *Fax:* 519-657-8173
darlene.howard@sympatico.ca

London: Brenda D. Barr - *1
257 Piccadilly St., London, ON N6A 1S3
Tel: 519-672-5953; *Fax:* 519-672-8736
brenda@barrfamilylaw.com

London: Bates Law Office - *1
Also Known As: Bates, Thomas A.
#1, 151 Pine Valley Blvd., London, ON N6K 3T6
Tel: 519-472-0330; *Fax:* 519-472-1814
tabates@rogers.com

London: Joanne G. Beasley & Associates - *2
Former Name: Joanne G. Beasley & Associates
593 Talbot St., London, ON N6A 2T2
Tel: 519-642-1520; *Fax:* 519-673-3868
info@beasleylawoffice.com

London: Beechie, Madison, Sawchuk LLP - *3
Former Name: Beechie, Madison, Sawchuk & Seabrook
439 Waterloo St., London, ON N6B 2P1
Tel: 519-673-1070; *Fax:* 519-439-4363

London: Behr Law Firm - *3
Former Name: Behr & Rady
#1105, 383 Richmond St., London, ON N6M 3C4
Tel: 519-438-4530; *Fax:* 519-679-6576

London: Belanger, Cassino, Coulston & Gallagher - *4
#153, 759 Hyde Park Rd., London, ON N6H 3S2
Tel: 519-472-6310; *Fax:* 519-657-5189

London: G.P. Belch
P.O. Box 5035, Stn. B, 300 Dufferin Ave., London, ON N6A 4L9
Tel: 519-661-4708; *Fax:* 519-661-5530
gbelch@london.ca

London: Belecky & Belecky - *2
95 Dufferin Ave., London, ON N6A 1K3
Tel: 519-673-5630; *Fax:* 519-667-4836
aj@belecky.ca; jf@belecky.ca

London: Brown, Beattie, O'Donovan LLP - *24
City Centre Tower, 380 Wellington St., 16th Fl., London, ON N6A 5B5
Tel: 519-679-0400; *Fax:* 519-679-6350
bboinfo@bbo.on.ca
www.bbo.on.ca

London: Mervin F. Burgard, Q.C. - *1
#203, 219 Oxford St. West, London, ON N6H 1S5
Tel: 519-679-9900; *Fax:* 519-679-8546

London: Campbell M. Dockstader - *1
36 Chapple Hill Rd., London, ON N6G 2H3
Tel: 519-657-4080; *Fax:* 519-657-2516

** indicates number of lawyers*

London: **Carlyle Peterson - *5**
#216, 700 Richmond St., London, ON N6A 5C7
Tel: 519-432-0632; *Fax:* 519-432-0634
cp@cplaw.com

London: **Rano Channan - *1**
68 Tamarack Cres., London, ON N6K 3J7

London: **Luigi E. Circelli - *1**
557 Talbot St., London, ON N6A 2S9
Tel: 519-673-1850; *Fax:* 519-673-4966
lcircelli@bellnet.ca

London: **Cohen Highley LLP - *22**
One London Pl., 255 Queens Ave., 11th Fl., London, ON N6A 5R8
Tel: 519-672-9330; *Fax:* 519-672-5960
hall@cohenhighley.com
www.cohenhighley.com

London: **Russell W. Cornett - *1**
499 McGarrell Dr., London, ON N6G 5K7
Tel: 519-675-0926;
russellwcornett@hotmail.com

London: **Cram & Associates - *4**
#514, 200 Queens Ave., London, ON N6A 1J3
Tel: 519-673-1670; *Fax:* 519-439-5011
www.cramassociates.comwww.facebook.com/pages/Cram-Associates/219463871414493, twitter.com/CramAssociates

London: **Crossan Ferguson Olanski LLP - *3**
629 Wellington St., London, ON N6A 3R8
Tel: 519-858-2222; *Fax:* 519-858-2323
Toll-Free: 877-772-2424
diana@strictlybusiness.ca

London: **William L. Dewar - *1**
479 Talbot St., London, ON N6A 2S4
Tel: 519-672-1830; *Fax:* 519-661-0095
wildew@on.aibn.com

London: **Ronald W. Dickie - *1**
#3237, 450 Talbot St., London, ON N6A 4K3
Tel: 519-679-9660; *Fax:* 519-667-3362
rwdickielaw@on.aibn.com

London: **Kenneth Duggan - *1**
#203, 111 Waterloo St., London, ON N6B 2M4
Tel: 519-672-5360; *Fax:* 519-433-6975
kvduggan@bellnet.ca

London: **Excalibur Communications - *1**
1653 Kathryn Dr., London, ON N6G 2R7
Tel: 519-439-0646; *Fax:* 519-439-3112
www.excaliburcommunications.ca

London: **Foster, Townsend, Graham & Associates - *15**
551 Waterloo St., London, ON N6B 2R1
Tel: 519-672-5272; *Fax:* 519-672-9313
Toll-Free: 888-354-0448
firm@ftgalaw.com
www.ftgalaw.com

London: **Frauts, Dobbie - *3**
Former Name: Dobson & Dobbie
585 Talbot St., London, ON N6A 2T2
Tel: 519-679-4000; *Fax:* 519-679-7700
info@frautsdobbie.ca

London: **Fryday, Murphy, Brown - *2**
#201, 145 Wharncliffe Rd. South, London, ON N6J 2K4
Tel: 519-679-8800; *Fax:* 519-673-3632
kfryday@londonlawyers.com

London: **David G. Fysh - *1**
520 Springbank Dr., London, ON N6J 1G8
Tel: 519-472-3974; *Fax:* 519-472-3756
david@davidfysh.com
www.davidfysh.com

London: **Giffen & Partners - *4**
465 Waterloo St., London, ON N6B 2P4
Tel: 519-679-4700; *Fax:* 519-432-8003
office@giffens.com

London: **Gordon B. Good - *1**
#710, 171 Queens Ave., London, ON N6A 5J7
Tel: 519-433-4663; *Fax:* 519-679-8080
gordongood@goodlawoffice.com

London: **J.G. Harding - *1**
635 Wellington St., London, ON N6A 3R8
Tel: 519-439-0641; *Fax:* 519-439-0643
j.harding@bmts.com

London: **Harrison Pensa LLP - *51**
P.O. Box 3237, 450 Talbot St., London, ON N6A 4K3
Tel: 519-679-9660; *Fax:* 519-667-3362
info@harrisonpensa.com
www.harrisonpensa.com

London: **Antin Jaremchuk - *1**
100 Fullarton St., London, ON N6A 1K1
Tel: 519-432-2417; *Fax:* 519-663-1165
jaremchuk@sympatico.ca

London: **Michael J. Lamb - *1**
#102, 101 Cherryhill Blvd., London, ON N6H 4S4
Tel: 519-645-1104; *Fax:* 519-645-1107
lamblaw@on.aibn.com

London: **Therese D.P. Landry Law Office - *1**
#319, 148 York St., London, ON N6A 1A9
Tel: 519-438-4111

London: **Paul F. Lepine - *1**
570 Queens Ave., London, ON N6B 1Y8
Tel: 519-432-4155; *Fax:* 519-432-6861
pflepine@mnsi.net

London: **Lerners LLP - London - *64**
P.O. Box 2335, 80 Dufferin Ave., London, ON N6A 4G4
Tel: 519-672-4510; *Fax:* 519-672-2044
lerner.london@lerners.ca
www.lerners.ca

London: **V. Libis - *1**
93 Dufferin Ave., London, ON N6A 1K3
Tel: 519-434-6821; *Fax:* 519-434-9515
valdis.libis@odyssey.on.ca

London: **John R. Lisowski - *1**
607 Queens Ave., London, ON N6B 1Y9
Tel: 519-679-5000; *Fax:* 519-673-1717

London: **Little & Jarrett - *5**
P.O. Box 2757, 412 King St., London, ON N6A 4H4
Tel: 519-672-8121; *Fax:* 519-432-0784

London: **Little, Inglis & Price - *4**
148 Wortley Rd., London, ON N6C 3P5
Tel: 519-672-5415; *Fax:* 519-672-3906
admin@lip.on.ca

London: **Lockyer Spence LLP - *1**
#600, 465 Richmond St., London, ON N6A 5P4
Tel: 519-675-1058; *Fax:* 519-675-1086

London: **Michael F. Loebach - *2**
#508, 171 Queens Ave., London, ON N6A 5J7
Tel: 519-439-3031; *Fax:* 519-439-3540
info@mloebachlaw.com

London: **MacKewn, Winder, Kirwin LLP - *4**
#300, 376 Richmond St., London, ON N6A 3C7
Tel: 519-672-2040; *Fax:* 519-672-6583
mwk@mwk.on.ca

London: **Nancy Z. Magguilli - *1**
PO Box 29002, RPO Westmount Mall, London, ON N6K 4L9
Tel: 519-641-6255; *Fax:* 519-641-6255

London: **Edward J. Mann - *1**
#605, 137 Dundas St., London, ON N6A 1E9
Tel: 519-672-8707; *Fax:* 519-660-4678
ejmann@on.aibn.com

London: **McKenzie Lake Lawyers LLP - *35**
Former Name: Ross Bennett & Lake; McKenzie Nash Bryant
300 Dundas St., London, ON N6B 1T6
Tel: 519-672-5666; *Fax:* 519-672-2674
info@mckenzielake.com
www.mckenzielake.com

London: **McNamara, Pizzale - *3**
#220, 200 Queens Ave., London, ON N6A 1J3
Tel: 519-434-2174; *Fax:* 519-642-7654
mcpizz@execulink.com

London: **Menear Worrad & Associates - *6**
100 Fullarton St., London, ON N6A 1K1
Tel: 519-672-7370; *Fax:* 519-663-1165
info@menearlaw.com
www.menearlaw.com

London: **Brian K. Morris - *1**
#36, 14 Cadeau Terrace, London, ON N6K 4X5
Tel: 519-461-4684;
brian.morris@sympatico.ca

London: **Armand Morrow - *1**
42 Hampton Cres., London, ON N6H 2N8
Tel: 519-471-7607; *Fax:* 519-471-9121

London: **Frederick A. Mueller - *1**
Former Name: Mueller & Reich
141 Wortley Rd., London, ON N6C 3P4
Tel: 519-673-1300; *Fax:* 519-673-1728
fred_mueller@rogers.com

London: **Barry F. Nelligan - *1**
#202, 145 Wharncliffe Rd. South, London, ON N6J 2K4
Tel: 519-438-1709; *Fax:* 519-438-1700

London: **Nicholson, Smith - *5**
295 Central Ave., London, ON N6B 2C9
Tel: 519-679-3366; *Fax:* 519-679-0958

London: **Suhas T. Nimkar - *1**
151 York St., London, ON N6A 1A8
Fax: 519-474-9578
Toll-Free: 866-551-5255
suhasnimkar@aol.com

London: **Michael R. Nyhof**
380 Queens Ave., London, ON N6B 1X6
Tel: 519-642-4015; *Fax:* 519-642-4034
michaelnyhof@on.aibn.com

London: **James R. O'Donnell - *1**
#16, 440 Wellington St., London, ON N6A 3P2
Tel: 519-673-0600; *Fax:* 519-439-3468
james@jamesodonnell.ca

London: **Patton Cormier & Associates - *4**
Former Name: Patton & Associates
#1512, 140 Fullarton St., London, ON N6A 5P2
Tel: 519-432-8282; *Fax:* 519-432-7285
apatton@pattoncormier.ca

London: **Payne Group International Inc. (PGi2) - *1**
145 Wakefield Cres., London, ON N5X 1Z6
Tel: 519-859-7442;
rpayne@PGi2.com

London: **Judith M. Potter - *1**
54 Hunt Club Dr., London, ON N6H 3Y3
Tel: 519-432-8811; *Fax:* 519-663-1165
jpotter@start.ca

London: **Peter J. Quigley - *1**
924 Oxford East, London, ON N5Y 3J9
Tel: 519-453-3393; *Fax:* 519-453-3341

London: **S. Michael Robertson - *1**
#105, 186 Albert St., London, ON N6A 1M1
Tel: 519-660-1147; *Fax:* 519-660-0840
smrobertson.lawyer@bellnet.ca

London: **Siskind, Cromarty, Ivey & Dowler LLP - *65**
Former Name: Siskinds LLP
P.O. Box 2520, 680 Waterloo St., London, ON N6A 3V8
Tel: 519-672-2121; *Fax:* 519-672-6065
Toll-Free: 877-672-2121
info@siskinds.com
www.siskinds.com

London: **Stambler & Mills - *1**
#1511, 148 Fullarton St., London, ON N6A 5P3
Tel: 519-672-6240; *Fax:* 519-433-9593

London: **Szemenyei Kerwin MacKenzie LLP**
Former Name: Bitz, Szemenyei, Ferguson & MacKenzie
P.O. Box 482, Stn. Lambeth, 2479 Main St., London, ON N6P 1R1
Tel: 519-652-1616; *Fax:* 519-652-1622

London: **L. Kent Thomas - *1**
11 Stanley St., London, ON N6C 1A9
Tel: 519-438-4181; *Fax:* 519-433-5557

London: **Thomson Mahoney Dobson Delorey - *6**
Former Name: Thomson Mahoney Elliott Delorey
#200, 145 Wharncliffe Rd., London, ON N6J 2K4
Tel: 519-673-1151; *Fax:* 519-673-3632
tmdd@londonlawyers.com

** indicates number of lawyers*

***London*: Underhill Joles - *1**
607 Princess Ave., London, ON N6B 2C1
Tel: 519-432-4644; *Fax:* 519-438-3936

***London*: Despina S. Valassis - *1**
579 Talbot St., London, ON N6A 2T2
Tel: 519-439-2768

***London*: Walker & Wood - *1**
60 Barons Ct., London, ON N6C 5J3
Tel: 519-672-3500; *Fax:* 519-672-2420
walkerwood@rogers.com

***London*: Watson Jacobs McCreary - *1**
Former Name: Jesin, Watson & McCreary
#14, 380 Adelaide St. North, London, ON N6B 3P6
Tel: 519-663-2296; *Fax:* 519-663-1034
mklug@bellnet.ca

***London*: Holly A. Watson - *1**
380 Queens Ave., London, ON N6B 1X6
Tel: 519-642-4015; *Fax:* 519-642-4034
hollywatson@on.aibn.com

***London*: Kenneth J. Williams - *1**
902 Adelaide St. North, London, ON N5Y 2M5
Tel: 519-641-2200; *Fax:* 519-641-7995
kwilliams@kenwlaw.ca

***London*: David Winninger - *1**
557 Talbot St., London, ON N6A 2S9
Tel: 519-858-3152; *Fax:* 519-858-3182

***Madoc*: Karen J. Yarrow - *1**
P.O. Box 670, 91 St. Lawrence St. East, Madoc, ON K0K 2K0
Tel: 613-473-2802; *Fax:* 613-473-4472
kyarrow@lks.net

***Manotick*: Chester Burtt & Associates Ltd.**
P.O. Box 1186, Manotick, ON K4M 1A9
Tel: 613-692-2525; *Fax:* 613-692-6149
info@cbal.ca
www.cbal.ca

***Manotick*: Saxony Canadian Consulting Corp. - *1**
1224 Rideau Bend Cres., Manotick, ON K4M 1A8
Tel: 613-692-2355; *Fax:* 613-692-7798
rfmacrae@yahoo.ca

***Manotick*: Glen F. Schruder**
1050 Hill St., Manotick, ON K4M 1J2
Tel: 613-692-2379

***Manotick*: Wilson Law Partners LLP - *3**
Also Known As: Wilson & Associates
P.O. Box 429, 5542 Main St., Manotick, ON K4M 1A4
Tel: 613-692-3547; *Fax:* 613-692-0826
andrew@wilsonlawpartners.com
www.wilsonlawpartners.com

***Maple*: Judith Holzman Law Offices - *1**
2126 Major Mackenzie Dr., Maple, ON L6A 1P7
Tel: 905-303-1070; *Fax:* 905-303-4364
Toll-Free: 866-233-0945
judith@jhlawoffices.com

***Maple*: M.D. Newman - *1**
62 Lancer Dr., Maple, ON L6A 1C9
Tel: 905-832-5602; *Fax:* 905-832-5446
mdnewman@rogers.com

***Markdale*: Dunlop, Johnson & Pust - *2**
P.O. Box 433, 21 Main St. East, Markdale, ON N0C 1H0
Tel: 519-986-2100; *Fax:* 519-986-2904
johnslaw@on.aibn.com; pustlaw@on.aibn.com

***Markdale*: Harris, Willis - *1**
P.O. Box 466, 45 Main St. West, Markdale, ON N0C 1H0
Tel: 519-986-2740; *Fax:* 519-986-4205
ewillis@bmts.com

***Markdale*: Rodney T. O'Halloran - *1**
P.O. Box 522, RR#7, Markdale, ON N0C 1H0
Tel: 519-986-1428; *Fax:* 519-986-1471

***Markham*: Elliot Berlin - *1**
#101, 16 Esna Park Dr., Markham, ON L3R 5X1
Tel: 905-470-9444; *Fax:* 905-470-9449
eberlin@sympatico.ca

***Markham*: Bigioni Barristers & Solicitors - *2**
#201, 6060 Hwy. 7 East, Markham, ON L3P 3A9
Tel: 905-294-5222; *Fax:* 905-294-1607
bigionibarristers@on.aibn.com

***Markham*: Marvin B. Bongard - *1**
Former Name: Bongard & Associate
P.O. Box 509, 10 Washington St., Markham, ON L3P 3R2
Tel: 905-294-7555; *Fax:* 905-294-8360
marvin@mbongard.com

***Markham*: Burstein & Greenglass LLP - *4**
#200, Royal Bank Bldg., 7481 Woodbine Ave., Markham, ON L3R 2W1
Tel: 905-475-1266; *Fax:* 905-475-7851
office@bglaw.ca

***Markham*: Timothy M. Carter - *1**
58 Pennock Cres., Markham, ON L3R 3M4
Tel: 905-479-8802; *Fax:* 905-479-4137
timcarter@sympatico.ca
www.employmentlawissues.com/bio_tim.phpwww.linkedin.com/profile/view?id=4098996

***Markham*: Cattanach Hindson Sutton VanVeldhuizen - *7**
52 Main St. North, Markham, ON L3P 1X5
Tel: 905-294-0666; *Fax:* 905-294-5688

***Markham*: CG Management & Communications Inc. - *2**
#200, 175 Commerce Valley Dr. West, Markham, ON L3T 7P6
Tel: 905-709-4424; *Fax:* 905-709-2664
ekim@cggroup.com

***Markham*: Anna Chung - *2**
#209, 80 Acadia Ave., Markham, ON L3R 9V1
Tel: 905-940-6802; *Fax:* 905-940-6804
Toll-Free: 877-213-2284

***Markham*: Ernest Dicker, Q.C. - *1**
10 Fairway Heights Cres., Markham, ON L3T 1K2
Tel: 905-889-5556; *Fax:* 905-889-3306

***Markham*: Sydney Gangbar, Q.C. - *1**
#303, 80 Tiverton Ct., Markham, ON L3R 0G4
Tel: 905-470-0272; *Fax:* 905-470-8365
sydneygangbar@rogers.com

***Markham*: E. Alan Garbe - *1**
7507 Kennedy Rd., Markham, ON L3R 0L8
Tel: 905-415-9100; *Fax:* 905-479-3625
eagarbe@garbe-law.com

***Markham*: Paul Gollom - *1**
7507 Kennedy Rd., Markham, ON L3R 0L8
Tel: 905-881-6200; *Fax:* 905-883-8381
pgollom@look.ca

***Markham*: Jozefacki, Fielding - *2**
#200, 4961 Hwy. 7 East, Markham, ON L3R 1N1
Tel: 905-940-3141; *Fax:* 905-940-3139
jozefackilaw@hotmail.com

***Markham*: Barry M. Kaufman - *1**
#308, 3950 - 14th Ave., Markham, ON L3R 0A9
Tel: 905-477-8848; *Fax:* 905-477-8489
barrykaufman@rogers.com

***Markham*: Anthea Koon - *1**
#232, Commerce Gate, 505 Highway 7 East, Markham, ON L3T 7T1
Tel: 905-889-0698; *Fax:* 905-889-8390
antheakoon@rogers.com

***Markham*: Alan J. Luftspring - *1**
#236, 7181 Woodbine Ave., Markham, ON L3R 1A3
Tel: 905-479-1200; *Fax:* 905-479-9769
alanluftspring@rogers.com
www.gtalawyer.com

***Markham*: Irene L. Matthews - *1**
#104, 7225 Woodbine Ave., Markham, ON L3R 1A3
Tel: 905-475-9716; *Fax:* 905-475-9142

***Markham*: Mingay & Vereshchak - *3**
81 Main St. North, Markham, ON L3P 1X7
Tel: 905-294-0550; *Fax:* 905-294-9141
info@mvlaw.net

***Markham*: G. Arthur Moad - *1**
#206, 5762 Hwy. 7, Markham, ON L3P 1A8
Tel: 905-294-6446; *Fax:* 905-294-4436
gamoad@on.aibn.com

***Markham*: R. Parnes - *1**
Markham Industrial Park, P.O. Box 3249, 4701 Hwy. 7., Markham, ON L3R 6G6
Tel: 905-477-5151; *Fax:* 905-477-6778

***Markham*: Theodore B. Rotenberg Barrister - *1**
#303, 80 Tiverton Ct., Markham, ON L3R 0G4
Tel: 905-479-3331; *Fax:* 905-479-5017
general@rogerlaw.com

***Markham*: Alan R. Smith - *1**
#207, 2800 - 14th Ave., Markham, ON L3R 0E4
Tel: 905-415-8858; *Fax:* 905-940-1285
alansmithlaw@on.aibn.com

***Markham*: Paul F. Smith - *1**
#202, 5762 Hwy. 7, Markham, ON L3P 1A8
Tel: 905-294-9955; *Fax:* 905-294-4004

***Markham*: A. Melvin Sokolsky - *1**
#3, 200 Riviera Dr., Markham, ON L3R 5M1
Tel: 905-944-9427; *Fax:* 905-479-7025

***Markham*: E. Bruce Solomon - *1**
7507 Kennedy Rd., Markham, ON L3R 0L8
Tel: 905-479-1900; *Fax:* 905-479-9793
ebs@markhamlaw.ca

***Markham*: D.M. Starzynski, Q.C. - *1**
#205, 16th Ave. Shopping Centre, 9275 Hwy. 48 North, Markham, ON L6E 1A3
Tel: 905-294-3891; *Fax:* 905-471-2550
Toll-Free: 877-411-0902
starzynski@sympatico.ca

***Markham*: Howard J. Stern - *1**
#308, 3621 Hwy. 7 East, Markham, ON L2R 0G6
Tel: 416-410-7880; *Fax:* 416-410-7880

***Markham*: Thomas & Pelman**
4701 Hwy. 7 East, Markham, ON L3R 1M7
Tel: 905-477-2233; *Fax:* 905-477-7668
thomasandpelman@thomasandpelman.com

***Markham*: Wilson, Vukelich LLP - *18**
#710, 60 Columbia Way, Markham, ON L3R 0C9
Tel: 905-940-8700; *Fax:* 905-940-8785
Toll-Free: 866-508-8700
information@wvllp.ca
www.wvllp.ca

***Markham*: Shirley Yee**
#200, 80 Acadia Ave., Markham, ON L3R 9V1
Tel: 905-940-6800; *Fax:* 905-305-7630
shirleyyeelaw@hotmail.com

***Markham*: Jack Zwicker - *1**
#306, 7100 Woodbine Ave., Markham, ON L3R 5J2
Tel: 905-470-2544; *Fax:* 905-470-2571
jackzwicker@rogers.com

***Marmora*: A.L. Philpot - *1**
P.O. Box 430, 65 Forsyth St., Marmora, ON K0K 2M0
Tel: 613-472-2245; *Fax:* 613-472-3310
bcomeau@countrylawyer.on.ca
www.countrylawyer.on.ca

***Matheson*: J.A. Barber - *1**
P.O. Box 189, 362 MacDougall St., Matheson, ON P0K 1N0
Tel: 705-273-2151; *Fax:* 705-273-2144

***Meaford*: Carol A. Allen - *1**
P.O. Box 3272, 54 Sykes St. South, Meaford, ON N4L 1A5
Tel: 519-538-9929; *Fax:* 519-538-9931
Toll-Free: 877-538-9929
carolallen@rogers.com

***Meaford*: Kopperud Hamilton - *1**
Former Name: Norman A. Kopperud Law Office
76 Sykes St. North, Meaford, ON N4L 1R2
Tel: 519-538-2044; *Fax:* 519-538-5323
Toll-Free: 877-593-1938
kopperudlaw@bmts.com
www.bluemountainlawyers.com

***Meaford*: Scheifele, Erskine & Renken - *4**
P.O. Box 3395, 39 Nelson St. West, Meaford, ON N4L 1A5
Tel: 519-538-2510; *Fax:* 519-538-1843
info@meafordlawyers.com

***Merrickville*: Douglas Coupar & Associates - *1**
RR#4, Merrickville, ON K0G 1N0
Tel: 613-269-3232; *Fax:* 613-269-3773

***Metcalfe*: Gary M. Chayko - *1**
P.O. Box 579, Metcalfe, ON K2P 1L5
Tel: 613-230-7260; *Fax:* 613-230-2163
gchayko@netscape.net

** indicates number of lawyers*

***Midland*: Chin & Orr Professional Corporation - *4**
382 King St., Midland, ON L4R 3M9
Tel: 705-526-5529; *Fax:* 705-526-3071
Toll-Free: 877-526-5529
law@chinandorr.com

***Midland*: Deacon Taws - *2**
476 Elizabeth St., Midland, ON L4R 1Z8
Tel: 705-526-3791; *Fax:* 705-526-2688
admin@deacontaws.com
www.deacontaws.com

***Midland*: Ferguson Barristers - *6**
531 King St., Midland, ON L4R 3N6
Tel: 705-526-1471; *Fax:* 705-526-1067
Toll-Free: 800-563-6348
www.facebook.com/group.php?gid=143074919075604
www.fergusonbarristers.cawww.twitter.com/fergusonlaw

***Midland*: HGR Graham Partners LLP - *13**
Former Name: Hacker Gignac Rice LLP
518 Yonge St., Midland, ON L4R 2C5
Tel: 705-526-2231; *Fax:* 705-526-0313
Toll-Free: 800-205-4052
info@hgrgp.ca
www.hgr.ca

***Midland*: Mark Kowalsky - *1**
P.O. Box 280, 8970 County Rd. #93, Midland, ON L4R 4K8
Tel: 705-526-1336; *Fax:* 705-526-8499

***Midland*: Prost Associates - *2**
P.O. Box 96, 323 Midland Ave., Midland, ON L4R 4K6
Tel: 705-526-9328; *Fax:* 705-526-1209
info@prostlaw.com
www.prostlwa.com

***Midland*: Wanda L. Warren & Associate - *2**
512 Dominion Ave., Midland, ON L4R 1P8
Tel: 705-528-1665; *Fax:* 705-526-3238
Toll-Free: 800-838-8706

***Milton*: Ingrid Hibbard - *1**
539 Moorelands Cres., Milton, ON L9T 4B2
Tel: 905-875-3828; *Fax:* 905-875-3829
ihibbard@pelangio.com

***Milton*: Hutchinson, Thompson, Henderson & Mott - *2**
264 Main St., Milton, ON L9T 1P2
Tel: 905-878-2841; *Fax:* 905-878-3937
lawoffice@lawmilton.com

***Milton*: D.I. Malcolm - *1**
6439 Hwy. 25 South, RR#1, Milton, ON L9T 2X5
Tel: 905-876-3033; *Fax:* 905-876-3448

***Milverton*: W. Stirling Kenny Law Office - *1**
11 Main St. North, Milverton, ON N0K 1M0
Tel: 519-595-8171; *Fax:* 519-271-7397

***Minden*: Donald J. Lange - *1**
Comp. 50, RR#2, Minden, ON K0M 2K0
Tel: 705-489-4974; *Fax:* 705-489-4975
donaldlange@donaldlange.com
www.donaldlange.com

***Mississauga*: Esther O. Abraham Law Office - *1**
#110A, 377 Burnhamthorpe Rd. East, Mississauga, ON L5A 3Y1
Tel: 905-270-3755; *Fax:* 905-270-3844
esther@dlaw.ca
www.dlaw.ca

***Mississauga*: Affiliated Customs Brokers Ltd. - *1**
6470 Northam Dr., Mississauga, ON L4V 1H9
Tel: 905-676-3936; *Fax:* 905-672-5335

***Mississauga*: David A. Aiken - *1**
#200, 39 Lake Shore Rd. East, Mississauga, ON L5G 1C9
Tel: 905-602-5230; *Fax:* 905-871-8507
d.aiken.law@davidaaiken.com

***Mississauga*: J. Paul Bannon - *2**
Former Name: Bannon & Falkeisen
#360, 33 City Centre Dr., Mississauga, ON L5B 2N5
Tel: 905-272-3412

***Mississauga*: Richard S. Barrett - *1**
1498 Lewisham Dr., Mississauga, ON L5J 3R4
Tel: 905-823-1487; *Fax:* 905-823-2529
lawyer@rogers.com
www.the-friendly-lawyer.com

***Mississauga*: N. Bartels - *1**
#304, 470 Hensall Circle, Mississauga, ON L5A 1X7
Tel: 905-276-8286

***Mississauga*: Paula L. Bateman, Barrister & Solicitor - *2**
6505 Mississauga Rd., #C, Mississauga, ON L5N 1A6
Tel: 905-567-4440; *Fax:* 905-821-1572

***Mississauga*: Stephen I. Beck - *1**
295 Matheson Blvd. East, Mississauga, ON L4Z 1X8
Tel: 905-568-8351; *Fax:* 905-568-9772
sbecklaw@on.aibn.com

***Mississauga*: Richard T. Bennett - *2**
82 Queen St. South., Mississauga, ON L5M 1K6
Tel: 905-826-1453; *Fax:* 905-826-7185
richardbennett@sprint.ca

***Mississauga*: Eugene J. Bhattacharya - *1**
295 Matheson Blvd. East, Mississauga, ON L4Z 1X8
Tel: 905-507-3796; *Fax:* 905-507-6011

***Mississauga*: Binsky Whittle - *1**
Former Name: The Law Office of Howard Binsky
#200, 2345 Stanfield Rd., Mississauga, ON L4Y 3R3
Tel: 905-270-8811; *Fax:* 905-270-2977
www.binskywhittle.com

***Mississauga*: George F. Brant - *1**
62 Queen St. South, Mississauga, ON L5M 1K4
Tel: 905-826-2511; *Fax:* 905-286-1335
gbrant@attglobal.net

***Mississauga*: Brian Chan Barrister, Solicitor & Notary Public - *1**
#42, 145 Traders Blvd. East, Mississauga, ON L4Z 3L3
Tel: 905-712-2888; *Fax:* 905-712-3838

***Mississauga*: Michael J. Bukovac - *1**
1325 Burnhamthorpe Rd. East, Mississauga, ON L4Y 3V8
Tel: 905-238-1411; *Fax:* 905-629-9277
michaelbukovac@on.aibn.com

***Mississauga*: Burych Lawyers - *3**
#204, 89 Queensway West, Mississauga, ON L5B 2V2
Tel: 905-896-8600; *Fax:* 905-896-9757
burychlawyers@bellnet.ca

***Mississauga*: Campbell Partners LLP - *4**
2624 Dunwin Dr., Mississauga, ON L5L 3T5
Tel: 905-828-2247; *Fax:* 905-828-4311
info@campbelllawyers.net
www.campbelllawyers.net

***Mississauga*: Larry R. Plener - *2**
Former Name: Larry R. Plener
2564 Confederation Pkwy., Mississauga, ON L4Z 1S1
Tel: 905-897-8611; *Fax:* 905-897-8807
lplener@sympatico.ca

***Mississauga*: Carey McCallum & Nimjee - *1**
1325 Burnhamthorpe Rd. East, Mississauga, ON L4Y 3V8
Tel: 905-624-6817; *Fax:* 905-624-0522

***Mississauga*: Thomas Carey - *1**
1325 Burnhamthorpe Rd. East, Mississauga, ON L4Y 3V8
Tel: 905-624-1149; *Fax:* 905-624-0522
tomcarey@bellnet.ca

***Mississauga*: J.C. Chapman - *1**
2572 Stanfield Rd., Mississauga, ON L4Y 1S2
Tel: 905-270-7034; *Fax:* 905-270-1001
jcchapman@on.aibn.com

***Mississauga*: Richard C. Chojnacki - *1**
#301, 29 Tannery St., Mississauga, ON L5N 1V1
Tel: 905-821-3644; *Fax:* 905-821-8355

***Mississauga*: L.R. Cutler - *1**
Former Name: Cutler/Goldberg LLP
#1201, 90 Burnhamthorpe Rd. West, Mississauga, ON L5B 3C3
Tel: 905-276-5200; *Fax:* 905-276-2193

***Mississauga*: Wieslawa Dabrowska - *1**
#405, 4310 Sherwoodtowne Blvd., Mississauga, ON L4Z 4C4
Tel: 905-281-0308; *Fax:* 905-281-3552
viesiad@istar.ca

***Mississauga*: Daigle & Hancock LLP - *4**
51 Village Centre Pl., Mississauga, ON L4Z 1V9
Tel: 905-273-3339; *Fax:* 905-273-5672
Toll-Free: 877-273-3339
lawyers@daiglehancock.com
www.daiglehancock.com

***Mississauga*: Arthur H. David - *1**
#6 & 12, 2145 Dunwin Dr., Mississauga, ON L5L 4L9
Tel: 905-828-2300; *Fax:* 905-828-4602
a.david@bellnet.ca

***Mississauga*: Douglas M. Davidson - *1**
#200, 1552 Dundas St. West, Mississauga, ON L5C 1E4
Tel: 905-279-3330; *Fax:* 905-279-2735

***Mississauga*: Day + Borg LLP - *2**
Former Name: Day, Michael J.
93 Queen St. South, Mississauga, ON L5M 1K7
Tel: 905-826-5670; *Fax:* 905-826-5673
www.dayborg.com

***Mississauga*: DeRusha Law Firm - *4**
#1, 1015 Matheson Blvd. East, Mississauga, ON L4W 3A4
Tel: 905-625-2874; *Fax:* 905-625-0614
info@derushalawfirm.com
www.derushalawfirm.com

***Mississauga*: Dicarlo, Wong & Pugliese Associates - *2**
#204, 1090 Dundas St. East, Mississauga, ON L4Y 2B8
Tel: 905-272-0303; *Fax:* 905-272-0081

***Mississauga*: Eades Law Office - *1**
7229 Pacific Circle, Mississauga, ON L5T 1S9
Tel: 905-795-4040; *Fax:* 905-564-2315

***Mississauga*: Richard Alan Fellman - *1**
#100, 46 Village Centre Pl., Mississauga, ON L4Z 1V9
Tel: 905-275-2231; *Fax:* 905-275-8323
rfellman@on.aibn.com

***Mississauga*: Michael J. Fisher - *1**
#4, 265 Queen St. South, Mississauga, ON L5M 1L9
Tel: 905-812-9700; *Fax:* 905-812-0770
mjfisher@globalserve.net

***Mississauga*: David A. Fram - *1**
810 Meadow Wood Road, Mississauga, ON L5J 2S6
Tel: 905-916-0130; *Fax:* 905-916-1600
david@davidfram.com
www.davidfram.com

***Mississauga*: Garvey & Garvey LLP - *3**
972 Clarkson Rd. South, Mississauga, ON L5J 2V7
Tel: 905-823-4400; *Fax:* 905-823-5153

***Mississauga*: Fabio Gazzola, Barrister & Solicitor - *1**
#6, 2145 Dunwin Dr., Mississauga, ON L5L 4L9
Tel: 905-820-1277; *Fax:* 905-828-4602
gazzolaf@bellnet.ca

***Mississauga*: J.M.P. Ghalioungui - *1**
#11, 4040 Creditview Rd.., Mississauga, ON L5C 3Y8
Tel: 905-820-4442; *Fax:* 905-820-4442

***Mississauga*: John L.Z. Gora - *1**
893 Beechwood Ave., Mississauga, ON L5G 4E3
Tel: 905-278-7678; *Fax:* 905-271-5568

***Mississauga*: Harris & Harris LLP - *8**
#300, 2355 Skymark Ave., Mississauga, ON L4W 4Y6
Tel: 905-629-7800; *Fax:* 905-629-4350
info@harrisandharris.com
www.harrisandharris.com

***Mississauga*: Jane Harvey Associates**
Square One Shopping Centre, 100 City Centre Dr., Mississauga, ON L5B 2C9
Tel: 905-272-2266; *Fax:* 905-270-2876
janehlaw@magma.ca
www.janeharveylawyers.com

***Mississauga*: Wm. G. Jeffery - *1**
#301, 8 Stavebank Rd. North, Mississauga, ON L5G 2T4
Tel: 905-278-7271; *Fax:* 905-278-7514

***Mississauga*: Kain & Ball - *3**
#240, 1900 Dundas St. West, Mississauga, ON L5K 1P9
Tel: 905-855-4888; *Fax:* 905-855-3760
kainandball@on.aibn.com

* *indicates number of lawyers*

***Mississauga*: Keel Cottrelle LLP - *6**
#104, 100 Matheson Blvd. East, Mississauga, ON L4Z 2G7
Tel: 905-890-7700;
kkozak@keelcottrelle.on.ca

***Mississauga*: Julian B. Keller - *1**
#301, 25 Watline Ave., Mississauga, ON L4Z 2Z1
Tel: 905-890-2211; *Fax:* 905-890-2246
juliankeller@rogers.com

***Mississauga*: Sami N. Kerba - *1**
1093 Lakeshore Rd. East, Mississauga, ON L5E 1E8
Tel: 905-274-6073; *Fax:* 905-274-9876
samikerba@nskerba.com

***Mississauga*: Keyser Mason Ball LLP, Barristers & Solicitors - *24**
#1600, 4 Robert Speck Pkwy., Mississauga, ON L4Z 1S1
Tel: 905-276-9111; *Fax:* 905-276-2298
kmb@kmblaw.com
www.kmblaw.com

***Mississauga*: Klein Law, Barristers, Mediators, Notaries - *3**
#38, 1100 Central Pkwy. West, Mississauga, ON L5C 4E5
Tel: 905-272-2540; *Fax:* 905-272-2100
contact@kleinlaw.ca
www.kleinlaw.ca

***Mississauga*: Kostyniuk & Bruggeman - *3**
#213, 1515 Matheson Blvd. East, Mississauga, ON L4W 2P5
Tel: 905-602-5551; *Fax:* 905-602-9775
rkostyniuk@rogers.com

***Mississauga*: S. Lenard Kotylo**
#1, P.O. Box 1067, Stn. B, 1105 Crestlawn Dr., Mississauga, ON L4Y 3W4
Tel: 905-282-0918

***Mississauga*: Kozlowski & Company - *1**
5065 Foresthill Drive, Mississauga, ON L5M 5A7
Tel: 905-542-7070; *Fax:* 905-542-3434

***Mississauga*: Malicki & Malicki - *1**
3020 Kirwin Ave., Mississauga, ON L5A 2K6
Tel: 905-279-6250; *Fax:* 905-279-3878
marek@malicki.ca

***Mississauga*: Marks & Ciraco - *2**
#303, 4310 Sherwoodtowne Blvd., Mississauga, ON L4Z 4C4
Tel: 905-712-8300; *Fax:* 905-712-8559
www.marksandciraco.com

***Mississauga*: Martin C. Schulz - *1**
Former Name: Schulz Pereira Fordjour
#500, 201 City Centre Dr., Mississauga, ON L5B 2T4
Tel: 905-897-2200; *Fax:* 905-897-1517
mschulz@bellnet.ca

***Mississauga*: Cindy McGoldrick - *1**
#103, 2691 Credit Valley Rd., Mississauga, ON L5M 7A1
Tel: 905-608-9967; *Fax:* 905-608-8206
cindy@cindymcgoldrick.com

***Mississauga*: Robert D. McIntyre, Q.C. - *1**
#410, 30 Eglinton Ave. West, Mississauga, ON L5B 3E7
Tel: 905-366-9700; *Fax:* 905-366-9707
rdm@ontlaw.com
www.ontlaw.com

***Mississauga*: Ronald F. Mossman - *1**
#300, 34 Village Centre Pl., Mississauga, ON L4Z 1V9
Tel: 905-848-4020; *Fax:* 905-848-4026
ronmossman@rmossman.com

***Mississauga*: D.M. Nathwani - *1**
#129, 1250 Mississauga Valley Blvd., Mississauga, ON L5A 3R6
Tel: 905-273-7887

***Mississauga*: R. Geoffrey Newbury - *1**
#106, 150 Lakeshore Rd. West, Mississauga, ON L5H 3R2
Tel: 905-271-9600; *Fax:* 905-271-1638
newbury@mandamus.org

***Mississauga*: Niebler, Liebeck**
1469 Indian Grove, Mississauga, ON L5H 2S5
Tel: 905-271-3232; *Fax:* 905-271-3677
niebler@on.aibn.com

***Mississauga*: O'Connor Zanardo - *2**
4275 Village Centre Ct., Top Fl., Mississauga, ON L4Z 1V3
Tel: 905-896-4370; *Fax:* 905-896-4926

***Mississauga*: O.J. Osmak - *1**
#126, Central Parkway Mall, 377 Burnhamthorpe Rd. East, Mississauga, ON L5A 3Y1
Tel: 905-277-0229; *Fax:* 905-277-4966
osmak@on.aibn.com

***Mississauga*: Ovenden & Ovenden - *2**
#204, 130 Dundas St. East, Mississauga, ON L5A 3V8
Tel: 905-270-8544; *Fax:* 905-273-7386

***Mississauga*: Pallett Valo LLP - *27**
#1600, 90 Burnhamthorpe Rd. West, Mississauga, ON L5B 3C3
Tel: 905-273-3300; *Fax:* 905-273-6920
Toll-Free: 800-323-3781
marketing@pallettvalo.com
www.pallettvalo.com

***Mississauga*: Petrillo Law Offices - *2**
#201, 2600 Skymark Ave., Unit 1, Mississauga, ON L4W 5B2
Tel: 905-949-9433; *Fax:* 905-949-1153
info@petrillolaw.com
www.petrillolaw.com

***Mississauga*: F. Polla - *1**
#100, 3643 Cawthra Rd., Mississauga, ON L5A 2Y4
Tel: 905-566-8640

***Mississauga*: Rawding, Lindsay - *2**
#201, 3415 Dixie Rd., Mississauga, ON L4Y 2B1
Tel: 905-625-4442; *Fax:* 905-624-0184

***Mississauga*: Terry D. Richardson - *1**
18 Mississauga Rd. North, Mississauga, ON L5H 2H4
Tel: 905-891-0011; *Fax:* 905-891-1410

***Mississauga*: Ridout & Maybee LLP, Intellectural Property & Technology Law Firm - *2**
#308, 1 City Centre Dr., Mississauga, ON L5B 1M2
Tel: 905-276-2300; *Fax:* 905-276-7687
mail@ridoutmaybee.com
www.ridoutmaybee.com

***Mississauga*: J. Saltzman**
#15, 7205 Goreway Dr., Mississauga, ON L4T 2T9
Tel: 905-671-1178; *Fax:* 905-671-8030
jerry_westwood@hotmail.com

***Mississauga*: Edgar R. Schink - *1**
#405, 130 Dundas St. East, Mississauga, ON L5A 3V8
Tel: 905-270-8882; *Fax:* 905-270-7665

***Mississauga*: Allan Shulman - *1**
2225 Erin Mills Pkwy., Mississauga, ON L5K 1T9
Tel: 905-822-3563; *Fax:* 905-822-6342
ashulman@on.aibn.com

***Mississauga*: John F. Silvester - *1**
#544, 33 City Centre Dr., Mississauga, ON L5B 2N5
Tel: 905-275-2588; *Fax:* 905-275-0714

***Mississauga*: Singh Lyn Ragonetti Bindal LLP - *3**
#52, 2355 Derry Rd. East, Mississauga, ON L5S 1V6
Tel: 905-293-9800; *Fax:* 905-293-9801
info@lawyers4u.ca

***Mississauga*: Speigel Nichols Fox LLP - *7**
#400, 30 Eglinton Ave. West, Mississauga, ON L5R 3E7
Tel: 905-366-9700; *Fax:* 905-366-9707
www.ontlaw.com

***Mississauga*: Tannahill, Lockhart & Clark Law LLP - *3**
#10, 5805 Whittle Rd., Mississauga, ON L4Z 2J1
Tel: 905-502-5770; *Fax:* 905-502-5009
www.tlcl.ca

***Mississauga*: Thompson, MacColl & Stacy - *9**
#5, 1020 Matheson Blvd. East, Mississauga, ON L4W 4J9
Tel: 905-625-5591; *Fax:* 905-238-3313

***Mississauga*: Brian M. Watson - *1**
#105, 3034 Palston Rd., Mississauga, ON L4Y 2Z6
Tel: 905-272-0942; *Fax:* 905-272-1682
watsonlaw@sympatico.ca

***Mississauga*: Annette Wilson - *1**
#203, 1325 Eglinton Ave. East, Mississauga, ON L4W 4L9
Tel: 905-602-1989; *Fax:* 905-602-8491

***Mississauga*: Michael Woods - *1**
#203, 120 Traders Blvd. East, Mississauga, ON L4Z 2H7
Tel: 905-568-3810; *Fax:* 905-568-1206
michaelwoods@on.aibn.com

***Mississauga*: Richard M. Woodside - *1**
2479 Burnford Trail, Mississauga, ON L5M 5E4
Tel: 905-567-4562

***Mississauga*: Janice E. Younker - *1**
1370 Hurontario St., Mississauga, ON L5G 3H4
Tel: 905-271-2784; *Fax:* 905-271-5960
younkerlaw@the-wire.com

***Mitchell*: Botsford Professional Corporation - *1**
Former Name: Sheldon L. Wood
P.O. Box 850, 24 Ontario Rd., Mitchell, ON N0K 1N0
Tel: 519-348-4731; *Fax:* 519-348-4107
blair@botsfordlaw.com

***Mitchell*: William E. Wilson - *1**
102 Ontario Rd., Mitchell, ON N0K 1N0
Tel: 519-348-8488; *Fax:* 519-348-4226
wewilson@ezlink.ca

***Monotick*: Alan C. Macleod - *1**
P.O. Box 1158, 5576 Dickinson St., Monotick, ON K4M 1A9
Tel: 613-692-4180; *Fax:* 613-692-0073

***Moosonee*: Keewaytinok Native Legal Services - *2**
P.O. Box 218, 40 Revillon Rd. North, Moosonee, ON P0L 1Y0
Tel: 705-336-2981; *Fax:* 705-336-2577
lantzp@lao.on.ca; khangkd@lao.on.ca
www.keewaytinok.org

***Morrisburg*: Gorrell, Grenkie, Leroy & Rémillard - *2**
Former Name: Gorrell, Grenkie, Leroy & Rémillard
P.O. Box 820, Stn. Morrisburg, 67 Main St., Morrisburg, ON K0C 1X0
Tel: 613-543-2922; *Fax:* 613-543-4228
info@yourlawfirm.ca
www.yourlawfirm.ca

***Morrisburg*: McInnis, MacEwen, Horner & Pietersma - *2**
Former Name: McInnis, MacEwen & Horner
P.O. Box 733, Morrisburg, ON K0C 1X0
Tel: 613-543-2946; *Fax:* 613-543-3867

***Mount Albert*: 2037770 Ontario Inc. - *1**
90 Shannon Rd., Mount Albert, ON L0G 1M0
Tel: 905-473-3418; *Fax:* 905-473-6846
rciano@campaignresearch.ca

***Mount Forest*: Deverell & Lemaich LLP - *2**
Former Name: Grant Deverell Lemaich & Barclay
P.O. Box 460, Stn. Mount Forest, 166 Main St. South, Mount Forest, ON N0G 2L0
Tel: 519-323-1600; *Fax:* 519-323-3877
info@northwellington-law.ca

***Mount Forest*: Fallis, Fallis & McMillan - *2**
150 Main St. South, Mount Forest, ON N0G 2L0
Tel: 519-323-2800; *Fax:* 519-323-4115
ffmlaw@wightman.ca

***Napanee*: C. F. Doreleyers - *2**
P.O. Box 398, Stn. Main, 35 Dundas St. East, Napanee, ON K7R 3P5
Tel: 613-354-3375; *Fax:* 613-354-5641

***Nepean*: Michael G. Carey - *1**
84 Centrepointe Dr., Nepean, ON K2G 6B1
Tel: 613-723-4774; *Fax:* 613-723-2377
careylawoffice@bellnet.ca

***Nepean*: Chiarelli Cramer Witteveen - *3**
Centrepointe Chambers, 92 Centrepointe Dr., Nepean, ON K2G 6B1
Tel: 613-723-9100; *Fax:* 613-723-9105
ccw@centrepointelaw.com

***Nepean*: Clermont Clausi Gardiner & Associates - *5**
1447 Woodroffe Ave., Nepean, ON K2G 1W1
Tel: 613-225-0037; *Fax:* 613-225-0921

***Nepean*: E. Max Cohen, Q.C. - *1**
24 Kitimat Cres., Nepean, ON K2H 7G5
Tel: 613-828-5855; *Fax:* 613-237-0510

***Nepean*: Doraty & Ferris**
Former Name: Doraty & LeBlanc
28 Northside Rd., Nepean, ON K2H 5Z3
Tel: 613-829-7171; *Fax:* 613-829-0244
inquiries@doratyferris.com

***Nepean*: JL Consulting - *1**
142F Valley Stream Dr., Nepean, ON K2H 9C6
Tel: 613-721-8904; *Fax:* 613-721-8918

** indicates number of lawyers*

***Nepean*: Landry, Vanier - *1**
90 Centrepointe Dr., Nepean, ON K2G 6B1
Tel: 613-226-3336; *Fax:* 613-226-8767
vanier@vanierlaw.on.ca

***Nepean*: MacKay & Sanderson - *2**
#201, 1580 Merivale Rd., Nepean, ON K2G 4B5
Tel: 613-238-6180; *Fax:* 613-238-3288

***Nepean*: Michael E. Mastronardi - *1**
12 Apache Cres., Nepean, ON K2E 6H7
Tel: 613-858-9158;
dmastr1213@rogers.com

***Nepean*: P3 Strategic Alliance Inc. - *1**
106 Starwood Rd., Nepean, ON K2G 1Z7
Fax: 905-476-8977
Toll-Free: 888-791-7834
cpitt@rogers.com

***Nepean*: Stephen A. Ritchie - *1**
92 Centrepointe Dr., Nepean, ON K2G 6B1
Tel: 613-224-6674; *Fax:* 613-723-9105
aritchie@allstream.net

***Nepean*: Jo-Anne E. Ward - *1**
17 Scout St., Nepean, ON K2C 4B9
Tel: 613-729-7667

***New Liskeard*: Ramsay Law Office - *2**
P.O. Box 160, 18 Armstrong St., New Liskeard, ON P0J 1P0
Tel: 705-647-4010; *Fax:* 705-647-4341
Toll-Free: 800-837-6648
ramsaypr@nt.net
www.nt.net/~ramsaypr

***Newcastle*: Valentine Lovekin - *1**
Former Name: Cureatz & Lovekin Law Office
35 King St., Newcastle, ON L1B 1H2
Tel: 905-987-3500; *Fax:* 905-987-3503
lovekin@lovekinlaw.com

***Newcastle*: Walters, Dizenbach, Ferguson - *3**
29 King Ave. East, Newcastle, ON L1B 1H3
Tel: 905-987-4735; *Fax:* 905-987-1061

***Newmarket*: Paul H. Caroline - *1**
#300, 16775 Yonge St., Newmarket, ON L3Y 8J4
Tel: 905-836-4018; *Fax:* 905-836-4020

***Newmarket*: Dunsmuir Advocates - *2**
P.O. Box 2003, Stn. Main, 17070 Yonge St., Newmarket, ON L3Y 6W4
Tel: 905-895-7741; *Fax:* 905-853-5851
www.dunsmuiradvocates.com

***Newmarket*: Mark Henry - *1**
105 Eagle St., Newmarket, ON L3Y 1J2
Tel: 905-898-2686; *Fax:* 905-898-3957

***Newmarket*: Hill Hunter Losell Law Firm LLP - *7**
#200, P.O. Box 324, Stn. Main, 17360 Yonge St., Newmarket, ON L3Y 4X7
Tel: 905-895-1007; *Fax:* 905-895-4064

***Newmarket*: Neal J. Kearney - *1**
#207, 1091 Gorham St., Newmarket, ON L3Y 8X7
Tel: 905-898-3012; *Fax:* 905-853-9894
kearneylaw@on.aibn.com

***Newmarket*: David Lakie - *1**
105 Eagle St., Newmarket, ON L3Y 1J2
Tel: 905-898-2686; *Fax:* 905-898-3957

***Newmarket*: Debra L. McNairn - *1**
#222, 465 Davis Dr., Newmarket, ON L3Y 7T9
Tel: 905-836-1371; *Fax:* 905-898-2050

***Newmarket*: Derrick McNamara - *1**
24 Hillview Dr., Newmarket, ON L3Y 4H9
Tel: 905-954-0593; *Fax:* 905-954-1827

***Newmarket*: Paul E. Montgomery - *1**
#300, 16775 Yonge St., Newmarket, ON L3Y 8J4
Tel: 905-836-4018; *Fax:* 905-836-4020
paulmontgomery@rogers.com

***Newmarket*: Murphy & Lewis - *2**
572 Davis Dr., Newmarket, ON L3Y 2P4
Tel: 905-836-4750; *Fax:* 905-836-6691
Toll-Free: 800-262-2659

***Newmarket*: Ramm Consultants Inc. - *1**
2944 Vivian Rd., Newmarket, ON L3Y 4W1
Tel: 905-715-7513;
tramm@rammconsultants.com

***Newmarket*: A. Schneider - *1**
291 Davis Dr., Newmarket, ON L3Y 2N6
Tel: 905-898-1342; *Fax:* 905-898-1344

***Newmarket*: Steinberg, Bruce & Paterson - *3**
#109, 1091 Gorham St., Newmarket, ON L3Y 7V1
Tel: 905-830-9940; *Fax:* 905-830-9246

***Newmarket*: Stiver Vale - *7**
195 Main St. South, Newmarket, ON L3Y 3Y9
Tel: 905-895-4571; *Fax:* 905-853-2958

***Niagara Falls*: Broderick & Partners - *7**
P.O. Box 897, 4625 Ontario Ave., Niagara Falls, ON L2E 6V6
Tel: 905-356-2621; *Fax:* 905-356-6904

***Niagara Falls*: David P. Czifra - *1**
P.O. Box 868, 4786 Queen St., Niagara Falls, ON L2E 6V6
Tel: 905-357-6633; *Fax:* 905-356-3635
czifra@vaxxine.com

***Niagara Falls*: Charles A. Galloway - *1**
5146 Victoria Ave., Niagara Falls, ON L2E 4E3
Tel: 905-356-2512; *Fax:* 905-356-2513

***Niagara Falls*: Margaret A. Hoy - *1**
P.O. Box 868, 4786 Queen St., Niagara Falls, ON L2E 6V6
Tel: 905-354-4414; *Fax:* 905-354-1272

***Niagara Falls*: D. Ceri Hugill - *1**
6304 Stonefield Park, Niagara Falls, ON L2J 4K1
Tel: 905-708-9529; *Fax:* 905-353-1790
resolver@cogeco.ca

***Niagara Falls*: S. James Knight, Q.C. - *1**
4683 Queen St., Niagara Falls, ON L2E 2L9
Tel: 905-356-1524; *Fax:* 905-357-9686

***Niagara Falls*: Patricia Lucas - *1**
4056 Dorchester Rd., Niagara Falls, ON L2E 6M9
Tel: 905-357-4510; *Fax:* 905-357-9757

***Niagara Falls*: Martin Sheppard Fraser LLP - Niagara Falls - *13**
P.O. Box 900, 4701 St. Clair Ave., 2nd Fl., Niagara Falls, ON L2E 6V7
Tel: 905-354-1611; *Fax:* 905-354-5540
Toll-Free: 800-263-2502
lawyers@martinshep.com
www.martinshep.com

***Niagara Falls*: D.J. McDonald - *1**
P.O. Box 726, Stn. Main, 4683 Queen St., Niagara Falls, ON L2E 6V5
Tel: 905-356-1524; *Fax:* 905-357-9686
danielmcdonald@bellnet.ca

***Niagara Falls*: McKay, Heath - *2**
#102, 4701 St. Clair Ave., Niagara Falls, ON L2E 3S9
Tel: 905-357-0660; *Fax:* 905-357-5680

***Niagara Falls*: G.F. McNab, Q.C. - *1**
4056 Dorchester Rd., Niagara Falls, ON L2E 6M9
Tel: 905-357-4510; *Fax:* 905-357-9757
mcnablucas@on.aibn.com

***Niagara Falls*: N. Minov - *1**
2455 Lepp Ave., Niagara Falls, ON L2J 2B9
Tel: 905-356-4420; *Fax:* 905-356-0333

***Niagara Falls*: James Rocca - *1**
4056 Dorchester Rd., Niagara Falls, ON L2E 6M9
Tel: 905-357-3730; *Fax:* 905-356-6185
jamesrocca@bellnet.com

***Niagara Falls*: Sharpe, Beresh & Gnys - *4**
Elgin Block, 4673 Ontario Ave., 3rd Fl., Niagara Falls, ON L2E 3R1
Tel: 905-357-5555; *Fax:* 905-357-5760
sharpe@sbglawfirm.com

***Niagara Falls*: Brian N. Sinclair, Q.C. - *1**
6617 Drummond Rd., Niagara Falls, ON L2G 4N4
Tel: 905-356-7755; *Fax:* 905-356-7772
evah@on.aibn.com

***Niagara Falls*: William Slovak, Q.C. - *1**
5627 Main St., Niagara Falls, ON L2G 5Z3
Tel: 905-374-6000; *Fax:* 905-374-9410
Toll-Free: 877-231-0011
mjs5627@hotmail.com

***Niagara Falls*: Malcolm A.F. Stockton - *1**
P.O. Box 868, Stn. Main, 4786 Queen St., Niagara Falls, ON L2E 6V6
Tel: 905-357-3500; *Fax:* 905-356-3635
stockton@iaw.com
www.iaw.com/~stockton

***Niagara Falls*: Guy Ungaro - *1**
#101, 3486 Portage Rd., Niagara Falls, ON L2J 2K4
Tel: 905-357-5310; *Fax:* 905-357-9677
guyungaro@hotmail.com

***Niagara Falls*: Brian C. Wilcox - *1**
6617 Drummond Rd., Niagara Falls, ON L2G 4N4
Tel: 905-358-0782; *Fax:* 905-356-7772
Toll-Free: 877-220-7211
brian@bcwlawoffice.com
www.bcwlawoffice.com

***Niagara on the Lake*: Richard J.W. Andrews - *1**
#201, 111A Garrison Village Dr., Niagara on the Lake, ON L0S 1J0
Tel: 905-468-0081; *Fax:* 905-468-0087
rjwandrews@on.aibn.com
www.adamsheritage.com/lawyer/

***Niagara on the Lake*: W.R. King - *1**
P.O. Box 900, 431 Mississauga St., Niagara on the Lake, ON L0S 1J0
Tel: 905-468-3272; *Fax:* 905-468-5441
kinglaw@bellnet.ca

***North Augusta*: Emerson Communications Inc. - *1**
12931 Land O'Nod, RR#3, North Augusta, ON K0G 1R0
Tel: 613-290-7905; *Fax:* 613-269-4866
eostiguy@magma.ca

***North Bay*: Birnie Law Firm - *1**
P.O. Box 100, Stn. Main, 116 McIntyre St. West, North Bay, ON P1B 8G8
Tel: 705-497-1900; *Fax:* 705-497-1700
m.c.b@birnielawfirm.ca

***North Bay*: Bowness & Murray - *2**
348 Fraser St., North Bay, ON P1B 3W7
Tel: 705-474-9680; *Fax:* 705-474-4218

***North Bay*: Clements, Barrister & Solicitor - *1**
Former Name: Tafel, Trussler & Eggert
477 Sherbrooke St., North Bay, ON P1B 2C2
Tel: 705-472-4890; *Fax:* 705-472-9612

***North Bay*: Colvin & Colvin Professional Corporation - *2**
P.O. Box 657, Stn. Main, 577 Main St. West, North Bay, ON P1B 8J5
Tel: 705-476-5161; *Fax:* 705-476-9902
Toll-Free: 877-268-8566
colvinlaw@cogeco.net

***North Bay*: Gorman Barristers - *1**
Thompson Building, 101 McIntyre St. West, North Bay, ON P1B 2Y5
Tel: 705-476-0500; *Fax:* 705-476-8054

***North Bay*: M. Lucie Laperriere - *1**
325 Ski Club Rd., North Bay, ON P1B 7R3
Tel: 705-495-8554; *Fax:* 705-495-6274
lr-law@efni.com

***North Bay*: Larmer Law Office - *1**
Former Name: Larmer & Larmer Barristers
335 Main St. West, North Bay, ON P1B 2T9
Tel: 705-476-5544; *Fax:* 705-476-0118
glarmer@larmer.ca
www.larmer.ca

***North Bay*: Lucenti, Orlando & Ellies Professional Corporation - *4**
P.O. Box 358, 373 Main St. West, North Bay, ON P1B 8H5
Tel: 705-472-9500; *Fax:* 705-472-4814
info@loellp.ca

***North Bay*: Robert J. Martyn**
374 Fraser St., North Bay, ON P1B 3W7
Tel: 705-476-7080; *Fax:* 705-476-8084

***North Bay*: James R. McIntosh - *1**
325 Main St. West, North Bay, ON P1B 2T9
Tel: 705-476-2500; *Fax:* 705-476-9347
maclaw@efni.com

** indicates number of lawyers*

***North Bay*: McLachlan Froud LLP - *2**
#202, 373 Main St. West, North Bay, ON P1B 2T9
Tel: 705-476-6333; *Fax:* 705-476-4397
hughmclachlan@sympatico.ca; jeffrey.froud@sympatico.ca

***North Bay*: Joe Sinicrope - *1**
495 Main St. West, North Bay, ON P1B 2V3
Tel: 705-495-1334; *Fax:* 705-495-7990
joesinicrope@neilnet.com

***North Bay*: Wallace Klein Partners in Law LLP - *7**
P.O. Box 37, 225 McIntyre St. West, North Bay, ON P1B 8G8
Tel: 705-474-2920; *Fax:* 705-474-1758
info@partnersinlaw.net

***North York*: Tilda M. Roll - *1**
#600, 1120 Finch Ave. West, North York, ON M3J 3H7
Tel: 416-665-6888; *Fax:* 416-665-8225
tmroll@aggsrlawyers.ca

***Oakville*: Douglas D. Baggs - *1**
P.O. Box 100, Stn. Main, 233 Robinson St., Oakville, ON L6J 4Z5
Tel: 905-842-8600; *Fax:* 905-842-8242
doug@dougbaggs.com
dougbaggs.com

***Oakville*: Stephen B. Collinson - *1**
457 Kerr St., Oakville, ON L6K 3C2
Tel: 905-842-1600; *Fax:* 905-842-2775

***Oakville*: John G. Cox - *1**
297 Church St., Oakville, ON L6J 1N9
Tel: 905-842-3211; *Fax:* 905-842-3765

***Oakville*: Diane F. Daly - *1**
#301, 165 Cross Ave., Oakville, ON L6J 0A9
Tel: 905-844-5883; *Fax:* 905-844-9765
dianedaly@dalylaw.ca
www.oakvillelaw.ca

***Oakville*: Richard B. Day - *1**
164 Trafalgar Rd., Oakville, ON L6J 3G6
Tel: 905-844-8581; *Fax:* 905-842-6166
rick@daylaw.ca

***Oakville*: J.B. Gardner - *1**
P.O. Box 249, 228 Lakeshore Rd. East, Oakville, ON L6J 5A2
Tel: 905-844-3218; *Fax:* 905-844-3699
jbg@quixnet.net

***Oakville*: Stuart W. Henderson - *1**
P.O. Box 249, 228 Lakeshore Rd. East, Oakville, ON L6J 5A2
Tel: 905-844-3218; *Fax:* 905-844-3699
swhenderson@on.aibn.com

***Oakville*: Brian W. King, Q.C. - *1**
#34, Hopedale Mall, 1515 Rebecca St., Oakville, ON L6L 5G8
Tel: 905-827-0808; *Fax:* 905-827-8380
bking@briankinglaw.com
www.briankinglaw.com

***Oakville*: Patrick M. Kirby - *1**
1373 Secord Ave., Oakville, ON L6L 2K9
Tel: 905-825-5277; *Fax:* 905-825-3178

***Oakville*: Law Offices of Charles W. Pley, Canada & USA Immigration Lawyers - *1**
#102, 2660 Sherwood Heights Dr., Oakville, ON L6J 7Y8
Tel: 905-829-2100; *Fax:* 905-829-2100
info@pleylaw.com
www.pleylaw.com

***Oakville*: Lush, Bowker Aird - *4**
P.O. Box 734, 261 Lakeshore Rd. East, Oakville, ON L6J 1H9
Tel: 905-844-0381; *Fax:* 905-849-4540
Toll-Free: 877-844-0381
lawyers@lushbowkeraird.on.ca

***Oakville*: Thomas H. Marshall, Q.C., Barristers & Solicitors - *3**
#205, 1540 Cornwall Rd., Oakville, ON L6J 7W5
Tel: 905-844-0464; *Fax:* 905-844-3983
sanderson@oakvillefamilylawyer.ca
www.oakvillefamilylawyer.ca

***Oakville*: Terri L. McCarthy - *1**
#3A, 418 North Service Rd. East, Oakville, ON L6H 5R2
Tel: 905-842-4223; *Fax:* 905-842-7401
tlm.law@on.aibn.com

***Oakville*: David L. McKenzie - *1**
#211, 277 Lakeshore Rd. East, Oakville, ON L6J 6J3
Tel: 905-845-7591; *Fax:* 905-845-8876

***Oakville*: Kathryn S. Naumetz, Law Office - *1**
263 Church St., Oakville, ON L6J 1N7
Tel: 905-845-2241; *Fax:* 905-845-0193

***Oakville*: Keith D. Nelson - *1**
#205, North (Rear) Entrance, 243 North Service Rd. West, Oakville, ON L6M 3E5
Tel: 905-338-8481; *Fax:* 905-338-0748
kdnelson@nelsonlawyer.com
www.nelsonlawyer.com

***Oakville*: O'Connor MacLeod Hanna LLP - *21**
700 Kerr St., Oakville, ON L6K 3W5
Tel: 905-842-8030; *Fax:* 905-842-2460
info@omh.ca
www.omh.ca

***Oakville*: P. William Perras, Jr. - *1**
#210, 1540 Cornwall Rd., Oakville, ON L6J 7W5
Tel: 905-827-2700; *Fax:* 905-827-2766
billperras@on.aibn.com

***Oakville*: David J. Pilo - *1**
#301, 88 Dunn St., Oakville, ON L6J 3C7
Tel: 905-338-2002; *Fax:* 905-338-3810
dpilo@on.aibn.com

***Oakville*: Policy Alliance Inc. - *1**
2030 Merchants Gate, Oakville, ON L6M 2Z8
Tel: 905-842-5910; *Fax:* 905-842-9885
youngt.policyalliance@cogeco.ca

***Oakville*: Ryrie, Kerr, Davidson - *2**
P.O. Box 100, Stn. Main, 233 Robinson St., Oakville, ON L6J 4Z5
Tel: 905-842-8600; *Fax:* 905-842-4774

***Oakville*: Shanahan, Martin A - *1**
#200, 2620 Bristol Circle, Oakville, ON L6H 6Z7
Tel: 905-829-2700

***Oakville*: Karen A. Thompson - *1**
#100, 251 North Service Rd. West, Oakville, ON L6M 3E7
Tel: 905-338-7941; *Fax:* 905-844-9765
karens@karenthompsonlaw.ca
www.karenthompsonlaw.ca

***Oakville*: Helen M. Thomson - *1**
#1160, 1011 Upper Middle Rd. East, Oakville, ON L6H 5Z9
Tel: 416-410-8895; *Fax:* 416-410-8895

***Oakville*: Townsend & Associates - *2**
Also Known As: Lynn Townend
Former Name: Townsend Renaud, Lynda J.
#10, 1525 Cornwall Rd., Oakville, ON L6J 0B2
Tel: 905-829-8600; *Fax:* 905-829-2035
lyn.townsend@ltownsend.ca

***Orangeville*: Mullin, Thwaites & Ward LLP - *4**
25 First St., Orangeville, ON L9W 2Z5
Tel: 519-941-4559; *Fax:* 519-941-4806
psprouleward@mtwlawoffice.com
www.mtwlawoffice.com

***Orangeville*: Parkinson & Parkinson - *1**
145 Broadway St., Orangeville, ON L9W 1K2
Tel: 519-941-3627; *Fax:* 519-941-3444
pp@parkinsonparkinson.ca

***Orangeville*: Peterson & Peterson**
P.O. Box 1607, 18 Lawton St., Orangeville, ON L9W 4X4
Tel: 705-356-9877; *Fax:* 705-356-7498
larryd.peterson@sympatico.ca

***Orangeville*: L. Anne Welwood - *1**
14 Zina St., Orangeville, ON L9W 1E1
Tel: 519-941-9710; *Fax:* 519-941-9244
aweldwood@welwoodlaw.com

***Orangeville*: Stephen F. White, Barrister & Solicitor - *1**
30 Mill St., Orangeville, ON L9W 2M3
Tel: 519-941-9440; *Fax:* 519-941-3803

***Orillia*: H. Robert Barlow, Q.C. - *1**
Stn. Main, 5 McLean Cr., RR#1, Orillia, ON L3V 6H1
Tel: 705-326-6881; *Fax:* 705-326-3063

***Orillia*: Crawford, McKenzie, McLean, Anderson & Duncan LLP - *7**
P.O. Box 520, Stn. Orillia, 40 Coldwater St. East, Orillia, ON L3V 6K4
Tel: 705-325-2753; *Fax:* 705-325-4913
mclaw@mclaw.ca

***Orillia*: Brian D. Kinnear - *1**
#108, P.O. Box 656, 17 Colborne St. East, Orillia, ON L3V 6K7
Tel: 705-323-9386; *Fax:* 705-323-9388
bkinnearlaw@on.aibn.com

***Orillia*: Lisa Welch Madden Law Firm - *1**
Former Name: Bourne, Jenkins & Mulligan
22 Matchedash St. N, Orillia, ON L3V 6K2
Tel: 705-325-6439; *Fax:* 705-325-7058
madden@lwmlaw.com

***Orillia*: Allan C. Parslow - *1**
212 John St., Orillia, ON L3V 3H7
Tel: 705-329-2223; *Fax:* 705-329-0433

***Orillia*: Russell Christie LLP - *7**
Former Name: Russell, Christie, Miller, Koughan, Winnitoy LLP
P.O. Box 158, 505 Memorial Ave., Orillia, ON L3V 6J3
Tel: 705-325-1326; *Fax:* 705-327-1811
rcmkw@russellchristie.com

***Orleans*: Brisebois & Webster - *2**
#103, 1803 St. Joseph Blvd., Orleans, ON K1C 6E7
Tel: 613-837-1140; *Fax:* 613-837-1689
brisebois webster@hotmail.com

***Orleans*: Canadian Diamond Consultants Inc. - *1**
890 Amyot Ave., Orleans, ON K1C 3A6
Tel: 613-424-7701; *Fax:* 613-424-7901
Toll-Free: 888-545-0260
c.d.c@rogers.com
www.canadiandiamondconsultants.ca

***Orleans*: Dust Evans Grandmaitre Professional Corporation - *5**
2589 St. Joseph Blvd., Orleans, ON K1C 1G4
Tel: 613-837-1010; *Fax:* 613-837-9670
Toll-Free: 800-379-6668
info@dustevans.com
www.dustevans.com

***Orleans*: Galarneau & Associates Professional Corp. - *4**
2831 St. Joseph Blvd., Orleans, ON K1C 1G6
Tel: 613-830-7111; *Fax:* 613-830-7108
bjg@galarneauassoc.com
www.galarneauassoc.com

***Orleans*: J & L Associates - *1**
1863 Des Epinettes Ave., Orleans, ON K1C 6N5
Tel: 613-355-9545;
gordonsharpe@aol.com

***Orleans*: Michael M. Johnson & Associates Inc. - *1**
1647 Sunview Dr., Orleans, ON K1C 5C6
Tel: 613-841-6685; *Fax:* 613-841-6686

***Orleans*: Brian Kelly Consulting - *1**
1596 St. Georges St., Orleans, ON K1E 2M9
Tel: 613-841-1395

***Orleans*: W.E. Robert Little & Associates Inc. - *1**
6158 Voyageur Dr., Orleans, ON K1C 2W3

***Orleans*: Marc Nadon - *1**
#101, 3009 St. Joseph Blvd., Orleans, ON K1E 1E1
Tel: 613-837-4437; *Fax:* 613-837-4204
info@marcnadon.ca

***Orleans*: On The Hill Consulting - *1**
611 Merkley Dr., Orleans, ON K4A 1S3
Tel: 613-875-1795;
phillips@telus.blackberry.ca

***Orleans*: Donald Partsch - *1**
1718 Des Sapins Gardens, Orleans, ON K1C 8E4
Tel: 613-837-3655;
donald.partsch@sympatico.ca

***Orleans*: Phillipe Henault Enterprises Inc. - *1**
1204 St-Moritz Ct., Orleans, ON K1C 2B3
Tel: 613-824-2184; *Fax:* 613-824-9534

***Orleans*: Sicotte Professional Corp. - *5**
Former Name: Sicotte & Associates
3009 St. Joseph Blvd., Orleans, ON K1E 1E1
Tel: 613-837-7408; *Fax:* 613-837-8015
admin@sicotte.ca

** indicates number of lawyers*

***Orleans*: Roger P. Trudel - *1**
2828 St. Joseph Blvd., Orleans, ON K1C 1G7
Tel: 613-837-2641; *Fax:* 613-830-5613
roger.trudel@on.aibn.com

***Orono*: W.K. Lycett, Q.C. - *1**
P.O. Box 87, 5301 Main St., Orono, ON L0B 1M0
Tel: 905-983-5007; *Fax:* 905-983-9022
wklycett@look.ca

***Oshawa*: Aleksandr G. Bolotenko - *1**
#978, Stn. A, 225 King St. East, Oshawa, ON L1H 7H2
Tel: 905-433-1176; *Fax:* 905-433-0283
agblaw.com

***Oshawa*: Boychyn & Boychyn - *1**
#1E, 57 Simcoe St. South, Oshawa, ON L1H 4G4
Tel: 905-576-2670; *Fax:* 905-576-0915
dboychyn@rogers.com

***Oshawa*: Julie Clark - *1**
P.O. Box 365, Stn. A, 32 Elgin St. East, Oshawa, ON L1H 7L5
Tel: 905-434-6411; *Fax:* 905-571-6114

***Oshawa*: Catherine Cornwall-Taylor - *1**
32 Elgin St. East, Oshawa, ON L1J 1T1
Tel: 905-434-6411; *Fax:* 905-571-6114

***Oshawa*: Creighton Victor Alexander Hayward Morison & Hall LLP - *5**
Also Known As: The Creighton Law Firm
Former Name: Hayward Morrison & Hall LLP
P.O. Box 26010, 235 King St. East, Oshawa, ON L1H 8R4
Tel: 905-723-3446; *Fax:* 905-432-2323
inquire@durhamlawyers.ca
www.durhamlawyers.ca

***Oshawa*: Diamond, Fischman & Pushman - *2**
P.O. Box 26008, Stn. 206, 179 King St. East, Oshawa, ON L1H 8R4
Tel: 905-723-5243; *Fax:* 905-436-6041
office@dflplaw.com

***Oshawa*: Elliott & Hughes - *2**
106 Stevenson Rd. South, Oshawa, ON L1J 5M1
Tel: 905-571-1774; *Fax:* 905-571-7706
Toll-Free: 877-272-5220

***Oshawa*: Diane M. England - *1**
167 Simcoe St. North, Oshawa, ON L1G 4S8
Tel: 905-721-1277; *Fax:* 905-721-1217
mail@dianeengland.com

***Oshawa*: Farquharson & Adamson - *1**
74 Simcoe St. South, Oshawa, ON L1H 4G6
Tel: 905-404-1947; *Fax:* 905-404-9050

***Oshawa*: Shan K. Jain, Q.C. - *1**
#2, 215 Simcoe St. North, Oshawa, ON L1G 4T1
Tel: 905-432-7787; *Fax:* 905-432-2343
jainc@sprint.ca

***Oshawa*: Kelly Greenway Bruce - *8**
Former Name: Kelly, Greenway, Bruce, Korb
P.O. Box 886, 114 King St. East, Oshawa, ON L1H 7N1
Tel: 905-723-2278; *Fax:* 905-432-2663
mail@oshawalawyers.com
www.oshawalawyers.com

***Oshawa*: Kitchen Kitchen Simeson McFarlane - *7**
P.O. Box 428, 86 Simcoe St. South, Oshawa, ON L1H 7L5
Tel: 905-579-5302; *Fax:* 905-579-6073
Toll-Free: 888-669-6446
mail@kksm.com

***Oshawa*: K.L. Lancaster - *1**
9 Ontario St., Oshawa, ON L1G 4Y9
Tel: 905-571-3901; *Fax:* 905-571-4241

***Oshawa*: Laskowsky & Laskowsky - *1**
73 Centre St. South, Oshawa, ON L1H 4A1
Tel: 905-579-0777; *Fax:* 905-576-9918

***Oshawa*: Mack, Kisbee & Greer - *3**
146 Simcoe St. North, Oshawa, ON L1G 4S7
Tel: 905-571-1400; *Fax:* 905-571-0735

***Oshawa*: Marks & Marks - *1**
#304, 17 King St. East, Oshawa, ON L1H 1A8
Tel: 905-728-5151; *Fax:* 905-433-4018

***Oshawa*: Richard J. Mazar Professional Corp. - *1**
#210, 419 King St. West, Oshawa, ON L1J 2K5
Tel: 905-571-2558; *Fax:* 905-571-3548
mazar@mazarlaw.com

***Oshawa*: Elaine M.F. McCallum - *1**
P.O. Box 1098, Stn. B, 174 Athol St. East, Oshawa, ON L1J 5Y9
Tel: 905-579-8866; *Fax:* 905-579-8913
Toll-Free: 888-579-5252
elainemfmccallum@on.aibn.com

***Oshawa*: Sharon A. Moote - *1**
Former Name: Moote & Cocchetto
#210, 200 Bond St. West, Oshawa, ON L1J 2L7
Tel: 905-432-7880; *Fax:* 905-432-7674

***Oshawa*: Joseph Neal - *1**
142 Simcoe St. North, Oshawa, ON L1G 4S7
Tel: 905-436-9015; *Fax:* 905-436-6098
jneal@oshawalawyers.ca

***Oshawa*: Josef Neubauer - *1**
106 Stevenson Rd. South, Oshawa, ON L1J 5M1
Tel: 905-433-1991; *Fax:* 905-433-7038

***Oshawa*: O'Brien, Balka & Elrick, Barristers & Solicitors - *6**
219 King St. East, Oshawa, ON L1H 1C5
Tel: 905-576-3402; *Fax:* 905-576-3915
Toll-Free: 866-245-5063
obe@oshawalaw.com
www.oshawalaw.com

***Oshawa*: Margot Poepjes - *1**
#217, 650 King St. East, Oshawa, ON L1H 1G5
Tel: 905-433-4020; *Fax:* 905-433-7028

***Oshawa*: Scott & Olver LLP - *3**
Former Name: Scott, Kimball, Olver
#4, 39 Bond St. East, Oshawa, ON L1G 1B2
Tel: 905-579-9400; *Fax:* 905-579-7400
scottolver@scottandolver.ca

***Oshawa*: Sosna & Burch - *3**
#8, 500 King St. West, Oshawa, ON L1J 2K9
Tel: 905-440-4759; *Fax:* 905-440-4764
sosna-burch@sosnaburch.com

***Oshawa*: Frank H.M. Stolwyk - *1**
57 Simcoe St. South, Unit 1-F, Oshawa, ON L1H 4G4
Tel: 905-576-8100; *Fax:* 905-579-6762
franks4950@aol.com

***Oshawa*: Strike, Salmers & Furlong - *3**
Former Name: Salmers, Strike & Furlong
P.O. Box 2096, Stn. A, 55 William St. East, Oshawa, ON L1H 7V4
Tel: 905-723-1101; *Fax:* 905-723-1157
allanfurlong@ssf-oshawa.com

***Oshawa*: Ronald L. Swartz - *1**
231 Simcoe St. North, Oshawa, ON L1G 4T1
Tel: 905-576-3392; *Fax:* 905-576-3397
rlswatrz@interlinks.net

***Oshawa*: David B. Thomas - *1**
28B Albert St., Oshawa, ON L1H 8S5
Tel: 905-576-5666; *Fax:* 905-576-5289

***Oshawa*: Martin Tweyman - *1**
#101, 19 Celina St., Oshawa, ON L1H 4M9
Tel: 905-571-1500; *Fax:* 905-571-7528
martin.tweyman.oshawa@bellnet.ca

***Oshawa*: Ronald F. Worboy - *1**
153 Simcoe St. North, Oshawa, ON L1G 4S6
Tel: 905-723-2288; *Fax:* 905-576-1355

***Oshawa*: Yanch & Yanch - *1**
#1D, P.O. Box 154, 57 Simcoe St. South, Oshawa, ON L1H 7L1
Tel: 905-728-9495; *Fax:* 905-721-8044
yanchfirm@hotmail.com

***Ottawa*: Douglas R. Adams - *1**
#1502, 222 Queen St., Ottawa, ON K1P 5V9
Tel: 613-238-8076; *Fax:* 613-238-5519

***Ottawa*: Addelman & Baum - *2**
Former Name: Baum, Douglas M.
#800, 85 Albert St., Ottawa, ON K1P 6A4
Tel: 613-237-2673; *Fax:* 613-237-8146
douglasmbaum@rogers.com

***Ottawa*: Ahmad-Yousuf & Assoc. - *3**
Former Name: Moore & Ahmad-Yousuf
#100, 180 Metcalfe St., Ottawa, ON K2P 1P5
Tel: 613-236-1111; *Fax:* 613-232-7763

***Ottawa*: AML Associates Inc. - *1**
10 Archer Sq., Ottawa, ON K1V 9Y8
Tel: 613-738-2000; *Fax:* 613-738-2358
ae.dumas@sympatico.ca

***Ottawa*: Anders, Young, Strong & Jonah - *4**
Former Name: Anders, Young & Jonah
#401, 1580 Merivale Rd., Ottawa, ON K2G 4B5
Tel: 613-224-1621; *Fax:* 613-224-8827

***Ottawa*: Andrews Robichaud - *6**
#500, 1306 Wellington St., Ottawa, ON K1Y 3B2
Tel: 613-237-1512; *Fax:* 613-237-9580
info@andrewsrobichaud.com
www.andrewsrobichaud.com

***Ottawa*: APCO Worldwide (Canada) - *2**
#703, 255 Albert St., Ottawa, ON K1P 6A9
Tel: 613-565-4242; *Fax:* 613-565-1937
www.apcoworldwide.com

***Ottawa*: Association House - *1**
#1860, 45 O'Connor St., Ottawa, ON K1P 1A4
Tel: 613-567-3638; *Fax:* 613-232-7148
gmcintosh@associationhouse.com

***Ottawa*: Augustine Bater Polowin LLP - *7**
#1100, 141 Laurier Ave. West, Ottawa, ON K1P 5J3
Tel: 613-569-9500; *Fax:* 613-569-9522
info@abplaw.com

***Ottawa*: Axion - *1**
#230, 196 Bradford St., Ottawa, ON K2B 5Z4
Tel: 613-369-4333; *Fax:* 613-726-8938
Toll-Free: 888-992-9466
info@axionplus.biz
www.axioninc.biz

***Ottawa*: Robert G. Bales - *1**
#200, 504 Kent St., Ottawa, ON K2P 2B9
Tel: 613-567-0674; *Fax:* 613-236-4064

***Ottawa*: Gary R. Barnes - *3**
#500, 200 Elgin St., Ottawa, ON K2P 1L5
Tel: 613-225-2529; *Fax:* 613-225-3930
barnesgary@rogers.com

***Ottawa*: Beament Green - *6**
979 Wellington Ave., Ottawa, ON K1Y 2X7
Tel: 613-241-3400; *Fax:* 613-241-8555
info@beament.com
www.beament.com

***Ottawa*: Bélanger Guy & Assoc. Inc. - *1**
#602, 250 City Centre Ave., Ottawa, ON K1R 6K7
Tel: 613-230-7175; *Fax:* 613-230-3799
bga@bga-inc.com

***Ottawa*: Jean Belanger - *1**
2230 Quinton St., Ottawa, ON K1H 6V3
Tel: 613-731-6362; *Fax:* 613-731-6199

***Ottawa*: Bell, Baker LLP - *12**
#500, 116 Lisgar St., Ottawa, ON K2P 0C2
Tel: 613-237-3444; *Fax:* 613-237-1413

***Ottawa*: Bell, Unger, Riley, Morris - *4**
24 Bayswater Ave., Ottawa, ON K1Y 2E4
Tel: 613-235-1266; *Fax:* 613-230-2727
rkriley@ottwaimmigration.com

***Ottawa*: Binavince & Associates Professional Corporation - *4**
Former Name: Binavince Smith.
116 Lisgar St., 6th Fl., Ottawa, ON K2P 0C2
Tel: 613-236-2199; *Fax:* 613-236-3136
lawyers@binavince.com
www.binavince.com

***Ottawa*: Blake, Cassels & Graydon LLP**
#2000, World Exchange Plaza, 45 Connor St., Ottawa, ON K1P 1A4
ottawa@blakes.com
www.blakes.com

***Ottawa*: John E. Bogue - *1**
#802, 200 Elgin St., Ottawa, ON K2P 1L5
Tel: 613-234-4901; *Fax:* 613-236-8906

** indicates number of lawyers*

***Ottawa*: Bosada & Associates - *1**
#222, 280 Metcalfe St., Ottawa, ON K2P 1R7
Tel: 613-563-1001; *Fax:* 613-563-1031
richard@bosada.ca

***Ottawa*: Bradley, Hiscock, McCracken - *5**
Former Name: Bradley, Hiscock
1581 Greenbank Rd., Ottawa, ON K2J 4Y6
Tel: 613-825-4585; *Fax:* 613-825-5101
bhlaw@bhlaw.ca

***Ottawa*: Alan S.J. Brass - *1**
#1002, 200 Elgin St., Ottawa, ON K2P 1L5
Tel: 613-238-5757; *Fax:* 613-688-1212

***Ottawa*: Brazeau Seller LLP - *17**
#750, 55 Metcalfe St., Ottawa, ON K1P 6L5
Tel: 613-237-4000; *Fax:* 613-237-4001
www.brazeauseller.com

***Ottawa*: C.P. Brett - *1**
70 Gloucester St., Ottawa, ON K2P 0A2
Tel: 613-230-2907; *Fax:* 613-235-4430
cpbrett@attglobal.net

***Ottawa*: Thomas W. Brooker - *1**
#208, 1400 Clyde Ave., Ottawa, ON K2G 3J2
Tel: 613-226-3265; *Fax:* 613-224-8943
tom@brookerlawoffice.ca

***Ottawa*: Bulger, Young - *3**
1493 Merivale Rd., Lower Level, Ottawa, ON K2E 5P3
Tel: 613-728-5881; *Fax:* 613-728-6158

***Ottawa*: Burton Katsepontes - *2**
#200, 283 Dalhousie St., Ottawa, ON K1N 7E5
Tel: 613-239-3064; *Fax:* 613-237-9181
npklaw@corpweb.net

***Ottawa*: Donald J. Byrne - *1**
#26, 1568 Carling Ave., Ottawa, ON K1Z 7M4
Tel: 613-722-5292; *Fax:* 613-729-6732
dbyrne@primus.ca

***Ottawa*: Callan-Honeywell LLP - *2**
418 Preston St., Ottawa, ON K1S 4N2
Tel: 613-729-2460; *Fax:* 613-729-1710
www.callanhoneywell.ca

***Ottawa*: Canadian Business Aviation Association**
#155, 955 Green Valley Cres., Ottawa, ON K2C 3V4
Tel: 613-236-5611; *Fax:* 613-236-2361
info@cbaa.com
www.cbaa-acaa.ca

***Ottawa*: Caparim International - *1**
37 Linden Terrace, Ottawa, ON K1S 1Z1
Tel: 613-563-3292; *Fax:* 613-563-2676

***Ottawa*: CapelleKane Immigration Lawyers Professional Corporation - *2**
#300, 311 Richmond Rd., Ottawa, ON K1Z 6X3
Tel: 613-230-7070; *Fax:* 613-230-9444
contact@capellekane.com
www.capellekane.com

***Ottawa*: Carraigtyr Consulting & Associates - *1**
799 Colson Ave., Ottawa, ON K1G 1R6
Tel: 613-260-2222; *Fax:* 613-260-2222
james100@rogers.com

***Ottawa*: Carroll & Wallace - *3**
#502, 66 Slater St., Ottawa, ON K1P 5H1
Tel: 613-236-5494; *Fax:* 613-232-7322
cwmlaw@cyberus.ca

***Ottawa*: Robert M. Chartrand - *1**
#101, 745B Montréal Rd., Ottawa, ON K1K 0T1
Tel: 613-745-9446; *Fax:* 613-745-0800

***Ottawa*: Edward Y.W. Cheung - *1**
#22, 5340 Canotek Rd., Ottawa, ON K1J 9C8
Tel: 613-748-9898; *Fax:* 613-748-1114
yw61@aol.com

***Ottawa*: Paul-Emile Chiasson - *1**
#600, 116 Lisgar St., Ottawa, ON K2P 0C2
Tel: 613-230-8800; *Fax:* 613-236-3136
pechiasson@sympatico.ca

***Ottawa*: Civica Inc. - *1**
45 O'Connor St., Ottawa, ON K1P 1A4
Tel: 613-232-0969; *Fax:* 613-447-2730
cwilson@civica.ca

***Ottawa*: Cogitare - *1**
2294 Courtice Ave., Ottawa, ON K1H 7G8
Tél: 613-733-6165; *Téléc:* 613-733-1105
bhubert@cogiscene.com

***Ottawa*: Conlin & McAlpin - *2**
1678 Bank St., Ottawa, ON K1V 7Y6
Tel: 613-737-4140; *Fax:* 613-737-7903
pconlin@conlinlaw.com

***Ottawa*: Rosalind Conway & Associate - *2**
#320, 185 Somerset St. West, Ottawa, ON K2P 0J2
Tel: 613-594-0300; *Fax:* 613-594-8111
rosalind.conway@magma.ca

***Ottawa*: Cooligan/Ryan LLP - *10**
#1100, 200 Elgin St., Ottawa, ON K2P 1L5
Tel: 613-236-0735; *Fax:* 613-238-3501
mail@colliganryan.com

***Ottawa*: Cordwood International Inc. - *1**
25 MacNabb Pl., Ottawa, ON K1L 8J5
Tel: 613-741-1615; *Fax:* 613-741-9388
ted.gibson@sympatico.ca

***Ottawa*: Crestview Public Affairs Inc. - *1**
#1510, 85 Albert St., Ottawa, ON K1P 6A4
Tel: 613-232-0462;
peter.naglik@crestviewpublicaffairs.com

***Ottawa*: DAI Inc. - *1**
#300, 67A Sparks St., Ottawa, ON K1P 5A5
Tel: 613-238-6317; *Fax:* 613-238-0007
ataylor@daigroup.ca

***Ottawa*: Deloitte & Touche LLP - *2**
#800, 100 Queen St., Ottawa, ON K1P 5T8
Tel: 613-236-2442; *Fax:* 613-236-2195
www.deloitte.com

***Ottawa*: T.M. Denton Consultants - *1**
37 Heney St., Ottawa, ON K1N 5V6
Tel: 613-789-5397; *Fax:* 613-789-5398
tmdenton@ftn.net

***Ottawa*: Dickie & Lyman Lawyers LLP - *2**
#640, 1600 Carling Ave., Ottawa, ON K1Z 1G3
Tel: 613-235-0101; *Fax:* 613-238-0101

***Ottawa*: DioGuardi Tax Law - *3**
#600, 100 Gloucester St., Ottawa, ON K2P 0A4
Tel: 613-237-2222; *Fax:* 613-237-9463
Toll-Free: 877-829-7902
pd@dioguarditaxlaw.com
www.taxrx.ca

***Ottawa*: Doucet McBride LLP - *12**
#100, 85 Plymouth St., Ottawa, ON K1S 3E2
Tel: 613-233-4474; *Fax:* 613-233-8868
lawyers@doucetmcbride.com
www.doucetmcbride.com

***Ottawa*: Doyle Salewski Inc. - *2**
404 Bank St., Ottawa, ON K2P 1Y5
Tel: 613-569-4444; *Fax:* 613-569-1116

***Ottawa*: Drache LLP - *5**
222 Somerset St. West, Ottawa, ON K2P 2G3
Tel: 613-233-2675; *Fax:* 613-233-6752

***Ottawa*: Dubuc/Osland - *3**
#706, 350 Sparks St., Ottawa, ON K1R 7S8
Tel: 613-236-3360; *Fax:* 613-236-3771

***Ottawa*: Daniel F. Dunlap - *1**
#5, 371A Richmond Rd., Ottawa, ON K2A 0E7
Tel: 613-722-7788; *Fax:* 613-722-8909
ddunlap@dunlaplaw.ca

***Ottawa*: Earnscliffe Strategy Group Inc. - *6**
#200, 46 Elgin St., Ottawa, ON K1P 5K6
Tel: 613-563-4455; *Fax:* 613-236-6173
www.earnscliffe.ca

***Ottawa*: Michael D. Edelson & Associates - *5**
#600, 200 Elgin St., Ottawa, ON K2P 1L5
Tel: 613-237-2290; *Fax:* 613-237-0071
mail@edelsonlaw.ca
www.edelsonlaw.ca

***Ottawa*: J.J. Mark Edwards - *1**
96 Helena St., Ottawa, ON K1Y 3N1
Tel: 613-722-2613; *Fax:* 613-722-9484
medwards@edwardslaw.ca

***Ottawa*: Emond Harnden - *25**
707 Bank St., Ottawa, ON K1S 3V1
Tel: 613-563-7660; *Fax:* 613-563-8001
Toll-Free: 888-563-7660
info@ehlaw.ca
www.ehlaw.ca

***Ottawa*: Bruce Engel Barrister & Solicitor - *2**
70 Gloucester St., 1st Fl., Ottawa, ON K2P 0A2
Tel: 613-235-6324; *Fax:* 613-235-7442
bruce.engel@rogers.com

***Ottawa*: Fanaian's Law Office - *1**
30 States Way, Ottawa, ON K2P 0Z6
Tel: 613-567-0833;
fanaian@hotmail.com

***Ottawa*: Farber & Robillard - *2**
330 Churchill Ave. North, Ottawa, ON K1Z 5B9
Tel: 613-722-9418; *Fax:* 613-722-5981

***Ottawa*: Pablo G.A. Fernandez-Davila - *1**
Former Name: Raymond A. Baumgarten
162 Laurier Ave. West, Ottawa, ON K1P 5J4
Tel: 613-565-8686; *Fax:* 613-565-8989
info@fernandez-davila.com

***Ottawa*: Finlayson & Singlehurst - *3**
70 Gloucester St., 4th Fl., Ottawa, ON K2P 0A2
Tel: 613-232-0227; *Fax:* 613-232-0542
fands@attglobal.net

***Ottawa*: Ann L. Flint - *1**
#203, 190 Somerset St. West, Ottawa, ON K2P 0J4
Tel: 613-594-5461; *Fax:* 613-594-5468

***Ottawa*: George Flumian - *1**
222 Argyle Ave., Ottawa, ON K2P 1B9
Tel: 613-236-8321; *Fax:* 613-230-6597

***Ottawa*: Fortey & Arbique - *2**
#210, 1335 Carling Ave., Ottawa, ON K1Z 8N8
Tel: 613-725-0303; *Fax:* 613-725-1292
info@forteyarbique.com

***Ottawa*: Francopol Inc. - *1**
1364 Ogden St., Ottawa, ON K1J 8C4
Tel: 613-796-5363; *Fax:* 613-235-2323
jctrottier@francopol.ca

***Ottawa*: Steven A. Fried - *1**
303 Waverly St., Ottawa, ON K2P 0V9
Tel: 613-233-4420; *Fax:* 613-288-1554
sfried@stevenfried.com

***Ottawa*: Susan Gahrns Law Office - *1**
116 Lisgar St., 6th Fl., Ottawa, ON K2P 0C2
Tel: 613-235-6299; *Fax:* 613-235-4704
law@gahrns.com

***Ottawa*: Goldberg Wiseman Stroud & Hollingsworth LLP, Barristers & Solicitors - *4**
Former Name: Goldberg Stroud LLP; Goldberg, Kronick & Stroud LLP
486 Gladstone Ave., Ottawa, ON K1R 5N8
Tel: 613-237-4922; *Fax:* 613-237-2920
info@gwshlaw.com
www.gsklaw.com

***Ottawa*: Donald R. Good - *2**
Merivale Depot, P.O. Box 5118, Ottawa, ON K2C 3H4
Tel: 613-228-9676; *Fax:* 613-228-7404
Toll-Free: 800-661-8837
farmlaw@on.aibn.com

***Ottawa*: Donald J. Gormley - *1**
#204, 190 Somerset St. West, Ottawa, ON K2P 0J4
Tel: 613-237-7726; *Fax:* 613-237-1977
donald.gormley@sympatico.ca

***Ottawa*: Goss, McCorriston, Stel - *3**
#203, 2430 Bank St., Ottawa, ON K1V 0T7
Tel: 613-738-0023; *Fax:* 613-738-1294

***Ottawa*: Government Policy Research Associates Inc. - *1**
#200, 265 Carling Ave., Ottawa, ON K1S 2E1
Tel: 613-235-5360

***Ottawa*: Government Strategies Corp. (GSC) - *1**
#200, 134 Sparks St., Ottawa, ON K1P 5B6
Tel: 613-230-6311; *Fax:* 613-230-1258

** indicates number of lawyers*

Ottawa: Mary Granskou Consulting - *1
101 Clearview Ave., Ottawa, ON K1Y 2L1
Tel: 613-722-6800;
granskou@magma.ca

Ottawa: Grant & Dawn - *4
226 MacLaren St., Ottawa, ON K2P 0L6
Tel: 613-235-2212; *Fax:* 613-235-5294

Ottawa: Geoffrey Grenville-Wood - *1
43 Florence St., Ottawa, ON K2P 0W6
Tel: 613-232-2688; *Fax:* 613-232-2680
geoffrey@grenvillewood.com

Ottawa: Grey, Clark, Shih & Associates Ltd. - *3
#901, 100 Sparks St., Ottawa, ON K1P 5B7
Tel: 613-238-7743; *Fax:* 613-238-0368

Ottawa: Gribbis Enterprises Ltd. - *1
20 Ellisson Way, Ottawa, ON K1G 4P6
Tel: 613-738-1632; *Fax:* 613-248-0110
jim.gribben@sympatico.ca

Ottawa: GS Government Consulting Services - *1
26 Maple Stand Way, Ottawa, ON K2G 6P4
Tel: 613-823-8079; *Fax:* 613-825-8592
gshields@magma.ca

Ottawa: David R. Habib - *1
18 Honeyood Ct., Ottawa, ON K1V 1Y4
Tel: 613-822-4100; *Fax:* 613-822-1698
habiblaw@rogers.com

Ottawa: John H. Hale Barrister & Solicitor
#203, 185 Somerset St., Ottawa, ON K2P 0J2
Tel: 613-230-4253; *Fax:* 613-230-6996

Ottawa: Brendan Hawley & Associates - *1
29 Taj Ct., Ottawa, ON K1G 5K7
Tel: 613-738-1016; *Fax:* 613-738-9123
brendan.hawley@sympatico.ca
www.brendanhawley.com

Ottawa: Hewitt, Hewitt, Nesbitt, Reid - *7
#604, Fuller Bldg., 75 Albert St., Ottawa, ON K1P 5E7
Tel: 613-563-0202; *Fax:* 613-563-0445
info@hewitts-law.com

Ottawa: Hillwatch Inc.
P.O. Box 4824, Stn. E, 3rd Ave., Ottawa, ON K1S 5H9
Tel: 613-238-8700; *Fax:* 866-310-4955
admin@hillwatch.com
www.hillwatch.com

Ottawa: Susan Hodgson - *1
#307, 150 Isabella St., Ottawa, ON K1S 1V7
Tel: 613-237-0505; *Fax:* 613-567-3559
susan@hodgsonlaw.ca

Ottawa: Honey/MacMillan - *3
146 Richmond Rd., Ottawa, ON K1Z 6W2
Tel: 613-722-2493; *Fax:* 613-722-2773
honeymac@rogers.com

Ottawa: Humphreys Public Affairs Group Inc. - *2
#1620, 130 Albert St., Ottawa, ON K1P 5G4
Tel: 613-230-3155; *Fax:* 613-236-2556
dhumphreys@hpag.ca
www.hpag.ca

Ottawa: ICG Defence Consultants Inc.
275 Slater St., Ottawa, ON K1P 5H9
Tel: 613-233-0848

Ottawa: Impact Public Affairs - *4
#910, 50 O'Connor St., Ottawa, ON K1P 6L2
Tel: 613-233-8906; *Fax:* 613-230-2669
cynthia@impactcanada.com

Ottawa: Industry Government Relations Group (IGRG) - *4
#1502, 85 Albert St., Ottawa, ON K1P 6A4
Tel: 613-232-1421; *Fax:* 613-232-9554

Ottawa: Inter/Sect Alliance Inc. - *1
#100, 408 Queen St., Ottawa, ON K1R 5A7
Tel: 613-276-3143; *Fax:* 613-235-5866
isa@intersectalliance.ca

Ottawa: Irh & Associates - *1
2388 Wyndale Cres., Ottawa, ON K1H 7A6
Tel: 613-737-4636; *Fax:* 613-233-9527
lhuneault@livingstonintl.com

Ottawa: Don Jarvis Consultants - *1
#202, 408 Queen St., Ottawa, ON K1R 5A7
Tel: 613-238-7809; *Fax:* 613-235-5866
djc@intersectalliance.ca

Ottawa: Jeffrey Bill - *1
#2701, CCT Building, 1125 Colonel By Dr., Ottawa, ON K1S 5R1
Tel: 613-244-7337; *Fax:* 613-244-1559

Ottawa: Karam Greenspon - *4
301 Elgin St., Ottawa, ON K2P 2N9
Tel: 613-232-9911; *Fax:* 613-232-5979

Ottawa: Kelly Santini LLP - *12
#2300, 66 Slater St., Ottawa, ON K1P 5H1
Tel: 613-238-6321; *Fax:* 613-233-4553

Ottawa: J.K. Kerr, Q.C. - *1
#404, 71 Bank St., Ottawa, ON K1P 5N2
Tel: 613-232-7902; *Fax:* 613-563-8067

Ottawa: Kiedrowski & Associates - *1
74 Iona St., Ottawa, ON K1Y 3L8
Tel: 613-724-3857; *Fax:* 613-724-3891
john.kiedrowski@sympatico.ca

Ottawa: KPMG - *1
#2000, 160 Elgin St., Ottawa, ON K2P 2P8
Tel: 613-212-2832; *Fax:* 613-212-2896
www.kpmg.ca

Ottawa: Laird, Sheena - *2
#110, 261 Cooper St., Ottawa, ON K2P 0G3
Tel: 613-232-3575; *Fax:* 613-232-6622
asselin7@bellnet.ca
www.asselinlaird.com

Ottawa: Langevin Morris LLP - *14
Former Name: Lewis Langevin LLP
190 O'Connor St., 9th Fl., Ottawa, ON K2P 2R3
Tel: 613-230-5787; *Fax:* 613-230-8563
general@langevinmorris.com
www.langevinmorris.com

Ottawa: Laveaux, Franck
Also Known As: Cabinet Laveaux Law Office
#215, 1725 St-Laurent Blvd., Ottawa, ON K1G 3V4
Tel: 613-523-0307; *Fax:* 613-523-0377
lex@laveaux.com
www.laveaux.com

Ottawa: Leadmark Consulting Group - *1
#1300, 155 Queen St., Ottawa, ON K1P 6L1
Tel: 613-232-2400; *Fax:* 613-232-2404
pauladdy@leadmarkconsulting.com

Ottawa: Louise M.S. LeBlanc - *1
29 Terrace Dr., Ottawa, ON K2H 9N3
Tel: 613-596-4256; *Fax:* 613-596-4235
lmsleblanc@sympatico.ca

Ottawa: Lois M. Leslie - *1
233 Bradford St., Ottawa, ON K2B 5Z5
Tel: 613-829-0108

Ottawa: Lightstone, Lyon
#420, 875 Carling Ave., Ottawa, ON K1S 5P1
Tel: 613-729-2460; *Fax:* 613-729-1710
lyon@lightcall.ca

Ottawa: Logres Inc. - *1
32 Langevin Ave., Ottawa, ON K1M 1E9
Tel: 613-851-1712;
cbyers@logresconsulting.com
www.logresconsulting.com

Ottawa: Lorimer Public Affairs
#201, 130 Albert St., Ottawa, ON K1P 5G4
Tel: 613-230-3156; *Fax:* 613-236-2556

Ottawa: Low, Murchison, LLP - *17
#200, 441 Maclaren St., Ottawa, ON K2P 2H3
Tel: 613-236-9442; *Fax:* 613-236-7942
lawyer@lowmurchison.com
www.lowmurchison.com

Ottawa: Macdonald, Affleck - *2
#104, 169 Lisgar St., Ottawa, ON K2P 0C3
Tel: 613-236-8712; *Fax:* 613-236-5145

Ottawa: MacKay & Sanderson - *2
#201, 1580 Merivale Rd., Ottawa, ON K2G 4B5
Tel: 613-238-6180; *Fax:* 613-238-3288

Ottawa: MacKinnon & Phillips - *8
#802, 200 Elgin St., Ottawa, ON K2P 1L5
Tel: 613-236-0662; *Fax:* 613-236-8906

Ottawa: Maclaren, Corlett - *8
#1625, 50 O'Connor St., Ottawa, ON K1P 6L2
Tel: 613-233-1146; *Fax:* 613-233-7190
mail@macorlaw.com
www.macorlaw.com

Ottawa: G. Carey MacLellan - *1
#1, 200 Cooper St., Ottawa, ON K2P 0G1
Tel: 613-232-9364; *Fax:* 613-230-3551

Ottawa: Carol Macleod & Associates Inc. - *1
#5, 156 St. Patrick St., Ottawa, ON K1N 5J8
Tel: 613-562-3938; *Fax:* 613-277-3930
contact@carolmacleod.com
www.carolmacleod.com

Ottawa: Mann & Partners LLP - *10
#612, 1600 Scott St., Ottawa, ON K1Y 4N7
Tel: 613-722-1500; *Fax:* 613-722-7677
www.mannlawyers.com

Ottawa: Howard Mann - *1
424 Hamilton Ave. South, Ottawa, ON K1Y 1E3
Tél: 613-729-0621; *Téléc:* 613-729-0306
hmann@ottawa.net

Ottawa: Marcus McNamara & Wilson - *4
#305, 185 Somerset St. West, Ottawa, ON K2P 0J2
Tel: 613-233-4083; *Fax:* 613-233-3132
marpar@sympatico.ca

Ottawa: Marks & Marks LLP - *1
#201, 190 Somerset St. West, Ottawa, ON K2P 0J4
Tel: 613-230-2123; *Fax:* 613-230-5707

Ottawa: Leonard Max, Q.C.
#201, 357 Preston St., Ottawa, ON K1S 4M8
Tel: 613-269-3872; *Fax:* 613-269-3581

Ottawa: Sean J. May - *1
#309, 185 Somerset St. West, Ottawa, ON K2P 0J2
Tel: 613-230-6524; *Fax:* 613-230-2705
smay@mayandkonyer.com

Ottawa: Mazerolle & Lemay - *6
#202, 1173 Cyrville Rd., Ottawa, ON K1J 7S6
Tel: 613-746-5700; *Fax:* 613-746-1783
www.mazerollelemay.com

Ottawa: MBM Intellectual Property Law LLP
Former Name: Marusyk Miller & Swain
270 Albert St., 14th Fl., Ottawa, ON K1P 5G8
Tel: 613-567-0762; *Fax:* 613-563-7671
mbm@mbm.com
www.mbm.com

Ottawa: McCann Law Offices - *4
#605, 200 Elgin St., Ottawa, ON K2P 1L5
Tel: 613-236-1410; *Fax:* 613-563-1367

Ottawa: McCloskey McCloskey - *2
#202, 5307 Canotek Rd., Ottawa, ON K1J 9M2
Tel: 613-745-0395; *Fax:* 613-745-8007
law@mccloskey.net

Ottawa: McDonald & Quinn - *1
#1, 1480 Woodward Ave., Ottawa, ON K1Z 7W6
Tel: 613-729-1005; *Fax:* 613-729-1176

Ottawa: McFadden, Fincham - *4
#606, 225 Metcalfe St., Ottawa, ON K2P 1P9
Tel: 613-234-1907; *Fax:* 613-234-5233
mail@mcfaddenfincham.com
www.mcfaddenfincham.com

Ottawa: McGuinty Law Offices Professional Corporation - *3
Former Name: McGuinty & McGuinty
1192 Rockingham Ave., Ottawa, ON K1H 8A7
Tel: 613-526-3858; *Fax:* 613-526-3187
reception@mcguintylaw.ca
www.mcguintylaw.com

Ottawa: Gordon C. McKechnie - *2
c/o Canadian Bank Note Company, 145 Richmond Rd., Ottawa, ON K1Z 1A1
Tel: 613-722-3421; *Fax:* 613-722-3334

Ottawa: Robert F. Meagher - *1
#502, 66 Slater St., Ottawa, ON K1P 5H1
Tel: 613-563-4278; *Fax:* 613-232-7322

** indicates number of lawyers*

***Ottawa*: Menzies & Coulson - *7**
111 Sherwood Dr., Ottawa, ON K1Y 3V1
Tel: 613-722-1313; *Fax:* 613-722-4712
Toll-Free: 888-722-1313
menzies@menziescoulson.com

***Ottawa*: John E. Merner - *3**
Former Name: Merner Burton Massie
136 Lewis St., Ottawa, ON K2P 0S7
Tel: 613-567-6093; *Fax:* 613-567-7164

***Ottawa*: Merovitz Potechin LLP - *8**
#301, 200 Catherine St., Ottawa, ON K2P 2K9
Tel: 613-563-7544; *Fax:* 613-563-4577
mplaw@mpottawa.com

***Ottawa*: Mile26 Strategy - *1**
#A, 40 Clarendon Ave., Ottawa, ON K1Y 0P2
Tel: 613-878-6784;
carlaventin@hotmail.com

***Ottawa*: Eric A. Milligan - *1**
#400, 45 Rideau St., Ottawa, ON K1N 5W8
Tel: 613-562-4077; *Fax:* 613-562-4102
milligan@delsysresearch.com

***Ottawa*: Miltons IP Professional Corporation - *6**
Former Name: Milton, Geller LLP
#700, 225 Metcalfe St., Ottawa, ON K2P 1P9
Tel: 613-567-7824; *Fax:* 613-567-4689
Toll-Free: 866-297-1179
info@miltonsip.com
www.miltonsip.com

***Ottawa*: Richard Minard - *1**
58 Clegg St., Ottawa, ON K1S 0H8
Tel: 613-237-6874; *Fax:* 613-234-1728
rminard@on.aibn.com

***Ottawa*: Mirsky, Pascoe - *3**
#300, 39 Robertson Rd., Ottawa, ON K2H 8R2
Tel: 613-828-2120; *Fax:* 613-596-0881

***Ottawa*: MM Inc. - *1**
#310, 81 Metcalfe St., Ottawa, ON K1P 6K7
Tel: 416-300-1322;
judithmoses@rogers.com

***Ottawa*: Moffat & Co., Macera & Jarzyna - *24**
Stn. D, 427 Laurier Ave. West, 12th Fl., Ottawa, ON K1R 7Y2
Tel: 613-238-8173; *Fax:* 613-235-2508
mail@macerajarzyna.com
www.macerajarzyna.com

***Ottawa*: Monachus Consulting - *1**
19 Elm St., Ottawa, ON K1R 6M9
Tel: 613-563-1357; *Fax:* 613-563-9277
afchambers@monachus.com

***Ottawa*: Christopher A. Moore Professional Corporation - *1**
63 Robert St., Ottawa, ON K2P 1G5
Tel: 613-230-9448; *Fax:* 613-230-3624
chalmo@istar.ca

***Ottawa*: More & McLeod - *1**
#212, 2249 Carling Ave., Ottawa, ON K2B 7E9
Tel: 613-820-7888; *Fax:* 613-820-3044
morelaw@bellnet.ca

***Ottawa*: Mount Clark Yemensky - *3**
#208, 1400 Clyde Ave., Ottawa, ON K2G 3J2
Tel: 613-226-8817; *Fax:* 613-224-8943

***Ottawa*: Kevin Murphy - *1**
#500, 200 Elgin St., Ottawa, ON K2P 1L5
Tel: 613-567-8248; *Fax:* 613-236-6958

***Ottawa*: Robert Elmo Murray - *1**
5 Kitimat Cres., Ottawa, ON K2H 7G4
Tel: 613-829-6773; *Fax:* 613-567-3559

***Ottawa*: Kenneth J. Naftel - *1**
#307, 150 Isabella St., Ottawa, ON K1S 1V7
Tel: 613-237-0505; *Fax:* 613-567-3559
ken@kennaftel.ca

***Ottawa*: Nelligan O'Brien Payne - *42**
#1500, 50 O'Connor, Ottawa, ON K1P 6L2
Tel: 613-238-8080; *Fax:* 613-238-2098
info@nelligan.ca
www.nelligan.ca

***Ottawa*: Nicol & Lazier - *2**
#400, 331 Cooper St., Ottawa, ON K2P 0G5
Tel: 613-232-4241; *Fax:* 613-236-9325

***Ottawa*: Niebergall & Grabowski - *2**
#200, 200 Elgin St., Ottawa, ON K2P 1L5
Tel: 613-232-8508; *Fax:* 613-232-9654
paulniebergall@rogers.com

***Ottawa*: Wanda Noel Barrister & Solicitor - *1**
171 Lanark Ave., Ottawa, ON K1Z 1C1
Tel: 613-729-6322; *Fax:* 613-729-7441
wanda.noel@sympatico.ca

***Ottawa*: Claire B. O'Connor - *1**
#101, 745B Montréal Rd., Ottawa, ON K1K 0T1
Tel: 613-745-9446; *Fax:* 613-745-0800
cboc@bellnet.ca

***Ottawa*: Michael B. Oliveira - *1**
#402, 280 Metcalfe St., Ottawa, ON K2P 1R7
Tel: 613-567-1016; *Fax:* 613-567-9126
moliveira@sprint.ca

***Ottawa*: Eugene L. Oscapella - *1**
70 MacDonald St., Ottawa, ON K2P 1H6
Tel: 613-238-5909; *Fax:* 613-238-2891
eugene@oscapella.ca

***Ottawa*: Joy C. Overtveld - *1**
284 Wellington St., Ottawa, ON K1A 0H8
Tel: 613-941-6805; *Fax:* 613-957-4019
overtvel@magma.ca
www.magma.ca/~overtvel/

***Ottawa*: P3 Collaborations - *1**
36 Sai Cres., Ottawa, ON K1G 5N8
Tel: 613-739-9971; *Fax:* 613-739-4815
info@p3collaborations.com
www.p3collaborations.com

***Ottawa*: Paradis, Jones, Horwitz, Bowles Associates - *4**
#900, 200 Elgin St., Ottawa, ON K2P 1L5
Tel: 613-238-5074; *Fax:* 613-230-3250

***Ottawa*: Parent, Carr - *2**
116 Lisgar St. 6th Fl., Ottawa, ON K2P 0C2
Tel: 613-567-1431; *Fax:* 613-567-1433

***Ottawa*: Parliamentary Group/Groupe Parlementaire - *3**
#400, 200 Elgin St., Ottawa, ON K2P 1L5
Tel: 613-860-0043; *Fax:* 613-235-7578
info@parlgroup.com
www.parliamentarygroup.com

***Ottawa*: Margaret J. Parlor - *1**
307 Greenview Ave., Ottawa, ON K2B 6A8
Tel: 613-828-3726

***Ottawa*: Francis K. Peddle - *1**
168 Henderson Ave., Ottawa, ON K1N 7P6
Tel: 613-232-1740; *Fax:* 613-232-0407
ftpeddle@bellnet.ca

***Ottawa*: Kimberley A. Pegg - *3**
#1, 200 Cooper St., Ottawa, ON K2P 0G1
Tel: 613-232-9331; *Fax:* 613-230-3551

***Ottawa*: Stephen M. Pender - *2**
116 Lisgar St., Ottawa, ON K2P 0C2
Tel: 613-569-0104; *Fax:* 613-235-4704
pender-leef@on.aibn.com

***Ottawa*: Perley-Robertson, Hill & McDougall LLP - *36**
#1400, 340 Albert St., Ottawa, ON K1R 0A5
Tel: 613-238-2022; *Fax:* 613-238-8775
Toll-Free: 800-268-8292
lawyers@perlaw.ca
www.perlaw.ca

***Ottawa*: Pfeiffer & Associates - *1**
157 McLeod St., Ottawa, ON K2P 0Z6
Tel: 613-238-4115; *Fax:* 613-563-8273
amy@pfeifferlaw.ca
www.pfeifferlaw.ca

***Ottawa*: Piazza, Brooks - *2**
Former Name: Piazza, Brooks & Siddons
#202, 309 Cooper St., Ottawa, ON K2P 0G5
Tel: 613-238-2244; *Fax:* 613-238-3382
ph@piazzalaw.com

***Ottawa*: Pinnacle Public Affairs - *1**
#1203, 275 Slater St., Ottawa, ON K1P 5H9
Tel: 613-594-8484;
pinnaclepublicaffairs.com

***Ottawa*: Plant Quinn Thiele - *7**
#700, 200 Elgin St., Ottawa, ON K2P 1L5
Tel: 613-563-1131; *Fax:* 613-230-8297
mquinn@pqtlaw.com
www.pqtlaw.com

***Ottawa*: Plaskacz & Associates - *1**
114 Crichton St., Ottawa, ON K1M 1V9
Tel: 613-244-6084;
plaskacz@plaskacz.com
www.plaskacz.com

***Ottawa*: Policy Insights Inc. - *3**
#402, 222 Queen St., Ottawa, ON K1P 5V9
Tel: 613-563-8078; *Fax:* 613-563-4284
info@policyinsights.com
www.policyinsights.com

***Ottawa*: Denis J. A. Pommainville - *1**
302 St. Patrick St., Ottawa, ON K1N 5K5
Tel: 613-241-7335; *Fax:* 613-241-5012
pommainville@bellnet.ca

***Ottawa*: Protocol Plus Inc. - *1**
10 Allendale Private, Ottawa, ON K2P 2G3
Tel: 613-795-4254;
raj@pearson-shoyama.ca

***Ottawa*: Prystupa Law Office - *2**
#203, 1419 Carling Ave., Ottawa, ON K1Z 7L6
Tel: 613-729-4669; *Fax:* 613-729-7768
admin@prystupalaw.ca
www.prystupalaw.ca

***Ottawa*: Public Affairs Counsel - *1**
177 Powell Ave., Ottawa, ON K1S 2A2
Tel: 613-292-0326; *Fax:* 613-235-9790
isabel.metcalfe@sympatico.ca

***Ottawa*: Public Affairs Strategy Group Inc. - *3**
#802, 350 Sparks St., Ottawa, ON K1R 7S8
Tel: 613-594-0202; *Fax:* 613-233-5880
info@pasq.net
www.deltamedia.ca/services/publicAffairs/index_e.asp

***Ottawa*: Public Knowledge Canada - *1**
855 Explorer Lane, Ottawa, ON K1C 2S3
Tel: 613-834-8435;
www.publicknowledge.ca

***Ottawa*: Helene Bruce Puccini - *1**
#307, 150 Isabella St., Ottawa, ON K1S 1V7
Tel: 613-230-6295; *Fax:* 613-567-3559
helene@puccini.ca

***Ottawa*: PvF Consulting - *1**
#200, 8 York St., Ottawa, ON K1N 5S6
Tel: 613-233-1633; *Fax:* 613-233-3889
info@pvfconsulting.com
www.pvfconsulting.com

***Ottawa*: Quinn Public Affairs**
1-215 Strathcona Ave., Ottawa, ON K1S 1X7
Tel: 613-231-5800;
info@quinnpublicaffairs.com
www.quinnpublicaffairs.com

***Ottawa*: Radnoff, Pearl LLP - *12**
Former Name: Radnoff, Pearl, Slover, Swedko, Dwoskin
100 Gloucester St., Ottawa, ON K2P 0A4
Tel: 613-594-8844; *Fax:* 613-594-9092
www.radnoffpearl.com

***Ottawa*: Ranger & Associés - *1**
#1000, 141 Laurier Ave. West, Ottawa, ON K1P 5J3
Tel: 613-234-2255; *Fax:* 613-234-2301

***Ottawa*: Rasmussen Starr Ruddy LLP - *11**
#660, 660 Carling Ave., Ottawa, ON K1Z 1G3
Tel: 613-232-1830; *Fax:* 613-232-2499
mail@rsrlaw.ca
www.rsrlaw.ca

** indicates number of lawyers*

Ottawa: **Raven, Cameron, Ballantyne, Yazbeck LLP - *10**
Former Name: Raven, Allen, Cameron & Ballantyne
1600 - 220 Laurier Ave. West, Ottawa, ON K1P 5Z9
Tel: 613-567-2901; *Fax:* 613-567-2921
info@ravenlaw.com
www.ravenlaw.com

Ottawa: **Rawson Group Initiatives Inc. - *2**
#300, 222 Argyle Ave., Ottawa, ON K2P 1B9
Tel: 613-236-7960; *Fax:* 613-230-6597

Ottawa: **Karen Ann Reid - *1**
#503, 200 Elgin St., Ottawa, ON K2P 1L5
Tel: 613-238-8777; *Fax:* 613-238-4824
kareid@istop.com

Ottawa: **Rick & Associates - *3**
Former Name: Harris & Rick Associates
#109, 591 March Rd., Ottawa, ON K2K 2M5
Tel: 613-592-0088; *Fax:* 613-592-3322
info@rickassociates.com
www.rickassociates.com

Ottawa: **Frank I. Ritchie - *1**
2253 Alta Vista Dr., Ottawa, ON K1H 7L9
Tel: 613-731-8288

Ottawa: **Larry A. Roine - *1**
#200, 2650 Queensview Dr., Ottawa, ON K2B 8H6
Tel: 613-820-8888; *Fax:* 613-820-8818

Ottawa: **Terrence M. Romanow - *1**
2038 Black Friars Rd., Ottawa, ON K2A 3K8
Tel: 613-722-8224; *Fax:* 613-722-0908

Ottawa: **Rothwell Group Inc. - *3**
#820, 45 O'Connor St., Ottawa, ON K1P 1A4
Tel: 613-567-6775; *Fax:* 613-567-6803
partners@rothwellgroup.ca
rothwellgroup.ca

Ottawa: **Ryk Oliver Corporation - *1**
1130 Castle Hill Cres., Ottawa, ON K2C 2A8
Tel: 613-723-2816; *Fax:* 613-723-5525
vaneyk@rogers.com

Ottawa: **Suzanne Sabourin - *1**
1633 Schouten Dr., Ottawa, ON K1E 2H9
Tel: 613-837-8546

Ottawa: **Sack Goldblatt Mitchell - *5**
Former Name: Engelmann Gottheil
#500, 30 Metcalfe St., Ottawa, ON K1P 5L4
Tel: 613-235-5327; *Fax:* 613-235-3041
mailbox@eglaw.com
www.sgmlaw.com

Ottawa: **Macey Schwartz - *1**
#1006, 75 Albert St., Ottawa, ON K1P 5E7
Tel: 613-236-1872; *Fax:* 613-236-8639
macey@bellnet.ca

Ottawa: **Scott & Coulson - *2**
#420, 1335 Carling Ave., Ottawa, ON K1Z 8N8
Tel: 613-725-3723; *Fax:* 613-729-8613

Ottawa: **Segal, Talarico, Habib, Molot LLP - *6**
#200, 2650 Queensview Dr., Ottawa, ON K2B 8H6
Tel: 613-820-8888; *Fax:* 613-820-8818
www.legal-team.com

Ottawa: **Sevigny Law Office - *2**
#1620, 344 Slater St., Ottawa, ON K1R 7Y3
Tel: 613-751-4459; *Fax:* 613-751-4471
info@sevignylaw.com

Ottawa: **Shapiro, Cohen - *6**
P.O. Box 3440, Stn. D, 112 Kent St., Ottawa, ON K1P 6P1
Tel: 613-232-5300; *Fax:* 613-563-9231
Toll-Free: 800-563-9390

Ottawa: **Sheppard & Claude - *2**
#200, 745A Montreal Rd., Ottawa, ON K1K 0T1
Tel: 613-748-3333; *Fax:* 613-748-1599
aclaude@sheppardclaude.ca

Ottawa: **Shields & Hunt - *6**
68 Chamberlain Ave., Ottawa, ON K1S 1V9
Tel: 613-230-3232; *Fax:* 613-230-1664
gjones@shields-hunt.com
www.shields-hunt.com

Ottawa: **Paula M. Smith - *1**
450 Laurier Ave. East, Ottawa, ON K1N 6R3
Tel: 613-565-0490

Ottawa: **Soloway, Wright LLP - *21**
#900, 427 Laurier Ave. West, Ottawa, ON K1R 7Y2
Tel: 613-236-0111; *Fax:* 613-238-8507
Toll-Free: 800-207-5880
info@solowaywright.com
www.solowaywright.com

Ottawa: **Wayne A. Stacey & Associates Ltd. - *1**
2145 Hubbard Cres., Ottawa, ON K1J 6L3
Tel: 613-745-9151;
wstacey@stacey.ca

Ottawa: **Steinberg Thompson d'Artois Rockman Summers - *5**
#1000, 150 Metcalfe St., Ottawa, ON K2P 1P1
Tel: 613-594-5996; *Fax:* 613-230-4161

Ottawa: **Stewart/Associates - *2**
#402, 200 Elgin St., Ottawa, ON K2P 1L5
Tel: 613-235-0453; *Fax:* 613-235-3304
stewartasso@travel-net.com

Ottawa: **Jennifer A. Stiell - *1**
#307, 150 Isabella St., Ottawa, ON K1S 1V7
Tel: 613-237-0505; *Fax:* 613-567-3559
jstiell@cyberus.ca

Ottawa: **Strategic Partners Group - *1**
#420, 1145 Hunt Club Rd., Ottawa, ON K1V 0Y3
Tel: 613-249-0611; *Fax:* 613-249-0421
mcuconato@rogers.blackberry.net

Ottawa: **The Strategy Project - *1**
38 Melgund Ave., Ottawa, ON K1S 2S2
Tel: 613-567-9592; *Fax:* 613-567-9561
jim@strategyproject.ca

Ottawa: **Summa Strategies Canada Inc. - *11**
#1000, 100 Sparks St., Ottawa, ON K1P 5B7
Tel: 613-235-1400; *Fax:* 613-235-1444
www.summa.ca

Ottawa: **Anna E. Sundin - *1**
276 Sunnyside Ave., Ottawa, ON K1S 0R8
Tel: 613-445-3183; *Fax:* 613-730-7484
asundin@storm.ca

Ottawa: **Michael W. Swinwood - *1**
346 Waverly Street, Ottawa, ON KP2 0W5
Tel: 613-563-7474; *Fax:* 613-256-8115
shagar@cyberus.ca

Ottawa: **Tactix Government Consulting Inc. - *7**
#700, World Exchange Plaza, 45 O'Connor St., Ottawa, ON K1P 1A4
Tel: 613-566-7053; *Fax:* 613-566-2026
www.tactix.ca

Ottawa: **Christopher C.C. Tan - *1**
70 Gloucester St., Ottawa, ON K2P 0A2
Tel: 613-235-2308; *Fax:* 613-235-6933

Ottawa: **Thomas & Partners - *3**
#360, 30 Metcalfe St., Ottawa, ON K1P 5L4
Tel: 613-232-7522; *Fax:* 613-232-7525
ottawa@thomasandpartners.com
www.thomasandpartners.com

Ottawa: **Tierney Stauffer - *11**
#510, 1600 Carling Ave., Ottawa, ON K1Z 0A1
Tel: 613-728-8057; *Fax:* 613-728-9866
www.tierneystauffer.com

Ottawa: **TL Maville & Associates Inc. - *1**
P.O. Box 5011, Ottawa, ON K2C 3H3
Tel: 613-727-0533; *Fax:* 613-727-1556
tom.maville@sympatico.ca

Ottawa: **Tunney, McMurray - *2**
#806, 200 Elgin St., Ottawa, ON K2P 1L5
Tel: 613-235-5660; *Fax:* 613-235-0805
tmbarry@rogers.com

Ottawa: **Gilad Vered - *1**
1801 Woodward Dr., Ottawa, ON K2C 0R3
Tel: 613-226-2000; *Fax:* 613-225-0391
gvered@arnon.ca

Ottawa: **Victor Ages Vallance LLP, Barristers & Solicitors - *8**
Former Name: Kimmel, Victor & Ages
112 Lisgar St., Ottawa, ON K2P 0C2
Tel: 613-238-1333; *Fax:* 613-238-8949
rfurtado@vavlawyers.com
www.vavlawyers.com

Ottawa: **Vincent Dagenais Gibson LLP/S.R.L. - *11**
#600, 325 Dalhousie St., Ottawa, ON K1N 7G2
Tel: 613-241-2701; *Fax:* 613-241-2599
susan.emmett@vdgjustice.ca

Ottawa: **Ian H. Warren - *1**
#2000, 150 Metcalfe St., Ottawa, ON K2P 1P1
Tel: 613-565-3813; *Fax:* 613-234-0418
jacklaw@storm.ca

Ottawa: **Wellington Strategy Group Inc. - *3**
#200, 8 York St., Ottawa, ON K1N 5S6
Tel: 613-594-0001; *Fax:* 613-594-8777

Ottawa: **Robert A. Whillans - *1**
540 Courtenay Ave., Ottawa, ON K2A 3B3
Tel: 613-238-1515; *Fax:* 613-238-1323

Ottawa: **Williams McEnery - *8**
Former Name: Williams, McEnery & Davis
169 Gilmour St., Ottawa, ON K2P 0N8
Tel: 613-237-0520; *Fax:* 613-237-3163
www.williamsmcenery.com

Ottawa: **David M. Wray - *1**
#310, P.O. Box 2760, Stn. D, 151 Slater St., Ottawa, ON K1P 5W8
Tel: 613-233-1322; *Fax:* 613-230-5168
dwray@wray-canada.com

Owen Sound: **Neil J. Arnold - *1**
935 - 2nd Ave. West, Owen Sound, ON N4K 4M8
Tel: 519-372-2218; *Fax:* 519-372-2599
neiljarnold@bmts.com

Owen Sound: **Ian C. Boddy - *1**
195 - 9th St. West, Owen Sound, ON N4K 3N5
Tel: 519-372-9886; *Fax:* 519-372-1091
ianboddy@bellnet.ca

Owen Sound: **Herbert E. Boyce - *1**
#103, Dominion Place, P.O. Box 968, 887 Third Ave. East, Owen Sound, ON N4K 6H6
Tel: 519-371-4160; *Fax:* 519-371-1604

Owen Sound: **Chander G. Chaddah - *1**
P.O. Box 965, 712 - 2 Ave. East, Owen Sound, ON N4K 6H6
Tel: 519-376-4343; *Fax:* 519-376-2547
www.cf-law.on.ca

Owen Sound: **Andrew E. Drury - *1**
#5B, 945 - 3 Ave. East, Owen Sound, ON N4K 2K8
Tel: 519-372-1850; *Fax:* 519-372-1602

Owen Sound: **D.A. Grace - *1**
P.O. Box 952, Stn. Main, 949 - 2 Ave. West, Owen Sound, ON N4K 4M8
Tel: 519-371-9370; *Fax:* 519-371-5747
dougrace@bmts.com

Owen Sound: **Greenfield & Barrie - *2**
P.O. Box 665, 142 - 10 St. West, Owen Sound, ON N4K 5R4
Tel: 519-376-4930; *Fax:* 519-376-4010
gblaw@btms.com

Owen Sound: **Kirby, Robinson, Treslan & Conlan - *6**
Former Name: Kirby, Gordon & Robinson
P.O. Box 730, 930 -1 Ave. West, Owen Sound, ON N4K 5W9
Tel: 519-376-7450; *Fax:* 519-376-8288
info@owensoundlawyers.com

Owen Sound: **Catherine A. Laing - *1**
P.O. Box 664, 935 - 2 Ave. West, Owen Sound, ON N4K 5R4
Tel: 519-371-2202; *Fax:* 519-376-4683
calaing@bellnet.ca

Owen Sound: **Alan E. Marsh - *1**
#102, P.O. Box 581, 345 - 8 St. East, Owen Sound, ON N4K 5R1
Tel: 519-371-8373; *Fax:* 519-371-8971
aemarsh@bmts.com

* indicates number of lawyers

***Owen Sound*: Middlebro' & Stevens LLP - *6**
P.O. Box 100, 1030 - 2 Ave. East, Owen Sound, ON N4K 5P1
Tel: 519-376-8730; *Fax:* 519-376-7135
ms@mslaw.ca
www.mslaw.ca

***Owen Sound*: Murray & Thomson - *2**
P.O. Box 1060, 912 - 2 Ave. West, Owen Sound, ON N4K 6K6
Tel: 519-376-6350; *Fax:* 519-376-0835
message@mtlaw.ca
www.mtlaw.ca

***Owen Sound*: Scott C. Vining - *1**
1199, 1st Avenue East, Owen Sound, ON N4K 2E2
Tel: 519-371-6210; *Fax:* 519-371-6238
vininglaw@brucetelecom.com

***Parry Sound*: Larry W. Douglas - *1**
22 Miller St., Parry Sound, ON P2A 1S8
Tel: 705-746-9471; *Fax:* 705-746-9606

***Parry Sound*: David A. Holmes - *1**
2 William St., Parry Sound, ON P2A 1V1
Tel: 705-746-4223; *Fax:* 705-746-6368
daholmes@cogeco.ca

***Parry Sound*: Lisa M. Lund Barrister & Solicitor - *1**
34 Mary St., Parry Sound, ON P2A 1E4
Tel: 705-746-4215; *Fax:* 705-746-5357
lisa.lund@lisalund.ca

***Parry Sound*: A. Wayne Piddington - *2**
97 James St., Parry Sound, ON P2A 1T7
Tel: 705-746-9365; *Fax:* 705-746-7159
newmanps@vianet.ca

***Parry Sound*: Powell, Cunningham, Grandy - *1**
88 James St., Parry Sound, ON P2A 1T9
Tel: 705-746-4207; *Fax:* 705-746-2945
pcg@cogeco.net

***Parry Sound*: D. Andrew Thomson - *1**
10 William St., Parry Sound, ON P2A 1V1
Tel: 705-746-5838; *Fax:* 705-746-4351
athomson@dathomsonbarrister.ca

***Pembroke*: Blair Jones Professional Corporation - *1**
Former Name: Kelly Kelly & Jones
1064 Pembroke St. West, Pembroke, ON K8A 5R4
Tel: 613-735-8226; *Fax:* 613-735-8474
joneslaw@magma.ca

***Pembroke*: Adrian R. Cleaver - *1**
P.O. Box 1147, 156 MacKay St., Pembroke, ON K8A 6Y6
Tel: 613-732-1377; *Fax:* 613-732-3889
acleaver@nrtco.net

***Pembroke*: B. Lynne Felhaber - *1**
#100, 77 Mary St., Pembroke, ON K8A 5V4
Tel: 613-735-6866; *Fax:* 613-735-6641

***Pembroke*: Glen Price, Lawyers - *2**
Former Name: Garretto & Price
P.O. Box 697, Stn. Main, 141A Lake St., Pembroke, ON K8A 6X9
Tel: 613-732-2883; *Fax:* 613-732-3436
Toll-Free: 877-732-2884
glenpricelawyer.com

***Pembroke*: Huckabone, O'Brien, Instance. Bradley, Lyle - *6**
Former Name: Huckabone, Shaw, O'Brien, Radley-Walters & Reimer
P.O. Box 487, 284 Pembroke St. East, Pembroke, ON K8A 6X7
Tel: 613-735-2341; *Fax:* 613-735-0920
admin@hsolawyers.com
www.hsolawyers.com

***Pembroke*: Johnson, Fraser & March - *3**
P.O. Box 366, Stn. Main, 259 Pembroke St. East, Pembroke, ON K8A 6X6
Tel: 613-735-0624; *Fax:* 613-735-0625
jfmlawyers@nrtco.net

***Pembroke*: R.B. Leach - *1**
224 Pembroke St. West, Pembroke, ON K8A 5N2
Tel: 613-732-4903; *Fax:* 613-732-0867

***Pembroke*: Quintal & Christinck - *2**
P.O. Box 205, 238 Pembroke St. East, Pembroke, ON K8A 3J7
Tel: 613-735-5777; *Fax:* 613-735-5935
quintal@nrtco.net

***Pembroke*: Roy C. Reiche - *1**
203 Nelson St., Pembroke, ON K8A 3N1
Tel: 613-735-2313; *Fax:* 613-735-2013

***Perth*: Greg W. Anderson - *1**
10 Market Sq., Perth, ON K7H 1V7
Tel: 613-267-9898; *Fax:* 613-267-2741
greg@greganderson.ca
www.greganderson.ca

***Perth*: Bond & Hughes Barristers & Solicitors - *2**
Former Name: James M. Bond
10 Market Sq., Perth, ON K7H 1V7
Tel: 613-267-1212; *Fax:* 613-267-7059
www.bondhughes.ca

***Perth*: John J.S. Chalmers - *1**
P.O. Box 2, Stn. Main, RR#3, Perth, ON K7H 3C5
Tel: 613-264-1505; *Fax:* 613-264-9259

***Perth*: Michael P. Reid - *1**
#202, Code's Mill, 53 Herriott St., Perth, ON K7H 1T5
Tel: 613-267-7280; *Fax:* 613-267-7285
mike@reidlaw.ca
www.reidlaw.ca

***Perth*: Rubino & Chaplin - *1**
P.O. Box 338, 10A Gore St. West, Perth, ON K7H 3E4
Tel: 613-267-5227; *Fax:* 613-267-3951
admin@rubinoandchaplin.ca

***Perth*: Kenneth W. Smith - *1**
P.O. Box 157, 27 Foster St., Perth, ON K7H 3E3
Tel: 613-267-5910; *Fax:* 613-264-0789
kenwsmith@on.aibn.com
www.kennethwsmith.com

***Perth*: Woodwark & Stevens - *2**
8 Gore St. West, Perth, ON K7H 2L6
Tel: 613-264-8080; *Fax:* 613-264-8084
info@woodwarkstevens.com
www.woodwarkstevens.com

***Peterborough*: Gary E. Ainsworth - *1**
#101, P.O. Box 1358, Stn. Main, 294 Rink St., Peterborough, ON K9J 7H6
Tel: 705-749-0628; *Fax:* 705-749-0633
gea@ainslaw.com
www.ainslaw.com

***Peterborough*: Richard Aitken - *1**
P.O. Box 2126, Stn. Main, 364 Water St., Peterborough, ON K9J 7Y4
Tel: 705-742-0440; *Fax:* 705-742-0889
raitkens@cgocable.net

***Peterborough*: R.W. Beninger - *1**
#205, P.O. Box 426, 261 George St. North, Peterborough, ON K9J 6Z3
Tel: 705-743-0065; *Fax:* 705-742-1867

***Peterborough*: W. Jelle Bosch - *1**
#203, P.O. Box 2364, 130 Hunter St. West, Peterborough, ON K9J 7Y8
Tel: 705-741-3630; *Fax:* 705-741-6339

***Peterborough*: John S. Crook - *1**
Former Name: Crook & Collins
#5, P.O. Box 1539, Stn. Main, 261 George St. North, Peterborough, ON K9J 7H7
Tel: 705-742-5415; *Fax:* 705-742-1867

***Peterborough*: H. Girvin Devitt - *1**
P.O. Box 1449, Stn. Main, 858 Chemong Rd., Peterborough, ON K9J 7H6
Tel: 705-742-5471;
devitt@nexicom.net

***Peterborough*: Douglas F. Walker Professional Corporation - *2**
243 Hunter St. W., Peterborough, ON K9H 2L4
Tel: 705-748-3012; *Fax:* 705-748-2746
www.dfwalker.com

***Peterborough*: Dunn & Dunn - *1**
469 Water St., Peterborough, ON K9H 3M2
Tel: 705-743-6460; *Fax:* 705-748-2675

***Peterborough*: Michael J. Dwyer - *1**
P.O. Box 958, 359 Aylmer St. North, Peterborough, ON K9J 7A5
Tel: 705-743-4221; *Fax:* 705-743-2187
mdwyer@bellnet.ca

***Peterborough*: Farquharson Daly - *1**
161 Hunter St. West, Peterborough, ON K9H 2L1
Tel: 705-742-9241; *Fax:* 705-741-1601

***Peterborough*: T.G. Gain - *1**
273 Water St., Peterborough, ON K9H 3P1
Tel: 705-749-6633; *Fax:* 705-749-9765
leygain@on.aibn.com

***Peterborough*: P. Douglas Galvin - *1**
#1, P.O. Box 1118, Stn. Main, 182 McDonnel St., Peterborough, ON K9J 7H4
Tel: 705-743-7500; *Fax:* 705-743-2336

***Peterborough*: Gowland, Boriss - *4**
P.O. Box 1629, 371 Reid St., Peterborough, ON K9H 4G4
Tel: 705-743-7252; *Fax:* 705-743-1850

***Peterborough*: Joan M. Guerin - *1**
#4, P.O. Box 1420, Stn. Main, 193 Simcoe St., Peterborough, ON K9J 7H6
Tel: 705-743-9087; *Fax:* 705-743-8528

***Peterborough*: William F. Hampton - *1**
219 Sherbrooke St., Peterborough, ON K9J 2N2
Tel: 705-876-6900; *Fax:* 705-876-6922

***Peterborough*: Harrison Law Office - *1**
P.O. Box 1916, 306 Stewart St., Peterborough, ON K9J 7X7
Tel: 705-741-5233; *Fax:* 705-741-2463
spharrison@trytel.net

***Peterborough*: James S. Hauraney - *1**
305 Reid St., Peterborough, ON K9J 3R2
Tel: 705-748-2333; *Fax:* 705-748-2618

***Peterborough*: A. John Hodgins - *1**
677 Brown Line, Peterborough, ON K9J 6X6
Tel: 416-251-9390; *Fax:* 416-251-0449
ajhodgins@hodginslaw.net

***Peterborough*: Howell Fleming LLP - *10**
P.O. Box 148, 415 Water St., Peterborough, ON K9J 6Y5
Tel: 705-745-1361; *Fax:* 705-745-6220
lkulatungam@howellfleming.com
www.howellfleming.com

***Peterborough*: Rod E. Johnston - *1**
P.O. Box 29, 521 George St. North, Peterborough, ON K9J 6Y5
Tel: 705-748-2244; *Fax:* 705-748-2540
info@rodjohnstonlaw.com

***Peterborough*: E.J. Jordan - *1**
P.O. Box 958, 359 Aylmer St. North, Peterborough, ON K9J 7A5
Tel: 705-743-4221; *Fax:* 705-743-2187

***Peterborough*: Lech, Lightbody & O'Brien - *2**
116 Hunter St. West, Peterborough, ON K9H 2K6
Tel: 705-742-3844; *Fax:* 705-742-0121
maryruth@hunterstreetlaw.com

***Peterborough*: Lillico Bazuk Kent Galloway - *4**
P.O. Box 568, 163 Hunter St. West, Peterborough, ON K9J 6Z6
Tel: 705-743-3577; *Fax:* 705-743-0013
lbkg@lbkglaw.com

***Peterborough*: Linda Willcox Whetung Professional Corporation - *1**
Former Name: Grant, Willcox Whetung
521 George St. North, Peterborough, ON K9J 6Y5
Tel: 705-743-6470; *Fax:* 705-743-3128
linda@lindawhetung.com

***Peterborough*: Lockington Lawless Fitzpatrick - *11**
P.O. Box 1146, 332 Aylmer St. North, Peterborough, ON K9J 7H4
Tel: 705-742-1674; *Fax:* 705-742-4677
info@locklaw.ca

***Peterborough*: J.M. Longworth - *1**
P.O. Box 1747, Stn. Main, 310 Rubidge St., Peterborough, ON K9J 7X6
Tel: 705-749-0100; *Fax:* 705-742-8718

***Peterborough*: John E. McGarrity - *1**
Stn. Main, 343 Stewart St., Peterborough, ON K9H 4A7
Tel: 705-743-1822; *Fax:* 705-743-4870
mcgarrity@trytel.net

** indicates number of lawyers*

***Peterborough*: McGillen Keay - *3**
Former Name: McGillen, Ayotte, Dupuis
#202, P.O. Box 1718, 140 King St., Peterborough, ON K9J 7X6
Tel: 705-748-2241; *Fax:* 705-748-9125
www.mcgillenkeay.com

***Peterborough*: McMichael, Davidson - *1**
64 Hunter St. West, Peterborough, ON K9H 2K4
Tel: 705-745-0571; *Fax:* 705-745-0411
lawoffice@mcmichaeldavidson.com

***Peterborough*: Moldaver & McFadden - *2**
121 George St. North, Peterborough, ON K9J 7H6
Tel: 705-743-1801; *Fax:* 705-743-0397

***Peterborough*: Christopher M. Spear - *1**
430 Sheridan St., Peterborough, ON K9H 3J9
Tel: 705-741-2144; *Fax:* 705-741-2712

***Peterborough*: Robert A. Stocker - *1**
174 Wallis Dr., Peterborough, ON K9J 6C3
Tel: 705-745-5786;
raslaw@cogeco.ca

***Peterborough*: Richard J. Taylor - *1**
P.O. Box 1963, Stn. Main, 306 Stewart St., Peterborough, ON K9J 7X7
Tel: 705-876-7791; *Fax:* 705-876-9280
taylorlaw@trytel.net

***Peterborough*: G.H. Usher - *1**
P.O. Box 327, 359 Aylmer St. North, Peterborough, ON K9J 6Z3
Tel: 705-743-4221; *Fax:* 705-743-8692

***Peterborough*: J. Ross Whittington - *1**
P.O. Box 327, 359 Aylmer St. North, Peterborough, ON K9J 6Z3
Tel: 705-743-4221; *Fax:* 705-743-8692

***Petrolia*: Robert B. Gray - *1**
#3, 4495 Petrolia Line, Petrolia, ON N0N 1R0
Tel: 519-882-0132; *Fax:* 519-336-3289

***Petrolia*: Wallace B. Lang - *1**
Former Name: Kilby & Lang
P.O. Box 700, 4245 Petrolia Lane, Petrolia, ON N0N 1R0
Tel: 519-882-0770; *Fax:* 519-882-3144

***Pickering*: G.W. Edmiston - *1**
1281 Commerce St., Pickering, ON L1W 1C7
Tel: 905-839-8270

***Pickering*: Alan Fisher - *1**
#824, 1880 Valley Farm Rd., Pickering, ON L1V 6B3
Tel: 905-839-7248

***Pickering*: J. Paul Fletcher - *1**
P.O. Box 667, Stn. Main, Pickering, ON L1V 3T3
Tel: 905-922-2027;
jpaulfletcherlaw@aol.com

***Pickering*: Brian R. Hawke - *1**
1 Evelyn Ave., Pickering, ON L1V 1N3
Tel: 905-509-5267; *Fax:* 905-509-5270
bhawke@on.aibn.com

***Pickering*: John G. Howes - *1**
#800, 1315 Pickering Pkwy., Pickering, ON L1V 7G5
Tel: 905-420-8628; *Fax:* 905-420-1073
Toll-Free: 800-373-6641
john@howeslaw.com

***Pickering*: Sherwood, Hunt - *2**
364 Kingston Rd., Pickering, ON L1V 1A2
Tel: 905-509-5500; *Fax:* 905-509-0070

***Pickering*: Harvey Storm - *1**
#8B, 1400 Bayly St., Pickering, ON L1W 3R2
Tel: 905-839-5121; *Fax:* 905-420-4062
Toll-Free: 888-876-5529
harvey@harveystorm.com
www.harveystorm.com

***Pickering*: Murray Stroud - *1**
356 Kingston Rd., Pickering, ON L1V 1A2
Tel: 905-509-1353; *Fax:* 905-509-2370
mstroud@stroudlaw.ca
www.stroudlaw.ca

***Pickering*: Tim Vanular Lawyers Professional Corporation - *2**
Former Name: Vanular, Timothy C.R.
#C10-C11, Brock North Plaza, 2200 Brock Rd. North, Pickering, ON L1X 2R2
Tel: 905-427-4886; *Fax:* 905-427-5542
Toll-Free: 800-243-4151
vanular@vanulaw.com
www.vanulaw.comhttp://www.facebook.com/pages/Tim-Vanular-Lawyers-Professional-Corporation/, www.twitter.com/Vanulaw, http://ca.linkedin.com/pub/tim-vanular/33/546/a93

***Pickering*: G.R. Wakefield - *1**
1 Evelyn Ave., Pickering, ON L1V 1N3
Tel: 905-509-5267; *Fax:* 905-509-5270
grwakefield@rogers.com

***Pickering*: Walker, Head - *8**
#800, Corporate Centre, 1315 Pickering Pkwy., Pickering, ON L1V 7G5
Tel: 905-839-4484; *Fax:* 905-420-1073
wlkhd@walkerhead.com
www.walkerhead.com

***Pickering*: J. Robert Wood & Associates - *1**
#419, 1400 The Esplanade North, Pickering, ON L1V 6V2
Tel: 905-837-9425; *Fax:* 905-837-9168
jrwood@rogers.com

***Picton*: Bruce F. Campbell - *1**
P.O. Box 1260, 194 Main St., Picton, ON K0K 2T0
Tel: 613-476-2366; *Fax:* 613-476-9821
bcampbl@kos.net

***Picton*: William M. Martin - *1**
P.O. Box 2160, 316 Main St., Picton, ON K0K 2T0
Tel: 613-476-2116; *Fax:* 613-476-8143

***Picton*: Shelagh M. Mathers - *1**
#4, 6 Talbot St., Picton, ON K0K 2T0
Tel: 613-476-2733; *Fax:* 613-476-6064
matherslaw@kos.net

***Picton*: Donald T. Mowat - *1**
P.O. Box 2290, 165 Main St., Picton, ON K0K 2T0
Tel: 613-476-3261; *Fax:* 613-476-4417

***Picton*: Walmsley & Walmsley - *1**
P.O. Box 1500, 340 Main St., Picton, ON K0K 2T0
Tel: 613-476-5516; *Fax:* 613-476-5725
walaw@kos.net

***Picton*: Jack H. Ward - *1**
P.O. Box 530, 51 Mary St., Picton, ON K0K 2T0
Tel: 613-476-3640; *Fax:* 613-476-3435

***Point Edward*: Fleck & Daigneault - *3**
#102, 704 Mara St., Point Edward, ON N7V 1X4
Tel: 519-337-5288; *Fax:* 519-337-5674
pascale@xcelco.on.ca

***Point Edward*: Peter Westfall - *1**
#104, 805 Christina St. North, Point Edward, Point Edward, ON N7V 1X6
Tel: 519-344-1155; *Fax:* 519-344-1842
pwestfall@bellnet.ca

***Port Colborne*: Brian N. Lambie - *1**
109 Adelaide St., Port Colborne, ON L3K 2W4
Tel: 905-835-8455; *Fax:* 905-835-5966

***Port Colborne*: Robt. H.H. Reilly - *1**
P.O. Box 127, Port Colborne, ON L3K 5V8
Tel: 905-835-1141; *Fax:* 905-835-2185

***Port Colborne*: John D. Tuck - *1**
P.O. Box 334, 84 West St., Port Colborne, ON L3K 5W1
Tel: 905-834-4525; *Fax:* 905-834-3254
pclaw@bellnet.ca

***Port Colborne*: Wilson, Opatovsky - *2**
P.O. Box 99, 190 Elm St., Port Colborne, ON L3K 5V7
Tel: 905-835-1163; *Fax:* 905-835-2171
Toll-Free: 888-288-8338

***Port Elgin*: George D. Gruetzner - *1**
P.O. Box 10, 667 Goderich St., Port Elgin, ON N0H 2C0
Tel: 519-832-2482; *Fax:* 519-389-4617

***Port Perry*: Michael L. Fowler - *2**
175 North St., Port Perry, ON L9L 1B7
Tel: 905-985-8411; *Fax:* 905-985-0029
mfowler@fowlerlaw.ca

***Prescott*: Richard M. Tobin - *1**
257 King St. West, PO Box 760, Prescott, ON K0E 1T0
Tel: 613-925-2853; *Fax:* 613-925-5741

***Rama*: Nahwegahbow, Corbiere - *3**
Former Name: Nahwegahbow, Nadjiwan, Corbiere
P.O. Box 46, 7410 Benson Side Rd., Rama, ON L0K 1T0
Tel: 705-325-0520; *Fax:* 705-325-7204
mail@nncfirm.ca

***Renfrew*: Sharon L. Anderson-Olmstead - *1**
117 Raglan St. South, Renfrew, ON K7V 1P8
Tel: 613-432-5898; *Fax:* 613-432-5899
sharon_anderson@bellnet.ca

***Renfrew*: Chown & Smith - *2**
297 Raglan St. South, Renfrew, ON K7V 1R6
Tel: 613-432-3669; *Fax:* 613-432-2874
admin@chownandsmith.com
www.chownandsmith.com

***Renfrew*: Lawrence E. Gallagher - *1**
33 Renfrew Ave. East, Renfrew, ON K7V 2W6
Tel: 613-432-8537; *Fax:* 613-432-8538
legallagher@nrtco.net

***Renfrew*: Joseph D. Legris Professional Corp. - *1**
248 Argyle St. South, Renfrew, ON K7V 1T7
Tel: 613-432-3689; *Fax:* 613-432-3936
jlegris@legrislaw.com
www.legrislaw.com

***Renfrew*: McNab, Stewart & Prince - *2**
117 Raglan St. South, Renfrew, ON K7V 1P8
Tel: 613-432-5844; *Fax:* 613-432-7832
dstewart@mcnablaw.com; tprince@mcnablaw.com
www.mcnablaw.com

***Richmond Hill*: Ronald A. Balinsky - *1**
96 Arnold Cres., Richmond Hill, ON L4C 3R8
Tel: 905-884-8161; *Fax:* 905-884-3155
rbalinsky@balinskylawfirm.com
www.balinskylawfirm.com

***Richmond Hill*: Peter D. Bouroukis - *1**
#411, 15 Wertheim Ct., Richmond Hill, ON L4B 3H7
Tel: 905-771-7030; *Fax:* 905-771-7027
pbouroukis@rogers.com

***Richmond Hill*: Jay Chauhan - *1**
#309, 330 Hwy. 7 East, Richmond Hill, ON L4B 3P8
Tel: 905-771-1235; *Fax:* 905-771-1237
jayadvocate@yahoo.ca
www.jaychauhan.com

***Richmond Hill*: Annie A. Cheng - *1**
#221A, 550 Hwy. 7 East, Richmond Hill, ON L4B 3Z4
Tel: 905-709-9988; *Fax:* 905-709-1885
aacheng@solutionsinlaw.ca

***Richmond Hill*: James H. Chow - *1**
#512, 330 Hwy. 7 East, Richmond Hill, ON L4B 3P8
Tel: 905-881-3363

***Richmond Hill*: Corinne M. Rivers - *1**
#104, 13311 Yonge St., Richmond Hill, ON L4E 3L6
Tel: 905-773-9911; *Fax:* 905-773-9927
corrine@cmrlaw.cawww.linkedin.com/pub/corinne-rivers/4/b44/65

***Richmond Hill*: Terry G. Hawtin - *1**
#301, 650 Hwy. 7 East, Richmond Hill, ON L4B 2N7
Tel: 905-709-9020; *Fax:* 905-709-4721
hawtin@hawtinlaw.ca

***Richmond Hill*: Alla Koren - *1**
12 Rollinghill Rd., Richmond Hill, ON L4E 4C1
Tel: 905-780-1500; *Fax:* 905-780-0070
akoren@rogers.com

***Richmond Hill*: John J. Lawlor Q.C. - *1**
#102, 10211 Yonge St., Richmond Hill, ON L4C 3B3
Tel: 905-884-9133; *Fax:* 905-884-9507
johnlawlor@on.aibn.com

***Richmond Hill*: Garry E. Levine - *1**
16 O'Connor Cres., Richmond Hill, ON L4C 7P3
Tel: 905-709-9444; *Fax:* 905-770-3782
glevine@rogers.com

***Richmond Hill*: Shirley K.T. Lo - *1**
#PH 10, 330 Hwy. 7 East, Richmond Hill, ON L4B 3P8
Tel: 905-707-5707; *Fax:* 905-707-5752
kshirleylo@hotmail.com

** indicates number of lawyers*

***Richmond Hill*: L.A. Lombardi & Co. Ltd. - *1**
#200, 66 West Beaver Creek, Richmond Hill, ON L4B 1G5
Tel: 416-924-9559; *Fax:* 416-924-7974

***Richmond Hill*: Malach & Fidler - *11**
#6, 30 Wertheim Ct., Richmond Hill, ON L4B 1B9
Tel: 905-889-1667; *Fax:* 905-889-1139
mf@netcom.ca

***Richmond Hill*: Parker Garber & Chesney - *1**
250 West Beaver Creek Rd., Richmond Hill, ON L4B 1C7
Tel: 905-764-0404; *Fax:* 905-764-0320

***Richmond Hill*: Paul Harte Professional Corporation, Barristers & Solicitors - *1**
#301, 1595 Sixteenth Ave., Richmond Hill, ON L4B 3N9
Tel: 905-709-7405; *Fax:* 905-763-2167
Toll-Free: 888-441-3341
pharte@hartelaw.com; mdamiano@hartelaw.com
www.hartelaw.com

***Richmond Hill*: Rohmer & Fenn - *3**
#503, Park Place Corporate Centre, 15 Wertheim Ct., Richmond Hill, ON L4B 3H7
Tel: 905-763-6690; *Fax:* 905-763-6699
firm@rohmerfenn.com

***Richmond Hill*: Barry Seltzer - *1**
#204, 9140 Leslie St., Richmond Hill, ON L4B 0A9
Tel: 905-475-9001; *Fax:* 905-475-9004
barry@barryseltzer.com

***Richmond Hill*: Virgilio, Vumbaca - *2**
#500, 1 Pearce St. West, Richmond Hill, ON L4B 3K3
Tel: 905-882-8666; *Fax:* 905-882-1082
jvirgilio@virgiliolaw.com

***Richmond Hill*: Gordon E. Watkin - *1**
#212A, Hillcrest Mall, 9350 Yonge St., Richmond Hill, ON L4C 5G2
Tel: 905-884-3778; *Fax:* 905-884-2655

***Ridgetown*: Edward T. Little - *1**
P.O. Box 700, 64 Main St. East, Ridgetown, ON N0P 2C0
Tel: 519-674-5436; *Fax:* 519-674-3352
etlittle@bellnet.ca

***Ridgetown*: Daniel B. Nicol - *1**
P.O. Box 700, 64 Main St. East, Ridgetown, ON N0P 2C0
Tel: 519-674-3372; *Fax:* 519-674-3352
dbnicol@pppoe.ca

***Ridgeway*: Community Legal Services of Niagara South - *1**
P.O. Box 430, 266 Ridge Rd., Ridgeway, ON L0S 1N0
Tel: 905-894-4775; *Fax:* 905-894-6101

***Ripley*: Crawford, Mill & Davies**
P.O. Box 100, 38 Queen St., Ripley, ON N0G 2R0
Tel: 519-395-2633; *Fax:* 519-395-4947
cmdripley@hurontel.ca

***Rockwood*: Douglas S. Black - *1**
P.O. Box 95, 118 Main St. South, Rockwood, ON N0B 2K0
Tel: 519-856-4555; *Fax:* 519-856-4680
dblacklaw@bellnet.ca

***Rockwood*: Judith P. Ryan**
P.O. Box 550, Rockwood, ON N0B 2K0
Tel: 519-856-2223; *Fax:* 519-856-2047
jpmryan@aol.com

***Sarnia*: Paul R. Beaudet - *1**
P.O. Box 2162, 251 Exmouth St., Sarnia, ON N7T 7L7
Tel: 519-337-1529; *Fax:* 519-336-2569
beaudet@ebtech.net
www.sarnia.com/beaudet

***Sarnia*: Terry L. Brandon - *1**
1069 London Rd., Sarnia, ON N7S 1P2
Tel: 519-337-4634; *Fax:* 519-337-5586
terrybrandon@sympatico.ca

***Sarnia*: Roderick Brown, Q.C. - *1**
555 Exmouth St., Sarnia, ON N7T 5P6
Tel: 519-336-7880; *Fax:* 519-336-6584
re_brown2927@hotmail.com

***Sarnia*: James J. Carpeneto - *1**
316 Christina St. North, Sarnia, ON N7T 5V5
Tel: 519-336-6955; *Fax:* 519-336-8401

***Sarnia*: W.M. Dawson, Q.C. - *1**
#201, 805 Christina St. North, Sarnia, ON N7V 1X6
Tel: 519-337-2321; *Fax:* 519-337-2466

***Sarnia*: Elliott & Porter - *2**
Former Name: Elliott, Porter, McFadyen & McFadyen
#101, St. Clair Corporate Centre, 265 Front St. North, Sarnia, ON N7T 7X1
Tel: 519-336-4600; *Fax:* 519-336-4640

***Sarnia*: George Murray Shipley Bell, LLP - *9**
P.O. Box 2196, 2 Ferry Dock Hill, Sarnia, ON N7T 7L8
Tel: 519-336-8770; *Fax:* 519-336-1811

***Sarnia*: Gray, Bruce, Cimetta (Cablo Cimetta Professional Corporation) - *4**
P.O. Box 2259, 1166 London Rd., Sarnia, ON N7T 7L7
Tel: 519-336-9700; *Fax:* 519-336-3289

***Sarnia*: C. Ed Gresham**
#203, 805 Christina St. North, Sarnia, ON N7V 1X6
Tel: 519-337-9224; *Fax:* 519-337-7440

***Sarnia*: David G. Hockin - *1**
#101, 265 Front St. North, Sarnia, ON N7T 7X1
Tel: 519-336-4357; *Fax:* 519-336-4367
lawyer@ebtech.net

***Sarnia*: Pamela J. McLeod - *1**
1350 L'Heritage Dr., Sarnia, ON N7S 6H8
Tel: 519-542-7714; *Fax:* 519-542-5577
mcleodlaw@ebtech.net

***Sarnia*: Robbins, Henderson & Davis - *4**
#201, 208 North Christina St., Sarnia, ON N7V 1X6
Tel: 519-344-5265; *Fax:* 519-344-1558

***Sarnia*: Raymond A. Whitnall - *1**
345 Christina St. North, Sarnia, ON N7T 5V6
Tel: 519-336-9460; *Fax:* 519-336-8366

***Sarnia*: Wyrzykowski & Robb - *2**
P.O. Box 2200, Stn. Main, Sarnia, ON N7T 7L7
Tel: 519-336-6118; *Fax:* 519-336-9550
orw@ebtech.net

***Sault Ste Marie*: Aiello, Pawelek - *2**
#102, 123 March St., Sault Ste Marie, ON P6A 2Z5
Tel: 705-946-8590; *Fax:* 705-946-8589

***Sault Ste Marie*: Allemano & Fitzgerald - *2**
P.O. Box 10, Sault Ste Marie, ON P6A 5L2
Tel: 705-942-0142; *Fax:* 705-942-7188

***Sault Ste Marie*: Bisceglia Dumanski Rasaiah LLP - *3**
747 Queen St. East, 2nd Fl., Sault Ste Marie, ON P6A 2A8
Tel: 705-942-5856; *Fax:* 705-942-6493
bdrlawfirm@bellnet.ca
www.bdlawfirm.ca

***Sault Ste Marie*: Kenneth R. Davies**
525 Wellington St. East, Sault Ste Marie, ON P6A 2M4
Tel: 705-256-7839; *Fax:* 705-942-8271

***Sault Ste Marie*: Ferranti & Chorney - *2**
189 East St., Sault Ste Marie, ON P6A 3C8
Tel: 705-949-6200; *Fax:* 705-949-6208

***Sault Ste Marie*: Hamilton, Nixon - *2**
P.O. Box 249, 67 Elgin St., Sault Ste Marie, ON P6A 5L8
Tel: 705-759-8498; *Fax:* 705-759-8781

***Sault Ste Marie*: Laidlaw, Paciocco, Melville - *3**
Former Name: Kelleher, Laidlaw, Paciocco, Melville
#604, 421 Bay St., Sault Ste Marie, ON P6A 1X3
Tel: 705-949-7790; *Fax:* 705-949-5816
paciocco@vianet.ca

***Sault Ste Marie*: O. Kennedy Lawson - *1**
#104, 473 Queen St. East, Sault Ste Marie, ON P6A 1Z5
Tel: 705-759-5030; *Fax:* 705-942-5309

***Sault Ste Marie*: Mathews, Dinsdale & Clark LLP**
#301, 369 Queen St., Sault Ste Marie, ON P6A 1Z4
Tel: 705-253-3711; *Fax:* 705-253-1102
vchiappella@mathewsdinsdale.com

***Sault Ste Marie*: Eric D. McCooeye - *1**
348 Albert St. East, Sault Ste Marie, ON P6A 2J6
Tel: 705-945-8868; *Fax:* 705-945-9051
smccooeye@shaw.ca

***Sault Ste Marie*: O'Neill Cresswell DeLorenzi Mendes - *6**
116 Spring St., Sault Ste Marie, ON P6A 3A1
Tel: 705-949-6901; *Fax:* 705-949-0618
info@saultlawyers.com
www.saultlawyers.com

***Sault Ste Marie*: Orazietti, Kwolek, Walz - *4**
128 March St., Sault Ste Marie, ON P6A 2Z3
Tel: 705-256-5601; *Fax:* 705-945-9427
soolaw@soonet.com

***Sault Ste Marie*: R.C. Peres, Q.C. - *1**
#104, 212 Queen St. East, Sault Ste Marie, ON P6A 5X8
Tel: 705-949-9411; *Fax:* 705-949-3759

***Sault Ste Marie*: William R. Scott - *1**
#202, 629A Queen St. East, Sault Ste Marie, ON P6A 2A6
Tel: 705-949-4333; *Fax:* 705-945-0958
wmrscottlaw@yahoo.com

***Sault Ste Marie*: Carol A. Shamess - *1**
181 March St., Sault Ste Marie, ON P6A 2Z6
Tel: 705-942-2580; *Fax:* 705-942-5048

***Sault Ste Marie*: Jack Squire - *1**
191 Northern Ave. East, Sault Ste Marie, ON P6B 4H8
Tel: 705-949-0162; *Fax:* 705-541-9616

***Sault Ste Marie*: T. Frederick Baxter, Barrister & Solicitor - *1**
Also Known As: McLeod, Baxter, Tremblay-Hall
494 Albert St. East, Sault Ste Marie, ON P6A 2K2
Tel: 705-759-0948; *Fax:* 705-759-2042

***Sault Ste Marie*: Walker, Thompson - *1**
#506, P.O. Box 428, 123 March St., Sault Ste Marie, ON P6A 5M1
Tel: 705-949-7806; *Fax:* 705-759-0457
walkerlaw@sympatico.ca

***Sault Ste Marie*: Willson, Carter - *2**
494 Albert St. East, Sault Ste Marie, ON P6A 2K2
Tel: 705-942-2000; *Fax:* 705-942-6511

***Sault Ste Marie*: Wishart Law Firm LLP - *6**
#500, 390 Bay St., Sault Ste Marie, ON P6A 1X2
Tel: 705-949-6700; *Fax:* 705-949-2465
wishart@wishartlaw.com
www.wishartlaw.com

***Scarborough*: Antflyck, Mazin Aulis LLP - *3**
Former Name: Antflyck & Mazin
1501 Ellesmere Rd., Scarborough, ON M1P 4T6
Tel: 416-431-1500; *Fax:* 416-431-1912
antflyckmazin@on.aibn.com

***Scarborough*: Stanley Baker - *1**
#700, 55 Town Centre Ct., Scarborough, ON M1P 4X4
Tel: 416-296-1794; *Fax:* 416-296-1259
stanleybaker@rogers.com

***Scarborough*: Andrea E.K. Chun - *1**
#700, One Corporate Plaza, 2075 Kennedy Rd., Scarborough, ON M1T 3V3
Tel: 416-754-3060; *Fax:* 416-754-3321
andreachun@bellnet.ca

***Schomberg*: Clarke G. Smith - *1**
#10, Brownsville Junction Plaza, 17250 Hwy. 27, Schomberg, ON L0G 1T0
Tel: 905-939-2344; *Fax:* 905-727-7096
cgsmith@rogers.com

***Seaforth*: Devereaux Murray LLP - *2**
P.O. Box 220, 77 Main St. South, Seaforth, ON N0K 1W0
Tel: 519-527-0850; *Fax:* 519-527-2324
c4thlaw@devereauxmurray.ca

***Seeleys Bay*: D.J. Atkinson - *1**
RR#1, Seeleys Bay, ON K0H 2N0
Tel: 613-382-2692

***Shelburne*: Courtney H. Foster**
P.O. Box 11, RR#4, Shelburne, ON L0N 1S8
Tel: 519-925-5854; *Fax:* 519-925-3159

***Shelburne*: Timmerman & Haskell - *2**
P.O. Box 216, 305 Owen Sound St., Shelburne, ON L0N 1S0
Tel: 519-925-2608; *Fax:* 519-925-2268

***Simcoe*: Brimage, Tyrrell, Van Severen & Homeniuk - *10**
21 Norfolk St. North, Simcoe, ON N3Y 4L1
Tel: 519-426-5840; *Fax:* 519-426-7515
law@brimage.com
www.brimage.com

** indicates number of lawyers*

***Simcoe*: Cline, Backus, Nightingale & McArthur, LLP - *8**
P.O. Box 528, Stn. Main, 39 Colborne St. North, Simcoe, ON N3Y 4N5
Tel: 519-426-6763; *Fax:* 519-426-2055
cbnmlaw@kwic.com
www.clinebackus.com

***Simcoe*: Cobb & Jones LLP - *7**
P.O. Box 548, 23 Argyle St., Simcoe, ON N3Y 4N5
Tel: 519-428-0170; *Fax:* 519-428-3105
cobblaw@cobbjones.ca
www.cobbjones.ca

***Simcoe*: William Mark Dresser - *1**
P.O. Box 103, Simcoe, ON N3Y 4K8
Tel: 519-426-8118; *Fax:* 519-426-8962
lawmark@sympatico.ca

***Simcoe*: Sheppard, MacIntosh, Lados & Nunn LLP - *4**
P.O. Box 677, 58 Peel St., Simcoe, ON N3Y 4T2
Tel: 519-426-1382; *Fax:* 519-426-1392
lawyers@sheppardmacintosh.com
www.sheppardmacintosh.com

***Simcoe*: Smelko Law Office - *1**
25 Norfolk St. North, Simcoe, ON N3Y 3N6
Tel: 519-426-1711; *Fax:* 519-426-7863
Toll-Free: 866-684-8527
smelkolaw@on.aibn.com

***Sioux Lookout*: Kevin W. Romyn - *1**
P.O. Box 99, 69 Queen St., Sioux Lookout, ON P8T 1A1
Tel: 807-737-2562; *Fax:* 807-737-2571
romynlaw@gosiouxlookout.com

***Smiths Falls*: G.W. Fournier - *1**
P.O. Box 752, 35 Daniel St., Smiths Falls, ON K7A 4W6
Tel: 613-283-8818; *Fax:* 613-283-8951

***Smiths Falls*: Howard Ryan Kelford Knott & Dixon, Barristers & Solicitors - *5**
2 Main St. East, Smiths Falls, ON K7A 1A2
Tel: 613-283-6772; *Fax:* 613-283-8840
Toll-Free: 888-852-5175
lthompson@smithsfallslaw.ca
www.smithsfallslaw.ca

***Smiths Falls*: Kirkland, Murphy & Kennedy Professional Corporation - *3**
Former Name: Kirkland, Murphy & Lee
P.O. Box 220, 15 Russell St. East, Smiths Falls, ON K7A 4T1
Tel: 613-283-0515; *Fax:* 613-283-8557
reception@smithsfallslawyers.com

***Smiths Falls*: Ross Cliffen & Morrison - *3**
Former Name: Ross & Cliffen
P.O. Box 804, 30 Russell St. East, Smiths Falls, ON K7A 4W6
Tel: 613-283-7331; *Fax:* 613-283-6792
rosslaw@ripnet.com
www.rossandcliffen.com

***Southampton*: Robert E. Forsyth - *1**
P.O. Box 420, 243 High St., Southampton, ON N0H 2L0
Tel: 519-797-3223; *Fax:* 519-797-3192
forsyth3@bmts.com

***St Catharines*: W.J. Garry Bracken - *1**
50 Dunvegan Rd., St Catharines, ON L2P 1H6
Tel: 905-988-9389; *Fax:* 905-685-1753
bracklaw@cogeco.ca

***St Catharines*: Chown, Cairns LLP - *17**
P.O. Box 760, 80 King St., St Catharines, ON L2R 6Y8
Tel: 905-688-4500; *Fax:* 905-688-0015
lawyers@chowlaw.com
www.chownlaw.com

***St Catharines*: Coy, Barch - *1**
46 Ontario St., St Catharines, ON L2R 5J4
Tel: 905-641-1146; *Fax:* 905-641-1148

***St Catharines*: Crossingham, Brady - *2**
P.O. Box 307, 63 Ontario St., St Catharines, ON L2R 6V2
Tel: 905-641-1621; *Fax:* 905-685-1461
cbm@vaxxine.com

***St Catharines*: Daniel & Partners LLP - *9**
Dominion Bldg., P.O. Box 24022, 39 Queen St., St Catharines, ON L2R 7P7
Tel: 905-688-9411; *Fax:* 905-688-5747
Toll-Free: 800-263-3650
lawyers@niagaralaw.ca

***St Catharines*: Mark F. Dedinsky - *1**
154 James St., 2nd Fl., St Catharines, ON L2R 5C5
Tel: 905-688-6275; *Fax:* 905-682-0264

***St Catharines*: Forster, Lewandowski & Cords - *2**
P.O. Box 1180, Stn. Main, 82 Lake St., St Catharines, ON L2R 7A7
Tel: 905-688-9110; *Fax:* 905-688-0901
Toll-Free: 866-715-9380
f.l.c@on.aibn.com

***St Catharines*: Ralph H. Frayne - *1**
Former Name: Freeman, Frayne & Hummell
9 Raymond St., St Catharines, ON L2R 2S9
Tel: 905-684-1147; *Fax:* 905-684-7147

***St Catharines*: Erik Grinbergs**
37 Church St., St Catharines, ON L2R 3B7
Tel: 905-688-9800; *Fax:* 905-684-0009
grinberg@vaxxine.com

***St Catharines*: John B. Hanna - *1**
P.O. Box 24044, Stn. Main, St Catharines, ON L2R 7P7
Tel: 905-687-9347; *Fax:* 905-687-3939

***St Catharines*: Heelis, Williams, Little & Almas LLP, Barristers & Solicitors - *6**
Also Known As: HWL&A
P.O. Box 1056, 14 Church St., St Catharines, ON L2R 7A3
Tel: 905-687-8200; *Fax:* 905-684-4844
rwilliam@14churchstlawoffice.com
www.14churchstlawoffice.com

***St Catharines*: Lancaster, Brooks & Welch LLP - *17**
Former Name: Lancaster, Mix & Welch
P.O. Box 790, 80 King St., St Catharines, ON L2R 6Z1
Tel: 905-641-1551; *Fax:* 905-641-1830
www.lbwlawyers.com

***St Catharines*: Legal Aid**
#302, P.O. Box 954, 110 James St., St Catharines, ON L2R 6Z4
Tel: 905-685-1012; *Fax:* 905-685-7202

***St Catharines*: Frank M. Marotta - *1**
21 Duke St., St Catharines, ON L2R 5W1
Tel: 905-688-5401; *Fax:* 905-688-6204
fmarotta@vaxxine.com

***St Catharines*: Martens, Lingard LLP - *7**
Former Name: Martens, Lingard, Maddalena, Robinson & Koke
195 King St., St Catharines, ON L2R 3J6
Tel: 905-687-6551; *Fax:* 905-687-6553
lawyers@martenslingard.ca

***St Catharines*: Paula McPherson - *1**
51 Hillcrest Ave., St Catharines, ON L2R 4Y3
Tel: 905-641-3457;
resolve@sympatico.ca

***St Catharines*: Tracy J. Middleton Collini - *1**
234 Vine St., St Catharines, ON L2M 4T1
Tel: 905-937-9229; *Fax:* 905-937-9228
collinilaw@msn.com

***St Catharines*: O'Neill & Radford - *1**
154 James St., St Catharines, ON L2R 7A3
Tel: 905-641-2633; *Fax:* 905-682-0264
bmradford@bellnet.ca

***St Catharines*: Ian G. Pearson - *1**
154 James St., 2nd Fl., St Catharines, ON L2R 5C5
Tel: 905-682-7882; *Fax:* 905-682-0264
ipearson@bellnet.ca

***St Catharines*: Sullivan, Mahoney LLP - *27**
P.O. Box 1360, 40 Queen St., St Catharines, ON L2R 6Z2
Tel: 905-688-6655; *Fax:* 905-688-5814
lawyers@sullivan-mahoney.com
www.sullivan-mahoney.com

***St Catharines*: Virginia L. Workman - *1**
#1004, 1 St. Paul, St Catharines, ON L2R 7L2
Tel: 905-704-0804; *Fax:* 905-704-4464
virginiaworkman@bellnet.ca

***St Marys*: William J. Galloway - *1**
P.O. Box 897, Stn. Main, 172 Queen St. East, St Marys, ON N4X 1B6
Tel: 519-284-2112; *Fax:* 519-284-3081

***St Thomas*: Jerome A. Collins - *1**
36 Hincks St., St Thomas, ON N5R 3N6
Tel: 519-633-3973; *Fax:* 519-633-7916

***St Thomas*: W.J. Glover, Law Office - *1**
Also Known As: Stafford Associates Crimical Law Office
P.O. Box 575, Stn. Main, 458 Talbot St., St Thomas, ON N5P 3V6
Tel: 519-633-2300; *Fax:* 519-633-0964
gloverlawyer@aol.com

***St Thomas*: Gunn & Associates - *5**
108 Centre St., St Thomas, ON N5R 2Z7
Tel: 519-631-0700; *Fax:* 519-631-1468
lawyers@gunn.on.ca
www.gunn.on.ca

***St Thomas*: Arnold B. Walker - *1**
4 Elgin St., St Thomas, ON N5R 3L6
Tel: 519-633-3273; *Fax:* 519-633-8585

***Stoney Creek*: Cicchi & Giangregorio - *2**
1-99 Hwy. 8, Stoney Creek, ON L8G 1C1
Tel: 905-664-6645; *Fax:* 905-664-6952

***Stoney Creek*: Coombs & Lutz - *1**
6 Lake Ave. South, Stoney Creek, ON L8G 1P3
Tel: 905-664-6341; *Fax:* 905-664-8966
lutz@bellnet.ca

***Stoney Creek*: Mary J. MacKinnon - *2**
Former Name: MacKinnon, Mary J.
860 Queenston Rd., Stoney Creek, ON L8G 4A8
Tel: 905-662-0046; *Fax:* 905-662-3339
info@mackinnonlaw.com
www.mackinnonlaw.com

***Stoney Creek*: Murray R. Mazza - *1**
426 Hwy. 8, Stoney Creek, ON L8G 1G2
Tel: 905-561-1444;
idseast@cogeco.net

***Stoney Creek*: O'Brien & Skrtich - *1**
26 King St. East, Stoney Creek, ON L8G 1J8
Tel: 905-662-2855; *Fax:* 905-662-8881

***Stoney Creek*: Mari-Anne Saunders - *1**
#303, 800 Queenston Rd., Stoney Creek, ON L8G 1A7
Tel: 905-664-6683; *Fax:* 905-664-4876

***Stouffville*: Button, Armstrong & Ness - *3**
P.O. Box 220, Stn. Main, 6361 Main St., Stouffville, ON L4A 7Z5
Tel: 905-640-3530; *Fax:* 905-640-7027
banlaw@rogers.com

***Stouffville*: Paul J. Crowe - *1**
#208, 86 Ringwood Dr., Stouffville, ON L4A 1C3
Tel: 905-640-8100; *Fax:* 905-640-6064
info@pauljcrowe.com
www.pauljcrowe.com

***Stratford*: John W. Buechler - *1**
488 Erie St., Stratford, ON N5A 2N6
Tel: 519-271-3520; *Fax:* 519-271-0097

***Stratford*: Michael F. Fair - *1**
24 Downie St., 2nd Fl., Stratford, ON N5A 6W3
Tel: 519-271-2912; *Fax:* 519-271-2732

***Stratford*: MBK Law LLP - *4**
Former Name: Barenberg, McDonald
42 Waterloo St., Stratford, ON N5A 4A7
Tel: 519-273-2734; *Fax:* 519-273-2713
info@mbklaw.ca

***Stratford*: Mountain Mitchell LLP - *7**
P.O. Box 846, 56 Albert St., Stratford, ON N5A 6W3
Tel: 519-271-6770; *Fax:* 519-271-9261
main@mountainmitchell.com
www.mountainmitchell.com

***Stratford*: Skinner, Dunphy & Bantle LLP - *4**
Former Name: Skinner, Rogerson, Dunphy
P.O. Box 542, 1 Ontario St., Stratford, ON N5A 6T7
Tel: 519-271-7330; *Fax:* 519-271-1762
thefirm@stratfordlaw.com

***Stratford*: L. Ray Waller - *1**
#103, P.O. Box 813, Stn. Main, 386 Cambria St., Stratford, ON N5A 6W1
Tel: 519-271-4420; *Fax:* 519-271-7833

***Strathroy*: Robert J. Dack - *1**
16 Front St. East, Strathroy, ON N7G 1Y4
Tel: 519-245-0370; *Fax:* 519-245-0523

** indicates number of lawyers*

***Strathroy*: Jones, Gibbons & Reis - *2**
39 Front St. West, Strathroy, ON N7G 1X5
Tel: 519-245-1110; *Fax:* 519-245-5859
jmr@webgate.net

***Strathroy*: Quinlan & Somerville - *2**
18 Front St. East, Strathroy, ON N7G 1Y4
Tel: 519-245-0342; *Fax:* 519-245-0108
lawyers@quinlansomerville.com

***Strathroy*: H.P. Ramkelawan - *1**
P.O. Box 254, Stn. Main, RR#5, Strathroy, ON N7G 3J2
Tel: 519-245-6074

***Strathroy*: George E. Sinker - *2**
53 Front St. West, Strathroy, ON N7G 1X6
Tel: 519-245-1144; *Fax:* 519-245-6090
gsinker@bellnet.ca

***Sudbury*: Michael G. Barnett - *1**
264 Elm St., Sudbury, ON P3C 1V4
Tel: 705-674-3210; *Fax:* 705-674-1265

***Sudbury*: William G. Beach - *1**
224 Applegrove St., Sudbury, ON P3C 1N3
Tel: 705-675-5685; *Fax:* 705-675-6601

***Sudbury*: Beckett, Huneault - *2**
135 Applegrove St., Sudbury, ON P3C 1N2
Tel: 705-673-9551; *Fax:* 705-673-0476

***Sudbury*: Gerald D. Brouillette - *1**
235 Elm St., Sudbury, ON P3C 1T8
Tel: 705-674-2822; *Fax:* 705-674-2975
gerry.brouillette@sympatico.ca

***Sudbury*: Conroy Trebb Scott Hurtubise LLP, Barristers, Solicitors - *6**
164 Elm St., Sudbury, ON P3C 1T7
Tel: 705-674-6441; *Fax:* 705-673-9567
Toll-Free: 800-627-1825
info@sudburylegal.com
www.sudburylegal.com

***Sudbury*: DeDiana, Eloranta & Longstreet - *1**
219 Pine St., Sudbury, ON P3C 1X4
Tel: 705-674-4289; *Fax:* 705-671-1047

***Sudbury*: Desmarais, Keenan LLP - *10**
#201, 62 Frood Rd., Sudbury, ON P3C 4Z3
Tel: 705-675-7521; *Fax:* 705-675-7390
Toll-Free: 800-290-5465
www.desmaraiskeenan.com

***Sudbury*: Hugh A. Doig, Q.C. - *1**
296 Larch St., Sudbury, ON P3B 1M2
Tel: 705-674-4213; *Fax:* 705-671-1652
doig@on.aibn.com

***Sudbury*: Robert L. Fabbro - *1**
#1, 54 Elgin St., Sudbury, ON P3E 3N2
Tel: 705-675-6620; *Fax:* 705-675-6655
robertfabbro@on.aibn.com

***Sudbury*: Brian N. Howe - *1**
235 Elm St. West, Sudbury, ON P3C 1T8
Tel: 705-674-8317; *Fax:* 705-674-2952

***Sudbury*: Elizabeth Kari - *1**
293 Elm St., 2nd Fl., Sudbury, ON P3C 1V6
Tel: 705-670-2770; *Fax:* 705-670-9172
ekari@cyberbeach.net

***Sudbury*: Donald Kuyek - *1**
229 Elm St. West, Sudbury, ON P3C 1T8
Tel: 705-675-1227; *Fax:* 705-675-5350
Toll-Free: 877-414-0311

***Sudbury*: Lacroix, Forest LLP/s.r.l. - *10**
Place Balmoral, 36 Elgin St., Sudbury, ON P3C 5B4
Tel: 705-674-1976; *Fax:* 705-674-6978
office@sudburylaw.com
www.sudburylaw.com

***Sudbury*: J. Robert LeBlanc - *1**
125 Durham St., 2nd Fl., Sudbury, ON P3E 3M9
Tel: 705-674-5858; *Fax:* 705-674-9137
bleblanc@cyberbeach.net

***Sudbury*: Patricia L. Meehan - *1**
293 Elm St. West, Sudbury, ON P3C 1V6
Tel: 705-674-2272; *Fax:* 705-674-5238
patricia.meehan@sympatico.ca

***Sudbury*: Mensour & Mensour - *2**
#101, 238 Elm St., Sudbury, ON P3C 1V3
Tel: 705-673-6787; *Fax:* 705-673-1418

***Sudbury*: Miller, Maki - *14**
176 Elm St., Sudbury, ON P3C 1T7
Tel: 705-675-7503; *Fax:* 705-675-8669
oharam@millermaki.com

***Sudbury*: Paquette & Renzini - *3**
#200, 1188 St. Jerome St., Sudbury, ON P3A 2V9
Tel: 705-560-2121; *Fax:* 705-560-8072
mail@paquette-renzini.ca

***Sudbury*: Parisé Law Office - *2**
58 Lisgar St., 2nd Fl., Sudbury, ON P3E 3L7
Tel: 705-674-4042; *Fax:* 705-674-4242
pariselaw@unitz.ca

***Sudbury*: Glenn E.J. Sandberg**
#200, 144 Elm St. West, Sudbury, ON P3C 1T7
Tel: 705-671-9922; *Fax:* 705-671-2107

***Sudbury*: Norman G. Stoner - *1**
#202, 124 Cedar St., Sudbury, ON P3E 1B4
Tel: 705-675-8307; *Fax:* 705-675-7245
ngslaw@bellnet.ca

***Sudbury*: Stanley J. Thomas - *1**
111 Durham St., Sudbury, ON P3E 3M9
Tel: 705-674-8306; *Fax:* 705-675-8466

***Sudbury*: Law Office of Serge F. Treherne - *1**
P.O. Box 1269, 144 Elm St. West, Sudbury, ON P3C 1T7
Tel: 705-670-9689; *Fax:* 705-670-9141
Toll-Free: 877-550-5616

***Sudbury*: Violette Law Offices - *1**
#1, 11 Elgin St., Sudbury, ON P3C 5B6
Tel: 705-674-1300; *Fax:* 705-671-1044
Toll-Free: 866-991-1300
office@violettelaw.com

***Sudbury*: Wilkins & Wilkins - *2**
P.O. Box 490, Stn. B, 176 Elm St., Sudbury, ON P3E 4P6
Tel: 705-675-1200

***Sundridge*: Michael A. Hardy & Associates - *2**
P.O. Box 1060, 105 Main St. East, Sundridge, ON P0A 1Z0
Tel: 705-384-5770; *Fax:* 705-384-5771
sunlaw@bellnet.ca

***Sutton*: Patrick J. Fahey Law Office - *2**
P.O. Box 487, 100 High St., Sutton, ON L0E 1R0
Tel: 905-722-3771; *Fax:* 905-722-9852
pat.pjf@rogers.com

***Thornhill*: Augustine M. Arrigo, Q.C. - *1**
48 Guardsman Rd., Thornhill, ON L3T 6L4
Tel: 905-889-6131

***Thornhill*: Leslie (Masood) Brown**
#225B, Commerce Gate, 505 Hwy. 7 East, Thornhill, ON L3T 7T1
Tel: 905-731-5083; *Fax:* 905-731-4078
les@torontolegalservices.ca

***Thornhill*: Edward L. Burlew - *1**
16 John St., Thornhill, ON L3T 1X8
Tel: 905-882-2422; *Fax:* 905-882-2431
Toll-Free: 888-486-5677

***Thornhill*: Law Office of Cosimo A. Crupi Barrister & Solicitor - *1**
Former Name: D'Andrea, Crupi
#302, 305 Renfrew Dr., Thornhill, ON L3R 9S7
Tel: 905-415-8900; *Fax:* 905-415-8902
cacrupi@crupilaw.ca
www.crupilaw.ca

***Thornhill*: Iain Stewart Cunningham - *1**
20 Cypress Point Ct., Thornhill, ON L3T 1V7
Tel: 905-764-7376; *Fax:* 905-707-5818

***Thornhill*: Stephen R. Dyment - *1**
#216, 2900 Steeles Ave. East, Thornhill, ON L3T 4X1
Tel: 905-882-1277; *Fax:* 905-882-8536

***Thornhill*: Fish & Associates Professional Corporation - *2**
7951 Yonge St., Thornhill, ON L3T 2C4
Tel: 905-881-1500; *Fax:* 905-881-6535
bfish@fishlaw.ca
www.familyfight.com

***Thornhill*: A.M. Flisfeder - *1**
45 Janesville Rd., Thornhill, ON L4J 6Z9
Tel: 416-469-0375; *Fax:* 416-469-0375
sgt_lafourse@sympatico.ca

***Thornhill*: Gregory J. Gaglione - *1**
#202, 7368 Yonge St., Thornhill, ON L4J 8H9
Tel: 416-882-0066; *Fax:* 416-882-2550

***Thornhill*: Elana P. Glass - *1**
149 Langtry Pl., Thornhill, ON L4J 8L6
Tel: 416-587-5680

***Thornhill*: Barry S. Greenberg - *1**
7626A Yonge St., Thornhill, ON L4J 1V9
Tel: 905-886-9535; *Fax:* 905-886-9540
bsgreenberg@rogers.com

***Thornhill*: Perry H. Gruenberger - *1**
#220, 8500 Leslie St., Thornhill, ON L3T 7M8
Tel: 905-764-6411; *Fax:* 905-886-6034

***Thornhill*: Seymour Iseman - *1**
Former Name: Iseman & Associate
#216, 2900 Steeles Ave. East, Thornhill, ON L3T 4X1
Tel: 905-881-8800; *Fax:* 905-881-7391
siseman@allstream.net

***Thornhill*: Arthur Lundy - *1**
#402, 300 John St., Thornhill, ON L3T 5W4
Tel: 905-886-3110; *Fax:* 905-886-0989

***Thornhill*: Carolyn L. MacDonald - *1**
14 Morgan Ave., Thornhill, ON L3T 1R1
Tel: 905-707-7723; *Fax:* 905-707-5818

***Thornhill*: Janet MacDougall - *1**
#202, 8108 Yonge St., Thornhill, ON L4J 1W4
Tel: 905-886-4907; *Fax:* 905-886-8070

***Thornhill*: R.G. Merritt - *1**
#205, 7089 Yonge St., Thornhill, ON L3T 2A7
Tel: 905-889-3430; *Fax:* 905-889-7290
rgmerritt@home.com

***Thornhill*: D. Todd Morganstein - *1**
#110, 8111 Yonge St., Thornhill, ON L3T 4V9
Tel: 905-881-8289; *Fax:* 905-881-2696

***Thornhill*: Roselyn Pecus - *1**
#310, 1 Promenade Circle, Thornhill, ON L4J 4P8
Tel: 905-709-8105; *Fax:* 905-709-8180

***Thornhill*: Tania Perlin**
#B10-137, 800 Steeles Ave. West, Thornhill, ON L4J 7L2
Tel: 416-225-5424; *Fax:* 416-225-3611

***Thornhill*: Raphael Barristers - *4**
#202, 1137 Centre St., Thornhill, ON L4J 3M6
Tel: 416-594-1812; *Fax:* 416-594-0868
Toll-Free: 877-217-1812
info@raphaelpersonalinjurylawyers.com
www.raphaelpersonalinjurylawyers.com

***Thornhill*: Thomas H. Riesz - *1**
#218, 180 Steeles Ave. West, Thornhill, ON L4J 2L1
Tel: 905-881-5609; *Fax:* 905-881-9859

***Thornhill*: Erwin S. Seltzer - *1**
9 MacArthur Dr., Thornhill, ON L4J 7T6
Tel: 905-731-7131

***Thornhill*: Ben Weinstein - *1**
#203, 1 Clark Ave. West, Thornhill, ON L4J 7Y6
Tel: 905-889-5364; *Fax:* 905-889-3231

***Thornhill*: Judith M. Wolf - *1**
#260, 1054 Centre St., Thornhill, ON L4J 8E5
Tel: 905-731-3372; *Fax:* 905-731-7913

***Thorold*: Jurmain Law Office - *2**
8A Clairmont St., Thorold, ON L2V 1R1
Tel: 905-227-2829; *Fax:* 905-227-9206
info@jurmainlaw.com
www.jurmainlaw.com

***Thorold*: John J. Simon - *1**
P.O. Box 505, Stn. Thorold, 7 Front St. North, Thorold, ON L2V 4W1
Tel: 905-227-9191; *Fax:* 905-227-7234
john_smith@hotmail.com

***Thorold*: Young, McNamara - *2**
18 Albert St. East, Thorold, ON L2V 1P1
Tel: 905-227-3777; *Fax:* 905-227-5988

** indicates number of lawyers*

***Thunder Bay*: Atwood Labine Arnone McCartney LLP - *7**
501 Donald St. East, Thunder Bay, ON P7E 6N6
Tel: 807-623-4342; *Fax:* 807-623-2098
asl@asl-law.com
www.alamlaw.ca

***Thunder Bay*: Marc L. Bode, Barrister & Solicitor - *1**
Former Name: Bode & Mackinnon
#816, 34 Cumberland St. North, Thunder Bay, ON P7A 4L3
Tel: 807-344-9444; *Fax:* 807-344-3420
marcbode@thaytel.net

***Thunder Bay*: David S. Bruzzese - *1**
#320, Marina Park Centre, 180 Park Ave., Thunder Bay, ON P7B 6J4
Tel: 807-344-1020; *Fax:* 807-344-1433
dsb.law@shawlink.ca

***Thunder Bay*: Buset & Partners LLP - *15**
1121 Barton St., Thunder Bay, ON P7B 5N3
Tel: 807-623-2500; *Fax:* 807-622-7808
Toll-Free: 866-532-8738
law@buset-partners.com
www.buset-partners.com

***Thunder Bay*: Carrel+Partners LLP - *13**
1136 Alloy Dr., Thunder Bay, ON P7B 6M9
Tel: 807-346-3000; *Fax:* 807-346-3600
Toll-Free: 800-263-0578
info@carrel.com
www.carrel.com

***Thunder Bay*: Cheadles LLP - *8**
Former Name: Cheadle Johnson Shanks MacIvor
#2000, P.O. Box 10429, 715 Hewitson St., Thunder Bay, ON P7B 6T8
Tel: 807-622-6821; *Fax:* 807-623-3892

***Thunder Bay*: Christie Potestio Freitag - *3**
#203, 920 Tungsten St., Thunder Bay, ON P7B 5Z6
Tel: 807-344-6651; *Fax:* 807-345-1105
potestio@chrpot.on.ca

***Thunder Bay*: Donald R. Colborne - *1**
Site 14, Comp 67, RR#13, Thunder Bay, ON P7B 5E4
Tel: 807-344-6628; *Fax:* 807-983-3079
colborne@microage-tb.com

***Thunder Bay*: Richard W. Courtis - *1**
#101, 1151 Barton St., Thunder Bay, ON P7B 5N3
Tel: 807-623-3000; *Fax:* 807-623-1251
Toll-Free: 877-266-6646
courtis@hotmail.com

***Thunder Bay*: Cupello & Company - *4**
#104, 105 South May St., Thunder Bay, ON P7E 1B1
Tel: 807-622-8201; *Fax:* 807-622-3755
Toll-Free: 888-223-0739
law@cupello-company.com

***Thunder Bay*: Erickson & Partners - *8**
Former Name: Erickson Larson
291 South Court St., Thunder Bay, ON P7B 2Y1
Tel: 807-345-1213; *Fax:* 807-345-2526
Toll-Free: 800-465-3912

***Thunder Bay*: Filipovic, Brothers & Conway - *5**
#20, Tomlinson Block, 8A North Cumberland St., Thunder Bay, ON P7A 4L1
Tel: 807-343-9090; *Fax:* 807-345-1397
Toll-Free: 800-760-8694

***Thunder Bay*: Dennis A. Forbes & Associates - *1**
155 Rupert St., Thunder Bay, ON P7B 3X2
Tel: 807-345-1250; *Fax:* 807-345-1250
dforbes@tbaytel.net
www.dennisforbes.com

***Thunder Bay*: Peter Heerema - *1**
44 Algoma St. South, Thunder Bay, ON P7B 3A9
Tel: 807-346-4053; *Fax:* 807-346-8714
peter.heerema@tbaytel.net

***Thunder Bay*: Illingworth & Illingworth - *2**
#201, 1151 Barton St., Thunder Bay, ON P7B 5N3
Tel: 807-623-7222; *Fax:* 807-622-5297
lawyers@tbaytel.net

***Thunder Bay*: Lac des Mille Lacs First Nation - *1**
#328, 1100 Memorial Ave., Thunder Bay, ON P7B 4A3
Tel: 807-622-9835; *Fax:* 807-622-9866
ldmlfn@tbaytel.net

***Thunder Bay*: Rick E. Lauder - *1**
217 Van Norman St., Thunder Bay, ON P7A 4B6
Tel: 807-683-4444; *Fax:* 807-345-0337
rick.lauder@shawbiz.ca
www.ricklauder.shawbiz.ca

***Thunder Bay*: Martin Scrimshaw Scott - *4**
Cumberland Park, 1 Cumberland St. South, Thunder Bay, ON P7B 2T1
Tel: 807-345-3600; *Fax:* 807-344-8152
msslaw@tbaytel.net

***Thunder Bay*: Thomas C. Mitton - *1**
123 South Brodie St., Thunder Bay, ON P7E 1B8
Tel: 807-623-4320; *Fax:* 807-622-8038
tcmitton@tbaytel.net

***Thunder Bay*: Peter Mrowiec - *1**
#816, 34 Cumberland St. North, Thunder Bay, ON P7A 4L3
Tel: 807-344-0099; *Fax:* 807-344-3420
pmlaw@tbaytel.net

***Thunder Bay*: Robert D. Mullen - *1**
Former Name: Macgillivray-Poirier & Mullen In Association
395 Fort William Rd., Thunder Bay, ON P7B 2Z3
Tel: 807-344-5848; *Fax:* 807-344-5877
rmullen@shawbiz.ca

***Thunder Bay*: Petrone Hornak Garofalo Mauro - *9**
76 Algoma St. North, Thunder Bay, ON P7A 4Z4
Tel: 807-344-9191; *Fax:* 807-345-8391
Toll-Free: 800-465-3988

***Thunder Bay*: A.D. Stewart - *1**
#112, 105 May St. North, Thunder Bay, ON P7C 3N9
Tel: 807-623-7852; *Fax:* 807-623-0014
astewart@807-city.on.ca

***Thunder Bay*: Frank Valente - *1**
#5-8A, 8 Cumberland St. North, Thunder Bay, ON P7A 4L1
Tel: 807-345-5225; *Fax:* 807-345-8400

***Thunder Bay*: Vauthier, Paivalainen - *1**
275 Bay St., Thunder Bay, ON P7B 1R7
Tel: 807-343-9394; *Fax:* 807-344-1562

***Thunder Bay*: Thomas G. Watkinson - *1**
123 Brodie St. South, Thunder Bay, ON P7E 1B8
Tel: 807-624-5605; *Fax:* 807-623-6096

***Thunder Bay*: Weiler, Maloney, Nelson - *11**
#201, 1001 William St., Thunder Bay, ON P7B 6M1
Tel: 807-623-1111; *Fax:* 807-623-4947
weilers@wmnlaw.com
www.weilers.ca

***Tilbury*: R.M. Jutras - *1**
P.O. Box 417, 50 Queen St. South, Tilbury, ON N0P 2L0
Tel: 519-682-3100; *Fax:* 519-682-3622

***Tilbury*: Taylor & Delrue - *3**
P.O. Box 459, 40 Queen St. South, Tilbury, ON N0P 2L0
Tel: 519-682-0164; *Fax:* 519-682-2777
taydel@cogeco.net

***Tillsonburg*: James G. Battin - *1**
25 Bidwell St., Tillsonburg, ON N4G 3T4
Tel: 519-688-9033; *Fax:* 519-688-9036
bidlaw@kwic.com

***Tillsonburg*: Gibson, Linton, Toth, Campbell & Bennett - *3**
P.O. Box 5, Stn. Main, 36 Broadway, Tillsonburg, ON N4G 4H3
Tel: 519-842-3658; *Fax:* 519-842-5001
gltcb@kwic.com

***Tillsonburg*: Groom & Szorenyi - *1**
36 Broadway, Tillsonburg, ON N4G 4H3
Tel: 519-842-4205; *Fax:* 519-842-4261

***Tillsonburg*: Jenkins & Gilvesy - *2**
Former Name: Morris, Jenkins & Gilvesy
P.O. Box 280, Stn. Main, 107 Broadway Street, Tillsonburg, ON N4G 4H5
Tel: 519-842-9017; *Fax:* 519-842-3394
http://www.linkedin.com/pub/lisa-gilvesy/9/622/65a

***Tillsonburg*: Mandryk, Stewart & Morgan - *3**
65 Bidwell St., Tillsonburg, ON N4G 3T8
Tel: 519-842-4228; *Fax:* 519-842-7659
mhlaw@oxford.net

***Timmins*: Sydney Brooks - *1**
Also Known As: Brooks & Associates
81 Balsam St. South, Timmins, ON P4N 2C9
Tel: 705-264-5341; *Fax:* 705-264-2550

***Timmins*: Carlesso Barazzutti - *2**
#204, Scotiabank Bldg., 3 Pine St. South, Timmins, ON P4N 2J9
Tel: 705-264-1374; *Fax:* 705-264-1450

***Timmins*: Suzanne Desrosiers - *1**
92 Spruce St. North, Timmins, ON P4N 6M8
Tel: 705-268-6492; *Fax:* 705-264-1940
sdesrosiers@peroonainternet.com

***Timmins*: Evans, Bragagnolo & Sullivan - *8**
120 Pine St. South, Timmins, ON P4N 2K4
Tel: 705-264-1285; *Fax:* 705-264-7424
ebslawyers@ebslawyers.com

***Timmins*: J.P. Huot - *1**
P.O. Box 1065, 36 Maple St. South, Timmins, ON P4N 7H9
Tel: 705-267-6464; *Fax:* 705-264-3260

***Timmins*: Petersen Consulting - *1**
136 Cedar St. South, Timmins, ON P4N 2G8
Tel: 705-264-5323; *Fax:* 705-268-0300
pcmanage@nt.net

***Timmins*: Racicot, Maisonneuve, Labelle, Cooper - *6**
15 Balsam St. South, Timmins, ON P4N 2C7
Tel: 705-264-2385; *Fax:* 705-268-3949
mlclaw@ntl.sympatico.ca

***Timmins*: Riopelle Griener Professional Corporation - *8**
#202, 85 Pine St. South, Timmins, ON P4N 2K1
Tel: 705-264-9591; *Fax:* 705-264-1393
Toll-Free: 866-624-1614
www.rglaw.cahttp://www.facebook.com/#!/RiopelleGriener

***Toronto*: Aaron & Aaron - *1**
#1400, 10 King St. East, Toronto, ON M5C 1C3
Tel: 416-364-9366; *Fax:* 416-364-3818
bob@aaron.ca
www.aaron.ca

***Toronto*: G.J. Abols - *1**
#8866, 700 Bay St., Toronto, ON M5G 1Z6
Tel: 416-598-8866; *Fax:* 416-971-7656

***Toronto*: Abrams & Krochak, Professional Corporation - *2**
Also Known As: Abrams & Krochak, Canadian Immigration Lawyers
#402, 250 Merton St., Toronto, ON M4S 1B1
Tel: 416-482-3387; *Fax:* 416-482-0647
askus@akcanada.com
www.abramsandkrochak.comwww.facebook.com/AKCanada, twitter.com/AbramsKrochak

***Toronto*: Adair Morse LLP - *19**
#1800, 1 Queen St. East, Toronto, ON M5C 2W5
Tel: 416-863-1230; *Fax:* 416-863-1241
info@adairmorse.com
www.adairmorse.com

***Toronto*: G. Chalmers Adams - *1**
#100, 1255 Yonge St., Toronto, ON M4T 1W6
Tel: 416-929-7232; *Fax:* 416-929-7225
info@gcadams.on.ca

***Toronto*: Adler Bytensky - *6**
#1708, 5000 Yonge St., Toronto, ON M2N 7E9
Tel: 416-365-3151; *Fax:* 416-365-0866
www.crimlawcanada.com

***Toronto*: Advocacy Centre for the Elderly - *5**
#701, 2 Carlton St., Toronto, ON M5B 1J3
Tel: 416-598-2656; *Fax:* 416-598-7924
www.advocacycentreelderly.org

***Toronto*: Advocate Placement Ltd. - *4**
#200, 1200 Bay St., Toronto, ON M5R 2A5
Tel: 416-927-9222; *Fax:* 416-927-8772
Toll-Free: 800-461-1275
resume@advocateplacement.com
www.advocateplacement.com

** indicates number of lawyers*

***Toronto*: Affleck Greene McMurty LLP - *13**
Former Name: Kelly Affleck Greene
#200, 365 Bay St., Toronto, ON M5H 2V1
Tel: 416-360-2800; *Fax:* 416-360-5960
info@agmlawyers.com
www.agmlawyers.com

***Toronto*: Agnew, Gladstone LLP - *2**
215 Carlton St., Toronto, ON M5A 2K9
Tel: 416-964-0021; *Fax:* 416-964-0744
yagnew@agnewgladstone.com
www.agnewgladstone.com

***Toronto*: Claudio R. Aiello - *1**
#900, 920 Yonge St., Toronto, ON M4W 3C7
Tel: 416-969-9900; *Fax:* 416-969-9060
claudio@aiellolaw.ca

***Toronto*: Irving J. Aiken - *1**
#1105, 65 Queen St. West, Toronto, ON M5H 2M5
Tel: 416-947-0199; *Fax:* 416-947-0379

***Toronto*: Jerome T. Albert**
921 Manning Ave., Toronto, ON M6G 2X5
Tel: 416-535-3173

***Toronto*: Alloway & Associates - *3**
290 Lawrence Ave. West, Toronto, ON M5M 1B3
Tel: 416-971-9293; *Fax:* 416-971-9349
email@alloway.net
www.alloway.net

***Toronto*: Alpert Law Firm - *2**
#900, 1 St. Clair Ave. East, Toronto, ON M4T 2V7
Tel: 416-923-0809; *Fax:* 416-923-1549
halpert@alpertlawfirm.ca
www.alpertlawfirm.ca

***Toronto*: Harriet Altman - *1**
68 Garnier Court, Toronto, ON M2M 4C9
Tel: 416-224-5240; *Fax:* 416-224-0360
Toll-Free: 877-224-5229

***Toronto*: Sheldon L. Altman - *1**
264B Adelaide St. East, Toronto, ON M5A 1N1
Tel: 416-929-1313; *Fax:* 416-929-1316
altmansheldon@aol.com
www.sheldonaltman.com

***Toronto*: Altwerger, Baker, Weinberg - *3**
#2901, P.O. Box 2450, 2300 Yonge St., Toronto, ON M4P 1E4
Tel: 416-480-1662; *Fax:* 416-480-0017
stevea@lexpertor.com

***Toronto*: Jaikrishin R. Ambwani - *1**
#330, 100 Cowdray Ct., Toronto, ON M1S 5C8
Tel: 416-754-4404; *Fax:* 416-754-7746
jack@jackambwani.com
www.jackambwani.com

***Toronto*: Julie Evelyn Amourgis - *1**
#800, 439 University Ave., Toronto, ON M5G 1Y8
Tel: 416-504-5844; *Fax:* 416-369-1723

***Toronto*: Anderson Bourdon Burgess**
#116, 295 The West Mall, Toronto, ON M9C 4Z4
Tel: 416-621-9644; *Fax:* 416-621-9668
anderson@andersonbb.com
www.andersonbb.com

***Toronto*: Dwight Anderson - *1**
1709 Bloor St. West, Toronto, ON M6P 4E5
Tel: 416-769-3522; *Fax:* 416-769-2302
dwightanderson@rogers.com

***Toronto*: Joan Anderson - *1**
#702, 100 Alexander St., Toronto, ON M4Y 1B9
Tel: 416-929-9909; *Fax:* 416-929-2367
anderson.j@sympatico.ca

***Toronto*: Andriessen & Associates - *4**
#900, 701 Evans Ave., Toronto, ON M9C 1A3
Tel: 416-620-7020; *Fax:* 416-620-1398
info@andriessen.ca
www.andriessen.ca

***Toronto*: Philip Anisman Barrister & Solicitor - *1**
#1704, 80 Richmond St. West, Toronto, ON M5H 2A4
Tel: 416-363-4200; *Fax:* 416-363-6200

***Toronto*: Dennis Apostolides - *1**
867 Danforth Ave., Toronto, ON M4J 1L7
Tel: 416-463-1147; *Fax:* 416-463-1762
apostolides@rogers.com

***Toronto*: Jerry Applebaum - *1**
36 Covington Rd., Toronto, ON M6A 1G1
Tel: 416-785-1140

***Toronto*: Armel, Gray LLP - *5**
#500, 390 Bay St., Toronto, ON M5H 2Y2
Tel: 416-362-1400; *Fax:* 416-362-1404

***Toronto*: D.W. Arn - *1**
380 Bathurst St., Toronto, ON M5T 2S6
Tel: 416-603-3658; *Fax:* 416-603-1144

***Toronto*: Aronovitch Macaulay Rollo LLP - *21**
251 King St. East, Toronto, ON M5A 1K2
Tel: 416-369-9393; *Fax:* 416-369-0665
info@amrlaw.ca
www.amrlaw.com

***Toronto*: Ara P. Arzumanian - *1**
Former Name: Levitt, Hoffman
#2200, 181 University Ave., Toronto, ON M5H 3M7
Tel: 416-777-1400; *Fax:* 416-777-1999
ara@businessandtechlaw.com
www.businessandtechlaw.com

***Toronto*: Harvey Ash - *1**
#900, 5799 Yonge St., Toronto, ON M2M 3V3
Tel: 416-250-0080; *Fax:* 416-225-1124
harveyash@lawyer.ca

***Toronto*: William Ash - *1**
#801, 55 Eglinton Ave. East, Toronto, ON M4P 1G8
Tel: 416-486-8751; *Fax:* 416-486-8789
willash@bellnet.ca

***Toronto*: Ashbourne & Caskey - *1**
2077 Lawrence Ave. West, Toronto, ON M9N 1H7
Tel: 416-247-6677; *Fax:* 416-247-3519

***Toronto*: Atherton Barristers - *1**
#1604, 55 University Ave., Toronto, ON M5J 2H7
Tel: 416-365-1030; *Fax:* 416-946-1619
Toll-Free: 866-237-1030
bcatherton@ablaw.com
www.athertonbarristers.com

***Toronto*: S.J. AvRuskin - *1**
66 Charles St. East., Toronto, ON M4Y 2R3
Tel: 416-922-4147; *Fax:* 416-922-8022

***Toronto*: Aylesworth LLP - *33**
Also Known As: Aylesworth
Ernst & Young Tower, TD Centre, P.O. Box 124, 222 Bay St., 18th Fl., Toronto, ON M5K 1H1
Tel: 416-777-0101; *Fax:* 416-865-1398
ekay@aylaw.com
www.aylesworth.com

***Toronto*: Denise Badley - *1**
#2, 2069 Danforth Ave., 2nd Fl., Toronto, ON M4C 1J8
Tel: 416-690-6195; *Fax:* 416-690-6271
dbadleylaw@rogers.com

***Toronto*: J. Waldo Baerg - *1**
#506, 372 Bay St., Toronto, ON M5H 2W9
Tel: 416-366-3705; *Fax:* 416-366-0157
waldobaerg@on.aibn.com

***Toronto*: Baker & Company - *4**
#3300, 130 Adelaide St. West, Toronto, ON M5H 3P5
Tel: 416-777-0100; *Fax:* 416-366-3992
info@bakerlawyers.com
www.bakerlawyers.com

***Toronto*: Baker & McKenzie LLP - *51**
#2100, Brookfield Place, P.O. Box 874, 181 Bay St., Toronto, ON M5J 2T3
Tel: 416-863-1221; *Fax:* 416-863-6275
www.bakernet.com

***Toronto*: Baker Schneider Ruggiero LLP - *8**
#1000, 120 Adelaide St. West, Toronto, ON M5H 3V1
Tel: 416-363-2211; *Fax:* 416-363-0645

***Toronto*: Gordon R. Baker, Q.C. - *1**
#1440, Exchange Tower, P.O. Box 426, 130 King St. West, Toronto, ON M5X 1E3
Tel: 416-365-7203; *Fax:* 416-365-7204
gord@gordbaker.com
www.gordbaker.com

***Toronto*: J. Anthony Baker - *1**
500 Danforth Ave., Toronto, ON M4K 1P6
Tel: 416-463-4411; *Fax:* 416-463-4562
baker@tonybakerlaw.com
www.tonybakerlaw.com

***Toronto*: Ahmad N. Baksh - *1**
#307, 1280 Finch Ave. West, Toronto, ON M3J 3K6
Tel: 416-667-1922; *Fax:* 416-667-0304
anbaksh@bellnet.ca

***Toronto*: John M. Banfill Q.C. - *1**
#300, 133 Berkeley St., Toronto, ON M5A 2X1
Tel: 416-365-0019; *Fax:* 416-365-0022
jmbanfill@bellnet.ca

***Toronto*: Banks & Starkman - *2**
#310, 200 Ronson Dr., Toronto, ON M9W 5Z9
Tel: 416-243-3394; *Fax:* 416-243-9692
lbanks@banksandstarkman.com
www.banksandstarkman.com

***Toronto*: J.R. Barrs - *1**
23 Bedford Road, Toronto, ON M5R 2J9
Tel: 416-366-6466; *Fax:* 416-364-2308

***Toronto*: Jacqueline R. Bart - *1**
#2200, Law Chambers, ING Tower, 181 University Ave., Toronto, ON M5H 3M7
Tel: 416-601-1346; *Fax:* 416-601-1357
jbart@canadianrelocationlaw.com
www.canadianrelocationlaw.com

***Toronto*: Basman, Smith - *19**
111 Richmond St. West, 8th Floor, Toronto, ON M5H 2G4
Tel: 416-365-0300; *Fax:* 416-365-9276
Toll-Free: 877-262-0001
info@basmansmith.com
www.basmansmith.com

***Toronto*: Bastedo, Stewart, Smith**
#1800, 180 Dundas St. West, Toronto, ON M5G 1Z8
Tel: 416-595-1916; *Fax:* 416-596-7538

***Toronto*: Batcher, Wasserman & Associates - *2**
#500, 718 Wilson Ave., Toronto, ON M3K 1E2
Tel: 416-635-6300; *Fax:* 416-635-6376
Toll-Free: 877-813-0820

***Toronto*: Bates Barristers - *4**
34 King Street East, 12th Floor, Toronto, ON M5C 2X8
Tel: 416-869-9898; *Fax:* 416-869-9405
info@batesbarristers.com
www.batesbarristers.com

***Toronto*: Beard, Winter - *47**
#701, 130 Adelaide St. West, Toronto, ON M5H 2K4
Tel: 416-593-5555; *Fax:* 416-593-7760
info@beardwinter.com
www.beardwinter.com

***Toronto*: Beber & Associates - *2**
#2900, 390 Bay St., Toronto, ON M5H 2Y2
Tel: 416-867-2280; *Fax:* 416-869-0321
www.beber.ca

***Toronto*: Sandra Bebris - *1**
#300, 1370 Don Mills Rd., Toronto, ON M3B 3N7
Tel: 416-510-1324; *Fax:* 416-441-0591
bebris@pathcom.com

***Toronto*: Steven Bellissimo - *1**
#1200, 439 University Ave., Toronto, ON M5G 1Y8
Tel: 416-362-6437; *Fax:* 416-972-9940
steve@sblaw.ca

***Toronto*: Bellmore & Moore - *5**
#1600, 393 University Ave., Toronto, ON M5G 1E6
Tel: 416-581-1818; *Fax:* 416-581-1279
www.bellmoreandmoore.com

***Toronto*: Belmont, Fine & Associates - *2**
#601, 1120 Finch Ave. West, Toronto, ON M3J 3H7
Tel: 416-661-2066; *Fax:* 416-661-2116
belmontfine@yahoo.com
www.belmontfine.com

***Toronto*: Bennett & Company - *2**
#1500, 151 Yonge Street, Toronto, ON M5C 2W7
Tel: 416-363-8688; *Fax:* 416-363-8083
bennett@ican.net
www.bennettonbankruptcy.ca

** indicates number of lawyers*

***Toronto*: Bennett Best Burn LLP - *12**
#1700, 150 York St., Toronto, ON M5H 3S5
Tel: 416-362-3400; *Fax:* 416-362-2211
info@bbburn.com
www.bbburn.com

***Toronto*: Benson Percival Brown - *17**
#800, 250 Dundas St. West, Toronto, ON M5T 2Z6
Tel: 416-977-9777; *Fax:* 416-977-1241
www.bensonpercival.com

***Toronto*: Bereskin & Parr - *55**
Scotia Plaza, 40 King St. West, 40th Fl., Toronto, ON M5H 3Y2
Tel: 416-364-7311; *Fax:* 416-361-1398
Toll-Free: 888-364-7311
info@bereskinparr.com
www.bereskinparr.com

***Toronto*: Bergel & Edson - *7**
#501, 1018 Finch Ave. West, Toronto, ON M3J 3L5
Tel: 416-663-2211; *Fax:* 416-663-2348
Toll-Free: 866-492-3743
www.bergeledson.com

***Toronto*: Max Berger Professional Law Corporation - *2**
#207, 1033 Bay St., Toronto, ON M5S 3A5
Tel: 416-969-9263; *Fax:* 416-969-9098
max@maxberger.ca
www.maxberger.ca

***Toronto*: Berkow, Cohen LLP - *6**
#400, 141 Adelaide St. West, Toronto, ON M5H 3L5
Tel: 416-364-4900; *Fax:* 416-364-3865
jberkow@berkowcohen.com
www.berkowcohen.com

***Toronto*: Bradley F. Berns - *1**
#902, 505 Consumers Rd., Toronto, ON M2J 4V8
Tel: 416-490-6456; *Fax:* 416-490-6439

***Toronto*: Bersenas Jacobsen Chouest Thomson Blackburn LLP - *10**
#201, 33 Yonge St., Toronto, ON M5E 1G4
Tel: 416-982-3800; *Fax:* 416-982-3801
info@lexcanada.com
www.lexcanada.com

***Toronto*: Myer Betel - *1**
7 Farrington Dr., Toronto, ON M2L 2B4
Tel: 416-447-4333; *Fax:* 416-447-3773
mbctel@rogers.com

***Toronto*: Lynn Bevan Professional Corporation - *1**
60 Oriole Rd., Toronto, ON M4V 2G1
Tel: 416-955-0400; *Fax:* 416-955-0410
lbevan@lynnbevan.com
www.lynnbevan.com

***Toronto*: Bhatia, Minipreet - *1**
#405, 3601 Victoria Park Ave., Toronto, ON M1W 3Y3
Tel: 416-493-1727; *Fax:* 416-756-3663

***Toronto*: Bigelow, Hendy - *4**
#200, 789 Don Mills Rd., Toronto, ON M3C 1T5
Tel: 416-429-3110; *Fax:* 416-429-3057
www.bigelowhendy.com

***Toronto*: Birchall Northey - *2**
533 College Street, Toronto, ON M6G 1A8
Tel: 416-860-1212; *Fax:* 416-860-1827
admin@birchallnorthey.com
www.birchallnorthey.com

***Toronto*: Peter Bird - *1**
31 Prince Arthur Dr., Toronto, ON M5R 1B2
Tel: 416-929-9408; *Fax:* 416-960-5456
peterbird@on.aibn.com

***Toronto*: Birenbaum & Bernstein - *2**
#104, 2801 Keele St., Toronto, ON M37 2G6
Tel: 416-633-3720; *Fax:* 416-633-4546

***Toronto*: Birenbaum, Steinberg, Landau, Savin & Colraine LLP - *9**
#1000, 33 Bloor St. East, Toronto, ON M4W 3H1
Tel: 416-961-4100; *Fax:* 416-961-2531
birenbaum@bslsc.com
www.bslsc.com

***Toronto*: Donald H. Bitter, Q.C. - *1**
#407, 600 Church St., Toronto, ON M4Y 2E7
Tel: 416-360-4357; *Fax:* 416-463-8259
notguilty@rogers.com

***Toronto*: Black, Sutherland LLP - *11**
Former Name: Black, Sutherland & Crabbe
#3425, P.O. Box 34, 130 Adelaide St. West, Toronto, ON M5H 3P5
Tel: 416-361-1500; *Fax:* 416-361-1674
Toll-Free: 866-902-7557
info@blacksutherland.com
www.blacksutherland.com

***Toronto*: Harry Blaier - *1**
#1800, Madison Centre, 4950 Yonge St., Toronto, ON M2N 6K1
Tel: 416-224-0200; *Fax:* 416-224-0758
hblaier@torlaw.com

***Toronto*: Edith M. Blake - *1**
75 The Donway West, Toronto, ON M3C 2E9
Tel: 416-445-0310; *Fax:* 416-445-0316

***Toronto*: Jonathan A. Bliss - *1**
370 Bloor St. East, Toronto, ON M4W 3M6
Tel: 416-927-9000; *Fax:* 416-927-9069
jonbliss@sympatico.ca

***Toronto*: Bloom & Lanys - *1**
#100, 250 Roehampton Ave., Toronto, ON M4P 1R9
Tel: 416-486-9913; *Fax:* 416-485-6054
Toll-Free: 877-835-7658
barb@bloom-lanys.com

***Toronto*: Joseph L. Bloomenfeld - *1**
#2110, 120 Adelaide St. West, Toronto, ON M5H 2C9
Tel: 416-363-7315; *Fax:* 416-363-7697

***Toronto*: Blouin, Dunn LLP - *8**
#1800, 155 University Ave., Toronto, ON M5H 3B7
Tel: 416-365-7888; *Fax:* 416-365-7988
info@blouindunn.com
www.blouindunn.com

***Toronto*: Bluestein & Pearlstein LLP - *3**
#1100, 121 King St. West, Toronto, ON M5H 3T9
Tel: 416-363-8844; *Fax:* 416-363-8807

***Toronto*: Blumberg Segal LLP - *6**
#1202, 390 Bay St., Toronto, ON M5H 2Y2
Tel: 416-361-1982; *Fax:* 416-363-8451
info@blumbergs.ca
www.blumbergs.ca

***Toronto*: Carla L. Bocci - *1**
#1917, 25 Adelaide St. East, Toronto, ON M5C 3A1
Tel: 416-365-2961; *Fax:* 416-365-1859

***Toronto*: Bodnaruk & Capone - *2**
#416, P.O. Box 49, 370 King St. West, Toronto, ON M5V 1J9
Tel: 416-593-7000; *Fax:* 416-593-5359

***Toronto*: Bogart Robertson & Chu - *4**
#1608, 141 Adelaide St. West, Toronto, ON M5H 3L5
Tel: 416-601-1991; *Fax:* 416-601-0006
contact@brclaw.com

***Toronto*: G.H. Bomza - *1**
#2303, 180 Dundas St. West, Toronto, ON M5G 1Z8
Tel: 416-598-2244; *Fax:* 416-598-3830
rosehallmgmt@bellnet.ca

***Toronto*: Sharon G.H. Bond - *1**
#100, 110 Eglinton Ave. West, Toronto, ON M4R 1A3
Tel: 416-483-5354; *Fax:* 416-483-5360
sghb@sharonbondlaw.com

***Toronto*: Ira E. Book - *1**
#200, 85 Scarsdale Rd., Toronto, ON M3B 2R2
Tel: 416-447-2665; *Fax:* 416-447-0066
ira@irabook.com

***Toronto*: Norman H.R. Borski, Q.C. - *1**
#201, 2256B Bloor St. West, Toronto, ON M6S 1N6
Tel: 416-766-2441

***Toronto*: Y.R. Botiuk, Q.C. - *2**
#212, 2323 Bloor St. West, Toronto, ON M6S 4W1
Tel: 416-763-4333; *Fax:* 416-763-0613

***Toronto*: Bougadis, Chang LLP - *3**
#600, 360 Bay St., Toronto, ON M5H 2V6
Tel: 416-703-2402; *Fax:* 416-703-2406
office@bcbarristers.com
www.bcbarristers.com

***Toronto*: T. Sam Boutzouvis - *1**
#501, 326 Richmond St. West, Toronto, ON M5V 1V3
Tel: 416-591-0111

***Toronto*: Mary E.E. Boyce - *1**
69 Elm St., Toronto, ON M5G 1H2
Tel: 416-591-7588; *Fax:* 416-971-9092

***Toronto*: Boyle & Co. LLP, Solicitors - *5**
#1900, 25 Adelaide St. East, Toronto, ON M5C 3A1
Tel: 416-867-8800; *Fax:* 416-867-8833
www.boyleco.com

***Toronto*: P.G. Bradley - *1**
1051 Tapscott Rd., Toronto, ON M1X 1A1
Tel: 416-298-0066; *Fax:* 416-299-8008
patrick@runnymede-dev.com

***Toronto*: L.A. Braithwaite, C.M., O.Ont., Q.C. - *1**
250 Wincott Dr., Toronto, ON M9R 2R5
Tel: 416-249-2288; *Fax:* 416-249-2280

***Toronto*: Brannan Meiklejohn Barristers - *2**
262 Avenue Rd., Toronto, ON M4V 2G7
Tel: 416-926-3797; *Fax:* 416-926-3712

***Toronto*: Brans, Lehun, Baldwin - *8**
#2401, 120 Adelaide St. West, Toronto, ON M5H 1T1
Tel: 416-601-1040; *Fax:* 416-601-0655
info@blbcdnlaw.com

***Toronto*: G.K.C. Braund, Q.C. - *1**
#204, 3333 Bayview Ave., Toronto, ON M2K 1G4
Tel: 416-223-0862; *Fax:* 416-223-4073

***Toronto*: Brauti Thorning LLP - *8**
#1800, 151 Yonge St., Toronto, ON M5C 2W7
Tel: 416-362-4567; *Fax:* 416-362-8410
www.btlegal.ca

***Toronto*: Philip E. Brent - *1**
#1160, 36 Toronto St., Toronto, ON M5C 2C5
Tel: 416-203-1449; *Fax:* 416-203-1772
brentayr@allstream.net

***Toronto*: Bresver, Grossman, Scheininger & Chapman - *5**
#2900, 390 Bay St., Toronto, ON M5H 2Y2
Tel: 416-869-0366; *Fax:* 416-869-0321

***Toronto*: Daniel J. Brodsky - *1**
11 Prince Arthur Ave., Toronto, ON M5R 1B2
Tel: 416-964-2618; *Fax:* 416-964-8305
brodsky@interlog.com

***Toronto*: Brown & Burnes - *6**
#1400, 390 Bay St., Toronto, ON M5H 2Y2
Tel: 416-366-7927; *Fax:* 416-363-9602
info@brownburnes.com
www.brownburnes.com

***Toronto*: Brown & Cohen Communications & Public Affairs Inc. - *2**
321 Brooke Ave., Toronto, ON M5M 2L4
Tel: 416-484-1132; *Fax:* 416-783-8177
info@brown-cohen.com
www.brown-cohen.com

***Toronto*: Brown & Korte Barristers - *12**
Former Name: Iacono Brown
130 Adelaide St. West, 31st Fl., Toronto, ON M5H 3P5
Tel: 416-869-0123; *Fax:* 416-869-0271
lawyers@brownandkorte.ca
www.brownandkorte.com

***Toronto*: Kenneth J. Brown - *1**
45 Mogul Dr., Toronto, ON M2H 2M8
Tel: 416-499-8005; *Fax:* 416-499-8048
k.j.brown@sympatico.ca

***Toronto*: M.H. Brown - *1**
38 Berwick Ave., Toronto, ON M5P 1H1
Tel: 416-487-5122; *Fax:* 416-487-5168
mel@browngroup.net

***Toronto*: Brown, Peck & Lubelsky - *4**
5287 Yonge St., Toronto, ON M2N 5R3
Tel: 416-223-8811; *Fax:* 416-223-8485

***Toronto*: G.J. Bruner - *1**
167 Danforth Ave., Toronto, ON M4K 1N2
Tel: 416-461-0983; *Fax:* 416-462-3347

***Toronto*: Anthony G. Bryant - *1**
#1706, 51 York Mills Road, Toronto, ON M2P 1B6
Tel: 416-927-7441; *Fax:* 416-413-0230
tbryant@istar.ca

** indicates number of lawyers*

Toronto: **Frederic L. Buckland - *1**
Former Name: Buckland Werbowys
1199 The Queensway, Toronto, ON M8Z 1R7
Tel: 416-236-0906; *Fax:* 416-236-1365
buckland@interlog.com

Toronto: **Buie Cohen LLP - *2**
Former Name: McPhail Buie & Cohen
#205, 250 Merton St., Toronto, ON M4S 1B1
Tel: 416-869-3400; *Fax:* 416-703-6522
cmbuie@buiecohen.com

Toronto: **J.J. Burke - *1**
#302, 2405 Lakeshore Blvd. West, Toronto, ON M8V 1C6
Tel: 416-252-9101;
jjburke@bellnet.ca

Toronto: **Harry R. Burkman - *1**
#2810, P.O. Box 129, 1 First Canadian Pl., Toronto, ON M5X 1A4
Tel: 416-364-3831; *Fax:* 416-364-3832
hburkman@burkman.com
www.burkman.com

Toronto: **Burnett & Jacobson - *3**
48 St. Clair Ave. West, Toronto, ON M4V 3C9
Tel: 416-922-8710; *Fax:* 416-964-5840

Toronto: **Burstein, Unger - *2**
Former Name: Paul Burstein & Associate
P.O. Box 180, 127 John St., Toronto, ON M5V 2E2
Tel: 416-204-1825; *Fax:* 416-204-1849
paul@127john.com

Toronto: **Bernard Burton - *1**
#410, 120 Carlton St., Toronto, ON M5A 4K2
Tel: 416-922-1263; *Fax:* 416-922-1963
bernardburton@chmlegal.com

Toronto: **Bury & Tarka - *2**
#1515, 390 Bay St., Toronto, ON M5H 2Y2
Tel: 416-363-9966; *Fax:* 416-363-4499

Toronto: **Bussin & Bussin - *3**
#1822, 181 University Ave., Toronto, ON M5H 3M7
Tel: 416-364-4925; *Fax:* 416-868-1818
bruce@bussinlaw.com

Toronto: **Paul Calarco - *1**
#1500, 700 Bay Street, Toronto, ON M5G 1Z6
Tel: 416-598-1948; *Fax:* 416-596-7629
pcalarco@on.aibn.com
www.paulcalarco.com

Toronto: **CaleyWray - *10**
#1205, 111 Richmond St. West, Toronto, ON M5H 2G4
Tel: 416-366-3763; *Fax:* 416-366-3293
mail@caleywray.com
www.caleywray.com

Toronto: **Campbell Strategies Inc. - *3**
95 Wellington St. West, Toronto, ON M5J 2N7
Tel: 416-368-7353; *Fax:* 416-368-9848
info@campbelstrategies.com
www.campbellstrategies.com

Toronto: **John R. Campbell, Q.C. - *2**
5 Douglas Crescent, Toronto, ON M4W 2E6
Tel: 416-924-9066; *Fax:* 416-961-0510
hkljrc@pathcom.com

Toronto: **G.H. Cancilla - *1**
#506, 372 Bay St., Toronto, ON M5H 2W9
Tel: 416-366-9504; *Fax:* 416-628-6628
ghc@cancillaw.com

Toronto: **John Cannings, Barristers - *5**
#400, 425 University Ave., Toronto, ON M5G 1T6
Tel: 416-591-0703; *Fax:* 416-591-0710
info@jcannings.com
www.jcannings.com/

Toronto: **Ruth Canton - *1**
2489 Bloor St. West, Toronto, ON M6S 1R6
Tel: 416-769-5759; *Fax:* 416-769-3132
Toll-Free: 888-838-7432

Toronto: **Rochelle F. Cantor - *1**
180 Spadina Rd., Toronto, ON M5R 2T8
Tel: 416-861-1625; *Fax:* 416-861-1466

Toronto: **Capp, Shupak - *5**
#1703, 2 St. Clair Ave. West, Toronto, ON M4V 1L5
Tel: 416-944-2313; *Fax:* 416-323-0697
shupak@cappshupak.com
www.marilynshupak.com

Toronto: **Cappell Parker LLP, Barristers & Solicitors - *2**
#1200, Toronto-Dominion Centre, 95 Wellington St. West, Toronto, ON M5J 2Z9
Tel: 416-367-0900; *Fax:* 416-367-0901
fecappell@cappell.com
www.cappell.com

Toronto: **Cappellacci DaRoza LLP - *2**
#500, 462 Wellington St. West, Toronto, ON M5V 1E3
Tel: 416-955-9500; *Fax:* 416-955-9503
ecappellacci@capplaw.ca
www.capplaw.ca

Toronto: **Caramanna, Friedberg LLP - *5**
#405, Lucliff Place, P.O. Box 144, 700 Bay St., Toronto, ON M5G 1Z6
Tel: 416-924-5969; *Fax:* 416-924-9973
info@cflaw.ca
www.cflaw.ca

Toronto: **Michael W. Caroline - *1**
#803, Waterpark Place, 10 Bay St., Toronto, ON M5J 2R8
Tel: 416-203-2250; *Fax:* 416-203-2280
mwc@michaelcaroline.com
www.michaelcaroline.com

Toronto: **John S.H. Carriere - *1**
#600, 330 Bay St., Toronto, ON M5H 2S8
Tel: 416-363-5594; *Fax:* 416-363-8492
johncarriere@bellnet.ca

Toronto: **C. Anthony Carroll - *1**
#1807, 8 King St. East, Toronto, ON M5C 1B5
Tel: 416-361-0522; *Fax:* 416-361-0248
carrollt@istar.ca

Toronto: **Carson, Gross, Christie, Knudsen - *5**
#600, 10 Carlson Ct., Toronto, ON M9W 6L2
Tel: 416-361-0900; *Fax:* 416-361-3459
info@cgck.com

Toronto: **G.M. Cass - *1**
Also Known As: Garry Cass
#302, 1200 Sheppard Ave. East, Toronto, ON M2K 2S5
Tel: 416-767-2277; *Fax:* 416-491-0273
www.garrycass.com

Toronto: **Ceresney, Weisberg Associates - *2**
#202, 4651 Sheppard Ave. East, Toronto, ON M1S 3V4
Tel: 416-291-7701; *Fax:* 416-291-1766

Toronto: **Chaitons LLP - *20**
Former Name: Chaiton & Chaiton
185 Sheppard Ave. West, Toronto, ON M2N 1M9
Tel: 416-222-8888; *Fax:* 416-222-8402
info@chaitons.com
www.chaiton.com

Toronto: **Chang & Boos - *5**
#1100, 77 Bloor St. West, Toronto, ON M5S 1M2
Tel: 416-362-6632; *Fax:* 416-362-1125
hchang@americanlaw.com
www.americanlaw.com

Toronto: **Evan Chang - *1**
#203, 1315 Lawrence Ave. East, Toronto, ON M3A 3R3
Tel: 416-449-1214; *Fax:* 416-449-9396
evan.c@sympatico.ca

Toronto: **Peter P. Chang - *1**
#2300, 2025 Sheppard Ave. East, Toronto, ON M2J 1V6
Tel: 416-497-1575; *Fax:* 416-497-2261
peterchang@rogers.com

Toronto: **Beverly C. Chapin-Hill - *1**
16 Neville Park Blvd., Toronto, ON M4E 3P6
Tel: 416-690-1832; *Fax:* 416-698-6041
bev@chapinandchapin.ca
www.chapinandchapin.com

Toronto: **Chapnick & Associates - *4**
228 Carlton St., Toronto, ON M5A 2L1
Tel: 416-968-2160; *Fax:* 416-975-9338
www.chapnickassociates.com

Toronto: **Chappell, Bushell, Stewart LLP - *8**
#3310, 20 Queen St. West, Toronto, ON M5H 3R3
Tel: 416-351-0005; *Fax:* 416-351-0002
info@cbslaw.to
www.chappellbushellstewart.com

Toronto: **Office of the Children's Lawyer - *23**
393 University Ave., 14th Fl., Toronto, ON M5G 1W9
Tel: 416-314-8000; *Fax:* 416-314-8050
www.attorneygeneral.jus.gov.on.ca/english/family/ocl/

Toronto: **Ronald W. Chisholm, Q.C. - *1**
#510, 330 University Ave., Toronto, ON M5G 1R7
Tel: 416-586-0777; *Fax:* 416-586-0267

Toronto: **Chitiz Pathak LLP - *15**
#1600, 320 Bay St. Ave., Toronto, ON M5H 4A6
Tel: 416-368-6200; *Fax:* 416-368-0300
info@chitizpathak.com
www.chitizpathak.com

Toronto: **Christopher E. Chop - *1**
#2000, 1 Queen St. East, Toronto, ON M5C 2W5
Tel: 416-601-4159; *Fax:* 416-601-0206
choplaw@gmail.com

Toronto: **Christies - *8**
Former Name: Christie, Saccucci, Matthews, Caskie & Chilco
#301, Confederation Sq., 20 Richmond St. East, Toronto, ON M5C 2R9
Tel: 416-367-0680; *Fax:* 416-367-0429
information@christie-lawyers.com
www.christie-lawyers.com

Toronto: **B.N. Christoff - *1**
#304, 3335 Yonge St., Toronto, ON M4N 2M1
Tel: 416-482-0990; *Fax:* 416-482-6511

Toronto: **Cipollone & Cipollone Barristers - *1**
#2100, 130 Adelaide St. West, Toronto, ON M5H 3P5
Tel: 416-368-5366; *Fax:* 416-368-5361

Toronto: **Dino J. Cirone - *1**
#2, 2084 Danforth Ave., Toronto, ON M4C 1J9
Tel: 416-423-8515; *Fax:* 416-423-4971

Toronto: **Civicworks Consulting Group Inc. - *1**
246 Sandringham Dr., Toronto, ON M3H 1G3
Tel: 416-587-7053; *Fax:* 416-636-0134
bobbywalman@rogers.com

Toronto: **S.G. Clapp - *1**
18 Erskine Ave., Toronto, ON M4P 1Y2
Tel: 416-484-4840; *Fax:* 416-484-0821
stanleyclapp@on.aibn.com

Toronto: **Deta J. Clark - *1**
#402, 5075 Yonge St., Toronto, ON M2N 6C6
Tel: 416-733-3135

Toronto: **Clark, Farb, Fiksel - *6**
188 Avenue Rd., Toronto, ON M5J 2J1
Tel: 416-599-7761; *Fax:* 416-324-4220
www.cfflaw.com

Toronto: **Clarke, Freeman, Miller & Ryan - *1**
1863 Danforth Ave., Toronto, ON M4C 1J3
Tel: 416-698-9323; *Fax:* 416-698-9110

Toronto: **Clean 16 Environmental Technologies Corp. - *1**
#6134, 2100 Bloor St. West, Toronto, ON M6S 5A5
Tel: 416-352-1973; *Fax:* 416-352-1973
info@clean16.com

Toronto: **L. Peter Clyne - *1**
#1709, 5650 Yonge St., Toronto, ON M2M 4G3
Tel: 416-922-0864; *Fax:* 416-922-6856
clynelaw@on.aibn.com

Toronto: **Robert G. Coates - *1**
#307, 120 Carlton St., Toronto, ON M5A 4K2
Tel: 416-925-6490; *Fax:* 416-925-4492
robert@rgcoates.com
www.rgcoates.com

Toronto: **Cohen & Associate - *2**
#801, 1 St. Clair Ave. East, Toronto, ON M4T 2V7
Tel: 416-323-0907; *Fax:* 416-324-8053
cohen@bellnet.ca

** indicates number of lawyers*

***Toronto*: M.V. Cohen - *1**
111 Richmond Street West, Toronto, ON M5H 2G4
Tel: 416-363-8366;
mvcohen2002@yahoo.ca

***Toronto*: Cohen, Sabsay LLP - *4**
#500, 350 Bay St., Toronto, ON M5H 2S6
Tel: 416-364-7436; *Fax:* 416-364-0083
cohen@cohensabsay.com
www.cohensabsay.com

***Toronto*: David Cohn - *1**
#301, 481 University Ave., Toronto, ON M5G 2E9
Tel: 416-777-1100; *Fax:* 416-364-2308

***Toronto*: John Collins - *1**
#400, 357 Bay St., Toronto, ON M5H 2R7
Tel: 416-364-9006; *Fax:* 416-862-7911
john.collins@on.aibn.com

***Toronto*: Conway Davis Gryski - *5**
#601, 130 Adelaide St. West, Toronto, ON M5H 3P5
Tel: 416-214-4554; *Fax:* 416-214-9915
Toll-Free: 877-559-4554
contactus@cdglaw.net
www.conwaydavisgryski.com

***Toronto*: Conway Kleinman Kornhauser LLP - *3**
Former Name: Conway Kornhauser & Gotlieb
#1102, 390 Bay St., Toronto, ON M5H 2Y2
Tel: 416-368-5400; *Fax:* 416-368-5454

***Toronto*: Cooper & Cooper - *1**
#208, 133 Richmond St. West, Toronto, ON M5H 2L3
Tel: 416-362-6459; *Fax:* 416-362-3139

***Toronto*: Allen M. Cooper - *1**
#101, 15 Elm St., Toronto, ON M5G 1H1
Tel: 416-977-8070; *Fax:* 416-977-8151

***Toronto*: Daniel Cooper Law Office - *1**
Former Name: Cooper Kingston LLP
193 Heath St. West, Toronto, ON M4V 1V3
Tel: 416-925-3772; *Fax:* 416-925-3457
daniel@dcooper.com

***Toronto*: Kirk J. Cooper - *1**
#308, 120 Carlton St., Toronto, ON M5A 4K2
Tel: 416-923-4277; *Fax:* 416-923-4144
kirkcooperlaw@rogers.com
www.kirkcooperlaw.com

***Toronto*: Cooper, Kleinman - *2**
3 Rowanwood Ave., Toronto, ON M4W 1Y5
Tel: 416-867-1400; *Fax:* 416-867-1873
gwcooper@cooperkleinman.ca

***Toronto*: Morris Cooper - *1**
99 Yorkville Ave., Toronto, ON M5R 3K5
Tel: 416-961-2626; *Fax:* 416-961-4000
cooper@cooperlaw.ca

***Toronto*: Robert A. Cooper - *1**
#208, 4211 Yonge St., Toronto, ON M2P 2A9
Tel: 416-222-8115; *Fax:* 416-222-8505

***Toronto*: Copeland Duncan - *2**
31 Prince Arthur Ave., Toronto, ON M5R 1B2
Tel: 416-964-8126; *Fax:* 416-960-5456
paulcope9@yahoo.com

***Toronto*: Jack Copelovici - *1**
Former Name: Copelovici & Hanuk
#204, 1220 Sheppard Ave. East, Toronto, ON M2K 2S5
Tel: 416-494-0910; *Fax:* 416-494-5480
jack@copel-law.com

***Toronto*: Barry S. Corbin - *1**
#2000, 393 University Ave., Toronto, ON M5G 1E6
Tel: 416-593-4200; *Fax:* 416-593-1352
barry.corbin@corbinestateslaw.com
www.corbinestateslaw.com

***Toronto*: Costa Law Firm - *5**
Former Name: David Costa & Associate
1015 Bloor St. West, Toronto, ON M6H 1M1
Tel: 416-535-6329; *Fax:* 416-535-4735
davidcosta@bell.blackberry.net
www.costalawfirm.ca

***Toronto*: Fernando D. Costa - *1**
#200, 1112 Dundas St. West, Toronto, ON M6J 1X2
Tel: 416-534-6357; *Fax:* 416-534-6219
fd.costa@bellnet.ca

***Toronto*: Costigan Horgan - *2**
#410, 120 Carlton St., Toronto, ON M5A 4K2
Tel: 416-922-8611; *Fax:* 416-922-1963
acostigan@chmlegal.com

***Toronto*: Counsel Public Affairs Inc. - *5**
#1606, 95 St. Clair West, Toronto, ON M4V 1N6
Tel: 416-920-0716; *Fax:* 416-352-6069
reception@counselpa.com
www.counselpa.com

***Toronto*: D.B. Cousins - *1**
#203, 425 University Ave., Toronto, ON M5G 1T6
Tel: 416-977-8871; *Fax:* 416-599-8075
david.b.cousins@bellnet.ca

***Toronto*: Coutts, Crane, Ingram - *7**
#700, 480 University Ave., Toronto, ON M5G 1V2
Tel: 416-977-0956; *Fax:* 416-977-5331
info@couttscrane.com
www.couttscrane.com

***Toronto*: Cowan & Cremer - *2**
#216, 214 King Street West, Toronto, ON M5H 3S6
Tel: 416-322-3671; *Fax:* 416-971-5520
cowancremer@sympatico.ca
www.cowancremer.com

***Toronto*: Ronald Cowitz - *1**
#308, 344 Bloor St. West, Toronto, ON M5S 3A7
Tel: 416-944-9594

***Toronto*: Christopher G. Cox - *1**
#209, 1711 McCowan Rd., Toronto, ON M1S 2Y3
Tel: 416-447-4274; *Fax:* 416-823-3215
cgcoxlaw@hotmail.com

***Toronto*: Cozen O'Connor - *8**
Former Name: Poss & Halfnight
#2000, 1 Queen St. East, Toronto, ON M5C 2W5
Tel: 416-361-3200; *Fax:* 416-361-1405

***Toronto*: F.H. Cremer - *1**
#201, 1593 Wilson Ave., Toronto, ON M3L 1A5
Tel: 416-244-5575; *Fax:* 416-247-3844

***Toronto*: Crewe & Marks - *2**
74 Riverdale Ave., Toronto, ON M4K 1C3
Tel: 416-967-9933; *Fax:* 416-967-9933
nsc@riv.com

***Toronto*: Frank D. Crewe - *2**
#500, 70 Bond St., Toronto, ON M5B 1X3
Tel: 416-362-2202; *Fax:* 416-363-9135

***Toronto*: Howard Crosner - *1**
#1400, 10 King St. East, Toronto, ON M5C 1C3
Tel: 416-947-0455; *Fax:* 416-364-3818
crosner77@eol.ca
www.crosner.com

***Toronto*: Leroy A. Crosse - *1**
#203, 705 Lawrence Ave. West, Toronto, ON M6A 1B4
Tel: 416-785-8338; *Fax:* 416-785-9369

***Toronto*: Crum-Ewing & Poliacik - *2**
56 Sheppard Ave. West, Toronto, ON M2N 1M2
Tel: 416-733-9292; *Fax:* 416-733-9654
poliacik@ceplaw.ca

***Toronto*: Cummings Cooper Schusheim & Berliner LLP - *6**
#408, 4110 Yonge St., Toronto, ON M2P 2B5
Tel: 416-512-9500; *Fax:* 416-512-9501
info@ccsb-law.com
www.ccsb-law.com

***Toronto*: Gino A.J. Cundari - *1**
1179 St. Clair Ave. West, Toronto, ON M6E 1B5
Tel: 416-654-9000; *Fax:* 416-654-6688

***Toronto*: Peter Cusimano, Barrister & Solicitor - *1**
Former Name: Cusimano & Cusimano
#100, 332 Sheppard Ave. East, Toronto, ON M2N 3B4
Tel: 416-222-0588; *Fax:* 416-222-0239
lawyer@cusimano.com
www.cusimano.com

***Toronto*: J. Jerome Cusmariu - *1**
1310 Dundas St. West, Toronto, ON M6J 1Y1
Tel: 416-533-1173; *Fax:* 416-533-0761
jcusmariu@on.aibn.com

***Toronto*: E.H. Cutler - *1**
#18A, 156 Duncan Mill Rd., Toronto, ON M3B 3N2
Tel: 416-449-4962; *Fax:* 416-449-5107
ernestcutler@bellnet.ca

***Toronto*: Andrew M. Czernik - *1**
#605, 920 Yonge St., Toronto, ON M4W 3C7
Tel: 416-920-4994; *Fax:* 416-920-5885
aczernik@on.aibn.com

***Toronto*: Czuma, Ritter - *2**
410 - 120 Carlton St., Toronto, ON M5A 4K2
Tel: 416-599-5799; *Fax:* 416-599-9981
michael@michaelczuma.com
www.michaelczuma.com

***Toronto*: E.L. D'Alimonte - *1**
#203, 1111 Albion Rd., Toronto, ON M9V 1A9
Tel: 416-741-5373

***Toronto*: Anthony D'Avella - *1**
#306, 4920 Dundas St. West, Toronto, ON M9A 1B7
Tel: 416-234-2198; *Fax:* 416-234-5142
anton.davella@on.aibn.com

***Toronto*: Dale & Lessmann LLP - *14**
#2100, 181 University Ave., Toronto, ON M5H 3M7
Tel: 416-863-1010; *Fax:* 416-863-1009
info@dalelessmann.com
www.dalelessmann.com

***Toronto*: Daniel F. Daly - *1**
#206, 20 Holly St., Toronto, ON M4S 3B1
Tel: 416-485-6700; *Fax:* 416-485-6711

***Toronto*: Damery & Mamak - *2**
101 Roncesvalles Ave., Toronto, ON M6R 2K9
Tel: 416-532-3349; *Fax:* 416-533-2967

***Toronto*: Danson, Recht, Voudouris LLP - *5**
Former Name: Danson, Recht & Freedman
#2000, 700 Bay St., Toronto, ON M5G 1Z6
Tel: 416-929-2200; *Fax:* 416-929-2192
www.drv-law.com

***Toronto*: Danson, Zucker & Connelly - *3**
#500, 70 Bond St., Toronto, ON M5B 1X3
Tel: 416-863-9955; *Fax:* 416-863-4896

***Toronto*: Daoust Vukovich LLP - *20**
#3000, 20 Queen St. West, Toronto, ON M5H 3R3
Tel: 416-597-6888; *Fax:* 416-597-8897
general@dv-law.com
www.dv-lew.com

***Toronto*: James Daris - *1**
#101, 8 Irwin Ave., Toronto, ON M4Y 1K9
Tel: 416-465-4973; *Fax:* 416-465-6042

***Toronto*: David Charles Barristers Professional Corp. - *4**
Former Name: David Eklove Charles
#800, 1200 Bay St., Toronto, ON M5R 2A5
Tel: 416-923-7407; *Fax:* 416-923-6070

***Toronto*: Davies Howe Partners - *10**
99 Spadina Ave., 5th Fl., Toronto, ON M5V 3P8
Tel: 416-977-7088; *Fax:* 416-977-8931
info@davieshowe.com
www.davieshowe.com

***Toronto*: Davies McLean Zweig Associates - *3**
1035 McNicoll Ave., Toronto, ON M1W 3W6
Tel: 416-756-7500; *Fax:* 416-512-1212

***Toronto*: Davis & Turk - *2**
#340, 1100 Sheppard Ave. West, Toronto, ON M3K 2B4
Tel: 416-630-5511; *Fax:* 416-630-7724

***Toronto*: Marie Davison - *1**
327 Eglinton Ave. East, Toronto, ON M4P 1L7
Tel: 416-486-9701; *Fax:* 416-483-1397

***Toronto*: De Faria & De Faria - *2**
872 Dundas St. West, Toronto, ON M6J 1V7
Tel: 416-603-4440; *Fax:* 416-603-4441

***Toronto*: De Ponte & Scalisi - *2**
#600, 155 Rexdale Blvd., Toronto, ON M9W 5Z8
Tel: 416-746-7829; *Fax:* 416-746-9335

***Toronto*: J.N. De Sommer - *1**
112 Adelaide St. East, Toronto, ON M5C 1K9
Tel: 416-341-7077; *Fax:* 416-368-2918
jndesommer@rbs.rogers.com

** indicates number of lawyers*

***Toronto*: Tilaka de Zoysa - *1**
#207, 2131 Lawrence Ave. East, Toronto, ON M1R 5G4
Tel: 416-752-2253; *Fax:* 416-752-6356

***Toronto*: Deacon, Spears, Fedson & Montizambert - *7**
#2900, 2300 Yonge St., Toronto, ON M4P 1E4
Tel: 416-489-5677; *Fax:* 416-489-7794
info@condolaw.to
www.condolaw.to

***Toronto*: Deeth Williams Wall LLP - *19**
#400, 150 York St., Toronto, ON M5H 3S5
Tel: 416-941-9440; *Fax:* 416-941-9443
info@dww.com
www.dww.com

***Toronto*: DelZotto, Zorzi LLP - *12**
4810 Dufferin St., #D, Toronto, ON M3J 5S8
Tel: 416-665-5555; *Fax:* 416-665-9653
info@dzlaw.com
www.dzlaw.com

***Toronto*: A.M. Dempsey, Q.C. - *1**
533 Queen St. East, Toronto, ON M5A 1V1
Tel: 416-364-6755; *Fax:* 416-364-7049

***Toronto*: Richard G.J. Desrocher - *1**
20 Leamington Ave., Toronto, ON M8Z 2W4
Tel: 416-236-5679; *Fax:* 416-236-7370

***Toronto*: Donald W. Devenney - *1**
#1106, 66 Spadina Rd., Toronto, ON M5R 2T4
Tel: 416-964-2687

***Toronto*: Deverett Law Offices - *2**
163 Willowdale Ave., Toronto, ON M2N 4Y7
Tel: 416-222-6789; *Fax:* 416-222-7605
info@deverettlaw.com
www.deverettlaw.com

***Toronto*: Jane H. Devlin - *1**
#701, 100 Adelaide St. West, Toronto, ON M5H 1S3
Tel: 416-366-3091; *Fax:* 416-366-0879
arbserv@istar.ca

***Toronto*: Devon Government Relations - *5**
Also Known As: Devon Group
#900, 1200 Bay St., Toronto, ON M5R 2A5
Tel: 416-504-5151; *Fax:* 416-504-5655
info@devongroup.ca
www.devongroup.ca

***Toronto*: Devry, Smith & Frank - *27**
#100, 95 Barber Greene Rd., Toronto, ON M3C 3E9
Tel: 416-449-1400; *Fax:* 416-449-7071
info@devrylaw.ca
www.devrylaw.ca

***Toronto*: Iqbal I. Dewji - *1**
#810, 255 Duncan Mill Road, Toronto, ON M3B 2H9
Tel: 416-449-9600; *Fax:* 416-449-9348
iimd@rogers.com

***Toronto*: DFH Public Affairs Ltd.**
Also Known As: Drysdale Forstner Hamilton Public Affairs Ltd.
#2400, P.O. Box 23, 120 Adelaide St. West, Toronto, ON M5H 1T1
Tel: 416-206-0118; *Fax:* 416-981-7711
info@dfhpublicaffairs.com
dfhpublicaffairs.com

***Toronto*: Philip J. Di Iorio Professional Corporation - *2**
Former Name: Philip J. Di Iorio
821 The Queensway, Toronto, ON M8Z 1N6
Tel: 416-253-1223; *Fax:* 416-253-0186

***Toronto*: Diamond & Diamond - *8**
#400, 700 Lawrence Ave. West, Toronto, ON M6A 3B4
Tel: 416-256-1600; *Fax:* 416-256-0100

***Toronto*: Michael R. Diamond - *1**
#200, 111 Eglinton Ave. East, Toronto, ON M4P 1H4
Tel: 416-482-2666; *Fax:* 416-482-4165
sndicator@sympatico.ca

***Toronto*: Dickson MacGregor Appell LLP - *9**
Former Name: Dickson, MacGregor, Appell & Burton
#306, 10 Alcorn Ave., Toronto, ON M4V 3A9
Tel: 416-927-0891; *Fax:* 416-927-0385
ellis@dicksonlawyers.com
www.dicksonlawyers.com

***Toronto*: Dimock Stratton LLP - *17**
P.O. Box 102, 20 Queen St. West, 32nd Fl., Toronto, ON M5H 3R3
Tel: 416-971-7202; *Fax:* 416-971-6638
firm@dimock.com
www.dimock.com

***Toronto*: Dion, Durrell & Associates - *2**
#2900, 250 Yonge St., Toronto, ON M5B 2L7
Tel: 416-408-2626; *Fax:* 416-408-3721
information@dion-durrell.com
www.dion-durrell.com

***Toronto*: H.J. Doan Barrister & Solicitor - *1**
18 Wild Briarway, Toronto, ON M2J 2L2
Tel: 416-491-2700; *Fax:* 416-502-9373

***Toronto*: Doane Phillips Yonge LLP - *3**
#300, 53 Jarvis St., Toronto, ON M5C 2H2
Tel: 416-366-3777; *Fax:* 416-366-9197

***Toronto*: C.H. Dolman, Q.C. - *1**
#102, 10 Milner Business Ct., Toronto, ON M1B 3C6
Tel: 416-754-8177; *Fax:* 416-754-8337
cdolman@rogers.com

***Toronto*: Leonard Domino & Associates - *5**
39 Delaware Ave., Toronto, ON M6H 2S8
Tel: 416-723-4499;
www.leonarddomino.com

***Toronto*: Brian P. Donnelly - *1**
#1509, 180 Dundas St. West, Toronto, ON M5G 1Z8
Tel: 416-597-2191; *Fax:* 416-597-9808

***Toronto*: J. Brian Donnelly - *1**
#201, 1165A St. Clair Ave. West, Toronto, ON M6E 1B2
Tel: 416-653-0311; *Fax:* 416-653-6653
jbd@jbdonnelly.com

***Toronto*: Dotsikas Hawtin Lawyers - *2**
#502, 1235 Bay St., Toronto, ON M5R 3K4
Tel: 416-925-1601; *Fax:* 416-925-4571
peter@dotsikaslaw.com

***Toronto*: Downtown Legal Services - *5**
655 Spadina Ave., Toronto, ON M5S 2H9
Tel: 416-934-4535; *Fax:* 416-934-4536
law.dls@utoronto.ca
www.dls.utoronto.ca

***Toronto*: William C. Draimin - *1**
#101, 45 St. Clair Ave. West, Toronto, ON M4V 1K9
Tel: 416-920-4605; *Fax:* 416-960-0698
wdraimin@draiminlaw.com

***Toronto*: Dranoff & Huddart - *2**
#314, 1033 Bay St., Toronto, ON M5S 3A5
Tel: 416-925-4500; *Fax:* 416-925-5197
info@dranoffhuddart.com
www.dranoffhuddart.com

***Toronto*: J. Blair Drummie - *1**
326 Richmond St. West, Toronto, ON M5V 1X2
Tel: 416-921-0915; *Fax:* 416-925-6181

***Toronto*: Du Markowitz LLP - *3**
#2000, Madison Centre, 4950 Yonge St., Toronto, ON M2N 6K1
Tel: 416-590-1900; *Fax:* 416-590-1600
info@dumarkowitz.com
www.dumarkowitz.com

***Toronto*: John Duncan & Associates - *3**
#701, The Fashion Bldg., 130 Spadina Ave., Toronto, ON M5V 2L4
Tel: 416-593-2513; *Fax:* 416-593-2514
info@duncanmorin.com
www.duncanmorin.com

***Toronto*: Thomas S. Dungey - *1**
46 Fairview Blvd., Toronto, ON M4K 1L9
Tel: 416-469-3088; *Fax:* 416-469-6739
tsdungey@rogers.com

***Toronto*: Lloyd T. Duong - *1**
2377 Dundas St. West, Toronto, ON M6P 1W7
Tel: 416-535-3463

***Toronto*: Norman L. Durbin - *1**
2530 Jane St., Toronto, ON M3L 1S1
Tel: 416-743-2345; *Fax:* 416-743-0645

***Toronto*: Dutton Brock LLP - *31**
Former Name: Dutton, Brock, MacIntyre & Collier
#1700, 438 University Ave., Toronto, ON M5G 2L9
Tel: 416-593-4411; *Fax:* 416-593-5922
info@duttonbrock.com
www.duttonbrock.com

***Toronto*: Diana C. Dzwiekowski - *1**
260 Willard Ave., Toronto, ON M6S 3R2
Tel: 416-762-7251; *Fax:* 416-762-7252

***Toronto*: East Toronto Community Legal Services - *4**
1320 Gerrard St. East, Toronto, ON M4L 3X1
Tel: 416-461-8102; *Fax:* 416-461-7497

***Toronto*: Eccleston LLP - *6**
Former Name: Movat, Eccleston
#3820, Toronto Dominion Centre, Box 230, 66 Wellington St. West, Toronto, ON M5K 1J3
Tel: 416-504-2722; *Fax:* 416-504-2686
www.ecclestonllp.com

***Toronto*: Ecclestone, Hamer, Poisson & Neuwald & Freeman - *5**
#900, 372 Bay St., Toronto, ON M5C 1J3
Tel: 416-365-7135; *Fax:* 416-365-2189
ecclchyk@idirect.com

***Toronto*: John M. Edgar - *1**
2901 Bloor St. West, Toronto, ON M8X 1B3
Tel: 416-231-3261; *Fax:* 416-231-8352

***Toronto*: George Edmonds, Q.C. - *1**
#700, 2 St. Clair Ave. West, Toronto, ON M4V 1L5
Tel: 416-955-0947; *Fax:* 416-863-3997
edmonds@interlog.com

***Toronto*: Egan LLP - *14**
Former Name: Donahue LLP
TD Centre, Ernst & Young Tower, P.O. Box 197, Stn. TD Centre, 222 Bay St., Toronto, ON M5K 1J7
Tel: 416-943-2400; *Fax:* 416-943-2735
www.ey.com/CA/; www.eganllp.com

***Toronto*: Elston Watt LLP - *4**
#2310, Bay-Wellington Tower, BCE Place, P.O. Box 792, 181 Bay St., Toronto, ON M5J 2T3
Tel: 416-977-9811; *Fax:* 416-977-9850
mail@elstonwatt.com

***Toronto*: Mitch Engel - *1**
#502, 1235 Bay St., Toronto, ON M5R 3K4
Tel: 416-944-8882; *Fax:* 416-925-4571
m.engel@rogers.com

***Toronto*: Enterprise Canada - *19**
#1202, 595 Bay St., Toronto, ON M5G 2C2
Tel: 416-586-1474; *Fax:* 416-586-1480
www.enterprisecanada.com

***Toronto*: Environics Communications Inc. - *2**
#900, 33 Bloor St. East, Toronto, ON M4W 3H1
Tel: 416-969-2702; *Fax:* 416-920-1822
communicate@environicspr.com
environicspr.comtwitter.com/environicspr

***Toronto*: Epstein Cole LLP - *25**
#2200, 393 University Ave., Toronto, ON M5G 1E6
Tel: 416-862-9888; *Fax:* 416-862-2142
www.epsteincole.com

***Toronto*: Norman Epstein - *1**
281 Eglinton Ave. East, Toronto, ON M4P 1L3
Tel: 416-225-5577; *Fax:* 416-483-5541

***Toronto*: Eric Lewis & Associates**
116 Parliament Street, Toronto, ON M5A 2Y8
Tel: 416-367-1918; *Fax:* 416-362-1918
lewis_smyth@hotmail.com

***Toronto*: J.A. Ermacora - *1**
75 Lowther Ave., Toronto, ON M5R 1C9
Tel: 416-961-5500; *Fax:* 416-961-9905
jermac@sympatico.ca

***Toronto*: Charles A. Eyton-Jones - *1**
1238 Kingston Rd., Toronto, ON M1N 1P3
Tel: 416-691-4529; *Fax:* 416-691-2563
info@eyton-jones.ca
www.eyton-jones.ca

***Toronto*: Fabian & Kaye - *2**
#103, 1210 Sheppard Ave. East, Toronto, ON M2K 1E3
Tel: 416-491-6411; *Fax:* 416-491-2219

** indicates number of lawyers*

***Toronto*: Fair & Siegel**
#1002, 250 Heath St. West, Toronto, ON M5P 3L4
Tel: 416-948-1652; *Fax:* 416-483-9228
msiegel@rogers.com

***Toronto*: Falconer Charney - *7**
8 Prince Arthur Ave., Toronto, ON M5R 1A9
Tel: 416-964-3408; *Fax:* 416-929-8179
falconercharney@fcbarristers.com
www.fcbarristers.com

***Toronto*: Ricardo G. Federico - *1**
#900, 920 Yonge St., Toronto, ON M4W 3C7
Tel: 416-928-1458; *Fax:* 416-322-3684

***Toronto*: Frederick S. Fedorsen - *2**
551 Gerrard St. East, Toronto, ON M4M 1X7
Tel: 416-463-6666; *Fax:* 416-463-8259
fred@fedorsennorth.com

***Toronto*: Jodi L. Feldman - *1**
#303, 21 St. Clair Ave. East, Toronto, ON M4T 1L9
Tel: 416-922-3233; *Fax:* 416-922-3234

***Toronto*: Jane L. Ferguson - *1**
#250, 1027 Yonge St., Toronto, ON M4W 2K9
Tel: 416-920-7533; *Fax:* 416-923-5576
jlferg@bellnet.ca

***Toronto*: Fernandes Hearn LLP - *9**
Also Known As: Fernandes, Hearn, Theall
#700, 155 University Ave., Toronto, ON M5H 3B7
Tel: 416-203-9500; *Fax:* 416-203-9444
info@fernandeshearn.com
www.fernandeshearn.com

***Toronto*: Field, Brown - *3**
5140 Yonge Street, Toronto, ON M7A 2K2
Tel: 416-595-1111; *Fax:* 416-595-7312

***Toronto*: Gerald Fields - *1**
#1800, P.O. Box 427, 130 King St. West, Toronto, ON M5X 1J8
Tel: 416-862-8000; *Fax:* 416-862-8001
Toll-Free: 888-268-6735
gfields@cornerstonegroup.com

***Toronto*: Filion Wakely Thorup Angeletti LLP - *26**
#2601, P.O. Box 32, 150 King St. West, Toronto, ON M5H 4B6
Tel: 416-408-3221; *Fax:* 416-408-4814
toronto@filion.on.ca
www.filion.on.ca

***Toronto*: Filmlegals Entertainment Law Service - *1**
7 Langley Ave., Toronto, ON M4K 1B4
Tel: 416-466-1487; *Fax:* 416-466-2548
mkrys@filmlegals.com
www.filmlegals.com

***Toronto*: Andrew Fine - *1**
#306, 1000 Finch Ave. West, Toronto, ON M3J 2V5
Tel: 416-785-9499

***Toronto*: Finkelstein & Associates - *1**
P.O. Box 23016, 437 Spadina Rd., Toronto, ON M5P 2W3
Tel: 416-487-2353; *Fax:* 416-487-1245

***Toronto*: Fireman Wolfe LLP - *7**
#415, P.O. Box 19, 55 St. Clair Ave. West, Toronto, ON M4V 2Y7
Tel: 416-967-9100; *Fax:* 416-967-1200
www.firemanlawyers.com

***Toronto*: Fisch & Antonette - *1**
Former Name: S.J. Antonette
419 College St., Toronto, ON M5T 1T1
Tel: 416-920-6312; *Fax:* 416-920-1780
josephyfisch@hotmail.com

***Toronto*: Joseph Y. Fisch - *2**
#1, 394 College St., Toronto, ON M5T 1S7
Tel: 416-920-6312; *Fax:* 416-920-1780
josephyfisch@hotmail.com

***Toronto*: Barry B. Fisher - *1**
#2000, 393 University Ave., Toronto, ON M5G 1E6
Tel: 416-585-2330; *Fax:* 416-585-2105
barryfisher@rogers.com

***Toronto*: R.A. Fisher - *1**
#309, 95 Barber Greene Rd., Toronto, ON M3C 3E9
Tel: 416-449-3004; *Fax:* 416-441-6898
royfisher@hotmail.com

***Toronto*: Donald R. Fiske - *1**
#665, West Tower, Clarica Centre, 3300 Bloor St. West, Toronto, ON M8X 2X8
Tel: 416-234-2177; *Fax:* 416-234-9039
fiske@bellnet.ca

***Toronto*: Fleischer & Kochberg - *1**
#203, 77 Finch Ave. West, Toronto, ON M2N 2H5
Tel: 416-223-8102; *Fax:* 416-223-9502
thefirm@relo-law.com
www.relo-law.com

***Toronto*: Fleming, Breen - *2**
370 Bloor St. East, Toronto, ON M4W 3M6
Tel: 416-927-9000; *Fax:* 416-927-9069
richard@defender.ca

***Toronto*: Fleming, White & Burgess - *2**
#1000, 2 Bloor St. West, Toronto, ON M4W 3E2
Tel: 416-961-2868; *Fax:* 416-961-2964
flemingwhite@bellnet.ca

***Toronto*: Fleury, Comery LLP - *4**
#104, 215 Morrish Rd., Toronto, ON M1C 1E9
Tel: 416-282-5754; *Fax:* 416-282-9906
thefirm@fleurcom.on.ca
www.fleurcom.on.ca

***Toronto*: Ronald Flom - *2**
#712, 2345 Yonge St., Toronto, ON M4P 2E5
Tel: 416-482-2777; *Fax:* 416-482-2599

***Toronto*: Fogler, Rubinoff LLP - *105**
#1200, Toronto-Dominion Centre, 95 Wellington St. West, Toronto, ON M5J 2Z9
Tel: 416-864-9700; *Fax:* 416-941-8852
Toll-Free: 866-861-9700
thefirm@foglers.com
www.foglers.com

***Toronto*: Forget & Matthews LLP, Barristers - *10**
#402, 214 King St. West, Toronto, ON M5H 3S6
Tel: 416-593-5400; *Fax:* 416-595-5400
infolaw@fmlaw.ca
www.fmlaw.ca

***Toronto*: R. Brian Foster Q.C. - *1**
#1, 16 Four Seasons Pl., Toronto, ON M9B 6E5
Tel: 416-695-2700; *Fax:* 416-695-3687
brianfoster@bellnet.ca

***Toronto*: Fournie Mickleborough LLP - *4**
Former Name: Rogers, Campbell, Mickleborough
#701, 90 Adelaide St. West, Toronto, ON M5H 3V9
Tel: 416-366-3999; *Fax:* 416-366-2860
rcm@companylawyers.com
www.companylawyers.com

***Toronto*: Kevin Fox, Barrister & Solicitor - *1**
Former Name: Fox Rovos
174 Davenport Rd., Toronto, ON M5R 1J2
Tel: 416-323-3252; *Fax:* 416-929-6885
kfox@davenportlaw.cawww.linkedin.com/pub/kevin-fox/17/97b/5 77

***Toronto*: Walter Fox - *3**
#312, 100 Richmond St. West, Toronto, ON M5H 3K6
Tel: 416-363-9238; *Fax:* 416-363-9230
fox@sympatico.ca

***Toronto*: Franco, Lento - *1**
Former Name: Franco, Lento, D'Alimonte
#504, 3200 Dufferin St., Toronto, ON M3K 2A7
Tel: 416-398-4044; *Fax:* 416-398-7396
ldlaw@total.net

***Toronto*: Fraser, Simms and Reid - *1**
#2, 15 John St., Toronto, ON M9N 1J2
Tel: 416-241-0111; *Fax:* 416-241-1911

***Toronto*: Harvey Freedman - *3**
#100, 79 Shuter St., Toronto, ON M5B 1B3
Tel: 416-363-1737; *Fax:* 416-861-9919
hfreedman@freedmans.ca

***Toronto*: Joel P. Freedman - *1**
#200, 3200 Dufferin St., Toronto, ON M6A 2T3
Tel: 416-248-6231; *Fax:* 416-241-0080
jpfreedman@freedmanlaw.com

***Toronto*: Norman J. Freedman, Q.C.**
#2150, 121 King St. West, Toronto, ON M5H 3T9
Tel: 416-815-7767; *Fax:* 416-815-7722

***Toronto*: Randall R. Friedland - *1**
#1301, 2200 Yonge St., Toronto, ON M4S 2C6
Tel: 416-932-4969; *Fax:* 416-932-0541
friedland@jodlaw.com

***Toronto*: J. Friedman, Q.C. - *1**
#202, 30 St. Clair Ave. West, Toronto, ON M4V 3A1
Tel: 416-515-0575; *Fax:* 416-515-0454
jack.friedman@bellnet.ca

***Toronto*: David G. Friend, Q.C. - *1**
#202, 3459 Sheppard Ave. East, Toronto, ON M1T 3K5
Tel: 416-754-0333; *Fax:* 416-292-0473
dfriend@bellnet.ca

***Toronto*: Fritz & Associates**
44 Upjohn Road, Toronto, ON M3B 2W1
Tel: 416-441-6747; *Fax:* 416-447-8588

***Toronto*: Fryer Levitt - *1**
#2, 421 Eglinton Ave. West, Toronto, ON M5N 1A4
Tel: 416-323-1377; *Fax:* 416-323-9355
jelevitt@fryerlevitt.com
www.fryerlevitt.com

***Toronto*: Harry Frymer - *1**
#320, 100 Richmond St. West, Toronto, ON M5H 3K6
Tel: 416-869-1073; *Fax:* 416-869-1840

***Toronto*: Derrick Fulton Barrister & Solicitor - *1**
#1515, 390 Bay St., Toronto, ON M5H 2Y2
Tel: 416-594-3338; *Fax:* 416-860-1474
dmfulton@istar.ca
home.istar.ca/~dmfulton/

***Toronto*: Fyshe McMahon LLP - *9**
Former Name: Page, Arnold LLP
#2000, 393 University Ave., Toronto, ON M5G 1E6
Tel: 416-977-1525; *Fax:* 416-977-1526

***Toronto*: F.A. Gabriel - *1**
#203, 425 University Ave., Toronto, ON M5G 1T6
Tel: 416-593-6621; *Fax:* 416-599-8075
fgabriel@bellnet.ca

***Toronto*: Laurie A. Galway - *1**
27 Prince Arthur Ave., Toronto, ON M5R 1B2
Tel: 416-413-9466; *Fax:* 416-960-1498
lauriegalway@27princearthur.com

***Toronto*: Douglas Gordon Garbig, A Professional Corporation - *1**
#3101, P.O. Box 52, 401 Bay St., Toronto, ON M5H 2Y4
Tel: 416-862-7822; *Fax:* 416-862-2568
garbig@garbig.com

***Toronto*: Gardiner Miller Arnold LLP - *6**
#1202, 390 Bay St., Toronto, ON M5H 2Y2
Tel: 416-363-2614; *Fax:* 416-363-8451
gmainfo@gmalaw.ca
www.gmalaw.ca

***Toronto*: Gardiner, Roberts LLP - *67**
#3100, Scotia Plaza, 40 King St. West, Toronto, ON M5H 3Y2
Tel: 416-865-6600; *Fax:* 416-865-6636
www.gardiner-roberts.com

***Toronto*: Garfin Zeidenberg LLP - *13**
#800, Yonge Norton Centre, 5255 Yonge St., Toronto, ON M2N 6P4
Tel: 416-512-8000; *Fax:* 416-512-9992
Toll-Free: 877-529-9910
gzinfo@gzlegal.com
www.gzlegal.com

***Toronto*: Susan W. Garfin - *1**
#2000, 393 University Ave., Toronto, ON M5G 1E6
Tel: 416-599-9933; *Fax:* 416-599-5497
garfin@rogers.com

***Toronto*: Garfinkle, Biderman - *19**
#801, Dundee Place, 1 Adelaide St. East, Toronto, ON M5C 2V9
Tel: 416-869-1234; *Fax:* 416-869-0547
www.garfinkle.com

***Toronto*: Gasee, Cohen & Youngman, Barrister & Solicitor - *6**
#200, 65 Queen St. West, Toronto, ON M5H 2M5
Tel: 416-363-3351; *Fax:* 416-363-0252
info@gcylaw.com
www.gcylaw.com

** indicates number of lawyers*

Toronto: Leon Gavendo - *1
#2000, Law Chambers, University Centre, 393 University Ave., Toronto, ON M5G 1E6
Tel: 416-585-3109; *Fax:* 416-585-9668
lgavendo@on.aibn.com

Toronto: L.B. Geffen - *1
#205, 2907 Kennedy Rd., Toronto, ON M1V 1S8
Tel: 416-292-6688; *Fax:* 416-292-6649
lgeffen@idirect.com

Toronto: Gelfand & Co. - *2
519 King St. West, Toronto, ON M5V 1K4
Tel: 416-929-4949; *Fax:* 416-929-1996
Toll-Free: 877-286-4296
lgelfand@gelfandandco.com

Toronto: Geller & Minster - *3
2 Keewatin Ave., Toronto, ON M4P 1Z8
Tel: 416-480-2200; *Fax:* 416-480-2693
geller@bellnet.ca

Toronto: Genest Murray LLP - *6
#700, 130 Adelaide St. West, Toronto, ON M5H 4C1
Tel: 416-368-8600; *Fax:* 416-360-2625
www.genestmurray.ca

Toronto: Basil L. Georgieff - *1
3543A St. Clair Ave. East, Toronto, ON M1K 1L6
Tel: 416-464-6888; *Fax:* 416-267-1452
basgeo@msn.com

Toronto: Lorne Gershuny - *1
1577 Bloor St. West, Toronto, ON M6P 1A6
Tel: 416-539-0989; *Fax:* 416-536-3618
lgershuny@hotmail.com

Toronto: Gertler & Associates - *2
5341 Dundas St. West, Toronto, ON M9B 1B1
Tel: 416-410-8613; *Fax:* 416-231-9492
www.gertlerandassociates.com

Toronto: Henry J. Gertner
4 Finch Ave. West, Toronto, ON M2N 6L1
Tel: 416-225-5992; *Fax:* 416-225-7611
gertnerlaw@bellnet.ca

Toronto: Ghose Law Office - *2
Also Known As: Bassanio Ghose Professional Corporation
Former Name: Ghose & Malhotra
#308, 1620 Albion Rd., Toronto, ON M9V 4B4
Tel: 416-744-1480; *Fax:* 416-744-9855
gmreception@bellnet.ca
www.gmlawoffice.ca

Toronto: Giffels Associates Limited - *1
30 International Blvd., Toronto, ON M9W 5P3
Tel: 461-675-5950; *Fax:* 461-675-4620
Toll-Free: 800-567-8918
stephen.obrien@giffels.com
www.giffels.com

Toronto: Gilbert & Yallen - *3
Former Name: Howard Gilbert
204 St. George St., 3rd Fl., Toronto, ON M5R 2N5
Tel: 416-927-0001; *Fax:* 416-927-0930

Toronto: Gilbert's LLP - *12
#2010, Toronto Dominion Centre, P.O. Box 301, 77 King st. West, Toronto, ON M5K 1K2
Tel: 416-703-1100; *Fax:* 416-703-7422
contact@gilbertslaw.ca
www.gilbertslaw.ca

Toronto: Gilbert, Wright & Kirby LLP - *9
#2302, P.O. Box 103, 401 Bay St., Toronto, ON M5H 2Y4
Tel: 416-363-3100; *Fax:* 416-363-1379
info@gwklaw.com
www.gwklaw.com

Toronto: Gilbertson Davis Emerson LLP - *8
#2020, 20 Queen St. West, Toronto, ON M5H 3R3
Tel: 416-979-2020; *Fax:* 416-979-1285
office@gilbertsondavis.com
www.gilbertsondavis.com

Toronto: John D. Gilfillan, Q.C. - *1
#1200, 8 King St. East, Toronto, ON M5C 1B5
Tel: 416-861-1881; *Fax:* 416-861-1737
gilfillan@interware.net

Toronto: Leslie M. Giroday - *1
190 Sixth St., Toronto, ON M8V 3A5
Tel: 416-255-1063; *Fax:* 416-251-8699
lmgiroday@sympatico.ca

Toronto: Glaholt LLP - *9
#800, 141 Adelaide St. West, Toronto, ON M5H 3L5
Tel: 416-368-8280; *Fax:* 416-368-3467
Toll-Free: 866-452-4658
bb@glaholt.com
www.glaholt.com

Toronto: Earl Glasner - *1
#320, 100 Richmond St. West, Toronto, ON M5H 3K6
Tel: 416-869-1076;
earlglasner@rogers.com

Toronto: Alan A. Glass - *1
#500, 1000 Finch Ave. West, Toronto, ON M3J 2V5
Tel: 416-667-9796; *Fax:* 416-667-8048

Toronto: Glass, Murray, Bianchi - *4
Former Name: Glass & Associates
50 Richmond St. East, 5th Fl., Toronto, ON M5C 1N7
Tel: 416-363-9295; *Fax:* 416-363-7659
lglass@glassassoc.com

Toronto: Louis Glatt - *1
2354 Danforth Ave., Toronto, ON M4C 1K7
Tel: 416-422-2107; *Fax:* 416-422-2606

Toronto: Global Ventures - *1
E3 - 296 Mill Rd., Toronto, ON M9C 4X8
Tel: 416-569-9306; *Fax:* 416-620-7768
consultrussi@aol.com

Toronto: Glober & Cohen, Associates - *3
114 Scollard St., Toronto, ON M5R 1G2
Tel: 416-324-9994; *Fax:* 416-324-0966

Toronto: Gluckstein & Associates LLP - *7
#301, P.O. Box 53, 595 Bay St., Toronto, ON M5G 2C2
Tel: 416-408-4252; *Fax:* 416-408-4235
Toll-Free: 866-308-7722
info@gluckstein.com
www.gluckstein.com

Toronto: Godfrey & Corcoran - *1
#702, 55 Queen St. East, Toronto, ON M5C 1R6
Tel: 416-363-0484; *Fax:* 416-363-0485
ccorcoran@idirect.com

Toronto: Sydney L. Goldenberg - *1
125 Highbourne Rd., Toronto, ON M5P 2J5
Tel: 416-482-3206; *Fax:* 416-482-8619

Toronto: Goldhar & Nemoy - *2
#214, 120 Carlton St., Toronto, ON M5A 4K2
Tel: 416-928-1488; *Fax:* 416-924-7166

Toronto: Avra Goldhar - *1
27 Abbeywood Trail, Toronto, ON M3B 3B4
Tel: 416-444-4378; *Fax:* 416-444-5721
agoldhar@rogers.com

Toronto: H.A. Goldkind - *1
#320, 100 Richmond St. West, Toronto, ON M5H 3K6
Tel: 416-366-5280

Toronto: Goldman Sloan Nash & Haber LLP - *25
#1600, 480 University Avenue, Toronto, ON M5G 1V6
Tel: 416-597-9922; *Fax:* 416-597-3370
welcome@gsnh.com
www.gsnh.com

Toronto: Jeffrey L. Goldman - *1
#500, 425 University Ave., Toronto, ON M5G 1T6
Tel: 416-597-9223; *Fax:* 416-977-5200
jglaw@aol.com

Toronto: Jeffrey W. Goldman - *1
#300, 3500 Dufferin St., Toronto, ON M3K 1N2
Tel: 416-787-1818; *Fax:* 416-787-1810
jeffreygoldman@goldmanlawoffice.com

Toronto: R.M. Goldman - *1
#301, 481 Univeristy Ave., Toronto, ON M5G 2E9
Tel: 416-977-8008; *Fax:* 416-364-2308
rgoldman@defender.ca

Toronto: Goldman, Spring, Kichler & Sanders - *7
#700, 40 Sheppard Ave. West, Toronto, ON M2N 6K9
Tel: 416-225-9400; *Fax:* 416-225-4805

Toronto: Goldstein & Grubner LLP - *2
#212, 3459 Sheppard Ave. East, Toronto, ON M1T 3K5
Tel: 416-292-0414; *Fax:* 416-292-4508
k.goldstein@rogers.com; igrubner@rogers.com
www.gglawyers.ca

Toronto: H.S. Goldstein - *1
#1202, P.O. Box 159, 4950 Yonge St., Toronto, ON M2N 6K1
Tel: 416-223-0600

Toronto: Goldstein, Rosen & Rassos LLP - *2
#102, 1648 Victoria Park Ave., Toronto, ON M1R 1P7
Tel: 416-757-4156; *Fax:* 416-757-9318
trassos@grrlaw.ca

Toronto: Golish & Golish - *2
21 Fairholme Avenue, Toronto, ON M6B 2W4
Tel: 416-789-2438; *Fax:* 416-789-2438

Toronto: David Gomes - *1
112 Adelaide St. East, Toronto, ON M5C 1K9
Tel: 416-361-0906; *Fax:* 416-368-2918
dgomes0604@rogers.com

Toronto: Goodman, Solomon & Gold - *3
#1500, 439 University Ave., Toronto, ON M5G 1Y8
Tel: 416-595-5555; *Fax:* 416-595-7020

Toronto: Stanley Goodman, Q.C. - *1
#1800, 4950 Yonge St., Toronto, ON M2N 6K1
Tel: 416-224-0224; *Fax:* 416-224-0758
stangoodman@torlaw.com

Toronto: Martin Z. Goose - *1
#504, 555 Burnhamthorpe Rd., Toronto, ON M9C 2Y3
Tel: 416-239-4811; *Fax:* 416-239-1707
martingoose@bellnet.ca

Toronto: Nathan Gotlieb - *1
#1800, Madison Centre, 4950 Yonge St., Toronto, ON M2N 6K1
Tel: 416-224-0200; *Fax:* 416-224-0758
ngotlieb@torlaw.com

Toronto: G.L. Gottlieb, Q.C. - *1
#309, 600 Bay St., Toronto, ON M5G 1M6
Tel: 416-977-3835; *Fax:* 416-977-3807
glgqc@interlog.com
www.glgqc.com

Toronto: Max A. Gould - *1
#1000, 30 St. Clair Ave. West, Toronto, ON M4V 3A1
Tel: 416-964-0290; *Fax:* 416-964-7102

Toronto: Michael J. Gould - *1
75 Bannatyne Dr., Toronto, ON M2L 2P2
Tel: 416-510-3030

Toronto: Graham Tobe - *1
#202, 1 Yorkdale Rd., Toronto, ON M6A 3A1
Tel: 416-256-1555; *Fax:* 416-256-0918

Toronto: D.J. Grant - *1
#412, 1220 Sheppard Ave. East, Toronto, ON M2K 2S5
Tel: 416-490-9206; *Fax:* 416-490-9949

Toronto: Deryk A. Gravesande - *1
2 Carlton Street, Toronto, ON M5B 1J3
Tel: 416-206-1110

Toronto: Green & Chercover - *15
30 St. Clair Ave. West, 10th Fl., Toronto, ON M4V 3A1
Tel: 416-968-3333; *Fax:* 416-968-0325
inquiry@greenchercover.ca
www.greenchercover.ca

Toronto: Green & Spiegel - *12
#2800, 390 Bay St., Toronto, ON M5H 2Y2
Tel: 416-862-7880; *Fax:* 416-862-1698

Toronto: David J. Green - *1
#1, 399 Spadina Ave., Toronto, ON M5T 2G6
Tel: 416-979-2333; *Fax:* 416-597-8966

Toronto: Weldon F. Green, Q.C. - *1
P.O. Box 151, 6 Portneuf Ct., Toronto, ON M5A 4E4
Tel: 416-364-4465; *Fax:* 416-364-3657
wfgreenco@on.aibn.com

Toronto: Donald M. Greenbaum, Q.C. - *1
5075 Yonge St., Toronto, ON M2N 6C6
Tel: 416-631-7504; *Fax:* 416-631-9895
baum@globility.com

** indicates number of lawyers*

Toronto: Greenberg & Levine - *2
2223 Kennedy Rd., Toronto, ON M1T 3G5
Tel: 416-292-6500; *Fax:* 416-292-6559
reception@greenbergandlevine.com
www.greenbergandlevine.com

Toronto: Greenberg, Jack - *1
#204, 181 Eglinton Ave. East, Toronto, ON M4P 1J4
Tel: 416-485-8833; *Fax:* 416-485-3246
jackgreenberg@greenberglawyers.ca

Toronto: Greenspan, White - *7
144 King St. East, Toronto, ON M5C 1G8
Tel: 416-366-3961; *Fax:* 416-366-7994
www.greenspanwhite.com

Toronto: Greenwoods Barristers & Solicitors - *2
#100, 3500 Dufferin St., Toronto, ON M3K 1N2
Tel: 416-638-4100; *Fax:* 416-638-3529
Toll-Free: 866-578-4100
agreenwd@greenwoodslaw.com
www.greenwoodslaw.com

Toronto: E.J. Gresik - *1
101 Scollard St., Toronto, ON M5R 1G4
Tel: 416-924-0781; *Fax:* 416-960-9650

Toronto: C. Grimanis - *1
799 Carlaw Avenue, Toronto, ON M4K 3E4
Tel: 416-469-1176; *Fax:* 416-469-4252

Toronto: Groia & Company Professional Corporation - *7
365 Bay St., 11th Fl., Toronto, ON M5H 2V1
Tel: 416-203-2115; *Fax:* 416-203-9231
postmaster@groiaco.com
www.groiaco.com

Toronto: Bernard Gropper - *1
#300, 261 Davenport Rd., Toronto, ON M5R 1K3
Tel: 416-962-3000; *Fax:* 416-487-3002
bgropper@gropperlaw.com

Toronto: C.H. Grosberg - *1
#205, 2907 Kennedy Rd., Toronto, ON M1V 1S8
Tel: 416-752-9745; *Fax:* 416-292-6649

Toronto: Grosso McCarthy Inc. - *2
P.O. Box 45, 200 Front Street West, 23rd Floor, Toronto, ON M5V 3K2
Tel: 416-362-6141; *Fax:* 416-362-6145
fgrosso@grossomccarthy.com
www.grossomccarthy.com

Toronto: Derek T. Ground - *1
16 Oakview Avenue, Toronto, ON M6P 3J2
Tel: 416-604-3434; *Fax:* 416-604-3596
derek.ground@sympatico.ca

Toronto: Grundy Cass Professional Corporation - *3
Former Name: Cass & Cass
#2310, Bay Wellington Tower, P.O. Box 792, 181 Bay St., Toronto, ON M5J 2T3
Tel: 416-849-8003; *Fax:* 416-849-8004

Toronto: Guberman Garson Immigration Lawyers - *5
Former Name: Guberman Garson Bush
#1920, 130 Adelaide St. West, Toronto, ON M5H 3P5
Tel: 416-363-1234; *Fax:* 416-363-8760
immlaw@ggilaw.com
www.ggilaw.com

Toronto: J.M. Guoba - *2
#211, 2425 Eglinton Ave. East, Toronto, ON M1K 5G8
Tel: 416-759-4500; *Fax:* 416-759-4510

Toronto: Peter F. Haber - *1
325 Mutual St., Toronto, ON M4Y 1X6
Tel: 416-961-0265; *Fax:* 416-961-1860
Toll-Free: 888-841-1104
peterhaber@rogers.com

Toronto: Lawrence Hadbavny - *1
Law Society of Upper Canada, 130 Queen St. West, Toronto, ON M5H 2N6
Tel: 416-947-3906; *Fax:* 416-644-4880
lhadbavn@lsuc.on.ca

Toronto: Michael P. Haddad - *2
208 Carlton St., Toronto, ON M5A 2L1
Tel: 416-926-8151; *Fax:* 416-927-9005
mhaddad@istar.ca

Toronto: Hahn & Maian - *2
664 Mount Pleasant Rd., Toronto, ON M4S 2N3
Tel: 416-486-9445; *Fax:* 416-486-1174
johnhahn@idirect.com

Toronto: Kenneth A. Hahn - *1
1078 Kipling Ave., Toronto, ON M9B 3M2
Tel: 416-231-3353; *Fax:* 416-231-6773

Toronto: Miles M. Halberstadt, Q.C. - *1
#200, 379 Dundas St. East, Toronto, ON M5A 2A6
Tel: 416-944-0441; *Fax:* 416-944-8330
mileshalberstadt@hotmail.com

Toronto: Hall Webber LLP Entertainment & New Media Law - *4
#400, 1200 Bay St., Toronto, ON M5R 2A5
Tel: 416-920-3849; *Fax:* 416-920-8373
mail@ent-law.com
www.ent-law.com

Toronto: David F. Halpenny - *1
#403, 111 Peter St., Toronto, ON M5V 2H1
Tel: 416-867-9208; *Fax:* 416-867-9139

Toronto: Allan S. Halpert - *2
37 Maitland St., Toronto, ON M4Y 1C8
Tel: 416-968-7733; *Fax:* 416-968-7192
allan@halpertlaw.com

Toronto: Munyonzwe Hamalengwa
#18A, 100 Westmore Dr., Toronto, ON M9V 5C3
Tel: 416-644-1106; *Fax:* 416-644-1126
mhamalengwa@sympatico.ca
www.munyonzwehamalengwa.ca

Toronto: Harvey L. Hamburg - *1
#215, 120 Carlton St., Toronto, ON M5A 4K2
Tel: 416-968-9054; *Fax:* 416-968-9023
hhamburg@sympatico.ca

Toronto: Michael A. Handler - *1
2950 Keele St., Toronto, ON M3M 2H2
Tel: 416-638-0680; *Fax:* 416-398-3007

Toronto: Hans & Hans - *1
17 Wembley Rd., Toronto, ON M6C 2E8
Tel: 416-960-5445; *Fax:* 416-924-7541
hansoff10@rogers.com

Toronto: Zakaul Haque - *1
#205, 1058A Albion Rd., Toronto, ON M9V 1A7
Tel: 416-743-6302; *Fax:* 416-743-4783

Toronto: George M. Harasymowycz - *1
#200, 2311 Bloor St. West, Toronto, ON M6S 1P1
Tel: 416-766-2472; *Fax:* 416-766-3297
george@haraslaw.com

Toronto: Murray P. Harrington - *1
285 Pitfield Rd., Toronto, ON M1S 1Z2
Tel: 416-299-0477; *Fax:* 416-299-7570

Toronto: David E. Harris - *1
#1900, 439 University Ave., Toronto, ON M5G 1Y8
Tel: 416-585-9329; *Fax:* 416-408-2372
delih@inforamp.net

Toronto: Ricki D. Harris - *2
#1800, 4950 Yonge St., Toronto, ON M2N 6K1
Tel: 416-224-0200; *Fax:* 416-224-0758
rdharris@torlaw.com

Toronto: Klaus Hartmann - *1
391 Willowdale Ave., Toronto, ON M2N 5A8
Tel: 416-590-0311; *Fax:* 416-590-0312

Toronto: Douglas G. Hatch - *1
#619, 4211 Yonge St., Toronto, ON M2P 2A9
Tel: 416-512-7521; *Fax:* 416-512-1946
dhatch@rogers.com

Toronto: Peter L. Hatch - *1
31 Prince Arthur Ave., Toronto, ON M5R 1B2
Tel: 416-972-6962; *Fax:* 416-960-5456

Toronto: Frederick Simon Hawa - *1
2267 Lakeshore Blvd. West, Toronto, ON M8V 3X2
Tel: 416-252-5190;
fredhawa@sympatico.ca

Toronto: John Hay & Associates - *1
#1207, 4003 Bayview Ave., Toronto, ON M2M 3Z8
Tel: 416-226-2049; *Fax:* 416-494-5586
john.hay@sympatico.ca

Toronto: Hazzard & Hore - *7
#1002, 141 Adelaide St. West, Toronto, ON M5H 3L5
Tel: 416-868-0074; *Fax:* 416-868-1468
info@hazardandhore.com
www.hazzardandhore.com

Toronto: Marian D. Hebb - *2
250 Merton Street, Toronto, ON M4S 1B1
Tel: 416-971-6618; *Fax:* 416-971-4144
mhebb@sympatico.ca

Toronto: Stephen H. Hebscher - *1
#1800, 4950 Yonge St., Toronto, ON M2N 6K1
Tel: 416-550-6554; *Fax:* 416-224-0758
crimlaw@torlaw.com

Toronto: E.S. Heiber - *1
#200, 70 Bond St., Toronto, ON M5B 1X3
Tel: 416-362-2768; *Fax:* 416-865-5328
esheiber@hvllp.com

Toronto: Heifetz, Crozier, Law - *5
#600, 10 King St. East, Toronto, ON M5C 1C3
Tel: 416-863-1717; *Fax:* 416-368-3133
dcrozier@hclaw.com
www.hclaw.com

Toronto: Julian Heller & Associates - *3
#1905, 120 Adelaide St. West, Toronto, ON M5H 1T1
Tel: 416-364-2404; *Fax:* 416-364-0793
jheller@hellerandassociates.on.ca

Toronto: Heller, Rubel - *9
#1902, 120 Adelaide St. West, Toronto, ON M5H 1T1
Tel: 416-863-9311; *Fax:* 416-863-9465
mshore@hellerrubel.com

Toronto: Hicks Morley Hamilton Stewart Storie LLP - *84
Also Known As: Hicks Morley
TD Tower, TD Centre, Box 371, P.O. Box 371, Stn. TD Centre, 66 Wellington St., 30th Fl., Toronto, ON M5K 1K8
Tel: 416-362-1011; *Fax:* 416-362-9680
www.hicksmorley.com

Toronto: High Park Advocacy Group - *5
303 Jane St., Toronto, ON M6S 3Z3
Tel: 416-535-2815; *Fax:* 416-531-4769
www.highparkgroup.com

Toronto: John L. Hill - *1
127 Bishop Ave., Toronto, ON M2M 1Z6
Tel: 416-226-3221; *Fax:* 416-226-3222
conlaw@pathcom.com

Toronto: Hiltz Szigeti LLP - *2
#906, 94 Cumberland St., Toronto, ON M5R 1A3
Tel: 416-968-6575; *Fax:* 416-968-3424
lawyers@hslaw.ca

Toronto: David Himelfarb - *1
#1400, 111 Richmond St. West, Toronto, ON M5H 2G4
Tel: 416-365-0303; *Fax:* 416-365-9276

Toronto: Hinkson Sachak Mcleod
Former Name: Steven M. Hinkson
#301, 366 Bay St., Toronto, ON M5H 4B2
Tel: 416-368-3476; *Fax:* 416-363-9917
shinkson@hinksonlaw.com

Toronto: Hitchman & Sprigings - *6
#5704, 40 King St. West, Toronto, ON M5H 3Y2
Tel: 416-777-2270; *Fax:* 416-777-2271
mail@hitchman.com
www.hitchman.com

Toronto: Hodder Barristers - *6
#2200, DBRS Tower, Adelaide Place, 181 University Ave., Toronto, ON M5H 3M7
Tel: 416-601-4818; *Fax:* 416-947-0909
info@hodderbarristers.com
www.torontolawyerlawfirm.com

Toronto: Hodgson Russ LLP - *3
#2309, P.O. Box 30, 150 King St. West, Toronto, ON M5H 1J9
Tel: 416-595-5100; *Fax:* 416-595-5021
info@hodgsonruss.com
www.hodgsonruss.com

Toronto: Hoffman, Sillery, Buckstein & Chuback - *3
#200, 1810 Avenue Rd., Toronto, ON M5M 3Z2
Tel: 416-787-1161; *Fax:* 416-787-3894

** indicates number of lawyers*

***Toronto*: Gerri C. Holder - *1**
#901, 701 Evans Ave., Toronto, ON M9C 1A3
Tel: 416-626-3069; *Fax:* 416-622-8952
gholder@rogers.com

***Toronto*: Christopher Holoboff - *1**
#500, 27 Queen St. East, Toronto, ON M5C 2M6
Tel: 416-868-0878; *Fax:* 416-868-0879
choloboff@aol.com

***Toronto*: Hooey, Remus - *6**
#400, 1 University Ave., 4th Floor, Toronto, ON M5J 2P1
Tel: 416-362-4000; *Fax:* 416-362-3646
hrlaw@hooeyremus.com
www.hooeyremus.com

***Toronto*: E.R. Hornstein - *1**
19 Relmore Rd., Toronto, ON M5P 2Y4
Tel: 416-901-7949

***Toronto*: Houser, Henry & Syron - *6**
#2000, 145 King St. West, Toronto, ON M5H 2B6
Tel: 416-362-3411; *Fax:* 416-362-3757
inquiries@houserhenry.com
www.houserhenry.com

***Toronto*: Howie, Sacks & Henry LLP - *12**
#2800, P.O. Box 4, 401 Bay St., Toronto, ON M5H 2Y4
Tel: 416-361-5990; *Fax:* 416-361-0083
Toll-Free: 877-474-5997
hsh@hshlawyers.com
www.hshlawyers.com

***Toronto*: John A. Howlett - *1**
36 Toronto Street, Toronto, ON M5C 2C5
Tel: 416-941-9444; *Fax:* 416-913-1444
jhowlett@bellnet.ca

***Toronto*: John P. Howorun - *1**
#1702, 360 Bay St., Toronto, ON M5H 2V6
Tel: 416-363-9355; *Fax:* 416-363-6371

***Toronto*: Hrycyna, Pothemont - *2**
#200, 1081 Bloor St. West, Toronto, ON M6H 1M5
Tel: 416-532-8006; *Fax:* 416-532-2666
taras.hycyna@bellnet.ca

***Toronto*: Hughes, Amys LLP - *28**
#200, 48 Yonge St., Toronto, ON M5E 1G6
Tel: 416-367-1608; *Fax:* 416-367-8821
Toll-Free: 800-565-1713
info@hughesamys.com
www.hughesamys.com

***Toronto*: Hughes, Dorsch, Garland, Coles LLP - *5**
#400, 365 Bay St., Toronto, ON M5H 2V1
Tel: 416-868-1300; *Fax:* 416-861-1147

***Toronto*: Edward F. Hung - *2**
#319, 1033 Bay St., Toronto, ON M5S 3A5
Tel: 416-926-8777; *Fax:* 416-926-1799
edhung@best-litigate.com
www.lawyersintoronto.com

***Toronto*: Susanne L. Hunter - *1**
31 Prince Arthur Ave., Toronto, ON M5R 1B2
Tel: 416-975-0388; *Fax:* 416-960-5456

***Toronto*: Peter D. Hutcheon - *1**
372 Bay St., Toronto, ON M5H 2W9
Tel: 416-515-2049; *Fax:* 416-929-3204
peter@tantech.com

***Toronto*: P.N.J. Hutchinson - *1**
#302, P.O. Box 68, 70 Dixfield Dr., Toronto, ON M9C 4J4
Tel: 416-621-4430;

***Toronto*: David L. Hynes - *1**
#2200, 181 University Ave., Toronto, ON M5H 3M7
Tel: 416-601-9299; *Fax:* 416-601-9311
dlh@davidlhynes.com

***Toronto*: Nick Iannazzo, Barrister & Solicitor - *1**
Former Name: Iannazzo Onizuka Associates
#500, 425 University Ave., Toronto, ON M5G 1T6
Tel: 416-598-2002; *Fax:* 416-598-8183
niannazzo@on.aibn.com

***Toronto*: ICF Consulting Canada Inc. - *1**
#808, 277 Wellington St. West, Toronto, ON M5V 3E4
Tel: 416-341-0990; *Fax:* 416-341-0383
info@icfi.com
www.icfi.com

***Toronto*: Iler, Campbell - *8**
#700, 890 Yonge St., Toronto, ON M4W 3P4
Tel: 416-598-0103; *Fax:* 416-598-3484
www.ilercampbell.com

***Toronto*: International Project & Protocol Services Inc. - *1**
307 St. Clements Ave., Toronto, ON M4R 1H3
Tel: 416-481-7623;
ipps@rogers.com
www.ipps.net

***Toronto*: Joan M. Irwin - *1**
#2200, P.O. Box 154, 4950 Yonge St., Toronto, ON M2N 6K1
Tel: 416-733-1992; *Fax:* 416-222-0021

***Toronto*: Alvin Isenberg - *2**
#804, 5075 Yonge St., Toronto, ON M2N 6C6
Tel: 416-225-5136; *Fax:* 416-225-6877
info@shumanlaw.ca
www.shumanlaw.ca

***Toronto*: Israel Foulon LLP - *3**
#200, 30A Hazleton Ave., Toronto, ON M5R 2E2
Tel: 416-640-1550; *Fax:* 416-640-1555
inquiries@israelfoulon.com
israelfoulon.com

***Toronto*: Cydney G. Israel - *1**
61 Saint Nicholas St., Toronto, ON M4Y 1W6
Tel: 416-962-6188; *Fax:* 416-925-0162

***Toronto*: Jackman, Waldman & Associates - *6**
281 Eglinton Ave. East, Toronto, ON M4P 1L3
Tel: 416-482-6501; *Fax:* 416-489-9618

***Toronto*: Carol E.F. Jackson - *1**
#900, 60 Yonge St., Toronto, ON M5E 1H5
Tel: 416-363-3292; *Fax:* 416-868-6381

***Toronto*: Jacobson & Jacobson - *2**
#222, 3089 Bathurst St., Toronto, ON M6A 2A4
Tel: 416-787-0611; *Fax:* 416-787-4873

***Toronto*: James, Siddall & Derzko - *4**
#1305, 55 Queen St. East, Toronto, ON M5C 1R6
Tel: 416-860-0166; *Fax:* 416-860-0041

***Toronto*: Elham Jamshidi - *1**
277 Richmond Street, Toronto, ON M5V 1X1
Tel: 416-586-0220

***Toronto*: Jane Finch Community Legal Services - *3**
#409, 1315 Finch Ave. West, Toronto, ON M3J 2G6
Tel: 416-398-0677; *Fax:* 416-398-7172
www.janefinchcommunitylegalservices.ca

***Toronto*: Janssen & Associates - *2**
89 Scollard St., Toronto, ON M5R 1G4
Tel: 416-929-1103; *Fax:* 416-929-9610

***Toronto*: Dale F. Jean-Pierre - *1**
#700, 55 Town Centre Crt., Toronto, ON M1P 4X4
Tel: 416-290-0560; *Fax:* 416-290-1259

***Toronto*: Jeffery, Robertson, Watson & Pendrith - *2**
#1812, 2 Carlton St., Toronto, ON M5B 1J3
Tel: 416-977-7700; *Fax:* 416-977-8570
nwatson@sympatico.ca

***Toronto*: John A. Johnson - *1**
697 The Queensway, Toronto, ON M8V 1L2
Tel: 416-503-4418

***Toronto*: Daphne Johnston - *1**
#2000, 393 University Ave., Toronto, ON M5G 1E6
Tel: 416-599-9635; *Fax:* 416-599-6043
Toll-Free: 800-364-5793
daphnejohnston@rogers.com

***Toronto*: Jones, Rogers LLP - *5**
#1600, 155 University Ave., Toronto, ON M5H 3B7
Tel: 416-361-0626; *Fax:* 416-361-6303
law@jonesrogers.ca

***Toronto*: Mary K.E. Joseph - *1**
113 Riverdale Ave., Toronto, ON M4K 1C2
Tel: 416-363-8048; *Fax:* 416-406-0038
mary@maryjoseph.ca

***Toronto*: Ron Jourard - *1**
#504, 3200 Dufferin St., Toronto, ON M6A 3B2
Tel: 416-398-6685; *Fax:* 416-398-7396
Toll-Free: 888-257-0002
jourard@defencelaw.com
www.defencelaw.com

***Toronto*: Robert W. Judge - *1**
44 Fairview Blvd., Toronto, ON M4K 1L9
Tel: 416-466-7007; *Fax:* 416-466-7050

***Toronto*: Steven W. Junger - *1**
#14, 620 Supertest Rd., Toronto, ON M3J 2M8
Tel: 416-787-7247; *Fax:* 416-787-3021
s.junger@sympatico.ca

***Toronto*: Juriansz & Li - *3**
#1709, North American Life Centre, 5650 Yonge St., Toronto, ON M2M 4G3
Tel: 416-226-2342; *Fax:* 416-222-6874

***Toronto*: Justice for Children & Youth - *6**
#1203, 415 Yonge St., Toronto, ON M5S 2T9
Tel: 416-920-1633; *Fax:* 416-920-5855
Toll-Free: 866-999-5329
info@jfcy.org
www.jfcy.org

***Toronto*: Kacaba & Associates - *2**
#440, 100 Richmond St. West, Toronto, ON M5H 3K6
Tel: 416-361-1777; *Fax:* 416-361-1776

***Toronto*: Kagan, Shastri - *6**
Former Name: Kagan, Zucker, Feldbloom, Shastri
188 Avenue Rd., Toronto, ON M5R 2J1
Tel: 416-368-2100; *Fax:* 416-368-8206

***Toronto*: The Kalen Group - *1**
262 Avenue Rd., Toronto, ON M4V 2G7
Tel: 416-929-7781; *Fax:* 416-929-7784
kalen@mrgeenjeans.ca

***Toronto*: Speros Kanellos - *1**
#202, 211 Consumers Rd., Toronto, ON M2J 4G8
Tel: 416-493-3100; *Fax:* 416-493-4377

***Toronto*: Chan Yeung Kang - *1**
#210, 280 Sheppard Ave. East, Toronto, ON M2N 3B1
Tel: 416-221-1417; *Fax:* 416-221-1732
cykanglaw@hotmail.com

***Toronto*: William Kaplan - *1**
#200, 70 Bond St., Toronto, ON M5B 1X3
Tel: 416-865-5341; *Fax:* 416-360-5746
william@williamkaplan.com
www.williamkaplan.com

***Toronto*: Kapoor Barristers - *2**
#210, 20 Adelaide St. East, Toronto, ON M5C 2T6
Tel: 416-363-2700; *Fax:* 416-368-6811
info@kapoorbarristers.com
www.kapoorbarristers.com

***Toronto*: Kappel Ludlow LLP - *2**
#1400, 439 University Ave., Toronto, ON M5G 1Y8
Tel: 416-408-4565; *Fax:* 416-408-4569
info@kappelludlow.com
www.kappelludlow.com

***Toronto*: Karta Strategy - *1**
#609, 45 Carlton St., Toronto, ON M5B 2H9
Tel: 416-506-0609;
info@kartastrategy.com
www.kartastrategy.com

***Toronto*: Joseph H. Kary - *1**
90A Isabella St., Toronto, ON M4Y 1N4
Tel: 416-929-9656; *Fax:* 416-363-2473

***Toronto*: Sheldon L. Kasman & Associate - *2**
#201, 1622 Eglinton Ave. West, Toronto, ON M6E 2G8
Tel: 416-789-1888; *Fax:* 416-789-5928
law@kasman.com
www.kasman.com

***Toronto*: Garen Kassabian - *1**
#203, 8 Sampson Mews, Toronto, ON M3C 0H5
Tel: 416-443-9494; *Fax:* 416-443-0575
garen@bellnet.ca

***Toronto*: Kavanagh Bateman & Baek LLP - *4**
Also Known As: Nobbs, Woods, Kavanagh & Bateman
#550, 141 Adelaide St. West, Toronto, ON M5H 3L5
Tel: 416-304-0600; *Fax:* 416-304-0669

***Toronto*: J.M. Kavanagh, Q.C. - *1**
#340, 100 Cowdray Ct., Toronto, ON M1S 5C8
Tel: 416-265-3560; *Fax:* 416-265-1944

** indicates number of lawyers*

Toronto: Robert C. Kay - *1
161 Bay Street, Toronto, ON M5J 2S1
Tel: 416-362-9999;

Toronto: D.H. Kayfetz - *1
99 South Dr., Toronto, ON M4W 1R7
Tel: 416-364-8131; *Fax:* 416-964-9009

Toronto: Keith & Kramer - *2
#404, 1200 Bay St., Toronto, ON M5R 2A5
Tel: 416-922-4417; *Fax:* 416-922-9328
tkeith@interlog.com

Toronto: Christina H. Kelk - *1
94 South Dr., Toronto, ON M4W 1R6
Tel: 416-966-1266; *Fax:* 416-966-2670
kelk@sympatico.ca

Toronto: Kelly & Lacy - *4
144 King St. East, 3rd Fl., Toronto, ON M5C 1G8
Tel: 416-362-3681; *Fax:* 416-366-1762
jennings@144king.com

Toronto: Kelly ADR Services - *1
Former Name: Kelly International Settlement Services Inc.
#200, 112 Adelaide St. East, Toronto, ON M5C 1K9
Tel: 416-362-8555; *Fax:* 416-362-8825
kjkelly@adrchambers.com

Toronto: H. Michael Kelly, Q.C. - *1
#200, 112 Adelaide St. East, Toronto, ON M5C 1K9
Tel: 416-960-3781; *Toll-Free:* 800-856-5154

Toronto: Evan N. Kenley - *1
#301, 1352 Bathurst St., Toronto, ON M5K 3H7
Tel: 416-932-1148; *Fax:* 416-932-1108

Toronto: M.L. Kerbel - *1
#1001, 65 Queen St. West, Toronto, ON M5H 2M5
Tel: 416-364-9532;
mlkerbel@sympatico.ca

Toronto: Shayne G. Kert - *1
370 Bloor St. East, Toronto, ON M4W 3M6
Tel: 416-863-0141; *Fax:* 416-927-9069

Toronto: Kestenberg Siegal Lipkus - *8
65 Granby St., Toronto, ON M5B 1H8
Tel: 416-597-0000; *Fax:* 416-597-6567
postmaster@ksllaw.com
www.ksllaw.com

Toronto: El-Farouk A. Khaki - *1
315 Mutual St., Toronto, ON M4Y 1X6
Tel: 416-925-7227; *Fax:* 416-925-2450
elfin925@rogers.com

Toronto: R.S. Kimel - *1
444 Adelaide St. West, Toronto, ON M5V 1S7
Tel: 416-703-1877; *Fax:* 416-504-9216

Toronto: King & King - *1
#2, 823 Millwood Rd., Toronto, ON M4G 1W3
Tel: 416-368-4678; *Fax:* 416-368-7234
aek@kingandking.net

Toronto: Kirkland Capital Corporation - *1
#105, 120 Rosedale Valley Rd., Toronto, ON M4W 1P8
Tel: 416-921-9992; *Fax:* 416-921-9998
info@kirklandcapital.com

Toronto: Don P. Kirsh - *1
#207, 3500 Dufferin St., Toronto, ON M3K 1N2
Tel: 416-630-6136; *Fax:* 416-630-6135
dkirsh@bellnet.ca
www.donkirsh.ca

Toronto: Sheila Kirsh - *1
#1812, 181 University Ave., Toronto, ON M5H 3M7
Tel: 416-367-1765; *Fax:* 416-594-0868
sheila@kirsh-law.com
www.kirsh-law.com

Toronto: Howard Joshua Kirshenbaum - *1
#17, 1140 Sheppard Ave. West, Toronto, ON M3K 2A2
Tel: 416-865-5339; *Fax:* 416-777-9255
kirshenbaum@msn.com

Toronto: Klaiman, Edmonds - *3
#1000, 60 Yonge St., Toronto, ON M5E 1H5
Tel: 416-867-9600; *Fax:* 416-867-9783
reception@klaimanedmonds.com
www.klaimanedmonds.com

Toronto: Judi E. Klein - *1
#104, 2552 Finch Ave. West, Toronto, ON M9M 2G3
Tel: 416-749-7747; *Fax:* 416-749-9190
judi-klein@look.ca
www.judieklein.supersites.ca

Toronto: Paula Knopf Arbitrations Ltd. - *1
4 Biggar Ave., Toronto, ON M6H 2N4
Tel: 416-652-1516; *Fax:* 416-652-2632
pkopf@allstream.net

Toronto: Joel B. Kohm - *1
#601, 18 Wynford Dr., Toronto, ON M3C 3S2
Tel: 416-510-1435; *Fax:* 416-510-0081
joel.kohm@rogers.com

Toronto: Marc Koplowitz Associates - *2
#2900, 390 Bay St., Toronto, ON M5H 2Y2
Tel: 416-368-1100; *Fax:* 416-368-1998
marc@koplaw.com

Toronto: Kopolovic, Strigberger - *1
#300, 69 Elm St., Toronto, ON M5G 1H2
Tel: 416-971-7272; *Fax:* 416-971-9092

Toronto: Korman & Company - *3
721 Queen St. East, Toronto, ON M4M 1H1
Tel: 416-465-4232; *Fax:* 416-465-6912
info@kormancompany.com
www.kormancompany.com

Toronto: Koroloff & Huckins - *2
#304, 1110 Sheppard Ave. East, Toronto, ON M2K 2W2
Tel: 416-229-6226; *Fax:* 416-229-6517

Toronto: Koskie Minsky - *36
#900, P.O. Box 52, 20 Queen St. West, Toronto, ON M5H 3R3
Tel: 416-977-8353; *Fax:* 416-977-3316
www.koskieminsky.com

Toronto: Kostyniuk & Greenside - *11
#300, 5468 Dundas St. West, Toronto, ON M9B 6E3
Tel: 416-762-8238; *Fax:* 416-762-5042
www.kostyniukandgreenside.com

Toronto: Kotler Law Firm - *1
#617, 1 Eglinton Ave. East, Toronto, ON M4P 3A1
Tel: 416-932-4949; *Fax:* 416-487-2992
hgk@koterlaw.ca

Toronto: Irwin Koziebrocki - *1
Also Known As: Levy Earl J QC Professional Corporation
#400, 100 Richmond St. West, Toronto, ON M5H 3K6
Tel: 416-364-7292; *Fax:* 416-364-7473
thekozman@aol.com

Toronto: Neil L. Kozloff - *1
#1900, 439 University Ave., Toronto, ON M5G 1Y8
Tel: 416-408-1114; *Fax:* 416-408-2372

Toronto: Alex Krakowitz - *1
#2200, P.O. Box 75, 1 Dundas St. West, Toronto, ON M5G 1Z3
Tel: 416-598-4626; *Fax:* 416-599-8341
Toll-Free: 800-410-1013
alex.krakowitz@lawpro.ca

Toronto: Kramer Henderson Sidlofsky LLP - *5
Former Name: Kramer Henderson
#2100, 120 Adelaide St. West, Toronto, ON M5H 1T1
Tel: 416-601-6820; *Fax:* 416-601-0712
info@kramerhenderson.com
www.kramerhenderson.com

Toronto: Krauss, Weinryb - *2
#1540, 5140 Yonge St., Toronto, ON M2N 6L7
Tel: 416-222-4446; *Fax:* 416-222-9788

Toronto: Gerald Kroll, Q.C. - *1
#1800, 4950 Yonge St., Toronto, ON M2N 6K1
Tel: 416-224-0200; *Fax:* 416-224-0758
kroll@torlaw.com

Toronto: Kuretzky Vassos - *9
#1404, 151 Yonge St., Toronto, ON M5C 2W7
Tel: 416-865-0504; *Fax:* 416-865-9567
info@kuretzkyvassos.com
www.kuretzkyvassos.com

Toronto: Helen Kurgatnikov Miller, Barrister & Solicitor - *1
#914, 1110 Finch Ave. West, Toronto, ON M3J 2T2
Tel: 416-665-4343

Toronto: Kvas Miller Everitt - *3
#3100, 3300 Bloor St. West, Toronto, ON M8X 2X3
Tel: 416-921-6558; *Fax:* 416-923-0760
kme@idirect.com
www.kmelawyers.com

Toronto: Grace F. Kwan - *1
90A Isabella St., 3rd Fl., Toronto, ON M4Y 1N4
Tel: 416-968-2014; *Fax:* 416-968-2054
gkwan@295.ca

Toronto: Wolfgang H. Kyser - *1
#310, 401 Queen's Quay West, Toronto, ON M5V 2Y2
Tel: 416-863-1053; *Fax:* 416-861-0191

Toronto: Stephen M. Labow - *1
#610, 480 University Ave., Toronto, ON M5G 1V2
Tel: 416-947-1172; *Fax:* 416-596-0808
stephen@labow.ca

Toronto: Lackman, Firestone Law Offices - *2
#511, 4576 Yonge Street, Toronto, ON M2N 6N4
Tel: 416-364-0020; *Fax:* 416-364-0389

Toronto: Lafontaine & Associates - *3
Former Name: Gregory L. Lafontaine
#506, 330 University Ave., Toronto, ON M5G 1R7
Tel: 416-204-1835; *Fax:* 416-204-1849
greg@127john.com

Toronto: Laishley Reed LLP - *6
#2000, 3 Church St., Toronto, ON M5E 1M2
Tel: 416-981-9401; *Fax:* 416-981-0060
info@laishleyreed.com
www.laishleyreed.com

Toronto: Tikam K. Lalla - *1
1203 Bloor St. West, Toronto, ON M6H 1N4
Tel: 416-532-2801; *Fax:* 416-532-4942

Toronto: D. Wayne Lalonde - *1
#2000, The Law Chambers, 393 University Ave., 20th Fl., Toronto, ON M5G 1E6
Tel: 416-585-2868; *Fax:* 416-593-4446
dwaynelalonde@lawchambers.com
www.lawchambers.com

Toronto: Mary L.F. Lam - *2
40 Binscarth Road, Toronto, ON M4W 1Y1
Tel: 416-383-0266; *Fax:* 416-383-0299
mary.lam@rogers.com

Toronto: Jack S. Lambert - *1
79 Edith Dr., Toronto, ON M4R 1Z1
Tel: 416-226-6333; *Fax:* 416-226-6344
jacklamlaw@rogers.com

Toronto: Garry E.J. Lamourie - *1
#2104, 180 Dundas St. West, Toronto, ON M5G 1Z8
Tel: 416-597-9828; *Fax:* 416-597-9808

Toronto: C. Robert Langdon, Q.C. - *1
140 Dinnick Cres., Toronto, ON M4N 1L8
Tel: 416-483-2887; *Fax:* 416-484-4306
c.robert.langdon@sympatico.ca

Toronto: Douglas G. Lash - *1
145 Glengrove Ave., Toronto, ON M4R 1P1
Tel: 416-932-2399; *Fax:* 416-932-9306
dlash@zebulongroup.com

Toronto: Wayne S. Laski - *1
#1800, 4950 Yonge St., Toronto, ON M2N 6K1
Tel: 416-224-0200; *Fax:* 416-224-0758
wlaski@wlaski.com

Toronto: Sam Laufer - *1
#3902, 44 Charles St. West, Toronto, ON M4Y 1R8
Tel: 416-922-9455; *Fax:* 416-923-8870
legitlaw@yahoo.com.au

Toronto: John V. Lawer, Q.C. - *1
#306, 40 St. Clair Ave. East, Toronto, ON M4T 1M9
Tel: 416-922-0737; *Fax:* 416-922-1896
johnv@johnvlawer.on.ca

Toronto: Lax O'Sullivan Scott Lisus LLP - *16
#1920, 145 King St. West, Toronto, ON M5H 1J8
Tel: 416-598-1744; *Fax:* 416-598-3730
www.counsel-toronto.com

Toronto: Laxton Glass LLP - *11
#200, 390 Bay St., Toronto, ON M5H 2Y2
Tel: 416-363-2353; *Fax:* 416-363-7112

* *indicates number of lawyers*

***Toronto*: Sheldon S. Lazarovitz - *1**
31 Westgate Blvd., Toronto, ON M3H 1N8
Tel: 416-638-6080; *Fax:* 416-638-6246
lazarovitz@rogers.com

***Toronto*: Timothy J. Leach - *1**
#309, 658 Danforth Ave., Toronto, ON M4J 5B9
Tel: 416-868-0265; *Fax:* 416-868-0478

***Toronto*: John Y.C. Lee - *1**
#418, 4002 Sheppard Ave. East, Toronto, ON M1S 1S6
Tel: 416-299-8900; *Fax:* 416-299-8232

***Toronto*: Julia Yuen-Nam Lee - *1**
825 Gerrard St. East, Toronto, ON M4M 1Y2
Tel: 416-466-6888

***Toronto*: Paul Lee & Associates - *7**
20 Maitland St., Toronto, ON M4Y 1C5
Tel: 416-961-2707; *Fax:* 416-961-5575
office@paullee.ca

***Toronto*: J.C. Lemire - *1**
#500, 70 Bond St., Toronto, ON M5B 1X3
Tel: 416-363-1097; *Fax:* 416-863-4896

***Toronto*: Lenczner Slaght Royce Smith Griffin LLP - *45**
#2600, 130 Adelaide St., West, Toronto, ON M5H 3P5
Tel: 416-865-9500; *Fax:* 416-865-9010
info@litigate.com
www.litigate.com

***Toronto*: George J. Leon - *1**
29 Berwick Ave., Toronto, ON M5P 1G9
Tel: 416-487-1385; *Fax:* 416-485-0437
gleon@idirect.com

***Toronto*: Thomas J. Leroy - *1**
#304, 375 University Ave., Toronto, ON M5G 2G1
Tel: 416-979-2352; *Fax:* 416-979-8562
leroyt@lao.on.ca

***Toronto*: Gérard Lévesque - *1**
184 Lake Promenade, Toronto, ON M8W 1A8
Tel: 416-253-0129; *Fax:* 416-253-4737

***Toronto*: Levine Associates - *3**
#1400, 10 King St. East, Toronto, ON M5C 1C3
Tel: 416-364-2345; *Fax:* 416-364-3818
shelleylevine@levlaw.com

***Toronto*: Lorne Levine - *1**
#305, 55 Eglinton Ave. East, Toronto, ON M4P 1G8
Tel: 416-483-1251; *Fax:* 416-483-1257

***Toronto*: Levine, Sherkin, Boussidan - *4**
#300, 23 Lesmill Rd., Toronto, ON M3B 3P6
Tel: 416-224-2400; *Fax:* 416-224-2408
www.lsblaw.com

***Toronto*: Levinson & Associates - *1**
#610, 480 University Ave., Toronto, ON M5G 1V2
Tel: 416-591-8484; *Fax:* 416-596-0808
levinson@levadvocate.net
www.levadvocate.net

***Toronto*: Levitan Lawyers - *1**
22 Soho St., Toronto, ON M5T 1Z7
Tel: 416-368-4600; *Fax:* 416-368-1166

***Toronto*: Sherry Levitan - *1**
#403, 1 Yorkdale Rd., Toronto, ON M6A 3A1
Tel: 416-784-1222; *Fax:* 416-784-0777
slevitan@bellnet.ca

***Toronto*: Shirley E. Levitan - *1**
69 Elm St., Toronto, ON M5G 1H2
Tel: 416-585-2626; *Fax:* 416-971-9092
shilev@idirect.com

***Toronto*: Levitt, Lightman, Dewar & Graham LLP - *3**
#1, 16 Four Seasons Pl., Toronto, ON M9B 6E5
Tel: 416-620-0362; *Fax:* 416-620-5158
flevitt@lldg.ca

***Toronto*: Alan D. Levy - *1**
75 Robert St., Toronto, ON M5S 2K4
Tel: 416-929-8282; *Fax:* 416-929-9895
alan@alanlevy.ca
www.alanlevy.ca

***Toronto*: E.J. Levy, Q.C. - *1**
#400, 100 Richmond St. West, Toronto, ON M5H 3K6
Tel: 416-364-7292; *Fax:* 416-364-7473

***Toronto*: Lewis & Associates - *5**
41 Madison Ave., Toronto, ON M5R 2S2
Tel: 416-924-2227; *Fax:* 416-924-9993
lewisassociates@eol.ca

***Toronto*: Andrew C. Lewis - *1**
#208, 90 Eglinton Ave. East, Toronto, ON M4P 2Y3
Tel: 416-322-7010; *Fax:* 416-483-2737
lewisac@bellnet.ca

***Toronto*: Joseph E. Lewis - *1**
#202, 327 Eglinton Ave. East, Toronto, ON M4P 1L7
Tel: 416-486-0084; *Fax:* 416-486-7363

***Toronto*: Raymond W.M. Li - *1**
#8, 4158 Kingston Rd., Toronto, ON M1E 2M6
Tel: 416-977-7773

***Toronto*: Susan M.C. Libanio - *1**
#617, 1 Summerhill Rd., Toronto, ON M8V 1R9
Tel: 416-533-6002; *Fax:* 416-533-6097
smel@rogers.com

***Toronto*: P. Yoel Lichtblau - *1**
499 Wilson Heights Blvd., Toronto, ON M3H 2V7
Tel: 416-633-2465; *Fax:* 416-398-3369
ylichtblau@rogers.com

***Toronto*: Lindenberg & Lindenberg - *2**
#100, 287 Eglinton Ave. East, Toronto, ON M4P 1L3
Tel: 416-484-8177; *Fax:* 416-322-0807

***Toronto*: Link Strategies Inc. - *1**
#910, P.O. Box 28, 1 Toronto St., Toronto, ON M5C 2V6
Tel: 416-368-0323; *Fax:* 416-368-6068
www.linkstrategies.ca

***Toronto*: John Liss - *1**
207 Brunswick Ave., Toronto, ON M5S 2M4
Tel: 416-968-2558; *Fax:* 416-961-7906

***Toronto*: John A.G. Lister - *1**
167 Danforth Ave., Toronto, ON M4K 1N2
Tel: 416-461-0983; *Fax:* 416-462-3347
jaglister@on.aibn.com

***Toronto*: Nadia Liva - *1**
15 Bedford Rd., Toronto, ON M5R 2J7
Tel: 416-598-0106; *Fax:* 416-868-0273
nadialiva@15bedford.com

***Toronto*: H. David Locke - *1**
#200, 37 Prince Arthur Ave., Toronto, ON M5R 1B2
Tel: 416-601-1525; *Fax:* 416-601-0392

***Toronto*: Paula V. Locke - *1**
#200, 37 Prince Arthur Ave., Toronto, ON M5R 1B2
Tel: 416-601-1525; *Fax:* 416-601-0392

***Toronto*: Lofranco Chagpar Barristers - *6**
Former Name: Rocco C. Lofranco, Barristers & Solicitors
#1300, 5255 Yonge St., Toronto, ON M2N 6P4
Tel: 416-223-8333; *Fax:* 416-223-3404
info@lofrancobarristers.com

***Toronto*: Gerald P. Logan - *1**
317 Grace St., Toronto, ON M6G 3A7
Tel: 416-535-8920; *Fax:* 416-537-6550

***Toronto*: Joachim M. Loh - *1**
#10, 3880 Midland Ave., Toronto, ON M1V 5K4
Tel: 416-609-8289; *Fax:* 416-609-8857
jmloh@jmlohlaw.com

***Toronto*: Lomer, Frost - Barristers - *2**
#1515, 180 Dundas St. West, Toronto, ON M5G 1Z8
Tel: 416-923-1900; *Fax:* 416-847-2564

***Toronto*: Loopstra Nixon LLP - *18**
#600, Woodbine Place, 135 Queens Plate Dr., Toronto, ON M9W 6V7
Tel: 416-746-4710; *Fax:* 416-746-8319
TheStraightAnswer@loonix.com
www.loopstranixon.com

***Toronto*: Francisco B. Luna - *1**
#1704, 2 Carlton St., Toronto, ON M5B 1J3
Tel: 416-977-3287; *Fax:* 416-977-1950
f.luna@on.aibn.com

***Toronto*: Karen D. Lundy - *1**
#2150, 1 Queen St. East, Toronto, ON M5C 2W5
Tel: 416-866-8858; *Fax:* 416-364-3866
karen.lundy@waldin.ca

***Toronto*: Lawrence M. Lychowyd - *1**
236A Bain Ave., Toronto, ON M4K 1G3
Tel: 416-466-8063; *Fax:* 416-694-3367
larrythelawyer@sympatico.ca
www.larrythelawyer.ca

***Toronto*: Michael M. Lynch, Q.C. - *1**
#414, Richmond Tower, 100 Richmond St. West, Toronto, ON M5H 3K6
Tel: 416-972-9828; *Fax:* 416-964-0823

***Toronto*: Bryan A. MacBride - *1**
#612, 55 Lombard, Toronto, ON M5C 2R7
Tel: 416-601-9222; *Fax:* 416-601-9223
bamc@rogers.com

***Toronto*: J.M. Macchione - *1**
#2000, 77 Bloor St. West, Toronto, ON M5S 1M2
Tel: 416-966-8373; *Fax:* 416-923-3654
janice.macchione@realstar.ca

***Toronto*: MacDonald & Partners LLP - *12**
90 Adelaide St. West, 3rd Fl., Toronto, ON M5H 3V9
Tel: 416-971-4802; *Fax:* 416-971-9584
famlaw@mpllp.com
www.macdonaldpartners.com

***Toronto*: MacDonald Group - *1**
4 Swanwick Ave., Toronto, ON M4E 1Z1
Tel: 416-937-6646

***Toronto*: Mary-Douglass MacDonald - *1**
122 Prince George Dr., Toronto, ON M9B 2Y2
Tel: 416-231-4899; *Fax:* 416-231-7306
mdmacdonald@rogers.com

***Toronto*: Mary E. MacInnes - *1**
25 McGlashan Ct., Toronto, ON M5M 4M6
Tel: 416-487-8210

***Toronto*: Carolyn A. MacLean - *1**
#102, 40 Isabella St., Toronto, ON M4Y 1N1
Tel: 416-925-4008; *Fax:* 416-920-0367

***Toronto*: Theresa M. MacLean - *1**
#202, 40 Isabella St., Toronto, ON M4Y 1N1
Tel: 416-964-9224; *Fax:* 416-920-0367

***Toronto*: Doug MacLeod, Barristor & Solicitor - *1**
#1700, 22 St Clair Ave. East, Toronto, ON M4T 2S3
Tel: 416-977-9894; *Fax:* 416-977-7337
doug@dougmacleod.com
www.dougmacleod.com

***Toronto*: Paul A. MacLeod - *1**
32 Elm St., Toronto, ON L3M 1H3
Tel: 905-945-9659; *Fax:* 905-945-0838
office@macleod-barr.com

***Toronto*: MacMaster, Poolman Law Office - *1**
Former Name: MacMaster, Poolman & Associates
#203, 150 Eglinton Ave. East, Toronto, ON M4P 1E8
Tel: 416-250-8387; *Fax:* 416-250-6233
info@macmasterpoolman.com
www.macmasterpoolman.com

***Toronto*: MacMillan Rooke Boeckle - *5**
#3005, P.O. Box 96, 401 Bay St., Toronto, ON M5H 2Y4
Tel: 416-360-1194; *Fax:* 416-360-8469
Toll-Free: 800-661-7606
info@macmillanrooke.com

***Toronto*: S.G.R. MacMillan - *1**
#2110, 120 Adelaide St. West, Toronto, ON M5H 1T1
Tel: 416-363-0100; *Toll-Free:* 877-363-0100
mail@sgrm.com
www.sgrm.com

***Toronto*: Dan Malamet - *1**
10 Audubon Ct., Toronto, ON M2N 1T9
Tel: 416-865-6952; *Fax:* 416-863-6275
dan.malamet@bakernet.com

***Toronto*: T.R. Anthony Malcolm - *1**
#601, 8 King St. East, Toronto, ON M5C 1B5
Tel: 416-864-1608; *Fax:* 416-864-1549
tram@tramalcolm.com

***Toronto*: Malo, Pilley & Lehman - *3**
Also Known As: Malo & Pilley
1067 Bloor St. West, Toronto, ON M6H 1M5
Tel: 416-534-3555; *Fax:* 416-534-7625

** indicates number of lawyers*

Toronto: **Mancia & Mancia - *1**
#601, 80 Richmond St. West, Toronto, ON M5H 2A4
Tel: 416-363-7422; *Fax:* 416-363-4975
cmancia@bellnet.ca

Toronto: **Harvey Mandel - *1**
#203, 55 Queen St. East, Toronto, ON M5C 1R6
Tel: 416-364-7717; *Fax:* 416-364-4813

Toronto: **Pierre F. Marchildon - *1**
#308, Dundas-Lambton Centre, 4195 Dundas St. West, Toronto, ON M8X 1Y4
Tel: 416-236-0686; *Fax:* 416-236-0650
Toll-Free: 866-236-0686
pfmlaw@on.aibn.com

Toronto: **Marcos Associates - *2**
1718 Dundas St. West, Toronto, ON M6K 1V5
Tel: 416-537-3151; *Fax:* 416-537-3153
emarcos@on.aibn.com

Toronto: **Paul E. Marcus**
York University, West Office Bldg., 4700 Keele St., Toronto, ON M3J 1P3
Tel: 416-650-8025; *Fax:* 416-650-8032
marcusp@yorkfoundation.yorku.ca
www.yorku.ca/foundation

Toronto: **June A. Maresca - *1**
#400, 2490 Bloor St. West, Toronto, ON M6S 1R4
Tel: 416-762-8617; *Fax:* 416-760-7338
jmaresca@on.aibn.com

Toronto: **Marin, Evans & Bell - *2**
#500, 200 Adelaide St. West, Toronto, ON M5H 1W7
Tel: 416-408-2177; *Fax:* 416-408-1718

Toronto: **Charles C. Mark, Q.C. - *1**
#2010, P.O. Box 28, 401 Bay St., Toronto, ON M5H 2Y4
Tel: 416-869-0929; *Fax:* 416-869-9118
ccmark@on.aibn.com

Toronto: **Markes Lawyers - *12**
Former Name: *Beach, Hepburn*
#506, 1090 Don Mills Rd., Toronto, ON M3C 3R6
Tel: 416-350-3500; *Fax:* 416-350-3510
amarkes@markeslawyers.com
www.markeslawyers.com

Toronto: **Markle, May, Phibbs - *8**
#300, 500 Sheppard Ave. East, Toronto, ON M2N 6H7
Tel: 416-593-4385; *Fax:* 416-593-4478

Toronto: **H. David Marks, Q.C. - *1**
#2150, 1 Queen St. East, Toronto, ON M5C 2W5
Tel: 416-863-1550; *Fax:* 416-863-9670
david.marks@waldin.ca

Toronto: **Larry M. Marshall - *1**
#1017, 250 Consumers Rd., Toronto, ON M2J 4V6
Tel: 416-497-2526; *Fax:* 416-497-3143
lmarshal@idirect.com

Toronto: **E.E. Marszewski - *1**
13 Maple Ave., Toronto, ON M4W 2T5
Tel: 416-927-1820; *Fax:* 416-967-4549
marszewski@aol.com

Toronto: **Calvin Martin, Q.C. - *1**
600 Church St., Toronto, ON M4Y 2E7
Tel: 416-922-5854; *Fax:* 416-944-0285
dvc14@calvinmartinqc.com
www.calvinmartinqc.com

Toronto: **Malcolm M. Martin - *1**
#310, 49 The Donway West, Toronto, ON M3C 3M9
Tel: 416-449-4111; *Fax:* 416-449-7879
mmartin@malcolmmartin.com

Toronto: **Martinello & Associates - *3**
#208, United Centre, 255 Duncan Mill Rd., Toronto, ON M3B 3H9
Tel: 416-510-8866; *Fax:* 416-449-9977
martinello@on.aibn.com

Toronto: **Alexander Martynowicz - *1**
#300, 940 The East Mall, Toronto, ON M9B 6J7
Tel: 416-622-9222; *Fax:* 416-622-0333

Toronto: **Ville K. Masalin - *1**
#309, 191 Eglinton Ave. East, Toronto, ON M4P 1K1
Tel: 416-484-9347; *Fax:* 416-484-9027

Toronto: **Masters & Masters - *2**
#440, 65 Queen St. West, Toronto, ON M5H 2M5
Tel: 416-361-1399; *Fax:* 416-361-6181
masterslaw@sympatico.ca
www.masterslaw.com

Toronto: **Gaetano P. Matteazzi - *1**
#100, 25 Morrow Ave., Toronto, ON M6R 2H9
Tel: 416-534-8881; *Fax:* 416-516-5305

Toronto: **Mark O. Mattson - *1**
17 Fenwood Heights, Toronto, ON M1M 2V6
Tel: 416-265-6548

Toronto: **McBride Wallace Laurent & Cord LLP - *7**
#200, 5464 Dundas St. West, Toronto, ON M9B 1B4
Tel: 416-231-6555; *Fax:* 416-231-6630

Toronto: **McCague, Peacock, Borlack, McInnis & Lloyd LLP - *24**
#2700, The Exchange Tower, P.O. Box 136, Stn. 1st, 130 King St. West, Toronto, ON M5X 1C7
Tel: 416-860-0001; *Fax:* 416-860-0003
general@mwph.com

Toronto: **D.V. McCarthy - *1**
#302, 885 Progress Ave., Toronto, ON M1H 3G3
Tel: 416-289-9620; *Fax:* 416-439-9553

Toronto: **Robert L. McClelland - *1**
#313, 2498 Yonge St., Toronto, ON M4P 2H8
Tel: 416-481-7360; *Fax:* 416-574-0429
ronmcc@ca.inter.net

Toronto: **McComb Dockrill - *2**
#2707, T-D Bank Tower, Toronto-Dominion Centre, P.O. Box 17, Stn. T-D Centre, Toronto, ON M5K 1A1
Tel: 416-366-1881; *Fax:* 416-366-0608
mccombdockrill@on.aibn.com

Toronto: **John D. McCrie - *1**
#9, 15 Belfield Rd., Toronto, ON M9W 1E8
Tel: 416-243-9501; *Fax:* 416-243-2990
johndmccrie@on.aibn.com

Toronto: **David J. McGhee - *1**
390 Bay St., 30th Fl., Toronto, ON M5H 2Y2
Tel: 416-362-9736; *Fax:* 416-362-9435
djmcghee@on.aibn.com

Toronto: **McGowan & Co. - *3**
Former Name: *McGowan, Elliott & Kim LLP*
#1400, 10 Bay St., Toronto, ON M5J 2R8
Tel: 416-350-2481; *Fax:* 416-363-1875

Toronto: **David R. McGregor - *1**
#316, 18 Wynford Dr., Toronto, ON M3C 3S2
Tel: 416-485-1123; *Fax:* 416-485-8742
dmseus@yahoo.ca

Toronto: **McIlroy & McIlroy Inc. - *1**
203 Riverside Dr., Toronto, ON M6S 4A8
Tel: 416-777-0447; *Fax:* 416-777-0436
www.mcilroy.com

Toronto: **McInnis, Nicoll - *2**
#507, 330 Bay St., Toronto, ON M5H 2S8
Tel: 416-362-1354; *Fax:* 416-362-1465

Toronto: **McIver & McIver - *2**
#700, 1 Richmond St. West, Toronto, ON M5H 3W4
Tel: 416-864-9000; *Fax:* 416-864-9190

Toronto: **Michael A. McKee - *1**
9 Elmlea Rd., Toronto, ON M9P 2M6
Tel: 416-928-6611; *Fax:* 416-928-9515
mckeelawoffice@yahoo.ca

Toronto: **McLean & Kerr LLP - *23**
#2800, 130 Adelaide St. West, Toronto, ON M5H 3P5
Tel: 416-364-5371; *Fax:* 416-366-8571
mail@mcleankerr.com
www.mcleankerr.com

Toronto: **Reginald M. McLean - *1**
1035 McNicoll Ave., Toronto, ON M1W 3W6
Tel: 416-512-1200; *Fax:* 416-512-1212
maclaw@bellnet.ca

Toronto: **McMaster, McIntyre & Smyth LLP, Barristers & Solicitors - *5**
2777 Dundas St. West, Toronto, ON M6P 1Y4
Tel: 416-769-4188; *Fax:* 416-769-4147
Toll-Free: 888-769-4188
mail@mmslawyers.com
www.mmslawyers.com

Toronto: **McPhadden, Samac, Merner, Barry - *4**
Former Name: McPhadden, Samac, Merner, Darling
#300, 8 King St. East, Toronto, ON M5C 1B5
Tel: 416-363-5195; *Fax:* 416-363-7485
reception@msmb.ca
www.msmb.ca

Toronto: **Deborah L. Meldazy - *1**
426 Davenport Rd., Toronto, ON M4V 1B5
Tel: 416-929-8524; *Fax:* 416-929-4042
dmeldazy@sympatico.ca

Toronto: **Menzies, von Bogen - *2**
1071B Bloor St. West, Toronto, ON M6H 1M5
Tel: 416-532-2833; *Fax:* 416-532-6553
Toll-Free: 877-218-0084
menzies2@on.aibn.com

Toronto: **Paul Mergler - *1**
1199 The Queensway, Toronto, ON M8Z 1R7
Tel: 416-232-9589; *Fax:* 416-232-9522
pabkon@interlog.com

Toronto: **E.H. Merifield - *1**
#2200, 4950 Yonge St., Toronto, ON M2N 6K1
Tel: 416-218-8381; *Fax:* 416-218-8384

Toronto: **Clarke A. Merritt - *2**
#3300, Box 33, 20 Queen St. West, Toronto, ON M5H 3R3
Tel: 416-971-3306; *Fax:* 416-971-4849
cmerrittl@aol.com

Toronto: **Michael G. McLachlan - *1**
Former Name: McLachlan Winter Freeman
#103, 30 St. Clair Ave. West, Toronto, ON M4V 3A1
Tel: 416-596-7077; *Fax:* 416-596-7629
mgmlaw1@gmail.com
www.mgmlaw.ca

Toronto: **David M. Midanik - *1**
34 Shaftesbury Ave., Toronto, ON M4T 1A1
Tel: 416-967-1603; *Fax:* 416-967-1604
david@midaniklawoffice.com
www.midaniklawoffice.com

Toronto: **Yaroslav Mikitchook - *1**
#509, 80 Richmond St. West, Toronto, ON M5H 2A4
Tel: 416-361-1668; *Fax:* 416-361-6140

Toronto: **Jack A. Mikolajko - *1**
#506, P.O. Box 31, 2333 Dundas St. West, Toronto, ON M9R 3A6
Tel: 416-538-8493; *Fax:* 416-538-2274
jmikolajko@bellnet.ca

Toronto: **Millar Kreklewetz LLP - *4**
Former Name: Millar Wyslobicky Kreklewetz LLP
24 Duncan St., 3rd Fl., Toronto, ON M5V 2B8
Tel: 416-864-6200; *Fax:* 416-864-6201
mkmail@taxandtradelaw.com
www.taxandtradelaw.com

Toronto: **Miller & Miller - *2**
1577 Bloor St. West, Toronto, ON M6P 1A6
Tel: 416-536-1159; *Fax:* 416-536-3618

Toronto: **Glen M.A. Miller - *1**
#211, 3850 Finch Ave. East, Toronto, ON M1T 3T6
Tel: 416-299-6785; *Fax:* 416-299-6204

Toronto: **Helen Miller - *1**
#914, 1110 Finch Ave. West, Toronto, ON M3J 2T2
Tel: 416-665-4343; *Fax:* 416-665-0110

Toronto: **Keith R. Millikin - *1**
#310, 200 Ronson Dr., Toronto, ON M9W 5Z9
Tel: 416-243-3394; *Fax:* 416-243-9692
kmillikin@banksandstarkman.com

Toronto: **Mills & Mills LLP - *25**
#700, 2 St. Clair Ave. West, Toronto, ON M4V 1L5
Tel: 416-863-0125; *Fax:* 416-863-3997
mills@millsandmills.ca
www.millsandmills.ca

** indicates number of lawyers*

Toronto: **Douglas J. Millstone - *1**
#309, 2100 Ellesmere Rd., Toronto, ON M1H 3B7
Tel: 416-289-7996; *Fax:* 416-289-7998
Toll-Free: 888-437-7996
dmilldtone@bellnet.ca
www.dmillstonelaw.com

Toronto: **Minden Gross Grafstein & Greenstein LLP - *50**
Also Known As: Minden Gross LLP
#2200, 145 King St. West, Toronto, ON M5H 4G2
Tel: 416-362-3711; *Fax:* 416-864-9223
dcarty@mindengross.com
www.mindengross.com

Toronto: **Paul Minz - *1**
#1, 3520 Pharmacy Ave., Toronto, ON M1W 2T8
Tel: 416-499-9350; *Fax:* 416-499-1463

Toronto: **Mircheff & Mircheff - *1**
#2B, 3030 Midland Ave., Toronto, ON M1S 5C9
Tel: 416-321-2885; *Fax:* 416-321-3345
mircheff@on.aibn.com

Toronto: **Misir, Patterson - *4**
880 St. Clair Ave. West, Toronto, ON M6C 1C5
Tel: 416-653-8600; *Fax:* 416-653-9639

Toronto: **Miskin Flancman & Frisch - *2**
1286 Kennedy Rd., Toronto, ON M1P 2L5
Tel: 416-752-2221; *Fax:* 416-752-8434
Toll-Free: 877-468-1120
miskflan@hotmail.com

Toronto: **Mitchell, Bardyn & Zalucky LLP - *13**
Also Known As: MBZ Law
#200, 3029 Bloor St. West, Toronto, ON M8X 1C5
Tel: 416-234-9111; *Fax:* 416-234-9114
info@mbzlaw.com

Toronto: **Heather Mitchell - *1**
#300, 165 Avenue Rd., Toronto, ON M5R 3S4
Tel: 416-927-6565; *Fax:* 416-975-3999
hhmitchell@heathermitchelllaw.com

Toronto: **M.J. Mitchell, Q.C. - *1**
#403, 1 Yorkdale Rd., Toronto, ON M6A 3A1
Tel: 416-362-0901; *Fax:* 416-781-3110
purlex@bellnet.ca

Toronto: **M.S. Mogil - *1**
#610, 4211 Yonge St., Toronto, ON M2P 2A9
Tel: 416-590-7999; *Fax:* 416-590-9998

Toronto: **Sai@#d Mohammedally - *1**
#B3, 45 Overlea Blvd., Toronto, ON M4H 1C3
Tel: 416-425-7695; *Fax:* 416-425-7596
saidmoha@bellnet.ca

Toronto: **Bernard J. Monaghan - *1**
#4084, 3080 Yonge St., Toronto, ON M4N 3N1
Tel: 416-486-9919; *Fax:* 416-486-1885

Toronto: **Barbara Morgan - *1**
#216, 4195 Dundas St. West, Toronto, ON M8X 1Y4
Tel: 416-234-8248; *Fax:* 416-234-8252

Toronto: **Morris & Morris LLP - *7**
#920, 390 Bay St., Toronto, ON M5H 2Y2
Tel: 416-366-2291; *Fax:* 416-366-5988

Toronto: **D.S. Morris - *1**
129 John St., Toronto, ON M5V 2E2
Tel: 416-977-4799; *Fax:* 416-977-4472

Toronto: **L.J. Morris - *1**
101 Scollard St., Toronto, ON M5R 1G4
Tel: 416-924-0711; *Fax:* 416-960-9650

Toronto: **Morrison Brown Sosnovitch - *12**
#910, P.O. Box 28, 1 Toronto St., Toronto, ON M5C 2V6
Tel: 416-368-0600; *Fax:* 416-368-6068
bizlaw@businesslawyers.com
www.businesslawyers.com

Toronto: **S.S. Moskowitz - *1**
740 Spadina Ave., Toronto, ON M5S 2J2
Tel: 416-961-8864; *Fax:* 416-961-7654

Toronto: **Mostyn & Mostyn - *4**
845 St. Clair Ave. West, 4th Fl., Toronto, ON M6C 1C3
Tel: 416-653-3819; *Fax:* 416-653-3891
info@mostyn.ca
www.mostyn.ca

Toronto: **Anthony Moustacalis - *1**
#1000, 121 Richmond St. West, Toronto, ON M5H 2K1
Tel: 416-363-2656; *Fax:* 416-363-4920

Toronto: **Henry Moyal - *1**
Also Known As: Moyal & Moyal
North American Centre, 8 Finch Ave. West, Toronto, ON M2N 6L1
Tel: 416-733-3193; *Fax:* 416-250-1818
Toll-Free: 888-847-2078
canada@moyal.com
www.moyal.com

Toronto: **Matthew Moyal - *1**
Also Known As: Moyal & Moyal
North American Centre, 8 Finch Ave. West, Toronto, ON M2N 6L1
Tel: 416-733-0330; *Fax:* 416-250-1818
moyal@idirect.com

Toronto: **Katrina L. Mulligan - *1**
#600, 1000 Finch Ave. West, Toronto, ON M3J 2V5
Tel: 416-518-1288; *Fax:* 416-650-1980
katrinamulligan@sympatico.ca

Toronto: **Murray & Gregory - *2**
160 John St., 3rd Fl., Toronto, ON M5V 2E5
Tel: 416-598-1643; *Fax:* 416-598-9520

Ottawa: **S.A. Murray Consulting Inc. (SAMCI) - *2**
336 MacLean St., Ottawa, ON K2P 0M6
Tel: 613-236-3383; *Fax:* 613-236-4184

Toronto: **S.A. Murray Consulting Inc. (SAMCI) - *3**
P.O. Box 594, 27 St Clair Ave. East, Toronto, ON M4T 2N4
Tel: 416-922-5152; *Fax:* 416-922-9870
www.samci.com

Toronto: **Elizabeth J. Nadeau - *1**
#600, 1000 Finch Ave. West, Toronto, ON M3J 2V5
Tel: 416-650-1011; *Fax:* 416-650-1980

Toronto: **J. Naumovich**
#101, 813 Broadview Ave., Toronto, ON M4K 2P8
Tel: 416-466-2119; *Fax:* 416-466-2581

Toronto: **Navigator Ltd. - *2**
British Colonial Bldg., 8 Wellington St. East, 3rd Fl., Toronto, ON M5E 1C5
Tel: 416-642-6440;
info@navltd.com
www.navltd.com

Toronto: **W.E.M. Naylor - *1**
#203, 637 College St., Toronto, ON M6G 1B5
Tel: 416-532-9940; *Fax:* 416-532-9983
naylor-william@on.aibn.com

Toronto: **Neal and Smith - *2**
#300, 3443 Finch Ave. East, Toronto, ON M1W 2S1
Tel: 416-494-4545; *Fax:* 416-494-4660
nealsmith@bellnet.ca
www.nealandsmith.com

Toronto: **Neinstein & Associates LLP - *8**
#700, 1200 Bay St., Toronto, ON M5R 2A5
Tel: 416-920-4242; *Fax:* 416-923-8358
Toll-Free: 866-920-4242
www.neinstein.com

Toronto: **C. Ann Nelson - *1**
#400, 2490 Bloor St. West, Toronto, ON M6S 1R4
Tel: 416-760-7076; *Fax:* 416-760-7338

Toronto: **Theodore Nemetz - *1**
#801, 1 St. Clair Ave. East, Toronto, ON M4T 2V7
Tel: 416-961-6560; *Fax:* 416-964-2494
nemetz@bellnet.ca

Toronto: **Newman Weinstock - *1**
#201, 3625 Dufferin St., Toronto, ON M3K 1Z2
Tel: 416-630-3220; *Fax:* 416-630-7632
rawein@on.aibn.com

Toronto: **Alexandra Ngan - *1**
#306, 1033 Bay St., Toronto, ON M5S 3A5
Tel: 416-925-3333; *Fax:* 416-925-3339

Toronto: **Metz L. Ngan - *1**
#209, 155 Gordon Baker Rd., Toronto, ON M2H 3N7
Tel: 416-502-9232; *Fax:* 416-502-3061
metznga@ipoline.com

Toronto: **Peter J. Ngan - *1**
#207, 738 Sheppard Ave. East, Toronto, ON M2K 1C4
Tel: 416-298-1828; *Fax:* 416-298-2186
pjngan@yahoo.ca
www.peterngan.com

Toronto: **Trang T. Nguyen - *1**
#12, 3875 Keele St., Toronto, ON M3J 3H5
Tel: 416-638-9422; *Fax:* 416-398-8358

Toronto: **Cynthia A. Nicholas - *1**
17 Annis Rd., Toronto, ON M1M 2Y8
Tel: 416-264-2875; *Fax:* 416-264-2330

Toronto: **Alexander R. Nicol - *1**
175 Rumsey Rd., Toronto, ON M4G 1P4
Tel: 416-467-7652; *Fax:* 416-425-4217

Toronto: **Howard Nightingale - *1**
#302, 4580 Dufferin St., Toronto, ON M3H 5Y2
Tel: 416-663-4423; *Fax:* 416-663-4424
Toll-Free: 877-224-8225
info@howardnightingale.com
www.howardnightingale.com

Toronto: **Noik & Associates - *4**
#400, 3410 Sheppard Ave. East, Toronto, ON M1T 3K4
Tel: 416-754-1020; *Fax:* 416-754-1784
bnoik@noik.com

Toronto: **O'Donohue & O'Donohue - *3**
#210, 330 Bay St., Toronto, ON M5H 2S8
Tel: 416-361-3231; *Fax:* 416-361-3472
mail@odonohue.ca

Toronto: **O'Neill, Browning, Pineau - *2**
#302, 372 Bay St., Toronto, ON M5H 2W9
Tel: 416-868-0544; *Fax:* 416-868-0724
browninglaw@rigers

Toronto: **O'Reilly, Moll - *1**
300 Main St., Toronto, ON M4C 4X5
Tel: 416-690-3324; *Fax:* 416-690-3330

Toronto: **Oiye, Henderson - *2**
#1812, 2 Carlton St., Toronto, ON M5B 1J3
Tel: 416-977-7700; *Fax:* 416-977-8570
alex@oiyehenderson.com

Toronto: **Olch, Torgov, Cohen LLP - *2**
#901, 111 Richmond St. West, Toronto, ON M5H 2G4
Tel: 416-363-8366; *Fax:* 416-363-0783
otc@otclaw.ca

Toronto: **Olthuis Kleer Townshend LLP - *1**
Former Name: Olthuis Kleer Townshend
229 College St., 3rd Fl., Toronto, ON M5T 1R4
Tel: 416-981-9330; *Fax:* 416-981-9350
tmckenna@oktlaw.com (General Inquiries)
www.oktlaw.com

Toronto: **Orbach, Katzman & Herschorn - *3**
#1001, 317 Adelaide St. West, Toronto, ON M5V 1P9
Tel: 416-967-6777; *Fax:* 416-967-1506
sender@okhlaw.ca

Toronto: **Mark M. Orkin, Q.C. - *1**
#1401, 111 Richmond St. West, Toronto, ON M5H 2G4
Tel: 416-363-4108; *Fax:* 416-365-9276
mmorkin@look.ca

Toronto: **Ormston, Bellissimo, Younan - *5**
#900, 1000 Finch Ave. West, Toronto, ON M3J 2V5
Tel: 416-787-6505; *Fax:* 416-787-0455

Toronto: **Samuel Osak - *1**
6 Bitteroot Rd., Toronto, ON M3H 4J4
Tel: 416-630-1041; *Fax:* 416-630-1043
sosak@sympatico.ca

Toronto: **M.A. Osborne - *1**
#201, 100 Sheppard Ave. West, Toronto, ON M2N 1M6
Tel: 416-225-1145; *Fax:* 416-225-0832

Toronto: **Oster Wolfman LLP - *4**
Former Name: Kerr, Oster & Wolfman
#200, 133 Berkeley St., Toronto, ON M5A 2X1
Tel: 416-365-7163; *Fax:* 416-365-1270
kow@kow.on.ca

Toronto: **Otis & Korman - *2**
41 Madison Ave., Toronto, ON M5R 2S2
Tel: 416-979-0670; *Fax:* 416-979-3778
korman@istar.ca

** indicates number of lawyers*

***Toronto*: Samy Ouanounou - *1**
#352, 1111 Finch Ave. West, Toronto, ON M3J 2E5
Tel: 416-222-3434; *Fax:* 416-222-3629
solaw@on.aibn.com

***Toronto*: Outerbridge Miller Sefton - *3**
#920, 4 King St. West, Toronto, ON M5H 1B6
Tel: 416-360-6182; *Fax:* 416-360-7729
info@omslaw.com
www.omslaw.com

***Toronto*: Owens, Wright - *12**
#300, 20 Holly St., Toronto, ON M4S 3B1
Tel: 416-486-9800; *Fax:* 416-486-3309
owenswright@owenswright.com

***Toronto*: Pace Law Firm - *12**
295 The West Mall, 6th Fl., Toronto, ON M9C 4Z4
Tel: 416-236-3060; *Fax:* 416-236-1809
Toll-Free: 877-236-3060
lawyers@pacelawfirm.com
www.pacelawfirm.com

***Toronto*: Pacey & Partners - *4**
Also Known As: Pacey, Dirks & Thiel LLP
Former Name: Pacey & Partners
#1610, 1 Queen St. East, Toronto, ON M5C 2W5
Tel: 416-868-0612; *Fax:* 416-868-3022

***Toronto*: Susanne I. Palmer - *1**
57 Huntley St., Toronto, ON M4Y 2L2
Tel: 416-924-0023;
partnering@sympatico.ca

***Toronto*: Demetrius Pantazis - *1**
#204, 1315 Lawrence Ave. East, Toronto, ON M3A 3R3
Tel: 416-469-5355; *Fax:* 416-469-8136
dpantazis@on.aibn.com

***Toronto*: Pape Barristers Professional Corporation - *4**
Also Known As: Pape, P.J.
#1910, P.O. Box 69, 1 Queen St. East, Toronto, ON M5C 2W5
Tel: 416-364-8765; *Fax:* 416-364-8855
pjp@papebarristers.com

***Toronto*: Papernick & Papernick - *1**
60 Purdon Dr., Toronto, ON M3H 4X1
Tel: 416-633-0043; *Fax:* 416-633-9488

***Toronto*: Allan Papernick, Q.C. - *1**
#203, 1200 Eglinton Ave. East, Toronto, ON M3C 1H9
Tel: 416-445-1273; *Fax:* 416-445-1678
apapernick@bellnet.ca

***Toronto*: Ado Park Q.C. - *1**
#604, 357 Bay St., Toronto, ON M5H 2T7
Tel: 416-363-4451; *Fax:* 416-363-9256

***Toronto*: Parkdale Community Legal Services - *6**
1266 Queen St. West, Toronto, ON M6K 1L3
Tel: 416-531-2411; *Fax:* 416-531-0885
mailbox@parkdalelegal.org
www.parkdalelegal.org

***Toronto*: Mary Lou Parker - *1**
#800, 2 St. Clair Ave. East, Toronto, ON M4T 2T5
Tel: 416-920-4708; *Fax:* 416-920-3819
mlparker@tor.axxent.ca

***Toronto*: Paterson, MacDougall LLP, Barristers, Solicitors - *13**
#900, P.O. Box 100, 1 Queen St. East, Toronto, ON M5C 2W5
Tel: 416-366-9607; *Fax:* 416-366-3743
bmacdoug@pmlaw.com
www.pmlaw.com

***Toronto*: Philip Patterson - *1**
#305, 1033 Bay St., Toronto, ON M5S 3A5
Tel: 416-968-9188; *Fax:* 416-925-2860
ppaterson@on.aibn.com

***Toronto*: Paul & Paul - *2**
Former Name: Paul & Kanellos
39 Hayden St., Toronto, ON M4Y 2P2
Tel: 416-968-1777; *Fax:* 416-968-1211
npaul@bellnet.ca

***Toronto*: J.G. Paul - *1**
#5, 1778 Bloor St. West, Toronto, ON M6P 3K4
Tel: 416-767-9919; *Fax:* 416-767-6272

***Toronto*: Murray E. Payne - *1**
3329 Bloor St. West, Toronto, ON M8X 1E7
Tel: 416-232-1242; *Fax:* 416-231-1280

***Toronto*: Peace, Burns, Halkiw & Manning LLP - *2**
#100, 25 Morrow Ave., Toronto, ON M6R 2H9
Tel: 416-533-1025; *Fax:* 416-516-5305

***Toronto*: Peirce, McNeely Associates - *3**
25 Lesmill Rd., Toronto, ON M3B 2T3
Tel: 416-449-2060; *Fax:* 416-449-2068

***Toronto*: Michael Pelensky - *1**
#300, 2 Toronto St., Toronto, ON M5C 2B6
Tel: 416-863-1300; *Fax:* 416-863-4942

***Toronto*: Penman Vona Professional Corporation, Barristers & Solicitors - *2**
Former Name: Penmam & Penman
#307A, 4195 Dundas St. West, Toronto, ON M8X 1Y4
Tel: 416-231-5696; *Fax:* 416-231-5697
gvona@penman.cawww.facebook.com/people/George-Vona/547477354, www.linkedin.com/pub/george-vona/5/243/7b4

***Toronto*: Glenn B. Peppiatt - *1**
939 Mt. Pleasant Rd., Toronto, ON M4P 2L7
Tel: 416-323-3232; *Fax:* 416-323-9350
peplaw@rogers.com

***Toronto*: Perks & Hanson - *2**
#901, 130 Adelaide St. West, Toronto, ON M5H 3P5
Tel: 416-362-3366; *Fax:* 416-362-3174
perks@perksandhanson.com

***Toronto*: James Perly Consulting Inc. - *1**
#1406, 168 King St. East, Toronto, ON M5A 4S4
Tel: 416-855-9130;
www.perlyconsulting.com

***Toronto*: Peters & Kestelman - *1**
245 Coxwell Ave., Toronto, ON M4L 3B4
Tel: 416-465-3561; *Fax:* 416-465-3563

***Toronto*: Petropoulos & Rapos - *1**
#305, 1920 Ellesmere Rd., Toronto, ON M1H 2V6
Tel: 416-431-5870; *Fax:* 416-289-4144
jami1@bellnet.ca

***Toronto*: V. Walter Petryshyn - *1**
1247 Dundas St. West, Toronto, ON M6J 1X6
Tel: 416-534-8431; *Fax:* 416-531-2455

***Toronto*: PGC Consultants Inc. - *1**
Also Known As: Peter G. Chubb
426 Sumach St., Toronto, ON M4X 1V5
Tel: 416-515-9312; *Fax:* 416-515-8884
peterchubb@rogers.com

***Toronto*: Phillips & Phillips - *1**
#2200, 181 University Ave., Toronto, ON M5H 3M7
Tel: 416-601-6802; *Fax:* 416-601-9590
brucenorth@phillipsandphillipslaw.com

***Toronto*: Douglas N. Phillips - *1**
13 Reno Dr., Toronto, ON M1K 2V5
Tel: 416-757-3445; *Fax:* 416-759-8036
dnplaw@rogers.com

***Toronto*: Picov & Kleinberg - *2**
#100, 110 Eglinton Ave. West, Toronto, ON M4R 1A3
Tel: 416-488-2100; *Fax:* 416-488-2794
kpicov@bellnet.ca

***Toronto*: L.A. Piller - *1**
#2200, 181 University Ave., Toronto, ON M5H 3M7
Tel: 416-601-1622; *Fax:* 416-363-7239
lpiller@pillerross.com
www.pillerross.com

***Toronto*: Jillian M. Pivnick - *1**
#410, 350 Lonsdale Rd., Toronto, ON M5P 1R6
Tel: 416-484-6306

***Toronto*: D.V. Pledge, Barrister & Solicitor - *1**
Former Name: Pledge & Associates
#203, 1013 Wilson Ave., Toronto, ON M3K 1G1
Tel: 416-630-8702; *Fax:* 416-630-8714
donnav.pledge@bellnet.ca
www.dvpledge.ca

***Toronto*: Harry Poch Environmental Lawyer - *1**
20 Beaverhall Dr., Toronto, ON M2L 2C7
Tel: 416-444-7971; *Fax:* 416-444-8971
harrypoch@rogers.com

***Toronto*: Policy Concepts - *1**
#404, 40 Holly St., Toronto, ON M4S 3C3
Tel: 416-922-6156; *Fax:* 416-922-4295
policyconcepts@on.aibn.com

***Toronto*: Stephen P. Ponesse - *1**
#3000, 390 Bay St., Toronto, ON M5H 2Y2
Tel: 416-361-3582; *Fax:* 416-368-7217
stephenponesse@on.aibn.com

***Toronto*: Porjes Walsh - *3**
Former Name: M. Dawn McConnell
#2200, 181 University Ave., Toronto, ON M5H 3M7
Tel: 416-601-0002; *Fax:* 416-363-1660
dawn.mcconnell@sympatico.ca

***Toronto*: Portland Group - *1**
#518, 1001 Bay St., Toronto, ON M5S 3A6
Tel: 416-413-9206;
trobson@rogers.com

***Toronto*: Don Poscente - *1**
683 Mt. Pleasant Rd., Toronto, ON M4T 1A8
Tel: 416-410-3333

***Toronto*: E.G. Posen - *1**
101 Brookview Dr., Toronto, ON M6A 2K5
Tel: 416-782-5344;
posen@pathcom.com

***Toronto*: Joseph M. Posen - *1**
517 Glengarry Ave., Toronto, ON M5M 1G2
Tel: 416-783-2494;
jposen@home.com

***Toronto*: Posesorski, Gary M. - *1**
5 Wembley Rd., Toronto, ON M6C 2E8
Tel: 416-780-9655; *Fax:* 416-783-4574

***Toronto*: Wietse G. Posthumus - *1**
#2700, West Tower, 55 Avenue Rd., Toronto, ON M5R 3L2
Tel: 416-929-3030; *Fax:* 416-961-9898

***Toronto*: Potts, Weisberg & Musil - *3**
#206, 90 Eglinton Ave. East, Toronto, ON M4P 2Y3
Tel: 416-485-7366; *Fax:* 416-485-7368
pwmlaw@interlog.com

***Toronto*: Powell Weir, Barristers & Solicitors - *2**
#506, 50 Gervais Dr., Toronto, ON M3C 1Z3
Tel: 416-441-6840; *Fax:* 416-441-0330
powlaw@interlog.com
www.powellweir.com

***Toronto*: Preisman, Kotnala - *2**
#302, 885 Progress Ave., Toronto, ON M1H 3G3
Tel: 416-439-9559; *Fax:* 416-439-9553

***Toronto*: C.G. Preobrazenski - *1**
#414, The Richmond Tower, 100 Richmond St. West, Toronto, ON M5H 3K6
Tel: 416-964-1717; *Fax:* 416-964-0823
marie@interware.com

***Toronto*: Stephen Price & Associates - *1**
#1708, 5000 Yonge St., Toronto, ON M2N 7E9
Tel: 416-365-0766; *Fax:* 416-365-0866

***Toronto*: Prime Strategies Group Inc. - *1**
#220, 156 Front St. West, Toronto, ON M5J 2L6
Tel: 416-313-3031;
vic@primestrat.com

***Toronto*: D.R. Proctor, Q.C. - *1**
#8A, 1921 Eglinton Ave. East, Toronto, ON M1L 2L6
Tel: 416-751-3958; *Fax:* 416-751-3770

***Toronto*: V.E. Purcell, Q.C. - *1**
6 Silverdale Cres., Toronto, ON M3A 3H1
Tel: 416-445-7600; *Fax:* 416-425-4310

***Toronto*: R.G. Pyne - *1**
3329 Bloor St. West, Toronto, ON M8X 1E7
Tel: 416-231-3339; *Fax:* 416-231-1280

***Toronto*: Quadra Consulting Group - *1**
26 Dalhousie St., Toronto, ON M5B 2A5
Tel: 416-364-0073; *Fax:* 416-362-7542
pmeyer@quadraconsultinggroup.com

***Toronto*: Quirk, McGillicuddy & Sutton - *1**
1604 Dufferin St., Toronto, ON M6H 3L7
Tel: 416-652-3543; *Fax:* 416-652-2730
fran@qmsutton.ca

** indicates number of lawyers*

Toronto: **R2B Strategies - *1**
145 Briar Hill Ave., Toronto, ON M4R 1H8
Tel: 416-435-8833; *Fax:* 416-481-3266

Toronto: **Rachlin & Wolfson LLP - *10**
#1500, 390 Bay St., Toronto, ON M5H 2Y2
Tel: 416-367-0202; *Fax:* 416-367-1820
enquiry@rachlinlaw.com
www.rachlinlaw.com

Toronto: **Danuta H. Radomski - *1**
351 Castlefield Ave., Toronto, ON M5N 1L4
Tel: 416-322-6134; *Fax:* 416-489-1462
dradomski@on.aibn.com

Toronto: **Ralph S Caswell - *1**
#1908, 150 York St., Toronto, ON M5H 3S5
Tel: 416-542-5400; *Fax:* 416-597-1479
caswell@barexpress.net

Toronto: **R. Sam Ramlall - *1**
#700, 5799 Yonge St., Toronto, ON M2M 3V3
Tel: 416-512-6465; *Fax:* 416-512-6042
rsamramlall@bellnet.ca

Toronto: **Rawana & Rawana Barristers & Solicitors - *2**
11721 Sheppard Ave. East, 2nd Fl., Toronto, ON M1B 1G3
Tel: 416-281-8505; *Fax:* 416-286-4353

Toronto: **Rayson & Associates - *4**
#302, 3845 Bathurst St., Toronto, ON M3H 3N2
Tel: 416-630-5600; *Fax:* 416-630-5906
erayson@rayson.ca

Toronto: **John L. Razulis - *1**
#219, 534 Lawrence Ave., Toronto, ON M6A 1A2
Tel: 416-787-1918; *Fax:* 416-787-7161
counsel@lawfulwork.ca
www.lawfulwork.ca

Toronto: **John H. Reble - *1**
Former Name: Reble, Ritchie, Green & Ketcheson
277 Glengrove Ave. West, Toronto, ON M5N 1W3
Tel: 416-485-9123;
jreble@istar.ca

Toronto: **The Refugee Law Office - *4**
#206, 375 University Ave., Toronto, ON M5G 2G1
Tel: 416-977-8111; *Fax:* 416-977-5567
rlo@lao.on.ca

Toronto: **Regan Desjardins LLP - *10**
Former Name: Regan Kram Desjardins LLP
#1502, P.O. Box 2069, 20 Eglinton Ave. West, Toronto, ON M4R 1K8
Tel: 416-601-1000; *Fax:* 416-601-9255
reception@rkdlaw.com
www.regandesjardins.com

Toronto: **T.S. Reiber Professional Corporation - *1**
#211, 1110 Sheppard Ave. East, Toronto, ON M2K 2W2
Tel: 416-927-9841; *Fax:* 416-975-1531
terry@reiber.ca

Toronto: **Reid, McLean & Scott - *1**
2938 Danforth Ave., Toronto, ON M4C 1M5
Tel: 416-699-1131; *Fax:* 416-699-1958

Toronto: **Mary P. Reilly - *2**
701 Coxwell Ave., Toronto, ON M4C 3C1
Tel: 416-461-7553; *Fax:* 416-461-2679

Toronto: **Reingold & Reingold - *1**
#4068, P.O. Box 17, 3080 Yonge St., Toronto, ON M4N 3N1
Tel: 416-483-3364; *Fax:* 416-440-1942
jrqc58@bellnet.ca

Toronto: **A.C.J. Reisler - *1**
161 Bridgeland Ave., Toronto, ON M6A 1Z1
Tel: 416-781-4002; *Fax:* 416-781-7797
areisler@wastecogroup.com

Toronto: **Stanley Reisman - *1**
#308, 360 Bloor St. West, Toronto, ON M5S 1X1
Tel: 416-961-8864; *Fax:* 416-961-7654

Toronto: **Reiter, Nemetz - *2**
#451, 1111 Finch Ave. West, Toronto, ON M3J 2E5
Tel: 416-665-1458; *Fax:* 416-665-0895

Toronto: **Rekai Frankel LLP - *6**
Former Name: Rekai Somerleigh Berezowski
33 Bloor St. East, 16th Fl., Toronto, ON M4W 3H1
Tel: 416-960-8876; *Fax:* 416-924-2371
eleanor@mobilitylaw.com
www.mobilitylaw.com

Toronto: **David J.M. Rendeiro**
#200, 1201 Dundas St. West, Toronto, ON M6J 1X3
Tel: 416-588-8000; *Fax:* 416-588-8002

Toronto: **Reznick, Parsons - *2**
#1917, 25 Adelaide St. East, Toronto, ON M5C 3A1
Tel: 416-863-6026; *Fax:* 416-863-9334

Toronto: **Lewis J. Richardson - *1**
#2000, 393 University Ave., Toronto, ON M5G 1E6
Tel: 416-599-1226; *Fax:* 416-962-9997

Toronto: **Richman & Richman - *1**
#404, 255 Duncan Mill Rd., Toronto, ON M3B 3H9
Tel: 416-510-1575; *Fax:* 416-510-1580
richman.richman@on.aibn.com

Toronto: **Nina S. Richmond - *1**
148 Brookdale Ave., Toronto, ON M5M 1P5
Tel: 416-489-4191; *Fax:* 416-489-5822
nina.richmond@rogers.com

Toronto: **D.S. Rickerd, Q.C. - *1**
21 Elm Ave., Toronto, ON M4W 1M9
Tel: 416-929-5177; *Fax:* 416-921-8322
drickerd@yorku.ca

Toronto: **Ricketts, Harris LLP - *12**
#816, Guardian of Canada Tower, 181 University Ave., Toronto, ON M5H 2X7
Tel: 416-364-6211; *Fax:* 416-364-1697
mail@rickettsharris.com
www.rickettsharris.com

Toronto: **Gerald Rifkin - *1**
#500, 1000 Finch Ave. West, Toronto, ON M3J 2V5
Tel: 416-667-9796; *Fax:* 416-667-8048

Toronto: **Riley, McGivney - *3**
#2300, 439 University Ave., Toronto, ON M5G 1Y8
Tel: 416-364-7611; *Fax:* 416-596-7562
mailbox@rileymclaw.ca

Toronto: **Riverdale Law Group - *3**
257 Danforth Ave., Toronto, ON M4K 1N2
Tel: 416-466-6264; *Fax:* 416-466-8465

Toronto: **Riverdale Mediation - *2**
257 Danforth Ave., Toronto, ON M4K 1N2
Tel: 416-466-6264; *Fax:* 416-466-8465
www.riverdalemediation.com

Toronto: **Roach, Schwartz & Associates, Barristers & Solicitors - *7**
688 St. Clair Ave. West, Toronto, ON M6C 1B1
Tel: 416-657-1465; *Fax:* 416-657-1511
www.roachschwartz.com

Toronto: **Robbins & Associates - *3**
#510, 481 University Ave., Toronto, ON M5G 2E9
Tel: 416-360-6530; *Fax:* 416-360-1056

Toronto: **William H. Roberts - *1**
#201, 34 Southport St., Toronto, ON M6S 3N3
Tel: 416-769-3162; *Fax:* 416-762-8972

Toronto: **Robertson & Keith - *1**
3464 Kingston Rd., Toronto, ON M1M 1R5
Tel: 416-261-1220; *Fax:* 416-261-1716

Toronto: **Robins, Appleby & Taub LLP - *20**
#2600, 120 Adelaide St. West, Toronto, ON M5H 1T1
Tel: 416-868-1080; *Fax:* 416-868-0306
www.robinsapplebyandtaub.com

Toronto: **James L. Robinson - *1**
2424 Bloor St. West, 2nd Fl., Toronto, ON M6S 1P9
Tel: 416-601-1411; *Fax:* 416-769-5365

Toronto: **Lawlor Rochester - *1**
#800, 141 Adelaide St. West, Toronto, ON M5H 3L5
Tel: 416-366-2267; *Fax:* 416-368-3467
bb@glaholt.com
www.glaholt.com

Toronto: **Rogers & Rowland - *1**
#400, 1235 Bay St., Toronto, ON M5R 3K4
Tel: 416-364-2333; *Fax:* 416-864-0271
mail@rogersrowland.com

Toronto: **Rogers Law Office - *1**
Also Known As: RLO
#3B, 4 Deer Park Cres., Toronto, ON M4V 2C3
Tel: 416-363-6626; *Fax:* 416-363-6628
file@rlo.ca
www.rlo.ca

Toronto: **Rogers, Moore - *18**
#1900, 181 University Ave., Toronto, ON M5H 3M7
Tel: 416-594-4500; *Fax:* 416-594-9100
rogersmoore@rogersmoore.com
www.rogersmoore.com

Toronto: **Nelson Roland - *1**
333 Adelaide St. West, 3rd Fl., Toronto, ON M5V 1R5
Tel: 416-351-1591; *Fax:* 416-340-9250
nroland@allstream.net

Toronto: **Norman W. Ronka, Law Office of - *1**
946 College St., Toronto, ON M6H 1A5
Tel: 416-969-0917; *Fax:* 416-905-8221

Toronto: **Law Office of Christopher J. Roper - *1**
#3300, The Cadillac Fairview Tower, 20 Queen St. West, Toronto, ON M5H 3R3
Tel: 416-368-6788; *Fax:* 416-368-5705
cjroper@interhop.net

Toronto: **Rose & Rose - *2**
#100, 1200 Sheppard Ave. East, Toronto, ON M2K 2S5
Tel: 416-590-9990; *Fax:* 416-590-9991

Toronto: **Rose, Persiko, Rakowsky, Melvin LLP - *2**
#600, 390 Bay St., Toronto, ON M5H 2Y2
Tel: 416-868-1900; *Fax:* 416-868-1708

Toronto: **Rosen & Company - *5**
#500, 350 Bay St., Toronto, ON M5H 2S6
Tel: 416-205-9700; *Fax:* 416-205-9970
johnrosen@rosenlaw.ca
www.rosenlaw.ca

Toronto: **Allan C. Rosen - *1**
#904, 27 Queen St. East, Toronto, ON M5C 2M6
Tel: 416-363-1601; *Fax:* 416-363-5620
acrosenlaw@rogers.com

Toronto: **Solomon L. Rosen - *1**
#1, 2933 Dufferin St., Toronto, ON M6B 3S7
Tel: 416-789-7133; *Fax:* 416-782-3507

Toronto: **Elliot F. Rosenberg - *1**
#201, 4949 Bathurst St., Toronto, ON M2R 1Y1
Tel: 416-512-7373; *Fax:* 416-512-7374
tlpress@patncom.com

Toronto: **Irving Rosenberg - *1**
#507, 1000 Finch Ave. West, Toronto, ON M3J 2V5
Tel: 416-398-0102; *Fax:* 416-398-0103
irose@on.aibn.com

Toronto: **Rosenblatt Associates - *2**
208 Adelaide St. West, 2nd Fl., Toronto, ON M5H 1W7
Tel: 416-644-4000; *Fax:* 416-861-1215
david@immigrate.net
www.immigrate.net

Toronto: **Stanley Rosenfarb - *1**
#800, 2001 Sheppard Ave. East, Toronto, ON M2J 4Z8
Tel: 416-494-4899; *Fax:* 416-494-3024
stan@srlaw.com

Toronto: **Larry H. Ross - *1**
#200, 609 Bloor St. West, Toronto, ON M6G 1K5
Tel: 416-535-6211; *Fax:* 416-535-7698

Toronto: **R.M. Ross - *1**
181 University Ave., 22nd Fl., Toronto, ON M5H 3M7
Tel: 416-601-1563; *Fax:* 416-363-7239
rross@pillerross.com

Toronto: **A.M. Rossman - *1**
#216, 801 York Mills Rd., Toronto, ON M3B 1X7
Tel: 416-444-2201; *Fax:* 416-444-0571

Toronto: **Cecil L. Rotenberg - *3**
#900, 1000 Finch Ave. West, Toronto, ON M3J 2V5
Tel: 416-449-8866; *Fax:* 416-510-9090
immigration@clrqc.com
www.clrqc.com

Toronto: **I. Robert Rotenberg - *1**
#1100, 11 King St. West, Toronto, ON M5H 4C7
Tel: 416-591-9100; *Fax:* 416-591-9008
rotenberg@sympatico.ca

** indicates number of lawyers*

Toronto: **Frank L. Roth - *1**
#500, 70 Bond St., Toronto, ON M5B 1X3
Tel: 416-963-8776; *Fax:* 416-863-4896
flr@bondlaw.net

Toronto: **Neal H. Roth - *1**
#401, 60 St. Clair Ave. East, Toronto, ON M4T 1N5
Tel: 416-351-7706; *Fax:* 416-351-7684
nealroth@on.aibn.com
www.nealroth.com

Toronto: **Rothman & Rothman - *1**
#638, 121 Richmond St. West, Toronto, ON M5H 2K1
Tel: 416-367-9901; *Fax:* 416-367-9979
rothman@sympatico.ca

Toronto: **Nancy-Gay Rotstein - *1**
#202, 40 Holly St., Toronto, ON M4S 3C3
Tel: 416-488-0800; *Fax:* 416-488-8350
nrotstein@municipal.ca

Toronto: **Roy Elliott Kim O'Connor LLP - *11**
#1400, 10 Bay St., Toronto, ON M5J 2R8
Tel: 416-362-1989; *Fax:* 416-362-6204
info@reko.ca
www.reko.ca

Toronto: **Rubenstein, Siegel - *2**
#402, 1200 Sheppard Ave. East, Toronto, ON M2K 2S5
Tel: 416-499-5252; *Fax:* 416-499-2290

Toronto: **Barry Rubinoff - *1**
488 Huron St., Toronto, ON M5R 2R3
Tel: 416-966-4884; *Fax:* 416-966-6768

Toronto: **Ruby & Edwardh - *7**
11 Prince Arthur Ave., Toronto, ON M5R 1B2
Tel: 416-964-9664; *Fax:* 416-964-8305

Toronto: **Ruderman, Shaw - *2**
#1820, P.O. Box 2037, 20 Eglinton Ave. West, Toronto, ON M4R 1K8
Tel: 416-484-8558; *Fax:* 416-484-6918
info@rudermanshaw.com

Toronto: **Victor E. Rudinskas - *1**
27 John St., 2nd Fl., Toronto, ON M9N 1J4
Tel: 416-240-0594; *Fax:* 416-248-5922
Toll-Free: 877-888-8390
vrudinskas@trebnet.com

Toronto: **George A. Rudnik - *1**
#1901, 260 Queens Quay West, Toronto, ON M5J 2N3
Tel: 416-927-7788; *Fax:* 416-925-9963

Toronto: **Rueter Scargall Bennett LLP - *7**
#4220, Box 226, 161 Bay St., Toronto, ON M5J 2S1
Tel: 416-869-9090; *Fax:* 416-869-3411

Toronto: **Martin K.I. Rumack - *1**
#202, 2 St. Clair Ave. East, Toronto, ON M4T 2T5
Tel: 416-961-3441; *Fax:* 416-961-1045
martin@martinrumack.com
www.martinrumack.com

Toronto: **Brian A. Rumanek - *1**
#204, 200 Evans Ave., Toronto, ON M8Z 1J7
Tel: 416-252-9115; *Fax:* 416-253-0494
thelawman@rogers.com

Toronto: **Richard E. Rusek - *1**
1623 Bloor St. West, Toronto, ON M6P 1A6
Tel: 416-533-8563

Toronto: **Rush, G.C.**
2970 Lake Shore Blvd. West, Toronto, ON M8V 1J7
Tel: 416-251-2291

Toronto: **C.H. Rutherford - *1**
#500, 1000 Finch Ave. West, Toronto, ON M3J 2V5
Tel: 416-667-9796

Toronto: **Rebecca J. Rutherford - *1**
#308, 100 Richmond St. West, Toronto, ON M5H 3K6
Tel: 416-598-3928; *Fax:* 416-947-1236

Toronto: **Ryder, Wright, Blair & Holmes LLP - *7**
333 Adelaide St. West, 3rd Fl., Toronto, ON M5V 1R5
Tel: 416-340-9070; *Fax:* 416-340-9250

Toronto: **Rye & Partners - *3**
#1200, 65 Queen St. West, Toronto, ON M5H 2M5
Tel: 416-362-4901; *Fax:* 416-362-8291
partners@ryeandpartners.com
www.ryeandpartners.com

Toronto: **Nadir Sachak - *1**
#301, 366 Bay St., Toronto, ON M5H 4B2
Tel: 416-363-7172; *Fax:* 416-363-9917
Toll-Free: 877-878-7206

Toronto: **Howard Saginur - *1**
#1510, 5140 Yonge St., Toronto, ON M2N 6L7
Tel: 416-512-1912; *Fax:* 416-512-1989
howard@saginur.com
www.saginur.com

Toronto: **F.G. Salehmohamed - *1**
#202, 747 Don Mills Rd., Toronto, ON M3C 1T2
Tel: 416-421-7000; *Fax:* 416-421-5388

Toronto: **M. Saltman Arbitrations Ltd. - *1**
#107, 100 Adelaide St. West, Toronto, ON M5H 2G4
Tel: 416-366-3091; *Fax:* 416-366-0879
arbserve@aol.com

Toronto: **Samis & Company - *16**
#1600, 400 University Ave., Toronto, ON M5G 1S5
Tel: 416-365-0000; *Fax:* 416-365-9993
info@samislaw.com
www.samislaw.com

Toronto: **Sanderson Entertainment Law - *2**
#201, 326 Richmond St. West, Toronto, ON M5V 1X2
Tel: 416-971-6616; *Fax:* 416-971-4144
info@sandersonlaw.ca
www.sandersonlaw.ca

Toronto: **Sandler, Gordon - *2**
#260, 1027 Yonge St., Toronto, ON M4W 2K9
Tel: 416-971-5102; *Fax:* 416-971-5305

Toronto: **Shil K. Sanwalka, Q.C. - *1**
#602, 18 Wynford Dr., Toronto, ON M3C 3S2
Tel: 416-449-7755; *Fax:* 416-449-6969
skslaw@sanwalka.org

Toronto: **Umberto Sapone - *2**
#201, P.O. Box 17, 3200 Dufferin St., Toronto, ON M6A 3B2
Tel: 416-789-2689; *Fax:* 416-789-0454

Toronto: **Dianne Saxe, Ph.D. - *3**
Also Known As: Saxe Law Office
248 Russell Hill Rd., Toronto, ON M4V 2T2
Tel: 416-962-5882; *Fax:* 416-962-8817
admin@envirolaw.com
www.envirolaw.comhttp://www.linkedin.com/in/envirolaw

Toronto: **J.F. Scandiffio - *1**
533 Queen St. East, Toronto, ON M5A 1V1
Tel: 416-364-6755; *Fax:* 416-364-7049

Toronto: **P.M. Scandiffio, Q.C. - *1**
#308, 344 Bloor St. West, Toronto, ON M5S 3A7
Tel: 416-515-1660; *Fax:* 416-515-1526

Toronto: **John J.M. Scarfe - *1**
27 Prince Arthurs Ave., Toronto, ON M5R 1B2
Tel: 416-410-4060; *Fax:* 416-960-1498
jscarfe@torontocriminallawyer.ca

Toronto: **Scher & De Angelis Professional Corp. - *2**
#210, 69 Bloor St. East, Toronto, ON M4W 1A9
Tel: 416-515-9686; *Fax:* 416-961-2534
scherde@interlog.com
www.interlog.com/~scherde

Toronto: **Lionel H. Schipper, Q.C. - *1**
#1010, 22 St. Clair Ave. East, Toronto, ON M4T 2S3
Tel: 416-923-7755; *Fax:* 416-961-7011

Toronto: **Simon Schneiderman - *1**
#1807, 8 King St. East, Toronto, ON M5C 1B5
Tel: 416-361-0680; *Fax:* 416-361-0248
clophie@aol.com

Toronto: **Schnurr Kirsh Schnurr Oelbaum Tator LLP - *7**
Former Name: Schnurr Kirsh Stephens
#1700, 65 Queen St., Toronto, ON M5H 2M5
Tel: 416-860-1057; *Fax:* 416-367-2502
www.estatelitigation.net

Toronto: **Cecil Schwartz - *1**
#2108, Madison Centre, P.O. Box 130, 4950 Yonge St., Toronto, ON M2N 6K1
Tel: 416-250-0083; *Fax:* 416-512-8275
cecil@cecilschwartz.com

Toronto: **Scott & Oleskiw - *2**
Former Name: Diane Oleskiw
#235, 215 Spadina Ave., Toronto, ON M5T 2C7
Tel: 416-591-9229; *Fax:* 416-591-9200
admin@scottoleskiw.com

Toronto: **B.M. Scully Barrister & Solicitor - *1**
31 Prince Arthur Ave., Toronto, ON M5R 1B2
Tel: 416-968-2456; *Fax:* 416-960-5456

Toronto: **Peter B. Scully - *1**
42 Heath St. West., Toronto, ON M4V 1T3
Tel: 416-929-2909; *Fax:* 416-929-2909
scullylaw@sympatico.ca

Toronto: **seclaw.ca - *1**
75 Lowther Ave., Toronto, ON MR 1C9
Tel: 416-535-0297; *Fax:* 416-535-0088
caspar@seclaw.ca

Toronto: **Gary L. Segal - *1**
#1000, 60 St. Clair Ave. West, Toronto, ON M4T 1N5
Tel: 416-967-5400; *Fax:* 416-967-7877
immigration@garysegal.com

Toronto: **Sennecke, Alexander Christian Erich**
#2401, 120 Adelaide St. West, Toronto, ON M5H 1T1
Tel: 416-410-2113; *Fax:* 416-410-9423
asennecke@sennecke.com

Toronto: **Seon Gutstadt Lash LLP - *6**
#1800, 4950 Yonge St., Toronto, ON M2N 6K1
Tel: 416-224-0224; *Fax:* 416-224-0758
boblash@torlaw.com
www.torlaw.com

Toronto: **Sera Associates - *2**
Former Name: Sera, Harrison Associates
#1800, 4950 Yonge St., Toronto, ON M2N 6K1
Tel: 416-222-7668; *Fax:* 416-224-0758

Toronto: **Frederick J. Shanahan - *1**
#414, 100 Richmond St. West, Toronto, ON M5H 3K6
Tel: 416-972-6449; *Fax:* 416-964-0823
f_shanny@hotmail.com

Toronto: **Lawrence N. Shapiro - *1**
#800, 2001 Sheppard Ave. East, Toronto, ON M2J 4Z8
Tel: 416-494-4899; *Fax:* 416-494-3024
lshapiro@tpg.to

Toronto: **David Share Associates - *4**
3442 Yonge St., Toronto, ON M4N 2M9
Tel: 416-488-9000; *Fax:* 416-488-9004
dshare@sharelawyers.com
www.sharelawyers.com

Toronto: **Sharma & Sharma - *2**
942 Gerrard St. East, Toronto, ON M4M 1Z2
Tel: 416-461-0467; *Fax:* 416-461-5817

Toronto: **Chet Sharma - *1**
#7, 1658 Victoria Park Ave., Toronto, ON M1R 1P7
Tel: 416-285-1550; *Fax:* 416-285-1698
chetsharma@aol.com

Toronto: **Shearman & Sterling LLP - *15**
#4405, Commerce Court West, P.O. Box 247, 199 Bay St., Toronto, ON M5L 1E8
Tel: 416-360-8484; *Fax:* 416-360-2958
www.shearman.com

Toronto: **Shekter, Dychtenberg LLP - *5**
#2900, 390 Bay St., Toronto, ON M5H 2Y2
Tel: 416-941-9995; *Fax:* 416-869-0321
richard@shekter.com

Toronto: **Shell Lawyers - *3**
Former Name: Shell Jacobs Lawyers
#401, 672 Dupont St., Toronto, ON M6G 1Z6
Tel: 416-539-0226; *Fax:* 416-539-0565
brian@shelllawyers.ca
www.shelllawyers.ca

Toronto: **Shelton Associates - *2**
#810, 439 University Ave., Toronto, ON M5G 1Y8
Tel: 416-977-8888; *Fax:* 416-977-1964

Toronto: **Sheppard Shalinksy Brown - *3**
488 Huron St., Toronto, ON M5R 2R3
Tel: 416-966-6885; *Fax:* 416-966-6837
Ysheppard@sfmlaw.com

* *indicates number of lawyers*

Toronto: Sheridan, Ippolito & Associates - *2
#506, 2 Jane St., Toronto, ON M6S 4W3
Tel: 416-763-3399; Fax: 416-763-3443
info@sheridanippolito.com
www.sheridanippolito.com

Toronto: Sherman, Brown, Dryer, Karol, Gold, Lebow - *1
Also Known As: Sherman Brown Barristers & Solicitors
#900, 5075 Yonge St., Toronto, ON M2N 6C6
Tel: 416-224-9800; Fax: 416-222-3091
cory@sanda.ca

Toronto: S.L. Sherman - *1
2645 Eglinton Ave. East, Toronto, ON M1K 2S2
Tel: 416-261-7161; Fax: 416-261-7163

Toronto: Sherrard Kuzz LLP - *8
#1500, 155 University Ave., Toronto, ON M5H 3B7
Tel: 416-603-0700; Fax: 416-603-6035
info@sherrardkuzz.com
www.sherrardkuzz.com

Toronto: Shibley Righton LLP - *32
#700, 250 University Ave., Toronto, ON M5H 3E5
Tel: 416-214-5200; Fax: 416-214-5400
Toll-Free: 877-214-5200
torontoinfo@shibleyrighton.com
www.shibleyrighton.com

Toronto: Alvin J. Shidlowski - *1
#1100, 20 Dundas St. West, Toronto, ON M5G 2G8
Tel: 416-591-9100; Fax: 416-591-9008
ajs7@rogers.com

Toronto: Shields O'Donnell MacKillop LLP - *11
Also Known As: Shields O'Donnell MacKillop LLP
Former Name: Hodgson Shields DesBrisay O'Donnell MacKillop Squire LLP
65 Queen St. West, 181th Fl., Toronto, ON M5H 2M5
Tel: 416-304-6400; Fax: 416-304-6406
info@djmlaw.ca
www.djmlaw.ca

Toronto: Bernard S. Shier - *1
219 Carlton St., Toronto, ON M5A 2L2
Tel: 416-923-8997; Fax: 416-923-8380

Toronto: Stanley I. Shier, Q.C. - *1
65 Queen St. West, 17th Fl., Toronto, ON M5H 2M5
Tel: 416-366-9591; Fax: 416-366-2107
stanleyshier@shierlaw.com

Toronto: O.B. Shime, Q.C. - *1
#200, 70 Bond St., Toronto, ON M5B 1X3
Tel: 416-366-8009; Fax: 416-365-7702
disputeservices@bellnet.ca

Toronto: Shamim Shivji - *1
#400, 144 Front St. West, Toronto, ON M5J 2L7
Tel: 416-599-5469;
sshivji@interlog.com

Toronto: E.I. Shoihet - *1
9 Cortleigh Blvd., Toronto, ON M4R 1K5
Tel: 416-863-9594

Toronto: Geary B. Shorser - *1
#2000, 393 University Ave., Toronto, ON M5G 1E6
Tel: 416-977-7749; Fax: 416-593-1352

Toronto: Ian C. Shoub - *1
1000 Finch Ave. West, 4th Fl., Toronto, ON M3J 2V5
Tel: 416-661-0990; Fax: 416-663-3236
ishoub@on.aibn.com

Toronto: Robert Shour - *1
#2000, 393 University Ave., Toronto, ON M5G 1E6
Tel: 416-977-4492; Fax: 416-977-4971
ralshour@on.aibn.com

Toronto: Louis D. Silver, Q.C. - *1
15 Silvergrove Rd., Toronto, ON M2L 2N5
Tel: 416-445-2795; Fax: 416-445-7243
louisdsilverqc@rogers.com

Toronto: Martin I. Silver - *1
#403, 1 Yorkdale Rd., Toronto, ON M6A 3A1
Tel: 416-781-5224; Fax: 416-781-3110
trilex@interlog.com

Toronto: Sheldon N. Silverman - *1
#638, 121 Richmond St. West, Toronto, ON M5H 2K1
Tel: 416-363-6295; Fax: 416-363-3047
ssilverman@sympatico.ca
www.sheldonsilverman.com

Toronto: Sim & McBurney - *10
330 University Ave., 6th Fl., Toronto, ON M5G 1R7
Tel: 416-595-1155; Fax: 416-595-1163

Toronto: Sim, Hughes, Ashton & McKay LLP - *9
330 University Ave., 6th Fl., Toronto, ON M5G 1R7
Tel: 416-595-1155; Fax: 416-595-1163
mailsim@sim-mcburney.com
www.sim-mcburney.com

Toronto: Monty M. Simmonds, Q.C. - *1
#1000, 2 St. Clair Ave. West, Toronto, ON M4V 1L5
Tel: 416-967-6706; Fax: 416-967-9483
services@medshire.com

Toronto: Michael S. Simrod - *1
#500, 1000 Finch Ave. West, Toronto, ON M3J 2V5
Tel: 416-667-0980;
msimrod@rogers.com

Toronto: Isaac Singer - *1
2424 Bloor St. West, Toronto, ON M6S 1P9
Tel: 416-766-1135; Fax: 416-769-5365
isinger@bellnet.ca

Toronto: Singer, Keyfetz, Crackower & Saltzman - *2
532 Eglinton Ave. East, Toronto, ON M4P 1N6
Tel: 416-488-6900; Fax: 416-488-7530

Toronto: Singer, Kwinter LLP - *8
#214, Polo Centre, 1033 Bay St., Toronto, ON M5S 3A5
Tel: 416-961-2882; Fax: 416-961-6760
Toll-Free: 866-285-6927
info@singerkwinter.com
www.singerkwinter.com

Toronto: Michael S. Singer - *1
#200, 4211 Yonge St., Toronto, ON M2P 2A9
Tel: 416-224-8383; Fax: 416-224-2408
michael.s.singer@gmail.com

Toronto: Yaso Sinnadurai - *1
#202, 2100 Ellesmere Rd., Toronto, ON M1H 3B7
Tel: 416-265-3456; Fax: 416-265-2770

Toronto: Regina Sinukoff Barrister & Solicitor - *1
#507, 1000 Finch Ave. West, Toronto, ON M3J 2V5
Tel: 416-739-7272; Fax: 416-739-7770
rsinukoff@on.aibn.com

Toronto: Steven H. Sinukoff - *1
#240, 118 Eglinton Ave. West, Toronto, ON M4R 2G4
Tel: 416-489-7997; Fax: 416-256-9244
stevensinukoff@bellnet.ca

Toronto: Michael Sitzer - *1
255 Lesmill Rd., Toronto, ON M3B 2V1
Tel: 416-391-2500; Fax: 416-391-3165
msitzer@sitzergroup.com

Toronto: Skadden, Arps, Slate, Meagher & Flom LLP - *9
Also Known As: Skadden Arps
#1750, P.O. Box 258, Stn. T-D Centre, 222 Bay St., Toronto, ON M5K 1J5
Tel: 416-777-4700; Fax: 416-777-4747

Toronto: Skapinker & Shapiro LLP - *2
#904, 180 Bloor St., Toronto, ON M5S 2V6
Tel: 416-214-1500; Fax: 416-214-0658
divorcelawyer@bellnet.ca
www.ontariofamilylaw.com

Toronto: Stewart Floyd Sklar - *1
#5, 1267A St. Clair Ave. West, 2nd Fl., Toronto, ON M6E 1B8
Tel: 416-654-6111; Fax: 416-654-6100

Toronto: S.H. Skolnik - *1
#318, 4002 Sheppard Ave. East, Toronto, ON M1S 4R5
Tel: 416-297-7300; Fax: 416-298-7142

Toronto: Steven Allen Skurka - *2
#205, 970 Lawrence Ave. West, Toronto, ON M6A 3B6
Tel: 416-787-6529; Fax: 416-787-7788
sskurka@ssclawyers.com

Toronto: Slater & Wells - *2
644 Evans Ave., Toronto, ON M8W 2W6
Tel: 416-259-4293; Fax: 416-259-1286

Toronto: Paul Slocombe - *1
387A Jane St., Toronto, ON M6S 3Z3
Tel: 416-762-0725; Fax: 416-762-6350

Toronto: Andrea M. Smart - *1
8 Rolston Ave., Toronto, ON M5A 3Z2
Tel: 416-961-8829; Fax: 416-961-8829

Toronto: Cindy L. Smith
#2104, 180 Dundas St. West, Toronto, ON M5G 1Z8
Tel: 416-408-0008; Fax: 416-597-9808

Toronto: K.D. Smith - *1
#500, 70 Bond St., Toronto, ON M5B 1X3
Tel: 416-361-0232; Fax: 416-863-4896

Toronto: Raymond I. Smith - *1
#1507, 8 King St. East., Toronto, ON M5C 1B5
Tel: 416-861-8695; Fax: 416-861-9074
raylaw@on.aibn.com

Toronto: Stanley Smither - *1
#B1, 309 Mt. Pleasant Rd., Toronto, ON M4T 2C2
Tel: 416-485-7511; Fax: 416-488-9028

Toronto: D.B. Snider - *1
978 Kingston Rd., Toronto, ON M4E 1S9
Tel: 416-699-0424; Fax: 416-699-0285

Toronto: Kenneth E. Snider - *1
#309, 2100 Ellesmere Rd., Toronto, ON M1H 3B7
Tel: 416-438-4515; Fax: 416-289-7998
ksnider@bellnet.ca

Toronto: Irving Snitman - *1
554 Annette St., Toronto, ON M6S 2C2
Tel: 416-767-0805; Fax: 416-767-4619
irv@irvingsnitman.com

Toronto: Solnik & Solnik Professional Corp. - *2
2991 Dundas St. West, Toronto, ON M6P 1Z4
Tel: 416-767-7506; Fax: 416-767-4738
manny@solnikandsolnik.com
www.solnikandsolnik.com

Toronto: Solomon, Grosberg LLP - *6
#1704, 55 University Ave., Toronto, ON M5J 2H7
Tel: 416-366-7828; Fax: 416-366-3513
lawyers@solgro.com

Toronto: J.J. Somjen - *2
#810, 1240 Bay St., Toronto, ON M5R 2A7
Tel: 416-922-8083; Fax: 416-922-4234
somjen@somjen.com

Toronto: Larry S. Sonenberg - *1
1123 Albion Rd., Toronto, ON M9V 1A9
Tel: 416-749-6000; Fax: 416-749-6004
Toll-Free: 877-388-5962
lssonenberg@on.aibn.com

Toronto: Sosa & Associates - *1
#600, 161 Eglinton Ave. East, Toronto, ON M4P 1J5
Tel: 416-480-2324; Fax: 416-480-2923

Toronto: Sotos LLP - *12
#1250, 180 Dundas St. West, Toronto, ON M5G 1Z8
Tel: 416-977-0007; Fax: 416-977-0717
info@sotosllp.com
www.sotosllp.com

Toronto: Spencer Law Firm - *1
Former Name: Spencer Romberg Associates
#300, 162 Cumberland St., Toronto, ON M5R 3N5
Tel: 416-967-1571; Fax: 416-966-1161

Toronto: Barry A. Spiegel - *1
#1202, 390 Bay St., Toronto, ON M5H 2Y2
Tel: 416-865-0330; Fax: 416-363-8451
barry@spieglaw.com

Toronto: Belva Spiel - *1
#402, 1670 Bayview Ave., Toronto, ON M4G 3C2
Tel: 416-486-1688; Fax: 416-486-2274

Toronto: Michael Spiro - *1
#207, 3625 Dufferin St., Toronto, ON M3K 1Z2
Tel: 416-630-1370; Fax: 416-633-2229

Toronto: Harvey Spring - *1
#488, 22 College St., Toronto, ON M5G 1K2
Tel: 416-967-0800; Fax: 416-967-2783
harveyspring@bellnet.ca

** indicates number of lawyers*

***Toronto*: C.A. Stafford - *1**
1036 Coxwell Ave., Toronto, ON M4C 3G5
Tel: 416-421-3211

***Toronto*: Jerome Stanleigh - *1**
#100, 20 York Mills Rd., Toronto, ON M2P 2C2
Tel: 416-924-0151; *Fax:* 416-924-2887
jerome@stanleigh.com

***Toronto*: James Stefoff - *1**
#1505, 80 Richmond St. West, Toronto, ON M5H 2A4
Tel: 416-366-7984

***Toronto*: Maxwell Steidman, Q.C. - *1**
#201, 1013 Wilson Ave., Toronto, ON M3K 1G1
Tel: 416-366-7661; *Fax:* 416-360-6868

***Toronto*: Larry C. Stein - *1**
#203, 2 Tippett Rd., Toronto, ON M3H 2V2
Tel: 416-636-8100; *Fax:* 416-636-6545

***Toronto*: Lorisa Stein - *1**
#800, 150 York St., Toronto, ON M5H 3S5
Tel: 416-596-8081;
lorisa@idirect.com
www.lorisastein.com

***Toronto*: Steinberg Morton Frymer - *14**
#1100, 5255 Yonge St., Toronto, ON M2N 6P4
Tel: 416-225-2777; *Fax:* 416-225-7112
smf@smflaw.com
www.smflaw.com

***Toronto*: James A. Stephenson, Q.C. - *1**
3 Daleberry Pl., Toronto, ON M3B 2A5
Tel: 416-383-1488

***Toronto*: Stern & Landesman - *3**
#1724, 390 Bay St., Toronto, ON M5H 2Y2
Tel: 416-869-3422; *Fax:* 416-869-3449

***Toronto*: Gary A. Stern - *1**
1938 Avenue Rd., Toronto, ON M5M 4A2
Tel: 416-780-0199; *Fax:* 416-780-0155
Toll-Free: 800-678-6705
gastern@torlaw.com

***Toronto*: Steven M. Fishbayn Barrister & Solicitor - *1**
100 Richmond St. West, Toronto, ON M5H 3K6
Tel: 416-361-9555; *Fax:* 416-862-7602

***Toronto*: Deborah L. Stewart - *1**
106 Glencairn Ave., Toronto, ON M4R 1M9
Tel: 416-226-9340; *Fax:* 416-226-5341

***Toronto*: Stikeman Keeley Spiegel Pasternack LLP - *4**
220 Bay St., 7th Fl., Toronto, ON M5J 2W4
Tel: 416-367-1930; *Fax:* 416-365-1813
info@stikeman.to
www.stikeman.to

***Toronto*: Stitt Feld Handy Group - *6**
Former Name: Stitt Feld Handy Houston
112 Adelaide St. East, Toronto, ON M5C 1K9
Tel: 416-307-0000; *Fax:* 416-307-0011
Toll-Free: 800-318-9741
contact@adr.ca
www.sfhgroup.com

***Toronto*: Stockwoods LLP - *12**
#2512, 150 King St. West, Toronto, ON M5H 1J9
Tel: 416-593-7200; *Fax:* 416-593-9345
www.stockwoods.ca

***Toronto*: Stone & Osborne - *2**
#201, 100 Sheppard Ave. West, Toronto, ON M2N 1M6
Tel: 416-225-1145; *Fax:* 416-225-0832

***Toronto*: Stone & Wenus - *2**
330 Broadview Ave., Toronto, ON M4M 2G9
Tel: 416-469-4125; *Fax:* 416-469-2877

***Toronto*: David S. Strashin - *1**
#702, 55 Eglinton Ave. East, Toronto, ON M4P 1G8
Tel: 416-482-8171; *Fax:* 416-485-4174

***Toronto*: StrategyCorp Inc. - *4**
Also Known As: Strategy Corp Toronto Inc.
145 King St. East, Toronto, ON M5C 2Y7
Tel: 416-864-7112; *Fax:* 416-864-7117
info@strategycorp.com
www.strategycorp.com

***Toronto*: Michael Strathman - *1**
219 Carlton St., Toronto, ON M5A 2L2
Tel: 416-922-2424; *Fax:* 416-923-8380
michael@strathmanlaw.ca

***Toronto*: Stringer, Brisbin, Humphrey Management Lawyers - *11**
#1100, 110 Yonge St., Toronto, ON M5C 1T4
Tel: 416-862-1616; *Fax:* 416-363-7358
Toll-Free: 866-821-7306
chumphrey@sbhlawyers.com
www.sbhlawyers.com

***Toronto*: John F. Stroz, Q.C. - *1**
2275 Dundas St. West, Toronto, ON M6R 1X6
Tel: 416-536-2131; *Fax:* 416-536-5451

***Toronto*: John S. Struthers - *1**
#501, 205 Richmond St. West, Toronto, ON M5V 1V3
Tel: 416-361-9609; *Fax:* 416-361-9443
jss@istar.ca

***Toronto*: J.A.F. Struyk - *1**
1144 Queen St. East, Toronto, ON M4M 1L1
Tel: 416-463-1188; *Fax:* 416-463-9020
strike@tcn.net

***Toronto*: Robert P. Sullivan - *1**
#1807, 8 King St. East, Toronto, ON M5C 1B5
Tel: 416-361-0390; *Fax:* 416-361-0248
rpsullivan@on.aibn.com

***Toronto*: S. Suppa - *1**
#10, 927 The Queensway, Toronto, ON M8Z 5Z7
Tel: 416-252-5688; *Fax:* 416-252-4511

***Toronto*: Sussex Strategy Group - *4**
#600, University Ave, Toronto, ON M5J 2H7
Tel: 416-961-6611; *Fax:* 416-961-9935
www.sussex-strategy.com

***Toronto*: Suter Law**
102 Annette St., Toronto, ON M6P 1N6
Tel: 416-760-0529; *Fax:* 416-769-0529

***Toronto*: Ian Sutherland Barrister & Solicitor - *1**
554 Annette St., Toronto, ON M6S 2C2
Tel: 416-763-0787; *Fax:* 416-763-0563
ian@sutherland.com
www.iansutherland.com

***Toronto*: Ralph A. Sutton - *1**
#1800, 4950 Yonge St., Toronto, ON M2N 6K1
Tel: 416-224-0200; *Fax:* 416-224-0758
rsutton@torlaw.com

***Toronto*: Swadron Associates - *6**
115 Berkeley St., Toronto, ON M5A 2W8
Tel: 416-362-1234; *Fax:* 416-362-1232
mail@swadron.com
www.swadron.com

***Toronto*: Kenneth P. Swan - *1**
#500, 70 Bond St., Toronto, ON M5B 1X3
Tel: 416-368-5279; *Fax:* 416-363-9135
kpswan@bondlaw.net

***Toronto*: Swanick & Associates - *5**
#101, 225 Duncan Mill Rd., Toronto, ON M3B 3K9
Tel: 416-510-1888; *Fax:* 416-510-1945

***Toronto*: H.A. Swartz - *2**
#106, 1120 Finch Ave. West, Toronto, ON M3J 3H7
Tel: 416-665-0600; *Fax:* 416-665-2848

***Toronto*: Lori M. Swartz**
#2200, P.O. Box 75, 1 Dundas St. West, Toronto, ON M5G 1Z3
Tel: 416-598-5899; *Fax:* 416-599-8341
Toll-Free: 800-410-1013
lori.swartz@lawpro.ca

***Toronto*: Eric J. Swetsky - *1**
25 Sylvan Valley Way, Toronto, ON M5M 4M4
Tel: 416-787-4376; *Fax:* 416-787-3538
www.advertisinglawyer.ca

***Toronto*: Mimi Tang - *1**
#202, 1210 Sheppard Ave. East, Toronto, ON M2K 1E3
Tel: 416-491-2929; *Fax:* 416-491-0990

***Toronto*: Tatham, Pearson - *3**
5524 Lawrence Ave. East, Toronto, ON M1C 3B2
Tel: 416-284-4749; *Fax:* 416-284-3086
Toll-Free: 800-970-5670
info@tathampearson.com

** indicates number of lawyers*

***Toronto*: Stanley Taube - *1**
#503, 33 Jackes Ave., Toronto, ON M4T 1E2
Tel: 416-513-1233

***Toronto*: Taveroff & Associates - *2**
#900, 2 Sheppard Ave. East, Toronto, ON M2N 5Y7
Tel: 416-221-9343; *Fax:* 416-221-8928

***Toronto*: Fred Tayar & Associates, Professional Corporation - *3**
#900, 20 Queen St. West, Toronto, ON M5H 3R3
Tel: 416-363-1800; *Fax:* 416-363-3356
fred@fredtayar.com

***Toronto*: Nicole J. Tellier - *2**
#200, 390 Dupont St., Toronto, ON M5R 1V9
Tel: 416-926-9669; *Fax:* 416-926-9079
ntellier@tellierlaw.com

***Toronto*: Stephen Thom - *1**
#500, 70 Bond St., Toronto, ON M5B 1X3
Tel: 416-364-3371; *Fax:* 416-863-4896

***Toronto*: Thomson, Rogers - *33**
#3100, 390 Bay St., Toronto, ON M5H 1W2
Tel: 416-868-3100; *Fax:* 416-868-3134
Toll-Free: 888-223-0448
info@thomsonrogers.com
www.thomsonrogers.com

***Toronto*: Ian Thornhill - *1**
#406, 255 Duncan Mill Rd., Toronto, ON M3B 3H9
Tel: 416-224-2004; *Fax:* 416-224-2101
ithornhilllaw@rogers.com

***Toronto*: Thornton Grout Finnigan LLP - *23**
#3200, Toronto-Dominion Centre, P.O. Box 329, 100 Wellington St. West, Toronto, ON M5K 1K7
Tel: 416-304-1616; *Fax:* 416-304-1313
info@tgf.ca
www.tgf.ca

***Toronto*: Thorsteinssons LLP Tax Lawyers - *20**
BCE Place, P.O. Box 786, 181 Bay St., 33rd Fl., Toronto, ON M5J 2T3
Tel: 416-864-0829; *Fax:* 416-864-1106
Toll-Free: 888-666-9998
managingpartner@thor.ca
www.thor.ca

***Toronto*: Lorne B. Tick - *1**
36 Elkpath Ave., Toronto, ON M2L 2W1
Tel: 416-444-9146; *Fax:* 416-444-9146
ltick@rogers.com

***Toronto*: Tikal's - *1**
178 St. George St., Toronto, ON M5R 2M7
Tel: 416-968-7070; *Fax:* 416-968-1876

***Toronto*: Philip Tinianov - *1**
#1800, 4950 Yonge St., Toronto, ON M2N 6K1
Tel: 416-363-0866; *Fax:* 416-224-0758
ptinianov@torlaw.com

***Toronto*: M.K. Titherington - *1**
46 Northcliffe Blvd., Toronto, ON M6H 3H2
Tel: 416-656-6465

***Toronto*: Tkatch & Associates - *2**
#488, 22 College St., Toronto, ON M5G 1K2
Tel: 416-968-0333; *Fax:* 416-968-0232
tkatchlaw@aol.com

***Toronto*: Norman W. Tomas - *1**
954A Royal York Rd., Toronto, ON M8X 2E5
Tel: 416-233-5567; *Fax:* 416-233-9779
ntomas@bellnet.ca

***Toronto*: James Tomlinson - *1**
#218A, 85 Ellesmere Rd., Toronto, ON M1R 4B9
Tel: 416-447-0476; *Fax:* 416-447-8611

***Toronto*: Mary Tomlinson - *1**
123 Glenrose Ave., Toronto, ON M4T 1K7

***Toronto*: Toomath & Associates - *1**
Also Known As: Toomath, E.H.
133 Berkeley St., 3rd Fl., Toronto, ON M5A 2X1
Tel: 416-869-0900; *Fax:* 416-366-4711

***Toronto*: Torkin Manes LLP - *76**
#1500, 151 Yonge St., Toronto, ON M5C 2W7
Tel: 416-863-1188; *Fax:* 416-863-0305
Toll-Free: 800-665-1555
info@torkinmanes.com
www.torkinmanes.com

***Toronto*: Paul G. Torrie - *2**
45 Saint Nicholas St., Toronto, ON M4Y 1W6
Tel: 416-964-9530; *Fax:* 416-925-8122
paul@global-adr.com

***Toronto*: Tough & Podrebarac LLP - *4**
#300, 166 Pearl St., Toronto, ON M5H 1L3
Tel: 416-348-7500; *Fax:* 416-348-7505

***Toronto*: Traub Moldaver - *5**
#1801, 4 King St. West, Toronto, ON M5H 1B6
Tel: 416-214-6500; *Fax:* 416-214-7275
Toll-Free: 877-727-6500

***Toronto*: Philip J. Traversy - *1**
#900, 2 Sheppard Ave. East, Toronto, ON M2N 5Y7
Tel: 416-221-9343; *Fax:* 416-221-8928
p.traversy@rogers.com

***Toronto*: T.J. Treloar - *1**
Former Name: Treloar, Mergler
#401, 302 The East Mall, Toronto, ON M9B 6C7
Tel: 416-232-2919; *Fax:* 416-232-9201

***Toronto*: Quoc Toan Trinh - *1**
1577 Bloor St. West, Toronto, ON M6P 1A6
Tel: 416-533-8987; *Fax:* 416-536-3618
trinhqtoan@on.aibn.com

***Toronto*: William M. Trudell - *2**
15 Bedford Rd., Toronto, ON M5R 2J7
Tel: 416-598-2019; *Fax:* 416-868-0273
wtrudell@15bedford.com

***Toronto*: Constantine Tsantis - *1**
69 Elm St., Toronto, ON M5G 1H2
Tel: 416-599-6689; *Fax:* 416-971-9092

***Toronto*: Maureen L. Tucker - *1**
43 Madawaska Ave., Toronto, ON M2M 2R1
Tel: 416-221-5122; *Fax:* 416-226-9737
Toll-Free: 877-580-2049
mltlaw@on.aibn.com

***Toronto*: Helen R. Turner - *1**
#1505, 80 Richmond St. West, Toronto, ON M5H 2A4
Tel: 416-366-7985; *Fax:* 416-366-4670

***Toronto*: Howard Ungerman - *1**
37 Maitland St., Toronto, ON M4Y 1C8
Tel: 416-924-4111; *Fax:* 416-924-4112

***Toronto*: Urquhart, Urquhart, Aiken & Medcof - *1**
#1505, 5140 Yonge St., Toronto, ON M2N 6L7
Tel: 416-595-1111; *Fax:* 416-595-7312
fieldbrown@bellnet.ca

***Toronto*: S. Van Duffelen - *1**
#100, 700 University Ave., Toronto, ON M5G 1Z5
Tel: 416-598-5667; *Fax:* 416-946-1180
vanduffelenlaw@on.aibn.com

***Toronto*: Michael B. Vaughan Q.C.**
#3100, 130 Adelaide St. West, Toronto, ON M5H 3P5
Tel: 416-363-9611; *Fax:* 416-363-9672
mbv@idirect.com

***Toronto*: Veritas Communications Inc. - *1**
#704, 161 Eglinton Ave. East, Toronto, ON M4P 1J5
Tel: 416-482-2248; *Fax:* 416-482-2292

***Toronto*: David R. Vine - *1**
#1604, 80 Richmond St. West, Toronto, ON M5H 2A4
Tel: 416-863-9341; *Fax:* 416-863-9342

***Toronto*: Mark H. Viner - *1**
541 Old Orchard Grove, Toronto, ON M5M 2G8
Tel: 416-785-7469; *Fax:* 416-785-1581
mviner@pathcom.com

***Toronto*: Julia M. Viva - *1**
58 Plymbridge Rd., Toronto, ON M2P 1A3
Tel: 416-488-7222; *Fax:* 416-489-6258

***Toronto*: James D. Vlasis - *1**
#240, 118 Eglinton Ave. West, Toronto, ON M4R 2G4
Tel: 416-920-3447; *Fax:* 416-920-3448
jamesvlasis@vlasislaw.com

***Toronto*: Wagman, Sherkin - *2**
#200, 756A Queen St. East, Toronto, ON M4M 1H4
Tel: 416-465-1102; *Fax:* 416-465-3941
charles_wagman@wagmansherkin.ca

***Toronto*: Waldin, de Kenedy - *3**
#2150, 1 Queen St. East, Toronto, ON M5C 2W5
Tel: 416-364-6761; *Fax:* 416-364-3866
waldin@waldin.ca

***Toronto*: Walker Poole Nixon LLP - *6**
#515, 5160 Yonge St., Toronto, ON M2N 6L9
Tel: 416-225-5160; *Fax:* 416-225-0072
info@wpnlaw.com
www.wpnlaw.com

***Toronto*: Bruce E. Walker - *2**
#205, 65 Wellesley St. East, Toronto, ON M4Y 1G7
Tel: 416-961-7451; *Fax:* 416-961-5966
bwalker@bwalkerlaw.com
www.bwalkerlaw.com

***Toronto*: Walker, Ellis - *2**
390 Bay St., 30th Fl., Toronto, ON M5H 1W2
Tel: 416-363-2144; *Fax:* 416-363-1541

***Toronto*: J.H.G. Wallace - *1**
551 Gerrard St. East, Toronto, ON M4M 1X7
Tel: 416-463-6666; *Fax:* 416-463-8259

***Toronto*: Walsh McLuskie Doyle - *4**
#2308, 180 Dundas St. West, Toronto, ON M5G 1Z8
Tel: 416-598-8177; *Fax:* 416-598-5466
firm@wmdlaw.net

***Toronto*: Walton Advocates - *5**
30 Hazelton Ave., Toronto, ON M5R 2E2
Tel: 416-489-3171; *Fax:* 416-489-9973

***Toronto*: Walton, Brigham & Kelly - *2**
301 Donlands Ave., Toronto, ON M4J 3R8
Tel: 416-425-4300; *Fax:* 416-425-4310
tkelly@bellnet.ca

***Toronto*: Wappel, Toome, Babits, Laar & Bell LLP - *6**
Also Known As: Toome Laar
#1801, 400 University Ave., Toronto, ON M5G 1S5
Tel: 416-598-1333; *Fax:* 416-598-5024

***Toronto*: Warren Bergman Associates - *2**
Former Name: Farb, Warren LLP
2925 Bathrust St., Toronto, ON M6S 3B1
Tel: 416-763-4183; *Fax:* 416-763-1310
Toll-Free: 877-763-4183
dwarren@warrenbergman.com

***Toronto*: Howard E. Warren - *1**
#802, 2 Sheppard Ave. East, Toronto, ON M2N 5Y7
Tel: 416-598-4777; *Fax:* 416-598-4316
hwarren@askhoward.com

***Toronto*: Robert D. Warren**
15 Bedford Rd., Toronto, ON M5R 2J7
Tel: 416-368-5393; *Fax:* 416-905-7736

***Toronto*: Wasser Resources Inc. - *1**
42 Arlstan Dr., Toronto, ON M3H 4V9
Tel: 416-638-1645;
www.wasserresources.com

***Toronto*: M.O. Watson - *1**
27 Whitehorn Cres., Toronto, ON M2J 3B1
Tel: 416-493-8541; *Fax:* 416-493-9042
barwat@rogers.com

***Toronto*: Weatherhead, Weatherhead - *2**
#500, 27 Queen St. East, Toronto, ON M5C 2M6
Tel: 416-362-1369; *Fax:* 416-362-5013
weatherhead@bellnet.ca

***Toronto*: J.H. Webster - *2**
2600 Danforth Ave., Toronto, ON M4C 1L3
Tel: 416-699-9644; *Fax:* 416-699-8905

***Toronto*: John David Webster, Q.C. - *1**
290 Lytton Blvd., Toronto, ON M5N 1R6
Tel: 416-489-6255

***Toronto*: John Weingust, Q.C. - *1**
Penthouse, 481 University Ave., 10th Fl., Toronto, ON M5G 2E9
Tel: 416-977-7786; *Fax:* 416-340-0064

***Toronto*: F. Sheldon Weinles - *1**
104 Caribou Rd., Toronto, ON M5N 2A9
Tel: 416-780-1330; *Fax:* 416-780-1331

***Toronto*: Joyce R. Weinman - *1**
#300, 20 Holly St., Toronto, ON M4S 3B1
Tel: 416-848-1019; *Fax:* 416-486-3309
joyce@jwdental.com
www.jwdental.com

***Toronto*: Gilbert Weinstock - *1**
#401, 1850 Victoria Park Ave., Toronto, ON M1R 1T1
Tel: 416-759-1354; *Fax:* 416-759-3256
gilbertweinstock@gmail.com

***Toronto*: WeirFoulds LLP - *78**
#1600, Exchange Tower, P.O. Box 480, 130 King St. West, Toronto, ON M5X 1J5
Tel: 416-365-1110; *Fax:* 416-365-1876
firm@weirfoulds.com
www.weirfoulds.com

***Toronto*: John Weisdorf, Q.C. - *1**
#1000, 121 Richmond St. West, Toronto, ON M5H 2K1
Tel: 416-861-1000; *Fax:* 416-861-8166

***Toronto*: Irwin Wenus - *1**
27 Acton Ave., Toronto, ON M3H 4G6
Tel: 416-633-5830

***Toronto*: Stephen Werbowyj Professional Corporation**
1199 The Queensway, Toronto, ON M8Z 1R2
Tel: 416-233-9461; *Fax:* 416-233-1524
werbowyj@bellnet.ca

***Toronto*: Ian D. Werker - *1**
#2000, 393 University Ave., Toronto, ON M5G 1E6
Tel: 416-593-7552; *Fax:* 416-593-0668
ian@werkerlaw.com

***Toronto*: West Scarborough Community Legal Services - *4**
#201, 2425 Eglinton Ave. East, Toronto, ON M1K 5G8
Tel: 416-285-4460; *Fax:* 416-285-1070

***Toronto*: Lawrence C. Wesson, Barrister & Solicitor - *1**
#710, 40 Sheppard Ave. West, Toronto, ON M2N 6K9
Tel: 416-225-7625; *Fax:* 416-225-1665

***Toronto*: Grace Westcott, Barrister & Solicitor - *1**
133 Laother Ave., Toronto, ON M5R 1E4
Tel: 416-489-2738; *Fax:* 416-489-1918
gw@westcottlaw.com

***Toronto*: Lionel B. White, Q.C. - *1**
65 Duggan Ave., Toronto, ON M4V 1Y1
Tel: 416-364-1127; *Fax:* 416-364-6903
lex.white@rogers.com

***Toronto*: Robin J. Wigdor - *1**
#901, 159 Frederick St., Toronto, ON M5A 4P1
Tel: 416-504-7237;
robin@wigdor.com
www.wigdor.com/robin/

***Toronto*: Willard & Devitt - *1**
155 Roncesvalles Ave., Toronto, ON M6R 2L3
Tel: 416-531-1136; *Fax:* 416-531-4096
robert@robertbeaumont.ca

***Toronto*: W.M. Sharpe - *3**
#307, 40 Wynford Dr., Toronto, ON M3C 1J5
Tel: 416-482-5321; *Fax:* 416-322-2083
wmsharpe@shippinglaw.ca
www.yachtsales.com/sharpe

***Toronto*: Paul T. Willis - *1**
#308, 120 Carlton St., Toronto, ON M5A 4K2
Tel: 416-926-9806; *Fax:* 416-926-9737
paul.t.willis@on.aibn.com

***Toronto*: Willms & Shier Environmental Lawyers LLP - *11**
#900., 4 King St. West, Toronto, ON M5H 1B6
Tel: 416-863-0711; *Fax:* 416-863-1938
info@willmsshier.com
www.willmsshier.com

***Toronto*: Willowdale Community Legal Services - *2**
#106, 245 Fairview Mall Dr., Toronto, ON M2J 4T1
Tel: 416-492-2437; *Fax:* 416-492-6281

** indicates number of lawyers*

Toronto: **Willson Lewis LLP, Barristers & Solicitors - *5**
#200, 1183 King St. West, Toronto, ON M6K 3C5
Tel: 416-534-9504; *Fax:* 416-534-9503
cwillson@willsonlewis.com
www.willsonlewis.com

Toronto: **David S. Wilson - *1**
#2000, 393 University Ave., Toronto, ON M5G 1E6
Tel: 416-943-1223; *Fax:* 416-943-1049
dswilson@davidswilsonlaw.com

Toronto: **Matthew F. Wilton & Associate**
127 John St., Toronto, ON M5V 2E2
Tel: 416-860-9889; *Fax:* 416-204-1849

Toronto: **Norman H. Winter - *1**
#801, 1 St. Clair Ave. East, Toronto, ON M4T 2V7
Tel: 416-964-0325; *Fax:* 416-964-2494
nw@nwinlaw.com

Toronto: **Wise & Associates Professional Corporation - *3**
Former Name: Wise, Roy
#201, 40 Scollard St., Toronto, ON M5R 3S1
Tel: 416-866-4144; *Fax:* 416-866-7946
roy.wise@wiseandassociates.com

Toronto: **G.R. Wise - *1**
3329 Bloor St. West, Toronto, ON M8X 1E7
Tel: 416-231-7399; *Fax:* 416-231-1280

Toronto: **Gary L. Wiseman - *1**
#1800, 4950 Yonge St., Toronto, ON M2N 6K1
Tel: 416-224-0200; *Fax:* 416-224-0758
gwiseman@idirect.com

Toronto: **L. Patricia Wong - *1**
#108, 14 Prince Arthur Ave., Toronto, ON M5R 1A9
Tel: 416-972-6957; *Fax:* 416-972-6427
werzy@planeteer.com

Toronto: **Newton Wong & Associates - *2**
#307, 1033 Bay St., Toronto, ON M5S 3A5
Tel: 416-971-9118; *Fax:* 416-971-7210

Toronto: **Wing H. Wong - *1**
#202, 4433 Sheppard Ave. East, Toronto, ON M1S 1V3
Tel: 416-298-6767; *Fax:* 416-298-3844

Toronto: **Cynthia J. Woods - *1**
#301, 2490 Bloor St. West, Toronto, ON M6S 1R4
Tel: 416-763-3065; *Fax:* 416-763-6876
info@woodslaw.ca
www.woodslaw.ca

Toronto: **Woolgar VanWiechen Ketcheson Ducoffe LLP - *9**
Former Name: Ducoffe, Stuart M.
#401, 70 The Esplanade, Toronto, ON M5E 1R2
Tel: 416-867-1666; *Fax:* 416-867-1434
www.woolvan.com

Toronto: **George A. Wootten, Q.C. - *1**
#901, 701 Evans Ave., Toronto, ON M9C 1A3
Tel: 416-621-7470; *Fax:* 416-621-6838

Toronto: **Wright & Associates - *5**
897 Kipling Ave., Toronto, ON M8Z 5H3
Tel: 416-236-7905; *Fax:* 416-236-5644
wright.associates@wnalaw.com

Toronto: **K.E. Wright - *1**
#1001, 65 Queen St. West, Toronto, ON M5H 2M5
Tel: 416-364-1157

Toronto: **Peter J. Wuebbolt - *1**
1554A Bloor St. West, Toronto, ON M6P 1A4
Tel: 416-516-4621; *Fax:* 416-516-1679

Toronto: **Sara Wunch - *1**
#1600, 480 University Ave., Toronto, ON M5T 1V6
Tel: 416-595-7001; *Fax:* 416-595-5663

Toronto: **Nicholas A. Xynnis - *1**
#400, 100 Richmond St. West, Toronto, ON M5H 3K6
Tel: 416-862-1010; *Fax:* 416-862-7602

Toronto: **Arthur Yallen**
204 St. George St., Toronto, ON M5R 2N5
Tel: 416-927-0001; *Fax:* 416-927-0930

Toronto: **John Yaremko, Q.C. - *1**
1 Connable Dr., Toronto, ON M5R 1Z7
Tel: 416-921-7158

Toronto: **Francesca E. Yaskiel - *1**
#903, 121 Richmond St. West, Toronto, ON M5H 2K1
Tel: 416-847-0847; *Fax:* 416-363-0263

Toronto: **Gerald B. Yasskin - *1**
#402, 1183 Finch Ave. West, Toronto, ON M3J 2G2
Tel: 416-667-0982; *Fax:* 416-665-4291

Toronto: **Yee & Lee - *2**
#109, 40 Wynford Dr., Toronto, ON M3C 1J5
Tel: 416-977-0091; *Fax:* 416-977-6335

Toronto: **David P. Yerzy - *1**
#108, 14 Prince Arthur Ave., Toronto, ON M5R 1A9
Tel: 416-972-6957; *Fax:* 416-972-6427
73203.2004@compuserve.com

Toronto: **Hyun Soo Yi - *1**
#204, 640 Bloor St. West, Toronto, ON M6G 1K9
Tel: 416-534-7711; *Fax:* 416-534-7714

Toronto: **Theodore C. Yoannou - *1**
#600, 1000 Finch Ave. West, Toronto, ON M3J 2V5
Tel: 416-650-1011; *Fax:* 416-650-1980
tedyoannou@hotmail.com

Toronto: **York Community Services**
1651 Keele St., Toronto, ON M6M 3W2
Tel: 416-653-5400; *Fax:* 416-653-8049
franklim@lao.on.ca

Toronto: **Joseph R. Young - *1**
#200, 20 Cumberland St., Toronto, ON M4W 1J5
Tel: 416-969-8887; *Fax:* 416-969-8866
jryoung@globalmigration.com

Toronto: **D.R. Zadorozny - *1**
#216, 4195 Dundas St. West, Toronto, ON M8X 1Y4
Tel: 416-239-2333; *Fax:* 416-239-1752
Toll-Free: 866-396-7251
drz@drzlaw.com

Toronto: **Silvie Zakuta - *1**
112 Adelaide St. East, Toronto, ON M5C 1K9
Tel: 416-923-1656; *Fax:* 416-368-2918
szakuta@aol.com

Toronto: **Zaldin & Fine - *3**
#1012, 111 Richmond St. West, Toronto, ON M5H 2G4
Tel: 416-868-1431; *Fax:* 416-868-6381
zalfin@ca.inter.net

Toronto: **Lawrence Zaldin - *1**
#424, 3600 Yonge St., Toronto, ON M4N 3R8
Tel: 416-488-1766; *Fax:* 416-488-3555
lzaldin@sympatico.ca

Toronto: **Zammit Semple LLP - *4**
#601, 130 Bloor St. West, Toronto, ON M5S 1N5
Tel: 416-923-2601; *Fax:* 416-923-1391

Toronto: **C. Zapf - *1**
2424 Bloor St. West, 2nd Fl., Toronto, ON M6S 1P9
Tel: 416-766-4208; *Fax:* 416-769-5365

Toronto: **M. David Zbarsky - *1**
#1001, 85 Thorncliffe Park Dr., Toronto, ON M4H 1L6
Tel: 416-421-6252; *Fax:* 416-467-6780

Toronto: **Zeldin, Collin - *1**
23 Bedford Rd., Toronto, ON M5R 2J9
Tel: 416-964-7914; *Fax:* 416-964-8067
collin@zecol.com

Toronto: **David L. Zifkin - *1**
90A Isabella St., 1st Fl., Toronto, ON M4Y 1N4
Tel: 416-927-7720; *Fax:* 416-964-9348
dzifkin@zifkin.com
www.zifkin.com

Toronto: **R. Zisman**
#307, 120 Carlton St., Toronto, ON M5A 4K2
Tel: 416-925-6490; *Fax:* 416-925-4492
rzisman@rgcoates.com

Toronto: **Howard G. Zweig - *1**
1035 McNicoll Ave., Toronto, ON M1W 3W6
Tel: 416-512-1201; *Fax:* 416-512-1212
zweiglaw@bellnet.ca

Toronton: **M.M. Jemmott, Q.C. - *1**
344 Dupont Street, Toronton, ON M5R 1V9
Tel: 416-975-0787;
marvajemmott@bellnet.ca

Tottenham: **Feehely, Gastaldi - *4**
P.O. Box 370, 5 Mill St. East, Tottenham, ON L0G 1W0
Tel: 905-936-4262; *Fax:* 905-936-5102
fg@feehelygastaldi.com

Tottenham: **Smith & Associates - *2**
P.O. Box 970, 23 Queen St. South, Tottenham, ON L0G 1W0
Tel: 905-936-4221; *Fax:* 905-936-4223

Trenton: **Bonn Law Office - *4**
Former Name: G.W. Bonn
80 Division St., Trenton, ON K8V 5S5
Tel: 613-392-9207; *Fax:* 613-392-6367
georgebonn@bonnlaw.com

Trenton: **Fleming Garrett Sioui - *5**
P.O. Box 397, Stn. Main, 21 Quinte St., Trenton, ON K8V 5R6
Tel: 613-965-6430; *Fax:* 613-965-6400
fgs@reach.net

Tweed: **L.G. Bryan - *1**
P.O. Box 669, 325 Victoria St. North, Tweed, ON K0K 3J0
Tel: 613-478-6100; *Fax:* 613-478-3485
lbryan@intranet.ca

Tweed: **Bart F. Lackie - *1**
2718 Mallbank Rd., RR#4, Tweed, ON K0K 3J0
Tel: 613-478-9940; *Fax:* 613-478-6061
bart@linesat.com

Unionville: **Susan M. Ambrose - *1**
105 Main St., Unionville, ON L3R 2G1
Tel: 905-477-0624; *Fax:* 905-477-5846
inquiries@lawgals.com

Unionville: **Janet L. Gillespie - *1**
178 Main St., Unionville, ON L3R 2G9
Tel: 905-479-6352; *Fax:* 905-479-1991
jlgillespie@rogers.com

Unionville: **Minken & Associates Professional Corporation - *5**
#200, 190 Main St., Unionville, ON L3R 2G9
Tel: 905-477-7011; *Fax:* 905-477-7010
Toll-Free: 866-477-7011
admin@minken.com
www.minken.com; www.employmentlawissues.ca

Unionville: **M.T.P. Wood - *1**
10050 Warden Ave., Unionville, ON L6C 1N3
Tel: 905-887-5999; *Fax:* 905-887-5826

Uxbridge: **Bailey & Sedore - *2**
11 Brock St. East, Uxbridge, ON L9P 1M4
Tel: 905-852-3363; *Fax:* 905-852-3480

Uxbridge: **Paul D. Fox - *1**
6749 Concession 6, RR#1, Uxbridge, ON L9P 1R1
Tel: 905-852-4560; *Fax:* 905-852-4435
paulfox@bellnet.ca

Uxbridge: **Randall B. Hoban - *1**
20 Bascom St., Uxbridge, ON L9P 1J3
Tel: 905-852-3666

Uxbridge: **P.D. Turner, Q.C. - *1**
P.O. Box 760, 63 Albert St., Uxbridge, ON L9P 1E5
Tel: 905-852-6196; *Fax:* 905-852-6197
doug@pdturner.com

Uxbridge: **Wilson Associates - *2**
22 Brock St. East, Uxbridge, ON L9P 1P1
Tel: 905-852-3353; *Fax:* 905-852-5120
lawyers@uxbridgelaw.com
www.uxbridgelaw.com

Vanier: **Equinox affaires publiques - *1**
C.P. 79163 RPO Vanier, Vanier, ON K1L 1A1
Tel: 819-613-2882; *Fax:* 888-237-4765
Toll-Free: 877-640-7933
info@equinoxinc.ca
www.equinoxinc.ca

Vaughan: **Bianchi, Presta - *9**
#300, 9100 Jane St., Vaughan, ON L4K 0A4
Tel: 905-738-1078; *Fax:* 905-738-0528
www.bianchipresta.com

Vaughan: **Bratty & Partners LLP - *14**
#200, 7501 Keele St., Vaughan, ON L4K 1Y2
Tel: 905-760-2600; *Fax:* 905-760-2900
info@bratty.com
www.bratty.com

* *indicates number of lawyers*

***Vaughan*: Drudi, Alexiou, Kuchar LLP - *4**
#307, 7050 Weston Rd., Vaughan, ON L4L 8G7
Tel: 905-850-6116; *Fax:* 905-850-9146

***Vaughan*: Fine & Deo - *7**
#300, 3100 Steeles Ave. West, Vaughan, ON L4K 3R1
Tel: 905-760-1800; *Fax:* 905-760-0050
Toll-Free: 888-346-3336
info@finedeo.com

***Vaughan*: Gambin RDQ LLP - *7**
#400, 3901 Hwy. 7, Vaughan, ON L4L 8L5
Tel: 905-264-7800; *Fax:* 905-264-7808

***Vaughan*: Enzo Salvatori - *1**
#4, 161 Pennsylvania Ave., Vaughan, ON L4K 1C3
Tel: 416-745-1777; *Fax:* 416-745-2220

***Vaughan*: Shiner Kent LLP - *3**
#203, 3800 Steeles Ave. West, Vaughan, ON L4L 4G9
Tel: 905-798-2929; *Fax:* 905-850-3397

***Vermilion Bay*: Shirley D. Gauthier - *1**
P.O. Box 490, Stn. Main, Vermilion Bay, ON P0V 2V0
Tel: 807-938-7984; *Fax:* 807-227-2902

***Walkerton*: D.A. Farr - *1**
P.O. Box 518, 229 Durham St. East, Walkerton, ON N0G 2V0
Tel: 519-881-1611; *Fax:* 519-881-1733
dfarr@wightman.ca

***Walkerton*: Magwood, Van De Vyvere, Thompson, & Grove-McClement LLP - *4**
#8280, P.O. Box 880, 215 Durham St., Walkerton, ON N0G 2V0
Tel: 519-881-3230; *Fax:* 519-881-3595
wmvt@bmts.com

***Wallaceburg*: Carscallen, Reinhart, Mathany, Maslak**
P.O. Box 409, Stn. Main, 619 James St., Wallaceburg, ON N8A 4X1
Tel: 519-627-2261; *Fax:* 519-627-1030

***Wallaceburg*: Hyde, Hyde & McGregor - *2**
233 Creek St., Wallaceburg, ON N8A 4C3
Tel: 519-627-2081; *Fax:* 519-627-1615

***Wasaga Beach*: Maurice Loton - *1**
P.O. Box 500, 802 Mosley St., Wasaga Beach, ON L9Z 2H4
Tel: 705-429-4332; *Fax:* 705-429-4683

***Wasaga Beach*: McNeill Law Office - *1**
Former Name: McNeill & Applegate
P.O. Box 550, 1014 Mosley St., Wasaga Beach, ON L9Z 1A5
Tel: 705-429-1776; *Fax:* 705-429-7095

***Waterdown*: A.S. Lonn - *1**
#23, 35 Main St. North, Waterdown, ON L0R 2H0
Tel: 905-689-6060; *Fax:* 905-689-9578
allan.lonn@on.aibn.com

***Waterford*: A. M. Lee Gaunt - *1**
Former Name: Driscoll & Gaunt
P.O. Box 580, Stn. Port Dover, 46 Main St. South, Waterford, ON N0A 1N0
Tel: 519-583-1411; *Fax:* 519-583-1110
leegaunt@kwic.com

***Waterford*: Birnie & Gaunt - *2**
P.O. Box 429, 70 Alice St., Waterford, ON N0E 1Y0
Tel: 519-443-8676; *Fax:* 519-443-5596

***Waterford*: C.A. Brennan - *1**
P.O. Box 1229, 19 Main St. South, Waterford, ON N0E 1Y0
Tel: 905-443-8643; *Fax:* 905-443-4489
neilbrennan@bellnet.ca

***Waterloo*: Amy, Appleby & Brennan - *3**
372 Erb St. West, Waterloo, ON N2L 1W6
Tel: 519-884-7330; *Fax:* 519-884-7390
aab-lawoffice@rogers.com

***Waterloo*: Richard C. Biggs - *1**
500 Dutton Dr., Waterloo, ON N2L 4C6
Tel: 519-886-1678; *Fax:* 519-886-1791
biggslaw@bellnet.ca

***Waterloo*: Chris & Volpini - *2**
375 University Ave. East, Waterloo, ON N2K 3M7
Tel: 519-888-0999; *Fax:* 519-888-0995
cvlaw@chrisvolpinilawyers.com

***Waterloo*: Dueck, Sauer, Jutzi & Noll LLP - *8**
Former Name: Dueck, Sauer, Jutzi & Noll
403 Albert St., Waterloo, ON N2L 3V2
Tel: 519-884-2620; *Fax:* 519-884-0254
tedd@dsjnlaw.com
www.dsjnlaw.com

***Waterloo*: W. Marlene Fitzpatrick - *1**
420 Weber St. North, Waterloo, ON N2L 4E7
Tel: 519-725-9500; *Fax:* 519-725-2379
marlenefitzpatrick@on.aibn.com

***Waterloo*: Haney, Haney & Kendall - *5**
P.O. Box 185, 41 Erb St. East, Waterloo, ON N2J 3Z9
Tel: 519-747-1010; *Fax:* 519-747-9323
hhk@haneylaw.com

***Waterloo*: Fred J. Heimbecker - *1**
295 Weber St. North, Waterloo, ON N2J 3H8
Tel: 519-886-1750; *Fax:* 519-886-0503
heim@bellnet.ca

***Waterloo*: William C. Hoskinson - *1**
P.O. Box 22103, 50 Westmount Rd. North, Waterloo, ON N2L 6J7
Tel: 519-571-1022; *Fax:* 519-743-0490

***Waterloo*: John E. Lang - *1**
21 Post Horn Place, Waterloo, ON N2L 5E8
Tel: 519-578-3330; *Fax:* 519-578-3337
johnelang@rogers.com

***Waterloo*: Kominek, Gladstone - *1**
#311, 55 Erb St. East., Waterloo, ON N2J 4K8
Tel: 519-886-1050; *Fax:* 519-747-9565
glynne.gladstone2@sympatico.ca

***Waterloo*: Eric M. Kraushaar - *1**
#5, 620 Davenport Rd., Waterloo, ON N2V 2C2
Tel: 519-886-0088; *Fax:* 519-746-1122
eric@churchill-homes.com

***Waterloo*: Paul W. Lang, Q.C. - *1**
347 Beechlawn Dr., Waterloo, ON N2L 5L8
Tel: 519-884-3382; *Fax:* 519-884-1073

***Waterloo*: Levesque & Deane - *2**
#5B, 490 Dutton Dr., Waterloo, ON N2L 6H7
Tel: 519-725-2929; *Fax:* 519-725-2920
debbie@kwlegal.com

***Waterloo*: Lowes, Salmon & Gadbois - *3**
500 Dutton Dr., Waterloo, ON N2L 4C6
Tel: 519-884-0800; *Fax:* 519-884-1026
Toll-Free: 877-258-2575
tlowes@watlaw.ca
www.watlaw.ca

***Waterloo*: Joe Mattes Barrister, Solicitor & Trademark Agent - *1**
#200, 24 Dupont St. East, Waterloo, ON N2J 2G9
Tel: 519-884-5600; *Fax:* 519-884-9963
joe@matteslaw.com

***Waterloo*: P.M. Miller - *1**
15 Westmount Rd. South, Waterloo, ON N2L 2K2
Tel: 519-884-1332; *Fax:* 519-884-1161

***Waterloo*: Oldfield, Greaves, D'Agostino & Billo - *6**
P.O. Box 16580, 172 King St. South, Waterloo, ON N2J 4X8
Tel: 519-576-7200; *Fax:* 519-576-0131
watlaw@watlaw.com

***Waterloo*: Petker & Associates - *3**
295 Weber St. North, Waterloo, ON N2J 3H8
Tel: 519-886-1204; *Fax:* 519-886-5674

***Waterloo*: James E. Pitcher - *1**
420 Weber St. North, Waterloo, ON N2J 4A7
Tel: 519-725-9444; *Fax:* 519-725-2379

***Waterloo*: Shortt, Hanbidge, Richardson & Welch - *4**
Former Name: Shortt, Hanbidge, Snider, Richardson & Welch
P.O. Box 550, Stn. Waterloo, 7 Union St. East, Waterloo, ON N2J 4B8
Tel: 519-579-5600; *Fax:* 519-579-2725
shs@shslaw.com

***Waterloo*: Sloan Strype LLP - *2**
P.O. Box 547, 92 Erb St. East, Waterloo, ON N2J 4B8
Tel: 519-886-1590; *Fax:* 519-886-8545
jsloan@sloanstrypelaw.com
www.sloanstrypelaw.com

***Waterloo*: Edward Roy Tschirhart - *1**
291 Faraday Ct., Waterloo, ON N2L 6A4
Tel: 519-880-1374; *Fax:* 519-880-8853
e.tschirhart@sympatico.ca

***Waterloo*: Barbara Wallace - *1**
326 Conservation Dr., Waterloo, ON N2V 1V3
Tel: 519-888-0599

***Waterloo*: Weir & Fedy - *2**
#105, 109 Erb St. West, Waterloo, ON N2L 1T4
Tel: 519-883-1844; *Fax:* 519-883-1845
jweir@weirfedy.com

***Waterloo*: White, Duncan & Linton LLP - *6**
P.O. Box 457, 45 Erb St. East, Waterloo, ON N2J 4B5
Tel: 519-886-3340; *Fax:* 519-886-8651

***Waterloo*: Whitney Consulting - *1**
145 Avondale Ave. South, Waterloo, ON N2L 2C5
Tel: 519-342-7457

***Watford*: Wallace B. Lang - *1**
5290 Nauvoo Rd., Watford, ON N0M 2S0
Tel: 519-876-2742; *Fax:* 519-876-2073

***Welland*: George C.M. Banks - *1**
P.O. Box 127, Stn. Main, 191 Division St., Welland, ON L3B 5P2
Tel: 905-735-1770; *Fax:* 905-735-7031
george.banks@bellnet.ca

***Welland*: Vince Bellantino - *1**
8 East Main St., Welland, ON L3B 3W3
Tel: 905-788-3881; *Fax:* 905-788-3885

***Welland*: Blackadder Green Marion Halinda & Wood LLP - *5**
P.O. Box 580, 136 East Main St., Welland, ON L3B 5R3
Tel: 905-735-3620; *Fax:* 905-735-1577

***Welland*: Flett Beccario, Barristers & Solicitors - *8**
P.O. Box 340, Stn. Main, 190 Division St., Welland, ON L3B 5P9
Tel: 905-732-4481; *Fax:* 905-732-2020
flett@flettbeccario.com
www.flettbeccario.com

***Welland*: William V. Frith - *1**
#301, P.O. Box 757, Stn. Main, 76 Division St., Welland, ON L3B 5R5
Tel: 905-735-7582; *Fax:* 905-735-0093
w_firth@iaw.com

***Welland*: Houghton, Sloniowski & Stengel - *3**
170 Division St., Welland, ON L3B 4A2
Tel: 905-734-4577; *Fax:* 905-732-3765
Toll-Free: 888-483-9770

***Welland*: Rodney J. Kajan - *1**
#102, P.O. Box 130, 60 King St., Welland, ON L3B 5P2
Tel: 905-732-1352; *Fax:* 905-732-0531

***Welland*: Kormos & Evans Law Office - *1**
14 Niagara St., Welland, ON L3C 1H9
Tel: 905-732-4424; *Fax:* 905-732-7574
markevans@on.aibn.com
www.markevanslaw.com

***Welland*: Anthony W. Pylypuk - *1**
P.O. Box 605, 80 King St., Welland, ON L3B 5R4
Tel: 905-735-2300; *Fax:* 905-735-9230
awpylypuk@pylypuk.com

***Welland*: Swayze & Swayze - *1**
P.O. Box 667, Stn. Main, 131 Division St., Welland, ON L3B 5R4
Tel: 905-734-4553; *Fax:* 905-734-8015
swayze@bellnet.ca

***Welland*: Talmage & DiFiore - *2**
P.O. Box 97, 221 Division St., Welland, ON L3B 5P2
Tel: 905-732-4477; *Fax:* 905-732-4718
talstradi@iaw.on.ca

***Welland*: Douglas R. Thomas - *1**
P.O. Box 564, Stn. Main, 9 Main St. East, Welland, ON L3B 5R3
Tel: 905-732-5529; *Fax:* 905-732-2211
thomform@iaw.on.ca

** indicates number of lawyers*

***Westport*: Barker Willson Professional Corporation - *3**
P.O. Box 309, 30 Main St., Westport, ON K0G 1X0
Tel: 613-273-3166; *Fax:* 613-273-3676
bwoffice@barkerwillson.com
www.barkerwillson.com

***Wheatley*: J.H. Eaton - *1**
26 Erie St. South, Wheatley, ON N0P 2P0
Tel: 519-825-7032; *Fax:* 519-825-9570
joyce.eaton@3web.net

***Whitby*: Donna C. Babbs Family Law Professional Corporation - *1**
P.O. Box 358, Stn. Main, 117 King St., Whitby, ON L1N 5S4
Tel: 905-668-7704; *Fax:* 905-665-9229

***Whitby*: Michael F. Boland - *1**
114 Green St., Whitby, ON L1N 4C8
Tel: 905-668-2606

***Whitby*: David J. Gillespie - *1**
P.O. Box 208, Stn. Main, 214 Dundas St. East, 2nd Fl., Whitby, ON L1N 5S1
Tel: 905-666-2221; *Fax:* 905-666-2344

***Whitby*: Stacy Howell**
#208, 420 Green St., Whitby, ON L1N 8R1
Tel: 905-668-7747; *Fax:* 905-668-7787
showell@bellnet.ca

***Whitby*: Jenkins & Newman - *3**
106 Colborne St. East, Whitby, ON L1N 1V8
Tel: 905-666-8588; *Fax:* 905-666-4873

***Whitby*: Johnston, Montgomery, Barristers & Solicitors - *2**
201 Byron St. South, Whitby, ON L1N 4P7
Tel: 905-666-2252; *Fax:* 905-430-0878
lphillips@lawwhitby.com
www.lawhitby.com

***Whitby*: Michaels & Michaels - *1**
#201, 1450 Hopkins St., Whitby, ON L1N 2C3
Tel: 905-665-7711; *Fax:* 905-430-9100
michaels_michaels@on.aibn.com

***Whitby*: Rosenberg, Pringle - *2**
#214, 185 Brock St. North, Whitby, ON L1N 4H3
Tel: 905-665-9594; *Fax:* 905-665-7124

***Whitby*: Edward P. Schein - *1**
107 Kent St., Whitby, ON L1N 4Y1
Tel: 905-666-1266; *Fax:* 905-668-2023

***Whitby*: Schneider, Howard - *1**
107 Kent St., Whitby, ON L1N 4Y1
Tel: 905-668-1677; *Fax:* 905-668-2023

***Whitby*: Siksay & Fraser - *2**
618 Athol St., Whitby, ON L1N 3Z8
Tel: 905-666-4772; *Fax:* 905-666-3233

***Whitby*: B.P. Stelmach - *1**
#5, 11 Stanely Ct., Whitby, ON L1N 8P9
Tel: 905-430-6611; *Fax:* 905-430-6828
stelmach@bellnet.ca

***Whitby*: Debra J. Sweetman - *1**
340 Byron St. South, Whitby, ON L1N 4P8
Tel: 905-666-8166; *Fax:* 905-666-8163
Toll-Free: 800-428-6944
debrajsweetman@aol.com

***Whitby*: Thomson Law Firm - *1**
P.O. Box 358, Stn. Main, 117 King St., Whitby, ON L1N 5S4
Tel: 905-668-7704; *Fax:* 905-668-1268

***Wiarton*: Peter Pegg - *1**
P.O. Box 569, 647 Berford St., Wiarton, ON N0H 2T0
Tel: 519-534-2011; *Fax:* 519-534-4494

***Winchester*: David J. Barnhart - *1**
P.O. Box 730, 489 Main St., Winchester, ON K0C 2K0
Tel: 613-774-2808; *Fax:* 613-774-5731

***Windsor*: Ballance & Melville - *2**
#100, 251 Goyeau St., Windsor, ON N9A 6V2
Tel: 519-255-1414; *Fax:* 519-255-7404
dawnmelville@bellnet.ca

***Windsor*: Barat, Farlam, Millson - *5**
#510, 251 Goyeau St., Windsor, ON N9A 6V2
Tel: 519-258-2424; *Fax:* 519-258-2451
bfm@bellnet.ca

***Windsor*: Bartlet & Richardes LLP - *13**
#1000, Canada Bldg., 374 Ouellette Ave., Windsor, ON N9A 1A9
Tel: 519-253-7461; *Fax:* 519-253-2321
mail@bartlet.com
www.bartlet.com

***Windsor*: Belowus Easton English - *3**
100 Ouellette Ave., 7th Fl., Windsor, ON N9A 6T3
Tel: 519-973-1900; *Fax:* 519-973-0225

***Windsor*: T. James Bennett - *1**
661 Champlain Dr., Windsor, ON N9E 1M6
Tel: 519-250-4397

***Windsor*: Anita M. Berecz - *1**
#304, 267 Pelissier St., Windsor, ON N9A 5N8
Tel: 519-258-8306; *Fax:* 519-258-4184
amberecz law@bellnet.ca

***Windsor*: Bondy, Riley, Koski - *2**
#310, 176 University Ave. West, Windsor, ON N9A 5P1
Tel: 519-258-1641; *Fax:* 519-258-1725
info@bondyriley.com

***Windsor*: A.J. Bradie - *2**
691 Ouellette Ave., Windsor, ON N9A 4J4
Tel: 519-255-1542; *Fax:* 519-255-9888
obrodie@mnsi.net

***Windsor*: Danny Branoff - *1**
912 Wyandotte St. East, Windsor, ON N9A 3J8
Tel: 519-258-4244; *Fax:* 519-258-4247

***Windsor*: Mario Carnevale Law Office - *2**
2488 McDougall Ave., Windsor, ON N8X 3N7
Tel: 519-969-8855; *Fax:* 519-969-0085

***Windsor*: Maria Carroccia - *1**
#602, Canada Bldg., 374 Ouellette Ave., Windsor, ON N9A 1A8
Tel: 519-258-0905; *Fax:* 519-258-8755
Toll-Free: 888-959-9917

***Windsor*: F. Michael Cervi - *1**
#400, 1500 Ouellette Ave., Windsor, ON N8X 1K7
Tel: 519-258-9494; *Fax:* 519-258-9985

***Windsor*: Chodola Reynolds Binder - *5**
720 Walker Rd., Windsor, ON N8Y 2N3
Tel: 519-254-6433; *Fax:* 519-254-7990
info@crblaw.cawww.facebook.com/pages/Windsor-Lawyers/130689596945631,
www.linkedin.com/company/chodola-reynolds-binder

***Windsor*: Clarks - *8**
#1200, Canada Bldg., 374 Ouellette Ave., Windsor, ON N9A 1A8
Tel: 519-254-4990; *Fax:* 519-254-2294
info@clarkslaw.com
www.clarkslaw.com

***Windsor*: Robert J. Comartin - *1**
350 Devonshire Rd., Windsor, ON N8Y 2L4
Tel: 519-253-7050; *Fax:* 519-253-7049

***Windsor*: Corrent & Macri - *5**
#201, 2485 Ouellette Ave., Windsor, ON N8X 1L5
Tel: 519-255-7332; *Fax:* 519-255-9123
mail@correntmacri.com

***Windsor*: Culmone Law, Barrister, Solicitor, Notary Public - *1**
410 Giles Blvd. East, Windsor, ON N9A 4C6
Tel: 519-258-3632; *Fax:* 519-977-1199
floro@culmonelaw.com
www.culmonelaw.com

***Windsor*: David Deluzio Law Firm - *1**
#200, 52 Chatham St. West, Windsor, ON N9A 5M6
Tel: 519-256-1994; *Fax:* 519-256-7233

***Windsor*: Robert M. DiPietro - *1**
#302, 380 Ouellette Ave., Windsor, ON N9A 6X5
Tel: 519-258-8248; *Fax:* 519-255-7685

***Windsor*: Jon Dobrowolski - *1**
#309, Westcourt Place, 251 Goyeau St., Windsor, ON N9A 6V2
Tel: 519-258-0034; *Fax:* 519-258-9133

***Windsor*: Donaldson, Donaldson, Greenaway - *5**
547 Devonshire Rd., Windsor, ON N8Y 2L6
Tel: 519-255-7333; *Fax:* 519-255-7173
ddglaw@on.aibn.com

***Windsor*: Ducharme Fox LLP - *13**
800 University Ave. West, Windsor, ON N9A 5R9
Tel: 519-259-1800; *Fax:* 519-259-1830
admin@ducharmefox.com

***Windsor*: Fazio & Associates - *4**
333 Wyandotte St. East, Windsor, ON N9A 3H7
Tel: 519-258-5030; *Fax:* 519-971-9051

***Windsor*: Julie Fodor - *1**
642 Windermere Rd., Windsor, ON N8Y 3E1
Tel: 519-256-8238; *Fax:* 519-258-5780
jfoder.law@bellnet.ca

***Windsor*: Gatti Law Professional Corporation - *2**
#400, 267 Pelissier St., Windsor, ON N9A 4K4
Tel: 519-258-1010; *Fax:* 519-258-0163
arg@argatti.com

***Windsor*: Goldstein DeBiase Manzocco, The Personal Injury Law Firm - *5**
#900, 176 University Ave. West, Windsor, ON N9A 5P1
Tel: 519-253-5242; *Fax:* 519-253-0218
gdm@thepersonalinjurylawfirm.net
www.thepersonalinjurylawfirm.net

***Windsor*: Goulin & Patrick - *2**
500 Windsor Ave., Windsor, ON N9A 6Y5
Tel: 519-258-8073; *Fax:* 519-977-0694
goulinpa@wincom.net

***Windsor*: Anthony J. Grassi - *1**
#322, 13300 Tecumseh Rd. East, Windsor, ON N8N 4R8
Tel: 519-739-1559;
anthonygrassi@bellnet.ca

***Windsor*: Greg Monforton and Partners - *7**
Former Name: Monforton, Robitaille, & Skipper
#1300, 100 Ouellette Ave., Windsor, ON N9A 6T3
Tel: 519-258-6490; *Fax:* 519-258-4104
Toll-Free: 800-663-1145
www.gregmonforton.com

***Windsor*: Neil M. Guttman**
#100, 215 Eugenie St. West, Windsor, ON N8X 2X7
Tel: 519-250-0130; *Fax:* 519-250-1772

***Windsor*: Jason P. Howie - *1**
350 Devonshire Rd., Windsor, ON N8Y 2L4
Tel: 519-973-1500; *Fax:* 519-973-9905
jason@jasonpaulhowie.com

***Windsor*: Kamin, Fisher, Burnett, Ziriada & Robertson - *5**
#200, 176 University Ave. West, Windsor, ON N9A 5P1
Tel: 519-252-1123; *Fax:* 519-977-6503
info@kaminlaw.ca

***Windsor*: Katzman, Wylupek - *5**
1427 Ouellette Ave., Windsor, ON N8X 1K1
Tel: 519-254-6324; *Fax:* 519-254-6774
www.katzman-wylupek.com

***Windsor*: Kerr & Kerr - *1**
#309, 251 Goyeau St., Windsor, ON N9A 2V2
Tel: 519-252-2211; *Fax:* 519-252-0132
Toll-Free: 888-772-9552
akerr@kerr-kerr.com

***Windsor*: Kirwin Partners LLP, Lawyers - *10**
423 Pelissier St., Windsor, ON N9A 4L2
Tel: 519-255-9840; *Fax:* 519-255-1413
www.kirwinpartners.com

***Windsor*: Kyrtsakas Law Office - *1**
5655 Tecumseh Rd. East, Windsor, ON N8T 1C8
Tel: 519-974-6303; *Fax:* 519-974-8644

***Windsor*: Lisa S. Labute - *1**
#407, 251 Goyeau St., Windsor, ON N9A 6V2
Tel: 519-252-6822; *Fax:* 519-252-2638
lslabute@mnsi.net

***Windsor*: Legal Assistance of Windsor - *3**
Former Name: Brian Rodenhurst
85 Pitt St. East, Windsor, ON N9A 2V3
Tel: 519-256-7831; *Fax:* 519-256-1387
www.uwindsor.ca/legalassistanceofwindsor

***Windsor*: Maleyko, D'hondt - *3**
#260, 2109 Ottawa St., Windsor, ON N8Y 1R8
Tel: 519-258-8220; *Fax:* 519-258-7788

** indicates number of lawyers*

Windsor: A.R. Mariotti - *1
#202, 176 University Ave. West, Windsor, ON N9A 5P1
Tel: 519-258-1931; *Fax:* 519-973-7575
arm.law@sympatico.ca

Windsor: Brenda A. McGinty - *1
518 Victoria Ave., Windsor, ON N9A 4M8
Tel: 519-255-1535; *Fax:* 519-255-1719

Windsor: McTague Law Firm LLP - *21
455 Pelissier St., Windsor, ON N9A 6Z9
Tel: 519-255-4300; *Fax:* 519-255-4360
info@mctaguelaw.com
www.mctaguelaw.com

Windsor: McWilliams & McWilliams - *1
#710, 100 Ouellette Ave., Windsor, ON N9A 6T3
Tel: 519-258-1100; *Fax:* 519-258-7384
mjmcwilliams@winlaw.ca

Windsor: Tullio Meconi - *1
349 Wyandotte St. East, Windsor, ON N9A 3H7
Tel: 519-252-7274;

Windsor: Donald D. Merritt - *1
#103, 525 Windsor Ave., Windsor, ON N9A 1J4
Tel: 519-258-8060; *Fax:* 519-258-9877

Windsor: Miller Canfield PLC - *21
Former Name: Miller Canfield Paddock & Stone LLP; Miller Canfield Paddock & Stone - Wilson Walker
#300, 443 Ouellette Ave., Windsor, ON N9A 6R4
Tel: 519-977-1555; *Fax:* 519-977-1566
www.millercanfield.com

Windsor: S. Frank Miller - *1
518 Victoria Ave., Windsor, ON N9A 4M8
Tel: 519-258-3044; *Fax:* 519-255-1719
frankmilleratlaw@earthlink.net

Windsor: Joana G. Miskinis - *1
518 Victoria Ave., Windsor, ON N9A 4M8
Tel: 519-254-3757; *Fax:* 519-255-1719

Windsor: Mousseau DeLuca McPherson Prince LLP - *11
#500, 251 Goyeau, Windsor, ON N9A 6V2
Tel: 519-258-0615; *Fax:* 519-258-6833
lawyers@mousseaulaw.com

Windsor: Michael P. O'Hearn - *1
#A-1, P.O. Box 1212, Stn. A, 75 Riverside Dr. East, Windsor, ON N9A 6P8
Tel: 519-255-1250; *Fax:* 519-971-9607
mike.ohearn@sympatico.ca

Windsor: John G. Ohler - *2
101 Tecumseh Rd. West, Windsor, ON N8X 1E8
Tel: 519-256-5496; *Fax:* 519-256-1492
ohlerlawfirm@bellnet.ca

Windsor: James W. Oxley
1854 Kildare Rd., Windsor, ON N8W 2W7
Tel: 519-258-7211

Windsor: D.R. Revait - *1
#209, Royal Windsor Terrace, 380 Pelissier, Windsor, ON N9A 6W8
Tel: 519-258-7030; *Fax:* 519-258-2629
derek.revait@bellnet.ca

Windsor: Salem & McCullough - *2
2828 Howard Ave., Windsor, ON N8X 3Y3
Tel: 519-966-3633; *Fax:* 519-972-7788

Windsor: Daniel W. Scott - *1
#302, 380 Ouellette Ave., Windsor, ON N9A 6X5
Tel: 519-258-8248

Windsor: Stephen L. Shanfield - *1
#333, 880 Ouellette Ave., Windsor, ON N9A 1C7
Tel: 519-258-3338; *Fax:* 519-258-3335
ssh@mnsi.net
www.shanfieldlaw.com

Windsor: Brian Sherwell - *1
827 Pillette Rd., Windsor, ON N8Y 3B4
Tel: 519-945-1109; *Fax:* 519-948-0003

Windsor: Shulgan Martini Marusic LLP - *7
Former Name: Martini Barile Marusic LLP
2491 Ouellette Ave., Windsor, ON N8X 1L5
Tel: 519-969-1817; *Fax:* 519-969-9655
info@smmbarristers.com

Windsor: Sorensen, Baker - *2
1600 Wyandotte St. East, Windsor, ON N8Y 1C7
Tel: 519-256-3111; *Fax:* 519-256-5468

Windsor: R. Craig Stevenson - *1
#18A, 25 Amy Croft Dr.., Windsor, ON N9K 1C7
Tel: 519-735-0777; *Fax:* 519-735-2999
rcslaw@mnsi.net
www.rcraigstevensonlawoffice.com

Windsor: Stipic Arpino - *3
1574 Ouellette Ave., Windsor, ON N8X 1K7
Tel: 519-258-3201; *Fax:* 519-258-2665
msa@mnsi.net

Windsor: Tamara Stomp & Associate - *2
721 Walker Rd., Windsor, ON N8Y 2N2
Tel: 519-948-9778; *Fax:* 519-948-9773
stomp@mnsi.net

Windsor: Sutts, Strosberg LLP - *20
#600, Westcourt Place, 251 Goyeau St., Windsor, ON N9A 6V4
Tel: 519-258-9333; *Fax:* 519-186-6613
www.strosbergco.com

Windsor: Michael V. Watters - *1
P.O. Box 7292, Stn. Sandwich, Windsor, ON N9C 3Z1
Tel: 519-253-6877; *Fax:* 519-253-9277

Windsor: G.V. Wortley - *1
2490 Talbot Rd., Windsor, ON N9H 1A6
Tel: 519-967-9410; *Fax:* 519-967-9431
wortley@jet2.net

Windsor: Martin Wunder, Q.C. - *1
#908, 100 Ouellette Ave., Windsor, ON N9A 6T3
Tel: 519-252-1121

Woodbridge: Gary A. Beaulne - *2
#401, 3700 Steeles Ave. West, Woodbridge, ON L4L 8K8
Tel: 905-850-5060; *Fax:* 905-850-5066
Toll-Free: 866-850-5006
garyabeaulne@hotmail.com

Woodbridge: F. Borgatti - *1
7135 Islington Ave., 2nd Fl., Woodbridge, ON L4L 1V9
Tel: 905-851-2883; *Fax:* 905-851-2887

Woodbridge: Bortolussi & Associates, Barristers & Solicitors - *3
#3, 100 Strada Dr., Woodbridge, ON L4L 5V7
Tel: 905-856-1816; *Fax:* 905-856-6682

Woodbridge: Roger Bourque - *1
#300, 3800 Steeles Ave. West, Woodbridge, ON L4L 4G9
Tel: 905-856-7101; *Fax:* 905-856-1524
rogerbourque@bellnet.ca

Woodbridge: Capo, Sgro, Dilena, Hemsworth, Mendicino - *7
#400, 7050 Weston Rd., Woodbridge, ON L4L 8G7
Tel: 905-850-7000; *Fax:* 905-850-7050

Woodbridge: Ralph Ciccia - *1
#400, 7050 Weston Rd., Woodbridge, ON L4L 8G7
Tel: 905-850-6408; *Fax:* 905-850-7050
rciccia@ciccia.ca

Woodbridge: Cosman, Gray LLP - *3
#104, 8 Director Ct., Woodbridge, ON L4L 3Z5
Tel: 905-850-3110; *Fax:* 905-850-3123
mark.cosman@cosmangray.com

Woodbridge: D'Alimonte Law - *1
#27, 4300 Steeles Ave. West, Woodbridge, ON L4L 4C2
Tel: 905-264-1553; *Fax:* 905-264-5450
jdalimonte@bellnet.ca

Woodbridge: Sean L.K. Daley - *1
#200, 4000 Steeles Ave. West, Woodbridge, ON L4L 4V9
Tel: 905-850-2002; *Fax:* 905-850-2007

Woodbridge: M. DiPaolo - *1
#400, 7050 Weston Rd., Woodbridge, ON L4L 8G7
Tel: 905-850-7575; *Fax:* 905-850-7050
mdipaolo@di-paolo.ca

Woodbridge: Anthony Gagliese - *1
#12, 5875 Hwy.#7, Woodbridge, ON L4L 8Z7
Tel: 905-264-1449; *Fax:* 905-264-3944
tony@sum-itclub.com

Woodbridge: John Lo Faso - *1
#600, 3700 Steeles Ave. West, Woodbridge, ON L4L 8K8
Tel: 905-856-3700; *Fax:* 905-850-9969
johnlofaso@westonlaw.ca

Woodbridge: Mancini Associates LLP - *3
#505, 7050 Weston Rd., Woodbridge, ON L4L 8G7
Tel: 905-851-7717; *Fax:* 905-851-7718

Woodbridge: Massimo Panicali - *1
#4, 253 Jevlan Dr., Woodbridge, ON L4L 7Z6
Tel: 905-850-2642; *Fax:* 905-850-8544
mass.pan-demonium@on.aibn.com

Woodbridge: Paradiso & Associates - *1
#504, 216 Chrislea Rd., Woodbridge, ON L4L 8S5
Tel: 905-850-6006; *Fax:* 905-850-5616
Toll-Free: 800-429-735
mail@paradisolaw.com
www.paradisolaw.com

Woodbridge: Piccin, Bottos - *5
#201, 4370 Steeles Ave. West, Woodbridge, ON L4L 4Y4
Tel: 905-850-0155; *Fax:* 905-850-0498

Woodbridge: Claudio Polsinelli - *1
#600, 3700 Steeles Ave. West, Woodbridge, ON L4L 8K8
Tel: 905-856-3700; *Fax:* 905-856-1213
claudio@westonlaw.ca

Woodbridge: Rigobon, Carli - *3
#401, 3700 Steeles Ave. West, Woodbridge, ON L4L 8K8
Tel: 905-850-5060; *Fax:* 905-850-5066
michael@rigoboncarli.com
www.rigoboncarli.com

Woodbridge: Felix Rocca - *1
#302, 7050 Weston Rd., Woodbridge, ON L4L 8G7
Tel: 905-851-7747; *Fax:* 905-851-7834
felixrocca@rogers.com

Woodbridge: Jack Rosati - *1
#206, 4550 Hwy. 7, Woodbridge, ON L4L 4Y6
Tel: 905-264-7566; *Fax:* 905-264-4054

Woodbridge: Rovazzi, Pallotta - *4
#901, 3700 Steeles Ave. West, Woodbridge, ON L4L 8K8
Tel: 905-850-2468; *Fax:* 905-850-4066
m.rovazzi@rplaw.ca

Woodbridge: Devi D. Sharma - *1
#625, 7050 Weston Rd., Woodbridge, ON L4L 8G7
Tel: 905-856-6404; *Fax:* 905-856-6264

Woodbridge: Stabile Professional Corporation - *2
Former Name: Stabile Partners
#905, 3700 Steeles Ave. West, Woodbridge, ON L4L 8K8
Tel: 905-851-6711; *Fax:* 905-851-5773
vista@stablaw.com

Woodbridge: Tanzola & Sorbara - *5
#101, 10 Director Ct., Woodbridge, ON L4L 7E8
Tel: 905-265-2252; *Fax:* 905-265-0667

Woodbridge: Turner, Brooks - *1
Former Name: Turner, Brooks Associates
#15, 4220 Steeles Ave. West, Woodbridge, ON L4L 3S8
Tel: 905-851-7110; *Fax:* 905-851-4229
sturner.barrister@bellnet.ca

Woodbridge: P.M. Valenti - *1
#300, West Bldg., 3800 Steeles Ave., Woodbridge, ON L4L 4G9
Tel: 905-850-8550; *Fax:* 905-850-9998

Woodstock: George H. Bishop - *1
32 Metcalf St., Woodstock, ON N4S 3E7
Tel: 519-539-8559; *Fax:* 519-539-2401
angie-bishoplaw@rogers.com

Woodstock: Debra A. Brown - *1
94 Graham St., Woodstock, ON N4S 6J7
Tel: 519-539-9870; *Fax:* 519-539-9248
debra@dabrownlaw.com

Woodstock: Peter H. Kratzmann - *1
48 Vansittart Ave., Woodstock, ON N4S 6E2
Tel: 519-537-2221; *Fax:* 519-537-5150
phklaw@primus.ca

** indicates number of lawyers*

***Woodstock*: Gordon Lemon - *3**
Former Name: Beatty Stock & Lemon
P.O. Box 336, 487 Princess St., Woodstock, ON N4S 7X6
Tel: 519-537-6629; *Fax:* 519-539-2459
info@beattylaw.on.ca

***Woodstock*: Gary D. McQuaid - *1**
380 Hunter St., Woodstock, ON N4S 4G2
Tel: 519-539-1310

***Woodstock*: White Coad LLP - *3**
P.O. Box 1059, 5 Wellington St. North, Woodstock, ON N4S 6P1
Tel: 519-421-1500; *Fax:* 519-539-6926
rcoad@whitecoad.com
www.whitecoad.com

***Woodstock*: R.B. Wolyniuk - *3**
P.O. Box 1233, 19 Riddell St., Woodstock, ON N4S 8R2
Tel: 519-539-7431; *Fax:* 519-539-4975

Prince Edward Island

***Alberton*: J. Allan Shaw, Law Corporation - *1**
P.O. Box 40, 479 Church St., Alberton, PE C0B 1B0
Tel: 902-853-3313; *Fax:* 902-853-3753

***Charlottetown*: Campbell Lea - *9**
P.O. Box 429, 15 Queen St., Charlottetown, PE C1A 7K7
Tel: 902-566-3400; *Fax:* 902-566-9266
office@campbelllea.com
www.campbelllea.com

***Charlottetown*: Carr, Stevenson & MacKay - *9**
Peake House, P.O. Box 522, 50 Water St., Charlottetown, PE C1A 7L1
Tel: 902-892-4156; *Fax:* 902-566-1377
csm@csmlaw.com
www.csmlaw.com/

***Charlottetown*: Kenneth A. Clark Law Office - *1**
#21, P.O. Box 2831, Stn. Central, 25 Queen St., Charlottetown, PE C1A 8C4
Tel: 902-566-9996; *Fax:* 902-566-9997

***Charlottetown*: Diamond & Associates - *3**
P.O. Box 39, Stn. Central, 224 Queen St., Charlottetown, PE C1A 7K2
Tel: 902-892-1200; *Fax:* 902-892-4848
diamond@isn.net

***Charlottetown*: Foster Hennessey MacKenzie - *3**
Former Name: Foster, O'Keefe
P.O. Box 38, Stn. Central, 129 Water St., Charlottetown, PE C1A 7K2
Tel: 902-892-3406; *Fax:* 902-368-8239

***Charlottetown*: Peter C. Ghiz - *1**
120 Prince St., Charlottetown, PE C1A 4R4
Tel: 902-628-6300; *Fax:* 902-628-6399
Toll-Free: 800-399-3221
peterghiz@peterghizlawyer.com

***Charlottetown*: Macnutt & Dumont - *4**
P.O. Box 965, 57 Water St., Charlottetown, PE C1A 7M4
Tel: 902-894-5003; *Fax:* 902-368-3782
info@macnuttdumont.ca

***Charlottetown*: Matheson & Murray - *8**
Former Name: Cox Hanson O'Reilly Matheson
#202, Queen Square, 119 Queen St., Charlottetown, PE C1A 4B3 Canada
Tel: 902-894-7051; *Fax:* 902-368-3762
info@mathesonandmurray.com
www.mathesonandmurray.com

***Charlottetown*: McInnes Cooper - *7**
#620, BDC Pl., 119 Kent St., Charlottetown, PE C1A 1N3
Tel: 902-368-8473; *Fax:* 902-368-8346
mcctn@mcinnescooper.com
www.mcinnescooper.com

***Charlottetown*: Philip Mullally Q.C. - *1**
P.O. Box 2560, Stn. Central, 51 University Ave., Charlottetown, PE C1A 8C2
Tel: 902-892-5452; *Fax:* 902-892-7013
pmullally@philipmullallylawoffice.com

***Charlottetown*: Paul J.D. Mullin Q.C. - *1**
P.O. Box 604, Stn. Central, 14 Great George St., Charlottetown, PE C1A 7L3
Tel: 902-368-3221; *Fax:* 902-894-7491
mullinlaw@pei.aibn.com

***Charlottetown*: Brenda J. Picard - *1**
PEI Legal Aid, P.O. Box 2000, Stn. Central, 40 Great George St., Charlottetown, PE C1A 7N8
Tel: 902-368-6043; *Fax:* 902-368-6122
bjpicard@gov.pe.ca

***Charlottetown*: Elizabeth S. Reagh Q.C. - *1**
17 West St., Charlottetown, PE C1A 3S3
Tel: 902-892-7667; *Fax:* 902-368-8629
reagh@isn.net

***Montague*: Alfred K. Fraser, Q.C. - *2**
P.O. Box 516, 554 Main St. North, Montague, PE C0A 1R0
Tel: 902-838-2041; *Fax:* 902-838-2754
pearle@akfraserlaw.com

***Mount Stewart*: Marlene R. Clarke Q.C. - *1**
P.O. Box 63, Mount Stewart, PE C0A 1T0
Tel: 902-676-2954; *Fax:* 902-676-2954

***Summerside*: Kathleen Loo Craig - *1**
P.O. Box 11, Stn. Main, Summerside, PE C1N 4P6
Tel: 902-887-2900; *Fax:* 902-887-2100

***Summerside*: David R. Hammond Q.C. - *1**
740A Water St. East, Summerside, PE C1N 5X1
Tel: 902-436-4267; *Fax:* 902-436-4268
dhammond@pei.aibn.com

***Summerside*: Lyle & McCabe - *2**
P.O. Box 300, 290 Water St., Summerside, PE C1N 4Y8
Tel: 902-436-4296; *Fax:* 902-436-4072
www.lylemccabelawoffice.com

***Summerside*: Stephen D.G. McKnight - *1**
P.O. Box 1570, Stn. Main, 494 Granville St., Summerside, PE C1N 4K4
Tel: 902-436-4851; *Fax:* 902-436-5063
stephen@keyandmcknight.com

***Summerside*: Robert McNeill - *1**
251 Water St., Summerside, PE C1N 1B5
Tel: 902-436-4847; *Fax:* 902-436-8183

Québec

***Alma*: Les Avocats Mario Bouchard Inc. - *3**
2340, au du Pont sud, RR#1, Alma, QC G8B 5V2
Tél: 418-668-7677; *Téléc:* 418-668-0539
mariob46@cgocable.ca
www.mariobouchard.com

***Alma*: Larouche, Lalancette, Pilote & Bouchard - *7**
723, ch du Pont-Taché nord, Alma, QC G8B 5B7
Tél: 418-662-6475; *Téléc:* 418-662-9239
www.llpb.ca

***Amos*: Ayotte Martineau McGuire Boyer - *2**
39A, av 1re ouest, Amos, QC J9T 1T7
Tél: 819-732-5258; *Téléc:* 819-732-0394

***Amos*: Bigué, avocats - *6**
Former Name: Bigué & Bigué
91, Première ave ouest, Amos, QC J9T 1T7
Tél: 819-732-8911; *Téléc:* 819-732-1470

***Amos*: Geoffroy, Matte, Kélada & Associés - *4**
4, rue Principale, Amos, QC J9T 2K6
Tél: 819-732-1698; *Téléc:* 819-732-7513
geoffroy.matte@sympatico.ca

***Anjou*: M.L. Anne Boutin - *1**
#2220, 7999, boul les Galeries d'Anjou, Anjou, QC H1M 1W9
Tél: 514-353-4411; *Téléc:* 514-353-4553
boutina@cadillacfairview.com

***Asbestos*: Denis Beaubien - *1**
601, boul Simoneau, Asbestos, QC J1T 4G7
Tél: 819-879-7177; *Téléc:* 819-879-2962
denis.beaubien@cgocable.ca

***Baie-Comeau*: Wullaert, Bachir, Tremblay, Bibeau et Trudeau - *4**
279, boul LaSalle, Baie-Comeau, QC G4Z 1T2
Tél: 418-294-8793; *Téléc:* 418-294-8258

***Baie-Saint-Paul*: Gagné Letarte - *16**
#205A, 11, rue St-Jean-Baptiste, Baie-Saint-Paul, QC G3Z 1M1
Tél: 418-435-6890; *Téléc:* 418-435-3082
www.gagneletarte.qc.ca

***Beauport*: Blouin & Associés - *3**
1217, av Royal, Beauport, QC G1E 2B2
Tél: 418-663-2931; *Téléc:* 418-663-3792
blouin@blouinetassocies.com
www.blouinetassocies.com

***Beloeil*: Bastien, Morand, Blanchette - *6**
201, boul Laurier, Beloeil, QC J3G 4G8
Tél: 450-467-5849; *Téléc:* 450-467-3152
Ligne sans frais: 877-467-5849
rbastien@avocatsbmb.com

***Beloeil*: Doré, Tourigny, Fiset & Associés - *5**
#314, 535, boul Sir-Wilfrid Laurier, Beloeil, QC J3G 5E9
Tél: 450-446-8474; *Téléc:* 450-467-7134

***Berthierville*: André Sylvestre**
1300, rue Notre Dame, Berthierville, QC J0K 1A0
Tél: 450-836-6213; *Téléc:* 450-836-7712
andre_sylvestre@bellnet.ca

***Boischatel*: JBRP & Associés Inc. - *1**
CP 141, 112 Montmorency, Boischatel, QC G0A 1H0
Tél: 418-822-2904; *Téléc:* 418-822-4192

***Boucherville*: Lecompte Deguire Avocats - *2**
1019, rue de la Ventrouze, Boucherville, QC J4B 5V3
Tél: 450-641-0065; *Téléc:* 450-641-3721
lecomptedeguire@videotron.ca

***Bromont*: Communications Anie Perrault - *1**
207, rue Martin, Bromont, QC J2L 3B3
Tél: 450-263-3728; *Téléc:* 450-263-3731
www.commap.ca

***Bromont*: Parabellum Communication Inc.**
170, rue Montcalm, Bromont, QC J2L 2C5
Tel: 450-534-2622; *Fax:* 450-534-2934
www.parabellum.ca

***Brossard*: Louis Hargreaves, Avocat - *1**
5480, croissant Beaumanoir, Brossard, QC J4Z 2G4
Tél: 450-462-3142; *Téléc:* 450-462-5881
louishargreaves@hotmail.com

***Buckingham*: Denis Montreuil - *1**
143, rue Joseph, Buckingham, QC J8L 1G3
Tél: 819-986-2701

***Cabano*: Annick Bédard - *1**
CP 370, 14, rue Pelletier, Cabano, QC G0L 1E0
Tél: 418-854-2206; *Téléc:* 418-854-0072

***Candiac*: Pierre Chenail & associés inc. - *1**
171, av de Deauville, Candiac, QC J5R 6X7
Tél: 450-724-3307; *Téléc:* 450-724-3308
pierre.chenail@videotron.ca

***Chandler*: Gaul & Associes - *1**
CP 757, Chandler, QC G0C 1K0
Tél: 418-689-2241

***Chibougamau*: Larouche & Girard, Avocats - *3**
127, rue des Forces armées, Chibougamau, QC G8P 3A1
Tel: 418-748-6468; *Fax:* 418-748-2323
larouchegirard@lino.com

***Chicoutimi*: Martin Côté, Avocat - *1**
CP 1475, Stn. Racine, 106, rue Garon, Chicoutimi, QC G7H 3C1
Tél: 418-543-3111; *Téléc:* 418-543-0753

***Chicoutimi*: Girard Allard Guimond Avocats - *3**
#202, 200, rue Racine est, Chicoutimi, QC G7H 1S1
Tél: 418-543-0725; *Téléc:* 418-543-1765
girardallardguimond@bellnet.ca

***Châteauguay*: Marie-Andrée Mallette - *1**
272, boul St-Jean-Baptiste, Châteauguay, QC J6K 3C2
Tél: 450-699-9499; *Téléc:* 450-699-9710
marieandreemallette@videotron.ca

***Cowansville*: Claude Boulet - *1**
#330, 104, rue du Sud, Cowansville, QC J2K 2X2
Tél: 450-263-0061; *Téléc:* 450-263-9468
c.boulet@endirect.qc.ca

***Cowansville*: Dontigny & Morin - *2**
Also Known As: Morin & Beauchesne
Former Name: Savoie, Morin & Dontigny
436, rue du Sud, Cowansville, QC J2K 2X7
Tél: 450-263-5458; *Téléc:* 450-263-7376

** indicates number of lawyers*

***Deschambault*: Bernatchez Associés - Avocats - *1**
Former Name: Yves Bernatchez
209, ch du Roy, Deschambault, QC G0A 1S0
Tél: 418-286-2287; *Téléc:* 418-286-6453
www.avoc.ca

***Dolbeau-Mistassini*: Bouchard Voyer Boily - *3**
Former Name: Bouchard & Voyer
1273, boul Wallberg, Dolbeau-Mistassini, QC G8L 1H3
Tél: 418-276-2234; *Téléc:* 418-276-3582
bvb@bellnet.ca

***Dolbeau-Mistassini*: Simard, Boivin, Lemieux - *4**
Former Name: Boivin, Lussier, Hébert
112, av de l'Église, Dolbeau-Mistassini, QC G8L 4W4
Tél: 418-276-2570; *Téléc:* 418-276-8797
Ligne sans frais: 877-276-2570
blh@blh.ca
www.sblavocats.com

***Donnacona*: Claude Dussault - *1**
299, rue Notre-Dame, Donnacona, QC G3M 1H1

***Dorval*: Amaron, Viberg & Pecho - *3**
#200, 280, av Dorval, Dorval, QC H9S 3H4
Tél: 514-636-4992; *Téléc:* 514-636-8122

***Dorval*: Francine Gagnon - *1**
545A, prom Lakeshore, Dorval, QC H9S 2B1
Tél: 514-631-6429; *Téléc:* 514-631-5606

***Drummondville*: Paul Biron, Avocat - *1**
Former Name: Biron, Nilsson
#202, 150, rue Marchand, Drummondville, QC J2C 4N1
Tél: 819-477-8741; *Téléc:* 819-477-7166

***Drummondville*: Roger Blais Avocat Inc - *2**
215, rue Lindsay, Drummondville, QC J2C 1N8
Tél: 819-477-2235; *Téléc:* 819-477-8674
blaisavocats@bellnet.ca

***Drummondville*: Boudreau, Méthot, Tourigny - *2**
Former Name: Boudreau, Méthot
83, rue St-Damase, Drummondville, QC J2B 6E5
Tél: 819-477-3517; *Téléc:* 819-477-0700

***Drummondville*: FBL - *1**
1325, boul Lemire, Drummondville, QC J2C 7X9
Tél: 819-477-1234; *Téléc:* 819-474-4757
benoit.laflamme@fbl.com

***Drummondville*: Hinse, Tousignant et Associés - *3**
360, rue Marchand, Drummondville, QC J2C 4N9
Tél: 819-477-3424; *Téléc:* 819-477-7728
Ligne sans frais: 888-488-3424
hinsetousignant@bellnet.ca
www.hinsetousignantavocats.com

***Drummondville*: Jutras et Associés - *5**
449, rue Hériot, Drummondville, QC J2B 1B4
Tél: 819-477-6321; *Téléc:* 819-474-5691
info@jutras.qc.ca
www.jutras.qc.ca

***Gatineau*: Jean-Paul Aubry - *1**
175, rue Champlain, Gatineau, QC J8X 3R3
Tél: 819-771-8645; *Téléc:* 819-771-9338

***Gatineau*: Christine M. Auger - *1**
177, rue Gamelin, Gatineau, QC J8Y 1W1
Tél: 819-770-4022; *Téléc:* 819-770-9729

***Gatineau*: Beaudry, Bertrand Avocats - *10**
Maison du Citoyen, 25, rue Laurier, 4e étage, Gatineau, QC J8X 4C8
Tel: 819-770-4880; *Fax:* 819-595-4979
avocats@beaudry-bertrand.com

***Gatineau*: Robert Bélanger, Avocat - *1**
307, boul Saint-Joseph, Gatineau, QC J8Y 3Y6
Tél: 819-771-6679; *Téléc:* 819-771-9675
robert.belanger.avocat@sympatico.ca

***Gatineau*: Françoise Boivin - *1**
Former Name: Bélec, Leteillier
#104, 160, boul de l'Hôpital, Gatineau, QC J8T 8J1
Tél: 819-243-7293; *Téléc:* 819-243-5913
francoiseboivin@videotron.ca

***Gatineau*: Boucher & Associés - *2**
768, boul Saint-Joseph, Gatineau, QC J8Y 4B8
Tél: 819-568-0041; *Téléc:* 819-568-4569

***Gatineau*: Dufour, Isabelle, Leduc, Bouthillette, Lapointe, Beaulieu - *9**
#301, 200, rue Montcalm, Gatineau, QC J8Y 3B5
Tel: 819-778-1870; *Fax:* 819-778-8860
dilblb@dilblb.com

***Gatineau*: Pierre Fontaine - *1**
25, rue Bernier, Gatineau, QC J8Z 1E7
Tél: 819-771-6578

***Gatineau*: Gaudreau - *2**
167, rue Notre-Dame-de-l'Ile, Gatineau, QC J8X 3T3
Tél: 819-770-7928; *Téléc:* 819-770-1424
bergeron.gaudreau@qc.aira.com

***Gatineau*: André Gingras, Avocat - *1**
30, rue Maricourt, Gatineau, QC J29 1R9
Tel: 819-595-4748; *Fax:* 819-772-4193
mariannamerica@videotron.ca

***Gatineau*: Alain Gourd Communications Inc. - *1**
22, ch Cochrane, Gatineau, QC J9H 2G2
Tél: 819-664-4487; *Téléc:* 819-684-0322
alain@gourdcommunications.com
www.gourdcommunications.com

***Gatineau*: Kehoe, Blais, Major - Avocats - *3**
#200, 344, boul Maloney est, Gatineau, QC J8P 7A6
Tél: 819-663-2439; *Téléc:* 819-663-4816
kbm@bellnet.ca

***Gatineau*: Lapointe, Cayen - *3**
#200, 370, boul Gréber, Gatineau, QC J8T 5R6
Tél: 819-568-0663; *Téléc:* 819-568-0226
lapointecayen@videotron.ca

***Gatineau*: Letellier & Associés - *7**
#127, 139, boul de l'Hôpital, Gatineau, QC J8T 8A3
Tél: 819-243-1336; *Téléc:* 819-243-9425
info@letellier.com
www.letellier.com

***Gatineau*: E. Wayne Lora - *2**
175, rue Champlain, Gatineau, QC J8X 3R3
Tél: 819-778-6511; *Téléc:* 819-770-5703
wlora@mac.com

***Gatineau*: Pharand Joyal - *5**
166, rue Wellington, Gatineau, QC J8X 2J4
Tél: 819-771-7781; *Téléc:* 819-771-0608
pharand.joyal@qc.aira.com

***Gatineau*: Ste-Marie & Lacombe - *2**
175, rue Champlain, Gatineau, QC J8X 3R3
Tél: 819-770-7800; *Téléc:* 819-770-5703

***Gatineau*: Sarrazin & Charlebois - *2**
162, rue Wellington, Gatineau, QC J8X 2J4
Tél: 819-770-4888; *Téléc:* 819-770-0712
sarrazin-charlebois@videotron.ca

***Gatineau*: Tobaccostat Canada - *1**
141 Frank-Robinson Ave., Gatineau, QC J9H 4A9
Tél: 819-684-0244; *Fax:* 819-684-9979
lmartial@magma.ca

***Gatineau*: Pierre Verreault - *1**
1-9, St-Dominique, Gatineau, QC J9A 1A1
Tél: 819-772-7757;
verreault@hotmail.com

***Gracefield*: Louise Major - *1**
40, rue Principale, Gracefield, QC J0X 1W0
Tél: 819-463-3477; *Téléc:* 819-463-4603
lmajor@notarius.net

***Granby*: Gaudet Galipeau Parcel - Avocats - *5**
Former Name: Gaudet & Associés
18, rue Court, Granby, QC J2G 4Y5
Tél: 450-777-1070; *Téléc:* 450-777-5960
gaudav@bellnet.ca

***Granby*: Daniel Laflamme - *1**
#200, 328, rue Principale, Granby, QC J2G 2W4
Tél: 450-372-3545

***Granby*: Gilles Viens - *1**
380, rue St-Jacques, Granby, QC J2G 3N6
Tél: 450-777-1312; *Téléc:* 450-777-8659
viensg@qc.aira.com

***Hampstead*: Judith Lifshitz - *1**
30, ch Belsize, Hampstead, QC H3X 3J8
Tél: 514-488-8561; *Téléc:* 514-488-0121

***Joliette*: Asselin & Asselin - Avocats - *4**
569, rue Archambault, Joliette, QC J6E 2W7
Tél: 450-755-5050; *Téléc:* 450-755-5111

***Joliette*: Boulard & Richer - Avocates - *2**
198, rue St-Joseph, Joliette, QC J6E 5C6
Tél: 450-753-8360; *Téléc:* 450-753-8359

***Joliette*: Ferland & Bélair - *3**
#150, 430, rue de Lanaudière, Joliette, QC J6E 7X1
Tél: 450-759-7412; *Téléc:* 450-759-5366
Ligne sans frais: 888-759-7412
avocats@ferlandbelair.ca

***Joliette*: Alain Généreux Avocat - *1**
400, rue Baby, Joliette, QC J6E 2W1
Tél: 450-752-6655; *Téléc:* 450-752-1098
alaingenereux@citenet.net

***Joliette*: Claudette Vincelette - *1**
Former Name: Vincelette, Marois
125, rue Beaudry nord, Joliette, QC J6E 6A4
Tél: 450-759-3958; *Téléc:* 450-756-2933
vincelet@primus.ca

***Jonquière*: Turcotte Fortin Cantin Marceau & Gagnon - *6**
Former Name: Turcotte, Fortin, Guay, Cantin & Marceau
CP 2040, Stn. Kenogami, 2106 Sainte-Famille, Jonquière, QC G7X 7X6
Tél: 418-547-2108; *Téléc:* 418-547-9519
tfcmg@bellnet.ca

***Kahnawake*: Mohawk Council of Kahnawake Legal Services - *4**
CP 720, Kahnawake, QC J0L 1B0
Tél: 450-632-7500; *Téléc:* 450-638-3663
legal@mck.ca
www.kahnawake.com

***L'Ile Perrot*: Aumais Chartrand - Avocats - *6**
#12, 100, boul Don Quichotte, L'Ile Perrot, QC J7V 6L7
Tél: 514-425-2233; *Téléc:* 514-453-0977
aumaischartrand@bellnet.ca
www.aumaischartrand.com

***La Malbaie*: Marie-Claude Dallaire - *1**
#220, CP 237, 251, rue John-Nairne, La Malbaie, QC G5A 1T7
Tél: 418-665-6417; *Téléc:* 418-665-6174
marieclaude.dallaire@ccjg.qc.ca

***Lac-Beauport*: Alain Baccigalupo - *1**
27, ch le Tour du Lac, Lac-Beauport, QC G0A 2C0
Tél: 418-849-0396; *Téléc:* 418-656-7861

***Lac-Mégantic*: Daniel Drouin - *1**
4927, rue Laval, Lac-Mégantic, QC G6B 1E2
Tél: 819-583-0787; *Téléc:* 819-583-4631
ddrouin@notarius.net

***Lac-Mégantic*: Monty, Coulombe**
5109 rue Frontenac, Lac-Mégantic, QC G6B 1H2
Tél: 819-583-3833; *Téléc:* 819-583-5673

***Lac-Simon*: Sylvie Savoie - *1**
Lac-Simon, QC J5A 2G9
Tél: 819-428-9366

***Lachine*: Communications Da Vinci - *1**
605, 36e av, Lachine, QC H8T 3L1
Tel: 514-713-3683;
www.davincicommunications.ca

***Lachine*: Laurier, Cêré & Couturier - *3**
356, 90e av, Lachine, QC H8R 2Z7
Tél: 514-363-0220; *Téléc:* 514-363-9495
laurierj@videotron.ca

***Lachine*: Louise Saint-Amour - *1**
#3, 1375, rue Notre-Dame, Lachine, QC H8S 2C9
Tél: 514-634-8243; *Téléc:* 514-634-3044
saintamourlouise@yahoo.ca

***Lachute*: William M.C. Steeves - *1**
18, boul de la Providence, Lachute, QC J8H 3K9
Tél: 450-562-2465; *Téléc:* 450-562-2467

***Lasalle*: Pascal Pillarella - *1**
#202, 7925, boul Newman, Lasalle, QC H8N 2N9
Tél: 514-364-3100; *Téléc:* 514-364-1604

** indicates number of lawyers*

***Laval*: Alepin Gauthier, Avocats - *13**
#601, 3080, boul Le Carrefour, Laval, QC H7T 2R5
Tél: 450-681-3080; *Téléc:* 450-681-1476
info@alepin.com
www.alepin.com

***Laval*: Allaire & Associés - *17**
#202, CP 422, Stn. St-Martin, 1333, boul Chomedey, Laval, QC H7V 3Z4
Tél: 450-978-5866; *Téléc:* 450-978-5871

***Laval*: Jean L. Beauchamp - *1**
405, rue Santerre, Laval, QC H7H 2X6
Tél: 450-628-6330; *Téléc:* 450-628-6389
jlbeauchamp@videotron.ca

***Laval*: Bélanger, Garceau - *2**
#309, 400, boul St-Martin ouest, Laval, QC H7M 3Y8
Tél: 450-669-1313; *Téléc:* 450-669-1122
belangergarceau@videotron.ca

***Laval*: Bertrand, Guerard & Bleau - *3**
134, boul. des Laurentides, Laval, QC H7G 2T3
Tél: 450-663-0851

***Laval*: François Bordeleau - *1**
60, rue Alexandre, Laval, QC H7G 3K9
Ligne sans frais: 877-975-2060

***Laval*: France Cormier - *1**
3682, rue Isabelle, Laval, QC H7P 4Z6
Tel: 450-622-7616; *Fax:* 450-622-5254
francecormier@videotron.ca

***Laval*: Dagenais, Poupart - *5**
#650, 2550, boul Daniel-Johnson, Laval, QC H7T 2L1
Tél: 450-978-2442; *Téléc:* 450-973-4010

***Laval*: Robert Dupuis - *1**
509, rue Lartigue, Laval, QC H7N 3T6
Tél: 450-663-5280; *Téléc:* 450-663-5281
Ligne sans frais: 866-663-5280
merobertdupuis_avocat@msn.com

***Laval*: Fournier, Diamond - *2**
#1102, 2500, boul Daniel-Johnson, Laval, QC H7T 2P6
Tél: 450-682-7011; *Téléc:* 450-686-8566

***Laval*: Michel B. Fournier - *1**
#204, 4150, boul St-Martin ouest, Laval, QC H7T 1C1
Tél: 450-686-2600; *Téléc:* 450-681-3642
mb.fournier@sympatico.ca

***Laval*: GTDS Inc. - *1**
Also Known As: Global Technologies for Defense & Security
#320, Place Lunebourg, 1200 Chomedey Blvd., Laval, QC H7V 3Z3
Tél: 514-993-8220; *Téléc:* 514-450-6883
marc.delahaut@gtdsinc.com

***Laval*: Lamarche, Pierre - *1**
237A, boul des Prairies, Laval, QC H7N 2T8
Tél: 450-667-9802; *Téléc:* 450-667-5740
plamarche@g1bonavocat.com
www.g1bonavocat.com

***Laval*: Jean Mignault - *1**
#2020, 400 Armand-Frapier, Laval, QC H7V 4B4
Tél: 514-332-4110; *Téléc:* 514-334-6043
jean.mignault@2020.net

***Laval*: Pierre Morin Conseil - *1**
#213, 3221, autorte 440 ouest, Laval, QC H7P 5P2
Tél: 450-680-1126; *Téléc:* 450-680-1889

***Laval*: NexPlan Expert inc. - *1**
Former Name: 9122-9203 Québec Inc.
200, pl. J.-J.-Joubert, Laval, QC H7G 4H6
Tél: 514-862-0682; *Téléc:* 450-669-0089

***Laval*: Turcotte, Nolet - *5**
#470, 500, boul St. Martin ouest, Laval, QC H7M 3Y2
Tél: 450-901-0151; *Téléc:* 450-901-0152
turcotte.nolet@qc.aira.com

***Longueuil*: Raymond Allard - *1**
1150, boul Marie-Victorin, Longueuil, QC J4G 2M4
Tél: 450-442-8600; *Téléc:* 450-463-1043
rallard@strsm.qc.ca

***Longueuil*: Archambault, Desjardins & Godin - *11**
1251, rue Beauregard, Longueuil, QC J4K 2M3
Tél: 450-674-4906; *Téléc:* 450-651-8644

***Longueuil*: Bernard, Brassard - Avocats - *13**
#200, 101, boul Roland-Therrien, Longueuil, QC J4H 4B9
Tél: 450-670-7900; *Téléc:* 450-670-0673
Ligne sans frais: 888-670-7900
commitment@bernard-brassard.com
www.bernard-brassard.com

***Longueuil*: Jacques Boissonnault - *1**
630, ch de Chambly, Longueuil, QC J4H 3L8
Tél: 514-831-3052; *Téléc:* 514-450-6512
Ligne sans frais: 866-462-3192
avocat.jb@videotron.ca

***Longueuil*: Dubois et Associés - *3**
#97, 45, Place Charles-Lemoyne, Longueuil, QC J4K 5G5
Tél: 450-646-2613; *Téléc:* 450-646-4225
duboisetassocies@videotron.ca

***Longueuil*: Monique Fortier - *2**
#95, 45, Place Charles Lemoyne, Longueuil, QC J4K 5G5
Tél: 450-651-4418

***Lorraine*: André J. Courtemanche - *1**
107, boul Val D'Ajol, Lorraine, QC J6Z 4G4
Tél: 450-582-4242; *Téléc:* 450-965-6958
acourtemanche@muridal.ca

***Lévis*: Lagueux Roy Gosselin - *4**
CP 1247, Stn. Lévis, 67, Côte-du-Passage, Lévis, QC G6V 6R8
Tél: 418-833-0311; *Téléc:* 418-833-1749
glrnotaires@notarius.net

***Lévis*: Pelletier D'Amours - *7**
Former Name: Pelletier, Kronstro@#m, Giguère
CP 3500, 6300, boul de la Rive sud, Lévis, QC G6V 6P9
Tél: 418-835-4944; *Téléc:* 418-835-8847
Ligne sans frais: 800-314-4944

***Magog*: Yves Messier - *1**
#100, 155 Principale ouest, Magog, QC J1X 2A7
Tel: 819-868-0714; *Fax:* 819-868-0746
yavocat@videotron.ca
www.quebeclegal.com

***Matane*: Deschenes & Doiron, Avocats, s.e.n.c. - *2**
352, av St-Jérôme, Matane, QC G4W 3B1
Tél: 418-562-2097; *Téléc:* 418-562-2926
dedoiron@globetrotter.qc.ca

***Mont-Joli*: Yvan Pelletier - *1**
CP 333, Stn. BureauChef, 1555, boul Jacques-Cartier, Mont-Joli, QC G5H 3L2
Tél: 418-775-4306;

***Mont-Laurier*: Roger Rancourt, Avocat - *1**
673, Carré Laurier, Mont-Laurier, QC J9L 2W4
Tél: 819-623-4485

***Mont-Laurier*: Simard, Deschênes et Barrette - *4**
445, rue du Pont, Mont-Laurier, QC J9L 2R8
Tél: 819-623-4259; *Téléc:* 819-623-9628

***Mont-Royal*: Consultations Delaney Inc. - *1**
101, av Dresden, Mont-Royal, QC H3P 3K1
Tél: 514-733-7754; *Téléc:* 514-733-0586
delaneyf@sympatico.ca

***Montmagny*: Robert Daveluy, Q.C. - *1**
#22, 46, rue St-Jean-Baptiste est, Montmagny, QC G5V 1J8
Tél: 418-248-1072

***Montmagny*: Marcel Guimont - *2**
CP 482, 25, rue du Palais-de-Justice, Montmagny, QC G5V 3S9
Tél: 418-248-1530; *Téléc:* 418-248-4157

***Montréal*: Adessky Lesage - *2**
#525, 4150, rue Ste-Catherine ouest, Montréal, QC H3Z 2Y5
Tél: 514-288-8070; *Téléc:* 514-288-8655
general@adesskylesage.com

***Montréal*: L'Agence Goodwin - *3**
#200, 839, rue Sherbrooke est, Montréal, QC H2L 1K6
Tél: 514-598-5252; *Téléc:* 514-598-1878
artistes@goodwin.agent.ca
www.agencegoodwin.com

***Montréal*: Joseph W. Allen - *1**
#203, 6855, av de l'Epée, Montréal, QC H3N 2C7
Tél: 514-274-9393; *Téléc:* 514-274-5614
jwallenimmlaw@bellnet.ca

***Montréal*: Amar & Associés - *3**
#1700, 770 Sherbrooke St., Montréal, QC H3B 1G1
Tél: 514-878-1532; *Téléc:* 514-878-4761
michael@amar.ca

***Montréal*: Claude F. Archambault - Avocat - *3**
50, rue Le Royer ouest, Montréal, QC H2Y 1W7
Tél: 514-845-4234; *Téléc:* 514-845-4236
www.claudefarchambault.pj.ca

***Montréal*: Arsenault, Lemieux - *2**
2328, rue Ontario est, Montréal, QC H2K 1W1
Tél: 514-527-8903; *Téléc:* 514-527-1410
arsenault.lemieux@qc.aira.com

***Montréal*: Andrew Barbacki - *1**
#2920, 500, place d'Armes, Montréal, QC H2Y 2W2
Tél: 514-397-1752; *Téléc:* 514-847-1212

***Montréal*: Baron Abrams - *9**
#200, 4141, rue Sherbrooke ouest, Montréal, QC H3Z 1B8
Tél: 514-935-7783; *Téléc:* 514-989-1811
info@baronabrams.com

***Montréal*: Barsalou Lawson - *10**
#1500, 2000, av McGill College, Montréal, QC H3A 3H3
Tel: 514-982-3355; *Fax:* 514-982-2550
www.barsalou.ca

***Montréal*: Howard A. Barza - *1**
#450, 2015, rue Peel, Montréal, QC H3A 1T8
Tél: 514-288-9322; *Téléc:* 514-288-2562

***Montréal*: Bastien & Champagne - *2**
#100, 6621, rue Sherbrooke est, Montréal, QC H1N 1C7
Tél: 514-253-0876; *Téléc:* 514-253-2578

***Montréal*: Jacques Bazinet - *1**
4276, rue Fabre, Montréal, QC H2J 3T6
Tél: 514-527-1702; *Téléc:* 514-597-1352

***Montréal*: BCF LLP - *61**
Also Known As: Brouillette Charpentier Fortin
1100, boul René-Lévesque ouest, 25e étage, Montréal, QC H3B 5C9
Tél: 514-397-8500; *Téléc:* 514-397-8515
info@bcf.ca
www.bcf.ca

***Montréal*: Beaudry Dessurealt - *3**
#304, 480, boul St-Laurent, Montréal, QC H2Y 3Y7
Tél: 514-282-0727; *Téléc:* 514-282-9363

***Montréal*: Diane Bélanger, Avocate - *2**
178, Jean-Talon est, Montréal, QC H2R 1S7
Tél: 514-597-9807; *Téléc:* 514-490-1807

***Montréal*: Bélanger, Sauvé - *73**
#1700, 1, Place Ville Marie, Montréal, QC H3B 2C1
Tel: 514-878-3081; *Fax:* 514-878-3053
info@belangersauve.com
www.belangersauve.com

***Montréal*: Peter J. Bellan - *1**
#1A, 5130, rue Charleroi, Montréal, QC H1G 2Z8
Tél: 514-955-0691; *Téléc:* 514-322-5069

***Montréal*: Edouard J. Belliardo - *1**
#701, 4, rue Notre-Dame est, Montréal, QC H2Y 188
Tél: 514-845-6253; *Téléc:* 514-845-8056

***Montréal*: Nicole Benchimol - *1**
#1200, 2015, rue Peel, Montréal, QC H3A 1T8
Tél: 514-844-1515; *Téléc:* 514-845-4472

***Montréal*: Bérard Avocats - *2**
417, rue des Seigneurs, 2e étage, Montréal, QC H3J 1X7
Tél: 514-934-1760; *Téléc:* 514-934-1212

***Montréal*: Berger & Winston - *2**
#1150, 615, boul René-Lévesque ouest, Montréal, QC H3B 1P5
Tél: 514-288-4177; *Téléc:* 514-876-1090
martin@bergerandwinston.com

***Montréal*: Jean Bernier - *1**
560, boul St Joseph est, Montréal, QC H2J 1J9
Tél: 514-849-2301; *Téléc:* 514-849-2309

***Montréal*: Elaine Bissonnette - *1**
3892, rue Monselet, Montréal, QC H1H 2C1
Tel: 514-323-8770; *Fax:* 514-323-8700
ebissonnette@sympatico.ca
www.avocatebissonnette.com

** indicates number of lawyers*

***Montréal*: Marc Bissonnette - *1**
#301, 4, rue Notre-Dame est, Montréal, QC H2Y 1B7
Tél: 514-871-8250; *Téléc:* 514-871-2892
marc.bissonnette@sympatico.ca

***Montréal*: Harry Blank - *1**
#1416, 1255, rue University, Montréal, QC H3B 3X1
Tél: 514-866-1125; *Téléc:* 514-866-6898
hablank@videotron.ca

***Montréal*: Harry J.F. Bloomfield - *1**
#1720, 1080, Côte du Beaver Hall Hill, Montréal, QC H2Z 1S8
Tél: 514-871-9571; *Téléc:* 514-397-0816
hbloomfield@fieldbloom.com
www.bloomfieldandassociates.ca

***Montréal*: Sonia, Bogdaniec - *1**
#47, 450, rue St-Gabriel, Montréal, QC H2Y 2Z9
Tél: 514-942-0471

***Montréal*: Rika Bohbot - *1**
#1511, 555, rue Chabanel ouest, Montréal, QC H2N 2J2
Tél: 514-385-3000; *Téléc:* 514-385-6625

***Montréal*: Boucher Harper - *7**
#610, 630, rue Sherbrooke ouest, Montréal, QC H3A 1E4
Tél: 514-878-1900; *Téléc:* 514-878-3679

***Montréal*: Pierre-Paul Boucher - *1**
7568, rue St-Denis, Montréal, QC H2R 2E6
Tél: 514-495-8900; *Téléc:* 514-495-8367

***Montréal*: François Bourdon - *1**
2308, rue Sherbrooke est, Montréal, QC H2K 1E5
Tél: 514-526-0821; *Téléc:* 514-521-5397

***Montréal*: Jacques Bourgault - *1**
7575, rue des Ecores, Montréal, QC H2E 2W5
Tél: 514-987-4534; *Téléc:* 514-522-8222

***Montréal*: Boyer, Gariépy - *4**
#200, 417, rue St-Nicolas, Montréal, QC H2Y 2P4
Tél: 514-287-9585; *Téléc:* 514-844-5243
boga@bellnet.ca

***Montréal*: Diane Brais - *1**
Former Name: Brais, Shindler
#700, 240, rue St-Jacques ouest, Montréal, QC H2Y 1L9
Tél: 514-985-5454; *Téléc:* 514-985-5433
braislaw@qc.aibn.com

***Montréal*: Braman Barbacki Moreau - *8**
#1300, 2001, av McGille College, Montréal, QC H3A 1G1
Tél: 514-286-1144; *Téléc:* 514-288-4773
bbminfo@bbmlex.com

***Montréal*: Sarto Brisebois - *2**
#710, 10, rue St-Jacques, Montréal, QC H2Y 1L3
Tél: 514-849-9444; *Téléc:* 514-849-0119

***Montréal*: Brisset Bishop -Avocats - *6**
#2020, 2020, rue University, Montréal, QC H3A 2A5
Tel: 514-393-3700; *Fax:* 514-393-1211
general@brissetbishop.com
www.brissetbishop.com

***Montréal*: Yvan Brodeur - *1**
#401, 31, rue St-Jacques, Montréal, QC H2Y 1K9
Tél: 514-849-5659; *Téléc:* 514-849-3633

***Montréal*: P.R. Brosseau**
#D90, 1321, rue Sherbrooke ouest, Montréal, QC H3G 1J4
Tél: 514-842-6066

***Montréal*: Jacques Brunet - *1**
#103, 3714, rue Ontario est, Montréal, QC H1W 1R9
Tél: 514-524-6638

***Montréal*: Rebecca Butovsky - *1**
3562, av de Vendome, Montréal, QC H4A 3M7
Tél: 514-484-2942

***Montréal*: Daniel Caisse - *3**
33, St-Jacques, 4e étage, Montréal, QC H2Y 1L3
Tél: 514-288-2250;
caisseetrichard@qc.aira.com

***Montréal*: Diane G. Cameron - *1**
#206, 4700, av Bonavista, Montréal, QC H3W 2C5
Tél: 514-483-2619; *Téléc:* 514-483-3616

***Montréal*: Campbell, Cohen, Leveille - *4**
#1802, 2, Place Alexis Nihon, 3500, boul de Maisonneuve ouest, Montréal, QC H3Z 3C1
Tél: 514-937-9445; *Téléc:* 514-937-2618

***Montréal*: Capital Hill Group/Groupe Capital Hill - *1**
#C-23, 1100, de la Gauchetière ouest, Montréal, QC H3B 2S2
Tel: 514-844-5530; *Fax:* 514-844-5165
info@capitalhill.ca

***Montréal*: Andre Carbonneau - *1**
2567, rue Ontario est, Montréal, QC H2K 1W6
Tél: 514-528-2626; *Téléc:* 514-528-2615
acarbonn@sprynet.com

***Montréal*: Pauline Cazelais, Q.C. - *1**
2339, Terrasse Guindon, Montréal, QC H1H 1L7
Tél: 514-522-5427

***Montréal*: Cerundolo & Maiorino - *2**
1807, rue Jean-Talon est, Montréal, QC H1E 1T4
Tél: 514-376-0335; *Téléc:* 514-376-6334

***Montréal*: Morris Chaikelson - *1**
4950, av Ponsard, Montréal, QC H3W 2A5
Tél: 514-482-1896; *Téléc:* 514-482-0359
chaimor@videotron.ca

***Montréal*: Chalifoux, Montpetit, Vaillancourt & Associés - *12**
Former Name: Chalifoux, Carette & Montpetit
#200, 28, rue Notre-Dame est, Montréal, QC H2Y 1B9
Tél: 514-842-1006; *Téléc:* 514-842-1811

***Montréal*: François Chapados - *1**
#2400, 1010, rue Sherbrooke ouest, Montréal, QC H3A 2T2
Tél: 514-844-2234; *Téléc:* 514-844-2087

***Montréal*: Charbonneau & Archambault - *2**
#2420, 500, place d'Armes, Montréal, QC H2Y 2W2
Tél: 514-842-0754

***Montréal*: Charness, Charness & Charness - *3**
#1100, 440, boul René-Lévesque ouest, Montréal, QC H2Z 1V7
Tel: 514-878-1808; *Fax:* 514-871-1149
char3law@bellnet.ca

***Montréal*: Maurice Chevalier - *1**
#1407, 3555, rue Berri, Montréal, QC H2L 4G4
Tél: 514-845-5551

***Montréal*: Choquette Beaupré Rheaume - *4**
#200, 5316, av du Parc, Montréal, QC H2V 4G7
Tél: 514-270-3192; *Téléc:* 514-270-8876

***Montréal*: Colby, Monet, Demers, Delage & Crevier - *16**
#2900, Tour McGill College, 1501, av McGill College, Montréal, QC H3A 3M8
Tel: 514-284-3663; *Fax:* 514-284-1961
cmddc@colby-monet.com
www.colby-monet.com

***Montréal*: Collu Communications Inc. - *1**
Former Name: Gabrielle Collu
3646, av Laval, Montréal, QC H2X 3C9
Tél: 514-844-7338; *Téléc:* 514-849-9689
collug@videotron.cawww.linkedin.com/pub/gabrielle-collu/5/a95/379

***Montréal*: Lulu Cornellier - *1**
#2821, 1, Place Ville Marie, Montréal, QC H3B 4R4
Tél: 514-842-1822; *Téléc:* 514-842-0052
lulucor@videotron.ca

***Montréal*: Benoit Côté - *1**
1252, rue Beaubien est, Montréal, QC H2S 1T9
Tél: 514-272-5755;
benoit.cote@bellnet.ca

***Montréal*: Couzin Taylor LLP - *3**
CP 4550, Stn. B, Montréal, QC H3B 5J3
Tél: 514-879-6600; *Téléc:* 514-879-2666
marcel.guilbault@ca.ey.com

***Montréal*: Cyr, Hamel, Bégin - *3**
Former Name: Jacques Cyr
#300, 13301, rue Sherbrooke est, Montréal, QC H1A 1C2
Tél: 514-642-2676; *Téléc:* 514-642-1663
jacquescyr@vocat.com
www.chbavocats.ca

***Montréal*: Daigneault, avocats inc. - *4**
Also Known As: Daigneault, Lawyers Inc.
Former Name: Robert Daigneault, Cabinet D'Avocats
#400, Place D'Youville, 353, rue Saint-Nicolas, Montréal, QC H2Y 2P1
Tél: 514-985-2929; *Téléc:* 514-985-0595
Ligne sans frais: 888-228-5834
enviro@daigneaultinc.com
www.daigneaultinc.com

***Montréal*: Jean-Louis Daunais - *1**
#100, 10550, rue Iberville, Montréal, QC H2B 2V1
Tél: 514-385-1601

***Montréal*: Davies Ward Phillips & Vineberg S.E.N.C.R.L., s.r.l. - *242**
Former Name: Phillips & Vineberg
1501, av McGill College, 26e étage, Montréal, QC H3A 3N9
Tél: 514-841-6400; *Téléc:* 514-841-6499
Ligne sans frais: 888-841-6400
jfournier@dwpv.com
www.dwpv.com

***Montréal*: De Grandpré Chait SENCRL-LLP - *62**
Former Name: De Grandpré Godin
#2900, 1000, rue de la Gauchetière ouest, Montréal, QC H3B 4W5
Tel: 514-878-4311; *Fax:* 514-878-4333
info@degrandpre.com
www.degrandpre.com

***Montréal*: Claude de la Madeleine - *1**
3600, boul Henri-Bourassa est, Montréal, QC H1H 1J4
Tél: 514-323-2112

***Montréal*: Charles Derome - *1**
5064, av du Parc, Montréal, QC H2V 4G1
Tél: 514-271-4700; *Téléc:* 514-271-4708
charles.derome@videotron.net

***Montréal*: Claude Des Marais - *1**
1206, boul St. Joseph, Montréal, QC H2J 1L6
Tél: 514-521-0047

***Montréal*: Suzanne Deschamps - *1**
1555, rue Peel, 14e étage, Montréal, QC H3A 3L8
Tél: 514-872-6215; *Téléc:* 514-872-6225
sdeschamps@ville.montreal.qc.ca

***Montréal*: Desjardins, Lapointe, Mousseau, Bélanger - *9**
#2185, 600, rue de la Gauchetière ouest, Montréal, QC H3B 4L8
Tél: 514-875-5404; *Téléc:* 514-875-5647
notaire@dlmb.ca
www.dlmb.ca

***Montréal*: Robert Desjardins - *1**
4515, rue Notre-Dame ouest, Montréal, QC H4C 1S3
Tél: 514-932-0819

***Montréal*: Desrosiers, Turcotte, Vanclair, Massicotte - *6**
Former Name: Desrosiers, Turcotte, Marachand, Massicotte
#503, 480, boul St. Laurent, Montréal, QC H2Y 3Y7
Tél: 514-387-9284; *Téléc:* 514-397-9922

***Montréal*: Donato Di Tullio - *1**
7647, boul Gouin est, Montréal, QC H1E 1A7
Tél: 514-648-1048; *Téléc:* 514-648-3288
ditullio@odyssee.net

***Montréal*: Doyon Izzi Nivoix - *6**
#501, 6455, rue Jean-Talon est, Montréal, QC H1S 3E8
Tél: 514-253-3338; *Téléc:* 514-251-0560
info@dinlex.com

***Montréal*: Druker Zilbert Schwartz - *5**
#605, 1255, carré Phillips, Montréal, QC H3B 3G5
Tél: 514-871-1300; *Téléc:* 514-871-1304

***Montréal*: Mario Du Mesnil - *2**
1595, rue St-Hubert, 4e étage, Montréal, QC H2L 3Z2
Tél: 514-526-6625; *Téléc:* 514-524-4341

***Montréal*: Duceppe, Théoret & Associés - *3**
1595, rue St-Hubert, 4e étage, Montréal, QC H2L 3Z2
Tél: 514-526-6621; *Téléc:* 514-524-4341

***Montréal*: Dugas & Legros - *2**
P.O. Box 1000, Stn. M, 4545, av Pierre-de-Coubertin, Montréal, QC H1V 3R2
Tel: 514-252-3137; *Fax:* 514-253-7156
juridique@loisirquebec.qc.ca

** indicates number of lawyers*

***Montréal*: Emile J. Fattal - *1**
#705, 1134, rue Ste-Catherine ouest, Montréal, QC H3B 1H4
Tél: 514-861-4545; *Téléc:* 514-874-1639
occidental@europe.com

***Montréal*: Jon M. Feldman - *1**
#1500, 1 Westmount Sq., Montréal, QC H3Z 2P9
Tel: 514-935-6222;
jfeldman@jlaw.ca

***Montréal*: Filteau & Belleau - *2**
Former Name: Filteau, Belleau, Normandeau & Daudelin
#301, 28, rue Notre-Dame est, Montréal, QC H2Y 1B9
Tél: 514-843-7877; *Téléc:* 514-499-1889

***Montréal*: Finkelberg, Light - *1**
#1200, 1, Westmount Sq., Montréal, QC H3Z 2P9
Tel: 514-932-7392; *Fax:* 514-932-0990
plight@sympatico.ca

***Montréal*: Fishman Flanz Meland Paquin SENCRL/LLP - *11**
Former Name: Goldstein, Flanz & Fishman SENCRL/LLP
#4100, 1250, boul René-Lévesque ouest, Montréal, QC H3B 4W8
Tel: 514-932-4100; *Fax:* 514-932-4170
info@ffmp.ca
www.ffmp.ca

***Montréal*: C.A. Fitzwilliam - *1**
#2821, 1, Place Ville Marie, Montréal, QC H3B 4R4
Tél: 514-940-5353;
cf@fitzwilliamlegal.com

***Montréal*: Frankel & Spina - *2**
#401, 60, rue St-Jacques, Montréal, QC H2Y 1L5
Tél: 514-849-3544; *Téléc:* 514-849-4457
plvspina@frankelspina.ca

***Montréal*: Franklin & Franklin - *2**
#545, 4141, rue Sherbrooke ouest, Montréal, QC H3Z 1B8
Tél: 514-935-3576; *Téléc:* 514-935-6862
info@franklinlegal.com

***Montréal*: Frumkin, Feldman & Glazman - *3**
#2270, Place du Canada, 1010, rue de la Gauchetière ouest, Montréal, QC H3B 2N2
Tél: 514-861-2812; *Téléc:* 514-861-6062

***Montréal*: Garceau Pasquin Pagé Viens - *15**
204, Place d'Youville, Montréal, QC H2Y 2B4
Tél: 514-845-5171; *Téléc:* 514-845-5578
lesavocats@procassur.com

***Montréal*: Gariepy, Marcoux, Richard, DuBois - *9**
#2420, 500, place d'Armes, Montréal, QC H2Y 2W2
Tél: 514-845-3533; *Téléc:* 514-845-9522
gmrd@gmrd.com

***Montréal*: Gasco Goodhue - *15**
Former Name: Gasco Goodhue Provost
#2100, 1080, côte du Beaver Hall, Montréal, QC H2Z 1S8
Tél: 514-397-0066; *Téléc:* 514-397-0393
lawyers@gasco.qc.ca
www.gasco.qc.ca

***Montréal*: Ulrich Gautier - *1**
#2350, 500, place D'Armes, Montréal, QC H2Y 2W2
Tél: 514-288-3344; *Téléc:* 514-288-3344
ugautier@videotron.ca

***Montréal*: Gendron, Carpentier, S.E.N.C - *2**
#300, 615, boul René-Lévesque ouest, Montréal, QC H3B 1P5
Tél: 514-395-4527; *Téléc:* 514-395-6031
cargen@bellnet.ca

***Montréal*: Gervais & Gervais - *1**
#2100, 500, place d'Armes, Montréal, QC H2Y 2W2
Tél: 514-288-4241; *Téléc:* 514-849-9984

***Montréal*: GGA Communications Inc. - *1**
Former Name: Gervais Gagnon Covington & Associes Inc.
#200, 606, rue Cathcart, Montréal, QC H3B 1K9
Tél: 514-393-9500; *Téléc:* 514-393-9324
www.ggacom.com

***Montréal*: Gingras Ouellet - *2**
4141, av Pierre-de-Coubertin, Montréal, QC H1V 3N7
Tél: 514-252-4638; *Téléc:* 514-252-6906

***Montréal*: Goldwater, Dubé, Family Law - *4**
#2310, 3500, de Maisonneuve ouest, Montréal, QC H3Z 3C1
Tél: 514-861-4367; *Téléc:* 514-861-7601
inquiries@goldwaterdube.com
www.goldwaterdube.com

***Montréal*: Gottlieb & Pearson - *9**
#1920, 2020, rue University, Montréal, QC H3A 2A5
Tél: 514-288-1744; *Téléc:* 514-288-6629
thibault@gottliebpearson.com

***Montréal*: Gouveia, Gouveia - *3**
#1704, 507, Place d'Armes, Montréal, QC H2Y 2W8
Tél: 514-844-0116; *Téléc:* 514-844-9053

***Montréal*: Elizabeth Greene - *1**
#650, 4141, rue Sherbrooke ouest, Montréal, QC H3Z 1B8
Tél: 514-934-4852; *Téléc:* 514-935-3559

***Montréal*: Gross, Pinsky - *11**
2, Place Alexis Nihon, 3500, boul de Maisonneuve ouest, Montréal, QC H3Z 3C1
Tel: 514-934-1333; *Fax:* 514-933-0810
gropin@grosspinsky.com

***Montréal*: Gurman, Crevier Inc. - *2**
#700, 125, rue Chabanel ouest, Montréal, QC H2N 1E4
Tél: 514-858-1118; *Téléc:* 514-858-1121
agurman@gurman-crevier.com

***Montréal*: Hadjis & Hadjis - *2**
#707, 1117, rue Ste-Catherine ouest, Montréal, QC H3B 1H9
Tél: 514-849-3526; *Téléc:* 514-849-1595

***Montréal*: Martine Hamel - *1**
#300, 13301, rue Sherbrooke est, Montréal, QC H1A 1C2
Tél: 514-642-4473; *Téléc:* 514-642-1663

***Montréal*: Hamilton, Cooper, Ashkenazy - *3**
#401, 4226, boul St-Jean, Montréal, QC H9G 1X5
Tél: 514-626-0266; *Téléc:* 514-626-0011
info@hcalaw.ca

***Montréal*: Handelman, Handelman & Schiller - *3**
#1610, 1255, rue Université, Montréal, QC H3B 3X3
Tél: 514-866-5071; *Téléc:* 514-866-4210
re@hhslaw.ca

***Montréal*: Hanna Glasz & Sher - *5**
#1750, 770, rue Sherbrooke ouest, Montréal, QC H3A 1G1
Tél: 514-284-9551; *Téléc:* 514-284-3419
briansher@qc.aibn.com

***Montréal*: Hébert, Downs, Lepage, Soulière & Carette - *6**
Former Name: Hébert & Bourque
#2830, 500, place d'Armes, Montréal, QC H2Y 2W2
Tél: 514-284-2351; *Téléc:* 514-284-2354
edowns@hdavocates.com
www.hdavocats.com

***Montréal*: Brent K. Hussey - *1**
#200, 280, av Droval, Montréal, QC H9S 3H4
Tél: 514-636-4992; *Téléc:* 514-636-8122
bkhussey@videotron.ca

***Montréal*: Hutchins Caron & Associates, Barristers & Solicitors - *5**
Also Known As: Hutchins Caron & Associates, Barristers & Solicitors
Former Name: Hutchins Grant & Associates; Hutchins, Soroka & Grant
#700, 485 rue McGill, Montréal, QC H2Y 2H4
Tel: 514-849-2403; *Fax:* 514-849-4907
Toll-Free: 877-849-2403
admin@hutchinslegal.ca
www.hutchinslegal.ca

***Montréal*: Michel A. Iacono, BA, BCL, LL.M. Avocat-Barrister & Solicitor - *1**
#2000, 300, rue Léo-Pariseau, Montréal, QC H2X 4B3
Tél: 514-288-1414

***Montréal*: J.R. Gagnon Affaires Publiques - *1**
Former Name: Gagnon, Jean-Rene
#106, 696, rue William, Montréal, QC H3C 1N9
Tél: 514-800-8008; *Téléc:* 514-800-1025
Ligne sans frais: 866-416-0960
itout.ca/fr/jrgagnon

***Montréal*: I.H. Kaufman - *1**
#711, 1117, rue Ste-Catherine ouest, Montréal, QC H3B 1H9
Tél: 514-282-7401; *Téléc:* 514-282-9209

***Montréal*: Kierans & Guay - *2**
#440, 606, rue Cathcart, Montréal, QC H3B 1K9
Tel: 514-866-3394; *Fax:* 514-866-3398

***Montréal*: Kliger & Kliger - *2**
#808, 1255, carré Phillips, Montréal, QC H3B 3G1
Tél: 514-281-1720; *Téléc:* 514-281-0678

***Montréal*: Kounadis Perreault - *3**
#2000, 300, av Leo-Pariseau, Montréal, QC H2X 4B3
Tél: 514-844-8631; *Téléc:* 514-844-6691

***Montréal*: Kugler Kandestin - *7**
#2101, 1, Place Ville-Marie, Montréal, QC H3B 2C6
Tél: 514-878-2861; *Téléc:* 514-875-8424
info@kugler-kandestin.com
www.kugler-kandestin.com

***Montréal*: Lucien Lachapelle - *1**
5971, rue St-Hubert, Montréal, QC H2S 2L8
Tél: 514-277-2164

***Montréal*: Gaetan Lagarde - *2**
#201, 1554, boul Mont-Royal est, Montréal, QC H2J 1Z2
Tél: 514-521-2442; *Téléc:* 514-525-5561
gaela@videotron.ca

***Montréal*: Lamarre Perron Lambert Vincent - *6**
#200, 480, boul St-Laurent, Montréal, QC H2Y 3Y7
Tél: 514-798-1515; *Téléc:* 514-798-5599

***Montréal*: Raymond Landry - *1**
#404, 505 boul René-Lévesque ouest, Montréal, QC H2Z 1Y7
Tel: 514-908-2171; *Fax:* 514-940-7044
rlandry@ca.inter.net

***Montréal*: Lapointe Rosenstein Marchand Melançon - *70**
Former Name: Lapointe Rosenstein; Marchand Melançon Forget
#1400, 1250, boul René-Lévesque ouest, Montréal, QC H3B 5E9
Tel: 514-925-6300; *Fax:* 514-925-9001
Toll-Free: 800-728-6228
www.lrmm.com

***Montréal*: LaTraverse Avocats - *4**
#1510, 1010, rue Sherbrooke ouest, Montréal, QC H3A 2R7
Tél: 514-938-1313; *Téléc:* 514-938-3691
latraverse@latraverse.ca
www.latraverse.ca

***Montréal*: Lazare & Altschuler - *2**
#2210, 1010, rue Sherbrooke ouest, Montréal, QC H3A 2R7
Tél: 514-878-3341; *Téléc:* 514-878-3314
lazare@lazalt.com

***Montréal*: Micheline Lebrun-Sylvestre - *1**
#305, 10500, boul de l'Acadie, Montréal, QC H4N 2V4

***Montréal*: John E. Lechter - *1**
#202, 2015, rue Drummond, Montréal, QC H3G 1W7
Tel: 514-845-4287; *Fax:* 514-845-1803

***Montréal*: Léger Robic Richard, S.E.N.C.R.L. - *23**
Also Known As: Robic
Centre CDP Capital, Bloc E, 8e étage, 1001, Square-Victoria, Montréal, QC H2Z 2B7
Tél: 514-987-6242; *Téléc:* 514-845-7874
info@robic.com
www.robic.ca

***Montréal*: Liebman & Associés**
#1500, 1, carré Westmount, Montréal, QC H3Z 2P9
Tél: 514-846-0666; *Téléc:* 514-935-2314
info@liebman.org
www.liebman.org

***Montréal*: Lord & Associes - *6**
#210, 1010, rue Ste-Catherine est, Montréal, QC H2L 2G3
Tél: 514-864-7313; *Téléc:* 514-864-7329

***Montréal*: Robert Loulou - *1**
#1, 7924, rue St-Denis, Montréal, QC H2R 2G1
Tél: 514-388-3511; *Téléc:* 514-388-3211

***Montréal*: Lozeau Gonthier Masse Richard - *8**
#1900, 1010, rue de la Gauchetière ouest, Montréal, QC H3B 2N2
Tél: 514-981-5600; *Téléc:* 514-981-5601
lgmr@ican.net

** indicates number of lawyers*

***Montréal*: Mannella & Associés - *3**
3055, boul de l'Assomption, Montréal, QC H1N 2H1
Tel: 514-899-5375; *Fax:* 514-899-0476
mannella@qc.aira.com

***Montréal*: Marchi, Bellemare - *5**
#200, 400, ave McGill, Montréal, QC H2Y 2G1
Tél: 514-288-5753; *Téléc:* 514-284-6606
marchibellemare.com

***Montréal*: Mario-Olivier Massie**
5400, boul Gouin ouest, Montréal, QC H4J 1C5
Tel: 514-338-2303; *Fax:* 514-338-3153

***Montréal*: Maynard & Zaor - *3**
#1101, 507, Place d'Armes, Montréal, QC H2Y 2W8
Tél: 514-288-1101; *Téléc:* 514-499-8548

***Montréal*: McConomy, Narvey, Green - *3**
Former Name: Narvey, Green & Lack
#1500, 1255, rue University, Montréal, QC H3B 3X2
Tél: 514-866-4466; *Téléc:* 514-866-4467

***Montréal*: McGilton Johnston Hodess - *3**
#1210, 2045, rue Stanley, Montréal, QC H3A 2V4
Tél: 514-842-1714; *Téléc:* 514-842-1718

***Montréal*: Melançon, Marceau, Grenier & Sciortino - *15**
#300, 1717, boul René-Lévesque est, Montréal, QC H2L 4T3
Tél: 514-525-3414; *Téléc:* 514-525-2803
www.mmgs.qc.ca

***Montréal*: Jean Mercier - *1**
#203, 4059, rue Hochelaga, Montréal, QC H1W 1K4
Tél: 514-252-0888

***Montréal*: Miller & Khazzam - *2**
#525, 4150, Ste-Catherine ouest, Montréal, QC H3Z 2Y5
Tél: 514-875-8040; *Téléc:* 514-875-8044

***Montréal*: Miller, Adel & Associés - *3**
#1210, 507, Place d'Armes, Montréal, QC H2Y 2W8
Tél: 514-845-4151; *Téléc:* 514-845-0306
aadel@adellaw.net

***Montréal*: Moisan Lasalle Perreault - *2**
#280, 450, rue Sherbrooke est, Montréal, QC H2L 1J8
Tél: 514-844-3077; *Téléc:* 514-844-1018
raymondelasalle@qc.aira.com

***Montréal*: Mondor, Rougeau, Lambert, Le Borgne - *6**
#200, 402, rue Notre-Dame est, Montréal, QC H2Y 1C8
Tél: 514-840-9119; *Téléc:* 514-840-0177

***Montréal*: Monette Barakett, Avocats S.E.N.C. - *25**
Former Name: Monette, Barakett, Lévesque, Bourque, Pedneault
#2100, 1010, rue de la Gauchetière ouest, Montréal, QC H3B 2R8
Tél: 514-878-9381; *Téléc:* 514-878-3957
monette@monette-barakett.com
www.monette-barakett.com

***Montréal*: Carmelo Morabito - *1**
#3001, 5095, rue Jean-Talon est, Montréal, QC H1S 3G4
Tél: 514-727-0332; *Téléc:* 514-727-9315
carmorab@total.net

***Montréal*: Myszka & Tepner - *2**
#204, 4781, av Van Horne, Montréal, QC H3W 1J1
Tél: 514-737-4069

***Montréal*: National Public Relations Inc.**
Also Known As: Cabinet de Relations Publiques National Inc.
#800, 2001, av McGill College, Montréal, QC H3A 1G1
Tel: 514-843-7171; *Fax:* 514-843-6976
info-mtl@national.ca
www.national.ca

***Montréal*: R.E. Notkin & Assoc. Inc. - *1**
4814 Cedar Cres., Montréal, QC H3W 2H9
Tel: 514-738-4271;
rnotkin@post.harvard.edu

***Montréal*: Nudleman Lamontagne - *2**
Former Name: Nudleman, Lamontagne & Grenier
#458, 1981, ave McGill College, Montréal, QC H3A 2W9
Tél: 514-866-6674; *Téléc:* 514-866-9822
info@nlglegal.ca

***Montréal*: O'Reilly & Associés - *4**
#1007, 1155, rue University, Montréal, QC H3B 3A7
Tél: 514-871-8117; *Téléc:* 514-871-9177

***Montréal*: Octane - *1**
417, rue Saint-Pierre, Montréal, QC H2Y 2M4
laucoin@octane-strategie.com

***Montréal*: Oligny & Jacques - *2**
#107, 1394, du Mont-Royal est, Montréal, QC H2J 1Y7
Tél: 514-871-2240; *Téléc:* 514-871-0874
oligny@generation.net

***Montréal*: Pateras & Iezzoni - *5**
#2314, 500, place d'Armes, Montréal, QC H2Y 2W2
Tél: 514-284-0860; *Téléc:* 514-843-7990
fgill@pateras-iezzoni.com

***Montréal*: Pearl & Associates - *3**
1170, Place du Frère André, 4e étage, Montréal, QC H3B 3C6
Tél: 514-861-1170; *Téléc:* 514-861-0850
Ligne sans frais: 866-710-1170
lawyers@pearlandassociates.com

***Montréal*: John J. Pepper, Q.C & Associates - *1**
#2500, 1155, boul René-Lévesque ouest, Montréal, QC H3B 2K4
Tél: 514-875-6565; *Téléc:* 514-843-8415

***Montréal*: Gregoire Perron & Assocjes - *1**
Former Name: Perron & Associés
84, rue Notre-Dame ouest, 5e étage, Montréal, QC H2Y 1S6
Tel: 514-285-6441; *Fax:* 514-285-8589
Toll-Free: 888-285-6441
gperron@videotron.ca

***Montréal*: Frederick R. Phillips - *1**
5511, place Bradford, Montréal, QC H3W 2M6
Tél: 514-733-8469

***Montréal*: Phillips, Friedman, Kotler - *18**
#900, Place du Canada, 1010, rue de la Gauchetière ouest, Montréal, QC H3B 2P8
Tél: 514-878-3371; *Téléc:* 514-878-3691
info@pfklaw.com
www.pfklaw.com/

***Montréal*: Marcel Plante - *1**
6984, rue St-Denis, Montréal, QC H2S 2S4
Tél: 514-272-8217

***Montréal*: Polak, Therrien, Turcotte - *1**
#1500, 1, carré Westmount, Montréal, QC H3Z 2P9
Tél: 514-935-6226; *Téléc:* 514-935-2314

***Montréal*: Polisuk Lord - *2**
#2650, 1155, boul René-Lévesque ouest, Montréal, QC H3B 4S5
Tél: 514-861-8546; *Téléc:* 514-861-1298
rwlord@polisuklord.com

***Montréal*: Pollack, Kravitz & Teitelbaum - *3**
Former Name: Pollack, Machlovitch, Kravitz & Teitelbaum
#1810, 1, carre Westmount, Montréal, QC H3Z 2P9
Tél: 514-905-1373; *Téléc:* 514-905-1377

***Montréal*: Pragmatis Inc. - *1**
730, boul Georges-Vanier, Montréal, QC H3J 2T3
Tel: 514-941-7125; *Fax:* 514-227-5430
mpoirier@pragmatis.biz

***Montréal*: Propre Compte - *1**
#1120, 555, boul René-Lévesque ouest, Montréal, QC H2Z 1B1
Tél: 514-874-1910; *Téléc:* 514-874-0953
jules.pleau@sympatico.ca

***Montréal*: Jacques Ranger - *1**
5694, av Laurendeau, Montréal, QC H4E 3W4
Tél: 514-766-0756

***Montréal*: Robinson Sheppard Shapiro LLP - *71**
#4600, 800, Place Victoria, Montréal, QC H4Z 1H6
Tel: 514-878-2631; *Fax:* 514-878-1865
info@rsslex.com
www.rsslex.com

***Montréal*: Rousseau, Gaudry - *3**
12675, rue Sherbrooke est, 2e étage, Montréal, QC H1A 3W7
Tél: 514-875-8243; *Téléc:* 514-875-9903
Ligne sans frais: 888-875-8243
rrousseau@rousseaugaudry.com
www.rousseaugaudry.com

***Montréal*: Leonard I. Sabloff & Associates - *1**
6600, route Trans-Canada, Montréal, QC H9R 4S2
Tel: 514-426-4626; *Fax:* 514-426-3977
sabloff@hotmail.com

***Montréal*: Johanne St. Pierre - *1**
#101, 1395, rue Fleury est, Montréal, QC H2C 1R7

***Montréal*: Jean Saulnier - *1**
7190, rue St-Denis, Montréal, QC H2R 2E2
Tél: 514-273-1525

***Montréal*: Bernard K. Schneider - *1**
#3, 6175, av d'Esplanade, Montréal, QC H2T 3A2
Tél: 514-277-6540; *Téléc:* 514-277-6554

***Montréal*: Anthony N. Schratz - *1**
#400, 630, rue Sherbrooke ouest, Montréal, QC H3A 1E4
Tél: 514-289-9362; *Téléc:* 514-289-9312
aschratz@bellnet.ca

***Montréal*: Seal Seidman G.P. - *4**
#1050, 2015, rue Drummond, Montréal, QC H3G 1W7
Tél: 514-842-8861; *Téléc:* 514-288-1708
lseidman@sealseidman.qc.ca

***Montréal*: Laizer Sirota - *1**
#305, 10, rue St-Jacques, Montréal, QC H2Y 1L3
Tél: 514-844-1123; *Téléc:* 514-844-4071

***Montréal*: Ian M. Solloway**
#1700, 700, rue Sherbrooke ouest, Montréal, QC H3A 1G1
Tel: 514-282-9144; *Fax:* 514-844-7290
sollow@videotron.ca

***Montréal*: Charles Louis Spector**
#1250, 505, boul René-Levesque ouest, Montréal, QC H2Z 1Y7
Tel: 514-878-2556; *Fax:* 514-954-5077

***Montréal*: Spiegel Sohmer Inc.**
#1203, 5, place Ville Marie, Montréal, QC H3B 2G2
Tél: 514-875-2100; *Téléc:* 514-875-8237
www.spiegelsohmer.com

***Montréal*: Arthur H. Steckler - *1**
#120, 5115, av de Gaspé, Montréal, QC H2T 3B7
Tél: 514-273-8891; *Téléc:* 514-273-1576

***Montréal*: Stein Monast, S.E.N.C.R.L.**
Former Name: Desjardins Ducharme S.E.N.C.R.L.
#2400, Tour de la Banque Nationale, 600, rue de la Gauchetière ouest, Montréal, QC H3B 4L8
Tél: 514-878-9411; *Téléc:* 514-878-4800
Ligne sans frais: 800-670-0102
www.desjardinsducharme.ca

***Montréal*: Stern & Blumer - *2**
#1825, CP 983, 300, av Leo-Pariseau, Montréal, QC H2W 2N1
Tél: 514-842-1133; *Téléc:* 514-842-3105

***Montréal*: Sternthal Katznelson Montigny - *9**
#1020, Place du Canada, 1010, rue de la Gauchetière ouest, Montréal, QC H3B 2N2
Tél: 514-878-1011; *Téléc:* 514-878-9195
info@skm.ca
www.skm.ca

***Montréal*: Sumbulian, Mark, Avocat / Advocate - *1**
Former Name: Sumbulian & Sumbulian; Sumbulian, Hayk
#1610, 1350, rue Sherbrooke ouest, Montréal, QC H3G 1J1
Tél: 514-281-1955; *Téléc:* 514-281-1956
sumbulian@bellnet.ca

***Montréal*: Talbot & Avocats - *2**
4519, rue St-Denis, Montréal, QC H2J 2L4
Tél: 514-849-2930; *Téléc:* 514-982-0716
liber-t@vigie.net

***Montréal*: Tassé & Vescio - *2**
Former Name: Tassé & Themens
2421, rue Allard, Montréal, QC H4E 2L3
Tél: 514-769-9654; *Téléc:* 514-769-7363

** indicates number of lawyers*

Montréal: **Tiger Goldman - *2**
#716, 1010, rue Sherbrooke ouest, Montréal, QC H3A 2R7
Tél: 514-284-8401; *Téléc:* 514-284-8408

Montréal: **Harvey Toulch - *1**
Former Name: Toulch & Associates
#406, 1117, rue Ste-Catherine ouest, Montréal, QC H3B 1H9
Tél: 514-849-1289; *Téléc:* 514-849-3101
hm@info-internet.net

Montréal: **Robert Toupin - *1**
1344, rue Jean-Talon est, Montréal, QC H2E 1S1
Tél: 514-278-5400; *Téléc:* 514-278-7584

Montréal: **Trudel Nadeau Avocats S.E.N.C.R.L. - *20**
#2500, Place du Parc, 300, av Léo-Pariseau, Montréal, QC H2X 4B7
Tél: 514-849-5754; *Téléc:* 514-499-0312
info@trudelnadeau.com
www.trudelnadeau.com

Montréal: **Tucci & Associés - *4**
Former Name: Sergio Tucci & Associates
201, rue St-Zotique est, Montréal, QC H2S 1L2
Tél: 514-271-0650; *Téléc:* 514-270-2164
tucci@tucci.ca
www.tucci.ca

Montréal: **Peter H. Turner - *1**
256, rue Devon, Montréal, QC H3R 1B9
Tél: 514-731-3544; *Téléc:* 514-737-3770

Montréal: **Unterberg, Carisse, Labelle, Dessureault, Lebeau & Petit - *4**
Former Name: Unterberg, Labelle, Lebeau
#700, 1980, rue Sherbrooke ouest, Montréal, QC H3H 1E8
Tél: 514-934-0841; *Téléc:* 514-937-6547
contact@utlnet.com

Montréal: **Woods & Partners - *16**
#1700, 2000, rue McGill College, Montréal, QC H3A 3H3
Tel: 514-982-4545; *Fax:* 514-284-2046
general@woods.qc.ca
www.litigationboutique.com

Montréal: **Zimmerman, Blitt - *2**
#410, 345, av Victoria, Montréal, QC H3Z 2N2
Tél: 514-483-2444; *Téléc:* 514-483-2477

New Carlisle: **Grenier, Grenier, Grenier - *3**
CP 519, New Carlisle, QC G0C 1Z0
Tél: 418-752-3308; *Téléc:* 418-752-6935
grenier1@globetrotter.qc.ca

New Carlisle: **St-Onge & Assels - *2**
CP 727, 100A, boul Gérard-D.-Levesque, New Carlisle, QC G0C 1Z0
Tél: 418-752-3351; *Téléc:* 418-752-2740
stonge_assels@globetrotter.net

Paspébiac: **Gilles Moulin - *1**
CP 880, Paspébiac, QC G0C 2K0
Tél: 418-752-2244

Pierrefonds: **Mark Anthony Ciarallo - *1**
4838, rue Oka, Pierrefonds, QC H9K 1H6
Tél: 514-696-7931; *Téléc:* 514-696-0548

Pointe-Claire: **Stanley Gelfand - *1**
#306, 189, boul Hymus, Pointe-Claire, QC H9R 1E9
Tél: 514-695-4542; *Téléc:* 514-695-7975

Québec: **Beaumont, Provencal, Breton - *5**
1756, rue Notre-Dame, Québec, QC G2E 3C5
Tél: 418-871-2955; *Téléc:* 418-871-7352

Québec: **Beauvais, Truchon Avocats - *28**
#200, CP 1000, 79, boul René-Lévesque est, Québec, QC G1R 4T4
Tél: 418-692-4180; *Téléc:* 418-692-5321
www.beauvaistruchon.com

Québec: **Bedard, Herman - *2**
#206, 51, rue des Jardins, Québec, QC G1R 4L6
Tél: 418-692-2425; *Téléc:* 418-692-2528

Québec: **Bélanger, Murray, Richard & Associés - *7**
Former Name: Bélanger & Associés
#520, 400, boul Jean-Lesage, Québec, QC G1K 8W1
Tél: 418-522-7000; *Téléc:* 418-522-8212
bmravocats@webnet.qc.ca

Québec: **André Bernatchez - *1**
#220, 157, rue des Chênes ouest, Québec, QC G1L 1K6
Tél: 418-628-4575

Québec: **Maurice Bernatchez - *1**
#2, 1460, av de la Verendrye, Québec, QC G1J 4V8
Tél: 418-667-7830

Québec: **Yvan Bilodeau - *1**
#180, 801, ch St-Louis, Québec, QC G1S 1C1
Tél: 418-686-4875; *Téléc:* 418-686-6160

Québec: **Boily Morency - *4**
#230, 70, rue Dalhousie, Québec, QC G1K 4B2
Tel: 418-694-0704; *Fax:* 418-694-2140
bomo@videotron.ca

Québec: **Bouchard Pagé Tremblay, S.E.N.C. - Avocats - *8**
6580, 1e av, Québec, QC G1H 2W4
Tél: 418-622-6699; *Téléc:* 418-628-1912
bouchardpagetremblay@oricom.ca
www.bouchardpagetremblay.com

Québec: **Robert Bouchard - *1**
#103, 30, av St-Denis, Québec, QC G1R 4B6
Tél: 418-694-4096; *Téléc:* 418-841-3690
rbouchard@groupeconscientia.com

Québec: **Roland Cote - *1**
1445, rue Maine, Québec, QC G1G 2J6

Québec: **David Interventions Stratégiques Inc. - *1**
Former Name: David Stratégies Marketing
#875, 4, ch Sainte-Foy, Québec, QC G1S 2K7
Tél: 418-682-3391; *Téléc:* 418-380-5535

Québec: **Dussault Lemieux Larochelle sencrl - *14**
Former Name: Brochet Dussault Lemieux Larochelle
#450, 2795, boul Laurier, Québec, QC G1V 4M7
Tél: 418-657-2424; *Téléc:* 418-657-1793
avocats@dllavocats.com

Québec: **Gagnon, Girard, Julian et Matte - *7**
#301, 1535, ch Ste-Foy, Québec, QC G1S 2P1
Tél: 418-681-0037; *Téléc:* 418-681-0539
ggjm@qc.aira.com

Québec: **La Société d'Avocats Garneau, Verdon, Michaud, Samson - *10**
67, rue Ste-Ursule, Québec, QC G1R 4E7
Tél: 418-692-3010; *Téléc:* 418-692-1742
gvm@qc.aira.com

Québec: **Giasson et Associés - *29**
#551, 2, rue des Jardins, Québec, QC G1R 4S9
Tél: 418-641-6156; *Téléc:* 418-641-6353
serge.giasson@ville.quebec.qc.ca

Québec: **Gosselin, Bussières, Bedard, Ouellet - *4**
#315, 400, boul Jean-Lesage, Québec, QC G1K 8W1
Tél: 418-529-9968; *Téléc:* 418-524-5243

Québec: **Grondin, Poudrier, Bernier - *36**
#900, 500, Grande Allée est, Québec, QC G1R 2J7
Tél: 418-683-3000; *Téléc:* 418-683-8784
Ligne sans frais: 800-463-5172
gpb@grondinpoudrier.com
www.grondinpoudrier.com

Québec: **Hodran Consultants Inc. - *1**
#305, 4, Jardins Merici, Québec, QC G1S 4M4
Tél: 514-571-2940;
gcardin@genomecanada.ca

Québec: **Joli-Cour Lacasse Avocats - *26**
Former Name: Pouliot L'Ecuyer
#600, 1134, Grande Allée Ouest, Québec, QC G1S 1E5
Tél: 418-681-7007; *Téléc:* 418-681-7100
communications@jolicoeurlacasse.com
www.jolicoeurlacasse.com

Québec: **Langlois Kronström Desjardins - *81**
#300, 801, Grande Allée ouest, Québec, QC G1S 1C1
Tel: 418-650-7000; *Fax:* 418-650-7075
Toll-Free: 888-650-7001
info@lkd.ca
www.langloiskronstromdesjardins.com

Québec: **Alain Lemieux, Affaires gouvernementales et publiques - *1**
Also Known As: AGP
Former Name: Affaires gouvernementales et publiques
912, Grande-Allée ouest, Québec, QC G1S 1C5
Tél: 418-682-3157; *Téléc:* 418-780-3824
lemieuxa@agpubliques.ca
www.agpubliques.ca

Québec: **Micheline Anne Montreuil - *1**
1050, rue François-Blondeau, Québec, QC G1H 2H2
Tél: 418-621-5032; *Téléc:* 418-621-5092
micheline@micheline.ca
www.micheline.ca

Québec: **Morency Avocats - *31**
Former Name: Pothier Delisle Societé D'Avocats
#400, 3075, ch des Quatre-Bourgeois, Québec, QC G1W 4X5
Tél: 418-651-9900; *Téléc:* 418-651-5184
avocats@morencyavocats.com
www.morencyavocats.com

Québec: **O'Brien, Avocats - *10**
#600, 140, Grande Allée est, Québec, QC G1R 5M8
Tél: 418-648-1511; *Téléc:* 418-648-9335
obrien@obrienavocats.qc.ca

Québec: **Siskinds Desmeules Avocats - *5**
#320, 43, rue Buade, Québec, QC G1R 4A2
Tél: 418-694-2009; *Téléc:* 418-694-0281
claude.desmeules@siskindsdesmeules.com

Québec: **Tremblay, Bois, Mignault & Lemay - *34**
#200, 1195, av Lavigerie, Québec, QC G1V 4N3
Tél: 418-658-9966; *Téléc:* 418-658-6100
Ligne sans frais: 800-807-9966
avocats@tremblaybois.qc.ca
www.tremblaybois.qc.ca

Repentigny: **Duval, Brochu, Tremblay & Associées - *2**
#201, 275B, rue Paradis, Repentigny, QC J6A 8H2
Tél: 450-581-2777; *Téléc:* 450-585-7565

Rimouski: **Jean Blouin - *1**
216, av de la Cathedrale, Rimouski, QC G5L 5J2

Rimouski: **Norman Dumais - *1**
#200, CP 998, Stn. Bureau-Chef, 97, rue St-Germain ouest, Rimouski, QC G5L 7E1
Tél: 418-723-3179; *Téléc:* 418-723-3195
dumais.avocat@globetrotter.net

Rimouski: **Laprise, Lacroix & Associes - *4**
#R0901, 9, rue Jules-A. Brillant, Rimouski, QC G5L 7E4
Tél: 418-722-5587; *Téléc:* 418-722-5949
raymond.lacroix@telus.com

Rivière-du-Loup: **Aide Juridique - *3**
Former Name: Giroux, LeBlond, Gaudette
#203, 37, rue de la Cour, Rivière-du-Loup, QC G5R 1J1
Tél: 418-862-1522; *Téléc:* 418-862-4528
bajrdl@ccjbslg.qc.ca

Rivière-du-Loup: **Belzile & Associés - *3**
#1027, 2, rue de la Cour, Rivière-du-Loup, QC G5R 4C3
Tél: 418-862-9460; *Téléc:* 418-862-9939

Rivière-du-Loup: **Rioux Bossé Massé Moreau - *6**
CP 487, 12, rue de la Cour, Rivière-du-Loup, QC G5R 3Z1
Tél: 418-862-3565; *Téléc:* 418-862-4408
rbmm@qc.aira.com
www.rbmm.qc.ca

Rosemère: **Indev Inc. - *1**
CP 533, Stn. Ste-Thérèse, 88, rue Jack-Rice, Rosemère, QC J7A 4Z1
Tél: 514-875-5475; *Téléc:* 514-875-5475
www.in-dev.ca

Rouyn-Noranda: **Denis Harvey - *1**
53, du Terminus ouest, Rouyn-Noranda, QC J9X 2P4
Tél: 819-262-2301; *Téléc:* 819-765-0653
dharvey@ccjat.qc.ca

Saint-Félicien: **Sandra Bouchard, Avocate - *1**
1082, rue Saint-Christophe, Saint-Félicien, QC G8K 1Z2
Tél: 418-679-5566; *Téléc:* 418-630-2111
sandbouc@destination.ca

** indicates number of lawyers*

***Saint-Georges*: Raymond Lessard - *1**
12285, av 1re, Saint-Georges, QC G5Y 2E2

***Saint-Hyacinthe*: Claude L. Bédard Avocat - *1**
1782, rue Girouard ouest, Saint-Hyacinthe, QC J2S 3A1
Tél: 450-774-2749; *Téléc:* 450-774-9533
claude.bedard@sympatico.ca

***Saint-Hyacinthe*: Brodeur, Boileau - *3**
Former Name: Brodeur, L'Ecuyer, Boileau
1700, rue Girouard ouest, Saint-Hyacinthe, QC J2S 3A1
Tél: 450-773-8566; *Téléc:* 450-778-3749

***Saint-Hyacinthe*: Sylvestre & Associés Avocats S.E.N.C. - *9**
#236, 1600, rue Girouard ouest, Saint-Hyacinthe, QC J2S 2Z8
Tél: 450-773-8445; *Téléc:* 450-773-2112
etude@avocatssylvestre.ca

***Saint-Jean-Port-Joli*: Les Avocats Blanchet Gaudreault - *2**
512, route de l'Eglise, Saint-Jean-Port-Joli, QC G0R 3G0
Tél: 418-598-7004; *Téléc:* 418-598-7390
blanchet.gaudreault@globetrotter.net

***Saint-Jean-sur-Richelieu*: Bérubé & Pion, SENCRL - *3**
Former Name: Bérubé Hébert
#225, 145, boul St-Joseph, Saint-Jean-sur-Richelieu, QC J3B 1W5
Tél: 450-359-7171; *Téléc:* 450-359-9957

***Saint-Jean-sur-Richelieu*: Paul Barry Gingras - *2**
Former Name: Gingras, Arsenault
229, rue Jacques-Cartier nord, Saint-Jean-sur-Richelieu, QC J3B 6T3
Tél: 450-347-0433; *Téléc:* 450-346-0099
gingras@qc.aira.com

***Saint-Jean-sur-Richelieu*: Lachance & Morin - *2**
108, rue St-Charles, Saint-Jean-sur-Richelieu, QC J3B 2C1
Tél: 450-346-4464

***Saint-Jean-sur-Richelieu*: Claude Lauzon - *1**
160, rue Longueuil, Saint-Jean-sur-Richelieu, QC J3B 6P1
Tél: 450-347-2344; *Téléc:* 450-347-4132

***Saint-Joseph-de-Beauce*: Cliche, Laflamme & Loubier - *6**
CP 160, 109, rue Verreault, Saint-Joseph-de-Beauce, QC G0S 2V0
Tél: 418-397-5264; *Téléc:* 418-397-5269
cliclafl@globetrotter.qc.ca

***Saint-Joseph-de-Beauce*: Giroux & Binette - *2**
#100, 700, av Robert-Cliche, Saint-Joseph-de-Beauce, QC G0S 2V0
Tél: 418-397-7288; *Téléc:* 418-397-7283

***Saint-Jérôme*: CRBI - *1**
461, de la Seigneurie, Saint-Jérôme, QC J5L 2K5
Tél: 450-530-7548;
crbi@videotron.ca

***Saint-Jérôme*: Lalonde Geraghty Riendeau Lapierre - *8**
44, rue De Martigny ouest, Saint-Jérôme, QC J7Z 2E9
Tél: 450-436-8022; *Téléc:* 450-436-5185
lalondegeraghty@lgrl.ca
www.lgrl.ca

***Saint-Jérôme*: Prévost Fortin D'Aoust - *30**
Former Name: Prévost Auclair Fortin D'Aoust
#400, 55, rue Castonguay, Saint-Jérôme, QC J7Y 2H9
Tel: 450-436-8244; *Fax:* 450-436-9735
info@pfdlex.com
www.pfdlex.com

***Saint-Lambert*: André Demers - *1**
439, av Notre-Dame, Saint-Lambert, QC J4P 2K5
Tél: 514-875-2007; *Téléc:* 514-466-7315

***Saint-Lambert*: Paul Joffe - *1**
360, av Putney, Saint-Lambert, QC J4P 3B6
Tél: 450-465-3654; *Téléc:* 450-465-5730
p.joffe@sympatico.ca

***Saint-Lambert*: L2i Solutions financières - *3**
Also Known As: L2i Financial Solutions
Former Name: Lagacé & Legault International Inc.
#200, 2015, rue Victoria, Saint-Lambert, QC J4S 1H1
Tel: 450-923-9381; *Fax:* 450-466-3919
info@solutionsL2i.com
solutionsl2i.com

***Saint-Lambert*: William Sullivan - *1**
147, ch Tiffin, Saint-Lambert, QC J4P 3E8
Tél: 514-397-1504; *Téléc:* 514-397-1505
wslaw@qc.aibn.com

***Saint-Laurent*: Applied R&D Technology & Funding Solutions Inc. - *1**
#406, 905, av Sainte-Croix, Saint-Laurent, QC H4L 5N9
Tel: 514-817-9312;
appliedrd@gmail.com
www.applied-rd.com

***Saint-Laurent*: Belanger, Fiore - *2**
#300, 685, boul Décarie, Saint-Laurent, QC H4L 5G4
Tél: 514-744-0825; *Téléc:* 514-744-9861
belanger.annie@videotron.ca; fiore.carole@vl.videotron.ca

***Saint-Laurent*: Gaston E. Bouchard - *1**
1015, rue Champigny, Saint-Laurent, QC H4L 4P3
Tél: 514-744-0918; *Téléc:* 514-345-4718

***Saint-Laurent*: Kravitz & Kravitz - *3**
#350, 750, boul Marcel-Laurin, Saint-Laurent, QC H4M 2M4
Tél: 514-748-2889; *Téléc:* 514-748-5191
kravitz@centra.ca

***Saint-Sauveur*: Jay Plante & Associates - *1**
300, ch de L'Ancienne Érablière, Saint-Sauveur, QC J0R 1R2
Tel: 514-261-8619; *Fax:* 514-450-2278

***Sainte-Anne-du-Lac*: Harmac du Lac Inc. - *1**
23, ch de L'Oseille, Sainte-Anne-du-Lac, QC J0R 1B0
Tél: 450-224-0289; *Téléc:* 450-224-0290
harmacdulac@sympatico.ca

***Sainte-Foy*: Claude Berlinguette - *1**
1429, rue du Nordet, Sainte-Foy, QC G2G 2C2
Tél: 418-871-1478

***Sainte-Julie*: Roland Boyer - *1**
69, av Mont Bruno, RR#3, Sainte-Julie, QC J3E 3A1
Tél: 450-649-3772; *Téléc:* 450-649-0101
rolandboyer@yahoo.com

***Sainte-Marie*: Sylvain, Parent, Gobeil - *4**
CP 40, 225, rue du College, Sainte-Marie, QC G6E 3B4
Tél: 418-387-2727; *Téléc:* 418-387-7070
spgs@globetrotter.net

***Sainte-Thérèse*: Marc H. Lamoreux - *1**
44, ch Cote St-Louis ouest, Sainte-Thérèse, QC J7E 2H7
Tél: 514-979-5918

***Salaberry-de-Valleyfield*: Les Avocats Rancourt, Legault & St-Onge - *6**
Former Name: Rancourt, Legault, Boucher & St-Onge
175, rue Salaberry, Salaberry-de-Valleyfield, QC J6T 2J1
Tél: 450-371-2221; *Téléc:* 450-371-2094
courrier@rancourtlegault.com
www.rancourtlegault.com

***Sept-Iles*: Besnier, Dion & Rondeau - *6**
865, boul Laure, Sept-Iles, QC G4R 1Y6
Tél: 418-962-9775; *Téléc:* 418-968-6806
besnier.avocats@cgocable.ca

***Sept-Iles*: Desrosiers & Associés - *3**
#201, 440, av Brochu, Sept-Iles, QC G4R 2W8
Tél: 418-962-7392; *Téléc:* 418-962-6100
desricar@globetrotter.qc.ca

***Shawinigan*: Pierre Dugré - *1**
305, 7e rue, Shawinigan, QC G9N 1C6
Tél: 819-537-8902; *Téléc:* 819-537-0267
Ligne sans frais: 877-744-0090
pierredugre@cgocable.ca

***Sherbrooke*: Claude R. Beauchamp - *1**
#101, 380, rue King ouest, Sherbrooke, QC J1H 1R4
Tél: 819-563-7733; *Téléc:* 819-563-7734

***Sherbrooke*: Pierre Belhumeur - *1**
#101, 380, rue King ouest, Sherbrooke, QC J1H 1R4
Tél: 819-566-1676; *Téléc:* 819-563-7734
pilul@interlinx.qc.ca

***Sherbrooke*: François Bouchard, Avocat - *1**
#610, 455, rue King ouest, Sherbrooke, QC J1H 6E9
Tél: 819-563-4898; *Téléc:* 819-563-5837
fbouchard@essagal.ca

***Sherbrooke*: Gerard G. Boudreau - *1**
2571, boul Portland, Sherbrooke, QC J1J 1V6
Tél: 819-562-0848; *Téléc:* 819-569-3580

***Sherbrooke*: Linda Boulanger - *1**
#3, 30, rue Vaudry, Sherbrooke, QC J1M 1B2
Tél: 819-820-2661; *Téléc:* 819-820-8330
lindaboulangeravocate@yahoo.ca

***Sherbrooke*: Jean-Claude Boutin - *1**
#100, 75, rue Wellington nord, Sherbrooke, QC J1H 5A9
Tél: 819-569-9933; *Téléc:* 819-822-0041

***Sherbrooke*: Delorme, LeBel, Bureau, s.e.n.c. - *7**
#100, 2355, rue King ouest, Sherbrooke, QC J1J 2G6
Tél: 819-566-6222; *Téléc:* 819-566-4221
dlb@dlbavocats.com

***Sherbrooke*: Drouin Lemieux - *2**
18, rue Wellington nord, Sherbrooke, QC J1H 5B7
Tél: 819-566-3939;
drouinlemieux@qc.aira.com

***Sherbrooke*: Fontaine, Panneton & Associes - *8**
#220, 2050, rue King ouest, Sherbrooke, QC J1J 2E8
Tél: 819-564-1222; *Téléc:* 819-822-2180
louis.panneton1@qc.aira.com

***Sherbrooke*: Gérin Custeau Francoeur - *3**
100, rue Richmond, Sherbrooke, QC J1H 6E1
Tél: 819-348-0274

***Sherbrooke*: Guenin Cormier Gallant Morin**
759, rue King est, Sherbrooke, QC J1G 1C6
Tel: 819-565-1808; *Fax:* 819-565-2729
gcgm@globetrotter.net

***Sherbrooke*: Hackett, Campbell, Bouchard - *4**
80, rue Peel, Sherbrooke, QC J1H 4K1
Tél: 819-565-7885; *Téléc:* 819-566-0888
info@hcblegal.com

***Sillery*: Hickson, Martin, Blanchard - *3**
Former Name: Hickson Noonan
1170, ch St-Louis, Sillery, QC G1S 1E5
Tél: 418-681-9671; *Téléc:* 418-527-6938
hickson.martin.blanchard@qc.aira.com

***Sorel*: Ally & Ally - *1**
53, rue George, Sorel, QC J3P 1B9
Tél: 450-743-7979; *Téléc:* 450-743-9821

***Sorel*: Carole Lepage - *1**
96, rue George, Sorel, QC J3P 1C3
Tél: 450-742-3766; *Téléc:* 450-742-1133
avocate@carolelepage.qc.ca

***St-Georges-de-Beauce*: Jérôme Poirier - *1**
Former Name: Lebel, Poirier
11720, 1re av, St-Georges-de-Beauce, QC G5Y 2C8
Tél: 418-228-3123; *Téléc:* 418-228-0494
jerome.poirier@globetrotter.net

***St-Léonard*: DiPace, Mercadente - *6**
#202, 5450, rue Jarry est, St-Léonard, QC H1P 1T9
Tél: 514-326-3300; *Téléc:* 514-326-4706
mercadante@videotron.net

***St-Romuald-d'Etchemin*: Huguette Gagnon - *1**
CP 2096, St-Romuald-d'Etchemin, QC G6W 5M3
Tél: 418-839-2045; *Téléc:* 418-839-2061
gagnonh@videotron.ca

***Ste-Thérèse-De-Blainville*: Brazeau, Grégoire & Cliche - *3**
72, rue Blainville ouest, Ste-Thérèse-De-Blainville, QC J7E 1X3
Tél: 514-430-1530; *Téléc:* 514-430-3607

***Trois-Rivières*: Roger Bellemare, Avocat - *2**
Former Name: Bellemare & Germain
5540, rue Decelles, Trois-Rivières, QC G8Y 6Y8
Tél: 819-376-7918; *Téléc:* 819-376-1425

***Trois-Rivières*: Biron, Spain & Associés - *3**
CP 444, 154, rue Radisson, Trois-Rivières, QC G9A 5G4
Tél: 819-375-4187; *Téléc:* 819-375-7395

** indicates number of lawyers*

***Trois-Rivières*: Braun & Bélisle - *2**
#4, 1185, rue Hart, Trois-Rivières, QC G9A 4S4
Tél: 819-691-1390; *Téléc:* 819-378-7344

***Trois-Rivières*: Godin, Boucher, Brunet, DuPlessis - *4**
CP 1474, Stn. Chef, 190, rue Bonaventure, Trois-Rivières, QC G9A 5L6
Tél: 819-379-5225; *Téléc:* 819-379-4545
godindenysp@qc.aira.com

***Trois-Rivières*: Louis Hénaire - *1**
Also Known As: Hénaire, Avocats
983, rue Hart, Trois-Rivières, QC G9A 4S3
Tél: 819-379-3355; *Téléc:* 819-379-1227

***Val-Bélair*: J. Michel Bouchard - *1**
1805, av Industrielle, Val-Bélair, QC G3K 1L8
Tél: 418-842-0996

***Val-d'Or*: Cossette & DuFour - *1**
795, 3e av, Val-d'Or, QC J9P 1S8
Tél: 819-825-2787; *Téléc:* 819-874-4160

***Valleyfield*: Droiun, Gingras, Robert & Toulouse - *4**
Former Name: Massé, Gingras, Robert & Toulouse
#200A, 30, av de Centenaire, Valleyfield, QC J6S 5X4
Tél: 450-370-3064; *Téléc:* 450-370-3068
ccjers.valleyfield@sympatico.ca

***Valleyfield*: Vachon, Martin & Besner - *3**
72, rue Montcalm, Valleyfield, QC J6T 2C9
Tél: 514-371-7771; *Téléc:* 514-371-2438
vachon@rocler.qc.ca

***Varennes*: Desjardins, Lessard - *2**
#203, 1950, boul René Gaultier, Varennes, QC J3X 1P5
Tél: 450-652-1830; *Téléc:* 450-652-3484

***Verdun*: Robert Beaudet - *2**
5331, rue Bannantyne, Verdun, QC H4H 1E8
Tél: 514-769-8527; *Téléc:* 514-769-7466

***Verdun*: Robert Church - *1**
82, boul William, Verdun, QC H3E 1R6
Tél: 514-765-8903; *Fax:* 514-765-3472

***Victoriaville*: Caron, Garneau, Bellavance - *3**
268, boul Bois Francs nord, Victoriaville, QC G6P 1G5
Tél: 819-758-8251; *Téléc:* 819-752-4520
avocatscg@bellnet.ca

***Westmount*: Aster & Aster - *2**
#410, 345, av Victoria, Westmount, QC H3Z 2N2
Tel: 514-483-2445; *Fax:* 514-483-0009
asterma@asterlaw.com
www.asterlaw.com

***Westmount*: Robert Berger - *1**
4269, rue Ste-Catherine ouest, Westmount, QC H3Z 1P7
Tél: 514-847-3667; *Téléc:* 514-847-0011
rberger@lexingtonrealties.ca

***Westmount*: Luisa Biasutti - *1**
#410, 4115, rue Sherbrooke ouest, Westmount, QC H3Z 1K9
Tél: 514-933-3838; *Téléc:* 514-933-2668
biasutti@groupeteq.com

***Westmount*: Paul B. Cohen - *1**
#809, 4000, boul de Maisonneuve ouest, Westmount, QC H3Z 1J9
Tel: 514-931-3691; *Fax:* 514-931-3637
paulcohen@bellnet.ca

***Westmount*: A. Barry Coleman - *1**
#660, 4141, rue Sherbrooke ouest, Westmount, QC H3Z 1B8
Tel: 514-935-5030; *Fax:* 514-935-3559

***Westmount*: Crestohl & Associates - *1**
#1200, 1, Carré Westmount, Westmount, QC H3Z 2P4
Tél: 514-932-7392; *Téléc:* 514-932-0990

***Westmount*: David & Touchette - *2**
#1800, 1 Westmount Sq., Westmount, QC H3Z 2P9
Tél: 514-871-8174; *Téléc:* 514-871-8052
mdavid@davidtouchette.com
www.davidtouchette.com

***Westmount*: M. Diamond & Associates Inc. - *3**
#400, 345, av Victoria, Westmount, QC H3Z 2N2
Tél: 514-483-2303; *Téléc:* 514-483-2373

***Westmount*: André R. Dorais Avocats - *3**
#2000, 1, carré Westmount, Westmount, QC H3Z 2P9
Tél: 514-938-0808; *Téléc:* 514-938-8888
adorais@ardavocats.com

***Westmount*: Me Linda Hammerschmid - *4**
#1290, 1 Westmount Sq., Westmount, QC H3Z 2P9
Tel: 514-846-1013; *Fax:* 514-846-1803

***Westmount*: Irving Mitchell Kalichman SENCRL/LLP Avocats Advocates - *8**
4119, rue Sherbrooke ouest, Westmount, QC H3Z 1A7
Tel: 514-935-4460; *Fax:* 514-935-2999

***Westmount*: Stein & Stein - *4**
4101, rue Sherbrooke ouest, Westmount, QC H3Z 1A7
Tel: 514-866-9806; *Fax:* 514-875-8218
law@steinandstein.com
www.steinandstein.com

***Westmount*: Rosalie Szewczuk - *1**
4420, rue Ste-Catherine ouest, Westmount, QC H3Z 1R2
Tel: 514-933-4453; *Fax:* 514-934-3134
rosiesz@videotron.ca

Saskatchewan

***Alameda*: Cundall, Baumgartner & Co.**
115 Fifth St., Alameda, SK S0C 0A0
Tel: 306-489-2216; *Fax:* 306-489-4602

***Assiniboia*: Lewans & Ford - *2**
P.O. Box 759, 228 Centre St., Assiniboia, SK S0H 0B0
Tel: 306-642-3543; *Fax:* 306-642-5777

***Assiniboia*: Marlin Law Office - *1**
P.O. Box 1088, 200 Centre St., Assiniboia, SK S0H 0B0
Tel: 306-642-3933; *Fax:* 306-642-5399
gmarlin@sk.sympatico.ca

***Assiniboia*: Mountain & Mountain - *2**
P.O. Box 459, 101 - 4 Ave. West, Assiniboia, SK S0H 0B0
Tel: 306-642-3866; *Fax:* 306-642-5848
lee.mountain@sasktel.net
mounl.sasktelwebsite.net/

***Biggar*: Busse Law Professional Corporation - *2**
Former Name: bmwlaw.sasktelwebsite.net
Credit Union Bldg., P.O. Box 669, 302 Main St., Biggar, SK S0K 0M0
Tel: 306-948-3346; *Fax:* 306-948-3366
busselaw@sasktel.net
www.busselaw.net

***Broadview*: Gary G. Moore - *1**
P.O. Box 610, 616 Main St., Broadview, SK S0G 0K0
Tel: 306-696-2454; *Fax:* 306-696-3105

***Brownlee*: Frederick R.C. Rawlings - *1**
P.O. Box 70, Brownlee, SK S0H 0M0
Tel: 306-759-2621

***Canora*: Rosowsky, Campbell & Seidle - *1**
P.O. Box 309, 115 - 2 Ave. West, Canora, SK S0A 0L0
Tel: 306-563-4250;
ros.cam@sk.sympatico.ca

***Davidson*: Dellene S. Church - *1**
P.O. Box 724, 200 Garfield St., Davidson, SK S0G 1A0
Tel: 306-567-5554; *Fax:* 306-567-2831
dsc-law@sasktel.net

***Estevan*: Kohaly & Elash - *2**
P.O. Box 580, 1312 - 4th St., Estevan, SK S4A 0X2
Tel: 306-634-3631; *Fax:* 306-634-6901
paulelash@kemlaw.sk.ca

***Estevan*: Komarnicki Trobert - *2**
#305, P.O. Box 725, 1133 - 4 St., Estevan, SK S4A 2A6
Tel: 306-634-2616; *Fax:* 306-634-9881
ktlaw@sasktel.net

***Estevan*: Orlowski Law Office - *2**
1215 - 5th St., Estevan, SK S4A 0Z5
Tel: 306-634-3353; *Fax:* 306-634-7714
orlowski.law@sasktel.net

***Eston*: Hughes Law Office - *1**
P.O. Box 729, 305 Main St. South, Eston, SK S0L 1A0
Tel: 306-962-4111; *Fax:* 306-962-3302
hugheseston@hotmail.com

***Fort Qu'appelle*: Halford Law Office - *1**
122 Boundary Avenue North, Fort Qu'appelle, SK S0G 1S0
Tel: 306-332-5661; *Fax:* 306-332-4293

***Gravelbourg*: Anderson & Company - *2**
Former Name: Louis E. Stringer
P.O. Box 1016, 209 Main St, Gravelbourg, SK S0H 1X0
Tel: 306-648-2582; *Fax:* 306-648-2501

***Humboldt*: Behiel, Will & Biemans - *4**
Former Name: Behiel, Munkler & Will
P.O. Box 878, 602 - 9 St., Humboldt, SK S0K 2A0
Tel: 306-682-2642; *Fax:* 306-682-5165
office_bmwlaw@sasktel.net
www.behielwill.com

***Indian Head*: KMP Law - *2**
523 Grand Ave., Indian Head, SK S0G 2K0
Tel: 306-695-2704;
kmplaw.com

***Kindersley*: Ard Law Office - *1**
P.O. Box 1898, 111 1 Avenue West, Kindersley, SK S0L 1S0
Tel: 306-463-2626; *Fax:* 306-463-4917
ard.law@sasktel.net

***Kindersley*: Sheppard & Millar - *2**
P.O. Box 1510, 113 - 1 Ave. East., Kindersley, SK S0L 1S0
Tel: 306-463-4647; *Fax:* 306-463-6133

***La Ronge*: Buckle Law Office - *1**
#1B, 1603 Bedford Dr., La Ronge, SK S0J 1L0
Tel: 306-425-5959; *Fax:* 306-425-2840

***Langenburg*: Layh & Associates - *2**
Former Name: Layh Law Office
Welke House, P.O. Box 250, 216 Road Ave. East, Langenburg, SK S0A 2A0
Tel: 306-743-5520; *Fax:* 306-743-5589
info@layhlaw.com
www.layhlaw.com

***Lloydminster*: Clements & Smith - *3**
#212, P.O. Box 440, Stn. Main, 5704 - 44 St., Lloydminster, SK S9V 0Y4
Tel: 780-875-7999; *Fax:* 780-875-1020
clements@bordercity.com

***Lloydminster*: Fox Wakefield - *2**
Former Name: Bennett Fox Wakefield
P.O. Box 50, 5105 - 49 St., Lloydminster, SK S9V 0Y6
Tel: 780-875-9105; *Fax:* 780-875-6748

***Meadow Lake*: Francis & Company - *2**
Former Name: Francis
P.O. Box 310, 822 - 9th Ave. West, Meadow Lake, SK S9X 1Y3
Tel: 306-236-5540; *Fax:* 306-236-5571
info@franciscolaw.ca
www.franciscolaw.ca

***Meadow Lake*: Gerald R. Perkins - *1**
#2, 132 Centre St., Meadow Lake, SK S9X 1Z7
Tel: 306-236-4040; *Fax:* 306-236-4878
perkinslawoffice@sasktel.net

***Melfort*: Annand Law Office - *2**
P.O. Box 69, 208 Main St., Melfort, SK S0E 1A0
Tel: 306-752-2707; *Fax:* 306-752-4484
info@annandlawoffice.com
www.annandlawoffice.com

***Melfort*: Kapoor Selnes Klimm - *3**
Former Name: Kapoor Selnes Klimm
417 Main St., Melfort, SK S0E 1A0
Tel: 306-752-5777; *Fax:* 306-752-2712

***Melfort*: Ronald Price-Jones - *1**
P.O. Box 129, #3 Hwy. East, Melfort, SK S0E 1A0
Tel: 306-752-5701; *Fax:* 306-752-2444
ronp-j@sasktel.net

***Melville*: Bell, Kreklewich & Company - *3**
P.O. Box 2000, 147 - 3 Ave. East, Melville, SK S0A 2P0
Tel: 306-728-5468; *Fax:* 306-728-4444
bell.kreklewich_bkc@sasktel.net

***Melville*: Schmidt Law Office - *1**
P.O. Box 160, 126 - 2nd Ave., Melville, SK S0A 2P0
Tel: 306-728-5481; *Fax:* 306-728-4201
s.lo@sasktel.net

** indicates number of lawyers*

***Moose Jaw*: Murray D. Acton - *1**
Also Known As: Acton Law Office
330 Main St. North, Moose Jaw, SK S6H 3J9
Tel: 306-694-0052; *Fax:* 306-691-0445
actonlaw@shaw.ca

***Moose Jaw*: Ron G. Bader - *1**
53 Stadecona St. West, Moose Jaw, SK S6H 1Z2
Tel: 306-691-5858; *Fax:* 306-691-5822
Toll-Free: 800-845-4748
ron@rgblaw.com

***Moose Jaw*: Curran & Fielding - *2**
#108, 54 Ominica St. West, Moose Jaw, SK S6H 1W9
Tel: 306-693-7181; *Fax:* 306-691-0187

***Moose Jaw*: Grayson & Company - *7**
Former Name: Grayson, Rushford, Cooper, Arendt, Cornea & Patterson
P.O. Box 908, 350 Langdon Cres., Moose Jaw, SK S6H 4P6
Tel: 306-693-6176; *Fax:* 306-693-1515
grayson@sasknet.net

***Moose Jaw*: Terrance Ocrane Law Office - *1**
#1, 53 Stadacona St. West, Moose Jaw, SK S6H 1Z2
Tel: 306-694-4922; *Fax:* 306-692-6386
ocranelawoffice@sasktel.net

***Moose Jaw*: B.A. Walper-Bossence Q.C. - *1**
84 Athabasca St. W, Moose Jaw, SK S6H 2B5
Tel: 306-693-7288; *Fax:* 306-692-6760
brendawalperlaw@shaw.ca
www.walperlaw.ca

***Moose Jaw*: Wheatley Law Firm - *1**
1357 Queen Crescent, Moose Jaw, SK S6H 7K7
Tel: 306-692-0113; *Fax:* 306-693-3230

***Moose Jaw*: Whittaker, Craik, MacLowich & Hughes - *2**
P.O. Box 1178, 109 Ominica St. West, Moose Jaw, SK S6H 4P9
Tel: 306-694-4677; *Fax:* 306-694-5747

***Moosomin*: Osman, Gordon & Co. - *6**
P.O. Box 280, 626 Carleton St., Moosomin, SK S0G 3N0
Tel: 306-435-3851; *Fax:* 306-435-3962

***Nipawin*: Carson Law Office - *1**
P.O. Box 1983, Nipawin, SK S0E 1E0
Tel: 306-862-5554;

***Nipawin*: Eremko & Eremko - *1**
P.O. Box 250, Nipawin, SK S0E 1E0
Tel: 306-862-4477

***Nipawin*: Taylor & Co. - *3**
P.O. Box 850, 117 - 1 Ave. East, Nipawin, SK S0E 1E0
Tel: 306-873-1865;
j.taylor_lawoffice@sasktel.net

***North Battleford*: Cawood Walker Demmans Baldwin - *4**
#201, P.O. Box 905, 1291 - 102 St., North Battleford, SK S9A 2Z3
Tel: 306-445-6177; *Fax:* 306-445-7076
cawood.et.al@sasktel.net

***North Battleford*: David Conroy - *1**
#101, 1351 - 101 St., North Battleford, SK S9A 0Z9
Tel: 306-445-3613; *Fax:* 306-445-9088
conroylaw@sasktel.net

***North Battleford*: Jones & Hudec - *6**
P.O. Box 1179, 10211 - 12 Ave., North Battleford, SK S9A 3K2
Tel: 306-446-2211; *Fax:* 306-446-3022
jhlaw@sasktel.net
www.joneshudec.com

***North Battleford*: Marusia A. Kobrynsky - *1**
10817 Meighen Cres., North Battleford, SK S9A 3L2
Tel: 306-445-8369; *Fax:* 306-446-3022
mkobrynsky@sasktel.net

***North Battleford*: Lindgren, Blais, Frank & Illingworth - *4**
P.O. Box 940, 1301 - 101 St., North Battleford, SK S9A 2Z3
Tel: 306-445-2421; *Fax:* 306-445-2313
mlbfh@sasktel.net
www.lbfilaw.com

***North Battleford*: Migneault Greenwood - *4**
1391 101st Street, North Battleford, SK S9A 2Y8
Tel: 306-445-4436; *Fax:* 306-445-6444
kevan@mglawoffice.com

***Preeceville*: Peet Law Firm - *1**
P.O. Box 1210, 17 First Ave. NW, Preeceville, SK S0A 3B0
Tel: 306-547-5590

***Prince Albert*: Balon Krishan - *3**
1335B - 2nd Ave. West, Prince Albert, SK S6V 5B2
Tel: 306-922-5151; *Fax:* 306-763-1755
bkm.law@sasktel.net

***Prince Albert*: Ron Cherkewich - *1**
#3, 27 - 11 St. West, Prince Albert, SK S6V 3A8
Tel: 306-764-1537; *Fax:* 306-763-0505
ron.cya@sasktel.net

***Prince Albert*: Eggum, Abrametz, Eggum - *4**
#101, 88 - 13th St. East, Prince Albert, SK S6V 1C6
Tel: 306-763-7441; *Fax:* 306-764-2882
klleggum@inet2000.com; petervabrametz@inet2000.com

***Prince Albert*: Holash Logue McCullagh Law Office - *3**
Former Name: Harradence Logue Holash; Holash Logue
1102 - 1 Ave. West, Prince Albert, SK S6V 4Y6
Tel: 306-764-4244; *Fax:* 306-764-4949

***Prince Albert*: Kirkby Law Office - *1**
#102, 1061 Central Ave., Prince Albert, SK S6V 4V4
Tel: 306-764-4673; *Fax:* 306-922-0434
kirkbylaw@sasktel.net

***Prince Albert*: Loewen & Klassen Law Office - *2**
1100 1st Avenue East, Prince Albert, SK S6V 2A7
Tel: 306-922-0212; *Fax:* 306-922-2422

***Prince Albert*: Sanderson Balicki Parchomchuk - *8**
110 - 11 St. East, Prince Albert, SK S6V 1A1
Tel: 306-764-2222; *Fax:* 306-764-2221
www.sbplaw.ca

***Prince Albert*: Stephens Law Office - *1**
Former Name: Stephens Arnot Heffernan
#3, 27 - 11th St. West, Prince Albert, SK S6V 3A8
Tel: 306-764-3456; *Fax:* 306-922-3772
www.stephenslaw.ca

***Prince Albert*: West, Siwak - *2**
1109 Central Ave., Prince Albert, SK S6V 4V7
Tel: 306-763-7467; *Fax:* 306-763-7469
west.siwak@sasktel.net

***Prince Albert*: Wilcox Zuk Law Office - *6**
20 - 12 St. West, Prince Albert, SK S6V 3B3
Tel: 306-922-4700; *Fax:* 306-922-0633
princealbert@mwzlaw.com

***Prince Albert*: Zatlyn Law Office - *5**
#231, 1061 Central Ave., Prince Albert, SK S6V 7N7
Tel: 306-922-1444; *Fax:* 306-922-5848
zatlyn@sasktel.net

***Regina*: Anderson Law Firm Professional Corporation - *1**
Former Name: Mellor & Anderson
#1400, 2002 Victoria Ave., Regina, SK S4P 0R7
Tel: 306-789-8868; *Fax:* 306-789-3366

***Regina*: Beke Law Firm - *1**
#200, 2040 McIntyre St., Regina, SK S4P 2R6
Tel: 306-569-9964;
bekelaw@sasktel.net

***Regina*: Bertram Scrivens MacLeod - *6**
Former Name: Martin & MacLeod
#1730, Avord Tower, 2002 Victoria Ave., Regina, SK S4P 0R7
Tel: 306-525-2737; *Fax:* 306-565-3244
office@bertramlaw.ca
www.bsmlaw.ca

***Regina*: Dahlem Findlay - *1**
2100 Smith St., Regina, SK S4P 2P2
Tel: 306-522-3631; *Fax:* 306-565-2616
don.findlay@sasktel.net
www.donfindlay.ca

***Regina*: Duchin, Bayda & Kroczynski - *4**
2515 Victoria Ave., Regina, SK S4P 0T2
Tel: 306-359-3131; *Fax:* 306-359-3372

***Regina*: Gates & Company - *5**
3132 Avonhurst Dr., Regina, SK S4R 3J7
Tel: 306-949-5544; *Fax:* 306-775-2995
office@gateslaw.ca

***Regina*: Elaine Germain - *1**
2269 Hamilton St., Regina, SK S4P 2E7
Tel: 306-525-8311; *Fax:* 306-565-2766

***Regina*: Gerrand Rath Johnson - *13**
Former Name: Gerrand Mulatz
#700, Toronto Dominion Bank Bldg., 1914 Hamilton St., Regina, SK S4P 3N6
Tel: 306-522-3030; *Fax:* 306-522-3555
grj@grj.ca
www.grj.ca

***Regina*: Griffin Toews Maddigan Brabant - *6**
Former Name: Griffin Toews Maddigan
1530 Angus St., Regina, SK S4T 1Z1
Tel: 306-525-6125; *Fax:* 306-525-5226
griffin.toews@sasktel.net

***Regina*: Cindy M. Haynes Law Office - *1**
4126 Wascana Ridge, Regina, SK S4V 2S1
Tel: 306-789-2242; *Fax:* 306-789-4950
cindym.haynes@cableregina.com

***Regina*: Jaques Law Office - *1**
1542 Albert St., Regina, SK S4P 2S4
Tel: 306-359-3041; *Fax:* 306-525-4173
jaques@hierlaw.com
www.hierlaw.com

***Regina*: Kanuka Thuringer LLP, Barristers & Solicitors - *24**
#1400, 2500 Victoria Ave., Regina, SK S4P 3X2
Tel: 306-525-7200; *Fax:* 306-359-0590
firm@kanukathuringer.com
www.kanukathuringer.com

***Regina*: KMP Law - *5**
2600 Victoria Ave., Regina, SK S4T 1K2
Tel: 306-761-6200; *Fax:* 306-761-6222
kmplaw.com

***Regina*: Kowalishen Law Firm - *1**
1954 Angus St., Regina, SK S4T 1Z6
Tel: 306-525-2385; *Fax:* 306-525-2386
kowalishenlaw@hotmail.com

***Regina*: MacKay & McLean - *3**
2042 Cornwall St., Regina, SK S4P 2K5
Tel: 306-569-1301; *Fax:* 306-569-8560
dgmackay@sasktel.net
www.mackaymclean.com/index

***Regina*: MacLean Keith - *4**
Nicol Ct., 2398 Scarth St., Regina, SK S4P 2J7
Tel: 306-757-1611; *Fax:* 306-757-0712

***Regina*: McCrank Stewart LLP - *11**
Former Name: Rendek McCrank; Stewart Johnson Brundige
#401, 1916 Dewdney Ave., Regina, SK S4R 1G9
Tel: 306-525-2191; *Fax:* 306-757-8138
www.msj.ca

***Regina*: McDougall Gauley - Regina - *33**
1500 - 1881 Scarth St., Regina, SK S4P 4K9
Tel: 306-757-1641; *Fax:* 306-359-0785
mramsay@mcdougallgauley.com
www.mcdougallgauley.com

***Regina*: Merchant Law Group LLP - Regina - *50**
#100, Saskatchewan Drive Plaza, 2401 Saskatchewan Dr., Regina, SK S4P 4H8
Tel: 306-359-7777; *Fax:* 306-522-3299
Toll-Free: 888-567-7777
merchant@merchantlaw.com
www.merchantlaw.com

***Regina*: Morgan, Khaladkar & Skinner - *2**
2510 - 13 Ave., Regina, SK S4P 0W2
Tel: 306-525-9191; *Fax:* 306-525-0006

***Regina*: Noble, Johnston & Associates - *4**
1143 Lakewood Ct. North, Regina, SK S4X 3S3
Tel: 306-949-5616; *Fax:* 306-775-2234
info@noblejohnston.com
www.noblejohnston.com

** indicates number of lawyers*

Regina: **Olive, Waller, Zinkhan & Waller - *18**
#1000, 2002 Victoria Ave., Regina, SK S4P 0R7
Tel: 306-359-1888; *Fax:* 306-352-0771
owzw@owzw.com
www.owzw.com

Regina: **Phillips & Co. - *3**
Holdane House, 2100 Scarth St., Regina, SK S4P 2H6
Tel: 306-569-0811; *Fax:* 306-565-3434
phillips.co@sasktel.net

Regina: **Ann Phillips - *1**
#205, 2022 Cornwall St., Regina, SK S4P 2K5
Tel: 306-791-2626; *Fax:* 306-352-2020
annphillips@attglobal.net

Regina: **Reimer & Canham - *2**
116 Albert St., Regina, SK S4R 2N2
Tel: 306-791-2503; *Fax:* 306-543-9655

Regina: **Sheppard, Braun, Muma - *2**
#204, 3988 Albert St., Regina, SK S4S 3R1
Tel: 306-586-6020; *Fax:* 306-586-8525
sbmlaw@sasktel.net

Regina: **Silversides & Cox - *2**
Former Name: Woloshyn & Company
180 Saskatchewan Pl., 1870 Albert St., Regina, SK S4P 4B7
Tel: 306-337-4560; *Fax:* 306-337-4568

Regina: **James Sirounis Law Office**
#100, 1150 Albert St., Regina, SK S4R 2R1
Tel: 306-569-7711

Regina: **Walker, Singer & McCannell - *3**
1872 Angus St., Regina, SK S4T 1Z4
Tel: 306-352-8109; *Fax:* 306-352-7339

Regina: **Willows Tulloch - *1**
Former Name: Willows Tulloch & Howe
533 Victoria Avenue, Regina, SK S4N 0P4
Tel: 306-924-8600; *Fax:* 306-924-8601
ntulloch@accesscom.ca

Regina: **Garrett Wilson Q.C. - *1**
2237 Smith St., Regina, SK S4P 2P5
Tel: 306-352-1641; *Fax:* 306-525-8884

Rosetown: **Aseltine Skelton & Turner - *2**
P.O. Box 1120, 314 Main St., Rosetown, SK S0L 2V0
Tel: 306-882-4244; *Fax:* 306-882-3969

Saskatoon: **A.S.K. Law - *3**
#210, 75 - 24th St. East, Saskatoon, SK S7K 0K3
Tel: 306-933-3933; *Fax:* 306-933-9505
www.asklaw.ca

Saskatoon: **Agnew & Company - *3**
279 - 3rd Avenue North, Saskatoon, SK S7K 2H8
Tel: 306-244-7966; *Fax:* 306-244-8010
agnewco@sasktel.net

Saskatoon: **Balfour Moss - *5**
#600, Princeton Tower, 123 - 2nd Ave. South, Saskatoon, SK S7K 7E6
Tel: 306-665-7844; *Fax:* 306-652-1586
balfourmoss.saskatoon@balfourmoss.com
www.balfourmoss.com

Saskatoon: **Bodnar Campbell - *2**
Former Name: Bodnar, Wanhella & Cutforth
#400, 245 - 3 Ave. South, Saskatoon, SK S7K 1M4
Tel: 306-664-3314; *Fax:* 306-664-3354
mbodnarlaw@sasktel.net

Saskatoon: **Brayford Shapiro - *2**
311 - 21 St. East., Saskatoon, SK S7K 0C1
Tel: 306-244-5656; *Fax:* 306-244-5644
www.shapirolaw.ca

Saskatoon: **Brent & Greenhorn - *2**
3026 Taylor St. East, Saskatoon, SK S7H 4J2
Tel: 306-955-9544; *Fax:* 306-955-2656
bandg@sasktel.net
www.lynnegreenhorn.com

Saskatoon: **Burlingham Cuelenaere Legal Prof. Corp. - *4**
1043 - 8 St. East, Saskatoon, SK S7H 0S2
Tel: 306-343-9581; *Fax:* 306-343-1947
burlinghamcuelenaere@sasktel.net

Saskatoon: **William J. Campbell - *1**
#100, 220 - 3 Ave. South, Saskatoon, SK S7K 1M1
Tel: 306-664-3314; *Fax:* 306-664-3354
wjcampbell@sasktel.net

Saskatoon: **Cuelenaere, Kendall, Katzman & Watson - *15**
#500, Standard Life Bldg., 128 - 4th Ave. South, Saskatoon, SK S7K 1M8
Tel: 306-653-5000; *Fax:* 306-652-4171
admin@cuelenaere.com
www.cuelenaere.com

Saskatoon: **Dufour Scott Phelps & Mason - *5**
#400, 135 - 21st St. East, Saskatoon, SK S7K 0B4
Tel: 306-244-2201; *Fax:* 306-244-2420
www.dufourlaw.com

Saskatoon: **Halyk Kennedy Knox - *3**
321 - 6 Ave. North, Saskatoon, SK S7K 2S3
Tel: 306-665-3434; *Fax:* 306-652-1915
halyk@sasktel.net

Saskatoon: **Marvin W. Henderson - *1**
1219 - 8th St. East, Saskatoon, SK S7H 0S5
Tel: 306-652-1234; *Fax:* 306-652-1235
mwhlaw@sasktel.net

Saskatoon: **Hnatyshyn Gough - *5**
#601, 402 - 21st St. East, Saskatoon, SK S7K 0C3
Tel: 306-653-5150; *Fax:* 306-652-5859
hglaw@hglaw.ca
www.hglaw.ca

Saskatoon: **Kloppenburg & Kloppenburg - *2**
#603, Princeton Tower, 123 - 2nd Ave. South, Saskatoon, SK S7K 7E6
Tel: 306-665-7600; *Fax:* 306-665-7800
juristen@kloppenburg.ca
www.kloppenburg.ca

Saskatoon: **KMP Law - *3**
#505, 333 - 3 Ave. North, Saskatoon, SK S7K 2M2
Tel: 306-652-8833; *Fax:* 306-652-3333
kmplaw.com

Saskatoon: **Koskie Helms - *2**
Former Name: Koskie & Company
#3, 501 Gray Ave., Saskatoon, SK S7N 2H8
Tel: 306-242-8478; *Fax:* 306-653-2120
firm@koskie.com
www.koskie.com

Saskatoon: **Leland Kimpinski LLP - *7**
#800, 230 - 22nd St. East, Saskatoon, SK S7K 0E9
Tel: 306-244-6686; *Fax:* 306-653-7008
info@lelandlaw.ca
www.lelandlaw.ca

Saskatoon: **MacDermid Lamarsh - *7**
301 - 3rd Ave. South, Saskatoon, SK S7K 1M6
Tel: 306-652-9422; *Fax:* 306-242-1554
macmarsh@macmarsh.com
www.macdermidlamarsh.com

Saskatoon: **MacLean Keith - *2**
#1300, 410 - 22 St. East, Saskatoon, SK S7K 5T6
Tel: 306-664-9200; *Fax:* 306-664-1960
maxleankeith@sk.sympatico.ca

Saskatoon: **Louis E. Martel - *1**
811 Bayview Cres., Saskatoon, SK S7V 1B7
Tel: 306-652-6830; *Fax:* 306-652-6836
martellawoffice@sasktel.net
www.martellawoffice.ca

Saskatoon: **Mathiason, Valkenburg - *1**
Former Name: Mathiason, Valkenburg & McLeod
#705, 230 - 22nd St. East, Saskatoon, SK S7K 0E9
Tel: 306-242-1202; *Fax:* 306-244-4423
mvm@sasktel.net

Saskatoon: **McKercher LLP - *59**
374 Third Ave. South, Saskatoon, SK S7K 1M5
Tel: 306-653-2000; *Fax:* 306-653-2669
info@mckercher.ca
www.mckercher.ca

Saskatoon: **Donald R. Morgan - *1**
#810, 410 - 22nd St. East, Saskatoon, SK S7K 5T6
Tel: 306-665-2666; *Fax:* 306-652-6646
morgan@donmorgan.ca

Saskatoon: **Nussbaum & Company - *2**
#204, 2102 - 8 St. East, Saskatoon, SK S7H 0V1
Tel: 306-955-8890; *Fax:* 306-955-1293
nussbaum@sasktel.net

Saskatoon: **Piche & Company - *1**
204-611 University Dr., Saskatoon, SK S7N 3Z1
Tel: 306-955-7667; *Fax:* 306-955-7727
Toll-Free: 866-234-3444
pichelaw@sasktel.net

Saskatoon: **Plaxton Gillies Barristers & Solicitors - *2**
Former Name: Walker, Plaxton & Co
#200, 402 - 21 St. East, Saskatoon, SK S7K 0C3
Tel: 306-653-1500; *Fax:* 306-664-6659
contactus@plaxtonlaw.com

Saskatoon: **Quon Ferguson - *2**
Former Name: Quon Ferguson Owens
#704, 224 - 4th Ave. South, Saskatoon, SK S7K 5M5
Tel: 306-665-8828; *Fax:* 306-665-8835

Saskatoon: **Rask & Company - *6**
#300, 402 - 21st St. East, Saskatoon, SK S7K 0C3
Tel: 306-242-2500; *Fax:* 306-242-2538
kim@rasklaw.com
www.rasklaw.com

Saskatoon: **Robertson Stromberg Pedersen LLP - *21**
Former Name: Robertson Stromberg
#600, Canada Building, 105 - 21st St. East, Saskatoon, SK S7K 0B3
Tel: 306-652-7575; *Fax:* 306-652-2445
Toll-Free: 800-667-0070
www.thinkrsplaw.com

Saskatoon: **Roe & Company - *6**
Former Name: Roe & Olson
#313, 220 - 3 Ave. South, Saskatoon, SK S7K 1M1
Tel: 306-244-9865; *Fax:* 306-934-6827
smurray@sasktel.net
http://www.roeandcompany.ca/

Saskatoon: **Rozdilsky, Baniak - *2**
#301, 220 - 3rd Ave. South, Saskatoon, SK S7K 1M1
Tel: 306-477-5408; *Fax:* 306-664-9992

Saskatoon: **Scharfstein Gibbings Walen & Fisher LLP - *12**
#500, Scotiabank Bldg., 111 - 2 Ave. South, Saskatoon, SK S7K 1K6
Tel: 306-653-2838; *Fax:* 306-652-4747
lawyers@scharfsteinlaw.com
www.scharfsteinlaw.com

Saskatoon: **Scott & Fehr Law Office - *4**
Former Name: Scott, Ludlow, Fehr
211 - 33rd St. West, Saskatoon, SK S7L 0V2
Tel: 306-955-6822; *Fax:* 306-955-6823
office@scottfehr.com

Saskatoon: **Sonnenschein Law Office - *1**
Lincoln's Inn, 313 - 20th St. East, Saskatoon, SK S7K 0A9
Tel: 306-652-4730; *Fax:* 306-653-5760
sonnenschein@sasktel.net

Saskatoon: **Stevenson Hood Thornton Beaubier LLP - *14**
#500, 123 - 2nd Ave. South, Saskatoon, SK S7K 7E6
Tel: 306-244-0132; *Fax:* 306-653-1118
info@shtb-law.com
www.shtb-law.com

Saskatoon: **Stooshinoff Law Office - *2**
#300, 416 - 21st St. East, Saskatoon, SK S7K 0C2
Tel: 306-653-9000; *Fax:* 306-653-5284
stooshinoff.law@sasktel.net

Saskatoon: **Wallace Meschishnick Clackson Zawada - *16**
#901, 119 - 4th Ave. South, Saskatoon, SK S7K 5X2
Tel: 306-933-0004; *Fax:* 306-933-2006
info@wmcz.com
www.wmcz.com

Saskatoon: **Steven J. Wilson - *1**
2120 York Ave., Saskatoon, SK S7J 1H8
Tel: 306-956-3345; *Fax:* 306-955-1699

** indicates number of lawyers*

***Shaunavon*: Coralie O. Geving - *1**
Also Known As: Geving Law Office
23 - 3 Ave. East, Shaunavon, SK S0N 2M0
Tel: 306-297-2205; *Fax:* 306-297-2411

***Swift Current*: Anderson & Company - *6**
P.O. Box 610, 51 - 1st Ave. NW, Swift Current, SK S9H 3W4
Tel: 306-773-2891; *Fax:* 306-778-3364
anderson.company@sasktel.net

***Swift Current*: Holland Law Office - *1**
P.O. Box 97, 262 - 2 Ave. NE, Swift Current, SK S9H 3V5
Tel: 306-773-0661; *Fax:* 306-773-9630

***Swift Current*: MacBean Tessem - *6**
Box 550, P.O. Box 550, 151 First Ave. NE, Swift Current, SK S9H 2B1
Tel: 306-773-9343; *Fax:* 306-778-3828
macbeantessem@macbeantessem.com
www.macbeantessem.com

***Swift Current*: McLaughlin, Forrester, Heinrichs - *3**
#9, P.O. Box 100, 244 - 1 Ave. NE, Swift Current, SK S9H 2B4
Tel: 306-773-7205; *Fax:* 306-773-9715
mfh.law@sasktel.net

***Turtleford*: D.S. Wooff - *1**
P.O. Box 99, Turtleford, SK S0M 2Y0
Tel: 306-845-2599

***Unity*: Hepting Neil & Jeanson - *3**
P.O. Box 600, 206 - 2nd Ave. West, Unity, SK S0K 4L0
Tel: 306-228-2631; *Fax:* 306-228-4449
hepting.neil@sasktel.net

***Wadena*: Marquette Law Firm - *1**
Former Name: Zawislak Marquette Law Firm
P.O. Box 699, 234 Main St. North, Wadena, SK S0A 4J0
Tel: 306-338-2554; *Fax:* 306-338-3131

***Weyburn*: NSWB Law Firm - *7**
P.O. Box 8, 319 Souris Ave. NE, Weyburn, SK S4H 2J8
Tel: 306-842-4654; *Fax:* 306-842-0522
law@nswb.com
www.nswb.com

***Wynyard*: Klebeck Law Office - *1**
P.O. Box 1120, 115 Ave. B East, Wynyard, SK S0A 4T0
Tel: 306-554-2523; *Fax:* 306-554-2099
klebeck.law.office@sasktel.net

***Wynyard*: Paulson & Ferraton - *1**
P.O. Box 460, 106 Main St., Wynyard, SK S0A 4T0
Tel: 306-554-2134; *Fax:* 306-554-2342
paulson.ferraton@sasktel.net

***Yorkton*: Stanatinos, Leland & Campbell LLP - *9**
P.O. Box 188, 36 - 4 Ave. North, Yorkton, SK S3N 2V7
Tel: 306-783-8541; *Fax:* 306-786-7484

***Yorkton*: Tourney, Dellow - *2**
#2, 16 - 3rd Ave. North, Yorkton, SK S3N 1B9
Tel: 306-782-2211; *Fax:* 306-782-2213
tourneydellow@sasktel.net

Yukon Territory

***Whitehorse*: Austring, Fendrick, Fairman & Parkkari - *8**
The Drury Bldg., 3081 - 3rd Ave., Whitehorse, YT Y1A 4Z7
Tel: 867-668-4405; *Fax:* 867-668-3710
Toll-Free: 800-661-0533
info@lawyukon.com
www.lawyukon.com

***Whitehorse*: Lackowicz & Hoffman - *6**
Former Name: Preston Lackowicz & Shier
#300, 204 Black St., Whitehorse, YT Y1A 2M9
Tel: 867-668-5252; *Fax:* 867-668-5251
lackowicz.shier@yukonlaw.com

***Whitehorse*: Macdonald & Company - *3**
#200, 204 Lambert St., Whitehorse, YT Y1A 3T2
Tel: 867-667-7885; *Fax:* 867-667-7600
gmacdonald@anton.yk.ca

** indicates number of lawyers*

SECTION 12
LIBRARIES

Library listings are arranged by province. Each province includes the following categories:

Regional Systems

Public Libraries

Archives

Library & Archives Canada / Bibliothèque et Archives Canada

395 Wellington St., Ottawa ON K1A 0N4
613-996-5115; Fax: 613-995-6274
Toll-Free 866-578-7777; TTY 613-992-6969
www.bac-lac.gc.ca
Librarian & Archivist of Canada, Daniel J. Caron
danielj.caron@bac-lac.gc.ca
Social Media: www.facebook.com/LibraryArchives; twitter.com/@LibraryArchives;www.youtube.com/user/LibraryArchiveCanada

Canadian Book Exchange Centre (CBEC): 613-952-8902; Fax: 613-954-9891; cbeccccel@bac-lac.gc.ca; www.collectionscanada.gc.ca/cbec-ccel/index-e.html; Symbol: OONL

Canadian Cataloguing in Publications Program (CIP): 819-994-6881; Fax: 819-997-7517; cip@lacbac.gc.ca; www.collectionscanada.ca/cip; Symbol: OONL; Manager, Monograph Cataloguing Section, Christine Alexander, christine.alexander@bac-lac.gc.ca

International Standard Numbers: 819-994-6872; Fax: 819-997-7517; isbn@lac-bac.gc.ca; www.collectionscanada.gc.ca/isn; Symbol: OONL; Maryse Plouffe, ISBN Supervisor, maryse.plouffe@bac-lac.gc.ca

Database Networks (Union Catalogue): 819-997-7990; Fax: 819-994-4388; union.catalogue@bac-lac.gc.ca; www.collectionscanada.gc.ca/union-catalogue/index-e.html; Symbol: OONL; OOA-Chief, Emilie Lowenberg

Jacob M. Lowy Collection: 613-995-7960; Fax: 613-943-1112; lowy@lac-bac.gc.ca; www.collectionscanada.gc.ca/lowy-collection/index-e.html; Symbol: OONL; Chief, Literary Arts: Monique Dupré, monique.dupre@bac-lac.gc.ca

Legal Deposit: 819-997-9565; Fax: 819-953-8508; legal.deposit@lac-bac.gc.ca; www.collectionscanada.ca/legal-deposit; Symbol: OONL; Manager, Diane Lanthier, diane.lanthier@bac-lac.gc.ca

Reference & Genealogy Division: 613-996-5115; Fax:613-995-6274; reference@lac-bac.gc.ca; www.collectionscanada.gc.ca/isn/041011-1000-e.html; www.collectionscanada.gc.ca/022; Symbol: OONL; OOA-Director, Antonio Lechasseur

Government Departments in Charge of Libraries

ALBERTA: Municipal Affairs, Public Library Services Branch, #803, Standard Life Centre, 10405 Jasper Ave., Edmonton, AB T5J 4R7, 780-427-4871; Fax: 780-415-8594, libraries@gov.ab.ca, www.municipalaffairs.alberta.ca/mc_libraries.cfm

BRITISH COLUMBIA: Ministry of Education, Public Library Services Branch, 620 Superior St., 2nd Fl., Victoria, BC V8V 2L7, 250-356-1791; Fax: 250-953-3225; Toll Free: 800-663-7051, llb@gov.bc.ca, www.bced.gov.bc.ca/pls; twitter.com/MyBCLibrary; Director of Library Services, Jacqueline van Dyck

MANITOBA: Culture, Heritage & Tourism Public Library Services Branch, #300, 1011 Rosser Ave., Brandon, MB R7A 0L5, 204-726-6590, Fax: 204-726-6868, pls@gov.mb.ca, www.gov.mb.ca/chc/pls/index - Director, Trevor Surgenor

NEW BRUNSWICK: New Brunswick Public Library Service, Place 2000, Provincial Office, 250 King St., Fredericton, NB E3B 9M9, 506-453-2354, Fax: 506-444-4064, dpetlinfo@gnb.ca, www.gnb.ca/003/index-e; Executive Director, Sylvie Nadeau

NEWFOUNDLAND & LABRADOR: Provincial Information & Library Resources Board, 48 St. George's Ave., Stephenville NL A2N 1K9, 709/643-0900, Fax: 709/643-0925, Email: shawntetford@nlpubliclibraries.ca, URL: www.nlpubliclibraries.ca - Executive Director, Shawn Tetford

NORTHWEST TERRITORIES: Northwest Territories Public Library Services, 75 Woodland Dr., Hay River NT X0E 1G1, 867-874-6531, Fax: 867-874-3321, Toll Free: 866-297-0232, www.nwtpls.gov.nt.ca -Territorial Librarian, Alison Hopkins, alison_hopkins@gov.nt.ca

NOVA SCOTIA: Nova Scotia Provincial Library, 770 Kempt Rd., Halifax NS B3K 4X8, 902/ 424-2457, Fax: 902/424-0633, Email: admin@nshpl.library.ns.ca, URL: www.library.ns.ca - Provincial Librarian, Jennifer Evans

NUNAVUT: Nunavut Public Library Services, PO Box 270, Baker Lake NU X0C 0A0, 867-793-3327, Fax: 867-793-3360, www.publiclibraries.nu.ca; Manager, Library Services, Ron Knowling

ONTARIO: Ministry of Tourism, Culture & Sport, Public Libraries Branch, #1700, 401 Bay Street, Toronto, ON M7A 0A7, 416-314-7627: Fax: 416-314-7635, www.mtc.gov.on.ca/en/libraries; Contact: Rod Sawyer, rod.sawyer@ontario.ca

PRINCE EDWARD ISLAND: Provincial Library Service, 89 Redhead Rd., PO Box 7500, Morell PE C0A 1S0, 902-961-7320, Fax: 902-961-7322, plshq@gov. pe.ca, www.library.pe.ca; twitter.com/PEILibrary; www.facebook.com/PEILibrary; Provincial Librarian, Kathleen Eaton, keeaton@gov.pe.ca

QUÉBEC: Ministère de la culture, des communications et de la condition féminine, Bibliothèque ministérielle - Direction de la coordination et du soutien à la gestion des programmes, Édifice Guy-Frégault, 225, Grande Allée est, Bloc C, RC, Québec QC G1R 5G5, 418-380-2325, Téle: 418-380-2326, www.mcc.gouv.qc.ca - Responsable: Jonathan Gailloux

SASKATCHEWAN: Provincial Library, 409A Park St., Regina, SK S4N 5B2, 306-787-2976, www.lib.sk.ca

YUKON: Public Library Services, Government of Yukon, Community Libraries, PO Box 2703, Whitehorse YT Y1A 2C6, 867-667-5239, Fax: 867-393-6333, Toll Free (in Yukon): 800-661-0408, whitehorse.library@gov.yk.ca, www.ypl.gov.yk.ca

Alberta

Regional Systems

Chinook Arch Regional Library System

2902 - 7th Ave. North, Lethbridge, AB T1H 5C6
Tel: 403-380-1500; *Fax:* 403-380-3550
Toll-Free: 888-458-1500
Other Numbers: ILL Desk: 403-942-8027; Toll-Free: 1-866-941-9262
arch@chinookarch.ab.ca
www.chinookarch.ab.ca
Social Media: twitter.com/chinooklibs; www.facebook.com/149361021750600

Maggie Macdonald, CEO
mmacdonald@chinookarch.ca
Robin Thiessen Hepher, Assistant Director
rthiessenhepher@chinookarch.ca
Terra Plato, Manager, Consulting Services
tplato@chinookarch.ca
Trevor Haugen, IT Team Leader
thaugen@chinookarch.ca

Marigold Library System

710 - 2nd St., Strathmore, AB T1P 1K4
Tel: 403-934-5334; *Fax:* 403-934-5331
Toll-Free: 855-934-5334
admin@marigold.ab.ca
www.marigold.ab.ca
Social Media: www.facebook.com/pages/Marigold-Library-System/143656909025785

Michelle Toombs, Director
michelle@marigold.ab.ca
Laura Taylor, Assistant Director
ltaylor@marigold.ab.ca
Margaret Newton, Manager, Bibliographic Services
margaret@marigold.ab.ca
Lynne Thorimbert, Manager, Service Delivery
lynne@marigold.ab.ca
Sandy Watson, Head, Acquisitions
sandy@marigold.ab.ca
Richard Kenig, Specialist, Information Technology & Network
compnet@marigold.ab.ca
Carlee Pilikowski, Communications Officer
carlee@marigold.ab.ca

Northern Lights Library System

5615 - 48 St., Elk Point, AB T0A 1A0
Tel: 780-724-2596; *Fax:* 780-724-2597
Toll-Free: 800-561-0387
info@nlls.ab.ca
www.nlls.ab.ca

Mircea Panciuk, Director
director@nlls.ab.ca
780-724-2596 ext. 236

Parkland Regional Library System

5404 - 56th Ave., Lacombe, AB T4L 1G1
Tel: 403-782-3850; *Fax:* 403-782-4650
Toll-Free: 800-567-9024
Other Numbers: Toll Free Fax: 800.555.5246
www.prl.ab.ca
Social Media: twitter.com/PrlLibrary; www.facebook.com/prl.library

Ronald Sheppard, Director
rsheppard@prl.ab.ca
Donna Williams, Assistant Director, Operations
dwilliams@prl.ab.ca
Marquita Bevans, Manager, Technical Services & Systems Librarian
mbevans@prl.ab.ca
Lauralee Gilmour, Manager, Interlibrary Loan Services
ill@prl.ab.ca
Susan Grieshaber-Otto, Manager, Consulting Services
sgrieshaberotto@prl.ab.ca
Tim Spark, Network Administrator
tspark@prl.ab.ca
Wayne Wedman, Cataloguer
wwedman@prl.ab.ca
Wendy Crews, Contact, Acquisitions
wcrews@prl.ab.ca
Doris Green, Contact, Direct Services, Audiobooks, Large Print, World Languages
direct.services@prl.ab.ca

Peace Library System

8301 - 110 St., Grande Prairie, AB T8W 6T2
Tel: 780-538-4656; *Fax:* 780-539-5285
Toll-Free: 800-422-6875
peacelib@peacelibrarysystem.ab.ca
www.peacelibrarysystem.ab.ca

Linda Duplessis, Director
ldupless@peacelibrarysystem.ab.ca
Carol Downing, Technical Services Manager
cdowning@peacelibrarysystem.ab.ca
780-538-4656
Padmini Ramaswamy, Network Administrator
pramaswa@peacelibrarysystem.ab.ca

Shortgrass Library System

2375 - 10th Ave. SW, Medicine Hat, AB T1A 8G2
Tel: 403-529-0550; *Fax:* 403-528-2473
director@shortgrass.ca
www.shortgrass.ca

Petra Mauerhoff, CEO & Director
petra@shortgrass.ca
Robert Batchelder, Assistant Director, Technical Services
bob@shortgrass.ca
Peggy Curthoys, Acquisitions Officer
peggy@shortgrass.ca

Yellowhead Regional Library

433 King St., Spruce Grove, AB T7X 2Y1
Tel: 780-962-2003; *Fax:* 780-962-2770
Toll-Free: 877-962-2003
yrlquery@yrl.ab.ca
www.yrl.ab.ca
Social Media: twitter.com/YRLnow

Kevin Dodds, Director
kdodds@yrl.ab.ca
780-982-2003 ext. 226
Wendy Sears Ilnicki, Assistant Director
wsears@yrl.ab.ca
780-962-2003 ext. 225

Public Libraries

Acadia Valley: Acadia Municipal Library

Warren Peers School, PO Box 6, Acadia Valley, AB T0J 0A0
Tel: 403-972-3744; *Fax:* 403-972-2000
aavalibrary@marigold.ab.ca
www.marigold.ab.ca/about/memberlibs/acadia.html

Maxine Booker, Chair
Brandi Peacock, Manager
Debbie Neilson, Library Assistant

Acme: Acme Municipal Library

610 Walsh Ave., Acme, AB T0M 0A0
Tel: 403-546-3879; *Fax:* 403-546-2248
aamlibrary@marigold.ab.ca
www.marigold.ab.ca/about/memberlibs/acme

Colleen Herrara, Library Manager
aamlibrary@marigold.ab.ca

Airdrie: **Airdrie Public Library**
#111, 304 Main St. South, Airdrie, AB T4B 3C3
Tel: 403-948-0600; *Fax:* 403-912-4002
info@airdriepubliclibrary.ca
www.airdriepubliclibrary.ca
Janine Jevne, Director
janine.jevne@airdriepubliclibrary.ca

Alberta Beach: **Alberta Beach Public Library**
4811 - 50th Ave., Alberta Beach, AB T0E 0A0
Tel: 780-924-3491; *Fax:* 780-924-3491
www.albertabeachlibrary.ca
Sylvia McGinley, Chair
Joanne Hilger, Secretary
Deb Hawkins-Stewart, Treasurer

Alder Flats: **Alder Flats Public Library**
Hwy. 13, Alder Flats, AB T0C 0A0
Tel: 780-388-3881; *Fax:* 780-388-3887
Other Numbers: 780-514-7639 (Off Hours); 780-388-0049 (Summer)
afpl@wrps.ab.ca
www.alderflatslibrary.ab.ca
Judy Miners, Library Director
780-388-3881

Alix: **Alix Public Library**
4928 - 50th St., Alix, AB T0C 0B0
Tel: 403-747-3233
alixpublic@libs.prl.ab.ca
alixpublic.prl.ab.ca
Beth Richardson, Librarian

Alliance: **Alliance Community Library**
101 - 1st Ave. East, Alliance, AB T0B 0A0
Tel: 780-879-3733
alliancelibrary@libs.prl.ab.ca
alliance.prl.ab.ca/index.htm
Tracy Rombough, Libary Manager
aplen7@telusplanet.net

Amisk: **Amisk Municipal Library**
5005 - 50 St., Amisk, AB T0B 0B0
Tel: 780-628-5457
amiskpubliclibrary@libs.prl.ab.ca
amisklibrary.prl.ab.ca
Carmen Toma, Library Manager

Andrew: **Andrew Municipal Public Library**
5021 - 50 St., Andrew, AB T0B 0C0
Tel: 780-365-3501; *Fax:* 780-365-3734
public@mcsnet.ca
www.andrewschool.ca
Hazel Anaka, Contact
hazel.anaka2@gmail.com
780-365-2434

Arrowwood: **Arrowwood Municipal Library**
22 Main St., Arrowwood, AB T0L 0B0
Tel: 403-534-3932; *Fax:* 403-534-3932
Toll-Free: 866-941-4177
help@arrowwoodlibrary.ca
www.arrowwoodlibrary.ca/client/arrowwood
Dorothy Way, Library Manager

Ashmont: **Ashmont Community Library**
Ashmont School, Main St., Ashmont, AB T0A 0C0
Tel: 780-726-3877; *Fax:* 780-726-3777
www.ashmontlibrary.ab.ca
Karen Duperron, Librarian

Athabasca: **Alice B. Donahue Library & Archives**
4716 - 48th St., Athabasca, AB T9S 2B6
Tel: 780-675-2735
www.athabascalibrary.ab.ca
Cynthia Graefe, Library Manager & Resource Sharing Contact
librarian@athabascalibrary.ab.ca

Banff: **Banff Public Library**
101 Bear St., Banff, AB T1L 1H3
Tel: 403-762-2661; *Fax:* 403-762-3805
banff_library@telusplanet.net
www.banfflibrary.ab.ca
Holly Nguyen, Librarian
Susanne Repstock, Assistant Librarian

Barnwell: **Barnwell Municipal Library**
490 Cottonwood St., Barnwell, AB T0K 0B0
Tel: 403-223-3626; *Toll-Free:* 866-941-4177
libbar@barnwelllibrary.ca
www.barnwelllibrary.ca/client/barnwell
Cindy Evanson, Library Manager
cevanson@barnwelllibrary.ca
403-223-3626

Barrhead: **Barrhead Public Library**
5103 - 53 Ave., Barrhead, AB T7N 1N9
Tel: 780-674-8519; *Fax:* 780-674-8520
plibrary@barrheadpubliclibrary.ca
www.barrheadpubliclibrary.ca
Elaine Dickie, Library Director

Bashaw: **Bashaw Municipal Library**
5112 - 52nd St., Bashaw, AB T0B 0H0
Tel: 780-372-4055; *Fax:* 780-372-4055
bashawlibrary@libs.prl.ab.ca
bashawlibrary.prl.ab.ca/
Cindy Hunter, Library Manager
780-372-4055

Bassano: **Bassano Memorial Library**
522 - 2nd Ave., Bassano, AB T0J 0B0
Tel: 403-641-4065; *Fax:* 403-641-4065
bmlcapic@eidnet.org
www.shortgrass.ca/bml

Bawlf: **David Knipe Memorial Library**
203 Hanson St., Bawlf, AB T0B 0J0
Tel: 780-373-3882
bawlflibrary.prl.ab.ca
Fern Reinke, Library Manager

Bear Canyon: **Bear Point Community Library**
PO Box 43, Bear Canyon, AB T0H 0B0
Tel: 780-595-3771; *Fax:* 780-595-3762
librarian@bearpointlibrary.ab.ca
www.bearpointlibrary.ab.ca
Tannis Bigam, Librarian

Beaumont: **Bibliothèque de Beaumont Library**
5700 - 49th St., Beaumont, AB T4X 1S7
Tel: 780-929-2665; *Fax:* 780-929-1291
www.beaumontlibrary.com
Martin Walters, Library Manager
martin@beaumontlibrary.com
Andrea Ciochetti, Program Coordinator
andrea@beaumontlibray.com

Beaverlodge: **Beaverlodge RCMP Centennial Library**
406 - 10th St., Beaverlodge, AB T0H 0C0
Tel: 780-354-2569; *Fax:* 780-354-3078
abarlibrary@telusplanet.net
www.beaverlodgelibrary.ab.ca
Shelly Longson, Library Manager

Beiseker: **Beiseker Municipal Library**
Old Railway Station, 601 - 1st Ave., Beiseker, AB T0M 0G0
Tel: 403-947-3230; *Fax:* 403-947-2146
abemlibrary@marigold.ab.ca
www.beisekerlibrary.ab.ca
Tracy Bell, Library Manager

Bentley: **Bentley Municipal Library**
5014 - 49 Ave., Bentley, AB T0C 0J0
Tel: 403-748-4626; *Fax:* 403-748-4627
bentleylibrary@libs.prl.ab.ca
bentleylibrary.prl.ab.ca
Tina Whitfield, Library Manager

Berwyn: **Berwyn W.I. Municipal Library**
5105 - 51st St., Berwyn, AB T0H 0E0
Tel: 780-338-3616; *Fax:* 780-338-3616
www.berwynlibrary.ab.ca
Kim Byard, Library Manager

Big Valley: **Big Valley Municipal Library**
29 - 1st Ave. South, Big Valley, AB T0J 0G0
Tel: 403-876-2642; *Fax:* 403-876-2401
bigvalleylibrary@prl.ab.ca
bvlibrary.prl.ab.ca
Janice E. Hermus, Librarian

Black Diamond: **Sheep River Community Library**
301 Center Ave., Black Diamond, AB T0L 0H0
Tel: 403-933-3278; *Fax:* 403-933-3278
abdsrclibrary@marigold.ab.ca
Muhammad Zia-Ul-Haque, Librarian
Eleanor Chinnick, Senior Librarian
Nadine Russell, Library Clerk

Blackfalds: **Blackfalds Public Library**
5018 Waghorn St., Blackfalds, AB T0M 0J0
Tel: 403-885-2343; *Fax:* 403-885-4353
Other Numbers: 403-885-6251 program room
library@blackfaldslibrary.com
www.blackfaldslibrary.com
Carley Binder, Librarian

Blairmore: **Crowsnest Pass Municipal Library - Blairmore**
2114 - 127 St., Blairmore, AB T0K 0E0
Tel: 403-562-8393; *Fax:* 403-562-8397
libbla@chinookarch.ab.ca
Judy Bradley, Librarian

Blue Ridge: **Blue Ridge Community Library**
24A Main St., Blue Ridge, AB T0E 0B0
Tel: 780-648-7323; *Fax:* 780-648-2348
www.yrl.ab.ca/about/lib/abrc.html
Mary Anne Lehman, Chair
Susan Curtis, Librarian
sucurtis@telusplanet.net

Bodo: **Bodo Public Library**
PO Box 93, Bodo, AB T0B 0M0
Tel: 780-753-6079; *Fax:* 780-753-8195
bodolibrary@libs.prl.ab.ca
www.prl.ab.ca/ABOD
Roxanna Wotschell, Library Manager

Bon Accord: **Bon Accord Public Library**
PO Box 749, Bon Accord, AB T0A 0K0
Tel: 780-921-2540; *Fax:* 780-921-2580
www.bonaccordlibrary.ab.ca
Dyvonna Inkster, Chair
Gayle Boyd, Library Manager
Joyce Curtis-Bonardi, Contact, Interlibrary Loans
Anita van der Leek, Contact, Programs

Bonanza: **Bonanza Municipal Library**
PO Box 53, Bonanza, AB T0H 0K0
Tel: 780-353-3067
librarian@bonanzalibrary.ca
www.bonanzalibrary.ca
Cindy Clarke, Chair

Bonnyville: **Bonnyville Municipal Library**
4804 - 49th Ave., Bonnyville, AB T9N 2J3
Tel: 780-826-3071; *Fax:* 780-826-2058
librarian@bonnyvillelibrary.ab.ca
www.bonnyvillelibrary.ab.ca
Ina Smith, Library Director
Linda Smiley, Assistant Library Manager
Kim Dechaine, Programmer
Brigitte Stewart, Contact, Public Services & Interlibrary Loan

Bow Island: **Bow Island Municipal Library**
510 Centre St., Bow Island, AB T0K 0G0
Tel: 403-545-2828; *Fax:* 403-545-6642
bowlib@shortgrass.ca
www.shortgrass.ca/bowisland/
Susan Andersen, Library Manager

Bowden: **Bowden Public Library**
1700 - 23rd St., Bowden, AB T0M 0K0
Tel: 403-224-3688; *Fax:* 403-224-2244
bowdenlibrary@libs.prl.ab.ca
bowdenlibrary.prl.ab.ca
Social Media: www.facebook.com/123488397714713
Verlie Weiss, President
Julie Brown, Library Manager

Boyle: **Boyle Public Library**
5002 - 3 St., Boyle, AB T0A 0M0
Tel: 780-689-4161; *Fax:* 780-689-5660
librarian@boylepublib.ab.ca
www.boylepublib.ab.ca
Katherine Bulmer, Library Manager

Breton: **Breton Public Library**
4916 - 50th Ave., Breton, AB T0C 0P0
Tel: 780-696-3740; *Fax:* 780-696-3590
bretonlibrary@yrl.ab.ca
www.bretonlibrary.ab.ca
Diane Shave, Library Director

Brocket: **Oldman River Cultural Centre Library**
PO Box 70, Brocket, AB T0K 0H0
Tel: 403-965-3939; *Fax:* 403-965-2289
Reg Crow Shoe, Director

Brooks: **Berry Creek Community School Library**
RR#2, Brooks, AB T1R 1E2
Tel: 403-566-3743; *Fax:* 403-566-3736
acclibrary@marigold.ab.ca
www.marigold.ab.ca/about/memberlibs/berrycreek
Susan Conners, Library Manager

***Brooks:* Brooks Public Library**
420 - 1st Ave. West, Brooks, AB T1R 1B9
Tel: 403-362-2947; *Fax:* 403-362-8111
brolib@shortgrass.ca
www.shortgrass.ca/bpl
Social Media: www.youtube.com/user/BrooksPublicLibrary; twitter.com/brookslibrary; www.facebook.com/BrooksPublicLibrary
Shannon Vossepoel, Head Librarian

***Brownfield:* Brownfield Community Library**
PO Box 63, Brownfield, AB T0C 0R0
Tel: 403-578-2247; *Fax:* 403-578-4208
brownfieldlibrary@libs.prl.ab.ca
brownfieldlibrary.prl.ab.ca
Darvy Gilbertson, Librarian

***Brownvale:* Brownvale Community Library**
PO Box 407, Brownvale, AB T0H 0L0
Tel: 780-597-2250

***Bruderheim:* Metro Kalyn Community Library**
5017 - 49th St., Bruderheim, AB T0B 0S0
Tel: 780-796-3032; *Fax:* 780-796-3032
librarian@bruderheimpl.ab.ca
www.bruderheimpl.ab.ca
Diana Mack, Community Librarian

***Cadogan:* Cadogan Public Library**
PO Box 10., Cadogan, AB T0B 0T0
Tel: 780-753-6933
cadoganlibrary.prl.ab.ca
Rochelle Scammell, Library Manager

***Calgary:* Calgary Public Library**
616 MacLeod Trail SE, Calgary, AB T2G 2M2
Tel: 403-260-2600
dear.library@calgarypubliclibrary.com
calgarypubliclibrary.com
Social Media: pinterest.com/calgarylibrary; twitter.com/calgarylibrary; www.facebook.com/pages/Calgary-Public-Library/49297786525
Gerry Meek, CEO
Ellen Humphrey, Assistant Director, Customer Services
Paul Lane, Assistant Director, Strategic Services
Scott Stanley, Senior Manager, Information Technology
Anne Sawa, Senior Manager, Support Services
Grant Kaiser, Senior Manager, Marketing & Development
Joye Hardman, Manager, Technical Services, Collections & Electronic Resources
Cathy Freer-Leszczynski, Manager, Community Services
Gerry Burger-Martindale, Customer Service Manager, Central Library
Evette Berry, Customer Service Manager, Circulation

***Calmar:* Calmar Public Library**
4705 - 50th Ave., Calmar, AB T0C 0V0
Tel: 780-985-3472; *Fax:* 780-985-2859
calmarlibrary@yrl.ab.ca
www.calmarpubliclibrary.ca
Carol Nystrom, Library Director
Susannah Kotyk, Library Assistant

***Camrose:* Camrose Public Library**
4710 - 50th Ave., Camrose, AB T4V 0R8
Tel: 780-672-4214; *Fax:* 780-672-9165
deb@libs.prl.ab.ca
cpl.prl.ab.ca
Social Media: twitter.com/CamroseLibrary1; www.facebook.com/CamroseLibrary
Anjah Howard, Chair

***Canmore:* Canmore Public Library**
950 - 8 Ave., Canmore, AB T1W 2T1
Tel: 403-678-2468; *Fax:* 403-678-2165
info@canmorelibrary.ab.ca
www.canmorelibrary.ab.ca
Don Pickard, Chair

***Carbon:* Carbon Municipal Library**
Community Centre, PO Box 70, Carbon, AB T0M 0L0
Tel: 403-572-3440
acarmlibrary@marigold.ab.ca
Faye Hecktor, Chair
Jay-Lynn Boutin, Library Manager

***Cardston:* Jim & Mary Kearl Library of Cardston**
25 - 3rd Ave. West, Cardston, AB T0K 0K0
Tel: 403-653-4775; *Fax:* 403-653-4716
help@cardstonlibrary.ca
Social Media: twitter.com/Chinooklibs
Donna Beazer, Library Manager
403-653-4707
Michele Snyder, Children's Programming Specialist

***Carmangay:* Carmangay & District Municipal Library**
414 Grand Ave., Carmangay, AB T0L 0N0
Tel: 403-643-3777; *Fax:* 403-643-3777
help@carmangaylibrary.ca
www.carmangaylibrary.ca/client/carmangay
Marian Schibbelhute, Library Manager

***Caroline:* Caroline Municipal Library**
5023 - 50 Ave., Caroline, AB T0M 0M0
Tel: 403-722-4060; *Fax:* 403-722-4070
carolinelibrary.prl.ab.ca
Norman Rose, Chair
Rita Collins, Library Co-Manager
Allison Hewitt, Library Co-Manager

***Carstairs:* Carstairs Public Library**
1402 Scarlett Ranch Rd., Carstairs, AB T0M 0N0
Tel: 403-337-3943; *Fax:* 403-337-3943
carstairs@libs.prl.ab.ca
www.carstairspublic.prl.ab.ca
Anne Strilchuk, Librarian
Joanne Merrick, Assistant

***Castor:* Castor Public Library**
5103 - 51 St., Castor, AB T0C 0X0
Tel: 403-882-3999
castorlibrary@libs.prl.ab.ca
castorlibrary.prl.ab.ca
Wendy Bozek, Library Manager

***Cereal:* Cereal & District Municipal Library**
415 Main St., Cereal, AB T0J 0N0
Tel: 403-326-3883
acermlibrary@marigold.ab.ca
Denise Reider, Library Manager

***Champion:* Champion Municipal Library**
2 Ave. South, Champion, AB T0L 0R0
Tel: 403-897-3099; *Fax:* 403-897-3098
help@championlibrary.ca
www.championlibrary.ca
Patty Abel, Librarian
Claudette Simons, Staff

***Chauvin:* Chauvin Municipal Library**
5200 - 4th Ave. North, Chauvin, AB T0B 0V0
Tel: 780-858-3746; *Fax:* 780-858-2392
www.chauvinmunicipallibrary.ab.ca

***Claresholm:* Claresholm Municipal Library**
211 - 49 Ave. West, Claresholm, AB T0L 0T0
Tel: 403-625-4168; *Fax:* 403-625-2939
help@claresholmlibrary.ca
www.claresholmlibrary.ca
Social Media: www.facebook.com/clarlibrary
Kathy Davies, Library Manager
Betty Hoare, Assistant Library Manager
Shelley Ford, Library Clerk & Program Coordinator
Chris Ann Anderson, Library Clerk
Brenda Fogarty, Library Clerk
Bea Kramer, Library Clerk

***Cleardale:* Menno Simons Public Library**
PO Bag 100, Cleardale, AB T0H 3Y0
Tel: 780-685-3623; *Fax:* 780-685-3665
gulas@prsd.ab.ca
Sylvia Gula, Librarian

***Clive:* Clive Public Library**
Clive Village Office, 5115 - 50 St., Clive, AB T0C 0Y0
Tel: 403-784-3131; *Fax:* 403-784-3131
clivelibrary@libs.prl.ab.ca
www.clivepublib.prl.ab.ca
Wanda Wagner, President
Sandra Ward, Librarian

***Coaldale:* Coaldale Public Library**
2014 - 18 St., Coaldale, AB T1M 1E9
Tel: 403-345-1340; *Fax:* 403-345-1342
help@coaldalelibrary.ca
www.coaldalelibrary.ca
Jane Franz, Librarian

***Cochrane:* Nan Boothby Memorial Library**
405 Railway St. West, Cochrane, AB T4C 2E2
Tel: 403-932-4353; *Fax:* 403-932-4385
nanboothby@home.com
www.cochranepubliclibrary.ca
Social Media: www.facebook.com/202620799775893

***Cold Lake:* Cold Lake Public Library**
5513B - 48 Ave., Cold Lake, AB T9M 1X9
Tel: 780-594-8828; *Fax:* 780-594-7787
www.library.coldlake.ab.ca
Social Media: twitter.com/CLPublicLibrary; www.facebook.com/groups/120871777954653
Christopher Stolfa, Chair
Mary Anne Penner, Library Director
director@library.coldlake.ab.ca

***Consort:* Consort Municipal Library**
Consort School, PO Box 456, Consort, AB T0C 1B0
Tel: 403-577-2501
aconmlibrary@marigold.ab.ca
Pat Rutledge, Chair
Marian Walsh, Library Manager

***Coronation:* Coronation Memorial Library**
5001 Royal St., PO Box 453, Coronation, AB T0C 1C0
Tel: 403-578-3445
coronationlibrary@libs.prl.ab.ca
Val Cornell, Chair
Margo McPhail, Librarian
Azusa Watson, Assistant Librarian

***Coutts:* Coutts Municipal Library**
218 - 1st Ave. South, Coutts, AB T0K 0N0
Tel: 403-344-3804; *Fax:* 403-344-3815
Sharon Wollersheim, Librarian
sharon.wollersheim@horizon.ab.ca

***Cremona:* Cremona Municipal Library**
Village of Cremona Municipal Bldg., 205 - 1 St. East, Cremona, AB T0M 0R0
Tel: 403-637-3100
cremonalibrary.prl.ab.ca
Sandra Herbert, Library Manager

***Crossfield:* Crossfield Municipal Library**
1026 Chisholm Ave., Crossfield, AB T0M 0S0
Tel: 403-946-4232; *Fax:* 403-946-4212
crossfield.library@telus.net
www.crossfieldlibrary.org
Social Media: twitter.com/CrossfieldLib; www.facebook.com/156681641025114
Lorea Anderson, Library Manager

***Czar:* Czar Municipal Library**
PO Box 127, Czar, AB T0B 0Z0
Tel: 780-857-3740; *Fax:* 780-857-2224
czarlibrary@libs.prl.ab.ca
Jackie Almberg, Library Manager

***Darwell:* Darwell Public Library**
Darwell Community Hall, #54, 225B Hwy. 765, Darwell, AB T0E 0L0
Tel: 780-892-3746; *Fax:* 780-892-3743
www.darwellpubliclibrary.ab.ca

***Daysland:* Daysland Public Library**
5130 - 50th St., Daysland, AB T0B 1A0
Tel: 780-679-7263
dayslandlibrary@libs.prl.ab.ca
dayslandlibrary.prl.ab.ca
Tara Mazur, Library Manager

***Debolt:* Debolt Public Library**
Alberta Ave., Debolt, AB T0H 1B0
Tel: 780-957-3770; *Fax:* 780-957-3770
librarian@deboltlibrary.ab.ca
www.deboltlibrary.ab.ca
Yvonne McIntyre, Library Manager

***Delburne:* Delburne Municipal Library**
2210 Main St., Delburne, AB T0M 0V0
Tel: 403-749-3848; *Fax:* 403-749-3848
delburnelibrary@libs.prl.ab.ca
delburnelibrary.prl.ab.ca/
Relda Chambers, Librarian

***Delia:* Delia Municipal Library**
Delia School, 205 - 3 Ave. North, Delia, AB T0J 0W0
Tel: 403-364-3777; *Fax:* 403-364-3805
adm.library@plrd.ab.ca
www.delialibrary.ca
Social Media: www.facebook.com/groups/228134655391
Barb Marshall, Chair
Leah Hunter, Library Manager

Devon: Devon Public Library
Devon Shopping Center, #101, 17 Athabasca Ave., Devon, AB T9G 1G5
Tel: 780-987-3720
www.devonpubliclibrary.ca
Social Media: www.facebook.com/110715152303134
Barry Fildes, Chair
Audrey Benjamin, Library Director
Linda Garez, Library Assistant
Holly Gilmour, Coordinator, Programs

Didsbury: Didsbury Municipal Library
2033 - 19 Ave., Didsbury, AB T0M 0W0
Tel: 403-335-3142; Fax: 403-335-3141
didsburylibrary@libs.prl.ab.ca
dml.prl.ab.ca
Inez Kosinski, Librarian
403-335-3142

Donalda: Donalda Municipal Library
5001 Main St., Donalda, AB T0B 1H0
Tel: 403-883-2345; Fax: 403-883-2022
donaldalibrary@libs.prl.ab.ca
donaldalibrary.prl.ab.ca
Susan Dahl, Library Manager

Drayton Valley: Drayton Valley Municipal Library
5120 - 50 St., Drayton Valley, AB T7A 1R7
Tel: 780-514-2228; Fax: 780-514-2532
www.draytonvalleylibrary.ca
Social Media: twitter.com/dvlibrary; www.facebook.com/dvlibrary
Lyndara Cowper-Smith, Chair
Nesen Naidoo, Director, Information Services & Economic Development
nnaidoo@draytonvalley.ca
Sandy Faunt, Librarian
sfaunt@draytonvalley.ca

Drumheller: Drumheller Public Library
224 Centre St., Drumheller, AB T0J 0Y0
Tel: 403-823-5382; Fax: 403-823-3651
drumlib@magtech.ca
www.drumhellerlibrary.ca
Social Media: www.facebook.com/group.php?gid=110077339080350
Linde Turner, Head Librarian
Debbie Laplante, Head, Technical Services

Duchess: Duchess Public Library
PO Box 88, Duchess, AB T0J 0Z0
Tel: 403-378-4369; Fax: 403-378-4369
manager@duchesspubliclibrary.ca
www.duchesspubliclibrary.ca
Shannon Vanderloh, Library Manager
Donna Billingsley, President

Duffield: Duffield Community Library
1 Main St., Duffield, AB T0E 0N0
Tel: 780-892-2644; Fax: 780-892-3344
duffieldlibrary@yrl.ab.ca
www.pcmlibraries.ab.ca/content/duffield-public-library
Social Media: www.facebook.com/pcmlibraries
Sandy Cornell, Chair
sacornell@uniserve.com
Kathy Conn, Library Manager
kconn@yrl.ab.ca

Duffield: Keephills Community Library
RR#1, Duffield, AB T0E 0N0
Tel: 780-731-0000; Fax: 780-731-2433
Other Numbers: 780-731-3965
www.keephillslibrary.ab.ca
Debbie Ramsay, Library Director
dramsay@psd70.ab.ca

Eaglesham: Eaglesham Public Library
PO Box 206, Eaglesham, AB T0H 1H0
Tel: 780-359-3792; Fax: 780-359-3745
www.eagleshamlibrary.ab.ca/
Norma Bolster, Contact

Eckville: Eckville Public Library
PO Box 492, Eckville, AB T0M 0X0
Tel: 403-746-3240; Fax: 403-746-2900
eckvillelibrary@libs.prl.ab.ca
www.prl.ab.ca/AECK
Carol Griner, Contact

Edberg: Edberg Public Library
48 First Ave. West, Edberg, AB T0B 1J0
Tel: 780-678-5606; Fax: 780-678-5606
www.edberglibrary.prl.ab.ca
Colleen Wack, Library Manager
Paulina Klevgaard, Library Assistant
Colin Wack, Library Assistant

Edgerton: Edgerton Public Library
5037 - 50 Ave., Box 180, Edgerton, AB T0B 1K0
Tel: 780-755-2666; Fax: 780-755-2667
www.edgertonlibrary.ab.ca
Mary Ann Sparks, Librarian
780-758-2666

Edmonton: Edmonton Public Library
7 Sir Winston Churchill Sq., Edmonton, AB T5J 2V4
Tel: 780-496-7000; Fax: 780-496-1885
Other Numbers: Customer Service: 780-496-7070
webmaster@epl.ca
www.epl.ca
Social Media: www.youtube.com/user/edmontonpl; twitter.com/EPLdotCA; www.facebook.com/EPLdotCA
Linda C. Cook, Chief Executive Officer
lcook@epl.ca
780-496-7050
Pilar Martinez, Executive Director, Public Services
pmartinez@epl.ca
780-496-5522
Joanne Griener, Executive Director, Management Services
jgriener@epl.ca
780-496-6822
Virginia Clevette, Manager, Centre for Reading & the Arts
780-496-7062
Mary Jane Bilsland, Manager, Information Services Division
780-442-6280
Kathleen Pine, Manager, Children's Division
780-496-7040

Edson: Edson Public Library
4726 - 8th Ave., Edson, AB T7E 1S8
Tel: 780-723-6691; Fax: 780-723-9728
www.edsonlibrary.ca
JoAnn Hooper, Library Manager
Gail Johnson, Chair

Elk Point: Elk Point Public Library
5123 - 50 Ave., Elk Point, AB T0A 1A0
Tel: 780-724-3737; Fax: 780-724-3739
www.elkpointlibrary.ab.ca
Daphne Schnurer, Librarian

Elnora: Elnora Public Library
210 Main St., Elnora, AB T0M 0Y0
Tel: 403-773-3966; Fax: 403-773-3922
elnoralibrary@libs.prl.ab.ca
elnoralibrary.prl.ab.ca/
Social Media: www.facebook.com/group.php?gid=62017158360
Wanda Strandquist, Library Manager
Tanis Westersund, Chair

Empress: Empress Municipal Library
PO Box 188, Empress, AB T0J 1E0
Tel: 403-565-3936; Fax: 403-565-2010
aemlibrary@marigold.ab.ca
Charl Vincent, Library Manager

Enchant: Enchant Community Library
PO Box 3000, Enchant, AB T0K 0V0
Tel: 403-739-3835; Fax: 403-739-2585
libenc@enchantlibrary.ca
www.enchantlibrary.ca/
Sharon Hagen, Librarian

Entwistle: Entwistle Municipal Library
5232 - 50th St., Entwistle, AB T0E 0S0
Tel: 780-727-3811; Fax: 780-727-2440
entwistlelibrary@yrl.ab.ca
www.pcmlibraries.ab.ca/content/entwistle-public-library

Evansburg: Evansburg & District Municipal Library
PO Box 339, Evansburg, AB T0E 0T0
Tel: 780-727-2030; Fax: 780-727-2060
www.evansburglibrary.ab.ca
Heather Nutbrown, Library Manager
Linda Mackoway, Library Director

Exshaw: Bighorn Library
2 Heart Mt. Dr., Exshaw, AB T0L 2C0
Tel: 403-673-3571; Fax: 403-673-3571
aexclibrary@marigold.ab.ca
www.bighornlibrary.ca
Social Media: twitter.com/bighornlibrary
Amanda Kelly, Chair
Rose Reid, Librarian

Fairview: Fairview Public Library
PO Box 248, Fairview, AB T0H 1L0
Tel: 780-835-2613; Fax: 780-835-2613
librarian@fairviewlibrary.ab.ca
www.fairviewlibrary.ab.ca/
Chris Burkholder, Librarian
librarian@fairviewlibrary.ab.ca
780-835-2613

Falher: Bibliothèque Dentinger/ Dentinger Library
CP 60, Falher, AB T0H 1M0
Tél: 780-837-2776; Téléc: 780-837-8755
www.peacelibrarysystem.ab.ca/Falher
Maureen Carter, Responsable

Flatbush: Flatbush Community Library
General Delivery, Flatbush, AB T0G 0Z0
Tel: 780-681-3756
librarian@flatbushlibrary.ab.ca
www.flatbushlibrary.ab.ca
Robin Lee Vance, Chair
Rose Herdman, Librarian
Deborah Kendze, Regional Librarian

Foremost: Foremost Municipal Library
103 - 1st Ave., Foremost, AB T0K 0X0
Tel: 403-867-3855
forlib@shortgrass-lib.ab.ca
www.shortgrass-lib.ab.ca/foremost/
Joanne Harty, Library Manager

Forestburg: Forestburg Municipal Library
4901 - 50th St., Forestburg, AB T0B 1N0
Tel: 780-582-4110; Fax: 780-582-4127
forestburglibrary@libs.prl.ab.ca
www.forestburg.ca/home/community_services/library
Judy Oberg, Librarian

Fort Assiniboine: Fort Assiniboine Public Library
Fort Assiniboine School, 35 State Ave., Fort Assiniboine, AB T0G 1A0
Tel: 780-584-2227; Fax: 780-674-8575
www.fortassiniboinelibrary.ab.ca
Irene Olson, Chair
Louise Davison, Library Manager
Doreen Lee, Library Clerk

Fort MacLeod: Fort MacLeod Municipal Library
PO Box 1479, Fort MacLeod, AB T0L 0Z0
Tel: 403-553-3880; Fax: 403-553-2643
Sharon Edwards, Librarian

Fort McMurray: Fort McMurray Public Library
151 MacDonald Dr., Fort McMurray, AB T9H 5C5
Tel: 780-743-7800; Fax: 780-743-5952
fmpl.ca
Social Media: twitter.com/fmpl_ab; www.facebook.com/fmpl.ca
Richard Salmons, Director
richard.salmons@fmpl.ca
780-743-7802
Mark Anthony, Manager, Technical Services
780-743-7810
Angela Gallant, Manager, Circulation Services
780-792-5137
Carolyn Murray, Marketing Manager
780-743-7807
Sara House, Manager, Adult Services
780-743-7036
Sharon Roberts, Manager, Children's Services
780-792-5136
Miranda Maguire, Contact
miranda.maguire@fmpl.ca

Fort Saskatchewan: Fort Saskatchewan Public Library
10011 - 102 St., Fort Saskatchewan, AB T8L 2C5
Tel: 780-998-4275; Fax: 780-992-3255
fsasklib@fspl.ca
www.fspl.ca
Social Media: twitter.com/FSaskLib; www.facebook.com/117991368229430
Matthew Fellows, Chair
Angela Kublik, Director
akublik@fspl.ca

Fort Vermilion: Fort Vermilion Community Library
5103 River Rd., Fort Vermilion, AB T0H 1N0
Tel: 780-927-4279; Fax: 780-927-4746
afvclibrary@platinum.ca
www.fvclibrary.com
Debbie Buckert, Library Manager

Fox Creek: Fox Creek Municipal - School Library
501 - 8 St., Fox Creek, AB T0H 1P0
Tel: 780-622-2343; Fax: 780-622-4160
foxcreeklibrary@yahoo.com
www.foxcreeklibrary.ca
Leslie Ann Sharkey, Head Librarian
Kerrianne Pasula, Librarian
Nicole Tyson, Library Technician

Galahad: Galahad Municipal Library
PO Box 25, Galahad, AB T0B 1R0
Tel: 780-583-3917; Fax: 780-583-3957
gallib@libs.prl.ab.ca
galahadpublic.prl.ab.ca/
Lori Wegenast, Librarian
Eden McDonald-Yale, Assistant

Gem: Gem Jubilee Library
PO Box 6, Gem, AB T0J 1M0
Tel: 403-641-3245

Gleichen: Gleichen & District Library Society
404 Main St., Gleichen, AB T0J 1N0
Tel: 403-734-2390; Fax: 403-734-2390
agmlibrary@marigold.ab.ca
www.marigold.ab.ca/about/memberlibs/gleichen
Amanda Gendron, President
Faydra Beard, Library Manager

Glenwood: Glenwood Municipal Library
PO Box 1156, Glenwood, AB T0K 2R0
Tel: 403-626-3660; Fax: 403-626-3660
help@glenwoodlibrary.ca
www.glenwoodlibrary.ca
Melissa Lybbert, Library Manager

Grande Cache: Grande Cache Municipal Library
10601 Shand Ave., Grande Cache, AB T0E 0Y0
Tel: 780-827-2081; Fax: 780-827-3112
www.grandecachelibrary.ab.ca
Laurel A. Kelsch, Library Director
laurkels@gyrd.ab.ca

Grande Prairie: Grande Prairie Public Library
#101, 9839 - 103 Ave., Grande Prairie, AB T8V 6M7
Tel: 780-532-3580; Fax: 780-538-4983
gplib@gppl.ab.ca
www.gppl.ab.ca
Social Media: twitter.com/GPPublicLibrary;
www.facebook.com/pages/Grande-Prairie-Public-Library/16350654747
Dawn Silver, Library Director
dsilver@gppl.ab.ca
780-357-7463
Serena Boyte-Hawryluk, Head of Children's & Youth Services
sboyte@gppl.ab.ca
780—35-7-74
Pam Chislett
pchislett@gppl.ab.ca
780-357-7474
Belinda Blackbourn, Technical Services Manager
bblackbourn@gppl.ab.ca
780-357-7460
Joan Taylor, Customer Services Manager
jtaylor@gppl.ab.ca
780-357-7452

Granum: Granum Public Library
310 Railway Ave., Granum, AB T0L 1A0
Tel: 403-687-3912; Fax: 403-687-3912
help@granumpubliclibrary.ca
www.granumpubliclibrary.ca

Grassland: Grassland Public Library
Hwy. 63, Grassland, AB T0A 1V0
Tel: 780-525-3733; Fax: 780-525-3750
librarian@grasslandlibrary.ab.ca
www.grasslandlibrary.ab.ca
Lori Zachkewich, Library Manager

Grassy Lake: Grassy Lake Public Library
PO Box 690, Grassy Lake, AB T0K 0Z0
Tel: 403-655-2232; Fax: 403-655-2259
help@grassylakelibrary.ca
www.grassylakelibrary.ca

Grimshaw: Grimshaw Municipal Library
5007 - 47 Ave., Grimshaw, AB T0H 1W0
Tel: 780-332-4553; Fax: 780-332-1250
www.grimshawlibrary.ab.ca
Linda Chmilar, Library Manager
lchmilar@grimshawlibrary.ab.ca
Vanessa Cowie, Assistant Librarian
ordering@grimshawlibrary.ab.ca

Gunn: Rich Valley Public Library
Rich Valley Community Hall, RR#1, Gunn, AB T0E 1A0
Tel: 780-967-3525
rvpublib@yrl.ab.ca
www.richvalleylibrary.ab.ca
Betti-Ann Laporte, Librarian

Hanna: Hanna Municipal Library
202 - 1st Ave. West, Hanna, AB T0J 1P0
Tel: 403-854-3865; Fax: 403-854-2772
library@hanna.ca
www.hanna.ca/library
Mary McKay, Library Director
C. Kelndorfer, ILL

Hardisty: Hardisty & District Public Library
5027 - 50 St., Hardisty, AB T0B 1V0
Tel: 780-888-3947; Fax: 780-888-3947
hardistylibrary@libs.prl.ab.ca
hardistylib.prl.ab.ca
Billi-Jo Wildeboer, Library Manager

Hay Lakes: Hay Lakes Municipal Library
106 Main St., Hay Lakes, AB T0B 1W0
Tel: 780-878-2665
haylakescontact@prl.ab.ca
haylakeslibrary.prl.ab.ca
Belinda Wegner, Library Manager
Tanya Reist, Chair

Hays: Hays Public Library
PO Box 36, Hays, AB T0K 1B0
Tel: 403-725-3744; Fax: 403-725-3744
help@hayslibrary.ca
www.hayslibrary.ca
Diane Wickenheiser, Library Manager

Heinsburg: Heinsburg Community Library
General Delivery, Heinsburg, AB T0A 1X0
Tel: 780-943-3913; Fax: 780-943-3773
heinsburglibrary@netscape.net
www.heinsburgcapsite.8k.com
Kelly Hovdestad, Library Clerk
kelly_hovdestad@sperd.ca
Rayma Isaac, Library Clerk

Heisler: Heisler Municipal Library
100 Haultain Ave., Heisler, AB T0B 2A0
Tel: 780-889-3999; Fax: 780-889-3999
heislerlibrary@libs.prl.ab.ca
www.prl.ab.ca/AHEI
Marvis Zimmer, Library Manager
Lorie Zimmer, Librarian

High Level: High Level Municipal Library
10601 - 103 St., High Level, AB T0H 1Z0
Tel: 780-926-2097; Fax: 780-926-4268
librarian@highlevellibrary.ab.ca
www.highlevellibrary.ab.ca
Jennilyn Boire, Library Director

High Prairie: High Prairie Municipal Library
4723 - 53 Ave., High Prairie, AB T0G 1E0
Tel: 780-523-3838; Fax: 780-523-3838
librarian@highprairielibrary.ab.ca
www.highprairielibrary.ab.ca
Janet Lemay, Library Manager
Angie Caughlin, Assistant Librarian (Interlibrary Loans)
Tracy Roberts, Assistant Librarian (Programming)

High River: High River Library
909 - 1st St. SW, High River, AB T1V 1A5
Tel: 403-652-2917; Fax: 403-652-7203
director@highriverlibrary.ca
www.highriverlibrary.ca
Deb Gardiner, Librarian

Hines Creek: Hines Creek Municipal Library
PO Box 750, Hines Creek, AB T0H 2A0
Tel: 780-494-3879; Fax: 780-494-3605
librarian@hinescreeklibrary.ab.ca
hinescreeklibrary.ab.ca
Sharon Nazarko, Librarian

Hinton: Hinton Municipal Library
803 Switzer Dr., Hinton, AB T7V 1V1
Tel: 780-865-2363; Fax: 780-865-4292
Other Numbers: Info Hotline: 780-865-6050
hettwild@hintonlibrary.org
www.hintonlibrary.org
Social Media:
www.facebook.com/pages/Hinton-Municipal-Library/117588374933796
Hetty Wilderdijk, Head Librarian
hettwild@hintonlibrary.org
780-865-6051

Holden: Holden Municipal Library
4912 - 50 St., Holden, AB T0B 2C0
Tel: 780-688-3838; Fax: 780-688-3838
librarian@holdenlibrary.ab.ca
www.holdenlibrary.ab.ca
Julianne Foster, Chair
Annette Chrystian, Library Clerk

Hughenden: Hughenden Public Library
7 Mackenzie Ave., Hughenden, AB T0B 2E0
Tel: 780-856-2435; Fax: 780-856-2435
hughendenlibrary.prl.ab.ca
Jennifer Johnson, Chair
Patricia Mackie, Library Manager
hughendenlibrary@libs.prl.ab.ca

Hussar: Hussar Municipal Library
102 - 2 St. NW, Hussar, AB T0J 1S0
Tel: 403-787-3788; Fax: 403-787-3922
ahumlibrary@marigold.ab.ca
www.marigold.ab.ca/about/memberlibs/hussar.html
Gay V. Harms, Library Manager

Hythe: Hythe Public Library
10013 - 100 St., Hythe, AB T0H 2C0
Tel: 780-356-3014; Fax: 780-356-2009
staff@hythelibrary.ab.ca
www.hythelibrary.ab.ca
Karen Bass, Library Manager

Innisfail: Innisfail Public Library
4949 - 49th St., Innisfail, AB T4G 1A5
Tel: 403-227-4407; Fax: 403-227-3122
innisfail@libs.prl.ab.ca
ipl.prl.ab.ca
Colleen Hayden, Librarian
chayden@libs.prl.ab.ca

Innisfree: Innisfree Public Library
Box 121, Innisfree, AB T0B 2G0
Tel: 780-724-2596
www.innisfreelibrary.ca

Irma: Irma Community Library
5012 - 51st Ave., Irma, AB T0B 2H0
Tel: 780-754-3746; Fax: 780-754-3802
www.irmalibrary.ca
Leah Larson, Library Manager
leah.larson@btps.ca

Irricana: Irricana Municipal Library
302 - 2 St., Irricana Sports Complex, Irricana, AB T0M 1B0
Tel: 403-935-4818; Fax: 403-935-4270
ailibrary@marigold.ab.ca
www.marigold.ab.ca/about/memberlibs/irricana.html
Laura Blanton, Library Manager

Keg River: Keg River Community Library
PO Box 3, Keg River, AB T0H 2G0
Tel: 780-981-2128; Fax: 780-981-2262
www.kegriverlibrary.ab.ca
Janice Freeman, Library Manager
Susan MacDougall, Library Staff
Betty Hasenack, Library Staff
Faye Van Oers Papirny, Library Staff

Killam: Killam Community Library
5017 - 49th Ave., Killam, AB T0B 2L0
Tel: 780-385-3032; Fax: 780-385-3698
www.killamlibrary.prl.ab.ca
Norm Savage, Library Manager

Kinuso: Kinuso Municipal Library
PO Box 60, Kinuso, AB T0G 1K0
Tel: 780-775-3694; Fax: 780-775-3650
kinusolibrary.ab.ca
Susan Moody, Librarian

Kitscoty: Kitscoty Hilltop Library
4910 - 51 St., Kitscoty, AB T0B 2P0
Tel: 780-846-2822; Fax: 780-846-2215
www.kitscotypubliclibrary.ab.ca/Home
Peggy Davies, Librarian

La Crete: La Crete Community Library
10001 - 99 Ave., La Crete, AB T0H 2H0
Tel: 780-928-3166; Fax: 780-928-3166
www.lacretelibrary.com
Helen Wiebe, Librarian

La Glace: La Glace Community Library
9924 - 97 Ave., La Glace, AB T0H 2J0
Tel: 780-568-4696; *Fax:* 780-568-4707
librarian@laglacelibrary.ab.ca
www.laglacelibrary.ab.ca
Evelyn Siebert, Library Head

Lac La Biche: Stuart MacPherson Library
McArthur Place, Lower Level, 10307 - 100 St., Lac La Biche, AB T0A 2C0
Tel: 780-623-7467; *Fax:* 780-623-7499
headlibrarian@stuartmacphersonlibrary.ca
Maureen Penn, Librarian

Lacombe: Mary C. Moore Public Library
#101, 5214 - 50 Ave., Lacombe, AB T4L 0B6
Tel: 403-782-3433; *Fax:* 403-782-3329
mcmpl@libs.prl.ab.ca
www.lacombelibrary.org
Social Media: www.facebook.com/MCMPL
Christina Petrisor, Head Librarian
403-782-9640

Lafond: Lafond Public Library
PO Box 20, Lafond, AB T0A 2G0
Tel: 780-645-2432; *Fax:* 780-645-2432
www.town.stpaul.ab.ca/places/Lafond-Public-Library_7216
Romona Logozar, Librarian

Lamont: Lamont Municipal Library
PO Box 180, Lamont, AB T0B 2R0
Tel: 780-895-2228; *Fax:* 780-895-2600
www.lamont.ca
Joanne Flaman, Public Librarian
Rose Konsorada, School Librarian

Leduc: Leduc Public Library
2 Alexandra Park, Leduc, AB T9E 4C4
Tel: 780-986-2637; *Fax:* 780-986-3462
www.leduclibrary.ca
Social Media: http://twitter/#!/LeducLibrary
Christine Brown, Head Librarian
cbrown@library.leduc.ab.ca
Angela Binnie, Information Services Coordinator
abinnie@library.leduc.ab.ca

Lethbridge: Lethbridge Public Library
810 - 5th Ave. South, Lethbridge, AB T1J 4C4
Tel: 403-380-7310; *Fax:* 403-329-1478
questions@lethlib.ca
www.lethlib.ca
Social Media: twitter.com/lethlib; www.facebook.com/lethlib
Donna Hunt, Board Chair
Todd Gnissios, Library Director & Chief Executive Officer

Linden: Linden Municipal Library
c/o Dr. Elliot School, Linden, AB T0M 1J0
Tel: 403-546-3757; *Fax:* 403-546-4220
almlibrary@marigold.ab.ca
www.marigold.ab.ca
Debbie Martin, Librarian
Danielle Malsbury, Assistant

Lloydminster: Lloydminster Public Library
5010 - 49th St., Lloydminster, AB T9V 0K2
Tel: 780-875-0850; *Fax:* 780-875-6523
Other Numbers: Reference Desk: 780-875-0877
info@lloydminster.info
www.lloydminster.info
Ronald Gillies, Head Librarian
hlib@lloydminster.info
Michele Duczek, Reference Librarian
mducek@lloydminster.info
780-875-0877

Lomond: Lomond Community Library
PO Box 290, Lomond, AB T0L 1G0
Tel: 403-792-3934; *Fax:* 403-792-3934
liblom@chinookarch.ab.ca
Mary McNamara, Librarian
liblom@chinookarch.ab.ca
403-792-3934

Longview: Longview Municipal Library
128 Morrison Place, Longview, AB T0L 1H0
Tel: 403-558-3927; *Fax:* 403-558-3927
alomlibrary@marigold.ab.ca
Joan Maxwell, Library Manager

Lougheed: Lougheed Public Library
5004 - 50 St., Lougheed, AB T0B 2V0
Tel: 780-386-2498
www.lougheed.prl.ab.ca
Barb McConnell, Library Manager

Magrath: Magrath Public Library
6N - 1 St. W., Magrath, AB T0K 1J0
Tel: 403-758-6498; *Fax:* 403-758-6442
www.magrathlibrary.ca
Charlotte Lester, Librarian
clester@magrathlibrary.ca

Manning: Manning Municipal Library
311 - 4th Ave. SE, Manning, AB T0H 2M0
Tel: 780-836-3054; *Fax:* 780-836-0071
librarian@manninglibrary.ab.ca
www.manninglibrary.ab.ca
Lesley Spry-Shandro, Head Librarian
780-836-3054
M.J. Lissack, Library Clerk, Genealogy
780-836-3054
Lori Jackson, Library Clerk, Programming
780-836-3054

Mannville: Mannville Municipal Library
5029, 50 St., Mannville, AB T0B 2W0
Tel: 230-663-3611; *Fax:* 780-763-3611
librarian@mannvillelibrary.ab.ca
www.mannvillelibrary.ab.ca
Theresa Myroniuk, Librarian

Marwayne: Marwayne Public Library
105 - 2nd St. South, Marwayne, AB T0B 2X0
Tel: 780-847-3930; *Fax:* 780-847-3796
librarian@marwaynelibrary.ab.ca
www.marwaynelibrary.ab.ca
Carmen Smart, Library Manager

Mayerthorpe: Mayerthorpe Public Library
4909 - 52nd St., Mayerthorpe, AB T0E 1N0
Tel: 780-786-2404; *Fax:* 780-786-4590
www.mayerthorpelibrary.ab.ca
Eleanor Mitchell, Librarian

McLennan: McLennan Municipal Library
19 - 1st Ave. NW, McLennan, AB T0H 2L0
Tel: 780-324-3767; *Fax:* 780-324-2288
librarian@mclennanlibrary.ab.ca
Carole Laboucan, Librarian

Medicine Hat: Medicine Hat Public Library
414 First St. SE, Medicine Hat, AB T1A 0A8
Tel: 403-502-8525; *Fax:* 403-502-8529
shelleyr@shortgrass.ca
Social Media: twitter.com/#!/mhpubliclibrary;
www.facebook.com/MHPublicLibrary
Shelley Ross, Chief Librarian
403-502-8528
Sheila Drummond, Head, Reference Services
403-502-8531
Carol Ann Cross-Roen, Head, Children's Services
403-502-8532
Hilary Munro, Head, Adult Services
403-502-8533
Annette ziegler, Manager, Circulation Services
403-502-8539

Milk River: Milk River Municipal Library
321 - 3rd Ave. NE, Milk River, AB T0K 1M0
Tel: 403-647-3793
mkrlib@chinookarch.ab.ca
www.chinookarch.ab.ca/chinookarch/
Lynn Bouldry, Librarian
lbouldry@milkriverlibrary.ca

Millarville: Millarville Community Library
Box 59, Millarville, AB T0L 1K0
Tel: 403-931-3919; *Fax:* 403-931-2475
amclibrary@marigold.ab.ca
Norma Dawson, Librarian

Millet: Millet Public Library
PO Box 30, Millet, AB T0C 1Z0
Tel: 780-387-5222
millet@yrl.ab.ca
www.milletlibrary.ca
Kristin Litke, Library Manager

Milo: Milo Municipal Library
116 Centre St., Milo, AB T0L 1L0
Tel: 403-599-3850; *Fax:* 403-599-3850
help@milolibrary.ca
www.milolibrary.ca
Joanne Monner, Librarian

Mirror: Mirror Public Library
5202 - 50 Ave., Mirror, AB T0B 3C0
Tel: 403-788-3044
mirrorlibrary@gmail.com

Heather Beamish, Librarian

Morrin: Morrin Municipal Library
Main St., Morrin, AB T0J 2B0
Tel: 403-772-3922; *Fax:* 403-772-3707
amomlibrary@marigold.ab.ca
M'liss Edwards, Library Manager

Myrnam: Myrnam Community Library
New Myrnam School, 5105 - 50 St., Myrnam, AB T0B 3K0
Tel: 780-366-3801; *Fax:* 780-366-2332
librarian@myrnamlibrary.ab.ca
www.myrnamlibrary.ab.ca
Ann Godziuk, Librarian
librarian@myrnamlibrary.ab.ca
780-366-3801

Nampa: Nampa Municipal Library
PO Box 509, Nampa, AB T0H 2R0
Tel: 780-322-3805; *Fax:* 780-322-3955
nlibrary@nampalibrary.ab.ca
Cathy Rasmussen, Librarian

Nanton: Nanton Municipal Library / Thelma Fanning Memorial Library
1907 - 21 Ave., Nanton, AB T0L 1R0
Tel: 403-646-5535; *Fax:* 403-646-2653
help@nantonlibrary.ca
www.nantonlibrary.ca
Social Media: www.flickr.com/photos/nanton_library;
www.facebook.com/pages/Nanton-Library/242719735785773

Neerlandia: Neerlandia Public Library
PO Box 10, Neerlandia, AB T0G 1R0
Tel: 780-674-5384; *Fax:* 780-674-2927
solthuis@phrd.ab.ca
www.neerlandialibrary.ab.ca/
Brenda Gelderman, Library Assistant
Dagmar Visser, Librarian

New Sarepta: New Sarepta Community Library
c/o New Sarepta Community High School, 5150 Center St., New Sarepta, AB T0B 3M0
Tel: 780-975-7513; *Fax:* 780-941-2224
newsareptalibrary@yrl.ab.ca
www.newsareptalibrary.ca
Willow Schnell, Library Director
Pearl Gregor, Chair

Newbrook: Newbrook Public Library
Box 208, Newbrook, AB T0A 2P0
Tel: 780-576-3772; *Fax:* 780-576-2115
librarian@newbrooklibrary.ab.ca
www.newbrooklibrary.ab.ca
Rose Alexander, Library Manager

Niton Junction: Green Grove Public Library
53521A Range Rd. 130, Niton Junction, AB T0E 1S0
Tel: 780-795-2474; *Fax:* 780-795-3933
www.greengrovelibrary.ab.ca
Toni Ice, Library Manager
toniice@gyrd.ab.ca
Lida Saulnier, Chair

Nordegg: Nordegg Public Library
General Delivery, Nordegg, AB T0M 2H0
Tel: 403-721-2339
nordegglibrary@libs.prl.ab.ca
Heather Clement, Librarian

Okotoks: Okotoks Public Library
7 Riverside Dr. West, Okotoks, AB T1S 1A6
Tel: 403-938-2220; *Fax:* 403-938-4317
assistant@okotokslibrary.ca
www.okotokslibrary.ca
Social Media: twitter.com/OkotoksLibrary;
www.facebook.com/OkotoksPublicLibrary
Tessa Nettleton, Director
403-938-2220
Caleigh Haworth, Assistant Librarian

Olds: Olds & District Municipal Library
5217 - 52 St., Olds, AB T4H 1H7
Tel: 403-556-6460; *Fax:* 403-556-6692
oml2@libs.prl.ab.ca
oml.prl.ab.ca
Lesley Winfield, Head Librarian
oml2libs.prl.ab.ca
403-556-6460

Onoway: **Onoway Public Library**
4808 - 51 St., Onoway, AB T0E 1V0
Tel: 780-967-2445; *Fax:* 780-967-2445
onowaylibrary@yrl.ab.ca
www.onowaylibrary.ab.ca
Kelly Huxley, Librarian
onowaylibrary@yrl.ab.ca
Lucy Strobl, Chair

Oyen: **Oyen Municipal Library**
105 - 3rd Ave. West, Oyen, AB T0J 2J0
Tel: 403-664-3580; *Fax:* 403-664-2520
aoymlibrary@marigold.ab.ca
www.townofoyen.com/oyen-municipal-library.html
Lois Bedwell, Board Chair
Tricia Fischbuch, Library Manager

Paradise Valley: **Three Cities Municipal Library**
PO Box 60, Paradise Valley, AB T0B 3R0
Tel: 780-745-2277; *Fax:* 780-745-2641
www.paradisevalleylibrary.ab.ca
Sandra Babcock, Library Contact
Library Contact

Peace River: **Peace River Municipal Library**
9807 - 97 Ave., Peace River, AB T8S 1H6
Tel: 780-624-4076; *Fax:* 780-624-4086
www.prmlibrary.ab.ca
Jennifer Straub, Acting Chair

Penhold: **Penhold & District Public Library**
#1 Waskasoo Ave., Penhold, AB T0M 1R0
Tel: 403-886-2636; *Fax:* 403-886-2638
penholdlibrary@libs.prl.ab.ca
penholdlibrary.prl.ab.ca
Myra Binnendyk, Head of Library
Karen Thomson, Assistant Librarian

Picture Butte: **Picture Butte Municipal Library**
120 - 4th St. South, Picture Butte, AB T0K 1V0
Tel: 403-732-4141; *Fax:* 403-732-4334
help@picturebuttelibrary.ca
www.picturebuttelibrary.ca
Linda Bexte, Library Manager

Pincher Creek: **Pincher Creek Municipal Library**
899 Main St., Pincher Creek, AB T0K 1W0
Tel: 403-627-3813; *Fax:* 403-627-2847
help@pinchercreeklibrary.ca
www.pinchercreeklibrary.ca
Social Media: twitter.com/pincherlibrary;
www.facebook.com/group.php?gid=42049238516
Janice Day, Library Manager

Plamondon: **Plamondon Municipal Library**
PO Box 630, Plamondon, AB T0A 2T0
Tel: 780-798-3852; *Fax:* 780-798-3860
headlibrarian@stuartmacphersonlibrary.ca
www.plamondonlibrary.ab.ca
Maureen Penn, Director, Library Services
Pam Lien, School Librarian

Ponoka: **Ponoka Jubilee Library**
5110 - 48 Ave., Ponoka, AB T4J 1J3
Tel: 403-783-3843
ponokalibrary.prl.ab.ca
Norma-Jean Colquhoun, Library Manager
Sharie Kuhl, Assistant Librarian
Jaclyn Berry, Programmer
Jenica Kostiuk, Coordinator, Summer Reading

Provost: **Provost Municipal Library**
5035 51 Ave., Provost, AB T0B 3S0
Tel: 780-753-2801
provostlibrary@libs.prl.ab.ca
provostlibrary.prl.ab.ca/
Colleen Vaughn, Library Supervisor

Radway: **Radway Public Library**
4915 - 50th St., Radway, AB T0A 2V0
Tel: 780-736-3548; *Fax:* 780-736-3858
librarian@radwaylibrary.ab.ca
www.radwaylibrary.ab.ca
Terrie-Lynne Rosa, Librarian
Sharon Krawchuk, Chair, County of Thorhild No. 7 Library Board

Rainbow Lake: **Rainbow Lake Municipal Library**
1 Atco Rd., Rainbow Lake, AB T0H 2Y0
Tel: 780-956-3656; *Fax:* 780-956-3858
librarian@rainbowlakelibrary.ab.ca
www.rainbowlakelibrary.ab.ca
Cheryl Edwards, Librarian
Mark Levy, Librarian

Rainier: **Alcoma Community Library**
c/o Alcoma School, Box 119, Rainier, AB T0J 2M0
Tel: 403-362-3741; *Fax:* 403-362-8897
aplcapic@eidnet.org
www.shortgrass.ca/acl

Ralston: **Graham Community Library**
R35 Dugway Dr., Community Centre, Ralston, AB T0J 2N0
Tel: 403-544-3670; *Fax:* 403-544-3814
grahamlib@yahoo.ca
www.grahamcommunitylibrary.ca
Stefanie Schranz, Librarian Manager
grahamlib@yahoo.ca

Raymond: **Raymond Public Library**
15 Broadway South, Raymond, AB T0K 2S0
Tel: 403-752-4785; *Fax:* 403-752-4710
rlibrary@chinookarch.ab.ca
www.raymondlibrary.ca
Faye Geddes, Librarian

Red Deer: **Red Deer Public Library**
4818 - 49th St., Red Deer, AB T4N 1T9
Tel: 403-346-4576
Other Numbers: 403-346-4688 (Children's department)
www.rdpl.org
Social Media: twitter.com/#!/rdpl;
www.facebook.com/reddeerpubliclibrary
Mike Todd, Chair
miket@aipins.ca
Dean Frey, Director
dfrey@rdpl.org
403-342-9102
Cory Stier, Assistant Director
403-342-9124
Donna Alberts, Librarian, Youth Services & Circulation
403-342-9114
Cynthia Belanger, Librarian, Adult Services
403-342-9104
Tatiana Poliakevitch, Librarian, Community Development
403-755-1130
Jen Waters, Librarian, Teen Services
403-755-1146
Celia Jaipaul, Coordinator, Family Literacy
403-755-1158
Lois Prostebby, Coordinator, Adult Literacy
403-346-2533
Kareena Fulton, Supervisor, Circulation
403-342-9108
Trish Klein, Supervisor, Readers' Services
403-342-9110

Redcliff: **Redcliff Public Library**
131 Main St. South, Redcliff, AB T0J 2P0
Tel: 403-548-3335
redlib@shortgrass.ca
www.shortgrass.ca/rpl

Redwater: **Redwater Public Library**
4915 - 48th St., Redwater, AB T0A 2W0
Tel: 780-942-3464
www.redwaterlibrary.ab.ca
Judy Dewald, Director, Library Services
director@redwaterlibrary.ab.ca

Rimbey: **Rimbey Municipal Library**
4938 - 50 Ave., Rimbey, AB T0C 2J0
Tel: 403-843-2841; *Fax:* 587-332-2614
rimbeylibrary.prl.ab.ca
Jean Keetch, Librarian
Shannon Kiss, Library Assistant

Rochester: **Rochester Community Library**
PO Box 309, Rochester, AB T0G 1Z0
Tel: 780-698-3970; *Fax:* 780-698-2290
tammy.morey@aspenview.org
www.rochesterlibrary.ab.ca
Tammy Morey, Librarian

Rocky Mountain House: **Rocky Mountain House Public Library**
4922 - 52nd St., Rocky Mountain House, AB T4T 1B1
Tel: 403-845-2042; *Fax:* 403-845-5633
armh@libs.prl.ab.ca
rmhlibrary.prl.ab.ca
Karen Paquette, Library Manager

Rockyford: **Rockyford Municipal & District Library**
Community Centre, Rockyford, AB T0J 2R0
Tel: 403-533-3964
armlibrary@marigold.ab.ca
www.rockyfordlibrary.ca
Jocelyne Kisko, Library Manager

Rolling Hills: **Rolling Hills Public Library**
302 - 4th St., Rolling Hills, AB T0J 2S0
Tel: 403-964-2186; *Fax:* 403-964-3659
rhlcapic@eidnet.org
www.shortgrass.ca/rhpl

Rosemary: **Rosemary Community Library**
Rosemary Academic Schoo, Block 6, Dahlia St., Rosemary, AB T0J 2W0
Tel: 403-378-4493; *Fax:* 403-378-4388
www.shortgrass.ca/rml/
Petra Mauerhoff, Chief Executive Officer
petra@shortgrass.ca
Bob Batchelder, Assistant Director, Technical Services
bob@shortgrass.ca

Rumsey: **Rumsey Community Library**
PO Box 113, Rumsey, AB T0J 2Y0
Tel: 403-368-3939
arumlibrary@marigold.ab.ca
Patty Steen, Librarian

Rycroft: **Rycroft Municipal Library**
PO Box 248, Rycroft, AB T0H 3A0
Tel: 780-765-3973; *Fax:* 780-765-2002
librarian@rycroftlibrary.ab.ca
www.rycroftlibrary.ab.ca

Ryley: **McPherson Public Library**
5113-50 St., Ryley, AB T0B 4A0
Tel: 780-663-3999; *Fax:* 780-663-3909
librarian@mcphersonlibrary.ab.ca
www.mcphersonlibrary.ab.ca

Sangudo: **Sangudo Public Library**
PO Box 524, Sangudo, AB T0E 2A0
Tel: 780-785-3431; *Fax:* 780-785-3179
www.sangudolibrary.ca
Cassandra Boll, Library Manager

Seba Beach: **Seba Beach Public Library**
PO Box 159, Seba Beach, AB T0E 2B0
Tel: 780-797-3940; *Fax:* 780-797-3800
www.sebabeachlibrary.ab.ca
Judy Mott, Library Manager

Sedgewick: **Sedgewick Municipal Library**
5011 - 51 Ave., Sedgewick, AB T0B 4C0
Tel: 780-384-3003; *Fax:* 780-384-3003
sedgewicklibrary@libs.prl.ab.ca
sedgpublib.prl.ab.ca
Judy Ferrier, Librarian

Sexsmith: **Sexsmith Shannon Library**
Sexsmith Civic Centre, 9917 - 99th Ave., Sexsmith, AB T0H 3C0
Tel: 780-568-4333; *Fax:* 780-568-7249
librarian@shannonlibrary.ab.ca
www.shannonlibrary.ab.ca
Sheryl Pelletier, Library Manager

Sherwood Park: **Strathcona County Library**
Community Centre, 401 Festival Lane, Sherwood Park, AB T8A 5P7
Tel: 780-410-8600; *Fax:* 780-467-6861
info@sclibrary.ab.ca
www.sclibrary.ab.ca
Social Media: www.flickr.com/photos/strathcona-county-library;
twitter.com/sc_library; twitter.com/sclbookmobile
Rob Butler, Chair
Sharon Siga, Library Director

Silver Valley: **Savanna Municipal Library**
PO Box 49, Silver Valley, AB T0H 3E0
Tel: 780-351-3771
www.savannalibrary.ca

Slave Lake: **Slave Lake Municipal Library**
101 Main St. East, First Floor, Slave Lake, AB T0G 2A0
Tel: 780-849-5250; *Fax:* 780-849-3275
librarian@slavelakelibrary.ab.ca
www.slavelakelibrary.ab.ca
Lori Herdzik, Librarian

Smith: **Smith Community Library**
PO Box 134, Smith, AB T0G 2B0
Tel: 780-829-2389; *Fax:* 780-829-2389
librarian@smithlibrary.ab.ca
www.smithlibrary.ab.ca

Smoky Lake: **Smoky Lake Municipal Public Library**
5010 - 50th St., Smoky Lake, AB T0A 3C0
Tel: 780-656-4212; *Fax:* 780-656-4212
www.smokylakelibrary.ab.ca
Melody Kaban, Library Manager

***Spirit River:* Spirit River Municipal Library**
PO Box 490, Spirit River, AB T0H 3G0
Tel: 780-864-4038; *Fax:* 780-864-3006
www.spiritriverlibrary.ab.ca

***Spruce Grove:* Spruce Grove Public Library**
Melcor Cultural Centre, 35 - 5th Ave., Spruce Grove, AB T7X 2C5
Tel: 780-962-4423; *Fax:* 780-962-4826
library@sgpl.ca
www.sgpl.ca
Social Media: www.youtube.com/user/SpruceGroveLibrary61; twitter.com/SG_Library; www.facebook.com/pages/Spruce-Grove-Public-Library/100622914545
Tammy Svenningsen, Library Director

***St Albert:* St Albert Public Library**
5 St Anne St., St Albert, AB T8N 3Z9
Tel: 780-459-1530; *Fax:* 780-458-5772
sapl@sapl.ab.ca
www.sapl.ab.ca
Pamela Forsyth, Director
pforsyth@sapl.ab.ca
780-459-1681
Peter Bailey, Head of Public Services
pbailey@sapl.ab.ca
780-459-1686
Pat Fader, Head of Technical Services
pfader@sapl.ab.ca
780-459-1684
Barbara Moreau, Children's Department Coordinator
bmoreau@sapl.ab.ca
780-459-1536
Wanda German, Circulation Services Manager
wgerman@sapl.ab.ca
780-459-1537

***St Isidore:* St Isidore Community Library/ Bibliothèque de St Isidore**
PO Box 1168, St Isidore, AB T0H 3B0
Tel: 780-624-8182; *Fax:* 780-624-8192
marielavoie@bibliothequestisidore.ab.ca
www.bibliothequestisidore.ab.ca/
Marie Lavoie, Chair & Librarian

***St Paul:* St Paul Municipal Library**
4802 - 53 St., St Paul, AB T0A 3A0
Tel: 780-645-4904; *Fax:* 780-645-5198
librarian@stpaullibrary.ab.ca
www.stpaullibrary.ab.ca

***Standard:* Standard Municipal Library**
822 The Broadway, Standard, AB T0J 3G0
Tel: 403-644-3995
astmlibrary@marigold.ab.ca
www.marigold.ab.ca/
Sharon Duffala, Librarian

***Stavely:* Stavely Municipal Library**
4823 - 49th St., Stavely, AB T0L 1Z0
Tel: 403-549-2190; *Fax:* 403-549-2190
help@stavelylibrary.ca
www.stavely.ca/Municipal_Library.htm
Cheryl Cochlan, Librarian

***Stettler:* Stettler Public Library**
6202 - 44th Ave., Stettler, AB T0C 2L1
Tel: 403-742-2292; *Fax:* 403-742-5481
spl@libs.prl.ab.ca
spl.prl.ab.ca
Social Media: www.facebook.com/group.php?gid=2492499282
Deborah Cryderman, Library Manager
Crystal Friars, Assistant Manager

***Stirling:* Stirling Municipal Library**
229 - 4th Ave., Stirling, AB T0K 2E0
Tel: 403-756-3665
Charlene Fletcher, Director, Library Services
libstir@chinookarch.ab.ca
Sheila Cooper-Bikman, Assistant
Shawna Hogenson, Assistant Librarian

***Stony Plain:* Stony Plain Public Library**
#112, 4613 - 52nd Ave., Stony Plain, AB T7Z 1E7
Tel: 780-963-5440; *Fax:* 780-963-1746
info@stonyplainlibrary.org
www.stonyplainlibrary.org
Social Media: twitter.com/stonyplainlib
Shauna Johnstone, Chair

***Strathmore:* Strathmore Municipal Library**
85 Lakeside Blvd., Strathmore, AB T1P 1A1
Tel: 403-934-5440; *Fax:* 403-934-1908
asmlibrary@marigold.ab.ca
www.strathmorelibrary.ca

***Sundre:* Sundre Municipal Library**
#2, 310 Centre St. North, Sundre, AB T0M 1X0
Tel: 403-638-4000; *Fax:* 403-638-5755
sundrelibrary@libs.prl.ab.ca
www.sundre.prl.ab.ca
Michael Baird, Library Manager

***Swan Hills:* Swan Hills Public Library**
5536 Main St., Swan Hills, AB T0G 2C0
Tel: 780-333-4505; *Fax:* 780-333-4551
www.swanhillslibrary.ab.ca
Nancy Keough, Head Librarian

***Sylvan Lake:* Sylvan Lake Public Library**
4715 - 50 Ave., Sylvan Lake, AB T4S 1C5
Tel: 403-887-2130; *Fax:* 403-887-0537
sylvan.library@libs.prl.ab.ca
www.sylvanlibrary.prl.ab.ca
Social Media: twitter.com/SylvanLib; www.facebook.com/group.php?gid=109719189059777
Shannon Sword, Librarian

***Taber:* Taber Public Library**
5415 - 50 Ave., Taber, AB T1G 1V2
Tel: 403-223-4343; *Fax:* 403-223-4314
libtab@taberlibrary.ca
www.www.taberlibrary.ca
Social Media: www.facebook.com/pages/Taber-Public-Library/21094305918
Fran Dogterom, Board Chair
Helen Jury, Library Co-Manager
hjury@taberlibrary.ca
Diane Zelenka, Library Co-Manager
dzelenka@taberlibrary.ca
Dawn Kondas, Program Coordinator
dkondas@taberlibrary.ca

***Thorhild:* Thorhild & District Municipal Library**
210 - 7 Ave., Thorhild, AB T0A 3J0
Tel: 780-398-3502; *Fax:* 780-398-3504
librarian@thorhildlibrary.ab.ca
www.thorhildlibrary.ab.ca
Rose Alexander, Library Manager

***Thorsby:* Thorsby Municipal Library**
PO Box 319, Thorsby, AB T0C 2P0
Tel: 780-789-3808; *Fax:* 780-789-3805
www.thorsbymunicipallibrary.ab.ca
Louise Normandeau, Library Director

***Three Hills:* Three Hills Municipal Library**
160 - 3rd Ave. South, Three Hills, AB T0M 2A0
Tel: 403-443-2360
athmlibrary@marigold.ab.ca
www.3hillslibrary.com
Wendy Cuffe, Head Librarian
Susan Hamm, Assistant Librarian

***Tilley:* Tilley Public Library**
PO Box 177, Tilley, AB T0J 3K0
Tel: 403-377-2233; *Fax:* 403-377-2097
www.shortgrass.ca/tpl

***Tofield:* Tofield Municipal Library**
5407 - 50 St., Tofield, AB T0B 4J0
Tel: 780-662-3838; *Fax:* 780-662-3929
librarian@tofieldlibrary.ca
www.tofieldlibrary.ca
Connie Forst, Library Manager

***Tomahawk:* Tomahawk Public Library**
Tomahawk School, #512, 6119 Township Rd., Tomahawk, AB T0E 2H0
Tel: 780-339-3935
tomahawklibrary@yrl.ab.ca
Social Media: www.facebook.com/pcmlibraries
Chris Goerz, Librarian
Monika Cappis, Chair, Parkland County Library Board

***Trochu:* Trochu Municipal Library**
317 Main St., Trochu, AB T0M 2C0
Tel: 403-442-2458
town.trochu.ab.ca
Sherie Campbell, Librarian

***Two Hills:* Alice Melnyk Public Library**
5009, 50 Ave., Two Hills, AB T0B 4K0
Tel: 780-657-3553; *Fax:* 780-657-3553
www.twohillslibrary.ab.ca
Elizabeth Wells, Library Manager & Resource Sharing Contact
librarian@twohillslibrary.ab.ca

***Valhalla Centre:* Valhalla Community Library**
PO Box 68, Valhalla Centre, AB T0H 3M0
Tel: 780-356-3834; *Fax:* 780-356-3834
librarian@valhallalibrary.ab.ca
www.valhallalibrary.ab.ca/
Gail Perry, Librarian
780-356-2382

***Valleyview:* Valleyview Municipal Library**
4804 - 50 Ave., Valleyview, AB T0H 3N0
Tel: 780-524-3033; *Fax:* 780-524-4563
www.valleyviewlibrary.ab.ca
Susanne Tremblay, Library Coordinator

***Vauxhall:* Vauxhall Public Library**
314 - 2nd Ave. North, Vauxhall, AB T0K 2K0
Tel: 403-654-2370; *Fax:* 403-654-2370
help@vauxhalllibrary.ca
www.vauxhalllibrary.ca
Social Media: twitter.com/Chinooklibs

***Vegreville:* Vegreville Centennial Library**
4709 - 50 St., Vegreville, AB T9C 1R1
Tel: 780-632-3491; *Fax:* 780-603-2338
library@vegreville.com
www.vegrevillelibrary.ab.ca
Social Media: www.facebook.com/Veglibrary
Kenneth Allan, Library Manager
780-632-3491
Jennie Barlott, Assistant Librarian

***Vermilion:* Vermilion Public Library**
5001 - 49th Ave., Vermilion, AB T9X 1B8
Tel: 780-853-4288; *Fax:* 780-853-1783
admin@vermilionpubliclibrary.ca
www.vermilionpubliclibrary.ca
Social Media: www.facebook.com/vermilionpl
Stuart Paul, Library Manager

***Veteran:* Veteran Municipal Library**
205 Luckow St., Veteran, AB T0C 2S0
Tel: 403-575-3915; *Fax:* 403-575-3870
www.thealbertalibrary.ab.ca
Nicole Larson, Librarian
Linda Schetzsle, Chair

***Viking:* Viking Municipal Library**
Viking Carena Complex, 5120 - 45 St., Viking, AB T0B 4N0
Tel: 780-336-4992; *Fax:* 780-336-4992
www.vikinglibrary.ab.ca
Social Media: www.facebook.com/pages/Viking-Municipal-Library/180715135371094
Marayann Wolosinka, Library Manager
Gina-Lee Hinton, Staff

***Vimy:* Vimy Community/School Library**
PO Box 29, Vimy, AB T0G 2J0
Tel: 780-961-3014; *Fax:* 780-961-2094
Pauline Despins, Librarian

***Vulcan:* Vulcan Municipal Library**
303 Centre St., Vulcan, AB T0L 2B0
Tel: 403-485-2571; *Fax:* 403-485-2571
help@vulcanlibrary.ca
www.vulcanlibrary.ca
Penny Allen, Library Manager
pallen@vulcanlibrary.ca
Cathie McNiven, Assistant Librarian
cmcniven@chinookarch.ab.ca

***Wabamun:* Wabamun Public Library**
Jubilee Hall, 5132 - 53 Ave., Wabamun, AB T0E 2K0
Tel: 780-892-2713; *Fax:* 780-892-7294
www.wabamunlibrary.ca
Betty Lalonde, Head Librarian

***Wainwright:* Wainwright Public Library**
921 - 3rd Ave., Wainwright, AB T9W 1C5
Tel: 780-842-2673; *Fax:* 780-842-2340
librarian@wainwrightlibrary.ab.ca
www.wainwrightlibrary.ab.ca
Jodi Dahlgren, Library Manager

Wandering River: **Wandering River Women's Institute Community Library**
Wandering River School, Wandering River, AB T0A 3M0
Tel: 780-771-3939
librarian@wanderingriverlibrary.ab.ca
www.wanderingriverlibrary.ab.ca
Jennifer Batiuk, Library Manager
780-623-0409

Warburg: **Warburg Public Library**
5212 50th Ave., Warburg, AB T0C 2T0
Tel: 780-848-2391; *Fax:* 780-848-2296
warburglibrary@yrl.ab.ca
www.warburglibrary.ab.ca
Gail O'Neil, Library Manager

Warner: **Warner Memorial Municipal Library**
206 - 3rd Ave., Warner, AB T0K 2L0
Tel: 403-642-3988; *Fax:* 403-642-3988
help@warnerlibrary.ca
www.warnerlibrary.ca
Andrea Tapp, Librarian
Jillian Hounssine, Substitute Librarian

Waskatenau: **Anne Chorney Public Library**
5125 - 51 St., Waskatenau, AB T0A 3P0
Tel: 780-358-2777; *Fax:* 780-358-2777
librarian@waskatenaulibrary.ab.ca
www.waskatenaulibrary.ab.ca
Goedele Kerckhof, Library Manager

Water Valley: **Water Valley Public Library**
PO Box 250, Water Valley, AB T0M 2E0
Tel: 403-637-3899
watervalleylibrary@libs.prl.ab.ca
www.watervalleycommunity.ca/library.html
Jaymee Shea, Librarian

Westlock: **Westlock Libraries**
#1, 10007 - 100 Ave., Westlock, AB T7P 2H5
Tel: 780-349-3060; *Fax:* 780-349-5291
info@westlocklibrary.ca
www.westlocklibrary.ca
Social Media: pinterest.com/westlocklibrary; twitter.com/westlocklibrary; www.facebook.com/westlocklibraries
Doug Whistance-Smith, Director
dwhistance@westlocklibrary.ca
Wendy Hodgson-Sadgrove, Assistant Director
hodgsonw@westlocklibrary.ca
Carey Whistance-Smith, Contact, Acquisitions, Cataloging, & Collections Maintenance
cwhistance@westlocklibrary.ca

Wetaskiwin: **Wetaskiwin Public Library**
5002 - 51st Ave., Wetaskiwin, AB T9A 0V1
Tel: 780-361-4446; *Fax:* 780-352-3266
library@wetaskiwin.ca
Manisha Khetarpal, Manager, Library Services
mkhetarpal@wetaskiwin.ca
Rachelle Kuzyk, Manager, Administrative Services
rkuzyk@wetaskiwin.ca

Whitecourt: **Whitecourt & District Public Library**
5201 - 49th St., Whitecourt, AB T7S 1N3
Tel: 780-778-2900; *Fax:* 780-778-2827
www.whitecourtlibrary.ab.ca
Richard Bangma, Head Librarian
780-778-2900

Wildwood: **Wildwood Public Library**
5112 - 50th St., Wildwood, AB T0E 2M0
Tel: 780-325-3882; *Fax:* 780-325-3920
www.wildwoodlibrary.ab.ca
Terrie Stone, Library Manager

Winfield: **Winfield Community Library**
PO Box 390, Winfield, AB T0C 2X0
Tel: 780-682-2423; *Fax:* 780-682-2490
winfieldlibrary@yrl.ab.ca
www.winfieldlibrary.ab.ca
Lorna Smith, Librarian
Maureen Webster, Library Assistant

Woking: **Woking Municipal Library**
PO Box 27, Woking, AB T0H 3V0
Tel: 780-774-3932
www.wokinglibrary.ca

Worsley: **Worsley & District Library**
216 Alberta Ave., Worsley, AB T0H 3W0
Tel: 780-685-3842; *Fax:* 780-685-3766
www.worsleylibrary.ab.ca
Colleen Rook, Librarian
Bonnie Bigam, Chair
780-685-2427

Wrentham: **Wrentham Library**
PO Box 111, Wrentham, AB T0K 2P0
Tel: 403-222-2485; *Fax:* 403-222-2101
libwren@chinookarch.ab.ca
Alice Cook, Library Supervisor

Youngstown: **Youngstown Municipal Library**
Main St., Youngstown, AB T0J 3P0
Tel: 403-779-3864; *Fax:* 403-779-3864
aymlibrary@marigold.ab.ca
Annette Lupuliak, Librarian

Zama City: **Zama Community Library**
PO Box 14, Zama City, AB T0H 4E0
Tel: 780-683-2888; *Fax:* 780-683-2889
www.zamacity.ca
Janet Forrest, Librarian

Archives

Athabasca: **Thomas A. Edge Archives & Special Collections**
Athabasca University, 1 University Dr., Athabasca, AB T9S 3A3
Tel: 780-675-6268; *Fax:* 780-675-6450
Toll-Free: 800-788-9041
karenl@athabascau.ca
www.athabascau.ca/archives

Banff: **The Banff Centre**
107 Tunnel Mountain Dr., Banff, AB T1L 1H5
Tel: 403-762-6265; *Fax:* 403-762-6266
library@banffcentre.ca
www.banffcentre.ca/library
Patrick Lawless, Managing Librarian
Patrick_Lawless@banffcentre.ca
403-762-6658
Jane Parkinson, Archivist
jane_parkinson@banffcentre.ca
403-762-6440
Suzanne Rackover, Music Librarian
Suzanne_Rackover@banffcentre.ca
406-762-6266

Banff: **Whyte Museum of the Canadian Rockies**
111 Bear St., Banff, AB T1L 1A3
Tel: 403-762-2291; *Fax:* 403-762-2339
archives@whyte.org
www.whyte.org
Elizabeth Kundert-Cameron, Librarian
ekc@whyte.org

Brooks: **Eastern Irrigation District**
550 Industrial Rd. West, Brooks, AB T1R 1B2
Tel: 403-362-1400; *Fax:* 403-362-6206
archive@eid.ab.ca
www.eid.ca/archives
Darlene Fisher, Contact, Records Management

Calgary: **Calgary Highlanders Regimental Museum & Archives**
4520 Crowchild Trail SW, Calgary, AB T3E 1T8
Tel: 403-974-2855
museum@calgaryhighlanders.com
www.calgaryhighlanders.com/organizations/museum/museum.htm
Mike Henry, Archvist

Calgary: **Calgary Sun**
2615 - 12th St. NE, Calgary, AB T2E 7W9
Tel: 403-250-4159; *Toll-Free:* 877-624-1463
research@sunmedia.ca
www.calgarysun.ca

Calgary: **Canadian Architectural Archives**
Taylor Family Digital Library, MacKimmie Library Tower, #520, 2500 University Dr. NW, Calgary, AB T2N 1N4
Tel: 403-220-7271; *Fax:* 403-210-3075
archives@ucalgary.ca
caa.ucalgary.ca

Calgary: **The City of Calgary**
Admin Bldg., 313 - 7th Ave. SE, Main Fl., Calgary, AB T2G 0J1
Tel: 403-268-8180; *Fax:* 403-268-6731
archives@calgary.ca
www.calgary.ca

Calgary: **Diocese of Calgary, Archives**
Synod Office, #180, 1209 59th Ave. SE, Calgary, AB T2H 2P6
Tel: 403-243-3673; *Fax:* 403-243-2182
diocese@calgary.anglican.ca
www.calgary.anglican.ca

Calgary: **Glenbow Museum**
130 - 9th Ave. SE, Calgary, AB T2G 0P3
Tel: 403-268-4197; *Fax:* 403-232-6569
Other Numbers: Archives, Phone: 403-268-4204
glenbow@glenbow.org
www.glenbow.org/collections/archives
Lindsay Moir, Librarian
Susan Kooyman, Archivist
Lynette Walton, Imperial Oil Archivist
lwalton@glenbow.org
403-268-4232

Calgary: **Heritage Park Society**
1900 Heritage Dr. SW, Calgary, AB T2V 2X3
Tel: 403-268-8500; *Fax:* 403-268-8501
info@heritagepark.ab.ca
www.heritagepark.ca
Social Media: www.facebook.com/pages/Heritage-Park/177397676028
Sylvia Harnden, Curator
403-268-8536

Calgary: **Legal Archives Society of Alberta**
#510, 919 - 11th Ave. SW, Calgary, AB T2R 1P3
Tel: 403-244-5510; *Fax:* 403-541-9102
lasa@legalarchives.ca
www.legalarchives.ca
Everett L. Bunnell, President
Stacy F. Kaufeld, Executive Director
Brenda McCafferty, Archivist

Calgary: **Lord Strathcona's Horse Regimental Museum**
4520 Crowchild Trail SW, Calgary, AB T2T 5J4
Tel: 403-974-2854; *Fax:* 403-974-2858
www.strathconas.ca/strathcona-museum
Social Media: twitter.com/LdSHRC

Calgary: **Naval Museum of Alberta**
1820 - 24 St. SW, Calgary, AB T2T 0G6
Tel: 403-242-0002; *Fax:* 403-240-1966
bhconnolly@rogers.com
Bruce Connolly, Assistant Curator

Calgary: **Sisters Faithful Companions of Jesus**
219 - 19th Ave. SW, Calgary, AB T2S 0C8
Tel: 403-228-3623; *Fax:* 403-541-9297
shc@fcjsisters.ca
www.fcjsisters.org
Social Media: twitter.com/fcjsisters; www.facebook.com/57766155162
Elizabeth Fitzgerald, Archivist

Calgary: **University of Calgary Archives**
Library Tower, 2500 University Dr. NW, 12th Fl., Calgary, AB T2N 1N4
Tel: 403-220-7271; *Fax:* 403-210-3075
uarc@ucalgary.ca
archives.ucalgary.ca

Calgary: **YouthLink Calgary**
316 - 7th Ave. SE, Calgary, AB T2G 4Z1
Tel: 403-206-4566
www.youthlinkcalgary.com
Social Media: twitter.com/YouthLinkCGY; www.facebook.com/YouthLinkCGY
Janet Pieschel, Executive Director
janet.pieschel@calgarypolice.ca
Gail Niinimaa, Administrator
gail.niinimaa@calgarypolice.ca

Cardston: **Cardston & District Historical Society**
89 - 3rd Ave. West, Cardston, AB T0K 0K0
Tel: 403-653-4726
H. Dale Lowry, Director

Edmonton: **Alberta & Northwest Conference, Archives**
c/o Provincial Archives of Alberta, 8555 Roper Rd., Edmonton, AB T6E 5W1
Tel: 780-427-8687; *Fax:* 780-427-4646

Edmonton: **Alberta Council**
11055 - 107th St. NW, Edmonton, AB T5H 2Z6
Tel: 780-424-5510; *Fax:* 780-426-1715
archives@albertagirlguides.com
www.albertagirlguides.ca

***Edmonton:* Canadian Moravian Archives**
612 - 111 St. SW, Edmonton, AB T6T 1H9
Tel: 780-440-3050; *Fax:* 780-463-2143
historical@moravian.ca
www.moravian.ca/docs/org.html
Bob Voelker, President
voelker@shaw.ca
William G. Brese, Contact

***Edmonton:* City of Edmonton Archives**
10440 - 108 Ave., Edmonton, AB T5H 3Z9
Tel: 780-496-8711; *Fax:* 780-496-8732
cms.archives@edmonton.ca
www.edmonton.ca/archives
Kim Christie-Milley, Reference Archivist

***Edmonton:* Edmonton Public Schools**
10425 - 99th Ave., Edmonton, AB T5K 0E5
Tel: 780-422-1970; *Fax:* 780-426-0192
archives@epsb.ca
archives.epsb.net

***Edmonton:* The Edmonton Sun**
#250, 4990 - 92nd Ave., Edmonton, AB T6B 3A1
Tel: 780-468-0100; *Toll-Free:* 877-624-1463
research@sunmedia.ca
www.edmontonsun.com
Social Media: twitter.com/Edmontonsun;
www.facebook.com/edmontonsun

***Edmonton:* Provincial Archives of Alberta**
8555 Roper Rd., Edmonton, AB T6E 5W1
Tel: 780-427-1750
paa@gov.ab.ca
www.culture.alberta.ca/paa
Social Media: www.flickr.com/photos/albertaculture;
twitter.com/#!/AlbertaCulture
Wayne Murdoch, Director, Collections Management Section
wayne.murdoch@gov.ab.ca
780-427-1767
Tom Anderson, Team Lead, Private Records
tom.anderson@gov.ab.ca
780-415-0700
Laurette Miller, FOIP Officer
jonathan.davidson@gov.ab.ca
780-644-7999
Gail Kudelik, President, Friends of the Provincial Archives of Alberta Society
780-427-1750

***Edmonton:* Ukrainian Canadian Archives & Museum of Alberta**
9543 - 110th Ave. NW, Edmonton, AB T5H 1H3
Tel: 780-424-7580; *Fax:* 780-420-5062
ucama@shaw.ca
www.ucama.com
Alexander Makar, Director

***Edmonton:* University of Alberta Archives**
#100, 8170 - 50th St., Edmonton, AB T6B 1E6
Tel: 780-466-6118; *Fax:* 780-466-5210
archive1@ualberta.ca
www.ualberta.ca/ARCHIVES/

***Jasper:* Jasper-Yellowhead Museum & Archives**
400 Bonhomme St., Jasper, AB T0E 1E0
Tel: 780-852-3013; *Fax:* 780-852-3240
archives@jaspermuseum.org
www.jaspermuseum.org
Social Media:
www.facebook.com/pages/Jasper-Museum/123561747657136
Dee Dee Bartlett, Archivist
Karen Byers, Archivist

***Lethbridge:* Sir Alexander Galt Museum & Archives**
502 - 1st St. South, Lethbridge, AB T1J 1Y4
Tel: 403-329-7302; *Fax:* 403-329-4958
Toll-Free: 866-320-3898
archives@galtmuseum.com
www.galtmuseum.com/archives.htm
Social Media: www.flickr.com/photos/galtmuseum;
twitter.com/GaltMuseum; www.facebook.com/GaltMuseum
Andrew Chernevych, Archivist

***Lethbridge:* University of Lethbridge Archives**
Library Bldg., Level 11, 4401 University Dr., Lethbridge, AB T1K 3M4
Tel: 403-329-2714
mike.perry@uleth.ca
www.uleth.ca/lib/archives/

***Medicine Hat:* Esplanade Arts & Heritage Centre**
401 - 1st St. SE, Medicine Hat, AB T1A 8W2
Tel: 403-502-8582; *Fax:* 403-502-8589
www.esplanade.ca/archives
Social Media: twitter.com/MedHatEsplanade;
www.facebook.com/MedHatEsplanade
Philip Pype, Archivist
phipyp@medicinehat.ca

***Millet:* Millet & District Historical Society**
c/o Millet & District Museum & Archives Room,, 5120 - 50 St., Millet, AB T0C 1Z0
Tel: 780-387-5558; *Fax:* 780-387-5548
info@milletmuseum.ca
www.milletmuseum.ca
Social Media: twitter.com/milletmuseum;
www.facebook.com/221092931274232
Tracey Leavitt, Executive Director, Curator
Jean Scott, Volunteer/Museum & Archives Manager

***Olds:* Mountain View Museum & Archives**
5038 - 50th St., Olds, AB T4H 1P6
Tel: 403-556-8464
info@oldsmuseum.ca
www.oldsmuseum.ca
Anne Lindsay, Museum Manager
manager@oldsmuseum.ca
Jeffery Kearney, Archivist

***Red Deer:* Red Deer & District Archives**
4525 - 47A Ave., Red Deer, AB T4N 6Z6
Tel: 403-309-8403; *Fax:* 403-340-8728
archives@reddeer.ca
Michael Dawe, City Archivist
Garth Clarke, Archivist
403-309-8403

***St Albert Place:* Musée Héritage Museum**
5 St Anne St., St Albert Place, AB T8N 3Z9
Tel: 780-459-1528
museum@artsheritage.ca
museeheritagemuseum.blogspot.com
Ann Ramsden, Director of Heritage

***Stony Plain:* The Multicultural Heritage Centre**
5411 - 51st St., Stony Plain, AB T7Z 1X7
Tel: 780-963-2777; *Fax:* 780-963-0233
info@multicentre.org
www.multicentre.org
Social Media: twitter.com/MultiCentre;
www.facebook.com/pages/Multicultural-Heritage-Centre
Judy Unterschultz, Executive Director
Rebecca Still, Museum and Archives
rebecca@multicentre.org

***Taber:* Taber & District Museum Society**
4702 - 50th St., Taber, AB T1G 2B6
Tel: 403-223-5708; *Fax:* 403-223-0529
Karen Ingram, Manager

***Wetaskiwin:* City of Wetaskiwin**
4904 - 51 St., Wetaskiwin, AB T9A 1L2
Tel: 780-361-4423; *Fax:* 780-361-4449
archives@wetaskiwin.ca
www2.wetaskiwin.ca/archives
Carolyn Hill, Archivist

British Columbia

Regional Systems

Cariboo Regional District Library
180 - 3rd Ave. North, #A, Williams Lake, BC V2G 2A4
Tel: 250-392-3630; *Toll-Free:* 800-665-1636
wlake@cariboord.bc.ca
www.cln.bc.ca
Colleen Swift, Manager, Library Services
cswift@cariboord.bc.ca

Fraser Valley Regional Library
34589 DeLair Rd., Abbotsford, BC V2S 5Y1
Tel: 604-859-7141; *Fax:* 604-852-5701
Toll-Free: 888-668-4141
www.fvrl.bc.ca
Social Media: www.youtube.com/user/FraserValleyLibrary;
twitter.com/readlearnplay;
www.facebook.com/FraserValleyLibrary
Rob O'Brennan, CEO
robert.obrennan@fvrl.bc.ca
Rita Penco, Director, Client Services
rita.penco@fvrl.bc.ca
Mary O'Callaghan, Director, Corporate Services
mary.ocallaghan@fvrl.bc.ca
Scott Hargrove, Director, Information Technology & Support Services
shargrove@fvrl.bc.ca
Brad Ferrick, Manager, Information Technology
brad.ferrick@fvrl.bc.ca
Cathy Wurtz, Manager, Human Resources
cathy.wurtz@fvrl.bc.ca
Mary Kierans, Manager, Support Services
mary.kierans@fvrl.bc.ca

IslandLink Library Federation
4153 Hawkes Ave., Victoria, BC V8Z 3Y9
Fax: 866-901-8509
Toll-Free: 888-256-5737
islandlink.bclibrary.ca

North Coast Library Federation
c/o Patti Chapman, Terrace Public Library, 4610 Park Ave., Terrace, BC V8G 1V6
Tel: 250-638-8177; *Fax:* 250-635-6207
coordinator@nclf.ca
nclf.ca
Billie Belcher, Chair
Patti Chapman, Secretary-Treasurer

North East Library Federation
PO Box 150, Hudson's Hope, BC V0C 1V0
Tel: 250-783-9414
manager@nelf.bclibrary.ca
nelf.bclibrary.ca
Barb Smith, Chair

Okanagan Regional Library
1430 KLO Rd., Kelowna, BC V1W 3P6
Tel: 250-860-4033; *Fax:* 250-861-8696
Other Numbers: 250-860-4652 (Telecirc for account access)
www.orl.bc.ca
Social Media: www.youtube.com/OKRegLibrary;
twitter.com/OKRegLib; www.facebook.com/OKRegLib
Ted Bacigalupo, Chair
Lesley Dieno, Executive Director
ldieno@orl.bc.ca
Barb Drake, Manager, Human Resources
bdrake@orl.bc.ca

Public Library InterLINK
#158, 5489 Byrne Rd., Burnaby, BC V5J 3J1
Tel: 604-437-8441; *Fax:* 604-437-8441
info@interlinklibraries.ca
www.interlinklibraries.ca
Rita Avigdor, Manager of Operations
rita.avigdor@interlinklibraries.ca
Colleen Smith, Audiobook Coordinator
colleen.smith@interlinklibraries.ca
604-517-8441

Southern Gulf Islands Community Libraries
BC
sgicl.bclibrary.ca

Thompson-Nicola Regional District Library System
#300, 465 Victoria St., Kamloops, BC V2C 2A9
Tel: 250-374-8866; *Fax:* 250-374-8358
admin@tnrd.ca
www.tnrd.ca
Social Media: www.facebook.com/TNRDLibrarySystem
Kevin Kierans, Director of Libraries
kevink@tnrdlib.ca

Vancouver Island Regional Library
6250 Hammond Bay Rd., Nanaimo, BC V9T 6M9
Tel: 250-758-4697; *Fax:* 250-758-2482
Toll-Free: 877-415-8475
Other Numbers: 250-753-1154 (Books By Mail)
info@virl.bc.ca
www.virl.bc.ca
Social Media: www.flickr/photos/virl; www.facebook.com/MyVIRL
Rosemary Bonanno, Executive Director
executivedirector@virl.bc.ca
250-729-2310
Elizabeth Wright, Manager, Systems Services
ewright@virl.bc.ca
250-729-2303
Laura Beswick, Manager, Collections & Support Services
lbeswick@virl.bc.ca
250-729-2321
Fiona Anderson, Director of Library Services
fanderson@virl.bc.ca
250-729-2311
Adrian Maas, Director of Finance
amaas@virl.bc.ca
250-729-2319

Harold Kamikawaji, Director of Human Resources
hkamikawaji@virl.bc.ca
250-729-2306

Public Libraries

***Alert Bay:* Alert Bay Public Library**
118 Fir St., Alert Bay, BC V0N 1A0
Tel: 250-974-5721; *Fax:* 250-974-5026
abplb@island.net
www.alertbay.com/library/
Sheila Jolliffe, Community Librarian

***Atlin:* Atlin Library**
Courthouse Bldg., 2nd St., Atlin, BC V0W 1A0
Linda Brown, Contact

***Bowen Island:* Bowen Island Public Library**
430 Bowen Trunk Rd., Bowen Island, BC V0N 1G0
Tel: 604-947-9788; *Fax:* 604-947-9788
info@bowenlibrary.ca
www.bowenlibrary.ca
Tina Nielsen, Librarian
tnielsen@bowenlibrary.ca

***Burnaby:* Burnaby Public Library**
6100 Willingdon Ave., Burnaby, BC V5H 4N5
Tel: 604-436-5427; *Fax:* 604-436-2961
Other Numbers: 604-293-0034 Telecirc
bpl@bpl.bc.ca
www.bpl.bc.ca
Social Media: twitter.com/burnabypl; www.facebook.com/burnabypubliclibrary
Edel Toner-Rogala, Chief Librarian
edel.toner-rogala@bpl.bc.ca
604-436-5431
Deb Thomas, Deputy Chief Librarian
deb.thomas@bpl.bc.ca
604-436-5432
Karen Steele, Librarian, Technical Services
karen.steele@bpl.bc.ca
604-436-5424
John Davenport, Librarian, Technical Services
jdavenpo@bpl.bc.ca
604-436-5435
Miriam Moses, Head, Technical Services, Acquisitions
miriam.moses@bpl.bc.ca
604-436-5435
May Chan, Head, Technical Services, Cataloguing
may.chan@bpl.bc.ca
604-436-5424
Greg Barkovich, Systems Supervisor
greg.barkovich@bpl.bc.ca
604-436-5437
Joyce Pinsker, Coordinator, Children & Youth Services
joyce.pinsker@bpl.bc.ca
604-436-5415

***Burns Lake:* Burns Lake Public Library**
585 Government St., Burns Lake, BC V0J 1E0
Tel: 250-692-3192; *Fax:* 250-692-7488
libraryn@burnslakelibrary.com
burnslake.bclibrary.ca
Linda L. Palmer, Head Librarian
Elaine Wiebe, Library Director
elaine@burnslakelibrary.com
Tenille Woskett, Assistant Director
tenille@burnslakelibrary.com

***Castlegar:* Castlegar & District Public Library**
1005 - 3rd St., Castlegar, BC V1N 2A2
Tel: 250-365-6611; *Fax:* 250-365-7765
info@castlegarlibrary.com
www.castlegarlibrary.com
Heather Maisel, Library Director
director@castlegarlibrary.com
250-365-7751
Julie Kalesnikoff, Librarian
julie@castlegarlibrary.com
Cheryl Babakaiff, Office Manager
cheryl@castlegarlibrary.com
Corinne Shortridge, Computer Technician
corinne@castlegarlibrary.com

***Chetwynd:* Chetwynd Public Library**
5012 - 46th St., Chetwynd, BC V0C 1J0
Tel: 250-788-2559; *Fax:* 250-788-2186
fasleson@pris.bc.ca
www.chetwyndpubliclibrary.com
Fay Asleson, Librarian
Jennifer Gosse, Chair

***Coquitlam:* Coquitlam Public Library**
575 Poirier St., Coquitlam, BC V3J 6A9
Tel: 604-937-4144; *Fax:* 604-937-4145
director@library.coquitlam.bc.ca
www.library.coquitlam.bc.ca
Social Media: twitter.com/CoqPubLib; www.facebook.com/175241429202024
Rhian Piprell, Director
rpiprell@library.coquitlam.bc.ca
604-937-4132
Silvana Harwood, Deputy Director
sharwood@library.coquitlam.bc.ca
604-937-4131
Mary Beth Folino, Circulation Supervisor
mfolino@library.coquitlam.bc.ca
604-937-4141
Deborah Duncan, Youth Services Coordinator
dduncan@library.coquitlam.bc.ca
604-937-4142
Jocelan Litton, Technical Services Coordinator
jlitton@library.coquitlam.bc.ca
604-937-4150
Kathy Marino, Collections Librarian
kmarino@library.coquitlam.bc.ca
604-937-4140
Kathleen Wyatt, Information Services Coordinator
kwayatt@library.coquitlam.bc.ca
604-937-4147
Nancy Collins, Systems Supervisor
systems@library.coquitlam.bc.ca
604-937-4151

***Cranbrook:* Cranbrook Public Library**
1212 - 2nd St. N, Cranbrook, BC V1C 4T6
Tel: 250-426-4063; *Fax:* 250-426-2098
staff@cranbrookpubliclibrary.ca
www.cranbrookpubliclibrary.ca
Ursula Brigl, Chief Librarian

***Crawford Bay:* Eastshore Community Library (Reading Centre)**
16234 King St., Crawford Bay, BC V0B 1E0
Tel: 250-227-6960

***Creston:* Creston & District Public Library**
531, 16th Ave. South, Creston, BC V0B 1G5
Tel: 250-428-4141; *Fax:* 250-428-4703
info@crestonlibrary.com
www.crestonlibrary.com
Social Media: twitter.com/intent/user?screen_name=crestonlibrary; www.facebook.com/pages/Creston-Public-Library/118409721541035
Joan Jeary, Chair

***Dawson Creek:* Dawson Creek Municipal Public Library**
1001 McKellar Ave., Dawson Creek, BC V1G 4W7
Tel: 250-782-4661; *Fax:* 250-782-4667
dclib@pris.ca
dawsoncreek.bclibrary.ca
Jenny Snyder, Head Librarian

***Dease Lake:* Dease Lake Reading Centre**
PO Box 237, Dease Lake, BC V0C 1L0
Tel: 250-771-3636
Carolyn Moore, Librarian

***Edgewater:* Edgewater Reading Centre**
PO Box 129, Edgewater, BC V0A 1E0
Tel: 250-347-9558

***Edgewood:* Inonoaklin Valley Reading Centre**
409 Monashee Ave., Edgewood, BC V0G 1J0
Tel: 250-269-7212; *Fax:* 250-269-7633
sbampton@hotmail.com
Susan Bampton, Librarian
sbampton@hotmail.com
Kathy Watson, Chair

***Elkford:* Elkford Public Library**
816 Michel Rd., Elkford, BC V0B 1H0
Tel: 250-865-2912; *Fax:* 250-865-2460
elklib1@yahoo.ca
www.elkfordlibrary.org
Diane Andrews, Head Librarian
elklib1@yahoo.ca
Rosalie Atherton, Library Clerk

***Fauquier:* Fauquier Reading Centre**
519 Willow St., Fauquier, BC V0G 1K0
Tel: 250-269-7348
Frank Poirier, Librarian

Karen Watson, Chair
karen.watson@canada.com
250-236-7390

***Fernie:* Fernie Heritage Library**
492 - 3rd Ave., Fernie, BC V0B 1M0
Tel: 250-423-4458; *Fax:* 250-423-7906
library@elkvalley.net
www.ferniheritagelibrary.com
Emma Dressler, Librarian

***Fort Nelson:* Fort Nelson Public Library**
Town Square, 5315 - 50th Ave. South, Fort Nelson, BC V0C 1R0
Tel: 250-774-6777; *Fax:* 250-774-6777
fnpl@fortnelson.bclibrary.ca
www.fortnelson.bclibrary.ca
Social Media: www.facebook.com/123316444364744
Flora Clark, Chair
Joan Davidson, Managing Librarian
Sylvia Bramhill, Assistant Librarian, Interlibrary Loans
Linda Novotny, Assistant Librarian, Technical Support
lnovotny@fortnelson.bclibrary.ca

***Fort St James:* Fort St James Public Library**
425 Manson St., Fort St James, BC V0J 1P0
Tel: 250-996-7431; *Fax:* 250-996-7484
fortlib@fsjames.com
fortstjames.bclibrary.ca
Diana Uhrich, Librarian
Jo-Anne Schemenauer, Assistant Librarian
Flora Arias Molina, Library Aide

***Fort St John:* Fort St John Public Library**
10015 - 100th Ave., Fort St John, BC V1J 1Y7
Tel: 250-785-3731; *Fax:* 250-785-7982
fortstjohn.bclibrary.ca
Kimberly Partanen, Head

***Fraser Lake:* Fraser Lake Public Library**
228 Endako Ave., Fraser Lake, BC V0J 1S0
Tel: 250-699-8888; *Fax:* 250-699-8899
fllibrarian@bcgroup.net
fraserlake.bclibrary.ca/
Audrey Fennema, Chief Librarian
Anne Mowry, Library Assistant
Hazel Thomas, Library Assistant

***Fruitvale:* Beaver Valley Public Library**
1847 - 1st St., Fruitvale, BC V0G 1L0
Tel: 250-367-7114; *Fax:* 250-367-7130
bvpublic@telus.net
beavervalley.bclibrary.ca
Marie Onyett, Head Librarian

***Galiano Island:* Galiano Island Community Library**
2540 Sturdies Bay Rd., Galiano Island, BC V0N 1P0
Tel: 250-539-2141
Other Numbers: Volunteer Chair: 250-539-2553
galianolibrary@shaw.ca
sgicl.bclibrary.ca/galiano
Social Media: www.facebook.com/galianolibrary

***Gibsons:* Gibsons & District Public Library**
470 South Fletcher Rd., Gibsons, BC V0N 1V0
Tel: 604-886-2130; *Fax:* 604-886-2689
www.gibsons.bclibrary.ca
Ms Michelle Southam, Chief Librarian
michelle.southam@gdpl.scrd.bc.ca
Pat Swadden, Assistant Librarian

***Grand Forks:* Grand Forks & District Public Library**
7342 - 5th St., Grand Forks, BC V0H 1H0
Tel: 250-442-3944; *Fax:* 250-442-2645
grandforks.bclibrary.ca
Heather Buzzell, Library Director
Amanda Deverson, Library Assistant

***Granisle:* Granisle Public Library**
#2 Village Sq., McDonald Ave., Granisle, BC V0J 1W0
Tel: 250-697-2713
library@granisle.net
granisle.bclibrary.ca
Sherry Smith, Chief Librarian

***Grasmere:* Grasmere Reading Centre**
PO Box 75, Grasmere, BC V0B 1R0
Tel: 250-887-3412; *Fax:* 250-887-3274
Bonnie Crosson, Head of Library

Greenwood: Greenwood Public Library
346 South Copper St., Greenwood, BC V0H 1J0
Tel: 250-445-6111; *Fax:* 250-445-6111
greenlib@shaw.ca
greenwood.bclibrary.ca
Judy Foucher, Community Librarian
Clare Folvik, Assistant Librarian

Hazelton: Hazelton & District Public Library
4255 Government St., Hazelton, BC V0J 1Y0
Tel: 250-842-5961; *Fax:* 250-842-2176
hazlib@bulkley.net
www.hazeltonlibrary.bc.ca
Eve Hope, Librarian

Houston: Houston Public Library
3150 - 14th St., Houston, BC V0J 1Z0
Tel: 250-845-2256; *Fax:* 250-845-2088
library.houston.ca
Toni McKilligan, Chief Librarian
Erna Vander Heide, Children's Librarian
Dana Giesbrecht, Library Assistant
Gail Conroy, Library Assistant

Hudson's Hope: Hudson's Hope Public Library
9905 Dudley Dr., Hudson's Hope, BC V0C 1V0
Tel: 250-783-9414; *Fax:* 250-783-5272
hh.ill@pris.ca
hudsonshope.bclibrary.ca

Invermere: Invermere Public Library
201 - 7th Ave., Invermere, BC V0A 1K0
Tel: 250-342-6416; *Fax:* 250-342-6416
invlibrary@cyberlink.bc.ca
invermere.bclibrary.ca
Elizabeth Robinson, Head Librarian

Kaslo: Kaslo & District Public Library
Kaslo Village Hall, Ground Fl., 413 - 4th St., Kaslo, BC V0G 1M0
Tel: 250-353-2942
info@kaslo.bclibrary.ca
www.kaslo.bclibrary.ca
Annie Reynolds, Coordinator, Library Services
areynolds@Kaslo.bclibrary.ca

Kimberley: Kimberley Public Library
115 Spokane St., Kimberley, BC V1A 2E5
Tel: 250-427-3112; *Fax:* 250-427-7157
staff@kimberleylibrary.net
kimberley.bclibrary.ca
Karin von Wittgenstein, Director

Kitimat: Kitimat Public Library
940 Wakashan Ave., Kitimat, BC V8C 2G3
Tel: 250-632-8985; *Fax:* 250-632-2630
kitimatlibrary@telus.net
www.kitimatpubliclibrary.org
Virginia Charron, Chief Librarian
vcharron@telus.net
Beverly Villemere, Assistant Librarian

Kitwanga: Gitanyow Independent School Reading Centre
PO Box 369, Kitwanga, BC V0J 2A0
Tel: 250-849-5528; *Fax:* 250-849-5870
Other Numbers: 250-849-5384 administration
Bernadette McLean, Chair

Lillooet: Lillooet & Area Public Library Association
930 Main St., Lillooet, BC V0K 1V0
Tel: 250-256-7944
lillooet.bclibrary.ca
Sheila Pfeifer, Chief Librarian
Steve Hempell, Technical Support
June Melhuish, Chair
250-256-7035

Lions Bay: Lions Bay Library (Reading Centre)
400 Centre Rd., Lions Bay, BC V0N 2E0
Tel: 604-921-6944

Mackenzie: MacKenzie Public Library
Recreation Centre, 400 Skeena Dr., Mackenzie, BC V0J 2C0
Tel: 250-997-6343; *Fax:* 250-997-5792
mackenziepubliclibrary@gmail.com
www.mackenzie.bclibrary.ca
Wanda Davis, Head Librarian

Madeira Park: Pender Harbour Reading Centre
12952 Madeira Park Rd., Madeira Park, BC V0N 2H0
Tel: 604-883-2983

Mayne Island: Mayne Island Public Library
411 Naylor Rd., Mayne Island, BC V0N 2J0
Tel: 250-539-2597
MIPL@shaw.ca
sgicl.bclibrary.ca/mayne
Judi Walker, Chair

McBride: McBride & District Public Library
241 Dominion St., McBride, BC V0J 2E0
Tel: 250-569-2411
library@mcbridebc.org
www.mcbride.bclibrary.ca
Naomi Balla-Boudreau, Library Director
Doreen Beck, Library Assistant
Dawn Phillips, Library Assistant
Martina Wall, Library Assistant

Midway: Midway Public Library
612 - 6th Ave., Midway, BC V0H 1M0
Tel: 250-449-2620; *Fax:* 250-449-2389
info@midwaylibrary.bc.ca
midway.bclibrary.ca
Stephanie Boltz, Librarian
info@midwaylibrary.bc.ca

Nakusp: Nakusp Public Library
92 - 6th Ave. NW, Nakusp, BC V0G 1R0
Tel: 250-265-3363; *Fax:* 250-265-3363
bna@netidea.com
nakusp.bclibrary.ca/
Sabina Iseli-Otto, Librarian
250-265-3363

Nelson: Nelson Municipal Library
602 Stanley St., Nelson, BC V1L 1N4
Tel: 250-352-6333; *Fax:* 250-354-1799
jstockdale@nelson.ca
nelson.bclibrary.ca
June Stockdale, Chief Librarian
Martha Scott, Assistant 3-Cataloguing
Nancy Radonich, Youth Services
Maureen Stoll, Assistant 2, Office Manager

New Denver: New Denver Reading Centre
PO Box 38, New Denver, BC V0G 1S0
Tel: 250-358-2221
Agnes Emary, Chair

New Westminster: New Westminster Public Library
716 - 6th Ave., New Westminster, BC V3M 2B3
Tel: 604-527-4660; *Fax:* 604-527-4674
listener@nwpl.ca
www.nwpl.ca
Julie Spurrell, Chief Librarian
spurrell@nwpl.ca
604-527-4675
Susan Buss, Interim Head, Reference Services
sbuss@nwpl.ca
604-527-4661
Marie McKee, Head of Technical Services
mmckee@nwpl.ca
604-527-4671
Ellen Heaney, Head of Children's Services
eheaney@nwpl.ca
604-527-4678

North Vancouver: North Vancouver City Library
120 West 14th St., North Vancouver, BC V7M 1N9
Tel: 604-998-3450; *Fax:* 604-983-3624
nvcl@cnv.org
www.cnv.org/nvcl
Social Media: twitter.com/#!/NorthVanCityLib; www.facebook.com/NorthVanCityLibrary?sk=wall
Jane Watkins, Chief Librarian
jwatkins@cnb.org
604-990-4226
Wai-Lin Chee, Deputy Chief Librarian
wchee@cnv.org
604-990-4222

North Vancouver: North Vancouver District Public Library
1277 Lynn Valley Rd., North Vancouver, BC V7J 2A1
Tel: 604-984-0286; *Fax:* 604-984-7600
Other Numbers: 604-984-0286 ext. 8140 (Circulation)
www.nvdpl.ca
Social Media: twitter.com/nvdpl; www.facebook.com/nvdpl
Areef Abraham, Chair
scoularh@nvdpl.ca
Heather Scoular, Director, Library Services
scoularh@nvdpl.ca
604-990-5800 ext. 8103
Michael DeKoven, Manager, Support Services
dekovenm@nvdpl.ca
604-990-5800 ext. 8120
Corinne McConchie, Manager, Technical Services
mconchiec@nvdpl.ca
604-990-5800 ext. 8113
Delores Weightman, Manager, Office & Human Resources
604-990-5800 ext. 8102
Heather Goodwin, Librarian, Home Service
604-990-5800 ext. 8124

Pemberton: Pemberton & District Public Library
Cottonwood St., Pemberton, BC V0N 2L0
Tel: 604-894-6916; *Fax:* 604-894-6917
library@pemberton.bclibrary.ca
pemberton.bclibrary.ca/community-info
Shannon Ellis, Library Director
sellis@pemberton.bclibrary.ca
Marilyn Marinus, Assistant Director
mmarinus@pemberton.bclibrary.ca
Niocole MacPhee, Children & Youth Services Coordinator
nmacphee@pemberton.bclibrary.ca
Valerie Fowler, Assistant Librarian
vfowler@pemberton.bclibrary.ca

Pender Island: Pender Island Public Library Association
4407 Bedwell Harbour Rd., Pender Island, BC V0N 2M0
Tel: 250-629-3722; *Fax:* 250-629-3788
pender.bclibrary.ca
Liz Testemale, Librarian
bpi.ill@gulfislands.com

Penticton: Penticton Public Library
785 Main St, Penticton, BC V2A 5E3
Tel: 250-770-7781
Other Numbers: InfoDesk: 250-770-7782; Kids' Library: 250-777-7783
library@summer.com
www.library.penticton.bc.ca
Larry R. Little, Chief Librarian
Karen Kellerman, Public Services Librarian
Shelley Murphy, Systems Librarian
Julia Cox, Youth Services Librarian

Piers Island: Piers Island Library
PO Box 2223, Piers Island, BC V8L 3S8
Tel: 250-656-0568
Other Numbers: 250-656-9697
piersislandreads@gmail.com
sgicl.bclibrary.ca/piers
Philippa White, Contact

Port Moody: Port Moody Public Library
100 Newport Dr., Port Moody, BC V3H 5C3
Tel: 604-469-4575; *Fax:* 604-469-4576
askthelibrary@portmoody.ca
library.portmoody.ca
Lynne Russell, Library Director

Pouce Coupe: Pouce Coupe Public Library
PO Box 75, Pouce Coupe, BC V0C 2C0
Tel: 250-786-5765
bpoc.ill@pris.bc.ca
www.poucecoupe.bclibrary.ca
Courtenay Johnston, Community Librarian
Patricia McDonald, Assistant Librarian

Powell River: Powell River Public Library
4411 Michigan Ave., Powell River, BC V8A 2S3
Tel: 604-485-4796; *Fax:* 604-485-5320
powellriverlibrary@shaw.ca
www.powellriverlibrary.ca
Stephanie Hall, Head Librarian

Prince George: Prince George Public Library
887 Dominion St., Prince George, BC V2L 5L1
Tel: 250-563-9251; *Fax:* 250-563-0892
www.lib.pg.bc.ca
Social Media: www.facebook.com/pglibrary
Allan Wilson, Chief Librarian
Marc Saunders, Manager, Public Services
Marjorie Tunney, Manager, Administrative Services

Prince Rupert: Prince Rupert Public Library
101 - 6th Ave. West, Prince Rupert, BC V8J 1Y9
Tel: 250-627-1345
info@princerupertlibrary.ca
www.princerupertlibrary.ca
Joe Zelwietro, Chief Librarian

Radium Hot Springs: **Radium Public Library**
#2, Main St. West, Radium Hot Springs, BC V0A 1M0
Tel: 250-347-2434
radiumpubliclibrary@hotmail.com
radium.bclibrary.ca
Social Media: www.facebook.com/RadiumPublicLibrary

Richmond: **Richmond Public Library**
#100, 7700 Minoru Gate, Richmond, BC V6Y 1R8
Tel: 604-231-6404
Other Numbers: Adult Ask Me Desk: 604-231-6413
www.yourlibrary.ca
Greg Buss, Chief Librarian & Secretary to the Board
Susan Walters, Deputy Chief Librarian
Mark Ellis, Manager, Information Technology
Wendy Jang, Coordinator, Multilingual Services
Virginia McCreedy, Coordinator, Children's Services
Shaneena Rahman, Coordinator, Circulation & Merchandising

Riondel: **Riondel Reading Centre**
PO Box 29, Riondel, BC V0B 2B0
Tel: 250-225-3570
Muriel Paquette, Chair

Roberts Creek: **Roberts Creek Community Library**
General Delivery, Roberts Creek, BC V0N 2W0
Tel: 604-886-2130

Rossland: **Rossland Public Library**
2180 Columbia Ave., Rossland, BC V0G 1Y0
Tel: 250-362-7611; *Fax:* 250-362-7138
rosslib@telus.net
rosslib.kics.bc.ca
Indira Wickremasinghe, Head Librarian
Lynn Amann, Children's Librarian & Assistant Librarian

Salmo: **Salmo Public Library**
PO Box 458, Salmo, BC V0G 1Z0
Tel: 250-357-2312; *Fax:* 250-357-2312
salmopubliclibrary@telus.net
salmo.bclibrary.ca
Amy Veysey, Library Director
salmopubliclibrary@telus.net

Salt Spring Island: **Salt Spring Island Public Library**
129 McPhillips Ave., Salt Spring Island, BC V8K 2T6
Tel: 250-537-4666; *Fax:* 250-537-4666
info@saltspringlibrary.com
saltspring.bclibrary.ca
Brigitte Peter-Cherneff, Chief Librarian
librarian@saltspringlibrary.com

Saturna Island: **Eddie Reid Memorial Library**
140 East Pt. Rd., Saturna Island, BC V0N 2Y0
Tel: 250-539-5312
library@saturnacan.net
sgicl.bclibrary.ca/saturna

Sechelt: **Sechelt Public Library**
5797 Cowrie St., Sechelt, BC V0N 3A0
Tel: 604-885-3260; *Fax:* 604-885-5183
info@sechelt.bclibrary.ca
www.sechelt.bclibrary.ca
Social Media: twitter.com/SecheltLibrary
Helen Prosser, Chief Librarian
Rose Toenders, Assistant Librarian
rose.toenders@sechelt.bclibrary.ca

Smithers: **Smithers Public Library**
3817 Alfred Ave., Smithers, BC V0J 2N0
Tel: 250-847-3043; *Fax:* 250-847-1533
contact@smitherslibrary.ca
smithers.bclibrary.ca
Social Media:
facebook.com/pages/Smithers-Public-Library/107866782746?ref=ts
Tracey Therrien, Library Director
ttherrien@smitherslibrary.ca

Sparwood: **Sparwood Public Library Association**
110 Pine Ave., Sparwood, BC V0B 2G0
Tel: 250-425-2299; *Fax:* 250-425-0229
sparwood.bclibrary.ca
James Bertoia, Head Librarian
jb@sparwoodlibrary.ca
250-425-2299

Squamish: **Squamish Public Library Association**
37907 - 2nd Ave., Squamish, BC V8B 0A7
Tel: 604-892-3110; *Fax:* 604-892-9376
www.squamish.bclibrary.ca
Social Media: twitter.com/squamishlibrary;
www.facebook.com/pages/Squamish-Public-Library/98609473295
Tara Franz, Chair

Stewart: **Stewart Public Library**
824 A Main St., Stewart, BC V0T 1W0
Tel: 250-636-2380; *Fax:* 250-636-2380
stewartpubliclibrary@gmail.com
www.stewart.bclibrary.ca
Galina Dyrant, Librarian
Anne Jefferson, Chair

Surrey: **Surrey Public Library**
City Centre Library, 3rd Fl., 10350 University Dr., Surrey, BC V3T 4B8
Tel: 604-598-7300; *Fax:* 604-598-7310
Other Numbers: Renewals: 604-502-6333
bsur@surrey.ca
www.surreylibraries.ca
Social Media: www.youtube.com/user/surreylibrary;
twitter.com/surreylibrary; www.facebook.com/surreylibraries
Melanie Houlden, Chief Librarian
mghoulden@surrey.ca
604-598-7305
Michael Ho, Manager, Administrative Services
mho@surrey.ca
604-598-7303
Stephanie Kurmey, Librarian, Collections Services
slkurmey@surrey.ca
604-598-7331

Taylor: **Taylor Public Library**
10008 - 104 Ave., Taylor, BC V0C 2K0
Tel: 250-789-9878; *Fax:* 250-789-3543
library@districtoftaylor.com
taylor.bclibrary.ca
Social Media:
www.facebook.com/group.php?gid=113819095313441
Sherry Murphy, Librarian

Terrace: **Terrace Public Library Association**
4610 Park Ave., Terrace, BC V8G 1V6
Tel: 250-638-8177; *Fax:* 250-635-6207
library@terracelibrary.ca
www.terracelibrary.ca
Patti Chapman, Chair
Margo Schiller, Chief Librarian

Trail: **Trail & District Public Library**
1051 Victoria St., Trail, BC V1R 3T3
Tel: 250-364-1731; *Fax:* 250-364-2176
director@traillibrary.com
www.traillibrary.com
Belinda Wilkinson, Director

Tumbler Ridge: **Tumbler Ridge Public Library**
340 Front St., Tumbler Ridge, BC V0C 2W0
Tel: 250-242-4778; *Fax:* 250-242-4707
www.tumblerridge.bclibrary.ca
Paula Coutts, Head Librarian
pcoutts@tumblerridgelibrary.net
Sharon Bray, Children's Services
sbray@tumblerridgelibrary.org
Jacob Fehr, Technical Services

Valemount: **Valemount Public Library**
1090A Main St., Valemount, BC V0E 2Z0
Tel: 250-566-4367; *Fax:* 250-566-4278
library@valemount.ca
valemount.bclibrary.ca
Wendy Cinnamon, Chief Librarian
Elli Haag, Assistant Librarian/Interlibrary Loan Librarian
Hollie Blanchette, Technology
Giovanna Gislimberti, Clerk

Vancouver: **Isaac Waldman Jewish Public Library**
Jewish Community Centre of Greater Vancouver, 950 West 41st Ave., Vancouver, BC V5Z 2N7
Tel: 604-257-5111; *Fax:* 604-257-5119
library@jccgv.bc.ca
www.jcclibrary.com
Karen Corrin, Librarian
Kelly Rae, Library Technician

Vancouver: **Vancouver Public Library**
350 West Georgia St., Vancouver, BC V6B 6B1
Tel: 604-331-3603
info@vpl.ca
www.vpl.ca
Sandra Singh, Chief Librarian
sandra.singh@vpl.ca
604-331-4003
Shelagh Flaherty, Director, Central Library
shelagh.flaherty@vpl.ca
604-331-4004
Diana Guinn, Director, Neighbourhood & Youth Services
diana.guinn@vpl.ca
604-331-4009
Eric Smith, Director, Corporate Services
eric.smith@vpl.ca
604-331-4018
Ingrid VanKemenade, Director, Human Resources
ingrid.vankemenade@vpl.ca
604-331-4052
Daphne Wood, Director, Planning & Development
daphne.wood@vpl.ca
604-331-4044
Jean Kavanagh, Manager, Marketing & Communications
jean.kavanagh@vpl.ca
604-331-3895

Vanderhoof: **Vanderhoof Public Library**
PO Bag 6000, Vanderhoof, BC V0J 3A0
Tel: 250-567-4060; *Fax:* 250-567-4458
vhpl@telus.net
www.vanderhoofpubliclibrary.com
Jane Gray, Librarian

Victoria: **Greater Victoria Public Library**
735 Broughton St., Victoria, BC V8W 3H2
Tel: 250-384-5222; *Fax:* 250-385-5971
TTY: 2504130364
Other Numbers: Reference: 250-382-7241
www.gvpl.ca
Social Media: twitter.com/gvpl
Maureen Sawa, CEO
msawa@gvpl.ca
250-413-0353
Lynne Jordan, Deputy CEO/Director of Strategic Development
jjordan@gvpl.ca
250-413-0354
Daniel Phillips, Manager, IT Solutions
dphillips@gvpl.ca
250-413-0357
Renée Bauert, Manager, Human Resources
rbauert@gvpl.ca
250-413-0359
Patricia Eaton, Manager, Public Services
peaton@gvpl.ca
250-413-0382

Victoria: **View Royal Public Library**
45B View Royal Ave., Victoria, BC V9B 1A6
Tel: 250-479-2723; *Fax:* 250-479-2723
vivr.ill@shaw.ca
members.shaw.ca/vivr.ill
Jim Powell, Chair

West Vancouver: **West Vancouver Memorial Library**
1950 Marine Dr., West Vancouver, BC V7V 1J8
Tel: 604-925-7400; *Fax:* 604-925-5933
Other Numbers: Art Gallery: 604-925-7407
info@westvanlibrary.ca
www.westvanlibrary.ca
Social Media: twitter.com/westvanlibrary;
www.facebook.com/WestVancouverMemorialLibrary
Jenny Benedict, Director, Library Services
jbenedict@westvanlibrary.ca
604-925-7424
Deb Hutchison Koep, Deputy Director & Head, Technology & Technical Services
dkoep@westvanlibrary.ca
604-925-7443
Cheryl McGregor, Head, Information Services
cmcgregor@westvanlibrary.ca
604-925-7439
Ellen Scoretz, Head, Circulation
escoretz@westvanlibrary.ca
604-925-7430
Lauren Henderson, Manager, Operations
lhenderson@westvanlibrary.ca
604-925-7431

Whistler: **Whistler Public Library**
4329 Main St., Whistler, BC V0N 1B4
Tel: 604-935-8433; *Fax:* 604-935-8434
info@whistlerlibrary.ca
www.whistlerlibrary.ca
Social Media: http://twitter.com/#!/WhistlerPL;
http://www.facebook.com/whistlerpubliclibrary
Elizabeth Tracy, Library Director
604-935-8438
Suzanne Thomas, Library Technician
sthomas@whistlerlibrary.ca
604-935-8433 ext. 8722
Beverly Newell, Community Librarian
bnewell@whistlerlibrary.ca

Danusia Smit, Circulation Manager
604-935-8433 ext. 8729
Nadine White, Public Services Librarian
604-935-8433 ext. 8725

Archives

Abbotsford: Matsqui-Sumas-Abbotsford Museum Archives
1B, 32320 George Ferguson Way, Abbotsford, BC V2T 6N4
Tel: 604-853-0313; Fax: 866-373-2771
prcoordinator.msamuseum@shawbiz.ca
www.abbotsford.net/msamuseum
Social Media:
www.facebook.com/profile.php?id=100001845282384
Dorothy Van der Ree, Executive Director
Christina Reid, Collections Manager
collectionsmanager@shawbiz.ca

Alert Bay: U'mista Cultural Centre
Front St., Alert Bay, BC V0N 1A0
Tel: 250-974-5403; Fax: 250-974-5499
Toll-Free: 800-690-8222
info@umista.ca
umista.org
Social Media: www.facebook.com/Umista.Cultural.Society
Sarah E. Holland, Executive Director
director@umista.ca
Juanita Johnston, Collections Manager
juanita@umista.ca

Ashcroft: Ashcroft Museum
402 Brink St., Ashcroft, BC V0K 1A0
Tel: 250-453-9232; Fax: 250-453-9664
museum@village.ashcroft.bc.ca
Helen Forster, Curator

Barkerville: Barkerville Historic Town
PO Box 19, Barkerville, BC V0K 1B0
Tel: 604-994-3332; Fax: 250-994-3435
Toll-Free: 888-994-3332
barkerville@barkerville.ca
www.barkerville.ca
Social Media: twitter.com/BarkervilleBC

Bella Bella: Heiltsuk Cultural Education Centre
PO Box 880, Bella Bella, BC V0T 1Z0
Tel: 250-957-2626; Fax: 250-957-2780
hcec04@yahoo.com
www.hcec.ca
Jennifer Carpenter, Director
jgcarp@hcec.ca
Terri Reid, Resource Centre Assistant
treid@hcec.ca

Burnaby: Nikkei National Museum & Cultural Centre
6688 Southoaks Cres., Burnaby, BC V5E 4M7
Tel: 604-777-7000; Fax: 604-777-7001
info@nikkeiplace.org
centre.nikkeiplace.org
Social Media: www.youtube.com/user/nikkeimuse;
twitter.com/nikkeimuse; www.facebook.com/NNMCC
A. Jensen, Collections Manager
ajensen@nikkeiplace.org
604-777-7000 ext. 140

Burnaby: Simon Fraser University Archives
#0400, Maggie Benston Student Services Centre,, 8888 University Dr., Simon Fraser University, Burnaby, BC V5A 1S6
Tel: 778-782-5433
britt@sfu.ca
www.sfu.ca/archives/

Campbell River: Museum at Campbell River
470 Island Hwy., Campbell River, BC V9W 2B7
Tel: 250-287-3103; Fax: 250-286-0109
general.inquiries@crmuseum.ca
www.crmuseum.ca
Sandra Parrish, Associate Director, Exhibits & Collection
sandra.parrish@crmuseum.ca
Linda Hogarth, Curator & Education Manager
linda.hogarth@crmuseum.ca

Castlegar: Selkirk College Archives
301 Frank Beinder Way, Castlegar, BC V1N 3J1
Tel: 250-365-1229; Fax: 250-365-7259
Toll-Free: 888-953-1133
bcs@selkirk.ca

Chilliwack: Chilliwack Archives
9291 Corbould St., Chilliwack, BC V2P 4A6
Tel: 604-795-9255; Fax: 604-795-5291
www.chilliwackmuseum.ca
Social Media: twitter.com/Chwkmusandarch
Ron Denman, Director
604-795-5210
Kelly Harms, Archivist

Chilliwack: Chilliwack Museum
45820 Spadina Ave., Chilliwack, BC V2P 1T3
Tel: 604-795-5210; Fax: 604-795-5291
cm_chin@dowco.com
chilliwack.museum.bc.ca/cm

Cranbrook: Canadian Museum of Rail Travel - Cranbrook Archives, Museum Landmark Foundation
57 Van Horne St. South, Cranbrook, BC V1C 4H9
Tel: 604-489-3918; Fax: 250-486-5744
mail@trainsdeluxe.com
www.trainsdeluxe.com
Garry Anderson, Executive Director/Archivist
mail@trainsdeluxe.com
250-489-3918

Cumberland: Cumberland Museum & Archives
2680 Dunsmuir Ave., Cumberland, BC V0R 1S0
Tel: 250-336-2445; Fax: 250-336-2321
info@cumberlandmuseum.ca
www.cumberlandmuseum.ca
Barbara Lemky, Curator

Delta: Delta Museum & Archives Society
4450 Clarence Taylor Cres., Delta, BC V4K 3W3
Tel: 604-940-3832; Fax: 604-946-5791
archives@deltamuseum.ca
www.deltamuseum.ca
Social Media:
www.facebook.com/DeltaMuseumAndArchivesSociety
Brenda Richmond, Archivist
Catharine McPherson, Assistant Archivist
Lea Edgar, Archival Attendant

Duncan: Cowichan Valley Museum & Archives
Duncan City Hall, 3rd Fl., Duncan, BC V9L 3Y2
Tel: 250-746-6612; Fax: 250-746-6612
cvmuseum.archives@shaw.ca
www.cowichanvalleymuseum.bc.ca
Kathryn Gagnon, Curator/Manager

Esquimalt: Township of Esquimalt
1149A Esquimalt Rd., Esquimalt, BC V9A 3N6
Tel: 250-412-8540; Fax: 250-412-8541
www.esquimalt.ca
Gregory Evans, Municipal Archivist

Fort Langley: Langley Centennial Museum & National Exhibition Centre
9135 King St., Fort Langley, BC V1M 2S2
Tel: 604-532-3536; Fax: 604-888-7291
information@langleymuseum.org
www.langleymuseum.org
Peter Tulumello, Manager, Cultural Services
ptulumello@tol.ca
Jane Lemke, Interim Curator, Arts & Heritage
jlemke@tol.ca
Jeff Chenatte, Educator, Arts & Heritage
jchenatte@tol.ca

Fort St John: Fort St John - North Peace Museum
9323 - 100th St., Fort St John, BC V1J 4N4
Tel: 250-787-0430; Fax: 250-787-0405
fsjmarchives@fsjmail.com
www.fsjmuseum.com

Fort Steele: Fort Steele Heritage Town
9851 Hwy. 93/95, Fort Steele, BC V0B 1N0
Tel: 250-417-6000; Fax: 250-489-2624
Info@FortSteele.bc.ca
fortsteele.ca
Social Media: www.facebook.com/fortsteeleheritagetown
Sally Struthers, General Manager
sally.struthers@fortsteele.bc.ca

Harrison Mills: Kilby Store & Farm
215 Kilby Rd., Harrison Mills, BC V0M 1L0
Tel: 604-796-9576; Fax: 604-796-9592
info@kilby.ca
www.kilby.ca
Bob Parliament, Area Manager
604-796-3859

Hazelton: 'Ksan Historical Village & Museum
PO Box 326, Hazelton, BC V0J 1Y0
Tel: 250-842-5544; Fax: 250-842-6533
Toll-Free: 877-842-5518
ksan@ksan.org
www.ksan.org

Kamloops: Kamloops Museum & Archives
207 Seymour St., Kamloops, BC V2C 2E7
Tel: 250-828-3576; Fax: 250-828-3760
museum@kamloops.ca
www.kamloops.ca/museum
Elizabeth Duckworth, Supervisor

Kamloops: Secwepemc Cultural Education Society
#311, 355 Yellowhead Hwy., Kamloops, BC V2H 1H1
Tel: 250-828-9749; Fax: 250-372-8833
www.secwepemc.org/museum/archives
Daniel Saul, Museum Manager
dsaul@kib.ca

Kaslo: Kootenay Lake Archives
312 - 4th St., Kaslo, BC V0G 1M0
Tel: 250-353-3204
archives@klhs.bc.ca
www.klhs.bc.ca/archives.htm
Elizabeth Scarlett, Archivist

Kelowna: Diocese of Kootenay, Archives
#201, 380 Leathead, Kelowna, BC V1X 1H8
Tel: 778-478-8310; Fax: 778-478-8314
admin@kootenay.info
www.kootenayanglican.ca/archives

Kelowna: Kelowna Public Archives
470 Queensway Ave., Kelowna, BC V1Y 6S7
Tel: 250-763-2417; Fax: 250-763-5722
archives@kelownamuseums.ca
www.kelownamuseums.ca/kelowna-public-archives.html
Social Media: twitter.com/kelownamuseums
Donna Johnson, Archivist
250-763-2417 ext. 25
Tara Hurley, Registrar & Archivist
registrar@kelownamuseums.ca
250-763-2417 ext. 29

Kitimat: Kitimat Centennial Museum & Archives
293 City Centre, Kitimat, BC V8C 1T6
Tel: 250-632-8950; Fax: 250-632-7429
kitimatmuseum@telus.net
www.kitimatmuseum.ca
Social Media:
www.facebook.com/pages/Kitimat-Museum-Archives/161440070544293
Louise Avery, Curator
Angela Eastman, Assistant Curator
aeastman.kitmuse@telus.net

Lake Cowichan: Kaatza Historical Society
125 South Shore Rd., Lake Cowichan, BC V0R 2G0
Tel: 250-749-6142; Fax: 250-749-3900
www.kaatzamuseum.ca
Barbara Simkins, Curator/Manager

Langley: Trinity Western University Archives
Norma Marion Alloway Library, Trinity Western University, 7600 Glover Rd., Upper Level, Langley, BC V2Y 1Y1
Tel: 604-513-2121; Fax: 604-513-2063
archives.twu.ca

Maple Ridge: Maple Ridge Museum & Community Archives
22520 - 116th Ave., Maple Ridge, BC V2X 0S4
Tel: 604-463-5311; Fax: 604-463-5317
www.mapleridgemuseum.org
Social Media:
www.flickr.com/photos/mrcommunityarchives/5902226789;
www.facebook.com/106860626035721
Allison White, Curator

Merritt: Nicola Tribal Association
#202, 2090 Coutlee Ave., Merritt, BC V1K 1B8
Tel: 250-378-4235; Fax: 250-378-9119
www.nicolatribal.com
Neil Todd, General Manager
Natasha Fountain, Manager, Research

Merritt: Nicola Valley Museum & Archives
1672 Tutill Crt., Merritt, BC V1K 1B8
Tel: 250-378-4145; Fax: 250-378-4145
nvma@uniserve.com
www.nicolavalleymuseum.org
Social Media: www.facebook.com/123292923631
Barb Watson, Office Administrator

Jo Atkinson, Assistant Administrator

***Mission:* Mission Community Archives**
33215 - 2nd Ave., Mission, BC V2V 4L1
Tel: 604-820-2621
mca@missionarchives.com
www.missionarchives.com
Valerie Billesberger, Archivist/Records Manager

***Nakusp:* Arrow Lakes Historical Society**
BC Hydro Bldg., 92B - 7th Ave. NW, Nakusp, BC V0G 1R0
Tel: 250-265-0110; *Fax:* 250-265-0110
Other Numbers: Off-Hours Phone: 250-265-3323
alhs@netidea.com
www.alhs-archives.com
Rosemarie Parent, President
miltrose@telus.net
Milton Parent, Historian
miltrose@telus.net

***Nelson:* Roman Catholic Diocese of Nelson**
402 West Richards St., Nelson, BC V1L 3K3
Tel: 250-352-6921; *Fax:* 250-352-1737
www.diocese.nelson.bc.ca
R.J. (Ron) Welwood, Contact
r-fwelwood@shaw.ca

***Nelson:* Touchstones Nelson Museum of Art & History**
502 Vernon St., Nelson, BC V1L 4E7
Tel: 250-352-9813; *Fax:* 250-352-9810
www.touchstonesnelson.ca/archives
Social Media: www.flickr.com/photos/touchstonesnelson;
www.facebook.com/group.php?gid=62908084663

***New Westminster:* Archives**
700 Royal Ave., New Westminster, BC V3M 5Z5
Tel: 604-527-5182; *Fax:* 604-527-5193

***New Westminster:* New Westminster Museum & Archives**
302 Royal Ave., New Westminster, BC V3L 1H7
Tel: 604-527-4640; *Fax:* 604-527-4641
museum@newwestcity.ca
www.newwestpcr.ca/culture/museum_and_archives
Social Media:
www.facebook.com/group.php?gid=107102786015526
Barry Dykes, Archivist
bdykes@newwestcity.ca
604-527-4642

***North Vancouver:* North Vancouver Museum & Archives**
Community History Centre, 3203 Institute Rd., North Vancouver, BC V7K 3E5
Tel: 604-990-3700
nvmac@dnv.org
www.northvanmuseum.ca/collections3.htm
Social Media: twitter.com/NorthVanMuseum;
www.facebook.com/NorthVancouverMuseumArchives
Janet Turner, Archivist
turnerj@dnv.org
Daien Ide, Reference Historian
ided@dnv.org

***Penticton:* Penticton Museum & Archives**
785 Main St., Penticton, BC V2A 5E3
Tel: 250-490-2451; *Fax:* 250-490-2442
www.pentictonmuseum.com
Peter Ord, Museum Manager
250-490-2452

***Port Alberni:* Alberni District Historical Society**
4255 Wallace St., Port Alberni, BC V9Y 3Y6
Tel: 250-723-2181; *Fax:* 250-723-1035
aadhs1@gmail.com
Judy Carlson, Volunteer Archivist
aadhs1@gmail.com

***Port Clements:* Port Clements Historical Society**
45 Bayview Dr., Port Clements, BC V0T 1R0
Tel: 250-557-4255; *Fax:* 250-557-4251
pcmuseum@island.net
www.portclementsmuseum.org

***Prince George:* Exploration Place**
333 Becott Place, Prince George, BC V2L 4V7
Tel: 250-562-1612; *Fax:* 250-562-6395
Toll-Free: 866-562-1612
curatorial@theexplorationplace.com.
www.theexplorationplace.com
Social Media: twitter.com/ExplorationPG;
www.facebook.com/TheExplorationPlace
Bob Campbell, Manager, Curatorial Services
bob@theexplorationplace.com
250-562-1612 ext. 230
Alisha Rubadeau, Assistant Curator
curatorial@theexplorationplace.com
Chad Hellenius, Assistant Archivist
archive@theexplorationplace.com

***Prince Rupert:* Prince Rupert City & Regional Archives**
424 Third Ave. West, Prince Rupert, BC V8J 1L7
Tel: 250-624-3326; *Fax:* 250-624-3706
info@princerupertarchives.ca
www.princerupertarchives.ca

***Quesnel:* Quesnel & District Museum & Archives**
705 Carson Ave., Quesnel, BC V2J 2B6
Tel: 250-992-9580; *Fax:* 250-992-9680
www.quesnelmuseum.ca
Elizabeth Hunter, Museum & Heritage Manager
ehunter@quesnel.ca
Leslie Middleton, Curatorial Assistant
leslie@quesnel.ca

***Revelstoke:* Revelstoke Museum & Archives**
PO Box 1908, Revelstoke, BC V0E 2S0
Tel: 250-837-3067; *Fax:* 250-837-3094
revelstokemuseum@telus.net
www.revelstokemuseum.ca
Cathy English, Curator
250-837-3067

***Richmond:* City of Richmond Archives**
7700 Minoru Gate, Richmond, BC V6Y 1R9
Tel: 604-247-8305; *Fax:* 604-231-6464
archives@richmond.ca
www.richmond.ca/cityhall/archives/about/about.htm
Bill Purver, Archivist

***Sooke:* Sooke Region Museum & Visitor Centre**
2070 Phillips Rd., Sooke, BC V9Z 0Y3
Tel: 250-642-6351; *Fax:* 250-642-7089
Toll-Free: 866-888-4748
info@sookeregionmuseum.com
www.sookeregionmuseum.com
Social Media:
www.facebook.com/group.php?gid=118482471530145
Joyce Linell, Contact

***Summerland:* Summerland Museum & Heritage Society**
9521 Wharton St., Summerland, BC V0H 1Z0
Tel: 250-494-9395; *Fax:* 250-494-9326
info@summerlandmuseum.org
www.summerlandmuseum.org
Sharon Stone, Administrator

***Surrey:* City of Surrey Archives**
17671 - 56 Ave., Surrey, BC V3S 1C9
Tel: 604-502-6459
archives@surrey.ca
www.surrey.ca/culture-recreation/2394.aspx
Social Media: twitter.com/SurreyArchives

***Terrace:* Diocese of Caledonia, Archives**
#201, 4716 Lazelle Ave., Terrace, BC V8G 1T2
Tel: 250-627-2243; *Fax:* 250-635-6026
calarch@citytel.net
www.caledonia.anglican.org

***Trail:* Trail Historical Society**
Trail City Hall, 1394 Pine Ave., 2nd Fl., Trail, BC V1R 4E6
Tel: 250-364-0829
history@trail.ca
www.trailhistory.com/archives.html
Sarah Benson, Director

***Vancouver:* BC Council**
1476 West 8th Ave., Vancouver, BC V6H 1E1
Tel: 604-714-6636; *Fax:* 604-714-6645
Toll-Free: 800-565-8111
info@bc-girlguides.org
www.bc-girlguides.org

***Vancouver:* British Columbia Conference, Archives**
6000 Iona Dr., Vancouver, BC V6T 1L4
Tel: 604-822-9589; *Fax:* 604-822-9212
united-archives@vst.edu
www.bc.united-church.ca/content/bob-stewart-archives-bc-confe
r

***Vancouver:* British Columbia Sports Hall of Fame & Museum**
777 Pacific Blvd. South, Vancouver, BC V6B 4Y8
Tel: 604-687-5520
sportsinfo@bcsportshalloffame.com
www.bcsportshalloffame.com
Social Media: twitter.com/BCSportsHall;
www.facebook.com/bcsportshall
Jason Beck, Curator
jason.beck@bssportshalloffame.com

***Vancouver:* City of Vancouver Archives**
1150 Chestnut St., Vancouver, BC V6J 3J9
Tel: 604-736-8561; *Fax:* 604-736-0626
archives@vancouver.ca
www.vancouver.ca/archives
Social Media: www.youtube.com/user/VancouverArchives;
twitter.com/VanArchives
Leslie Mobbs, City Archivist & Director, Records & Archives Division
leslie.mobbs@vancouver.ca

***Vancouver:* Diocese of New Westminster and the Ecclesiastical Province of British Columbia and the Yukon, Archives**
6000 Iona Dr., Vancouver, BC V6T 1L4
Tel: 604-822-9583; *Fax:* 604-822-9212
anglican-archives@vst.edu
www.anglicanarchivesvancouver.com

***Vancouver:* Institute of Indigenous Government / Union of BC Indian Chiefs**
#500, 342 Water St., Vancouver, BC V6B 1B6
Tel: 604-684-0231; *Fax:* 604-684-5726
library@ubcic.bc.ca
www.ubcic.bc.ca/department/library.htm
Social Media: twitter.com/#!/UBCIC; www.facebook.com/UBCIC
Kim Lawson, Archivist/Librarian
library@ubcic.bc.ca
604-684-0241
Jennifer Cole, Head, Technical Services/Acquisitions
library@ubcic.bc.ca
604-684-0241

***Vancouver:* Jewish Historical Society of BC**
6184 Ash St., Vancouver, BC V5Z 3G9
Tel: 604-257-5199
info@jewishmuseum.ca
www.jewishmuseum.ca
Jennifer Yuhasz, Archivist

***Vancouver:* Roman Catholic Archdiocese of Vancouver**
150 Robson St., Vancouver, BC V6B 2A7
Tel: 604-683-0281; *Fax:* 604-683-4288
www.rcav.org/archives
Anthea Seles, Records Manager/Archivist
aseles@rcav.bc.ca
604-683-0281 ext. 302

***Vancouver:* Satellite Video Exchange Society**
1965 Main St., Vancouver, BC V5T 3C1
Tel: 604-872-8337; *Fax:* 604-876-1185
info@videoout.ca
www.vivomediaarts.com
Emma Hendrix, General Manager
admin@vivomediaarts.com
Sharon Bradley, Coordinator, Distribution
604-872-8449

***Vancouver:* University of British Columbia Archives**
Irving K. Barber Learning Centre, University of British Columbia, 1961 East Mall, Vancouver, BC V6T 1Z1
Tel: 604-822-5877; *Fax:* 604-822-9587
www.library.ubc.ca/archives

***Vancouver:* Vancouver Ballet Society**
677 Davie St., 6th Fl., Vancouver, BC V6B 2G6
Tel: 604-681-1425
www.vancouverballetsociety.ca/Archives
Leslie Nadon, Administrator
vbs@telus.net
Maureen Allen, Library & Archives Chair

***Vernon:* Greater Vernon Museum & Archives**
3009 - 32nd Ave., Vernon, BC V1T 2L8
Tel: 250-542-3142; *Fax:* 250-542-5358
archives@vernonmuseum.ca
www.vernonmuseum.ca
Barbara Bell, Archivist
Liz Ellison, Database Manager & Assistant to the Archivist
ellison@vernonmuseum.ca

***Victoria:* City of Victoria Archives**
8 Centenial Sq., Victoria, BC V8W 1P6
Tel: 250-361-0375; *Fax:* 250-361-0394
archives@victoria.ca
victoria.ca/EN/main/departments/legislative-services/archives.html

***Victoria:* Diocese of British Columbia, Archives**
900 Vancouver St., Victoria, BC V8V 3V7
Tel: 250-386-7781; *Fax:* 250-386-4013
Toll-Free: 800-582-8627
darchives@bc.anglican.ca
diocesanarchivesbc.com

***Victoria:* Roman Catholic Diocese of Victoria**
#1, 4044 Nelthorpe St., Victoria, BC V8X 2A1
Tel: 250-479-1331; *Fax:* 250-479-5423
chancery@rcdvictoria.org
www.rcdvictoria.org
Social Media: twitter.com/RCDVictoria
Michael Lapierre, Vicar-General
mlapierre@cdvictoria.org
250-479-1331

***Victoria:* Saanich Municipal Archives**
3100 Tillicum Rd., Victoria, BC V9A 6T2
Tel: 250-475-1775; *Fax:* 250-388-7819
archives@saanich.ca
www.saanicharchives.ca
Social Media: www.facebook.com/137902079636927
Caroline Duncan, Municipal Archivist
250-475-1775 ext. 3478
Sonia Nicholson, Archives Specialist
250-475-1775 ext. 3479
Evelyn Wolfe, Archives Specialist
250-475-1775 ext. 3477

***Victoria:* Sisters of St Ann**
1550 Begbie St., Victoria, BC V8R 1K8
Tel: 250-592-0685; *Fax:* 250-592-0234
www.sistersofsaintanne.org/bc
Mickey King, Archivist

***West Vancouver:* West Vancouver Archives**
680 - 17th St., West Vancouver, BC V7V 3T2
Tel: 604-925-7298; *Fax:* 604-925-5915
archives@westvancouver.ca
www.wvma.net
Shaunna Moore, District Archivist

***White Rock:* White Rock Museum & Archives Society**
14970 Marine Dr., White Rock, BC V4B 1C4
Tel: 604-541-2222; *Fax:* 604-541-2223
whiterockarchives@telus.net
www.whiterock.museum.bc.ca
Hugh Ellenwood, Community Historian & Archives Manager
604-541-2225
Jasmine Moore, Coordinator, Collections & Exhibits
whiterockcollections@telus.net
604-541-2230

Manitoba

Regional Systems

Border Regional Library
312 - 7th Ave., Virden, MB R0M 2C0
Tel: 204-748-3862; *Fax:* 204-748-3862
brlibrary.cimnet.ca
Linda Grant-Braybrook, Librarian

Evergreen Regional Library
55 First Ave., Gimli, MB R0C 1B0
Tel: 204-642-7912; *Fax:* 204-642-8319
gimli.library@mts.net
www.erlibrary.ca
Valerie Eyolfson, Head Librarian
gimli.library@mts.net
204-642-7912
Karen Gottfried, Assistant Librarian
gimli.library@mts.net
204-642-7912
Sandy Reykdal, Assistant Librarian
gimli.library@mts.net
204-642-7912

Lac du Bonnet Regional Library
PO Box 216, Lac du Bonnet, MB R0E 1A0
Tel: 204-345-2653; *Fax:* 204-345-6827
mldb@mts.net
Vickie Short, Head Librarian
Janice Hoffman, Assistant Librarian
Lisa Rand, Assistant Librarian
Pat Loeppry, Library Clerk

Lakeland Regional Library
318 Williams Ave., Killarney, MB R0K 1G0
Tel: 204-523-4949
lrl@mts.net
www.lakelandregionallibrary.ca
Gloria Kinsley, Librarian

Manitou Regional Library
418 Main St., Manitou, MB R0G 1G0
Tel: 204-242-3134; *Fax:* 204-242-3184
manitoulibrary@mts.net
www.manitouregionallibrary.ca
Bev Boote, Head Librarian

Parkland Regional Library
504 Main St. North, Dauphin, MB R7N 1C9
Tel: 204-638-6410; *Fax:* 204-638-9483
prlhq@parklandlib.mb.ca
www.parklandlib.mb.ca
Jean-Louis Guillas, Director
jguillas@parklandlib.mb.ca

South Central Regional Library
160 Main St., Winkler, MB R6W 2P8
Tel: 204-325-7174; *Fax:* 204-331-1847
headlib@scrlibrary.mb.ca
www.scrlibrary.mb.ca
Social Media: www.facebook.com/scrllibrary
Mary Toma, Head Librarian
headlib@srclibrary.mb.ca
204-325-5864
Esther Penner, Head of Technical Services
techserv@scrlibrary.mb.ca

Southwestern Manitoba Regional Library
149 Main St., Melita, MB R0M 1L0
Tel: 204-522-3923
www.swmblib.wix.com/library-page

Western Manitoba Regional Library/ Brandon Public Library
#1, 710 Rosser Ave., Brandon, MB R7A 0K9
Tel: 204-727-6648; *Fax:* 204-727-4447
brandon@wmrl.ca
www.wmrl.ca
Social Media: twitter.com/wmrlibrary
Kathy Thornborough, Chief Librarian
kathy@wmrl.ca
Shelley Mortensen, Assistant Librarian
shelley@wmrl.ca

Public Libraries

***Baldur:* Regional Municipality of Argyle Public Library**
627 Elizabeth St. East, Baldur, MB R0K 0B0
Tel: 204-535-2314; *Fax:* 204-535-2242
rmargyle@gmail.com
Cheri McLaren

***Beausejour:* Brokenhead River Regional Library**
427 Park Ave., Beausejour, MB R0E 0C0
Tel: 204-268-7570; *Fax:* 204-268-7570
brrlibr@MTS.net
www.efree.mb.ca/brrl/home.html
Debbie Winnicki, Head Librarian

***Boissevain:* Boissevain & Morton Regional Library**
436 South Railway St., Boissevain, MB R0K 0E0
Tel: 204-534-6478; *Fax:* 204-534-3710
mbom@mts.net
bmlibrary.ca

***Carman:* Boyne Regional Library**
15 - 1st Ave. SW, Carman, MB R0G 0J0
Tel: 204-745-3504
boynereg@mts.net
www.boyneregionallibrary.com
Sandra Yeo, Head Librarian
Diane Cohoe, Assistant Librarian
illbrl@hotmail.com

***Cartwright:* Cartwright Branch Library**
483 Veteran Dr., Cartwright, MB R0K 0L0
Tel: 204-529-2261
cartlib@mts.net
www.lakelandregionallibrary.ca
Andrea Trembath, Branch Librarian

***Churchill:* Churchill Public Library**
Town Centre Complex, 181 Laverendrye Ave., Churchill, MB R0B 0E0
Tel: 204-675-2731; *Fax:* 204-675-2934

***Deloraine:* Bren Del Win Centennial Library**
311 North Railway Ave. West, PO Box 584, Deloraine, MB R0M 0M0
Tel: 204-747-2415; *Fax:* 204-747-3446
bdwlib@mts.net
Helen Schoenbaert, Chair
Lorraine Stovin, Librarian

***Eriksdale:* Eriksdale Public Library**
9 Main St., Eriksdale, MB R0C 0W0
Tel: 204-739-2668; *Fax:* 204-739-2668
epl1@mts.net
www.eriksdalepl.org
Rita L. Cushnie, Librarian
epl1@mts.net

***Flin Flon:* Flin Flon Public Library**
58 Main St., Flin Flon, MB R8A 1J8
Tel: 204-687-3397; *Fax:* 204-687-4233
ffpl@mts.net
www.flinflonpubliclibrary.ca
Cindy McLean, Library Administrator
Buz Trevor, Library Board Chair

***Gillam:* Bette Winner Public Library**
PO Box 400, Gillam, MB R0B 0L0
Tel: 204-652-2617; *Fax:* 204-652-2617
library@townofgillam.com
Social Media:
www.facebook.com/group.php?gid=160167924017586
Ricci Bangle, Head Librarian

***Headingley:* Headingley Public Library**
49 Alboro St., Headingley, MB R4J 1A3
Tel: 204-888-5410; *Fax:* 204-831-7207
hml@mymts.net
www.headingleylibrary.ca
Joan Spice, Head Librarian
Alison Au, Library Assistant
Kathie MacIsaac, Library Assistant

***Holland:* Victoria Municipal Library**
PO Box 371, Holland, MB R0G 0X0
Tel: 204-526-2011
victlib@goinet.ca

***Ile-des-Chênes:* Bibliothèque Ritchot - Ile-des-Chênes**
École Gabrielle-Roy, CP 581, Ile-des-Chênes, MB R0A 0T0
Tél: 204-878-2147; *Téléc:* 204-878-3495
ritchotlib@hotmail.com
www.richot.com/libraries.htm
Louise Durand, Bibliothécaire

***La Broquerie:* Bibliothèque Saint-Joachim Library**
29, Normandeau Bay, La Broquerie, MB R0A 0W0
Tel: 204-424-9533; *Fax:* 204-424-5610
bsjl@bsjl.ca
www.bsjl.ca
Yolande Tétrault, Présidente, Conseil d'administration
Rolande Durand, Bibliothécaire
204-424-9533

***Lundar:* The Pauline Johnson Public Library**
23 Main St., Lundar, MB R0C 1Y0
Tel: 204-762-5367; *Fax:* 204-762-5367
mlpj@mts.net

***Lynn Lake:* Lynn Lake Centennial Library**
PO Box 1127, Lynn Lake, MB R0B 0W0
Tel: 204-356-8222
Margaret Thomson, Librarian

***MacGregor:* North Norfolk MacGregor Regional Library**
35 Hampton St. East, MacGregor, MB R0H 0R0
Tel: 204-685-2796; *Fax:* 204-685-2478
maclib@mts.net
www.northnorfolk.ca
Antoinette Blankvoort, Head Librarian
Bernice Albers, Assistant Librarian
204-685-2294

***Minnedosa:* Minnedosa Regional Library**
45 - 1st Ave. SE, Minnedosa, MB R0J 1E0
Tel: 204-867-2585; *Fax:* 204-867-6140
mmr@mts.net
www.discoverminnedosa.ca
Social Media: www.facebook.com/103641533063836

Linda Cook, Librarian
Lisa Bilcowski, Assistant Librarian

***Morris:* Valley Regional Library**
141 Main St. South, Morris, MB R0G 1K0
Tel: 204-746-2136
valleylib@mts.net
www.valleylibrary.ca
Dinne DeKezel, Librarian
204-746-2136
Diane Ali, Assistant Librarian
Jane Stevenson, Head Volunteer
Meredith Loewen, Volunteer
Rikki Bergstresser, Student Librarian

***Norway House:* Ayamiscikawikamik Public Library**
General Delivery, Norway House, MB R0B 1B0
Tel: 204-359-6047; *Fax:* 204-642-7151
Violet Ouellette, Librarian

***Notre-Dame-de-Lourdes:* Bibliothèque Père Champagne / Père Champagne Library**
44, rue Rodgers, CP 399, Notre-Dame-de-Lourdes, MB R0G 1M0
Tel: 204-248-2386
ndbiblio@yahoo.ca
bpcl.fbmb.ca/en/home/
Gisèle Théroux, Responsable

***Pilot Mound:* Pilot Mound Library**
219 Broadway Ave. West, Pilot Mound, MB R0G 1P0
Tel: 204-825-2035
pmlibrary@mymts.net
www.pilotmoundlibrary.ca
Allison MacAulay, Librarian

***Pinawa:* Pinawa Public Library**
Community Centre, Vanier Ave., Pinawa, MB R0E 1L0
Tel: 204-753-2496; *Fax:* 204-753-2770
email@pinawapubliclibrary.com
www.pinawapubliclibrary.com
Marg Stokes, Head Librarian
plibrary@sdwhiteshell.mb.ca
204-753-2496
Audrey Miller, Library Assistant
plibrary@sdwhiteshell.mb.ca
204-753-2496
Donna Schofield, Library Assistant
plibrary@sdwhiteshell.mb.ca
204-753-2496

***Portage la Prairie:* Portage la Prairie Regional Library**
40B Royal Rd. North, Portage la Prairie, MB R1N 1V1
Tel: 204-857-4271; *Fax:* 204-239-4387
portlib@portagelibrary.com
www.portagelibrary.com
Percy Gregoire-Voskamp, Head Librarian

***Rapid City:* Rapid City Regional Library**
125 - 3rd Ave., Rapid City, MB R0K 1W0
Tel: 204-826-2732
rcreglib@mts.net
216.130.92.162/Default.htm
Shirley Martin, Head Librarian

***Reston:* Reston District Library**
220 - 4th St., Reston, MB R0M 1X0
Tel: 204-877-3673
restonlb@yahoo.ca

***Rivers:* Prairie Crocus Regional Library**
137 Main St., Rivers, MB R0K 1X0
Tel: 204-328-7613
pcrl@mts.net
www.prairiecrocuslibrary.ca
Dora M. Irvine, Librarian

***Rossburn:* Rossburn Regional Library**
53 Main St. North, Rossburn, MB R0J 1V0
Tel: 204-859-2687; *Fax:* 204-859-2687
rrl@mts.net
www.rossburnregionallibrary.ca
Stephanie Parkinson, Librarian/Book-Keeper
rrl@mts.net
Ivy Phelps, Library Assistant
rrl@mts.net

***Russell:* Russell & District Regional Library**
339 Main St., Russell, MB R0J 1W0
Tel: 204-773-3127
ruslib@mts.net
www.russellmb.com/s-library
Louise Sidoryk, Library Technician

***Saint-Claude:* Bibliothèque Saint-Claude / St. Claude Library**
50 - 1st St., Saint-Claude, MB R0G 1Z0
Tel: 204-379-2524
stclib@mts.net
www.stclaude.ca
Lynn Gobin, Librarian

***Selkirk:* Red River North Regional Library**
303 Main St., Selkirk, MB R1A 1S7
Tel: 204-482-3522; *Fax:* 204-482-6166
library@ssarl.org
www.ssarl.org
Ken Kuryliw, Director, Library Services
kkuryliw@ssarl.org
Lorraine Smith, Technical Services Coordinator
lsmith@ssarl.org
Katherine Anderson, Public Services & Information Technology Coordinator
kanderson@ssarl.org

***Shilo:* Shilo Community Library**
Bldg. T 100, Notre Dame & French, Box 177, Shilo, MB R0K 2A0
Tel: 204-765-2590
shilocommunitylibrary@yahoo.ca
Social Media: www.facebook.com/group.php?gid=7280251236

***Snow Lake:* Snow Lake Community Library**
Joseph H. Kerr School, 201 Cherry Ave., Snow Lake, MB R0B 1M0
Tel: 204-358-2322; *Fax:* 204-358-2116
www.snowlake.com
Vivian Bennett, Librarian
204-358-2833

***Somerset:* Somerset Library/ Bibliothèque Somerset**
289 Carlton Ave., Somerset, MB R0G 2L0
Tel: 204-744-2170
Lucille Labossiere, Librarian
204-744-2860

***Souris:* Glenwood & Souris Regional Library**
#18, 114 - 2nd St. South, Souris, MB R0K 2C0
Tel: 204-483-2757
frontdesk@sourislibrary.mb.ca
sourislibrary.mb.ca
Gayle O'Greysik, Chair
Connie Bradshaw, Librarian
Lynda Luptak, Assistant Librarian

***St Jean Baptiste:* Bibliothèque Montcalm Library**
113B - 2nd Ave., St Jean Baptiste, MB R0G 2B0
Tel: 204-758-3137; *Fax:* 204-758-3574
biblio@atrium.ca
www.rmofmontcalm.com/bibliothequemontcalmlibrary
Diane Bérard, Bibliothécaire
dmtberard@hotmail.com

***St Pierre Jolys:* Jolys Regional Library / Bibliothèque régionale Jolys**
505 Hébert Ave., St Pierre Jolys, MB R0A 1V0
Tel: 204-433-7729; *Fax:* 204-433-7412
stplibrary@jrlibrary.mb.ca
www.jrlibrary.mb.ca

***St. Georges:* Bibliothèque Allard Library**
104086 PTH 11, St. Georges, MB R0E 1V0
Tel: 204-367-8443; *Fax:* 204-367-1780
info@allardlibrary.com
www.allardlibrary.com
Social Media: www.facebook.com/group.php?gid=144949018850811
Diane Dubé, Citizen Rep RM of Alexander - Chairperson

***Ste Rose du Lac:* Ste Rose Regional Library**
General Delivery, Ste Rose du Lac, MB R0L 1S0
Tel: 204-447-2527
sroselib@mts.net
www.steroseregionallibrary.info
Elaine Chaput, Head Librarian
Sonia Houde, Assistant Librarian
Tara Dubord, Technical Services

***Ste-Anne-des-Chênes:* Bibliothèque Ste-Anne Library**
16, rue de l'Eglise, Ste-Anne-des-Chênes, MB R5H 1H8
Tél: 204-422-9958; *Téléc:* 204-422-9958
steannelib@steannemb.ca
bibliosteannelib.8m.com/cac_en.html
Monica Ball, Bibliothécaire
Clément Charrière, Président
Norbert Ritchot, Secrétaire
steannelib@steannemb.ca
Mimi Pattyn, Trésorière
steannelib@steannemb.ca

***Steinbach:* Jake Epp Library**
255 Elmdale St., Steinbach, MB R5G 0C9
Tel: 204-326-6841; *Fax:* 204-326-6859
jakeepplibrary@yahoo.com
www.jakeepplibrary.com
Loraine Trudeau, Head Librarian
jakeepplibrary@yahoo.com
204-326-6841

***Stonewall:* South Interlake Regional Library**
419 Main St., Stonewall, MB R0C 2Z0
Tel: 204-467-8415; *Fax:* 204-467-9809
sirl@mts.net
www.sirlibrary.com
Darlene Dallman, Head Librarian

***Swan River:* North-West Regional Library**
610 - 1st St. North, Swan River, MB R0L 1Z0
Tel: 204-734-3880; *Fax:* 204-734-3880
nwrl@mts.net
www.swanriverlibrary.ca
June McKenzie, Head Librarian

***The Pas:* The Pas Regional Library**
53 Edwards Ave., The Pas, MB R9A 1R2
Tel: 204-623-2023; *Fax:* 204-623-4594
library@mts.net
www.thepasregionallibrary.com
Lauren Wadelius, Library Administrator
Keith Paquette, Head Librarian
Kristin Nolan, Library Assistant

***Thompson:* Thompson Public Library**
81 Thompson Dr. North, Thompson, MB R8N 0C3
Tel: 204-677-3717; *Fax:* 204-778-5844
info@thompsonlibrary.com
www.thompsonlibrary.com
Cheryl Davies, Administrator
admin@thompsonlibrary.com

***Winnipeg:* MFL Occupational Health Centre**
#102, 275 Broadway, Winnipeg, MB R3C 4M6
Tel: 204-949-0811; *Fax:* 204-956-0848
Toll-Free: 888-843-1229
mflohc@mflohc.mb.ca
www.mflohc.mb.ca/mflohc_folder/information_&_resources.html
Tiffany Pau, Library Coordinator
204-949-7909

***Winnipeg:* Winnipeg Public Library**
251 Donald St., Winnipeg, MB R3C 3P5
Tel: 204-986-6472; *Fax:* 204-942-5671
TTY: 2049863485
wpl.city.winnipeg.mb.ca/library/
Rick Walker, Manager of Library Services
rwalker@winnipeg.ca
Vera Andrysiak, Central Services Coordinator
vandrysiak@winnipeg.ca
204-986-6458
Betty Parry, Support Services Coordinator
bparry@winnipeg.ca
204-986-5002
Kathleen Williams, Outreach Services Coordinator
kwilliam@winnipeg.ca
204-986-4255
Bruno Legal, Marketing Coordinator
blegal@winnipeg.ca
204-986-4334
Carol Mahe, Branch Services Coordinator
cmahe@winnipeg.ca
204-986-6473

Archives

***Boissevain:* Boissevain Community Archives**
436 South Railway St., Boissevain, MB R0K 0E0
Tel: 204-534-6478; *Fax:* 204-534-3710
mbom@mts.net
bmlibrary.ca/resources/community-archives
Michelle Scott, Archivist

***Brandon:* Brandon General Museum and Archives Inc.**
19 9th St., Brandon, MB R7A 4A3
Tel: 204-717-1514
bgmainfo@wcgwave.ca
www.brandon.ca/council-information/bgma/museum-overview
Stephanie Doerksen, Museum Coordinator

Brandon: **Diocese of Brandon, Archives**
PO Box 21009, W.E.P.O., Brandon, MB R7B 3W8
Tel: 204-727-7550; *Fax:* 204-727-4135
diobran@mts.net
www.dioceseofbrandon.org

Brandon: **Magnacca Research Centre**
122 - 18th St., Brandon, MB R7A 5A4
Tel: 204-727-1722; *Fax:* 204-727-1722
dalymuseum@wcgwave.ca
www.dalyhousemuseum.ca/archives.htm
Social Media: twitter.com/DalyHouseMuseum;
www.facebook.com/dalyhouse
Eileen Trott, Archivist

Brandon: **X11 Manitoba Dragoons & 26 Field Regiment Museum**
Brandon Armoury, 1116 Victoria Ave., 1st Fl., Brandon, MB R7A 1B2
Toll-Free: 888-728-2559
26fdlibrary@wcgwave.ca
www.12mbdragoons.com
Ed McArthur, Curator
26fdregCurator@wcgwave.ca
204-726-3498
Gord Sim, Researcher
sim.gordo@gmail.com
204-727-7691

Carberry: **Carberry Plains Archives**
115 Main St., Carberry, MB R0K 0H0
Tel: 204-834-6614; *Fax:* 204-834-6604
cparchives@mts.net
www.mts.net/~archives/
Penny Shaw, Archivist
cparchives@mts.net

Churchill: **Diocese of Churchill - Hudson Bay**
Eskimo Museum, 242 La Verendrye Ave., Churchill, MB R0B 0E0
Tel: 204-675-2252
Lorraine Brandson, Curator

Flin Flon: **Flin Flon Archives**
58 Main St., Flin Flon, MB R8A 1J8
Tel: 204-687-3397; *Fax:* 204-687-4233
ffpl@mts.net
Phyllis Stadnick, Administrator

Killarney: **J.A.V. David Museum**
414 Williams Ave., Killarney, MB R0K 1G0
Tel: 204-523-7325
Other Numbers: Off season, Phone: 204-523-8836

Leaf Rapids: **Leaf Rapids Community Archives**
PO Box 190, Leaf Rapids, MB R0B 1W0
Tel: 204-473-2742; *Fax:* 204-473-2566
lrlib@mts.net
leafrapidslibrary.tripod.com
Lisa Everton, Archivist
lrpl@mts.net
204-473-2742

MacGregor: **Archives**
35 Hampton St. East, MacGregor, MB R0H 0R0
Tel: 204-685-2094; *Fax:* 204-685-2616

Selkirk: **Selkirk Mental Health Centre Archives Collection Inc.**
825 Manitoba Ave., Selkirk, MB R1A 2B5
Tel: 204-482-3810
smhc-archives.com

Shilo: **Royal Canadian Artillery Museum / Le Musée de l'artillerie du Canada**
Building N, Canadian Forces Base Shilo, 118 Patricia Rd., Shilo, MB R0K 2A0
Tel: 204-765-3000
stag@mts.net
www.rcamuseum.com
Kirsten Smith, Contact
kirsten.smith@forces.gc.ca

Steinbach: **Mennonite Heritage Village**
231 PTH 12 North, Steinbach, MB R5G 1T8
Tel: 204-326-9661; *Fax:* 204-326-5046
Toll-Free: 800-280-8741
info@mhv.ca
www.mhv.ca
Social Media:
www.facebook.com/pages/Mennonite-Heritage-Village/1079972 72562045
Roland Sawatzky, Senior Curator
rolands@mhv.ca
204-326-9661

Thompson: **Heritage North Museum**
162 Princeton Dr., Thompson, MB R8N 2A4
Tel: 204-677-2216; *Fax:* 204-677-8953
hnmuseum@mts.net
www.heritagenorthmuseum.ca/
Tanna Teneycke, Executive Director

Winnipeg: **Archevêché de St-Boniface**
622, av Taché, Winnipeg, MB R2H 0G3
Tél: 204-237-9851
secretariat@archsaintboniface.ca
Yolande Comeau, Secrétaire de la chancelerie

Winnipeg: **Archives des Soeurs Grises, St Boniface / Grey Nun Archives, St-Boniface**
151 Despins St., Winnipeg, MB R2H 0L7
Tél: 204-237-8941; *Téléc:* 204-237-3466

Winnipeg: **Archives of Manitoba/ Archives du Manitoba**
#130, 200 Vaughan St., Winnipeg, MB R3C 1T5
Tel: 204-945-3971; *Fax:* 204-948-2008
Toll-Free: 800-617-3588
archives@gov.mb.ca
www.gov.mb.ca/chc/archives

Winnipeg: **Centre for Mennonite Brethren Studies**
1310 Taylor Ave., Winnipeg, MB R3M 3Z6
Tel: 204-669-6575; *Fax:* 204-654-1865
Toll-Free: 888-669-6575
www.mbconf.ca/mbstudies/index.en.html
Ken Reddig, Director
kreddig@mbconf.ca
Conrad Stoesz, Archivist
cstoesz@mbconf.ca

Winnipeg: **City of Winnipeg**
380 William Ave., Winnipeg, MB R3A 0J1
Tel: 204-986-5325; *Fax:* 204-986-7133
www.winnipeg.ca

Winnipeg: **Costume Museum of Canada**
109 Pacific Ave., Winnipeg, MB R3B 0M1
Tel: 204-989-0072; *Fax:* 204-989-0074
Social Media:
www.facebook.com/pages/Costume-Museum-of-Canada/948974 56640
Brenda Hamer, Collections Coordinator

Winnipeg: **Diocese of Rupert's Land, Archives**
935 Nesbitt Bay, Winnipeg, MB R3T 1W6
Tel: 204-992-4203; *Fax:* 204-992-4219
Toll-Free: 866-693-4418
archives@rupertsland.ca
rupertsland.ca

Winnipeg: **Fire Fighters Historical Society of Winnipeg**
56 Maple St., Winnipeg, MB R3B 0Y8
Tel: 204-942-4817; *Fax:* 204-885-1306
firemuseum@gatewest.net
www.winnipegfiremuseum.ca
Barbara Kuryluk, Curator
kuryluk@gatewest.net
204-942-4817
Ted Kuryluk, President
204-888-8021
Terry Brisley, Vice-President
204-222-5045
William Mitchell, Director
204-256-1007

Winnipeg: **Fort Garry Horse Museum & Archives**
551 Machray Ave., Winnipeg, MB R2W 1A8
Tel: 204-586-6298; *Fax:* 204-582-0370
www.fortgarryhorse.ca
Larry Lajeunesse, Museum Chairman
204-582-0370
Gordon Crossley, Museum Director

Winnipeg: **Grand Lodge of Manitoba Archives**
420 Corydon Ave., Winnipeg, MB R3L 0N8
Tel: 204-832-6062; *Fax:* 204-284-3527
rkiv@mts.net
www.mbgrandlodge.com/masonic-resource-center/archives
Allan G. Brock, Grand Archivist
rkiv@mts.net

Winnipeg: **Jewish Heritage Centre of Western Canada**
#C140, 123 Doncaster St., Winnipeg, MB R3N 2B2
Tel: 204-477-7461; *Fax:* 204-477-7465
jewishheritage@jhcwc.org
www.jhcwc.org/impa.php

Winnipeg: **Manitoba & Northwestern Ontario Conference, Archives**
The University of Winnipeg Library, 515 Portage Ave., Winnipeg, MB R3B 2E9
Tel: 204-783-0708; *Fax:* 204-786-1824
www.mnwo.united-church.ca

Winnipeg: **Manitoba Council**
#213, 530 Century St., Winnipeg, MB R3H 0Y4
Tel: 204-774-4475; *Fax:* 204-774-9271
Toll-Free: 800-565-8111
info@girlguides.mb.ca
www.girlguides.mb.ca

Winnipeg: **Manitoba Museum**
190 Rupert Ave., Winnipeg, MB R3B 0N2
Tel: 204-988-0662; *Fax:* 204-942-3679
info@manitobamuseum.ca
www.manitobamuseum.ca
Cindi Steffan, Manager, Information Services
csteffan@manitobamuseum.ca

Winnipeg: **Mennonite Heritage Centre**
600 Shaftesbury Blvd., Winnipeg, MB R3P 0M4
Tel: 204-888-6781; *Fax:* 204-831-5675
Toll-Free: 866-888-6785
archives@mennonitechurch.ca
www.mennonitechurch.ca/programs/archives
Alf Redekopp, Director
aredekopp@mennonitechurch.ca
Connie Wiebe, Archives Secretary
cwiebe@mennonitechurch.ca
Conrad Stoesz, Archivist
cstoesz@mennonitechurch.ca

Winnipeg: **Rainbow Resource Centre**
170 Scott St., Winnipeg, MB R3L 0L3
Tel: 204-474-0212; *Fax:* 204-478-1160
info@rainbowresourcecentre.org
www.rainbowresourcecentre.org/library
Chad Smith, Executive Director
executivedirector@rainbowresourcecentre.org
204-284-3404
Sarah Dack, Coordinator, Information & Intake Assessment

Winnipeg: **Service des archives**
200, av de la Cathédrale, Winnipeg, MB R2H 0H7
Tél: 204-233-0210; *Téléc:* 204-237-3240
archives@ustboniface.mb.ca
www2.ustboniface.ca/cusb/archives

Winnipeg: **Sisters of Our Lady of the Missions / Religieuses de Notre Dame des Missions**
St Edward's Convent, Provincial Office, 800 Adele Ave, Winnipeg, MB R3E 0K6
Tel: 204-774-5067
www.rndm.org/

Winnipeg: **Soeurs Missionnaires Oblates du Sacré-Coeur et de Marie Immaculée / Missionary Oblate Sisters of the Sacred Heart & of Mary Immaculate**
Missionary Oblate Sisters of Saint Boniface, #111, 420 rue DesMeurons, Winnipeg, MB R2H 2N9
Tél: 204-233-7287; *Téléc:* 204-235-7418
generaladministration@missionaryoblatesisters.ca
www.missionaryoblatesisters.ca
Thérèse Bilodeau, Archiviste

Winnipeg: **Transcona Historical Museum**
141 Regent Ave. West, Winnipeg, MB R2C 1R1
Tel: 204-222-0423; *Fax:* 204-222-0208
info@transconamuseum.mb.ca
www.transconamuseum.mb.ca
Social Media:
www.youtube.com/user/TransconaMuseum/videos;
www.facebook.com/transconamuseum
Alanna Horejda, Co-Curator
Erin McIntyre, Co-Curator

Winnipeg: **Ukrainian Catholic Church Archeparchy of Winnipeg**
233 Scotia St., Winnipeg, MB R2V 1V7
Tel: 204-338-7801; *Fax:* 204-339-4006
nataliacurator@yahoo.ca
www.archeparchy.ca

Gloria Romaniuk, Archivist
Natalia Radawetz, Museum Curator

***Winnipeg:* Ukrainian Cultural & Educational Centre**
184 Alexander Ave. East, Winnipeg, MB R3B 0L6
Tel: 204-942-0218; *Fax:* 204-943-2857
ucec@mts.net
www.oseredok.org

***Winnipeg:* Ukrainian Cultural & Educational Centre Archives**
184 Alexander Ave. East, Winnipeg, MB R3B 0L6
Tel: 204-942-0218; *Fax:* 204-943-2857
ucec@mts.net
www.oseredok.org

***Winnipeg:* Western Canada Aviation Museum**
Hangar T-2, 958 Ferry Rd., Winnipeg, MB R3H 0Y8
Tel: 204-786-5503; *Fax:* 204-775-4761
info@wcam.mb.ca
www.wcam.mb.ca

New Brunswick

Regional Systems

AWK Library Regional Office / Région de bibliothèques AWK
#201, 644 Main St., Moncton, NB E1C 1E2
Tel: 506-869-6032; *Fax:* 506-869-6022
annette.selmes@gnb.ca
www.gnb.ca

Tina Bourgeois, Regional Director
tina.bourgeois@gnb.ca
506-869-6030
Nadine Goguen, Assistant Regional Director
nadine.goguen2@gnb.ca
506-869-6031
Robin Illsley, Public Services Librarian
robin.illsley@gnb.ca
506-869-6007
Karen Armstrong, Technical Services Librarian
karen.armstrong@gnb.ca
506-869-6034

Chaleur Library Region / Région de bibliothèques Chaleur
113A Roseberry St., Campbellton, NB E3N 2G6
Tel: 506-789-6599; *Fax:* 506-789-7318
www1.gnb.ca

Sarah Kilfoil, Regional Director
sarah.kilfoil@gnb.ca
Georgette Lavail, Acting Assistant Regional Director
georgette.lavail@gnb.ca
Jennifer Iannuzzelli, Acting Public Services Librarian
jennifer.iannuzzelli@gnb.ca
Vacant , Techinical Services Librarian
Debbie Mann, Administrative Assistant
debbie.mann@gnb.ca
506-789-7325
Shirley Savoie, Regional Office Secretary
shirley.savoie@gnb.ca
506-789-6599

Fundy Library Regional Office / Région de bibliothèques de Fundy
1 Market Sq., Saint John, NB E2L 4Z6
Tel: 506-643-7222; *Fax:* 506-643-7225
lucy.harrigan@gnb.ca
www.gnb.ca

Ian A. Wilson, Regional Director
ian.wilson@gnb.ca
506-643-7242
Alexandra Brooks, Assistant Regional Director
Alexandra.brooks@gnb.ca
506-643-7233
Jean Cunningham, Public Services Librarian
jean.cunningham@gnb.ca
506-643-7230
Gayle DuJohn, Regional Office Secretary
gayle.dujohn@gnb.ca
506-643-7222
Lucy Harrigan, Administrative Assistant
lucy.harrigan@gnb.ca
506-643-7235
Carole May, Administrative Assistant
carole.may@gnb.ca
506-643-7235
Joel Goudreau, Technical Support Analyst
joel.goudreau@gng.ca
506-643-2924
Vacant, Technical Services Librarian
506-643-7226
Pamela Galbraith, Library Assistant, Technical Services
pam.galbraith@gnb.ca
506-643-7245
Melanie Hatfield, Library Assistant, Technical Services
melanie.hatfield@gnb.ca
506-643-7245
Mary Melanson, Library Clerk, Technical Services
mary.melanson@gnb.ca
506-643-7244
Karen Merritt, Library Clerk, Technical Services
karen.merritt@gnb.ca
506-643-7244

Haut Saint-Jean Library Region / Région de bibliothèques Haut Saint-Jean
#102, 15 rue de l'Église, Edmunston, NB E3V 1J3
Tel: 506-735-2074; *Fax:* 506-735-2193
www.gnb.ca/publiclibraries

Michelle Bourque, Public Services Librarian
506-735-2550
Patrick Provencher, Technical Services Librarian
506-735-2611

Haut-Saint-Jean Library Regional Office / Région de bibliothèques Haut-Saint-Jean
540 Principale St., Saint-Basile, NB E7C 1J5
Tel: 506-263-3423; *Fax:* 506-263-3425
www.gnb.ca

Johanne Jacob, Regional Director
johanne.jacob@gnb.ca
Patrick Provencher, Assistant Regional Director
patrick.provencher@gnb.ca
Pauline Grondin, Regional Office Secretary
pauline.grondin@gnb.ca

York Library Region / Région de bibliothèques York
C, 80 Bishop Drive, Fredericton, NB E3C 1B2
Tel: 506-453-5380; *Fax:* 506-457-4878
www1.gnb.ca/0003/library.asp?Code=YF

Jill Foster, Regional Director
jill.foster@gnb.ca
506-453-5380
Bill Mitchell, Assistant Regional Director
bill.mitchell@gnb.ca
506-457-7271
Joyce Newman, Librarian, Technical Services
joyce.newman@gnb.ca
506-444-2606

Public Libraries

***Atholville:* Bibliothèque publique d'Atholville / Atholville Public Library**
275, rue Notre-Dame, Atholville, NB E3N 4T1
Tél: 506-789-2914; *Téléc:* 506-789-2056
biblioda@gnb.ca

Nicole Richard, Gestionnaire

***Bas-Caraquet:* Bibliothèque publique de Bas-Caraquet / Bas-Caraquet Public Library**
8185-2, rue St-Paul, Bas-Caraquet, NB E1W 6C4
Tél: 506-726-2775; *Téléc:* 506-726-2770
bibliobc@gnb.ca

Rémy Levesque, Gestionnaire (par intérim)

***Bathurst:* Bibliothèque publique Smurfit-Stone / Smurfit-Stone Public Library**
#1, 150, rue St. George, Bathurst, NB E2A 1B5
Tél: 506-548-0706; *Téléc:* 506-548-0708
bibliocn@gnb.ca

Dayna DeBenedet, Directrice

***Beresford:* Bibliothèque publique Mgr-Robichaud / Mgr. Robichaud Public Library**
#3, 855, rue Principale, Beresford, NB E8K 1T3
Tél: 506-542-2704; *Téléc:* 506-542-2714
bibliomr@gnb.ca

Tanya Eindiguer, Gestionnaire par intérim
tanya.eindiguer@gnb.ca
Jocelyne Poirier, Aide-bibliothécaire
jocelyne.poirier@gnb.ca
Thérèse Chedore, Aide-bibliothécaire
therese.chedore@gnb.ca
Thérèse Chedore, Aide-bibliothécaire
therese.chedore@gnb.ca

***Boiestown:* Boiestown Community - School Library**
Upper Miramichi Regional High School, #1, 3466 Rte. 625, Boiestown, NB E6A 1C8
Tel: 506-369-2022; *Fax:* 506-369-2023
boiestown.library@gnb.ca
www.gnb.ca

Gail Ross, Library Manager

***Bouctouche:* Bibliothèque publique Gérald-Leblanc / Gérald Leblanc Public Library**
#100, 84, boul Irving, Bouctouche, NB E4S 3L4
Tél: 506-743-7263; *Téléc:* 506-743-7263
bibliopb@gnb.ca
www1.gnb.ca/0003/bibliotheque.asp?Code=AB

Michele-Ann Goguen, Responsable

***Campbellton:* Bookmobile North**
113A Roseberry St., Campbellton, NB E3N 2G6
Tel: 506-789-7339; *Fax:* 506-789-7318
bibliobusnord.bookmobilenorth@gnb.ca

Cindy Bovenizer, Acting Supervisor

***Campbellton:* Campbellton Centennial Library / Bibliothèque du Centenaire de Campbellton**
#100, 19 Aberdeen St., Campbellton, NB E3N 2J6
Tel: 506-753-5253; *Fax:* 506-753-3803
bibliocc@gnb.ca

Jocelyn Paquette, Library Director
Tanya Eindiguer, Head, Reference Services
Colette Arseneault, Circulation Supervisor

***Caraquet:* Bibliothèque publique Mgr-Paquet / Mgr. Paquet Public Library**
10A, du rue Colisée, Caraquet, NB E1W 1A5
Tél: 506-726-2681; *Téléc:* 506-726-2685
bibliock@gnb.ca

Carole Hébert, Gestionnaire

***Chipman:* Chipman Public Library**
8 King St., Chipman, NB E4A 2H3
Tel: 506-339-5852; *Fax:* 506-339-9804
chipman.publiclibrary@gnb.ca
www.gnb.ca

Krista Blyth, Library Manager

***Dalhousie:* Bibliothèque du centenaire de Dalhousie / Dalhousie Centennial Library**
403, rue Adelaide, Dalhousie, NB E8C 1B6
Tél: 506-684-7370; *Téléc:* 506-684-7374
bibliocd@gnb.ca

Sandra B. Carter, Gestionnaire

***Dieppe:* Bibliothèque publique de Dieppe / Dieppe Public Library**
333, av Acadie, Dieppe, NB E1A 1G9
Tél: 506-877-7945; *Téléc:* 506-877-7910
bibliopd@gnb.ca
www1.gnb.ca/0003/bibliotheque.asp?Code=AD

Emanuela Chiriac, Directrice

***Doaktown:* Doaktown Community - School Library**
Doaktown Consolidated High School, 430 Main St., Doaktown, NB E9C 1E8
Tel: 506-365-2018; *Fax:* 506-365-2019
dtcslib@gnb.ca
www.gnb.ca

Belva Brown, Library Manager

***Dorchester:* Dorchester Public Library**
3516 Cape Rd., Dorchester, NB E4K 2X5
Tel: 506-379-3032; *Fax:* 506-379-3033
DorchPL@gnb.ca
www1.gnb.ca/0003/library.asp?Code=AO

Krista Johansen, Library Manager

***Edmundston:* Mgr. W.J. Conway Public Library / Bibliothèque publique Mgr-W.-J. Conway**
33, Irène St., Edmundston, NB E3V 1B7
Tel: 506-735-4713; *Fax:* 506-737-6848
biblioed@gnb.ca, www.gnb.ca

Robert Daigle, Library Director
Michelle Bourque, Librarian, Young Adult & Adult Services
Jewel McLatchy, Librarian, Children's Services
Pierre Van Eeckhout, Librarian, Reference Services
Louis Roy, Supervisor, Circulation

***Florenceville:* Andrew & Laura McCain Public Library / Bibliothèque publique Andrew-et-Laura-McCain**
8 McCain St., Florenceville, NB E7L 3H6
Tel: 506-392-5294; *Fax:* 506-392-8108
florenpl@gnb.ca
www.gnb.ca

Julie Craig, Library Manager

***Fredericton:* Dr. Marguerite Michaud Library / Bibliothèque Dr Marguerite Michaud**
Centre communautaire Sainte-Anne, 715 Priestman St., Fredericton, NB E3B 5W7
Tél: 506-453-7100; *Téléc:* 506-453-3958
BiblioDMM@gnb.ca
www.franco-fredericton.com/bibliomm
Françoise Caron, Librarian
Lorraine Suley, Assistant Librarian
Lorraine Suley

***Fredericton:* Fredericton - Nashwaaksis Public - School Library**
324 Fulton Ave., Fredericton, NB E3A 5J4
Tel: 506-453-3241; *Fax:* 506-444-4129
nashwaaksis.library@gnb.ca
www.gnb.ca

***Fredericton:* Fredericton Public Library**
12 Carleton St., Fredericton, NB E3B 5P4
Tel: 506-460-2800; *Fax:* 506-460-2801
FtonPub@gnb.ca
www.gnb.ca
Brian R. Steeves, Library Director
Stephanie Furrow, Head, Reference Services
Jessica Larocque, Children's Librarian
Leslie Cockburn, Coordinator, Young Adult & Adult Services
Sheila Grondin-Lyons, Supervisor, Circulation

***Fredericton:* York Bookmobile**
4 Carleton St., Fredericton, NB E3B 5P4
Tel: 506-453-5380; *Fax:* 506-457-4878
york.bookmobile@gnb.ca
www.gnb.ca
Maria Whitlock, Supervisor, Bookmobile

***Grand Falls:* Grand Falls Public Library / Bibliothèque publique de Grand-Sault**
Town Hall, #201, 131 Pleasant St., Grand Falls, NB E3Z 1G6
Tel: 506-475-7781; *Fax:* 506-475-7783
gfplib@gnb.ca
www.gnb.ca
Émilie Lefrançois, Library Director

***Grand Manan:* Grand Manan Library**
1144 Rte. 776, Grand Manan, NB E5G 4E8
Tel: 506-662-7099; *Fax:* 506-662-7094
GrandMananLibrary@gnb.ca
www1.gnb.ca/0003/library.asp?Code=FG
Kendra Neves, Manager

***Hartland:* Dr. Walter Chestnut Public Library / Bibliothèque publique Dr-Walter-Chestnut**
#1, 395 Main St., Hartland, NB E7P 2N3
Tel: 506-375-4876; *Fax:* 506-375-6816
hartlandl@gnb.ca
www.gnb.ca
Jean Haywood, Library Manager

***Harvey:* Harvey Community Library**
Harvey High School, 2055 Rte. 3, Harvey, NB E6K 1L1
Tel: 506-366-2206; *Fax:* 506-366-2210
harvey.library@gnb.ca
www.gnb.ca
Joanne Cole, Library Manager

***Hillsborough:* Hillsborough Public Library**
#2, 2849 Main St., Hillsborough, NB E4H 2X7
Tel: 506-734-3722; *Fax:* 506-734-3711
Hillsborough.publiclibrary@gnb.ca
www1.gnb.ca/0003/library.asp?Code=AH
Barbara Alcorn, Library Manager
Hillsborough.publiclibrary@gnb.ca
506-734-3722

***Kedgwick:* Kedgwick Public Library / Bibliothèque publique de Kedgwick**
116 Notre-Dame St., #P, Kedgwick, NB E8B 1H8
Tel: 506-284-2757; *Fax:* 506-284-4557
bibliopk@gnb.ca
www.gnb.ca
Louise Lang-Levesque, Library Manager

***Lamèque:* Bibliothèque publique de Lamèque / Lamèque Public Library**
46, rue du Pêcheur nord, Lamèque, NB E8T 1J3
Tél: 506-344-3262; *Téléc:* 506-344-3263
bibliopl@gnb.ca
Jeanne-Mance Noël, Gestionnaire

***McAdam:* McAdam Public Library**
Municipal Bldg., 146 Saunders Rd., McAdam, NB E6J 1L2
Tel: 506-784-1403; *Fax:* 506-784-1402
mcadam.library@gnb.ca
www.gnb.ca
Anthony Dickinson, Library Manager

***Memramcook:* Memramcook Public Library/Bibliothèque publique de Memramcook**
#1, 540, rue Centrale, Memramcook, NB E4K 3S6
Tel: 506-758-4029; *Fax:* 506-758-4030
bibliopm@gnb.ca
www.memramcook.com/public_library.cfm
Jocelyne LeBlanc, Library Manager
bibliopm@gnb.ca
506-758-4029

***Minto:* Minto Public Library**
Municipal Bldg., #2, 420 Pleasant Dr., Minto, NB E4B 2T3
Tel: 506-327-3220; *Fax:* 506-327-3041
minto.publiclibrary@gnb.ca
www.gnb.ca
Mary Lambropoulos, Library Manager

***Miramichi:* Miramichi - Médiathèque Père-Louis-Lamontagne**
Centre communautaire Carrefour Beausoleil, 300 Beaverbrook Rd., Miramichi, NB E1V 1A1
Tél: 506-627-4084; *Téléc:* 506-627-4592
mediathequeP@gnb.ca
www.mpll.nb.ca
Geneviève Thériault, Library Director
Gaétane Niles, Assistant Librarian

***Miramichi:* Miramichi - Newcastle Public Library**
100 Fountain Head Lane, Miramichi, NB E1V 4A1
Tel: 506-623-2450; *Fax:* 506-623-2335
Npublib@gnb.ca
www.gnb.ca
Catherine Reid, Library Director

***Mirimichi:* Miramichi - Chatham Public Library**
24 King St., Mirimichi, NB E1N 2N1
Tel: 506-773-6274; *Fax:* 506-773-6963
chathmpl@gnb.ca
www.gnb.ca
Jennifer Wilcox, Library Director

***Moncton:* Moncton Public Library / Bibliothèque publique de Moncton**
#101, 644 Main St., Moncton, NB E1C 1E2
Tel: 506-869-6000; *Fax:* 506-869-6040
mplib@gnb.ca
www.monctonpubliclibrary.ca
Chantale Bellemare, Library Director
mplib@gnb.ca
506-869-6000
Thérèse Arseneault, Head of Reference Services
506-869-6037
Nancy Cohen, Children's Librarian
Evelyn Whitehead, Young Adult and Adult Services Coordinator

***Nackawic:* Nackawic Public - School Library / Bibliothèque publique-scolaire de Nackawic**
30 Landegger Dr., Nackawic, NB E6G 1E9
Tel: 506-572-2136; *Fax:* 506-575-2336
nackawic.library@gnb.ca
www.gnb.ca
Paulette Tonner, Library Manager

***Oromocto:* Oromocto Public Library**
54 Miramichi Rd., Oromocto, NB E2V 1S2
Tel: 506-357-3329; *Fax:* 506-357-5161
oromocto.publiclibrary@gnb.ca
www.gnb.ca
Muriel M. Morton, Library Director

***Perth-Andover:* Perth-Andover Public Library / Bibliothèque publique de Perth-Andover**
642 East Riverside Dr., Perth-Andover, NB E7H 1Z6
Tel: 506-273-2843; *Fax:* 506-273-1913
paplib@gnb.ca
www.gnb.ca
Tammie Wright, Library Manager

***Petit-Rocher:* Bibliothèque publique de Petit-Rocher / Petit-Rocher Public Library**
#110, 702, rue Principale, Petit-Rocher, NB E8J 1V1
Tél: 506-542-2744; *Téléc:* 506-542-2745
bibliopr@gnb.ca
Sonia Godin, Gestionnaire

***Petitcodiac:* Petitcodiac Public Library**
#101, 6 Kay St., Petitcodiac, NB E4Z 4K6
Tel: 506-756-3144; *Fax:* 506-756-3142
Petitcodiac.PublicLibrary@gnb.ca
www1.gnb.ca/0003/library.asp?Code=AE
Cathy MacDonald, Library Manager
Petitcodiac.PublicLibrary@gnbcca
506-756-3144

***Plaster Rock:* Plaster Rock Public - School Library / Bibliothèque publique-scolaire de Plaster Rock**
290A Main St., Plaster Rock, NB E7G 2C6
Tel: 506-356-6018; *Fax:* 506-356-6019
prplib@gnb.ca
www.gnb.ca
Carolyn Knowlton, Branch Manager

***Port Elgin:* Port Elgin Public Library**
1 Station St., Port Elgin, NB E4M 1C6
Tel: 506-538-2118; *Fax:* 506-538-2126
PortEPL@gnb.ca
www1.gnb.ca/0003/library.asp?Code=AT
Kathleen Grigg, Library Manager
PortEPL@gnb.ca
506-538-2118

***Quispamsis:* Kennebecasis Public Library**
1 Landing Ct., Quispamsis, NB E2E 4R2
Tel: 506-849-5314; *Fax:* 506-849-5318
info@kvlibrary.org
www.kvlibrary.org
Leslye McVicar, Director

***Richibucto:* Bibliothèque publique de Richibucto / Richibucto Public Library**
9376, rue Main, Richibucto, NB E4W 4C9
Tél: 506-523-7851; *Téléc:* 506-523-7851
bibliori@gnb.ca
Sylvie Bourque, Acting Library Manager

***Riverview:* Riverview Public Library**
34 Honour House Ct., Riverview, NB E1B 3Y9
Tel: 506-387-2108
riverview.publiclibrary@gnb.ca
www.townofriverview.ca
Social Media: www.facebook.com/riverviewpubliclibrary
Lynn Cormier, Librarian
lynn.cormier@gnb.ca
506-387-2108

***Sackville:* Sackville Public Library**
66 Main St., Sackville, NB E4L 4A7
Tel: 506-364-4915; *Fax:* 506-364-4915
spublib@gnb.ca
www1.gnb.ca/0003/library.asp?Code=AK
Allan J. Alward, Library Manager
spublib@gnb.ca
506-364-4915

***Saint John:* Le Cormoran Library**
67 Ragged Point Rd., Saint John, NB E2K 5C3
Tel: 506-658-4610; *Fax:* 506-658-3984
BiblioLC@gnb.ca
Mireille Mercure, Director
mireille.mercure@gnb.ca

***Saint John:* Saint John Free Public Library, East Branch**
#2, 545 Westmorland Pl., Saint John, NB E2J 2G5
Tel: 506-643-7250; *Fax:* 506-696-5354
EastBranch.PublicLibrary@gnb.ca
Emily King, Branch Manager
Deborah Eves, Staff
Melissa Hanley, Staff
Patty Martin, Staff
Julie McGrath, Staff

***Saint John:* Saint John Free Public Library, Main Branch**
1 Market Sq., Saint John, NB E2L 4Z6
Tel: 506-643-7220; *Fax:* 506-643-7225
sjfpl@gnb.ca
www.gnb.ca/0003/regions/saint_john_main_branch.asp
Joann Hamilton-Barry, City Librarian
Keith MacKinnon, Head, Reference Services
Heather McKend, Children's Librarian
Carole MacFarquhar, Young Adult & Adult Librarian

***Saint John:* Saint John Free Public Library, West Branch**
621 Fairville Blvd., Saint John, NB E2M 4X5
Tel: 506-643-7260; *Fax:* 506-672-1752
westbranch.publiclibrary@gnb.ca

Robin Sexton-Mayes, Branch Manager

***Saint-Antoine:* Bibliothèque publique de Saint-Antoine / Saint-Antoine Public Library**
11, av Jeanne d'Arc, Saint-Antoine, NB E4V 1H2
Tél: 506-525-4028; *Téléc:* 506-525-4199
bibliosa@gnb.ca
www1.gnb.ca
Paulette Léger, Gestionnaire de bibliothèque

***Saint-Basile:* Haut Saint-Jean-Bookmobile**
540 Principale St., Saint-Basile, NB E7C 1J5
Tel: 506-263-3426; *Fax:* 506-263-3437
bibliobus-hsj@gnb.ca
www.gnb.ca
Andrée Boutot-Cyr, Supervisor, Bookmobile

***Saint-François-de-Madawaska:* Mgr. Plourde Public Library / Bibliothèque publique Mgr-Plourde**
15 Bellevue St., Saint-François-de-Madawaska, NB E7A 1A4
Tel: 506-992-6052; *Fax:* 506-992-6047
stfplib@gnb.ca
www.gnb.ca
Bertin Nadeau, Library Manager

***Saint-Léonard:* Dr. Lorne J. Violette Public Library / Bibliothèque publique Dr.-Lorne-J.-Violette**
180 St-Jean St., Saint-Léonard, NB E7E 2B9
Tel: 506-423-3025; *Fax:* 506-423-3026
stlplib@gnb.ca
www.gnb.ca
Nathalie Nadeau-Plourde, Library Manager

***Saint-Quentin:* La Moisson Public Library / Bibliothèque publique La Moisson de Saint-Quentin**
Municipal Bldg., 206 Canada St., Saint-Quentin, NB E8A 1H1
Tel: 506-235-1955; *Fax:* 506-235-1957
biblioIm@gnb.ca
www.bibliothequesaint-quentin.com
Hélène DuRepos Thériault, Library Manager

***Salisbury:* Salisbury Public Library**
3215 Main St., Salisbury, NB E4J 2K7
Tel: 506-372-3240; *Fax:* 506-372-3261
salisbury.publiclibrary@gnb.ca
www.salisburynb.ca/
Social Media: www.facebook.com/SalisburyPublicLibrary
Kathy MacDonald, Library Manager
506-372-3240

***Shediac:* Bibliothèque publique de Shediac / Shediac Public Library**
#100, 290, rue Main, Shediac, NB E4P 2E3
Tél: 506-532-7014; *Téléc:* 506-532-8400
bibliosh@gnb.ca
biblioshediaclibrary.ca
Gabrielle LeBlanc, Responsable
bibliosh@gnb.ca
506-532-7014

***Shippagan:* Bibliothèque publique Laval-Goupil / Laval-Goupil Public Library**
128, rue Mgr-Chiasson, Shippagan, NB E8S 1X7
Tél: 506-336-3920; *Téléc:* 506-336-3921
bibliops@gnb.ca
Pauline Godin, Gestionnaire

***St Andrews:* Ross Memorial Library**
110 King St., St Andrews, NB E5B 1Y6
Tel: 506-529-5125; *Fax:* 506-529-5129
standrpl@gnb.ca
www.rossmemlibrary.org
Lesley Wells, Library Manager

***St Stephen:* St Croix Public Library**
11 King St., St Stephen, NB E3L 2C1
Tel: 506-466-7529; *Fax:* 506-466-7574
ststeppl@gnb.ca
www.gnb.ca/publiclibraries
Elva Hatt, Library Manager

***Stanley:* Stanley Community Library**
#2, 28 Bridge St., Stanley, NB E6B 1B2
Tel: 506-367-2492; *Fax:* 506-367-2764
stanley.library@gnb.ca
www.gnb.ca
Kelly Dickinson, Library Manager

***Sussex:* Sussex Regional Library**
46 Magnolia Ave., Sussex, NB E4E 2H2
Tel: 506-432-4585; *Fax:* 506-432-4583
sussexpl@gnb.ca

***Tracadie-Sheila:* Bibliothèque publique de Tracadie-Sheila / Tracadie-Sheila Public Library**
3620, rue Principale, Tracadie-Sheila, NB E1X 1C9
Tél: 506-394-4005; *Téléc:* 506-394-4009
bibliots@gnb.ca
Graeme Peters, Directeur

***Welshpool:* Campobello Public Library**
3 Welshpool St., Welshpool, NB E5E 1G3
Tel: 506-752-7082; *Fax:* 506-752-7083
Social Media: www.facebook.com/group.php?gid=16314039207
Stephanie Milbury, Library Manager
506-752-1013

***Woodstock:* L.P. Fisher Public Library / Bibliothèque publique L.-P.-Fisher**
679 Main St., Woodstock, NB E7M 2E1
Tel: 506-325-4777; *Fax:* 506-325-4811
lpfisher.library@gnb.ca
www.gnb.ca
Jonathan Tait, Library Manager

Archives

***Bathurst:* Herman J. Good, VC, Canadian Legion**
575 St Peters Ave., Bathurst, NB E2A 2Y5
Tel: 506-546-3135
historicplaces@pc.gc.ca
www.historicplaces.ca/en/rep-reg/place-lieu.aspx?id=5457
Ron Fortier, Curator
506-546-4751

***Bouctouche:* Musée de Kent**
150, ch du Couvent, Bouctouche, NB E4S 3C1
Tél: 506-743-5005
admin@museedekent.ca
www.museedekent.ca/
Pierre Cormier, Directeur

***Dalhousie:* Restigouche Regional Museum**
115 George St., Dalhousie, NB E8C 1R6
Tel: 506-684-7490; *Fax:* 506-684-7490
gurrm@nbnet.nb.ca
www.restimuse.org/dalhousie.html
Bill Clarke, Contact

***Edmundston:* Centre de documentation et d'études Madawaskayennes**
165, boul Hébert, Edmundston, NB E3V 2S8
Tél: 506-737-5058; *Téléc:* 506-737-5373
www.umce.ca/biblio/cdem/
Guy Lefrançois, Responsable
glefranc@umce.ca

***Fredericton:* Provincial Archives of New Brunswick / Archives provinciales du Nouveau-Brunswick**
University of New Brunswick, Bonar Law-Bennett Bldg., 23 Dineen Dr., Fredericton, NB E3B 5H1
Tel: 506-453-2122; *Fax:* 506-453-3288
provincial.archives@gnb.ca
www.gnb.ca/Archives
Marion Beyea, Director & Archivist
Marion.Beyea@gnb.ca
506-444-4021
Dean Lund, Manager, Conservation
Dean.Lund@gnb.ca
506-444-6724
Dale R. Cogswell, Manager, Government Records
Dale.Cogswell@gnb.ca
506-457-3512
Fred Farrell, Manager, Photographs, Public Sector
Fred.Farrell@gnb.ca
506-444-4146

***Fredericton:* University of New Brunswick Archives & Special Collections Dept**
Harriet Irving Library, 5 Macaulay Lane, Fredericton, NB E3B 5H5
Tel: 506-453-4748; *Fax:* 506-453-4595
archives@unb.ca
www.lib.unb.ca/archives/

***Grand Falls:* Grand Falls Museum / Musée de Grand-Sault**
#142 Court St.aska Rd., Grand Falls, NB E01 1M0
Tel: 506-473-5265
www.museevirtuel-virtualmuseum.ca
Anne Rideout Côté, President, Grand Falls Historical Society

***Grand Manan:* Grand Manan Museum**
1141 Rte. 776, Grand Manan, NB E5G 4E9
Tel: 506-662-3424
gmadmin@grandmananmuseum.ca
www.grandmananmuseum.ca
M.J. Edwards, Director/Curator

***Miramichi:* St Michael's Museum & Genealogical Centre**
10 Howard St., Miramichi, NB E1N 3A7
Tel: 506-773-3277; *Fax:* 506-778-5156
mmuseum@nbnet.nb.ca

***New Maryland:* Diocese of Fredericton, Archives**
33 Alban St., New Maryland, NB E3C 1E4
Tel: 506-459-3637; *Fax:* 506-453-3288
www.fredericton.anglican.org

***Sackville:* Maritime Conference, Archives**
32 York St., Sackville, NB E4L 4R4
Tel: 506-536-0998; *Fax:* 506-536-2900
www.marconf.ca/archives.htm

***Sackville:* Mount Allison University Archives**
Ralph Pickard Bell Library, 49 York St., Sackville, NB E4L 1C6
Tel: 506-364-2563; *Fax:* 506-364-2617
archives@mta.ca
www.mta.ca/library/archives/index.htm

***Saint John:* New Brunswick Museum**
277 Douglas Ave., Saint John, NB E2K 1E5
Tel: 506-643-2322; *Fax:* 506-643-2360
Toll-Free: 888-268-9595
archives@nbm-mnb.ca
www.nbm-mnb.ca
Social Media: twitter.com/nbmmnb; www.facebook.com/nbmmnb
Felicity Osepchook, Head
felicity.osepchook@nbm-mnb.ca
506-643-2324

***Saint John:* Roman Catholic Diocese of Saint John**
1 Bayard Dr., Saint John, NB E2L 3L5
Tel: 506-653-6807; *Fax:* 506-653-6812
archives@dioceseofsaintjohn.org
www.dioceseofsaintjohn.org
Mary McDevitt, Archivist

***Saint John:* Saint John Jewish Historical Museum**
91 Leinster St., Saint John, NB E2L 1J2
Tel: 506-633-1833; *Fax:* 506-642-9926
sjjhm@nbnet.nb.ca
personal.nbnet.nb.ca/sjjhm
Katherine Biggs-Craft, Curator

***Shippagan:* Société historique Nicolas-Denys**
Université de Moncton, Campus de Shippagan, 218, boul J.-D.-Gauthier, Shippagan, NB E8S 1P6
Tél: 506-336-3461; *Téléc:* 506-336-3434
shnd@umcs.ca
www2.umoncton.ca/cfdocs/cea/reseau/centre9.html
Philippe Basque, Président
Nathalie Lanteigne, Responsable

***St Andrews:* Charlotte County Historical Society, Inc.**
123 Frederick St., St Andrews, NB E5B 1Z1
Tel: 506-529-4248
contact@ccarchives.ca
www.ccarchives.ca

***St Martins:* Quaco Museum Archives**
236 Main St., St Martins, NB E5R 1B8
Tel: 506-833-2553
Other Numbers: 506-833-4740
curator@quaco.ca
www.quaco.ca/index.html

***Woodstock:* Carleton County Historical Society**
128 Connell St., Woodstock, NB E7M 1L5
Tel: 506-328-9706; *Fax:* 506-328-2942
cchs@nb.aibn.com
www.cchs-nb.ca

Newfoundland & Labrador

Regional Systems

Newfoundland & Labrador Public Libraries - Central Division
6 Bell Pl., Gander, NL A1V 1X2
Tel: 709-651-5356; *Fax:* 709-256-2194

Patricia Parsons, Central Division Manager
pparsons@nlpl.ca
709-651-5351
Michelle Stuckless, Librarian

Newfoundland & Labrador Public Libraries - West Newfoundland-Labrador Division
5 Union St., Corner Brook, NL A2H 5M7
Tel: 709-634-7333; *Fax:* 709-634-7313
www.nlpl.ca
Sanford Chilcote, Manager
schilcote@nlpl.ca

Provincial Information & Library Resources Board - Eastern Division
Arts & Culture Centre, St. John's, NL A1B 3A3
Tel: 709-737-3508; *Fax:* 709-737-3571
johnwhite@nlpl.ca
www.nlpl.ca
John White, Division Manager
johnwhite@nlpl.ca
709-737-3508

Public Libraries

***Arnold's Cove:* Arnold's Cove Public Library**
5 Highliner Dr., Arnold's Cove, NL A0B 1A0
Tel: 709-463-8707
gsmith@nlpl.ca
www.nlpl.ca
Gwen Smith, Librarian

***Baie Verte:* Baie Verte Public Library**
Hwy. 410, Baie Verte, NL A0K 1B0
Tel: 709-532-8361
www.nlpl.ca
Eileen Cooper, Library Technician
ecooper@nlpl.ca

***Bay Roberts:* Bay Roberts Public Library**
76 Cross Rd., Bay Roberts, NL A0A 1G0
Tel: 709-786-9629
mclarke@nlpl.ca
www.nlpl.ca
Marilyn Clarke, Librarian

***Bell Island:* Bell Island Public Library**
Provincial Government Bldg., 20 Bennett St., Bell Island, NL A0A 4H0
Tel: 709-488-2413
www.nlpl.ca
John White, Manager, Easter Division
johnwhite@nlpl.ca
709-737-3508
Lois Clarke, Library Technician
lclarke@nlpl.ca

***Bishop's Falls:* Bishop's Falls Public Library**
PO Box 329, Bishop's Falls, NL A0H 1C0
Tel: 709-258-6244
cstanley@nlpl.ca
www.nlpl.ca
Cora Stanley, Librarian

***Bonavista:* Bonavista Memorial Public Library**
PO Box 400, Bonavista, NL A0C 1B0
Tel: 709-468-2185
bwilton@nlpl.ca
www.nlpl.ca
Brenda Wilton, Librarian

***Botwood:* Botwood Kinsmen Public Library**
240 Water St., Botwood, NL A0H 1E0
Tel: 709-257-2091
www.nlpl.ca
Social Media: www.facebook.com/277034772326408
Phyllis Coates, Library Technician
pcoates@nlpl.ca

***Brigus:* Brigus Public Library**
General Delivery, Brigus, NL A0A 1K0
Tel: 709-528-3156
www.nlpl.ca
Raelene Wall, Librarian

***Buchans:* Buchans Public Library**
Lakeside Academy, Buchans Hwy., PO Box 99, Buchans, NL A0H 1G0
Tel: 709-672-3859
www.nlpl.ca
Dawn Pennell, Librarian
dpennell@nlpl.ca

***Burgeo:* Burgeo Public Library**
1 School Rd., Burgeo, NL A0M 2H0
Tel: 709-886-2730
www.nlpl.ca.ca
Freda MacDonald, Library Technician
fmacdonald@nlpl.ca

***Burin:* Burin Public Library**
PO Box 219, Burin, NL A0E 1G0
Tel: 709-891-1924
www.nlpl.ca
Patricia Peddle, Librarian
ppeddle@nlpl.ca

***Cape St George:* Cape St George Public Library**
879 Oceanview Dr., Cape St George, NL A0N 1T1
Tel: 709-644-2852
www.nlpl.ca
Elizabeth Cornect, Librarian
ecornect@nlpl.ca

***Carbonear:* Carbonear Public Library**
PO Box 928, Carbonear, NL A1Y 1C4
Tel: 709-596-3382
www.nlpl.ca
Maureen Snow, Librarian
msnow@nlpl.ca

***Carmanville:* Carmanville Public Library**
Phoenix Academy, 95-97 Main St., PO Box 105, Carmanville, NL A0G 1N0
Tel: 709-534-2370
www.nlpl.ca
Kay Butt, Librarian

***Cartwright:* Cartwright Public Library**
PO Box 330, Cartwright, NL A0K 1V0
Tel: 709-938-7219
hclark@nlpl.ca
www.nlpl.ca
Hilda Clark, Library Technician

***Catalina:* Catalina (Joseph E. Clouter) Public Library**
PO Box 69, Catalina, NL A0C 1J0
Tel: 709-469-3045
www.nlpl.ca
Kimberley Johnson, Librarian
kjohnson@nlpl.ca

***Centreville:* Intertown Public Library**
c/o Centreville Academy, 2 Memory Lane, PO Box 100, Centreville, NL A0G 4P0
Tel: 709-678-2700
vrogers@nlpl.ca
www.nlpl.ca
Veronica Rogers, Librarian

***Change Islands:* Change Islands Public Library**
c/o A.R. Scammell Academy, Main St. North, PO Box 129, Change Islands, NL A0G 1R0
Tel: 709-621-5566
www.nlpl.ca
Christine Hoffe, Librarian
choffe@nlpl.ca

***Channel-Port-aux-Basques:* Port aux Basques Public Library**
PO Box 790, Channel-Port-aux-Basques, NL A0M 1C0
Tel: 709-695-3471; *Fax:* 709-695-3471
bingram@nlpl.ca
www.nlpl.ca
Brenda Ingram, Library Technician

***Churchill Falls:* Churchill Falls Public Library**
PO Box 160, Churchill Falls, NL A0R 1A0
Tel: 709-925-3281; *Fax:* 709-925-3487
cyoung@nlpl.ca
www.nlpl.ca
Social Media:
www.facebook.com/group.php?gid=169595486419342
Loretta Bryant, Library Technician

***Clarenville:* Clarenville Public Library**
98 Manitoba Dr., Clarenville, NL A5A 1K7
Tel: 709-466-7634
www.nlpl.ca
Social Media: www.facebook.com/152981014757509
Tanya MacLean, Librarian
tmaclean@nlpl.ca

***Conception Bay South:* Conception Bay South Public Library**
110 Conception Bay Hwy., Conception Bay South, NL A1W 3A5
Tel: 709-834-4241
www.nlpl.ca
Bertha Rideout, Librarian
brideout@nlpl.ca

***Cormack:* Cormack Public Library**
280A Veterans Dr., Cormack, NL A8A 2R4
Tel: 709-635-7022; *Fax:* 709-635-7022
www.nlpl.ca
Social Media: www.facebook.com/205158306213208
Marie Morris, Librarian
mmorris@nlpl.ca

***Corner Brook:* Corner Brook Public Library**
4 West St., Corner Brook, NL A2H 0C1
Tel: 709-634-0013
www.cornerbrooklibrary.org
Social Media: www.facebook.com/CornerBrookPublicLibrary
Jessica Prince, Librarian

***Cow Head:* Cow Head Public Library**
119 Main St., Cow Head, NL A0K 2A0
Tel: 709-243-2467
www.nlpl.ca
Nora Shears, Librarian
nshears@nlpl.ca

***Daniels Harbour:* Daniels Harbour Public Library**
15 Church Lane, Daniels Harbour, NL A0K 2C0
Tel: 709-898-2283
www.nlpl.ca
Social Media: www.facebook.com/110178682390214
Sharon Humber, Librarian
shumber@nlpl.ca

***Deer Lake:* Deer Lake Public Library**
4 Poplar Rd., Deer Lake, NL A8A 1Z4
Tel: 709-635-3671
www.nlpl.ca
Social Media: www.facebook.com/130449280349655
Worneta Cramm, Librarian
wcramm@nlpl.ca

***Doyles:* Codroy Valley Public Library**
General Delivery, Doyles, NL A0N 1J0
Tel: 709-955-3158
www.nlpl.ca
Judy Gillis, Librarian
jgillis@nlpl.ca

***Fogo:* Fogo Island Public Library**
Main St. PO Box 40, Fogo, NL A0G 2B0
Tel: 709-266-2210; *Fax:* 709-266-2384
www.nlpl.ca
Elizabeth Blundon, Librarian

***Fortune:* Fortune Public Library**
Municipal Centre, Temple St., PO Box 400, Fortune, NL A0E 1P0
Tel: 709-832-0232
www.nlpl.ca
Fay Herridge, Librarian
fherridge@nlpl.ca

***Fox Harbour PB:* Fox Harbour Public Library**
PO Box 139, Fox Harbour PB, NL A0B 1V0
Tel: 709-227-2135
www.nlpl.ca
Catherine Murray, Librarian
cmurray@nlpl.ca

***Gambo:* Gambo Public Library**
6 Centennial Rd., Gambo, NL A0G 1T0
Tel: 709-674-5052
www.nlpl.ca
Desiree Hopkins, Library Technician

***Gander:* Gander Public & Resource Library**
6 Bell Pl., Gander, NL A1V 1X2
Tel: 709-651-5356
mstuckless@nlpl.ca
www.nlpl.ca
Social Media:
www.facebook.com/pages/Gander-Public-Library/169210156452499
Michelle Stuckless, Library Technician

Garnish: **Garnish (Greta Hollett) Memorial Library**
PO Box 40, Garnish, NL A0E 1T0
Tel: 709-826-2371
www.nlpl.ca
Linda Nolan, Librarian
lnolan@nlpl.ca

Gaultois: **Gaultois Public Library**
Town Hall, Valley Rd., PO Box 10, Gaultois, NL A0H 1N0
Tel: 709-841-3311
www.nlpl.ca

Glenwood: **Glenwood Public Library**
26 Main St., Glenwood, NL A0G 2K0
Tel: 709-679-5700
www.nlpl.ca
Kelly Gillingham, Librarian
kgillingham@nlpl.ca

Glovertown: **Alexander Bay Public Library**
Glovertown Academy, Penney's Brook Rd., Glovertown, NL A0G 2L0
Tel: 709-533-6688
www.nlpl.ca
Rose Sweetapple, Librarian
rsweetapple@nlpl.ca

Grand Bank: **Grand Bank Public Library**
PO Box 1000, Grand Bank, NL A0E 1W0
Tel: 709-832-0310
www.nlpl.ca
Jane Matthews, Librarian

Grand Falls-Windsor: **Harmsworth Public Library**
Gordon Pinsent Centre for the Arts, 1 Cromer Ave., Grand Falls-Windsor, NL A2A 1W9
Tel: 709-489-2303; *Fax:* 709-489-9328
www.nlpl.ca
Madonna Crant, Librarian
mcrant@nlpl.ca

Greenspond: **Greenspond Memorial Library**
PO Box 70, Greenspond, NL A0G 2N0
Tel: 709-269-3434
www.nlpl.ca
Cindy Blackwood, Librarian
cblackwood@nlpl.ca

Happy Valley-Goose Bay: **Melville Public Library**
Elizabeth Goudie Bldg., 141 Hamilton River Rd., Happy Valley-Goose Bay, NL A0P 1E0
Tel: 709-896-8045
hskoglund@nlpl.ca
www.nlpl.ca
Hyra Skoglund, Library Tecnician

Harbour Breton: **Harbour Breton Public Library**
PO Box 569, Harbour Breton, NL A0H 1P0
Tel: 709-885-2165
www.nlpl.ca
Denise Whittle, Librarian

Harbour Grace: **Harbour Grace Public Library**
PO Box 40, Harbour Grace, NL A0A 2M0
Tel: 709-596-3894
www.nlpl.ca
Doreen Quinn, Librarian
dquinn@nlpl.ca

Hare Bay: **Hare Bay Public Library**
Jane Collins Academy, 22 Anstey's Rd., Hare Bay, NL A0G 2P0
Tel: 709-537-2391; *Fax:* 709-537-2374
www.nlpl.ca
Jane Rogers-Willis, Librarian

Harry's Harbour: **Harry's Harbour Public Library**
PO Box 65, Harry's Harbour, NL A0J 1E0
Tel: 709-624-5464
www.nlpl.ca
Ellen King, Librarian
eking@nlpl.ca

Hermitage: **Hermitage Public Library**
John Watkins Academy, PO Box 159, Hermitage, NL A0H 1S0
Tel: 709-883-2421
bwillmott@nlpl.ca
www.nlpl.ca
Bernice Willmott, Library Technician

Holyrood: **Holyrood Public Library**
PO Box 263, Holyrood, NL A0A 2R0
Tel: 709-229-7852
www.nlpl.ca
Social Media: www.facebook.com/pages/Holyrood-Public-Library/256371237757317
Marianne King, Librarian

Kings Point: **Tilley Memorial Public Library**
PO Box 100, Kings Point, NL A0J 1J0
Tel: 709-268-2282
pbowers@nlpl.ca
www.nlpl.ca
Patsy Bowers, Library Technician

L'Anse au Loup: **Labrador South Public Library**
General Delivery, L'Anse au Loup, NL A0K 3L0
Tel: 709-927-5542
podell@nlpl.ca
www.nlpl.ca
Pauline O'Dell, Library Technician

La Scie: **La Scie Public Library**
Town Hall, La Scie, NL A0K 3M0
Tel: 709-675-2004
www.nlpl.ca
Karen Drover, Library Technician

Labrador City: **Labrador City Public Library**
306 Hudson Dr., Labrador City, NL A2V 1L5
Tel: 709-944-2190; *Fax:* 709-944-3674
www.nlpl.ca
Trudy Andrews, Library Technician
tandrews@nlpl.ca

Lark Harbour: **Lark Harbour (Blow-Me-Down) Public/School Library**
St. James All Grade School, Main St., Lark Harbour, NL A0L 1H0
Tel: 709-681-2147
www.nlpl.ca
Lesley Sheppard, Library Technician

Lewisporte: **Lewisporte Public Library**
PO Box 1179, Lewisporte, NL A0G 3A0
Tel: 709-535-2519
jsnow@nlpl.ca
www.nlpl.ca
Bobbi Benson, Librarian

Lourdes: **Lourdes Public/School Library**
82 Main St., Lourdes, NL A0N 1R0
Tel: 709-642-5388
pwoodrow@nlpl.ca
www.nlpl.ca
Patricia Woodrow, Library Technician

Lumsden: **Lumsden Public Library**
Lumsden School Complex, PO Box 119, Lumsden, NL A0G 3E0
Tel: 709-530-2617
kstagg@nlpl.ca
www.nlpl.ca
Kay Stagg, Librarian

Marystown: **Marystown Public Library**
Sacred Heart Elementary School, Marystown, NL A0E 2M0
Tel: 709-279-1507
www.nlpl.ca
Patricia Mayo, Library Technician

Mount Pearl: **Mount Pearl (Ross King) Memorial Public Library**
65 Olympic Dr., Mount Pearl, NL A1N 5H6
Tel: 709-368-3603
ygillard@nlpl.ca
www.nlpl.ca
Yvonne Gillard, Library Technician

Musgrave Harbour: **John B. Wheeler Public Library**
PO Box 130, Musgrave Harbour, NL A0G 3J0
Tel: 709-655-2730
eabbott@nlpl.ca
www.nlpl.ca
Eunice Abbott, Library Technician

Norris Arm: **Norris Arm Public Library**
65 Norris Ave., PO Box 100, Norris Arm, NL A0G 3M0
Tel: 709-653-2531
lrowsell@nlpl.ca
www.nlpl.ca
Leona Rowsell, Librarian

Norris Point: **Norris Point Public Library**
PO Box 129, Norris Point, NL A0K 3V0
Tel: 709-458-3368
jsamms@nlpl.ca
www.nlpl.ca
Judy Samms, Library Technician

North West River: **North West River Library & CAP Site**
PO Box 410, North West River, NL A0P 1M0
Tel: 709-497-8705; *Fax:* 709-497-8705
nwrvollibrary@hotmail.com
northwestriverlibrary.weebly.com
Social Media: www.facebook.com/groups/122067064513337
Wendy Mitchell, Librarian
Isobel Watts, Contact
isowatts@nf.sympatico.ca

Old Perlican: **Old Perlican Public Library**
PO Box 265, Old Perlican, NL A0A 3G0
Tel: 709-587-2028
www.nlpl.ca
Cathy Hatch, Library Technician

Pasadena: **Pasadena Public Library**
Town Council Building, 16 - 10th Ave., Pasadena, NL A0L 1K0
Tel: 709-686-2792
www.nlpl.ca

Placentia: **Placentia Public Library**
PO Box 119, Placentia, NL A0B 2Y0
Tel: 709-227-3621
dbowering@nlpl.ca
www.nlpl.ca
Doris Bowring, Library Technician

Point Leamington: **Point Leamington Public Library**
Point Leamington, NL A0H 1Z0
Tel: 709-484-3541
bwarford@nlpl.ca
www.nlpl.ca
Beverley Warford, Librarian

Port au Port: **Port au Port Public Library**
PO Box 220, Port au Port, NL A0N 1T0
Tel: 709-648-2472; *Fax:* 709-648-9512
jclarke@nlpl.ca
www.nlpl.ca
Janice Clarke, Library Technician
Wanda Martin, Staff

Port Saunders: **Port Saunders (Ingornachoix) Public Library**
PO Box 59, Port Saunders, NL A0K 4H0
Tel: 709-861-3690
ebiggin@nlpl.ca
www.nlpl.ca
Evelyn Biggin, Library Technician

Pouch Cove: **Pouch Cove Public Library**
PO Box 40, Pouch Cove, NL A0A 3L0
Tel: 709-335-2652
lbragg@nlpl.ca
www.nlpl.ca
Laura Bragg, Library Technician
Laura Noseworthy, Library Technician

Ramea: **Ramea Public Library**
c/o St. Boniface All Grade School, 10 School Rd., Ramea, NL A0N 2J0
Tel: 709-625-2344
flushman@nlpl.ca
www.nlpl.ca
Frances Lushman, Library Technician

Robert's Arm: **Robert's Arm Public Library**
PO Box 119, Robert's Arm, NL A0J 1R0
Tel: 709-652-3100
hsuley@nlpl.ca
www.robertsarm.com/library.html
Helen Suley, Librarian

Rocky Harbour: **Rocky Harbour Public Library**
Gros Morne Academy, 5 Parson's Lane, Rocky Harbour, NL A0K 4N0
Tel: 709-458-2900
www.nlpl.ca
Judy Samms, Library Technician

***Seal Cove WB:* Seal Cove Public Library**
Seal Cove Town Council, Council Rd., Seal Cove WB, NL A0K 5E0
Tel: 709-531-2505
kpinksen@nlpl.ca
www.nlpl.ca
Karen Pinksen, Librarian

***Sop's Arm:* Sop's Arm Public Library**
Main St., General Delivery, Sop's Arm, NL A0K 5K0
Tel: 709-482-2225
dwhite@nlpl.ca
www.nlpl.ca
Diane White, Library Technician

***Southern Harbour:* Southern Harbour Public Library**
Community Centre, Municipal Dr., Southern Harbour, NL A0B 3H0
Tel: 709-463-8814
www.nlpl.ca
Social Media: facebook.com/pages/Southern-Harbour-Public-Library/18762611126927
Bride Whiffen, Librarian

***Springdale:* Springdale Public Library**
Indian River High School, PO Box 1414, Springdale, NL A0J 1T0
Tel: 709-673-4169
www.nlpl.ca
Judy Hamilton, Librarian

***St Alban's:* St Alban's Public Library**
Town Hall Building, Main St., St Alban's, NL A0H 2E0
Tel: 709-538-3034
www.nlpl.ca
Kerri-Ann Snook, Librarian

***St Anthony:* St Anthony Public Library**
PO Box 129, St Anthony, NL A0K 4S0
Tel: 709-454-3025
jelliott@nlpl.ca
www.nlpl.ca
Jocelyn Elliott, Library Technician

***St Bride's:* Cape Shore Public Library**
Council Bldg. Main Rd, St Bride's, NL A0B 2Z0
Tel: 709-337-2360
www.nlpl.ca
Jacqueline Nash, Library Technician

***St Fintans:* St Fintan's (Bay St George South) Public/School Library**
PO Box 70, St Fintans, NL A0N 1Y0
Tel: 709-645-2186; *Fax:* 709-645-2780
www.nlpl.ca
Leanda Shears, Librarian

***St George's:* St George's Public Library**
Town Office, 93 mainÆSt., St George's, NL A0N 1Z0
Tel: 709-647-3808
www.nlpl.ca
Joan Downey, Library Technician

***St Lawrence:* St Lawrence Public Library**
St. Lawrence Academy, St Lawrence, NL A0E 2V0
Tel: 709-873-2650
www.nlpl.ca
Social Media: facebook.com/pages/St-Lawrence-Public-Library/149095271806633
Vicki Lockyer, Library Technician

***St Lunaire-Griquet:* St Lunaire-Griquet Public Library**
General Delivery, St Lunaire-Griquet, NL A0K 2X0
Tel: 709-623-2904
mbussey@nlpl.ca
www.nlpl.ca
Mae Bussey, Library Technician

***St. John's:* St John's Public Libraries**
Arts & Culture Centre, 125 Allendale Rd., St. John's, NL A1B 3A3
Tel: 709-737-2133; *Fax:* 709-737-2660
reference@nlpl.ca
Social Media: www.facebook.com/pages/A-C-Hunter-Public-Library/218044514923543
Michelle Walters, Manager
michellewalters@nlpubliclibraries.ca
709-737-3946

***Stephenville:* Newfoundland & Labrador Public Libraries**
48 St Georges Ave., Stephenville, NL A2N 1K9
Tel: 709-643-0900; *Fax:* 709-643-0925
illstaff@nlpl.ca
www.nlpl.ca
Shawn Tetford, Executive Director
stetford@nlpl.ca
709-643-0902
Lynn Cuff, Director, Regional Services
lcuff@nlpl.ca
709-643-0922
Andrew Hunt, Director, Financial Services
ahunt@nlpl.ca
709-643-0904
John White, Eastern Divisional Manager
johnwhite@nlpl.ca
709-737-3508
Newman George, Director, Information Technology
ngeorge@nlpl.ca
709-643-0911
Patricia Parsons, Central Divisional Manager
pparsons@nlpl.ca
709-651-5351
Michelle Walters, St. John's Manager
mwalters@nlpl.ca
709-737-3946

***Stephenville:* Stephenville (Kindale) Public Library**
45 Carolina Ave., Stephenville, NL A2N 3P8
Tel: 709-643-4262
www.nlpl.ca
Monica White, Library Technician

***Stephenville Crossing:* Stephenville Crossing Public Library**
Town Council Office, Stephenville Crossing, NL A0N 2C0
Tel: 709-646-2600
yyoung@nf.aibn.com
www.nlpl.ca

***Summerford:* Summerford Public Library**
Summerford Community Bldg., Main St., Summerford, NL A0G 4E0
Tel: 709-629-3244
www.nlpl.ca
Mavis Boyd, Librarian

***Torbay:* Torbay Public Library**
1288A Torbay Rd., Torbay, NL A1K 1B2
Tel: 709-437-6571
www.nlpl.ca
Marcia Deibel, Library Technician

***Trepassey:* Trepassey Public Library**
PO Box 183, Trepassey, NL A0A 4B0
Tel: 709-438-2224
www.nlpl.ca
Patricia McCormack, Library Technician

***Twillingate:* Twillingate Public Library**
J.M. Olds Collegiate, 97 Main St., Twillingate, NL A0G 4M0
Tel: 709-884-2353
www.nlpl.ca
Barbara Hamlyn, Librarian

***Victoria:* Victoria Public Library**
Victoria Municipal Centre, 2nd Fl., Main Rd., RR #74, Victoria, NL A0A 4G0
Tel: 709-596-3682
www.nlpl.ca
Shona Colbourne, Library Technician

***Wabush:* Wabush Public Library**
PO Box 179, Wabush, NL A0R 1B0
Tel: 709-282-3479; *Fax:* 709-282-3479
pstrickland@nlpl.ca
www.nlpl.ca
Paulette Strickland, Library Technician

***Wesleyville:* New-Wes-Valley Public Library**
PO Box 70, Lester Pearson High, Main St., Wesleyville, NL A0G 4R0
Tel: 709-536-5777
www.nlpl.ca
Beverley Hounsell, Librarian

***Whitbourne:* Whitbourne Public Library**
PO Box 400, Whitbourne, NL A0B 3K0
Tel: 709-759-2461
www.nlpl.ca
Social Media: facebook.com/pages/Whitbourne-Public-Library/144844512243474
Gloria Somerton, Library Technician

***Winterton:* Winterton Public Library**
PO Box 119, Winterton, NL A0B 3M0
Tel: 709-583-2119
www.nlpl.ca
Betty Pitcher, Library Technician

***Woody Point:* Woody Point (Edgar L. Roberts Memorial) Library**
PO Box 179, Woody Point, NL A0K 1P0
Tel: 709-453-2556
www.nlpl.ca
Michelle Harris, Librarian

Archives

***Bonavista:* Bonavista Historical Society**
PO Box 2957, Bonavista, NL A0C 1B0
Tel: 709-468-7747; *Fax:* 709-468-2495
bonavistaarchives@nf.aibn.com
www.townofbonavista.com
Chrystal Fudge, Contact

***Botwood:* Botwood Heritage Society Archive**
PO Box 490, Botwood, NL A0H 1E0
Tel: 709-257-2071; *Fax:* 709-257-3330
botwoodheritage@hotmail.com
Social Media: www.facebook.com/pages/Botwood-Heritage-Society/21744933206
Everett Elliott, Volunteer Archivist
709-257-4134

***Corner Brook:* Diocese of Western Newfoundland, Archives**
25 Main St., Corner Brook, NL A2H 1C2
Tel: 709-639-8712; *Fax:* 709-639-1636
dsown@nf.aibn.com
westernnewfoundland.anglican.org

***Happy Valley-Goose Bay:* Them Days Incorporated**
3 Courte Manche St., Happy Valley-Goose Bay, NL A0P 1E0
Tel: 709-896-8531; *Fax:* 709-896-4970
themdays@themdays.com
www.themdays.com
Melanie Blackmore, Administrator
administrator@themdays.com

***Harbour Grace:* Conception Bay Museum**
PO Box 298, Harbour Grace, NL A0A 2M0
Tel: 709-596-0506
www.hrgrace.ca/museum.html
Peggy Fahey, Curator

***Musgrave Harbour:* Fisherman's Museum**
4 Marine Dr., Musgrave Harbour, NL A0G 3J0
Tel: 709-655-2589; *Fax:* 709-655-2064
bantinghti@nf.aibn.com
www.musgraveharbour.com/museum.html
Mitzie Abbott, Town Clerk
709-655-2119

***St. John's:* City of St John's Archives**
495 Water St., 3rd Fl., St. John's, NL A1C 5M2
Tel: 709-576-8167; *Fax:* 709-576-8254
archives@stjohns.ca
www.stjohns.ca/cityservices/archives/index.jsp
Social Media: twitter.com/CityofStJohns; www.facebook.com/cityofstjohns
Helen Miller, Archivist

***St. John's:* Congregation of Sisters of Mercy of Newfoundland**
Littledale Complex, Waterford Bridge Rd., St. John's, NL A1C 5P5
Tel: 709-726-7320; *Fax:* 709-726-4414
Other Numbers: Alternataive number: 709-726-4414
mercy.generalate@nf.sympatico.ca
www.sistersofmercynf.org
Elizabeth Davis, Congregational Leader

***St. John's:* Diocese of Eastern Newfoundland & Labrador, Archives**
19 King's Bridge Rd., St. John's, NL A1C 3K4
Tel: 709-576-6728; *Fax:* 709-576-7122
archives@anglicanenl.net
www.anglican.nfol.ca

St. John's: Maritime History Archive
Henrietta Harvey Bldg., Memorial University, #1013, 320 Elizabeth Ave., St. John's, NL A1C 5S7
Tel: 709-864-8428; Fax: 709-864-3123
mha@mun.ca
www.mun.ca/mha/

St. John's: MUN Folklore & Language Archive
#ED4038, G.A. Hickman Bldg., St. John's, NL A1B 3X8
Tel: 709-864-8401; Fax: 709-864-4718
munfla@mun.ca
www.mun.ca/folklore/munfla

St. John's: Newfoundland & Labrador Conference, Archives
320 Elizabeth Ave., St. John's, NL A1B 1T9
Tel: 709-754-0372; Fax: 709-754-8336
ucarchives@nfld.net
www.united-church.ca/local/archives

St. John's: Newfoundland Historical Society
Churchill Square, St. John's, NL A1B 4J9
Tel: 709-722-3191; Fax: 709-722-9035
nhs@nf.aibn.com
www.nlhistory.ca
Larry Coady, President
lcoady@nl.rogers.com
Fred Smith, Vice-President

St. John's: Presentation Congregation Archives
Cathedral Sq., Presentation Convent, St. John's, NL A1C 5L4
Tel: 709-753-7291; Fax: 709-753-1578
prescong@nf.aibn.com
Mary Perpetua Kennedy, Archivist
perpetuakennedy@hotmail.com
Patricia Whittle, Assistant Archivist
bozowhittle@yahoo.com

St. John's: Provincial Archives of Newfoundland & Labrador
9 Bonaventure Ave., PO Box 1800, Stn. C, St. John's, NL A1C 5P9
Tel: 709-757-8030; Fax: 709-757-8031
archives@therooms.ca
www.therooms.ca/archives
Greg Walsh, Provincial Archivist

St. John's: Queen's College
Archives & Special Collections, Queen Elizabeth II Library, Memorial University of Newfoundland, St. John's, NL A1B 3Y1
Tel: 709-864-4349; Fax: 709-864-2153
Toll-Free: 877-753-0116
archives@mun.ca
www.mun.ca/queens

St. John's: Roman Catholic Archdiocese of St John's
49 Bonaventure Ave, St. John's, NL A1C 5N5
Tel: 709-726-3660
www.rcsj.org

St. John's: Sport Archives of Newfoundland & Labrador
The Rooms Provincial Archives Division, 9 Bonaventure Ave., PO Box 1800, Stn. C, St. John's, NL A1C 5P9
Tel: 709-757-8088; Fax: 709-757-8031
SANL@therooms.ca
www.therooms.ca/archives/sports_archives.asp
Linda Murphy, Volunteer Archivist
Frances Horwood, Volunteer Archivist

Trinity TB: Trinity Historical Society Archives
Lester-Garland House, 3rd Fl., Trinity TB, NL A0C 2S0
Tel: 709-464-3599; Fax: 709-464-3599
info@trinityhistoricalsociety.com
www.trinityhistoricalsociety.com
Clarence Dewling, Archivist

Wesleyville: Bonavista North Regional Museum & Gallery
12 Memorial Dr., Wesleyville, NL A0G 4R0
Tel: 709-536-2110; Fax: 709-536-3039
museum@nf.aibn.com
bonavistanorth.blogspot.ca
Social Media: twitter.com/BonavistaNorth
Duke Kelloway, Contact
Janet Davis, Contact

Northwest Territories

Regional Systems

NWT Public Library Services
75 Woodland Dr., Hay River, NT X0E 1G1
Tel: 867-874-6531; Fax: 867-874-3321
Toll-Free: 866-297-0232
www.ece.gov.nt.ca/Public_Library_Services/index
Alison Hopkins, Territorial Librarian
alison_hopkins@gov.nt.ca
867-874-3531
Brian Dawson, Head, Technical Services
brian_dawson@gov.nt.ca
867-874-6531

Public Libraries

Fort Simpson: John Tsetso Memorial Library
PO Box 258, Fort Simpson, NT X0E 0N0
Tel: 867-695-3276; Fax: 867-695-3276
si_library@gov.nt.ca
www.ece.gov.nt.ca/Public_Library_Services/CommunityLibraries.html
Lorraine Ocko, Librarian
867-695-3275

Fort Smith: Mary Kaeser Library
170 McDougal Rd., Fort Smith, NT X0E 0P0
Tel: 867-872-2296
www.mklibrary.ca/
Social Media: www.facebook.com/MKLibrary
Jeri Miltenberger, Local Librarian
jeri_miltenberger@gov.nt.ca

Hay River: Hay River Dene Reserve Community Library
Chief Sunrise Education Centre, Hay River, NT X0E 1G4
Tel: 867-874-2128; Fax: 867-874-3678
Other Numbers: 867-874-6444
Barbara Berlinguette, Contact
Kevin Lafferty, Interlibrary Loans Clerk
kevin_lafferty@gov.nt.ca

Hay River: Northwest Territories Centennial Library
75 Woodland Dr., Hay River, NT X0E 1G1
Tel: 867-874-6486; Fax: 867-874-3834
www.nwtpls.gov.nt.ca
Christine Gyapay, Local Librarian
christine_gyapay@gov.nt.ca

Inuvik: Inuvik Centennial Library
100 MacKenzie Rd., Inuvik, NT X0E 0T0
Tel: 867-777-8620; Fax: 867-777-8621
IK_Library@gov.nt.ca
www.inuvik.ca/townhall/library.html
Beverly Garven, Head Librarian

Norman Wells: Norman Wells Community Library
PO Box 97, Norman Wells, NT X0E 0V0
Tel: 867-587-2956; Fax: 867-587-2193
normanwells_library@gov.nt.ca
Lori Shapansky, Local Librarian

Tulita: Tulita Community Library
General Delivery, Tulita, NT X0E 0K0
Tel: 867-588-4471; Fax: 867-588-4908
Darlene Etchinelle, Librarian

Yellowknife: Yellowknife Public Library
Centre Square Mall, 5022 - 49th St., 2nd Fl., Yellowknife, NT X1A 3R8
Tel: 867-920-5642; Fax: 867-920-5671
library@yellowknife.ca
www.yellowknife.ca
Social Media: www.facebook.com/187241917965175
Deborah Bruser, Library Manager
dbruser@yellowknife.ca
867-669-3401
Kris Solowy, Library Technician
ksolowy@yellowknife.ca
867-669-3402
Jennifer Knowlan, Public Service Librarian
jknowlan@yellowknife.ca
867-920-5642

Archives

Fort Smith: Northern Life Museum National Exhibition Centre
110 King St., Fort Smith, NT X0E 0P0
Tel: 867-872-2859; Fax: 867-872-5808
www.nwtresearch.com/canoe/museum.htm
Kevin Brunt, Curator of Collections
curator@auroranet.net.ca
Laurie Young, Manager

Nova Scotia

Regional Systems

Annapolis Valley Regional Library
26 Bay Rd., Bridgetown, NS B0S 1C0
Tel: 902-665-2995; Fax: 902-665-4899
Toll-Free: 866-922-0229
www.valleylibrary.ca
Social Media: www.facebook.com/AVRLibrary
Frances Newman, Regional Librarian
Charlotte Janes, Head, Systems & Administration

Cape Breton Regional Library
50 Falmouth St., Sydney, NS B1P 6X9
Tel: 402-562-3279; Fax: 902-564-0765
Other Numbers: 902-562-3279 (Bookmobile services)
inssc@nssc.library.ns.ca
www.cbrl.ca
Social Media: twitter.com/CBRLibrary; www.facebook.com/pages/Cape-Breton-Regional-Library/296649443707
Claire Detheridge, Chair
Faye MacDougall, Regional Librarian
fmacdoug@nssc.library.ns.ca
Ian R. MacIntosh, Deputy Regional Librarian & Collections Librarian
imacinto@nssc.library.ns.ca
Theresa MacDonald, Librarian, Technical Services
tmacdona@nssc.library.ns.ca
Clare MacKillop, Supervisor, Cape Breton County Branch Libraries
cmackill@nssc.library.ns.ca
Amanda Andrews, Supervisor, Victoria County Library Services
aandrews@nssc.library.ns.ca
Rosalie Gillis, Coordinator, Community Support
rgillis@nssc.library.ns.ca
Tara MacNeil, Coordinator, Programs
tmacneil@nssc.library.ns.ca

Cumberland Regional Library
21 Acadia St., Amherst, NS B4H 4W3
Tel: 902-667-2135; Fax: 902-667-1360
information@cumberlandpubliclibraries.ca
www.crl.library.ns.ca
Social Media: twitter.com/CumberlandPL; www.facebook.com/195505467145534
Robert Angel, Chair
Beth Clinton, Chief Librarian & Board Secretary
Denise Corey, Deputy Chief Librarian
Chantelle Taylor, Youth Services Librarian
Peggy Sperry, Contact, Books By Mail
902-667-2135 ext. 229

Eastern Counties Regional Library
390 Murray St., Mulgrave, NS B0E 2G0
Tel: 902-747-2597; Fax: 902-747-2500
Toll-Free: 855-787-7323
www.ecrl.library.ns.ca
Social Media: www.facebook.com/153045861388306
Laura Emery, Chief Librarian
Patricia McCormick, Contact
Mildred Carrigan, Library Assistant, Inter-Library Loans
mcarriga@nsme.library.ns.ca
Lana Hadley, Accounts Administrator
bookkeep@nsme.library.ns.ca

Halifax Public Libraries
60 Alderney Dr., Dartmouth, NS B2Y 4P8
Tel: 902-490-5744; Fax: 902-490-5889
Other Numbers: 902-490-5753 (Accounts); 903-490-5710 (Research)
asklib@halifaxpubliclibraries.ca
www.halifaxpubliclibraries.ca
Social Media: twitter.com/hfxpublib; www.facebook.com/hfxpublib
Leo McKenna, Chair
Judith Hare, Chief Executive Officer
Susan McLean, Deputy CEO & Director, Public Services
Francisca Goldsmith, Director, Branch Services

Bruce Gorman, Director, Information Technology & Collection Management
Al LeBlanc, Director, Finance & Facilities
Cathy Maddigan, Director, Human Resources
Paula Saulnier, Director, Corporate Research & Development
Darlene Beck, Regional Manager, Reference Services
Karen Dahl, Regional Manager, Youth Services
Heather MacKenzie, Regional Manager, Services to Older Adults
Sarah Wenning, Regional Manager, Reader's Services
Kevin Crick, Manager, Information Technology
Denis Cunningham, Manager, Communications & Marketing
Tracey Jones, Manager, Literacy, ESL, & Diversity Services
Debbie LeBel, Manager, Collection Development

Pictou-Antigonish Regional Library
PO Box 276, New Glasgow, NS B2H 5E3
Fax: 902-755-6775
Toll-Free: 866-779-7761
estackho@nsngp.library.ns.ca
www.parl.ns.ca
Eric Stackhouse, Chief Librarian, Systems Librarian, & Board Secretary
Fred Popowich, Deputy Chief & Technical Services Librarian
Kristel Fleuren-Hunter, Children's Services Librarian
Trecia Schell, Community Services Librarian
Fern MacDonald, Manager, User Services
Melanie Pauls, Coordinator, Community Access to Technology

South Shore Regional Library
547 King St., Bridgewater, NS B4V 1B3
Tel: 902-543-2548; *Fax:* 902-543-8191
Toll-Free: 877-455-2548
info@southshorepubliclibraries.ca
www.southshorepubliclibraries.ca
Social Media: twitter.com/@ssplibraries; www.facebook.com/southshorepubliclibraries
Troy Myers, Chief Executive Officer & Chief Librarian
Jeff Mercer, Librarian

Western Counties Regional Library
405 Main St., Yarmouth, NS B5A 1G3
Tel: 902-742-2486; *Fax:* 902-742-6920
insy@nsy.library.ns.ca (Interlibrary loans)
www.westerncounties.ca
Social Media: www.youtube.com/irwhite62; twitter.com/wcrlibrary; www.facebook.com/62520112493
Gary Archibald, Chair
ansy@nsy.library.ns.ca
Erin Comeau, Regional Library Director
ecomeau@nsy.library.ns.ca
Joanne Head, Deputy Director
jhead@nsy.library.ns.ca
Richard Beharriell, Coordinator, Library Services
rbeharriell@nsy.library.ns.ca
Deborah Duke, Coordinator, Library Services
dduke@nsy.library.ns.ca
Yvonne LeBlanc, Manager, Office
ansy@nsy.library.ns.ca
Ian White, Manager, Public Relations
iwhite@nsy.library.ns.ca
Scott MacMullen, Supervisor, Maintenance, Buildings & Vehicles & System Administrator
smacmull@nsy.library.ns.ca
Carol Surette, Bookkeeper
csurette@nsy.library.ns.ca

Public Libraries

Colchester-East Hants Public Library
754 Prince St., Truro, NS B2N 1G9
Tel: 902-895-0235; *Fax:* 902-895-7149
Toll-Free: 888-632-9088
anstc@nstc.library.ns.ca
cehlibrary.ednet.ns.ca
Janet Pelley, Library Director
Lesley Brann, Administrator, Adult & Outreach Services
Lynda Marsh, Administrator, Youth Services
Bill Morgan, Administrator, Automated & Technical Services
Norma Johnson-MacGregor, Librarian, Electronic Services

Archives

***Amherst:* Cumberland County Museum & Archives**
150 Church St., Amherst, NS B4H 3C4
Tel: 902-667-2561; *Fax:* 902-667-0996
ccma@cumberlandcountymuseum.com
www.cumberlandcountymuseum.com
Social Media: www.facebook.com/group.php?gid=148688355199338
Shirley Nickerson, Manager/Curator
902-667-2561

***Annapolis Royal:* Historic Restoration Society of Annapolis County**
136 St. George St., Annapolis Royal, NS B0S 1A0
Tel: 902-532-7754; *Fax:* 902-532-0700
historic@ns.aliantzinc.ca
www.annapolisheritagesociety.com
Social Media: twitter.com/odellmuseum
Barry Moody, Chair

***Antigonish:* Antigonish Heritage Museum**
20 East Main St., Antigonish, NS B2G 2E9
Tel: 902-863-6160
www.parl.ns.ca/aheritage
Jocelyn Gillis, Manager

***Antigonish:* St Francis-Xavier University Archives**
Angus L. Macdonald Library, Antigonish, NS B2G 2W5
Tel: 902-867-2201; *Fax:* 902-867-5153
archives@stfx.ca
www.stfx.ca

***Baddeck:* Alexander Graham Bell National Historic Site/ Lieu Historique National Alexander Graham Bell**
559 Chebucto St., Baddeck, NS B0E 1B0
Tel: 902-295-2069; *Fax:* 902-295-3496
TTY: 9022951512
eddy.kennedy@pc.gc.ca
www.bell.capebretonu.ca/index.asp.
Eddy Kennedy, Site Manager

***Barrington:* Cape Sable Historical Society Centre**
2402 Hwy. 3, Barrington, NS B0W 1E0
Tel: 902-637-2185
barmuseumcomplex@eastlink.ca
www.capesablehistoricalsociety.com/
Brenda Maxwell, Archives Manager
maxwelbm@gov.ns.ca

***Bridgetown:* Bridgetown & Area Historical Society**
12 Queen St., Bridgetown, NS B0S 1C0
Tel: 902-665-4530
www.jameshousemuseum.com
Frances Nixon, Museum Administrator

***Bridgewater:* DesBrisay Museum**
130 Jubilee Rd., Bridgewater, NS B4V 3X9
Tel: 902-543-4033; *Fax:* 902-543-4713
museum@bridgewater.ca
www.desbrisaymuseum.ca
Social Media: www.facebook.com/pages/DesBrisay-Museum/190907454254694
Linda Bedford, Curator
lbedford@bridgewater.ca

***Canso:* Canso Historical Society**
c/o Whitman House Museum, 1297 Union St., Canso, NS B0H 1H0
Tel: 902-366-2170
cansotouristbureau@ns.sympatico.ca
www.guysboroughcountyheritage.ca

***Centreville:* Archelaus Smith Museum**
915 Hwy. 330, Centreville, NS B0W 1P0
Tel: 902-745-2642
blancherossoconnell@hotmail.com
www.archelaus.org/index.html
Charla Strang, Treasurer
902-745-0428
Blanche O'Connell, President
blancherossoconnell@hotmail.com
902-745-2642
Willamae Ross, Secretary
902-745-3343

***Cherry Brook:* Black Cultural Centre for Nova Scotia**
10 Cherry Brook Rd., Cherry Brook, NS B2Z 1A8
Tel: 902-434-6223; *Fax:* 902-434-2306
Toll-Free: 800-465-0767
contact@bccns.com
www.bccns.com
Social Media: www.youtube.com/bccnsvideo
Henry V. Bishop, Curator
Russell Grosse, Operations Manager

***Church Point:* St Mary's Museum/ Le Musée Sainte Marie**
1713 Hwy 1, Church Point, NS B0W 1M0
Tel: 902-769-2378; *Fax:* 902-769-0048
www.museeeglisesaintemariemuseum.ca
Blanche Forrest, Secretary, Museum Committee

***Dartmouth:* Cole Harbour Rural Heritage Society**
471 Poplar Dr., Dartmouth, NS B2W 4L2
Tel: 905-434-0222
farm.museum@ns.aliantzinc.ca
coleharbourfarmmuseum.ca

***Dartmouth:* Dartmouth Heritage Museum Society**
26 Newcastle St., Dartmouth, NS B2Y 3M5
Fax: 902-464-8210
www.dartmouthheritagemuseum.ns.ca
Social Media: www.facebook.com/pages/Dartmouth-Heritage-Museum/205574426126756
Lisa O'Neill, Executive Director
lisaoneill@bellaliant.com
902-464-2916
Crystal Martin, Curator
martinc@bellaliant.com
902-464-2004

***Halifax:* Canadian Broadcasting Corporation (Halifax)/ Société Radio-Canada (Halifax)**
PO Box 3000, Halifax, NS B3J 3E9
Tel: 902-420-4160; *Fax:* 902-420-4281
www.novascotia.cbc.ca
Doug Kirby, Media Library Coordinator
doug.kirby@cbc.ca

***Halifax:* Canadian Museum of Immigration at Pier 21**
1055 Marginal Rd., Halifax, NS B3H 4P7
Tel: 902-425-7770; *Fax:* 902-423-4045
Toll-Free: 855-526-4721
info@pier21.ca
www.pier21.ca
Cara MacDonald, Manager, Reference Services
reference@pier21.ca
902-420-6655
Steve Schwinghamer, Historian
research@pier21.ca
902-420-6646
Cassidy Bankson, Researcher & Coordinator, Oral History
oralhistory@pier21.ca
902-425-7770 ext. 241

***Halifax:* Diocese of Nova Scotia & Prince Edward Island**
2571 MacDonald St., Halifax, NS B3L 3G3
Tel: 902-420-0717; *Fax:* 902-425-0717
archives@nspeidiocese.ca, www.nspeidiocese.ca

***Halifax:* Nova Scotia Archives & Records Management**
6016 University Ave., Halifax, NS B3H 1W4
Tel: 902-424-6060; *Fax:* 902-424-0628
nsarm@gov.ns.ca
www.gov.ns.ca/nsarm
Social Media: www.youtube.com/NSArchives; twitter.com/NS_Archives; www.facebook.com/novascotiaarchives
W. Brian Speirs, Provincial Archivist

***Halifax:* Nova Scotia Sport Hall of Fame**
#446, 1800 Argyle St., Halifax, NS B3J 3N8
Tel: 902-421-1266; *Fax:* 902-425-1148
sporthalloffame@eastlink.ca
www.novascotiasporthalloffame.com
Social Media: twitter.com/NSSHF; www.facebook.com/116064731766960
Bill Robinson, Executive Director
bill@nsshf.com
Shane Mailman, Facility & Communications Manager
shane@nsshf.com

***Halifax:* Saint Mary's University Archives**
Patrick Power Library, 923 Robie St., 3rd Fl., Halifax, NS B3H 3C3
Tel: 902-420-5508; *Fax:* 902-420-5561
www.smu.ca/administration/archives

***Halifax:* Shambhala Archives**
1084 Tower Rd., Halifax, NS B3H 2Y5
Tel: 902-420-1118; *Fax:* 902-423-2750
archives@shambhala.org
www.archives.shambhala.org

***Halifax:* Sisters of Charity of St. Vincent de Paul - Halifax**
Sisters of Charity Centre, 215 Seton Rd., Halifax, NS B3M 0C9
Tel: 902-406-8136; *Fax:* 902-457-3506
archives@schalifax.ca
www.schalifax.ca
Patti Bannister, Congregational Archivist

Halifax: **University Archives & Special Collections**
c/o Killam Memorial Library, 6225 University Ave., Halifax, NS B3H 4H8
Tel: 902-494-3615; *Fax:* 902-494-2062
duasc@dal.ca
libraries.dal.ca/collections/archives_special_collections

Kentville: **King's County Historical Society**
c/o The Genealogy & Family History Committee, The Kings County Museum, 37 Cornwallis St., Kentville, NS B4N 2E2
Tel: 902-678-6237; *Fax:* 902-678-2764
genealogy@okcm.ca
www.okcm.ca
Social Media: twitter.com/Kings_Co_Museum;
www.facebook.com/kingscountymuseum

Liverpool: **Thomas H. Raddall Research Centre**
109 Main St., Liverpool, NS B0T 1K0
Tel: 902-354-4058; *Fax:* 902-354-2050
rafusela@gov.ns.ca
www.raddallresearchcentre.com
Linda Rafuse, Director
rafusela@gov.ns.ca
902-354-4058
Kathy Stitt, Administrative Assistant
stittkim@gov.ns.ca

Louisbourg: **Fortress of Louisbourg**
259 Park Service Rd., Louisbourg, NS B1C 2L2
Tel: 902-733-2280; *Fax:* 902-733-2362
fortress.uccb.ns.ca

Maplewood: **Parkdale-Maplewood Community Museum**
3005 Barss Corner Rd., RR#1, Maplewood, NS B0R 1A0
Tel: 902-644-2893; *Fax:* 902-644-3422
Other Numbers: Off-season: 902-644-2375
p-mcm@hotmail.com
parkdale.ednet.ns.ca
Social Media: www.facebook.com/94020106181
Barbara Gail Wentzell, Curator
Donna Arenburg, Museum Assistant

Middleton: **Macdonald Museum**
21 School St., Middleton, NS B0S 1P0
Tel: 902-825-6116; *Fax:* 902-825-0531
macdonald.museum@ns.sympatico.ca
www.macdonaldmuseum.ca
Alison Brathwaite, Librarian & Curatorial Assistant

Parrsboro: **Parrsborough Shore Historical Society**
1155 Whitehall Rd., Parrsboro, NS B0M 1S0
Tel: 902-254-2376
ottawa.house@ns.sympatico.ca
www.ottawahousemuseum.ca
Susan Clarke, Facility Manager
Conrad Byers, Historian

Pictou: **Hector Exhibit Centre & Archives**
86 Haliburton Rd., Pictou, NS B0K 1H0
Tel: 902-485-4563; *Fax:* 902-485-5213
pcghs@gov.ns.ca
www.rootsweb.com/~nspcghs/
Social Media: twitter.com/HectorCentre;
www.facebook.com/pages/Hector-Exhibit-Centre/234152123269050
Marlene Chisholm, Researcher
marlene.chisholm@ns.sympatico.ca

Port Hastings: **Port Hastings Historical Museum & Archives**
24 Rte 19, Port Hastings, NS B9A 1M1
Tel: 902-625-1295
office@porthastingsmuseum.ca
www.porthastingsmuseum.ca
Bob MacEachern, Historical Society President
Maxine Smith, Secretary

Shearwater: **Shearwater Aviation Museum**
12 Wing Shearwater, Shearwater, NS B0J 3A0
Tel: 902-720-2165; *Fax:* 902-720-2037
library@shearwateraviationmuseum.ns.ca
www.shearwateraviationmuseum.ns.ca
Social Media: twitter.com/YAWmuseum;
www.facebook.com/shearwateraviationmuseum
Christine Dunphy, Librarian/Archivist
902-720-2165

Shelburne: **Shelburne County Museum**
20 Dock St., Shelburne, NS B0T 1W0
Tel: 902-875-3219; *Fax:* 902-875-4141
shelburne.museum@ns.sympatico.ca
www.historicshelburne.com
Finn Bower, Curator
Betty Stoddard, Assistant Curator/Office Manager

Sydney: **Beaton Institute**
1250 Grand Lake Rd., Sydney, NS B1M 1A2
Tel: 902-563-1329; *Fax:* 902-562-8899
beaton@cbu.ca
www.cbu.ca/beaton

Truro: **Colchester Historical Society Museum and Archives**
29 Young St., Truro, NS B2N 3W3
Tel: 902-895-6284; *Fax:* 902-895-9530
archivist@colchesterhistoreum.ca
colchesterhistoreum.ca
Nan D. Harvey, Archivist
Penny Lighthall, Curator

Tusket: **Argyle Township Court House Archives**
8162 Hwy. 3, Tusket, NS B0W 3M0
Tel: 902-648-2493; *Fax:* 902-648-2537
pcrowell@argylecourthouse.com
www.argylecourthouse.com
Peter Crowell, Municipal Historian & Archivist
pcrowell@argylecourthouse.com

Windsor: **West Hants Historical Society**
281 King St., Windsor, NS B0N 2T0
Tel: 902-798-4706
whhs@ns.aliantzinc.ca
www.westhantshistoricalsociety.ca
Social Media:
www.facebook.com/group.php?gid=141349919273121

Wolfville: **Esther Clark Wright Archives (Atlantic Baptist Archives)**
PO Box 4, Wolfville, NS B4P 2R6
Tel: 902-585-1011; *Fax:* 902-585-1748
library.acadiau.ca/archives/

Yarmouth: **Yarmouth County Historical Society**
22 Collins St., Yarmouth, NS B5A 3C8
Tel: 902-742-5539; *Fax:* 902-749-1120
ycarchives@eastlink.ca
yarmouthcountymuseum.ednet.ns.ca
Social Media: www.facebook.com/group.php?gid=92402018979
Nadine Gates, Director & Curator
ycmuseum@eastlink.ca
Jamie Serran, Archivist
ycarchives@eastlink.ca

Ontario

Regional Systems

Ontario Library Service North/ Service des bibliothèques de l'Ontario nord
334 Regent St., Sudbury, ON P3C 4E2
Tel: 705-675-6467; *Fax:* 705-675-2285
Toll-Free: 800-461-6348
Other Numbers: Fax Toll-Free: 800-398-8890
www.olsn.ca
Social Media: www.facebook.com/olsnorth
Leanne Clendening, Chief Executive Offcier
lclendening@olsn.ca
705-675-6467 ext. 209
Ghyslain Sabourin, Deputy Chief Executive Officer
gsabourin@olsn.ca
705-675-6467 ext. 208
Marjatta Asu, Service Team Lead, Skills Development
masu@olsn.ca
Serge Aubin, Service Team Lead, Technology & Innovation
saubin@olsn.ca
Karen Thistle, Service Team Lead, Capacity Building
kthistle@olsn.ca
Mette Kruger, Archival Librarian, First Nation Repository Pilot Project
mkruger@olsn.ca
705-692-9990

Southern Ontario Library Service (SOLS)
#902, 111 Peter St., Toronto, ON M5H 2H1
Tel: 416-961-1669; *Fax:* 416-961-5122
Toll-Free: 800-387-5765
www.sols.org
Laurey Gillies, CEO
lgillies@sols.org
Daryl Novak, Director, Operations
dnovak@sols.org

Public Libraries

Addison: **Elizabethtown-Kitley Township Public Library**
6544 New Dublin Rd., RR#2, Addison, ON K0E 1A0
Tel: 613-498-3338; *Fax:* 613-345-7235
mail@elizabethtown-kitley.on.ca
www.elizabethtown-kitley.on.ca/library.htm
C. Hoy, Chair
Ruth Blanchard, Chief Executive Officer

Ajax: **Ajax Public Library**
55 Harwood Ave. South, Ajax, ON L1S 2H8
Tel: 905-683-4000; *Fax:* 905-683-6960
libraryinfo@ajax.ca
www.ajaxlibrary.ca
Jennifer Brown, Chair
Donna Bright, Chief Librarian/CEO
905-683-4000 ext. 8825
Dan Gioiosa, Support Services Manager
905-683-4000 ext. 8824
Cindy Poon, Public Service Manager
cindy.poon@ajax.ca
905-683-4000 ext. 8801
Sarah Dodge, Information Services Coordinator
sarah.dodge@ajax.ca
905-683-4000 ext. 8802

Ajax: **United Way Durham Region**
#9, 114 Old Kingston Rd., Ajax, ON L1T 2Z9
Tel: 905-686-0606; *Fax:* 905-436-6414
Toll-Free: 866-436-6910
informdurham@bellnet.ca
www.informdurham.com
Cathy Gowland, Manager, Information Services

Alban: **French River Public Library / Bibliothèque publique de la Rivière-des-français**
796 Chemin/Hwy 64, Alban, ON P0M 1A0
Tel: 705-857-1771; *Fax:* 705-857-1392
frenchriver_publiclibrary@yahoo.ca
www.olsn.ca/frenchriverpl/index
Suzanne Duval, Chair

Alliston: **New Tecumseth Public Library**
17 Victoria St. East, Alliston, ON L9R 1V6
Tel: 705-435-5651; *Fax:* 705-435-0750
www.ntpl.ca
Social Media:
www.facebook.com/group.php?gid=139887459474221
Mark Gagnon, Chief Executive Officer
mgagnon@ntpl.ca
705-435-0250

Almonte: **Mississippi Mills Public Library**
155 High St., Almonte, ON K0A 1A0
Tel: 613-256-1037
visitinglibrary@mississippimills.ca
www.mississippimills.ca/library
Peter Nelson, Chief Librarian
pnelson@mississippimills.ca
Monica Blackburn, Deputy & Children's Librarian
mblackburn@mississippimills.ca
Margo Hay-Goodings, Contact, Visiting Library Service

Angus: **Essa Public Library**
#1, 8505 County Road 10, Angus, ON L0M 1B1
Tel: 705-424-6531; *Fax:* 705-424-5512
essalib@essa.library.on.ca
www.essa.library.on.ca
Social Media: twitter.com/essalibrary;
www.facebook.com/essapubliclibrary
Janine Harris-Wheatley, CEO
ceoadmin@essa.library.on.ca
705-424-2679
Shaun Fox, Coordinator of Public Service
Angie Wishart, Coordinator of Support Services

Apsley: **North Kawartha Public Library**
175 Burleigh St., Apsley, ON K0L 1A0
Tel: 705-656-4333; *Fax:* 705-656-2538
info@northkawarthalibrary.com
www.northkawarthalibrary.com
Social Media: twitter.com/NorthKawartha;
www.facebook.com/NorthKawartha
Carolyn Amyotte, Chair
Shannon Hunter, Chief Executive Officer
s.hunter@northkawartha.on.ca
Debbie Hall, Librarian, Apsley & Woodview Branches
d.hall@northkawarthalibrary.com
Susan Suhr, Coordinator, Technical Services, Apsley & Woodview Branches
s.suhr@northkawarthalibrary.com

Linda Fierheller, Clerk

***Arnprior:* Arnprior Public Library**
21 Madawaska St., Arnprior, ON K7S 1R6
Tel: 613-623-2279; *Fax:* 613-623-0281
library@arncap.com
www.arnprior.library.on.ca
Social Media: www.facebook.com/197513506955476
Neil Salminen, Chair
Karen DeLuca, Chief Librarian
Carolyn Swayze, Children & Teen Services Librarian

***Astorville:* East Ferris Public Library / Bibliothèque publique d'East Ferris**
1257 Village Rd., PO Box 160, Astorville, ON P0H 1B0
Tel: 705-752-2042; *Fax:* 705-752-0365
efpl@ontera.net
www.olsn.ca/east_ferrispl
Jennifer Laporte, CEO
Norma McQuoid, Co-Chair
Jennifer Laporte, Chief Executive Officer
Connie Lortie, Library Assistant

***Athens:* Township of Athens Public Library**
5 Central St., Athens, ON K0E 1B0
Tel: 613-924-2048
athenspl@bellnet.ca
www.athenslibrary.ca
Julianna McAleese, Chair
Freda Schaafsma, Head Librarian
Hennie Janssens, Children's Librarian

***Atherley:* Ramara Township Public Library**
5482 Hwy. 12 South, Atherley, ON L3V 6H7
Tel: 705-325-5776; *Fax:* 705-325-8176
info@ramarapubliclibrary.org
www.ramarapubliclibrary.org
Jane Banfield, CEO

***Atikokan:* Atikokan Public Library**
Civic Centre, Atikokan, ON P0T 1C0
Tel: 807-597-4406; *Fax:* 807-597-1514
jlewis@aplibrary.org
www.aplibrary.org
Jonathan Lewis, CEO/Librarian
jlewis@aplibrary.org
807-594-4406
Tracey Sinclair, Head of Children's Services
tsinclair@nwconx.net

***Aurora:* Aurora Public Library**
15145 Yonge St., Aurora, ON L4G 1M1
Tel: 905-727-9494; *Fax:* 905-727-9374
Other Numbers: Telecirc 905-727-0314
www.library.aurora.on.ca
Social Media: www.facebook.com/aurorapubliclibrary
Louise Procter Maio, CEO
lproctermaio@library.aurora.on.ca
905-727-9494 ext. 221

***Bala:* Wahta Mohawks Public Library**
2664, Muskoka Rd. #38, Bala, ON P0C 1A0
Tel: 705-756-2354; *Fax:* 705-756-2376
www.wahta.ca/programs.htm
Shirley Sahanatien, CEO

***Bancroft:* Bancroft Public Library**
14 Flint St., Bancroft, ON K0L 1C0
Tel: 613-332-3380; *Fax:* 613-332-5473
info@bancroftpubliclibrary.ca
www.bancroftpubliclibrary.ca
Noreen Tinney, Chair
Vanessa Holm, CEO/Library Manager
Beverly Creighton, Librarian/InterLibrary Loan Officer
Shirley McRandall, Library Collection Maintenance Officer
Pat Lavoy, Library Events Officer

***Barrie:* Barrie Public Library**
60 Worsley St., Barrie, ON L4M 1L6
Tel: 705-728-1010; *Fax:* 705-728-4322
Other Numbers: Ext. 7020 (Adult Information Desk)
barlib@barrie.ca
www.library.barrie.on.ca
Social Media: twitter.com/BPL_inthecity;
www.facebook.com/pages/Barrie-Public-Library/4560242280
Al Davis, Director of Library Services
adavis@barrie.ca
705-728-1010 ext. 7500
Jaime Griffis, Manager, Branch & Public Services
jgriffis@barrie.ca
705-728-1010 ext. 7009
Shonna Froebel, Manager, Adult Information Services
sfroebel@barrie.ca
705-728-1010 ext. 7007
Jane Salmon, Manager, Children's & Youth Services
jsalmon@barrie.ca
705-728-1010 ext. 7017
Khuan Seow, Manager, Information Technology
kseow@barrie.ca
705-728-1010 ext. 7010
Chris Vanderkruys, Manager, Development, Marketing & Communications
cvanderkruys@barrie.ca
705-728-1010 ext. 7137
Heather Betz, Business Officer
hbetz@barrie.ca
705-728-1010 ext. 7006

***Barry's Bay:* Barry's Bay & Area Public Library**
19474 Opeongo Line, Barry's Bay, ON K0J 1B0
Tel: 613-756-2000; *Fax:* 613-756-2000
bblibry@bellnet.ca
library.barrys-bay.ca
Karen Filipkowski, CEO/Head Librarian

***Baysville:* Lake of Bays Public Library**
Community Centre, 10 University Ave., Baysville, ON P0B 1A0
Tel: 705-767-2361; *Fax:* 705-767-2361
www.lakeofbayslibrary.ca
David Johnstone, Chair
Linda Lacroix, CEO
linla@vianet.on.ca

***Beachburg:* Township of Whitewater Region Public Library**
20 Cameron St., Beachburg, ON K0J 1C0
Tel: 613-582-7090
libraries.whitewaterregion.ca
Marilyn Labow, CEO/Chief Librarian
mlabow@nrtco.net

***Beamsville:* Lincoln Public Library**
4996 Beam St., Beamsville, ON L0R 1B0
Tel: 905-563-7014; *Fax:* 905-563-1810
info@lincoln.library.on.ca
www.lincoln.library.on.ca
Social Media: www.facebook.com/115678635175024
John Kralt, Chair
Jill Nicholson, CEO
Janice Coles, Deputy CEO
Elisabeth Peters, Children's Services Coordinator

***Bear Island:* Temagami First Nation Public Library / Bibliothèque publique de Tribu Temagami**
General Delivery, Bear Island, ON P0H 1C0
Tel: 705-237-8876; *Fax:* 705-237-8959
www.temagamifirstnation.ca/
Virginia Mackenzie, CEO
705-237-8876

***Bearskin Lake:* Bearskin Lake Public Library / Bibliothèque Publique de Bearskin**
General Delivery, Bearskin Lake, ON P0V 1E0
Tel: 807-363-2518; *Fax:* 807-363-1066
Other Numbers: Alternate Phone: 807-363-2598
Rodney McKay, Chief

***Beaverton:* Brock Township Public Libraries**
401 Simcoe St., Beaverton, ON L0K 1A0
Tel: 705-426-9283; *Fax:* 705-426-9353
info@brocklibraries.ca
www.brocklibraries.ca
Social Media: twitter.com/brocklibrary;
www.facebook.com/201312729933754
Joe Allin, Chair
joe.allin@doblecom.net
705-357-3969
Susan Dalton, CEO
susandalton@brocklibraries.ca
705-426-5052 ext. 22
Lori Mitchell, Administration Technician
lorimitchell@brocklibraries.ca

***Belleville:* Belleville Public Library**
254 Pinnacle St., Belleville, ON K8N 3B1
Tel: 613-968-6731; *Fax:* 613-968-6841
Other Numbers: Telecirc: 613-968-4708
www.bellevillelibrary.com
Social Media: twitter.com/BellevillePL;
www.facebook.com/219197338115817
Trevor Pross, CEO
tpross@bellevillelibrary.com
613-968-6731 ext. 2222
Holly Dewar, Manager, Public Services
hdewar@bellevillelibrary.com
613-968-6731 ext. 2241
Fanny Tom, Head of Circulation
ftom@bellevillelibrary.com
613-968-6731 ext. 2243
Soyoung Lee, Children's Librarian
slee@bellevillelibrary.com
613-968-6731 ext. 2246
Susan Holland, Gallery Curator
gallery@bellevillelibrary.com
613-986-6731 ext. 2239

***Birch Island:* Whitefish River First Nation Public Library**
46 Bay of Islands Rd., Birch Island, ON P0P 1A0
Tel: 705-285-0028; *Fax:* 705-285-4532
whitefishriverfirstnationlibrary@hotmail.com
www.whitefishriver.ca/admin/public_library.htm
Gregor Jocko, CEO/Librarian
705-285-0028

***Blenheim:* Caldwell First Nation Library**
RR#2, 10297 Talbot Rd., Blenheim, ON N0P 1A0
Tel: 519-676-5499
Larry Johnson, Chief

***Blind River:* Blind River Public Library / Bibliothèque de Blind River**
8 Woodward Ave., Blind River, ON P0R 1B0
Tel: 705-356-7616
brpl@onlink.net
www.olsn.ca/blindriverlibrary

***Blind River:* Mississauga First Nation Public Library**
148 Village Rd., Blind River, ON P0R 1B0
Tel: 705-356-5335; *Fax:* 705-356-4206
mfnlibrary@onlink.net
www.onlink.net/~mfnlib/library.htm
Sherry Caibaiosai, Librarian

***Bolton:* Caledon Public Library**
150 Queen St. South, Bolton, ON L7E 1E3
Tel: 905-587-1400; *Fax:* 905-857-8280
bolton@caledon.library.on.ca
www.caledon.library.on.ca
Social Media: www.youtube.com/user/caledonpubliclibrary;
twitter.com/caledonlibrary; www.facebook.com/304312508343
Virginia DiLauro, Chair
Bill Manson, CEO/Chief Librarian
bmanson@caledon.library.on.ca
519-927-5662
Gillian Booth-Moyle, Contact, Technical Services
gboothmoyle@caledon.library.on.ca
905-584-1456 ext. 224
Mary Maw, Contact, Communications & Programming
mmaw@caledon.library.on.ca
905-857-1400 ext. 228
Kelley Potter, Contact, Juvenile & Young Adult Services
kpotter@caledon.library.on.ca
905-857-1400 ext. 238
Mojgan Schmalenberg, Contact, Technology Services
mschmale@caledon.library.on.ca
905-857-1400 ext. 237
Sharon Wilson, Contact, Adult Collections & Reference
swilson@caledon.library.on.ca
905-857-1400 ext. 232

***Bonfield:* Bonfield Public Library**
365 Hwy. 531, Bonfield, ON P0H 1E0
Tel: 705-776-2396; *Fax:* 705-776-1154
bpl@ontera.net
www.ontera.net/~bpl
Greg Boxwell, Chair

***Borden:* Borden Public & Military Library / Bibliothèque publique et militaire de Borden**
Bldg. E-102, 41 Kapyong Rd., Borden, ON L0M 1C0
Tel: 705-424-1200
www.borden.forces.gc.ca/998/89/46/52-eng.asp
Donald Allen, Chief Librarian

***Bowmanville:* Clarington Public Library**
163 Church St., Bowmanville, ON L1C 1T7
Tel: 905-623-7322
Other Numbers: 905-623-7322, ext. 731 (Interlibrary loans)
info@clarington-library.on.ca
www.clarington-library.on.ca
Social Media: www.youtube.com/ClaringtonPL;
twitter.com/ClaringtonLib;
www.facebook.com/ClaringtonPublicLibrary
Edith Hopkins, Library Director
ehopkins@clarington-library.on.ca
905-623-7322 ext. 2702

Linda Delgrande, Manager, Support Services
ldelgrande@claringtonlibrary.on.ca
905-623-7322 ext. 2703
Lindsay Flood, Manager, Administrative Services
lflood@clarington-library.on.ca
905-623-7322 ext. 2704
Sarah Vaisler, Manager, Marketing
svaisler@clarington-library.on.ca
905-623-7322 ext. 2705
Darlene McCann, Coordinator, Circulation Services
dmccann@clarington-library.on.ca
905-623-7322 ext. 2717

***Bracebridge:* Bracebridge Public Library**
94 Manitoba St., Bracebridge, ON P1L 2B5
Tel: 705-645-4171; *Fax:* 705-645-6551
bracelib@vianet.on.ca
www.bracebridge.library.on.ca
Social Media: twitter.com/bracebridgepl;
www.facebook.com/BracebridgePublicLibrary
Bob Taylor, Chair
Cathryn Rodney, CEO/Chief Librarian
Carolyn Dawkins, Library Assistant/Office Manager
Nancy Beasley, Interlibrary Loan Coordinator
Cindy Buhne, Children's & Youth Services Librarian

***Bradford:* Bradford West Gwillimbury Public Library**
425 Holland St. West, Bradford, ON L3Z 0J2
Tel: 905-775-3328; *Fax:* 905-775-1236
bwgmailbox@bradford.library.on.ca
www.bradford.library.on.ca
Social Media: www.facebook.com/203251287495
Milt Calder, Chair
Liz Fenwick, Chief Executive Officer
905-775-3328 ext. 6101
Nina Cunniff, Information Services Librarian
Kim Perry, Circulation Supervisor
905-775-3328 ext. 6106

***Brampton:* Brampton Library**
65 Queen St. East, Brampton, ON L6W 3L6
Tel: 905-793-4636
TTY: 866-959-999
info@bramlib.on.ca
www.bramlib.on.ca
Cathy Matyas, CEO
cmatyas@bramlib.on.ca
905-793-4636 ext. 4311
Lesley Bates, Director, Corporate Services
lbates@bramlib.on.ca
905-793-4636 ext. 4361
Susan Tolja, Acquisition Specialist
stolja@bramlib.on.ca
905-793-4636 ext. 4119
Jason Baty, Director, Information Technology
jbaty@bramlib.on.ca
905-793-4636 ext. 4107
Lisa Lipton, Director, Service Development
llipson@bramlib.on.ca
905-793-4636 ext. 4368
Monika Conduit, Coordinator, Children's Services
mconduit@bramlib.on.ca
905-793-4636 ext. 4325

***Brantford:* Brantford Public Library**
173 Colborne St., Brantford, ON N3T 2G8
Tel: 519-756-2220; *Fax:* 519-756-4979
info@brantford.library.on.ca
brantford.library.on.ca
Social Media: www.youtube.com/user/BrantfordLibrary;
twitter.com/BtfdLibrary; www.facebook.com/112507975464133
Penny MacKenzie, Chair
penny_mackenzie@hotmail.com
519-753-9887
Rose Vespa, Chief Executive Officer
rvespa@brantford.library.on.ca
519-756-2220 ext. 319
Kathryn Drury, Manager, Information Services
kdrury@brantford.library.on.ca
519-756-2220 ext. 309
Alaa El-Talmas, Manager, Access & Materials Management
aeltalmas@brantford.library.on.ca
519-756-2220 ext. 314
David Harvie, Manager, Technology Development & Support
dharvie@brantford.library.on.ca
519-756-2220 ext. 307

***Bridgenorth:* Smith-Ennismore-Lakefield Public Library**
836 Charles St., Bridgenorth, ON K0L 1H0
Tel: 705-292-5065; *Fax:* 705-292-6695
www.mypubliclibrary.ca
Kathleen Charlton, Library Programming Coordinator
kcharlton@mypubliclibrary.ca
Joan MacDonald, Librarian
jmacdonald@mypubliclibrary.ca

***Brighton:* Brighton Public Library**
35 Alice St., Brighton, ON K0K 1H0
Tel: 613-475-2511; *Fax:* 613-475-3453
brightonpl@gmail.com
www.brighton.library.on.ca
Bob Burke, Chair
bpburke@sympatico.ca
Maureen Venton, CEO
Sharon Bugg, Assistant Librarian
Jeni Dyment, Contact, Children's Library

***Britt:* Britt Public Library**
841 Riverside Dr., Britt, ON P0G 1A0
www.olsn.ca/BrittPL
Barbara Wohleber, Chief Executive Officer

***Britt:* Magnetawan First Nation Public Library/ Bibliothèque publique de Première Nation de Magnetawan**
Magnetawan First Nation Band Office, 10 Regional Rd., Hwy. 529 North, RR #1, Britt, ON P0G 1A0
Tel: 705-383-2477; *Fax:* 705-383-2566
mfnlibrary@hotmail.com
Wanda Noganosh, CEO

***Brockville:* Augusta Township Public Library**
4500 County Rd. 15, RR#2, Brockville, ON K6V 5T2
Tel: 613-926-2449; *Fax:* 613-926-0441
augusta@augustalibrary.com
www.augustalibrary.com
Jacquie Kelly, Chair
Angie Knights, Librarian
Linda Parrott, Librarian

***Brockville:* Brockville Public Library**
23 Buell St., Brockville, ON K6V 5T7
Tel: 613-342-3936; *Fax:* 613-342-9598
info@brockvillelibrary.ca
www.brockvillelibrary.ca
Social Media: twitter.com/BrockvillePL;
www.facebook.com/BrockvillePublicLibrary
Margaret Wicklum, Chair
Stephen Elliot, Interim CEO & Chief Librarian
613-342-3936 ext. 22
Cindy Fischer, Office Manager
cindy@brockvillelibrary.ca
613-342-3936 ext. 27
Margie Bentley, Contact, Homebound Service & Local History Files
margie@brockvillelibrary.ca
613-342-3936 ext. 21
Lisa Cirka, Contact, Children's & Young Adult Services
lisa@brockvillelibrary.ca
613-342-3936 ext. 21
Laura Julien, Contact, Interlibrary Loan & Book Club Service
interlibrary@brockvillelibrary.ca
613-342-3936 ext. 21
Amanda Robinson, Contact, Audit Information Services, IT Dept. & Webmaster
amanda@brockvillelibrary.ca
613-342-3936 ext. 24

***Bruce Mines:* Bruce Mines & Plummer Additional Union Public Library**
33 Desbarats St., Bruce Mines, ON P0R 1C0
Tel: 705-785-3370; *Fax:* 705-785-3370
bmpa@ontera.net
www.brucemines andplummerlibrary.ca
Lorelee Gordon, CEO/Librarian
Jackie Bloye, Clerk

***Buckhorn:* Galway-Cavendish & Harvey Township Public Library**
5 George St., Buckhorn, ON K0L 1J0
Tel: 705-657-3695; *Fax:* 705-657-3695
www.galwaycavendishharveylibrary.ca
Social Media:
www.facebook.com/group.php?gid=374519655929786
Maria Bradburn, Chief Executive Officer
mbradburn@nexicom.net

***Burks Falls:* Burks Falls, Armour & Ryerson Union Public Library**
39 Copeland St., Burks Falls, ON P0A 1C0
Tel: 705-382-3327; *Fax:* 705-382-3327
info@burksfallslibrary.com
www.burksfallslibrary.com
Social Media: www.facebook.com/151818654228
Sandy Henshall, CEO

***Burlington:* Burlington Public Library**
2331 New St., Burlington, ON L7R 1J4
Tel: 905-639-3611; *Fax:* 905-681-7277
www.bpl.on.ca
Social Media: www.youtube.com/user/BPLStaffer;
twitter.com/BurlingtonPL;
www.facebook.com/pages/Burlington-Public-Library/245349649340
Carrie Brooks-Joiner, Chair
905-639-3611 ext. 1103
Maureen Barry, CEO
barrym@bpl.on.ca
905-639-3611 ext. 1100
Rick Craig, Director, Finance & Facilities
craigr@bpl.on.ca
905-639-3611 ext. 1102
Linda Dobson, Director, Human Resources
dobsonl@bpl.on.ca
905-693-3611 ext. 1104
Andrea Gordon, Interim Director, Service Development
gordona@bpl.on.ca
905-639-3611 ext. 1101
Judy Hyland, Director, Service Delivery
hylandj@bpl.on.ca
905-639-3611 ext. 1105

***Calabogie:* Greater Madawaska Public Library**
4984 Calabogie Rd., Calabogie, ON K0J 1H0
Tel: 613-752-2317; *Fax:* 613-752-2617
Other Numbers: Alternate Phone: 613-752-1720
library@greatermadawaska.com
www.townshipofgreatermadawaska.com/library
Social Media:
www.facebook.com/GreaterMadawaskaPublicLibrary
Meriah Caswell, CEO/Librarian

***Callander:* Callander Public Library**
30 Catherine St., Callander, ON P0H 1H0
Tel: 705-752-2544; *Fax:* 705-752-2819
apeden@ontera.net
www.mycallander.ca/library/library-home/
Alison Peden, CEO
705-752-2544

***Cambridge:* Cambridge Libraries & Galleries**
1 North Sq., Cambridge, ON N1S 2K6
Tel: 519-621-0460; *Fax:* 519-621-2080
www.cambridgelibraries.ca
Social Media: www.facebook.com/161803547206997
Colin Carmichael, Chair
board@cambridgelibraries.ca
Greg Hayton, CEO
ghayton@cambridgelibraries.ca
Mary Misner, Gallery Director
mmisner@cambridgegalleries.ca
Cathy Kiedrowski, Head, Information & Technical Services
ckiedrowski@cambridgelibraries.ca
Helen Kelly, Head, Children's Services
hkelly@cambridgelibraries.ca

***Campbellford:* Trent Hills Public Library**
98 Bridge St. East, Campbellford, ON K0L 1L0
Tel: 705-653-3611; *Fax:* 705-653-4611
campbellford@trenthillslibrary.ca
www.trenthillslibrary.ca
Donna Wilson, CEO

***Carleton Place:* Carleton Place Public Library**
101 Beckwith St., Carleton Place, ON K7C 2T3
Tel: 613-257-2702
carletonlibdsl@vianet.ca
www.carletonplace.ca
Social Media: twitter.com/Carleton_Place;
www.facebook.com/CarletonPlaceTownHall
Janet Baril, Librarian

***Cartier:* Cartier Public Library / Bibliothèque publique de Cartier**
Lansdowne St., PO Box 1000, Cartier, ON P0M 1J0
Tel: 705-965-2481
Joanne Ederer, Chief Executive Officer

Casselman: **Bibliothèque publique de Casselman / Casselman Public Library**
764, rue Brébeuf, Casselman, ON K0A 1M0
Tél: 613-764-5505; *Téléc:* 613-764-5507
bibliotheque@casselman.ca
www.bibliocasselman.ca
Michel Gérin, Président
Rachel Boucher, Directrice

Castleton: **Cramahe Township Public Library**
Castleton Town Hall, 1780 Percy St., Castleton, ON K0K 1M0
Tel: 905-344-7320
castleton@cramahelibrary.ca
www.cramahelibrary.ca
Mary Ryback, Chair
mryback@sympatico.ca

Chapleau: **Chapleau Public Library**
20 Pine St. East, Chapleau, ON P0M 1K0
Tel: 705-864-0852; *Fax:* 705-864-0295
www.chapleaucapsite.zoomshare.com
Maureen Travis, Chief Librarian
Gisele Robitaille, Assistant Librarian
Cassandra Comte, Assistant Librarian

Chatham: **Chatham-Kent Public Library**
120 Queen St., Chatham, ON N7M 2G6
Tel: 519-354-2940; *Fax:* 519-354-2602
cklibrary@chatham-kent.ca
www.chatham-kent.ca/PublicLibraries/Pages/Home.aspx
Social Media: www.youtube.com/user/CKPublicLibrary; twitter.com/cklibrary; www.facebook.com/ChatKentPubLib
Diane Daly, Chair
Kathryn D. Goodhue, CEO/Chief Librarian
kathryng@chatham-kent.ca
519-354-2940 ext. 241
Tania Sharpe, Coordinator, Public Services
tanias@chatham-kenet.ca
519-354-2940 ext. 242
Robin Stewart, Coordinator, Branch & Children's Services
robins@chatham-kent.ca
519-354-2940 ext. 236
Heidi Wyma, Coordinator, Support Services
heidiw@chatham-kent.ca
519-354-2940 ext. 257

Christian Island: **Beausoleil First Nation Library**
150 Mkade Kegwin Miikaan, Christian Island, ON L9M 0A9
Tel: 705-247-2255; *Fax:* 705-247-2772
bfnlibrary@hotmail.com
www.olsn.ca/bfnlibrary

Clinton: **Huron County Library**
77722B London Rd., Hwy. 4 South, RR#5, Clinton, ON N0M 1L0
Tel: 519-482-5457; *Fax:* 519-482-7820
libraryadmin@huroncounty.ca
www.huroncounty.ca/library
Dorothy Kelly, Chair
Beth Ross, County Librarian
Meighan Wark, Branch Services Librarian
mwark@huroncounty.ca

Cobalt: **Cobalt Public Library / Bibliothèque publique du Cobalt**
30 Lang St., Cobalt, ON P0J 1C0
Tel: 705-679-8120; *Fax:* 705-679-8120
cobaltlibrary@ontera.net
cobaltlibrary.com
Margaret Leaper, Chief Executive Officer

Cobourg: **Cobourg Public Library**
200 Ontario St., Cobourg, ON K9A 5P4
Tel: 905-372-9271; *Fax:* 905-372-4538
info@cobourg.library.on.ca
www.cobourg.library.on.ca
Social Media: twitter.com/cobourgPL; www.facebook.com/CobourgPubliclibrary
Charmaine Lindsay, Chief Executive Officer
clindsay@cobourg.library.on.ca
905-372-9271 ext. 6200
Bonnie Symons, Manager, Public Services
Heather Viscount, Manager, Access Services

Cochrane: **Cochrane Public Library / Bibliothèque publique de Cochrane**
178 - 4th Ave., Cochrane, ON P0L 1C0
Tel: 705-272-4178; *Fax:* 705-272-4165
library@cochraneontario.com
www.olsn.ca/cochrane
Social Media: www.facebook.com/CochraneLibrary
Christina Noël-Blazecka, Chief Executive Officer

Coe Hill: **Wollaston & Limerick Public Library**
2149 Hwy. 620, Coe Hill, ON K0L 1P0
Tel: 613-337-5183; *Fax:* 613-337-5183
info@wollaston-limericklibrary.ca
www.wollaston-limericklibrary.ca
Elizabeth Hans Flanagan, Chair
Bonnie Purdy, CEO
Bonnie Weise, Library Assistant

Coldwater: **Coldwater Memorial Public Library**
31 Coldwater Rd., Coldwater, ON L0K 1E0
Tel: 705-686-3601; *Fax:* 705-686-3741
library@coldwater.library.on.ca
www.coldwater.library.on.ca
Adah Silk, Chair

Collingwood: **Collingwood Public Library**
55 Ste. Marie St., Collingwood, ON L9Y 0W6
Tel: 705-445-1571; *Fax:* 705-445-3704
www.collingwoodpubliclibrary.ca
Social Media: www.facebook.com/collingwoodpubliclibrary
Paul Dulmage, Chair
Lynda Reid, Director, Library Services
lreid@collingwood.ca
Ruth Branget, Coordinator, Accessibility & Audiovisual Materials
rbranget@collingwood.ca
705-445-1571 ext. 6224

Constance Lake: **Constance Lake First Nation Public Library**
2 Musko St., Constance Lake, ON P0L 1B0
Tel: 705-463-1199; *Fax:* 705-463-2077
suthliz@clfn.on.ca
Lizzie Sutherland, CEO
suthliz@clfn.on.ca

Cornwall: **Akwesasne Cultural Centre**
c/o Mohawk Council of Akwesasne, Cornwall, ON K6H 5T3
Tel: 518-358-2240; *Fax:* 518-358-2649
Other Numbers: Cornwall, Phone: 613-575-2250; Fax: 613-575-2181
info@akwesasneculturalcenter.org
akwesasneculturalcenter.org/library
Glory Cole, Director
coleg@northnet.org
Bernadine Boots, ILL/Reference Clerk

Cornwall: **Cornwall Public Library (Ontario) / Bibliothèque publique de Cornwall**
45 Second St. East, Cornwall, ON K6H 5V1
Tel: 613-932-4796; *Fax:* 613-932-2715
generalmail@library.cornwall.on.ca
www.library.cornwall.on.ca
Social Media: twitter.com/CornwallPubLibr
Jacqueline Houde, Chair
Dawn Kiddell, CEO & Chief Librarian
dkiddell@cornwall.library.on.ca
Abigail MacLean, Head, Administration
amaclean@library.cornwall.on.ca
Stephanie McMartin, Head, Information Systems & Technical Services
smcmartin@library.cornwall.on.ca
Daphne Morris, Head, Adult Services
dfmorris@library.cornwall.on.ca
Lyne Lapalme, Head, Youth & Children's Services
llapalme@library.cornwall.on.ca
Pierre Dufour, Coordinator, Communications &Pprograms
pdufour@library.cornwall.on.ca

Cornwall: **Stormont, Dundas & Glengarry County Library / Bibliothèque des comtés unis Stormont, Dundas et Glengarry**
#106, 26 Pitt St., Cornwall, ON K6J 3P2
Tel: 613-936-8777; *Fax:* 613-936-2532
generalinfo@sdglibrary.ca
www.sdglibrary.ca
Social Media: www.youtube.com/user/SDGcountylibrary; www.facebook.com/pages/SDG-County-Library/250998401616550
Bill McGimpsey, Chair
mcgimpsey@ontarioeast.net
Karen Franklin, Manager, Library Services
kfranklin@sdglibrary.ca
613-936-8777 ext. 211
Maureen Stephens, Technical Services Coordinator, Acquisitions & Cataloguing
mstephens@sdglibrary.ca
613-936-8777 ext. 225
Lucia Digirolamo, Secretary
ldigirolamo@sdglibrary.ca
613-936-8777 ext. 221

Curve Lake: **Curve Lake First Nation Public Library**
22 Winookeedaa St., Curve Lake, ON K0L 1R0
Tel: 705-657-3217; *Fax:* 705-657-8708
clfnlibrary@gmail.com
www.clfnpubliclibrary.webs.com
Susie V. Taylor, CEO
705-657-8045 ext. 217
Patricia Taylor, Librarian
705-657-3217

Cutler: **Serpent River First Nation Public Library**
49 Village Rd., Cutler, ON P0P 1B0
Tel: 705-844-2009; *Fax:* 705-844-2736
ljones.srfn@ontera.net
Patricia Squires, Librarian

Deep River: **Deep River Public Library**
55 Ridge Rd., Deep River, ON K0J 1P0
Tel: 613-584-4244
www.deepriverlibrary.ca
Tom Wiwcharuk, Chief Executive Officer
twiwcharuk@deepriverlibrary.ca

Deep River: **Laurentian Hills Public Library**
34465 Hwy. 17, RR#1, Deep River, ON K0J 1P0
Tel: 613-584-2714; *Fax:* 613-584-9145
library@laurentianhills.ca
library.laurentianhills.ca
Maureen L. Bakewell, CEO

Deseronto: **Deseronto Public Library**
358 Main St., Deseronto, ON K0K 1X0
Tel: 613-396-2744
info@deserontopubliclibrary.ca
www.deserontopubliclibrary.ca
Social Media: www.facebook.com/people/Deseronto-Dpl/100001832929682
Don Simpson, Chair
Frances Smith, CEO & Librarian
Ruth Sager, Librarian Assistant

Deseronto: **Kanhiote / Tyendinaga Territory Public Library**
1658 York Rd., RR#1, Deseronto, ON K0K 1X0
Tel: 613-967-6264; *Fax:* 613-396-3627
kanhiote@gmail.com
www.kanhiote.ca
Karen Lewis, CEO

Devlin: **Naicatchewenin First Nations Library**
Rainy Lake Indian Reserve, RR#1, Devlin, ON P0W 1C0
Tel: 807-486-3407; *Fax:* 807-486-3704
naicatcheweninfirstnation.ca
Darlene Smith, Director of Administration
darlene.smith@bellnet.ca

Dobie: **Dobie Public Library**
92 McPherson St., Dobie, ON P0K 1B0
Tel: 705-568-8951; *Fax:* 705-568-8951
publib@nt.net
Dianne Quinn, CEO

Dokis: **Dokis First Nation Public Library**
930 Main St., Dokis, ON P0M 2K0
Tel: 705-763-2511; *Fax:* 705-763-2765
dokislibrary@hotmail.com
www.dokisfirstnation.com
Tanya Restoule, Librarian

Dorion: **Dorion Public Library**
170 Dorion Loop Rd., Dorion, ON P0T 1K0
Tel: 807-857-2318; *Fax:* 807-857-2203
dorlib@tbaytel.net
www.dorionpubliclibrary.ca
Betty Chambers, Head Librarian
Claudia Hubbard, Assistant
Lee Harris, Assistant
Valerie Modin, Chair

Douglas: **Admaston-Bromley Public Library**
Hwy. 60, Douglas, ON K0J 1S0
Tel: 613-649-2576; *Fax:* 613-649-2676
info@admastonbromleylibrary.com
www.admastonbromleylibrary.com
Social Media: www.facebook.com/120297281409518
Mallorie Lascelle, Head Librarian
Jane Wouda, Library Assistant, CAP & Children's Programs

***Douro:* Douro-Dummer Public Library / Bibiothèque publique de Douro-Dummer**
435 Fourth Line, Douro, ON K0L 1S0
Tel: 705-652-8599
library@dourodummer.on.ca
www.dourodummer.on.ca/library
Social Media: www.youtube.com/DouroDummerLibrary; twitter.com/DDPLibrarian

Edna Latone, Librarian

***Dryden:* Dryden Public Library**
36 Van Horne Ave., Dryden, ON P8N 2A7
Tel: 807-223-1475; *Fax:* 807-223-4312
library@dryden.ca
www.dryden.ca/city_services/library
Social Media: twitter.com/DrydenLibrary; www.facebook.com/322522094446779

Kim Vares, Chair
kvares@shaw.ca
Lucille Ayers, Vice-Chair
layers@drytel.net
Sandra Weitzel, CEO

***Dubreuilville:* Bibliothèque publique de Dubreuilville / Dubreuilville Public Library**
120 Magpie St., Dubreuilville, ON P0S 1B0
Tél: 705-884-1435; *Téléc:* 705-884-1437
Ligne sans frais: 877-637-8010
dpl@dubreuilville.ca

Brigitte Tremblay, Directrice

***Dunchurch:* Whitestone Hagerman Memorial Public Library**
2206 Hwy. 124, Dunchurch, ON P0A 1G0
Tel: 705-389-3311; *Fax:* 705-389-3311
whitestonelibrary@vianet.ca
www.olsn.ca/whitestonelibrary
Social Media: www.facebook.com/group.php?gid=10486481029

Lori Guillemette, Library Administrator
Joe-Anne McMillan, Library Clerk

***Dundalk:* Southgate Public Library**
80 Proton St. North, Dundalk, ON N0C 1B0
Tel: 519-923-3248
southgatepl@bmts.com
southgate-library.com

Dianne Dean, CEO
southgatepl@bmts.com

***Dunnville:* Haldimand County Public Library**
111 Broad St. East, Dunnville, ON N1A 1E8
Tel: 905-774-7595; *Fax:* 905-774-4294
library@haldimandcounty.on.ca
www.haldimandcounty.on.ca

Pat MacDonald, Chair
Debra Jackson, CEO
905-318-3272 ext. 6115
Paul Diette, Deputy CEO
905-318-3272 ext. 6111

***Durham:* West Grey Library System**
240 Garafraxa St. North, Durham, ON N0G 1R0
Tel: 519-369-2107; *Fax:* 519-369-9966
info@westgreylibrary.com
www.westgreylibrary.com
Social Media: www.facebook.com/pages/West-Grey-Teens/294716850569475; www.facebook.com/west.greylibrary

Lacy Russell, CEO/Chief Librarian
Kim Priestman, Durham Branch Librarian
Kendra Hawley, Children's Librarian

***Eabamet Lake:* Fort Hope First Nation Public Library**
PO Box 297, Eabamet Lake, ON P0T 1L0
Tel: 807-242-8421; *Fax:* 807-242-1592

***Ear Falls:* Ear Falls Public Library**
2 Willow Cres., Ear Falls, ON P0V 1T0
Tel: 807-222-3209; *Fax:* 807-222-3432
efpl@hotmail.com
www.olsn.ca/earfallspl

Becky Bergman, Library Coordinator

***Earlton:* Township of Armstrong Public Library / Bibliothèque publique d'Armstrong**
35 - 10th St., Earlton, ON P0J 1E0
Tel: 705-563-2717; *Fax:* 705-563-2093
earltonlibrary@ntl.sympatico.ca
www.olsn.ca/armstrong

Ghislaine Gravel, Head Librarian
Bernice Lockhart, Assistant Librarian
blockhart@ntl.sympatico.ca

***Eganville:* Bonnechere Union Public Library**
74A Maple St., Eganville, ON K0J 1T0
Tel: 613-628-2400; *Fax:* 613-628-5377
info@bonnechereupl.com
www.bonnechereupl.com

Jennifer Coleman-Davidson, CEO/CFO
ceo@bonnechereupl.com

***Elgin:* Rideau Lakes Public Library**
26 Halladay St., PO Box 189, Elgin, ON K0G 1E0
Tel: 613-359-5334; *Fax:* 613-359-5418
elgin@rideaulakeslibrary.ca
www.rideaulakeslibrary.ca
Social Media: twitter.com/rideaulibrary1; www.facebook.com/rideaulakespubliclibrary

Sue Warne, Library CEO
swarren@ripnet.com
Doug Franks, Library Chair
djfranks@uottawa.ca

***Elk Lake:* Elk Lake Public Library**
First St., Elk Lake, ON P0J 1G0
Tel: 705-678-2340; *Fax:* 705-678-2340
elklake@ontera.net
www.elklake.ca/communityservice.html

Peggy Verrier, CEO
elklake@ontera.net
705-678-2340
Heidi Foley, Assistant Librarian

***Elliot Lake:* Elliot Lake Public Library**
Algo Centre Mall, 151 Ontario Ave., Elliot Lake, ON P5A 2T2
Tel: 705-461-7204; *Fax:* 705-461-9464
www.elliotlakelibrary.com

Pat McGurk, Interim CEO
705-461-7204 ext. 2801

***Emo:* Emo Public Library**
Jessie St., Emo, ON P0W 1E0
Tel: 807-482-2575; *Fax:* 807-482-2575
emolib@bellnet.ca
www.twspemo.on.ca

Shirley Sheppard, Librarian
Kathy Leek, Assistant Librarian & Electronic Data Assistant

***Emsdale:* Perry Township (Emsdale) Public Library**
25 Joseph St., Emsdale, ON P0A 1J0
Tel: 705-636-5454; *Fax:* 705-636-5454
perrylib@ontera.net
www.olsn.ca/library/perry/index.htm
Social Media: www.facebook.com/191662771194

Patricia Aitchison, Head Librarian
Margriet Fetterley, Assistant

***Englehart:* Englehart Public Library / Bibliothèque publique d'Englehart**
#809, 71 - 4th Ave., Englehart, ON P0J 1H0
Tel: 705-544-2100; *Fax:* 705-544-2238
techepl@ontera.net
www.englehartpubliclibrary.ca

Munroe Burton, Chair
Sharon Williams, Librarian/CEO
Liz Robitaille, Clerk
Sharon Antonucci, Clerk

***Espanola:* Espanola Public Library**
245 Avery Dr., Espanola, ON P5E 1S4
Tel: 705-869-2940; *Fax:* 705-869-6463
library@town.espanola.on.ca
www.espanola.library.on.ca

Charles Grayson, Chief Librarian

***Essex:* Essex County Library**
#101, 360 Fairview Ave. West, Essex, ON N8M 1Y3
Tel: 519-776-5241; *Fax:* 519-776-6851
www.essexcountylibrary.ca
Social Media: twitter.com/EssexCountyLib; www.facebook.com/pages/Essex-County-Library/109132675785815

Janet Woodbridge, Chief Librarian, CEO
jwoodbridge@essexcountylibrary.ca
J. Franklin-McInnis, Deputy Chief Librarian/Manager of Branches
jfranklin@essexcountylibrary.ca

***Fauquier:* Bibliothèque publique de Fauquier-Strickland / Fauquier-Strickland Public Library**
25, rue Grzela, Fauquier, ON P0L 1G0
Tél: 705-339-2521; *Téléc:* 705-339-2421
biblioff@vianet.ca
www.olsn.ca

Jocelyne Ratté, Directrice générale
Claude Tremblay Blais, Aide-bibliothécaire

***Fergus:* Wellington County Library**
552 Wellington Rd. 18, RR#1, Fergus, ON N1M 2W3
Tel: 519-846-0918; *Fax:* 519-846-2066
www.county.wellington.on.ca

Murray McCabe, Chief Librarian
murraym@wellington.ca
519-846-0918 ext. 6224
Janice Ellison, Contact, Administration
janicee@wellington.ca
519-846-0918 ext. 6227
Elaine Salter, Contact, Cataloguing
elaines@wellington.ca
519-846-0918 ext. 6223
Deanna Stevens, Contact, Interlibrary Loan
deannas@wellington.ca
519-846-0918 ext. 6225

***Flesherton:* Grey Highlands Public Library**
101 Highland Dr., Flesherton, ON N0C 1E0
Tel: 519-924-2241; *Fax:* 519-924-2562
flepub@bmts.com
www.greyhighlandspubliclibrary.com
Social Media: www.facebook.com/120056264709502

Jim Harrold, Chair
Wilda Allen, CEO/Chief Librarian

***Flinton:* Addington Highlands Public Library**
927 Flinton Rd., Flinton, ON K0H 1P0
Tel: 613-333-1091
flintonl@hotmail.com
www.addingtonhighlandspubliclibrary.ca
Social Media: www.facebook.com/445455308804599

Carol Lessard, Chair
June Phillips, CEO & Head Librarian

***Foleyet:* Foleyet Public Library**
145 Sherry St., Foleyet, ON P0M 1T0
Tel: 705-899-2280

***Fonthill:* Pelham Public Library**
43 Pelham Town Sq., Fonthill, ON L0S 1E0
Tel: 905-892-6443; *Fax:* 905-892-3392
admin@pelhamlibrary.on.ca
www.pelhamlibrary.on.ca
Social Media: www.facebook.com/pelham.ibrary

Stephanie Stowe, CEO
sstowe@pelhamlibrary.on.ca
905-892-6443
Marsha Hunt, Deputy CEO
mhunt@pelhamlibrary.on.ca
Elaine Anderson, Public Service Coordinator
eanderson@pelhamlibrary.on.ca
Jennifer Bennett, Children & Youth Services Coordinator
jbennett@pelhamlibrary.on.ca
Melanie Taylor-Ridgway, Community Services Coordinator
mtaylorridgway@pelhamlibrary.on.ca

***Forest:* Chippewas of Kettle & Stony Point Library**
RR#2, 6218 Indian Lane, Forest, ON N0N 1J0
Tel: 519-786-2955; *Fax:* 519-786-6904
ksplibrary@yahoo.com
www.kspeducation.com

Beverly Bressette, Administrative Assistant, Hillside School

***Fort Erie:* Fort Erie Public Library**
136 Gilmore Rd., Fort Erie, ON L2A 2M1
Tel: 905-871-2546; *Fax:* 905-871-2191
www.forterie.library.on.ca
Social Media: twitter.com/fepl; www.facebook.com/pages/Fort-Erie-Public-Library/135750286529152

Ann McLaughlin, Chair
board@forterie.library.on.ca
Craig Shufelt, Chief Executive Officer
cshufelt@forterie.library.on.ca
905-871-2546 ext. 303
Maria Brigantino, Business Administrator
mbrigantino@forterie.library.on.ca
905-871-2546 ext. 307
Michael Schell, Systems Administrator
mschell@forterie.library.on.ca
905-871-2546 ext. 301
Joel Nash, Coordinator, Public Services
jnash@forterie.library.on.ca
905-871-2546 ext. 310
Amy Roebuck, Coordinator, Community Services
aroebuck@forterie.library.on.ca
905-871-2546 ext. 309

Fort Frances: Fort Frances Public Library
363 Church St., Fort Frances, ON P9A 1C9
Tel: 807-274-9879; *Fax:* 807-274-4496
msedgwick@fort-frances.com
library.fort-frances.com
Margaret Sedgwick, Librarian

Gananoque: Gananoque Public Library
100 Park St., Gananoque, ON K7G 2Y5
Tel: 613-382-2436
gplp@bellnet.ca
www.gananoque.ca/community-services/public-services/library
Social Media: twitter.com/townofgananoque;
www.facebook.com/TownOfGananoque
John Love, Librarian

Garden River: Garden River First Nation Public Library
14 Syrette Lake Rd., Garden River, ON P6A 5K9
Tel: 705-946-3933; *Fax:* 705-946-0413
Irene Gray, Chief Executive Officer
irene.gray@gardenriver.ca

Garden Village: Nipissing First Nation Public Library
36 Semo Rd., Garden Village, ON P2B 3K2
Tel: 705-753-2050; *Fax:* 705-753-0571
glennab@nfn.ca
Glenna Beaucage, CEO

Georgetown: Halton Hills Public Library
9 Church St., Georgetown, ON L7G 2A3
Tel: 905-873-2681; *Fax:* 905-873-6118
www.library.hhpl.on.ca
Social Media: www.youtube.com/user/haltonhillspubliclib;
twitter.com/HaltonHillsPL; www.facebook.com/12169735434
Jay Jackson, Chair
Jane Diamanti, Director
jane.diamanti@haltonhills.ca
905-873-2681 ext. 2501
Geoffrey Cannon, Deputy Director, Library Services
geoff.cannon@haltonhills.ca
905-873-2681 ext. 2513
Douglas Davey, Children's & Youth Advocate
douglas.davey@haltonhills.ca
905-873-2681 ext. 2508
Beverley King, Adult Services Librarian
kingb@hhpl.on.ca
905-873-2681 ext. 2522
Clare Hanman, Technical Services Librarian
clare.hanman@haltonhills.ca
905-873-2681 ext. 2512

Geraldton: Greenstone Public Library
405 Second St. West, Geraldton, ON P0T 1M0
Tel: 807-854-2421; *Fax:* 807-854-2421
greenstonepl@hotmail.com
www.olsn.ca/greenstone/
Mari Mannisto, CEO
greenstonepl@hotmail.com

Gilmour: Tudor & Cashel Baverstock Memorial Public Library
371 Weslemkoon Lake Rd., Gilmour, ON K0L 1W0
Tel: 613-474-1096; *Fax:* 613-474-0664
www.tudorandcashel.com
Mary Hawkins, CEO, Secretary-Treasurer, & Librarian
Barb Sanderson, Assistant Librarian

Gogama: Gogama Public Library / Bibliothèque publique de Gogama
Low Ave., Gogama, ON P0M 1W0
Tel: 705-894-2448
glibrary@onlink.net
Sue Primeau, Volunteer Head Librarian

Gogama: Mattagami First Nation Public Library
PO Box 99, Gogama, ON P0M 1W0
Tel: 705-894-2003; *Fax:* 705-894-2386
mjnms@hotmail.com
www.olsn.ca
Patsy Mckay, CEO
msh@onlink.net
705-894-2003

Golden Lake: Algonquins of Pikwakanagan Library
c/o 1657A Mishomis Inamo, Pikwakanagan, Golden Lake, ON K0J 1X0
Tel: 613-625-2402; *Fax:* 613-625-2332
library@pikwakanagan.ca
algonquinsofpikwakanagan.com/library.php
Estelle Amikons, Librarian

Gore Bay: Gore Bay Union Public Library
15 Water St., Gore Bay, ON P0P 1H0
Tel: 705-282-2221; *Fax:* 705-282-2221
gorebaylibrary@gorebaycable.com
www.olsn.ca/gorebay
Margaret Lane, Chair
Johanna Allison, CEO

Grafton: Alnwick-Haldimand Public Libraries
10836 County Rd. #2, Grafton, ON K0K 2G0
Tel: 905-349-2822; *Fax:* 905-349-3259
alnhald@alnwickhaldimand.ca
www.alnwickhaldimand.ca
Carol Dempsey, Chief Executive Officer

Grand Valley: Grand Valley Public Library
4 Amaranth St. East, Grand Valley, ON L0N 1G0
Tel: 519-928-5622; *Fax:* 519-928-2586
grandvalleylibrary@primus.ca
www.grandvalley.org
Shann Leighton, CEO
shannleighton@primus.ca
Angela Legue, Chair, Library Board
alegue@sympatico.ca
Trish Hamilton, Library Assistant
Tracy Kelly, Library Assistant, Children's Services
tkelly@primus.ca
Tammy Park, Library Assistant
Joanne Stevenson, Library Assistant, ILL
jostevenson@primus.ca

Gravenhurst: Gravenhurst Public Library
180 Sharpe St. West, Gravenhurst, ON P1P 1J1
Tel: 705-687-3382; *Fax:* 705-687-7016
library@gravenhurst.ca
www.gravenhurst.ca/library
Social Media: twitter.com/gravenhurstlib;
www.facebook.com/242143099195701
Marg Nicholson, Chair
Rita Orr, CEO/Chief Librarian

Grimsby: Grimsby Public Library
18 Carnegie Lane, Grimsby, ON L3M 1Y1
Tel: 905-945-5142
gen-library@town.grimsby.on.ca
www.town.grimsby.on.ca/Library
Social Media: twitter.com/GrimsbyLibrary;
www.facebook.com/236752953060009
Linda Henry, Board Chair
Lita Barrie, CEO/Chief Librarian & Secretary-Treasurer

Guelph: Guelph Public Library
100 Norfolk St., Guelph, ON N1H 4J6
Tel: 519-824-6220
webmaster@library.guelph.on.ca
www.library.guelph.on.ca
Social Media: www.youtube.com/user/GuelphPublicLibrary;
twitter.com/GuelphLibrary;
www.facebook.com/155431451134898
Jennifer Mackie, Chair
Kitty Pope, CEO
Mary Ellen Cann, Contact, Interlibrary Loans
Andrea Curtis, Contact, Children's Programs & Services
Glenda Duffin, Contact, Extension Services
Steven Kraft, Contact, Adult Information Services & Circulation
Darcy Hiltz, Archivist

Hagersville: Mississaugas of the New Credit First Nation Public Library
2789 Missisauga Rd., RR#6, Hagersville, ON N0A 1H0
Tel: 905-768-5686; *Fax:* 905-768-4592
www.newcreditfirstnation.com
Cynthia Jamieson, Executive Director
cjamieson@newcreditfirstnation.com

Haileybury: Temiskaming Shores Public Library
545 Lakeshore Rd., Haileybury, ON P0J 1K0
Tel: 705-672-3707; *Fax:* 705-672-5966
haillib@ontera.net
www.temisklibrary.com
Social Media: www.facebook.com/TemiskamingShoresLibrary
Roger Oblin, Chair
Rebecca Hunt, Library CEO & Haileybury Branch Librarian

Haliburton: Haliburton County Public Library
78 Maple Ave., Haliburton, ON K0M 1S0
Tel: 705-457-2241; *Fax:* 705-457-9586
info@haliburtonlibrary.ca
www.haliburtonlibrary.ca
Social Media: www.facebook.com/216747128340069
Nancy McLuskey, Chair
Bessie Sullivan, CEO/County Librarian

Susan Robinson, Supervisor, Community Partnerships & Administration
Sherrill Sherwood, Supervisor, Collections Development & Promotions
Catherine Coles, Branch Services Librarian

Hamilton: Hamilton Public Library
55 York Blvd., Hamilton, ON L8R 3K1
Tel: 905-546-3200; *Fax:* 905-546-3202
TTY: 9055463474
Other Numbers: System-wide Circulation, Phone: 905-546-3425
askhpl@hpl.ca
www.hpl.ca
Social Media: pinterest.com/hamiltonlibrary;
twitter.com/HamiltonLibrary;
www.facebook.com/hamiltonpubliclibrary
George Geczy, Chair
Paul Takala, Chief Librarian
ptakala@hpl.ca
905-546-3215
Robin Hewitt, Director, Finance & Facilities
rhewitt@hpl.ca
905-546-3200 ext. 3226
Lisa DuPelle, Director, Human Resources
ldupelle@hpl.ca
905-546-3200 ext. 3290
Rebecca Raven, Director, Public Service
rraven@hpl.ca
905-546-3200 ext. 3455
Michael Ciccone, Director, Collections
mciccone@hpl.ca
905-546-3200 ext. 3213
Sue Beattie, Manager, Circulation, Bookmobiles
Darcy Glidden, Manager, Online Public Services

Hanover: Hanover Public Library
451 - 10th Ave., Hanover, ON N4N 2P1
Tel: 519-364-1420; *Fax:* 519-364-1747
hanpub@hanover.ca
hanoverlibrary.ca
Social Media: www.facebook.com/185150051536615;
twitter.com/hanoverlibrary;
www.facebook.com/216793488339895
Agnes Rivers-Moore, Chief Librarian
arm@hanover.ca

Havelock: Havelock-Belmont-Methuen Township Public Library
13 Quebec St., Havelock, ON K0L 1Z0
Tel: 705-778-2621; *Fax:* 705-778-2621
habellib@nexicom.net
www.hbmlibrary.on.ca
Sandra Harris, CEO/Chief Librarian

Hawkesbury: Bibliothèque publique de Hawkesbury / Hawkesbury Public Library
550 Higginson St., Hawkesbury, ON K6A 1H1
Tél: 613-632-0106; *Téléc:* 613-636-2097
info@bibliotheque.hawkesbury.on.ca
www.bibliotheque.hawkesbury.on.ca
Yvon Leonard, Président
Lynn Belle-Isle, Directrice générale
Nathalie St-Jacques, Bibliotechnicienne
Jennifer Beaulieu, Bibliotechnicienne
Michel Bruneau, Commis à la référence

Hearst: Bibliothèque publique de Hearst / Hearst Public Library
801 George St., Hearst, ON P0L 1N0
Tel: 705-372-2843; *Fax:* 705-372-2833
hearstpl@ontera.net
www.bibliohearst.on.ca
Francine Daigle, Director, Library Services
Julie Portelance, Library Services Technician

Hermon: Carlow-Mayo Public Library
124 Fort Stewart Rd., Hermon, ON K0L1C0
Tel: 613-332-2544
carlowmayopl@gmail.com
www.carlowmayopubliclibrary.ca
Laurie Cannon, Chief Executive Officer

Heron Bay: Ojibways of the Pic Rivers First Nation Public Library
21 Rabbit Dr., Heron Bay, ON P0T 1R0
Tel: 807-229-0630; *Fax:* 807-229-1944
prfnpublic@picriver.com
www.picriver.com
Glenda Michano-Nabigon, Chief Executive Officer
gmichano_nabigon@hotmail.com

Hilton Beach: Hilton Union Public Library
3085 Marks St., Hilton Beach, ON P0R 1G0
Tel: 705-246-2557; *Fax:* 705-000-0000

Holland Landing: East Gwillimbury Public Library
19513 Yonge St., Holland Landing, ON L9N 1P2
Tel: 905-836-6492; *Fax:* 905-836-6499
info@egpl.ca
www.egpl.ca
Social Media: www.facebook.com/24029821550
Loretta Whiteman, Chair
Michelle Alleyne, Acting CEO

Hornepayne: Hornepayne Township Public Library
68 Front St., Hornepayne, ON P0M 1Z0
Tel: 807-868-2332; *Fax:* 807-868-3111
hpl1@ontera.net
www.olsn.ca/hornepayne
Cheryl Dane, Chair
Linda Kahara, CEO
lkahara@ontera.net
Tena Hopps, Circulation Clerk
Margarita LeFort, Circulation Clerk

Huntsville: Huntsville Public Library
7 Minerva St. East, Huntsville, ON P1H 1W4
Tel: 705-789-5232
www.huntsvillelibrary.net
Social Media: www.facebook.com/161708837282455
Barb Stephen, Chair
Deborah Duce, Chief Executive Officer & Chief Librarian
705-789-5232 ext. 3407
Roberta Green, Contact, Interlibrary Loan & Technical Services
705-789-5232 ext. 3405
Julie Manczak, Contact, Adult & Senior Services
705-789-5232 ext. 3410
Amber McNair, Contact, Youth Services - Children & Teens
705-789-5232 ext. 3406

Ignace: Ignace Public Library
36 Main St., Ignace, ON P0T 1T0
Tel: 807-934-2280; *Fax:* 807-934-6452
ceoignacelibrary@gmail.com
www.olsn.ca/ignace
Pam Greenwood, CEO & Chief Librarian
Sherrill Musclow, Chair

Innisfil: Innisfil Public Library
967 Innisfil Beach Rd., Innisfil, ON L9S 1V3
Tel: 705-431-7410; *Fax:* 705-431-4898
lakeshore@innisfil.library.on.ca
www.innisfil.library.on.ca
Social Media: www.youtube.com/user/InnsfilLibrary;
twitter.com/InnisfilPL; www.facebook.com/InnisfilPublicLibrary
Susan Downs, Chief Librarian & CEO
sdowns@innisfil.library.on.ca
Jayne Asselstine, Deputy Chief Librarian & Recording Secretary
Kathy Hammer, Children's Services Librarian
khammer@innisfil.library.on.ca
Debra Mann, Reference Librarian
dmann@innisfil.library.on.ca

Iron Bridge: Huron Shores Public Library
10 John St., Iron Bridge, ON P0R 1H0
Tel: 705-843-2192; *Fax:* 705-843-2035
huronshores@onlink.net
www.olsn.ca/huronshores
Terri Beharriell, CEO/Librarian
Tim McDougall, CAP Chair

Iroquois Falls: Bibliothèque publique d'Iroquois Falls Public Library
725 Synagogue St., Iroquois Falls, ON P0K 1G0
Tel: 705-232-5722; *Fax:* 705-232-7166
ifpl@ontera.net
www.olsn.ca/iroquoisfallsp/
Lina Tremblay-Joseph, CEO
Diane Gagnon, Assistant Librarian
Carole Rioux, Clerk

Kagawong: Billings Township Public Library
18 Upper St., Kagawong, ON P0P 1J0
Tel: 705-282-2944
billings@xplornet.com
Beth Gordon, CEO

Kakabeka Falls: Conmee Public Library
Conmee Community Centre, 19 Holland Rd. West, RR#1, Kakabeka Falls, ON P0T 1W0
Tel: 807-475-5229
conmeelibrary@msn.com
www.conmee.com/library.shtml

Kapuskasing: Kapuskasing Public Library / Bibliothèque publique de Kapuskasing
24 Mundy Ave., Kapuskasing, ON P5N 1P9
Tel: 705-335-3363; *Fax:* 705-335-2464
kaplibrary@ntl.sympatico.ca
Social Media:
www.facebook.com/pages/Kapuskasing-Public-Library/1232403
94393542
Cecile Langlois, Librarian

Kearney: Kearney & Area Public Library
8 Main St., Kearney, ON P0A 1M0
Tel: 705-636-5849; *Fax:* 705-636-7060
kearneylibrary@hotmail.com
www.olsn.ca/kearney
Brandi Nolan, CEO/Librarian

Keene: Otonabee-South Monaghan Public Library
3252 County Rd. 2, Keene, ON K0L 2G0
Tel: 705-295-6814
keene_library@nexicom.net
www.otosoumon.library.on.ca
Social Media: twitter.com/LibraryOtonSMon;
www.facebook.com/OSMLIBRARY
Michael Gillespie, Chair
705-295-6156
Carolanne Nadeau, Chief Executive Officer

Kemptville: North Grenville Public Library
1 Water St., Kemptville, ON K0G 1J0
Tel: 613-258-4711; *Fax:* 613-258-4134
info@ngpl.ca
www.ngpl.ca
Social Media: twitter.com/NGPLStaff;
www.facebook.com/NorthGrenvillePL
Jim Armour, Chair
jarmour@summa.ca; armourj@cogeco.ca
613-258-7577
Susan Higgins, CEO
shiggins@ripnet.com
Patricia Evans, Head, Interlibrary Loan Dept.
pevans@ripnet.com
Sue Bergeron, Children's & Teen's Programmer
kids@ngpl.ca

Kenora: City of Kenora Public Library
24 Main St. South, Kenora, ON P9N 1S7
Tel: 807-467-2081; *Fax:* 807-467-2085
maeisler@kenora.ca
www.kenorapubliclibrary.org
Erin Roussin, Head Librarian
eroussin@kenora.ca
Lori Jackson, Head of Reference
ljackson@kenora.ca
Cathy Peacock, Assistant Librarian
cpeacock@kenora.ca
Marg Eisler, Online Contact, Interlibrary Loan
maeisler@kenora.ca
Kelly Wald, Adult Services
kwald@kenora.ca
Crystal Alcock, Childrens Services
cralcock@kenora.ca
Lee Spicer, Technical Services
lspicer@kenora.ca
Pat Kornas, Circulation
pkornas@kenora.ca

Keswick: Georgina Public Libraries
90 Wexford Dr., Keswick, ON L4P 3P7
Tel: 905-476-7233; *Fax:* 905-476-8724
www.georgina-library.com
Social Media: www.flickr.com/photos/44103929@N07;
twitter.com/georginalibrary; www.facebook.com/GeorginaPL
Paul Nicholls, Chair
paul.e.nicholls@gmail.com
Mary Baxter, CEO/Director, Library Services & eBranch Head
mbaxter@georgina.ca
905-476-7233 ext. 101
Bev Walsh, Children's & Teen's Services Librarian
bwalsh@georgina.ca
905-476-5762 ext. 107

Killaloe: Killaloe & District Public Library
1 John St., Killaloe, ON K0J 2A0
Tel: 613-757-2211; *Fax:* 613-757-3634
killaloelibrary@maskcom.ca
www.killaloe-hagarty-richards.ca/library/default.htm
Social Media: twitter.com/KillaloeLibrary;
www.facebook.com/166579606709402
Lee LaFont, Chair
Nicole Zummach, Librarian/CEO
Pat Foran, Library Clerk

King City: King Township Public Library
1970 King Rd., King City, ON L7B 1A6
Tel: 905-833-5101; *Fax:* 905-833-0824
www.king-library.on.ca
Social Media: twitter.com/KingLibraries
Adele Reid, Contact
a.reid@king-library.on.ca
Rona O'Banion, CEO/Chief Librarian
r.obanion@king-library.on.ca
Sharon Bentley, Deputy CEO
s.bentley@king-library.on.ca
905-939-2102
Kelley England, Manager, Children's & Young Adult Services
k.england@king-library.on.ca
Adele Reid, Manager, King City & Library Budgets
a.reid@king-library.on.ca

Kingston: Kingston Frontenac Public Library
130 Johnson St., Kingston, ON K7L 1X8
Tel: 613-549-8888; *Fax:* 613-549-8476
www.kfpl.ca
Social Media: twitter.com/KFPL;
www.facebook.com/KingstonFrontenacPL
Claudette Richardson, Chair
Patricia Enright, CEO/Chief Librarian
Doug Brown, Director, Facilities & Projects
Barbara Love, Director, Branch Operations
Shelagh Quigley, Director, Human Resources
Lester Webb, Director, Outreach & Technology

Kirkland Lake: Teck Centennial Library
10 Kirkland St. East, Kirkland Lake, ON P2N 1P1
Tel: 705-567-7966; *Fax:* 705-568-6303
library@tkl.ca
www.olsn.ca/kirklandlakepl/
Cheryl Lafreniere, Chief Librarian

Kirkland Lake: Teck Centennial Library (Kirkland Lake)
10 Kirkland St. East, Kirkland Lake, ON P2N 1P1
Tel: 705-567-7966; *Fax:* 705-568-6303
www.olsn.ca/kirklandlakepl
Cheryl Lafreniere, Head Librarian

Kitchener: Kitchener Public Library
85 Queen St. North, Kitchener, ON N2H 2H1
Tel: 519-743-0271; *Fax:* 519-743-1261
TTY: 8776144832
Other Numbers: InfoLink: 519-743-7502
askus@kpl.org
www.kpl.org
Social Media: www.facebook.com/kplteensread;
twitter.com/KitchLibrary; www.facebook.com/kitchenerlibrary
Dan Carli, Chair
Sonia Lewis, CEO
sonia.lewis@kpl.org
519-743-0271 ext. 244
Lesa Balch, Senior Manager, Service Development
lesa.balch@kpl.org
519-743-0271 ext. 231
Sabina Franzen, Senior Manager, Administration
sabina.franzen@kpl.org
519-743-0271 ext. 240
Ann Wood, Senior Manager, Public Services
ann.wood@kpl.org
519-743-0271 ext. 234

Lanark: Lanark Highlands Public Library
75 George St., 2nd Fl., Lanark, ON K0G 1K0
Tel: 613-259-3068
lanarklib@perth.igs.net
www.lanarklibrary.ca
Ken Sinclair, Chair
Wanda Proulx, CEO
Romalda Park, Assistant Librarian

Lansdowne: Leeds & the Thousand Islands Public Library
1B Jessie St., Lansdowne, ON K0E 1L0
Tel: 613-659-3885; *Fax:* 613-659-4192
leeds.admin@ltipl.net
www.ltipl.net
Social Media: twitter.com/ltipl;
www.facebook.com/leeds1000islandspubliclibrary
Pat Stephenson, Chair
Vacant , CEO
Lisa Marston, Contact
lisa@ltipl.net

Larder Lake: Larder Lake Public Library / Bibliothèque publique de Larder Lake
Larder Lake Municipal Comples, 69 Fourth Ave., Larder Lake, ON P0K 1L0
Tel: 705-643-2222; *Fax:* 705-643-2222
www.larderlakepubliclibrary.ca
Social Media: www.facebook.com/pages/Larder-Lake-Public-Library/196291357068815
Tracey Reid, Board Chair
Patricia Bodick, Librarian

Latchford: Latchford Public Library
66 Main St., Latchford, ON P0J 1N0
Tel: 705-676-2030
lpl@ontera.net
Edith Robillard, CEO
Jacki Perry, Children's Services
Perry Livingston, ILL
Georgina Garreau, Reference Services

Lindsay: City of Kawartha Lakes Public Library
190 Kent St. West, Lindsay, ON K9V 2Y6
Tel: 705-324-9411; *Fax:* 705-878-1859
Toll-Free: 888-822-2225
libraryadministration@city.kawarthalakes.on.ca
www.city.kawarthalakes.on.ca/residents/library-services
Barbara Truax, Chair
Kevin Williams, CEO
kwilliams@city.kawarthalakes.on.ca
705-324-9411 ext. 1307
Linda Kent, Chief Librarian
lkent@city.kawarthalakes.on.ca
705-324-9411 ext. 1260

Listowel: North Perth Public Library
260 Main St. West, Listowel, ON N4W 1A1
Tel: 519-291-4621; *Fax:* 519-291-2235
npl@northperth.library.on.ca
www.northperth.library.on.ca
Social Media: www.facebook.com/NorthPerthPublicLibrary
Paul Horn, Chair
Rebecca Dechert Sage, Chief Executive Officer
rsage@northperth.library.on.ca
Sherri Berfelz, Coordinator, Public Service
SBerfelz@northperth.library.on.ca
Jennifer Cummings, Library Technician
jcummings@northperth.library.on.ca
Andrew Epplett, Library Assistant, Adult Services
AEpplett@northperth.library.on.ca
Christine Koeber, Library Assistant, Circulation
ckoeber@northperth.library.on.ca
Andrea Yungblut, Library Assistant, Interlibrary Loan
ayungblut@northperth.library.on.ca

Little Current: Aundeck Omni Kaning First Nation Public Library
13 Hill St., Little Current, ON P0P 1K0
Tel: 705-368-3696
mcgrawn@aokfn.com
Norma McGraw, Librarian

Little Current: Northeastern Manitoulin & the Islands Public Library
50 Meredith St. West, Little Current, ON P0P 1K0
Tel: 705-368-2444; *Fax:* 705-368-0708
nemilib@vianet.on.ca
www.olsn.ca/nemi/
Judith Kift, Librarian & CEO
Brittany Morphet, CAP Youth Worker

London: London Public Library
251 Dundas St., London, ON N6A 6H9
Tel: 519-661-4600; *Fax:* 519-663-9013
TTY: 5194328835
Other Numbers: Employment Resource Centre: 519-661-5100, ext. 5834
info@lpl.london.on.ca
www.londonpubliclibrary.ca
Social Media: www.youtube.com/user/LondonPublicLibrary; twitter.com/londonlibrary; www.facebook.com/londonlibrary
Josh Morgan, Chair
josh.morgan@lpl.london.on.ca
Susanna Hubbard Krimmer, CEO
susanna.krimmer@lpl.london.on.ca
519-661-5143
Margaret Mitchell, Deputy CEO
margaret.mitchell@lpl.london.on.ca
519-661-5134
Anne Baker, Director, Planning & Research
anne.baker@lpl.london.on.ca
519-661-5114
Tom Travers, Director, Information Technology Services
tom.travers@lpl.london.on.ca
519-661-6403
Margaret Wilkinson, Director, Customer Services & Branch Operations
margaret.wilkinson@lpl.london.on.ca
519-661-5100 ext. 5135
Ellen Hobin, Manager, Marketing & Communications
ellen.hobin@lpl.london.on.ca
519-661-6403
Julie Brandl, Children's & Youth Services Coordinator
David McCord, Coordinator, Collections Management
david.mccord@lpl.london.on.ca

M'Chigeeng: M'Chigeeng First Nation Public Library
18 Lakeview Dr., M'Chigeeng, ON P0P 1G0
Tel: 705-377-5540; *Fax:* 705-377-5080
Sandra Bayer, CEO
705-377-5540

MacTier: Township of Georgian Bay Public Library
12 Muskoka Rd., MacTier, ON P0C 1H0
Tel: 705-375-5430
info@gbpl.ca
www.gbpl.ca
Social Media: www.facebook.com/200394210063297
Barbara Swyers, Chief Executive Officer
705-756-8851

Madoc: Madoc Public Library
20 Davidson St., Madoc, ON K0K 2K0
Tel: 613-473-4456
www.madocpubliclibrary.com
Gayle Ketcheson, Chair
Susan Smith, Librarian
Terry Pritchard, Assistant Librarian

Magnetawan: Magnetawan Public Library
Municipal Building, 4304 North Sparks St., Magnetawan, ON P0A 1P0
Tel: 705-387-4411; *Fax:* 705-387-0636
magcap@ontera.net
www.magnetawanlibrary.ca
Social Media: www.facebook.com/pages/Magnetawan-Public-Library/41591429313
Pauline Chirstianson, Board Chair
Bonnie Davidson, CEO & Head Librarian
Lorinda Makoviczki, Library Assistant

Mallorytown: Front of Yonge Public Library
76 County Rd. 5 South, Mallorytown, ON K0E 1R0
Tel: 613-923-1790; *Fax:* 613-923-2691
foylibrary@ripnet.com
www.library.frontofyonge.com
Donna Hunt, Chief Executive Officer

Manitouwadge: Manitouwadge Public Library
Community Centre, Manitouwadge, ON P0T 2C0
Tel: 807-826-3913; *Fax:* 807-826-4640
Janis Lamothe, Librarian/CEO

Manitowaning: Assiginack Public Library
25 Spragge St., Manitowaning, ON P0P 1N0
Tel: 705-859-2110; *Fax:* 705-859-3010
aplgoodtomes@email.com
www.assiginacklibrary.org
Debbie Robinson, CEO/Librarian

Marathon: Marathon Public Library
22 Peninsula Rd., Marathon, ON P0T 2E0
Tel: 807-229-0740; *Fax:* 807-229-3336
tneedham@tbaytel.net
www.marathon.ca/article/public-library-178.asp
Tamara Needham, Head Librarian

Markham: Markham Public Library
6031 Hwy. 7, Markham, ON L3P 3A7
Tel: 905-513-7977; *Fax:* 905-471-6015
comments@markham.library.on.ca
www.markhampubliclibrary.ca
Social Media: www.facebook.com/group.php?gid=132151853488105
Catherine Biss, Chief Executive Officer
cbiss@markham.library.on.ca
905-513-7977 ext. 5999
Moe Hosseini-Ara, Director, Service Excellence
mhosse@markham.library.on.ca
905-513-7977 ext. 5997
Larry Pogue, Director, Administration & Operational Support
lpogue@markham.library.on.ca
905-513-7977 ext. 5986
Deborah Walker, Director, Library Strategy & Innovation
dwalker@markham.library.on.ca
905-513-7977 ext. 4414
Andrea Cecchetto, Manager, Learning & Growth
acecch@markham.library.on.ca
905-513-7977 ext. 4997
Suliang Feng, Manager, Virtual Services
sfeng@markham.library.on.ca
905-513-7977 ext. 4625
Verna Gilchrist, Manager, Technical Services & C3 Support
vgilchrist@markham.library.on.ca
905-513-7977 ext. 3011
Diane Macklin, Manager, Marketing & Community Development
dmacklin@markham.library.on.ca

Markstay: Markstay Public Library
7 Pioneer St. East, Markstay, ON P0M 2W0
Tel: 705-507-2612
www.olsn.ca/markstay-warrenpl

Marmora: Marmora & Lake Public Library
37 Forsyth St., Marmora, ON K0K 2M0
Tel: 613-472-3122
info@marmoralibrary.ca
www.marmoralibrary.ca
Social Media: www.facebook.com/marmoralibrary
Joan Kennedy, Chair
Sheryl Price, Chief Executive Officer
Tammie Adams, Assistant Librarian

Massey: Sables Spanish River Public Library Board
Massey & Township Public Library, 185 Grove St., Massey, ON P0P 1P0
Tel: 705-865-2641; *Fax:* 705-865-2641
infomasseylibrary@gmail.com
www.masseylibrary.com
Elizabeth Gamble, CEO & Treasurer
Ruth DeClerck, Assistant Librarian

Massey: Sagamok Anishnawbek Public Library
4007 Espaniel, Massey, ON P0P 1P0
Tel: 705-865-2034; *Fax:* 705-865-3307
Colleen Eshkakogan, CEO

Matheson: Black River-Matheson Public Library
352 Second St., Matheson, ON P0K 1N0
Tel: 705-273-2760
info@blackrivermatheson.com
www.blackriver-matheson.com/library-p13.php
Karen Ukrainetz, CEO/Librarian

Mattawa: Mattawa (John Dixon) Public Library
370 Pine St., Mattawa, ON P0H 1V0
Tel: 705-744-5550; *Fax:* 705-744-1714
mplibrary@efni.com
users.efni.com/~mplibrary/
Lise Moore Asselin, CEO
Lynne Pellerin, Reference & Technical Services
Nicole Leblanc, Interlibrary Loans

Mattice: Mattice - Val Côté Public Library / Bibliothèque publique de Mattice - Val Côté
500 Hwy. 11, Mattice, ON P0L 1T0
Tel: 705-364-5301; *Fax:* 705-364-6431
biblimat@ntl.sympatico.ca
www.olsn.ca/mattice-valcote
Michelle Salonen, Chief Executive Officer
Nancy Boucher, Library Assistant

Maynooth: Hastings Highlands Public Library
33011 Hwy 62 North, Maynooth, ON K0L 2S0
Tel: 613-338-2262; *Fax:* 613-338-3292
info@hastingshighlandspubliclibrary.ca
www.hastingshighlandspubliclibrary.ca
Social Media: www.facebook.com/HastingsHighlandsPublicLibrary
Penny Anderson, Chair
Kimberly McMunn, CEO/Librarian
Kristin Seaborn, Assistant Librarian
Deb Jeffrey, Program/Volunteer Coordinator
Wendy Keating, Communtiy Program Coordinator

McKellar: McKellar Township Public Library
701 Hwy. 124, McKellar, ON P0G 1C0
Tel: 705-389-2611; *Fax:* 705-389-2611
mckellarlib@vianet.ca
www.mckellarpubliclibrary.ca
Joan Ward, Librarian
jward@post.library.on.ca
Terri Short, Staff
asterken@post.library.on.ca

Meaford: **Meaford Public Library**
15 Trowbridge St. West, Meaford, ON N4L 1V4
Tel: 519-538-1060; *Fax:* 519-538-1808
info@meafordlibrary.on.ca
www.meafordlibrary.on.ca
Social Media: www.facebook.com/meafordpubliclibrary
Cathie Lee, Acting CEO
Michael Crowley, Children's Coordinator
Lynne Fascinato, Contact, Interlibrary Loan
David Port, Chair

Merrickville: **Merrickville Public Library**
446 Main St. West, Merrickville, ON K0G 1N0
Tel: 613-269-3326; *Fax:* 613-269-3326
merrickville_library@bellnet.ca
www.village.merrickville-wolford.on.ca/mpl/index.html
Mary Kate Laphen, Librarian

Midhurst: **Simcoe County Library Co-Operative**
County Administration Centre, 1110 Hwy. 26, Midhurst, ON L0L 1X0
Tel: 705-726-9300; *Fax:* 705-727-4253
library@simcoe.ca
www.county.simcoe.on.ca/dpt/lib/index.htm
Gayle Hall, Chief Librarian

Midhurst: **Springwater Township Public Library**
12 Finlay Mill Rd., Midhurst, ON L0L 1X0
Tel: 705-737-5650; *Fax:* 705-737-3594
midhurst.library@springwater.ca
www.olsn.ca/springwater/index.asp
Lynn Patkau, Chief Librarian

Midland: **Midland Public Library**
320 King St., Midland, ON L4R 3M6
Tel: 705-526-4216; *Fax:* 705-526-1474
www.midlandlibrary.com
Social Media: twitter.com/midland_library;
www.facebook.com/midlandlibrary
John E. Swick, Chair
Bill Molesworth, Chief Executive Officer
bmolesworth@town.midland.on.ca
Betty Fullerton, Head, Technical Services
Gail Griffith, Head, Adult & Information Services
Bonnie Reynolds, Head, Juvenile Services

Millbrook: **Cavan Monaghan Libraries**
Old Millbrook School, 1 Dufferin St., Millbrook, ON L0A 1G0
Tel: 705-932-2919; *Fax:* 705-932-4019
www.cavanmonaghanlibraries.ca
Social Media: twitter.com/CMLibraries;
www.facebook.com/CavanMonaghanLibraries

Milton: **Milton Public Library**
1010 Main St. East, Milton, ON L9T 6H7
Tel: 905-875-2665; *Fax:* 905-875-4324
TTY: 905-875-155
information@mpl.on.ca
www.mpl.on.ca
Social Media: twitter.com/Milton_Library
Ken Jacobsen, Chair
h_kjaco@cogeco.ca
Leslie Fitch, Chief Executive Officer
leslie.fitch@mpl.on.ca
905-875-2665 ext. 3252

Milverton: **Perth East Public Library**
19 Mill St. East, Milverton, ON N0K 1M0
Tel: 519-595-8395; *Fax:* 519-595-2943
pel@pcin.on.ca
www.pertheast.library.on.ca
Patti Henhoeffer, CEO
phenhoeffer@pcin.on.ca

Mindemoya: **Central Manitoulin Public Libraries**
6020 Hwy. 542, Mindemoya, ON P0P 1S0
Tel: 705-377-5334; *Fax:* 705-377-5585
bookworm@amtelecom.net
www.centralmanitoulin.ca
Sandra Strong, Chair
Claire Cline, CEO/Chief Librarian
Mel Delange, Library Assistant
Geraldine Carlisle, Library Assistant

Mine Centre: **Seine River First Nation Public Library**
Mine Centre, ON P0W 1H0
Tel: 807-599-2870; *Fax:* 807-599-2871
Glenda Potson, Librarian
gpotson@fort-frances.lakeheadu.ca
Susan Johnson, Head, Reference

Mississauga: **Mississauga Library System**
301 Burnhamthorpe Rd. West, Mississauga, ON L5B 3Y3
Tel: 905-615-3500; *Fax:* 905-615-3625
library.info@mississauga.ca
www.mississauga.ca/portal/residents/library
Don Mills, Director, Library Services
don.mills@mississauga.ca
905-615-3200 ext. 3601
Debbie MacDonald, Manager, Shared Services
debbie.macdonald@mississauga.ca
905-615-3200 ext. 2112
Anne Murphy, Manager, Area 1 (Central Library)
anne.murphy@mississauga.ca
905-615-3200 ext. 4520

Mitchell: **West Perth Public Library**
105 St. Andrew St., Mitchell, ON N0K 1N0
Tel: 519-348-9234; *Fax:* 519-348-4540
wpl@pcin.on.ca
www.westperth.library.on.ca
Social Media: www.facebook.com/310691049146
Charles Fitzsimmons, Chair
Caroline Shewburg, Chief Librarian

Mobert: **Pic Mobert First Nation Public Library**
General Delivery, Mobert, ON P0M 2J0
Tel: 807-822-1594; *Fax:* 807-822-1578
principal@picmobert.ca

Moonbeam: **Bibliothèque publique de Moonbeam / Moonbeam Public Library**
53, av St-Aubin, Moonbeam, ON P0L 1V0
Tel: 705-367-2462; *Fax:* 705-367-2120
biblio@moonbeam.ca
biblio.moonbeam.ca
Gisèle Belisle, Directrice-Responsable
Angèle Albert, Directrice adjointe

Morson: **Big Grassy First Nation Public Library**
PO Box 453, Morson, ON P0W 1J0
Tel: 807-488-5916; *Fax:* 807-488-5345
bglibrary@bgfn.on.ca
www.bgfn.on.ca/library.htm
Kitty Gale, Librarian

Muncey: **Chippewas of the Thames**
RR#1, 328 Chippewa Rd., Muncey, ON N0L 1Y0
Tel: 519-289-2176; *Fax:* 519-289-2230
Arlene Elm, Librarian

Murillo: **Oliver Paipoonge Public Library**
1 Baxendale Rd., Murillo, ON P0T 2G0
Tel: 807-935-2729
www.olsn.ca/OliverPaipoonge
Maxine McCulloch, CEO
mmcculloch@post.library.on.ca

Napanee: **Lennox & Addington County Library**
97 Thomas St. East, Napanee, ON K7R 4B9
Tel: 613-354-4883; *Fax:* 613-354-3112
infoservices@lennox-addington.on.ca
www.lennox-addington.on.ca/library/location-and-hours.html
Mary Anne Evans, Director, Information Services
mevans@lennox-addington.on.ca
613-354-4883 ext. 238
Daphne Gardiner, Acting Systems Administrator
dgardiner@lennox-addington.on.ca
613-354-4883 ext. 372
Julie Wendland, Reference Assistant
jwendland@lennox-addington.on.ca
613-354-4883 ext. 371
Coleen McFarlane, Technical Assistant
cmcfarlane@lennox-addington.on.ca
613-354-4883 ext. 232

Naughton: **Whitefish Lake First Nation Public Library**
c/o Band Offices, 25 Reserve Rd., Naughton, ON P0M 2M0
Tel: 705-692-1102; *Fax:* 705-692-5010
library@wlfn.com
www.wlfn.com
Mary Fraser, Librarian

Nestor Falls: **Ojibways of Onigaming First Nation Public Library**
Mikinaak Onigaming School, 212 Mikinaak Rd., Nestor Falls, ON P0X 1K0
Tel: 807-484-2612; *Fax:* 807-484-2352
onigamingfn@yahoo.com
Geraldine Kelly, Librarian

Newmarket: **Newmarket Public Library**
438 Park Ave., Newmarket, ON L3Y 1W1
Tel: 905-953-5110; *Fax:* 905-953-5104
npl@newmarketpl.ca
www.newmarketpl.ca
Social Media: www.youtube.com/user/NewmarketLibrary;
twitter.com/newmarktlibrary;
www.facebook.com/pages/Newmarket-Public-Library/247080242075
Wendy Van Straten, Chair
Todd Kyle, Chief Executive Officer
Linda Peppiatt, Deputy Chief Executive Officer
Simon Chong, Contact, Systems
Heather Halliday, Contact, Adult Services
Susan Hoffman, Contact, Children's Services
Jennifer Leveridge, Contact, Community Services
Michael Russell, Contact, Digital Services

Niagara Falls: **Niagara Falls Public Library**
4848 Victoria Ave., Niagara Falls, ON L2E 4C5
Tel: 905-356-8080; *Fax:* 905-356-7004
Other Numbers: Children's Department, Phone: 905-356-4053
nfpl@nflibrary.ca
www.nflibrary.ca
Monika Seymour, Chief Librarian
Susan DiBattista, Manager, Public Services
Janet Martin, Manager, Audiovisual & Technical Services
Keith Muma, Manager, Buildings & Property
Andrew Porteus, Manager, Reference & Information Services
Inge Saczkowski, Manager, Children's Services

Niagara on the Lake: **Niagara on the Lake Public Library**
10 Anderson Lane, Niagara on the Lake, ON L0S 1J0
Tel: 905-468-2023; *Fax:* 905-468-3334
www.notlpubliclibrary.org
Social Media: pinterest.com/notlpl; twitter.com/notl_library;
www.facebook.com/210765253379
C. Simpson, CEO
csimpson@notl.org
Debbie Smith, Assistant Library Manager
debbiesmith@notl.org
Laura Tait, Library Assistant
ltait@notl.org

Nipigon: **Nipigon Public Library**
52 Front St., Nipigon, ON P0T 2J0
Tel: 807-887-3142; *Fax:* 807-887-3142
nipigonpl@tbaytel.net
www.nipigon.net/content/Nipigon_Public_Library
Social Media: twitter.com/nipigon;
www.facebook.com/NipigonTownship
Sumiye Sugawara, Library Technician/CEO

Nobel: **Shawanaga First Nation Public Library**
2 Church St., Nobel, ON P0G 1G0
Tel: 705-366-2526; *Fax:* 705-366-2740
csousa_20@hotmail.com
Chelsie Sousa, CEO
csousa_20@hotmail.com

North Bay: **North Bay Public Library**
271 Worthington St. East, North Bay, ON P1B 1H1
Tel: 705-474-4830
library@cityofnorthbay.ca
www.cityofnorthbay.ca/library
Paul Walker, CEO
Rebecca Larocque, Head, Reference, AV & Systems
Judith Bouman, Head, Technical & Adult Services
Robert Boisvert, Head, French Services
Nora Elliott-Coutts, Deputy CEO & Head, Children's Services

Norwood: **Asphodel-Norwood Public Library**
2363 County Rd. #45, Norwood, ON K0L 2V0
Tel: 705-639-2228
norwood@anpl.org
www.anpl.org
Social Media: www.facebook.com/175172212505525

Oakville: **Oakville Public Library**
120 Navy St., Oakville, ON L6J 2Z4
Tel: 905-815-2042; *Fax:* 905-815-2024
Other Numbers: Renewals & Holds, Phone: 905-815-2044
oplreference@oakville.ca
www.opl.on.ca
Social Media: twitter.com/OakvilleLibrary;
www.facebook.com/pages/Oakville-Public-Library/184886721537133
Charlotte Meissner, Chief Executive Officer & Director, Corporate Services
cmeissner@oakville.ca
905-815-2031

Janice Kullas, Director, Service Planning & Development
jkullas@oakville.ca
905-815-2035
Pearl Raju, Director, Digital Access & Development
praju@oakville.ca
905-815-2027
Melissa Cameron, Manager, Marketing & Development
melissaCameron@oakville.ca
905-815-2014
Michael Hodgins, Manager, Community Information
mhodgins@oakville.ca
905-815-2042 ext. 5069
Randy Kisch, Manager, Library Systems
rkisch@oakville.ca
905-815-2042 ext. 5066
Susan Kun, Manager, Adult Collections
skun@oakville.ca
905-815-2036
Lorna Young, Manager, Bibliographic Services
lyoung@oakville.ca
905-815-2042 ext. 5168
Florence De Dominicis, Branch Manager
fdedominicis@oakville.ca
905-815-2042 ext. 5041

Ohsweken: Six Nations Public Library
1679 Chiefswood Rd., Ohsweken, ON N0A 1M0
Tel: 519-445-2954; *Fax:* 519-445-2873
info@snpl.ca
www.snpl.ca
Sabrina Redwing Saunders, CEO
saunders@snpl.ca

Opasatika: La Bibliothèque d'Opasatika / Opasatika Public Library
6, rue St-Antione, Opasatika, ON P0L 1Z0
Tél: 705-369-3421; *Téléc:* 705-369-3098
opasatikabiblio@hotmail.ca
opasatika.net
Joanne Lallier, Bibliothécaire

Orangeville: Orangeville Public Library
1 Mill St., Orangeville, ON L9W 2M2
Tel: 519-941-0610; *Fax:* 519-941-4698
TTY: 519-942-051
infolibrary@orangeville.ca
www.orangeville.library.on.ca
Social Media: twitter.com/orangevilleont;
www.facebook.com/pages/Orangeville-Ontario/359934204153
Rick Schwarzer, Chief Executive Officer
Pam Johnson, Coordinator, Public Services
pjohnson@orangeville.ca
519-941-0610 ext. 5232

Orillia: Orillia Public Library
36 Mississaga St. West, Orillia, ON L3V 3A6
Tel: 705-325-2338; *Fax:* 705-327-1744
Other Numbers: Circulation: 705-325-2552; Child Svs.: 705-325-2559
info@orilliapubliclibrary.ca
www.orilliapubliclibrary.ca
Social Media: twitter.com/orillialibrary;
www.facebook.com/OrilliaPublicLibrary
Gay Guthrie, Chair
Suzanne Campbell, Chief Executive Officer
Kelli Absalom, Contact, Adult Services
Joyce Dempsey, Contact, Circulation Services
David Rowe, Contact, Technical Services & Systems
Amanda Sist, Contact, Children's Services
Jayne Turvey, Contact, Community Services

Oshawa: Oshawa Public Library
65 Bagot St., Oshawa, ON L1H 1N2
Tel: 905-579-6111; *Fax:* 905-433-8107
www.oshawalibrary.on.ca
Social Media: www.youtube.com/user/OshawaLibraryTV;
twitter.com/OshawaLibraries/librarytweets;
www.facebook.com/pages/Oshawa-Public-Library/137995122909368
Kim O'Reilly, Manager, Children & Youth Services
koreilly@oshawalibrary.on.ca
905-579-6111 ext. 5232
Joseph Sansalone, Manager, Adult Information Services
jsansalone@oshawalibrary.on.ca
905-579-6111 ext. 5220
Margaret Wallace, Manager, Customer & Circulation Services
mwallace@oshawalibrary.on.ca
905-579-6111 ext. 5253

Ottawa: Ottawa Public Library / Bibliothèque publique d'Ottawa
120 Metcalfe St., Ottawa, ON K1P 5M2
Tel: 613-580-2945
Other Numbers: Infoservice: 613-580-2940
www.biblioottawalibrary.ca
Social Media: www.flickr.com/photos/bpo-opl;
twitter.com/opl_bpo; www.facebook.com/groups/2376591023
Danielle McDonald, Chief Executive Officer
Danielle.McDonald@biblioottawalibrary.ca
Elaine Condos, Division Manager, Facilities & Business Services
Elaine.Condos@biblioottawalibrary.ca
Monique E. Désormeaux, Division Manager, Service Excellence
Monique.Désormeaux@biblioottawalibrary.ca
Jennifer Stirling, Division Manager, System Wide Services & Innovation
Jennifer.Stirling@biblioottawalibrary.ca
Nelly Beylouni-Zamat, Manager, Diversity & Accessibility Services
Nelly.Beylouni-Zamat@biblioottawalibrary.ca
Monique Brûlé, Manager, Collection Management
Monique.Brule@biblioottawalibrary.ca
Craig Ginther, Manager, Innovation, Continuous Improvement, & Digital Services
Craig.Ginther@biblioottawalibrary.ca
Maureen McEvoy, Manager, Communications & Community Relations
Maureen.Mcevoy@biblioottawalibrary.ca
Anna Mould, Manager, Staff Development & Service Excellence
Anna.Mould@ottawa.ca
Matthew Pritz, Manager, Business Services & Strategic Coordination
Matthew.Pritz@ottawa.ca
Richard Stark, Manager, Library Facilities, Planning, & Development
Richard.Stark@biblioottawalibrary.ca
Jane Venus, Manager, Lifelong Learning & Literacy
Jane.Venus@biblioottawalibrary.ca
Line Gravelle, Main Branch Manager
line.gravelle@biblioottawalibrary.ca

Owen Sound: Owen Sound & North Grey Union Public Library
824 - 1st Ave. West, Owen Sound, ON N4K 4K4
Tel: 519-376-6623; *Fax:* 519-376-7170
library@owensound.library.on.ca
www.owensound.library.on.ca
Social Media: www.facebook.com/OSNGUPL
Cindy Weir, Chief Librarian/CEO
Chris Carmichael, Technical Services & Systems Manager
carmichc@owensound.library.on.ca
Beth Hall, Administrative & Public Services Manager
bhall@owensound.library.on.ca
Nadia Danyluk, Children & Youth Services Librarian
ndanyluk@owensound.library.on.ca
Tim Nicholls-Harrison, Adult & Community Learning Services Manager
tnicholls-harrison@owensoundd.library.on.ca

Paris: County of Brant Public Library
12 William St., Paris, ON N3L 1K7
Tel: 519-442-2433; *Fax:* 519-442-7582
www.brant.library.on.ca
Gay Kozak Selby, CEO
Larry Stewart, Chair, Library Board
Christine Scrivener, Branch Coordinator

Parry Sound: Parry Sound Public Library
29 Mary St., Parry Sound, ON P2A 1E3
Tel: 705-746-9601; *Fax:* 705-746-9601
pspl@vianet.ca
www.pspl.on.ca
Social Media:
www.facebook.com/group.php?gid=346576685525
Selena Martin, Assistant Librarian

Parry Sound: Seguin Township Public Library
15 Humphrey Dr., Parry Sound, ON P2A 2W8
Tel: 705-732-4526; *Fax:* 705-732-4526
humphreylibrary@cogeco.net
www.olsn.ca/seguin/page5.html
Patricia Coles, Chief Executive Officer
pcoles@cogeco.net
Ruth Smith, Branch Head

Parry Sound: Wasauksing First Nation Public Library
1508 Geewadin Rd, Lane G, Parry Sound, ON P2A 2X1
Tel: 705-746-2531; *Fax:* 705-746-5984
librarian@wasauksing.ca
firstnation.ca/wasauksing/wasauksing-public-library
Fran King, CEO

Tina Tabobandung, Education Director
705-726-2531

Pawitik: Naotkamegwanning First Nation Public Library
General Delivery, Pawitik, ON P0X 1L0
Tel: 807-226-5710; *Fax:* 807-226-1066
nfnpl2010@live.ca
Janelle Crow, Chief Executive Officer

Pembroke: Pembroke Public Library
237 Victoria St., Pembroke, ON K8A 4K5
Tel: 613-732-8844; *Fax:* 613-732-1116
fineprint@pembrokelibrary.ca
www.pembroke.library.on.ca
Social Media: www.facebook.com/30360225984
Margaret Mau, CEO/Secretary-Treasurer
mmau@pembrokelibrary.ca

Penetanguishene: Penetanguishene Public Library
24 Simcoe St., Penetanguishene, ON L9M 1R6
Tel: 705-549-7164; *Fax:* 705-549-3932
www.penetanguishene.library.on.ca
Cynthia Coté, CEO
ccote@penetanguishene.library.on.ca
Jenet Ryan, Head, Public & Technical Services
jryan@penetanguishene.library.on.ca
705-549-7164

Perth: Perth & District Union Public Library
30 Herriott St., Perth, ON K7H 1T2
Tel: 613-267-1224; *Fax:* 613-267-7899
info@perthunionlibrary.ca
www.perthunionlibrary.ca
Elizabeth Goldman, CEO/Head Librarian
egoldman@perthunionlibrary.ca

Petawawa: Petawawa Public Library
16 Civic Centre Rd., Petawawa, ON K8H 3H5
Tel: 613-687-2227; *Fax:* 613-687-2527
info@petawawapubliclibrary.ca
www.petawawapubliclibrary.ca
Social Media: twitter.com/Petawawalibrary;
www.facebook.com/pages/Petawawa-Public-Library/102474823136454
C.M. Goldsmith, Librarian

Peterborough: Peterborough Public Library
345 Aylmer St. North, Peterborough, ON K9H 3V7
Tel: 705-745-5382; *Fax:* 705-745-8958
comments@city.peterborough.on.ca
www.peterborough.library.on.ca
Social Media: www.facebook.com/PeterboroughLibrary
Becky Rogers, CEO
brogers@city.peterborough.on.ca
705-745-5382 ext. 2380
Laura Gardner, Collection Development Librarian
lgardner@city.peterborough.on.ca
705-745-5382 ext. 2361
Marisa Giuliani, Access Services Librarian
mgiuliani@city.peterborough.on.ca
705-745-5382 ext. 2351
Betty-Kay Murray, Children's Librarian
bmurray@city.peterborough.on.ca
705-745-5382 ext. 2370
Karen Bisschop, Information Services Librarian
kbisschop@peterborough.on.ca
705-745-5382 ext. 2352

Philipsburg: Region of Waterloo Library
2017 Nafziger Rd., RR#2, Philipsburg, ON N3A 3H4
Tel: 519-575-4590; *Fax:* 519-634-5371
libhq@region.waterloo.ca
www.rwl.library.on.ca
Social Media: www.facebook.com/176350209088438
Lucille Bish, Director, Community Services
blucille@region.waterloo.ca
519-575-4499
Katherine Seredynska, Manager, Public Services
skath@region.waterloo.ca
Kelly Bernstein, Manager, Information Services
kbernstein@region.waterloo.ca

Pickerel: Henvey Inlet First Nation Public Library
354B Pickerel River Rd., Pickerel, ON P0G 1J0
Tel: 705-857-2331; *Fax:* 705-857-3021
www.firstnation.ca/henvey-inlet/henvey-inlet-public-library
Debbie Fox, Chief Executive Officer
maheengun12@hotmail.com
705-857-2331 ext. 225

***Pickering:* Pickering Public Library**
1 The Esplanade, Pickering, ON L1V 6K7
Tel: 905-831-6265; *Fax:* 905-831-6927
Toll-Free: 888-831-6266
TTY: 9058312789
Other Numbers: Renewals: 905-831-8209
help@picnet.org
www.picnet.org
Social Media: www.youtube.com/user/PickeringLibrary; twitter.com/pickeringpublib; www.facebook.com/PPLibrary
Cathy Grant, CEO
cathyg@picnet.org
905-831-6265 ext. 6236
Elaine Bird, Director of Support Services
elaineb@picnet.org
905-831-6265 ext. 6231
Kathy Williams, Director of Public Services
kathyw@picnet.org
905-831-6265 ext. 6251

***Picton:* County of Prince Edward Public Library**
208 Main St., Picton, ON K0K 2T0
Tel: 613-476-5962; *Fax:* 613-476-3325
frdesk@peclibrary.org
www.peclibrary.org
Barbara Sweet, CEO
Dianne Cranshaw, Assistant CEO & Contact, Interlibrary Loan
613-399-2023
Krista Richardson, Manager, Archives
613-399-2023
Kate Konkin, Coordinator, Seniors Programs
613-476-5962
Eric Pierce, Coordinator, Information Technology & Computer Training
613-476-5962
Liz Zylstra, Coordinator, Youth Programs
613-476-5962
Christine Renaud, Branch Manager
crenaud@peclibrary.org
613-476-5962

***Port Carling:* Township of Muskoka Lakes Libraries**
69 Joseph St., Port Carling, ON P0B 1J0
Tel: 705-765-5650; *Fax:* 705-765-0422
pclib@muskoka.com
users.muskoka.com/library
Social Media: twitter.com/MuskokaLakesPL; www.facebook.com/group.php?gid=155634271143907
Linda McAuley, Chair
Sheila Durand, Chief Executive Officer & Chief Librarian
Nancy Doran, Library Assistant
Cathy Duck, Library Assistant
Lorna MacFarlane, Library Assistant
Barb Neibert, Library Assistant

***Port Colborne:* Port Colborne Public Library**
310 King St., Port Colborne, ON L3K 4H1
Tel: 905-834-6512; *Fax:* 905-835-5775
library@portcolborne.ca
www.portcolbornelibrary.org
Social Media: www.facebook.com/pages/Port-Colborne-Public-Library/340178134131
Jennifer R. Parry, Director of Library Services
Derek Miller, Chair
Robert Heil, Chief Administrative Office
CAO@portcolborne.ca

***Port Elgin:* Bruce County Public Library**
1243 MacKenzie Rd., Port Elgin, ON N0H 2C6
Tel: 519-832-6935; *Fax:* 519-832-9000
library.brucecounty.on.ca
Social Media: www.facebook.com/138293532885246
Ken MacLeod, CEO
kmacleod@brucecounty.on.ca
Jo-Ann Alexander, Audiovisual Coordinator
jalexander@brucecounty.on.ca
Dan Blacklock, Collection Development Coordinator
dblacklock@brucecounty.on.ca
Donna Morey, Interlibrary Loan Coordinator
dmorey@brucecounty.on.ca
Shirley Morningstar, Information Services Coordinator
smorningstar@brucecounty.on.ca
Christine Wood, Technical Services Coordinator
cwood@brucecounty.on.ca

***Port Hope:* Port Hope Public Library**
31 Queen St., Port Hope, ON L1A 2Y8
Tel: 905-885-4712; *Fax:* 905-885-4181
library@porthope.ca
www.phpl.ca
Social Media: www.facebook.com/pages/Port-Hope-Public-Library/301945576498428
Barbara J. Stephenson, Chief Librarian
bstephenson@porthpe.ca
Alison M.B. Houston, Deputy Chief Librarian
ahouston@porthope.ca

***Port Loring:* Port Loring & District (Argyle) Public Library**
11767 Hwy. 522, Port Loring, ON P0H 1Y0
Tel: 705-472-8170; *Fax:* 705-757-3284
ArgyleCommunityLibrary@hotmail.com
www.olsn.ca/argylecommunitylibrary/index.html
Marla Booth, Library Services

***Port McNicoll:* Tay Township Public Libraries**
715 - 4th Ave., Port McNicoll, ON L0K 1R0
Tel: 705-534-3511; *Fax:* 705-534-3511
pmlibrary@tay.ca
www.tay.library.on.ca
Heather Delong, Head Librarian
hdelong@tay.ca
Allison Thompson, CEO
athompson@tay.ca
705-534-7248 ext. 240
Robert Coryell, Chair
dcoryell@rogers.com

***Port Perry:* Mississaugas of Scugog Island First Nation Library**
Health & Resource Centre, 22600 Island Rd., Port Perry, ON L9L 1B6
Tel: 905-985-1826; *Fax:* 905-985-7958
library@scugogfirstnation.com
Joan Wood, Library & CAP Worker
jwood@scugogfirstnation.com

***Port Perry:* Scugog Memorial Public Library**
231 Water St., Port Perry, ON L9L 1A8
Tel: 905-985-7686; *Fax:* - - 210
info@scugoglibrary.ca
www.scugoglibrary.ca
Social Media: twitter.com/ScugogLibrary; www.facebook.com/scugoglibrary
Betty Somerville, Chair
Amy Caughlin, Chief Librarian
acaughlin@scugoglibrary.ca

***Port Rowan:* Port Rowan Public Library**
1034 Main St., Port Rowan, ON N0E 1M0
Tel: 519-586-3201; *Fax:* 519-586-3297
norfolk.library@norfolkcounty.ca
www.ncpl.ca
Marsha Johnstone, Librarian

***Powassan:* Powassan & District Union Public Library**
324 Clark St., Powassan, ON P0H 1Z0
Tel: 705-724-3618; *Fax:* 705-724-5525
mrosset@ontera.net
powlib.www2.onlink.net
Social Media: twitter.com/powassanlibrary; www.facebook.com/powassanlibrary
Marie Rosset, CEO

***Prescott:* Prescott Public Library**
360 Dibble St. West, Prescott, ON K0E 1T0
Tel: 613-925-4340; *Fax:* 613-925-0100
library@prescott.ca
www.prescott.ca/residential/library
Jane McGuire, Chief Librarian/CEO
Susen Kaylo Raas, Assistant Librarian
Linda Doris, Library Assistant
Roxanne Brown, Library Assistant

***Rainy River:* Rainy River Public Library**
334 - 4th St., Rainy River, ON P0W 1L0
Tel: 807-852-3375; *Fax:* 807-852-3375
libraryrr@gmail.com
www.rainyriverlibrary.com
Michael Dawber, Librarian/CEO

***Rama:* Chippewas of Rama First Nation Public Library**
6147 Rama Rd., Rama, ON L3V 6H6
Tel: 705-325-3611; *Fax:* 705-325-2801
sherryl@ramafirstnation.ca
Sarah Cunningham, Libary Coordinator
sarahc@ramafirstnation.ca
705-325-3611 ext. 1405
Shelley Snache, Children's Services
shelley.snache@mnjikaning.ca
705-325-3611 ext. 1437

***Red Lake:* Red Lake Public Library**
117 Howey St., Red Lake, ON P0V 2M0
Tel: 807-727-2230; *Fax:* 807-727-2230
rllib212@yahoo.com
www.nwconx.net/rllib

***Red Rock:* Red Rock Public Library**
42 Salls St., Red Rock, ON P0T 2P0
Tel: 807-886-2558; *Fax:* 807-886-2558
rrocklib@gmail.com
www.olsn.ca/redrock/
Sandra Parker, Librarian

***Redbridge:* Phelps Public Library**
42 Old Mill Rd., RR#1, Redbridge, ON P0H 2A0
Tel: 705-663-2720
Beverly Reynolds, Librarian

***Renfrew:* Renfrew Public Library**
13 Railway Ave. East, Renfrew, ON K7V 3A9
Tel: 613-432-8151; *Fax:* 613-432-7680
renlib@renfrew.library.on.ca
www.town.renfrew.on.ca/library/
Social Media: twitter.com/intent/user?screen_name=renfrewreads; www.facebook.com/pages/Renfrew-Public-Library/291766994831
Bettijane O'Neill, Chief Librarian
Susan Klinck, Head, Children Services

***Richards Landing:* St Joseph Township Public Library**
PO Box 9, Richards Landing, ON P0R 1J0
Tel: 705-246-2353; *Fax:* 705-246-2353
sjtlibrary@ontera.net
stjosephisland.net
Sharon Thomas, Librarian/Treasurer/CEO

***Richmond Hill:* Richmond Hill Public Library**
1 Atkinson St., Richmond Hill, ON L4C 0H5
Tel: 905-884-9288; *Fax:* 905-884-6544
Other Numbers: Administrative: 905-770-0310
www.rhpl.richmondhill.on.ca
Social Media: twitter.com/rhpltweets; www.facebook.com/rhpl.news
Louise Procter Maio, CEO
Catherine Charles, Corporate Relations Officer
ccharles@rhpl.ca
905-770-0310 ext. 300

***Rockland:* Clarence-Rockland Public Library / Bibliothèque publique de Clarence-Rockland**
#2, 1525 du Parc Ave., Rockland, ON K4K 1C3
Tel: 613-446-5680; *Fax:* 613-446-1497
biblioinfo@biblibclarence-rockland.ca.
www.clarence-rockland.com
Nancie Bolduc, President, Library Board
Daniel Noel, Chief Executive Officer
Danielle Denis, Libary Technician

***Roseneath:* Alderville Learning Centre & Library**
11696 Second Line Rd., Roseneath, ON K0K 2X0
Tel: 905-352-2488; *Fax:* 905-352-1080
Other Numbers: Learning Centre, Phone: 905-352-2793
aldervillelearningcentre@eagle.ca
www.aldervillelearningcentre.com/index.php/library.html
Dona Wigmore, Librarian
Keri Gray, Learning Centre Coordinator

***Russell:* Bibliothèque publique du Canton de Russell/ Russell Township Public Library**
1053 Concession St., Box 280, Russell, ON K4R 1E1
Tel: 613-445-5331; *Fax:* 613-443-8014
mylibrary@russellbiblio.on.ca
www.russellbiblio.on.ca
Social Media: www.flickr.com/photos/russellbiblio; twitter.com/russellbiblio; www.facebook.com/159607974060274
Claire Dionne, CEO
claire.dionne@russellbiblio.com
613-445-5331
Joanne Yelle, Responsable, Services technique
joanne.yelle@russellbiblio.com
613-443-3636
Hélène Quesnel, Branch Head
helene.quesnel@russellbiblio.com
613-445-5331

Sachigo Lake: **Sachigo Lake First Nation Public Library**
c/o Martin McKay Memorial School, Sachigo Lake, ON P0V 2P0
Tel: 807-595-2526; *Fax:* 807-595-1305
Annie Tait, Chief Executive Officer
taitannie@gmail.com

Saint-Isidore: **Bibliothèque publique de la municipalité de La Nation/ Nation Municipality Public Library**
25, rue de l'Aréna, Saint-Isidore, ON K0C 2B0
Tel: 613-524-2252; *Fax:* 613-524-2545
biblioinfo@nationmun.ca
www.nationmunbiblio.ca
Social Media: www.flickr.com/photos/librarybooks; twitter.com/BiblioLaNation; www.facebook.com/109251539103571
France Lamoureux, Présidente
flamoureux@nationmun.ca
Jeanne Leroux, Directrice général
jeanneleroux@nationmun.ca
Monique Thèorêt Quesnel, Bibliotechnienne, Services techniques
mquesnel@nationmun.ca
Lyne Paquette, Assistante de bibliothèque
lpaquette@nationmun.ca

Saugeen: **Saugeen First Nation Library**
812 French Bay Rd., Saugeen, ON N0H 2L0
Tel: 519-797-5986; *Fax:* 519-797-5987
sfnlibrary@bmts.com
Theresa Gill, CEO

Sault Ste Marie: **Batchewana First Nation**
236 Frontenac St., Sault Ste Marie, ON P6A 5K9
Tel: 705-759-0914; *Fax:* 705-759-9171
Toll-Free: 877-236-2632
www.batchewana.ca
Alexandra Syrette, Communication Coordinator
705-759-0914 ext. 208

Sault Ste Marie: **Prince Township Library / Bibliothèque publique du Canton Prince**
3042 Second Line West, Sault Ste Marie, ON P6A 6K4
Tel: 705-779-3653; *Fax:* 705-779-2725
ptpl@twp.prince.on.ca
www.olsn.ca/princetownship/index.html
Margaret Christenson, Librarian

Sault Ste Marie: **Sault Ste Marie Public Library**
50 East St., Sault Ste Marie, ON P6A 3C3
Tel: 705-759-5230
Other Numbers: 705-759-5242 (Admin.); 705-759-5231 (Account info.)
www.ssmpl.ca
Christopher Rous, Chair
Elizabeth Rossnagel, Director, Public Libraries
e.rossnagel@cityssm.on.ca
Mark Jones, Acting Head, Technical Services & Circulation
m.jones@cityssm.on.ca
Roxanne Rissanen, Acting Head, Public Services
r.rissanen@cityssm.on.ca
Matthew MacDonald, Children's Librarian
m.macdonald@cityssm.on.ca
Julie Ringrose, Adult Services Librarian
j.ringrose@cityssm.on.ca

Savant Lake: **Savant Lake Community Library**
General Delivery, Savant Lake, ON P0V 2S0
Tel: 807-584-2242; *Fax:* 807-584-2272
Barbara Smith, Principal

Schreiber: **Schreiber Public Library**
314 Scotia St., Schreiber, ON P0T 2S0
Tel: 807-824-2477; *Fax:* 807-824-2996
libinfo@schreiber.ca
www.schreiberlibrary.ca
Social Media: www.youtube.com/user/schreiberlibrary; www.facebook.com/160900397294463
Rona Godin, Chair
Donna Mikeluk, Head Librarian
Linda Williamson, Assistant Librarian

Shannonville: **Tyendinaga Township Public Library**
852 Melrose Rd., RR#1, Shannonville, ON K0K 3A0
Tel: 613-967-0606; *Fax:* 613-967-0606
tyendinagatwplibrary@xplornet.ca
www.ttpl.ca
Tanya Stapley-Wilson, Librarian/CEO

Shelburne: **Shelburne Public Library**
201 Owen Sound St., Shelburne, ON L0N 1S0
Tel: 519-925-2168; *Fax:* 519-925-6555
info@shelburnelibrary.ca
www.shelburnelibrary.ca
Social Media: www.facebook.com/pages/Shelburne-Public-Library/195224210500255
Rose Dotten, CEO/Head Librarian
rdotten@shelburnelibrary.ca

Sheshegwaning: **Sheshegwaning Public Library**
1125 Sheshegwaning St., Sheshegwaning, ON P0P 1X0
Tel: 705-283-3014; *Fax:* 705-283-4038
debracada@hotmail.com
www.olsn.ca/sheshegwaning
Debra Cada, CEO
debracada@hotmail.com

Shoal Lake: **Iskutewisakaggun #39 First Nation Community Public Library**
Kejick Post Office, Shoal Lake, ON P0X 1E0
Tel: 807-733-3621; *Fax:* 807-733-3635
i_ross38@hotmail.com
Irene Ross, CEO
i_ross38@hotmail.com

Simcoe: **Norfolk County Public Library**
46 Colborne St. South, Simcoe, ON N3Y 4H3
Tel: 519-426-3506; *Fax:* 519-426-0657
www.ncpl.ca
Social Media: twitter.com/norfolklibrary; www.facebook.com/NorfolkLibrary
Bill Hett, Chief Executive Officer
bill.hett@norfolkcounty.ca
519-426-3506 ext. 1253
Heidi Goodale, Manager, Collection Development & Technology
heidi.goodale@norfolkcounty.ca
519-426-3506 ext. 1250
Marsha Johnstone, Manager, Programming & Communications
marsha.johnstone@norfolkcounty.ca
519-426-3506 ext. 1252
Pat Reidy, Manager, Facilities & Operations
pat.reidy@norfolkcounty.ca
519-426-3506 ext. 1251
Janet Cowan, Coordinator, Administration
janet.cowan@norfolkcounty.ca
519-426-3506 ext. 1258

Sioux Lookout: **Sioux Lookout Public Library**
21 - 5th Ave., Sioux Lookout, ON P8T 1B3
Tel: 807-737-3660; *Fax:* 807-737-4046
info@slpl.on.ca
www.slpl.on.ca
Wendy MacDonald, Chief Executive Officer & Chief Librarian

Sioux Narrows: **Sioux Narrows Public Library**
Sioux Narrows Public School, Hwy 71, Sioux Narrows, ON P0X 1N0
Tel: 807-226-5204; *Fax:* 807-226-5712
library@kmts.ca
Alice Motlong, Head Librarian
807-226-5204

Smiths Falls: **Smiths Falls Public Library**
81 Beckwith St. North, Smiths Falls, ON K7A 2B9
Tel: 613-283-2911; *Fax:* 613-283-9834
smithsfallslibrary@vianet.ca
www.smithsfallslibrary.ca
William Widenmaier, Chair
Karen Schecter, Chief Librarian
Elizabeth Lavender, Assistant Librarian
Debra Kuehl, Children's Librarian

Smithville: **West Lincoln Public Library**
Town Hall Complex, 318 Canboro St., Smithville, ON L0R 2A0
Tel: 905-957-3756
smithville@westlincolnlibrary.ca
www.westlincolnlibrary.ca
Social Media: twitter.com/WLPLibrary; www.facebook.com/pages/West-Lincoln-Library/119491941625
Catharine Vaughan, CEO

Smooth Rock Falls: **Smooth Rock Falls Public Library / Bibliothèque publique de Smooth Rock Falls**
120 Ross Rd., Smooth Rock Falls, ON P0L 2B0
Tel: 705-338-2318; *Fax:* 705-338-2330
smooth@ntl.sympatico.ca
www.townofsmoothrockfalls.ca
Lise Gagnon, CEO
Lynne Pelletier, Contact, ILL & Children's Services

South River: **South River-Machar Union Public Library**
63 Marie St., South River, ON P0A 1X0
Tel: 705-386-0222; *Fax:* 705-386-0222
osrmlibrary@hotmail.com
www.olsn.ca/srmupl
Social Media: www.facebook.com/288691530122
Jan Heinonen, Chief Executive Officer
Jo-Ann Long, Assistant Librarian

Southwold: **Oneida Community Library**
2315 Keystone Pl., Southwold, ON N0L 2G0
Tel: 519-652-3977
Corey Nicholas, CEO

Spanish: **Spanish Public Library / Bibliothèque publique du Spanish**
8 Trunk Rd., Spanish, ON P0P 2A0
Tel: 705-844-2555; *Fax:* 705-844-2555
library@town.spanish.on.ca
www.town.spanish.on.ca/pages/library.asp
Hanne Sauvé, Chief Librarian
library@town.spanish.on.ca
705-844-2555
Jannifer MacPhail, Front Desk

Spencerville: **Edwardsburgh / Cardinal Public Library**
5 Henderson St., Spencerville, ON K0E 1X0
Tel: 613-658-5575
library@spencerville.ca
www.spencervillelibrary.ca
Kathy Colwell, Head Librarian

St Catharines: **St Catharines Public Library**
54 Church St., St Catharines, ON L2R 7K2
Tel: 905-688-6103; *Fax:* 905-688-6292
admin@stcatharines.library.on.ca
www.stcatharines.library.on.ca
Social Media: twitter.com/stcathlibrary; www.facebook.com/298407173635
Lilita Stripnieks, CEO
lstripnieks@stcatharines.library.on.ca
Jack Foster, Business Administrator
jfoster@stcatharines.library.on.ca
David Bott, Manager, IT & Networks
dbott@stcatharines.library.on.ca
John Dunn, Manager, Technical Services & ILS
jdunn@stcatharines.library.on.ca
Diane Andrusko, Manager, Adult Information Services
dandrusko@stcatharines.library.on.ca
Ann McKenzie, Manager, Children's & Community Services
amckenzie@stcatharines.library.on.ca
Anna Chiota, Manager, Branch Services
achiota@stcatharines.library.on.ca
Anne Penfold, Manager, Circulation Services
apenfold@stcatharines.library.on.ca

St Charles: **St. Charles Public Library**
22 Ste. Anne St., St Charles, ON P0M 2W0
Tel: 705-867-5332; *Fax:* 705-867-2511
stcharles-library@yahoo.ca
cap-pac.8m.com
Nicole Lafontaine, Chief Librarian
stcharles-library@yahoo.ca
705-867-5332
Carol Vaillant, Assistant Librarian

St Marys: **St Marys Public Library**
15 Church St. North, St Marys, ON N4X 1B4
Tel: 519-284-3346; *Fax:* 519-284-2630
libraryinfo@stmaryspubliclibrary.ca
www.townofstmarys.com/public-library
Social Media: twitter.com/stmaryspl; www.facebook.com/group.php?gid=33345900699
Yunmi Hwang, Chief Executive Officer
yhwang@town.stmarys.on.ca
Jan McClelland, Library Technician
jmcclelland@town.stmarys.on.ca
Karen Coddington, Library Clerk, Children's Programs
Merley Wheaton, Library Clerk, Programs

St Thomas: **St Thomas Public Library**
153 Curtis St., St Thomas, ON N5P 3Z7
Tel: 519-631-6050; *Fax:* 519-631-1987
rdenham@st-thomas.library.on.ca
www.st-thomas.library.on.ca
Social Media: www.facebook.com/302831323082900
Rudi Denham, CEO / Head Librarian
rdenham@st-thomas.library.on.ca
Paul Blower, Head, Reference/Adult Services
pblower@st-thomas.library.on.ca

Heather Robinson, Head, Children & Teens Services
hrobinson@st-thomas.library.on.ca
Terri Scott, Acting Head of Circulation
tscott@st-thomas.library.on.ca

St. Thomas: Elgin County Library
450 Sunset Dr., St. Thomas, ON N5R 5V1
Tel: 519-631-1460; *Fax:* 519-631-9209
sloponen@elgin-county.on.ca
www.library.elgin-county.on.ca
Sandi Loponen, Library Coordinator
sloponen@elgin-county.on.ca
Dalene Van Zyl, Reference Resource Person
dvanzyl@elgin-county.on.ca
Susan Morrell, Reference Resource Person
smorrell@elgin-county.on.ca

Stayner: Clearview Public Library
201 Huron St., Stayner, ON L0M 1S0
Tel: 705-428-3595
interlibraryloans@clearview.ca
www.clearview.library.on.ca
Social Media:
www.facebook.com/pages/Clearview-Public-Library/285803031750
Diane Kelly, Chair
7054663251

Stirling: Stirling-Rawdon Public Library
43 Front St., Stirling, ON K0K 3E0
Tel: 613-395-2837
www.stirlinglibrary.com
Social Media: www.facebook.com/172294119529138
Sue Winfield, CEO/Head Librarian
sue@stirlinglibrary.com
Theresa Brennan, Assistant Librarian
Jaye Bannon, Children's Librarian

Stonecliffe: Head, Clara & Maria Township Public Library
15 Township Hall Rd., Stonecliffe, ON K0J 2K0
Tel: 613-586-2526; *Fax:* 613-586-2596
hcmlibra@xplornet.com
www.hcmpubliclibrary.ca
Gayle Watters, CEO/Librarian

Stouffville: Whitchurch-Stouffville Public Library
30 Burkholder St., Stouffville, ON L4A 4K1
Tel: 905-642-7323; *Fax:* 905-640-1384
Toll-Free: 888-603-4292
cnordheimerjames@whitchurch-library.on.ca
www.whitchurch-library.on.ca
Social Media: twitter.com/WhitStoufLibrar; www.facebook.com/WSPLibrary
Maurice Smith, Chair
Carolyn Nordheimer James, CEO/Secretary-Treasurer
905-642-7323 ext. 223
Catherine Sword, Coordinator, Public Services
905-642-7323 ext. 224
Anne Houle, Coordinator, Children & Youth Services
905-642-7323 ext. 228
Marcia Jackson-Friginette, Coordinator, Technical Services
905-642-7323 ext. 222

Stratford: Stratford Public Library
19 St Andrew St., Stratford, ON N5A 1A2
Tel: 519-271-0220; *Fax:* 519-271-3843
askspl@pcin.on.ca
www.stratford.library.on.ca
Social Media: pinterest.com/splibrary; twitter.com/SPLibrary; www.facebook.com/stratfordpubliclibrary
Geoff Williams, Chair
Sam Coghlan, Library Director & CEO
scoghlan@pcin.on.ca
519-271-0220 ext. 15
Wendy Hicks, Deputy Director
whicks@pcin.on.ca
519-271-0220 ext. 36
Sonya Fischer, Customer Services Librarian
sfischer@pcin.on.ca
519-271-0220 ext. 24
David Harvie, Systems Librarian
dharvie@pcin.on.ca
519-271-0220 ext. 29
Theresa Talsma, Interlibrary Loans Technician
ttalsma@pcin.on.ca
519-271-0220 ext. 23
Shauna Thomas, Sunday Services Supervisor
sthomas@pcin.on.ca
519-271-0220 ext. 58

Strathroy: Middlesex County Library
34B Frank St., Strathroy, ON N7G 2R4
Tel: 519-245-8237; *Fax:* 519-245-8238
www.middlesex.library.on.ca
Lindsay Brock, Director, Information Services
lbrock@middlesex.ca
519-245-8237 ext. 4022
Chris Harrington, Reference Librarian
Patti Wallace, Children's Librarian
519-245-8237 ext. 4027
Heather Cadman, Library Technician, Web site
519-245-8237 ext. 4023
Stan MacKenzie, Library Technician, Interlibrary Loans
519-245-8237 ext. 4026
Ann Pilon, Library Technician, Requests
519-245-8237 ext. 4025
Pamela Warzecha, Library Technician, Special Services
519-245-8237 ext. 4021

Stratton: Stratton Community Library
11331 Hwy. 11, Stratton, ON P0W 1N0
Tel: 807-483-5455
Anna H.M. Boily, Clerk-Treasurer

Sturgeon Falls: West Nipissing Public Library / Bibliothèque publique de Nipissing Ouest
#107, 225 Holditch St., Sturgeon Falls, ON P2B 1T1
Tel: 705-753-2620; *Fax:* 705-753-2131
mail@wnpl.ca
www.wnpl.ca
Carole Marion, Chief Executive Officer
cmarion@wnpl.ca
Frances Cockburn, Head, Archives
fcockburn@wnpl.ca

Sudbury: Greater Sudbury Public Library / Bibliothèque publique du grand Sudbury
74 Mackenzie St., Sudbury, ON P3C 4X8
Tel: 705-673-1155; *Fax:* 705-673-6145
www.sudbury.library.on.ca
Social Media: www.facebook.com/group.php?gid=19877797824
Martin Lajeunesse, Chair
(Roy) Hannu Piironen, Vice-Chair

Sundridge: Sundridge-Strong Union Public Library
110 Main St., Sundridge, ON P0A 1Z0
Tel: 705-384-7311; *Fax:* 705-384-7311
sslibrary@hotmail.com
www.olsn.ca/sundridgestronglibrary
Denise Rogers, Librarian

Sutton West: Chippewas of Georgina Island First Nation Public Library
Joseph Snake Rd., RR#2, Sutton West, ON L0E 1R0
Tel: 705-437-4328; *Fax:* 705-437-4597
Karen Foster, CEO
karenfoster@knet.ca
705-437-4327
Lynn Mooney, Literacy Coordinator
705-437-4327

Tehkummah: Tehkummah Township Public Library
Municipal Offices Bldg., RR#1, Tehkummah, ON P0P 2C0
Tel: 705-859-3301; *Fax:* 705-859-2605
tehklib@yahoo.ca
Judy McDermid, CEO

Temagami: Temagami Public Library
Welcome Centre, 7 Lakeshore Dr., Temagami, ON P0H 2H0
Tel: 705-569-2945
library@temagami.ca
www.temagami.library.on.ca
Shelley Rowland, Chief Executive Officer & Librarian

Terrace Bay: Terrace Bay Public Library
13 Selkirk Ave., Terrace Bay, ON P0T 2W0
Tel: 807-825-3315; *Fax:* 807-825-1249
terracebaypl@hotmail.com
terracebay.library.on.ca
Social Media:
www.facebook.com/group.php?gid=116263591747005
Mary Deschatelets, CEO
807-825-3315 ext. 234
Jean Fenton, Assistant Librarian
807-825-3315 ext. 222

Thamesville: Delaware Nation Public Library
RR#3, Thamesville, ON N0P 2K0
Tel: 519-692-3411; *Fax:* 519-692-5522
Other Numbers: Alternate Phone: 519-692-3936
Darryl Stonefish, CEO
dkstonefi@yahoo.ca

Thessalon: Thessalon First Nation Public Library
RR#2, PO Box 9, Thessalon, ON P0R 1L0
Tel: 705-842-1258; *Fax:* 705-842-2332
thessalonfirstnationlibrary@hotmail.com
Julie Bisaillon, Chief Executive Officer
bisaillon_julie@hotmail.com

Thessalon: Thessalon Union Public Library
187 Main St., Thessalon, ON P0R 1L0
Tel: 705-842-2306; *Fax:* 705-842-5690
library@thesslibcap.com
www.thesslibcap.com
Social Media:
www.facebook.com/group.php?gid=104998919541074; twitter.com/ThessalonPublic; www.facebook.com/104998919541074
Sandra McKee, CEO/Librarian
Sharon Couvillon, Contact, Technical Services

Thornbury: The Blue Mountains Public Library
173 Bruce St. South, Thornbury, ON N0H 2P0
Tel: 519-599-3681; *Fax:* 519-599-7951
libraryinfo@thebluemountains.ca
www.thebluemountainslibrary.ca
Cathy Innes, Chair
Carol Cooley, CEO
Elisa Chandler, Coordinator, Technical Services
Jennifer Perks, Coordinator, Children & Youth Services
Donna St. Jacques, Coordinator, Desk Services
Emma Barker, Library Assistant, Administrative Services

Thorold: Thorold Public Library
14 Ormond St. North, Thorold, ON L2V 1Y8
Tel: 905-227-2581; *Fax:* 905-227-2311
thoroldpubliclibrary@cogeco.net
www.thoroldpubliclibrary.ca
Social Media:
www.facebook.com/pages/Thorold-Public-Library/156082714436307
Patti Bronson, Chief Librarian
pbronson@cogeco.net
905-227-2581
Tony Vandermaas, Chair
Cheryl Bowman, Contact, Information Desk

Thunder Bay: Thunder Bay Public Library
285 Red River Rd., Thunder Bay, ON P7B 1A9
Tel: 807-345-8275; *Fax:* 807-344-5119
Other Numbers: 807-624-4200 (Reference); 807-344-7138 (Renewals)
adults@tbpl.ca (Adult services)
www.tbpl.ca
Social Media: www.facebook.com/TBayPL
George Saarinen, Chair
gsaarinen@tbpl.ca
Barb Philp, Acting CEO/Chief Librarian
bphilp@tbpl.ca
807-684-6802
Tina Tucker, Director, Community Development
ttucker@tbpl.ca
807-684-6813
Yvonne Wodell, Director, Human Resources
ywodell@tbpl.ca
807-684-6806
Joanna Aegard, Head, Virtual Library Services
jaegard@tbpl.ca
807-684-6819
Stephen Hurrell, Head, Automated Support Systems
shurrell@tbpl.ca
807-684-6807
Angela Meady, Head, Children's & Youth Services
ameady@tbpl.ca
807-684-6810
Ruth Hamlin-Douglas, Acting Head, Adult Services
rhamlin-douglas@tbpl.ca
807-624-4206
Sylvia Renaud, Head, Technical Services
srenaud@tbpl.ca
807-684-6808
Jesse Roberts, Head, Reference Services
jroberts@tbpl.ca
807-624-4203

Tillsonburg: Tillsonburg Public Library
2 Library Lane, Tillsonburg, ON N4G 2S7
Tel: 519-842-5571; *Fax:* 519-842-2941
publiclibrary@tillsonburg.ca
library.tillsonburg.ca/polaris/default.aspx
Matthew Scholtz, Librarian
mscholtz@web.ocl.net

***Timmins:* Timmins Public Library / Bibliothèque municipale de Timmins**
320 Second Ave., Timmins, ON P4N 8A4
Tel: 705-360-2623
tpl.timmins.ca
Judith Heinzen, CEO
tpl_4@timmins.ca
705-360-8520
Elaine De Bonis, Assistant Director
elaine.debonis@timmins.ca
705-360-8517
Teresa Woodrow, Head, Support Services
teresa.woodrow@timmins.ca
705-360-8523
Chantal Benson, Head, Technical Support & Services
chantal.benson@timmins.ca
705-360-8518

***Toronto:* Holocaust Eduation Centre**
Sarah & Chaim Neuberger Holocaust Education Centre, UJA Federation, 4600 Bathurst St., 4th Fl., Toronto, ON M2R 3V3
Tel: 416-635-2996
www.holocaustcentre.com/AnitaEkstein
Anna Skorupsky, Librarian
askorupsky@ujafed.org

***Toronto:* Toronto Public Library**
789 Yonge St., Toronto, ON M4W 2G8
Tel: 416-393-7000; *Fax:* 416-393-7083
TTY: 4163937030
www.torontopubliclibrary.ca
Social Media: www.youtube.com/torontopubliclibrary; twitter.com/torontolibrary; www.facebook.com/torontopubliclibrary
Linda MacKenzie, Director, Research & Reference Libraries
lmackenzie@torontopubliclibrary.ca
416-393-7133
Ron Dyck, Director, Information Technology & Facilities
rdyck@torontopubliclibrary.ca
416-393-7104
Katherine Palmer, Director, Planning & Policy
kpalmer@torontopubliclibrary.ca
416-395-5602
Linda Hazzan, Director, Communications, Programming & Engagement
lhazzan@torontopubliclibrary.ca
416-393-7214
Anne Bailey, Director, Branch Libraries
abailey@torontopubliclibrary.ca
416-397-5944
Vickery Bowles, Director, Collections Management & City-Wide Services
vbowles@torontopubliclibrary.ca
416-395-5506
Dan Keon, Director, Human Resources
dkeon@torontopubliclibrary.ca
416-395-5850
Heather Rumball, President/Director of Development, Toronto Public Library Foundation
hrumball@torontopubliclibrary.ca
416-393-7134

***Trenton:* Quinte West Public Library**
7 Creswell Dr., Trenton, ON K8V 6X5
Tel: 613-394-3381; *Fax:* 613-394-2079
Other Numbers: 613-394-3381, ext. 3322 (Circulation services)
info.qwpl@city.quintewest.on.ca
www.library.quintewest.ca
Social Media: www.facebook.com/QuinteWestPublicLibrary
Bob Wannamaker, Chair
Rita Turtle, Chief Exectuive Officer
rturtle.qwpl@city.quintewest.on.ca
613-394-3381 ext. 3315
Robert Amesse, Coordinator, Adult Information & Reference
ramesse.qwpl@city.quintewest.on.ca
613-394-3381 ext. 3325
Rosemary Kirby, Contact, Children's Information & Reference
rkirby.qwpl@city.quintewest.on.ca
613-394-3381 ext. 3311
Linda Lafond, Contact, Interlibrary Loan Information
illo.qwpl@city.quintewest.on.ca
613-394-3381 ext. 3316
Kim Vivian, Contact, Homeward Bound
kvivian.qwpl@city.quintewest.on.ca
613-394-3381 ext. 3325

***Tweed:* Municipality of Tweed Public Library**
230 Metcalf St., Tweed, ON K0K 3J0
Tel: 613-478-1066; *Fax:* 613-478-6457
tweedlibrary@vianet.ca
tweedlibrary.ca
Social Media: www.facebook.com/pages/Tweed-Public-Library/11074565565 7043
Catherine Anderson, CEO

***Uxbridge:* Uxbridge Township Public Library**
9 Toronto St. South, Uxbridge, ON L9P 1P7
Tel: 905-852-9747
uxlib@powergate.ca
www.uxlib.com
Social Media: www.flickr.com/photos/uxbridgepubliclibrary; twitter.com/uxbridgelibrary; www.facebook.com/pages/Uxbridge-Public-Library/1817175818 70540
Alexandra Hartmann, CEO / Chief Librarian
ahartmann@uxlib.com
905-852-9747 ext. 26
Pamela Noble, Outreach/Program Coordinator
pnoble@uxlib.com
905-852-9747 ext. 24
Leslie Nagle, Contact, Interlibrary Loans
leslie.nagle@uxlib.com
905-852-9747 ext. 27

***Val Rita:* Val Rita-Harty Public Library / Bibliothèque municipale de Val Rita-Harty**
106, rue Gouvernement, Val Rita, ON P0L 2G0
Tel: 705-335-8700; *Fax:* 705-335-8700
bibliovalrita@hotmail.com
www.valharty.ca
Cecile Lamontagne, Présidente du conseil bibliothèque

***Vankleek Hill:* Champlain Township Public Library / Bibliothèque Champlain**
94 Main St. East, PO Box 520, Vankleek Hill, ON K0B 1R0
Tel: 613-678-2216; *Fax:* 613-678-2216
library@champlaintwplibrary.ca
www.champlaintwplibrary.ca
Lise Béliveau, Chair
Lynda Poyser, CEO & Head Librarian
lpoyser@champlaintwplibrary.ca
Diane Bourgault, Circulation Clerk & Library Assistant
dianeb@champlaintwplibrary.ca
Margaret MacMillan, Circulation Clerk & Library Assistant
marg@champlaintwplibrary.ca
Cynthia Martin, Circulation Clerk & Library Assistant
cynthia@champlaintwplibrary.ca

***Vaughan:* Vaughan Public Libraries**
900 Clark Ave. West, Vaughan, ON L4J 8C1
Tel: 905-653-7323; *Fax:* 905-709-1530
www.vaughanpl.info
Social Media: pinterest.com/vaughanpl; twitter.com/vaughanpl; www.facebook.com/pages/Vaughan-Public-Libraries/133050006 764886
Margie Singleton, Chief Executive Officer
margie.singleton@vaughan.ca
905-653-7323 ext. 4101
Aleksandra Dowiat Vine, Director, Planning & Communication
aleksandra.dowiat-vine@vaughan.ca
905-653-7323 ext. 4120
Marilyn Guy, Director, Operations
marilyn.guy@vaughan.ca
905-653-7323 ext. 4114
Sandy Vander Werff, Director, Finance
sandy.vanderwerff@vaughan.ca
905-653-7323 ext. 4104
Terri Watman, Director, Service Delivery
terri.watman@vaughan.ca
905-653-7323 ext. 4124

***Virginiatown:* McGarry Township Public Library / Bibliothèque publique de McGarry**
1 - 27 St., Virginiatown, ON P0K 1X0
www.mcgarrypubliclibrary.8m.com
Anne-Marie Boucher, CEO/Librarian

***Wainfleet:* Wainfleet Township Public Library**
31909 Park St., Wainfleet, ON L0S 1V0
Tel: 905-899-1277; *Fax:* 905-899-2495
www.wainfleetlibrary.ca
Lorrie Atkinson, CEO
latkinson@wainfleetlibrary.ca
Leanne Good, Library Programmer
lgood@wainfleetlibrary.ca
Cheryl Davis-Catchpaw, Secretary/Library Clerk
cdavis-catchpaw@wainfleetlibrary.ca
Dariusz Zelichowski, IT/Systems Specialist
wainweb@township.wainfleet.org

***Walker's Point:* Walker's Point Volunteer Community Book Exchange**
Walker's Point Community Centre, 1074 Walker's Point Rd., Walker's Point, ON P0C 1M0
Tel: 705-687-9965

***Wallaceburg:* Bkejwanong First Nation Public Library**
Walpole Island First Nation, 136 Tecumseh Road, RR #3, Wallaceburg, ON N8A 4K9
Tel: 519-627-7034; *Fax:* 519-627-7035
library@wifn.org
www.bkejwanonglibrary.ca
Social Media: www.facebook.com/bkejwanong.fnpl
Summer Sands-Macbeth, Librarian/CEO
Stephanie Lallean, Library Assistant

***Wasaga Beach:* Wasaga Beach Public Library**
120 Glenwood Dr., Wasaga Beach, ON L9Z 2K5
Tel: 705-429-5481; *Fax:* 705-429-5481
wblibrary@georgian.net
www.wasagabeach.library.on.ca
Jackie Beaudin, CEO
705-429-5481 ext. 2404

***Waterloo:* Waterloo Public Library**
35 Albert St., Waterloo, ON N2L 5E2
Tel: 519-886-1310; *Fax:* 519-886-7936
TTY: 18667863941
Other Numbers: TeleRenew: 519-886-5480
www.wpl.ca
Social Media: www.youtube.com/user/WaterlooLibrary; twitter.com/waterloolibrary; www.facebook.com/124917584192823
Laurie Clarke, CEO
lclarke@wpl.ca
519-886-1310 ext. 123
Gloria Van Eek-Meijers, Deputy CEO
gvaneek@wpl.ca
519-886-1310 ext. 125
Alannah d'Ailly, Manager, Library Collections
adailly@wpl.ca
519-886-1310 ext. 127
Sue Klopchic, Human Resources
jobs@wpl.ca
519-889-1310 ext. 164

***Wawa:* Michipicoten First Nation Public Library**
107 Hiawatha Dr., RR#1, Wawa, ON P0S 1K0
Tel: 705-856-1993; *Fax:* 705-856-1642
library@michipicoten.com
www.michipicoten.com
Lee-Ann Andre-Swanson, Chief Executive Officer

***Wawa:* Wawa Public Library**
40 Broadway Ave., Wawa, ON P0S 1K0
Tel: 705-856-2062; *Fax:* 705-856-1488
Other Numbers: Circulation Desk, ext. 290
mtpl@wawa.cc
www.mtpl.on.ca
Jayne Griffith, Head Librarian
jgriffith@wawa.cc
705-856-2062 ext. 291
Barb McCullough, Assistant Librarian
Jude Charbonneau, Circulation Technician
Joanne DeVries, Circulation Technician

***Weagamow Lake:* North Caribou First Nation Public Library**
PO Box 158, Weagamow Lake, ON P0V 2Y0
Tel: 807-469-1288; *Fax:* 807-469-1132
beatricekanate@knet.ca
Beatrice Kanate, CEO

***Welland:* Welland Public Library**
50 The Boardwalk, Welland, ON L3B 6J1
Tel: 905-734-6210; *Fax:* 905-734-8955
www.welland.library.on.ca
Social Media: twitter.com/wellandlib; www.facebook.com/wellandpubliclibrary
Janet C. Booth, CEO & Secretary-Treasurer
jbooth@welland.library.on.ca
905-734-6210 ext. 2500
Qingyi (Ken) Su, Coordinator, Information Services
qksu@welland.library.on.ca
905-734-6210 ext. 2503
Stephen Hanns, Manager, Public Services
shanns@welland.library.on.ca
905-734-6210 ext. 2502

Barbara Murphy, Manager, Support Services
bmurphy@welland.library.on.ca
905-734-6210 ext. 2501
Daniella Liebregts, Coordinator, Children's & Youth Services
dliebreghts@welland.library.on.ca
905-734-6210 ext. 2508

Wendover: Bibliothèque publique du Canton d'Alfred et Plantagenet / Alfred & Plantagenet Public Library
3104, av du Quai, Wendover, ON K0A 3K0
Tél: 613-673-2923
biblio_dg@yahoo.ca
www.alfred-platagenet.com
Catherine Bélisle, Directrice
Anne St-Pierre, Aide

Westport: Westport Public Library
3 Spring St., Westport, ON K0G 1X0
Tel: 613-273-3223; *Fax:* 613-273-3223
library@rideau.net
village.westport.on.ca/about-westport/westport-public-library
Social Media: www.facebook.com/155845464448129
Ruth Pedherney, Chair
Pamela Stuffles, CEO

Whitby: Whitby Public Library
405 Dundas St. West, Whitby, ON L1N 6A1
Tel: 905-668-6531; *Fax:* 905-668-7445
Other Numbers: Holds & Renewals, Phone: 905-430-7913
admin@whitbylibrary.on.ca
www.whitbylibrary.on.ca
Social Media: www.youtube.com/whitbypubliclibrary; twitter.com/whitbylibrary; www.facebook.com/whitbylibrary
Claude Lavoie, Chair
wplboard@whitbylibrary.on.ca
Ian Ross, CEO/Chief Librarian
ianross@whitbylibrary.on.ca
Rhonda Jessup, Public Services Manager
rjessup@whitbylibrary.on.ca
Elaine Yatulis Dobbin, Manager, Technical Services & Systems Support
Michelle Frenette, Manager, Support Services

White River: White River Public Library
123 Superior St., White River, ON P0M 3G0
Tel: 807-822-1113; *Fax:* 807-822-1113
wrlib@nwconx.net
www.whiteriverlibrary.com
Jan Ramage, CEO

Whitedog: Wabaseemoong First Nation Public Library
General Delivery, Whitedog, ON P0X 1P0
Tel: 807-927-2000; *Fax:* 807-927-2176

Whitney: South Algonquin Public Library
PO Box 208, Whitney, ON K0J 2M0
Tel: 613-637-5471; *Fax:* 613-637-5471
whitlib@northcom.net
www.olsn.ca/southalgonquin
Charlene Alexander, CEO
613-637-5471
Cynthia Haskin, Branch Library
madlib@northcom.net
613-637-1099

Wiarton: Ninda Kikaendjigae Wigammik Library
25 Maadookii Subdivision, RR#5, Wiarton, ON N0H 2T0
Tel: 519-534-1508; *Fax:* 519-534-2130
www.nawash.ca/index.cfm?page=library
Daphne Johnston, Supervisor
daphnejohnston@nawashfn.ca

Wikwemikong: Wikwemikong First Nation Public Library
34A Henry St., Wikwemikong, ON P0P 2J0
Tel: 705-859-2692; *Fax:* 705-859-3851
wikylibrary@hotmail.com
www.olsn.ca/wpl
Sheri Mishibinijima, Librarian
smish@amtelecom.net

Windsor: Windsor Public Library
850 Ouellette Ave., Windsor, ON N9A 4M9
Tel: 519-255-6770; *Fax:* 519-255-7207
TTY: 519-255-720
wpl@city.windsor.on.ca
www.windsorpubliclibrary.com
Social Media: twitter.com/windsorpublib; www.facebook.com/windsorpl
Nancy Peel, Manager
npeel@windsorpubliclibrary.com
519-255-6770
Barry Holmes, CEO

Woodstock: Oxford County Library
Oxford County Administration Bldg., 21 Reeve St., Woodstock, ON N4S 7Y3
Tel: 519-539-9800; *Fax:* 519-485-4028
cap@ocl.net (CAP e-mail)
www.ocl.net
Social Media: www.facebook.com/OxfordCountyLibrary
Margaret Lupton, Chair
mlupton@zorra.on.ca
519-475-4443
Lisa Miettinen, Chief Executive Officer & Chief Librarian
lmiettinen@ocl.net
519-539-9800
Cristina McLaren, Librarian, Branch Services
cmclaren@ocl.net
Susan Gillespie, Cataloguer
sgillespie@ocl.net

Woodstock: Woodstock Public Library
445 Hunter St., Woodstock, ON N4S 4G7
Tel: 519-539-4801; *Fax:* 519-539-5246
gbaumbach@woodstock.library.on.ca
www.woodstock.library.on.ca
Social Media: www.facebook.com/myWPL
Brian Crockett, Chair
Gary Baumbach, CEO/Chief Librarian
gbaumbach@woodstock.library.on.ca
Susan Start, Head, Information & Adult Services
sstart@woodstock.library.on.ca
Darlene Pretty, Head, Children's & Youth Services
dpretty@woodstock.library.on.ca
Carolyn Veenstra, Head, Circulation Services
cmveenstra@woodstock.library.on.ca
Karen Scott, eBranch Manager
kscott@woodstock.library.on.ca
Judi Meadows, Administration & Room Bookings
jmeadows@woodstock.library.on.ca

Wyoming: Lambton County Library Headquarters
787 Broadway St., Wyoming, ON N0N 1T0
Tel: 519-845-3324; *Fax:* 519-845-0700
Toll-Free: 866-324-6912
Other Numbers: 519-845-3324, ext. 428 (Home Library Service)
www.lclmg.org
Social Media: twitter.com/LamLib; www.facebook.com/271179146270568
Robert Tremain, General Manager
robert.tremain@county-lambton.on.ca
519-845-0801 ext. 5236
Susie Beynon, Public Services Manager
susie.beynon@county-lambton.on.ca
Carol Gardiner, Branch Services Manager
carol.gardiner@county-lambton.on.ca
Krystyna Stalmach, Technical Services Manager
krystyna.stalmach@county-lambton.on.ca

Archives

Alexandria: Glengarry Historical Society
PO Box 416, Alexandria, ON K0C 1A0
Tel: 613-347-7192
archives@glengarryhistoricalsociety.com
www.glengarryhistoricalsociety.com
David G. Anderson, Contact
anderson@glen-net.ca

Ameliasburgh: Quinte Educational Museum & Archives
13 Coleman St. Group Box 14, Ameliasburgh, ON K0K 1A0
Tel: 613-966-5501
info@qema1978.com
www.qema1978.com/
Dan Rainey, President
danrainey@qema1978.com

Amherstburg: Marsh Collection Society
235A Dalhousie St., Amherstburg, ON N9V 1W4
Tel: 519-736-9191; *Fax:* 519-736-7166
mcschin@mnsi.net
www.marshcollection.org
Jennifer MacLeod, Archivist
mcschin@mnsi.net
519-736-9191

Amherstburg: North American Black Historical Museum
277 King St., Amherstburg, ON N9V 2C7
Tel: 519-736-5433; *Fax:* 866-622-4672
Toll-Free: 800-713-6336
nabhm@mnsi.net
www.blackhistoricalmuseum.org
Philip H. Alexander, President

Arnprior: Arnprior & McNab-Braeside Archives
21B Madawaska St., Arnprior, ON K7S 1R6
Tel: 613-623-0001; *Fax:* 613-623-0001
adarchives@hotmail.com
www.adarchives.org

Aylmer: Aylmer & District Museum Association
14 East St., Aylmer, ON N5H 1W2
Tel: 519-773-9723; *Fax:* 519-773-9723
aylmermuseum@amtelecom.net
www.amtelecom.net/~aylmermuseum
Pat Zimmer, Curator

Bayfield: Bayfield Archives Room
20 Main St. North, Bayfield, ON N0M 1G0
bayarchives@tcc.on.ca
www.bayfieldhistorical.ca
Elaine Sturgeon, Archivist

Beachville: County of Oxford Archives
12 Vine St., Beachville, ON N0J 1A0
Tel: 519-539-9800; *Fax:* 519-423-1964
archives@oxfordcounty.ca
www.oxfordcounty.ca/archives
Mary Gladwin, Archivist
mgladwin@oxfordcounty.ca
519-426-1928 ext. 210
Liz Mayville, Assistant Archivist
519-423-1928 ext. 209

Bowmanville: Clarington Museums & Archives
Sarah Jane Williams Heritage Centre, 62 Temperance St., Bowmanville, ON L1C 3A8
Tel: 905-623-2734; *Fax:* 905-623-5684
claringtonmuseums.archives@rogers.com
www.claringtonmuseums.com
Martha Rutherford Conrad, Administrator
claringtonmuseums@rogers.com
Charles Taws, Archivist

Brampton: Region of Peel Art Gallery, Museum, & Archives
The Peel Heritage Complex, 9 Wellington St. East, Brampton, ON L6W 1Y1
Tel: 905-791-4055; *Fax:* 905-451-4931
www.peelregion.ca/heritage
Social Media: www.flickr.com/photos/peelheritage; www.facebook.com/visitPAMA
Claire Loughheed, Manager
905-791-4055 ext. 3637
Diane Allengame, Archivist
905-791-4055 ext. 3629
Brian Gilchrist, Reference Archivist
905-791-4055 ext. 3630
Marty Brent, Supervisor, Museum & Archive Services
905-791-4055 ext. 4676

Brantford: Brant Historical Society
57 Charlotte St., Brantford, ON N3T 2W6
Tel: 519-752-2483; *Fax:* 519-752-1931
information@brantmuseum.ca
www.brantmuseum.ca
Social Media: www.youtube.com/user/branthistorical; twitter.com/branthistorical; www.facebook.com/BrantHistoricalSociety
Erin Dee-Richard, Curator
Lisa Anderson, Education Officer

Bridgenorth: Smith Ennismore Historical Society
826 Ward St., Bridgenorth, ON K0L 1H0
Tel: 705-292-9430
feedback@sehs.on.ca
sehs.on.ca/hlc.htm
John Harris, President

Brockville: Brockville Museum
5 Henry St., Brockville, ON K6V 6M4
Tel: 613-342-4397; *Fax:* 613-342-7345
Other Numbers: Leeds/Grenville Genealogical Society: 613-342-7773
museum@brockville.com
www.brockvillemuseum.com

Amy Whitehorne, Museum Educator
awhitehorne@brockville.com
Margaret Mulkins, Librarian, Leeds & Grenville Genealogical Society
cmulkins@bell.net

Burlington: Joseph Brant Museum
1240 North Shore Blvd. East, Burlington, ON L7S 1C5
Tel: 905-634-3556; *Fax:* 905-634-4498
Toll-Free: 888-748-5386
www.museumsofburlington.com
Social Media: twitter.com/BurlingtonMuse
Barbara E. Teatero, Director
teaterob@burlington.ca
Paul Stone, Curator of Collections
stonep@burlington.ca
Brianne Crites, Curatorial Assistant
critesb@burlington.ca

Cambridge: Cambridge Archives
46 Dickson St., 2nd Fl., Cambridge, ON N1R 1T7
Tel: 519-740-4680; *Fax:* 519-623-0058
archives@cambridge.ca
www.cambridge.ca/city_clerk/city_archives
Jim Quantrell, Archivist
quantrellj@city.cambridge.on.ca
519-740-4680 ext. 4610

Cannington: Cannington & Area Historical Society
PO Box 196, Cannington, ON L0E 1E0
Tel: 705-432-2430; *Fax:* 705-432-2909
Ted Foster, President

Chatham: Chatham-Kent Museum
75 William St. North, Chatham, ON N7M 4L4
Tel: 519-360-1998; *Fax:* 519-354-4170
CKccc@chatham-kent.ca
www.chatham-kent.ca
Social Media: www.facebook.com/pages/The-Cultural-Centre/2315010202339 0
Stephanie Suitor, Curator
stephanies@chatham-kent.ca

Combermere: Madonna House
2888 Dafoe Rd. RR#2, Combermere, ON K0J 1L0
Tel: 613-756-3713; *Fax:* 613-756-0211
archives@madonnahouse.org
www.madonnahouse.org/tour/vianney_house.html
Social Media: www.youtube.com/MadonnaHouseCanada; twitter.com/madonnahouse; www.facebook.com/MadonnaHouse

Delhi: Delhi Tobacco Museum & Heritage Centre
200 Talbot Rd., Delhi, ON N4B 2A2
Tel: 519-582-0278; *Fax:* 519-582-0122
delhi.museum@norfolkcounty.ca
www.delhimuseum.ca
Judy A. Livingstone, Curator/Director
Heather Gerrard, Museum Assistant

Fergus: Wellington County Museum & Archives
0536 County Rd. 18, RR#1, Fergus, ON N1M 2W3
Tel: 519-846-0916; *Fax:* 519-846-9630
karen@wcm.on.ca
www.wcm.on.ca
Karen Wagner, Archivist
karen@wcm.on.ca

Fort Frances: Fort Frances Museum & Cultural Centre
259 Scott St., Fort Frances, ON P9A 1G8
Tel: 807-274-7891; *Fax:* 807-274-4103
ffmuseum@fort-frances.com
museum.fort-frances.com

Gatineau: Canadian Museum of Nature/ Musée canadien de la nature
1740, ch Pink, Gatineau, ON J9J 3N7
Tel: 613-364-4042; *Fax:* 613-364-4026
cmnlib@mus-nature.ca
nature.ca/en/research-collections/library-archives
Chantal Dussault, Head, Archives, Records & Library
cdussault@mus-nature.ca
613-364-4047

Georgetown: Esquesing Historical Society
9 Church St., Georgetown, ON L7G 2A3
Tel: 905-877-9510
www.esquesinghistoricalsociety.ca/archives.html
Stephen Blake, President, Esquesing Historical Society
905-877-8251
J. Mark Rowe, Archivist
mrowe6@cogeco.ca

Gloucester: Gloucester Archives Branch
4550 Bank St., Gloucester, ON K1T 3W6
Tel: 613-822-2076
archives@ottawa.ca
ottawa.ca/archives

Goderich: Huron County Museum Archives
110 North St., Goderich, ON N7A 2T8
Tel: 519-524-2686; *Fax:* 519-524-1922
www.huroncounty.ca/museum
Beth Ross, County Librarian & Director, Cultural Services
bross@huroncounty.ca
Patricia Hamilton, Museum Curator
phamilton@huroncounty.ca

Gravenhurst: Gravenhurst Archives
Gravenhurst Public Library, 180 Sharpe St. West, Gravenhurst, ON P1P 1J1
Tel: 705-687-3382
library@gravenhurst.ca
www.surenet.net/~glib
Rita Orr, Chief Executive Officer & Chief Librarian
Marion Fry, Volunteer Archivist

Guelph: Guelph Civic Museum
52 Norfolk St., Guelph, ON N1H 4H8
Tel: 519-836-1221; *Fax:* 519-836-5280
museum@guelph.ca
www.guelph.ca/museum
Social Media: twitter.com/guelphmuseums
Bev Dietrich, Curator
bev.dietrich@guelph.ca
519-836-1221 ext. 2774
Kathleen Wall, Assistant Curator
kathleen.wall@guelph.ca
519-836-1221 ext. 2776

Haliburton: Haliburton Highlands Museum
PO Box 389, Haliburton, ON K0M 1S0
Tel: 705-457-2760
info@haliburtonhighlandsmuseum.com
www.haliburtonhighlands.com/museum
Thomas Ballantine, Director
Stephen Hill, Curator

Hamilton: Canadian Baptist Archives/ Archives baptistes canadiennes
c/o McMaster Divinity College, 1280 Main St. West, Hamilton, ON L8S 4K1
Tel: 905-525-9140
cbarch@mcmaster.ca
www.macdiv.ca/students/baptistarchives.php
Gordon Heath, Director
Adam McCulloch, Archivist
amccull@mcmaster.ca
905-525-9140 ext. 23511

Hamilton: Diocese of Niagara, Archives
Division of Archives & Research Collections, McMaster University Library,, 1280 Main St. West, Hamilton, ON L8S 4L6
Tel: 905-525-9140; *Fax:* 905-522-0691
archives@mcmaster.ca
library.mcmaster.ca/archives/anglican

Hamilton: Hamilton Public Library
55 York Blvd., 3rd Fl., Hamilton, ON L8N 4E4
Tel: 905-546-3408

Keewatin: Diocese of Keewatin, Archives
915 Ottawa St., Keewatin, ON P0X 1C0
Tel: 807-547-3353; *Fax:* 807-547-3356
dioceseofkeewatin@shaw.ca
www.dioceseofkeewatin.ca

Kenora: Lake of the Woods Museum
300 Main St. South, Kenora, ON P9N 3X5
Tel: 807-467-2105; *Fax:* 807-467-2109
museum@kmts.ca
www.lakeofthewoodsmuseum.ca
Lori Nelson, Director
Riley Sleeman, Collections/Education Coordinator
Wendy Midgard, Finance/Temp. Ex. Coordinator

Kingston: Diocese of Ontario, Archives
90 Johnston St., Kingston, ON K7L 1X7
Tel: 613-544-4774; *Fax:* 613-547-3745
archives@ontario.anglican.ca
www.ontario.anglican.ca

Kingston: Fort Henry National Historic Site of Canada Museum
PO Box 213, Kingston, ON K7L 4V8
Tel: 613-542-7388; *Fax:* 613-542-3054
Toll-Free: 800-437-2233
getaway@parks.on.ca
www.forthenry.com
Ron Ridley, Curator

Kingston: The International Hockey Hall of Fame & Museum
277 York St., Kingston, ON K7L 4V6
Tel: 613-544-2355; *Fax:* 613-544-2844
info@ihhof.com
www.ihhof.com
Mark Potter, President
mark.potter@ihhof.com

Kingston: Marine Museum of the Great Lakes at Kingston
55 Ontario St., Kingston, ON K7L 2Y2
Tel: 613-542-2261; *Fax:* 613-542-0043
marmus@marmuseum.ca
www.marmuseum.ca
Maurice Smith, Curator Emeritus

Kingston: Queen's University Archives
Kathleen Ryan Hall, 11 Medical Quadrangle, Kingston, ON K7L 3N6
Tel: 613-533-2378; *Fax:* 613-533-6403
archives@queensu.ca
archives.queensu.ca

Kingston: Religious Hospitallers of St. Joseph, St Joseph Province
16 Manitou Cres. East, Kingston, ON K7N 1B2
Tel: 613-389-0275; *Fax:* 613-384-6978
reg.archives@bellnet.ca
Rodney Carter, Archivist

Kingston: Sisters of Providence of St. Vincent de Paul
1200 Princess St., Kingston, ON K7M 3C9
Tel: 613-544-4525; *Fax:* 613-531-9805
archives@providence.ca
www.providence.ca
Social Media: twitter.com/srsofprovidence
Veronica Stienburg, Archivist

Kitchener: Grace Schmidt Room of Local History
85 Queen St. North, Kitchener, ON N2H 2H1
Tel: 519-743-0271

Kitchener: Waterloo Region Museum
10 Huron Rd., Kitchener, ON N2P 2R7
Tel: 519-748-1914; *Fax:* 519-748-0009
TTY: 5195754608
waterlooregionmuseum@regionofwaterloo.ca
waterlooregionmuseum.com/doon-heritage-village.aspx
Stacy McLennan, Registrar/Researcher
smclennan@regionofwaterloo.ca
519-748-1914 ext. 3268

Kleinburg: McMichael Canadian Art Collection/ Collection McMichael d'Art Canadien
10365 Islington Ave., Kleinburg, ON L0J 1C0
Tel: 905-893-1121; *Fax:* 905-893-2588
library@mcmichael.com
www.mcmichael.com
Linda Morita, Librarian/Archivist
lmorita@mcmichael.com

Listowel: Listowel Branch
260 Main St. West, Listowel, ON N4W 1A1
Tel: 519-291-1598; *Fax:* 519-291-2128
listowelarchives@pcin.on.ca
www.stratfordpertharchives.on.ca

London: Diocese of Huron Verschoyle Philip Memorial Archives
Huron University College, 1349 Western Rd., London, ON N6G 1H3
Tel: 519-645-7956; *Fax:* 519-645-8669
archives@huron.anglican.ca
www.archives.diohuron.org

London: Ivey Family London Room
251 Dundas St., London, ON N6A 6H9
Tel: 519-661-4600

London: J.J. Talman Regional Collection
D.B. Weldon Library, University of Western Ontario, 1151 Richmond St., London, ON N6A 3K7
Tel: 519-661-2111
www.lib.uwo.ca/archives/talman.shtml

London: London & Middlesex Country Branch Library
Grosvenor Lodge Coach House, 1017 Western Rd., London, ON N6G 1G5
Tel: 519-641-4025
londonmiddlesex.ogs.on.ca

London: Museum London
421 Ridout St. North, London, ON N6A 5H4
Tel: 519-661-0333; *Fax:* 519-661-2559
jcewan@museumlondon.ca
www.museumlondon.ca/
Janette Cousins Ewan, Art Registrar

London: The Royal Canadian Regiment Museum
Wolseley Hall, Wolseley Barracks, 701 Oxford St. East, London, ON N5Y 4T7
Fax: 519-660-5344
www.theroyalcanadianregiment.ca/thercrmuseum/index.html
Georgiana Stanciu, Director & Curator
519-660-5275 ext. 5015

London: University of Western Ontario Archives
Archives & Research Collections Centre, University of Western Ontario, 1151 Richmond St., London, ON N6A 3K7
Tel: 519-661-2111; *Fax:* 519-850-2979
www.lib.uwo.ca/archives

Midland: Huronia Museum
549 Little Lake Park, Midland, ON L4R 4P4
Tel: 705-526-2844; *Fax:* 705-527-6622
director@huroniamuseum.com
www.huroniamuseum.com
Jamie Hunter, Curator
Nicole Henderson, Collections Manager

Milton: Halton Region Museum
5181 Kelso Rd., RR#3, Milton, ON L9T 2X7
Tel: 905-875-2200; *Fax:* 905-876-4322
Toll-Free: 866-442-5866
museum@halton.ca
www.halton.ca/museum
Social Media: www.facebook.com/HaltonRegionMuseum
Michele Finn, Information Coordinator

Minesing: County of Simcoe
1149 Hwy. 26, RR#2, Minesing, ON L0L 1Y2
Tel: 705-726-9331; *Fax:* 705-725-5341
Toll-Free: 866-893-9300
archives@simcoe.ca
www.simcoe.ca/dpt/arc/index.htm
Bruce Beacock, County Archivist
bruce.beacock@simcoe.ca
Ellen Millar, Assistant Archivist
ellen.millar@simcoe.ca

Mississauga: Pentecostal Assemblies of Canada
2450 Milltower Ct., Mississauga, ON L5N 5Z6
Tel: 905-542-7400; *Fax:* 905-542-7313
archives@paoc.org
www.paoc.org/about/archives
Marilyn Stroud, Archivist
mstroud@paoc.org

Mitchell: Mitchell Branch
7D Frances St., Mitchell, ON N0K 1N0
Tel: 519-348-8817; *Fax:* 519-348-9805
mitchellarchives@pcin.on.ca
www.stratfordpertharchives.on.ca

Napanee: Lennox & Addington County Museum & Archives
97 Thomas St. East, Napanee, ON K7R 4B9
Tel: 613-354-3027; *Fax:* 613-354-1005
archives@lennox-addington.on.ca
lennox-addington.on.ca/museum-and-archives/overview
Jane Foster, Manager
nmuseum@lennox-addington.on.ca
613-354-3027 ext. 23
Shelley Respondek, Archivist
archives@lennox-addington.on.ca

Niagara on the Lake: Niagara Historical Research Centre
c/o Niagara on the Lake Public Library, 10 Anderson Lane, Niagara on the Lake, ON L0S 1J0
Tel: 905-468-2023; *Fax:* 905-468-3334
www.notlpubliclibrary.org/localhistory.php
Social Media: pinterest.com/notlpl; www.facebook.com/group.php?gid=210765253379
Cathy Simpson, Chief Executive Officer
csimpson@notl.org
Linda Gula, Head of Reference
historylinda@yahoo.ca
905-468-2023

Niagara on the Lake: Shaw Festival Theatre Foundation Library
PO Box 774, 10 Queen's Parade, Niagara on the Lake, ON L0S 1J0
Tel: 905-468-2153; *Fax:* 905-468-5438
Toll-Free: 800-657-1106
www.shawfest.com
Nancy Butler, Head Librarian

North Bay: Discovery North Bay Museum
100 Ferguson St., North Bay, ON P1B 1W8
Tel: 705-476-2323; *Fax:* 705-476-9300
info@heritagenorthbay.com
www.discoverynorthbay.weebly.com/index
Jennifer Bell, Director
education@heritagenorthbay.com

Rideau Archives Branch
6581 Fourth Line Rd., North Gower, ON K0A 2T0
Tel: 613-489-2926
rideauarchives@ottawa.ca
ottawa.ca/archives

North Gower: Rideau Archives Branch
6581 Fourth Line Rd., North Gower, ON K0A 2T0
Tel: 613-489-2926
rideauarchives@ottawa.ca
ottawa.ca/archives

North York: Toronto Catholic District School Board Archives and Record Management
80 Sheppard Ave. East, North York, ON M2N 6E8
Tel: 416-222-8282; *Fax:* 416-229-5345
www.tcdsb.org

Norwich: Norwich & District Historical Society
91 Stover St. North, RR#3, Norwich, ON N0J 1P0
Tel: 519-863-3638; *Fax:* 519-863-2343
norwichdhs@execulink.com
www.norwichdhs.ca
Mary Beth Start, Curator/Archivist
Janet Hilliker, Archivist

Oil Springs: Oil Museum of Canada
2324 Kelly Rd., Oil Springs, ON N0N 1P0
Tel: 519-834-2840; *Fax:* 519-834-2840
oil.museum@county-lambton.on.ca
www.lclmg.org/lclmg/Museums/tabid/53/Default.aspx
Connie Bell, Manager
connie.bell@county-lambton.on.ca

Orillia: Mariposa Folk Foundation
10 Peter St. South, Orillia, ON L3V 5A9
Tel: 705-326-3655; *Fax:* 705-326-5963
www.mariposafolk.com
Social Media: twitter.com/#!/mariposafolk; www.facebook.com/MariposaFolkFestivalOfficial
Paulette Kirkey, President

Orillia: Stephen Leacock Museum
50 Museum Dr., Orillia, ON L3V 7T9
Tel: 705-329-1908; *Fax:* 705-326-5578
Toll-Free: 705-326-5578
www.leacockmuseum.com
Craig Metcalf, Director

Oshawa: Oshawa Community Museum & Archives
1450 Simcoe St. South, Lakeview Park, Oshawa, ON L1H 8S8
Tel: 905-436-7624; *Fax:* 905-436-7625
info@oshawamuseum.org
www.oshawamuseum.org
Social Media: twitter.com/oshawamuseum; www.facebook.com/21181410334
Melissa Cole, Curator

Oshawa: Robert McLaughlin Gallery
Civic Centre, 72 Queen St., Oshawa, ON L1H 3Z3
Tel: 905-576-3000; *Fax:* 905-576-9774
communications@rmg.on.ca
www.rmg.on.ca
Social Media: www.youtube.com/RMGOshawa; twitter.com/theRMG; www.facebook.com/TheRMG
Barb Duff, Library Services Coordinator
bduff@rmg.on.ca
Linda Jansma, Curator
ljansma@rmg.on.ca
905-576-3000 ext. 111
Sonya Jones, Curatorial Assistant, Bouckley Photography Collection
sjones@rmg.on.ca
905-576-3000 ext. 110

Ottawa: Archives & Special Collections
#039, 65 University Private, Ottawa, ON K1N 6N5
Tel: 613-562-5910; *Fax:* 613-562-5133
www.biblio.uottawa.ca

Ottawa: Archives Deschâtelets
175, rue Main, Ottawa, ON K1S 1C3
Tel: 613-237-0580; *Fax:* 613-232-4064
ardescha@yahoo.ca

Ottawa: Bank of Canada Archives
234 Wellington St., Ottawa, ON K1A 0G9
Tel: 613-782-8673; *Fax:* 613-782-7387
archives@bankofcanada.ca
www.bankofcanada.ca/archives

Ottawa: Bytown Railway Society
PO Box 47076, Ottawa, ON K1B 5P9
Tel: 613-745-1201; *Fax:* 613-745-1201
info@bytownrailwaysociety.ca
www.bytownrailwaysociety.ca

Ottawa: C. Robert Craig Memorial Library
Ottawa City Archives, 100 Tallwood Dr., Ottawa, ON K2G 4R7
knowlesdc@bell.net
www.ovar.ca/CraigLibrary/craiglib.htm
Dave Knowles, President & Librarian

Ottawa: Canadian Institute of Geomatics/ Association canadienne des sciences géomatiques
#100D, 900 Dynes Rd., Ottawa, ON K2C 3L6
Tel: 613-224-9851; *Fax:* 613-224-9577
www.cig-acsg.ca
Carol E. Railer, Manager, Production & Advertising for Geomatica
editgeo@magma.ca

Ottawa: Canadian Intergovernmental Conference Secretariat/ Secrétariat des conférences intergouvernementales Canadiennes
222 Queen St., 10th Fl., Ottawa, ON K1P 5V9
Tel: 613-995-4310; *Fax:* 613-947-4336
info@scics.gc.ca
www.scics.gc.ca
Bernard Latulippe, Director,Information Management
613-995-4203
Jane Dubé, Head, Information Management

Ottawa: Canadian Ski Hall of Fame & Museum
#9, 2420 Bank St., Ottawa, ON K1V 8S1
Tel: 613-722-3584
info@skimuseum.ca
www.skimuseum.ca
Social Media: www.facebook.com/pages/Canadian-Ski-Museum/59397511258
Ivo Krupka, Chair
Don Runge, Director, Publications

Ottawa: Canadian Women's Movement Archives/ Archives canadiennes du mouvement des femmes
Archives Special Collections, Morisset Hall, University of Ottawa, #039, 65 University Pvt, Ottawa, ON K1N 6N5
Tel: 613-562-5213
referenc@uottawa.ca
www.biblio.uottawa.ca
Lucie Desjardins, Archivist

Ottawa: Centre de recherche en histoire religieuse du Canada/ Research Centre in Religious History of Canada
Saint Paul University, 223 Main St., Ottawa, ON K1S 1C4
Tél: 613-236-1393; *Téléc:* 613-782-3005
Ligne sans frais: 800-637-6859
crh-rc-rhc@ustpaul.ca
www.ustpaul.ca
Pierre Hurtubise, Directeur

Ottawa: City of Ottawa Archives/ Archives municipales d'Ottawa
100 Tallwood Dr., Ottawa, ON K2G 4R7
Tel: 613-580-2857; *Fax:* 613-580-2614
archives@ottawa.ca
ottawa.ca/archives
Serge Barbe, City Archivist
serge.barbe@ottawa.ca
613-580-2424 ext. 13683

Ottawa: Diocese of Ottawa, Archives
71 Bronson Ave., Ottawa, ON K1R 6G6
Tel: 613-232-7126; *Fax:* 613-232-7088
archives@ottawa.anglican.ca
www.ottawa.anglican.ca/Archives

Ottawa: Eastern Ontario Chapter (EOC)
c/o John Lund and Theresa Sorel, City of Ottawa Archives, City of Ottawa, 200 Laurier Ave. West, Ottawa, ON K1P 1J1
www.aao-archivists.ca

Ottawa: Friends of Library & Archives Canada
395 Wellington St., Ottawa, ON K1A 0N4
Tel: 613-992-8304; *Fax:* 613-943-2343
Other Numbers: 813-943-1544
friends.amis@lac-bac.gc.ca
www.friendsoflibraryandarchivescanada.ca
Daniel J. Caron, Librarian and Archivist of Canada
Marianne Scott, President

Ottawa: Montréal & Ottawa Conference, Archives
c/o City of Ottawa Archives, 100 Tallwood Dr., Ottawa, ON K2G 4R7
Tel: 613-580-2424; *Fax:* 613-580-2614
archives@ottawa.ca
www.montrealandottawaconference.ca

Ottawa: National Archival Appraisal Board/ Conseil national d'évaluation des archives
c/o CCA, #501, 130 Albert St., Ottawa, ON K1P 5G4
Tel: 613-565-1222; *Fax:* 613-565-5445
Toll-Free: 866-254-1403
naab@archivescanada.ca
www.naab.ca
Louise Pilon, Administrator
lpilon@archives.ca

Ottawa: Oblats de Marie Immaculée
175 Main St., Ottawa, ON K1S 1C3
Tél: 613-237-0580; *Téléc:* 613-237-4064
ardescha@yahoo.ca
Andre Dubois, Archiviste
ardescha@yahoo.ca
Gérard Landreville, Autre personnel
Luc Fortin, Autre personnel

Ottawa: Ottawa Jewish Archives
21 Nadolny Sachs Private Lane, Ottawa, ON K2A 1R9
Tel: 613-798-4696; *Fax:* 613-798-4695
archives@jewishottawa.com
www.jewishottawa.com
Social Media: www.facebook.com/JFedOttawa
Laurie Dougherty, Archivist
ldougherty@jewishottawa.com

Ottawa: Parent Finders of Canada & Parent Finders of Ottawa
PO Box 21025, Ottawa South Postal Outlet, Ottawa, ON K1S 5N1
Tel: 613-730-8305; *Fax:* 613-730-0345
pfncr@yahoo.com
www.parentfindersottawa.ca
Patricia McCarron, President

Ottawa: Roman Catholic Archdiocese of Ottawa/ Corporation Episcopale Catholique Romaine d'Ottawa
1247 Kilborn Pl., Ottawa, ON K1H 6K9
Tel: 613-738-5025; *Fax:* 613-738-0130
archottawa.ca
Eugene Margeson, Archivist
emargeson@archottawa.ca

Ottawa: The Royal College of Physicians & Surgeons of Canada
774 Echo Dr., Ottawa, ON K1S 5N8
Tel: 613-730-8177; *Fax:* 613-730-2410
Toll-Free: 800-668-3740
archives@royalcollege.ca
www.royalcollege.ca/public
Tammi Pettigrew, Administrator Library/Archives/Central Records

Ottawa: St. Paul University Archives
175, rue Main, Ottawa, ON K1S 1C3
Tél: 613-237-0580; *Téléc:* 613-232-4064
archives@ustpaul.ca

Ottawa: Scouts Canada
1345 Baseline Rd., Ottawa, ON K2C 0A7
Tel: 613-224-5131; *Fax:* 613-224-3571
Toll-Free: 888-855-3336
helpcentre@scouts.ca
www.scouts.ca

Wilfred H. Bradley Reference Library
71 Bronson Ave., Ottawa, ON K1R 6G6
Tel: 613-232-7124; *Fax:* 613-232-7088
archives@ottawa.anglican.ca
www.ottawa.anglican.ca/Archives
Glenn J. Lockwood, Archivist

Ottawa: Wilfred H. Bradley Reference Library
71 Bronson Ave., Ottawa, ON K1R 6G6
Tel: 613-232-7124; *Fax:* 613-232-7088
archives@ottawa.anglican.ca
www.ottawa.anglican.ca/Archives

Owen Sound: Grey Roots Museum & Archives
102599 Grey Rd. 18, RR#4, Owen Sound, ON N4K 5N6
Tel: 519-376-3690; *Fax:* 519-376-4654
Toll-Free: 877-473-9766
info@greyroots.com
www.greyroots.com/collections-research
Karin Noble, Archivist
karin.noble@greyroots.com
Kate Jackson, Assistant Archivist
kate.jackson@greyroots.com

Pembroke: Grey Sisters of the Immaculate Conception
Marguerite Centre, 700 MacKay St., Pembroke, ON K8A 1G6
Tel: 613-732-9916; *Fax:* 613-735-2048
Jacquelyn Wolgemuth, Head Librarian

Perth: The Perth Museum & Archives
11 Gore St. East, Perth, ON K7H 1H4
Tel: 613-267-1947; *Fax:* 613-267-5635
www.town.perth.on.ca
Karen Rennie, Heritage Manager/Curator
Debbie Sproule, Recording Secretary

Peterborough: Peterborough Museum & Archives
Ashburnham Memorial Park, 300 Hunter Hunter St. East, Peterborough, ON K9H 6Y5
Tel: 705-743-5180; *Fax:* 705-743-2614
archives@peterboroughmuseumandarchives.ca
www.peterboroughmuseumandarchives.ca
Social Media: www.facebook.com/pages/Peterborough-Museum-Archives/112608310308
Mary Charles, City Archivist

Peterborough: Trent University Archives
Bata Library, Symons Campus, 1600 West Bank Dr., 1st Fl., Peterborough, ON K9J 7B8
Tel: 705-748-1011
archives@trentu.ca
www.trentu.ca/library/archives

Prescott: Grenville County Historical Society
500 Railway Ave., Prescott, ON K0E 1T0
Tel: 613-925-0489
gchs@ripnet.com
web.ripnet.com/~gchs
Bonnie Gaylord, Research Chair

Sault Ste Marie: Sault Ste Marie & 49th Field Regiment R.C.A. Historical Society, Sault Ste Marie Museum
690 Queen St. East, Sault Ste Marie, ON P6A 2A4
Tel: 705-759-7278; *Fax:* 705-759-3058
heritage@saultmuseum.com
www.saultmuseum.com
Kim Forbes, Curator & Director

Simcoe: Norfolk Historical Society
109 Norfolk St. South, Simcoe, ON N3Y 2W3
Tel: 519-426-1583; *Fax:* 519-426-1584
office@norfolklore.com
www.norfolklore.com
Scott Gillies, Curator

Southampton: Bruce County Museum & Cultural Centre
33 Victoria St. North, Southampton, ON N0H 2L0
Tel: 519-797-2080; *Fax:* 519-797-2191
Toll-Free: 866-318-8889
archives@brucecounty.on.ca
www.brucemuseum.ca
Barbara Ribey, Director & Curator
bribey@brucecounty.on.ca
519-797-2080 ext. 110
Ann-Marie Collins, Archivist
acollins@brucecounty.on.ca
519-797-2080 ext. 114
Lisa Luscombe, Collections Assistant
lluscombe@brucecounty.on.ca
519-797-2080
Susan Schlorff, Archival Assistant
sschlorff@brucecounty.on.ca
519-797-2080 ext. 129
Deb Sturdevant, Archival Assistant
dsturdevant@brucecounty.on.ca
519-797-2080

St Catharines: Niagara Peninsula Branch Library
PO Box 2224, St Catharines, ON L2M 7R8
www.ogs.on.ca/niagara/default.htm

St Catharines: St Catharines Museum at Lock 3
1932 Welland Canals Pkwy., St Catharines, ON L2R 7K6
Tel: 905-984-8880; *Fax:* 905-984-6910
Toll-Free: 800-305-5134
TTY: 9056884889
museum@stcatharines.ca
www.stcatharines.ca
Social Media: twitter.com/stcmuseum; www.facebook.com/stcatharinesmuseum
Kathleen Powell, Supervisor & Curator
kpowell@stcatharines.ca
905-688-5601 ext. 5250

St Catharines: Special Collections & Archives
James A. Gibson Library, Brock University, 500 Glenridge Ave., 10th Fl., St Catharines, ON L2S 3A1
Tel: 905-688-5550; *Fax:* 905-988-5490
libspcl@brocku.ca
www.brocku.ca/library/collections/special-collections-archives

Stratford: Stratford Shakespeare Festival
350 Douro St., Stratford, ON N5A 3ST
Tel: 519-271-0055; *Fax:* 519-271-1040
Toll-Free: 800-561-1233
www.stratfordfestival.ca
Social Media: www.flickr.com/photos/48668126@N07/; twitter.com/stratfest; www.facebook.com/StratfordFestival
Francesca Marini, Archives Director
fmarini@stratfordshakespearefestival.com
519-271-0055 ext. 4301
Beth Knazook, Photo Archivist
eknazook@stratfordshakespearefestival.com
519-271-0055 ext. 4311
Christine Schindler, Coordinator, Archives
cschindler@stratfordshakespearefestival.com
519-271-0055 ext. 4328
Nora Polley, Archives Assistant
npolley@stratfordshakespearefestival.com
519-271-0055 ext. 4315

Stratford: Stratford-Perth Archives
24 St Andrew St., Stratford, ON N5A 1A3
Tel: 519-271-0531; *Fax:* 519-273-5746
sparchives@perthcounty.ca
www.stratfordpertharchives.on.ca
Betty Jo Belton, Archivist
519-271-0531 ext. 250

Sudbury: Diocese of Moosonee, Archives
J.N. Desmarais Library, Laurentian University, 935 Ramsey Lake Rd., Sudbury, ON P3E 2C6
Tel: 705-675-1151; *Fax:* 705-675-4877
archives@laurentian.ca
www.laurentian.ca/library

***Teeterville:* Teeterville Pioneer Museum**
194 Teeter St., Teeterville, ON N0E 1S0
Tel: 519-426-5870; *Fax:* 519-428-3069
Other Numbers: Summer Hours, Phone: 519-443-4400
teeterville.museum@norfolkcounty.ca
www.teetervillemuseum.ca
Social Media: www.facebook.com/teetervillemuseum
Judy A. Livingstone, Curator & Director

***Thunder Bay:* City of Thunder Bay**
235 Vickers St. North, Thunder Bay, ON
Tel: 807-625-2270; *Fax:* 807-622-4212
archives@thunderbay.ca
www.thunderbay.ca
Matt Szybalski, Manager, Corporate Records & City Archivist
807-625-3390

***Thunder Bay:* Northwestern Ontario Sports Hall of Fame**
219 May St. South, Thunder Bay, ON P7E 1B5
Tel: 807-622-2852; *Fax:* 807-622-2736
nwosport@tbaytel.net
www.nwosportshalloffame.com
Social Media: www.youtube.com/user/nwosport;
www.facebook.com/259816551287
Diane Imrie, Executive Director
Kathryn Dwyer, Curator

***Thunder Bay:* Thunder Bay Historical Museum**
425 Donald St. East, Thunder Bay, ON P7E 5V1
Tel: 807-623-0801; *Fax:* 807-622-6880
info@thunderbaymuseum.com
www.thunderbaymuseum.com
Thorold Tronrud, Curator

***Toronto:* Anglican General Synod Archives**
80 Hayden St., Toronto, ON M4Y 3G2
Tel: 416-924-9199; *Fax:* 416-968-7983
archives@national.anglican.ca
www.anglican.ca/resources/gsarchives
Nancy Hurn, Librarian

***Toronto:* Archives of Ontario**
134 Ian Macdonald Blvd., Toronto, ON M7A 2C5
Tel: 416-327-1600; *Fax:* 416-327-1999
Toll-Free: 800-668-9933
reference@ontario.ca
www.archives.gov.on.ca
Miriam McTiernan, Archivist of Ontario
miriam.mctiernan@ontario.ca
416-327-1602
Michael Johnson, Director, Archives Management & Information Storage
michael.johnson1@ontario.ca
416-327-1577

***Toronto:* Art Gallery of Ontario/ Musée des beaux-arts de l'Ontario**
317 Dundas St. West, Toronto, ON M5T 1G4
Tel: 416-979-6642; *Fax:* 416-979-6602
library_archives@ago.net
www.ago.net
Social Media: twitter.com/agotoronto;
www.facebook.com/AGOToronto
Karen McKenzie, Chief Librarian
karen_mckenzie@ago.net

***Toronto:* Arts & Letters Club**
14 Elm St., Toronto, ON M5G 1G7
Tel: 416-597-0223; *Fax:* 416-597-9544
info@artsandlettersclub.ca
www.artsandlettersclub.ca
Scott James, Archivist

***Toronto:* Bergendal Collection of Mediaeval Manuscripts**
15 Duncan St., Toronto, ON M5H 3P9
Tel: 416-925-8044; *Fax:* 416-925-3631
bergendalcoll@sympatico.ca
www3.sympatico.ca/bergendalcoll
Joseph Pope, Curator

***Toronto:* Brothers of the Christian Schools Archives**
131 Farnham Ave., Toronto, ON M4V 1H7
Tel: 416-929-7878; *Fax:* 416-929-1277
wfarrell@rogers.com
Walter Farrell, F.S.C., Archivist
wfarrell@rogers.com

***Toronto:* Burgee Data Archives**
117 Airdrie Rd., Toronto, ON M4G 1M6
Tel: 416-423-9979; *Fax:* 416-423-9979
Peter B. Edwards, Director

***Toronto:* Canadian Children's Book Centre**
#217, 40 Orchard View Blvd., Toronto, ON M4R 1B9
Tel: 416-975-0010; *Fax:* 416-975-8970
info@bookcentre.ca
www.bookcentre.ca/library
Charlotte Teeple, Executive Director
charlotte@bookcentre.ca
Meghan Howe, Library Coordinator
meghan@bookcentre.ca

***Toronto:* Canadian Lesbian & Gay Archives**
34 Isabella St., Toronto, ON M4Y 1N1
Tel: 416-777-2755
queeries@clga.ca
www.clga.ca
Social Media: twitter.com/clgarchives;
www.facebook.com/CLGArchives
Robert Windrum, President

***Toronto:* Canadian Opera Company/ La compagnie d'opéra canadienne**
227 Front St. East, Toronto, ON M5A 1E8
Tel: 416-306-2328; *Fax:* 416-363-5584
info@coc.ca
www.coc.ca
Social Media: twitter.com/canadianopera;
www.facebook.com/canadianoperacompany
Birthe Joergensen, Archivist
birthej@coc.ca

***Toronto:* Canadian Royal Heritage Trust**
Fealty Heritage Centre, #206A, 3050 Yonge St., Toronto, ON M4N 2K4
Tel: 416-482-4909; *Fax:* 416-544-8082
kg3library@crht.ca
www.crht.ca/Resources

***Toronto:* City of Toronto Archives**
255 Spadina Rd., Toronto, ON M5R 2V3
Tel: 416-397-0778; *Fax:* 416-392-9685
archives@toronto.ca
www.toronto.ca/archives

***Toronto:* Clara Thomas Archives & Special Collections**
#305, Scott Library, 4700 Keele St., Toronto, ON M3J 1P3
Tel: 416-736-5442; *Fax:* 416-650-8039
archives@yorku.ca
www.library.yorku.ca/cms/archivesspecialcollections

***Toronto:* College of Physicians & Surgeons of Ontario**
80 College St., Toronto, ON M5G 2E2
Tel: 416-967-2600; *Fax:* 416-961-3330
Toll-Free: 800-268-7096
feedback@cpso.on.ca
www.cpso.on.ca

***Toronto:* Digital Archives**
c/o CBC Digital Archives Website, PO Box 500, Stn A, Toronto, ON M5V 1E6
Toll-Free: 866-306-4636
TTY: 8662206045
archives@cbc.ca
www.cbc.ca/archives

***Toronto:* Diocese of Toronto, Archives**
135 Adelaide St. East, Toronto, ON M5C 1L8
Tel: 416-363-6021; *Fax:* 416-363-7678
Toll-Free: 800-668-8932
manicholls@toronto.anglican.ca
www.toronto.anglican.ca

***Toronto:* Diocese of Toronto, St James' Cathedral Archives**
65 Church St., Toronto, ON M5C 2E9
Tel: 416-364-7865
archives@stjamescathedral.on.ca
www.stjamescathedral.on.ca

***Toronto:* Etobicoke Historical Society**
c/o Montgomery's Inn, 4709 Dundas St. West, Toronto, ON M9A 1A8
www.etobicokehistorical.com
Denise Harris, President
denise.harris@sympatico.ca
Robert Given, Historian Emeritus

***Toronto:* Exhibition Place**
200 Princes' Blvd., Toronto, ON M6K 3C3
Tel: 416-263-3600
info@explace.on.ca
www.explace.on.ca
Social Media: twitter.com/explaceTO;
www.facebook.com/pages/Exhibition-Place/159377337482707
Linda Cobon, Manager, Records & Archives

***Toronto:* The Film Reference Library**
TIFF Bell Lightbox, 350 King St. West, Toronto, ON M5V 3X5
Tel: 416-967-1517; *Fax:* 416-967-0628
www.tiff.net/filmreferencelibrary
Sylvia Frank, Director
Eve Goldin, Library Manager
egoldin@tiffg.ca

***Toronto:* General Archives of the Basilian Fathers**
95 St Joseph St., Toronto, ON M5S 2R9
Tel: 416-921-7861; *Fax:* 416-921-8357
archives@basilian.org
www.basilian.org
James E. Rent, CSB, Archivist

***Toronto:* George Brown College Archives**
Casa Loma Campus, #F-103, 500 MacPherson Ave., Toronto, ON M5R 1X1
Tel: 416-415-5000; *Fax:* 416-415-4772
archives.georgebrown.ca

***Toronto:* Hockey Hall of Fame**
400 Kipling Ave., Toronto, ON M8V 3L1
Tel: 416-360-7735; *Fax:* 416-251-5770
acquisitions@hhof.com
www.hhof.com/html/ResCentre/rc00
Miragh Bitove, Archivist & Collections Registrar
mbitove@hhof.com
Craig Campbell, Manager, Resource Centre & Archives
campbellc@hhof.com
Steve Poiner, Coordinator, HHOF Images & Archival Services
Spoiner@hhof.com
Izak Westgate, Manager, Outreach Exhibits & Assistant Curator
Iwestgate@hhof.com

***Toronto:* Holy Blossom Temple**
1950 Bathurst St., Toronto, ON M5P 3K9
Tel: 416-789-3291
www.holyblossom.org
Social Media:
www.facebook.com/pages/Holy-Blosson-Temple/98017462501
David Hart, Archivist
Sheila Smolkin, Archivist

***Toronto:* Institute of the Blessed Virgin Mary in North America (Loretto Sisters)**
101 Mason Blvd., Toronto, ON M5M 3E2
Tel: 416-487-5543; *Fax:* 416-485-9884
ibvmadm@rogers.com
www.ibvm.ca/
Juliana Dusel, IBVM, Archivist

***Toronto:* King Louis XIV Memorial Archives**
Fealty Heritage Centre, #206A, 3050 Yonge St., Toronto, ON M4N 2K4
Tel: 416-482-4909; *Fax:* 416-544-8082
archives@crht.ca

***Toronto:* Montgomery's Inn Museum**
4709 Dundas St. West, Toronto, ON M9A 1A8
Tel: 416-394-8113; *Fax:* 416-394-6027
Randall Reid, Program Director

***Toronto:* Multicultural History Society of Ontario**
John M. Kelly Library, St. Michael's College, University of Toronto, 113 St. Joseph's St., 1st Fl., Toronto, ON M5S 3C2
mhso.mail@utoronto.ca
www.mhso.ca
Pasang Thackchhoe, Contact

***Toronto:* National Ballet of Canada/ Ballet national du Canada**
470 Queens Quay West, Toronto, ON M5V 3K4
Tel: 416-345-9686; *Fax:* 416-345-8323
anevile@national.ballet.ca
www.national.ballet.ca/thecompany/archives/
Adrienne Nevile, Archives Coordinator

***Toronto:* Ontario Genealogical Society**
Gladys Allison Canadiana Rm., North York Central Library, 6th Fl., 5120 Yonge St., Toronto, ON M2N 5N9
Tel: 416-395-5623; *Fax:* 416-489-9803
lchester@ogs.on.ca
www.ogs.on.ca

L.A. Chester, Chair
V. Lynham, Technician

***Toronto:* The Ontario Jewish Archives**
Sherman Campus, UJA Federation of Greater Toronto, 4600 Bathurst St., Toronto, ON M2R 3V2
Tel: 416-635-2883; *Fax:* 416-849-1006
oja1@ujafed.org
www.ontariojewisharchives.org
Dora Solomon, Director
Melissa Caza, Archivist
George Wharton, Archivist
Donna Bernardo-Ceriz, Assistant Archivist

***Toronto:* The Presbyterian Church in Canada**
50 Wynford Dr., Toronto, ON M3C 1J7
Tel: 416-441-1111; *Toll-Free:* 800-619-7301
a
www.presbyterianarchives.ca
Kim Arnold, Archivist & Records Administrator
karnold@presbyterian.ca
416-441-1111 ext. 310
Bob Anger, Assistant Archivist
bangar@presbyterian.ca
416-441-1111 ext. 266

***Toronto:* Queen's Own Rifles of Canada Regimental Museum**
c/o Casa Loma, 1 Austin Terrace, Toronto, ON M5R 1X8
qorassociationtoronto@gmail.com
www.qor.com/social/museum.html
Peter A. Sigmundson, Curator
Capt. P.A. Simundson

***Toronto:* Queen's York Rangers (1st American Regiment) Museum**
CFA Fort York, 660 Fleet St. West, Toronto, ON M5V 1A9
Tel: 416-203-4600
rhq@qyrang.ca
www.qyrang.ca
Diane Kruger, Curator
rhq@qyrang.org

***Toronto:* Reuben & Helene Dennis Museum**
1700 Bathurst St., Toronto, ON M5P 3K3
Tel: 416-781-3514; *Fax:* 416-781-0150
museum@beth-tzedec.org
www.beth-tzedec.org/museum/

***Toronto:* Roman Catholic Archdiocese of Toronto**
Catholic Pastoral Centre, #505, 1155 Yonge St., Toronto, ON M4T 1W2
Tel: 416-934-3400; *Fax:* 416-934-3444
archives@archtoronto.org
www.archtoronto.org/archives
Marc Lerman, Archivist
mlerman@archtoronto.org
416-934-3400 ext. 505

***Toronto:* The Royal Canadian Yacht Club**
141 St George St., Toronto, ON M5R 2L8
Tel: 416-967-7245; *Fax:* 416-967-5710
heritage@rcyc.ca
www.rcyc.ca
Sylvia Parsons, Receptionist
switchboard@rcyc.ca
416-967-7245

***Toronto:* St John's Rehabilitation Hospital**
c/o Administration, 285 Cummer Ave., Toronto, ON M2M 2G1
Tel: 416-226-6780; *Fax:* 416-226-6265
www.stjohnsrehab.com

***Toronto:* St Joseph's Health Centre (Toronto) Archives**
30 The Queensway, Toronto, ON M6R 1B5
Tel: 416-530-6389; *Fax:* 416-530-6836

***Toronto:* The Salvation Army**
26 Howden Rd., Toronto, ON M1R 3E4
Tel: 416-285-4344; *Fax:* 416-285-7763
heritage_centre@can.salvationarmy.org
www.salvationist.ca/about-us/history/museum-archives
Social Media: twitter.com/salvationist
John Carew, Director
David Pitcher, Coordinator, Research

***Toronto:* Scarboro Mission Society**
2685 Kingston Rd., Toronto, ON M1M 1M4
Tel: 416-261-7135; *Fax:* 416-261-0820
Toll-Free: 800-260-4815
info@scarboromissions.ca
www.scarboromissions.ca
John Carten, Councillor
jcarten@scarboromissions.ca

***Toronto:* Scarborough Historical Society**
6282 Kingston Rd., Toronto, ON M1C 1K9
Tel: 416-995-6930; *Fax:* 416-282-9482
www.scarboroughhistorical.com/archives
Richard Schofield, Archivist

***Toronto:* Scotiabank Group Archives & Fine Art Department**
44 King St. West, 19th Fl. East, Toronto, ON M5H 1H1
archives@scotiabank.com
www.scotiabank.com/ca/en/0,,467,00

***Toronto:* Sculptors Society of Canada/ La Société des sculpteurs du Canada**
500 Church St., Toronto, ON M4Y 2C8
Tel: 647-435-5858
gallery@cansculpt.org
www.cansculpt.org
Karen Stoskopf Harding, Archivist

***Toronto:* Sesquicentennial Museum & Archives**
263 McCaul St., Toronto, ON M5T 1W7
Tel: 416-397-3680; *Fax:* 416-397-3685
greg.mckinnon@tdsb.on.ca

***Toronto:* The Sisterhood of St. John the Divine Convent**
233 Cummer Ave., Toronto, ON M2M 2E8
Tel: 416-226-2201; *Fax:* 416-226-2131
convent@ssjd.ca
www.ssjd.ca/convent.html
Joyce Bodley, Contact

***Toronto:* Sisters of St. Joseph of Toronto**
101 Thorncliffe Park Dr., Toronto, ON M4H 1M2
Tel: 416-467-8070; *Fax:* 416-429-7921
info@csj-to.ca
www.csj-to.ca
Linda Wicks, Archivist

***Toronto:* Sisters Servants of Mary Immaculate**
5 Austin Terrace, Toronto, ON M5R 1Y1
Tel: 416-924-7422; *Fax:* 416-928-9261
ssmi.org@rogers.com
www.ssmi.org
Frances Byblow, Contact

***Toronto:* Tartu Institute**
300 Bloor St. West, Toronto, ON M5B 1W4
vemu@tartucollege.ca
www.tartuinstitute.ca
Piret Noorhani, Head Archivist
piret@tartucollege.ca
416-925-9405
Roland Weiler, Archivist
rweiler7@cogeco.ca
905-627-3856

***Toronto:* Todmorden Mills Heritage Museum & Art Centre**
67 Pottery Rd., Toronto, ON M4K 2B9
Tel: 416-396-2819
todmorden@toronto.ca
www.toronto.ca/culture/museums/todmorden.htm

***Toronto:* Toronto Port Authority**
60 Harbour St., Toronto, ON M5J 1B7
Tel: 416-863-2011; *Fax:* 416-863-4830
www.torontoport.com/corporate_archives.asp?id=37

***Toronto:* The Toronto Sun**
333 King St. East, Toronto, ON M5A 3X5
Tel: 416-947-2258
research@sunmedia.ca
www.torontosun.com
Julie Kirsh, Director, Electronic Information & News Research

***Toronto:* Toronto Symphony Orchestra**
212 King St. West, 6th Fl., Toronto, ON M5H 1K5
Tel: 416-593-7769; *Fax:* 416-977-2912
archives@tso.ca
www.tso.ca
Social Media: twitter.com/TorontoSymphony; www.facebook.com/pages/Toronto-Symphony-Orchestra/52219459772
John Dunn, Volunteer Archivist

***Toronto:* Toronto-Dominion Bank Archives Department**
#1704, 110 Yonge St., Toronto, ON M5C 1T4
Tel: 416-982-8848; *Fax:* 416-499-6609

***Toronto:* United Church of Canada Archives**
3250 Bloor St. West, Toronto, ON M8X 2Y4
Tel: 416-231-7680; *Fax:* 416-231-3103
Toll-Free: 800-268-3781
archives@united-church.ca
www.united-church.ca/local/archives/on
Social Media: www.facebook.com/UnitedChurchCda
Sharon P. Larade, Chief Archivist

***Toronto:* University of Toronto, Archives & Records Management Services**
Thomas Fisher Rare Book Library, 120 St George St., 4th Fl., Toronto, ON M5S 1A5
Tel: 416-978-5344; *Fax:* 416-946-5343
utarms@list.library.utoronto.ca
utarms.library.utoronto.ca

***Toronto:* University of Toronto, Trinity College**
6 Hoskin Ave., Toronto, ON M5S 1H8
Tel: 416-978-2019; *Fax:* 416-978-2797
archives@trinity.utoronto.ca
www.trinity.utoronto.ca/Library_Archives/Archives

***Toronto:* University of Toronto, University College**
Humphrey Milnes Rm., Laidlaw Wing, 15 King's College Circle, Toronto, ON M5S 3H7
Tel: 416-978-8154; *Fax:* 416-971-2059

***Toronto:* Upper Canada College Archives**
200 Lonsdale Rd., Toronto, ON M4V 1W6
Tel: 416-488-1125; *Fax:* 416-484-8612
www.ucc.on.ca
Jill M.D. Spellman, Archivist
jspellman@ucc.on.ca

***Toronto:* Weston Historical Society**
1901 Weston Rd., Toronto, ON M9N 3P1
Tel: 416-249-6663; *Fax:* 416-241-2299
westonhistoricalsociety@rogers.com
www.welcometoweston.ca
Mary Lou Ashbourne, President
mashbour@idirect.com
416-247-4354
Eva Ferguson, Contact
fergusone@rogers.com
416-235-0845

***Toronto:* York Pioneer & Historical Society**
2482 Yonge St., Toronto, ON M4P 3E3
Tel: 416-483-0907
yorkpioneers@gmail.com
www.yorkpioneers.org
John Marshall, Archivist

***Tweed:* Tweed & Area Heritage Centre**
40 Victoria St. North, Tweed, ON K0K 3J0
Tel: 613-478-3989; *Fax:* 613-478-6457
tweedheritageinfo@on.aibn.com
www.ruralroutes.com/tweedhistoricalsociety
Evan Morton, Curator

***Uxbridge:* Uxbridge Historical Centre**
7239 Concession 6, Uxbridge, ON L9P 1N5
Tel: 905-852-5854; *Fax:* 905-852-5854
museum@town.uxbridge.on.ca
www.uxlib.com/museum
Social Media: twitter.com/#%21/UxbridgeMuseum; www.facebook.com/uxbridgehistoricalcentre
Allan McGillivray, Curator
museum@town.uxbridge.on.ca
905-852-5854

***Vaughan:* City of Vaughan Archives**
City Hall, Main Fl., 2141 Major Mackenzie Dr., Vaughan, ON L6A 1T1
Tel: 905-832-2281
archives@city.vaughan.on.ca
www.city.vaughan.on.ca/culture_recreation/archives/index.cfm

***Vernon:* Osgoode Township Historical Society & Museum**
7814 Lawrence St., Vernon, ON K0A 3J0
Tel: 613-821-4062; *Fax:* 613-821-3140
oths@magma.ca
osgoodemuseum.ca
Social Media: twitter.com/osgoodemuseum; www.facebook.com/125725207465630
Robin Cushnie, Museum Manager
manager@osgoodemuseum.ca
Ann Robinson, Administrator
administration@osgoodemuseum.ca

***Waterford:* The Waterford & Townsend Historical Society**
Spruce Row Museum, 159 Nichol St., Waterford, ON N0E 1Y0
Tel: 519-443-4211; *Fax:* 519-443-5640
sprucerow.museum@norfolkcounty.on.ca
www.wths.weebly.com/index

***Waterloo:* Evangelical Lutheran Church in Canada**
75 University Ave. West, Waterloo, ON N2J 3C5
Tel: 519-884-1970
erichrwschultz@aol.com
www.easternsynod.org

***Waterloo:* Mennonite Archives of Ontario**
Conrad Grebel University College, 140 Westmount, Rd. North, Waterloo, ON N2L 3G6
Tel: 519-885-0220; *Fax:* 519-885-0014
marchive@uwaterloo.ca
grebel.uwaterloo.ca/mao/index
Sam Steiner, Librarian & Archivist
steiner@library.uwaterloo.ca

***Waterloo:* Special Collections & Archives**
Dana Porter Library, 200 University Ave. West, Waterloo, ON N2L 3G1
Tel: 519-888-4567; *Fax:* 519-888-4322
www.lib.uwaterloo.ca/discipline/SpecColl/Special1.html

***Waterloo:* Wilfrid Laurier University Archives**
75 University Ave. West, 1st Fl., Waterloo, ON N2L 3C5
Tel: 519-884-0710; *Fax:* 519-884-8023
www.library.wlu.ca/libinfo/dept/spar.html

***Wellington:* Prince Edward County Archives**
261 Main St., Wellington, ON K0K 3L0
Tel: 613-399-2023
archives@peclibrary.org
www.peclibrary.org/pecarchivess31.php
Krista Richardson, Archives Manager, County of Prince Edward Archives

***Whitby:* Town of Whitby Archives**
c/o Whitby Public Library, 405 Dundas St., Whitby, ON L1N 6A1
Tel: 905-668-6531; *Fax:* 905-668-7445
archives@whitbylibrary.on.ca
www.whitbylibrary.on.ca
Social Media: www.flickr.com/people/whitbyarchives
Brian Winter, Archivist

Whitby Archives
405 Dundas St.West, Whitby, ON L1N 6A1
Tel: 905-668-6531; *Fax:* 905-668-7445
archives@whitbylibrary.on.ca
www.whitbylibrary.on.ca/archives
Social Media: www.flickr.com/photos/whitbyarchives
Brian Winter, Town Archivist

***Whitby:* Whitby Archives**
405 Dundas St.West, Whitby, ON L1N 6A1
Tel: 905-668-6531; *Fax:* 905-668-7445
archives@whitbylibrary.on.ca
www.whitbylibrary.on.ca/archives

***Windsor:* Assumption University Archives**
400 Huron Church Rd., Windsor, ON N9C 2J9
Tel: 519-973-7033; *Fax:* 519-973-7089
info@assumptionu.ca
www.assumptionu.ca
Cécile Bertrand, Secretary to the President
cbertrand@assumptionu.ca

***Windsor:* Serbian Heritage Museum**
6770 Tecumseh Rd. East, Windsor, ON N8T 1E6
Tel: 519-944-4884; *Fax:* 519-974-3963
members.tripod.com/swo_heritage/serbian.htm

***Windsor:* Windsor's Community Museum/ Le Musée communautaire de Windsor**
François Baby House, 254 Pitt St. West, Windsor, ON N9A 5L5
Tel: 519-253-1812; *Fax:* 519-253-0919
wmuseum@city.windsor.on.ca
www.citywindsor.ca
Hugh Barrett, Coordinator, Education & Volunteers
hbarrett@city.windsor.on.ca

Prince Edward Island

Regional Systems

Prince Edward Island Public Library Service
89 Red Head Rd., Morell, PE C0A 1S0
Tel: 902-961-7320; *Fax:* 902-961-7322
plshq@gov.pe.ca
www.library.pe.ca
Social Media: twitter.com/#!/PEILibrary; www.facebook.com/PEILibrary
Kathleen Eaton, Provincial Librarian
keeaton@gov.pe.ca
Gary Ramsay, Reference Librarian
gwramsay@gov.pe.ca
902-368-4643
Liam O'Hare, Systems Librarian
lfohare@gov.pe.ca
902-961-7322
Barbara Kissick, Youth Services Librarian
bjkissick@gov.pe.ca
902-368-4641
Nichola Cleaveland, Government Services Librarian
nacleave@gov.pe.ca
902-398-4653

Public Libraries

***Abram-Village:* Bibliothèque publique d'Abram-Village**
a/s École Évangéline, RR#3, Abram-Village, PE C0B 2E0
Tél: 902-854-7268; *Téléc:* 902-854-2981
abram@gov.pe.ca
www.library.pe.ca
Doris Arsenault, Branch Library Technician

***Alberton:* Alberton Public Library**
460 Main St., Alberton, PE C0B 1B0
Tel: 902-853-3049
alberton@gov.pe.ca
www.library.pe.ca
Kelly Gillis, Branch Library Technician

***Borden:* Borden-Carleton Public Library**
244 Borden Ave., Borden, PE C0B 1X0
Tel: 902-437-6492
borden-carleton@gov.pe.ca
www.library.pe.ca
Sharon Leard, Branch Library Technician

***Breadalbane:* Breadalbane Public Library**
4023 Dixon Rd., Breadalbane, PE C0A 1E0
Tel: 902-964-2520
breadalbane@gov.pe.ca
www.library.pe.ca
Joan Sutton, Branch Library Technician

***Charlottetown:* Bibliothèque publique Dr. J. Edmond Arsenault**
5 Acadian Dr., Charlottetown, PE C1C 1M2
Tél: 902-368-6092
carrefour@gov.pe.ca
www.library.pe.ca

***Charlottetown:* Confederation Centre Public Library**
PO Box 7000, Charlottetown, PE C1A 8G8
Tel: 902-368-4642; *Fax:* 902-368-4652
ccpl@gov.pe.ca
www.library.pe.ca
Trina O'Brien Leggott, Chief Librarian

***Cornwall:* Cornwall Public Library (PEI)**
39 Lowther Dr., Cornwall, PE C0A 1H0
Tel: 902-629-8415
cornwall@gov.pe.ca
www.library.pe.ca
Wheatley Pam, Branch Library Technician

***Crapaud:* Crapaud Public Library**
20424 Trans Canada Hwy., Crapaud, PE C0A 1J0
Tel: 902-658-2297
crapaud@gov.pe.ca
www.library.pe.ca
Luann Molyneaux, Branch Library Technician

***Georgetown:* Georgetown Genevieve Soloman Memorial Library**
36 Kent St., Georgetown, PE C0A 1L0
Tel: 902-652-2832
georgetown@gov.pe.ca
www.library.pe.ca
Mary Cameron, Branch Library Technician

***Hunter River:* Hunter River Public Library**
19816 Rte. 2, Hunter River, PE C0A 1N0
Tel: 902-964-2800
hunter_river@gov.pe.ca
www.library.pe.ca
Elisa Brown-Martel, Branch Library Technician

***Kensington:* Kensington Public Library**
55 Victoria St., Kensington, PE C0B 1M0
Tel: 902-836-3721
kensington@gov.pe.ca
www.library.pe.ca
Stephanie Campbell, Branch Library Technician

***Kinkora:* Kinkora Public Library**
45 Anderson St., Kinkora, PE C0B 1N0
Tel: 902-887-2172
kinkora@gov.pe.ca
www.library.pe.ca
Catherine Arsenault, Branch Library Technician

***Montague:* Montague Public Library**
273 Queen's Rd., Montague, PE C0A 1R0
Tel: 902-838-2928
montague@gov.pe.ca
www.library.pe.ca
Swarna Chandrasekera, Branch Library Technician

***Morell:* Morell Public Library**
89 Red Head Rd., Morell, PE C0A 1S0
Tel: 902-961-3389
morell@gov.pe.ca
www.library.pe.ca
Maria Van De Cappelle, Branch Library Technician

***Mount Stewart:* Mount Stewart Public Library**
104 Main St., Mount Stewart, PE C0A 1T0
Tel: 902-676-2050
mtstewart@gov.pe.ca
www.library.pe.ca
Maria Van De Cappelle, Branch Library Technician

***Murray Harbour:* Murray Harbour Public Library**
1381 Main St., Murray Harbour, PE C0A 1V0
Tel: 902-962-3875
murray_harbour@gov.pe.ca
www.library.pe.ca
Kaye MacLean, Branch Library Technician

***Murray River:* Murray River Leona Giddings Memorial Library**
1066 McInnis Rd., Murray River, PE C0A 1V0
Tel: 902-962-2667
murray_river@gov.pe.ca
www.library.pe.ca
Kaye MacLean, Branch Library Technician

***O'Leary:* O'Leary Public Library**
18 Community St., O'Leary, PE C0B 1V0
Tel: 902-859-8788
www.library.pe.ca
Nancy McNally, Branch Library Technician

***Souris:* Souris Public Library**
75 Main St., Souris, PE C0A 2B0
Tel: 902-687-2157; *Fax:* 902-687-4426
souris@gov.pe.ca
www.library.pe.ca
Kathy MacEwen, Branch Library Technician

***St. Peters:* St. Peters Public Library**
1968 Cardigan Rd., St. Peters, PE C0A 2A0
Tel: 902-961-3415
www.library.pe.ca
Ann MacInnis, Branch Library Technician

Stratford: **Stratford Public Library (PEI)**
57 Bunbury Rd., Stratford, PE C1B 1T8
Tel: 902-569-7441
stratford@edu.pe.ca
www.library.pe.ca
Jane McKinney, Branch Library Technician

Summerside: **Bibliothèque J.-Henri-Blanchard**
5, av Maris Stella, Summerside, PE C1N 3Y5
Tél: 902-432-2748; *Téléc:* 902-888-1686
blanchard@gov.pe.ca
www.library.pe.ca
Juanita Lewis, Branch Library Technician

Summerside: **Summerside Rotary Library**
192 Water St., Summerside, PE C1N 1B1
Tel: 902-436-7323; *Fax:* 902-888-8055
summerside@gov.pe.ca
www.library.pe.ca
Jean-François Savaria, Branch Librarian

Tignish: **Tignish Public Library**
103 School St., Tignish, PE C0B 2B0
Tel: 902-882-7363
tignish@gov.pe.ca
www.library.pe.ca
Diane McCue, Branch Library Technician

Tyne Valley: **Tyne Valley Public Library**
19 Allen Rd., Tyne Valley, PE C0B 2C0
Tel: 902-831-2928
tyne_valley@gov.pe.ca
www.library.pe.ca
Carolyn Millar, Branch Library Technician

Archives

Charlottetown: **Prince Edward Island Public Archives & Records Office**
Hon. George Coles Building, 4th Fl., 175 Richmond St., Charlottetown, PE C1A 7M4
Tel: 902-368-4290
archives@gov.pe.ca
www.gov.pe.ca/archives
Jill MacMicken Wilson, Provincial Archivist
jswilson@gov.pe.ca
902-368-4351
Ann-Marie McIsaac, Provincial Records Manager
902-368-6093

Charlottetown: **University of Prince Edward Island Archives**
Robertson Library, 550 University Ave., Charlottetown, PE C1A 4P3
Tel: 902-894-2802; *Fax:* 902-628-4305
www.upei.ca/library

Québec

Regional Systems

Réseau BIBLIO de l'Abitibi-Témiscamingue-Nord-du-Québec
20, av Québec, Rouyn-Noranda, QC J9X 2E6
Tél: 819-762-4305; *Téléc:* 819-762-5309
info@reseaubiblioatnq.qc.ca
www.reseaubiblioduquebec.qc.ca/portail/index.aspx?page=2&RID=1
Louis Dallaire, Directeur général
louis.dallaire@reseaubiblioatnq.qc.ca
Louise Julien, Responsable, Traitment documentaire
louise.julien@crsbpat.qc.ca
Lidia Turgeon, Responsable, Services administratifs
lidia.turgeon@crsbpat.qc.ca
Chantal Baril, Responsable, Soutien professionnel
chantal.baril@crsbpat.qc.ca

Réseau BIBLIO de l'Estrie
4155, rue Brodeur, Sherbrooke, QC J1L 1K4
Tél: 819-565-9744; *Téléc:* 819-565-9157
crsbpe@reseaubiblioestrie.qc.ca
www.reseaubiblioestrie.qc.ca
Joelle Thivierge, Directrice générale
jthivierge@reseaubiblioestrie.qc.ca
819-565-9744 ext. 102
France Lachance, Service à la clientele
flachance@reseaubiblioestrie.qc.ca
819-565-9744 ext. 103
Françoise Desprès, Prêt entre bibliothèques
fdespres@reseaubiblioestrie.qc.ca
819-565-9744 ext. 105

Réseau BIBLIO de l'Outaouais
2295, rue Saint-Louis, Gatineau, QC J8T 5L8
Tél: 819-561-6008; *Téléc:* 819-561-6767
biblio@crsbpo.qc.ca
www.reseaubiblioduquebec.qc.ca/portail/index.aspx?page=2&RID=8
Sylvie Thibault, Directrice générale
sylvie.thibault@crsbpo.qc.ca
Claudette Deschênes, Agente de bureau
claudette.deschenes@crsbpo.qc.ca
Jonathan Careau, Coordonnateur du soutien technique aux bibliothèques
jonathan.careau@crsbpo.qc.ca

Réseau BIBLIO de la Capitale-Nationale et de la Chaudière-Appalaches
3189, rue Albert-Demers, Charny, QC G6X 3A1
Tél: 418-832-6166; *Téléc:* 418-832-6168
Ligne sans frais: 866-446-6166
info@reseaubibliocnca.qc.ca
www.reseaubiblioduquebec.qc.ca/portail/index.aspx?page=2&RID=9
Isabelle Poirier, Directrice générale
ipoirier@reseaubibliocnca.qc.ca
Daniel Jubinville, Technicienne en documentation
djubinville@reseaubibliocnca.qc.ca
Marc Hébert, Agent culturel
mhebert@reseaubibliocnca.qc.ca

Réseau BIBLIO de la Côte-Nord
59, rue Napoléon, Sept-Iles, QC G4R 5C5
Tél: 418-962-1020; *Téléc:* 418-962-5124
biblio@reseaubibliocn.qc.ca
www.reseaubiblioduquebec.qc.ca/portail/index.aspx?page=2&RID=3
Jean-Roch Gagnon, Directeur général
jrgagnon@reseaubibliocn.qc.ca
Chantal Hould, Responsable, Services techniques
chantalh@reseaubibliocn.qc.ca

Réseau BIBLIO de la Gaspésie-Iles-de-la-Madeleine
31, rue des Écoliers, Cap-Chat, QC G0J 1E0
Tél: 418-786-5597; *Téléc:* 418-786-2024
info@reseaubibliogim.qc.ca
www.reseaubiblioduquebec.qc.ca/portail/index.aspx?page=2&RID=4
Julie Blais, Directrice générale
julie.blais@reseaubibliogim.qc.ca
Monique Demers, Bibliothécaire, soutien aux bibliothèques affiliées
monique.demers@reseaubibliogim.qc.ca
Carole Bernatchez, Technicienne en documentation
carole.bernatchez@reseaubibliogim.qc.ca

Réseau BIBLIO de la Montérégie
275, rue Conrad-Pelletier, La Prairie, QC J5R 4V1
Tél: 450-444-5433; *Téléc:* 450-659-3364
crsaide@reseaubibliomonteregie.qc.ca
www.reseaubibliomonteregie.qc.ca
Jacqueline Labelle, Directrice générale
jlabelle@reseaubibliomonteregie.qc.ca
Josée Audet, Directrice, Services techniques
josee.audet@reseaubibliomonteregie.qc.ca
Annie Bonneyville, Conseillère aux bibliothèques affiliées

Réseau BIBLIO des Laurentides
29, rue Brissette, Sainte-Agathe-des-Monts, QC J8C 3L1
Tél: 819-326-6440; *Téléc:* 819-326-0885
info@crsbpl.qc.ca
www.reseaubiblioduquebec.qc.ca/portail/index.aspx?page=2&RID=5
JoAnne Turnbull, Directrice générale
jturnbull@crsbpl.qc.ca
Julie Filion, Directrice, Soutien aux bibliothèques
jfilion@crsbpl.qc.ca
Norbert Morveau, Directeur, Soutien informatique
nmorneau@crsbpl.qc.ca
Claire Dufresne, Bibliothécaire

Réseau BIBLIO du Bas-Saint-Laurent
465, rue St-Pierre, Rivière-du-Loup, QC G5R 4T6
Tél: 418-867-1682; *Téléc:* 418-867-3434
crsbp@crsbp.net
www.reseaubibliobsl.qc.ca
Jacques Côté, Directeur général
jacques.cote@crsbp.net
Josée Brulotte, Bibliothécaire, directrice soutien au réseau
josee.brulotte@crsbp.net

Réseau BIBLIO du Centre-du-Québec, de Lanaudière et de la Mauricie
3125, rue Girard, Trois-Rivières, QC G8Z 2M4
Tél: 819-375-9623; *Téléc:* 819-375-0132
Ligne sans frais: 877-324-2546
crsbp@reseaubibliocqlm.qc.ca
www.reseaubibliocqlm.qc.ca
Hélène Arseneau, Directrice générale
helene.arseneau@reseaubibliocqlm.qc.ca
Michelle Vallée, Directrice, Services aux bibliothèques
michelle.vallee@reseaubibliocqlm.qc.ca
Valérie Simard, Directrice, Service techniques coopératifs
valerie.simard@reseaubibliocqlm.qc.ca
Lauren Duchemin, Directrice, Services administratifs
lauren.duchemin@reseaubibliocqlm.qc.ca
Francine Allen, Responsable, Choix et traitement
francine.allen@reseaubibliocqlm.qc.ca

Public Libraries

Acton Vale: **Bibliothèque Acton Vale**
1093A, rue Saint-André, Acton Vale, QC J0H 1A0
Tél: 450-546-2703; *Téléc:* 450-642-1165
acton.vale@reseaubibliomonteregie.qc.ca
Sophia Bédard, Responsable

Aguanish: **Bibliothèque d'Aguanish**
106, rue Jacques-Cartier, Aguanish, QC G0G 1A0
Tél: 418-533-2323; *Téléc:* 418-533-2012
www.reseaubiblioduquebec.qc.ca
Normande Blais, Responsable
418-533-2352

Albanel: **Bibliothèque publique d'Albanel**
153A, Principale, Albanel, QC G8M 3J3
Tél: 613-279-5762
albanel@reseaubiblioslsj.qc.ca
Marguerite Dubeau, Responsable
613-279-5800
Hélène Theberge, Assistante
613-279-3381

Albertville: **Bibliothèque d'Albertville**
1058, rue Principale, Albertville, QC G0J 1A0
Tél: 418-756-6015
biblio.albert@crsbp.net
www.reseaubiblioduquebec.qc.ca
Danielle Berger, Responsable

Alma: **Bibliothèque municipale d'Alma**
500, rue Collard ouest, Alma, QC G8B 1N2
Tél: 418-669-5140; *Téléc:* 418-669-5089
bibliotheque@ville.alma.qc.ca
www.almabibliotheque.com
Média social: www.facebook.com/biblio.alma
Emile Guertin, Responsable
emile.guertin@ville.alma.qc.ca

Alma: **Bibliothèque publique de Delisle**
221, rue des Bruyères, Alma, QC G8E 1J9
Tél: 418-668-2697
delisle@reseaubiblioslsj.qc.ca
Ghislain Girard, Responsable
418-480-3396

Alma: **Bibliothèque publique de Saint-Coeur-de-Marie**
5791 avenue du Pont nord, Alma, QC G8E 1X1
Tél: 418-347-3729; *Téléc:* 418-347-3697
stcoeur@reseaubiblioslsj.qc.ca
www.reseaubiblioduquebec.qc.ca/portail/index.aspx?page=3&BID=558
Martine Gobeil, Responsable
Sylvie Larouche, Adjointe
Joanne Duperre, Secrétaire
Julie Dallaire, Trésorière

Amherst: **Bibliothèque de Saint-Rémi**
124, rue St-Louis, Amherst, QC J0T 2L0
Tél: 819-687-3372; *Téléc:* 819-687-8430
amherst@municipalite.amherst.qc.ca
www.reseaubiblioduquebec.qc.ca
Hélène Dion, Directrice adjointe
hdion@municipalite.amherst.qc.ca

Amqui: **Bibliothèque Madeleine-Gagnon**
24, promenade de l'Hôtel de Ville, Amqui, QC G5J 3E1
Tél: 418-629-4242; *Téléc:* 418-629-4090
bibliotheque@ville.amqui.qc.ca
www.ville.amqui.qc.ca

***Angliers:* Bibliothèque d'Angliers**
14, rue Baie Miller, Angliers, QC J0Z 1A0
Tél: 819-949-4351; *Téléc:* 819-949-4321
angliers@reseaubiblioatnq.qc.ca
www.reseaubiblioduquebec.qc.ca
Manon Corbin, Responsable
Magalie Corbin-Boivin, Bénévole
Lyna Pine, Bénévole
Amélya Urrutiaguer, Bénévole

***Armagh:* Bibliothèque municipale d'Armagh**
9, rue de la Salle, Armagh, QC G0R 1A0
Tél: 418-466-3004; *Téléc:* 418-466-2409
armabib@globetrotter.qc.ca
www.reseaubiblioduquebec.qc.ca/armagh
Sylvie Chabot, Responsable
Annette Chamberland, Adjointe

***Arntfield:* Bibliothèque de Arntfield**
15, rue Fugère, Arntfield, QC J0Z 1B0
Tél: 819-279-2241; *Téléc:* 819-279-2481
arntfield@reseaubiblioatnq.qc.ca
www.reseaubiblioduquebec.qc.ca
Jeannine Drouin, Responsable
819-279-2329

***Arundel:* Bibliothèque d'Arundel/ Arundel Library**
2, rue du Village, Arundel, QC J0T 1A0
Tél: 819-687-8246; *Téléc:* 819-687-8760
biblio@municipalite.arundel.qc.ca
www.reseaubiblioduquebec.qc.ca
Fran Jones, Responsable

***Asbestos:* Bibliothèque municipale d'Asbestos**
351, boul Saint-Luc, Asbestos, QC J1T 2W4
Tél: 819-879-7171; *Téléc:* 819-879-2343
bibliasbestos@cgocable.ca
ville.asbestos.qc.ca/bibliotheque-municipale.html
Julie Fontaine, Responsable

***Aston-Jonction:* Bibliothèque d'Aston-Jonction**
210, rue Lemire, Aston-Jonction, QC G0Z 1A0
Téléc: 819-226-3459
biblio070@reseaubibliocqlm.qc.ca
www.reseaubiblioduquebec.qc.ca
Léa Houle, Responsable

***Auclair:* Bibliothèque Auclair**
777, rue du Clocher, Auclair, QC G0L 1A0
Tél: 418-899-0417
biblio.auclair@crsbp.net
www.reseaubiblioduquebec.qc.ca
Cécile Castonguay, Responsable

***Aumond:* Bibliothèque de Aumond**
679, rue Principale, Aumond, QC J0W 1W0
Tél: 819-449-4006; *Téléc:* 819-449-7448
Diane Guénette, Responsable

***Baie-Comeau:* Bibliothèque municipale Alice-Lane**
6, av Radisson, Baie-Comeau, QC G4Z 1W4
Tél: 418-296-8304; *Téléc:* 418-296-8328
vbc@ville.baie-comeau.qc.ca
Yvon Grondin, Superviseur responsable
ygrondin@ville.baie-comeau.qc.ca
418-396-8361

***Baie-des-Sables:* Bibliothèque de Baie-des-Sables**
190, rue de La Mer, Baie-des-Sables, QC G0J 1C0
Tél: 418-772-6218
biblio.sables@crsbp.net
www.reseaubiblioduquebec.qc.ca
Monique Roy, Responsable

***Baie-du-Febvre:* Bibliothèque de Baie-du-Febvre**
23, rue de l'Église, Baie-du-Febvre, QC J0G 1A0
Tél: 450-783-6484; *Téléc:* 450-783-2235
biblio032@reseaubibliocqlm.qc.ca
www.reseaubiblioduquebec.qc.ca
Lise Laforce, Responsable

***Baie-Johan-Beetz:* Bibliothèque Baie-Johan-Beetz**
16, rue Tanguay, Baie-Johan-Beetz, QC G0G 1B0
Tél: 418-539-0125; *Téléc:* 418-539-0205
munbjb@globetrotter.net
www.reseaubiblioduquebec.qc.ca/baie-johan-beetz

***Baie-Saint-Paul:* Bibliothèque René-Richard**
9, rue Forget, Baie-Saint-Paul, QC G3Z 1T4
Tél: 418-435-5858; *Téléc:* 418-435-0010
bibliobsp@charlevoix.net
www.baiestpaul.com/bibliotheque/
Denise Ouellet, Responsable
Hélène Simard, Adjointe

***Baie-Sainte-Catherine:* Bibliothèque Ali-Baba**
308, rue Leclerc, Baie-Sainte-Catherine, QC G0T 1A0
Tél: 418-237-4241; *Téléc:* 418-237-4223
www.reseaubiblioduquebec.qc.ca/baie-sainte-catherine
Patricia Ouellet, Responsable

***Baie-Trinité:* Bibliothèque de Baie-Trinité**
3, rue St-Joseph, Baie-Trinité, QC G0H 1A0
Tél: 418-939-2231; *Téléc:* 418-939-2616
www.reseaubiblioduquebec.qc.ca
Ghislaine Harvey, Responsable
ghislhar@hotmail.com
418-939-2535

***Barraute:* Bibliothèque Barraute**
600, 1re Rue, Barraute, QC J0Y 1A0
Tél: 819-734-6762; *Téléc:* 819-734-6762
barraute@reseaubiblioatnq.qc.ca
Claire Voyer, Responsable

***Bassin:* Bibliothèque de L'Ile-du-Havre-Aubert**
#104, 280, ch de Bassin, Bassin, QC G4T 0B5
Tél: 418-937-2279; *Téléc:* 418-937-5558
bibliohavre@muniles.ca
www.reseaubiblioduquebec.qc.ca
Christiane Turbide, Responsable

***Batiscan:* Bibliothèque municipale de Batiscan**
791-2, place de la Solidarité, Batiscan, QC G0X 1A0
Tél: 819-840-0600; *Téléc:* 819-362-3174
biblio025@reseaubibliocqlm.qc.ca
www.reseaubiblioduquebec.qc.ca

***Beaconsfield:* Bibliothèque de Beaconsfield**
303, boul Beaconsfield, Beaconsfield, QC H9W 4A7
Tél: 514-428-4460; *Téléc:* 514-428-4477
bibliotheque@beaconsfield.ca
www.beaconsfield.ca/fr/services-de-la-bibliotheque
Michèle Janis, Chef de division
michele.janis@beaconsfield.ca
514-482-4400 ext. 4482
Beverley Gilbertson, Chef bibliothécaire
beverley.gilbertson@beaconsfield.ca
514-428-4400 ext. 4466
Anne Bourel, Responsable, service du prêt
anne.bourel@beaconsfield.ca
514-428-4400 ext. 4472
Beverley Price, Responsable, services techniques
beverley.price@beaconsfield.ca
514-428-4400 ext. 4474

***Beaucanton:* Bibliothèque Beaucanton**
2709, boul McDuff, #C, Beaucanton, QC J0Z 1H0
Tél: 819-941-2686; *Téléc:* 819-941-2686
beaucanton@reseaubiblioatnq.qc.ca
www.reseaubiblioduquebec.qc.ca
Célyne Beauchamp, Responsable

***Beauceville:* Bibliothèque Madeleine-Doyon**
100, Place de l'Église, Beauceville, QC G5X 1X3
Tél: 418-774-2466; *Téléc:* 418-774-2499
biblio@ville.beauceville.qc.ca
www.reseaubiblioduquebec.qc.ca/beauceville
Sheina Simoneau, Responsable
Brigitte Veilleux, Adjointe

***Beauharnois:* Bibliothèque Dominique-Julien**
#100, 600, rue Ellice, Beauharnois, QC J6N 3P7
Tél: 450-429-3546; *Téléc:* 450-429-3820
Marielle Vinet, Responsable

***Beaulac-Garthby:* Bibliothèque de Saints-Martyrs-Canadiens**
13, ch du Village, Beaulac-Garthby, QC G0Y 1B0
Tél: 819-344-5171
biblio157@reseaubibliocqlm.qc.ca
www.reseaubiblioduquebec.qc.ca
Pierre L. Ramsay, Responsable
Thérèse Lemay, Bénévole

***Beaumont:* Bibliothèque Luc-Lacourcière**
64, ch du Domaine, Beaumont, QC G0R 1C0
Tél: 418-837-2658; *Téléc:* 418-837-2658
bibl.l.lacourciere@videotron.ca
www.reseaubiblioduquebec.qc.ca/beaumont/
Nicole Maheu, Responsable

***Beaupré:* Bibliothèque La Plume d'oie**
11298, rue de La Salle, Beaupré, QC G0A 1E0
Tél: 418-827-8483; *Téléc:* 418-827-3818
bibliotheque@ville.beaupre.qc.ca
www.reseaubiblioduquebec.qc.ca/beaupre/
Charlotte Bouchard, Responsable

***Bedford:* Bibliothèque Léon-Maurice-Côté**
52, rue Du Pont, Bedford, QC J0J 1A0
Tél: 450-248-4625
bedford@reseaubibliomonteregie.qc.ca
Renée Dallaire, Responsable
Estelle Messier, Co-responsable
Andrée Beaudoin, Responsable, PIB

***Belcourt:* Bibliothèque de Belcourt**
219A, rue Communautaire, Belcourt, QC J0Y 2M0
Tél: 819-737-8894; *Téléc:* 819-737-4084
belcourt@reseaubiblioatnq.qc.ca
www.reseaubiblioduquebec.qc.ca/belcourt
Guylaine Labbée, Responsable

***Bellecombe:* Bibliothèque de Bellecombe**
2471, rte des Pionniers, Bellecombe, QC J0Z 1K0
Tél: 819-797-8302; *Téléc:* 819-797-6585
bellecombe@reseaubiblioatnq.qc.ca
www.reseaubiblioduquebec.qc.ca/bellecombe
Gaétane Morrissette, Responsable

***Belleterre:* Bibliothèque de Belleterre**
265, 1e av, Belleterre, QC J0Z 1L0
Tél: 819-722-2052; *Téléc:* 819-722-2527
belleterre@reseaubiblioatnq.qc.ca
www.reseaubiblioduquebec.qc.ca/belleterre
Claudette Rioux Gauthier, Responsable

***Beloeil:* Bibliothèque municipale de Beloeil**
620, rue Richelieu, Beloeil, QC J3G 5E8
Tél: 450-467-7872; *Téléc:* 450-467-3257
biblio@ville.beloeil.qc.ca
Johanne Guèvremont, Directrice
biblio@ville.beloeil.qc.ca
450-467-7872
Hélène Fournier, Technicienne en documentation

***Berthier-sur-Mer:* Bibliothèque Camille-Roy**
5, rue du Couvent, Berthier-sur-Mer, QC G0R 1E0
Tél: 418-259-2353; *Téléc:* 418-259-2038
biblcamr@globetrotter.qc.ca
www.reseaubiblioduquebec.qc.ca
Jocelyne Guimont, Responsable
418-259-2622

***Biencourt:* Bibliothèque de Biencourt**
#1, 2, rue Saint-Marc, Biencourt, QC G0K 1T0
Tél: 418-499-1041
biblio.biencourt@crsbp.net
www.reseaubiblioduquebec.qc.ca

***Blainville:* Bibliothèque municipale de Blainville**
1000, ch du Plan-Bouchard, Blainville, QC J7C 3S9
Tél: 450-434-5370; *Téléc:* 450-434-5378
bibliotheque@ville.blainville.qc.ca
www.ville.blainville.qc.ca
Patrick Toupin, Directeur, Loisirs et développement communautaire

***Blue Sea:* Bibliothèque Blue Sea**
2, ch Blue Sea, Blue Sea, QC J0X 1C0
Tél: 819-463-2261; *Téléc:* 819-463-4345
admbluesea@crsbpo.qc.ca
www.reseaubiblioduquebec.qc.ca/bluesea
Isabelle Gauthier, Responsable

***Bois-Franc:* Bibliothèque de Bois-Franc**
466, rte 105, Bois-Franc, QC J9E 3A9
Tél: 819-441-0645; *Téléc:* 819-449-4407
admboisfranc@crsbpo.qc.ca
www.reseaubiblioduquebec.qc.ca/BoisFranc
Francine Marenger, Bibliothécaire

***Boisbriand:* Bibliothèque municipale de Boisbriand**
901, boul. de la Grande-Allée, Boisbriand, QC J7G 1W6
Tél: 450-435-7466; *Téléc:* 450-435-0627
slegault@ville.boisbriand.qc.ca
Stéphane Legault, Directeur

***Bonaventure:* Bibliothèque Françoise-Bujold**
95A, av Port-Royal, Bonaventure, QC G0C 1E0
Tél: 418-534-4238; *Téléc:* 418-534-4336
bonapret@globetrotter.net
Thérèse Arsenault, Responsable

***Boucherville:* Bibliothèque Montarville-Boucher-De la Bruère**
501, ch du Lac, Boucherville, QC J4B 6V6
Tél: 450-449-8650; *Téléc:* 450-449-6865
bibliothèque@boucherville.ca
www.boucherville.ca
Média social: twitter.com/boucherville_;
www.facebook.com/pages/Ville-de-Boucherville/47679369584

***Bouchette:* Bibliothèque de Bouchette**
36, rue Principale, Bouchette, QC J0X 1E0
Tél: 819-465-2555; *Téléc:* 819-465-2318
admbouchette@crsbpo.qc.ca
www.reseaubiblioduquebec.qc.ca/Bouchette
Janick Patry, Responsable

***Boulanger:* Bibliothèque publique de Sainte-Jeanne-d'Arc**
400, rue Verreault, Boulanger, QC G0W 1E0
Tél: 418-276-1189
jeanne@reseaubiblioslsj.qc.ca
www.reseaubiblioduquebec.qc.ca
Madelaine Tremblay, Responsable

***Brigham:* Bibliothèque municipale de Brigham**
118, avenue des Cèdres, Brigham, QC J2K 4K4
Tél: 450-266-0500
brigham@reseaubibliomonteregie.qc.ca
www.reseaubiblioduquebec.qc.ca
Céline Vaillancourt, Responsable
rbcv@endirect.qc.ca
450-263-6677

***Bristol:* Bibliothèque de Bristol/ Bristol Library**
32, ch Aylmer, Bristol, QC J0X 1G0
Tél: 819-647-5555; *Téléc:* 819-647-2424
admbristol@crsbpo.qc.ca
www.reseaubiblioduquebec.qc.ca/Bristol
Kelly Dowe, Responsable

***Brossard:* Bibliothèque de Brossard (Georgette-Lepage)**
7855, av San-Francisco, Brossard, QC J4X 2A4
Tél: 450-923-6350; *Téléc:* 450-923-7042
bibliotheque@brossard.ca
www.ville.brossard.qc.ca/biblio
Média social: www.youtube.com/user/bibliobrossard; twitter.com/Bibliobrossard; www.facebook.com/bibliobrossard
Jacques-André Chartrand, Président
Suzanne Payette, Représentante de la bibliothèque

***Brownsburg-Chatham:* Bibliothèque de Brownsburg-Chatham**
200, rue MacVicar, Brownsburg-Chatham, QC J8G 2Z6
Tél: 450-533-5355
biblio@brownsburgchatham.ca
www.reseaubiblioduquebec.qc.ca
Brigitte Bowen, Responsable

***Bryson:* Bibliothèque de Bryson**
833, rue Principale, Bryson, QC J0X 1H0
Tél: 819-648-2543; *Téléc:* 819-648-5297
admbryson@crsbpo.qc.ca
www.commercepontiac.ca/services/libraries.html

***Brébeuf:* Bibliothèque M.-A. Grégoire-Coupal**
#2, 217, rte 323, Brébeuf, QC J0T 1B0
Tél: 819-425-9833
biblio@brebeuf.ca
www.brebeuf.ca/brebeuf_bibliotheque.html
Ginette Bernard, Responsable

***Buckingham:* Bibliothèque municipale de Buckingham**
181, rue Joseph, Buckingham, QC J8L 1G6
Tél: 819-595-7461
Lise Robitaille, Responsable
819-986-4211
Carole Larocque, Technicienne en documentation
819-986-4214

***Buckland:* Bibliothèque Biblio Buck**
4340, rue Principale, Buckland, QC G0R 1G0
Tél: 418-789-3119; *Téléc:* 418-789-3119
www.buckland.qc.ca
Claude Gignac, Responsable
Diane Laflamme, Adjointe
Lise Hudon, Responsable de l'animation

***Béarn:* Bibliothèque de Béarn**
38, rue Principale nord, Béarn, QC J0Z 1G0
Tél: 819-726-2251; *Téléc:* 819-726-2121
bearn@reseaubiblioatnq.qc.ca
www.reseaubiblioduquebec.qc.ca/bearn
Annie Drolet, Responsable

***Bécancour:* Bibliothèque publique de Bécancour**
1295, av Nicolas-Perrot, Bécancour, QC G9H 1A1
Tél: 819-294-4455
www.becancour.net/fr/activites_et_loisirs/reseau_des_bibliotheques

***Bégin:* Bibliothèque publique de Bégin**
120B, rue Tremblay, Bégin, QC G0V 1B0
Tél: 418-672-4503
begin@reseaubiblioslsj.qc.ca
Marie-Joseph Thérriault, Responsable

***Cabano:* Bibliothèque Cabano**
14A, du Vieux Chemin, Cabano, QC G0L 1E0
Tél: 418-845-5568; *Téléc:* 418-854-0118
biblio.cabano@crsbp.net
Huguette Nadeau, Responsable
biblio.cabano@crsbp.net
418-854-5568 ext. 200

***Cadillac:* Bibliothèque Cadillac**
15, 1ère av est, Cadillac, QC J0Y 1C0
Tél: 819-759-3606; *Téléc:* 819-759-3607
cadillac@reseaubiblioatnq.qc.ca
www.crsbpat.qc.ca/cadillac/
Rita Maranda, Responsable

***Calixa-Lavallée:* Bibliothèque municipale de Calixa-Lavallée**
771, rang Beauce, Calixa-Lavallée, QC J0L 1A0
Tél: 450-583-5417
calixa.lavallee@reseaubibliomonteregie.qc.ca
www.reseaubiblioduquebec.qc.ca
Nicole Jacques, Responsable

***Campbell's Bay:* Bibliothèque de Campbell's Bay/Litchfield**
4, rue Patterson, Campbell's Bay, QC J0X 1K0
Tél: 819-648-5676; *Téléc:* 819-648-2045
biblio-cb@mrcpontiac.qc.ca
www.reseaubiblioduquebec.qc.ca/CampbellsBay
Média social: www.facebook.com/172200822806575
Jean-Pierre Landry, Directeur général

***Candiac:* Bibliothèque municipale de Candiac**
Centre Claude-Hébert, 59, ch Haendel, Candiac, QC J5R 1R7
Tél: 450-635-6032; *Téléc:* 450-635-0900
biblio@ville.candiac.qc.ca
www.ville.candiac.qc.ca
Patricia Lemieux, Directrice

***Cantley:* Bibliothèque municipale de Cantley**
8, ch River, Cantley, QC J8V 2Z9
Tél: 819-827-3434; *Téléc:* 819-827-4328
biblio@bibliocantley.qc.ca
www.bibliocantley.qc.ca
Bibiane Rondeau, Coordonnatrice
Melanie Vigneault, Adjointe

***Cap-aux-Meules:* Bibliothèque de Cap-aux-Meules**
#3, 315, ch Principal, Cap-aux-Meules, QC G4T 1E2
Tél: 418-986-6821; *Téléc:* 418-986-5446
bibliocamiles@hotmail.com
Suzanne Chevrier, Responsable

***Cap-Chat:* Bibliothèque La ruche littéraire**
27, des Écoliers, Cap-Chat, QC G0J 1E0
Tél: 418-786-2068
bbocchat@globetrotter.qc.ca
Carmeline Langlais, Responsable
418-786-2149

***Cap-d'Espoir:* Bibliothèque de Cap-d'Espoir**
52, rue du Curé-Poirier, Cap-d'Espoir, QC G0C 1G0
Tél: 418-782-2921; *Téléc:* 418-782-2590
bbocesp@ville.perce.qc.ca
www.reseaubiblioduquebec.qc.ca
Marie-Lise Rail, Responsable

***Cap-Saint-Ignace:* Bibliothèque Léo-Pol-Morin**
100, Place de l'Église, Cap-Saint-Ignace, QC G0R 1H0
Tél: 418-246-3037; *Téléc:* 418-246-5663
biblicap@globetrotter.qc.ca
www.reseaubiblioduquebec.qc.ca/cap-saint-ignace
Lyne Gobeil, Responsable
Lyne Richard, Adjointe

***Cap-Santé:* Bibliothèque municipale de Cap-Santé**
15, rue Marie-Fitzbach, Cap-Santé, QC G0A 1L0
Tél: 418-285-6891; *Téléc:* 418-285-0009
capsante@globetrotter.qc.ca
www.reseaubiblioduquebec.qc.ca/cap-sante
Francine Germain, Responsable

***Caplan:* Bibliothèque Jeanne-Ferlatte**
17, boul Perron est, Caplan, QC G0C 1H0
Tél: 418-388-2545; *Téléc:* 418-388-2429
bibliocaplan@hotmail.com
Colette Bertrand, Responsable

***Capucins:* Bibliothèque de Capucins**
294, rte du Village, Capucins, QC G0J 1H0
Tél: 418-786-2013
bbocapu@globetrotter.net
www.reseaubiblioduquebec.qc.ca
Jeannine Harrisson, Responsable

***Carleton-sur-Mer:* Bibliothèque Gabrielle-Bernard-Dubé**
774, boul Perron, Carleton-sur-Mer, QC G0C 1J0
Tél: 418-364-7103
livre1@globetrotter.net
Julie Poulin, Responsable

***Causapscal:* Bibliothèque de Causapscal**
3, Place de la Fabrique, Causapscal, QC G0J 1J0
Tél: 418-756-3522
biblio.causap@crsbp.net
www.reseaubiblioduquebec.qc.ca
Thérèse Audit, Responsable

***Chambly:* Bibliothèque municipale de Chambly**
1691, rue Bourgogne, Chambly, QC J3L 1Y8
Tél: 450-658-2711; *Téléc:* 450-447-4525
biblio@ville.chambly.qc.ca
www.ville.chambly.qc.ca/index.php/bibliotheque
Carole Mainville-Bériault, Directrice
cmberiault@ville.chambly.qc.ca
450-658-0674

***Chambord:* Bibliothèque publique de Chambord**
72-1, boul de la Montagne, Chambord, QC G0W 1G0
Tél: 418-342-6274
chambord@reseaubiblioslsj.qc.ca
Andrée Chiasson, Responsable
Kathy Lemay, Responsable

***Champlain:* Bibliothèque de Champlain**
963, rue Notre-Dame, Champlain, QC G0X 1C0
Tél: 819-840-0407; *Téléc:* 819-295-3032
biblio005@reseaubibliocqlm.qc.ca
www.reseaubiblioduquebec.qc.ca
Isabelle Vézina, Responsable

***Chandler:* Bibliothèque municipale-scolaire de Chandler**
183, rue Commerciale ouest, Chandler, QC G0C 1K0
Tél: 418-689-3808; *Téléc:* 418-689-3639
giselec@globetrotter.net
www.reseaubiblioduquebec.qc.ca
Gisele Cyr, Directeur

***Chapais:* Bibliothèque publique de Chapais**
45, 5e av, Chapais, QC G0W 1H0
Tél: 418-745-3244
chapais@reseaubiblioslsj.qc.ca
www.reseaubiblioduquebec.qc.ca
Line Lambert, Responsable

***Charette:* Bibliothèque de Charette (Armance-Samson)**
390, rue Saint-Édouard, Charette, QC G0X 1E0
Tél: 819-221-2095
biblio023@reseaubibliocqlm.qc.ca
www.reseaubiblioduquebec.qc.ca
Louise Gélinas, Responsable

***Charlemagne:* Bibliothèque Camille-Laurin de Charlemagne**
84, rue du Sacré-Coeur, Charlemagne, QC J5Z 1W8
Tél: 450-581-7243; *Téléc:* 450-581-0597
biblio@ville.charlemagne.qc.ca
www.ville.charlemagne.qc.ca/biblio.htm
Christine Arel, Responsable
biblio@ville.charlemagne.qc.ca
450-581-7243 ext. 36
Julie Savoie, Technicienne en documentation
450-581-7243 ext. 34
Lise Boissonneault, Commis
450-581-7243 ext. 23
Karine Carufel, Commis
450-581-7243 ext. 23

***Chazel:* Bibliothèque municipale de Chazel**
343, rue Principale, Chazel, QC J0Z 1N0
Tél: 819-333-3262
chazel.ao.ca
Hélène Charrois, Coordonnatrice

***Chelsea:* Bibliothèque de Chelsea / Chelsea Library**
100, ch Old Chelsea, Chelsea, QC J9B 1C1
Tél: 819-827-4019
bibliotheque@chelsea.ca
www.chelsea.ca
Média social:
www.facebook.com/pages/Chelsea-Library/117427068307837
Béatrice O'Byrne, Bibliothécaire

***Chertsey:* Bibliothèque de Chertsey**
333, av de l'Amitié, Chertsey, QC J0K 3K0
Tél: 450-882-4738
mpicard@municipalite.chertsey.qc.ca
www.reseaubiblioduquebec.qc.ca
Monique Picard, Responsable
mpicard@municipalite.chertsey.qc.ca

***Chesterville:* Bibliothèque de Chesterville**
474, rue de l'Acceuil, Chesterville, QC G0P 1J0
Tél: 819-382-2997
biblio146@reseaubibliocqlm.qc.ca
www.reseaubiblioduquebec.qc.ca
Louise Lefebvre, Responsable

***Chevery:* Bibliothèque de Chevery**
CP 92, Chevery, QC G0G 1G0
Tél: 418-787-2244; *Téléc:* 418-787-2241
www.reseaubiblioduquebec.qc.ca
Ana Osborne, Responsable

***Chibougamau:* Bibliothèque municipale de Chibougamau**
601, 3e rue, Chibougamau, QC G8P 3A2
Tél: 418-748-2497; *Téléc:* 418-748-2980
bibliotheque@ville.chibougamau.qc.ca
www.ville.chibougamau.qc.ca
Lise Matte, Bibliotechnicienne
lisematte@ville.chibougamau.qc.ca
418-748-2497

***Chicoutimi:* Bibliothèque de Chicoutimi**
155, rue Racine est, Chicoutimi, QC G7H 1R5
Tél: 418-698-5350; *Téléc:* 418-698-5359
webbiblio@ville.saguenay.qc.ca
www.ville.saguenay.qc.ca
Anne Lebel, Chef de division, Bibliothèques de Saguenay
anne.lebel@ville.saguenay.qc.ca
Claude Dumais, Responsable, Bibliothèques de l'arrond. de Chicoutimi
claude.dumais@ville.saguenay.qc.ca
Isabelle Nepton, Responsable de l'Animation
isabelle.nepton@ville.saguenay.qc.ca

***Chicoutimi:* Bibliothèque de Rivière-du-Moulin**
1410, rue des Cèdres, Chicoutimi, QC G8A 2E6
Tél: 418-698-3226
webbiblio@ville.saguenay.qc.ca
www.ville.saguenay.qc.ca
Anne Lebel, Chef de division, Bibliothèques de Saguenay
anne.lebel@ville.saguenay.qc.ca
Claude Dumais, Responsable, Bibliothèques de l'arrond. de Chicoutimi
claude.dumais@ville.saguenay.qc.ca
Ginette Tremblay, Responsable de la bibliothèque

***Chute-aux-Outardes:* Bibliothèque de Chute-aux-Outardes**
4, rue de l'École, Chute-aux-Outardes, QC G0H 1C0
Tél: 418-567-2535; *Téléc:* 418-567-4478
bibliotheque.desjardins@csestuaire.qc.ca
www.reseaubiblioduquebec.qc.ca
Manon Finn, Responsable

***Chute-Saint-Philippe:* Bibliothèque de Chute-Saint-Philippe**
592, ch du Progrès, Chute-Saint-Philippe, QC J0W 1A0
Tél: 819-585-3397; *Téléc:* 819-585-4949
bibliotheque@chute-saint-philippe.ca
www.reseaubiblioduquebec.qc.ca/chute-saint-philippe
Françoise St-Amour, Responsable
819-585-3397 ext. 27

***Chénéville:* Bibliothèque Chénéville / Lac-Simon**
77, rue Hôtel-de-Ville, Chénéville, QC J0V 1E0
Tél: 819-428-3583; *Téléc:* 819-428-4838
biblio.cheneville@mrcpapineau.com
www.reseaubiblioduquebec.qc.ca/Cheneville
Madeleine Tremblay, Responsable

***Châteauguay:* Bibliothèque municipale de Châteauguay**
25, boul Maple, Châteauguay, QC J6J 3P7
Tél: 450-698-3080; *Téléc:* 450-698-3077
biblio@ville.chateauguay.qc.ca
www.ville.chateauguay.qc.ca
Céline Lussier, Chef, Division bibliothèque
celine-lussier@ville.chateauguay.qc.ca
450-698-3095
Véronique Marcotte, Bibliothécaire, Référence
veronique.marcotte@ville.chateauguay.qc.ca
450-698-3094
Marie-France Martel, Technicienne en documentation
450-698-3086
Michel St-Onge, Technicien en documentation
450-698-3087
Jocelyne Brunet, Technicienne en documentation
450-698-3084

***Clarenceville:* Bibliothèque municipale de Saint-Georges-de-Clarenceville**
1340, ch Middle, Clarenceville, QC J0J 1B0
Tél: 450-294-3200
clarenceville@reseaubibliomonteregie.qc.ca
Nestor Rassart, Responsable
Ginette Fournel, Responsable, PIB

***Clermont:* Bibliothèque municipale de Clermont**
11, rue Jean Talon, Clermont, QC G4A 1A4
Tél: 418-439-2903; *Téléc:* 418-439-4889
www.reseaubiblioduquebec.qc.ca/clermont
Ginette Simard, Responsable

***Clerval:* Bibliothèque de Clerval**
579, rue du Village, Clerval, QC J0Z 1R0
Tél: 819-783-2069; *Téléc:* 819-783-2640
clerval@reseaubiblioatnq.qc.ca
Germaine Thibault, Responsable

***Cloridorme:* Bibliothèque de Cloridorme**
472, rte 132, Cloridorme, QC G0E 1G0
Tél: 418-395-2609; *Téléc:* 418-395-2228
munclori@globetrotter.qc.ca
www.reseaubiblioduquebec.qc.ca
Marie Dufresne, Responsable

***Cloutier:* Bibliothèque de Cloutier**
531, rte 391 sud, Cloutier, QC J0Z 1S0
Tél: 819-797-8613; *Téléc:* 819-797-1299
cloutier@reseaubiblioatnq.qc.ca
www.reseaubiblioduquebec.qc.ca
Rachel Jutras, Responsable

***Cléricy:* Bibliothèque de Cléricy**
8002A, rue du Souvenir, Cléricy, QC J0Z 1P0
Tél: 819-797-7110; *Téléc:* 819-637-2133
clericy@reseaubiblioatnq.qc.ca
www.reseaubiblioduquebec.qc.ca/cléricy
Lise Robin Boucher, Responsable

***Coaticook:* Bibliothèque Françoise-Maurice de Coaticook**
34, rue Main est, Coaticook, QC J1A 1N2
Tél: 819-849-4013; *Téléc:* 819-849-0479
biblcoat@bibliotheque.coaticook.qc.ca
bibliotheque.culturecoaticook.qc.ca
Média social: www.facebook.com/10055338813?sk=notes
Patrick Falardeau, Directeur, Conseil d'administration

***Colombier:* Bibliothèque de Colombier**
570, rue Principale, Colombier, QC G0H 1P0
Tél: 418-565-3013; *Téléc:* 418-565-3289
bibliocolombier@hotmail.com
Isabelle Maltais, Responsable

***Coteau-du-Lac:* Bibliothèque Jules-Fournier**
3, rue du Parc, Coteau-du-Lac, QC J0P 1B0
Tél: 450-763-2763; *Téléc:* 450-763-2495
bibliotheque@coteau-du-lac.com
www.coteau-du-lac.com/services-et-citoyens/bibliotheque
Christine Gauthier, Responsable
Sylvie Cloutier, Préposée au prêt

***Cowansville:* Bibliothèque Gabrielle-Giroux-Bertrand**
171, rue Principale, Cowansville, QC J2K 3L9
Tél: 450-263-4071; *Téléc:* 450-263-7477
biblio129@reseaubibliomonteregie.qc.ca
www.reseaubiblioduquebec.qc.ca; www.cowansville.org
Brigitte Messier, Responsable

***Crabtree:* Bibliothèque de Crabtree**
59, 16e rue, Crabtree, QC J0K 1B0
Tél: 450-754-4332
biblio114@reseaubibliocqlm.qc.ca
www.reseaubiblioduquebec.qc.ca
Média social: www.facebook.com/186371856677
Marjolaine Bertrand, Responsable
450-754-4332

***Côte-Saint-Luc:* Bibliothèque publique Eleanor London Côte-Saint-Luc**
5851, boul Cavendish, Côte-Saint-Luc, QC H4W 2X8
Tél: 514-485-6900; *Téléc:* 514-485-6966
reference@cotesaintluc.org
www.elcslpl.org
Média social:
www.facebook.com/group.php?gid=123100031035453
Janine West, Directrice de la bibliothèque
jwest @ cotesaintluc.org
514-485-6900 ext. 4202

***Danford Lake:* Bibliothèque de l'Alleyn-et-Cawood**
#10, ch Jondee, Danford Lake, QC J0X 1P0
Tél: 819-467-2941; *Téléc:* 819-467-3133
admalleyncawood@crsbpo.qc.ca
www.reseaubiblioduquebec.qc.ca/Alleyn-et-Cawood

***Danville:* Bibliothèque municipale de Danville**
Hôtel de Ville, Danville, QC J0A 1A0
Tél: 819-839-3236; *Téléc:* 819-839-2918
biblio053@reseaubiblioestrie.qc.ca
www.reseaubiblioduquebec.qc.ca
Daniel Hinse, Responsable

***Daveluyville:* Bibliothèque de Daveluyville**
436, 5e Rue, Daveluyville, QC G0Z 1C0
Tél: 819-367-3645; *Téléc:* 819-367-3550
biblio057@reseaubibliocqlm.qc.ca
www.reseaubiblioduquebec.qc.ca
Jacqueline B. Pépin, Responsable

***Delson:* Bibliothèque municipale de Delson**
1, 1e av, Delson, QC J5B 1M9
Tél: 450-632-1050
delson@reseaubibliomonteregie.qc.ca
www.reseaubiblioduquebec.qc.ca
Lyne Croussette, Responsable

***Desbiens:* Bibliothèque publique de Desbiens**
1058, rue Marcellin, local 2, Desbiens, QC G0W 1N0
Tél: 418-346-5739
desbiens@reseaubiblioslsj.qc.ca
www.reseaubiblioduquebec.qc.ca/portail/index.aspx?page=3&BID=532
Régine Brassard, Responsable

***Deschaillons-sur-St-Laurent:* Bibliothèque de Deschaillons-sur-Saint-Laurent**
1042A, rue Marie-Victorin, Deschaillons-sur-St-Laurent, QC G0S 1G0
Tél: 819-292-2483; *Téléc:* 819-292-3194
biblio101@reseaubibliocqlm.qc.ca
www.reseaubiblioduquebec.qc.ca
Odette Gilbert, Responsable

***Deschambault-Grondines:* Bibliothèque Du Bord de l'Eau**
115, rue de l'Église, Deschambault-Grondines, QC G0A 1S0
Tél: 418-286-6938; *Téléc:* 418-286-6511
bibdesch@globetrotter.qc.ca
www.reseaubiblioduquebec.qc.ca/deschambault/
Jacqueline Gignac, Responsable
Marlène Gariépy, Adjointe
418-286-6491
Marie-Claude Gauthier, Responsable, Extranet
418-286-6491
Madeleine Bouillé, Responsable, Animation
Diane Genest, Responsable, Échanges
Isabelle Petit, Responsable, Collection locale

***Deux-Montagnes:* Bibliothèque de Deux-Montagnes / Deux-Montagnes Library**
200, rue Henri-Dunant, Deux-Montagnes, QC J7R 4W6
Tél: 450-473-2702; *Téléc:* 450-473-2816
biblio@ville.deux-montagnes.qc.ca
bibliotheque.ville.deux-montagnes.qc.ca
Johanne Chaput, Responsable, Activités culturelles
jchaput@ville.deux-montagnes.gc.ca
Mireille Brodeur, Commis
mbrodeur@ville.deux-montagnes.qc.ca
Guylaine Lemire, Technicienne en documentation
glemire@ville.deux-montagnes.qc.ca

Louise St-Laurent, Technicienne en documentation
lsaint-laurent@ville.deux-montagnes.qc.ca

Dolbeau-Mistassini: Bibliothèque de Dolbeau-Mistassini
175, 4e av, Dolbeau-Mistassini, QC G8L 2W6
Tél: 418-276-1317; *Téléc:* 418-276-8188
www.dolbeau.biblio.qc.ca
Pauline Lapointe, Responsable
plapointe@ville.dolbeau-mistassini.qc.ca
Liette Caron, Technicienne en documentation
lcaron@ville.dolbeau-mistassini.qc.ca
Annie Lamontagne, Technicienne en documentation
alamontagne@ville.dolbeau-mistassini.qc.ca

Dollard-des-Ormeaux: Bibliothèque de Dollard-des-Ormeaux
12001, boul De Salaberry, Dollard-des-Ormeaux, QC H9B 2A7
Tél: 514-684-1496; *Téléc:* 514-684-9569
bibliotheque@ddo.qc.ca
www.ville.ddo.qc.ca
Média social: www.facebook.com/biblioddo
Shamim Kassam, Information Resource Specialist
shamim_kassam@transalta.com
403-267-3636
Cheryl McNeil, Information Resource Specialist
cheryl_mcneil@transalta.com
403-267-7675
Carol Thiessen, Information Resource Specialist
carol_thiessen@transalta.com
403-267-7651

Dorval: Bibliothèque de Dorval
1401, ch du Bord-du-Lac, Dorval, QC H9S 2E5
Tél: 514-633-4170; *Téléc:* 514-633-4177
biblio@ville.dorval.qc.ca
www.ville.dorval.qc.ca

Dosquet: Bibliothèque La Bouquinerie/Dosquet
1, rue Viger, Dosquet, QC G0S 1H0
Tél: 418-728-3994; *Téléc:* 418-728-3338
www.reseaubiblioduquebec.qc.ca/dosquet
France Laflamme, Responsable
Lise Martineau, Responsable, PIB
Gaétan Labbé, Responsable, Échanges
Édith Gosselin, Responsable, Collection locale

Drummondville: Bibliothèque municipale Côme-Saint-Germain
545, rue des Écoles, Drummondville, QC J2B 1J6
Tél: 819-478-6573; *Téléc:* 819-478-0399
biblio@ville.drummondville.qc.ca
www.ville.drummondville.qc.ca
Joceline-Andrée Turcotte, Chef de division
jturcotte@ville.drummondville.qc.ca
819-478-6588
Michel LeBlanc, Technicien en documentation
819-474-8841
Suzanne Pelletier, Technicienne en documentation
spelletier@ville.drummondville.qc.ca
819-474-8882
Natalie Bissonnette, Bibliothécaire
nbissonnette@ville.drummondville.qc.ca

Duhamel: Bibliothèque Duhamel
1899, rue Principale, Duhamel, QC J0V 1G0
Tél: 819-428-7100; *Téléc:* 819-428-1941
admduhamel@crsbpo.qc.ca
www.reseaubiblioduquebec.qc.ca/Duhamel/
Roselyne Bernard, Responsable
Marylou Bernard, Bénévole
Pearl Fillion, Bénévole

Dunham: Bibliothèque municipale de Dunham/ Dunham Municipal Library
3638, rue Principale, Dunham, QC J0E 1M0
Tél: 450-295-2621
dunham@reseaubibliomonteregie.qc.ca
www.reseaubiblioduquebec.qc.ca
Marie Bonneville, Responsable

Duparquet: Bibliothèque Duparquet
54, rue Principale, Duparquet, QC J0Z 1W0
Tél: 819-948-2455; *Téléc:* 819-948-2266
duparquet@reseaubiblioatnq.qc.ca
www.crsbpat.qc.ca/duparquet/
Lise Baron, Responsable

Dupuy: Bibliothèque de Dupuy
63, rue Principale, Dupuy, QC J0Z 1X0
Tél: 819-783-2147; *Téléc:* 819-783-2147
dupuy@reseaubiblioatnq.qc.ca
www.reseaubiblioduquebec.qc.ca/dupuy
Huguette Huot, Responsable

Durham-Sud: Bibliothèque de Durham-Sud
77, rue de l'Église, Durham-Sud, QC J0H 2C0
Tél: 819-858-1156; *Téléc:* 819-858-2044
biblio153@reseaubibliocqlm.qc.ca
Jacques Boyer, Responsable

Dégelis: Bibliothèque Élisabeth-Turgeon
663, 6e rue ouest, Dégelis, QC G5T 1Y3
Tél: 418-853-2332
biblio.degelis@crsbp.net
www.reseaubiblioduquebec.qc.ca
Gertrude Leclerc, Responsable

East Broughton: Bibliothèque La Bouquinerie/East Broughton/Sacré-Coeur-de-Jésus
372A, av du Collège, East Broughton, QC G0N 1G0
Tél: 418-427-4900; *Téléc:* 418-427-3514
bouquinerie@eastbroughton.com
www.reseaubiblioduquebec.qc.ca/eastbroughton/
Lynda Laplante, Responsable

Entrelacs: Bibliothèque d'Entrelacs
2351, ch Entrelacs, Entrelacs, QC J0T 2E0
Tél: 450-228-2529; *Téléc:* 450-228-4866
biblient@entrelacs.com
www.entrelacs.com/biblio_frame.htm
Suzanne Larivière, Responsable

Esprit-Saint: Bibliothèque d'Esprit-Saint
121, rue des Érables, Esprit-Saint, QC G0K 1A0
Tél: 418-779-2016
biblio.esprit@crsbp.net
www.reseaubiblioduquebec.qc.ca
Sylvie Boucher, Responsable

Fabre: Bibliothèque Le Coquelicot de Fabre
620, av de l'Église, Fabre, QC J0Z 1Z0
Tél: 819-634-2745; *Téléc:* 819-634-2646
fabre@reseaubiblioatnq.qc.ca
www.reseaubiblioduquebec.qc.ca/fabre
Jacinthe Breton Desrochers, Responsable

Farnham: Bibliothèque de Farnham inc.
479, rue de l'Hôtel de Ville, Farnham, QC J2N 2H3
Tél: 450-293-3375; *Téléc:* 450-293-2989
bibliofarnham@bellnet.ca
bibliofarnham.ca
Dino Coudé, Responsable

Fassett: Bibliothèque Fassett/Notre-Dame-de-Bonsecours
19, rue Gendron, Fassett, QC J0V 1H0
Tél: 819-423-6943; *Téléc:* 819-423-5388
admfassett@crsbpo.qc.ca
www.reseaubiblioduquebec.qc.ca/Fassett/
Nathalie Frenière, Responsable
Gabrielle Lefaivre, Bénévole

Fatima: Bibliothèque de Fatima
#2, 730, ch des Caps, Fatima, QC G4T 2T3
Tél: 418-986-4736
biblio.fatima@hotmail.com
www.reseaubiblioduquebec.qc.ca
Thérèse Harvie, Responsable

Ferme-Neuve: Bibliothèque de Ferme-Neuve
144, 12e rue, Ferme-Neuve, QC J0W 1C0
Tél: 819-587-3102
bibliotheque@municipalite.ferme-neuve.qc.ca
www.reseaubiblioduquebec.qc.ca
Andrée Quevillon, Responsable

Fermont: Bibliothèque publique de Fermont
100, place Daviault, Fermont, QC G0G 1J0
Tél: 418-287-3227; *Téléc:* 418-287-3274
biblio@villedefermont.qc.ca
Aline Martel, Responsable

Forestville: Bibliothèque municipale de Forestville
10, 10e rue, Forestville, QC G0T 1E0
Tél: 418-587-4483; *Téléc:* 418-587-2458
biblioforestville@globetrotter.net
www.reseaubiblioduquebec.qc.ca
Roger Dumont, Responsable

Fort-Coulonge: Bibliothèque de Fort-Coulonge
134, rue Principale, Fort-Coulonge, QC J0X 1V0
Tél: 819-683-3421; *Téléc:* 819-683-3627
biblio.fc@fortcoulonge.qc.ca
www.fortcoulonge.qc.ca
Pierrette Lafrenière, Responsable

Fortierville: Bibliothèque de Fortierville
198A, rue de la Fabrique, Fortierville, QC G0S 1J0
Tél: 819-287-4309; *Téléc:* 819-287-5922
biblio015@reseaubibliocqlm.qc.ca
Denise Lemay, Responsable
Diane Perreault, Bénévole
Adrienne Nault, Bénévole

Fossambault-sur-le-Lac: Bibliothèque municipale de Fossambault-sur-le-Lac ("La Source")
145, rue Gingras, Fossambault-sur-le-Lac, QC G3N 0K2
Tél: 418-875-3133; *Téléc:* 418-875-3544
fossam@coopcscf.com
www.fossambault-sur-le-lac.com
Monique Blouin, Responsable
418-875-2876

Franquelin: Bibliothèque municipale de Franquelin
27, rue des Érables, Franquelin, QC G0H 1E0
Tél: 418-294-6170; *Téléc:* 418-296-6946
www.reseaubiblioduquebec.qc.ca
Steeve Grenier, Responsable

Fugèreville: Bibliothèque de Fugèreville
33A, rue Principale, Fugèreville, QC J0Z 2A0
Tél: 819-748-2276; *Téléc:* 819-748-2422
fugereville@reseaubiblioatnq.qc.ca
www.reseaubiblioduquebec.qc.ca/fugereville
Gaétane Cloutier, Responsable

Gallichan: Bibliothèque La Gallithèque
207, ch de la Rivière ouest, Gallichan, QC J0Z 2B0
Tél: 819-787-6301
gallichan@mrcao.qc.ca
gallichan.ao.ca
Brigitte Rivard, Responsable

Gallix: Bibliothèque municipale de Gallix
524, av Lapierre, Gallix, QC G0G 1L0
Tél: 418-766-3264
www.reseaubiblioduquebec.qc.ca
Lyne Porlier, Responsable

Gaspé: Bibliothèque Alma-Bourget-Costisella
10, Côte Cater, Gaspé, QC G4X 1V2
Tél: 418-368-2104; *Téléc:* 418-368-8532
biblio.gaspe@globetrotter.net
Adrienne Bisson, Responsable

Gaspé: Bibliothèque de Cap-aux-Os
1826, boul Forillon, Gaspé, QC G4X 6L4
Tél: 418-368-2104; *Téléc:* 418-368-6810
www.reseaubiblioduquebec.qc.ca
Rita Beaudin, Responsable

Gaspé: Bibliothèque de L'Anse-au-Griffon
465, boul du Griffon, Gaspé, QC G4X 6A3
Tél: 418-368-2104; *Téléc:* 418-368-6837
bboaag@globetrotter.qc.ca
www.reseaubiblioduquebec.qc.ca
Camille Malouin, Responsable

Gaspé: Bibliothèque de L'Anse-à-Valleau
9, rue Mathurin, Gaspé, QC G4X 4A8
Tél: 418-368-2104
www.reseaubiblioduquebec.qc.ca
Priscillia Poirier, Responsable
priscillia.poirier@globetrotter.qc.ca

Gaspé: Bibliothèque de Petit-Cap
439, boul Petit-Cap, Gaspé, QC G4X 4L1
Tél: 418-368-2104
bibliopetitcap@globetrotter.net
www.reseaubiblioduquebec.qc.ca
Philomène Cloutier, Responsable

Gaspé: Bibliothèque de Saint-Majorique
3-1, montée de Corte-Réal, Gaspé, QC G4X 6R7
Tél: 418-368-2104
biblio.stmajorique@globetrotter.net
www.reseaubiblioduquebec.qc.ca
Gracia Cabot, Responsable

***Gatineau:* Bibliothèque municipale de Gatineau**
#317, 144, boul de l'Hôpital, Gatineau, QC J8T 7S7
Tél: 819-595-7460; *Téléc:* 819-243-2399
Ligne sans frais: 800-299-2002
bibliotheque@gatineau.ca
www.ville.gatineau.qc.ca/bibliotheque.htm
Média social: www.flickr.com/photos/38625711@N06/sets; twitter.com/bibliogatineau; www.facebook.com/bibliogatineau
Carole Laguë, Chef de division
lague.carole@gatineau.qc.ca
819-243-2345 ext. 2548

***Gethsémani:* Bibliothèque de La Romaine**
École Marie-Sarah, Poste Restante, Gethsémani, QC G0G 1M0
Tél: 418-787-2241
www.reseaubiblioduquebec.qc.ca

***Girardville:* Bibliothèque publique de Girardville**
180, rue Principale, Girardville, QC G0W 1R0
Tél: 418-258-3222; *Téléc:* 418-258-3473
girardv@reseaubiblioslsj.qc.ca
Francine Lambert, Responsable
418-258-3222
Carolle Lalancette, Co-responsable

***Godbout:* Bibliothèque municipale de Godbout**
102B, rue Alexandre, Godbout, QC G0H 1G0
Tél: 418-568-7702; *Téléc:* 418-568-7356
biblio.godbout@hotmail.com
www.reseaubiblioduquebec.qc.ca
Caroline Morin, Responsable
curbymorin@globetrotter.net
418-568-7420

***Gracefield:* Bibliothèque de Gracefield**
3, rue de la Polyvalente, Gracefield, QC J0X 1W0
Tél: 819-463-1180; *Téléc:* 819-463-4236
admgracefield@crsbpo.qc.ca
www.reseaubiblioduquebec.qc.ca/Gracefield
Denise Pelletier Rochon, Responsable

***Granby:* Bibliothèque Paul-O.-Trépanier**
11, rue Dufferin, Granby, QC J2G 2T8
Tél: 450-776-8320; *Téléc:* 450-776-8313
Other Numbers: Horaire (btc vocale): (450) 776-8310
bibliotheque@ville.granby.qc.ca
www.biblio.ville.granby.qc.ca/bibliotheque/
Linda Laberge, Responsable
llaberge@ville.granby.qc.ca
Lyne Plourde, Bénévole

***Grand-Mère:* Bibliothèque Hélène-B. Beauséjour**
650, 8e rue, Grand-Mère, QC G9T 6K1
Tél: 819-538-5555
bibliotheque@ville.shawinigan.qc.ca
www.shawinigan.qc.ca
Charlotte Lecours, Responsable des bibliothèques
819-536-7211 ext. 501

***Grand-Remous:* Bibliothèque de Grand-Remous**
1508, rte Transcanadienne, Grand-Remous, QC J0W 1E0
Tél: 819-438-2168; *Téléc:* 418-438-2364
admgrandremous@crsbpo.qc.ca
www.reseaubiblioduquebec.qc.ca/Grand-Remous
Lise Fraser, Responsable

***Grande-Entrée:* Bibliothèque de Grande-Entrée**
214, route 199, Grande-Entrée, QC G4T 7A4
Tél: 418-985-2288; *Téléc:* 418-985-2149
biblioge@muniles.ca
www.reseaubiblioduquebec.qc.ca
Raoul Cyr, Responsable

***Grande-Rivière:* Bibliothèque La Détente/Grande-Rivière**
210, rue du Carrefour, Grande-Rivière, QC G0C 1V0
Tél: 418-385-3833; *Téléc:* 418-385-2290
Marie-Paule Berger, Responsable

***Grande-Vallée:* Bibliothèque de Grande-Vallée**
3, rue St-François-Xavier est, Grande-Vallée, QC G0E 1K0
Tél: 418-393-2166; *Téléc:* 418-393-2274
bbogrval@globetrotter.net
www.reseaubiblioduquebec.qc.ca
Gaétanne Normand, Responsable
normandg@hotmail.com

***Grandes-Bergeronnes:* Bibliothèque Les Bergeronnes**
514, rue du Boisé, Grandes-Bergeronnes, QC G0T 1G0
Tél: 418-232-1134; *Téléc:* 418-232-6602
Ninon Marty, Responsable

***Grandes-Piles:* Bibliothèque de Grandes-Piles**
650, 4e av, Grandes-Piles, QC G0X 1H0
Tél: 819-533-3697; *Téléc:* 819-538-6947
biblio030@reseaubibliocqlm.qc.ca
www.reseaubiblioduquebec.qc.ca
Line Blanchard, Responsable

***Grenville:* Bibliothèque de Grenville**
18, rue Tri-Jean, Grenville, QC J0V 1J0
Tél: 819-242-2585; *Téléc:* 819-242-5891
biblio@grenville.ca
www.reseaubiblioduquebec.qc.ca/grenville
Céline Joly, Responsable
Hélène Joly, Bénévole au comptoir de prêts

***Grenville-sur-la-Rouge:* Bibliothèque de Calumet**
435, rue Principale, Grenville-sur-la-Rouge, QC J0V 1B0
Tél: 819-242-8088; *Téléc:* 819-242-1232
biblio5@crsbpl.qc.ca
www.reseaubiblioduquebec.qc.ca
Judy Smith, Responsable

***Grenville-sur-la-Rouge:* Bibliothèque de Pointe-au-Chêne**
2714, rte 148, Grenville-sur-la-Rouge, QC J0V 1B0
Tél: 819-242-0298
bibpac@hawknet.ca
www.reseaubiblioduquebec.qc.ca
Johanne Nantel, Responsable

***Grondines:* Bibliothèque L'Ardoise**
525, ch Sir-Lomer-Gouin, Grondines, QC G0A 1W0
Tél: 418-268-8359; *Téléc:* 418-268-5553
bibligron@csportneuf.qc.ca
www.reseaubiblioduquebec.qc.ca/grondines/
Guylaine Rivard, Responsable
Michelle Trottier, Adjointe

***Gros-Morne:* Bibliothèque de Gros-Morne**
1, rue de l'Église ouest, Gros-Morne, QC G0E 1L0
Tél: 418-797-2610
www.reseaubiblioduquebec.qc.ca

***Grosse-Ile:* Bibliothèque de Grosse-Ile**
448, ch Principal, Grosse-Ile, QC G4T 6A8
Tél: 418-986-2885; *Téléc:* 418-985-2955
Natasha Joncas, Responsable

***Guyenne:* Bibliothèque de Guyenne**
1255-F, rang 5, Guyenne, QC J0Y 1L0
Tél: 819-732-9128; *Téléc:* 819-732-0904
guyenne@reseaubiblioatnq.qc.ca
www.reseaubiblioduquebec.qc.ca/guyenne
Francine Simard, Responsable

***Guérin:* Bibliothèque de Guérin**
516A, rue St-Gabriel, Guérin, QC J0Z 2E0
Tél: 819-784-7024; *Téléc:* 819-784-7026
guerin@reseaubiblioatnq.qc.ca
www.reseaubiblioduquebec.qc.ca/guerin
Sylvie Laverdière, Responsable

***Ham-Nord:* Bibliothèque de Ham-Nord**
474, rue Principale, Ham-Nord, QC G0P 1A0
Tél: 819-344-2805; *Téléc:* 819-344-2806
biblio150@reseaubibliocqlm.qc.ca
www.reseaubiblioduquebec.qc.ca

***Harrington Harbour:* Bibliothèque de Harrington Harbour**
CP 7, Harrington Harbour, QC G0G 1N0
Tél: 418-787-2244; *Téléc:* 418-787-2241
www.reseaubiblioduquebec.qc.ca
Judi Ransom, Responsable

***Havre-aux-Maisons:* Bibliothèque de Havre-aux-Maisons**
37, ch Central, Havre-aux-Maisons, QC G4T 5H1
Tél: 418-969-2100
biblioham@muniles.ca
www.reseaubiblioduquebec.qc.ca
Marcel Thériault, Responsable

***Havre-Saint-Pierre:* Bibliothèque municipale de Havre-St-Pierre**
1045, rue Dulcinée, Havre-Saint-Pierre, QC G0G 1P0
Tél: 418-538-3301; *Téléc:* 418-538-3439
biblio.havrest-pierre@globetrotter.net
www.reseaubiblioduquebec.qc.ca
Nicole Cormier, Responsable

***Hemmingford:* Bibliothèque municipale d'Hemmingford / Hemmingford Community Library**
552, av Goyette, Hemmingford, QC J0L 1H0
Tél: 450-247-0010
hemmingford@reseaubibliomonteregie.qc.ca
www.reseaubiblioduquebec.qc.ca
Elizabeth Nicholls, Responsable

***Henryville:* Bibliothèque municipale d'Henryville**
#104, 854, rue St-Jean-Baptiste, Henryville, QC J0J 1E0
Tél: 450-299-1165
henryville@reseaubibliomonteregie.qc.ca
www.reseaubiblioduquebec.qc.ca
Mathieu Fortin, Responsable

***Honfleur:* Bibliothèque La Livrothèque**
320, rue Saint-Jean, Honfleur, QC G0R 1N0
Tél: 418-885-8212; *Téléc:* 418-885-9195
livro@globetrotter.qc.ca
www.reseaubiblioduquebec.qc.ca/honfleur/
Isabelle Roussy, Responsable
Nathalie Beaudoin, Adjointe
Lyne Fournier, Responsable, Collection locale
Nicole Morin, Responsable, PIB

***Hope Town:* Bibliothèque de Hope Town**
224, rte 132, Hope Town, QC G0C 2K0
Tél: 418-752-3848; *Téléc:* 418-752-2434
www.reseaubiblioduquebec.qc.ca
Lynda McWhirter, Responsable

***Huberdeau:* Bibliothèque d'Huberdeau**
101, rue Du Pont, Huberdeau, QC J0T 1G0
Tél: 819-687-1164; *Téléc:* 819-687-8808
biblio@municipalite.huberdeau.qc.ca
www.reseaubiblioduquebec.qc.ca
Suzanne Fortin, Responsable
Brenda Gaudreault, Bénévole
Bernard Dervillez, Bénévole
Huguette Deslauriers, Bénévole

***Huntingdon:* Little Green Library / La Petite Bibliothèque Verte**
6 Hunter St., Huntingdon, QC J0S 1H0
Tel: 450-264-4872
Laura Smith, President
Ola Proudfoot, Cataloguer
Mary Quinnel, Head, Acquisistions (English)
Evelyne Latreille, Head, Acquisitions (French)

***Hérouxville:* Bibliothèque de Hérouxville**
1060, rue Saint-Pierre, Hérouxville, QC G0X 1J0
Tél: 418-365-7337; *Téléc:* 418-365-7041
biblio090@reseaubibliocqlm.qc.ca
www.reseaubiblioduquebec.qc.ca
Julie L'Heureux, Responsable

***Ile-du-Grand-Calumet:* Bibliothèque Ile-du-Grand-Calumet**
2, rue Brizard, Ile-du-Grand-Calumet, QC J0X 1J0
Tél: 819-648-5966; *Téléc:* 819-648-2659
admcalumet@crsbpo.qc.ca
www.reseaubiblioduquebec.qc.ca/Grand-Calument/
Chantal Corriveau, Responsable

***Inverness:* Bibliothèque de Inverness (L'Inverthèque)**
1801, rue Dublin, Inverness, QC G0S 1K0
Tél: 418-453-2867; *Téléc:* 418-453-2554
biblio145@reseaubibliocqlm.qc.ca
www.reseaubiblioduquebec.qc.ca

***Issoudun:* Bibliothèque La Rêverie/Notre-Dame-de-Sacré-Coeur-d'Issoudun**
268, rue Principale, Issoudun, QC G0S 1L0
Tél: 418-728-9061; *Téléc:* 418-728-2303
www.reseaubiblioduquebec.qc.ca/issoudun
Carole Couture, Responsable
Rosaline Croteau, Responsable, PIB

***Jonquière:* Bibliothèque d'Arvida**
2850, Place Davis, Jonquière, QC G7X 7W7
Tél: 418-699-6068; *Téléc:* 418-699-6046
celine.verreault@ville.saguenay.qc.ca
www.ville.saguenay.qc.ca
Anne Lebel, Chef de division, Bibliothèques de Saguenay
anne.lebel@ville.saguenay.qc.ca
Luc Lepage, Responsable, Bibliothèques de l'arrond. de Jonquière
luc.lepage@ville.saguenay.qc.ca
Monique Laprise, Responsable de l'Animation
monique.laprise@ville.saguenay.qc.ca

***Jonquière:* Bibliothèque de Kénogami**
3825, rue de Montcalm, Jonquière, QC G7X 1V8
Tél: 418-698-5350
webbiblio@ville.saguenay.qc.ca
ville.saguenay.qc.ca
Anne Lebel, Chef de division, Bibliothèques de Saguenay
anne.lebel@ville.saguenay.qc.ca
Luc Lepage, Responsable, Bibliothèques de l'arrond. de Jonquière
luc.lepage@ville.saguenay.qc.ca
Monique Laprise, Responsable de l'Animation
monique.laprise@ville.saguenay.qc.ca

***Kiamika:* Bibliothèque de Kiamika**
3, ch Valiquette, Kiamika, QC J0W 1G0
Tél: 819-585-3225; *Téléc:* 819-585-3992
biblio@kiamika.ca
Nanette Sirois, Responsable

***Kingsey Falls:* Bibliothèque de Kingsey Falls**
13, rue Caron, Kingsey Falls, QC J0A 1B0
Tél: 819-363-3818
biblio040@reseaubibliocqlm.qc.ca
Suzanne Boulet, Responsable

***Kinnear's Mills:* Bibliothèque La Boukinnerie**
120, rue des Églises, Kinnear's Mills, QC G0N 1K0
Tél: 418-424-0082; *Téléc:* 418-424-3015
www.reseaubiblioduquebec.qc.ca
Michelle Bernier-Pageau, Responsable
Gaétane Malo, Responsable des PIB

***Kirkland:* Bibliothèque de Kirkland**
17100, boul Hymus, Kirkland, QC H9J 2W2
Tél: 514-630-2726; *Téléc:* 514-630-2716
www.ville.kirkland.qc.ca
Sonia Djevalikian, Chef de division
SDjevalikian@ville.kirkland.qc.ca
514-694-4100 ext. 3200

***Knowlton:* Bibliothèque Commémorative Pettes / Pettes Memorial Library**
276, ch Knowlton, Knowlton, QC J0E 1V0
Tél: 450-243-6128; *Téléc:* 450-243-5272
pettes.ca

***L'Anse-Saint-Jean:* Bibliothèque publique de L'Anse-St-Jean**
3, rue du Couvent, L'Anse-Saint-Jean, QC G0V 1J0
Tél: 418-272-2633
anse@reseaubiblioslsj.qc.ca
www.reseaubiblioduquebec.qc.ca
Germaine Boudreault, Responsable
Marie Thibeault, Adjointe

***L'Ascension:* Bibliothèque de l'Ascension**
4, rue Principale ouest, L'Ascension, QC J0T 1W0
Tél: 819-275-1546; *Téléc:* 819-275-1546
bibliotheque@municipalite-lascension.qc.ca
www.reseaubiblioduquebec.qc.ca/l'ascension
Monique Turpin, Responsable
Danielle Tremblay, Adjointe

***L'Ascension:* Bibliothèque publique de L'Ascension**
900, 4e av est, L'Ascension, QC G0W 1Y0
Tél: 418-347-3482; *Téléc:* 418-347-4253
ascens@reseaubiblioslsj.qc.ca
www.reseaubiblioduquebec.qc.ca/portail/index.aspx?page=3&BI D=528
Diane Tremblay, Coordonnatrice

***L'Assomption:* Bibliothèque Christian-Roy**
375, rue St-Pierre, L'Assomption, QC J5W 2B6
Tél: 450-589-5671; *Téléc:* 450-589-6882
bibliotheque@ville.lassomption.qc.ca
www.ville.lassomption.qc.ca/cbiblio.html
Marjolaine Bertrand, Bibliothécaire
450-589-5671 ext. 237

***L'Assomption:* Les Bibliothèques publiques de Laval-Laurentides-Lanaudière**
375, rue St-Pierre, L'Assomption, QC J5W 1A1
Tél: 450-589-5671; *Téléc:* 450-589-6882
bibliotheque@ville.lassomption.qc.ca
www.bplll.qc.ca
Stéphane Legault, Président

***L'Isle-aux-Coudres:* Bibliothèque 'Pour la suite du monde'**
1026, ch des Coudriers, L'Isle-aux-Coudres, QC G0A 3J0
Tél: 418-438-2602; *Téléc:* 418-438-2750
www.reseaubiblioduquebec.qc.ca/coudres
Claudine Hovington, Responsable
418-438-2602

***L'Isle-aux-Grues:* Bibliothèque La Rose des Vents/L'Isle-aux-Grues**
107, ch de la Volière, L'Isle-aux-Grues, QC G0R 1P0
Tél: 418-248-8060; *Téléc:* 418-248-4680
Lisette Painchaud, Responsable
418-248-4687

***L'Isle-Verte:* Bibliothèque de Notre-Dame-des-Sept-Douleurs**
ch de l'Ile, L'Isle-Verte, QC G0L 1K0
Tél: 418-898-3451
biblio.douleurs@crsbp.net
www.reseaubiblioduquebec.qc.ca

***L'Islet:* Bibliothèque Jean-Paul-Bourque/L'Islet-sur-Mer**
16, rte des Pionniers est, L'Islet, QC G0R 2B0
Tél: 418-247-7576; *Téléc:* 418-247-5009
www.reseaubiblioduquebec.qc.ca/l'islet-sur-mer/
Jacqueline C. Kirouac, Responsable
Hélène St-Pierre, Adjointe

***L'Islet:* Bibliothèque Léon-Laberge**
#1, 284, boul Nilus-Leclerc, L'Islet, QC G0R 2C0
Tél: 418-247-5345; *Téléc:* 418-247-5085
bleonl@globetrotter.qc.ca
www.reseaubiblioduquebec.qc.ca/l'islet/
Madeleine Gagnon, Responsable
Johanne Dessureault, Responsable, Animation

***L'Épiphanie:* Bibliothèque de L'Épiphanie**
83, rue Amireault, L'Épiphanie, QC J5X 1A1
Tél: 450-588-4470
biblio061@reseaubibliocqlm.qc.ca
www.reseaubiblioduquebec.qc.ca
Nathalie L'Espérance, Responsable

***L'Étang-du-Nord:* Bibliothèque de l'Étang-du-Nord**
1589, ch Étang-du-Nord, L'Étang-du-Nord, QC G4T 3C1
Tél: 418-986-3321; *Téléc:* 418-986-6231
georgettenoelchev@hotmail.com
Georgette Chevarie, Responsable

***La Baie:* Bibliothèque de La Baie**
1911, 6e av, La Baie, QC G7B 1S1
Tél: 418-698-5350; *Téléc:* 418-697-5087
webbiblio@ville.saguenay.qc.ca
www.ville.saguenay.qc.ca
Anne Lebel, Chef de division, Bibliothèques de Saguenay
anne.lebel@ville.saguenay.qc.ca
Céline Verreault, Responsable, Bibliothèques de l'arrond. de La Baie
celine.verreault@ville.saguenay.qc.ca
Virginie Beaudoin, Responsable de l'Animation
virginie.beaudoin@ville.saguenay.qc.ca

***La Conception:* Bibliothèque de La Conception**
1373, boul du Centenaire, La Conception, QC J0T 1M0
Tél: 819-686-3016; *Téléc:* 819-686-5808
biblio@municipalite.laconception.qc.ca
www.reseaubiblioduquebec.qc.ca
Manuela Brassard-Erba, Responsable

***La Corne:* Bibliothèque de La Corne**
324, rte 111, La Corne, QC J0Y 1R0
Tél: 819-799-2365; *Téléc:* 819-799-3571
lacorne@reseaubiblioatnq.qc.ca
www.reseaubiblioduquebec.qc.ca/la corne
Chantal Lessard, Responsable

***La Doré:* Bibliothèque publique de la Doré**
4450, des Peupliers, La Doré, QC G8J 1E5
Tél: 418-256-3992; *Téléc:* 418-256-3992
www.reseaubiblioduquebec.qc.ca/portail/index.aspx?page=3&BI D=541
Colombe Tremblay, Responsable

***La Macaza:* Bibliothèque de La Macaza**
53, rue des Pionniers, La Macaza, QC J0T 1R0
Tél: 819-275-2077; *Téléc:* 819-275-3429
biblio-lamacaza@bellnet.ca
Nicole Ayotte, Responsable
nicoleayotte1@hotmail.com
Ghislaine Plouffe, Adjointe

***La Malbaie:* Bibliothèque Laure-Conan**
395, rue St-Etienne, La Malbaie, QC G5A 1S8
Tél: 418-665-6027; *Téléc:* 418-665-6481
ville.lamalbaie.qc.ca/fr/bibliotheques/
Marie-Claire Fortin, Directrice

***La Malbaie:* Bibliothèque municipale de Cap-à-l'Aigle**
768, rue Saint-Raphaël, La Malbaie, QC G5A 2P2
Tél: 418-665-7596; *Téléc:* 418-665-7597
Louise Belley, Responsable
Marie-Claire Tremblay, Responsable, Échanges

***La Minerve:* Bibliothèque de La Minerve**
8, rue Mailloux, La Minerve, QC J0T 1S0
Tél: 819-274-2313; *Téléc:* 819-274-2031
laminerve@crsbpl.qc.ca
www.municipalite.laminerve.qc.ca
Marcelle Grégoire, Responsable

***La Motte:* Bibliothèque de La Motte**
349, ch St-Luc, La Motte, QC J0Y 1T0
Tél: 819-732-0505; *Téléc:* 819-727-4248
lamotte@reseaubiblioatnq.qc.ca
www.reseaubiblioduquebec.qc.ca/la motte
Nicole Richard, Responsable

***La Pocatière:* Bibliothèque municipale de La Pocatière**
#4, 900, 6e av, La Pocatière, QC G0R 1Z0
Tél: 418-856-3459
biblio.pocati@crsbp.net
www.reseaubiblioduquebec.qc.ca
Sylvie Dionne, Responsable

***La Prairie:* Bibliothèque Léo-Lecavalier**
Complexe Saint-Laurent, 500, rue Saint-Laurent, La Prairie, QC J5R 5X2
Tél: 450-444-6710; *Téléc:* 450-444-6708
biblio@ville.laprairie.qc.ca
www.ville.laprairie.qc.ca/bibliotheque
Brigitte Tremblay, Responsable

***La Reine:* Bibliothèque La Reine**
1, 3e av ouest, La Reine, QC J0Z 2L0
Tél: 819-947-5271; *Téléc:* 819-947-5271
lareine@reseaubiblioatnq.qc.ca
Angèle Thouin, Responsable
Jeannine Blais, Bénévole
Pierrette East, Bénévole

***La Sarre:* Bibliothèque municipale Richelieu de La Sarre**
Maison de la culture, 195, rue Principale, La Sarre, QC J9Z 1Y3
Tél: 819-333-2294; *Téléc:* 819-333-2296
slafleur@ville.lasarre.qc.ca
www.ville.lasarre.qc.ca/culture/fr/lecture/details.cfm?ID=7
Média social: www.facebook.com/333704643348589
Lise Gaignard, Directrice
lgaignard@ville.lasarre.qc.ca
Noëlline Marcoux, Technicienne
nmarcoux@ville.lasarre.qc.ca

***La Trinité-des-Monts:* Bibliothèque de La Trinité-des-Monts**
12, rue Principale ouest, La Trinité-des-Monts, QC G0K 1B0
Tél: 418-779-2272
biblio.trinite@crsbp.net
www.reseaubiblioduquebec.qc.ca

***La Tuque:* Bibliothèque municipale, Ville de La Tuque**
375, rue St-Joseph, La Tuque, QC G9X 1L5
Tél: 819-523-3100; *Téléc:* 819-523-4487
bibliotheque@ville.latuque.qc.ca
www.ville.latuque.qc.ca
Alain Michaud, Bibliothécaire
Julie Gravel, Technicienne en documentation
jgravel@ville.latuque.qc.ca

***Labelle:* Bibliothèque de Labelle**
1, rue Dupont, Labelle, QC J0T 1H0
Tél: 819-681-3371; *Téléc:* 819-686-3820
labelle@crsbpl.qc.ca
Nathalie Robson, Responsable
labelle@crspbl.qc.ca

***Labrecque:* Bibliothèque publique de Labrecque**
3425, rue Ambroise, Labrecque, QC G0W 2S0
Tél: 418-481-1618; *Téléc:* 418-481-2022
labrecque@reseaubiblioslsj.qc.ca
www.reseaubiblioduquebec.qc.ca/portail/index.aspx?page=3&BI D=537
Denise Villeneuve, Responsable
418-481-1327
Christine Jean, Bénévole
418-481-1377

Audrey Néron, Bénévole
418-481-1465

***Lac-a-la-Croix:* Bibliothèque publique de Lac-à-la-Croix**
#002, 335, de Rouillac, Lac-a-la-Croix, QC G8G 2B5
Tél: 418-349-8133
lac.croix@reseaubiblioslsj.qc.ca
www.reseaubiblioduquebec.qc.ca
Guylaine Dufour, Responsable

***Lac-au-Saumon:* Bibliothèque Bertrand-Leblanc**
20, Place de la Municipalité, Lac-au-Saumon, QC G0J 1M0
Tél: 418-778-3008
biblio.saumon@crsbp.net
www.reseaubiblioduquebec.qc.ca

***Lac-aux-Sables:* Bibliothèque de Lac-aux-Sables**
820, rue Saint-Alphonse, Lac-aux-Sables, QC G0X 1M0
Tél: 418-336-3238; *Téléc:* 418-336-2500
biblio045@reseaubibliocqlm.qc.ca
www.reseaubiblioduquebec.qc.ca
Louise Veillette, Responsable

***Lac-Beauport:* Bibliothèque L'Écrin**
46, ch du Village, Lac-Beauport, QC G0A 2C0
Tél: 418-849-6133; *Téléc:* 418-849-0361
ecrin@ccapcable.com
www.reseaubiblioduquebec.qc.ca/lac-beauport
Claudette Robillard, Responsable
Jocelyne Bradett, Adjointe
Claudette Baker, Adjointe

***Lac-Bouchette:* Bibliothèque publique de Lac-Bouchette**
#110, 258, rue Principale, Lac-Bouchette, QC G0W 1V0
Tél: 418-348-9302
lac.bouchett@reseaubiblioslsj.qc.ca
www.reseaubiblioduquebec.qc.ca/portail/index.aspx?page=3&BID=539
Lucie Paradis, Responsable

***Lac-Cayamant:* Bibliothèque municipale de Cayamant**
6, ch Lachapelle, Lac-Cayamant, QC J0X 1Y0
Tél: 819-463-3587; *Téléc:* 819-463-4020
admcayamant@crsbpo.qc.ca
www.reseaubiblioduquebec.qc.ca/Cayamant
Suzanne Vallières, Responsable

***Lac-des-Aigles:* Bibliothèque Lac-des-Aigles**
75A, rue Principale, Lac-des-Aigles, QC G0K 1V0
Tél: 418-779-2300
biblio.aigles@crsbp.net
Lise Leblanc, Responsable
418-779-2330

***Lac-des-Iles:* Bibliothèque de Saint-Aimé-du-Lac-des-Iles**
877, ch Diotte, Lac-des-Iles, QC J0W 1J0
Tél: 819-597-4174; *Téléc:* 819-597-2554
biblio59@crsbpl.qc.ca
www.reseaubiblioduquebec.qc.ca
Pierrette D. Pilotte, Responsable

***Lac-des-Loups:* Bibliothèque Lac-des-Loups (La Pêche)**
275, rue Pontbriand, Lac-des-Loups, QC J0X 3K0
Tél: 819-456-3222; *Téléc:* 819-456-4534
admlac-des-loups@crsbpo.qc.ca
www.reseaubiblioduquebec.qc.ca/Lac-Des-Loups
Michelle Archambault, Responsable

***Lac-des-Plages:* Bibliothèque Lac-des-Plages**
2053, ch Tour-du-Lac, Lac-des-Plages, QC J0T 1K0
Tél: 819-426-2391; *Téléc:* 819-426-2085
admdesplages@crsbpo.qc.ca
www.reseaubiblioduquebec.qc.ca/Lac-Des-Plages
Micheline Tessier, Responsable

***Lac-des-Seize-Iles:* Bibliothèque de Lac-des-Seize-Iles**
47, de l'Église, Lac-des-Seize-Iles, QC J0T 2M0
Tél: 450-226-9942
biblio@xplornet.com
www.reseaubiblioduquebec.qc.ca/lac-des-seize-iles
Anne Bates, Responsable
Lucille Pelletier, Adjointe

***Lac-des-Écorces:* Bibliothèque de Lac-des-Écorces**
570, boul St-François, Lac-des-Écorces, QC J0W 1H0
Tél: 819-585-2555
bibliolde@lacdesecorces.ca
www.reseaubiblioduquebec.qc.ca
Nicole Thériault, Responsable
Karolle Thériault, Adjointe

***Lac-des-Écorces:* Bibliothèque de Val-Barrette**
135, rue St-Joseph, Lac-des-Écorces, QC J0W 1H0
Tél: 819-585-3131; *Téléc:* 819-585-4915
bibliovb@lacdesecorces.ca
Nicole Thériault, Responsable
ntheriault001@hotmail.com
819-585-2490
Sylvie Giguère, Bénévole
819-585-3803

***Lac-du-Cerf:* Bibliothèque de Lac-du-Cerf**
15, rue Émard, Lac-du-Cerf, QC J0W 1S0
Tél: 819-597-4163; *Téléc:* 819-597-4163
biblio@lac-du-cerf.ca
www.reseaubiblioduquebec.qc.ca
Francine Boismenu-St-Louis, Responsable

***Lac-Etchemin:* Bibliothèque L'Élan**
208A, 2e av, Lac-Etchemin, QC G0R 1S0
Tél: 418-625-5325; *Téléc:* 418-625-3175
biblio@sogetel.net
www.reseaubiblioduquebec.qc.ca/lac-etchemin
Jacques Gagnon, Responsable
jgagnon@sogetel.net
Germaine Godbout, Responsable, PIB
418-625-7796

***Lac-Kénogami:* Bibliothèque de Lac-Kénogami**
3000, ch de l'Église, Lac-Kénogami, QC G7X 7V6
Tél: 418-695-4717; *Téléc:* 418-547-6158
webbiblio@ville.saguenay.qc.ca
www.ville.saguenay.qc.ca
Caroline Tremblay, Responsable
Monique Laprise, Responsable, l'Animation
monique.laprise@ville.saguenay.qc.ca
Luc Lepage, Responsable, Bibliothèques de l'arrond. de Jonquière
luc.lepage@ville.saguenay.qc.ca
Anne Lebel, Chef de division, Bibliothèques de Saguenay
anne.lebel@ville.saguenay.qc.ca

***Lac-Mégantic:* Bibliothèque municipale de Lac-Mégantic**
5086, rue Frontenac, Lac-Mégantic, QC G6B 1H3
Tél: 819-583-0876; *Téléc:* 819-583-0878
www.bibliomegantic.qc.ca
Daniel Lavoie, Directeur/Bibliothécaire
direction@bibliomegantic.qc.ca
Nancy Giroux, Technicienne en documentation
nancy@bibliomegantic.qc.ca
Annie Trudel, Technicienne en documentation
annie@bibliomegantic.qc.ca
Denise Grenier, Préposée à la saisie de données
denise@bibliomegantic.qc.ca
Natalie Rosa, Commis au comptoir, Entretien

***Lac-Saguay:* Bibliothèque de Lac-Saguay**
257A, rte 117, Lac-Saguay, QC J0W 1L0
Tél: 819-278-3972; *Téléc:* 819-278-0260
info@lacsaguay.qc.ca
www.reseaubiblioduquebec.qc.ca
Micheline Bouliane, Responsable
Denise Lachance, Adjointe

***Lac-Saint-Paul:* Bibliothèque de Lac-Saint-Paul**
384, rue Principale, Lac-Saint-Paul, QC J0W 1K0
Tél: 819-587-4283; *Téléc:* 819-587-4892
biblio52@crsbpl.qc.ca
www.reseaubiblioduquebec.qc.ca/lac-saint-paul
Charlaine Miller, Responsable
819-587-4379

***Lac-Sainte-Marie:* Bibliothèque municipale de Lac-Sainte-Marie**
8, rue Laramée, Lac-Sainte-Marie, QC J0X 1Z0
Tél: 819-467-3779; *Téléc:* 819-467-4826
admstemarie@crsbpo.qc.ca
www.reseaubiblioduquebec.qc.ca/Lac-Ste-Marie
Marie-Paule Bertrand, Bibliothécaire

***Lac-Supérieur:* Bibliothèque de Lac-Supérieur**
1277, ch du Lac-Supérieur, Lac-Supérieur, QC J0T 1J0
Tél: 819-681-3370; *Téléc:* 819-688-3010
biblio@muni.lacsuperieur.qc.ca
www.reseaubiblioduquebec.qc.ca
Thérèse Gaucher, Responsable

***Lac-à-la-Tortue:* Bibliothèque de Lac-à-la-Tortue**
1082, 37e av, Lac-à-la-Tortue, QC G0X 1L0
Tél: 819-538-5882
www.shawinigan.ca
Charlotte Lecours, Responsable des bibliothèques

***Lac-Édouard:* Bibliothèque de Lac-Édouard**
195, rue Principale, Lac-Édouard, QC G0X 3N0
Tél: 819-653-2238; *Téléc:* 819-653-2238
biblo024@reseaubibliocqlm.qc.ca
www.reseaubiblioduquebec.qc.ca
Sonia Cloutier, Responsable

***Lachute:* Bibliothèque Jean-Marc-Belzile**
378, rue Principale, Lachute, QC J8H 1Y2
Tél: 450-562-4578; *Téléc:* 450-562-1431
biblio@ville.lachute.qc.ca
www.ville.lachute.qc.ca/bibliotheque
Émilie Paquin, Chef de service de la bibliothèque et des activités culturelles
epaquin@ville.lachute.qc.ca
450-562-3781 ext. 255
Chantal Bélisle, Technicienne en documentation
cbelisle@ville.lachute.qc.ca
450-562-3781 ext. 214
Joanne Desjardins, Commis de la bibliothèque
jdesjardins@ville.lachute.qc.ca
450-562-3781 ext. 264

***Lacolle:* Bibliothèque municipale de Lacolle**
3, rue de Collège, Lacolle, QC J0J 1J0
Tél: 450-515-8050
www.lacolle.com/services.html
Linda Corbière, Responsable

***Laforce:* Bibliothèque Laforce**
703, rue Principale, Laforce, QC J0Z 2J0
Tél: 819-722-2461; *Téléc:* 819-722-2462
laforce@reseaubiblioatnq.qc.ca
Lise Bray, Responsable

***Lamarche:* Bibliothèque publique de Lamarche**
102, rue Principale, Lamarche, QC G0W 1X0
Tél: 418-481-2861
lamarche@reseaubiblioslsj.qc.ca
www.reseaubiblioduquebec.qc.ca
Rose Perron-Tremblay, Responsable

***Landrienne:* Bibliothèque Landrienne**
158, rue Principale est, Landrienne, QC J0Y 1V0
Tél: 819-732-4357; *Téléc:* 819-732-3866
landrienne@crsbpo.qc.ca
www.reseaubiblioduquebec.qc.ca/landrienne
Linda Perron, Responsable
819-732-4357

***Lanoraie:* Bibliothèque de Lanoraie (Ginette-Rivard-Tremblay)**
#100, 12, rue Louis-Joseph-Doucet, Lanoraie, QC J0K 1E0
Tél: 450-887-1100; *Téléc:* 450-836-5229
biblio060@reseaubibliocqlm.qc.ca
Jacques Gagné, Responsable

***Larouche:* Bibliothèque publique de Larouche**
709, rue Gauthier, Larouche, QC G0W 1Z0
Tél: 418-695-2201
larouche@reseaubiblioslsj.qc.ca
www.reseaubiblioduquebec.qc.ca/portail/index.aspx?page=3&BID=543
Lucette Douillard, Directrice

***Laterrière:* Bibliothèque de Laterrière**
6167, rue Notre-Dame, Laterrière, QC G7N 1A1
Tél: 418-698-5350; *Téléc:* 418-678-2647
webbiblio@ville.saguenay.qc.ca
www.ville.saguenay.qc.ca
Anne Lebel, Chef de division, Bibliothèques de Saguenay
anne.lebel@ville.saguenay.qc.ca
Claude Dumais, Responsable, Bibliothèques de l'arrond. de Chicoutimi
claude.dumais@ville.saguenay.qc.ca
Lise Tremblay, Responsable de la bibliothèque

***Latulipe:* Bibliothèque Latulipe-et-Gaboury**
#5, rue du Carrefour Nord, Latulipe, QC J9Z 2N0
Tel: 819-747-4521
latulipe@reseaubiblioatnq.qc.ca
www.reseaubiblioduquebec.qc.ca/latulipe

***Laurier-Station:* Bibliothèque Wilfrid Laurier**
147, rue Saint-Denis, Laurier-Station, QC G0S 1N0
Tél: 418-728-5939; *Téléc:* 418-728-4801
bwlaurier@globetrotter.net
www.reseaubiblioduquebec.qc.ca/bay-station
Nancy Dubois, Responsable
Melissa Bouchard, Adjointe
Normande Bergeron, Responsable des échanges

***Laurierville:* Bibliothèque de Laurierville**
148A, rue Grenier, Laurierville, QC G0S 1P0
Tél: 819-365-4913; *Téléc:* 819-365-4936
biblio122@reseaubibliocqlm.qc.ca
Aline Desrochers, Responsable

***Laval:* Bibliothèques Ville de Laval**
1535, boul Chomedey, Laval, QC H7V 3Z4
Tél: 450-662-4343; *Téléc:* 450-978-5833
adm-biblio@ville.laval.qc.ca
www.ville.laval.qc.ca
Média social: twitter.com/Laval331; www.facebook.com/bibliothequeslaval
Paul Lemay, Dir. Serv. de vie communautaire, culture et communications
p.lemay@ville.laval.qc.ca
Jean-François Roulier, Chef de division
j-f.roulier@ville.laval.qc.ca
450-978-6888 ext. 5848
Ghislaine Bélanger, Chef de division
450-978-6888 ext. 5982

***Lavaltrie:* Bibliothèque de Lavaltrie**
241, Saint-Antoine-Nord, Lavaltrie, QC J5T 2G7
Tél: 450-586-2921; *Téléc:* 450-586-0124
biblio011@reseaubibliocqlm.qc.ca
Brigitte Richer, Directrice
Lise Pigeon, Adjointe
Manon Beauchamp, Coordonnatrice, Accès Internet

***Laverlochère:* Bibliothèque de Laverlochère**
3, rue Principale sud, Laverlochère, QC J0Z 2P0
Tél: 819-765-2549; *Téléc:* 819-765-2089
laverlochere@reseaubiblioatnq.qc.ca
www.reseaubiblioduquebec.qc.ca/laverlochere
Lauriane Rivest, Responsable

***Lebel-sur-Quévillon:* Bibliothèque Lebel-sur-Quévillon**
500, Place Quévillon, Lebel-sur-Quévillon, QC J0Y 1X0
Tél: 819-755-4826; *Téléc:* 819-755-8124
lebel@reseaubiblioatnq.qc.ca
Mona Savard, Responsable

***Leclercville:* Bibliothèque Aux Rayons d'Or**
166, rue de l'Église, Leclercville, QC G0S 2K0
Jeannine Beaudet, Responsable
Francine B. Demers, Responsable des statistiques, Secrétaire

***Lefebvre:* Bibliothèque de Lefebvre**
193, 10e rang, Lefebvre, QC J0H 2C0
Tél: 819-394-3354; *Téléc:* 819-394-2782
biblio081@reseaubibliocqlm.qc.ca
www.reseaubiblioduquebec.qc.ca

***Lejeune:* Bibliothèque de Lejeune**
69, rue de la Grande-Coulée, Lejeune, QC G0L 1S0
Tél: 418-855-2428
biblio.lejeune@crsbp.net
www.reseaubiblioduquebec.qc.ca

***Lemieux:* Bibliothèque de Lemieux**
526, rue de l'Eglise, Lemieux, QC G0X 1S0
Tél: 819-283-2506
biblio138@reseaubibliocqlm.qc.ca
www.reseaubiblioduquebec.qc.ca
Lucie Blanchette, Responsable

***Lennoxville:* Bibliothèque publique de Lennoxville/ Lennoxville Public Library**
101, rue Queen, Lennoxville, QC J1M 1J7
Tél: 819-562-4949; *Téléc:* 819-563-3705
bibliolen@gmail.com
www.lennoxvillelibrary.ca
Barbara Gosselin, Responsable

***Les Coteaux:* Bibliothèque municipale Des Coteaux**
65, rte 338, Les Coteaux, QC J7X 1A2
Tél: 450-267-1414; *Téléc:* 450-267-3532
coteaux@reseaubibliomonteregie.qc.ca
Lucie Hamel, Responsable
Carole Labelle, Adjointe

***Les Cèdres:* Bibliothèque municipale de Les Cèdres**
1060, ch du Fleuve, Les Cèdres, QC J7T 1A1
Tél: 450-452-4363
cedres@reseaubibliomonteregie.qc.ca
www.reseaubiblioduquebec.qc.ca
Odette Marois, Responsable
omarois@ville.lescedres.qc.ca

***Les Escoumins:* Bibliothèque municipale des Escoumins**
12, rue Boily, Les Escoumins, QC G0T 1K0
Tél: 418-233-3097; *Téléc:* 418-233-3273
escobiblio@globetrotter.qc.ca
Odile Boisvert, Responsable

***Les Méchins:* Bibliothèque municipale de Les Méchins**
164, rue Principale, Les Méchins, QC G0J 1T0
Tél: 418-729-1346
biblio.lesmechins@mrcdematane.qc.ca
www.lesmechins.com
Louise Farand, Responsable
418-729-1346

***Les Éboulements:* Bibliothèque Félix-Antoine-Savard**
248B, rue du Village, Les Éboulements, QC G0A 2M0
Tél: 418-489-2990; *Téléc:* 418-635-2520
bibliotheque@leseboulements.com
www.reseaubiblioduquebec.qc.ca/leseboulements/
Philippe Naud, Responsable

***Longue-Pointe-de-Mingan:* Bibliothèque de Longue-Pointe-de-Mingan**
878, ch du Roi, Longue-Pointe-de-Mingan, QC G0G 1V0
Tél: 418-949-2053; *Téléc:* 418-949-2166
Andrée Legault, Responsable

***Longueuil:* Bibliothèques publiques de Longueuil**
1100, rue Beauregard, Longueuil, QC J4K 2L1
Tél: 450-463-7180; *Téléc:* 450-646-8874
www.longueuil.ca/bibliotheques/
Micheline Perreault, Chef du Service des bibliothèques
micheline.perreault@ville.longueuil.qc.ca
450-463-7100 ext. 7244
Marjolaine Millette, Chef des opérations, service au public et marketing
marjolaine.millette@ville.longueuil.qc.ca
450-463-7100 ext. 3160
Martin Dubois, Chef des opérations, services techniques et technologie
martin.dubois@ville.longueuil.qc.ca
450-463-7100 ext. 2479

***Lorraine:* Bibliothèque municipale de Lorraine**
31, boul de Gaulle, Lorraine, QC J6Z 3W9
Tél: 450-621-1071
bibliotheque@ville.lorraine.qc.ca
www.ville.lorraine.qc.ca
Paulette Gouroff, Directrice
450-621-1071

***Lorrainville:* Bibliothèque Lorrainville**
2, rue St-Jean-Baptiste est, Lorrainville, QC J0Z 2R0
Tél: 819-625-2464; *Téléc:* 819-625-2380
lorrainville@reseaubiblioatnq.qc.ca
www.lorrainville.ca
Alain Guimond, Responsable

***Lotbinière:* Bibliothèque 'Au fil des pages'**
30, rue Joly, local 100, Lotbinière, QC G0S 1S0
Tél: 418-796-2912; *Téléc:* 418-796-2198
www.reseaubiblioduquebec.qc.ca/lotbiniere
Lucille Beaudet, Responsable
Gisèle Bouchard, Responsable, PEB
Diane Cadoret, Responsable, Échanges
Denise Chrétien, Responsable, Collection locale
Hélène Gagnon, Responsable, Statistiques
Ginette Auger, Responsable, Extranet

***Lourdes-de-Blanc-Sablon:* Bibliothèque de Blanc-Sablon**
20, rue Mgr Scheffer, Lourdes-de-Blanc-Sablon, QC G0G 1W0
Tél: 418-461-2030; *Téléc:* 418-461-2529
www.reseaubiblioduquebec.qc.ca
Vincent Joncas, Responsable

***Low:* Bibliothèque municipale de Low**
4A, ch D'Amour, Low, QC J0X 2C0
Tél: 819-422-3218; *Téléc:* 819-422-3796
admlow@crsbpo.qc.ca
www.reseaubiblioduquebec.qc.ca/Low
Lise Legros, Responsable

***Luskville-Pontiac:* Bibliothèque de Luskville**
2024, rte 148, Luskville-Pontiac, QC J0X 2G0
Tél: 819-455-2370; *Téléc:* 819-455-9756
admluskville@crsbpo.qc.ca
www.reseaubiblioduquebec.qc.ca/Luskville
Louise Ramsay, Responsable

***Lyster:* Bibliothèque de Lyster (Graziella-Ouellet)**
2375, rue Bécancour, Lyster, QC G0S 1V0
Tél: 819-389-5787; *Téléc:* 819-389-5981
biblio144@reseaubibliocqlm.qc.ca
Pierrette Fradette, Responsable

***Macamic:* Bibliothèque de Colombourg**
705, Rang 2-3 ouest, Macamic, QC J0Z 2S0
Tél: 819-333-5783; *Téléc:* 819-333-1075
colombourg@reseaubiblioatnq.qc.ca
www.reseaubiblioduquebec.qc.ca/colombourg
Noëlla Royer, Responsable

***Macamic:* Bibliothèque de Macamic**
34A, 6e av ouest, Macamic, QC J0Z 2S0
Tél: 819-782-4604; *Téléc:* 819-782-4464
macamic@reseaubiblioatnq.qc.ca
www.reseaubiblioduquebec.qc.ca/macamic
Ginette Labbé, Responsable

***Madeleine-Centre:* Bibliothèque Jacques-Ferron**
104, rue Principale, Madeleine-Centre, QC G0E 1P0
Tél: 418-393-3269; *Téléc:* 418-393-2869
bbostema@globetrotter.qc.ca
Carole Giroux, Responsable

***Magog:* Bibliothèque municipale d'Omerville**
65, rue St-Jacques ouest, Magog, QC J1X 4H4
Tél: 819-868-6679
biblio078@reseaubiblioestrie.qc.ca
www.reseaubiblioduquebec.qc.ca
Monique Saint-Onge, Responsable

***Magog:* Bibliothèque municipale Memphrémagog**
61, rue Merry nord, Magog, QC J1X 2E7
Tél: 819-843-1330; *Téléc:* 819-843-1594
biblio@ville.magog.qc.ca
www.ville.magog.qc.ca
Diane Boulé, Responsable/Bibliothécaire
dianeb@abacom.com
Luc Grenier, Technicien en documentation
lukg@abacom.com

***Malartic:* Bibliothèque Malartic**
640, De la Paix, Malartic, QC J0Y 1Z0
Tél: 819-757-3611; *Téléc:* 819-757-3084
malartic@reseaubiblioatnq.qc.ca
Maurice Bélanger, Responsable

***Manawan:* Bibliothèque de Manawan**
470, rue Otapi, Manawan, QC J0K 1M0
Tél: 819-971-1379; *Téléc:* 819-971-1266
biblio067@reseaubibliocqlm.qc.ca
Janette Ottawa, Responsable

***Mandeville:* Bibliothèque municipale de Mandeville**
162A, rue Desjardins, Mandeville, QC J0K 1L0
Tél: 514-835-2055
bibliomandeville@intermonde.net
www.mandeville.qc.ca/bibliotheque
Monique Bessette, Coordonnatrice

***Maniwaki:* Bibliothèque de Maniwaki/Déléage/Egan-Sud**
14, rue Comeau, Maniwaki, QC J9E 2R8
Tél: 819-449-2738; *Téléc:* 819-449-7626
admmaniwaki@crsbpo.qc.ca
www.reseaubiblioduquebec.qc.ca/Maniwaki/
Colette Archambault, Responsable
Jacqueline Martin, Adjointe

***Manseau:* Bibliothèque de Manseau**
200A, rue Roux, Manseau, QC G0X 1V0
Tél: 819-356-2450; *Téléc:* 819-356-2721
biblio084@reseaubibliocqlm.qc.ca
www.reseaubiblioduquebec.qc.ca
Denise Bernier, Responsable

***Mansfield:* Bibliothèque Mansfield-et-Pontefract**
314, rue Principale, Mansfield, QC J0X 1R0
Tél: 819-683-3491; *Téléc:* 819-683-3590
admmansfield@crsbpo.qc.ca
www.reseaubiblioduquebec.qc.ca/Mansfield
Martine Laroche, Responsable

***Maria:* Bibliothèque Noël-Audet**
475, rue des Chardonnerets, Maria, QC G0C 1Y0
Tél: 418-759-3832; *Téléc:* 418-759-5035
bbomaria@globetrotter.qc.ca
www.reseaubiblioduquebec.qc.ca
Sylvie Boudreau, Responsable

Marieville: **Bibliothèque Commémorative Desautels**
1801, rue du Pont, Marieville, QC J3M 1J7
Tél: 450-460-4444; *Téléc:* 450-460-3526
biblio126@reseaubibliomonteregie.qc.ca
www.ville.marieville.qc.ca/bibliotheque/
Daniel Lalonde, Responsable
d.lalonde@ville.marieville.qc.ca

Marsoui: **Bibliothèque de Marsoui**
2, rue des Écoliers, Marsoui, QC G0E 1S0
Tél: 418-288-5508
michelle.cote@globetrotter.net
www.reseaubiblioduquebec.qc.ca
Michelle Côté, Responsable

Mascouche: **Bibliothèque municipale de Mascouche**
3015, ave des Ancêtres, Mascouche, QC J7K 1X6
Tél: 450-474-4159; *Téléc:* 450-474-3410
biblio@ville.mascouche.qc.ca
www.ville.mascouche.qc.ca
Sarah Germain, Bibliothécaire professionnelle
sgermain@ville.mascouche.qc.ca

Mashteuiatsh: **Bibliothèque publique de Mashteuiatsh**
507, rue Uapileu, Mashteuiatsh, QC G0W 2H0
Tél: 418-275-2473; *Téléc:* 418-275-0097
masht@reseaubibliosIsj.qc.ca
www.reseaubiblioduquebec.qc.ca/portail/index.aspx?page=3&BID=545
Johane Langlais, Responsable
Johane Langlais, Bibliotechnicienne

Maskinongé: **Bibliothèque de Maskinongé**
11, rue Marcel, Maskinongé, QC J0K 1N0
Tél: 819-227-4656
biblio059@reseaubibliocqlm.qc.ca
www.reseaubiblioduquebec.qc.ca
Andrée Livernoche, Responsable

Massueville: **Bibliothèque municipale de Massueville/St-Aimé**
846A, rue de l'Église, Massueville, QC J0G 1K0
Tél: 450-788-3120
aime@reseaubibliomonteregie.qc.ca
www.reseaubiblioduquebec.qc.ca
Claire Berger, Responsable

Matane: **Bibliothèque municipale de Matane (Fonds de Solidarité FTQ)**
Complexe culturel Joseph-Rouleau, #2, 520, av Saint-Jérôme, Matane, QC G4W 3B5
Tél: 418-562-9233; *Téléc:* 418-566-2064
biblio@ville.matane.qc.ca
www.ville.matane.qc.ca/bibliotheque_municipale
Lise Whittom Grenier, Responsable
l.grenier@ville.matane.qc.ca

Matapédia: **Bibliothèque de Matapédia**
5, rue Hôtel-de-Ville, Matapédia, QC G0J 1V0
Tél: 418-865-2917; *Téléc:* 418-865-2828
bbomatap@globetrotter.net
www.reseaubiblioduquebec.qc.ca
Julie Michaud, Responsable
418-865-2135

Mercier: **Bibliothèque municipale de Mercier**
16, rue du Parc, Mercier, QC J6R 1E5
Tél: 450-692-6780; *Téléc:* 450-691-6529
danielmorin@bibliothequedemercier.qc.ca
Daniel Morin, Responsable
daniel.morin@bibliothequedemercier.qc.ca

Messines: **Bibliothèque de Messines**
3, ch de la Ferme, Messines, QC J0X 2J0
Tél: 819-465-2637; *Téléc:* 819-465-2943
admmessines@crsbpo.qc.ca
www.reseaubiblioduquebec.qc.ca/Messines
Claire Lacroix, Responsable

Mirabel: **Bibliothèque municipale de Mirabel**
17710, rue du Val-d'Espoir, Mirabel, QC J7J 1V7
Tél: 450-475-2011
biblio@ville.mirabel.qc.ca
www.ville.mirabel.qc.ca
Média social: www.facebook.com/152931024748094
Sarah Germain, Directrice
s.germain@ville.mirabel.qc.ca
450-475-2082
Carole Gaudet, Technicienne en documentation
c.gaudet@ville.mirabel.qc.ca
Diane Girouard, Technicienne en documentation
d.girouard@ville.mirabel.qc.ca
Fanny Laberge, Technicienne en documentation
f.laberge@ville.mirabel.qc.ca
Sylvie Labelle, Secrétaire
s.labelle@ville.mirabel.qc.ca

Moisie: **Bibliothèque de Moisie**
250, ch des Forges, Moisie, QC G0G 2B0
Tél: 418-927-2279
www.reseaubiblioduquebec.qc.ca/moisie
Nancy Malenfant, Personne-ressource

Mont-Brun: **Bibliothèque Mont-Brun**
955, rue Principale, Mont-Brun, QC J0Z 2Y0
Tél: 819-637-7101; *Téléc:* 819-637-2374
montbrun@reseaubiblioatnq.qc.ca
www.crsbpat.qc.ca/montbrun/
Noëlla Thibault, Responsable
Gisèle Guilbert Rodrigue, Bénévole

Mont-Carmel: **Bibliothèque Odile-Boucher**
22, rue de la Fabrique, Mont-Carmel, QC G0L 1W0
Tél: 418-498-3500
biblio.carmel@crsbp.net
Denise Chamberland, Responsable
418-498-3492

Mont-Joli: **Bibliothèque Jean-Louis-Desrosiers**
1477, boul Jacques-Cartier, Mont-Joli, QC G5H 2V5
Tél: 418-775-4106; *Téléc:* 418-775-4037
julie.belanger@ville.mont-joli.qc.ca
ville.mont-joli.qc.ca
Julie Bélanger, Responsable
julie.belanger@ville.mont-joli.qc.ca

Mont-Laurier: **Bibliothèque de Des Ruisseaux**
1269, boulevard Des Ruisseaux, Mont-Laurier, QC J9L 0H6
Tél: 819-623-6748; *Téléc:* 819-623-6810
desruisseaux@crsbpl.qc.ca
www.reseaubiblioduquebec.qc.ca
Louise Paquette, Responsable

Mont-Laurier: **Bibliothèque de Mont-Laurier**
385, rue Du Pont, Mont-Laurier, QC J9L 2R5
Tél: 819-623-1833; *Téléc:* 819-623-7079
bibliotheque.mont-laurier@tlb.sympatico.ca
www.reseaubiblioduquebec.qc.ca
Edith Whear, Responsable

Mont-Laurier: **Bibliothèque de Val-Limoges**
3620, chemin Val-Limoges, RR6, Mont-Laurier, QC J9L 3G6
Tél: 819-623-9124
vallimoges@crsbpl.qc.ca
www.reseaubiblioduquebec.qc.ca
Louise Paquette, Responsable

Mont-Louis: **La Bibliothèque Liratou de Mont-Louis**
1, 1e av ouest, Mont-Louis, QC G0E 1T0
Tél: 418-797-2310; *Téléc:* 418-797-2928
www.reseaubiblioduquebec.qc.ca
Annie-France Létourneau, Responsable

Mont-Saint-Hilaire: **Bibliothèque Armand-Cardinal**
150, rue du Centre Civique, Mont-Saint-Hilaire, QC J3H 3M8
Tél: 450-467-2854; *Téléc:* 450-446-5879
bibliotheque@villemsh.ca
www.ville.mont-saint-hilaire.qc.ca
Francine Ledoux-Nadeau, Bibliothécaire
francine.ledoux.nadeau@ville.mont-saint-hila

Mont-Saint-Michel: **Bibliothèque de Mont-Saint-Michel**
94, rue de l'Église, Mont-Saint-Michel, QC J0W 1P0
Tél: 819-587-3093
biblio55@lino.com
www.reseaubiblioduquebec.qc.ca
Lucette Castonguay, Responsable

Mont-Saint-Pierre: **Bibliothèque Kevin Pouliot-Bernatchez**
102, rue Cloutier, Mont-Saint-Pierre, QC G0E 1V0
Tél: 418-797-2898; *Téléc:* 418-797-2307
bbomtsp@globetrotter.net
Karine Sergerie, Responsable

Mont-Tremblant: **Bibliothèque Samuel-Ouimet**
1147, rue de St-Jovite, Mont-Tremblant, QC J8E 1V1
Tél: 819-425-8614; *Téléc:* 819-425-1391
biblio.samuel-o@villedemont-tremblant.qc.ca
www.villedemont-tremblant.qc.ca
Gabriel Lemelin, Responsable
Isabelle Carriere, Secrétaire
icarriere@villedemont-tremblant.qc.ca

Montbeillard: **Bibliothèque Montbeillard**
551, rue du Village, Montbeillard, QC J0Z 2X0
Tél: 819-797-7110; *Téléc:* 819-797-2390
montbeillard@reseaubiblioatnq.qc.ca
Diane St-Onge, Responsable

Montcalm: **Bibliothèque de Montcalm**
30, rte du Lac-Rond Nord, Montcalm, QC J0T 2V0
Tél: 819-687-2575; *Téléc:* 819-687-2374
biblio@municipalite.montcalm.qc.ca
www.reseaubiblioduquebec.qc.ca/montcalm
Pierre Nadeau, Responsable

Montcerf-Lytton: **Bibliothèque Montcerf-Lytton**
16, rue Principale nord, 2e étage, Montcerf-Lytton, QC J0W 1N0
Tél: 819-449-2065; *Téléc:* 819-449-7310
admmontcerf@crsbpo.qc.ca
www.reseaubiblioduquebec.qc.ca/Montcerf/
Christine Ménard, Responsable

Montebello: **Bibliothèque de Montebello**
240A, rue Bonsecours, Montebello, QC J0V 1L0
Tél: 819-423-6213; *Téléc:* 819-423-5703
admmontebello@crsbpo.qc.ca
www.reseaubiblioduquebec.qc.ca/Montebello/
Mariette Côté, Responsable

Montpellier: **Bibliothèque de Montpellier**
4B, rue du Bosquet, Montpellier, QC J0V 1M0
Tél: 819-428-3663; *Téléc:* 819-428-1221
admmontpellier@crsbpo.qc.ca
www.reseaubiblioduquebec.qc.ca/Montpellier/
Claudette Riopel, Responsable

Montréal: **Bibliothèque et centre d'informatique Atwater / Atwater Library & Computer Centre**
1200, av Atwater, Montréal, QC H3Z 1X4
Tél: 514-935-7344; *Téléc:* 514-935-1960
info@atwaterlibrary.ca
www.atwaterlibrary.ca
Média social:
www.facebook.com/Atwaterlibraryandcomputercentre
Lynn Verge, Executive Director
lverge@atwaterlibrary.ca
514-935-7344
Aude McDermott, Library Manager
amcdermott@atwaterlibrary.ca
Tanya Mayhew, Administration and Development Manager
tmayhew@atwaterlibrary.ca

Montréal: **Bibliothèque Reginald J.P. Dawson**
1967, boul Graham, Montréal, QC H3R 1G9
Tél: 514-734-2966; *Téléc:* 514-734-3089
denis.chouinard@ville.mont-royal.qc.ca
www.ville.mont-royal.qc.ca/index.php?id=112
Denis Chouinard, Chef de division
denis.chouinard@ville.mont-royal.qc.ca
514-734-2966

Montréal: **The Fraser-Hickson Institute / Institut Fraser-Hickson**
#100, 16, av Westminster nord, Montréal, QC H4X 1Z1
Tel: 514-489-5301
info@fraserhickson.ca
www.fraserhickson.qc.ca
Frances W. Ackerman, Library Director & Secretary to the Board

Montréal: **Jewish Public Library (Montréal) / La Bibliothèque publique juive (Montréal)**
1, carré Cummings Sq., 5151, Côte Ste-Catherine Rd., Montréal, QC H3W 1M6
Tel: 514-345-2627; *Fax:* 514-345-6477
info@jplmontreal.org
www.jewishpubliclibrary.org
Eva Raby, Executive Director
Kathy Diamond, Reference Librarian
Eddie Paul, Head, Bibliographic & Information Services
Allan Oberman, Head of Information & Administrative Services
Shannon Hodge, Archivist
archives@jplmontreal.org
514-345-2027

Montréal: **Réseau des bibliothèques publiques de Montréal**
801, rue Brennan (Pavillon Prince), 5e étage, Montréal, QC H2C 0G4
Tél: 514-872-5923; *Téléc:* 514-872-4911
bibliomontreal.com
Média social: www.flickr.com/photos/bibliomontreal; twitter.com/Bibliomontreal, twitter.com/bibliojeunes; www.facebook.com/bibliomontreal

Louise Guillemette-Labory, Directrice-associée
lglabory@ville.montreal.qc.ca
Luc Jodoin, Chef de division, Planification et développement réseau
Michel Claveau, Chef de division, Activités regroupées
Monique Khouzam, Chef de division, Programme et services aux arrondissements

Morin-Heights: **Bibliothèque de Morin-Heights**
823, ch du Village, Morin-Heights, QC J0R 1H0
Tél: 450-226-3232
bibliomh@cgocable.ca
www.morinheights.com
Audrey Gibeault, Responsable

Murdochville: **Bibliothèque de Murdochville**
635, 5e rue, Murdochville, QC G0E 1W0
Tél: 418-784-2866; *Téléc:* 418-784-2607
bbomurd@globetrotter.net
www.reseaubiblioduquebec.qc.ca
Sonia Dunn, Responsable

Métabetchouan-Lac-à-la-Croi: **Bibliothèque publique de Métabetchouan**
87, rue Saint-André, Métabetchouan-Lac-à-la-Croi, QC G8G 1Z2
Tél: 418-349-8495
metabet@reseaubibliosIsj.qc.ca
www.reseaubiblioduquebec.qc.ca
Hélène Lachance, Responsable
418-349-3517

Métis-sur-Mer: **Bibliothèque Métis-sur-Mer**
3, 162, rue Principale, Métis-sur-Mer, QC G0J 1S0
Tél: 418-936-3231
biblio.metis@crsbp.net
www.reseaubiblioduquebec.qc.ca/metis-sur-mer

Namur: **Bibliothèque Namur/ Namur Library**
331, rue Hôtel-de-Ville, Namur, QC J0V 1N0
Tél: 819-426-2457; *Téléc:* 819-426-3074
admnamur@crsbpo.qc.ca
www.reseaubiblioduquebec.qc.ca/Namur/
Tammie Leggett, Responsable

Napierville: **Bibliothèque municipale de Napierville**
290, rue St-Alexandre, Napierville, QC J0J 1L0
Tél: 450-245-0030; *Téléc:* 450-245-3777
napierville@reseaubibliomonteregie.qc.ca
www.reseaubiblioduquebec.qc.ca
Viviane Leroux, Responsable

Natashquan: **Bibliothèque de Natashquan**
29, ch d'en Haut, Natashquan, QC G0G 2E0
Tél: 418-726-3362; *Téléc:* 418-726-3698
natashb@globetrotter.net
www.reseaubiblioduquebec.qc.ca
Cindy Carbonneau, Responsable

Neuville: **Bibliothèque Félicité-Angers**
760, rte 138, Neuville, QC G0A 2R0
Tél: 418-876-2023; *Téléc:* 418-876-3349
www.reseaubiblioduquebec.qc.ca/neuville
Diane Forgues-Michaud, Responsable

New Richmond: **Bibliothèque du Vieux-Couvent**
99, Place Suzanne-Guité, New Richmond, QC G0C 2B0
Tél: 418-392-7070; *Téléc:* 418-392-5331
biblio@villenewrichmond.com
www.reseaubiblioduquebec.qc.ca
Chantal Cormier, Responsable

Newport: **Bibliothèque de Newport**
208, rte 132, Newport, QC G0C 2A0
Tél: 418-777-2523; *Téléc:* 418-689-3639
bbonewpt@globetrotter.qc.ca
www.reseaubiblioduquebec.qc.ca
Dolores Bouchard, Responsable

Nicolet: **Bibliothèque de Nicolet**
116, rue Evariste-Lecompte, Nicolet, QC J3T 1E6
Tél: 819-293-6007; *Téléc:* 819-293-6767
biblio072@reseaubibliocqlm.qc.ca
www.reseaubiblioduquebec.qc.ca
Serge Rousseau, Responsable

Nicolet: **Bibliothèque Solidarité rurale**
204, 85, rue Notre-Dame, Nicolet, QC J3T 1V8
Tél: 819-293-6825; *Téléc:* 819-293-4181
www.reseaubiblioduquebec.qc.ca/solidarite-rurale

Nominingue: **Bibliothèque de Nominingue**
2112, ch du Tour du Lac, Nominingue, QC J0W 1R0
Tél: 819-278-3384; *Téléc:* 819-278-4967
biblio51@crsbpl.qc.ca
www.reseaubiblioduquebec.qc.ca/nominingue
Nicole Jorg, Responsable

Normandin: **Bibliothèque municipale de Normandin**
1156, rue Valois, Normandin, QC G8M 3Z8
Tél: 418-274-2241; *Téléc:* 418-274-2241
bibliotheque@ville.normandin.qc.ca
www.normandin.biblio.qc.ca/
Thérèse Cloutier, Présidente
Bruno Forget, Responsable
bibliotheque@ville.normandin.qc.ca

Normétal: **Bibliothèque Normétal**
36A, rue Principale, Normétal, QC J0Z 3A0
Tél: 819-788-2505; *Téléc:* 819-788-2730
normetal@reseaubiblioatnq.qc.ca
www.crsbpat.qc.ca/normetal/
Annie Lamoureux, Responsable

North Hatley: **Bibliothèque de North Hatley / North Hatley Library**
165, rue Main, North Hatley, QC J0B 2C0
Tél: 819-842-2110
biblio@nhlibrary.qc.ca
www.nhlibrary.qc.ca
Annie Potter, Responsable

Notre-Dame-de-Ham: **Bibliothèque de Notre-Dame-de-Ham**
25, rue de l'Église, Notre-Dame-de-Ham, QC G0P 1C0
Tél: 819-344-5010
biblio149@reseaubibliocqlm.qc.ca
France McSween, Responsable

Notre-Dame-de-la-Merci: **Bibliothèque de Notre-Dame-de-la-Merci**
1900, Montée de la Réserve, Notre-Dame-de-la-Merci, QC J0T 2A0
Tél: 819-424-2152; *Téléc:* 819-424-7347
biblio42@crsbpl.qc.ca
www.reseaubiblioduquebec.qc.ca
Célina Riopel, Responsable

Notre-Dame-de-la-Paix: **Bibliothèque Notre-Dame-de-la-Paix**
10, rue Saint-Jean-Baptiste, Notre-Dame-de-la-Paix, QC J0V 1P0
Tél: 819-522-6610; *Téléc:* 819-522-6710
admpaix@crsbpo.qc.ca
www.reseaubiblioduquebec.qc.ca/Notre-Dame-de-la-Paix
Suzon Côté, Responsable

Notre-Dame-de-la-Salette: **Bibliothèque de Notre-Dame-de-la-Salette**
68, rue des Saules, Notre-Dame-de-la-Salette, QC J0X 2L0
Tél: 819-766-2872; *Téléc:* 819-766-2983
admsalette@crsbpo.qc.ca
www.reseaubiblioduquebec.qc.ca/Notre-Dame-de-la-Salette
Nathalie Joannette, Conseillère

Notre-Dame-de-Lorette: **Bibliothèque publique de Notre-Dame-de-Lorette**
Couvent Maria-Goretti, 22, rue Principale, Notre-Dame-de-Lorette, QC G0W 1B0
Tél: 418-276-3941
ndlorette@reseaubibliosIsj.qc.ca
www.reseaubiblioduquebec.qc.ca/portail/index.aspx?page=3&BID=547
Georgette Bouchard, Responsable

Notre-Dame-de-Lourdes: **Bibliothèque Notre-Dame-de-Lourdes**
3971, rue Principale, Notre-Dame-de-Lourdes, QC J0K 1K0
Tél: 450-759-7864
bibliondl@intermonde.net
www.notredamedelourdes.ca/services-biblio.asp
Johanne Vincent, Responsable

Notre-Dame-de-Montauban: **Bibliothèque de Notre-Dame-de-Montauban**
550, rue des Loisirs, Notre-Dame-de-Montauban, QC G0X 1W0
Tél: 418-336-1211; *Téléc:* 418-336-2353
biblio058@reseaubibliocqlm.qc.ca
www.reseaubiblioduquebec.qc.ca
Denise Villemure, Responsable

Notre-Dame-de-Pontmain: **Bibliothèque de Notre-Dame-de-Pontmain**
15, rue Notre-Dame, Notre-Dame-de-Pontmain, QC J0W 1S0
Tél: 819-597-2382
bibliotheque@munpontmain.qc.ca
www.reseaubiblioduquebec.qc.ca
Francine Leclair, Responsable

Notre-Dame-de-Portneuf: **Bibliothèque La Découverte/Notre-Dame-de-Portneuf**
500A, rue Notre-Dame, Notre-Dame-de-Portneuf, QC G0A 2Z0
Tél: 418-286-4452; *Téléc:* 418-286-8150
www.reseaubiblioduquebec.qc.ca/portneuf
Johanne Savard, Responsable
johannesavard@hotmail.ca
418-286-3509

Notre-Dame-des-Monts: **Bibliothèque La Girouette**
87, rue Notre-Dame, Notre-Dame-des-Monts, QC G0T 1L0
Téléc: 418-439-0883
www.reseaubiblioduquebec.qc.ca/monts/
Marie-Paule Boudreault, Responsable
Johanne Tremblay, Responsable, Échanges
Michel Turcotte, Responsable de l'animation

Notre-Dame-des-Pins: **Bibliothèque Le Signet/Notre-Dame-des-Pins**
2755, 1e av, Notre-Dame-des-Pins, QC G0M 1K0
Tél: 418-774-9454
www.reseaubiblioduquebec.qc.ca/pins/
Lyette Roy, Responsable
Claire Maranda, Adjointe
Denise Bégin, Responsable, PIB

Notre-Dame-du-Bon-Conseil: **Bibliothèque de Notre-Dame-du-Bon-Conseil**
541, rue Notre-Dame, Notre-Dame-du-Bon-Conseil, QC J0C 1A0
Tél: 819-336-2967
biblio096@reseaubibliocqlm.qc.ca
www.reseaubiblioduquebec.qc.ca
Véronique Montesinos, Responsable

Notre-Dame-du-Lac: **Bibliothèque Notre-Dame-du-Lac**
681, rue Commerciale, Notre-Dame-du-Lac, QC G0L 1X0
Tél: 418-899-6004
biblio.ndlac@crsbp.net
Judith Pellerin, Responsable
418-899-6045

Notre-Dame-du-Laus: **Bibliothèque de Notre-Dame-du-Laus**
4, rue de l'Église, Notre-Dame-du-Laus, QC J0X 2M0
Tél: 819-767-2772
biblio057@crsbpl.qc.ca
www.reseaubiblioduquebec.qc.ca
Francine Boisvert, Responsable

Notre-Dame-du-Nord: **Bibliothèque Notre-Dame-du-Nord**
15, rue Desjardins, Notre-Dame-du-Nord, QC J0Z 3B0
Tél: 819-723-2695; *Téléc:* 819-723-2483
nord@reseaubiblioatnq.qc.ca
Carmen Laliberté, Responsable

Notre-Dame-du-Portage: **Bibliothèque de Notre-Dame-du-Portage**
539, rte du Fleuve, Notre-Dame-du-Portage, QC G0L 1Y0
Tél: 418-862-9163
biblio.portage@crsbp.net
www.reseaubiblioduquebec.qc.ca

Nouvelle: **Bibliothèque de Nouvelle**
470, rue Francoeur, Nouvelle, QC G0C 2E0
Tél: 418-794-2253; *Téléc:* 418-794-2254
bbonouv@globetrotter.net
www.reseaubiblioduquebec.qc.ca
Louise Leblanc, Responsable

Noyan: **Bibliothèque municipale de Noyan / Noyan Public Library**
1312, ch de la Petite-France, Noyan, QC J0J 1B0
Tél: 450-294-2175
noyan@reseaubibliomonteregie.qc.ca
Claude Jeunehomme, Responsable

Nédélec: **Bibliothèque de Nédélec**
68, rue Principale, Nédélec, QC J0Z 2Z0
Tél: 819-784-3351; *Téléc:* 819-784-2126
nedelec@reseaubiblioatnq.qc.ca
www.reseaubiblioduquebec.qc.ca/nedelec

Jacqueline Aylwin, Responsable

***Obedjiwan:* Bibliothèque d'Obedjiwan**
22, rue Tcikatnaw, Obedjiwan, QC G0W 3B0
Tél: 819-974-1221; *Téléc:* 819-974-1224
biblio065@reseaubibliocqlm.qc.ca
www.reseaubiblioduquebec.qc.ca
Rachelle Chachai, Responsable

***Odanak:* Bibliothèque de Odanak**
58, rue Waban-Aki, Odanak, QC J0G 1H0
Tél: 514-568-0107; *Téléc:* 514-568-0107
biblio139@reseaubibliocqlm.qc.ca
www.reseaubiblioduquebec.qc.ca/Portail/index.aspx?page=3&BID=195
Marie-Chantal Bouchard, Responsable

***Old Fort Bay:* Bibliothèque de Old Fort**
Livraison Generale, Old Fort Bay, QC G0G 2G0
Tél: 418-379-2911; *Téléc:* 418-379-2959
René Fequet, Responsable

***Ormstown:* Bibliothèque municipale d'Ormstown**
85, rue Roy, Ormstown, QC J0S 1K0
Tél: 450-829-3249
ormstown@reseaubibliomonteregie.qc.ca
Madeleine Robidoux, Responsable

***Otter Lake:* Bibliothèque Otter Lake**
340, av Martineau, Otter Lake, QC J0X 2P0
Tél: 819-453-7344; *Téléc:* 819-453-7311
admotterlake@crsbpo.qc.ca
www.reseaubiblioduquebec.qc.ca/OtterLake/
Esther Dubeau, Responsable

***Packington:* Bibliothèque Packington**
115, rue Soucy, Packington, QC G0L 1Z0
Tél: 418-853-5362; *Téléc:* 418-853-6427
biblio.packing@crsbp.net
Denis Moreau, Responsable

***Padoue:* Bibliothèque de Padoue**
215, rue Beaulieu, Padoue, QC G0J 1X0
Tél: 418-775-8188
biblio.padoue@crsbp.net
Cécile Ouellet Caron, Responsable

***Palmarolle:* Bibliothèque Palmarolle**
115, rue Principale, Palmarolle, QC J0Z 3C0
Tél: 819-787-3459; *Téléc:* 819-787-2412
palmarolle@reseaubiblioatnq.qc.ca
Ghislaine Bégin, Responsable

***Papineauville:* Bibliothèque de Papineauville**
294, rue Papineau, Papineauville, QC J0V 1R0
Tél: 819-427-5511
admpapineau@crsbpo.qc.ca
www.reseaubiblioduquebec.qc.ca/Papineauville
Suzanne Gauthier, Responsable

***Parisville:* Bibliothèque de Parisville**
1260, rue St-Jacques, Parisville, QC G0S 1X0
Tél: 819-292-2644; *Téléc:* 819-292-2214
biblio103@reseaubibliocqlm.qc.ca
Jeannine Boucher, Responsable

***Paspébiac:* Bibliothèque de Paspébiac**
95, boul Gérard-D.-Levesque Ouest, Paspébiac, QC G0C 2K0
Tél: 418-752-2277; *Téléc:* 418-752-6747
pretpas@globetrotter.qc.ca
www.reseaubiblioduquebec.qc.ca
Noula Castilloux, Responsable

***Percé:* Bibliothèque de Percé**
137, rte 132, Percé, QC G0C 2L0
Tél: 418-782-5305; *Téléc:* 418-782-5487
bboperce@ville.perce.qc.ca
www.reseaubiblioduquebec.qc.ca
Pierrette Cloutier, Responsable

***Petit-Saguenay:* Bibliothèque publique de Petit-Saguenay**
50, rue Tremblay, Petit-Saguenay, QC G0V 1N0
Tél: 418-272-3083
petitsag@reseaubiblioslsj.qc.ca
www.reseaubiblioduquebec.qc.ca/portail/index.aspx?page=3&BID=549
Aurore Gagné, Responsable

***Petite-Rivière-St-François:* Bibliothèque Gabrielle-Roy/Petite-Rivière-Saint-François**
1069, rue Principale, Petite-Rivière-Saint-François, QC G0A 2L0
Tél: 418-632-5895; *Téléc:* 418-632-5886
biblioprsf@hotmail.com
www.reseaubiblioduquebec.qc.ca/petite-riviere
Suzanne Lapointe, Responsable
Viviane Guay, Adjointe
Esther Bouchard, Responsable, Échanges/Collection locale
Martine Lavoie, Responsable, Animation

***Petite-Vallée:* Bibliothèque de Petite-Vallée**
45, rue Principale, Petite-Vallée, QC G0E 1Y0
Tél: 418-393-2949; *Téléc:* 418-393-2949
bibliopv@globetrotter.net
www.reseaubiblioduquebec.qc.ca
Lorraine Lachance, Responsable

***Pierreville:* Bibliothèque de Notre-Dame-de-Pierreville**
48, rue Principale, Pierreville, QC J0G 1J0
Tél: 450-568-2087
biblio142@reseaubibliocqlm.qc.ca
www.reseaubiblioduquebec.qc.ca
Maryse Boisvert, Responsable
450-568-2090
Dominique Boisvert, Bénévole
450-568-6788

***Pierreville:* Bibliothèque de Pierreville (Jean-Luc-Précourt)**
26, rue Ally, Pierreville, QC J0G 1J0
Tél: 450-568-3500; *Téléc:* 450-568-0689
biblio051@reseaubibliocqlm.qc.ca
www.reseaubiblioduquebec.qc.ca
Chantale Bellamy, Responsable

***Pincourt:* Bibliothèque de Pincourt/ Pincourt Library**
225, boul Pincourt, Pincourt, QC J7V 9T2
Tél: 514-425-1104; *Téléc:* 514-425-6668
bibliotheque@villepincourt.qc.ca
www.villepincourt.qc.ca
Média social: www.facebook.com/villedepincourt
Sylvie de Repentigny, Régisseure
514-425-1104 ext. 6242
Mireille Péladeau, Technicienne en documentation

***Plaisance:* Bibliothèque de Plaisance**
281, rue Desjardins, Plaisance, QC J0V 1S0
Tél: 819-427-1189; *Téléc:* 819-427-5015
admplaisance@crsbpo.qc.ca
www.reseaubiblioduquebec.qc.ca/Plaisance
Martine Prud'homme, Responsable

***Plessisville:* Bibliothèque municipale de la Ville de Plessisville**
1800, rue Saint-Calixte, Plessisville, QC G6L 1R6
Tél: 819-362-6628; *Téléc:* 819-362-6421
bibliotheque@ville.plessisville.qc.ca
www.ville.plessisville.qc.ca/fr/content/heures_biblio.aspx
Suzanne Bédard, Responsable
sbedard@ville.plessisville.qc.ca
819-362-6628

***Pointe-aux-Outardes:* Bibliothèque de Pointe-aux-Outardes**
481, ch Principale, Pointe-aux-Outardes, QC G0H 1H0
Tél: 418-567-9529; *Téléc:* 418-567-4409
biblipao@globetrotter.net
Guylaine Chouinard, Responsable

***Pointe-Calumet:* Bibliothèque La Sablière**
190, 41e Av, Pointe-Calumet, QC J0N 1G2
Tél: 450-473-6991; *Téléc:* 450-473-6571
bibliotheque@municipalite.pointe-calumet.qc.ca
www.reseaubiblioduquebec.qc.ca
Brigitte Lessard, Responsable
b.lessard@municipalite.point-calumet.qc.ca
Louise Charron, Adjointe

***Pointe-Claire:* Bibliothèque publique de Pointe-Claire**
100, av Douglas-Shand, Pointe-Claire, QC H9R 4V1
Tél: 514-630-1218; *Téléc:* 514-630-1261
bibliotheque@ville.pointe-claire.qc.ca
www.ville.pointe-claire.qc.ca/fr_1046_index
Céline Laperrière, Chef de division, Bibliothèque
laperrierec@ville.pointe-claire.qc.ca
514-630-1218 ext. 1217

***Pointe-des-Cascades:* Bibliothèque Adrienne Demontigny-Clément**
52, ch du Fleuve, Pointe-des-Cascades, QC J0P 1M0
Tél: 450-455-5310
pointe.cascades@reseaubibliomonteregie.qc.ca
Camille St-Marseille, Responsable
Johane Séguin Poirier, Adjointe

***Pointe-Lebel:* Bibliothèque de Pointe-Lebel**
255, rue Granier, Pointe-Lebel, QC G0H 1N0
Tél: 418-589-2424; *Téléc:* 418-589-6154
www.reseaubiblioduquebec.qc.ca/pointe-lebel
Lise Therrien, Responsable
418-589-2424

***Pointe-à-la-Croix:* Bibliothèque de La Petite-Rochelle**
44A, rue Lasalle, Pointe-à-la-Croix, QC G0C 1L0
Tél: 418-788-1305
biblio.41@hotmail.com
www.reseaubiblioduquebec.qc.ca
Lise P. Young, Responsable

***Pont-Rouge:* Bibliothèque Auguste-Honoré-Gosselin**
41, rue du Collège, Pont-Rouge, QC G3H 3A4
Tél: 418-873-4067; *Téléc:* 418-873-4141
Other Numbers: Bureau: 418-873-4052
bibliopontrouge@hotmail.com
www.ville.pontrouge.qc.ca
Denyse Simard, Responsable
Nancy Talbot, Commis de bibliothèque
Odile Germain, Préposée entretien
Murielle Darveau, Responsable, Activités culturelles
Réjeanne Brousseau, Responsable, Collection locale
Yves Germain, Responsable, Statistiques

***Pontiac:* Bibliothèque municipale de Quyon**
12, rue Saint-John, Pontiac, QC J0X 2V0
Tél: 819-458-1227; *Téléc:* 819-458-9756
www.reseaubiblioduquebec.qc.ca/Quyon
Bernadette Milks, Coordonnateur

***Port-Cartier:* Bibliothèque municipale de Port-Cartier (Le Manuscrit)**
21, rue des Cèdres, Port-Cartier, QC G5B 2W5
Tél: 418-766-3366; *Téléc:* 418-766-3561
bportcar@globetrotter.qc.ca
www.villeport-cartier.com
Stéphan Harvey, Régisseur culturel
418-766-3854
Chantal Maltais, Bibliotechnicienne

***Port-Menier:* Bibliothèque municipale de l'Ile d'Anticosti**
38, ch des Forestiers, Port-Menier, QC G0G 2Y0
Tél: 418-535-0381
biblioanticosti@xplornet.com
Wendy Tremblay, Responsable
418-535-0048

***Portneuf-sur-Mer:* Bibliothèque de Portneuf-sur-Mer**
170, rue Principale, Portneuf-sur-Mer, QC G0T 1P0
Tél: 418-238-5303; *Téléc:* 418-238-5319
annie.morin@bellnet.ca
Annie Morin, Sec.-trés., Portneuf-sur-Mer
Christine Olivier, Responsable

***Poularies:* Bibliothèque Poularies**
990, rue Principale, Poularies, QC J0Z 3E0
Tél: 819-782-5159; *Téléc:* 819-782-5063
poularies@reseaubiblioatnq.qc.ca
Sophie Dallaire, Responsable

***Price:* Bibliothèque de Price**
1, rue du Centre, Price, QC G0J 1Z0
Tél: 418-775-5596
biblio.price@crsbp.net
www.reseaubiblioduquebec.qc.ca

***Princeville:* Bibliothèque de Princeville (Madeleine-Bélanger)**
140, rue Saint-Jean-Baptiste sud, Princeville, QC G6L 5A5
Tél: 819-364-5071
biblio079@reseaubibliocqlm.qc.ca
Madeleine Beaudoin, Responsable

***Préissac Nord:* Bibliothèque de Préissac-des-Rapides**
6, rue Des Rapides, Préissac Nord, QC J0Y 2E0
Tél: 819-732-4938; *Téléc:* 819-732-4909
preissacn@reseaubiblioatnq.qc.ca
www.reseaubiblioduquebec.qc.ca/preissac-des-rapides
Huguette Béland, Responsable

Préissac Sud: **Bibliothèque de Preissac Sud**
186, av du Lac, Préissac Sud, QC J0Y 2E0
Tél: 819-759-4138; *Téléc:* 819-759-4138
preissacs@reseaubiblioatnq.qc.ca
www.reseaubiblioduquebec.qc.ca/preissac sud
Yolande P. Gagné, Responsable

Prévost: **Bibliothèque Jean-Charles-Des Roches**
2945, boul du Curé-Labelle, Prévost, QC J0R 1T0
Tél: 450-224-8888
biblio@ville.prevost.qc.ca
www.reseaubiblioduquebec.qc.ca
Christian Schryburt, Responsable

Péribonka: **Bibliothèque publique de Péribonka**
296A, Édouard-Niquet, Péribonka, QC G0W 2G0
Tél: 418-374-2890; *Téléc:* 418-374-2491
peribonk@reseaubiblioslsj.qc.ca
www.reseaubiblioduquebec.qc.ca/portail/index.aspx?page=3&BID=548
Cynthia Gauthier, Responsable
418-374-2831
Line Fortin, Acquisitions
Chantale Néron, Acquisitions
Johane Hudon, Retards

Québec: **Réseau des bibliothèques de la Ville de Québec**
350, rue Saint-Joseph est, Québec, QC G1K 3B2
Tél: 418-641-6789; *Téléc:* 418-641-6787
Other Numbers: Référence: 418-641-6789, poste 221
courrier@institutcanadien.qc.ca
www.bibliothequesdequebec.qc.ca
Marie Goyette, Directrice
418-641-6789 ext. 246
Marik Trépanier, Responsable
Anne-Christine Félicité, Coordonnatrice
Marie-Eve St-Hilaire Richard

Ragueneau: **Bibliothèque municipale Amaury-Tremblay**
13, rue des Loisirs, Ragueneau, QC G0H 1S0
Tél: 418-567-8453; *Téléc:* 418-567-2344
www.reseaubiblioduquebec.qc.ca
Édith Martel, Responsable

Ragueneau: **Bibliothèque Ragueneau**
13, rue des Loisirs, Ragueneau, QC G0H 1S0
Tél: 418-567-2291; *Téléc:* 418-567-2344
biblio@municipalite.ragueneau.qc.ca
www.reseaubiblioduquebec.qc.ca/ragueneau

Ravignan: **Bibliothèque Liratu**
108A, rue de l'Église, Ravignan, QC G0R 2L0
Téléc: 418-267-5930
www.reseaubiblioduquebec.qc.ca/saint-louis-de-gonzague/
Yollande Rancourt-Bilodeau, Responsable

Rawdon: **Bibliothèque de Rawdon (Alice-Quintal)**
3643, rue Queen, Rawdon, QC J0X 1S0
Tél: 450-834-2596
biblio076@reseaubibliocqlm.qc.ca
www.reseaubiblioduquebec.qc.ca
Renée Lalonde, Responsable

Repentigny: **Bibliothèque municipale de Repentigny**
p, Place d'Evry, Repentigny, QC J6A 8H7
Tél: 450-470-3420; *Téléc:* 450-470-3079
bibliotheque@ville.repentigny.qc.ca
www.ville.repentigny.qc.ca/bibliotheque
Chantal Brodeur, Chef de division, bibliothèques
brodeurc@ville.repentigny.qc.ca
Julie-Anne D'Aoust, Chef de division adjoint, services au public
Marie Eve Lima, Chef de section, développement et promotion

Richelieu: **Bibliothèque municipale Simonne-Monet-Chartrand**
200, boul Richelieu, Richelieu, QC J3L 3R4
Tél: 450-658-1157
richelieu@reseaubibliomonteregie.qc.ca
www.villederichelieu.org
Claude Monast, Responsable
Manon Auclair, Responsable, Échanges et Animation

Richmond: **Bibliothèque municipale de Richmond-Cleveland**
820, rue Gouin, Richmond, QC J0B 2H0
Tél: 819-826-5814; *Téléc:* 819-826-5547
bibliothequercm@ville.richmond.qc.ca
www.ville.richmond.qc.ca/biblio.htm
Suzanne Nault, Responsable

Rigaud: **Bibliothèque municipale de Rigaud**
102, St Pierre, Rigaud, QC J0P 1P0
Tél: 450-451-8841; *Téléc:* 450-451-8845
biblio@ville.rigaud.qc.ca
www.ville.rigaud.qc.ca/
Isabelle Guérard, Coordonnatrice
biblio@ville.rigaud.qc.ca
450-451-8841
Anne-Marie Fournier, Commis

Rimouski: **Bibliothèque de Le Bic**
149, rue Sainte-Cécile-du-Bic, Rimouski, QC G0L 1B0
Tél: 418-736-5325
biblio.lebic@crsbp.net
www.reseaubiblioduquebec.qc.ca
Martine Fournier, Bibliothécaire

Rimouski: **Bibliothèque de Sainte-Blandine**
22, rue Lévesque, Rimouski, QC G5N 5S6
Tél: 418-735-5055
biblio.blandine@crsbp.net
www.reseaubiblioduquebec.qc.ca

Rimouski: **Bibliothèque Lisette-Morin**
110, rue de l'Évêché E, Rimouski, QC G5L 7C7
Tél: 418-724-3164; *Téléc:* 418-724-3139
bibliotheque.lisette-morin@ville.rimouski.qc.ca
ville.rimouski.qc.ca/fr/citoyens/bibliotheques/lisettemorin.html
Nicole Gagnon, Responsable

Rimouski: **Bibliothèque Pointe-au-Père**
315, av Thomas-Dionne, Rimouski, QC G5M 1M7
Tél: 418-722-4748
biblio.pere@crsbp.net
Ginette Ménard, Responsable

Ripon: **Bibliothèque de Ripon**
31, rue Coursol, Ripon, QC J0V 1V0
Tél: 819-983-2000; *Téléc:* 819-983-1327
admripon@crsbpo.qc.ca
www.reseaubiblioduquebec.qc.ca/Ripon
Céline Derouin, Responsable

Rivière-au-Tonnerre: **Bibliothèque de Rivière-au-Tonnerre**
473, rue Jacques-Cartier, Rivière-au-Tonnerre, QC G0G 2L0
Tél: 418-465-2255; *Téléc:* 418-465-2956
crsbp@globetrotter.net
Marie-Josée Lapierre, Responsable

Rivière-du-Loup: **Bibliothèque municipale Françoise-Bédard**
67, rue du Rocher, Rivière-du-Loup, QC G5R 1J8
Tél: 418-862-4252
bibliotheque@ville.riviere-du-loup.qc.ca
www.ville.riviere-du-loup.qc.ca/biblio
Sylvie Michaud, Bibliothécaire responsable
sylvie.michaud@ville.riviere-du-loup.qc.ca
418-867-6669
Marie-France April, Technicienne en documentation
418-867-6670
Annie Rodrigue, Technicienne en documentation (aide à la recherche)
annie.rodrigue@ville.riviere-du-loup.qc.ca
418-862-6529
Isabelle Moffet, Coordonnatrice à l'animation
isabelle.moffet@ville.riviere-du-loup.qc.ca
418-867-6668

Rivière-Héva: **Bibliothèque Rivière-Héva**
15A, rue du Parc, Rivière-Héva, QC J0Y 2H0
Tél: 819-735-2306; *Téléc:* 819-735-4251
www.reseaubiblioduquebec.qc.ca/portail/index.aspx?page=3&BID=821
Nicole Turcotte, Responsable
Claire Julien, Bénévole

Rivière-Pentecôte: **Bibliothèque de Rivière-Pentecôte**
4344, rue Jacques-Cartier, Rivière-Pentecôte, QC G0H 1R0
Tél: 418-799-2143; *Téléc:* 418-799-2263
www.reseaubiblioduquebec.qc.ca
Hélène Jean, Responsable

Rivière-Rouge: **Bibliothèque de Sainte-Véronique**
2167, boul Fernand-Lafontaine, Rivière-Rouge, QC J0T 1T0
Tél: 819-275-3759; *Téléc:* 819-275-3759
bibliovero@riviere-rouge.ca
www.reseaubiblioduquebec.qc.ca
Claire Cochet, Responsable
Nicole Lefebvre, Bénévole
Rita Radermaker, Bénévole
Denise Ranger, Bénévole
Suzanne Ranger-Dubé, Bénévole

Rivière-à-Claude: **Bibliothèque de Rivière-à-Claude**
520, rue Principale est, Rivière-à-Claude, QC G0E 1Z0
Tél: 418-797-2455
mcrioux@globetrotter.net
www.reseaubiblioduquebec.qc.ca
Marie-Claude Rioux, Responsable

Rivière-Éternite: **Bibliothèque publique de Rivière Eternité**
404, rue Principale, Rivière-Éternite, QC G0V 1P0
Tél: 418-272-1052
eternite@reseaubiblioslsj.qc.ca
www.reseaubiblioduquebec.qc.ca
Lucie Gagné, Responsable

Roberval: **Bibliothèque Georges-Henri-Lévesque**
829, boul St-Joseph, Roberval, QC G8H 2L6
Tél: 418-275-0202; *Téléc:* 418-275-7045
ville.roberval.qc.ca/biblio/contact.htm
Tania Loisirs, Directrice
tdesbiens@ville.roberval.qc.ca
Lise Morin, Secrétaire
lmorin@ville.roberval.qc.ca

Rock Forest: **Bibliothèque du secteur de Rock Forest**
968, rue du Haut-Bois sud, Rock Forest, QC J1N 2C8
Tél: 819-823-8676; *Téléc:* 819-823-8345
Bibliotheque.rockforest@ville.sherbrooke.qc.ca
www.ville.sherbrooke.qc.ca
Mèdia social: twitter.com/#!/VilleSherbrooke

Rosemère: **Bibliothèque municipale H J Hemens de Rosemère**
339, rue Grande-Côte, Rosemère, QC J7A 1K2
Tél: 450-621-6132; *Téléc:* 450-621-6131
biblio@ville.rosemere.qc.ca
ville.rosemere.qc.ca/biblio
Marc Bineault, Bibliothécaire - Chef de service
mbineault@ville.rosemere.qc.ca
514-621-6132
Ginette Corbeil Rivet, Responsable, Services techniques et référence

Rougemont: **Bibliothèque municipale de Rougemont**
839, rue Principale, Rougemont, QC J0L 1M0
Tél: 450-469-3213
rougemont@reseaubibliomonteregie.qc.ca
Simone Tétrault, Responsable
450-469-3452
Francine Chalifoux, Bénévole

Rouyn-Noranda: **Biblio Rollet**
12570, boul Rideau, Rouyn-Noranda, QC J0Z 3J0
Tél: 819-797-7110; *Téléc:* 819-493-1210
rollet@reseaubiblioatnq.qc.ca
www.crsbpat.qc.ca/rollet/
Liliane Monderie, Responsable

Rouyn-Noranda: **Bibliothèque de Beaudry**
6884, boul Témiscamingue, Rouyn-Noranda, QC J9Y 1N1
Tél: 819-797-2543; *Téléc:* 819-797-2108
beaudry@reseaubiblioatnq.qc.ca
Marguerite Petit, Responsable

Rouyn-Noranda: **Bibliothèque Destor**
7292, rang du parc, Rouyn-Noranda, QC J9Y 0C8
Tél: 819-637-2279; *Téléc:* 819-637-5512
destor@reseaubiblioatnq.qc.ca
www.reseaubiblioduquebec.qc.ca/destor
Rita Tremblay, Responsable
Guylaine Pelletier, Adjointe

Rouyn-Noranda: **Bibliothèque municipale de Rouyn-Noranda**
201, av Dallaire, Rouyn-Noranda, QC J9X 4T5
Tél: 819-762-0944; *Téléc:* 819-797-7564
info@biblrn.qc.ca
www.biblrn.qc.ca
Joël Lacoursière, Directeur général
joel.lacoursiere@biblrn.qc.ca
Ginette Montigny, Responsable, Services techniques
ginette.montigny@biblrn.qc.ca
Diane Brazeau, Secrétaire de direction
diane.brazeau@biblrn.qc.ca

Roxton Pond: **Bibliothèque municipale de Roxton Pond**
905, rue Saint-Jean, Roxton Pond, QC J0E 1Z0
Tél: 450-372-6991
roxton.pond@reseaubibliomonteregie.qc.ca
www.reseaubiblioduquebec.qc.ca
Diane Blanchard, Responsable

Rémigny: **Bibliothèque de Rémigny**
1304, ch de l'Église, Rémigny, QC J0Z 3H0
Tél: 819-761-2331; *Téléc:* 819-761-2421
remigny@reseaubiblioatnq.qc.ca
www.reseaubiblioduquebec.qc.ca/rémigny
Jocelyne Savignac, Responsable

Sabrevois: **Bibliothèque municipale de Sainte-Anne-de-Sabrevois**
1218, rte 133, Sabrevois, QC J0J 2G0
Tél: 450-346-0899
sabrevois@reseaubibliomonteregie.qc.ca
www.reseaubiblioduquebec.qc.ca
Guylaine Marchand, Responsable

Sacré-Coeur-Saguenay: **Bibliothèque de Sacré-Coeur**
89-A, Principale nord, Sacré-Coeur-Saguenay, QC G0T 1Y0
Tél: 418-236-4621; *Téléc:* 418-236-9144
www.reseaubiblioduquebec.qc.ca
Vanessa Deschênes, Responsable
vandeschenes@hotmail.com

Saint-Adelphe: **Bibliothèque de Saint-Adelphe (Roger-Fontaine)**
150, rue Baillargeon, Saint-Adelphe, QC G0X 2G0
Tél: 418-322-6634; *Téléc:* 418-322-5434
biblio004@reseaubibliocqlm.qc.ca
www.reseaubiblioduquebec.qc.ca
Lyne Deshaies, Responsable

Saint-Adolphe-d'Howard: **Bibliothèque de Saint-Adolphe-d'Howard**
1881, ch du Village, Saint-Adolphe-d'Howard, QC J0T 2B0
Tél: 819-327-2117; *Téléc:* 819-327-2282
biblio24@crsbpl.qc.ca
www.reseaubiblioduquebec.qc.ca
Vickie Vandal, Responsable

Saint-Aimé-des-Lacs: **Bibliothèque La Plume d'Or**
123B, rue Principale, Saint-Aimé-des-Lacs, QC G0T 1S0
Tél: 418-439-2229
www.reseaubiblioduquebec.qc.ca/lacs
Hélène Perron, Responsable
Monique Gravel, Adjointe/Responsable Animation/Extranet

Saint-Alban: **Bibliothèque Biblio-Chut!/Saint-Alban**
179, rue Principale, Saint-Alban, QC G0A 3B0
Tél: 418-268-3557; *Téléc:* 418-268-5073
www.reseaubiblioduquebec.qc.ca/saint-alban
Monette Perreault, Responsable
Lise Pleau, Adjointe

Saint-Alexis-de-Matapédia: **Bibliothèque de Saint-Alexis-de-Matapédia**
190, rue Principale, Saint-Alexis-de-Matapédia, QC G0J 2E0
Tél: 418-299-2520; *Téléc:* 418-299-3011
plateau1@globetrotter.net
www.reseaubiblioduquebec.qc.ca
Rachel Lebrun, Responsable

Saint-Alexis-de-Montcalm: **Bibliothèque de Saint-Alexis**
232, rue Principale, Saint-Alexis-de-Montcalm, QC J0K 1T0
Tél: 450-839-7277; *Téléc:* 450-831-2108
biblio110@reseaubibliocqlm.qc.ca
France Parent, Responsable

Saint-Alexis-des-Monts: **Bibliothèque de Saint-Alexis-des-Monts (Léopold-Bellemare)**
105, rue Hôtel-de-Ville, Saint-Alexis-des-Monts, QC J0K 1V0
Tél: 819-265-3598
biblio028@reseaubibliocqlm.qc.ca
Danielle Gagnon, Responsable

Saint-Alphonse-de-Caplan: **Bibliothèque de A B C du savoir**
134A, rue Principale ouest, Saint-Alphonse-de-Caplan, QC G0C 2V0
Tél: 418-388-5577; *Téléc:* 418-388-2435
bbostal@globetrotter.net
www.reseaubiblioduquebec.qc.ca
Roselyn Onraet, Responsable

Saint-Alphonse-de-Granby: **Bibliothèque municipale de Saint-Alphonse-de-Granby**
360, rue Principale, Saint-Alphonse-de-Granby, QC J0E 2A0
Tél: 450-375-7229; *Téléc:* 450-375-4570
alphonse@reseaubibliomonteregie.qc.ca
Julie Fortin, Responsable
Annie Lessard, Responsable, Animation/Administration

Saint-Alphonse-Rodriguez: **Bibliothèque de Saint-Alphonse-Rodriguez (Docteur-Jacques-Olivier)**
20, rue de la Plage, Saint-Alphonse-Rodriguez, QC J0K 1W0
Tél: 450-883-2264; *Téléc:* 450-883-3959
biblio062@reseaubibliocqlm.qc.ca
Lina Laforest, Responsable

Saint-Amable: **Maison de la culture Jacqueline Gemme**
575, rue Principale, Saint-Amable, QC J0L 1N0
Tél: 450-649-3555; *Téléc:* 450-649-0203
amable@reseaubibliomonteregie.qc.ca
www.reseaubiblioduquebec.qc.ca
France Therrien, Responsable

Saint-Ambroise: **Bibliothèque publique de Saint-Ambroise**
156, rue Gaudreault, Saint-Ambroise, QC G7P 2J9
Tél: 418-672-2253
stambr@reseaubiblioslsj.qc.ca
www.reseaubiblioduquebec.qc.ca
Carole Gagné, Responsable

Saint-André-Avellin: **Bibliothèque de Saint-André-Avellin**
532, rue Charles-Auguste Montreuil, Saint-André-Avellin, QC J0V 1W0
Tél: 819-983-2840; *Téléc:* 819-983-2344
admavellin@crsbpo.qc.ca
www.reseaubiblioduquebec.qc.ca/St-Andre-Avellin
Adéodat Bernard, Responsable

Saint-André-de-Kamouraska: **Bibliothèque de Saint-André**
126, rue Principale, Saint-André-de-Kamouraska, QC G0L 2H0
Tél: 418-493-2649
biblio.andre@crsbp.net
www.reseaubiblioduquebec.qc.ca

Saint-André-de-Restigouche: **Bibliothèque de Saint-André-de-Restigouche**
163, rue Principale, Saint-André-de-Restigouche, QC G0J 1G0
Tél: 418-865-2234; *Téléc:* 418-865-1393
TTY: 4188651393
m.st.and.restigouche@globetrotter.net
www.reseaubiblioduquebec.qc.ca
Blandine Parent, Responsable

Saint-Anicet: **Bibliothèque municipale de Saint-Anicet**
1547, rte 132, Saint-Anicet, QC J0S 1M0
Tél: 450-264-9431; *Téléc:* 450-264-3544
anicet@reseaubibliomonteregie.qc.ca
Carmen Bourgoyne, Responsable

Saint-Antoine-de-Tilly: **Bibliothèque La Corne de brume**
943, rte de L'Église, Saint-Antoine-de-Tilly, QC G0S 2C0
Tél: 418-886-2603
www.reseaubiblioduquebec.qc.ca/tilly
Hughes Lansac, Responsable
Jean-Marc Dumas, Adjoint
Reine Bourassa, Responsable, PIB
Louise Bernier, Responsable, Échanges

Saint-Antoine-sur-Richelieu: **Bibliothèque Hélène-Dupuis-Marion**
#2, 1060, rue du Moulin Payet, Saint-Antoine-sur-Richelieu, QC J0L 1R0
Tél: 450-787-3140; *Téléc:* 450-787-2852
antoine@reseaubibliomonteregie.qc.ca
Nicole Villiard, Responsable

Saint-Antonin: **Bibliothèque Paradis du Livre**
261, rue Principale, Saint-Antonin, QC G0L 2J0
Tél: 418-867-2353; *Téléc:* 418-862-3268
biblio.antonin@crsbp.net
Hélène Léveillé, Responsable

Saint-Apollinaire: **Bibliothèque Au Jardin des livres/Saint-Apollinaire**
#102, 94, rue Principale, Saint-Apollinaire, QC G0S 2E0
Tél: 418-881-2447; *Téléc:* 418-881-4152
bibliotheque@st-apollinaire.com
www.reseaubiblioduquebec.qc.ca/saint-apollinaire
Denise Olivier, Responsable
Francine Leclerc, Adjointe au responsable
Francine Rousseau, Secrétaire-relationniste
Karine Bernier, Trésorière

Saint-Arsène: **Bibliothèque Saint-Arsène**
49, rue de l'Église, Saint-Arsène, QC G0L 2K0
Tél: 418-867-2205
biblio.arsene@crsbp.net
Suzanne Michaud, Responsable

Saint-Athanase: **Bibliothèque Saint-Athanase**
6081, ch de l'Église, Saint-Athanase, QC G0L 2L0
Tél: 418-859-1143
biblio.athanase@crsbp.net
Diane Dumont, Responsable

Saint-Aubert: **Bibliothèque Charles-E.-Harpe**
14, rue des Loisirs, Saint-Aubert, QC G0R 2R0
Tél: 418-598-3623; *Téléc:* 418-598-3369
bibliaub@videotron.qc.ca
www.reseaubiblioduquebec.qc.ca/saint-aubert/
Céline Bélanger, Responsable

Saint-Augustin: **Bibliothèque publique de St-Augustin**
710, rue Principale, Saint-Augustin, QC G0W 1K0
Tél: 418-374-1084
augustin@reseaubiblioslsj.qc.ca
www.reseaubiblioduquebec.qc.ca
Rosette Savard, Responsable

Saint-Augustin-Saguenay: **Bibliothèque de Saint-Augustin**
École de Saint-Augustin, 710, rue Principale, Saint-Augustin-Saguenay, QC G0W 1K0
Tél: 418-374-1084; *Téléc:* 418-947-2533
augustin@reseaubiblioslsj.qc.ca
www.reseaubiblioduquebec.qc.ca
Pauline Fortin, Responsable

Saint-Barthélemy: **Bibliothèque de Saint-Barthélemy**
601 rue Dusablé, Saint-Barthélemy, QC J0K 1X0
Tél: 450-885-3232; *Téléc:* 450-885-2165
www.saint-barthelemy.ca
Média social: www.facebook.com/104244999653520
Louise Belhumeur, Responsable

Saint-Basile: **Bibliothèque Au fil des mots**
41, rue Caron, Saint-Basile, QC G0A 3G0
Tél: 450-537-2022
biblio@saintbasile.qc.ca
www.reseaubiblioduquebec.qc.ca
Andréanne Legault, Responsable

Saint-Basile: **Bibliothèque Au fil des mots/Saint-Basile**
41, rue Caron, Saint-Basile, QC G0A 3G0
Tél: 418-329-2858; *Téléc:* 418-329-3743
biblio@saintbasile.qc.ca
www.reseaubiblioduquebec.qc.ca/saint-basile
Lise Bélanger, Responsable
Juliette Bourgoin, Adjointe
Josée Marcotte, Responsable, PIB
Denise Hardy, Responsable, Échanges

Saint-Basile-le-Grand: **Bibliothèque Roland Leblanc**
40, rue Savaria, Saint-Basile-le-Grand, QC J3N 1L8
Tél: 450-461-8085; *Téléc:* 450-461-8089
bibliotheque@ville.saint-basile-le-grand.qc.ca
www.bibliothequesaintbasile.qc.ca
France Goyette, Directrice

Saint-Benjamin: **Bibliothèque La Détente/Saint-Benjamin**
440, rue du Collège, Saint-Benjamin, QC G0M 1N0
Tél: 418-594-8189; *Téléc:* 418-594-6068
www.reseaubiblioduquebec.qc.ca/saint-benjamin
Régine Perras, Responsable
418-594-5635

Saint-Benoît-Labre: **Bibliothèque L'Envolume**
216, rte 271, Saint-Benoît-Labre, QC G0M 1P0
Tél: 418-228-9250; *Téléc:* 418-228-0518
biblstbe@globetrotter.qc.ca
www.reseaubiblioduquebec.qc.ca/saint-benoit-labre/
Josette Labbé, Responsable
Suzanne Legroulx, Responsable, Échanges/Animation
Carmen Quirion, Responsable, PIB

Saint-Bernard: **Bibliothèque Liratout/Saint-Bernard**
540, rue Vaillancourt, Saint-Bernard, QC G0S 2G0
Tél: 418-475-4669; *Téléc:* 418-475-4602
bibliost-bernard@nouvellebeauce.com
www.reseaubiblioduquebec.qc.ca/saint-bernard
Carolle Larochelle, Responsable

Saint-Bernard-de-Michaudvil: **Bibliothèque municipale de Saint-Bernard-de-Michaudville**
390, rue Principale, Saint-Bernard-de-Michaudvil, QC J0H 1C0
Tél: 450-792-3190; *Téléc:* 450-792-3591
bernard.sud@reseaubibliomonteregie.qc.ca
Marie-Sylvie Lavallée, Responsable

Saint-Blaise-sur-Richelieu: **Bibliothèque municipale de Saint-Blaise-sur-Richelieu**
#6, 795, rue des Loisirs, Saint-Blaise-sur-Richelieu, QC J0J 1W0
Tél: 450-291-5944; *Téléc:* 450-291-5095
blaise@reseaubibliomonteregie.qc.ca
Laure Desrochers, Responsable

Saint-Bonaventure: **Bibliothèque de Saint-Bonaventure**
110, rue Cyr, Saint-Bonaventure, QC J0C 1C0
Tél: 819-396-1676; *Téléc:* 819-396-2335
biblio120@reseaubibliocqlm.qc.ca
www.reseaubiblioduquebec.qc.ca
Gisèle Corbin, Responsable

Saint-Boniface: **Bibliothèque de Saint-Boniface**
155, rue Langevin, Saint-Boniface, QC G0X 2L0
Tél: 819-535-3330; *Téléc:* 819-535-1242
biblio021@reseaubibliocqlm.qc.ca
www.reseaubiblioduquebec.qc.ca
Chantal Gélinas, Responsable

Saint-Bruno: **Bibliothèque publique de Saint-Bruno**
550, rue des 4H, Saint-Bruno, QC G0W 2L0
Tél: 418-343-2007
stbruno@reseaubiblioslsj.qc.ca
www.reseaubiblioduquebec.qc.ca/portail/index.aspx?page=3&BID=556
Denise Martel, Responsable
418-343-3488

Saint-Bruno-de-Guigues: **Bibliothèque de Saint-Bruno-de-Guigues**
23B, rue Principale nord, Saint-Bruno-de-Guigues, QC J0Z 2G0
Tél: 819-728-2910; *Téléc:* 819-728-2404
guigues@reseaubiblioatnq.qc.ca
www.reseaubiblioduquebec.qc.ca/s
Louise Gagnon, Responsable

Saint-Bruno-de-Kamouraska: **Bibliothèque des Brulots**
6, rue Du Couvent, Saint-Bruno-de-Kamouraska, QC G0L 2M0
Tél: 418-856-7053
biblio.bruno@crsbp.net
www.reseaubiblioduquebec.qc.ca

Saint-Bruno-de-Montarville: **Bibliothèque municipale de Saint-Bruno-de-Montarville**
82, boul Seigneurial ouest, Saint-Bruno-de-Montarville, QC J3V 5N7
Tél: 450-645-2950; *Téléc:* 450-441-8485
bibliotheque@stbruno.ca
Jean-Marc Lynch, Bibliothécaire en chef
jean-marc.lynch@ville.stbruno.qc.ca
450-653-2443 ext. 2850

Saint-Calixte: **Bibliothèque de Saint-Calixte**
6250, rue Hôtel-de-Ville, Saint-Calixte, QC J0K 1Z0
Tél: 450-222-2782; *Téléc:* 450-222-2789
biblio@mscalixte.qc.ca
www.reseauibliodquebec.qc.ca/saint-calixte
Madeleine Vézina, Responsable
Gisèle D'Amours, Adjointe

Saint-Casimir: **Bibliothèque Jean-Charles-Magnan**
510, boul de la Montagne, Saint-Casimir, QC G0A 3L0
Tél: 418-339-2909; *Téléc:* 418-339-3105
jcmagnan@csportneuf.qc.ca
www.reseaubiblioduquebec.qc.ca/saint-casimir/
Ange-Aimée Asselin, Responsable
Nicole Tessier, Responsable, PIB

Saint-Charles-de Bourget: **Bibliothèque publique de Saint-Charles-de-Bourget**
362, rue Principale, Saint-Charles-de Bourget, QC G0V 1G0
Tél: 418-672-1082; *Téléc:* 418-672-4403
stcharle@reseaubiblioslsj.qc.ca
www.reseaubiblioduquebec.qc.ca
Isabelle Néron, Responsable
418-672-1082
Joanne Vallière, Bénévole
Natalie Harvey, Bénévole
Louise Breton, Bénévole
Claire Chayer, Bénévole
Isabelle Forgues, Bénévole

Saint-Charles-de-Drummond: **Club de Lecture Centre Réal-Rochefort/Saint-Charles-de-Drummond**
565, rue Victorin, Saint-Charles-de-Drummond, QC J2C 1C1
Tél: 819-477-2326; *Téléc:* 819-477-0697
ccsc@ville.drummondville.qc.ca
Guylaine Dion-Daneault, Responsable

Saint-Charles-Garnier: **Bibliothèque de Saint-Charles-Garnier**
38, de Saint-Charles-Garnier, Saint-Charles-Garnier, QC G0K 1K0
Tél: 418-798-4820
biblio.garnier@crsbp.net
www.reseaubiblioduquebec.qc.ca

Saint-Clet: **Bibliothèque municipale de Saint-Clet**
25, rue Piché, Saint-Clet, QC J0P 1S0
Tél: 450-465-3175
clet@reseaubibliomonteregie.qc.ca
www.reseaubiblioduquebec.qc.ca
Brigitte Lalonde, Responsable

Saint-Clément: **Bibliothèque de Saint-Clément**
25A, rue Saint-Pierre, Saint-Clément, QC G0L 2N0
Tél: 418-963-2258; *Téléc:* 418-963-2619
biblio.clement@crsbp.net
www.reseaubiblioduquebec.qc.ca
Thérèse St-Pierre, Responsable

Saint-Cléophas: **Bibliothèque de Saint-Cléophas**
356, rue Principale, Saint-Cléophas, QC G0J 3N0
Tél: 418-536-3915
biblio.cleophas@crsbp.net
www.reseaubiblioduquebec.qc.ca
Hélène Dumont, Responsable
Linda Hudon, Bénévole

Saint-Cléophas-de-Brandon: **Bibliothèque de Saint-Cléophas-de-Brandon**
750, rue Principale, Saint-Cléophas-de-Brandon, QC J0K 2A0
Tél: 450-889-5683; *Téléc:* 450-889-8007
biblio107@reseaubibliocqlm.qc.ca
www.reseaubiblioduquebec.qc.ca
Marie-Line Gingras, Responsable

Saint-Colomban: **Bibliothèque de Saint-Colomban**
347, montée de l'Église, Saint-Colomban, QC J5K 1B1
Tél: 450-436-1453; *Téléc:* 450-432-1863
biblio@st-colomban.qc.ca
www.reseaubiblioduquebec.qc.ca
Média social:
www.facebook.com/group.php?gid=133415300034333
Lucie Jubinville, Directrice

Saint-Constant: **Bibliothèque municipale de Saint-Constant**
85, Mtée Saint-Régis, Saint-Constant, QC J5A 1X8
Tél: 450-638-2010; *Téléc:* 450-632-9399
bibliotheque@ville.saint-constant.qc.ca
www.ville.saint-constant.qc.ca/Citoyens/bibliotheque.asp
Nathalie Groulx, Responsable

Saint-Cuthbert: **Bibliothèque de Saint-Cuthbert**
1891, rue Principale, Saint-Cuthbert, QC J0K 2C0
Tél: 450-836-4852; *Téléc:* 450-836-4833
biblio126@reseaubibliocqlm.qc.ca
Pierre-Yvon Laporte, Responsable
Julie Rémillard, Adjointe
Cécile Rémillard, Bénévole
450-836-2146
Monique Lepage, Bénévole

Saint-Cyprien: **Bibliothèque de Saint-Cyprien (Alphonse-Desjardins)**
187, rue Principale, Saint-Cyprien, QC G0L 2P0
Tél: 418-963-2226
biblio.cyprien@crsbp.net
www.reseaubiblioduquebec.qc.ca
Ginette Gagné, Responsable

Saint-Cyprien-des-Etchemins: **Bibliothèque municipale de Saint-Cyprien**
399, rue Principale, Saint-Cyprien-des-Etchemins, QC G0R 1B0
Tél: 418-383-3476; *Téléc:* 418-383-5269
Sandy DeBlois, Responsable

Saint-Célestin: **Bibliothèque de Saint-Célestin (Claude-Bouchard)**
450B, rue Marquis, Saint-Célestin, QC J0C 1G0
Tél: 819-229-3403
biblio130@reseaubibliocqlm.qc.ca
www.reseaubiblioduquebec.qc.ca
Nicole Cameron, Responsable

Saint-Côme: **Bibliothèque de Saint-Côme**
1677, 55e rue, Saint-Côme, QC J0K 2B0
Tél: 450-883-2726; *Téléc:* 450-883-6431
biblio054@reseaubibliocqlm.qc.ca
www.reseaubiblioduquebec.qc.ca
Josée Blanchard, Responsable

Saint-Côme-Linière: **Bibliothèque municipale de Saint-Côme-Linière**
1375, 18e rue, Saint-Côme-Linière, QC G0M 1J0
Tél: 418-685-3825; *Téléc:* 418-685-2566
bibliostcome@hotmail.com
www.reseaubiblioduquebec.qc.ca/saint-come
Chantal Poulin, Responsable
Laurette Thompson, Adjointe

Saint-Damase: **Bibliothèque municipale de Saint-Damase**
113, rue St-Étienne, Saint-Damase, QC J0H 1J0
Tél: 418-797-3341
damase@reseaubibliomonteregie.qc.ca
Hélène Simard, Responsable

Saint-Damase-de-l'Islet: **Bibliothèque municipale de Saint-Damase-de-l'Islet**
28, rue de Village est, Saint-Damase-de-l'Islet, QC G0R 2X0
Tél: 418-598-9370; *Téléc:* 418-598-9396
stdamase3@hotmail.com
Sylvie Cloutier, Responsable

Saint-Damase-de-Matapédia: **Bibliothèque de Saint-Damase-de-Matapédia**
18, av du Centenaire, Saint-Damase-de-Matapédia, QC G0J 2J0
Tél: 418-776-2103
biblio.damase@crsbp.net
www.reseaubiblioduquebec.qc.ca
Edith Deschênes, Responsable

Saint-Damien: **Bibliothèque de Saint-Damien**
2045, rue Taschereau, Saint-Damien, QC J0K 2E0
Tél: 450-835-7519; *Téléc:* 450-835-5538
biblio041@reseaubibliocqlm.qc.ca
www.reseaubiblioduquebec.qc.ca
Josée St-Martin, Responsable

Saint-Damien-de-Buckland: **Bibliothèque Le Bouquin d'Or/Saint-Damien-de-Buckland**
75, rue Saint-Gérard, Saint-Damien-de-Buckland, QC G0R 2Y0
Tél: 418-789-2127; *Téléc:* 418-789-2125
www.reseaubiblioduquebec.qc.ca/saint-damien
Marielle Dion-Jobin, Responsable de la bibliothèque
418-789-2125

Saint-Denis: **Bibliothèque de Saint-Denis**
5, rue 287, Saint-Denis, QC G0L 2R0
Tél: 418-498-2968
biblio.denis@crsbp.net
www.reseaubiblioduquebec.qc.ca
Doris Rivard, Responsable

Saint-Didace: **Bibliothèque de Saint-Didace**
530A, rue Principale, Saint-Didace, QC J0K 2G0
Tél: 450-835-3933; *Téléc:* 450-835-0602
biblio@saint-didace.com
www.saint-didace.com
Monique Guay, Coordonnatrice
450-835-4184 ext. 8205

Saint-Dominique: **Bibliothèque municipale de Saint-Dominique**
488, Saint-Dominique, Saint-Dominique, QC J0H 1L0
Tél: 450-771-0256
dominique@reseaubibliomonteregie.qc.ca
Manon Denault, Responsable

Saint-Donat: **Bibliothèque de Saint-Donat**
510, rue Desrochers, Saint-Donat, QC J0T 2C0
Tél: 819-424-3044; *Téléc:* 819-424-5020
biblio@saintdonat.ca
www.reseaubiblioduquebec.qc.ca/saint-donat
Anita Desmeules, Responsable
Joanne Riopel, Adjointe

Saint-Donat: **Bibliothèque de Saint-Donat**
101, rue Bérubé, Saint-Donat, QC G0K 1L0
Tél: 418-739-3368
biblio.donat@crsbp.net
www.reseaubiblioduquebec.qc.ca

Saint-Edmond-les-Plaines: **Bibliothèque publique de Saint-Edmond**
561, rue Principale, Saint-Edmond-les-Plaines, QC G0W 2M0
Tél: 418-274-2591; *Téléc:* 418-274-5629
stedmond@reseaubiblioslsj.qc.ca
Lucie Coté, Responsable

Saint-Edouard-de-Lotbinière: **Bibliothèque municipale de Saint-Édouard-de-Lotbinière**
105, rue de L'École, Saint-Edouard-de-Lotbinière, QC G0S 1Y0
Tél: 418-796-2433; *Téléc:* 418-796-2228
Patricia McDonald, Responsable
Diane Chabot, Secretaire-trésorière
Pierre Luc Daigle, Responsable des activités

Saint-Elphège: **Bibliothèque de Saint-Elphège (La Bouquinerie)**
227A, rue de l'Église, Saint-Elphège, QC J0G 1J0
Tél: 450-568-7339; *Téléc:* 450-568-0288
biblio007@reseaubibliocqlm.qc.ca
www.reseaubiblioduquebec.qc.ca

Saint-Elzéar: **Bibliothèque de Saint-Elzéar**
144, ch Principal, Saint-Elzéar, QC G0C 2W0
Tél: 418-534-4314; *Téléc:* 418-534-2626
www.reseaubiblioduquebec.qc.ca
Lucille Ferlatte, Responsable

Saint-Elzéar: **Bibliothèque de Saint-Elzéar (Saint-Elzéar-de-Témiscouata)**
144, ch Principale, Saint-Elzéar, QC G0L 2W0
Tél: 418-534-4314; *Téléc:* 418-534-2626
bostelz@globetrotter.net
www.reseaubiblioduquebec.qc.ca
Thérèse Sirois, Responsable

Saint-Esprit: **Bibliothèque de Saint-Esprit (Alice-Parizeau)**
45, rue des Écoles, Saint-Esprit, QC J0K 2L0
Tél: 450-831-2274; *Téléc:* 450-839-6070
biblio125@reseaubibliocqlm.qc.ca
Diane Lamarre, Responsable

Saint-Eugène: **Bibliothèque publique de Saint-Eugène**
469, du Pont, Saint-Eugène, QC G0W 1B0
Tél: 418-276-7790
steugene@reseaubiblioslsj.qc.ca
www.reseaubiblioduquebec.qc.ca
Lise Lavoie, Responsable
Pauline Dumont, Adjointe

Saint-Eugène-de-Guigues: **Bibliothèque de Saint-Eugène-de-Guigues**
4, 1ère av ouest, Saint-Eugène-de-Guigues, QC J0Z 3L0
Tél: 819-785-4441; *Téléc:* 819-785-2301
eugene@reseaubiblioatnq.qc.ca
www.reseaubiblioduquebec.qc.ca/St-Eugene
Lorraine Falardeau, Responsable

Saint-Eustache: **Bibliothèque municipale Guy-Bélisle**
80, boul Arthur-Sauvé, Saint-Eustache, QC J7R 2H7
Tél: 450-974-5035; *Téléc:* 450-974-5054
ngrimard@ville.saint-eustache.qc.ca
biblio.ville.saint-eustache.qc.ca
Nicole Grimard, Responsable
ngrimard@ville.saint-eustache.qc.ca
Danielle Touchette, Technicienne, Animation/Référence
France Genest, Bibliothécaire adjointe
Rina Dupuis, Préposée acquisitions

Saint-Eusèbe: **Bibliothèque de Saint-Eusèbe**
222B, rue Principale, Saint-Eusèbe, QC G0L 2Y0
Tél: 418-899-0194
biblio.eusebe@crsbp.net
www.reseaubiblioduquebec.qc.ca
Gisèle Lebrun Bolduc, Responsable
Sébastien Meunier, Adjoint

Saint-Fabien: **Bibliothèque de Saint-Fabien**
30, 7e Ave., Saint-Fabien, QC G0L 2Z0
Tél: 418-869-2602
biblio.fabien@crsbp.net
www.reseaubiblioduquebec.qc.ca
Raynald Beaulieu, Responsable

Saint-Fabien-de-Panet: **Bibliothèque Fabiothèque/Saint-Fabien-de-Panet**
199, rue Bilodeau, Saint-Fabien-de-Panet, QC G0R 2J0
Tél: 418-249-4417; *Téléc:* 418-249-2507
www.reseaubiblioduquebec.qc.ca/saint-fabien-de-panet
Michèle Thibodeau, Responsable
418-249-2732

Saint-Faustin-Lac-Carré: **Bibliothèque du Lac**
64, rue de la Culture, Saint-Faustin-Lac-Carré, QC J0T 1J1
Tél: 819-688-5434; *Téléc:* 819-688-5644
bibliodulac@municipalite.stfaustin.qc.ca
Marielle Jacques, Responsable
Nicole Morel, Commis aux prêts
819-688-2645

Saint-Ferdinand: **Bibliothèque de Saint-Ferdinand (Onil-Garneau)**
620, rue Notre-Dame, Saint-Ferdinand, QC G0N 1N0
Tél: 418-428-9607
biblio049@reseaubibliocqlm.qc.ca
Lucie Lamontagne, Responsable

Saint-Ferréol-les-Neiges: **Bibliothèque Aux Sources/Saint-Ferréol-les-Neiges**
33, rue de l'Église, Saint-Ferréol-les-Neiges, QC G0A 3R0
Tél: 418-826-3540; *Téléc:* 418-826-0489
www.reseaubiblioduquebec.qc.ca/saint-ferreol
Lucie Bédard, Responsable
Louisette Bédard, Responsable, l'Animation

Saint-Flavien: **Bibliothèque La Flaviethèque/Saint-Flavien**
6, rue Caux, Saint-Flavien, QC G0S 2M0
Tél: 418-728-0025; *Téléc:* 418-728-4190
biblifla@globetrotter.qc.ca
www.reseaubiblioduquebec.qc.ca/saint-flavien
Carole Turgeon, Responsable

Saint-Fortunat: **Bibliothèque municipale de Saint-Fortunat**
173, rue Principale, Saint-Fortunat, QC G0P 1G0
Tél: 418-344-5399
www.reseaubiblioduquebec.qc.ca/saint-fortunat
Huguette Garneau, Responsable

Saint-François-d'Assise: **Bibliothèque de Saint-François-d'Assise**
457, ch Central, Saint-François-d'Assise, QC G0J 2N0
Tél: 418-299-2099; *Téléc:* 418-299-3037
munstfrs@globetrotter.net
Monelle Gallant, Responsable

Saint-François-de-Sales: **Bibliothèque publique de Saint-François-de-Sales**
255, rue de l'Église, Saint-François-de-Sales, QC G0W 1M0
Tél: 418-348-9444
franco@reseaubiblioslsj.qc.ca
www.reseaubiblioduquebec.qc.ca/portail/index.aspx?page=3&BI D=563
Myriam Simard, Responsable
418-348-6736

Saint-François-du-Lac: **Bibliothèque de Saint-François-du-Lac**
480, rue Notre-Dame, Saint-François-du-Lac, QC J0G 1M0
Tél: 450-568-1130
bibliotheque@saint-francois-du-lac.ca
www.saint-francois-du-lac.ca/bibliotheque_saint-francois.php
Ghislaine Lachapelle, Responsable

Saint-Fulgence: **Bibliothèque publique de Saint-Fulgence**
12, Saint-Basile, Saint-Fulgence, QC G0V 1S0
Tél: 418-615-0059
stfulgence@reseaubiblioslsj.qc.ca
www.reseaubiblioduquebec.qc.ca/portail/index.aspx?page=3&BI D=564
Lina Tremblay, Responsable
418-674-2440

Saint-Félicien: **Bibliothèque municipale de Saint-Félicien**
#200, 1209, boul Sacré Coeur, Saint-Félicien, QC G8K 2R5
Tél: 418-679-2100; *Téléc:* 418-679-1449
biblio@ville.stfelicien.qc.ca
www.stfelicien.biblio.qc.ca
Johanne Laprise, Responsable
Francine Ménard, Technicienne en documentation

Saint-Félicien: **Bibliothèque publique de Saint-Méthode**
3159, rue de la Sainte-Méthode, Saint-Félicien, QC G8K 3C2
Tél: 418-679-0757
stmethode@reseaubiblioslsj.qc.ca
Thérèse Fortin, Responsable

Saint-Félix-d'Otis: **Bibliothèque publique de Saint-Félix-d'Otis**
455, rue Principale, Saint-Félix-d'Otis, QC G0V 1M0
Tél: 418-544-1144
stfelix@reseaubiblioslsj.qc.ca
www.reseaubiblioduquebec.qc.ca/portail/index.aspx?page=3&BI D=562
Nathalie Simard, Responsable

Saint-Félix-de-Kingsey: **Bibliothèque de Saint-Félix-de-Kingsey**
6115B, rue Principale, Saint-Félix-de-Kingsey, QC J0B 2T0
Tél: 819-848-1400
biblio152@reseaubibliocqlm.qc.ca
www.reseaubiblioduquebec.qc.ca
Pauline Roy, Responsable

Saint-Félix-de-Valois: **Bibliothèque de Saint-Félix-de-Valois**
4863, rue Principale, Saint-Félix-de-Valois, QC J0K 2M0
Tél: 450-889-5589; *Téléc:* 450-889-7911
biblio010@reseaubibliocqlm.qc.ca
Suzie Thériault, Responsable

Saint-Gabriel-de-Brandon: **Bibliothèque de Saint-Gabriel (Au fil des pages)**
53, rue Beausoleil, Saint-Gabriel-de-Brandon, QC J0K 2N0
Tél: 450-835-2212; *Téléc:* 450-835-1493
biblio013@reseaubibliocqlm.qc.ca
Noëlla Ganley, Responsable

Saint-Gabriel-de-Rimouski: **Bibliothèque Le Bouquinier**
103, rue Leblanc, Saint-Gabriel-de-Rimouski, QC G0K 1M0
Tél: 418-798-8310; *Téléc:* 418-798-4108
biblio.gabriel@crsbp.net
www.reseaubiblioduquebec.qc.ca
Nicole Leblanc, Responsable
Julie Lepage, Bénévole
Julie Lavoie, Bénévole

Saint-Germain: **Bibliothèque de Saint-Germain**
506, rue de la Fabrique, Saint-Germain, QC G0L 3G0
Tél: 418-492-5767
biblio.germain@crsbp.net
www.reseaubiblioduquebec.qc.ca
Simone Lévesque, Responsable

Saint-Germain-de-Grantham: **Bibliothèque de Saint-Germain-de-Grantham (Le Signet)**
299, rue Notre-Dame, Saint-Germain-de-Grantham, QC J0C 1K0
Tél: 819-395-2644
biblio100@reseaubibliocqlm.qc.ca
www.reseaubiblioduquebec.qc.ca
Louise Gaillard-Simoneau, Responsable

Saint-Gervais: **Bibliothèque Faubourg de la Cadie**
36A, rue de la Fabrique est, Saint-Gervais, QC G0R 3C0
Tél: 418-887-3628; *Téléc:* 418-887-3628
www.reseaubiblioduquebec.qc.ca/saint-gervais
Micheline Trudel, Responsable
Louisette Toussaint, Adjointe
Mariette Labrecque, Responsable, Animation

Saint-Gilles: **Bibliothèque Le Signet**
1540, rue du Couvent, Saint-Gilles, QC G0S 2P0
Tél: 418-888-5178; *Téléc:* 418-888-5486
www.reseaubiblioduquebec.qc.ca/saint-gilles
Pascale Bélanger, Responsable
Nicole Aubert, Adjointe

Saint-Guillaume: **Bibliothèque de Saint-Guillaume**
106, rue Saint-Jean-Baptiste, Saint-Guillaume, QC J0C 1L0
Tél: 819-396-3754; *Téléc:* 819-396-0184
biblio087@reseaubibliocqlm.qc.ca
www.reseaubiblioduquebec.qc.ca
Jocelyne Taillon, Responsable

Saint-Guy: **Bibliothèque de Saint-Guy**
54, ch Principal, Saint-Guy, QC G0K 1W0
Tél: 418-963-1490
biblio.guy@crsbp.net
Nathalie Belisle, Responsable

***Saint-Gédéon:* Bibliothèque publique de Saint-Gédéon**
208, Dequen, Saint-Gédéon, QC G0W 2P0
Tél: 418-345-8001
stgedeon@reseaubiblioslsj.qc.ca
www.reseaubiblioduquebec.qc.ca
Carole Gagnon, Responsable

***Saint-Henri-de-Lévis:* Bibliothèque La Reliure/Saint-Henri**
123, rue Belleau, Saint-Henri-de-Lévis, QC G0R 3E0
Tél: 418-882-0694; *Téléc:* 418-882-0302
bibhenri@globetrotter.qc.ca
www.reseaubiblioduquebec.qc.ca/saint-henri
Céline Labrecque, Responsable

***Saint-Henri-de-Taillon:* Bibliothèque publique de Saint-Henri-de-Taillon**
420, rue Principale, Saint-Henri-de-Taillon, QC G0W 2X0
Tél: 418-669-6001; *Téléc:* 418-347-1138
sthenri@reseaubiblioslsj.qc.ca
www.reseaubiblioduquebec.qc.ca
Chantale Fortin, Responsable
418-347-1513

***Saint-Hilarion:* Bibliothèque aux Quatre Vents de Saint-Hilarion**
#247, ch Principal, local 1, Saint-Hilarion, QC G0A 3V0
Tél: 418-489-2999
biblioquatrevents@gmail.com
www.reseaubiblioduquebec.qc.ca/saint-hilarion

***Saint-Hippolyte:* Bibliothèque de Saint-Hippolyte**
871, chemin des Hauteurs, Saint-Hippolyte, QC J8A 3P4
Tél: 450-224-4137; *Téléc:* 450-224-9927
bibliosthip@bellnet.ca
Élise Chaumont, Responsable
Joanne Bonneau, Adjointe

***Saint-Honoré-de-Chicoutimi:* Bibliothèque publique de Saint-Honoré**
100, rue Paul-Aimé Hudon, Saint-Honoré-de-Chicoutimi, QC G0V 1L0
Tél: 418-673-3790
biblio@ville.sthonore.qc.ca
www.reseaubiblioduquebec.qc.ca/portail/index.aspx?page=3&BID=567
Hélène Chaput, Coordonnatrice

***Saint-Honoré-de-Témiscouata:* Bibliothèque Les Moussaillons**
6, rue de l'Église, Saint-Honoré-de-Témiscouata, QC G0L 3K0
Tél: 418-854-8450
biblio.honore@crsbp.net
www.reseaubiblioduquebec.qc.ca
Hélène Paradis, Responsable
Dominique Viel, Responsable, Promotion
418-497-2696

***Saint-Hugues:* Bibliothèque municipale de Saint-Hugues**
207, rue Saint-Germain, Saint-Hugues, QC J0H 1N0
Tél: 450-794-2630; *Téléc:* 450-794-2630
hugues@reseaubibliomonteregie.qc.ca
www.reseaubiblioduquebec.qc.ca
Marie Bernier Lavigne, Responsable

***Saint-Hyacinthe:* Médiathèque maskoutaine**
2720, rue Dessaulles, Saint-Hyacinthe, QC J2S 2V7
Tél: 450-773-1830; *Téléc:* 450-773-3398
www.mediatheque.qc.ca
Média social: www.facebook.com/mediathequemaskoutaine
Yves Tanguay, Directeur
tanguayy@mediatheque.qc.ca
450-773-1830 ext. 23
Sonia de Bonville, Responsable, Services publics Bibliothèque T.-A.-St-Germain
debonvilles@mediatheque.qc.ca
450-773-1830 ext. 25
Marie-France Pineault, Secrétaire administrative
pineaultmf@mediatheque.qc.ca
450-773-1830 ext. 21

***Saint-Ignace-de-Loyola:* Bibliothèque de Saint-Ignace-de-Loyola**
621, rue de l'Église, Saint-Ignace-de-Loyola, QC J0K 2P0
Tél: 450-836-3376; *Téléc:* 450-836-1400
biblio156@reseaubiblioclqlm.qc.ca
www.reseaubiblioduquebec.qc.ca
Andrée Bergeron, Responsable

***Saint-Irénée:* Bibliothèque Adolphe-Basile-Routhier**
136, rue Principale, Saint-Irénée, QC G0T 1V0
Téléc: 418-452-8221
www.reseaubiblioduquebec.qc.ca/saint-irenee
Micheline Mongrain, Responsable
Denise Gauthier, Adjointe
Claudia Boudreault, Responsable des concours

***Saint-Isidore:* Bibliothèque Laurette-Nadeau-Parent**
101, rue des Aigles, Saint-Isidore, QC G0S 2S0
Tél: 418-882-6470
www.reseaubiblioduquebec.qc.ca/saint-isidore

***Saint-Isidore:* Bibliothèque municipale de Saint-Isidore**
5, rue Boyer, Saint-Isidore, QC J0L 2A0
Tél: 450-454-9871
isidore@reseaubibliomonteregie.qc.ca
Ginette Goyette, Responsable
Louisette Paré, Responsable, PIB
Nicole Dubuc, Responsable, Échanges

***Saint-Jacques:* Bibliothèque municipale Marcel-Dugas**
16, rue Maréchal, Saint-Jacques, QC J0K 2R0
Tél: 450-839-3926; *Téléc:* 450-839-2387
biblio@st-jacques.org
www.st-jacques.org/bibli/index
Francine Roy-Gaudet, Responsable

***Saint-Jacques-de-Leeds:* Bibliothèque La Ressource**
425, rue Principale, Saint-Jacques-de-Leeds, QC G0N 1J0
Tél: 418-424-3181; *Téléc:* 418-424-0126
www.reseaubiblioduquebec.qc.ca/leeds/
Louise Dionne, Responsable
Martine Bolduc, Responsable, PIB
Sylvie Tanguay, Responsable, Échanges

***Saint-Jacques-le-Mineur:* Bibliothèque municipale de Saint-Jacques-le-Mineur**
89, rue Principale, Saint-Jacques-le-Mineur, QC J0J 1Z0
Tél: 450-347-1888; *Téléc:* 450-347-5754
jacques@reseaubibliomonteregie.qc.ca
Benoît D'Avignon, Responsable

***Saint-Janvier-de-Joly:* Bibliothèque Adrien-Lambert/Saint-Janvier-de-Joly**
729, rue des Loisirs, Saint-Janvier-de-Joly, QC G0S 1M0
Tél: 418-728-2984; *Téléc:* 418-728-2984
adrienlambert1936@hotmail.com
www.reseaubiblioduquebec.qc.ca/joly
Marielle Sylvain, Responsable
mariebouffonsylvain@hotmail.com
Monique Turmel, Adjointe

***Saint-Jean-Baptiste:* Bibliothèque municipale de Saint-Jean-Baptiste**
3090, rue Principale, Saint-Jean-Baptiste, QC J0L 2B0
Tél: 450-467-1786
jean.baptiste@reseaubibliomonteregie.qc.ca
Sylvie Sweeney, Responsable

***Saint-Jean-Chrysostome:* Bibliothèques Lévis**
959, rue de l'Hôtel-de-Ville, Saint-Jean-Chrysostome, QC G6Z 2N8
Tél: 418-835-4982; *Téléc:* 418-839-2640
bibliolevis@ville.levis.qc.ca
bibliotheques.ville.levis.qc.ca
Suzanne Rochefort, Chef du service des bibliothèques
srochefort@ville.levis.qc.ca

***Saint-Jean-de-Brébeuf:* Bibliothèque Saint-Jean-de-Brébeuf(Bibliothèque Bibliomagie)**
844, rue de l'Église, Saint-Jean-de-Brébeuf, QC G6G 0A1
Tél: 418-453-2571; *Téléc:* 418-453-2339
www.reseaubiblioduquebec.qc.ca/saint-jean-de-brebeuf
Solange Bolduc, Responsable

***Saint-Jean-de-Dieu:* Bibliothèque de Saint-Jean-de-Dieu**
32, rue Principale sud, Saint-Jean-de-Dieu, QC G0L 3M0
Tél: 418-963-3529
biblio.jeandieu@crsbp.net
www.reseaubiblioduquebec.qc.ca
Francine Rioux, Responsable

***Saint-Jean-de-Matha:* Bibliothèque de Saint-Jean-de-Matha**
81, rue Sainte-Louise, Saint-Jean-de-Matha, QC J0K 2S0
Tél: 450-886-5855
biblio047@reseaubiblioclqlm.qc.ca
www.reseaubiblioduquebec.qc.ca
Nicole Léonard, Responsable

***Saint-Jean-Port-Joli:* Bibliothèque Marie-Bonenfant/Saint-Jean-Port-Joli**
7B, place de l'Église, Saint-Jean-Port-Joli, QC G0R 3G0
Tél: 418-598-3187; *Téléc:* 418-598-3085
biblio.stjean@globetrotter.net
www.reseaubiblioduquebec.qc.ca/joli
Gilberte Picard, Responsable
Évangéline Dionne, Adjointe
Azeline Leblanc, Responsable, l'Animation
Thérèse Morneau, Responsable, PIB

***Saint-Jean-sur-Richelieu:* Bibliothèques municipales de Saint-Jean-sur-Richelieu**
180, rue Laurier, Saint-Jean-sur-Richelieu, QC J3B 7B2
Tél: 450-357-2111; *Téléc:* 450-357-2055
www.ville.saint-jean-sur-richelieu.qc.ca
Camille Bricault, Chef, Division bibliothèques
Lise Gosselin, Bibliothécaire responsable
France Gagnon, Bibliotechnicienne
f.gagnon@ville.saint-jean-sur-richelieu.qc.c
Yvan Tourigny, Bibliotechnicien
Sylvette Toutant, Bibliothécaire responsable
Julie Roy, Bibliotechnicienne
Lucie Gauthier, Bibliotechnicienne

***Saint-Joseph-de-Beauce:* Bibliothèque de Saint-Joseph-de-Beauce**
139-100, rue Sainte-Christine, Saint-Joseph-de-Beauce, QC G0S 2V0
Tél: 418-397-6160; *Téléc:* 418-397-5715
www.reseaubiblioduquebec.qc.ca/saint-joseph-de-beauce
Gilberte Doyon, Responsable
Gina Poulin, Adjointe
Marie-Reine Vézina, Responsable, Échanges/PIB
Lise Bourque, Responsable, Animation

***Saint-Joseph-de-Kamouraska:* Bibliothèque de Saint-Joseph-de-Kamouraska**
298-A, rue Principale est, Saint-Joseph-de-Kamouraska, QC G0L 3P0
Tél: 418-493-2658
biblio.joseph@crsbp.net
www.reseaubiblioduquebec.qc.ca
Sébastien Simard, Responsable

***Saint-Joseph-de-Lepage:* Bibliothèque de Saint-Joseph-de-Lepage**
70, rue de la Rivière, Saint-Joseph-de-Lepage, QC G5H 3N8
Tél: 418-775-4607
biblio.lepage@crsbp.net
www.reseaubiblioduquebec.qc.ca
Noëlla Dupont, Responsable
Jacqueline Roy, Bénévole
Nathalie Roy, Bénévole

***Saint-Joseph-du-Lac:* Bibliothèque de Saint-Joseph-du-Lac**
70, Montée du Village, Saint-Joseph-du-Lac, QC J0N 1M0
Tél: 450-623-7833; *Téléc:* 450-623-2889
biblio64@crsbpl.qc.ca
www.reseaubiblioduquebec.qc.ca
Hélène Caron, Responsable
hcaron@ssdl.qc.ca
450-623-1072 ext. 4
Francine Carbonneau, Adjointe
450-623-7633

***Saint-Jude:* Bibliothèque St-Jude**
940, rue de Centre, Saint-Jude, QC J0H 1P0
Tél: 450-792-2164
Daniele Boulanger, Responsable

***Saint-Julien:* Bibliothèque municipale de Saint-Julien**
794, ch Saint-Julien, Saint-Julien, QC G0N 1B0
Tél: 418-423-3410; *Téléc:* 418-423-3410
bibliotheque@st-julien.ca
www.reseaubiblioduquebec.qc.ca/saint-julien
Yolande Poirier, Responsable
Yannick Gouin, Responsable, PIB

***Saint-Juste-du-Lac:* Bibliothèque de Saint-Juste-du-Lac**
37, ch Principal, Saint-Juste-du-Lac, QC G0L 3R0
Tél: 418-899-0374
biblio.juste@crsbp.net
Jeanne Benoist, Responsable

***Saint-Juste-du-Lac:* Bibliothèque Lots-Renversés**
Route 295, Saint-Juste-du-Lac, QC G0L 1V0
Tél: 418-899-0375
biblio.lotsren@crsbp.net
Leslie Bingham, Responsable

***Saint-Justin:* Bibliothèque de Saint-Justin**
1281, rue Gérin, Saint-Justin, QC J0K 2V0
Tél: 819-227-2775; *Téléc:* 819-227-4876
biblio056@reseaubibliocqlm.qc.ca
www.reseaubiblioduquebec.qc.ca
Josianne Messier, Responsable

***Saint-Jérôme:* Bibliothèque Marie-Antoinette-Foucher**
101, place du Curé-Labelle, Saint-Jérôme, QC J7Z 1X6
Tél: 450-432-0569; *Téléc:* 450-436-1211
www.ville.saint-jerome.qc.ca/pages/
Chantal Paquin, Bibliothécaire
cpaquin@villesaint-jerome.qc.ca
450-436-1512 ext. 3350

***Saint-Lambert:* Bibliothèque municipale de Saint-Lambert**
490, av Mercille, Saint-Lambert, QC J4P 2L5
Tél: 450-466-3910; *Téléc:* 450-923-6512
bibliotheque@saint-lambert.ca
Guylaine Pellerin, Directrice
guylaine.pellerin@ville.saint-lambert.qc.ca
405-466-3889 ext. poste
Caroline Régis, Bibliothécaire

***Saint-Lazare:* Bibliothèque Biblio-Culture**
116B, rue de la Fabrique, Saint-Lazare, QC G0R 3J0
Tél: 418-883-2551; *Téléc:* 418-883-2551
biblio-st-lazare@globetrotter.net
www.reseaubiblioduquebec.qc.ca/saint-lazare
Raoul Laflamme, Responsable
laflammer@globetrotter.net
418-883-3005
Anna-Marie Chabot-Laverdière, Adjointe
Johanne Allard, Responsable, Animation

***Saint-Liboire:* Bibliothèque municipale de Saint-Liboire**
21, Place Mauriac, Saint-Liboire, QC J0H 1R0
Tél: 450-793-4751
liboire@reseaubibliomonteregie.qc.ca
Julie Girouard, Responsable

***Saint-Liguori:* Bibliothèque de Saint-Liguori**
741, rue Principale, Saint-Liguori, QC J0K 2X0
Tél: 450-753-4446; *Téléc:* 450-753-4638
biblio006@reseaubibliocqlm.qc.ca
www.reseaubiblioduquebec.qc.ca
Jeanne Gagné-Richard, Responsable

***Saint-Lin-Laurentides:* Bibliothèque de Saint-Lin-Laurentides**
920, 12e av, Saint-Lin-Laurentides, QC J5M 2W2
Tél: 450-439-2486; *Téléc:* 450-439-1525
biblio@saint-lin-laurentides.com
www.reseaubiblioduquebec.qc.ca/saint-lin-laurentides
Jocelyne Dufort, Responsable
Danielle Gravel, Adjointe

***Saint-Louis-de-Blandford:* Bibliothèque de Saint-Louis-de-Blandford**
80, rue Principale, Saint-Louis-de-Blandford, QC G0Z 1B0
Tél: 819-364-7007; *Téléc:* 819-364-2781
biblio116@reseaubibliocqlm.qc.ca
Françoise Lafond, Responsable

***Saint-Louis-de-Gonzague:* Bibliothèque municipale de Saint-Louis-de-Gonzague**
140, rue Principale, Saint-Louis-de-Gonzague, QC J0S 1T0
Tél: 450-371-9411; *Téléc:* 450-371-7428
louis.gonzague@reseaubibliomonteregie.qc.ca
www.reseaubiblioduquebec.qc.ca
Marie-Andrée Demers, Responsable

***Saint-Louis-du-Ha!Ha!:* Bibliothèque de Saint-Louis-du-Ha!Ha!**
234, rue Commerciale, Saint-Louis-du-Ha!Ha!, QC G0L 3S0
Tél: 418-854-4031
biblio.louis@crsbp.net
www.reseaubiblioduquebec.qc.ca
Laurette Lavoie, Responsable

***Saint-Luc-de-Bellechasse:* Bibliothèque L'Éveil/Saint-Luc-de-Bellechasse**
115, rue de la Fabrique, Saint-Luc-de-Bellechasse, QC G0R 1L0
Tél: 418-636-2776; *Téléc:* 418-636-2776
bibliotheque@sogetel.net
www.reseaubiblioduquebec.qc.ca/saint-luc
Lisette Bilodeau, Responsable

***Saint-Luc-de-Vincennes:* Bibliothèque de Saint-Luc-de-Vincennes**
660, rue Principale, Saint-Luc-de-Vincennes, QC G0X 3K0
Tél: 819-295-3608; *Téléc:* 819-295-3782
biblio097@reseaubibliocqlm.qc.ca
www.reseaubiblioduquebec.qc.ca
Louise Lemire, Responsable
819-295-3603

***Saint-Ludger-de-Milot:* Bibliothèque publique de Saint-Ludger-de-Milot**
739, rue Gaudreault, Saint-Ludger-de-Milot, QC G0W 2B0
Tél: 418-373-2568; *Téléc:* 418-373-2554
stludger@reseaubiblioslsj.qc.ca
www.reseaubiblioduquebec.qc.ca/portail/index.aspx?page=3&BID=568
Karine Boutot, Responsable

***Saint-Léon-le-Grand:* Bibliothèque de Saint-Léon-le-Grand (Bas-Saint-Laurent)**
241, rue Gendron, Saint-Léon-le-Grand, QC G0J 2W0
Tél: 418-743-2914
biblio.granleon@crsbp.net
www.reseaubiblioduquebec.qc.ca
Lise Fournier, Responsable

***Saint-Léon-le-Grand:* Bibliothèque de Saint-Léon-le-Grand (Mauricie)**
44, rue de la Fabrique, Saint-Léon-le-Grand, QC J0K 2W0
Tél: 819-228-3236; *Téléc:* 819-228-8088
biblio029@reseaubibliocqlm.qc.ca
www.reseaubiblioduquebec.qc.ca
Diane Lavergne, Responsable

***Saint-Léonard-d'Aston:* Bibliothèque de Saint-Léonard-d'Aston (Lucille-M.-Desmarais)**
146, rue des Écoles, Saint-Léonard-d'Aston, QC J0C 1M0
Tél: 819-399-3368
biblio089@reseaubibliocqlm.qc.ca
Sylvie Turmel, Responsable

***Saint-Léonard-de-Portneuf:* Bibliothèque Biblio 'Fleur de lin'**
260, rue Pettigrew, Saint-Léonard-de-Portneuf, QC G0A 4A0
Tél: 418-337-3961; *Téléc:* 418-337-6742
www.reseaubiblioduquebec.qc.ca/saint-leonard
Ginette Paquet, Responsable
Hélène Cantin, Adjointe
Marie-Paule Langlois, Responsable, PIB
Carole Perron, Responsable, Statistiques

***Saint-Malachie:* Bibliothèque J.-A.-Kirouac**
1184, rue Principale, Saint-Malachie, QC G0R 3N0
Tél: 418-642-5127; *Téléc:* 418-642-2231
jakir@globetrotter.qc.ca
www.reseaubibliodequebec.qc.ca/saint-malachie/
Louise Guénette, Responsable
Francine Moore, Responsable, PIB
Mariette Labrecque, Responsable, Animation

***Saint-Marc-du-Lac-Long:* Bibliothèque Saint-Marc-du-Lac-Long**
14A, rue de l'Église, Saint-Marc-du-Lac-Long, QC G0L 1T0
Tél: 418-893-1075; *Téléc:* 418-893-1339
biblio.laclong@crsbp.net
Jeanne-D'Arc Poliquin, Responsable

***Saint-Marc-sur-Richelieu:* Bibliothèque municipale Archambault-Trépanier/Saint-Marc-sur-Richelieu**
102, rue de la Fabrique, Saint-Marc-sur-Richelieu, QC J0L 2E0
Tél: 450-584-2258
marc@reseaubibliomonteregie.qc.ca
www.reseaubiblioduquebec.qc.ca
Nancy Bélanger, Responsable

***Saint-Marcel:* Bibliothèque municipale de Saint-Marcel**
375, rue Taché est, Saint-Marcel, QC G0R 3R0
Tél: 418-356-2691; *Téléc:* 418-356-2820
www.saintmarcel.qc.ca
Solange Pelletier, Responsable
418-356-2635
Bélanger Laurence, Responsable
418-356-5554

***Saint-Marcel-de-Richelieu:* Bibliothèque Saint-Marcel-de-Richelieu**
#2, 1060, rue des Ormes, Saint-Marcel-de-Richelieu, QC J0L 1R0
Tél: 450-794-2832; *Téléc:* 450-794-1140
Nicole Beauchamp, Responsable
450-794-2706

***Saint-Marcellin:* Fautoulire**
336, rte 234, Saint-Marcellin, QC G0K 1R0
Tél: 418-798-8164
biblio.marcellin@crsbp.net
www.reseaubiblioduquebec.qc.ca
Nathalie Girard, Responsable

***Saint-Mathias-sur-Richelieu:* Bibliothèque municipale de Saint-Mathias-sur-Richelieu**
50, rue Lussier, Saint-Mathias-sur-Richelieu, QC J3L 6A4
Tél: 450-447-0679
mathias@reseaubibliomonteregie.qc.ca
www.reseaubiblioduquebec.qc.ca
France Desautels, Responsable

***Saint-Mathieu:* Bibliothèque municipale de Saint-Mathieu**
299, ch Saint-Édouard, Saint-Mathieu, QC J0L 2H0
Tél: 450-659-9528
mathieu@reseaubibliomonteregie.qc.ca
Danielle Routhier, Responsable

***Saint-Mathieu-de-Beloeil:* Bibliothèque municipale Ryane-Provost**
5000, rue des Loisirs, Saint-Mathieu-de-Beloeil, QC J3G 2C9
Tél: 450-467-7490
mathieu.beloeil@reseaubibliomonteregie.qc.ca
www.reseaubiblioduquebec.qc.ca
Claude Monast, Responsable

***Saint-Mathieu-de-Rioux:* Bibliothèque de Saint-Mathieu-de-Rioux**
41, rue de l'Église, Saint-Mathieu-de-Rioux, QC G0L 3T0
Tél: 418-738-3057
biblio.mathieu@crsbp.net
www.reseaubiblioduquebec.qc.ca
Michelyne Caron, Responsable

***Saint-Mathieu-du-Parc:* Bibliothèque de Saint-Mathieu-du-Parc (Micheline H.- Gélinas)**
600, ch Saint-Marc, Saint-Mathieu-du-Parc, QC G0X 1N0
Tél: 819-532-2345
biblio093@reseaubibliocqlm.qc.ca
www.reseaubiblioduquebec.qc.ca
Suzie Parent, Responsable

***Saint-Maurice:* Bibliothèque de Saint-Maurice**
1380, rue Notre-Dame, Saint-Maurice, QC G0X 2X0
Tél: 819-378-7315
biblio026@reseaubibliocqlm.qc.ca
www.reseaubiblioduquebec.qc.ca
Aline Hamois, Responsable

***Saint-Michel:* Bibliothèque municipale Claire-Lazure**
440, place Saint-Michel, Saint-Michel, QC J0L 2J0
Tél: 450-454-7995
michel@reseaubibliomonteregie.qc.ca
www.reseaubiblioduquebec.qc.ca
Lucie Longtin, Responsable

***Saint-Michel-de-Bellechasse:* Bibliothèque Benoît-Lacroix**
8, av Saint-Charles, Saint-Michel-de-Bellechasse, QC G0R 3S0
Tél: 418-884-2766; *Téléc:* 418-884-2866
biblistmic@globetrotter.net
www.reseaubiblioduquebec.qc.ca/saint-michel
Gilbert Théberge, Responsable

***Saint-Michel-des-Saints:* Bibliothèque de Saint-Michel-des-Saints (Antonio-Saint-Georges)**
390B, rue Matawin, Saint-Michel-des-Saints, QC J0K 3B0
Tél: 450-833-5471
biblio044@reseaubibliocqlm.qc.ca
www.reseaubiblioduquebec.qc.ca
Cécile Baudouard, Responsable

***Saint-Michel-du-Squatec:* Bibliothèque Alma-Durand**
149, rue St-Joseph, CP 104, Saint-Michel-du-Squatec, QC G0L 4H0
Tél: 418-855-2708; *Téléc:* 418-855-5228
biblio.squatec@crsbp.net
Céline Morin, Responsable
Linda Cyr, Bénévole

***Saint-Modeste:* Bibliothèque municipale de Saint-Modeste**
312, rue Principale, Saint-Modeste, QC G0L 3W0
Tél: 418-867-2352
biblio.modeste@crsbp.net
www.reseaubiblioduquebec.qc.ca
Solange Chouinard, Responsable

***Saint-Médard:* Bibliothèque de Saint-Médard**
1, rue Principale est, Saint-Médard, QC G0L 3V0
Tél: 418-963-1588
biblio.medard@crsbp.net
www.reseaubiblioduquebec.qc.ca
Andrée Beaulieu, Responsable

***Saint-Narcisse:* Bibliothèque de Saint-Narcisse (Gérard-Desrosiers)**
509, rue Massicotte, Saint-Narcisse, QC G0X 2Y0
Tél: 418-328-4430; *Téléc:* 418-328-4348
biblio001@reseaubibliocqlm.qc.ca
www.reseaubiblioduquebec.qc.ca
Rose-Alice Lafontaine, Responsable
Louise Lafontaine, Adjointe

***Saint-Narcisse-de-Beaurivag:* Bibliothèque municipale de Saint-Narcisse-de-Beaurivage**
510, rue de l'École, Saint-Narcisse-de-Beaurivag, QC G0S 1W0
Tél: 418-475-6464; *Téléc:* 418-475-6880
biblio.st-narcisse@globetrotter.net
www.reseaubiblioduquebec.qc.ca/saint-narcisse
Monique Arlen, Responsable
418-475-6750

***Saint-Nazaire:* Bibliothèque publique de St-Nazaire**
220, rue Principale, Saint-Nazaire, QC G0W 2V0
Tél: 418-662-1422; *Téléc:* 418-662-5467
nazaire@reseaubibliosIsj.qc.ca
www.reseaubiblioduquebec.qc.ca/portail/index.aspx?page=3&BID=570
Manon Tremblay, Responsable

***Saint-Nazaire-d'Acton:* Bibliothèque municipale de Saint-Nazaire-d'Acton**
715, rue des Loisirs, Saint-Nazaire-d'Acton, QC J0H 1V0
Tél: 819-392-2090
nazaire@reseaubibliomonteregie.qc.ca
Maryse Pelland, Responsable

***Saint-Noël:* Bibliothèque de Saint-Noël**
12, rue Saint-Joseph est, Saint-Noël, QC G0J 3A0
Tél: 418-776-2549
biblio.noel@crsbp.net
www.reseaubiblioduquebec.qc.ca
Diane Leclerc, Responsable

***Saint-Nérée:* Bibliothèque Biblio Du Centenaire**
2139, route Principale, Saint-Nérée, QC G0R 3V0
Tél: 418-243-3649; *Téléc:* 418-243-2136
www.reseaubiblioduquebec.qc.ca/saint-neree
Francine Nadeau, Responsable
Suzanne Corlay, Adjointe

***Saint-Odilon:* Bibliothèque L'Intello/Saint-Odilon-de-Cranbourne**
111, rue de l'Hôtel-de-Ville, Saint-Odilon, QC G0S 3A0
Tél: 418-464-4803; *Téléc:* 418-464-4800
www.reseaubiblioduquebec.qc.ca/saint-odilon
Mariette Vachon, Responsable
418-464-2463
Sylvie Drouin, Responsable, PIB/Extranet
418-464-4134
Odile Ruel, Responsable, Échanges
Lucille Carbonneau, Responsable, Collection locale
418-464-2972
Dany Lessard, Responsable, Statistiques
418-464-4260

***Saint-Omer:* Bibliothèque de Saint-Omer**
106B, rte 132 est, Saint-Omer, QC G0C 2Z0
Tél: 418-364-6485
bibliostomer@globetrotter.net
www.reseaubiblioduquebec.qc.ca
Line Arsenault, Responsable

***Saint-Ours:* Bibliothèque municipale de Saint-Ours**
2636, rue de l'Immaculée-Conception, Saint-Ours, QC J0G 1P0
Tél: 450-785-2779
ours@reseaubibliomonteregie.qc.ca
www.reseaubiblioduquebec.qc.ca
Lucie Grenier, Responsable

***Saint-Pacôme:* Bibliothèque de Saint-Pacôme**
201, boul Bégins, Saint-Pacôme, QC G0L 3X0
Tél: 418-315-0579
biblio.pacome@crsbp.net
www.reseaubiblioduquebec.qc.ca
Marc Bélanger, Responsable

***Saint-Pamphile:* Bibliothèque Marie-Louise-Gagnon/Saint-Pamphile**
3, rue Elgin sud, Saint-Pamphile, QC G0R 3X0
Tél: 418-356-5403; *Téléc:* 418-356-5502
pamphile@globetrotter.net
www.saintpamphile.ca
Micheline Leclerc, Responsable

***Saint-Pascal:* Bibliothèque de Saint-Pascal**
470, rue Notre-Dame, Saint-Pascal, QC G0L 3Y0
Tél: 418-492-2312
biblio.pascal@crsbp.net
www.reseaubiblioduquebec.qc.ca
Cécile Joseph, Responsable

***Saint-Patrice-de-Beaurivage:* Bibliothèque Florence-Guay/Saint-Patrice-de-Beaurivage**
470, du Manoir, Saint-Patrice-de-Beaurivage, QC G0S 1B0
Tél: 418-596-2439; *Téléc:* 418-596-2430
borivage@globetrotter.qc.ca
www.reseaubiblioduquebe.qc.ca/saint-patrice
Claire Béland, Responsable
450-596-3074

***Saint-Paul de l'île-aux-Noi:* Bibliothèque municipale Lucile-Langlois-Éthier**
959C, rue Principale, Saint-Paul de l'île-aux-Noi, QC J0J 1G0
Tél: 450-291-5585
paul.ile.noix@reseaubibliomonteregie.qc.ca
www.reseaubiblioduquebec.qc.ca
Roger Langlois, Responsable

***Saint-Paul-d'Industrie:* Bibliothèque de Saint-Paul**
18, boul Brassard, Saint-Paul-d'Industrie, QC J0K 3E0
Tél: 450-759-3333; *Téléc:* 450-759-6396
biblio071@reseaubibliocqlm.qc.ca
www.reseaubiblioduquebec.qc.ca
Isabelle Plouffe, Responsable

***Saint-Paul-de-la-Croix:* Bibliothèque de Saint-Paul-de-la-Croix**
1-B, rue du Parc, Saint-Paul-de-la-Croix, QC G0L 3Z0
Tél: 418-898-3095
biblio.croix@crsbp.net
www.reseaubiblioduquebec.qc.ca
Johanne Lagacé, Responsable
Diane Dubé, Bénévole
418-898-2006
Marjolaine April, Bénévole
Isabelle Lagacé, Bénévole
Jacinthe Dionne, Bénévole
418-898-2179

***Saint-Paulin:* Bibliothèque de Saint-Paulin (Jeannine-Julien)**
3051, rue Bergeron, C.P. 39, Saint-Paulin, QC J0K 3G0
Tél: 819-268-2425; *Téléc:* 819-268-2890
biblio118@reseaubibliocqlm.qc.ca
www.reseaubiblioduquebec.qc.ca
Lucie Marcouiller, Responsable

***Saint-Philippe:* Bibliothèque Saint-Philippe/Le Vaisseau d'Or**
2223, rte Édouard VII, Saint-Philippe, QC J0L 2K0
Tél: 450-659-7701; *Téléc:* 450-659-5354
bibliotheque@municipalite.saint-philippe.qc.ca
www.municipalite.saint-philippe.qc.ca
Line Thibodeau, Responsable

***Saint-Philippe-de-Néri:* Bibliothèque Claude-Béchard**
11, rue de l'Église, Saint-Philippe-de-Néri, QC G0L 4A0
Tél: 418-551-0314
biblio.philip@crsbp.net
www.reseaubiblioduquebec.qc.ca
Mariette Dumais, Responsable

***Saint-Philippe-de-Néri:* Bibliothèque Claude-Béchard**
11 de la Côte, Saint-Philippe-de-Néri, QC G0L 4A0
Tél: 418-551-0314
biblio.philip@crsbp.net
www.reseaubiblioduquebec.qc.ca/claude-bechard

***Saint-Philémon:* Bibliothèque des Sous-Bois**
1460, rue St-Louis, Saint-Philémon, QC G0R 4A0
Tél: 418-469-2443
www.reseaubiblioduquebec.qc.ca/saint-philemon

***Saint-Pie:* Bibliothèque municipale de Saint-Pie**
309, rue Notre-Dame, Saint-Pie, QC J0H 1W0
Tél: 450-772-2332; *Téléc:* 450-772-2332
pie@reseaubibliomonteregie.qc.ca
Danielle Massé, Responsable

***Saint-Pie-de-Guire:* Bibliothèque de Saint-Pie-de-Guire**
445C, rue Principal, Saint-Pie-de-Guire, QC J0G 1R0
Tél: 450-784-0232
biblio132@reseaubibliocqlm.qc.ca
www.reseaubiblioduquebec.qc.ca
Sylvie Courchesne, Responsable

***Saint-Pierre-de-Broughton:* Bibliothèque Maurice-Couture/Saint-Pierre-de-Broughton**
6, du Couvent, Saint-Pierre-de-Broughton, QC G0N 1T0
Tél: 418-424-3450; *Téléc:* 418-424-0389
biblio.m.couture@cgocable.ca
www.reseaubiblioduquebec.qc.ca/broughton
Brigitte Routhier, Responsable

***Saint-Pierre-de-l'Ile-d'Orl:* Bibliothèque Oscar-Ferland**
515, rte des Prêtres, Saint-Pierre-de-l'Ile-d'Orl, QC G0A 4E0
Tél: 418-828-2962; *Téléc:* 418-828-2855
www.reseaubiblioduquebec.qc.ca/saint-pierre/
Lisette Grégoire, Responsable
Guylaine Pichette, Adjointe
Claudine Rouleau, Responsable, Échanges

***Saint-Pierre-les-Becquets:* Bibliothèque de Saint-Pierre-les-Becquets**
108, rue des Loisirs, Saint-Pierre-les-Becquets, QC G0X 2Z0
Tél: 819-263-0797; *Téléc:* 819-263-2622
biblio086@reseaubibliocqlm.qc.ca
Francine Bergeron, Responsable

***Saint-Placide:* Bibliothèque de Saint-Placide**
73, rue de l'Église, Saint-Placide, QC J0V 2B0
Tél: 450-258-1780; *Téléc:* 450-258-0364
biblio@municipalite.saint-placide.qc.ca
www.reseaubiblioduquebec.qc.ca
Danielle Le Moëligou, Responsable
450-258-42

***Saint-Polycarpe:* Bibliothèque municipale de Saint-Polycarpe**
7, rue Ste-Catherine, Saint-Polycarpe, QC J0P 1X0
Tél: 450-265-3444; *Téléc:* 450-265-3010
polycarpe@reseaubibliomonteregie.qc.ca
www.reseaubiblioduquebec.qc.ca
Suzanne Poirier, Responsable
450-265-3043

***Saint-Prime:* Bibliothèque publique de Saint-Prime**
616, rue Principale, Saint-Prime, QC G8J 1T4
Tél: 418-251-4976
stprime@reseaubibliosIsj.qc.ca
www.reseaubiblioduquebec.qc.ca/portail/index.aspx?page=3&BID=571
Claudette Tremblay, Responsable
Suzanne Aubin, Secrétaire-trésorière

***Saint-Prosper:* Bibliothèque de Saint-Prosper (Livresque)**
371, rue de l'Église, Saint-Prosper, QC G0X 3A0
Tél: 418-328-4219; *Téléc:* 418-328-4219
biblio012@reseaubibliocqlm.qc.ca
www.reseaubiblioduquebec.qc.ca
Christiane Couture, Responsable

***Saint-Raphaël:* Bibliothèque Jeannine-Marquis-Garant**
88, rue du Foyer, Saint-Raphaël, QC G0R 4C0
Tél: 418-243-3437; *Téléc:* 418-243-2605
www.reseaubiblioduquebec.qc.ca/saint-raphael/
René Bouchard, Responsable

***Saint-René-de-Matane:* Bibliothèque de Saint-René-de-Matane**
178, av Saint-René, Saint-René-de-Matane, QC G0J 3E0
Tél: 418-224-1339
www.municipalite.st-rene-matane.qc.ca

***Saint-Robert:* Bibliothèque municipale de Saint-Robert**
1, Aggée-Pelletier, Saint-Robert, QC J0G 1S0
Tél: 450-782-2562
robert@reseaubibliomonteregie.qc.ca
Mariette Latour, Responsable

***Saint-Roch-de-l'Achigan:* Bibliothèque de Saint-Roch-de-l'Achigan**
30, rue Dr Wilfrid-Locat nord, Saint-Roch-de-l'Achigan, QC J0K 3H0
Tél: 450-588-5838; *Téléc:* 450-588-4478
biblio109@reseaubibliocqlm.qc.ca
www.reseaubiblioduquebec.qc.ca

Jocelyne Allard, Responsable

***Saint-Roch-de-Mékinac:* Bibliothèque de Saint-Roch-de-Mékinac**
1216, rue Principale, Saint-Roch-de-Mékinac, QC G0X 2E0
Tél: 819-646-5635
biblio033@reseaubibliocqlm.qc.ca
www.reseaubiblioduquebec.qc.ca
Claudia Klaus, Responsable

***Saint-Roch-de-Richelieu:* Bibliothèque municipale de Saint-Roch-de-Richelieu**
1111, rue du Parc, Saint-Roch-de-Richelieu, QC J0L 2M0
Tél: 450-785-2755
roch@reseaubibliomonteregie.qc.ca
Hélène Jackson, Responsable

***Saint-Roch-des-Aulnaies:* Bibliothèque Bibli-Aulnaies/Saint-Roch-des-Aulnaies**
1028, de la Seigneurie, Saint-Roch-des-Aulnaies, QC G0R 4E0
Tél: 418-856-7045; *Téléc:* 418-354-2059
www.reseaubiblioduquebec.qc.ca/aulnaies
Louise Filion, Responsable
louloufilion@hotmail.com
418-354-2233
Marcelle Dubé, Adjointe
Monique Belzile, Responsable, Échanges

***Saint-Rosaire:* Bibliothèque de Saint-Rosaire**
9, rue St-Pierre, Saint-Rosaire, QC G0Z 1K0
Tél: 819-795-4861; *Téléc:* 819-795-4861
biblio088@reseaubibliocqlm.qc.ca
www.reseaubiblioduquebec.qc.ca
Jacques Dubois, Responsable

***Saint-Rémi:* Bibliothèque municipale de Saint-Rémi**
25, rue Saint-Sauveur, Saint-Rémi, QC J0L 2L0
Tél: 450-454-3993; *Téléc:* 450-454-4083
bibliotheque@ville.saint-remi.qc.ca
www.ville.saint-remi.qc.ca/05bibliotheque
Monique Black, Technicienne en documentation

***Saint-Samuel:* Bibliothèque de Saint-Samuel**
143, rue de l'Église, Saint-Samuel, QC G0Z 1G0
Tél: 819-353-1242; *Téléc:* 819-353-1499
biblio137@reseaubibliocqlm.qc.ca
www.reseaubiblioduquebec.qc.ca
Noëlla Grondin, Responsable
Pierrette Doucet, Adjointe
biblio137@telwarwick.net

***Saint-Sauveur:* Bibliothèque de Saint-Sauveur**
33, av de l'Église, Saint-Sauveur, QC J0R 1R0
Tél: 450-227-2669; *Téléc:* 450-227-3362
biblio.st-sauveur@cgocable.ca
www.reseaubiblioduquebec.qc.ca
Claudette St-Jacques, Responsable

***Saint-Simon:* Bibliothèque de Saint-Simon**
39, rue de l'Église, Saint-Simon, QC G0L 4C0
Tél: 418-738-2249
biblio.simon@crsbp.net
www.reseaubiblioduquebec.qc.ca
France Beauchesne, Responsable
Gisèle Desharnais, Bénévole
Jocelyn Rioux, Bénévole
418-738-2344

***Saint-Simon:* Bibliothèque municipale Lise-Bourque-St-Pierre**
46, rue des Loisirs, Saint-Simon, QC J0H 1Y0
Tél: 450-798-2276
simon@reseaubibliomonteregie.qc.ca
Claire Bousquet, Responsable
450-798-2624

***Saint-Siméon:* Bibliothèque municipale de Saint-Siméon**
505A, rue Saint-Laurent, Saint-Siméon, QC G0T 1X0
Tél: 418-638-2691; *Téléc:* 418-638-5145
www.reseaubiblioduquebec.qc.ca/saint-simeon
Lyse Leblond, Responsable

***Saint-Siméon-de-Bonaventure:* Bibliothèque de Saint-Siméon**
116, rue Bélanger, Saint-Siméon-de-Bonaventure, QC G0C 3A0
Tél: 418-534-2606; *Téléc:* 418-534-3830
bbostsim@globetrotter.net
www.reseaubiblioduquebec.qc.ca
Huguette Lepage, Responsable
hlepage@globetrotter.net
418-534-3928

***Saint-Stanislas:* Bibliothèque publique de Saint-Stanislas**
953, rue Principale, Saint-Stanislas, QC G8L 7B4
Tél: 418-276-4476; *Téléc:* 418-276-4476
stanisla@reseaubiblioslsj.qc.ca
www.reseaubiblioduquebec.qc.ca/portail/index.aspx?page=3&BID=572
Line Laprise, Responsable

***Saint-Stanislas-de-Kostka:* Bibliothèque Saint-Stanislas-de-Kostka**
117, rue Centrale, Saint-Stanislas-de-Kostka, QC J0S 1W0
Tél: 450-370-4650
Christiane Blanchard, Responsable
Manon Demeule, Responsable, achats

***Saint-Sulpice:* Bibliothèque de Saint-Sulpice**
215, rue des Loisirs, Saint-Sulpice, QC J5W 6C9
Tél: 450-589-7816
biblio133@reseaubibliocqlm.qc.ca
www.reseaubiblioduquebec.qc.ca
Julie Parent, Responsable

***Saint-Sylvestre:* Bibliothèque municipale de Saint-Sylvestre**
824, rue Principale, Saint-Sylvestre, QC G0S 3C0
Tél: 418-596-2427; *Téléc:* 418-596-2384
Isabelle Gagnon, Responsable
munisylvestre@globetrotter.net
418-596-3400

***Saint-Sylvère:* Bibliothèque de Saint-Sylvère**
260, rte de l'École, Saint-Sylvère, QC G0Z 1H0
Tél: 819-285-2699; *Téléc:* 819-285-2040
biblio037@reseaubibliocqlm.qc.ca
www.reseaubiblioduquebec.qc.ca
Linda Searles, Responsable

***Saint-Sébastien:* Bibliothèque municipale de Saint-Sébastien**
595, rue de La Fabrique, Saint-Sébastien, QC G0Y 1M0
Tél: 819-652-2727
biblio092@reseaubiblioestrie.qc.ca
www.st-sebastien.com
Eric Bernier, Responsable

***Saint-Séverin:* Bibliothèque de Saint-Séverin**
1986, Place du Centre, Saint-Séverin, QC G0X 2B0
Tél: 418-365-5844; *Téléc:* 418-365-7544
biblio008@reseaubibliocqlm.qc.ca
www.reseaubiblioduquebec.qc.ca
Sylvie Brouillette, Responsable

***Saint-Séverin-de-Beauce:* La Voluthèque**
900, rue des Lacs, Saint-Séverin-de-Beauce, QC G0N 1V0
Tél: 418-426-2423; *Téléc:* 418-426-1274
biblicle@oricom.ca
www.reseaubiblioduquebec.qc.ca/saint-severin
Cécile Couture, Responsable
Maryse Trépanier, Personnes-ressources du Résseau Biblio
René Leduc, Représentant désigné

***Saint-Sévère:* Bibliothèque de Saint-Sévère (Denise L. Noël)**
47, rue Principale, Saint-Sévère, QC G0X 3B0
Tél: 819-264-5656; *Téléc:* 819-264-6013
biblio119@reseaubibliocqlm.qc.ca
www.reseaubiblioduquebec.qc.ca
Jocelyne Lavigne, Responsable

***Saint-Tharcisius:* Bibliothèque de Saint-Tharcisius**
55, rue Principale, Saint-Tharcisius, QC G0J 3G0
Tél: 418-629-4727
biblio.tharci@crsbp.net
www.reseaubiblioduquebec.qc.ca
Maryse Rioux, Responsable

***Saint-Thomas-de-Joliette:* Bibliothèque de Saint-Thomas (Jacqueline-Plante)**
#941, 10, rue Principale, Saint-Thomas-de-Joliette, QC J0K 3L0
Tél: 450-759-8173; *Téléc:* 450-759-2530
biblio117@reseaubibliocqlm.qc.ca
www.reseaubiblioduquebec.qc.ca
Média social: www.facebook.com/group.php?gid=159259607457177
Brigitte Brunet, Responsable

***Saint-Thomas-Didyme:* Bibliothèque publique de Saint-Thomas-de-Didyme**
31-1, av du Moulin, Saint-Thomas-Didyme, QC G0W 1P0
Tél: 418-274-4034
thomas@reseaubiblioslsj.qc.ca
Denise Bergeron, Responsable

***Saint-Théodore-d-Acton:* Bibliothèque autonome de Saint-Théodore-d'Acton**
1803, rue Principale, Saint-Théodore-d-Acton, QC J0H 1Z0
Tél: 450-546-5643
www.st-theodore.com

***Saint-Tite:* Bibliothèque de Saint-Tite (Marielle-Brouillette)**
330, rue du Moulin, Saint-Tite, QC G0X 3H0
Tél: 418-365-6203
biblio017@reseaubibliocqlm.qc.ca
www.reseaubiblioduquebec.qc.ca
Noëlla Gauthier, Responsable

***Saint-Ubalde:* Bibliothèque Guy-Laviolette**
400, rue de l'Aréna, Saint-Ubalde, QC G0A 4L0
Tél: 418-277-2124; *Téléc:* 418-277-2055
www.reseaubiblioduquebec.qc.ca/saint-ubalde/
Odile Tessier, Responsable
Claire Morissette, Responsable, Échanges

***Saint-Valentin:* Bibliothèque municipale de Saint-Valentin**
790, 4e Ligne, Saint-Valentin, QC J0J 2E0
Tél: 450-291-3948
valentin@reseaubibliomonteregie.qc.ca
www.reseaubiblioduquebec.qc.ca/valentin/
Réjane Hébert Olivier, Responsable

***Saint-Vallier:* Bibliothèque Marie-Josephte-Corrivaux**
365, av de l'Église, Saint-Vallier, QC G0R 4J0
Tél: 418-884-3190; *Téléc:* 418-884-2454
www.reseaubiblioduquebec.qc.ca/saint-vallier
Monique Rochefort, Responsable
Suzanne Alain, Adjointe

***Saint-Valérien:* Bibliothèque de Saint-Valérien**
159, rue Principale, Saint-Valérien, QC G0L 4E0
Tél: 418-736-8170
biblio.valerien@crsbp.net
www.reseaubiblioduquebec.qc.ca
Chantal Paquet, Responsable

***Saint-Valère:* Bibliothèque de Saint-Valère**
2A, rue du Parc, Saint-Valère, QC G0P 1M0
Tél: 819-353-3464; *Téléc:* 819-353-3465
biblio127@reseaubibliocqlm.qc.ca
www.reseaubiblioduquebec.qc.ca
Hélène Provencher-Hébert, Responsable

***Saint-Vianney:* Bibliothèque de Saint-Vianney**
170-B, av Centrale, Saint-Vianney, QC G0J 3J0
Tél: 418-629-4082
biblio.vianney@crsbp.net
Estelle Allaire, Responsable

***Saint-Victor:* Bibliothèque Biblio Luc-Lacourcière**
287, rue Marchand, Saint-Victor, QC G0M 2B0
Tél: 418-588-6689; *Téléc:* 418-588-6855
www.reseaubiblioduquebec.qc.ca/saint-victor/
Marc Bélanger, Responsable
Noelline Jacques, Adjointe

***Saint-Wenceslas:* Bibliothèque de Saint-Wenceslas**
1240, rue Principale, Saint-Wenceslas, QC G0Z 1J0
Tél: 819-224-4055
biblio073@reseaubibliocqlm.qc.ca
www.reseaubiblioduquebec.qc.ca
Jeanne Champagne, Responsable

***Saint-Zotique:* Bibliothèque municipale de Saint-Zotique**
1250, rue Principale, Saint-Zotique, QC J0P 1Z0
Tél: 450-267-3689
dg@st-zotique.com
www.st-zotique.com
Ginette Léger, Responsable

***Saint-Zénon:* Bibliothèque de Saint-Zénon (Danièle-Bruneau)**
6191, rue Principale, Saint-Zénon, QC J0K 3N0
Tél: 450-884-0328; *Téléc:* 450-884-5285
biblio048@reseaubibliocqlm.qc.ca
www.reseaubiblioduquebec.qc.ca
Simone L. Boisvert, Responsable

***Saint-Zéphirin-de-Courval:* Bibliothèque de Saint-Zéphirin-de-Courval**
950, rue des Loisirs, Saint-Zéphirin-de-Courval, QC J0G 1V0
Tél: 450-564-2401; *Téléc:* 450-564-2339
biblio092@reseaubibliocqlm.qc.ca
www.reseaubiblioduquebec.qc.ca
Angèle Lefebvre, Responsable

Saint-Édouard: **Bibliothèque municipale de Saint-Édouard**
405B, Montée Lussier, Saint-Édouard, QC J0L 1Y0
Tél: 450-454-2056
edouard@reseaubibliomonteregie.qc.ca
www.reseaubiblioduquebec.qc.ca
Fleurette Michaud, Responsable

Saint-Édouard-de-Maskinongé: **Bibliothèque de Saint-Édouard-de-Maskinongé**
3851, rue Notre-Dame, Saint-Édouard-de-Maskinongé, QC J0K 2H0
Tél: 819-268-2883
biblio123@reseaubibliocqlm.qc.ca
www.reseaubiblioduquebec.qc.ca
Hélène Robert, Responsable

Saint-Élie-de-Caxton: **Bibliothèque de Saint-Élie-de-Caxton**
50, ch des Loisirs, Saint-Élie-de-Caxton, QC G0X 2N0
Tél: 819-221-2839
biblio115@reseaubibliocqlm.qc.ca
www.reseaubiblioduquebec.qc.ca
Charline Plante, Responsable

Saint-Éloi: **Bibliothèque de Saint-Éloi**
456, rue Principale, Saint-Éloi, QC G0L 2V0
Tél: 418-898-2734
biblio.eloi@crsbp.net
www.reseaubiblioduquebec.qc.ca
Rachel Tardif, Responsable

Saint-Émile-de-Suffolk: **Bibliothèque de Saint-Émile-de-Suffolk**
299, route des Cantons, Saint-Émile-de-Suffolk, QC J0V 1Y0
Tél: 819-426-2987; *Téléc:* 819-426-3447
biblio.stemile@mrcpapineau.com
www.reseaubiblioduquebec.qc.ca
Georgette Haineault, Responsable

Saint-Éphrem-de-Beauce: **Bibliothèque La Voûte de l'Imaginaire**
#14, 34, rte 281 Sud, Saint-Éphrem-de-Beauce, QC G0M 1R0
Tél: 418-484-4848
www.reseaubiblioduquebec.qc.ca/saint-ephrem

Saint-Épiphane: **Bibliothèque de Saint-Épiphane**
216, rue du Couvent, Saint-Épiphane, QC G0L 2X0
Tél: 418-862-0052
biblio.epiphane@crsbp.net
www.reseaubiblioduquebec.qc.ca
Jacqueline Jalbert, Responsable

Saint-Étienne-de-Beauharnoi: **Bibliothèque municipale de Saint-Étienne-de-Beauharnois**
430, rue de l'Église, Saint-Étienne-de-Beauharnoi, QC J0S 1S0
Tél: 450-429-6384; *Téléc:* 450-429-6384
etienne@reseaubibliomonteregie.qc.ca
www.reseaubiblioduquebec.qc.ca
Carole Lalande, Responsable
Francine Boyer, Gestion du PIB et Administration des systèmes informatiques

Saint-Étienne-des-Grès: **Bibliothèque de Saint-Étienne-des-Grès**
#300, 190, rue Saint-Honoré, Saint-Étienne-des-Grès, QC G0X 2P0
Tél: 819-299-3854
biblio019@reseaubibliocqlm.qc.ca
www.reseaubiblioduquebec.qc.ca
Denis Boisvert, Responsable

Saint-Étienne-des-Grès: **Bibliothèque de Saint-Thomas-de-Caxton**
332, rue des Loisirs, Saint-Étienne-des-Grès, QC G0X 2P0
Tél: 819-296-3004
biblio105@reseaubibliocqlm.qc.ca
www.reseaubiblioduquebec.qc.ca
France Bournival, Responsable

Sainte-Adèle: **Bibliothèque Claude-Henri-Grignon**
170, rue Morin, Sainte-Adèle, QC J8B 2P7
Tél: 450-229-2921; *Téléc:* 450-229-2283
Stéphanie Lachaine, Responsable
slachaine@ville.sainte-adele.qc.ca

Sainte-Adèle: **Bibliothèque Jean-Baptiste-Rolland**
1200, rue Claude-Grégoire, Sainte-Adèle, QC J8B 1E9
Tél: 450-229-2921; *Téléc:* 450-229-2283
Stéphanie Lachaine, Responsable
slachaine@ville.sainte-adele.qc.ca
Suzanne Legault, Adjointe

Sainte-Agathe-de-Lotbinière: **Bibliothèque municipale Rayons d'Art**
402A, rue Gosford ouest, Sainte-Agathe-de-Lotbinière, QC G0S 2A0
Tél: 418-599-2830; *Téléc:* 418-599-2905
rayons@coopsteagathe.com
www.reseaubiblioduquebec.qc.ca/sainte-agathe
Denise Allard-Martineau, Responsable

Sainte-Agathe-des-Monts: **Bibliothèque municipale de Sainte-Agathe-des-Monts**
10, rue St-Donat, Sainte-Agathe-des-Monts, QC J8C 1P5
Tél: 819-326-4595
culture@ville.sainte-agathe-des-monts.qc.ca
ville.sainte-agathe-des-monts.qc.ca/fr/services-bibliotheque.php

Sainte-Angèle-de-Monnoir: **Bibliothèque Sainte-Angèle-de-Monnoir**
1, rue des Loisirs, Sainte-Angèle-de-Monnoir, QC J0L 1P0
Tél: 450-460-3644

Sainte-Angèle-de-Mérici: **Bibliothèque de Sainte-Angèle-de-Mérici**
23, rue de la Fabrique, Sainte-Angèle-de-Mérici, QC G0J 2H0
Tél: 418-775-8321
biblio.merici@crsbp.net
www.reseaubiblioduquebec.qc.ca

Sainte-Angèle-de-Prémont: **Bibliothèque de Sainte-Angèle-de-Prémont**
2451, rue Camirand, Sainte-Angèle-de-Prémont, QC J0K 1R0
Tél: 819-268-5079; *Téléc:* 819-268-5536
biblio124@reseaubibliocqlm.qc.ca
www.reseaubiblioduquebec.qc.ca
Denis Beauregard, Responsable

Sainte-Anne-de-Bellevue: **Bibliothèque de Sainte-Anne-de-Bellevue**
40, rue Saint-Pierre, Sainte-Anne-de-Bellevue, QC H9X 1Y6
Tél: 514-457-1940; *Téléc:* 514-457-7146
anne.bellevue@reseaubibliomonteregie.qc.ca
www.reseaubiblioduquebec.qc.ca

Sainte-Anne-de-la-Pérade: **Bibliothèque de Sainte-Anne-de-la-Pérade (Armand-Goulet)**
100, rue de la Fabrique, Sainte-Anne-de-la-Pérade, QC G0X 2J0
Tél: 418-325-2216; *Téléc:* 418-325-3070
biblio014@reseaubibliocqlm.qc.ca
www.reseaubiblioduquebec.qc.ca
Cécile Fortier, Responsable

Sainte-Anne-des-Lacs: **Bibliothèque de Sainte-Anne-des-Lacs**
723 chemin Ste-Anne-des-Lacs, Sainte-Anne-des-Lacs, QC J0R 1B0
Tél: 450-224-8332; *Téléc:* 450-224-8672
www.reseaubiblioduquebec.qc.ca
Hélène Limoges, Responsable

Sainte-Anne-des-Monts: **Bibliothèque municipale Blanche-Lamontagne**
120, 7e rue ouest, Sainte-Anne-des-Monts, QC G4V 2L2
Tél: 418-763-3810; *Téléc:* 418-763-3400
bbosadm@globetrotter.qc.ca
www.villesainte-anne-des-monts.qc.ca/html/biblio.php
Monique Campion
418-763-3810

Sainte-Anne-des-Plaines: **Bibliothèque publique de Sainte-Anne-des-Plaines**
155, rue des Cèdres, Sainte-Anne-des-Plaines, QC J0N 1H0
Tél: 450-478-4337; *Téléc:* 450-478-6733
biblio.sadp@videotron.ca
www.ville.ste-anne-des-plaines.qc.ca/biblio/
Sylviane Dubé, Directrice

Sainte-Anne-du-Lac: **Bibliothèque de Sainte-Anne-du-Lac**
1B, rue St-François-Xavier, Sainte-Anne-du-Lac, QC J0W 1V0
Tél: 819-586-2051; *Téléc:* 819-586-2203
bibsadl@tlb.sympatico.ca
www.reseaubiblioduquebec.qc.ca
Sylvie Giard, Responsable
Suzanne Lévesque, Adjointe
Claudette Bigras, Bénévole
819-586-2094
Nicole Bélisle, Bénévole
819-586-2408

Sainte-Aurélie: **Bibliothèque Le Maillon**
151B, ch des Bois-Francs, Sainte-Aurélie, QC G0M 1M0
Tél: 418-593-3021; *Téléc:* 418-593-3961
maillon@sogetel.net
www.reseaubiblioduquebec.qc.ca/sainte-aurelie/
JoAnne Leclerc, Responsable
Christiane Giguère, Adjointe

Sainte-Barbe: **Bibliothèque municipale Lucie Benoît**
468, ch de l'Église, Sainte-Barbe, QC J0S 1P0
Tél: 450-371-2424
barbe@reseaubibliomonteregie.qc.ca
Lucie Benoît, Responsable

Sainte-Brigide-d'Iberville: **Bibliothèque de Sainte-Brigide-d'Iberville**
Centre municipal, 510, 9e rang, Sainte-Brigide-d'Iberville, QC J0J 1X0
Tél: 450-293-4604; *Téléc:* 450-293-1243
administration@sainte-brigide.qc.ca
www.sainte-brigide.qc.ca
Francine Belzile, Responsable

Sainte-Brigitte-de-Laval: **Bibliothèque Le Trivent**
3, rue du Couvent, Sainte-Brigitte-de-Laval, QC G0A 3K0
Tél: 418-666-4666; *Téléc:* 418-825-3114
trivent.bibli@csdps.qc.ca
www.reseaubiblioduquebec.qc.ca/sainte-brigitte/
Marie-Ôve Joubert, Responsable
Carole Gagnon, Adjointe

Sainte-Brigitte-des-Saults: **Bibliothèque de Sainte-Brigitte-des-Saults**
400, rue Principale, Sainte-Brigitte-des-Saults, QC J0C 1E0
Tél: 819-336-4460; *Téléc:* 819-336-4410
biblio043@reseaubibliocqlm.qc.ca
www.reseaubiblioduquebec.qc.ca
Jocelyne Guérin, Responsable
Jocelyne Guilbault, Bénévole

Sainte-Béatrix: **Bibliothèque de Sainte-Béatrix**
Pavillon du Village, Sainte-Béatrix, QC J0K 1Y0
Tél: 450-883-2245; *Téléc:* 450-883-1772
administration@stebeatrix.com
www.sainte-beatrix.com
Micheline Thibault, Responsable

Sainte-Catherine: **Bibliothèque publique de Sainte-Catherine**
5365, boul St-Laurent, Sainte-Catherine, QC J5C 1A6
Tél: 450-632-0590; *Téléc:* 450-632-9908
bibliotheque@ville.sainte-catherine.qc.ca
www.ville.sainte-catherine.qc.ca/francais/biblio_accueil.html
Lise Forcier, Directrice
lise.forcier@ville.sainte-catherine.qc.ca

Sainte-Christine: **Bibliothèque municipale de Sainte-Christine**
629, rue des Loisirs, Sainte-Christine, QC J0H 1H0
Tél: 819-858-2828
christine@reseaubibliomonteregie.qc.ca
www.reseaubiblioduquebec.qc.ca
Rosalie Proulx, Responsable

Sainte-Claire: **Bibliothèque municipale de Sainte-Claire**
55, rue de la Fabrique, Sainte-Claire, QC G0R 2V0
Tél: 418-883-2275; *Téléc:* 418-883-3845
msclaire@globetrotter.qc.ca
www.municipalite.sainte-claire.qc.ca
Marielle Gosselin, Responsable
gosselin_marie@globetrotter.net

Sainte-Clotilde-de-Beauce: **Bibliothèque Jeanne-Édith-Audet**
307, rue du Couvent, Sainte-Clotilde-de-Beauce, QC G0N 1C0
Tél: 418-427-2181; *Téléc:* 418-427-2637
pp307@hotmail.com
www.reseaubiblioduquebec.qc.ca/sainte-clotilde
Paulette Pomerleau, Conseillère
Angèle Grenier, Responsable au prêt (adm.)
418-427-2392
Jocelyne G. Prévost, Responsable des statistiques (adm.)
418-427-5151
Suzanne Therrien, Responsable des PIB (sec. adm.)
418-427-2558

***Sainte-Cécile-de-Lévrard:* Bibliothèque de Sainte-Cécile-de-Lévrard**
234, rue Principale, Sainte-Cécile-de-Lévrard, QC G0X 2M0
Tél: 819-263-0368; *Téléc:* 819-263-2104
biblio113@reseaubibliocqlm.qc.ca
www.reseaubiblioduquebec.qc.ca
Yvette Demers, Responsable

***Sainte-Cécile-de-Masham:* Bibliothèque de Sainte-Cécile-de-Masham (La Pêche)**
5, rue Principale ouest, Sainte-Cécile-de-Masham, QC J0X 2W0
Tél: 819-456-2627; *Téléc:* 819-456-4228
admmasham@crsbpo.qc.ca
www.reseaubiblioduquebec.qc.ca/Masham
Gisèle Duguay, Responsable

***Sainte-Elisabeth-de-Proulx:* Bibliothèque publique de Sainte-Elisabeth-de-Proulx**
1254, rue Principale, Sainte-Elisabeth-de-Proulx, QC G8M 4V2
Tél: 418-276-9494
elisabeth@reseaubiblioslsj.qc.ca
www.reseaubiblioduquebec.qc.ca/portail/index.aspx?page=3&BID=574
Rosanne Carrier-Simard, Responsable

***Sainte-Elizabeth:* Bibliothèque de Sainte-Elisabeth (Françoise-Allard-Bérard)**
2270, rue Principale, Sainte-Elizabeth, QC J0K 2J0
Tél: 450-759-2875
biblio068@reseaubibliocqlm.qc.ca
www.reseaubiblioduquebec.qc.ca
Josette Lamontagne, Responsable

***Sainte-Eulalie:* Bibliothèque de Sainte-Eulalie**
757A, rue des Bouleaux, Sainte-Eulalie, QC G0Z 1E0
Tél: 819-225-8069; *Téléc:* 819-225-4078
biblio074@reseaubibliocqlm.qc.ca
www.reseaubiblioduquebec.qc.ca
Marjolaine Rheault, Responsable
819-225-4434

***Sainte-Famille:* Bibliothèque municipale de Sainte-Famille/Saint-François-de-l'île-d"Orléans**
3912-1, ch Royal, Sainte-Famille, QC G0A 3P0
Tél: 418-666-4666; *Téléc:* 418-829-2513
biblio@munstefamille.org
www.reseaubiblioduquebec.qc.ca
Ernest Labranche, Responsable

***Sainte-Flavie:* Bibliothèque Olivar-Asselin**
505, rte de la Mer, Sainte-Flavie, QC G0J 2L0
Tél: 418-775-7050
biblio.flavie@crsbp.net
www.reseaubiblioduquebec.qc.ca
Liz Fortin, Responsable

***Sainte-Florence:* Bibliothèque de Sainte-Florence**
29, rue des Loisirs, Sainte-Florence, QC G0J 2M0
Tél: 418-756-5079
biblio.florence@crsbp.net
www.reseaubiblioduquebec.qc.ca
Gaétane Morin, Responsable

***Sainte-Françoise:* Bibliothèque de Sainte-Françoise (Bas-Saint-Laurent)**
31, rue Principale, Sainte-Françoise, QC G0L 3B0
Tél: 418-851-3878
biblio.francoise@crsbp.net
www.reseaubiblioduquebec.qc.ca
Édith Rioux, Responsable

***Sainte-Françoise:* Bibliothèque de Sainte-Françoise (Centre-du-Québec)**
563, rue Principale, Sainte-Françoise, QC G0S 2N0
Tél: 819-287-5838
biblio104@reseaubibliocqlm.qc.ca
www.reseaubiblioduquebec.qc.ca
Diane Bélanger, Responsable

***Sainte-Germaine-Boulé:* Bibliothèque de Sainte-Germaine-Boulé**
240, rue Roy, Sainte-Germaine-Boulé, QC J0Z 1M0
Tél: 819-787-6477; *Téléc:* 819-787-6477
boule@reseaubiblioatnq.qc.ca
www.reseaubiblioduquebec.qc.ca/ste-germaine-boule
Odette Rancourt Audet, Responsable

***Sainte-Hedwidge-de-Roberval:* Bibliothèque publique de Sainte-Hedwidge**
1090, rue Principale, Sainte-Hedwidge-de-Roberval, QC G0W 2R0
Tél: 418-275-4318
hedwidge@reseaubiblioslsj.qc.ca
www.reseaubiblioduquebec.qc.ca
Michelle Morin, Responsable
418-275-4963
Marie Gagnon, Représentante municipale
Josée-Anne Rodrigue, Bénévole
Hélène Langlais, Bénévole
Denise Bonneau, Bénévole
Dominique Harvey, Bénévole
Caroline Privé, Bénévole
Guy Privé, Bénévole
Carole-Anne Morin, Bénévole

***Sainte-Hélène:* Bibliothèque de Sainte-Hélène**
707, rue du Couvent, Sainte-Hélène, QC G0L 3J0
Tél: 418-492-3819
biblio.helene@crsbp.net
www.reseaubiblioduquebec.qc.ca
Lucie Bérubé, Responsable

***Sainte-Hélène-de-Bagot:* Bibliothèque municipale de Sainte-Hélène-de-Bagot**
384, 6e av, Sainte-Hélène-de-Bagot, QC J0H 1M0
Tél: 450-791-2618
helene@reseaubibliomonteregie.qc.ca
www.reseaubiblioduquebec.qc.ca
France Vachon, Responsable

***Sainte-Hénédine:* Bibliothèque La Détente/Sainte-Hénédine**
111, rue Principale, Sainte-Hénédine, QC G0S 2R0
Tél: 418-935-3993; *Téléc:* 418-935-3113
biblsthe@globetrotter.qc.ca
www.reseaubiblioduquebec.qc.ca/sainte-henedine/
Doris Drouin-Dubreuil, Responsable
Jocelyne Cyr, Adjointe
Louise Bédard, Responsable, PIB
Lise Dion, Responsable, Collection locale

***Sainte-Irène:* Bibliothèque de Sainte-Irène**
362, rue de la Fabrique, Sainte-Irène, QC G0J 1P0
Tél: 418-629-5705
biblio.irene@crsbp.net
www.reseaubiblioduquebec.qc.ca
Sylvie Chenel, Responsable

***Sainte-Julie:* Bibliothèque municipale de Sainte-Julie**
1600, ch du Fer-à-Cheval, Sainte-Julie, QC J3E 2M1
Tél: 450-922-7070; *Téléc:* 450-922-7077
biblio@ville.sainte-julie.qc.ca
Marie-Hélène Parent, Bibliothécaire en chef
mhparent@ville.sainte-julie.qc.ca
450-922-7115 ext. 7071

***Sainte-Julienne:* Bibliothèque Gisèle-Paré**
2550, rue Marcel-Masse, Sainte-Julienne, QC J0K 2T0
Tél: 450-831-3811; *Téléc:* 450-831-4433
biblio43@crsbpl.qc.ca
www.reseaubiblioduquebec.qc.ca/sainte-julienne
Marielle Rompré, Responsable
Carmen Vézina, Adjointe

***Sainte-Justine:* Bibliothèque Roch-Carrier**
250, rue Principale, Sainte-Justine, QC G0R 1Y0
Tél: 418-383-5399
bibliorochcarrier@sogetel.net
www.reseaubiblioduquebec.qc.ca/roch-carrier

***Sainte-Louise:* Bibliothèque Idée-Lire**
506, rue Principale, Sainte-Louise, QC G0R 3K0
Tél: 418-354-7730
www.reseaubiblioduquebec.qc.ca/sainte-louise
Jacqueline Lizotte, Responsable

***Sainte-Luce:* Bibliothèque de Luceville**
67, rue Saint-Pierre est, Sainte-Luce, QC G0K 1P0
Tél: 418-739-3534
biblio.luceville@crsbp.net
www.reseaubiblioduquebec.qc.ca

***Sainte-Luce:* Bibliothèque de Sainte-Luce**
1, 200 rue Langlois, Sainte-Luce, QC G0K 1P0
Tél: 418-739-4024
biblio.luce@crsbp.net
www.reseaubiblioduquebec.qc.ca
Luc Bourassa, Responsable

***Sainte-Lucie-de-Beauregard:* Bibliothèque A la Bouquinerie**
21, rte des Chutes, Sainte-Lucie-de-Beauregard, QC G0R 3L0
Tél: 418-223-3122; *Téléc:* 418-223-3121
www.reseaubiblioduquebec.qc.ca/sainte-lucie
Huguette Rouillard, Responsable
418-223-3613

***Sainte-Madeleine:* Bibliothèque municipale de Sainte-Madeleine**
1040A, rue Saint-Simon, Sainte-Madeleine, QC J0H 1S0
Tél: 450-795-3959; *Téléc:* 450-795-3736
madeleine@reseaubibliomonteregie.qc.ca
www.reseaubiblioduquebec.qc.ca
Cathy Collins, Responsable

***Sainte-Marguerite:* Biblio La Bouquine**
235, rue Saint-Jacques, Sainte-Marguerite, QC G0S 2X0
Tél: 418-935-7089; *Téléc:* 418-935-3709
www.reseaubiblioduquebec.qc.ca/sainte-marguerite/
Adrienne Gagné, Responsable

***Sainte-Marguerite:* Bibliothèque de Sainte-Marguerite**
15, rue de la Vérendrye, Sainte-Marguerite, QC G0J 2Y0
Tél: 418-756-3364
biblio.margot@crsbp.net
www.reseaubiblioduquebec.qc.ca
Colette Marquis, Responsable

***Sainte-Marie:* Bibliothèque Honorius-Provost**
80, rue St-Antoine, Sainte-Marie, QC G6E 4B8
Tél: 418-387-2240; *Téléc:* 418-387-2454
jacques.filiatrault@sainte-marie.ca
www.ville.sainte-marie.qc.ca
Jacques Filiatrault, Responsable

***Sainte-Marie-de-Blandford:* Bibliothèque de Sainte-Marie-de-Blandford**
492, rue des Bosquets, Sainte-Marie-de-Blandford, QC G0X 2W0
Tél: 819-283-2127; *Téléc:* 819-283-2169
biblio108@reseaubibliocqlm.qc.ca
www.reseaubiblioduquebec.qc.ca
Carmen Bilodeau, Responsable

***Sainte-Marie-Salomé:* Bibliothèque de Sainte-Marie-Salomé**
121, rue Viger, Sainte-Marie-Salomé, QC J0K 2Z0
Tél: 450-839-6212; *Téléc:* 450-753-5236
biblio050@reseaubibliocqlm.qc.ca
www.reseaubiblioduquebec.qc.ca
Diane Éthier, Responsable

***Sainte-Marthe-sur-le-Lac:* Bibliothèque municipale de Sainte-Marthe-sur-le-Lac**
3003, ch Oka, Sainte-Marthe-sur-le-Lac, QC J0N 1P0
Tél: 450-974-7111; *Téléc:* 450-974-7110
www.saintemarthesurlelac.qc.ca/contenu.aspx?page=154
Micheline Aloi, Commis senior
450-947-7111

***Sainte-Monique:* Bibliothèque de Sainte-Monique**
247, rue Principale, Sainte-Monique, QC J0G 1N0
Tél: 819-289-2051; *Téléc:* 819-289-2344
biblio052@reseaubibliocqlm.qc.ca
www.reseaubiblioduquebec.qc.ca
Pierrette Beauchemin, Responsable

***Sainte-Monique-Lac-St-Jean:* Bibliothèque publique de Sainte-Monique**
138, rue Honfleur, Sainte-Monique-Lac-St-Jean, QC G0W 2T0
Tél: 418-347-4391
monique@reseaubiblioslsj.qc.ca
www.reseaubiblioduquebec.qc.ca/portail/index.aspx?page=3&BID=577
Normande Gauthier, Directrice

***Sainte-Mélanie:* Bibliothèque de Sainte-Mélanie (Louise-Amélie-Panet)**
940, rue Principale, Sainte-Mélanie, QC J0K 3A0
Tél: 450-889-5871
biblio111@reseaubibliocqlm.qc.ca
www.reseaubiblioduquebec.qc.ca
Martin Alarie, Responsable

***Sainte-Paule:* Bibliothèque de Sainte-Paule**
102, rue Banville, Sainte-Paule, QC G0J 3C0
Tél: 418-737-1378
biblio.paule@crsbp.net
www.reseaubiblioduquebec.qc.ca
Carmen Côté-D'Amour, Responsable

Sainte-Perpétue: **Bibliothèque de Sainte-Perpétue**
2504, rang St-Joseph, Sainte-Perpétue, QC J0C 1R0
Tél: 819-336-6275
www.sainte-perpetue.com
Louiselle Robichaud, Responsable

Sainte-Pétronille: **Bibliothèque municipale de Sainte-Pétronille**
3, ch de l'Église, Sainte-Pétronille, QC G0A 4C0
Tél: 418-828-2270; *Téléc:* 418-828-1364
bibliospetro@qc.aira.com
www.reseaubiblioduquebec.qc.ca/sainte-petronille
Lise Paquet, Responsable

Sainte-Rita: **Bibliothèque Sainte-Rita**
23, rue de L'Église est, Sainte-Rita, QC G0L 4G0
Tél: 418-963-2967
biblio.rita@crsbp.net
www.reseaubiblioduquebec.qc.ca
Lucille Turcotte, Responsable

Sainte-Rose-de-Watford: **Bibliothèque municipale de Sainte-Rose-de-Watford**
693, rue Carrier, Sainte-Rose-de-Watford, QC G0R 4G0
Tél: 418-267-5812; *Téléc:* 418-267-5812
biblioste-rose@sogetel.net
www.sainterosedewatford.qc.ca
Lisette Gagnon, Responsable
jlcya@sogetel.net
418-267-5721
Nicole Bédard, Adjointe

Sainte-Rose-du-Nord: **Bibliothèque publique de Ste-Rose-du-Nord**
126, rue Descente-des-Femmes, Sainte-Rose-du-Nord, QC G0V 1T0
Tél: 418-675-2250
ste-rose@reseaubiblioslsj.qc.ca
www.reseaubiblioduquebec.qc.ca/portail/index.aspx?page=3&BID=578
Lise Clermont, Responsable

Sainte-Sabine: **Bibliothèque Sabithèque**
#203, 4, rue St-Charles, Sainte-Sabine, QC G0R 4H0
Tél: 418-383-5788; *Téléc:* 418-383-5488
www.reseaubiblioduquebec.qc.ca/sainte-sabine/
Micheline Cyr, Responsable
Solange Mercier, Adjointe

Sainte-Sophie-de-Lévrard: **Bibliothèque de Sainte-Sophie-de-Lévrard**
184A, rue St-Antoine, Sainte-Sophie-de-Lévrard, QC G0X 3C0
Tél: 819-288-0334; *Téléc:* 819-288-5804
biblio102@reseaubibliocqlm.qc.ca
www.reseaubiblioduquebec.qc.ca
Daniel Désilets, Responsable

Sainte-Thérèse: **Bibliothèque municipale de Sainte-Thérèse**
150, boul du Séminaire, Sainte-Thérèse, QC J7E 1Z2
Tél: 450-434-1440; *Téléc:* 450-434-6070
biblio@sainte-therese.ca
www.ville.sainte-therese.qc.ca/biblio
Lise Thériault, Directrice
l.theriault@sainte-therese.ca

Sainte-Thècle: **Bibliothèque de Sainte-Thècle**
301, rue St-Jacques, Sainte-Thècle, QC G0X 3G0
Tél: 418-289-3717; *Téléc:* 418-289-3014
biblio016@reseaubibliocqlm.qc.ca
www.reseaubiblioduquebec.qc.ca
Thérèse Lemelin, Responsable

Sainte-Ursule: **Bibliothèque de Sainte-Ursule (C.-J. Magnan)**
215, rue Lessard, Sainte-Ursule, QC J0K 3M0
Tél: 819-228-0735; *Téléc:* 819-228-8326
biblio031@reseaubibliocqlm.qc.ca
Suzanne Pilon, Responsable
Lisette Bergeron, Bénévole
Dominique Côté, Bénévole

Sainte-Victoire-de-Sorel: **Bibliothèque municipale de Sainte-Victoire-de-Sorel**
519, ch Ste-Victoire, Sainte-Victoire-de-Sorel, QC J0G 1T0
Tél: 450-782-3111
victoire@reseaubibliomonteregie.qc.ca
www.reseaubiblioduquebec.qc.ca
Micheline Lamoureux, Responsable
Josée Paquette, Responsable, Échanges
Lucille Ayotte, Responsable, Collection locale

Sainte-Élizabeth-de-Warwick: **Bibliothèque de Sainte-Élizabeth-de-Warwick**
228, rue Principale, Sainte-Élizabeth-de-Warwick, QC J0A 1M0
Tél: 819-358-2429; *Téléc:* 819-358-9192
biblio141@reseaubibliocqlm.qc.ca
www.reseaubiblioduquebec.qc.ca
Christiane Luscher, Responsable
819-358-6980
Céline Parenteau, Adjointe
Denise Gagnon, Bénévole
Pierrette Martel Leblanc, Bénévole
Cécile Morin, Bénévole

Sainte-Émélie-de-l'Énergie: **Bibliothèque de Sainte-Émélie-de-l'Énergie**
241, rue Coutu, Sainte-Émélie-de-l'Énergie, QC J0K 2K0
Tél: 450-886-3823; *Téléc:* 450-886-9175
biblio053@reseaubibliocqlm.qc.ca
www.reseaubiblioduquebec.qc.ca
Diane Durand, Responsable

Sayabec: **Bibliothèque Quilit**
8B, rue Keable, Sayabec, QC G0J 3K0
Tél: 418-536-5431
biblio.sayabec@crsbp.net
www.reseaubiblioduquebec.qc.ca
Thérèse Arsenault, Responsable

Scott: **Bibliothèque municipale de Scott**
1, rue 8e, Scott, QC G0S 3G0
Tél: 418-386-2736; *Téléc:* 418-387-1837
munscott@globetrotter.net
www.reseaubiblioduquebec.qc.ca/scott
Roger Pigeon, Responsable
Bédard Jacinthe, Adjointe

Senneterre: **Bibliothèque de Senneterre**
121, 1e rue Est, Senneterre, QC J0Y 2M0
Tél: 819-737-8829; *Téléc:* 819-737-4215
senneterre@reseaubiblioatnq.qc.ca
www.reseaubiblioduquebec.qc.ca/senneterre
Denise Dufour, Responsable

Sept-Iles: **Bibliothèque Louis-Ange-Santerre**
500, av Jolliet, Sept-Iles, QC G4R 2B4
Tél: 418-964-3355; *Téléc:* 418-964-3353
www.ville.sept-iles.qc.ca
Média social: www.facebook.com/229438240426807
Sylvie Pelletier, Superviseure
sylvie.pelletier@ville.sept-iles.qc.ca

Shannon: **Bibliothèque municipale de Shannon**
50, rue St-Patrick, Shannon, QC G0A 4N0
Tél: 418-844-1622; *Téléc:* 418-844-2111
biblio@cableshannon.com
www.reseaubiblioduquebec.qc.ca
Brigitte Olivier, Responsable
Marie-Josée Monderie, Adjointe
Germaine Pelletier, Responsable, Collection locale

Shawinigan: **Bibliothèque Fabien-LaRochelle**
550, av de l'Hôtel-de-Ville, Shawinigan, QC G9N 6V3
Tél: 819-536-7218; *Téléc:* 819-536-0808
bibliotheque@ville.shawinigan.qc.ca
www.shawinigan.ca
Charlotte Lecours, Responsable des bibliothèques

Shawville: **Bibliothèque Shawville/Clarendon/Thorne / Shawville/Clarendon/Thorne Library**
356, rue Main, Shawville, QC J0X 2Y0
Tél: 819-647-3732; *Téléc:* 819-647-3732
admshawville@crsbpo.qc.ca
www.reseaubiblioduquebec.qc.ca/ShawvilleClarendon
Jennifer Davies, Responsable

Sherbrooke: **Bibliothèque municipale Éva-Senécal**
450, rue Marquette, Sherbrooke, QC J1H 1M4
Tél: 819-821-5860; *Téléc:* 819-822-6110
bibliotheque@ville.sherbrooke.qc.ca
www.ville.sherbrooke.qc.ca
Linda Travis, Chef, Section bibliothèque
819-821-5862
Luce Mathieu, Responsable, Référence
819-821-5598
André Bruneau, Bibliothécaire, Acquisitions
819-821-5595
Luce Marquis, Bibliothécaire, Catalogage
819-821-5464
Jeanne Desautels, Bibliothécaire, Acquisitions
819-821-5594

Shipshaw: **Bibliothèque de Shipshaw (Rivage)**
4281-A, rue des Pins, Shipshaw, QC G7P 1L8
Tél: 418-542-3982; *Téléc:* 418-542-6231
webbiblio@ville.saguenay.qc.ca
www.ville.saguenay.qc.ca
Lyne Racine, Responsable

Shipshaw: **Bibliothèque de Shipshaw (Rivière)**
4281-A, rue des Pins, Shipshaw, QC G7P 1L8
Tél: 418-542-3982; *Téléc:* 418-542-6231
webbiblio@ville.saguenay.qc.ca
www.ville.saguenay.qc.ca
Ginette Tremblay, Responsable

Sorel-Tracy: **Bibliothèque municipale de Sorel-Tracy**
3015, Place des loisirs, Sorel-Tracy, QC J3R 5S5
Tél: 450-780-5600
www.ville.sorel-tracy.qc.ca
Guy Desjardins, Régisseur, Culture & Bibliothèque

Sorel-Tracy: **Bibliothèque municipale de Sorel-Tracy**
145, rue George, Sorel-Tracy, QC J3P 1C7
Tél: 450-780-5600
www.ville.sorel-tracy.qc.ca
Guy Desjardins, Régisseur, Culture & Bibliothèque

St-Alexandre-de-Kamouraska: **Bibliothèque Saint-Alexandre**
480, av de l'École, St-Alexandre-de-Kamouraska, QC G0L 2G0
Tél: 418-495-3123
biblio.alexi@crsbp.net
Hélène Therrien, Responsable

St-Barnabé-Nord: **Bibliothèque de Saint-Barnabé**
70, rue Duguay, St-Barnabé-Nord, QC G0X 2K0
Tél: 819-264-2085; *Téléc:* 819-264-2079
biblio027@reseaubibliocqlm.qc.ca
www.reseaubiblioduquebec.qc.ca
Luc Gélinas, Responsable

St-Charles-de-Bellechasse: **Bibliothèque Jacques-Labrie/Saint-Charles-de-Bellechasse**
2829A, av Royale, St-Charles-de-Bellechasse, QC G0R 2T0
Tél: 418-887-6561; *Téléc:* 418-887-6779
biblstch@globetrotter.qc.ca
www.reseaubiblioduquebec.qc.ca/saint-charles
Manon Larochelle, Responsable
Louise Cantin, Adjointe

St-David-de-Falardeau: **Bibliothèque publique Saint-David-de-Falardeau**
124, boul St-David, St-David-de-Falardeau, QC G0V 1C0
Tél: 418-673-6395
stdavid@reseaubiblioslsj.qc.ca
www.reseaubiblioduquebec.qc.ca
Francine Allard, Responsable

St-Dominique-du-Rosaire: **Bibliothèque de St-Dominique-du-Rosaire**
235, rue Principale, St-Dominique-du-Rosaire, QC J0Y 2K0
Tél: 819-727-4144; *Téléc:* 819-727-4344
dominique@reseaubiblioatnq.qc.ca
www.reseaubiblioduquebec.qc.ca/st-dominique
Marcelle Gravelle, Responsable
Lucie Mercier, Adjointe
Isabelle Payette, Adjointe

St-François-Xavier-de-Viger: **Bibliothèque de Saint-François-Xavier-de-Viger**
125, rue Principale, St-François-Xavier-de-Viger, QC G0L 3C0
Tél: 418-497-2302
biblio.xavier@crsbp.net
www.reseaubiblioduquebec.qc.ca
Diana Morin, Responsable

St-Jean-de-l'Ile-d'Orléans: **Bibliothèque municipale de Saint-Jean-de-l'Ile-d'Orléans**
10, ch des Côtes, St-Jean-de-l'Ile-d'Orléans, QC G0A 3W0
Tél: 418-829-3336; *Téléc:* 418-829-0997
biblio.vm@sympatico.ca
Françoise Laberge, Responsable
Nicole Pelchat, Responsable, Acquisitions

St-Lambert-Desmeloizes: **Bibliothèque de St-Lambert**
509B, rte du 5e & 8e rang, St-Lambert-Desmeloizes, QC J0Z 1V0
Tél: 819-788-2491; *Téléc:* 819-788-2491
lambert@reseaubiblioatnq.qc.ca
www.reseaubiblioduquebec.qc.ca/st-lambert
Jeanne D'Arc Fluet, Responsable

St-Laurent-de-l'Ile-d'Orléa: **Bibliothèque David-Gosselin/Saint-Laurent-de-l'Ile-d'Orléans**
#1, 1330, ch Royal, St-Laurent-de-l'Ile-d'Orléa, QC G0A 3Z0
Tél: 418-828-2529; *Téléc:* 418-828-2170
bibliosaintlaurentiledorleans@gmail.com
www.reseaubiblioduquebec.qc.ca/saint-laurent
Guy Delisle, Responsable
guy.delisle2@gmail.com

St-Nazaire-d'Acton: **Bibliothèque municipale de St-Nazaire-d'Acton**
715, rue des Loisirs, St-Nazaire-d'Acton, QC G0R 3T0
Tél: 418-392-2090
nazaire@reseaubibliomonteregie.qc.ca
www.reseaubiblioduquebec.qc.ca
René Blais, Responsable
Jacinthe Bruneau, Adjointe

St-Pierre-de-la-Riv.-du-Sud: **La Volumineuse**
620, rue Principale, St-Pierre-de-la-Riv.-du-Sud, QC G0R 4B0
Tél: 418-248-8031; *Téléc:* 418-241-1477
biblstpi@globetrotter.qc.ca
www.reseaubiblioduquebec.qc.ca/saint-pierre-r-s
Georgette Roy, Responsable
groy45@globetrotter.net
418-248-2319

St-Stanislas: **Bibliothèque Saint-Stanislas (Émile-Bordeleau)**
33A, rue du Pont, St-Stanislas, QC G0X 3E0
Tél: 819-840-0703; *Téléc:* 418-328-4121
biblio002@reseaubibliocqlm.qc.ca
www.reseaubiblioduquebec.qc.ca
Ghislaine B. Asselin, Responsable

Stanbridge East: **Bibliothèque Denise-Larocque-Duhamel / Denise Larocque Duhamel Library**
12A, rue Maple, Stanbridge East, QC J0J 2H0
Tél: 450-248-4662
stanbridge@reseaubibliomonteregie.qc.ca
Nicole L'Heureux, Responsable

Standon: **Bibliothèque l'Étincelle**
514B, rue Principale, Standon, QC G0R 4L0
Tél: 418-642-2708; *Téléc:* 418-642-2570
etincel@globetrotter.qc.ca
www.reseaubiblioduquebec.qc.ca/saint-leon
Mario Grenier, Responsable
Odette Genest, Adjointe
Michel Lacasse, Responsable, PEB
Céline Lafontaine, Responsable, Échanges
Claire Rathé, Responsable, Collection locale

Stanstead: **Haskell Free Library Inc.**
1 Church St., Stanstead, QC J0B 3E2
Tel: 819-876-2471; *Fax:* 802-873-3634
Other Numbers: Derby Line Phone: 802/873-3022
www.haskellopera.org
Nancy Rumery, Director of Library, Head Librarian
802-873-3022 ext. 201

Ste-Catherine-de-la-J-Carti: **Bibliothèque Anne-Hébert**
22, rue Louis-Jolliet, Ste-Catherine-de-la-J-Carti, QC G3N 2V3
Tél: 418-875-2171; *Téléc:* 418-875-2699
bibliotheque@villescjc.com
www.reseaubiblioduquebec.qc.ca/cartier
Geneviève Roger, Responsable

Ste-Geneviève-de-Batiscan: **Bibliothèque de Sainte-Geneviève-de-Batiscan (Clément-Marchand)**
2, rue du Centre, Ste-Geneviève-de-Batiscan, QC G0X 2R0
Tél: 418-363-2261
biblio036@reseaubibliocqlm.qc.ca
www.reseaubiblioduquebec.qc.ca
Nicole Lahaie, Responsable

Ste-Geneviève-de-Berthier: **Bibliothèque de Sainte-Geneviève-de-Berthier (Léo-Paul-Desrosiers)**
391, rang de la Rivière-Bayonne sud, Ste-Geneviève-de-Berthier, QC J0K 1A0
Tél: 450-836-4333; *Téléc:* 450-836-7260
biblio066@reseaubibliocqlm.qc.ca
www.reseaubiblioduquebec.qc.ca
Gabrielle Desjardins, Responsable

Ste-Gertrude-Mannville: **Bibliothèque de Sainte-Gertrude**
391, rte 395, Ste-Gertrude-Mannville, QC J0Y 2L0
Tél: 819-727-2244; *Téléc:* 819-727-2244
gertrude@crsbpat.qc.ca
Geneviève Michaud, Responsable
Colette Dumais, Responsable, Demandes spéciales

Ste-Hélène-de-Mancebourg: **Bibliothèque de Sainte-Hélène-de-Mancebourg**
459, ch Rangs 2 et 3, Ste-Hélène-de-Mancebourg, QC J0Z 2T0
Tél: 819-333-4609; *Téléc:* 819-333-9591
mancebourg@reseaubiblioatnq.qc.ca
www.reseaubiblioduquebec.qc.ca
Émilienne Jérôme, Responsable
819-333-5766

Ste-Jeanne-d'Arc: **Bibliothèque de Sainte-Jeanne-d'Arc**
207, rue Principale, Ste-Jeanne-d'Arc, QC G0J 2T0
Tél: 418-776-5814
biblio.jeanne@crsbp.net
www.reseaubiblioduquebec.qc.ca
Pauline Proulx, Responsable

Ste-Lucie-des-Laurentides: **Bibliothèque de Sainte-Lucie-des-Laurentides**
2057, ch des Hauteurs, Ste-Lucie-des-Laurentides, QC J0T 2J0
Tél: 819-326-3228
biblio@municipalite.sainte-lucie-des-laurentides.qc.ca
www.municipalite.sainte-lucie-des-laurentides.qc.ca
Lorraine Beauchamp, Responsable

Ste-Marcelline-de-Kildare: **Bibliothèque de Sainte-Marcelline-de-Kildare**
435, 1ère av Pied-de-la-Montagne, Ste-Marcelline-de-Kildare, QC J0K 2Y0
Tél: 450-883-2241; *Téléc:* 450-883-2242
biblio135@reseaubibliocqlm.qc.ca
www.reseaubiblioduquebec.qc.ca
Gisèle Labine, Responsable
Nicole Perreault, Adjointe

Ste-Marguerite-du-Lac-Masso: **Bibliothèque de Sainte-Marguerite-Estérel**
4, rue des Lilas, Ste-Marguerite-du-Lac-Masso, QC J0T 1L0
Tél: 450-228-4442; *Téléc:* 450-228-4442
biblio031@crsbpl.qc.ca
www.reseaubiblioduquebec.qc.ca/sainte-marguerite-esterel
Joane Grandmaison, Responsable

Ste-Séraphine: **Bibliothèque de Sainte-Séraphine**
2660, rue Centre communautaire, Ste-Séraphine, QC J0A 1E0
Tél: 819-336-3222; *Téléc:* 819-336-3800
biblio085@reseaubibliocqlm.qc.ca
www.reseaubiblioduquebec.qc.ca
Monique Raîche, Responsable

Ste-Thérèse-de-la-Gatineau: **Bibliothèque municipale de Sainte-Thérèse-de-la-Gatineau**
29, rue Principale, Ste-Thérèse-de-la-Gatineau, QC J0X 2X0
Tél: 819-449-7964; *Téléc:* 819-449-2194
admtherese@crsbpo.qc.ca
www.reseaubiblioduquebec.qc.ca/Ste-Therese-de-la-Gatineau
Josée Riel, Coordonnatrice

Stoneham: **Bibliothèque Jean-Luc-Grondin**
325, ch du Hibou, Stoneham, QC G0A 4P0
Tél: 418-848-3399; *Téléc:* 418-848-1748
jlgrondin@sympatico.ca
www.reseaubiblioduquebec.qc.ca/stoneham/
Gaétane St-Laurent, Responsable
Mireille Bélanger, Responsable, PIB

Sutton: **Bibliothèque municipale de Sutton**
19, rue Highland, Sutton, QC J0E 2K0
Tél: 450-538-5843; *Téléc:* 450-538-4286
sutton@reseaubibliomonteregie.qc.ca
www.reseaubiblioduquebec.qc.ca
Lisa Charbonneau, Responsable

Tadoussac: **Bibliothèque municipale de Tadoussac**
162, des Jésuites, Tadoussac, QC G0T 2A0
Tél: 418-235-4446; *Téléc:* 418-235-4433
ville@tadoussac.com
www.tadoussac.com/fr/loisirs/bibliotheque-municipale-de-tadoussac
Johanne Hovington, Responsable
jojohovington@hotmail.com

Taschereau: **Bibliothèque de Taschereau**
50B, rue Morin, Taschereau, QC J0Z 3N0
Tél: 819-796-2219; *Téléc:* 819-796-3226
taschereau@reseaubiblioatnq.qc.ca
www.reseaubiblioduquebec.qc.ca/taschereau
Francine Laplante, Responsable

Terrasse-Vaudreuil: **Bibliothèque Terrasse-Vaudreuil**
74, 7e av, Terrasse-Vaudreuil, QC J7V 3M9
Tél: 514-425-0430
Huguette Noël, Responsable

Terrebonne: **Bibliothèque publique de Terrebonne**
3425, place Camus, Terrebonne, QC J6Y 1L2
Tél: 450-961-2001
www.ville.terrebonne.qc.ca/loisirs_bibliotheques-publiques.php
Céline Paquette, Coordonnatrice aux bibliothèques
celine.paquette@ville.terrebonne.qc.ca

Thetford Mines: **Bibliothèque publique de Black Lake**
Polyvalente de Black Lake, 499, St-Désiré, Thetford Mines, QC G6H 1L7
Tél: 418-423-4291; *Téléc:* 418-423-4909
Carmen Poulin, Agente de bureau

Thurso: **Bibliothèque de Thurso/Lochaber-Partie-Ouest/Lochaber**
341A, rue Victoria, Thurso, QC J0X 3B0
Tél: 819-985-3479; *Téléc:* 819-386-0134
admthurso@crsbpo.qc.ca
www.reseaubiblioduquebec.qc.ca/Thurso
Lysette Boyer, Responsable

Tingwick: **Bibliothèque de Tingwick**
1266, rue St-Joseph, Tingwick, QC J0A 1L0
Tél: 819-359-3225; *Téléc:* 819-359-2233
biblio083@reseaubibliocqlm.qc.ca
www.reseaubiblioduquebec.qc.ca
Lyse Brochu, Responsable

Tourville: **Bibliothèque municipale de Tourville**
946, Principale, Tourville, QC G0R 4M0
Tél: 418-359-2106; *Téléc:* 418-359-3671
municipal.tourville@globetrotter.net
Ghislaine Legros, Responsable
418-359-2192

Tring-Jonction: **Bibliothèque Livre-en-train**
208, rue Principale, Tring-Jonction, QC G0N 1X0
Tél: 418-426-1500
www.reseaubiblioduquebec.qc.ca/tring-jonction

Trois-Pistoles: **Bibliothèque Anne-Marie-D'Amours**
145, rue de l'Aréna, Trois-Pistoles, QC G0L 4K0
Tél: 418-851-2374; *Téléc:* 418-851-3567
www.ville-trois-pistoles.ca
Karen Dionne, Responsable
k.dionne@ville-trois-pistoles.ca
418-851-2374
Frédéric Jean, Directeur, Loisirs et communications
f.jean@ville-trois-pistoles.ca
418-851-1995

Trois-Rives: **Bibliothèque de Saint-Joseph-de-Mékinac**
258, rue St-Joseph, Trois-Rives, QC G0X 2C0
Tél: 819-646-5686; *Téléc:* 819-646-5686
biblio034@reseaubibliocqlm.qc.ca
www.reseaubiblioduquebec.qc.ca
Georgette Doucet, Responsable

Trois-Rivières: **Bibliothèques de Trois-Rivières**
1425, place de l'Hôtel-de-Ville, Trois-Rivières, QC G9A 5L9
Tél: 819-372-4615
bibliotheque@v3r.net
www.biblio.v3r.net
Julie Moreau, Chef d'équipe
jmoreau@v3r.net
Odette Pelletier, Coordination, Services techniques
opelletier@v3r.net
819-372-4641 ext. 4251

Très-Saint-Rédempteur: **Bibliothèque municipale de Très-Saint-Rédempteur**
769, rte Principale, Très-Saint-Rédempteur, QC J0P 1P1
Tél: 450-451-5203
redempteur@reseaubibliomonteregie.qc.ca
www.reseaubiblioduquebec.qc.ca
Carolle Lalonde, Responsable

Témiscamingue: **Bibliothèque de Témiscamingue**
40, rue Boucher, Témiscamingue, QC J0Z 3R0
Tél: 819-627-3273; *Téléc:* 819-627-3019
biblioTEM@hotmail.com
www.temiscaming.net/bibliotheque
Suzelle Plante, Responsable
Claudie Gaudet, Responsable écolière

Tête-à-la-Baleine: **Bibliothèque municipale de Tête-à-la-Baleine**
Centre Communautaire, Municipalité de la Côte-Nord-du-Golfe-du-Saint-Laurent, Tête-à-la-Baleine, QC G0G 2W0
Tél: 418-787-2244; *Téléc:* 418-787-2241
www.reseaubiblioduquebec.qc.ca
Olive Marcoux, Responsable

Upton: **Bibliothèque municipale d'Upton**
784, rue Saint-Éphrem, Upton, QC J0H 2E0
Tél: 450-549-4537
Francine Savoie, Responsable
450-549-4564

Val-Alain: **Bibliothèque L'Hiboucou**
1198, rue de l'Église, Val-Alain, QC G0S 3H0
Tél: 418-744-3313; *Téléc:* 418-744-3222
www.reseaubiblioduquebec.qc.ca/val-alain/
Karine Fleury, Responsable

Val-Brillant: **Bibliothèque Val-Brillant**
11, rue Saint-Pierre ouest, Val-Brillant, QC G0J 3L0
Tél: 418-742-3711
biblio.brillant@crsbp.net
Adrienne Aubut, Responsable

Val-d'Espoir: **Bibliothèque de Val-d'Espoir**
1240, 5e Rang est, Val-d'Espoir, QC G0C 3G0
www.reseaubiblioduquebec.qc.ca
Lorraine Dallaire, Responsable

Val-d'Or: **Bibliothèque municipale de Val-d'Or**
600, 7e rue, Val-d'Or, QC J9P 3P3
Tél: 819-824-2666; *Téléc:* 819-825-3062
www.ville.valdor.qc.ca
Olivier Barrette, Responsable
barretto@ville.valdor.qc.ca
Colette Gobeil, Bibliotechnicienne
gobeilc@ville.valdor.qc.ca
819-824-2666
Diane Naud, Bibliotechnicienne
naudd@ville.valdor.qc.ca
819-824-2666

Val-David: **Bibliothèque de Val-David**
1355, rue de l'Académie, Val-David, QC J0T 2N0
Tél: 819-324-5678; *Téléc:* 819-322-6327
Ligne sans frais: 888-322-7030
bibliotheque@valdavid.com
www.valdavid.com/citoyens-loisirs-biblio.php
Nicole Gagne, Responsable

Val-des-Bois: **Bibliothèque de Val-des-Bois/Bowman**
593, rte 309, Val-des-Bois, QC J0X 3C0
Tél: 819-454-2280; *Téléc:* 819-454-2211
biblio.valdesbois@mrcpapineau.com
www.reseaubiblioduquebec.qc.ca/Val-des-Bois
Shirley Raymond, Responsable

Val-des-Lacs: **Bibliothèque Val-des-Lacs**
349, ch Val-des-Lacs, Val-des-Lacs, QC J0T 2P0
Tél: 819-326-5624; *Téléc:* 819-326-7065
bibliotheque@municipalite.val-des-lacs.qc.ca

Val-des-Monts: **Bibliothèque de Perkins (Val-des-Monts)**
17, ch du Manoir, Val-des-Monts, QC J8N 7E8
Tél: 819-671-1476; *Téléc:* 819-457-4141
admperkins@crsbpo.qc.ca
www.reseaubiblioduquebec.qc.ca/Perkins
Denise Cécyre, Responsable

Val-des-Monts: **Bibliothèque de Poltimore/Denholm (Val-des-Monts)**
2720, rte Principale, Val-des-Monts, QC J8N 3B6
Tél: 819-457-4467; *Téléc:* 819-457-4141
bibliopoltimore@crsbpo.qc.ca
www.reseaubiblioduquebec.qc.ca/Poltimore
France Landry, Responsable

Val-des-Monts: **Bibliothèque de Saint-Pierre-de-Wakefield (Val-des-Monts)**
24, ch du Parc, Val-des-Monts, QC J8N 4H8
Tél: 819-457-1911; *Téléc:* 819-457-9113
admstpierre@crsbpo.qc.ca
www.reseaubiblioduquebec.qc.ca/St-Pierre-de-Wakefield
Colette Prud'Homme, Responsable

Val-Morin: **Bibliothèque Francine Paquette**
6160, rue Morin, Val-Morin, QC J0T 2R0
Tél: 819-324-5672
biblio@val-morin.ca
www.reseaubiblioduquebec.qc.ca
Jacqueline Leonard, Responsable

Val-Paradis: **Bibliothèque de Val-Paradis**
1865-A, ch des Rangs 1 et 10, Val-Paradis, QC J0Z 3S0
Tél: 819-941-2046; *Téléc:* 819-941-2485
paradis@reseaubiblioatnq.qc.ca
www.reseaubiblioduquebec.qc.ca
Renée Bégin, Responsable

Val-Saint-Gilles: **Bibliothèque de Val-Saint-Gilles**
801, rue Principale, Val-Saint-Gilles, QC J0Z 3T0
Tél: 819-333-5676; *Téléc:* 819-333-3116
gilles@reseaubiblioatnq.qc.ca
www.reseaubiblioduquebec.qc.ca
Nicole Richer, Responsable

Valcourt: **Bibliothèque publique Yvonne L. Bombardier**
1002, rue J.A. Bombardier, Valcourt, QC J0E 2L0
Tél: 450-532-2250; *Téléc:* 450-532-5807
bylb@fjab.qc.ca
www.centreculturelbombardier.com/bibliotheque.htm
Média social: www.facebook.com/CentreCulturelBombardier
Karine Corbeil, Directrice
k.corbeil@fjab.qc.ca

Varennes: **Bibliothèque Jacques-Lemoyne-de-Sainte-Marie**
2221, boul René-Gaultier, Varennes, QC J3X 1E3
Tél: 450-652-3949
ville.varennes.qc.ca/activites-bibliotheque/bibliotheque
Michèle Lamoureux, Bibliothécaire

Vaudreuil-Dorion: **Bibliothèque municipale de Vaudreuil-Dorion**
51, rue Jeannotte, Vaudreuil-Dorion, QC J7V 6E6
Tél: 450-455-5588; *Téléc:* 450-455-5653
biblio@ville.vaudreuil-dorion.qc.ca
www.ville.vaudreuil-dorion.qc.ca
Michel Vallée, Directeur, Arts et Culture
Hélène Diamond, Chef de division - Bibliothèque
Dominique D'Amour, Technicienne en documentation
Jean Gagnon, Technicien en documentation

Vendée: **Bibliothèque de Vendée**
1816, ch du Village, Vendée, QC J0T 2T0
Tél: 819-681-3372
bibliovendee@municipalite.amherst.qc.ca
www.reseaubiblioduquebec.qc.ca
Jeannine Dallaire, Responsable

Verchères: **Bibliothèque municipale-scolaire Dansereau-Larose**
36, rue Dalpé, Verchères, QC J0L 2R0
Tél: 450-583-3309; *Téléc:* 450-583-3637
biblio@ville.vercheres.qc.ca
www.reseaubiblioduquebec.qc.ca/vercheres

Victoriaville: **Bibliothèque Charles-Édouard-Mailhot**
2, rue de l'Ermitage, Victoriaville, QC G6P 6T2
Tél: 819-758-8441; *Téléc:* 819-758-9432
www.bibliomcq.qc.ca/victoriaville
Louise Grondines, Directrice
louise.grondines@ville.victoriaville.qc.ca

Ville-Marie: **Bibliothèque Ville-Marie 'La Bouquine'**
50, rue Notre-Dame de Lourdes, Ville-Marie, QC J9V 1X9
Tél: 819-629-2881
villemarie@reseaubiblioatnq.qc.ca
www.reseaubiblioatnq.qc.ca/villemarie/
Cécile Boily, Responsable

Villebois: **Bibliothèque de Villebois**
3889, rue de l'Église, Villebois, QC J0Z 3V0
Tél: 819-941-2040; *Téléc:* 819-941-2685
villebois@reseaubiblioatnq.qc.ca
www.reseaubiblioduquebec.qc.ca/villebois
Marie-Pierre Desbiens, Responsable
Nathalie Simard, Adjointe

Wakefield: **Wakefield Library / Bibliothèque de Wakefield (La Pêche)**
20 Valley Dr., Wakefield, QC J0X 3G0
Tel: 819-459-3266; *Fax:* 819-459-8832
contact@wakefieldlibrary.ca
Sue Graham, Coordinator

Warwick: **Bibliothèque de Warwick (P.-Rodolphe-Baril)**
181, rue St-Louis, Warwick, QC J0A 1M0
Tél: 819-358-4325; *Téléc:* 819-358-4326
bibliowarwick@cablevision.com
www.reseaubiblioduquebec.qc.ca
France Gendron, Responsable
819-358-4325
Diane Provencher, Animatrice et préposée aux prêts
Collette Lavasseur-Desroche

Waterloo: **Bibliothèque publique de Waterloo / Waterloo Public Library**
650, rue de la Cour, Waterloo, QC J0E 2N0
Tél: 450-539-2268
biblio@cacwaterloo.qc.ca
Gisèle Dupuis, Responsable

Weedon: **Bibliothèque Saint-Gérard**
#249 A, rue Principale, Weedon, QC J0B 3J0
Tél: 819-877-5704
biblio024@reseaubiblioestrie.qc.ca

Wemotaci: **Bibliothèque de Wemotaci**
CP 222, Wemotaci, QC G0X 3R0
Tél: 819-666-2232; *Téléc:* 819-666-2233
biblio064@reseaubiblioqlm.qc.ca
www.reseaubiblioduquebec.qc.ca
Yvette Niquay, Responsable

Wentworth-Nord: **Bibliothèque de Wentworth-Nord**
3470, rte Principale, Wentworth-Nord, QC J0T 1Y0
Tél: 450-226-2416
information@bibliowentworthnord.org

Westmount: **Bibliothèque publique de Westmount**
4574, rue Sherbrooke ouest, Westmount, QC H3Z 1G1
Tél: 514-989-5299
Other Numbers: 514-989-5368 (Audiovisuel)
refdesk@westmount.org (Référence)
www.westlib.org/library
Média social: www.facebook.com/bibliowestmount
Julie-Anne Cardella, Directrice
jacardella@westmount.org
514-989-5429
Wendy Wayling, Bibliothécaire des enfants
wwayling@westmount.org
514-989-5357
Benoît Morin, Bibliothécaire de référence
bmorin@westmount.org
514-989-5517

Wickham: **Bibliothèque de Wickham**
893, rue Moreau, Wickham, QC J0C 1S0
Tél: 819-398-6878; *Téléc:* 819-398-7166
biblio154@reseaubiblioqlm.qc.ca
www.reseaubiblioduquebec.qc.ca
Pierrette Courchesne, Responsable

Windsor: **Bibliothèque municipale Patrick-Dignan de Windsor**
52, rue St-Georges, Windsor, QC J1S 1J5
Tél: 819-845-7115; *Téléc:* 819-845-5516
bibliwin@abacom.com
www.bibliotheque.windsor.qc.ca
Jacynthe Dubois, Technicienne en documentation
duboisj2@abacom.com

Wotton: **Bibliothèque Wotton**
#398 Mgr. l'Heureaux, Wotton, QC J0A 1N0
Tél: 819-828-0693; *Téléc:* 819-828-3594
biblio055@reseaubiblioestrie.qc.ca

Yamachiche: **Bibliothèque de Yamachiche (J.-Alide-Pellerin)**
440, rue Sainte-Anne, Yamachiche, QC G0X 3L0
Tél: 819-296-3580; *Téléc:* 819-296-3542
biblio020@reseaubiblioqlm.qc.ca
www.reseaubiblioduquebec.qc.ca
Hélène Larose, Responsable

Archives

Alma: **Société d'histoire du Lac-Saint-Jean**
1671, av du Pont nord, Alma, QC G8B 5G2
Tél: 418-668-2606; *Téléc:* 418-668-5851
Ligne sans frais: 866-668-2606
info@shlsj.org
www.shlsj.org
Gaston Martel, Archiviste et directeur

Amos: **Société d'histoire d'Amos**
Édifice de la Maison de la culture, 222, 1e av est, Amos, QC J9T 1H3
Tél: 819-732-6070; *Téléc:* 819-732-3242
societe.histoire@cableamos.com
www.societehistoireamos.com
Pierrette Blais, Archiviste

Baie-Comeau: **Société historique de la Côte-Nord**
9, av Marquette, Baie-Comeau, QC G4Z 1K4
Tél: 418-296-8228; *Téléc:* 418-294-4187
shcn@globetrotter.net
www.shcote-nord.org
Média social:
www.facebook.com/group.php?gid=215657145115493
Pierre Frenette, Président
Marc Champagne, Secrétaire
marcus_spartacus@hotmail.com
Catherine Pellerin, Directrice-archiviste
catherine.pellerin@shcote-nord.org

Baie-Comeau: **Ville de Baie-Comeau**
19, av Marquette, Baie-Comeau, QC G4Z 1K5
Tél: 418-296-8898; *Téléc:* 418-296-8194
lpineault@ville.baie-comeau.qc.ca
Sylvain Ouellet, Greffier
souellet@ville.baie-comeau.qc.ca

Cap-de-la-Madeleine: **Sanctuaire Notre-Dame du Cap**
626, rue Notre-Dame, Cap-de-la-Madeleine, QC G8T 4G9
Tél: 819-374-2441; *Téléc:* 819-374-2890
courrier@ndc-cap.com
sanctuaire-ndc.ca
Média social: www.facebook.com/193784683998487

Chambly: **Société d'histoire de la Seigneurie de Chambly**
2445, rue Bourgogne, Chambly, QC J3L 2A5
Tél: 450-658-2666
shsc@societehistoirechambly.org
www.societehistoirechambly.org
Paul-Henri Hudon, Président

Chicoutimi: **Evêché de Chicoutimi**
602, rue Racine est, Chicoutimi, QC G7H 1V1
Tél: 418-543-0783; *Téléc:* 418-543-2141
diocese.chicoutimi@videotron.net
www.evechedechicoutimi.qc.ca
Raynald Côté, Chancelier
raynald.cote@evechedechicoutimi.qc.ca

Chicoutimi: **Séminaire de Chicoutimi**
679, rue Chabanel, Chicoutimi, QC G7H 1Z7
Tél: 418-549-0190; *Téléc:* 418-549-1524
lycee.seminaire@lycee-sdec.qc.ca
www.sdec.qc.ca
Clément-Jacques Simard, Archiviste

Chicoutimi: **Société historique du Saguenay**
930, rue Jacques Cartier est, Chicoutimi, QC G7H 7K9
Tél: 418-549-2805; *Téléc:* 418-698-3758
shs@shistoriquesaguenay.com
www.shistoriquesaguenay.com
Louise Bouchard, Directrice générale

Gaspé: **Centre d'archives du Musée de la Gaspésie**
80, boul de Gaspé, Gaspé, QC G4X 1A9
Tel: 418-368-1534; *Fax:* 418-368-1535
archives@museedelagaspesie.ca
www.museedelagaspesie.ca/cag/french/index.htm
Social Media: www.youtube.com/user/musee1534;
twitter.com/MG1534
Sébastien Lévesque, Directeur général
direction@museedelagaspesie.ca
Jeannot Bourdages, Archiviste
archives@museedelagaspesie.ca

Gatineau: **Archives municipales de la Ville de Gatineau**
855, boul de la Gappe, Gatineau, QC J8T 8H9
Tél: 819-243-2329; *Téléc:* 819-243-2341
archives@ville.gatineau.qc.ca
www.ville.gatineau.qc.ca/archives/
Bernard Savoie, Responsable, Chef, Section gestion des documents et des archives
Michelyne Mongeon, Archiviste
Louise Bisson, Analyste

Gatineau: **Centre de l'Outaouais**
855, boul de la Gappe, Gatineau, QC J8T 8H9
Tél: 819-568-8798; *Téléc:* 819-568-5933
archives.gatineau@banq.qc.ca

Gatineau: **Western Québec School Board**
15, rue Katimavik, Gatineau, QC J9J 0E9
Tel: 819-864-2336; *Fax:* 819-684-1328
Toll-Free: 800-363-9111
wqsb@wqsb.qc.ca
www.wqsb.qc.ca

Granby: **Société d'histoire de la Haute-Yamaska**
135, rue Principale, Granby, QC J2G 2V1
Tél: 450-372-4500
info@shhy.org
www.shhy.org
Richard Racine, Directeur général, archiviste
richard.racine@shhy.info
Johanne Rochon, Responsable de la diffusion, archiviste
johanne.rochon@shhy.info

Jonquière: **La Commission scolaire de la Jonquière**
3644, rue Saint-Jules, Jonquière, QC G7X 7X4
Tél: 418-542-7551; *Téléc:* 418-542-1505
sgeneral@csjonquiere.qc.ca
www.csjonquiere.qc.ca
Christian St-Gelais, Secrétaire général
Serge LeBlanc, Agent d'administration
serge.leblanc@csjonquiere.qc.ca
418-695-1801

Jonquière: **Service de gestion des documents et des archives**
2505, rue St-Hubert, Jonquière, QC G7X 7W2
Tél: 418-547-2191; *Téléc:* 418-547-6965

Knowlton: **Brome County Historical Society**
130, ch Lakeside, Knowlton, QC J0E 1V0
Tel: 450-243-6782
bchs@endirect.qc.ca
www.bromemuseum.com

La Pocatière: **Evêché de Sainte-Anne-de-la-Pocatière**
#1200, 4, av Painchaud, La Pocatière, QC G0R 1Z0
Tél: 418-856-1811; *Téléc:* 418-856-5863
librairie@diocese-ste-anne.net
www.diocese-ste-anne.net/
Céline Hudon, Archiviste
819-856-1811 ext. 131
Doris Laplante, Chancelier
418-856-1811 ext. 122

La Pocatière: **Société historique de la Côte-du-Sud**
100, 4e av Painchaud, La Pocatière, QC G0R 1Z0
Tél: 418-856-2104
archsud@bellnet.ca
www.shcds.org
François Taillon, Directeur, Centre des archives

La Prairie: **Archives des Frères de l'Instruction chrétienne**
870, ch de Saint-Jean, La Prairie, QC J5R 2L5
Tél: 450-659-1922; *Téléc:* 450-659-3717
François Boutin, Archiviste
boutinf@jdlm.qc.ca
François Boutin, Archviste
Albert Pruneau, Collaborateur
André Lemire, Collaborateur
Gaston Roy, Collaborateur

La Prairie: **Société d'histoire de La Prairie de la Magdeleine**
249, rue Sainte-Marie, La Prairie, QC J5R 1G1
Tél: 450-659-1393
histoire@laprairie-shlm.com
www.laprairie-shlm.com/
Edith Gagnon, secrétaire-coordonnatrice

Lac-aux-Sables: **Société d'histoire de Lac-aux-Sables et d'Hervey-Jonction**
40, rue Bourassa, Lac-aux-Sables, QC G0X 1M0
Tél: 418-336-2918
www.rabaska.com/histoire/lacauxsables.htm
Annie Gauthier, Responsable
anik3@globetrotter.net

Lac-Etchemin: **Société du patrimoine de Sainte-Justine-de-Langevin**
212E, 2e av, Lac-Etchemin, QC G0R 1S0
Tél: 418-625-1231; *Téléc:* 418-625-5980
etchemin@eccetera.com
Ghislain Royer, Archiviste

Lac-Mégantic: **Société d'histoire et du patrimoine de la région de Mégantic**
5086, rue Frontenac, Lac-Mégantic, QC G6B 1H3
Tél: 819-583-0876; *Téléc:* 819-583-0878
direction@bibliomegantic.qc.ca
www.bibliomegantic.qc.ca
Daniel Lavoie, Bibliothécaire

Lachine: **Musée de Lachine**
1, ch du Musée, Lachine, QC H8S 4L9
Tél: 514-634-3478; *Téléc:* 514-637-6784
museedelachine@lachine.ca
lachine.ville.montreal.qc.ca/musee

Laval: **Frères des écoles chrétiennes, Montréal**
300, ch du Bord-de-l'Eau, Laval, QC H7X 1S9
Tél: 450-689-4151; *Téléc:* 450-689-6260
archives@delasalle.qc.ca
Louis-Marie Côté, Archiviste
archives@delasalle.qc.ca
Claude Gadoury, Personnel

Laval: **Société d'histoire et de généalogie de l'Ile Jésus**
4290, boul Samson, Laval, QC H7W 2G9
Tél: 450-681-9096; *Téléc:* 450-686-8270
info@shgij.org
www.shgij.org

Lennoxville: **Lennoxville-Ascot Historical & Museum Society**
9 Speid St., Lennoxville, QC J1M 1Z3
Tel: 819-564-0409; *Fax:* 819-564-8951
lrider@uplands.ca
http://www.museevirtuel-virtualmuseum.ca/
Lillian Rider, Head of Archives

Lennoxville: **Montréal & Ottawa Conference, Archives**
Old Library, McGreer Hall, Bishop's University, Lennoxville, QC J1M 1Z7
Tel: 819-822-9600; *Fax:* 819-822-9661
etrc2@ubishops.ca
www.montrealandottawaconference.ca

Longueuil: **Soeurs des Saints Noms de Jésus et de Marie, Longueuil**
80, rue Saint-Charles est, Longueuil, QC J4H 1A9
Tél: 450-651-8104; *Téléc:* 450-651-8636
archivessnjm@yahoo.ca
www.snjm.org/French2/archivefr.htm
Yvonne Painchaud, Archiviste

Magog: **Société d'histoire du Lac Memphrémagog / Historic Society of Lake Memphremagog**
95, rue Merry nord, local 024, Magog, QC J1X 2E7
Tél: 819-868-6779
info@histoiremagog.com
www.histoiremagog.com
Jérémy Parentert, Président

Montréal: **The Archive of the Jesuits in Canada / Archives des jésuites au Canada**
25, rue Jarry ouest, Montréal, QC H2P 1S6
Tel: 514-387-2541; *Fax:* 514-387-5637
archives@jesuites.org
www.jesuites.org/archives
Bruce Henry, Director
Christian Lacombe, Librarian
Jacques Monet, Historian
Jasmin Miville Allard, Contact, Art Collection

Montréal: **Archives de Montréal**
#108R, 275, rue Notre-Dame est, Montréal, QC H2Y 1C6
Tél: 514-872-1173; *Téléc:* 514-872-3475
consultation_archives@ville.montreal.qc.ca
www.ville.montreal.qc.ca
Média social: www.youtube.com/user/ArchivesMtl;
twitter.com/Archives_Mtl;
www.facebook.com/groups/86029182129
Denys Chouinard, Chef de la section des archives

Montréal: **Archives provinciales des Capucins et Bibliothèque franciscaine provinciale des Capucins**
3650, boul de la Rousselière, Montréal, QC H1A 2X9
Tél: 514-642-5391; *Téléc:* 514-642-5033
sacre-coeur@videotron.ca
Godefroy-C. Dévost, Bibliothécaire-Archiviste
514-642-5391 ext. 345
France Guilbert, Technicienne en documentation
514-642-5391 ext. 347

Montréal: **Bank of Montreal**
129, rue Saint-Jacques, étage D, Montréal, QC H2Y 1L6
Tel: 514-877-6810; *Fax:* 514-877-7341
yolaine.toussaint@bmo.com
Yolaine Toussaint, Archivist
yolaine.toussaint@bmo.com

Montréal: **Bell Canada / Le Service de la documentation historique**
6055 Monkland Ave., 2nd Fl., Montréal, QC H4A 1H3
Tel: 514-870-5214; *Fax:* 514-484-4429

Montréal: **Canadian Centre for Architecture Archives**
1920, rue Baile, Montréal, QC H3H 2S6
Tel: 514-939-7011; *Fax:* 514-939-7020
ref@cca.qc.ca
www.cca.qc.ca/en/collection/archives

Montréal: **Canadian Jewish Congress, Charities Committee / Congrès juif canadien, Comité des charités**
1590, av Docteur Penfield, Montréal, QC H3G 1C5
Tel: 514-931-7531
archives@cjccc.ca
www.cjccc.ca
Norma Joseph, Chair, CJCCC National Archives
Janice Rosen, Director, CJCCC National Archives
Helene Vallee, Archives Assistant

Montréal: **Canadian Pacific Archives/ Archives chemin de fer Canadien Pacifique**
910, rue Peel, Montréal, QC H3C 3E4
Tel: 514-395-5135; *Fax:* 514-395-5135
archives@cpr.ca
www.cpheritage.com

Montréal: **Centre d'Archives de Montréal, de Laval, de Lanaudière, des Laurentides, de la Montérégie**
535, av Viger est, Montréal, QC H2L 2P3
Tél: 514-873-1100; *Téléc:* 514-873-2980

Montréal: **Centre de documentation (gestion)**
Pavillon Hubert-Aquin, local A-R170, 400, rue Ste-Catherine est, Montréal, QC H2L 2C5
Tél: 514-987-6114; *Téléc:* 514-987-3542
bibliotheques@uqam.ca
www.bibliotheques.uqam.ca

Montréal: **Centre de recherche de l'Oratoire Saint-Joseph**
3800, ch Queen Mary, Montréal, QC H3V 1H6
Tél: 514-733-8211; *Téléc:* 514-733-9735
biblio@osj.qc.ca
www.saint-joseph.org/fr_1117_index.php

Montréal: **Concordia University Archives**
Hall Bldg., #1015, 1455, boul de Maisonneuve ouest, Montréal, QC H3G 1M8
Tel: 514-848-2424; *Fax:* 514-848-2857
archives.concordia.ca
Marie-Pierre Aubé, Director, Records Management & Archives
Marie-Pierre.Aube@concordia.ca
514-848-2424 ext. 7776
Nathalie Hodgson, Archivist/Records Officer, Historial Archives
Nathalie.Hodgson@concordia.ca
514-848-2424 ext. 5851
Rachel Marion, Archivist/Records Officer, Records Management
Rachel.Marion@concordia.ca
514-848-2424 ext. 3487

Montréal: **Congrégation de Notre-Dame de Montréal**
2330, rue Sherbrooke ouest, Montréal, QC H3H 1G8
Tél: 514-931-5891; *Téléc:* 514-931-2915
cndarchives@cnd-m.com

Montréal: **Congrégation de Ste-Croix, Montréal**
4994, ch Côte-des-Neiges, Montréal, QC H3V 1A4
Tél: 514-735-1526; *Téléc:* 514-735-7813
administrationprov@religieuxcsc.qc.ca
www.ste-croix.qc.ca/index.php
Marie-Josée Vadnais, Archiviste
514-735-1526 ext. 420

Montréal: **Diocese of Montréal and the Ecclesiastical Province of Canada, Archives**
1444 av Union, Montréal, QC H3A 2B8
Tel: 514-843-6577; *Fax:* 514-843-6344
archives@montreal.anglican.ca
montreal.anglican.ca

Montréal: **Division de la gestion de documents et des archives**
Pavillon Roger-Gaudry, Université de Montréal, #615E, 2900, boul Édouard-Montpetit, Montréal, QC H3T 1J4
Tél: 514-343-6023
Other Numbers: Référence: 514-343-2251
archives@archiv.umontreal.ca
www.archiv.umontreal.ca

Montréal: **Frères de St Gabriel, Province de Montréal**
1601, boul Gouin est, Montréal, QC H2C 1C2
Tél: 514-387-7337; *Téléc:* 514-387-0735
fsgarchives@bellnet.ca
www.saintgabriel.ca
Philippe Geoffrion, Archiviste

Montréal: **The Gazette**
200, 1010, rue Ste-Catherine ouest, Montréal, QC H3B 5L1
Tel: 514-987-2412; *Fax:* 514-987-2433
library@thegazette.canwest.com
www.montrealgazette.com/index.html
Social Media: twitter.com/#!/mtlgazette;
www.facebook.com/montrealgazette
Michael Porritt, Library Administrator
mporritt@thegazette.canwest.com

Montréal: **Montréal & Ottawa Conference, Archives**
225 - 50e av, Montréal, QC H8T 2T7
Tel: 514-634-7015; *Fax:* 514-634-7015
moarchivesucc@gmail.com
www.montrealandottawaconference.ca

Montréal: **Montréal Holocaust Memorial Centre / Centre commémoratif de l'holocauste à Montréal**
Cummings House, 5151, chemin de la Côte-Sainte-Catherine, Montréal, QC H3W 1M6
Tel: 514-345-2605; *Fax:* 514-344-2651
info@mhmc.ca
www.mhmc.ca
Social Media: www.facebook.com/78382729139
Bill Surkis, Executive Director

Montréal: **Musée d'art contemporain de Montréal Archives des collections**
185, rue Sainte-Catherine ouest, Montréal, QC H2X 3X5
Tél: 514-847-6226; *Téléc:* 514-874-6292
info@macm.org

Montréal: **Musée McCord/ McCord Museum**
690, rue Sherbrooke ouest, Montréal, QC H3A 1E9
Tel: 514-398-7100; *Fax:* 514-398-5045
nora.hague@mccord.mcgill.ca
www.musee-mccord.qc.ca
Christian Vachon, Director, Collection Management
Cynthia Cooper, Head, Collections and Research
Céline Widmer, Curator, Hisotry and Archives

Montréal: **L'Oratoire St-Joseph du Mont-Royal**
3800, ch Queen-Mary, Montréal, QC H3V 1H6
Tél: 514-733-8211; *Téléc:* 514-733-9735
Ligne sans frais: 677-672-8647
biblio@osj.qc.ca
www.saint-joseph.org
Mèdia social: www.facebook.com/osaintjoseph
Daniel Picot, Directeur du centre de recherche et documentation OSJ
514-733-8211 ext. 2331

Montréal: **Pères Dominicains, Montréal**
2715, ch. de la Côte-Sainte-Catherine, Montréal, QC H3T 1B6
Tél: 514-341-2244; *Téléc:* 514-341-3233
archives@dominicains.ca
www.dominicains.ca
Luc Aubin, Archiviste provincial

Montréal: **Port de Montréal/ Port of Montreal**
Édifice du port de Montréal, 2100, av Pierre-Dupuy, aile 1, Montréal, QC H3C 3R5
Tél: 514-283-7011; *Téléc:* 514-283-0829
Other Numbers: Emergency number: 514-283-6911
info@port-montreal.com
www.port-montreal.com
Denise Duguay, Archiviste/Superviseur, Gestion des documents
duguayd@port-montreal.com
514-283-7009

Montréal: **Séminaire de Saint-Sulpice de Montréal**
116, rue Notre-Dame ouest, Montréal, QC H2Y 1T2
Tél: 514-849-6561; *Téléc:* 514-286-9021
ucss.archives@sulpc.org
www.sulpc.org/sulpc_univers_culturel_archives_en.php
Marc Lacasse, Coordinateur
Marc Lacasse, Archiviste, Coordinateur du service
lacasse@cam.org

Montréal: **Soeurs Grises de Montréal**
138, rue Saint-Pierre, Montréal, QC H2Y 2L7
Tél: 514-842-9411; *Téléc:* 514-842-0142
www.sgm.qc.ca
Suzanne Morin, Responsable des archives

Montréal: **Vidéographe inc**
4550, rue Garnier, Montréal, QC H2J 3S7
Tél: 514-521-2116; *Téléc:* 514-521-1676
info@videographe.qc.ca
www.videographe.qc.ca
Mèdia social: twitter.com/Videographe;
www.facebook.com/pages/Vidéographe/124501969721
Fortner Anderson, CEO
fanderson@videographe.qc.ca
Denis Vaillancourt, Charge de projets
denisvaillancourt@videographe.qc.ca

Nicolet: **Séminaire de Nicolet**
#110, 900, boul Louis-Fréchette, Nicolet, QC J3T 1V5
Tél: 819-293-4838; *Téléc:* 819-293-4543
seminairedenicolet@archives-seminaire-nicolet.qc.ca
archives-seminaire-nicolet.qc.ca
Marie Pelletier, Archiviste
m.pelletier@archives-seminaire-nicolet.qc.ca

Nicolet: **Les Soeurs de l'Assomption de la Sainte-Vierge**
251, rue Saint-Jean Baptiste, Nicolet, QC J3T 1X9
Tél: 819-293-2011; *Téléc:* 819-293-8315
archives@sasv.ca
www.sasv.ca/english/archives.php
Rose-Aimee Richard, Principal Archivist

Oka: **Société d'histoire d'Oka**
2017, ch d'Oka, Oka, QC J0N 1E0
Tél: 450-479-8556; *Téléc:* 450-479-8556
www.histoiredoka.ca
Réjeanne Cyr, Présidente

Oka: **Tsi Ronterihwanonhnha ne Kanienkeha / Kanehsatake Resource Centre**
407 St Michel, Oka, QC J0N 1E0
Tel: 450-479-1651; *Fax:* 450-479-8587
Other Numbers: 450-479-1783
kononkwe@inbox.com
Hilda Nicholas, Director

Outremont: **Fondation Lionel-Groulx**
261, av Bloomfield, Outremont, QC H2V 3R6
Tél: 514-271-4759; *Téléc:* 514-271-6369
info@fondationlionelgroulx.org
www.fondationlionelgroulx.org
Robert Boily, Directeur général
Yves Devin, Bibliothécaire
514-271-4759 ext. 226
Marie Léveillé, Archiviste principale
514-271-4759 ext. 225
François Dumas, Archiviste de référence
514-271-4759 ext. 224

Pierrefonds: **Montréal Arrondissement Pierrefonds/Roxboro**
13665, boul Pierrefonds, Pierrefonds, QC H9A 2Z4
Tel: 514-624-1124; *Fax:* 514-624-1300
amallaire@villemontreal.qc.ca
Anne-Marie Allaire, Archiviste
amallaire@villemontreal.qc.ca
514-624-1011

Québec: **Les Archives de la Ville de Québec**
350, rue St-Joseph est, 4e étage, Québec, QC G1K 3B2
Tél: 418-641-6214
greffearchives@ville.quebec.qc.ca
ville.quebec.qc.ca/en/apropos/portrait/archives_historiques.aspx
Sylvain Ouellet, Director of the Registry and Archives

Québec: **Archives des Augustines du Monastère de l'Hôpital Général de Québec**
260, boul Langelier, Québec, QC G1K 5N1
Tél: 418-692-0461; *Téléc:* 418-692-2668
denisrobitaille@augustines.ca
www.augustines.ca
Denis Robitaille, Chargé de projet
denisrobitaille@augustines.ca
Claire Gagnon, Archiviste

Québec: **Archives du Séminaire de Québec**
9, rue de Vieille-Université, CP 460, Haute-Ville, Québec, QC G1R 4R7
Tél: 418-643-2158; *Téléc:* 418-692-5206
Ligne sans frais: 866-710-8031
archives@mcq.org

***Québec:* Centrale des syndicats du Québec**
#100, 320, rue St-Joseph est, Québec, QC G1K 9E7
Tél: 418-649-8888; *Téléc:* 418-649-8800
documentation@csq.qc.net
www.csq.qc.net
François Gagnon, Conseiller
gagnon.francois@csq.qc.net

***Québec:* Division des Archives**
#Pavillon Jean-Charles Bonenfant, #5489, 2345 allée des Bibliothèques, Québec, QC G1K 0A6
Tél: 418-656-3722; *Téléc:* 418-656-3826
Other Numbers: Administration: 416-656-2131 ext 3722
division.archives@sg.ulaval.ca
www.archives.ulaval.ca

***Québec:* Église catholique de Québec**
#114, 1073, boul René-Lévesque ouest, Québec, QC G1S 4R5
Tél: 418-688-1211; *Téléc:* 418-688-1399
fabriques@ecdq.org
fabriques.ecdq.org
Rémy Gagnon, Responsable
remy.gagnon@ecdq.org

***Québec:* Fonds Ancien, Bibliothèque du Séminaire de Québec**
9, rue de Vieille-Université, CP 460, Haute-Ville, Québec, QC G1R 4R7
Tél: 418-643-2158; *Téléc:* 418-692-5206
Ligne sans frais: 866-710-8031
archives@mcq.org

***Québec:* Monastère des Augustines de l'Hôtel-Dieu de Québec**
75, rue des Remparts, Québec, QC G1R 3R9
Tél: 418-692-0461; *Téléc:* 418-692-2668
denisrobitaille@augustines.ca
www.augustines.ca
Claire Gagnon, Archiviste
François Rousseau, Archiviste

***Québec:* Musée de la Civilisation**
85, rue Dalhousie, Québec, QC G1K 8R2
Tél: 418-643-2158; *Téléc:* 418-646-9705
Ligne sans frais: 866-710-8031
documentation@mcq.org
www.mcq.org
Mèdia social: www.facebook.com/museedelacivilisation
Danielle Aubin, Responsable
Pierrette Lafond, Technicienne
418-643-2158 ext. 400
Martine Malenfant, Technicienne
mmalenfant@mcq.org
Martine Malenfant, Technicienne
mmalenfant@mcq.org

***Québec:* Musée du Royal 22e Régiment / Museum of the Royal 22e Régiment**
La Citadelle, 1, Côte de la Citadella, Québec, QC G1R 4V7
Tel: 418-694-2815; *Fax:* 418-694-2853
information@lacitadelle.qc.ca
www.lacitadelle.qc.ca
Social Media:
www.youtube.com/user/museeroyal?blend=5&ob=5;
www.facebook.com/193043460745807
Madeleine Béland, Archiviste des collections
mbeland@lacitadelle.qc.ca

***Québec:* Pères Eudistes**
6125, av 1 est, Québec, QC G1H 2V9
Tél: 418-626-6494; *Téléc:* 418-628-8774
www.eudistes.org/archives.htm
André Samson, Responsable

***Québec:* Religieux de St-Vincent-de-Paul (Canada)**
2555, ch Ste-Foy, Québec, QC G1V 1T8
Tél: 418-650-3441; *Téléc:* 418-650-5459
relsv.qc.ca/relsv
Pierre Grenier, Responsable
pierre.grenier@relsv.qc.ca

***Québec:* Société d'histoire de Sainte-Foy**
CP 8586, Québec, QC G1V 4N5
Tél: 418-654-4275
Michel Germain, Vice-Président
418-653-3215

***Québec:* Soeurs de Saint-Joseph-de-Saint-Vallier, Québec**
560, ch Sainte-Foy, Québec, QC G1S 2J6
Tél: 418-681-7361; *Téléc:* 418-683-4440
archives.st-joseph@sympatico.ca
www.saint-joseph-fed.org
Louise Talbot, Responsable
Marie-Claude Lavoie

***Québec:* Soeurs Servantes du Saint-Coeur-de-Marie, Québec**
30, av des Cascades, Québec, QC G1E 2J8
Tél: 418-663-6280
Madeleine Lamothe, Archiviste

***Québec:* Soeurs Ursulines de Québec**
2, rue du Parloir, Québec, QC G1R 4M5
Tél: 418-683-0671
archivesmg@ursulines-uc.com
www.ursulines-uc.com/
Marie Marchand, Responsable, Archives
archurs.qc@bellnet.com
418-695-2523 ext. 254

***Repentigny:* Commission scolaire des Affluents, Affaires corporatives et gestion de l'information**
80, rue Jean-Baptiste-Meilleur, Repentigny, QC J6A 6C5
Tél: 450-492-9400; *Téléc:* 450-492-3720
archives@csaffluents.qc.ca
www.csaffluents.qc.ca
Jacques Dufour, Secrétaire général et directeur des communications
jacques.dufour@sg.csaffluents.qc.ca
450-492-9400 ext. 1310
Viviane Rondeau, Régisseuse
viviane.rondeau@rm.csaffluents.qc.ca
450-492-9400 ext. 1370

***Rigaud:* Archives Collège Bourget**
65, rue St-Pierre, Rigaud, QC J0P 1P0
Tél: 450-451-0815; *Téléc:* 450-451-4171
biblio@collegebourget.qc.ca

***Rimouski:* Archevêché de Rimouski**
34, rue de l'Évêché ouest, Rimouski, QC G5L 4H5
Tél: 418-723-3320; *Téléc:* 418-722-8978
Sylvain Gosselin, Archiviste
418-723-3320 ext. 128

***Rimouski:* Bibliothèque**
#J-330, 300, Allée des Ursulines, Rimouski, QC G5L 3A1
Tél: 418-723-1986; *Téléc:* 418-724-1621

***Rimouski:* Centre d'archives du Bas-St-Laurent et de la Gaspésie-îles-de-la-Madeleine**
Édifice Louis-Joseph-Moreault, 337, rue Moreault, Rimouski, QC G5L 1P4
Tél: 418-727-3500; *Téléc:* 418-727-3739
archives.rimouski@banq.qc.ca

***Rivière-du-Loup:* Commission scolaire de Kamouraska - Rivière du Loup**
464, rue Lafontaine, Rivière-du-Loup, QC G5R 3Z5
www.cskamloup.qc.ca
Mèdia social: twitter.com/cskamloup;
www.facebook.com/cskamloup.qc.ca

***Rouyn-Noranda:* Centre d'Abitibi-Témiscamingue et Nord-du-Québec**
27, rue du Terminus ouest, Rouyn-Noranda, QC J9X 2P3
Tél: 819-763-3484; *Téléc:* 819-763-3480
archives.rouyn@banq.qc.ca

***Saguenay:* Centre d'archives du Sauguenay-Lac-Saint-Jean**
930, rue Jacques-Cartier est, C-103, Saguenay, QC G7H 7K9
Tél: 418-698-3516; *Téléc:* 418-698-3758
archives.saguenay@banq.qc.ca

***Saint-Hyacinthe:* Centre d'histoire de Saint-Hyacinthe**
650, rue Girouard est, Saint-Hyacinthe, QC J2S 2W2
Tél: 450-774-0203; *Téléc:* 450-250-8127
infos@chsth.com
www.chsth.com
Anne-Marie Charuest, Archiviste
Luc Cordeau, Archiviste

***Saint-Jean-sur-Richelieu:* Société d'histoire du Haut-Richelieu**
203, rue Jacques Cartier nord, Saint-Jean-sur-Richelieu, QC J3B 6Z4
Tél: 450-358-5220
shhr@qc.aira.com
www.genealogie.org/club/shhr
Mèdia social:
www.facebook.com/group.php?gid=199604623393992
Nicole Poulin, Responsable

***Saint-Joseph-de-Beauce:* Société du patrimoine des Beaucerons / Beauce Historical Society**
#400, 139, rue Sainte-Christine, Saint-Joseph-de-Beauce, QC G0S 2V0
Tel: 418-397-6379; *Fax:* 418-397-6379
spb@axion.ca
www.culture-quebec.qc.ca/patrimoine-beauce
Rolland Bouffard, Président
Daniel Carrier, Archiviste

***Saint-Jérome:* Commission scolaire de la Rivière-du-Nord**
995, rue Labelle, Saint-Jérome, QC J7Z 5N7
Tél: 450-438-3131
tremblayr@csrdn.qc.ca
www.csrdn.qc.ca
Rémi Tremblay, Secrétaire général

***Saint-Jérome:* La Compagnie de Jésus**
175, boul des Hauteurs, Saint-Jérome, QC J7Z 5E7
Tél: 450-438-3593; *Téléc:* 450-438-6617
Andre Gendron, Bibliothécaire
Martine Proulx, Responsable, services techniques

***Saint-Laurent:* Arrondissement de Saint-Laurent**
777, boul Marcel-Laurin, Saint-Laurent, QC H4M 2M7
Tel: 514-855-6000; *Fax:* 514-855-4121
chevrier.josee@ville.saint-laurent.qc.ca
Josée Chevrier, Coordonnatrice, Gestion de documents
chevrier.josee@ville.saint-laurent.qc.ca
Yves Drolet, Commis, gestion de documents
drolet.yves@ville.saint-laurent.gc.ca
514-855-6000 ext. 4073

***Saint-Laurent:* Soeurs de Sainte-Croix, Saint-Laurent**
905, rue Basile-moreau, Saint-Laurent, QC H4L 4A1
Tél: 514-747-1892
Suzanne Gratton, Archiviste

***Sainte-Agathe-des-Monts:* Commission scolaire des Laurentides**
13, rue Sainte-Antoine, Sainte-Agathe-des-Monts, QC J8C 2C3
Tél: 819-326-0333; *Téléc:* 819-326-2121
www.cslaurentides.qc.ca
Marie-Josée Lorion, Secrétaire générale/Directrice, communications
secretariat.general@cslaurentides.qc.ca
819-326-0333 ext. 2006
Michel Goyer, Technicien en documentation
goyerm@cslaurentides.qc.ca
819-326-0333 ext. 2032

***Sainte-Anne-de-Beaupré:* Pères rédemptoristes, Sainte-Anne-de Beaupré**
10018, av Royale, Sainte-Anne-de-Beaupré, QC G0A 3C0
Tél: 418-827-4629
info@redemptoristes.ca
www.redemptoristes.ca
Samuel Baillargeon, Archiviste

***Sept-Iles:* Centre de la Côte-Nord**
#190-2, 700, boul Laure, Sept-Iles, QC G4R 1Y1
Tél: 418-964-8434; *Téléc:* 418-964-8500

***Shawinigan:* Commission scolaire de l'Énergie**
2072, rue Gignac, Shawinigan, QC G9N 6V7
Tél: 819-539-6971; *Téléc:* 819-539-7797
Ligne sans frais: 888-711-0013
www.csenergie.qc.ca
Luce Marion, Bibliothécaire
lmarion@csenergie.qc.ca
Minique Champagne, Technicienne

***Sherbrooke:* Archevêché de Sherbrooke**
130, rue de la Cathédrale, Sherbrooke, QC J1H 4M1
Tél: 819-563-9934; *Téléc:* 819-562-0125
bibliotheque@diocesedesherbrooke.org
www.diosher.org
Huguette Lachance Pinard, Services des archives

***Sherbrooke:* Centre d'archives de l'Estrie**
#401, 225, rue Frontenac, Sherbrooke, QC J1H 1K1
Tél: 819-820-3010; *Téléc:* 819-820-3146
archives.sherbrooke@banq.qc.ca

***Sherbrooke:* Commission scolaire de la Région-de-Sherbrooke**
2955, boul de l'Université, Sherbrooke, QC J1K 2Y3
Tél: 819-822-5540; *Téléc:* 819-822-5530
www.csrs.qc.ca
Mèdia social: twitter.com/cssherbrooke

Diane Boivin, Analyste en gestion documentaire
819-843-9266

***Sherbrooke:* Département des archives**
275, rue Dufferin, Sherbrooke, QC J1H 4M5
Tél: 819-821-5406; *Téléc:* 819-821-5417
info@histoiresherbrooke.com
www.histoiresherbrooke.com/

***Sherbrooke:* Diocese of Quebec, Archives**
Library, Bishop's University, 2600, rue College, Sherbrooke, QC J1M 0C8
Tel: 819-822-9600; *Fax:* 819-822-9644
www.ubishops.ca/library_info/lib-old.htm

***Sherbrooke:* Montréal & Ottawa Conference, Archives**
c/o Centre régional de l'Estrie, Archives nationales du Québec, #401, 225, rue Frontenac, Sherbrooke, QC J1H 1K1
Tel: 819-820-3010; *Fax:* 819-820-3146
anq.sherbrooke@banq.qc.ca
www.montrealandottawaconference.ca

***Sherbrooke:* Société d'histoire de Sherbrooke**
275, rue Dufferin, Sherbrooke, QC J1H 4M5
Tél: 819-821-5406; *Téléc:* 819-821-5417
info@histoiresherbrooke.com
www.histoiresherbrooke.com/
Hélène Liard, Archiviste
helene.liard@histoiresherbrooke.com

***Sorel-Tracy:* Société historique Pierre-de-Saurel inc**
6A, rue Saint-Pierre, Sorel-Tracy, QC J3P 3S2
Tél: 450-780-5739; *Téléc:* 450-780-5743
histoire.archives@shps.qc.ca
www.soreltracyregion.net
Luc Poirier, Président du Conseil d'Administration
president@shp.qc.ca

***Stanbridge East:* Missisquoi Historical Society**
Cornell Bldg., Missisquoi Museum, 2, rue River, Stanbridge East, QC J0J 2H0
Tel: 450-248-3153; *Fax:* 450-248-0420
info@missisquoimuseum.ca
www.museemissisquoi.ca
Judy Antle, Archivist
jantle@museemissisquoi.ca
450-248-3153
Heather Darch, Curator
hdarch@museemissisquoi.ca
450-248-3153

***Stanstead:* Stanstead Historical Society/ Société historique de Stanstead**
535, rue Dufferin, Stanstead, QC J0B 3E0
Tel: 819-876-7322; *Fax:* 819-876-7936
archives@colbycurtis.ca
www.colbycurtis.ca/eng/archives.html

***Thetford Mines:* Société des archives historiques de la région de l'Amiante**
671, boul Frontenac ouest, Thetford Mines, QC G6G 1N1
Tél: 418-338-8591; *Téléc:* 418-338-3498
archives@cegepth.qc.ca
www.sahra.qc.ca
Stéphane Hamann, Directeur - Archiviste
Marie-Josée Poirier, Technicienne en documentation

***Trois-Rivières:* Centre d'Archives de la Mauricie et Centre-du-Québec**
#208, 225, rue des Forges, Trois-Rivières, QC G9A 2G7
Tél: 819-371-6015; *Téléc:* 819-371-6158
archives.trois-rivieres@banq.qc.ca

***Trois-Rivières:* Evêché de Trois-Rivières**
362, Bonaventure, Trois-Rivières, QC G9A 2B3
Tél: 819-374-1432; *Téléc:* 819-379-2496
archives@evechetr.org
diocese-trois-rivieres.org
Denise Maltais, Archiviste diocésaine
819-379-1432 ext. 2308

***Trois-Rivières:* Service des archives et des collections**
3351, boul des Forges, Trois-Rivières, QC G8Z 1T7
Tél: 819-376-5030
mario.audet@uqtr.ca

***Trois-Rivières:* Soeurs Ursulines, Trois-Rivières**
784, rue des Ursulines, Trois-Rivières, QC G9A 5B5
Tel: 819-375-6039; *Fax:* 819-691-0490
urstr.archives@cgocable.ca
www.ursulines-uc.com/musees.php#a_tr
Claude Jutras, Directeur du service des archives

***Trois-Rivières:* Ville de Trois-Rivières**
1325 place de l'Hôtel-de-Ville, Trois-Rivières, QC G9A 5H3
Tél: 819-372-4647; *Téléc:* 819-372-4648
archives@v3r.net
www.laville.v3r.net

***Val-d'Or:* Société d'histoire et de généalogie de Val-d'Or**
600, 7e rue, Val-d'Or, QC J9P 3P3
Tél: 819-825-6352; *Téléc:* 819-825-3062
Louiselle Alain, Présidente

***Victoriaville:* Commission scolaire des Bois-Francs**
40, boul Bois-Francs, Victoriaville, QC G6P 6S5
Tél: 819-758-6453; *Téléc:* 819-758-5827
mprovencher@csbf.qc.ca
www.csbf.qc.ca
Michael Provencher, Secrétariat général
lgingras@csbf.qc.ca
819-758-6453 ext. 22010

***Westmount:* Avataq Cultural Institute**
#360, 4150, rue Ste-Catherine ouest, Westmount, QC H3Z 2Y5
Tel: 514-989-9031; *Fax:* 514-989-8789
Toll-Free: 800-361-5029
avataq@avataq.qc.ca
www.avataq.qc.ca
Christelle Cuillert, Archivist
christelle@avataq.qc.ca
514-989-9031 ext. 241
Nancyanne Grey, Contact
514-989-9031 ext. 291

Saskatchewan

Regional Systems

Chinook Regional Library
1240 Chaplin St. West, Swift Current, SK S9H 0G8
Tel: 306-773-3186; *Fax:* 306-773-0434
chinook@chinook.lib.sk.ca
www.chinooklibrary.ca/chinook.htm
Michael J. Keaschuk, Director
Myra Leyshon, Assistant Director

Lakeland Library Region (Saskatchewan)
1302 - 100th St., North Battleford, SK S9A 0V8
Tel: 306-445-6108; *Fax:* 306-445-5717
info@lakeland.lib.sk.ca
www.lakeland.lib.sk.ca
Social Media: www.facebook.com/pages/Lakeland-Library-Region/144591632312109
Annmarie Hillson, Regional Librarian

Palliser Regional Library
366 Coteau St. West, Moose Jaw, SK S6H 5C9
Tel: 306-693-3669; *Fax:* 306-692-5657
webmaster@palliser.lib.sk.ca
www.palliserlibrary.ca
Jan Smith, Director & Systems Librarian
Arwen Rudolph, Rural Branch Supervisor
Wanda Burton, Office Manager
Melissa Silzer-Frank, Contact, Interlibrary Loan & Technical Support

Parkland Regional Library
PO Box 5049, Yorkton, SK S3N 3Z4
Tel: 306-783-7022; *Fax:* 306-782-2844
pstroud@parkland.lib.sk.ca
www.parkland.lib.sk.ca
Deirdre Crichton, Regional Library Director
dcrichton@parkland.lib.sk.ca
S. Temoin, Assistant Regional Librarian
stemoin@parkland.lib.sk.ca
L. Corbett, Business Manager
office@parkland.lib.sk.ca
M. Patrick, Systems/ Database Administrator
mpatrick@parkland.lib.sk.ca
P. Anderson, Technician, Acquisitions & Bibliographic Control
panderso@parkland.lib.sk.ca
B. Eckhart, Technician, Interlibrary Loan
beckhart@parkland.lib.sk.ca
P. Stroud, Contact, Information Services
pstroud@parkland.lib.sk.ca

Southeast Regional Library
49 Bison Ave., Weyburn, SK S4H 0H9
Tel: 306-848-3100; *Fax:* 306-842-2665
library.srl@southeast.lib.sk.ca
www.southeast.lib.sk.ca
Allan Johnson, CEO & Library Director
allan@southeast.lib.sk.ca

Wapiti Regional Library
145 - 12th St. East, Prince Albert, SK S6V 1B7
Tel: 306-764-0712; *Fax:* 306-922-1516
wapiti@panet.pa.sk.ca
www.panet.pa.sk.ca
Kevin Phillip, Acting Regional Director

Wheatland Regional Library
806 Duchess St., Saskatoon, SK S7K 0R3
Tel: 306-652-5077; *Fax:* 306-931-7611
Toll-Free: 866-652-5077
admin@wheatland.sk.ca
www.wheatland.sk.ca
Rena Bartsch, Director
rbartsch@wheatland.sk.ca
306-652-4182
Joanne Hardy, Administrative Services Manager
jhardy@wheatland.sk.ca
306-652-5077
Kim Hebig, Assistant Director & Manager, Central Branch
khebig@wheatland.sk.ca
306-652-4183
Saache Heinrich, Youth Services Manager
sheinrich@wheatland.sk.ca
306-652-4184

Public Libraries

***Aberdeen:* Aberdeen Library**
201 Thompson St., Aberdeen, SK S0K 0A0
Tel: 306-253-4349
aberdeen.library@wheatland.sk.ca
www.wheatland.sk.ca/branches_aberdeen.html
Laura Favreau , Librarian

***Admiral:* Admiral Branch Library**
PO Box 152, Admiral, SK S0N 0B0
Tel: 306-297-4040
www.chinooklibrary.ca/admiral.htm
Shannon Wallis, Librarian

***Air Ronge:* Senator Myles Venne School Public Library**
Box 268, Air Ronge, SK S0J 3G0
Tel: 306-425-2478; *Fax:* 306-425-2815
Edna Mirasty, Librarian
smvs09@sk.sympatico.ca
306-425-2478
Betsy Dorion, Library Assistant

***Alameda:* Alameda Branch Library**
200 - 5th St., Alameda, SK S0C 0A0
Tel: 306-489-2066
alameda@southeast.lib.sk.ca
www.southeast.lib.sk.ca/home.html
Dee Anne Schiestel, Chair
Diane Miller, Librarian

***Allan:* Allan Library**
216 Main St., Allan, SK S0K 0C0
Tel: 306-257-4222
allan.library@wheatland.sk.ca
www.wheatland.sk.ca
Sandra Wilson, Library Contact

***Arcola:* Arcola Branch Library**
127 Main St., Arcola, SK S0C 0G0
Tel: 306-455-2321
arcola@southeast.lib.sk.ca
hip.southeast.lib.sk.ca/Southeast/Docs/arcola
Shauna Forester, Librarian

***Assiniboia:* Assiniboia & District Public Library**
201 - 3rd Ave. West, Assiniboia, SK S0H 0B0
Tel: 306-642-3631; *Fax:* 306-642-5622
assiniboia@palliser.lib.sk.ca
www.palliserlibrary.ca
Carol Munro, Branch Librarian

***Avonlea:* Avonlea Branch Library**
201 Main St. West, Avonlea, SK S0H 0C0
Tel: 306-868-2076; *Fax:* 306-868-2221
avonlea@palliser.lib.sk.ca
www.palliserlibrary.ca
Sheryl Ursu, Librarian
Erica Miller, Branch Librarian

Balgonie: **Balgonie Branch Library**
129 Railway St., Balgonie, SK S0G 0E0
Tel: 306-771-2332
balgonie@southeast.lib.sk.ca
www.southeast.lib.sk.ca
Donna Janke, Librarian

Battleford: **Battleford Branch Library**
201 - 22nd St., Battleford, SK S0M 0E0
Tel: 306-937-2646; *Fax:* 306-937-6631
battleford.lib@lakeland.lib.sk.ca
www.lakeland.lib.sk.ca
Rita Kuntz, Branch Librarian

Beauval: **Beauval Public Library**
PO Bag 9000, Beauval, SK S0M 0G0
Tel: 306-288-2022; *Fax:* 306-288-2202
sb@pnls.lib.sk.ca
Carol Edguist, Librarian

Beechy: **Beechy Library**
PO Box 154, Beechy, SK S0L 0C0
Tel: 306-859-2032
beechy.library@wheatland.sk.ca
www.beechysask.ca/library.htm
Lois Meaden, Branch Library Staff Contact

Bengough: **Bengough Branch Library**
301 Main St., Bengough, SK S0C 0K0
Tel: 306-268-2022
bengough@southeast.lib.sk.ca
www.southeast.lib.sk.ca/branches
Fay Adam, Branch Librarian

Bethune: **Bethune Branch Library**
Community Hall, 524 East St., Bethune, SK S0G 0H0
Tel: 306-638-3046; *Fax:* 306-638-3102
bethune@palliser.lib.sk.ca
www.palliserlibrary.ca
Robbie Curtis, Librarian

Bienfait: **Bienfait Branch Library**
414 Main St., Bienfait, SK S0C 0M0
Tel: 306-388-2995; *Fax:* 306-388-2223
bienfait@southeast.lib.sk.ca
www.southeast.lib.sk.ca
Bonnie Gibson, Librarian

Big River: **Dore Lake Book Deposit**
c/o Hamlet of Dore Lake, Big River, SK S0J 0E0
Tel: 306-832-4528
northern.dore@sasktel.net

Biggar: **Biggar Lionel A. Jones Library**
202 - 3rd Ave. West, Biggar, SK S0K 0M0
Tel: 306-948-3911
biggar.library@wheatland.sk.ca
Darlene Stainbrook, Community Librarian
Ruth Hall, Assistant Community Librarian

Borden: **Borden Library**
303 - 1st Ave., Borden, SK S0K 0N0
Tel: 306-997-2220
borden.lib@lakeland.lib.sk.ca
Cyndy Fairbrother, Librarian
Diane Sylvester, Librarian

Briercrest: **Briercrest Branch Library**
Community Center, Main St., Briercrest, SK S0H 0K0
Tel: 306-799-2137
briercrest@palliser.lib.sk.ca
www.palliserlibrary.ca
Eileen Jeffery, Chair
Lisa Nestman, Branch Librarian

Broadview: **Broadview Branch Library**
515 Main St., Broadview, SK S0G 0K0
Tel: 306-696-2414
broadview@southeast.lib.sk.ca
hip.southeast.lib.sk.ca/Southeast/Docs/broadview.html
Pat Gerke, Chair
Christine Judy, Branch Librarian
Donna Driedger, Assistant Librarian

Broadview: **Kahkewistahaw First Nation**
PO Box 609, Broadview, SK S0G 0K0
Tel: 306-696-3291; *Fax:* 306-696-3201
Toll-Free: 888-691-0188
education@kahkewistahaw.com
www.kahkewistahaw.com
Iris Taypotat, Resource Coordinator

Bruno: **Bruno Branch Library**
522 Main St., Bruno, SK S0K 0S0
Tel: 306-369-2353
bruno.library@wheatland.sk.ca
www.wheatland.sk.ca/branches_bruno.html

Buffalo Narrows: **Wisewood Public Library**
PO Box 309, Buffalo Narrows, SK S0M 0J0
Tel: 306-235-4240; *Fax:* 306-235-4452
wisewoodlibrary@nlsd113.net
wisewoodpubliclibrary.blogspot.ca
Darlene Petit, School Librarian
Loni McCuaig, Public Librarian
sbn@pnls.lib.sk.ca
306-235-4520
Melissa Laprise, Part-Time Librarian

Carlyle: **Carlyle Branch Library**
119 Souris Ave. West, Carlyle, SK S0C 0R0
Tel: 306-453-6120
carlyle@southeast.lib.sk.ca
hip.southeast.lib.sk.ca/Southeast/Docs/carlyle.html
Lauren Hume, Chair
306-453-2824
Rita Kyle, Librarian

Carnduff: **Carnduff Branch Library**
Carnduff Education Complex, 506 Anderson Rd., Carnduff, SK S0C 0S0
Tel: 306-482-3255
carnduff@southeast.lib.sk.ca
Elizabeth Henger, Chair
306-482-3270
Marjorie Johnson, Librarian
Darlene Davis, School Librarian
Agnes Kimler, School Librarian

Cochin: **Cochin Book Depository**
Hwy. 4, PO Box 190, Cochin, SK S0M 0L0
Tel: 306-386-1148; *Fax:* 306-386-2305
cochin.lib@lakeland.lib.sk.ca
Judy Smith, Contact

Coleville: **Coleville Library**
R.M. Bldg., PO Box 45, Coleville, SK S0L 0K0
Tel: 306-965-2551
coleville.library@wheatland.sk.ca
www.wheatland.sk.ca/branches_coleville
Wendy Bahm, Branch Library Staff Contact

Colonsay: **Colonsay Library**
RM Bldg., PO Box 172, Colonsay, SK S0K 0Z0
Tel: 306-255-2232
colonsay.library@wheatland.sk.ca
www.wheatland.sk.ca/branches_colonsay.html

Conquest: **Conquest Branch Library**
Conquest Community Centre, PO Box 130, Conquest, SK S0L 0L0
Tel: 306-856-4555
conquest.library@wheatland.sk.ca
www.wheatland.sk.ca/branches_conquest.html

Coronach: **Coronach Branch Library**
111A Center St., Coronach, SK S0H 0Z0
Tel: 306-267-3260
coronach@palliser.lib.sk.ca
www.palliserlibrary.ca
Social Media: www.facebook.com/50610228952
Janel Korbo, Chair
Marlene McBurney, Branch Librarian
Giselle Wilson, Assistant Librarian

Craik: **Craik Branch Library**
611 - 1st Ave., PO Box 339, Craik, SK S0G 0V0
Tel: 306-734-2388
craik@palliser.lib.sk.ca
www.palliserlibrary.ca
Crystal Stinson, Chair
Jo McAlpine, Branch Librarian

Cut Knife: **Cut Knife Community Branch Library**
115 Broad St., PO Box 595, Cut Knife, SK S0M 0N0
Tel: 306-398-2342
cutknife.lib@lakeland.lib.sk.ca
www.lakeland.lib.sk.ca

Dalmeny: **Dalmeny Branch Library**
301 Railway Ave., PO Box 850, Dalmeny, SK S0K 1E0
Tel: 306-254-2119
dalmeny.library@wheatland.sk.ca
www.wheatland.sk.ca
Dana Perkins, Librarian

Davidson: **Davidson Branch Library**
314 Washington Ave., PO Box 754, Davidson, SK S0G 1A0
Tel: 306-567-2022; *Fax:* 306-567-2081
davidson@palliser.lib.sk.ca
www.palliserlibrary.ca
Dianne Murfitt, Chair
September Brooke, Librarian
Debbie Shearwood, Assistant

Delisle: **Delisle Library**
201 - 1st St. West, Delisle, SK S0L 0P0
Tel: 306-493-8288
delisle.library@wheatland.sk.ca
www.wheatland.sk.ca/branches_delisle.html

Denzil: **Denzil Branch Library**
Brooks Ave., PO Box 188, Denzil, SK S0L 0S0
Tel: 306-358-2118; *Fax:* 306-358-4828
denzil.lib@lakeland.lib.sk.ca
www.lakeland.lib.sk.ca
Carrie McKee, Librarian

Dinsmore: **Dinsmore Branch Library**
Town Office, 100 Main St., PO Box 369, Dinsmore, SK S0L 0T0
Tel: 306-846-2011
dinsmore.library@wheatland.sk.ca
www.wheatland.sk.ca/branches_dinsmore.html
Mary McBain, Community Librarian
Carol Greuel, Assistant Librarian
Mary Jones, Assistant Librarian

Dodsland: **Dodsland Branch Library**
135 - 2nd Ave., PO Box 100, Dodsland, SK S0L 0V0
Tel: 306-356-2180
dodsland.library@sasktel.net
www.wheatland.sk.ca
Coralie DeBusschere, Librarian

Drake: **Drake Library**
Francis St., Drake, SK S0K 1H0
Tel: 306-363-2101
drake.library@wheatland.sk.ca
www.wheatland.sk.ca/branches_drake.html

Dundurn: **Dundurn Branch Library**
PO Box 626, Dundurn, SK S0K 1K0
Tel: 306-492-2366
dundurn.library@wheatland.sk.ca
www.wheatland.sk.ca/branches_dundurn.html
Candace Myers, Branch Head

Eatonia: **Eatonia Branch Library**
PO Box 100, Eatonia, SK S0L 0Y0
Tel: 306-967-2224
eatonia.library@wheatland.sk.ca
www.townofeatonia.com/services/library
Sandy Guidinger, Chair
Debbie Tweten, Branch Library Staff Member
Garnet Nunweiler, Library Assistant
Melanie Rudy, Library Assistant

Edam: **Edam Library**
1000 Main St., Edam, SK S0M 0V0
Tel: 306-397-2223; *Fax:* 306-397-2626
edam.lib@lakeland.lib.sk.ca
Trudy McMurphy, Administrator, Village of Edam
edamvill@sasktel.net
306-397-2223

Elbow: **Elbow Branch Library**
402 Minto St., Elbow, SK S0H 1J0
Tel: 306-854-2220
elbow@palliser.lib.sk.ca
www.palliserlibrary.ca
Janice Scrimbitt, Branch Librarian

Elrose: **Elrose Branch Library**
Town Office, PO Box 185, Elrose, SK S0L 0Z0
Tel: 306-378-2808
elrose.library@wheatland.sk.ca
www.wheatland.sk.ca/branches_elrose.html

Estevan: **Estevan Public Library**
701 Souris Ave. North, Estevan, SK S4A 2T1
Tel: 306-636-1620; *Fax:* 306-634-5830
estevan@southeast.lib.sk.ca
estevanlibrary.weebly.com
Social Media: twitter.com/#!/estevanlibrary;
www.facebook.com/EstevanPublicLibraryBranch
Kate-Lee Donohoe, Branch Manager
kdonohoe@southeast.lib.sk.ca

***Eston:* Eston Branch Library**
218 Main St., Eston, SK S0L 1A0
Tel: 306-962-3513
eston.library@wheatland.sk.ca
www.wheatland.sk.ca

***Fillmore:* Fillmore Branch Library**
51 Main St., Fillmore, SK S0G 1N0
Tel: 306-722-3369
fillmore@southeast.lib.sk.ca
Tracey Jones, Librarian
Jeanette Shotter, Librarian

***Fort Qu'appelle:* Fort Qu'Appelle Branch Library**
140 Company Ave. South, Fort Qu'appelle, SK S0G 1S0
Tel: 306-332-6411
fort.quappelle@southeast.lib.sk.ca
www.fortquappelle.com/library
Holly Smith, Librarian
306-332-6411

***Fort Qu'appelle:* Standing Buffalo Branch Library**
PO Box 248, Fort Qu'appelle, SK S0G 1S0
Tel: 306-332-4414
Eleice Bear, Librarian

***Gainsborough:* Gainsborough Branch Library**
401 Railway, Gainsborough, SK S0C 0Z0
Tel: 306-685-2229
gainsborough@southeast.lib.sk.ca
Marjorie Johnson, Librarian

***Glaslyn:* Glaslyn Library**
182 Main St., Glaslyn, SK S0M 0Y0
Tel: 306-342-4748; *Fax:* 306-342-4748
glaslyn.lib@lakeland.lib.sk.ca
www.lakeland.lib.sk.ca
Jody Seifert, Librarian

***Glenavon:* Glenavon Branch Library**
311 Railway Ave., Glenavon, SK S0G 1Y0
Tel: 306-429-2180
glenavon@southeast.lib.sk.ca
hip.southeast.lib.sk.ca/Southeast/Docs/glenavon.html
Heather Wozniak, Librarian

***Goodsoil:* Goodsoil Library**
301 Main St. North, Goodsoil, SK S0M 1A0
Tel: 306-238-2155; *Fax:* 306-238-2155
goodsoil.lib@lakeland.lib.sk.ca
www.lakeland.lib.sk.ca
Jolynn Berlinger, Librarian
306-238-2155

***Grenfell:* Grenfell Branch Library**
710 Desmond Ave., Grenfell, SK S0G 2B0
Tel: 306-697-2455
grenfell@southeast.lib.sk.ca
hip.southeast.lib.sk.ca/Southeast/Docs/grenfell
Ann Neuls, Librarian
Eunice Wolfe, Library Assistant

***Hafford:* Hafford Library**
17 Main St., Hafford, SK S0J 1A0
Tel: 306-549-2373; *Fax:* 306-549-2333
haffordlibrary@hotmail.com
Carol Herman, Librarian

***Hague:* Hague Library**
210 Railway St., Hague, SK S0K 1X0
Tel: 306-225-4326
hague.library@wheatland.sk.ca
www.wheatland.sk.ca/branches_hague.html
Lynn Williamson, Branch Librarian
hague.library@sasktel.net

***Hanley:* Hanley Branch Library**
112A Lincoln St., Hanley, SK S0G 2E0
Tel: 306-544-2546
hanley.library@wheatland.sk.ca
www.wheatland.sk.ca/branches_hanley
Ann Rogers, Branch Librarian

***Herschel:* Stranraer Commemmorative Library**
Veteran Ave., Herschel, SK S0L 1L0
Tel: 306-377-2144; *Fax:* 306-377-2023
stranraer.library@wheatland.sk.ca
Charlene Bradley, Branch Library Staff

***Holdfast:* Holdfast Branch Library**
125 Roberts Street, Holdfast, SK S0G 2H0
Tel: 306-488-2000
holdfast@palliser.lib.sk.ca
www.palliserlibrary.ca/holdfast/holdfast.htm
Tammy Bilsky, Librarian

***Ile-a-la-Crosse:* Rossignol Elementary Community School**
Ile-a-la-Crosse, SK S0M 1C0
Tel: 306-833-2010; *Fax:* 306-833-2322
lborgerson@icsd.ca
Valerie Gardiner, School Librarian
vgardiner@icsd.ca
306-833-2010

***Imperial:* Imperial Branch Library**
Town Office, Main St., 310 Royal St., Imperial, SK S0G 2J0
Tel: 306-963-2272
imperial@palliser.lib.sk.ca
www.palliserlibrary.ca/imperial/imperial.htm
Donalda MacLellan, Branch Librarian

***Indian Head:* Indian Head Branch Library**
419 Grand Ave., Indian Head, SK S0G 2K0
Tel: 306-695-3922
indian.head@southeast.lib.sk.ca
www.southeast.lib.sk.ca

***Island Lake:* Island Lake Library**
Island Lake First Nations School, Island Lake, SK S0M 3G0
Tel: 306-837-4868; *Fax:* 306-837-4558
sli.ill@lakeland.lib.sk.ca

***Kenaston:* Kenaston Library**
PO Box 309, Kenaston, SK S0G 2N0
Tel: 306-252-2130
kenaston.library@wheatland.sk.ca
www.wheatland.sk.ca/branches_kenaston.html
Faye McVeigh, Branch Librarian
Vicki Gowler, Library Assistant

***Kennedy:* Kennedy Branch Library**
235 Scott St., Kennedy, SK S0G 2R0
Tel: 306-538-2020
kennedy@southeast.lib.sk.ca
www.southeast.lib.sk.ca
Amy Hewson, Librarian

***Kerrobert:* Kerrobert Library**
Nain St. South, Kerrobert, SK S0L 1R0
Tel: 306-834-5211; *Fax:* 306-834-2633
kerrobert.library@wheatland.sk.ca

***Kindersley:* Kindersley Library**
104 Princess St., Kindersley, SK S0L 1S2
Tel: 306-463-4141
kindersley.library@wheatland.sk.ca
www.kindersley.ca
Marilyn Shea, Librarian

***Kipling:* Kipling Branch Library**
207 - 6th Ave., Kipling, SK S0G 2S0
Tel: 306-736-2911
kipling@southeast.lib.sk.ca
www.www.southeast.lib.sk.ca
Sharon Ovans, Board Chair
Sheila Robertson, Librarian

***Kyle:* Kyle Public Library**
116 Centre St., Kyle, SK S0L 1T0
Tel: 306-375-2566
kyle.library@wheatland.sk.ca
www.wheatland.sk.ca/branches_kyle.html
Elva Akister, Community Librarian
Jan Rein, Assistant

***La Ronge:* Pahkisimon Nuyeáh Library System**
118 Avro Pl., La Ronge, SK S0J 1L0
Tel: 306-425-4525; *Fax:* 306-425-4572
Toll-Free: 866-396-8818
pnlsoffice@pnls.lib.sk.ca
www.pnls.lib.sk.ca
Audrey Mark, Director
ae.mark@ pnls.lib.sk.ca
Jocelyn Provost, Library Coordinator
jprovost@ pnls.lib.sk.ca
Harriet Roy, Assistant Director
hroy@pnls.lib.sk.ca

***La Ronge:* La Ronge Public Library**
PO Box 5680, La Ronge, SK S0J 1L0
Tel: 306-425-2160; *Fax:* 306-425-3883
sla@pnls.lib.sk.ca
www.pnls.lib.sk.ca/laronge/
Rosemary Loeffler, Library Administrator
r.loeffler.sla@pnls.lib.sk.ca
Jocelyn Mark, Contact, Interlibrary Loans
jmark@pnls.lib.sk.ca

***Lake Alma:* Lake Alma Branch Library**
Hwy. 18, Lake Alma, SK S0C 1M0
Tel: 306-447-2061; *Fax:* 306-447-2061
lake.alma@southeast.lib.sk.ca
www.southeast.lib.sk.ca
Bernice Bloor, Librarian

***Lampman:* Lampman Branch Library**
302 Main St., Lampman, SK S0C 1N0
Tel: 306-487-2202
lampman@southeast.lib.sk.ca
www.southeast.lib.sk.ca
Martha Engel, Librarian

***Landis:* Landis Library**
100 Princess St., Landis, SK S0K 2K0
Tel: 306-658-2177
landis.library@wheatland.sk.ca
www.wheatland.sk.ca/branches_landis.html
Vera Halter, Branch Librarian

***Langham:* Langham Library**
PO Box 697, Langham, SK S0K 2L0
Tel: 306-283-4362
langham.library@wheatland.sk.ca
www.wheatland.sk.ca/branches_langham.html
Dean Buhr, Community Librarian
Pat C. Wood, Chair

***Lanigan:* Lanigan Library**
PO Box 70, Lanigan, SK S0K 2M0
Tel: 306-365-2472
lanigan.library@wheatland.sk.ca
www.wheatland.sk.ca/branches_lanigan.html
Fran Nugent, Branch Library Staff Contact
Harvey Nugent, Branch Assistant

***Lashburn:* Lashburn Branch Library**
95 Main St., Lashburn, SK S0M 1H0
Tel: 306-285-4144
lashburn.lib@lakeland.lib.sk.ca
www.lakeland.lib.sk.ca

***Livelong:* Livelong Branch Library**
PO Box 161, Livelong, SK S0M 1J0
Tel: 306-845-3395
livelong.lib@lakeland.lib.sk.ca
Inga Sample, Librarian

***Loon Lake:* Loon Lake Branch Library**
PO Box 216, Loon Lake, SK S0M 1L0
Tel: 306-837-2186
loonlake.lib@lakeland.lib.sk.ca
www.lakeland.lib.sk.ca
Gwen Lindstrom, Librarian
loonlake.lib@lakeland.lib.sk.ca

***Loreburn:* Loreburn Branch Library**
528 Main St., Loreburn, SK S0H 2S0
Tel: 306-644-2026
loreburn@palliser.lib.sk.ca
www.palliserlibrary.ca/loreburn/loreburn.htm
Sue Ann Abbott, Branch Librarian

***Lucky Lake:* Lucky Lake Library**
101 - 1st Ave. South, Lucky Lake, SK S0L 1Z0
Tel: 306-858-2246
luckylake.library@wheatland.sk.ca
www.wheatlandlibrary.sk.ca
Elaine Ylioja, Community Librarian
Caroline Duhaime, Assistant Community Librarian

***Lumsden:* Lumsden Branch Library**
20 - 3rd Ave., Lumsden, SK S0G 3C0
Tel: 306-731-1431
lumsden@southeast.lib.sk.ca
www.lumsden.ca/
Sheila Felix, Librarian

***Luseland:* Luseland Library**
510 Grand Ave., Luseland, SK S0L 2A0
Tel: 306-372-4808
luseland.library@wheatland.sk.ca
www.wheatland.sk.ca
Diane Hurford, Branch Library Staff Contact
Ellen-May Anthony, Chair

***Macklin:* Macklin Branch Library**
5001 Press Ave., Macklin, SK S0L 2C0
Tel: 306-753-2933; *Fax:* 306-753-3234
macklin.lib@lakeland.lib.sk.ca
www.lakeland.lib.sk.ca
Colleen Allen, Librarian

Maidstone: **Maidstone Branch Library**
#102B, 108 - 1st Ave. West, Maidstone, SK S0M 1M0
Tel: 306-893-4153; *Fax:* 306-893-4153
maidstone.lib@lakeland.lib.sk.ca
www.lakeland.lib.sk.ca

Makwa: **Makwa Branch Library**
Box 10, General Delivery, Makwa, SK S0M 1N0
Tel: 306-236-3995
makwa.lib@lakeland.lib.sk.ca
Michelle Boehler, Branch Librarian
306-236-3995

Manor: **Manor Library**
23 Main St., Manor, SK S0C 1R0
Tel: 306-448-2266
manor@southeast.lib.sk.ca
www.southeast.lib.sk.ca
Tracy Brimmer, Board Chair
306-448-2028
Rita Kyle, Librarian
Helen Hortness, Library Assistant

Marsden: **Marsden Branch Library**
#104 Centre St., Marsden, SK S0M 1P0
Tel: 306-826-5666; *Fax:* 306-826-5666
marsden.lib@lakeland.lib.sk.ca
www.lakeland.lib.sk.ca
Denise Polkinghorne, Librarian

Marshall: **Marshall Branch Library**
13 Main St., Marshall, SK S0M 1R0
Tel: 306-387-6155; *Fax:* 306-387-6555
marshall.lib@lakeland.lib.sk.ca
Holly Gauthier, Librarian

Martensville: **Martensville Library**
PO Box 1180, Martensville, SK S0K 2T0
Tel: 306-956-7311
martensville.library@wheatland.sk.ca
www.wheatland.sk.ca/branches_martensville.html
Marla Skomar, Head Librarian
Heather Braun, Contact
Stacey Brooman, Contact

Maryfield: **Maryfield Branch Library**
21 Barrows St., Maryfield, SK S0G 3K0
Tel: 306-646-2148
maryfield@southeast.lib.sk.ca
www.southeast.lib.sk.ca
Doris Erickson, Librarian
Doreen Jurkovic, Librarian

Mayfair: **Mayfair Branch Library**
Mayfair Central School, Mayfair, SK S0M 1S0
Tel: 306-246-4465
mayfair.lib@lakeland.lib.sk.ca
Janet Cherwinski, Librarian

Maymont: **Maymont Library**
PO Box 102, Maymont, SK S0M 1T0
Tel: 306-389-2006
maymont.lib@lakeland.lib.sk.ca
www.lakeland.lib.sk.ca
Cassandra Mireau, Regional Librarian
cmireau@lakeland.lib.sk.ca
306-445-6108 ext. 226

Meadow Lake: **Meadow Lake Library**
320 Centre St., PO Box 9000, Meadow Lake, SK S9X 1V8
Tel: 306-236-5396; *Fax:* 306-236-6282
meadowlake.lib@lakeland.lib.sk.ca
www.lakeland.lib.sk.ca
Tara Million, Librarian

Meath Park: **Meath Park Branch Library**
PO Box 122, Meath Park, SK S0J 1T0
Tel: 306-929-2133; *Fax:* 306-929-2401
Kathryn Hughes, Branch Librarian

Medstead: **Medstead Branch Library**
209 Second Ave., Medstead, SK S0M 1W0
Tel: 306-342-4609
medstead.lib@lakeland.lib.sk.ca
www.lakeland.lib.sk.ca
Nissa Shields, Librarian

Meota: **Meota Library**
PO Box 214, Meota, SK S0M 1X0
Tel: 306-892-2004
meota.lib@lakeland.lib.sk.ca
Deborah Pearce, Librarian
Juliette Tebay, Substitute Librarian

Mervin: **Mervin Branch Library**
11 Main St., Mervin, SK S0M 1Y0
Tel: 306-845-2784; *Fax:* 306-845-3563
Dawn Simkins, Librarian
306-845-2784

Meskanaw: **Meskanaw Paperback Deposit**
General Delivery, Meskanaw, SK S0K 2W0
Tel: 306-864-3730

Midale: **Midale Branch Library**
PO Box 185, Midale, SK S0C 1S0
Tel: 306-458-2263
midale@southeast.lib.sk.ca
Lydia Duncan, Librarian

Milden: **Milden Library**
PO Box 7, Milden, SK S0L 2L0
Tel: 306-935-4600
milden.library@wheatland.sk.ca
www.wheatland.sk.ca/branches_milden.html
Sandra Frey, Library Assistant

Milestone: **Milestone Library**
112 Main St., Milestone, SK S0G 3L0
Tel: 306-436-2112
milestone@southeast.lib.sk.ca
Diana Cook, Librarian

Montmartre: **Montmartre Regional Library**
136 Central, Montmartre, SK S0G 3M0
Tel: 306-424-2029
montmartre@southeast.lib.sk.ca
Lillian Ripplinger, Librarian

Montreal Lake: **Montreal Lake Community Library**
PO Box 150, Montreal Lake, SK S0J 1Y0
Tel: 306-663-5602; *Fax:* 306-663-5652
sml@pnls.lib.sk.ca
Blanche Bird, Librarian

Moose Jaw: **Moose Jaw Public Library**
461 Langdon Cres., Moose Jaw, SK S6H 0X6
Tel: 306-692-2787; *Fax:* 306-692-3368
reference.smj@sasktel.net
www.moosejawlibrary.ca
Karon Selzer, Head Librarian
Greg Salmer, Asst. Head Librarian
gsalmer@moosejawlibrary.ca
Laura Shtern, Children's Librarian
childrens.smj@sasktel.net

Moosomin: **Moosomin Branch Library**
701 Main St., Moosomin, SK S0G 3N0
Tel: 306-435-2107
moosomin@southeast.lib.sk.ca
Christie McGonigal, Librarian

Mortlach: **Mortlach Branch Library**
Main St., Mortlach, SK S0H 3E0
Tel: 306-355-2202
mortlach@palliser.lib.sk.ca
www.palliserlibrary.ca
Linda Locke, Branch Librarian

Mossbank: **Mossbank Branch Library**
Box 422, 310 Main St., Mossbank, SK S0H 3G0
Tel: 306-354-2474; *Fax:* 306-692-5657
mossbank@palliser.lib.sk.ca
www.palliserlibrary.ca/mossbank/mossbank.htm
Debbie Sullivan, Branch Librarian

Neilburg: **Neilburg Branch Library**
108 Centre St., Neilburg, SK S0M 2C0
Tel: 306-823-4234
neilburg.lib@lakeland.lib.sk.ca
Sharon Schempp, Librarian

Nokomis: **Nokomis Library**
PO Box 38, Nokomis, SK S0G 3R0
Tel: 306-528-2251
nokomis.library@wheatland.sk.ca
Teresda Strachan, Librarian

North Battleford: **North Battleford Library**
1392 - 101st St., North Battleford, SK S9A 1A2
Tel: 306-445-3206; *Fax:* 306-445-6454
ref.desk@lakeland.lib.sk.ca
www.northbattlefordlibrary.com
Social Media:
www.facebook.com/group.php?gid=164895500216624
Karne Sabraw, Library Manager
librarian.northbattleford@lakeland.lib.sk.ca

North Battleford: **Saskatchewan Hospital Branch Library**
PO Box 39, North Battleford, SK S9A 2X8
Tel: 306-446-6863; *Fax:* 306-446-6810
saskhospital.lib@lakeland.lib.sk.ca
www.lakeland.lib.sk.ca
Rita Kuntz, Branch Librarian

Odessa: **Odessa Branch Library**
328 1st Ave., Odessa, SK S0G 3S0
Tel: 306-957-2020
odessa@southeast.lib.sk.ca
Sheila Leurer, Librarian

Ogema: **Ogema Branch Library**
117 Main St., Ogema, SK S0C 1Y0
Tel: 306-459-2985
ogema@southeast.lib.sk.ca
hip.southeast.lib.sk.ca/Southeast/Docs/ogema.html
Valerie Dunn, Librarian

Osler: **Osler Library**
228 Willow Dr., Osler, SK S0K 3A0
Tel: 306-239-4774; *Fax:* 306-239-2194
oslerlibrary@yourlink.ca
www.wheatland.sk.ca/branches_osler.html
Tina Remple, Branch Head

Oungre: **Oungre Branch Library**
Lyndale School, Oungre, SK S0C 1Z0
Tel: 306-456-2662; *Fax:* 306-456-2250
oungre@southeast.lib.sk.ca
www.southeast.lib.sk.ca
Carri Clarke, Librarian

Outlook: **Outlook Library**
505 Franklin St. South, Outlook, SK S0L 2N0
Tel: 306-867-8823; *Fax:* 306-867-1831
outlook.library@wheatland.sk.ca
www.wheatland.sk.ca

Oxbow: **Oxbow Branch Library/Ada Staples Library**
516 Prospect Ave., Oxbow, SK S0C 2B0
Tel: 306-483-5175; *Fax:* 306-483-2276
oxbow@southeast.lib.sk.ca
www.oxbow.ca
Shirley Berntson, Librarian
Shirley Berntson, Assistant Librarian

Pangman: **Pangman Library**
120 Mergens St., Pangman, SK S0C 2C0
Tel: 306-442-2119
pangman@southeast.lib.sk.ca
www.southeast.lib.sk.ca
Carolyn Colbow, Librarian

Paradise Hill: **Paradise Hill Branch Library**
104 - 2nd Ave., Paradise Hill, SK S0M 2G0
Tel: 306-344-4741
paradisehill.lib@lakeland.lib.sk.ca
www.lakeland.lib.sk.ca
Dianne Palsich, Branch Librarian

Paynton: **Paynton Branch Library**
Paynton, SK S0M 2J0
Tel: 306-895-2175
paynton.lib@lakeland.lib.sk.ca
www.lakeland.lib.sk.ca
Linda Peterson, Librarian
Marion McDougall, Head of Reference
204-895-2173

Pelican Narrows: **Tawowikamik Public Library**
PO Box 100, Pelican Narrows, SK S0P 0E0
Tel: 306-632-2022; *Fax:* 306-632-2022
spn@pnls.lib.sk.ca
Margaret Brass, Head Librarian
306-632-2161
Merle Michel, School Library Clerk
Angie McLeod, Public Library Clerk
Josephine Custer, Public Library Clerk

Perdue: **Perdue Library**
Perdue Comm. Complex, 10th St., Perdue, SK S0K 3C0
Tel: 306-237-4227
perdue.library@sasktel.net
www.wheatland.sk.ca/branches_perdue.html

Pierceland: **Pierceland Library**
Main St., Pierceland, SK S0M 2K0
Tel: 306-839-2166
pierceland.lib@lakeland.lib.sk.ca
www.lakeland.lib.sk.ca
Ann Hill, Librarian

Pilot Butte: Pilot Butte Branch Library
PO Box 668, Pilot Butte, SK S0G 3Z0
Tel: 306-781-3403
pilot.butte@southeast.lib.sk.ca
Sharon Millie, Librarian

Plenty: Plenty Library
PO Box 70, Plenty, SK S0L 2R0
Tel: 306-932-4455
plenty.library@wheatland.sk.ca
www.wheatland.sk.ca/branches_plenty.html
Lynn Halter, Branch Library Staff Contact

Qu'Appelle: Qu'Appelle Branch Library
PO Box 450, Qu'Appelle, SK S0G 4A0
Tel: 306-699-2902
quappelle@southeast.lib.sk.ca
www.southeast.lib.sk.ca
Elizabeth Fries, Librarian

Rabbit Lake: Rabbit Lake Branch Library
PO Box 146, Rabbit Lake, SK S0M 2L0
Tel: 306-824-2089
rabbitlake.lib@lakeland.lib.sk.ca
www.lakeland.lib.sk.ca
Marlene Martens, Librarian
Melita Hildebrand, Assistant Librarian

Radisson: Radisson Branch Library
329 Main St., Radisson, SK S0K 3L0
Tel: 306-827-4521
radisson.lib@lakeland.lib.sk.ca
www.lakeland.lib.sk.ca
Shirley Hosegood, Branch Librarian
Kaylla Maxwell, Substitute Librarian

Radville: Radville Branch Library
522 Healy Ave., Radville, SK S0C 2G0
Tel: 306-869-2742
radville@southeast.lib.sk.ca
www.southeast.lib.sk.ca
Shannon Bourassa, Librarian

Redvers: Redvers Library
53B Railway Ave., Redvers, SK S0C 2H0
Tel: 306-452-3255
redvers@southeast.lib.sk.ca
www.southeast.lib.sk.ca
Janet Dauvin, Librarian

Regina: Regina Public Library
2311 - 12th Ave., Regina, SK S4P 0N3
Tel: 306-777-6000; Fax: 306-949-7260
Other Numbers: 306-777-6120 (Info Svs); 306-777-6024 (ILL)
www.reginalibrary.ca
Social Media: www.flickr.com/photos/reginapubliclibrary; www.facebook.com/ReginaPublicLibrary
Jeff Barber, CEO & Library Director
jbarber@reginalibrary.ca
306-777-6099
Julie McKenna, Deputy Library Director
jmckenna@reginalibrary.ca
306-777-6074
André Gagnon, Manager, Collections and Programming
andre@reginalibrary.ca
306-777-6071
Gail Kruger, Head, Finance & Administration
gkruger@reginalibrary.ca
306-777-6060
Curtis Collins, Director, Dunlop Art Gallery
ccollins@reginalibrary.ca
306-777-6045
Tony Playter, Manager, Marketing & Communications
tplayter@reginalibrary.ca
306-777-6015
Robert Reynolds, Manager, Information Technology
rreynolds@reginalibrary.ca
306-777-6056
Sheila Fillon, Interim Director, Public Service
sfillon@reginalibrary.ca
306-777-6222
Jeff Grant, Manager, Human Resources & Administrator
jgrant@reginalibrary.ca
306-777-6072
Julie Arie, Manager, Virtual Services
jarie@reginalibrary.ca
306-777-6142
Joan Niedermayer, Executive Office Liaison
jniedermayer@reginalibrary.ca
306-777-6150
Barry Donaldson, Manager, Physical Plant
bdonaldson@reginalibrary.ca
306-777-6052

Regina Beach: Regina Beach Branch Library
133 Donovel Cres., Regina Beach, SK S0G 4C0
Tel: 306-729-2062
regina.beach@southeast.lib.sk.ca
www.southeast.lib.sk.ca
Lorie Gejdos, Acting Librarian
Debbie Arsenault

Riverhurst: Riverhurst Branch Library
The Village Square, 324 Teck St., Riverhurst, SK S0H 3P0
Tel: 306-353-2130
riverhurst@palliser.lib.sk.ca
www.palliserlibrary.ca/riverhurst/riverhurst.htm
Winnie Hockman, Board Chair
Donna Miner, Librarian

Rocanville: Rocanville Branch Library
218 Ellice St., Rocanville, SK S0A 3L0
Tel: 306-645-2088
rocanville@southeast.lib.sk.ca
www.southeast.lib.sk.ca
Kim Gulka, Board Chair
Carol Greening, Librarian
Shirley Duce, Library Assistant
Jamie Smigelski, Library Assistant

Rockglen: Rockglen Branch Library
1018 Centre St., Rockglen, SK S0H 3R0
Tel: 306-476-2350
rockglen@palliser.lib.sk.ca
www.palliserlibrary.ca
Kendra Loucks, Board Chair
Angela Stewart, Branch Librarian

Rosetown: Rosetown Library
#201, 5 Ave. East, Rosetown, SK S0L 2V0
Tel: 306-882-3566
rosetown.library@wheatland.sk.ca
www.wheatland.sk.ca
Lydia Hare, Manager

Rosthern: Rosthern Library
1029 6th St., Rosthern, SK S0K 3R0
Tel: 306-232-5377
rosthern.library@wheatland.sk.ca
www.rosthern.com/town_services/library.html
Agnes Epp, Librarian
Andy Lehmann, Library Staff
Elsie Lehmann, Library Staff
Lillian Gervais, Library Staff

Rouleau: Rouleau Branch Library
204 Main St., Rouleau, SK S0G 4H0
Tel: 306-776-2322
rouleau@palliser.lib.sk.ca
www.palliserlibrary.ca/rouleau/rouleau.htm
Dee Colibaba, Branch Librarian

Saskatoon: Saskatoon Public Library
311 - 23rd St. East, Saskatoon, SK S7K 0J6
Tel: 306-975-7558; Fax: 306-975-7542
illreps@saskatoonlibrary.ca
www.saskatoonlibrary.ca
Zenon Zuzak, Director of Libraries
z.zuzak@saskatoonlibrary.ca
306-975-7575
Bryan Foran, Manager, Branch & Technical Sevices
b.foran@saskatoonlibrary.ca
Anne Craggs, Manager, Public Services, Planning & Development
a.craggs@saskatoonlibrary.ca
Cinda Romuldietz, Manager, Information Technology Services
c.romuldietz@.saskatoonlibrary.ca

Sedley: Sedley Branch Library
224 Broadway, Sedley, SK S0G 4K0
Tel: 306-885-4505; Fax: 306-885-4506
sedley@southeast.lib.sk.ca
Julie Lapointe, Librarian
306-885-4738
Connie Perras, Librarian
306-885-2228

Sonningdale: Sonningdale Library
PO Box 40, Sonningdale, SK S0K 4B0
Tel: 306-237-7603
sonningdale.library@wheatland.sk.ca
www.wheatland.sk.ca/branches_sonningdale.html
Connie Guiness, Branch Library Staff Contact
Lynn Ross, Chair

Speers: Speers Branch Library
Main St., Speers, SK S0M 2V0
Tel: 306-246-4866
speers.lib@lakeland.lib.sk.ca
Maureen Kachmarski, Branch Librarian

Spruce Home: Spruce Home Branch Library
General Delivery, Spruce Home, SK S0J 2N0
Tel: 306-764-8377

St Walburg: St Walburg Library
124 Main St., St Walburg, SK S0M 2T0
Tel: 306-248-3250; Fax: 306-248-3278
stwalburg.lib@lakeland.lib.sk.ca
www.lakeland.lib.sk.ca
Valerie L'Heureux, Librarian

Stanley Mission: Keethanow Public Library
PO Box 70, Stanley Mission, SK S0J 2P0
Tel: 306-635-2104; Fax: 306-635-2050
l.ratt.ssk@pnls.lib.sk.ca
Lucy Ratt, Branch Librarian

Stoughton: Stoughton Branch Library
232 Main St., Stoughton, SK S0G 4T0
Tel: 306-457-2484
stoughton@southeast.lib.sk.ca
www.southeast.lib.sk.ca
Sharlet Coderre, Librarian

Tugaske: Tugaske Branch Library
106 Ogema St., Tugaske, SK S0H 4B0
Tel: 306-759-2215; Fax: 306-759-2253
tugaske@palliser.lib.sk.ca
www.palliserlibrary.ca/tugaske/tugaske.htm
Sarah McKen, Branch Librarian
Manon Bueckert, Assistant Branch Librarian

Turtleford: Thunderchild Branch Library
PO Box 39, Turtleford, SK S0M 2Y0
Tel: 306-845-2071
Susan Wapass, Librarian

Turtleford: Turtleford Branch Library
212 Main St., Turtleford, SK S0M 2Y0
Tel: 306-845-2074
turtleford.lib@lakeland.lib.sk.ca
www.lakeland.lib.sk.ca
Hilma Copeland, Branch Librarian
Dianne Brett, Branch Librarian

Unity: Unity Library
Town Office Complex, Unity, SK S0K 4L0
Tel: 306-228-2802
unity.library@wheatland.sk.ca
www.wheatland.sk.ca/branches_unity.html
Michelle Schumack, Branch Library Staff Contact
Rhelda Winterhalt, Chair
JoAnn Coid, Assistant

Vibank: Vibank Branch Library
101 - 2nd Ave., Vibank, SK S0G 4Y0
Tel: 306-762-2270
vibank@southeast.lib.sk.ca
www.southeast.lib.sk.ca
Betty Kuntz, Librarian
vibank@southeast.lib.sk.ca
306-762-2270

Viscount: Viscount Library
PO Box 117, Viscount, SK S0K 4M0
Tel: 306-944-2155
viscount.library@wheatland.sk.ca
www.wheatland.sk.ca/branches_viscount.html
Carol Brown, Librarian

Waldheim: Waldheim Branch Library
PO Box 446, Waldheim, SK S0K 4R0
Tel: 306-945-2221
waldheim.ca/category/library
Lynn McDonald, Librarian

Wapella: Wapella Branch Library
519 South Railway St., Wapella, SK S0G 4Z0
Tel: 306-532-4419
wapella@southeast.lib.sk.ca
www.southeast.lib.sk.ca
Sharon Matheson, Librarian
306-532-4419
Nancy Knutson, Librarian

***Warman:* Warman Library**
101 Klassen St., Warman, SK S0K 4S0
Tel: 306-933-4387
warman.library@wheatland.sk.ca
www.wheatland.sk.ca
Social Media: www.facebook.com/pages/Warman-Library/125784437506962
Margaret-Ann Janzen, Community Librarian

***Waskesiu Lake:* Waskesiu Lake Library**
1225 Montreal, Waskesiu Lake, SK S0J 2Y0
Tel: 306-663-5999

***Watrous:* Watrous Library**
306 Main St., Watrous, SK S0K 4T0
Tel: 306-946-2244
watrous.library@wheatland.sk.ca
townofwatrous.com/library.htm
Kathleen Kimmig, Community Librarian
Toni Ambrose, Assistant
Judy Beauparlant, Assistant

***Wawota:* Wawota Branch Library**
308 Railway Ave., Wawota, SK S0G 5A0
Tel: 306-739-2375
wawota@southeast.lib.sk.ca
Social Media: www.facebook.com/286787141339067
Maureen Jensen, Librarian

***Weyburn:* Weyburn Public Library**
45 Bison Ave. NE, Weyburn, SK S4H 0H9
Tel: 306-842-4352; *Fax:* 306-842-1255
weyburn@southeast.lib.sk.ca
wcapqlx.sasktelwebhosting.com/wpl
Social Media: twitter.com/WeyburnPublic; www.facebook.com/189593097722161
Kam Teo, City Librarian
Ilene Lequyere, Library Assistant

***White City:* White City Branch Library**
12 Ramm Ave., White City Community Centre, White City, SK S0G 5B0
Tel: 306-781-2118
white.city@southeast.lib.sk.ca
www.southeast.lib.sk.ca/branches.html
Lori Lee Harris, Branch Librarian
Shayna Hordos, Assistant Librarian

***Whitewood:* Whitewood Library**
731 Lalonde St., Whitewood, SK S0G 5C0
Tel: 306-735-4233
whitewood@southeast.lib.sk.ca
Irene Blyth, Librarian

***Wilkie:* Wilkie Library**
202 - 2nd Ave. East, Wilkie, SK S0K 4W0
Tel: 306-843-2616
wilkie.library@wheatland.sk.ca
Terri Dueck, Branch Library Staff Contact
Frances Love, Chair

***Willow Bunch:* Willow Bunch Branch Library**
2 Ave. F South, Willow Bunch, SK S0H 4K0
Tel: 306-473-2393
willowbunch@palliser.lib.sk.ca
www.palliserlibrary.ca
Social Media: www.facebook.com/223931024328192
Jeanette Mondor, Chair
Barb Gibbons, Branch Librarian

***Windthorst:* Windthorst Branch Library**
202 Angus St., Windthorst, SK S0G 5G0
Tel: 306-224-2159
windthorst@southeast.lib.sk.ca
Jill Taylor, Librarian

***Wolseley:* Wolseley Branch Library**
Bldg. 500, Front St., Wolseley, SK S0G 5H0
Tel: 306-698-2221
wolseley@southeast.lib.sk.ca
www.southeast.lib.sk.ca
Sharon Jeeves, Librarian
Susan Campbell, Librarian

***Wood Mountain:* Wood Mountain Branch Library**
2nd Ave. West, Wood Mountain, SK S0H 4L0
Tel: 306-266-2110
woodmountain@palliser.lib.sk.ca
www.palliserlibrary.ca
Gus Gere, Branch Librarian

***Yellow Grass:* Yellow Grass Branch Library**
213 Souris St., Yellow Grass, SK S0G 5J0
Tel: 306-465-2574
yellow.grass@southeast.lib.sk.ca
Betty Guest, Librarian

***Young:* Young Library**
114 Main St., Young, SK S0K 4Y0
Tel: 306-259-2227
young.library@wheatland.sk.ca
www.wheatland.sk.ca/branches_young.html
Gisele Camber, Branch Library Staff Contact
Elaine Raskell, Chair

Archives

***Duck Lake:* Duck Lake Historical Museum**
5 Anderson Ave., Duck Lake, SK S0K 1J0
Tel: 306-467-2057; *Toll-Free:* 866-467-2057
duckmuf@sasktel.net
www.dlric.org/museum.html
Céline Perillat, Curator

***Prince Albert:* Diocese of Saskatchewan, Archives**
1308 - 5th Ave. East, Prince Albert, SK S6V 2H7
Tel: 306-763-2455; *Fax:* 306-764-5172
archives@sasktel.net
www.skdiocese.com/archives/

***Prince Albert:* Orra Sheldon Resource Centre**
1308 - 5th Ave. East, Prince Albert, SK S6V 2H7
Tel: 306-763-2455; *Fax:* 306-764-5172
www.skdiocese.com/archives

***Prince Albert:* Prince Albert Historical Society**
10 River St. East, Prince Albert, SK S6V 8A9
Tel: 306-764-2992
historypa@citypa.com
www.historypa.com
Social Media: www.facebook.com/PrinceAlbertHistoricalSociety; twitter.com/historypa

***Regina:* Diocese of Qu'Appelle, Archives**
Saskatchewan Archives Board, University of Regina, 303 Hillsdale St., Regina, SK S4P 1B8
Tel: 306-787-4068; *Fax:* 306-787-1197
quappelle.anglican.ca/index.php/archives-records

***Regina:* RCMP Heritage Centre / Centre du Patrimoine de la GRC**
5907 Dewdney Ave., Regina, SK S4T 0P4
Tel: 306-522-7333; *Toll-Free:* 866-567-7267
info@rcmphc.com
www.rcmpheritagecentre.com
Rhonda Lamb, Manager
306-522-7333 ext. 3017
Jodi Ann Eskritt, Curator
306-522-7333 ext. 3004

***Regina:* Regina Firefighters' Museum**
1205 Ross Ave., Regina, SK S4P 3C8
Tel: 306-777-7830; *Fax:* 306-777-6807

***Regina:* Saskatchewan Archives Board**
3303 Hillsdale St., Regina, SK S4S 6W9
Tel: 306-787-4068; *Fax:* 306-787-1197
Other Numbers: Information Management Inquiry Line: 306-787-0734
info.regina@archives.gov.sk.ca
www.saskarchives.com
Trevor J.D. Powell, Chair, The Saskatchewan Archives Board of Directors
Linda McIntyre, Provincial Archivist

***Regina:* Saskatchewan Genealogical Society**
#110, 1514 - 11th Ave., Regina, SK S4P 0H2
Tel: 306-780-9207; *Fax:* 306-780-3615
sgslibrary@sasktel.net
www.saskgenealogy.com
Megen Ashcroft, Librarian
sgslibrary@sasktel.net
Linda Dunsmore-Porter, Executive Director
ed.sgs@sasktel.net
Lisa Warner, Contact

***Regina:* University Archives & Special Collections**
Dr. John Archer Library, #107, 3737 Wascana Pkwy., Regina, SK S4S 0A2
Tel: 306-585-4014; *Fax:* 306-585-4493
archives@uregina.ca
www.uregina.ca/library/services/archives

***Saskatoon:* City of Saskatoon Archives**
88 - 24th St., Saskatoon, SK S7K 0K4
Tel: 306-975-7811; *Fax:* 306-975-2612
www.saskatoon.ca
Social Media: www.youtube.com/saskatooncitynews; twitter.com/cityofsaskatoon; www.facebook.com/saskatooncitynews
J. Jeffrey O'Brien, City Archivist
306-657-8725

***Saskatoon:* Diocese of Saskatoon, Archives**
Synod Office, PO Box 1965, Saskatoon, SK S7K 3S5
Tel: 306-244-5651; *Fax:* 306-933-4606
anglicanarchivist@sastel.net
www.anglicandiocesesaskatoon.com

***Saskatoon:* Local History Room**
311 - 23rd St. East, Saskatoon, SK S7K 0J6
Tel: 306-975-7578; *Fax:* 306-975-7542

***Saskatoon:* Mohyla Institute**
1240 Temperance St., Saskatoon, SK S7N 0P1
Tel: 306-653-1944; *Fax:* 306-653-1902
www.mohyla.ca
Social Media: www.facebook.com/StPetroMohylaInstitute

***Saskatoon:* Saskatchewan Synod, Archives**
114 Seminary Cres., Saskatoon, SK S7N 0X3
Tel: 306-244-2474; *Fax:* 306-664-8677
sksynod@elcic.ca
www.sasksynod.elcic.ca

***Saskatoon:* Saskatoon Office**
Murray Bldg., 3 Campus Dr., Saskatoon, SK S7N 5A4
Tel: 306-933-5832; *Fax:* 306-933-7305
info.saskatoon@archives.gov.sk.ca
www.saskarchives.com

***Saskatoon:* University Archives**
#301 Main Library, 3 Campus Dr., University of, Saskatchewan, Saskatoon, SK S7N 5A4
Tel: 306-966-6028
university.archives@usask.ca
www.usask.ca/archives

***Verigin:* National Doukhobour Heritage Village Inc.**
PO Box 99, Verigin, SK S0A 4H0
Tel: 306-542-4441
ndhv@yourlink.ca
www.ndhv.ca

***Weyburn:* Soo Line Historical Society**
411 Industrial Lane, Weyburn, SK S4H 2L2
Tel: 306-842-2922; *Fax:* 306-842-2922
slhm@sasktel.net
www.silver.sasktelwebsite.net/index.html
Social Media: www.facebook.com/pages/Soo-Line-Historical-Museum/118758801502753;

Yukon Territory

Public Libraries

***Destruction Bay:* Destruction Bay Volunteer Branch Library**
General Delivery, Destruction Bay, YT Y0B 1H0
Tel: 867-841-5161

***Mayo:* Keno City Volunteer Branch Library**
Site 1, Box 17, Mayo, YT Y0B 1M0
Tel: 867-995-2394

***Whitehorse:* Yukon Public Libraries**
1171 - 1st St., Whitehorse, YT Y1A 2C6
Tel: 867-667-5239; *Fax:* 867-393-6333
Toll-Free: 800-661-0408
Other Numbers: 867-667-3668 (Reference); 867-667-5228 (Programs)
whitehorse.library@gov.yk.ca
www.ypl.gov.yk.ca
Social Media: www.facebook.com/yukonpubliclibraries
Hans Ott, Chair
wplboard@yahoo.ca
Julie Ourom, Director
867-667-5447

Archives

***Dawson:* Dawson City Museum**
595 Fifth Ave., Dawson, YT Y0B 1G0
Tel: 867-993-5291; *Fax:* 867-993-5839
info@dawsonmuseum.ca
www.dawsonmuseum.ca
Social Media: twitter.com/dcmuseum;
www.facebook.com/pages/Dawson-City-Museum/118073228250444

Laura Mann, Executive Director
867-993-5291 ext. 1
Molly MacDonald, Archives Coordinator
867-993-5291 ext. 4

***Whitehorse:* Yukon Tourism & Culture**
400 College Dr., Whitehorse, YT Y1A 2C6
Tel: 867-667-5321; *Fax:* 867-393-6253
Toll-Free: 800-661-0408
yukon.archives@gov.yk.ca
www.yukonarchives.ca

Ian Burnett, Territorial Archivist
ian.burnett@gov.yk.ca
867-667-5275
Cheryl Charlie, Archives Reference Assistant
cheryl.charlie@gov.yk.ca
867-667-8064
Peggy D'Orsay, Archives Librarian
Peggy.Dorsay@gov.yk.ca
867-667-5625
Vacant , Accessions Archivist
867-667-5333
Wendy Sokolon, Government Records Archivist
wendy.sokolon@gov.yk.ca
867-667-5926
Leslie Buchan, Private Records Archivist
lesley.buchan@gov.yk.ca
867-667-5641

SECTION 13
PUBLISHING

Publishers

Book Publishers

Aardvark Enterprises (Div. of Speers Investments Ltd.)
204 Millbank Dr. SW, Calgary, AB T2Y 2H9
Tel: 403-256-4639;
ISBNs: 0-921057; ISSN: 0831-1919
Publishers of poems, short stories & how-to books
J. Alvin Speers, President

AB collector publishing
5835 Grant St., Halifax, NS B3H 1C9
Tel: 902-429-5768; Fax: 506-385-1981
Toll-Free: 888-748-5514
darklady@nbnet.nb.ca
www.abcollectorpublishing.ca
Publisher of poetry, short stories, biography, drama, works relating to photography, ceramics, art & history, in English, French, German
Astrid Brunner, Publisher

Abbeyfield Publishers
Owned By: Bill Belfontaine Ltd.
 # 304, 160 Balmoral Ave., Toronto, ON M4V 1J7
Tel: 416-925-6458; Fax: 416-925-4165
Toll-Free: 866-370-9407
info@whiteknightbooks.ca
www.whiteknightbooks.ca
Bill Belfontaine, Publisher

ABC Publishing
Owned By: Augsburg Fortress Canada
80 Hayden St., Toronto, ON M4Y 3G2
Tel: 416-924-9199; Fax: 416-968-7983
www.abcpublishing.com
ISBNs: 0-919030, 0-919891, 0-921846
The premier source for Anglican prayer & hymn books, Path books, & parish programming materials & other resources for Church leaders, the Anglican Book Centre & its publishing unit, ABC Publishing, merged with Augsburg Fortress Canada in 2007.

Academic Printing & Publishing
5349 Chute Lake Rd., Kelowna, BC V1W 4Y1
Tel: 250-764-5030; Fax: 778-477-5664
academicpublishing@shaw.ca
www.academicprintingandpublishing.com
ISBNs: ISSNs: 0003-6390; 1206-5269; 1206-3696
Publishers of scholarly books & journals, with emphasis on Philosophy
Roger A. Shiner, Director

Acadiensis Press
Campus House, University of New Brunswick, PO Box 4400, Fredericton, NB E3B 5A3
Tel: 506-453-4978;
acadnsis@unb.ca
www.lib.unb.ca/Texts/Acadiensis
ISBNs: ISSN: 0044-5871
Publisher of ACADIENSIS: The Journal of the History of the Atlantic Region, & books on the culture & history of Atlantic Canada
Dr. David Frank, Managing Editor

Acorn Press
PO Box 22024, Charlottetown, PE C1A 9J2
Tel: 902-221-1061;
info@acornpresscanada.com
www.acornpresscanada.com
Social Media:
twitter.com/AcornPress
www.facebook.com/pages/The-Acorn-Press/1466243853 54176?re
ISBNs: 1-894838014-9; 1-894838-16-5-64
Publishing books about Prince Edward Island, with emphasis on Prince Edward Island authors, Acorn Press lists works of fiction, poetry, folklore, history & literature for children
Laurie Brinklow, Publisher

Addison-Wesley Publishers Ltd.
Previous Name: Copp Clark Ltd.
Owned By: Pearson Canada
PO Box 580, 26 Prince Andrew Pl., Toronto, ON M3C 2T8
Tel: 416-447-5101; Fax: 416-443-0948
Toll-Free: 800-387-8028
www.pearsoncanada.ca
ISBNs: 9780321531193; 9780321510105
Addison-Wesley, a Pearson imprint, is a key publisher of technical resources of particular interest to computer programmers, engineers & system administrators. Academic titles include astronomy, mathematics & statistics, economics & finance
MR Allan T. Reynolds, President & CEO, Pearson Canada

Agogic Publishing
#406, 109 - 10 St., New Westminster, BC V3M 3X7
Tel: 604-290-2692; Fax: 604-540-4419
agogic@iglide.net
www.agogic.biz
ISBNs: 1-896595
Publishers of learner's guides for guitar

Alexander Press
2875, av Douglas, Montréal, QC H3R 2C7
Tel: 514-738-5517; Fax: 514-738-4718
Toll-Free: 866-303-5517
alexanderpress@gmail.com
www.alexanderpress.com
ISBNs: 1-896800
Publishes Christian Orthodox books & media in Greek, English & French

Alpine Book Peddlers
#140, 405 Bow Meadows Cres., Canmore, AB T1W 2W8
Tel: 403-678-2280; Fax: 403-678-2840
alpinebk@aeontech.ca
ISBNs: 0-9699368, 0-9692631, 0-919934, 0-9692457; SAN: 1187546
John Blum

Alter Ego Editions
5922, rue Jeanne-Mance, Montréal, QC H2V 4S8
Tel: 514-276-7429; Fax: 514-276-7429
books@alterego.montreal.qc.ca
www.alterego.montreal.qc.ca
ISBNs: 1-896743
Small independent French-Language publisher

The Alternate Press
Owned By: Life Media
#52, B2-125 The Queensway, Toronto, ON M8Y 1H6
altpress@lifemedia.ca
www.lifemedia.ca/altpress
ISBNs: 0-920118-04-6; 978-0-920118-15-3;0-920118-00-3
An imprint of Life Media, The Alternate Press publishes materials promoting home schooling & natural learning, natural parenting, natural business (home-based & green), & poetry
Wendy Priesnitz, Publisher
Ron Priesnitz, Publisher

The Althouse Press
Faculty of Education, University of Western Ontario, 1137 Western Rd., London, ON N6G 1G7
Tel: 519-661-2096; Fax: 519-661-3714
press@uwo.ca
www.edu.uwo.ca/althousepress
ISBNs: 0-920354; SAN: 115-1142
Dr. Greg Dickinson, Director
K. Butson, Contact, kbutson@uwo.ca

Amethyst House Book Publishers
6 Sunderland Cres., Scarborough, ON M1H 2V3
Tel: 416-431-1339;
www.amethysthouse.com

Annick Press Ltd.
15 Patricia Ave., Toronto, ON M2M 1H9
Tel: 416-221-4802; Fax: 416-221-8400
annickpress@annickpress.com
www.annickpress.com
Social Media: www.youtube.com/AnnickPress
twitter.com/AnnickPress
www.facebook.co m/AnnickPress
ISBNs: 0-920236, 920303, 1-55037; SAN: 115-0065
Publishers of fiction and nonfiction for children and young adults. Editorial offices in Toronto and Vancouver.
Rick Wilks

Anvil Press
PO Box 3008 MPO, Vancouver, BC V6B 3X5
Tel: 604-876-8710;
info@anvilpress.com
www.anvilpress.com
Social Media:
twitter.com/AnvilPress
www.facebook.com/AnvilPress
ISBNs: 1-895636
Brian Kaufman, Publisher

Apple Press Publishing
810 Landresse Ct., Newmarket, ON L3X 1M6
Tel: 905-853-7979; Fax: 905-853-1175
Toll-Free: 866-222-8883
info@applepressbooks.com
ISBNs: 0-919972
George Quinn, President, 905-853-7979

Aquila Communications Ltd.
2642, rue Diab, Saint-Laurent, QC H4S 1E8
Tel: 514-338-1065; Fax: 514-338-1948
Toll-Free: 800-667-7071
info2@aquilacommunications.com
www.aquilacommunications.com
ISBNs: 0-88510, 2-89054; SAN: 115-2483, 115-8295
Publishes French as a Second Language reading materials from grades 4 through college
Mike Kelada, Vice-President & General Manager
Sami Kelada, President/CEO

Arbeiter Ring Publishing
#201E, 121 Osborne St., Winnipeg, MB R3L 1Y4
Tel: 204-942-7058; Fax: 204-944-9198
info@arbeiterring.com
www.arbeiterring.com
ISBNs: 1-894037
Publishers of books on contemporary politics, culture, and social issues.

Argenta Friends Press
Press Rd., Naksup, BC V0G 1R0
Tel: 250-366-4314; Fax: 250-366-4314
afp@look.ca
ISBNs: 0-920367
Pat Cattermole

Ariane Editions Inc.
#110, 1209, rue Bernard ouest, Outremont, QC H2V 1V7
Tél: 514-276-2949; Téléc: 514-279-4121
info@ariane.qc.ca
www.ariane.qc.ca
ISBNs: 2-920987
Martine Vallée
Marc Vallée

Armdale Publications
#203, 10544 - 106 St. NW, Edmonton, AB T5J 2M4
Tel: 780-429-1073; Fax: 780-425-5844
armadale@global-serve.net
Winston Mohabir
Haloshini Naideo, Manager

Arsenal Pulp Press Ltd.
#101, 211 East Georgia St., Vancouver, BC V6A 1Z6
Tel: 604-687-4233; Fax: 604-687-4283
info@arsenalpulp.com
www.arsenalpulp.com
Social Media:
twitter.com/arsenalpulp
www.facebook.com/arsenalpulp
ISBNs: 0-88978, 1-55152; SAN: 115-0847
Publisher with over 200 titles in print, including literary fiction & non-fiction; cultural & gender studies; gay, lesbian & multicultural literature; cookbooks & guidebooks.
Robert Ballantyne, Associate Publisher
Brian Lam, Publisher
Cynara Geisser, Marketing Director

Art Global
384, av Laurier ouest, Montréal, QC H2V 2K7
Tél: 514-272-6111; Téléc: 514-272-8609
kermoyan@edirom.com
ISBNs: 2-920718
Ara Kermoyan

Art Metropole
788 King St. West, Toronto, ON M5V 1N6
Tel: 416-703-4400; Fax: 416-703-4404
info@artmetropole.com
www.artmetropole.com
ISBNs: 0-920956; SAN: 156-9902
Publishers of art books & publications
A.A. Bronson, Director

Artel Educational Resources Ltd.
5528 Kingsway, Burnaby, BC V5H 2G2
Tel: 604-435-4949; Fax: 604-435-1955
Toll-Free: 800-665-9255
info@arteleducational.ca
www.arteleducational.ca
ISBNs: SAN: 116-029X
Publishes educational resources for schools, institutions, home schoolers & the general public; Includes material for all levels of education, ESL & Special Education

Vern Milani, President

Artery Enterprises Ltd.
PO Box 3302, Langley, BC V3A 4R6
Tel: 604-534-8122; Fax: 604-534-8124
Toll-Free: 888-333-1006
info@artery.ca
www.artery.ca
ISBNs: 0-920431; SAN: 117-0198

Artextes Éditions / Centre d'information Artexte
#508, 460, rue Sainte-Catherine ouest, Montréal, QC H3B 1A7
Tél: 514-874-0049; Téléc: 514-874-0316
info@artexte.ca
www.artexte.ca
Publishes critical anthologies, monographs & references dealing with visual, media & interdisciplinary art
François Dion, Director

Artistic Warrior
#207, 2475 Dobbin Rd., #22, West Kelowna, BC V4T 2E9
publisher@artisticwarrior.com
www.artisticwarrior.com
Publisher of new & emerging Canadian authors with a focus on BC authors.
Darcy Nybo, Publisher

Asquith House Limited/Michael Preston Associates
94 Asquith Ave., Toronto, ON M4W 1J8
Tel: 416-925-3577; Fax: 416-925-8823
Toll-Free: 800-646-6858
m.preston@sympatico.ca
ISBNs: SAN: 115-4915
Publishes educational books, reading programs, maps & globes
M. Preston
P. Preston

Asteroid Publishing Inc.
PO Box 3, Richmond Hill, ON L4C 4X9
Tel: 416-352-1561;
info@asteroidpublishing.ca
asteroidpublishing.ca
Social Media:
www.twitter.com/asteroidpublish
Publisher of literary fiction & non-fiction books.

Athabasca University Press
Edmonton Learning Centre, Peace Hills Trust Tower, #1200, 10011 - 109 St., Edmonton, AB T5J 3S8
Tel: 780-497-3412; Fax: 780-421-3298
aupress@athabascau.ca
www.aupress.ca
Social Media: www.youtube.com/user/aupresst
twitter.com/au_press
www.facebook.com/pa ges/AU-Press/189461926898
ISBNs: 0-919737
Walter Hildebrandt, Director, director.aupress@athabascau.ca

Athena Books
47 Sarrazin Way, Ottawa, ON K2J 4A5
Tel: 613-825-6986;
athena@magma.ca
www.magma.ca/~athena
ISBNs: 1-895520
Robert Allan Stewart, President

Augsburg Fortress Publishers Canadian Office
500 Trillium Dr., Kitchener, ON N2G 4Y4
Tel: 519-748-2200; Fax: 519-748-9835
Toll-Free: 800-265-6397
info@afcanada.com
www.afcanada.com
Social Media: www.youtube.com/user/AugsburgFortress
www.twitter.com/augsburgfortres
www.facebook.com/augsburgfortress
The publishing wing of the Evangelical Lutheran Church in America, Augsburg Fortress also services the Evangelical Lutheran Church in Canada & publishes Bibles, Bible study resources, multicultural materials, music, & seasonal & special occasion books.
Larry N. Willard, Canadian Operations Director

Augustine Hand Press
62 Walter Copp Cres., Winnipeg, MB R2K 4H6
ISBNs: 0973151900, 0973151919

Aviation Publishers Co. Ltd.
PO Box 1361 B, Ottawa, ON K1P 5R4
Tel: 613-244-8280; Fax: 613-244-8281
info@aviationpublishers.com
www.aviationpublishers.com
ISBNs: 0-9690054
Publishers of the ground school flight training manual "From the Ground Up" as well as other books on flight training & aeronautical theory.
William N. Peppler, President
Graeme Peppler, General Manager

Aviation World
Previous Name: Aero Training Products Inc.
195 Carlingview Dr., Toronto, ON M9W 5E8
Tel: 416-674-5959; Fax: 416-574-5915
Toll-Free: 800-668-1987
www.aviationworld.net/index.php
Social Media:
twitter.com/AW_Canada
www.facebook.com/aviationworld
Training materials for pilots & technicians

Backroad Mapbooks
Owned By: Mussio Ventures Ltd.
#106, 1500 Hartley Ave., Coquitlam, BC V3K 7A1
Tel: 604-521-6277; Fax: 604-521-6260
Toll-Free: 877-520-5670
info@backroadmapbooks.com; hr@backroadmapbooks.com
www.backroadmapbooks.com
Other information: GPS Maps, E-mail: gps@backroadmapbooks.com
Backroad Mapbooks produces up-to-date outdoor recreation Canadian maps & guidebooks.
Russell Mussio, President, rmussio@backroadmapbooks.com
Chris Taylor, Vice-President & Manager, National Sales, ctaylor@backroadmapbooks.com
Andrew Allen, Contact, Mapping Department, aallen@backroadmapbooks.com

Bacon & Hughes Limited
#30, 81 Auriga Dr., Ottawa, ON K2E 7Y5
Tel: 613-226-8136; Fax: 613-226-8121
Toll-Free: 800-563-2468
sales@baconandhughes.ca
www.baconandhughes.ca
Bacòn & Hughes Limited provides learning resources from early childhood to the secondary level. Teacher resources & French literature are also available.

Bahá'¡ Distribution Service
Previous Name: Unity Arts Inc.
#9, 945 Middlefield Rd., Toronto, ON M1V 5E1
Tel: 416-609-9900; Fax: 416-609-9600
Toll-Free: 800-465-3287
orders@bahaibooksonline.com
www.bahaibooksonline.com

Banff Centre Press
The Banff Centre, PO Box 1020, 107 Tunnel Mountain Dr., Banff, AB T1L 1H5
Tel: 403-762-6410; Fax: 403-762-6277
Toll-Free: 800-565-9989
press@banffcentre.ca
www.banffcentre.ca/press; boulderpavement.ca/issue007
Social Media:
twitter.com/BanffCentreLit
www.facebook.com/TheBanffCentre
The Banff Centre Press publishes books of contemporary art, culture, & literature.
Steven Smith, Director, steven_smith@banffcentre.ca
Leanne Johnson, Managing Editor, leanne_johnson@banffcentre.ca

The Battered Silicon Dispatch Box
PO Box 204, Shelburne, ON L0N 1S0
Tel: 519-925-3027; Fax: 519-925-3482
gav@bmts.com
www.batteredbox.com
ISBNs: 1-55246
Publishers of Sherlock Holmes and other out-of-print works by Canadian & international authors
George A. Vanderhurgh

Battle Street Books
175 Battle St., Kamloops, BC V2C 2L1
Tel: 250-372-1119; Fax: 250-372-1830
info@battlestreetbooks.com
www.battlestreetbooks.com
Battle Street Books publishes the novels, plays, & short stories of British Columbia writer, Ernest Langford.

BC Decker Inc.
PO Box 620 LCD 1, #310, 69 John St. South, Hamilton, ON L8N 3K7
Tel: 905-522-7017; Toll-Free: 800-568-7281
customercare@bcdecker.com
www.bcdecker.com
BC Decker publishes the ACP Medicine & ACS Surgery book products in both print & digital editions, as well as ten specialty medical journals, to serve the informational needs of health care professionals & students.

Béliveau Éditeur
Anciennement Éditions Sciences et Culture inc.; Iris Diffusion
920, rue Jean-Neveu, Longueuil, QC J4G 2M1
Tél: 450-679-1933; Téléc: 450-679-6648
admin@beliveauediteur.com
www.beliveaueditеur.com
ISBNs: 2-89092
Spécialités: Affaires, finances, biographies, psychologie et sciences humaines, religion, mathématiques, physique, chimie
Mathieu Béliveau, Président-directeur général

Bendall Books Educational Publishers
PO Box 115, Mill Bay, BC V0R 2P0
Tel: 250-743-2946; Fax: 250-743-2910
admin@bendallbooks.com
www.bendallbooks.com
Bendall Books is a publisher & distributor of educational materials for the college & university sector.
Raymond Bendall, Publisher

The Best of Bridge Publishing Ltd.
#800, 120 Eglington Ave. E, Toronto, ON M4P 1E2
Tel: 416-322-6552; Fax: 416-322-6936
bestofbridge@robertrose.ca
www.bestofbridge.com
ISBNs: 0-9690425
Publishers of cookbooks
Joan Wilson, President

Betelgeuse Books
#516, 3044 Bloor St. West, Toronto, ON M8X 2Y8
Betelgeuse@sympatico.ca
www.maxpages.com/betelgeuse
Betelgeuse Books publishes books about northern Canada.

Between the Lines (BTL)
#277, 401 Richmond St. West, Toronto, ON M5V 3A8
Tel: 416-535-9914; Fax: 416-535-1484
Toll-Free: 800-718-7201
info@btlbooks.com
www.btlbooks.com
Between the Lines provides books with critical perspectives on culture, economics, & society.
Amanda Crocker, Editorial Coordinator, editor@btlbooks.com
Paula Brill, Marketing & Promotion Coordinator, Marketing & Promotion
Voula Kraniou, Financial Coordinator
Jennifer Tiberio, Design & Production Coordinator

Biblioasis
PO Box 92, Emeryville, ON N0R 1C0
Tel: 519-968-2206; Fax: 519-250-5713
info@biblioasis.com
www.biblioasis.com
Social Media:
twitter.com/biblioasis
www.facebook.com/groups/2409174840
Publisher of poetry, fiction & non-fiction.
Daniel Webb, Publisher/Editor, dwells@biblioasis.com

Bibliothèque nationale du Québec
2275, rue Holt, Montréal, QC H2G 3H1
Tél: 514-873-1100; Téléc: 514-873-9312
Ligne sans frais: 800-363-9028
info@bnquebec.ca
www.bnquebec.ca
ISBNs: 2-550, 2-551
Lise Bissonnette, Présidente et directrice générale

Black Moss Press
2450 Byng Rd., Windsor, ON N8W 3E8
Tel: 519-252-2551;
www.blackmosspress.com
Social Media:
www.facebook.com/group.php?gid=118907923236
The literary press publishes Canadian literature, including poetry & short story anthologies.
Marty Gervais, President

Black Rose Books
CP 1258 Place du Parc, Montréal, QC H2W 2R3
Ligne sans frais: 800-565-9523
info@blackrosebooks.net
www.blackrosebooks.net
Black Rose Books publishes critical writing on topics such as philosophy, politics, history, sociology, & hte environment.
Robert Dollins, Editorial Administrator

Blue Heron Press
160 Greenlees Dr., Kingston, ON K7K 6P4
Tel: 613-549-4334;
info@blueheronpress.ca
www.blueheronpress.ca
The literary press specializes in Canadian literature.

Bodhi Publishing
PO Box 144, Kinmount, ON K0M 2A0
kcw@bodhipublishing.org
www.bodhipublishing.netfirms.com
Other information: E-mail, Orders: www.bodhipublishing.org
The charitable organization publishes books by Venerable Namgyal Rinpoche.

BookLand Press
#600, 15 Allstate Pkwy., Markham, ON L3R 5B4
books@booklandpress.com
www.booklandpress.com
Social Media:
www.twitter.com/booklandpress

Boomerang Éditeur Jeunesse inc.
33, rue de Chenonceau, Blainville, QC J7B 1P6
Tél: 450-430-3259; Téléc: 450-430-4607
info@boomerangjeunesse.com
www.boomerangjeunesse.com
Resources for children

Borealis Book Publishers
8 Mohawk Cres., Nepean, ON K2H 7G6
Tel: 613-829-0150; Fax: 613-829-7783
Toll-Free: 877-696-2585
drt@borealispress.com
www.borealispress.com
Borealis Book Publishers consists of Borealis Books, Tecumseh Books, Publishing Advisors Inc., Journal of Canadian Poetry, Canadian Critical Editions, & the Parliamentary Handbook / Répertoire Parlementaire Canadien.

Boston Mills Press
c/o Firefly Books, 66 Leek Cres., Richmond Hill, ON L4B 1H1
Tel: 416-499-8412; Fax: 416-499-8313
Toll-Free: 800-387-6192
service@fireflybooks.com
ISBNs: 0-919783; 0-919822
Boston Mills Press publishes nonfiction books for adults, including nature, history, travel, & transportation titles. It is a client publisher of Firefly Books.

Bradley Publications
2352 Smith St., Regina, SK S4P 2P6
Tel: 306-525-3305; Fax: 306-757-1810

Breakwater Books Ltd.
Previous Name: Summerhill Books
PO Box 2188, 1 Stamp's Lane, St. John's, NL A1C 6E6
Tel: 709-722-6680; Fax: 709-753-0708
Toll-Free: 800-563-3333
info@breakwaterbooks.com
www.breakwaterbooks.com
Social Media:
twitter.com/BreakwaterBooks
ISBNs: 0-919519, 0-920911, 1-55081; SAN 115-0154
Newfoundland's first publishing house; specializing in educational & curriculum materials, and resources with an emphasis on the history & unique culture of Newfoundland & Labrador
Rebecca Rose, President

Brendan Kelly Publishing Inc.
2122 Highview Dr., Burlington, ON L7R 3X4
Tel: 905-335-3359; Fax: 905-335-5104
mail@brendankellypublishing.com
www.brendankellypublishing.com
ISBNs: 1-895997, 0-9695244
Specialists in the subject areas of mathematics, business, sports & psychology
Brendan Kelly, President

Breton Books & Music
RR#1, Wreck Cove, NS B0C 1H0
Tel: 902-539-5140; Fax: 902-539-9117
Toll-Free: 800-565-5140
bretonbooks@ns.sympatico.ca
www.capebretonbooks.com
ISBNs: 1-895415
Showcasing Cape Breton authors
Ronald Caplan, President

Brick Books
PO Box 20081, 431 Boler Rd., London, ON N6K 4G6
Tel: 519-657-8579;
brick.books@sympatico.ca
www.brickbooks.ca
Social Media: www.youtube.com/brickbooks
twitter.com/brickbooks
www.facebook.com/brickbooks
ISBNs: 0-919626, 1-894078; SAN: 115-0162
Small literary press devoted to the work of Canadian poets
Kitty Lewis, General Manager

Brindle & Glass Publishing Ltd.
340 - 1105 Pandora Ave., Victoria, BC V8V 3P9
Tel: 250-360-0829; Fax: 250-386-0829
info@brindleandglass.com
www.brindleandglass.com
Social Media:
twitter.com/BrindleAndGlass
www.facebook.com/BrindleandGlass
Publish a set of books: regional and national titles; new editions of books that should still be available; books for adults and for young readers; fiction, drama and poetry.
Ruth Linka, Publisher

Broadview Press
PO Box 1243, #5, 280 Perry St., Peterborough, ON K9J 7H5
Tel: 705-743-8990; Fax: 705-743-8353
customerservice@broadviewpress.com
www.broadviewpress.com
Social Media:
twitter.com/broadviewpress
www.facebook.com/pages/Broadview-Press/316561361724692
ISBNs: 0-921149, 1-55111; SAN: 115-6772
With additional offices in Guelph, Nanaimo, Wolfville & Calgary; specializing in English Studies & Philosopy
Don LePan, President

Broken Jaw Press Inc. (MAPP)
Previous Name: Maritimes Arts Projects Productions
PO Box 596 A, Fredericton, NB E3B 5A6
Tel: 506-454-5127; Fax: 506-454-5134
editors@brokenjaw.com
www.brokenjaw.com
Social Media: brokenjawpress.blogspot.ca
ISBNs: 0-921411, 1-896647, 1-55391; SAN: 117-1437
Joe Blades, Publisher

Broquet inc. / Broquet Publishing Company Inc.
97-B, Montee des Bouleaux, Saint-Constant, QC J5A 1A9
Tel: 450-638-3338; Fax: 450-638-4338
info@broquet.qc.ca
www.broquet.qc.ca
ISBNs: 2-89000
Antoine Broquet, Éditeur

The Brucedale Press
Owned By: Broad Horizons Books
PO Box 2259, Port Elgin, ON N0H 2C0
Tel: 519-832-6025;
brucedale@bmts.com
www.bmts.com/~brucedale
ISBNs: 0-9698716, 1-896922
Specializing in Bruce Peninsula & Queen's Bush writers, artists & photographers
Anne Duke Judd, Contact

Bungalo Books
#100, 17 Elk Ct., Kingston, ON K7M 7A4
Tel: 613-374-2494; Fax: 613-389-2351
bungalo@pokeweed.com; bungalo@cgocable.net
www.bungalobooks.com
ISBNs: 0-921285
Books for children
John Bianchi, President, john@johnbianchi.com
Frank B. Edwards, Publisher

Bunker to Bunker Books
PO Box 914 T, Calgary, AB T2H 2H4
Tel: 403-512-2123;
bunkertobunkerbooks@yahoo.com
www.bunkertobunkerbooks.com
ISBNs: 0-9699039
Military firearms books, British & Canadian military collectible books, WW II history
Geoff Todd, Contact

Burgher Books
#504, 555 Richmond St. West, Toronto, ON M5V 3B1
Tel: 416-504-3471; Fax: 416-504-6604
info@burgher.com

BuschekBooks
PO Box 74053, 5 Beechwood Ave., Ottawa, ON K1M 2H9
Tel: 613-744-2589; Fax: 613-744-2967
contact@buschekbooks.com
www.buschekbooks.com
ISBNs: 0-9699904, 1-894543
John Buschek, Publisher

Butterworths Canada Ltd.
Head Office
Owned By: LexisNexis Canada
#700, 123 Commerce Valley Dr. East, Markham, ON L3T 7W8
Tel: 905-479-2665; Toll-Free: 800-668-6481
media@lexisnexis.ca; customerservice@lexisnexis.ca
www.butterworths.ca
ISBNs: 0-409
Now a part of LexisNexis Canada, Butterworths' catalogue focuses on Canadian law. Vancouver Office: #920, 355 Burrard St., Vancouver, BC, V6C 2G8, Tel.: 604-684-1462. Ottawa Office: #700, 112 Kent St., Ottawa, ON, K1P 5P2, Tel.: 613-238-3499. Toronto Office: #400, 905 King St. West, Toronto, ON, M6K 3G9, Tel.: 416-862-7656. Montréal Office: #111, 215 rue St. Jacques, Montréal, QC, H2Y 1M6.

Caitlin Press Inc.
8100 Alderwood Rd., Halfmoon Bay, BC V0N 1Y1
Tel: 604-885-9194; Toll-Free: 877-964-4953
www.caitlin-press.com
ISBNs: 1-894759, 0-920576; SAN: 115-2793
Specializing in BC authors, poetry, stories of the Central Interior and in works by and about BC women.
Vici Johnstone, Publisher & Owner, vici@caitlin-press.com

Callawind Publications Inc. / Publications Callawind inc.
#179, 3551, boul St. Charles, Kirkland, QC H9H 3C4
Tel: 514-685-9109; Fax: 514-685-7952
info@callawind.com
www.callawind.com
ISBNs: 1-896511
Specializing in cookbooks & children's books; also available in the U.S. from #200, 4501 Forbes Blvd., Lanham, MD, 20706, Tel: 800-462-6420, www.bibliodistribution.com.
Marcy Claman, President

Cambridge University Press
66 Pine St. South, Port Hope, ON L1A 3G1
Tel: 905-885-9315; Fax: 905-885-9332
Toll-Free: 877-406-5248
toronto@cambridge.org
www.cambridge.org
ISBNs: 0-521; SAN: 281-3769
Cambridge U. Press publishes academic & educational writing from arouns the world, currently over 2500 titles and 200 journals per year. Vancouver office: c/o Curriculum Plus, 40407 Ayr Dr., Box 2319, Vancouver, BC, V0N 3G0, Tel: 800-660-1244, Email: ian.sutherland@shaw.ca
Pamela Robinson, Sales Representative, probinson@cambridge.org

Canada Law Book Inc.
Owned By: The Cartwright Group Ltd.
240 Edward St., Aurora, ON L4G 3S9
Tel: 905-841-6472; Fax: 905-841-5085
Toll-Free: 800-263-2037
www.canadalawbook.ca
ISBNs: 0-88804
Specializing in legal resources (print & online), & current awareness services
Stuart Morrison, President, The Cartwright Group Ltd.
Ruth Epstein, VP, Canada Law Book LL.B.

Canadian Bible Society
10 Carnforth Rd., Toronto, ON M4A 2S4
Tel: 416-757-4171; Fax: 416-757-3376
Toll-Free: 800-465-2425
info@biblesociety.ca
www.biblesociety.ca
Social Media:
www.facebook.com/CanadianBibleSociety
ISBNs: 0-88834; SAN: 112-5559
The Society translates, publishes & distributes the Bible throughout Canada

Rev. Ted Seres, National Director, tseres@biblesociety.ca
Dennis Hillia, Director, Operations, dhillis@biblesociety.ca

Canadian Centre for Community Renewal (CCCR) / Centre canadien pour le renouveau communautaire
Previous Name: Centre for Community Enterprise
PO Box 1161 A, Port Alberni, BC V9Y 7M1
Toll-Free: 888-255-6779
communityrenewal.ca
Social Media:
twitter.com/communityrenewa
www.facebook.com/Canadiancentreforcommunityrenewal
ISBNs: 1-895818
CCCR publishes i4, an ejournal with information on the principles of community economic development. The online catalogue carries nearly 600 articles, papers and books available in pdf.
Mike Lewis, Executive Director
Don McNair, Editor & Publisher, mcnair@cedworks.com

Canadian Circumpolar Institute CCI Press
1 - 42 Pembina Hall, University of Alberta, Edmonton, AB T6G 2H8
Tel: 403-492-4512; Fax: 403-492-1153
ccinst@gpu.srv.ualberta.ca
www.uofaweb.ualberta.ca/polar/
ISBNs: 1-896445, 0-919058
Elaine Maloney, Managing Editor, elaine.maloney@ualberta.ca
Cindy S. Mason, Business Manager, 780-492-4512, cindy.mason@ualberta.ca

Canadian Educators' Press
1230 White Clover Way, Mississauga, ON L5V 1K7
Tel: 905-826-0578;
cepress@sympatico.ca
ISBNs: 1-896191
CEP publishes titles related to Canadian law and law enformcement.
Silma Deonarine, Manager

Canadian Government Publishing
350 Albert St., 4th Fl., Ottawa, ON K1A 0S5
Tel: 613-941-5995; Fax: 613-998-1450
Toll-Free: 800-635-7943
publications@pwgsc.gc.ca
publications.gc.ca
ISBNs: 0-660, 0-662; SAN: 115-2882
The official publisher for the Government of Canada, CGP publishes priced documents in print, Braille, and large-print formats and on a variety of subjects, such as health, finance, science and education, among others. These publications include books, serials, monographs, maps, pamphlets, and information kits. Formats also include online publishing and electronic publications.

The Canadian Institute for Law, Theology & Public Policy
89 Douglasview Rise SE, Calgary, AB T2Z 2P5
Tel: 403-720-8714; Fax: 403-720-8746
ciltpp@cs.com
www.ciltpp.com
ISBNs: 1-896363
Publishes books and taps which seek to integrate in depth the Christian faith with public policy issues
Will Moore, President

Canadian Institute of Chartered Accountants (CICA)
277 Wellington St. West, Toronto, ON M5V 3H2
Tel: 416-977-3222; Fax: 416-977-8585
www.cica.ca
ISBNs: 1-55385, 0-88800
Published material includes resources for accountants & accounting students.
Doug Baker, Chair FCA
Kevin Dancey, President & CEO FCA, 416-204-3333, Fax: 416-204-3405, kevin.dancey@cica.ca
Peter Hoult, Director, Information & Productivity, 416-204-3330, peter.hoult@cica.ca

Canadian Institute of Resources Law
#3353 MFH, University of Calgary, 2500 University Dr. NW, Calgary, AB T2N 1N4
Tel: 403-220-3200; Fax: 403-282-6182
cirl@ucalgary.ca
www.cirl.ca
ISBNs: 0-919269; SAN: 115-2904
The Institute publishes the results of its research & proceedings of conferences that it sponsors, on the topic of Natural Resources Law. Titles include, "Canada Energy Law Service."
Richard Neufeld, Chair
J. Owens Saunders, Executive Director, 403-220-3975, josaunde@ucalgary.ca

Canadian Institute of Strategic Studies
#702, 165 University Ave., Toronto, ON M5H 3B8
Tel: 416-322-8128; Fax: 416-322-8129
info@ciss.ca
www.ciss.ca
ISBNs: 1-894736, 0-919769; SAN: 115-2912
The Institute publishes books, papers & journals devoted to the research & analysis of Canadian Military Affairs, security affairs & international relations in general.
Sen. Hugh Segal, Chair
Alex Morrison, President

Canadian Institute of Ukrainian Studies Press (CIUS Press)
University of Toronto, #308, 256 McCaul St., Toronto, ON M5T 1W5
Tel: 416-978-6934; Fax: 416-978-2672
cius@chass.utoronto.ca
www.ciuspress.com
ISBNs: 0-920862, 1-895571, 1-894301, 1-894865; SAN: 115-2920
The Institute is the publishing arm of the Canadian Institute of Ukranian Studies. It focuses on original research in English on Ukrainian history, language, literature, contemporary Ukraine, and Ukrainians in Canada. It also publishes English translations of Ukrainian monographs and memoirs.
Dr. Zenon Kohut, Director, CIUS

Canadian International Council (CIC)
#064S, 1 Devonshire Pl., Toronto, ON M5S 3K7
Tel: 416-946-7209; Fax: 416-946-7319
Toll-Free: 800-668-2442
info@opencanada.org
www.opencanada.org
Social Media: www.youtube.com/user/onlinecicvideos
twitter.com/TheCIC
www.facebook.c om/CanadianInternationalCouncil
ISBNs: 0-9866175; SAN: 115-2890
CIC is a non-partisan, nationwide research council which publishes content on Canada's foreign policy.
Jim Balsillie, Chair
Jennifer Jeffs, President
Laura Sunderland, Communications Officer, lsunderland@onlinecic.org

Canadian Museum of Civilization
100 Laurier St., Gatineau, QC K1A 0M8
Tel: 819-776-8387; Fax: 819-776-8535
Toll-Free: 800-555-5621
publications@civilization.ca
www.civilization.ca
ISBNs: 0-660; SAN: 115-4532
Together with the Canadian War Museum, the CMC publishes a range of books, papers, essays, journals and reports with a focus on Canadian history, prehistory & civilization for both adults and children.
Victor Rabinovitch, President & CEO, 819-776-7116, victor.rabinovitch@civilization.ca
Chantal Schryer, VP, Public Affairs & Publishing, 819-776-8499, chantal.schryer@civilization.ca
Stéphanie Verner, Media Relations Officer, 819-776-7169, stephanie.verner@civilization.ca

Canadian Paperbacks Publishing Ltd.
17 Gwynne Ave., Ottawa, ON K1Y 1X1
Tel: 613-722-1171;
ISBNs: 0-919554
This is the publisher of "A Dictionary of Canadian Artists," a resource of biographies. The copyright of this 8-volume series however was sold to the National Gallery of Canada (www.gallery.ca) in 2007, where the project continues online.
Colin S. MacDonald, President

Canadian Plains Research Center Press (CPRCP Press)
University of Regina, 3737 Wascana Parkway, Regina, SK S4S 0A2
Tel: 306-585-4758; Fax: 306-585-4699
Toll-Free: 866-874-2257
canadian.plains@uregina.ca
www.cprcpress.ca
ISBNs: 0-88977; SAN: 115-0278
The CPRCP Press is publishing arm of the University of Regina. It publishes scholarly manuscripts on aspects of life in the Prairie region, as well as non-fiction trade titles concerning the Prairies.
Harry Diaz, Executive Director, harry.diaz@uregina.ca
Brian Mlazgar, Publications Manager, 306-585-4795, brian.mlazgar@uregina.ca

Canadian Scholars' Press Inc. (CSPI)
#801, 180 Bloor St. West, Toronto, ON M5S 2V6
Tel: 416-929-2774; Fax: 416-929-1926
info@cspi.org
www.cspi.org
ISBNs: 1-55130, 0-921627, 1-894184
CSPI is an independent publisher of texts, scholarly works, and titles that present themes and issues of interest to the general Canadian market. It also imprints Women's Press and Sumach Press, both with a focus on feminist work which contributes to the social identity of Canada, and also Kellom Books which carries poetry, fiction and non-fiction by men.
Andrew Wayne, President, awayne@cspi.org
Rick Walker, VP, Book Publishing, rick.walker@cspi.org
Drew Hawkins, VP, Custom Publishing, dhawkins@cspi.org

Canadian University Press
#503, 920 Yonge St., Toronto, ON M4W 3C7
Tel: 416-962-2287; Fax: 416-966-3699
Toll-Free: 866-250-5595
president@cup.ca
www.cup.ca
Social Media:
twitter.com/canunipress
Canadian University Press is a national, non-profit co-operative, owned and operated by more than 80 student newspapers from coast to coast.
Sam Brooks, President, 416-962-2287 x229
Arshy Mann, National Bureau Chief, 416-962-2287 x230, national@cup.ca

Canadian Urban Institute / Institut urbain du Canada
PO Box 612, #402, 555 Richmond St. W, Toronto, ON M5V 3B1
Tel: 416-365-0816; Fax: 416-365-0650
cui@canurb.com
www.canurb.com
Social Media:
twitter.com/canurb
www.facebook.com/265253496954
ISBNs: 1-895446
Terry Cooke, Chair
Michael Fenn, Interim President & CEO, 416-365-0816, X-233, mfenn@canurb.com

Canadian Water Resources Association (CWRA) / Association canadienne des ressources hydriques
1401 - 14th St., Lethbridge, AB T1H 2W6
Tel: 403-317-0017;
www.cwra.org
ISBNs: 1-896513, 0-9694535
CWRA publishes journals, books & reports on water resources in Canada. Titles include the quarterly publication, Canadian Water Resources Journal, the newsletter, Water News.
Rick Ross, Executive Director, fjross@telusplanet.net

CANAV Books
51 Balsam Ave., Toronto, ON M4E 3B6
Tel: 416-698-7559; Fax: 416-693-4344
www.canavbooks.com
ISBNs: 0-9690703, 0-91022; SAN: 115-3021
Publishers of books on aviation history
Larry Milberry, Publisher, larry@canavbooks.com

Can-Ed Media Ltd.
43 Moccasin Trail, Toronto, ON M3C 1Y5
Tel: 416-445-3900; Fax: 416-445-9976
canedmedia@sympatico.ca
ISBNs: 0-920102; SAN: 170-0073
Specializes in dance & fitness recordings & instruction books

Cape Breton University Press
Previous Name: University College of Cape Breton Press
PO Box 5300, 1250 Grand Lake Rd., Sydney, NS B1P 6L2
Tel: 902-563-1955; Fax: 902-563-1177
cbu_press@cbu.ca
www.cbu.ca/press
Social Media:
twitter.com/cbupress
www.facebook.com/CapeBretonUniversityPress
ISBNs: 0-920336, 1-897009; SAN: 115-5458
Publishing arm of Cape Breton University.
Mike R. Hunter, Editor-in-Chief, mike_hunter@cbu.ca

Capemara Communications Inc.
4623 William Head Rd., Victoria, BC V9C 3Y7
Tel: 250-474-3935; Fax: 250-478-3979
Toll-Free: 800-661-0368
info@capamara.com
capamara.com
This publisher offers specialty magazines and trade newspapers for various industries in Canada and around the world. Titles

include: Aquaculture, Hatchery International, Small Farm Canada, Crane & Hoist Canada.

Captus Press
 # 14-15, 1600 Steeles Ave. West, Concord, ON L4K 4M2
Tel: 416-736-5537; Fax: 416-736-5793
info@captus.com
www.captus.com
ISBNs: 0-921801, 1-895712, 1-896691, 1-55322
Captus is a publisher of textbooks which provide a Canadian context for university and college courses in the subjects of business, law, disability studies, and Aboriginal economic development.
Randy Hoffman, President

Carraig Books / Livres Carraig
CP 8733, Sainte-Foy, QC G1V 4N6
Tél: 418-651-5918;
carraigbooks@sympatico.ca
ISBNs: 0-9690805, 0-9698581
The company specializes in books on Quebec-Irish history with titles including, "Eyewitness - Grosse Ile - 1847," "The Shamrock Trail, Tracing the Irish in Quebec City."
Marianna O'Gallagher, m.ogallagher@sympatico.ca

Carswell
Owned By: Thomson Reuters
One Corporate Plaza, 2075 Kennedy Rd., Toronto, ON M1T 3V4
Tel: 416-609-8000; Fax: 416-298-5094
Toll-Free: 800-387-5351
carswell.comments@thomson.com
www.carswell.com
ISBNs: 0-459, 0-7798, 0-88820; SAN: 115-0316
Carswell publishes directories, including the Lexpert Legal Directory, Tax & Accounting, Business, Compliance & International.
Don Van Meer, President/CEO

CBC Learning
Previous Name: CBC Non-Broadcast Sales
PO Box 500 A, 205 Wellington St. West, Toronto, ON M5W 1E6
Tel: 416-205-6384; Fax: 416-205-2376
Toll-Free: 866-999-3072
cbclearning@cbc.ca
www.cbceds.ca
ISBNs: 0-660; SAN: 115-2777
Publishes resources related to CBC programs & programming

CCH Canadian Limited
Owned By: Wolters Kluwer
#300, 90 Sheppard Ave. East, Toronto, ON M2N 3A1
Tel: 416-224-2224; Fax: 416-224-2243
Toll-Free: 800-268-4522
cservice@cch.ca; support@cch.ca
www.cch.ca
ISBNs: 1-55367, 1-55141, 0-88796, 1-55496; SAN: 115-2785
Publishers of professional information products involving tax, accounting, law, financial planning & human resources
Ian Rhind, President/CEO
Allan Orr, VP, Finance & Administration, aorr@cch.ca

Cedar Cave Books
PO Box 180, Newmarket, ON L3Y 4X1
Fax: 905-895-7613
Toll-Free: 866-895-9296
info@cedarcave.com
www.cedarcave.com/
Cedar Cave Books are self-publishers of a number of non-fiction books, with titles including "Yoga for Cats," & "Florida, Eh?"

Centax Books & Distribution
Owned By: Printwest
1150 - 8th Ave., Regina, SK S4R 1C9
Tel: 306-359-7580; Fax: 800-823-6829
Toll-Free: 800-667-5595
centax@printwest.com
www.centaxbooks.com
ISBNs: 0-919845, 1-895292, 1-894022, 1-897010
Together with its sister company, Publishing Solutions, Centax produces and markets cookbooks, RCMP history books, business and family management books, family lifestyle, gardening, self-help and sports books.
Dan Marce, General Manager, d.marce@printwest.com
Tracy Wilson, Office Manager, t.wilson@printwest.com
Margo Embury, Director, Operations, m.embury@printwest.com

Centre for Addiction & Mental Health (CAMH)
Previous Name: Addiction Research Foundation
33 Russell St., Toronto, ON M5S 2S1
Tel: 416-595-6059; Fax: 416-593-4694
Toll-Free: 800-661-1111
publications@camh.net
www.camh.net
Other information: 1-800-463-627
ISBNs: 0-88868, 1-77052; SAN 115-0081
CAMH publishes resources for therapists, doctors, nurses, front-line workers, and other professionals in the fields of addictions & mental health. Materials include research papers, pamphlets, newsletters and journals.

Centre for the Grief Journey
PO Box 201, 2-3415 Dixie Rd., Mississauga, ON L4Y 4J6
Tel: 905-624-8080; Fax: 905-624-6742
info@griefjourney.com
www.griefjourney.com
Social Media: www.youtube.com/user/Griefjourney
www.facebook.com/groups/315946219470

The company produces resources to support the grieving process.
Dr. Bill Webster, Contact, bwebster@griefjourney.com

Centre FORA
#0103, 450, av Notre-Dame, Sudbury, ON P3C 5K8
Tél: 705-524-3672; Téléc: 705-524-8535
Ligne sans frais: 888-814-4422
info@centrefora.on.ca
www.centrefora.on.ca
ISBNs: 2-921706
Centre francophone d'édition en éducation de base des adultes, et de diffusion de matériel éducatif pour tout âge. Service d'édition: coordination de projects, production, impression, rédaction, etc. Service de diffusion. Bureaux: Sudbury, North Bay.
Liane Romain, Executive Director, lianer@centrefora.on.ca

Centre franco-ontarien de ressources pédagogiques

435, rue Donald, Ottawa, ON K1K 4X5
Tél: 613-747-8000; Téléc: 613-747-2808
Ligne sans frais: 877-742-3677
cforp@cforp.ca
www.cforp.on.ca; www.librairieducentre.com
Médias sociaux:
twitter.com/CFORP
Centre multiservices en éducation; développement, édition; production multimedia; programmation; formation professionnelle; imprimerie
Gilles Leroux, Directeur général, x253, robert.arseneault@cforp.on.ca

Céthial Books for Children (Canada) Inc.
Anciennement Céthial & Bossche Productions Inc
CP 252 Mount Royal, Montréal, QC H3P 3C5
Tél: 514-278-3333; Ligne sans frais: 800-238-4425
cethial@cethial.com; info@cethial.com
www.cethial.com
ISBNs: 1-55274, 1-896933

CGS Communications, Inc.
Previous Name: Canadian Guidance Services
2521 Nicklaus Ct., Burlington, ON L7M 4V1
Tel: 905-332-0083; Fax: 905-319-1641
info@cgscommunications.com
www.cgscommunications.com
ISBNs: 0-929079
Published materials include books on career/educational planning and scholarship informaton.

CHA Press
17 York St., Ottawa, ON K1N 9L6
Tel: 613-241-8005; Fax: 613-241-5055
custserv@cha.ca
www.cha.ca/cart/catalog/cha-publications.html
ISBNs: 0-919100, 1-896151
Pamela C. Fralick, President & CEO

The Charlton Press
PO Box 820 Willowdale B, Toronto, ON M2K 2R1
Tel: 416-488-1418; Fax: 416-488-4656
Toll-Free: 800-442-6042
chpress@charltonpress.com
www.charltonpress.com
ISBNs: 0-88968; SAN: 115-0235
Publishers of catalogues on 20th century collectables including coins, bank notes & others
W.K. Cross, Publisher

Chenelière Éducation
Anciennement Éditions de la Chenelière inc.
7001, boul St-Laurent, Montréal, QC H2S 3E3
Tél: 514-273-1066; Téléc: 514-276-0324
Ligne sans frais: 800-565-5531
info@cheneliere-education.ca
www.cheneliere.ca
ISBNs: 2-89310, 2-89461
Y compris Groupe Beauchemin, Gaëtan Morin Éditeur, et les Publications Graficor
Jacques Rochefort, Président-directeur général, jrochefort@cheneliere.ca
Michel Carl Perron, Vice-président, Production, mcperron@cheneliere.ca

Chestnut Publishing Group Inc.
#610, 4005 Bayview Ave, Toronto, ON M2M 3Z9
Tel: 416-224-5824; Fax: 416-224-0595
sharkstark@sympatico.ca
www.chestnutpublishing.com
ISBNs: 1-894601, 0-9731237, 0-9689552, 0-9688946
CPG publishes educational material for both adult & children, ESL materials, as well as novels & teacher's guides targeted at reluctant readers. It has 4 imprints: Chestnut Publishing, High Interest Publishing (HIP), Lynx Publishing and Patnor Books with its New Start Suspense Series.
Stanley Starkman, President, 416-224-5824, sharkstark@sympatico.ca

Claudiere Books
#3, 402 McLeod St., Ottawa, ON K2P 1A6
info@chaudierebooks.com
www.chaudierebooks.com
Social Media: www.myspace.com/chaudierebooks
twitter.com/ChaudiereBooks
Jennifer Mulligan, Publisher/Production Manager/Business Manager, jennifer@chaudierebooks.com
Robert McLennan, Publisher/Senior Editor, rob@chaudierebooks.com

Clifford Ford Publications
#15, 120 Walnut Ct., Ottawa, ON K1R 7W2
Tel: 613-237-0550;
crford@cliffordfordpublications.ca
www.cliffordfordpublications.ca
ISBNs: 0-919883
This is a publisher of a wide range of sheet music, including Canadian historical anthologies, choral collections and pedagogical music, as well as those works composed by Clifford Ford.

CNIB
1929 Bayview Ave., Toronto, ON M4G 3E8
Tel: 416-486-2500; Fax: 416-480-7700
Toll-Free: 800-563-2642
info@cnib.ca
www.cnib.ca
ISBNs: 0-616, 0-921122
CNIB reproduces materials in alternative formats, including DAISY audio, Braille

Coach House Books
401 Huron St., Toronto, ON M5S 2G5
Tel: 416-979-2217; Fax: 416-977-1158
Toll-Free: 800-367-6360
mail@chbooks.com
www.chbooks.com
Social Media: www.flickr.com/photos/42290717@N07
twitter.com/coachhousebooks
www.fac ebook.com/groups/2260058751
ISBNs: 1-55245, 1-897439, 1-77056
Coach House Books publishes Canadian content across a variety of fields: fiction, poetry, art & architecture, drama & performing arts, children's, social science & travel, including a series of books about Toronto. It has been nominated for a slew of literary awards, such as Griffin Poetry Prizes, Governor General's Awards, Trillium Book Awards, and the Ontario Premier's Award for Excellence in the Arts.
Stan Bevington, Publisher, stan@chbooks.com
Alana Wilcox, Editorial Director, alana@chbooks.com

Codasat Canada Ltd.
3122 Blenheim St., Vancouver, BC V6K 4J7
Tel: 604-228-9952; Fax: 604-222-2965
www.codasat.com
In addition to inventory management services, Codasat offers sales & distribution services to small & medium-sized publishers wishing to sell books in the Canadian market.
Sandra Hargreaves, Co-owner

Colombo & Company
42 Dell Park Ave., Toronto, ON M6B 2T6
Tel: 416-782-6853; Fax: 416-782-0285
jrc@colombo.ca
www.colombo.ca
ISBNs: 1-894540, 0-9695092, 1-896308
This is the publishing imprint for books by John Robert Colombo & colleagues, including poetry & poetry anthologies, Canadiana, reference works & quotation collections, mysteries, humour & translations.
John Robert Colombo, Publisher

Commodore Books
6079 Academic Quadrangle, English Dept., Simon Fraser University, 8888 University Dr., Burnaby, BC V5A 1S6
Tel: 778-782-4988; Fax: 604-291-5737
info@commodorebooks.com
www.commodorebooks.com
The first and only black literary press in western Canada.

Commoners' Publishing Society Inc.
631 Tubman Cres., Ottawa, ON K1V 8L5
Tel: 613-523-2444; Toll-Free: 866-890-9489
cheriton@on.aibn.com
www.commonerspublishing.com
ISBNs: 0-88970; SAN: 115-0243
Although by no means limited to men's issues, Commoners' publishes books on parenting, marriage and divorce policy from a male perspective.
Glenn Cheriton, President

The Communication Project
9 Lobraico Lane, Whitchurch-Stouffville, ON L4A 7X5
Tel: 905-640-8914; Fax: 905-640-2922
Toll-Free: 800-772-7765
tcp@tcpnow.com
www.tcppress.com
ISBNs: 1-896232
A research & education group, with an independent press, dedicated to quality books for children & adults in the areas of literacy, science education, life course, & intergenerational relationships

Community Legal Education Ontario (CLEO) / Éducation juridique communautaire Ontario
#600, 119 Spadina Ave., Toronto, ON M5V 2L1
Tel: 416-408-4420; Fax: 416-408-4424
cleo@cleo.on.ca
www.cleo.on.ca
ISBNs: 0-88903; SAN: 115-3110
CLEO is a community legal clinic specializing in public legal education and publishing booklets, pamphlets, fact sheets & manuals, all written in clear language for people with low incomes, immigrants & refugees, seniors, injured workers, & women. Topics include workers' rights, landlord & tenant law, immigration law, family law, consumer rights, & women's rights. Most publications are available in French, and some are available in other languages. MOst are free of charge.
Nicole Osbourne James, Editor & Production Coordinator

Company's Coming Publishing Limited
2311 - 96 St., Edmonton, AB T6N 1G3
Tel: 780-450-6223; Fax: 780-450-1857
info@companyscoming.com
www.companyscoming.com
Social Media:
www.facebook.com/pages/Companys-Coming/59216157574
ISBNs: 1-896891, 1-897069, 1-895455, 0-9690695, 0-9693322, 1-897477
Publishes an extensive array of cookbooks, including a selection of series, with Kids Cooking, Pint Size, & Focus as examples. In addition, Company's Coming publishes a series of craft books.
Grant Lovig, President & Publisher
Gail Lovig, Vice-President, Marketing & Distribution
Kim Hamilton, Marketing Coordinator, 780-450-6223, X-264, kimh@companyscoming.com

Continental Records Company Ltd.
PO Box 7, Streetsville, ON L5M 2B7
Tel: 905-813-9544; Fax: 905-812-4993
Toll-Free: 800-494-6129
conrecs@gocontinental.com
www.gocontinental.com
ISBNs: 0-920325
In addition to selling 45 RPM records & unique oldies on CD, Continental Records publishes chart books and music books. Titles include The Record & CD Collector's Directory. The company also offers The Directory of Canadian Recruiters, a compilation of employment firms & organizations.
Neil Patte, President

Continuing Legal Education Society of British Columbia (CLEBC)
#500, 1155 West Pender St., Vancouver, BC V6E 2P4
Tel: 604-669-3544; Fax: 604-669-9260
Toll-Free: 800-663-0437
custserv@cle.bc.ca
www.cle.bc.ca
Social Media:
twitter.com/clebc
www.facebook.com/clebc
ISBNs: 1-55258, 0-86504; SAN: 115-3153
CLEBC specializes in books, papers, case digests & manuals for the legal profession, covering a variety of practice areas including aboriginal law, administrative law, criminal law, family law, labour, real estate, tax and more. An online subscription service is also available. They offer 100+ live courses per year, video repeats, live webinars, CLE-TV courses.
Ronald G. Friesen, CEO, 604-893-2114, rfriesen@cle.bc.ca
Dennis Cole, Director, Finance & Administration, 604-893-2102, dcole@cle.bc.ca
Susan Munro, Director, Publications, 604-893-2106, smunro@cle.bc.ca
Rob Seto, Director, Programs, 604-893-2111, rseto@cle.bc.ca
Michael Kaine, Director, Information Technology, 604-893-2131, mkaine@cle.bc.ca

Copp Clark Professional
Owned By: Pearson Plc
#1, 1675 Sismet Rd., Mississauga, ON L4W 4K8
Tel: 905-238-2882; Fax: 905-238-3413
Toll-Free: 877-389-3378
info@coppclark.com
www.coppclark.com
ISBNs: 0-7730, 0-273
The oldest, continuously active publisher in Canada, Copp Clark publishes resources for the financial trading community, authoritative reference data on holiday observances.
Ronald S. Marr, President & Publisher
Grace D'Alfonso, Editorial Director

Cormorant Books Inc.
390 Steelcase Rd. East, Markham, ON L3R 1G2
Tel: 905-475-5571;
www.cormorantbooks.com
Social Media: www.youtube.com/user/cormorantbooks
www.twitter.com/cormorantbooks
www.facebook.com/pages/Cormorant-Books/27 6145292065
ISBNs: 0-920953, 1-896951, 1-897151; SAN: 115-4176
Cormorant Books specializes in fiction emerging Canadian writers, reissues of Canadian literary classics, and English translations of works by Quebec writers. There is a selection of gay & lesbian literature, as well as non-fiction titles, including historical biographies and memoirs.
Marc Coté, President & Publisher

Coteau Books
Owned By: Thunder Creek Publishing Cooperative
2517 Victoria Ave., Regina, SK S4P 0T2
Tel: 306-777-0170; Fax: 306-522-5152
Toll-Free: 800-440-4471
coteau@coteaubooks.com
www.coteaubooks.com
Other information: www.goodreads.com/profile/Coteau_Books
Social Media: pinterest.com/coteaubooks
twitter.com/CoteauBooks
www.facebook.com/pages/Coteau-Books/21207050660
ISBNs: 0-919926, 1-55050
Coteau Books is a not-for-profit, cooperatively run press specializing in fiction, poetry, drama & fiction for young readers, with some emphasis on Saskatchewan writers.
Nik L. Burton, Managing Editor
Amber Goldie, Marketing Manager

Crabtree Publishing Company
616 Welland Ave., St. Catharines, ON L2M 5V6
Tel: 905-682-5221; Fax: 800-355-7166
Toll-Free: 800-387-7650
custserv@crabtreebooks.com
www.crabtreebooks.com
ISBNs: 0-7787, 0-86505, 1-4271; SAN: 115-1436
With offices in the U.S., Canada, the U.K. and Australia, Crabtreespecializes in children's non-fiction work & educational products on many curriculum subjects. Material is published in an audio format and in several languages, including Spanish and French. Imprints include: A Bobbie Kalman Book; Leaps and Bounds Books; and Look, Listen, & Learn.
Lisa Antonsen, National Account Manager
Peter Crabtree, President

Cranberry Tree Press
#173, 5060 Tecumseh Rd. East, Windsor, ON N8T 1C1
Fax: 519-945-6207
mail@cranberrytreepress.com
www.cranberrytreepress.com
ISBNs: 0-9681325, 0-9684218, 1-894668
Cranberry Tree Press is a contract, co-operative publishing service with editors & designers on staff.
Lenore Langs, Publisher & Editor

Creative Book Publishing Ltd.
PO Box 8660 A, St. John's, NL A1B 3T7
Tel: 709-748-0813; Fax: 709-579-6511
nlbooks@transcontinental.ca
www.creativebookpublishing.ca
ISBNs: 0-920021, 1-895387, 1-894294, 1-897174, 0-920884
Creative Book Publishing specializes in works by Newfoundland & Labrador authors, promoting them to national & international markets. Genres include fiction, poetry, memoirs, history, women's studies and more. Books are published under 3 imprints: Creative Publishers, Killick Press, & Tuckamore Books.
Russell Wangersky, General Manager, rwanger@thetelegram.com
Donna Francis, Editor & Marketing Manager, donna.francis@transcontinental.ca

Crisp Learning Canada
Previous Name: Reid Publishing Ltd.
Owned By: Course Technology, a Thomson company
60 Briarwood Ave., Mississauga, ON L5G 3N6
Tel: 905-274-5678; Fax: 905-278-2801
Toll-Free: 800-446-4797
info@crisplearning.ca
www.crisplearning.ca
ISBNs: 0-921601; SAN: 116-0478
Crisp Learning publishes a library of books & training manuals specializing in: communication, conflict resolution, presentation skills, telephone skills, sales & marketing, customer service, managing, organizational development, and personal improvement.
Stephen Connolly, President, steveconnolly@homeroom.ca

Cross Canada Books
354 Wellesley St. East, Toronto, ON M4X 1H3
Tel: 416-925-7807; Fax: 416-925-9946
Toll-Free: 800-473-4078
doug.fisher@sympatico.ca
ISBNs: 0-920400
Book distributor

Crown Publications Inc.
PO Box 9452 Prov Govt, 563 Superior St., Victoria, BC V8W 9V7
Tel: 250-387-6409; Fax: 250-387-1120
Toll-Free: 800-663-6105
crownpub@gov.bc.ca
www.crownpub.bc.ca
ISBNs: 0-9696417
Crown Publications is the authorized distributor of British Columbia acts, regulations & related legislative publications, and an authorized agent for Canadian Federal Government publications.
Sherry Brown, Director, 250-356-6876, sherry.brown@gov.bc.ca
Wendy Pope, Manager, 250-356-5392, wendy.pope@gov.bc.ca

Culture Concepts Books
69 Ashmount Cres., Toronto, ON M9R 1C9
Tel: 416-245-8119; Fax: 416-245-3383
cultureconcepts@rogers.com
www.cultureconceptsbooks.ca
ISBNs: 0-921472
Culture Concepts Books publishes fiction titles and academic titles in adult education, food, nutrition and culture. Also offered are professional editing services & manuscript evaluation, selected literary agency & book production.
Thelma Barer-Stein, President

Cyclops Press
#1, 164 Browning Ave., Toronto, ON M4K 1W5
mail@cyclopspress.com
www.cyclopspress.com
ISBNs: 1-894177
An independent, artist-run, multimedia, literary micro- publisher specializing in poetry, novels, feature films & videos, CDs, interdisciplinary art projects. Material is distributed through Signature Editions, www.signature-editions.com.
Clive Holden
Alissa York

Dance Collection Danse Publishing
145 George St., Toronto, ON M5A 2M6
Tel: 416-365-3233; Toll-Free: 800-665-5320
talk@dcd.ca
www.dcd.ca
Social Media:
www.twitter.com/DanceCollection
www.facebook.com/pages/Dance-Collection-Danse/14927618346
ISBNs: 0-929003
Publisher of "Dance Collection Danse Magazine," & books on dance.
Francisco Alvarez, Chair

Database Directories
588 Dufferin St., London, ON N6B 2A4
Tel: 519-433-1666; Fax: 519-430-1131
mail@databasedirectory.com
www.databasedirectory.com
ISBNs: 1-896537
Publisher of current contact information on Canadian schools, libraries, book retailers & municipalities
Lesley Classic, CEO

David C. Cook Distribution Canada
Owned By: David C. Cook Publishing
PO Box 98, 55 Woodslee Ave., Paris, ON N3L 3E5
Toll-Free: 800-263-2664
custserv@davidccook.ca
www.davidccook.ca
ISBNs: SAN: 170-0197
Distribution wing of David C. Cook Publishing, Colorado Springs, CO. Specializing in Christian literature & communication resources
Greg Tombs, Managing Director, Global Distribution

Davus Publishing
150 Norfolk St. South, Simcoe, ON N3Y 2W2
Tel: 519-426-2077; Fax: 519-426-0105
davuspub@sympatico.ca
www.davuspublishing.com
ISBNs: 0-915317
Featuring the works of David Beasley, and Major John Richardson, Canada's first novelist.
David R. Beasley, President & Publisher, davuspub@sympatico.ca

DC Books
PO Box 666 St. Laurent, 950, rue Décarie, Montréal, QC H4L 4V9
Tel: 514-939-3990; Fax: 514-939-0569
Toll-Free: 800-591-6250
dcbooks@videotron.ca
www.dcbooks.ca
ISBNs: 0-919688, 1-897190; SAN: 115-8988
DC Books publishes poetry & prose with innovative Canadian emphasis, histories, memoirs, & drama. Also offered are Railfare DC Books about railways & Moosehead Anthology. The house is a Member of the Association of English Editors of Quebec, & the Literary Press Group.
Keith Henderson, Managing Editor

Depository Services Program
350 Albert St., 5th Fl., Ottawa, ON K1A 0S5
Tel: 613-941-5995; Fax: 613-941-2410
Toll-Free: 800-635-7943
publications@pwgsc.gc.ca
publications.gc.ca
ISBNs: 0-660, 0-662; SAN: 115-2882
The official publisher for the Government of Canada, CGP publishes priced documents in print, Braille, and large-print formats and on a variety of subjects, such as health, finance, science and education, among others. These publications include books, serials, monographs, maps, pamphlets, and information kits. Formats also include online publishing and electronic publications.

Detselig Enterprises Ltd.
c/o Temeron Books Inc., #210, 1220 Kensington Rd. NW, Calgary, AB T2N 3P5
Tel: 403-283-0900; Fax: 403-283-6947
contact@brusheducation.ca
www.temerondetselig.com
ISBNs: 0-920490, 1-55059; SAN: 115-0324
Specializing in general trade & academic books written by authors from Canada, the U.S., Austria and The Netherlands
T.E. Giles, President

Deux Voiliers Publishing
Gatineau, QC
Tel: 819-684-7688;
deuxvoiliers@gmail.com
sites.google.com/site/deuxvoilierspublishing
A small print press specializing in first-time Canadian novelists.
Ian Thomas Shaw, Owner

Diffusion Dimedia inc.
539, boul Lebeau, Saint-Laurent, QC H4N 1S2
Tel: 514-336-3941; Fax: 514-331-3916
general@dimedia.qc.ca
www.dimedia.qc.ca
Diffuse & distribue des livres de langue française au Canada
Johanne Paquette, Contact

Diffusion du Livre Mirabel
DétenteurÉditions du Renouveau Pédagogique Inc.
5757, rue Cypihot, Saint-Laurent, QC H4S 1R3
Tél: 514-334-2690; Téléc: 514-334-4720
Ligne sans frais: 800-263-3678
erpidlm@erpi.com
www.erpi.com
ISBNs: 0-88527
Division d'Éditions du Renouveau Pédagogique Inc.; livres jeunesse & imagerie, informatique, littérature, livres de cuisine, bandes dessinées
Normand Cleroux, Président

Diffusion Inter-Livres
1703, rue Belleville, Lemoyne, QC J4P 3M2
Tél: 450-465-0037; Téléc: 450-923-8966
ligueqc@cam.org
www.inter-livres.ca
Joël Coppieter

Doubleday Canada Ltd.
c/o Random House of Canada Limited, #300, One Toronto St., Toronto, ON M5C 2V6
Tel: 416-364-4449; Fax: 416-364-6863
Toll-Free: 000-000-0000
www.randomhouse.ca
ISBNs: 0-385; SAN: 115-0340
Doubleday Canada is an imprint of Random House of Canada, publishing high quality Canadian literary & commercial fiction from new & established writers, memoirs, history, business, & social & political journalism
John Neale, President
Evaughn Moffat, Vice-President, Sales & Marketing

Douglas & McIntyre Publishing Group
#201, 2323 Quebec St., Vancouver, BC V5T 4S7
Tel: 604-254-7191; Fax: 604-254-9099
Toll-Free: 800-667-6902
dm@dmpibooks.com
dmpibooks.com
Social Media:
www.youtube.com/user/dmdouglasmac?feature=mhum
www.facebook.com/DMPublis hers
ISBNs: 0-88894, 1-55054, 1-55365; SAN: 115-1886, 115-026X
Specializing in Canadian fiction & non-fiction.
Mark Scott, President
Scott McIntyre, CEO

Dovehouse Editions Inc.
1890 Fairmeadow Cres., Ottawa, ON K1H 7B9
Tel: 613-731-7601; Fax: 613-731-7601
www.dovehouse.ca
ISBNs: 0-919473, 1-895537
Publishers of The Carleton Renaissance Plays in Translation Series, as well as other works in Renaissance Studies; Publications of the Barnabe Riche Society; University of Toronto Italian Studies; and Ottawa Hispanic Studies
Dr. Donald Beecher, Editor

Dragon Hill Publishing Ltd.
5474 Thibault Wynd NW, Edmonton, AB T6R 3P9
Tel: 780-239-4996;
info@dragonhillpublishing.com
www.dragonhillpublishing.com
ISBNs: 1-896124
Publishing for the popular adult and youth markets, in the subject areas of self-help, biography, success guides, and traditional cultures
Gary Whyte, Publisher

Drawn & Quarterly
PO Box 48056, Montréal, QC H2V 4S8
Tel: 514-279-2221;
info@drawnandquarterly.com
www.drawnandquarterly.com
ISBNs: 1-896597
Publisher of comic books & graphic novels.
Chris Oliveros, Publisher, chris@drawnandquarterly.com

DreamCatcher Publishing Inc.
55 Canterbury St., Saint John, NB E2L 2C6
Tel: 506-632-4008; Fax: 506-632-4009
info@dreamcatcherpublishing.ca
www.dreamcatcherpublishing.ca
ISBNs: 1-894372
Specializing in Maritime writers, fiction & non-fiction for children & adults
Elizabeth Margaris, Publisher

Dundurn Group
#500, 3 Church St., Toronto, ON M5E 1M2
Tel: 416-214-5544; Fax: 416-214-5556
info@dundurn.com
www.dundurn.com
Social Media:
twitter.com/dundurnpress
www.facebook.com/dundurnpress

Duval Education / Duval Éducation
Anciennement Duval House Publishing/Les Éditions Duval
DétenteurNelson Education Ltd.
#100, 233 Dunbar Ave., Montreal, QC H3P 2H4
Tél: 514-932-8229; Téléc: 514-932-9175
Ligne sans frais: 888-932-8229
duvalhouse@duvalhouse.com
www.duvalhouse.com
ISBNs: 1-55220, 1-895850
Educational resources in English & French, ESL materials, Aboriginal resources
Simon de Jocas, Vice President, simon.dejocas@nelson.com

eastendbooks
45 Fernwood Park Ave., Toronto, ON M4E 3E9
Tel: 416-691-6816; Fax: 416-691-2414
info@eastendbooks.com
www.eastendbooks.com
ISBNs: 1-896973
A small-press with an Ontario focus, publishing material in a range of subjects, including fiction, travel, current events, modern jazz
Jeanne MacDonald

Écrits des Forges
992-A, rue Royale, Trois-Rivières, QC G9A 4H9
Tél: 819-840-8492;
ecritsdesforges.com
ISBNs: 2-89046
Poésie, et essais en poésie
Stéphane Despatie, Director général

ECW Press (ECW)
#200, 2120 Queen St. East, Toronto, ON M4E 1E2
Tel: 416-694-3348; Fax: 416-698-9906
info@ecwpress.com
www.ecwpress.com
Social Media:
www.facebook.com/ecwpress
Jack David, Co-Publisher, Business, Sports, Mysteries, jack@ecwpress.com
Jannifer Knoch, Editor, jenk@ecwpress.com

ECW Press
#200, 2120 Queen St. East, Toronto, ON M4E IE2
Tel: 416-694-3348; Fax: 416-698-9906
info@ecwpress.com
www.ecwpress.com
ISBNs: 1-55022, 0-920802, 1-920763; SAN: 115-1274
Publishers of Essays on Canadian Writing, & a diverse selection of contemporary poetry, fiction, writings on culture & politics, biography
Jack David, Co-publisher
Crissy Boylan, Managing Editor

EDIMAG inc.
CP 325 Rosemont, Montréal, QC H1X 3B8
Tél: 514-522-2244; Téléc: 514-522-6301
info@edimag.com
www.edimag.com
ISBNs: 2-921735, 2-89542
Santé, alimentation & recettes, environnement, connaissances pratiques, jeux & sport, loisirs
Pierre Nadeau, Éditeur

Éditions Actualisation
Place du Parc, #2200, 300, rue Léo-Pariseau, Montréal, QC H2X 4B3
Tél: 514-284-2622; Téléc: 514-284-2625
Ligne sans frais: 877-688-0101
admin@actualisation.com
www.actualisation.com

Matériel pour animer des formations, destiné aux formateurs, éducateurs et conseillers en ressources humaines: guides, manuels, questionnaires. Québec: Centre de la technologie, 1995, rue Frank Carrel, bureau 102, 418-688-0100.
Louis Fortin, Président MBA, louis.fortin@actualisation.com

Éditions Anne Sigier inc.
DétenteurÉditions Médiaspaul
a/s Éditions Médiaspaul, 3965, boul Henri-Bourassa est, Montréal, QC H1H 1L1
Tél: 514-322-7341; Téléc: 514-322-4281
mediaspaul@mediaspaul.qc.ca
www.annesigier.qc.ca
ISBNs: 2-89129
Bibles, livres de spiritualité chrétienne, beaux-livres
Anne Sigier
Jacques Sigier

Éditions Arts, Lettres et Techniques inc.
12, rue Northcote, Hampstead, QC H3X 1P5
Tél: 514-747-4784;
ISBNs: 0-921137
Droit, médecine, techniques, sciences, arts
Jacqueline Irali, Présidente

Les Éditions Behaviora inc.
CP 91, 151, ch Bellevue, Eastman, QC J0E 1P0
Tél: 450-297-0515; Téléc: 450-297-0516
behaviora@sympatico.ca
www.behaviora.qc.ca
ISBNs: 2-7629
Ouvrages de psychologie, de pédagogie, & de sciences sociales
Dr. Rodrigue Otis

Éditions Bellarmin
DétenteurÉditions Fides
a/s Éditions Fides, 306, rue Saint-Zotique est, Montréal, QC H2S 1L6
Tél: 514-745-4290; Téléc: 514-745-4299
editions@fides.qc.ca
www.fides.qc.ca
ISBNs: 0-88502, 2-89007
Michel Maillé, Directeur général

Les Éditions Brault et Bouthillier / Brault & Bouthillier Publishing
4823, rue Sherbrooke ouest, Montréal, QC H3Z 1G7
Tél: 514-932-9466; Téléc: 514-932-5929
Ligne sans frais: 866-750-9466
editions@ebbp.ca
www.ebbp.ca
ISBNs: 0-88537, 2-7615
Manuels scolaires, ouvrages pédagogiques/parascolaires; français et anglais
Jean Brault, Président
Yves Brault, Vice-président
Paul Beullac, Éditeur

Les Éditions Cap-aux-Diamants
#212, 3, rue de la Vieille-Université, Québec, QC G1R 5K1
Tél: 418-656-5040; Téléc: 418-656-7282
revue.cap-aux-diamants@hst.ulaval.ca
www.capauxdiamants.org
ISBNs: 2-920069
Yves Beauregard, revue.cap-aux-diamants@hst.ulaval.ca

Les Éditions CEC inc.
Une compagnie de Quebecor Media
DétenteurQuebecor Media
9001, boul Louis-H.-La Fontaine, Anjou, QC H1J 2C5
Tél: 514-351-6010; Téléc: 514-351-3534
Ligne sans frais: 800-363-0494
infoped@ceceditions.com
www.editionscec.com
ISBNs: 0-7751, 2-7617
Ouvrages pour tous les ordres d'enseignement - manuels scolaires, ouvrages de référence, grammaires, anthologies littéraires

Éditions CERES
CP 1089 B, Montréal, QC H5B 3K9
Tél: 514-937-7138; Téléc: 514-937-9875
editionsceres@gmail.ca
www.editionsceres.ca
ISBNs: 0-919089
Les éditions CERES publient exclusivement des livres érudits
C. Stéfane

Les Éditions Chouette
#B-238, 1001, rue Lenoir, Montréal, QC H4C 2Z6
Tél: 514-925-3325; Téléc: 514-925-3323
info@editions-chouette.com
www.chouettepublishing.com
Livres Caillou
Christine L'Heureux, Présidente-fondatrice

Les Éditions Cornac
Anciennement Les Éditions du Loup de Gouttière
5, rue Sainte-Ursule, Québec, QC G1R 4C7
Tél: 418-692-0377; Téléc: 418-692-0605
editionscornac.com
ISBNs: 2-921310, 2-89529
Livres jeunesse; poésie; essais; albums illustrés; a pour mission d'encourager l'expression des Premières Nations
Michel Brûlé, Éditeur, michel@editionscornac.com

Les Éditions de l'Hexagone
Une compagnie de Quebecor Media
DétenteurQuebecor Media/Groupe VML
1010, rue de la Gauchetière est, Montréal, QC H2L 2N5
Tél: 514-523-7993; Téléc: 514-282-7530
adpcommandes@messageries-adp.com
www.edhexagone.com
ISBNs: 2-89006, 2-89295
Littérature québécoise
Danielle Fournier, Directrice

Les Éditions de l'Homme
Une compagnie de Quebecor Media
DétenteurQuebecor Media
955, rue Amherst, Montréal, QC H2L 3K4
Tél: 514-523-1182; Téléc: 514-597-0370
adpcommandes@messagies-adp.com
www.editions-homme.com
ISBNs: 2-7619, 2-89005, 2-89006
Livres de sciences humaines
Pierre Lespérance, Président
Pierre Bourdon, Vice-président à l'édition

Éditions de l'Instant même
865, av Moncton, Québec, QC G1S 2Y4
Tél: 418-527-8690; Téléc: 418-681-6780
info@instantmeme.com
www.instantmeme.com
ISBNs: 2-921197, 2-9800635, 2-89502
Romans, essais, nouvelles
Marie Taillon, Directrice générale

Les Éditions de L'IQRC/Les Presses de l'Université Laval
Pavillon Maurice-Pollack, #3103, 2305, rue de l'Université, Québec, QC G1V 0A6
Tél: 418-656-2803; Téléc: 418-656-3305
Ligne sans frais: 800-859-7474
presses@pul.ulaval.ca
www.pulaval.com
ISBNs: 2-89224
Américana, bioéthique critique, cinéma et société, culture québécoise, éducation, géographie, histoire sociale, lectures, politique
Denis Dion, Directeur général

Les Éditions de la courte échelle
5243, boul Saint-Laurent, Montréal, QC H2T 1S4
Tél: 514-274-2004; Téléc: 514-270-4160
info@courteechelle.com
www.courteechelle.com
ISBNs: 2-89021; SAN: 116-0249
Un leader de la littérature jeunesse francophone - livres pour les trois à six ans; collection adulte
Hélène Derome, Présidente/Éditrice

Éditions de la Paix
127, rue Lussier, Saint-Alphonse-de-Granby, QC J0E 2A0
Tél: 450-375-4765; Téléc: 450-375-4765
info@editpaix.qc.ca
www.editpaix.qc.ca
Jeunesse, patrimoine, romans, poésie, spiritualité
Jean-Paul Tessier, Président-directeur général

Les Éditions de la Pleine Lune
223, 34e av, Lachine, QC H8T 1Z4
Tél: 514-637-6366; Téléc: 514-637-6366
editpllune@videotron.ca
www.pleinelune.qc.ca
ISBNs: 2-89024
Ouvrages québécois et canadiens
Marie-Madeleine Raoult, Directrice

Éditions de Mortagne
CP 116, Boucherville, QC J4B 5E6
Tél: 450-641-2387; Téléc: 450-655-6092
info@editionsdemortagne.com
www.editionsdemortagne.com
ISBNs: 2-89074
Biographies, romans, collection 'Lime et citron', guides pratiques, santé, psychologie, astrologie, motivation
Max Permingeat, Président

Les Éditions des Plaines
CP 123, Saint-Boniface, MB R2H 3B4
Tél: 204-235-0078; Téléc: 204-233-7741
admin@plaines.mb.ca
www.plaines.ca
Médias sociaux:
www.facebook.com/editionsdesplaines
ISBNs: 0-920944, 2-921353, 2-89611
La maison s'applique à donner la parole aux écrivains de l'Ouest canadien
Joanne Therrien, Éditrice en chef Plaines Éducation, direction@plaines.mb.ca

Les Éditions du Blé
340, boul Provencher, Saint-Boniface, MB R3H 0G7
Tél: 204-237-8200; Téléc: 204-233-8182
direction@editionsduble.ca
www.livres-disques.ca/editions_ble/home/index .cfm
ISBNs: 0-920640, 2-921347
La première maison d'édition francophone de l'Ouest canadien; ouvrages des auteurs de la région - poésie, romans, essais, théâtre, livres pour enfants & adolescents
Lucien Chaput

Éditions du Bois-de-Coulonge
1140, av De Montigny, Sillery, QC G1S 3T7
Tél: 418-683-6332; Téléc: 418-683-6332
www.ebc.qc.ca
ISBNs: 2-9801397
Services aux collectivités & vente directe au grand public
Richard Leclerc, Propriétaire Ph.D., rleclerc@ebc.qc.ca

Éditions du Boréal
4447, rue Saint-Denis, Montréal, QC H2J 2L2
Tél: 514-287-7401; Téléc: 514-287-7664
boreal@editionsboreal.qc.ca
www.editionsboreal.qc.ca
ISBNs: 2-89052, 0-7646
Fiction, poésie, essais, histoire, biographies, livres pratiques, collections jeunesse
Pascal Assathiany, Directeur général

Éditions du Nordir
Dép des lettres française, Université d'Ottawa, 60, rue Université, Ottawa, ON K1N 6N5
Tél: 819-243-1253; Téléc: 819-243-6201
lenordir@sympatico.ca
www.livres-disques.ca/editions_nordir
ISBNs: 0-921272
Biographies, études littéraires, poésie, réflexions sociales

Les Éditions du Noroît
#202, 4609, rue d'Iberville, Montréal, QC H2H 2L9
Tél: 514-727-0005; Téléc: 514-723-6660
lenoroit@lenoroit.com
www.lenoroit.com
ISBNs: 2-89018
Livres de poésie et essais littéraires
Mylene Durand, Contact, mylenedurand@lenoroit.com

Les Éditions du Remue-Ménage inc.
#501, 110, rue Ste-Thérèse, Montréal, QC H2Y 1E6
Tél: 514-876-0097; Téléc: 514-876-7951
info@editions-remuemenage.qc.ca
www.editions-remuemenage.qc.ca
ISBNs: 2-89091
Livres sur les femmes: biographie, culture, développement international, éducation, études féministes, poésie, politique, santé
Rachel Bédard, Éditrice

Éditions du Renouveau Pédagogique inc.
Anciennement Editions Pierre Tisseyre
5757, rue Cypihot, Saint-Laurent, QC H4S 1R3
Tél: 514-334-2690; Téléc: 514-334-4720
Ligne sans frais: 800-263-3678
info@erpi.com
www.erpi.com
ISBNs: 2-7613
Maison d'édition scolaire; matériel didactique pour tous les niveaux d'enseignement
Normand Cléroux, Président

Les Éditions du Septentrion
1300, av Maguire, Québec, QC G1T 1Z3
Tél: 418-688-3556; Téléc: 418-527-4978
sept@septentrion.qc.ca
www.septentrion.qc.ca
Spécialisée en histoire, archéologie, science politique, ethnographie, et aux sciences humaines
Denis Vaugeois, Président

Les Éditions du Trécarré
Une compagnie de Quebecor Media
DétenteurQuebecor Media
La Tourelle, #800, 1055, boul René-Lévesque est, Montréal, QC H2L 4S5
Tél: 514-849-5259; Téléc: 514-849-1388
adpcommandes@messageries-adp.com
www.edtrecarre.com
ISBNs: 2-89249, 2-89568
Livres pratiques (cuisine, santé); cahiers d'exercices; littérature jeunesse
Marc Laberge, Président
Colette Laberge, Redactrice en chef

Éditions du Vermillon
305, rue Saint-Patrick, Ottawa, ON K1N 5K4
Tél: 613-241-4032; Téléc: 613-241-3109
leseditionsduvermillon@rogers.com
www.leseditionsduvermillion.com
ISBNs: 0-919925, 1-895873, 1-894547, 1-897058
Romans, poésie, bandes dessinées, guides pédagogiques, essais
Monique Bertoli, Directrice générale

Éditions Fides
306, rue Saint-Zotique est, Montréal, QC H2S 1L6
Tél: 514-745-4290; Téléc: 514-745-4299
maillem@fides.qc.ca
www.fides.qc.ca
ISBNs: 2-7621
Littérature (collection de poche 'Bibliothèque québécoise'), essais, livres religieux, ouvrages de référence, beaux livres; collection Éditions Bellarmin
Michel Maillé, Directeur général

Les Éditions Flammarion Ltée
375, av Laurier ouest, Montréal, QC H2V 2K3
Tél: 514-277-8807; Téléc: 514-278-2085
info@flammarion.qc.ca
www.flammarion.qc.ca
ISBNs: 2-89077
Une maison d'édition généraliste
Jean-Michel Sivry, Président

Éditions Ganesha
CP 484 Youville, Montréal, QC H2P 2W1
Tél: 450-641-2395; Téléc: 450-641-2989
courriel@editions-ganesha.qc.ca
www.editions-ganesha.qc.ca
Ouvrages diverses: philosophie, religion/cultes, psychologie
André Beaudoin
Lucie Cournoyer

Les Éditions Héritage
300, rue Arran, Saint-Lambert, QC J4R 1K5
Tél: 514-875-0327; Téléc: 514-672-1481
Ligne sans frais: 888-228-1498
ISBNs: 2-7625, 0-7773
Luc Payette, Président

Éditions Hurtubise inc
1815, av De Lorimier, Montréal, QC H2K 3W6
Tél: 514-523-1523; Téléc: 514-523-9969
Ligne sans frais: 800-361-1664
www.editionshurtubise.com
Médias sociaux:
www.youtube.com/profile?user=livreshmh#grid/uploads
twitter.com/_Hurtubise
www.facebook.com/EditionsHurtubise
ISBNs: 2-89045, 2-89428
Littérature, beaux livres, jeunesse, éducation
Hervé Foulon, Président-directeur général

Les Éditions JCL inc. / JCL Publishing
930, rue Jacques-Cartier est, Chicoutimi, QC G7H 7K9
Tél: 418-696-0536; Téléc: 418-696-3132
jcl@jcl.qc.ca
www.jcl.qc.ca
ISBNs: 2-89431, 2-920176
Éditeur généraliste: romans, histoire, culture, jeunesse
Jean-Claude Larouche, Président, jclarouche@jcl.qc.ca

Les Éditions JML inc.
1150, ch des Patriotes nord, Mont-St-Hilaire, QC J3G 4S6
Tél: 450-536-1565; Téléc: 450-536-2565
infos@editionsjml.com
www.editionsjml.com
ISBNs: 2-89234
Cahiers de préparation de cours, cahiers de titulariat, relevés de notes, relevés d'absences

Éditions l'Artichaut inc.
355, rue Dubé, Rimouski, QC G5L 4W6
Tél: 418-723-1554; Téléc: 418-725-4828
artichaut@editionslartichaut.com
www.editionslartichaut.com
ISBNs: 2-921288; 2-922998
Matériel didactique axé sur le développement des compétences en langue française (niveaux primaire, secondaire)
Ginette Tremblay, Propriétaire

Les Éditions La Pensée Inc.
4370, rue de l'Hôtel de Ville, Montréal, QC H2W 2H5
Tél: 514-848-9042; Téléc: 514-848-9836
Ligne sans frais: 800-667-5442
administration@editions-lapensee.qc.ca
www.editions-lapensee.qc.ca
Marc-Aimé Guérin, President

Les Éditions le Griffon d'argile
7649, boul Wilfrid-Hamel, Sainte-Foy, QC G2G 1C3
Tél: 418-871-6898; Téléc: 418-871-6818
Ligne sans frais: 800-268-6898
admin@griffondargile.com
www.griffondargile.com
ISBNs: 2-920210, 2-920922, 2-89443
André Gosselin

Les Éditions le Renouveau Charlesbourg inc.
DétenteurInstitut Pie X
CP 87605 Charlesbourg, 870, carré de Tracy est, Québec, QC G1G 5W6
Tél: 418-628-3445; Téléc: 418-624-2277
Ligne sans frais: 877-628-3445
info@editionslerenouveau.com
www.editionslerenouveau.com
Guide de lecture de la Bible, ouvrages du domaine religieux, musique, objets religieux
Jacques Roy, Responsable

Éditions Les 400 Coups
#B550, 1001, rue Lenoir, Montréal, QC H4C 2Z6
Tél: 514-381-1422; Téléc: 514-487-8811
info@editions400coups.com
www.editions400coups.ca
Médias sociaux:
twitter.com/Les400coups
www.facebook.com/editionsles400coups
ISBNs: 2-920993, 2-89540
Albums jeunesse, livres d'art, bandes dessinées. Publient également sous les noms de Mille-Iles, de Zone convective, et de Mécanique générale
Myriam Comtois, Responsable, Communications, m.comtois@editions400coups.com

Éditions Liber
2318, rue Bélanger, Montréal, QC H2G 1C8
Tél: 514-522-3227; Téléc: 514-522-2007
info@editionsliber.org
www.editionsliber.org
ISBNs: 2-921569, 2-89578
Études & essais en philosophie, sciences humaines, littérature
Giovanni Calabrese, Directeur

Éditions Libre Expression
Une compagnie de Quebecor Media
DétenteurQuebecor Media
La Tourelle, #800, 1055, boul. René-Lévesque E, Montréal, QC H2L 4S5
Tél: 514-849-5259; Téléc: 514-849-1388
www.edlibreexpression.com
ISBNs: 2-89111, 2-7648
Fiction, biographie, essais, histoire, culture, guides, beaux livres, livres de poche

Les Éditions Logiques
Une compagnie de Quebecor Media
Anciennement Logidisque inc.
DétenteurQuebecor Media
La Tourelle, #800, 1055, boul René-Lévesque est, Montréal, QC H2L 4S5
Tél: 514-849-5259; Téléc: 514-849-1388
adpcommandes@messageries-adp.com
www.edlogiques.com

ISBNs: 2-89381
Gestion des affaires, économie, pédagogie, psychologie populaire, philosophie, sociologie

Éditions Marie-France ltée
9900, av des Laurentides, Montréal, QC H1H 4V1
Tél: 514-329-3700; Téléc: 514-329-0630
Ligne sans frais: 800-563-6644
editions@marie-france.qc.ca
www.marie-france.qc.ca
Médias sociaux: www.linkedin.com/company/1234624
twitter.com/EdMarieFrance
www.faceboo k.com/editions.marie.france
ISBNs: 2-89168
Informatique, littérature, mathématique, français, français immersion
Jean H. Lachapelle, Président

Éditions MultiMondes
930, rue Pouliot, Québec, QC G1V 3N9
Tél: 418-651-3885; Téléc: 418-651-6822
Ligne sans frais: 800-840-3029
multimondes@multim.com
www.multim.com
ISBNs: 2-921146, 2-89544
Environnement, santé, jeunesse, muséologie, pédagogie, science et technologie
Jean-Marc Gagnon, Président, jmgagnon@multim.com
Lise Morin, Vice-présidente, lmorin@multim.com

Éditions Paulines
5610, rue Beaubien est, Montréal, QC H1T 1X5
Tél: 514-253-5610; Téléc: 514-253-1907
editions@paulines.qc.ca
www.paulines.qc.ca
ISBNs: 0-920912
Ouvrages de spiritualité

Les Éditions Perce-Neige ltée
#22, 140 Botsford St., Moncton, NB E1C 4X4
Tél: 506-383-4446; Téléc: 506-857-2064
perceneige@nb.aibn.com
perceneige.recf.ca
ISBNs: 2-920221
Essais historiques, études littéraires, contes traditionnels et récits, poésie, romans
Paul Bourque, Directeur général

Éditions Phidal inc./Phidal Publishing Inc.
5740, rue Ferrier, Montréal, QC H4P 1M7
Tel: 514-738-0202; Fax: 514-738-5102
Toll-Free: 800-738-7349
customer@phidal.com
www.phidal.com
ISBNs: 2-89393, 2-7643
Ouvrages pour enfants
Albert Soussan, Président

Éditions Prise de Parole
#205, 109, rue Elm, Sudbury, ON P3C 1T4
Tél: 705-675-6491; Téléc: 705-673-1817
prisedeparole@bellnet.ca
www.livres-disques.ca/prise_parole/
ISBNs: 0-920814, 0-921573, 2-89423
Bandes dessinées, beaux livres, contes traditionnels, enfants, ados, études littéraires, poésie, revues, romans
Denise Truax, Directrice générale, prisedeparole@bellnet.ca
Sylvie Lessard, Agente de commercialisation, pdpcommercialisation@bellnet.ca
Alain Mayotte, Directeur administratif, pdpadministration@bellnet.ca

Les Éditions Québec Amérique
329, rue de la Commune ouest, 3e étage, Montréal, QC H2Y 2E1
Tél: 514-499-3000; Téléc: 514-499-3010
courrier@quebec-amerique.com
www.quebec-amerique.com
ISBNs: 0-88552, 2-89037, 2-7644
Ouvrages de référence, littérature, jeunesse
Jacques Fortin, CEO

Les Éditions Quebecor
Une compagnie de Quebecor Media
DétenteurQuebecor Media
7, ch Bates, Montréal, QC H2V 4V7
Tél: 514-270-1746; Téléc: 514-270-5313
simard.jacques@quebecoreditions.com
www.quebecoreditions.com
ISBNs: 0-88617, 2-89089, 2-9801107
Affaires, alimentation, astrologie, biographie, guides pratiques, littérature, santé, sports, nouvel âge
Jacques Simard, Éditeur

Les Éditions Reynald Goulet inc.
40, rue Mireault, Repentigny, QC J6A 1M1
Tél: 450-654-2626; Téléc: 450-654-5433
Ligne sans frais: 800-663-3021
info@goulet.ca
www.goulet.ca
ISBNs: 2-89377
Ouvrages de bureautique, d'informatique, de dessin assisté par ordinateur, et l'autoformation au niveau post-secondaire
Reyald Goulet, Président & Dir. général

Les Éditions SMG inc.
#203, 5365, boul Jean XXIII, Trois-Rivières, QC G8Z 4A6
Tél: 819-376-5650; Téléc: 819-373-2904
ISBNs: 2-89094

Les Éditions Stanké
Une compagnie de Quebecor Media
Détenteur Quebecor Media
La Tourelle, #800, 1055, boul René-Lévesque Est, Montréal, QC H2L 4S5
Tél: 514-849-5259; Téléc: 514-849-1388
info@groupelibrex.com
www.edstanke.com
ISBNs: 2-7604, 0-88566
Ouvrages grand public: romans, essais, récits
Alain Stanké, Président & Dir.-gén.
Patrick Leimgruber, Directeur commercial

Les Éditions Thémis
Faculté de droit, Université de Montréal, CP 6128 Centre-Ville, Montréal, QC H3C 3J7
Tél: 514-343-6627; Téléc: 514-343-6779
info@editionsthemis.com
www.themis.umontreal.ca
ISBNs: 2-920376, 2-89400; SAN: 115-8252
Livres juridiques; Revue juridique Thémis
Stéphane Rousseau, Président et Dir. général

Les Éditions Un Monde différent ltée
#101, 3905, rue Isabelle, Brossard, QC J4Y 2R2
Tél: 450-656-2660; Téléc: 450-659-9328
Ligne sans frais: 800-443-2582
info@umd.ca
www.umd.ca
ISBNs: 2-89225, 2-92000
Traductions et adaptations de best-sellers américains, ouvrages d'auteurs canadiens et internationaux
Michel Ferron, Éditeur

Les Éditions Vents d'Ouest
185, rue Eddy, Gatineau, QC J8X 2X2
Tél: 819-770-6377;
info@ventsdouest.ca
www.ventsdouest.ca
Ado, histoire, romans, essais, nouvelles
Melvin Jomphe, Président

Les Éditions XYZ inc. / XYZ Publishing
1815, av De Lorimier, Montréal, QC H2K 3W6
Tél: 514-525-2170; Téléc: 514-525-7537
info@editionsxyz.com
www.editionsxyz.com
Médias sociaux:
www.youtube.com/profile?user=livreshmh#grid/upload/
twitter.com/editions xyz
www.facebook.com/EditionsXYZ
ISBNs: 2-89261 French; 0-9683601 Eng.
Dominique Lemay, Directrice générale, dominique.lemay@editionsxyz.com
André Vanasse, Conseiller littéraire, andre.vanasse@editionsxyz.com

Éditions Yvon Blais
DétenteurThomson Reuters
CP 180, Cowansville, QC J2K 3H6
Tél: 450-266-1086; Téléc: 450-263-9256
Ligne sans frais: 800-363-3047
editionsyvonblais.professeurs@thomsonreuters.com
www.editionsyvonblais.c om
ISBNs: 2-89451
Éditeur juridique; textes des conférences des formations continues du Barreau du Québec; fiscalité; ressources humaines
Yvon Blais, Président

EDU Reference Publishers Direct Inc.
Previous Name: EDU Reference Distribution; C. Kirkness Press
#3, 109 Woodbine Downs Blvd., Toronto, ON M9W 1Y6
Tel: 416-674-8622; Fax: 416-674-6215
eduref@edureference.com
www.edureference.com
ISBNs: 0-86596, 0-04150
A distributor - bringing publishers & buyers in the Canadian education community together
Orland Kirkness, President

Educa Books
Previous Name: Educa Library Services
PO Box 2694 D, Ottawa, ON K1P 5W6
Tel: 613-738-2163; Fax: 613-247-0256
educa2@yahoo.com
educa0.tripod.com/edu/
ISBNs: 1-895959, 1-55394
Specialists in dictionaries, reference books, language learning resources
L. Martin

EGS Press
#118, 283 Danforth Ave., Toronto, ON M4K 1N2
Tel: 416-829-8014;
info@egspress.com
www.egspress.com
ISBNs: 0-9685330
Publisher of research material in the fields of media, the arts & therapy from the European Graduate School, Switzerland, & the annual journal "Poiesis: A Journal of the Arts & Communication."
Stephen K. Levine, Editor-in-Chief

8th House Publishing
Montréal, QC
Tel: 438-338-8657;
info@8thHousePublishing.com
www.8thHousePublishing.com
Social Media: www.youtube.com/user/8thHouseBooks
www.facebook.com/pages/8th-House-Publ ishing/72137082479
Publisher of fiction.

Ekstasis Editions
PO Box 8474 Main, Victoria, BC V8W 3S1
Tel: 250-361-9941; Fax: 250-385-3378
Toll-Free: 866-361-9951
ekstasis@islandnet.com
www.ekstasiseditions.com
Ekstasis Editions is a literary publisher of fiction, poetry, criticism, & nonfiction books about spirituality. Children's books are published under the Cherubim Books imprint. Over 200 titles have been published.

Elsevier Canada
905 King St. West, 4th Fl., Toronto, ON M6K 3G9
Tel: 416-253-3640; Fax: 416-255-5456
Toll-Free: 866-896-3331
cs.canada@elsevier.com
www.elsevier.ca; www.lb.ca
ISBNs: 0-3230, 0-3974, 0-3998, 0-4430, 0-4160, 1-5566, 1-5605,
Robert Dingee

emc notes, inc.
PO Box 61507, 1119 Fennell St. E., Hamilton, ON L8T 5A1
Tel: 905-575-4449; Fax: 866-551-5382
Toll-Free: 77-246-1763
sales@emcnotes.com
www.emcnotes.com
Publishers of music curriculum products.

Emond Montgomery Publications Limited
60 Shaftesbury Ave., Toronto, ON M4T 1A3
Tel: 416-975-3925; Fax: 416-975-3924
Toll-Free: 888-837-0815
info@emp.ca; orders@emp.ca
www.emp.ca
ISBNs: 0-920722, 1-55239
Specialists in legal publishing & textbooks
D. Paul Emond, President/CEO

Empyreal Press
PO Box 1708, Champlain, NY
skarwood@videotron.ca
www.skarwood.com
ISBNs: 0-921852
An independent literary press, specializing in new & established Canadian writers of poetry, prose & non-fiction
Geoffrey Isherwood, CEO

Environmental Law Centre
#800, 10025 - 106 St., Edmonton, AB T5J 1G4
Tel: 780-424-5099; Fax: 780-424-5133
Toll-Free: 800-661-4238
elc@elc.ab.ca
www.elc.ab.ca
ISBNs: 0-921503
Publishing objective information about environmental & natural resources law & policy
Cindy Chiasson, Executive Director, cchiasson@elc.ab.ca

Ergo Books
PO Box 1439 B, London, ON N6A 5M2
Tel: 519-432-4357;
ergopro@ergobooks.com
www.ergobooks.com
ISBNs: 0-920516; SAN: 115-3374
Specializing in fiction, poetry, humour, local history & memoirs by Southwestern Ontario writers
Winston G. Schell, Publisher

Essence Publishing
20 Hanna Ct., Belleville, ON K8P 5J2
Tel: 613-962-0234; Fax: 613-962-3055
Toll-Free: 800-238-6376
info@essence-publishing.com
www.essencegroup.com
ISBNs: 1-896400, 1-894169, 1-55306
Specializing in short-run publishing, with emphasis on Christian themes & perspectives

Everyday Publications Inc.
310 Killaly St. West, Port Colborne, ON L3K 6A6
Tel: 905-834-5552; Fax: 905-834-8045
books@everydaypubications.org
www.everydaypublications.org
ISBNs: 0-88873, 0-919586; SAN: 115-3398
Specializing in books about the Bible, in English, French, Spanish, Portuguese, Swahili & Chinese
R.E. Harlow, Publisher

Exile Editions Ltd.
134 Eastbourne Ave., Toronto, ON M5P 2G6
Fax: 416-969-9556
info@exileeditions.com
www.exileeditions.com
ISBNs: 1-550960, 0-920428; SAN: 115-3404
Specializing in fiction, poetry, drama, non-fiction & translations, from established and new writers
Michael Callaghan, Publisher

Exportlivre
289, boul Desaulniers, Saint-Lambert, QC J4P 1M8
Tel: 450-671-3888; Fax: 450-671-2121
order@exportlivre.com
www.exportlivre.com
Book export agency, handling orders for books in English & French in the areas of trade & non-trade publications, children's fiction & non-fiction, scientific & technical books, textbooks, scholarly publications & government publications
Thomas Déri, Directeur

Federation of Ontario Naturalists (FON)
#201, 366 Adelaide St. West, Toronto, ON M5V 1R9
Tel: 416-444-8419; Fax: 416-444-9866
Toll-Free: 800-440-2366
info@ontarionature.org
www.ontarionature.org
Publisher of ON Nature; other resources available through the online Shop
Caroline Schultz, Executive Director

Fernwood Publishing Co. Ltd.
PO Box 5, 32 Oceanvista Lane, Site 2A, Black Point, NS B0J 1B0
Tel: 204-474-2958; Fax: 204-475-2813
info@fernpub.ca
www.fernwoodpublishing.ca
Social Media:
twitter.com/fernpub
www.facebook.com/fernwood.publishing?ref=sgm
ISBNs: 1-895686, 1-55266
Errol Sharpe, Publisher/Editor, errol@fernpub.ca
Nancy Malek, Promotions, promotions@fernpub.ca

Fifth House Publishers
Owned By: Fitzhenry & Whiteside Limited
195 Allstate Pkwy., Markham, ON L3R 4T8
Fax: 800-260-9777
Toll-Free: 800-387-9776
bookinfo@fitzhenry.ca
www.fifthhousepublishers.ca
Social Media:
twitter.com/FifthHouseBooks
ISBNs: 0-920079, 1-894004, 1-894856, 1-895618; SAN: 115-1134
Specializing in non-fiction with a Western Canadian emphasis
Stephanie Stewart, Publisher, stewart@fifthhousepublishers.ca

Firefly Books Ltd.
66 Leek Cres., Richmond Hill, ON L4B 1H1
Tel: 416-499-8412; Fax: 416-499-8313
Toll-Free: 800-387-6192
service@fireflybooks.com
www.fireflybooks.com
Other information: Toll-Free Fax: 800-450-0391
Firefly Books publishes non-fiction books & distributes non-fiction & children's books.
Rob Lidstone, Contact, Sales Operations, Data Export, & Website, rlidstone@fireflybooks.com
Parisa Michailidis, Contact, Special & Corporate Sales, parisa@fireflybooks.com
Ann Quinn, Contact, Schools & Libraries, annq@fireflybooks.com
Diane Vanderkooy, Contact, Rights, dianevan@fireflybooks.com

Fisher House Publishers
PO Box 51582, Provo, UT
fisherhousejohn@hotmail.com
www.fisherhouse.com
ISBNs: 1-896255
John R. Fisher Ph.D

Fitzhenry & Whiteside Limited
195 Allstate Pkwy., Markham, ON L3R 4T8
Tel: 905-477-9700; Fax: 800-260-9777
Toll-Free: 800-387-9776
godwit@fitzhenry.ca
www.fitzhenry.ca
Social Media:
twitter.com/FitzWhits
www.facebook.com/FitzWhits
ISBNs: 0-55041, 0-88902, 1-55005, 1-894004, 1-895618, 0-7737, 0
Specializing in history, biography, poety, sports, photography, reference resources, and children's and young adult material.
Owner of Red Deer Press Inc., and Fifth House Publishers
Sharon Fitzhenry, President, sfitz@fitzhenry.ca

Flanker Press Ltd.
PO Box 2522 C, #2, 57 Old Pennywell Rd., St. John's, NL A1C 6K1
Tel: 709-739-4477; Fax: 709-739-4420
Toll-Free: 866-739-4420
info@flankerpress.com
www.flankerpress.com
Social Media:
twitter.com/FlankerPress
www.facebook.com/pages/Flanker-Press-Ltd/430191950460
ISBNs: 0-9698767, 1-894463
Specializing in regional Newfoundland & Labrador historical fiction & non-fiction titles; imprints include Pennywell Books, & Brazen Books
Garry Cranford, President

Fleurbec
198, ch de la Grande-Grillade, Saint-Henri-de-Lévis, QC G0R 3E0
Tél: 418-882-0843; Téléc: 418-882-6133
melilot@sympatico.ca
www.fleurbec.com
ISBNs: 2-920174
Guides d'identification, ouvrages scientifiques, guide culinaire - plantes sauvages, flore
Gisèle Lamoureux, Dirigeante

Folklore Publishing
9731 - 42 Ave. NW, Edmonton, AB T6E 5P8
Tel: 780-435-2376; Fax: 780-435-0674
fboer@folklorepublishing.com
www.folklorepublishing.com
History
Faye Boer, Publisher

Formac Publishing Company Limited
5502 Atlantic St., Halifax, NS B3H 1G4
Tel: 902-421-7022; Fax: 902-425-0166
Toll-Free: 800-565-1975
orderdesk@formac.ca
www.formac.ca
ISBNs: 0-88780, 0-921921; SAN: 115-1371
Publishers & distributors
James Lorimer, Publisher

49th Avenue Press
Previous Name: Vancouver Community College Press
100 West 49th Ave., Vancouver, BC V5Y 2Z6
Tel: 604-323-5374; Fax: 604-323-5597
lholmes@langara.bc.ca
www.bendallbooks.com
ISBNs: 1-896661
Linda Holmes, President

The Fraser Institute
1770 Burrard St., 4th Fl., Vancouver, BC V6J 3G7
Tel: 604-688-0221; Fax: 604-688-8539
Toll-Free: 800-665-3558
info@fraserinstitute.ca
www.fraserinstitute.ca
ISBNs: 0-88975; SAN: 115-3498
Offices in Vancouver, Calgary, Toronto, Montreal; engaged in research & publication with emphasis on economics, public policy and other issues that affect Canadians
Mark Mullins, Executive Director

Frederick Harris Music Co. Ltd.
#1, 5865 McLaughlin Rd., Mississauga, ON L5R 1B8
Tel: 905-501-1595; Fax: 905-501-0929
Toll-Free: 800-387-4013
fhmc@frederickharris.com
www.frederickharris.com
Darlene Dunn, Customer Service Representative

Freehand Books
#515, 815 1st St. SW, Calgary, AB T2P 1N3
Tel: 403-452-5662;
customerservice@broadviewpress.com
www.freehand-books.com
Social Media:
twitter.com/fhbooks
www.facebook.com/freehandbooks
Kelsey Attard, Managing Editor, kattard@broadviewpress.com

Friday 501
Previous Name: Wolf Creek Books
PO Box 31599, Whitehorse, YT Y1A 6L2
Tel: 867-668-3501; Fax: 867-668-4472
info@friday501.com
www.friday501.com

Friday Circle
Dept. of English, University of Ottawa, Ottawa, ON K1N 6N5
Tel: 613-562-5800; Fax: 613-562-5990
fridaycircle@uottawa.ca
www.fridaycircle.uottawa.ca
ISBNs: 1-896362, 1-9697391
Publishing works by faculty, students & alumni of the Creative Writing Program, University of Ottawa
Seymour Mayne, Co-editor

Frog Hollow Press
1758 Armstrong Ave., Victoria, BC V8R 5S6
Tel: 250-595-3607; Fax: 250-595-3607
carylpeters@telus.net
www.froghollowpress.com
Caryl Peters, Publisher

Frontenac House
1138 Frontenac Ave. SW, Calgary, AB T2T 1B6
Tel: 403-245-8588;
connect@frontenachouse.com
frontenachouse.com
Rose Scollard, Owner
David Scollard, Owner

Fulcrum Publishing Inc.
508 Lawrence Ave. West, Toronto, ON M6A 1A1
Tel: 416-504-0504; Fax: 416-256-3002
Toll-Free: 866-688-0504
info@fulcrum.ca
fulcrum.ca
Specializes in trade magazines catering to small business owners.
Alan Fogel, Publisher, afogel@fulcrum.ca
Russell Hoffman, Genreal Manager, rhoffman@fulcrum.ca

Full Blast Productions
70 Allan Dr., St. Catherines, ON L2N 1E9
Fax: 905-937-2657
Toll-Free: 877-355-2578
fbp@cogeco.ca
www.fullblastproductions.mybisi.com
ISBNs: 1-895451
Publisher of English & Spanish language teaching resources

Fundy Guild Inc.
Fundy National Park, #2, 8642, RR#114, Fundy National Park, NB E4H 4V2
Tel: 506-887-6094; Fax: 506-887-6008
info@fundyguild.ca
www.fundyguild.ca
ISBNs: 0-920383
Publishes books related to the bay of Fundy & Fundy National Park
Beulah Michelin

Gaspereau Press
47 Church Ave., Kentville, NS B4N 2M7
Tel: 902-678-6002; Fax: 902-678-7845
Toll-Free: 877-230-8232
info@gaspereau.com
www.gaspereau.com
ISBNs: 1-894031
Specializing in contemporary literature by emerging & established Canadian authors, with publishing & printing under one roof
Gary Dunfield, Co-publisher
Andrew Steeves, Co-publisher

General Store Publishing House (GSPH)
PO Box 415, 499 O'Brien Rd., Renfrew, ON K7A 4A6
Tel: 613-432-7697; Fax: 613-432-7184
Toll-Free: 800-465-6072
submissions@gsph.com
www.gsph.com
ISBNs: 0-919431, 1-896182, 1-894263, 1-897113 SAN: 115-6853
Tim Gordon, President

Georgetown Publications Inc.
34 Armstrong Ave., Georgetown, ON L7G 4R9
Tel: 905-873-8498; Fax: 888-595-3009
Toll-Free: 888-595-3008
info@georgetownpublications.com
www.georgetownpublications.com
Social Media:
twitter.com/georgetownpubl
www.facebook.com/pages/Georgetown-Publications/2020572398
ISBNs: 0-9731994, 0-9733149
Distributor for Allison & Busby, American Girl Pubishing, Hampton Roads Publishing, & Large Print Press, among others

Gilpin Publishing
PO Box 597, Alliston, ON L9R 1V7
Tel: 705-424-6507; Fax: 705-424-6507
mail@gilpin.ca
www.gilpin.ca
ISBNs: 0-921046; SAN: 119-6162
Music publishing - MP3s, CDs, piano methods, instrumental & choral arrangements, sheet music
Wayne Gilpin, Publisher

The Ginger Press
848 - 2 Ave. East, Owen Sound, ON N4K 2H3
Tel: 519-376-4233; Fax: 519-376-9871
Toll-Free: 800-463-9937
maryann@gingerpress.com
www.gingerpress.com
ISBNs: 0-921773
A bookshop, café, & publishing house, specializing in Owen Sound & area writers & subjects
Maryann Thomas, Publisher

Godwin Books
1212 Hampshire Rd., Victoria, BC V8S 4T1
Tel: 250-414-0215; Fax: 250-414-0216
rthomson@islandnet.com
www.godwinbooks.com
ISBNs: 0-9696774
Featuring books by Robert Thomson & George Godwin
Robert Stuart Thomson, Editor

Good Medicine Books
PO Box 844, Skookumchuck, BC V0B 2E0
canadiancaboose@yahoo.com
goodmedicinefoundation.com
ISBNs: 0-920698
Good Medicine Cutural Foundation publishes a collection of material on a theme of trains, as well documentation & accounts on First Nations People, in particular, the Pikunni.
Adolf Hungry Wolf, Publisher

Goose Lane Editions
Previous Name: Fiddlehead Poetry Books
#330, 500 Beaverbrook Ct., Fredericton, NB E3B 5X4
Tel: 506-450-4251; Fax: 506-459-4991
Toll-Free: 888-926-8377
info@gooselane.com
www.gooselane.com
ISBNs: 0-919197, 0-86492, 0-920110; SAN: 115-3420
Small independent publisher of high-quality, award-winning books.
Susanne Alexander, Publisher, s.alexander@gooselane.com

Gordon Soules Book Publishers Ltd.
1354-B Marine Dr., West Vancouver, BC V7T 1B5
Tel: 604-922-6588; Fax: 604-688-5442
books@gordonsoules.com
www.gordonsoules.com
ISBNs: 0-919574, 1-894661, 0-920045; SAN: 115-0987
Publisher of self-help, health, fitness & natural medicine books; cookbooks; tarot decks & tarot books; travel books & maps
Gordon Soules, President

Granville Island Publishing
#212, 1656 Duranleau St., Vancouver, BC V6H 3S4
Tel: 604-688-0320; Fax: 604-668-0132
Toll-Free: 877-688-0320
info@granvilleislandpublishing.com
www.granvilleislandpublishing.com
Social Media:
twitter.com/GIPLbooks
Granville Island Publishing manages book projects for clients such as individuals, corporations, & other orgnaizations.
Jo Blackmore, Publisher

Grass Roots Press
Owned By: Literacy Services of Canada Ltd.
6520 - 82 Ave., Main Fl., Edmonton, AB T6B 0E7
Tel: 780-413-6491; Fax: 780-413-6582
Toll-Free: 888-303-3213
info@grassrootsbooks.net
www.grassrootsbooks.net
Social Media:
www.facebook.com/pages/Grass-Roots-Press/18724182463501
3
Specializing in adult literacy & ESL resources
Dr Pat Campbell, President, pat@grassrootsbooks.net
Lisa Zohar, Manager, lisa@grassrootsbooks.net
Linda Kita-Bradley, linda@grassrootsbooks.net

Great Plains Publications Ltd.
#345, 955 Portage Ave., Winnipeg, MB R3G 0P9
Tel: 204-475-6799;
info@greatplains.mb.ca
www.greatplains.mb.ca
Social Media:
twitter.com/GreatPlainsPub
www.facebook.com/GreatPlainsPublications
ISBNs: 0-9697804, 1-894283
Specializing in the best books from the Prairies & authors from across Canada
Gregg Shilliday, Publisher

Green Dragon Press
#1009, 2267 Lakeshore Blvd. West, Toronto, ON M8V 3X2
Tel: 416-251-6366; Fax: 416-251-6365
www3.sympatico.ca/equity.greendragonpress
ISBNs: 1-896781
Publishes books & materials on women's equity

Grey House Publishing Canada
#301 - 555 Richmond St. West, Toronto, ON M5V 3B1
Tel: 416-644-6479; Fax: 416-644-1904
Toll-Free: 866-433-4739
info@greyhouse.ca
www.greyhouse.ca
Other information: circ.greyhouse.ca
Social Media:
www.linkedin.com/company/grey-house-publishing-canada
twitter.com/greyhousecanada
www.facebook.com/GreyHouseCanada
ISBNs: 978-1-59237
Publishers of a number of comprehensive Canadian directories including the Canadian Almanac & Directory, Associations Canada, Libraries Canada & the Canadian Parliamentary Guide.
Bryon Moore, General Manager
Tannys Williams, Managing Editor

Greystone Books
#201, 2323 Quebec St., Vancouver, BC V5T 4S7
Tel: 604-254-7191; Fax: 604-254-9099
Toll-Free: 800-667-6902
dm@dmpibooks.com
www.dmpibooks.com/greystone-books
Social Media:
twitter.com/greystonetravel
www.facebook.com/GreystoneBooks
Books about nature, the environment, travel, sports, popular culture & current issues.
Rob Sanders, Publisher

Grolier
#570, 1700, boul Laval, Laval, QC H7S 2N6
Tel: 450-667-5497; Fax: 450-667-7694
Toll-Free: 800-563-3231
customerservice@grolier.qc.ca
www.grolier.ca
ISBNs: 0-7172; SAN 115-3668
Publisher of children's books

Groundwood Books
#801, 110 Spadina Ave., Toronto, ON M5V 2K4
Tel: 416-363-4343; Fax: 416-363-1017
www.houseofanansi.com
Social Media:
www.facebook.com/groundwoodbooks
ISBNs: 0-88899; SAN 115-0391
Publisher of children's books in English & Spanish
Patricia Aldana, Publisher

Groupe Éducalivres inc. - Éditions Études Vivantes
Anciennement Éditions Agence d'Arc
955, rue Bergar, Laval, QC H7L 4Z6
Tél: 514-334-8466; Téléc: 514-334-8387
Ligne sans frais: 800-567-3671
commentaires@educalivres.com
www.educalivres.com
ISBNs: 2-7607, 0-88586, 0-289022, 0-03-92

Groupe Fides Inc.
#100, 7333, place des Roseraies, Anjou, QC H1M 2X6
Tél: 514-745-4290; Téléc: 514-745-4299
editions@groupefides.com
www.groupefides.com
Médias sociaux:
twitter.com/editionsFides
www.facebook.com/pages/%C3%89ditions-Fides/34420228231178
ISBNs: 2-89137, 2-89035, 2-7621, 2-923694, 2-923989
Maison d'édition dont les spécialités sont : ouvrages de fiction, de référence, de spiritualité, essais, beaux livres, manuels d'énseignment collégial et universitaire.
Stéphane Lavoie, Directeur général, stephane.lavoie@groupefides.com
Guylaine Girard, Directrice de l'édition, Éditions Fides, guylaine.girard@groupefides.com
Luc Tousignant, Directeur de l'édition, Fides éducation, luc.tousignant@groupefides.com

Groupe Modulo
Previous Name: Modulo Publisher
#300, 233, av Dunbar, Montréal, QC H3P 2H4
Tel: 514-738-9818; Fax: 514-738-5838
Toll-Free: 888-738-9818
www.moduloediteur.com
ISBNs: 2-89113, 2-920210, 2-920922, 2-89443, 2-920190, 2-921363
Éditeur au préscolaire et au primaire
Jean Bouchard, Directeur général

GTK Press
#109, 18 Wynford Dr., Toronto, ON M3C 3S2
Tel: 416-385-1313; Fax: 416-385-1319
Toll-Free: 866-485-7737
info@gtkpress.com
www.gtkpress.com
ISBNs: 1-894318, 1-55137
Publisher of curriculum resources, notably science, technology, mathematics
K.L. Kwong, President

Guérin éditeur ltée
4501, rue Drolet, Montréal, QC H2T 2G2
Tél: 514-842-3481; Téléc: 514-842-4923
Ligne sans frais: 800-398-8337
france.larochelle@guerin-editeur.qc.ca
www.guerin-editeur.qc.ca
ISBNs: 2-7601
L'éditeur des écoles. Groupe Guérin: Guérin, éditeur limitée, Les Éditions La Pensée Inc., et LIDEC Inc.
Marc-Aimé Guérin, President

Guernica Editions Inc.
489 Strathmore Blvd., Toronto, ON M4C 1N8
Tel: 416-658-9888; Fax: 416-657-8885
Toll-Free: 800-565-9523
guernicaeditions@cs.com
www.guernicaeditions.com
ISBNs: 0-919349, 2-89135, 0-920717, 1-55071; SAN: 115-0421
Michael Mirolla, Editor-in-Chief/Publisher

Guy Saint-Jean Éditeur
3440, boul Industriel, Laval, QC H7L 4R9
Tél: 450-663-1777; Téléc: 450-663-6666
info@saint-jeanediteur.com
www.saint-jeanediteur.com
ISBNs: 2-920340, 2-89455
Guides pratiques sur la santé, la psychologie populaire, le sport, le jardinage; beaux-livres; littérature; Green Frog Publishing (www.greenfrogpublishing.com) et MarieGray (www.mariegray.com)
Nicole Saint-Jean

GWEV Publishing Inc.
PO Box 565, Stittsville, ON K2S 1A6
Tel: 613-831-9154; Fax: 613-831-4291
Toll-Free: 866-747-3797
Sylvia@gwevpublishing.com
www.gwevpublishing.com
ISBNs: 0-9681414, 0-9731300
Publisher of children's books
Sylvia Vincent, Publisher, sylvia@gwevpublishing.com

H.B. Fenn & Company Ltd.
34 Nixon Rd., Bolton, ON L7E 1W2
Tel: 905-951-6600; Fax: 905-951-6601
Toll-Free: 800-267-3366
sales@hbfenn.com
www.hbfenn.com
ISBNs: 0-919768, 1-55168; SAN: 115-1746
Book distributor
Harold B. Fenn, President

Hades Publications, Inc.
PO Box 1414 M, Calgary, AB T2P 2L6
Tel: 403-254-0160; Fax: 403-254-0456
admin@hadespublications.com
www.trickster.com
ISBNs: 0-919230, 0-921298
Publishes books and other materials on Magic, Illusion, Conjuring & Variety Arts
Brian Hades, Publisher

Hagios Press
PO Box 33024, Regina, SK S4T 7X2
Tel: 306-522-5055;
hagiospress@accesscomm.ca
www.hagiospress.com
Social Media:
twitter.com/hagiospress
www.facebook.com/pages/Hagios-Press/260545 433980082
Publisher of poetry, art books, short-fiction, and literary non-fiction, with a particular focus on books that advance a spiritual connection with the world.

Hancock House Publishers Ltd.
19313 Zero Ave., Surrey, BC V3S 9R9
Tel: 604-538-1114; Fax: 604-538-2262
Toll-Free: 800-938-1114
sales@hancockhouse.com
www.hancockhouse.com
ISBNs: 0-88839, 0-91954; SAN: 115-3730
Publishers of wildlife & nature books
David Hancock, President

Hans Schafler & Co. Ltd.
#2, 1184 Speers Rd., Oakville, ON L6L 2X4
Tel: 905-827-2949; Fax: 905-827-2524
Toll-Free: 877-646-9323
info@schafler.com
www.schafler.com
Publishes curriculum books for schools
Lisbeth Schafler

Happy Landings
851 Heritage Dr., RR#4, Merrickville, ON K0G 1N0
Tel: 613-269-2552; Fax: 613-269-3962
books@happylandings.com
www.happylandings.com
ISBNs: 0-9697322
Publisher of aviation books by Garth Wallace
Liz Wallace, Publisher

Harbour Publishing Co. Ltd.
PO Box 219, Madeira Park, BC V0N 2H0
Tel: 604-883-2730; Fax: 604-883-9451
Toll-Free: 800-667-2988
info@harbourpublishing.com
www.harbourpublishing.com
Social Media:
twitter.com/Harbour_Publish
www.facebook.com/group.php?gid=2284749935
ISBNs: 0-920080, 1-55017
Specializing in BC authors & books of the Pacific Northwest

Howard White, President

Harlequin Enterprises Limited
225 Duncan Mill Rd., Toronto, ON M3B 3K9
Tel: 416-445-5860; Fax: 416-445-8655
Toll-Free: 800-387-0112
customer_ecare@harlequin.ca
www.eharlequin.com
ISBNs: 0-373, 1-55166, 0-778; SAN: 115-3749
Specializing in series romance & fiction for women
Katherine Orr, Vice President, Public Relations

HarperCollins Canada Ltd.
2 Bloor St. East, Toronto, ON M4W 1A8
Tel: 416-975-9334; Fax: 416-975-5223
Toll-Free: 800-387-0117
hcorder@harpercollins.com
www.harpercollins.ca
ISBNs: SAN: 150-026X
Canadian imprints include Avon, Greenwillow Books, HarperAudio, HarperBusiness, HarperLargePrint, William Morrow, among many others; specializing in Canadian fiction & non-fiction, for adults & children

Hartley & Marks Publishers
3661 Broadway West, Vancouver, BC V6R 2B8
Tel: 800-277-5887; Fax: 800-707-5887
info@hartleyandmarks.com
www.hartleyandmarks.com
ISBNs: 0-88179; SAN: 115-3757

Hedgerow Press
PO Box 2471, Sidney, BC V8L 3Y3
Tel: 250-656-9320;
hedgep@telus.net
www.hedgerowpress.com
Joan Coldwell, Publsiher

Herald Press
Owned By: Mennonite Publishing Network
#C8, 490 Dutton Dr., Waterloo, ON N2L 6H7
Tel: 519-747-5722; Fax: 519-747-5721
Toll-Free: 800-245-7894
hpcan@mph.org
www.heraldpress.com
ISBNs: 0-8361; SAN: 116-0931
The trade publishing division of Mennonite Publishing Network; specializing in resources with emphasis on the Anabaptist perspective, biblical studies, mission, family & church life
Ron Rempel, Publisher, Canadian Branch

Heritage House Publishing Co. Ltd.
#340, 1105 Pandora Ave., Victoria, BC V8V 3P9
Tel: 604-574-7067; Fax: 604-574-9942
Toll-Free: 800-665-3302
heritage@heritagehouse.ca
www.heritagehouse.ca
Social Media:
www.facebook.com/pages/Heritage-House-Publishing/15190894
ISBNs: 0-919214, 1-895811, 1-894384; SAN: 115-8287
Specializing in Western Canadian non-fiction subjects & authors
Rodger Touchie, President/Publisher

HikingCamping.com
PO Box 8563, Canmore, AB T1W 2V3
Fax: 866-431-3894
nomads@hikingcamping.com
www.hikingcamping.com
Social Media:
twitter.com/nomadhikers
Specializing in guidebooks for hikers & campers, works of inspiration, insight & philosophy, & photography

Historical Trails West/Historical Research Centre
1115 - 8th Ave. South, Lethbridge, AB T1J 1P7
Tel: 403-328-3824;
hrc@ourheritage.net
www.ourheritage.net
Specializing in books & resources of Western Canadian interest
Bruce A. Haig, Director

Hogrefe & Huber Publishers
1543 Bayview Ave., Toronto, ON M4G 3B5
Tel: 416-482-6339; Fax: 416-617-354
Toll-Free: 800-228-3749
hhpub@hogrefe.com
www.hogrefe.com
ISBNs: 0-88937, 0-920887; SAN: 115-379X
Specializing in resources in the areas of applied & experimental psychology, health, pharmacology, psychiatry & neurosciences
DR G.-J. Hogrefe, Publisher

House of Anansi Press
Owned By: Stoddart Publishing
#801, 110 Spadina Ave., Toronto, ON M5V 2K4
Tel: 416-363-4343; Fax: 416-363-1017
Toll-Free: 800-663-5714
customerservice@houseofanansi.com
www.houseofanansi.com
Social Media: youtube.com/HouseOfAnansi
twitter.com/houseofanansi
www.facebook.com/houseofanansi?ref=ts
ISBNs: 0-88784; SAN: 115-0391
Specializing in new & established Canadian writers of fiction, non-fiction & poetry, & French-Canadian works in translation
Sarah MacLachlan, President
Lynn Henry, Publisher

House of Parlance
5230 Marguerite St., Vancouver, BC V6M 3K2
www.houseofparlance.com
Cathy Barrett, Co-founder

Human Kinetics Canada
#100, 475 Devonshire Rd., Windsor, ON N8Y 2L5
Tel: 519-971-9500; Fax: 519-971-9797
Toll-Free: 800-465-7301
info@khcanada.com
www.humankinetics.com

Humanitas
228, de la Lande, Rosemère, QC J4A 4J1
Tél: 450-965-6624; Téléc: 450-965-8839
humanitas@cyberglobe.net
www.editionshumanitas.com
ISBNs: 2-89396, 2-9800950
Art, poésie, romans, essais, théâtre
Constantin Stoiciv

Hungry I Books
#215, 1590 Dr. Penfield Ave., Montréal, QC H3G 1C5
Tel: 514-848-2424;
cjs@alcor.concordia.ca
portico.concordia.ca/jchair/en/publications/hungryibooks.htm
Hungry I Books is a publishing arm of the Institute for Canadian Jewish Studies.

Hyperion Press Limited
300 Wales Ave., Winnipeg, MB R2M 2S9
Tel: 204-256-9204;
tamos@mts.net
ISBNs: 0-920534, 1-895340, 1-895569; SAN: 115-124X
Dr. Marvis Tutiah, President
Arlene Osen, Vice President

Imago Press
30 Laws St., Toronto, ON M6P 2Y7
Tel: 416-604-9741;
imagorediron@rogers.com
www.imagorediron.ca
ISBNs: 0-920489, 0-9697555
Marshall Hryciuk

Inanna Publications and Education Inc.
210 Founders College, York University, 4700 Keele Street, Toronto, ON M3J 1P3
Tel: 416-736-5356; Fax: 416-736-5765
inanna.publications@inanna.ca
www.inanna.ca
Independent feminist press.
Luciana Ricciutelli, Editor-in-Chief, luciana@inanna.ca

Inclusion Press International
47 Indian Trail, Toronto, ON M6R 1Z8
Tel: 416-658-5363; Fax: 416-658-5067
inclusionpress@inclusion.com
www.inclusion.com
ISBNs: 1-895418
Resource materials with emphasis on diversity, inclusion & community, for educational institutions, government agencies, human service agencies, First Nations organizations
Jack Pearpoint, Co-publisher
Marsha Forest, Co-publisher

Inner City Books
PO Box 1271 Q, Toronto, ON M4T 2P4
Tel: 416-927-0355; Fax: 416-924-1814
info@innercitybooks.net
www.innercitybooks.net
ISBNs: 0-919123, 1-894574; SAN: 115-3870
Publishers of studies in Jungian Psychology by Jungian Analysts.
Daryl Sharp, President

Insomniac Press
520 Princess Ave., London, ON N6B 2B8
www.insomniacpress.com
ISBNs: 1-895837, 1-894663
Independent press that publishes non-fiction, poetry & fiction
Mike O'Connor, Publisher, mike@insomniacpress.com
Dan Varrette, Managing Editor, dan@insomniacpress.com

Institut de recherches psychologiques, inc. / Institute of Psychological Research Inc.
34, rue Fleury ouest, Montréal, QC H3L 1S9
Tél: 514-382-3000; Téléc: 514-382-3007
Ligne sans frais: 800-363-7800
info@i-r-p.ca
www.i-r-p.ca
ISBNs: 0-88509, 2-89109
Robert Chevrier

The Institute for Research on Public Policy / L'Institut de recherche en politiques publiques
#200, 1470, rue Peel, Montréal, QC H3A 1T1
Tel: 514-985-2461; Fax: 514-985-2559
irpp@irpp.org
www.irpp.org
ISBNs: 0-920380, 0-88645; SAN: 115-3889, 115-0537
Specializing in research & publication with emphasis on Canadian public policy, Canadian federalism, economic policy, international relations; publisher of Policy Options journal
Suzanne Ostiguy McIntyre, Vice President, Operations
Mel Cappe, President

Institute for Risk Research
University of Waterloo, 200 University Ave. West, Waterloo, ON N2L 3G1
Tel: 519-888-4567; Fax: 519-725-4834
irr-neram@uwaterloo.ca
www.irr-neram.ca
ISBNs: 0-88898, 0-9696747, 0-9684982
Along with The Network for Environmental Risk Assessment and Management (NERAM), the Institute for Risk Research specializes in research & publications in the areas of risk, risk management for the environment, human health, industrial safety & transportation
Dr. John Shortreed, Executive Committee

Institute of Intergovernmental Relations
Room 301, School of Policy Studies, Queen's University, Kingston, ON K7L 3N6
Tel: 613-533-2080; Fax: 613-533-6868
iigr@iigr.ca
www.iigr.ca
ISBNs: 0-88911, 1-55339
Specializing in research & publication, with emphasis on Canadian federalism, intergovernmental relations, constitutional reform & social union
Thomas J. Courchene, Director

International Development Research Centre (IDRC) / Le Centre de recherches pour le développement international
PO Box 8500, 150 Kent St., Ottawa, ON K1G 3H9
Tel: 613-236-6163; Fax: 613-563-2476
pub@idrc.ca
www.idrc.ca
ISBNs: 0-88936, 1-55250
Publishers of IDRC Bulletin, & resources with emphasis on international development, sustainable development, food, health, social issues
Bill Carman, Senior Communications Advisor, Publishing

International Institute for Sustainable Development
161 Portage Ave. East, 6th Fl., Winnipeg, MB R3B 0Y4
Tel: 204-958-7700; Fax: 204-958-7710
info@iisd.org
www.iisd.org
ISBNs: 1-895536
Specializing in books & other materials with emphasis on the IISD's institutional & research history. Offices in Ottawa, New York & Geneva
David Runnalls, President & CEO
Stuart Slayen, Manager, Publishing & Communications

International Press Publications Inc.
#21, 90 Nolan Ct., Markham, ON L3R 4L9
Tel: 905-946-9588; Fax: 905-946-9590
sales@ippbooks.com
www.ippbooks.com
ISBNs: SAN: 170-0049
"Specialists in directories on all subjects from all over the world; largest distributors of books on career guidance, general reference, research, text books, dictionaries; free search for rare & out-of-print books from any country"

Bali Sethi, President

Irwin Law Inc.
#206, 14 Duncan St., Toronto, ON M5H 3G8
Tel: 416-862-7690; Fax: 416-862-9236
Toll-Free: 888-314-9014
www.irwinlaw.com
ISBNs: 1-55221
Jeffrey Miller, Publisher

Is Five Press
Owned By: Is Five Foundation
#200, 161 Eglinton Ave. East, Toronto, ON M4P 1J5
Tel: 416-480-2408; Fax: 416-480-2546
tom@isfive.com
www.isfive.com
ISBNs: 0-920934; SAN: 115-3943
Specializing in books, manuals & curriculum resources in social & environmental subject areas; other services include writing, design, translation & editing

ISER Books
Facilities Management Building, Room FM-2005A, Memorial University, St. John's, NL A1C 5S7
Tel: 709-737-3453; Fax: 709-737-4342
iser-books@mun.ca
www.mun.ca/iser
ISBNs: 1-894725, 0-919666; SAN: 115-3897
Al Potter, Manager

Island Studies Press
University of Prince Edward Island, 550 University Ave., Charlottetown, PE C1A 4P3
Tel: 902-566-0386; Fax: 902-566-0756
iis@upei.ca
www.upei.ca
ISBNs: 0-919013
Publisher of books on the history, literature, culture and environment of Prince Edward Island

ITMB Publishing Ltd.
530 West Broadway, Vancouver, BC V5Z 1E9
Tel: 604-879-3621; Fax: 604-879-4521
itmb@itmb.com
www.itmb.com
ISBNs: 0-921463, 1-895907, 1-55341; SAN: 112-6997
Publisher of travel maps
Jack Joyce, President

J. Gordon Shillingford Publishing Inc.
Previous Name: The Muses' Company
PO Box 86 Corydon Ave., Winnipeg, MB R3M 3S3
Tel: 204-779-6967; Fax: 204-779-6970
jgshill@allstream.net
jgshillingford.com
ISBNs: 1-896239, 0-919754, 0-969761, 0-920486, 0-968942
Primarily a literary publisher; publishes on average 14 titles/year.
J. Gordon Shillingford, President
Karen Green, Marketing Director
Glenda MacFarlane, Drama Editor
Catherine Hunter, Poetry Editor

J.C. George Enterprises
577 Mount Pleasant Rd., Toronto, ON M4S 2M5
Tel: 416-483-4353; Fax: 416-791-8586
mgfa@interlog.com
ISBNs: 0-921369
Publishes educational materials & books

J.E.S.L. Educational Products
58 Glen Park Ave., Toronto, ON M6B 2C2
Tel: 416-785-7941; Fax: 416-785-7941
jesl@rogers.com
www.interlog.com/~jesl
ISBNs: 0-9691264, 0-9684362
Publishes Jewish educational materials
Edmond Y. Lipsitz

Jack The Bookman Ltd.
#4, 1150 Kerrisdale Blvd., Newmarket, ON L3Y 8Z9
Tel: 905-836-5999; Fax: 905-836-1152
Toll-Free: 800-563-5168
jackthebookman@sympatico.ca
www.jackthebookman.com
Library wholesalers
Scott Davey, Vice-President

James Lorimer & Co. Ltd., Publishers
#1002, 317 Adelaide St. W, Toronto, ON M5V 1P9
Tel: 416-362-4762; Fax: 416-362-3939
Toll-Free: 800-565-1975
info@lorimer.ca
www.lorimer.ca
Social Media:
www.facebook.com/LorimerBooks
ISBNs: 0-88862, 1-55028; SAN: 115-1134
Lynn Schellenberg, Acquisitions Editor, acquisitions@lorimer.ca
Faye Smailes, Children's Book Editor, childrenseditor@lorimer.ca
James Lorimer, Publisher, jlorimer@lorimer.ca
Allison McDonald, Editorial & Marketing Coordinator, promotion@lorimer.ca

Jesperson Publishing
See Breakwater Books,
ISBNs: 1-894377, 0-921692, 0-920502
Clyde Rose, Publisher

John Markham & Associates
11210 Elderberry Way, Sidney, BC V8L 5J6
Tel: 250-655-1823; Fax: 250-655-1826
Toll-Free: 800-865-1826
jma@jamtags.com

John Wiley & Sons Canada Ltd.
#400, 5353 Dundas St. W, Toronto, ON M9B 6H8
Tel: 416-236-4433; Fax: 416-236-4447
Toll-Free: 800-567-4797
canada@wiley.com
www.wiley.com
ISBNs: 0-471; SAN: 115-1185
William J. Pesce, President & CEO
Timothy B. King, Sr. Vice-President, Planning & Development
Bill Zerter, Chief Operating Officer, John Wiley & Sons Canada, Ltd.

John Wiley & Sons Inc.
111 River St., Hoboken, NJ
Tel: 201-748-6000; Fax: 201-748-6088
info@wiley.com
www.wiley.com
Ellis E. Cousens, Executive Vice President, Chief Financial & Operations Officer
William J. Arlington, Sr. Vice President, Human Resources
Gary M. Rinck, Sr. Vice President, Human Resources

Johnson Gorman Publishers
2003 - 35 Ave. SW, Calgary, AB T2T 2E2
Tel: 403-246-7956; Fax: 403-246-8926
ISBNs: 0-921835; SAN: 115-0871
Dennis Johnson

Johnstone Training & Consultation (JTC) Inc.
PO Box 1927, Kemptville, ON K0G 1J0
Tel: 613-258-3092; Fax: 613-258-9971
Toll-Free: 888-408-6647
jtcinc@jtcinc.ca
www.jtcinc.ca
ISBNs: 1-895271
Resource materials for not-for-profits & charities
Laura Kelly

Jordan Music Productions
Previous Name: Sarah Jordan Publishing
RPO Lakeport, PO Box 28105, 600 Ontario St., St Catharines, ON L2N 7P8
Tel: 905-938-9555; Fax: 905-938-9970
Toll-Free: 800-567-7733
sjordan@sara-jordan.com
www.SongsThatTeach.com
Social Media: www.myspace.com/funtoteach
twitter.com/SongsThatTeach
www.facebook.com/406506519407554
ISBNs: 1-895523, 1-894262, 1-533860; SAN: 118-959X
Publisher & producer of educational songs & music

Juris Analytica Publishing Inc.
604 - 10080 Jasper Ave., Edmonton, AB T5J 1V9
Tel: 780-420-9010; Fax: 780-420-9030
ISBNs: 0-9698958

The Kashtan Press
22 Gretna Green, Kingston, ON K7M 3J2
Tel: 613-546-8364;
luciuk@luciuk.ca
luciuk.ca/kashtanpress.html
ISBNs: 1-896354
Primarily Ukranian & Ukranian/Canadian History
Dr. Lubomyr Luciuk

Kegedonce Press
Neyaashiinigmiing, Chippewas of Nawash First Nation, RR #7, Owen Sound, ON N4K 6V5
www.kegedonce.com
Social Media:
twitter.com/KegedoncePress
www.facebook.com/?ref=logo#!/Kegedonce
Publishes the work of Indigenous writers nationally and internationally.
Kateri Akiwenzie-Damm, Owner/Managing Editor

Ken Haycock & Associates Inc
Previous Name: Rockland Press
#343, 101-1001 West Broadway, Vancouver, BC V6H 4E4
Tel: 604-925-0266; Fax: 604-925-0566
admin@kenhaycock.com
www.kenhaycock.com
ISBNs: 0-920175
Ken Haycock, Publisher
Michelle Rudert, Director, Client Services

Keng Seng Enterprises Inc.
#103, 4000, rue St-Ambroise, Montréal, QC H4C 2C7
Tel: 514-939-3971; Fax: 514-989-1922
canada@kengseng.com
www.kengseng.com
ISBNs: 1-895494
David Chen, President

Kerrwil Publications Ltd.
#800, 2 St. Clair Ave. E, Toronto, ON M4T 2T5
Tel: 416-622-6736; Fax: 416-695-0453
www.kerrwil.com

Kids Can Press Ltd.
Owned By: Corus Entertainment Inc.
29 Birch Ave., Toronto, ON M4V 1E2
Tel: 416-925-5437; Fax: 416-960-5437
Toll-Free: 800-265-0884
info@kidscan.com
www.kidscanpress.com
ISBNs: 0-919964, 0-55337, 1-55074; SAN: 115-4001
Specializes in children's literature & children's books
Lisa Lyons, President

Kindred Productions
1310 Taylor Ave., Winnipeg, MB R3M 3Z6
Tel: 204-669-6575; Fax: 204-654-1865
Toll-Free: 800-545-7322
kindred@mbconf.ca
www.kindredproductions.com
ISBNs: 0-919797, 0-921788, 1-894791
Publishing & distribution arm of the Mennonite Bretheren Churches in North America.
Marilyn Hudson, Director

Kirkton Press Ltd.
396 Grills Rd., RR#1, Baltimore, ON K0K 1C0
Tel: 905-349-3443; Fax: 905-349-3420
Toll-Free: 800-332-3663
kirkton@eagle.ca
www.breakingtheviciouscycle.info
ISBNs: 0-9692768
Publishers of "The Vicious Cycle" series of diet/health books.
Elaine Gottschall, President
Herbert Gottschall, Vice-President

Kitchener News Company Ltd.
PO Box 274 Waterloo, 455 Dutton Dr., Waterloo, ON N2J 4A4
Tel: 519-884-3710; Fax: 519-885-4640
Toll-Free: 800-265-8839
www.kitnews.com
ISBNs: 0-394
Educational books & mass market paperbacks

Knopf Canada
Owned By: Random House of Canada, Ltd.
#210, 33 Yonge St., Toronto, ON M5E 1G4
Tel: 416-777-9477; Fax: 416-777-9470
ISBNs: 0-394, 0-676
Louise Dennys, Publisher

Koala Books of Canada Ltd.
14327 - 95A Ave., Edmonton, AB T5N 0B6
Tel: 780-452-5149; Fax: 780-452-5149
ISBNs: SAN: 169-9385
John Carolan, General Manager, jcarolan@nucleus.com
Vera Lech, Secretary/Treasurer

Kugh Enterprises
PO Box 31821, Whitehorse, YT Y1A 6L3
Tel: 867-633-2118;
gkarpes@northwestel.net
www.yukonweb.com/tourism/kugh
ISBNs: 1-896
Publisher of Wilderness books about the Yukon.
Gus Karpes

Lambrecht Publications
1763 Maple Bay Rd., Duncan, BC V9L 5N6
Tel: 250-748-8722; Fax: 250-748-8722
Toll-Free: 877-774-4372
ISBNs: 0-919383; SAN: 115-057X
H. Lambrecht, Publisher

Lancaster House
#200, 17 Dundonald St., Toronto, ON M4Y 1K3
Tel: 416-977-6618; Fax: 416-977-5873
Toll-Free: 888-298-8841
lan@lancasterhouse.com
www.lancasterhouse.com
ISBNs: 0-920450
Publishes information & hosts conferences in the areas of labour & employment law.
Paul Wollaston, General Manager
Vanessa Scott, Editorial Coordinator
Cristina Santos, Production Coordinator/Database Administrator
Norma Nixon, Manager, Customer Service & Database

LandOwner Resource Centre
PO Box 599, 5524 Dickinson St., Manotick, ON K4M 1A5
Tel: 613-692-3571; Fax: 613-692-0831
info@lrconline.com
www.lrconline.com
ISBNs: 0-9680992
Publishes information on forestry, agriculture, wildlife, water, soil and other land management issues.

Laurier Books Ltd.
PO Box 2694 D, Ottawa, ON K1P 5W6
Tel: 613-738-2163; Fax: 613-247-0256
educa2@yahoo.com
educa0.tripod.com/edu
ISBNs: 1-895959, 1-55394; SAN: 168-2806
Publishers of Educational Books, Foreign Language Dictionaries; French Language Dictionaries; Native American Books & Native Languages; Asian Studies books
Marthe Lalwani

Lazara Press
PO Box 2269 Main, Vancouver, BC V6B 3W2
Tel: 604-872-1134; Fax: 604-874-6661
www.lazarapress.ca
ISBNs: 0-920999
Small, progressive publishing house located in Vancouver. Publishers of poetry, literature, broadsides & chapbooks. Committed to publishing & distributing works that might not otherwise be available.
Penny Goldsmith, Owner/Founder

Leaf Press
PO Box 416, Lantzville, BC V0R 2H0
ursulavaira@leafpress.ca
www.leafpress.ca
Social Media:
www.facebook.com/Leaf.Press
Poetry chapbook publisher.

Learnxs Press
5050 Yonge St., Toronto, ON M2N 5N8
Tel: 416-397-3911;
learnxs.foundation@tbsb.on.ca
ISBNs: 0-920020; SAN: 115-4060
Publishing house for the production & sale of innovative learning materials in conjunction with the Toronto District School Board.
Ross Richardson, Production Manager

Left Field Press
3105 Cowie Rd., Hornby Island, BC V0R 1Z0
Tel: 250-335-0005;
info@leftfieldpress.com
www.leftfieldpress.com
Dan Bruiger, Editor

Leméac Éditeur
4609, rue d'Iberville, 1er étage, Montréal, QC H2H 2L9
Tél: 514-524-5558; Téléc: 514-524-3145
lemeac@lemeac.com
www.lemeac.com
ISBNs: 2-7609, 0-7761
Notre politique éditoriale essentiellement à caractère littéraire s'inscrit surtout dans les domaines du roman, du théâtre contemporain, de l'essai, de la biographie de personalités ayant marqué le secteur culturel.
Lise P. Bergevin, Directrice générale

LexisNexis Canada Inc.
Previous Name: Lexis Nexis Butterworths; Butterworths Canada Ltd
#700, 123 Commerce Valley Dr. East, Markham, ON L3T 7W8
Tel: 905-479-2665; Fax: 905-479-2826
Toll-Free: 800-668-6481
info@lexisnexis.ca
www.lexisnexis.ca
ISBNs: 0-409, 0-433; SAN: 115-2750
Provider of invormation & services to law professionals, corporations, government & academic institutions through online products.
Michael Pilmer, President & CEO

Libra Information Services
PO Box 353 A, 18 Eastern Ave. Lower Level, Toronto, ON M5W 1C2
Tel: 416-364-0050; Fax: 416-364-0606
libra@web.ca
www.web.ca/~libra
Publishers of material on Innovative Health Care methods, and for Social Investors & Conscious Consumers

Librairie Gallimard de Montréal
3700, boul Saint-Laurent, Montréal, QC H2X 2V4
Tél: 514-499-2012; Téléc: 514-499-1535
info@gallimardmontreal.com
www.gallimardmontreal.com

Librairie Wilson & Lafleur Ltée
40, rue Notre-Dame est, Montréal, QC H2Y 1B9
Tél: 514-875-6326; Téléc: 514-875-8356
Ligne sans frais: 800-363-2327
libraire@wilsonlafleur.com
www.wilsonlafleur.com
ISBNs: 2-89127
Éditeur en droit et législation
Claude Wilson

Library Bound
#6-7, 75 Rankin Ave., Waterloo, ON N2V 1W2
Tel: 519-885-3233; Fax: 519-885-2662
Toll-Free: 800-363-4728
lbi@librarybound.com
www.librarybound.com
ISBNs: SAN: 116-9203
Also provide services for shelf-ready materials
Heather Bindseil, President, 5198853233 ext.28, heatherb@librarybound.com
Lisa Bendig, Accounting Department, lisab@librarybound.com
Ron Stadnik, Print Collections Development, 5198853233 ext.26, ron@librarybound.com

Lidec Inc.
4350, av de l'Hôtel-de-Ville, Montréal, QC H2W 2H5
Tel: 514-843-5991; Fax: 514-843-5252
Toll-Free: 800-350-5991
lidec@lidec.qc.ca
www.lidec.qc.ca
ISBNs: 2-7608, 0-7762
La maison Lidec fut fondée par les Frères des écoles chrétiennes pour répondre aux besoins de l'éducation, puis achetée en 1985 par le Groupe Guérin. Lidec se spécialise dans le matériel scolaire de tous les niveaux et de toutes les disciplines. La maison publie des manuels de base et du matériel complémentaire pour l'enseignement primaire, secondaire, collégial et universitaire adaptés aux différents programmes du Ministère de l'Éducation du Québec et des autres provinces canadiennes.
Marc-Aimé Guérin, President

Life Cycle Books Ltd.
#20, 1149 Bellamy Rd. N, Toronto, ON M1H 1H7
Fax: 866-690-8532
Toll-Free: 800-880-5860
canorders@lifecyclebooks.com
www.lifecyclebooks.com
ISBNs: 0-919225; SAN: 115-8417
Publisher of pro-life & abstinence books and other educational materials.

Lingo Media Inc.
#703, 151 Bloor St. West, Toronto, ON M5S 1S4
Tel: 416-927-7000; Fax: 416-927-1222
Toll-Free: 866-927-7011
mkraft@lingomedia.com
www.lingomedia.com
Develops and publishes English Language Learning materials for use in China.
Michael Kraft, mkraft@lingomedia.com
Khurram Qureshi, kqureshi@lingomedia.com

Linguatech éditeur inc.
CP 26026 Salaberry, Montréal, QC H3M 1L0
Tél: 514-336-5207; Téléc: 514-336-4736
linguatechediteur@bellnet.ca
home.ican.net/~lingua
ISBNs: 2-920342
Publications: dictionnaires et vocabulaires; Actes de congrès; Ouvrages didactiques; Langues de spécialité
André Dubuc, Président
Robert Dubuc, Vice-Président
Odette Dubuc, Secrétaire

Little Brick Schoolhouse Inc.
PO Box 84001, 1235 Trafalgar Rd., Oakville, ON L6H 3J0
Tel: 905-844-4669; Fax: 905-690-3400
schoolhouse@cogeco.ca
www.littlebrick.com
ISBNs: 0-919788
Publisher of Educational entertainment products dealing with Canadian & American History.
Robert Livesey, President

Lobster Press Limited
1620, rue Sherbrooke ouest, #C & D, Montréal, QC H3H 1C9
Tel: 514-904-1100; Fax: 514-904-1101
marketing@lobsterpress.com
www.lobsterpress.com
ISBNs: 1-894222, 1-897073, 2-922435
Publisher of children's books
Alison Fripp, President & Publisher
Meghan Nolan, Editor
Stephanie Hindley, Director, Marketing
Ruth Joseph, Office Manager

Lone Pine Publishing
10145 - 81 Ave., Edmonton, AB T6E 1W9
Tel: 780-433-9333; Fax: 780-433-9646
Toll-Free: 800-661-9017
info@lonepinepublishing.com
www.lonepinepublishing.com
ISBNs: 0-919433, 1-55105; SAN: 115-4125
Focus as a regional publisher in the Rocky Mountains, West Coast & Great Lakes. Focus on nature, outdoor recreation & popular history.
Shane Kennedy, President
Nancy Foulds, Senior Editor
David Cleary, Director of Sales & Marketing

Loon Books Publishing
722 Lipton St., Winnipeg, MB R3E 2L3
Tel: 204-772-2527; Fax: 204-783-6944
loonbooksltd@yahoo.ca
loonbooks.ca

Lorraine Greey Publications Limited
#303, 56 The Esplanade, Toronto, ON M5E 1A7
Tel: 416-422-3995;
Lorraine Durham Greey, President

Louise Courteau, éditrice inc.
481, Lac St-Louis est, Saint-Zénon, QC J0K 3N0
Tél: 450-884-5958; Téléc: 450-884-5913
presse@louisdecourteau.com
www.louisdecorteau.com
Louise Courteau, Éditrice

Loyal Colonies Press
304 Olympus Ave., Kingston, ON K7M 4T9
Tel: 613-389-0866;
tvincent@can.rogers.com
www.bibliofiles.ca/lc_index.cfm
ISBNs: 0-929832
Publishers of history books, largely biographies of Canadians; Publishes roughly 2 books per year.
Thomas B. Vincent, Proprietor

Lugus Publications Ltd.
48 Falcon St., Toronto, ON M4S 2P5
Tel: 416-322-5113; Fax: 416-484-9512
gethin@la-rampa.com
ISBNs: 0-921633, 1-896266
Publishes Children's books and other books & pamphlets.
Annual sales of $200,000 - $350,000
Gethin James, Manager

Lyalta Publishing
#1403, 2 St. SW, Calgary, AB T2R 0W7
Tel: 403-233-2558; Toll-Free: 888-322-2558
www.lyaltapublishing.com
ISBNs: 0-9699101, 0-9681761
Assists individuals and small organizations in self-publishing
Lyle Manery, Founder

Lynx Images Inc.
PO Box 5961 A, Toronto, ON M5W 1P4
Tel: 416-925-8422; Fax: 416-925-8352
website@lynximages.com
www.lynximages.com
ISBNs: 0-9698427, 1-894073
Documentary Film production company & publisher. Publishes books dealing with Canadian History & companion books to documentaries.
Russell Floren, President
Barbara Chisolm, Vice-President, Publishing

Maa Press
1-4925 Marello Rd., Nelson, BC V1L 6X4
info@maapress.ca
www.maapress.ca
K. Linda Kivi

MacKenzie Art Gallery
3475 Albert St., Regina, SK S4S 6X6
Tel: 306-584-4285; Fax: 306-569-8191
sandra.nixon@uregina.ca
www.mackenzieartgallery.ca
ISBNs: 1-896470
Publishes books about visual arts and Canadian & local artists

Madison Press Books
#200, 1000 Yonge St., Toronto, ON M4Y 2K2
Tel: 416-923-5027; Fax: 416-923-9708
info@madisonpressbooks.com
www.madisonpressbooks.com
Independent publishers of illustrated non-fiction titles; Catalog includes a number of international best-sellers including Robert D. Ballard's 'Discovery of the Titanic'; Also publish children's books & custom publishing programs for corporate clients
Oliver Salzmann, Publisher, ext. 223, osalzmann@madisonpressbooks.com
Alison Maclean, Associate Publisher, amaclean@madisonpressbooks.com

Madonna House Publications
Madonna House, 2888 Dafoe Rd., Combermere, ON K0J 1L0
Tel: 613-756-3728; Fax: 613-756-0103
Toll-Free: 888-703-7110
publications@madonnahouse.org
www.madonnahouse.org/publications
ISBNs: 0-921440
Non-profic Catholic Christian publisher of religious books, audiobooks, videos, music & cards.
Linda Lambeth

Malcolm Lester & Associates
22 St. Clair Ave. E, 14th Fl., Toronto, ON M4T 2S3
Tel: 416-928-2637; Fax: 416-944-3122
malcolm@malcolmlester.com
www.malcolmlester.com
ISBNs: 1-9659415
Publisher & publishing consultant; Develop books for other publishers; Develops custom books for corporate clients, individuals & organizations.
Malcolm Lester, malcolm@malcolmlester.com
Andrea Knight, andrea@malcolmlester.com

Mansfield Press
25 Mansfield Ave., Toronto, ON M6J 2A9
Tel: 416-532-2086;
info@mansfieldpress.net
www.mansfieldpress.net
Social Media:
twitter.com/MansfieldPress
www.facebook.com/group.php?gid=5479869165
Denis De Klerck, Publisher, denis@mansfieldpress.net

Map Art
70 Bloor St. East, Oshawa, ON L1H 3M2
Tel: 905-436-2525; Toll-Free: 877-231-6277
info@mapart.com
www.mapart.com
Leading publishers of Maps, Atlases, Wall Maps & Street Guides.

Marcus Books
301 Petheram Pl., Newmarket, ON L3X 1J8
Tel: 905-478-2201;
thomas.rieder@sympatico.ca
ISBNs: 0-919951; SAN: 115-4249
Thomas Rieder, President

Marshall Cavendish
#3, 109 Woodbine Downs Rd., Toronto, ON M9W 6Y1
Tel: 416-674-8622; Fax: 416-674-6215
info@edureference.com
www.marshallcavendish.com
ISBNs: 0-7614
Publishes educational, home & library reference & non-fiction titles.
Orland Kirkness

Marvin Melnyk Associates Ltd
PO Box 220, Queenston, ON L0S 1L0
Tel: 905-262-4964; Fax: 905-262-4974
Toll-Free: 800-682-0029
meljack@niagara.com
ISBNs: 0-919803; SAN: 115-4281
John O. Fritz, Vice-President
Marvin Melnyk, President

Master Point Press
331 Douglas Ave., Toronto, ON M5M 1H2
Tel: 416-781-0351; Fax: 416-781-1831
info@masterpointpress.com
www.masterpointpress.com
ISBNs: 0-9698461, 1-894154, 1-897106
Publisher of a variety of books on the topic of the card game Bridge; also publishes books on other games, as well as software
Ray Lee, President
Linda Lee, Co-owner

MasterAthlete Book Publishing Group Ltd.
75 Main St., Mount Albert, ON L0G 1M0
Tel: 905-473-9714; Fax: 905-473-9715
ISBNs: 0-921016; SAN: 118-3613
Liz Roach, President

MBooks of BC
Richmond Gardens, #307, Birchwood Ct., 6311 Gilbert Rd., Richmond, BC V7C 3V7
Tel: 778-822-3864;
jrmbooks@hotmail.com
www.mbooksofbc.com
ISBNs: 0-9694933
MBooks of BC has published books by Joe Ruggier (Publisher / Author) as well as titles by many other authors (mostly poets) using print-on-demand technology.
Joe M. Ruggier, Managing Editor, Publisher, Author

McArthur & Company
#241, 67 Mowat Ave., Toronto, ON M6K 3E3
Tel: 416-408-4007; Fax: 416-408-4081
info@mcarthur-co.com
www.mcarthur-co.com
Social Media: www.youtube.com/mcarthurandco
www.twitter.com/McArthurCo/
www.facebook
.com/pages/McArthur-Company-Publishing/271238
ISBNs: 1-55278; SAN: 117-9713
Publisher & distributor of Canadian & international fiction & non-fiction; Publisher of 63 best-sellers & 21 #1 bestsellers.
Kim McArthur, President, Publisher
Jim Palmeieri, Director, Finance

McClelland & Stewart Ltd. (M&S)
5th Fl., 75 Sherbourne St., Toronto, ON M5A 2P9
Tel: 416-598-1114; Fax: 416-598-7764
Toll-Free: 800-788-1074
mail@mcclelland.com
www.mcclelland.com
ISBNs: 0-7710; SAN: 115-4192
Publisher of over 100 titles annually, both fiction & non-fiction. Publishers of authors such as Margaret Atwood, Alistair MacLeod, Rohinton Mistry & Jane Urquhart. Publishers of political memoirs, including Pierre Elliott Trudeau's.
Douglas J. Pepper

McGill-Queen's University Press
Previous Name: Carleton University Press Inc
#1720, 1010, rue Sherbrooke ouest, Montréal, QC H3A 2R7
Tel: 514-398-3750; Fax: 514-398-4333
Toll-Free: 877-864-8477
mqup@mcgill.ca
www.mqup.mcgill.ca
Social Media:
twitter.com/scholarmqup
www.facebook.com/McGillQueens
ISBNs: 0-88629, 0-7735, 0-88911, 1-55339; SAN: 106-4206
Publisher of non-fiction books, with over 1800 books in print and numerous awards & bestsellers.
Philip Cercone, Executive Director & Senior Editor, 514-398-3750, philip.cercone@mcgill.ca
John Zucchi, Deputy Senior Editor, 514-398-2056, john.zucchi@mcgill.ca
Joan McGilvray, Coordinating Editor, 514-398-3922, joan.mcgilvray@mcgill.ca
Joanne Pisano, Permissions & Rights Coordinator, 514-398-2068, joanne.pisano@mcgill.ca

McGill-Queen's University Press
Queen's University, 144 Barrie St., Kingston, ON K7L 3N6
Tel: 613-533-2155; Fax: 613-533-6822
mqup@post.queensu.ca
www.mqup.mcgill.ca
ISBNs: 0-7735
Donald H. Akenson, Senior Editor
Kyla Madden, Deputy Senior Editor, 6kmm3@queensu.ca

McGraw-Hill Ryerson Limited
300 Water St., Whitby, ON L1N 9B6
Tel: 905-430-5000; Fax: 905-430-5020
Toll-Free: 800-565-5758
cs_queries@mcgrawhill.ca
www.mcgrawhill.ca
ISBNs: 0-07; SAN: 115-060X
Publishers of a large quantity of education materials, including textbooks
John Dill, President/CEO

MDAG Publishing
8035 Redtail Ct., Surrey, BC V3W 0N4
Tel: 604-502-0796;
contact@mdag.com
www.mdag.com/publishing
ISBNs: 0-9682039
Released tools & publications produced by the Minesite Drainage Assessment Group

Mediacorp Canada Inc.
21 New St., Toronto, ON M5R 1P7
Tel: 416-964-6069; Fax: 416-964-3202
info@mediacorp.ca
www.mediacorp.ca
ISBNs: 0-9681447, 1-894450
Publishers of data & publications regarding employment, employers & labour

The Mercury Press
Previous Name: Aya Press
PO Box 672 P, Toronto, ON M5S 2Y4
Tel: 416-531-4338; Fax: 416-531-0765
Toll-Free: 800-591-6250
contact@themercurypress.ca
www.themercurypress.ca
ISBNs: 0-920544, 1-55128; SAN: 115-009X
Publishers of poetry, fiction, murder mysteries & non-fiction by Canadian authors

Messageries ADP inc.
Une compagnie de Quebecor Media
DétenteurQuebecor Media
955, rue Amherst, Montréal, QC H2L 3K4
Tél: 514-523-1182; Téléc: 514-521-4434
Ligne sans frais: 800-361-4806
www.messageries-adp.com
Diffuseur et distributeur de livres francophones au Canada; partenaire de 139 maisons d'édition québécoises, françaises, belges et suisses

Michelin North America (Canada) Inc.
Travel Publications, #510, 2540, boul Daniel Johnson, Laval, QC H7T 2T9
Toll-Free: 800-361-8236
ISBNs: 2-06; SAN: 115-0618
Publishes maps & travel guides
Jack Haugh

Mile Oak Publishing Inc.
#81, 20 Mineola Rd. East, Mississauga, ON L5G 4N9
Tel: 905-274-4356;
mile_oak@compuserve.com
www.i75online.com
ISBNs: 1-896819
Publishers of the "Along Interstate-75" travel guide.
Dave Hunter, Publisher

Mini Mocho Press
Owned By: 7
PO Box 57424 Jackson, Hamilton, ON L8P 4X2
Tel: 905-523-1518;
jamesstrecker@sympatico.ca
ISBNs: 0-921980
Publishes a catalog of 26 titles featuring primarily authors from Southern Ontario

James Strecker

Misthorn Press
Comp. 11, Site 660, RR#6, Courtenay, BC V9N 8H9
Tel: 250-335-2237; Fax: 250-338-8469
ISBNs: 0-9680159

MLR Editions Canada
Dept. of English & Film Studies, Wilfrid Laurier Univ, Waterloo, ON N2L 3C5
Tel: 519-576-6068;
ISBNs: 0-9692539
Paul Tiessen, Publisher, ptiessen@wlu.ca

MOD Publishing
4 Fairview Blvd., Toronto, ON M4K 1L9
Tel: 416-466-9275; Fax: 416-466-7493
jean.weihs@rogers.com
www.modpublishing.com
ISBNs: 0-9684559, 0-9683974, 1-894461
Publishes supplemental educational aids that covers material not covered within current cirriculum

Modus Vivendi
Anciennement Les Éditions Modus Vivendi inc
55 rue Jean-Talon Ouest, Montréal, QC H2R 2W8
Tél: 514-272-0433; Téléc: 514-272-7234
info@modusaventure.com
www.modusaventure.com
ISBNs: 2-921556, 2-92155, 2-89523, 2-922148 (Presses Aventure)
Publishers of non-fiction books covering topics such as arts & crafts, cooking, food & wine, diet & health, games & activities, home renovations and others.
Jean Poitras, Editeur

Monarch Books of Canada
5000 Dufferin St., Toronto, ON M3H 5T5
Tel: 416-663-8231; Fax: 416-736-1702
Toll-Free: 800-404-7404
customer_service@monarchbooks.ca
www.monarchbooks.ca
Specializes in distributing Children's books, Teacher Resources, Special Needs, Sports, Reference and more, from a wide range of publishers, as well as bestselling audiobook titles.

Mondia éditeurs inc.
105, rue de Martigny ouest, Saint-Jérome, QC J7Y 2G2
Tél: 514-438-8479; Téléc: 514-884-8307
ISBNs: 0-88556, 2-89114, 0-9861676

Money Jar Publishing
#2021, 642 Sheppard Ave. East, Toronto, ON M2K 1B9
Tel: 416-223-7312;
millyard@rogers.com
ISBNs: 0-9695889
John Millyard, Owner

Montréal Museum of Fine Arts / Musée des beaux-arts de Montréal
CP 3000 H, Montréal, QC H3G 2T9
Tél: 514-285-2000;
flavoie@mbamtl.org
www.mbamtl.org; www.mmfa.qc.ca
ISBNs: 2-89192
Francine Lavoie, Head, Publishing, flavoie@mbamtl.org

Moonprint Press
PO Box 293, Winnipeg, MB R3C 2G9
Tel: 204-237-5504;
Diane Driedger, Co-Publisher
Cecile Guillemot, Co-Publisher

Moose Enterprise Book & Theatre Play Publishing
684 Walls Side Rd., Sault Ste Marie, ON P6A 5K6
Tel: 705-779-3331; Fax: 705-779-3331
Toll-Free: 888-826-6698
mooseenterprises@on.aibn.com
www.moosehidebooks.com
ISBNs: 0-9698319, 0-9681852, 0-9684909, 0-9686086, 1-894650
Local publishers of plays, children's short stories, non-fiction & fiction works.
Richard Mousseau, Publisher, rmousseau@moosehidebooks.com

Mosaic Press
#1, 1252 Speers Rd., Oakville, ON L6L 5N9
Tel: 905-825-2130; Fax: 905-825-2130
info@mosaic-press.com
www.mosaic-press.com
ISBNs: 0-88962; SAN: 115-4362, 115-4370
Publishes over 20 original titles each year, with a back catalog of over 500 books covering all genres. Literature; The Arts; Social Studies & International Studies
Howard Aster, Publisher

Mother Tongue Publishing Ltd.
290 Fulford-Ganges Rd., Salt Spring Island, BC V8K 2K6
Tel: 250-537-4155; Fax: 250-537-4725
info@mothertonguepress.com
www.mothertonguepublishing.com
Social Media:
www.facebook.com/153416691391280
ISBNs: 1-896949, 0-9698904
Publishers of local authors as well as books on British Columbia art history, art & literature.

Moving to Magazines Ltd.
Previous Name: Moving Publications Ltd.
Owned By: Homes Publishing Group
178 Main St., Unionville, ON L3R 2G9
Tel: 905-479-0641; Toll-Free: 800-363-4663
info@movingto.com
www.movingto.com
Social Media:
www.facebook.com/pages/Moving-To-Magazines/11258237542805
ISBNs: 1-895020
Publishers of the "Moving to" series of publications geared towards people moving to new cities in Canada.
Anita Wood, President/Publisher

Multicultural History Society of Ontario
43 Queen's Park Cres. East, Toronto, ON M5S 2C3
Tel: 416-979-2973; Fax: 416-979-7947
ISBNs: 0-919045
Publishers of a number of journals and non-fiction books dealing with Multicultural History in Ontario

Munsey Music
PO Box 511, Richmond Hill, ON L4C 4Y8
Tel: 905-737-0208; Fax: 905-737-0208
info@MunseyMusic.com
www.MunseyMusic.com
ISBNs: 0-9697066, 0-9685152; SAN: 116-967X
Terence Munsey, President

Native Law Centre
University of Saskatchewan, #160, Law Bldg., 15 Campus Dr., Saskatoon, SK S7N 5A6
Tel: 306-966-6189; Fax: 306-966-6207
native.law@usask.ca
www.usask.ca/nativelaw/
ISBNs: 0-88880; SAN: 115-4540
Publishers of materials relating to First Nations & Aboriginal Law in Canada.
Zandra Wilson, Publications Editor, 3069666192, zandra.wilson@usask.ca

Nelson Education Ltd.
1120 Birchmount Rd., Toronto, ON M1K 5G4
Tel: 416-752-9100; Fax: 416-752-8101
Toll-Free: 800-668-0671
inquire@nelson.com
www.nelson.com
ISBNs: 0-176; SAN: 115-0669
Canada's leading Educational Publisher. Publishes K-12 textbooks and educational products, as well as higher education, professional learning & business education publications
William D. Rieders, Acting President
Michael Andrews, CFO
Beverly Buxton, Vice-President, School Division
James Reeve, Vice-President, Higher Education Division

New Society Publishers
PO Box 189, Gabriola Island, BC V0R 1X0
Tel: 250-247-9737; Fax: 250-247-7471
Toll-Free: 800-567-6772
info@newsociety.com
www.newsociety.com
Social Media:
twitter.com/NewSocietyPub
www.facebook.com/NewSocietyPublishers
ISBNs: 1-55092, 0-86571
Progressive publishing company that specializes in books about activism & ecological sustainability
Rob Sanders, Publisher

New Star Books Ltd.
#107, 3477 Commercial St., Vancouver, BC V5N 4E8
Tel: 604-738-9429; Fax: 604-738-9332
info@newstarbooks.com
www.newstarbooks.com
ISBNs: 0-919573, 0-921586, 1-55420; SAN: 115-1908
Publishes 6-10 titles annually covering politically- and socially-based non-fiction as well as fiction, poetry and books on local history & culture.
Rolf Maurer, President/Publisher

New World Publishing
PO Box 36075, Halifax, NS B3J 3S9
Tel: 902-576-2055; Fax: 902-576-2095
Toll-Free: 877-211-3334
nwp1@eastlink.ca
www.newworldpublishing.com
ISBNs: 1-895814
Francis Mitchell, Managing Editor

NeWest Publishers Ltd.
#201, 8540 - 109 St., Edmonton, AB T6G 1E6
Tel: 780-432-9427; Fax: 780-433-3179
Toll-Free: 866-796-5473
info@newestpress.com
www.newestpress.com
Social Media:
twitter.com/newestpress
www.facebook.com/group.php?gid=5242749678
ISBNs: 0-920316, 0-920897, 1-896300
Western regional press publishing 10-12 books annually
Paul Matwychuk, General Manager

Newport Bay Publishing Limited
356 Cyril Owen Pl., Victoria, BC V9E 2B6
Tel: 250-479-4616; Fax: 250-479-3836
info@newportbay.ca
www.newportbay.ca/publishing
ISBNs: 0-921513
Publishers of a small number of books covering the following subjects: biography, world governance, alternative economics, alternative health and medicine, home and garden, media/journalism, Native peoples, nature/environment, philosophy, social sciences, and women/feminism.
Donna Lindenberg

Nightwood Editions
PO Box 1779, Gibsons, BC V0N 1V0
Toll-Free: 800-667-2988
info@nightwoodeditions.com
www.nightwoodeditions.com
Social Media:
twitter.com/nightwooded
www.facebook.com/pages/Nightwood-Editions/250167265022217
ISBNs: 0-88971; SAN: 115-2661
Publishers of new poetry & fiction by Canadian writers; Also publishes non-fiction works

Nimbus Publishing Ltd.
Previous Name: Petheric Press Ltd.
PO Box 9166, 3731 MacKintosh St., Halifax, NS B3K 5M8
Tel: 902-455-4286; Fax: 902-455-5440
Toll-Free: 800-646-2879
info@nimbus.ns.ca
www.nimbus.ca
Social Media: www.youtube.com/user/NimbusPublishing
www.twitter.com/NimbusPub
www.fa cebook.com/nimbuspub
ISBNs: 0-920852, 0-921054, 1-55109; SAN: 115-0685
Terrilee Bulger, Sales & Marketing Manager, tbulger@nimbus.ns.ca
John S. Marshall, President

North Shore Publishing Inc.
2351 Sinclair Circle, Burlington, ON L7P 3C1
Tel: 905-336-2364; Fax: 905-336-5110
info@canadianheritagebooks.com
www.canadianheritagebooks.com
ISBNs: 1-896899
Publishers of local heritage books in Southern Ontario

Northern Canada Mission Distributors
PO Box 3030, Prince Albert, SK S6V 7V4
Tel: 306-764-3388; Fax: 306-764-3390
ncmd@ncem.ca
www.ncem.ca
ISBNs: 0-920731, 1-896968
William Dyck

The North-South Institute / L'Institut Nord-Sud
#200, 55 Murray St., Ottawa, ON K1N 5M3
Tel: 613-241-3535; Fax: 613-241-7435
nsi@nsi-ins.ca
www.nsi-ins.ca
ISBNs: 1-896770; SAN: 115-4605
Publishers of findings made by the North-South Institute
Roy Culpepper, President, rculpepper@nsi-ins.ca

Ann Weston, Vice-President & Coordinator of Research, aweston@nsi-ins.ca

Novalis Publishing
#400, 10 Lower Spadina Ave., Toronto, ON M5V 2Z2
Tel: 416-363-3303; Fax: 416-363-9409
Toll-Free: 877-702-7773
books@novalis.ca
www.novalis.ca
Social Media: www.youtube.com/user/novalisbooks
twitter.com/bayardcanada
www.face book.com/pages/Novalis-Books/122209491151036
ISBNs: 2-89088, 2-89507; SAN: 115-4621
Religious publishing house in the Catholic Tradition; Publishes in the areas of liturgy, prayer, spirituality, sacramental practice, catechetics, religious education and personal growth.
Joesph Sinasac, Publishing Director, joseph.sinasac@novalis.ca
Grace Deutsch, Editorial Director, grace.deutsch@novalis.ca

Now Or Never Publishing
#1101, 1003 Pacific St., Vancouver, BC V6E 4P2
www.nonpublishing.com
Social Media:
www.facebook.com/noworneverpublishing

NRC Research Press
National Research Council of Canada, 1200 Montreal Rd., Bldg. M-55, Ottawa, ON K1A 0R6
Tel: 613-993-9084; Fax: 613-952-7656
pubs@nrc-cnrc.gc.ca.
pubs.nrc-cnrc.gc.ca
Publishes research findings conducted by the National Research Council of Canada
Cameron Macdonald, Director, Publishing

Oasis Press
38 Nina St., Toronto, ON M5R 1Z4
Tel: 416-534-5124; Fax: 416-537-8421
allenmorgan@sympatico.ca
oasispress.allenmorgan.com
ISBNs: 1-895092
Publishers of story collections for children
Allen Morgan

Oberon Press
#205, 145 Spruce St., Ottawa, ON K1R 6P1
Tel: 613-238-3275; Fax: 613-238-3275
oberon@sympatico.ca
www.oberonpress.ca
ISBNs: 0-88750, 0-7780; SAN: 115-0723
Publishers of fiction by Canadian Authors. Publishes 10 new titles annually, and has 650 titles in print.
Nicholas Macklem, President

OCAPT Business Books
27 Donna Marie Dr., Welland, ON L3C 2X7
Tel: 905-735-2967; Fax: 905-788-0839
Toll-Free: 888-579-3013
ocapt@iaw.on.ca
www.ocapt.com
ISBNs: 0-915299, 1-56327, 0-527, 0-9667843
Publishes books & visual learning products for the manufacturing & service industries
Gail Grimaldi

Oolichan Books
PO Box 2278, Fernie, BC V0B 1M0
Tel: 250-423-6113;
info@oolichan.com
www.oolichan.com
Social Media:
twitter.com/OolichanBooks
www.facebook.com/pages/Oolichan-Books/18 1252759556
ISBNs: 0-88982; SAN: 115-4680
Publishes poetry, fiction & non-fiction titles including literary criticism, memoirs & books on regional history
Randal Macnair, Publisher
Ron Smith, Managing Editor
Pat Smith, Consulting Editor

Orca Book Publishers Canada
PO Box 5626 B, Victoria, BC V8R 6S4
Fax: 877-408-1551
Toll-Free: 800-210-5277
orca@orcabook.com
www.orcabook.com
Social Media:
twitter.com/orcabook
www.facebook.com/OrcaBook
ISBNs: 0-920501, 1-55143; SAN: 115-7485
Publishers of children's books; with ovr 350 titles in print & 60 new titles per year. Picturebooks, Early chapter books, teen novels

Bob Tyrrell, Editorial Director
Andrew Wooldridge, Publisher
Dayle Sutherland, Marketing Director
Melanie Jeffs, Office Manager

Organisation for Economic Cooperation & Development (OECD)
#650, 2001 L St. NW, Washington, DC
Tel: 202-785-6323; Fax: 202-785-0350
Toll-Free: 800-456-6323
washington.contact@oecd.org
www.oecdwash.org
ISBNs: 92-64
Sandra Wilson, Head, Center for Public Affairs

Our Schools/Our Selves
107 Earl Grey Rd., Toronto, ON M4J 3L6
Tel: 416-463-6978; Fax: 416-463-6978
Toll-Free: 800-565-1975
satu.repo@utoronto.ca
ISBNs: 0-921908
Satu Repo

Owl's Head Press
8500 Main St., Alma, NB E4H 1M7
Tel: 506-887-2073;
ISBNs: 0-920635

Owlkids Books
Previous Name: Maple Tree Press Inc.
#400, 10 Lower Spadina Ave., Toronto, ON M5V 2Z2
Tel: 416-340-2700; Fax: 416-340-9769
owlkids@owlkids.com
owlkidsbooks.com
Social Media:
twitter.com/owlkids
www.facebook.com/owlkids
ISBNs: 0-919872, 0-920775, 1-895688, 1-897066, 1-894379; SAN: 1
Publishers of non-fiction books for children covering a wide variety of topics including Sports, Humor, Science, Crafts, Canada, History & Culture.

Oxford University Press - Canada
#204, 8 Sampson Mews, Toronto, ON M3C 0H5
Tel: 416-441-2941; Fax: 416-444-0427
Toll-Free: 800-387-8020
customer.service@oup.com
www.oupcanada.com
ISBNs: 0-19; SAN: 115-731
One of the oldest publishing companies in the world; Publishers of non-fiction & educational material
David Stover, President
Wendy Moran, Associate Vice-President/Director, Creative Services
David Steele, Vice-President/Director, School Division

P.D. Meany Publishers
145 Westminster Ave., Toronto, ON M6R 1N8
Tel: 416-516-2903; Fax: 416-516-7632
info@pdmeany.com
www.pdmeany.com
ISBNs: 0-88835; SAN: 115-4273
Publishers of a variety of fiction & non-fiction titles
Pierrek L'Abbé

Pacific Edge Publishing Ltd.
1773 El Verano Dr., Gabriola, BC V0R 1X6
Tel: 250-247-9093; Fax: 250-247-9083
Toll-Free: 800-668-8806
info@pacificedgepublishing.com
www.pacificedgepublishing.com
ISBNs: 1-895110
Publisher & distributor of educational resources for K-12 teachers.
Chris Sherwood

Pacific Educational Press
University of British Columbia, 411-2389 Health Sciences Mall, Vancouver, BC V6T 1Z3
Tel: 604-822-5385; Fax: 604-822-6603
pep.sales@ubc.ca
pacificedpress.ca
Social Media:
twitter.com/PacificEdPress
ISBNs: 0-88865, 1-895766; SAN: 115-1266
Publishing house of the Faculty of Education at the University of British Columbia; Publishes educational resources
Catherine Edwards, Director

Pandora Press
33 Kent Ave., Kitchener, ON N2G 3R2
Tel: 519-745-1560; Fax: 519-578-1826
Toll-Free: 866-696-1678
bookshop.pandorapress.com
ISBNs: 0-9698762, 0-9685543, 1-894710
Angie Hostetler, Manager, angie@pandorapress.com

Paperplates Books
19 Kenwood Ave., Toronto, ON M6C 2RB
Tel: 416-651-2551; Fax: 416-651-2910
paper@perkolator.com
www.paperplates.org
Small Publishing House; Publishes short fiction & personal essays
Bernard Kelly
Cary Fagan

Parkland Publishing
501 Mount Allison Pl., Saskatoon, SK S7H 4A9
Tel: 306-242-7731;
info@parklandpublishing.com
www.parklandpublishing.com
Social Media:
www.facebook.com/pages/Parkland-Publishing/1612394872512 7
Publishes non-fiction books about Saskatchewan, hiking in Saskatchewan & trivia about Saskatchewan
Robin Kaplan, Co-founder
Arlene Kaplan, Co-founder

Pathway Publishers
RR#4, Aylmer, ON N5H 2R3
ISBNs: 0-919374
Amish & Anabaptist Publishing House

Pearson Canada Inc.
Previous Name: Prentice-Hall Canada; Addison-Wesley Publishers
Owned By: Pearson Canada
26 Prince Andrew Pl., Don Mills, ON M3C 2T8
Tel: 416-447-5101; Fax: 416-443-0948
Toll-Free: 800-263-9965
www.pearsoncanada.ca
ISBNs: 9780131113497; 9780131228436; 9780131280397
A Pearson Canada imprint, Pearson Education Canada Inc. is the largest publisher of print & electronic curriculum materials in Canada
MR Allan T. Reynolds, President & CEO, Pearson Canada

Pedlar Press
PO Box 26 P, 191 Madison Ave., Toronto, ON M5S 2S6
Tel: 416-534-2011; Fax: 416-535-9677
ISBNs: 0-9681884, 0-9686522, 0-9732140

Pegasus Publishing
PO Box 26, Causeway Rd., Site 19, Seaforth, NS B0J 1N0
Tel: 902-827-3204;
jenniblackmore@eastlink.ca
ISBNs: 0-9692552
Jenni Blackmore

Pembroke Publishers Limited
538 Hood Rd., Markham, ON L3R 3K9
Tel: 905-477-0650; Fax: 905-477-3691
Toll-Free: 800-997-9807
mary@pembrokepublishers.com
www.pembrokepublishers.com
Social Media:
www.twitter.com/PembrokePublish
www.facebook.com/PembrokePublishers
ISBNs: 0-921217, 1-55138
Publisher of educational resources for parents & teachers covering: Reading & Writing; Grammar & Speaking; Thinking & drama; Classroom management & major issues in education
Claudia Connolly, General Manager
Mary Macchiusi, President

Pemmican Publications Inc.
150 Henry Ave., Winnipeg, MB R3B 0J7
Tel: 204-589-6346; Fax: 204-589-2063
pemmican@pemmican.mb.ca
www.pemmicanpublications.ca
ISBNs: 0-91943, 0-921827; SAN: 115-1657
Published more than 150 titles, including history, biography, Canadian cultural and linguistic studies, adult fiction, poetry and illustrated stories for young and early readers. Pemmican is the only dedicated Metis publishing house in Canada.
Andreen Hourie, Managing Editor

Pendas Productions
525 Canterbury Rd., London, ON N6G 2N5
Tel: 519-434-8555;
pendas@pennkemp.ca
www.pennkemp.ca
ISBNs: 0-920820
Gavin Stairs

Penguin Books Canada Ltd.
Owned By: Pearson Canada
#700, 90 Eglinton Ave. East, Toronto, ON M4P 2Y3
Tel: 416-925-2249; Fax: 416-925-0068
info@penguin.ca
www.penguin.ca
ISBNs: 9781592403691; 9780140260670; 9780142004272
Penguin Books Canada is a division of Pearson Canada, & publishes paperback & hardcover books in a range of subjects, for adults & children. Winner of the 2008 Canadian Booksellers Association Publisher of the Year Award
MR David Davidar, President
MS Yvonne Hunter, Director, Publicity & Marketing

Penumbra Press
PO Box 20011, Newcastle, ON L1B 1M3
Tel: 613-692-5590;
john@penumbrapress.ca
www.penumbrapress.com
Social Media:
twitter.com/Penumbra_Press
ISBNs: 0-921254, 0-929806, 1-894131; SAN: 115-0774
Small fine-art & literary publishing house; Publishes Northern and Native literatures; children's literature; poetry; translations of Scandinavian literature; history; mythology; art books
John Flood, President, john@penumbrapress.ca

Phaidon Press Inc.
14 Glenwood Ave., Toronto, ON M6P 3C6
Tel: 416-761-1755; Fax: 416-761-9316
enquiries@phaidon.com
www.phaidon.com
Publisher of books on the visual arts

Picasso Publications Inc.
#3904, 10080 Jasper Ave., Edmonton, AB T5J 1V9
Tel: 780-420-1070; Fax: 780-420-0475
sales@picassopublications.com
ISBNs: 1-55279

Pippin Publishing Corp.
PO Box 242 Don Mills, Toronto, ON M3C 2S2
Tel: 416-510-2918; Fax: 416-510-3359
jld@pippinpub.com
www.pippinpub.com
ISBNs: 0-88751; SAN: 115-3293
Jonathan Lovat Dickson

Playwrights Canada Press
Previous Name: Playwrights Union of Canada
#202, 269 Richmond St. West, Toronto, ON M5V 1X1
Tel: 416-703-0013; Fax: 416-408-3402
info@playwrightscanada.com
www.playwrightscanada.com
Social Media:
twitter.com/PlayCanPress
www.facebook.com/PLCNP
ISBNs: 0-88754, 0-919834
Publishes roughly 32 books of plays, theatre history & criticism annually
Angela Rebeiro, Project Coordinator, editor@playwrightscanada.com
Annie Gibson, Publisher

Pokeweed Press
#337, 829 Norwest Rd., Kingston, ON K7P 2N3
Tel: 613-374-2494;
publisher@pokeweed.com
www.pokeweed.com
ISBNs: 1-894323
Frank B. Edwards, Publisher

Polar Bear Press
35 Price Andrew Pl., Toronto, ON M3C 2H2
Tel: 416-449-4000; Fax: 416-449-9924
Toll-Free: 800-490-4049
north49@idirect.com
ISBNs: 1-896757

Polestar Book Publishers
An Imprint of Raincoast Books, 9050 Shaughnessy St., Vancouver, BC V6P 6E5
Tel: 604-323-7100; Fax: 604-323-2600
Toll-Free: 800-663-5714
info@raincoast.com
www.raincoast.com
ISBNs: 0-919591, 1-896095
Michelle Benjamin, Publisher

Pontifical Institute of Mediaeval Studies, Dept. of Publications
59 Queen's Park Cres. East, Toronto, ON M5S 2C4
Tel: 416-926-7142; Fax: 416-926-7258
pontifex@chass.utoronto.ca
www.pims.ca
ISBNs: 0-88844; SAN: 115-0804
Small University Press publishing the results of research carried out by all medievalists
Rev. James K. McConica, President CSB, OC

Porcupine's Quill Inc.
PO Box 160, 68 Main St., Erin, ON N0B 1T0
Tel: 519-833-9158; Fax: 519-833-9845
pql@sentex.net
porcupinesquill.ca
Social Media:
twitter.com/porcupinesquill
www.facebook.com/theporcupinesquill
ISBNs: 0-88984; SAN: 115-0820
Small publishing house, Publishers of Canadian poetry & literature
Tim Inkster, Publisher
Elke Inkster, Publisher

Portage & Main Press
Previous Name: Peguis Publishers Limited
#100, 318 McDermot Ave., Winnipeg, MB R3A 0A2
Tel: 204-987-3500; Fax: 866-734-8477
Toll-Free: 800-667-9673
books@pandmpress.com
www.portageandmainpress.com
ISBNs: 0-919566, 1-89110, 1-895411, 1-55379
Publishers of educational books & resources for teachers
Catherine Gerbosi, President

Potlatch Publications Limited
30 Berryhill Ave., Waterdown, ON L0R 2H4
Tel: 905-689-2104; Fax: 905-689-1632
robtnielsen@aol.com
www.angelfire.com/on3/potlatch
ISBNs: 0-919676; SAN: 115-1355
Robert Nielsen, President

Pottersfield Press
83 Leslie Rd., East Lawrencetown, NS B2Z 1P8
Tel: 902-827-4517; Fax: 902-455-3652
Toll-Free: 800-646-2879
www.pottersfieldpress.com
ISBNs: 0-919001, 1-895900; SAN: 115-0790
Publishers of a number of non-fiction books, including local history & geography; memoirs; & biographies
Lesley Choyce

Power Engineering Books Ltd.
7 Perron St., St Albert, AB T8N 1E3
Tel: 780-458-3155; Fax: 780-460-2530
Toll-Free: 800-667-3155
sales@powerengbooks.com
www.powerengbooks.com
ISBNs: SAN: 115-4850
Andrew Benko

Prairie House Books
PO Box 84007 Market Mall, Calgary, AB T3A 5C4
Tel: 403-202-5438; Fax: 403-202-5437
phbooks@telusplanet.net
english-idioms.net/wm/main.cgi
ISBNs: 1-895012
Wayne Magnuson, Editor/Publisher

Prentice-Hall Canada Inc.
Previous Name: Ginn Publishing Canada Inc.
Owned By: Pearson Canada
26 Prince Andrew Place, Don Mills, ON M3C 2T8
Tel: 416-447-5101; Fax: 416-443-0948
cdn_ordr@prenhall.com
www.pearsoncanada.ca
ISBNs: 9780137149445; 9780205608171
A Pearson Canada (Pearson Education) imprint.
MR Allan T. Reynolds, President & CEO, Pearson Canada

The Press of the Nova Scotia College of Art & Design
5163 Duke St., Halifax, NS B3J 3J6
Tel: 902-444-9600; Fax: 902-425-2420
thepress@nscad.ns.ca
www.nscad.ns.ca/press/press_relaunched.php
ISBNs: 0-919616
Publishers of scholarly works in the fields of contemporary art, craft & design
Susan McEachern, Editorial Director
Eric MacDonald, Manager

Les Presses de l'Université de Montréal
306, rue Saint-Zotique est, Montréal, QC H2S 1L6
Tél: 514-343-6933; Téléc: 514-343-2232
pum@umontreal.ca
www.pum.umontreal.ca
Médias sociaux:
twitter.com/umontreal_news
ISBNs: 2-7606
A pour mandat le diffusion des résultats de la recherche universitaire (livres, revues, édition électronique); la transférence des connaissances scientifiques à un large public; participation à la vie de la Cité; et contribution au rayonnement national et international de l'Université de Montréal
Antoine Del Busso, Directeur général, delbussa@pum.umontreal.ca

Presses de l'Université du Montréal
#6010, 3744, rue Jean-Brillant, Montréal, QC H3T 1P1
Tél: 418-657-4399; Téléc: 418-657-2096
Ligne sans frais: 800-859-7474
pum@umontreal.ca
www.pum.umontreal.ca
Médias sociaux:
twitter.com/PressesUdeM
ISBNs: 0-7770, 2-7605, 2-920073
Antoine Del Busso, Directrice générale

Les Presses de l'Université Laval
#3103, Pavillon Maurice-Pollack, 2305, rue de l'Université, Québec, QC G1V 0A6
Tél: 418-656-2803; Téléc: 418-656-3305
presses@pul.ulaval.ca
www.pulaval.com
Médias sociaux: www.youtube.com/user/PressesUL
www.facebook.com/pulaval
ISBNs: 2-7637, 2-89224
Ouvrages didactiques, manuels, travaux savants; diffuseur et distributeur
Denis Dion, Directeur général, denis.dion@pul.ulaval.ca
Louise Saint-Michel, Secrétaire, louise.saint-michel@pul.ulaval.ca

Presses Inter Universitaires
PO Box 36, Cap-Rouge, QC G1Y 3C6
Tel: 418-657-6050; Fax: 418-657-7630
ISBNs: 2-89441

The Prince Edward Island Museum & Heritage Foundation
2 Kent St., Charlottetown, PE C1A 1M6
Tel: 902-368-6600; Fax: 902-368-6608
mhpei@gov.pe.ca
www.peimuseum.com
ISBNs: 0-920434

Probe International
225 Brunswick Ave., Toronto, ON M5S 2M6
Tel: 416-964-9223; Fax: 416-964-8239
www.probeinternational.org
ISBNs: 0-919849, 1-85383, 0-7656

Productive Publications
PO Box 7200 A, Toronto, ON M5W 1X8
Tel: 416-483-0634; Fax: 416-322-7434
productivepublications@rogers.com
www.productivepublications.ca
ISBNs: 0-920847, 1-896210, 1-55270; SAN: 117-1712
Iain Williamson, Owner

Prosveta Inc.
3950 Albert Mines, Canton-de-Hatley, QC J0B 2C0
Tel: 819-564-8212; Fax: 819-564-1823
Toll-Free: 800-854-8212
prosveta@prosveta-canada.com
www.prosveta-canada.com
ISBNs: 1-895978
Publishers of books related to philosophy & meditation authored by Omraam Mikhael Aivanhov
Huguette Paquin, Vice-Presidente

Psycan Corporation
#12, 120 West Beaver Creek Rd., Richmond Hill, ON L4B 1L2
Tel: 905-731-8795; Fax: 905-731-5029
Toll-Free: 800-263-3558
mail@psycan.com
www.psycan.com
Family-owned & operated publisher of eductional & clinical resources

Ptarmigan Press
1372 - 16th Ave., Campbell River, BC V9W 2E1
Tel: 250-286-0878; Fax: 250-286-9749
info@kaskgraphics.com
www.kaskgraphics.com/ptarmigan/
ISBNs: 0-919537; SAN: 116-0281
Small publishing house; Publisher of non-fiction covering Fishing; Hiking; Local history; Autobiography; Cooking; How To; Health; Sexual Abuse
Ann Kask

Public Works & Government Services Canada - Depository Services Program / Travaux public et services gouvernement aux Canada
Previous Name: Canada Communications Group Publishing
350 Albert St., 4th Fl., Ottawa, ON K1A 0S5
Tel: 613-993-1695; Fax: 613-941-2410
dsp-psd@pwgsc.gc.ca
dsp-psd.pwgsc.gc.ca
ISBNs: 0-662, 0-660; SAN: 115-2882
Publishes federal government publications and distribute them to oublic & academic libraries.
Christine Leduc, Director, 6139965959

Publications Ontario
50 Grosvenor St., Toronto, ON M7A 1N8
Tel: 416-326-5300; Fax: 416-613-566
Toll-Free: 800-668-9938
www.publications.serviceontario.ca
ISBNs: 0-7743, 0-7729, 0-7778
Publishers of government publications, including driver's handbook, fire codes, building codes, agricultural publications, employment standards & occupational health & safety
Marg Munro, Manager
Eric Steeves, Director

Publishers Group Canada
Previous Name: Publishers Group West
#300, 76 Stratford St., Toronto, ON M6J 2S1
Tel: 416-934-9900; Fax: 416-934-1410
Toll-Free: 800-747-8147
info@pgcbooks.ca
www.pgcbooks.ca
Social Media:
twitter.com/pgcanada
www.facebook.com/pages/Publishers-Group-Canada/16271343 24
ISBNs: SAN: 117-0171
Distributors of a large number of non-fiction, fiction & children's books for a large number of publishers.
Graham Fidler, Exec. Vice-President, ext. 203, graham@pgcbooks.ca
Suzanne Wice, Director, Sales & Marketing, ext. 207, suzanne@pgcbooks.ca

Purich Publishing Ltd.
PO Box 23032 Market Mall, Saskatoon, SK S7J 5H3
Tel: 306-373-5311; Fax: 306-373-5315
purich@sasktel.net
www.purichpublishing.com
ISBNs: 1-895830
Publishers of books dealing with Aboriginal & Social Justice Issues; Law & Western Canadian History; Focus on the university, college & reference market
K. Bolstad
D. Purich

Qualitas Publishing
195 Cardiff Dr. NW, Calgary, AB T2K 1S1
Tel: 403-618-3830;
info@qualitaspublishing.com
www.qualitaspublishing.com

Quarry Press
20 Hatter St., Kingston, ON K7M 2L5
Tel: 613-548-8429; Fax: 613-548-1556
ISBNs: 0-919627, 1-55082; SAN: 115-4958
Bob Hilderley, Publisher

Quattro Books
89 Pinewood Ave., Toronto, ON M6C 2V2
Tel: 647-748-7484;
www.quattrobooks.ca
Social Media: www.youtube.com/quattrobooks
twitter.com/quattrobooks
www.facebook.com/group.php?gid=132166700599&ref=ts
Allan Briesmaster, Vice-Presidnet/Publisher, allan@quattrobooks.ca

Québec dans le Monde
CP 8503 Sainte-Foy, #404, 1001, route de l'Eglise, Québec, QC G1V 4N5
Tél: 418-659-5540; Téléc: 418-659-4143
info@quebecmonde.com
www.quebecmonde.com
ISBNs: 2-921309, 2-89525, 2-9801130; SAN: 116-8657
Denis Turcotte, Directeur général

Québec Science Éditeur
#300, 4388, rue St-Denis, Montréal, QC H2J 2L1
Tél: 514-843-6888; Téléc: 514-843-4897
courrier@quebecscience.qc.ca
www.cybersciences.com
ISBNs: 2-920073
Jean-Yves Poirier, jypoirier@velo.qc.ca
Raymond Lemieux, Rédacteur en chef

Quintin Publishers / Éditions Michel Quintin
PO Box 340, 4770, rue Foster, Waterloo, QC J0E 2N0
Tel: 450-539-3774; Fax: 450-539-4905
info@editionsmichelquintin.ca
editionsmichelquintin.ca
Social Media:
twitter.com/EditionsQuintin
www.facebook.com/EditionsQuintin
ISBNs: 2-920438, 2-89435; SAN: 116-5356
Michel Quintin, Président-directeur général
Johanne Ménard, Édition scientifique, jmenard@editionsmichelquintin.ca
Mélanie Roy, Coordonnatrice, production, info@editionsmichelquintin.ca

Rainbird Press
4890 Mackenzie St., Vancouver, BC V6L 2R6
rainbirdpress@gmail.com
m_bullock.tripod.com, www.latremouille.com/mbullock
ISBNs: 0-9690504, 0-9684894
Publishers of the poetry of Michael Bullock.
Lori-Ann Latremouille

Raincoast Books Distribution Ltd.
2440 Viking Way, Richmond, BC V6V 1N2
Tel: 604-448-7100; Fax: 800-365-3770
Toll-Free: 800-663-5714
info@raincoast.com
www.raincoast.com
Other information: distribution@raincoast.com
Social Media: www.linkedin.com/company/879232?trk=tyah
twitter.com/RaincoastBooks
ww w.facebook.com/raincoastbooks
ISBNs: 0-920417, 1-895714, 1-55192, 1-896095, 0-919591; SAN 115
Full-service book distributor and former publisher (Publishing operations closed in January of 2008).
Allan MacDougall, President/CEO

Random House of Canada Ltd. Editorial & Publicity Offices
Previous Name: Ballantine-Fawcett Books
#300, 1 Toronto St., Toronto, ON M5C 2V6
Tel: 416-364-4449; Fax: 416-364-6863
ISBNs: 0-394, 0-679; SAN: 115-088X
Louise Dennys, Vice-President

Random House of Canada Ltd.
2775 Matheson Blvd. East, Mississauga, ON L4W 4P7
Tel: 905-624-0672; Fax: 905-624-6217
Toll-Free: 800-668-4247
www.randomhouse.com
ISBNs: 0-394, 0-679 0-449, 0-553 0-385 0-7704, 0-676; SAN: 201-
Large publisher of best-selling & award-winning books; distributor of many international authors
Brad Martin, President & COO
David Kent, Publisher
Katheleen Bain, Vice-President, Sales & Marketing

Rattling Books
Tors Cove, NL A0A 4A0
Tel: 709-334-3911;
www.rattlingbooks.com
Social Media: myspace.com/rattlingbooks
www.facebook.com/group.php?gid=2427995853
Audio Book publisher.

Reach for Unbleached!
Attn. D. Broten, PO Box 39, Whaletown, BC V0P 1Z0
Tel: 250-935-6992;
dbroten@rfu.org
www.rfu.org
ISBNs: 0-9680431
Publishers of environmental education material about paper & pulp mill monitoring

Reader's Digest Association (Canada) Ltd.
1100, boul René Levesque ouest, Montréal, QC H3B 5H5
Tel: 514-940-0751; Fax: 514-940-3637
Toll-Free: 866-736-3382
trade@readersdigest.ca
www.readersdigest.ca
ISBNs: 0-88850; SAN 115-0898, 115-4974
Andrea C. Martin, President/CEO

Red Deer Press
195 Allstate Parkway, Markham, ON L3R 4T8
Toll-Free: 800-387-9776
bookinfo@fitzhenry.ca
www.reddeerpress.com
ISBNs: 0-88995; SAN: 115-0871
Publishes picture books, junior, juvenile, Young Adult fiction and non-fiction and adult non-fiction titles. Was purchased by Fitzhenry & Whiteside in 2005.
Richard Dionne, Publisher, dionne@reddeerpress.com
Peter Carver, Children's Editor

Reference Press
PO Box 70, Teeswater, ON N0G 2S0
Tel: 519-392-6634; Fax: 519-392-6634
refpress@wcl.on.ca
www.libris.ca/refpress
ISBNs: 0-919981; SAN: 115-687X
Publisher of Canadian reference materials & software for use in school & public libraries
Gordon Ripley

Reflections
PO Box 178, Gabriola, BC V0R 1X0
Tel: 250-247-8685;
ISBNs: 0-9692570

Renouf Publishing Co. Ltd. / Éditions Renouf limitées
#22, 1010 Polytek St., Ottawa, ON K1J 9J3
Tel: 613-745-2665; Fax: 613-745-7660
Toll-Free: 866-767-6766
orders@renoufbooks.com
www.renoufbooks.com
ISBNs: 0-88852; SAN: 170-8066
Publishers of over 35 international organizations' publiations & documents
Gordon Grahame, President
Avrum Kerzner, Comptroller
Brigid Grahame, General Manager

Repository Press
137 Lyon St. South, Prince George, BC V2M 3K7
Tel: 250-562-7074; Fax: 250-561-7094
harris@cnc.bc.ca
ISBNs: 0-920104; SAN: 115-5016
John Harris, Publisher/Editor
Vivien Lougheed, Publisher

The Resource Centre Inc.
PO Box 190, Waterloo, ON N2J 3Z9
Tel: 519-885-0826; Fax: 519-747-5629
Toll-Free: 800-923-0330
sales@theresourcecentre.com
www.theresourcecentre.com
ISBNs: 0-920701; SAN: 115-5032
Publishers of educational resources, including books on ESL, Language & Writing among other subjects
N. Gridgeman, President

Riverwood Publishers Ltd.
471 Eagle St., Newmarket, ON L3Y 1K7
Tel: 905-853-8887; Fax: 905-853-3330
Toll-Free: 800-561-2674
info@riverwoodpub.com
www.riverwoodpub.com

ISBNs: 1-895121; SAN: 116-1288
Publishers of children's books & Canadian distributors of Usborne Books, a respected children's book publisher.
Ron Charlesworth, President

Robert Davies Multimedia Publishing / Éditions multimedia Robert Davies inc.
Previous Name: L'Etincelle editeur inc.
9 Parkside Pl., Montréal, QC H3Z 1T3
Tel: 514-934-5433; Fax: 514-937-8765
Toll-Free: 800-481-2440
rdppub@rdppub.com
www.rdppub.com
ISBNs: 1-895854, 1-55207, 2-89019, 2-89462
Robert Davies, Publisher

Robert Rose Inc.
120 Eglington Ave. E, Toronto, ON M4P 1E2
Tel: 416-322-6552; Fax: 416-322-6936
www.fireflybooks.com/RR.html
ISBNs: 1-896503, 0-7788
Publishers of cookbooks; Distributed by Firefly Books
Robert J. Dees

Robin Brass Studio Inc.
PO Box 335 R, Montréal, QC H2S 2R0
Tel: 514-272-7463; Fax: 514-272-7971
rbrass@sympatico.ca
www.rbstudiobooks.com
ISBNs: 1-896941; SAN: 115-5040
Small publishing house producing primarily non-fiction, especially within the area of military history & other Canadian history; Also designs and produces books under contract for other publishers & organizations

Rocky Mountain Books
406 - 13th Ave. NE, Calgary, AB T2E 1C2
Tel: 604-574-7067; Fax: 604-881-7068
Toll-Free: 800-665-3302
distribution@heritagehouse.ca
www.rmbooks.com
Social Media: www.youtube.com/rmbooks1
twitter.com/rmbooks
www.facebook.com/rmboo ks
ISBNs: 0-921102; SAN: 115-5040
Publisher of outdoor activity guidebooks, historical accounts of Canadian mountaineering and other adventures, biographies & related non-fiction
Don Gorman, Publisher, don@rmbooks.com

Ronsdale Press
Previous Name: Cacanadadada Press
3350 West 21st Ave., Vancouver, BC V6S 1G7
Tel: 604-738-4688; Fax: 604-731-4548
ronsdale@shaw.ca
www.ronsdalepress.com
Social Media:
twitter.com/ronsdalepress
www.facebook.com/ronsdalepress
ISBNs: 0-921870, 1-55380; SAN: 116-2454
Publishers of fiction, poetry, regional history, biography & autobiography, books of ideas about Canada, as well as children's books.
Ronald B. Hatch, Director

Roseway Publishing Co. Ltd.
32 Oceanvista Lane, Site 2A, Box 5, Black Point, NS B0T 1B0
Tel: 902-857-1388; Fax: 902-857-1328
info@rosewaypublishing.ca
www.rosewaypublishing.com, www.selfpublishingspecialists.com
ISBNs: 0-9694180, 1-896496
Small publishing house; Publishes plays & fiction & non-fiction books of local interest
Kathleen K. Tudor, Owner/Manager

Routledge/Taylor & Francis Group
7625 Empire Dr., Florence, KY
Tel: 859-727-5000; Fax: 800-248-4724
Toll-Free: 800-634-7064
orders@taylorandfrancis.com
www.routledge.com, www.taylorandfrancis.com
ISBNs: 0-415, 0-87830
Publishers of educational & academic resources for the college/university market. Distributor is Login Canada, www.lb.ca.

The Rowman & Littlefield Publishing Group
Canadian Sales Office, 10 Cushendun Rd., Toronto, ON M1E 2B3
Tel: 416-282-3592;
donmacivor@rogers.com
www.rowmanlittlefield.com
Canadian sales office for large international publisher focusing on non-fiction books for the academic market

The Royal Astronomical Society of Canada
136 Dupont St., Toronto, ON M5R 1V2
Tel: 416-924-7973; Fax: 416-924-2911
Toll-Free: 844-626-2665
mempub10001@rasc.ca
www.rasc.ca
Publishes journals and guides to astronomy
Jo Taylor, Membership & Publications Clerk

Rubicon Publishing Inc.
PO Box 69596, Oakville, ON L6J 7R4
Tel: 905-849-8777; Fax: 905-849-7579
contact@rubiconpublishing.com
www.rubiconpublishing.com
ISBNs: 0-921156; SAN: 115-432X
Publisher of educational resources for students and educators for grades K-12.
Kimberley Wulf
Maggie Goh

Safety Sense Enterprises
PO Box 9512 T, Ottawa, ON K1G 3V2
Tel: 613-830-9342; Fax: 613-830-4284
ISBNs: 0-9695568
Hon. Heward Graffley, President/CEO

Salal Press
PO Box 36060, Victoria, BC V9A 7J5
Tel: 250-384-0305; Fax: 250-384-0351
salal@horizon.bc.ca
ISBNs: 1-894012
Small publisher of novels and non-fiction books
Clare Thorbes

Sandhill Publishing
#4, 3308 Appaloosa Rd., Kelowna, BC V1V 2G9
Tel: 250-491-1446; Fax: 250-491-4066
Toll-Free: 800-667-3848
info@sandhillbooks.com
www.sandhillbooks.com
ISBNs: 0-920923; SAN: 115-2181
Distributor for Small Press & Independent Publishers
Nancy Wise

Saunders Book Company
PO Box 308, 199 Campbell St., Collingwood, ON L9Y 3Z7
Tel: 705-445-4777; Fax: 705-445-9569
Toll-Free: 800-461-9120
info@saundersbook.ca
www.saundersbook.ca
ISBNs: SAN: 169-9768
Publishers of books for educational books & fiction for K-12 schools & libraries
John Saunders, President
James Saunders, Sales, james.saunders@saundersbook.ca

Scholar's Choice
PO Box 7214, 2323 Trafalgar St., London, ON N5Y 5S7
Tel: 519-453-7470; Fax: 519-455-2853
Toll-Free: 800-265-1095
sales@scholarschoice.ca
www.scholarschoice.ca
ISBNs: 0-88809; SAN: 170-0014
Publisher & retailer of educational materials
Scott Webster, President
Cindy Webster, Executive Vice-President

Scholastic Canada Ltd. / Éditions Scholastic
175 Hillmount Rd., Markham, ON L6C 1Z7
Tel: 905-887-7323; Fax: 905-887-1131
custsev@scholastic.ca
www.scholastic.ca
ISBNs: 0-590; SAN: 115-5164
Leading publishers & distributors of children's books & educational materials in French & English
Iole Lucchese, Co-President
Linda Goswell, Co-President

School Book Fairs Limited
2201 Dunwin Dr., Mississauga, ON L5L 1X2
Tel: 905-828-6620; Fax: 905-828-2761
Toll-Free: 800-268-4557
sbf@sbfmedia.com
www.sbfmedia.com
ISBNs: 0-921932; SAN 115-5083
Publisher & distributor of mass market & trade paperbacks for schools; Also publish educational resource books

Scroll Press
10575 Lakeside Place, Prince George, BC V2K 5M7
Tel: 250-967-4365;
dee@scrollpress.com
scrollpress.com
Publishes novels and collections of short stories.

Second Story Press
#401, 20 Maud St., Toronto, ON M5S 2R4
Tel: 416-537-7850; Fax: 416-537-0588
info@secondstorypress.ca
secondstorypress.ca
Social Media:
twitter.com/_secondstory
www.facebook.com/pages/Second-Story-Press /10623359005
ISBNs: 0-929005, 1-896764; SAN: 115-1134
Publishers of roughly 8 titles per sesaon, spanning adult fiction & non-fiction; children's fiction, non-fiction & picture books; Young Adult fiction & non-fiction. Special interest areas include Judaica, Ability Issues, Coping with Cancer & Queer rights
Margie Wolf, President

Self-Counsel Press Ltd.
1481 Charlotte Rd., North Vancouver, BC V7J 1H1
Tel: 604-986-3366; Fax: 604-986-3947
Toll-Free: 800-663-3007
orders@self-counsel.com
www.self-counsel.com
ISBNs: 0-88908, 1-55180; SAN: 115-0545
Publisher of self-help law books & books for small business
Diana R. Douglas, President

September Dreams Publishing
PO Box 44085 Southcentre PO, 9419 Fairmount Dr. SE, Calgary, AB T2J 7C5
Tel: 403-519-7418;
viktor@septemberdreams.com
www.septemberdreams.com
ISBNs: 0-9695763
Publishers of four books covering business, computer, humour & lifestyle
Viktor E. Oey
Rudy W. Oey

Septembre éditeur inc.
CP 9425 Sainte-Foy, 2825, ch des Quatre-Bourgeois, Québec, QC G1V 4B8
Tél: 418-658-7272; Téléc: 418-652-0986
Ligne sans frais: 800-361-7755
serviceclientele@septembre.com
www.septembre.com
ISBNs: 2-930433, 2-89471
Matériel didactique; éducation; emplois; formation; littérature jeunesse; management; ressources humaines; métiers; orientation; outils pédagogiques
Martin Rochette, Président-directeur général

Seraphim Editions
54 Bay St., Woodstock, ON N4S 3K9
Tel: 519-290-5509; Fax: 519-290-5509
info@seraphimeditions.com
www.seraphimeditions.com
Maureen Whyte, Publisher

Services documentaires multimedia inc.
#620, 5650, rue d'Iberville, Montréal, QC H2GH3L 3T1
Tél: 514-382-0895; Téléc: 514-384-9139
informations@sdm.qc.ca
www.sdm.qc.ca
ISBNs: 2-89059, 0-88523
Denis Lévesque, Directeur Général
Claude Jourdain, Direction de l'info. et du dév. tech.
Diane Dallaire-Talbot, Directrice, l'Exploration

Shard Press
102 Garnet Ave., Toronto, ON M6G 1V7
Tel: 416-538-2679; Fax: 416-538-2679
info@shard.com
www.shard.com
ISBNs: 0-9696455
Cyril Chen

Sheltus & Picard Inc.
CP 1321, Bedford, QC J0J 1A0
Tél: 450-248-7319; Téléc: 450-248-2057
cp.jas.rm@acbm.net
ISBNs: 0-9696296
Small publisher specializing in local history
J.A. Sheltus, President/CEO
C. Picard, Vice-President & Editor

Shoreline Press
23, rue Sainte-Anne, Sainte-Anne-de-Bellevue, QC H9X 1L1
Tel: 514-457-5733; Fax: 514-457-5733
shoreline@sympatico.ca
www.shorelinepress.ca
ISBNs: 0-9695180, 0-9698752, 1-896754; SAN 116-9564
Independent press publishing specializing in memoirs & titles of local interest
Judy Isherwood, Owner & Publisher

Sierra Club Books
85 Second St., 2nd Fl., San Francisco, CA
Tel: 415-977-5500; Fax: 415-977-5799
booksinfo@sierraclub.org
www.sc.org/books/

Signature Editions
Previous Name: Nuage Editions.
PO Box 206 Corydon, Winnipeg, MB R3M 3S7
Tel: 204-779-7803; Fax: 204-779-6970
signature@allstream.net
www.signature-editions.com
ISBNs: 0-921833, 1-897109; SAN: 115-0723
Karen Haughian, Publisher

Simon & Schuster Canada
#600, 625 Cochrane Dr., Markham, ON L3R 9R9
Tel: 905-943-9942; Fax: 905-943-9026
Toll-Free: 800-268-3216
info@simonandschuster.ca
www.simonsayscanada.com
ISBNs: 1-55525, 0-38224, 0-945299; SAN: 115-4788
Publishers of a large catalog of books covering all aspects of fiction & non-fiction
Deborah Woods, President
Susan Stoddart, Chair

Simply Read Books Inc.
#501, 5525 West Blvd., Vancouver, BC V6M 3W6
Tel: 604-727-2960; Fax: 604-263-5707
info@simplyreadbooks.com
www.simplyreadbooks.com
Publishers of fiction for children & young adults

Sinai Multi-lingual Books
7356 Ontario St., Vancouver, BC V5X 3B8
Tel: 604-327-6694; Fax: 604-327-6694
info@booksm.com
www.booksm.com
ISBNs: 1-896277
Publishes books in English, French, Arabic, Chinese, German, Russian & Spanish
Cynthia Wong

Singing Shield Productions
104 Ray Blvd., Thunder Bay, ON P7B 4C4
Tel: 807-344-8355; Fax: 807-344-8355
pebarr@tbaytel.net
ISBNs: 0-9691717; SAN: 115-5784
Elinor Barr

Sister Vision Press
101 Dewson St., Toronto, ON M6H 1H4
Tel: 416-533-9353;
ISBNs: 0-920813, 1-896705
Stephanie Martin
Makeda Silvera

Snowapple Press
PO Box 66024 Heritage, Edmonton, AB T6J 6T4
Tel: 403-437-0191; Fax: 403-437-0191
ISBNs: 1-895592
Guy Tessier, Publisher

Socadis Inc.
420, rue Stinson, Ville Saint-Laurent, QC H4N 3L7
Tel: 514-331-3300; Fax: 514-745-3282
Toll-Free: 800-361-2847
socinfo@socadis.com
www.socadis.com

Society to Overcome Pollution
716 St. Ferdinand, Montréal, QC H4C 2T2
Tel: 514-932-7267;

Sono Nis Press
PO Box 260, Winlaw, BC V0G 2J0
Tel: 250-226-0077; Fax: 250-226-0074
Toll-Free: 800-370-5228
books@sononis.com
www.sononis.com
A literary house specializing in poetry, fiction & regional non-fiction.

Sound & Vision Publishing Ltd.
#103, 109 Beech Ave., Toronto, ON M4E 3H5
www.soundandvision.com
ISBNs: 0-920151; SAN: 115-0979
Publishers of books about contemporary music & music history
Geoff Savage, Publisher

Spotted Cow Press
4216 - 121 St., Edmonton, AB T6J 1Y8
Tel: 780-434-3858;
jmartin@spottedcowpress.ca
www.spottedcowpress.ca

Statistics Canada
c/o Circulation Management, 120 Parkdale Ave., Ottawa, ON K1A 0T6
Tel: 613-951-7277; Fax: 613-951-1584
Toll-Free: 800-700-1033
order@statcan.ca
www.statcan.ca
ISBNs: 0-660, 0-662
Publishes research and information conducted by Statistics Canada

Steller Press Ltd.
3122 Blenheim St., Vancouver, BC V6K 4J7
Tel: 604-222-2955; Fax: 604-222-2965
info@stellerpress.com
www.stellerpress.com
ISBNs: 1-894143
Regional publisher; focusing on books for the Pacific Northwest & Lower Mainland

Stoneycroft Publishing
PO Box 1710, RR#1, Yarmouth, NS B5A 4A5
Tel: 902-742-2667;
stuarttrask@eastlink.ca
ISBNs: 1-896269
Gwen G. Trask

Studio Word
Previous Name: Studio Word Processing Ltd.
228 Park Ridge Cl., Camrose, AB T4V 4P1
Tel: 780-672-2551; Fax: 780-672-5887
studioword@studioword.com
www.studioword.com
ISBNs: 0-969, 0-968, 1-894361
Publishes training manuals for popular software applications
Lois Larson, Owner

Subway Books Ltd.
#203, 1819 Pendrell St., Vancouver, BC V6G 1T3
Tel: 604-488-1388;
ISBNs: 0-9681660
Publishes books on social issues, non-fiction topics, biographies & poetry

Sumach Press
180 Bloor St. West, Toronto, ON M5S 2V6
Tel: 416-929-2964; Fax: 416-929-1926
info@sumachpress.com
threeoclockpress.com/sumachpress
Social Media:
twitter.com/3oclockpress
www.facebook.com/pages/Three-OClock-Press/139452176099151
ISBNs: 1-894549, 1-896764, 0-929005; SAN: 115-1134
Publishers of feminist writing
Lois Pike

Summerthought Publishing
PO Box 2309, Banff, AB T1L 1C1
Tel: 403-762-0535; Fax: 403-762-3095
info@summerthought.com
www.summerthought.com
ISBNs: 0-919934; SAN: 115-2149
Specializing in the publication of Canadian Rockies non fiction books.
Andrew Hempstead, Publisher

Summit Educational Services
PO Box 149, Richmond Hill, ON L4C 4X9
Tel: 905-883-9427; Fax: 905-770-8576
Toll-Free: 800-741-5956
admin@summit-ed.com
www.summit-ed.com
ISBNs: 1-895187
Arlene Marks, President

Sun-Scape Enterprises Ltd.
290 Healey Rd., Bolton, ON L7E 1C9
Tel: 905-951-3155; Fax: 905-951-9712
ISBNs: 0-919842
Kenneth George Mills

Sybertooth Inc.
59 Salem St., Sackville, NB E4L 4J6
sybertooth.ca
A publisher of fiction, non-fiction, poetry, and plays.

Talon Books Ltd.
PO Box 2076, 278 East 1st Ave., Vancouver, BC V6B 3S3
Tel: 604-444-4889; Fax: 604-444-4119
Toll-Free: 888-445-4176
info@talonbooks.com
www.talonbooks.com
Social Media:
twitter.com/Talonbooks
www.facebook.com/pages/Talonbooks/139312703339
ISBNs: 0-88922; SAN: 115-5334; Telebook: S1150391
Publishers specializing in poetry, drama & literary criticism. Also publishes fiction & non-fiction
Kevin Williams, President/Publisher, kevin@talonbooks.com
Greg Gibson, Managing Editor, production@talonbooks.com

Tanager Press
145 Troy St., Mississauga, ON L5G 1S8
contact@tanagerpress.com
www.tanagerpress.com
ISBNs: 1-895410
Publishes resources for those learning guitar & musical theory
N. Ledwidge
J. Neveleff

Tantalas Books
PO Box 255, 10 Towers Ave., Gander, NL A1V 1W6
Tel: 709-656-8833; Fax: 709-651-3849
ISBNs: 0-9695519

Taylor & Francis
325 Chestnut St., 8th Fl., Philadelphia, PA
Tel: 215-625-8900; Fax: 215-625-2940

TechnoKids Inc.
2097 Bates Common, Burlington, ON L7R 0A5
Fax: 905-631-9113
Toll-Free: 800-221-7921
information@technokids.com
www.technokids.com
Social Media: www.technokids.com/blog
twitter.com/technokidsinc
www.facebook.com/ technokidscomputercurriculum
ISBNs: 1-894995
Publisher of technology cirriculum for schools. Publish K-12 Microsoft Office technology projects. Over 60 titles available.

Temeron Books Inc.
#210, 1220 Kensington Rd. NW, Calgary, AB T2N 3P5
Tel: 403-283-0900; Fax: 403-283-6947
temeron@telusplanet.net
www.temerondetselig.com
ISBNs: 1-895510, 1-55059, 0-920490; SAN: 115-0324
Publishers of educational resources in the fields of psychology, social & political science; history, biography & memoirs; Health; K9 Training & Information; Living & Social Interaction
T.E. Giles, President

Ten Speed Press
c/o Hornblower Books, #1202, 200 Woolner Ave., Toronto, ON M6N 1Y4
Tel: 416-461-7973; Fax: 416-461-0365
Toll-Free: 800-404-4446
alan@tenspeed.ca
www.tenspeed.com/canada.htm
ISBNs: 0-89815, 1-58008, 0-89087, 1-883672, 1-58246, 1-58761

Terrific Titles for Young Readers
52 Hazelton Ave, Toronto, ON M5R 2E2
Tel: 416-921-9557;

Theytus Books
Green Mountain Rd., Lot 45, RR#2, Comp. 8, Site 50, Penticton, BC V2A 6J7
Tel: 250-493-7181; Fax: 250-493-5302
info@theytus.com
www.theytus.com
Social Media:
www.facebook.com/245963905424764
ISBNs: 0-919441, 1-894778; SAN: 115-1517
Aboriginal-owned & operated publishing house; Focus is on

publishing books of Aboriginal literature, children's books, history, culture, politics & educational materials
Sarah Dickie, Operations Manager, operations@theytus.com

Thistledown Press Ltd.
118 - 20th St. West, Saskatoon, SK S7M 0W6
Tel: 306-244-1722; Fax: 306-244-1762
tdpress@thistledownpress.com
www.thistledownpress.com
Social Media:
twitter.com/ReadThistledown
www.facebook.com/pages/Thistledown-Press/115752538043
ISBNs: 0-920066, 1-894345, 0-920633, 1-895449
Publishes poetry & fiction for adults & young adults by Canadian writers; Also publishes resources for teachers
Allan Forrie, Publisher, editorial@thistledownpress.com
Jackie Forrie, Publishing & Production Manager

Thomas Allen & Son Ltd.
390 Steelcase Rd. East, Markham, ON L3R 1G2
Tel: 905-475-9126; Fax: 905-475-4255
Toll-Free: 800-458-5504
info@t-allen.com
www.thomas-allen.com
ISBNs: 0-919028, 088762; SAN: 115-1762
Publishers of award-winning bestsellers; Publish a small, highly-focused list of no more than 10-12 books a year, both fiction & non-fiction
T.J. Allen

Thompson Educational Publishing, Inc.
20 Ripley Ave., Toronto, ON M6S 3N9
Tel: 416-766-2763; Fax: 416-766-0398
Toll-Free: 877-366-2763
publisher@thompsonbooks.com
thompsonbooks.com
ISBNs: 1-55077; SAN: 115-0391
Publishes educational texts in the social sciences & humanities
Keith Thompson, President
Faye Thompson, Vice-President, faye@thompsonbooks.com

Three O'Clock Press
#801, 180 Bloor St. West, Toronto, ON M5S 2V6
Tel: 416-929-2964; Fax: 416-929-1926
info@threeoclockpress.com
threeoclockpress.com
Social Media:
twitter.com/3oclockpress
www.facebook.com/pages/Three-OClock-Press/139452176099151
Feminist writing.

Tikka Books
PO Box 203, Chambly, QC J3L 4B3
Tel: 450-658-6205;
leila@tikkabooks.com
www.tikkabooks.com
ISBNs: 1-896106; 0-921993
Independent publishing house
Leila Pelposaari, Publisher

Timeless Books
#423, 215 Spadina Ave., Toronto, ON M5T 2C7
Tel: 416-644-1030; Fax: 416-644-0116
contact@timeless.org
www.timeless.org
ISBNs: 0-931454, 2-9044616
Publishers of teachings on yoga, including poetry & spiritual biography; Also publishes classic books & audio
Andrew Wedman, Publisher, andrew@timeless.org
Clea McDougall, Editor, clea@timeless.org
Kendra Ward, Managing Editor, kendra@timeless.org

Times Mirror Professional Publishing
Previous Name: Mosby Yearbook
130 Flaska Dr., Markham, ON L6G 1B8
Tel: 905-470-6739; Fax: 905-470-0050
ISBNs: 0-8016; SAN: 115-4389

TouchWood Editions Ltd.
Previous Name: Horsdal & Schubart Publishers Ltd.
340 - 1105 Pandora Ave., Victoria, BC V8V 3P9
Tel: 250-360-0829; Fax: 250-386-0829
info@touchwoodeditions.com
www.touchwoodeditions.com
Social Media:
twitter.com/TouchWoodEd
www.facebook.com/TouchWoodEditions
ISBNs: 0-920663, 1-894898
Publishes books with a focus on history, historical fiction, biography, food, nautical subjects, mysteries & art/architecture
Ruth Linka, Publisher

Tradewind Books
#202, 1807 Maritime Mews, Vancouver, BC V6H 3W7
Tel: 604-662-4405; Fax: 604-730-0454
tradewindbooks@eudoramail.com
www.tradewindbooks.com
Social Media:
twitter.com/tradewindbooks
www.facebook.com/pages/Tradewind-Books/164946283181
ISBNs: 1-896580
Publishers of children's literature recognized internationally
Michael Katz

Tralco Educational Services Inc.
#101, 1030 Upper James St., Hamilton, ON L9C 6X6
Tel: 905-575-5717; Fax: 905-575-1783
Toll-Free: 888-487-2526
sales@tralco.com
www.tralco.com
ISBNs: 0-921376, 1-894738, 1-55409
Publishes supplementary materials for second-language education; Publishes in French, German, Spanish, ESL & Italian. Also produces activity books, videos, audio cassettes, games & software
Karen Traynor, President

Tree Frog Press Ltd.
10144 - 89 St., Edmonton, AB T5H 1P7
Tel: 780-429-1947;
www.bookpublishers.ab.ca/members/treefrog.html
ISBNs: 0-88967; SAN: 115-1053
Involved in custom book production for self-publishers & organizations & families
Allan Shute, Editor & Publisher

Tree House Press Inc.
#2, 110 Lansing Dr., Hamilton, ON L8W 3A1
Fax: 905-574-0228
Toll-Free: 800-776-8733
contact@treehousepress.com
www.treehousepress.com
ISBNs: 1-895165
Publishes educational resources specifically made for each province's educational standards

Trent University. Academic Skills Centre
Trent University, PO Box 4800, 1600 West Bank Dr., Peterborough, ON K9J 7B8
Tel: 705-748-1720; Fax: 705-748-1830
acdskills@trentu.ca
www.trentu.ca/academicskills
ISBNs: 0-9693668, 1-894674

Tri-Fold Books (Distributor)
141 King St., Guelph, ON N1E 4P7
Tel: 519-821-9901; Fax: 519-821-5333
Toll-Free: 800-572-2300
info@trifoldbooks.com
ISBNs: SAN: 106-4320
Douglas N. Cass, Owner

Trifolium Books Inc.
A Fitzhenry & Whiteside Company, 195 Allstate Pkwy., Markham, ON L3R 4T8
Tel: 905-477-9700; Fax: 905-477-9179
Toll-Free: 800-387-9776
bookinfo@fitzhenry.ca
www.fitzhenrty.ca
ISBNs: 1-895579, 1-55244
Publishes practical resources in science, technology, information technology, mathematics, careers, general business and life skills, for schools (elementary and secondary), trade professional and reference and library markets.
Sharon Fitzhenry

Trillistar Books
PO Box 30059 Parkgate, North Vancouver, BC V7H 2Y5
Tel: 778-433-5340;
editor@trillistar.com
trillistar.com
Books to alter the cultural landscape through evolving ideas, both educational and aesthetic.

Trout Lily Press
940 Holly Ave., Winnipeg, MB R3T 1W5
www.sju.ca/troutlily/
Very small independent publisher of poetry & prose

TSAR Publications
PO Box 6996 A, Toronto, ON M5W 1X7
Tel: 416-483-7191; Fax: 416-486-0706
inquiries@tsarbooks.com
www.tsarbooks.com
Social Media:
twitter.com/TSARbooks
www.facebook.com/pages/TSAR-Publications/211176882248465
ISBNs: 0-929661, 1-894770
Publishes 6-8 titles of fiction, poetry & non-fictoin (literary criticism, history) annually.

Tumbleweed Press
#4, 1853A Avenue Rd., Toronto, ON M5M 2G3
Tel: 416-781-4010; Fax: 416-781-2764
info@tumblebooks.com
www.tumbleweed-press.com
ISBNs: 0-9683303, 0-9680678
Custom publishers of children's books to be used for marketing purposes

Tundra Books
75 Sherbourne St., 5th Fl., Toronto, ON M5A 2P9
Tel: 416-598-4786; Toll-Free: 800-788-1074
tundra@mcclelland.com
www.tundrabooks.com
Imprint of McClelland & Stewart.
Kathy Lowinger, Publisher

TUNS Press
Faculty of Architecture & Planning, Dalhousie University, PO Box 1000, Halifax, NS B3J 2X4
Tel: 902-494-3925; Fax: 902-423-6672
tuns.press@dal.ca
tunspress.dal.ca
ISBNs: 0-929112
Publishing arm of the Faculty of Architecture & Planning at Dalhousie University

Turnstone Press
#018, 100 Arthur St., Winnipeg, MB R3B 1H3
Tel: 204-947-1555; Fax: 204-942-1555
editor@turnstonepress.com
www.turnstonepress.com
ISBNs: 0-88801; SAN: 115-1096
Publishers of fiction, literary criticism, poetry & non-fiction; Imprints include Turnstone Press which publishes mysteries, thrillers & noir fiction
Manuela David, Managing Editor
Patrick Gunter, Marketing Director

Ulverscroft Large Print (Canada) Ltd.
PO Box 80038, Burlington, ON L7L 6B1
Tel: 905-637-8734; Fax: 905-333-6788
Toll-Free: 888-860-3365
ulpbcan@worldchat.com
www.ulverscroft.com
ISBNs: 0-7089
Publishers of large print books, producing 84 large print books monthly.
Diane van Veen

Ulysses Travel Guides / Éditions Ulysse
4176, rue Saint-Denis, Montréal, QC H2W 2M5
Tel: 514-843-9447; Fax: 514-843-9448
info@ulysses.ca
www.ulyssesguides.com
ISBNs: 2-921444, 2-89464; SAN: 115-7167
Publishers of Canadian travel guides covering all areas of the country with a focus on Québec
Daniel Desjardins

Umberto Press
PO Box 42086, 2300 Oak Bay Ave., Victoria, BC V8R 6T4
Tel: 250-721-7239; Fax: 250-592-6463

United Church Publishing House
#300, 3250 Bloor St. West, Toronto, ON M8X 2Y4
Tel: 416-231-5931; Fax: 416-231-3103
Toll-Free: 800-288-7365
bookpub@united-church.ca
www.united-church.ca/ucph
ISBNs: 0-919000, 1-55134; SAN: 111-6002
Rebekah Chevalier, Director, Publishing
P, 4162317680 ext 4034, rchevali@united-church.ca

University Extension Press
#237 Williams Bldg., University of Saskatchewan, 221 Cumberland Ave. N, Saskatoon, SK S7N 1M3
Tel: 306-966-5558; Fax: 306-966-5567
extension.press@usask.ca
www.extension.usask.ca
Perry Millar, Managing Editor

Bertram Wolfe, Director

University of Alberta Press
Ring House 2, University of Alberta, Edmonton, AB T6G 2E1
Tel: 780-492-3662; Fax: 780-492-0719
www.uap.ualberta.ca

ISBNs: 0-88864; SAN: 118-9794
Linda D. Cameron, Director, 7804920717, linda.cameron@ualberta.ca

University of British Columbia Press
2029 West Mall, Vancouver, BC V6T 1Z2
Tel: 604-822-5959; Fax: 604-822-6083
Toll-Free: 877-377-9378
frontdesk@ubcpress.ca
www.ubcpress.ca

ISBNs: 0-7748; SAN: 115-1118
Publishing branch of the University of British Columbia; Largest scholarly press in Western Canada; Publishes 50-60 books annually with over 800 published since establishment; Specialties include political science, native studies, forestry, Asian studies, Canadian history, environmental studies, planning & urban studies.
R. Peter Milroy, Director

University of Calgary Press
2500 University Dr. NW, Calgary, AB T2N 1N4
Tel: 403-220-7578; Fax: 403-282-0085
Toll-Free: 800-663-5714
ucpress@ucalgary.ca
www.uofcpress.com

ISBNs: ISBN: 0-919813, 1-895176, 1-55238; SAN: 115-0871
Publishing arm of the University of Calgary
Donna Livingstone, Director, 403-220-3511, livingsd@ucalgary.ca
Karen Buttner, Editorial Secretary, 403-220-3979, kbuttner@ucalgary.ca
John King, Senior Editor, 403-220-4208, jking@ucalgary.ca
Peter Enman, Editor, 403-220-2606, enman@ucalgary.ca

University of Manitoba Press
301 St. John's College, University of Manitoba, Winnipeg, MB R3T 2M5
Tel: 204-474-6465; Fax: 204-474-7566
uofm_press@umanitoba.ca
www.umanitoba.ca/publications/uofmpress

ISBNs: 0-88755; SAN: 115-5474
Publishing arm of the University of Manitoba; Publishes 6-8 scholarly works annually; Best known for Native History, Canadian History, Native Studies & Canadian literary studies.
David Carr, Director, 2044749242, carr@cc.umanitoba.ca
Cheryl Miki, Marketing Coordinator, 2044749495, miki@cc.umanitoba.ca
Pat Sanders, Managing Editor, 2044747338, sandersp@cc.umanitoba.ca

University of Ottawa Press (UOP/PUO) / Presses de l'Université d'Ottawa
542 King Edward Ave., Ottawa, ON K1N 6N5
Tel: 613-562-5246; Fax: 613-562-5247
Toll-Free: 800-565-9523
puo-uop@uottawa.ca
www.press.uottawa.ca
Social Media:
twitter.com/uOttawaPress
www.facebook.com/uOttawaPress

ISBNs: 0-7766, 2-7603
Canada's oldest French Language university press & the only Bilingual University press in North America.
Lara Mainville, Director

University of Toronto Centre of Criminology
14 Queen's Park Cres. West, Toronto, ON M5S 3K9
Tel: 416-978-7124; Fax: 416-978-4195
criminology.publications@utoronto.ca
www.criminology.utoronto.ca

ISBNs: 0-919584
In-house publishing facility to showcase research of Centre faculty & graduate students
Rita Donelan, Assistant to the Director

University of Toronto Press
#700, 10 St. Mary St., Toronto, ON M4Y 2W8
Tel: 416-978-2239; Fax: 416-978-4738
Toll-Free: 800-565-9523
publishing@utpress.utoronto.ca
www.utpress.utoronto.ca

ISBNs: ISBN: 0-8020; SAN: 115-1134, 115-3234
Publishing arm of the University of Toronto
Anne Laughlin, Managing Editor, 4169782239 ext236, alaughlin@utpress.utoronto.ca
Charley LaRose, Publications Co-ordinator, 4169782239 ext237, clarose@utpress.utoronto.ca

Up Here Publishing Ltd.
Previous Name: Outcrop, The Northern Publishers
#800, 4920 - 52th St., Yellowknife, NT X1A 3T1
Tel: 867-766-6710; Fax: 867-873-9876
Toll-Free: 866-572-1757
www.uphere.ca
Ronne Heming, Vice-President, ronne@outcrop.com

Véhicule Press
CP 125 Place du Parc, Montréal, QC H2W 4A3
Tél: 514-844-6073; Téléc: 514-844-7543
vp@vehiculepress.com
www.vehiculepress.com
Médias sociaux:
www.twitter.com/VehiculePress
www.facebook.com/VehiculePress?ref=h l

ISBNs: 0-919890, 1-55065; SAN: 115-1150
Simon Dardick, Co-Publisher
Nancy Marrelli, Co-Publisher

Vesta Publications Ltd.
PO Box 1641, Cornwall, ON K6H 5R9
Tel: 613-932-7735;
vesta@primus.ca

ISBNs: 0-919806, 1-55065; SAN: 115-5520
Stephen Gill, Editor

Visual Arts Ontario
#225, 215 Spadina Ave., Toronto, ON M5T 2C7
Tel: 416-591-8883; Fax: 416-591-2432
info@vao.org
www.vao.org

ISBNs: 0-920708; SAN: 115-5539
Publishes materials that address the interests of visual artists in Ontario
Hennie L. Wolff

VLB Éditeur
Une compagnie de Quebecor Media
Anciennement Editions Quinze
DétenteurQuebecor Media
1010, rue de la Gauchetière est, Montréal, QC H2L 2N5
Tél: 514-523-7993; Téléc: 514-282-7530
adpcommandes@messageries-adp.com
www.edvlb.com

ISBNs: 2-89005
Martin Balthazar, Éditeur

Voyageur Publishing
1474 Clayton Rd., RR1, Almonte, ON K0A 1A0
Tel: 613-256-9435; Fax: 613-256-9435
info@voyageurpublishing.ca
www.voyageurpublishing.ca/

ISBNs: 0-921842
Publishers of Canadian History books with a Christian Perspective
Liz Jefferson, Promotions Contact

Wall & Emerson, Inc.
205 Bethune College, 4700 Keele St., Toronto, ON M3J 1P3
Tel: 416-467-8685; Fax: 416-352-5368
Toll-Free: 877-409-4601
wall@wallbooks.com
www.wallbooks.com

ISBNs: 1-895131, 0-921332; SAN: 116-0486
Client publisher of the University of Toronto Press; Publishes textbooks for universities & colleges, primarily in adult education, science, history of science, mathematics, English as a second language, and industrial engineering
Byron E. Wall, President

Warwick Publishing
#200, 161 Frederick St., Toronto, ON M5A 4P3
Tel: 416-596-1555; Fax: 416-596-1520
nick@warrickgp.com
www.warwickgp.com

ISBNs: 1-895629, 1-894020, 1-894622
Publishes daily interest, non-fiction trade books with a focus on sports, food & drink, and personal finance.
Nick Pitt

Waterloo Music Co. Ltd.
3 Regina St. North, Waterloo, ON N2J 4A5
Tel: 519-886-4990; Fax: 519-886-4999

ISBNs: 0-88909, 0-88797; SAN: 157-9363
William Brubacher, President

Weigl Educational Publishers Ltd.
6325 - 10 St. SE, Calgary, AB T2H 2Z9
Tel: 403-233-7747; Fax: 403-233-7769
info@weigl.com
www.weigl.com

ISBNs: 0-9690637, 0-919879, 1-896990; SAN: 115-1312, 115-5536
Publishers of educational resources & books
Linda Weigl, President & Publisher

West Coast Paradise Publishing
PO Box 2093 Main, Sardis, BC V2R 1A5
Tel: 604-824-9528; Fax: 604-824-9541
rya@shaw.ca
rg.anstey.ca

ISBNs: 0-9697494, 1-896779, 1-897031
Self-publishers of over 50 books by Robert G. Anstey
Yvonne Anstey

White Knight Books
Previous Name: White Knight Publications
Owned By: Bill Belfontaine Ltd.
#304, 160 Balmoral Ave., Toronto, ON M4V 1J7
Tel: 416-925-6548; Fax: 416-925-4165
info@whiteknightbooks.ca
www.whiteknightbooks.ca

ISBNs: 978-1-89745-603-3
Publisher of books in a range of subject areas, including Biography; Business; Canadian History; Education; Health & Medicine; Humour; Personal Finance; Poetry; Self-Help; Travel. For White Knight Book Distribution Services Ltd., consult www.whiteknightbookdistribution.com
Bill Belfontaine, Publisher
Karen Thomas, Creative Director, White Knight Books, design@whiteknightbooks.ca
Bill Husion, Sales Consultant, White Knight Distribution Services Lt
Jody Hronek, Special Sales, White Knight Book Distribution Services

Whitecap Books Ltd.
Owned By: Fitzhenry & Whiteside Ltd.
351 Lynn Ave., North Vancouver, BC V7J 2C4
Tel: 604-980-9852; Fax: 604-980-8197
whitecap@whitecap.ca
www.whitecap.ca

ISBNs: 1-895099, 1-55110, 1-55285; SAN: 115-1290
Currently publishes more than 300 Canadian & foreign titles; Primary emphasis is in the areas of food & wine, but also publish children's fiction & non-fiction; travel sports & transportation.
Michael Burch, President
Nick Rundall, Vice-President

Whitlands Publishing Ltd.
4444 Tremblay Dr., Victoria, BC V8N 4W5
Tel: 250-477-0192;
info@whitlands.com
www.whitlands.com

ISBNs: 0-9685061, 0-9734383
Publishers of novels by J. Robert Whittle

Wilfrid Laurier University Press
75 University Ave. West, Waterloo, ON N2L 3C5
Tel: 519-884-0710; Fax: 519-725-1399
press@wlu.ca
www.wlupress.wlu.ca

ISBNs: 0-88920; SAN: 115-1525
Publishing arm of Wilfrid Laurier University; Publishes 28-30 titles annually in the fields of history, literature, sociology, social work, life writing, film and media studies, aboriginal studies, women's studies, philosophy, & religious studies
Brian Henderson, Director, x6123, brian@press.wlu.ca
Lisa Quinn, Acquisitions Editor, x2843, quinn@press.wlu.ca
Rob Kohlmeier, Managing Editor, x6119, rob@press.wlu.ca

Wilson et Lafleur
40, rue Notre-Dame, Montréal, QC H2Y 1B9
Tél: 514-875-6326; Téléc: 514-875-8356
librarie@wilsonlafleur.com
www.wilsonlafleur.com

ISBNs: 2-89127
Claude Wilson, Président

Windflower Communications
67 Flett Ave., Winnipeg, MB R2K 3N3
Tel: 204-668-7475; Fax: 204-661-8530
Toll-Free: 800-465-6564
windflower@brandtfamily.com

ISBNs: 1-895308
Publishes 2-4 books annually
Gilbert G. Brandt, President
Susan Brandt, Vice-President
SuAnn Brandt Goertzen, Manager, Wholesale Division

Winding Trail Press
5201 Dufferin St., Toronto, ON M3H 5T8
Tel: 613-443-4484; Fax: 800-221-9985
Toll-Free: 800-565-9523
contact@windingtrailpress.com
windingtrailpress.geliefan.net/index.shtml
Publishes Canadian literature and non-fiction.
Ruth Bradley-St. Cyr, Publisher

Winslow Publishing
PO Box 38012, 550 Eglinton Ave. West, Toronto, ON M5N 3A8
Tel: 416-789-4733;
winslow@interlog.com
www.winslowpublishing.com
ISBNs: 0-921199
Michelle West

Wolsak & Wynn Publishers Ltd.
#102, 69 Hughson St. North, Hamilton, ON L8R 1G5
Tel: 905-972-9885; Fax: 905-972-8589
info@wolsakandwynn.ca
www.wolsakandwynn.ca
ISBNs: 0-919897
Publishers mostly poetry and non-fiction.
Noelle Allen, Publisher

Women's Press
#801, 180 Bloor St. West, Toronto, ON M5S 2V6
Tel: 416-929-2774; Fax: 416-929-1926
info@womenspress.ca
www.womenspress.ca
ISBNs: 0-88961, 0-921881, 0-7737, 0-921556; SAN: 115-5628
Publishes high-quality feminist writing
Jack Wayne, President, jwayne@cspi.org
Megan Mueller, Editorial Director, meganmueller@cspi.org

Wood Lake Publishing Inc.
9025 Jim Bailey Rd., Kelowna, BC V4V 1R2
Tel: 250-766-2778; Fax: 250-766-2736
Toll-Free: 800-299-2926
info@woodlake.com
www.woodlakebooks.com
Social Media: www.youtube.com/woodlakepublishing
twitter.com/woodlakebooks
www.faceb ook.com/WoodLakePublishingInc
ISBNs: 1-55145, 1-896836; SAN: 117-7436
Publishers of religious books and religious education tools.
Imprints: WoodLake | Northstone | CopperHouse | Seasons of the Spirit | The Best of Whole People of God Online.
Lois Huey Heck, Marketing Manager
Bonnie Schlosser, Publisher

Word of Mouth Production
299 Booth Ave., Toronto, ON M4M 2M7
Tel: 416-462-0670; Fax: 416-462-0682
mail@torontofunplaces.com
www.torontofunplaces.com
Social Media: torontofunplaces.blogspot.ca
twitter.com/NathaliePrezeau
ISBNs: 0-9684432
Publishes a directory of recreation activities to do in the GTA and southern Ontario.
Nathalie Prézeau

Wordwrights Canada
PO Box 456 O, Toronto, ON M4A 2P1
Tel: 416-752-0689; Fax: 416-752-0689
wordwrights@sympatico.ca
www.wordwrights.ca
ISBNs: 0-920835
Wordwrights Canada provides resources for writers, including the online course Lessons in Writing the Poem, and publishes books and eBooks.
Susan Ioannou, Director

Work 4 Projects Ltd.
CP 400, Succ Victoria, Westmount, QC H3Z 2V8
Tel: 514-489-4941; Fax: 514-489-5505

Wuerz Publishing Ltd.
895 McMillan Ave., Winnipeg, MB R3M 0T2
Tel: 204-956-0308; Fax: 204-956-5053
ISBNs: 0-929963
Steve Wuerz

YYZ Books
#140, 401 Richmond St. West, Toronto, ON M5V 3A8
Tel: 416-598-4546; Fax: 416-598-2282
yyz@yyzartistsoutlet.org
www.yyzartistsoutlet.org
ISBNs: 0-920397
Publishes a variety of current writing focusing on art & culture

Zygote Publishing
PO Box 4049, Edmonton, AB T6E 4S8
Tel: 780-439-7580; Fax: 780-439-7529
publish@zygotepublishing.com
www.zygotepublishing.com

Magazine & Newspaper Publishers

AgMedia Inc.
Previous Name: AgMedia Co-operative Inc.
58 Teal Dr., Guelph, ON N1C 1G4
Tel: 519-763-4044; Fax: 519-763-4482
www.betterfarming.com

Alberta Business Research Ltd
112 25 Chisholm Ave., St. Albert, AB T8N 5A5
Tel: 780-429-1610; Fax: 780-421-7677

Andrew John Publishing
#220, 115 King St. West, Dundas, ON L9H 1V1
Tel: 905-628-4309; Fax: 866-849-1266
Toll-Free: 877-245-4080
info@andrewjohnpublishing.com
www.andrewjohnpublishing.com
Andrew John Publishing Inc. is a trade oriented publishing house with a focus on health sciences and specializing in association and society publishing. They publish, for example, "Wavelength", "Caslpo", "Canadian Hearing Report", "College Contact" and "Listen Ecoute".

Annex Publishing & Printing Inc.
Previous Name: AIS Communications Ltd.
PO Box 530, 105 Donly Dr. South, Simcoe, ON N3Y 4N5
Tel: 519-429-3966; Fax: 519-429-3094
Toll-Free: 800-265-2827
salesprint@annexweb.com
www.annexweb.com
Michael Fredericks, President & CEO, mfredericks@annexweb.com
Diane Kleer, VP Production/Group Publisher, dkleer@annexweb.com

Armadale Publications Inc.
PO Box 1193 Main PO, 203 10544 106SE, Edmonton, AB T5H 2X6
Tel: 780-429-1073;
armadale@global-serve.net
www.albertaoilandgas.com
Cal Kelly, Editor

August Communications Ltd.
225-530 Century St., Winnipeg, MB R3H 0Y4
Tel: 204-957-0265; Fax: 204-957-0217
Toll-Free: 888-573-1136
Gladwyn D. Nickel, Publisher

Bale Communications Inc.
#1463, 1011 Upper Middle Rd. East, Oakville, ON L6H 5Z9
Tel: 416-252-9400; Fax: 416-252-8002
info@adnews.com
www.adnews.com
Bale Communications publishes Adnews, a Canadian publication that offers daily advertising & marketing news.
Rob Bale, Publisher
Derek Winkler, Editor

Battlefords Publishing Ltd.
892 - 104th St., North Battleford, SK S9A 1M9
Tel: 306-445-7261; Fax: 306-445-3223
Toll-Free: 866-549-9979
battlefords.publishing@sasktel.net
Battlefords Publishing Ltd. is a newspaper & web printing company.
Alana Schweitzer, Publisher

Baum Publications Ltd.
#201, 2323 Boundary Rd., Vancouver, BC V5M 4V8
Tel: 604-291-9900; Fax: 604-291-1906
circulation@baumpub.com
www.baumpub.com
Baum Publications Ltd. publishes specialty trade publications, such as Contractors Magazine, Heavy Equipment Guide, Oil & Gas Product News, & Recycling Product News.
Engelbert J. Baum, President, ebaum@baumpub.com
Ken Singer, Publisher & Vice-President, ksinger@baumpub.com
Melvin Date Chong, Controller & Vice-President, mdatechong@baumpub.com
Tina Anderson, Manager, Production, tanderson@baumpub.com

Baxter Publications Inc.
310 Dupont St., Toronto, ON M5R 1V9
Tel: 416-968-7252; Fax: 416-968-2377
baxgroup@baxter.net; humanres@baxter.net
www.baxter.net
Baxter Publications is the publisher of education products & travel industry products. Services include web design & development, web hosting, & digital publishing.

Bayard Presse Canada Inc.
4475, rue Frontenac, Montréal, QC H2H 2S2
Tel: 514-522-3936; Fax: 514-522-1761
www.bayardcanada.ca

Becker Associates
Previous Name: Publishing & Printing Services
#202, 10 Morrow Ave., Toronto, ON M6R 2J1
Tel: 416-538-1650; Fax: 416-489-1713
info@beckerassociates.ca
www.beckerassociates.ca
Other information: Montréal Phone: 514-274-0742
Social Media:
www.facebook.com/pages/Becker-Associates/123404977701883
Becker Associates offers services such as editorial management, production management, & web-based publishing for publications & scholarly journals.
Adam Becker, President, Publications & Web, abecker@beckerassociates.ca

Black Press
818 Broughton St., Victoria, BC V8W 1E4
Tel: 250-381-9171; Fax: 250-381-9172
www.blackpress.ca
Publishes over 100 newspapers throughout British Columbia

Breton Communications Inc.
#202, 495 boul. St-Martin ouest, Laval, QC H7M 1Y9
Tel: 450-629-6005; Fax: 450-629-6044
breton.com@bretoncom.com
www.bretoncom.com
Martine Breton, President, martine@bretoncom.com

Brunico Communications Ltd.
#100, 366 Adelaide St. West, Toronto, ON M5V 1R9
Tel: 416-408-2300; Fax: 416-408-0870
brunico@magic.ca
www.brunico.com
Through print, electronic publications and industry events, Brunico connects indicituals and organizations, building communities specializing in the entertainment and marketing sectors. Brunico Marketing Inc., the California subsidiary of Brunico Communications Ltd., produces Brunico's entertainment and marketing conferences in New York, Washington, Los Angeles and other U.S. cities.

Business Information Group (BIG)
Previous Name: Southam Business Communications Inc.
80 Valleybrook Dr., Toronto, ON M3B 2S9
Tel: 416-442-5600; Fax: 416-442-2191
Toll-Free: 800-668-2374
www.businessinformationgroup.ca
ISBNs: 1-55257, 0-919217, 0-919378, 0-9693221, 0-911448
Specializes in business magazines, directories and databases.
Bruce Creighton, President

Byrne Publishing Group Inc
#10 - 1753 Dolphin Ave., Kelowna, BC V1Y 8A6
Tel: 250-861-5399; Fax: 250-868-3040
Toll-Free: 888-311-1119
info@okanaganlife.com
www.okanaganlife.com

Cameron Publications Ltd.
42 Borden Ave., Dartmouth, NS B3B 1C8
Tel: 902-468-1635; Fax: 902-468-1623

Campbell Communications Inc.
PO Box 5310, 1218 Langley St., 3rd Fl., Victoria, BC V8R 6S4
Tel: 250-388-7231; Fax: 250-385-3563
focusadmin@shaw.ca
www.focusonline.ca
ISBNs: 1-895297
Publisher of FOCUS Magazine
Leslie Campbell, Publisher & Editor

Canada Wide Media Limited
Previous Name: Canada Wide Magazines & Communications Ltd.
4180 Lougheed Hwy., 4th Fl., Burnaby, BC V5C 6A7
Tel: 604-299-7311; Fax: 604-299-9188
cwm@canadawide.com
www.canadawide.com
Canada Wide Media provides a range of media services and products, in printed publications and digital media.
Peter Legge, President & Publisher LL.D, plegge@canadawide.com
Heather Parker, Senior Vice-President CGA, hparker@canadawide.com
Samantha Legge, Vice-President, Marketing, slegge@canadawide.com
Corinne Smith, Vice-President, Production, csmith@canadawide.com

Canadian Arctic Resources Committee
488 Gladstone Ave, Ottawa, ON K1N 8V4
Tel: 613-759-4284; Fax: 613-237-3845
Toll-Free: 866-949-9006
www.carc.org
ISBNs: ISSN: 0380-5522
Publisher of Northern Perspectives journal, & other publications dealing with the long-term environmental and social wellbeing of northern Canada and its peoples. Yellowknife office: 5003 - 48 St., P.O. Box 1705, Yellowknife, NT, X1A 2P3, Email: davidg@carc.org.
Charles Birchall, Chair
Jan Glyde, Contact, janglyde@carc.org

Canadian Committee on Labour History
Peace Hills Trust Tower, Athabasca University, 1200, 10011 - 109 St., Edmonton, AB T5J 3S8
cclh@athabascau.ca
www.cclh.ca
ISBNs: 0-9692060, 0-9695835, 1-894000; SAN: 115-4168
Publisher of Labour/Le Travail: Journal of Canadian Labour Studies, as well as books & bulletins around the subject of labour history.
Alvin Finkel, President, alvinf@athabascau.ca
Rhonda Hinther, Vice-President, rhonda.hinther@civilization.ca
Gregory S. Kealey, Treasurer, gkealey@unb.ca

Canadian Controlled Media Communications
#101, 5397 Eglinton Ave. West, Toronto, ON M9C 5K6
Tel: 416-928-2909; Fax: 416-966-1181
Toll-Free: 800-320-6420
www.ccmc.ca
CCMC is a sports and entertainment marketing company with ventures in publishing, radio and television, internet, event production and media creation. Published products include SCOREGolf and CFL Illustrated.

Canadian Energy Research Institute
#150, 3512 - 33rd St. NW, Calgary, AB T2L 2A6
Tel: 403-282-1231; Fax: 403-284-4181
ceri@ceri.ca
www.ceri.ca
ISBNs: 0-920522, 1-896091; SAN: 115-2866
CERI is an independent, not-for-profit research establishment created through a partnership of industry, academia, and government. It aims to provide relevant, objective economic research in energy and related environmental issues. CERI's publications are categorized into Studies and Periodicals. Studies are reports published by the Institute on completion of study projects.
Peter Howard, Interim President & CEO, 403-220-2379, phoward@ceri.ca

Canadian Home Publishers
#120, 511 King St. West, Toronto, ON M5V 2Z4
Tel: 416-593-0204; Fax: 416-591-1630
chheditorial@canhomepub.com
www.houseandhome.com
Social Media:
www.facebook.com/houseandhomemagazine
Lynn Reeves, President & Publisher
Kirby Miller, VP & General Manager

Canadian Institute of Mining, Metallurgy & Petroleum (CIM) / Institut canadien des mines, de la métallurgie et du pétrol
#1250, 3500 boul de Maisonneuve ouest, Westmount, QC H3Z 3C1
Tel: 514-939-2710; Fax: 514-939-2714
cim@cim.org
www.cim.org
ISBNs: 1-894475, 0-919086, 1-926872
Chris Twigge-Molecey, President, 905-403-3926, Fax: 905-855-7629, ctwigge-molecey@hatch.ca
Jean Vavrek, Executive Director, ext. 1301, Fax: 514-939-2714, jvavrek@cim.org
Angela Hamlyn, Dir., Media & Communications, ext. 1303, ahamlyn@cim.org

Canadian Medical Association
1867 Alta Vista Dr., Ottawa, ON K1G 5W8
Tel: 613-731-9331; Fax: 613-565-5471
Toll-Free: 866-971-9171
pubs@cmaj.ca
www.cmaj.ca; www.cma.ca
ISBNs: 1-894391, 0-920169, 1-897490
The Association publishes the Canadian Medical Association Journal (CMAJ) in print and online. CMAJ showcases innovative research and ideas aimed at improving health. It publishes original clinical research, analyses and reviews, news and editorials.

Canstar Community News Ltd.
Owned By: FP Canadian Newspapers
1355 Mountain Ave., Winnipeg, MB R2X 3B6
Tel: 204-697-7000;
Published titles include such community newspapers as The Herald, The Lance, The Metro and The Times.

Carswell
Owned By: Thomson Reuters
One Corporate Plaza, 2075 Kennedy Rd., Toronto, ON M1T 3V4
Tel: 416-609-8000; Fax: 416-298-5094
carswell.customerrelations@thomson.com
www.carswell.com
ISBNs: 0-459, 0-7798, 0-88820
Carswell publishes information and electronic research solutions to the legal, tax, finance, accounting and human resources markets. Its material is integrated information available in a range of formats, including books, looseleaf services, journals, newsletters, CD-ROMS and online.
Don Van Meer, President & CEO

CHMM Inc.
#4, 951 Denison St., Markham, ON L3R 3W9
Tel: 905-305-6155; Fax: 905-305-6255
comments@solidwastemag.com
www.solidwastemag.com
The company publishes Solid Waste & Recycling Magazine, providing environmental information to industry and government. Topics include: Recycling, Diversion, Composting, The Haulers Page, Landfill Technology, Equipment, Regulation Roundup, and Final Analysis. The publication is available to qualified Canadians for free.

Chronicle Companies
#306, 555 Burnhamthorpe Rd., Toronto, ON M9C 2Y3
Tel: 416-916-2476; Fax: 416-352-6199
Toll-Free: 866-632-4766
health@chronicle.org
chronicle.ca
ISBNs: 0-9685848
This is a privately-held independent producer of periodicals, newsletters, websites and information for medical practitioners, and for the pharmaceutical and biotech industries. Publications include, "The Chronicle of Cancer Therapy," "The Chronicle Neurology Network," and "The Skin Book."
R.Allan Ryan, Editorial Director, allan.ryan@chronicle.ca

CLB Media Inc.
Owned By: The Cartwright Group Ltd.
240 Edward St., Aurora, ON L4G 3S9
Tel: 905-727-0077; Fax: 905-727-0017
www.clbmedia.ca
CLB Media properties include more than 26 business-to-business publications and web sites in such fields as industrial/manufacturing, logging/milling, workplace management, security and automotive.

CMP Publications
PO Box 34097, Halifax, NS B3J 3S1
Tel: 902-425-1320; Fax: 902-425-1325
cmp@cmppublications.com
www.cmppublications.com
ISBNs: 0-9693595, 0-9739494
The company is dedicated to researching, publishing and / or distributing information and books related to the natural and social sciences. Titles include themes on fisheries, agriculture, construction, environment, recycling and more.

Cottage Life Books
54 St. Patrick St., Toronto, ON M5T 1V1
Tel: 416-599-2000; Fax: 416-599-0500
Toll-Free: 877-874-5253
clmag@cottagelife.com
www.cottagelife.com
ISBNs: 0-9696922
In addition to keeping a website with a plethora of information about cottage lifestyle, the company publishes Cottage Life magazine and distributes a small selection of cottage-related books.
Al Zikovitz, Publisher, zikovitz@cottagelife.com
Stacie Smith, Media Contact, 416-910-8112, smithcommunications@sympatico.ca

Craig Kelman & Associates
2020 Portage Ave., Winnipeg, MB R3J 0K4
Tel: 866-985-9780; Fax: 866-985-9799
info@kelman.ca
www.kelman.ca
Social Media: www.linkedin.com/company/1058679
www.facebook.com/Kelman.Publishing
Craig Kelman & Associates is a contract publisher of magazines, directories, & newsletters.
Chris Kelman, Contact, 866-985-9781, chris@kelman.ca

CTC Communications Corp.
#102, 155A Matheson Blvd. West, Mississauga, ON L5R 3L5
Tel: 905-712-3636; Fax: 905-712-2935
info@ctccomm.com
www.ctccomm.com

Dakota Design & Advertising Ltd.
Bay 114, 3907 - 3A St. NE, Calgary, AB T2E 6S7
Tel: 403-250-1128; Fax: 403-250-1194

Les Éditions Apex inc. / Apex Publications Inc.
185, rue Saint-Paul, Québec, QC G1K 3W2
Tél: 418-692-2110; Téléc: 800-664-2739
Ligne sans frais: 800-905-7468
info@photolife.com
www.photolife.com
Éditeur de périodiques: "Photo Life", et "Photo Solution"
Valérie Racine, Rédactrice en chef, editor@photolife.com

Les Editions du Journal de l'Assurance
#100, 321, rue de la Commune ouest, Montréal, QC H2Y 2E1
Tél: 514-289-9595; Téléc: 514-289-9527
reception@journal-assurance.ca
www.journal-assurance.ca
Publications: "FlashFinance.ca", "Le Journal de l'assurance", "CarrièresAssurance.ca", "Le Congrès de l'assurance et de l'investissement", "QuébecInc.", et "The Insurance & Investment Journal".
Serge Therrien, Président et éditeur, serge.therrien@journal-assurance.ca

Les Éditions forestières
#203, 1175, rue Lavigerie, Québec, QC G1V 4P1
Tél: 418-877-4583; Téléc: 418-877-6449
www.lemondeforestier.ca
Publication: Le journal "Le Monde forestier"
Guy Lavoie, Directeur général, direction@lemondeforestier.ca

Les Éditions Héritage
300, rue Arran, Saint-Lambert, QC J4R 1K5
Tél: 514-875-0327; Téléc: 450-672-5448
information@editionsheritage.com
www.editionsheritage.com
Luc Payette, Président

Éditions Infopresse inc.
4310, boul St-Laurent, Montréal, QC H2W 1Z3
Tél: 514-842-5873; Téléc: 514-842-2422
redaction@infopresse.com
www.infopresse.com
Médias sociaux:
www.facebook.com/Infopresse
"Le Portail du marketing, de la publicité et des communications."
Bruno Gautier, Président et éditeur
Sandrine Archambault, Directrice générale, frederic.bruniquel@infopresse.com

Les Éditions Rogers limitée
Anciennement Maclean Hunter Publishing
800, 1200, av McGill College, Montréal, QC H3B 4G7
Tél: 514-845-5141;
www.leseditionsrogers.ca
Ken Whyte, Président/Chef de la direction

Editions Versicolores inc.
1320 Saint-Joseph Blvd., Québec, QC G2K 1G2
Tel: 418-628-8690; Fax: 418-628-0524

Egress Enterprises Inc
3901 Anderson Rd., Kelowna, BC V1X 7V8
Tel: 250-765-3886; Fax: 877-725-1488

English Literary Studies (ELS)
Dept. of English, University of Victoria, PO Box 3070, Victoria, BC V8W 3W1
Tel: 250-721-7237; Fax: 250-721-6498
hedyt@uvic.ca
www.engl.uvic.ca
ISBNs: 0-920604; SAN: 115-3366
Hedy Miller

L'Escale Nautique
Anciennement Les Productions Maritimes
175, rue Saint-Paul, Québec, QC G1K 3W2
Tél: 418-692-3779; Téléc: 418-694-6904
production@escalenautique.qc.ca
www.escalenautique.qc.ca
Le leader de la presse nautique au Québec; publications y compris le journal "L'Escale nautique", et "Guide du tourisme nautique"
Michel Veilleux, Directeur général

Family Communications Inc. / Communications Famille inc.
65 The East Mall, Toronto, ON M8Z 5W3
Tel: 416-537-2604; Fax: 416-538-1794
Family Communications is Canada's largest privately-held, independent publisher of women's magazines, holding a leading position in Canada's bridal, new parent and home buying markets through its flagship titles: Today's Bride, Best Wishes, Mon Bébé, Expecting, C'est Pour Quand?, The Baby & Child Care Encyclopedia, Parents Canada and Canadian Home Planning.
Manon Le Moyne, Editeur

Farm Business Communications
PO Box 9800, 1666 Dublin Ave., Winnipeg, MB R3H 0H1
Tel: 204-954-1400; Fax: 204-945-4142
Bob Willcox, Publisher, 204-944-5751, bob.willcox@fbcpublishing.com
John Morriss, Associate Publisher / Editorial director, 204-944-5754, john.morriss@fbcpublishing.com

Formula Media Group
#4, 447 Speers Rd., Oakville, ON L6K 3S7
Tel: 905-842-6591; Fax: 905-842-4432
Toll-Free: 800-693-7986

Globe Interactive
Previous Name: Globe Information Services
Owned By: CTVGlobemedia
444 Front St. West, Toronto, ON M5V 2S9
Tel: 416-585-5250; Fax: 416-585-5249
Toll-Free: 800-268-9128
www.theglobeandmail.com
ISBNs: 0-921925
Publisher of The Globe & Mail daily newspaper, in print & online
Jim Sheppard, Executive Editor, Online News

Groupe Bomart
#204, 905 Michèle-Bohec, Blainville, QC J7C 5J6
Tél: 450-435-3131; Téléc: 450-435-3884
www.bomartgroup.com
Spécialisée dans l'édition de magazines dans le domaine du camionnage, de transport, de la logistique et des affaires

Groupe Constructo
#200, 1500, boul Jules-Poitras, Saint-Laurent, QC H4N 1X7
Tél: 514-745-5720; Téléc: 514-339-2267
Ligne sans frais: 800-363-0910
www.constructo.ca
Manon Bouchard, Marketing contact, 514-856-6609, manon.bouchard@trancontinental.ca

Groupe Magazines S.A. Inc.
#300, 275, boul des Braves, Terrebonne, QC J6W 3H6
Tel: 450-964-7590;

GSA Publishing Group
201 - 1945 West 4th Ave., Vancouver, BC V6J 1M7
Tel: 604-689-2909; Fax: 604-689-2989
sales@gsapublishing.com
www.gsapublishing.com
Social Media:
www.twitter.com/gsatravelmag
www.facebook.com/gsatravelmag
Travel magazine for travel agents.
Frank Cumming, Publisher, publisher@gsapublishing.com

Herald Publishing Co.
PO Box 280, Dundalk, ON N0C 1B0
Tel: 519-923-2203; Fax: 519-923-2747
www.herald-publishing.com

HOMES Magazine
Previous Name: Homes for Sale Magazine Ltd.
178 Main St., Unionville, ON L3R 2G9
Tel: 905-479-4663; Fax: 905-479-4482
Toll-Free: 800-363-4663
info@homesmag.com
www.homesmag.com
Various publications including Homes Magazine, Active Adult Magazine, Condo Life Magazine, Moving To Magazines, Ontario Design Trade Sourcebook, and Renovation and Decor Magazine.
Michael Rosset, Publisher
Risë Levy, Editor
Natalie Armstrong, Circulation Manager

Homes Publishing Group (HPG)
178 Main St., Unionville, ON L3R 2G9
Tel: 905-479-4663; Toll-Free: 800-363-4663
info@homesmag.com
www.homespublishinggroup.com
Social Media:
twitter.com/HOMESPublishing
www.facebook.com/pages/HOMES-Publishing-Group/11773177455
Homes Publishing Group publishes titles such as "Homes Magazines", "Active Adult Magazine", "Condo Life Magazine", and "Moving To Magazines".
Toni Pettit, Editor, editortoni@gmail.com

Horse Publications Group
Previous Name: Corinthian Publishing Co. Ltd.
PO Box 670, 225 Industrial Pkwy. South, Aurora, ON L4G 4J9
Tel: 905-727-0107; Fax: 905-841-1530
Toll-Free: 800-505-7428
editor@horse-canada.com
www.horse-canada.com
Publications includes Horse Sport, Horse-Canada & Canadian Thoroughbred, and Horsepower.
Jennifer Anstey, Publisher, Staff, janstey@horse-canada.com
Susan Stafford, Mangaging Editor (Horse Sport), Staff, editor@horse-canada.com
Lee Benson, Mangaging Editor (Horse-Canada), Staff, info@horse-canada.com
Jennifer Morrison, Mangaging Editor (Canadian Thoroughbred), Staff, teditor@horse-canada.com

IG Publications Ltd.
PO Box 3090, 101 Owl St., Banff, AB T1L 1C7
Tel: 403-760-3484;
igpub@telusplanet.net
www.igpublications.com
Publishes travel information for B.C.

Insurancewest Media Ltd.
PO Box 3311 Terminal, Vancouver, BC V6B 3Y3
Tel: 604-874-1001; Fax: 604-874-3922
manager@insurancewest.ca
www.insurancewest.ca
Publishes a variety of publications such as "The BC Broker", "Insurancewest", "Alberta Insurance Directory", and "British Columbia Insurance Directory".

Investment Executive Inc.
100 - 25 Sheppard Ave. West, Toronto, ON M2N 6S7
Tel: 416-227-8266; Fax: 416-218-3624
Toll-Free: 888-366-4200
support@investmentexecutive.com
www.investmentexecutive.com

Ishcom Publications Ltd.
#201, 2065 Dundas St. East, Mississauga, ON L4X 2W1
Tel: 905-206-0150; Fax: 905-206-9972
Toll-Free: 800-201-8596

Issues Ink
#403, 313 Pacific Ave., Winnipeg, MB R3A 0M2
Tel: 204-453-1965; Fax: 204-475-5247
issues@issuesink.com
www.issuesink.com
Issues Ink is a Winnipeg-based publishing and consulting company with extensive experience in the agricultural sector.
Shawn Brook, President

Journal la Nouvelle Édition
Anciennement L'Edition Commerciale
2030 boul Pie-IX, Montréal, QC H1V 2C8
Tél: 514-257-1000; Téléc: 514-257-7505
www.journaledition.com
"Journal des gens d'affaires de Montréal"; actualités économiques
Alain Dulong, Président/Éditeur, a.dulong@journaledition.com

JuneWarren-Nickle's Energy Group
Previous Name: JuneWarren Publishing Ltd.
816 - 55 Ave. NE, 2nd Fl., Calgary, AB T2E 6Y4
Tel: 403-209-3500; Fax: 403-245-8666
Toll-Free: 800-387-2446
www.nickles.com
Social Media:
www.facebook.com/92980312678
Bill Whitelaw, Publisher

Kenilworth Publishing
#710, 15 Wertheim Ct., Richmond Hill, ON L4B 3H7
Tel: 905-771-7333; Fax: 905-771-7336
Toll-Free: 800-409-8688
www.kenilworth.com

Kerrwil Publications Ltd.
538 Elizabeth St., Midland, ON L4R 2A3
www.kerrwil.com

Key Media Inc. (KMI)
#800, 312 Adelaide St. West, Toronto, ON M5V 1R2
Tel: 416-644-8740; Fax: 416-203-9083
www.kmipublishing.com
Specializes in business-to-business and consumer publications.

Kingston Publications
Owned By: Sun Media Corporation
18 St. Remy Pl., Kingston, ON K7K 6C4
Tel: 613-549-8442; Fax: 613-389-7507
www.kingstonpublications.com
Liza Nelson, Publisher, 613-549-8442 ext 135
Jane Deacon, Editor, 613-549-8442 ext 108

Koocanusa Publications Inc.
#100, 100 - 7th Ave. South, Cranbrook, BC V1C 2J4
Tel: 250-426-7253; Fax: 250-426-4125
Toll-Free: 800-663-8555
info@kpimedia.com
www.koocanusapublications.com
Magazine and directory publishing.
Keith Powell, Publisher, keith@kpimedia.com

Kostuch Media Ltd.
Previous Name: Kostuch Publications Ltd.
101-23 Lesmill Rd., Toronto, ON M3B 3P6
Tel: 416-447-0888;
www.kostuchmedia.com
Publisher serving the foodservice and hospitality markets in Canada such as "Foodservice and Hospitality" and "Hotelier".
Kostuch Mitch, President and Group Publisher, mkostuch@foodservice.ca
Rosanna Caira, Editor and Publisher, rcaira@foodservice.ca

Kylix Media Inc
5165, rue Sherbrooke Ouest, Montréal, QC H4A 1T6
Tél: 514-481-5892; Téléc: 514-481-9699

Landscape Ontario Horticultural Trades Association
7856 - 5th Line South, RR#4, Milton, ON L9T 2X8
Tel: 416-848-7575; Fax: 905-875-3942
Toll-Free: 800-265-5656
www.horttrades.com
Publisher of Landscape Ontario magazine.
Shawna Barrett, Communications Coordinator, sbarrett@landscapeontario.com
Lee Ann Knudsen, Publisher, lak@landscapeontario.com

LexisNexis Canada Ltd.
#700, 123 Commerce Valley Dr. East, Markham, ON L3T 7W8
Tel: 905-479-2665; Toll-Free: 800-668-6481
customerservice@lexisnexis.ca
www.lexisnexis.ca

Lighthouse Publishing Ltd
353 York St., Bridgewater, NS B4V 3K2
Tel: 902-543-2457; Fax: 902-543-2228
Lynn Hennigar, General Manager

Martin Charlton Communications
Previous Name: Charlton Communications
#300, 1914 Hamilton St., Regina, SK S4N 3N6
Tel: 306-584-1000; Fax: 306-352-4110
www.martincharlton.ca
This is a public relations consultant with services including writing, graphic design, media training, communications planning, among others.

McLeish Communications Inc.
1, rue Pacifique, Sainte-Anne-de-Bellevue, QC H9X 1C5
Tel: 514-457-2347; Fax: 514-457-2147
Lumina Fillion, Editor & Art Director

MediaEdge Inc.
5255 Yonge St., Toronto, ON M2N 6P4
Tel: 416-512-8186; Fax: 416-512-8344
robertt@mediaedge.ca
www.mediaedge.ca
Publications including Building Strategies, Canadian Apartment Magazine, CondoBusiness, Construction Business, & Design Quarterly.
Kevin Brown, President

Mediconcept Inc.
#300, 3333, boul Cote-Vertu, Saint-Laurent, QC H4R 2N1
Tel: 514-331-4561; Fax: 514-336-1129
info@mediconcept.ca
www.mediconcept.ca

Mercury Publications Ltd.
1740 Wellington Ave., Winnipeg, MB R3H 0E8
Tel: 204-954-2085; Fax: 204-954-2057
Toll-Free: 800-337-6372
mp@mercury.mb.ca
www.mercury.mb.ca
Specializes in business-to-business communications.
Frank Yeo, President & CEO, fyeo@mercury.mb.ca

Metro Guide Publishing
1300 Hollis St., Halifax, NS B3J 1T6
Tel: 902-420-9943; Fax: 902-429-9058
publishers@metroguide.ca
www.metroguidepublishing.ca
Sheila Blair, Publisher

Moorshead Magazines Ltd.
#500, 505 Consumers Rd., Toronto, ON M2J 4V8
Toll-Free: 888-326-2476
www.moorshead.com
Publications include Family Chronicle; Internet-genealogy; History Magazine.

Multi-Vision Publishing Inc.
#1100, 655 Bay St., Toronto, ON M5G 2K4
Tel: 416-595-9944; Fax: 416-595-7217

National Research Council of Canada - NRC Research Press
Bldg. M-55, 1200 Montréal Rd., Ottawa, ON K1A 0R6
Tel: 613-993-0362; Fax: 613-952-7656
pubs@nrc-cnrc.gc.ca
www.nrc-cnrc.gc.ca
Publisher of scholarly journals since 1929. They are part of the Canada Institute for Scientific and Technical Information and publish 16 journals, monographs, conference proceedings, and allied publications.
Bruce P. Dancik, Editor-in-Chief, pubs@nrc-cnrc.gc.ca

Naylor (Canada) Inc.
Previous Name: Naylor Communications Ltd.
Owned By: Naylor, LLC
#300, 1630 Ness Ave., Winnipeg, MB R3J 3X1
Fax: 204-947-2047
Toll-Free: 800-665-2456
www.naylor.com
Social Media: www.linkedin.com/company/naylor-publications
twitter.com/naylorllc
www .facebook.com/naylorllc
Provides customized association marketing communications, including magazines, member directories, online buyers' guides, e-newsletters, digital magazines, show guides, & event marketing & promotion materials. Publications includes "Icon," "The Clarifier," "Who's Who," "Connections," "Pace," & "Association Leadership."
Robert Thompson, Publisher

The Neepawa Press
Previous Name: Sundance Publications Ltd.
PO Box 939, 423 Mountain Ave., Neepawa, MB ROJ 1HO
Tel: 204-476-2309; Fax: 204-476-5802
office@neepawapress.com
www.neepawapress.com
Publications such as the Neepawa Press.
Jack Gibson, Publisher, gibson@neepawapress.com

News Canada Inc.
Head Office
#509, 920 Yonge St., Toronto, ON M4W 3C7
Tel: 416-599-9900; Fax: 416-599-9700
Toll-Free: 888-855-6397
www.newscanada.com
Provides print editors with feature news stories of interest to their readers, as well as video & radio segments for broadcasters.
Ruth Douglas, President/Publisher

Norris-Whitney Communications Inc.
#7, 23 Hannover Dr., St Catharines, ON L2W 1A3
Tel: 905-641-3471; Fax: 888-665-1307
info@nor.com
www.nor.com
Norris-Whitney Communications Inc. is an international communications company specializing in the music, audio, and lighting fields.

North Huron Publishing Inc.
PO Box 429, 404 Queen St., Blyth, ON N0M 1H0
Tel: 519-523-4311; Fax: 519-523-9140
Publications include; The Citizen, The Rural Voice, and Stops Along the Way.

North Island Publishing Ltd.
Previous Name: North Island Sound Ltd.
#8, 1606 Sedlescomb Dr., Mississauga, ON L4X 1M6
Tel: 905-625-7070; Fax: 905-625-4856
Toll-Free: 800-331-7408
www.northisland.ca
Sandy Donald, Publisher
Doug Bennet, Editor

North Superior Publishing Inc.
1402- 590 Beverly St., Thunder Bay, ON P7B 5N3
Tel: 807-623-2348; Fax: 807-623-7515
nspinc@tbaytel.net
www.northsuperiorpublishing.com
Publishes "Golfing News", "Business", and "Snowmobile News".
Sylvia Gomez, Sales Rep, 807-623-2348, sylvia@northsuperiorpublishing.com

Northern Star Communications Ltd.
900 - 6 Ave. SW, 5th Fl., Calgary, AB T2P 3K2
Tel: 403-263-6881; Fax: 403-263-6886
Toll-Free: 800-052-6417
editor@northernstar.ab.ca
www.northernstar.ab.ca
Four oilpatch magazines- "The Roughneck", "Energy Processing Canada", "Propane Canada" and "The Roughneck Buy and Sell", as well as the annual "Alberta Gas Plant Directory" and volume one of the "Roughneck Joke Book".
Scott , Publisher, scott@northernstar.ab.ca

Ontario Association of Certified Engineering Technicians & Technologists
#404, 10 Four Seasons Pl., Toronto, ON M6B 6H7
Tel: 416-621-9621; Fax: 416-621-8694
info@oacett.org
www.oacett.org
Social Media:
twitter.com/oacett
www.facebook.com/OACETT
OACETT is dedicated to excellence in the engineering & applied science technology profession in a manner that serves & protects the public interest. The association publishes The Ontario Technologist.

The Ontario Historical Society
34 Parkview Ave., Toronto, ON M2N 3Y2
Tel: 416-226-9011; Fax: 416-226-2740
ohs@historicalsociety.ca
www.ontariohistoricalsociety.ca
Social Media:
www.facebook.com/pages/The-Ontario-Historical-Society/146

OP Publishing Ltd.
#500, 200 West Esplanade, North Vancouver, BC V7M 1A4
Tel: 604-998-3310; Fax: 604-998-3320
Toll-Free: 800-816-0747
info@oppublishing.com
www.oppublishing.com
Publishes magazines such as "Fishing", "Cottage", "Pacific Yachting", "Western Sportsman", "Outdoor Edge", "Canadian Aviator", "BC Marine Parks Guide", and "BC Fishing".
Mark Yelic, Publisher

OT Communications
1025-101 Sixth Ave. SW, Calgary, AB T2P 3P4
Tel: 403-264-3270; Fax: 403-264-3276
Toll-Free: 800-465-0322
info@otcommunications.com
www.otcommunications.com

Our Kids Publications Ltd.
4242 Rockwood Rd., Mississauga, ON L4W 1L8
Toll-Free: 877-272-1845
info@ourkids.net
www.ourkids.net
Magazine "Our Kids Go to Camp" is devoted to helping parents find the right camp for their children and "Our Kids Go To School" is devoted to helping parents find the "best education for their kids".
Agatha Stawicki, Director, Marketing & Advertising

Parents Canada Group
Owned By: Family Communications Inc.
Tel: 416-537-2604; Fax: 416-538-1794
amyb@parentscanada.com
www.parentscanada.com
Social Media:
twitter.com/#%21/ParentsCanada
www.facebook.com/ParentsCanada
Donald G. Swinburne, President

Parkhurst Publishing
Previous Name: C.M.E. Publishing
400 McGill St., 3rd Fl., Montréal, QC H2Y 2G1
Tel: 514-397-8833; Fax: 514-397-0228
www.parkpub.com
ISBNs: 0-9688648, 0-9698972, 0-9732870
Parkhurst is a medical publishing house providing a wide range of medical media journals and educational communications to physicians and patients. Toronto office: 416-489-8045.

Perks Publications Inc.
3 Kennett Dr., Whitby, ON L1P 1L5
Tel: 905-430-7267; Fax: 905-430-6418
Toll-Free: 877-880-4877
mike@perkspub.com
www.perkspub.com
Publishes Trade Magazines, Journals, Periodicals, and News Letter for Associations across the county.
Tanja Nowotny, Editor/Art Director, 905-697-8905, Fax: 905-697-2596, tanja@perkspub.com

Pink Triangle Press
#1600, 2 Carlton St., Toronto, ON M5B 1J3
Tel: 416-925-5221; Fax: 416-925-4817
pinktrianglepress.com

Playhouse Publications
Bell Tower, #950, 10104 - 103 Ave., Edmonton, AB T5J 0H8
Tel: 780-423-5834; Fax: 780-413-6185
info@playhousepublications.ca
www.playhousepublications.ca
An affiliate of Suggitt Publishing Ltd., specializing in playbills for theatre & opera companies.

Post City Magazines Inc.
30 Lesmill Rd., Toronto, ON M3B 2T6
Tel: 416-250-7979; Fax: 416-250-1737
editorial@postcity.com
www.postcity.com
Lorne London, Publisher, lornelondon@postcity.com

Postmedia Network Inc.
Owned By: Postmedia Network Canada Corp.
1450 Don Mills Rd., Toronto, ON M3B 3R5
Tel: 416-383-2300;
www.postmedia.com
Social Media: www.linkedin.com/company/1191505?trk=tyah
twitter.com/postmedianet
www.facebook.com/Postmedia
The company is a publisher by circulation of paid English-language daily newspapers. Titles include: National Post, Vancouver Sun, Edmonton Journal, Calgary Herald, Star Phoenix, Ottawa Citizen, (Montréal) Gazette. Online titles include Canada.comand Dose.ca.
Ron Osborne, Chair
Paul Godfrey, President & CEO
Doug Lamb, Executive VP & CFO
Gillian Akai, VP, Legal Affairs, 416-383-2550, gakai@postmedia.com

Powershift Communications Inc.
245 Fairview Mall Dr., 5th Fl., Toronto, ON M2J 4T1
Tel: 416-494-1066; Fax: 416-494-2536
dbm@powershift.ca
www.powershift.ca
A business-to-business publishing corporation.

Publicor Une Div De Comms Inc
Previous Name: Publicor
7, ch Bates, Outremont, QC H2V 4V7
Tel: 514-270-1100; Fax: 514-270-5395
Andre Vilder, Editor

Pulsus Group Inc.
2902 South Sheridan Way, Oakville, ON L6J 7L6
Tel: 905-829-4770; Fax: 905-829-4799
pulsus@pulsus.com
www.pulsus.com
Privately owned Canadian company which publishes "The Canadian Journal of Cardiology", "The Canadian Journal of Gastroenterology", "The Canadian Journal of Infectious Diseases & Medical Microbiology", "The Canadian Journal of Plastic Surgery", "Canadian Respiratory Journal", "Pain Research & Management", "Paediatrics & Child Health", and "Experimental & Clinical Cardiology".
LeBlanc Ann, Vice-President, 905-829-4770 ext 124
Lisa Robb, Director of Advertising Sales, 905-829-4770 ext 143

Robins Southern Printing (1990) Ltd.
1320 - 36 St. North, Lethbridge, AB T1H 5H8
Tel: 403-328-5114; Fax: 403-328-5443

Rogers Publishing Ltd.
333 Bloor St. East, 6th Fl., Toronto, ON M4W 1G9
Tel: 416-764-2000;
www.rogerspublishing.ca
Publications include "Canadian Business", "Chatelaine", "Flare", "Todays' Parents", "Macleans", "Money Sense", "Profit", "Marketing", "Lou Lou" and "Ontario Out of Doors" as well as Quebec magazines "L'actualité", "Le Bulletin", "Châtelaine", et "Lou Lou".
Ken Whyte, President

Salon Communications Inc.
#1902, 365 Bloor St. East, Toronto, ON M4W 3L4
Tel: 416-869-3131; Fax: 416-869-3008

Solstice Publishing Inc.
47 Soho Sq., Toronto, ON M5T 2Z2
Toll-Free: 800-263-5295
Publisher of Ski Canada Magazine.

STA Communications Inc.
#310, 6500 Trans-Canada Hwy., Pointe-Claire, QC H9R 0A5
Tel: 514-695-7623; Fax: 514-695-8554
www.stacommunications.com
Journals include "Diagnosis", "CME", "Clinicien", Cardiology", and"Pharmaceutical".
Paul Brand, Contact (Montreal office), 541-695-8393 ext.220, paulb@sta.ca

Stone & Cox Ltd.
500-111 Peter St., Toronto, ON M5V 2H1
Tel: 416-599-0772;
Cathy St Pierre, Contact, 416-599-0772 ext 103, Fax: 416-599-0867, cathysp@cdnins.com

Suggitt Publishing Ltd.
Bell Tower, #950, 10104 - 103 Ave., Edmonton, AB T5J 0H8
Tel: 780-413-6163; Fax: 780-413-6185
Toll-Free: 877-784-4488
reception@suggitt.com
www.suggitt.com
Other information: Alternate Fax: 780-428-6100
Consumer magazines.
Tom Suggitt, President & CEO, tom@suggitt.com
Rob Suggitt, President & CFO, rob@suggitt.com

Sun Media Corp.
Previous Name: Bowes Publishing Ltd.
333 King St. East, Toronto, ON M5A 3X5
Tel: 416-350-6159;
sunnewsnetwork@qmisales.ca
www.sunmedia.ca/SunMedia

Sunrise Publishing
2213B Hanselman Ct., Saskatoon, SK S7L 6A8
Tel: 306-244-5668; Fax: 306-244-5679
Toll-Free: 800-247-5743
sunrisepublish.com

Swan Erickson Publishing Inc.
#355, 4261 - A14 Highway #7 East, Markham, ON L3R 9W6
Tel: 905-723-2233; Fax: 905-436-0813

Taylor Publishing Group (TPG)
#2, 1121 Invicta Dr., Oakville, ON L6H 2R2
Tel: 905-844-8218;
www.taylorpublishinggroup.com
William Taylor, Owner & Publisher

Thornhill Publications Ltd.
#16, 7780 Woodbine Ave., Markham, ON L3R 2N7
Tel: 905-475-1743; Fax: 905-475-1029

Town Media Inc.
Previous Name: Town Publishing Inc.
1074 Cooke Blvd., Burlington, ON L7T 4A8
Tel: 905-634-8003; Fax: 905-634-7661
TM.info@sunmedia.ca
www.townmedia.ca
A division of Sun Media.

Trajan Publishing Corp.
PO Box 28103 Lakeport, #10, 600 Ontario St., St Catharines, ON L2N 7P8
Tel: 905-646-7744; Fax: 905-646-0995
Toll-Free: 800-408-0352
office@tranjan.ca
www.trajan.com
Produces "Antique & Collectibles Showcase" and "Canadian Coin News& Canadian Stamp News".
Bret Evans, Editor, bret@trajan.ca

Transcontinental Inc.
General Management
3315, 1 Place Ville Marie, Montréal, QC H3B 3N2
Tel: 514-954-4000; Fax: 514-954-4016
Toll-Free: 800-387-0825
www.tctranscontinental.com
Social Media:
twitter.com/tctranscontinen
www.facebook.com/tc.transcontinental
Publishes a variety of magazines, newspapers, and books. Magazines include Canadian Living, Coup de pouce, Elle Canada and Style at home. Also publishes a variety of books and educational materials.
François Olivier, President & CEO

Transcontinental Publications G.T. Inc.
Western Publications
#500, 2608 Granville St., Vancouver, BC V6H 3V3

Transcontinental Specialty Publications
#609, 1888 Brunswick St., Halifax, NS B3J 3J8
Tel: 902-468-8027; Fax: 902-425-8118
www.tctranscontinental.com

Tribute Publishing Inc.
71 Barber Greene Rd., Toronto, ON M3C 2A2
Tel: 416-445-0544; Fax: 416-445-2894
generalinfo@tribute.ca
www.tribute.ca
Entertainment magazine

TVA Publications
Previous Name: Trustar Ltd
Owned By: Québecor Média
1010, rue de Sérigny, Longueuil, QC J4K 5G7
Tel: 514-848-7000; Fax: 514-848-9854
Toll-Free: 888-535-8634
abomag@tvapublications.com
www.tvapublications.com

University of Calgary Press
2500 University Dr. NW, Calgary, AB T2N 1N4
Tel: 403-220-7578; Fax: 403-282-0085
ucpmail@ucalgary.ca
www.uofcpress.com
Donna Livingstone, Director, 403-220-3511, livingsd@ucalgary.ca

University of Toronto Press Inc.
#700, 10 Mary St., Toronto, ON M4Y 2W8
Tel: 416-978-2239; Fax: 416-978-4738
www.utpress.utoronto.ca
Publishes a variety of journals including "Bookbird: a journal of international children's literature", "The Canadian Journal on Aging", "The Canadian Journal of Information and Library Sciences", "Eighteenth Century Fiction","SIMILE: Studies in Media and Information Literacy Education", and "Ulimate Reality and Meaning".
John Yates, Presidnet/Publisher, jyates@utpress.utoronto.ca

Velo Québec Éditions
1251, rue Rachel est, Montréal, QC H2J 2J9
Tél: 514-521-8356; Téléc: 514-521-5711
Médias sociaux:
twitter.com/VeloQuebec
www.facebook.com/VeloQuebec

Youngblood Publishing
#404, 4580 Dufferin St., North York, ON M3H 5Y2
Tel: 416-665-7333; Fax: 416-665-7226

Youth Culture Inc.
85 Kildonan Dr., Toronto, ON M8W 2X2
Tel: 416-595-1313; Fax: 416-595-1312
info@youthculture.com
www.youthculture.com
Social Media:
twitter.com/vervegirlmag
www.facebook.com/vervegirlcanada
Magazines are directed and marketed towards teens and "tweens".
Kaaren Whitney-Vernon, President, CEO, and Group Publisher, kaaren@youthculture.com
Joanna Whitney, Editor, joanna@youthculture.com

Newspapers

Alberta

Daily Newspapers in Alberta

Calgary: Calgary Herald
Owned By: Postmedia Network Inc.
PO Box 2400 M, 215 - 16 St. SE, Calgary, AB T2P 0W8
Tel: 403-235-7100; Fax: 403-235-7379
Toll-Free: 800-327-9219
calgaryherald@reachcanada.com
www.calgaryherald.com
Social Media: www.linkedin.com/company/calgary-herald
twitter.com/calgaryherald
w ww.facebook.com/yycherald
Circulation: 550,000 Frequency: Morning
Peter Menzies, General Manager
Guy Huntingford, Publisher
Fax: 403-235-7575
ghuntingford@calgaryherald.com
Lorne Motley, Editor-in-chief
403-235-7546
lmotley@calgaryherald.com

Calgary: Calgary Sun
Owned By: Sun Media Corp.
2615 - 12 St. NE, Calgary, AB T2E 7W9
Tel: 403-410-1010; Fax: 403-250-4176
cal-circulation@sunmedia.ca; cal-news@sunmedia.ca
www.calgarysun.com
Other information: Classified, E-mail: calgarysun.classifieds@sunmedia.ca
Social Media:
twitter.com/calgarysun
www.facebook.com/pages/The-Calgary-Sun/131068450250444
Frequency: Morning
Jose Rodriguez, Editor in Chief, jose.rodriguez@sunmedia.ca
Martin Hudson, Managing Editor, martin.hudson@sunmedia.ca
Ty Pilson, Assistant Managing Editor, Ty.pilson@sunmedia.ca
Dave Naylor, City Editor, dave.naylor@sunmedia.ca
Todd Saelhof, Sports Editor, todd.saelhof@sunmedia.ca
Kevin Williamson, Showbiz Editor, kevin.williamson@sunmedia.ca

Edmonton: The Edmonton Journal
Owned By: Postmedia Network Inc.
PO Box 2421 , 10006 - 101 St., Edmonton, AB T5J 0S1
Tel: 780-429-5100
library@edmontonjournal.com(reprints)
www.edmontonjournal.com
Other information: Customer Service: 780-498-5500; Classified Advertising: 780-428-1234
Social Media:
twitter.com/EJ_News; twitter.com/EJ_Life; twitter.com/EJ_Arts
www.facebook.com/edmontonjournal
A print edition & a digital edition are available.
John Connolly, Publisher, jconnolly@edmontonjournal.com
Lucinda Chodan, Editor-in-Chief, lchodan@edmontonjournal.com
Stephanie Coombs, Managing Editor, scoombs@edmontonjournal.com
Paul Cashman, Editor, Business, pcashman@edmontonjournal.com
Donna Christensen, Editor, Community, dchristensen@edmontonjournal.com
Craig Ellingson, Editor, Sports, cellingson@edmontonjournal.com
Kathy Kerr, Editor, Content & Sunday Reader, kkerr@edmontonjournal.com
David Howell, Editor, City, dhowell@edmontonjournal.com
Randy Mark, Editor, Photo Assignment, rmark@edmontonjournal.com
Kerry Powell, Editor, Digital, kpowell@edmontonjournal.com
Keri Sweetman, Editor, Arts & Life, ksweetman@edmontonjournal.com

Barb Wilkinson, Deputy Editor, Innvoation & Engagement, bwilkinson@edmontonjournal.com
Joe Celino, Vice-President, Production, Systems, Reader Sales & Service, jcelino@edmontonjournal.com
Gail Matheson, Vice-President, Human Resources & Finance, gmatheson@edmontonjournal.com
Joseph Wuest, Vice-President, Advertising, Sales & Marketing, jwuest@edmontonjournal.com

Edmonton: Edmonton Sun
Owned By: Sun Media Corp.
#250, 4990 - 92 Ave., Edmonton, AB T6B 3A1
Tel: 780-468-0100
research@sunmedia.ca
www.edmontonsun.com
Other information: News tips, E-mail: edm-citydesk@sunmedia.ca
Social Media: twitter.com/Edmontonsun
www.facebook.com/edmontonsun
Frequency: Morning
Steve Serviss, Editor-in-chief, Steve.Serviss@sunmedia.ca
Donna Harker, Managing Editor, donna.harker@sunmedia.ca
Nicole Bergot, City Editor, nicole.bergot@sunmedia.ca
Jennifer Bill, National Life Editor, jennifer.bill@sunmedia.ca
Tom Braid, Photo Editor, tom.braid@sunmedia.ca

Fort McMurray: Fort McMurray Today
Owned By: Sun Media Corp.
PO Box 4008 , 8550 Franklin Ave., Fort McMurray, AB T9H 3G1
Tel: 780-743-8186; Fax: 780-715-3820
www.fortmcmurraytoday.com
Social Media: www.facebook.com/pages/Fort-McMurray-Today/13093416031779
Circulation: Mon.-Tues., 5,500; Wed.-Thurs., 10,300; Fri., 7,300; Sat., 20,000 Frequency: Afternoon/evening, Mon.-Sat.
Mary Ann Kostiuk, Publisher
Jessica MacIntosh, Managing Editor

Grande Prairie: Daily Herald-Tribune
Owned By: Sun Media Corp.
PO Box 3000 , 10604 - 100 St., Grande Prairie, AB T8V 6V4
Tel: 780-532-1110; Fax: 780-532-2120
www.dailyheraldtribune.com
Social Media: twitter.com/GPHeraldTribune
www.facebook.com/DailyHeraldTribune
Circulation: 8,384 M-Th; 12,830 F Frequency: Monday-Friday; Afternoon
Fred Rinne, Editor-in-Chief, fred.rinne@sunmedia.ca

Lethbridge: Lethbridge Herald
PO Box 670 , 504 - 7th St. South, Lethbridge, AB T1J 3Z7
Tel: 403-328-4411; Fax: 403-328-4536
www.lethbridgeherald.com
Social Media: www.youtube.com/user/lethbridgeherald
twitter.com/Leth_Herald
www.face book.com/LethbridgeHerald
Circulation: 18,950, Sun.-Thu.; 23,213, Fri., 20,386, Sat.
Frequency: Morning
Coleen Campbell, General Manager & Vice-President
403-328-4003
ccampbell@abnewsgroup.com
Doyle MacKinnon, Managing Editor, dmackinnon@lethbridgeherald.com

Medicine Hat: Medicine Hat News
PO Box 10 , 3257 Dunmore Rd. SE, Medicine Hat, AB T1A 7E6
Tel: 403-527-1101; Fax: 403-528-5696
www.medicinehatnews.com
Social Media: www.youtube.com/user/MedicineHatNews
twitter.com/medicinehatnews
www.facebook.com/pages/Medicine-Hat-News/196589917022152
Mike Hertz, Publisher

Red Deer: Red Deer Advocate
2950 Bremner Ave., Red Deer, AB T4R 1M9
Tel: 403-343-2400
mypaper@reddeeradvocate.com
www.reddeeradvocate.com
Other information: Newsroom: editorial@reddeeradvocate.com
Social Media: twitter.com/RedDeerAdvocate
Circulation: 16,000
The newspaper employs more than 160 people.

Other Newspapers in Alberta

Airdrie: Airdrie City View
Owned By: Great West Newspapers
#403, 2903 Kingview Blvd., Airdrie, AB T4A 0C4
Tel: 403-948-1885; Fax: 403-948-2554
sales@airdrie.greatwest.ca
www.airdriecityview.com
Circulation: 16,987 Frequency: Fridays
Cameron Christianson, Publisher

Airdrie: Airdrie Echo
112 1st Ave. NE, Airdrie, AB T4B 0R6
Tel: 403-948-7280; Fax: 403-912-2341
www.airdrieecho.com
The Airdrie Echo is a member of Canoe Sun Media Community Newspapers.

Athabasca: Athabasca Advocate
Owned By: Great West Newspapers, LP
4917B - 49th St., Athabasca, AB T9S 1C5
Tel: 780-675-9222; Fax: 780-675-3143
advocate@athabasca.greatwest.ca
www.athabascaadvocate.com
Other information: Subscriptions & Classified Ads: reception@athabasca.greatwest.ca
Social Media: twitter.com/athaadvocate
www.facebook.com/pages/The-Athabasca-Advocate/12260854447
Circulation: 3,490 Frequency: Tuesday
The newspaper serves the Alberta communities of Athabasca & Boyle, & the surrounding area.
Ross Hunter, Publisher, rhunter@athabasca.greatwest.ca
Meghan McIvor, Manager, Production, production@athabasca.greatwest.ca
Tara Shapransky, Reporter & Photographer
Cheryl Major, Representative, Display Advertising
Melissa Hall, Contact, Classifieds, Subscriptions, & Accounts Receivable

Banff: The Banff Crag & Canyon
Owned By: Canoe Sun Media
201 Bear St., 2nd Fl., Banff, AB T1W 1N8
Tel: 403-762-2453; Fax: 403-762-5274
www.banffcragandcanyon.com
Circulation: 6,970 Frequency: Tuesday
Kim Oliver, Publisher
Dave Husdal, Editor

Banff: Canmore Leader
21 Bear St., 2nd Fl., Banff, AB T1L 1H2
Tel: 403-762-2453; Fax: 403-762-5274
www.canmoreleader.com
Social Media: twitter.com/canmoreleader
Frequency: Tuesday
The Canmore Leader is a member of Canoe Sun Media Community Newspapers.

Barrhead: Barrhead Leader
Previous Name: Barrhead News
PO Box 4520 , 5015 - 51 St, Barrhead, AB T7N 1A4
Tel: 780-674-3823; Fax: 780-674-6337
www.barrheadleader.com
Social Media: www.youtube.com/barrheadleader
twitter.com/barrheadleader
www.facebook.com/pages/Barrhead-Leader/205029536182859?sk
Circulation: 4,000 Frequency: Weekly
Carol Farnalls, Publisher
Marcus Day, Editor
Amy Newton, Manager, Sales
Les Dunford, Senior Writer, Town & Country

Bassano: Bassano Times
PO Box 78 , Bassano, AB T0J 0B0
Tel: 403-641-3636; Fax: 403-641-3952
Frequency: Weekly

Beaumont: La Nouvelle Beaumont News
4908 - 50 Ave., Beaumont, AB T4X 1J9
Tel: 780-929-6632; Fax: 780-929-6634
www.thebeaumontnews.ca
The Beaumont News is a member of Canoe Sun Media Community Newspapers.

Beaverlodge: Beaverlodge Advertiser
PO Box 628 , Beaverlodge, AB T0H 0C0
Tel: 780-354-2460; Fax: 780-354-2460
Frequency: Wednesday

Blairmore: Crowsnest Pass Herald
Crowsnest Mall, PO Box 960 , 12925 - 20th Ave., Blairmore, AB T0K 0E0
Tel: 403-562-2248; Fax: 403-562-8379
news@passherald.ca; tips@passherald.ca
www.passherald.ca
Frequency: Tuesday
Gail Sygutek, Co-Owner
Trevor Slapak, Co-Owner & Editor
Lisa Sygutek, Publisher
Mike Chambers, Manager, Production
Willy Sygutek, Manager, Circulation
Lindsay Goss, Reporter
Betty Walmsley, Contact, Advertising Sales

Blairmore: Crowsnest Pass Promoter
PO Box 1019 , 13343 - 20 Ave., Blairmore, AB T0K 0E0
Tel: 403-562-8884; Fax: 403-562-2242
www.crowsnestpasspromoter.com
Social Media: www.facebook.com/pages/Crowsnest-Pass-Promoter/1814472319
Frequency: Weekly
The Crowsnest Pass Promoter is a member of Canoe Sun Media Community Newspapers.

Bonnyville: Bonnyville Nouvelle
5304 - 50 Ave., Bonnyville, AB T9N 1Y4
Tel: 780-826-3876; Fax: 780-826-7062
nouvelle@bonnyville.greatwest.ca
www.bonnyvillenouvelle.ca
Other information: Advertising, E-mail: advertising@bonnyville.greatwest.ca
Social Media: www.facebook.com/pages/Bonnyville-Nouvelle/294955134326
Frequency: Tuesday
The Bonnyville Nouvelle serves communities in northeastern Alberta, including Bonnyville, Cold Lake, Ardmore, La Corey, Fort Kent, Glendon, & Iron River.
Clare Gauvreau, Publisher
Melissa Barr, Editor & Reporter
Nora Chachula, Manager, Production
Brandon MacLeod, Sports Reporter
Amber Cook, Sales Associate
Breanna Ernst, Sales Associate

Bow Island: The 40-Mile County Commentator
Previous Name: County Commentator & Cypress Courier
Owned By: Alta Newspaper Group
PO Box 580 , 147 - 5th Ave., Bow Island, AB T0K 0G0
Tel: 403-545-2258; Fax: 403-545-6886
www.bowislandcommentator.com
Circulation: 5,842
Coleen Campbell, Publisher
403-545-2258
ccampbell@tabertimes.com

Brooks: Brooks & County Chronicle
PO Box 1568 Main, Brooks, AB T1R 1C4
Tel: 403-793-2252; Fax: 403-793-2288
thepaper@telusplanet.net
www.brooksinthenews.com
Social Media: www.facebook.com/group.php?gid=179545068732938
Circulation: 11,401 Frequency: Sunday
The newspaper serves Brooks, Alberta & the surrounding communities.
M. Joan Brees, Publisher & Editor

Brooks: Brooks Bulletin
Owned By: Nesbitt Publishing Co. Ltd.
PO Box 1450 , 124 - 3rd St. West, Brooks, AB T1R 1C3
Tel: 403-362-5571; Fax: 403-362-5080
editor@brooksbulletin.com
www.brooksbulletin.com
Frequency: Weekly

Calgary: Le Chinook
Détenteur: ViaPlus Communication Inc.
32 - 805 5ème ave SW, Calgary, AB T2P 0N6
Tél: 403-232-5488;Téléc: 403-232-5489
nouvelles@lechinook.com
www.lechinook.com
Tirage: 10 000 Fréquence: Mensuel; français
Agathe Fillion

Camrose: Camrose Booster
4925 - 48 St., Camrose, AB T4V 1L7
Tel: 780-672-3142; Fax: 780-672-2518
ads@camrosebooster.com
www.camrosebooster.com
Circulation: 12,941 Frequency: Tuesday

Blain Fowler, Publisher, mcfoul@cable-lynx.net
Berdie Fowler, Editor

Camrose: Camrose Canadian
4610 - 49 Ave., Camrose, AB T4V 0M6
Tel: 780-672-4421; Fax: 780-672-5323
editor@camrosecanadian.com
www.camrosecanadian.com
Social Media:
twitter.com/CamroseCanadian
www.facebook.com/CamroseCanadian
Frequency: Weekly
The Camrose Canadian is a member of Canoe Sun Media Community Newspapers.

Canmore: Rocky Mountain Outlook
Owned By: Great West Newspapers, LP
PO Box 8610 , #201, 1001 - 6th Ave., Canmore, AB T1W 2V3
Tel: 403-609-0220
www.rmoutlook.com
Social Media:
twitter.com/rmoutlook
www.facebook.com/pages/Rocky-Mountain-Outlook/1131460020
4
Circulation: 9,387 Frequency: Thursday
The newspaper serves the communities of Banff, Lake Louise, Canmore, & Kananaskis.
Jason Lyon, Publisher, jlyon@outlook.greatwest.ca
Dave Whitfield, Editor, dwhitfield@outlook.greatwest.ca
Craig Douce, Photojournalist, jbrisbane@outlook.greatwest.ca
Erin Buehler, Contact, Sales, swhite@outlook.greatwest.ca

Cardston: Temple City Star
PO Box 2060 , 311 Main St., Cardston, AB T0K 0K0
Tel: 403-653-4664; Fax: 403-653-3162
info@templecitystar.net
www.templecitystar.net
Frequency: Thursday
Robert T. Smith, Owner & Publisher
Lindy S. Pehrson, Editor
Deane Haynes, Office Manager
Tracy Weasel Fat, Production & Web Master

Carstairs: Carstairs Courier
PO Box 114 , 320 - 10th St. South, Carstairs, AB T0M 0N0
Tel: 403-337-2806; Fax: 403-337-3160
www.carstairscourier.ca
Social Media:
twitter.com/carstairscourie
Frequency: Tuesday

Castor: Castor Advance
Owned By: Black Press Group Ltd.
PO Box 120 , Castor, AB T0C 0X0
Tel: 403-882-4044
stetnews@telusplanet.net
Frequency: Weekly

Claresholm: Claresholm Local Press
PO Box 520 , 4913 - 2nd St. West, Claresholm, AB T0L 0T0
Tel: 403-625-4474; Fax: 403-625-2828
clpprint@telus.net
www.claresholmlocalpress.ca
Social Media:
www.facebook.com/pages/Claresholm-Local-Press/6361231890
0
Frequency: Weekly
The newspaper serves the Alberta communities of Claresholm, Stavely, & Granum.
Roxanne Thompson, Owner & Publisher
Rob Vogt, Editor
J.W. (Bill) Schnarr, Reporter & Photographer
Julie Hutchinson, Website Manager & Graphic Designer
Amanda Zimmer, Manager, Production

Coaldale: Sunny South News
Owned By: Alta Newspaper Group Limited Partnership
PO Box 30 , Coaldale, AB T1M 1M2
Tel: 403-345-3081
www.sunnysouthnews.com
Circulation: 3,845 Frequency: Weekly; Tuesday
Serves the towns of Coaldale and Picture Butte as well as the villages and hamlets within the County of Lethbridge.
Coleen Campbell, Publisher
403-545-2258
ccampbell@tabertimes.com

Cochrane: Cochrane Eagle
Owned By: Great West Newspapers, LP
126A River Ave., Cochrane, AB T4C 2C2
Tel: 403-932-6588; Fax: 403-851-6520
letters@cochrane.greatwest.ca
www.cochraneeagle.com
Other information: Advertising, E-mail:
advertising@cochrane.greatwest.ca
Circulation: 12,540 Frequency: Wednesday
Jack Tennant, Publisher, jtennant@cochrane.greatwest.ca
Derek Clouthier, Editor, dclouthier@cochrane.greatwest.ca
Brenda Tennant, Manager, Advertising, btennant@cochrane.greatwest.ca
Lindsay Seewalt, Reporter, lseewalt@cochrane.greatwest.ca
Brendan Nagle, Reporter, Sports, sports@cochrane.greatwest.ca
Jeremy Broadfield, Photographer, photo@cochrane.greatwest.ca
Carrie Anderson, Contact, Administration & Circulation, classifieds@cochrane.greatwest.ca
Jodi Collins, Contact, Accounting, accounting@cochrane.greatwest.ca
Theresa Lewis, Contact, Production, production@cochrane.greatwest.ca

Cochrane: Cochrane Times
206 - 5th Ave. West, Bay 8, Cochrane, AB T4C 1X4
Tel: 403-932-3500; Fax: 403-932-3935
www.cochranetimes.com
Frequency: Wednesday
The Cochrane Times is a member of Canoe Sun Media Community Newspapers.

Cold Lake: Cold Lake Sun
PO Box 268 , #1, 5121 - 50th Ave., Cold Lake, AB T9M 1P1
Tel: 780-594-5881; Fax: 780-594-2120
www.coldlakesun.com
Social Media:
twitter.com/ColdLakeSun
The Cold Lake Sun is a member of Canoe Sun Media Community Newspapers. A PDF version of the newspaper is produced each week.
Donna Ritco, Publisher

Cold Lake: The Courier
Centennial Bldg. #67, PO Box 6190 Forces, Cold Lake, AB T9M 2C5
Tel: 780-594-5206; Fax: 780-594-2139
thecourier@telus.net
www.thecouriernewspaper.ca
Frequency: Weekly
The Courier serves the military community of Cold Lake, Alberta.
Connie Lavigne, Courier Manager, Connie.Lavigne@forces.gc.ca
Karen Parker, Editor & Reporter
Vicki Gregory, Production Coodinator & Graphic Designer
Debbie Green, Contact, Administration & Sales

Consort: Consort Enterprise
PO Box 129 , Consort, AB T0C 1B0
Tel: 403-577-3337; Fax: 403-577-3611
www.consortenterprise.com
Frequency: Weekly
The Consort Enterprise serves the Alberta communities of Consort, Monitor, Altario, Veteran, Kirriemuir, & Compeer.

Coronation: East Central Alberta Review
PO Box 70 , 4923 Victoria Ave., Coronation, AB T0C 1C0
Tel: 403-578-4111; Fax: 403-578-2088
admin@ecareview.com; advertise@ecareview.com
www.ecareview.com
Other information: Marketing: advertise@ecareview.com
Joyce Webster, Publisher & Editor, publisher@ecareview.com
Brenda Schimke, Editor
Pamela Johnson, Office & Web Manager
Jennifer Chernishenko, Reporter, news1@ecareview.com

Didsbury: Didsbury Review
PO Box 760 , 2017 - 19th Ave., Didsbury, AB T0M 0W0
Tel: 403-335-3301; Fax: 403-335-8143
readers@Didsbury.greatwest.ca
www.didsburyreview.ca
Social Media:
twitter.com/didsburyreview
Frequency: Tuesday

Drayton Valley: Western Review
PO Box 6960 , 4905 - 52 Ave., Drayton Valley, AB T7A 1S3
Tel: 780-542-5380; Fax: 780-542-9200
www.draytonvalleywesternreview.com
Social Media:
www.facebook.com/group.php?gid=269245220567
Frequency: Tuesday
The Drayton Valley Western Review is a member of Canoe Sun Media Community Newspapers. A digital edition of the newspaper is also produced each week.

Drumheller: Drumheller Mail
PO Box 1629 , 515 Hwy. 10 East, Drumheller, AB T0J 0Y0
Tel: 403-823-2580; Fax: 403-823-3864
information@drumhellermail.com
www.drumhellermail.com
Social Media:
twitter.com/DrumhellerMail
www.facebook.com/drumhellermail
Frequency: Wednesday
Ossie Sheddy, Publisher
O. (Bob) Sheddy IIII, Editor

Edmonton: Edmonton Examiner
Previous Name: West Edmonton Examiner
Owned By: Bowes Publishers Ltd.
#250, 4990 - 92 Ave., Edmonton, AB T6B 3A1
Tel: 780-453-9001; Fax: 780-451-4574
edm.advertisinginfo@sunmedia.ca
www.edmontonexaminer.com
Social Media:
twitter.com/edm_examiner
www.facebook.com/pages/Edmonton-Examiner/275284275634
Frequency: Wednesday
The Edmonton Examiner is a member of Canoe Sun Media Community Newspapers. Each week, seven versions of the newspaper are published for seven city zones. The newspaper employs over 90 people.
John Caputo, Publisher, jcaputo@edmontonexaminer.com
Scott Haskins, Editor, shaskins@edmontonexaminer.com
Ted Dakin, Manager, Advertising Sales, tdakin@edmontonexaminer.com
Michael Staley, Manager, Circulation, michael.staley@sunmedia.ca

Edmonton: Le Franco
#312, 8627 - 91 St., Edmonton, AB T6C 3N1
Tel: 780-465-6581; Fax: 780-469-1129
journal@lefranco.ab.ca
www.lefranco.ab.ca
Other information: Administration: administration@lefranco.ab.ca
Social Media:
www.facebook.com/pages/Le-Franco-journal/225495297491230
Le Franco is a French language newspaper for readers in Edmonton & the surrounding area.
Étienne Alary, Director, direction@lefranco.ab.ca
Lysane Sénécal Mastropaolo, Journaliste, redaction@lefranco.ab.ca

Edson: Edson Leader
PO Box 6330 , 4820 - 3rd Ave., Edson, AB T7E 1T8
Tel: 780-723-3301; Fax: 780-723-5171
leadernews@telusplanet.net
www.edsonleader.com
Social Media:
www.facebook.com/pages/The-Edson-Leader/13200235685103
1
Frequency: Monday
The Edson Leader is a member of Canoe Sun Media Community Newspapers. A PDF version of the newspaper is produced each week.

Edson: The Weekly Anchor
PO Box 6870 , 5040 - 3rd Ave., Edson, AB T7E 1V2
Tel: 780-723-5787; Fax: 780-723-5725
anchorwk@telusplanet.net
www.weeklyanchor.com
Circulation: 5,307 / week Frequency: Monday
The independent newspaper serves the Alberta communities of Edson, Robb, Evansburg, Marlboro, Entwistle, Nojack, Wildwood, Carrot Creek, Peers, & Niton Junction.

Elk Point: Elk Point Review
Owned By: Glacier Media Inc.
PO Box 309 , 4809 - 50 Ave., Elk Point, AB T0A 1A0
Tel: 780-724-4087; Fax: 780-645-2346
journal@st.paul.greatwest.ca
Circulation: 617 Frequency: Weekly
The mewspaper serves the Alberta community of Elk Point & the surrounding area.
Clair Gauvreau, Publisher

Fairview: Fairview Post
PO Box 1900 , 10118 - 110 St., Fairview, AB T0H 1L0
Tel: 780-835-4925; Fax: 780-835-4227
fairviewpost.editor@sunmedia.ca
www.fairviewpost.com
Social Media:
twitter.com/fairviewpost
www.facebook.com/fairviewpost
The Fairview Post is a member of Canoe Sun Media Community Newspapers. A digital edition of the newspaper is available each week.

Falher: Smoky River Express
PO Box 644 , 217 Main St. SW, Falher, AB T0H 1M0
Tel: 780-837-2585; Fax: 780-837-2102
www.smokyriverexpress.com
Social Media:
www.facebook.com/SmokyRiverExpress
The newspaper serves the Municipal District of Smoky River.
Mary Burgar, Publisher, spn@cablecomet.com
Kevin Laliberte, Editor, sreeditor@telus.net
Richard Froese, Reporter, srexpres@telus.net

Fort MacLeod: Macleod Gazette
Owned By: Macleod Gazette (2001) Limited
PO Box 720 , 310 - 24th St., Fort MacLeod, AB T0L 0Z0
Tel: 403-553-3391; Fax: 403-553-2961
ftmgazet@telusplanet.net
www.fortmacleodgazette.com
Frequency: Weekly
Frank McTighe, Publisher & Editor
Emily McTighe, Manager, Advertising
Sharon Monical, Contact, Production

Fort Saskatchewan: Fort Saskatchewan Record
Owned By: Sun Media Corp.
#168, 10404 - 99 Ave., Fort Saskatchewan, AB T8L 3W2
Tel: 780-998-7070; Fax: 780-998-5515
www.fortsaskatchewanrecord.com
Other information: Business:
business@fortsaskatchewanrecord.com
Circulation: 9,174 Frequency: Thursday
Allison Smith, Manager, Distribution
780-998-7070 ext. 28
distribution@fortsaskatchewanrecord.com
MaryAnn Kochan, Multimedia Account Executive, Advertising
780-998-7070 ext. 31
maryann@fortsaskatchewanrecord.com

Grande Cache: Grande Cache Mountaineer Publishing Ltd.
PO Box 660 , 203 Pine Plaza, Grande Cache, AB T0E 0Y0
Tel: 780-827-3539; Fax: 780-827-3530
gcnews@telus.net
grandecachenews.awna.com
Social Media:
www.facebook.com/158809672750
Circulation: 1,296 Frequency: Tuesday
Noel Edey, Publisher
Arthur Veitch, Editor

Grande Prairie: Peace Country Sun
10604 - 100 St., Grande Prairie, AB T8V 6V4
Tel: 780-532-1110; Fax: 780-532-2120
www.peacecountrysun.com
Social Media:
twitter.com/peacecountrysun
www.facebook.com/PeaceCountrySun
Frequency: Weekly
The Peace Country Sun is a member of Canoe Sun Media Community Newspapers.

Grimshaw: Mile Zero News
PO Box 1010 , 4905 Railway Ave., Grimshaw, AB T0H 1W0
Tel: 780-332-2215; Fax: 780-332-4380
Circulation: 1,292 Frequency: Wednesday

Hanna: Hanna Herald
PO Box 790 , Hanna, AB T0J 1P0
Tel: 403-854-3366; Fax: 403-854-3256
www.hannaherald.com
Social Media:
www.facebook.com/pages/Hanna-Herald/134487243289016
Frequency: Wednesday
The Hanna Herald is a member of Canoe Sun Media Community Newspapers. A PDF version of the newspaper is produced each week.
Shawn Cornell, Publisher, shawn.cornell@sunmedia.ca
Jackie Gold-Irwin, Editor, jackie.gold@sunmedia.ca
David Feil, Multimedia Journalist, david.feil@sunmedia.ca
Krista Kittler, Manager, Office, krista.kittler@sunmedia.ca
Deanne Cornell, Contact, Advertising & Sales, deanne.cornell@sunmedia.ca

High Level: The Echo
10006 - 97 St., High Level, AB T0H 1Z0
Tel: 780-926-2000; Fax: 780-926-2001
echo@mackreport.ab.ca
Circulation: 1,599 Frequency: Weekly; Wednesday
Tom Mihaly, Publisher

High Prairie: South Peace News
PO Box 1000 , 4901 - 51st Ave., High Prairie, AB T0G 1E0
Tel: 780-523-4484; Fax: 780-523-3039
www.southpeacenews.com
Social Media:
twitter.com/SouthPeaceNews
Frequency: Wednesday
Mary Burgar, Publisher, spn@cablecomet.com
Chris Clegg, Editor, statsmanchris@hotmail.com
Mac Olsen, Reporter, macolsen@telus.netail.com
Alicia Boisson, Sales Representative, southpeacenews@hotmail.com

High River: High River Times
618 Centre St. South, High River, AB T1V 1E9
Tel: 403-652-2034; Fax: 403-652-3962
placeit.sun@classifiedextra.ca(classifieds)
www.highrivertimes.com
Circulation: 7,145 Frequency: Tuesday, Friday
The High River Times is a member of Canoe Sun Media Community Newspapers. The newspaper serves the Alberta communities of High River, Cayley, Blackie, & Longview.
Nancy Middleton, Publisher, nancy.middleton@sunmedia.ca
Craig Baird, Editor, craig.baird@sunmedia.ca
Kaire Davis, Manager, Office
Heather Keller, Manager, Advertising, heather.keller@sunmedia.ca

Hinton: Hinton Parklander
387 Drinnan Way, Hinton, AB T7V 2A3
Tel: 780-865-3115; Fax: 780-865-1252
news@hintonparklander.com
www.hintonparklander.com
Social Media:
www.facebook.com/group.php?gid=113936721972274
Frequency: Weekly
The Hinton Parklander is a member of Canoe Sun Media Community Newspapers. The newspaper serves the town of Hinton in Alberta & its surrounding area.
Terry Thachuk, Publisher
Eric Plummer, Editor
Craig Palmer, Reporter

Innisfail: Innisfail Province
Owned By: Glacier Media Inc.
4932 - 49th St., Innisfail, AB T4G 1N2
Tel: 403-227-3477; Fax: 403-227-3330
province@innisfail.greatwest.ca
www.innisfailprovince.com
Social Media:
twitter.com/innisfailprovin
Circulation: 8,203 Frequency: Tuesday
Ray Brinson, Publisher
Lea Smaldon, Managing Editor
Michaela Johnstone, Editor

La Crete: The Northern Pioneer
Owned By: Mackenzie Report Inc.
PO Box 571 , 10303 - 100 St., La Crete, AB T0H 2H0
Tel: 780-928-4000; Fax: 780-928-4001
pioneer@mackreport.ab.ca
Circulation: 1,120 Frequency: Wednesday
The Northern Pioneer serves the Alberta communities of La Crete & Fort Vermilion.
Tom Mihaly, Publisher & Editor

Lac La Biche: Lac La Biche Post
Owned By: Glacier Media Inc.
PO Box 508 , 10211 - 101 St., Lac La Biche, AB T0A 2C0
Tel: 780-623-4221; Fax: 780-623-4230
www.laclabichepost.com
Social Media:
www.facebook.com/group.php?gid=157459007605036
Circulation: 2,886 Frequency: Tuesday
Rob McKinley, Publisher
Iona Wolstenholme, Manager, Sales
Alina Smirnova, Reporter & Photographer

Lacombe: Lacombe Globe
Owned By: Sun Media Corp.
5022 - 50th St., Lacombe, AB T4L 1W8
Tel: 403-782-3498; Fax: 403-782-5850
www.lacombeglobe.com
Circulation: 2,911 Frequency: Tuesday
Mary-Ann Kostiuk, Publisher
Lisa Joy, Editor

Lamont: Lamont Farm 'n' Friends
Owned By: W & E Cowley Publishing Ltd.
PO Box 800 , Lamont, AB T0B 2R0
Tel: 780-943-2032; Fax: 780-942-2515
redwater@shaw.ca
www.cowleynewspapers.com/farm-n-friends
Circulation: 19,394 Frequency: Friday
Ed Cowley, Publisher & Editor

Leduc: Leduc Representative
4504 - 61 Ave., Leduc, AB T9E 3Z1
Tel: 780-986-2271; Fax: 780-986-6397
www.leducrep.com
Frequency: Friday
The Leduc Representative is a member of Canoe Sun Media Community Newspapers. The newspaper serves Leduc & Leduc County in Alberta.

Lethbridge: Lethbridge Shopper
234 - 12th St. B North, Lethbridge, AB T1H 2K7
Tel: 403-329-8225; Fax: 403-329-8211
www.shoppergroup.com
Frequency: Weekly
The Lethbridge Shopper serves Lethbridge & the surrounding area.

Lloydminster: Lloydminster Meridian Booster
Owned By: Sun Media Corp.
5714 - 44th St., Lloydminster, AB T9V 0B6
Tel: 780-875-3362; Fax: 780-875-3423
www.meridianbooster.com
Circulation: 43,041 Frequency: Monday, Wednesday, Friday
Shaun Jessome, Publisher
Dana Smith, Managing Editor

Manning: Banner Post
PO Box 686 , Manning, AB T0H 2M0
Tel: 780-836-3588; Fax: 780-836-2820
Frequency: Wednesday
The Banner Post serves Manning, Alberta & the surrounding area.

Medicine Hat: Medicine Hat Shopper
922 Allowance Ave. SE, Medicine Hat, AB T1A 3G7
Tel: 403-527-5777; Fax: 403-526-7352
www.shoppergroup.com
Frequency: Weekly
Classified advertisements also appear on the web site.
Ron Heizelman, General Manager

Morinville: Morinville Free Press
Owned By: W & E Cowley Publishing Ltd.
PO Box 3005 , 10126 - 100 Ave., Morinville, AB T8R 1R9
Tel: 780-939-3309; Fax: 780-939-3093
morinville@shaw.ca
www.cowleynewspapers.com
Frequency: Tuesday, Friday
The newspaper serves residents of Alberta's Sturgeon County.

Morinville: The Morinville News
PO Box 3135 , Morinville, AB T8R 1S1
Tel: 780-800-3619
editor@morinvillenews.com
morinvillenews.com
Social Media:
twitter.com/MorinvilleNews
www.facebook.com/pages/MorinvilleNewsco m/116150388429696
Stephen A. Dafoe, Owner & Publisher

Nanton: Nanton News
Owned By: Sun Media Corp.
PO Box 429 , Nanton, AB T0L 1R0
Tel: 403-646-2023; Fax: 403-646-2848
natnews@telusplanet.net
www.nantonnews.com
Circulation: 1,012 Frequency: Wednesday
Nancy Middleton, Publisher

Okotoks: Okotoks Western Wheel
PO Box 150 , 9 McRae St., Okotoks, AB T1S 2A2
Tel: 403-938-6397; Fax: 403-938-2518
www.westernwheel.com
Frequency: Weekly
Paul Rockley, Publisher, prockley@greatwest.ca
Darlene Casten, Editor
Bruce Campbell, Sports Editor
Diana Locke, Sales Representative, dlocke@okotoks.greatwest.ca

Jackie Moore, Contact, Advertising, jmoore@okotoks.greatwest.ca

Olds: Mountain View Gazette
Owned By: Great West Newspapers, LP
5013 - 51 St., Olds, AB T4H 1P6
Tel: 403-556-7510; Fax: 403-556-7515
www.mountainviewgazette.ca
Social Media: twitter.com/mtnviewgazette
Circulation: 23,000 Frequency: Tuesday
Alberta's Mountain View & Red Deer Counties are served by the Mountain View Gazette.
John Gleeson, Contact
403-556-7510 ext 223

Olds: The Olds Albertan
5013 - 51 St., Olds, AB T4H 1P6
Tel: 403-556-7510; Fax: 403-556-7515
www.oldsalbertan.ca
Social Media: twitter.com/oldsalbertan
Circulation: 6,900 Frequency: Tuesday
The free newspaper serves the Alberta communities of Olds, Wimborne, Torrington, & Bowden & the surrounding region.
Murray Elliott, Publisher, melliott@olds.greatwest.ca

Oyen: Oyen Echo
PO Box 420 , 109 - 6th Ave. East, Oyen, AB T0J 2J0
Tel: 403-664-3622; Fax: 403-664-3622
www.oyenecho.ca
Frequency: Tuesday

Peace River: Peace River Record-Gazette
Owned By: Sun Media Corp.
10009 - 100 Ave., Peace River, AB T8S 1S6
Tel: 780-624-2591; Fax: 780-624-8600
www.prrecordgazette.com
Circulation: 2,834 Frequency: Tuesday
Scott Fitzpatrick, Publisher

Pincher Creek: Pincher Creek Echo
Owned By: Sun Media Corp.
PO Box 1000 , 714 Main St., Pincher Creek, AB T0K 1W0
Tel: 403-627-3252; Fax: 403-627-3949
www.pinchercreekecho.com
Circulation: 2,432 Frequency: Friday
Kathy Taylor, Publisher

Ponoka: Ponoka News
Owned By: Black Press Group Ltd.
PO Box 4217 , 5019A - 50th Ave., Ponoka, AB T4J 1R6
Tel: 403-783-3311; Fax: 403-783-6300
editorial@ponokanews.com
www.ponokanews.com
Circulation: 6,000 Frequency: Wednesday
Free weekly publication
George Brown, Editor
Judy Dick, Manager, manager@ponokanews.com

Provost: Provost News
PO Box 180 , 5111 - 50th St., Provost, AB T0B 3S0
Tel: 780-753-2564; Fax: 780-753-6117
provost_news@awna.com; advertising@provostnews.ca
www.provostnews.ca
Frequency: Weekly
Richard Holmes, Managing Editor, rcholmes@agt.net
Heather Allen, Contact, Service

Red Deer: Red Deer Express
Owned By: Black Press Group Ltd.
#121, 5301 - 43 St., Red Deer, AB T4N 1C8
Tel: 403-346-3356
advertising@reddeerexpress.com
www.reddeerexpress.com
Social Media: twitter.com/reddeerexpress
www.facebook.com/pages/The-Red-Deer-Express-News-Wire/121
Circulation: 30,000+ Frequency: Wednesday
The Red Deer Express is a community newspaper & online news source that serves Red Deer & central Alberta.
Erin Fawcett, Reporter, efawcett@reddeerexpress.com
Mark Weber, Reporter, mweber@reddeerexpress.com
Karissa Hansen, Contact, Classified Ad Sales, classifieds@reddeerexpress.com

Red Deer: Red Deer Life
2950 Bremner Ave., Red Deer, AB T4R 1M9
Tel: 403-343-2400
www.reddeeradvocate.com
Circulation: 26,000+ Frequency: Sunday
The community newspaper is delivered to homes in Red Deer & rural regions.

Redwater: The Review
Owned By: W & E Cowley Publishing Ltd.
PO Box 850 , 4720 - 50 Ave., Redwater, AB T0A 2W0
Tel: 780-942-2023; Fax: 780-942-2515
redwater@shaw.ca
www.cowleynewspapers.com
Redwater's The Review serves residents in the Counties of Smoky Lake & Thorhild.

Rimbey: Rimbey Review
Owned By: Black Press Group Ltd.
PO Box 244 , 5001 - 50 Ave., Rimbey, AB T0C 2J0
Tel: 403-843-4909
www.rimbeyreview.com
Circulation: 14,500 Frequency: Tuesday
The free community newspaper provides news & information to readers in Rimbey & west central Alberta.
Michele Rosenthal, Publisher, manager@rimbeyreview.com
George Brown, Editor, editor@rimbeyreview.com
Treena Mielke, Reporter, reporter@rimbeyreview.com
Susan Whitecotton, Contact, Classifieds, sales@rimbeyreview.com

Rocky Mountain House: The Mountaineer
4814 - 49 St., Rocky Mountain House, AB T4T 1S8
Tel: 403-845-3334; Fax: 403-845-5570
www.mountaineer.bz
Social Media: twitter.com/RMH_Mountaineer
www.facebook.com/RMHMountaineer
Frequency: Weekly
The newspapers covers news from Clearwater County, the Town of Rocky Mountain House, & the Village of Caroline.
Glen Mazza, Publisher, publish@mountaineer.bz
Stu Salkeld, Editor, editor@mountaineer.bz
Gail Krabben, Manager, Production, production@mountaineer.bz
Dianne McLaren, Manager, Advertising, advertising@mountaineer.bz
Bernie Visotto, Manager, Office, class@mountaineer.bz

Rycroft: The Central Peace Signal
PO Box 250 , Rycroft, AB T0H 3A0
Tel: 780-765-3604
Circulation: 2,722 Frequency: Tuesday
Danny Zahara, Publisher

Sedgewick: The Community Press
PO Box 99 , 4917 - 50 St., Sedgewick, AB T0B 4C0
Tel: 780-385-6693; Fax: 780-385-3107
news@thecommunitypress.com
www.thecommunitypress.com
Other information: Billing, Phone: 780-384-3641; Advertising: ads@thecommunitypress.com
Social Media: twitter.com/CPresstweet
www.facebook.com/pages/The-Community-Press/95868706526?re
Frequency: Weekly
The newspaper serves Alberta's Flagstaff County & the surrounding region. The Community Press is part of a multi-newspaper collective known as Caribou Publishing.
Eric Anderson, Publisher
Leslie Cholowsky, Editor
Jae Robbins, Reporter & Sales Executive
Steven LaFantaisie, Administrator, Classifieds Composition
Karen Ruzicka, Administrator

Sherwood Park: Sherwood Park News
Owned By: Sun Media Corp.
168 Kaska Rd., Sherwood Park, AB T8A 4G7
Tel: 780-464-0033; Fax: 780-464-8512
www.sherwoodparknews.com
Frequency: Tuesday, Friday
The two newspapers, Sherwood Park News & Strathcona County This Week, merged in 2007 to become Sherwood Park - Strathcona County News. The newspaper is a member of Canoe Sun Media Community Newspapers.
Michael Di Massa, Editor, michael.dimassa@sunmedia.ca
Stacey Lozinski, Manager, Regional Sales, stacey@sherwoodparknews.com
Calli Forbes, Reporter, calli.forbes@sunmedia.ca
Ben Proulx, Reporter, ben.proulx@sunmedia.ca
Shane Jones, Sports Reporter, shane.jones@sunmedia.ca
Dawn Zapotoski, Contact, Distribution / Circulation
780-464-0033 ext 262
distribution@sherwoodparknews.com

Slave Lake: Lakeside Leader
PO Box 849 , 103 - 3rd St. NE, Slave Lake, AB T0G 2A0
Tel: 780-849-4380; Fax: 780-849-3903
lsleader@telusplanet.net
www.lakesideleader.com
Mary Burgar, Publisher, spn@cablecomet.com
Joe McWilliams, Editor
Tamara Leslie, Manager, Sales & Production
Caezer Ng, Reporter
Perri Walker, Office Administrator

Slave Lake: Slave Lake Scope
PO Box 1130 , Slave Lake, AB T0G 2A0
Tel: 780-849-4350; Fax: 780-479-8363
Toll-Free: 888-318-5555
scopepub3@shaw.ca
www.slavelakescope.com
Frequency: Weekly

Smoky Lake: Smoky Lake Signal
Owned By: Smoky Signal Press Ltd.
PO Box 328 , 4924 - 50 St., Smoky Lake, AB T0A 3C0
Tel: 780-656-4114; Fax: 780-656-4361
signal@mcsnet.ca
www.smokylake.com
Frequency: Wednesday
Nathan Taylor, Publisher

Spruce Grove: Calmar Community Voice
E.J. Lewchuck & Associates Ltd., PO Box 3595 , Bay C, 45 South Ave., Spruce Grove, AB T7X 3A8
Tel: 780-962-9228; Fax: 780-962-1021
news@com-voice.com
www.com-voice.com
Circulation: 3,000 Frequency: Every other Tue.
Elaine Lewchuck, Publisher

Spruce Grove: Community Voice
c/o E.J. Lewchuck & Associates Ltd., PO Box 3595 Main, 45 South Ave., Bay C, Spruce Grove, AB T7X 3A8
Tel: 780-962-9228; Fax: 780-962-1021
news@com-voice.com; sales@com-voice.com
www.com-voice.com
Other information: Classifieds, Phone: 780-962-9229
Frequency: Weekly

Spruce Grove: The Grove Examiner
Owned By: Sun Media Corp.
75 South Ave., Spruce Grove, AB T7X 3B4
Tel: 780-962-4257; Fax: 780-962-0658
www.sprucegroveexaminer.com
Circulation: 9,342 Frequency: Friday
Rita Sharek, Publisher

Spruce Grove: The Stony Plain Reporter
Owned By: Sun Media Corp.
75 South Ave., Spruce Grove, AB T7X 3B4
Tel: 780-962-4257; Fax: 780-962-0658
www.stonyplainreporter.com
Circulation: 9,636 Frequency: Friday
Inez Scheideman, Publisher

Spruce Grove: Wabamun Community Voice
PO Box 3595 , 45 South Ave., Bay C, Spruce Grove, AB T7X 3A8
Tel: 780-962-9228; Fax: 780-962-1021
news@com-voice.com; sales@com-voice.com
www.com-voice.com
Frequency: Weekly

St Albert: St. Albert Gazette
Owned By: Grest West Newspaper Group Ltd.
340 Carleton Dr., St Albert, AB T8N 7L3
Tel: 780-460-5500; Fax: 780-460-8220
www.stalbertgazette.com
Social Media: twitter.com/StAlbertGazette
Circulation: 44,142 Frequency: Wednesday, Saturday
Brian Bachynski, Publisher, bbachynski@greatwest.ca
John Korobanik, Editor
780-460-5510
jkorobanik@stalbert.greatwest.ca

St Paul: St. Paul Journal
PO Box 159 , 4813 - 50th Ave., St Paul, AB T0A 3A0
Tel: 780-645-3342; Fax: 780-645-2346
www.spjournal.com
Social Media: www.youtube.com/user/JournalStaff
StPaulJournal
www.facebook.com/pages /St-Paul-Journal/312421611441?ref=t

Frequency: Tuesday
The community newspaper provides news & information about the County & Town of St. Paul.
Claire Gauvreau, Publisher, cgauvreau@greatwest.ca
Janani Whitfield, Editor, jwhitfield@stpaul.greatwest.ca
Marge Smith, Manager, Production, msmith@stpaul.greatwest.ca
Claire Turcotte-Joly, Sales Associate, cjoly@stpaul.greatwest.ca
Mandy Paradis, Contact, Circulation & Subscriptions, mparadis@stpaul.greatwest.ca

Stettler: Stettler Independent
Owned By: Prairie Newspaper Group Division of Black Press
PO Box 310 , 4810 - 50th Ave., Stettler, AB T0C 2L0
Tel: 403-742-2395; Fax: 403-742-8050
www.stettlerindependent.com
Frequency: Wednesday
John MacNeil, Editor, editor@stettlerindependent.com
Richard Froese, Reporter, reporter@stettlerindependent.com
Les Stulberg, Reporter, reporter2@stettlerindependent.com
Kaysi Strome, Representative, Sales, sales2@stettlerindependent.com

Strathmore: The Strathmore Standard
Owned By: Sun Media Corp.
136 - 2nd Ave., Strathmore, AB T1P 1K2
Tel: 403-934-3021; Fax: 403-934-5011
www.strathmorestandard.com
Circulation: 5,512 Frequency: Thursday
Gary Hickling, Editor

Sundre: Sundre Round-Up
Owned By: Great West Newspapers, LP
PO Box 599 , 103 - 2 St. NW, Sundre, AB T0M 1X0
Tel: 403-638-3577; Fax: 403-638-3077
www.sundreroundup.ca
Social Media: twitter.com/sundreroundup
Frequency: Tuesday
Sundre Round Up is one of six newspapers published by Mountain View Publishing, which is a subsidiary of Great West Newspapers LP. The newspaper features information from the town of Sundre & the surrounding region in west central Alberta.

Swan Hills: Swan Hills Grizzly Gazette
Owned By: Grizzly Gazette (1990) Inc.
PO Box 1000 , 4924 Plaza Ave., Swan Hills, AB T0G 2C0
Tel: 780-333-2100; Fax: 780-333-2111
sgazette@telusplanet.net
Frequency: Tuesday
Carol Webster, Publisher

Sylvan Lake: Eckville Echo
#103, 5020 - 50A St., Sylvan Lake, AB T4S 1R2
Tel: 403-887-2331; Fax: 403-887-2081
Toll-Free: 888-882-2331
www.eckvilleecho.com
Other information: Toll-Free Fax: 1-888-999-2081
Circulation: 2,500 Frequency: Thursday
Sylvan Lake News Ltd. publishes the Eckville Echo.
Michele Rosenthal, Publisher, publisher@sylvanlakenews.com
Cathy Lange, Manager, sales@eckvilleecho.com
Cheryl Hyvonen, Contact, Front Office, admin@sylvanlakenews.com

Sylvan Lake: Sylvan Lake News
#103, 5020 - 50A St., Sylvan Lake, AB T4S 1R2
Tel: 403-887-2331
www.sylvanlakenews.com
Other information: Classifieds, Phone: 403-309-3300
Circulation: 7,350 Frequency: Friday
News is presented from the town of Sylvan Lake & the surrounding region, from Red Deer to Benalto.
Michele Rosenthal, Publisher, publisher@sylvanlakenews.com
Steve Dills, Editor, editor@sylvanlakenews.com
Cathy Lange, Sales Manager, Classifieds, sales@sylvanlakenews.com
Aleisha Bosch, Reporter, features@sylvanlakenews.com

Taber: The Taber Times
Owned By: Alta Newspaper Group Limited Partnership
4822 - 53 St., Taber, AB T1G 1W4
Tel: 403-223-2266; Fax: 403-223-1408
tabads@my403.com
www.tabertimes.com
Circulation: 3,322 Frequency: Weekly; Wednesday
Garrett Simmons, Editor
403-223-2266
gsimmons@tabertimes.com
Coleen Campbell, Publisher

Three Hills: The Capital
Owned By: Capital Printers Ltd.
411 Main St., Three Hills, AB T0M 2A0
Tel: 403-443-5133; Fax: 403-443-7331
info@threehillscapital.com
www.threehillscapital.com
Frequency: Weekly
The Capital is also available through electronic subscription.
Timothy J. Shearlaw, Publisher & Editor
Jay Shearlaw, Manager, Production
Grant Alford, Reporter & Photographer
Debi Moon, Reporter & Photographer
Barb Widmer, Administrative Clerk

Tofield: Tofield Mercury
PO Box 150 , 5312 - 50th St., Tofield, AB T0B 4J0
Tel: 780-662-4046; Fax: 780-662-3735
adsmercury@gmail.com
www.tofieldmerc.com
Social Media: twitter.com/tofieldmercury
www.facebook.com/pages/Tofield-Mercury/281508 385201719
Circulation: 1,643 Frequency: Tuesday
The newspaper is part of Caribou Publishing. It serves the Alberta communities of Tofield, Ryley, & Holden & the surrounding region.
Kerry Anderson, Publisher
Patricia Harcourt, Editor
Michelle Pinon, Reporter
Michelle Anderson, Administrator, Accounts Payable

Two Hills: Two Hills & County Chronicle
PO Box 668 , 4708 - 50 St., Two Hills, AB T0B 4K0
Tel: 780-657-2524; Fax: 780-657-2534
Circulation: 1,500 Frequency: Tuesday
Ruven Rajoo, Publisher
Sonny Rajoo, Editor

Valleyview: Valley Views
PO Box 787 , 4713 - 50th St., Valleyview, AB T0H 3N0
Tel: 780-524-3490; Fax: 780-524-4545
valleynews@valleyviews.ca
www.valleyviews.ca
Circulation: 1,400 Frequency: Wednesday
Online & print subscriptions are available.
Joan Plaxton, Publisher & Editor
S. Palmer, Manager, Production
Betty Kobe, Manager, Office
Brett Patterson, Reporter

Vauxhall: Vauxhall Advance
Owned By: Alta Newspaper Group Limited Partnership
PO Box 302 , 516 - 2nd Ave. North, Vauxhall, AB T0K 2K0
Tel: 403-654-2122
www.vauxhalladvance.com
Circulation: 865 Frequency: Weekly; Thursday
Coleen Campbell, Publisher

Vegreville: Vegreville News Advertiser
PO Box 810 , 5110 - 50 St., Vegreville, AB T9C 1R9
Tel: 780-632-2861; Fax: 780-632-7981
Toll-Free: 800-522-4127
news@newsadvertiser.com; editor@newsadvertiser.com
www.newsadvertiser.com
Other information: Classifieds, E-mail: ads@newsadvertiser.com
Frequency: Weekly
Dan Beaudette, Publisher & Editor, dan@newsadvertiser.com
Michael Simpson, Editorial Manager, michael@newsadvertiser.com
Brett Ewaschuk, Manager, Production, brett@newsadvertiser.com

Vegreville: Vegreville Observer
PO Box 489 , 5106 - 50 St., Vegreville, AB T9C 1R6
Tel: 780-632-2353; Fax: 780-632-3235
Toll-Free: 800-522-4127
vegrevilleobserver@digitalweb.net
www.vegobserver.com
Frequency: Weekly
Gloria Elly, Office Manager

Vermilion: Vermilion Standard
Owned By: Sun Media Corp.
4917 - 50 Ave., Vermilion, AB T9X 1A6
Tel: 780-853-5344; Fax: 780-853-5203
www.vermilionstandard.com
Circulation: 2,722 Frequency: Tuesday
Dan Macpherson, Publisher and General Manager

Veteran: Veteran Eagle
PO Box 462 , 210 Lucknow St., Veteran, AB T0C 2S0
Tel: 403-575-3892; Fax: 403-575-3938
veteagle@veterancable.net
Social Media: www.facebook.com/pages/Veteran-Eagle/341029685921764
Frequency: Weekly

Viking: The Weekly Review
PO Box 240 , 5311 - 50th St., Viking, AB T0B 4N0
Tel: 780-336-3422; Fax: 780-336-3223
vikingreview@gmail.com
www.weeklyreview.ca
Social Media: twitter.com/vikingweekly
www.facebook.com/pages/Viking-Weekly-Review/1307946669448
Circulation: 1,700 Frequency: Weekly
The newspaper reports on the Alberta communities of Viking, Ryley, Kinsella, Irma, Holden, & Bruce. Both regular & online subscriptions are available. The Weekly Review is part of Caribou Publishing.
Kerry Anderson, Owner & Publisher
Lorraine Poulsen, Managing Editor
Jackie Jeffrey, Manager, Production & Sales

Vulcan: The Vulcan Advocate
Owned By: Sun Media Corp.
112 - 3rd Ave., Vulcan, AB T0L 2B0
Tel: 403-485-2036; Fax: 403-485-6938
www.vulcanadvocate.com
Circulation: 2,095 Frequency: Wednesday
Nancy Middleton, Publisher
Catherine Pooley, Editor, Pooley

Wainwright: Wainwright Edge
Owned By: Star News Inc.
1027 - 3rd Ave., Wainwright, AB T9W 1T6
Tel: 780-842-4465; Fax: 780-842-2760
classifieds@starnews.ca
www.starnews.ca
Circulation: 6,820 Frequency: Friday
Roger Holmes, Publisher, roger@starpress.ca
Patrick Moroz, Associate Publisher & Manager, Sales, patrick@starnews.ca
Kelly Clemmer, Editor-in-Chief, kelly@starnews.ca
Rodney Oracheski, Editor, Sports, rod@starnews.ca
Terry Hunka, Manager, Composition, terry@starnews.ca
Sandy Olejnik, Manager, Finance, sandy@starnews.ca
Carrie Baumgartner, Graphic Designer, carrie@starnews.ca
Sherry Schatz, Contact, Sales & Promotions, sherry@starnews.ca

Wainwright: Wainwright Star
Owned By: Star News Inc.
1027 - 3rd Ave., Wainwright, AB T9W 1T6
Tel: 780-842-4465; Fax: 780-842-2760
info@starnews.ca; classifieds@starnews.ca
www.starnews.ca
Frequency: Tuesday
Rogers Holmes, Publisher, roger@starpress.ca
Patrick Moroz, Associate Publisher & Sales Manager, patrick@starnews.ca
Kelly Clemmer, Editor-in-Chief, kelly@starnews.ca
Rodney Oracheski, Sports Editor, rod@starnews.ca
Terry Hunka, Manager, Composition, terry@starnews.ca
Sandy Olejnik, Manager, Finance, sandy@starnews.ca
Carrie Baumgartner, Graphic Designer, carrie@starnews.ca

Westlock: Westlock News
Owned By: Great West Newspapers, LP
9871 - 107th St., Westlock, AB T7P 1R9
Tel: 780-349-3033; Fax: 780-349-3677
www.westlocknews.com
Social Media: www.youtube.com/user/WestlockNews
twitter.com/westlocknews
www.faceboo k.com/pages/Westlock-News/130628693670762
Circulation: 3,850 Frequency: Weekly
The town & county of Westlock & the village of Clyde are served by the newspaper.
George Blais, Publisher
Tim Bryant, Reporter
Doug Neuman, Reporter
Anne Baxandall, Contact, Advertising
Shawna Mayne, Contact, Production
Carol Van Ruskenveld, Contact, Front Office

Wetaskiwin: The Wetaskiwin Times
Owned By: Sun Media Corp.
5013 - 51rd St., Wetaskiwin, AB T9A 1L4
Tel: 780-352-2231; Fax: 780-352-4333
www.wetaskiwintimes.com
Circulation: 10,316 Frequency: Monday

Brian Bentt, Publisher

Whitecourt: Maythorpe Freelancer
Owned By: Sun Media Corp.
PO Box 630 , 4732 - 50 Ave., Whitecourt, AB T7S 1N7
Tel: 780-778-3977; Fax: 780-778-6459
www.mayerthorpefreelancer.com
Circulation: 1,254 Frequency: Wednesday
Jim Gray, Publisher

Whitecourt: The Whitecourt Star
Owned By: Sun Media Corp.
PO Box 630 , 4732 - 50th Ave., Whitecourt, AB T7S 1N7
Tel: 780-778-3977; Fax: 780-778-6459
www.whitecourtstar.com
Circulation: 2,844 Frequency: Wednesday
Pam Allain, Publisher

British Columbia

Daily Newspapers in British Columbia

Burnaby: Metro Vancouver
Head Office
4330 Kingsway, Burnaby, BC V5H 4G8
Tel: 604-602-1002; Fax: 866-254-6504
www.metrovancouver.org
Circulation: 145,000
Mary Kemmis, Publisher/Managing Director

Dawson Creek: Dawson Creek Daily News
Previous Name: Peace River Block News
Owned By: Glacier Media Inc.
901 - 100th Ave., Dawson Creek, BC V1G 1W2
Tel: 250-782-4888; Fax: 250-782-6770
www.dawsoncreekdailynews.ca
Social Media:
twitter.com/DawsonCreekNews
www.facebook.com/pages/Dawson-Creek-Daily-News/2011033299
Circulation: 1,900
Alison McMeans, Managing Editor, editor@dcdn.ca
Rick Sadick, Director, Advertising, rsadick@dcdn.ca
Margot Owens, Manager, Circulation, circulation@dcdn.ca
Rick Davison, Assistant Editor, Sports, sports@dcdn.ca
Megan Gorecki, Assistant Editor, News, news@dcdn.ca
Tracy Keller, Supervisor, Composition, compose@dcdn.ca

Fort St. John: Alaska Highway News
Owned By: Glacier Media Inc.
9916 - 98th St., Fort St. John, BC V1J 3T8
Tel: 250-785-5631; Fax: 250-785-3522
circulation@ahnfsj.ca
www.alaskahighwaynews.ca
Social Media:
twitter.com/AHNnewspaper
www.facebook.com/pages/Alaska-Highway-News/20106280659083
Circulation: 4,400
The Alaska Highway News covers Fort St. John, Farmington, Cecil Lake, Baldonnel, Goodlow, Hudson's Hope, Charlie Lake, Taylor, Montney, Rose Prairie, & North Pine.
Alison McMeans, Managing Editor, editor@ahnfsj.ca
Ryan Wallace, Manager, Advertising, rwallace@ahnfsj.ca
Aleisha Hendry, Assistant Editor, ahendry@ahnfsj.ca
Lynn Novack, Contact, Classified Ads & Circulation, classifieds@ahnfsj.ca

Kamloops: The Daily News
Owned By: Glacier Media Inc.
393 Seymour St., Kamloops, BC V2C 6P6
Tel: 250-372-2331; Fax: 250-372-0823
circulation@kamloopsnews.ca
www.kamloopsnews.ca
Other information: News: kamloopsnews@telus.net; Advertising: sales@kamloopsnews.ca
Social Media:
twitter.com/kamnews
www.facebook.com/kamnews?v=wall&ref=ts
Circulation: 12,237
The Daily News of Kamloops is available in print & online. In addition to local news, specialized content includes Real Estate Weekly, Motoring, Spotlight, & Variety.
Tim Shoults, Publisher
250-371-6100
tshoults@kamloopsnews.ca
Mel Rothenburger, Editor
250-371-6152
mrothenburger@kamloopsnews.ca
Mike Cornell, Editor, News
250-371-6145
Gregg Drinnan, Editor, Sports
250-371-6154
Mark Rogers, Editor, New Media
250-371-6149
Kevin Dergez, Director, Advertising
250-371-6128
kdergez@kamloopsnews.ca
Rick Major, Director, Reader Sales & Services
250-371-6176
rmajor@kamloopsnews.ca

Kelowna: The Daily Courier
Owned By: Continental Newspapers Canada Ltd.
550 Doyle Ave., Kelowna, BC V1Y 7V1
Tel: 250-762-4445; Fax: 250-762-3866
Toll-Free: 800-585-7653
letters@ok.bc.ca; city.desk@ok.bc.ca(news tips)
www.kelownadailycourier.ca
Other information: Classifieds, Phone: 250-763-3228; Circulation: 250-763-4000
Social Media:
twitter.com/KelownaCourier
www.facebook.com/KelownaDailyCourier
The Daily Courier is distributed Monday to Friday, & the Okanagan Saturday & the Okanagan Sunday are distributed on weekends.
Terry Armstrong, Group Publisher
250-470-0721
terry.armstrong@ok.bc.ca
Willy Kerntopf, Vice-President, Operations
250-470-0705
willy.kerntopf@ok.bc.ca
Jon Manchester, Managing Editor
250-470-0741
jon.manchester@ok.bc.ca
Pat Bulmer, City Editor
250-470-0739
pat.bulmer@ok.bc.ca
David Wylie, Night Editor
250-470-0778
david.wylie@ok.bc.ca
Brenda Babinski, Director, Human Resources
250-470-0760
brenda.babinski@ok.bc.ca
Krista Frasz, Director, Advertising
250-470-0761
krista.frasz@ok.bc.ca
John Park, Director, Circulation
250-470-0795
john.park@ok.bc.ca
Michael Grundy, Manager, Business
250-470-0776
michael.grundy@ok.bc.ca

Kimberley: The Daily Bulletin
335 Spokane St., Kimberley, BC V1A 1Y9
Tel: 250-427-5333; Fax: 250-427-5336
bulletin@cyberlink.bc.ca
www.dailybulletin.ca
Social Media:
www.facebook.com/TownsmanBulletin
Circulation: 1,660
Karen Johnston, Publisher
Carolyn Grant, Editor Editor
Nicole Koran, Contact, Advertising, bulletinads@cyberlink.bc.ca

Nanaimo: Nanaimo Daily News
Owned By: Glacier Media Inc.
#B1, 2575 McCullough Rd., Nanaimo, BC V9S 5W5
Tel: 250-729-4200
circulation@nanaimodailynews.com
www.nanaimodailynews.com
Other information: Subscription & delivery enquiries, Phone: 250-729-4266
Social Media:
twitter.com/NanaimoDaily
www.facebook.com/pages/Nanaimo-Daily-News/150301821648264
Circulation: 6,325
The Nanaimo Daily News serves central Vancouver Island.
Hugh Nicholson, Publisher, HNicholson@glaciermedia.ca
Cale Cowan, Managing Editor, CCowan@nanaimodailynews.com
Josh Aldrich, Editor, Sports, JAldrich@nanaimodailynews.com
Dustin Walker, Editor, Digital, DWalker@nanaimodailynews.com
Paul Walton, Editor, News, PWalton@nanaimodailynews.com
Lynn Welburn, Editor, Entertainment, LWelburn@nanaimodailynews.com
Rachel Mason, Manager, Business, RMason@nanaimodailynews.com
Andrea Rosato-Taylor, Manager, Advertising, ARosato-Taylor@nanaimodailynews.com
Trixi Agrios, Director, Classified Advertising, classifieds@van.net
Les Gould, Director, Reader Sales, LGould@nanaimodailynews.com

Penticton: Penticton Herald
Previous Name: Penticton Press
Owned By: Continental Newspapers Canada Ltd.
#101, 186 Nanaimo Ave. West, Penticton, BC V2A 1N4
Tel: 250-492-4002; Fax: 250-492-2403
www.pentictonherald.ca
Other information: Classified, Phone: 250-493-4332; Circulation: 250-493-6737
Social Media:
twitter.com/pentictonherald
www.facebook.com/pentictonherald
The Herald is delivered Monday to Friday. The Okanagan, which is published jointly with The Daily Courier of Kelowna, is delivered on Saturday & Sunday.
André Martin, General Manager & Contact, Online Advertising, andre.martin@pentictonherald.ca
James Miller, Managing Editor, editor@pentictonherald.ca
Cherie Morgan, General Manager, Accounting, cherie.morgan@pentictonherald.ca
Shannon Huggard, Manager, Circulation, cherie.morgan@pentictonherald.ca
John Moorhouse, Reporter, News, john.moorhouse@pentictonherald.ca
David Crompton, Reporter, Sports, david.crompton@pentictonherald.ca

Port Alberni: Alberni Valley Times
Owned By: Glacier Media Inc.
4918 Napier St., Port Alberni, BC V9Y 3H5
Tel: 250-723-8171; Fax: 250-723-0586
news@avtimes.net
www.avtimes.net
Social Media:
twitter.com/albernitimes
www.facebook.com/AVTimes?sk=wall
Circulation: 4,600 M-Th; 5,900 F
The newspaper reaches communities in the Alberni Valley on Vancouver Island Monday to Friday.
Cale Cowan, Managing Editor, CCowan@avtimes.net
Cindy Donovan, Manager, Production, CDonovan@avtimes.net
Debbie Reid, Manager, Business, DReid@avtimes.net
Pam Craig, Contact, Display Ads, PCraig@avtimes.net
John Richardson, Contact, Circulation & Subscriptions, JRichardson@avtimes.net
Heather Thomson, Contact, News & Sports, HThomson@avtimes.net

Prince George: Prince George Citizen
Owned By: Glacier Interactve Media
PO Box 5700 , 150 Brunswick St., Prince George, BC V2L 5K9
Tel: 250-562-2441; Fax: 250-562-7453
info@pgcitizen.ca
www.princegeorgecitizen.com
Social Media:
twitter.com/pgcitizen
www.facebook.com/pages/the-Prince-George-Cit izen/30700145
Circulation: 16,011 Frequency: Monday
Del Laverdure, Publisher

Trail: Trail Daily Times
1163 Cedar Ave., Trail, BC V1R 4B8
Tel: 250-368-8551
newsroom@traildailytimes.ca
www.traildailytimes.ca
Social Media:
twitter.com/traildailytimes
www.facebook.com/pages/Trail-Daily-Times/138 321642898882
The British Columbia communities of Trail, Rossland, Montrose, Warfiels, & Fruitvale are served by the newspaper.
Barb Blatchford, Publisher & Sales Manager, publisher@trailtimes.ca
Guy Bertrand, Editor, editor@trailtimes.ca
Michelle Bedford, Manager, Circulation, circulation@trailtimes.ca
Tammy Crockett, Office Manager, accounting@trailtimes.ca
Jim Bailey, Reporter, sports@trailtimes.ca
Val Rossi, Reporter, newsroom@trailtimes.ca
Jeanine Margoreeth, Contact, Classifieds, nationals@trailtimes.ca

Vancouver: The Province
Owned By: Postmedia Network Inc.
#1, 200 Granville St., Vancouver, BC V6C 3N3
Tel: 604-605-2000; Fax: 604-605-2914
Toll-Free: 800-663-2662
subscribe@theprovince.com; tabtips@theprovince.com
www.theprovince.com
Other information: Letters to the Editor, E-mail: provletters@theprovince.com
Social Media: www.youtube.com/theprovinceonline
twitter.com/theprovince
www.faceb ook.com/TheProvince
The Province is a tabloid that publishes daily, except for Saturdays & holidays.
Wayne Moriarty, Editor-in-chief

Vancouver: Sing Tao Daily
Owned By: Torstar Corporation
1296 Kingsway, Vancouver, BC V5V 3E1
news.singtao.ca
News is presented in Cantonese for Chinese Canadians.
Amy Mui, Contact, Advertising, amui@singtao.ca

Vancouver: The Vancouver Sun
Pacific Newspaper Group Inc., #1, 200 Granville St., Vancouver, BC V6C 3N3
Tel: 604-605-2000; Fax: 604-605-2914
Toll-Free: 800-663-2662
sunnewstips@vancouversun.com
www.vancouversun.com
Social Media: pinterest.com/vancouversun
twitter.com/VanSunReporters/vancouver-sun- master-list
www.facebook.com/pages/The-Vancouver-Sun/7116517082
Circulation: 161,000 Mon.-Thu., 174,000 Fri., 57,669 Sat.-Sun.
Frequency: Morning
Dennis Skulsky, Publisher
Patricia Graham, Editor-in-chief

Victoria: Times Colonist
Previous Name: British Colonist; Victoria Daily Times
Owned By: Glacier Media Inc.
2621 Douglas St., Victoria, BC V8T 4M2
Tel: 250-380-5211; Fax: 250-380-5353
Toll-Free: 800-663-6384
customerservice@timescolonist.com
www.timescolonist.com
Other information: Classified Inquiries, E-mail: classified@timescolonist.com
Social Media:
twitter.com/timescolonist
www.facebook.com/timescolonist
Circulation: 57,367 Tu, W, Th, Sa, Su; 61,414 F
The Times Colonist appears in print Tuesday to Sunday, & news is available onine each day.
Bob McKenzie, Publisher
250-380-5202
bmckenzie@timescolonist.com
Dave Obee, Editor-in-Chief
250-380-5201
dobee@timescolonist.com
Brian Drewry, Editor, Sports
250-380-5344
bdrewry@timescolonist.com
Phil Jang, Editor, News
250-995-4443
pjang@timescolonist.com
Darron Kloster, Editor, Business
250-380-5235
dkloster@timescolonist.com
Bruce MacKenzie, Editor, City
250-380-5314
dpaulson@timescolonist.com
Dave Paulson, Editor, Features
250-380-5346
dpaulson@timescolonist.com
Bruce Cousins, Director, Reader Sales & Service
250-380-5274
bcousins@timescolonist.com
Steve Majorki, Director, Production
250-995-4417
smajorki@timescolonist.com
Catherine McConnell, Director, Finance
250-995-4426
cmcconnell@timescolonist.com
Jim Ritchie, Director, Human Resources
250-995-4432
jritchie@timescolonist.com
David Whitman, Director, Advertising
250-380-5289
dwhitman@timescolonist.com
Shannon Kowalko, Manager, Marketing & Promotions
250-380-5379
skowalko@timescolonist.com

Other Newspapers in British Columbia

100 Mile House: 100 Mile House Free Press
Owned By: Black Press Group Ltd.
PO Box 459 , 100 Mile House, BC V0K 2E3
Tel: 250-395-2219; Fax: 250-395-3939
www.100milefreepress.net
Social Media:
twitter.com/100mile
www.facebook.com/pages/100-Mile-Free-Press/117 25299835404
Frequency: Wednesday
The 100 Mile House Free Press covers the South Cariboo region, from Lac la Hache to Clinton.
Chris Nickless, Publisher & Manager, Sales, publisher@100milefreepress.net
Ken Alexander, Editor, newsroom@100milefreepress.net
Heather Nelson, Contact, Advertising Sales, heather@100milefreepress.net

Abbotsford: Abbotsford News
34375 Gladys Ave., Abbotsford, BC V2S 2H5
Tel: 604-853-1144
newsroom@abbynews.com; publisher@abbynews.com
www.abbynews.com
Social Media:
twitter.com/abbynews
www.facebook.com/myabbynews
Full printed editions of the newspaper are also available online.
Andrew Franklin, Publisher, publisher@abbynews.com
Andrew Holota, Editor, newsroom@abbynews.com
Alana Green, Manager, Creative Services, alana@abbynews.com
Kevin Hemery, Manager, Circulation, circulation@abbynews.com
Jenn Schotts, Assistant Manager, Advertising, jenn@abbynews.com

Abbotsford: Abbotsford Times
Owned By: Glacier Media Inc.
30887 Peardonville Rd., Abbotsford, BC V2T 6K2
Tel: 604-854-5244; Fax: 604-854-5541
editorial@abbotsfordtimes.com
www.abbotsfordtimes.com
Other information: Classified Ads: classified@abbotsfordtimes.com
Circulation: 45,409 Frequency: Semi-weekly
Local news from Abbottsford & Mission, British Columbia is covered.
Darren McDonald, Editor, dmcdonald@abbotsfordtimes.com
Shaulene Burket, Contact, Advertising, sburkett@abbotsfordtimes.com
Jean Konda-Witte, Contact, Photography, Jkonda-Witte@abbotsfordtimes.com

Agassiz: Agassiz-Harrison Observer
Owned By: Black Press Group Ltd.
PO Box 129 , 7167 Pioneer Ave., Agassiz, BC V0M 1A0
Tel: 604-796-4300
ads@ahobserver.com
www.agassizharrisonobserver.com
Social Media:
twitter.com/agassizobserver
www.facebook.com/AgassizHarrisonObserver
Circulation: 6,000+ Frequency: Friday
Community news from Agassiz, Harrison Hot Springs, & Hope, is featured in the newspaper.
Andrew Franklin, Publisher, publisher@abbynews.com
Jessica Peters, Editor, news@ahobserver.com
Chris Blank, Manager, Sales, ads@ahobserver.com

Aldergrove: Aldergrove Star
Previous Name: Aldergrove Echo
Owned By: Black Press Group Ltd.
27118 Fraser Hwy., Aldergrove, BC V4W 3P6
Tel: 604-856-8303
newsroom@aldergrovestar.com
www.aldergrovestar.com
Social Media:
twitter.com/aldergrovestar
www.facebook.com/pages/Aldergrove-Star/186177 368124190
Circulation: 11,000 Frequency: Weekly
Dwayne Weidendorf, Publisher, publisher@aldergrovestar.com
Kurt Langmann, Editor & Columnist
Janice Reid, Sales Consultant, sales@aldergrovestar.com

Armstrong: Okanagan Advertiser
PO Box 610 , 3400 Okanagan St., Armstrong, BC V0E 1B0
Tel: 250-546-3121
subscribe@okadvertiser.com
www.okanaganadvertiser.com
Other information: Enderby Office, Phone: 250-838-6017
Frequency: Wednesday
The Okanagan Advertiser serves the British Columbia communities of Armstrong, Enderby, & the Spallumcheen Valley.

Ashcroft: Ashcroft-Cache Creek Journal
Previous Name: The Ashcroft Journal; British Columbia Mining Journal
Owned By: Black Press Group Ltd.
PO Box 190 , 130 - 4th St., Ashcroft, BC V0K 1A0
Tel: 250-453-2261
editorial@accjournal.ca
www.ash-cache-journal.com
Social Media:
twitter.com/ashcroftnews
www.facebook.com/group.php?gid=272576022776823
Frequency: Weekly
Subscriptions are available for print & the online edition.
Terry Daniels, Publisher & Contact, Sales, sales@accjournal.ca
Wendy Coomber, Editor, editorial@accjournal.ca
Anne Blake, Contact, Production, production@accjournal.ca

Barriere: Barriere Star Journal
Previous Name: Barriere Bulletin
Owned By: Black Press Group Ltd.
PO Box 1020 , Barriere, BC V0E 1E0
Tel: 250-672-5611
news@starjournal.net
www.starjournal.net
Social Media:
twitter.com/barrierenews
www.facebook.com/pages/Barriere-Star-Jour nal/233231670068
Frequency: Monday
Al Kirkwood, Publisher & Manager, Sales, al@starjournal.net
Jill Hayward, Editor, news@starjournal.net
Margaret Houben, Reporter, Classified Manager, & Office Clerk, office@starjournal.net

Bowen Island: Undercurrent
Owned By: Black Press Group Ltd.
PO Box 130 , Bowen Island, BC V0N 1G0
Tel: 604-947-2442
www.bowenislandundercurrent.com
Social Media:
www.facebook.com/pages/Bowen-Island-Undercurrent/2920532 0
Circulation: 949 Frequency: Friday
A print edition & e-edition of the newspaper are available.
Susanne Martin, Editor, editor@bowenislandundercurrent.com
Janis Treleaven, Contact, Ad Sales, ads@bowenislandundercurrent.com

Burnaby: Burnaby NewsLeader
Owned By: Black Press Group Ltd.
7438 Fraser Park Dr., Burnaby, BC V5J 5B9
Tel: 604-438-6397
newsroom@burnabynewsleader.com
www.burnabynewsleader.com
Social Media:
twitter.com/burnabynews
www.facebook.com/burnabynews
Frequency: Wednesday, Friday
The newspaper publishes a print & online edition.
Jean Hincks, Publisher, publisher@burnabynewsleader.com
Chris Bryan, Editor & Columnist, editor@burnabynewsleader.com
Mario Bartel, Web Editor & Photographer, photo@burnabynewsleader.com

Burnaby: Burnaby Now
Owned By: Glacier Media Inc.
#201A, 3430 Brighton Ave., Burnaby, BC V5A 3H4
Tel: 604-444-3451
distribution@burnabynow.com
www.burnabynow.com
Other information: Production Department, E-mail: production@burnabynow.com
Frequency: Wednesday, Friday
Brad Alden, Publisher
604-444-3010
Pat Tracy, Editor
604-444-3007
editorial@burnabynow.com
Lara Graham, Contact, Advertising
604-444-3030

Burnaby: The Now
Owned By: Glacier Media Inc.
#201A, 3430 Brighton Ave., Burnaby, BC V5A 3H4
Tel: 604-444-3451
distribution@thenownews.com
www.thenownews.com
Other information: Classified Advertising, E-mail: classified@van.net
Circulation: 53,016 Frequency: Wednesday, Friday
News is provided for the British Columbia communities of Coquitlam, Anmore, Port Moody, Port Coquitlam, & Belcarra.
Brad Alden, Publisher
604-444-3010
publisher@thenownews.com
Leneen Robb, Editor
604-444-3090
editorial@thenownews.com
Gary Slavin, Manager, Production
604-444-3039
gslavin@van.net
Catherine Ackerman, Contact, Advertising
604-444-3070
cackerman@thenownews.com

Burnaby: The Record
Owned By: Glacier Media Inc.
#201A, 3430 Brighton Ave., Burnaby, BC V5A 3H4
Tel: 604-444-3451; Fax: 604-444-3460
production@royalcityrecord.com
www.royalcityrecord.com
Other information: Classified, Phone: 604-444-3000; Circulation: 604-942-3081
Social Media:
twitter.com/TheRecord
www.facebook.com/RoyalCityRecord
Circulation: 16,000+ Frequency: Wednesday, Friday
The community newspaper focuses upon New Westminster, British Columbia.
Brad Alden, Publisher
604-444-3010
Pat Tracy, Editor
604-444-3007
editorial@royalcityrecord.com
Lara Graham, Contact, Advertising
604-444-3030
display@royalcityrecord.com

Burns Lake: Lakes District News
PO Box 309 , 23 - 3rd Ave., Burns Lake, BC V0J 1E0
Tel: 250-692-7526
newsroom@ldnews.net
www.ldnews.net
Social Media:
twitter.com/burnslakenews
www.facebook.com/pages/Lakes-District-News/150 52412501865
Circulation: 1,800 Frequency: Wednesday
Laura Blackwell, Publisher & Contact, Advertising, laura@ldnews.net

Campbell River: Campbell River Mirror
Owned By: Black Press Group Ltd.
#104, 250 Dogwood St., Campbell River, BC V9W 5Z5
Tel: 250-287-9227
editor@campbellrivermirror.com
www.campbellrivermirror.com
Social Media:
twitter.com/crmirror
www.facebook.com/pages/Campbell-River-Mirror/251551 478191
Circulation: 16,000+ Frequency: Semi-weekly
News is presented from Campbell River & the central region of Vancouver Island. The newspaper is available in print & as an e-edition.
Zena Williams, Publisher, publisher@campbellrivermirror.com
Alistair Taylor, Managing Editor, editor@campbellrivermirror.com
Paul Rudan, News Editor & Columnist, paulr@campbellrivermirror.com
Shelley Quewezance, Manager, Circulation, circulation@campbellrivermirror.com
Kristen Douglas, Reporter, Photographer, & Columnist, kristend@campbellrivermirror.com

Campbell River: Courier-Islander
Owned By: Glacier Media Inc.
1040 Cedar St., Campbell River, BC V9W 5B5
Tel: 250-287-7464; Fax: 250-287-8891
classifieds@van.net
www.courierislander.com
Social Media:
twitter.com/courierislander
Frequency: Wednesday, Friday
Neil Cameron, Publisher & Editor, editor@courierislander.com
Marilyn Kirby, Manager, Business & Circulation, mkirkby@courierislander.com
Paul Somerville, Manager, Advertising, psomerville@courierislander.com

Castlegar: Castlegar News
Owned By: Black Press Group Ltd.
#2, 1810 - 8th Ave., Castlegar, BC V1N 2Y4
Tel: 250-365-6397
newsroom@castlegarnews.com
www.castlegarnews.com
Social Media:
twitter.com/castlegarnews
www.facebook.com/castlegarnews
Circulation: 6,537 Frequency: Thursday
A print edition & an e-edition are available. The free newspaper is distributed from Genelle to Playmor Junction, British Columbia.
Chris Hopkyns, Publisher, publisher@castlegarnews.com
Jim Sinclair, Editor
Cindy Amaral, Manager, Production, creative@castlegarnews.com
Theresa Hodge, Manager, Office, classifieds@castlegarnews.com
Craig Lindsay, Reporter, reporter@castlegarnews.com

Chetwynd: Chetwynd Echo
5016 - 50th Ave., Chetwynd, BC V0C 1J0
Tel: 250-788-2246
editor@chetwyndecho.net
www.chetwyndecho.net
Social Media:
twitter.com/ChetwyndEcho
www.facebook.com/pages/Chetwynd-Echo/1618 98250528779
Frequency: Weekly
The newspaper is available in print & online.

Chilliwack: Chilliwack Progress
Owned By: Black Press Group Ltd.
45860 Spadina Ave., Chilliwack, BC V2P 6H9
Tel: 604-702-5550
www.theprogress.com
Social Media:
twitter.com/theprogress
www.facebook.com/chilliwackprogress
Liz Lynch, Publisher, publisher@theprogress.com
Gregg Knill, Editor & Columnist, editor@theprogress.com
Jenna Hauck, Photojournalist, photo@theprogress.com
Louise Meger, Contact, Circulation, circulation@theprogress.com

Chilliwack: Chilliwack Times
Owned By: Glacier Media Inc.
45951 Tretheway Ave., Chilliwack, BC V2P 1K4
Tel: 604-792-9117; Fax: 604-792-9300
editorial@chilliwacktimes.com
www.chilliwacktimes.com
Other information: Classifieds, Phone: 604-795-4417
Social Media:
twitter.com/chilliwacktimes
www.facebook.com/ChilliwackTimes
Frequency: Tuesday, Thursday
Ken Goudswaard, Editor, kgoudswaard@chilliwacktimes.com
Nick Bastaja, Contact, Advertising, nbastaja@chilliwacktimes.com
Lisa Ellis, Contact, Distribution, Lellis@chilliwacktimes.com

Clearwater: North Thompson Times
Owned By: Black Press Group Ltd.
Brookfield Mall, #14, 74 Young Rd., Clearwater, BC V0E 1N1
Tel: 250-674-3343
newsroom@clearwatertimes.com
www.clearwatertimes.com
Social Media:
twitter.com/clearwaternews
www.facebook.com/pages/Clearwater-Times/30206 6023142345
Circulation: 1,250 Frequency: Monday
The weekly community newspaper covers events in Clearwater, Upper Clearwater, Wells Gray Park, Blue River, Roundtop, Avola, East Blackpool, Vavenby, & Birch Island, British Columbia.
Al Kirkwood, Publisher & Manager, Sales, classifieds@clearwatertimes.com
Keith McNeill, Editor, newsroom@clearwatertimes.com
Tom Fletcher, Columnist, tfletcher@blackpress.ca
Yevonne Cline, Contact, Classified, classifieds@clearwatertimes.com

Courtenay: Comox Valley Echo
Owned By: Glacier Media Inc.
407D - 5th St., Courtenay, BC V9N 1J7
Tel: 250-334-4722; Fax: 250-334-3172
echo@comoxvalleyecho.com
www.comoxvalleyecho.com
Social Media:
twitter.com/comoxvalleyecho
www.facebook.com/ComoxValleyEcho?v=wal l
Circulation: 22,948 Frequency: Tuesday, Friday
The newspaper covers the Vancouver Island communities of Courtenay, Cumberland, Comox, Black Creek, Denman, Merville, Fanny Bay, Royston, & the Hornby Islands.
Dave MacDonald, Publisher, dvmac@comoxvalleyecho.com
Debra Martin, Editor, dmartin@comoxvalleyecho.com
Keith Currie, Manager, Advertising Sales, kcurrie@comoxvalleyecho.com
Deb Fowler, Manager, Business, dfowler@comoxvalleyecho.com
Ryan Getz, Manager, Production, rgetz@comoxvalleyecho.com
Hedi MacDonald, Manager, Circulation, circ@comoxvalleyecho.com

Courtenay: Comox Valley Record
Owned By: Black Press Group Ltd.
765 McPhee Ave., Courtenay, BC V9N 2Z7
Tel: 250-338-5811
editor@comoxvalleyrecord.com
www.comoxvalleyrecord.com
Social Media:
twitter.com/cvrecord
www.facebook.com/pages/Comox-Valley-Record-Newsroom /17335
Frequency: Semi-weekly
The newspaper is available in print & online.
Joanna Ross, Publisher, salesmgr@comoxvalleyrecord.com
Mark Allan, Editor & Columnist, editor@comoxvalleyrecord.com
Earle Couper, Editor, Sports, sports@comoxvalleyrecord.com
Erin Haluschak, Photographer & Reporter, photos@comoxvalleyrecord.com
Susan Granberg, Manager, Production, production@comoxvalleyrecord.com
Terry Marshall, Contact, Circulation, circulation@comoxvalleyrecord.com

Cranbrook: Cranbrook Daily Townsman
Previous Name: Cranbrook Courier
822 Cranbrook St. North, Cranbrook, BC V1C 3R9
Tel: 250-426-5201; Fax: 250-426-5003
advertising@dailytownsman.com
www.dailytownsman.com
Social Media:
www.facebook.com/TownsmanBulletin
Frequency: Monday - Friday
The Wednesday newspaper is distributed to communities throughout British Columbia's Columbia Valley.
Karen Johnston, Publisher
Barry Coulter, Editor
250-426-5201 ext 210
barry@dailytownsman.com
Jenny Leiman, Manager, Office
Dan Mills, Representative, Advertising
Trevor Crawley, Contact, Sports
Stephanie Bennett, Contact, Circulation

Cranbrook: Kootenay News Advertiser
Owned By: Black Press Group Ltd.
1510 - 2nd St. North, Cranbrook, BC V1C 3L2
Tel: 250-489-3455
editor@kootenayadvertiser.com
www.kootenayadvertiser.com
Social Media:
twitter.com/cranbrooknews
www.facebook.com/pages/Kootenay-News-Advertise r/110173431
Circulation: 22,744
Darcy Wiebe, Publisher, darcy@kootenayadvertiser.com

Creston: Creston Valley Advance
Owned By: Black Press Group Ltd.
PO Box 1279 , 1018 Canyon St., Creston, BC V0B 1G0
Tel: 250-428-2266; Fax: 250-428-3320
editor@crestonvalleyadvance.ca
www.crestonvalleyadvance.ca
Social Media:
twitter.com/crestonadvance
www.facebook.com/cvadvance?v=wall
Circulation: 3,500 Frequency: Weekly
Serving the communities of Creston, Erickson, Lister, Canyon, Yahk, West Creston and Wynndel, as well as the East Shore of Kootenay Lake.
Brian Lawrence, Editor, editor@crestonvalleyadvance.ca

Lorne Eckersley, Publisher, publisher@crestonvalleyadvance.ca

Delta: South Delta Leader
Owned By: Black Press Group Ltd.
#7, 1363 - 56 St., Delta, BC V4L 2P7
Tel: 604-948-3640
editor@southdeltaleader.com
www.southdeltaleader.com
Social Media:
twitter.com/sdleader
www.facebook.com/sdleader
Circulation: 16,500 Frequency: Friday
The community newspaper is available in print & online. The print edition is delivered to homes & businesses in Tsawwassen, Ladner, & Tilbury, British Columbia.
Chrissie Bowker, Publisher, publisher@southdeltaleader.com
Philip Raphael, Editor
Kristine Salzmann, Reporter, reporter@southdeltaleader.com
Jane Ilott, Contact
Sarah Kelloway, Contact, Creative Services

Duncan: Cowichan News Leader
Owned By: Black Press Group Ltd.
#2, 5380 Trans Canada Hwy., Duncan, BC V9L 6W4
Tel: 250-746-4471
www.cowichannewsleader.com
Social Media:
twitter.com/duncannews
www.facebook.com/group.php?gid=196266000414293
News & information is provided about British Columbia's Cowichan Valley.
Bill Macadam, Publisher & Sales Manager, publisher@cowichannewsleader.com
John McKinley, Managing Editor, editor@cowichannewsleader.com
Don Bodger, Sports Editor, sports@cowichannewsleader.com
Lara Stuart, Manager, Circulation, circulation@cowichannewsleader.com
Andrew Leong, Photographer
Kim Sayer, Office Supervisor, office@cowichannewsleader.com

Duncan: Cowichan News Leader Pictorial
Owned By: Black Press Group Ltd.
#2, 5380 Trans Canada Hwy., Duncan, BC V9L 6W4
Tel: 250-746-4471; Fax: 250-746-8529
editor@cowichannewsleader.com
www.cowichannewsleader.com
Social Media:
twitter.com/duncannews
www.facebook.com/group.php?gid=196266000414293
Circulation: 21,423 W; 23,406 F; 44,829 total Frequency: Wednesday, Friday
The newspaper covers Vancouver Island's Cowichan Valley.
Bill Macadam, Publisher & Manager, Sales, publisher@cowichannewsleader.com
John McKinley, Managing Editor
Don Bodger, Editor, Sports, sports@cowichannewsleader.com
Lara Stuart, Manager, Circulation, circulation@cowichannewsleader.com
Kim Sayer, Supervisor, Office, office@cowichannewsleader.com

Fernie: Fernie Free Press
Owned By: Black Press Group Ltd.
PO Box 2350 , Fernie, BC V0B 1M0
Tel: 250-423-4666; Fax: 250-423-3110
Toll-Free: 866-337-6437
freepres@shawcable.com
www.thefreepress.ca
Social Media:
twitter.com/FernieFreePress
www.facebook.com/freepressbc
Circulation: 1,851 Frequency: Weekly; Thursday
Serves Elkford, Fernie, Sparwood and the South Country.
Dave Hamilton, Publisher, publisher@thefreepress.ca

Fort Nelson: Fort Nelson News
PO Box 600 , #3, 4448 - 50th Ave. North, Fort Nelson, BC V0C 1R0
Tel: 250-774-2357; Fax: 250-774-3612
www.fortnelsonnews.ca
Social Media:
twitter.com/fortnelsonnews
www.facebook.com/fortnelsonnews
Frequency: Weekly
Judith Kenyon, Editor, editorial@fnnews.ca
Leah Edmunds, Manager, Advertising, ads@fnnews.caews.ca
Cindy Bye, Contact, Subscriptions

Fort St James: Caledonia Courier
Owned By: Black Press Group Ltd.
PO Box 1298 , Fort St James, BC V0J 1P0
Tel: 250-996-8482
newsroom@caledoniacourier.com
www.caledoniacourier.com
Social Media:
twitter.com/fortstjamesnews
www.facebook.com/pages/Caledonia-Courier/207583255934276
Circulation: 1,000 Frequency: Weekly
Pam Berger, Publisher & Manager, Sales, advertising@ominecaexpress.com
Ruth Lloyd, Editor, newsroom@caledoniacourier.com
Betty Johnson, Manager, Classified, Circulation, & Front Office, office@ominecaexpress.com
Wendy Haslam, Contact, Production Department

Fort St John: The Northerner
9916 - 98A Ave., Fort St John, BC V1J 3T8
Tel: 250-785-5631
www.thenortherner.ca
Frequency: Friday

Fort St. John: North Peace Express
9916 - 98th St., Fort St. John, BC V1J 3T8
Tel: 250-785-5631; Fax: 250-785-3522
Circulation: 10,400 Frequency: Weekly
William Julian, Publisher

Gabriola: Gabriola Sounder
PO Box 62 , #1, 510 North Rd., Gabriola, BC V0R 1X0
Tel: 250-247-9337; Fax: 250-247-8147
derek@soundernews.com
www.soundernews.com
Circulation: 3,580 Frequency: Monday
Derek Kilbourn, Editor, derek@soundernews.com
Sarah Holmes, Publisher, sarah@soundernews.com

Gold River: The Record
PO Box 279 , Gold River, BC V0P 1G0
Tel: 250-283-2324
record@island.net
www.island.net/~record
Social Media:
www.facebook.com/pages/The-Record/131808520232076?sk=wall
Frequency: Bi-weekly; Wedmesday
The Record is an independent newspaper that serves the Nootka Sound communities of British Columbia. Both print & web editions are available.
Lynne West, Associate Publisher
Jerry West, Editor

Grand Forks: Boundary Weekender
7255 Riverside Dr., Grand Forks, BC V0H 1H5
Tel: 250-442-2191

Grand Forks: Grand Forks Gazette
Owned By: Black Press Group Ltd.
PO Box 700 , Grand Forks, BC V0H 1H0
Tel: 250-442-2191; Fax: 250-442-3336
editor@grandforksgazette.ca
www.grandforksgazette.ca
Social Media:
twitter.com/grandforksgaz
www.facebook.com/pages/Grand-Forks-Gazette/17401365933631
Circulation: 2,807 Frequency: Weekly; Wednesday
Jackie Metcalfe, Publisher
Karl Yu, Editor

Greenwood: Boundary Creek Times Mountaineer
Previous Name: Boundary Creek Times
Owned By: Bennett Publishing Ltd.
PO Box 99 , Greenwood, BC V0H 1J0
Tel: 250-445-2233; Fax: 250-445-2243
bctimes@direct.ca
Circulation: 1,894 Frequency: Friday
Chuck Bennett, Publisher

Hagensborg: Coast Mountain News (CMN)
PO Box 250 , 1290 Hwy. 20, Hagensborg, BC V0T 1H0
Tel: 250-982-2696; Fax: 250-982-2512
CMNews@caribooadvisor.com
Circulation: 1,150 Frequency: Every other Thu.

Hope: Hope Standard
Owned By: Black Press Group Ltd.
PO Box 1090 , 540 Wallace St., Hope, BC V0X 1L0
Tel: 604-869-2421
www.hopestandard.com
Social Media:
twitter.com/hopestandard
www.facebook.com/HopeStandard
Frequency: Wednesday
Andrew Franklin, Publisher, publisher@hopestandard.com
Kerrie-Ann Schoenit, Editor, news@hopestandard.com
Pattie Desjardins, Contact, Advertising Sales, sales@hopestandard.com
Janice McDonald, Contact, Classified Advertising, classifieds@hopestandard.com

Houston: Houston Today Newspaper
Owned By: Black Press Group Ltd.
3232 Hwy. 16, Houston, BC V0J 1Z1
Tel: 250-845-2890
newsroom@houston-today.com
www.houston-today.com
Social Media:
twitter.com/houstonnews1
www.facebook.com/pages/Houston-Today/230245473700891
Frequency: Wednesday
Andrew Hudson, Reporter

Invermere: The Valley Echo
Owned By: Black Press Group Ltd.
PO Box 70 , 530 - 13th St., Invermere, BC V0A 1K0
Tel: 250-342-9216
editor@invermerevalleyecho.com
www.invermerevalleyecho.com
Social Media:
twitter.com/TheValleyEcho
www.facebook.com/InvermereValleyEcho
Frequency: Weekly
The Valley Echo serves the British Columbia communities of Invermere, Fairmont Hot Springs, Windermere, Radium Hot Springs, & Wilmer.
Marilyn Berry, Publisher, marilyn@invermerevalleyecho.com
Nicole Trigg, Editor, editor@invermerevalleyecho.com
Jess de Groot, Manager, Production, production@invermerevalleyecho.com
Andrea Klassen, Reporter

Kamloops: Kamloops This Week
Owned By: Black Press Group Ltd.
1365B Dalhousie Dr., Kamloops, BC V2C 5P6
Tel: 250-374-7467
www.kamloopsthisweek.com
Social Media:
twitter.com/kamthisweek
www.facebook.com/kamloopsthisweek
Frequency: Wednesday, Friday
Kelly Hall, Publisher, publisher@kamloopsthisweek.com
Christopher Foulds, Managing Editor & Columnist, editor@kamloopsthisweek.com
Jack Bell, Manager, Sales, sales@kamloopsthisweek.com
Dave Eagles, Photographer, dave_eagles@kamloopsthisweek.com

Kelowna: Capital News
Owned By: Black Press Group Ltd.
2495 Enterprise Way, Kelowna, BC V1X 7K2
Tel: 250-763-3212
nlark@kelownacapnews.com
www.kelownacapnews.com
Social Media:
twitter.com/kelownacapnews
www.facebook.com/newskelowna
Frequency: Tuesday, Thursday, Friday
Kelowna & its surrounding communities of Peachland, the Westside, & Lake Country are served by the newspaper.
Karen Hill, Publisher, khill@kelownacapnews.com
Barry Gerding, Managing Editor & Columnist, bgerding@kelownacapnews.com
Alistair Waters, Assistant Editor, awaters@kelownacapnews.com
Glenn Beaudry, Manager, Circulation, gbeaudry@kelownacapnews.com
Sean Connor, Photographer, photodesk@kelownacapnews.com

Kelowna: Westside Weekly
550 Doyle Ave., Kelowna, BC V1Y 7V1
Tel: 250-470-0748
westside@ok.bc.ca
www.kelownadailycourier.ca
Social Media:
www.facebook.com/westsideweekly

Circulation: 16,334 Su; 13,687 Th Frequency: Sunday, Thursday
The Westside Weekly serves West Kelowna, Peachland, & the Westbank First Nation.
Terry Armstrong, Group Publisher
Dave Trifunov, Editor

Keremeos: The Review
Owned By: Black Press Group Ltd.
PO Box 130 , 605 - 7th Ave., Keremeos, BC V0X 1N0
Tel: 250-499-2653; Fax: 250-499-2645
www.keremeosreview.com
Social Media:
twitter.com/keremeosnews
www.facebook.com/pages/Keremeos-Review/14483434 8947774
Circulation: 955 Frequency: Thursday
Mark Walker, Publisher, mwalker@blackpress.ca
Tammy Sparkes, Associate Publisher, publisher@keremeosreview.com
Steve Arstad, Editor, news@keremeosreview.com
Tammy Hartfield, Manager, Composing, ads@keremeosreview.com
Sandi Nolen, Representative, Advertising Sales, sales@keremeosreview.com

Kitimat: Northern Sentinel
Owned By: Black Press Group Ltd.
626 Enterprise Ave., Kitimat, BC V8C 2E4
Tel: 250-632-6144
newsroom@northernsentinel.com
www.northernsentinel.com
Social Media:
twitter.com/kitimatnews
www.facebook.com/pages/Kitimat-Northern-Sentinel /20302058
Circulation: 2,000 Frequency: Wednesday
Louisa Genzale, Publisher & Contact, Ad Management, publisher@northernsentinel.com
Cameron Orr, Editor, newsroom@northernsentinel.com
Nancy Knight, Contact, Classifieds, classifieds@northernsentinel.com

Ladner: Delta Optimist
Owned By: Glacier Media Inc.
#207, 4840 Delta St., Ladner, BC V4K 2T6
Tel: 604-946-4451; Fax: 604-946-5680
production@delta-optimist.com
www.delta-optimist.com
Other information: Classifieds, Phone: 604-630-3300; Distribution: 604-249-3332
Social Media:
twitter.com/DeltaOptimist
www.facebook.com/pages/Delta-Optimist/128177527229189
Frequency: Wednesday, Friday
The newspaper covers community news & events in Ladner & Tsawwassen.
Ted Siba, Publisher, tsiba@delta-optimist.com
Ted Murphy, Editor, tmurphy@delta-optimist.com
Trixi Agrios, Manager, Classified, tagrios@postmedia.com
Trish Factor, Manager, Office, pfactor@delta-optimist.com
Dave Hamilton, Manager, Sales, dhamilton@delta-optimist.com

Ladysmith: Ladysmith-Chemainus Chronicle
Owned By: Black Press Group Ltd.
PO Box 400 , 341 - 1st Ave., Ladysmith, BC V9G 1A3
Tel: 250-245-2277
www.ladysmithchronicle.com
Social Media:
twitter.com/LC_Chronicle
www.facebook.com/group.php?gid=173359166022754
Frequency: Weekly
A print edition & an e-edition of the newspaper are available.
Teresa McKinley, Publisher, publisher@ladysmithchronicle.com
Lindsay Chung, Editor, editor@ladysmithchronicle.com
Doug Kent, Manager, Production
Colleen Wheeler, Manager, Circulation & Office
Niomi Pearson, Reporter, news@ladysmithchronicle.com

Lake Country: Lake Country Calendar
Owned By: Black Press Group Ltd.
#3, 3370 Beaver Lake Rd., Lake Country, BC V4V 1S7
Tel: 250-766-4688; Fax: 250-766-4645
production@lakecountrynews.net
www.lakecountrycalendar.com
Other information: Classifieds & Community Events, E-mail: classified@lakecountrynews.net
Social Media:
twitter.com/winfieldnews
www.facebook.com/pages/Lake-Country-Calendar/30 1407309875
Circulation: 4,055 Frequency: Wednesday
The area covered by the Lake Country Calendar includes the communities of Winfield, Oyama, Okanagan Centre, & Carr's Landing.
Barry Gerding, Editor, newsroom@lakecountrynews.net

Lake Cowichan: Lake Cowichan Gazette
Owned By: Black Press Group Ltd.
PO Box 10 , 170 Cowichan Lake Rd., Lake Cowichan, BC V0R 2G0
Tel: 250-749-4383
office@lakecowichangazette.com
www.lakecowichangazette.com
Social Media:
twitter.com/lakecowichannew
www.facebook.com/pages/Lake-Cowichan-Gazette /117628711667
Circulation: 789 Frequency: Wednesday
Local news is provided for the British Columbia communities of Lake Cowichan, Honeymoon Bay, Caycuse, Skutz Falls, Youbou, & Mesachie Lake. A print edition & an e-dition of the newspaper are available.
Dennis Skalicky, Publisher & Editor, publisher@lakecowichangazette.com
Karen Brouwer, Office Manager

Langley: Langley Advance
Owned By: Glacier Media Inc.
#112, 6375 - 202nd St., Langley, BC V2Y 1N1
Tel: 604-534-8641; Fax: 604-534-0824
www.langleyadvance.com
Social Media:
twitter.com/LangleyAdvance
Circulation: 40,400 Frequency: Tuesday, Thursday
The City of Langley, Langley Township, & Cloverdale are served by the newspaper.
Ryan McAdams, General Manager, rmcadams@langleyadvance.com
Bob Groeneveld, Editor, editorial@langleyadvance.com
Shannon Balla, Manager, Sales, sballa@langleyadvance.com
Jackie McKinley, Contact, Delivery, jmckinley@langleyadvance.com

Langley: Langley Times
Owned By: Black Press Group Ltd.
20258 Fraser Hwy., Langley, BC V3A 4E6
Tel: 604-533-4157
newsroom@langleytimes.com
www.langleytimes.com
Social Media:
twitter.com/langleytimes
www.facebook.com/pages/Langley-Times/1204 74554691065
Circulation: 38,000 Frequency: Tuesday, Thursday
Dwane Weidendorf, Publisher, publisher@langleytimes.com
Frank Bucholtz, Editor, newsroom@langleytimes.com

Lantzville: The Lantzville Log
PO Box 214 , Lantzville, BC V0R 2H0
Tel: 250-390-5336; Fax: 250-390-2847
editor@thelog.ca
www.thelog.ca
Circulation: 2,000 Frequency: 11 times a year
Julie Winkel, Owner & Publisher

Lazo: 19 Wing Comox Totem Times
Building #45, Wing Headquarters, PO Box 1000 Main, 19 Wing Comox, Lazo, BC V0R 2K0
Tel: 250-339-2541
totemtimes@gmail.com
Frequency: Bi-weekly; Tuesday
The newspaper is distributed at 19 Wing in the Comox Valley, Canadian Forces bases throughout Canada, & Canadian Forces deployments around the world.
Robert Hatch, Managing Editor, robert.hatch@forces.gc.ca
Gillian Ottaway, Graphics Designer, totemtimes@gmail.com
Leah Hyrko, Representative, Advertising & Sales, leah.totemtimes@shaw.ca

Lillooet: Bridge River-Lillooet News
Owned By: Glacier Interactive Media
PO Box 709 , 979 Main St., Lillooet, BC V0K 1V0
Tel: 250-256-4219; Fax: 250-256-4210
Toll-Free: 877-300-8569
lillooetnews@cablelan.net
www.lillooetnews.net
Social Media:
twitter.com/lillooetnews
www.facebook.com/BridgeRiverLIllooetNews
Circulation: 1,581 Frequency: Wednesday
Nicole Palfy, Publisher, npalfy@lillooetnews.net
Wendy Fraser, Editor, editor@lillooetnews.net

Lumby: Lumby Valley Times
PO Box 408 , 2062 Park Ave., Lumby, BC V0E 2G0
Tel: 250-307-0163
lvt@telus.net
www.lumbyvalleytimes.ca
Circulation: 2,700 Frequency: Weekly; Fri.
Rod Neufeld, Publisher

Mackenzie: Mackenzie Times
PO Box 609 , #125, 403 Mackenzie Blvd., Mackenzie, BC V0J 2C0
Tel: 250-997-6675; Fax: 250-997-4747
ads@mackenzietimes.com; news@mackenzietimes.com
Circulation: 1,000 Frequency: Wednesday
Jackie Benton, Editor

Maple Ridge: Maple Ridge - Pitt Meadows Times
#2, 22345 North Ave., Maple Ridge, BC V2X 8T2
Tel: 604-463-2281; Fax: 604-463-9943
twitter.com/mapleridgetimes
www.mrtimes.com
Other information: Classified Advertising, Phone: 604-998-0218
Social Media:
www.facebook.com/group.php?gid=153740064640252
Circulation: 30,000 Frequency: Tuesday, Friday
The newspaper is a division of Postmedia Nework Inc.
Spencer Levan, Publisher, slevan@mrtimes.com
Bob Groeneveld, Editor, bgroeneveld@mrtimes.com
Roxanne Hooper, Assistant Editor, rhooper@mrtimes.com
Shannon Balla, Manager, Sales, sballa@mrtimes.com
Ralph DeAdder, Advertising Representative, rdeadder@mrtimes.com
Wendy Bradley, Contact, Delivery, wbradley@van.net

Maple Ridge: The News
Owned By: Black Press Group Ltd.
22328 - 119th Ave., Maple Ridge, BC V2X 2Z3
Tel: 604-467-1122
newsroom@mapleridgenews.com
www.mapleridgenews.com
Social Media:
newsroom@mapleridgenews.com
www.facebook.com/MapleRidgeNews
Circulation: 34,000+ Frequency: Wednesday, Friday
The News is distributed in the communities of Maple Ridge & Pitt Meadows, British Columbia. An e-edition is also available.
Jim Coulter, Publisher, publisher@mapleridgenews.com
Michael Hall, Editor, editor@mapleridgenews.com
Carly Ferguson, Manager, Advertising & Creative Services, admanager@mapleridgenews.com
Brian Yip, Manager, Circulation, circulation@mapleridgenews.com

Merritt: Merritt Herald
Owned By: Black Press Group Ltd.
PO Box 9 , 2090 Granite Ave., Merritt, BC V1K 1B8
Tel: 250-378-4241; Fax: 250-378-6818
www.merrittherald.com
Social Media:
twitter.com/merrittherald
www.facebook.com/pages/Merritt-Herald/30030671 6649720
Frequency: Tuesday, Thursday
News, community events, & sports are presented from Merritt & the Nicola Valley.
Kelly Hall, Publisher, publisher@merrittherald.com
Jade Swartzberg, Editor, newsroom@merrittherald.com
Theresa Arnold, Manager, Operations, production@merrittherald.com
Carol Soames, Manager, Office & Classifieds, classifieds@merrittherald.com

Mission: Mission City Record
Owned By: Black Press Group Ltd.
33047 First Ave., Mission, BC V2V 1G2
Tel: 604-826-6221
www.missioncityrecord.com
Social Media:
twitter.com/missionrecord
www.facebook.com/pages/Mission-Record/12307945 1105629
Circulation: 10,000+ Frequency: Thursday
A print edition & an e-edition are available.
Andrew Franklin, Publisher, publisher@missioncityrecord.com
Jason Roessle, Editor, news@missioncityrecord.com
Carol Aun, Editor, Arts, arts@missioncityrecord.com
Adrian MacNair, Reporter, arts@missioncityrecord.com
Crystal Orchison, Contact, Advertising, crystal@missioncityrecord.com

Nakusp: Arrow Lakes News
Owned By: Black Press Group Ltd.
PO Box 189 , 203 Broadway, Nakusp, BC V0G 1R0
Tel: 250-265-3823
www.arrowlakesnews.com
Social Media:
twitter.com/nakuspnews
www.facebook.com/pages/Arrow-Lakes-News/118259024876158
Circulation: 1,200 Frequency: Thursday
The British Columbia communities of Naskusp, New Denver, Trout Lake, Silverton, Burton, Fauquier, Arrow Park, & Edgewood are served by the newspaper.
Mavis Cann, Publisher & Manager, Ads, publisher@arrowlakesnews.com
Claire Paradis, Editor, newsroom@arrowlakesnews.com
Sharon Bamber, Contact, Classifieds, sales@arrowlakesnews.com

Nanaimo: Harbour City Star
Owned By: Glacier Media Inc.
c/o Nanaimo Daily News, 2575 McCullough Rd., #B1, Nanaimo, BC V9S 5W5
Tel: 250-729-4200; Fax: 250-729-4256
www.nanaimodailynews.com
Other information: Classifieds, Phone: 250-729-4222; Circulation: 250-729-4266
Circulation: 33,974 Frequency: Friday
Curt Duddy, Publisher, cduddy@nanaimodailynews.com
Cale Cowan, Managing Editor, ccowan@nanaimodailynews.com
Kathleen Fletcher, Manager, Production, kfletcher@nanaimodailynews.com
Angela Kephart, Manager, Business, akephart@nanaimodailynews.com
Andrea Rosato-Taylor, Manager, Advertising, arosato-taylor@nanaimodailynews.com
Wayne Kuss, Director, Reader Services, wkuss@nanaimodailynews.com

Nanaimo: Nanaimo News Bulletin
Owned By: Black Press Group Ltd.
777 Poplar St., Nanaimo, BC V9S 2H7
Tel: 250-753-3707
editor@nanaimobulletin.com
www.nanaimobulletin.com
Social Media:
twitter.com/nanaimobulletin
www.facebook.com/nanaimobulletin
Circulation: 30,000 Frequency: Tuesday, Thursday, Saturday
The Nanaimo New Bulletin is available in print & online.
Maurice Donn, Publisher, publisher@nanaimobulletin.com
Chris Hamlyn, Assistant Editor, news@nanaimobulletin.com
Greg Sakaki, Editor, Sports, sports@nanaimobulletin.com
Jessica Kalser, Manager, Circulation, circulation@nanaimobulletin.com
Sean McCue, Manager, Sales, salesmgr@nanaimobulletin.com
D. Paterson, Manager, Production, production@nanaimobulletin.com
Chris Bush, Photographer, photos@nanaimobulletin.com

Nelson: Express
554 Ward St., Nelson, BC V1L 1S9
Tel: 250-354-3910; Fax: 250-352-5075
Toll-Free: 800-665-3288
express@expressnews.bc.ca
www.expressnews.ca
Other information: Editorial, Phone: 250-354-1118
Social Media: www.youtube.com/user/expressnewsupdate
www.facebook.com/group.php?gid=28 1836361276
Frequency: Weekly
Nelson Becker, Publisher

Nelson: Nelson Star
Owned By: Black Press
514 Hall St., Nelson, BC V1L 1Z2
Tel: 250-352-1890
www.nelsonstar.com
Circulation: 7,898 Frequency: Wednesday, Friday
Chuck Bennett, Regional Publisher, chuckbennett@blackpress.ca
Karen Bennett, Manager, Operations, advertising@nelsonstar.com
Bob Hall, Editor, bob@nelsonstar.com
Selina Birk, Sales Associate, classifieds@nelsonstar.com
Kevin Berggren, Contact, Creative Services, creative@nelsonstar.com
Elizabeth Simmons, Contact, Circulation, circulation@nelsonstar.com

North Vancouver: North Shore News
Owned By: Glacier Media Inc.
#100, 126 East 15th St., North Vancouver, BC V7L 2P9
Tel: 604-985-2131; Fax: 604-985-3227
distribution@nsnews.com
www.nsnews.com
Other information: Classified, Phone: 604-630-3300; Real Estates Ads: 604-985-6982
Social Media:
twitter.com/NorthShoreNews
www.facebook.com/northshorenews
Frequency: Sunday, Wednesday, Friday
Doug Foot, Publisher
604-998-3550
dfoot@nsnews.com
Terry Peters, Managing Editor
604-998-3530
tpeters@nsnews.com
Dee Dhaliwal, Director, Sales & Marketing
604-998-3520
ddhaliwal@nsnews.com
Rick Anderson, Manager, Real Estate
604-998-3580
randerson@nsnews.com
Shari Hughes, Manager, Creative Services
604-998-3570
shughes@nsnews.com

Oliver: Oliver Chronicle
PO Box 880 , 36083 - 97th St., Oliver, BC V0H 1T0
Tel: 250-498-3711; Fax: 250-498-3966
www.oliverchronicle.com
Frequency: Wednesday
Both paper & online editions are available.
Susan Valentine, Publisher, publisher@oliverchronicle.com
Lyonel Doherty, Editor, editor@oliverchronicle.com
Alana Gulick, Contact, Accounting, office@oliverchronicle.com
Kelly Hall, Contact, Production, ads@oliverchronicle.com
Susan Valentine, Contact, Sales, sales@oliverchronicle.com

Osoyoos: Osoyoos Times
PO Box 359 , 8712 Main St., Osoyoos, BC V0H 1V0
Tel: 250-495-7225; Fax: 250-495-6616
ads@osoyoostimes.com
www.osoyoostimes.com
Frequency: Wednesday
Chris Stodola, Publisher & National Sales Manager, Commercial Printing, printing@osoyoostimes.com
Mathew White, Reporter & Photographer, reporter@osoyoostimes.com
Jocelyn Merit, Office Administrator, admin@osoyoostimes.com
Sherry Anderson, Contact, Newspaper Circulation & Delivery
Ken Baker, Contact, Advertising Sales & Layout, sales@osoyoostimes.com

Parksville: Parksville Qualicum News
Owned By: Black Press Group Ltd.
PO Box 1180 , #4, 154 Middleton Ave., Parksville, BC V9P 2H2
Tel: 250-248-4341
www.pqbnews.com
Social Media:
twitter.com/parksvillenews
www.facebook.com/PQBNews
Frequency: Semi-weekly
The Parksville Qualicum News is available inprint & online. The newspaper serves the City of Parksville, the Town of Qualicum Beach, & the Vancouver Island communities of Deep Bay, Qualicum Bay, Errington, Hilliers, Coombs, & Whiskey Creek.
Peter McCully, Publisher, publisher@pqbnews.com
Steven Heywood, Editor, editor@pqbnews.com
Neil Horner, Asistant Editor & Columnist, news@pqbnews.com
Lissa Alexander, Reporter, reporter@pqbnews.com
Auren Ruvinsky, Reporter, writer@pqbnews.com
Peggy Sidbeck, Manager, Production, production@pqbnews.com
Brittany Pearce, Representative, Advertising
250-905-0015

Peachland: The Peachland Signal
PO Box 800 , #3, 4478 Third St., Peachland, BC V0H 1X0
Tel: 250-767-2004; Fax: 250-767-3306
signal@cablelan.net
Circulation: 1,308 Frequency: Weekly
Darren Bayrack, Publisher

Peachland: Peachland View
4437 - 3rd St., Peachland, BC V0H 1X7
Tel: 250-767-7771
publisher.peachlandview@shaw.ca
www.peachlandview.com
Circulation: 3,100 Frequency: Friday
The independently owned, free community newspaper is distributed to Peachland's residences & businesses, as well as businesses in Westbank.
Susan Valentine, Group Publisher, publisher@oliverchronicle.com
Joanne Layh, Editor, editor@peachlandview.ca
Constance Roth, Manager, Sales, sales@peachlandview.ca

Pender Island: Island Tides
PO Box 55 , Pender Island, BC V0N 2M1
Tel: 250-629-3660; Fax: 250-629-3838
islandtides@islandtides.com; news@islandtides.com
www.islandtides.com
Circulation: 18,000 Frequency: Bi-weekly; Thursday
Island Tides presents news & views from British Columbia's west coast. The newspaper is available around the Strait of Georgia.
Christa Grace-Warrick, Publisher

Penticton: Penticton Western News
Owned By: Black Press Group Ltd.
2250 Camrose St., Penticton, BC V2A 8R1
Tel: 250-492-3636
region@pentictonwesternnews.com
www.pentictonwesternnews.com
Other information: Classified Department, E-mail: classifieds@pentictonwesternnews.com
Social Media:
twitter.com/pentictonnews
www.facebook.com/pentictonnews
Frequency: Wednesday, Friday
News, sports, & entertainment in Penticton & the South Okanagan are covered by the newspaper.
Mark Walker, Publisher, mwalker@blackpress.ca
Dan Ebenal, Editor & Columnist, editor@pentictonwesternnews.com
Emanuel Sequeira, Sports Editor & Columnist, sports@pentictonwesternnews.com
Larry Mercier, Manager, Sales, larry@pentictonwesternnews.com
Kirk Myltoft, Composing Manager, Creative Services, kirk@pentictonwesternnews.com
Mark Oleksyn, Manager, Circulation, circulation@pentictonwesternnews.com
Mark Brett, Photographer, photos@pentictonwesternnews.com

Port Alberni: Pennyworth
Owned By: Glacier Media Inc.
4918 Napier St., Port Alberni, BC V9Y 3H5
Tel: 250-729-4290
Circulation: 10,500 Frequency: Thursday
Pennyworth offers free classifieds.
Curt Duddy, Publisher, CDuddy@nanaimodailynews.com
Cale Cowan, Managing Editor, CCowan@avtimes.net
Cindy Donovan, Manager, Production, CDonovan@avtimes.net
Debbie Reid, Manager, Business, DReid@avtimes.net
Pam Craig, Contact, Display Ads, PCraig@avtimes.net
Tamie Macey, Contact, Classified Ads, TMacey@avtimes.net
John Richardson, Contact, Circulation & Subscriptions, JRichardson@avtimes.net

Port Coquitlam: The Tri-City News
Owned By: Black Press Group Ltd.
1405 Broadway St., Port Coquitlam, BC V3C 6L6
Tel: 604-525-6397
www.tricitynews.com
Social Media:
twitter.com/tricitynews
www.facebook.com/pages/The-Tri-City-News/73945744787
Frequency: Wednesday, Friday
The newpaper covers happenings in the British Columbia communities of Port Coquitlam, Coquitlam, Anmore, Port Moody, & Belcarra.
Nigel Lark, Publisher, publisher@tricitynews.com
Richard Dal Monte, Editor, newsroom@tricitynews.com
Diane Strandberg, Reporter & Assistant Editor, dstrandberg@tricitynews.com
Don Layfield, Manager, Sales, admanager@tricitynews.com
Kim Yorston, Manager, Circulation, circulation@tricitynews.com

Port Hardy: North Island Gazette
Owned By: Black Press Group Ltd.
PO Box 458 , Port Hardy, BC V0N 2P0
Tel: 250-949-6225
viads@bcclassified.com(classified advertising)
www.northislandgazette.com
Social Media:
twitter.com/nigazette
www.facebook.com/pages/North-Island-Gazette/1889892344453
Circulation: 2,500 Frequency: Thursday
The newspaper serves the northern part of Vancouver Island, including the communities of Port McNeill, Port Hardy, Port Alice, Sointula, & Alert Bay.
Sandy Grenier, Publisher, office@northislandgazette.com

J.R. Rardon, Editor, editor@northislandgazette.com
Marlene Parkin, Manager, Production, production@northislandgazette.com
Aidan O'Toole, Reporter, reporter@northislandgazette.com
Lisa Harrison, Representative, Sales, sales@northislandgazette.com

Powell River: Powell River Peak
4400 Marine Ave., Powell River, BC V8A 2K1
Tel: 604-485-5313; Fax: 604-485-5007
admin@prpeak.com
www.prpeak.com
Social Media:
twitter.com/Peak_Aboo
www.facebook.com/pages/Peak-Publishing/16876744017 3
Circulation: 11,680 Frequency: Weekly; Wednesday (Weekend Shopper; Friday)
Joyce Carlson, Publisher
Laura Walz, Editor

Prince George: Prince George Free Press
Owned By: Black Press Group Ltd.
1773 South Lyon St., Prince George, BC V2N 1T3
Tel: 250-564-0005; Fax: 250-562-0025
editor@pgfreepress.com
pgfreepress.com
Social Media:
twitter.com/pgfreepress
www.facebook.com/pages/Prince-George-Free-Press/140123662
Circulation: 59,590 Frequency: Bi-weekly; Wed., Fri.
Dennis Chapman, Publisher
Darlene Osborne, General Manager
Bill Phillips, Editor

Princeton: Similkameen News Leader
PO Box 956 , 226A Bridge St., Princeton, BC V0X 1W0
Tel: 250-295-4149; Fax: 250-295-4103
Toll-Free: 888-350-9969
editor@thenewsleader.ca
www.thenewsleader.ca
Other information: Advertising Department, E-mail: ads@thenewsleader.ca
Circulation: 1,400 Frequency: Monday
The tabloid newspaper is distributed in the Similkameen Valley, including Princeton, Cawston, Coalmont, Keremeos, Hedley, & Tulameen.
W. George Elliott, Publisher, george@thenewsleader.ca
Brenda Engel, Office Administrator, brenda@thenewsleader.ca

Princeton: Similkameen Spotlight
Owned By: Black Press Group Ltd.
PO Box 340 , 282 Bridge St., Princeton, BC V0X 1W0
Tel: 250-295-3535
advertising@similkameenspotlight.com
www.similkameenspotlight.com
Social Media:
twitter.com/similkameennews
www.facebook.com/pages/Similkameen-Spotlight/125668670529
The Similkameen Spotlight serves the Similkameen Valley, including Coalmont, Princeton, Tulameen, Keremeos, & Hedley.
Lisa Carleton, Associate Publisher, lisa@similkameenspotlight.com
Michaela Garstin, Editor
Wendy Bentley, Manager, Classifieds, classifieds@similkameenspotlight.com

Queen Charlotte: Queen Charlotte Islands Observer
PO Box 205 , 623 - 7th St., Queen Charlotte, BC V0T 1S0
Tel: 250-559-4680; Fax: 250-559-8433
Toll-Free: 888-529-4747
observer@haidagwaii.ca
www.qciobserver.com

Quesnel: Cariboo Observer
Owned By: Black Press Group Ltd.
188 Carson Ave., Quesnel, BC V2J 2A8
Tel: 250-992-2121
editor@quesnelobserver.com
www.quesnelobserver.com
Social Media:
twitter.com/quesnelnews
www.facebook.com/pages/Quesnel-Cariboo-Observer/258929627
News is provided about Quesnel & area, British Columbia.
Tracey Roberts, Publisher & Manager, Sales, publisher@quesnelobserver.com
Autumn MacDonald, Editor, editor@quesnelobserver.com
Jonas Gagnon, Reporter, Sports, sports@quesnelobserver.com

Revelstoke: Revelstoke Times Review
Owned By: Black Press Group Ltd.
PO Box 20 , 518 - 2nd St. West, Revelstoke, BC V0E 2S0
Tel: 250-837-4667
www.revelstoketimesreview.com
Social Media:
twitter.com/revelstoketimes
www.facebook.com/RevelstokeTimesReview
Circulation: 1,800 Frequency: Wednesday
The Revelstoke Review, which was founded in 1914, merged with the Revelstoke Times in 2003 to create the Revelstoke Times Review.
Mavis Cann, Publisher, mavis@revelstoketimesreview.com
Aaron Orlando, Editor, editor@revelstoketimesreview.com
Fran Carlson, Manager, Office, circulation@revelstoketimesreview.com
Rob Stokes, Contact, Production, production@revelstoketimesreview.com

Richmond: Richmond Review
Owned By: Black Press Group Ltd.
#1, 3671 Viking Way, Richmond, BC V6V 2J5
Tel: 604-247-3700
news@richmondreview.com
www.richmondreview.com
Other information: Newsroom, Phone: 604-247-3730; Classified Advertising: 604-575-5555
Social Media:
twitter.com/richmondreview
www.facebook.com/richmondreview
Circulation: 93,849 / week Frequency: Wednesday, Friday
Mary Kemmis, Publisher, publisher@richmondreview.com
Bhreandain Clugston, Editor
Don Fennell, Editor, Sports, sports@richmondreview.com
Jaana Bjork, Manager, Creative Services, jaana@richmondreview.com
Rachael Finkelstein, Manager, Circulation, circulation@richmondreview.com
Elana Gold, Assistant Manager, Advertising, admanager@richmondreview.com

Salmon Arm: Salmon Arm Observer
Owned By: Black Press Group Ltd.
171 Shuswap St., Salmon Arm, BC V1E 4H7
Tel: 250-832-2131
newsroom@saobserver.net
www.saobserver.net
Social Media:
twitter.com/salmonarm
www.facebook.com/pages/Salmon-Arm-Observer/126369231201
Frequency: Wednesday
Tracy Hughes, Editor & Columnist, newsroom@saobserver.net
Penny Brown, Contact, Advertising Sales, pennyjb@saobserver.net

Salmon Arm: The Shuswap Market News
Owned By: Black Press Group Ltd.
171 Shuswap St., Salmon Arm, BC V1E 4H7
Tel: 250-832-2131
www.saobserver.net
Frequency: Friday
The Shuswap Market News is a free paper.
Tracy Hughes, Editor & Columnist, newsroom@saobserver.net
Sherry Kaufmam, Contact, Advertising Sales, sherry@saobserver.net

Salt Spring Island: Gulf Islands Driftwood
Owned By: Black Press Group Ltd.
328 Lower Ganges Rd., Salt Spring Island, BC V8K 2V3
Tel: 250-537-9933
info@driftwoodgimedia.com
www.gulfislandsdriftwood.com
Social Media:
twitter.com/gidriftwood
www.facebook.com/gulfislandsdriftwood
Frequency: Weekly
The community newspaper is available in print & online. The Gulf Island Driftwood serves the British Columbia islands of Mayne, Salt Spring, Pender, Saturna, & Galiano.
Amber Ogilvie, Publisher, aogilvie@gulfislandsdriftwood.com
Gail Sjuberg, Managing Editor, gsjuberg@gulfislands.net
Lorraine Sullivan, Manager, Production, production@gulfislands.net

Sechelt: Coast Reporter
Previous Name: Coast Independant
Owned By: Glacier Interactive Media
PO Box 1388 , 5485 Wharf Rd., Sechelt, BC V0N 3A0
Tel: 604-885-4811; Fax: 604-885-4818
www.coastreporter.net
Social Media:
twitter.com/coast_reporter
www.facebook.com/coastreporter
Circulation: 13,123 Frequency: Fri.
Peter Kvarnstrom, Publisher, pkvarnstrom@coastreporter.net

Sicamous: Eagle Valley News
Owned By: Black Press Group Ltd.
PO Box 113 , 1133 Parksville St., Sicamous, BC V0E 2V0
Tel: 250-836-2570; Fax: 250-836-2661
classifieds@eaglevalleynews.com
www.eaglevalleynews.com
Circulation: 942 Frequency: Wednesday
J. Thomson

Sidney: Peninsula News Review
Previous Name: Sidney Review
Owned By: Black Press Group Ltd.
#6, 9843 Second St., Sidney, BC V8L 3C7
Tel: 250-656-1151
www.peninsulanewsreview.com
Social Media:
twitter.com/peninsulanews
www.facebook.com/PeninsulaNewsReview
The newspaper serves the British Columbia communities of Sidney, North Saanich, & Central Saanich.
Jim Parker, Publisher, publisher@peninsulanewsreview.com
Erin Cardone, Editor, editor@peninsulanewsreview.com
Arlene Smith, Manager, Circulation, circulation@peninsulanewsreview.com
Devon MacKenzie, Reporter, reporter@peninsulanewsreview.com

Smithers: Interior News
Owned By: Black Press Group Ltd.
PO Box 2560 , 3764 Broadway, Smithers, BC V0J 2N0
Tel: 250-847-3266; Fax: 250-847-2995
advertising@interior-news.com
www.interior-news.com
Social Media:
twitter.com/smithersnews
www.facebook.com/pages/Smithers-Interior-News/22646570738
Circulation: 3,838 Frequency: Wednesday
Vic Swan, Publisher

Sooke: Sooke News Mirror
Owned By: Black Press Group Ltd.
#112, 6660 Sooke Rd., Sooke, BC V9Z 0A5
Tel: 250-642-5752
www.sookenewsmirror.com
Social Media:
twitter.com/sookenews
www.facebook.com/SookeNewsMirror
Frequency: Wednesday
The Sooke News Mirror serves the District of Sooke & its surrounding area.
Rod Sluggett, Publisher, publisher@sookenewsmirror.com
Pirjo Raits, Editor, editor@sookenewsmirror.com
Sharron Ho, Reporter, news@sookenewsmirror.com
Harla Eve, Contact, Office Administration, office@sookenewsmirror.com
Joan Gamache, Advertising Representative & Contact, Circulation, sales@sookenewsmirror.comm
Frank Kaufman, Contact, Production, creative@sookenewsmirror.com

Squamish: Squamish Chief
Owned By: Glacier Interactive Media
PO Box 3500 , 38117 - 2nd Ave., Squamish, BC V8B 0B9
Tel: 604-892-9161; Fax: 604-892-8483
sales@squamishchief.com
www.squamishchief.com
Circulation: 3,866 Frequency: Friday
David Burke, Editor, dburke@squamishchief.com
Laila Michell, Publisher, lmichell@squamishchief.com

Summerland: Summerland Review
Owned By: Black Press Group Ltd.
PO Box 309 , Summerland, BC V0H 1Z0
Tel: 250-494-5406
www.summerlandreview.com
Social Media:
twitter.com/summerlandnews
www.facebook.com/pages/Summerland-Review/149061881826182
A print edition & an e-edition are available.

Mark Walker, Publisher, mwalker@blackpress.ca
John Arendt, Editor, news@summerlandreview.com
Barbara Manning Grimm, Writer & Photographer, sports@summerlandreview.com
Nan Cogbill, Manager, Circulation & Classified, class@summerlandreview.com
Jo Freed, Manager, Sales, ads@summerlandreview.com

Surrey: Cloverdale Reporter
Owned By: Black Press Group Ltd.
17586 - 56A Ave., Surrey, BC V3S 1G3
Tel: 604-575-2405
editor@cloverdalereporter.com
www.cloverdalereporter.com
Social Media:
twitter.com/cloverdalenews
www.facebook.com/CloverdaleReporter
Circulation: 21,451 Frequency: Friday
News is reported from the Cloverdale area of Surrey, British Columbia in both print & e-editions.
Ursula Maxwell-Lewis, Founding Editor & Columnist
Jennifer Lang, Editor
604-575-2400
Lyliane Ward, Consultant, Advertising
604-575-2423
sales@cloverdalereporter.com

Surrey: The Indo-Canadian Voice
#8338, 120 St., Surrey, BC V3W 3N4
Tel: 604-502-6100; Fax: 604-501-6111
editor@voiceonline.com
www.voiceonline.com
Circulation: 15,000 Frequency: Weekly
Vinnie Combow, General Manager, rcombow@gmail.com

Surrey: The Leader
Owned By: Black Press Group Ltd.
#200, 5450 - 152nd St., Surrey, BC V3S 5J9
Tel: 604-575-2744
newsroom@surreyleader.com
www.surreyleader.com
Social Media:
twitter.com/surreyleader
www.facebook.com/surreyleader
Frequency: Tuesday, Thursday
The Leader covers news for Surrey & North Delta, British Columbia. Editions are available in print & online.
Jim Mihaly, Publisher, publisher@surreyleader.com
Paula Carlson, Editor, pcarlson@surreyleader.com
Sheila Reynolds, Assistant Editor, sreynolds@surreyleader.com
Jeff Nagel, Regional Reporter, jnagel@surreyleader.com
Boaz Joseph, Multimedia Journalist, bjoseph@surreyleader.com

Surrey: The Link
#101, 13463 - 78th Ave., Surrey, BC V3W 0A8
Tel: 604-591-5160; Fax: 604-591-2113
ads@thelinkpaper.ca
www.thelinkpaper.ca
Paul R. Dhillon, Editor-in-chief, editor@thelinkpaper.ca

Surrey: The Now
#201, 7889 - 132nd St., Surrey, BC V3W 4N2
Tel: 604-572-0064
delivery@thenownewspaper.com
www.thenownewspaper.com
Other information: Distribution, Phone: 604-534-6493; Classifieds: 604-444-3000
Social Media:
twitter.com/TheNowNewspaper
www.facebook.com/thesurreynow
Circulation: 120,000 Frequency: Tuesday, Friday
The area covered by the newspaper includes Surrey, Whiterock, & Noth Delta, British Columbia.
Marlyn Graziano, Publisher, mgraziano@thenownewspaper.com
Beau Simpson, Editor, bsimpson@thenownewspaper.com

Surrey: The Peace Arch News
Owned By: Black Press Group Ltd.
#200, 2411 - 160 St., Surrey, BC V3S 0C8
Tel: 604-531-1711
www.peacearchnews.com
Social Media:
twitter.com/whiterocknews
www.facebook.com/pages/Peace-Arch-News/135146319865795
Circulation: 37,000+ Frequency: Tuesday, Thursday
The Peace Arch News serves communities on the Semiahmoo Peninsula, including South Surrey & White Rock.
Rita Walters, Publisher, publisher@peacearchnews.com
Lance Peverley, Editor & Columnist
604-542-7402
lpeverley@peacearchnews.com
Jim Chmelyk, Manager, Creative Services
604-542-7420
jim@peacearchnews.com
Marilou Pasion, Manager, Circulation
604-542-7430
marilou@peacearchnews.com

Terrace: Terrace Standard
Owned By: Black Press Group Ltd.
3210 Clinton Ave., Terrace, BC V8G 5R2
Tel: 250-638-7283; Fax: 250-638-8432
www.terracestandard.com
Social Media:
twitter.com/terracestandard
www.facebook.com/pages/Terrace-Standard/1715 47382936857
Circulation: 8,400 Frequency: Wednesday
The newspaper employs fifteen staff members in its Terrace office.
Rod Link, Publisher & Editor, newsroom@terracestandard.com
Brian Lindenbach, Manager, Sales, brianl@terracestandard.com
Margaret Speirs, Community Reporter, newsroom@terracestandard.com

Tumbler Ridge: Tumbler Ridge News
#120, 230 Main St., Tumbler Ridge, BC V0C 2W0
Tel: 250-242-5343; Fax: 250-242-5340
mail@tumblerridgenews.com
www.tumblerridgenews.com
Social Media:
www.facebook.com/TumblerRidgeNews
Circulation: 1,500 Frequency: Wednesday
Loraine Funk, Publisher
Trent Ernst, Editor, editor@tumblerridgenews.com
Dorothy Zunti, Manager, sales@tumblerridgenews.com
Roxanne Braam, Contact, Classifieds

Ucluelet: Tofino-Ucluelet Westerly News
Owned By: Glacier Media Inc.
PO Box 317 , #1, 1920 Lyche Rd., Ucluelet, BC V0R 3A0
Tel: 250-726-7029; Fax: 250-726-4282
office@westerlynews.ca; reporter@westerlynews.ca
www.canada.com/westerly
Other information: Classified Advertising, E-mail: classifieds@van.net
Social Media:
www.facebook.com/group.php?gid=198056156972097
Circulation: 1,225 Frequency: Thursday
Lisa Stewart, Publisher & Editor, Lstewart@westerlynews.ca

Valemount: The Valley Sentinel
PO Box 688 , 1012 Commercial Dr., Valemount, BC V0E 2Z0
Tel: 250-566-4425; Fax: 250-566-4528
Toll-Free: 800-226-2129
ads@thevalleysentinel.com
www.thevalleysentinel.com
Social Media: www.linkedin.com/company/the-valley-sentinel
Frequency: Wednesday
The Valley Sentinel Robson Valley communities, including Valemount & McBride.
Andrea Scholz, Publisher, publisher@thevalleysentinel.com
Daniel Betts, Editor, editor@thevalleysentinel.com
Deanna Mickelow, Contact, Sales, insertions@thevalleysentinel.com

Vancouver: Apna Roots
PO Box 2296 , Vancouver, BC V6B 3W5
Tel: 604-599-5408; Fax: 604-599-5415
indo@telus.net
www.apnaroots.com
Circulation: 15,000 Frequency: Bi-Weekly
Rue Hayer Bains, Publisher

Vancouver: Country Life in BC
1120 East 13th Ave., Vancouver, BC V5T 2M1
Tel: 250-871-0001; Fax: 250-871-0003
countrylifeinbc@shaw.ca
www.countrylifeinbc.com
Frequency: Monthly
Country Life in BC provides agricultural news for farmers in British Columbia.
Peter Wilding, Publisher & Editor
604-871-0001; Fax: 604-871-0003
David Schmidt, Associate Editor
604-793-9193
davidschmidt@shaw.ca
Cathy Glover, Contact
604-328-3814; Fax: 604-946-5919
cathyglover@telus.net

Vancouver: L'Express du Pacifique
#227A, 1555, 7e av ouest, Vancouver, BC V6J 1S1
Tél: 604-736-3734;Téléc: 604-736-3740
administration@lexpress.org
www.lexpress.org
Tirage: 1 800 Fréquence: Lundi; aux deux semaines
Stéphanie Descôteaux
Raphael Perdrau, directeur de la publication
Cécil Lepage, journaliste

Vancouver: Indo-Canadian Times
PO Box 2296 , Vancouver, BC V6B 3W5
Tel: 604-599-5408; Fax: 604-599-5415
indo@telus.net
www.indocanadiantimes.com
Circulation: 32,000 Frequency: Weekly; Wednesday; Punjabi
Rupinder Hayer, Publisher

Vancouver: Jewish Independent
Previous Name: Jewish Western Bulletin
#99, 291 East 2nd Ave., Vancouver, BC V5T 1B8
Tel: 604-689-1520
editor@jewishindependent.ca
jewishindependent.ca
Social Media:
www.facebook.com/pages/Jewish-Independent/1835431450065 90
Circulation: 5,000 Frequency: Weekly

Vancouver: The Vancouver Courier
Owned By: Glacier Media Inc.
1574 - West 6th Ave., Vancouver, BC V6J 1R2
Tel: 604-738-1411
delivery@vancourier.com; releases@vancourier.com
www.vancourier.com
Other information: Community Events: events@vancourier.com
Social Media:
www.facebook.com/TheVancouverCourierNewspaper
Circulation: 123,250 Frequency: Wednesday, Friday
Emily Jubb, Publisher
604-630-3521
ejubb@vancourier.com
Barry Link, Editor, blink@vancourier.com
Don Delayem, Director
604-630-3523
ddelayen@vancourier.com

Vancouver: WestEnder
Owned By: Black Press Group Ltd.
#280, 1770 Burrard St., Vancouver, BC V6J 3G7
Tel: 604-606-8686
www.westender.com
Social Media:
twitter.com/wevancouver
www.facebook.com/WEVancouver
Frequency: Thursday
Anne Devereaux, Publisher
604-742-8684
publisher@wevancouver.com
Martha Perkins, Editor & Columnist
604-742-8695
editor@wevancouver.com
Andrea Warner, Listings Editor
604-742-8698
listings@wevancouver.com
Kelsey Klassen, Reporter
604-742-8699
kelsey@wevancouver.com
Miguel Black, Manager, Distribution
604-742-8676
circulation@wevancouver.com
Gail Nugent, Manager, Sales
604 742-8678
admanager@wevancouver.com

Vancouver: Westside Revue
1736A East 33rd Ave., Vancouver, BC V5N 3E2
Tel: 604-327-1665
Circulation: 7,600 Frequency: Bi-weekly
Rod Raglin, Publisher & Editor

Vanderhoof: Omineca Express
Owned By: Black Press Group Ltd.
PO Box 1007 , 150 Columbia St. West, Vanderhoof, BC V0J 3A0
Tel: 250-567-9258; Fax: 250-567-2070
newsroom@ominecaexpress.com
www.ominecaexpress.com
Social Media:
twitter.com/vanderhoofnews
www.facebook.com/pages/Vanderhoof-Omineca-Express/11349 81

Circulation: 2,300 Frequency: Wednesday
The newspaper serves the British Columbia communities of Vanderhoof, Fraser Lake, & Fort Fraser.
Pam Berger, Publisher & Manager, Sales, publisher@ominecaexpress.com
Christina Millington, Editor, newsroom@ominecaexpress.com
Ruth Lloyd, Reporter
250-996-8482
newsroom@ominecaexpress.com
Wendy Haslam, Contact, Production Department, wendy@ominecaexpress.com
Betty Johnson, Contact, Front Office, Circulation Sales & Classified Sales, office@ominecaexpress.com

Vernon: The Morning Star
Owned By: Black Press Group Ltd.
4407 - 25th Ave., Vernon, BC V1T 1P5
Tel: 250-545-3322
newsroom@vernonmorningstar.com
www.vernonmorningstar.com
Social Media:
twitter.com/vernonnews
www.facebook.com/pages/Vernon-Morning-Star/19250709412252
Circulation: 30,000+ Frequency: Sunday, Wednesday, Friday
News is covered in the North Okanagan communities of Vernon, Oyama, Cherryville, Lavington, Coldstream, Silver Star, Armstrong, Falkland Lumby, Enderby, North Westside, Grindrod, Kingfisher, Ashton Creek, Mabel Lake, the Okanagan Indian Band, Spallumcheen, & the Splatsin First Nation.
Ian Jensen, Publisher, publisher@vernonmorningstar.com
Glenn Mitchell, Managing Editor & Columnist, glenn@vernonmorningstar.com
Kristin Froneman, Entertainment Editor & Columnist, entertainment@vernonmorningstar.com
Roger Knox, Web Editor & Columnist, roger@vernonmorningstar.com
Kevin Mitchell, Sports Editor, sports@vernonmorningstar.com
Tammy Stelmachowich, Manager, Circulation, circulation@vernonmorningstar.com
Alan Tomiak, Manager, Sales, alan@vernonmorningstar.com
Carol Williment, Manager, Classified, classifieds@vernonmorningstar.com
Lisa VanderVelde, Photographer, lisa@vernonmorningstar.comtar.com

Victoria: Goldstream News Gazette
Owned By: Black Press Group Ltd.
PO Box 7310 D, #117, 777 Goldstream Ave., Victoria, BC V9B 2X4
Tel: 250-478-9552
www.goldstreamgazette.com
Social Media:
twitter.com/goldstreamnews
www.facebook.com/GoldstreamNewsGazette
Frequency: Wednesday, Friday
The West Shore communities of Langford, Metchosin, Colwood, & View Royal on Vancouver Island are served by the newspaper. The Goldstream News Gazette is available in print & online.
Penny Sakamoto, Publisher, publisher@goldstreamgazette.com
Kevin Laird, Editorial Director, klaird@blackpress.ca
Jim Zeeben, Editor, editor@goldstreamgazette.com
Bruce Hogarth, Director, Circulation, distribution@vicnews.com

Victoria: Lookout
c/o CFB Esquimalt, PO Box 17000 Forces, 1522 Esquimalt Rd., Victoria, BC V9A 7N2
Tel: 250-363-3014; Fax: 250-363-3015
frontoffice@lookoutnewspaper.com
www.lookoutnewspaper.com
Social Media:
twitter.com/Lookout_news
www.facebook.com/lookout.newspaper
Frequency: Monday
The newspaper contains news & information about the Canadian Navy.
Melissa Atkinson, Publisher, melissa.atkinson@forces.gc.ca
Shelley Lipke, Writer, shelley.lipke@forces.gc.ca
Raquel Tirado, Supervisor, Office Accounts, raquel.tirado@forces.gc.ca
Ivan Groth, Sales Representative, sales@lookoutnewspaper.com
Francisco Cumayas, Contact, Production Department, production@lookoutnewspaper.com

Victoria: Oak Bay News
Previous Name: Oak Bay Star
Owned By: Black Press Group Ltd.
818 Broughton St., Victoria, BC V8W 1E4
Tel: 250-598-4123
viads@bcclassified.com(classifid advertising)
ww.oakbaynews.com
Social Media:
twitter.com/oakbaynews
www.facebook.com/OakBayNews
Frequency: Wednesday, Friday
Penny Sakamoto, Publisher, publisher@oakbaynews.com
Kevin Laird, Editorial Director, klaird@blackpress.ca
Laura Lavin, Editor, editor@oakbaynews.com
Bruce Hogarth, Director, Circulation, distribution@vicnews.com
Oliver Sommer, Director, Sales, osommer@blackpress.ca
Don Denton, Photo Supervisor, ddenton@vicnews.com
Christine van Reeuwyk, Reporter, cvanreeuwyk@oakbaynews.com

Victoria: Saanich News
Owned By: Black Press News Group Ltd.
818 Broughton St., Victoria, BC V8W 1E4
Tel: 250-920-2090
www.saanichnews.com
Social Media:
twitter.com/saanichnews
www.facebook.com/saanichnews
News is featured from the Vancouver Island municipality of Saanich. A print & an e-edition are available.
Penny Sakamoto, Publisher, publisher@saanichnews.com
Kevin Laird, Editorial Director, editor@saanichnews.com
Edward Hill, Editor, editor@saanichnews.com
Bruce Hogarth, Director, Circulation, distribution@vicnews.com
Don Denton, Photo Supervisor, ddenton@vicnews.com

Victoria: Victoria News
Owned By: Black Press Group Ltd.
818 Broughton St., Victoria, BC V8W 1E4
Tel: 250-386-3484
editor@vicnews.com
www.vicnews.com
Social Media:
twitter.com/victorianews
www.facebook.com/victorianews
News is provided about Victoria & Equimalt, British Columbia. An e-edition is available.
Penny Sakamoto, Publisher, psakamoto@blackpress.ca
Don Descoteau, Editor, editor@vicnews.com
Bruce Hogarth, Director, Circulation, distribution@vicnews.com
Oliver Sommer, Director, Sales, osommer@blackpress.ca

Whistler: The Whistler Question
Owned By: Glacier Interactive Media
#353, 4370 Lorimer Rd., Whistler, BC V0N 1B4
Tel: 604-932-5131; Fax: 604-932-2862
Toll-Free: 877-419-8866
smatches@whistlerquestion.com
www.whistlerquestion.com
Social Media:
twitter.com/whistlernews
www.facebook.com/whistlerquestion
Circulation: 10,000 Frequency: Thursday
Serves the communities of Whistler, Pemberton, and Mt. Currie with select distribution in Greater Vancouver.
Stephanie Matches, Publisher, smatches@whistlerquestion.com
Tanya Foubert, Editor, tanya@whistlerquestion.com

Williams Lake: The Cariboo Advisor
Owned By: Black Press Group Ltd.
68 North Broadway Ave., Williams Lake, BC V2G 1C1
Tel: 250-398-5516
Social Media:
www.facebook.com/pages/The-Cariboo-Advisor/28414815494687
Circulation: 8,769 Frequency: Wednesday
Kathy McLean, Publisher
Rob DeMone, Editor

Williams Lake: Williams Lake Tribune
Owned By: Black Press Group Ltd.
188 North First Ave., Williams Lake, BC V2G 1Y8
Tel: 250-392-2331
editor@wltribune.com
www.wltribune.com
Social Media:
twitter.com/williamslnews
www.facebook.com/pages/Williams-Lake-Tribune/232460703435
Frequency: Tuesday, Thursday; Friday (Tribune Weekend)
The Williams Lake Tribune employs 45 full & part-time people.
Lisa Bowering, Publisher & Manager, Advertising, publisher@wltribune.com
Erin Hitchcock, Editor, editor@wltribune.com
Gaeil Farrar, Community Editor, community@wltribune.com
Beth Walton, Contact, Classifieds, classifieds@wltribune.com

Business in British Columbia

Vancouver: Sounding Board
Business in Vancouver Media Group/Board of Trade
World Trade Center, #400, 999 Canada Pl., Vancouver, BC V6C 3E1
Tel: 604-681-2111; Fax: 604-681-0437
editor@boardoftrade.com
www.boardoftrade.com/publicationsresources/sounding-board.aspx
Social Media:
twitter.com/BoardofTrade
www.facebook.com/VancouverBoardofTrade
Circulation: 12,500 Frequency: 12 times a year
As the official monthly publication of The Vancouver Board of Trade, the Sounding Board newspaper provides analysis and discussion of regional and national issues facing the business community.
Katherine Butler, Marketing, kbutler@biv.com
Greg Hoekstra, Editor

Manitoba

Daily Newspapers in Manitoba

Brandon: Brandon Sun
Owned By: FP Canadian Newspapers LP
501 Rosser Ave., Brandon, MB R7A 0K4
Tel: 204-727-2451
circ@brandonsun.com; opinion@brandonsun.com
www.brandonsun.com
Other information: Classified Advertising, Phone: 204-571-7400; Newsroom: 204-571-7430
Social Media:
twitter.com/thebrandonsun
www.facebook.com/thebrandonsun
Circulation: 15,000
The Brandon Sun publishes seven day a week & serves Brandon & southwestern Manitoba.
Eric Lawson, Publisher
204-571-7401
James O'Connor, Managing Editor
204-571-7431
Jim Lewthwaite, Editor, City
204-571-7430
James Shewaga, Editor, Sports
204-571-7402
Glen Parker, Director, Sales & Marketing
204-571-7424
Andrew Kean, Manager, Information Technology
204-571-7378
Kevin Wardle, Manager, Circulation
204-571-7405
Kara Morrice, Supervisor, Graphic Design
204-571-7452
Lori Timms, Supervisor, Customer Service
204-571-7387
Jonathan Kirkup, Controller
204-571-7406

Flin Flon: The Reminder
Owned By: Glacier Media Inc.
10 North Ave., Flin Flon, MB R8A 0T2
Tel: 204-687-3454
ads@ffdailyreminder.com
Circulation: 1,600 M, W; 1,900 F Frequency: Monday, Wednesday, Friday
Communities served by The Reminder include Flin Flon, Denare Beach, Snow Lake, Creighton, & Cranberry Portage, Manitoba.
Randy Daneliuk, Publisher, rdaneliuk@ffdailyreminder.com
Jonathon Naylor, Editor, news@ffdailyreminder.com
Carl Hill, Contact, Production, chill@ffdailyreminder.com
Karen MacKinnon, Contact, Sales, kmackinnon@ffdailyreminder.com

Portage la Prairie: Portage Daily Graphic
Previous Name: Herald Leader Press
Owned By: Sun Media Corp.
1941 Saskatchewan Ave. West, Portage la Prairie, MB R1N 3B4
Tel: 204-857-3427; Fax: 204-239-1270
events@cpheraldleader.com
www.portagedailygraphic.com
Social Media:
twitter.com/TheDailyGraphic
www.facebook.com/pages/Portage-Daily-Graphic/217303238304
Circulation: 4,300
Barry Clayton, Publisher, barry.clayton@sunmedia.ca

Winnipeg: Winnipeg Free Press
Owned By: FP Canadian Newspapers LP
1355 Mountain Ave., Winnipeg, MB R2X 3B6
Tel: 204-697-7000; Fax: 204-697-7412
letters@freepress.mb.ca(letters to the editor)
www.winnipegfreepress.com
Other information: News Tips: city.desk@freepress.mb.ca
Social Media: www.youtube.com/user/WinnipegFreePress
twitter.com/WinnipegNews
www.fa cebook.com/winnipegfreepress
Circulation: 123,300
Bob Cox, Publisher
204-697-7362
Paul Samyn, Editor
204-697-7295
Steve Pona, Associate Editor & Business Editor
204-697-7264
Mike Aporius, Editor, Photos
204-697-7304
Steve Lyons, Editor, Sports
204-697-7285
Shane Minkin, Editor, Entertainment & Life
204-697-7308
John Sullivan, Editor, Travel
204-697-7293
Laurie Finley, Vice-President
204-697-7164

Winnipeg: The Winnipeg Sun
Owned By: Sun Media Corp.
1700 Church Ave., Winnipeg, MB R2X 3A2
Tel: 204-632-2780
wpgsun.citydesk@sunmedia.ca
www.winnipegsun.com
Social Media:
twitter.com/WinnipegSun
www.facebook.com/wpgsun
Circulation: 45,407 Mon.-Sat., 58,712 Sun. Frequency: Morning
Stephen Riley, CEO & Publisher, stephen.ripley@sunmedia.ca

Other Newspapers in Manitoba

Altona: The Red River Valley Echo
Owned By: Sun Media Corp.
PO Box 700 , Altona, MB R0G 0B0
Tel: 204-324-5001; Fax: 204-324-1402
www.altonaecho.com
Circulation: 6,400 Frequency: Friday
Rick Reimer, General Manager

Baldur: Baldur-Glenboro Gazette
Previous Name: Baldur Gazette; Baldur Gazette News
PO Box 280 , 223 Elizabeth Ave., Baldur, MB R0K 0B0
Tel: 204-535-2127; Fax: 204-535-2350
gazette@mts.net
www.baldur-glenborogazette.ca
Other information: Glenboro Office, Phone: 204-827-2343, E-mail: gazette2@mts.net
Circulation: 1,649 Frequency: Tuesday
The Baldur Gazette News amalgamated with the Glenboro Gazette in 2003 to create the Baldur-Glenboro Gazette. The newspaper serves the southwestern Manitoba communities of Baldur, Glenboro, Belmont, Glenora, Cypress River, Stockton, Ninette, Wawanesa, & Treesbank.
Mike Johnson, Co-Publisher & Editor
Travis Johnson, Co-Publisher & Assistant Editor
Maria Berry, Contact, Local Display & Classified Advertising
Joy Johnson, Contact, Accounting

Beausejour: The Clipper Weekly
Owned By: Clipper Publishing Corp.
PO Box 2033 , 27A - 3rd St. South, Beausejour, MB R0E 0C0
Tel: 204-268-4700; Fax: 204-268-3858
mail@clipper.mb.ca
www.clipper.mb.ca
Social Media:
www.facebook.com/group.php?gid=227001374012429
Circulation: 13,000+ Frequency: Monday
Community news is provided to the North Eastman Region of Manitoba, including the communities of Beausejour, Dugald, Tyndall, Whitemouth, Oakbank, Anola, Garson, & Lac du Bonnet.
Kim MacAulay, Publisher, macaulay@clipper.mb.ca
Mark T. Buss, Editor, news@clipper.mb.ca
Jennifer Kuhn, Manager, Office
Traci Klimchuk, Contact, Display Advertising, traci@clipper.mb.ca

Boissevain: Boissevain Recorder
Boissevain Recorder Inc., PO Box 220 , 425 South Railway St., Boissevain, MB R0K 0E0
Tel: 204-534-6479; Fax: 204-534-2977
subscribe@therecorder.ca; news@therecorder.ca
www.therecorder.ca
Other information: Classified Advertising: classifieds@therecorder.ca
Circulation: 1,300 Frequency: Friday
Lorraine Houston, Editor, editor@therecorder.ca
Paul Rayner, Reporter, prayner@therecorder.ca
Dawn Maynes, Contact, Circulation & Accounts, mail@therecorder.ca
Christie Paskewitz-Smith, Contact, Advertising & Printing, ads@therecorder.ca

Brandon: Westman Journal
Previous Name: Wheat City Journal
Owned By: Glacier Interactive Media
315 College Ave., Unit D, Brandon, MB R7A 1E7
Tel: 204-725-0209; Fax: 204-725-3021
info@wheatcityjournal.ca
www.westmanjournal.com
Social Media:
twitter.com/ChrisTataryn
www.facebook.com/pages/Westman-Journal/22 2064044474022
Circulation: 20,000 Frequency: Thursday (Weekly).
Lorraine Dillabough, Editor, newsroom@wheatcityjournal.ca

Carberry: Carberry News-Express
Carberry News-Express Ltd., PO Box 220 , 34 Main St., Carberry, MB R0K 0H0
Tel: 204-834-2153; Fax: 204-834-2714
info@carberrynews.ca
www.carberrynews.ca
Other information: Classified Advertising: classifieds@carberrynews.ca
Circulation: 972 Frequency: Monday
Bernice Lupton, Publisher
Lori Flett, Acccount Administrator, lori@carberrynews.ca
Betty Reynolds, Contact, Printing Quotes
Eva Rutz, Contact, Advertising, ads@carberrynews.ca

Carman: The Valley Leader
Owned By: Sun Media Corp.
PO Box 70 , Carman, MB R0G 0J0
Tel: 204-745-2051; Fax: 204-745-3976
www.carmanvalleyleader.com
Circulation: 5,852 Frequency: Friday
Rick Reimer, Publisher

Cartwright: Southern Manitoba Review
PO Box 249 , Cartwright, MB R0K 0L0
Tel: 204-529-2342
cartnews@mts.net
www.southernmanitobareview.com
Circulation: 867 Frequency: Thursday
Vicky M. Wallace, Publisher

Darlingford: The Southern Shopper & Review
RR#2, Darlingford, MB R0G 0L0
Tel: 204-362-2666; Fax: 204-246-2018
southernshopper@mts.net
www.southernshopperonline.ca
Frequency: Semi-monthly
The Southern Shopper & Review serves communities in southern Manitoba.

Dauphin: Dauphin Herald
Previous Name: The Weekly News; The Spectator; Dauphin Herald & Press
PO Box 548 , 120 - 1st Ave. NE, Dauphin, MB R7N 1A5
Tel: 204-638-4420; Fax: 204-638-8760
dherald@mts.net
www.dauphinherald.com
Circulation: 5,800 Frequency: Tuesday
Shawn Bailey, Editor, psbailey@mts.net
Mandy Carberry, Manager, Circulation & Distribution, dhcirc@mts.net
Bob Gilroy, Manager, Print Shop, dhprintshop@mts.net
Brent Wright, Manager, Advertising, dherald@mts.net
Shannon Drewniak, Consultant, Classified Advertising, dhclass@mts.net
Amanda Neiman, Consultant, Display Advertising, dherald@mts.net
Debbie Brezden, Contact, Accounting, dh.debbie@mts.net

Deloraine: Deloraine Times & Star
Owned By: Glacier Media Inc.
PO Box 407 , 122 Broadway St. North, Deloraine, MB R0M 0M0
Tel: 204-747-2249; Fax: 204-747-3999
Circulation: 787 Frequency: Friday
Judy Wells, Publisher, cpocket@mts.net
Marlene Tibury, Contact, Sales
204-522-3491
ads.cpocket@mts.net

Emerson: The Southeast Journal
PO Box 68 , 17 Main St., Emerson, MB R0A 0L0
Tel: 204-373-2493; Fax: 204-373-2084
sej@mts.net
www.southeastjournal.ca
Circulation: 3,064 Frequency: Saturday
News is covered in the Manitoba communities of Emerson, Morris, Dominion City, Tolstoi, Woodmore, Riverside/Rosenort, & Ridgeville.
Brenda Piett, Co-Publisher & Contact, Sales & Circulation
Don Piett, Co-Publisher & Editor

Grandview: Grandview Exponent
Owned By: Chaloner Publishers
PO Box 39 , Grandview, MB R0L 0Y0
Tel: 204-546-2555; Fax: 204-546-3081
expos@mts.net
www.grandviewexponent.com
Circulation: 1,178 Frequency: Tuesday
Clayton Chaloner, Publisher & Editor

Killarney: The Guide
Struth Publishing Ltd., PO Box 670 , 336 Park St. East, Killarney, MB R0K 1G0
Tel: 204-523-4611; Fax: 204-523-4445
ads@killarneyguide.ca
www.killarneyguide.ca
Circulation: 1,655 Frequency: Friday
The newspaper is available in print & online.
Jay Struth, Editor, news@killarneyguide.ca
Curt Struth, Manager, Printing & Advertising, printing@killarneyguide.ca

Lac du Bonnet: The Beausejour Review
Owned By: Sun Media Corp.
PO Box 910 , Lac du Bonnet, MB R0E 1A0
Tel: 204-345-8611; Fax: 204-345-6344
info@valleytimes.ca
www.beausejourreview.com
Circulation: 6,904 Frequency: Fri.
Lana Meier, Publisher

Lac du Bonnet: Lac du Bonnet Leader
Owned By: Sun Media Corp.
PO Box 910 , Lac du Bonnet, MB R0E 1A0
Tel: 204-345-8611; Fax: 204-345-6344
www.lacdubonnetleader.com
Circulation: 5,013 Frequency: Friday
Lana Meier, Publisher

Manitou: Manitou Western Canadian
Owned By: BKS Publishing Ltd.
PO Box 190 , 424 Ellis Ave. East, Manitou, MB R0G 1G0
Tel: 204-242-2555; Fax: 204-242-3137
Circulation: 1,305 Frequency: Tuesday
Grant Howatt, Publisher

Melita: Melita New Era
Owned By: Corner Pocket Publishing Ltd.
PO Box 820 , 128 Main St. South, Melita, MB R0M 1L0
Tel: 204-522-3491; Fax: 204-522-3648
Circulation: 1,219 Frequency: Friday
The newspaper serves southwestern Manitoba & southeastern Saskatchewan.
G. Longmuir, Manager, cpocket@mts.net
Marlene Tilbury, Contact, Sales, ads.cpocket@mts.net

Minnedosa: Minnedosa Tribune
PO Box 930 , 14 - 3rd Ave. SW, Minnedosa, MB R0J 1E0
Tel: 204-867-3816; Fax: 204-867-5171
www.minnedosatribune.com
Circulation: 2,737 Frequency: Friday
Darryl Holyk, Publisher & Editor, editor@minnedosatribune.com
Camille McTavish, Office Manager & Contact, Classifieds, class@minnedosatribune.com

Richard Davies, Reporter & Photographer, reporter@minnedosatribune.com
Heather Hopkins, Contact, Graphic Design & Ad Sales, adsales@minnedosatribune.com

Morden: The Morden Times
Owned By: Sun MediaÆCorp.
104 - 8th St., Morden, MB R6M 1Y7
Tel: 204-822-4421; Fax: 204-822-4079
www.mordentimes.com
Circulation: 6,798 Frequency: Friday
Rick Reimer, Publisher

Neepawa: Neepawa Banner
Owned By: 325945 (Mantioba) Ltd.
PO Box 699 , 243 Hamilton St., Neepawa, MB R0J 1H0
Tel: 204-476-3401; Fax: 204-476-5073
Toll-Free: 888-436-4242
twitter.com/NeepawaBanner
www.neepawabanner.com
Social Media: www.youtube.com/TheNeepawaBanner
twitter.com/NeepawaBanner
www.face book.com/neepawabanner
Circulation: 8,297 Frequency: Friday
Ken Waddell, Owner, Publisher, & Contact, Sales, kwaddell@neepawabanner.com
Kate Jackman-Atkinson, Reporter & Photographer, news@neepawabanner.com
Neils Mack, Administrator, Production, pages@neepawabanner.com
Kay De'Ath, Contact, Accounts & Circulation, accounts@neepawabanner.com
Lanny Stewart, Contact, Sports, sports@neepawabanner.com
James Underwood, Contact, Graphic & Web Design, creative@neepawabanner.com
Sandra Unger, Contact, Front Desk, print@neepawabanner.com

Neepawa: Neepawa Press
Owned By: Glacier Media Inc.
PO Box 939 , 423 Mountain Ave., Neepawa, MB R0J 1H0
Tel: 204-476-2309; Fax: 204-476-5802
office@neepawapress.com
www.neepawapress.com
Other information: Classified Advertising, E-mail: classified@neepawapress.com
Circulation: 6,745 Frequency: Wednesday
Brent Fitzpatrick, Regional Publisher, pub@sasktel.net
Darren Graham, General Manager, advertising@neepawapress.com
Kaiten Critchlow, Reporter, kaitencritchlow@neepawapress.com
Jean Seaborn, Manager, Office, office@neepawapress.com

Pilot Mound: The Sentinel Courier
PO Box 179 , 13 Railway St. South, Pilot Mound, MB R0G 1P0
Tel: 204-825-2772; Fax: 204-825-2439
sentinel@sentinelcourier.com
www.sentinelcourier.com
Circulation: 1,100 Frequency: Tuesday
The Sentinel Courier serves the Manitoba communities of Pilot Mound, Clearwater, Mariapolis, La Riviere, & Crystal City.
Susan Peterson, Publisher

Portage la Prairie: Central Manitoba Shopper & News
1943 Saskatchewan Ave. West, Portage la Prairie, MB R1N 0R7
Tel: 204-857-7582; Fax: 204-239-5437
cmshopper@shawcable.com
Frequency: Weekly

Reston: Reston Recorder
Owned By: Glacier Media Inc.
PO Box 10 , 330 - 4th St., Reston, MB R0M 1X0
Tel: 204-877-3321; Fax: 204-522-3648
Circulation: 619 Frequency: Friday
Dolores Caldwell, Manager, cpocket@mts.net
Donna Anderson, Contact, Sales, ads.cpocket@mts.net

Rivers: Rivers Banner
Owned By: 3259545 (Manitoba) Ltd.
PO Box 70 , Rivers, MB R0K 1X0
Tel: 204-328-7494; Fax: 204-328-5212
info@riversbanner.com
www.riversbanner.com
Circulation: 1,671 Frequency: Friday
Sheila Runions, General Manager

Roblin: Roblin Review
PO Box 938 , 119 - 1st Ave., Roblin, MB R0L 1P0
Tel: 204-937-8377; Fax: 204-937-8212
rreview@mts.net; reviewads@mts.net
www.theroblinreview.com
Circulation: 1,812 Frequency: Tuesday
Ed Doering, Editor & Reporter

Russell: Russell Banner
PO Box 100 , 455 Main St. North, Russell, MB R0J 1W0
Tel: 204-773-2069; Fax: 204-773-2645
www.russellbanner.com
Circulation: 1,552 Frequency: Tuesday
Terrie Welwood, Editor & Reporter, rbeditor@mts.net
Cindy Ruston, Contact, Advertising, rbanner@mts.net
Jessica Shaw, Contact, Subscriptions & Accounts, russellbanner@mts.net

Selkirk: The Selkirk Journal
Owned By: Sun Media Corp.
510 Greenwood Ave., Selkirk, MB
Tel: 204-467-2421; Fax: 204-482-3336
www.selkirkjournal.com
Circulation: 18,363 Frequency: Friday
Lana Meier, Publisher

Shilo: Shilo Stag
PO Box 5000 Main, CFB Shilo, Shilo, MB R0K 2A0
Tel: 204-765-3000; Fax: 204-765-3814
stag@mts.net
cg.cfpsa.ca/cg-pc/Shilo/EN/InformationandFAQ/Newspapers
Social Media:
www.facebook.com/ShiloSTAG
Circulation: 3,000 Frequency: Bi-weekly; Thursday
The Canadian Forces newspaper serves the military & civilian communities of CFB Shilo, Wawanesa, Sprucewoods, Cottonwoods, & Douglas.
Mike McEwan, General Manager
Jules Xavier, Managing Editor
Quinn Roberts, Assistant Editor & Base Photographer
Jillian Driessen, Production Assistant
Jennifer Roehl, Advertising Representative

Shoal Lake: Crossroads This Week
Previous Name: Birtle Eye-Witness
Owned By: Nesbitt Publishing Company Ltd.
PO Box 160 , 353 Station Rd., Shoal Lake, MB R0J 1Z0
Tel: 204-759-2644; Fax: 204-759-2521
ctwnews@mts.net
www.crossroadsthisweek.com
Circulation: 2,799 Frequency: Weekly; Fridays
Greg Nesbitt, Publisher

Souris: Souris Plaindealer
PO Box 488 , Souris, MB R0K 2C0
Tel: 204-483-2070; Fax: 204-483-3866
Circulation: 778 Frequency: Friday
Darci Semeschuk, Manager
204-483-2070
cpocket@mts.net
Marlene Tilbury, Contact, Sales
204-522-3491
ads.cpocket@mts.net

St-Boniface: La Liberté
PO Box 190 , St-Boniface, MB R2H 3B4
Tel: 204-237-4823; Fax: 204-231-1998
Toll-Free: 800-523-3355
la-liberte@la-liberte.mb.ca
www.la-liberte.mb.ca/le-journal
Social Media:
www.youtube.com/user/LaLiberteMB?feature=mhum
twitter.com/LaLiberteMB
www.facebook.com/LaLiberteManitoba
Frequency: Weekly
La Liberté is a French language newspaper.
Sophie Gaulin, Editor, redaction@la-liberte.mb.ca
Lysiane Romain, Assistant Editor & Coordinator, Special Projects
Véronique Togneri, Production Manager & Graphics Specialist
Sylvie Laurencelle-Vermette, Officer, Communications & Marketing

Steinbach: The Carillon
377 Main St., Steinbach, MB R5G 1A5
Tel: 204-326-3421; Fax: 204-326-4860
info@thecarillon.com
www.thecarillon.com
Other information: Advertising, E-mail: ads@thecarillon.com
Circulation: 7,357 Frequency: Thursday
The Carillon serves Steinbach southeastern Manitoba. Derksen Printers & Publishers publishes the newspaper.
Glenn Buffie, Publisher & General Manager, gbuffie@thecarillon.com
Peter Dyck, Editor, pdyck@thecarillon.com
Terry Frey, Editor, Sports, tfrey@thecarillon.com
Carol Martens, Editor, Community News, cmartens@thecarillon.com
Alvin Derksen, Manager, Advertising Sales, aderksen@thecarillon.com
Kelsey Wynn, Manager, Circulation, kwynn@thecarillon.com

Stonewall: The Interlake Spectator
Owned By: Sun Media Corp.
486 Main St., Stonewall, MB R0C 2Z0
Tel: 204-642-2421
www.interlakespectator.com
Circulation: 14,341 Frequency: Friday
Lana Meier, Publisher

Stonewall: The Stonewall Argus & Teulon Times
Owned By: Sun Media Corp.
PO Box 190 , 486 Main St., Stonewall, MB R0C 2Z0
Tel: 204-467-2421; Fax: 204-467-5967
stonewallargusteulontimes.com
Circulation: 3,731 Frequency: Friday
Lana Meier, Publisher

Swan River: Swan Valley Star & Times
Owned By: The Gilroy Publishing Group
PO Box 670 , 704 Main St., Swan River, MB R0L 1Z0
Tel: 204-734-3858; Fax: 204-734-4935
info@starandtimes.ca; office@starandtimes.ca
www.starandtimes.ca
Circulation: 3,700 Frequency: Tuesday
Brian Gilroy, Publisher & General Manager, brian@starandtimes.ca
Twyla Machan, Editor, editor@starandtimes.ca
Jackie Hamelin Mayuk, Reporter & Photographer, reporter@starandtimes.ca
Kelley Hagglund, Contact, Classified Advertising, classifieds@starandtimes.ca

The Pas: Opasquia Times
PO Box 750 , 148 Fischer Ave., The Pas, MB R9A 1K8
Tel: 204-623-3435; Fax: 204-623-5601
opads@mts.net(advertising)
www.opasquiatimes.com
Other information: Classified Advertising, E-mail: opclass@mts.net
Circulation: 2,800 Frequency: Wednesday, Friday
Opasquia Times presents news & information from the Opaskwayak Cree Nation, The Pas, the Rural Municipality of Kelsey, & the surrounding region.
Brian Gilroy, Publisher
Jennifer Cook, General Manager, optimes@mts.net
Trent Allen, Editor, opnews@mts.net
Devon Parker, Reporter & Photographer, opsports@mts.net

Thompson: Nickel Belt News
Owned By: Glacier Media Inc.
PO Box 887 , 141 Commercial Pl., Thompson, MB R8N 1N8
Tel: 204-677-4534
Circulation: 7,000 Frequency: Friday
The Nickel Belt News is a free publication that circulates in Thompson & throughout northern Manitoba.
Brent Fitzpatrick, Publisher
Lynn Taylor, General Manager, generalmanager@thompsoncitizen.net
John Barker, Editor, editor@thompsoncitizen.net

Thompson: Thompson Citizen
Owned By: Glacier Media Inc.
PO Box 887 , 141 Commercial Pl., Thompson, MB R8N 1N8
Tel: 204-677-4534; Fax: 204-677-3681
ads@thompsoncitizen.net
www.thompsoncitizen.net
Social Media:
twitter.com/ThompsonCitizen
Circulation: 4,500 Frequency: Wednesday
Brent Fitzpatrick, Regional Publisher, pub@sasktel.net
Lynn Taylor, General Manager, generalmanager@thompsoncitizen.net
John Barker, Editor, editor@thompsoncitizen.net
Ryan Lynds, Manager, Production, production@thompsoncitizen.net
Matt Durnan, Reporter, news@thompsoncitizen.net
Ian Graham, Contact, Sports, sports@thompsoncitizen.net
Brianne Richard, Contact, Classified Advertising, classified@thompsoncitizen.net
Laura Skoreyko, Contact, Sales & Display / Local Advertising, laura@thompsoncitizen.net

Treherne: The Times
PO Box 50 , 194 Broadway St., Treherne, MB R0G 2V0
Tel: 204-723-2542; Fax: 204-723-2754
trehernetimes@mts.net
www.trehernetimes.ca
Circulation: 2,700 Frequency: Weekly
The Times circulates in the Manitoba rural municipalities of South Norfolk, Victoria, Lorne, & Grey. The newspaper is available in print & online.
Gary Lodwick, Editor

Virden: Virden-Empire Advance
Owned By: Glacier Media Inc.
PO Box 250 , #4, 585 Seventh Ave., Virden, MB R0M 2C0
Tel: 204-748-3931; Fax: 204-748-1816
empire12@mts.net
Circulation: 2,459 Frequency: Friday
The newspaper serves the southwestern Manitoba communities of Virden, Elkhorn, Oak Lake, Reston, Pipestone, Miniota, Kenton, & Lenore.
Gail Longmuir, Manager, gail.empire@mts.net
Dianne Hanson, Manager, Sales, empire12@mts.net
Wade Branston, Contact, Production, empire12@mts.net
Trish Peters, Contact, Accounting, accounts.empire@mts.net

Winkler: The Winkler Times
Owned By: Canoe Sun Media
PO Box 1356 , Winkler, MB R6W 4B3
Tel: 204-325-4771; Fax: 204-325-5059
www.winklertimes.com
Circulation: 6,531 Frequency: Friday
Rick Reimer, Publisher

Winnipeg: Headingley Headliner
1355 Mountain Ave., Winnipeg, MB R2X 3B6
Tel: 204-697-7009; Fax: 204-953-4300
www.winnipegfreepress.com/our-communities/headliner
Circulation: 5,500 Frequency: Friday
Michelle Pereira, Publisher
John Kendle, Editor

Winnipeg: The Herald
1355 Mountain Ave., Winnipeg, MB R2X 3B6
Tel: 204-697-7009; Fax: 204-953-4300
classifieds@canstarnews.com
www.winnipegfreepress.com/our-communities/he rald
Circulation: 40,485 Frequency: Wednesday
Michelle Pereira, Publisher & Manager, Sales
204-697-7044
John Kendle, Managing Editor
204-697-7093

Winnipeg: The Jewish Post & News
#11, 395 Berry St., Winnipeg, MB R3J 1N6
Tel: 204-694-3332; Fax: 204-694-3916
jewishp@mymts.net
www.jewishpostandnews.com
Circulation: 2,779 Frequency: Weekly
The newspaper features local news & news from Israel, as well as features & opinions of interest to the Jewish community.
Bernie Bellan, Publisher
Matt Bellan, Publisher & Editor

Winnipeg: The Lance
1355 Mountain Ave., Winnipeg, MB R2X 3B6
Tel: 204-697-7009; Fax: 204-953-4300
www.winnipegfreepress.com/our-communities/lance
Circulation: 36,235 Frequency: Wednesday
Michelle Pereira, Publisher
John Kendle, Editor

Winnipeg: The Metro
1355 Mountain Ave., Winnipeg, MB R2X 3B6
Tel: 204-697-7009; Fax: 204-953-4300
www.winnipegfreepress.com/our-communities/metro
Circulation: 34,499 Frequency: Wednesday
Michelle Pereira, Publisher & Manager, Sales
204-697-7044
John Kendle, Managing Editor
204-697-7093

Winnipeg: The Times
1355 Mountain Ave., Winnipeg, MB R2X 3B6
Tel: 204-697-7009; Fax: 204-953-4300
www.winnipegfreepress.com/our-communities/times
Circulation: 36,208 Frequency: Wednesday
Michelle Pereira, Publisher & Sales Manager
204-697-7044
John Kendle, Managing Editor
204-697-7093

Winnipeg: The Voxair
PO Box 17000 Forces, #105, Bldg. 63, 17 Wing Winnipeg, Winnipeg, MB R3J 3Y5
Tel: 204-833-2500; Fax: 204-833-2809
voxair@mymts.net
www.thevoxair.ca
Social Media:
www.facebook.com/thevoxair
Frequency: Bi-weekly; Wednesday
The Voxair is a community newspaper for Royal Canadian Air Force personnel at 17 Wing Winnipeg.
LCol J.R. Zuorro, Editor-in-Chief
Rick Harris, Managing Editor
Michael Sherby, Voxair Manager, Michael.Sherby@forces.gc.ca
Alison Dickey, Photojournalist & Coordinator, Production
Maureen Walls, Coordinator, Sales
Capt. Jordan Woodman, Wing Public Affairs Officer

New Brunswick

Daily Newspapers in New Brunswick

Caraquet: L'Acadie Nouvelle
CP 5536 , 476, boul St-Pierre ouest, Caraquet, NB E1W 1B7
Tél: 506-727-4444;Téléc: 506-727-7620
Ligne sans frais: 800-561-2255
infos@acadienouvelle.com
www.capacadie.com
Autre information: Bureau de Dieppe, Téléphone: 506-383-1955, Télécopieur: 506-383-7440
Médias sociaux:
twitter.com/capacadie
www.facebook.com/acadienouvelle
Tirage: 16 000
Le journal L'Acadie Nouvelle est le seul quotidien francophone du Nouveau-Brunswick.
Francis Sonier, Éditeur-directeur général, francis.sonier@acadiemedia.com
Gaétan Chiasson, Directeur de la salle des nouvelles, gaetan.chiasson@acadienouvelle.com
René Chiasson, Directeur régional des ventes, Imprimerie et projets spéciaux, rene.chiasson@acadiemedia.com
Jean-Charles Gallant, Directeur régional des ventes, Journal et Internet, jean-charles.gallant@acadiemedia.com
Denis Jean, Directeur des opérations, denis.jean@acadiemedia.com
André Wilson, Directeur marketing et innovation, andre.wilson@acadiemedia.com

Fredericton: The Daily Gleaner
Owned By: Brunswick News Inc.
PO Box 3370 , 984 Prospect St. West, Fredericton, NB E3B 2T8
Tel: 506-452-6671; Fax: 506-452-7405
Toll-Free: 800-565-9399
www.telegraphjournal.com
Frequency: Morning
The Daily Gleaner serves Fredericton & the surrounding region with local & international news.

Moncton: Times & Transcript
Previous Name: The Moncton Times; The Moncton Transcript
Owned By: Brunswick News Inc.
PO Box 1001 , 939 Main St., Moncton, NB E1C 8P3
Tel: 506-859-4905 Toll-Free: 800-322-3329
www.telegraphjournal.com
Frequency: Morning
Subscriptions are available for the print & online editions.

Saint John: The Telegraph-Journal
Owned By: Brunswick News Inc.
PO Box 2350 , 210 Crown St., Saint John, NB E2L 3V8
Toll-Free: 800-222-9710
www.telegraphjournal.com
The Telegraph-Journal is a source for local news from Saint John & for provincial news about the New Brunswick government & issues. The newspaper is distributed throughout New Brunswick.

Other Newspapers in New Brunswick

Bathurst: The Northern Light
Owned By: Brunswick News Inc.
355 King Ave., Bathurst, NB E2A 1P4
Tel: 506-546-4491; Fax: 506-546-1491
www.telegraphjournal.com
Circulation: 3,549 Frequency: Tuesday
Maurice Aube, Publisher
Greg Mulock, Editor

Campbellton: The Tribune
Owned By: Brunswick News Inc.
PO Box 486 , 6 Shannon St., Campbellton, NB E3N 3G9
Tel: 506-753-4413; Fax: 506-759-9595
www.telegraphjournal.com
Circulation: 3,109 Frequency: Friday
Subscriptions are available for both the print & online edition,
Peter MacIntosh, Publisher
Tim Jaques, Editor

Edmundston: Le Journal Madawaska
Détenteur: Brunswick News Inc.
20, rue St. François, Edmundston, NB E3V 1E3
Tél: 506-735-5575;Téléc: 506-735-8086
www.telegraphjournal.com
Fréquence: mercredi; français

Grand Falls: The Victoria Star
Owned By: Brunswick News Inc.
PO Box 7363 , 229 Broadway Blvd., Grand Falls, NB E3Z 2K1
Tel: 506-473-3083
www.telegraphjournal.com
Circulation: 2,347 Frequency: Wednesday
The Victoria Star provides community news & information to the northwestern New Brunswick town of Grand Falls & Victoria County.
Matt Hemphill, Publisher
Mark Rickard, Editor

Grand Sault: La Cataracte
CP 7363 , 229, boul Broadway, Grand Sault, NB E3Z 2K1
Tél: 506-473-3083
Tirage: 5 300 Fréquence: Wed.
Don Calhoun, Publisher

Hampton: The Hampton Herald
242 Main St., Hampton, NB E5N 6B8
Tel: 506-832-5613; Fax: 506-832-3353
info@ossekeag.ca
www.ossekeag.ca
Circulation: 7,450 Frequency: Bi-weekly
The newspaper is distributed in the Town of Hampton & the neighbouring communities of Hatfield Point, Titusville, Belleisle, Smithtown, Bloomfield, Norton, Nauwigewauk, & Bloomfield.
Debbie Hickey, Co-Owner & Operator, Ossekeag Publishing
Mike Hickey, Co-Owner & Operator, Ossekeag Publishing

Hampton: The Sussex Herald
242 Main St., Hampton, NB E5N 6B8
Tel: 506-832-5613; Fax: 506-832-3353
Toll-Free: 888-289-2555
info@ossekeag.ca
www.ossekeag.ca
Circulation: 10,794 Frequency: Bi-weekly
The Sussex Herald serves Sussex, New Brunswick & the neighbouring communities of Petitcodiac, Havelock, Cambridge-Narrows, Apohaqui, & Salisbury.
Debbie Hickey, Co-Owner & Operator, Ossekeag Publishing
Mike Hickey, Co-Owner & Operator, Ossekeag Publishing

Miramichi: Miramichi Leader
Owned By: Brunswick News Inc.
PO Box 500 , 175 General Manson Way, Miramichi, NB E1V 3M6
Tel: 506-622-2600
www.telegraphjournal.com
Frequency: Monday, Wednesday; Friday (Miramichi Weekend)
The Miramichi Leader & the Miramichi Weekend provide news for residents of New Brunswick's Miramichi Valley.
Bill MacIntosh, Publisher
Gail Savoy, Editor

Oromocto: The Post-Gazette
Owned By: Brunswick News Inc.
281 Restigouche Rd., Oromocto, NB E2V 2H5
Tel: 506-357-9813
Circulation: 15,500 Frequency: Thursday
The greater Fredericton area of New Brunswick is served by Oromocto's community newspaper.
Shelley Wood, Publisher
Heather Gratton, Editor

Richibucto: L'Étoile de Kent
#2, 9406, rue Principale, Richibucto, NB E4W 4E1
Tél: 506-523-6231;Téléc: 506-523-6520
redaction@journaletoile.com
Fréquence: Weekly, Thursday
Mario Tardiff

Sackville: Sackville Tribune Post
Owned By: Transcontinental Inc.
80 Main St., Sackville, NB E4L 4A7
Tel: 506-536-2500; Fax: 506-536-4024
www.sackvilletribunepost.com
Social Media:
www.facebook.com/pages/Sackville-Tribune-Post/14581003216
Circulation: 2,392 Frequency: Wednesday
Richard Russell, Publisher
Scott Doherty, Editor

Shediac: Le Moniteur Acadien
CP 5191 , Shediac, NB E4P 8T9
Tél: 506-532-6680;Téléc: 506-532-6681
moniteur@rogers.com
www.moniteuracadien.com
Tirage: 5 200 Fréquence: Hebdomadaire; français
Gilles Hache, Éditeur

St Stephen: International Money Saver
179A King St., St Stephen, NB E3L 2E4
Tel: 506-466-5072; Fax: 506-466-5717
moneysav@nbnet.nb.ca
Circulation: 15,000 Frequency: Saturday

St Stephen: St. Croix Courier
PO Box 250 , Milltown Blvd., St Stephen, NB E3L 2X2
Tel: 506-466-3220; Fax: 506-466-9950
www.stcroixcourier.com
Circulation: 3,324 Tu; 2,193 F Frequency: Tuesday; Friday (Courier Weekend)
Vern Faulkner, Editor
506-466-9952
editor@stcroixcourier.ca
Heather Cunningham, Director, Advertising
506-466-9951
heather@stcroixcourier.ca
Shelley McKeeman, Director, Business Operations
506-466-9954
shelley@stcroixcourier.ca

Sussex: Kings County Record
Owned By: Brunswick News Inc.
593 Main St., Sussex, NB E4E 7H5
Tel: 506-433-1070; Fax: 506-432-3532
www.telegraphjournal.com
Frequency: Tuesday; Friday (Kings County Record Weekender)
David Kelly, Editor

Woodstock: Bugle-Observer
Previous Name: The Bugle; The Observer
Owned By: Brunswick News Inc.
110 Carleton St., Woodstock, NB E7M 1E4
Tel: 506-328-8863
www.telegraphjournal.com
Social Media:
twitter.com/BugleObserver1
Frequency: Tuesday; Friday (Bugle-Observer Weekend)
The Bugle-Observer provides news to New Brunswick's Carleton County.
Peter Macintosh, Publisher
Devon Judge, Editor

Newfoundland & Labrador

Daily Newspapers in Newfoundland & Labrador

Corner Brook: The Western Star
Owned By: Transcontinental Inc.
PO Box 460 , 106 West St., Corner Brook, NL A2H 6E7
Tel: 709-634-4348; Fax: 709-634-9824
newsroom@thewesternstar.com
www.thewesternstar.com
Other information: Advertising, Fax: 709-637-4675
Social Media: www.youtube.com/thewesternstardotcom
twitter.com/western_star
www.face book.com/thewesternstar
Circulation: 52,500 / weekly
The Western Star provides news & information for Corner Brook & western Newfoundland.
Trina Burden, Publisher & General Manager, tburden@thewesternstar.com
Troy Turner, Managing Editor, tturner@thewesternstar.com
Chris Noseworthy, Editor, Social Media & Web, cnoseworthy@thewesternstar.com
Bill Boland, Manager, Operations, bboland@thewesternstar.com
Karen Brinson, Manager, Marketing, kbrinson@thewesternstar.com
Gloria Hunt, Manager, Advertising, ghunt@thewesternstar.com
Janet Maynard, Manager, Finance, jmaynard@thewesternstar.com

St. John's: The Telegram
Owned By: Transcontinental Inc.
PO Box 86 , 430 Topsail Rd., St. John's, NL A1E 4N1
Tel: 709-364-6300; Fax: 709-364-3939
telegram@thetelegram.com; circ@thetelegram.com
www.thetelegram.com
Other information: Advertising, Phone: 709-748-0829; News Tips: 709-364-2323
Social Media:
twitter.com/StJohnsTelegram
www.facebook.com/StJohnsTelegram
Charles Stacey, Publisher & General Manager, cstacey@thetelegram.com
Kerry Hann, Managing Editor, khann@thetelegram.com
Pam Frampton, Associate Managing Editor, pframpton@thetelegram.com
Dan Helmbold, Associate News Editor, dhelmbold@thetelegram.com
Robin Short, Editor, Sports, sports@thetelegram.com
Gerry Carew, Director, Digital Products & Operations, gcarew@thetelegram.com
Keith Connolly, Manager, Advertising, kconnolly@thetelegram.com
Leo Gosse, Manager, Sales & Marketing, lgosse@thetelegram.com
Ian Kirby, Manager, Production, ikirby@thetelegram.com
Don Mackey, Manager, Mailroom, dmackey@thetelegram.com

Other Newspapers in Newfoundland & Labrador

Carbonear: The Compass
Owned By: Transcontinental Inc.
PO Box 760 , 176 Water St., Carbonear, NL A1Y 1C3
Tel: 709-596-6458; Fax: 709-596-1700
www.cbncompass.ca
Circulation: 3,638 Frequency: Tuesday
Kevin Hiscock, General Manager, NL Weeklies, khiscock@cbncompass.ca
Terry Roberts, Senior Editor, editor@cbncompass.ca
Bill Bowman, Editor, editor@cbncompass.ca
Nicholas Mercer, Reporter, nmercer@cbncompass.ca
Amanda Pike, Coordinator, Sales & Circulation, apike@cbncompass.ca
Shelleen Emberley, Representative, Customer Service & Circulation, semberley@cbncompass.ca
Daphne Hearnley, Representative, Advertising Sales, dhearn@cbncompass.ca

Channel-Port-aux-Basques: The Gulf News
Owned By: Transcontinental Inc.
PO Box 1090 , 17 Grand Bay Rd., Channel-Port-aux-Basques, NL A0M 1C0
Tel: 709-695-3671; Fax: 709-695-7901
editor@gulfnews.ca
www.gulfnews.ca
Circulation: 2,506 Frequency: Monday
The Gulf News provides news & information to Channel-Port-aux-Basques & communities in southwestern Newfoundland & Labrador.
Brodie Thomas, Editor
Corinna Yates, Reporter, reporter@gulfnews.ca
Charlene Blackmore, Manager, Circulation, circulation@gulfnews.ca
Michelle Mercer, Advertising Sales Executive, adsales@gulfnews.ca

Clarenville: The Packet
Owned By: Transcontinental Inc.
8B Thompson St., Clarenville, NL A5A 1Y9
Tel: 709-466-2243; Fax: 709-466-2717
editor@thepacket.ca
www.thepacket.ca
Circulation: 4,242 Frequency: Thursday
Newfoundland & Labrador communities on Trinity Bay, Bonavista Bay, & Placentia Bay are served by The Packet.
Barbara Dean-Simmons, Editor, editor@thepacket.ca
Bonnie Goodyear, Manager, Business, bgoodyear@thepacket.ca
Natalie Montague, Circulation Representative, nmontague@thepacket.ca

Gander: The Beacon
Owned By: Transcontinental Inc.
PO Box 420 , 61 Elizabeth Dr., Gander, NL A1V 1W8
Tel: 709-256-4371; Fax: 709-256-3826
info@ganderbeacon.ca
www.ganderbeacon.ca
Social Media:
www.facebook.com/pages/The-Beacon/111859792188557
Circulation: 5,300 Frequency: Thursday
The newspaper serves the town of Gander & communities in the Terra Nova & Bonavista North regions of Newfoundland & Labrador.
Kevin Higgins, Editor, khiggins@ganderbeacon.ca
Matt Molloy, Editor, Sports, mmolloy@ganderbeacon.ca
Terri Saunders, Reporter, tsaunders@ganderbeacon.ca
Marilyn Puddicombe, Coordinator, Provincial Circulation, mpuddicombe@ganderbeacon.ca
Paula Clark, Senior Account Executive, pclark@ganderbeacon.ca
Lori Anstey, Circulation Representative, circulation@ganderbeacon.ca

Grand Falls-Windsor: Advertiser
Owned By: Transcontinental Inc.
PO Box 129 , Grand Falls-Windsor, NL A2A 2J4
Tel: 709-489-2162; Fax: 709-489-4817
editor@advertisernl.ca
www.gfwadvertiser.ca
Circulation: 1,926 M; 2,330 Th; 4,256 total Frequency: Monday, Thursday
Renell LeGrow, Editor, editor@advertisernl.ca
Krysta Colbourne, Associate Editor, kcolbourne@gfwadvertiser.ca
Sue Hickey, Reporter & Photographer, shickey@advertisernl.ca
Kitty Dean, Office Manager, kitty.dean@transcontinental.ca
Karla King, Sales Executive, kingk@gfwadvertiser.ca

Happy Valley-Goose Bay: The Labradorian
Owned By: Transcontinental Inc.
PO Box 39 B, 2 Hillcrest Rd., Happy Valley-Goose Bay, NL A0P 1E0
Tel: 709-896-3341; Fax: 709-896-8781
www.thelabradorian.ca
Circulation: 1,828 Frequency: Monday
The newspaper serves coastal & central Labrador.
Jamie Lewis, Editor, editor@thelabradorian.ca
Alicia Elson, Reporter, reporter@thelabradorian.ca
Sharon Gallant, Business Manager, Sales, sgallant@thelabradorian.ca
Melissa Rumbolt, Contact, Circulation, mrumbolt@thelabradorian.ca

Harbour Breton: The Coaster
Owned By: Transcontinental Inc.
PO Box 298 , 30-42 Canada Dr., Harbour Breton, NL A0H 1P0
Tel: 709-885-2379; Fax: 709-885-2393
editor@thecoaster.ca
www.thecoaster.ca
Other information: Advertising, Phone: 709-885-2378, Fax: 709-885-2393
Social Media:
twitter.com/coasternl
Circulation: 1,493 Frequency: Tuesday
The community newspaper serves the Coast of Bays of Newfoundland & Labrador.
Clayton Hunt, Manager & Editor
John Power, Sales Executive, ads@thecoaster.ca

Labrador City: The Aurora
Owned By: Transcontinental Inc.
PO Box 423 , Labrador City, NL A2V 2K7
Tel: 709-944-2957; Fax: 709-944-2958
www.theaurora.ca
Circulation: 1,554 Frequency: Monday
The Aurora serves residents of western Labrador.
Jamie Lewis, Editor, editor@theaurora.ca
Ty Dunham, Reporter
Paula Hillier, Office Manager, phillier@theaurora.ca
Linda French, Representative, Advertising & Sales, ads@theaurora.ca

Lewisporte: The Pilot
Owned By: Transcontinental Inc.
PO Box 1210 , 151 Main St., Lewisporte, NL A0G 3A0
Tel: 709-535-6910; Fax: 709-535-8640
editor@pilotnl.ca
www.lportepilot.ca
Circulation: 3,016 Frequency: Wednesday
The Pilot serves the Lewisporte - Twillingate area of Newfoundland & Labrador.
Karen Wells, Editor
Pam Snow, Reporter & Photographer, psnow@pilotnl.ca
Joanne Chaffey, Office Manager & Contact, Sales, jchaffey@pilotnl.ca

Marystown: The Southern Gazette
Owned By: Transcontinental Inc.
PO Box 1116 , Ville Marie Dr., Marystown, NL A0E 2M0
Tel: 709-279-3188; Fax: 709-279-2628
www.southerngazette.ca
Circulation: 3,120 Frequency: Tuesday
George Macvicar, Manager & Editor, editor@southerngazette.ca

Paul Herridge, Reporter & Photographer, pherridge@southerngazette.ca
Maxine Drake, Consultant, Sales, mdrake@southerngazette.ca

Paradise: The Shoreline News
PO Box 3065 , Paradise, NL A1L 3W2
Tel: 709-834-2169
tsnews@nf.aibn.com
www.theshorelinenews.com
Circulation: 16,000 Frequency: Saturday
The Shoreline News serves the residents of Paradise, Conception Bay South, Conception Bay Centre, & St. Mary's Bay. Subscriptions are available for both the print & online editions of the newspaper.
Frank Petten, Publisher

Placentia: The Charter
Owned By: Transcontinental Inc.
PO Box 450 , Placentia, NL A0B 2Y0
Tel: 709-227-5240; Fax: 709-227-3892
adsales@thecharter.ca
www.thecharter.ca
Circulation: 4,636 Frequency: Thursday
Elizabeth MacDonald, Editor

Springdale: The Nor'Wester
Owned By: Transcontinental Inc.
PO Box 28 , 4 Juniper Lane, Springdale, NL A0J 1T0
Tel: 709-673-3721; Fax: 709-673-4171
info@thenorwester.ca; adsales@thenorwester.ca
www.thenorwester.ca
Circulation: 2,570 Frequency: Thursday
Rudy Norman, Editor
709-252-2954
editor@thenorwester.ca
Christine Saunders, Manager, Office & Circulation
709-673-3721

St. Anthony: The Northern Pen
Owned By: Transcontinental Inc.
PO Box 520 , 10-12 North St., St. Anthony, NL A0K 4S0
Tel: 709-454-2191; Fax: 709-454-3718
info@northernpen.ca
www.northernpen.ca
Social Media:
twitter.com/northernpen
Circulation: 4,144 Frequency: Monday
Newfoundland & Labrador's northern peninsula & southern Labrador are served by The Northern Pen newspaper.
Kevin Hiscock, General Manager, NL Weeklies, khiscock@cbncompass.ca
Kathy Parsons, Manager, Advertising, kparsons@northernpen.ca
Frances Reardon, Manager, Office & Circulation, freardon@northernpen.ca
Wavey Pilgrim, Account Executive, wpilgrim@northernpen.ca

St-Jean: Le Gaboteur
#254, 65 chemin Ridge, St-Jean, NL A1B 4P5
Tél: 709-753-9585;Téléc: 709-753-9586
gaboteur@nf.sympatico.ca
www.gaboteur.ca
Médias sociaux: www.youtube.com/Legaboteur
www.facebook.com/gaboteur
Tirage: 1 000 Fréquence: Bi-mensuel; français

Stephenville: The Georgian
Owned By: Transcontinental Inc.
PO Box 283 , 43 Main St., Stephenville, NL A2N 2Z4
Tel: 709-643-4531; Fax: 709-643-5041
info@thegeorgian.ca
www.thegeorgian.ca
Other information: Advertising, Phone: 709-643-4531, Fax: 709-643-5041
Circulation: 1,423 Frequency: Monday
Christopher Vaughan, Editor, editor@thegeorgian.ca
Frank Gale, Reporter, reporter@thegeorgian.ca
Julie Power, Representative, Customer Service
Gloria Hunt, Contact, Advertising & Marketing, adsales@thegeorgian.ca

Northwest Territories

Other Newspapers in Northwest Territories

Fort Smith: Slave River Journal
Owned By: Cascade Publishing Limited
PO Box 990 , 207 McDougall Rd., Fort Smith, NT X0E 0P0
Tel: 867-872-2784
news@norj.ca
www.srji.com
Circulation: 1,346 Frequency: Wednesday
Don Jaque, Publisher, don@norj.ca
Meagan Wohlberg, Managing Editor, news@norj.ca

Hay River: The Hub
Owned By: Northern News Services Ltd.
8-4 Courtoreille St., Hay River, NT X0E 1G2
Tel: 867-874-6577; Fax: 867-874-2679
advertise@hayriverhub.com
www.hayriverhub.com
Other information: Classified Advertising, E-mail: classifieds@hayriverhub.com
Social Media:
twitter.com/hayriverhub
www.facebook.com/hayriverhub
Frequency: Weekly
Chris Brodeur, Publisher

Yellowknife: L'Aquilon
CP 456 , Yellowknife, NT X1A 2N4
Tél: 867-873-6603;Téléc: 867-873-6663
ykjournaliste@northwestel.net
www.aquilon.nt.ca
Tirage: 1,000 Fréquence: Vendredi; français
Alain Bessette, Publisher

Yellowknife: Deh Cho Drum
Owned By: Northern News Services Ltd.
PO Box 2820 , Yellowknife, NT X1A 2R1
Tel: 867-695-3786; Fax: 867-695-3766
dehchodrum@nnsl.com
www.nnsl.com/dehcho/dehcho.html
Social Media:
twitter.com/nnslonline
www.facebook.com/NnslOnline
Circulation: 1,458 Frequency: Thu.
Petra Ehrke, Manager, National/Territorial Advertising

Yellowknife: Den Cho Drum
Owned By: Northern News Services Ltd.
PO Box 2820 , Yellowknife, NT X1A 2R1
Tel: 867-873-4031; Fax: 867-873-8507
nnsl@nnsl.com; circulation@nnsl.com
www.nnsl.com/dehcho
Other information: Advertising: advertising@nnsl.com; Editorial: editorial@nnsl.com
Social Media:
twitter.com/nnslonline
www.facebook.com/NnslOnline
Circulation: 1,269 Frequency: Thursday
Jack (Sig) Sigvaldson, Publisher
Michael Scott, General Manager
Bruce Valpy, Managing Editor
Petra Ehrke, Manager, Advertising

Yellowknife: Nunavut News North
Owned By: Northern News Services Ltd.
PO Box 2820 , 5108 - 50th St., Yellowknife, NT X1A 2R1
Tel: 867-873-4031; Fax: 867-873-8507
advertising@nnsl.com
www.nnsl.com/publish/nunavutpromo.html
Circulation: 6,592 Frequency: Weekly; Monday
Jack Sigvaldason, Publisher

Yellowknife: NWT News North
Owned By: Northern News Services Ltd.
PO Box 2820 , 5108 - 50th St., Yellowknife, NT X1A 2R1
Tel: 867-873-4031; Fax: 867-873-8507
nnsl@nnsl.com
www.nnsl.com/nwtnewsnorth/nwt.html
Social Media:
twitter.com/nnslonline
www.facebook.com/NnslOnline
Circulation: 9,158 Frequency: Monday
Jack (Sig) Sigvaldason, Publisher
Bruce Valpy, Managing Editor, editorial@nnsl.com

Yellowknife: Yellowknifer
Owned By: Northern News Services Ltd.
PO Box 2820 , 5108 - 50th St., Yellowknife, NT X1A 2R1
Tel: 867-873-4031; Fax: 867-873-8507
editorial@nnsl.com
www.nnsl.com/publish/yellowkniferpromo.html
Circulation: 5,220 W; 5,875 F; 11,095 Total Frequency: Bi-weekly; Wednesday, Friday
J.W. Sigvaldason, Publisher

Nova Scotia

Daily Newspapers in Nova Scotia

Amherst: Amherst Daily News
Owned By: Transcontinental Inc.
Town Square, PO Box 280 , 147 South Albion St., Amherst, NS B4H 2X2
Tel: 902-667-5102; Fax: 902-667-0419
www.amherstdaily.com
Other information: Advertising, Phone: 902-661-5439, Fax: 902-667-0419
Social Media:
www.facebook.com/pages/Amherst-Daily-News/131375826905362
Circulation: 4,500
Richard Russell, Group Publisher, Transcontinental Nova Scotia Media Group Inc., rrussell@ngnews.ca
Darrell Cole, Managing Editor, dcole@amherstdaily.com
Gladys Coish, Manager, Regional Sales, gcoish@amherstdaily.com
Greg Landry, Manager, Operations, glandry@amherstdaily.com
Joni Johnson, Clerk, Circulation, jjohnson@amherstdaily.com

Halifax: The Chronicle-Herald
Owned By: Halifax Herald Ltd.
PO Box 610 , 2717 Joseph Howe Dr., Halifax, NS B3J 2T2
Tel: 902-426-2811
Social Media:
twitter.com/chronicleherald
www.facebook.com/thechronicleherald
Sarah Dennis, President & Chief Executive Officer
Mary Lou Croft, Executive Vice-President
Bryan Duffy, Vice-President, Finance
Bob Howse, Editor in Chief
Nancy Cook, Director, Sales
Shawn Woodford, Director, Marketing & Product Development

New Glasgow: The News
Owned By: Transcontinental Inc.
PO Box 159 , 352 East River Rd., New Glasgow, NS B2H 5E2
Tel: 902-752-3000
news@ngnews.ca; classified@ngnews.ca
www.ngnews.ca
Other information: Newsroom, Phone: 902-928-3514; Classifieds: 902-928-3515
Social Media:
www.facebook.com/pages/The-News/137537789618902
Nova Scotia's Pictou County is served by the daily newspaper.
Richard Russell, Group Publisher, Transcontinental Nova Scotia Media Group Inc., rrussell@ngnews.ca
Dave Chaulker, District Manager, Reader Sales & Service
902-928-3517
Mark Graham, Manager, Advertising Sales, mgraham@ngnews.ca

Sydney: Cape Breton Post
Owned By: Transcontinental Inc.
PO Box 1500 , 255 George St., Sydney, NS B1P 6K6
Tel: 902-564-5451; Fax: 902-562-7077
news@cbpost.com; edit@cbpost.com
www.capebretonpost.com
Other information: Advertising, Phone: 902-563-3847, Fax: 902-564-6280
Social Media:
twitter.com/capebretonpost; twitter.com/cbpost_sports
www.facebook.com/thecapebretonpost
The Cape Breton Post is Cape Breton Island's only local daily newspaper.
Anita DeLazzer, Publisher & General Manager, adelazzer@cbpost.com
Tom Ayers, Director, Editorial, tayers@cbpost.com
Helen MacCoy, Director, Reader Sales & Distribution, hmaccoy@cbpost.com
Scott MacQuarrie, Manager, Sales, smacquarrie@cbpost.com
Shaun Robinson, Manager, Business & Operations, srobinson@cbpost.com

Truro: Truro Daily News
Owned By: Transcontinental Inc.
PO Box 220 , 6 Louise St., Truro, NS B2N 5C3
Tel: 902-893-9405; Fax: 902-895-6104
Toll-Free: 800-939-4992
news@trurodaily.com
www.trurodaily.com
Other information: Newsroom, Phone: 902-896-7527; Classified Advertising: 902-896-7529
Social Media:
www.facebook.com/pages/Truro-Daily-News/108404435879900

Circulation: 7,100
The newspaper covers Truro, Tatamagouche, & Colchester County.
Carl Fleming, Managing Editor, cfleming@trurodaily.com
Joey Smith, Night Editor & Reporter, jsmith@trurodaily.com
Matt Veno, Editor, Sports, mveno@trurodaily.com
Michelle MacLeod, District Manager, Reader Sales & Service, mmacleod@trurodaily.com
Bruce Pearson, Manager, Advertising, bpearson@trurodaily.com
Judi Wellington, Supervisor, Advertising Retail, jwellington@trurodaily.com

Other Newspapers in Nova Scotia

Amherst: The Citizen-Record
Owned By: Transcontinental Inc.
147 South Albion St., Amherst, NS B4H 2X2
Tel: 902-667-5102; Fax: 902-667-0419
www.cumberlandnewsnow.com
Other information: Advertising, Phone: 902-661-5439
Frequency: Thursday
In 2011, The Citizen & The Record community newspapers merged to create The Citizen-Record. The newspaper covers Nova Scotia's Cumberland County. The Citizen-Record is available in print & online.
Richard Russell, Group Publisher, Transcontinental Nova Scotia Media Group Inc.
902-896-7526
rrussell@ngnews.ca
Christopher Gooding, Co-Editor
902-597-3731
Andrew Wagstaff, Co-Editor
902-661-5440
Gladys Coish, Regional Manager, Sales, gcoish@amherstdaily.com

Antigonish: The Casket
Owned By: Casket Printing & Publishing Company
88 College St., Antigonish, NS B2G 2L7
Tel: 902-863-4370; Fax: 902-863-1943
www.thecasket.ca
Social Media:
twitter.com/casketeditor
www.facebook.com/pages/The-Casket-Newspaper/99987897299
Circulation: 4,064 Frequency: Wednesday
The Casket serves the town & county of Antigonish in Nova Scotia.
Mary Jane McDonald, General Manager, mjm@thecasket.ca
Brian Lazzuri, Managing Editor, editor@thecasket.ca
Gail MacDougall, Editor, Sports, gailmacdougall@thecasket.ca
Dave Roberts, Representative, Advertising, csr@thecasket.ca
Tena McGrath, Contact, Circulation & Subscriptions, subscriptions@thecasket.ca
Greg Walsh, Contact, Graphic Design, graphicdesign@thecasket.ca

Bass River: The Shoreline Journal
Previous Name: West Colchester Free Press
PO Box 41 , RR#1, Bass River, NS B0M 1B0
Tel: 902-647-2968
www.theshorelinejournal.com
Social Media:
twitter.com/mauricerees
www.facebook.com/theshorelinejournal
Circulation: 1,363 Frequency: Monthly
The community newspaper serves Nova Scotia's Fundy Shore, including the communities of Bass River, Truro, Parrsboro, Belmont, Masstown, Debert, & Onslow.
Dorothy Rees, Co-Manager
Maurice Rees, Co-Manager, maurice@theshorelinejournal.com

Bridgetown: Monitor-Examiner
Previous Name: Bridgetown Monitor
PO Box 250 , Bridgetown, NS B0S 1C0
Tel: 902-665-4041
Frequency: Weekly

Digby: The Digby County Courier
Owned By: Transcontinental Inc.
124 Water St., Digby, NS B0V 1A0
Tel: 902-245-4715; Fax: 902-245-6136
info@digbycourier.ca
www.digbycourier.ca
Circulation: 1,374 Frequency: Thursday
John DeMings, Editor, editor@digbycourier.ca
Leanne Delong, Reporter, ldelong@digbycourier.ca
Chris Frost, Representative, Sales, cfrost@digbycourier.ca

Enfield: The Enfield Weekly Press
Owned By: Advocate Media Inc.
287 Hwy. 2, Enfield, NS B2T 1C9
Tel: 902-883-3181; Fax: 902-883-3180
editor@enfieldweeklypress.com
www.enfieldweeklypress.com
Circulation: 1,877 Frequency: Wednesday
Leith Orr, Publisher, leith@advocatemediainc.com

Enfield: The Laker
Owned By: Advocate Media Inc.
287 Hwy. 2, Enfield, NS B2T 1C9
Tel: 902-883-3181; Fax: 902-883-3180
advertising@enfieldweeklypress.com
www.thelaker.ca
Social Media:
twitter.com/TheLakerNews
Circulation: 8,400 Frequency: Monthly
The community newspaper serves Nova Scotia's Lakes area, including Waverley, Windsor Junction, Beaver Bank, Fall River, & Wellington. The Laker is published the first week of each month.
Leith Orr, Publisher, leith@advocatemediainc.com
Abby Cameron, Editor, editor@enfieldweeklypress.com
Scott MacKinnon, Manager, Advertising, scott@advocatemediainc.comom
Angela Isenor, Contact, Design & Production, design@enfieldweeklypress.com
Danielle Shreenan, Contact, Classified & Circulation, admin@enfieldweeklypress.com

Greenwood: The Aurora
PO Box 99 , 14 Wing, Greenwood, NS B0P 1N0
Tel: 902-765-1494; Fax: 902-765-1717
www.auroranewspaper.com
Circulation: 5,900 Frequency: Monday
The Aurora is a free newspaper that serves the personnel of 14 Wing Greenwood, Nova Scotia.
Stephen R. Boates, Managing Editor, editor@auroranewspaper.com
Capt. John Pulchny, Editorial Advisor, john.pulchny@forces.gc.ca
Brian Graves, Coordinator, Production, production@auroranewspaper.com
Anne Kempton, Contact, Business & Advertising, marketing@auroranewspaper.com
John Steeves, Administrative Clerk, frontdesk@auroranewspaper.com

Guysborough: Guysborough Journal
Owned By: Addington Publications
PO Box 210 , 48 Main St., Guysborough, NS B0H 1N0
Tel: 902-533-2851; Fax: 902-533-2750
news@guysboroughjournal.ca
www.guysboroughjournal.com
Other information: Subscriptions, E-mail: subscribe@guysboroughjournal.ca
Circulation: 1,250 Frequency: Wednesday
The community newspaper covers Nova Scotia's Guysborough County. Print & digital editions are available.
Helen Murphy, Publisher, Manager, & Editor
Sharon Heighton, Manager, Office & Circulation
Dorothy Ostewig, Coordinator, Production
Navneet Kaur, Contact, Advertising, advertising@guysboroughjournal.ca

Halifax: The Coast
5567 Cunard St., Halifax, NS B3K 1C5
Tel: 902-422-6278; Fax: 902-425-0013
frontdesk@thecoast.ca; coast@thecoast.ca
www.thecoast.ca
Social Media:
twitter.com/TwitCoast
www.facebook.com/TheCoastHalifax
Circulation: 24,000 Frequency: Thursday
The Coast is an independent, locally owned paper that features news, reports on the arts, & movie, theatre, music, gallery, & museum listings for Halifax, Nova Scotia. The free newspaper is distributed each week at over 650 locations. The Coast is a member of the international Association of Alternative Newsweeklies.
Catherine Salisbury, President, cathsalis@thecoast.ca
Christine Oreskovich, Publisher, christineo@thecoast.ca
Kyle Shaw, Editor, editor@thecoast.ca
Tim Bousquet, Editor, News, timb@thecoast.ca
Stephanie Johns, Editor, Arts, arts@thecoast.ca
Tara Thorne, Editor, Listings, listings@thecoast.ca
Megan Fildes, Manager, Production, meganf@thecoast.ca
Christa Harrie, Manager, Promotions & Marketing, christah@thecoast.ca
Audra McKenna, Manager, Office, audram@thecoast.ca
Jessica Tasker, Manager, Distribution, distribution@thecoast.ca
Bethany Stout, Director, Advertising, bethanys@thecoast.ca
Loukas Crowther, Senior Production Designer, loukasc@thecoast.ca

Inverness: The Inverness Oran
PO Box 100 , 15767 Central Ave., Inverness, NS B0E 1N0
Tel: 902-258-2253; Fax: 902-258-2632
www.oran.ca
Circulation: 4,500 Frequency: Wednesday
Rankin MacDonald, President & Editor, editor@oran.ca
Eleanor MacDonald, Publisher & Secretary
Bill Dunphy, Editor, Sports
Inez Forbes, Manager, Advertising, inez@oran.ca
Frank MacDonald, Treasurer
Ann Morrison, Accountant, ann@oran.ca
Kelly MacGillivray, Contact, Advertising & Circulation
Diane Mouland, Contact, Production

Kentville: The Kings County Advertiser
Owned By: Transcontinental Inc.
#6, 28 Aberdeen St., Kentville, NS B4N 2N1
Tel: 902-681-2121; Fax: 902-681-0830
events@kentvilleadvertiser.ca
www.kingscountynews.ca
Social Media:
twitter.com/KingsNSnews
Circulation: 3,505 Frequency: Tuesday
Jennifer Vardy-Little, Editor, jlittle@kingscountynews.ca
Jennifer Hoegg, Associate Editor, jhoegg@kingscountynews.ca
Sheila Donovan, Representative, Sales, sdonovan@kingscountynews.ca

Kentville: Kings County Register
Owned By: Transcontinental Media Inc.
#6, 28 Aberdeen St., Kentville, NS B4N 2N1
Tel: 902-681-2121; Fax: 902-681-0830
events@kentvilleadvertiser.ca
www.kingscountynews.ca
Circulation: 2,186 Frequency: Wed.

Liverpool: The Queens County Advance
Owned By: Transcontinental Inc.
271 Main St., Liverpool, NS B0T 1K0
Tel: 902-354-3441; Fax: 902-354-2455
info@theadvance.ca
www.theadvance.ca
Social Media:
www.linkedin.com/company/the-queens-county-advance
Circulation: 1,655 Frequency: Tuesday
Aethne Hinchliffe, Reporter, aethne@theadvance.ca
Nick Moase, Reporter, nmoase@theadvance.ca
Kathy Greene, Representative, Sales, kgreene@theadvance.ca

Lunenburg: Lunenburg County Progress
Owned By: Lighthouse Publishing Ltd
PO Box 340 , 108 Montague St., Lunenburg, NS B0J 2C0
Tel: 902-643-8863; Fax: 902-634-3572
mail@southshorenow.ca
southshorenow.ca
Social Media:
www.youtube.com/user/southshorenowca/featured
twitter.com/southshorenow
www.facebook.com/pages/southshorenow/171604385422
Frequency: Wednesday
Lynn Hennigar, President
Vernon Dickie, Editor

Meteghan River: Le Courrier de la Nouvelle-Écosse
9250, rte 1, Meteghan River, NS B0W 2L0
Tél: 902-769-3078;Téléc: 902-769-3869
adminstration@lecourrier.com
www.lecourrier.com
Tirage: 1,325 Fréquence: vendredi
Denise Comeau-Desautels, Directrice générale; Rédactrice en chef; Directrice, des ventes
Stephanie LeBlanc, Chef de production, production@lecourrier.com
Rachid Hertouch, Journaliste, journaliste@lecourrier.com
Susan Comeau, Responsable, publicite@lecourrier.com

Middleton: The Annapolis County Spectator
Owned By: Transcontinental Inc.
PO Box 880 , 87 Commercial St., Middleton, NS B0S 1P0
Tel: 902-825-3457; Fax: 902-825-6707
info@annapolisspectator.ca
www.annapoliscountyspectator.ca
Circulation: 2,077 Frequency: Thursday
Larry Powell, Editor, editor@annapolisspectator.ca
Heather Killen, Reporter, hkillen@annapolisspectator.ca
Al Simpson, Representative, Sales, hkillen@annapolisspectator.ca

Oxford: The Oxford Journal
PO Box 10 , 111 Rideau St., Oxford, NS B0M 1P0
Tel: 902-447-2051; Fax: 902-447-2055
www.oxfordjournal.ca
Circulation: 2,500 Frequency: Wedmesday
The Oxford Journal serves central & eastern Cumberland County in Nova Scotia.
Paul Marchant, Publisher

Pictou: The Advocate
Owned By: Advocate Media Inc.
PO Box 1000 , 21 George St., Pictou, NS B0K 1H0
Tel: 902-485-8014; Fax: 902-752-4816
www.pictouadvocate.com
Social Media:
twitter.com/pictouadvocate
www.facebook.com/pages/The-Pictou-Advocate/11 500838191033
Circulation: 2,758 Frequency: Wednesday
Leith Orr, Publisher, leith@advocatemediainc.com
Jackie Jardine, Editor, editor@pictouadvocate.com
Scott MacKinnon, Manager, Advertising, scott@advocatemediainc.com

Pictou: The Light
Owned By: Advocate Media Inc.
21 George St., Pictou, NS B0K 1H0
Tel: 902-956-8099; Fax: 902-257-2832
circul@advocateprinting.ns.ca(circulation)
www.tatamagouchelight.com
Other information: Subscriptions, Phone: 902-485-8014; Advertising: 902-657-2593
Social Media:
twitter.com/TheLightNews
Circulation: 5,000 Frequency: Monthly; Wednesday
The Light is a free newspaper that provides news & information to the Nova Scotia communities of Tatamagouche, Pugwash, Malagash, Earltown, River John, Wentworth, & Wallace.
Leith Orr, Publisher, leith@advocatemediainc.com
Scott MacKinnon, Manager, Advertising, scott@advocatemediainc.com

Port Hawkesbury: The Reporter
Owned By: Reporter Publishing Ltd.
2 MacLean Ct., Port Hawkesbury, NS B9A 3K2
Tel: 902-625-3300; Fax: 902-625-1701
www.porthawkesburyreporter.com
Social Media:
twitter.com/thereporternews
Circulation: 4,390 Frequency: Tuesday, Friday
Rick Cluett, Publisher, rickc@porthawkesburyreporter.com
Anne Cluett, Manager, Advertising, annec@porthawkesburyreporter.com

Shelburne: The Shelburne County Coast Guard
Owned By: Transcontinental Inc.
164 Water St., Shelburne, NS B0T 1W0
Tel: 902-875-3244; Fax: 902-875-3454
info@thecoastguard.ca
www.thecoastguard.ca
Social Media:
www.facebook.com/group.php?gid=237796249638696
Frequency: Weekly
Greg Bennett, Editor, editor@thecoastguard.ca
Amy Woolvett, Reporter, amywoolvett@thecoastguard.ca
Samantha O'Grady, Representative, Sales, sogrady@thecoastguard.ca

Windsor: The Hants Journal
Owned By: Transcontinental Inc.
73 Gerrish St., Windsor, NS B0N 2T0
Tel: 902-798-8371; Fax: 902-798-5451
info@hantsjournal.ca
www.hantsjournal.ca
Social Media:
twitter.com/HantsJournal
www.facebook.com/pages/The-Hants-Journal/132834 683453645
Circulation: 2,313 Frequency: Thursday
The Hants Journal covers Windsor, Hantsport, & Hants County in Nova Scotia.
Carole Morris-Underhill, Editor, editor@hantsjournal.ca
Ashley Thompson, Reporter, athompson@hantsjournal.ca
Michele White, Representative, Sales, mwhite@hantsjournal.ca

Yarmouth: The Yarmouth County Vanguard
Owned By: Transcontinental Inc.
2 Second St., Yarmouth, NS B5A 4B1
Tel: 902-742-7111; Fax: 902-742-2311
info@thevanguard.ca
www.thevanguard.ca
Other information: Advertising, Fax: 902-742-6527
Circulation: 4,180 Frequency: Tuesday
Fred A. Hatfield, Managing Editor, editor@thevanguard.ca
Tina Comeau, Associate Editor, tcomeau@thevanguard.ca
Patrick Dempsey, Representative, Sales, pdempsey@thevanguard.ca

Nunavut

Other Newspapers in Nunavut

Iqaluit: Nunatsiaq News
Owned By: Nortext Publishing Corporation
PO Box 8 , Iqaluit, NU X0A 0H0
Tel: 867-979-5357; Fax: 867-979-4763
editor@nunatsiaqonline.ca; ads@nunatsiaqonline.ca
www.nunatsiaqonline.ca
Other information: Advertising, Toll-Free: 1-800-263-1452, ext. 131, Fax: 1-800-417-2474
Social Media:
twitter.com/nunatsiaqnews
www.facebook.com/pages/Nunatsiaq-News/100174284441
Circulation: 6,357 Frequency: Friday
The newspaper of the eastern Arctic is published weekly in English & Inuktitut. Nunatsiaq Online is also available each day.
Steven Roberts, Publisher
Jim Bell, Editor

Yellowknife: Kivalliq News
Owned By: Northern News Services Ltd.
PO Box 2820 , Yellowknife, NU X1A 2R1
Tel: 867-873-4031; Fax: 867-873-8507
advertising@nnsl.com
www.nnsl.com/publish/kivpromo.html
Circulation: 1,746 Frequency: Weekly; Wed.
Petra Ehrke, Advertising Manager

Ontario

Daily Newspapers in Ontario

Barrie: Innisfil Examiner
571 Bayfield St., Barrie, ON L4M 4Z9
Tel: 705-726-6537; Fax: 705-726-5148
www.innisfilexaminer.ca
Circulation: 10,558 Frequency: Evening, Mon.-Sat.
David Zilstra, Publisher, david.zilstra@sunmedia.ca
Tom Villemaire, Editor, tom.villemaire@sunmedia.ca

Belleville: The Belleville Intelligencer
Owned By: Sun Media Corp.
#535, 199 Front St., Belleville, ON K8N 5H5
Tel: 613-962-9171; Fax: 613-962-9652
newsroom@intelligencer.ca
www.intelligencer.ca
Social Media:
twitter.com/theintell
www.facebook.com/pages/The-Belleville-Intell igencer/24122
Circulation: Mon.-Fri., Sun. 16,998; Sat. 18,000 Frequency: Afternoon
Bill Gilsky, Managing Editor, bill.glisky@sunmedia.ca

Brantford: The Brantford Expositor
Owned By: Sun Media Corp.
#1, 195 Henry St., Bldg. 4, Brantford, ON N3S 5C9
Tel: 519-756-2020; Fax: 519-756-3285
www.brantfordexpositor.ca
Social Media:
twitter.com/theexpositor
www.facebook.com/BrantfordExpositor
Circulation: 22,082 Frequency: Morning
John Chambers, Editor, john.chambers@sunmedia.ca

Brockville: Recorder & Times
Owned By: Sun Media Corp.
2479 Parkedale Ave., Brockville, ON K6V 3H2
Tel: 613-342-4441; Fax: 613-342-4456
Toll-Free: 800-267-4434
www.recorder.ca
Social Media:
twitter.com/recordertimes
www.facebook.com/recorder.newsroom
Circulation: 13,500 Frequency: Evening, Mon.-Sat.
Liza Nelson, Publisher, liza.nelson@sunmedi.ca
Derek Gordanier, Managing Editor, derek.gordanier@sunmedia.ca

Chatham: Chatham Daily News
Owned By: Sun MNedia Corp.
138 King St. West, Chatham, ON N7M 1E3
Tel: 519-354-2000; Fax: 519-354-3448
www.chathamdailynews.ca
Social Media:
twitter.com/ChathamNews
www.facebook.com/pages/The-Chatham-Daily-News/51 305137016
Circulation: 13,373 Frequency: Evening
Dean Muharrem, Publisher, dean.muharrem@sunmedia.ca

Cobourg: Cobourg Daily Star
Owned By: Sun Media Corp.
99 King St. West, Cobourg, ON K9A 4L1
Tel: 905-372-0131; Fax: 905-372-4966
www.northumberlandtoday.com
Social Media:
twitter.com/northumbtoday
www.facebook.com/NorthumberlandToday
Circulation: 4,503 Frequency: Evening
Mark Holmes, Publisher, mark.holmes@sunmedia.ca
Sharie Lynn Fleming, Managing Editor, sharielynn.fleming@sunmedia.ca

Coburg: Port Hope Evening Guide
Owned By: Sun Media Corp.
99 King St. West, Coburg, ON K9A 4L1
Tel: 905-372-0131; Fax: 905-372-4966
www.northumberlandtoday.com
Social Media:
twitter.com/northumbtoday
www.facebook.com/NorthumberlandToday
Sharie Lyn Fleming, Managing Editor, sharielynn.fleming@sunmedia.ca
Mark Holmes, Publisher, mark.holmes@sunmedia.ca

Cornwall: Cornwall Standard-Freeholder
Owned By: Sun Media Corp.
1150 Montreal Rd., Cornwall, ON K6H 1E2
Tel: 613-933-3160; Fax: 613-933-7521
www.standard-freeholder.com
Social Media:
twitter.com/northumbtoday
www.facebook.com/pages/Standard-Freeholder/114 748981826
Circulation: 14,800 Frequency: Morning, Mon.-Sat.
Milton Ellis, Publisher, milton.ellis@sunmedia.ca
Brian Dryden, Managing Editor, Brian.Dryden@sunmedia.ca

Fort Frances: Daily Bulletin
PO Box 339 , 116 - 1st St. East, Fort Frances, ON P9A 3M7
Tel: 807-274-5373; Fax: 807-274-7286
Toll-Free: 800-465-8508
news@fortfrances.com
www.fftimes.com
Social Media:
twitter.com/fftimes
Circulation: 2,500 Frequency: Afternoon
J.R. Cumming, Publisher, jcumming@fortfrances.com
Mike Behan, Editor, mbehan@fortfrances.com

Guelph: The Guelph Mercury
Owned By: Metroland Media Group Ltd.
#8, 14 Macdonell St., Guelph, ON N1H 6P7
Tel: 519-823-6060 Toll-Free: 866-871-9868
editor@guelphmercury.com
www.guelphmercury.com
Circulation: 40,578 Frequency: Evening
Phil Andrews, Managing Editor, pandrews@guelphmercury.com

Hamilton: The Hamilton Spectator
Previous Name: The Burlington Spectator
44 Frid St., Hamilton, ON L8N 3G3
Tel: 905-526-3333; Fax: 905-526-1395
Toll-Free: 800-263-6902
www.thespec.com
Social Media:
twitter.com/TheSpec
Circulation: 103,664 Mon.-Fri., 118,606 Sat. Frequency: Evening
Dana Robbins, Publisher, pcollins@thespec.com

Kenora: Daily Miner & News
Owned By: Sun Media Corp.
PO Box 1620 , 33 Main St. South, Kenora, ON P9N 3X7
Tel: 807-468-5555; Fax: 807-468-4318
www.kenoradailyminerandnews.com
Social Media:
twitter.com/Kenora_Daily
www.facebook.com/pages/Kenora-Daily-Miner-News/ 1615816705
Circulation: 4,000 Frequency: Evening
Mitch Wolfe, Publisher, mitch.wolfe@sunmedia.ca

Kingston: The Kingston Whig-Standard
Owned By: Sun Media Corp.
6 Cataraqui St., Kingston, ON K7L 4Z7
Tel: 613-544-5000; Fax: 613-530-4122
whig.local@sunmedia.ca
www.thewhig.com
Social Media:
www.facebook.com/KingstonWhigStandard
Circulation: 27,695 Mon.-Fri., 38,822 Sat. Frequency: Morning & evening
Ron Laurin, Publisher, ron.laurin@sunmedia.ca
Derek Shelly, Editor, derek.shelly@sunmedia.ca

Kirkland Lake: Northern Daily News
Osprey Media Group, PO Box 1030 , 8 Duncan Ave., Kirkland Lake, ON P2N 3L4
Tel: 705-567-5321; Fax: 705-567-6162
news@northernnews.ca
www.northernnews.ca
Circulation: 5,800 Frequency: Evening
Joe O'Grady, Managing Editor

Kitchener: The Record
Previous Name: Kitchener-Waterloo Record
Owned By: Metroland West Media Group
160 King St. East, Kitchener, ON N2G 4E5
Tel: 519-894-2231; Fax: 519-894-3912
www.therecord.com
Circulation: 81,702 Frequency: Morning, 6 days a week
Lynn Haddrall, Editor-in-Chief
Paul McCuaig, Publisher

Lindsay: Lindsay Post
Owned By: Sun Media Corp.
17 William St. South, Lindsay, ON K9V 3A3
Tel: 705-324-2113; Fax: 705-324-0174
linretail@thepost.ca
www.thepost.ca
Social Media:
twitter.com/thelindsaypost
www.facebook.com/thelindsaypost
Circulation: 5,500 Frequency: Morning
Gordon Brewerton, Publisher, gordon.brewerton@sunmedia.ca
Jason Bain, Editor, jason.bain@sunmedia.ca

London: The London Free Press
Owned By: Canoe Sun Media Corp.
PO Box 2280 , 369 York St., London, ON N6A 4G1
Tel: 519-679-1111; Fax: 800-265-4105
Toll-Free: 800-365-4167
letters@lfpress.com
www.lfpress.com
Social Media:
twitter.com/lfpress
www.facebook.com/lfpress
Circulation: 91,716 Sun.-Fri., 110,223 Sat. Frequency: Morning
Joe Ruscitti, Editor-in-chief
519-667-4524
joe.ruscitti@sunmedia.ca

Niagara Falls: Niagara Falls Review
Owned By: Sun Media Corp.
4801 Valley Way, Niagara Falls, ON L2E 1W4
Tel: 905-358-5711; Fax: 905-356-0785
www.niagarafallsreview.ca
Social Media:
twitter.com/niafallsreview
www.facebook.com/niagarafallsreview
Circulation: 17,000 Frequency: Morning
Steven Gallagher, Editor, steven.gallagher@sunmedia.ca

North Bay: North Bay Nugget
Owned By: Sun Media Corp.
259 Worthington St. West, North Bay, ON P1B 3B5
Tel: 705-472-3200; Fax: 705-472-1438
nbay.news@sunmedia.ca
www.nugget.ca
Social Media:
twitter.com/northbaynugget
www.facebook.com/NBNugget
Circulation: 29,000 Frequency: Evening, Mon.-Fri.; morning, Sat.
Dan Johnson, Publisher, dan.johnson@sunmedia.ca
Steve Hardy, Managing Editor, steve.hardy@sunmedia.ca

Orillia: Orilla Packet & Times
Owned By: Sun Media Corp.
#15, 425 West St. North, Orillia, ON L3V 7R2
Tel: 705-325-1355; Fax: 705-325-4033
www.orilliapacket.com
Social Media:
twitter.com/OrilliaPacket
www.facebook.com/pages/The-Orillia-Packet-Time s/120034318
Circulation: 13,092
Randy Lucenti, Regional Editor, randy.lucenti@sunmedia.ca
Nathan Taylor, City Editor, nathan.taylor@sunmedia.ca

Ottawa: Le Droit
CP 8860 T, #222, 47 Clarence St., Ottawa, ON K1N 3J9
Tél: 613-562-0111;Téléc: 613-562-7572
www.lapresse.ca.ca/droit
Médias sociaux:
twitter.com/CybLeDroit
www.facebook.com/CybLeDroit
Tirage: 33 281 lun.-ven., 40 638 sam. Fréquence: Matin; français
Jacques Pronovost, Editeur/Président
Andre Larocque, Rédacteur

Ottawa: Metro Ottawa
#402, 116 Albert St., Ottawa, ON K1P 5G3
Tel: 613-236-5058; Fax: 866-253-2024
ottawalistings@metronews.ca
metronews.ca/news/ottawa
Other information: Toll Free Fax: 1-866-253-2024
Circulation: 60,000
Dara Mottahed, Publisher

Ottawa: The Ottawa Citizen
PO Box 5020 , 1101 Baxter Rd., Ottawa, ON K2C 3M4
Tel: 613-829-9100; Fax: 613-726-1198
Toll-Free: 800-267-6100
copydesk@ottawacitizen.com
www.ottawacitizen.com
Circulation: 129,852 Mon.-Fri., 161,901 Sat., 129,749 Sun.
Gerry Nott, Publisher & Editor-in-Chief, gnott@ottawacitizen.com

Ottawa: The Ottawa Sun
Previous Name: Ottawa Sun and Sunday Sun
Owned By: Canoe Sun Media
PO Box 9729 T, Ottawa, ON K1G 5H7
Tel: 613-739-7000; Fax: 613-739-8041
oped@sunpub.com
www.ottawasun.com
Social Media:
twitter.com/ottawasuncom
www.facebook.com/OttawaSun
Circulation: 128,200 Mon.-Fri., 86,600 Sat., 74,000 Sun. Frequency: Morning
Mitchell Axelrad, Editor-in-chief, mitchell.axelrad@sunmedia.ca
Rick Gibbons, Publisher, rick.gibbons@sunmedia.ca

Owen Sound: Owen Sound Sun Times
Owned By: Sun Media Corp.
290 - 9th St. East, Owen Sound, ON N4K 1N7
Tel: 519-376-2250; Fax: 519-372-1861
osst.news@sunmedia.ca
www.owensoundsuntimes.com
Social Media:
twitter.com/OwenSoundST
www.facebook.com/pages/Owen-Sound-Sun-Time s/1058115027839
Circulation: 24,198 Frequency: Evening
Cheryl McMenemy, Publisher, cheryl.mcmenemy@sunmedia.ca
Doug Edgar, Managing Editor, doug.edgar@sunmedia.ca

Pembroke: Pembroke Daily Observer
Previous Name: Pembroke Observer
Owned By: Sun Media Corp.
100 Crandall, Pembroke, ON K8A 0B1
Tel: 613-732-3691; Fax: 613-732-1022
pem.editorial@sunmedia.ca
www.thedailyobserver.ca
Social Media:
twitter.com/Pemobserver
www.facebook.com/TheDailyObserver
Circulation: 5,950 Frequency: Evening
Peter Lapinskie, Managing Editor, Peter.Lapinskie@sunmedia.ca
Jim Kwiatkowski, Publisher, Jim.kwiatkowski@sunmedia.ca

Peterborough: Peterborough Examiner
Owned By: Sun Media Corp.
PO Box 3890 , 60 Hunter St. East, Peterborough, ON K9J 3L4
Tel: 705-745-4641; Fax: 705-745-3361
exam.newsroom@sunmedia.ca
www.thepeterboroughexaminer.com
Social Media:
twitter.com/PBoroexaminer
www.facebook.com/pages/Peterborough-Examiner/1556386678 34
Circulation: 25,453 Mon.-Sat., 23,367 Sun. Frequency: Morning
Gordon Brewerton, Publisher, gordon.brewerton@sunmedia.ca
Jim Hendry, Managing Editor, jim.hendry@sunmedia.ca

Sarnia: Sarnia Observer
Owned By: Sun Media Corp.
140 South Front St., Sarnia, ON N7T 7M8
Tel: 519-344-3641; Fax: 519-332-2951
editorial@theobserver.ca
www.theobserver.ca
Social Media:
twitter.com/sarniaObserver
www.facebook.com/pages/The-Sarnia-Obser ver/15113891159723
Circulation: 22,415 Frequency: Monday-Friday evening; Saturday morning
Daryl Smith, Publisher, daryl.smith@sunmedia.ca
Rod Hilts, Managing Editor, rod.hilts@sunmedia.ca

Sault Ste Marie: Sault Star
Owned By: Sun Media Corp.
145 Old Garden River Rd., Sault Ste Marie, ON P6A 5M5
Tel: 705-759-3030; Fax: 705-759-5947
ssmstar@saultstar.com
www.saultstar.com
Social Media:
twitter.com/SaultStar
www.facebook.com/SaultStar
Circulation: 20,003, Mon. - Sat. Frequency: Evening (morning Sat.)
Lou Maulucci, Publisher, lou.maulucci@sunmedia.ca
Frank Rupnik, Managing Editor, frank.rupnik@sunmedia.ca

Simcoe: Simcoe Reformer
Previous Name: Tuesday Times Reformer
Owned By: Sun Media Corp.
PO Box 370 , 50 Gilberston Dr., Simcoe, ON N3Y 4L2
Tel: 519-426-5710
www.simcoereformer.ca
Social Media:
twitter.com/simcoe_reformer
www.facebook.com/simcoereformer
Circulation: 19,630 Frequency: Tuesday
Sue Downs, Managing Editor, sdowns@bowesnet.com

St Catharines: The St Catharines Standard
Owned By: Sun Media Corp.
17 Queen St., St Catharines, ON L2R 5G5
Tel: 905-684-7251; Fax: 905-684-6032
standard@stcatharinesstandard.ca
www.stcatharinesstandard.ca
Social Media:
twitter.com/stcatstandard
www.facebook.com/stcatharinesstandard
Circulation: 33,000 Mon.-Fri., 47,000 Sat. Frequency: Afternoon
Wendy Metcalfe, Managing Editor, wendy.metcalfe@sunmedia.ca
Judy Bullis, Publisher, judy.bullis@sunmedia.ca

St Thomas: The St Thomas Times-Journal
Owned By: Sun Media Corporation
16 Hincks St., St Thomas, ON N5R 5Z2
Tel: 519-631-2790
www.stthomastimesjournal.com
Social Media:
twitter.com/Timesjournal
www.facebook.com/stthomastimesjournal
Circulation: 7,971 Frequency: Evening
Bev Ponton, Publisher, bev.ponton@sunmedia.ca
Ian McCallum, Managing Editor, ian.mccallum@sunmedia.ca

Stratford: Stratford Beacon-Herald
Owned By: Sun Media Corp.
789 Erie St., Stratford, ON N4Z 1A1
Tel: 519-271-2220
www.stratfordbeaconherald.com
Social Media:
twitter.com/ThebeaconHerald
www.facebook.com/stratfordbeaconherald
Circulation: 11,457 Frequency: Daily
Dave Carter, Publisher, dave.carter@sunmedia.ca

Sudbury: The Sudbury Star
Owned By: Sun Media Corp.
33 MacKenzie St., Sudbury, ON P3B 1Y6
Tel: 705-674-5271; Fax: 705-674-0624
editorial@thesudburystar.com
www.thesudburystar.com
Social Media:
www.twitter.com/sudburystar
www.facebook.com/thesudburystar
Circulation: 26,333 Mon.-Sat., 23,960 Sun. Frequency: Morning
Brian MacLeod, Managing Editor, brian.macleod@sunmedia.ca
Bruce Cowan, Publisher, bruce.cowan@sunmedia.ca

Thunder Bay: The Chronicle-Journal
Previous Name: Times-News
Horizon Operations (Canada) Ltd., 75 South Cumberland St., Thunder Bay, ON P7B 1A3
Tel: 807-343-6200; Fax: 807-345-3582
editor@chroniclejournal.com
www.chroniclejournal.com
Social Media:
twitter.com/cj_thunderbay
www.facebook.com/chroniclejournal
Frequency: 29,110 Mon.-Fri.; 31,764 Sat.; 26,513 Sun.
Brian Dryden, Managing Editor
Colin Bruce, Publisher

Timmins: Timmins Daily Press
Owned By: Sun Media Corp.
187 Cedar St. South, Timmins, ON P4N 7G1
Tel: 705-268-5050; Fax: 705-268-7373
news@thedailypress.ca
www.timminspress.com
Social Media:
twitter.com/TimminsPress
www.facebook.com/pages/Timmins-Daily-Press/12792333394420
Circulation: 13,541 Frequency: Morning
Lisa Wilson, Publisher, lisa.wilson@sunmedia.ca
Thomas Perry, Managing Editor, thomas.perry@sunmedia.ca

Toronto: Daily Racing Form (DRF)
47 Voyageur Ct. North, Toronto, ON M9W 4Y2
Tel: 416-798-1911; Fax: 416-798-1919
www.drf.com
Social Media:
twitter.com/DRFInsidePost
www.facebook.com/racingform
Circulation: 3,570 Mon., 5,529 Tue.-Fri. 9,558 Sat., 8,465 Sun.
Frequency: Morning
Bill Tallon, Editor

Toronto: The Globe & Mail
Owned By: CTVglobemedia Publishing Inc.
444 Front St. West, Toronto, ON M5V 2S9
Tel: 416-585-5600; Fax: 416-585-5102
www.theglobeandmail.com
Circulation: 316,428 Frequency: Morning, Mon. to Sat.; also Report on Business Magazine, Globe Television
Phillip Crawley, Publisher & CEO
John Stackhouse, Editor-in-chief, jstackhouse@globeandmail.com

Toronto: Metro Toronto
Previous Name: Metro Today
625 Church St., 6th Fl., Toronto, ON M4Y 2G1
Tel: 416-486-4900; Fax: 416-482-8097
Toll-Free: 888-916-3876
www.metronews.ca
Circulation: 220,000
Greg Lutes, Publisher

Toronto: National Post
300-1450 Don Mills Rd., Toronto, ON M3B 3R5
Tel: 416-383-2300; Fax: 416-383-2305
www.nationalpost.com
Social Media: pinterest.com/nationalpost
twitter.com/nationalpost
www.facebook.co m/NationalPost
Frequency: Monday-Friday (175,238); Saturday (217,115)
Gordon Fisher, President
Douglas Kelly, Publisher
Mark Spencer, Vice-President, Advertising Sales
Jonathan Harris, Vice-President, Digital Media
Santina Zito, Vice-President, Operations
Stephen Meurice, Editor-in-chief

Toronto: Toronto 24 hours
Owned By: Sun Media Corp.
333 King St. East, Toronto, ON M5A 3X5
Tel: 416-350-6400; Fax: 416-350-6523
eedition.toronto.24hrs.ca
Circulation: 238,612
Bob Harris, Publisher

Toronto: The Toronto Star
Owned By: Toronto Star Newspapers Ltd.
One Yonge St., Toronto, ON M5E 1E6
Tel: 416-367-4500; Fax: 416-869-4328
city@thestar.ca
www.thestar.com
Social Media:
twitter.com/TorontoStar
www.facebook.com/torontosta
Circulation: 390,163 Mon.-Fri., 566,706 Sat., 347,790 Sun.
Frequency: Morning, 2 editions
John D. Cruickshank, Publisher
Michael Cooke, Editor, lettertoed@thestar.ca

Toronto: The Toronto Sun
Owned By: Canoe Sun Media Corp.
Sun Media Corp., 333 King St. East, Toronto, ON M5A 3X5
Tel: 416-947-2222; Fax: 416-368-0374
www.torontosun.com
Social Media:
twitter.com/TheTorontoSun
www.facebook.com/pages/Toronto-Sun/18952 6659635
Circulation: 179,004, Mon.-Fri., 151,101, Sat., 311,689, Sun.
Frequency: Morning
Mike Power, Publisher
James Wallace, Editor-in-chief, james.wallace@sunmedia.ca

Welland: Welland Tribune
Previous Name: Welland-Port Colborne Tribune
Owned By: Sun Media Corp.
228 East Main St., Welland, ON L3B 5P5
Tel: 905-732-2411
welland.tribune@sunmedia.ca
www.wellandtribune.ca
Social Media:
twitter.com/wellandtribune
www.facebook.com/wellandtribune
Circulation: 14,260
Ken Koyama, Publisher, Ken.Koyama@sunmedia.ca

Windsor: The Windsor Star
167 Ferry St., Windsor, ON N9A 4M5
Tel: 519-255-5743; Fax: 519-255-5515
letters@windsorstar.com
www.windsorstar.com
Circulation: 72,514 Mon.-Fri., 82,127 Sat. Frequency: Morning
John Coleman, Editor
519-255-5531

Woodstock: Woodstock Sentinel-Review
Previous Name: Woodstock-Ingersoll Daily Sentinel Review
Owned By: Sun Media Corp.
16 Brock St., Woodstock, ON N4S 3B4
Tel: 519-537-2341
www.woodstocksentinelreview.com
Social Media:
twitter.com/woodstocksr
www.facebook.com/sentinelreview
Circulation: 9,600 Frequency: Evening; supplement - CoverStory (weekly, circ. 15,200)
Andrea DeMeer, Publisher, andrea.demeer@sunmedia.ca

Other Newspapers in Ontario

Ailsa Craig: Middlesex Banner
Owned By: Banner Publications
PO Box 433 , 175 Main St., Ailsa Craig, ON N0M 1A0
Tel: 519-293-1095; Fax: 519-293-1095
editor@banner.on.ca
www.banner.on.ca
Circulation: 1,170 Frequency: Weekly; Wednesdays
Brad Harness, Publisher

Ajax: Ajax/Pickering News Advertiser
Owned By: Metroland Media Group Ltd.
130 Commercial Ave., Ajax, ON L1S 2H5
Tel: 905-683-5110; Fax: 905-683-7363
www.durhamregion.com/community/ajax
Social Media:
twitter.com/newsdurham
www.facebook.com/newsdurham
Circulation: Wed., Thurs. - 51,400; Fri. - 50,400 Frequency: 3 times a week
Tim Whittaker, Publisher
Joanne Burghardt, Editor

Alexandria: Glengarry News
Owned By: Glengarry News Ltd.
PO Box 10 , 3 Main St., Alexandria, ON K0C 1A0
Tel: 613-525-2020; Fax: 613-525-3824
gnews@glengarrynews.ca
www.glengarrynews.ca
Social Media:
www.facebook.com/pages/The-Glengarry-News/128432023877168
Circulation: 6,242 Frequency: Wednesday
Kevin Macdonald, President
Jeff Korenko, Publisher
Steven Warburton, Managing Editor

Alliston: Alliston Herald
Owned By: Metroland Media Group Ltd.
PO Box 280 , #22, 169 Dufferin St. South, Alliston, ON L9R 1E6
Tel: 705-435-6228; Fax: 705-435-3342
www.simcoe.com/community/alliston
Circulation: 21,870 Frequency: Weekly
Joe Anderson, Publisher

Atikokan: Atikokan Progress
Owned By: Atikokan Printing (1994) Ltd.
PO Box 220 , 109 Main St. East, Atikokan, ON P0T 1C0
Tel: 807-597-2731; Fax: 807-597-6103
progress@nwon.com
www.atikokanprogress.ca
Social Media:
www.facebook.com/pages/Atikokan-Progress/1015015585517024
Circulation: 1,513 Frequency: Monday
Eve Shine, Publisher
Michael P. McKinnon, Editor

Aurora: The Auroran
#8, 15213 Yonge St., Aurora, ON L4G 1L8
Tel: 905-727-3300
support@theauroran.com(technical department)
www.auroran.com
Circulation: 19,284 Frequency: Tuesday
The Auroran is an independent community newspaper.
Bob Ince, General Manager & Contact, Advertising, bob@auroran.com
Cynthia Proctor, Manager, Production, cynthia@auroran.com
Zach Shoub, Manager, Operations, zach@auroran.com
Brock Weir, Editor, brock@auroran.com

Aylmer: Aylmer Express
Owned By: Aylmer Express
PO Box 160 , 390 Talbot St. East, Aylmer, ON N5H 2R9
Tel: 519-773-3126; Fax: 519-773-3147
Toll-Free: 800-465-9433
www.aylmerexpress.com
Circulation: 3,886 Frequency: Wednesday
John Hueston, Publisher

Ayr: The Ayr News
PO Box 1173 , 40 Piper St., Ayr, ON N0B 1E0
Tel: 519-632-7432; Fax: 519-632-7743
inquiries@ayrnews.ca
www.ayrnews.ca
Circulation: 3,588 Frequency: Weekly; Wednesday
James W. Schmidt, Publisher, jw.schmidt@ayrnews.ca
John P. Schmidt, Editor, jp.schmidt@ayrnews.ca

Bancroft: Bancroft This Week
Previous Name: Bancroft Times
254 Hastings St., Bancroft, ON K0L 1C0
Tel: 613-332-2002; Fax: 613-332-1710
bancroft-times@sympatico.ca
www.bancroftthisweek.com
Circulation: 4,971 Frequency: Thursday
John Bauman, Publisher
613-332-2002 ext 37

Barrie: Barrie Advance
Owned By: Metroland Media Group Ltd.
21 Patterson Rd., Barrie, ON L4N 7W6
Tel: 705-726-0573; Fax: 705-726-9350
www.simcoe.com
Circulation: 112,078 Frequency: Wednesday, Friday
Lori Martin, Regional Manager & Editor, lmartin@simcoe.com

Barrie: Barrie Examiner
Owned By: Sun Media Corp.
571 Bayfield St., Barrie, ON L4M 4Z9
Tel: 705-726-6537; Fax: 705-726-5148
www.thebarrieexaminer.com
Social Media:
twitter.com/BarrieExaminer
www.facebook.com/pages/Barrie-Examiner/335403 395723
David Zilstra, Publisher, david.zilstra@sunmedia.ca
Brian Rodnick, Editor, brian.rodnick@sunmedia.ca

Barrie: Super Shopper, Buy, Trade & Sell
Previous Name: Trade & Sell
124 Brock St., Barrie, ON L4N 2M2
Tel: 705-726-6015; Fax: 705-726-6015
Toll-Free: 877-777-8820
feedback@buysell.com
www.supershopper.com
Circulation: 13,271 Frequency: Thursday
Laurie Crosson

Barrys Bay: Barry's Bay This Week
Owned By: Sun Media Corp.
41 Bay St., Barrys Bay, ON K0J 1B0
Tel: 613-756-2944; Fax: 613-756-2994
bbtw.newsroom@sunmedia.ca
www.barrysbaythisweek.com
Social Media:
twitter.com/bbaythisweek
www.facebook.com/barrysbaythisweek
Circulation: 2,642 Frequency: Wednesday
Johnd Bauman, Publisher, john.bauman@sunmedia.ca
Jenn Watt, Editor, jenn.watt@sunmedia.ca

Beamsville: Lincoln Post Express
PO Box 400 , 4309 Central Ave., Beamsville, ON L0R 1B0
Tel: 905-563-5393; Fax: 905-563-7977
Circulation: 16,000 Frequency: Weekly
Tim Dundas, Publisher
Tom Wilkinson, Editor

Beamsville: West Niagara News
Previous Name: Grimsby/West Lincoln Independent
Owned By: Sun Media Corp.
PO Box 400 , 4991 King St., Beamsville, ON L0R 1B0
Tel: 905-563-5393; Fax: 905-563-7977
www.westniagaranews.ca
Social Media:
twitter.com/WestNiagaraNews
www.facebook.com/pages/West-Niagara-News/204 327962894
Circulation: 45,526 Frequency: Wednesday, Friday
Tim Dundas, Publisher,
tdundas@niagaracommunitynewspapers.com

Beeton: Beeton/New Tecumseth Times
Previous Name: Tottenham Times, New Tecumseth Times
Owned By: Simcoe-York Printing and Publishing Ltd.
34 Main St. West, Beeton, ON L0G 1A0
Tel: 905-729-2287; Fax: 905-729-2541
admin.syp@rogers.com
www.newtectimes.com
Circulation: 2,490 Frequency: Wed.
John Archibald, Publisher
Wendy Soloduik, News Editor

Beeton: Innisfil Scope
Owned By: Simcoe-York Printing & Publishing Ltd.
PO Box 310 , 34 Main St. West, Beeton, ON L0G 1A0
Tel: 905-729-2287; Fax: 905-729-2541
Toll-Free: 888-559-2287
editor@innisfilscope.com
www.innisfilscope.com
Circulation: 11,755 Frequency: Wednesday
John Archibald, General Manager
Bruce Haire, Publisher

Beeton: King Weekly Sentinel
Previous Name: King Township Sentinel
Owned By: Simcoe-York Printing & Publishing Ltd.
34 Main St., Beeton, ON L0G 1A0
Tel: 905-729-2287; Fax: 905-729-2541
www.kingsentinel.com
Circulation: 6,499 Frequency: Wed.
Mark Pavilons, Editor, editor@kingsentinel.com

Beeton: Woodbridge Advertiser
PO Box 379 , 2 Main St. West, Beeton, ON L0G 1A0
Tel: 905-729-4501 Toll-Free: 888-285-4501
wa@csolve.net
www.ontariosauctionpaper.com
Circulation: 5,500 Frequency: Thu.
Karl Mallette, Publisher

Belleville: Belleville Shopper's Market
PO Box 446 , 365 North Front St., Belleville, ON K8N 5A5
Tel: 866-541-6757; Fax: 866-757-0227
www.shoppersmarket.on.ca
Circulation: 42,800 Frequency: Saturday
Charles Parker, General Manager

Blenheim: Blenheim News-Tribune
Owned By: Blenheim Publishers
PO Box 160 , 62 Talbot St. West, Blenheim, ON N0P 1A0
Tel: 519-676-3321; Fax: 519-676-3454
tribune@southkent.net
Circulation: 2,548 Frequency: Wednesday
Peter Laurie, Editor

Blyth: The Citizen
Owned By: North Huron Publishing Co. Inc.
PO Box 429 , Blyth, ON N0M 1H0
Tel: 519-523-4792; Fax: 519-523-9140
info@northhuron.on.ca
www.northhuron.on.ca
Circulation: 1,976 Frequency: Thursday
Keith Roulston, Publisher
Bonnie Gropp, Editor

Bolton: Caledon Citizen
Owned By: Caledon Publishing Ltd.
25 Queen St., Bolton, ON L7E 1C1
Tel: 905-857-6626; Fax: 905-857-6363
www.caledoncitizen.com
Circulation: 9,814 Frequency: Wednesday
Bruce Haire, Editor, editor@caledoncitizen.com

Bolton: Caledon Enterprise
Previous Name: Bolton Entrprise
Owned By: Metroland Media Group Ltd.
PO Box 99 , #4A, 12612 Hwy. 50, Bolton, ON L7E 5T1
Tel: 905-454-4344
www.metroland.com
Circulation: 28, 054 Frequency: Wednesday 13,193; Saturday 14,861
Bill Anderson, General Manager

Bracebridge: Bracebridge Examiner
Owned By: Metroland Media Group Ltd.
34 E.P. Lee Dr., Bracebridge, ON P1L 1V2
Tel: 705-645-8771; Fax: 705-645-1718
examnews@muskoka.com
www.cottagecountrynow.ca/community/southmuskoka
Social Media:
www.facebook.com/examinerbannernews
Circulation: 5,500 Frequency: Weekly; Wednesday
Joe Anderson, Publisher

Bracebridge: Muskoka Sun
Owned By: Metroland Media
34 E.P. Lee Dr., Bracebridge, ON P1L 1V2
Tel: 705-645-8771; Fax: 705-645-1718
sun@muskoka.com
www.cottagecountrynow.ca/topic/MuskokaSun
Social Media:
twitter.com/TheMuskokaSun
Circulation: 11,000 Frequency: Weekly
Joe Anderson, Publisher

Bracebridge: The Muskokan
Owned By: Metroland Media
PO Box 1049 , 34 E.P. Lee Dr., Bracebridge, ON P1L 1V2
Tel: 705-645-8771; Fax: 705-645-1718
www.cottagecountrynow.ca/topic/Muskokan
Circulation: 20,000 Frequency: Weekly; Thursday
Jack Tynan, Editor
Joe Anderson, Publisher

Bradford: Bradford West Gwillimbury Times
PO Box 1570 , 74 John St. West, Bradford, ON L3Z 2B8
Tel: 905-775-4471; Fax: 905-775-4489
www.bradfordtimes.ca
Circulation: 11,000 Frequency: Saturday
Miriam King, Editor
905-775-4471 ext 223
David Zilstra, Publisher
905-775-4471 ext 263

Bridgebridge: Gravenhurst Banner
Owned By: Metroland Media Group Ltd.
34 E.P. Lee Dr., Bridgebridge, ON P1L 1V2
Tel: 705-687-6674
www.cottagecountrynow.ca/community/southmuskoka
Social Media:
www.facebook.com/examinerbannernews/examinerbannernews
Circulation: 3,043 Frequency: Wednesday
Joe Anderson, Publisher

Brighton: The Independent
Owned By: Metroland Media
PO Box 1030 , 1 Young St., Brighton, ON K0K 1H0
Tel: 613-475-0255; Fax: 613-475-4546
www.metroland.com
Circulation: 18,505 Frequency: Wednesday
Stasha Conolly, Publisher

Brockville: St. Lawrence EMC
7712 Kent Blvd., Brockville, ON K6V 7H6
Tel: 613-342-0305; Fax: 613-498-0307
Toll-Free: 866-242-0262
www.emcstlawrence.ca
Social Media:
twitter.com/emcnews
www.facebook.com/emcnewspaper
Circulation: 28,330 Frequency: Thursday
Duncan Weir, Vice-President, Publishing, dweir@perfprint.ca
Ryland Coyne, Editor, rcoyne@perfprint.ca
Gavin Beer, Regional Manager, Sales, gbeer@perfprint.ca
Lori Sommerdyk, Manager, Distribution,
lsommerdyk@theemc.ca

Burks Falls: Almaguin News
Previous Name: Burks Falls-Powasson Almaguin News
Owned By: Metroland Media Group Ltd.
59 Ontario St., Burks Falls, ON P0A 1C0
Tel: 705-382-9996; Fax: 705-382-9997
Toll-Free: 800-731-6397
www.almaguinnews.com
Circulation: 3,783 Frequency: Wednesday
Joe Anderson, Publisher
Bruce Hickey, Editor

Burlington: Burlington Post
Owned By: Metroland Media Group Ltd.
#1, 5040 Mainway, Burlington, ON L7L 7G5
Tel: 905-632-4444; Fax: 905-632-9162
www.insidehalton.com/community/burlington
Circulation: 46,777 W, 57,619 F, 46,781 Su Frequency: Wednesday, Friday, Sunday
Niel Oliver, Publisher

Caledonia: Grand River Sachem
Owned By: Metroland Media Group Ltd.
3 Sutherland St. West, Caledonia, ON N3W 1C1
Tel: 905-765-4441; Fax: 905-765-3651
news@sachem.ca; advertising@sachem.ca
www.sachem.on.ca
Circulation: 18,110 Frequency: Friday
Neil Dring, Publisher & Editor, ndring@sachem.ca

Cambridge: Cambridge Times
Owned By: Metroland Media Group Ltd.
#1-4, 475 Thompson Dr., Cambridge, ON N1T 2K7
Tel: 519-623-7395; Fax: 519-623-9155
www.cambridgetimes.ca
Circulation: 127,025 Frequency: Tuesday, Thursday, Friday
Peter Winkler, Publisher

Cannington: Brock Citizen
Owned By: Metroland Media Group Ltd.
20 Cameron St. East, Cannington, ON L0E 1E0
Tel: 705-432-8842; Fax: 705-432-2942
www.mykawartha.com
Circulation: 7,110 Frequency: Friday
Bruce Danford, Publisher, bdanford@mykawartha.com
Scott Howard, Editor, showard@mykawartha.com

Carleton Place: Carleton Place EMC & Canadian-Gazette
Owned By: Metroland Media Group Ltd.
53 Bridge St., Carleton Place, ON K7C 2V2
Tel: 613-257-1303; Fax: 613-257-7373
www.yourottawaregion.com/community/ruralsouth
Frequency: Weekly
In 2011, The Carleton Place EMC & The Canadian merged to create the Carleton Place EMC & Canadian-Gazette newspaper.

Mike Mount, Publisher
Ryland Coyne, Managing Editor
Gregory Esnard, Director, Circulation
Andrea Harding, Manager, Advertising

Chatham: Chatham This Week
Owned By: Sun Media Corp.
138 King St. West, Chatham, ON N7M 1E3
Tel: 519-351-7331; Fax: 519-351-7774
don.robinet@sunmedia.ca
www.chathamthisweek.com
Social Media:
twitter.com/ctw_news
www.facebook.com/pages/Chatham-This-Week/1119 10658860951
Circulation: 18,550 Frequency: Wednesday
Jimr Blake, Editor, Jim.blake@sunmedia.ca

Chatham: Chatham-Kent Pennysaver
Owned By: Sun Media Corp.
138 King St. West, 2nd Fl., Chatham, ON N7M 1E3
Tel: 519-351-4362; Fax: 519-351-7774
Toll-Free: 877-351-7331
www.chathampennysaver.com
Circulation: 26,000
Dean Muharrem, Publisher & General Manager, deanm@bowesnet.com

Chatham: Wallaceburg Courier Press
Owned By: Sun Media Corp.
138 King St. West, Chatham, ON N7M 1E3
Tel: 519-351-7331; Fax: 519-351-7334
www.wallaceburgcourierpress.com
Social Media:
twitter.com/w_courierpress
www.facebook.com/pages/Wallaceburg-Courier-Press/15259469
Circulation: 11,168 Frequency: Wed.
Dean Muharrem, Publisher, dean.muharrem@sunmedia.ca
Jim Blake, Editor, Jim.blake@sunmedia.ca

Chesterville: Chesterville Record
Owned By: Etcetera Publications
PO Box 368 , 7 King St., Chesterville, ON K0C 1H0
Tel: 613-448-2321 Toll-Free: 866-307-3541
chestervillerecord.com
Circulation: 1,941 Frequency: Wednesday
Robin Morris, Publisher

Chesterville: The Villager
Previous Name: Russell Villager
Owned By: County Media
7 King St. St., Chesterville, ON K0C 2K0
Tel: 613-445-3804
adsrussellvillager@gmail.com
russellvillager.com
Social Media:
www.facebook.com/TheRussellVillager
Circulation: 989 Frequency: Wed.
Serving Russell Village and Township and surrounding areas.
Robin Morris, Managing Publisher

Clinton: Clinton News-Record
Owned By: Sun Media Corp.
53 Albert St., Clinton, ON N0M 1L0
Tel: 519-482-3443
www.clintonnewsrecord.com
Social Media:
twitter.com/clintonnewsreco
www.facebook.com/ClintonNewsRecord
Circulation: 2,438 Frequency: Wednesday
Neil H. Clifford, Publisher, neil.clifford@sunmedia.ca
Cheryl Heath, Editor, clinton.news@sunmedia.ca

Cobden: Cobden Sun
Owned By: The Cobden Sun Ltd.
PO Box 100 , Crawford St., Cobden, ON K0J 1K0
Tel: 613-646-2380; Fax: 613-628-3291
Circulation: 1,374 Frequency: Wednesday
Ron Tracey, Publisher

Cobourg: The Northumberland News
Owned By: Metroland Media Group Ltd.
#212, 884 Division St., Cobourg, ON K9A 5V6
Tel: 905-373-7355; Fax: 905-373-4719
northnews@northumberlandnews.com
www.northumberlandnews.com
Social Media:
twitter.com/north_news
www.facebook.com/Northnews
Circulation: 22,800 Frequency: Thursday, Friday
The Ontario communities of Cobourg & Port Hope, & the Townships of Cramahe, Hamilton, & Alnwick/Haldimand are served by The Northumberland News.
Tim Whittaker, Publisher
Joanne Burghardt, Editor in Chief
Crystal Crimi, Managing Editor, ccrimi@northumberlandnews.com
Fred Eismont, Director, Advertising
Abe Fakhourie, Manager, Distribution
Lillian Hook, Manager, Office
Peter Dounoukos, Senior Sales Representative, pdounoukos@northumberlandnews.com
Carol Chapple, Contact, Classifieds, cchapple@northumberlandnews.com
Layla Dounoukos, Contact, Distribution, ldounoukos@northumberlandnews.com

Cochrane: Cochrane Times-Post
Previous Name: Cochrane Times
Owned By: Sun Media Corp.
143 - 6th Ave., Cochrane, ON P0L 1C0
Tel: 705-272-3344; Fax: 705-272-3434
www.cochranetimespost.com
Circulation: 2,200 Frequency: Fri.
Wayne Major, Publisher

Collingwood: Collingwood/Wasaga Beach Connection
Previous Name: Collingwood Connection
Owned By: Metroland Media Group Ltd.
#B, 11 Ronell Cres., Collingwood, ON L9Y 4J6
Tel: 705-444-1875; Fax: 705-444-1876
www.simcoe.com
Circulation: 19,640 Frequency: Friday
Carol Lamb, Regional General Manager, clamb@simcoe.com
Larry Culham, Editor

Collingwood: The Enterprise-Bulletin
Owned By: Sun Media Corp.
77 Simcoe St., Collingwood, ON L9Y 3J9
Tel: 705-445-4611; Fax: 705-444-6477
www.theenterprisebulletin.com
Social Media:
twitter.com/EnterpriseBulle
www.facebook.com/theenterprisebulletin?sk=ap p_2309869772
Circulation: 18,591 Frequency: Wednesday, Friday; also Enterprise-Bulletin This Week (Fri., circ. 13,652)
Doreen Sykes, Publisher, doreen.sykes@sunmedia.ca
Morgan Ian Adams, Managing Editor, ian.adams@sunmedia.ca

Cornwall: Le Journal
113 rue de Montréal, Cornwall, ON K6H 1B2
Tél: 613-938-1433;Téléc: 613-938-2798
pub@eap.on.ca
Tirage: 2,300 Fréquence: Jeudi; français
Roger Duplantie, President

Cornwall: Seaway News
Owned By: J.G.F. Holdings Inc.
29 - 2nd St. East, Cornwall, ON K6H 1Y2
Tel: 613-933-0014; Fax: 613-933-0024
diane@cornwallseawaynews.com
www.cornwallseawaynews.com
Circulation: 34,964 Frequency: Friday
Rick Shaver, Editor & General Manager, rshaver@conwallseawaynews.com
Todd Lihou, Editor, todd.lihou@tc.tc

Deep River: North Renfrew Times
Owned By: Deep River Community Assn. Inc.
PO Box 310 , 21 Champlain St., Deep River, ON K0J 1P0
Tel: 613-584-4161; Fax: 613-584-1062
nrt@magma.ca
www.northrenfrewtimes.com
Circulation: 2,226 Frequency: Wednesday
Terry Myers, Editor-in-Chief

Delhi: Delhi News-Record
Owned By: Sun Media Corp.
237 Main St., Delhi, ON N4B 2M4
Tel: 519-582-2510
www.delhinewsrecord.com
Social Media:
twitter.com/DelhiNewsRecord
www.facebook.com/DelhiNewsRecord
Circulation: 1,447 Frequency: Wednesday
Merv Hawkins, Publisher, mhawkins@sunmedia.ca

Dorchester: Dorchester Signpost
Owned By: Dorchester Signpost
15 Bridge St., Dorchester, ON N0L 1G2
Tel: 519-268-7337; Fax: 519-268-3260
info@dorchestersignpost.com
www.dorchestersignpost.com
Circulation: 2,370 Frequency: Wednesday
Fred Huxley, Publisher

Drayton: The Community News
Owned By: W.H.A. Publications Ltd.
PO Box 189 , 41 Wellington St. North, Drayton, ON N0G 1P0
Tel: 519-638-3066; Fax: 519-638-3066
Toll-Free: 800-708-9555
editor@wellingtonadvertiser.com
www.wellingtonadviser.com
Circulation: 4,689 Frequency: Friday
W.H. Adsett, Publisher

Dryden: Dryden Observer
Owned By: Alex Wilson Coldstream Ltd.
PO Box 3009 , 32 Colonization Ave, Dryden, ON P8N 2Y9
Tel: 807-223-2381; Fax: 807-223-2907
Toll-Free: 800-465-7230
www.drydenobserver.ca
Circulation: 3,945 Frequency: Wednesday
Chris Marchand, Editor
807-221-7334

Dundalk: Dundalk Herald
Owned By: Dundalk Herald Publishing
PO Box 280 , 260 Main St. East, Dundalk, ON N0C 1B0
Tel: 519-923-2203; Fax: 519-923-2747
herald.news@bmts.com
dundalkherald.ca
Circulation: 2,053 Frequency: Wednesday
Matthew Walls, Publisher
Mary Fowler, Editor

Dundalk: The Flesherton Advance
PO Box 280 , 260 Main St. East, Dundalk, ON N0C 1B0
Tel: 519-923-2203; Fax: 519-923-2747
herald.news@bmts.com; herald.ads@bmts.com
www.dundalkherald.ca
Frequency: Wednesday
Matt Walls, Publisher
Cathy Walls, General Manager

Dundas: Dundas Star News
Owned By: Metroland Media Group Ltd.
47 Cootes Dr., Dundas, ON L9H 1B5
Tel: 905-523-4014
www.dundasstarnews.com
Circulation: 18,047 Frequency: Friday
Neil Oliver, Publisher

Dundas: Stoney Creek News
Owned By: Metroland Media Group Ltd.
47 Cootes Dr., Dundas, ON L9H 1B5
Tel: 905-523-4014; Fax: 905-664-3102
www.hamiltonnews.com
Circulation: 29,791 Frequency: Fri.
Neil Oliver, Publisher

Dunnville: Dunnville Chronicle
Owned By: Sun Media Corp.
131 Lock St. East, Dunnville, ON N1A 1J6
Tel: 905-774-7632; Fax: 905-774-5744
www.dunnvillechronicle.ca
Social Media:
twitter.com/DunnChronicle
www.facebook.com/dunnvillechronicle
Circulation: 2,642 Frequency: Wednesday; also CoverStory (Sat.)
Judy Bulls, Publisher, judy.bullis@sunmedia.ca

Eganville: Eganville Leader
Owned By: The Eganville Leader Publishing Ltd.
150 John St., Eganville, ON K0J 1T0
Tel: 613-628-2332; Fax: 613-628-3291
leader@nrtco.net
www.eganvilleleader.com
Circulation: 4,931 Frequency: Wednesday
Ron Tracey, Co-Publisher
Gerald Tracey, Editor & Co-Publisher

Elliot Lake: Elliot Lake Standard
Owned By: Sun Media Corp.
14 Hillside Dr. South, Elliot Lake, ON P5A 1M6
Tel: 705-848-7195; Fax: 705-848-0249
news@elliotlakestandard.ca
www.elliotlakestandard.ca
Social Media:
twitter.com/ELStandard
www.facebook.com/pages/Elliot-Lake-Standard/1186295215427
Circulation: 4,564 Frequency: Wednesday

Elmira: Elmira Independent
Owned By: Metroland Media Group Ltd.
PO Box 128 , 13A Industrial Dr., Elmira, ON N3B 2Z5
Tel: 519-669-5155; Fax: 519-669-5928
editor@elmiraindependent.com
www.elmiraindependent.com
Circulation: 3,320 Frequency: Friday
Doug Rowe, General Manager
519-291-1660 ext 116

Elmira: Observer
20B Arthur St., North, Elmira, ON N3B 1Z9
Tel: 519-669-5790; Fax: 519-669-5753
Toll-Free: 888-966-5942
info@woolwichobserver.com
www.observerxtra.com
Other information: Advertising, E-mail:
sales@woolwichobserver.com
Social Media: www.flickr.com/photos/observerxtra
twitter.com/woolwichnews
www.facebo
ok.com/pages/The-Woolwich-Observer/43581142285
Circulation: 15,073 Frequency: Saturday
The community newspaper serves Woolwich & Wellesley Townships in Ontario.
Joe Merlihan, Publisher
Steve Kannon, Editor

Erin: Erin Advocate
Owned By: Metroland Media Group Ltd.
#5, 8 Thompson Cres., Erin, ON N0B 1T0
Tel: 519-833-9603; Fax: 519-833-9605
www.metroland.com
Circulation: 2,200 Frequency: Wednesday
Joan Murray, Editor

Espanola: Mid-North Monitor
Owned By: Sun Media Corp.
#1, 48 Mead Blvd., Espanola, ON P5E 1E8
Tel: 705-869-0588; Fax: 705-869-0587
www.midnorthmonitor.com
Circulation: 3,492 Frequency: Wednesday

Essex: Essex Free Press
Owned By: The Essex Free Press Limited
PO Box 115 , 16 Centre St., Essex, ON N8M 2Y1
Tel: 519-776-4268; Fax: 519-776-4014
essexfreepress@on.aibn.com
sxfreepress.com
Circulation: 3,460 Frequency: Wednesday
Richard Parkinson, Editor & Co-Publisher

Etobicoke: Bloor West Villager
Previous Name: The Villager
Owned By: Metro Land Media Group
307 Humberline Dr., Etobicoke, ON M9W 5V1
Tel: 416-675-4390; Fax: 416-675-9262
insidetoronto.com/community/bloorwestparkdale
Circulation: 42,351 Frequency: Fri.
Dave Harvey, Contact

Exeter: Exeter Times-Advocate
Owned By: Metroland Media Group Ltd.
PO Box 850 , 365 Main St., Exeter, ON N0M 1S0
Tel: 519-235-1331; Fax: 519-235-0766
www.southwesternontario.ca
Circulation: 3,775 Frequency: Wednesday
Deb Lord, Manager

Fergus: Fergus News Express
Previous Name: Ferguse-Elora News Express
Owned By: Metroland Media Group Ltd.
204, Andrew St. West, Fergus, ON N1M 2W7
Tel: 519-843-1310; Fax: 519-843-1334
www.southwesternontario.ca
Circulation: 3,587 Frequency: Wednesday
Francis Bauer, Editor
519-843-1310 ext 107

Fergus: The Wellington Advertiser
Owned By: W.H.A. Publications Ltd.
905 Gartshore St., Fergus, ON N1M 2W8
Tel: 519-843-5410; Fax: 519-843-7607
www.wellingtonadvertiser.com
Circulation: 39,071 Frequency: Friday
W.H. Adsett, Publisher

Fonthill: The Voice
#8, 209 Hwy. 20 East, Fonthill, ON L0S 1E6
Tel: 905-892-8690; Fax: 905-892-0823
classified@thevoiceofpelham.ca
www.thevoiceofpelham.ca
Circulation: 8,437 Frequency: Wednesday
Sarah Murrell, Editor, editor@thevoiceofpelham.ca
Leslie Chiappetta, Manager, Office, office@thevoiceofpelham.ca
Warren Mason, Contact, Advertising Sales, advertising@thevoiceofpelham.ca

Fort Erie: Fort Erie Times
Previous Name: Fort Erie Times Review
Owned By: Sun Media Corp.
PO Box 1219 , #1, 450 Garrison Rd., Fort Erie, ON L2A 1N2
Tel: 905-871-3100; Fax: 905-871-5243
kris.dube@sunmedia.ca
www.forterietimes.com
Circulation: 12,043 Frequency: Saturday
Myra Robertson, Manager
905-871-3100 x202
myra.robertson@sunmedia.ca

Fort Frances: Fort Frances Times
Owned By: Fort Frances Times Ltd.
116 - 1st St. East, Fort Frances, ON P9A 3M7
Tel: 807-274-5373; Fax: 807-274-7286
Toll-Free: 800-465-8508
fftimes.com
Circulation: 5,240 Frequency: Wednesday
Jim Cumming, Publisher
Mike Behan, Editor

Foxboro: Belleville EMC
Owned By: Metroland Media Group Ltd.
PO Box 155 , 244 Ashley St., Foxboro, ON K0K 2B0
Tel: 613-966-2034; Fax: 613-966-8747
www.emcbelleville.com
Social Media:
twitter.com/emcnews
www.facebook.com/emcnewspaper
Circulation: 23,146 Frequency: Thursday
Mike Mount, Vice-President & Regional Publisher
Duncan Weir, Group Publisher, dweir@perfprint.ca
Ryland Coyne, Regional Managing Editor
Terry Bush, Managing Editor, tbush@theemc.ca
Gregory Esnard, Director, Circulation

Gananoque: Gananoque Reporter
Owned By: Sun Media Corp.
79 King St. East, Gananoque, ON K7G 1E8
Tel: 613-382-2156; Fax: 613-382-3010
editor@gananoquereporter.com
www.gananoquereporter.com
Social Media:
twitter.com/GanReporter
www.facebook.com/pages/Gananoque-Reporter/197634110311
48
Circulation: 3,616 Frequency: Wednesday
Liza Nelson, Publisher, liza.nelson@sunmedi.ca

Georgetown: Georgetown Independent/Free Press
Owned By: Metroland Media Group Ltd.
#29, 280 Guelph St., Georgetown, ON L7G 4B1
Tel: 905-873-0301; Fax: 905-873-0398
www.independentfreepress.com
Circulation: 42,299 Frequency: Wednesday, Friday
John McGhie, Managing Editor, jmcghie@theifp.ca
Ken Nugent, Publisher

Geraldton: Times Star
Owned By: Time Star Publishing
401 Main St., Geraldton, ON P0T 1M0
Tel: 807-854-1919; Fax: 807-854-1682
tstar@astrocom-on.com
Circulation: 1,293 Frequency: Wednesday
Stephane Parent, Publisher

Glencoe: Transcript & Free Press
Owned By: Hayter-Walden Publications Inc.
PO Box 400 , 243 Main St., Glencoe, ON N0L 1M0
Tel: 519-287-2615; Fax: 519-287-2408
tfp@execulink.com
Circulation: 2,069 Frequency: Wednesday
Dale Hayter, Publisher
Marie Williams-Gagnon, Editor

Gloucester: L'Express d'Orléans / Orleans Express
#30, 5300 Canotek Rd., Gloucester, ON K1J 8R7
Tél: 613-744-4800;Téléc: 613-744-8232
www.expressottawa.ca
Tirage: 36,500 Fréquence: Mardi; français
Madeleine Joanisse, Éditeur
Florence Bolduc, Rédacteur en chef

Goderich: The Goderich Signal-Star
Owned By: Sun Media Corp.
120 Huckins St., Goderich, ON N7A 3X8
Tel: 519-524-2614; Fax: 519-524-9175
www.goderichsignalstar.com
Social Media:
twitter.com/goderichsignals
www.facebook.com/pages/Goderich-Signal-Star/ 284282905213

Circulation: 5,530 Frequency: Wed; also Focus (every other Fri.)
Linda Leblan, Publisher, linda.leblanc@sunmedia.ca
Andy Bader, Editor, andy.bader@sunmedia.ca

Grand Bend: The Lakeshore Advance
Owned By: Sun Media Corp.
58 Ontario St. North, Grand Bend, ON N0M 1T0
Tel: 519-238-5383; Fax: 519-238-5131
lakeshore.advance@sunmedia.ca
www.lakeshoreadvance.com
Social Media:
twitter.com/lakeshoreadvanc
www.facebook.com/pages/Lakeshore-Advance/1808979619584
69
Circulation: 1,587 Frequency: Wed.
Neil H. Clifford, Publisher, neil.clifford@sunmedia.ca
Lynda Hillman-Rapley, Editor, lakeshore.advance@sunmedia.ca

Gravenhurst: Muskoka Today
PO Box 34 , Gravenhurst, ON P1P 1H5
Tel: 705-687-5777 Toll-Free: 800-240-2329
news@muskokatoday.com
www.muskokatoday.com
Circulation: 10,000
Lois Cooper, Editor
Mark Clairmont, Publisher

Guelph: The Guelph Tribune
Owned By: Metroland Media Group Ltd.
#1, 27 Woodlawn Rd. West, Guelph, ON N1H 1G8
Tel: 519-763-3333; Fax: 519-763-4814
www.guelphtribune.ca
Circulation: 84,356 Frequency: Tuesday 39,808, Friday 44,548

Chris Clark, Editor
519-763-3333 ext 230

Haliburton: Haliburton Echo
Previous Name: Haliburton County Echo
Owned By: Sun Media Corp.
146 Highland St., Haliburton, ON K0M 1S0
Tel: 705-457-1037; Fax: 705-457-3275
info@haliburtonecho.on.ca
www.haliburtonecho.ca
Social Media:
twitter.com/haliburtonecho
www.facebook.com/HaliburtonEcho
Circulation: 4,302 Frequency: Tuesday
John Bauman, Publisher, john.bauman@sunmedia.ca
Jenn Watt, Editor, jenn.watt@sunmedia.ca

Hamilton: Le Régional
Hamilton Branch
970 rue King Est, Hamilton, ON L8M 1C4
Tél: 905-549-7002;Téléc: 905-790-9127
info@leregional.com
www.leregional.com
Tirage: 10,000 Fréquence: Mercredi
Christiane Beaupré, Rédactrice en chef

Hanover: The Post (Hanover)
Owned By: Sun Media Corp.
413 - 18th Ave., Hanover, ON N4N 3S5
Tel: 519-364-2001; Fax: 519-364-6950
postedit@thepost.on.ca
www.thepost.on.ca
Social Media:
twitter.com/hanoverthepost
www.facebook.com/pages/The-Post-Hanover/28286 2818943
Patrick Bales, Managing Editor, patrick.bales@sunmedia.ca
Marie David, Publisher, marie.david@sunmedia.ca

Harrow: Harrow News
Owned By: Harrownews Publishing Co. Inc.
PO Box 310 , 563 Queen St., Harrow, ON N0R 1G0
Tel: 519-738-2542; Fax: 519-738-3874
harnews@mnsi.net
Circulation: 1,300 Frequency: Weekly; Tuesday
Cecil MacKenzie, Publisher & Co-Editor
Gary MacKenzie, Co-Editor

Hawkesbury: Le Carillon
Détenteur: La Comp. D'Edition Andre Paquette Inc.
CP 1000 , 1100 Aberdeen, Hawkesbury, ON K6H 3H1
Tél: 613-632-4155;Téléc: 613-632-6122
nouvelles@eap.on.ca
editionap.ca/en/node/30
Tirage: 19,587 Fréquence: Mercredi; français
Yvan Joly, Directeur

Hawkesbury: Le/The Regional
124, rue Principale est, Hawkesbury, ON K6A 1A3
Tel: 613-632-0112; Fax: 613-632-0277
Toll-Free: 888-477-3566
pub@le-regional.ca; news@le-regional.ca
www.le-regional.ca
Circulation: 32,800 Frequency: Fri.; English & French
André Cayer
Sylvain Roy

Hawkesbury: Tribune-Express édition Ontario
Previous Name: Hawkesbury Tribune/Express
PO Box 1000 , 1100 Aberdeen, Hawkesbury, ON K6H 3H1
Tel: 613-632-4155; Fax: 613-632-8601
nouvelles@eap.on.ca
Circulation: 23,750 Frequency: Friday; English & French
Roger Duplantie

Hearst: Le Nord
CP 2320 , 813, rue Georges, Hearst, ON P0L 1N0
Tél: 705-372-1233;Téléc: 705-362-5954
lenord@lenord.on.ca
www.lenord.on.ca
Médias sociaux:
www.facebook.com/pages/Journal-Le-Nord-de-Hearst/14860381
Tirage: 3000 Fréquence: Mercredi; français et anglais
André Bolduc, Rédacteur-en-chef
Omer Cantin, Éditeur/Publisher
705-372-1233
ocantin@lenord.on.ca

Huntsville: Huntsville Forester
Owned By: Metroland Media Group Ltd.
11 Main St. West, Huntsville, ON P1H 2C5
Tel: 705-789-5541; Fax: 705-789-9381
www.cottagecountrynow.ca
Circulation: 6,305 Frequency: Wednesday
Joe Anderson, Publisher

Ingersoll: Ingersoll Times
Owned By: Sun Media Corp.
19 King St. West, Ingersoll, ON N5C 2J2
Tel: 519-485-3631; Fax: 519-485-6652
jennifer.vandermeer@sunmedia.ca
www.ingersolltimes.com
Social Media:
twitter.com/IngersollTimes
www.facebook.com/IngersollTimes
Circulation: 2,235 Frequency: Wednesday
Andrea DeMeer, Publisher, ademeer@bowesnet.com
Jennifer Vandermeer, Editor, jennifer.vandermeer@sunmedia.ca

Iroquois Falls: The Enterprise
Owned By: William C. Cavell Enterprises Ltd.
PO Box 834 , 727 Synagogue St., Iroquois Falls, ON P0K 1G0
Tel: 705-232-4081
Circulation: 2,345 Frequency: Thursday
W.C. Cavell, Publisher

Kapuskasing: Kapuskasing Times
Owned By: Sun Media Corp.
51 Riverside Dr., Kapuskasing, ON P5N 1A7
Tel: 705-335-2283; Fax: 705-337-1222
kaptimes.news@sunmedia.ca
www.kapuskasingtimes.com
Social Media:
twitter.com/northerntimes
www.facebook.com/pages/The-Northern-Times/1365879097003
33
Frequency: Vendredi; aussi Le/The Weekender (Vendredi)
Wayne Major, Publisher, wayne.major@sunmedia.ca

Kenora: Lake of the Woods Enterprise
Owned By: Sun Media Corp.
33 Main St., Kenora, ON P9N 3X7
Tel: 807-468-5555; Fax: 807-468-4318
info@kenoraenterprise.com
www.lotwenterprise.com
Circulation: 9,400 Frequency: Saturday
Jim Blight

Keswick: Georgina Advocate
Owned By: Metroland Media Group Ltd.
184 Simcoe Ave., Keswick, ON L4P 2C9
Tel: 905-476-7753; Fax: 905-476-5785
www.yorkregion.com
Circulation: 16,757 Frequency: Thursday
Ian Proudfoot, Publisher

Kincardine: The Independent
Owned By: Kincardine Publishing Company Ltd.
PO Box 1240 , 840 Queen St., Kincardine, ON N2Z 2Z4
Tel: 519-396-3111; Fax: 519-396-3899
indepen@bmts.com
www.independent.on.ca
Circulation: 2,203 Frequency: Wednesday
Eric Howald, Publisher

Kincardine: Kincardine News
Owned By: Sun Media Corp.
719 Queen St., Kincardine, ON N2Z 1Z9
Tel: 519-396-2963; Fax: 519-396-6865
kincardine.news@sunmedia.ca
www.kincardinenews.com
Social Media:
twitter.com/Kincardinenews
www.facebook.com/pages/Kincardine-News/120117654724117
Circulation: 3,736 Frequency: Wednesday
Marie David, Publisher, marie.david@sunmedia.ca
Troy Patterson, Editor, kincardine.news@sunmedia.ca

Kingston: Kingston This Week
Owned By: Sun Media Corp.
18 St Remy Place, Kingston, ON K7K 6C4
Tel: 613-389-7400; Fax: 613-389-6443
news@kingstonthisweek.com
www.kingstonthisweek.com
Social Media:
twitter.com/ktwchat
www.facebook.com/pages/Kingston-This-Week/92511562310
Circulation: 97,444 Frequency: Tuesday, Friday
Lori Mitchell, Publisher, lori.mitchell@sunmedia.ca

Kingsville: Kingsville Reporter
Owned By: Postmedia Community Publishing
17 Chestnut St., Kingsville, ON N9Y 1J9
Tel: 519-733-2211; Fax: 519-733-6464
kingsreporter@emporium.ca
Circulation: 2,350 Frequency: Weekly; Tuesday
Greg Sims, Publisher

Kitchener: Guelph Review
Previous Name: Guelph Pennysaver
685 Wabanaki Dr., Kitchener, ON N2C 2G3
Tel: 866-960-0636; Fax: 519-894-5401
www.guelphpennysaver.com
Circulation: 47,300 Frequency: Friday
Rocky Nash, General Manager

Kitchener: Kitchener-Waterloo Review
Previous Name: Pennysaver
Owned By: Sun Media Corp.
685 Wabanaki Dr., Kitchener, ON N2C 2G3
Tel: 519-894-1400; Fax: 519-894-5401
www.k-wreview.ca
Social Media:
twitter.com/kwreview
www.facebook.com/KWReview
Bonnie Frank, Publisher, bonnie.frank@sunmedia.ca

Lakefield: Lakefield Herald
Previous Name: Katchewanooka Herald
Owned By: Lakefield Herald Ltd.
PO Box 1000 , 74 Bridge St., Lakefield, ON K0L 2H0
Tel: 705-652-6594; Fax: 705-652-6912
Toll-Free: 877-652-5114
info@lakefieldherald.com
www.lakefieldherald.com
Circulation: 1,036 Frequency: Friday
Simon Conolly, Publisher

Leamington: The Leamington Post
Owned By: Sun Media Corp.
75 Oak West, Leamington, ON N8H 2B2
Tel: 519-326-4434; Fax: 519-326-2171
leamington.post@sunmedia.ca
www.leamingtonpost.ca
Social Media:
twitter.com/leamingtonpost
www.facebook.com/LeamingtonPost
Circulation: 5,000 Frequency: Wednesday; also Leamington Shopper (Sat., circ. 17,000)
Shannon Ricker, Publisher, shannon.ricker@sunmedia.ca
Jim Blake, Editor, jim.blake@sunmedia.ca

Lindsay: Kawartha Lakes This Week
Owned By: Metroland Media Group Ltd.
192 David St., Lindsay, ON K9V 4Z4
Tel: 705-324-8600; Fax: 705-324-5694
www.mykawartha.com
Bruce Danford, Publisher, bdanford@mykawartha.com

Listowel: Listowel Banner & Independent Plus
Owned By: Metroland Media Group Ltd.
PO Box 97 , 185 Wallace Ave. North, Listowel, ON N4W 3H2
Tel: 519-291-1660; Fax: 519-291-3771
www.southwesternontario.ca
Circulation: 3,480 Frequency: Wednesday; also Independent & Independent Plus (Fri.)
Bill Huether, General Manager
Patrick Raftis, Editor

Little Current: The Manitoulin Expositor
Previous Name: The Manitoulin West Recorder
Owned By: Manitoulin Publishing Co. Ltd.
PO Box 369 , Little Current, ON P0P 1K0
Tel: 705-368-2744; Fax: 705-368-3822
www.manitoulin.ca
Circulation: 1,961 Frequency: Friday
Rick McCutcheon, Publisher

London: London Pennysaver
369 York St., London, ON N6A 4G1
Tel: 519-685-2020; Fax: 519-667-4573
pennyreaderads@londonpennysaver.com
www.londonpennysaver.com
Circulation: 144,000 Frequency: Friday
Marj Bastow, General Manager

London: The Londoner
Owned By: Sun Media Corp.
1147 Gainsborough Rd., London, ON N6H 5L5
Tel: 519-673-5005; Fax: 519-673-4624
www.thelondoner.ca
Social Media:
twitter.com/londoneronline
www.facebook.com/LondonerOnline
Circulation: 107,623 Frequency: Wed.
Linda LeBlanc, Publisher, linda.leblanc@sunmedia.ca
Don Biggs, Editor, don.biggs@sunmedia.ca

Lucknow: Lucknow Sentinel
Owned By: Sun Media Corp.
619 Campbell St., Lucknow, ON N0G 2H0
Tel: 519-528-2822; Fax: 519-528-3529
lucknow.editorial@sunmedia.ca
www.lucknowsentinel.com
Social Media:
twitter.com/LucknowSentine1
www.facebook.com/LucknowSentinel
Circulation: 1,639 Frequency: Wednesday
Linda LeBlanc, Publisher, linda.leblanc@sunmedia.ca
Andy Bader, Editor, andy.bader@sunmedia.ca

Manotick: Barrhaven Independent
Owned By: The Morris Group
1165 Beaverwood Rd., Manotick, ON K4M 1A5
Tel: 613-825-9858; Fax: 613-692-3758
advert@bellnet.ca; newsfile@bellnet.ca
www.barrhavenindependent.on.ca
Social Media:
www.facebook.com/pages/Barrhaven-Independent/1423932758
16
Circulation: 17,625 Frequency: Weekly
Jeffrey Morris, Publisher & Editor

Manotick: Manotick Messenger
Owned By: The Morris Group
PO Box 567 , 1165 Beaverwood Rd., Manotick, ON K4M 1A5
Tel: 613-692-6000; Fax: 613-692-3758
publish@bellnet.ca; newsfile@bellnet.ca
www.manotickmessenger.on.ca
Other information: Classified Advertising, Phone: 613-925-4265
Circulation: 13,928 Frequency: Thursday
Beth Morris, Owner
Jeff Morris, Publisher
Bev McRae, Journalist & Photographer
Gary Coulombe, Representative, Advertising, advert@bellnet.ca

Markham: Markham Economist & Sun
Owned By: Metroland Media Group Ltd.
#115, 50 McIntosh Dr., Markham, ON L3R 9T3
Tel: 905-294-2200; Fax: 905-294-1538
www.yorkregion.com
Circulation: 179,476 Frequency: Tuesday, Thursday, Saturday
Ian Proudfoot, Publisher
Dave Teetzel, Editor

Mattawa: Mattawa Recorder
PO Box 67 , 341 McConnell St., Mattawa, ON P0H 1V0
Tel: 705-744-5361; Fax: 705-744-5361
recorder@bellnet.ca
mattawa.ca
Circulation: 1,050 Frequency: Sunday
Heather Edwards, Contact

Meaford: Blue Mountains Courier-Herald
Previous Name: The Courier Herald
Owned By: Metroland Media
68 Sykes St. North, Meaford, ON N4L 1R2
Tel: 519-599-3760; Fax: 519-538-5028
simcoe.com/community/bluemountains
Circulation: 1,100 Frequency: Wed.; also Meaford Express (Wed., circ. 2,521)
Kathy Taylor, Publisher

Meaford: Meaford Express
Owned By: Metroland Media Group Ltd.
68 Sykes St. North, Meaford, ON N4L 1R2
Tel: 519-538-1421; Fax: 519-538-5028
www.simcoe.com/community/meaford
Social Media:
www.facebook.com/TheMeafordExpress
Circulation: 1,421 Frequency: Wednesday
Joe Anderson, Publisher
Craig Widdifield, Managing Editor
Maureen Christie, Regional Manager, Advertising
Stephen Hall, Manager, Production
Lori McNabb, Manager, Distribution

Midland: Midland & Penetanguishene Mirror
Previous Name: Penetanguishene Mirror
Owned By: Metroland Media Group Ltd.
488 Dominion Ave., Midland, ON L4R 1P6
Tel: 705-527-5500; Fax: 705-527-5467
simcoe.com/community/midland
Circulation: 14,026 W; 19,404 F Frequency: Wednesday, Friday
Travis Mealing, Editor

Midland: Midland Free Press
Previous Name: Penetanguishene Free Press
Owned By: Sun Media Corp.
PO Box 37 , #4, 845 King St., Midland, ON L4R 0B7
Tel: 705-526-5431; Fax: 705-526-1771
freepress@midlandfreepress.com
www.midlandfreepress.com
Social Media:
twitter.com/midlandfreepres
www.facebook.com/midlandfreepress?sk=wall
Circulation: 6,657 Frequency: Tuesday, Friday
Amanda Woodman, General Manager, amanda.woodman@sunmedia.ca

Mildmay: Mildmay Town Crier Weekly
Owned By: Mildmay Town and Country Crier
100 Elora St., Mildmay, ON N0G 2J0
Tel: 519-367-2681; Fax: 519-367-5417
thecrier@wightman.ca
tiffanyweb.bmts.com
Circulation: 1,800 Frequency: Wednesday
John H. Hafermehl, Publisher

Millbrook: Millbrook Times
Owned By: Millbrook Times
PO Box 285 , 5 Lisa Court, Millbrook, ON L0A 1G0
Tel: 705-932-3001; Fax: 705-932-3377
Circulation: 1,816 Frequency: Thu.
Beverley Martin, Publisher

Milton: Milton Canadian Champion
Owned By: Metroland Media Group Ltd.
555 Industrial Dr., Milton, ON L9T 5E1
Tel: 905-878-2341
www.insidehalton.com
Circulation: 38,934 Frequency: Tuesday, Friday
Karen Smith, Editor

Minden: Minden Times
Owned By: Sun Media Corp.
PO Box 97 , #2, 2 IGA Rd., Minden, ON K0M 2K0
Tel: 705-286-1288; Fax: 705-286-4768
www.mindentimes.ca
Social Media:
twitter.com/mindentimes
www.facebook.com/MindenTimes
Circulation: 2,891 Frequency: Wednesday
Jenn Watt, Editor, jenn.watt@sunmedia.ca
John Bauman, Publisher, john.bauman@sunmedia.ca
Don Smith, Publisher

Mississauga: Mississauga News
Owned By: Metroland Media Group Ltd.
3145 Wolfedale Rd., Mississauga, ON L5C 3A9
Tel: 905-273-8111; Fax: 905-277-0146
www.mississauga.com
Social Media:
twitter.com/MissiNewsRoom
www.facebook.com/MissiNewsRoom
Circulation: 150,000 Frequency: Tri-weekly
The News is a perennial newspaper award winner, including best newspaper in Ontario & Canada, on several occasions. The Mississauga News is delivered three times a week to houses. A separate edition called The Mississauga News This Week is delivered Thursdays to apartments.
Ken Nugent, Publisher, knugent@metroland.com
Rob Leuschner, General Manager, rleuschner@metroland.com
Gerry Timbers, Managing Editor, gtimbers@mississauga.net

Mississauga: The Weekly Voice
#206, 2985 Drew Rd., Mississauga, ON L4T 0A4
Tel: 905-795-8282; Fax: 905-795-9801
info@weeklyvoice.com
www.weeklyvoice.com
Circulation: 10,300 W; 30,300 Sa; 40,600 total Frequency: Wednesday, Saturday
The free newspaper presents information & views of intererst to the South Asian community of the Greater Toronto Area. The Weekly Voice is distributed at major South Asian grocery stores, transit stations, libraries, & community centres.
Sudhir Anand, Publisher, sudhir@weeklyvoice.com
Binoy Thomas, Editor in Chief
Dhruv Ghosh, General Manager, dhruv@weeklyvoice.com
Harsimrat Panfer, Contact, Classifieds, admin@weeklyvoice.com
Asha Singhh, Contact, Accounts, accounts@weeklyvoice.com

Mitchell: Mitchell Advocate
Owned By: Sun Media Corp.
42 Montreal St., Mitchell, ON N0K 1N0
Tel: 519-348-8431; Fax: 519-348-8836
www.mitchelladvocate.com
Social Media:
twitter.com/mitchellpaper
www.facebook.com/pages/The-Mitchell-Advocate/274629353636
Circulation: 2,479 Frequency: Wednesday
Andy Bader, Publisher/Editor, andy.bader@sunmedia.ca

Morrisburg: Morrisburg Leader
Owned By: The Morrisburg Leader Ltd.
PO Box 891 , Morrisburg, ON K0C 1X0
Tel: 613-543-2987
info@morrisburgleader.ca
www.morrisburgleader.ca
Circulation: 2,111 Frequency: Wednesday
Sam Laurin, Publisher & Editor
Bonnie McNairn, Managing Editor

Mount Forest: Arthur Enterprise-News
Owned By: Metroland Media Group Ltd.
PO Box 130 , 277 Main St. South, Mount Forest, ON N0G 2L0
Tel: 519-323-1550; Fax: 519-323-4548
www.southwesternontario.ca
Circulation: 748 Frequency: Friday
Lynne Turner, General Manager & Editor, lturner@mountforest.com

Mount Forest: Mount Forest Confederate
Owned By: Metroland Media Group Ltd.
PO Box 130 , 277 Main St. South, Mount Forest, ON N0G 2L0
Tel: 519-323-1550; Fax: 519-323-4548
www.mountforest.com
Circulation: 2,649 Frequency: Wednesday
Lynne Pinnegar, Publisher

Napanee: Napanee Beaver
Owned By: 543570 Ont. Inc.
72 Dundas St. East, Napanee, ON K7R 1H9
Tel: 613-354-6641; Fax: 613-354-2622
www.napaneebeaver.com
Circulation: 2,385 Frequency: Wednesday
Jean Morrison, Publisher
Seth Duchene, Editor

Napanee: The Napanee Guide
Owned By: Sun Media Corp.
#11, 2 Dairy Ave., Napanee, ON K7R 3T1
Tel: 613-354-6648; Fax: 613-354-6708
www.napaneeguide.com
Social Media:
twitter.com/napaneeguide
www.facebook.com/groups/208529789177838
Circulation: 14,101 Frequency: Friday
Ron Laurin, Publisher, ron.laurin@sunmedia.ca

Nepean: Alta Vista Canterbury News
Previous Name: Alta Vista News
Owned By: Ottawa News Publishing
#3B, 15 Antares Dr., Nepean, ON K2E 7Y9
Tel: 613-723-5970; Fax: 613-723-1862
Circulation: 36,000 Frequency: Every other Thu.; also Britannia/Lincoln Heights News, Carlingwood/Baseline News, Glebe & Ottawa South News, Westboro/Hampton Park News
Michael Wollock, Publisher
Tom Collins, Editor

Nepean: Nepean / Barrhaven EMC
Owned By: Metroland Media Group Ltd.
80 Colonnade Rd. North, Nepean, ON K2E 7L2
Tel: 613-224-3330; Fax: 613-224-2265
www.yourottawaregion.com; www.emcbarrhaven.ca
Social Media:
twitter.com/emcnews
www.facebook.com/emcnewspaper
Circulation: 48,172 Frequency: Thursday
In 2011, the Nepean / Barrhaven EMC merged with the Nepean & Barrhaven editions of Ottawa This Week.
Mike Mount, Vice-President & Regional Publisher
Patricia Lonergan, Managing Editor
Tom O'Malley, Digital Manager
Gregory Esnard, Director, Circulation
Carly McGhie, Coordinator, Advertising

Nepean: Stittsville News
Owned By: Metroland Media Group Ltd.
#4, 80 Colonnade Rd., Nepean, ON K2E 7L2
Tel: 613-224-3330; Fax: 613-224-2265
metroland.com/Communities/100094/Stittsville_News_EMC
Circulation: 1,935 Frequency: Tuesday
Bryan Wiltsie, Publisher

New Hamburg: New Hamburg Independent
Owned By: Metroland Media Group Ltd.
77 Peel St., New Hamburg, ON N3A 1E7
Tel: 519-662-1240; Fax: 519-662-3521
Toll-Free: 800-563-3578
editor@newhamburgindependent.ca
www.newhamburgindependent.ca
Circulation: 3,060 Frequency: Wed.
Neil Oliver, Publisher
Cal Bosveld, Publisher

New Liskeard: The Temiskaming Speaker
Owned By: Temiskaming Printing Co.
PO Box 580 , 18 Wellington St., New Liskeard, ON P0J 1P0
Tel: 705-647-6791; Fax: 705-647-9669
www.northernontario.ca
Circulation: 4,840 Frequency: Wed.
Dave Armstrong, Publisher

Newmarket: Newmarket Era Banner
Previous Name: Era Banner
Owned By: Metroland Media Group Ltd.
580B Steven Ct., Newmarket, ON L3Y 4X1
Tel: 905-773-7627; Fax: 905-853-5379
www.yorkregion.com
Circulation: 174,637 Frequency: Tuesday, Thursday, Sunday
Debora Kelly, Editor-in-Chief
Ian Proudfoot, Regional General Manager

Niagara Falls: Niagara Falls Review
Previous Name: Niagara Falls News
Owned By: Sun Media Corp.
4949 Victoria Ave., Niagara Falls, ON L2E 4C7
Tel: 905-357-2440; Fax: 905-357-1620
www.niagarafallsreview.ca
Social Media:
twitter.com/niafallsreview
www.facebook.com/niagarafallsreview
Steven Gallagher, Managing Editor
905-358-5711 x1129
steven.gallagher@sunmedia.ca

Niagara Falls: Niagara Shopping News
Owned By: Sun Media
4949 Victoria Ave., Niagara Falls, ON L2E 4C7
Tel: 905-357-2440; Fax: 905-357-1620
mark.munson@sunmedia.ca
www.niagarashoppingnews.ca/webapp/sitepages
Circulation: 29,650 Frequency: Friday
Mark Munson

Nipigon: Nipigon-Red Rock Gazette
Owned By: Lakeshore Community Publishing Ltd.
PO Box 1057 , 145 Railway St., Nipigon, ON P0T 2J0
Tel: 807-887-3583; Fax: 807-887-3720
Circulation: 1,008 Frequency: Tuesday
Linda Harbison, Publisher

North York: Canadian Jewish News Head Office
Owned By: Canadian Jewish News
 # 205, 1500 Don Mills Rd., North York, ON M3B 3K4
Tel: 416-391-1836; Fax: 416-391-0829
www.cjnews.com
Social Media:
twitter.com/TheCJN
www.facebook.com/TheCJN
Circulation: 41,302 Frequency: Thur.
Gary Laforet, General Manager
Mordechai Ben-Dat, Editor

Oakville: Milton Shopping News
c/o The Shopping News, 467 Speers Rd., 2nd Fl., Oakville, ON L6K 3S4
Tel: 905-878-8855; Fax: 905-878-6727
smillen@haltonsearch.com
miltonshoppingnews.com
Circulation: 18,700 Frequency: Weekly; Thursday
Lars Melander, General Manager
905-337-5555

Oakville: Oakville Beaver
Owned By: Metroland Media Group Ltd.
467 Speers Rd., Oakville, ON L6K 3S4
Tel: 905-845-3824
www.insidehalton.com; www.metroland.com
Social Media:
twitter.com/oakvillebeaver
Circulation: 139,631 Frequency: Wed., Fri., Sun.; also North News (Fri.), & Oakville Marketplace (Tue.)
Oakville's community newspaper; print and online editions
Neil Oliver, Publisher
Jill David, Editor-in-Chief

Oakville: Oakville Shopping News
1158 South Service Rd. West, Oakville, ON L6L 5T7
Tel: 905-827-2244; Fax: 905-827-2308
Circulation: 46,500 Frequency: Wed., Fri.
Bill Whitaker Sr.

Oakville: Oakville Today
Owned By: Metroland Media Group Ltd.
467 Speers Rd., 2nd Fl., Oakville, ON L6K 3S4
Tel: 905-825-2229; Fax: 905-825-8315
www.insidehalton.com/community/oakvilletoday
Circulation: 32,438 Frequency: Thursday
The newspaper is delivered to residences in northern Oakville.
Neil Oliver, Publisher
Lars Melander, General Manager
Charlene Hall, Manager, Circulation
Sandy Pare, Manager, Business
Pete Steuneberg, Manager, Production

Ohsweken: Tekawennake - Six Nations & New Credit
PO Box 130 , Ohsweken, ON N0A 1M0
Tel: 519-753-0077
teka@tekanews.com
www.tekanews.com
Circulation: 2,500 Frequency: Wednesday
Scott Smith

Orangeville: Orangeville Banner
Owned By: Metroland Media Group Ltd.
37 Mill St., Orangeville, ON L9W 2M4
Tel: 519-941-1350; Fax: 519-941-9600
www.orangeville.com
Circulation: 19,115 Tue.; 23,055 Fri. Frequency: Tuesday, Friday
Bill Anderson, General Manager
Richard Vivian, Managing Editor

Orangeville: Orangeville Citizen
Owned By: Claridge Community Newspaper Ltd.
10 - 1st St., Orangeville, ON L9W 2C4
Tel: 519-941-2230; Fax: 519-941-9361
www.citizen.on.ca
Circulation: 11,983 Frequency: Thursday
Tom Claridge, Editor
Alan Claridge, Publisher

Orillia: Orillia Today
Owned By: Metroland Media Group Ltd.
25 Ontario St., Orillia, ON L3V 6H2
Tel: 705-329-2058; Fax: 705-329-2059
www.simcoe.com
Circulation: 41,430 Frequency: Wed., Fri.
Maureen Christie, Regional General Manager

Orono: Orono Weekly Times
Owned By: Orono Weekly Times
PO Box 209 , 5310 Main St., Orono, ON L0B 1M0
Tel: 905-983-5301
oronotimes@rogers.com
visitorono.com/orono-weekly-times
Social Media:
www.facebook.com/oronotimes
Circulation: 1,067 Frequency: Wed.
Margaret Zwart, Publisher

Oshawa: Oshawa Express Newspaper
600 Thornton Rd. South, Oshawa, ON L1J 6W7
Tel: 905-571-7334; Fax: 905-571-0255
editor@oshawaexpress.ca
www.oshawaexpress.ca
Social Media:
www.facebook.com/pages/The-Oshawa-Express/218913348146817
Circulation: 35,000 Frequency: Weekly

Oshawa: Oshawa/Whitby/Clarington This Week, Canadian Statesman
Owned By: Metroland Media Group Ltd.
865 Farewell Ave., Oshawa, ON L1H 7L5
Tel: 905-579-4400; Fax: 905-579-2238
www.durhamregion.com
Circulation: 147,467 Frequency: Wed., Fri., Sun.
Tim Whittaker, Publisher
Chris Bovie, Editor-in-chief

Ottawa: Centretown News
St. Patrick's Building, #303, 1125 Colonel By Dr., Ottawa, ON K1S 5B6
Tel: 613-520-7410; Fax: 613-520-4068
ctown@carleton.ca
www.centretownnews.ca
Other information: Advertising, E-mail: ctownads@carleton.ca
Social Media:
twitter.com/CentretownNews
Circulation: 17,000 Frequency: Bi-weekly; Friday
The content of Centretown News is produced by third & fourth year students from Carleton University's School of Journalism & Communication. The community newspaper is delivered to homes & businesses in the Ottawa-Carleton region between September & April.
Klaus Pohle, Publisher
Alison Foster, Editor
Toni Baggos, Editor, Photos
Layla Cameron, Editor, Insight
Mitch Goldenberg, Editor, Sports
Chris Herhalt, Editor, Online
Lindsay Jolivet, Editor, News
Alex Paterson, Editor, Business
Christine Sirois, Editor, Arts
Brad Clouthier, Manager, Advertising

Ottawa: The Hill Times
Owned By: The Hill Times Publishing Inc.
69 Sparks St., Ottawa, ON K1P 5A5
Tel: 613-232-5952; Fax: 613-232-9055
www.thehilltimes.ca
Social Media:
twitter.com/thehilltimes
www.facebook.com/thehilltimes
Circulation: 12,947 Frequency: Monday
Political newspaper.
Andrew Morrow, General Manager
613-688-8844
amorrow@hilltimes.com
Kate Malloy, Editor
613-688-8838
kmalloy@hilltimes.com

Ottawa: Ottawa South EMC
Owned By: Performance Printing Ltd.
Ottawa EMC Group, #103, 57 Auriga Dr., Ottawa, ON K2E 8B2
Tel: 613-723-5970; Fax: 613-723-1862
www.emcottawasouth.ca/news
Social Media:
twitter.com/emcnews
www.facebook.com/emcnewspaper
Frequency: Weekly
Mike Tracy, Publisher
613-283-3182 x164
dweir@perfprint.ca
Melissa Touchey
613-688-1489
mtouhey@thenewsemc.ca

Ottawa: The Star
Owned By: Transcontinental Media Inc.
#200, 1400 St. Laurent Blvd., Ottawa, ON K1K 4H4
Tel: 613-744-4800; Fax: 613-744-1976
thestar@transcontinental.ca
Circulation: 35,000 Frequency: Tuesday
Terry Tyo, Publisher

Palmerston: Minto Express
Previous Name: Harriston Review
Owned By: Metroland Media Group Ltd.
PO Box 757 , 171 William St., Palmerston, ON N0G 2P0
Tel: 519-343-2440; Fax: 519-343-2267
www.southwesternontario.ca
Circulation: 1,260 Frequency: Tuesday
Bill Huether, General Manager
519-291-1660 ext 103

Paris: The Paris Star
Owned By: Sun Media Corp.
#3, 3 Elm St., Paris, ON N3L 2L6
Tel: 519-442-7866; Fax: 519-442-3100
www.parisstaronline.com
Social Media:
twitter.com/ParisStar
www.facebook.com/pages/The-Paris-Star/114234 248620217
Circulation: 1,638 Frequency: Wed.
Cheryl Philips, Publisher, cheryl.philips@sunmedia.ca
Michael Peeling, Editor, parisedit@bowesnet.com

Parkhill: Forest Standard
Owned By: Hayter-Walden Publications Inc.
PO Box 400 , Parkhill, ON N0M 2K0
Tel: 519-786-5242; Fax: 519-786-4884
standard@execulink.com
hayterwalden.com
Circulation: 2,481 Frequency: Thursday
Dale Hayter, Publisher

Parkhill: Parkhill Gazette
Owned By: Hayter-Walden Publications Inc.
PO Box 400 , 165 King St., Parkhill, ON N0M 2K0
Tel: 519-294-6264; Fax: 519-294-6391
Circulation: 1,177 Frequency: Thursday
Dale Hayter, Publisher

Parry Sound: Parry Sound Beacon Star
Owned By: Metroland Media Group Ltd.
PO Box 370 , 67 James St., Parry Sound, ON P2A 1T6
Tel: 705-746-2104; Fax: 705-746-8369
www.parrysoundbeaconstar.com
Circulation: 3,688 Frequency: Saturday
Fred Heidman, General Manager

Parry Sound: Parry Sound North Star
Owned By: Metroland Media Group Ltd.
PO Box 370 , 67 James St., Parry Sound, ON P2A 2X4
Tel: 705-746-2104
www.cottagecountrynow.ca
Social Media:
www.facebook.com/PSNorthStar
Circulation: 4,500 Frequency: Wed.
Fred Heidman, General Manager

Penetanguishene: Le Goût de Vivre
343, rue Lafontaine, RR#3, Penetanguishene, ON L9M 1R3
Tél: 705-533-3349;Téléc: 705-533-3422
legoutdevivre@bellnet.ca
legoutdevivre.com
Tirage: 1 000 Fréquence: 1er et 3e jeudi du mois; français

Perth: Perth Courier
Owned By: Metroland Media Group Ltd.
39 Gore St. East, Perth, ON K7H 1H4
Tel: 613-267-1100; Fax: 613-267-3986
www.metroland.com/Communities/100090/Perth_Courier
Circulation: 4,836 Frequency: Wed.
John W. Clement, Publisher
Ian Gray, Editor

Petawawa: Petawawa Post
Bldg. P-106, Petawawa, ON K8H 2X3
Tel: 613-687-5511; Fax: 613-588-6966
petawawapost@bellnet.ca
www.psppetawawa.com/petawawapost.cfm
Circulation: 7,700 Frequency: Tuesday
Bruce Peever, Manager, bruce.peever@forces.qc.ca

Peterborough: Peterborough This Week
Owned By: Metroland Media Group Ltd.
884 Ford St., Peterborough, ON K9J 5V3
Tel: 705-749-3383; Fax: 705-749-0074
www.mykawartha.com
Social Media: pinterest.com/rellman
twitter.com/kawarthanews
www.facebook.com/mykawartha.peterboroughnews
Circulation: 96,277 Frequency: Wed., Fri.
Bruce Danford, Publisher, bdanford@mykawartha.com

Petrolia: The Petrolia Topic
Owned By: Sun Media Corp.
140 Front St. South, Petrolia, ON N7T 7M8
Tel: 519-336-1100; Fax: 519-336-1833
www.petroliatopic.com
Social Media:
twitter.com/petroliatopic
www.facebook.com/pages/Petrolia-Topic/15152106 1568151
Circulation: 2,422 Frequency: Wed.
Daryl Smith, Publisher, daryl.smith@sunmedia.ca

Picton: Picton Gazette
Owned By: Picton Gazette
267 Main St., Picton, ON K0K 2T0
Tel: 613-476-3201; Fax: 613-476-3464
gazette@connect.reach.net
www.pictongazette.com
Circulation: 2,170 Frequency: Wed.; The Picton Gazette Regional (Sat., circ. 10,602)
Jean M. Morrison, Publisher
Adam Bramburger, Editor

Port Dover: Port Dover Maple Leaf
Owned By: Port Dover Maple Leaf Limited
PO Box 70 , 351 Main St., Port Dover, ON N0A 1N0
Tel: 519-583-0112; Fax: 519-583-3200
info@inportdover.com
www.inportdover.com
Circulation: 3,163 Frequency: Wed.
Stan Morris, Publisher

Port Elgin: Shoreline Beacon
Previous Name: Shoreline News
Owned By: Sun Media Corp.
694 Goderich St., Port Elgin, ON N0H 2C0
Tel: 519-832-9001; Fax: 519-389-4793
shorelinebeacon.news@sunmedia.ca
www.shorelinebeacon.com
Social Media:
twitter.com/shorelinebeacon
www.facebook.com/shorelinebeacon?sk=wall
Circulation: 4,510 Frequency: Wed.
Kiera Merria, Publisher, kiera.merriam@sunmedia.ca
Patrick Bales, Editor, patrick.bales@sunmedia.ca

Port Perry: Port Perry Star
Owned By: Metroland Media Group Ltd.
188 Mary St., Port Perry, ON L9L 1B7
Tel: 905-985-7383; Fax: 905-985-4160
www.metroland.com/Communities/100390/Port_Perry_Star
Circulation: 23,400 Frequency: Wed., Fri.
Tim Whittaker, Publisher

Prescott: Prescott Journal
Owned By: St. Lawrence Printing Co. Ltd.
PO Box 549 , 231 King St. West, Prescott, ON K0E 1T0
Tel: 613-925-4265; Fax: 613-925-2837
newsfile@bellnet.ca
www.prescottjournal.com
Circulation: 2,441 Frequency: Wed.
Lisa D. Taylor, Publisher

Rainy River: Rainy River Record
Owned By: Fort Frances Times Ltd.
PO Box 280 , 312 - 3rd St., Rainy River, ON P0W 1L0
Tel: 807-852-3366; Fax: 807-852-4434
info@rainyriverrecord.com
www.rainyriverrecord.com
Circulation: 788 Frequency: Tuesday
J.R. Cumming, Publisher
Ken Johnston, Editor

Rainy River: The Westend Weekly
PO Box 66 , Rainy River, ON P0W 1L0
Tel: 807-852-3815; Fax: 807-852-1863
westernweekly@tbaytel.net
www.westendweekly.ca
Circulation: 8,600 Frequency: Wed.
Jacquie Dufresne, Editor-in-chief

Renfrew: Renfrew Mercury
Previous Name: Renfrew Mercury/Mercury Weekender
Owned By: Metroland Media Group Ltd.
35 Opeongo Rd., Renfrew, ON K7V 1A8
Tel: 613-432-3655; Fax: 613-432-6689
www.metroland.com/communities/100092/renfrew_mercury
Circulation: 4,006 Frequency: Tuesday
Fred Runge, Publisher
Lucy Hass, Editor

Renfrew: Renfrew Weekender
Previous Name: Renfrew News
Owned By: Metroland Media Group Ltd.
35 Opeongo Rd., Renfrew, ON K7V 4A8
Tel: 613-432-3655; Fax: 613-432-6689
Circulation: 14,795 Frequency: Friday
Lucy Hass, Editor
Fred Runge, Publisher
Derek Walter, General Manager

Richmond Hill: The Liberal
Owned By: Metroland Media Group Ltd.
50 East Beaver Creek Rd., Richmond Hill, ON L4B 1G6
Tel: 905-881-3373; Fax: 905-881-9924
www.yorkregion.com
Circulation: 197,459 Frequency: Tuesday 45,443; Thursday 76,048; Sunday 75,968
Ian Proudfoot, Publisher
Debora Kelly, Editor-in-chief

Ridgetown: The Ridgetown Independent News
PO Box 609 , 1 Main St., Ridgetown, ON N0P 2C0
Tel: 519-674-5205; Fax: 519-674-2573
Circulation: 1,971 Frequency: Wednesday
Jim Brown, Owner & Publisher
Gord Brown, General Manager
Barb Brown, Editor

Rockland: Le Journal Vision
PO Box 897 , 1579 Laurier St., Rockland, ON K4K 1L5
Tel: 613-446-6456; Fax: 613-446-1381
Toll-Free: 800-365-9970
vision@eap.on.ca
Social Media:
www.facebook.com/group.php?gid=199878750108078
Circulation: 26,800 Frequency: Weekly
The newspaper is bilingual.
Paulo Casimiro, Editor, paulo.casimiro@eap.on.ca

Sarnia: The Sarnia & Lambton County This Week
Previous Name: Sarnia This Week
Owned By: Sun Media Corp.
140 front St. South, Sarnia, ON N7T 7M8
Tel: 519-336-1100; Fax: 519-336-1833
www.sarniathisweek.com
Social Media:
twitter.com/STW_Heather
www.facebook.com/185718368129719
Circulation: 24,026 Frequency: Wed.
Daryl Smith, Publisher, daryl.smith@sunmedia.ca
Jim Blake, Editor, jim.blake@sunmedia.ca

Sault Ste Marie: Sault Ste Marie This Week
Owned By: Sun Media Corp.
2 Towers St., Sault Ste Marie, ON P6A 2T9
Tel: 705-949-6111; Fax: 705-942-8596
www.saultthisweek.com
Circulation: 34,047 Frequency: Wed.
Fred Bright, Publisher

Schreiber: Terrace Bay Schreiber News
312 Manitoba St., Schreiber, ON P0T 2S0
Tel: 807-824-2021; Fax: 807-824-2162
Circulation: 3,500+ Frequency: Tuesday
The Ontario community newspaper publishes local stories of interest to readers in Terrace Bay, Schreiber, Rossport, & the surrounding area.

Seaforth: The Huron Expositor
Owned By: Sun Media Corp.
8 Main St., Seaforth, ON N0K 1W0
Tel: 519-527-0240; Fax: 519-527-2858
www.seaforthhuronexpositor.com
Social Media:
twitter.com/C4thExp
www.facebook.com/TheHuronExpositor
Circulation: 2,020 Frequency: Wed.
Neil H. Clifford, Publisher, neil.clifford@sunmedia.ca
Susan Hundertmark, Editor, seaforth.news@sunmedia.ca

Shelburne: Shelburne Free Press & Economist
Owned By: Claridge Community Newspapers Ltd.
PO Box 100 , Shelburne, ON L0N 1S0
Tel: 519-925-2832; Fax: 519-925-5500
www.citizen.on.ca
Circulation: 2,108 Frequency: Thursday
Thomas Claridge, Publisher

Sioux Lookout: Sioux Lookout Bulletin
Owned By: 948892 Ontario Inc.
PO Box 1389 , 40 Front St., Sioux Lookout, ON P8T 1B9
Tel: 807-737-3209; Fax: 807-737-3084
office@siouxbulletin.com
www.siouxbulletin.com
Circulation: 4,444 Frequency: Wed.
Dick MacKenzie, Editor, dick@siouxbulletin.com

Sioux Lookout: Wawatay News
Owned By: Wataway Native Communications Society
Wawatay Native Communications Society, PO Box 1180 , 16 Fifth Ave., Sioux Lookout, ON P8T 1B7
Tel: 807-737-2951; Fax: 807-737-3224
editor@wawatay.on.ca
www.wawatay.on.ca
Circulation: 9,050 Frequency: Every other Thu.; English, Ojibwe & Cree
Bryan Phelan, Publisher and General Manager

Smiths Falls: Smiths Falls Record News
Owned By: Performance Printing Ltd.
PO Box 158 , 65 Lorne St., Smiths Falls, ON K7A 4T1
Tel: 613-283-3182; Fax: 613-283-7480
Circulation: 11,000 Frequency: Tuesday
Duncan Weir, Publisher

St Catharines: Thorold Niagara News
Owned By: Sun Media Corp.
17 Queen St., St Catharines, ON L2R 5G5
Tel: 905-688-4332; Fax: 905-688-6313
stcatharinesnews@bellnet.ca
www.thoroldedition.ca
Social Media:
twitter.com/ThoroldNews
www.facebook.com/pages/Thorold-Niagara-New s/1003918167460
Circulation: 6,827 Frequency: Wed.
Tim Dundas, Publisher,
tdundas@niagaracommunitynewspapers.com

St Marys: St Marys Journal-Argus
Owned By: Metroland Media Group Ltd.
PO Box 1030 , 11 Wellington St. North, St Marys, ON N4X 1B7
Tel: 519-284-2440; Fax: 519-284-3650
www.stmarys.com
Circulation: 2,621 Frequency: Wed.
Laura Payton, Editor
Doug Rowe, Regional General Manager

St Thomas: Elgin County Market
Owned By: Sun Media Corp.
16 Hincks St., St Thomas, ON N5R 5Z2
Tel: 519-631-3782; Fax: 519-631-3759
www.elgincountymarket.com
Circulation: 30,600
Linda Axelson, Publisher

Stoney Creek: Ancaster News
Owned By: Metroland Media Group Ltd.
333 Arvin Ave., Stoney Creek, ON L8E 2M6
Tel: 905-664-8800; Fax: 905-523-4014
www.hamiltonnews.com/community/ancaster
Circulation: 12,591 Frequency: Friday
Debra Downey, Editor, ddowney@hamiltonnews.com

Stoney Creek: Hamilton Mountain News
Owned By: Metroland Media Group Ltd.
333 Arvin Ave., Stoney Creek, ON L8E 2M6
Tel: 905-523-4014
www.hamiltonmountainnews.com
Circulation: 48,883 Frequency: Friday
John Rousseau, Associate Publisher

Stouffville: Stouffville Sun-Tribune
Previous Name: Stouffville Tribune
Owned By: Metroland Media Group Ltd.
6290 Main St., Stouffville, ON L4A 1H2
Tel: 905-640-2612; Fax: 905-640-8778
www.yorkregion.com
Circulation: 18,374 Frequency: Thu., Sat.
Ian Proudfoot, Publisher
Debora Kelly, Editor-in-chief

Stratford: Inside Stratford / Perth
PO Box 23016 , 285 Lorne Ave. East, Stratford, ON N5A 7V8
Tel: 519-272-0051; Fax: 519-272-0067
Circulation: 24,000+ Frequency: Weekly
The community newspaper serves Stratford & Perth County.
Richard Johnson, Publisher & Editor

Stratford: Stratford Gazette
Owned By: Metroland Media Group Ltd.
#106, 10 Downie St., Stratford, ON N5A 7K4
Tel: 519-271-8002; Fax: 519-271-5636
www.southwesternontario.ca/community/stratford-gazette
Circulation: 19,500 Frequency: Thursday
Doug Rowe, Regional Managing Editor
Laura Payton, General Manager
Laura Carter, Manager, Distribution

Strathroy: Strathroy Age Dispatch
Owned By: Sun Media Corp.
73 Front St. West, Strathroy, ON N7G 1X6
Tel: 519-245-2370; Fax: 519-245-1647
www.strathroyagedispatch.com
Social Media:
twitter.com/AgeDispatch
www.facebook.com/pages/Strathroy-Age-Dispatch/12
098118126
Circulation: 4,070 Frequency: Wed.
Linda LeBlanc, Publisher, linda.leblanc@sunmedia.ca
Don Biggs, Editor, don.biggs@sunmedia.ca

Sturgeon Falls: Sturgeon Falls Tribune
Owned By: 1102282 Ontario Inc.
206 King St., Sturgeon Falls, ON P2B 1R7
Tel: 705-753-2930; Fax: 705-753-5231
tribune@westnipissing.com
www.westnipissing.com/Tribune/Home.html
Circulation: 2,661 Frequency: Tuesday; English & French
Suzanne Gammon, Publisher

Sudbury: Journal Le Voyageur
336, rue Pine, Sudbury, ON P3C 5L1
Tél: 705-673-3377;Téléc: 705-673-5854
Ligne sans frais: 866-688-7027
levoyageur@levoyageur.ca
www.levoyageur.ca
Tirage: 8 700 Fréquence: Mercredi; français
Paul Lefebvre, Contact

Sudbury: Northern Life
Owned By: Laurentian Media Group
158 Elgin St., Sudbury, ON P3E 3N5
Tel: 705-673-5667; Fax: 705-673-4652
www.northernlife.ca
Circulation: 90,727 Frequency: Wed., Fri.
Abbas Homayed, Publisher

Tavistock: Tavistock Gazette
Owned By: Tavistock Gazette Ltd.
PO Box 70 , 119 Woodstock South, Tavistock, ON N0B 2R0
Tel: 519-655-2341; Fax: 519-655-3070
gazette@tavistock.on.ca
www.tavistock.on.ca
Circulation: 1,323 Frequency: Wed.
William Gladding, Publisher

Tecumseh: Lakeshore News
Previous Name: North Essex News
Owned By: Postmedia Community Publishing
1116 Lesperance Rd., Tecumseh, ON N8N 1X2
Tel: 519-735-2080; Fax: 519-735-2082
lakeshorenews@postmedia.com
www.windsoressexnews.com/LakeshoreNews.aspx
Circulation: 1,759 Frequency: Wednesday

Tecumseh: LaSalle Post
Owned By: Postmedia Community Publishing
1116 Lesperance Rd., Tecumseh, ON N8N 1X2
Tel: 519-735-2080; Fax: 519-735-2082
lasallepost@postmedia.com
www.windsoressexnews.com/LasallePost.aspx
Circulation: 9,768 Frequency: Wed.
Gary Baxter, Publisher

Tecumseh: Shoreline Week
Owned By: Postmedia Community Publishing
1614 Lesperance Rd., Tecumseh, ON N8N 1Y2
Tel: 519-735-2080; Fax: 519-735-2082
shorelineweek@postmedia.com
www.windsoressexnews.com
Circulation: 15,024 Frequency: Wed.
Gary Baxter, Publisher

Thamesville: Thamesville Herald
PO Box 580 , 65 London Rd., Thamesville, ON N0P 2K0
Tel: 519-692-3825
Circulation: 772 Frequency: Wed.
Allison Humphrey, Publisher

Thessalon: The North Shore Sentinel
Owned By: Rankin Publications
359 River Rd. North, Thessalon, ON P0R 1L0
Tel: 705-842-2504; Fax: 705-842-2679
ns-sentinel@bellnet.ca
Circulation: 2,315 Frequency: Wed.
Randy Rankin, Publisher

Thorold: Grimsby Lincoln News
Owned By: Metroland Media Group Ltd.
#1, 3550 Schmon Pkwy., Thorold, ON L2V 4Y6
Tel: 905-688-2444
www.niagarathisweek.com/community/grimsby
Circulation: 165,000 Frequency: Wednesday, Friday
The Grimsby Lincoln News is a free tabloid newspaper.
Neil Oliver, Publisher
David Bos, General Manager
Joel Billinghurst, Manager, Production
Melissa Duemo, Manager, Business
Tracy Travis-Scott, Manager, Circulation
Dave Hawkins, Director, Advertising

Thorold: Niagara This Week
Owned By: Metroland Media Group Ltd.
#1B, 3300 Merrittville Hwy., Thorold, ON L2V 4Y6
Tel: 905-688-2444
www.niagarathisweek.com
Circulation: 342,000 Frequency: Wed., Fri.
Mike Williscraft, Director of Editorial

Thunder Bay: Thunder Bay's Source
Owned By: Thunder Bay Post Inc.
87 North Hill St., Thunder Bay, ON P7A 5V6
Tel: 807-346-2600; Fax: 807-345-9923
www.tbnewswatch.com
Circulation: 48,000 Frequency: Fri.
Leith Dunick, Publisher

Tilbury: Tilbury Times
Owned By: Postmedia Community Publishing
40 Queen St. South, Tilbury, ON N0P 2L0
Tel: 519-682-0411; Fax: 519-682-3633
tilburytimes@postmedia.com
www.windsoressexnews.com/TilburyTimes.aspx
Circulation: 1,962 Frequency: Wed.
Gary Baxter, Publisher
Bob Odette, Associate Editor

Tillsonburg: Tillsonburg News
Owned By: Sun Media Corp.
25 Townline Rd., Tillsonburg, ON N4G 4H6
Tel: 519-688-6397
www.tillsonburgnews.com
Social Media:
twitter.com/TillsonburgNews
www.facebook.com/TillsonburgNews
Circulation: 10,201 Frequency: Wed.
Merv Hawkins, Publisher, merv.hawkins@sunmedia.ca
Kim Novak, Editor, kim.novak@sunmedia.ca

Timmins: Les Nouvelles
187, rue Cedar, Timmins, ON P4N 7G1
Tél: 705-268-2955
lesnouv@vianet.ca
journaux.apf.ca/lesnouvelles
Fréquence: Mercredi; français
Doris Bouchard, Editor
Bruce Cowan, Publisher

Timmins: Timmins Times
Owned By: Sun Media Corp.
815 Pine St. South, Timmins, ON P4N 8S3
Tel: 705-268-6252; Fax: 705-268-2255
www.timminstimes.com
Circulation: 37,416 Frequency: Wed., Fri.
Heather Duhns, Managing Editor
Linda Leblanc, Publisher

Tobermory: The Bruce Peninsula Press
PO Box 89 , 39 Legion St., Tobermory, ON N0H 2R0
Tel: 519-596-2658; Fax: 519-596-8030
Toll-Free: 800-794-4480
info@tobermorypress.com
www.tobermorypress.com
Circulation: 2,946
The community newspaper serves the northern Bruce Peninsula.
John Francis, Publisher & Editor
Trudy Watson, Contact, Advertising & Sales

Toronto: Annex Gleaner
581 Bloor St. West, Toronto, ON M6G 1K3
Tel: 416-504-6987; Fax: 416-504-8792
gleanereditor@gmail.com
www.gleanernews.ca
Other information: Display & Classified Advertising, E-mail:
gleanerpub@gmail.com
Social Media:
twitter.com/gleanernews
Circulation: 33,500 Frequency: Monthly
Community news is provided to Toronto western downtown neighbourhood. The Annex Gleaner is a free publication that is delivered to residents & businesses.
Rebecca Payne, Editor-in-Chief
Justin Crann, Contributing Editor, justin.gleaner@gmail.com
Monika Warzecha, Online Editor, monika.gleaner@gmail.com

Toronto: The Bay Street Times
#514, 5334 Yonge St., Toronto, ON M2N 6V1
Tel: 416-949-6332; Fax: 416-997-6697
editor@baystreetimes.com
www.baystreettimes.com
Frequency: Monthly

Toronto: Beach Metro Community News
2196 Gerrard St. East, Toronto, ON M4E 2C7
Tel: 416-698-1164; Fax: 416-698-1253
admin@beachmetro.com
www.beachmetro.com
Social Media: www.youtube.com/BeachMetroNews
twitter.com/BeachMetroNews
www.facebook .com/BeachMetroNews?v=wall
Circulation: 30,000 Frequency: 22 times a year
Sheila Blinoff, General Manager, admin@beachmetro.com
Jon Muldoon, Editor, editor@beachmetro.com

Toronto: Bloor West Villager
Owned By: Metroland Media Group Ltd.
307 Humberline Dr., Toronto, ON M9W 5V1
Tel: 416-675-4390; Fax: 416-675-9262
www.insidetoronto.com/community/bloorwestparkdale
Social Media:
twitter.com/BWVillager
Circulation: 34,154 Frequency: Thursday
The Toronto neighbourhoods of Bloor West, Roncesvalles, & The Juncion are served by the newspaper.
Ian Proudfoot, Publisher
Peter Haggert, Editor in Chief
Grace Peacock, Managing Editor
Warren Elder, Director, Advertising
Katherine Bernal, Manager, Production

Toronto: Downtown Bulletin
Previous Name: Toronto St. Lawrence & Downtown Community Bulletin
Owned By: Community Bulletin Newspaper Group Inc.
#121, 260 Adelaide St. East, Toronto, ON M5A 1N1
Tel: 416-929-0011
info@communitybulletin.ca
www.thebulletin.ca/cbulletin
Circulation: 57,000 Frequency: Monday, Monthly
Frank Touby, Editor
Paulette Touby, Publisher

Toronto: East York Mirror
Owned By: Metroland Media Group Ltd.
100 Tempo Ave., Toronto, ON M2H 3S5
Tel: 416-493-4400; Fax: 416-493-6190
www.insidetoronto.com/community/eastyork
Social Media:
twitter.com/EastYorkMirror
Circulation: 34,845 Frequency: Thursday
The newspaper covers the Toronto neighbourhoods of East York, Riverdale, & Leaside.
Ian Proudfoot, Publisher
Alan Shackleton, Managing Editor
Tim Corcoran, Regional Director, Advertising
Katherine Bernal, Manager, Production

Toronto: Etobicoke Guardian
Previous Name: Etobicoke Advertiser-Guardian
Owned By: Metroland Media Group Ltd.
307 Humberline Dr., Toronto, ON M9W 5V1
Tel: 416-675-4390; Fax: 416-675-9262
www.metroland.com/Communities/100057/Etobicoke_Guardian
Circulation: 138,838 Frequency: Wed., Fri.
Peter Haggert, Editor-in-chief
Ian Proudfoot, Publisher
Marg Middleton, General Manager

Toronto: L'Express
888 ave. Eastern, Toronto, ON M4L 1A3
Tél: 416-465-2107;Téléc: 416-465-3778
info@lexpress.to
www.lexpress.to
Tirage: 20,000 Fréquence: Mardi; français; et: L'Observateur, London; L'Information, Hamilton/Burlington & Le Courrier d'Oshawa, Métro Courrier
D.P. Mazare

Toronto: Hi-Rise
#121, 95 Leeward Glenway, Toronto, ON M3C 2Z6
Tel: 416-424-1393; Fax: 416-467-8262
sec.valdunn@vif.com
www.hi-risenews.com
Circulation: 60,000 Frequency: Monthly
Valerie Dunn

Toronto: North York Mirror
Owned By: Metroland Media Group Ltd.
100 Tempo Ave., Toronto, ON M2H 3S5
Tel: 416-493-4400
www.insidetoronto.com/community/northyork
Social Media:
twitter.com/NorthYorkMirror
Circulation: 96,836 Frequency: Thursday, Friday
The community newspaper is deistributed to homes in the former city of North York, Ontario.
Betty Carr, Publisher
Marg Middleton, General Manager
Paul Futhey, Managing Editor
Tim Corcoran, Regional Director, Advertising
Warren Elder, Director, Advertising
Katherine Bernal, Manager, Production

Toronto: Our Toronto Free Press
#202, 49 Elm St., Toronto, ON M5G 1H1
Tel: 416-977-0183
letters@torontofreepress.com
www.torontofreepress.com
Frequency: Tuesday
Judi McLeod, Editor & Owner

Toronto: Scarborough Mirror
Owned By: Metroland Media Group Ltd.
100 Tempo Ave., Toronto, ON M2H 3S5
Tel: 416-493-4400
insidetoronto.com/community/scarborough
Circulation: 227,965 Frequency: Wed., Fri.
Alan Shackleton, Managing Editor
Peter Haggert, Editor-in-chief
Ian Proudfoot, Publisher
Marg Middleton, General Manager

Toronto: Share
658 Vaughan Rd., Toronto, ON M6E 2Y5
Tel: 416-656-3400; Fax: 416-656-3711
share@interlog.com
www.sharenews.com
Social Media:
twitter.com/sharenews
www.facebook.com/pages/Share-Newspaper/35798374757 7821
Circulation: 50,000 Frequency: Weekly
Serves the Black and Caribbean community in the GTA.
Arnold A. Auguste, Publisher

Toronto: Toronto Street News
c/o LoveCry, 1024 Queen St. East, Toronto, ON M4M 1K4
Tel: 416-406-0099
vpflet@hotmail.com
www.torontostreetnews.com
Circulation: 3,000 Frequency: Weekly
Available free to homeless, handicapped, underemployed and dying so that they can sell for income.
Victor Fletcher, Publisher

Toronto: Town Crier
Owned By: Multimedia Nova Corporation
101 Wingold Ave., Toronto, ON M6B 1P8
Tel: 416-785-4300; Fax: 416-488-3671
info@MyTownCrier.ca
www.towncrieronline.ca
Social Media:
twitter.com/mytowncrier
www.facebook.com/TownCriersTownSports
Frequency: Monthly; nine separate newspapers: Bayview Mills TC, Bloor-Annex TC (circ. 30,000); Beach Riverdale TC (circ. 30,000); Leaside-Rosedale TC (circ. 25,000); North Toronto TC (circ. 30,000) Forest Hill T
Eric McMillan, Managing Editor
Lori Abittan, President & Publisher

Toronto: Village Living Magazines
Toronto,
Toll-Free: 866-933-1652
villagelivingmagazine.ca
Social Media: pinterest.com/villagelivinmag
twitter.com/villagelivinmag
www.facebook .com/VillageLivingMagazines
Frequency: Bi-Monthly
Free community newspaper serving the areas of Forest Hill, Hillcrest Village, Wychwood Heights, Regal Heights, and Upper Village.

Toronto: The Women's Post
51 Wolseley St., Toronto, ON M5T 1A4
Tel: 416-645-7038; Fax: 416-645-7046
www.womenspost.ca
Circulation: 71,818 Frequency: Bi-monthly
Sarah Whatmough-Thomson, Editor

Toronto: York Guardian
100 Tempo Ave., Toronto, ON M2H 3S5
Tel: 416-493-4400
wwww.insidetoronto.com/news
Circulation: 26,016 Frequency: Thursday
The newspaper is delivered to homes in Toronto.
Ian Proudfoot, Publisher
Paul Futhey, Managing Editor
Warren Elder, Director, Advertising
Katherine Bernal, Manager, Production

Trenton: The Community Press
5 Cresswell Dr., Trenton, ON K8V 6H5
Tel: 613-392-6501; Fax: 613-392-0505
www.communitypress.ca
Social Media:
twitter.com/community_press
www.facebook.com/TheCommunityPress
Circulation: 44,367 Frequency: Thursday
THe Community Press is a member of Canoe Sun Media Community Newspapers.
Maureen Keeler, Publisher, maureen.keeler@sunmedia.ca
Bill Glisky, Regional Managing Editor, bill.glisky@sunmedia.ca
Janet Richards, City Editor, janet.richards@sunmedia.ca

Trenton: Trentonian
Owned By: Sun Media Corp.
5 Cresswell Dr., Trenton, ON K8V 6H5
Tel: 613-392-6501; Fax: 613-392-0505
tren.newsroom@sunmedia.ca
www.trentonian.ca
Social Media:
twitter.com/TheTrentonian
www.facebook.com/pages/The-Trentonian/16 4324826919177
Circulation: 6,642 Frequency: Monday, Wednesday, Friday
Maureen Keeler, Publisher, maureen.keeler@sunmedia.ca

Tweed: Tweed News
Owned By: Tweed News Publishing Co. Ltd.
PO Box 550 , 242 Victoria St. North, Tweed, ON K0K 3J0
Tel: 613-478-2017; Fax: 613-478-2749
info@thetweednews.ca
www.thetweednews.ca
Circulation: 1,111 Frequency: Wed.
Rodger Hanna, Publisher & Editor
Roseann Trudeau, Circulation Manager

Uxbridge: Times-Journal
Previous Name: Uxbridge Times-Journal
Owned By: Metroland Media Group Ltd.
PO Box 459 , 16 Bascom St., Uxbridge, ON L9P 1M9
Tel: 905-852-9141; Fax: 905-852-9341
www.durhamregion.com
Circulation: 16,941 Frequency: Wed, Fri.
Tim Whittaker, Publisher, jpirone@durhamregion.com

Vankleek Hill: The Review
Previous Name: Vankleek Hill Review
Owned By: The Review (996963 Ontario Inc.)
PO Box 160 , 76 Main St. East, Vankleek Hill, ON K0B 1R0
Tel: 613-678-3327; Fax: 613-937-2591
Toll-Free: 877-678-3327
review@thereview.ca
www.thereview.on.ca
Circulation: 3,662 Frequency: Wed.; English & French
Louise Sproule, Publisher, lsproule@thereview.ca
Richard Mahoney, Editor

Vaughan: Vaughan Citizen
Owned By: Metroland Media Group Ltd.
#29, 8611 Weston Rd., Vaughan, ON L4L 9P1
Tel: 905-264-8703; Fax: 905-264-9453
www.yorkregion.com/community/vaughan
Circulation: 49,404 Su; 50,702 Th; 100,106 total Frequency: Sunday, Thursday
Ian Proudfoot, Publisher
Kim Champion, Editor
John Willems, Regional General Manager
Robert Lazurko, Manager, Business

Virgil: Niagara Advance
Owned By: Sun Media Corp.
PO Box 430 , 1501 Niagara Stone Rd., Virgil, ON L0S 1T0
Tel: 905-468-3283; Fax: 905-468-3137
www.niagaraadvance.ca
Social Media:
twitter.com/NiagaraAdvance
www.facebook.com/pages/Niagara-Advance/121004 834576571
Circulation: 7,331 Frequency: Saturday
Tim Dundas, Publisher,
tdundas@niagaracommunitynewspapers.com
Penny Coles, Editor

Walkerton: Walkerton Herald-Times
Owned By: Metroland Media Group Ltd.
PO Box 190 , 10 Victoria St., Walkerton, ON N0G 2V0
Tel: 519-881-1600; Fax: 519-881-0276
www.southwesternontario.ca
Circulation: 2,200 Frequency: Wed.
John McPhee, General Manager

Wallaceburg: Wallaceburg News
538 James St., Wallaceburg, ON N8A 2N9
Tel: 519-627-2557; Fax: 519-627-1261
www.thewallaceburgnews.ca
Frequency: Wed.
Wayne Snider, Managing Editor
Daryl Smith, Publisher

Wasaga Beach: Stayner Sun
Owned By: Metroland Media Group Ltd.
#10, 1 Market Lane, Wasaga Beach, ON L9Z 0B6
Tel: 705-428-2638; Fax: 705-422-2446
www.simcoe.com
Circulation: 1,128 Frequency: Wed.
Joe Anderson, Publisher

Wasaga Beach: Staynor Sun
Previous Name: Angus-Borden Sun
Owned By: Metroland Media
#10, 1 Market Lane, Wasaga Beach, ON L9Z 0B6
Tel: 705-428-2638; Fax: 705-428-6909
www.simcoe.com/community/stayner
Circulation: 1650 Frequency: Weekly
Joe Anderson, Publisher
Craig Widdifield, Managing Editor

Wasaga Beach: The Wasaga Sun
Owned By: Metroland Media Group Ltd.
#10, 1 Market Lane, Wasaga Beach, ON L9Z 2B9
Tel: 705-429-1688; Fax: 705-422-2446
www.simcoe.com/community/wasagabeach
Circulation: 8,004 Frequency: Wednesday
Joe Anderson, Publisher
Craig Widdifield, Managing Editor
Scott Woodhouse, Assignment Editor
Mary Ellis, Director, Business
Kent Feagan, Director, Production
Heather Harris, Director, Distribution

Waterdown: Flamborough Review
Owned By: Metroland Media Group Ltd.
PO Box 20 , 30 Main St. North, Waterdown, ON L0R 2H0
Tel: 905-689-4841; Fax: 905-689-3110
www.flamboroughreview.com
Circulation: 13,662 Frequency: Fri.

Waterloo: Waterloo Chronicle
Owned By: Metroland Media Group Ltd.
#20, 279 Weber St. North, Waterloo, ON N2J 3H8
Tel: 519-886-2830; Fax: 519-886-9383
www.waterloochronicle.ca
Circulation: 31,564 Frequency: Wednesday (weekly)
Neil Oliver, Publisher

Watford: Watford Guide-Advocate
Owned By: Hayter-Walden Publications Inc.
PO Box 99 , 5292 Nauvoo Rd., Watford, ON N0M 2S0
Tel: 519-876-2809; Fax: 519-876-2322
guideadvocate@execulink.com
Circulation: 1,160 Frequency: Thursday (weekly).
Dale Hayter, Publisher

Wawa: Wawa Print & Litho Inc.
Previous Name: Wawa/Algoma News Review
PO Box 528 , 33 Ste-Marie St., Wawa, ON P0S 1K0
Tel: 705-856-2267; Fax: 705-856-4952
Toll-Free: 800-461-9209
Circulation: 1,060 Frequency: Wed.
W. Robert Avis, Publisher & Editor
Krystal Gignac, Advertising Manager

West Lorne: The West Elgin Chronicle
Owned By: Sun Media Corp.
168 Main St., West Lorne, ON N0L 2P0
Tel: 519-768-2220; Fax: 519-768-2221
jesse.cnockaert@sunmedia.ca
www.thechronicle-online.com
Social Media:
twitter.com/WE_TheChronicle
www.facebook.com/TheWestElginChronicle
Frequency: Thu.
Bev Ponton, Publisher
519-631-2790 x242
bev.ponton@sunmedia.ca
Ian McCallum, Editor
519-631-2790 x248
ian.mccallum@sunmedia.ca

Westport: The Review-Mirror
PO Box 130 , 43 Bedford St., Westport, ON K0G 1X0
Tel: 613-273-8000; Fax: 613-273-8001
Toll-Free: 800-387-0796
info@review-mirror.com; editor@review-mirror.com
www.review-mirror.com
Other information: News Tips: newsroom@review-mirror.com
Circulation: 1,625 Frequency: Thursday
The Review Mirror serves Westport, the Rideau Valley, & the Rideau Lakes in Ontario. Print & electronic subscriptions are available.
Howard Crichton, Publisher & Managing Editor
Margaret Brand, Reporter & Photographer, mbrand@review-mirror.com
Marco Smits, Reporter & Photographer, msmits@review-mirror.com
Louise Haughton, Contact, Office, lhaughton@review-mirror.com
Bill Ritchie, Contact, Advertising Sales, advertising@review-mirror.com

Wheatley: Wheatley Journal
Owned By: Wheatley Journal
PO Box 10 , 14 Talbot West, Wheatley, ON N0P 2P0
Tel: 519-825-4541; Fax: 519-825-4546
Circulation: 946 Frequency: Wed.
Sheila McBrayne, Editor

Wiarton: Wiarton Echo
Owned By: Sun Media Corp.
573 Berford St., Wiarton, ON N0H 2T0
Tel: 519-534-1560; Fax: 519-534-4616
www.wiartonecho.com
Social Media:
twitter.com/wiartonecho
www.facebook.com/pages/Wiarton-Echo/334537 066702
Circulation: 2,593 Frequency: Wed.
Keith Gilbert, Publisher/Editor, keith.gilbert@sunmedia.ca

Winchester: Winchester Press
Owned By: Manotick Messenger Inc.
PO Box 399 , 545 Lawrence St., Winchester, ON K0C 2K0
Tel: 613-774-2524; Fax: 613-774-3967
www.winchesterpress.on.ca
Circulation: 9,964 Frequency: Wed.
Beth Morris, Owner & President
Amanda Smith-Millar, Editor, news@winchesterpress.on.co

Windsor: The Amherstburg Echo
Owned By: Sun Media Corp.
4525 Rhodes Dr., Windsor, ON N8W 5R8
Tel: 519-966-4500; Fax: 519-966-3660
www.amherstburgecho.com
Social Media:
twitter.com/echo_ron
www.facebook.com/pages/Amherstburg-Echo/18145 3438559762
Circulation: 8,283 Frequency: Tuesday
Shannon Ricker, Publisher, shannon.ricker@sunmedia.ca

Windsor: Journal Le Rempart
Anciennement: Le Rempart
7515, ch. Forest Glade, Windsor, ON N8T 3P5
Tél: 519-948-4139;Téléc: 519-948-0628
info@lerempart.ca
www.lerempart.ca
Tirage: 1 000 Fréquence: Mercredi; français
Denis Poirier, Publisher

Windsor: Windsor Pennysaver
4525 Rhodes Dr., Windsor, ON N8W 5R8
Tel: 519-966-4500; Fax: 519-966-3660
classified@windsorpennysaver.com
www.windsorpennysaver.com
Circulation: 119,000 Frequency: Fri.
Shannon Ricker, Publisher
Rod Hilts, Regional Managing Editor

Wingham: Wingham Advance-Times
Owned By: Metroland Media Group Ltd.
PO Box 390 , 5 Diagonal Rd., Wingham, ON N0G 2W0
Tel: 519-357-2320; Fax: 519-357-2900
www.southwesternontario.ca
Circulation: 1,988 Frequency: Wed.
Pauline Kerr, Editor
Bill Huether, General Manager

Woodstock: Norwich Gazette
Owned By: Sun Media Corp.
8 Brock St., Woodstock, ON N4S 3B4
Tel: 519-537-2341
norwich.gazette@sunmedia.ca
www.norwichgazette.ca
Social Media:
twitter.com/NorwichGazette
www.facebook.com/NorwichGazette
Circulation: 1,433 Frequency: Wed.
Andrea DeMeer, Publisher, ademeer@bowesnet.com
Jennifer Vandermeer, Editor, jennifer.vandermeer@sunmedia.ca

Woodstock: Oxford Shopping News
16 Brock St., Woodstock, ON N4S 3B4
Tel: 519-537-6657; Fax: 519-537-8542
www.oxfordshoppingnews.com
Circulation: 28,284 Frequency: Tuesday
Pat Logan, Publisher

Ethnic in Ontario

Brampton: Gujarat Express
Corporate Office, 20 Eldwood Pl., Brampton, ON L6V 3N3
Tel: 905-457-7096; Fax: 905-457-7096
abgujaratexpress@yahoo.ca
www.gujaratexpress.ca
Frequency: Weekly
Gujarat Express serves new immigrants to Canada & the South Asian community.
Amit Bhatt, Publisher & Editor
Haresh Kumar, Sub Editor
Chinmay Dave, Contact, Sales & Marketing

University in Ontario

Belleville: QNet News
Owned By: Loyalist College
PO Box 4200 , Belleville, ON K8N 5B9
Tel: 613-969-1913; Fax: 613-962-1376
Toll-Free: 888-569-2547
www.qnetnews.ca
Social Media:
www.facebook.com/qnetnews
Frequency: Weekly
Loyalist College newspaper.

Hamilton: The Satellite
Owned By: Mohawk College
135 Fennell Ave. West, G108K, Hamilton, ON L8N 3T2
Tel: 905-575-2183; Fax: 905-575-2385
satellite.editor@mohawkcollege.ca
www.satelliteonline.ca
Mohawk College newspaper.

Kingston: The Navigator
Owned By: St. Lawrence College
King & Portsmouth, 100 Portsmouth Ave., Kingston, ON K7L 5A6
Tel: 613-544-5400; Fax: 613-545-3923
www.stlawrencecollege.ca
Social Media:
www.facebook.com/stlawrencecollege.ca?1=1&iMenuID=5
St. Lawrence College newspaper.

Kitchener: Spoke
Owned By: Conestoga College
299 Doon Valley Dr., Kitchener, ON N2G 4M4
Tel: 519-748-5220; Fax: 519-748-3505
www.conestogac.on.ca/
Conestoga College newspaper

London: The Interrobang
Owned By: Fanshawe College
PO Box 7005 , 1001 Fanshawe College Blvd., London, ON N5Y 5R6
Tel: 519-452-4430; Fax: 519-452-4420
www.fanshawec.ca
Frequency: Weekly
Fanshawe College newspaper.

Oakville: The Sheridan Sun
Owned By: Sheridan College Institute of Technology & Advanced Learning
Trafalgar Road Campus, PO Box 2500 Main, 1430 Trafalgar Rd., Oakville, ON L6L 7T7
Tel: 905-845-9430; Fax: 905-815-4148
infosheridan@sheridaninstitute.ca
www.sheridancollege.ca
Sheridan College Institute of Technology & Advanced Learning newspaper.

Oshawa: The Chronicle
Owned By: Durham College
PO Box 385 , 2000 Simcoe St. North, Oshawa, ON L1H 7K4
Tel: 905-721-2000; Fax: 905-721-3113
www.durhamcollege.ca
Durham College newspaper.

Ottawa: The Charlatan
Owned By: Carleton University
Unicentre Building, Rm. 531, 1125 Colonel By Dr., Ottawa, ON K1S 5B6
Tel: 613-520-6680
editor.charlaton@gmail.com
www.charlatan.ca
Social Media:
twitter.com/CharlatanLive
www.facebook.com/CharlatanLive
Carleton University newspaper.

Peterborough: The Three Penny Beaver
Owned By: Sir Sandford Fleming College
Sutherland Campus, 599 Brealey Dr., Peterborough, ON K9J 7B1
Tel: 705-749-5530; Fax: 705-749-5507
Toll-Free: 866-353-6464
info@flemingc.on.ca
flemingcollege.ca
Sir Sandford Fleming College newspaper.

Sarnia: Lion's Tale
Owned By: Lambton College
1457 London Rd., Sarnia, ON N7S 6K4
Tel: 519-542-7751
info@lambton.on.ca
www.lambton.on.ca
Social Media:
twitter.com/LionsTale
www.facebook.com/LambtonCollegeSAC
Lambton College newspaper.

St Catharines: Brock Press
Owned By: Brock University
Alumni Student's Centre, Rm. 204a, 500 Glenridge Ave., St Catharines, ON L2S 3A1
Tel: 905-688-5550; Fax: 905-984-4853
editor@brockpress.com
www.brockpress.com
Brock University newspaper.

Sudbury: The Shield
Owned By: Cambrian College of Applied Arts & Technology
1400 Barrydowne Rd., Sudbury, ON P3A 3V8
Tel: 705-566-8101 Toll-Free: 800-461-7145
The.Shield@cambriancollege.ca
www.cambrianshield.com
Social Media:
twitter.com/cambrianshield
www.facebook.com/groups/134154158785/
Cambrian College of Applied Arts & Technology newspaper.

Thunder Bay: The Argus
Owned By: Lakehead University
953 Oliver Rd., Thunder Bay, ON P7B 5E1
Tel: 807-766-7251
www.theargus.ca
Lakehead University newspaper.

Thunder Bay: Opus
Owned By: Confederation College
PO Box 398 , 1450 Nakina Dr., Thunder Bay, ON P7C 4W1
Tel: 807-475-6110; Fax: 807-623-4512
Toll-Free: 800-465-5493
www.confederationc.on.ca
Confederation College newspaper

Toronto: The Buzz
Owned By: Seneca College of Applied Arts & Technology
c/o Newnham Campus, 1750 Finch Ave. East, Toronto, ON M2J 2X5
Tel: 416-491-5050
buzzinfo@senecac.on.ca
www.senecacollege.ca
Seneca College of Applied Arts & Technology newspaper.

Toronto: Dialog Newspaper
Owned By: George Brown College
PO Box 1015 B, Toronto, ON M5T 2T9
Tel: 416-415-2000 Toll-Free: 800-265-2002
info@gbrownc.on.ca
studentassociation.ca/dialog-editions
Frequency: Monthly, from Aug to April
George Brown College newspaper.
Mick Sweetman, Publications & Communications Coordinator, sapccoord@georgebrown.ca

Toronto: EtCetera
Owned By: Humber Institute of Technology and Advanced Learning
North Campus, 205 Humber College Blvd., Toronto, ON M9W 5L7
Tel: 416-675-3111; Fax: 416-675-2427
enquiry@humber.ca
www.humber.ca
Humber Institute of Technology and Advanced Learning newspaer.

Toronto: The Underground
Owned By: University of Toronto at Scarborough
1265 Military Trail, SL-234, Toronto, ON M1C 1A4
Tel: 416-287-7054
info@the-underground.ca
www.the-underground.ca
Social Media:
twitter.com/utscUNDERGROUND
University of Toronto at Scarborough newspaper.
Ranziba Nehrin, Editor-in-Chief, editor@the-underground.ca

Welland: Niagara News
Owned By: Niagara College
Welland Campus, 300 Woodlawn Rd., Welland, ON L3C 7L3
Tel: 905-735-2211; Fax: 905-736-6000
news@niagaracollege.ca
www.niagaracollege.ca/newspaper
Niagara College newspaper.

Windsor: The Converged Citizen
Owned By: St. Clair College
South Campus, 2000 Talbot Rd. West, Windsor, ON N9A 6S4
Tel: 519-972-2727; Fax: 519-972-3811
media.converged@gmail.com
www.convergedcitizen.com
St. Clair College newspaper.
Jason Viau, Staff Member

Prince Edward Island

Daily Newspapers in Prince Edward Island

Charlottetown: The Guardian
Previous Name: The Evening Patriot
Owned By: Transcontinental Media Inc.
PO Box 760 , 165 Prince St., Charlottetown, PE C1A 4R7
Tel: 902-629-6000; Fax: 902-566-3808
Toll-Free: 800-267-6397
comments@theguardian.pe.ca
www.theguardian.pe.ca
Social Media:
twitter.com/peiguardian
www.facebook.com/PEI.Guardian
Circulation: 21,023 Frequency: Morning
Don Brander, Publisher
Gary MacDougall, Managing Editor

Summerside: Journal Pioneer
Owned By: Transcontinental Media Inc.
PO Box 2480 , 316 Water St., Summerside, PE C1N 4K5
Tel: 902-436-2121
newsroom@journalpioneer.com
www.journalpioneer.com
Circulation: 10,257 Frequency: Evening
Brad Works, Managing Editor
902-432-8212
bworks@journalpioneer.com
Sandy Rundle, Publisher
902-432-8203; Fax: 902-436-3736

Other Newspapers in Prince Edward Island

Montague: The Eastern Graphic
Owned By: Island Press Limitd
567 Main St. South, Montague, PE C0A 1R0
Tel: 902-838-2515; Fax: 902-838-4392
subscribe@peicanada.com; accounts@peicanada.com
peicanada.com/content/eastern_graphic
Social Media:
www.facebook.com/peicanada
Circulation: 5,700 Frequency: Weekly
The publication covers news for eastern Prince Edward Island.
Paul MacNeill, Publisher, paul@peicanada.com
Heather Moore, Editor, editor@peicanada.com
Jan MacNeill, Manager, Advertising, jan@peicanada.com
Aura Lee Shepard, Coordinator, Production, auralee@peicanada.com
Sharon Riley, Account Executive, sharon@peicanada.com

Montague: West Prince Graphic
Owned By: Island Press Ltd.
PO Box 790 , 567 Main St., Montague, PE C0A 1R0
Tel: 902-838-2515; Fax: 902-838-4392
Toll-Free: 800-806-5443
accounts@peicanada.com
www.peicanada.com
Social Media:
twitter.com/graphicnews
Circulation: 6,016 Frequency: Weekly; Wed.
Paul MacNeill, Publisher
902-838-2515 x 201
paul@peicanada.com

Summerside: La Voix Acadienne
5, av Maris Stella, Summerside, PE C1N 6M9
Tél: 902-436-6005;Téléc: 902-888-3976
pub@lavoixacadienne.com
www.lavoixacadienne.com
Médias sociaux:
twitter.com/lavoixacadienne
www.facebook.com/pages/La-Voix-Acadienne/246332682050424
Tirage: 1 100 Fréquence: Mercredi; français
Marcia Enman, Directrice général

Québec

Daily Newspapers in Québec

Granby: La Voix de L'Est
76, rue Dufferin, Granby, QC J2G 9L4
Tél: 450-375-4555;Téléc: 450-777-7221
redaction@lavoixdelest.qc.ca
www.lavoixdelest.ca
Médias sociaux:
twitter.com/lavoixdelest
www.facebook.com/lavoixdelest
François Beaudoin, Directeur de l'information, fbeaudoi@lavoixdelest.qc.ca

Montréal: Le Devoir
2050, rue de Bleury, 9e étage, Montréal, QC H3A 3M9
Tél: 514-985-3333;Téléc: 514-985-3390
redaction@ledevoir.com
www.ledevoir.com
Tirage: 24 582 lun.-ven., 39 084 sam. Fréquence: Matin; français
Josée Boileau, Rédactrice-en-chef

Montréal: Le Journal de Montréal
Détenteur: Sun Media Corp.
4545, rue Frontenac, Montréal, QC H2H 2R7
Tél: 514-521-4545
www.journaldemontreal.com
Médias sociaux:
twitter.com/JdeMontreal
www.facebook.com/jdemontreal
Tirage: 265 573 lun.-ven., 316 457 sam., 265 610 dim.
Fréquence: Matin; français
Lyne Robitaille, Présidente et Éditrice

Montréal: The Montréal Gazette
Anciennement: The Gazette
Détenteur: Postmedia Network Inc.
#200, 1010 St. Catherine St. West, Montréal, QC H3B 5L1
Tél: 514-987-2222;Téléc: 514-987-2399
www.montrealgazette.com
Médias sociaux:
www.facebook.com/montrealgazette
Tirage: 148,000 Mon.-Fri.; 217,000 Sat.; 138,000 Sun.
Raymond Brassard, Managing Editor
514-987-2508

Montréal: La Presse
7, rue St-Jacques, Montréal, QC H2Y 1K9
Tél: 514-285-7000;Téléc: 514-285-6808
www.cyberpresse.ca
Tirage: 185 609 lun.-ven., 268 236 sam., 194 012 dim.
Fréquence: Matin; français
Guy Crevier, Président et éditeur
Éric Trottier, Vice-président et éditeur adjoint

Montréal: Quotidien 24 heures Montréal
#5, 800 Square Victoria, Montréal, QC H4Z 0A3
Tél: 514-393-1010;Téléc: 514-373-2400
24info@quebecormedia.com
www.24hmontreal.canoe.ca
Tirage: 134,691
Lucie Ludec, VP, lucie.leduc@sunmedia.ca

Québec: Le Soleil
CP 1547 Terminus, 410, boul Charest est, Québec, QC G1K 7J6
Tél: 418-686-3394;Téléc: 418-686-3374
redaction@lesoleil.com
www.cyberpresse.ca/le-soleil
Tirage: 181 380 Fréquence: Matin; français
Claude Gagnon, Président & éditeur
Raymond Tardif, Éditeur adjoint

Saguenay: Le Quotidien
1051, boul Talbot, Saguenay, QC G7H 5C1
Tél: 418-545-4474;Téléc: 418-690-8824
redaction@lequotidien.com
www.lapresse.ca/le-quotidien
Tirage: 29 131 Fréquence: Matin; français
Michel Simard, Président et éditeur

Sainte-Marie: EditionBeauce.com
Détenteur: Publications Beauce-Nord Inc.
234, rue Baronet, Sainte-Marie, QC G6E 2R1
Tél: 418-387-1205;Téléc: 418-387-1364
repertoire@editionbeauce.com
www.editionbeauce.com
Médias sociaux:
twitter.com/editionbeauce
www.facebook.com/editionbeauce

Sherbrooke: The Record
PO Box 1200 , 1195 Galt East, Sherbrooke, QC J1G 1Y7
Tel: 819-569-9525; Fax: 819-821-3179
www.sherbrookerecord.com
Social Media:
www.facebook.com/sherbrookerecord
Circulation: 25,135 Frequency: Monday-Friday
Sharon McCully, Publisher, outletjournal@sympatico.ca
Daniel Coulombe, Editor, dcoulombe@sherbrookerecord.com

Sherbrooke: La Tribune
Détenteur: Gesca Limitée
1950, rue Roy, Sherbrooke, QC J1K 2X8
Tél: 819-564-5466 Ligne sans frais: 800-567-6955
abonnement@latribune.qc.ca
www.lapresse.ca/la-tribune
Médias sociaux:
twitter.com/tribune1910
www.facebook.com/quotidienlatribune
Tirage: 32 000 lun.-ven., 42 000 sam. Fréquence: Matin; français
Louise Boisvert, Présidente et éditrice

Trois-Rivières: Le Nouvelliste
Détenteur: Gesca Limitée
CP 668 , 1920, rue Bellefeuille, Trois-Rivières, QC G9A 3Y2
Tél: 819-376-2501 Ligne sans frais: 877-933-2506
abonnement@lenouvelliste.qc.ca
www.lapresse.ca/le-nouvelliste
Tirage: 43 000 lun.-ven., 46 000 sam. Fréquence: Matin; français
Alain Turcotte, Rédactrice-en-chef
Raymond Tardif, Éditeur

Vanier: Le Journal de Québec
Détenteur: Sun Media Corp.
450, rue Bechard, Vanier, QC G1M 2E9
Tél: 418-683-1573;Téléc: 418-683-8886
commentaires@journaldequebec.com
www.journaldequebec.com
Médias sociaux:
twitter.com/JdeQuebec
www.facebook.com/JdeQuebec
Tirage: 98 490 lun.-ven., 121 943 sam., 100 575304 dim.
Fréquence: Matin; français
Louise Cordeau, Éditeur et Chef de la direction,
louise.cordeau@journaldequebec.com

Other Newspapers in Québec

Acton Vale: La Pensée de Bagot
Détenteur: DBC Communications inc.
800, rue de Roxton, Acton Vale, QC J0H 1A0
Tél: 450-546-3271;Téléc: 450-546-3491
publicite@lapensee.qc.ca
www.lapensee.qc.ca
Tirage: 14,797 Fréquence: Dimanche
Michel Dorais, Directeur, mdorais@lapensee.qc.ca
Benoit Chartier, Éditeur

Alma: Le Lac Saint-Jean
#01, 100, rue St-Joseph sud, Alma, QC G8B 7A6
Tél: 418-668-4545;Téléc: 418-668-8522
redaction_alma@tc.tc
www.lelacstjean.com
Tirage: 19 716 Fréquence: Samedi
Gaston Martin

Amos: Le Citoyen de L'Harricana
Détenteur: Les Hebdos Régionaux Québecor Média
92, rue Principale Sud, Amos, QC J9T 2J6
Tél: 819-732-6531;Téléc: 819-732-3764
www.hebdosregionaux.ca/abitibi-temiscamingue
Caroline Couture, Éditrice,
caroline.couture@quebecormedia.com

Asbestos: Les Actualités
Détenteur: Les Hebdos Régionaux Québecor Média
572, 1è ave, Asbestos, QC J1T 4R4
Tél: 819-879-6681;Téléc: 819-879-7235
nathalie.hurdle@quebecormedia.com
www.hebdosregionaux.ca/estrie/les-actu alites
Médias sociaux:
twitter.com/LesActualites
www.facebook.com/actuasbestos
Tirage: 14 800 Fréquence: Samedi
Carole Pellerin, Éditeur, carole.pellerin@quebecormedia.com

Baie-Comeau: Plein Jour de Baie-Comeau
Anciennement: Plein-Jour Charlevoix, Le Plein-Jour en Haute Côte-Nord
Détenteur: Les Hebdos Régionaux Québecor Média
#309, 625, boul Laflèche, Baie-Comeau, QC G5C 1C5
Tél: 418-589-5900;Téléc: 418-589-8216
raphael.hovington@hebdosquebecor.com
www.hebdosregionaux.ca/est-du-quebe c/plein-jour-de-baie-comeau
Médias sociaux:
twitter.com/PJbaiecomeau
www.facebook.com/pleinjourbaiecomeau
Tirage: 16 366 Fréquence: Vendredi; aussi Plein jour sur la Manicouagan (mercredi, tirage 15 866)
Sebastien Rouillard, Éditeur,
sebastien.rouillard@hebdosquebecor.com

Baie-Saint-Paul: L'Hebdo Charlevoisien
Détenteur: Néomedia
45, Raymond Mailloux, Baie-Saint-Paul, QC G3Z 1W2
Tél: 418-435-0220;Téléc: 418-435-3349
reception@charlevoix.net
www.charlevoixendirect.com
Tirage: 13 033 Fréquence: Saturday
Charles Warren, Directeur
418-665-1299
charles@hebdocharlevoisien.ca
Guy Charlebois, Directeur de production, hebdo@charlevoix.net

Beaulac-Garthby: Le Contact de Beaulac-Garthby
CP 58 , 9, rue de la Chapelle, Beaulac-Garthby, QC G0Y 1BO
Tél: 418-458-2737;Téléc: 418-458-1142
contactbg2002@yahoo.ca
www.beaulac-garthby.com
Tirage: 355
Andree Sautier, Redactrice-en-chef
Serge Frederick, President

Beaupré: L'Autre Voix
#101, 10 989, boul Ste-Anne, Beaupré, QC G0A 1E0
Tél: 418-827-1511;Téléc: 418-827-1513
redaction.lautrevoix@transcontinental.ca
www.lautrevoix.com
Mathieu Tremblay, Éditeur

Beloeil: L'Oeil Régional
Détenteur: Les Hebdos Régionaux Québecor Média
393, boul Sir-Wilfrid-Laurier, Beloeil, QC J3G 4H6
Tél: 450-467-1821;Téléc: 450-467-3087
redaction@oeilregional.com
ww.hebdosregionaux.ca/monteregie/loeil-region al
Médias sociaux:
www.facebook.com/oeilregional
Tirage: 30 000 Fréquence: Samedi
Guy Gilbert Jr., Éditeur, guy.gilbert@quebecormedia.com

Boucherville: Journal La Relève Inc.
Détenteur: Transcontinental Media Inc.
528, rue St-Charles, Boucherville, QC J4B 3M5
Tél: 450-641-4844;Téléc: 450-641-4849
lareleve@lareleve.qc.ca
www.lareleve.qc.ca
Tirage: 54 650 Fréquence: Jeudi et Vendredi
Bernard Desmarteau, Représentant

Boucherville: La Seigneurie
Détenteur: Les Hebdos Régionaux Québecor Média
391, boul de Montagne, Boucherville, QC J4B 1B7
Tél: 450-641-3360;Téléc: 450-655-9752
www.hebdosregionaux.ca/monteregie/la-seigneurie
Médias sociaux:
www.facebook.com/laseigneurie
Tirage: 29 421 Fréquence: Samedi
Serge Landry, Éditeur
450-655-5556
serge.landry@quebecormedia.com

Cantley: L'Écho de Cantley
188, montée de la Source, Boite 1, Comp. 9, Cantley, QC J8V 3J2
Tél: 819-827-2828
dg@echocantley.ca
www.echocantley.ca
Tirage: 2 400
Chantal Turcottoe, President, presidente@echocantley.ca

Cap-aux-Meules: Le Radar
CP 8183 , 110 ch. Gros-Cap, Cap-aux-Meules, QC G4T 1R3
Tél: 418-986-2345;Téléc: 418-986-6358
Ligne sans frais: 866-986-2345
leradar@lino.com
www.leradar.qc.ca
Médias sociaux:
www.facebook.com/radar.hebdomadaire
Tirage: 3 000 Fréquence: Vendredi; français
Achille Hubert, Éditeur, editeur@leradar.qc.ca
Pierre-Luc Richard, Rédactrice-en-chef,
redacteur@leradar.qc.ca

Chambly: Le Journal de Chambly
Détenteur: Les Hebdos Régionaux Québecor Média
CP 175 , 1685, rue Bourgogne, Chambly, QC J3L 1Y8
Tél: 450-658-6516;Téléc: 450-658-3785
www.hebdosregionaux.ca/monteregie/le-journal-de-chambly
Médias sociaux:
twitter.com/JournalChambly
www.facebook.com/journaldechambly
Tirage: 21 237 Fréquence: Mardi
Daniel Noiseux, Éditeur, daniel.noiseux@quebecormedia.com

Charlesbourg: Charlesbourg Express
Détenteur: Transcontiniental Media Inc.
Médias-Transcontinental, #900, 1265, boul Charest ouest, Charlesbourg, QC G1N 4V4
Tél: 418-686-6400;Téléc: 418-686-4841
redaction_quebec@tc.tc
www.charlesbourgexpress.com
Médias sociaux:
twitter.com/quebechebdo
Tirage: 30 100 Fréquence: Samedi
Lilianne Laprise, Éditrice

Châteauguay: Le Soleil de Châteauguay
Anciennement: Le Soleil du Samedi
Détenteur: Les Hebdos Régionaux Québecor Média
82, boul Salaberry sud, Châteauguay, QC J6J 4J6
Tél: 450-692-8552;Téléc: 450-692-3460
www.hebdosregionaux.ca/monteregie/le-soleil-de-chateauguay
Médias sociaux:
twitter.com/cybersoleil
www.facebook.com/cybersoleil

Tirage: 28 197 Fréquence: Samedi
Robert Fichaud, Éditeur, robert.fichaud@quebecormedia.com

Chibougamau: Le Jamésien
Détenteur: Les Hebdos Régionaux Québecor Média
317, 3e rue, Chibougamau, QC G8P 1N4
Tél: 418-748-6406;Téléc: 418-748-2421
www.hebdosregionaux.ca/saguenay-lac-st-jean/la-sentinelle-et-l e-jamesien
Tirage: 10,000 Fréquence: Samedi
Ralph Pilote, Directeur général Québecor Média
Saguenay-Lac-Saint-Jea, ralph.pilote@quebecormedia.ca

Chibougamau: La Sentinelle
Détenteur: Les Hebdos Régionaux Québecor Média
317, 3e rue, Chibougamau, QC G8P 1N4
Tél: 418-748-6406;Téléc: 418-748-2421
www.hebdosregionaux.ca/saguenay-lac-st-jean/la-sentinelle-et-l e-jamesien
Tirage: 10,000 Fréquence: Samedi
Ralph Pilote, Directeur général Québecor Média
Saguenay-Lac-Saint-Jea, ralph.pilote@quebecormedia.ca

Coaticook: Le Progrès de Coaticook
Détenteur: Transcontinental Media Inc.
72, rue Child, Coaticook, QC J1A 2B1
Tél: 819-849-9846;Téléc: 819-849-1041
www.leprogres.net
Tirage: 8 600 Fréquence: Samedi
Monique Côté, Éditrice, monique.cote@tc.tc
Dany Jacques, Chef de pupitre,
dany.jacques@transcontinental.ca

Courcelette: Journal Adsum
CP 1000 Forces, #515, Garnison Valcartier, Courcelette, QC G0A 4Z0
Tél: 418-844-5000;Téléc: 418-844-6934
adsum@forces.gc.ca
www.journaladsum.com
Tirage: 5 500 Fréquence: 22 fois par année
Caroline Charest, caroline.charest@forces.gc.ca

Daveluyville: Causeur
CP 1083 , Daveluyville, QC G0Z 1C0
Tél: 819-605-0063
lecauseur@hotmail.com
www.ville.daveluyville.qc.ca/causeur_journal_municipal.php
Médias sociaux:
www.facebook.com/pages/Le-Causeur/351233864932287
Tirage: 1 100 Fréquence: Mensuel
Patricia Mercier, Présidente

Delson: Le Reflet
Détenteur: Les Hebdos Régionaux Québecor Média
11, rte 132, Delson, QC J5B 1G9
Tél: 450-635-9146;Téléc: 450-635-4619
info@lereflet.qc.ca
www.hebdosregionaux.ca/monteregie/le-reflet
Médias sociaux:
www.facebook.com/journallereflet
Tirage: 31 700 Fréquence: Samedi
Robert Fichaud, Éditeur, robert.fichaud@quebecormedia.com
Hélène Gingras, Directrice de l'information,
helene.gingras@quebecormedia.com

Disraéli: Le Cantonnier
888, rue St-Antoine, Disraéli, QC G0N 1E0
Tél: 418-449-1888;Téléc: 418-449-1889
lecantonnier@lino.com
www.lecantonnier.com
Jean-Denis Grimard, Rédacteur en chef

Dolbeau-Mistassini: Journal Nouvelles Hebdo
1741, des Pins, Dolbeau-Mistassini, QC G8L 1M9
Tél: 418-276-6211;Téléc: 418-276-6166
redaction.dolbeau@tc.tc
www.nouvelleshebdo.com
Médias sociaux:
twitter.com/NouvellesHebdo
www.facebook.com/Nouvelleshebdo?ref=ts& sk=wall
Tirage: 13 369
Claudia Turcotte, Directrice des ventes, claudia.turcotte@tc.tc

Donnacona: Le Courrier de Portneuf
CP 1030 , 276, rue Notre-Dame, Donnacona, QC G3M 1G7
Tél: 418-285-0211 Ligne sans frais: 866-577-0211
www.courrierdeportneuf.com
Tirage: 31 953 Fréquence: Samedi
Josee-Anne Fiset, Directrice general,
josee-anne.fiset@courrierdeportneuf.com

Dorval: The Chronicle
Détenteur: Transcontinental Media Inc.
#303, 455, boul Fénelon, Dorval, QC H9S 5T8
Tél: 514-636-7314;Téléc: 514-636-7317
info.chronicle@transcontinental.ca
www.westislandchronicle.com
Médias sociaux:
twitter.com/WestIslandChron
www.facebook.com/wichronicle
Tirage: 14 800 Fréquence: Wed.
Denis Therrien, Publisher, denis.therrien@tc.tc
Marc Lalonde, Editor-in-chief, marc.lalonde@tc.tc

Dorval: Cités Nouvelles / City News
Détenteur: Transcontinental Media Inc.
#303, 455, boul Fenelon, Dorval, QC H9S 5T8
Tél: 514-636-7314;Téléc: 514-636-7317
citesnouvelles@tc.tc
www.citesnouvelles.com
Médias sociaux:
twitter.com/CitesNouvelles
www.facebook.com/CitesNouvelles
Tirage: 55 000 Fréquence: Sunday; English & French

Dorval: Magazine Ile des Soeurs / Nuns Island Magazine
Détenteur: Transcontinental Media Inc.
#303, 455, boul Fénelon, Dorval, QC H9S 5T8
Tél: 514-636-7314;Téléc: 514-636-7315
redaction_lemagazineids@tc.tc
www.lemagazineiledessoeurs.com
Médias sociaux:
twitter.com/LeMagazineIDS
www.facebook.com/278830125519919
Tirage: 8 091 Fréquence: Wed.; English & French
Patricia-Ann Beaulieu, Éditrice, patriciaann.beaulieu@tc.tc
Normand Sauvé, Chef de pupitre, normand.sauve@tc.tc

Dorval: Le Messager de LaSalle
Owned By: Transcontinental Media Inc.
#303, 455, boul Fénelon, Dorval, QC H9S 5T8
Tél: 514-636-7314; Fax: 514-636-7315
redaction_messagerlasalle@tc.tc
www.messagerlasalle.com
Social Media:
twitter.com/MessagerLaSalle
www.facebook.com/166724190111906
Circulation: 32 200 Frequency: Sunday; English & French
Patricia-Ann Beaulieu, Éditrice, patriciaann.beaulieu@tc.tc
Normand Sauvé, Chef de pupitre, normand.sauve@tc.tc

Dorval: Le Messager Lachine Dorval
Détenteur: Transcontinental Media Inc.
#303, 455, boul Fénelon, Dorval, QC H9S 5T8
Tél: 514-636-7314;Téléc: 514-636-7315
redaction_lachine-dorval@transcontinental.ca
www.messagerlachine.com
Médias sociaux:
twitter.com/MessagerLachine
www.facebook.com/pages/Le-Messager-Lachine-Dorval/166241
8
Tirage: 23 100 Fréquence: Sunday; English & French
Michel Bessette, Éditeur

Dorval: Le Messager Verdun
Détenteur: Transcontinental Media Inc.
#303, 455, boul Fénelon, Dorval, QC H9S 5T8
Tél: 514-636-7314;Téléc: 514-636-7315
redaction_verdun@tc.tc
www.messagerverdun.com
Médias sociaux:
twitter.com/MessagerVerdun
www.facebook.com/379058848771978
Tirage: 24 500 Fréquence: Sunday; English & French
Patricia-Ann Beaulieu, Éditrice, patriciaann.beaulieu@tc.tc
Normand Sauvé, Chef de pupitre, normand.sauve@tc.tc

Dorval: La Voix Pop
Anciennement: La Voix Populaire
Détenteur: Transcontinental Media Inc.
#303, 455, boul Fénelon, Dorval, QC H9S 5T8
Tél: 514-636-7314;Téléc: 514-636-7315
redaction_lavoixpop@tc.tc
www.lavoixpopulaire.com
Médias sociaux:
twitter.com/VoixPop
www.facebook.com/lavoixpop
Tirage: 23 500 Fréquence: Dimanche
Patricia-Ann Beaulieu, Éditrice, patriciaann.beaulieu@tc.tc
Normand Sauvé, Chef de pupitre, normand.sauve@tc.tc

Drummondville: L'Express
Détenteur: Transcontinental Media Inc.
1050, rue Cormier, Drummondville, QC J2C 2N6
Tél: 819-478-8171;Téléc: 819-478-4306
www.journalexpress.ca
Tirage: 46 089 Fréquence: Dimanche
Johanne Marceau, Éditeur, johanne.marceau@tc.tc
Lise Tremblay, Chef de pupitre, lise.tremblay@tc.tc

Drummondville: L'Impact de Drummondville
Détenteur: Les Hebdos Régionaux Québecor Média
2345, rue St-Pierre, Drummondville, QC J2C 5A7
Tél: 819-445-7000;Téléc: 819-445-7001
www.hebdosregionaux.ca/estrie/limpact
Jean Crépeau, Éditeur, jean.crepeau@quebecormedia.com

Egan-Sud: La Gatineau
Détenteur: Les Éditions La Gatineau Ltée
135-B, route 105, Egan-Sud, QC J9E 3A9
Tél: 819-449-1725;Téléc: 819-449-5108
reception@lagatineau.com
www.lagatineau.com
Tirage: 11100 Fréquence: Vendredi; français
Denise Carrière, Directrice, direction@lagatineau.com

Farnham: L'Avenir & des Rivières
221, rue Principale est, Farnham, QC J2N 1L5
Tél: 450-293-3138
caroline.dolce@tc.tc
www.laveniretdesrivieres.com
Tirage: 14 390 Fréquence: Samedi

Fermont: Journal le Trait D'Union du Nord
850 Place Daviault, local 159, Fermont, QC G0G 1J0
Tél: 418-287-3655;Téléc: 418-287-3874
info.journaltdn@gmail.com
www.journaltdn.ca
Tirage: 1 700
Sandra Carter, Directrice générale
Véronique Dumais, Rédactrice en chef et journaliste

Forestville: Journal Haute Côte-Nord Ouest
#100, 31 rte 138 ouest, Forestville, QC G0T 1E0
Tél: 418-587-2090;Téléc: 418-587-6407
information@journalhautecotenord.com
www.journalhautecotenord.com
Tirage: 6 285 Fréquence: Vendredi
Luc Brisson, Éditeur, luc.brisson@journalhautecotenord.com

Fort-Coulonge: Pontiac Journal du Pontiac / Le Journal de Pontiac
289, Manoir Mansfield, #RR 148, Fort-Coulonge, QC J0X 1V0
Tél: 819-683-3582;Téléc: 819-683-2977
editor@journalpontiac.com
Tirage: 9,319 Fréquence: Bi-weekly
Dana Bertrand, Circulation Manager, notice@journalpontiac.com
Fred Ryan, Publisher, abawqp@bulletinaylmer.com

Gaspé: L'Aviron
Détenteur: Les Hebdos Régionaux Québecor Média
144, rue Jacques Cartier, Gaspé, QC G4X 1M9
Tél: 506-753-7637
www.hebdosregionaux.ca/est-du-quebec/lecho-de-la-baie-et-lavi
ron
Tirage: 6,100 Fréquence: Vendredi
Bernard Johnson, Éditeur,
bernard.johnson@hebdosquebecor.com

Gaspé: L'Écho de la Baie
Détenteur: Les Hebdos Régionaux Québecor Média
144, rue Jacques Cartier, Gaspé, QC G4X 1M9
Tél: 418-392-5083;Téléc: 418-392-6605
echodelabaie@hebdosquebecor.com
www.hebdosregionaux.ca/est-du-quebec/lec
ho-de-la-baie-et-laviron
Médias sociaux:
twitter.com/LEchoDeLaBaie
www.facebook.com/echobaie
Fréquence: Dimanche
Bernard Johnson, Éditeur,
bernard.johnson@hebdosquebecor.com

Gaspé: Le Havre
Détenteur: Les Hebdos Régionaux Québecor Média
144, rue Jacques Cartier, Gaspé, QC G4X 1M9
Tél: 418-689-6686
havre@hebdosquebecor.com
www.hebdosregionaux.ca/est-du-quebec/le-havre
Médias sociaux:
twitter.com/LeHavre
www.facebook.com/lehavre
Tirage: 6,100 Fréquence: Vendredi
Bernard Johnson, Éditeur,
bernard.johnson@hebdosquebecor.com

Gaspé: Le Pharillon
Détenteur: Les Hebdos Régionaux Québecor Média
144, rue Jacques-Cartier, Gaspé, QC G4X 1M9
Tél: 418-368-3242
pharillon@hebdosquebecor.com
www.hebdosregionaux.ca/est-du-quebec/le-pharillon
Médias sociaux:
twitter.com/LePharillon
www.facebook.com/pharillon
Tirage: 8 618 Fréquence: Dimanche
Alain Saint-Amand, Directeur régional Bas Saint-Laurent / Gaspésie, alain.saint-amand@quebecormedia.com
Bernard Johnson, Éditeur,
bernard.johnson@hebdosquebecor.com

Gatineau: Aylmer Bulletin
#C-10, 181, rue Principale, Gatineau, QC J9H 6A6
Tel: 819-684-4755; Fax: 819-684-6428
Toll-Free: 800-486-7678
www.bulletinaylmer.com
Circulation: 21,885 Frequency: Wed.
Lynne Lavery, Office Manager, l.lavery@bulletinaylmer.com
Fred Ryan, Editor, abawqp@videotron.ca

Gatineau: Le Bulletin
Détenteur: Transcontinental Media Inc.
435, rue Principale, Gatineau, QC J8L 2G8
Tél: 819-986-5089;Téléc: 819-986-2073
yannick.boursier@tc.tc
www.lebulletin.net
Tirage: 11 351 Fréquence: Dimanche
Michel Blais, Éditeur

Gatineau: L'Etoile de l'Outaouais
Détenteur: Transcontinental Media Inc.
160, boul de l'Hôpital, Gatineau, QC J8T 8J1
Tél: 819-568-7544;Téléc: 819-568-7038
redaction.outaouais@transcontinental.ca
www.letudiantoutaouais.ca
Tirage: 34 324 Fréquence: Mercredi

Gatineau: La Revue
Anciennement: La Revue de Gatineau
Détenteur: Transcontinental Media Inc.
#160, boul de l'Hôpital, Gatineau, QC J8T 8J1
Tél: 819-568-7736;Téléc: 819-568-7038
boursiery@transcontinental.ca
www.journallarevue.com
Tirage: 41 174 Fréquence: Mercredi
Yves Blondin, Éditeur

Gatineau: West Québec Post
#C-10, 181, rue Principale, Gatineau, QC J9H 6A6
Tel: 819-684-4755; Fax: 819-684-6428
Toll-Free: 800-486-7678
editor@westquebecpost.com
www.lowdownonline.com/tag/west-quebec-post
Circulation: 9,065 Frequency: Weekly
Lynne Lavery, Manager, l.lavery@bulletinaylmer.com
Fred Ryan, Publisher, abawqp@videotron.ca

Granby: Granby Express
Anciennement: Samedi Express
#5, 398, rue Principale, Granby, QC J2G 2W6
Tél: 450-777-4515
stephanie.macfarlane@tc.tc
www.granbyexpress.com
Médias sociaux:
www.facebook.com/GranbyExpress
Tirage: 39 500 Fréquence: Hebdomadaire
Cathy Bernard, Éditrice, cathy.bernard@tc.tc

Grande-Vallée: Journal le Phare
Anciennement: Le Phare, l'autre vision
1A, rue du Vieux Pont Est, Grande-Vallée, QC G0E 1K0
Tél: 418-393-2205
www.journallephare.org
Médias sociaux:
www.facebook.com/pages/Journal-le-Phare/225905758286
Tirage: 1 325
Noël-Denis Samson, Président

Hudson: Hudson/St. Lazare Gazette
Previous Name: Lake of Two Mountains Gazette
Owned By: Lake of Two Mountains Gazette Ltd.
PO Box 70 , 397 Main Rd., Hudson, QC J0P 1H0
Tel: 450-458-5482; Fax: 450-458-3337
hudsongazette@videotron.ca
www.hudsongazette.com
Social Media:
www.facebook.com/437408105332
Circulation: 16,000 Frequency: Wed.
First English Quebec weekly on the web.

Huntingdon: The Gleaner/La Source
Détenteur: Les Hebdos Régionaux Québecor Média
66, rue Châteauguay, Huntingdon, QC J0S 1H0
Tél: 450-264-5364;Téléc: 450-264-9521
www.hebdosregionaux.ca/monteregie/the-gleaner-la-source
Tirage: 3,328
Sheri Graham, Éditrice,
sheri.sheri.graham@quebecormedia.com

Joliette: L'Action
Détenteur: Transcontinental Media Inc.
342, Beaudry nord, Joliette, QC J6E 6A6
Tél: 450-759-3664;Téléc: 450-759-3190
infolanaudiere@tc.tc
www.laction.com
Tirage: 46 700 Fréquence: Dimanche

Joliette: Le Journal de Joliette
Détenteur: Les Hebdos Régionaux Québecor Média
1075, boul Firestone, 5e étage, Joliette, QC J6E 6X6
Tél: 450-960-2424;Téléc: 450-960-2626
journaljoliette@hebdosquebecor.com
www.hebdosregionaux.ca/rive-nord/le-j ournal-de-joliette
Médias sociaux:
twitter.com/JdeJoliette
www.facebook.com/jdejoliette
Jean Curadeau, Éditeur, jean.curadeau@quebecormedia.com

Jonquière: Le Réveil
Détenteur: Les Hebdos Régionaux Québecor Média
1, rue Mont Sainte-Claire, Jonquière, QC G7X 7W4
Tél: 418-695-2601;Téléc: 418-695-1391
redaction.reveil@hebdosquebecor.com
www.hebdosregionaux.ca/saguenay-lac- st-jean/le-reveil
Médias sociaux:
twitter.com/LeReveil
www.facebook.com/lereveil
Tirage: 70 529 Fréquence: Dimanche
Ralph Pilote, Directeur général Québecor Média Saguenay-Lac-Saint-Jea, ralph.pilote@quebecormedia.ca

Knowlton: Brome County News
Owned By: Sherbrooke Record
5 Victoria, Knowlton, QC J0E 1V0
Tel: 450-242-1188; Fax: 450-243-5155
Toll-Free: 800-463-9525
www.sherbrookerecord.com/brome
Social Media:
www.facebook.com/sherbrookerecord
Circulation: 12,307 Frequency: Wed.
Daniel Coulombe, Editor, dcoulombe@sherbrookerecord.com
Sharon McCully, Publisher, outletjournal@sympatico.ca

L'Islet: Le Hublot
135, rue Notre-Dame, L'Islet, QC G0R 2B0
Tél: 418-247-3333;Téléc: 418-247-3336
clochers@globetrotter.net
www.lehublot.ca
Tirage: 1 735 Fréquence: Last Thurs. of the month
Guylaine Hudon, Directrice Générale

La Sarre: Le Citoyen Abitibi-Ouest
Détenteur: Les Hebdos Régionaux Québecor Média
56, 6e avanue est, La Sarre, QC J9Z 1L8
Tél: 819-333-5507;Téléc: 819-333-4537
www.hebdosregionaux.ca/abitibi-temiscamingue
Joël Caya, Éditeur, joel.caya@quebecormedia.com

La Tuque: L'Écho de La Tuque
Détenteur: Transcontinental Media Inc.
324, rue St-Joseph, La Tuque, QC G9X 1L2
Tél: 819-523-6141;Téléc: 819-523-6143
redaction_latuque@transcontinental.ca
www.lechodelatuque.com
Tirage: 6 802
Michel Scarpino, Directeur du journal

Lac-Etchemin: La Voix du Sud
1516A, rte 277, Lac-Etchemin, QC G0R 1S0
Tél: 418-625-7471;Téléc: 418-625-5200
Ligne sans frais: 866-325-8649
redaction_lacetchemin@tc.tc
www.lavoixdusud.com
Tirage: 22 434 Fréquence: Samedi
Caroline Gilbert, Éditeur, caroline.gilbert@tc.tc

Lac-Mégantic: L'Écho de Frontenac
5040, boul des Vétérans, Lac-Mégantic, QC G6B 2G5
Tél: 819-583-1630;Téléc: 819-583-1124
www.echodefrontenac.com
Médias sociaux:
twitter.com/echodefrontenac
www.facebook.com/308170576707
Tirage: 9 134 Fréquence: Dimanche; français
Gaétan Poulin, Éditeur
Rémi Tremblay, Rédacteur-en-chef

Lachenaie: Le Trait d'Union
#210, 1300, Grande Allée, Lachenaie, QC J6W 4M4
Tél: 450-964-4400;Téléc: 450-964-4403
letraitdunion@transcontinental.ca
www.letraitdunion.com

Lachute: L'Argenteuil
Détenteur: La Compagnie d'édition André Paquette inc
52, rue Principale, Lachute, QC J8H 3A8
Tél: 450-562-2494;Téléc: 450-562-1434
argenteuil@eap.on.ca
editionap.ca/fr/node/34
Tirage: 15 000 Fréquence: Mercredi; français
François Leblanc, Directeur, francois.leblanc@eap.on

Lachute: Progrès Watchman
Anciennement: The Watchman
52, rue Principale, Lachute, QC J8H 3A8
Tél: 450-562-8593
Tirage: 13 000 Fréquence: Samedi
Evelyne Bergeron, Editor

Laval: Courrier Laval
Détenteur: Transcontinental Media Inc.
#200, 2700, av Francis-Hughes, Laval, QC H7S 2B9
Tél: 450-667-4360;Téléc: 450-667-0845
redactionlaval@tc.tc
www.courrierlaval.com
Médias sociaux:
twitter.com/lecourrierlaval
www.facebook.com/courrierlaval
Tirage: 108 375 Fréquence: Dimanche; aussi Courrier du Jeudi
Claude Labelle, Éditeur

Laval: L'Écho de Laval
Détenteur: Les Hebdos Régionaux Québecor Média
900, boul St-Martin ouest, Laval, QC H7S 2K9
Tél: 450-575-2000;Téléc: 450-575-2020
redaction.echolaval@hebdosquebecor.com
www.hebdosregionaux.ca/rive-nord/ lecho-de-laval
Médias sociaux:
twitter.com/LEchodeLaval
www.facebook.com/écholaval
Eric Mercier, Éditeur, eric.mercier@quebecormedia.com

Laval: The Laval News
#304, 3860 boul Notre-Dame, Laval, QC H7V 1S1
Tel: 450-978-9999; Fax: 450-687-6330
lavalnews.ca
Circulation: 28,965 Frequency: Thu.
George Bakoyannis, Publisher, georgeb@the-news.ca

Laval: Nouvelles Parc-Extension News
#304, 3860, boul Notre-Dame, Laval, QC H7V 1S1
Tel: 450-978-9999; Fax: 450-687-6330
editor@the-news.ca
www.px-news.com
Frequency: Saturday; English & French
George Bakoyannis, Co-Publisher, General Director, georgeb@the-news.ca
George S. Guzmas, Co-Publisher, Advertising Director, georgeg@the-news.ca

Laval: Vivre
828 - av 79, Laval, QC H7V 3J1
Tél: 450-973-8787;Téléc: 450-973-8414
poste@ccvm.org
www.ccvm.org
Tirage: 1 000 Fréquence: 4 fois par an
Manon Rousseau, Directrice

Lennoxville: The Townships Sun
PO Box 28 , Lennoxville, QC J1M 1Z3
Social Media:
twitter.com/TownshipsSun
Circulation: 696 Frequency: Monthly

Lévis: Le Peuple Lévis
Anciennement: Le Peuple-Tribune
Détenteur: Les Hebdos Régionaux Québecor Média
#103B, 5790, boul Étienne-Dallaire, Lévis, QC G6V 8V6
Tél: 418-833-9398;Téléc: 418-833-8177
redaction.levis@hebdosquebecor.com
www.hebdosregionaux.ca/chaudiere-appa laches/le-peuple-levis
Médias sociaux:
twitter.com/LePeupleLevis
www.facebook.com/peuplelevis
Tirage: 57 087 Fréquence: Samedi
Paul Lessard, Éditeur, paul.lessard@quebecormedia.com

Lévis: Le Peuple Lotbinière
#103B, 5790, boul Étienne-Dallaire, Lévis, QC G6V 8V6
Tél: 418-728-2131;Téléc: 418-728-4819
redaction.lotbiniere@hebdosquebecor.com
www.peuplelotbiniere.com
Médias sociaux:
twitter.com/Plotbiniere
www.facebook.com/plotbiniere
Tirage: 12 390 Fréquence: Dimanche; français
Mélanie Labrecque, Éditeur,
redaction.lotbiniere@hebdosquebecor.com

Lingwick: Le Reflet du Canton de Lingwick
#306, 72, rte 108, Lingwick, QC J0B 2Z0
Tél: 819-877-3560
info@lereflet.org
lereflet.org
Fréquence: 9/an
Daniel Pezat, Président

Longueuil: Brossard-Eclair
Détenteur: Les Hebdos Régionaux Québecor Média
267, rue Saint-Charles ouest, Longueuil, QC J4H 1E3
Tél: 450-646-3333;Téléc: 450-674-0205
www.hebdosquebecor.com/bre/index_bre.asp
Tirage: 23 880 Fréquence: Mardi; French & English
Lucie Masse, Rédacteur-en-chef
450-616-8080
lucie.masse@quebecormedia.com

Longueuil: Le Courrier du Sud
Détenteur: Les Hebdos Régionaux Québecor Média
267, rue Saint-Charles ouest, Longueuil, QC J4H 1E3
Tél: 450-646-3333;Téléc: 450-674-0205
publicite@courrierdusud.com
www.hebdosregionaux.ca/monteregie/le-courrie r-du-sud
Médias sociaux:
twitter.com/LeCourrierDuSud
www.facebook.com/lecourrierdusud
Tirage: 127 350
Lucie Masse, Éditrice, lucie.masse@quebecormedia.com

Longueuil: Le Journal de Saint-Hubert
Détenteur: Les Hebdos Régionaux Québecor Média
267, rue Saint-Charles ouest, Longueuil, QC J4H 1E3
Tél: 450-646-3333;Téléc: 450-674-0205
Tirage: 28 000 Fréquence: Mercredi
Lucie Masse, Rédacteur, lucie.masse@quebecormedia.com

Longueuil: Le Magazine de Saint-Lambert
Détenteur: Les Hebdos Régionaux Québecor Média
267, rue Saint-Charles ouest, Longueuil, QC J4H 1E3
Tél: 450-646-3333;Téléc: 450-674-0205
www.hebdosregionaux.ca/monteregie/le-magazine-de-saint-lambert
Lucie Masse, Éditrice, lucie.masse@quebecormedia.com

Longueuil: Point Sud
#200, 24, rue De Gentilly, Longueuil, QC J4H 1Y8
Tél: 450-677-2626;Téléc: 450-442-2663
info@pointsud.ca
www.pointsud.ca
Médias sociaux:
twitter.com/Point_Sud
www.facebook.com/pointsud

Louiseville: L'Écho de Maskinongé
Anciennement: L'Écho D'Autray et de Maskinongé
43, St-Louis, Louiseville, QC J5V 2C7
Tél: 819-228-5532;Téléc: 819-228-9379
redaction_em@transcontinental.ca
www.lechodemaskinonge.com

Tirage: 27 200 Fréquence: Dimanche
André Lamy, Directeur
Pierre-Louis Paquin, Chef de pupitre à l'information

Magog: Le Reflet du Lac
Détenteur: Transcontinental Media Inc.
#104, 101, rue Du Moulin, Magog, QC J1X 4A1
Tél: 819-843-3500;Téléc: 819-843-3085
Ligne sans frais: 866-637-5236
www.lerefletdulac.com
Médias sociaux:
www.facebook.com/LeRefletduLac
Tirage: 23 359 Fréquence: Samedi
Monique Côté, Éditrice, monique.cote@tc.tc
Dany Jacques, Chef de pupitre, dany.jacques@tc.tc

Malartic: Le Courrier de Malartic
CP 4020 , Malartic, QC J0Y 1Z0
Tél: 819-757-4712;Téléc: 819-757-4712
Tirage: 1 200 Fréquence: Mardi; français
Denyse Roberge, Éditrice

Maniwaki: Le Choix
Détenteur: Les Hebdos Régionaux Québecor Média
139, rue Principale sud, Maniwaki, QC J9E 1Z8
Tél: 819-441-2225;Téléc: 819-623-7148
www.hebdosregionaux.ca/laurentides/le-choix
Denis Labelle, Éditeur, denis.labelle@quebecormedia.com

Matane: L'Avant-Poste
Détenteur: Les Hebdos Régionaux Québecor Média
305, rue de la Gare, Matane, QC G4W 3J2
Tél: 418-629-3443;Téléc: 418-629-2919
avant-poste@hebdosquebecor.com
www.hebdosregionaux.ca/est-du-quebec/lava nt-poste
Médias sociaux:
twitter.com/LAvantPoste
www.facebook.com/lavantposte
Tirage: 8 815 Fréquence: Saturday
Jean Gagnon, Éditeur, jean.gagnon@hebdosquebecor.com

Matane: Le Riverain
Détenteur: Les Hebdos Régionaux Québecor Média
305, rue de la Gare, Matane, QC G4W 3J2
Tél: 418-764-2809;Téléc: 418-562-4607
www.hebdosregionaux.ca/est-du-quebec/le-riverain
Tirage: 5,749 Fréquence: Dimanche
Jean Gagnon, Éditeur, jean.gagnon@hebdosquebecor.com

Matane: La Voix Gaspesienne
Détenteur: Les Hebdos Régionaux Québecor Média
#107, 305, rue de la Gare, Matane, QC G4W 3J2
Tél: 418-562-4040;Téléc: 418-562-4607
voixgaspesienne@hebdosquebecor.com
www.hebdosregionaux.ca/est-du-quebec/
la-voix-gaspesienne-et-la-voix-de-la-m
Médias sociaux:
twitter.com/VoixGaspeMatane
www.facebook.com/voixgaspematane
Tirage: 5 013 Fréquence: Mercredi; aussi La Voix du dimanche
Alain Saint-Amand, Directeur régional Bas Saint-Laurent / Gaspésie, alain.saint-amand@quebecormedia.com
Jean Gagnon, Éditeur, jean.gagnon@hebdosquebecor.com

Mont-Laurier: L'Écho de la Lievre
Détenteur: Les Hebdos Régionaux Québecor Média
369, boul Albiny-Paquette, Mont-Laurier, QC J9L 1K5
Tél: 819-623-5250;Téléc: 819-623-7148
redaction.montlaurier@hebdosquebecor.com
www.hebdosregionaux.ca/laurenti des/lecho-de-la-lievre
Médias sociaux:
twitter.com/LEchoDeLaLievre
www.facebook.com/lecholievre
Tirage: 16 000 Fréquence: Samedi
André Guillemette, Directeur général régional Laurentides, andre.guillemette@quebecormedia.com
Denis Labelle, Éditeur, denis.labelle@quebecormedia.com

Mont-Tremblant: L'Information du Nord Mont-Tremblant
Détenteur: Les Hebdos Régionaux Québecor Média
1107, rue de Saint-Jovite, Mont-Tremblant, QC J8E 3J9
Tél: 819-425-8658;Téléc: 819-425-7713
info.nord@hebdosquebecor.com
www.hebdosregionaux.ca/laurentides/linforma
tion-du-nord-mont-tremblant
Médias sociaux:
twitter.com/linfodunordmt
www.facebook.com/linfodunordmt
Tirage: 14 300 Fréquence: Vendredi
Johanne Régimbald, Éditrice,
johanne.regimbald@quebecormedia.com

Mont-Tremblant: L'Information du Nord Sainte-Agathe
Détenteur: Les Hebdos Régionaux Québecor Média
1107, rue de Saint-Jovite, Mont-Tremblant, QC J8E 3J9
Tél: 819-425-8658;Téléc: 819-425-7713
info.nord@hebdosquebecor.com
www.hebdosregionaux.ca/laurentides/linforma
tion-du-nord-sainte-agathe
Médias sociaux:
twitter.com/linfodunordsa
www.facebook.com/linfodunordsa
Johanne Régimbald, Éditrice,
johanne.regimbald@quebecormedia.com

Mont-Tremblant: L'Information du Nord Valée de la Rouge
Détenteur: Les Hebdos Régionaux Québecor Média
1107, rue de Saint-Jovite, Mont-Tremblant, QC J8E 3J9
Tél: 819-425-8658;Téléc: 819-425-7713
www.hebdosregionaux.ca/laurentides/linformation-du-nord-vallee
-de-la-rouge
Johanna Régimbald, Éditrice,
johanne.regimbald@quebecormedia.com

Montmagny: L'Oie Blanche
70, rue de l'Anse, Montmagny, QC G5V 3S7
Tél: 418-248-8820;Téléc: 418-248-4033
oieblanc.presse@globetrotter.net
www.oieblanc.com
Médias sociaux:
twitter.com/oieblanc
www.facebook.com/166453626708427
Tirage: 19 672 Fréquence: Samedi

Montmagny: Le Peuple Côte-du-Sud
Détenteur: Les Hebdos Régionaux Québecor Média
#200, 80, boul Taché est, Montmagny, QC G5V 3S7
Tél: 418-248-0415;Téléc: 418-248-2377
www.hebdosregionaux.ca/chaudiere-appalaches/le-peuple-cote-sud
Tirage: 21 073 Fréquence: Samedi
Claudette Tardif, Éditrice, claudette.tardif@quebecormedia.com

Montréal: L'Avenir de l'Est
#210, 8770 boul Langelier, Montréal, QC H1P 3C6
Tél: 514-899-5888;Téléc: 514-899-5001
redaction_est@tc.tc
www.avenirdelest.com
Médias sociaux:
twitter.com/avenirdelest
www.facebook.com/avenirdelest
Tirage: 42 314
Véronique Gauthier, Éditrice

Montréal: Le Couac
6940, rue Jogues, Montréal, QC H4E 2W8
Tél: 514-596-1017
info@lecouac.org
www.lecouac.org

Montréal: Échos du Vieux-Montréal
165, rue St-Paul ouest, Montréal, QC H2Y 1Z5
Tél: 514-844-2133;Téléc: 514-844-5858
Tirage: 15 000
Denise Di Candido, Chief Editor
Vincent Di Candido, Président

Montréal: Le Faubourg
210, 8770 blvd Langelier, Montréal, QC H1P 3C6
Tél: 514-899-5888;Téléc: 514-899-5001
redactioncentre@tc.tc
www.faubourgvillemarie.ca
Myriam Poirier, Contact

Montréal: Greek Canadian Reportage
8060, rue Birnam, Montréal, QC H3N 2T7
Tel: 514-279-7772
pages.globetrotter.net/gcradb
Circulation: 15,000 Frequency: Weekly
Anthony Bartzakos, Publisher & Editor

Montréal: L'Informateur de Rivières-Des-Prairies
Détenteur: Transcontinental Media Inc.
#210, 8770 boul. Langelier, Montréal, QC H1P 3C6
Tél: 514-899-5888;Téléc: 514-899-5001
redaction_est@tc.tc
www.linformateurrdp.com
Médias sociaux:
twitter.com/LinformateurRDP
www.facebook.com/linformateurrdp
Véronique Gauthier, Éditrice
Marie-Josée Chouinard, Directrice de l'information

Montréal: Journal de la rue
4237, rue Ste-Catherine est, Montréal, QC H1V 1X4
Tél: 514-256-9000;Téléc: 514-256-9444
journal@journaldelarue.ca
www.cafegraffiti.net
Tirage: 60 000 Fréquence: 6 fois par an
Raymond Viger, Redacteur en chef,
raymondviger@journaldelarue.ca

Montréal: Journal de Rosemont
Détenteur: Transcontinental Media Inc.
#210, 8770, boul Langelier, Montréal, QC H1P 3C6
Tél: 514-899-5888;Téléc: 514-899-5001
redaction_est@tc.tc
www.journalderosemont.com
Médias sociaux:
twitter.com/JournalRosemont
www.facebook.com/JournaldeRosemont
Tirage: 59 588
Sylvia Cerasi, Rédactrice-en-chef
Sylviane Lussier, Éditrice

Montréal: Journal L'Itinéraire
2103, rue Sainte-Catherine est, 3e étage, Montréal, QC H2K 2H9
Tél: 514-597-0238;Téléc: 514-597-1544
itineraire@itineraire.ca
itineraire.ca
Médias sociaux: www.youtube.com/user/itineraire1
twitter.com/LItineraire
www.facebook. com/pages/Itinéraire/115888658426315
Tirage: 13 000 Fréquence: bimensuel
Jocelyne Sénécal, Directrice des ressources humines
Serge Lareault, Directeur général

Montréal: Montréal Express
Anciennement: Nouvelles de l'Est
Détenteur: Transcontinental Media Inc.
#210, 8770 boul Langelier, Montréal, QC H1P 3C6
Tél: 514-899-5885
redaction_est@tc.tc
www.montrealexpress.ca
Tirage: 24 629

Montréal: Le Plateau
Détenteur: Transcontinental Media Inc.
#210, 8770, boul Langelier, Montréal, QC H1P 3C6
Tél: 514-899-5888;Téléc: 514-899-5001
Ligne sans frais: 866-637-5236
redaction_est@tc.tc
www.leplateau.com
Médias sociaux:
twitter.com/Journalplateau
www.facebook.com/journalduplateau
Tirage: 34 132
Stéphane Desjardins, Éditeur
Josianne Desjardins, Rédacteur-en-chef

Montréal: Westmount Examiner
Owned By: Transcontinental Inc.
#210, 245, av Victoria, Montréal, QC H3Z 2M6
Tel: 514-484-5610; Fax: 514-484-6028
Toll-Free: 866-637-5236
examiner@transcontinental.ca
www.westmountexaminer.com
Social Media:
twitter.com/WestmountExam
Frequency: Weekly

Natashquan: Le Portageur
CP 40 , 50, ch d'en haut, Natashquan, QC G0G 2E0
Tél: 418-726-3736;Téléc: 418-726-3714
leportageur.jimdo.com
Tirage: 548 Fréquence: Mercredi
Nicole Lessard

New Carlisle: The Gaspé Spec
Détenteur: Sea-Coast Publications Inc.
CP 99 , 128, boul Gerard D. Levesque, New Carlisle, QC G0C 1Z0
Tél: 418-752-5400;Téléc: 418-752-6932
specs@globetrotter.net
www.gaspespec.com
Autre information: Alternate Phone: 418-752-5070
Tirage: 3,022 Fréquence: Sunday
Sharon Renouf-Farrell, Publisher
Gilles Gagné, News Editor

Nicolet: Le Courrier-Sud
Anciennement: Nicolet Courrier-Sud
Détenteur: Transcontinental Media Inc.
Medias Trancontinental, 3255, rue Marie Victorin, Nicolet, QC J3T 1X5
Tél: 819-293-4551
redaction_cs@tc.tc
www.lecourriersud.com
Tirage: 21 105 Fréquence: Dimanche
Mathieu Allard, Directeur de journal, mathieu.allard@tc.tc
Marie-Eve Veillette, Chef de pupitre

Outremont: L'Express d'Outremont & Mont-Royal
Anciennement: L'Express d'Outremont/de Mont-Royal
Détenteur: Transcontinental Media Inc.
#203, 1500, boul Jules-Poitras, Outremont, QC H4N 1X7
Tél: 514-855-1292;Téléc: 514-855-1855
redactionexpress@transcontinental.ca
www.expressoutremont.com
Médias sociaux:
twitter.com/InfoOutremontMR
www.facebook.com/372191966155544
Tirage: 28 748 Fréquence: Jeudi, hebdo
Mario Marois, Éditeur
Marilaine Bolduc-Jacob, Rédactrice en chef

Préissac: L'Alliance de Preissac
180, av du Lac, RR 1, Préissac, QC J0Y 2E0
Tél: 819-759-4141;Téléc: 819-759-4142
journalalliance.preissac@cablevision.qc.ca
Tirage: 1 000 Fréquence: Mensuel
Estelle Gelot, Présidente

Québec: L'Actuel
Détenteur: Transcontinental Media Inc.
#900, 1265, boul Charest ouest, Québec, QC G1N 4V4
Tél: 418-686-6400;Téléc: 418-686-4841
redaction_quebec@tc.tc
www.lactuel.com
Médias sociaux:
twitter.com/quebechebdo
www.facebook.com/lactuel
Tirage: 38 000 Fréquence: Samedi

Québec: L'Appel
#900, 1265, boul Charest ouest, Québec, QC G1N 4V4
Tél: 418-686-6400;Téléc: 418-686-1086
redaction_quebec@tc.tc
www.lappel.com
Tirage: 52 000 Fréquence: Samedi
Lilianne Laprise, Éditrice

Québec: Beauport Express
Détenteur: Transcontinental Media Inc.
Hebdos Transcontinental à Québec, #900, 1265, boul Charest ouest, Québec, QC G1N 4V4
Tél: 418-686-6400;Téléc: 418-686-1086
redaction_quebec@tc.tc
www.beauportexpress.com
Médias sociaux:
twitter.com/quebechebdo
www.facebook.com/quebechebdo
Tirage: 38 700 Fréquence: Hebdomadaire
Lilianne Laprise, Éditrice
Louis Mercier, Directeur général régional
Lynda Drouin, Directrice administrative

Québec: Journal Droit de Parole
266, Saint-Vallier Ouest, Québec, QC G1K 1K2
Tél: 418-648-8043
droitdeparole.org
Tirage: 15 000 Fréquence: bi-hebdomadaire
Gilles Simard, Rédacteur-en-chef
Claude Giguère, Journaliste

Québec: Journal Jacques-Cartier
Owned By: Transcontinental Media Inc.
Médias-Transcontinental, #900, 1265, boul Charest ouest, Québec, QC G1N 4V4
Tel: 418-686-3036; Fax: 418-686-1086
redaction_quebec@transcontinental.ca
www.lejacquescartier.com
Social Media:
twitter.com/quebechebdo
www.facebook.com/quebechebdo
Circulation: 9,500 Frequency: au 2 mois
Lilianne Laprise, Éditrice

Québec: Journal le Carrefour
715, rue Saint-Bernard, Québec, QC G1N 1J4
Tél: 418-649-0775
carrefour@webnet.qc.ca
www.carrefourdequebec.com
Tirage: 72 500 Fréquence: Dimanche
Martin Claveau, Éditeur
Nicolas Godbout, Rédacteur-en-chef

Québec: Quebec Chronicle-Telegraph
Owned By: 1764 Publications Inc.
#218, 1040 av Belvédère, Québec, QC G1S 3G3
Tel: 418-650-1764; Fax: 418-650-5172
info@qctonline.com
www.qctonline.com
Social Media:
www.facebook.com/64677421759
Circulation: 1,854 Frequency: Wed.
Ray Stanton, Editor/Publisher, editor@qctonline.com

Québec: Québec Express
Détenteur: Transcontinental Media Inc.
Médias-Transcontinental, #900, 1265, boul Charest ouest, Québec, QC G1N 4V4
Tél: 418-686-6400;Téléc: 418-686-1086
redaction_quebec@tc.tc
www.lequebecexpress.com
Médias sociaux:
twitter.com/quebechebdo
www.facebook.com/quebechebdo
Tirage: 38 000
Lilianne Laprise, Éditrice

Québec: La Quête
729, Côte d'Araham, Québec, QC G1R 1A2
Tél: 418-649-2388;Téléc: 418-649-7770
Tirage: 3 000
Bernard Hélie, Coordonnateur

Repentigny: L'Écho de Repentigny
Détenteur: Les Hebdos Régionaux Québecor Média
#4, 544, boul Notre-Dame, Repentigny, QC J6A 2T8
Tél: 450-932-4782;Téléc: 450-932-4794
echorepentigny@quebecormedia.com
www.hebdosregionaux.ca/rive-nord/lecho- de-repentigny
Médias sociaux:
twitter.com/LEchodeRepen
www.facebook.com/echorepentigny
Martin Gravel, Éditeur, martin.gravel@quebecormedia.com

Repentigny: Hebdo Rive Nord
Anciennement: L'Artisan
1004, rue Notre-Dame, Repentigny, QC J5Y 1S9
Tél: 450-581-5120;Téléc: 450-581-4515
equiperedaction@transcontinental.ca
www.hebdorivenord.com

Repentigny: Hebdo Rive-Nord
1004, rue Notre-Dame, Repentigny, QC J5Y 1S9
Tél: 450-581-5120;Téléc: 450-581-4515
equiperedaction@transcontinental.ca
www.hebdorivenord.com
Tirage: 46 457 Fréquence: Dimanche
Yannick Boulanger, Éditeur

Richelain: Journal Servir
Garnison St-Jean, CP 100 Bureau Chef, Richelain, QC J0J 1R0
Tél: 450-358-7099;Téléc: 450-358-7423
www.journalservir.com
Tirage: 3 300 Fréquence: English & French
Gaëtane Dion, Rédactrice-en-chef

Rimouski: L'Avantage Votre Journal
Détenteur: Transcontinental Media Inc.
183, St-Germain ouest, Rimouski, QC G5L 4B8
Tél: 418-722-0205;Téléc: 418-723-4237
Ligne sans frais: 877-722-4237
bgleeson@lavantage.qc.ca
www.lavantage.qc.ca
Médias sociaux: www.youtube.com/user/journallavantage
twitter.com/lavantageqcca
www.fa cebook.com/pages/LAvantage/311812224673
Tirage: 40 586 Fréquence: Vendredi
Jean Mercier, Éditeur, jean.mercier@tc.tc

Rimouski: Le Progrès Écho
Anciennement: Le Progrès Echo Dimanche
Détenteur: Les Hebdos Régionaux Québecor Média
CP 3217 , 217, av Léonidas, Rimouski, QC G5L 9G6
Tél: 418-721-1212;Téléc: 418-723-1855
www.hebdosregionaux.ca/est-du-quebec/le-rimouskois-et-progres-echo
Tirage: 30 492 Fréquence: Dimanche
Marc Pitre, Éditeur, marc.pitre@quebecormedia.com

Rimouski: Le Rimouskois
Détenteur: Les Hebdos Régionaux Québecor Média
CP 3217 , 271, av Le¢nidas, Rimouski, QC G5L 9G6
Tél: 418-721-1212;Téléc: 418-723-1855
www.hebdosregionaux.ca/est-du-quebec/le-rimouskois-et-progres-echo
Tirage: 24 059 Fréquence: Mercredi
Alain Saint-Amand, Directeur régional Bas Saint-Laurent / Gaspésie, alain.saint-amand@quebecormedia.com
Marc Pitre, Éditeur, marc.pitre@quebecormedia.com

Rivière-du-Loup: Info Dimanche
72, rue Fraser, Rivière-du-Loup, QC G5R 1C6
Tél: 418-862-1911;Téléc: 418-862-6165
journal@infodimanche.com
www.infodimanche.com
Médias sociaux: www.youtube.com/infodimanche
twitter.com/infodimanche
www.facebook. com/infodimanche
Tirage: 29 118 Fréquence: Dimanche
Michel Chalifour, Éditeur, michel@infodimanche.com
Mario Pelletier, Rédacteur-en-chef, journalistes@infodimanche.com

Rivière-du-Loup: Info Dimanche
72, rue Fraser, Rivière-du-Loup, QC G5R 1C6
Tél: 418-862-1911;Téléc: 418-862-6165
journal@infodimanche.com
www.infodimanche.com
Tirage: 30 000 Fréquence: Dimanche
Mario Pelletier, Rédacteur en chef, journalistes@infodimanche.com

Rivière-du-Loup: L'Information
Détenteur: Les Hebdos Régionaux Québecor Média
55-A, rue de l Hôtel-de-ville, Rivière-du-Loup, QC G5R 1L4
Tél: 418-775-4381;Téléc: 418-775-7768
info.montjoli@hebdosquebecor.com
www.hebdosregionaux.ca/est-du-quebec/li nformation
Médias sociaux:
twitter.com/Linformation
www.facebook.com/infomontjoli
Tirage: 10 500 Fréquence: Dimanche
Francis Desrosiers, Éditeur, francis.desrosiers@quebecormedia.com

Rivière-du-Loup: Saint-Laurent Portage
Anciennement: Le Portage
Détenteur: Les Hebdos Régionaux Québecor Média
55-A, rue de l Hôtel-de-ville, Rivière-du-Loup, QC G5R 1L4
Tél: 418-862-1774;Téléc: 418-862-4387
gilles.lebel@hebdosquebecor.com
www.hebdosregionaux.ca/est-du-quebec/le-saint-laurent-portage
Médias sociaux:
twitter.com/SLPortage
www.facebook.com/slportage
Tirage: 39 000 Fréquence: Dimanche
Francis Desrosiers, Éditeur, francis.desrosiers@quebecormedia.com

Roberval: L'Etoile du Lac
Détenteur: Transcontinental Media Inc.
#101, 797 boul. Saint-Joseph, Roberval, QC G8H 2L4
Tél: 418-275-2911;Téléc: 418-275-2834
redaction_roberval@tc.tc
www.letoiledulac.com
Médias sociaux:
www.twitter.com/letoiledulac
www.facebook.com/letoiledulac
Tirage: 14 158 Fréquence: Samedi
Daniel Migneault, Rédacteur en chef, daniel.migneault@tc.tc

Rouyn-Noranda: Le Citoyen Rouyn-Noranda
Anciennement: Le Citoyen
Détenteur: Les Hebdos Régionaux Québecor Média
1, rue du Terminus est, Rouyn-Noranda, QC J9X 3B5
Tél: 819-762-4361;Téléc: 819-797-2450
www.hebdosregionaux.ca/abitibi-temiscamingue
Tirage: 18 760 Fréquence: Dimanche; supplement, Journal du Nord-Ouest
Joël Caya, Éditeur, joel.caya@quebecormedia.com

Rouyn-Noranda: Ensemble pour bâtir
CP 424 , 200, rue Leblanc, Rouyn-Noranda, QC J0Z 1Y0
Tél: 819-768-2568
ensemblepb1@tlb.sympatico.ca
www.journal-ensemble.org
Tirage: 1 400
Diane Gaudet-Bergeron, Présidente

Rouyn-Noranda: La Frontière
Détenteur: Les Hebdos Régionaux Québecor Média
1, rue du Terminus est, Rouyn-Noranda, QC J9X 3B5
Tél: 819-762-4361;Téléc: 819-797-2450
redaction.rouyn@hebdosquebecor.com
www.hebdosregionaux.ca/abitibi-temisc amingue
Médias sociaux:
twitter.com/lafrontiere
www.facebook.com/lafrontiere
Tirage: 5 626 Fréquence: Mercredi
Joël Caya, Éditeur, joel.caya@quebecormedia.com

Saguenay: Le Progrès Dimanche
1051, boul Talbot, Saguenay, QC G7H 5C1
Tél: 418-545-4474
redaction@lequotidien.com
www.lapresse.ca/le-quotidien/progres-dimanche
Tirage: 44 500 Fréquence: Dimanche
Michel Sinard, Éditeur

Saint-André-Avellin: La Petite-Nation
Détenteur: Transcontinental Media Inc.
3A, rue Principale, Saint-André-Avellin, QC J0V 1W0
Tél: 819-983-2725;Téléc: 819-983-6844
yannick.boursier@tc.tc
www.lapetitenation.com
Tirage: 9 600 Fréquence: Dimanche

Saint-Basile-le-Grand: L'Action Régionale
Détenteur: Les Hebdos Régionaux Québecor Média
#101, 155, boul Sir-Wilfrid-Laurier, Saint-Basile-le-Grand, QC J3N 1A9
Tél: 450-441-7252;Téléc: 450-441-4497
direction@journallactionregionale.com
www.hebdosregionaux.ca/monteregie/ laction-regionale
Médias sociaux:
www.facebook.com/journallactionregionale
Isabelle Bergeron, Éditrice,
direction@journallactionregionale.com

Saint-Bruno: Les Versants
1488, rue Montarville, Saint-Bruno, QC J3V 3T5
Tél: 450-441-5300
info@versants.com
www.versants.com
Tirage: 18 000
Philippe Clair, Éditeur, pclair@versants.com

Saint-Bruno-de-Kamouraska: Le Trait d'Union de St-Bruno
CP 10 , 4, rue du Couvent, Saint-Bruno-de-Kamouraska, QC G0L 2M0
Tél: 418-492-2612;Téléc: 418-492-9076
mun.stbrunokam@globetrotter.net
www.stbrunokam.qc.ca
Constance Gagné, Présidente

Saint-Bruno-de-Montarville: Le Journal de Saint-Bruno/Saint-Basile
Détenteur: Les Hebdos Régionaux Québecor Média
1507, rue Roberval, Saint-Bruno-de-Montarville, QC J3V 3P8
Tél: 450-653-3685;Téléc: 450-653-6967
lecteurs@journaldest-bruno.qc.ca
www.hebdosregionaux.ca/monteregie/le-jo urnal-de-saint-bruno
Médias sociaux:
twitter.com/JournalStBruno
www.facebook.com/journaldestbruno
Tirage: 14 900 Fréquence: Samedi
Sylvain Bouchard, Éditeur,
sylvain.bouchard@quebecormedia.com

Saint-Denis-de-Brompton: Le Saint-Denisien
CP 244 , Saint-Denis-de-Brompton, QC J0B 2P0
Tél: 819-340-1371
stdenisi@abacom.com
www.lesaintdenisien.ca
Tirage: 1 175
Michel Bibeau, Président et éditeur en chef
819-846-2119

Saint-Donat: Journal Altitude
365, rue Principale, Saint-Donat, QC J0T 2C0
Tél: 819-424-2610;Téléc: 819-424-3615
journalaltitude@cgocable.ca
www.st-donat.com/journal.html
Tirage: 3,700 Fréquence: Vendredi; français
Martin Lafortune, Contact

Saint-Eustache: La Concorde
53, rue Saint-Eustache, Saint-Eustache, QC J7R 2L2
Tél: 450-472-3440;Téléc: 450-472-1638
infojournaux@groupejcl.com
www.leveil.com
Médias sociaux:
www.facebook.com/JOURNAL.LEVEIL
Tirage: 45 300 Fréquence: Mercredi; aussi L'Eveil (dimanche; tirage 37 400)
Jean-Claude Langlois, Président-Éditeur
Jean-François Legault, Directeur, Ventes,
jflegault@groupejcl.com

Saint-Eustache: L'Éveil
53, rue St-Eustache, Saint-Eustache, QC J7R 2L2
Tél: 450-472-3440;Téléc: 450-472-1638
infojournaux@groupejcl.com
www.leveil.com
Médias sociaux:
www.facebook.com/JOURNAL.LEVEIL
Tirage: 45 720 Fréquence: Samedi
Jean-Claude Langlois, Éditeur

Saint-Félicien: Le Point du Saint-Jean
Détenteur: Les Hebdos Régionaux Québecor Média
1258, boul Sacré-Cour, Saint-Félicien, QC G8K 2R2
Tél: 418-695-2601;Téléc: 418-695-1391
www.hebdosregionaux.ca/saguenay-lac-st-jean/le-point-du-lac-st-jean
Médias sociaux:
twitter.com/PointLacStJean
www.facebook.com/pointlacstjean
Ralph Pilote, Directeur général Québecor Média Saguenay-Lac-Saint-Jea, ralph.pilote@quebecormedia.ca

Saint-François-de-la-Rivière du Sud: L'Écho de St-François
534, ch St-François ouest, Saint-François-de-la-Rivière du Sud, QC G0R 3A0
Tél: 418-259-2177
echosf@videotron.ca
Tirage: 675 Fréquence: Mensuel
Lorraine Lamonde, Présidente

Saint-Georges-de-Beauce: L'Éclaireur Progrès
Détenteur: Les Hebdos Régionaux Québecor Média
710, 98e rue, Saint-Georges-de-Beauce, QC G5Y 8G1
Tél: 418-228-8858;Téléc: 418-227-0268
redaction.saintgeorges@hebdosquebecor.com
www.hebdosregionaux.ca/chaudiere-appalaches/leclaireur-progres
Médias sociaux:
twitter.com/EclairProgres
www.facebook.com/leclaireurprogres
Tirage: 28 700 Fréquence: Mercredi, Vendredi
Gilbert Bernier, Éditeur, gilbert.bernier@quebecormedia.com

Saint-Georges-de-Beauce: Le Progrès de Bellechasse-Etchemins
Détenteur: Les Hebdos Régionaux Québecor Média
710, 98e rue, Saint-Georges-de-Beauce, QC G5Y 8G1
Tél: 418-476-7784;Téléc: 418-476-5068
andre.boutin@quebecormedia.com
www.hebdosregionaux.ca/chaudiere-appalaches/le-progres-de-bellechasse
Médias sociaux:
twitter.com/pbellechasse
www.facebook.com/pbellechasse
Gilbert Bernier, Éditeur, gilbert.bernier@quebecormedia.com

Saint-Hippolyte: Le Sentier
CP 135 , Saint-Hippolyte, QC J8A 3P5
Tél: 450-563-1975;Téléc: 450-563-1059
redaction@journal-le-sentier.org
www.journal-le-sentier.org
Tirage: 4 000
Denise Marcoux, Présidente, variatxt@sympatico.ca

Saint-Hyacinthe: Le Clairon Regional de St-Hyacinthe
Détenteur: DBC Communications inc.
655, av Ste-Anne, Saint-Hyacinthe, QC J2S 5G4
Tél: 450-773-6028;Téléc: 450-773-3115
redaction@leclairon.qc.ca
www.leclairon.qc.ca
Tirage: 33 985 Fréquence: Samedi
Benoit Chartier, Éditeur

Saint-Hyacinthe: Le Courrier de Saint-Hyacinthe
Détenteur: DBC Communications inc.
655, rue Ste-Anne, Saint-Hyacinthe, QC J2S 5G4
Tél: 450-773-6028;Téléc: 450-773-3115
redaction@lecourrier.qc.ca
www.lecourrier.qc.ca
Médias sociaux:
twitter.com/LeCourrier1853
Tirage: 13 605 Fréquence: Mercredi; français
Benoit Chartier, Éditeur
Martin Bourassa, Rédacteur en chef et éditorialiste,
mbourassa@lecourrier.qc.ca

Saint-Jean-Port-Joli: L'Attisée
Maison Communautaire Joly, CP 954 , #22, 318, rue Verreault, 2e étage, Saint-Jean-Port-Joli, QC G0R 3G0
Tél: 418-598-9590;Téléc: 418-598-7588
journal.attisee@videotron.ca
www.lattisee.com
Tirage: 2700
Benoit Lévesque, Éditeur

Saint-Jean-sur-Richelieu: Le Canada Français
84, rue Richelieu, Saint-Jean-sur-Richelieu, QC J3B 6X3
Tél: 450-347-0323;Téléc: 450-347-4539
canadaf@canadafrancais.com
www.canadafrancais.com
Médias sociaux:
www.facebook.com/lecanadafrancais
Tirage: 18 955 Fréquence: Mercredi; aussi Le Richelieu Dimanche (dimanche)
Gilles Lévesque, Rédacteur en chef

Saint-Jean-sur-Richelieu: L'Écho de Saint-Jean-sur-Richelieu
Détenteur: Les Hebdos Régionaux Québecor Média
#102B, 81, rue Richelieu bureau, Saint-Jean-sur-Richelieu, QC J3B 6X2
Tél: 450-653-5295
sjr.redaction@quebecormedia.com
www.hebdosregionaux.ca/monteregie/lecho-de-saint-jean-sur-richelieu
Médias sociaux:
twitter.com/LEchoSaintJean
www.facebook.com/lechosaintjean
Denis Tétreault, Éditeur, denis.tetreault@quebecormedia.com

Saint-Jérome: L'Écho du Nord
Détenteur: Les Hebdos Régionaux Québecor Média
179, rue St-Georges, Saint-Jérome, QC J7Z 4Z8
Tél: 450-436-5887;Téléc: 450-436-5904
redaction.st-jerome@hebdosquebecor.com
www.hebdosregionaux.ca/laurentides/lecho-du-nord-et-le-mirabel
Médias sociaux:
twitter.com/EchoNordMirabel
www.facebook.com/echonordmirabel
Tirage: 7 500 Fréquence: Mercredi
Andre Juteau, Éditeur
Claude Lamarche, Rédacteur-en-chef

Saint-Jérome: Journal Le Nord
Anciennement: L'Annonceur
Détenteur: Transcontinental Media Inc.
393, boul des Laurentides, Saint-Jérome, QC J7Z 4L9
Tél: 450-438-8383;Téléc: 450-438-4174
mychel.lapointe@transcontinental.ca
www.journallenord.com
Tirage: 40 012 Fréquence: Mercredi

Saint-Jérome: Le Mirabel
Détenteur: Les Hebdos Régionaux Québecor Média
179, rue St-Georges, Saint-Jérome, QC J7Z 4Z8
Tél: 450-436-8200;Téléc: 450-436-5904
redaction.st-jerome@hebdosquebecor.com
www.hebdosregionaux.ca/laurentides/lecho-du-nord-et-le-mirabel
Médias sociaux:
twitter.com/EchoNordMirabel
www.facebook.com/echonordmirabel
Tirage: 39 430 Fréquence: Samedi
André Guillemette, Éditeur / Directeur général régional des Laurentides, andre.guillemette@quebecormedia.com

Saint-Laurent: Courrier Ahuntsic
Détenteur: Transcontinental Media Inc.
#203, 1500, boul Jules-Poitras, Saint-Laurent, QC H4N 1X7
Tél: 514-855-1292;Téléc: 514-855-1855
courrierahuntsic@transcontinental.ca
www.courrierahuntsic.com
Médias sociaux:
twitter.com/InfoAhuntsicBC
www.facebook.com/courrierahuntsicbc

Fréquence: Dimanche

Saint-Laurent: Le Journal de Mont-Royal
Détenteur: Transcontinental Media Inc.
#203, 1500, boul Jules-Poitras, Saint-Laurent, QC H4N 1X7
Tél: 514-855-1292;Téléc: 514-855-1855
redactionexpress@transcontinental.ca
www.expressoutremont.com
Médias sociaux:
twitter.com/InfoOutremontMR
www.facebook.com/372191966155544

Saint-Laurent: Les Nouvelles Saint-Laurent / Saint-Laurent News
Détenteur: Transcontinental Media Inc.
#203, 1500, boul Jules-Poitras, Saint-Laurent, QC H4N 1X7
Tél: 514-855-1292;Téléc: 514-855-1855
nouvellessaint-laurent@tc.tc
www.nouvellessaint-laurent.com
Médias sociaux:
twitter.com/InfoStLaurent
www.facebook.com/NouvellesSaintLaurent
Tirage: 27 499 Fréquence: Sunday; English & French

Saint-Laurent: Progrés Villeray
Détenteur: Transcontinental Media Inc.
#203, 1500, boul Jules-Poitras, Saint-Laurent, QC H4N 1X7
Tél: 514-855-1292;Téléc: 514-855-1855
redactionprogres@transcontinental.ca
www.leprogresvilleray.com
Médias sociaux:
twitter.com/InfoVillerayPE
www.facebook.com/ProgresVillerayParcExtension
Tirage: 22 576

Saint-Laurent: The Suburban
Owned By: Michael Publishing Co. Inc.
#105, 7575 Trans-Canada Hwy., Saint-Laurent, QC H4T 1V6
Tel: 514-484-1107; Fax: 514-484-9616
www.thesuburban.com
Circulation: West End: 64,000; West Island: 41,000; East End: 25,000 Frequency: Wed.: West End, West Island; Thu.: East End
Michael Sochaczevski, Publisher
Sari Medicoff, Operations Manager

Saint-Pamphile: L'Écho d'en Haut
#209, 35, rue Principale, Saint-Pamphile, QC G0R 3X0
Tél: 418-356-5491;Téléc: 418-356-5491
info@echodenhaut.org
www.echodenhaut.org
Tirage: 2 915
Diane Bérubé, Directrice Générale

Saint-Pascal: Le Placoteux
491, av d'Anjou, Saint-Pascal, QC G0L 3Y0
Tél: 418-492-2706;Téléc: 418-492-9706
association@leplacoteux.qc.ca
www.leplacoteux.com
Médias sociaux:
www.facebook.com/LePlacoteux
Tirage: 17 469 Fréquence: Dimanche
Bruno Lacroix, Editeur, association@leplacoteux.com

Saint-Pierre-de-l'île-d'Orléans: Autour de l'île
115, 517 rte des Prêtes, Saint-Pierre-de-l'île-d'Orléans, QC G0A 4E0
Tél: 418-828-0330;Téléc: 418-828-0741
autourdelile@videotron.ca
www.autourdelile.com
Tirage: 3 400 Fréquence: Mensuel
Hélène Bayard, Rédactrice-en-chef

Saint-Sauveur: Le Journal des Pays D'en Haut La Vallée
Détenteur: Les Hebdos Régionaux Québecor Média
#104, 94, de la Gare, Saint-Sauveur, QC J0R 1R6
Tél: 450-227-4646;Téléc: 450-227-8144
redaction.lavallee@hebdosquebecor.com
www.hebdosregionaux.ca/laurentides
/le-journal-des-pays-den-haut-la-vallee
Médias sociaux:
twitter.com/JdesPaysdEnHaut
www.facebook.com/journalpdh
Tirage: 23 000 Fréquence: Mercredi
André Guillemette, Éditeur / Directeur général régional des Laurentides, andre.guillemette@quebecormedia.com

Saint-Siméon: Le Goéland
CP 250 , 127, boul Perron ouest, Saint-Siméon, QC G0C 3A0
Tél: 418-534-2026;Téléc: 418-534-4353
Tirage: 610
Antoinette Arsenault, Éditrice

Saint-Tite: L'Hebdo Mekinac-des Chenaux
CP 4057 , Saint-Tite, QC G0X 3H0
Tél: 819-537-5111;Téléc: 819-537-5471
Ligne sans frais: 866-637-5236
redaction.hmc@transcontinental.ca
www.lhebdomekinacdeschenaux.com
Médias sociaux:
www.facebook.com/hebdomekinacdeschenaux
Tirage: 13 081 Fréquence: Samedi; français
Nancy Allaire, Éditeur

Sainte-Anne-des-Plaines: Le Point d'Impact
194B, boul Sainte-Anne, Sainte-Anne-des-Plaines, QC J0N 1H0
Tél: 450-478-3538
journallepoint@qc.aira.com
www.journallepoint.com
Tirage: 6 000 Fréquence: Samedi

Sainte-Brigitte-de-Laval: Le Lavalois
CP 1020 , Sainte-Brigitte-de-Laval, QC G0A 3K0
Tél: 418-907-7172;Téléc: 418-907-7172
www.lelavalois.com
Tirage: 1 300 Fréquence: irregulier
Lucille Thomassin, Présidente, lucille@ccapcable.com

Sainte-Geneviève-de-Batis: Le Bulletin des Chenaux
44, chemin Rivière-à-Veillet, Sainte-Geneviève-de-Batis, QC G0X 2R0
Tél: 819-840-3091;Téléc: 418-362-2861
info@lebulletindeschenaux.com
www.lebulletindescheneaux.com
Médias sociaux:
twitter.com/BullDesChenaux
www.facebook.com/pages/Bulletin-des-Chenaux/2130995187272
Tirage: 9 000
Patrick Pepin, Directrice générale

Sainte-Julie: L'Information Sainte-Julie
Détenteur: Les Hebdos Régionaux Québecor Média
566, rue Jules-Choquet, Sainte-Julie, QC J3E 1W6
Tél: 450-649-0719;Téléc: 450-649-7748
www.hebdosregionaux.ca/monteregie/linformation-de-sainte-julie
Médias sociaux:
www.facebook.com/infodestejulie
Tirage: 19 363 Fréquence: Samedi
Sylvain Bouchard, Éditeur, sylvain.bouchard@quebecormedia.com
Nathalie Gilbert, Directrice de l'information, nathalie.gilbert@quebecormedia.com

Sainte-Marie-de-Beauce: Beauce Média
Détenteur: Les Hebdos Régionaux Québecor Média
1147, boul Vachon nord, Sainte-Marie-de-Beauce, QC G6E 3B6
Tél: 418-387-8000;Téléc: 418-387-4495
redaction.bmedia@hebdosquebecor.com
www.hebdosregionaux.ca/chaudiere-app alaches/beauce-media
Médias sociaux:
twitter.com/BeauceMedia
www.facebook.com/beaucemedia
Tirage: 16 807 Fréquence: Lundi
Lise Doyon, Éditrice, lise.doyon@hebdosquebecor.com

Sainte-Thérèse: L'Écho de la Rive-Nord
Détenteur: Les Hebdos Régionaux Québecor Média
#208, 204, boul Labelle, Sainte-Thérèse, QC J7E 2X7
Tél: 450-818-7575;Téléc: 450-818-7582
redaction.echorivenord@hebdosquebecor.com
www.hebdosregionaux.ca/rive-no rd/lecho-de-la-rive-nord
Médias sociaux:
twitter.com/LEchoRiveNord
www.facebook.com/lechorivenord
Serge Cameron, Éditeur, serge.cameron@quebecormedia.com

Sainte-Thérèse: L'Écho de Saint-Eustache
Détenteur: Les Hebdos Régionaux Québecor Média
#208, 204, boul Labelle, Sainte-Thérèse, QC J7E 2X7
Tél: 450-818-7575;Téléc: 450-818-7582
redaction.saint-eustache@hebdosquebecor.com
www.hebdosregionaux.ca/rive- nord/lecho-de-saint-eustache
Médias sociaux:
twitter.com/LEchoStEustache
www.facebook.com/lechosteustache
Serge Cameron, Éditeur, serge.cameron@quebecormedia.com

Sainte-Thérèse: Journal Le Courrier
Anciennement: Courrier Le Courrier
Détenteur: Transcontinental Media Inc.
190, boul Curé-Labelle, Sainte-Thérèse, QC J7E 2X5
Tél: 450-434-4144;Téléc: 450-434-3142
louis.sauvageau@transcontinental.ca
www.journallecourrier.com
Médias sociaux:
twitter.com/journalcourrier
www.facebook.com/JournalCourrier
Tirage: 55 472 Fréquence: Samedi
Louis Sauvageau, Éditeur
André Juteau, Directeur général régional
Linda Veilleux, Directrice administrative

Sainte-Thérèse: Le Nord Info
Détenteur: Transcontinental Media Inc.
50B, rue Turgeon, Sainte-Thérèse, QC J7E 3H4
Tél: 450-435-6537;Téléc: 450-435-0588
infojournaux@groupejcl.com
www.nordinfo.com
Médias sociaux:
twitter.com/NordInfoVoix
www.facebook.com/NordInfoCom
Tirage: 57 000 Fréquence: Samedi
Jean-Claude Langlois, Président-Éditeur

Sainte-Thérèse: La Voix des Milles-Iles
50B, rue Turgeon, Sainte-Thérèse, QC J7E 3H4
Tél: 450-435-6537;Téléc: 450-435-0588
infojournaux@groupejcl.com
www.nordinfo.com
Médias sociaux:
twitter.com/NordInfoVoix/journaliste
www.facebook.com/NordInfoCom
Tirage: 57 000 Fréquence: Mercredi
Jean-Claude Langlois, Éditeur

Saint-Étienne-des-Grès: Le Stéphanois
CP 282 , 1260, rue St-Alphonse, Saint-Étienne-des-Grès, QC G0X 2P0
Tél: 819-535-2089;Téléc: 819-535-5118
lestephanois@cgocable.ca
www.lestephanois.ca
Tirage: 1 700
Gérard Levesque, Président
819-655-0307

Salaberry-de-Valleyfield: Le Journal Saint-François
Détenteur: Les Hebdos Régionaux Québecor Média
20, rue Académie, Salaberry-de-Valleyfield, QC J6T 6M9
Tél: 450-371-6222;Téléc: 450-371-7254
www.hebdosregionaux.ca/monteregie/le-journal-saint-francois
Médias sociaux:
www.facebook.com/journalsaintfrancois
Tirage: 31 000
Diane Dumont, Éditrice, diane.dumont@quebecormedia.com

Salaberry-de-Valleyfield: Le Soleil de Valleyfield
Anciennement: Le Soleil de Salaberry-de-Valleyfield
Détenteur: Les Hebdos Régionaux Québecor Média
20, rue Académie, Salaberry-de-Valleyfield, QC J6T 6M9
Tél: 450-373-8555;Téléc: 450-373-8666
www.hebdosregionaux.ca/monteregie/le-soleil-de-valleyfield
Médias sociaux:
www.facebook.com/soleilvalleyfield
Tirage: 30 200
Diana Dumont, Éditrice, diane.dumont@quebecormedia.com

Sept-Iles: Le Nord-Est
Détenteur: Les Hebdos Régionaux Québecor Média
365, boul Laure, Sept-Iles, QC G4R 1Y2
Tél: 418-962-9441
redaction.septiles@hebdosquebecor.com
www.hebdosregionaux.ca/est-du-q uebec/le-nord-est
Médias sociaux:
twitter.com/JournalNordEst
www.facebook.com/lenordest
Tirage: 13 510 Fréquence: Dimanche; aussi Le Nord-Est Plus (mercredi)
Catherine Martin, Éditrice, catherine.martin@hebdosquebecor.com

Sept-Iles: Le Port-Cartois
Détenteur: Les Hebdos Régionaux Québecor Média
781, boul Laure, Sept-Iles, QC G4R 1Y2
Tél: 418-766-5321;Téléc: 418-766-5329
redaction.portcartois@hebdosquebecor.com
www.hebdosregionaux.ca/est-du-q uebec/le-port-cartois
Tirage: 3 600 Fréquence: Dimanche
Catherine Martin, Éditrice, catherine.martin@hebdosquebecor.com

Shawinigan: L'Écho de Shawinigan
Détenteur: Les Hebdos Régionaux Québecor Média
#101, 795, 5e rue, Shawinigan, QC G9N 1G2
Tél: 819-731-0327;Téléc: 819-731-0328
nouvelles.shawinigan@quebecormedia.com
www.hebdosregionaux.ca/mauricie/l echo-de-shawinigan
Médias sociaux:
twitter.com/lechoshawinigan
www.facebook.com/lechoshawinigan
Hugues Carpentier, Éditeur,
hugues.carpentier@quebecormedia.com

Shawinigan: L'Hebdo du St-Maurice
CP 10 , 2102, av Champlain, Shawinigan, QC G9N 6T8
Tél: 819-537-5111;Téléc: 819-537-5471
redaction_shawinigan@transcontinental.ca
www.lhebdodustmaurice.com
Tirage: 30 511 Fréquence: Samedi; français
Michel Matteau, Éditeur

Shawville: The Equity
Owned By: Pontiac Printshop Ltd.
133 Centre St., Shawville, QC J0X 2Y0
Tel: 819-647-2204; Fax: 819-647-2206
news@theequity.ca
www.theequity.ca
Social Media: www.youtube.com/equitynewspaper
twitter.com/equitynewspaper
www.facebo ok.com/EquityNewspaper
Circulation: 3,362
Heather Dickson, Publisher
Andrea Cranfield, Editor, editor@theequity.ca

Sherbrooke: Entrée Libre
#317, 187, rue Laurier, Sherbrooke, QC J1H 4Z4
Tél: 819-821-2270;Téléc: 819-566-2664
journal@entreelibre.info
www.entreelibre.info
Médias sociaux:
www.facebook.com/pages/Journal-Entr%C3%A9e-Libre/100568
95
Tirage: 9 000 Fréquence: huit fois par année; 8-16 pa
Produit par le collectif du même nom selon une démarche d'éducation populaire autonome, est accessible aux gens du quartier centre-sud-ouest de Sherbrooke.
Claude Dostie, Rédacteur en chef
819-565-4798

Sherbrooke: Le Haut Saint-François
#105, 175, rue Queen, Sherbrooke, QC J1M 1K1
Tél: 819-563-1001
redaction@estrieplus.com
www.estrieplus.com
Médias sociaux:
www.facebook.com/EstriePlus
Tirage: 17 500 Fréquence: 20 fois par an
Maxime Doyon, Président

Sherbrooke: L'Info
CP 157 , Succursale Saint-Élie d'Orford, Sherbrooke, QC J1R 1A1
Tél: 819-820-9663
journalinfo@cooptel.qc.ca
linfodesaintelie.org/Site_Journal_Linfo/Bienvenue.html
Tirage: 3966
Alain Béliveau, Président

Sherbrooke: Le Journal de Magog
Détenteur: Les Hebdos Régionaux Québecor Média
3330, rue King ouest, Sherbrooke, QC J1L 1C9
Tél: 819-565-7777;Téléc: 819-565-4650
redaction.magog@hebdosquebecor.com
www.hebdosregionaux.ca/estrie/le-jour nal-de-magog
Autre information: 819-575-7575
Médias sociaux:
twitter.com/JdeMagog
www.facebook.com/jdemagog
Sarah Beaulieu, Directrice générale Quebecor Media Estrie,
sarah.beaulieu@quebecormedia.com

Sherbrooke: Le Journal de Sherbrooke
Détenteur: Les Hebdos Régionaux Québecor Média
3330 rue King ouest, Sherbrooke, QC J1L 1C9
Tél: 819-565-7777;Téléc: 819-565-4650
redaction.sherbrooke@hebdosquebecor.com
www.hebdosregionaux.ca/estrie/le -journal-de-sherbrooke
Autre information: 819-575-7575
Médias sociaux:
twitter.com/jdesherbrooke
www.facebook.com/journaldesherbrooke
Sarah Beaulieu, Directrice générale Quebecor Media Estrie,
sarah.beaulieu@quebecormedia.com

Sherbrooke: La Nouvelle de Sherbrooke
1950, rue Roy, Sherbrooke, QC J1K 2X8
Tél: 819-564-5450
redaction@latribune.qc.ca
www.lapresse.ca/la-tribune/la-nouvelle
Médias sociaux:
twitter.com/HebdoLaNouvelle
Tirage: 47 000 Fréquence: Mercredi
Céline Maheu, Éditrice
Denis Duchaine, Rédacteur-en-chef

Shipshaw: Journal La Vie d'Ici
4681, rue Saint-Léonard, Shipshaw, QC G7P 1J4
;Téléc: 418-213-0701
informations@laviedici.com
www.laviedici.com
Claire Duchesne, Présidente
Denys Claveau, Co-Directeur, Photographe
Nadine Boily, Chroniqueur

Sorel-Tracy: Les 2 Rives et La Voix
Détenteur: Les Hebdos Régionaux Québecor Média
58, rue Charlotte, Sorel-Tracy, QC J3P 1G3
Tél: 450-742-9408;Téléc: 450-742-2493
www.hebdosregionaux.ca/monteregie/les-2-rives-et-la-voix
Médias sociaux:
www.facebook.com/les2rives
Tirage: 28 000 Fréquence: Mardi
Pierre Plante, Éditeur, pierre.plante@quebecormedia.com
Louise Grégoire-Racicot, Rédactrice-en-chef

St-Charles-de-Bellechasse: Au fil de la Boyer
8B ave Commerciale, St-Charles-de-Bellechasse, QC G0R 2T0
Tél: 418-948-0741
laboyer@laboyer.com
www.laboyer.com
Médias sociaux:
www.facebook.com/journal.la.boyer
Tirage: 1 000
Jean-Pierre Paré, Éditeur

St-Fabien-de-Panet: Le Réveil
199B, rue Bilodeau, St-Fabien-de-Panet, QC G0R 2J0
Tél: 418-249-2128;Téléc: 418-249-2507
lereveil@sogetel.net
Fréquence: Mensuel
Thérèse Bilodeau, Présidente

St-Laurent: Courrier Bordeaux-Cartierville
Détenteur: Transcontinental Media Inc.
#203, 1500, boul Jules-Poitras, St-Laurent, QC H4N 1X7
Tél: 514-855-1292;Téléc: 514-855-1855
veronique.leduc@transcontinental.ca
www.courrierahuntsic.com
Médias sociaux:
twitter.com/InfoAhuntsicBC
www.facebook.com/courrierahuntsicbc
Tirage: 17 237 Fréquence: Dimanche

St-Léonard: Le Flambeau de l'Est
#210, 8770, boul Langelier, St-Léonard, QC H1P 3C6
Tél: 514-899-5888;Téléc: 514-899-5001
redaction_est@tc.tc
www.flambeaudelest.com
Médias sociaux:
twitter.com/Flambeaudelest
www.facebook.com/leflambeaudelest
Stéphane Desjardins, Éditeur

St-Léonard: Guide de Montréal-Nord
Détenteur: Transcontinental Media Inc.
#210, 8770, boul Lanaelier, St-Léonard, QC H1P 3C6
Tél: 514-899-5888;Téléc: 514-899-5001
redaction_est@tc.tc
www.guidemtlnord.com
Médias sociaux:
twitter.com/Guidemtlnord
www.facebook.com/guidemtlnord
Tirage: 32 841
Véronique Gauthier, Éditrice

St-Léonard: Le Guide Montréal-Nord
#210, 8770, boul Langelier, St-Léonard, QC H1P 3C6
Tél: 514-899-5888;Téléc: 514-899-5001
redaction_est@tc.tc
www.guidemtlnord.com
Médias sociaux:
twitter.com/Guidemtlnord
www.facebook.com/guidemtlnord
Véronique Gauthier, Éditrice

St-Léonard: Progrès Saint-Léonard
Détenteur: Transcontinental Media Inc.
#212, 8770, boul Langelier, St-Léonard, QC H1P 3C6
Tél: 514-899-5888;Téléc: 514-899-5984
redaction_est@tc.tc
www.progresstleonard.com
Médias sociaux:
twitter.com/progresstleo
www.facebook.com/progresstleonard
Tirage: 30 592 Fréquence: Mercredi
Véronique Gauthier, Éditrice
Jacques Boulanger, Éditeur

St-Pierre-du-Sud: Le Pierr'Eau
645, 2eme av, St-Pierre-du-Sud, QC G0R 4B0
Tél: 418-248-8277;Téléc: 418-248-7068
journal@stpierrerivieresud.ca
www.pierreau.ca
Myriam Poulin, Directrice

Stanstead: Stanstead Journal
269 Dufferin St., Stanstead, QC J0B 3E2
Tél: 819-876-7514 Ligne sans frais: 800-567-1259
reception@stanstead-journal.com
www.stanstead-journal.com
Tirage: 2 700 Fréquence: Wed.
Jean-Yves Durocher, President & Publisher,
jy.durocher@stanstead-journal.com

Témiscaming: Contact
CP 566 , 32, rue Simon, Témiscaming, QC J0Z 3R0
Tél: 819-627-9050;Téléc: 819-627-1794
contact@cablevision.qc.ca
temiscamingcontact.org
Tirage: 1 000 Fréquence: Bilingual
Elaine Ouellet, Rédactrice-en-chef

Terrebonne: La Revue de Terrebonne
231, rue Ste-Marie, Terrebonne, QC J6W 3E4
Tél: 450-964-4444;Téléc: 450-471-1023
larevue@larevue.qc.ca; ventes@larevue.qc.ca
www.larevue.qc.ca
Autre information: Montréal: 514-990-7314
Médias sociaux:
www.linkedin.com/pub/gilles-bordonado/12/a66/556
twitter.com/revueterreb onne
www.facebook.com/revueterrebonne
Tirage: 57 800 Fréquence: Mercredi
Gilles Bordonado, Président-Directeur général,
gbordonado@larevue.qc.ca

Thetford Mines: Le Courrier Frontenac
CP 789 , 541, boul Smith nord, Thetford Mines, QC G6G 5V3
Tél: 418-338-5181;Téléc: 418-338-5482
courrier.frontenac@tc.tc
www.courrierfrontenac.com
Tirage: 22 256 Fréquence: Mercredi
Pascal Gourdeau, Rédacteur-en-chef, pascal.gourdeau@tc.tc

Trois-Rivières: L'Écho de Trois-Rivières
Détenteur: Les Hebdos Régionaux Québecor Média
3625, boul du Chanoine-Moreau, Trois-Rivières, QC G9Y 5N6
Tél: 819-731-0327;Téléc: 819-731-0328
www.hebdosregionaux.ca/mauricie/lecho-de-trois-rivieres
Médias sociaux:
twitter.com/lecho3rivieres
www.facebook.com/lecho3rivieres
Philippe Châtillon, Éditeur,
philippe.chatillon@quebecormedia.com

Trois-Rivières: L'Hebdo-Journal
Détenteur: Transcontinental Media Inc.
#205, 525, rue Barkoff, Trois-Rivières, QC G8T 2A5
Tél: 819-379-1490;Téléc: 819-379-0705
reception.hj@transcontinental.ca
www.lhebdojournal.com
Tirage: 48 900 Fréquence: Samedi
Alain Bernard, Éditeur, alain.bernard@tc.tc
Carole Béliveau, Secrétaire de direction, carole.beliveau@tc.tc

Trois-Rivières: Le Tour d'y voir
991, rue Champflour, Trois-Rivières, QC G9A 1Z8
Tél: 819-371-9393
leblanc@ecof.qc.ca
www.tdv.qc.ca
Tirage: 1 000
Marie-Pierre Leblanc

Val-David: Le Journal Ski-se-dit
2600, rue Monty, Val-David, QC J0T 2N0
Tél: 819-322-7969;Téléc: 819-322-7904
ski-se-dit@cgocable.ca
www.ski-se-dit.info

Tirage: 3 000 Fréquence: Mensuel
Françoise Gilbert, Présidente

Val-d'Or: Le Citoyen de la Vallée de l'Or
Détenteur: Les Hebdos Régionaux Québecor Média
1462, rue de la Québécoise, Val-d'Or, QC J9P 5H4
Tél: 819-825-3755;Téléc: 819-825-0361
www.hebdosregionaux.ca/abitibi-temiscamingue
Fréquence: Dimanche
Caroline Couture, Éditrice,
caroline.couture@quebecormedia.com

Val-d'Or: Les Echos Abitibiens
Détenteur: Les Hebdos Régionaux Québecor Média
1462, rue de la Québécoise, 2e étage, Val-d'Or, QC J9P 5H4
Tél: 819-825-3755;Téléc: 819-825-0361
redaction.valdor@hebdosquebecor.com
www.hebdosregionaux.ca/abitibi-temis camingue
Médias sociaux:
twitter.com/LechoAbitibien
www.facebook.com/lechoabitibien
Tirage: 17 700 Fréquence: Mercredi; (Amos, Lasarre, Malartic, Matagami)
Caroline Couture, Éditrice,
caroline.couture@quebecormedia.com

Val-des-Monts: Journal l'Envol
Anciennement: L'Envol des Monts
12, Potvin, Val-des-Monts, QC J8N 7B2
Tél: 819-671-1502;Téléc: 819-671-7463
envol.desmonts@sympatico.ca
Tirage: 11 500 Fréquence: Mensuel
Nicole A. Thibodeau, Contact

Valleyfield: Journal Le Suroît
#201, 52, rue Nicholson, Valleyfield, QC J6T 4M8
Tél: 450-371-8051;Téléc: 450-371-4237
Ligne sans frais: 877-371-8051
journal@media-sudouest.com
www.publications-sudouest.com/regional.html

Vaudreuil-Dorion: L'Étoile
Anciennement: 1ère Édition du Sud-Ouest
Détenteur: Transcontinental Media Inc.
469, av St-Charles, Vaudreuil-Dorion, QC J7V 2N4
Tél: 450-455-6111;Téléc: 450-455-3028
webmestre@hebdosdusuroit.com
www.journalletoile.com
Médias sociaux:
twitter.com/journalletoile
www.facebook.com/journalletoile
Angèle M. Prévost, Éditrice, directrice générale,
aprevost@hebdosdusuroit.com

Vaudreuil-Dorion: Première Édition
Détenteur: Transcontinental Media Inc.
469, av St-Charles, Vaudreuil-Dorion, QC J7V 2N4
Tél: 450-455-7955;Téléc: 450-455-3028
webmestre@hebdosdusuroit.com
www.journalpremiereedition.com
Médias sociaux:
twitter.com/journal1edition
www.facebook.com/journalpremiereedition
Angèle M. Prévost, Éditrice, directrice générale

Victoriaville: L'Écho de Victoriaville
Détenteur: Les Hebdos Régionaux Québecor Média
106, boul Bois-Francs nord, Victoriaville, QC G6P 1E7
Tél: 819-604-6686;Téléc: 819-604-6398
www.hebdosregionaux.ca/estrie/lecho-de-victoriaville
Jean Crépeau, Éditeur, jean.crepeau@quebecormedia.com

Victoriaville: La Nouvelle de Victoriaville
43, rue Notre-Dame est, 2e étage, Victoriaville, QC G6P 3Z4
Tél: 819-758-6211;Téléc: 819-758-0417
redaction_victo@transcontinental.ca
www.lanouvelle.net
Tirage: 42 074 Fréquence: Dimanche
Sylvie Côté, Éditrice
Manon Samson, Rédactrice-en-chef

Victoriaville: La Nouvelle Union
Anciennement: L'Union
43, rue Notre-Dame est, Victoriaville, QC G6P 3Z4
Tél: 819-759-6211;Téléc: 819-758-2759
redaction_victo@transcontinental.ca
www.lanouvelle.net
Tirage: 25 968 Fréquence: Hebdomadaire; Mercredi
Sylvie Côté, Éditrice
Manon Samson, Rédactrice-en-chef

Ville-Marie: Journal Le Reflet
Anciennement: Le Témiscamien
22, rue Sainte-Anne, Ville-Marie, QC J9V 2B7
Tél: 819-622-1313;Téléc: 819-622-1333
reflet@journallereflet.com
www.journallereflet.com
Tirage: 8 500 Fréquence: Mercredi
Karen Lachapelle, Directrice générale, dg@journallereflet.com

Wakefield: The Low Down to Hull & Back News
Owned By: Performance Printing Ltd.
PO Box 99 , 815 Riverside Dr., Wakefield, QC J0X 3G0
Tel: 819-459-2222; Fax: 819-459-3831
general@lowdownonline.com
www.lowdownonline.com
Social Media:
twitter.com/TrevorGreenway; twitter.com/lucyannescholey
www.facebook.com/152335818154890
Circulation: 2,990 Frequency: Wed.
Nikki Mantell, Publisher, nmantell@lowdownonline.com
Liette Robert, General Manager

Windsor: L'Etincelle
193, rue St-Georges, Windsor, QC J1S 1J7
Tél: 819-845-2705;Téléc: 819-845-5520
journal@letincelle.qc.ca
www.letincelle.qc.ca
Tirage: 10 500 Fréquence: Mercredi
Claude Frenette, Éditeur, cfrenette@letincelle.qc.ca
Chantal Darveau, Directrice, cdarveau@letincelle.qc.ca

Saskatchewan

Daily Newspapers in Saskatchewan

Moose Jaw: Moose Jaw Times-Herald
Owned By: Transcontinental Inc.
44 Fairford St. West, Moose Jaw, SK S6H 1V1
Tel: 306-692-6441
editorial@mjtimes.sk.ca
www.mjtimes.sk.ca
Circulation: 59,220 / week
The Times-Herald is published Monday to Saturday. On Sunday, Moose Jaw This Week is available. The newspaper provides local content & it also subscribe to the Saskatchewan News Network & the Canadian Press.
Rob Clark, Publisher & General Manager
306-692-1262; Fax: 306-692-2101
rob.clark@mjtimes.sk.ca
Lesley Sheppard, Managing Editor
306-692-1262; Fax: 306-692-2101
Katherine Davies, Director, Digital Products & Operations,
Katherine.Davies@transcontinental.ca
Judy Ellis, Manager, Classifieds, classifieds@mjtimes.sk.ca
Glenn Haug, Manager, Advertising, glenn.haug@mjtimes.sk.ca
Doug Lix, Manager, Circulation, doug.lix@mjtimes.sk.ca
Polly Veroba, Manager, Business, pveroba@mjtimes.sk.ca

Prince Albert: Prince Albert Daily Herald
Owned By: Transcontinental Inc.
30 - 10th St. East, Prince Albert, SK S6V 0Y5
Tel: 306-764-4276; Fax: 306-763-3331
editorial@paherald.sk.ca
www.paherald.sk.ca
Other information: Advertising, Phone: 306-764-4276, ext. 238, Fax: 306-763-6747
Social Media:
www.facebook.com/pages/Prince-Albert-Daily-Herald/1405868
John Morash, Publisher, john.morash@paherald.sk.ca
Perry Bergson, Editor, perry.bergson@paherald.sk.ca
Lorraine Brassard, Manager, Circulation,
Lorraine.brassardr@paherald.sk.ca
Mitzi Munro, Manager, Advertising, mmunro@paherald.sk.ca
Terry Munro, Coordinator, Information Technology & Web Site,
tmunro@paherald.sk.ca
Robyn Nagy, Contact, Classifieds, rnagy@paherald.sk.ca
Jolene Vanstone, Contact, Accounting,
jvanstone@paherald.sk.ca

Regina: The Leader-Post
PO Box 2020 , 1964 Park St., Regina, SK S4P 3G4
Tel: 306-781-5211; Fax: 306-565-8812
www.leaderpost.ca
Social Media:
twitter.com/leaderpost
www.facebook.com/reginaleaderpost
Circulation: 70,203 Frequency: Afternoon
Greg MacLean, Publisher
Bob Hughes, Editor

Saskatoon: The StarPhoenix
Previous Name: The Saskatoon Phoenix; Saskatoon Capital; Daily Star; Daily Phoenix
Owned By: Postmedia Network Inc.
204 - 5th Ave. North, Saskatoon, SK S7K 2P1
Tel: 306-657-6397; Fax: 306-657-6437
Toll-Free: 800-667-2002
readerservice@thestarphoenix.com
www.thestarphoenix.com
Other information: Advertising, Phone: 306-657-6340, Fax: 306-657-6208
Social Media:
twitter.com/thestarphoenix
www.facebook.com/thestarphoenix
Six editions of the newspapers are published each week. TheStarPhoenix.comoffers news each day.
Rick Fraser, Vice-President, Saskatchewan Sales & Marketing
Linda Evans, Manager, Classifieds,
advertising@thestarphoenix.com
Marsha Seivewright, Manager, Integrated Advertising Sales,
mseivewright@thestarphoenix.com
John Grainger, City Coordinator, Newsroom,
citydesk@thestarphoenix.com
Sherry Dyck, Supervisor, Business Development,
sdyck@thestarphoenix.com

Other Newspapers in Saskatchewan

Assiniboia: Assiniboia Times
Owned By: Glacier Media Group Ltd.
PO Box 910 , 410 - 1st Ave. East, Assiniboia, SK S0H 0B0
Tel: 306-642-5901; Fax: 306-642-4519
Circulation: 4,300 Frequency: Fri.
Joyce Simard, Publisher, joyce@assiniboiatimes.ca

Biggar: The Biggar Independent
PO Box 40 , 102 - 3rd Ave. West, Biggar, SK S0K 0M0
Tel: 306-948-3344; Fax: 306-948-2133
info@biggarindependent.ca
www.biggarindependent.ca
Circulation: 1,683 Frequency: Monday
Daryl Hasein, Co-Publisher
Margaret Hasein, Co-Publisher
Kevin Brautigam, Editor
Urla Tyler, Consultant, Advertising, tip@sasktel.net
Delta Fay Cruickshank, Contact, Production

Canora: The Canora Courier
Owned By: Glacier Media Inc.
123 First Ave. East, Canora, SK S0A 0L0
Tel: 306-563-5131; Fax: 306-563-5131
canoracourier@sasktel.net
Circulation: 1,383 Frequency: Wednesday
The Saskatchewan town of Canora & the villages in its municipal district are served by the weekly newspaper.
Ken Lewchuk, General Manager, k.lewchuk@sasktel.net
Gary Lewchuk, Editor
Dan Daoust, Contact, Sales, sales.canoracourier@sasktel.net
Sonia Lewchuk, Contact, Administration,
office.canoracourier@sasktel.net

Canora: Kamsack Times
Owned By: Glacier Media Inc.
123 First Ave. East, Canora, SK S0A 0L0
Tel: 306-563-5131; Fax: 306-563-5131
kamacktimes@sasktel.net
Circulation: 1,566 Frequency: Thursday
The Times presents community affairs for the towns of Norquay & Kamsack, as well as nearby villages & hamlets.
Ken Lewchuk, General Manager, k.lewchuk@sasktel.net
William Koreluik, Editor
Dan Daoust, Contact, Sales, sales.canoracourier@sasktel.net

Canora: Norquay North Star
PO Box 746 , 123 First Ave. East, Canora, SK S0A 0L0
Tel: 306-563-5131; Fax: 306-563-6144
Circulation: 762 Frequency: Weekly
Ken Sopkow, Publisher & Editor

Canora: The Preeceville Progress
Owned By: Glacier Media Inc.
PO Box 746 , 123 First Ave. East, Canora, SK S0A 0L0
Tel: 306-563-5131; Fax: 306-563-5131
Circulation: 1,079 Frequency: Thursday
The towns of Preeceville & Sturgis, plus nearby villages & hamlets, are served by The Preeceville Progress.
Ken Lewchuk, General Manager, k.lewchuk@sasktel.net
Gary Lewchuk, Editor, k.lewchuk@sasktel.net
Dan Daoust, Contact, Sales

Carlyle: Carlyle Observer
Owned By: Glacier Interactive Media
PO Box 160 , 132 Main St., Carlyle, SK S0C 0R0
Tel: 306-453-2525; Fax: 306-453-2938
observer@sasktel.net
www.carlyleobserver.com
Circulation: 3,076 Frequency: Fri.
Cindy Moffatt, General Manager

Carnduff: Gazette Post-News
PO Box 220 , 106 Broadway St., Carnduff, SK S0C 0S0
Tel: 306-482-3252; Fax: 306-482-3373
gazettepost.news@sasktel.net
Circulation: 1,144 Frequency: Weekly
Flora Grass, General Manager
Bill Grass, Editor

Coronach: Triangle News
Owned By: Transcontinental Inc.
PO Box 689 , Coronach, SK S0H 0Z0
Tel: 306-267-3381
trianglenews@sasktel.net
www.trianglenews.sk.ca
Circulation: 927 Frequency: Monday
The Triangle News serves the community of Coronach with a weekly newspaper & a daily web site.
Rob Clark, Group Publisher, rob.clark@mjtimes.sk.ca
Kelly Elder, Contact, Editorial & Sales
Denise Skinner, Contact, Office & Sales

Craik: Craik Weekly News
PO Box 360 , 221 Third St., Craik, SK S0G 0V0
Tel: 306-734-2313; Fax: 306-734-2789
craiknews@sasktel.net
Circulation: 880 Frequency: Monday
Harve Friedel, Editor

Cut Knife: Highway 40 Courier
PO Box 639 , 200 Steele St., Cut Knife, SK S0M 0N0
Tel: 306-398-4901; Fax: 306-398-4909
ckcouriernews@sasktel.net
Circulation: 505 Frequency: Wednesday
Lorie Gibson, Publisher & Editor

Davidson: The Davidson Leader
PO Box 786 , 205 Washington Ave., Davidson, SK S0G 1A0
Tel: 306-567-2047; Fax: 306-567-2900
theleaderonline@gmail.com
www.leaderonline.ca
Social Media:
twitter.com/davidsonleader
www.facebook.com/DavidsonLeader
Circulation: 1,294 Frequency: Monday
The Davidson Leader covers the Saskatchewan communities of Davidson, Kenaston, Elbow, Imperial, Bladworth, Dundurn, Craik, & Loreburn. The newspaper is available in print & as as e-paper.
Tara de Ryk, Publisher & Editor

Esterhazy: The Miner-Journal
PO Box 1000 , 606 Veterans Ave., Esterhazy, SK S0A 0X0
Tel: 306-745-6669; Fax: 306-745-2699
miner.journal@sasktel.net
www.minerjournal.com
Circulation: 1,390 Frequency: Monday
The Miner-Journal covers news for the Saskatchewan communities of Esterhazy, Bredenbury, Stockholm, Langenburg, Dubuc, Churchbridge, Atwater, Rocanville, Bangor, Gerald, Spy Hill, Yarbo, & Tantallon.
Brenda Matchett, Publisher
Christina Holmberg, General Manager
Helen Solmes, Editor

Estevan: Estevan Lifestyles
Owned By: Glacier Interactive Media
PO Box 816 , 300 Kensington Ave., Estevan, SK S4A 2A7
Tel: 306-634-5112; Fax: 306-634-2588
lifestyles@sasktel.net
www.sasklifestyles.com
Social Media:
www.facebook.com/lifestyles.estevan
Circulation: 7,918 Frequency: Fri.
Teresa Howie, Publisher
David Willberg, Editor

Estevan: Estevan Mercury
Owned By: Glacier Interactive Media
PO Box 730 , 68 Souris Ave. North, Estevan, SK S4A 2A6
Tel: 306-634-2654; Fax: 306-634-3934
classifieds@estevanmercury.ca
www.estevanmercury.ca
Social Media:
twitter.com/estevan_mercury
www.facebook.com/EstevanMercury
Circulation: 3,308 Frequency: Wed.
Brant Kersey, General Manager, bkersey@estevanmercury.ca

Estevan: The Southeast Trader Express
Owned By: Glacier Media Group Ltd.
PO Box 730 , 68 Souris Ave. North, Estevan, SK S4A 2A6
Tel: 306-634-2654; Fax: 306-634-3934
mercury_merc1@sasktel.net
www.estevanmercury.ca
Circulation: 9236 Frequency: Friday
Peter Ng, Publisher

Eston: The Press Review
Owned By: Jamac Publishing Ltd.
PO Box 787 , 112 Main St. West, Eston, SK S0L 1A0
Tel: 306-962-3221; Fax: 306-962-4445
estonpress@sasktel.net
Circulation: 910 Frequency: Tuesday
Stewart Crump, Publisher & General Manager
Tim Crump, Editor

Foam Lake: Foam Lake Review
PO Box 550 , 325 Main St., Foam Lake, SK S0A 1A0
Tel: 306-272-3262; Fax: 306-272-4521
review.foamlake@sasktel.net
Circulation: 1,399 Frequency: Monday
Bob Johnson, Publisher & Editor

Fort Qu'Appelle: Fort Qu'Appelle Times
PO Box 940 , Fort Qu'Appelle, SK S0G 1S0
Tel: 306-332-5526; Fax: 306-332-5414
Circulation: 1,278 Frequency: Tuesday
Sandra Huber, Publisher
Linda Aspinall, Editor

Gravelbourg: Gravelbourg Tribune
PO Box 1017 , 611 Main St., Gravelbourg, SK S0H 1X0
Tel: 306-648-3479; Fax: 306-648-2520
gravelbourgtribune@sasktel.net
Circulation: 1,212 Frequency: Monday
Paul Boisvert, Publisher & Editor, trib.editorial@sasktel.net

Grenfell: The Broadview Express
Owned By: Transcontinental Inc.
PO Box 189 , Grenfell, SK S0G 2B0
Tel: 306-697-2722
sunnews@sasktel.net
www.grenfellsun.sk.ca
Circulation: 525 Frequency: Monday
Rob Clark, Group Publisher, rob.clark@mjtimes.sk.ca
Dwayne Stone, Publisher, sunnews@sasktel.net
Annie Savage, Reporter, sunnews@sasktel.net

Grenfell: Grenfell Sun
Owned By: Transcontinental Inc.
PO Box 189 , Grenfell, SK S0G 2B0
Tel: 306-697-2722
sunnews@sasktel.net
www.grenfellsun.sk.ca
The newspaper covers happenings in Grenfell & the surrounding area.
Rob Clark, Group Publisher, rob.clark@mjtimes.sk.ca
Dwayne Stone, Publisher
Annie Savage, Reporter

Gull Lake: The Gull Lake Advance
PO Box 628 , 1462 Conrad Ave., Gull Lake, SK S0N 1A0
Tel: 306-672-3373; Fax: 306-672-3573
glad12@sasktel.net
Social Media:
www.facebook.com/pages/Gull-Lake-Advance/12667570734475
9
Circulation: 1,162 Frequency: Tuesday
The weekly newspaper provides news & information for Gull Lake & southwestern Saskatchewan.
John Peters, Publisher

Herbert: Herbert Herald
PO Box 399 , 716 Herbert Ave., Herbert, SK S0H 2A0
Tel: 306-784-2422; Fax: 306-784-3246
herbertherald@sasktel.net
Circulation: 1,519 Frequency: Tuesday
Rhonda Ens, Owner

Hudson Bay: Hudson Bay Post Review
Owned By: Glacier Media Group Ltd.
20 Railway Ave., Hudson Bay, SK S0E 0Y0
Tel: 306-865-2771; Fax: 306-865-2340
Circulation: 1,325 Frequency: Wed.
Brent Fitzpatrick, Publisher, pub@sasktel.net

Humboldt: Humboldt Journal
Owned By: Glacier Ventures Inc.
PO Box 970 , 535 Main St., Humboldt, SK S0K 2A0
Tel: 306-682-2561; Fax: 306-682-3322
humboldt.journal@sasktel.net
www.humboldtjournal.ca
Circulation: 10,650 Frequency: Sunday, Wednesday; also, Humboldt Trader Regional (Sun.)
Brent Fitzpatrick, Publisher, pub@sasktel.net
Mary Ann Reith, General Manager, journal.admgr@sasktel.net
Keri Dalman, Editor, humboldt.journal@sasktel.net

Indian Head: Indian Head - Wolseley News
PO Box 70 , 508 Grand Ave., Indian Head, SK S0G 2K0
Tel: 306-695-3565; Fax: 306-695-3448
ihwnews@sasktel.net
Circulation: 1,344 Frequency: Monday
Jodi Gendron, Publisher & Editor

Ituna: The Ituna News
Owned By: Foam Lake Review Ltd.
PO Box 413 , 303 Main St. North, Ituna, SK S0A 1N0
Tel: 306-795-2412; Fax: 306-795-3621
news.ituna@sasktel.net
Circulation: 759 Frequency: Monday
Bob Johnson, Publisher
Susan Antonishyn, Editor

Kindersley: The Clarion
PO Box 1150 , 919 Main St., Kindersley, SK S0L 1S0
Tel: 306-463-4611; Fax: 306-463-6505
ads.jamac@gmail.com
Circulation: 1,765 Frequency: Wednesday
Stewart Crump, Publisher

Kindersley: Kerrobert Citizen
Owned By: Jamac Publishing
PO Box 1150 , 919 Main St., Kindersley, SK S0L 1S0
Tel: 306-463-4611; Fax: 306-463-6505
ads.jamac@gmail.com
Circulation: 469 Frequency: Wednesday
Stewart Crump, Publisher
Kevin McBain, Editor

Kindersley: West Central Crossroads
Owned By: Jamac Publishing
PO Box 1150 , 919 Main St., Kindersley, SK S0L 1S0
Tel: 306-463-4611; Fax: 306-463-6505
ads.jamac@gmail.com
Circulation: 14,902 Frequency: Friday
Stewart Crump, Publisher

Kipling: Kipling Citizen
Owned By: Glacier Media Inc.
PO Box 329 , 521 Main St., Kipling, SK S0J 2S0
Tel: 306-736-2535; Fax: 306-736-8445
Circulation: 1,200+ Frequency: Friday
News & advertising from the Saskatchewan communities of Kipling, Corning, Peebles, Kennedy, Wawota, Windthorst, Glenavon, & Langbank are featured in the Kipling Citizen.
Laura Kish, General Manager
Terry Curzon, Representative, Advertising Sales

La Ronge: La Ronge Northerner
Owned By: Glacier Media Group
PO Box 1350 , 715 La Ronge Ave., La Ronge, SK S0J 1L0
Tel: 306-425-3344; Fax: 306-425-2827
ads.northerner@sasktel.net
www.townoflaronge.ca/TheNortherner
Circulation: 1,383 Frequency: Weekly; Thursday
Brenda Fitch, Publisher

Langenburg: The Four-Town Journal
PO Box 68 , 102 Carl Ave. West, Langenburg, SK S0A 2A0
Tel: 306-743-2617; Fax: 306-743-2299
fourtown@sasktel.net
Circulation: 1,366 Frequency: Wednesday
Langenburg, Saltcoats, Bredenbury, & Churchbridge are the communities served by The Four-Town Journal.
Bill Johnston, Publisher & Editor
Lynda Johnston, Contact, Office

Lanigan: Lanigan Advisor
PO Box 1029 , 42 Main St., Lanigan, SK S0K 2M0
Tel: 306-365-2010; Fax: 306-365-3388
laniganadvisor@sasktel.net
Circulation: 942 Frequency: Monday
Linda Mallett, Publisher & Editor

Lumsden: Lumsden Waterfront Press Regional Newspaper
PO Box 507 , 635 James St. North, Lumsden, SK S0G 3C0
Tel: 306-731-3143; Fax: 306-731-2277
watpress@sasktel.net
www.waterfrontpress.com
Circulation: 4,098 Frequency: Thursday
Lucien Chouinard, Co-Publisher & Editor
Jacqueline Chouinard, Co-Publisher & Editor

Macklin: Macklin Mirror
Owned By: Holmes Publishing
PO Box 100 , 4701 Main St., Macklin, SK S0L 2C0
Tel: 306-753-2424; Fax: 306-753-2424
macklinmirror@sasktel.net
Circulation: 937 Frequency: Wednesday
Robert Brost, Editor

Maple Creek: Maple Creek News
Owned By: Alta Newspaper Group Limited Partnership
PO Box 1328 , 116 Harder St., Maple Creek, SK S0N 1N0
Tel: 306-662-2133; Fax: 306-662-3092
editorial@maplecreeknews.com
www.maplecreeknews.com
Social Media:
twitter.com/maplecreeknews
www.facebook.com/pages/Maple-Creek-News/150542211683094
Circulation: 2,500 Frequency: Thursday
Angela Litke, Manager

Meadow Lake: The Meadow Lake Progress
Owned By: Sun Media Corp.
114a Centre St., Meadow Lake, SK S9X 1Y6
Tel: 306-236-5265; Fax: 306-236-3130
www.meadowlakeprogress.com
Circulation: 2,703 Frequency: Sunday
Donna Ritco, Publisher

Meadow Lake: Northern Pride
219 Centre St., Meadow Lake, SK S9X 1Z4
Tel: 306-236-5353; Fax: 306-236-5962
northern.pride@sasktel.net
www.northernprideml.com
Circulation: 3,992 Frequency: Tuesday
The newspaper serves Meadow Lake & northwestern Saskatchewan.
Terry Villeneuve, Publisher
John King, Editor

Melfort: The Melfort Journal
Owned By: Sun Media Corp.
PO Box 1300 , Melfort, SK S0E 1A0
Tel: 306-752-5737; Fax: 306-752-5358
www.melfortjournal.com
Circulation: 2,774 Frequency: Tuesday
Ken Sorenson, Publisher, Advertising
Ken Sorenson, General Manager
Greg Wiseman, Editor

Melville: Melville Advance
PO Box 1420 , 218 - 3rd Ave. West, Melville, SK S0A 2P0
Tel: 306-728-5448; Fax: 306-728-4004
melvilleadvance@sasktel.net
www.melvilleadvance.com
Circulation: 2,610 Frequency: Wednesday
Print & online subscriptions are available.
Mark Orosz, Co-Publisher & Manager, Advertising
Lin Orosz, Co-Publisher & Contact, Editorial, editor.melvilleadvance@sasktel.net
Ben Clark, News Reporter
Darcy Gross, Sports Reporter, sports.melvilleadvance@sasktel.net
Lloyd Schmidt, Computer Graphic Artist, sports.melvilleadvance@sasktel.net

Moose Jaw: The Moose Jaw Times Herald
Previous Name: Moose Jaw This Week
44 Fairford St. West, Moose Jaw, SK S6H 1V1
Tel: 306-692-6441; Fax: 306-692-2101
editorial@mjtimes.sk.ca
www.mjtimes.sk.ca
Social Media:
twitter.com/MJTimesHerald
Rob Clark, General Manager & Publisher
306-691-1254; Fax: 3066922101
rob.clark@mjtimes.sk.ca
Lesley Sheppard, Managing Editor

Moosomin: The World-Spectator
PO Box 250 , 624 Main St., Moosomin, SK S0G 3N0
Tel: 306-435-2445; Fax: 306-435-3969
world_spectator@sasktel.net
www.world-spectator.com
Other information: Advertising, E-mail: ads@world-spectator.com
Social Media:
www.facebook.com/worldspectator
Circulation: 3,360 Frequency: Monday
The following Saskatchewan communities are served by The World-Spectator: Moosomin, Wawota, Maryfield, Tantallon, St. Lazare, Elkhorn, Fleming, Manson, Kennedy, Rocanville, Wapella, Spy Hill, Welwyn, McAuley, Kola, Kelso, Fairlight, & Langbank.
Kevin Weedmark, Publisher & Editor, kevin@world-spectator.com

Nipawin: The Nipawin Journal
Previous Name: Nipawin N.E. Region Community Booster.
Owned By: Sun Media Corp.
117 - 1st St. West, Nipawin, SK S0E 1E0
Tel: 306-862-4618; Fax: 306-862-4566
www.nipawinjournal.com
Circulation: 3,115 Frequency: Wed.
Ryan Kiedowski, Editor
Kathy McAuley, Publisher

Nokomis: Last Mountain Times
Owned By: Last Mountain Times Ltd.
PO Box 340 , 103 - 1st Ave. West, Nokomis, SK S0G 3R0
Tel: 306-528-2020; Fax: 306-528-2090
editor@lastmountaintimes.ca
Circulation: 1220 Frequency: Weekly; Tuesday
David Degenstien, Owner/Editor/Publisher

Nokomis: The Market Connection
PO Box 340 , Nokomis, SK S0G 3R0
Tel: 306-528-2020; Fax: 306-528-2090
editor@lastmountaintimes.ca
Circulation: 31,000 Frequency: 9 times a year; third Tues. of every month
The Market Connection is published concurrently with an issue of Last Mountain Times.
Dave Degenstien, Publisher/Editor/Owner

North Battleford: The Battlefords News-Optimist
PO Box 1029 , 892 - 104 St., North Battleford, SK S9A 3E6
Tel: 306-445-7261; Fax: 306-445-3223
Toll-Free: 866-549-9979
battlefords.publishing@sasktel.net
www.newsoptimist.ca
Other information: Sales, Fax: 306-445-1977; Composition, Fax: 306-445-7281
Social Media:
twitter.com/BfordsNewsOpt
Frequency: Wednesday; Friday (Regional Optimist)
Alana Schweitzer, Publisher, newsoptimist.alana@sasktel.net
Becky Doig, Editor, newsoptimist.editor@sasktel.net
John Cairns, Staff Reporter, newsoptimist.john@sasktel.netet
Trent Cey, Sports Reporter, newsoptimist.sports@sasktel.net
Chris Walls, Manager, Advertising Sales, chris@newsoptimist.ca
Bonnie Sisler, Contact, Classifieds, adtakers@newsoptimist.ca

North Battleford: Maidstone Mirror
Owned By: Battlefords Publishing Ltd.
PO Box 1029 , 892 - 104th St., North Battleford, SK S9A 3E6
Tel: 306-445-7261; Fax: 306-445-3223
Toll-Free: 866-549-9979
battlefords.publishing@sasktel.net
battlefords.publishing@sasktel.net
Circulation: 777 Frequency: Weekly
John Webster, Publisher
Becky Doig, Editor

Outlook: The Outlook
Owned By: Glacier Media Inc.
PO Box 1717 , 108 Saskatchewan Ave. East, Outlook, SK S0L 2N0
Tel: 306-867-8262; Fax: 306-867-9556
theoutlook@sasktel.net
Circulation: 1,770 Frequency: Friday
The Outlook offers news & information to west central Saskatchewan.
Delwyn Luedtke, General Manager & Contact, Sales
Tim Holtorf, Contact, Production, out.production@sasktel.net
Derek Ruttle, Contact, News, druttle@sasktel.ca

Oxbow: The Oxbow Herald
Owned By: Transcontinental Inc.
219 Main St., Oxbow, SK S0C 2B0
Tel: 306-483-2323
oxbow.herald@sasktel.net
www.oxbowherald.sk.ca
Circulation: 990 Frequency: Monday
The Oxbow Herald reports the happenings of Oxbow, Saskatchewan & the surrounding area through a weekly newspaper & a daily web site.
Rob Clark, Group Publisher, rob.clark@mjtimes.sk.ca
Ken Pedlar, Publisher
Lizz Bottrell, Contact, Editorial, lizz@oxbowherald.sk.ca
Lorena Wolensky, Contact, Advertising, lorena@oxbowherald.sk.ca

Pierceland: The Beaver River Banner
PO Box 700 , Pierceland, SK S0M 2K0
Tel: 306-839-4496; Fax: 306-839-2306
br.banner@sasktel.net
www.beaverriverbanner.com
Circulation: 1,715 Frequency: Weekly; Tuesday
Brad Harrison, Publisher/Editor

Radville: Radville & Deep South Star
Owned By: Transcontinental Inc.
PO Box 370 , Radville, SK S0C 2G0
Tel: 306-869-2202; Fax: 306-869-2533
circulation@rdstar.sk.ca
www.rdstar.sk.ca
Circulation: 619 Frequency: Thursday
Rob Clark, Group Publisher, rob.clark@mjtimes.sk.ca
Melissa Aspen, Contact, Advertising
Kathy Gudnason, Contact, Editorial, editorial@rdstar.sk.ca

Redvers: Redvers Optimist
Owned By: Glacier Media Inc.
PO Box 490 , 10 Broadway St., Redvers, SK S0C 2H0
Tel: 306-452-3363; Fax: 306-452-6408
the.optimist@sasktel.net
Social Media:
www.facebook.com/RedversOptimist
Circulation: 932 Frequency: Saturday
Evelyn Smith, Office Manager
Ellen Skulmoski, Contact, Sales

Regina: Journal L'eau vive
Détenteur: La Coopérative de publ. fransaskoises
2200, rue Edgar, Regina, SK S4N 3K9
Tél: 306-347-0481;Téléc: 306-565-3450
Ligne sans frais: 888-644-3236
direction@accesscomm.ca
nonprofits.accesscomm.ca/leauvive/web/accueil.html
Tirage: 1,400 Fréquence: Thursday
Claude Shink, Directeur/Rédacteur

Regina: Sunday Post
Previous Name: Regina Sun
Owned By: The Leader-Post
PO Box 2020 , 1964 Park St., Regina, SK S4P 3G4
Tel: 306-565-8250; Fax: 306-565-8350
Frequency: Weekly
A free weekly newspaper focusing on features, analysis and lengthier, weekend-style reads.

Rosetown: Rosetown Eagle
Owned By: Rosetown Publishing Co. Ltd.
PO Box 130 , Rosetown, SK S0L 2V0
Tel: 306-882-4202; Fax: 306-882-4204
editor.eagle@gmail.com
Circulation: 2,190 Frequency: Monday
Danny Pagé, General Manager

Rosthern: Saskatchewan Valley News
Previous Name: The Enterprise
PO Box 10 , Rosthern, SK S0K 3R0
Tel: 306-232-4865; Fax: 306-232-4694
Toll-Free: 800-601-7858
info@saskvalleynews.com
www.saskvalleynews.com
Circulation: 1,969 Frequency: Thursday
The Saskatchewan Valley News covers Rosthern & rural communities in the surrounding area.
Renay Kowalczyk, General Manager & Editor

Shaunavon: The Shaunavon Standard
Owned By: Alta Newspaper Group Limited Partnership
PO Box 729 , Shaunavon, SK S0N 2M0
Tel: 306-297-4144; Fax: 306-297-3357
www.theshaunavonstandard.com
Social Media:
twitter.com/The_SStandard

Circulation: 1,700 Frequency: Tuesday
Paul MacNeil, Editor, standard@sasktel.net

Shellbrook: Shellbrook Chronicle
Owned By: Pepperfram Limited Publications
PO Box 10 , Shellbrook, SK S0J 2E0
Tel: 306-747-2442; Fax: 306-747-3000
chads@shellbrookchronicle.com(advertising)
www.shellbrookchronicle.com
Circulation: 4,234 Frequency: Friday
The following Saskatchewan communities are covered by the Shellbrook Chronicle: Shellbrook, Debden, Parkside, Marcelin, Holbein, Mayview, Mont Nebo, Canwood, Big River, Leask, & Blaine Lake.
C.J. Pepper, Publisher
Brad Dupuis, Editor, chnews@shellbrookchronicle.com
Madeleine Wrigley, Contact, Advertising Sales, chroniclesales@sasktel.net
Cheryl Mason, Contact, Reception & Bookkeeping

Shellbrook: Spiritwood Herald
Owned By: Pepperfram Limited Publications
PO Box 10 , 44 Main St., Shellbrook, SK S0J 2E0
Tel: 306-747-2442; Fax: 306-747-3000
Social Media:
www.facebook.com/pages/Spiritwood-Herald/253716234680672
Circulation: 2,620 Frequency: Friday
Clark Pepper, Publisher
John Young, Editor

Swift Current: The Southwest Booster
Owned By: Transcontinental Inc.
30 - 4th Ave. NW, Swift Current, SK S9H 3X4
Tel: 306-773-9321; Fax: 306-773-9136
www.swbooster.com
Social Media:
www.facebook.com/pages/The-Southwest-Booster/163689647007
Circulation: 19,100 Frequency: Weekly
Bob Watson, General Manager, bwatson@swbooster.com
Scott Anderson, Managing Editor, sanderson@swbooster.com
Bridget Denys, Manager, Business, bdenys@swbooster.com
Mark Soper, Manager, Sales, msoper@swbooster.com
Morgan Reil, Supervisor, Commercial Print, mreil@swbooster.com
Steven Mah, Sports Reporter, smah@swbooster.com
Valerie McLearn, Coordinator, Ads, vmclearn@swbooster.com

Tisdale: Tisdale Recorder & Parkland Review
Owned By: Glacier Media Group Ltd.
PO Box 1660 , 1004 - 102nd Ave., Tisdale, SK S0E 1T0
Tel: 306-873-4515; Fax: 306-873-4712
Social Media:
www.facebook.com/199458986756467
Circulation: 13,288 Frequency: Wed.
Brent Fitzpatrick, Publisher, pub@sasktel.net

Unity: The Northwest Herald
PO Box 309 , 321 Main St., Unity, SK S0K 4L0
Tel: 306-228-2267; Fax: 306-228-2767
northwest.herald@sasktel.net
www.estevanmercury.ca/section/northwest
Circulation: 505 Frequency: Wednesday
Neil Thom, Editor, editorial@website.com
Debbie Barr, Prepress Manager, prepress@website.com
Lorraine Betker, Accountant, editorial@website.com

Wadena: Wadena News
Owned By: Bruce W. Squires and Alison J. Squires
PO Box 100 , 101 - 1st St. NE, Wadena, SK S0A 4J0
Tel: 306-338-2231
wadena.news@sasktel.net
Circulation: 3,114 Frequency: Weekly; Wed.
Bruce Squires, Co-Publisher
Alison Squires, Co-Publisher

Wakaw: Wakaw Recorder
Owned By: Dwaymar Enterprises Ltd.
PO Box 9 , 224 - 1st St. South, Wakaw, SK S0K 4P0
Tel: 306-233-4325
Circulation: 2,203 Frequency: Weekly; Wednesday
Dwayne Biccum, Publisher

Warman: The Country Press
PO Box 880 , 520 Central St. West, Warman, SK S0K 4S0
Tel: 306-934-6191; Fax: 306-668-8250
countrypress@sasktel.net
Circulation: 12,818 Frequency: Wednesday
C. Lynn Handford, Publisher & Editor

Watrous: Watrous Manitou
Owned By: 101026460 Saskatchewan Ltd.
PO Box 100 , Watrous, SK S0K 4T0
Tel: 306-946-3343; Fax: 306-946-2026
watrous.manitou@sasktel.net
www.thewatrousmanitou.com
Social Media:
www.facebook.com/thewatrousmanitou
Circulation: 1730 Frequency: Weekly; Mondays
Nicole Lay, Publisher
Robin Lay, Publisher

Weyburn: Weyburn Review
Owned By: Glacier Interactive Media
PO Box 400 , 904 East Ave., Weyburn, SK S4H 2K4
Tel: 306-842-7487; Fax: 306-842-0282
production@weyburnreview.com
www.weyburnreview.com
Social Media:
twitter.com/WeyburnReview
www.facebook.com/pages/Weyburn-Review/100299633382446
Circulation: 4,200 Frequency: Wed.
Darryl Ward, Publisher
Patricia Ward, Editor-in-chief

Weyburn: Weyburn This Week
115 - 2nd St. NE, Weyburn, SK S4H 0T7
Tel: 306-842-3900; Fax: 306-842-2515
weyburnthisweek@sasktel.net
www.weyburnthisweek.com
Other information: Advertising, E-mail: advertisingthisweek@sasktel.net
Circulation: 5,861 Frequency: Friday
The free publication covers local news & events in Weyburn & surrounding communities in southeastern Saskatchewan.
Andrea Heath, Manager & Representative, Sales
Jennifer LaCharite, Reporter, editorialthisweek@sasktel.net
Frances Cartier, Contact, Administration
Leslie Dempsey, Contact, Graphic Design

Whitewood: Whitewood Herald
PO Box 160 , 708 South Railway St., Whitewood, SK S0G 5C0
Tel: 306-735-2230; Fax: 306-735-2899
herald@whitewoodherald.com
www.whitewoodherald.com
Circulation: 831 Frequency: Monday
Chris Ashfield, Publisher
Donna Beutler, Office Manager
Marlene Carefoot, Contact, Advertising

Wolseley: Wolseley Bulletin
PO Box 89 , 219 Poplar St., Wolseley, SK S0G 5H0
Tel: 306-698-2271; Fax: 306-698-2808
unos@sasktel.net
www.saskfarmnews.com/id6.html
Circulation: 500 Frequency: Friday
The Wolseley Bulletin is distributed in the following communities: Wolseley, Glenavon, Indian Head, Qu'Appelle, Grenfell, Montmartre, Sintaluta, & Regina.
Rick Dahlman, Publisher & Editor, rdahlman@sk.sympatico.ca

Wynyard: Wynyard Advance/Gazette
PO Box 10 , 117 Ave. B East, Wynyard, SK S0A 4T0
Tel: 306-554-2224; Fax: 306-554-3226
Circulation: 1,556 Frequency: Monday
Bob Johnson, Publisher
Leanne Dumont, Editor

Yorkton: The News Review Extra
Owned By: Glacier Interactive Media
18 - 1st Ave. North, Yorkton, SK S3N 1J4
Tel: 306-783-7355; Fax: 306-783-9138
info@yorktonnews.com
www.yorktonnews.com
Social Media:
twitter.com/yorktonnews
www.facebook.com/yorkton.newsreview
Circulation: 6,700 Frequency: Bi-weekly
Ken Chyz, Publisher, kenchyz@yorktonnews.com

Yorkton: Yorkton This Week
Owned By: Glacier Interactive Media
PO Box 1300 , 20 - 3rd Ave. North, Yorkton, SK S3N 2X3
Tel: 306-782-2465; Fax: 306-786-1898
sales@yorktonthisweek.com
www.yorktonthisweek.com
Social Media:
twitter.com/yorktonthisweek
www.facebook.com/pages/Yorkton-This-Week/168910973121215
Circulation: 4,680 Frequency: Wed.
Neil Thom, Publisher & General Manager

Yukon Territory

Daily Newspapers in Yukon Territory

Whitehorse: The Whitehorse Star
2149 - 2nd Ave., Whitehorse, YT Y1A 1C5
Tel: 867-668-2060; Fax: 867-668-7130
star@whitehorsestar.com
www.whitehorsestar.com
Circulation: Mon.-Thu. 2,900; Fri. 4,200 Frequency: Weekdays
Jackie Pierce, Publisher
Jim Butler, Editor
403/667-4481

Other Newspapers in Yukon Territory

Whitehorse: L'Aurore boréale
Association Franco-Yukonnaise, 302, rue Strickland, Whitehorse, YT Y1A 2K1
Tél: 867-667-2931;Téléc: 867-667-2932
auroredir@afy.yk.ca
www.afy.yk.ca
Médias sociaux:
www.facebook.com/AFY.Yukon
Tirage: 945 Fréquence: Bi-mensuel; français
Marie-Claude Nault, Coordonnatrice de la publicité, aurorepub@afy.yk.ca
Thibaut Rondel, Journaliste, journaliste@afy.yk.ca
Cécile Girard, Directrice, auroredir@afy.yk.ca

Whitehorse: Yukon News
Owned By: Media North Limited
211 Wood St., Whitehorse, YT Y1A 2E4
Tel: 867-667-6285; Fax: 867-668-3755
editor@yukon-news.com
www.yukon-news.com
Social Media:
twitter.com/yukon_news
www.facebook.com/pages/Yukon-News/186396428426
Circulation: Mon 5,248 Wed. 5,613, Fri 7,243; Total 18,104.
Steve Robertson, Publisher, stever@yukon-news.com
John Thompson, Editor, johnt@yukon-news.com

Magazine Name Index

D

E

X

Y

Z

Magazines

Business

Advertising, Marketing, Sales

Adnews Insight Magazine
Owned By: Bale Communications Inc.
#1463, 1011 Upper Middle Rd., Oakville, ON L6H 5Z9
Tel: 416-252-9400; Fax: 416-252-8002
info@adnews.com
Frequency: 4 times a year
Robert A. Bale, Publisher
Derek Winkler, Editor

Adnews Online Daily
Owned By: Bale Communications Inc.
#1463, 1011 Upper Middle Rd. East, Oakville, ON L6H 5Z9
Tel: 416-252-9400; Fax: 416-252-8002
info@adnews.com
Circulation: 33,000 Frequency: Daily
Robert Bale, Publisher

Blitz Magazine Inc
1360 Bathurst St., Toronto, ON M5R 3H7
; Fax: 647-435-0304
Toll-Free: 888-952-5478
editor@blitzmagazine.com
Circulation: 10,000 Frequency: 6 times a year
Media communications magazine, delivered nation-wide
Troy Weston, Editor-in-chief

Boards
#500, 366 Adelaide St. West, Toronto, ON M5V 1R9
Tel: 416-408-2300; Fax: 416-408-0870
Toll-Free: 866-262-7371
drankin@brunico.com
Circulation: 11,250
Russell Goldstein, Publisher, rgoldstein@brunico.com
Rae Ann Fera, Editor, raeann@boardsmag.com

Buyer News - International Edition
Owned By: Powershift Communications Inc.
c/o Powershift Communications Inc., 245 Fairview Mall Dr., 5th Fl., Toronto, ON M2J 4T1
Tel: 416-494-1066; Fax: 416-494-2536
info@powershift.ca
Frequency: 8 times a year
Dante Piccinin, Publisher & Editorial Directo,
homeimprovement@rogers.com

Canadian Advertising Rates & Data
Owned By: Rogers Publishing Ltd.
1 Mount Pleasant Rd., 7th Fl., Toronto, ON M4Y 2Y5
Tel: 416-764-1620; Fax: 416-764-1721
Toll-Free: 800-265-3561
aileen.beloso@rci.rogers.com
Circulation: 2,100 Frequency: Monthly
Bruce Richards, Publisher,
bruce.richards@cardonline.rogers.com
Artemis Hall, Editor, 416-764-1785, artemis.hall@rci.rogers.com

Canadian Direct Marketing News
#302, 137 Main St. North, Markham, ON L3P 1Y2
Tel: 905-201-6600; Fax: 905-201-6601
Toll-Free: 800-688-1838
Circulation: 8,058 Frequency: Monthly, plus annual directory of suppliers & annual directories The List of Lists...The DM Industry Sourcebook & the Canadian Call Centre Industry Directory
Amy Bostock, Editor, amy@dmn.ca
Mark Henry, Ad Sales
Steve Lloyd, Publisher & President

The Chronicle of Healthcare Marketing
Owned By: Chronicle Information Resources Ltd.
#306, 555 Burnhamthorpe Rd., Toronto, ON M9C 2Y3
Tel: 416-916-2476; Fax: 416-352-6199
Toll-Free: 866-632-4766
health@chronicle.org
Circulation: 2,159 Frequency: 9 times a year
Mitchell Shannon, Publisher
R. Allan Ryan, Editorial Director

Contact
Canadian Professional Sales Assn., #400, 655 Bay St., Toronto, ON M5G 2K4
Tel: 416-408-2685; Fax: 416-408-2684
Toll-Free: 888-267-2772
Circulation: 37,125 Frequency: bi-monthly
Bernadette Johnson, Editor
Harvey Copeman, Vice-President, Sales & Marketing

Direct Marketing News
Owned By: Lloydmedia, Inc.
#302, 137 Main St. North, Markham, ON L3P 1Y2
Tel: 905-201-6600 Toll-Free: 800-668-1838
Circulation: 7,300 Frequency: Monthly
Amy Bostock, Editor, amy@dmn.ca

Imprint Canada
#16, 190 Marycroft Ave., Woodbridge, ON L4L 5Y2
Tel: 905-856-2600; Fax: 905-856-2667
Toll-Free: 877-895-7022
feedback@imprintcanada.com
Social Media:
twitter.com/imprint_canada
Circulation: 6,700
Tony Muccilli, Publisher

Infopresse (IP)
Détenteur: Éditions Infopresse inc.
4310, boul Saint-Laurent, Montréal, QC H2W 1Z3
Tél: 514-842-5873;Téléc: 514-842-2422
redaction@infopresse.com
Médias sociaux:
twitter.com/infopresse
Tirage: 7 500 Fréquence: 10 fois par an
Bruno Gautier, Président et éditeur
Arnaud Granata, Vice-président, directeur, et rédacteur en chef

Kidscreen
#500, 366 Adelaide St. West, Toronto, ON M5V 1R9
Tel: 416-408-2300; Fax: 416-408-0870
Toll-Free: 800-543-4512
Social Media:
twitter.com/kidscreen
www.facebook.com/pages/Kidscreen/21921612484 8853
Circulation: 11,500 Frequency: Monthly
Jocelyn Christie, Vice-President & Publisher,
jchristie@brunico.com
Lana Castleman, Editor, lcastleman@brunico.com

Marketing Magazine
Owned By: Rogers Publishing Ltd.
1 Mount Pleasant Rd., Toronto, OM M4Y 2Y5
Tel: 416-596-5853; Fax: 416-596-3482
bppgservice@rci.rogers.com
Social Media:
www.facebook.com/MarketingMagCanada
Circulation: 7,292 Frequency: 17 issues a year
Lucy Collin, Publisher, 416-764-1582
Tom Gierasimczuk, Editor-in-Chief, 416-764-1603

Marketwire
Previous Name: Matthews Media Directories
PO Box 403, #900, 25 York St., Toronto, ON M5J 2V5
Tel: 416-362-0885; Fax: 416-362-6669
Toll-Free: 888-299-0338
Michael J. Nowlan, President & CEO

The National List of Advertisers
Owned By: Rogers Publishing Ltd.
1 Mount Pleasant Rd., 8th Fl., Toronto, ON M4Y 2Y5
Tel: 416-764-1620 Toll-Free: 800-265-3561
aileen.beloso@rci.rogers.com
Circulation: 1,467 Frequency: Quarterly
Artemis Hall, Editor

Sign Media
Owned By: Kenilworth Publishing
#710, 15 Wertheim Crt., Richmond Hill, ON L4B 3H7
Tel: 905-771-7333; Fax: 905-771-7336
Toll-Free: 800-409-8688
editor@signmedia.ca
Social Media:
www.twitter.com/signmediacanada
www.linkedin.com/groups/Sign-Media-Canad a-magazine-386611
Circulation: 11,016 Frequency: 7 times a year
Ellen Kral, Publisher
Blair Adams, Editorial Director
Erik Tolles, Sales Manager

Silver Screen
383 Lawrence Ave. West, Toronto, ON M5M 1B9
Tel: 416-488-3393; Fax: 416-488-5217
malcolm@msilver.com
Social Media:
twitter.com/MalcolmSilver
www.facebook.com/malcolm.silver.33
Circulation: 1,800
Occassional newletter containing information about downtown Toronto real estate.
Malcolm Silver, Publisher

Strategy
Owned By: Brunico Communications
#100, 366 Adelaide St. West, Toronto, ON M5V 1R9
Tel: 416-408-2300; Fax: 416-408-0870
Toll-Free: 888-278-6426
Social Media:
www.twitter.com/strategyonline
www.facebook.com/pages/Strategy/217 618361606458
Circulation: 13,152 Frequency: Monthly
Russell Goldstein, Executive Publisher, rgoldstein@brunico.com
Mary Maddever, Editor, mmaddever@brunico.com

Architecture

Award Magazine
Owned By: Canada Wide Magazines & Communications Ltd.
4180 Lougheed Hwy., Burnaby, BC V5C 6A7
Tel: 604-299-7311; Fax: 604-299-9188
cwm@canadawide.com
Circulation: 26,000 Frequency: 6 times a year
Shannon Miller, Editor, smiller@canadawide.com
Peter Legge, Publisher

Canadian Architect
Owned By: Business Information Group
80 Valleybrook Dr., Toronto, ON M3B 2S9
Tel: 416-510-6806; Fax: 416-510-5140
Toll-Free: 800-268-7742
editors@canadianarchitect.com
Circulation: 10,323 Frequency: Monthly
Tom Arkell, Publisher, 416-510-6806,
tomarkell@canadianarchitect.com

Construction Canada
Owned By: Kenilworth Publishing
#710, 15 Wertheim Crt., Richmond Hill, ON L4B 3H7
Tel: 905-771-7333; Fax: 905-771-7336
Toll-Free: 800-409-8688
Circulation: 12,109 Frequency: Bi-monthly
Ellen Kral, Publisher
Blair Adams, Editorial Director
Cora Golden, Sales Director

Info-Link
#270, 3044 Bloor St. West, Toronto, ON M8X 2Y8
Tel: 416-604-7552; Fax: 416-604-2545
Frequency: 4 times a year

Sustainable Architecture & Building Magazine
Owned By: Janam Publications
81, rue Leduc, Gatineau, QC J8X 3A7
Tel: 819-778-5040; Fax: 819-595-8553
Social Media:
www.youtube.com/user/SABmagazine?feature=mhum
twitter.com/SABMagazine
www.facebook.com/sabmagcanada
Don Griffith, Publisher, dgriffith@sabmagazine.com
Jim Taggart, Editor, architext@telus.net

Arts, Art & Antiques

Arabella
Owned By: Arabella Publications Inc.
PO Box 246, Queenston, ON L0S 1L0
Tel: 289-296-0510
admin@arabelladesign.com
Social Media:
www.facebook.com/107077652659400
Debra Usher, Editor-in-Chief

Automobile, Cycle, & Automotive Accessories

L'Automobile
Détenteur: Business Information Group
Tirage: 12 829 Fréquence: 6 fois par an; français
Marc Gadbois, Éditeur, 416-510-6776,
mgadbois@lautomobile.ca
Michel Poirier-Defoy, Rédacteur senior, 541-942-8463,
mpoirierdefoy@lautomobile.ca

Automotive Parts & Technology
c/o Newcom Business Media Inc., 451 Attwell Dr., Toronto, ON M9W 5C4
Tel: 416-614-0955; Fax: 416-614-2781
info@aptmag.ca
Jim Glionna, Publisher

Automotive Service Data Book
Owned By: Business Information Group
Tel: 416-445-6641; Fax: 416-442-2261
Frequency: Annually, December
David Booth, Editor

Bike Trade Canada
#200, 260 Spadina Ave., Toronto, ON M5T 2E4
Tel: 416-977-2100; Fax: 416-977-9200
Toll-Free: 866-977-3325
info@pedalmag.com
Circulation: 5,000 Frequency: 3 times a year
Benjamin A. Sadavoy, Publisher & Editor
Sarah Carlin, Circulation

Bodyshop
Owned By: Business Information Group
80 Valleybrook Rd., Toronto, ON M3B 2S9
Tel: 416-510-6763; Fax: 416-442-2213
Circulation: 11,917 Frequency: 6 times a year
Andrew Ross, Publisher, aross@bodyshopbiz.com
JD Ney, Editor, jdney@bodyshopbiz.com

Canadian Auto World
Owned By: Metro Land Media Group Ltd.
c/o Formula Media Group, #4, 447 Speers Rd., Oakville, ON L6K 3S7
Tel: 905-842-6591; Fax: 905-842-4432
Toll-Free: 800-693-7986
Circulation: 4,529 Frequency: 6 times a year
Jack Hayes, jhayes@metroland.com

Canadian Cycling Magazine
Owned By: Gripped Publishing Inc.
#510, 344 Bloor St., Toronto, ON M5S 3A7
Tel: 416-927-0774; Fax: 416-927-1491
Toll-Free: 800-567-0444
info@gripped.com
Social Media:
twitter.com/CDNCyclingMag
www.facebook.com/cyclingmag
Sam Cohen, Publisher, sam@gripped.com

Canadian Technician
451 Attwell Dr., Toronto, ON M9W 5C4
Tel: 416-614-0955; Fax: 416-614-2781
Mark Vreugdenhill, Publisher
Allan Janssen, Editor

Collision Quarterly
Automotive Retailer Publishing Company Ltd., #1, 8980 Fraserwood Ct., Burnaby, BC V5J 5H7
Tel: 604-432-7987; Fax: 604-432-1756
publish@ara.bc.ca
Circulation: 6,179 Frequency: Quarterly
Kara Cunningham, Publisher & Editor
Kelly Johnston, Circulation Manager, arastaff@ara.bc.ca

Collision Repair Magazine
c/o Media Matters, 645 Ossington Ave., Toronto, ON M6G 3T6
Tel: 416-628-8344
Social Media:
twitter.com/CollisionMag
Darryl Simmons, Publisher
Mike Davey, Editor

dandyhorse
#903, 22 Close Ave., Toronto, ON M5K 2V4
Tel: 416-822-7910
subscribe@dandyhorsemagazine.com
Social Media: dandyhorsemagazine.com/blog/
www.twitter.com/dandyhorse
www.facebook.com/pages/Dandyhorse-Magazine/11617638512626
Tammy Thorne, Editor-in-Chief, tammy@dandyhorsemagazine.com

Jobber News
Owned By: Business Information Group
80 Valleybrook Dr., Toronto, ON M3B 2S9
Tel: 416-510-6763 Toll-Free: 800-268-7742
Social Media:
twitter.com/jobbernews
Circulation: 11,136 Frequency: Monthly
Andrew Ross, Publisher, 416-510-6763, aross@jobbernews.com

Octane
Owned By: Fulcrum Publishing Inc.
Fulcrum Publications, #201, 508 Lawrence Ave. West, Toronto, ON M5A 1A1
Tel: 416-504-0504; Fax: 416-256-3002
Toll-Free: 866-688-0504
ehoffman@fulcrum.ca
Circulation: 9,000 Frequency: 6 times a year

Service Station & Garage Management
Owned By: Business Information Group
80 Valleybrook Dr., Toronto, ON M3B 2S9
Tel: 416-510-6776 Toll-Free: 800-268-7742
Circulation: 31,200 Frequency: Monthly
Marc Gadbois, Publisher, marc@ssgm.com

Taxi News
38 Fairmount Cres., Toronto, ON M4L 2H4
Tel: 416-466-2328; Fax: 416-466-4220
john@taxinews.com
Circulation: 9,800 Frequency: Monthly
John Duffy, Publisher
William McOuat, Editor

Aviation & Aerospace

Airforce
c/o Airforce Productions Ltd., PO Box 2460 D, #400, 222 Somerset St. West, Ottawa, ON K1P 5W6
Tel: 613-232-2303; Fax: 613-232-2156
Toll-Free: 866-351-2322
vjohnson@airforce.ca
Circulation: 16,526 Frequency: 4 times a year
Vic Johnson, Editor

Bombardier Magazine
Owned By: Spafax
#101, 1179 King St. West, Toronto, ON M6K 3C5
Tel: 416-350-2425; Fax: 416-350-2440
experiencemagazine@spafax.com
Natasha Mekhail, Editor, nmekhail@spafax.com

Canadian Aviator Magazine
Previous Name: Aviator Magazine
Owned By: OP Publishers
#500, 200 West Esplanade, Vancouver, BC V6Z 2T1
Tel: 604-998-3310 Toll-Free: 800-867-0474
canadianaviator@xplornet.com
Circulation: 16,000 Frequency: 6 times a year
Includes Aviators Blue Pages, a directory of aviation business, products, services and attractions.
Mark Yelic, Publisher
Russ Niles, Editor, canadianaviator@xplornet.com

Canadian Plane Trade
Previous Name: Canada Flight
71 Bank St., 7th Fl., Ottawa, ON K1P 5N2
Tel: 613-236-4901; Fax: 613-236-8646
Circulation: 18,000 Frequency: Monthly; includes: Canadian Homebuilt Aircraft News, Canadian Ultralight News, Executive Flight News, Seaplane News, Aircraft Maintenance Engineers News, Canadian Plane Trade, Aviation Museum News
Michel Hell, Publisher, Editor, editorial@copanational.org

Helicopters
Owned By: Annex Publishing & Printing Inc.
PO Box 530, 105 Donly Dr. South, Simcoe, ON N3Y 4N5
Tel: 519-429-3966; Fax: 519-429-3094
Toll-Free: 800-265-2827
Social Media:
twitter.com/Helicopters_Mag
Frequency: 5 times a year
Coverage of commercial, corporate, general and military rotary-wing aviation in Canada and around the world.
Matt Nichols, Editor, 416-725-5637, mnicholls@annexweb.com

ICAO Journal
International Civil Aviation Organization, 999, rue University, Montréal, QC H3C 5H7
Tel: 514-954-8219; Fax: 514-954-6077
icaohq@icao.int
Circulation: 15,000 Frequency: 6 issues a year; English, French & Spanish editions
Eric MacBurnie, Editor

Wings
Owned By: Annex Publishing & Printing Inc.
PO Box 530, 105 Donly Dr. South, Simcoe, ON N3Y 4N5
Tel: 519-429-3966; Fax: 519-429-3094
Toll-Free: 800-265-2827
Social Media:
twitter.com/@wings_magazine
Frequency: 6 times a year
Matt Nicholis, Editor, 416-725-5637, mnicholls@annexweb.com

Baking & Bakers' Supplies

Bakers Journal
Owned By: Annex Publishing & Printing Inc.
PO Box 530, 105 Donly Dr. South, Simcoe, ON N3Y 4N5
Tel: 519-429-3966; Fax: 519-429-3094
Toll-Free: 800-265-2827
Social Media:
twitter.com/BakersJournal
Circulation: 6,800 Frequency: 10 times a year
Martin McAnulty, Publisher, mmcanulty@annexweb.com
Laura Aiken, Editor, 416-522-1595, laiken@annexweb.com

Barbers & Beauticians

Canadian Hairdresser Magazine
1300 Bay St., 2nd Fl., Toronto, ON M5R 3K8
Tel: 416-923-1111
info@canhair.com
Social Media:
twitter.com/canhair
www.facebook.com/pages/Canadian-Hairdresser-Magazine/1504
Circulation: 30,112 Frequency: 10 times a year
Joan Harrison, CEO & Editorial Director

Salon Magazine
Owned By: Salon Communications Inc.
#1902, 365 Bloor St. East, Toronto, ON M4W 3L4
Tel: 416-869-3131; Fax: 416-869-3008
Social Media:
twitter.com/Salon_Magazine
www.facebook.com/SalonMag
Circulation: 35,000 Frequency: 8 times a year; English & French
Melissa Hill, Editor-in-Chief, melissa@salonmagazine.ca
Laura Dunphy, President/Publisher, laura@salonmagazine.ca

Boating & Yachting

Boating Business
Owned By: Formula Publications Ltd.
Tel: 905-842-6591; Fax: 905-842-6843
Circulation: 5,375 Frequency: 6 times a year
J. Scott Robinson, Publisher
Valerie Tryer, Circulation Coordinator

Poker Runs America Magazine
Owned By: Taylor Publishing Group
#2, 1121 Invicta Dr., Oakville, ON L6H 2R2
Tel: 905-844-8218; Fax: 905-844-8219
Toll-Free: 800-354-9145
info@pokerrunsamerica.com
Social Media: www.youtube.com/user/steveeditor123
twitter.com/pokerrunamerica
www.fa cebook.com/PokerRunsAmerica

Books

Access
c/o Ontario Library Association, #201, 50 Wellington St., Toronto, ON M5E 1C8
Tel: 416-363-3388; Fax: 416-941-9581
Toll-Free: 866-873-9867
info@accessola.com
Circulation: 4,500 Frequency: 4 times a year
Lori Knowles, Editor

Canadian Bookseller
Canadian Booksellers Association, #902, 1255 Bay St., Toronto, ON M5R 2A9
Tel: 416-467-7883; Fax: 416-467-7886
Toll-Free: 866-788-0790
enquiries@cbabook.org
Circulation: 2,500 Frequency: 6 times a year
Bill McOuat, Editor, wjmc@rogers.com

Feliciter
c/o Canadian Library Association, #400, 1150 Morrison Dr., Ottawa, ON K2H 8S9
Tel: 613-232-9625; Fax: 613-563-9895
info@cla.ca
Social Media:
www.linkedin.com/groups?gid=4137241&trk=myg_ugrp_ovr
twitter.com/cla_web
www.facebook.com/CanadianLibraryAssociation
Circulation: 3,800 Frequency: Bi-monthly
Kelly Moore, Executive Director, 613-232-9625 x306, kmoore@cla.ca

Brides, Bridal

Weddings & Honeymoons
65 Helena Ave., Toronto, ON M6G 2H3
Tel: 416-653-4986; Fax: 416-653-2291
barwed@rogers.com
Circulation: 30,000 Frequency: 3 pa
Joyce Barshow, Publisher & Editor-in-chief

Broadcasting

Broadband & Content Mediacaster
Previous Name: Cablecaster
Owned By: Business Information Group
80 Valleybrook Dr., Toronto, ON M3B 2S9
Tel: 416-510-6878; Fax: 416-510-5140
Toll-Free: 800-268-7742
Circulation: 6,800 Frequency: 12 times a year
James Cook, Publisher, 416-510-6871, jcook@mediacastermagazine.com
Lee Rickwood, Editor, 416-510-6865, lrickwood@mediacastermagazine.com

Broadcast Dialogue
18 Turtle Path, Site 1, Box 150, Brechin, ON L0K 1B0
Tel: 705-484-0752
broadcastdialogue@rogers.com
Circulation: 7,200
Howard Christensen, Publisher, howard@broadcastdialogue.com
Barry Hamelin, Executive Director, barry@broadcastdialogue.comm

Broadcaster
Owned By: Business Information Group
80 Valleybrook Dr., Toronto, ON M3B 2S9
Tel: 416-510-6865; Fax: 416-510-5134
Toll-Free: 800-268-7742
editor@broadcastermagazine.com
Circulation: 7,670 Frequency: 8 pa
James A. Cook, Publisher, 416-510-6871, jcook@broadcastermagazine.com

Playback
Owned By: Brunico Communications
#500, 366 Adelaide St. West, Toronto, ON M5V 1R9
Tel: 416-408-2300; Fax: 416-408-0870
Toll-Free: 888-278-6426
Social Media:
twitter.com/PlaybackOnline
www.facebook.com/playbackonline
Circulation: 9,052 Frequency: 25 times a year
Russell Goldstein, President & CEO, rgoldstein@brunico.com
Mary Maddever, Vice-President & Editorial Director, mmaddever@brunico.com

Building & Construction

Alberta Construction Magazine
#300, 5735 - 7 St. NE, Calgary, AB T2E 8V3
Tel: 403-265-3700; Fax: 403-265-3706
Toll-Free: 888-563-2946
marketing@junewarren.com
Circulation: 8,500 Frequency: 6 times a year; also Alberta Constuction Association Membership Roster & Buyers' Guide (annual, May)
Chaz Osburn, Editor

Alberta Construction Magazine
Previous Name: Alberta Construction Service & Supply Directory
Owned By: JuneWarren-Nickle's Energy Group
816 - 55 Ave. NE, 2nd Fl., Calgary, AB T2E 6Y4
Tel: 403-209-3500; Fax: 403-245-8666
Toll-Free: 800-387-2446
Circulation: 8,500 Frequency: Quarterly
Agnes Zalewski, Publisher

Atlantic Construction Journal
Transcontinental Specialty Publications, #609, 1888 Brunswick St., Dartmouth, NS B3J 3J9
Tel: 902-468-8027; Fax: 902-468-2425
Toll-Free: 800-537-5507
acj@hfnews.ca
Circulation: 15,000 Frequency: 4 times a year
Naster Tracz, Senior Account Executive
Ken Partridge, Editor

BSDA Newsmagazine
Building Supply Dealers Assn. of BC, #2, 19299 - 94th Ave., Surrey, BC V4N 4E6
Tel: 604-513-2205; Fax: 604-513-2206
Toll-Free: 888-711-5656
Circulation: 1,000 Frequency: 4 times a year
George Tracy

Building & Construction Trades Today
PO Box 186, 27 St. Clair Ave. East, Toronto, ON M4T 2M1
Tel: 416-944-1217; Fax: 416-944-0133
hize@earthlink.net
Circulation: 2,000-2,500 Frequency: 8 times a year
Alan Heisey, Publisher
Jason Kieffer, Editor

Building Magazine
Owned By: Business Information Group
#800, 12 Concorde Place, Toronto, ON M3C 2J4
Tel: 416-442-5600; Fax: 416-442-2191
Toll-Free: 800-668-2374
Circulation: 10,737 Frequency: 6 times a year
Tom Arkell, Senior Publisher, 416-510-6806, tomarkell@canadianarchitect.com

Canadian Apartment Magazine
Owned By: MediaEdge Inc.
Tel: 416-512-8186 Toll-Free: 866-216-0860
Social Media: www.linkedin.com/groups?gid=3987507
twitter.com/cdnapartmentmag
www.fa cebook.com/cammediaedge
Circulation: 7,000 Frequency: 6 times a year
Scott Anderson, Editor, scotta@mediaedge.ca
Steve McLinden, Publisher, stevem@mediaedge.ca
Paul Murphy, Publisher, paulm@mediaedge.ca

Canadian Contractor
Owned By: Business Information Group
80 Valleybrook Dr., Toronto, ON M3B 2S9
Tel: 416-442-5600
Frequency: Monthly
Stephen Dempsey, Publisher, 416-442-5600 x 6780, sdempsey@bizinfogroup.ca
Stephen Payne, Editor, 416-442-5600 x 6784, rkoci@bizinfogroup.ca

Canadian Property Management (CPM)
Owned By: MediaEdge Inc.
Tel: 416-512-8186 Toll-Free: 866-216-0860
Social Media: www.linkedin.com/groups?home=&gid=3987537
twitter.com/CDNPropMgmt
www. facebook.com/cpmmediaedge
Circulation: 12,504 Frequency: 8 times a year
Sean Foley, Publisher, seanf@mediaedge.ca
Barbara Carss, Editor-in-Chief, barbc@mediaedge.ca

CondoBusiness
Owned By: MediaEdge Inc.
Tel: 416-512-8186 Toll-Free: 866-216-0860
Social Media: www.linkedin.com/groups?gid=3987591
twitter.com/condobusiness
www.face book.com/condomediaedge
Circulation: 2,500 Frequency: 8 times a year
Steve McLinden, Publisher, stevem@mediaedge.ca
Scott Anderson, Editor, scotta@mediaedge.ca

Construire
L'Association de la Construction du Québec, 9200, boul Métropolitain est, Montréal, QC H1K 4L2
Tél: 514-354-4339;Téléc: 514-354-8292
Ligne sans frais: 888-868-3424
repcomm@videotron.ca; info@prov.acq.org
Tirage: 27 000 Fréquence: 6 fois par an; français
Pierre Leduc, Directeur commercial

Daily Commercial News
Previous Name: Daily Commercial News & Construction Record
Reed Construction Data, 500 Hood Rd., 4th Fl., Markham, ON L3R 9Z3
Tel: 905-752-5471; Fax: 905-752-5450
christine.takashima@reedbusiness.com
Circulation: 4,000 Frequency: Daily
Mark Casaletto, Publisher

Equipment Journal
Pace Publishing Limited, #6, 5160 Explorer Dr., Mississauga, ON L4W 4T7
Tel: 905-629-7500; Fax: 905-629-7988
Toll-Free: 800-667-8541
office@equipmentjournal.com
Social Media:
twitter.com/EJmike
Circulation: 23,500 Frequency: 17 issues a year, every 3 weeks
John Baker, Publisher, admin@equipmentjournal.com

Formes
6718, rue Chambord, Montréal, QC H2G 3C3
Tél: 514-736-7637;Téléc: 514-272-3477
info@formes.ca
Fréquence: 6 fois par an

Heavy Equipment Guide
Owned By: Baum Publications Ltd.
Baum Publications Ltd., 124 - 2323 Boundary, Vancouver, BC V5M 4V8
Tel: 604-291-9900; Fax: 604-291-1906
Circulation: 21,000 Frequency: 10 times a year
Engelbert J. Baum, Publisher
Lawrence Buser, Editor, lbuser@baumpub.com

Home Builder Magazine
4819, boul St. Charles, Pierrefonds, QC H9H 3C7
Tel: 514-620-2200; Fax: 514-620-6300
homebuilder@work4.ca
Circulation: 26,418 Frequency: 6 times a year
Nachmi Artzy, Publisher

Journal Constructo
#200, 1500, boul Jules-Poitras, Saint-Laurent, QC H4N 1X7
Tél: 514-745-5720;Téléc: 514-339-2267
Ligne sans frais: 800-363-0910
Tirage: 2 611 Fréquence: 80 fois par an; français
Anik Girard, Éditeur
Marie Vaillancourt, Chef de L'Information

Le Journal de L'Habitation
Détenteur: Médias-Transcontinental
Médias-Transcontinental, #900, 1265, boul Charest ouest, Québec, QC G1N 4V4
Tél: 418-686-6400;Téléc: 418-686-4841
redaction_quebec@transcontinental.ca
Tirage: 28 000 Fréquence: 2 times a month
Yvon Lallier, Éditeur

Journal of Commerce
#101, 4299 Canada Way, Burnaby, BC V5G 1H3
Tel: 604-412-2260 Toll-Free: 800-794-6913
jocinfo@reedbusiness.com
Social Media: www.linkedin.com/groups?gid=1867398
twitter.com/JOC_Canada
www.faceboo k.com/pages/Journal-of-Commerce/117845964137
Circulation: 1,800 Frequency: 2 times a week

LBMAO Reporter
The Lumber & Building Materials Association of Ontario (LMBAO), #27, 5155 Spectrum Way, Mississauga, ON L4Z 5A1
Tel: 905-625-1084 Toll-Free: 888-365-2626
jmoquin@lbmao.on.ca
Circulation: 1,750 Frequency: 6 times a year
Joanne Moquin, jmoquin@lbmao.on.ca

On-Site
Owned By: Business Information Group
80 Valleybrook Dr., Toronto, ON M3B 2S9
Tel: 416-510-6794; Fax: 416-510-5140
Circulation: 21,000 Frequency: 7 times a year
Serving the commercial construction industry.
Corinne Lynds, Editor, clynds@on-sitemag.com
Peter Leonard, Publisher, pleonard@on-sitemag.com

Ontario Home Builder
Owned By: Ontario Home Builders' Association
#101, 20 Upjohn Rd., North York, ON M3B 2V9
Tel: 416-443-1545; Fax: 416-443-9982
Toll-Free: 800-387-0109
info@ohba.ca
Circulation: 8,084 Frequency: 5 times a year
Wayne Nanciso, Publisher

Ottawa Construction News
Tel: 613-224-3460; Fax: 613-224-1076
Toll-Free: 888-432-3555
Circulation: 12,000 Frequency: 12 times a year
Mark Buckshon, Publisher
Terry Tinkess, Editor

Québec Habitation
5930, boul Louis-H.-Lafontaine, Anjou, QC H1M 1S7
Tél: 514-353-9960;Téléc: 514-352-5259
Ligne sans frais: 800-468-8160
info@quebec-habitation.com
Tirage: 30 000 Fréquence: 6 fois par an; français
Jean Garon, Rédactrice-en-chef, jeangaron@videotron.ca

Sanitation Canada
Owned By: Perks Publications Inc.
3 Kennett Dr., Whitby, ON L1P 1L5
Tel: 905-430-7267; Fax: 905-430-6418
Toll-Free: 877-880-4877
Circulation: 5,134 Frequency: 6 times a year
Michael Nosko, Publisher

Toronto Construction News
Reed Construction Data, 500 Hood Rd., 4th Fl., Markham, ON L3R 9Z3
Tel: 905-752-5408; Fax: 905-750-5450
Toll-Free: 800-465-6475
Circulation: 4,000 Frequency: 7 times a year
Patrick McConnell, Publisher

Business & Finance

Advisor's Edge
Owned By: Rogers Publishing Ltd.
1 Mount Pleasant Rd., Toronto, ON M4Y 2Y5
Tel: 416-764-3859; Fax: 416-764-3943
safiya.bulbulia@rci.rogers.com
Social Media:
twitter.com/advisorca
Circulation: 35,963 Frequency: 10 times a year
Advisor's Edge magazine is an independent Canadian publication focused solely on the information needs of Canadian retail financial advisors (brokers, financial planners, insurance specialists, mutual fund salespeople and bank-based consultants). With a strong emphasis on practice management, the magazine helps advisors stay on top of industry trends, investment insurance products and strategies, as well as marketing and client relationship best practices
Donna Kerry, Publisher, donna.kerry@rci.rogers.com
Philip Porado, Executive Editor, philip.porado@rci.rogers.com

Les Affaires
Détenteur: Transcontinental Media Inc.
1100, boul René-Lévesque ouest, 24e étage, Montréal, QC H3B 4X9
Tél: 514-392-9000;Téléc: 514-392-1586
Ligne sans frais: 800 361 7215
lesaffaires@cdsglobal.ca
Médias sociaux:
twitter.com/la_lesaffaires
www.facebook.com/pages/lesaffairescom/100306918236
Tirage: 90 000 Fréquence: 52 fois par an; français; aussi Affaires 500, PME, Affaires plus (10 fois par an, 93 288)
Il est reconnu pour sa couverture des grandes sociétés canadiennes, des petites et moyennes entreprises québécoises, de l'économie canadienne et des affaires publiques. La moitié de son contenu est consacrée aux finances personnelles et aux placements avec diverses pages spécialisées, des tableaux et des graphiques.
Michel Lord, Éditeur
Jean-Paul Gagné, Rédacteur-en-chef,
pierre.marcoux@transcontinental.ca

Affaires Plus Magazine
Détenteur: Transcontinental Media Inc.
1100, boul René-Lévesque 24e étage, Montréal, QC H3B 4X9
Tél: 514-392-9000;Téléc: 514-392-4726
aplus@transcontiental.ca
Médias sociaux:
twitter.com/la_lesaffaires
Tirage: 88 806 Fréquence: 12 fois par an; français
Créé en 1978, le magazine Affaires PLUS est le magazine d'affaires au plus fort tirage et au plus fort lectorat au Québec. C'est aussi la plus personnelle des publications d'affaires de Médias Transcontinental. Le magazine est bâti autour de trois axes: mon argent, ma carrière, ma vie, qui déterminent à la fois le positionnement et le contenu d'Affaires PLUS
Stéphane Labrèche, Rédacteur en chef,
stephane.labreche@transcontinental.ca

Alberta Venture
10259 - 105 St., Edmonton, AB T5J 1E3
Tel: 780-990-0839; Fax: 780-425-4921
Toll-Free: 866-227-4276
admin@albertaventure.com
Circulation: 40,800 Frequency: 10 times a year
Alberta Venture is the only province-wide magazine that keeps you informed about Alberta's business community. Covers trends, issues, people and events that set the pace for Canada's fastest growing economy
Ruth Kelly, Editor

Atlantic Business Magazine
PO Box 2356 C, 197 Water St., St. John's, NL A1C 6E7
Tel: 709-726-9300; Fax: 709-726-3013
Circulation: 33,000 Frequency: 6 times a year
Founded in 1989, Atlantic Business Magazine is an independently owned, bi-monthly glossy publication that covers all areas of business within the four Atlantic provinces.
Hubert Hutton, Publisher,
hhutton@atlanticbusinessmagazine.com
Dawn Chafe, Editor, dchafe@atlanticbusinessmagazine.com

Avantages
Détenteur: Les Éditions Rogers limitée
1200, ave McGill College, 8e étage, Montréal, QC H3B 4G7
Tél: 514-843-5141;Téléc: 514-843-2180
abonnement.avantages@rci.rogers.com
Médias sociaux:
twitter.com/revueavantages
www.facebook.com/revueavantages
Tirage: 5,056 Fréquence: 8 fois par an; français
Simeon Goldstein, Rédacteur-en-chef,
Simeon.Goldstein@avantages.rogers.com
Garth Thomas, Éditeur, Garth.Thomas@advisor.rogers.com

Backbone Magazine
c/o Publimedia Communications Inc., 187 Rondoval Cres., North Vancouver, BC V7N 2W6
Tel: 905-918-0567; Fax: 604-986-5309
info@backbonemag.com
Circulation: 115,000 Frequency: 6 times per year
Backbone magazine's aim is to provide business people with a tangible tool to enhance the way they do business in Canada's New Economy
Steve Dietrich, Publisher, sdietrich@backbonemag.com
Peter Wolchak, Editor, pwolchak@backbonemag.com

BCBusiness Magazine
Owned By: Canada Wide Magazines & Communications Ltd.
4180 Lougheed Hwy. 4th Fl., Burnaby, BC V5C 6A7
Tel: 604-299-7311; Fax: 604-299-9188
Toll-Free: 800-663-0518
cwm@canadawide.com
Social Media: www.youtube.com/user/BCBusinessOnline
twitter.com/bcbusiness
www.faceb ook.com/bcbusiness
Circulation: 26,000 Frequency: Monthly
An authoritative voice on the province's business scene, BCBusiness goes beyond the headlines to give readers valuable, relevant insights into today's trends and issues
Peter Legge, Publisher, ttjaden@canadawide.com
David Jordan, Editor, djordan@canadawide.com
John Bucher, Editor, jbucher@canadawide.com

Benefits & Pensions Monitor
Owned By: Powershift Communications Inc.
#501, 245 Fairview Mall Dr., Toronto, ON M2J 4T1
Tel: 416-494-1066, Fax: 416-494-2536
info@powershift.ca
Circulation: 21,840 Frequency: 8 times a year
The magazine also publishees interactive online issues.
John McLaine, Publisher & Editorial Director,
jmclaine@powershift.ca
Joe Hornyak, Executive Editor, jhornyak@powershift.ca

Benefits Canada
Owned By: Rogers Publishing Ltd.
1 Mount Pleasant Rd., 12th Fl., Toronto, ON M4Y 2Y5
Tel: 416-764-3915; Fax: 416-764-3938
Circulation: 16,807 Frequency: 12 times a year; English & French
Provides information and analysis on pensions, benefits, healthcare and investments to key decision-makers who manage employer-sponsored pension and benefits plans. The publication targets the plan sponsor community, particularly those employers with more than 500 employees
Garth Thomas, Publisher, 416-764-3806,
garth.thomas@rci.rogers.com
Rehana Begg, Editor, 416-764-3823,
rehana.begg@rci.rogers.com

BIZ Magazine
Previous Name: BIZ Hamilton/Halton Business Report; Hamilton Business Report
Owned By: Town Media Inc.
1074 Cooke Blvd, Hamilton, ON L7T 4A8
Tel: 905-522-6117; Fax: 905-529-2242
info@townmedia.ca
Circulation: 24,000 Frequency: 4 times a year
Business publication in the Hamilton/Burlington region, with award-winning features, profiles, real-life photography and controversial opinions
Arend Kirsten, Editor

The Bottom Line
Owned By: LexisNexis Canada Ltd.
#700, 123 Commerce Valley Dr. East, Markham, ON L3T 7W8
Tel: 905-479-2665; Fax: 905-479-6460
Toll-Free: 800-461-3275
adam.malik@lexisnexis.ca
Circulation: 30,428 Frequency: 16 times a year
The Bottom Line is an independent and specialized business periodical that keeps accredited professional accountants, financial managers, and consultants abreast of news, trends, and technology within the industry
Ann McDonagh, Publisher
Robert Kelly, Managing Editor
Adam Malik, Assistant & Layout Editor

Business Central Magazine
#304, 4820 Gaetz Ave., Red Deer, AB T4N 4A4
Tel: 403-309-5587; Fax: 403-346-3044
Circulation: 5,000 Frequency: 6 times a year
Donald C. Sylvester, Publisher & Editor

Business Examiner Vancouver Island
Previous Name: Business Examiner - South Island Edition
#200, 3060 Cedar Hill Rd., Victoria, BC V8T 3J5
Tel: 250-381-3926; Fax: 250-381-5606
Circulation: 14,400 Frequency: 24 times a year
Mark MacDonald, mark@businessexaminer.net
Joanne Iormetti, joanne@businessexaminer.net

The Business Executive
1193 Lindsay Dr., Oakville, ON L6M 3B8
Tel: 416-806-4158; Fax: 905-811-1857
t.peters@busexec.com
Circulation: 30,000 Frequency: monthly
The Business Executive is Southern Ontario's only business-to-business newspaper published on a monthly basis. The Business Executive is divided into sections to allow the readers to pick and choose subjects of most interest to them. Some of the sections include: Real Estate & Construction, Finance, Business News, People and Lifestyles, Computers and Technology, International Trade & Travel.
Thomas Peters, Publisher, t.peters@busexec.com
Wendy Peters, Editor, wpeters@busexec.com

Business in Calgary
#1025, 101 - 6th Ave. SW, Calgary, AB T2P 3P4
Tel: 403-264-3270; Fax: 403-264-3276
Toll-Free: 800-465-0322
info@businessincalgary.com
Circulation: 30,735 Frequency: Monthly
Articles about the people, trends and events that make Calgary a prominent business centre in the west.
Derek Sankey, Editor, editor@businessincalgary.com
Pat Ottmann, Publisher, pat@businessincalgary.comcom
Tim Ottmann, Publisher, tim@businessincalgary.comcom

Business London
Previous Name: London Business Magazine
Owned By: Sun Media Corp..
PO Box 7400, London, ON N5Y 4X3
Tel: 519-471-2907; Fax: 519-473-7859
editorial@businesslondon.ca
Circulation: 12,000 Frequency: Monthly
The Magazine provides unparalleled behind-the-scenes coverage, chronicling companies on the move and putting faces to faceless events.
Gord Delamont, Publisher, 519-471-2907 x281,
gord.delamont@sunmedia.ca

Business Vancouver Island Head Office
Previous Name: Business Examiner - North
25 Cavan St., Nanaimo, BC V9R 2T9
Fax: 250-758-2668
Toll-Free: 866-758-2684
merv@businessexaminer.net
Circulation: 14,000 Frequency: Monthly
Steve Weatherbee, Editor

Businest
#810, 630, Sherbrooke ouest, Montréal, QC H3A 1E4
Tél: 514-866-3131;Téléc: 514-866-3030
inforeseauselect@tc.tc
Tirage: 20 100 Fréquence: Mensuel; français
Publication qui couvre de domaine des affaires, et dessert les professionnels, les entreprises et les gens d'affaires le territoire de La Pocatière aux Ies-de-la-Madeleine, et la Côte-Nord
Ernie Wells, Rédacteur-en-chef

CA Magazine
277 Wellington St. West, Toronto, ON M5V 3H2
Tel: 416-977-3222; Fax: 416-204-3409
CAmagazine@cica.ca
Circulation: 72,500 Frequency: 10 times a year; English & French
CAmagazine is published by the Canadian Institute of Chartered Accountants (CICA) ten times a year. Articles about careers in chartered accounting are featured while current issues are discussed and explained. The magazine also deals with a wide variety of business topics from the Chartered Accountant's perspective
Christian Bellavance, Editor-in-chief

Canada Japan Journal
Previous Name: Canada Japan Business Journal
Japan Advertising Ltd., #410, 1199 West Pender St., Vancouver, BC V6E 2R1
Tel: 604-688-2486; Fax: 604-688-1487
Toll-Free: 888-245-2549
japanad@telus.net
Circulation: 15,750 Frequency: Monthly; Japanese
Taka Aoki, Editor

Canadian Business
Owned By: Rogers Publishing Ltd.
1 Mount Pleasant Rd. 11th Fl., Toronto, ON M4Y 2Y5
Tel: 416-764-1200; Fax: 416-764-1255
adsales@canadianbusiness.com
Social Media:
twitter.com/CDNbusinessmag
www.facebook.com/canadianbusinessmagazine
Circulation: 80,064 Frequency: 19 issues per year
Canadian Business, Canada's best-selling business magazine, captures the attention of Canada's business leaders with topical, timely stories that matter to corporate managers and executives. Written for an audience with an orientation to the future, its compelling insight inspires readers to capitalize on change
Joe Chidley, Editor
Deborah Rosser, Publisher

Canadian Business Franchise/L'entreprise
c/o Kenilworth Media Inc., #710, 15 Wertheim Ct., Richmond Hill, BC L4B 3H7
Tel: 905-771-7333; Fax: 905-771-7336
Toll-Free: 800-409-8688
editor@franchiseinfo.ca
Social Media:
www.twitter.com/FranchiseFYI
www.facebook.com/CanadianBusinessFranchiseM agazine
Frequency: Bi-monthly
Features articles on franchise advice from bankers, lawyers and franchise specialists.
Colin Bradbury, Publisher & Editor
Tuesday Royko, Editorial Assistant

Canadian Capital
Owned By: Rogers Publishing Ltd.
Tel: 416-764-3802
bppgservice@rci.rogers.com
Phillip Porado, Editor, Philip.porado@rci.rogers.com

Canadian German Trade
#1500, 480 University Ave., Toronto, ON M5G 1V2
Tel: 416-598-3355; Fax: 416-598-1840
info.toronto@germanchamber.ca
Circulation: 2,500 Frequency: 6 times a year
Covers news concerning the Canadian and German economy, special articles which are of interest to the Canadian and German business community, as well as updated economic datanews concerning the Canadian and German economy, special articles which are of interest to the Canadian and German business community, as well as updated economic data
Sonya Deevy, Contact

Canadian Investment Review
Owned By: Rogers Publishing Ltd.
1 Mount Pleasant Ave., 12th Fl., Toronto, ON M4Y 2Y5
Tel: 416-764-3867; Fax: 416-764-3934
Circulation: 4,700 Frequency: 4 times a year
Forum for academics, institutional investors and industry practitioners to exchange ideas on the capital markets, investment and economic theory, and the related sociology and demographics.
Caroline Cakebread, Editor, caroline.cakebread@rogers.com
Garth Thomas, Publisher

The Canadian Manager
Canadian Institute of Management, 15 Collier St., Lower Level, Barrie, ON L4M 1G5
Tel: 705-725-8926; Fax: 705-725-8196
Toll-Free: 800-387-5774
office@cim.ca
Circulation: 4,500 Frequency: Quarterly
The Canadian Manager is published 4 times per year by the Canadian Institute of Management, with a readership over 12,000 (approx.)
Anna Victoria Wong, Editor/Manager, awong@baseconsulting.ca

Canadian Not-For-Profit News
Owned By: Carswell
One Corporate Plaza, 2075 Kennedy Rd., Toronto, ON M1T 3V4
Tel: 416-609-8000; Fax: 416-298-5094
Frequency: Monthly
Source of current information on the tax implications and practical considerations relating to the most relevant and timely issues surrounding registered charities and other non-profit organizations

The Canadian Taxpayer
Owned By: Carswell
c/o Carswell, One Corporate Plaza, 2075 Kennedy Rd., Toronto, ON M1T 3V4
Tel: 416-609-8000; Fax: 416-298-5082
Toll-Free: 800-387-5164
carswell.orders@thomson.com
Circulation: 1,000 Frequency: 24 times per year
The Taxpayer is the flagship publication of the Canadian Taxpayers Federation (CTF). It is published six times a year and contains comprehensive updates on CTF happenings and accomplishments around the country. It features articles written by CTF researchers and spokespersons. Guest editorial writers also contribute to this publication.
Robert Freeman, Vice-President

Canadian Treasurer
Owned By: Lloydmedia, Inc.
137 Main St. North, 3rd Fl., Markham, ON L3P 1Y2
Tel: 905-201-6600; Fax: 905-201-6601
Toll-Free: 800-668-1838
Mark Henry, Editor, mark@canadiantreasurer.com

Central Nova Business News
Truro & District Chamber of Commerce, 605 Prince St., Truro, NS B2N 5B6
Tel: 902-895-6328
tim@trurochamber.com
Social Media:
twitter.com/TruroCoC
Circulation: 1,500 Frequency: Monthly
The official Publication of the Truro and District Chamber of Commerce
Tim Ticker, Exectuive Director

CGA Magazine
c/o Certified General Accountants, #100, 4200 North Fraser Way, Burnaby, BC V5J 5K7
Tel: 604-669-3555; Fax: 604-689-5845
Toll-Free: 800-663-1529
cgamagazine@cga-canada.org
Other information: Subscriptions, E-mail: subscription@cga-canada.org
Circulation: 75,000 Frequency: 6 pa
Contents include articles about professional accountancy & news from the business & regulatory sectors.
Lorriane Pitt, Publisher
Anya Levykh, Managing Editor
Lily Claydon, Director, Art
Gavin Carroll, Coordinator, Advertising & Assistant Director, Art
Doris Hollett, Coordinator, Production & Editorial Assistant
Ingrid Mueller, Specialist, National Advertising Sales, 416-226-4862, imueller@cga-canada.org

Chamber Vision
Owned By: Metro Guide Publishing
Greater Moncton Chamber of Commerce, #200, 1273 Main St., Moncton, NB E1C 0P4
Tel: 506-857-2883
info@gmcc.nb.ca
Social Media:
twitter.com/MonctonChamber
www.facebook.com/GreaterMonctonChamberOfCommerce
Circulation: 5000 Frequency: 6 times a year

CMA Management Magazine
Previous Name: CMA Magazine
c/o Society of Management Accountants of Canada, Miss. Exec., #1400, One Robert Speck Pkwy., Mississauga, ON L4Z 3M3
Tel: 905-949-4200; Fax: 905-949-0888
Toll-Free: 800-263-7622
info@cma-canada.org
Circulation: 48,000 Frequency: bi-monthly; English & French
Management is an outstanding business magazine specifically tailored to help you make informed business decisions and give you a strategic advantage. It provides effective, practical solutions to your most pressing business challenges. It features the latest trends in management strategies with sharp, fresh editorial and attention-grabbing design.
David Fletcher, Publisher
Robert Colman, Editor-in-chief

Commerce & Industry
Mercury Publications Ltd.
Owned By: Mercury Publications Ltd.
1740 Wellington Ave., Winnipeg, MB R3H 0E8
Tel: 204-954-2085; Fax: 204-954-2057
Toll-Free: 800-337-6372
Circulation: 18,154 Frequency: bi-monthly
A national publication focused on the industrial, manufacturing, resource, transportation and construction sectors. Each issue offers a large variety of sector analysis, in-depth company profiles and reports on key areas of interest to the magazine's target audience.
Al Kaglik, National Account Manager, al@mercury.mb.ca
Frank Yeo, Publisher
Edna Saito, Production Manager

Commerce News: The Voice of Business in Edmonton
Edmonton Chamber of Commerce, #700, 9990 Jasper Ave. NW, Edmonton, AB T5J 1P7
Tel: 780-426-4620; Fax: 780-424-7946
info@edmontonchamber.com
Circulation: 26,000 Frequency: 11 pa
The official publication of the Edmonton Chamber of Commerce is Commerce News. The publication covers business issues & is of interest to Edmonton's business community, community leaders, & Chamber of Commerce members.
Serap Ozturk, Contact, Advertising, Venture Publisbing Inc., sozturk@venturepublishing.ca

Conseiller
Détenteur: Les Éditions Rogers limitée
1200, ave McGill College, 8e étage, Montréal, QC H3B 4G7
Tél: 514-843-5141;Téléc: 514-843-2180
abonnement.avantages@rci.rogers.com
Tirage: 9,173 Fréquence: 10 fois par an; français
Saskia Ouaknine, Rédactrice en chef, Saskia.Ouaknine@rci.rogers.com

Contact Management
Owned By: Lloydmedia, Inc.
137 Main St. North, 3rd Fl., Markham, ON L3P 1Y2
Tel: 905-201-6600; Fax: 905-201-6601
Toll-Free: 800-668-1838
Circulation: 5,300 Frequency: Quarterly
Amy Bostock, Editor, amy@contactmanagement.ca

The Corporate Ethics Monitor
PO Box 54034, Toronto, ON M6A 3B7
Tel: 416-783-6776; Fax: 416-783-7386
info@ethicscan.ca
Circulation: 400 Frequency: Bi-monthly
Each sixteen page issue of Corporate Ethics Monitor is laden with articles and stories that deal with recognizing and enhancing ethics in the workplace. Expect to find original research, timely articles, provocative perspectives, and practical ideas. The reporting on comparative business practices reflects dozens of hours of interviews, data base retrieval, fact checking and preparation of tables, charts and profiles.

Daily Business Buzz
Owned By: Transcontinental Media
#609, 1888 Brunswick St., Halifax, NS B3J 3J8
Tel: 902-425-8255; Fax: 902-425-8118
Circulation: 17,000 Frequency: Daily online
Daily business news for the Atlantic Canada region. The Daily Business Buzz is a spin-off of the Nova Scotia Business Journal.
Ken Partridge, Senior Editor
Peter Coleman, Senior Account Executive

Defined Benefit Monitor
Owned By: Powershift Communications Inc.
245 Fairview Mall Dr., 5th Fl., Toronto, ON M2J 4T1
Tel: 416-494-1066

Frequency: 2 times a year
Sent to a portion of Benefits & Pensions Monitor's circulation list.
John L. McLaine, Publisher & Editorial Director, jmclaine@powershift.ca

Defined Contribution Monitor
Owned By: Powershift Communications Inc.
245 Fairview Mall Dr., 5th Fl., Toronto, ON M2J 4T1
Tel: 416-494-1066
Frequency: 2 times a year
Sent to a portion of Benefits & Pensions Monitor's circulation list.
John L. McLaine, Publisher & Editorial Director, jmclaine@powershift.ca

L'Edition Le Journal des Gens d'Affaires
Détenteur: L'Edition Commerciale
Tél: 514-257-1000;Téléc: 514-257-7505
Tirage: 29 700
Carole Le Hirez, Rédacteur-en-chef
Lise Thériault, Éditeur

Entreprendre
Editions Qualité Performante inc., #660, 1600, boul St-Martin est, Laval, QC H7G 4R8
Tél: 450-669-8373;Téléc: 450-669-9078
Ligne sans frais: 800-479-1777
message@entreprendre.ca
Tirage: 45 000 Fréquence: 10 fois par an; français
Le magazine Entreprendre rejoint un auditoire exceptionnel de décideurs du monde des affaires. Outil d'information qui développe des références et éclaire la nature profonde de l'entrepreneurship au Québec
Edmond Bourque, Publisher

Exchange Magazine for Business
#10, 160 Frobisher Dr., Waterloo, ON N2V 2B1
Tel: 519-886-0298; Fax: 519-886-6409
Circulation: 17,500 Frequency: 8 times a year
Covers business news in the Kitchener-Waterloo area
Jon Rohr, Editor-in-chief

Finance et Investissement
Owned By: Transcontinental Media Inc.
1100, boul René-Lévesque ouest, 24e étage, Montréal, QC H3B 4X9
Tel: 514-392-9000; Fax: 514-392-4726
redaction@finance-investissement.com
Circulation: 30,000 Frequency: irregulier
Depuis son lancement en novembre 1999, le journal Finance et Investissement est devenu la source d'information privilégiée des représentants en épargne collective, des conseillers en valeurs mobilières, des conseillers en sécurité financière et des planificateurs financiers
Sylvain Bedard, Publisher, sylvain.bedard@transcontinental.ca

Financial Post Business Magazine
Previous Name: National Post Business
#300, 1450 Don Mills Rd., Toronto, ON M3B 3R5
Tel: 416-383-2300; Fax: 416-383-2305
Toll-Free: 800-267-6568
Social Media:
twitter.com/FinPostMagazine
www.facebook.com/pages/Financial-Post-Magazine/2252405808
Circulation: 289,000 Frequency: 12 times a year
Terence Corcoran, Managing Editor

FlashFinance
#100, 321, rue de la Commune, Montréal, QC H2Y 2E1
Tel: 514-289-9595; Fax: 514-289-9527
flash@flashfinance.ca
Circulation: 2 000 Frequency: Weekly
Outil privilégié d'information du monde de l'assurance et de la finance, FlashFinance.cajoint des milliers de dirigeants de compagnies d'assurance, de propriétaires de cabinets, de directeurs de courtage, et de conseillers financiers
Hubert Roy, Rédactor, hubert.roy@flashfinance.ca

Franchise Canada Directory
Canadian Franchise Association, #116, 5399 Eglinton Ave. West, Toronto, ON M9C 5K6
Tel: 905-625-2896; Fax: 905-625-9076
Toll-Free: 800-665-4232
info@cfa.ca
Frequency: Annually
John Schofield, Editor

FranchiseCanada Magazine
Canadian Franchise Association, #116, 5399 Eglinton Ave. West, Toronto, ON M9C 5K6
Tel: 416-695-2896; Fax: 416-695-1950
Toll-Free: 800-665-4232
info@cfa.ca
Circulation: 6,000 Frequency: bi-monthly
A bi-monthly magazine geared at entrepreneurs interested in acquiring a franchise. Franchise Canada Magazine will contain top-notch editorial from leading authorities in the industry as well as countless tips on how to establish a successful franchise.
John Scofield, Editor

GST & Commodity Tax
Owned By: Carswell
One Corporate Plaza, 2075 Kennedy Rd., Toronto, ON M1T 3V4
Tel: 416-609-8000; Fax: 416-298-5094
The exclusive source for what leading experts are saying about the latest developments in GST, federal and provincial sales and commodity taxes, and customs and excise duties

Halton Business Times
#1, 5040 Mainway, Burlington, ON L7L 7G5
Tel: 905-632-4444; Fax: 905-632-9162
thepost@worldchat.com
Circulation: 12,000 Frequency: 12 times a year
Ian Oliver, Publisher
Karen Smith, Editor

Huronia Business Times
21 Patterson Rd., Barrie, ON L4N 7W6
Tel: 705-726-0573; Fax: 705-726-9350
Circulation: 12,000 Frequency: Monthly
Purchased by Metroland Business Publications in September of 1998, Huronia Business Times, and its sister publication the Mississauga Business Times, was formerly owned by North Island Publishing from 1992-1998. Metroland also publishes five other Business Times newspapers in southern Ontario
Martin Melbourne, Editor, mmelbourne@simcoe.com

Info-ACAIQ
Anciennement: ACAIQ Magazine
Association des courtiers et agents immobilier du Québec, #300, 6300, rue Auteuil, Brossard, QC J4Z 3P2
Tél: 450-676-4800;Téléc: 450-676-7801
Ligne sans frais: 800-440-5110
Tirage: 16 000
L'Info ACAIQ est le journal des professionnels du courtage immobilier du Québec. Il couvre divers sujets relatifs à l'application de la Loi sur le courtage immobilier, aux règlements de la profession, au marché immobilier en plus de questions d'ordre juridique et déontologique reliées à la pratique du courtage immobilier

Investment Executive (IE)
Owned By: Transcontinental Media Inc.
#100, 25 Sheppard Ave. West, Toronto, ON M2N 6S7
Tel: 416-733-7600; Fax: 416-218-3624
Toll-Free: 888-366-4200
editorial@investmentexecutive.com
Circulation: 120,000 Frequency: 16 times a year
Investment Executive is Canada's national newspaper for financial service industry professionals. Topics such as mutual funds, investment research, technology, estate planning, tax, building relationships with clients and developing products and services for the client of the future.
Tessa Wilmott, Editor-in-chief, twilmott@investmentexecutive.com

Investor's Digest of Canada
MPL Communications Inc., #700, 133 Richmond St. West, Toronto, ON M5H 3M8
Tel: 416-869-1177; Fax: 416-869-0616
Toll-Free: 800-504-8846
customers@mplcomm.com
Circulation: 42,912 Frequency: 24 times a year
Devoted to uncovering profitable opportunities in every area of investing, using the insights of Canada's leading investment professionals
Michael Popovich, Editor
Barrie Martland, Publisher

Italcommerce
Italian Chamber of Commerce in Canada, #1150, 550, rue Sherbrooke ouest, Montréal, QC H3A 1B9
Tel: 514-844-4249; Fax: 514-844-4875
Toll-Free: 800-263-4372
info.montreal@italchambers.net
Frequency: 3 times a year; French, English & Italian
A pour mission de promouvoir et soutenir les échanges commerciaux entre le Québec, le Canada et l'Italie. Le magazine est diffusé au Canada, en Italie ainsi que dans 60 autres pays où on retrouve des chambres de commerce italiennes
Pasquale Iacobacci, Managing Editor

Ivey Business Journal
c/o Richard Ivey School of Business, University of Western Ontario, London, ON N6A 3K7
Tel: 519-661-4222
ibjonline@ivey.uwo.ca
Circulation: 12,013 Frequency: 6 times a year
Covers articles about e-business, managing uncertainty, knowledge management, marketing, strategy and other topics that managers need to know more about to steer their firms to success.
Ed Pearce, Publisher
Stephen Bernhut, Editor, 416-923-9945, sbernhut@ivey.ca

Le Journal du Conseiller
Détenteur: Les Éditions Rogers limitée
1200, ave McGill College, 8e étage, Montréal, QC H3B 4G7
Tél: 514-843-5141;Téléc: 514-843-2180
Donna Kelly
Yves Bonneau

Kootenay Business Magazine
Owned By: Koocanusa Publications Inc.
#100, 100 - 7th Ave. South, Crawbrook, BC V1C 2J4
Tel: 250-426-7253; Fax: 250-426-4125
Toll-Free: 800-663-8555
Social Media: www.flickr.com/photos/kootenaybusiness
twitter.com/kootbusiness
Circulation: 9,400 Frequency: 6 times a year
Kootenay Business magazine is free to businesses within the Kootenay/ Columbia/ Boundary/ Revelstoke area.
Keith Powell, Publisher, publisher@kpimedia.com

Manitoba Business Magazine
#508, 294 Portage Ave., Winnipeg, MB R3C 0B9
Tel: 204-943-2940; Fax: 204-943-2942
mbmsales@shaw.ca
Circulation: 8,000 Frequency: 10 times a year
Ritchie Gage, Editor

Marketplace Magazine
65 Dewdney Ave., 2nd Fl., Winnipeg, MB R3B 0E1
Tel: 204-992-3402; Fax: 204-475-3003
Circulation: 13,000 Frequency: 12 times a year
Jon Waldman, Editor, 204-992-3402

mbot Magazine
Previous Name: Business Bulletin
Mississauga Board of Trade, #701, 77 City Centre Dr., Mississauga, ON L5B 1M5
Tel: 905-273-6151; Fax: 905-273-4937
info@mbot.com; advertising@mbot.com
Social Media: www.youtube.com/user/MBOTMississauga
twitter.com/mbotontario
www.faceb ook.com/MississaugaBoardofTrade
Circulation: 5,000 Frequency: 11 times a year
Business news & updates on MBOT activities.
Sheldon Leiba, President & CEO, Mississauga Board of Trade, sleiba@mbot.com

Mingle
Owned By: Apeeling Orange Design Communications
15 Alderney Dr., Dartmounth, NS B2Y 2N2
Tel: 902-446-8231
Social Media: www.youtube.com/user/MingleLive
twitter.com/MingleMagazine
www.faceboo k.com/groups/36560444626
Circulation: 6,000
Jacquie Thillaye, Editor

The MOMpreneur
Calgary, AB
info@themompreneur.com
Social Media:
twitter.com/MompreneurCan
www.facebook.com/MompreneurMag?ref=ts
Frequency: 6 times a year
Frances Wright, CEO, ceo@themompreneur.com

MoneySense
Owned By: Rogers Publishing Ltd.
1 Mount Pleasant Rd., 11th Fl., Toronto, ON M4Y 2Y5
Tel: 416-764-1400; Fax: 416-764-1376
service@moneysense.ca
Social Media: www.youtube.com/MoneySenseMagazine
twitter.com/MoneySenseMag
www.faceb ook.com/MoneySenseMagazine
Circulation: 800,000 Frequency: 7 times a year
Personal finance magazine.
Jonathan Chereau, Editor
Julie Osborne, Publisher

Motivated
101 Ira Needles Blvd., Waterloo, ON N2J 3Z4
Social Media: www.youtube.com/motivatedmagazine
twitter.com/motivatedonline
www.facebook.com/MotivatedMagazine
Includes inspiring articles from leaders, entrepreneurs, & everyday people with the goal of motivating readers towards success in their business & personal lives.
Lisa Holba, Publisher

National Post Business, FP 500
Previous Name: National Post 500; The Financial Post 500
#300, 1450 Don Mills Rd., Toronto, ON M3B 3R5
Tel: 416-383-2300; Fax: 416-383-2305
Toll-Free: 800-267-6568
Circulation: 289,000 Frequency: Annually, June
Ranking of Canada's largest corporations
Brian Banks, Editor

North Country Business
PO Box 180, Bracebridge, ON P1L 1T6
Tel: 705-646-1314; Fax: 705-645-6424
mm.info@sunmedia.ca
Circulation: 5,259 Frequency: monthly
Donald Smith, Publisher

Northern Ontario Business
Laurentian Publishing Co., 158 Elgin St., Sudbury, ON P3E 3N5
Tel: 705-673-5705; Fax: 705-673-9542
Toll-Free: 800-757-2766
info@nob.on.ca
Circulation: 10,000 Frequency: Monthly
Northern Ontario Business is printed every month and is the only publication devoted to the region's business community
Patricia Mills, Publisher, pmills@nob.on.ca
Kelly Louiseize, Managing Editor, kellyl@nob.on.ca

Nova Scotia Business Journal
c/o TC Media, #609, 1888 Brunswick St., Halifax, NS B3J 3J8
Tel: 902-425-8255
Circulation: 70,000 Frequency: Monthly
The publication covers business events & issues that affect Nova Scotia's business environment.
Ken Partridge, Senior Editor
Barb McCay Cashin, Editor
Ian Ross, Manager, Sales
David Schaffner, Designer
Jodie Purchase, Coordinator, Advertising

Office@Home
PO Box D-79, Bowen Island, BC V0N 1G0
Tel: 604-947-2275; Fax: 604-947-0633
officeathome@dowco.com
Frequency: 4 times a year
Dave Sharrock, Publisher
Dale Gagne, Editor

Ontario Industrial Magazine
#1159, 1011 Upper Middle Rd. East, Oakville, ON L6H 5Z9
Tel: 416-446-1404; Fax: 416-446-0502
Toll-Free: 800-624-2776
sales@oim-online.com
Circulation: 20,000 Frequency: Monthly
OIM provides the very latest information about manufacturing technology, material handling products, industrial equipment & services, financial management and general business news
Keith Laverty, Publisher
Bill Bryson, Editorial Advisor

Ottawa Business Journal
PO Box 3814 C, Ottawa, ON K1Y 4J8
Tel: 613-238-1818
editor@obj.ca
Social Media:
twitter.com/obj_news
www.facebook.com/pages/Ottawa-Business-Journal/1313985714
Circulation: 16,300 Frequency: Bi-weekly
Ottawa Business Journal is the leading source of local business news and information for Canada's national capital region. Every Monday, the newspaper provides authoritative and in-depth news coverage on the sectors that comprise Ottawa's vibrant business scene, ranging from technology to commercial real estate and corporate finance to hospitality.
Michael Curran, Publisher

Partners, Italy & Canada
Italian Chamber of Commerce of Toronto, #201F, 622 College St., Toronto, ON M6G 1B6
Tel: 416-789-7169; Fax: 416-789-7160
info.toronto@italchambers.net
Circulation: 12,000 Frequency: Quarterly
partners is the official publication of the Italian Chamber of Commerce of Toronto. Published quarterly, the magazine features editorials and special reports written by international experts and tackles themes such as business ethics, design, multiculturalism, foreign trade, arts and entertainment. Through interviews and company profiles, partners is the voice of the Canadian, Italian and international business community.
Corrado Paina, Editorial Director, paina@italchambers.ca
Emily Saso, Managing Editor, saso@italchambers.ca

Payments Business
Owned By: Lloydmedia, Inc.
137 Main St. North, 3rd Fl., Markham, ON L3P 1Y2
Tel: 905-201-6600; Fax: 905-201-6601
Toll-Free: 800-668-1838
Circulation: 100,000
Leslee Mason, Editor, leslee@paymentsbusiness.ca

Port of Halifax
Owned By: Metro Guide Publishing
1300 Hollis St., Halifax, NS B3J 1T6
Tel: 902-420-9943; Fax: 902-429-9058
mross@metroguide.ca
Circulation: 20,000
Port of Halifax Magazine features information about the Port of Halifax along with stories of interest to the international shipping community
Patty Baxter, Publisher, 902-420-9943 ext 231, publishers@metroguide.ca

Private Wealth Canada
Owned By: Powershift Communications Inc.
c/o Powershift Communications Inc., 245 Fairview Mall Dr., 5th Fl., Toronto, ON M2J 4T1
Tel: 416-494-1066; Fax: 416-494-2536
info@powershift.ca
Circulation: 1,200
Provides financial & lifestyle information for senior executives.
Brian McKerchar, Publisher
Joe Hornyak, Executive Editor
Heather Field, Director, Online Initiatives, webpromos@powershift.ca

Profit
Owned By: Rogers Publishing Ltd.
One Mount Pleasant Rd., 11th Fl., Toronto, ON M4Y 2Y5
Tel: 416-764-1402; Fax: 416-764-1404
Social Media:
twitter.com/profit_magazine
www.facebook.com/PROFITmagazine
Circulation: 184,000 Frequency: 6 times a year
Topics of entrepreneural business and economics.
Deborah Rosser, Publisher

Progress
Previous Name: Atlantic Progress
#1201, 1660 Hollis St., Halifax, NS B3J 1V7
Tel: 902-494-0999; Fax: 902-494-0997
progress@progressmedia.ca
Social Media:
twitter.com/progressmedia
www.facebook.com/ProgressMediaGroup
Circulation: 26,513 Frequency: 10 times a year
Pamela Scott Crace, Editor

Québec Enterprise
269, ch de la Grande Côte, Rosemère, QC H7A 1J2
Tél: 450-420-8408;Téléc: 450-970-2205
magazine@quebecenterprise.com
Tirage: 20,520 Fréquence: 5 fois par an; français
Magazine d'affaires couvrant les activités industrielles de toutes les régions du Québec

Québec Franchise & Occasions d'Affaires
Anciennement: Québec Franchise & Microfranchise
CP 32189, St-André, QC H2L 4Y5
Tél: 514-383-0034;Téléc: 514-383-0057
JD@Quebec-Franchise.qc.ca
Tirage: 10 000 copies Fréquence: 6 times a year, French, 25% English
Spécialisé dans la franchise et les opportunités d'affaires au Québec et au Canada
Jacques Desforges, Editor

Québec inc
Anciennement: Magazine Finance
#100, 321, rue de la Commune ouest, Montréal, QC H2Y 2E1
Tél: 514-289-9595;Téléc: 514-289-9527
quebecinc@quebecinc.ca
Tirage: 33 231 Fréquence: 8 fois par an
Magazine pour gens d'affaires du Québec
Serge Therrien, Rédacteur en chef, serge.therrien@quebecinc.ca

Report on Business Magazine (ROB)
c/o The Globe and Mail, 444 Front St. West, Toronto, ON M5V 2S9
Tel: 416-585-5000
newsroom@globeandmail.com
Frequency: 11 times a year
Canada's premier business magazine is distributed nationwide with The Globe and Mail to targeted circulation. The thought-provoking and important business stories reach an influential and educated audience. As a pro-business, pro-Canada and pro-reader magazine, it charts the path of business like no other publication in this country
Philip Crawley, Publisher and CEO

Revue Commerce
Détenteur: Transcontinental Media Inc.
1100, boul René-Lévesque ouest, 24e étage, Montréal, QC H3B 4X9
Tél: 514-392-9000;Téléc: 514-392-2026
Tirage: 37,766 Fréquence: Mensuel; français
Magazine d'actualité qui couvre le monde des affaires
Diane Bérar, Rédactrice en chef

Rotman
Owned By: Rotman School of Management
105 St. George St., Toronto, ON M5S 3E6
Tel: 416-946-0103
Frequency: Quarterly
Karen Christensen, Editor-in-Chief, christen@rotman.utoronto.ca

Senior Executive
Previous Name: Canadian Government Executive
Beacon Publishing Inc., 2150 Fillmore Cres., Ottawa, ON K1J 6A4
Tel: 613-747-1138; Fax: 613-747-7319
publisher@seniorexec.ca
Circulation: 20,000 Frequency: bi-monthly
Senior Executive magazine features informative articles on topics such as: management techniques; service improvement;business developments; success stories; best practices; IM and IT; innovative use of technology; financial management; personal finance; innovative organizational approaches; modern comptrollership; risk management; policy issues; personnel and retention issues; stress management; transformations; horizontal management;and partnering innovations/successes/challenges between business and government.
John Kiska, Associate Editor
Jonathan Calof, Associate Editor
Chris MacLean, Managing Editor, !cmaclean@seniorexec.ca!
John Kiska, Associate Editor

SOHO Business Report
Previous Name: Home Business Report
439A Marmont St., Coquitlam, BC V3K 4S4
Tel: 604-936-5815; Fax: 604-936-5805
Toll-Free: 888-963-5815
Circulation: 40,000 Frequency: 4 times a year
SOHO Business Report is a quarterly magazine begun in 1989, when the SOHO-based business phenomenon was just a "blip" on the screen of public consciousness. It originated in Abbotsford, British Columbia, Canada from the home of founding publisher Barbara Mowat. Starting as a small newsletter, it first started as The B.C. Home Business Report, and was designed to help link home-based businesses across the province, providing the lone entrepreneur with practical tips and sensible advice on running their business. The newsletter was in demand, and soon other regional editions followed in Alberta and Ontario. Then in 1994, Home Business Report went national. After all these years, it was time for the magazine to enter its teenage growth spurt and the SOHO Business Report emerged as a celebration of over a decade and a half of helping entrepreneurs
Chad Thiessen, Publisher

Thompson's World Insurance News
PO Box 1027, Waterloo, ON N2J 4S1
Tel: 519-579-2500; Fax: 519-745-7321
mpub@sympatico.ca
Frequency: Weekly
Canada's only independent weekly for p&c insurance professionals, has been the industry's most trusted news source for more than a decade
Mark Publicover, Managing Editor

Thunder Bay Business
Owned By: North Superior Publishing Inc.
1402-590 Beverly St., Thunder Bay, ON P7B 6H1
Tel: 807-623-2348; Fax: 807-623-7515
nspinc@tbaytel.net

Circulation: 5,000 Frequency: Monthly
Northwestern Ontario business publication.
Scott Sumner, Publisher & Editor

Trade & Commerce
1700 Church Ave., Winnipeg, MB R2X 3A2
Tel: 204-632-2606; Fax: 204-694-3040
tcommerce@wpgsun.com
Circulation: 10,000 Frequency: 4 times a year
Trade & Commerce magazine produces annual "Market Surveys" on all Canadian provinces and territories, that review overall economic performance and highlight investment and growth opportunities in specific communities. Each of the year's five issues also profiles leading companies operating within the surveyed regions. The Access Americas section features attractive U.S. and international locations for Canadian business and industrial expansion. Distributed nationally to top managers in Canada fastest growing companies
George Mitchell, Publisher

Camping & Outdoor Recreation

RV Lifestyle Magazine
Owned By: Taylor Publishing Group
#2, 1121 Invicta Dr., Oakville, ON L6H 2R2
Tel: 905-844-8218; Fax: 905-844-5032
info@rvlifemag.com
Social Media: www.flickr.com/groups/rvadventures
Frequency: 7 issues per year
William E. Taylor, Publisher
Peter Tasler, Editor-in-chief, editor@rvlifemag.com

Celtic

Irish Connections Canada
Owned By: O'Loghlin Communications Inc.
121 Decarie Circle, Toronto, ON M9B 3J6
Tel: 416-621-7373
Frequency: 3 times per year
Eamonn O'Loghlin, Editor/Publisher, olcomm@rogers.com

Chemicals & Chemical Process Industries

Canadian Chemical News / L'Actualité chimique canadienne
c/o The Chemical Institute of Canada, #550, 130 Slater St., Ottawa, ON K1P 6E2
Tel: 613-232-6252; Fax: 613-232-5862
Toll-Free: 888-542-2242
editorial@accn.ca
Circulation: 5,500 Frequency: 10 times a year
Michelle Piquettee, Editor-in-chief
Heather Dana Munroe, Managing Editor

Canadian Process Equipment & Control News
#29, 588 Edward Ave., Richmond Hill, ON L4C 9Y6
Tel: 905-770-8077; Fax: 905-770-8075
cpe@cpecn.com
Circulation: 24,127 Frequency: 6 times a year
Jerry Cook, Editor, jcook@jcook@cpecn.com

Industrial Process Products & Technology
Owned By: Swan Erickson Publishing Inc.
#355, 4261 - A14 Highway #7 East, Markham, ON L3R 9W6
Tel: 905-475-4231
Circulation: 24,190 Frequency: 6 times a year
Michael Swan, Publisher, 905-649-8966, mswan@ippt.ca
Glen Scholry, Editor, 905-642-1215, gscholey@ippt.ca

Clothing & Accessories

Canadian Apparel Magazine
Canadian Apparel Federation, #504, 124 O'Connor St., Ottawa, ON K1P 5M9
Tel: 416-493-3912
kait@trendsmagazine.ca
Circulation: 25,466 Frequency: bi-monthly
Bob Kirke, Publisher
Marsha Ross, Managing Editor

Style
#701, 555 Richmond St. West, Toronto, ON M5V 3B1
Circulation: 12,000 Frequency: 5 times a year
Rod Morris, Publisher
Leslie Wu, Editor

Computing & Technology

CIO Canada
Owned By: It World Canada Inc.
#302, 55 Town Centre Ct., Toronto, ON M1P 4X4
Tel: 416-290-0240; Fax: 416-290-0238
general@itworldcanada.com
Circulation: 8,000 Frequency: 12 times a year
Shane Schick, Editor, sschick@itworldcanada.com

Computer Dealer News
Owned By: IT World Canada Inc.
#302, 55 Town Centre Crt., Scarborough, ON M1P 4X4
Tel: 416-290-0240
info@itbusiness.ca
Circulation: 18,859 Frequency: 18 times a year
Paolo Del Nibletto, Editor, pdelnibletto@itworldcanada.com

Computer World Canada
Owned By: IT World Canada Inc.
#302, 55 Town Centre Ct., Toronto, ON M1P 4X4
Tel: 416-290-0240; Fax: 416-290-0238
general@itworldcanada.com
Circulation: 40,000 Frequency: 25 times a year
Dan McLean, Publisher
Greg Enright, Editor

ConnectIT
17 Moodie Dr., Richmond Hill, ON L4C 8C9
Tel: 905-763-1200; Fax: 905-886-6216
Toll-Free: 800-465-2059

Direction Informatique
Détenteur: IT World Canada Inc.
#1502, 505, René Lévesque ouest, Montreal, QC H2Z 1Y7
Tél: 514-876-9964
redaction@directioninformatique.com
Médias sociaux:
www.linkedin.com/groups/Direction-Informatique-2744942
twitter.com/direc tioninfo
www.facebook.com/DirectionInformatique?sk=wall
Tirage: 17 939 Fréquence: 10 fois par an; français
Denis Lalonde, Rédacteur en chef, dlalonde@directioninformatique.com
Jean-François Ferland, Journaliste, jfferland@directioninformatique.com
Brad McBride, Directeur des Ventes, bmcbride@itworlcanada.com

eChannelLine Daily News
Previous Name: Computer Reseller News
17 Moodie Dr., Richmond Hill, ON L4C 8C9
Tel: 905-763-1200; Fax: 905-886-6216
Toll-Free: 800-465-2059
Circulation: 36,000 Frequency: daily
Steve Wexler, Editor-in-chief, Special Projects

Network World Canada
Owned By: IT World Canada Inc.
#302, 55 Town Centre Ct., Toronto, ON M1P 4X4
Tel: 416-290-0240; Fax: 416-290-0238
general@itworldcanada.com
Circulation: 16,000 Frequency: 24 times a year
Michael Martin, Editor

Technologies for Worship Magazine
3891 Holborn Rd., Queensville, ON L0G 1R0
Tel: 905-473-9822; Fax: 905-473-9928
info@tfwm.com
Social Media:
twitter.com/tfwm
www.facebook.com/TechnologiesForWorshipMagazine
Circulation: 30,000 Frequency: bi-monthly
Shelagh Rogers, Founder
Kevin Rogers Cobus, Editor

Conventions & Meetings

Meeting Places
BIV Media Group, #500, 1155 West Pender St., Vancouver, BC V6E 2P4
Tel: 604-688-2398; Fax: 604-688-6058
kbutler@biv.com
Circulation: 13,000
Paul Harris, Editor
Gail Clark, Publisher

Meetings + Incentive Travel (M+IT)
Previous Name: Conventions Meetings Canada
Owned By: Business Information Group
80 Valleybrook Dr., Toronto, ON M3B 2S9
Tel: 416-442-5600; Fax: 416-764-1419
Social Media:
twitter.com/meetingscanada
www.facebook.com/MeetingsCanada
Circulation: 130,000
Stephen Dempsey, Publisher

Cosmetics

Cosmetics Magazine / Cosmetiques
Owned By: Rogers Publishing Ltd.
1 Mount Pleasant Rd., 8th Fl., Toronto, ON M4Y 2Y5
Tel: 416-764-1664; Fax: 416-764-1704
Social Media:
twitter.com/cosmeticsmag#
www.facebook.com/pages/Cosmetics-Magazine/280002595351473
Circulation: 10,691 (5,400 Cosmetiques) Frequency: 6 times a year; also Cosmetiques (4 fois par an; français; 1992)
James R. Hicks, Publisher, 416-764-1664, jim.hicks@cosmetics.rogers.com
Kristen Vinakmens, Editor, 416-764-1680, kristen.vinakmens@cosmetics.rogers.com

The Kit
Owned By: Toronto Star Newspapers Limited
#204, 1 Yonge St., Toronto, ON M5E 1E6
Tel: 416-945-8700
info@thekit.ca
Social Media: pinterest.com/thekit/pins/
twitter.com/thekit
www.facebook.com/TheKITmag
Frequency: Monthly
Giorgina Bigioni, Publisher

Credit

The Atlantic Co-operator: The Voice of the Co-operative Movement in Atlantic Canada
123 Halifax St., Moncton, NB E1C 8N5
Tel: 506-858-6617; Fax: 506-858-6615
editor@theatlanticco-operator.coop
Frequency: Bi-monthly
Published by Atlantic Co-operative Publishers Limited, The Atlantic Co-operator provides news & information about the co-operative movement in Atlantic Canada.

Culture, Current Events

Eighteen Bridges
Owned By: Venture Publishing Inc.
Canadian Literature Centre, 4-115 Humanities Centre, University of Alberta, Edmonton, AB T6G 2E5
ebmag@ualberta.ca
Social Media:
www.twitter.com/eighteenbridges
Curtis Gillespie, Editor

Hush
Vancouver, BC
editor@hushmagazine.ca
Social Media: www.youtube.com/user/HushMagazine
twitter.com/HUSHvancouver
www.facebo ok.com/HushVancouver
Barb Sligl, Editor

The Walrus
Owned By: Walrus Foundation
#101, 19 Duncan St., Toronto, ON M5H 3H1
Tel: 416-971-5004 Toll-Free: 866-236-0475
info@walrusmagazine.com
Social Media:
twitter.com/walrusmagazine
www.facebook.com/thewalrusmagazine
Circulation: 60,000 Frequency: 10 times a year
Shelley Ambrose, Executive Director & Publisher, 416-971-5004 x 236, shelley.ambrose@walrusmagazine.com

Dentistry

Canadian Journal of Dental Hygiene
Previous Name: Probe
c/o Canadian Dental Hygienists Assn., 96 Centrepointe Dr., Ottawa, ON K2G 6B1
Tel: 613-224-5515; Fax: 613-224-7283
Toll-Free: 800-267-5235
info@cdha.ca
Social Media:
twitter.com/theCDHA
www.facebook.com/theCDHA
Circulation: 11,400 Frequency: 6 times a year
Susan A. Ziebarth, Executive Director
Susanne Sunell, Scientific Editor

Denturism Canada - The Journal of Canadian Denturism / Denturologie Canada
Owned By: Craig Kelman & Associates Ltd.
2020 Portage Ave., 3rd Fl., Winnipeg, MB R3J 0K4
Tel: 204-985-9780; Fax: 204-985-9795
dacdenturist@bellnet.ca

Circulation: 1,909 Frequency: 4 times a year
Hussein Amery, Editor-in-Chief, ameryhk@telus.net
Cheryl Parisien, Managing Editor, cheryl@kelman.ca

Journal de l'Ordre des dentistes du Québec
Anciennement: Journal Dentaire du Québec
Ordre des dentistes du Québec, 625, boul René-Lévesque ouest, 15e étage, Montréal, QC H3B 1R2
Tél: 514-875-8511;Téléc: 514-875-9049
journal@odq.qc.ca
Tirage: 5500 Fréquence: 6 fois par an; French
Dr. Denis Forest, Rédacteur

Journal of the Canadian Dental Association / Journal de l'Association Dentaire Canadienne
1815 Alta Vista Dr., Ottawa, ON K1G 3Y6
Tel: 613-523-1770
reception@cda-adc.ca
Circulation: 19,600 Frequency: 11 times a year; English & French
Dr. John O'Keefe, Editor

Manitoba Dentist
Cutting Edge Communications, #2, 1248 Pembina Hwy., Winnipeg, MB
Tel: 204-669-2377; Fax: 204-669-2336
jparcells@cecommunications.ca
Circulation: 1,700 Frequency: Annually
Jamie Parcells, Publisher

Ontario Dentist Journal (ODA)
c/o Ontario Dentist Association, 4 New St., Toronto, ON M5R 1P6
Tel: 416-922-3900; Fax: 416-922-9005
info@oda.ca
Social Media:
www.facebook.com/pages/Canadian-Dental-Health/2034526896 6
Circulation: 7,000 Frequency: 10 times a year
Julia Kuipers, Managing Editor

Oral Health
Owned By: Business Information Group
80 Valleybrook Dr., Toronto, ON M3B 2S9
Tel: 416-510-6785; Fax: 416-510-5140
Toll-Free: 800-268-7742
Other information: Toll Free: U.S. 1-800-387-0273
Circulation: 17,200 Frequency: Monthly
Melissa Summerfield, Publisher, 416-510-6781, msummerfield@oralhealthjournal.com
Andrea M. Smith, Editorial Director, cwilson@oralhealthjournal.com

Directories & Almanacs

Almanach du Peuple
Détenteur: Malcolm Média
#213, 3100, boul de la Concorde Est, Laval, QC H7E 2B8
Tél: 450-665-0271
adv-pub.media@videotron.ca
Tirage: 125 000 Fréquence: Annuellement; français
Luc Lemay, Éditeur
Robert Ferland, Directeur, Marketing

Canadian Forces Base Kingston Official Directory
Owned By: Kingston Publications
18 St. Remy Place, Kingston, ON K7K 6C4
Tel: 613-549-8442; Fax: 613-389-7507
Circulation: 3,500 Frequency: Annually, March; English & French
Liza Nelson, Publisher, 613-549-8442 ext 132

Frasers
Previous Name: Frasers Canadian Trade Directory
Owned By: Business Information Group
80 Valleybrook Dr., Toronto, ON M3B 2S9
Tel: 416-442-5600; Fax: 416-510-5140
Toll-Free: 888-297-7195
info@canadianmanufacturing.com
Circulation: 6,000; 15,000 CD-Rom Frequency: Annually, March
Michael Ouellette, Editor, MOuellette@canadianmanufacturing.com

Sources
#201, 812A Bloor St. West, Toronto, ON M6G 1A5
Tel: 416-964-7799; Fax: 416-964-8763
sources@sources.ca
Circulation: 14,000 Frequency: 2 times a year
Ulli Diemer, Publisher

Drugs

L'actualité pharmaceutique
Détenteur: Éditions Rogers Media
1200, ave McGill College, 8e étage, Montréal, QC H3B 4G7
Tél: 514-843-2105;Téléc: 514-843-2183
Tirage: 8,046 Fréquence: 10 fois par an; français
Caroline Bélisle, Éditeur
Caroline Baril, Rédacteur

The Canadian Journal of Hospital Pharmacy / Le Journal canadien de la pharmacie hospitalière
The Cdn. Society of Hospital Pharmacists, #3, 30 Concourse Gate., Ottawa, ON K2E 7V7
Tel: 613-736-9733; Fax: 613-736-5660
cjhpedit@cshp.ca
Circulation: 3,200 Frequency: 7 times a year; English & French
Mary Ensom, Editor

Canadian Pharmaceutical Journal
1785 Alta Vista Dr., Ottawa, ON K1G 3Y6
Tel: 613-523-7877; Fax: 613-523-2332
Toll-Free: 800-917-9489
info@pharmacists.ca
Circulation: 18,076 Frequency: 6 times a year
Leesa D. Bruce, Publisher
Renée Dykeman, Managing Editor
Rosemary R. Killeenn, Editor

Le Pharmactuel
L'Association des pharmaciens des établissements de santé, #320, 4050, rue Molson, Montréal, QC H1VH3A 1T1
Tél: 514-286-0776;Téléc: 514-286-1081
info@apesquebec.org
Médias sociaux:
twitter.com/pharmactuel
www.facebook.com/pages/Pharmactuel/3799274 15393855
Tirage: 1 800 Fréquence: 5 fois par an
Julie Méthot, Rédactrice en chef, redaction@pharmactuel.com

Pharmacy Business
Owned By: Fulcrum Publishing
508 Lawrence Ave. West, North York, ON M6A 1A1
Tel: 416-504-0504; Fax: 416-256-3002
Toll-Free: 866-688-0504
Social Media:
twitter.com/Pharma_Biz
Serving the retail pharaceutical industry.
Jane Auster, Editor, jauster@fulcrum.ca

Pharmacy Practice
Owned By: Rogers Publishing Ltd.
1 Mount Pleasant Rd., Toronto, ON M4Y 2Y5
Tel: 416-764-3926; Fax: 416-764-3931
rosalind.stefanac@pharmacygroup.rogers.com
Circulation: 17,193 Frequency: 8 times a year
Vicki Wood, Editor
Jackie Quemby, Publisher

Québec Pharmacie
Détenteur: Rogers Publishing Ltd.
1200, av McGill College, 8e étage, Montréal, QC H3B 4G7
Tél: 514-843-2569;Téléc: 514-843-2183
Tirage: 8,025 Fréquence: 8 fois par an; français
Hélène Blanchette, Editor

Education

Agenda
c/o Ontario English Catholic Teachers' Association, #400, 65 St. Clair Ave. East, Toronto, ON M4T 2Y8
Tel: 416-925-2493; Fax: 416-925-7764
Toll-Free: 800-268-7230
a.oconnor@oecta.on.ca
Circulation: 46,000 Frequency: Sept.-June monthly (7 times during school year)
Aleda O'Connor, Director, Communications

The ATA Magazine
The Alberta Teachers' Association, Barnett House, 11010 - 142 St., Edmonton, AB T5N 2R1
Tel: 780-447-9400; Fax: 780-455-6481
Toll-Free: 800-232-7208
government@teachers.ab.ca
Circulation: 42,100 Frequency: 4 times a year
Timothy Johnston, Editor
Raymond Gariépy, Associate Editor

Canadian Association of University Teachers (CAUT Bulletin) ACPPU
2705 Queensview Dr., Ottawa, ON K2B 8K2
Tel: 613-820-2270; Fax: 613-820-2417
acppu@caut.ca
Social Media:
twitter.com/CAUT_ACPPU
www.facebook.com/CAUT.ACPPU
Circulation: 46,000 Frequency: 10 times a year
Greg Allain, President
James Turk, Executive Director, 613-820-2270, turk@caut.ca
Liza Duhaime, Managing Editor, 613-726-5197, duhaime@caut.ca

Education Forum
c/o Ontario Secondary School Teachers' Federation, 60 Mobile Dr., Toronto, ON M4A 2P3
Tel: 416-751-8300; Fax: 416-751-7079
Toll-Free: 800-267-7867
Circulation: 49,323 Frequency: 3 times a year
Renate Brandon, Advertising Director
Marianne Clayton, Assistant Editor
Janice Grant, Traffic Coordinator
Pierre Côté, Editor

Education Today
Ontario Public School Boards Assn., 439 University Ave. 18th Fl., Toronto, ON M5G 1Y8
Tel: 416-340-2540; Fax: 416-340-7571
webmaster@opsba.org
Circulation: 3,500 Frequency: 3 times a year
Catherine Watson, Editor, cwatson@opsba.org

Educational Digest
Owned By: Zanny Ltd.
11966 Woodbine Ave., Gormley, ON L0H 1G0
Tel: 905-887-5048; Fax: 905-887-0764
Circulation: 76,000 Frequency: Quarterly
Janet Gardiner, Publisher

ESL in Canada Directory
PO Box 75117, 20 Bloor St. East, Toronto, ON M4W 3T3
Tel: 416-608-4194; Fax: 416-513-0026
Frequency: 2 times a year
Ross McBride, Production Manager

Green Teacher
95 Robert St., Toronto, ON M5S 2K5
Tel: 416-960-1244; Fax: 416-925-3474
info@greenteacher.com
Social Media:
twitter.com/GreenTeacherMag
www.facebook.com/GreenTeacherMagazine
Circulation: 7,200 Frequency: Quarterly
Green Teacher magazine offers perspectives on the role of education in creating a sustainable future, practical articles and ready to use activities for various age levels, and reviews of dozens of new educational resources.
Tim Grant, Co-Editor
Gail Littlejohn, Co-Editor

The Manitoba Teacher
c/o The Manitoba Teachers' Society, McMaster House, 191 Harcourt St., Winnipeg, MB R3J 3H2
Tel: 204-888-7961; Fax: 204-831-0877
Toll-Free: 800-262-8803
Circulation: 17,500 Frequency: 7 pa (September; October / November; December; January / February; March; April / May; June)
The Manitoba Teachers' Society is the professional & collective bargaining representative for 15,000 educators in the province. The Manitoba Teacher is the society's newsmagazine.
George Stephenson, Publications Editor & Manager, Website
Matea Tuhtar, Contact, Advertising

Professionally Speaking / Pour parler profession
Ontario College of Teachers, 101 Bloor St. East, Toronto, ON M5S 0A2
Tel: 416-961-8800; Fax: 416-961-8822
Toll-Free: 888-534-2222
ps@oct.ca
Circulation: 218,570 Frequency: 4 times a year
Richard Lewko, Publisher
Philip Carter, Editor

Quebec Home & School News
Québec Federation of Home & School Associations, #560, 3285, boul Cavendish, Montréal, QC H4B 2L9
Tél: 514-481-5619;Téléc: 514-481-5610
Ligne sans frais: 888-808-5619
info@qfhsa.org
Médias sociaux:
twitter.com/QFHSA
www.facebook.com/QFHSA
Tirage: 7,600 distribution; 5,900 paid distribution Fréquence: 4 times a year
Notorized publications data as of Sept. 2005
Donna Norris, President
Helen Koeppe, Editor

Teach Magazine
#321, 1655 Dupont St., Toronto, ON M6P 3T1
info@teachmag.com
Circulation: 22,000 Frequency: 5 times a year
Wili Liberman, Publisher & Editor

University Affairs / Affaires universitaires
c/o Assn. of Universities & Colleges of Canada, #600, 350 Albert St., Ottawa, ON K1R 1B1
Tel: 613-563-1236; Fax: 613-563-9745
ua@aucc.ca
Circulation: 18,153 Frequency: 10 times a year; English & French
Christine Tausig Ford, Publisher
Peggy Berkowitz, Editor

Electrical Equipment & Electronics

Cabling Networking Systems (CNS)
Previous Name: Cabling Systems
Owned By: Business Information Group
80 Valleybrook Dr., Toronto, ON M3B 2S9
Tel: 416-510-5111 Toll-Free: 800-268-7742
Circulation: 10,313 Frequency: 6 times a year
Maureen Levy, Publisher, mlevy@cnsmagazine.com
Paul Barker, Editor, pbarker@cnsmagazine.com

Electrical Business
Owned By: Annex Publishing & Printing Inc.
PO Box 775, 222 Edward St., Aurora, ON L4G 1W5
Tel: 519-429-3966; Fax: 519-429-3094
Toll-Free: 800-265-2827
Social Media:
twitter.com/ebmag
Circulation: 18,000 Frequency: 10 times a year
John MacPherson, Publisher, jmacpherson@annexweb.com
Anthony Capkun, Editor, acapkun@annexweb.com

Electrical Line
Owned By: Pacific Media Publishing Inc.
Pacific Media Publishing Inc., 1785 Emerson Crt., North Vancouver, BC V7H 2Y6
Tel: 604-924-3661; Fax: 604-924-3662
Circulation: 20,000 Frequency: Bi-Monthly
Ken Buhr, Editor/Publisher

Électricité Québec
Anciennement: Le Maître Electricien
5925, boul Decarie, Montréal, QC H3W 3C9
Tél: 514-738-2184;Téléc: 514-738-2192
Ligne sans frais: 800-361-9061
info@cmeq.org
Tirage: 9 834 Fréquence: 6 fois par an; français
Hélène Rioux, Éditrice et rédactrice-en-chef

Electricity Today
Hurst Communications, #215, 1885 Clements Rd., Pickering, ON L1W 3V4
Tel: 905-686-1040; Fax: 905-686-1078
hq@electricityforum.com
Circulation: 23,000 Frequency: 8 times a year
Randolph Hurst, Publisher, rwh@rogers.com

EP&T
Owned By: Business Information Group
80 Valleybrook Dr., Toronto, ON M3B 2S9
Tel: 416-442-5600; Fax: 416-510-5134
info@ept.ca
Circulation: 24,000 Frequency: 8 times a year; also EP&T's Electrosource Product Reference Guide & Telephone Directory (annually, Jan.)
Robert Luton, Publisher
Stephen Law, Editor, 416-510-5208, slaw@ept.ca

Emergency Services

Canadian Paramedicine
Previous Name: Canadian Emergency News
PO Box 579, Drumheller, AB T0J 0Y0
Tel: 403-823-5969
cp@emsnews.com
Social Media:
twitter.com/#!/CdnParamedicine
www.facebook.com/CanadianParamedicine
Circulation: 4,000 Frequency: 6 times a year
Lyle Blumhagen, Publisher/Editor

Engineering

Aggregates & Roadbuilding Magazine
PO Box 530, 105 Donly Dr. South, Simcoe, ON N3Y 4N5
Tel: 519-429-3966; Fax: 519-429-3094
Toll-Free: 800-265-2827
Social Media:
twitter.com/RockToRoad
Circulation: 11,400 Frequency: 7 times a year
Scott Jamieson, Publisher / Editor, sjamieson@annexweb.com

Annuaire Téléphonique de la Construction du Québec
CP 590, 22, rue St-Charles, Sainte-Thérèse, QC J7E 2A4
Tél: 450-437-1600;Téléc: 450-437-0723
optilog@optilog.com
Tirage: 7 200 Fréquence: Annuellement; français
Michel Vaudrin, Éditeur & Rédacteur

Canadian Consulting Engineer
Owned By: Business Information Group
80 Valleybrook Dr., Toronto, ON M3B 2S9
Tel: 416-510-5119; Fax: 416-510-5134
Toll-Free: 800-268-7742
Social Media:
twitter.com/beata_o
Circulation: 8,476 Frequency: 7 times a year
Covers all engineering disiplines and all geographical areas.
Maureen Levy, Publisher, 416-510-5111, mlevy@ccemag.com
Bronwen Parsons, Editor, bparsons@ccemag.com

Construction Alberta News
PO Box 48109, St Albert, AB T8N 5B3
Tel: 780-460-8004; Fax: 866-860-1639
admin@conaltanews.com
Frequency: 2 times a year

Engineering Dimensions
#101, 40 Sheppard Ave. West, Toronto, ON M2N 6K9
Tel: 416-224-1100; Fax: 416-224-8168
Toll-Free: 800-339-3716
Other information: Toll Free Fax: 1-800-268-0496
Circulation: 68,000 Frequency: Bi-Monthly
Connie Mucklestone, Publisher
Nicole Axworthy, Editor, naxworthy@peo.on.ca

Geomatica
Previous Name: CISM Journal
Canadian Institute of Geomatics, #100, 900 Dynes Rd., Ottawa, ON K2C 3L6
Tel: 613-224-9851; Fax: 613-224-9577
editgeo@magma.ca
Social Media:
www.linkedin.com/groups?gid=1095187&trk=myg_ugrp_ovr
Circulation: 910 Frequency: 4 times a year; English & French
Geomatica is dedicated to the dissemination of information on technical advances in the geomatics sciences.
Jean Thie, Editor, 819 459-3719, jean.thie@ecoinformatics.com

Innovation: Journal of the Association of Professional Engineers & Geoscientists of BC
c/o Association of Professional Engineers & Geoscientists of BC, #200, 4010 Regent St., Burnaby, BC V5C 6N2
Tel: 604-430-8035; Fax: 604-430-8085
Toll-Free: 888-430-8035
apeginfo@apeg.bc.ca
Circulation: 25,712 Frequency: Bi-monthly
Information is published that is of interest to British Columbia's engineering & geoscience professionals, industry & government representatives, & members of educational institutions.
Melinda Lau, Managing Editor, mlau@apeg.bc.ca
Gillian Cobban, Contact, Advertising, advertising@apeg.bc.ca

The Ontario Technologist
#404, 10 Four Seasons Place, Toronto, ON M9B 2C4
Tel: 905-727-0077; Fax: 905-727-0017
arush@clbmedia.ca
Social Media:
twitter.com/OACETT
www.facebook.com/OACETT
Circulation: 21,240 Frequency: 6 times a year
Publication of the Ontario Association of Certified Engineering Technicians and Technologists.
Angela Rush, Sales Representative

The PEG
APEGGA, Scotia One, #1500, 10060 Jasper Ave. NW, Edmonton, AB T5J 4A2
Tel: 780-426-3990; Fax: 780-425-1877
Toll-Free: 800-661-7020
glee@apega.ca
Circulation: 47,000 Frequency: 5 times a year
Official, legislated publication of APEGA.
George Lee, Managing Editor

PLAN
Ordre des ingenieurs du Québec, Gare Windsor, #350, 1100, rue de la Gauchetière ouest, Montréal, QC H3B 2S2
Tél: 514-845-6141;Téléc: 514-845-1833
Ligne sans frais: 800-461-6141
Tirage: 49 000 Fréquence: 9 fois par an; français
Daniel Boismenu, Editeur
Geneviève Terreault, Coordonatrice
France Cadieux, Publicité

Plan Canada
Canadian Institute of Planners, #801, 116 Albert St., Ottawa, ON K1P 5G3
Tel: 613-237-7526; Fax: 613-237-7045
Toll-Free: 800-207-2138
general@cip-icu.ca
Circulation: 4,715 Frequency: Quarterly
Michele Garneau, Publisher
Mark Seasons, Chair, Editorial Board

Publiquip Inc.
Anciennement: Publiquip/Roucam
490, Gilles Villeneuve, Berthierville, QC J0C 1A0
Tél: 450-836-3666 Ligne sans frais: 800-361-5295
services_clients@publiquip.com
Tirage: 43 506 Fréquence: Mensuel; français
Gilles Chevigny, Éditeur

Supply Post
#105, 26730 - 56th Ave., Langley, BC V4W 3X5
Tel: 604-607-5577; Fax: 604-607-0533
Toll-Free: 800-663-4802
editorial@supplypost.com
Social Media:
twitter.com/supplypost
www.facebook.com/pages/Supply-Post-Newspaper/173647662651
Circulation: 16,500+ Frequency: 12 pa
The publication is of interest to persons involved in the construction equipment, trucking, forestry, mining, oil & gas, & marine industries.
Jeff Watson, Manager, jeff.watson@supplypost.com
Tanya Lee, Contact, Editorial Contributions & Classified Ad Sales, tanya.lee@supplypost.com
Christine Mazur, Contact, Subscriptions, circulation@postpublishers.com
Gary Mazur, Contact, Sales & IT, gary.mazur@supplypost.com
Debra Watson, Contact, Accounts & Billing, debra.watson@postpublishers.com

Environment & Nature

Ecoforestry
Previous Name: International Journal of Ecoforestry
Ecoforestry Institute Society, PO Box 5070 B, Victoria, BC V8R 6N3
Tel: 250-595-0655
journal@ecoforestry.ca
Frequency: quarterly
Journal looks at issues relating to the forestry industry using a low-impact approach to forest management. Its goal is to increase public awareness of ecoforestry by working with community organizations, offering workshops to the public and providing information.

ehscompliance.ca
Previous Name: Environmental Compliance Report & the Occupational Health & Safety
Owned By: Business Information Group
80 Valleybrook Dr., Toronto, ON M3B 2S9
Tel: 416-422-2122; Fax: 416-510-5133
Toll-Free: 800-668-2374
customercare@bizinfogroup.ca
Frequency: Monthly
A monthly national newsletter that examines the developments and amendments in Canadian environmental law. It gives its readers commentary on new legislation, proposed environmental

bills, changing environmental legislation, and all other issues affecting enviromental law policies in Canada.
Lidia Lubka, Editor/Publisher, llubka@ecolog.com

EnviroLine
PO Box 77042 Chinatown, 4905 - 23 Ave. NW, Calgary, AB T2G 5J8
Tel: 403-263-3272; Fax: 403-263-3280
enviroline@shaw.ca
Circulation: 500 Frequency: 20 times a year
Provides Western Canadian resource industries with reviews of important and up-to-date environmental issues.
Mark Lowey, Publisher & Editor

Environmental Reviews
Owned By: NRC Research Press
NRC Research Press, Bldg. M-55, 1200 Montreal Rd., Ottawa, ON K1A 0R6
Tel: 613-990-7873; Fax: 613-952-7656
pubs@nrcresearchpress.com
Circulation: 300 Frequency: Annually
Publication presents reviews on a range of environmental issues and topics, emphasizing the effects humans have on natural and manmade ecosystems. Topics investigated in this publication include climate change, air and marine pollution, erosion and agroforestry.
John P. Smol, Editor

Recycling Product News
Owned By: Baum Publications Ltd.
Baum Publications Ltd., #201, 2323 Boundary Rd., Vancouver, BC V5M 4V8
Tel: 604-291-9900; Fax: 604-291-1906
ebaum@baumpub.com
Circulation: 18,000 Frequency: 8 times a year
Publication focuses on products, technologies services and industry news in recycling and waste management, ranging from composting to scrap metal.
Engelbert J. Baum, Publisher
Keith Barker, Editor, kbarker@baumpub.com

Vecteur Environnement
#220, 911, rue Jean-Talon est, Montréal, QC H2R 1V5
Tél: 514-270-7110;Téléc: 514-270-7154
vecteur@reseau-environnement.com
Tirage: 4 000 Fréquence: 5 fois par an; français
Revue de l'industrie, des sciences et techniques de l'environnement du Québec; publiée par RÉSEAU environnement
Martine Boivin, Rédactrice-en-chef

Fashion

Zink
#2, 94, Ste-Therese, Montréal, QC H2Y 3V5
Tel: 514-759-7702
zinknews@zinkmediagroup.com
Social Media: www.youtube.com/user/ZinkMag
twitter.com/ZINKMagazine
www.facebook.com/ZinkMagazine
Frequency: Monthly
Sheriff J. Ishak, Editor-in-Chief/Publisher/CEO

Fire Protection

Atlantic Firefighter
Hilden Publishing Ltd., #456, 6 - 295 Queen St. East, Brampton, NS L6W 4S6
Toll-Free: 800-555-2514
info@atlanticfirefighter.ca
Circulation: 6,200 Frequency: 11 times a year
Jennifer Brown, Publisher & Editor

Canadian Firefighter & EMS Quarterly
Previous Name: EMS Quarterly
PO Box 530, 105 Donly Dr. South, Simcoe, ON N3Y 4N5
Tel: 519-429-3966; Fax: 519-429-3094
Toll-Free: 800-265-2827
Social Media:
twitter.com/fireincanada
www.facebook.com/firefightingincanada
Circulation: 7,500 Frequency: 4 times a year
Martin McAnulty, Publisher
Laura King, Editor, 289-259-8077, lking@annexweb.com

Fire Fighting in Canada
Owned By: Annex Publishing & Printing Inc.
PO Box 530, 105 Donly Dr. South, Simcoe, ON N3Y 4N5
Tel: 519-429-3966; Fax: 519-429-3094
Toll-Free: 800-265-2827
fire@annexweb.com
Circulation: 5,200 Frequency: 8 times a year
Educating and informing fire chiefs, senior officers and firefighters in municipal, industrial and military fire departments across the country.
Laura King, Editor, 289-259-8077, lking@annexweb.com
Martin J. McAaulty, Publisher

Fisheries

Aquaculture North America
Previous Name: Northern Aquaculture
Owned By: Capamara Communications
4623 William Head Rd., Victoria, BC V9J 1R3
Tel: 250-474-3982; Fax: 250-478-3979
info@capamara.com
Circulation: 3,600 Frequency: 12 times a year
Peter Chettleburgh, Publisher

Atlantic Fisherman
162 Trider Cres., Dartmouth, NS B3B 1R6
Tel: 902-422-4990; Fax: 902-422-4278
editorial@advocatemediainc.com
Other information: E-mail, classified & circulation:
atlfisherman@advocatemediainc.com
Frequency: Monthly
Atlantic Fisherman serves the commercial fishing industry across the Maritimes & in Newfoundland & Labrador.
Leith Orr, Publisher, leith@advocatemediainc.com
Suzanne Rent, Editor, leith@advocatemediainc.com
James Croke, Advertising Executive, james@advocatemediainc.com
Deryck Richardson, Advertising Executive, deryck@advocatemediainc.com

The Sou'Wester
Owned By: Trancontinental Media Inc.
2 Second St., Yarmouth, NS B5A 4B1
Tel: 902-681-2121; Fax: 902-681-0830
info@souwester.ca
Circulation: 10,500 Frequency: 12 times a year
Tina Comeau, Editor

Floor Coverings

Coverings
Owned By: W.I. Media
PO Box 84 Cheltenham, Caledon, ON L7C 3L7
Tel: 647-290-3673; Fax: 905-998-0095
Circulation: 7,100 Frequency: 8 times a year
Kerry Knudsen, Publisher/Editor, 647-274-0507, Fax: 905-998-0095

Surface
2105, rue de Salaberry, St-Bruno-de-Montarville, QC J3V 4N7
Tél: 450-441-4243;Téléc: 450-441-6997
Tirage: 5 500 Fréquence: 5 fois par an; français
Marcel Soury, Rédacteur-en-chef

Florists

Canadian Florist
Previous Name: Canadian Florist, Greenhouse & Nursery
Owned By: Annex Publishing & Printing Inc.
PO Box 530, 105 Donly Dr. South, Simcoe, ON N3Y 4N5
Tel: 519-429-3966; Fax: 519-429-3094
Toll-Free: 800-265-2827
dmccarthy@annexweb.com
Social Media:
twitter.com/canadianflorist
www.facebook.com/CanadianFlorist
Circulation: 5,394 Frequency: 8 times per year
Brandi Cowen, Editor, bcowen@annexweb.com
Scott Jamieson, Publisher, sjamieson@annexweb.com

Food & Beverage

L'Actualité Alimentaire
Anciennement: Le Monde Alimentaire
Détenteur: Édikom inc.
615, Notre-Dame, Saint-Lambert, QC J4P 2K8
Tél: 514-990-6967
Tirage: 5 000
Martin Lemire, Vice-président, développement des affaires, mlemire@edikom.ca

Canadian Pizza Magazine
Owned By: Annex Publishing & Printing Inc.
PO Box 530, 105 Donly Dr. South, Simcoe, ON N3Y 4N5
Tel: 519-429-3966; Fax: 519-429-3094
Toll-Free: 800-265-2827
Social Media:
twitter.com/cdnpizzamag
Circulation: 9,500 Frequency: 8 times a year
Martin McAnulty, Publisher, mmcanulty@annexweb.com
Laura Aiken, Editor, laiken@annexweb.com

Food in Canada
Owned By: Business Information Group
80 Valleybrook Dr., Toronto, ON M3B 2S9
Tel: 416-442-5600; Fax: 416-510-5140
Toll-Free: 888-297-7195
info@canadianmanufacturing.com
Circulation: 9,200 Frequency: 9 times a year
Ingrid Eilbracht, Publisher, 416-510-6775, IEilbracht@foodincanada.com

Grocery Business
PO Box 4085, 390 Queens Quay West, Toronto, ON M5V 3A6
Tel: 416-817-5278
DanBordun@grocerybusiness.ca
Social Media:
twitter.com/GroceryBusiness
Karen Jones, Publisher/Editor, 416-561-4744, KarenJames@grocerybusiness.ca
Kevin Smith, Publisher/Editor, 416-569-5005, KevinSmith@grocerybusiness.ca

Independent Convenience News (ICN)
Owned By: Fulcrum Publishing Inc.
#201, 508 Lawrence Ave. West, Toronto, ON M6A 1A1
Tel: 416-504-0504 Toll-Free: 866-688-0504

Le Must
Détenteur: Édikom inc.
Édikom inc., 615, av Notre-Dame, Saint-Lambert, QC J4P 2K8
Tél: 514-990-6967 Ligne sans frais: 877-875-6878
info@edikom.ca
Médias sociaux:
twitter.com/LEmustWeb
www.facebook.com/LEmustalimentaire
Martin Lemire, Vice-président, développement des affaires, mlemire@edikom.ca

Your Convenience Manager (YCM)
Owned By: Fulcrum Publishing Inc.
#201, 508 Lawrence Ave. West, Toronto, ON M6A 1A1
Tel: 416-504-0504 Toll-Free: 866-688-0504

Your Foodservice Manager
Owned By: Fulcrum Publishing Inc.
#201, 508 Lawrence Ave. West, Toronto, ON M6A 1A1
Tel: 416-504-0504 Toll-Free: 866-688-0504
yfmfeedback@fulcrum.ca
Circulation: 26,000
Jane Auster, Editor

Footwear

Canadian Footwear Journal
Previous Name: Footwear Forum
Owned By: Shoetrades Publications
Tel: 514-457-8787; Fax: 514-457-5832
cfj@shoetrades.com
Circulation: 7,000 Frequency: 8 times a year; plus Retail Buyers' Guide (annual), Shoemaking Buyers' Guide (annual)
Shirley Boake, Associate Publisher
Barbara McLeish, Editor

Forest & Lumber Industries

Canadian Forest Industries
Owned By: Annex Publishing & Printing Inc.
PO Box 530, 105 Donly Dr. South, Simcoe, ON N3Y 4N5
Tel: 519-429-3966; Fax: 519-429-3094
Toll-Free: 800-265-2827
jcft@qc.aira.com
Circulation: 14,600 Frequency: Bi-monthly
Scott Jamieson, Publisher, sjamieson@annexweb.com
John Tenpenny, Editor, 905-713-4351, jtenpenny@annexweb.com

Canadian Wood Products
Owned By: Annex Business Media
PO Box 530, 105 Doly Dr. South, Simcoe, ON N3Y 4K5
; Fax: 519-429-3094
Toll-Free: 888-599-2228
subscribe@woodbusiness.ca
Circulation: 7,340 Frequency: 6 times a year
Scott Jamieson, Publisher, sjamieson@annexweb.com
John Tenpenny, Editor, jtenpenny@annexweb.com

Directory of Ontario Home Improvement Retailers & Their Suppliers
Previous Name: Directory of Ontario Lumber & Building Materials Retailers, Buyers' Gu
Lumber & Building Materials Association of Ontario (LBMAO), #27, 5155 Spectrum Way, Mississauga, ON L4W 5A1
Tel: 905-625-1084; Fax: 905-625-3006
Toll-Free: 888-365-2626
jmoquin@lbmao.on.ca
Social Media:
twitter.com/LBMAO
www.facebook.com/lbmao
Frequency: Annually, October

The Forestry Chronicle
c/o The Canadian Ecology Centre, PO Box 99, 6905 Hwy. 17 West, Mattawa, ON P0H 1V0
Tel: 705-744-1715; Fax: 705-744-1716
admin@cif-ifc.org
Circulation: 3,000 Frequency: Bi-Monthly
A professional and scientific forestry journal.
Roxanne M. Comeau, Publisher

Logging & Sawmilling Journal
211 East 1st St., North Vancouver, BC V7L 1B4
Tel: 604-990-9970; Fax: 604-990-9971
stanhope@forestnet.com
Social Media:
www.facebook.com/group.php?gid=108109979252130
Circulation: 13,000+ Frequency: 7 pa
The journal is free to forestry related businesses. Information is published about forest management, logging, sawmilling, transportation, road & bridge construction, & wood manufacturing.

Madison's Canadian Lumber Directory
Owned By: KetaDesign Productions Inc.
PO Box 2486, #209, 980 West 1st St., Vancouver, BC V6B 3W7
Tel: 604-984-6838
madrep@direct.ca
Social Media:
twitter.com/KetaK
Circulation: 1,200 Frequency: Annually, Spring
Kéta Kosman, Editor

Mid-Canada Forestry & Mining
Previous Name: Mid-Canada Woodlands; Central Woodlands
Owned By: Craig Kelman & Associates Ltd.
2020 Portage Ave., 3rd Fl., Winnipeg, MB R3J 0K4
Tel: 204-985-9780; Fax: 204-985-9795
Circulation: 4,500 Frequency: 4 times a year
Terry Ross, Editor, terry@kelman.ca

Le Monde forestier
Anciennement: Le Coopérateur forestier
Détenteur: Les Editions forestières
#203, 1175, av Lavigerie, Québec, QC G1V 4P1
Tél: 418-877-4583;Téléc: 418-877-6449
Médias sociaux:
twitter.com/MondeForestier
www.facebook.com/LeMondeForestier
Tirage: 15 000 Fréquence: 10 fois par an; français
Guy Lavoie, Directeur général, direction@lemondeforestier.ca
Roger Robitaille, Directeur des ventes, roger@lemondeforestier.ca

Opérations forestières et de scierie
Détenteur: Annex Publishing & Printing Inc.
CP 530, 105 Donly Dr. South, Simcoe, ON N3Y 4N5
Tél: 519-429-3966;Téléc: 519-429-3094
Ligne sans frais: 800-265-2827
info@forestcommunications.com
Tirage: 5 436 Fréquence: 4 fois par an; français
Mariève Paradis, Rédacteur, mparadis@annexweb.com

Yardstick
Owned By: Naylor (Canada) Inc.
c/o Naylor (Canada) Inc., #300, 1630 Ness Ave., Winnipeg, MB R3J 3X1
Tel: 204-975-0434; Fax: 204-949-9092
Toll-Free: 800-665-2456
wrla@naylor.com
Circulation: 1,669 Frequency: 6 times a year; also WRLA Directory & Buyers' Guide (annually, Jan.)
Jonah O'Neill, Editor

Funeral Service

The Canadian Funeral Director Magazine
HPL Publishers Ltd., 178 McQuay Blvd., Whitby, ON L1P 1L5
Tel: 905-666-8011
info@thefuneralmagazine.com
Frequency: Monthly
Scott Hillier, Publisher & Editor, scott@thefuneralmagazine.com

Canadian Funeral News
#1025, 101 - 6th Ave. SW, Calgary, AB T2P 3P4
Tel: 403-264-3270; Fax: 403-264-3276
Toll-Free: 800-465-0322
info@otcommunications.com
Frequency: 12 pa
The journal provides news, articles, profiles, & columns for funeral service professionals throughout Canada.
Pat Ottmann, Publisher, pat@businessincalgary.com
Tim Ottmann, Associate Publisher, tim@businessincalgary.com
Lisa Johnston, Editor, isjoh@telus.net
Kenji Doshida, Director, Art, kenji@businessincalgary.com
Ena Kazic, Executive, Sales, ena@otcommunications.com

Network
#1025, 101 - 6th Ave. SW, Calgary, AB T2P 3P4
Tel: 403-264-3270; Fax: 403-264-3276
Toll-Free: 800-465-0322
info@otcommunications.com
Frequency: 6 pa
The magazine covers topics such as cemetery management, cremation, & monument designing & building.
Pat Ottmann, Publisher, pat@businessincalgary.com
Tim Ottman, Associate Publisher, tim@businessincalgary.com
Lisa Johnston, Editor, lisjoh@telus.net
Kenji Doshida, Director, Art, kenji@businessincalgary.com
Ena Kazic, Executive, Sales, ena@otcommunications.com

Fur Trade

Canadian Trapper
32 Willoughby Dr., St Albert, AB T8N 3R3
Tel: 780-459-4734; Fax: 780-459-4731
Frequency: 6 pa
Published by Coyote Communications Inc., the magazine offers trapper education & news about the Canadian fur industry.
Becky McIntosh, Publisher & Editor

Gardening & Garden Equipment

Canadian Garden Centre & Nursery
Owned By: Annex Publishing & Printing Inc.
PO Box 530, 105 Donly Dr. South, Simcoe, ON N3Y 4N5
Tel: 519-429-3966; Fax: 519-429-3094
Toll-Free: 800-265-2827
Circulation: 4,000 Frequency: 5 times a year
Brandi Cowen, Editor, bcowen@annexweb.com
Scott Jamieson, Publisher, sjamieson@annexweb.com

Greenhouse Canada
Owned By: Annex Publishing & Printing Inc.
PO Box 530, 105 Donly Dr. South, Simcoe, ON N3Y 4N5
Tel: 519-429-3966; Fax: 519-429-3094
Toll-Free: 800-265-2827
greenhouse@annexweb.com
Circulation: 5,500 Frequency: Monthly
Dave Harrison, Editor

Gifts

CGTA Retail News
Canadian Gift & Tableware Association, 42 Voyager Ct. South, Toronto, ON M9W 5M7
Tel: 416-679-0170; Fax: 416-679-1868
Toll-Free: 800-611-6100
retailnews@cgta.org
Social Media:
twitter.com/RetailNewsMag
www.facebook.com/RetailNewsMagazine
Circulation: 16,529 Frequency: bi-monthly
Tom Foran, Publisher, tforan@cgta.org
Erica Kirkland, Editor, erica@cgta.org

Gifts & Tablewares
Owned By: Business Information Group
80 Valleybrook Dr., Toronto, ON M3B 2S9
Tel: 416-510-6870; Fax: 416-510-5134
Toll-Free: 800-268-7742
Social Media: www.youtube.com/gtwebtveditor
Circulation: 15,010 Frequency: 7 times a year
Stephen Dempsey, Publisher, 416-510-6870, sdempsey@bizinfogroup.ca
Lori Smith, Editor, 416-442-5600 x 3238, lsmith@gifts-and-tablewares.com

Glass

Glass Canada
Owned By: Annex Publishing & Printing Inc.
PO Box 530, 105 Donly Dr. South, Simcoe, ON N3Y 4N5
Tel: 519-429-3966; Fax: 519-429-3094
Toll-Free: 800-265-2827
ais@aiscommunications.net
Circulation: 5,800 Frequency: 6 times a year
Chris Skalkos, Editor
Peter Phillips, Publisher

Government

Government Purchasing Guide
Kenilworth Media Inc., #710, 15 Wertheim Ct., Richmond Hill, ON L4B 3H7
Tel: 905-771-7333; Fax: 905-771-7336
Toll-Free: 800-409-8688
sales@gpgmag.ca
Circulation: 10,220 Frequency: 6 times a year
Ellen Kral, Publisher
Cora Golden, Director, Sales
Blair Adams, Editorial Director

Municipal Redbook
Owned By: Reed Construction Data
c/o Reed Construction Data, #101 - 4299 Canada Way, Burnaby, ON V5G 1H3
Tel: 604-433-8164; Fax: 604-433-9549
Toll-Free: 888-878-2121
Circulation: 2,000 Frequency: Annually

Municipal World
42860 Sparta Line, Union, ON N0L 2L0
Tel: 519-633-0031; Fax: 519-633-1001
mwadmin@municipalworld.com
Social Media:
twitter.com/Municipaljobs
www.facebook.com/MunicipalWorld
Circulation: 8,000 Frequency: Monthly
Susan Gardner, Executive Editor
Nick Smith, Contact, nick@municipalworld.com

Optimum Online: The Journal of Public Sector Management
The Summit Group, #100, 263 Holmwood Ave., Ottawa, ON K1S 2P8
Tel: 613-688-0763; Fax: 613-688-0767
Circulation: 10,000
Gilles Paquet, Editor

Parliamentary Names & Numbers
Sources, #201, 812A Bloor St. West, Toronto, ON M6G 1L9
Tel: 416-964-7799; Fax: 416-964-8763
sources@sources.ca
Circulation: 500 Frequency: 2 times a year
Ulli Diemer, Publisher

Urba
Union des municipalitiés de Québec, #680, 680, rue Sherbrooke ouest, Montréal, QC H3A 2M7
Tél: 514-282-7700;Téléc: 514-282-8893
Médias sociaux:
twitter.com/UMQuebec
Tirage: 6 600 Fréquence: 6 fois par an; français
Laurent Paul Ménard, Rédacteur

Graphic Arts

Applied Arts
Previous Name: Electronic Link
#411, 18 Wynford Dr., Toronto, ON M3C 3S2
Tel: 416-510-0909; Fax: 416-510-0913
art@appliedartsmag.com
Circulation: 12,000 Frequency: 6 times a year
Roberta Heckhausen, Publisher, rosetta@appliedartsmag.com
Peter Giffen, Editor, editor@appliedartsmag.com

The Graphic Exchange
Brill Communications Inc., 125 John St., Toronto, ON M5V 2E2
Tel: 416-533-6425
mail@gxo.com
Circulation: 13,394 Frequency: 6 times a year
Dan Brill, Publisher & Editor

Uppercase
#204, 100 - 7th Ave. SW, Calgary, AB T2P 0W4
Tel: 403-283-5318
Social Media: www.linkedin.com/in/janinevangool
twitter.com/uppercasemag
Janine Vangool, Publisher/Editor/Designer, janine@uppercasemagazine.com

Grocery Trade

L'Alimentation
7063, rue Saint-Denis, Montréal, QC H2S 2S5
Tél: 514-271-6922;Téléc: 514-271-1308
dbeaudin@l-alimentation.com
Tirage: 16,300 Fréquence: 10 fois par an; français
Diane Beaudin, Éditrice, dbeaudin@l-alimentation.com

Canadian Grocer
Owned By: Rogers Publishing Ltd.
1 Mount Pleasant Rd., Toronto, ON M4Y 2Y5
; Fax: 416-764-1523
Toll-Free: 800-268-9119
Circulation: 16,905 Frequency: 10 times a year
Jennifer Litterick, Publisher, 416-764-1665, jennifer.litterick@canadiangrocer.rogers
Rob Gerlsbeck, Editor, 416-764-1679, rob.gerlsbeck@canadiangrocer.rogers.com

Western Grocer
Owned By: Mercury Publications Ltd.
1740 Wellington Ave., Winnipeg, MB R3H 0E8
Tel: 204-954-2085; Fax: 204-954-2057
Toll-Free: 800-337-6372
mp@mercury.mb.ca
Circulation: 16,005 Frequency: 6 times a year
Robin Bradley, Associate Publisher/Sales Manager, robin@mercury.mb.ca

Hardware Trade

Hardware Merchandising
Owned By: Business Information Group
80 Valleybrook Dr., Toronto, ON M3B 2S9
Tel: 416-442-5600; Fax: 416-510-5134
Toll-Free: 800-268-7742
Social Media:
twitter.com/HardwareMagCa
Circulation: 14,881 Frequency: 6 times a year
Serves the home improvement retailing industry.
Stephen Dempsey, Publisher, 416-510-6780, Fax: 416-510-5140, SDempsey@bizinfogroup.ca
Lori Smith, Editor, lsmith@hardwaremagazine.ca

Home Improvement Retailing
Owned By: Powershift Communications Inc.
Powershift Communications Inc., #501, 245 Fairview Mall Dr., Toronto, ON M2J 4T1
Tel: 416-494-1066; Fax: 416-494-2536
info@powershift.ca
Circulation: 15,500 Frequency: 6 times a year
Dante Piccinin, Publisher, homeimprovement@rogers.com

Quart de Rond
Assn. des détaillants de matériaux de construction du Québec, #200, 476, rue Jean-Neveu, Longueuil, QC J4G 1N8
Tél: 450-646-5842;Téléc: 450-646-6171
information@aqmat.org
Tirage: 3 200 Fréquence: 8 fois par an; français

Health & Medical

L'Actualité Médicale
Détenteur: Éditions Rogers Media
1200, ave McGill College, 8e étage, Montréal, QC H3B 4G7
Tél: 514-843-5141;Téléc: 514-843-2183
Tirage: 16,626 Fréquence: 23 fois par an; français
Catherine Choquette, Rédactrice

The Alberta Doctors' Digest
Alberta Medical Association, 12230 - 106 Ave. NW, Edmonton, AB T5N 3Z1
Tel: 780-482-2626; Fax: 780-482-5445
Toll-Free: 800-270-9680
amamail@albertadoctors.org
Social Media:
twitter.com/Albertadoctors
Circulation: 8,300 Frequency: Bi-Monthly
Dr. Dennis W. Jirsch, Editor

British Columbia Medical Journal
c/o BC Medical Association, #115, 1665 West Broadway, Vancouver, BC V6J 5A4
Tel: 604-638-2815; Fax: 604-638-2917
Toll-Free: 800-972-2262
journal@bcma.bc.ca
Circulation: 10,500 Frequency: 10 times a year
Jay Draper, Managing Editor M.D., JDraper@bcma.bc.ca

Canadian Association of Radiologists Journal (CARJ/JACR) / Journal l'assn canadienne des radiologistes
Owned By: Canadian Medical Association
Department of Radiology, HHSC - MUMC Site, 1200 Main St. West, Hamilton, ON L8N 3Z5
; Fax: 905-521-1390
JournalsOnlineSupport-usa@elsevier.com
Circulation: 1,800 Frequency: 5 times a year; English & French
Emphasizes medical education and continuing professional development fo r radiologists
Dr. Craig Coblentz, Editor-in-chief

Canadian Chiropractor
Owned By: Annex Publishing & Printing Inc.
PO Box 530, 105 Donly Dr. South, Simcoe, ON N3Y 4N5
Tel: 519-429-3966; Fax: 519-429-3094
Toll-Free: 800-265-2827
Circulation: 5,800 Frequency: 8 times a year
Maria DiDanieli, Editor, mdidanieli@annexweb.com
Martin McAnulty, Publisher, mmcanulty@annexweb.com

Canadian Family Physician
College of Family Physicians of Canada, 2630 Skymark Ave., Mississauga, ON L4W 5A4
Tel: 905-629-0900; Fax: 905-629-0893
Toll-Free: 800-387-6197
CFPmedia@cfpc.ca
Circulation: 35,000 Frequency: Monthly
Kathryn Harrington, Managing Editor

Canadian Geriatrics Journal
Previous Name: Geriatrics Today: Journal of Canadian Geriatrics Society
The Canadian Geriatrics Society, #6, 20 Crown Steel Dr., Markham, ON L3R 9X9
Tel: 905-415-9161; Fax: 905-415-0071
Toll-Free: 866-247-0086
Circulation: 15,500 Frequency: 4 times a year
John D. Birkby, Publisher

Canadian Health & Lifestyle
Owned By: Rogers Publishing Ltd.
1 Mount Pleasant Rd., 7th Fl., Toronto, ON M4Y 2Y5
Tel: 416-764-1888; Fax: 416-764-1493
Social Media:
www.facebook.com/canadianhealthandlifestyle
Circulation: 394,807 Frequency: Quarterly
Barbara Goodman, Editor-in-Chief, editor@healthandlifestyle.rogers.com
Angela Jones, Publisher, angela.jones@rci.rogers.com

Canadian Healthcare Manager
Owned By: Rogers Publishing Ltd.
1 Mount Pleasant Rd., Toronto, ON M4Y 2Y5
Tel: 416-764-2000; Fax: 416-764-3930
Circulation: 11,400 Frequency: 4 times a year
Simon Hally, Publisher & Editor
Alison Webb, Publisher

Canadian Healthcare Technology
#207, 1118 Centre St., Thornhill, ON L4J 7R9
Tel: 905-709-2330; Fax: 905-709-2258
info2@canhealth.com
Circulation: 12,715 Frequency: 8 times a year
Jerry Zeidenberg, Publisher

Canadian Journal of Anesthesia / Journal Canadien d'Anesthésie
c/o Canadian Anesthesiologists' Society, #208, 1 Eglinton Ave. East, Toronto, ON M4P 3A1
Tel: 416-480-0602; Fax: 416-480-0320
cja_office@cas.ca
Social Media:
www.twitter.com/CASUpdate
Circulation: 5,000 Frequency: Monthly
Dr. Donald R. Miller, Editor
Carolyn Gillis, Associate Editor

Canadian Journal of Cardiology
Owned By: Elsevier Inc.
Canadian Cardiovascular Society, #1403, 222 Queen St., Toronto, ON K1P 5V9
Tel: 613-569-3407; Fax: 613-569-6574
Toll-Free: 877-569-3407
Circulation: 15,500 Frequency: 14 times a year
The official journal of the Canadian Cardiovascular Society (CCS).
Dr. Stanley Nattel, Editor, stanley.nattel@icm-mhi.org
Jane Grochowski, Publisher, j.grochowski@elsevier.com

Canadian Journal of Continuing Medical Education (CME)
Owned By: STA Communications Inc.
6500 Trans-Canada Hwy., Pointe-Claire, QC H9R 0A5
Tel: 514-695-7623; Fax: 514-695-8554
cme@sta.ca
Circulation: 35,544 Frequency: 12 times a year
Robert E. Passaretti, Publisher

The Canadian Journal of Diagnosis
Owned By: STA Communications Inc.
6500 Trans-Canada Hwy., Pointe-Claire, QC H9R 0A5
Tel: 514-695-7623; Fax: 514-695-8554
diagnosis@sta.ca
Circulation: 35,266 Frequency: Monthly
Robert Passaretti, Publisher

Canadian Journal of Dietetic Practice & Research / Revue canadienne de la pratique et de la recherche en diété
#604, 480 University Ave., Toronto, ON M5G 1V2
Tel: 416-596-0857; Fax: 416-596-0603
Circulation: 5,305 Frequency: Quarterly; French & English
Marsha Sharp, CEO

Canadian Journal of Emergency Medicine (CJEM/JCMU) / Journal canadien de la médecine d'urgence
Owned By: Decker Publishing
628 Cowan Circle, Pickering, ON L1W 3K7
Tel: 613-523-3343; Fax: 613-523-0190
Toll-Free: 800-463-1158
cjem@rogers.com
Circulation: 4,000 Frequency: 6 times a year
Dr. Jim Ducharme, Editor-in-Chief

Canadian Journal of Gastroenterology / Journal Canadien de Gastroenterologie
Owned By: Pulsus Group Inc.
2902 South Sheridan Way, Oakville, ON L6J 7L6
Tel: 905-829-4770; Fax: 905-829-4799
pulsus@pulsus.com
Circulation: 13,700 Frequency: Monthly
Official journal of the Canadian Association of Gastroenterology and the Canadian Association for the Study of the Liver.
Subrata Ghosh, Editor-in-chief

Canadian Journal of Infectious Diseases & Medical Microbiology
Owned By: Pulsus Group Inc.
2902 South Sheridan Way, Oakville, ON L6J 7L6
Tel: 905-829-4770; Fax: 905-829-4799
pulsus@pulsus.com
Circulation: 8,800 Frequency: 6 times a year
Official journal of Medical Microbiology and Infectious Disease Canada (AMMI Canada).
JM Conly, Editor-in-chief

Canadian Journal of Medical Laboratory Science (CJMLS)
Cdn. Society for Medical Laboratory Science, PO Box 2830 LCD 1, Hamilton, ON L8N 3N8
Tel: 905-528-8642; Fax: 905-528-4968
Toll-Free: 800-263-8277
info@csmls.org
Circulation: 16,000 Frequency: bi-monthly; English & French editions
Journal available only to members
Alison McLennan, Publisher

Canadian Journal of Medical Radiation Technology / Le Journal Canadien des Techniques en Radiation Médicale
Canadian Assn. of Medical Radiation Technologists, 85 Albert St., 10th Fl., Ottawa, ON K1P 6A4
Tel: 613-234-0012; Fax: 613-234-1097
Toll-Free: 800-463-9729
Circulation: 10,468 Frequency: 4 times a year; English & French
CAMRT Journal available only to members
Christiane Ménard, Director of Communications

The Canadian Journal of Occupational Therapy / Revue canadienne d'ergothérapie
Carleton Technology & Training Centre, #3400, 1125 Colonel By Dr., Ottawa, ON K1S 5R1
Tel: 613-523-2268; Fax: 613-523-2552
Toll-Free: 800-434-2268
publications@caot.ca
Circulation: 7,000 Frequency: 5 times a year; English & French
Marcia Finlayson, Editor

Canadian Journal of Ophthalmology (CJO)
c/o Canadian Ophthalmological Society, #610, 1525 Carling Ave., Ottawa, ON K1Z 8R9
Tel: 613-729-6779; Fax: 613-729-7209
Toll-Free: 800-267-5763
Circulation: 1,300 Frequency: 7 times a year
Phil Hooper, Editor-in-Chief MD, FRSCSC

The Canadian Journal of Plastic Surgery / Journal canadien de chirurgie plastique
Owned By: Pulsus Group Inc.
2902 South Sheridan Way, Oakville, ON L6J 7L6
Tel: 905-829-4770; Fax: 905-829-4799
pulsus@pulsus.com
Circulation: 5,200 Frequency: 4 times a year; English with French abstracts
Official journal of the Canadian Society of Plastic Surgeons, the Canadian Society for Aesthetic (Cosmetic) Plastic Surgery, Groupe pour l'Avancement de la Microchirurgie Canada, and the Canadian Society for Surgery of the Hand (Manus Canada).
Dr. P.E. Wyshynski, Editor-in-chief
Robert B. Kalina, Publisher

Canadian Journal of Public Health (CJPH) / Revue canadienne de santé publique
Canadian Public Health Association, #300, 1565 Carling Ave., Ottawa, ON K1Z 8R1
Tel: 613-725-3769; Fax: 613-725-9826
cjph@cpha.ca
Circulation: 2,300 Frequency: Bi-monthly; English & French
Gilles Paradis, Hon. Scientific Editor
Elinor Wilson, Executive Managing Editor

Canadian Journal of Rural Medicine (CJRM) / Journal canadien de la médecine rurale
Owned By: Canadian Medical Association
Canadaian Medical Association, 1867 Alta Vista Dr., Ottawa, ON K1G 5W8
Tel: 613-731-9331; Fax: 613-523-0937
cjrm@cjrm.net
Circulation: 7,000 Frequency: 4 times a year
Peter Hutten-Czapski, Editor M.D.

Canadian Journal of Surgery (CJS/JCC) / Journal canadien de chirurgie
Owned By: Canadian Medical Association
1867 Alta Vista Dr., Ottawa, ON K1G 5W8
Tel: 613-731-9331; Fax: 613-523-0937
Toll-Free: 800-267-9703
pubs@cma.ca
Circulation: 2,900 Frequency: 6 times a year; English & French
A peer reviewed journal meeting the medical education needs of Canada's surgical specialists
Garth L. Warnick, Co-Editor M.D., Garth.Warnock@vch.ca
Edward J. Harvey, Co-Editor M.D., edward.harvey@muhc.mcgill.ca

Canadian Medical Association Journal (CMAJ/JAMC) / Journal de l'Association médicale canadienne
Owned By: Canadian Medical Association
1867 Alta Vista Dr., Ottawa, ON K1G 5W8
Fax: 613-565-5471
Toll-Free: 866-971-9171
pubs@cma.ca
Social Media:
twitter.com/CMAJ_News
www.facebook.com/CMAJ.JAMC
Circulation: 62,000 Frequency: 25 times a year; English; some French
For Canadian physicians; reflects the complexities of modern medical practice through concise reports on original research, peer commentaries and review articles.
John Fletcher, Editor-in-Chief

Canadian Nursing Home
c/o Health Media Inc., PO Box 45566, 2397 King George Blvd., Surrey, BC V4A 9N3
Tel: 604-535-7933
info@nursinghomemagazine.ca
Circulation: 3,000 Frequency: 4 times a year
Agnes Forster, Publisher
Frank Fagan, Editor

Canadian Respiratory Journal
Owned By: Pulsus Group Inc.
Pulsus Group Inc, 2902 South Sheridan Way, Oakville, ON L6J 7L6
Tel: 905-829-4770; Fax: 905-829-4799
Toll-Free: 866-879-4770
pulsus@pulsus.com
Circulation: 15,600 Frequency: 8 times a year
Official journal of the Canadian Thoracic Society.
Robert B. Kalina, Publisher
Peter Paré, Editor-in-chief

The Chronicle of Cardiovascular & Internal Medicine
Owned By: Chronicle Information Resources Ltd.
#306, 555 Burnhamthorpe Rd., Toronto, ON M9C 2Y3
Tel: 416-916-2476; Fax: 416-352-6199
Toll-Free: 866-632-4766
health@chronicle.org
Circulation: 5,843 Frequency: 6 times a year
Mitchell Shannon, Publisher
R. Allan Ryan, Editorial Director

The Chronicle of Neurology & Psychiatry
Owned By: Chronicle Information Resources Ltd.
#306, 555 Burnhamthorpe Rd., Toronto, ON M9C 2Y3
Tel: 416-916-2476; Fax: 416-352-6199
Toll-Free: 866-632-4766
health@chronicle.org
Circulation: 6,189 Frequency: 9 times a year
Mitchell Shannon, Publisher
R. Allan Ryan, Senior Editor

The Chronicle of Skin & Allergy
Owned By: Chronicle Information Resources Ltd.
#306, 555 Burnhamthorpe Rd., Toronto, ON M9C 2Y3
Tel: 416-916-2476; Fax: 416-352-6199
Toll-Free: 866-632-4766
health@chronicle.org
Circulation: 7,045 Frequency: 9 times a year
R. Allan Ryan, Senior Editor
Mitchell Shannon, Publisher

The Chronicle of Urology & Sexual Medicine
Owned By: Chronicle Information Resources Ltd.
#306, 555 Burnhamthorpe Rd., Toronto, ON M9C 2Y3
Tel: 416-916-2476; Fax: 416-352-6199
Toll-Free: 866-632-4766
health@chronicle.org
Circulation: 5,020 Frequency: 6 times a year
The Chronicle of Urology & Sexual Medicine is a scientific newspaper providing news and information on practical therapeutics and clinical progress in urology and sexual medicine.
Mitchell Shannon, Publisher
R. Allan Ryan, Senior Editor

Clinical & Investigative Medicine (CIM) / Médecine clinique et expérimentale
Canadian Society for Clinical Investigation Head Office, 774 Echo Dr., Ottawa, ON K1S 5N8
Circulation: 1,000 Frequency: 6 times a year
Dr. Jonathan Angel, Editor M.D., jangel@ohri.ca
Dr. Peter D. Bevan, Support Contact Ph.D., cimsupport@mac.com

Clinical & Refractive Optometry
Previous Name: Practical Optometry
Owned By: Mediconcept Inc.
#201, 3535 St. Charles Blvd., Kirkland, QC H9H 5B9
Tel: 514-426-5150; Fax: 514-426-3442
Circulation: 3,065 Frequency: 12 times a year
Official journal of the Canadian Society of Clinical and Refractive Optometry.
Lawrence Goldstein, Publisher, lgoldstein@mediconconcept.ca
Mary D. Lemme, Managing Editor, mdilemme@mediconcept.ca

Clinicien plus
Détenteur: STA Communications Inc.
#306, 955 Boul. St. John, Pointe-Claire, QC H9R 5K3
Tél: 514-695-8393;Téléc: 514-695-8554
clinicien@sta.ca
Tirage: 12 149 Fréquence: Mensuel; français
Robert Passaretti, Éditeur

Coup d'oeil
Breton Communications Inc., #202, 495, boul St-Martin ouest, Laval, QC H7M 1Y9
Tél: 450-629-6005;Téléc: 450-629-6044
Ligne sans frais: 888-462-2112
info@bretoncom.com
Tirage: 4,055 Fréquence: mensuel
Martine Breton, President

CrossCurrents: The Journal of Addiction & Mental Health
Centre for Addiction & Mental Health, 33 Russell St., Toronto, ON M5S 2S1
jacquelyn_waller-vin@camh.net
Circulation: 3,000 Frequency: 4 times a year
Hema Zbogar, Editor

Dental Chronicle
Owned By: Chronicle Information Resources Ltd.
#306, 555 Burnhamthorpe Rd., Toronto, ON M9C 2Y3
Tel: 416-916-2476; Fax: 416-352-6199
Toll-Free: 866-632-4766
health@chronicle.org
Circulation: 33,682 Frequency: 6 times a year
Mitchell Shannon, Publisher
R. Allan Ryan, Senior Editor

Dental Practice Management
Previous Name: Dental Guide
Owned By: Business Information Group
80 Valleybrook Dr., Toronto, ON M3B 2S9
Tel: 416-510-6785; Fax: 416-510-5140
Toll-Free: 800-268-7742
Other information: Toll Free: U.S. 1-800-387-0273
Circulation: 18,700 Frequency: 4 times a year
Catherine Wilson, Editor, cwilson@oralhealthjournal.com

Doctor's Review
Owned By: Parkhurst Publishing
400 McGill, 3rd Fl., Montréal, QC H2Y 2G1
Tel: 514-397-8833 Toll-Free: 800-663-7403
editors@doctorsreview.com
Circulation: 40,000 Frequency: Monthly
Monthly travel and lifestyle journal.
David Elkins, Publisher
Annarosa Sabbadini, Editor

doctorNS
Previous Name: Medical Society of Nova Scotia DoctorsNS; Medical Society of Nova Scot
Doctors Nova Scotia, 5 Spectacle Lake Dr., Dartmouth, NS B3B 1X7
Tel: 902-468-1866; Fax: 902-468-6578
info@doctorsns.com
Social Media:
twitter.com/Doctors_NS
Circulation: 3,000 Frequency: 10 times a year
Kelly Stoddard, Editor

Drug Rep Chronicle
Owned By: Chronicle Information Resources Ltd.
#306, 555 Burnhamthorpe Rd., Toronto, ON M9C 2Y3
Tel: 416-916-2476; Fax: 416-352-6199
Toll-Free: 866-632-4766
health@chronicle.org

Drugstore Canada
Owned By: Rogers Publishing Ltd.
1 Mount Pleasant Rd., Toronto, ON M4Y 2Y5
Tel: 416-764-2000; Fax: 416-764-3930
Circulation: 16,703 Frequency: 10 times a year

Experimental & Clinical Cardiology
Owned By: Pulsus Group Inc.
Pulsus Group Inc, 2902 South Sheridan Way, Oakville, ON L6J 7L6
Tel: 905-829-4770; Fax: 905-829-4799
Official journal of the International Academy of Cardiovascular Sciences.
Robert B. Kalina, Publisher
Dr. B. Ost'ádal, Editor-in-chief

Fitness Business Canada
30 Mill Pond Dr., Georgetown, ON L7G 4S6
Tel: 905-873-0850; Fax: 905-873-8611
fbc@fitnet.ca
Graham Longwell, Publisher
Barb Gormley, Managing Editor

FMWC Newsletter
Federation of Medical Women of Canada, 780 Echo Dr., Ottawa, ON K1S 5R7
Tel: 613-569-5881; Fax: 613-569-4432
Toll-Free: 877-771-3777
fmwcmain@fmwc.ca
Circulation: 1,000 Frequency: 3 times a year
Gail Beck, President

Guide to Canadian Healthcare Facilities
Previous Name: Canadian Hospital Association Buyer's Guide
c/o Canadian Healthcare Association, 17 York St., Ottawa, ON K1N 9J6
Tel: 613-241-8005; Fax: 613-241-9481
Circulation: 1,300 Frequency: annual
Eleanor Sawyer, Director, Publishing
Nola Haddadian, Managing Editor

HEALTHbeat
#319, 9768 - 170 St., Edmonton, AB T5T 5L4
Toll-Free: 800-727-0782
Circulation: 40,000 Frequency: 12 times a year
Jan Henry, Publisher

Healthcare Management FORUM / Forum gestion des soins de santé
Canadian College of Health Service Executives, 292 Somerset St. West, Ottawa, ON K2P 0J6
Tel: 613-235-7218; Fax: 613-235-5451
Toll-Free: 800-363-9056
Circulation: 3,500 Frequency: Quarterly
Laurie Wilson, Managing Editor, 613-235-7218, editor@sympatico.ca

Hospital News, Canada
Trader Media Corp, 15 Apex Rd., Toronto, ON M6A 2V6
Tel: 416-781-5516; Fax: 416-781-5499
info@hospitalnews.com
Circulation: 32,650 Frequency: Monthly
Julie Abelsohn, Publisher

The Journal of Current Clinical Care
info@healthplexus.net
Social Media: www.facebook.com/pages/HealthPlexus-and-JCCC/1729668593 96
Frequency: 6 times a year
Michael Yasny, Publisher
Kristin Casady, Editorial Director

Journal of Otolaryngology
Owned By: Decker Publishing
#310, 69 John St. South, Hamilton, ON L8N 3K7
Tel: 905-522-8526; Fax: 905-522-9273
Toll-Free: 855-647-6511
customercare@deckerpublishing.com
Circulation: 1,113 Frequency: 6 times a year

Journal of Psychiatry & Neuroscience (JPN) / Revue de psychiatrie & de neuroscience
Owned By: Canadian Medical Association
1867 Alta Vista Dr., Ottawa, ON K1G 5W8
Tel: 613-731-9331; Fax: 613-523-0937
Toll-Free: 800-267-9703
jpn@cma.ca
Circulation: 7,200 Frequency: 6 times a year, English & French
P. Boksa, Co-Editor M.D.
R. Joober, Co-Editor M.D.

The Journal of Rheumatology
Journal of Rheumatology Publishing Co. Ltd., #901, 365 Bloor St. East, Toronto, ON M4W 3L4
Tel: 416-967-5155; Fax: 416-967-7556
jrheum@jrheum.com
Social Media: twitter.com/jrheum
www.facebook.com/journalofrheumatology
Circulation: 3,500 Frequency: Monthly
Duncan A. Gordon, Editor-in-chief

Journal of the Canadian Chiropractic Association
#600, 30 St Patrick St., Toronto, ON M5T 3A3
Tel: 416-585-7902; Fax: 416-585-2970
Toll-Free: 877-222-9303
Circulation: 5,384 Frequency: 4 times a year
Dr. Allan Gotlib, Editor, agotlib@chiropracticcanada.ca

Journal SOGC
c/o Society of Obstetrician & Gynaecology of Canada, 780 Echo Dr., Ottawa, ON K1P 5J3
Tel: 613-730-4192; Fax: 613-730-4314
Toll-Free: 800-561-2416
helpdesk@sogc.com
Circulation: 9,970 Frequency: 13 times a year; English with French abstracts
Timothy Rowe, Editor in Chief

Long Term Care
Ontario Long Term Care Association, #202, 345 Renfrew Dr., Markham, ON L3R 9S9
Tel: 905-470-8995; Fax: 905-470-9595
info@oltca.com
Circulation: 6,000 Frequency: Quarterly

Massage Therapy Canada
Owned By: Annex Publishing & Printing Inc.
PO Box 530, 105 Donly Dr. South, Simcoe, ON N3Y 4N5
Tel: 519-429-3966; Fax: 519-429-3094
Toll-Free: 800-265-2827
Circulation: 5,800 Frequency: 4 times a year
Maria DiDanieli, Editor, 289-259-1408, mdidanieli@annexweb.com

MedActuel FMC
Anciennement: Medactuel-FMC
c/o Éditions Santé Rogers media, 1001, boul de Maisonneuve ouest, 10e étage, Montréal, QC H3A 3E1
Tél: 514-843-2140;Téléc: 514-845-2063
medactuelfmc@lactualite.com
Tirage: 10 000 Fréquence: 10 fois par an
Greg Buie, Éditeur
Catherine Choquette, Rédactrice en chef, choquette@lactualite.com

Le Médecin du Québec
Quebec Federation of General Practitioners, #1000, 1440, rue St-Catherine ouest, Montréal, QC H3G 1R8
Tél: 514-878-1911;Téléc: 514-878-4455
Ligne sans frais: 800-361-8499
info@fmoq.org
Médias sociaux: www.youtube.com/lafmoq
twitter.com/OMNIPRATICIENS
www.facebook.com/laf moq
Tirage: 14,000 Fréquence: Mensuel; français
Louise Roy, Rédacteur M.D.

Médecine/sciences
#800, 500, Sherbrooke ouest, Montréal, QC H3A 3C6
Tél: 514-288-2247;Téléc: 514-288-0520
Tirage: 2 007 Fréquence: 10 fois par an
Michel Bergeron, Directeur général

The Medical Post
Owned By: Rogers Publishing Ltd.
1 Mount Pleasant Rd., Toronto, ON M4Y 2Y5
Tel: 416-764-3887; Fax: 416-764-1207
info@medicalpost.rogers.com
Circulation: 47,715 Frequency: 23 times a year
Janet Smith, Publisher
Colin Leslie, Editor-in-Chief

Nutrition - Science en Evolution
Previous Name: Diététique en Action
#1220, 2155, rue Guy, Montréal, QC H3H 2R9
Tel: 514-393-3733; Fax: 514-393-3582
Toll-Free: 888-393-8528
Circulation: 2,500 Frequency: 3 times a year; French
Paul-Guy Duhamel, President

Obesity Surgery
PO Box 1002, 5863 Leslie St., Toronto, ON M2H 1J8
Tel: 416-224-5055; Fax: 416-224-5455
journal@obesitysurgery.com
Social Media: twitter.com/clinmedjournals
Circulation: 2,300 Frequency: 12 times a year
Victoria Ferrara, Editor, victoria.ferrara@springer.com

Obstetrics & Gynaecology Canada
Previous Name: Obstetrics & Gynaecology 2000
Owned By: CTC Communications Corp.
Circulation: 10,000 Frequency: 4 times a year
Michael E. Farley, Publisher
Kathy Pearsall, Managing Editor

Occupational Therapy Now / Actualités ergothérapiques
CTTC Bldg., #3400, 1125 Coloney By Dr., Ottawa, ON K1S 5R1
Tel: 613-523-2268; Fax: 613-523-2552
Toll-Free: 800-434-2268
otnow@caot.ca
Social Media: www.facebook.com/CAOT.ca
Circulation: 6,500 Frequency: 6 times a year; English and French
Fern Swedlove, Editor

Oncology Exchange
Owned By: Parkhurst Publishing
400, rue McGill, 3e étage, Montréal, QC H2Y 2G1
Tel: 514-397-8833; Fax: 514-397-0228
Circulation: 6,000 Frequency: Quarterly
Devon Phillips, Editor, phillips@parkpub.com

Ontario Medical Review
Ontario Medical Assn., #900, 150 Bloor St., Toronto, ON M5S 3C1
Tel: 416-599-2580; Fax: 416-340-2232
Toll-Free: 800-268-7215
kim_secord@oma.org
Social Media: twitter.com/OntariosDoctors
www.facebook.com/Ontariosdoctors?v=wall
Circulation: 31,000 Frequency: 11 times a year
Jeff Henry, Editor
Elizabeth Petruccelli, Managing Editor
Kim Secord, Circulation Manager

Optical Prism
Nusand Publishing Inc., #1113, 250 the East Mall, Toronto, ON M9B 6L3
Tel: 416-233-2487; Fax: 416-233-1746
info@opticalprism.ca
Social Media: pinterest.com/opticalprism
twitter.com/opticalprism
www.facebook.co m/OpticalPrismMagazine
Circulation: 10,609 Frequency: 10 times a year
Robert May, Publisher
Sarah McGoldrick, Editor, smcgoldrick@opticalprism.ca

Opti-Guide
Breton Communications Inc., #202, 495, boul St-Martin ouest, Laval, QC H7M 1Y9
Tel: 450-629-6005; Fax: 450-629-6044
Toll-Free: 888-462-2112
info@bretoncom.com
Circulation: 5,481 Frequency: Annually
Martine Breton, President/Publisher, martine@bretoncom.com

L'Optométriste
Association des optométristes du Québec, #740, 1265, rue Berri, Montréal, QC H2L 4X4
Tél: 514-288-6272;Téléc: 514-288-7071
aoq@aoqnet.qc.ca
Tirage: 4 400 Fréquence: 6 fois par an; français

Paediatrics & Child Health
Owned By: Pulsus Group Inc.
Pulsus Group Inc, 2902 South Sheridan Way, Oakville, ON L6J 7L6
Tel: 905-829-4770; Fax: 905-829-4799
Toll-Free: 866-879-9770
pulsus@pulsus.com
Circulation: 14,500 Frequency: 10 times a year
Official journal of the Canadian Paediatric Society.
Robert Kalina, Publisher
Dr. Noni MacDonald, Editor
Dr. N. MacDonald, Editor

Pain Research & Management
Previous Name: Pain Research Management
Owned By: Pulsus Group Inc.
Pulsus Group Inc., 2902 South Sheridan Way, Oakville, ON L6J 7L6
Tel: 905-829-4770; Fax: 905-829-4799
Toll-Free: 866-879-4770
pulsus@pulsus.com
Circulation: 15,300 Frequency: 4 times a year
Official journal of the Canadian Pain Society.
Robert Kalina, Publisher
Dr. Kenneth D. Craig, Editor

Parkhurst Exchange
Owned By: Parkhurst Publishing
400, rue McGill, 3e étage, Montréal, QC H2Y 2G1
Tel: 514-397-8833; Fax: 514-397-0228
Toll-Free: 800-663-7403
parkex@parkpub.com
Circulation: 39,453 Frequency: 12 times a year
Monthly GP/FP journal.
Madeleine Pantais, Publisher

Perspectives in Cardiology
Owned By: STA Communications Inc.
#310, 6500 Trans-Canada Hwy., Pointe-Claire, QC H9R 0A5
Tel: 514-695-7623; Fax: 514-695-8554
Circulation: 15,270 Frequency: 10 times a year
Robert Passaretti, Publisher

Physiotherapy Canada
Owned By: University of Toronto Press
5201 Dufferin St., Toronto, ON M3H 5T8
Tel: 416-667-7777; Fax: 416-667-7881
editor@physiotherapy.ca
Circulation: 9,500 Frequency: 4 times a year
Dina Brooks, Scientific Editor PhD, dina.brooks@utoronto.ca

Psychology Ontario
Previous Name: Psychology Canada
c/o Ontario Psychological Association, #403, 21 St. Clair Ave. East, Toronto, ON M4T 1L8
Tel: 416-961-5552; Fax: 416-961-5516
info@psych.on.ca
Circulation: 1,450 Frequency: Quarterly
Dr. Mario Cappelli, Editor
Sandra Traub, Publication Manager

Rehab & Community Care Medicine
Previous Name: Rehab & Community Care Management
#803, 255 Duncan Mill Rd., Toronto, ON M3B 3H9
Tel: 416-421-7944; Fax: 416-421-8418
Toll-Free: 800-798-6282
Circulation: 20,500 Frequency: Quarterly
Caroline Tapp-McDougall, Publisher & Editor-in-Chief, caroline@bcsgroup.com
Helmut Dostal, Managing Editor, dostal@bcsgroup.com

Stitches: The Journal of Medical Humour
Owned By: Stitches: the Journal of Medical Humour
Aurora, ON
Circulation: 38,652 Frequency: Bi-monthly
Michael Moriarty, Publisher
Randall Willis, Editor

Synergie
Anciennement: ARTERE
#400, 505, boul de Maisonneuve ouest, Montréal, QC H3A 3C2
Tél: 514-842-4861;Téléc: 514-282-4289
Ligne sans frais: 800-361-4661
anne.lepine@aqesss.qc.ca
Médias sociaux:
twitter.com/aqesss
Tirage: 6 212 Fréquence: 10 fois par an; français
Guylaine Boucher, Rédactrice, guylaine.boucher@aqesss.qc.ca

Urology Times of Canada
Owned By: CTC Communications Corp.
#200, 2110 Matheson Blvd. West, Mississauga, ON L5R 3L5
Tel: 905-712-3636; Fax: 905-712-1679
info@ctccomm.com
Circulation: 4,800 Frequency: bi-monthly
Mike Farley, Publisher
K. Pearsall, Managing Editor
Karen Tousignant, Advertising

Heating, Plumbing, Air Conditioning

Contracting Canada Magazine
1697 Kelsey Ct., Mississauga, ON L5L 3J8
Tel: 905-569-2777; Fax: 905-569-2444
don@contractingcanada.com
Circulation: 29,000 Frequency: 4 times a year
Contracting Canada's editorial focus is on the latest industry innovations including products, service and troubleshooting techniques, system design and installation profiles, sales and marketing features. Departments include field service and installation tips, technical advice from industry experts, the latest innovations and applications of products, tools and instruments for contractors.
Don B. Beaulieu, Publisher & Editorial Director

Heating Plumbing Air Conditioning
Owned By: Business Information Group
80 Valleybrook Dr., Toronto, ON M3B 2S9
Tel: 416-442-5500; Fax: 416-510-5140
Social Media:
twitter.com/hpacmag
Circulation: 16,312 Frequency: 7 times a year; also Buyers Guide (annually, Aug.)
Peter Leonard, Publisher, 416-510-6847, PLeonard@hpacmag.com
Kerry Turner, Editor, 416-510-5218, KTurner@hpacmag.com

Inter-mécanique du bâtiment (CMMTQ)
8175, boul St-Laurent, Montréal, QC H2P 2M1
Tél: 514-382-2668;Téléc: 514-382-1566
Ligne sans frais: 800-465-2668
Tirage: 6 000 Fréquence: 10 fois par an; français
André Dupuis, Rédacteur-en-chef

Plumbing & HVAC Product News
Previous Name: HVAC Refrigeration; Plumbing, Piping & Heating Magazine
Owned By: Newcon Business Media
451 Attwell Dr., Toronto, ON M9W 5C4
Tel: 416-614-0955; Fax: 416-614-8861
Circulation: 17,982 Frequency: 6 times a year
Simon Blake, Editor, simon@plumbingandhvac.ca
Mark Vreugdenhil, Publisher, mark@plumbingandhvac.ca

Homes

Montreal Home
#2001, 1 Place Ville Marie, Montréal, QC H3B 2C4
Tel: 514-448-6714
info@montrealhomemag.com
Frequency: English and French

Hotels & Restaurants

Atlantic Restaurant News
Owned By: Ishcom Publications Ltd.
#301, 2065 Dundas St. West, Mississauga, ON L4X 2W1
Tel: 905-206-0150; Fax: 905-206-9972
Toll-Free: 800-201-8596
Circulation: 5,500 Frequency: 6 times a year
Steve Isherwood, Publisher, sisherwood@can-restaurantnews.com

Bar & Beverage Business
Owned By: Mercury Publications Ltd.
Tel: 204-954-2085; Fax: 204-954-2057
mp@mercury.mb.ca
Circulation: 17,063 Frequency: 6 times a year
Frank Yeo, Publisher
Kelly Gray, Editor

BC Restaurant News
British Columbia Restaurant & Foodservices Association, 439 Helmcken St., Vancouver, BC V6B 2E6
Tel: 604-669-2239; Fax: 604-669-6175
Toll-Free: 877-669-2239
info@bcrfa.com
Frequency: 8 times a year
Jason McRobbie, Editor

Canadian Lodging News
Owned By: Ishcom Publications Ltd.
#201, 2065 Dundas St. East, Mississauga, ON L4X 2W1
Tel: 905-206-0150; Fax: 905-206-9972
Toll-Free: 800-201-8596
Circulation: 9,000 Frequency: 10 times a year
Steven Isherwood, Publisher, sisherwood@can-lodgingnews.com

Chef & Grocer
Previous Name: Le Chef
252, Rte. St-André, Saint-Étienne-de-Lauzon, QC G6J 1E8
Tel: 418-831-5317; Fax: 418-831-5172
Toll-Free: 800-363-1727
info@chefandgrocer.com
Circulation: 25,105 Frequency: Monthly; Bilingual
Maurice LeBlanc, Publisher, mleblanc@chefandgrocer.com
Eric Buteau, Editor-in-chief, ebuteau@chefandgrocer.com

Foodservice & Hospitality
Previous Name: Canadian Hotel & Restaurant Product News
Owned By: Kostuch Publications Ltd.
#101, 23 Lesmill Rd., Toronto, ON M3B 3P6
Tel: 416-447-0888; Fax: 416-447-5333
mkostuch@foodservice.ca
Social Media:
twitter.com/fsworld
www.facebook.com/pages/Foodserviceworldcom/114297021936?v
Circulation: 25,120 Frequency: 12 times a year
Mitch Kostuch, President/Publisher
Rosanna Caira, Associate Publisher/Editor

Hotelier
Owned By: Kostuch Publications Ltd.
#101, 23 Lesmill Rd., Toronto, ON M3B 3P6
Tel: 416-447-0888; Fax: 416-447-5333
rcaira@foodservice.ca
Circulation: 9,000 Frequency: 8 times a year
Mitch Kostuch, President
Rosanna Caira, Editor & Publisher

Ontario Restaurant News
Owned By: Ishcom Publications Ltd.
#201, 2065 Dundas St. East, Mississauga, ON L4X 2W1
Tel: 905-206-0150; Fax: 905-206-9972
Toll-Free: 800-201-8596
Circulation: 16,500 Frequency: Monthly
Steven Isherwood, Publisher, sisherwood@can-restaurantnews.com

Pacific Prairie Restaurants News
Previous Name: Western Hospitality News
Owned By: Ishcom Publications Ltd.
#201, 2065 Dundas St. East, Mississauga, ON M6R 1W8
Tel: 905-206-0150; Fax: 905-206-9972
Toll-Free: 800-201-8596
lwu@can-restaurantnews.com
Circulation: 14,000 Frequency: 6 times a year
Steven Isherwood, Publisher, 905-206-0150 x236
Leslie Wu, Editor, 905-206-0150 x227

Western Hotelier
Owned By: Mercury Publications Ltd.
c/o Mercury Publications, 1740 Wellington Ave., Winnipeg, MB R3H 0E8
Tel: 204-979-6071; Fax: 204-954-2057
david@mercury.mb.ca
Circulation: 5,200 Frequency: 5 times a year
Frank Yeo, Publisher
Kelly Gray, Editor, editorial@mercury.mb.ca
Kristi Balon, Editorial Coordinator, editorial@mercury.mb.ca

Western Restaurant News
Owned By: Mercury Publications Ltd.
1740 Wellington Ave., Winnipeg, MB R3H 0E8
Tel: 204-954-2085; Fax: 204-954-2057
Toll-Free: 800-337-6372
Circulation: 14,523 Frequency: 6 times a year
Elaine Dufault, Associate Publisher/Sales Manager, elaine@mercury.mb.ca
Kelly Gray, Editor, editorial@mercury.mb.ca

Housewares

HomeStyle Magazine
Lorell Communication Inc., 146 Cavendish Ct., Oakville, ON L6J 5S2
Tel: 905-338-0799; Fax: 905-338-5657
info@homestylemag.ca
Frequency: Bi-monthly
Laurie O'Halloran, Publisher & Editor, laurie@homestylemag.ca

Human Resources

Canadian HR Reporter
Owned By: Thomson Reuters Canada Ltd.
1 Corporate Plaza, 2075 Kennedy Rd., Toronto, ON M1T 3V4
Tel: 416-609-3800; Fax: 416-298-5031
Toll-Free: 800-387-5164
Circulation: 10,800 Frequency: 22 times a year
John Hobel, Publisher & Editor, 416-298-5197, john.hobel@thomsonreuters.com

HR Professional Magazine
Previous Name: Human Resources Professional
Owned By: Naylor (Canada) Inc.
c/o Naylor (Canada) Inc., #300, 1630 Ness Ave., Winnipeg, MB R3J 3X1
; Fax: 204-947-2047
Toll-Free: 800-665-2456
Social Media:
twitter.com/HRProMag
www.facebook.com/HRProfessionalMag
Circulation: 18,000 Frequency: 6 times a year
Laurie Blake, Editor, 905-235-5414, lblake@naylor.com

Industrial & Industrial Automation

Canadian Electronics
Owned By: Annex Publishing & Printing Inc.
222 Edward St., Aurora, ON LaG 1W6
Tel: 905-727-0077; Fax: 905-727-0017
Toll-Free: 800-265-2827
subscribe@electronicsincanada.com
Social Media:
twitter.com/cdnelectronics
Circulation: 18,135 Frequency: 4 times a year
Klaus Pirker, Publisher, 905-726-4670, kpirker@annexweb.com
Mike Edwards, Editorial Director, 905-713-4389, medwards@annexweb.com

Canadian Industrial Equipment News
Owned By: Business Information Group
80 Valleybrook Dr., Toronto, ON M3B 3S9
Tel: 416-442-5600
Circulation: 20,464 Frequency: Monthly
Michael King, Publisher, 416-510-5107, mking@cienmagazine.com
Olga Markovich, Editor, 416-510-5113, omarkovich@cienmagazine.com
Dianne Rakoff, Circulation Manager

Energy Management
Owned By: Annex Publishing & Printing Inc.
222 Edward St., Aurora, ON LAG 1W6
Tel: 905-727-0077; Fax: 905-727-0017
Toll-Free: 800-265-2827
Social Media:
twitter.com/manageurenergy
Circulation: 18,135 Frequency: Monthly
John MacPherson, Publisher, jmacpherson@annexweb.com
Anthony Capkun, Editor, acapkun@annexweb.com

Le Journal Industriel du Québec
800-1200 ave McGill College, Montréal, QC H3B 4G7
Tél: 450-785-2590;Téléc: 450-785-2591
Tirage: 20 000 Fréquence: 10 fois par an; français
Yvan Gauthier, Publisher

Manufacturing Automation
Previous Name: Manufacturing & Process Automation
Owned By: Annex Publishing & Printing Inc.
222 Edward St., Aurora, ON L4G 1W6
Tel: 905-727-0077; Fax: 905-727-0017
Toll-Free: 800-265-2827
Social Media:
twitter.com/automationmag
Circulation: 19,020 Frequency: 7 times a year
Klaus Pirker, Publisher, publisher@automationmag.com
Mary Del Ciancio, Editor, editor@automationmag.com

MCI
Détenteur: P.A.P. Communication inc.
P.A.P. Communications Inc., 1627, boul Bastien, Québec, QC G2K 1H1
Tél: 418-623-3383;Téléc: 418-623-5033
Ligne sans frais: 800-387-3383
info@magazinemci.com
Médias sociaux:
twitter.com/MagazineMci
www.facebook.com/pages/Magazine-MCI/212557108776939
Tirage: 23 000 Fréquence: 6 fois par an; français
Bernard Gauthier, Rédacteur en chef

Plant
Owned By: Business Information Group
80 Valleybrook Dr., Toronto, ON M3B 2S9
Tel: 416-422-5600; Fax: 416-510-5140
info@canadianmanufacturing.com
Circulation: 30,000 Frequency: Monthly
Joe Terrett, Editor, 416-442-5600 x 3215, JTerrett@plant.ca

Plant Engineering & Maintenance (PEM)
Owned By: Annex Publishing & Printing Inc.
222 Edward St., Aurora, ON L4G 1W6
Tel: 905-727-0077; Fax: 905-727-0017
Toll-Free: 800-265-2827
Social Media:
twitter.com/PEM_Maintenance
Circulation: 18,000 Frequency: 6 times a year
John MacPherson, Publisher, jmacpherson@annexweb.com
André Voshart, Editor, lnacht@annexweb.com

Produits pour l'industrie québécoise
Détenteur: Annex Publishing & Printing Inc.
222 Edward St., Aurora, ON L4G 1W6
Tél: 905-727-0077;Téléc: 905-727-0017
Ligne sans frais: 888-743-3551
Fréquence: 5 fois par an; français
Nigel Bishop, Éditeur, nbishop@annexweb.com
Rob Colman, Rédacteur, rcolman@annexweb.com

Industrial Safety

Accident Prevention
Industrial Accident Prevention Assn (IAPA)., #300, 5110 Creekbank Rd., Mississauga, ON L4W 0A1
Tel: 905-614-4272; Fax: 905-614-1414
Toll-Free: 800-316-4272
apmag@iapa.ca
Circulation: 12,500 Frequency: 5 times a year
Scott Williams, Editor

Canadian Occupational Safety
Owned By: Thomson Reuters Canada Limited
Tel: 905-727-0077; Fax: 905-727-0017
Social Media:
www.twitter.com/cosmagazine
www.facebook.com/104930002952393
Circulation: 12,600 Frequency: 6 times a year
Cocoe Horsley, Publisher
Mari-Len De Guzman, Editor,
mari-len.deguzman@thomsonreuters.com

Le groupe de communication Sansectra Inc.
#201, 85, rue Saint-Charles ouest, Longueuil, QC J4H 1C5
Tél: 450-651-2855
travail.sante@sympatico.ca
Tirage: 3000 Fréquence: Mars, juin, septembre, décembree & Guide-Source; français
Huguette Beauchamp, Directrice générale, 450-651-2855

OHS Canada Magazine (OH&S Canada)
Previous Name: Occupational Health & Safety Canada
Owned By: Business Information Group
80 Valleybrook Dr., Toronto, ON M3B 2S9
Tel: 416-442-2122; Fax: 416-442-2191
Toll-Free: 800-268-7742
orders@ohscanada.com
Circulation: 10,587 Frequency: 8 times a year
Peter Boxer, Publisher, 416-510-5102, pboxer@ohscanada.com
Angela Stelmakowich, Editor, 416-510-5115,
jlian@ohscanada.com

Insurance

Alberta Insurance Directory
Insurancewest Media Ltd.
Owned By: Insurancewest Media Ltd.
PO Box 3311 Terminal, 661 Market Hill, Vancouver, BC V5Z 4B5
Tel: 604-874-1001; Fax: 604-874-3922
manager@insurancewest.ca
Circulation: 1,555 Frequency: Annually
The directory, started in 1982, is considered the recognized reference authority. It contains full, accurate and up-to-date listings in Alberta of 600 general insurance broker offices, 100 independent adjusting offices, 280 general and life insurer offices, and 50 insurance association and government-related offices. In addition, 2700 senior insurance personnel are listed and cross-referenced; 100 trades and suppliers also included. The 230-page coil-bound book is used primarily by general insurance brokers, adjusters and insurers in Alberta.
Linda Helme, Publisher & Editor & Advertising Sales
Bill Earle, Publisher & Editor & Advertising Sales

BC Broker: The Voice of the P&C Insurance Industry in B.C.
c/o Insurancewest Media Ltd., PO Box 3311 Terminal, 661 Market Hill, Vancouver, BC V6B 3Y3
Tel: 604-874-1001; Fax: 604-874-3922
manager@insurancewest.ca
Circulation: 4,500+ Frequency: Bi-monthly
The trade publication is sent to general insurance brokers who are members of the Insurance Brokers Association of British Columbia. BC Broker is also distributed to general insurance companies, independent adjusters, lawyers, & suppliers. A digital edition is also available. Each issue of BC Broker features an educational article on a technical insurance topic & columns from the association's president & chief staff executive.
Fran Burnside, Manager, Publications & Contact, Magazine Advertising Sales, 604-875-7762, fburnside@insurancewest.ca
Trudy Lancelyn, Managing Editor, 604-606-8008,
tlancelyn@ibabc.org
Will Wong, Director, Art, 604-874-1001

British Columbia Insurance Directory
Insurancewest Media Ltd.
Owned By: Insurancewest Media Ltd.
PO Box 3311 Terminal, 661 Market Hill, Vancouver, BC V5Z 4B5
Tel: 604-874-1001; Fax: 604-874-3922
manager@insurancewest.ca
Circulation: 2,563 Frequency: Annually, April
The directory, started in 1964, is considered the recognized reference authority. It contains full, accurate and up-to-date listings in B.C. of 950 general insurance broker offices, 160 independent adjusting offices, 250 general and life insurer offices, and 60 insurance association and government-related offices. In addition, 5000 senior insurance personnel are listed and cross-referenced; 200 trades and suppliers also included. The 340-page coil-bound book is used primarily by general insurance brokers, adjusters and insurers in B.C.
Bill Earle, Editor & Publisher & Advertising Sales
Jim Bensley, Editor & Publisher & Advertising Sales

Canadian Insurance Claims Directory
University of Toronto Press
Owned By: University of Toronto Press Inc.
#700, 10 St Mary St., Toronto, ON M4Y 2W8
Tel: 416-978-2239; Fax: 416-978-4738
Toll-Free: 800-565-9523
publishing@utpress.untoronto.ca
Circulation: 1,500 Frequency: Annually, May
This directory is to facilitate the forwarding of insurance claims throughout Canada and the United States. Its subscribers are adjusters, firms specializing in counsel to the insurance industry, insurance companies, and industrial and government offices.
Gwen Peroni, Editor

Canadian Insurance Top Broker
Owned By: Rogers Publishing Ltd.
1 Mount Pleasant Rd., Toronto, ON M4Y 2Y5
Tel: 416-764-1323
canadianinsurance@rci.rogers.com
Circulation: 15,441 Frequency: 10 issues per year
Focus on the property and casualty insurance market.
Mia Williamson, Publisher
Daryl Angier, Editor

Canadian Underwriter
Owned By: Business Information Group
80 Valleybrook Dr., Toronto, ON M3B 2S9
; Fax: 416-510-6809
Toll-Free: 800-268-7742
Social Media:
www.linkedin.com/groups?gid=2940726&trk=myg_ugrp_ovr
twitter.com/CdnUnde rwriter
www.facebook.com/CanadianUnderwriter?ref=mf
Circulation: 10,061 Frequency: Monthly; also Rehabilitation & Medical Services Guide, Litigation Services Guide, Insurance Marketer, Annual Statistical Issue, Ontario Insurance Directory
Canadian Underwriter is a professional Insurance and Risk Management magazine covering all aspects of Canada's property and casualty Insurance Market.
David Gambrill, Editor, 416-510-6796,
david@canadianunderwriter.ca
Steve Wilson, Senior Publisher, 416-510-6800,
steve@canadianunderwriter.ca

Forum
Previous Name: CAIFA Forum
c/o Advocis, #209, 390 Queens Quay West, Toronto, ON M5V 3A2
Tel: 416-444-5251; Fax: 416-444-8031
Toll-Free: 800-563-5822
kdoucet@advocis.ca
Circulation: 18,100 Frequency: Monthly
Peter Wilmshurst, Publisher
Kristin Doucet, Editor

General Insurance Register
Owned By: Rogers Publishing Ltd.
Tel: 416-764-1451
deokie.ramnarine@rci.rogers.com
Circulation: 5,500 Frequency: Annually, January
Lists insurance Adjusters, Appraisers, Legal firms in Canada; Consultants, Engineering, Investigation, Rehabilitation, Replacement, Restoration & other services companies; also lists Brokers, Intermediaries & Managing Agents

The Insurance & Investment Journal / Journal de L'Assurance
Owned By: Les Editions du Journal de l'Assurance
#100, 321 Rue de la Commune West, Montreal, QC H2Y 2E1
Tel: 514-289-9595; Fax: 514-289-9527
reception@insurance-journal.ca
Circulation: 15 500 Frequency: 10 times a year
The Insurance Journal targets financial advisors, life insurance producers, financial planners, and general insurance brokers in Canada. The magazine publishes news and examines trends in the development of insurance and financial products, such as group and individual insurance, disability insurance, mutual funds, segregated funds, health care management, and information technology. Published 10 times per year.
Serge Therrien, Publisher, serge.therrien@insurance-journal.ca
Donna Glasgow, Editor-in-Chief,
donna.glasgow@insurance-journal.ca

Insurancewest
Insurancewest Media Ltd.
Owned By: Insurancewest Media Ltd.
PO Box 3311 Terminal, 661 Market Hill, Vancouver, BC V5Z 4B5
Tel: 604-874-1001; Fax: 604-874-3922
Toll-Free: 800-888-8811
manager@insurancewest.ca
Circulation: 6,000 Frequency: 6 times a year
Launched in 1996, this bi-monthly magazine (formerly a quarterly) circulates to 6000 in Canada's four western provinces - virtually every insurance industry decision-maker in the west. Insurancewest is about insurance people and companies
Bill Earle, Publisher & Editor & Advertising Sales
Jim Bensley, Publisher & Editor & Advertising Sales

Le Journal de l'Assurance
Détenteur: Les Editions du Journal de l'Assurance
#100, 321, rue de la Commune Ouest, Montréal, QC H2Y 2E1
Tél: 514-289-9595;Téléc: 514-289-9527
reception@journal-assurance.ca
Tirage: 64 000 Fréquence: 10 fois par an; français

Serge Therrien, Président et éditeur, serge.therrien@journal-assurance.ca
Hubert Roy, Rédacteur en chef, hubert.roy@journal-assurance.ca

Ontario Insurance Directory
Owned By: Business Information Group
80 Valleybrook Dr., Toronto, ON M3B 2S9
Tel: 416-442-2122; Fax: 416-442-2191
Toll-Free: 800-668-2374
Circulation: 3,500 Frequency: Annually, December
Personal address and telephone book dedicated solely to the Ontario insurance industry.
Steve Wilson, Senior Publisher

Interior Design & Decor

Azure
#601, 460 Richmond St. West, Toronto, ON M5V 1Y1
Tel: 416-203-9674; Fax: 416-203-9842
azure@azureonline.com
Circulation: 30,000 Frequency: 8 times a year
Sergio Sgaramella, Publisher
Catherine Osborne, Senior Editor
Nelda Rodger, Editor

Canadian Facility Management & Design
#338, 4195 Dundas St. West, Toronto, ON M8X 1Y4
Tel: 416-236-5856; Fax: 416-236-5219
cfm@sympatico.ca
Circulation: 6,538 Frequency: 6 times a year
Arvid Stonkus, Publisher & Production Manager

Canadian Interiors
Owned By: Business Information Group
800, 12 Concorde Place, Toronto, ON M3C 4J2
Tel: 416-442-5600; Fax: 416-442-2191
Toll-Free: 800-668-2374
Circulation: 11,847 Frequency: 6 times a year
Martin Spreer, Publisher, 416-510-6766, mspreer@canadianinteriors.com

Ontario Design
Owned By: Homes Publishing Group
178 Main St., Unionville, ON L3R 2G9
Tel: 905-479-4663 Toll-Free: 800-363-4663
info@ontariodesigntrade.com
Social Media: www.facebook.com/148850138470077
Circulation: 12,000 Frequency: Annually
Michael Rosset, Publisher

Jewellery & Giftware

Canadian Jeweller
#1106, 60 Bloor St. West, Toronto, ON M4W 3B8
Tel: 416-203-7900; Fax: 416-703-6392
Toll-Free: 888-358-8185
editorial@gorgmgo.com
Social Media: twitter.com/cj_mag
Circulation: 8152 Frequency: 7 times a year
Olivier Felicio, Publisher, olivier@rivegauchemedia.com
Erin Poredos, Creative Business Coordinator, erin@gorgmgo.com

Ever Magazine
#1106, 60 Bloor St. West, Toronto, ON M4W 3B8
Tel: 416-203-7900; Fax: 416-703-6392
sales@gorgmgo.com
Social Media: twitter.com/EverMagazine
www.facebook.com/pages/Ever-Magazine/1501 36948395161
Canadian jewellery magazine.

Jewellery Business
Owned By: Kenilworth Publishing Inc.
#710, 15 Wertheim Crt., Richmond Hill, ON L4B 3H7
Tel: 905-771-7333; Fax: 905-771-7336
Toll-Free: 800-409-8688
editor@jewellerybusiness.com
Social Media: www.linkedin.com/groups?gid=4069559&trk=hb_side__g
twitter.com/jewellery bizmag
Circulation: 8,079 Frequency: 6 times a year

Journalism

L'edition Nouvelles
8030, rue Marie Lefranc, Laval, QC H7Y 2C2
Tel: 450-962-7610; Fax: 450-962-7092
Toll-Free: 866-639-7226
Circulation: 1 451 Frequency: mensuel
Ruth Douglas, President & Publisher

Media
Canadian Association of Journalists, PO Box 280, Brantford, ON N3T 5M8
Tel: 613-526-8061; Fax: 613-521-3904
Circulation: 4,000 Frequency: Quarterly
David McKie, Publisher

News Canada / L'Édition Nouvelles
Owned By: News Canada Inc.
Tel: 416-599-9900; Fax: 416-599-9700
Toll-Free: 888-855-6397
Frequency: Monthly
Ruth Douglas, President/Publisher

Landscaping

Hortwest
c/o BC Landscape & Nursery Association, #102, 5783 - 176A St., Surrey, BC V3S 6S6
Circulation: 1,250 Frequency: 10 times a year
Karen DeJong, Managing Editor
Barb Nelson, Manager, Advertising, b-nelson@telus.net

Landscape Ontario
Previous Name: Horticulture Review
Owned By: Landscape Ontario Horticultural Trades Association
7856 - 5th Line South, #RR4, Milton, ON L9T 2X8
Tel: 416-848-7575; Fax: 905-875-3942
Toll-Free: 800-265-5656
Circulation: 2,300 Frequency: Monthly
Lee Ann Knudson, Publisher
Allan Dennis, Editor, adennis@landscapeontario.com

Landscape Trades
Owned By: Landscape Ontario Horticultural Trades Association
7856 - 5th Line South, RR #4, Milton, ON L9T 2X8
Tel: 905-875-1805; Fax: 905-875-0183
Toll-Free: 800-265-5656
Circulation: 8,226 Frequency: 9 times a year
Sarah Willis, Editorial Director, 647-723-5424, sarahw@landscapeontario.com

Landscaping & Groundskeeping
Owned By: Baum Publications Ltd.
Baum Publications Ltd., 124 - 2323 Boundary, Vancouver, BC V5M 4V8
Tel: 604-291-9900; Fax: 604-291-1906
Circulation: 14,229 Frequency: 6 times a year
Engelbert Baum, Publisher
Lee Toop, Editor, ltoop@baumpub.com

Prairie Landscape Magazine
#200, 10331 - 178 St., Calgary, AB T5S 1R5
Tel: 780-489-1991; Fax: 780-444-2152
prairielandscape@shaw.ca
Circulation: 950 Frequency: 6 pa
The magazine targets persons involved in the following businesses in Manitoba, Saskatchewan, & Alberta: retail & wholesale nurseries, greenhouse operators, sod farms, grounds maintenance, landscape contractors, arborists, & municipal goverments.
Nigel Bowes, Managing Editor

Québec Vert
Détenteur: Editions Versicolores inc.
1320, boul. Saint-Joseph, Québec, QC G2K 1G2
Tél: 418-628-8690;Téléc: 418-628-0524
Ligne sans frais: 800-463-1576
Tirage: 3 167 Fréquence: 8 fois par an; français
Claire Bélisle, Éditeur

Turf & Recreation
275 James St., Delhi, ON N4B 2B2
Tel: 519-582-8873; Fax: 519-582-8877
Toll-Free: 800-525-6825
turf@on.aibn.com
Circulation: 15,000 Frequency: 7 times a year
Bart Crandon, Publisher, turf.bart@on.aibn.com
Brenda Bozso, Administrative & Circulation Manager, turf.brenda@on.aibn.com

Laundry & Dry Cleaning

Fabricare Canada
PO Box 968, Oakville, ON L6J 5E8
Tel: 905-337-0516
Frequency: 6 pa
Fabricare Canada features news about the textile care industry, business ideas, environmental issues, & information about new products. Summaries in French & Korean are included in each issue. The publication is a member off the Canadian Cleaners & Launderers Allied Trades Association.
Marcia Todd, Publisher
Becca Anderson, Assistant Editor
Bill Goodbrand, Contact, Advertising Production & Sales, 905-849-1853

Legal

The Advocate
#103, 1529 West 6th Ave., Vancouver, BC V6J 1R1
Tel: 604-737-8274
info@vancouverbar.ca
Circulation: 12,000 Frequency: Bi-monthly
Published by the Vancouver Bar Association, The Advocate is of interest to members of the legal profession, the judiciary, courthouses, & law schools in British Columbia & abroad. The Advocate features legal news & commentary.
Lynda Roberts, Administrator

Briefly Speaking
c/o Ontario Bar Association, #300, 20 Toronto St., Toronto, ON M5C 2B8
Tel: 416-869-1047; Fax: 416-869-1390
Toll-Free: 800-668-8900
ccrocker@oba.org
Circulation: 13,000 Frequency: 3 times a year; English & French
The official, bilingual learned legal journal of the Ontario Bar Association.
Catherine Brennan, Editor

Canadian Bar Review / La Revue du Barreau canadien
c/o Canadian Bar Foundation, #500, 865 Carling Ave., Ottawa, ON K1S 5S8
Tel: 613-237-2925; Fax: 613-237-0185
Toll-Free: 800-267-8860
review@cba.org
Circulation: 36,200 on-line Frequency: 3 times a year; English & French
The official, bilingual learned legal journal of the CBA, the Canadian Bar Review is published online three times a year. Fully searchable archives of the Bar Review, dating back to 1923, are available in PDF format. The Review directly meets the educational objective of the CBA. It is frequently cited in the Supreme Court of Canada and boasts an international reputation for quality and excellence.
Prof. Beth Bilson, Editor-in-chief

Canadian Corporate Counsel Association Magazine (CCCA)
Owned By: Rogers Publishing Ltd.
#410, 20 Toronto Street, Toronto, ON M3C 2B8
Tel: 416-869-0522; Fax: 416-869-0946
ccca@ccca-cba.org
Social Media: twitter.com/CCCA_News
Circulation: 10,511 Frequency: 4 times a year
Forum for in-house counsel to advance the development of their practice of law.
Stefanie MacDonald, Publisher
Jordan Furlong, Editor

Le Journal du Barreau
445, boul St-Laurent, Montréal, QC H2Y 3T8
Tél: 514-954-3400;Téléc: 514-954-3464
Ligne sans frais: 800-361-8495
journaldubarreau@barreau.qc.ca
Médias sociaux: twitter.com/BarreauduQuebec
www.facebook.com/barreauduquebec
Tirage: 28,000 Fréquence: 12 fois par an; français
Le Journal du Barreau, édité par le Service des communications, est la publication phare du monde juridique québécois. Il traite de l'évolution de l'exercice de la profession d'avocat, de différents domaines du droit, du système judiciaire et des aspects du droit liés aux enjeux de société
Virginie Savard, Assistante en communications

Law Times
Owned By: Thomson Reuters Canada Ltd.
One Corporate Plaza, 2075 Kennedy Rd., Toronto, ON M1T 3V4
Tel: 416-298-5141; Fax: 416-649-7870
Social Media: twitter.com/lawtimes
Circulation: 12,700 Frequency: 40 times a year
Ontario's source of legal affairs news and commentary. News Flash: Our weekly coverage offers analysis and insight into the legal profession's key players, news events and court rulings. Focus Sections: Each issue explores in detail a topic of compelling interest to Ontario's legal profession. Our focus

sections cover topics as diverse as computer software, private investigators and forensic services
Gail J. Cohen, Editorial Director, 416-649-9928
Glen Kouth, Editor, 416-641-9554

The Lawyers Weekly
Owned By: LexisNexis Canada Ltd.
#700, 123 Commerce Valley Dr., Markham, ON L3T 7W8
Tel: 905-479-2665; Fax: 905-479-6460
Toll-Free: 800-668-6481
Circulation: 21,400 Frequency: 48 times a year
Published since 1983, The Lawyers Weekly was the first newspaper for the Canadian legal profession. It serves the national market with bureaus in Ottawa and Toronto and correspondents across the country. Published 48 times a year, The Lawyers Weekly provides lawyers with information essential to maintaining and building a successful practice in today's competitive business environment.
Tim Wilbur, Managing Editor
Gary Rodrigues, Publisher
Rob Kelly, Editor-in-Chief

McGill Law Journal / Revue de droit de McGill
3644 Peel St., Montréal, QC H3A 1W9
Tel: 514-398-7397; Fax: 514-398-7360
journal.law@mcgill.ca
Social Media:
twitter.com/McGill_LJ
www.facebook.com/pages/McGill-Law-Journal/187527307932696
Circulation: 1,330 Frequency: 4 times a year; English & French
The McGill Law Journal is an academic legal journal established in 1952 by the students of the McGill University Faculty of Law. More than fifty years later, and still entirely student-run, we remain committed to the advancement of legal scholarship in both the common and civil law. Amongst university law journals, McGill's is especially unique as a result of its bilingual, bijuridical character, and its success as the most frequently quoted university law journal by the Supreme Court of Canada.
Laure Prévost, Managing Editor

Le Monde Juridique
642, Pierre-Tétreault, Montréal, QC H1L 4Y5
Tél: 514-353-3549
agmonde@videotron.ca
Tirage: 10 000 Fréquence: 10 fois par an; français
Magazine des juristes du Québec
André Gagnon, Rédacteur en chef B.A., LLL

National
Owned By: Rogers Publishing Ltd.
#500, 865 Carling Ave., Ottawa, ON K1S 5S8
Tel: 613-237-2925; Fax: 613-237-0185
Toll-Free: 800-267-8860
national@cba.org
Circulation: 37,000 Frequency: 9 times a year; English & French
National is the official magazine of the Canadian Bar Association. It tracks and analyzes the latest trends and developments in the law, provides practice and career information to lawyers, informs members of CBA activities and explores issues of importance to Canadian law practitioners
Stefanie MacDonald, Publisher
Beverley Spencer, Editor-in-Chief, beverleys@cba.org

Ontario Legal Directory
Previous Name: Toronto Legal Directory
University of Toronto Press, #700, 10 St. Mary St., Toronto, ON M4Y 2W8
Tel: 416-667-7810; Fax: 416-667-7881
publishing@utpress.utoronto.ca
Circulation: 5,500 Frequency: Annually, February
Accuracy and completeness of detail have characterized the Ontario Legal Directory since 1925, when the first annual edition of the Toronto Legal Directory was published. With over 30,000 listings of lawyers, law firms, federal and provincial courts and government offices, each complete with names, addresses, telephone and fax numbers, and e-mail and web addresses, the Ontario Legal Directory places all the information you need right at your fingertips. The Blue Pages put governments and courts information right up front, organized in easy-to-find categories with thumb-tab indexing.
Lynn N. Browne, Editor

The Ontario Reports
Owned By: LexisNexis Canada Ltd.
#700, 123 Commerce Valley Dr. East, Markham, ON L3T 7WB
Tel: 905-479-2665; Fax: 905-479-3758
Toll-Free: 800-668-6481
info@lexisnexis.ca
Frequency: Weekly
Published by the Law Society of Upper Canada through LexisNexis Canada, the Ontario Reports, Third Series provides in full text, leading cases decided at all levels of Ontario courts. Published 52 times per year, the soft cover parts also contain official Law Society notices (i.e., Practice Directions), government notices of interest to the legal profession, fee schedules, lawyers announcements and advertising. A personally addressed copy is sent to each of the Law Society's members each Friday.
Sarojini Pillay, Editor

Osgoode Hall Law Journal
Osgoode Hall Law School of York University, 4700 Keele St., Toronto, ON M3J 1P3
Tel: 416-736-5354; Fax: 416-736-5869
journal@osgoode.yorku.ca
Circulation: 1,500 Frequency: Quarterly, plus index; English or French
The Journal has acquired a reputation for excellence in publishing scholarly articles that represent a wide range of perspectives about law and legal institutions
Stepan Wood, Editor-in-chief, swood@osgoode.yorku.ca
Lara Kinkartz, Managing Editor

The Scrivener Magazine
PO Box 44, #1220, 625 Howe St., Vancouver, BC V6C 2T6
Tel: 604-681-4516; Fax: 604-681-7258
Toll-Free: 800-663-0343
scrivener@notaries.bc.ca
Circulation: 6,000 Frequency: 4 times a year
The Scrivener is published quarterly by The Society of Notaries Public of British Columbia. Celebrates the Notary's role in drafting, communicating, authenticating, and getting the facts straight. Strives to publish articles about points of law and the Notary profession for the education and enjoyment of its members, their Allied Professionals, and the public
Val Wilson, Editor-in-chief

Lighting

Professional Lighting & Production
Owned By: Norris-Whitney Communications Inc.
#7, 23 Hannover Dr., St Catharines, ON L2W 1A3
Tel: 905-641-3471; Fax: 905-665-1307
info@nor.com
Social Media:
www.twitter.com/plpmag
www.facebook.com/professionallighting
Circulation: 10,200 Frequency: 4 times a year
Jim Norris, Publisher

Machinery Maintenance

Machinery & Equipment MRO
Owned By: Business Information Group
80 Valleybrook Dr., Toronto, ON M3B 2S9
Tel: 416-510-5600; Fax: 416-510-5134
Toll-Free: 800-387-0273
broebuck@mromagazine.com
Social Media:
twitter.com/mromagazine
Circulation: 18,000 Frequency: 6 times a year
Machinery & Equipment MRO was founded to serve the industrial aftermarket (maintenance, repair and operations).
Nick Naunheimer, Publisher, nnaunheimer@mromagazine.com
Bill Roebuck, Editor & Associate Publisher, broebuck@mromagazine.com
Eric Achilles Cousineau, Sales Manager, eachilles@mromagazine.com

Materials Handling & Distribution

Gestion & Logistique
Détenteur: Les Editions Bomart ltée
Tél: 450-435-3131;Téléc: 450-435-3884
Tirage: 10 104 Fréquence: 10 fois par an
Pierre Gravel, Président & éditeur
Eric Cloutier, Directeur de la rédaction

Materials Management & Distribution (MM&D)
Owned By: Business Information Group
80 Valleybrook Dr., Toronto, ON M3B 2S9
Tel: 416-442-5600; Fax: 416-510-5140
Toll-Free: 888-297-7195
info@canadianmanufacturing.com
Circulation: 19,000 Frequency: Monthly; also Data Capture Communication & Commerce (4 times a year)
Supply chain magazine covering information management & transportation
Emily Atkins, Editor/Publisher, 416-510-5130, EAtkins@mmdonline.com

Metalworking

Canadian Metalworking
Owned By: Business Information Group
80 Valleybrook Dr., Toronto, ON M3B 2S9
Tel: 416-442-5600; Fax: 416-510-5140
Toll-Free: 888-297-7195
info@canadianmanufacturing.com
Circulation: 20,500 Frequency: 10 times a year
Steve Devonport, Publisher, 416-510-5125, SDevonport@canadianmetalworking.com
Jim Anderton, Editor, 416-510-5148, janderton@canadianmetalworking.com

Metalworking Production & Purchasing
Owned By: Annex Publishing & Printing Inc.
PO Box 775, 222 Edward St., Aurora, ON L4G 1W6
Tel: 905-727-0071; Fax: 905-727-0017
Toll-Free: 800-265-2827
Social Media:
twitter.com/metalworkingCA
Circulation: 20,000 Frequency: 6 times a year; also The Canadian Machine Tool Dealer
Nigel Bishop, Publisher
Robert Colman, Editor

Military

Canadian Defence Review
PO Box 305, 21 Main St., Markham, ON L3P 3J8
Tel: 905-554-4586
info@canadiandefencereview.com
Social Media:
twitter.com/CDRmagazine
Circulation: 10,470 Frequency: 6 times a year
Peter A. Kitchen, Publisher
Nick Stephens, Managing Editor
Dianne Osadchuk, Circulation Manager

Mining

Canadian & American Mines Handbook
Owned By: Business Information Group
80 Valleybrook Dr., Toronto, ON M3B 2S9
Tel: 416-442-5600; Fax: 416-510-5138
Toll-Free: 800-668-2374
mineshandbook@northernminer.com
Frequency: Annually, November
Doug Donnelly, Publisher
Diane Giancola, Editor

Canadian Miner
285 Lynn Ave., North Vancouver, BC V7J 2C3
Tel: 604-980-0794; Fax: 604-980-7123
Toll-Free: 800-570-3366
editor@canadianminingnews.com
Circulation: 3,250 Frequency: 4 times a year
Michael J. McGrath, Editor

Canadian Mining Journal
Owned By: Business Information Group
80 Valleybrook Dr., Toronto, ON M3B 2S9
Tel: 416-510-6891; Fax: 416-510-5138
Toll-Free: 800-268-7742
Circulation: 10,045 Frequency: 9 times a year
Russell Noble, Editor, 416-510-6891, rnoble@canadianminingjournal.com
Robert Seagraves, Publisher, 416-510-6891, rseagraves@canadianminingjournal.com

CIM Magazine
Previous Name: CIM Bulletin
Owned By: Canadian Institute of Mining, Metallurgy & Petroleum
#1250, 3500, boul de Maisonneuve ouest, Westmount, QC H3Z 3C1
Tel: 514-939-2710; Fax: 514-939-2714
cim@cim.org
Circulation: 10,822 Frequency: 8 times a year
Angela Hamlyn, Editor-in-Chief, ahamlyn@cim.org

FP Survey-Mines & Energy
Previous Name: The Financial Post Survey of Mines & Energy Resources
Owned By: Owen Media Partners Inc.
#208, 2085 Hurontario St., Mississauga, ON L5A 4G1
Tel: 905-290-1818; Fax: 905-290-1760
Toll-Free: 800-206-6548
owenmediainfo@owen-media.com
Circulation: 4,300 Frequency: Annually, August

Mineral Exploration
Owned By: Canada Wide Magazines & Communications Ltd.
4180 Lougheed Hwy., 4th Fl., Burnaby, BC V5C 6A7
Tel: 604-299-7311; Fax: 604-299-9188
mineralexplorationsubs@canadawide.com
Circulation: 6,400 Frequency: 4 times a year
Kirsten Rodenhizer, Editorial Coordinator, krodenhizer@canadawide.com

Mining Sourcebook
Owned By: Business Information Group
80 Valleybrook Dr., Toronto, ON M3B 2S9
Tel: 416-510-6891; Fax: 416-510-5138
Circulation: 5,861 Frequency: Annually, November
Ray Perks, Publisher, rperks@canadianminingjournal.com

The Northern Miner
Owned By: Business Information Group
80 Valleybrook Dr., Toronto, ON M3B 2S9
Tel: 416-510-6768; Fax: 416-510-5138
Toll-Free: 800-668-2374
northernminer2@northernminer.com
Social Media: twitter.com/northernminer/
Circulation: 16,874 Frequency: Weekly
Doug Donnelly, Publisher, 416-442-2098, ddonnelly@northernminer.com

The Prospector: Investment & Exploration News
#104, 333 East First St., North Vancouver, BC V7L 4W9
Tel: 604-639-5495; Fax: 604-990-1093
sales@theprospectornews.com
Other information: Editorial, E-mail: editor@theprospectornews.com
Frequency: 6 pa
Published by Foxtrot Communications Ltd., The Prospector includes industry analysis, company profiles, boardroom reports, & enviromental information.

Motor Trucks & Buses

L'Écho du Transport
Détenteur: Les Editions Bomart ltée
#204, 905, Michèle-Bohec, Blainville, QC J7C 5J6
Tél: 450-435-3131;Téléc: 450-435-3884
Tirage: 25,500 Fréquence: 10 fois par an; français
Pierre Gravel, Éditeur, pgravel@bomartgroup.com
Eric Clouter, Rédacteur-en-chef, ecloutier@bomartgroup.com

The Manitoba Trucking Guide for Shippers
Previous Name: Manitoba Ship-by-Truck Directory
Owned By: Craig Kelman & Associates Ltd.
Tel: 204-985-9791
info@trucking.mb.ca
Circulation: 1,000 Frequency: Annually

Over the Road
18 Parkglen Dr., Ottawa, ON K2G 3G9
Tel: 613-224-9947; Fax: 613-224-8825
otr@otr.on.ca
Circulation: 21,000 Frequency: 12 times a year
Peter Charboneau, Publisher, peter@otr.on.ca

Today's Trucking
c/o New Communications Group Inc., 451 Attwell Dr., Toronto, ON M9W 5C4
Tel: 416-614-2200; Fax: 416-614-8861
rolf@todaystrucking.com
Circulation: 30,000 Frequency: 10 times a year
Rolf Lockwood, Publisher, rolf@todaystrucking.com
Peter Carter, Editor

Truck News, Truck West & Motortruck
Owned By: Business Information Group
80 Valleybrook Dr., Toronto, ON M3B 2S9
Tel: 416-510-5123; Fax: 416-510-5143
Toll-Free: 800-268-7742
Social Media: twitter.com/LouSmyrlis
www.facebook.com/trucknews
Circulation: 20,477 Frequency: 6 times a year
Lou Smyrlis, Editorial Director, 416-510-6881, lou@TransportationMedia.ca
Adam Ledlow, Managing Editor, adam@transportationmedia.ca

La Voix du vrac
#235, 670, rue Bouvier, Québec, QC G2J 1A7
Tél: 418-623-7923;Téléc: 418-623-0448
revue@ancai.com
Tirage: 8,400 Fréquence: 6 fois par an; français
Alain Simard, Éditeur

Western Canada Highway News
Owned By: Craig Kelman & Associates Ltd.
Tel: 204-985-9785; Fax: 204-985-9795
Toll-Free: 866-985-9785
info@kelman.ca
Other information: Toll-Free Fax: 1-866-985-9799
Circulation: 4,000 Frequency: 4 times a year
Official publication of the Alberta Motor Transport Association (AMTA), Saskatchewan Trucking Association (STA), & Manitoba Trucking Association (MTA).
Craig Kelman, Publisher
Terry Ross, Editor, terry@kelman.ca

Music

Canadian Music Trade
Owned By: Norris-Whitney Communications Inc.
Norris-Whitney Communications, #7, 23 Hannover Dr., St Catharines, ON L2W 1A3
Tel: 905-641-1512; Fax: 905-641-1648
Toll-Free: 877-746-4692
press@nor.com
Social Media: www.twitter.com/cdnmusictrade
www.facebook.com/canadianmusictrade
Circulation: 3,500 Frequency: 6 times a year
Serving Canadian music dealers and suppliers.
Jim Norris, Publisher

Music Directory Canada (MDC)
Owned By: Norris-Whitney Communications Inc.
#7, 23 Hannover Dr., St Catharines, ON L2W 1A3
Tel: 905-641-3471 Toll-Free: 800-265-8481
mdc@nor.com
Social Media: www.twitter.com/mdcanada
www.facebook.com/musicdirectorycanada
Circulation: 6,000
Jim Norris, Publisher

Professional Sound
Owned By: Norris-Whitney Communications Inc.
#7, 23 Hannover Dr., St Catharines, ON L2W 1A3
Tel: 905-641-3471; Fax: 905-641-1648
mail@nor.com
Social Media: www.youtube.com/D2EEA06A387113CE
twitter.com/profsound
www.facebook .com/professionalsound
Circulation: 10,400 Frequency: 6 times a year
Jim Norris, Publisher

Nursing

Alberta RN
College & Association of Registered Nurses of Alberta, 11620 - 168 St., Edmonton, AB T5M 4A6
Tel: 780-451-0043; Fax: 780-452-3276
Toll-Free: 800-252-9392
carna@nurses.ab.ca
Circulation: 28,000 Frequency: 9 times a year
Margaret Ward-Jack, Managing Editor
Rachel Champagne, Editor

Canadian Journal of Cardiovascular Nursing (CJCN)
c/o Canadian Council of Cardiovascular Nurses, 774 Echo Dr., Ottawa, ON K1S 5N8
Tel: 613-735-0952; Fax: 613-735-7983
david@cccn.can
Circulation: 700 Frequency: Quarterly
CJCN, the official publication of the Canadian Council of Cardiovascular Nurses.
Nicole Parent, Editor
Paula Price, Editor

Canadian Nurse
Canadian Nurses Assn., 50 Driveway, Ottawa, ON K2P 1E2
Tel: 613-237-2133; Fax: 613-237-3520
Toll-Free: 800-361-8404
info@canadian-nurse.com
Circulation: 120,815 Frequency: 9 times a year
Lisa Brazeau, Editor-in-chief, editor@canadian-nurse.com

Canadian Oncology Nursing Journal
Owned By: Pappin Communications
The Victoria Centre, 84 Isabella St., Pembroke, ON K8A 5S5
Tel: 613-735-0952; Fax: 613-735-7983
info@pappin.com
Circulation: 1,000 Frequency: 4 times a year; English & French
Bruce M. Pappin, Managing Editor
Dr. Heather Porter, Editor-in-chief

Infirmière canadienne
Canadian Nurses Assn., 50, rue Driveway, Ottawa, ON K2P 1E2
Tél: 613-237-2159;Téléc: 613-237-3520
Ligne sans frais: 800-361-8404
info@canadian-nurse.com
Tirage: 3 000 Fréquence: 9 fois par an
Lucille Auffrey, Editor-in-chief

Newsbulletin
Saskatchewan Registered Nurses' Association, 2066 Retallack St., Regina, SK S4S 7X5
Tel: 306-359-4200; Fax: 306-525-0849
Toll-Free: 800-667-9945
info@srna.org
Circulation: 10,000 Frequency: 5 times a year
Shirley McKay, Director Registrar

Perspective Infirmière
Anciennement: L'Infirmière du Québec; Nursing Québec
4200, boul Dorchester ouest, Montréal, QC H3Z 1V4
Tél: 514-935-2501;Téléc: 514-935-2055
Ligne sans frais: 800-363-6048
revue@oiiq.org
Médias sociaux: www.flickr.com/people/ordreinf
twitter.com/OIIQ
www.facebook.com/Ordre .infirmieres.infirmiers.Quebec
Tirage: 66 913 Fréquence: 6 fois par an; français
Marlène Lavoie, Secrétaire de rédaction, MLavoie@oiiq.org
Lyse Savard, Rédactrice, lyse.savard@oiiq.org

Registered Nurse Journal
#1600, 438 University Ave., Toronto, ON M5G 2K8
Tel: 416-599-1925; Fax: 416-599-1926
Toll-Free: 800-268-7199
Circulation: 24,000 Frequency: 6 times a year
Marion Zych, Publisher, mzych@rnao.ca

The Registered Practical Nursing Journal
Previous Name: The Care Connection
Bldg. 4, #200, 5025 Orbitor Dr., Mississauga, ON L4W 4Y5
Tel: 905-602-4664; Fax: 905-602-4666
Toll-Free: 877-602-4664
editor@rpnao.org
Social Media: twitter.com/rpnao
www.facebook.com/RPNAO
Circulation: 5,500 Frequency: 4 times a year
Joanne Young Evans, Executive Director

Santé Québec
Anciennement: l'Infirmière auxiliaire
Ordre des infirmières & infirmiers auxiliaires du Québec, 531, rue Sherbrooke est, Montréal, QC H2L 1K2
Tél: 514-282-9511;Téléc: 514-282-0631
Ligne sans frais: 800-283-9511
oiiaq@oiiaq.org
Tirage: 23 000 Fréquence: 3 fois par an; français et anglais
Catherine-Dominique Nantel, Rédactrice-en-chef & Éditrice

Packaging

Canadian Packaging
Owned By: Business Information Group
80 Valleybrook Dr., Toronto, ON M3B 2S9
Tel: 416-442-5600; Fax: 416-510-5140
Toll-Free: 888-297-7195
info@canadianmanufacturing.com
Circulation: 13,626 Frequency: 9 times a year
Stephen Dean, Publisher, 416-510-5198, SDean@canadianpackaging.com
George Guidoni, Editor, 416-510-5227, GGuidoni@canadianpackaging.com

Petroleum, Oil & Gas

Air Water Land
Owned By: JuneWarren-Nickle's Energy Group
816 - 55 Ave. NE, 2nd Fl., Calgary, AB T2E 6Y4
Tel: 403-209-3500; Fax: 403-245-8666
Toll-Free: 800-387-2446
Circulation: 10,000 Frequency: Annually

Alberta Oil & Gas Directory
Owned By: Armadale Publications Inc.
Tel: 780-429-1073; Fax: 780-425-5844
armadale@nucleus.com
Circulation: 10,000 Frequency: Annually
Haloshini Naidoo, Manager
Winston Mohabir, Publisher

Canadian Oil Register
#300, 999 - 8 St. SW, Calgary, AB T2R 1N7
Tel: 403-209-3500; Fax: 403-245-8666
Frequency: Weekly

Canadian Oilpatch Technology Guidebook & Directory
Previous Name: Canadian Oilfield Service & Supply Directory
Owned By: JuneWarren-Nickle's Energy Group
816 - 55 Ave. NE, 2nd Fl., Calgary, AB T2E 6Y4
Tel: 403-209-3500; Fax: 403-245-8666
Toll-Free: 800-387-2446
Circulation: 10,000 Frequency: Annually; August
Bill Whitelaw, Publisher

Canadian Petroleum Contractor
Owned By: Fulcrum Publishing Inc.
#201, 508 Lawrence Ave. West, Toronto, ON M6A 1A1
Tel: 416-504-0504 Toll-Free: 866-688-0504
Circulation: 1,000 Frequency: Quarterly

Earth Resources
Previous Name: Ocean Resources
Owned By: Metro Guide Publishing
1300 Hollis St., Halifax, NS B3J 1T6
Tel: 902-422-4990; Fax: 902-422-4728
Frequency: 8 times a year
Suzanne Rent, Editor, srent@metroguide.ca

Energy Processing Canada
Owned By: Northern Star Communications Ltd.
900 - 6th Avenue SW, 4th Fl., Calgary, AB T2P 3K2
Tel: 403-263-6881; Fax: 403-263-6886
Toll-Free: 800-526-4177
energy@northernstar.ab.ca
Circulation: 9,866 Frequency: 6 times a year
Serving the hydrocarbons processing related industries.
Scott Jeffrey, Publisher, scott@northernstar.ab.ca

Heavy Oil & Oilsands Guidebook
Owned By: JuneWarren-Nickle's Energy Group
816 - 55 Ave. NE, 2nd Fl., Calgary, AB T2E 6Y4
Tel: 403-209-3500; Fax: 403-245-8666
Toll-Free: 800-387-2446
Circulation: 15,000 Frequency: Annual
Agnes Zalewski, Publisher

The Journal of Canadian Petroleum Technology
Eau Claire Place II, #900, 521 - 3rd Ave. SW, Calgary, AB T2P 3T3
Tel: 403-930-5454; Fax: 403-930-5470
specal@spe.org
Social Media: www.youtube.com/user/2012SPE?feature=mhee
twitter.com/SPE_Events
www.f acebook.com/spemembers
Circulation: 3,800 Frequency: 12 times a year
Stephen A. Holditch, Editor-in-Chief

New Technology Magazine
Owned By: JuneWarren-Nickle's Energy Group
816 - 55 Ave. NE, 2nd Fl., Calgary, AB T2E 6Y4
Tel: 403-209-3500; Fax: 403-245-8666
Toll-Free: 800-387-2446
Circulation: 7,000 Frequency: 10 times a year
Maurice Smith, Editor

Oil & Gas Inquirer
Owned By: JuneWarren-Nickle's Energy Group
816 - 55 Ave. NE, 2nd Fl., Calgary, AB T2E 6Y4
Tel: 403-209-3500; Fax: 403-245-8666
Toll-Free: 800-387-2446
marketing@junewarren.com
Circulation: 10,000 Frequency: 10 times per year
Janet Howes, Editor

The Oil & Gas Magazine (OGM)
PO Box 668, Blaketown, NL A0B 1C0
Tel: 709-759-3800; Fax: 709-582-3408
info@theogm.com
Social Media:
www.linkedin.com/groups/OGM-4035069?gid=4035069
twitter.com/theogmonline
www.facebook.com/TheOGM
Frequency: Bi-monthly
Bill Abbott, Editor

Oil & Gas Network (OGN)
#300, 840 - 6th Ave. SW, Calgary, AB T2P 3E5
Tel: 403-503-0460; Fax: 403-206-7753
jrr@oilgas.net
Social Media:
twitter.com/oilgasnetwork
Circulation: 15,900 Frequency: Bi-Monthly
John Robertson, Editor, jrr@oilgas.net

Oil & Gas Product News
Owned By: Baum Publications Ltd.
Baum Publications Ltd., 124 - 2323 Boundary, Vancouver, BC V5M 4V8
Tel: 604-291-9900; Fax: 604-291-1906
Circulation: 10,708 Frequency: 6 times a year
Lee Toop, Editor, ltoop@baumpub.com

Oilsands Review
Owned By: JuneWarren-Nickle's Energy Group
816 - 55 Ave. NE, 2nd Fl., Calgary, AB T2E 6Y4
Tel: 403-209-3500; Fax: 403-245-8666
Toll-Free: 800-387-2446
Circulation: 10,000 Frequency: Monthly
Deborah Jaremko, Editor

Oilweek
Owned By: JuneWarren-Nickle's Energy Group
816 - 55 Ave. NE, 2nd Fl., Calgary, AB T2E 6Y4
Tel: 403-209-3500; Fax: 403-245-8666
Toll-Free: 800-387-2446
Circulation: 10,000 Frequency: Monthly
Darrell Stonehouse, Managing Editor
Bill Whitelaw, Publisher

Profiler
Owned By: JuneWarren-Nickle's Energy Group
816 - 55 Ave. NE, 2nd Fl., Calgary, AB T2E 6Y4
Tel: 403-209-3500; Fax: 403-245-8666
Toll-Free: 800-387-2446
Frequency: 4 times a year

Propane-Canada
Owned By: Northern Star Communications Ltd.
900 - 6th Avenue SW, 4th Fl., Calgary, AB T2P 3K2
Tel: 403-263-6881; Fax: 403-263-6886
Toll-Free: 800-526-4177
propane@northernstar.ab.ca
Circulation: 8,800 Frequency: 6 times a year
Scott Jeffrey, Publisher, scott@northernstar.ab.ca

The Roughneck
Owned By: Northstar Communications Inc.
900 - 6th Avenue SW, 4th Fl., Calgary, AB T2P 3K2
Tel: 780-263-6881; Fax: 780-423-6886
Toll-Free: 800-526-4177
roughneck@northernstar.ab.ca
Scott Jeffrey, Publisher, scott@northernstar.ab.ca

The Roughneck Buy & Sell
Owned By: Northstar Communications Inc.
900 - 6th Avenue SW, 4th Fl., Calgary, AB T2P 3K2
Tel: 780-263-6881; Fax: 780-423-6886
Toll-Free: 800-526-4177
buyandsell@northernstar.ab.ca
Circulation: 10,000 Frequency: 12 times a year

Photography

Photo Life
185, rue St-Paul, Québec, QC G1K 3W2
;Téléc: 800-664-2739
Ligne sans frais: 800-905-7468
editor@photolife.com
Tirage: 10 000 Fréquence: 6 fois par an; français
Valérie Racine, Rédacteur en Chef, write@photolife.com
Guy Poirier, gpoirier@photolife.com

Photo Life Buyers' Guide
Previous Name: National Photo Buyers' Guide
Owned By: Apex Publications Inc.
185, rue St-Paul, Québec, QC G1K 3W2
Toll-Free: 800-905-7468
info@photolife.com
Other information: Toll Free Fax: 1-800-664-2739
Social Media:
twitter.com/PhotoLifeMag
www.facebook.com/pages/Photo-Life-Magazine/13775363291636
Circulation: 65,000 Frequency: Annually
Valerie Racine, Editor, write@photolife.com
Guy Poirier, Publisher, gpoirier@photolife.com

PhotoLife
Previous Name: Master Guide
185 St-Paul St., Québec, QC G1K 3W2
Tel: 418-692-2110; Fax: 418-692-3392
Toll-Free: 800-905-7468
Other information: Toll Free Fax: 1-800-644-2739
Circulation: 6,500 Frequency: Annually
Guy J. Poirier, Publisher
Xavier Bonacassi, Editor

Plastics

Canadian Plastics
Owned By: Business Information Group
80 Valleybrook Dr., Toronto, ON M3B 2S9
Tel: 416-442-5600; Fax: 416-510-5143
Toll-Free: 800-268-7742
Circulation: 10,402 Frequency: 12 times a year
Judith Nancekivell, Senior Publisher, 416-510-5116, jnancekivell@canplastics.com

Canadian Plastics Directory & Buyer's Guide
Owned By: Business Information Group
80 Valleybrook Dr., Toronto, ON M3B 2S9
Tel: 416-442-5600; Fax: 416-510-5134
Toll-Free: 800-268-7742
Circulation: 10,959 Frequency: Annually
Judith Nancekivell, Publisher, jnancekivell@canplastics.com
Mark Stephen, Editor, mstephen@canplastics.com

Police

Blue Line Magazine
#254, 12A - 4981 Hwy. 7 East, Markham, ON L3R 1N1
Tel: 905-640-3048; Fax: 905-640-7547
blueline@blueline.ca
Circulation: 12,000 Frequency: 10 times a year
Morley S. Lymburner, Publisher/Editor
Mark Reesor, Senior Editor

Tour of Duty
Previous Name: News & Views
Toronto Police Assn., 180 Yorkland Blvd., Toronto, ON M2J 1R5
Tel: 416-491-4301; Fax: 416-494-4948
information@tpa.ca
Circulation: 9,245 Frequency: Monthly

Power & Power Plants

Nuclear Canada Yearbook
Canadian Nuclear Association, #1610, 130 Albert St., Ottawa, ON K1P 5G4
Tel: 613-237-4262; Fax: 613-237-0989
Circulation: 3,500 Frequency: Annually
Colin Hunt, Publisher & Editor

Printing & Publishing

Canadian Magazines Canadiene
#700, 425 Adelaide St. West, Toronto, ON M5V 3C1
Tel: 416-504-0274; Fax: 416-504-0437
cmceditorial@magazinescanada.ca
Social Media: cmcblog.magazinescanada.ca
Resource for publishing professionals.
Chantal Tranchemontagne, Editor-in-Chief

Estimators' & Buyers' Guide
Owned By: North Island Publishing Ltd.
#8, 1606 Sedlescomb Dr., Mississauga, ON L4X 1M6
Tel: 905-625-7070; Fax: 905-625-4856
Toll-Free: 800-331-7408
Frequency: Annually
Alexander Donald, Publisher

Graphic Arts Magazine
72 Main St., Mount Albert, ON L0G 1M0
; Fax: 905-830-9345
Toll-Free: 877-513-3999
joe@graphicartsmagazine.com
Social Media:
www.linkedin.com/company/graphic-arts-magazine
twitter.com/graphicarts
www.facebook.com/pages/Graphic-Arts-Magazine/140386003309
Circulation: 11,200 Frequency: 10 times a year
Joe Mulcahy, Publisher
Scott Bury, Editor

Graphic Monthly
Owned By: North Island Publishing Ltd.
#8, 1606 Sedlecomb Dr., Mississauga, ON L4X 1M6
Tel: 905-625-7070; Fax: 905-625-4856
Toll-Free: 800-331-7408
Circulation: 10,000 Frequency: 6 times a year
Alexander Donald, Publisher, s.donald@northisland.ca
Filomena Tamburri, Editor, ftamburri@graphicmonthly.ca

Livre d'ici
#55, 222, Cours Dominion, Montréal, QC H3J 2X1
Tel: 514-933-8033; Fax: 514-933-7958
publicite@livre-dici.qc.ca

Circulation: 1,600
Jacques Therriault, Publisher

Le Maître Imprimeur
5400, rue Chemin, Saint-Laurent, QC H4S 1P6
Tél: 514-388-9311;Téléc: 514-388-0188

Tirage: 5 000 Fréquence: 10 fois par an; français
Christine Veznia, Éditeur

Product Engineering & Design

Design Engineering
Owned By: Business Information Group
80 Valleybrook Dr., Toronto, ON M3B 2S9
Tel: 416-442-5600; Fax: 416-510-5140
Toll-Free: 888-297-7195
info@canadianmanufacturing.com
Circulation: 19,000 Frequency: 8 times a year
Alan Macpherson, Associate Publisher,
AMacPherson@design-engineering.com
Mike Mcleod, Editor, MMcLeod@design-engineering.com

Design Product News
Owned By: Annex Publishing & Printing Inc.
222 Edward St., Aurora, ON L4G 1W6
Tel: 905-727-0077; Fax: 905-727-0017
Toll-Free: 800-265-2827
Social Media:
www.dpncanada.com
Circulation: 20,000 Frequency: 6 times a year
Nigel Bishop, Publisher, nbishop@annexweb.com
Mike Edwards, Editor, medwards@annexweb.com

Pulp & Paper

Pulp & Paper Canada
Owned By: Business Information Group
80 Valleybrook Dr., Toronto, ON M3B 2S9
Tel: 416-510-5140 Toll-Free: 800-268-7742
media@pulpandpapercanada.com
Circulation: 9,698 Frequency: Monthly; also Annual Directory (Dec.)
Jim Bussiere, Publisher, jim@pulpandpapercanada.com
Cindy Macdonald, Editor

Purchasing

Canadian Trade Index
#208, 2085 Hurontario St., Mississauga, ON L5A 4G1
Tel: 905-290-1818; Fax: 905-361-0140
Toll-Free: 800-206-6548
customerservice@ctidirectory.com
Frequency: Annually, May
Hugh Owen, President

Purchasing B2B
Owned By: Business Information Group
80 Valleybrook Dr., Toronto, ON M3B 2S9
Tel: 416-442-5600; Fax: 416-510-5140
Toll-Free: 888-297-7195
info@canadianmanufacturing.com
Circulation: 19,292 Frequency: 10 times a year
Dorothy Jakovina, Publisher, 416-510-6899,
djakovina@bizinfogorup.ca

Real Estate

Canadian Appraiser / L'Évaluateur Canadien
#3C, 2020 Portage Ave., Winnipeg, MB R3J 0K4
Tel: 204-985-9780; Fax: 866-985-9799
info@kelman.ca
Circulation: 5,961 Frequency: 4 times a year
Craig Kelman, Editor

Canadian Mortgage Professional (CMP)
Owned By: Key Media Inc.
#800, 312 Adelaide St. West, Toronto, ON M5V 1R2
Tel: 416-644-8740; Fax: 416-203-9083
Circulation: 10,000 Frequency: Monthly
Vernon Jones, Editor, vernon.jones@kmimedia.ca

Canadian Property Guide
Previous Name: Canadian Industrial Property Guide
#1000, 33 Yonge St., Toronto, ON M5E 1S9
Tel: 416-359-2550; Fax: 416-359-2538
cmildon@royallepage.com
Circulation: 70,000 Frequency: Bi-annual
Caroline Mildon

Espace Montréal
#9235, 800, rue de la Gauchetière ouest, Montréal, QC H5A 1K6
Tél: 514-879-1559
espace@espaceqc.com
Tirage: 10 000 Fréquence: 4 fois par an
Andrew Cross, Publisher & Editor

Espace Québec
#9235, 800, de la Gauchetière ouest, Montréal, QC H5A 1K6
Tél: 418-523-0523 Ligne sans frais: 800-232-9846
espace@espaceqc.com
Tirage: 5 000 Fréquence: 2 fois par an
Andrew Cross, Éditeur/Rédacteur

REM: Real Estate Magazine
#1178, 2255B Queen St. East, Toronto, ON M4E 1G3
Tel: 416-425-3504; Fax: 416-406-0882

Social Media:
www.twitter.com/REM_Online
www.facebook.com/pages/REM-Real-Estate-Magazine/9723353 10
Circulation: 50,000 Frequency: 12 times a year
Heino Molls, Publisher, heino@remonline.com
Jim Adair, Editor, jim@remonline.com

The Western Investor
Business in Vancouver Media Group, #501, 1155 West Pender St., Vancouver, BC V6E 2P4
Tel: 604-669-8500; Fax: 604-669-2154
Toll-Free: 800-661-6988
subscribe@westerninvestor.com
Social Media:
twitter.com/westerninvestor
Circulation: 16,000 Frequency: Monthly
Cheryl Carter, Publisher, 604-608-5109
Frank O'Brien, Editor, 604-669-8500

Rental & Leasing Equipment

Canadian Rental Service
Owned By: Annex Publishing & Printing Inc.
PO Box 530, 105 Donly Dr. South, Simcoe, ON N3Y 4N5
Tel: 519-429-3966; Fax: 519-429-3094
Toll-Free: 800-265-2827
Social Media:
twitter.com/CRSmagazine
www.facebook.com/pages/Canadian-Rental-Service/1716104629
Circulation: 3,543 Frequency: 9 times a year
Patrick Flannery, Editor, 226-931-0545,
pflannery@annexweb.com

Contractors Magazine
Previous Name: Contractors Rental
Owned By: Baum Publications Ltd.
Baum Publications Ltd., 124 - 2323 Boundary, Vancouver, BC V5M 4V8
Tel: 604-291-9900; Fax: 604-291-1906
Circulation: 14,021 Frequency: 6 times a year
Engelbert Baum, Publisher
Lawrence Buser, Editor, lbuser@baumpub.com

Retailing

Canadian Retailer
#800, 1255 Bay St., Toronto, ON M5R 2A9
Tel: 416-922-6678; Fax: 416-922-8011
Toll-Free: 888-373-8245
info@retailcouncil.org
Circulation: 15,000 Frequency: 6 times a year
The official publication of Retail Council of Canada.
Theresa Rogers, Editor-in-chief
Diane Brisebois, Publisher

Monday Report on Retailers & Shopping Centre News
Owned By: Rogers Publishing Ltd.
1 Mount Pleasant Rd., 7th Fl., Toronto, ON M4Y 2Y5
Tel: 416-764-1722
Frequency: Weekly
Canada's premier information resource for people seeking in-depth, up to-date data on the retail, food service and shopping centre industries in Canada
Pamela Kirk, General Manager

Science, Research & Development

Bio Business
#202, 30 Beaver Creek Rd. East, Richmond Hill, ON L4B 1J2
Tel: 905-886-5040; Fax: 905-886-6615
Toll-Free: 800-613-6353
cforbes@jesmar.com
Circulation: 15,000 Frequency: 4 times a year
Christopher Forbes, Publisher

Biochemistry & Cell Biology / Biochimie & biologie cellulaire
Owned By: National Research Council of Canada - NRC Research Press
National Research Council of Canada, Ottawa, ON K1A 0R6
Tel: 613-993-0362; Fax: 613-952-7656
pubs@nrc-cnrc.gc.ca
Circulation: 1,150 Frequency: Bi-monthly; English & French
Cameron Macdonald, Director
Bruce P. Dancik, Editor
Judy Busnarda, Managing Editor

Camford Chemical Report
38 Groomsport Cres., Toronto, ON M1T 2K9
Tel: 416-740-5604; Fax: 416-291-3406
ccr@camfordinfo.com
Social Media:
twitter.com/cheminfo
Frequency: 50 times a year
Bob Douglas, Publisher

Canadian Geotechnical Journal / Revue canadienne de géotechnique
Owned By: National Research Council of Canada - NRC Research Press
c/o NRC Research Press, Bldg. M-55, 1200 Montreal Rd., Ottawa, ON K1A 0R6
Tel: 613-998-9432; Fax: 613-952-7656
cgj@nrcresearchpress.com
Circulation: 2,600 Frequency: monthly; English & French
Ian Moore, Associate Editor
Bruce P. Dancik, Editor
Bushra Waheed, Managing Editor

Canadian Journal of Botany / Revue canadienne de botanique
Owned By: National Research Council of Canada - NRC Research Press
c/o NRC Research Press, Bldg. M-55, 1200 Montreal Rd., Ottawa, ON K1A 0R6
Tel: 613-998-9432; Fax: 613-952-7656
botany@nrcresearchpress.com
Circulation: 1,550 Frequency: Monthly; English & French
Christian R. Lacroix, Editor PhD

Canadian Journal of Chemistry / Revue canadienne de chimie
Owned By: National Research Council of Canada - NRC Research Press
c/o NRC Research Press, Bldg. M-55, 1200 Montreal Rd., Ottawa, ON K1A 0R6
Tel: 613-998-9432; Fax: 613-952-7656
cjc@nrcresearchpress.com
Circulation: 1,700 Frequency: Monthly; English & French
Dr. Robert H. Lipson, Senior Editor
Judy Buscarda, Managing Editor

Canadian Journal of Civil Engineering / Revue canadienne de génie civil
Owned By: National Research Council of Canada - NRC Research Press
NRC Research Press, Bldg. M-55, 1200 Montreal Rd., Ottawa, ON K1A 0R6
Tel: 613-998-9432; Fax: 613-952-7656
cjce@nrcresearchpress.com
Circulation: 3,200 Frequency: bi-monthly; English & French
Dr. Tarek Sayed, Editor
Dr. Mike Bartlett, Editor
Bushra Waheed, Managing Editor

Canadian Journal of Earth Sciences / Revue canadienne des sciences de la Terre
Owned By: National Research Council of Canada - NRC Research Press
NRC Research Press, Bldg. M-55, 1200 Montreal Rd., Ottawa, ON K1A 0R6
Tel: 613-998-9432; Fax: 613-952-7656
cjes@nrcresearchpress.com
Circulation: 2,400 Frequency: Monthly; English & French
Dr. John Greenough, Editor PhD

Canadian Journal of Fisheries & Aquatic Science / Journal canadien des sciences halieutiques et aquatiques
NRC Research Press, 1200 Montreal Rd., Bldg. M-55, Ottawa, ON K1A 0R6
Tel: 613-998-9432; Fax: 613-952-7656
cjfas@nrcresearchpress.com
Circulation: 2,400 Frequency: Monthly

Don Jackson, Editor PhD
Rolf D. Vinebrooke, Editor PhD

Canadian Journal of Forest Research / Revue canadienne de recherche forestière
Owned By: National Research Council of Canada - NRC Research Press
NRC Research Press, Bldg. M-55, 1200 Montreal Rd., Ottawa, ON K1A 0R6
Tel: 613-998-9432; Fax: 613-952-7656
cjfr@nrcresearchpress.com
Circulation: 900 Frequency: Monthly; English & French
Daniel Kneeshaw, Editor PhD
Pierre Bernier, Editor PhD

Canadian Journal of Microbiology / Revue canadienne de microbiologie
Owned By: National Research Council of Canada - NRC Research Press
NRC Research Press, Bldg. M-55, 1200 Montreal Rd., Ottawa, ON K1A 0R6
Tel: 613-998-9432; Fax: 613-952-7656
cjm@nrcresearchpress.com
Circulation: 1,675 Frequency: Monthly; English & French
James J. Germida, Editor
Harry G. Deneer, Editor

Canadian Journal of Physics / Revue canadienne de physique
Owned By: National Research Council of Canada - NRC Research Press
NRC Research Press, Bldg. M-55, 1200 Montreal Rd., Ottawa, ON K1A 0R6
Tel: 613-998-9432; Fax: 613-952-7656
cjp@nrcresearchpress.com
Circulation: 850 Frequency: Monthly; English & French
Dr. Michael Steinitz, Editor

Canadian Journal of Physiology & Pharmacology / Revue canadienne de physiologie & pharmacologie
Owned By: National Research Council of Canada - NRC Research Press
c/o NRC Research Press, Bldg. M-55, 1200 Montreal Rd., Ottawa, ON K1A 0R6
Tel: 613-998-9432; Fax: 613-952-7656
cjpp@nrcresearchpress.com
Circulation: 975 Frequency: Monthly; English & French
Dr. Donald D. Smyth, Editor
Dr. Grant Pierce, Editor

Canadian Journal of Zoology / Revue canadienne de zoologie
Owned By: National Research Council of Canada - NRC Research Press
NRC Resarch Press, Bldg. M-55, 1200 Montreal Rd., Ottawa, ON K1A 0R6
Tel: 613-998-9432; Fax: 613-952-7656
cjz@nrcresearchpress.com
Circulation: 1,250 Frequency: Monthly; English & French
M.B. Fenton, Editor PhD
Helga Guderley, Editor PhD

Genome / Génome
Owned By: National Research Council of Canada - NRC Research Press
NRC Research Press, Bldg. M-55, 1200 Montreal Rd., Ottawa, ON K1A 0R6
Tel: 613-998-9432; Fax: 613-952-7656
genome@nrcresearchpress.com
Circulation: 1,350 Frequency: bi-monthly; English & French
Arthur J. Hilliker, Editor PhD
G. Brian Golding, Editor PhD

LAB Business
Previous Name: Laboratory Business
#202, 30 East Beaver Creek Rd., Richmond Hill, ON L4B 1J2
Tel: 905-886-5040; Fax: 905-886-6615
cforbes@jesmar.com
Social Media:
twitter.com/biolabmag
www.facebook.com/biolabmag
Circulation: 30,250 Frequency: 5 times a year
Christopher Forbes, Publisher, cforbes@jesmar.com

Laboratory Buyers Guide
Owned By: Business Information Group
80 Valleybrook Dr., Toronto, ON M3B 2S9
Tel: 416-510-6835 Toll-Free: 800-268-7742
Circulation: 20,000 Frequency: Annually
Leslie Burt, Publisher, lburt@labcanada.com
Nestor Gula, Editor, ngula@labcanada.com

Laboratory Product News
Owned By: Business Information Group
80 Valleybrook Dr., Toronto, ON M3B 2S9
Tel: 416-510-6835; Fax: 416-510-5140
Toll-Free: 800-268-7742
Circulation: 20,000 Frequency: 6 times a year
Leslie Burt, Publisher, lburt@labcanada.com

The Microscopical Society of Canada Bulletin
c/o Dept. of Physics, Acadia University, Wolfville, NS B4P 2R6
Tel: 902-585-1318
Circulation: 650 Frequency: 4 times a year
Nadi Braidy, Editor, nadi.braidy@usherbrooke.ca

OSMT Advocate
#402, 234 Eglinton Ave. East, Toronto, ON M4P 1K5
Tel: 416-485-7660; Fax: 416-485-7660
Toll-Free: 800-461-6768
osmt@osmt.org
Social Media:
twitter.com/osmt2011
www.facebook.com/217098608317170
Circulation: 3,000 Frequency: Annual
Blanca McArthur, Executive Director, bmcarthur@osmt.org

Physics in Canada (PIC) / La Physique au Canada
#112, McDonald Bldg., 150 Louis Pasteur Ave., Ottawa, ON K1N 6N5
Tel: 613-562-5614; Fax: 613-562-5615
capmgr@uottawa.ca
Circulation: 1,623 Frequency: 6 times a year; French & English
Béla Jo¢s, Editor

Security

Canadian Security
Owned By: Annex Publishing & Printing Inc.
222 Edward St., Aurora, ON L4G 1W6
Tel: 905-727-0077; Fax: 905-727-0017
Toll-Free: 800-265-2827
sfenninger@clbmedia.ca
Social Media:
twitter.com/securityed
Circulation: 13,000 Frequency: 6 times a year
Neil Sutton, Editor
Peter Young, Publisher

Security Products & Technology News
Owned By: Annex Publishing & Printing Inc.
222 Edward St., Aurora, ON L4G 1W6
Tel: 905-727-0077; Fax: 905-727-0017
Toll-Free: 800-265-2827
Social Media:
twitter.com/SecurityEd
Circulation: 13,000 Frequency: 8 times a year
Source of information for dealers, installers, system integrators, resellers and specifiers working in the Canadian security industry.
Peter Young, Publisher, 905-713-4344, peter@sptnews.ca
Paul Grossinger, Editor, 905-713-4387, pgrossinger@annexweb.com

Shipping & Marine

BC Shipping News
#300, 1275 West 6th Ave., Vancouver, BC V6H 1A6
Tel: 604-893-8800; Fax: 604-708-1920
info@bcshippingnews.com
Social Media: www.linkedin.com/company/bc-shipping-news
twitter.com/bcshipping
Frequency: 10 pa
A subsidiary of McIvor Communications Inc., BC Shipping News provides information about Canada's west coast commercial marine industry. The magazine is of interest to port & terminal operators, shipbuilders & repairers, ship owners & operators, trade association representatives, & government representatives. Both print & digital editions are available.
Jane McIvor, Contact, Subscriptions & Advertising, jane@bcshippingnews.com

Canadian Sailings
#304, av 185 Dorval, Dorval, QC H9S 5J9
Tel: 514-934-0373; Fax: 514-934-4708
devonv@greatwhitepublications.ca
Social Media:
www.twitter.com/CanSailings
www.facebook.com/pages/Canadian-Sailings-Magazine/2187715
Circulation: 9,000 Frequency: Weekly
Joyce Hammock, Publisher & Editor, jhammock@canadiansailings.ca

Social Welfare

Charity Times Magazine
#11, 6221 Hwy. 7, Vaughan, ON L4H 0K8
Tel: 905-851-6800; Fax: 905-851-6225
Social Media:
www.facebook.com/pages/Charity-Times-Magazine/81165429690
Frequency: 6 times per year
Joe Plati, Publisher, jplati@charitytimesmagazine.ca
Cameron Wood, Editor, cwood@charitytimesmagazine.ca

Sporting Goods & Recreational Equipment

Golf Business Canada
#105, 955 Green Valley Cres., Ottawa, ON K1C 3V4
Tel: 613-226-3616; Fax: 613-226-4148
ngcoa@ngcoa.ca
Circulation: 4,000 Frequency: 4 times a year
Nathalie Lavallée, Chief Operating Officer, 613-226-3616 ext 15

Piscines & Spas
Détenteur: Kenilworth Media Inc.
#710, 15 Wertheim Crt., Richmond Hill, ON L4B 3H7
Tél: 905-771-7333;Téléc: 905-771-7336
Ligne sans frais: 800-409-8688
editor@poolspamarketing.com
Médias sociaux:
twitter.com/PoolSpaMktg
Fréquence: Deux fois par année
Piscines & Spas est également la publication officielle du 'Salon Splash', le salon professionnel qui se tient chaque année à l'automne au Québec.

Pool & Spa Marketing
Owned By: Kenilworth Media Inc.
#710, 15 Wertheim Crt., Richmond Hill, ON L4B 3H7
Tel: 905-771-7333; Fax: 905-771-7336
Toll-Free: 800-409-8688
richard@poolspamarketing.com
Social Media:
twitter.com/PoolSpaMktg
Circulation: 8,000 Frequency: 7 times a year
Richard Hubbard, Publisher

Pools, Spas & Patios
Owned By: Kenilworth Media Inc.
#710, 15 Wertheim Crt., Richmond Hill, ON L4B 3H7
Tel: 905-771-7333; Fax: 905-771-7336
Toll-Free: 800-409-8688
editor@poolsspaspatios.com
Social Media:
twitter.com/poolsspaspatios
www.facebook.com/PoolsSpasPatiosmagazine
Frequency: Annually

Sports & Recreation

Canadian Running
Owned By: Gripped Publishing Inc.
#510, 344 Bloor St., Toronto, ON M5S 3A7
Tel: 416-927-0774; Fax: 416-927-1491
Toll-Free: 800-567-0444
info@runningmagazine.ca
Social Media:
twitter.com/CanadianRunning
www.facebook.com/CanadianRunningMagazine
Mihira Lakshman, Editor-in-Chief, mihira@runningmagazine.ca

iRun
Owned By: Great River Media Inc.
PO Box 3814, C, Ottawa, ON M5S 3A7
Tel: 613-238-1818
editor@iRun.ca
Social Media: www.youtube.com/user/iRunNation
twitter.com/irunnation
www.facebook.com/iRunMagazine
Circulation: 60,000 Frequency: 6 times a year
Mark Sutcliffe, Group Publisher
Ray Zahab, Editor-in-Chief

Poker Player Magazine
Owned By: HeadsUp Entertainment Inc.
#1739, 246 Stewart Green SW, Calgary, AB T3H 3C8
Tel: 403-269-9039; Fax: 403-269-9060
Kelly B. Kellner, President/Founder/COO

Sportsnet
Owned By: Rogers Publishing Ltd.
1 Mount Pleasant Rd., Toronto, ON M4Y 2Y5
Social Media:
twitter.com/Sportsnet
www.facebook.com/sportsnet

Circulation: 100,000 Frequency: 26 times a year
Steve Maich, Publisher
Brandon Kirk, Editor

Triathlon Magazine Canada
Owned By: Gripped Publishing Inc.
#510, 344 Bloor St., Toronto, ON M5S 3A7
Tel: 416-927-8198; Fax: 416-927-1491
Toll-Free: 800-567-0444
info@triathlonmagazine.ca
Social Media:
twitter.com/CanadianRunning
www.facebook.com/CanadianRunningMagazine
Kevin Mackinnon, Editor-in-Chief, kevin@triathlonmagazine.ca

Telecommunications

Canadian New Media
#1800, 160 Elgin St., Ottawa, ON K2P 2P7
Tel: 613-230-1984; Fax: 613-230-3793
James Lewis, Editor

Wireless Telecom
#1110, 130 Albert St., Ottawa, ON K1P 5G4
Tel: 613-233-4888; Fax: 613-233-2032
info@cwta.ca
Circulation: 7,273 Frequency: 3 times a year

Television, Radio, Video & Home Appliances

Marketnews Magazine
Bomar Publishing Inc., #102, 701 Evans Ave., Toronto, ON M9C 1A3
Tel: 416-667-9945; Fax: 416-667-0609
mail@marketnews.ca
Circulation: 11,200 Frequency: Monthly
John Thomson, Associate Publisher, jtomson@marketnews.ca
Bob Grierson, Publisher, bgrierson@marketnews.ca
Robert Franner, Editor, rfranner@marketnews.ca
Erik Devantier, Creative Director

Media Names & Numbers
#201, Bloor St. West., Toronto, ON M6G 1L9
Tel: 416-964-7799; Fax: 416-964-8763
sources@sources.ca
Circulation: 500 Frequency: Annually
Ulli Diemer, Publisher

Première Video Magazine
#100, 102 Atlantic Ave., Toronto, ON M6K 1X9
Tél: 416-539-8800;Téléc: 416-539-8511
sbachir@spmedia.ca
Tirage: 7,900 Fréquence: Monthly
Salah Bachir, President

Textiles

Canadian Textile Journal / La Revue du Textile
#3000 Boullé St., Saint-Hyacinthe, QC J2S 1H9
Tel: 450-778-1870; Fax: 450-778-3901
Toll-Free: 877-288-8378
info@gcttg.com
Circulation: 2,500 Frequency: Quarterly
Martin Filteau, First Vice-President, Textile Division, mfilteau@gcttg.com

The Textile Journal
3000, rue Boulle, Saint-Hyacinthe, QC J2S 1H9
Tel: 450-778-1870; Fax: 450-778-9016
rleclerc@ctt.ca
Roger Leclerc

Toys

Toys & Games (T&G)
Owned By: Playtonic Communications
Playtonic Communications, PO Box 94084, 3409 Yonge St., Toronto, ON M4N 3R1
Tel: 416-487-1869
editor@toysandgamesmagazine.ca
Social Media:
www.facebook.com/pages/Toys-Games-Magazine/12429854431907
Circulation: 5,000 Frequency: 6 times a year
Graham Kennedy, Publisher

Transportation, Shipping & Distribution

Atlantic Construction & Transportation Journal
Previous Name: Atlantic Transportation Journal
Owned By: Transcontinental Specialty Publications/Holiday Media
#609, 1888 Brunswick St., Halifax, NS B3J 3J8
Tel: 902-468-8027; Fax: 902-425-8118
ken.partridge@transcontinental.ca
Circulation: 12,500 Frequency: 4 times a year
Jeff Nearing, General Manager

Canadian Automotive Fleet
#206, 1001 Champlain Ave., Burlington, ON L7L 5Z4
Tel: 289-288-9994; Fax: 289-288-9996
Toll-Free: 877-870-0055
caf@fleetbusiness.com
Social Media: www.youtube.com/CAFMagazine
twitter.com/CanAutoFleet
Circulation: 12,474 Frequency: 7 times a year
Keith McLaughlin, Publisher, kmclaughlin@fleetbusiness.com
Mario Cywinski, Editor & Provincial Manager, mario@fleetbusiness.com

Canadian Transit Forum
#710, 15 Wertheim Ct., Richmond Hill, ON L4B 3H7
Tel: 905-771-7333; Fax: 905-771-7336
ellenkrai@kenilworth.com
Circulation: 1,800 Frequency: 6 times a year
Ellen Krai, Publisher

Canadian Transportation Logistics
Owned By: Business Information Group
80 Valleybrook Dr., Toronto, ON M3B 2S9
Tel: 416-510-5108; Fax: 416-510-5134
Circulation: 17,665 Frequency: 11 times a year
Nick Krukowski, Publisher, nick@ctl.ca
Lou Smyrlis, Editorial Director, lou@TransportationMedia.ca

Maritime Magazine
Owned By: Les Productions Maritimes
#200, 4493, Sherbrooke ouest, Westmount, QC H3Z 1E7
Tel: 514-937-9009; Fax: 514-937-9088
marketing@maritimemag.com
Circulation: 11,000 Frequency: 4 times a year; French & English
Covers Marine Transport Industry
Leo Ryan, Rédacteur en chef, lryan@maritimemag.com

Repertoire Transport & Logistique
Détenteur: Les Editions Bomart ltée
Tél: 450-435-3131;Téléc: 450-435-3884
Eric Cloutier, Directeur de la rédaction

Routes et Transports
A.Q.T.R., #200, 1255, rue University, Montréal, QC H3B 3B2
Tél: 514-523-6444;Téléc: 514-523-2666
info@aqtr.qc.ca
Tirage: 3 500 Fréquence: 4 fois par an; français
Jean Auden, Editor

Travel

Bulletin Voyages
78 boul Saint-Joseph Ouest, Montréal, QC H2T 2P4
Tél: 514-287-9773;Téléc: 514-842-6180
Tirage: 9 062 Fréquence: Hebdomadaire; français
Jean-Pierre Kerten, Éditeur

Canada Journal
KLR Communications, 44 Cameron Cres., Toronto, ON M4G 1Z8
Tel: 416-487-0166; Fax: 416-487-2452
mail@canadajournal.ca
Circulation: 27,000 Frequency: bi-weekly; German
Klaus Ruland, Publisher/Editor

Canadian Travel Press
Owned By: Baxter Publishing Co
310 Dupont St., Toronto, ON M5R 1V9
Circulation: 13,000 Frequency: Thu.- weekly; summer - bi-weekly
David McClung, President
Edith Baxter, Editor

Canadian Traveller
#201, 2080 Hartley Ave., Coquitlam, BC V3K 6W5
Tel: 604-699-9990; Fax: 604-699-9993
Toll-Free: 866-699-9933
administration@canadiantraveller.net
Social Media:
twitter.com/cantravelmag
Circulation: 14,782 Frequency: Monthly
Rex Armstead, Publisher/Editor, rexa@canadiantraveller.net
Janice Strong, Editor, janices@canadiantraveller.net
Brad Liski, Associate Publisher, bradl@canadiantraveller.net

GSA: The Travel Magazine for Western Canada
Owned By: GSA Publishing Group
#201, 1945 West 4th Ave., Vancouver, BC V6J 1M7
Tel: 604-689-2909
office@gsapublishing.com
Social Media:
www.twitter.com/gsatravelmag
www.facebook.com/gsatravelmag
Circulation: 5,100 Frequency: 26 times a year
Frank Cumming, Publisher, publisher@gsapublishing.com
Vickie Sam Paget, Editor, editor@gsapublishing.com

Le Magazine l'agent de voyages inc.
CP 38, Anjou, QC H1K 4G5
Tél: 514-881-9637;Téléc: 514-881-8292
info@planisphere.qc.ca
Tirage: 8 500 Fréquence: 7 fois par an; français
Michel Villeneuve, Éditeur

Personnel Guide to Canada's Travel Industry
Owned By: Baxter Publishing Co
Tel: 416-968-7252; Fax: 416-968-2377
pg@baxter.net
Circulation: 3,000 Frequency: 2 times a year
David McClung, President

Revue Voyage en Groupe / Group Travel
Anciennement: Voyage en Groupe
590, ch St-Jean, La Prairie, QC J5R 2L1
Tél: 450-444-5870
voyageengroupe@bellnet.ca
Tirage: 13 000 Fréquence: 6 fois par an; français
Monique Papineau, Éditrice

Tourisme Plus
#301, 11800, 5e av, Montréal, QC H1E 7C1
Tél: 514-881-8583;Téléc: 514-881-8292
production@planisphere.qc.ca
Tirage: 9 200 Fréquence: 46 fois par an; français
Michel Villeneuve, Rédacteur-en-chef

Travel Courier
Owned By: Baxter Publishing Co
310 Dupont St., Toronto, ON M5R 1V9e
Tel: 416-968-7252; Fax: 416-968-2377
Circulation: 11,191 Frequency: Weekly, Thu.
Edith Baxter, Editor-in-chief

Travelweek
Concepts Travel Media Ltd., #100, 282 Richmond St. East, Toronto, ON M5A 1P4
Tel: 416-365-1500; Fax: 416-365-1504
Toll-Free: 800-727-1429
travelweek@travelweek.ca
Circulation: 12,420 Frequency: Weekly
Patrick Dineen, Editor

Vending & Vending Equipment

Canadian Vending & Office Coffee Service Magazine
Previous Name: Canadian Vending
Owned By: Annex Publishing & Printing Inc.
PO Box 530, 105 Donly Dr. Aouth, Simcoe, ON N3Y 4N5
Tel: 519-429-3966; Fax: 519-429-3094
Toll-Free: 800-265-2827
Circulation: digital only Frequency: 10 times a year
Stefanie Wallace, Editor, swallace@annexweb.com

Veterinary

The Canadian Veterinary Journal / La Revue Vétérinaire Canadienne
c/o Canadian Veterinary Medical Association, 339 Booth St., Ottawa, ON K1R 7K1
Tel: 613-236-1162; Fax: 613-236-9681
Toll-Free: 800-567-2862
admin@cvma-acmv.org
Circulation: 5,500 Frequency: Monthly; English & French
The Canadian Veterinary Journal, published by the Canadian Veterinary Medical Association, is the 'voice of veterinary medicine in Canada'.
Carlton Gyles, Editor-in-chief

Journal Le Vétérinarius
Anciennement: Le Vétérinarius
#200, 800, av Sainte-Anne, Saint-Hyacinthe, QC J2S 5G7
Tél: 450-774-1427;Téléc: 450-774-7635
omvq@omvq.qc.ca
Tirage: 2 500 Fréquence: 6 fois par an; français
Mathieu Bilodeau, Rédacteur-en-chef

Water & Wastes Treatment

Canadian Environmental Protection
Owned By: Baum Publications Ltd.
Baum Publications Ltd., 124 - 2323 Boundary, Vancouver, BC V5M 4V8
Tel: 604-291-9900; Fax: 604-291-1906
ebaum@baumpub.com
Circulation: 20,127 Frequency: 8 times a year
Lee Toop, Editor, ltoop@baumpub.com

Environmental Science & Engineering Magazine
Environmental Science & Engineering Publications Inc., #30, 220 Industrial Pkwy. South, Aurora, ON L4G 3V6
Tel: 905-727-4666; Fax: 905-841-7271
Toll-Free: 888-254-8769
Circulation: 19,000 Frequency: 6 times a year
Steve Davey, Publisher & Editor, steve@esemag.com

Ground Water Canada
Previous Name: Canadian Water Well
Owned By: Annex Publishing & Printing Inc.
PO Box 530, 105 Donly Dr. South, Simcoe, ON N3Y 4N5
Tel: 519-429-3966; Fax: 519-429-3094
Toll-Free: 800-265-2827
Social Media:
twitter.com/groundwatermag
Circulation: 3,842 Frequency: 4 times a year
Serves the water well and geothermal industries.
Laura Aiken, Editor, 416-522-1595, laiken@annexweb.com

Hazardous Materials Management Magazine
80 Valleybrook Dr., Toronto, ON M3B 2S9
Circulation: 14,048 Frequency: Bi-monthly
Guy Crittenden, Editor, 800-268-7742 ext3580, gcrittenden@hazmatmag.com
Brad O'Brien, Publisher, bobrien@hazmatmag.com

Maritime Provinces Water & Wastewater Report
Transcontinental Media, PO Box 41001, Dartmouth, NS B2Y 4P7
Tel: 902-749-2525; Fax: 902-742-2311
jonesh@transcontinental.ca
Circulation: 2,567 Frequency: 4 times a year
Barb McCay Cashin, Editor

Solid Waste & Recycling Magazine
Previous Name: Solid Waste Management
Owned By: Business Information Group
80 Valleybrook Dr., Toronto, ON M3B 2S9
Tel: 416-510-6798; Fax: 416-510-5133
Toll-Free: 800-268-7742
Circulation: 10,000 Frequency: 6 times a year
Brad O'Brien, Publisher, bobrien@solidwastemag.com
Guy Crittenden, Editor, gcrittenden@solidwastemag.com

Woodworking

2 x 4
Editions C.R. Inc., PO Box 1010, Victoriaville, QC G6P 8Y1
Tel: 819-752-4243; Fax: 819-382-2970
c-roy@ivic.qc.ca
Circulation: 8,000 Frequency: 4 times a year; English & French
Claude Roy, Publisher
Bernard Gauthier, Editor, info@bernardgauthier.com

Woodworking
Owned By: Kleiser Media Inc.
#203, 520 Riverside Dr., Toronto, ON M6S 4B5
Tel: 416-763-3653
info@kleisermedia.com
Circulation: 11,190 Frequency: 6 times a year
Bert Kleiser, Publisher, 416-763-3653, Bert@kleisermedia.com
Stephan Kleiser, Editor, Stephan@kleisermedia.com

Consumer

Advertising, Marketing, Sales

Adbusters
1234 - West 7th Ave., Vancouver, BC V6H 1B7
Tel: 604-736-9401; Fax: 604-737-6021
Toll-Free: 800-663-1243
info@adbusters.org
Circulation: 120,000 Frequency: 6 times a year
Kalle Lasn, Publisher

Sparksheet
contact@sparksheet.com
Social Media: www.youtube.com/user/sparksheettv
www.twitter.com/sparksheet
www.faceb ook.com/pages/Sparksheet/185418500634
Circulation: 120,000 Frequency: 6 times a year
For media and marketing professionals
Dan Levy, Editor

Airline Inflight

enRoute
Détenteur: Spafax Canada
#707, 4200 boul. St-Laurent, Montréal, QC H2W 2R2
Tél: 514-844-2001;Téléc: 514-844-6001
info@enroutemag.net
Tirage: 149,478 Fréquence: Monthly; English & French
Ilana Weitzman, Editor-in-Chief

Animals

Animals' Voice
Ontario SPCA, 16586 Woodbine Ave., RR#3, Newmarket, ON L3Y 4V8
Tel: 905-898-7122; Fax: 905-853-8643
info@ospca.on.ca
Circulation: 100,000 Frequency: 2 times a year
Katie Leonard, Contact, kleonard@ospca.on.ca

Canine Review
PO Box 53236 Marlborough, Calgary, AB T2A 7L9
Tel: 403-236-0557 Toll-Free: 866-236-0557
editor@caninereview.ca
Circulation: 2,000 Frequency: 10 pa
Lisa Ricciotti, Editor, 877-811-3699, editor@caninereview.ca
Merla Thomson, Publisher, 403-236-0557, merla@caninereview.ca

Dogs Dogs Dogs
Owned By: Dogs Dogs Dogs Multimedia
#103, 2192 Queen St. East, Toronto, ON M4E 1E6
Tel: 416-693-0918; Fax: 416-691-9784
info@dogsdogsdogs.ca; advertising@dogsdogsdogs.ca
Social Media: M4E 1E6
twitter.com/dddogsmedia
www.facebook.com/pages/Dogs-Dogs-Dogs-Multimedia/28541235
Circulation: 12,000 / issue Frequency: 5 pa
Dogs Dogs Dogs contains advice, reviews, & stories for persons interested in dogs. The newspaper is available through subscription & at veterinary clinics, shelters, & pet supply retailers in the Greater Toronto Area.

Magazine Animal
Détenteur: TVA Publications
7, ch Bates, Outremont, QC H2V 4V7
Tél: 514-848-7164 Ligne sans frais: 888-535-8634
Fréquence: 10 fois par an
Chantal Brousseau, Rédactrice en chef, chantal.brousseau@tvapublications.com

Modern Dog
#202, 343 Railway St., Vancouver, BC V6A 1A4
Tel: 604-734-3131; Fax: 604-734-3031
Toll-Free: 866-734-3131
info@moderndogmagazine.com
Social Media:
www.twitter.com/ModernDogMag
www.facebook.com/moderndogmagazine?v=wall
Frequency: 4 times a year
Connie Wilson, Editor-in-chief

Pets Magazine
Owned By: Simmons Publishing
c/o Simmons Publishing, 32 Foster Cres., Whitby, ON L1R 1W1
Tel: 905-665-9669; Fax: 905-665-9249
Toll-Free: 877-738-7624
editor@petsmagazine.ca
Circulation: 36,565 Frequency: 6 pa

Pets Quarterly Magazine
85 Trowbridge St. West, Meaford, ON N4L 1G4
Tel: 519-538-1418; Fax: 519-538-4017
info@capmagazines.ca
Circulation: 53,800 Frequency: 4 pa
Kelly Chase, Editor
Adrienne Ramsay, Manager, Advertising
Jim Eaton, Publisher

Arts, Art & Antiques

Border Crossings
#500, 70 Arthur St., Winnipeg, MB R3B 1G7
Tel: 204-942-5778; Fax: 204-949-0793
Toll-Free: 866-825-7165
bordercrossings@mts.net
Circulation: 5,500 Frequency: 4 pa
Meeka Walsh, Editor
Robert Enright, Editor-at-large

C Magazine
Previous Name: C international contemporary art magazine
C The Visual Arts Foundation, PO Box 5 B, Toronto, ON M5T 2T2
Tel: 416-539-9495; Fax: 416-539-9903
Toll-Free: 800-745-6312
info@cmagazine.com
Social Media:
twitter.com/cmagazineart
www.facebook.com/cmagazineart
Circulation: 3,000 Frequency: 4 pa

Canadian Art
#320, 215 Spadina Ave., Toronto, ON M5T 2C7
Tel: 416-368-8854; Fax: 416-368-6135
Toll-Free: 800-222-4762
info@canadianart.ca
Circulation: 23,500 Frequency: 4 pa
Richard Rhodes, Editor
Bryne McLaughlin, Managing Editor

Dance International
The Vancouver Ballet Society, Level 6, 677 Davie St., Vancouver, BC V6B 2G6
Tel: 604-681-1525; Fax: 604-681-7732
Editor@DanceInternational.org
Social Media:
twitter.com/DIMagazine
www.facebook.com/pages/Dance-International/12875748380447
Circulation: 4,000 Frequency: 4 pa
Maureen Riches, Editor

Downhome
Previous Name: Downhomer Magazine
43 James Lane, St. John's, NL A1E 3H3
Tel: 709-726-5113; Fax: 709-726-2135
Toll-Free: 888-588-6353
mail@downhomer.com
Social Media:
twitter.com/downhomelife
www.facebook.com/downhomelife
Circulation: 225,000 Frequency: Monthly
Ron Young, Publisher

ETC Montréal
#250, 1435, rue St-Alexandre, Montréal, QC H3A 2G4
Tél: 514-848-1125;Téléc: 514-848-0071
etc.artactuel@videotron.ca
Tirage: 2 500 Fréquence: 4 fois par an
Isabelle Lelarge, Rédacteur-en-chef, etc.lelarge@videotron.ca

Galleries West
#301, 690 Princeton Way SW, Calgary, AB T2P 5J9
Tel: 403-234-7097; Fax: 403-243-4649
publisher@gallerieswest.ca
Frequency: 3 times a year
Jennifer MacLeod, Editor

Inter, art actuel
Anciennement: Intervention
Les Éditions intervention, 345, rue du Pont, Québec, QC G1K 6M4
Tél: 418-529-9680;Téléc: 418-529-6933
infos@inter-lelieu.org
Médias sociaux: www.youtube.com/user/intervention22
twitter.com/lelieuinter
www.facebo ok.com/lelieu.actualite
Tirage: 1 200 Fréquence: 3 fois par an
Richard Martel, Coordination artistique, programmation@inter-lelieu.org

Inter, art actuel
345, rue du Pont, Québec, QC G1K 6M4
Tél: 418-529-9680;Téléc: 418-529-6933
infos@inter-lelieu.org
Médias sociaux: www.youtube.com/user/intervention22
twitter.com/LeLieuInter
www.facebo ok.com/inter.art.actuel
Tirage: 1 200 Fréquence: 3 times a year
Inter, art actuel est une revue culturelle disséminant diverses formes de l'art actuel: performance, art action, installation, poésie, manouvre, multimédia, etc.
Nathalie Perreault, Coordinator

Muse
Canadian Museums Assn., #400, 280 Metcalfe St., Ottawa, ON K2P 1R7
Tel: 613-567-0099; Fax: 613-233-5438
Circulation: 2,500 Frequency: 6 pa; English & French

Muzik Etc./Drums Etc.
753, rue Ste-Hélène, Longueuil, QC J4K 3R5
Tel: 450-651-4257; Fax: 450-670-8683
Circulation: 30,000 Frequency: bimestriel
Sofi Gamache, Editor in Chief, 450-674-1114
Ralph Angelillo, Editor in Chief, 450-928-1726

Ontario Craft
Previous Name: Craftnews
Designers Walk, 990 Queen St. West, Toronto, ON M6J 1H1
Tel: 416-925-4222; Fax: 416-925-4223
info@craft.on.ca
Circulation: 2,500 Frequency: 2 pa
Deborah Kirkegaard, Program & Development Officer

Parachute
info@parachute.ca; editions@parachute.ca
Circulation: 4,000 Frequency: 4 pa
The magazine halted production in 2007, but back issues can be ordered online.
Chantal Pontbriand, Directrice, c.pontbriand@parachute.ca

Qui Fait Quoi
CP 64002 Le Gardeur, 4841, rue Jeanne, Montréal, QC H2V 4J6
Tél: 514-842-5333;Téléc: 514-495-1069
info@qfq.com
Tirage: 7,000 Fréquence: 9 times a year
Steeve Laprise, Rédacteur en chef / éditeur, redaction@qfq.com

ROM
Previous Name: Rotunda
c/o Royal Ontario Museum, 100 Queen's Park, Toronto, ON M5S 2C6
Tel: 416-586-5758; Fax: 416-586-5649
Circulation: 27,000 Frequency: 3 pa
Sandra Piller, Executive Editor

Slate
155 King St. East, Kingston, ON K7L 2Z9
Tel: 613-542-3717; Fax: 613-542-1447
Toll-Free: 800-871-8093
info@slateartguide.com
Circulation: 12,000 Frequency: 8 pa
Allan Lochhead, Publisher, allan@slateartguide.com

Spirale
6742, rue Saint-Denis, Montréal, QC H2S 2S2
Tél: 514-934-5651;Téléc: 514-934-6390
spiralemagazine@yahoo.com
Tirage: 1 500
Pierre L'Hérault, Direction

Take One
#482, 283 Danforth Ave., Toronto, ON M4K 1N2
Tel: 416-944-1096; Fax: 416-465-4356
takeone@interlog.com
Social Media:
twitter.com/NorthernStarsca
www.facebook.com/nstarseditor
Circulation: 5,000 Frequency: 4 times a year
Wyndham Wise, Publisher

Vie des Arts
#603, 5605 av. De Gaspé, Montréal, QC H2T 2A4
Tél: 514-282-0205;Téléc: 514-282-0235
admin@viedesarts.com
Médias sociaux: www.youtube.com/user/ViedesArtsMagzine
Tirage: 3 386 Fréquence: 4 fois par an; français avec section en anglais
Anne Charpentier, Rédacteur, redaction@viedesarts.com

Westbridge Art Market Report
Owned By: Westbridge Publications Ltd.
1737 Fir St., Vancouver, BC V6J 5J9
Tel: 604-736-1014; Fax: 604-734-4944
info@westbridge-fineart.com
Anthony R. Westbridge, Publisher & Editor

Automobile, Cycle, & Automotive Accessories

Canadian Biker
PO Box 4122, Victoria, BC V8X 3X4
Tel: 250-384-0333; Fax: 250-384-1832
canbike@canadianbiker.com
Circulation: 20,000 Frequency: 10 pa
Len Creed, President
John Molony, Publisher, office@canadianbiker.com

Canadian Classics & Performance
33534 Western Rd. #RR 2, Mount Pleasant, PE C0B 1J0
Tel: 902-831-2733; Fax: 902-831-2385
Toll-Free: 866-976-8666
canadianclassic@xplornet.com
Circulation: 11,000 Frequency: 12 times a year
Dale Lidstone, Publisher

CarGuide
Owned By: Formula Publications Ltd.
#4, 447 Speers Rd., Oakville, ON L6K 3S7
Tel: 905-842-6591; Fax: 905-842-4432
Toll-Free: 800-693-7986
Circulation: 333,043 Frequency: 6 pa; English & French editions
Jackson Hayes, Editor, jhayes@metroland.com

Cycle Canada
Détenteur: LC Média Inc.
200, 1895 boul de l'Industrie, St-Mathieu-de-Beloeil,
Tél: 450-444-5773;Téléc: 514-444-6773
Ligne sans frais: 866-522-5656
Tirage: 38,000 Fréquence: 10 pa
Costa Mouzouris, Editor
Jean Lemieux, Publisher

Lemon-Aid New Car Buyer's Guide / Roulez sans vous faire rouler
c/o Automobile Protection Association, 292, St-Joseph Blvd. West, Montréal, QC H2V 2N7
Tel: 514-272-5555; Fax: 514-273-0797
apamontreal@apa.ca
Frequency: Annual
Online magazine that summarizes road test data, customer reviews, mechanic reviews, manufacturer data and government reports to help consumers choose a car.

Luxury Vehicles Magazine
Previous Name: The Professional's Guide to Luxury Vehicles
#143, 99 Bronte Rd., Oakville, ON L6L 3B7
Tel: 416-410-9795
Delando@HawthorneCap.ca
Social Media:
www.linkedin.com/company/luxury-vehicles-magazine
Circulation: 160,000 Frequency: Quarterly
John D. Duncan, Publisher
Bob English, Editor, 519/833-2089

Le Monde de l'Auto / The Car Guide
Owned By: LC Média inc.
LC Média inc., #200, 1895, boul de l'Industrie, Saint-Mathieu-de Beloeil, QC J3G 4S5
Tel: 450-464-1479; Fax: 450-464-8271
Toll-Free: 866-522-5656
abonnement@lcmedia.ca
Social Media:
twitter.com/thecarguide
www.facebook.com/thecarguide

Le Monde du VTT
215, rue Principale, Saint-Amable, QC J0L 1N0
Tirage: 9 560 Fréquence: 6 times a year
Richard Jetté, Éditeur

Motocycliste
c/o Fédération Motocycliste du Québec, #460, 9675, Papineau, Montréal, QC H2B 3C8
Tél: 514-252-8121;Téléc: 514-252-7857
fmq@fmq.qc.ca
Tirage: 15 500 Fréquence: 5 fois par an

MOTOMAG
1730 - 55e av, Lachine, QC H8T 3J5
Tél: 514-631-6550;Téléc: 514-631-0591
Médias sociaux:
facebook.com/pages/Moto-Magazine-Actualités-essais-motos-
Tirage: 11 234 Fréquence: 6 fois par an
Genevieve Pepin, Chief Editor
Michel Crepault, Publisher

Old Autos
PO Box 250, 348 Main St., Bothwell, ON N0P 1C0
Tel: 519-695-2303; Fax: 519-695-3716
Toll-Free: 800-461-3457
info@oldautos.ca
Circulation: 19,263 Frequency: 24 pa
Murray McEwan, Publisher/Editor

Pole Position
553, rue Calixa-Lavallée, Beloeil, QC J3G 4B6
Tel: 450-464-4076; Fax: 450-464-7742
info@poleposition.ca
Circulation: 16,625 Frequency: 8 times a year
Marie-Lyse Tremblay, Contact, marielyse@poleposition.ca

PRN Motorsport Magazine
Previous Name: Performance Racing News
44 Prince Andrew Pl., Toronto, ON M3C 2H4
Tel: 416-922-7223; Fax: 416-964-1836
info@prnmag.com
Social Media:
twitter.com/prnmag
www.facebook.com/PRNMAG
Circulation: 11,691 Frequency: 12 pa
Tim Rutledge, General Manager & Managing Editor, trutledge@ppgpubs.com

Vancouver International Auto Show Program
Owned By: Carling Media
Carling Media, #115, 1641 Lonsdale Ave., North Vancouver, BC V7M 2J5
Tel: 604-612-6237
editorial@carlingmedia.com
Circulation: 50,000 Frequency: 1 issue per year; English and Chinese
Distributed free to visitors of the Vancouver International Auto Show that runs the last week of March into early April.
Glen Ringdal, Publisher

Vélo Mag
Détenteur: Velo Québec Éditions
Maison des Cyclistes, 1251, rue Rachel est, Montréal, ON H2J 2J9
Tél: 514-521-8356;Téléc: 514-521-5711
Ligne sans frais: 800-567-8356
velomag@velo.qc.ca
Médias sociaux:
twitter.com/velomag_
www.facebook.com/pages/Vélo-Mag/341952746621
Tirage: 15 000 Fréquence: 6 fois par an; français
Jacques Sennechael, Rédacteur-en-chef
Pierre Sormay, Éditeur

World of Wheels
Owned By: Metroland Printing Publishing & Distribution
c/o Formula Media Group, #4, 447 Speers Rd., Oakville, ON L6K 3S7
Tel: 905-842-6591; Fax: 905-842-4432
Social Media:
twitter.com/wow_mag
Circulation: 26,099 Frequency: 6 pa

Aviation & Aerospace

Canadian Aviation Historical Society Journal
PO Box 2700 D, Ottawa, ON K1P 5W7
Tel: 416-410-9774; Fax: 416-923-3425
cahsnatsec@cahs.ca
Social Media:
twitter.com/CanAvHistSoc
www.facebook.com/118513138246225
Circulation: 1,000 Frequency: Quarterly
Chapters located in Calgary, Manitoba, Montréal, New Brunswick, Ottawa, PEI, Regina, Toronto and Vancouver.
Bill March, CAHS Editor, cahsnatpub@cahs.ca
Gary Williams, President, 306-543-8123, g.m.williams@sasktel.net
Danielle Metcalfe-Chenail, Vice President
Rachel Lea Heide, Treasurer
Don MacNeil, Membership

Babies & Mothers

The Baby & Child Care Encyclopaedia
Owned By: Parents Canada Group
Tel: 416-537-2604; Fax: 416-538-1794
admin@parentscanada.com
Circulation: 100,000 Frequency: 2 pa (May & Nov.)
Donald G. Swinburne, Publisher

The Compleat Mother - The Magazine of Pregnancy, Birth & Breastfeeding
PO Box 38033, Calgary, AB T3K 5G9
Tel: 403-255-0246
thecompleatmother@shaw.ca
Circulation: 8,000 Frequency: 4 pa
Angela van Son, Distributor

Parents Canada
Owned By: Parents Canada Group
Tel: 416-537-2604; Fax: 416-538-1794
amyb@parentscanada.com
Social Media:
twitter.com/#%21/ParentsCanada
www.facebook.com/ParentsCanada

Parents Canada Best Wishes
Owned By: Parents Canada Group
Tel: 416-537-2604; Fax: 416-538-1794
Toll-Free: 866-457-3320
admin@parentscanada.com
Circulation: 142,260 Frequency: 2 pa (May & Nov.)
Donald G. Swinburne, Publisher
Susan Pennell-Sebekos, Editor, susanp@parentscanada.com

Parents Canada C'est Pour Quand?
Détenteur: Parents Canada Group
2260, des Patriotes, Laval, QC H7L 3K8
Tél: 450-622-0091;Téléc: 450-622-0099
mlemoyne@qc.aira.com
Tirage: 43 000 Fréquence: 2 fois par an; français
Manon Le Moyne, Éditrice & Rédactrice-en-chef

Parents Canada Expecting
Owned By: Parents Canada Group
Tel: 416-537-2604; Fax: 416-538-1794
Toll-Free: 866-457-3320
admin@parentscanada.com

Parents Canada Labour & Birth Guide
Owned By: Parents Canada Group
Tel: 416-537-2604; Fax: 416-538-1794
Toll-Free: 866-457-3320
admin@parentscanada.com

Parents Canada Mon Bébé
Détenteur: Parents Canada Group
2260, des Patriotes, Laval, QC H7L 3K8
Tél: 450-622-0091;Téléc: 450-622-0099
Tirage: 43 000 Fréquence: 2 fois par an; français
Manon Le Moyne, Éditrice & Rédactrice-en-chef

Parents Canada Naissance
Détenteur: Parents Canada Group
2260, des Patriotes, Laval, QC H7L 3K8
Tél: 450-622-0091;Téléc: 450-622-0099
Fréquence: Français

Poupon
Anciennement: Mère Nouvelle
Détenteur: Les Éditions Rogers limitée
1200, ave McGill College, 8e étage, Montréal, QC H3B 4G7
Tél: 514-843-5141
Tirage: 34,500 Fréquence: 2 fois par an
French magazine for new parents.
Holly Bennett, Rédactrice

Today's Parent Newborn
Owned By: Rogers Publishing Ltd.
1 Mount Pleasant Rd., 8th Fl., Toronto, ON M4Y 2Y5
Tel: 416-764-2883; Fax: 416-764-2801
Circulation: 112,900 Frequency: 2 pa
Guide for the first months with a new baby.
Rosemary Munroe, Publisher

Today's Parent Pregnancy
Previous Name: Great Expectations
Owned By: Rogers Publishing Ltd.
1 Mount Pleasant Rd., 8th Fl., Toronto, ON M4Y 2Y5
Tel: 416-764-2883; Fax: 416-764-2801
Circulation: 131,725 Frequency: 3 pa
Holly Bennett, Editor
Rosemary Munroe, Publisher

Today's Parent Toronto
Owned By: Rogers Publishing Ltd.
1 Mount Pleasant Rd., 8th Fl., Toronto, ON M4Y 2Y5
Tel: 416-764-2883; Fax: 416-764-2801
Circulation: 55,000 Frequency: Monthly
Alison Wood, Editor
Rosemary Munroe, Publisher

Boating & Yachting

Boat Guide
Owned By: Formula Publications Ltd.
Tel: 905-842-6591; Fax: 905-842-6843
boatbiz@idirect.ca
Circulation: 60,000 Frequency: 2 pa
Scott Robinson, Publisher
Lizanne Madigan, Editor

Boating East Cruising & Waterway Lifestyle Guide
c/o Ontario Travel Guides, PO Box 483, Westport, ON K0G 1X0
Tel: 800-324-6052; Fax: 800-317-2549
info@ontariotravelguides.com
Social Media:
twitter.com/RideauWaterway
www.facebook.com/group.php?gid=13041157700880 2
Circulation: 25,000 / annually Frequency: Annually
The guide covers the major waterways of Eastern Ontario & upstate New York.

Boats & Places
Previous Name: Today's Boating
#13, 130 Saunders Rd., Barrie, ON L4N 9A8
Tel: 705-725-4669; Fax: 705-725-4669
info@boatsandplaces.com
Circulation: 24,692 Frequency: 6 times per year
Brian Minton, Publisher
Amanda Dyer Comission, Editor

Canadian Yachting
Kerrwil Publications Limited, #201, 49 Bathurst St., Toronto, ON M5V 2P2
Circulation: 24,500 Frequency: 6 pa
Elizabeth Kerr, Publisher, 416-258-9948, eakerr@kerrwill.com
Andy Adams, Managing Editor, 416-574-7313, aadams@kerrwill.com

L'Escale Nautique
Détenteur: Les Productions Maritimes
535, route de la Montagne, Notre-Dame-du-Portage, QC G0L 1Y0
Tél: 418-863-5055;Téléc: 418-850-4674
redaction@escalenautique.qc.ca
Médias sociaux:
www.facebook.com/pages/LEscale-Nautique/283699044980203
Tirage: 12 000 Fréquence: 4 fois par an, plus guide nautique; français
Michel Sacco, Rédacteur-en-chef

Gam on Yachting
#1, 5650 Tomken R., Mississauga, ON L4W 4P1
Tel: 416-368-1559; Fax: 416-368-2831
gam@gamonyachting.com
Circulation: 13,500 Frequency: 8 pa
John Grainger, Publisher & Editor, 905-465-0458, editor@gameyachting.com

Ontario Sailor Magazine
Previous Name: Lake Ontario Sailor Magazine
91 Hemmingway Dr., Courtice, ON L1E 2C2
Tel: 905-434-7409; Fax: 905-434-1654
sails@istar.ca
Circulation: 10,000 Frequency: 7 times a year
Sandra McDowell, Publisher
Greg McDowell, Managing Editor

Pacific Yachting
Owned By: OP Publishing Ltd.
#500, 200 West Esplanade, Vancouver, BC V6Z 2T1
Tel: 604-998-3310 Toll-Free: 800-867-0474
subscriptions@oppublishing.com
Social Media: pinterest.com/pacificyachting
twitter.com/pacificyachting
www.facebook .com/pacificyachtingmagazine
Circulation: 16,975 Frequency: Monthly
Mark Yelic, Publisher
Dale Miller, Editor, 604-998-3323, Fax: 604-998-3320

Les Plaisanciers
Détenteur: Power Boating Canada Magazine
#310, 970, Montée de Liesse, Saint-Laurent, QC H4T 1W7
Tél: 514-856-0788;Téléc: 514-856-0790
Tirage: 20 000 Fréquence: 5 fois par an; français
Roy Baird, Sr., Publisher

Port Hole / Le Hublot
c/o Canadian Power & Sail Squadrons, 26 Golden Gate Ct., Toronto, ON M1P 3A5
Tel: 416-293-2438; Fax: 416-293-2445
Toll-Free: 888-277-2628
hqg@cps-ecp.ca
Circulation: 28,000 Frequency: 4 pa; English & French
Joan Eyolfson Cadham, Editor-in-chief

Power Boating Canada
Owned By: Taylor Publishing Group
#2, 1121 Invicta Dr., Oakville, ON L6H 2R2
; Fax: 905-844-5032
Toll-Free: 800-354-9145
editor@powerboating.com
Social Media:
twitter.com/Power_Boating
www.facebook.com/231865076875417
Frequency: 7 pa
William Taylor, Publisher
Steve Fennel, Editor

Québec Yachting
Anciennement: Québec Yachting Voile & Moteur
Tél: 450-663-4141;Téléc: 450-668-7511
Ligne sans frais: 866-433-3553
quebecyachting@quebecyachting.ca
Tirage: 10 500 Fréquence: 6 fois par an; français
Daniel Hébert, Co-Editor
Nicole Bonneville, Co-Editor

Windsport Magazine
SBC Media Inc., #3266, 2255B Queen St. East, Toronto, ON M4E 1G3
Tel: 416-406-2400; Fax: 416-406-0656
info@windsport.com
Social Media:
twitter.com/windsport
www.facebook.com/pages/Windsport-Magazine/148182847219
Circulation: 26,000 Frequency: 4 pa
John Bryja, Editor

Books

Amphora
c/o Alcuin Society, PO Box 3216, Vancouver, BC V6B 3X8
Tel: 604-937-3293
info@alcuinsociety.com
Social Media: blog.alcuinsociety.com
twitter.com/alcuin
www.facebook.com/alcuinsociety
Circulation: 340 Frequency: 3 times a year; spring, summer, fall
Amphora, the Alcuin Society's journal, presents original articles, interviews and departments focusing on the world of the book arts: collecting, typography, typesetting, calligraphy, papermaking, ornamentation, illustration, printing and binding.
Howard Greaves, Chair, amphora@alcuinsociety.com

BC BookWorld
A.R.T. BookWorld Productions, 3516 West 13th Ave., Vancouver, BC V6R 2S3
Tel: 604-736-4011; Fax: 604-736-4011
bookworld@telus.net
Circulation: 100,000 Frequency: 4 times a year
Alan Twigg, Publisher
David Lester, Editor

Brides, Bridal

Mariage Québec
Détenteur: St Joseph Media
#1301, 1155, rue Université, Montréal, QC H3B 3A7
Tél: 514-284-2552;Téléc: 514-284-4492
info@mariagequebec.com
Médias sociaux:
www.facebook.com/magazinemariagequebec
Tirage: 22 915 Fréquence: 2 fois par an; français
Denyse Clermont, Éditrice
Claude LaFramboise, Directeur de la direction

Ottawa Wedding
Owned By: Coyle Publishing
67 Neil Ave., Stittsville, ON K2S 1B9
Tel: 613-271-8903; Fax: 613-271-8905
Social Media:
www.twitter.com/ottweddingmag
www.facebook.com/OttawaWeddingMagazine
Circulation: 10,000 Frequency: 2 times a year
George W. Coyle, Publisher, gcoyle@coylepublishing.com
Pat den Boer, Editor, editor@coylepublishing.com

Sposa Magazine
c/o Jasmin Publishing, 55 York St., Toronto, ON M5J 1R7
Tel: 416-364-5899; Fax: 416-364-5996
Circulation: 50,000 Frequency: 2 pa
Gulshan Sippy, Editor

Today's Bride
Owned By: Family Communications Inc.
65 The East Mall, Toronto, ON M8Z 5W3
Tel: 416-537-2604; Fax: 416-538-1794
sales@canadianbride.com
Social Media:
twitter.com/Todaysbridemag
www.facebook.com/todaysbridemagcanada
Circulation: 99, 361 Frequency: 2 pa
Donald G. Swinburne, Publisher

WeddingBells
Owned By: St Joseph Media
#320, 111 Queen St. East, Toronto, ON M5C 1S2
Tel: 416-364-3333; Fax: 416-594-3374
feedback@weddingbells.ca
Social Media:
twitter.com/WeddingbellsMag
www.facebook.com/WeddingbellsMag
Circulation: 103,500 Frequency: 2 pa
Offices in Toronto, Vancouver, Calgary, Leduc, Winnipeg, Ottawa and Montréal.
Alison McGill, Editor-in-Chief

Business & Finance

Business in Vancouver
102 East 4th Ave., Vancouver, BC V5T 1G2
Tel: 604-688-2398; Fax: 604-688-1963
Social Media:
www.linkedin.com/company/business-in-vancouver
twitter.com/bizinvancouver
www.facebook.com/BIVMG
Circulation: 62,000 Frequency: Weekly, Tue.
Paul Harris, Publisher

Canadian MoneySaver
#700, 55 King St. West, Kitchener, ON N2G 4W1
Tel: 519-772-7632
moneyinfo@canadianmoneysaver.ca
Social Media:
www.facebook.com/pages/Canadian-Money-Saver/2391936895
075
Circulation: 69,700 Frequency: 9 pa
Canadian MoneySaver is an acclaimed investment advisory with a recognized reputation for providing a trustworthy and down-to-earth service since 1981. Canadian MoneySaver publishes monthly with three double issues (July/August, November/December and March/April).
Dale Ennis, Publisher/Editor-in-Chief

Canadian Shareowner Magazine
#806, 4 King St. West, Toronto, ON M5H 1B6
Tel: 416-595-9600
Circulation: 20,876 Frequency: 6 pa
Periodical offering a proprietary Stock Selection Guide to find stocks in which subscribers ought to consider investing
John T. Bart, Publisher & Editor

Niagara Magazine Group
Previous Name: Business Niagara Magazine
17 Queen St., St Catharines, ON L2R 5G5
Tel: 905-682-4509; Fax: 905-682-8219
Circulation: 20,000
Released bi-monthly by Osprey Media Group Inc., Business Niagara Magazine reaches over 20,000 registered businesses and is geared to everyone from a one-person operation to a large publicly traded organization.
Mishka Balsom, Publisher

Pensez-y bien!
Les Éditions EJS, 13, ch du Pied-de-Roi, Lac Beaufort, QC G3B 1N6
Tél: 418-686-1940;Téléc: 418-871-0972
fbegin@ejs.qc.ca
Tirage: 150 000 Fréquence: trimestriel; français
Les articles présentent et expliquent les services et les produits financiers
France Bégin, Éditeur

The Wire Report
Owned By: The Hill Times Publishing Inc.
69 Sparks Street Rd., Ottawa, ON K1P 5A5
Tel: 613-232-5952; Fax: 613-232-9055
roneill@hilltimes.com
Social Media:
twitter.com/thewirereport
Circulation: 60,000 Frequency: Weekly
Anne Marie Creskey, Publisher, 613-232-5952, acreskey@hilltimes.com
Simon Doyle, Editor, 613-232-5952, sdoyle@thewirereport.ca

Camping & Outdoor Recreation

Camping Caravaning
#100, 1560, rue Eiffel, Boucherville, QC J4B 5Y1
Tél: 450-650-3722;Téléc: 450-650-3721
Ligne sans frais: 877-650-3722
magazine@fqcc.ca
Tirage: 46 000 Fréquence: 8 fois par an
Louise Saindon, Président
André Rivest, Éditeur
Louise Gagnon, Directrice de la publication

Camping in Ontario
Ontario Private Campground Assn., #206, 305 Milner Ave., Toronto, ON M1B 3V4
Tel: 416-820-2714; Fax: 647-352-0900
Toll-Free: 877-672-2226
opca@campinginontario.ca
Circulation: 200,000 Frequency: Annually, January
Beth Potter, Executive Director

explore
Quarto Communications, 54 St. Patrick St., Toronto, ON M5T 1V1
Tel: 416-599-2000; Fax: 416-599-0800
Toll-Free: 877-874-5253
explore@explore-mag.com
Social Media:
twitter.com/explore_mag
www.facebook.com/exploremag
Circulation: 30,000 Frequency: 6 pa; 0714-816X
Al Zikovitz, Publisher
James Little, Editor

RV Gazette
Explorer RV Club, #6, 328 Mill St., Beaverton, ON L0K 1A0
; Fax: 705-426-1403
Toll-Free: 800-999-0819
info@rvgazette.com
Circulation: 13,304 Frequency: bi-monthly
Marcia Anderson, General Manager

Vie en Plein Air
Détenteur: Camping Canada Magazine
#310, 970, Montée de Liesse, Saint-Laurent, QC H4T 1W7
Tél: 514-856-0787;Téléc: 514-856-0790
Tirage: 20 000 Fréquence: 4 fois par an; français
Claude Leonard, Éditeur

Children's

chickaDEE
Owned By: Owlkids Books
#400, 10 Lower Spadina Ave., Toronto, ON M5V 2Z2
Tel: 416-340-2700; Fax: 416-340-9769
Toll-Free: 800-551-6957
chickadee@owlkids.com
Circulation: 95,000 Frequency: 10 pa
Mary Vincent, Publisher

Chirp
Owned By: Owlkids Books
#400, 10 Lower Spadina Ave., Toronto, ON M5V 2Z2
Tel: 416-340-2700; Fax: 416-340-9769
Toll-Free: 800-551-6957
chirp@owlkids.com
Circulation: 75,000 Frequency: 10 times a year
Sarah Trusty, Assistant Editor

Les Débrouillards
Publications BLD inc., 4475, rue Frontenac, Montréal, QC H2H 2S2
Tél: 514-844-2111;Téléc: 514-278-3030
scientifix@lesdebrouillards.com
Tirage: 37 000 Fréquence: 5 fois par an; français
Félix Maltais, Éditeur
Isabelle Vaillancourt, Rédactrice-en-chef

Les Explorateurs
Publications BLD inc., 4475, rue Frontenac, Montréal, QC H2H 2S2
Tél: 514-844-2111;Téléc: 514-278-3030
lesexplorateurs@lesdebrouillards.com
Tirage: 24,000 Fréquence: 11 fois par an; français
Félix Maltais, Éditeur
Sarah Perreault, Rédactrice en chef

The Hospital Activity Book for Children
Owned By: Suggitt Publishing Ltd.
Bell Tower, #950, 10104 - 103 Ave., Edmonton, AB T5J 0H8
; Fax: 877-463-6185
Toll-Free: 877-413-6163
reception@habfc.com
Activity books for children ages 4-12 who are undergoing medical treatment.
Stephen Kathnelson, President, stephen@habfc.com
Melanie Smith, General Manager, St. John's Office, melanie@habfc.com

J'Aime Lire
Détenteur: Bayard Presse Canada Inc.
4475, rue Frontenac, Montréal, QC H2H 2S2
Tél: 514-844-2111;Téléc: 514-278-3030
Ligne sans frais: 800-313-3020
redaction@bayardpresse.qc.ca
Tirage: 23 000
Suzanne Spino, Directrice générale

Kayak: Canada's History Magazine for Kids
Bryce Hall, Main Fl., 515 Portage Ave., Winnipeg, MB R3B 2E9
Tel: 204-988-9300; Fax: 204-988-9309
Toll-Free: 866-952-3444
info@kayakmag.ca
Circulation: 16,000 Frequency: 4 times a year

Kids Tribute
Owned By: Tribute Publishing Inc.
71 Barber Greene Rd., Toronto, ON M3C 2A2
Tel: 416-445-0544; Fax: 416-445-2894
generalinfo@tribute.ca
Circulation: 300,000 Frequency: 4 pa
Sandra Stewart, Publisher & Editor

kidsworld Magazine
#301, 177 Danforth Ave., Toronto, ON M4K 1N2
Circulation: 300,000 Frequency: 5 pa
Michael Sheasgreen, Publisher

The Magazine / Le Magazine Interdit aux Adultes
Previous Name: The Magazine not for Kids
643 Queen St. East, Toronto, ON M4M 1G4
Tel: 416-778-8727; Fax: 416-778-8726
Toll-Free: 866-622-0022
vocals@themagazine.ca
Social Media: www.youtube.com/magisodes
twitter.com/TheMagazineHQ
www.facebook.com/T heMagazineHQ
Circulation: 3,800,000 Frequency: Bi-monthly
Eric Conroy, Publisher

OWL Magazine
Owned By: Owlkids Books
#400, 10 Lower Spadina Ave., Toronto, ON M5V 2Z2
Tel: 416-340-2700; Fax: 416-340-9769
Toll-Free: 800-551-6957
owlkids@cdsglobal.ca
Circulation: 75,000 Frequency: 10 pa
Craig Battle, Associate Editor

Zamoof!
Owned By: Dream Wave Publishing Inc.
544 Spruceview Place South., Kelowa, BC V1V 2P7
Tel: 250-762-9624; Fax: 905-946-1679
Toll-Free: 877-762-9624
mail@zamoofmag.com
Social Media: www.youtube.com/user/Zamoofmag
twitter.com/zamoof
www.facebook.com/pag
es/ZAMOOF-Magazine/202494399778717?sk
Frequency: 6 pa

City Magazine

Avenue
RedPoint Media Group Inc., #105, 1210 - 20th Ave. SE, Calgary, AB T2G 1M8
Tel: 403-240-9055; Fax: 403-240-9059
info@redpointmedia.ca
Circulation: 27,000 Frequency: 10 times a year
Gary Davies, Publisher, gdavies@redpointmedia.ca
Jennifer Hamilton, Managing Editor, jhamilton@redpointmedia.ca
Kathe Lemon, Editor, klemon@redpointmedia.ca

Bayview Post
30 Lesmill Rd., Toronto, ON M3B 2T6
Tel: 416-250-7979; Fax: 416-250-1737
editorial@postcity.com; advertising@postcity.com
Other information: Classified Advertising, E-mail: classifieds@postcity.com
Social Media:
twitter.com/PostCity
www.facebook.com/PostCityMagazines

Circulation: 25,000 Frequency: Monthly
The magazine features news, articles, & advertising of interest to persons of Toronto's Bayview neighbourhood.
Lorne London, Publisher, lornelondon@postcity.com
Laurie McGillivray, Associate Publisher, lauriemcgillivray@postcity.com
Andrew Mannsbach, Associate Publisher, Sales, andrewmannsbach@postcity.com
Ron Johnson, Editor, ronjohnson@postcity.com
Lisa London-Shiffman, Vice-President, Sales, LisaLondon@postcity.com
Dorothy Chudzinski, Managing Art Director, DorothyChudzinski@postcity.com
Lynne London, Director, Advertising, LynneLondon@postcity.com
Janice Fletcher, Controller, JaniceFletcher@postcity.com

Escarpment Views
Owned By: 1826789 Ontario Inc.
50 Ann St., Georgetown, ON L7G 2V2
Tel: 905-877-9665
Frequency: Quarterly
The magazine is dedicated to Ontario's Niagara Escarpment community.
Gloria Hildebrandt, Editor, 905-873-2834

The False Creek News
661A Market Hill, Vancouver, BC V5Z 4B5
Tel: 604-876-6770
mail@thefalsecreeknews.com
Other information: News, E-mail: news@thefalsecreeknews.com
Circulation: 25,000
The False Creek News features reports & information about local issues, arts, & entertainment. The magazine is of interest to residents of Vancouver's False Creek, Fairview Slopes, & Granville Island neighbourhoods. Copies of the magazine are distributed to homes, businesses, & community centres.
M. Juma, Publisher
S. Bowell, Editor
N. Ebrahim, Manager, Advertising, adsales@thefalsecreeknews.com
G. Jiwa, Manager, Administration
A. Rattanshi, Accountant
A. Thobhani, Contact, Circulation

Fast Forward Weekly
Owned By: Great West Newspapers
1204 - 20th Ave. SE, Calgary, AB T2G 1M8
Tel: 403-244-2235; Fax: 403-244-1431
info@ffwd.greatwest.ca
Social Media:
twitter.com/FFWDWeekly
Circulation: 24,000 Frequency: Weekly; Thursdays
Fred Bye, Publisher, fbye@ffwd.greatwest.ca
Drew Anderson, Editor, danderson@ffwd.greatwest.ca

The Georgia Straight
1701 West Broadway St., Vancouver, BC V6J 1Y3
Tel: 604-730-7000; Fax: 604-730-7010
contact@straight.com; gs.info@straight.com
Circulation: 804,000+ Frequency: Weekly
Dan McLeod, Publisher/Editor, 604/730-7088

The Grid
1 Yonge Street, 2nd Floor, Toronto, ON M5E 1E6
Tel: 416-364-1300
letters@thegridto.com
Social Media: www.youtube.com/user/TheGridTO
twitter.com/TheGridTo
www.facebook.com/thegridto
Frequency: Weekly
Lianne George, Editor, lianne@thegridto.com

Le Guide Prestige Montréal
#700, 2160, de la Montagne, Montréal, QC H3G 2T3
Tél: 514-982-9823;Téléc: 514-289-9160
info@prestipresse.com
Tirage: 150,000 Fréquence: 4 times a year; English & French
Publication officielle de l'Association des hôtels du grand Montréal distribuée exclusivement dans les 76 hôtels membres, Le Guide Prestige Montréal répertorie à l'intention des visiteurs tout ce qu'il y a à voir et à faire à Montréal.
Steve Robins, Executive Vice President, steve@prestipresse.com
André Ducharme, Editor-in-chief

Hamilton Magazine
Previous Name: Hamilton This Month
Owned By: Town Media Inc.
Town Media, 1074 Cooke Blvd., Burlington, ON L7T 4A8
Tel: 905-634-8003; Fax: 905-634-7661
info@townmedia.ca
Social Media:
twitter.com/hamiltonmag
www.facebook.com/HamiltonMag
Circulation: 39,901 Frequency: 5 pa
Donna Gardener, Publisher, donna.gardener@sunmedia.ca
Marcd Skulnick, Editor, marc.skulnick@sunmedia.ca

HighGrader
PO Box 20055, Timmins, ON P4N 1A5
Tel: 705-266-4950
highgrader@nt.net
Circulation: 2,500
Brit Griffin, Publisher

Hour Community
Communications Voir Inc., 355, rue Ste-Catherine ouest, 7e étage, Montréal, QC H3B 1A5
Tel: 514-848-0777; Fax: 514-848-9004
Toll-Free: 877-631-8647
info@hour.ca
Social Media:
twitter.com/hourmontreal
www.facebook.com/HourMontreal
Circulation: 49,000 Frequency: 52 pa
Jamie O'Meara, Editor-in-chief

International Guide, Victoria
Previous Name: International Guide, Calgary
Owned By: IG Publications Ltd.
2392 Mt St Michael Rd., Saanichton, BC V8M 1T7
Tel: 250-727-1098; Fax: 250-652-8646
visitorschoice@shaw.ca
Social Media: www.youtube.com/user/VCIG11
twitter.com/visitorsinfo
www.facebook.com/ visitorsinfo
Circulation: 18,000
Wayne Kehoe, Publisher
Cherie Rautio, Editor

Island Times Magazine
PO Box 956, Parksville, BC V9P 2G9
Tel: 250-228-0995; Fax: 250-586-4405
publisher@islandtimesmagazine.ca
Social Media:
www.facebook.com/islandtimesmagazine.ca
Vancouver Island lifestyles magazine.
Jolene Aarbo, Publisher
Julie McManus, Editor

Kingston Life Magazine
18 St. Remy Pl., Kingston, ON K7K 6C4
Tel: 613-549-8442; Fax: 613-549-4333
Frequency: 4 times a year
Mary Laflamme, Publisher

Lethbridge Living
1518 - 3rd Ave. S, Lethbridge, AB T1J 0K8
Tel: 403-381-1454; Fax: 403-330-3075
editor@lethbridgeliving.com
Social Media:
twitter.com/Lethliving
www.facebook.com/lethbridge.living
Circulation: 17,000 Frequency: 6 times a year
Focus on the people and diversity of cultures in Lethbridge and Southern Alberta.
Martin Oordt, Editor
Mary Oordt, Managing Editor

London City Life Magazine
1147 Gainsborough Rd., London, ON N6H 5L5
Tel: 519-471-2907; Fax: 519-473-7859
editorial@londoncitylife.ca
Circulation: 31,000 Frequency: 6 pa
Gord Delamont, Publisher & Editor, 519-471-2907 ext 286

Monday Magazine
Owned By: Black Press Group Ltd.
818 Broughton St., Victoria, BC V8W 1E4
Tel: 250-382-6183
editorial@mondaymag.com
Social Media:
twitter.com/mondaymag
www.facebook.com/MondayMagazine
Frequency: Weekly
The magazine of Victoria, British Columbia presents alternative news & entertainment information. Print & e-editions are available.
Penny Sakamoto, Publisher, publisher@mondaymag.com
Grant McKenzie, Editor, editor@mondaymag.com
Janet Gairdner, Manager, janet@mondaymag.com
Mary Ellen Green, Contact, Arts, arts@mondaymag.com
Danielle Pope, Contact, News, news@mondaymag.com

Moving to Magazines T.O. / Emménager-à
Previous Name: Moving to & Around
Owned By: Homes Publishing Group
178 Main St., Unionville, ON L3R 2G9
Tel: 905-479-4663 Toll-Free: 800-363-4663
info@movingto.com
Social Media:
www.facebook.com/pages/Moving-To-Magazines/11258237542805
Circulation: 240,000 Frequency: Annually, or bi-annual issues cover all major Canadian cities & areas; 2 bilingual issues, Montréal, Ottawa/Hull
Michael Rosset

Niagara Life Magazine (a division of Downtowner Publications Inc.)
Previous Name: The Downtowner
#1, 3300 Merrittville Hwy., Thorold, ON L2V 4Y6
Tel: 905-641-1984; Fax: 905-641-0682
niagaralife@on.aibn.com
Circulation: 45,000 Frequency: 8 times a year
Katherine Nadeau, Editor-in-Chief
Gail Todd, Managing Editor

Northword Magazine
PO Box 817, 3864 2nd Ave., Smithers, BC V0J 2N0
Tel: 250-847-4600; Fax: 250-847-4668
Toll-Free: 866-632-7688
Frequency: 4 times a year

Now
189 Church St., Toronto, ON M5B 1Y7
Tel: 416-364-1300; Fax: 416-364-1166
web@nowtoronto.com
Social Media:
twitter.com/nowtoronto
www.facebook.com/nowmagazine
Circulation: 108,779 Frequency: Weekly; Thursday
Alice Klein, Editor/CEO
Michael Hollett, Editor/Publisher

Off-Centre Magazine
Schwebs Bridge, #RR1, C58, Falkland, BC V0E 1W0
Tel: 250-379-2124; Fax: 250-379-2124
off-centre@off-centre.ca
Circulation: 17,000 Frequency: Monthly
Leanne Allen, Publisher

Okanagan Life
c/o Byrne Publishing Group, #10, 1753 Dolphin Ave., Kelowna, BC V1Y 8A6
Tel: 250-861-5399; Fax: 250-868-3040
Toll-Free: 888-311-1119
info@okanaganlife.com; editorial@okanaganlife.com
Other information: Subscriptions, E-mail: subscribe@okanaganlife.com
Social Media:
twitter.com/OkanaganLifeMag
www.facebook.com/pages/Okanagan-Life-Magazine/15090795829
Circulation: 22,000
Contents include information about personalities, food, travel, & recreation in British Columbia's Okanagan region.
Paul Byrne, Publisher & Editor, paul@okanaganlife.com
Laurie Carter, Senior Editor, laurie@okanaganlife.com
Mishell Raedeke, Creative Director, mishell@okanaganlife.com
Wendy Letwinetz, Contact, Administration, wendy@okanaganlife.com

Ottawa City Magazine
St. Joseph Media Inc., 43 Eccles St., Ottawa, ON K1R 6S3
Tel: 613-230-0333
feedback@stjosephmedia.com
Social Media:
twitter.com/ottawamag
www.facebook.com/OttawaMag
Circulation: 35,500 Frequency: 7 times a year
Sarah Brown, Editor, sbrown@stjosephmedia.com
Harvey Chartrand, Editor

Ottawa Life Magazine
301 Metcalfe, Lower Level, Ottawa, ON K2P 1S3
Tel: 613-688-5433; Fax: 613-688-1994
info@ottawalife.com
Social Media:
twitter.com/ottawalifers
www.facebook.com/pages/Ottawa-Life-Magazine/1123843988222
Harvey Chartrand, Editor

The Ottawa X Press
704 Somerset St. West, Ottawa, ON K1R 6P6
Tel: 613-237-8226; Fax: 613-237-8220
Toll-Free: 866-255-5516
info@ottawaexpress.ca
Social Media:
twitter.com/ottawaxpress
www.facebook.com/ottawaxpress
Circulation: 63,500 Frequency: Weekly, Thu.
Guillaume Moffet, Managing Editor

Pique Newsmagazine
Owned By: Pique Publishing Inc.
#103, 1390 Alpha Lake Rd., Whistler, BC V0N 1B1
Tel: 604-938-0202; Fax: 604-938-0201
mail@piquenewsmagazine.com
Social Media:
twitter.com/piquenews
www.facebook.com/PiqueNewsmagazine
Circulation: 16,500 Frequency: Weekly, Fri.
Bob Barnett, Publisher, bob@piquenewsmagazine.com
Clare Ogilvie, Editor, edit@piquenewsmagazine.com

Planet S
Owned By: Hullabaloo Publishing Ltd.
#409, 135-21st St. East, Saskatoon, SK S7K 0B4
Tel: 306-651-3423; Fax: 306-651-3428
reception@planetsmag.com
Social Media:
twitter.com/PlanetSMagazine
www.facebook.com/pages/Planet-S-Magazine/407 16663512
Circulation: 60,000
Chris Kirkland, Editor, editor@planetsmag.com

the prairie dog
#201, 1836 Scarth St., Regina, SK S4P 2G3
Tel: 306-757-8522; Fax: 306-352-9686
reception@prairiedogmag.com
Circulation: 16,000 Frequency: Bi-weekly
April Bourgeois, Publisher
Stephen Whitworth, Editor

Profile Kingston
PO Box 91, Kingston, ON K7L 4V6
Tel: 613-546-6723; Fax: 613-546-0707
editor@profilekingston.com
Circulation: 16,000 Frequency: 6 times a year
Bonnie Golomb, Publisher

Spacing
Owned By: Spacing Media
#309, 720 Bathurst St., Toronto, ON M5S 2R4
Tel: 416-644-1017
info@spacing.ca
Social Media: www.flickr.com/groups/spacingmagpool
twitter.com/spacing
Matthew Blackett, Publisher/Creative Director, matt@spacing.ca
Todd Harrison, Managing Editor, toddharrison@spacing.ca

Thornhill Post
30 Lesmill Rd., Toronto, ON M3B 2T6
Tel: 416-250-7979; Fax: 416-250-1737
editorial@postcity.com; advertising@postcity.com
Other information: Classified Advertising, E-mail:
classifieds@postcity.com
Social Media:
twitter.com/PostCity
www.facebook.com/PostCityMagazines
Circulation: 25,000 Frequency: Monthly
The magazine serves Thornhill, Ontario by featuring news & information about local people, places, events, restaurants, & shopping.
Lorne London, Publisher, lornelondon@postcity.com
Laurie McGillivray, Associate Publisher, lauriemcgillivray@postcity.com
Andrew Mannsbach, Associate Publisher, Sales, andrewmannsbach@postcity.com
Ron Johnson, Editor, ronjohnson@postcity.com
Lisa London-Shiffman, Vice-President, LisaLondon@postcity.com
Dorothy Chudzinski, Managing Art Director, DorothyChudzinski@postcity.com
Lynne London, Director, Advertising, LynneLondon@postcity.com
Janice Fletcher, Controller, JaniceFletcher@postcity.com

Thunder Bay Guest Magazine
Owned By: Dougall Media
87 North Hill St., Thunder Bay, ON P7A 5V6
Tel: 804-346-2600; Fax: 807-345-9923
Circulation: 12,469 Frequency: 9 pa
Richard Sadick, Publisher

Toronto Events Calendar
Previous Name: Toronto Events Planner
#460, 20 Eglinton Ave. East, Toronto, ON M4P 1A9
Tel: 416-782-5699; Fax: 416-787-9299
info@torontoeventscalendar.com
Frequency: 2 pa; January, June
R.S. Diamond, Editor
Sybil Levine, Publisher

Toronto Life
Toronto Life, Urban Group, St. Joseph Media Corp, Queen Richmond Centre, Toronto, ON M5C 1S2
Tel: 416-364-3333; Fax: 416-861-1169
editorial@torontolife.com
Social Media:
twitter.com/toronto_life
www.facebook.com/torontolife
Circulation: 91,692 Frequency: Monthly
John Macfarlane, Editor

UPtown Magazine
1355 Mountain Ave., Winnipeg, MB R2X 3B6
Tel: 204-949-4370; Fax: 204-949-4376
feedback@uptownmag.com
Social Media:
twitter.com/UptownMag
www.facebook.com/uptownmag
Circulation: 17,000 Frequency: Weekly
John Kendle, Editor, 204-697-7093, john.kendle@freepress.mb.ca
Michelle Pereira, Publisher, 204-697-7044, michelle.pereira@canstarnews.com

Vancouver Magazine
Owned By: Transcontinental Media Inc.
Transcontinental Publishing, #560, 2608 Granville St., Vancouver, BC V6H 3V3
Tel: 604-877-7732; Fax: 604-877-4848
mail@vancouvermagazine.com
Circulation: 48,000 Frequency: 10 pa
Kim Peacock, Publisher
John Burns, Editor-in-chief

Victoria Boulevard
Owned By: Boulevard Lifestyles Inc.
Boulevard Lifestyles Inc., 1845B Fort St., Victoria, BC V8R 1J6
Tel: 250-598-8111; Fax: 250-598-3183
Info@VictoriaBoulevard.com
Social Media:
twitter.com/boulevardmag
www.facebook.com/BoulevardMagazine
Circulation: 45,000 Frequency: Bi-monthly
Evelyn Butler, Publisher

Village Post
30 Lesmill Rd., Toronto, ON M3B 2T6
Tel: 416-250-7979; Fax: 416-250-1737
editorial@postcity.com; advertising@postcity.com
Other information: Classified Advertising, E-mail:
classifieds@postcity.com
Social Media:
twitter.com/PostCity
www.facebook.com/PostCityMagazines
Circulation: 25,000 Frequency: Monthly
The Forest Hill & Yorkville neighbourhoods of Toronto are served by The Village Post, which features reports on local news, people, & lifestyles.
Lorne London, Publisher, lornelondon@postcity.com
Laurie McGillivray, Associate Publisher, lauriemcgillivray@postcity.com
Andrew Mannsbach, Associate Publisher, Sales, andrewmannsbach@postcity.com
Ron Johnson, Editor, ronjohnson@postcity.com
Lisa London-Shiffman, Vice-President, LisaLondon@postcity.com
Dorothy Chudzinski, Managing Art Director, DorothyChudzinski@postcity.com
Lynne London, Director, Advertising, LynneLondon@postcity.com
Janice Fletcher, Controller, JaniceFletcher@postcity.com

Visitors' Choice, BC
102 East 4th Ave., Vancouver, BC V5T 1G2
Tel: 604-608-5180; Fax: 604-608-5181
Toll-Free: 800-867-5141
editor@visitorschoice.com
Social Media:
twitter.com/VisitorsChoice
facebook.com/VisitorsChoice
Circulation: 795,000 Frequency: 3 pa
Publishes vistor's guides for 12 communities in BC.
Fawn Duchaine, Publisher, 604-340-5819, fduchaine@visitorschoice.com

Voilà Québec
#201, 735, boul Wilfrid-Hamel, Québec, QC G1M 2R1
Tél: 418-694-1272;Téléc: 418-694-1119
info@voilaquebec.com
Tirage: 70,000 Fréquence: 4 pa; English & French
Louis-Georges Jalbert, Président/éditeur, louis@voilaquebec.com
Manon Gauvreau, Directrice de l'administration, comptabilite@voilaquebec.com

Voir Gatineau-Ottawa
#200, 396, rue Cooper, Ottawa, ON K2P 2H7
Tél: 613-237-8226;Téléc: 613-237-8220
info@gatineau.voir.ca
Fréquence: Hebdomadaire, français
Céline Lebrun, Directeur général
Guillaume Moffet, Rédactrice-en-chef

Voir Montréal
375, rue Ste-Catherine ouest, 7e étage, Montréal, QC H3B 1A5
Tél: 514-848-0805;Téléc: 514-848-9004
Ligne sans frais: 877-631-8647
info@mtl.voir.ca
Médias sociaux: me.voir.ca
twitter.com/voir
www.facebook.com/journalvoir
Tirage: 102 000
Simon Jodoin, Rédacteur-en-chef

Voir Québec
#100, 735, rue Saint-Joseph est, Québec, QC G1K 3C6
Tél: 418-522-7777;Téléc: 418-522-7779
Ligne sans frais: 877-632-8647
info@qc.voir.ca
Tirage: 41 725 Fréquence: Hebdomadaire; français, aussi Voir Québec City; 52 par an
Michel Fortin, Directeur général
Simon Jodoin, Rédacteur-en-chef

Where Calgary
Owned By: St Joseph Media
1131 Kensington Rd. NW, 2nd Fl., Calgary, AB T2N 3P4
Tel: 403-299-1888
abrunnhofer@where.ca
Circulation: 46,500 Frequency: Bi-monthly
Brian French, Publisher

Where Edmonton
Owned By: St Joseph Media
#1, 930 - 50 St., Edmonton, AB T6B 2L5
Tel: 780-465-3362
editor@whereedmonton.com
Circulation: 33,240 Frequency: 6 times a year
Rob Tanner, Publisher

Where Halifax
Owned By: St Joseph Media
1300 Hollis St., Halifax, NS B3J 1T6
Tel: 902-420-9943
tadams@metroguide.ca
Circulation: 220,000 Frequency: 10 pa
Sheila Blair-Reid, Publisher

Where Ottawa
Previous Name: Where Ottawa-Hull
Owned By: St Joseph Media
43 Eccles St., Ottawa, ON K1R 6S3
Tel: 613-230-0333
kbraginetz@where.ca
Circulation: 19,081 Frequency: Monthly
Melanie Scott, Editor
Dianne Wing, Publisher

Where Toronto/Mississauga/Muskoka
Owned By: St Joseph Media
#320, 111 Queen St. East, Toronto, ON M5C 1S2
Tel: 416-364-3333 Toll-Free: 800-387-1156
lluong@where.ca
Circulation: 74,988 Frequency: Monthly

Anne Gibson, Editor-in-chief

Where Victoria
Previous Name: Victoria Today
Owned By: St Joseph Media
818 Broughton St., Victoria, BC V8W 1E4
Tel: 250-383-3633
editor@wherevictoria.com
Circulation: 64,320 Frequency: 6 pa
Anna Scolnick, Publisher

Where Winnipeg
Owned By: St Joseph Media
#400, 112 Market Ave., Winnipeg, MB R3B 0P4
Tel: 204-943-4439
erin@bestmarketing.com
Circulation: 33,708 Frequency: 6 pa
Brad Hughes, Editor-in-chief
Laurie Hughes, Publisher

Windsor Life Magazine
#318, 5060 Tecumseh Rd. East, Windsor, ON N8T 1C1
Tel: 519-979-5433; Fax: 519-979-9237
Circulation: 79,373 Windsor & Essex County Frequency: 8 times a year
Robert E. Robinson, Publisher
Hal Sullivan, Editor

Computing & Technology

Atout Micro
CP 240, Saint-Isidore, QC G0S 2S0
Tél: 418-882-5214 Ligne sans frais: 866-826-1089
atout@atoutmicro.ca
Autre information: Sans frais: 1-866-826-1089
Médias sociaux:
twitter.com/AtoutMicro
Tirage: 8000
François Picard, Éditeur & Rédacteur en chef

We Compute
1232 Kingston Rd., Scarborough, ON M1N 1P3
Tel: 416-481-1955; Fax: 416-481-2819
Circulation: 150,000 Frequency: 12 times a year
Eric Macmillan, Editor
George Bachir, Publisher

Cosmetics

Glow
Owned By: St Joseph Media
#320, 111 Queen St. East, Toronto, ON M5C 1S2
Tel: 416-364-3333; Fax: 416-594-3374
shoppersoptimum@shoppersdrugmart.ca
Social Media: pinterest.com/glowmag
twitter.com/glowcanada
www.facebook.com/GlowMag
Frequency: 6 times a year; English & French
Juliette Baxter, Editor-in-Chief

Culture, Current Events

Broken Pencil
PO Box 203 P, Toronto, ON M5S 2S7
Tel: 416-204-1700
editor@brokenpencil.com
Circulation: 3,000 Frequency: 4 times a year
Devoted exclusively to underground culture and the independent arts.
Lindsay Gibb, Editor, editor@brokenpencil.com

Edges: New Planetary Patterns
655 Queen St. East, Toronto, ON M4M 1G4
Tel: 416-691-2316; Fax: 416-691-2491
Toll-Free: 877-691-1422
ica@icacan.org
Circulation: 12,000 Frequency: 3 pa
Fred Simons, Executive Director
Leah Taylor, Editor

Fuse
#454, 401 Richmond St. West, Toronto, ON M5V 3A8
Tel: 416-340-8026
info@fusemagazine.org
Social Media:
twitter.com/fusemag
www.facebook.com/FUSEartculturepolitics
Circulation: 3,300 Frequency: 4 pa
Gina Badger, Editorial Director
Izida Zorde, Associate Editor
Christal Pshyk, Managing Director, christal@fusemagazine.ca

HELLO!
Owned By: Rogers Publishing Ltd.
1 Mount Pleasant Rd., 8th Fl., Toronto, ON M4Y 2Y5
Tel: 416-764-2863; Fax: 416-764-2866
Social Media:
twitter.com/HELLOCanada
www.facebook.com/138543579563513
Circulation: 137,025 Frequency: 46 issues per year

Maisonneuve
PO Box 53527, 1051 boul Decarie, St Laurent, QC H4L 5J9
Tel: 514-482-5089
business@maisonneuve.org
Social Media: technorati.com
twitter.com/maisonneuvemag
www.facebook.com/maisonneuvemagazine
Frequency: Quarterly

The Newfoundland Herald
Owned By: Skylab Media Group
PO Box 2015, Logy Bay Rd., St. John's, NL A1C 5R7
Tel: 709-726-7060; Fax: 709-726-6971
letters@nfldherald.com
Circulation: 17,000 Frequency: Weekly
Mark Dwyer, Managing Editor, 709-570-5212, mdwyer@nfldherald.com

Plaid
Tel: 416-998-1202
info@plaidmag.com
Social Media:
twitter.com/PlaidMagazine
www.facebook.com/PlaidMagazine
Frequency: 2 pa
Odessa Paloma Parker, Editor, odessa@plaidmag.com

Saltscapes Publishing Inc.
c/o Saltscapes, #209, 30 Damascus Rd., Bedford, NS B4A 0C1
Tel: 902-464-7258; Fax: 902-464-3755
Circulation: 40,000 Frequency: 6 times a year
Jim Gourlay, Publisher
Heather White, Editor

Up & Coming
Toronto, ON
Frequency: Quarterly
Erotic lifestyle magazine featuring essays, and photo spreads for adults.
Mike Feswick, Owner

Directories & Almanacs

Black Pages Directory
1390 Eglinton Ave. West, Toronto, ON M6C 2E4
Tel: 416-784-3002; Fax: 416-784-5719
info@blackpages.ca
Frequency: Annually
Black Pages Directory Canada is a comprehensive guide to Canada's Black and Caribbean community. While this guide was created to help you find products, services and activities within our community, it serves as a valuable resource of information about Canada's Black and Caribbean community.

Drugs

Drugs & Addiction Magazine
Owned By: Suggitt Publishing Ltd.
Bell Tower, #950, 10104 - 103 Ave., Edmonton, AB T5J 0H8
Toll-Free: 866-421-5999
reception@dafacts.com
A teaching tool given free to young people in order to educate them about the dangers of drug abuse.
Stephen Kathnelson, President, stephen@dafacts.com
Melanie Smith, General Manager, melanie@dafacts.com
Elana Sures, Author

Education

Life Learning Magazine
Life Media, #52, B2-125 Queensway, Toronto, ON MBY 1H6
publisher@lifelearningmagazine.com
Social Media:
twitter.com/LifeLearningMag
www.facebook.com/LifeLearningMagazine
Circulation: 10,000 Frequency: Bi-monthly; digital
Rolf Priesnitz, Publisher

Entertainment

The Buzz
160 Richmond St., Charlottetown, PE C1A 1H9
Tel: 902-628-1958
buzzon@eastlink.ca
Social Media: www.youtube.com/BUZZpei
twitter.com/buzzpei
www.facebook.com/thebuzzpei
Circulation: Sept.-June - 15,000; July-Aug. - 26,000 Frequency: Monthly
Peter Richards, Managing Editor, 902-628-1958

CineAction: Radical Film Criticism & Theory
#705, 40 Alexander St., Toronto, ON M4Y 1B5
Tel: 416-964-3534
cineaction@cineaction.ca
Circulation: 4,000 Frequency: 3 pa
Robin Wood
Susan Morrison

Cinema Scope
465 Lytton Blvd., Toronto, ON M5N 1S5
Tel: 416-889-5430
info@cinema-scope.com
Social Media:
twitter.com/CinemaScopeMag
www.facebook.com/pages/Cinema-Scope-Magazine/205268252835
Frequency: 4 pa
Mark Peranson, Publisher & Editor
Andrew Tracy, Managing Editor

Cineplex Magazine
Owned By: Cineplex Media
102 Atlantic Ave., Toronto, ON M6K 1X9
Tel: 416-539-8800; Fax: 416-539-8511
theresa.mcvean@cineplex.com
Circulation: 700,000 Frequency: Monthly

En Primeur
71 Barber Greene Rd., Toronto, ON M3C 2A2
Tél: 416-445-0544;Téléc: 416-445-2894
Tirage: 105,000
Sandra I. Stewart, Publisher

En Primeur Jeunesse
Détenteur: Tribute Publishing Inc.
c/o Tribute Entertainment Media Group, 71 Barber Greene Rd., Toronto, ON M3C 2A2
Tél: 416-445-0544;Téléc: 416-445-2894
Tirage: 50 000 Fréquence: 4 fois par an; français

Magazine Le Clap
#370, 2360, ch Ste-Foy, Sainte-Foy, QC G1V 4H2
Tél: 418-653-2470;Téléc: 418-653-6018
leclap@clap.ca; redaction@clap.ca
Médias sociaux:
twitter.com/cinema_leclap
www.facebook.com/cinemaleclap
Tirage: 100 000 Fréquence: 7 fois par an; français

Playboard
Archway Publishers, #4, 15255 - 36 Ave., Surrey, BC V3S 0Y4
Tel: 778-294-5881; Fax: 778-294-5882
info@playboardmag.com
Circulation: 15,000 Frequency: 10 pa
Playboard is prominently displayed and distributed free in all of the Vancouver Civic theatres, the Arts Club Theatres, the Richmond Gateway
Alan Slater, Publisher & Editor

Scene Magazine (SCENE)
PO Box 27048, 35 Hammond Cres., London, ON N5X 3X5
Tel: 519-642-4780; Fax: 519-642-0737
news@scenemagazine.com
Circulation: 77,000 Frequency: 25 pa
Bret Downe, Publisher & Editor-in-chief, bret@scenemagazine.com
Alma Bernardo Downe, Coordinator, alma@scenemagazine.com

Star Système
Détenteur: TVA Publications
1010, rue de Sérigny, 4e étage, Longueuil, QC J4K 5G7
Tél: 514-370-5823;Téléc: 514-270-7079
Ligne sans frais: 888-535-8634
Fréquence: 51 fois par an

Teen Tribute
Owned By: Tribute Publishing Inc.
71 Barber Greene Rd., Toronto, ON M3C 2A2
Tel: 416-445-0544; Fax: 416-445-2894
advertising@tribute.ca
Social Media:
twitter.com/tributemag
Circulation: 300,000 Frequency: 4 times a year
Robin Stevenson, Editor
Sandra Stewart, Publisher

Tribute Magazine
Owned By: Tribute Publishing Inc.
71 Barber Greene Rd., Toronto, ON M3C 2A2
Tel: 416-445-0544; Fax: 416-445-2894
generalinfo@tribute.ca
Social Media:
twitter.com/tributemag
Circulation: 500,450 Frequency: 9 pa
Sandra Stewart, Editorial Director

View Weekly
Previous Name: View Magazine
370 Main St. West, Hamilton, ON L8P 1K3
Tel: 905-527-3343; Fax: 905-527-3721
info@viewmag.com
Circulation: 30,000 Frequency: Weekly
Rob Kilpatrick, Editor-in-chief
Sean Rosen, Publisher, seanr@viewmag.com

Visitor Magazine
PO Box 41030, Waterloo, ON N0K 3K0
Tel: 519-886-2831; Fax: 519-886-6409
advertise@exchangemagazine.com
Circulation: 100,000
John Rohr, Publisher, jon.rohr@exchangemagazine.com

Vue Weekly
Owned By: Postvue Publishing Inc
#200, 11230 - 119th St. NW, Edmonton, AB T5G 2X3
Tel: 780-426-1996; Fax: 780-426-2889
Social Media: www.youtube.com/vueonline
twitter.com/vueweekly
www.facebook.com/vueweekly
Circulation: 24,274 Frequency: Weekly
Eden Munro, Managing Editor/Associate Publisher, eden@vueweekly.com
Ron Garth, Publisher & Editor, ron@vueweekly.com

Environment & Nature

Alternatives Journal: Canadian Environmental Ideas & Action
Previous Name: Alternatives Journal: Environmental Thought, Policy & Action
c/o Faculty of Environmental Studies, University of Waterloo, 200 University Ave. West, Waterloo, ON N2L 3G1
Tel: 519-888-4442; Fax: 519-746-0292
Toll-Free: 866-437-2587
infoalternativesjournal.ca
Circulation: 4,500 Frequency: 6 pa
A theme-based publication dedicated to illustrating the relationships between the environment and social justice, politics and the economy. It looks at the challenges and issues related to the interaction of humanity and the environment, and the responses to those issues.
Nicola Ross, Executive Editor

The Atlantic Salmon Journal
Atlantic Salmon Federation, PO Box 5200, St Andrews, NB E5B 3S8
Tel: 506-529-4581; Fax: 506-529-1070
Toll-Free: 800-565-5666
Circulation: 11,000 Frequency: 4 times a year
This magazine is the world's oldest publication regarding conservation-minded salmon angling and protection of the species.
Martin Silverstone, Editor, martinsilverstone@videotron.ca

British Columbia Environmental Report
Owned By: Canadian Environmental Network (CEN)
c/o British Columbia Environmental Network, #122, 718-333 Brooksbank Ave., North Vancouver, BC V7J 3V6
Tel: 604-515-1969
editor@ecobc.org; network@bcen.bc.ca
The British Columbia Environmental Report is a journal which features news, analysis, events, & reviews about British Columbia environmental topics.
Dave Stevens, Chair, Board of Directors
Chris Blake, Executive Coordinator

Canadian Geographic
PO Box 923 Main, #200, 1155 Lola St., Ottawa, ON L3P 0B8
Tel: 613-745-4629 Toll-Free: 800-267-0824
Social Media: www.youtube.com/user/CanadianGeographic
twitter.com/CanGeoMag
www.face book.com/canadiangeographic
Circulation: 222,000 Frequency: 6 times a year
Publication aims to promote Canada both to Canadians and around the world. It looks at issues relating to the nature and wildlife within Canada, and what can be done to preserve the natural Canadian landscape.
John L. Thomson, CEO & Publisher
Rick Boychuk, Editor

Canadian Wildlife
Owned By: Canadian Wildlife Federation
350 Michael Cowpland Dr., Kanata, ON K2M 2W1
Tel: 613-599-9594; Fax: 613-599-4428
Toll-Free: 800-563-9453
info@cwf-fcf.org
Frequency: bi-monthly
Aimed at both teenagers and adults, this magazine covers issues relating to Canadian and international wildlife, and reports on the work of the Canadian Wildlife Federation.

Environmental Science & Engineering Magazine
#30, 220 Industrial Parkway South, Aurora, ON L4G 3V6
Tel: 905-727-4666; Fax: 905-841-7271
Circulation: 19,000 Frequency: bi-monthly
This publicationis the largest documentary magazine in Canada and has articles on various environmental issues, including air pollution, water filtration, hazerdous waste, alternative energy, greenhouse gasses, among others; available only to subscribers.
Steve Davey, Editor & Publisher, steve@esemag.com

Green Living Magazine
Key Publishers Company Ltd., 66 The Esplanade, Toronto, ON M5E 1A6
Tel: 416-360-0044; Fax: 416-642-1711
Toll-Free: 866-934-0044
info@green-living.ca
Social Media:
twitter.com/GreenLivingPage
www.facebook.com/GreenLivingPage
Circulation: 150,000 Frequency: quarterly
Green Living Magazine attempts to promote living a green lifestyle to its readers by providing information about organics, health, the environment and eco-consumer products. They support sustainable and healthy living and publicizing the green message.
Laurie Simmonds, Publisher

Journal of Environmental Engineering & Science
Owned By: National Research Council of Canada
NRC Research Press, 1200 Montreal Rd., Bldg. M-55, Ottawa, ON K1A 0R6
Tel: 613-990-7873; Fax: 613-952-7656
Toll-Free: 800-668-1222
pubs@nrcresearchpress.com
Frequency: bi-monthly
This publication provides a forum for the discussion of environmental engineering & science research. Topics this journal explores include environmental engineering, physical & analytical sciences, life sciences related to environmental issues, health sciences, & oceanography.

La Maison du 21e siècle
2955, rue du Domaine-du-lac-Lucerne, Sainte-Adèle, QC J8B 3K9
Tél: 450-228-1555
info@maisonsaine.ca
Médias sociaux:
www.linkedin.com/pub/andré-fauteux/b/128/912
twitter.com/Maison21e
www.facebook.com/maisonsaine
Fréquence: 4 fois par an
André Fauteux, Éditeur

Natural Life
Previous Name: Earthkeeper Magazine
Life Media, #52, B2-125 The Queensway, Toronto, ON M8Y 1H6
info@LifeMedia.ca
Circulation: 35,000 Frequency: 6 pa
This independently owned magazine has an international focus on providing intelligent and in-depth practical information on issues such as healthy cooking, organic gardening, sustainable homes, natural parenting, wellness and natural healing, eco-leisure and eco-travel and sustainable business.
Wendy Priesnitz, Editor
Rolf Priesnitz, Publisher

Nature Canada
c/o Nature Canada, #300, 75 Albert St., Ottawa, ON K1P 5E7
Tel: 613-562-3447; Fax: 613-562-3371
Toll-Free: 613-562-3371
info@naturecanada.ca
Social Media: www.youtube.com/user/NatureCanada1
www.facebook.com/NatureCanada
Circulation: 26,400 Frequency: 4 pa
The mission of this magazine is to protect nature, its diversity and the processes that sustain it, and does this by providing information regarding several environmental topics including bird conservation, wilderness protection, endangered species and national parks. The publication supports community-based efforts to protect wildlife; encourages the development of an effective network of parks and protected areas across Canada; and promoting biodiversity in Canada and abroad.

ON Nature
Head Office
Previous Name: Seasons
#612, 214 King St. West, Toronto, ON M5H 3S6
Tel: 416-444-8419; Fax: 416-444-9866
Toll-Free: 800-440-2366
info@ontarionature.org
Circulation: 14,500 Frequency: 4 pa
ON Nature attempts to bring its readers closer to nature by providing information about Ontario's natural areas and wildlife, and by providing insight into current environmental issues. Magazine features articles by nature specialists, colour photography, information regarding wilderness travel and up-to-date news on conservation battles.
Caroline Schultz, Executive Director
Victoria Foote, Editor

Québec Oiseaux
CP 1000 M, 4545, av Pierre-De Coubertin, Montréal, QC H1V 3R2
Tél: 514-252-3190
Médias sociaux: www.youtube.com/user/QOiseaux
www.twitter.com/quebecoiseaux
www.facebo ok.com/quebecoiseaux
Tirage: 7 928 Fréquence: 4 fois par an
Michel Préville, Rédacteur-en-chef

Solid Waste & Recycling
80 Valleybrook Dr., Toronto, ON M3B 2S9
Tel: 416-510-6798; Fax: 416-510-5133
Toll-Free: 800-268-7742
Circulation: 9,426 Frequency: 6 times a year
This publication dicusses all issues and topics pertaining to recyling and waste management.

Watershed Sentinel
c/o Watershed Sentinel Educational Society, PO Box 1270, Comox, BC V9M 7Z8
Tel: 250-339-6117
editor@watershedsentinel.ca
Social Media:
www.facebook.com/pages/Watershed-Sentinel/106472301541
Circulation: 3,500 Frequency: 6 pa
This West Coast publication covers both bioregional and global perspectives on topics such as the environment, health and sustainability.
Delores Broten, Publisher & Editor

Women & Environments International Magazine
Previous Name: Women & Environments; WE International
HNES Building, #234, York University, 4700 Keele St., Toronto, ON M3J 1P3
Tel: 416-736-2100; Fax: 416-736-5679
weimag@yorku.ca
Circulation: 2,000 Frequency: 2 pa
Publication examines the relationships between women and the environment from a feminist perspective. It provides a forum for academic research and theory, professional practice and community experience and covers topics such as ecology and environmental activism, community development, childcare, and urban and rural agriculture.
Prabha Khosla
Reggie Modlich

Families

BC Parent Magazine
PO Box 72086, Sasamat RPO, Vancouver, BC V6R 4P2
Tel: 604-221-0366
bcparent@shaw.ca
Circulation: 50,000 Frequency: 9 times a year
Elizabeth Shaffer, Editor, eshaffer@telus.net

Calgary's Child Magazine
#723, 105-150 Crowfoot Cres. NW, Calgary, AB T3G 3T2
Tel: 403-241-6066; Fax: 403-286-9731
calgaryschild@shaw.ca
Circulation: 70,000 Frequency: 6 times a year
Ellen Percival, Publisher & Editor

City Parent
Owned By: Metroland Media
#4, 447 Speers Rd., Oakville, ON L6K 3S7
Tel: 905-842-6591
dpells@cityparent.com
Social Media: www.facebook.com/cityparent
Circulation: 77,785 Frequency: 12 times a year
Jane Muller, Editor-in-chief, jmuller@metroland.com

Divorce Magazine
#1179, 2255B Queen St. East, Toronto, ON M4E 1G3
Tel: 416-368-8853; Fax: 416-368-4978
Toll-Free: 888-217-9538
Social Media: www.myspace.com/divorcemagazine
twitter.com/divorcemagazine
www.fac ebook.com/divorcemagazine
Circulation: 170,000 Frequency: 4 times a year
Dan Couvrette, CEO & Publisher, danc@divorcemag.com
Dinh Nguven, Editor, dinh@divorcemarketinggroup.com

Edmonton's Child Magazine
Owned By: Gryphon Publishing
PO Box 369, 9768 - 170 St., Edmonton, AB T5T 5L4
Tel: 780-484-3360; Fax: 780-486-1844
Toll-Free: 866-484-3360
info@edmontonschild.com
Social Media: www.twitter.com/edmontonschild
www.facebook.com/edmontonschild
Circulation: 30,000 Frequency: Monthly
Kerri Leland, Editor, editor@edmontonschild.com

Enfants Québec
Détenteur: Les Éditions Rogers limitée
300, rue Arran, Saint-Lambert, QC J4R 1K5
Tél: 514-875-9612
serviceclient@editionsheritage.com
Médias sociaux: www.facebook.com/pages/Enfants-Qu%C3%A9bec/1650279035 1870
Tirage: 60,506 Fréquence: 8 fois par an; français
Eve Christian, Rédactrice
Sylvie Payette, Éditrice

Fit Parent
Toronto, ON
info@fitparentmagazine.com
Frequency: 6 times per year
Craig Knight, Publisher, craig@fitparentmagazine.com

Island Parent Magazine
#A-10, 830 Pembroke St., Victoria, BC V8T 1H9
Tel: 250-388-6905; Fax: 250-388-6920
Toll-Free: 888-372-0862
mail@islandparent.ca
Social Media: twitter.com/islandparent
www.facebook.com/IslandParent
Circulation: 20,000 Frequency: Monthly
Paul Abra, Publisher
Mada Johnson, Editor

Our Kids Go to Camp
Owned By: Our Kids Publications Ltd.
4242 Rockwood Rd., Mississauga, ON L4W 1L8
Toll-Free: 877-272-1845
info@ourkids.net
Circulation: 200,000 Frequency: Annually
Agatha Stawicki, Managing Editor

Our Kids Go to School
Owned By: Our Kids Publications Ltd.
4242 Rockwood Rd., Mississauga, ON L4W 1L8
Tel: 905-272-1843; Fax: 905-272-0474
Toll-Free: 877-272-1845
info@ourkids.net
Social Media: www.youtube.com/ourkidsnet
www.twitter.com/ourkidsnet
www.facebook.com/ourkidsnet
Circulation: 250,000 Frequency: Annually
Agatha Stawicki, Publisher

Owlkids
Previous Name: Tree Home Family
Owned By: Owlkids Books
#400, 10 Lower Spadina Ave., Toronto, ON M5V 2Z2
Tel: 800-551-6957; Fax: 905-946-0410
owlkids@cdsglobal.ca
Circulation: 66,768 Frequency: 6 times a year
Mary Beth Leatherdale, Editor

Pomme d'Api Québec
Détenteur: Bayard Presse Canada Inc.
c/o Bayard Jeunesse Canada, 4475, rue Frontenac, Montréal, QC H2H 2S2
Tél: 514-844-2111;Téléc: 514-278-3030
redaction@bayardpresse.qc.ca
Tirage: 16 000
Suzanne Spino, Directrice générale

7 Jours
Détenteur: TVA Publications
1010, rue de Sérigny, 4e étage, Longueuil, QC J4K 5G7
Tél: 514-848-7000;Téléc: 514-848-7070
Ligne sans frais: 800-367-0667
7jours@tva-publications.com
Médias sociaux: twitter.com/7jours
www.facebook.com/magazine7Jours
Tirage: 121 540 Fréquence: Hebdomadaire
Luc de Sève, Éditeur et directeur

Today's Parent
Owned By: Rogers Publishing Ltd.
1 Mount Pleasant Rd., 8th Fl., Toronto, ON M4Y 2Y5
Tel: 416-764-2883; Fax: 416-764-2894
editors@todaysparent.com
Social Media: www.facebook.com/TodaysParent
Circulation: 160,056 Frequency: Monthly
Rosemary Munroe, Publisher
Karine Ewart, Editr-in-Chief

Today's Parent Baby and Toddler / Bout de Chou
Previous Name: Mon Enfant
Owned By: Les Éditions Rogers limitée
1200, av McGill College, 8e étage, Montréal, QC H3B 4G7
Tel: 514-845-5141
Circulation: 131,050 (40,700 Bout de Chou) Frequency: 2 pa; English (2 fois par an; français)
For parents with kids aged 0-3.

Fashion

Clin d'oeil
Détenteur: TVA Publications
Tél: 514-848-7164;Téléc: 514-270-7079
clindoeil@publicor.ca
Médias sociaux: twitter.com/Mag_clindoeil
www.facebook.com/group.php?gid=61535490997
Tirage: 60 372 Fréquence: Mensuel; français
Claire Syril, Éditeur
Mitsou Gélinas, Directeur de la publication

Dolce Magazine
Owned By: DOLCE Publishing Inc.
DOLCE Publishing Inc., #30, 111 Zenway Blvd., Vaughan, ON L4H 3H9
Tel: 905-264-6789; Fax: 905-264-3787
Toll-Free: 888-683-6523
Social Media: twitter.com/dolcemag
www.facebook.com/pages/Dolce-Vita-Magazine/24 838319308
Circulation: 290,000
Michelle Zerillo-Sosa, Publisher & Editor-in-chief, michelle@dolce.ca

Fashion Magazine
Owned By: St Joseph Media
St. Joseph Media, #320, 111 Queen St. East, Toronto, ON M5C 1S2
Tel: 416-364-3333; Fax: 416-594-3374
Toll-Free: 800-757-3977
Social Media: pinterest.com/fashionmagazine
twitter.com/FashionCanada
www.faceboo k.com/fashioncanada
Circulation: 124,927 Frequency: 10 times a year
Ceri Marsh, Editor-in-chief
Michelle Bilodeau, Assoc. Editor
Giorgina Bigioni, Publisher

Flare
Owned By: Rogers Publishing Ltd.
1 Mount Pleasant Rd., 8th Fl., Toronto, ON M4Y 2Y5
Tel: 416-764-2863; Fax: 416-764-2866
Social Media: flarefashion.tumblr.com
twitter.com/FLAREfashion
www.facebook.com/FLAREFashion
Circulation: 124,646 Frequency: Monthly
Miranda Purves, Editor-in-Chief
Melissa Ahlstrand, Publisher

Good Life Connoisseur
#317, 1489 Marine Dr., West Vancouver, BC V7T 1B8
Tel: 604-925-0313 Toll-Free: 888-925-0313
Social Media: twitter.com/GLConnoisseur
www.facebook.com/GoodLifeConnoisseur
Frequency: 4 times a year
Terry Tremaine, Publisher & Editor

LOULOU
Owned By: Rogers Publishing Ltd.
#1700, 1200 McGill College Ave., Montréal, QC H3B 4G7
Tel: 514-843-2189; Fax: 514-843-2189
julia.cyboran@loulou.rogers.com
Social Media: twitter.com/louloumagazine
www.facebook.com/LOULOUMagazine
Circulation: 146,001 Frequency: 8 times a year; English & French
Marie-José Desmarais, Publisher

LOULOU
Détenteur: Éditions Rogers Media
#1700, 1200, av McGill College, Montréal, QC H3B 4G7
Tél: 514-843-2189;Téléc: 514-843-2189
julia.cyboran@loulou.rogers.com
Médias sociaux: twitter.com/MagazineLOULOU
Tirage: 73,883 Fréquence: 8 times a year; English & French
Marie-Joseé Desmarais, Publisher/Editor
Claude LaFramboise, Executive Editor

Nuvo Magazine
3055 Kingsway, Vancouver, BC V5R 5J8
Tel: 604-899-9380; Fax: 604-899-1450
Toll-Free: 877-205-6886
Frequency: 4 times a year
Jim Tobler, Editor

Fifty-Plus Adults

Active Adult
Owned By: Homes Publishing Group
178 Main St., Unionville, ON L3R 2G9
Tel: 905-479-4663 Toll-Free: 800-363-4663
nsicilia@homesmag.com
Social Media: twitter.com/HOMESPublishing
www.facebook.com/pages/activeadultmagcom/150 770131613956?
Circulation: 100,000 Frequency: 3 times a year
Michael Rosset, Publisher
Patrick Tivy, Editor

Be Fabulous!
11604 - 113 Ave., Edmonton, AB T5G 0J6
Tel: 780-470-0749; Fax: 780-470-0751
info@fabulousat50.com
Social Media: www.youtube.com/user/Befabulousat50?feature=mhum
twitter.com/Fabat50
w ww.facebook.com/#%21/pages/FABULOUS50/86887170329
Magazine for baby boomer women over 50.
Dianna Bowes, Editor, editor@fabulousat50.com

Bel Age
Détenteur: Transcontinental Media Inc.
#900, 2001, rue University, Montreal, QC H3A 2A6
Ligne sans frais: 800-780-0181
belage@transcontinental.ca
Médias sociaux: www.facebook.com/belagemagazine
Tirage: 145 872 Fréquence: 11 fois par an; français
Lucie Desaulniers, Rédactrice en chef

Comfort Life
Owned By: Our Kids Publications Ltd.
Tel: 905-272-1843; Fax: 905-272-0474
Toll-Free: 877-272-1845
info@comfortlife.ca
Social Media: www.youtube.com/comfortlifetv
www.twitter.com/comfortlife
www.facebook .com/comfortlife.ca
Circulation: 30,000 Frequency: Annually
Agatha , Publisher

Community Resource Directory
Owned By: Egress Enterprises Inc
Tel: 250-765-3886; Fax: 250-765-7346
info@communityresourcedirectories.com
Frequency: Annual
Joel A. Rickard, Publisher

The Edmonton Senior
Owned By: Alberta Business Research Ltd
Alberta Business Research, #112, 25 Chisholm Ave., St Albert, AB T8N 1N3
Tel: 780-429-1610; Fax: 780-421-7677
Toll-Free: 866-425-3722
seniorsgotravel@shaw.ca
Other information: Toll-Free Fax: 866-425-3714
Circulation: 60,000 Frequency: 12 times a year
Lorne Silverstein, Publisher
Colin Smith, Editor

Fifty-Five Plus
c/o Coyle Publishing Inc., 67 Neil Ave., Stittsville, ON K2S 1B9
Tel: 613-271-8903; Fax: 613-271-8905
Social Media:
twitter.com/55mag
ww.facebook.com/Fiftyfiveplus
Circulation: 45,000 Frequency: 8 times a year
George Coyle, Publisher
Pat den Boer, Editor

Focus 50+
#13-215, 4 Alliance Blvd., Barrie, ON L4M 5J1
Tel: 705-735-2144
Circulation: 11,500 Frequency: Monthly
Focus 50+ is published monthly by Focus Plus Inc. and is distributed free of charge to drop-off points throughout Simcoe County.
Taylor Ledden, Editor
Jeanneke Van Hattem, Publisher

Good Times
Owned By: Transcontinental Media Inc.
#900, 2001 University St., Montréal, QC H3A 2A6
Toll-Free: 888-290-1466
editor@goodtimes.ca
Circulation: 157,086 Frequency: 11 times a year
Marray Lewis, Editor-in-Chief, editor@goodtimes.ca

The Independent Times
Previous Name: The Independent Senior
Owned By: Foxtrot Communications
#104 - 333 East First St., North Vancouver, BC V7L 4W9
Tel: 604-639-5495; Fax: 604-990-1093
mfox@nucleus.com
Circulation: 50,000 Frequency: Monthly
K. Gordon, Publisher
Kevin Dale McKeown, Managing Editor, editor@theindependenttimes.com

Kerby News
1133 - 7th Ave. SW, Calgary, AB T2P 1B2
Tel: 403-265-0661; Fax: 403-705-3211
kerbynews@kerbycentre.com
Circulation: 25,000 Frequency: Monthly
Barry Whitehead, Editor

The Montrealer
342 Ballantyne North, Montreal Lake, QC H4X 2C5
Tel: 514-369-7000
editor@themontrealeronline.com
Social Media:
www.facebook.com/themontrealeronline
Circulation: 30,000 Frequency: Monthly
Peter Kerr, Publisher

The Senior Paper
PO Box 1010 Main, Regina, SK S4P 3B2
Tel: 306-525-8988
The publication is of interest to persons over sixty years of age. Submissions of classified advertising, special events, & milestones are welcomed. Print & electronic issues are available.

The Seniors Choice
PO Box 41075, South RPO, Lake Country, BC V4V 1Z7
Tel: 250-765-5911; Fax: 888-265-7532
pat@seniorschoice.com
Circulation: 15,000 Frequency: Monthly
James E. Archibald, Publisher
Patricia Archibald, Editor

The Seniors Review
#B2, 11 Bond St., St Catharines, ON L2R 4Z4
Tel: 905-687-9861; Fax: 905-687-6911
Toll-Free: 800-627-3111
Circulation: 40,000
David Irwin, Publisher
Carol Anderson, Editor

The Silver Pages
24 Cherryhill Dr., Grimsby, ON L3M 3B5
Tel: 905-309-1525; Fax: 905-309-1524
info@thesilverpages.ca
Social Media:
www.linkedin.com/company/the-silver-pages
www.facebook.com/TheSilverPage s
Circulation: 50,000 Frequency: 6 times a year
John Bauslaugh, Publisher
Tim Miller, Editorial Director

The Times
Previous Name: Seniors Today; Prime Times News
Owned By: Canstar Community News
1355 Mountain Ave., Winnipeg, MB R2X 3B6
Tel: 204-697-7009; Fax: 204- 95-3430
Circulation: 10,000 Frequency: 24 times a year
Michelle Pereira, Publisher
John Kendle, Editor

Virage
CP 1000 M, 4545, av Pierre-de-Coubertin, Montréal, QC H1V 3R2
Tél: 514-252-3017;Téléc: 514-252-3154
info@fadoq.ca
Tirage: 215 027 Fréquence: trimestriel
Martine Langlois, Éditrice
Lyne Rémillard, Rédacteur-en-chef

Zoomer Magazine
Previous Name: CARP Magazine
30 Jefferson Ave., Toronto, ON M6K 1Y4
Tel: 416-363-5562; Fax: 416-363-7693
comment@zoomermag.com
Other information: www.zoomers.ca
Social Media:
twitter.com/zoomermag
www.facebook.com/ZoomerMag
Circulation: 20,000 Frequency: Monthly
Susan Boyd, Editor-in-Chief

Fishing & Hunting

Alberta Fishing Guide
#6C, 5571 - 45 St., Red Deer, AB T4N 1L2
Tel: 403-347-5079; Fax: 403-341-5454
Circulation: 27,825 Frequency: Annually, March
Barry Mitchell, Publisher

Aventure chasse et pêche
332, rue Veilleux, Saint-Simon-les-Mines, QC G0M 1K0
Tel: 418-774-4443; Fax: 418-774-4444
cregimbald@qacp.com
Circulation: 50,600 Frequency: 4 times a year
Claude Regimbald, Marketing Manager
Denis Lapointe, Production Manager

Bateaux de pêche
#310, 970, Montée de Liesse, Saint-Laurent, QC H4T 1W7
Tel: 514-856-0787; Fax: 514-856-0790
Circulation: 18,000
Roy Baird, Publisher

BC Outdoors Sport Fishing
Previous Name: BC Fishing Recreation Guide & Atlas
Owned By: OP Publishing Ltd.
#900, 1080 Howe St., Vancouver, BC V6Z 2T1
Toll-Free: 800-898-8811
info@oppublishing.com
Social Media:
twitter.com/BCOutdoors
www.facebook.com/group.php?gid=4086426581
Circulation: 15,000 Frequency: Annually
Mark Yelic, Publisher, myelic@outdoorgroupmedia.com
Mike Mitchell, Editor, 604-820-6453, mmitchell@outdoorgroupmedia.com

The Canadian Fly Fisher
Tel: 613-836-8295
info@jencor.ca
Chris Marshall, Editor

Island Angler
30 Acacia Ave., Nanaimo, BC V9R 3L4
Tel: 250-753-2227; Fax: 250-753-2295
Circulation: 15,000
Andrew Kolasinski, Publisher, kolapub@yahoo.ca

Ontario Out of Doors
PO Box 8500, Peterborough, ON K9J 0B4
Tel: 705-748-0076; Fax: 705-748-9577
mail@ontariooutofdoors.com
Social Media: www.youtube.com/oodmag
twitter.com/oodmag
www.facebook.com/oodmag
Circulation: 92,026 Frequency: 10 times a year
John Kerr, Editor-in-Chief

Outdoor Canada
#100, 54 St. Patrick St., Toronto, ON M5T 1V1
Tel: 416-599-2000
walsh@outdoorcanada.ca
Social Media:
twitter.com/OutdoorCanada
www.facebook.com/outdoorcanada
Circulation: 82,574 Frequency: 8 times a year
Patrick Walsh, Editor
Jaqueline Howe, Publisher

The Outdoor Edge
Owned By: Outdoor Group Media
c/o Keywest Marketing Ltd., #202, 9644 - 54 Avenue, Edmonton, AB T6E 5V1
Toll-Free: 800-898-8811
info@outdoorgroupmedia.com
Circulation: 54,517 Frequency: 6 times a year
Mark Yelic, Publisher

Sentier Chasse-Pêche
#201 1650, rue Michelin, Laval, QC H7L 4R3
Tél: 450-665-0271;Téléc: 450-665-2974
Ligne sans frais: 800-563-6738
abonnement@sentierchassepeche.com
Tirage: 80 000 Fréquence: 11 fois par an; français
Louis Turbide, Rédacteur, louis.turbide@sentierchassepeche.com

Western Sportsman
Owned By: OP Publishing Ltd.
#202, 9644 - 54th Ave., Edmonton, AB T6E 5V1
Tel: 780-643-3961 Toll-Free: 800-898-8811
info@outdoorgroupmedia.com
Circulation: 25,933 Frequency: 6 times a year
Dave Webb, Editor, 780-643-3963, editor@westernsportsman.com
Mark Yelic, Publisher, 780-643-3962, myelic@outdoorgroupmedia.com

Food & Beverage

Appeal
Owned By: Canada Wide Magazines & Communications Ltd.
Tel: 604-299-7311; Fax: 604-299-9188
cwm@canadawide.com
Circulation: 230,000 Frequency: 2 times a year
Kim Mah, Editor
Peter Legge, Publisher

La Barrique
Détenteur: Kylix Media Inc
#414, 5165, rue Sherbrooke Ouest, Montréal, QC H4A 1T6
Tél: 514-481-5892
Tirage: 12 000 Fréquence: 6 fois par an; français
Aldo Parise, Rédacteur-en-chef adjoint
Nick Hamilton, Rédacteur-en-chef
Marylin Barker, Directrice de tirage

BC Wine Trails
2250 Camrose St., Penticton, BC V2A 8R1
Tel: 250-492-3636
Circulation: 15,000 Frequency: 4 times a year
Dani Greene, Manager

Coup de Pouce
Détenteur: Transcontinental Media Inc.
1100, boul René-Lévesque ouest, 24e étage, Montréal, QC H3B 4X9
Tél: 514-392-9000 Ligne sans frais: 800-528-3836
Médias sociaux: twitter.com/coupdepouce_mag
www.facebook.com/coupdepouce
Fréquence: 5 fois par an; français
Francine Tremblay, Éditrice
France Lefebvre, Rédacteur

Elite Wine, Food & Travel Magazine
Previous Name: Enoteca Wine & Food Magazine
PO Box 37, #5, 23 McCleary Ct., Concord, ON L4K 1B2
Tel: 905-760-1724; Fax: 905-760-1718
editor@elitewinefoodtravel.com
Circulation: 10,000 Frequency: 4 times a year
Anna Cavaliere, Editor

Flavours
Owned By: BIV Media Group
124 Braemar Ave., Winnipeg, MB R2H 2K7
Tel: 204-953-0291; Fax: 866-957-0217
Toll-Free: 888-573-1136
gcrosbie@flavoursmagazine.ca
Social Media: twitter.com/FlavoursMag
www.facebook.com/FlavoursWesternCanada
Frequency: 4 times a year
Available exclusively through the Manitoba Liquor Marts, Saskatchewan's Liquor and Gaming Authority stores, Preferred Alberta Liquor Store outlets and the Alliance of Beverage Licensees, BC License Retail Stores.
Brandon Boone, Editor-in-chief, b.boone@flavoursmagazine.ca
Fawn Duchaine, Publisher, FDuchaine@biv.com

Food & Drink
Liquor Control Board of Ontario, 55 Lakeshore Blvd. East, Toronto, ON M5E 1A4
Tel: 416-365-5900; Fax: 416-365-5935
Toll-Free: 800-668-5226
Circulation: 500,000 Frequency: bi-monthly; English & French
Judy Dunn, Editor
Wayne Leek, Publisher

Fresh Juice
Previous Name: Homemakers
Owned By: Transcontinental Media Inc.
#100, 25 Sheppard Ave. West, Toronto, ON M2N 6S7
Tel: 905-733-7600
letters@canadianliving.com
Social Media: twitter.com/FreshJuiceCA
www.facebook.com/FreshJuiceCA
Crys Stewart, Content Director
Lynn Chambers, Publsiher

Le Guide Cuisine
Détenteur: Communication Duocom
Communication Duocom Inc., #201, 72 B, rue Sainte-Anne, Sainte-Anne-de-Bellevue, QC H9X 1L8
Tél: 514-457-0144;Téléc: 514-457-0226
Ligne sans frais: 800-558-5508
info@leguidecuisine.com
Tirage: 45,000 Fréquence: 5 times a year
Nicolas Vallée, Éditeur

InterVin Insider
Owned By: Town Media Inc.
1074 Cooke Blvd., Burlington, ON L7T 4A8
Tel: 905-634-8003; Fax: 905-634-7661
Social Media: twitter.com/intervin
www.facebook.com/intervin
Frequency: 7 issues per year
Publication of the InterVinWine Awards.

Taste
2625 Rupert St., Vancouver, BC V5M 3T5
Tel: 604-252-3000
communications@bcldb.com
Magazine for BC Liquor.

Tidings
Previous Name: WineTidings
Owned By: Kylix Media Inc
Tel: 905-886-6641
signup@tidingsmag.com
Social Media: twitter.com/QuenchByTidings
Circulation: 35,000 Frequency: 8 times a year
Aldo Parise, Editor-in-chief

Toronto Wine & Cheese Show Guide
#4, 447 Speers Rd., Oakville, ON L6K 3S4
Tel: 905-842-6591; Fax: 905-842-6843
Toll-Free: 800-693-7986
Social Media: twitter.com/WineCheeseShow
www.facebook.com/WineandCheeseShow
Circulation: 33,500 Frequency: 1 times a year
Janet Gardiner, Publisher

Vines
Owned By: Town Media Inc.
1074 Cooke Blvd., Burlington, ON L7T 4A8
Tel: 905-634-8003; Fax: 905-634-7661
tm.info@sunmedia.ca
Social Media: twitter.com/VinesMag
www.facebook.com/VinesMag
Frequency: 7 issues per year
Aimed at Canadians interested in wine.
Donna Gardener, Publisher, donna.gardener@sunmedia.ca

Fraternal, Service Clubs, Associations

KIN Magazine
c/o Kin Canada (Kinsmen & Kinette Clubs of Canada), PO Box 3460, 1920 Rogers Dr., Cambridge, ON N3H 5C6
Tel: 519-653-1920; Fax: 519-650-1091
Toll-Free: 800-742-5546
kinhq@kincanada.ca
Social Media: twitter.com/kincanada
www.facebook.com/kincanada
Circulation: 10,000 Frequency: 3 print (Feb., June, Oct.); 3 online (April, Aug. & Dec.)
Michelle Rickard, Editor

Mensa Canada Communications
Mensa Canada Society, PO Box 1570, Kingston, ON K7L 5C8
Tel: 613-547-0824; Fax: 613-531-0626
mensa@eventsmgt.com
Circulation: 2,100 Frequency: 6 times a year
Phyrne Parker, President

Papyrus Magazine
c/o Rameses Temple, A.A.O.N.M.S., 3100 Keele St., Toronto, ON M3M 2H4
Tel: 416-633-6317; Fax: 416-633-6345
Circulation: 7,200 Frequency: 6 times a year
Otto Yoworski, Editor

The Sentinel
c/o Loyal Orange Association, 94 Sheppard Ave. West, Toronto, ON M2N 1M5
Tel: 416-223-1690; Fax: 416-223-1324
Circulation: 4,000 Frequency: 4 times a year
Jeremy Dowdell, Editor

Gardening & Garden Equipment

Alberta Gardener
Owned By: Pegasus Publications Inc.
130A Cree Cres., Winnipeg, MB R3J 3W1
Tel: 204-940-2700; Fax: 204-940-2727
Toll-Free: 888-680-2008
info@pegasuspublications.net
Social Media: www.facebook.com/AlbertaGardener
Circulation: 6,628 Frequency: 6 times a year

BC Home & Garden
Owned By: Canada Wide Media Limited
4180 Lougheed Hwy., 4th Fl., Burnaby, BC V5C 6A7
Tel: 604-299-7311; Fax: 604-299-9188
Toll-Free: 800-663-0518
Circulation: 35,000
In 2012, GardenWise magazine & BC Home magazine combined to create BC Home & Garden magazine. The publication offers garden & landscape ideas, design trends, & style advice.
Samantha Legge, Publisher, 604-473-0378, slegge@canadawide.com
Rhea Attar, Director, Sales Operations, rattar@canadawide.com

Canadian Gardening
Owned By: Transcontinental Media Inc.
#100, 25 Sheppard Ave. West, Toronto, ON M2N 6S7
Tel: 416-733-7600
Social Media: www.youtube.com/user/CanadianGardening
twitter.com/CDNGardening
www.fa cebook.com/canadiangardening

Circulation: 153,000 Frequency: 8 times a year
Aldona Satterthwaite, Editor-in-chief
Jacqueline Howe, Publisher

Canadian Organic Grower
Previous Name: Eco-Farm & Garden
39 McArthur, Level 1-3, Ottawa, ON K1L 8L7
Tel: 613-216-0741; Fax: 613-236-0743
Toll-Free: 888-375-7383
office@cog.ca
Social Media: www.twitter.com/CanadianOrganic
www.facebook.com/CanadianOrganic
Circulation: 2,500 Frequency: 4 times a year
Janet Wallace, Editor, janet@cog.ca

Fleurs, plantes et jardins
Détenteur: Transcontinental Media Inc.
1100, boul René-Lévesque ouest, Montréal, QC H3B 4X9
Tél: 418-686-3036
fpj@tc.tc
Médias sociaux: twitter.com/fleursplantesja
www.facebook.com/fleursplantesjardins
Tirage: 55 506 Fréquence: 9 fois par an; français
Francine Tremblay, Éditeur
Sophie Banford, Rédacteur

Garden Making
Owned By: Inspiring Media Inc.
#204, 111B Garrison Village Dr. #RR 3, Niagara on the Lake, ON L0S 1J0
Tel: 416-932-5075; Fax: 866-857-4262
Toll-Free: 877-832-1444
publisher@gardenmaking.com
Social Media: www.youtube.com/gardenmaking
www.twitter.com/gardenmaking
www.facebook .com/gardenmaking
Circulation: 22,960 Frequency: Quarterly
Beckie Fox, Editor-in-Chief, editor@gardenmaking.com

Gardening Life
Previous Name: Toronto Life Gardens
Owned By: St Joseph Media
#120, 511 King St. West, Toronto, ON M5V 2Z4
Tel: 416-593-0204; Fax: 416-591-1630
Toll-Free: 800-559-8868
mail@canhomepub.com
Circulation: 95,797 Frequency: 6 times a year
Giorgina Bigioni, Publisher
Caren Watkins, Editor-in-chief

Gardens Central
PO Box 2680, #M6, 601 West Broadway, Vancouver, BC V6B 3W8
Tel: 604-879-4991; Fax: 604-879-5110
Toll-Free: 800-263-1088
grow@gardenswest.com
Social Media: twitter.com/gardenscentral
www.facebook.com/gardenscentral
Circulation: 40,000 Frequency: 9 times a year

Gardens East
PO Box 2680, #M6, 601 West Broadway, Vancouver, BC V6B 3W8
Tel: 604-879-4991; Fax: 604-879-5110
Toll-Free: 800-263-1088
grow@gardenswest.com
Social Media: www.facebook.com/gardenseast
Circulation: 40,000 Frequency: 9 times a year

Gardens West
PO Box 2680, #M6, 601 West Broadway, Vancouver, BC V6B 3W8
Tel: 604-879-4991; Fax: 604-879-5110
Toll-Free: 800-263-1088
grow@gardenswest.com
Social Media: twitter.com/gardens_west
www.facebook.com/gardenswest
Circulation: 40,000 Frequency: 9 times a year
Dorothy Horton, Publisher/Editor

Manitoba Gardener
Owned By: Pegasus Publications Inc.
130A Cree Cres., Winnipeg, MB R3J 3W1
Tel: 204-940-2700; Fax: 204-940-2727
Toll-Free: 888-680-2008
info@pegasuspublications.net
Social Media: www.facebook.com/ManitobaGardener

Circulation: 6,628 Frequency: 6 times a year
Dorothy Dobbie, Publisher
Joan Cohen, Editor

Ontario Gardener
Owned By: Pegasus Publications Inc.
130A Cree Crescentn St., Winnipeg, MB R3J 3W1
Tel: 204-940-2700; Fax: 204-940-2727
Toll-Free: 888-680-2008
info@pegasuspublications.net
Social Media:
www.facebook.com/OntarioGardener
Frequency: 6 times a year
Shauna Dobbie, Publisher & Editor

Gay/Lesbian

fab Magazine
Owned By: Pink Triangle Press
#1600, 2 Carlton St., Toronto, ON M5B 1J3
Tel: 416-925-5221; Fax: 416-925-4817
Social Media:
twitter.com/fabmagazine
Circulation: 31,000 Frequency: 26 times a year
Brandon Matheson, Publisher & Editor,
brandonmatheson@fabmagazine.com

Index: Gay & Lesbian Business Directory
Owned By: Pink Triangle Press
#1600, 2 Carlton St., Toronto, ON M5B 1J3
Tel: 416-925-5221; Fax: 416-925-4817
index@xtra.ca
Circulation: 34,000 Frequency: Annually
Directories for Vancouver, Toronto and Ottawa.

Perceptions
PO Box 8581, Saskatoon, SK S7K 6K7
Tel: 306-244-1930; Fax: 306-665-1280
perceptions@shaw.ca
Circulation: 1,500
Gens Hellquist, Publisher

Xtra!
Owned By: Pink Triangle Press
2 Carlton St., Toronto, ON M5B 1J3
Tel: 416-925-6665; Fax: 416-925-6674
Toll-Free: 800-268-9872
Info.Toronto@Xtra.ca
Social Media: www.youtube.com/user/xtraonline
www.twitter.com/xtra_canada
www.facebo ok.com/xtra.ca
Circulation: 42,000
Brandon Matheson, Publisher & Editor-in-chief,
Brandon.Matheson@xtra.ca

Xtra! (Ottawa)
Previous Name: Capital Xtra
#503, 251 Bank St., Ottawa, ON K2P 1X3
Tel: 613-237-7133; Fax: 613-237-6651
Social Media:
twitter.com/Xtra_OTT
Circulation: 17,000 Frequency: Monthly
Brandon Matheson, Publisher & Editor-in-chief

Xtra! (Vancouver)
Owned By: Pink Triangle Press
#501, 1033 Davie St., Vancouver, BC V6E 1M7
Tel: 604-684-9696; Fax: 604-684-9697
Social Media:
twitter.com/Xtra_VAN
Circulation: 22,000 Frequency: Bi-weekly
Ken Hickling, Publisher, ken.hickling@xtra.ca

General Interest

Access Magazine
Trafalgar Publications, 79 Portsmouth Dr., Toronto, ON M1C 5C8
Tel: 416-335-0747; Fax: 416-335-0748
crossfire@accessmag.com
Circulation: 150,000 Frequency: 10 times a year
Sean Plummer, Editor

Active Living
Previous Name: Disability Today
2276 Rosedene Rd., St Ann's, ON L0R 1Y0
Tel: 905-957-6016; Fax: 905-957-6017
activeliv@aol.com
Circulation: 50,000 Frequency: 4 times a year, plus Active Living's Buyers' Guide Product & Service Directory (annual)
Kimberley Barrada, Editor
Jeffrey Tiessen, Publisher

L'Agora
CP 96, Ayer's Cliff, QC J0B 1C0
Tél: 819-849-6360
editeurs@agora.homovivens.org
Tirage: 10 000
Hélène Laberge, Rédactrice-en-chef
Jacques Dufresne, Éditeur

Alberta Views
#208, 320 - 23 Ave. SW, Calgary, AB T2S 0J2
Tel: 403-243-5334; Fax: 403-243-8599
Toll-Free: 877-212-5334
avadmin@albertaviews.ab.ca
Circulation: 20,000 Frequency: 8 times a year
Jackie Flanagan, Publisher & Editor

Best Health
Owned By: Reader's Digest Magazines (Canada) Ltd.
1100, boul René Lévesque ouest, Montréal, QC H3B 5H5
Toll-Free: 800-465-0780
Social Media: pinterest.com/besthealthmag/
twitter.com/besthealthmag
www.facebook.co m/besthealth
Circulation: 100,000 Frequency: 8 pa
Our Canada features reader-written stories & photographs.

CAA Magazine
Owned By: Totem Communications Group Inc.
Totem Communications Group Inc., 37 Front St. East, Toronto, ON M5E 1B3
Tel: 416-360-7339; Fax: 416-640-6164
caamagazine@totembrandstories.com
Social Media:
twitter.com/CAAMagazine
Frequency: Quarterly
Tracy Howard, Editor

Canadian Immigrant Magazine
8508 Ash St., Vancouver, BC V6P 3S4
Tel: 604-872-0102
Frequency: monthly

Canadian Newcomer
222 Parkview Hill Cres., Toronto, ON M4B 1R8
Tel: 416-406-4719
feedback@cnmag.ca
Frequency: Bi-monthly theme issues, daily features
Online magazine discussing employment, housing, lifestyle, health, finance, education & media in Canada
Dale Sproule, Publisher, dale@cnmag.ca

Contact
Cité Universitaire, Université Laval, 2325, rue de L'Université, Québec, QC G1V 0A6
Tél: 418-656-7266;Téléc: 418-656-2809
magazine.contact@dap.ulaval.ca
Tirage: 37 125 Fréquence: 3 fois par an; français
Louise Desautels, Rédactrice en chef

Continuité
82, Grande-Allée ouest, Québec, QC G1R 2G6
Tél: 418-647-4525;Téléc: 418-647-6483
continuite@magazinecontinuite.qc.ca
Tirage: 5 000 Fréquence: 4 fois par an; français
Josiane Ouellet, Rédactrice en chef,
redaction@magazinecontinuite.qc.ca

The Country Connection
Owned By: Pinecone Publishing
691 Pinecrest Rd., Boulter, ON K0L 1G0
Tel: 613-332-3651
Social Media:
www.facebook.com/pages/The-Country-Connection/1571661377
0
Circulation: 5,000 Frequency: 4 times a year
Gus Zylstra, Publisher & Managing Editor

Dernière heure
Détenteur: TVA Publications
7, chemin Bates, Outremont, QC H2V 4V7
Tél: 514-848-7000;Téléc: 514-270-7079
dh@tva-publications.com
Tirage: 30 000 Fréquence: Hebdomadaire; français

Digital Journal Magazine
PO Box 1046, Toronto, ON M5C 2K4
Tel: 416-410-9675
Social Media:
www.facebook.com/digitaljournal
Christopher A. Hogg, Editor-in-chief

être en ligne
Anciennement: R.G.
CP 222 C, 1613, rue Amherst, Montréal, QC H2L 4K1
Tél: 514-521-3873;Téléc: 514-523-2214
info@rgmag.com
Médias sociaux:
twitter.com/etremag
www.facebook.com/pages/Magazine-Etre/133489396662525
Tirage: 11 500
Antoine Aubert, Rédactor, antoine@etremag.com

Focus Magazine
Previous Name: Focus on Women
Victoria, BC
Tel: 250-388-7231
focuspublish@shaw.ca
Circulation: 360,000 Frequency: Monthly
Focus is a monthly print magazine that's been serving Victoria for over 24 years.
Leslie Campbell, Publisher

Fugues
1212, St-Hubert, Montréal, QC H2L 3Y8
Tél: 514-848-1854;Téléc: 514-845-7645
redaction@fugues.com
Médias sociaux:
twitter.com/Fuguesmagazine
www.facebook.com/fugues
Tirage: 50,000 Fréquence: 14 times a year
Maurice Nadeau, Publisher

Georgian Bay Today
PO Box 186, 27 St. Clair Ave. East, Toronto, ON M4T 2M1
Tel: 416-944-1217; Fax: 416-944-0133
hize@earthlink.net
Circulation: 2,000 Frequency: 4 times a year
An independent, quarterly, newspaper/magazine. It offers information, features, news, opinion, illustration and advertising to link all who spend weekends hereabouts (call them "recreationists"), residents and tourists around the shore of Georgian Bay and related lakelands.
Arthur Gron, Editor, arthurgron@web.ca
Alan Heisey, Publisher

Going Natural
Federation of Canadian Naturists, PO Box 81128 D, Ancaster, ON L9G 4X1
Tel: 905-304-4836; Fax: 905-304-4837
editor@fcn.ca
Circulation: 2,500 Frequency: 4 times a year
Dr. Paul Rapoport, Editor

Humanist Perspectives
Previous Name: Humanist in Canada
Owned By: Canadian Humanist Publications
PO Box 3769 C, Ottawa, ON K1Y 4J8
CHPboard@humanistperspectives.org
Circulation: 1,500 Frequency: 4 times a year
Carl Dow, Editor, editor@humanistperspectives.org

Kindred Spirits Chronicles
Previous Name: Kindred Spirits of PEI
110 Queen St., Charlottetown, PE C1A 4B1
Tel: 902-368-2663 Toll-Free: 800-665-2663
hello@annestore.ca
Circulation: Online Frequency: Monthly
Poetry & short stories related to rural PEI at the turn of the 20th century, as well as articles on Lucy Maud Montgomery. The Chronicles are published online.
George Campbell, Publisher & Editor

Lambert
#10, 426, rue Victoria, Saint-Lambert, QC J4P 2H9
Tél: 450-465-0789;Téléc: 450-465-8128
lambert@lookommunication.com
Médias sociaux:
twitter.com/magazinelambert
www.facebook.com/MagazineLambert
Fréquence: 6 times a year; French
Marcel Renaud, marcelr@magazinelambert.com

Legion Magazine
Canvet Publications Ltd., 86 Aird Pl., Ottawa, ON K2L 0A1
Tel: 613-591-0116; Fax: 613-591-0146
editor@legionmagazine.com
Social Media:
www.facebook.com/pages/Legion-Magazine/169253049780364
Circulation: 313,217 Frequency: 6 times a year
Mac Johnston, Editor & General Manager

Living Safety / Famille Avertie
c/o Canada Safety Council, 1020 Thomas Spratt Place, Ottawa, ON K1G 5L5
Tel: 613-739-1535; Fax: 613-739-1566
csc@safety-council.org
Circulation: 25,000 Frequency: 4 times a year
Jack A. Smith, General Manager

Le Lundi
Détenteur: TVA Publications
1010, rue de Sérigny, 4e étage, Longueuil, QC J4K 5G7
Tél: 514-848-7000;Téléc: 514-848-9854
Tirage: 27 589 Fréquence: Hebdomadaire; français
Sylvie Bourgeault, Publisher

Magazine Prestige
305, boul René-Lévesque ouest, Québec, QC G1S 1S1
Tél: 418-683-5333;Téléc: 418-683-2899
info@magazineprestige.com
Médias sociaux:
www.facebook.com/MagazinePRESTIGE?ref=stream
Fréquence: 11 fois par an
Marie-Josée Turcotte, Rédacteur-en-chef, redaction@magazineprestige.com

Muskoka Magazine
Owned By: Cottage Country Communications
PO Box 180, #12, 440 Ecclestone Dr., Bracebridge, ON P1L 1T6
Tel: 705-646-1314; Fax: 705-645-6424
mm.info@sunmedia.ca
Social Media:
www.facebook.com/muskokamagazine
Circulation: 14,550 Frequency: 10 times a year
Sandy Lockhart, Editor
Donald Smith, Publisher & Editor

Nouvelles CSQ
Anciennement: Nouvelles CEQ
Centrale des syndicats du Québec, 9405, rue Sherbrooke est, Montréal, QC H1L 6P3
Tél: 514-356-8888;Téléc: 514-356-9999
Ligne sans frais: 800-465-0897
Médias sociaux: www.youtube.com/user/csqvideos
twitter.com/csq_centrale
www.facebook.c om/lacsq
Tirage: 103 000 Fréquence: 5 fois par an; français
Louise Rochefort, Directrice

On the Bay Magazine
Owned By: Transcontinental Media Inc.
#201, 186 Hurontario St., Collingwood, ON L9Y 4T4
Tel: 705-444-9192; Fax: 705-444-5658
Toll-Free: 888-282-2014
info@onthebaymagazine.com
Social Media:
www.facebook.com/pages/On-The-Bay-Magazine/249445781903
Frequency: 6 times a year
Janet Lees, Editor, jlees@onthebaymagazine.com
Jeffrey Shearer, Publisher, jshearer@onthebaymagazine.com

Our Canada
1100, boul René Lévesque ouest, Montréal, QC H3B 5H5
Toll-Free: 800-465-0780
Frequency: 6 pa
Our Canada features reader-written stories & photographs.

Pacific Rim Magazine
c/o Langara College, 100 West 49th Ave., Vancouver, BC V5Y 2Z6
Tel: 604-323-5432
Circulation: 18,000
Darren Bernaerdt, Publisher

Protégez-Vous
CP 190 Place d'Armes, #305, 2120, rue Sherbrooke est, Montréal, QC H2Y 3G7
Tél: 514-873-3000;Téléc: 514-223-7160
Ligne sans frais: 866-895-7186
courrier@protegez-vous.ca
Médias sociaux:
twitter.com/ProtegezVous
www.facebook.com/protegezvous.ca
Tirage: 151 145 Fréquence: 12 fois par an; français
David Clerk, Contact

Reader's Digest / Sélection du Reader's Digest
1100, boul René Lévesque ouest, Montréal, QC H3B 5H5
Tel: 514-940-0751; Fax: 514-940-3637
Toll-Free: 800-465-0780
customerservice@readersdigest.ca
Social Media:
twitter.com/readersdigestca
www.facebook.com/readersdigestcanada
Circulation: 1,200,000 Frequency: Monthly; English & French editions
Andrea C. Martin, President & CEO
Antoni Cioffi, Vice-President & CFO
Mathieu Péloquin, Vice-President, Marketing
Linda Melrose, Production Manager

Safarir
37, boul des Laurentides, Laval, QC H7G 2S3
Tél: 514-380-1202
Médias sociaux:
twitter.com/safarirmag
www.facebook.com/safarir
Fréquence: 12 fois par an; français
Sylvain Bolduc, Fondateur

Sélection du Reader's Digest
Anciennement: Sélection
1100, boul René Lévesque ouest, Montréal, QC H3B 5H5
Tél: 514-940-0751;Téléc: 514-940-3637
Ligne sans frais: 888-459-3333
Médias sociaux:
twitter.com/selectionrd
selection.readersdigest.ca
Tirage: 242,970 Fréquence: Monthly
Robert Goyette, Rédacteur-en-chef

University of Toronto Magazine
University of Toronto, J. Robert S. Prichard Alumni House, 21 King's College Circle, Toronto, ON M5S 3J3
Tel: 416-946-3192; Fax: 416-978-3958
Toll-Free: 800-463-6048
uoft.magazine@utoronto.ca
Social Media:
twitter.com/uoftmagazine
www.facebook.com/pages/U-of-T-Magazine/17602252 9092653
Circulation: 300,000 Frequency: Quarterly
Scott Anderson, Editor & Manager, scott.anderson@utoronto.ca

Up Here
Previous Name: Up Here: Life at the top of the World
PO Box 1350, Yellowknife, NT X1A 2N9
Tel: 867-766-6710; Fax: 867-873-9876
Toll-Free: 866-572-1757
subscribe@uphere.ca
Circulation: 24,827 Frequency: 8 times a year
Aaron Spitzer, Editor, aaron@uphere.ca

Western Living
Owned By: Transcontinental Media Inc.
#560, 2608 Granville St., Vancouver, BC V6H 3V3
Tel: 604-877-7732 Toll-Free: 800-363-3272
wlmail@westernlivingmagazine.com
Social Media: pinterest.com/westernliving/
twitter.com/Western_Living
www.facebook.c om/WesternLivingMagazine
Circulation: 165,000 Frequency: 10 times a year
Lri Chalmers, Publisher
Anicka Quin, Editor-in-Chief

Western Standard
#201, 2512 - 1st Ave. NW, Calgary, AB T2N 0C2
Tel: 403-701-3045
info@westernstandard.ca
Frequency: Bi-weekly
Conservative news & commentary from a Western Canadian perspective.

Westworld Alberta
Owned By: Canada Wide Magazines & Communications Ltd.
Alberta Motor Association, PO Box 8180 South, Edmonton, AB T6H 5X9
Tel: 604-299-7311; Fax: 604-299-9188
Toll-Free: 800-642-3810
cwm@canadawide.com
Circulation: 540,000 Frequency: 5 times a year
Peter Legge, Publisher
Kirsten Rodenhizer, Editor, krodenhizer@canadawide.com

Westworld British Columbia
Owned By: Canada Wide Magazines & Communications Ltd.
British Columbia Automobile Association, PO Box 6680, Vancouver, BC V6B 4L4
Tel: 604-268-5555 Toll-Free: 800-663-1956
cwm@canadawide.com
Circulation: 476,301 Frequency: 4 times a year
Peter Legge, Publisher
Anne Rose, Editor

Westworld Saskatchewan
Owned By: Canada Wide Magazines & Communications Ltd.
CAA Saskatchewan, 200 Albert St. North, Regina, SK S4R 5E2
Tel: 604-299-7311; Fax: 604-299-9188
Toll-Free: 877-564-6222
cwm@canadawide.com
Circulation: 120,000 Frequency: 4 times a year
Peter Legge, Publisher
Sheila Hansen, Editor, shansen@canadawide.com

Health & Medical

Abilities Magazine
c/o Canadian Abilities Foundation, #401, 340 College St., Toronto, ON M5T 3A9
Tel: 416-923-1885; Fax: 416-923-9829
info@abilities.ca
Circulation: 45,000 Frequency: 4 times a year
Jaclyn Law, Managing Editor
Raymond D. Cohen, Editor-in-chief

Alive Magazine
Alive Publishing Group Inc., #100 - 12751 Vulcan Way, Richmond, BC V6V 3C8
Fax: 800-663-6597
Toll-Free: 800-663-6580
info@alive.com
Social Media: plus.google.com/115031422972901434935/posts
twitter.com/aliveHealth
ww w.facebook.com/alive.health.wellness
Circulation: 250,000 Frequency: Monthly
Topics include health, wellness, natural health.

beyond fitness
#1025, 1200, Chomedey, Laval, QC H7V 3Z3
Tel: 450-973-4863; Fax: 450-973-7856
pm@videotron.ca
Circulation: 150,000 Frequency: 11 times a year
Pierre Martineau, President & Publisher
Laura Warf, Fitness Editor
André Thibault, Administration & Circulation Manager

Caregiver Solutions
Previous Name: Canada's Family Guide to Home Health Care & Wellness Solutions
Owned By: BCS Communications Ltd.
#803, 255 Duncan Mill Rd., Toronto, ON M3B 3H9
Tel: 416-421-7944; Fax: 416-421-8418
Toll-Free: 800-798-6282
Social Media:
www.facebook.com/CaregiverSolutions
Circulation: 30,000 Frequency: 4 times a year
Caroline Tapp-McDougall, Publisher, caroline@bcsgroup.com

Common Ground Magazine
Owned By: Common Ground Publishing Corp.
#204, 4381 Fraser St., Vancouver, BC V5V 4G4
Tel: 604-733-2215; Fax: 604-733-4415
Toll-Free: 800-365-8897
admin@commonground.ca
Circulation: 70,000 Frequency: 12 times a year
Joseph Roberts, Publisher & Senior Editor

Diabetes Dialogue
#1400, 522 University Ave., Toronto, ON M5G 2R5
Toll-Free: 800-226-8464
Membership@diabetes.ca
Circulation: 45,510 Frequency: Quarterly
Marg Churchill, Marketing, mchurchill@keithhealthcare.com

Family Health
PO Box 2421, 10006 - 101 St., Edmonton, AB T5J 2S6
Fax: 780-498-5661
fhonline@familyhealthonline.ca
Circulation: 97,000 Frequency: 4 times a year
Robert Clarke, Publisher

Future Health
c/o Canadians for Health Research, PO Box 126, Westmount, QC H3Z 2T1
Tel: 514-398-7478; Fax: 514-398-8361
Circulation: 2,000 Frequency: 4 times a year; English, some French
Tim Lougheed, Chair, Canadians for Health Research

Healthcare Information Management & Communications Canada
Owned By: Healthcare Computing & Communications Canada, Inc
11755 - 108 Avenue, Edmonton, AB T5H 1B8
Tel: 780-489-4521; Fax: 780-489-3290
healthcare@shaw.ca
Circulation: 6,000 Frequency: Quarterly
Steven A. Huesing, Publisher & Editor

HeartBeat
PO Box 1, Site 100, RR#1, Carvel, AB T0E 0H0
Tel: 780-380-2910; Fax: 780-892-3401
Circulation: 4,600 Frequency: 4 times a year
Pauline Newman, Publisher

Impact Magazine
2007 - 2nd St. SW, Calgary, AB T2S 1S4
Tel: 403-228-0605; Fax: 403-228-0627
info@impactmagazine.ca
Frequency: Bi-monthly
Elaine Kupser, Publisher, elaine@impactmagazine.ca
Chris Welner, Editor, editor@impactmagazine.ca

Mosaic Mond, Body and Spirit Magazine
#209, 10715 - 124 St., Edmonton, AB T5M 0H2
Tel: 780-447-3667; Fax: 780-939-0588
mosaicmagazine@shaw.ca
Social Media:
www.facebook.com/218630024830514
Circulation: 75,000 Frequency: Quarterly
Holistic medicine.
Connie Brisson, Publisher/Editor

Vision Magazine
Breton Communications Inc., #202, 495, boul St-Martin ouest, Laval, QC H7M 1Y9
Tel: 450-629-6005; Fax: 450-629-6044
Toll-Free: 888-462-2112
info@bretoncom.com
Circulation: 11,435 Frequency: 6 times a year
Martine Breton, Présidente, martine@bretoncom.com

Vitalité Québec Mag
1025 - 1200 Chomeday, Laval, QC H7V 3Z3
Téléc: 450-973-7856
Médias sociaux:
www.facebook.com/profile.php?id=100003109059533
Tirage: 40 000 Fréquence: 10 fois par an; français
André Thibault, Directeur, Administration et diffusion
Monick Juliette Élie, Rédacteur-en-chef
Pierre Martineau, Président

Vitality Magazine: Toronto's Monthly Wellness Journal
356 Dupont St., Toronto, ON M5R 1V9
Tel: 416-964-0528; Fax: 416- -
editorial@vitalitymagazine.com
Circulation: 52,000 Frequency: 10 times a year
Julia Woodford, Editor

WHOLifE Journal
PO Box 278, Kamsack, SK S0A 1S0
Tel: 306-542-3616; Fax: 306-542-3619
Toll-Free: 800-780-3564
editor@wholife.com
Circulation: 17,000 Frequency: 6 times a year
Covers natural health & wellness for body, mind & spririt, plus environmental issues
Melva Armstrong, Publisher

History & Genealogy

Canada's History Magazine
Previous Name: The Beaver: Canada's History Magazine
Bryce Hall, Main Fl., 515 Portage Ave., Winnipeg, MB R3B 2E9
Tel: 204-988-9300; Fax: 204-988-9309
Toll-Free: 866-952-3444
editors@canadashistory.ca
Social Media:
twitter.com/canadashistory
www.facebook.com/CanadasHistory
Circulation: 45,000 Frequency: 6 times a year
Deborah Morrison, President/CEO, dmorrison@canadashistory.ca

Family Chronicle
Owned By: Moorshead Magazines Ltd.
#312, 505 Consumers Rd., Toronto, ON M2J 4V8
Tel: 416-491-3699; Fax: 416-491-3996
Toll-Free: 888-326-2476
admin@familychronicle.com
Social Media:
www.facebook.com/117640134975204
Frequency: 6 times a year
Edward Zapletal, Editor & Publisher, edward@moorshead.com

Heritag e/Patrimoine
190 Bronson Ave., Ottawa, ON K1R 6H4
Tel: 613-237-1066; Fax: 613-237-5987
heritagecanada@heritagecanada.org
Frequency: 4 times a year
Carolyn Quinn, Editor

The Loyalist Gazette
R.R. # 1, Indian River, ON K0L 2B0
Tel: 416-591-1783; Fax: 416-591-7506
Circulation: 2,500 Frequency: 2 times a year
Robert McBride, Editor

Newfoundland and Labrador Studies
Previous Name: Joseph R. Smallwood Centre for Newfoundland Studies
Memorial University of Newfoundland, St. John's, NL A1C 5S7
Tel: 709-737-7474; Fax: 709-737-7560
nlstudies@mun.ca
Bi-annual, interdisciplinary journal about the society & culture of Newfoundland & Labrador
Al Potter

OHS Bulletin
Owned By: The Ontario Historical Society
34 Parkview Ave., Toronto, ON M2N 3Y2
Tel: 416-226-9011 Toll-Free: 866-955-2755
izzo@ontariohistoricalsociety.ca
Social Media:
www.facebook.com/pages/The-Ontario-Historical-Society/146
Circulation: 2,500 Frequency: 5 times a year
Sheila Creighton, Editor
Patricia K. Neal, Executive Director

Hobbies

The Canadian Amateur
CARF Publications, #217, 720 Belfast Rd., Ottawa, ON K1G 0Z5
Tel: 613-244-4367; Fax: 613-244-4369
Toll-Free: 877-273-8304
rachq@rac.ca
Circulation: 7,200 Frequency: 6 times a year
Alan Griffin

Canadian Coin News
Owned By: Trajan Publishing Corp.
PO Box 28103 Lakeport, 600 Ontario St., St. Catherines, ON L2N 7P8
Tel: 905-646-7744; Fax: 905-646-0995
Toll-Free: 800-408-0352
Circulation: 8,500 Frequency: 26 times a year
Bret Evans, Managing Editor & Associate Publisher
Hans Niedermair, News Editor

Canadian Railway Modeller
c/o North Kildonan Publications, PO Box 35087 Henderson, 963 Henderson Hwy., Winnipeg, MB R2K 4J9
Tel: 204-668-0168; Fax: 204-669-9821
Circulation: 25,000 Frequency: 6 times a year
Morgan B. Turney, Editor
John Longhurst, Editor

Canadian Stamp News
Owned By: Trajan Publishing Corp.
PO Box 28103 Lakeport, 600 Ontario St., St. Catherines, ON L2N 7P8
Tel: 905-646-7744; Fax: 905-646-0995
Toll-Free: 800-408-0352
Circulation: 5,000 Frequency: 26 times a year
Paul Winkler, Publisher
Bret Evans, Editor

Comics & Games Monthly
#20, 225 Sterling Rd., Toronto, ON M6R 2B2
media@cgmagazine.ca
Social Media:
www.twitter.com/cgmonthly
www.facebook.com/ComicsGamingmagazine
Frequency: Monthly
Brendan Frye, Editor-in-Chief, bfrye@cgmagazine.ca

ÉCHEC+
c/o La Fédération Québécoise des Échecs, CP 1000 M, 4545, av Pierre-De Coubertin, Montréal, QC H1V 3R2
Tél: 514-252-3034;Téléc: 514-251-8038
info@fqechecs.qc.ca
Médias sociaux:
twitter.com/fqechecs
www.facebook.com/fqechecs
Tirage: 2 000 Fréquence: 6 fois par an; français
Louis Morin, Rédacteur

Metalcraft
345 Munster Ave., Toronto, ON M8Z 3C6
Tel: 416-232-0330; Fax: 416-234-1516
info@metalcraftmag.com
Frequency: 4 times a year
Nestor Gula, Editor

Model Aviation Canada
#9, 5100 South Service Rd., Burlington, ON L7L 6A5
Tel: 905-632-9808; Fax: 905-632-3304
Toll-Free: 855-359-6222
maachq@on.aibn.com
Circulation: 12,600 Frequency: 6 times a year
Ronald R. Dodd, President

Philatélie Québec
275, rue Bryant, Sherbrooke, QC J1J 3E6
editions_ddr@videotron.ca
Tirage: 1 500 Fréquence: 6 fois par an; français
Guy Desrosiers, Editeur

Quilter's Connection
Previous Name: Connections for Quilters Newsletter
PO Box 51065 Crest Centre, Burnaby, BC V3N 5B9
Tel: 604-290-3454; Fax: 604-540-2231
info@quiltersconnection.ca
Social Media:
www.twitter.com/QltrsConnection
www.facebook.com/QuiltersConnectionMagaz ine
Frequency: Quarterly

Railfan Canada
PO Box 35087 Henderson, 963 Henderson Hwy, Winnipeg, MB R2K 4J9
Tel: 204-668-0168; Fax: 204-669-9821
editor@railfancanada.ca
Frequency: Monthly
Railroad photography.

Homes

ARIDO Journal
#220, 6 Adelaide St. East, Toronto, ON M5C 1H6
Tel: 416-921-2127; Fax: 416-921-3660
Toll-Free: 800-334-1180
ltheoret@arido.on.ca
Circulation: 4,000
Lori Theoret, Publisher

Canadian Home & Country
Previous Name: Century Home
#100, 25 Sheppard Ave. West, Toronto, ON M2N 6S7
Tel: 416-733-7600
Social Media:
www.facebook.com/styleathome
Circulation: 140,000 Frequency: 7 times a year
Erin McLaughlin, Editor

Canadian Home Workshop
c/o Quarto Communications, 54 St. Patrick St., Toronto, ON M5T 1V1
Tel: 416-599-2000 Toll-Free: 800-465-6183
Social Media: www.youtube.com/user/canadianhomeworkshop
twitter.com/chwmag
www.faceb ook.com/canadianhomeworkshop
Frequency: 6 times a year
Canadian Home Workshop magazine provides information about woodworking & home improvement. Features include do-it-yourself projects & reviews of tools & products.
Douglas Thomson, Editor
Randy Craig, Director, Advertising & Marketing
Amy McCleverty, Director, Art
Jodi Brooks, Manager, Production

Heather Maxwell-Tufford, Manager, Circulation

Canadian Homes & Cottages
Previous Name: Homes & Cottages
The In-Home Show, #4, 2650 Meadowvale Blvd., Mississauga, ON L5N 6M5
Tel: 905-567-1440; Fax: 905-567-1442

Circulation: 79,099 Frequency: 6 times a year
Steven Griffin, Publisher
Janice Naisby, Editor-in-chief

Canadian House & Home
Canadian Home Publishers, #120, 511 King St. West, Toronto, ON M5V 2Z4
Tel: 416-593-0204; Fax: 416-591-1630
Toll-Free: 800-559-8868
Social Media:
twitter.com/HouseandHome
www.facebook.com/houseandhomemagazine
Circulation: 249,124 Frequency: 10 times a year
Lynda Reeves, Publisher
Cobi Ladner, Editor

Canadian Living
Owned By: Transcontinental Media Inc.
#100, 25 Sheppard Ave. West, Toronto, ON M2N 6S7
Tel: 905-733-7600
letters@canadianliving.com
Social Media:
twitter.com/canadianliving
www.facebook.com/canadianliving
Circulation: 533,370 Frequency: 12 times a year
Debbie Gibson, Publisher

Chez Soi
Anciennement: Décoration Chez-Sol
Détenteur: TVA Publications
7, ch Bates, Outremont, QC H2V 4V7
Tél: 514-848-7164;Téléc: 514-270-7079

Tirage: 576 000 Fréquence: 10 fois par an; français

Condo Life Magazine
178 Main St., Unionville, ON L3R 2G9
Tel: 905-479-4663 Toll-Free: 800-363-4663
info@homesmag.com
Circulation: 140,000
Michael Rosset, Publisher
Toni Pettit, Editor

Cottage Life
54 Patrick St., Toronto, ON M5T 1V1
Tel: 416-599-2000; Fax: 416-599-0800
Toll-Free: 877-874-5253
letters@cottagelife.com
Social Media: youtube.com/CottageLifeMagazine
twitter.com/CottageLifeMag
www.faceboo k.com/cottagelife
Circulation: 70,000 Frequency: 6 times a year
Al Zikovitz, Publisher
Penny Caldwell, Editor

Cottage Magazine
Owned By: OP Publishing Ltd.
#500, 200 West Esplanade, Nnorth Vancouver, BC V6Z 2T1
Tel: 604-998-3310 Toll-Free: 800-867-0474
subscriptions@cottagemagazine.com
Circulation: 13,195 Frequency: 6 times a year
Mark Yelic, Publisher
Peter Robson, Editor, 604-998-3327

The Cottager
PO Box 40, Victoria Beach, MB R0E 2C0
Tel: 204-756-8381; Fax: 204-756-2662
editor@thecottager.com
Social Media:
www.facebook.com/pages/The-Cottager/137410736323877
Circulation: 10,000 Frequency: 5 times a year
Glenn Halgren
Cathy Halgren, Circulation

Décormag
Trancontinental Media, 1100, boul. René-Lévesque Ouest, 24e étage, Montréal, QC H3A 4X9
Tél: 514-392-9000;Téléc: 514-848-9779
redaction@decormag.com
Médias sociaux:
twitter.com/decormagdeco
www.facebook.com/decormag
Tirage: 84 542 Fréquence: 11 fois par an; français
Marie-Christine Tremblay, Édimestre
Michèle Dubreuil, Directrice

Del Condominium Life
4800 Dufferin St., Toronto, ON M3H 5S9
Tel: 416-739-5143; Fax: 416-661-4538

Circulation: 32,500 Frequency: 3 times a year
Patricia MacKellar, Editor/Production Manager

Designer Showcase
Owned By: Metro Guide Publishing
1300 Hollis St., Halifax, NS B3J 1T6
Tel: 902-420-9943; Fax: 902-429-9058
jgillard@metroguide.ca
Circulation: 8,000
Patty Baxter, Publisher, 902-420-9943 ext 231, publishers@metroguide.ca
Dana Edgar, Production Coordinator, 902-420-9943 ext 247, dedgar@metroguide.ca

East Coast Living
Owned By: Metro Guide Publishing
1300 Hollis St., Halifax, NS 3J 1T6
Tel: 902-420-9943; Fax: 902-429-9058
publishers@metroguide.ca
Circulation: 34,100 Frequency: 2 times a year
Trevor Adams, Managing Editor, 902-420-9943 ext 229, tadams@metroguide.ca
Janice Hudson, Editor, 902-420-9943 ext 221, jhudson@metroguide.ca
Patty Baxter, Publisher, 902-420-9943 ext 231, publishers@metroguide.ca
Dana Edgar, Production Coordinator, 902-420-9943 ext 231, dedgar@metroguide.ca

Home Digest
1416 Stonehampton Ct., Pickering, ON L1V 7C9
Tel: 905-509-9900 Toll-Free: 855-550-5577
home_digest@rogers.com
Social Media: www.onlinehomedigest.com
twitter.com/Home_Digestmag
www.facebook.co m/HomeDigestmag
Circulation: 700,000 Frequency: 4 times a year
Barry Holmes, Publisher
William Roebuck, Editor

Homes Magazine
Owned By: Homes Publishing Group
178 Main St., Unionville, ON L3R 2G9
Tel: 905-479-4663 Toll-Free: 800-363-4663
info@homesmag.com
Social Media:
twitter.com/HOMESPublishing
www.facebook.com/pages/homesmagcom/122876181095771?ref=ts
Circulation: 100,000 Frequency: 9 times a year
Michael Rosset, Publisher
Toni Pettit, Editor, editortoni@gmail.com

Les Idées de ma maison
Détenteur: TVA Publications
7, Chemin Bates, Outremont, QC H2V 4V7
Tél: 514-848-7000;Téléc: 514-270-7079
Médias sociaux:
twitter.com/Mag_IdeesMaison
www.facebook.com/Lesideesdemamaison
Tirage: 65 493 Fréquence: 10 fois par an; français

Les idées Réno-Dépôt
Anciennement: Les Idées de ma maison
Détenteur: TVA Publications
7, Chemin Bates, Outremont, QC H2V 4V7
Tél: 514-848-7164;Téléc: 514-270-7079
Tirage: 50 000 Fréquence: 4 fois par an; français

Maison d'Aujourd'hui
3390, boul Crémazie est, Montréal, QC H2A 1A4
Tél: 514-729-0000;Téléc: 514-729-2552
courriel@maisonmax.com
Tirage: 50 000 Fréquence: semi-annuel
Phillippe Massé, Président

Planimage Magazines
Previous Name: Over 500 Home Plans
#105, 1501, rue Ampere, Boucherville, QC J4B 5Z5
Tel: 450-641-7526; Fax: 450-641-6688
Toll-Free: 800-752-6744
contact@planimage.com
Social Media: www.planimage.com/blog
twitter.com/planimage
www.facebook.com/Planimag e
Circulation: 30 000 Frequency: 6 times a year
Daniel Therrien, Publisher & Editor

Proven & Popular Home Plans
Owned By: Giroux Publishing
Tel: 250-493-0942 Toll-Free: 800-361-7526
plan@westhomeplanners.com
Circulation: 10,000 Frequency: Annually

Real Estate Victoria
818 Broughton St., Victoria, BC V8W 1E4
Tel: 250-381-9171; Fax: 250-381-9172
rev@revweekly.com
Circulation: 20,000 Frequency: Weekly, Thursday
David Black, President/CEO, rebecca@blackpress.ca
Rick O'Connor, Chief Operating Officer, coconnor@blackpress.ca

Renovation & Decor Magazine
Owned By: Homes Publishing Group
178 Main St., Unionville, ON L3R 2G9
Tel: 905-479-4663 Toll-Free: 800-363-4663
info@renoanddecor.com
Social Media:
twitter.com/HOMESPublishing
www.facebook.com/pages/renoanddecorcom/153184468041814?re
Circulation: 75,000
Catherine Daley, Publisher, cdaley.homes@gmail.com

Rénovation Bricolage
Détenteur: TVA Publications
1010, rue de Serigny, Longueil, QC J4K 5G7
Tél: 514-848-7000;Téléc: 514-848-9854
Ligne sans frais: 888-535-8634
renobrico@tvapublications.com
Médias sociaux:
twitter.com/mag_renobrico
www.facebook.com/RenovationBricolage
Tirage: 33 270 Fréquence: 9 fois par an; français
Claude Leclerc, Éditeur/Rédacteur

Renovation Contractor
Owned By: The Caruk Media Group
#201, 5500 North SErvice Rd., Burlington, ON L7L 6W6
Tel: 647-367-0073; Fax: 289-997-8260
Social Media: www.linkedin.com/company/1968664
www.facebook.com/renocontractor.ca
Serves small- and medium-sized home renovators.
Jim Caruk, Editor-in-Chief, jim@renocontractor.ca
Allan Britnell, Managing Editor, allan@renocontractor.ca

Style at Home: Canada's Decorating Magazine
Previous Name: Canadian Select Homes
Owned By: Transcontinental Media Inc.
#100, 25 Sheppard Ave. West, Toronto, ON M2N 6S7
Tel: 416-733-7600; Fax: 416-218-3632
letters@styleathome.com
Social Media: www.youtube.com/user/StyleAtHomeMagazine
twitter.com/StyleAtHome
www.f acebook.com/styleathome
Circulation: 235,000 Frequency: Monthly
Jacqueline Howe, Publisher
Gail Johnston Habs, Editor

Toronto Home
#1801, 1 Young St., Toronto, ON M5E 1W7
Toll-Free: 855-335-7745
info@torontohomemag.com

Votre Maison
Détenteur: TVA Publications
7, ch Bates, Outremont, QC H2V 4V7
Tél: 514-848-7164;Téléc: 514-270-7079
Fréquence: 12 fois par an; français

Horses, Riding & Breeding

Atlantic Horse & Pony
PO Box 1509, Liverpool, NS B0T 1K0
Tel: 902-354-5411
Circulation: 4,000 Frequency: 6 times a year
Dirk van Loon, Editor

Canadian Arabian Registry/News
Previous Name: Canadian Arabian News
#113, 37 Athabascan Ave., Sherwood Park, AB T8A 4H3
Tel: 780-416-4990; Fax: 780-416-4860
cahr@cahr.ca
Circulation: 2,200 Frequency: 4 times a year
Nicole Toren, Editor
Shari Christie, Administrator/Registrar

Canadian Horse Annual
Owned By: Horse Publications Group
PO Box 670, Aurora, ON L4G 4J9
Tel: 905-727-0107; Fax: 905-841-1530
Toll-Free: 800-505-7428
info@horse-canada.com
Frequency: Annually
Jennifer Anstey, Publisher, janstey@horse-canada.com

Canadian Horse Journal - Central & Atlantic Edition
Previous Name: Pacific Horse Journal
PO Box 2190, Sidney, BC V8L 3S8
Tel: 250-655-8883; Fax: 250-655-8913
Toll-Free: 800-299-3799
sales@horsejournals.com
Social Media:
www.linkedin.com/company/horse-community-journals
twitter.com/HORSEJourn als
www.facebook.com/CanadianHorseJournal
Circulation: 20,000 Frequency: 12 times a year
ON to Maritimes, plus ON Equestrian Federation News

Canadian Horse Journal - Pacific & Prairie Edition
Previous Name: Pacific Horse Journal
PO Box 2190, Sidney, BC V8L 3S8
Tel: 250-655-8883; Fax: 250-655-8913
Toll-Free: 800-299-3799
sales@horsejournals.com
Social Media:
www.linkedin.com/company/horse-community-journals
twitter.com/HORSEJourn als
www.facebook.com/CanadianHorseJournal
Circulation: 20,000 Frequency: 12 times a year
BC to MB, plus Horse Council BC Newsletter
Kathy Smith, Publisher/Editor

The Canadian Sportsman
PO Box 129, 9405 Plank Rd., Straffordville, ON N0J 1Y0
Tel: 519-866-5558; Fax: 519-866-5596
gfoerster@canadiansportsman.ca
Frequency: Bi-weekly
Gary Foerster, Publisher
Dave Briggs, Editor

Canadian Thoroughbred
Owned By: Horse Publications Group
PO Box 670, Aurora, ON L4G 4J9
Tel: 905-727-0107; Fax: 905-841-1530
Toll-Free: 800-505-7428
info@horse-canada.com
Circulation: 4,500 Frequency: 6 times a year
Jennifer Anstey, Publisher, janstey@horse-canada.com
Jennifer Morrison, Editor, dolphin12@rogers.com

Courrier Hippique
CP 1000 M, 4545, av Pierre-de-Coubertin, Montréal, QC H1V 3R2
Tél: 514-252-3030;Téléc: 514-252-3165
courrier@hippique.qc.ca
Médias sociaux:
www.facebook.com/pages/Courrier-Hippique/312091372180708
Tirage: 7 000 Fréquence: 6 times a year
Nathalie Laberge, Rédactrice-en-chef, redaction@hippique.qc.ca

Horse & Country Canada
#203, 23 - 845 Dakota St., Winnipeg, MB R2M 5M3
Tel: 204-256-7467; Fax: 204-257-2467
contact@horsecountry.ca
Social Media:
www.facebook.com/pages/Horse-Country/140013221802?ref=ts
Circulation: 12,000 Frequency: 8 times a year
Linda Hazelwood, Publisher & Editor

Horse Sport
Owned By: Horse Publications Group
PO Box 670, Aurora, ON L4G 4J9
Tel: 905-727-0107; Fax: 905-841-1530
Toll-Free: 800-505-7428
info@horse-canada.com
Social Media:
twitter.com/horsesport_mag
www.facebook.com/HorseSport
Circulation: 10,000 Frequency: 12 times a year
Jennifer Anstey, Publisher, janstey@horse-canada.com
Susan Stafford, Editor, editor@horse-canada.com

Horse-Canada
Previous Name: Canadian Horseman
Owned By: Horse Publications Group
PO Box 670, Aurora, ON L4G 4J9
Tel: 905-727-0107; Fax: 905-841-1530
Toll-Free: 800-505-7428
info@horse-canada.com
Social Media:
twitter.com/horsecanada
www.facebook.com/HorseCanadaMagazine
Circulation: 17,000 Frequency: 6 times a year
Jennifer Anstey, Publisher, janstey@horse-canada.com
Amy Harris, Editor, hceditor@horse-canada.com

Horsepower Magazine
Owned By: Horse Publications Group
PO Box 670, Aurora, ON L4G 4J9
Tel: 905-727-0107 Toll-Free: 800-505-7428
ftdesk@horse-canada.com
Circulation: 16,000 Frequency: 6 times a year
Published as a special pull-out in Horse-Canada Magazine.
Jennifer Anstey, Publisher, janstey@horse-canada.com
Susan Stafford, Editor, fearless.editor@gmail.com

Horses All
629 Evermeadow Rd. SW, Calgary, AB T2Y 4W8
Tel: 403-608-2238 Toll-Free: 800-665-0502
Social Media:
www.facebook.com/pages/Horses-All-Magazine/1759807358442
3
Circulation: 7,000 Frequency: Monthly
Craig Couillard, Publisher, 403-200-1019,
craig.couillard@fbcpublishing.com

Racing Quarterly
Owned By: Horse Publications Group
PO Box 670, Aurora, ON L4G 4J9
Tel: 905-727-0107; Fax: 905-841-1530
Toll-Free: 800-505-7428
info@horse-canada.com
Frequency: Quarterly
Lee Benson, Editor, lbenson@xplornet.com

The Rider
PO Box 10072, 27 Legend Crt., Ancaster, ON L9K 1P2
Tel: 905-648-2035; Fax: 905-648-6977
Toll-Free: 877-743-3715
barry@therider.com
Circulation: 7,000 Frequency: Monthly
Aidan Finn, Editor

Trot
c/o Standardbred Canada, 2150 Meadowvale Blvd., Mississauga, ON L5N 6R6
Tel: 905-858-3060
Frequency: Monthly
Chris Roberts, Manager & Editor

Interior Design & Decor

Homefront
#803, 255 Duncan Mill Rd., Toronto, ON M3B 3H9
Tel: 416-421-7944; Fax: 416-421-8418
Toll-Free: 800-798-6282
Circulation: 35,000 Frequency: 4 times a year
Helmut Dostal, Publisher
Caroline Tapp-McDougall, Editor-in-Chief

Plaisirs de Vivre/Living in Style
Previous Name: Résidences
#208, 1800, rue Notre-Dame ouest, Montréal, QC H3J 1M1
Tel: 514-982-9823; Fax: 514-289-9160
pdv@prestipresse.com
Circulation: 70,198 Frequency: 6 times a year; English & French
Peter Weiss, Publisher
Céline Tremblay, Editor-in-chief

Labour, Trade Unions

Our Times
Owned By: Our Times Publishing Inc.,
#407, 15 Gervais Dr., Toronto, ON M3C 1Y8
Tel: 416-703-7661; Fax: 416-703-9094
Toll-Free: 800-648-6131
office@ourtimes.ca
Social Media:
twitter.com/OurTimesMag
www.facebook.com/ourtimesmagazine
Circulation: 8,000 Frequency: 6 times a year
Independent labour magazine.
Lorraine Endicott, Editor

Socialist Worker
PO Box 339 E, Toronto, ON M6H 4E3
Tel: 416-972-6391; Fax: 416-972-6319
sworker@sympatico.ca
Circulation: 2,000 Frequency: 24 times a year
Paul Kellogg, Editor

Literary

The Antigonish Review
PO Box 5000, St. Francis Xavier University, Antigonish, NS B2G 2W5
Tel: 902-867-3962; Fax: 902-867-5563
tar@stfx.ca
Circulation: 900 Frequency: 4 times a year
Bonnie McIsaac, Office Manager
Gerald Trites, Editor

ARC: Canada's National Poetry Magazine
PO Box 81060, Ottawa, ON K1P 1B1
Tel: 613-729-3550
arc@arcpoetry.ca
Social Media:
twitter.com/arcpoetry
www.facebook.com/pages/Arc-Poetry-Magazine/131264640283
36
Circulation: 1,200 Frequency: 2 times a year
Anita Lahey, Editor
Pauline Conley, Managing Editor

Brick: A Literary Journal
PO Box 537 Q, Toronto, ON M4T 2M5
Tel: 416-593-9684; Fax: 416- -
info@brickmag.com
Circulation: 2,200 Frequency: 2 times a year
M. Redhill

Canadian Notes & Queries
PO Box 92, Emerville, ON N0R 1A0
Tel: 519-968-2206; Fax: 519-250-5713
info@notesandqueries.ca
Circulation: 500 Frequency: 2 times a year
Tim Inkster, Publisher
John Metcalf, Editor

The Capilano Review
2055 Purcell Way, North Vancouver, BC V7J 3H5
Tel: 604-984-1712
contact@thecapilanoreview.ca
Circulation: 900 Frequency: 3 times a year
Brook Houglum, Editor

The Claremont Review
4980 Wesley Rd., Victoria, BC V8Y 1Y9
Tel: 250-658-5221; Fax: 250-658-5387
lmoran@telus.net
Social Media:
www.facebook.com/groups/273911722449/
Circulation: 1,000 Frequency: 2 times a year
Susan Stenson, Editor
Linda Moran, Managing Editor

Contemporary Verse 2
#502, 100 Arthur St., Winnipeg, MB R3B 1H3
Tel: 204-949-1365; Fax: 204-942-1555
cv2@mts.net
Circulation: 650 Frequency: 4 times a year
Clarise Foster, Managing Editor

Descant
Descant Arts & Letters Foundation, PO Box 314 P, 50 Baldwin St., Toronto, ON M5S 2S8
Tel: 416-593-2557; Fax: 416-593-9362
info@descant.on.ca
Social Media:
twitter.com/DescantMagazine
Circulation: 1,200 Frequency: 4 times a year
Karen Mulhallen, Editor

Exile
134 Eastbourne Ave., Toronto, ON M5P 2G6
Tel: 416-485-4885
exq@exilequarterly.com
Social Media:
twitter.com/WPTwits
Frequency: Quarterly
Michael Callaghan, Publisher
Barry Campos, Editor-in-Chief

The Fiddlehead
Owned By: University of New Brunswick
University of New Brunswick, Campus House, PO Box 4400 A, 11 Garland Ct., Fredericton, NB E3B 5A3
Tel: 506-453-3501
fiddlehd@unb.ca
Social Media:
www.facebook.com/174825212565312
Circulation: 1,000 Frequency: 4 times a year
Ross Leckie, Editor

Geist
Owned By: Geist Foundation
#210, 111 West Hastings St., Vancouver, BC V6B 1H4
Tel: 604-681-9161; Fax: 604-677-6319
Toll-Free: 888-434-7834
geist@geist.com, letters@geist.com
Social Media:
twitter.com/geistmagazine
www.facebook.com/geist.mag
Circulation: 8,000 Frequency: 4 times a year
Stephen Osborne, Editor, editor@geist.com

Grain
PO Box 67, Saskatoon, SK S7K 3K1
Tel: 306-244-2828; Fax: 306-244-0255
grainmag@sasktel.net
Social Media:
www.facebook.com/189449391085557
Circulation: 1,700 Frequency: 4 times a year
Rilla Friesen, Editor

Little Brother
Toronto, ON
info@littlebrothermagazine.com
Social Media:
twitter.com/yourlb
www.facebook.com/littlebrothermagazine
Frequency: 4 issues per year
Collection of essays and short stories.
Emily M. Keeler, Editor

The Malahat Review
University of Victoria, PO Box 1700 CSC, 3800 Finnerty Road (Ring Road), D262, Victoria, BC V8W 2Y2
Tel: 250-721-8524; Fax: 250-472-5051
malahat@uvic.ca
Social Media:
twitter.com/malahatreview
www.facebook.com/pages/The-Malahat-Review/154705264550
Circulation: 1,000 Frequency: 4 times a year
John Barton, Editor

Matrix
#502, 1400, boul de Maisonneuve ouest, Montréal, QC H3G 1M8
Tel: 514-848-2357; Fax: 514-848-4501
info@matrixmagazine.org
Social Media:
twitter.com/matrixmagazine
www.facebook.com/pages/Matrix-Magazine/279322 025424646
Circulation: 1,500 Frequency: 4 times a year
Jon Paul Florentino, Editor

The New Quarterly
c/o St. Jerome's University, 290 Westmount Rd. North, Waterloo, ON N2L 3G3
Tel: 519-884-8111; Fax: 519-884-5759
info@tnq.ca
Circulation: 1,000 Frequency: 4 times a year
Covers Canadian writers & writing
Kim Jernigan, Editor

Nuit blanche
#403, 1026, rue St-Jean, Québec, QC G1R 1R7
Tél: 418-692-1354;Téléc: 418-692-1355
nuitblanche@nuitblanche.com
Médias sociaux:
twitter.com/nuitblanchemag
Fréquence: 4 fois par an; français
Anne-Marie Guérineau, Directrice

On Spec Magazine
The Copper Pig Writers' Society, PO Box 4727, Edmonton, AB T6E 5G6
Tel: 780-413-0215; Fax: 780-413-1538
onspec@onspec.ca
Social Media:
www.twitter.com/onspecmagazine
www.facebook.com/groups/2395098260
Circulation: 2,000 Frequency: 4 times a year
Diane Walton, Managing Editor

paperplates
19 Kenwood Ave., Toronto, ON M6C 2R8
Tel: 416-651-2551; Fax: 416-651-2910
magazine@paperplates.org
Frequency: 4 issues a year
Bernard Kelly, Publisher & Editor

Prairie Fire
Owned By: Prairie Fire Press Inc.
Prairie Fire Press Inc., #423, 100 Arthur St., Winnipeg, MB R3B 1H3
Tel: 204-943-9066; Fax: 204-942-1555
prfire@mts.net
Circulation: 1,500 Frequency: 4 times a year
Features new Canadian writing.
Andris Taskans, Editor
Heidi Harms, Associate Editor

Prairie Journal
Prairie Journal Press, PO Box 68073, 28 Crawford Terrace NW, Calgary, AB T3G 3N8
prairiejournal@yahoo.com
Circulation: 750 Frequency: 2 times a year
A. Burke

Prism International
Buch., #E462, Dept. of Creative Writing, UBC, 1866 Main Mall, Vancouver, BC V6T 1Z1
Tel: 604-822-2514; Fax: 604-822-3616
prismcirculation@gmail.com
Social Media:
www.facebook.com/prism.mag.5
Circulation: 1,200 Frequency: 4 times a year
Jen Neale, Executive Editor, Circulation & Promotion, 604-822-2514, Fax: 604-822-3616, prismcirculation@gmail.com
Sierra Gemma, Executive Editor, Finance, 604-822-2514, Fax: 604-822-3616, prismfinances@gmail.com

Rampike Magazine
c/o Dept. of English, University of Windsor, 401 Sunset Ave., Windsor, ON N9B 3P4
Tel: 519-253-3000; Fax: 519-971-3676
jirgins@uwindsor.ca
Circulation: 4,000 Frequency: 2 times a year
Karl E. Jirgins, Editor/Publisher

sub-TERRAIN Magazine
PO Box 3008 MPO, Vancouver, BC V6B 3X5
Tel: 604-876-8710
subter@portal.ca
Social Media:
twitter.com/subterrain
www.facebook.com/subTerrain
Circulation: 3,500 Frequency: 3 issues a year
Brian Kaufman, Editor

West Coast Line
Owned By: West Coast Review Publishing Society
West Coast Review Publishing Society, Simon Fraser University, 6079 Academic Quadrangle, 8888 University Dr., Burnaby, BC V5A 1S6
Tel: 778-782-4988; Fax: 778-782-5737
wcl@sfu.ca
Circulation: 800 Frequency: Quarterly
Glen Lowry, Managing Editor

White Wall Review
Ryerson Literary Society, c/o Department of English, Jorgenson Hall, 350 Victoria St., 5th Fl., Toronto, ON M5B 2K3
Tel: 416-977-9924; Fax: 416-977-7709
aleeloy@arts.ryerson.ca
Anne Marie Lee-Loy

Men's

Highrise Magazine
info@highrisemag.com
Frequency: 4 times a year
Cynthia Cully, Editor-in-chief

Sharp Magazine
Owned By: Contempo Media Inc.
#100, 370 Queen's Quay West, Toronto, ON M5V 3J3
Tel: 416-591-0093 Toll-Free: 866-815-1441
sales@sharpmagazine.ca
Social Media: www.linkedin.com/company/1729850?trk=tyah
www.twitter.com/sharpmagazine
www.facebook.com/Sharpformen
Frequency: Bi-Monthly
Jeremy Freed, Editor-in-Chief, jeremy@contempomedia.ca

Military

Esprit de Corps
#204, 1066 Somerset St. West, Ottawa, ON K1Y 4T3
Tel: 613-725-5060; Fax: 613-725-1019
Toll-Free: 800-361-2791
espritdecorp@idirect.com
Circulation: 15,000
Scott Taylor, Publisher

Mining

Canadian Mining Magazine
Owned By: Matrix Group Publishing Inc.
#300, 52 Donald St., Winnipeg, MB R3C 1L6
; Fax: 866-244-2544
Toll-Free: 866-999-1299
Social Media:
twitter.com/cminingmagazine
www.facebook.com/CanadianMiningMagazin e
Frequency: Quarterly
Maurice LaBorde, Publisher, mlaborde@matrixgroupinc.ne
Shannon Savory, Editor-in-Chief, ssavory@matrixgroupinc.net

Music

Beatlology Magazine
#90, 260 Adelaide St. East, Toronto, ON M5A 1N1
Andrew Croft, Publisher, publisher@beatlology.com
Charles Iscove, Editor, editor@beatlology.com

Canadian Musician
Owned By: Norris-Whitney Communications Inc.
#7, 23 Hannover Dr., St Catharines, ON L2W IA3
Tel: 905-641-3471; Fax: 888-665-1307
Toll-Free: 877-746-4692
mail@nor.com
Social Media: pinterest.com/cdnmusician/
twitter.com/cdnmusician
www.facebook.com/cdnmusician
Circulation: 27,000 Frequency: 6 times a year
Jim Norris, Publisher

Country Music News
PO Box 7323 Vanier Terminal, Ottawa, ON K1L 8E4
Circulation: 6,500 Frequency: Monthly
Larry Delaney, Publisher & Editor, Larry@CountryMusicNews.ca

Crescendo
Toronto Musicians' Assn., #500, 15 Gervais Dr., Toronto, ON M3C 1Y8
Tel: 416-421-1020; Fax: 416-421-7011
Toll-Free: 800-463-6333
info@tma149.ca
Circulation: 4,000 Frequency: 3 times a year
Allan MacMillan, Publisher
Brian Blain, Managing Editor

Exclaim!
849A Bloor St. W., Toronto, ON M6G 1M3
Tel: 416-535-9735; Fax: 416-535-0566
exclaim@exclaim.ca
Social Media:
twitter.com/exclaimdotca
www.facebook.com/exclaimdotca
Circulation: 100,000 Frequency: 11 pa
Coverage of new music across all genres.
Ian Danzig, Publisher, ian@exclaim.ca

Musicworks
Owned By: Musicworks Society of Ontario Inc
#358, 401 Richmond St. West, Toronto, ON M5V 3A8
Tel: 416-977-3546; Fax: 416-977-4181
Toll-Free: 877-977-3546
sound@musicworks.ca
Circulation: 3,000 Frequency: 3 times a year; English & French
Musicworks is dedicated to contemporary experimental music. Each issue includes a CD featuring music by artists appearing in the magazine.
Gayle Young, Publisher, gayle@musicworks.ca
Michelle Roy, Editor, editor@musicworks.ca

Opera Canada
#244, 366 Adelaide St. East, Toronto, ON M5A 3X9
Tel: 416-363-0395 Toll-Free: 800-222-5097
editorial@operacanada.ca
Circulation: 5,575 Frequency: 4 times a year
Wayne Gooding, Editor

La Scena Musicale / The Music Scene
5409, rue Waverly, Montréal, QC H2T 2X8
Tel: 514-948-2520
info@scena.org
Social Media:
twitter.com/lascena
www.facebook.com/groups/4470026401/
Circulation: 42,000
Wah Keung Chan, Éditeur & Rédacteur-en-chef, wkchan@lascena.org

TRIBE Magazine
358 Danforth Ave., Toronto, ON M4K 3Z2
Tel: 416-778-4115; Fax: 416-405-9473
editor@tribe.ca
Circulation: 35,000 Frequency: 10 times a year
Alex Dordevic, Publisher/Editor

WHOLENOTE: Toronto's Music, Classical & New
#503, 720 Bathurst St., Toronto, ON M5S 2R4
Tel: 416-603-3786; Fax: 416-603-4791
info@thewholenote.com
Social Media:
twitter.com/thewholenote
www.facebook.com/pages/The-WholeNote/1397343369 57
Circulation: 36,000
Allan Pulker, Publisher

News

L'Actualité
Détenteur : Éditions Rogers Media
1200, av McGill College, 8e étage, Montréal, QC H3B 4G7
Tél: 514-843-2564;Téléc: 514-843-2186
redaction@lactualite.rogers.com
Médias sociaux:
twitter.com/Lactualite
www.facebook.com/lactualite
Tirage: 160,070 Fréquence: 20 fois par an; français
Carole Beaulieu, Rédactrice

Columbia Journal
PO Box 2633 Main, Vancouver, BC V6B 3W8
Tel: 604-266-6552; Fax: 604-267-3342
editor@columbiajournal.ca
Circulation: 20,000 Frequency: 12 times a year
Jim Lipkovits, Editor
Marco Procaccini, Editor

Le Courrier Parlementaire
Owned By: Publications Mass-Media inc.
30, Grande-Allée ouest, Québec, QC G1R 2G6
Tel: 418-640-4211
editeur@courrierparlementaire.com
Social Media:
twitter.com/CourrierPar
Denis Massicotte, Publisher

Embassy
Owned By: The Hill Times Publishing Inc.
69 Sparks Street Rd., Ottawa, ON K1P 5A5
Tel: 613-232-5952; Fax: 613-232-9055
news@embassymag.ca
Social Media:
twitter.com/EMBASSYMagazine
Circulation: 60,000 Frequency: Weekly; Wednesday
Issues of foreign policy.
Anne Marie Creskey, Publisher, acreskey@embassymag.ca

Inroads
3777 Kent Ave., #A, Montréal, QC H3S 1N4
Tel: 514-731-8383; Fax: 519-662-3594
inroadsmagazine@ymail.com
Frequency: 2 times a year
Robert Chodos, Managing Editor, leischod@rogers.com

Maclean's
Owned By: Rogers Publishing Ltd.
1 Mount Pleasant Rd., 11th Fl., Toronto, ON M4Y 2Y5
Tel: 416-764-1300; Fax: 416-764-1332
Toll-Free: 800-268-9119
service@macleans.ca
Social Media:
twitter.com/MacleansMag
www.facebook.com/MacleansMagazine
Circulation: 330,203 Frequency: Weekly
Penny Hicks, Publisher
Mark Stevenson, Editor

The Mirror
901 - 100th Ave., Dawson Creek, BC V1G 1W2
Tel: 250-782-4888; Fax: 250-782-6770
Frequency: Friday
The Mirror is a newsmagazine which is printed each week by the Dawason Creek Daily News. The magazine is distributed in Dawson Creek, Chetwynd, & Tumbler Ridge.
Daniel Przybylski, Publisher, publisher@dcdn.ca

Photography

Blackflash
Buffalo Berry Press, PO Box 7381 Main, 12 - 23rd St. East, 2nd Fl., Saskatoon, SK S7K 4J3
Tel: 306-374-5115; Fax: 306-665-6568
editor@blackflash.ca
Circulation: 1,300 Frequency: 3 times a year
John Shelling, Managing Editor

Ciel Variable
Anciennement: CV Photo; Productions Ciel Variable
#204, 661, rue Rose-de-Lima, Montréal, QC H4C 2L7
Tél: 514-390-1193;Téléc: 514-390-8802
info@cielvariable.ca
Médias sociaux:
www.facebook.com/magazinecielvariable
Tirage: 1,850 Fréquence: 4 times a year; English & French
Jacques Doyen, Rédacteur en chef et directeur

Photo Life
Previous Name: Photo Digest
Owned By: Apex Publications
185, rue St-Paul, Québec, QC G1K 3W2
Fax: 800-664-2739
Toll-Free: 800-905-7468
info@photolife.com
Other information: Toll Free Fax: 1-800-664-2739
Social Media:
twitter.com/PhotoLifeMag
www.facebook.com/photolifemag
Circulation: 55,000 Frequency: 6 times a year
Guy Poirier, Publisher, gpoirier@photolife.com
Valérie Racine, Editorial Director, editor@photolife.com

Political

bout de papier
#412, 47 Clarence St., Ottawa, ON K1N 9K1
Tel: 613-241-1391; Fax: 613-241-5911
boutdepapier@pafso.com
Circulation: 2,800 Frequency: 4 times a year; English & French
Debra Hulley, Managing Editor

Briarpatch
2138 McIntyre St., Regina, SK S4P 2R7
Tel: 306-525-2949; Fax: 306-565-3430
info@briarpatchmagazine.com
Circulation: 2,000 Frequency: 8 times a year
Shayna Stock, Publisher, publisher@briarpatchmagazine.com
Dave Oswald Mitchell, Managing Editor, editor@briarpatchmagazine.com

Canadian Dimension
#2E, 91 Albert St., Winnipeg, MB R3B 1G5
Tel: 204-957-1519; Fax: 204-943-4617
Toll-Free: 800-737-7051
sales@canadiandimension.com
Social Media:
twitter.com/CDN_Dimension
www.facebook.com/CDNDimension
Circulation: 3,500 Frequency: 6 times a year (including 2 double issues)
Cy Gonick, Publisher & Coordinating Editor, editor@canadiandimension.com

Dialogue Magazine
Previous Name: Westcoast Logger
Gabriel Communications, 6227 Groveland Dr., Nanaimo, BC V9V 1B1
Tel: 250-758-9877; Fax: 250-758-9855
dialogue@dialogue.ca
Circulation: 700 Frequency: Bi-monthly
Volunteer-based, non-profit publishing.
Maurice J. King, President & Publisher
Janet Hicks, Editor

Parliament Now
Owned By: The Hill Times Publishing Inc.
69 Sparks Street Rd., Ottawa, ON K1P 5A5
Tel: 613-232-5952; Fax: 613-232-9055
news@parliamentnow.ca

Peace Magazine
PO Box 248 P, Toronto, ON M5S 2S7
Tel: 416-588-8748
office@peacemagazine.org
Social Media:
twitter.com/peace_mag
www.facebook.com/pages/Peace-Magazine/224393994267274
Circulation: 2,500 Frequency: 4 times a year
Metta Spencer, Chair, mspencer@web.net

This Magazine
Red Maple Foundation, #417, 401 Richmond St. West, Toronto, ON M5V 3A8
Tel: 416-979-9429 Toll-Free: 877-999-8447
editor@this.org
Social Media: quote.this.org/
twitter.com/thismagazine
www.facebook.com/thismagazine
Circulation: 8,000 Frequency: 6 times a year
Lauren McKeon, Editor, 416-979-8400
Lisa Whittington-Hill, Publisher, 416-979-9429

Printing & Publishing

Devil's Artisan: A Journal of the Printing Arts
c/o The Porcupine's Quill, PO Box 160, 68 Main St., Erin, ON N0B 1T0
Tel: 519-833-9158; Fax: 519-833-9845
elke@porcupinesquill.ca
Circulation: 800 Frequency: 2 times a year
Tim Inkster, Publisher
Don McLeod, Editor

Quill & Quire
#320, 111 Queen St. East, Toronto, ON M5C 1S2
Tel: 416-364-3333; Fax: 416-595-5415
Social Media:
itunes.apple.com/ca/podcast/quill-quire/id475815029
twitter.com/quillandquire
www.facebook.com/quillandquire
Frequency: 10 times per year
Magazine of the Canadian book trade.
Stuart Woods, Editor, swoods@quillandquire.com
Alison Jones, Publisher/Advertising Sales, ajones@quillandquire.com

Real Estate

Canadian Real Estate Wealth
Owned By: Key Media Inc.
#800, 312 Adelaide St. West, Toronto, ON M5V 1R2
Tel: 416-644-8740; Fax: 416-203-9083
subscriptions@kmimedia.ca
Social Media:
twitter.com/CanRealEstMag
facebook.com/Canadianrealestatemag
Frequency: Monthly
Nila Sweeney, Editor, nila.sweeney@keymedia.com.au

Homes & Land Magazine
Owned By: Suggitt Publishing Ltd.
Bell Tower, #950, 10104 - 103 Ave., Edmonton, AB T5J 0H8
Toll-Free: 866-702-2120
Real estate listings for provinces across Canada.
Tom Suggitt, President & CEO, tom@suggitt.com

Religious & Denominational

The Anglican
135 Adelaide St. East, Toronto, ON M5C 1L8
Tel: 416-363-6021
Frequency: Monthly
Stuart Mann, Editor

Anglican Journal
c/o Anglican Church of Canada, 80 Hayden St., Toronto, ON M4Y 3G2
Tel: 416-924-9192; Fax: 416-921-4452
editor@national.anglican.ca
Social Media:
twitter.com/anglicanjournal
www.facebook.com/anglicanjournal
Circulation: 160,000 Frequency: 10 times a year
Janet Thomas, Editorial Assistant
Leanne Larmontoin, Editor

BC Christian News
#200, 20316 - 56th Ave., Langley, BC V3A 3Y7
Tel: 604-534-1444; Fax: 604-534-2970
admin@canadianchristianity.com
Circulation: 37,000 Frequency: Monthly

Flyn Ritchie, Publisher & Editor, editor@canadianchristianity.com
David Dawes, Managing Editor, ddawes@canadianchristianity.com

Canada Lutheran
#302, 393 Portage Ave., Winnipeg, MB R3B 3H6
Tel: 204-984-9177; Fax: 204-984-9185
Toll-Free: 888-786-6707
canaluth@elcic.ca
Social Media:
www.facebook.com/CanadianLutherans
Circulation: 14,000 Frequency: 8 times a year
The magazine of the Evangelical Lutheran Church in Canada.
Susan McIlveen, Managing Editor, editor@elcic.ca

Canadian Mennonite
Previous Name: Mennonite Reporter
#C5, 490 Dutton Dr., Waterloo, ON N2L 6H7
Tel: 519-884-3810; Fax: 519-884-3331
Toll-Free: 800-378-2524
letters@canadianmennonite.org
Circulation: 17,000 Frequency: 24 times a year
Timothy Miller Dyck, Editor

Catholic Insight
PO Box 625 Adelaide, 31 Adelaide St. East, Toronto, ON M5C 2J8
Tel: 416-204-9601; Fax: 416-204-1027
admin@catholicinsight.com
Circulation: 3,700 Frequency: 11 times a year
Fr. Alphonse de Valk, Publisher

The Catholic Register
#401, 1155 Yonge St., Toronto, ON M4T 1W2
Tel: 416-934-3410; Fax: 416-934-3409
web@catholicregister.org
Social Media:
twitter.com/catholicregistr
www.facebook.com/thecatholicregister
Circulation: 33,000 Frequency: 47 times a year
Joseph Sinasac, Editor

Christian Courier
5 Joanna Dr., St Catharines, ON L2N 1V1
Tel: 905-682-8311 Toll-Free: 800-969-4838
admin@christiancourier.ca
Social Media:
twitter.com/ChrCourier
Circulation: 2,500 Frequency: Bi-weekly
Harry DerNederlanden, Editor-in-chief

ChristianCurrent
PO Box 725, Winnipeg, MB R3C 2K3
Tel: 204-982-2060; Fax: 204-947-5632
Brian Koldyk, Publisher
Robert White, Managing Editor

ChristianWeek
PO Box 725, #204, 424 Logan Ave., Winnipeg, MB R3C 2K3
Tel: 204-982-2060; Fax: 204-947-5632
Toll-Free: 800-263-6695
admin@christianweek.org
Social Media:
twitter.com/christianweek
www.facebook.com/ChristianWeek
Circulation: 5,000 Frequency: Every other Tue., except every 3 weeks in Dec.
Doug Koop, Editorial Director

Clarion
1 Beghin Ave., Winnipeg, MB R2J 3X5
Tel: 204-663-9000; Fax: 204-633-9202
admin@premierprinting.ca
Circulation: 3,000 Frequency: Bi-weekly
W. Gortemaker, Publisher

Diocesan Times
c/o Diocese of NS & PEI, 5732 College St., Halifax, NS B3H 1X3
diocesantimes@gmail.com
Frequency: Monthly, excpet July & August
The Diocesan Times, serving Anglicans in Nova Scotia and Prince Edward Island.

Edmonton Jewish News
#207, 11460 Jasper Ave., Edmonton, AB T7K 0A1
Tel: 780-421-7966; Fax: 780-424-3951
ejnews@telus.net
Circulation: 2,000
David Moser, Publisher

Faith Today
c/o The Evangelical Fellowship of Canada, PO Box 5885 W Beaver Creek, #103, Leslie St., Richmond Hill, ON L4B 0B8
Tel: 905-479-5885; Fax: 905-479-4742
Toll-Free: 866-302-3362
efc@evangelicalfellowship.ca
Social Media:
www.facebook.com/FaithToday
www.facebook.com/FaithToday
Circulation: 20,000 Frequency: 6 times a year
Gail Reid, Managing Editor
Bruce Clemenger, Publisher

Gospel Herald
c/o Gospel Herald Foundation, 5 Lanking Blvd., Toronto, ON M4J 4W7
Tel: 416-461-7406; Fax: 416-424-1850
subscription@gospelherald.org
Circulation: 1,320 Frequency: Monthly
Wayne Turner, Editor
Max E. Craddock, Managing Editor

Huron Church News
190 Queens Ave., London, ON N6A 6H7
Tel: 519-434-6893; Fax: 519-673-4151
Toll-Free: 800-919-1115
huron@huron.anglican.ca
Bishop Bruce Howe, Publisher
David Parson, Editor

Island Catholic News
PO Box 5424 LCD 9, Victoria, BC V8R 6S4
Tel: 250-727-9429
admin@islandcatholicnews.ca
Circulation: 2,000 Frequency: Monthly
Marnie Butler, Senior Editor
Patrick Jamieson, Managing Editor

Jewish Free Press
Owned By: Jewish Free Press Inc.
8411 Elbow Dr. SW, Calgary, AB T2V 1K8
Tel: 403-252-9423; Fax: 403-255-5640
jewishfp@telus.net
Circulation: 2,000 Frequency: Semi-monthly
Richard Bronstein, Publisher

The Jewish Tribune
Previous Name: The Covenant
15 Hove St., Toronto, ON M3H 4Y8
Tel: 416-633-6224; Fax: 416-630-2159
Circulation: 60,000 Frequency: weekly
Norm Gordner, Editor

Living Light News
#200, 5306 - 89th St., Edmonton, AB T6E 5P9
Fax: 780-468-6872
Toll-Free: 800-932-0555
shine@livinglightnews.org
Circulation: 50,000 Frequency: Bi-Monthly
Jeff Caporale, Editor-in-chief

London Jewish Community News
536 Huron St., London, ON N5Y 4J5
Tel: 519-673-3310; Fax: 519-673-1161
Frequency: quarterly

Mennonite Brethren Herald
1310 Taylor Ave., Winnipeg, MB R2M 3Z6
Tel: 204-654-5760; Fax: 204-654-1865
Toll-Free: 888-669-6575
mbherald@mbconf.ca
Social Media:
twitter.com/MB_Herald
www.facebook.com/MBHerald
Circulation: 17,500 Frequency: Monthly
Karla Braun, Assistant Editor
Laura Kalmar, Editor
Helga Kasdorf, Manager, Circulation & Advertising

The New Brunswick Anglican
115 Church St., Fredericton, NB E3B 4C8
Tel: 506-459-1801
awatts@nbnet.nb.ca
Social Media:
www.facebook.com/dfton
Circulation: 10,000 Frequency: 10 times a year
Ana Watts, Communications Officer

The New Freeman
The Diocese of Saint John, 1 Bayard Dr., Saint John, NB E2L 3L5
Tel: 506-653-6806; Fax: 506-653-6818
tnf@nbnet.nb.ca
Circulation: 7,480 Frequency: Weekly

Margie Trafton, Editor

Niagara Anglican
c/o Anglican Diocese of Niagara, Cathedral Place, 252 James St. North, Hamilton, ON L8R 2L3
Tel: 905-527-1316
dihutton@mountaincable.com
Circulation: 16,175 Frequency: Monthly exc. July & Aug.
Christopher Grabiec, Editor

L'Oratoire / The Oratory
3800, ch Queen Mary, Montréal, QC H3V 1H6
Tél: 514-733-8211
abonnement@osj.qc.ca
Tirage: 7,500 anglais; 42,000 français Fréquence: 3 fois par an

Ottawa Jewish Bulletin
21 Nadolny Sachs, Ottawa, ON K2A 1R9
Tel: 613-798-4696; Fax: 613-798-4730
bulletin@ottawajewishbulletin.com
Circulation: 2,500 Frequency: 19 times a year

Outlook
6184 Ash St., Vancouver, BC V5Z 3G9
Tel: 604-324-5101; Fax: 604-325-2470
cjoutlook@telus.net
Frequency: 6 times a year
Carl Rosenberg, Editor-in-chief

Prairie Messenger
PO Box 190, 100 College Dr., Muenster, SK S0K 2Y0
Tel: 306-682-1772; Fax: 306-682-5285
pm@stpeterspress.ca
Circulation: 7,000 Frequency: 46 times a year
Maureen Weber, Editor, pm.canadian@stpeterspress.ca

Presbyterian Record
50 Wynford Dr., Toronto, ON M3C 1J7
Tel: 800-619-7301; Fax: 416-441-2825
record@presbyterianrecord.ca
Circulation: 42,000 Frequency: Monthly exc. Aug.
David Harris, Editor

Salvationist
Previous Name: The War Cry
2 Overlea Blvd., Toronto, ON M4H 1P4
Toll-Free: 800-725-2769
Social Media:
twitter.com/salvationist
www.facebook.com/salvationistmagazine
Circulation: 20,000 Frequency: Monthly
Maj. Ken Smith, Editor

Seven
c/o ChristianWeek, PO Box 725, #204, 424 Logan Ave., Winnipeg, MB R3A 0R4
Tel: 204-982-2060; Fax: 204-947-5632
Toll-Free: 800-263-6695
admin@christianweek.org
Frequency: Bi-Monthly

Shalom
#508, 5670 Spring Garden Rd., Halifax, NS B3J 1H6
Tel: 902-422-7491; Fax: 902-425-3722
atlanticjewishcouncil@theajc.ns.ca
Circulation: 1,400 Frequency: 3 times a year
Edna LeVine, Editor

Studies in Religion / Sciences Religieuses
Owned By: SAGE Publications
#347 Arts, University of Alberta, Edmonton, AB T6G 2E6
Tel: 780-492-4876; Fax: 418-659-4563
Circulation: 1,400 Frequency: Quarterly
Francis Lady, Editor-in-chief, 780-492-4876, francis.landy@ualberta.ca
Timothy Pettipiece, Managing Editor, tpettipi@hotmail.com

Testimony
The Penetecostal Assemblies of Canada, 2450 Milltower Ct., Mississauga, ON L5N 5Z6
Tel: 905-542-7400
testimony@paoc.org
Circulation: 14,000 Frequency: Monthly
Stacey McKenzie, Editor

The United Church Observer
478 Huron St., Toronto, ON M5R 2R3
Tel: 416-960-8500; Fax: 416-960-8477
Social Media:
www.facebook.com/pages/United-Church-Observer/1276051239 1
Circulation: 80,000 Frequency: 11 times a year

Muriel Duncan, Editor

La Voix Sépharade
#216, 1, carré Cummings, Montréal, QC H3W 1M6
Tél: 514-733-4998;Téléc: 514-733-3158
info@csuq.org
Tirage: 6,000 Fréquence: 4 fois par an
Danielle Glanz, Directeur, 514-733-4998 x 3183, dglanz@csuq.org

Western Catholic Reporter
8421 - 101 Ave., Edmonton, AB T6A 0L1
Tel: 780-465-8030; Fax: 780-465-8031
wcr@wcr.ab.ca
Circulation: 37,015 Frequency: 44 times a year
Glen Argan, Managing Editor

Science, Research & Development

Découvrir: La revue de la recherche
Anciennement: Interface
Association francophone pour le savoir, 425, rue de la Gauchetière est, Montréal, QC H2L 2M7
Tél: 514-849-0045;Téléc: 514-849-5558
decouvrir@acfas.ca
Médias sociaux:
twitter.com/_Acfas
www.facebook.com/33532707807
Tirage: 10 000 Fréquence: 6 fois par an; français
Johanne Lebel, Édimestre & rédactrice en chef, johanne.lebel@acfas.ca

Québec Science (QS)
Détenteur: Vélo Québec
1251, rue Rachel est, Montréal, QC H2J 2J9
Tél: 514-521-8356 Ligne sans frais: 800-567-8356
courrier@quebecscience.qc.ca
Médias sociaux:
twitter.com/quebecscience
www.facebook.com/pages/Quebec-Science/28025722 6593
Tirage: 32 000 Fréquence: 10 fois par an; français
Raymond Lemieux, Rédacteur-en-chef, r.lemieux@quebecscience.qc.ca

Revue Spectre
9601, rue Colbert, Anjou, QC H1J 1Z9
Tel: 514-948-6422; Fax: 514-948-6423
camille.turcotte@apsq.org
Circulation: 3,000
Diane Poulin, Editor-in-chief

Social Welfare

Canadian Social Work & CASW Bulletin / Travail social canadien et Bulletin de l'ACTS
Previous Name: The Social Worker
Myropen Publications Ltd., #402, 383 Parkdale Ave., Ottawa, ON K1Y 4R4
Tel: 613-729-6668; Fax: 613-729-9608
casw@casw-acts.ca
Circulation: 16,000 Frequency: English/French; 3 times a year
Eugenia Repetur Moreno, Executive Director

Community Action: Canada's Community Service Newspaper
41 Marbury Cres., Toronto, ON M3A 2G3
Tel: 416-449-6766; Fax: 416-444-5850
comact@interlog.com
Circulation: 12,010 Frequency: 11 times a year
Leon Kumove, Publisher

Perception
Canadian Council on Social Development, PO Box 13713, Kanata, ON K2K 1X6
Tel: 613-236-8977; Fax: 613-482-7970
taillon@ccsd.ca
As of January 2007, Perception will no longer be offered as a subscription; instead, it will be part of the benefits package available exclusively to their members.
Nancy Perkins, Communications Coordinator

WhyNot Magazine
Canadian Foundation for Physically Disabled Persons, #265, 6 Garamond Crt., Toronto, ON M3C 1Z5
Tel: 416-760-7351; Fax: 416-760-9405
whynot@sympatico.ca
Frequency: 3 times a year
Dedicated to its three main events: Great Valentine Gala, Rolling Rampage and The Terry Fox Hall of Fame.
Bill McQuat, Editor
Vim Kochhar, Publisher
Larry Allen, Editor

Sports & Recreation

Athletics: Canada's National Track & Field/Running Magazine
#211, 3 Concorde Gate, Toronto, ON M3C 3N7
Tel: 416-426-7215; Fax: 416-426-7358
ontrack@eol.ca
Circulation: 4,000 Frequency: 8 times a year
John Craig, Editor
Cecil Smith, Managing Director

BC Hockey Now
#300, 92 Lonsdale Ave., North Vancouver, BC V7M 2E6
Tel: 604-990-1432; Fax: 604-990-1433
Frequency: 18 times a year; also Alberta Hockey Now & Ontario Hockey Now
Don McIntosh, Publisher, dmcintosh@hockeynow.ca
Andrew Chong, Editor, andrewchong@hockeynow.ca

Below the Belt Boxing Magazine
#1712, 1478 Pilgrims Way, Oakville, ON L6M 3G7
Tel: 416-336-1947
dameon@belowthebelt.tv

Canadian Cyclist
7 Barker St., Paris, ON N3L 2H4
Tel: 519-442-7905
news@canadiancyclist.com
Social Media:
twitter.com/cdncyclist
Circulation: 8,000
Tracy Harkness, Publisher
Robert Jones, Editor

Canadian Rodeo News
272245, RR#2, Airdrie, AB T4A 2L5
Tel: 403-945-7393; Fax: 403-945-0936
editor@rodeocanada.com
Circulation: 4,000 Frequency: Monthly
Darell Hartlen, Editor

Coast & Kayak Magazine
Previous Name: Wavelength
Wild Coast Publishing, PO Box 24 A, Nanaimo, BC V9R 5K4
Tel: 250-244-6437; Fax: 866-654-1937
Toll-Free: 866-984-6437
kayak@coastandkayak.com
Frequency: Quarterly
The publication presents information about kayaking, paddlesports, & coastal recreation. The magazine is available at retail outlets & through paddling clubs, guides, & manufacturers on the west coast of Canada & the United States.
John Kimantas, Editor, editor@coastandkayak.com

Crown
Mississauga, ON
info@crownmagonline.com
Social Media: www.youtube.com/user/Crownmagonline
twitter.com/crownmagazine
www.face book.com/groups/30306464460/
Relating to Canadian high school basketball.
Gilbert Muako-Jones
Tariq Sbiet

The Curling News
PO Box 53103, 10 Royal Orchard Blvd., Thornhill, ON L3T 7R9
Tel: 905-997-3348 Toll-Free: 800-605-2875
sweep@sweepmag.com
Social Media:
twitter.com/curling
Frequency: 6 times a year; Nov.-April

Diver Magazine
PO Box 38529, 241 East 1st St., North Vancouver, BC V7M 3N1
Tel: 604-988-0711; Fax: 604-988-0747
Toll-Free: 877-974-4333
russell@divermag.com
Social Media:
twitter.com/divermag
www.facebook.com/divermagazine
Circulation: 7,000 Frequency: 8 times a year
Phil Nuytten, Publisher
Virginia Cowell, Editor

Flagstick Golf Magazine
Owned By: Bauder Media Group Inc.
8197 Parkway Rd., Ottawa, ON K0A 2P0
Tel: 613-821-0888; Fax: 613-821-4888
Toll-Free: 877-503-0888
info@flagstick.com
Social Media: www.youtube.com/flagstickgolf
www.twitter.com/flagstick
www.facebook.c om/flagstick
Circulation: 20,000 Frequency: 7 times a year
Jeff Bauder, Publisher, jbauder@flagstick.com
Scott MacLeod, Editor, scotmac@flagstick.com

Golf Guide
16410 - 137 Ave. NW, Edmonton, AB T5V 1R6
Tel: 780-447-2128; Fax: 780-447-1933
Frequency: Annually, April
Paul McCracken, Publisher

Golf International
12305 blvd Métropolitain est, Montréal, QC H1B 5R3
Tél: 514-645-2040;Téléc: 514-645-5508
Tirage: 50 000 Fréquence: 5 fois par an; français
Richard Beaudry, Président-éditeur, rbeaudry@ovationmedias.com

Golf West
Previous Name: Golf the West
Owned By: Koocanusa Publications Inc.
#100, 100 - 7th Ave. South, Cranbrook, BC V1C 2J4
Tel: 250-426-7253; Fax: 250-426-4125
info@kpimedia.com
Social Media: www.flickr.com/photos/golfwest
twitter.com/@golfwestmag
Circulation: 30,000 Frequency: Annually, Spring
Keith G. Powell, Publisher, keith@kpimedia.com
Kerry Shelborn, Editor, kerry@kpimedia.com

Hockey Magazine
Owned By: Suggitt Publishing Ltd.
Bell Tower, #950, 10104 - 103 Ave., Edmonton, AB T5J 0H8
Tel: 780-425-3642; Fax: 780-413-6185
reception@hockeymagazine.net
Minor league hockey coverage; separate magazines for Edmonton & Calgary.

Hockey News
Transcontinental Media Inc., #100, 25 Sheppard Ave. West, Toronto, ON M2N 6S7
Tel: 416-227-8237 Toll-Free: 888-361-9768
Social Media: www.youtube.com/user/THNTV
twitter.com/thehockeynews
www.facebook.com/thehockeynews
Circulation: 103,350 Frequency: 42 times a year
Gerald McGroarty, Publisher & Editor-in-chief

Le Journal Québec Quilles / Bowling Québec
2930, rue Desmarteau, Montréal, QC H1L 4N7
Tél: 514-351-5224
qcquilles@videotron.ca
Fréquence: 5 fois par an; français
Yves Larocque, Éditeur

The Leader
#100, 1345 Baseline Rd., Ottawa, ON K2C 0A7
Tel: 613-224-5131; Fax: 613-224-5982
smuehlherr@scouts.ca
Circulation: 38,000 Frequency: 10 times a year
Susan Muehlherr, Executive Editor

MARCHE-Randonnée
c/o Fédération Québécoise de la Marche, CP 1000 M, 4545, ave. Pierre-De Coubertin, Montréal, QC H1V 3R2
Tél: 514-252-3157;Téléc: 514-252-5137
Ligne sans frais: 866-252-2065
Tirage: 8 225 Fréquence: trimestriel
Raymond Dulude, Advertising
Daniel Pouplot, Production Manager
Louise Giroux, Co-ordinatrice

Motoneige Québec
4545, av Pierre-de-Coubertin, Montréal, QC H1V 0B2
Tél: 514-252-3076;Téléc: 514-254-2066
info@fcmq.qc.ca
Tirage: 65 000 Fréquence: 4 fois par an; français
Yves Ouellet, Rédacteur en chef indépendant

Newfoundland Sportsman
Previous Name: Outdoor Sportsman
PO Box 13754 A, 36 Pippy Pl., St. John's, NL A1B 4G5
Toll-Free: 877-754-3515
customerservice@newfoundlandsportsman.com
Social Media:
www.facebook.com/newfoundlandsportsman
Circulation: 14,621 Frequency: 6 times a year
Dwight J. Blackwood, Publisher
Gordon Follett, Editor

Northwestern Ontario Golfing News
Owned By: North Superior Publishing Inc.
North Superior Publishing Inc., 1145 Barton St., Thunder Bay, ON P7B 5N3
Tel: 807-623-2348; Fax: 807-623-7515
Circulation: 2,000 Frequency: 5 times a year
Scott Sumner, Publisher & Editor

Northwestern Ontario Snowmobile News
Owned By: North Superior Publishing Inc.
North Superior Publishing Inc., Thunder Bay, ON
Tel: 807-623-2348; Fax: 807-623-7515
nspinc@tbaytel.net
Circulation: 2,000 Frequency: 7 times a year
Scott A. Summer, Publisher & Editor

Ontario Golf
Owned By: Sun Media Inc.
Town Media, 1074 Cooke Blvd., Burlington, ON L7T 4A8
Tel: 905-634-8003; Fax: 905-634-7661
info@townmedia.ca
Social Media: www.youtube.com/ontariogolf
twitter.com/OntarioGolfMag
www.facebook .com/ontariogolf
Circulation: 55,000 Frequency: 4 times a year
Donna Gardener, Publisher, dgardener@townmedia.ca
Ted McIntyre, Editor, tedbits@golfontario.ca

Ontario Tennis
Ontario Tennis Association, #200, 1 Shoreham Dr., Toronto, ON M3N 3A7
Tel: 416-514-1100; Fax: 416-514-1112
Toll-Free: 800-387-5066
ota@tennisontario.com
Social Media: www.youtube.com/user/otatv1
twitter.com/#!/tennisontario
www.facebook. com/OntarioTennisAssociation
Circulation: 20,000 Frequency: 3 times a year
James H. Boyce, Executive Director

Pacific Golf and Alberta Golf
Previous Name: Pacific Golf Magazine
Owned By: Canada Wide Magazines & Communications Ltd.
c/o Canada Wide Media Ltd., 4180 Lougheed Hwy., 4th Fl., Burnaby, BC V5C 6A7
Tel: 604-299-7311; Fax: 604-299-9188
cwm@canadawide.com
Circulation: 25,000 Frequency: Trimestriel
Peter Legge, Publisher
Stephen Thomas, General Sales Manager

Pedal Magazine / SkiTrax Magazine
#200, 260 Spadina Ave., Toronto, ON M5T 2E4
Tel: 416-977-2100; Fax: 416-977-9200
Toll-Free: 866-977-3325
info@pedalmag.com
Circulation: 18,000 Frequency: 6 pa
Benjamin Sadavoy, Publisher & Editor

Québec Soccer
6900, rue St-Denis, 2e étage, Montréal, QC H2S 2S2
Tél: 514-278-6399;Téléc: 514-278-9737
journal@quebecsoccer.com
Tirage: 150 000 Fréquence: 11 fois par an; français
Pascal Cifarelli, Éditeur/fondateur/directeur
Pablo Ferreri, Directeur géneral

Riders West
Previous Name: Ski& Ride West
Owned By: Koocanusa Publications Inc.
#100, 100 - 7th Ave. South, Cranbrook, BC V1C 2J4
Tel: 250-426-7253; Fax: 250-426-4125
Toll-Free: 800-663-8555
info@kpimedia.com
Social Media: www.flickr.com/photos/snoriders/
twitter.com/riderswest
Circulation: 32,000 Frequency: 5 times per year
Jeff Cummings, Editor
Keith G. Powell, Publisher

SBC Skateboard Magazine
#3266, 2255B Queen St. East, Toronto, ON M4E 1G3
Toll-Free: 800-223-6197
info@sbcskateboard.com
Social Media:
twitter.com/sbcskateboard
www.facebook.com/SBCSkateboardMagazine
Circulation: 25,000 Frequency: 5 times a year
Steve Jarrett, Publisher
Ryan Stutt, Managing Editor

SCORE - Canada's Golf Magazine
Owned By: Canadian Controlled Media Communications
#101, 5397 Eglinton Ave. West, Toronto, ON M9C 5K6
Tel: 416-928-2909; Fax: 416-966-1181
Toll-Free: 800-320-6420
info@scoregolf.com
Circulation: 142,438 Frequency: 6 times a year
Kim Locke, President & Publisher
Bob Weeks, Editor

SCORE Golf Québec
Détenteur: Canadian Controlled Media Communications
#101, 5397 Eglinton Ave. West, Toronto, ON M9C 5K6
Tél: 416-928-2909;Téléc: 416-966-1181
info@scoregolf.com
Tirage: 35,000 Fréquence: 4 fois par an
Peter Robinson, Editor, robinson@scoregolf.com
Kim Locke, Publisher

Ski Canada
Previous Name: Sunsports
Owned By: Solstice Publishing Inc.
47 Soho Sq., Toronto, ON M5T 2Z2
Tel: 416-595-1252; Fax: 416-595-7255
Toll-Free: 888-666-9754
info@skicanadamag.com
Social Media:
twitter.com/skicanadamag
www.facebook.com/SkiCanadaMag
Circulation: 40,733 Frequency: 6 times a year
Iain MacMillan, Editor
Paul Green, Publisher

Ski Press/Ski Presse
1395, rue Marie-Victorin, Saint-Bruno, QC J3V 6B7
Tél: 450-653-1033
patwells@skipressmag.com
Médias sociaux:
twitter.com/skipresse_mag
www.facebook.com/pages/SkipressWorld/108500488806
Tirage: 182,000 Fréquence: 4 times a year
Jean Marc Blais, Publisher
Jules Older, Editor-in-chief, English version

SkiTrax
#200, 260 Spadina Ave., Toronto, ON M5T 2E4
Tel: 416-977-2100; Fax: 416-977-9200
Toll-Free: 866-754-8729
info@skitrax.com
Social Media:
twitter.com/skitrax
www.facebook.com/pages/SkiTrax/115966559512?sk=wall
Circulation: 30,000 Frequency: 4 times a year
Benjamin Sadavoy, Publisher

Sledworthy Magazine
13 Pippy Place, St. John's, NL A1C 1V7
Tel: 709-690-2609
info@sledworthy.com
Social Media: www.youtube.com/user/SledworthyMagazine
twitter.com/Sledworthy
www.facebook.com/pages/Sledworthy-Magazine/253014
76142394
Circulation: 30,000
Andrew Goldsworthy, Editor-in-Chief, andrew@sledworthy.com

Sno Riders West
Owned By: Koocanusa Publications Inc.
#100, 100 - 7th Ave. South, Cranbrook, BC V1C 2J4
Tel: 250-426-7253; Fax: 250-426-4125
Toll-Free: 800-663-8555
info@kpimedia.com
Social Media: www.flickr.com/photos/snoriders
twitter.com/snoriders
www.facebook.com/pages/SnoRiders/100894413330321
Frequency: 5 times a year; fall (41,000), winter (30,000), mid-winter (32,000), spring (32,000), summer (32,000)
Kerry Shellborn, Editor, editor@kpimedia.com
Keith G. Powell, Publisher, publisher@kpimedia.com

Snowboard Canada Magazine
SBC Media, #3266, 2255B Queen St. East, Toronto, ON M4E 1G3
Tel: 416-406-2400; Fax: 416-406-0656
Social Media:
twitter.com/snowboardcanada
www.facebook.com/SnowboardCanada
Circulation: 73,000 Frequency: 4 times a year
Steve Jarrett, Publisher

Sporting Scene
22 Maberley Cres., West Hill, ON M1C 3K8
Tel: 416-284-0304
sportingscene@sympatico.ca
Other information: Mobile: 416-272-1789
Circulation: 24,000 Frequency: 11 times a year
Peter Martens, Publisher & Editor-in-chief

Squash Life
c/o Squash Ontario, 3 Concorde Gate, Toronto, ON M3C 3N7
Tel: 416-426-7201; Fax: 416-426-7393
Social Media:
twitter.com/SquashOntario
www.facebook.com/SquashOntario
Circulation: 5,000 Frequency: 3 times a year
Sherry Funston, Executive Director & Managing Editor

Supertrax International
#187, 762 Upper James St., Hamilton, ON L9C 3A2
Tel: 905-286-2135; Fax: 705-286-6308
Toll-Free: 800-905-8729
info@supertraxmag.com
Other information: USA, Phone: 1-888-946-4666
Frequency: 4 pa
Supertrax International is a snowmobile magazine.

Swim News
356 Sumach St., Toronto, ON M4X 1V4
Circulation: 4,300 Frequency: 10 times a year
N.J. Thierry, Publisher

Volleyball Canada Magazine
Previous Name: True North Volleyball Magazine
#202, 5510 Canotek Rd., Gloucester, ON K1J 9J5
Tel: 613-748-5681; Fax: 613-748-5727
info@volleyball.ca
Circulation: 35,000 Frequency: 4 times a year
Greg Smith, Publisher

Wakeboard SBC Magazine
#3266, 2255B Queen St. East, Toronto, ON M4E 1G3
Tel: 416-406-2400; Fax: 416-406-0656
info@sbcmedia.com
Circulation: 36,000 Frequency: 2 times a year
Steve Jarrett, Publisher

Television, Radio, Video & Home Appliances

Audio Ideas Guide
#12, 860 Dufferin St., King City, ON L7B 1K5
Tel: 905-833-7177; Fax: 905-833-7178
mail@audio-ideas.on.ca
Frequency: Quarterly
Andrew Marshall, Editor/Publisher, andrew@audio-ideas.com

The Inner Ear
Owned By: TIEMedia
Tel: 905-294-5570
info@innerearmag.com
Social Media:
www.facebook.com/innerearmagazine
Circulation: 16,000 Frequency: 4 times a year
Ernie Fisher, Editor

Spécial téléromans
Détenteur: TV Hebdo
Trustmedia, 7, ch Bates, Outremont, QC H2V 4V7
Tél: 514-848-7000;Téléc: 514-843-7070
tvhebdo@tvapublications.com
Tirage: 46 000 Fréquence: 2 fois par an; français
Louis Lalande, Vice-President

StarWeek Magazine
c/o Toronto Star, One Yonge St., Toronto, ON M5E 1E6
Tel: 416-869-4244; Fax: 416-869-4103
canderson@thestar.ca
Circulation: 645,181 Frequency: Weekly; Sat.
Part of the Toronto Star's Saturday edition.
Gord Stimmell, Editor

Sunday Sun Television Magazine
Calgary Sun, 2615 - 12 St. NE, Calgary, AB T2E 7W9
Tel: 403-250-4220; Fax: 403-250-4258
cal-circulation@sunmedia.ca
Circulation: 63,794 Frequency: Weekly
Jose Rodriguez, Editor-in-Chief, jose.rodriguez@sunmedia.ca

Sunday Sun Television Magazine
c/o Edmonton Sun, #250, 4990 - 92 Ave., Edmonton, AB T6B 3A1
Tel: 780-468-0100
edm-citydesk@sunmedia.ca
Circulation: 95,860 Frequency: Weekly
Steve Serviss, Editor-in-Chief, steve.serviss@sunmedia.ca

Télé Horaire
c/o Le Journal de Montréal, 4545, rue Frontenac, Montréal, QC H1H 2R7
Tél: 514-521-4545;Téléc: 514-525-4416
Ligne sans frais: 800-361-9415
services@quebecormedia.com
Médias sociaux:
twitter.com/JdeMontreal
www.facebook.com/jdemontreal
Tirage: 326 440 Fréquence: Hebdomadaire; français
Lyne Robitaille, Présidente et éditrice

Télé Horaire (Québec)
c/o Le Journal de Québec, 450, ave Béchard, Québec, QC G1M 2E9
Tél: 418-683-1573;Téléc: 418-683-8886
commentaires@journaldequebec.com
Médias sociaux:
twitter.com/JdeQuebec
www.facebook.com/JdeQuebec
Tirage: 126 689 Fréquence: Hebdomadaire; français
Louise Cordeau, Éditrice et chef de la direction, louise.cordeau@journaldequebec.com

TV Guide
Owned By: Bell Media
Social Media:
twitter.com/TVGuideCanada
www.facebook.com/TVGuideCanada
Circulation: 281,955 Frequency: Weekly
Amber Dowling, Editor
Caroline Andrews, Publisher

TV Hebdo
Détenteur: TVA Publications
Tél: 514-848-7000;Téléc: 514-270-7070
tvhebdo@tvapublications.com
Médias sociaux:
twitter.com/tvhebdo
www.facebook.com/tvhebdo
Tirage: 123 670 Fréquence: Hebdomadaire
Louis Lalande, Vice-Président

TV Times, Calgary Herald
PO Box 2400 M, 215 - 16th St. SE, Calgary, AB T2P 0W8
Tel: 403-235-7323; Fax: 403-235-7379
Toll-Free: 800-372-9219
calgaryherald@reachcanada.com
Circulation: 150,000

TV Times, Edmonton
10006 - 101 St., Edmonton, AB T5J 0S1
Tel: 780-429-5100; Fax: 780-429-5500
Circulation: 150,000
Linda Hughes, Publisher
Allan Mayer, Editor-in-chief

TV Week Magazine (TVW)
Owned By: Canada Wide Magazines & Communications Ltd.
4180 Lougheed Hwy., 4th Fl., Burnaby, BC V5C 6A7
Tel: 604-299-7311; Fax: 604-299-9188
Toll-Free: 800-663-0518
cwm@canadawide.com
Social Media: pinterest.com/bcliving
twitter.com/bc_living
www.facebook.com/bcliving
Circulation: 75,000 Frequency: Weekly
Peter Legge, Publisher
Brent Furdyk, Editor, bfurdyk@canadawide.com

Travel

Above & Beyond Magazine
PO Box 683, Mahone Bay, NS B0J 2E0
Tel: 613-599-4190; Fax: 613-599-4191
Toll-Free: 877-227-2842
Circulation: 20,000 Frequency: 6 pa
Tom Koelbel, Publisher & Editor

Bear Country
1475 West Walsh St., Thunder Bay, ON P7E 4X6
Tel: 807-474-2636; Fax: 807-474-2658
pgresham@bearskinairlines.com
Circulation: 10,000 Frequency: 4 times a year
Patti Gresham, Production Manager & Editor

British Columbia Magazine
Previous Name: Beautiful British Columbia Magazine
1803 Douglas St., 3rd Fl., Victoria, BC V8T 5C3
Tel: 250-356-5860; Fax: 250-356-5896
Toll-Free: 800-663-7611
orders@bcmag.ca
Other information: Toll Free Fax: 1-800-308-4533
Circulation: 125,000 Frequency: 4 times a year
Don Foxford, Publisher
Anita Willis, Editor, editor@bcmag.ca

Dreamscapes Travel & Lifestyle Magazine
Previous Name: American Express Dreamscapes
3 Bluffwood Dr., Toronto, ON M2H 3L4
Tel: 416-497-5353; Fax: 416-497-0871
Toll-Free: 888-700-4464
dreamscapesmagazine@rogers.com
Circulation: 110,000 Frequency: 8 times a year
Sandra Kitchen, Publisher
Donna Vieira, Editor
Joe Turkel, President & Group Publisher

Espaces
#205, 911, rue Jean-Talon est, Montréal, QC H2R 1V5
Tél: 514-277-3477;Téléc: 514-277-3822
Ligne sans frais: 888-277-6718
info@espaces.qc.ca
Tirage: 50 000 Fréquence: bimestriel
Marie Eisenmann, Rédactrice en chef

Family Getaways
Owned By: Our Kids Publications Ltd.
4242 Rockwood Rd., Mississauga, ON L4W 1L8
Tel: 905-272-1843; Fax: 905-272-0474
fun@ourkids.net
Circulation: 100,000 Frequency: annual
Agatha Stawicki, Managing Editor

Geo Plein Air
Détenteur: Velo Québec Éditions
1251, rue Rachel est, Montréal, QC H2J 2J9
Tél: 514-521-8356 Ligne sans frais: 800-567-8356
Médias sociaux:
twitter.com/geopleinair_
www.facebook.com/pages/Geo-Plein-Air/3518 22425904
Tirage: 25 358 Fréquence: 7 fois par an; français
Magazine québécois de la nature et de l'aventure
Pierre Sormany, Éditeur
Nathalie Schneider, Rédactrice en chef

Greater Halifax Visitor Guide
Owned By: Metro Guide Publishing
1300 Hollis St., Halifax, NS B3J 1T6
Tel: 902-420-9943; Fax: 902-429-9058
publishers@metroguide.ca
Circulation: 240,000 Frequency: Annually
Sheila Blair, Publisher

Horizon Travel Magazine
#210, 2150 Winston Park Dr., Oakville, ON L6H 5V1
Tel: 905-257-1020
horizon@horizontravelmag.com
Social Media:
twitter.com/horizontravmag
www.facebook.com/pages/Horizon-Travel-Magazine/1718715761
Horizon Travel Magazine is a travel & lifestyle magazine.

Key to Kingston
Owned By: Sun Media Corporation
Kingston Publications, 18 St. Remy Place, Kingston, ON K7K 6C4
Tel: 613-549-8442; Fax: 613-389-7507
Circulation: 22,500 Frequency: 8 pa
Mary Laflamme, Publisher
Liza Nelson, Publisher, 613-549-8442 ext 132
Jane Deacon, Editor, 613-549-8442 ext 108

The Laurentians Tourist Guide / Les Laurentides Guide Touristique
#14, 142, rue de la Chapelle, Mirabel, QC J7J 2C8
Tel: 450-436-8532
info-tourisme@laurentides.com
Social Media:
www.facebook.com/pages/Tourisme-Laurentides/139848066744
Circulation: 73,000, English edition; 202,000, French edition
Frequency: Annually; English & French editions
Diane Leblond, General Manager

99 North Magazine
Owned By: Canada Wide Magazines & Communications Ltd.
4180 Lougheed Hwy., Burnaby, BC V5C 6A7
Circulation: 100,000 Frequency: 2 times a year
Samantha Legge, General Manager

Outpost: Canada's Travel Magazine
#207, 250 Augusta Ave., Toronto, ON M5T 2L7
Tel: 416-972-6635
info@outpostmagazine.com
Social Media:
twitter.com/OutpostMagazine
www.facebook.com/Outpostmagazine
Circulation: 28,000 Frequency: Bi-monthly
Matthew Robinson, Publisher, matt@outpostmagazine.com
Deborah Sanborn, Editor, deborah@outpostmagazine.com

Rocky Mountain Visitor's Magazine
Previous Name: Kootenay Visitor's Magazine
Owned By: Koocanusa Publications Inc.
#100, 100 - 7th Ave. South, Cranbrook, BC V1C 2J4
Tel: 250-426-7253; Fax: 250-426-4125
Toll-Free: 800-663-8555
publisher@kpimedia.com
Circulation: 40,000 May; 30,000 Nov. Frequency: Semi-annually
Jeff Cummings, Editor
Keith G. Powell, Publisher

Saskatchewan Vacation Guide
Tourism Saskatchewan, 189-1621 Albert St., Regina, SK S4P 2S5
Tel: 306-787-9685; Fax: 306-787-0715
Toll-Free: 877-237-2273
Circulation: 195,000 Frequency: annually

Touring Magazine
Owned By: Canadian Automobile Association
c/o Transcontinental S.E.N.C., #100, 25 Sheppard Ave. West, Toronto, ON M2N 6S7
Tel: 416-847-8548
info@transcontinentalcustom.com
Circulation: 608,000 Frequency: 4 times a year; English & French

The Travel Society Magazine
147 Liberty St., Toronto, ON M6K 3G3
Tel: 416-926-0111
member@thetravelsociety.com
Social Media:
twitter.com/TTravelSociety
www.facebook.com/thetravelsociety
Circulation: 7,000
Nigel D. Raincock, Publisher
Ann Wallace, Editor

Where Canadian Rockies
Previous Name: Where Rocky Mountains
Owned By: St Joseph Media
1131 Kensington Rd. NW, 2nd Fl., Calgary, AB T2N 3P4
Tel: 403-299-1881
editor@rmvpublications.com
Circulation: 240,000 summer; 145,000 winter Frequency: 2 pa; English with some Japanese
Jack Newton, Publisher

Where Vancouver/Whistler
Owned By: St Joseph Media
#510, 1755 West Broadway, Vancouver, BC V6J 4S5
Tel: 604-736-5586; Fax: 604-736-3465
sradford@where.ca
Circulation: 53,000 Frequency: Monthly
Peggie Terry, Publisher

University & Student Publications

Dal News
Dalhousie University, Halifax, NS B3H 4R2
Tel: 902-494-2541; Fax: 902-494-3561
dalhousie.review@dal.ca
Social Media:
www.facebook.com/DalhousieUniversity
Frequency: Monthly

Women's & Feminist

L'Actuelle
1043, rue Tiffin, Longueuil, QC J4P 3G7
Tél: 450-442-3983;Téléc: 450-442-4363
cerfer@videotron.ca
Médias sociaux:
www.facebook.com/283417910957
Tirage: 50 000 Fréquence: 5 fois par an; français
Publication officielle des Cercles de Fermières du Québec (CFQ)

Canadian Guider
c/o Girl Guides of Canada, 50 Merton St., Toronto, ON M4S 1A3
Tel: 416-487-5281; Fax: 416-487-5570
cdnguider@girlguides.ca
Circulation: 30,891 Frequency: 3 times a year
Deborah Del Duca

Canadian Woman Studies / Les Cahiers de la Femme
210 Founders College, York University, 4700 Keele St., Toronto, ON M3J 1P3
Tel: 416-736-5356; Fax: 416-736-5765
cwscf@yorku.ca
Circulation: 5,000 Frequency: 4 times a year
Luciana Ricciutelli, Editor

Chatelaine
Owned By: Rogers Publishing Ltd.
1 Mount Pleasant Rd., 8th Fl., Toronto, ON M4Y 2Y5
Tel: 416-764-1888; Fax: 416-764-2891
Toll-Free: 800-268-6812
lise.ravary@chatelaine.com
Social Media: pinterest.com/chatelainemag
twitter.com/chatelainemag
www.facebook.com/ChatelaineMagazine
Circulation: 536,447 Frequency: Monthly
Jane Francisco, Editor-in-Chief
Laurie Jennings, Executive Editor

Châtelaine
Détenteur: Rogers Publishing Ltd.
1200, av McGill College, Montréal, QC H3B 4G7
Tél: 514-845-5141;Téléc: 514-843-2185
abonner@chatelaine.com
Médias sociaux:
twitter.com/chatelaine_qc
www.facebook.com/ChatelaineQc
Tirage: 160,070 Fréquence: Mensuel; français

Clin d'Oeil (FA)
Détenteur: Publicor
7, Chemin Bates, Outremont, QC H2V 4V7
Tél: 514-270-1100;Téléc: 514-270-9618
Médias sociaux:
twitter.com/Mag_clindoeil
Tirage: 56 030 Fréquence: Mensuel; français

Edmonton Woman
Owned By: Alberta Business Research Ltd
Alberta Business Research Ltd., #112, 25 Chisholm Ave., St Albert, AB T8N 1N3
Tel: 780-429-1610; Fax: 780-421-7677
contact@edmontonwoman.com
Circulation: 25,000 Frequency: 6 times a year
Fisal Asiff, Publisher
Colin Smith, Editor-in-chief

elevate magazine
Owned By: Salon Communications Inc.
#1902, 365 Bloor St. East, Toronto, ON M4W 3L4
Tel: 416-869-3131; Fax: 416-869-3008
letters@elevatemagazine.com
Social Media:
www.facebook.com/ElevateMagazine
Daniela Glacco, Publisher, daniela@elevatemagazine.com
Marissa Ponikowski, Editor-in-chief, marissa@elevatemagazine.com

Elle Canada
Owned By: Transcontinental Media Inc.
#100, 25 Sheppard Ave. West, Toronto, ON M2N 6S7
Tel: 416-733-7600
Social Media: www.youtube.com/user/ellecanadacom
twitter.com/ellecanada
www.facebook .com/ellecanada
Jacqueline Howe, Publisher
Noreen Flanagan, Sr. Editor

Elle Québec
Détenteur: Transcontinental Media Inc.
Publications Transcontinental-Hachette, 1100 René-Lévesque ouest, 24e étage, Montréal, QC H3B 4X9
Tél: 514-499-0491;Téléc: 514-848-9779
Médias sociaux: www.youtube.com/user/ElleQc
twitter.com/ellequebec
www.facebook.com/ellequebec
Tirage: 88 398 Fréquence: Mensuel; français
Francine Tremblay, Éditrice
Sylvie Poirier, Rédactrice-en-chef

Femme Plus
Anciennement: L'Essentiel
Détenteur: TVA Publications
Tél: 514-270-1100;Téléc: 514-270-9618
femme@tva-publications.com
Tirage: 466924 Fréquence: Mensuel; français
Sandra Cliche, Éditrice

Magazine les Ailes de la mode
#677, rue Ste-Catherine Ouest, Montréal, QC H3A 3S8
Tél: 514-282-4537
Tirage: 29 751 Fréquence: 6 fois par an
Claude Fortin, Éditeur
Julie Brisson, Rédactrice-en-chef
Camille Roberge, Rédactrice

More
Owned By: Transcontinental Media Inc.
#100, 25 Sheppard Ave. West, Toronto, ON M2N 6S7
Tel: 416-733-7600
Social Media: www.youtube.com/user/MoreMagazineCanada
twitter.com/more_ca
www.facebo ok.com/MoreMagazineCanada

Orah Magazine
Canadian Hadassah-WIZO, #900, 1310, av Greene, Montréal, QC H3Z 2B8
Tel: 514-937-9431; Fax: 514-933-6483
info@chw.ca
Social Media: www.youtube.com/user/CHWOrganization
twitter.com/CHWdotCA
www.faceb ook.com/CanadianHadassahWIZO
Circulation: 14,000 Frequency: 2 times a year
Marla Dan, Executive Editor & Nat'l President
Alina Ianson, Editor-in-Chief & Nat'l Exec. Dir.

Room
Previous Name: Room of One's Own
PO Box 46160 D, Vancouver, BC V6J 5G5
contactus@roommagazine.com
Social Media:
twitter.com/RoomMagazine
Circulation: 1,100 Frequency: 4 times a year

Women of Influence
#550, 36 Lombard St., Toronto, ON M5C 2X3
Tel: 416-923-1688; Fax: 416-923-2862
Toll-Free: 800-354-3303
info@womenofinfluenceinc.ca
Social Media:
www.linkedin.com/company/women-of-influence-inc.
twitter.com/womenofinfl nce
www.facebook.com/womenofinfluenceinc
Circulation: 20,000 Frequency: Quarterly
Carolyn Lawrence, President/CEO, clawrence@womenofinfluenceinc.ca
Carolyn Patricia Grisols, Managing Editor, cpgrisold@womenofinfluenceinc.ca

Youth

The Canadian Leader
Canyouth Publications, #100, 1345 Baseline Rd., Ottawa, ON K2C 0A7
Tel: 613-224-5131; Fax: 613-224-3571
leader@scouts.ca
Circulation: 37,000 Frequency: 10 times a year
Ross Francis, Executive Editor

Cool! Le magazine qui bouge
Détenteur: TVA Publications
1010, rue de Sérigny, 4e étage, Longueuil, QC J4K 5G7
Tél: 514-370-5823;Téléc: 514-270-7079
cool@tva-publications.com
Tirage: 62 000 Fréquence: 12 fois par an
Marie-Claude Bonneau, Director

Cream World
Toronto, ON
info@creamworld.ca
Social Media:
twitter.com/creamworldmag
Marcus S., Publisher/Founder

Faze Magazine
#2400, 4936 Yonge St., Toronto, ON M2N 6S3
Tel: 416-222-3060
info@faze.ca
Social Media:
twitter.com/FazeMagazine
www.facebook.com/FazeMagazine
Frequency: 5 times a year
Lorraine Zander, Editor-in-Chief

girlworks
Owned By: girls media inc.
PO Box 91559, 47 Main St. South, Georgetown, ON L7G 5M9
Social Media:
www.facebook.com/pages/girlworks-media-inc/151751732682
Frequency: Bi-monthly
Janet Kim, Contact, jkim@girlworks.ca

Vervegirl
Owned By: Youth Culture Inc.
85 Kildonna Dr., Toronto, ON M1N 3B9
Tel: 416-595-1313; Fax: 888-707-6298
Circulation: 178,851 Frequency: 8 times a year
Kaaren Whitney-Vernon, Group Publisher & Sales
Joanna Whitney, Editor

Youthink
4180 Lougheed Hwy., 4th Fl., Burnaby, BC V5C 6A7
Tel: 604-299-7311; Fax: 604-299-9188
cwm@canadawide.com
Social Media:
twitter.com/youthinkmag
www.facebook.com/youthinkmag?ref=ts
Circulation: 69,987 Frequency: Monthly
Janine Verreault, Editor

Ethnic

Aboriginal

Alberta Native News
#207, 11460 Jasper Ave., Edmonton, AB T5K 0M1
Tel: 780-421-7966; Fax: 780-424-3951
editor@albertanativenews.com
Circulation: 14,000 Frequency: 12 times a year
David Moser, Publisher

Alberta Sweetgrass
The Aboriginal Multi-Media Society, 13245 - 146 St., Edmonton, AB T5L 4S8
Tel: 780-455-2700; Fax: 780-455-7639
market@ammsa.com
Social Media:
twitter.com/windspeakernews
www.facebook.com/windspeakernews
Circulation: 7,000 Frequency: Monthly
Bert Crowfoot, Publisher
Shari Narine, Editor

First Nations Free Press
363 Sioux Rd., Sherwood Park, AB T8A 4W7
Tel: 780-449-1803; Fax: 780-449-1807
Frequency: Monthly
Flo Baker, Publisher

The First Perspective & The Drum
Taiga Communications Inc., PO Box 299, Peguis, MB R0C 3J0
Tel: 204-645-4214
staff@rezxchange.net
Circulation: 10,000 Frequency: Monthly
James Wastasecoot, Publisher
Len Kruzenga, Editor

Ha-Shilth-Sa
PO Box 1383, Port Alberni, BC V9Y 7M2
Tel: 250-724-5757; Fax: 250-723-0463
Circulation: 3,100
Denise Ambrose, Regional Reporter
Annie Watts, Office Manager

Inuvik Drum
PO Box 2820, Yellowknife, NT X1A 2R1
Tel: 867-873-4031; Fax: 867-873-8507
nnsl@nnsl.com
Social Media:
twitter.com/nnslonline
www.facebook.com/pages/NNSLcom/118071834921181
Circulation: 1,634
Jack Sigvaldson, Publisher
Bruce Valpy, Managing Editor, editorial@nnsl.com
Petra Ehrke, National/Territorial Manager, advertising@nnsl.com

Ktuqcqakyam Newsletter
7468 Mission Rd., Cranbrook, BC V1C 7E5
Tel: 250-489-2464
Circulation: 700 Frequency: Bi-monthly
Donna Kraus-Hagerman, Contact

Mi'kmaq-Maliseet Nation News
PO Box 1590, 72 Church Rd., Truro, NS B2N 5V3
Tel: 902-895-2039; Fax: 902-893-3030
Toll-Free: 877-895-2038
info@mmnn.ca
Frequency: Monthly
Don Julien, Publisher
Art Stevens, Managing Editor

The Nation: The News & Cultural Magazine of the James Bay Cree
c/o Beesum Communications Inc., #403, 4529 Clark, Montréal, QC H2T 2T3
Tel: 514-272-3077; Fax: 514-278-9914
beesum@beesum-communications.com
Circulation: 6,730 Frequency: 26 times a year; English & James Bay Cree
Aaron MacDevitt, Sales Representative

Native Journal
PO Box 57096, 2020 Sherwood Dr., Sherwood Park, AB T8A 5L7
Tel: 780-448-9693; Fax: 780-448-9694
Toll-Free: 866-526-8688
elaine@nativejournal.ca
Circulation: 70,000 Frequency: Monthly
Elaine Shuflita, Publisher
Lisa Doucet, Publisher, njeditor@shaw.ca

Native Youth News
363 Sioux Rd., Sherwood Park, AB T8A 4W7
Tel: 780-449-1803; Fax: 780-449-1807
Toll-Free: 800-830-1803
fnfpltd@teleusplanet.net
Frequency: Monthly
Flo Baker, Publisher

Natotawin
PO Box 10880, Opaskwayak, MB R0B 2J0
Tel: 204-627-7066
gabriel.constant@opaskwayak.ca
Circulation: 1,000 Frequency: Weekly
Gabriel Constant, Editor

New Breed Magazine
c/o Gabriel Dumont Institute, #2, 604 - 22nd St. West, Saskatoon, SK S7M 5W1
Tel: 306-657-5716; Fax: 306-244-0252
Circulation: 1,000 Frequency: 3 times a year
Darren Préfontaine
David Morin
Karon Shmon

Nunavut News/North
c/o Northern News Services Ltd., PO Box 2820, Yellowknife, NT X1A 2R1
Tel: 867-873-4031; Fax: 867-873-8507
nnsl@nnsl.com
Frequency: Weekly
J.W. (Sig) Sigvaldason, Publisher
Mike Scott, General Manager

Raven's Eye
13245 - 146 St., Edmonton, AB T5L 4S8
Tel: 780-455-2700; Fax: 780-455-7639
Circulation: 6,500 Frequency: Monthly
Bert Crowfoot, Publisher

Saskatchewan Sage
13245 - 146 St., Edmonton, AB T5L 4S8
Tel: 780-455-2700; Fax: 780-455-7639
Toll-Free: 800-661-5469
market@ammsa.com
Circulation: 6,000 Frequency: Monthly
Bert Crowfoot, Publisher

Cheryl Petten, Editor

Secwepemc News, The Voice of the Shuswap Nation
Secwepemc Cultural Education Society, 274A, Halston Connector Rd., Kamloops, BC V2H 1J9
Tel: 778-471-5789; Fax: 778-471-5792
Circulation: 5,000 Frequency: Monthly
Kathy Manuel, Managing Editor

Turtle Island News
PO Box 329, 2208 Chiefswood Rd., Hagersville, ON N0A 1M0
Tel: 519-445-0868; Fax: 519-445-0865
news@theturtleislandnews.com
Social Media:
twitter.com/TurtleIslandnew
www.facebook.com/TurtleIslandNews?ref=nf
Circulation: 20,000 Frequency: Weekly
National native newspaper.
Lynda Powless, Publisher & Editor, lynda@theturtleislandnews.com

Western Native News Ltd.
#330, 10036 Jasper Ave, Edmonton, AB T5J 1J2
Tel: 780-421-7966; Fax: 780-424-3951
nativenews@telus.net
Frequency: Monthly
David Moser, Publisher
Deborah Shatz, Editor

Windspeaker
The Aboriginal Multi-Media Society (AMMSA), 13245 - 146 St., Edmonton, AB T5L 4S8
Tel: 780-455-2700; Fax: 780-455-7639
market@ammsa.com
Social Media:
twitter.com/windspeakernews
www.facebook.com/windspeakernews
Circulation: 25,500 Frequency: Monthly
Aboriginal news source.
Bert Crowfoot, CEO & Publisher
Debora Steel, Editor

African-Canadian & Caribbean Canadian

Caribbean Camera
#212, 55 Nugget Ave., Toronto, ON M1S 3L1
Tel: 416-412-2905; Fax: 416-412-2134
Circulation: 35,000 Frequency: Weekly; 2 editions: Montreal & Toronto
Raynier Maharaj, Editor

Hawarya
Owned By: African Network Inc.
PO Box 66036, 1116 Wilson Ave., Toronto, ON M3M 1G7
Tel: 416-459-5964; Fax: 905-799-2193
hawarya.publications@sympatico.ca
Frequency: Monthly; Ethiopian
African news, especially Ethiopian.
Muluken Muchie, Editor, editor@hawarya.net

The Jamaican Weekly Gleaner
The Gleaner Company (Canada) Inc, 1390 Eglinton Ave. West, Toronto, ON M6C 2E4
Tel: 416-784-3002; Fax: 416-784-5719
Toll-Free: 800-233-9540
gleanercan@gleanerna.com
Social Media:
twitter.com/jamaicagleaner
www.facebook.com/TheJamaicaGleaner
Circulation: 110,000 Frequency: Weekly; also The Jamaican Weekly Star, The Black Pages Directory
Maxwell Wynter, General Manager
Yulanda Gordon, Editor

Pride News Magazine
52 Morecambe Gate, Toronto, ON M1W 2N6
Tel: 416-492-2476; Fax: 416-492-2477
pridenews@bellnet.ca
Circulation: 25,000
Michael Van Cooten, Publisher & Editor

Word: Toronto's Urban Culture Magazine
#123, 4-2880 Queen St. East, Brampton, ON L6S 6H4
Tel: 905-799-1630; Fax: 905-799-2788
info@wordmag.com
Circulation: 160,000 Frequency: 9 times a year
Angela Baldassarre, Editor
Phillip Vassell, Publisher

Arabic

Al-Mughtarib Weekly Newspaper
PO Box 48113, 60 Dundas St. East, Mississauga, ON L5A 4G8
Fax: 905-949-0117
Toll-Free: 866-771-9358
Frequency: Weekly
Saleh Rafai, Editor-in-chief

Al-Mustakbal
#200, 1305, Mazurette, Montréal, QC H4N 1G8
Tel: 514-334-0909; Fax: 514-332-5419
info@almlustakbal.com
Circulation: 12,000
Serves the Arab community.
Joseph Nakhlé, Editeur
Ibrahim Ghorqyebo, Rédacteur-en-chef

Arab Guide
368 Queen St. East, 2nd Fl., Toronto, ON M5A 1T1
Tel: 416-362-0304; Fax: 416-861-0238
Circulation: 5,000
E. Elgamal, Editor
F. Ahmed, Publisher

Arab News International
602 Millwood Rd., Toronto, ON M5A 1K8
Tel: 416-362-0307; Fax: 416-861-0238
info@arabnews.ca
Frequency: Bi-weekly
Salah Allam, Publisher
Eynass El Masri, Managing Editor

Arabbusiness International
368 Queen St. East, 2nd Fl., Toronto, ON M5A 1T1
Tel: 416-362-0304; Fax: 416-861-0238
allam@octoline.com
Circulation: 6,000
S. Allam, Publisher
N. Soliman, Editor & Manager, Advertising

ARC Arabic Journal
368 Queen St. East, Toronto, ON M5A 1T1
Tel: 416-362-0304; Fax: 416-861-0238
Circulation: 5,000
Emad Nafeh, Editor

Canadian Asian News
852 Preston Manor Dr., Mississauga, ON L5V 2L6
Tel: 905-502-5585; Fax: 905-502-5585
asiannews@rogers.com
Circulation: 150,000 Frequency: Bi-weekly; 32 pa
Dilnoor Panjwani

El-Mahroussa Magazine
Egyptian Canadian Friendship Association Inc., 879, av Saint-Charles, Chomedey, Laval, QC H7V 3T5
Tél: 450-687-0273;Téléc: 450-505-1908
Tirage: 12,000 Fréquence: 12 issues a year; Arabic & French
Nancy Youssef, Chief of Staff

El-Masri Newspaper
879, av St-Charles, Chomedey, Laval, QC H7V 3T5
Tél: 450-687-0273;Téléc: 450-505-1908
info@el-masrionline.com
Tirage: 12,000 Fréquence: Bi-weekly; Arabic & French
Adel Iskander, General Director

The Iran Star
#205, 72 Steeles Ave. West, Thornhill, ON L4J 1A1
Tel: 905-763-9770; Fax: 905-763-9771
iranstar@iranstar.com
Circulation: 12,500
Bijan Binesh, Editor-in-chief
Shahram Binesh, Editor & Coordinator

Voice of Egypt in Canada
1274, Dupont, Laval, QC H7Y 1T5
Tel: 514-288-0188; Fax: 514-288-1944
georgesaad@videotron.ca
Frequency: 4 times a year
George Saad, Editor-in-chief

Armenian

Abaka
Tekeyan Armenian Cultural Association of Montréal, 825, rue Manoogian, Saint-Laurent, QC H4N 1Z5
Tel: 514-747-6680; Fax: 514-747-6162
centretekeyan@bellnet.ca
Social Media:
www.facebook.com/303091173093256

Circulation: 1,000 Frequency: Weekly; Tabloid; Armenian, French & English
Arsène Mamourian, Editor

Horizon
3401, rue Olivar-Asselin, Montréal, QC H4J 1L5
Tel: 514-332-3757; Fax: 514-332-4870
Circulation: 2,000
Vahakn Karakashian, Editor

Lradou Newsletter
3401, rue Olivar-Asselin, Montréal, QC H4J 1L5
Tel: 514-333-1616
Frequency: Annually

Pourastan
Parish Council of St. Gregory, 615, av Stuart, Outremont, QC H2V 3H2
Tel: 514-279-3066; Fax: 514-279-8008
sourpkrikor@qc.aibn.com
Circulation: 700 Frequency: irregulier
Father Boyajan

Bulgarian

Bulgarian Horizons
5312 Dundas St. West, Toronto, ON M9B 1B3
Tel: 416-962-7100; Fax: 416-962-7101
Circulation: 2,000
Maxim Bozhilov, Editor

Celtic

Celtic Life International
PO Box 8805 A, Halifax, NS B3K 5M4
Tel: 902-835-2358; Fax: 902-835-0080
info@CelticLife.ca
Social Media: www.youtube.com/user/celticlifeint
twitter.com/celticlife
www.facebook .com/pages/CelticLifeca/41377434690
Frequency: 4 times a year

Chinese

Chinese Canadian Times
2528 Bayview Ave., Toronto, ON M2L 2Y4
Tel: 416-445-7815; Fax: 416-447-9791
web@cctimes.ca
Frequency: Weekly; Chinese
Publication for Chinese Canadians.

The Chinese Journal
Previous Name: Canadian Chinese Times
10553A - 97 St., Edmonton, AB T5H 2L4
Tel: 780-424-0213; Fax: 780-428-7117
chinesejournal@telusplanet.net
Circulation: 7,000 Frequency: Weekly
Vicki Lim, Publisher
Grace Chi, Editor

The Chinese Press
Previous Name: Eastern Chinese Press Inc.
1123, rue Clark, 2e étage, Montréal, QC H2Z 1K3
Tel: 514-397-9969; Fax: 514-397-9929
Circulation: 25,000 Frequency: Weekly
Crescent Chau, Publisher/Editor

Herald Monthly
#28, 300 Steelcase Rd. West, Markham, ON L3R 2W2
Tel: 905-944-1777; Fax: 905-944-1778
toronto@cchc.org
Circulation: 76,000 Frequency: Monthly; first Wed. of the month
Herald Monthly is a free broadsheet monthly Chinese newspaper.
Helena Lee, Chief Editor

Ming Pao Daily News
1355 Huntingwood Dr., Scarborough, ON M1S 3J1
Tel: 416-321-0088; Fax: 416-321-9663
advert@mingpaotor.com
Circulation: 73,000 M; 62,000 Tu; 71,000 W-Th; 66,000 F; 97,000 Sa Frequency: Daily; Cantonese
Hong Kong news serving the Greater Toronto Area.
Jeannie Lee, Regional General Manager
Frankie Chow, Manager, Advertising

Modesty Magazine
#115, 18 Crown Steel Dr., Markham, ON L3R 9X8
Tel: 905-513-1232; Fax: 905-513-0483
modestygroup@rogers.com
Circulation: 10,000 Frequency: Chinese
Ivy Lee, Publisher & Editor

The New Star Times
#206, 150 Consumers Rd., North York, ON M2J 1P9
Tel: 416-491-8401
Frequency: Weekly; Fridays; Mandarin
Serves Mandarin-speaking immigrants in Toronto.

Popular Lifestyle & Entertainment Magazine (PLEM)
3248 Cambie St., Vancouver, BC V5Z 2W4
Tel: 604-872-1285; Fax: 604-872-0677
info@plem.com
Social Media:
www.facebook.com/iPLEM
Circulation: 75,953 Frequency: Monthly; Chinese
Patrick Wong, President & Editor-in-chief
Amanda Pi, Managing Editor
Lorna Chan, Account Executive

Les Presses Chinoises
1123, rue Clark, Montréal, QC H2Z 1K3
Tél: 514-397-9969;Téléc: 514-397-9929
Tirage: 25 000 Fréquence: Weekly
Amy Tsang

Rice Paper
PO Box 74174 Hillcrest, Vancouver, BC V5V 5C8
Tel: 604-872-3464
info@ricepapermagazine.ca
Social Media:
twitter.com/ricepapermag
www.facebook.com/ricepaper
Circulation: 3,000 Frequency: 4 times a year
Ray Hsu, Editor-in-chief

Sing Tao Daily
417 Dundas St. West, Toronto, ON M5T 1G6
Tel: 416-596-8140; Fax: 416-599-6688
singtaoadmin@singtao.ca
Frequency: Daily; Chinese
Chinese daily newspaper.
Robert Lang, Chief Editor

World Journal (Toronto)
#9, 7755 Warden Ave., Markham, ON L3R 0N3
Tel: 416-778-0888; Fax: 416-778-1037
webmaster@worldjournal.com
Circulation: 30,000 Frequency: Daily; Chinese
Paul Chang, Editor-in-chief
David Ting, President

World Journal (Vancouver)
2288 Clark Dr., Vancouver, BC V5N 3G8
Tel: 604-876-1338
bcwebmaster@worldjournal.com
Frequency: Daily; Chinese
Kuo-Liang Swei, Editor
Richard Lin, President

Dutch

De Nederlandse Courant
1945 Four Seasons Dr., Burlington, ON L7P 2Y3
Tel: 905-333-3615
Circulation: 2,700 Frequency: Bi-weekly; 25 pa; Dutch & English
Theo Luykenaar, Publisher, publisher@denederlandsecourant.com
Bas Opdenkelder, Editor, editor@denederlandsecourant.com

Dutch
Owned By: Mokeham Publishing Inc.
PO Box 20203, 457 Ellis St., Penticton, BC V2A 8M1
Tel: 250-492-3002
info@dutchthemag.com
Social Media:
twitter.com/dutchthemag
www.facebook.com/dutchthemag
A magazine in English about The Netherlands & the Dutch.
Tom , Editor, editor@dutchthemag.com

Estonian

Estonian World Review
Previous Name: Eesti Eleo
3 Madison Ave., Toronto, ON M5R 2S2
Tel: 416-733-4550; Fax: 416-733-0944
ewr@eesti.ca
Circulation: 2,300 Frequency: Weekly; Estonian
Elle Puusaag, Editor
Juri Laansoo, General Manager

Filipino

Filipiniana News
1531 Queen St. West, Toronto, ON M6R 1A5
Tel: 416-534-7836; Fax: 416-535-9491
filipiniananews@rogers.com
Circulation: 10,000 Frequency: Monthly

Filipino Journal
46 Pincarrow Rd., Winnipeg, MB R3Y 1E3
Tel: 204-489-8894; Fax: 204-489-1575
info@filipinojournal.com
Social Media: www.flickr.com/photos/Filipino_Journal
www.facebook.com/FilipinoJournalF ans
Circulation: 4,500 Frequency: 24 pa

The North American Filipino Star
5320-A, rue Queen Mary, Penthouse, Montréal, QC H3X 1T7
Tel: 514-485-7861
market@filipinostar.org
Circulation: 15,000 Frequency: Monthly
Zenaida Ferry-Kharroubi, Publisher & Chief Editor

The Philippine Reporter
PO Box 44529, 2682 Eglinton Ave. East, Scarborough, ON M1K 5K2
Tel: 416-461-8694; Fax: 416-461-7399
philreporter@gmail.com
Circulation: 10,000 Frequency: Bi-monthly; 24 pa
Serves the Filipino-Canadian community.
Hermie Garcia, Editor

Finnish

Kanadan Sanomat
Owned By: Vapaa Sana Press Ltd.
#308, 191 Eglinton Ave. East, Toronto, ON M4P 1K1
Toll-Free: 800-618-1584
markus@vapaasana.com
Social Media:
twitter.com/finnishcdnCom
Circulation: 2,500 Frequency: Weekly

German

Albertaner
3635 - 28th St., Edmonton, AB T6T 1N4
Tel: 780-465-7526; Fax: 780-465-3140
ajoop@planet.eon.net
Circulation: 3,500
Arnim Joop, Publisher & Editor

Der Bote
Mennonite Church Canada, 600 Shaftesbury Blvd., Winnipeg, MB R3P 0M4
Tel: 204-888-6781; Fax: 204-831-5675
Toll-Free: 866-888-6785
Circulation: 3,300 Frequency: Bi-weekly
Ingrid Jamzen, Editor

Deutsche Zeitung
Previous Name: Deutsche Presse B.C.
85 Inglis St., Ayr, ON N0B 1E0
Tel: 519-632-7700; Fax: 519-632-8700
Toll-Free: 888-749-0606
deutschezt@golden.net
Circulation: 7,500 Frequency: Weekly; German
Erhard Matthaes, Editor

Die Mennonitische Post
383 Main St., Steinbach, MB R5G 1Z4
Tel: 204-326-6790
mennpost@mts.net
Social Media:
www.facebook.com/pages/Die-Mennonitische-Post/4732462627
1
Circulation: 5,000 Frequency: 23 pa

Echo Germanica
118 Tyrrel Ave., Toronto, ON M6G 2G5
Tel: 416-652-1332; Fax: 416-658-6909
info@echoworld.com
Circulation: 16,000
Sybille Forster-Rentmeister, Publisher/Editor-in-chief

German Canadian Business & Trade Directory
PO Box 106, 2255B Queen St. East, Toronto, ON M4E 1G3
Tel: 416-465-9957; Fax: 416-465-8169
Circulation: 5,000
Eva Wazda, Publisher

Greek

Greek Canadian Tribune / Ellinokanadiko Vima
7835, av Wiseman, Montréal, QC H3N 2N8
Tel: 514-272-6873; Fax: 514-272-3157
info@bhma.net
Circulation: 13,000 Frequency: Weekly; Greek & English
Christos Manikis, Publisher & Editor

Greek Press
6 Chester Ave., Toronto, ON M4K 2Z9
Tel: 416-465-3243; Fax: 416-604-2480
info@greekpress.ca
Circulation: 6,000 Frequency: Bi-weekly
Constantine Kranias, Publisher/Editor

Hellenic Hamilton News
#2, 8 Morris Ave., Hamilton, ON L8L 1X7
Tel: 905-549-9208; Fax: 905-549-7935
Circulation: 5,300 Frequency: Monthly; Greek
Panos Andronidis, Publisher & Editor

Patrides, A North American Review
PO Box 266 O, 70 Wynford Dr., Toronto, ON M3C 2S2
Tel: 416-921-4229; Fax: 416-921-0723
Circulation: 160,000 Frequency: Bi-weekly
Thomas S. Saras, Editor-in-Chief
Kathy Saras, Executive Managing Editor

Hungarian

Kanadai-amerikai Magyarság / Canadian American Hungarians
#103, 747 St Clair Ave. West, Toronto, ON M6C 4A4
Tel: 416-656-8361; Fax: 416-651-2442
info@kanadaimagyarsag.ca
Frequency: Weekly: English, Magyar
Csaba Gaal, Editor & Manager

New Hungarian Voice
PO Box 74527 Kitsilano, Vancouver, BC V6K 4P4
nhv@newhungarianvoice.com
Frequency: Quarterly; English
Peter Czink, Editor-in-Chief

Icelandic

Logberg -Heimskringla
#100, 283 Portage Ave., Winnipeg, MB R3B 2B5
Tel: 204-284-5686; Fax: 204-284-7099
Toll-Free: 866-564-2374
linda@lh-inc.ca
Circulation: 2,000 Frequency: 24 times per year; English & Icelandic
Joan Eyolfson Cadham, Editor, joan@lh-inc.ca

Italian

Corriere Canadese
c/o Multimedia Nova Corporation, 101 Wingold Ave., Toronto, ON M6B 1P8
Tel: 416-785-4300; Fax: 416-785-7350
Social Media:
twitter.com/CorriereCom
www.facebook.com/CorriereCanadese
Frequency: Daily
Corriere Canadese is an Italian language publication.
Paola Bernardini, Managing Editor
Lori Abittan, General Manager/COO
Elena Caprile, Editor-in-chief

Corriere Canadese / Tandem
Owned By: Multimedia Nova Corporation
101 Wingold Ave., Toronto, ON M6B 1P8
Tel: 416-785-4300; Fax: 416-488-3671
Toll-Free: 877-503-5077
Frequency: Weekly
The English language publication features Italian news from Canada & Italy. Corriere Canadese / Tandem is the weekend edition of Corriere Canadese.
Daniel Iannuzzi, Founder
Paola Bernardini, Editor-in-Chief
Francesco Veronesi, Managing Editor
Nicola Sparano, Sport Editor

Corriere Italiano
Owned By: Transcontinental Media Inc.
1500, boul Jules-Poitras, Montréal, QC H4N 1X7
Tel: 514-855-1292; Fax: 514-855-1855
corriereitaliano@transcontinental.ca
Social Media:
twitter.com/CorriereItalian
Circulation: 20 500 Frequency: Weekly
Fabrizio Intravaia, Editor, fabrizio.intravaia@transcontinental.ca
Matilde Salvatore, Editor, matilde.salvatore@transcontinental.ca

Il Cittadino Canadese
#710, 6020, rue Jean Talon est, Montréal, QC H1S 3B1
Tel: 514-253-2332; Fax: 514-253-6574
journal@cittadinocanadese.com
Circulation: 15,000 Frequency: Weekly
Antonina Mormina, Publisher
Vittorio Giordano, Editor

Il Rincontro / La Recontre
6675, av Wilderton, Montréal, QC H3S 2L8
Tel: 514-739-4213; Fax: 514-344-8238
Social Media:
www.facebook.com/198534390236066
Circulation: 11,500 Frequency: Monthly; Italian
Tony Vellone, Editor, tony.vellone@videotron.ca

Lo Specchio/Vaughan
#101, 166 Woodbridge Ave., Woodbridge, ON L4L 2S7
Tel: 905-856-2823; Fax: 905-856-2825
editorial@lospecchio.com
Circulation: 28,000 Frequency: Weekly; Fridays
Sergio Tagliavini, Editor

L'Ora Di Ottawa
203 Louisa St., Ottawa, ON K1R 6Y9
Tel: 613-232-5689; Fax: 613-563-2573
info@loradiottawa.ca
Circulation: 2,115 Frequency: Weekly
Paolo Siraco, Managing Editor

Japanese

Nikkei Voice
6 Garamond Ct., Toronto, ON M3C 1Z5
Tel: 416-386-0287; Fax: 416-386-0136
nikkeivoice.editors@gmail.com
Frequency: Monthly
Frank Moritsugu, Publisher

Korean

Korea Central Daily
655 Bloor St. West, Toronto, ON M6G 1L1
Tel: 416-533-5533; Fax: 416-533-5500
Hyo Kim, Publisher
James Lim, Editor-in-Chief

The Korea Times Daily
287 Bridgeland Ave., Toronto, ON M6A 1Z6
Tel: 416-787-1111; Fax: 416-781-7777
Social Media:
twitter.com/ktimesca
www.facebook.com/ktimesca
Circulation: 17,000 Frequency: 6 pa; Korean
Woon Y. Kim, Editor-in-chief
Lawrence M. Kim, Publisher

Latin American

El Mundo Latino News
Godwick Dr., Mississauga, ON L5N 7X4
Tel: 905-306-7929; Fax: 905-279-2702
Circulation: 10,000 Frequency: Weekly
Ana Griselda Romero, Publisher

El Popular
2413 Dundas St. West, Toronto, ON M6P 1X3
Tel: 416-531-2495; Fax: 416-531-7187
editor@diarioelpopular.com
Frequency: Weekly
Eduardo Uruena, Publisher

Lithuanian

Teviskes Ziburiai/Lights of Homeland
2185 Stavebank Rd., Mississauga, ON L5C 1T3
Tel: 905-275-4672; Fax: 905-290-9802
tevzib@rogers.com
Circulation: 2,800 Frequency: Weekly
P. Gaida, Editor-in-chief
J. Kuras, Chair

Multicultural

Community Digest / Nouvelles Communautaires
British Columbia Edition, #216, 1755 Robson St., Vancouver, BC V6G 3B7
Tel: 604-875-8313
mail@communitydigest.ca; news@communitydigest.ca
Other information: Advertising: adsales@communitydigest.ca
Frequency: Weekly (in three editions - British Columbia, Alberta, & Ontario)
The multicultural newsmagazine is available in English & French. It promotes bilingualism & cultural trade & harmony.
N. Ebrahim, Publisher
Steve Bowell, Managing Editor
G. Jiwa, Manager, Business

Community Digest / Nouvelles Communautaires
Alberta Edition, #660, 3545 - 32nd Ave. NE, Calgary, AB T1Y 6M6
Tel: 403-271-8275
mail@communitydigest.ca; news@communitydigest.ca
Other information: Advertising: adsales@communitydigest.ca
Frequency: Weekly (in three editions - British Columbia, Alberta, & Ontario)
The multicultural magazine encourages cultural harmony. Issues are available in English & French.
N. Ebrahim, Publisher
A. Thobhani, Alberta Bureau Chief

Ethno-Cultural Networker
129 Browning Blvd., Winnipeg, MB R3K 0L1
Tel: 204-774-3569; Fax: 204-783-2029
Circulation: 7000 Frequency: Monthly
Vinod Moudgill, Editor

Peel Multicultural Scene
Peel Multicultural Council, 6630 Turner Valley Rd., Mississauga, ON L5N 2P1
Tel: 905-819-1144; Fax: 905-542-3950
pmcgeneral@peelmc.com
Social Media:
youtube.com/peelpmc
www.facebook.com/profile.php?id=15988712827
Circulation: 400

Persian

Shahrvand Publications Ltd.
#304, 505 Highway 7 East, Toronto, ON L3T 7T1
Tel: 905-764-7022; Fax: 905-764-5919
news@shahrvand.com
Circulation: 30,000 Frequency: Tuesday, Friday
Farsi newspaper
Hassan Zerehi, Editor-in-chief

Polish

Czas/Polish Times
207 Cathedral Ave., Winnipeg, MB R2W 0X2
Tel: 204-582-4392; Fax: 204-582-4392
czaspol@mts.net
Circulation: 651 Frequency: Weekly
Krystyna Gajda, President

Glos Polski/Polish Voice
71 Judson St., Toronto, ON M8Z 1A4
Tel: 416-201-9601
glospolski@bellnet.ca
Circulation: 6,000 Frequency: Weekly
Wieslaw Maglera, Editor-in-chief

Polish Business Directory
777C The Queensway, Toronto, ON M8Z 1N4
Tel: 416-255-9182; Fax: 416-255-9893
Toll-Free: 877-742-9455
mail@master.on.ca
Circulation: 50,000 Frequency: annually
Martin Chlapowski
Robert Wagner, rwagner@master.on.ca

Portuguese

Alem-Fronteiras
585 Queen St. South, Kitchener, ON N2G 1W9
Tel: 519-745-3233; Fax: 519-745-3395
legacytr@golden.net
Circulation: 1,000

Sol Portugues/Portuguese Sun
977 College St., Toronto, ON M6H 1A6
Tel: 416-538-1788; Fax: 416-538-7953
sol@solnet.com
Circulation: 12,000 Frequency: Weekly
Antonio Perinu, Publisher
Alice Perinu, Editor-in-chief

Voice Portuguese-Canadian Newspaper
Owned By: SOL Printing & Publishing
1278 Dundas St. West, Toronto, ON M6J 1X7
Tel: 416-534-3177; Fax: 416-588-6441
voice@voicenews.ca
Frequency: Weekly

Joaquim R. Baptista, Publisher & Editor

A Voz de Portugal
4231, boul St-Laurent, Montréal, QC H2W 1Z4
Tel: 514-284-1813; Fax: 514-284-6150
Toll-Free: 866-684-1813
jornal@avozdeportugal.com
Circulation: 10,000 Frequency: Weekly
Sylvio Martins, Editor, sylviomartins@avozdeportugal.com

Russian

Nasha Gazeta
#1073, 40-1110 Finch Ave. West, Toronto, ON M3J 3M2
Tel: 647-435-8619
nashacanada@yahoo.ca
Circulation: 10,000 Frequency: Weekly
G. Kukuy, President
T. Sergeeva, Managing Editor
I. Toutchinski, Editor-in-chief

Serbian

Bratstvo Srpsko
Owned By: Fraternity Publishing
425 Jane St., Toronto, ON M6S 3Z7
Tel: 416-769-7181
Circulation: 2,250 Frequency: Monthly
William Durovic, Editor-in-chief
Tania Nuttall, Editor

Kisobran
#368, 3495 Cambie St., Vancouver, BC V5Z 4R3
Tel: 604-731-9446
redakcija@kisobran.com
Circulation: 4,000 Frequency: monthly
Dragan Andrejevic, Publisher

Slovak, Czech

Novy Domov
Masaryk Memorial Institute Inc., 450 Scarborough Golf Club Rd., Toronto, ON M1G 1H1
Tel: 416-439-9557
novydomov@masaryktown.org
Frequency: Bi-weekly
Jan Rotbauer, Editor

Satellite 1-416
ABE, PO Box 176 E, Toronto, ON M6H 4E2
Tel: 416-530-4222; Fax: 416-530-0069
abe@zpravy.ca
Circulation: 1,600
Ales Brezina, Publisher & Editor

South Asian

Ahmadiyya Gazette Canada
10610 Jane St., Maple, ON L6A 3A2
Tel: 905-303-4000; Fax: 905-832-3220
gazette@ahmadiyya.ca
Frequency: English, French & Urdu
Hasan Muhammad Khan, Editor-in-chief, editor@ahmadiyyagazette.ca
S.H. Hadi, Urdu Editor
M. Nadeem A. Siddiq, Editor

Al-Hilal/Crescent
338 Hollyberry Trail, Toronto, ON M2H 2P6
Tel: 416-493-4374; Fax: 416-493-4374
lowaisi@rogers.com
Circulation: 4,200 Frequency: Bi-monthly
M.L. Owaisi, Publisher
Farida Abdullah, Editor

Bazm
4248, rue Hugo, Pierrefonds, QC H9H 2V7
Tel: 514-620-2041; Fax: 419-828-7613
bazm1989@yahoo.ca
Frequency: Monthly
Saira Watsy, Publisher & Chief Editor
Itaat Wasty, Sr. Editor

Desi News
17600 Yonge St., Newmarket, ON L3Y 8J1
Tel: 416-695-4357
desinews@rogers.com
Circulation: 30,000 Frequency: Monthly
G.A. Easwar, Publisher
Shagorika Easwar, Editor

Eastern News
119 Royal West Dr., Brampton, ON L6X 0V4
Tel: 905-216-2085; Fax: 905-216-2065
mkhan@theeasternnews.com
Circulation: 7,500 Frequency: 24 pa
Masood Khana
Masood Khan, Editor

India Journal
#11, 2355 Derry Rd. East, Mississauga, ON L5S 1V6
Tel: 905-405-0420; Fax: 905-405-0428
Circulation: 22,000
Harjinder Singh, Publisher

Indo Caribbean World
312 Brownridge Dr., Thornhill, ON L4J 5X1
Tel: 905-738-5005; Fax: 905-738-3927
indocaribbeanworld@gmail.com
Circulation: 30,000 Frequency: 2 times per month
Harry Ramkhelawan, Publisher & Editor

Indo-Canadian Voice
Previous Name: Indo-Canadian Awaaz
8338 - 120 St., Surrey, BC V3W 3N4
Tel: 604-502-6100; Fax: 604-501-6111
Circulation: 10,000 Frequency: weekly
Vinnie Combow, Editor
Rajesh Gupta, Publisher

Journal Apna Watan
4021, boul Notre Dame, Laval, QC H7W 1S8
Tel: 514-798-2838
apnawatan2002@yahoo.com
Circulation: 5,000 Frequency: Monthly
Arshad Randhawa, Editor

Pakeeza International
Owned By: Directories International Limited
PO Box 84021, 1235 Trafalgar Road, Oakville, ON L6H 3J0
Tel: 905-337-3030; Fax: 905-338-1364
info@pakeezainternational.com
Social Media:
twitter.com/pakeezaintl
www.facebook.com/PakeezaInternational
Circulation: 6,000 Frequency: Wednesday; Urdu
Pakeeza International and The South Asian Voice are distributed in over 200 South Asian grocery stores, convenience stores, Mosques, and shops across the GTA. This includes Burlington, Oakville, Mississauga, Milton, Vaughan, Toronto (Etobicoke, Scarborough, North York, Downtown), Markham, Ajax, Pickering, and Brampton.
Sabih Mansoor, Publisher & Editor

Sanjh Savera/Dust and Dawn
7405 Kimbel St., Mississauga, ON L4T 3M6
Tel: 905-789-7787; Fax: 905-789-7717
info@sanjhsavera.com
Circulation: 15,000
Nirmal Hansa, Publisher

The South Asian Voice
Previous Name: Indo Pak Community Voice
Owned By: Directories International Limited
1235 Trafalgar Rd., Oakville, ON L6H 3J0
Tel: 905-337-3030; Fax: 905-338-1364
southasianvoice@mansoor.com
Circulation: 6,000 Frequency: Wednesday; English
Sabih Mansoor, Publisher

Thamilar Thakaval
PO Box 3 F, Toronto, ON M4Y 2L4
Tel: 416-920-9250; Fax: 416-921-6576
Circulation: 5,000 Frequency: Monthly
Thiru S. Thiuchelvam, Editor-in-chief

The Times of Sri Lanka
58 Sundial Cres., Toronto, ON M4A 2J8
Tel: 416-445-5390; Fax: 647-342-2967
timeslanka@rogers.com
Social Media:
www.facebook.com/timeslanka.tsl?ref=tn_tnmn
Circulation: 20,000 Frequency: TradeWinds e-Magazine is published monthly
Upali Obeyesekere, Managing Editor, 416-418-2207, upaliobey@rogers.com

The Weekly Voice
#206, 2985 Drew Rd., Mississauga, ON L4T 0A4
Tel: 907-958-2821; Fax: 905-795-9801
info@weeklyvoice.com
Circulation: 50,000
Binoy Thomas, Editor

Spanish

La Voz de Montreal
#112, 6225, Place Northcrest, Montréal, QC H3S 2T5
Tel: 514-253-2739; Fax: 514-343-9697
lavoz@sympatico.ca
Circulation: 15,000 Frequency: Monthly
Gilberto Miranda, Director

Swedish

Scandinavian Press
1294 - 7th Ave. West, Vancouver, BC V6H 1B6
Tel: 604-731-6381; Fax: 604-731-2292
office@nordicway.com
Frequency: 4 times a year
Anders Neumuller, Publisher & Editor, anders@nordicway.com

Swedish Press
1294 - 7th Ave. West, Vancouver, BC V6H 1B6
Tel: 604-731-6381; Fax: 604-731-2292
office@nordicway.com
Social Media:
twitter.com/SwedishPress
Circulation: 6,000 Frequency: Monthly; English & Swedish
Anders Neumuller, Publisher & Editor

Ukrainian

"Homin Ukrainy" Publishing Co. Ltd.
83 Christie St., Toronto, ON M6G 3B1
Tel: 416-516-2443; Fax: 416-516-4033
homin@on.aibn.com
Circulation: 1,000 Frequency: Weekly; Ukrainian & English
M. Shepetyk, Publisher
O. Romanyshyn, Editor

Moloda Ukraina
12 Minstrel Dr., Toronto, ON M8Y 3G4
Tel: 416-255-8604
Walentina Rodak, Contact

Novy Shliakh/New Pathway
New Pathway Publishers Ltd., 145 Evans Ave., Toronto, ON M5Z 5X8
Tel: 416-960-3424; Fax: 416-960-1442
npweekly@look.ca
Circulation: 4,500 Frequency: Weekly; also New Pathway Almanac (annual)
Leslie Salnick, President

Progress Ukrainian Catholic News
233 Scotia St., Winnipeg, MB R2V 1V7
Tel: 204-338-7801; Fax: 204-339-4006
Circulation: 4,900
Rev. Mikhail Kouts, Associate Editor
Lydia Firman, Business Manager
Most Rev. Richard Soo, Managing Editor SJ

Ukrainian News
PO Box 38006 Capilano, Edmonton, AB T6A 3Y6
Tel: 780-488-3693; Fax: 780-488-3859
ukrnews@shaw.ca
Circulation: 3,274 Frequency: Bi-weekly; English & Ukrainian
Marco Levytsky, Publisher & Editor
Vitaly Shevchenko, Chief, KYIV Bureau
Irene Hladki, Manager, Advertising & Production

Visnyk/The Herald
9 St. John's Ave., Winnipeg, MB R2W 1G8
Tel: 204-586-3093; Fax: 204-582-5241
Toll-Free: 877-586-3093
visnyk@uocc.ca
Circulation: 10,000 Frequency: Monthly; English & Ukrainian
Rev. Andrew Jarmus, Editor-in-chief

Vietnamese

Lang Van
250 North Service Rd., RR#2, Grimsby, ON L3M 4E8
Tel: 905-607-8010; Fax: 905-607-8011
tapchilangvan@yahoo.com
Circulation: 5,000
Nguyen Huu Nghia, Publisher/Editor-in-chief

Thôi Bâo/Time News
1114 College St., Toronto, ON M6H 1B6
Tel: 416-925-8607; Fax: 416-925-0695
Circulation: 14,500 Frequency: Weekly
Lee Nguyen, Manager
Dave Nguyen, Publisher

Vietnam Time Magazine Edmonton
PO Box 284 Main, 202 - 10711 - 107 Ave. NW, Edmonton, AB T5J 2J1
Tel: 780-429-4781; Fax: 780-429-4781
thoibao@telus.net
Circulation: 1,500
Thanh Nguyen, Publisher

Farm

Farm Publication

Aberdeen Angus World
PO Box 177, Stavely, AB T0L 1Z0
Tel: 403-549-2234; Fax: 403-549-2207
office@angusworld.ca
Aberdeen Angus World is the official publication of the Canadian Angus Association. The magazine contains information about the improvement of the Angus breed.
Dave Callaway, Editor & Publisher
Jan Lee, Associate Editor, 403-948-6053, jlee@chicoranches.com

Acrobiomass
Owned By: Annex Publishing & Printing Inc.
PO Box 530, 105 Donly Dr. South, Simcoe, ON N3Y 4N5
Tel: 519-429-3966; Fax: 519-429-3094
Toll-Free: 800-265-2827
Social Media:
twitter.com/AgAnnex
All-digital publication covering the emerging agro-biomass sector in all its forms.

The Ad-Viser
Farm Press Ltd., 1320 - 36th St. North, Lethbridge, AB T1H 5H8
Tel: 403-328-5114; Fax: 403-328-5443
Toll-Free: 877-328-0048
adsales@farmpressltd.com
Circulation: 20,159 Frequency: Every other Thu.
Jeff Sarich, Publisher

AGDealer Magazine
Owned By: Farm Business Communications
1666 Dublin Ave., Winnipeg, MB R3H 0H1
Tel: 204-954-1400; Fax: 204-954-1422
admin@agdealer.com
Social Media:
twitter.com/AGCanadadotcom
www.facebook.com/pages/AGCanadacom/1716 31800662

Agri Digest
PO Box 512, Sorrento, BC V0E 2W0
agridigest@fairpoint.net
Social Media: www.linkedin.com/company/agridigest-online
twitter.com/agridigest
www. facebook.com/AgriDigestOnline
The journal examines issues in agriculture.
Fran Bach, Contact, Advertising

Agricom
2474 Champlain St., Clarence Creek, ON K0A 1N0
Tél: 613-488-2651;Téléc: 613-488-2541
info.agricom@lavoieagricole.ca
Tirage: 5 000 Fréquence: 22 times a year
Pierre Glaude, Publisher

Alberta Beef
#202, 2915 - 19 St. NE, Calgary, AB T2E 7A2
Tel: 403-250-1090; Fax: 403-291-9546
info@beefnews.com
Circulation: 8,700 Frequency: 12 times a year
Garth McClintock, Publisher

Alberta Farmers Express
Previous Name: Alberta Express
Owned By: Farm Business Communications
1666 Dublin Ave., Winnipeg, MB R3H 0H1
Tel: 204-954-1400; Fax: 204-954-1422
Social Media:
twitter.com/AGCanadadotcom
www.facebook.com/pages/AGCanadacom/171631800662
Circulation: 29,500 Frequency: 12 times per year
Will Verboven, Editor, will.verboven@fbcpublishing.com
Dave Bedard, Daily News Editor, daveb@fbcpublishing.com

Barley Country
c/o Alberta Barley Commission, #200, 3601A - 21 St. NE, Calgary, AB T2E 6T5
Tel: 403-291-9111; Fax: 403-291-0190
Toll-Free: 800-265-9111
abbarley@albertabarley.com
Circulation: 35,000 Frequency: 4 times a year
Terry Bullick, Editor, tbullick@telusplanet.net
Nikki Barnes, Advertising, Project Coordinator

BC Dairy Directory
PO Box 724, Summerland, BC V0H 1Z0
Tel: 250-496-5707; Fax: 250-496-5132
Toll-Free: 888-324-7347
info@bcdairydirectory.com
Circulation: 1,450 Frequency: Annually, June
Karin McCarty, Editor

Beef in B.C. Inc.
c/o B.C. Cattlemen's Association, #4, 10145 Dallas Dr., Kamloops, BC V2C 6T4
Tel: 250-573-3611; Fax: 250-573-5155
beefinbc@kamloops.net
Circulation: 2,200 Frequency: 7 times a year
Bob France, Editor

Better Farming
Owned By: AgMedia Inc.
Tel: 519-763-4044; Fax: 519-763-4482
publisher@betterfarming.com
Circulation: 43,000
Paul Nolan, Publisher & Advertising Director
Don Stoneman, Senior Staff Editor, 519-654-9106, Fax: 519-654-9357, dstoneman@betterfarming.com
Robert Irwin, Managing Editor, 613-678-2232, Fax: 613-678-5993, rirwin@betterfarming.com

Better Pork
Owned By: AgMedia Inc.
Tel: 519-763-4044; Fax: 519-763-4482
Circulation: 6,403 Frequency: 6 times a year

Le Bulletin des Agriculteurs
#320, 1, Place du Commerce, Ile-des-Soeurs, QC H3E 1A2
Tél: 514-766-9554;Téléc: 514-766-2665
Tirage: 24 000 Fréquence: Mensuel; français
Yvon Therien, Éditeur, yvon.therien@lebulletin.com

CAAR Communicator
Previous Name: WFCD Communicator
628 - 70 Arthur St., Winnipeg, MB R3B 1G7
Tel: 204-989-9300; Fax: 204-989-9306
Toll-Free: 800-463-9323
info@caar.org
Social Media:
twitter.com/CdnAgRetail
Circulation: 4,700 Frequency: 5 times a year
Publication of the Canadian Association of Agri-Retailers.
Lynda Nicol, Contact, 204-989-9305, lynda@caar.org

Canadian Ayrshire Review
c/o The Ayrshire Breeders' Association of Canada, 4865, boul Laurier ouest, Saint-Hyacinthe, QC J2S 3V4
Tel: 450-778-3535; Fax: 450-778-3531
info@ayrshire-canada.com
Circulation: 1,500 Frequency: Bi-monthly; English & French
Linda Ness, Business Manager

Canadian Biomass Magazine
Owned By: Annex Publishing & Printing Inc.
PO Box 530, 105 Donly Dr. South, Simcoe, ON N3Y 4N5
Tel: 519-429-3966; Fax: 519-429-3094
Toll-Free: 800-265-2827
Social Media:
twitter.com/AgAnnex
Frequency: Bi-monthly
Scott Jamieson, Editorial Director, 519-429-5180, sjamieson@annexweb.com
John Tenpenny, Editor, 905-713-4351, jtenpenny@annexweb.com

Canadian Cattlemen: The Beef Magazine
Owned By: Farm Business Communications
PO Box 9800, 1666 Dublin AVe., Winnipeg, MB R3C 3K7
Tel: 204-944-5753; Fax: 204-942-8463
Circulation: 21,000 Frequency: 13 editions, annually
Gren Winslow, Editor, 204-944-5753, gren@fbcpublishing.com

Canadian Guernsey Journal
Canadian Guernsey Assn., 5653 Hwy 6, RR#5, Guelph, ON N1H 6J2
Tel: 519-836-2141; Fax: 519-763-6582
info@guernseycanada.ca
Circulation: 250 Frequency: annual
Vivianne M. Macdonald, Managing Editor

Canadian Hereford Digest
5160 Skyline Way NE, Calgary, AB T2E 6V1
Tel: 403-275-2662; Fax: 403-295-1333
Toll-Free: 888-836-7242
info@herefordddigest.com
Social Media:
twitter.com/CAN_Hereford
Circulation: 2,500; 8,000 (commercial issue) Frequency: 7 times a year; English & French
Brad Dubeau, Director, Communications

The Canadian Horsetrader
PO Box 219, Dutton, ON N0L 1J0
Tel: 519-762-3993
pams@wwdc.com
Social Media:
www.linkedin.com/pub/horse-trader-magazine/50/870/165
twitter.com/Hor seTraderMag
www.facebook.com/horsetradermag
Circulation: 10,000 Frequency: Monthly

Canadian Jersey Breeder
#9, 350 Speedvale Ave. West, Guelph, ON N1H 7M7
Tel: 519-821-1020
info@jerseycanada.com
Circulation: 1,400 Frequency: 5 times a year
Ryan Barrett, Editor

Canadian Poultry Magazine
Owned By: Annex Publishing & Printing Inc.
PO Box 530, 105 Donly Dr. South, Simcoe, ON N3Y 4K5
Tel: 519-429-3966; Fax: 519-429-3094
Toll-Free: 800-265-2827
Social Media:
twitter.com/canadianpoultry
Circulation: 5,300 Frequency: 12 times a year
Kristy Nudds, Editor, knudds@annexweb.com
Marilyn White, Sales Manager, mwhite@annexweb.com

Canola Digest
Canola Council of Canada, #400, 167 Lombard Ave., Winnipeg, MB R3B 0T6
Tel: 204-982-2100 Toll-Free: 866-834-4378
admin@canolacouncil.org
Circulation: 40,000 Frequency: 4 times a year
Jay Whetter, Communications Manager, whetterj@canolacouncil.org.

Canola Guide
Owned By: Farm Business Communications
1666 Dublin Ave., Winnipeg, MB R3H 0H1
Tel: 204-944-5569; Fax: 204-944-5562
Circulation: 26,012 Frequency: 4 times a year
Cory Bourdeau'hui, Editor

Charolais Banner
124 Shannon Rd., Regina, SK S4S 4B1
Tel: 306-546-3940; Fax: 306-546-3942
charolaisbanner@sasktel.net
Social Media:
twitter.com/CharolaisBanner/statuses/178291270366662656
Circulation: 1,000 Frequency: 5 times a year
Helge By, Publisher

Le Coopérateur Agricole
CP 500 Youville, Montréal, QC H2P 2W2
Tél: 514-384-6450;Téléc: 514-858-2025
cooperateur@lacoop.coop
Tirage: 20 718 Fréquence: 10 fois par an; français
André Léger, Publicités, andre.leger@lacoop.coop
Patrick Dupuis, Rédacteur-en-chef

Country Guide
Owned By: Farm Business Communications
1666 Dublin Ave., Winnipeg, MB R3H 0H1
Tel: 204-944-5754; Fax: 204-942-8463
Circulation: 20000 Frequency: Monthly
Eastern and Western editions
Tom Button, Editor, tbutton@twinbanks.com

Dairy Update
Owned By: Farm Business Communications
1666 Dublin Ave., Winnipeg, MB R3H 0H1
Tel: 204-944-5569; Fax: 204-944-5562
Circulation: 44,405 Frequency: 9 times a year
G. Winslow, Editor

Drainage Contractor
Owned By: Annex Publishing & Printing Inc.
PO Box 530, 105 Donly Dr. South, Simcoe, ON N3Y 4N5
Tel: 519-429-3966; Fax: 519-429-3094
Toll-Free: 800-265-2827
Circulation: 8,871 Frequency: Annually; November
Ed Cosman, Contact, ecosman@annexweb.com

Eastern Ontario Agrinews
PO Box 368, 7 King St., Chesterville, ON K0C 1H0
Tel: 613-448-2321; Fax: 613-448-3260
rm@agrinewsinteractive.com
Circulation: 14,000 Frequency: Monthly
Robin R. Morris, Publisher

Farm Focus
Owned By: Transcontinental Inc.
#609, 1888 Brunswick St., Halifax, NS B3J 3J8
Tel: 902-749-2525; Fax: 902-742-2311
Jeff Nearing, Publisher & General Manager
Heather Jones, Editor, editor@atlanticfarmfocus.ca
David Schaffner, Designer, david.schaffner@transcontinental.ca
Jennifer Lalonde, Representative, Advertising Sales, jennifer.lalonde@transcontinental.ca

Farming for Tomorrow
Previous Name: Farm Light & Power
#200, 2161 Scarth St., Regina, SK S4P 2H8
Toll-Free: 866-525-4338
info@farmingfortomorrow.ca
Other information: Toll Free Fax: 1-888-213-9999
Circulation: 67,400 Frequency: 2 times a year
Tom Bradley, Editor/Publisher

Feather Fancier Newspaper
5739 Telfer Rd., Sarnia, ON N7T 7H2
Tel: 519-542-6859; Fax: 519-542-4168
featherfancier@ebtech.net
Circulation: 1,800 Frequency: 11 times a year
Paul Monteith, Editor & Publisher

Fruit & Vegetable Magazine
Previous Name: Canadian Fruitgrower
Owned By: Annex Publishing & Printing Inc.
PO Box 530, 105 Donly Dr. South, Simcoe, ON N3Y 4N5
Tel: 519-429-3966; Fax: 519-429-3094
Toll-Free: 800-265-2827
fruitedit@annexweb.com
Social Media: twitter.com/FruitVeggieMag
Circulation: 7,000 Frequency: 8 times a year
Diane Kleer, Publisher
Marg Land, Editor, mland@annexweb.com

Germination
Owned By: Issues Ink
#301, 313 Pacific Ave., Winnipeg, MB R3A 0M2
Tel: 877-710-3222
Social Media: twitter.com/germinationmag
www.facebook.com/GerminationMag
Circulation: 5,700
Germination is the first and only magazine aimed specifically at Canada's seed industry.
Shawn Brook, President

Gestion et Technologie Agricoles
Détenteur: DBC Communications inc.
655, av Sainte-Anne, Saint-Hyacinthe, QC J2S 5G4
Tél: 450-773-6028;Téléc: 450-773-3115
publicite@courrierclarion.qc.ca
Tirage: 20 000 Fréquence: 11 fois par an; français

Grainews
Owned By: Farm Business Communications
1666 Dublin Ave., Winnipeg, MB R3H 0H1
Tel: 204-944-5567; Fax: 204-944-5562
Toll-Free: 800-665-1362
Social Media: www.facebook.com/pages/AGCanadacom/171631800662
Circulation: 32,000 Frequency: 18 times a year
Leeann Minogue, Acting Editor, 306-861-2678, leeann.minogue@fbcpublishing.com

Holstein Journal
#301, 9040 Leslie St., Richmond Hill, ON L4B 3M4
Tel: 905-886-4222; Fax: 905-886-0037
Circulation: 4,900 Frequency: Monthly; English & French
G. Peter English, Publisher, peter@holsteinjournal.com
Bonnie Cooper, Editor, bonnie@holsteinjournal.com

iDeal Equipment Magazine
Owned By: Farm Business Communications
1666 Dublin Ave., Winnipeg, MB R3H OH1
Tel: 204-954-1400; Fax: 204-954-1422
Social Media: twitter.com/AGCanadadotcom
www.facebook.com/pages/AGCanadacom/171631800662

The Island Farmer
PO Box 790, 567 Main St., Montague, PE C0A 1R0
Tel: 902-838-2515; Fax: 902-838-4392
Toll-Free: 800-806-5443
andy@peicanada.com
Social Media: twitter.com/graphicnews
Circulation: 2,244 Frequency: Bi-weekly
Paul MacNeill, Publisher
Andy Walker, Editor

The Limousin Leader
Bollum Marketing, PO Box 10, Site 11, RR#1, Airdrie, AB T4B 2A3
Tel: 403-948-4768; Fax: 403-948-7531
rhonda@limousinleader.com
Frequency: 4 times a year
Randy Bollum, Editor

Ma Revue de machinerie agricole
Section Rouge Média Inc., 468, boul Roland-Therrien, Longueuil, QC J4H 4E3
Tél: 450-677-2556;Téléc: 450-677-4099
info@marevueagricole.com
Tirage: 35 000 Fréquence: 11 fois par an; français
Louise Gionet, Directeure des ventes publicitaires

Manitoba Co-Operator
Owned By: Farm Business Communications
1666 Dublin Ave., Winnipeg, MB R3H 0H1
Tel: 204-944-5569; Fax: 204-944-5562
Circulation: 11,939 Frequency: Weekly; supplements Seed Manitoba (annual); Yield Manitoba (annual)
Laura Rance, Editor, 204-792-4382, laura@fbcpublishing.com

Manitoba Farmers' Voice
Owned By: Craig Kelman & Associates Ltd.
c/o Keystone Agricultural Producers, #203, 1700 Ellice Ave., Winnipeg, MB R3H 0B1
Tel: 204-697-1140; Fax: 204-697-1109
communications@kap.mb.ca
Frequency: 4 times a year
Cheryl Parisien, Managing Editor, cheryl@kelman.ca

Manitoba FarmLIFE
#300, 2050 Cume Blvd., Brandon, MB R7A 5Y1
Toll-Free: 888-756-5459
Circulation: 28,000 Frequency: 26 times a year
Dale Coulter, Manager

Manure Manager
Owned By: Annex Publishing & Printing Inc.
PO Box 530, 105 Donly Dr. South, Simcoe, ON N3Y 4N5
Tel: 519-429-3966; Fax: 519-429-3094
Toll-Free: 800-265-2827
Social Media: twitter.com/ManureManager
Frequency: 8 times a year
Manure handling industry across North America.
Marg Land, Editor, mland@annexweb.com

The Northern Horizon
901 - 100th Ave., Dawson Creek, BC V1G 1W2
Tel: 250-782-4888; Fax: 250-782-6300
Circulation: 28,000 Frequency: Bi-weekly; Friday
The agricultural publication serves British Columbia, north central Alberta, & the Alberta Peace Region.
Dan Przybylski, Manager, Sales, publisher@dcdn.ca

Northwest Farmer Rancher
PO Box 1029, 892 - 104th St., North Battleford, SK S9A 3E6
Tel: 306-445-7621; Fax: 306-445-3223
battlefords.publishing@sasktel.net
Circulation: 15,000+ Frequency: 7 pa
The magazine targets agricultural producers in northwestern Saskatchewan.
Chris Walls, Manager, Advertising Sales, chris@newsoptimist.ca

Ontario Beef
Ontario Cattlemen's Assn., 130 Malcolm Rd., Guelph, ON N1K 1B1
Tel: 519-824-0334; Fax: 519-824-9101
leaanne@cattle.guelph.on.ca
Circulation: 20,000 Frequency: 5 times a year
Lianne Appleby, Editor
Donna Corbet, Circulation Manager

Ontario Beef Farmer
Owned By: Sun Media Corp.
PO Box 7400, London, ON N5Y 4X3
Fax: 519-473-2256
Toll-Free: 877-358-7773
ontariofarmer.nationals@sunmedia.ca
Circulation: 10,310 Frequency: Bi-monthly
Paul Mahon, Publisher & Editor, paul.mahon@sunmedia.ca

Ontario Dairy Farmer
Owned By: Sun Media Corp.
PO Box 7400, London, ON N5Y 4X3
Fax: 519-473-2256
Toll-Free: 877-358-7773
Circulation: 7,445 Frequency: 8 times a year
Paul Mahon, Publisher

Ontario Farmer
Owned By: Sun Media Corp.
PO Box 7400, London, ON N5Y 4X3
Fax: 519-473-2256
Toll-Free: 877-358-7773
Circulation: 32,127 Frequency: Weekly, Tue.
Paul Mahon, Editor

Ontario Hog Farmer
Owned By: Sun Media Corp.
PO Box 7400, London, ON N5Y 4X3
Fax: 519-473-2256
Toll-Free: 877-358-7773
Circulation: 4,830 Frequency: 8 times a year
Paul Mahon, Publisher

Ontario Milk Producer
Dairy Farmers of Ontario, 6780 Campobello Rd., Mississauga, ON L5N 2L8
Tel: 905-821-8970; Fax: 905-821-3160
questions@milk.org
Circulation: 10,791 Frequency: Monthly
Bill Dimmick, Editor

Porc Québec
Anciennement: Porc Québec - Québec Hog Industry Magazine
555, boul Roland Therrien, Longueuil, QC J4H 4E9
Tél: 450-679-0530;Téléc: 450-679-0102
porcquebec@upa.qc.ca
Tirage: 3 000 Fréquence: 5 times a year
Nathalie Hansen, Directrice
Audrey Gendron, Rédactrice en chef, agendron@upa.qc.ca

Prairie Farmer
Previous Name: The Agri Times
PO Box 1356, Winkler, MB R6W 4B3
Tel: 204-325-4771; Fax: 204-325-5059
Toll-Free: 888-565-8357
Circulation: 26,000 Frequency: 25 times a year
Rick Reimer, Publisher

Prairie Hog Country
PO Box 5536, Leduc, AB T9E 2A1
Tel: 780-986-0962; Fax: 780-980-9640
hogcountry@shaw.ca
Circulation: 4,800 Frequency: bi-monthly
Calvin Daniels, Copy Editor
Laurie Brandly, Publisher

Le Producteur de lait québécois
Fédération des producteurs de lait du Québec, 555, boul Roland Thérrien, Longueuil, QC J4H 3Y9
Tél: 450-679-0530;Téléc: 450-679-5899
fplq@upa.qc.ca
Tirage: 9 338 Fréquence: 10 fois par an; français

Producteur Plus
CP 147, Farnham, QC J2N 2R4
Tél: 450-293-3145;Téléc: 450-293-8383
info@producteurplus.com
Tirage: 18 644 Fréquence: 8 fois par an; français
Léonard Pigeon, Éditeur et Rédacteur-en-chef

Québec Farmers' Advocate
#255, 555, boul Roland-Therrien, Longueuil, QC J4H 4E7
Tel: 450-679-0540; Fax: 450-463-5291
qfa@upa.qc.ca
Circulation: 3,000 Frequency: Monthly

Regional Country News
Previous Name: The Farm Gate
Owned By: Metroland Printing Publishing & Distribution
11 Wellington St. North, St Marys, ON N4X 1B7
Tel: 519-284-2440
Circulation: 18,000 Frequency: Monthly
Stew Slater, Editor, 519-284-1155 ext 105
Bill Huether, Publisher
Laura Payton, Editor, 519-284-2440

Rural Roots
PO Box 126, Beaverlodge, AB T0H 0C0
editor@ruralrootsmagazine.ca

Frequency: Quarterly
The magazine features accounts of rural lifestyles & communities in western Canada. Topics include farming, farm family business ventures, horticulture, livestock, wildlife, conservation, history, antiques, hobbies, country homes & adventures. Rural Roots is distributed to subscribers, and it can be found at agribusinesses, farmers' markets, & tourist centres.

The Rural Voice
Owned By: North Huron Publishing Ltd.
PO Box 429, Blyth, ON N0M 1H0
Tel: 519-523-4792; Fax: 519-523-9140
info@northhuron.on.ca
Circulation: 13,293 Frequency: Monthly
Keith Roulston, Publisher

Saskatchewan Farm Life
2206A Ave. C North, Saskatoon, SK S7L 6C3
Tel: 306-384-3276; Fax: 306-668-6164
Toll-Free: 888-924-6397
Frequency: Bi-weekly
The magazine provides information for farmers & ranchers in Saskatchewan. A classified section is included.
Don Moores, Publisher

seed.ab.ca
Owned By: Issues Ink
5030 - 50 St., Lacombe, AB T4L 1W8
Tel: 403-782-8022; Fax: 866-798-1826
Toll-Free: 877-710-3222
marketing@issuesink.com
Circulation: 64,000
seed.ab.cais Alberta's source for seed, offering the latest variety information, complete crop evaluations, comprehensive grower directories, trends, issues, and more.
Lorena Pahl, General Manager, 403-325-0081, lorena.pahl@seed.ab.ca

Sheep Canada
1489 Rte. 560, Deerville, NB E7K 1W7
Tel: 506-328-3599; Fax: 506-328-8165
Toll-Free: 888-241-5124
gallivan@sheepcanada.com
Social Media:
www.facebook.com/pages/Sheep-Canada-magazine/253659158039
Frequency: 4 times a year
Dr. Cathy Gallivan, Editor

Simmental Country
#13, 4101 - 19 St. NE, Calgary, AB T2E 7C4
Tel: 403-250-7979; Fax: 403-250-5121
Toll-Free: 866-860-6051
mcartwright@simmental.com
Circulation: 1,800 Frequency: Monthly
The official publication of the Canadian Simmental Association with up to-date information and articles that are of interest to both Purebred and Commercial Cattlemen.

La Terre de chez nous
#100, 555, boul Roland Therrien, Longueuil, QC J4H 3Y9
Tél: 450-679-8483;Téléc: 450-670-4788
Ligne sans frais: 877-679-7809
Médias sociaux: youtube.com/terredecheznous
twitter.com/laterreca
www.facebook.com/lat erreca
Tirage: 38,620 Fréquence: Hebdomadaire; français
Loïc Hamon, Rédacteur-en-chef

Top Crop Manager
Owned By: Annex Publishing & Printing Inc.
PO Box 530, 105 Donly Dr. South, Simcoe, ON N3Y 4N5
Tel: 519-429-3966; Fax: 519-429-3094
Toll-Free: 800-265-2827
Social Media:
twitter.com/TopCropMag
Frequency: 8 Western/year, 7 Eastern/year, 1 Potatoes/year
Magazine of crop production and technology, a specialty agricultural trade publication.
Sara Avoledo, Eastern Editor, savoledo@annexweb.com
Bruce Barker, Western Editor, bruce@haywirecreative.ca

Union Farmer Quarterly
National Farmers Union, 2717 Wentz Ave., Saskatoon, SK S7K 4B6
Tel: 306-652-9465; Fax: 306-664-6226
nfu@nfu.ca
Social Media:
twitter.com/NFUcanada
Circulation: 5,000 Frequency: 4 times a year
Terry Pugh, Editor

Voice of the Farmer
PO Box 459, 16 Bascom St., Uxbridge, ON L9P 1M9
Tel: 905-852-9141; Fax: 905-852-9341
Frequency: Biweekly; also - Voice of the: Huron Farmer, Kent Farmer, Lambton Farmer, Middlesex Farmer, Elgin Farmer, Perth Farmer, Oxford Farmer, Waterloo Farmer; monthly Voice of: York Farmer, Durham Farmer, Vi
Mary Forbes, Publishing Manager

Western Dairy Farmer Magazine
Owned By: Sun Media Corp.
Ontario Farmer, PO Box 7300, London, ON N5Y 4X3
Tel: 780-986-2271; Fax: 780-986-6397
Toll-Free: 877-358-7773
ontariofarmer.advertising@sunmedia.ca
Circulation: 6,962 Frequency: 6 times a year

Western Hog Journal
Alberta Pork Industry Services, 4828 - 89 St., Edmonton, AB T6E 5K1
Tel: 780-474-8288; Fax: 780-479-5128
Toll-Free: 877-247-7675
info@albertapork.com
Circulation: 4,315 Frequency: 4 times a year
Bernie Peet, Editor, 403-782-3776, whj@albertapork.com

Western Horse Review
Previous Name: Northern Horse Review
#814, 3545 - 32 Ave. NE, Calgary, AB T1Y 6M6
Social Media:
twitter.com/westernhorserev
www.facebook.com/pages/Western-Horse-Review/178276713247
Circulation: 15,000 Frequency: 11 pa
Ingrid Schulz, Co-Publisher & Editor, ingrids@efirehose.net
Danya Sapergia, Editor, editorial@westernhorsereview.com

The Western Producer
PO Box 2500, 2310 Millar Ave., Saskatoon, SK S7K 2C4
Tel: 306-665-3544; Fax: 306-934-2401
Toll-Free: 800-667-6978
subscriptions@producer.com; newsroom@producer.com
Other information: Advertising, E-mail: advertising@producer.com
Social Media:
twitter.com/westernproducer
Frequency: Weekly
The agricultural publication is of interest to farmers & ranchers in western Canada. News & information is included about rural life, technology, production, livestock, markets, & finance. News bureaus are located in Ottawa, Brandon, Winnipeg, Saskatoon, Regina, Calgary, & Camrose.
Joanne Paulson, Editor, joanne.paulson@producer.com
Brian Cross, Editor, Supplements, brian.cross@producer.com
Terry Fries, Editor, News, terry.fries@producer.com
Michelle Houlden, Editor, Graphics, michelle.houlden@producer.com
D'Arce McMillan, Editor, Markets & Agri-Finance, darce.mcmillan@producer.com
Karen Morrison, Editor, Farm Living, karen.morrison@producer.com
Michael Raine, Editor, Farm Management, michael.raine@producer.com
Catherine Rumanick, Editor, Layout, catherine.rumanick@producer.com
Paul Yanko, Editor, Website, paul.yanko@producer.com
Kelly Berg, Director, Advertising, 306-665-3524, kelly.berg@producer.com
Robert Magnell, Creative Director, 306-665-9629, robert.magnell@producer.com
Jack Phipps, Director, Marketing, 306-665-3520, jack.phipps@producer.com
Shauna Brand, Manager, Classifieds, 306-665-3536, shauna.brand@producer.com
Rhett Soveran, Manager, Marketing, Digital, & New Media, 306-665-3545, rhett.soveran@producer.com
Gwen Thompson, Supervisor, Subscriptions, 306-665-3596, gwen.thompson@producer.com
Brenda McPhail, Librarian, brenda.mcphail@producer.com

Food & Beverage

Flavourful
Owned By: Issues Ink
#301, 313 Pacific Ave., Winnipeg, MB R3A 0M2
Tel: 204-453-1965
Frequency: 2 times a year
Distributed through Canadian embassies and used as a tool by participants in missions to Canada's key agri-food markets such as the U.S., Japan, European Union, Mexico, and China.

Spud Smart
Owned By: Issues Ink
#301, 313 Pacific Ave., Winnipeg, MB R3A 0M2
Tel: 204-453-1965; Fax: 204-475-5247
Social Media:
twitter.com/SpudSmartMag
www.facebook.com/SpudSmart
Spud Smart is the primary publication in the Canadian potato industry.
Julienne Isaacs, Editor, 204-453-1965 x810, jisaacs@issuesink.com

Industrial & Industrial Automation

Resource Engineering & Maintence (REM)
Owned By: Annex Publishing & Printing Inc.
PO Box 530, 105 Donly Dr. South, Simcoe, ON N3Y 4N5
Tel: 519-429-3966; Fax: 519-429-3094
Toll-Free: 800-265-2827
André Voshart, Editor, 905-726-4655, avoshart@annexweb.com

Scholarly

Health & Medical

Canadian Journal of Neurological Sciences
c/o Canadian Neurological Sciences Federation, #709, 7015 MacLeod Trail SW, Calgary, AB T2H 2K6
Tel: 403-229-9544; Fax: 403-229-1661
Circulation: 1,500 Frequency: Bi-monthly
The journal is the official publication of the four member societies of the Canadian Neurological Sciences Federation: Canadian Neurological Society (CNS), Canadian Neurosurgical Society (CNSS), Canadian Association of Child Neurology (CACN), & the Canadian Society of Clinical Neurophysiologists (CSCN). Peer reviewed articles about the neurosciences are published in the Canadian Journal of Neurological Sciences. The journal is circulated to society members, non-members, & institutions in Canada & around the world.
Cindy Leschyshyn, CJNS Editorial Coordinator, 403-229-9575, cindy-leschyshyn@cjns.org
Maggie McCallion, CJNS Designer & Coordinator, Production, maggie-mccallion@cjns.org
Dan Morin, Contact, Advertising

Literary

The Dorchester Review
#204, 1066 Somerset St. West, Ottawa, ON K1Y 4T3
info@dorchesterreview.ca
A historical and literary review.

Event
c/o Douglas College, PO Box 2503, New Westminster, BC V3L 5B2
Tel: 604-527-5293; Fax: 604-527-5095
event@douglascollege.ca
Social Media:
www.facebook.com/douglascollege
Circulation: 1,250 Frequency: Every 3 months
Poetry and prose magazine.
Elizabeth Bachinsky, Editor
Nikki Reimer, Managing Editor
Ian Cockfield, Editor

Scholarly Publication

Acadiensis: Journal of the History of the Atlantic Region / Revue d'Histoire de la Région Atlantique
Campus House, University of New Brunswick, PO Box 4400 A, Fredericton, NB E3B 5A3
Tel: 506-453-4978; Fax: 506-453-5068
acadiensis@unb.ca
Circulation: 900 Frequency: 2 times a year; English & French
Bill Parenteau, Editor
Nicole Lang, Editor, nlang@umce.ca
Stephen Dutcher, Managing Editor, nlang@umce.ca

Annals of Air & Space Law / Annales de droit aérian et spatial
Institute & Centre of Air & Space Law, McGill University, 3661, rue Peel, Montréal, QC H3A 1X1
Tel: 514-398-5095; Fax: 514-398-8197
edannals.law@mcgill.ca
Circulation: 1,000 Frequency: annually
Prof.Dr. Paul S. Dempsey, Editor

Anthropologica
Wilfrid Laurier University Press, 2-139 DAWB, 75 University Ave. West, Waterloo, ON N2L 3C5
Tel: 519-884-0710; Fax: 519-725-1399
press@wlu.ca

Circulation: 625 Frequency: 2 times a year
Dr. Leslie Jermyn, Managing Editor, ljermyn@chass.utoronto.ca
Andrew Lyons, Editor-in-chief, andrewpaullyons@gmail.com

Arctic
c/o Arctic Institute of North America, University of Calgary, 2500 University Dr. NW, Calgary, AB T2N 1N4
Tel: 403-220-7515; Fax: 403-282-4609
kmccullo@ucalgary.ca
Circulation: 1,500 Frequency: 4 times a year
Dr. Karen McCullough, Editor, 403/220-4049
Dr. Benoît Beauchamp, Executive Director, 403/220-7516

ARIEL - A Review of International English Literature
Department of English, University of Calgary, 2500 University Dr. NW, Calgary, AB T2N 1N4
Tel: 403-220-4657; Fax: 403-289-1123
ariel@ucalgary.ca
Circulation: 850 Frequency: 4 times a year
Michael T. Clarke, Co-Editor, michael.t.clarke@ucalgary.ca
Faye Halpern, Co-Editor, fhalpern@ucalgary.ca

Atlantis: A Women's Studies Journal
Institute for the Study of Women, Mount Saint Vincent Univer, Halifax, NS B3M 2J6
Tel: 902-457-6319; Fax: 902-443-1352
atlantis@msvu.ca
Circulation: 500 Frequency: 2 times a year
Linda Kealey, General Editor
Annalee Lepp, General Editor
Katherine Side, General Editor

BC Studies: The British Columbian Quarterly
Buchanan E, #162, 1866 Main Mall, Vancouver, BC V6T 1Z1
Tel: 604-822-3727; Fax: 604-822-0606
info@bcstudies.com
Circulation: 700 Frequency: 4 times a year
Leanne Coughlin, Editor

Canadian Ethnic Studies Journal / Études Ethniques au Canada
University of Manitoba, 410 Fletcher Argue Building, Winnipeg, MB R3T 2N2
Tel: 204-474-8493; Fax: 204-474-7653
ces@cc.umanitoba.ca
Circulation: 1,800 Frequency: 3 times a year
Fully refereed, interdisciplinary journal devoted to the study of ethnicity, immigration, inter-group relations, and the history and cultural life of ethnic groups in Canada.
Jo-Anne Cleaver, Editor

Canadian Foreign Policy Journal / La Politique étrangère du Canada
5306 River Building, Norman Paterson School of International Affairs, 1125 Colonel By Dr., Ottawa, ON K1S 5B6
Tel: 613-520-6655; Fax: 613-520-2889
international_affairs@carleton.ca
Frequency: 3 times a year
Online ISSN is 2157-0817
David Carment, Editor
Kevin Arthur, Managing Editor

The Canadian Historical Review
Owned By: University of Toronto Press Inc.
c/o University of Toronto Press Inc., 5201 Dufferin St., Toronto, ON M3H 5T8
Tel: 416-667-7810; Fax: 416-667-7881
chr@utpress.utoronto.ca
Circulation: 1,700 Frequency: 4 times a year; English & French
Ken Cruikshank, Co-Editor
Sylvie Dépatie, Co-Editor

Canadian Journal of Development Studies / Revue canadienne d'études du développement
c/o School for International Studies, Simon Fraser University, #7200, 515 West Hastings St., Vancouver, BC V6B 5K3
Tel: 778-782-7148
cjds@sfu.ca
Circulation: 500 Frequency: 4 times a year, plus 1 special issue; English & French
Henry Veltmeyer, Co-Editor
Scott Simon, Co-Editor

Canadian Journal of Economics / Revue canadienne d'economique
PO Box 35006, 1221, Fleury est, Montréal, QC H2C 3K4
Tel: 646-257-5906
journals@economics.ca
Circulation: 3,200 Frequency: 4 times a year
David Green, Managing Editor

Canadian Journal of Higher Education / La revue canadienne d'enseignemnet supérieur
c/o Canadian Society for the Study of Higher Education, #204, 260 Dalhousie St., Ottawa, ON K1N 7E4
Tel: 613-241-0018; Fax: 613-241-0019
The peer reviewed journal publishes articles about the structure & processes of the Canadian higher education system. Book reviews are also included in the journal.
Lesley Andres, Editor, 604-822-8943, lesley.andres@ubc.ca

Canadian Journal of History (CJH) / Annales canadiennes d'histoire
Dept. of History, University of Saskatchewan, 9 Campus Dr., Saskatoon, SK S7N 5A5
Tel: 306-966-5794; Fax: 306-966-5852
cjh@duke.usask.ca
Circulation: 725 Frequency: 3 times a year
Linda Dietz, Managing Editor

The Canadian Journal of Information & Library Science
Owned By: University of Toronto Press Inc.
5201 Dufferin St., Toronto, ON M3H 5T8
Tel: 416-667-7810; Fax: 416-667-7881
journals@utpress.utoronto.ca
Circulation: 400 Frequency: 4 times a year
Lynne McKechnie, Editor

Canadian Journal of Law & Society (CJLS/RCDS) / Revue Canadienne Droit et Société
Dept des sciences juridiques, UQAM, CP 8888 Centre-Ville, Montréal, QC H3C 3P8
Tél: 514-987-3000;Téléc: 514-987-4784
Tirage: 700 Fréquence: Biennially; English & French
Dawn Moore, Managing Editor, dawn_moore@carleton.ca

Canadian Journal of Linguistics / Revue Canadienne de Linguistique
Owned By: University of Toronto Press Inc.
5201 Dufferin St., Toronto, ON M3H 5T8
Tel: 416-667-7810; Fax: 416-667-7881
journals@utpress.utoronto.ca
Circulation: 900 Frequency: 4 times a year
Rose-Marie Dechaine, Editor

Canadian Journal of Mathematics
CMS, 5201 Dufferin St., Toronto, ON M3H 5T8
Tel: 416-667-7810; Fax: 416-667-7881
journals@utpress.utoronto.ca
Circulation: 1,225 Frequency: Bi-monthly
James B. Carrell, Editor
Nassif Ghoussoub, Editor

Canadian Journal of Philosophy
Owned By: University of Calgary Press
Tel: 403-220-3514; Fax: 403-282-0085
ucpmail@ucalgary.ca
Circulation: 875 Frequency: 4 times a year plus supplementary volume
Michael Stingl, Editorial Board Coordinator

Canadian Journal of Program Evaluation / La Revue canadienne d'évaluation de programme
155 College St., Toronto, ON M5T 3M7
Tel: 416-978-3901; Fax: 416-946-0346
cjpe@evaluationcanada.ca
Circulation: 1,900 Frequency: Bi-annually; English & French
Robert Schwartz, Director of Evaluation & Monitoring Ph.D.

Canadian Journal of Psychiatry
#701, 141 Laurier Ave. West, Ottawa, ON K1P 5J3
Tel: 613-234-2815; Fax: 613-234-9857
cjp@cpa-apc.org
Circulation: 6,100 Frequency: 12 times a year
Dr. Joel Paris, Editor-in-chief

Canadian Journal of Psychoanalysis / Revue canadienne de psychanalyse
Becker Associates, #202, 10 Morrow Ave., Toronto, ON M6R 2J1
Tel: 416-538-1650; Fax: 416-489-1713
cjp-rcp@qc.aira.com
Circulation: 650 Frequency: Bi-annually
Charles Levin, Editor, charleslevin@videotron.ca

Canadian Journal of Women & The Law (CJWL/RFD) / Revue Femmes et Droit
Previous Name: Revue juridique la femme et la droit
5210 Dufferin St., Toronto, ON M3H 5T8
Tel: 416-667-7810; Fax: 416-667-7881
Frequency: 2 times a year; English & French
Debra Parkes, English Language Co-Editor
Louise Langevin, French Language Co-Editor/Corédactrice francophone

Canadian Journal on Aging / La Revue Canadienne du Vieillissement
Owned By: Cambridge University Press
A124 Sedgewick Building, PO Box 1700 CSC, Victoria, BC V8W 2Y2
Tel: 416-667-7810; Fax: 416-667-7881
Circulation: 1,600 Frequency: 4 times a year; English & French
Mark W. Rosenberg, Editor

Canadian Literature
Owned By: University of British Columbia
c/o University of British Columbia, Anthropology & Sociology Building, #8, 6303 Marine Dr. NW, Vancouver, BC V6T 1Z1
Tel: 604-822-2780
can.lit@ubc.ca
Social Media:
twitter.com/canadianlit
www.facebook.com/group.php?gid=17013685211
Circulation: 1,200 Frequency: 4 times a year
Joël Castonguay-Bélanger, Editor
Margery Fee, Editor

Canadian Mathematical Bulletin
Owned By: University of Toronto Press Inc.
5201 Dufferin St., Toronto, ON M3H 5T8
Tel: 416-667-7810; Fax: 416-667-7881
journals@utpress.utoronto.ca
Circulation: 775 Frequency: 4 times a year
Maung Min-Oo, Editor-in-chief
Andrew J. Nicas, Editor-in-chief

Canadian Modern Language Review (CMLR/RCLV) / Le Revue canadienne des langues vivantes
Owned By: University of Toronto Press Inc.
5201 Dufferin St., Toronto, ON M3H 5T8
Tel: 416-667-7810; Fax: 416-667-7881
journals@utpress.utoronto.ca
Circulation: 1,000 Frequency: 4 times a year; English & French
Larry Vandergrift, Co-Editor
Tracey Derwing, Co-Editor

Canadian Poetry: Studies, Documents, Reviews
Dept. of English, University of Western Ontario, Richmond St. North, London, ON N6A 3K7
Tel: 519-673-1164; Fax: 519-661-3776
canadianpoetry@uwo.ca
Circulation: 400 Frequency: 2 times a year; spring/fall, fall/winter
D.M.R. Bentley, Editor, dbentley@uwo.ca
R.J. Shroyer, Associate Editor, shroyer@uwo.ca

Canadian Public Administration (CPA/APC) / Administration publique du Canada
#401, 1075 Bay St., Toronto, ON M5S 2B1
Tel: 416-924-8787; Fax: 416-924-4992
Circulation: 3,600 Frequency: 4 times a year
Barbara Wake Carroll, Editor

Canadian Public Policy / Analyse de Politique
PO Box 35006, 1221, Fleury est, Montréal, QC H2C 3K4
Tel: 646-257-5906
cpp.adp@gmail.com
Circulation: 1,500 Frequency: 4 times a year; English & French
Herb Emery, Managing Editor, hemery@ucalgary.ca

Canadian Review of American Studies
Owned By: University of Toronto Press Inc.
5201 Dufferin St., Toronto, ON M3H 5T8
Tel: 416-667-7810; Fax: 416-667-7881
journals@utpress.utoronto.ca
Circulation: 400 Frequency: 3 times a year; English & French
Priscilla Walton, Editor

Canadian Review of Sociology / Revue Canadienne de sociologie
PO Box 98014, 2126 Burnhamthorpe Rd. West, Mississauga, ON L5L 5V4
Tel: 416-660-4378
office@csa-scs.ca
Social Media:
twitter.com/csa_sociology
www.facebook.com/pages/Canadian-Sociological-Association
Circulation: 1,428 Frequency: Quarterly; French & English
Harley Dickinson, Managing Editor

Canadian Theatre Review
Owned By: University of Toronto Press Inc.
5201 Dufferin St., Toronto, ON M3H 5T8
Tel: 416-667-7810; Fax: 416-667-7881
journals@utpress.utoronto.ca
Circulation: 650 Frequency: 4 pa
Ann Wilson, Co-Editor
Rick Knowles, Co-Editor
Harry Lane, Co-Editor
Reid Gilbert, Co-Editor
Catherine Graham, Co-Editor
Andrew Houston, Co-Editor

Cartographica
Owned By: University of Toronto Press Inc.
5201 Dufferin St., Toronto, ON M3H 5T8
Tel: 416-667-7810; Fax: 416-667-7881
journals@utpress.utoronto.ca
Circulation: 900 Frequency: 4 times a year
Jeremy Crampton, Co-Editor
Roger Wheate, Co-Editor
Clifford Wood, Co-Editor

Eighteenth-Century Fiction
Owned By: University of Toronto Press Inc.
5201 Dufferin St., Toronto, ON M3H 5T8
Tel: 416-667-7810; Fax: 416-667-7881
Toll-Free: 800-221-9985
journals@utpress.utoronto.ca
Social Media: www.facebook.com/utpjournals
Circulation: 750 Frequency: Quarterly
Jacqueline Langille, Managing Editor
Peter Walmsley, Co-Editor
Eugene Zuroski, Co-Editor

Energy Studies Review
c/o MIES, KTH 330, McMaster University, Hamilton, ON L8S 4M4
Tel: 905-525-9140; Fax: 905-777-8344
Frequency: 2 times a year
Prof. Joseph A. Doucet, Editor

Environments: A Journal of Interdisciplinary Studies
Geography & Environmental Studies, Wilfred Laurier University, 75 University Ave. West, Waterloo, ON N2L 3C5
Circulation: 400 Frequency: 3 times a year
D. Scott Slocombe, Editor, sslocomb@wlu.ca

INFOR
Owned By: University of Toronto Press Inc.
5201 Dufferin St., Toronto, ON M3H 5T8
Tel: 416-667-7810; Fax: 416-667-7881
journals@utpress.utoronto.ca
Circulation: 400 Frequency: 4 times a year
Bernard Gendron, Editor

International Journal
Owned By: Canadian International Council
c/o Canadian International Council, #064S, 1 Devonshire Place, Toronto, ON M5S 3K7
Tel: 416-667-7810
ij@opencanada.org
Social Media: www.tumblr.com/register/follow/internationaljournal
Circulation: 1,300 Frequency: 4 times a year
Scholarly publication on international relations.
David Haglund, Co-Editor
Joseph Jodcel, Co-Editor

Intersections : Canadian Journal of Music/Revue canadienne de musique
PO Box 507 Q, Toronto, ON M4T 2M5
Tel: 416-483-7282; Fax: 416-489-1713
Circulation: 400 Frequency: 2 times a year; French and English
Prof. Mary Woodside, Editor
François de Médicis, Rédacteur

Jeunesse: Young People, Texts, Cultures (CCL) / Littérature Canadienne pour la Jeunesse
Centre for Research in Young People's Texts and Cultures, University of Winnipeg, 515 Portage Ave., Winnipeg, MB R3B 2E9
Tel: 204-786-9351; Fax: 204-774-4134
jeunesse@uwinnipeg.ca
Circulation: 900 Frequency: Bi-annually; English & French
Jeunesse has an expanded mandate to publish research on and to provide a forum for discussion about, cultural productions for, by, and about young people. Especially interested in the cultural functions and representations of "the child."
Marie Davis, Editor, 204-786-9185, m.reimer@uwinnipeg.ca
Larissa Wodtke, Managing Editor, 204-786-9351, l.wodtke@uwinnipeg.ca

Journal of Baha'i Studies / La Revue des Études Bahá'¡es/La Revista des Estudios Bahá'¡
34 Copernicus St., Ottawa, ON K1N 7K4
Tel: 613-233-1903; Fax: 613-233-3644
Circulation: 2,000 Frequency: Biannual; English, French & Spanish
Anne Furlong, Editor

Journal of Canadian Art History / Annales d'histoire de l'art canadien
c/o EV-3.819, Concordia University, 1455, boul de Maisonneuve ouest, Montréal, QC H3G 1M8
Tel: 514-848-2424; Fax: 514-848-4584
JCAH@alcor.concordia.ca
Circulation: 550 Frequency: 2 times a year; English & French
Sandra Paikowsky, Publisher
Martha Langford, Editor-in-Chief

Journal of Canadian Poetry
Circulation: 350 Frequency: Annually
David Staines, Editor

Journal of Canadian Studies / Revue d'Études Canadiennes
University of Toronto Press - Journals Division, 5201 Dufferin St., Toronto, ON M3H 5T8
Tel: 416-667-7810; Fax: 416-667-7881
journals@utpress.utoronto.ca
Circulation: 1,300 Frequency: 4 times a year; English & French
Robert M. Campbell
Kerry Cannon, Managing Editor

Journal of Law & Social Policy / Revue des lois et des politiques sociales
Clinic Resource Office, Legal Aid Ontario, #41, 425 Adelaide St. West, Toronto, ON M5V 3C1
Tel: 416-204-5408; Fax: 416-204-5422
Toll-Free: 800-668-8258
jlsp@lao.on.ca
Circulation: 230 Frequency: Annually
Margaret Capes, Editor
Andrew Bolter, Editor

Journal of Scholarly Publishing
Owned By: University of Toronto Press Inc.
University of Toronto Press - Journals Division, 5201 Dufferin St., Toronto, ON M3H 5T8
Tel: 416-667-7810; Fax: 416-667-7881
journals@utpress.utoronto.ca
Circulation: 800 Frequency: Quarterly
Tom Radko, Editor

Journal of Ukrainian Studies
University of Toronto, #302, 256 McCaul St., Toronto, ON M5T 1W5
Tel: 416-978-8669; Fax: 416-978-2672
r.senkus@utoronto.ca
Circulation: 250 Frequency: Semi-annually (and occasionally as a double or quadruple issue)
Roman Senkus, Editor

Labour, Capital & Society / Travail, capital et société
c/o Suzanne Dansereau, International Development Studies, Saint Mary's University, Halifax, NS B3H 3C3
journallcs-tcs@smu.ca
Frequency: Semi-annually
The bilingual, refereed journal focuses on labour issues in Asia, Africa, the Middle East, Latin America, & the Caribbean.
Suzanne Dansereau, Editor

Labour/Le Travail
Owned By: Athabasca University Press
c/o Canadian Committee on Labour History, Athabasca University, Peace Hills Trust Tower, #1200, 10011 - 109 St., Edmonton, AB T5J 3S8
Tel: 709-737-2144; Fax: 709-737-4342
cclh@athabascau.ca
Circulation: 1,000 Frequency: 2 times a year; English & French
Bryan D. Palmer, Editor-in-chief
Irene Whitfield, Managing Editor, 709/737-3453

Material Culture Review / Revue de la culture matérielle
Previous Name: Material History Review
c/o University of Cape Breton, PO Box 5300, 1250 Grand Lake Rd., Sydney, NS B1P 6L2
Tel: 902-563-1990; Fax: 902-563-1910
mcr_rcm@cbu.ca
Circulation: 400 Frequency: 2 times a year
Richard MacKinnon, Managing Editor, 902-563-1284, richard_mackinnon@cbu.ca

McGill Journal of Education / Revue des sciences de l'éducation McGill
c/o Faculty of Education, McGill University, 3700, rue McTavish, Montréal, QC H3A 1Y2
Tel: 514-398-4246
mje.education@mcgill.ca
Circulation: 500 Frequency: 3 times a year; English & French
Stephen Peters, Managing Editor

McMaster Journal of Theology & Ministry
c/o McMaster Divinity College, McMaster University, 1280 Main St. West, Hamilton, ON L8S 4K1
Tel: 905-525-9140; Fax: 905-577-4782
mjtm@mcmaster.ca
Frequency: annual
Wendy J. Porter, Editor

Modern Drama
Owned By: University of Toronto Press Inc.
5201 Dufferin St., Toronto, ON M3H 5T8
Tel: 416-667-7810; Fax: 416-667-7881
journals@utoronto.ca
Circulation: 1,700 Frequency: Quarterly
Alan Ackerman, Editor

The Monograph
Ontario Association for Geographic & Environmental Education, #202, 10 Morrow Ave., Toronto, ON M6R 2J1
Tel: 416-538-1650; Fax: 416-489-1713
journals@interlog.com
Circulation: 800 Frequency: 4 times a year
Gary Birchall, Editor

Mosaic: A Journal for the Interdisciplinary Study of Literature
#208, Tier Bldg., University of Manitoba, Winnipeg, MB R3T 2N2
Tel: 204-474-9763; Fax: 204-474-7584
mosaic_journal@umanitoba.ca
Circulation: 900 Frequency: 4 times a year
Andrée-Ann Boisvert, Production Manager, umboisva@cc.umanitoba.ca
Jackie Pantel, Business, Submissions & Systems Manager
Dr. Dawne McCance, Editor

Mouseion, Journal of the Classical Association of Canada / Revue de la Societé canadienne des études classiques
Department of Classics, Memorial University of Newfoundland, St. John's, NL A1C 5S7
Tel: 709-737-7914
mouseion@mun.ca
Frequency: 3 pa
Articles & reviews about classical studies are published in both English & French. One issue each year is devoted to the study of archaeology.
Brad Levett, Editor, 709-864-8595, Fax: 709-864-3670
Guy Chamberland, Associate Editor, Roman History & French Language, 705-673-1730, Fax: 705-673-4979
Craig Maynes, Associate Editor, Latin Literature, 709-864-7914, Fax: 709-864-3670
Myles McCallum, Associate Editor, Archaeology, 902-420-5815, Fax: 902-491-8694
Kathryn Simonsen, Associate Editor, Greek History & Book Reviews, 709-737-8531, Fax: 709-864-3670
Hans vanderLeest, Associate Editor, Archaeology, 709-364-2557

Newfoundland & Labrador Studies
Faculty of Arts Publications, Memorial University of Newfoundland, #MS 1004, 297 Mt. Scio Rd., St. John's, NL A1B 4L6
Tel: 709-737-2144; Fax: 709-737-4342
nlstudies@mun.ca
Circulation: 350 Frequency: 2 times a year; English & French
Ron Rompkey, Chair
Irene Whitfield, Managing Editor

Ontario History
Owned By: The Ontario Historical Society
Ontario Historical Society, 34 Parkview Ave., Willowdale, ON M2N 3Y2
Tel: 416-226-9011; Fax: 416-226-2740
ohs@ontariohistoricalsociety.ca
Circulation: 1,200 Frequency: Annually
Dr. Tory Tronrud, Editor, oh@thunderbaymuseum.com

Pacific Affairs
c/o University of British Columbia, #376, 1855 West Mall, Vancouver, BC V6T 1Z2
Tel: 604-822-6508; Fax: 604-822-9452
enquiry@pacificaffairs.ubc.ca
Social Media: twitter.com/PacificAffairs
Circulation: 1,600 Frequency: 4 times a year
Publishes scholarly articles of contemporary Asia and Pacific.
Hyung Gu Lynn, Editor, hlynn@exchange.ubc.ca
Carolyn Grant, Managing Editor, cgrant@pacificaffairs.ubc.ca

The Philantropist / Le Philanthrope
c/o CCSP Press, Simon Fraser University, 515 West Hastings St., Vancouver, BC V6B 5K3
Tel: 604-984-8105
managing_editor@thephilanthropist.ca
Circulation: 450 Frequency: 4 times a year
Marilyn Bittman, Editor

Policy Options / Options politiques
Inst. for Research on Public Policy, #200, 1470, rue Peel, Montréal, QC H3A 1T1
Tel: 514-985-2461
irpp@irpp.org
Social Media: www.youtube.com/user/IRPP1972
twitter.com/irpp
www.facebook.com/pag es/IRPP/157517894283753
Circulation: 2,000 Frequency: 10 times a year
L. Ian MacDonald, Editor

Prairie Forum
Canadian Plains Research Center, University of Regina, 3737 Wascana Pkwy., Regina, SK S4S 0A2
Tel: 306-585-4795; Fax: 306-585-4699
Toll-Free: 866-874-2257
canadian.plains@uregina.ca
Social Media: twitter.com/cprcpress
Circulation: 300 Frequency: 2 times a year
Dr. Howard Leeson, Editor

Queen's Quarterly
Queen's University, 144 Barrie St., Kingston, ON K7L 3N6
Tel: 613-533-2667; Fax: 613-533-6822
queens.quarterly@queensu.ca
Circulation: 3,000 Frequency: 4 times a year
Dr. Boris Castel, Editor
Joan Harcourt, Literary Editor

Relational Child & Youth Care Practice
Previous Name: Journal of Child & Youth Care
Malaspina University-College, ASTEC Bldg., 900 Fifth St., Nanaimo, BC V9R 5S5
Tel: 250-753-3245; Fax: 250-740-6466
rcycp@mala.bc.ca
Circulation: 450 Frequency: 4 times a year
Gerry Fewster, Founding Editor
Carol Stuart, Managing Editor
Dr. T. Garfat, Co-Editor

Renaissance & Reformation / Renaissance et réforme
c/o Iter, #7009, 130 St George St., Toronto, ON M5S 1A5
Tel: 416-978-7074; Fax: 416-978-1668
iter.renref@utoronto.ca
Circulation: 700 Frequency: 4 times a year
Pascale Duhamel, Editor

Resources for Feminist Research
Ontario Institute for Studies in Education/University of Toronto, 252 Bloor St. West, Toronto, ON M5S 1V6
Tel: 416-978-2033; Fax: 416-926-4725
rfr@utoronto.ca
Circulation: 2,000 Frequency: 2 times a year
Feminist Peer-reviewed Academic Journal.
Philinda Masters, Editor

Revue canadienne de linguistique appliquée / Canadian Journal of Applied Linguistics
Institut des langues secondes, Université d'Ottawa, 600 King Edward, Ottawa, ON K1N 6N5
Tél: 613-562-5743;Téléc: 613-562-5126
hknoerr@uottawa.ca
Fréquence: 2 fois par an
Hélène Knoerr, Editor

Revue Le Médecin Vétérinaire du Québec
Ordre des médecins vétérinaires du Québec, #200, 800, av Ste-Anne, Saint-Hyacinthe, QC J2S 5G7
Tél: 450-774-1427;Téléc: 450-774-7635
omvq@omvq.qc.ca
Tirage: 2 500 Fréquence: 4 fois par an; français
Jean Piérard, Rédacteur-en-chef d.m.v.

Russell: The Journal of Bertrand Russell Studies
Previous Name: Russell: The Journal of the Bertrand Russell Archives
The Bertrand Russell Research Centre, Mills Memorial Library L108, Hamilton, ON L8S 4L6
Tel: 905-525-9140; Fax: 905-522-1277
russjour@mcmaster.ca
Circulation: 400 Frequency: 2 times a year
Kenneth Blackwell, Editor

Scientia Canadensis - Journal of the History of Cdn. Science, Technology & Medicine
Canadian Science & Technology Historical Association, PO Box 8502 T, Ottawa, ON K1G 3H9
Circulation: 200 Frequency: Annually
Stéphane Castonguay, Editor-in-chief

Scrivener Creative Review
c/o McGill University, 853, rue Sherbrooke ouest, Montréal, QC H3A 2T6
Tel: 514-398-6588; Fax: 514-398-8146
scrivener.creative.review@gmail.com
Social Media: www.facebook.com/groups/6726676175
Circulation: 500 Frequency: Annually
Klara du Plessis, Editor

Seminar
Owned By: University of Toronto Press Inc.
University of Toronto Press - Journals Division, 5201 Dufferin St., Toronto, ON M3H 5T8
Tel: 416-667-7810; Fax: 416-667-7881
journals@utpress.utoronto.ca
Circulation: 770 Frequency: Quarterly
Raleigh Whitinger, Editor

Social History / Histoire Sociale
Owned By: University of Toronto Press Inc.
5201 Dufferin St., Toronto, ON M3H 5T8
Tel: 416-667-7810; Fax: 416-667-7881
journals@utpress.utoronto.ca
Circulation: 500 Frequency: Semi-annually
Chad Gaffield, Editor
Gordon Darroch, Editor

Studies in Canadian Literature / Études en littérature canadienne
Campus House, PO Box 4400, 11 Garland Ct., Fredericton, NB E3B 5A3
Tel: 506-453-3501; Fax: 506-453-5069
scl@unb.ca
Circulation: 500 Frequency: 2 times a year
John Clement Ball, Editor, jball@unb.ca
Kathryn Taglia, Managing Editor
Jennifer Andrews, Editor, jandrews@unb.ca

Studies in Political Economy: A Socialist Review
Carleton University, Dunton Tower, 1125 Colonel By Dr., Ottawa, ON K1S 5B6
Tel: 613-520-2600; Fax: 613-520-3713
spe@carleton.ca
Circulation: 600 Frequency: 2 times a year
Hélène Pellerin

Theatre Research in Canada / Recherches théâtrales au Canada
Graduate Centre for Study of Drama, University of Toronto, 214 College St., 3rd Fl., Toronto, ON M5T 2Z9
Fax: 416-971-1378
tric.rtac@utoronto.ca
Circulation: 350 Frequency: Semi-annually; English & French
Bruce Barton, Editor

The Tocqueville Review / La Revue Tocqueville
Owned By: University of Toronto Press Inc.
5201 Dufferin St., Toronto, ON M3H 5T8
Tel: 416-667-7781; Fax: 416-667-7881
journals@utpress.utoronto.ca
Circulation: 400 Frequency: Bi-annually
Michel Forsé, Co-Editor
Françoise Mélonio, Co-Editor
Laurence Gullec, Co-Editor
Cheryl Welch, Co-Editor

TOPIA: Canadian Journal of Cultural Studies
240 Vanier College, York University, 4700 Keele St., Toronto, ON M3J 1P3
Tel: 416-736-2100; Fax: 416-736-5640
topia@yorku.ca
Circulation: 300 Frequency: 2 times a year
Jody Berland, Editor

Transcultural Psychiatry
Previous Name: Transcultural Psychiatric Research Review
Psychiatry Dept., McGill University, 1033, av des Pins ouest, Montréal, QC H3A 1A1
Tel: 514-398-7302; Fax: 514-375-1459
transcultural.psychiatry@mcgill.ca
Circulation: 500 Frequency: 4 times a year
Laurence J. Kirmayer, Editor M.D.
Sing Lee, Associate Editor M.D.
Roland Littlewood, Associate Editor M.D., PhD
Leslie Swartz, Associate Editor PhD

Ultimate Reality & Meaning
Owned By: University of Toronto Press Inc.
5201 Dufferin St., Toronto, ON M3H 5T8
Tel: 416-667-7810; Fax: 416-667-7881
journals@utpress.utoronto.ca
Circulation: 380 Frequency: Quarterly
John F. Perry, Editor
J. Patrick Mohr, Executive Editor

University of Toronto Law Journal
Owned By: University of Toronto Press Inc.
5201 Dufferin St., Toronto, ON M3H 5T8
Tel: 416-667-7810; Fax: 416-667-7881
journals@utpress.utoronto.ca
Circulation: 700 Frequency: Quarterly
Karen Knop, Editor

University of Toronto Quarterly
Owned By: University of Toronto Press Inc.
University of Toronto Press - Journals Division, 5201 Dufferin St., Toronto, ON M3H 5T8
Tel: 416-667-7810; Fax: 416-667-7881
journals@utpress.utoronto.ca
Circulation: 1,100 Frequency: Quartlerly
Brian Corman, Editor

Urban History Review / Revue d'Histoire Urbaine
Owned By: Becker Associates
#202, 10 Morrow Ave., Toronto, ON M6R 2J1
Tel: 416-538-1630; Fax: 416-489-1713
info@urbanhistoryreview.ca
Circulation: 400 Frequency: 2 times a year
Alan Gordon, Co-Editor
Claire Poitras, Co-Editor

Windsor Review
c/o Dept. of English, University of Windsor, Chrysler Hall North, 401 Sunset Ave., Windsor, ON N9B 3P4
Tel: 519-253-3000; Fax: 519-971-3676
uwrevu@uwindsor.ca
Social Media: twitter.com/windsorreview
Circulation: 500 Frequency: Bi-annually
Alistair MacLeod, Editor, Fiction
Susan Holbrook, Editor, Poetry
Alex McKay, Editor, Visual Arts
Marty Gervais, Managing Editor

University

Student Guides

Acces Media
#31, 1124, ch Marie-Anne est, Montréal, QC H2J 2B7
Tel: 514-524-1182; Fax: 514-524-7771
Toll-Free: 800-391-1182
info@accesmedia.com
Circulation: 300,000
Edgar Donelle

Welcome Back Student Magazine
Kingston Publications, PO Box 1352, #205, 111 Princess St., Kingston, ON K7L 5C6
Tel: 613-549-8442; Fax: 613-549-4333
mowens@kingstonpublications.com
Circulation: 18,500 Frequency: Annually
Mary Laflamme, Publisher & Editor

University & Student Publications

L'Accent
Détenteur: Cégep de Rimouski
60, rue de l'Évêché ouest, Rimouski, QC G5L 4H6
Tél: 418-723-1880;Téléc: 418-724-4961
Ligne sans frais: 800-463-0617
infoscol@cegep-rimouski.qc.ca

L'AccrO
Détenteur: Cégep de Saint-Hyacinthe
3000, av Boullé, Saint-Hyacinthe, QC J2S 1H9
Tél: 450-773-6800;Téléc: 450-773-9971
info@cegepsth.qc.ca
Fréquence: Mensuel

L'Afficheur
Détenteur: Cégep de Limoilou
1300, 8e av, Québec, QC G1J 5L5
Tél: 418-647-6600;Téléc: 418-647-6798
lafficheur@climoilou.qc.ca

Algonquin Times
Owned By: Algonquin College
Algonquin College, 1385 Woodroffe Ave., Rm. N209, Ottawa, ON K2G 1V8
Tel: 613-727-4723; Fax: 613-727-7743
times@algonquincollege.com
Frequency: Bi-weekly
Algonquin College newspaper.
Kris Lapenskie, Online Editor

The Aquinian
Owned By: St. Thomas University
PO Box 4400 A, Fredericton, NB E3B 5G3
Tel: 506-452-0532; Fax: 506-452-0617
admin@theaq.net
Social Media:
twitter.com/aquinian
www.facebook.com/aquinian
St. Thomas University newspaper.
Liam McGuire, Editor-in-Chief, eic@theaq.net

The Argosy
Owned By: Mount Allison University
Wallace- McCain Student Centre, #386, 62A York St., Sackville, NB E4L 1H3
Tel: 506-364-2300
argosy@mta.ca
Social Media:
twitter.com/The_Argosy
www.facebook.com/TheArgosy
Frequency: Weekly; Thursadys
Mount Allison University's Independent Student Newspaper Since 1872
Dan Wortman, Managing Editor
Julie Stephenson, Editor

Arthur
Owned By: Trent University
#104, 751 George St., Peterborough, ON K9H 7P5
Tel: 705-745-3535; Fax: 705-745-3534
editors@trentarthur.ca
Trent University newspaper.
James Burrows, Editor
Ariel Sharratt, Editor

The Artichoke
Owned By: Winter's College, York University
#004, 4700 Keele St., Toronto, ON M3J 1P3
Tel: 416-736-5128
wintersfreepress@winterscouncil.com
Social Media:
twitter.com/artichokebywfp
www.facebook.com/pages/Artichoke-Magazine/131605956923469
Frequency: Monthly
Student magazine for Winter's College at York University.
Lindsay Presswell, Editor, editor@wintersfreepress.com

The Athenaeum
Owned By: Acadia University
Student Union Bldg., PO Box 6002, #512, 50 Acadia St., Wolfville, NS B4P 2R5
Tel: 902-585-2147
Social Media:
twitter.com/athonline
Acadia University newspaper.
Vanessa Gallant, Editor-in-Chief, eic@acadiau.ca

Le Bagou
Détenteur: Cégep du Vieux Montréal
255, rue Ontario est, Montréal, QC H2X 1X6
Tél: 514-982-3437;Téléc: 514-982-3400

Bandersnatch
Détenteur: Cégep John Abbott
CP 2000, 21275, rue Lakeshore, Sainte-Anne-de-Bellevue, QC H9X 3L9
Tél: 514-457-6610;Téléc: 514-457-1655
bandersnatch@johnabbott.qc.ca

Le Bonjour
Détenteur: Cégep de Sorel-Tracy
3000, boul Tracy, Sorel-Tracy, QC J3R 5B9
Tél: 450-742-6651;Téléc: 450-742-1878
info@cegepst.qc.ca

Bricklayer
Owned By: Red Deer College
PO Box 5005, 100 College Blvd., Red Deer, AB T4N 5H5
Tel: 403-342-3300; Fax: 403-340-8940
Red Deer College newspaper.

Brunswickan
Owned By: University of New Brunswick
PO Box 4400 A, #35, 21 Pacey Dr., Fredericton, NB E3B 5A3
Tel: 506-447-3388
University of New Brunswick newspaper.
Sandy Chase, Editor-in-Chief, editor@thebruns.ca

Bulletin d'information du Collège Ahuntsic (BICA)
Détenteur: Cégep d'Ahuntsic
9155, rue St-Hubert, Montréal, QC H2M 1Y8
Tél: 514-389-5921 Ligne sans frais: 866-389-5921
bica@collegeahuntsic.qc.ca

The Cadre
Owned By: University of Prince Edward Island
W.A. Murphy Student Centre, 550 University Ave., Charlottetown, PE C1A 2N6
Tel: 902-566-0629; Fax: 902-566-0979
editor@thecadre.ca
Social Media: www.tumblr.com/register/follow/upeicadre
twitter.com/thecadre
Frequency: Weekly, during the academic year
University of Prince Edward Island newspaper.
Garrett Curley, Editor-in-Chief, editor@thecadre.ca

The Campus
Owned By: Université Bishop's
PO Box 5000, 2600 College St., Sherbrooke, QC J1M 1Z7
Tel: 819-822-9600; Fax: 819-822-9661
liaison@ubishops.ca
Social Media: www.youtube.com/user/bishopsuniversity
twitter.com/ubishops
www.facebo ok.com/bishops
Frequency: Bi-weekly; Thursday, during academic year

Caper Times
Previous Name: The 60th Meridian
Owned By: Cape Breton University
c/o Cape Breton University (CBU), PO Box 5300, 1250 Grand Lake Rd., Sydney, NS B1P 6L2
Tel: 902-563-1473
editor@capertimes.ca
Cape Breton University newspaper.
Lucy MacDonald, Editor-in-Chief

Capilano Courier
Owned By: Capilano College
2055 Purcell Way, North Vancouver, BC V7J 3H5
Tel: 604-984-4949
editor@capilanocourier.com
Capilano College newspaper.
JJ Brewis, Editor-in-Chief

The Carillon
Owned By: The University of Regina
227 Riddell Centre, 3737 Wascana Pkwy., Regina, SK S4S 0A2
Tel: 306-586-8867
editor@carillonregina.com
Social Media:
twitter.com/the_carillon
www.facebook.com/carillon.newspaper
Frequency: 11 times a year; Thursdays
The University of Regina newspaper.
Dietrich Neu, Editor-in-Chief, editor@carillonregina.com

The Cascade
Owned By: University of the Fraser Valley (UFV)
33844 King Rd., Abbotsford, BC V2S 7M8
Tel: 604-854-4529
Social Media:
twitter.com/ufvcascade
University of the Fraser Valley (UFV) newspaper.
Paul Esau, Editor-in-Chief, esau@ufvcascade.ca

The Cord
Owned By: Wilfrid Laurier University
75 University Ave. West, Waterloo, ON N2L 3C5
Tel: 519-884-0710
Social Media:
twitter.com/cordnews
www.facebook.com/pages/The-Cord/113605339652
Frequency: Weekly
Wilfrid Laurier University newspaper.
Justin Fauteux, Editor, 519-884-0710 x3563, jfauteux@thecord.ca

The Crown
Owned By: Redeemer University College
777 Garner Rd. East, Ancaster, ON L9K 1J4
Tel: 905-648-2131
managing.editor@thecrown.ca
Redeemer University College newspaper.
Ben Reid, Editor-in-Chief

D.E.C. express
Détenteur: Cégep de Baie-Comeau
537, boul Blanche, Baie-Comeau, QC G5C 2B2
Tél: 418-589-5707;Téléc: 418-589-9842
Ligne sans frais: 800-463-2030
Médias sociaux:
twitter.com/cegepbaiecomeau
www.facebook.com/cegepbaiecomeau

Daily Bulletin
Previous Name: UW Gazette
Owned By: University of Waterloo
200 University Ave. West, Waterloo, ON N2L 3G1
Tel: 519-888-4567
bulletin@uwaterloo.ca
Social Media:
twitter.com/uwdailybulletin
Frequency: Daily; online
University of Waterloo newspaper.
Brandon Sweet, Editor

L'Écho
Détenteur: Collège de Lévis
9, rue Monseigneur Gosselin, Lévis, QC G6V 5K1
Tél: 418-833-1249;Téléc: 418-833-7055
fondation@collegedelevis.qc.ca
Fréquence: Semestriel
Pierre Bélanger, Directeur, belpier28@gmail.com

The Echo
Owned By: Vanier College
821, av Ste-Croix, Saint-Laurent, QC H4L 3X9
Tel: 514-744-7500; Fax: 514-744-7023
echo@fclass.vaniercollege.qc.ca
Vanier College newspaper.
Caroline Zemokhol, Editor-in-Chief

Échorridor
Détenteur : Cégep d'Alma
675, boul Auger ouest, Alma, QC G8B 2B7
Tél: 418-668-2387;Téléc: 418-668-6841
college@calma.qc.ca
Fréquence: Quinzomadaire

L'Éclipse
Détenteur: Cégep Saint-Jean-sur-Richelieu
CP 1018, 30, boul du Séminaire, Saint-Jean-sur-Richelieu, QC J3B 5J4
Tél: 450-347-5301;Téléc: 450-347-3329
communications@cstjean.qc.ca
Fréquence: Hebdomadaire

Eclosion
Détenteur: Cégep de Sainte-Foy
#M-106, 2410, ch Ste-Foy, Sainte-Foy, QC G1V 1T3
Tél: 418-658-5389;Téléc: 418-658-6798
j.leclosion@gmail.com

The Endeavour
Owned By: Lethbridge Community College
#TE3225, 3000 College Dr. South, Lethbridge, AB T1K 1L6
Tel: 403-320-3301; Fax: 403-317-3582
endeavour@lethbridgecollege.ab.ca
Social Media:
twitter.com/LCEndeavour
www.facebook.com/174217563573
Lethbridge Community College newspaper.
Anne Raslask, Publisher

L'Entremetteur
Détenteur: Cégep de l'Outaouais
Campus Gabrielle-Roy, Cégep-Outaouais, 333, boul Cité-des-Jeunes, Hull, QC J8Y 6M4
Tél: 819-770-4012;Téléc: 819-770-8167

The Eyeopener
Owned By: Ryerson University
55 Gould St., Toronto, ON M5B 1E9
Tel: 416-979-5262
editor@theeyeopener.com
Social Media:
twitter.com/theeyeopener
www.facebook.com/pages/The-Eyeopener/32810756867
Frequency: Monthly
The Eyeopener is Ryerson University's independent student newspaper.
Lee Richardson, Editor-in-Chief, 416-979-5000

La FlaMèche
Détenteur: Cégep de l'Abitibi-Témiscamingue
425, boul du Collège, Rouyn-Noranda, QC J9X 5E5
Tél: 819-762-0931;Téléc: 819-762-2071
Ligne sans frais: 866-234-3728
Fréquence: Hebdomadaire

Folia Montana
Owned By: Mount Saint Vincent University
166 Bedford Hwy., Halifax, NS B3M 2J6
Tel: 902-457-6117; Fax: 902-457-6498
Social Media:
www.facebook.com/people/Alumnae-Relations/651842399
Circulation: 17,000 Frequency: Bi-Annually
Mount Saint Vincent University alumni newspaper.

Folio
Owned By: University of Alberta
General Services Bldg., 6th Fl., 114 St. - 89 Ave., Edmonton, AB T6G 2H1
Tel: 780-492-2325; Fax: 780-492-2997
University of Alberta newspaper.
Michael Brown, Acting Editor, 780-492-9407, michael.brown@ualberta.ca

Le Front
Détenteur: Université de Moncton
18, ave Antonine-Maillet, Moncton, NB E1A 3E9
Tél: 506-863-2012;Téléc: 506-858-4524
lefront@umoncton.ca
Médias sociaux:
www.facebook.com/164290830264753

The Fulcrum
Détenteur: University of Ottawa
631 King Edward Ave., Ottawa, ON K1N 6N5
Tél: 613-562-5261;Téléc: 613-562-5259
Médias sociaux: www.flickr.com/photos/thefulcrum/
twitter.com/The_Fulcrum
www.facebook .com/UofOFulcrum
The Fulcrum is the independent English-language student newspaper at the University of Ottawa.
Mercedes Mueller, Editor-in-Chief, 613-562-5261, editor@thefulcrum.ca

Gargoyle
Owned By: University College
15 King's College Circle, F6, Toronto, ON M5S 3H7
Tel: 416-946-0941
ucgargoyle@gmail.com
Social Media:
twitter.com/ucgargoyle
University College newspaper.
Angjielin Hila, Editor-in-Chief
Carla Mesa Guzzo, Editor-in-Chief

The Gateway
Owned By: University of Alberta
#3-04, Student Union Bldg., Edmonton, AB T6G 2J7
Tel: 780-492-5168; Fax: 780-492-6665
biz@gateway.ualberta.ca
Social Media: www.youtube.com/user/thegatewaymultimedia
twitter.com/the_gateway
www. facebook.com/TheGatewayOnline
Frequency: Weekly; Wednesdays, during the academic year; 3 issues in the spring/summer
The Gateway is the official student newspaper at the University of Alberta.
Ryan Bromsgrove, Editor-in-Chief, 780-492-5168, eic@gateway.ualberta.ca

The Gauntlet
Owned By: The University of Calgary
MacEwan Student Centre, #319, 2500 University Dr. NW, Calgary, AB T2N 1N4
Tel: 403-220-7750
editor@thegauntlet.ca
Social Media:
twitter.com/gauntletuofc
www.facebook.com/uofcgauntlet
The University of Calgary newspaper.
Erin Shumlich, Editor-in-Chief, 403-220-7752, eic@thegauntlet.ca

The Gazette
Owned By: University of Western Ontario
#263, University Community Centre, London, ON N6A 3K7
Tel: 519-661-3580
editor@westerngazette.ca
Social Media:
twitter.com/uwogazette
Circulation: 11,000 Frequency: 4 times a week; Tues.-Fri.
The Gazette is the student newspaper at the University of Western Ontario in London, Ontario, Canada.
Gloria Dickie, Editor-in-Chief

Gazette
Owned By: Dalhousie University
Student Union Building, #312, 6136 University Ave., Halifax, NS B3H 4J2
Tel: 902-494-1280
editor@dalgazette.com
Social Media:
twitter.com/dalgazette
www.facebook.com/DalGazette
Dalhousie University newspaper.
Dylan Matthias, Editor-in-Chief

The Georgian Eye
Owned By: Georgian College
One Georgian Dr., Barrie, ON L4M 3X9
Tel: 705-728-1968; Fax: 705-722-5123
georgianeye@gmail.com
Social Media:
twitter.com/georgianeye
www.facebook.com/pages/Georgian-Eye/189699 477762452
Georgian College newspaper. The new Georgian Eye Blog is an online site for students to write about things that interest them and comment on other students rants or raves.

La Gifle
Détenteur: Cégep de Trois-Rivières
CP 97, 3500, rue De Courval, Trois-Rivières, QC G9A 5E6
Tél: 819-376-1721;Téléc: 819-693-8023
communications@cegeptr.qc.ca
Médias sociaux: plus.google.com/109162921820608962493
twitter.com/cegeptr
www.facebook .com/cegeptr

Golden Ram
Owned By: Nova Scotia Agricultural College
PO Box 550, Truro, NS B2N 5E3
Tel: 902-895-3963; Fax: 902-895-1203
goldenram@nsac.ca
Nova Scotia Agricultural College newspaper.
Katherine Mitchell, Editor
Matthew Morrison, Editor

The Gradzette
Owned By: University of Manitoba
221 University Centre, Winnipeg, MB R3T 2N2
Tel: 204-474-9181; Fax: 204-474-7560
gradzette@umgsa.ca
Social Media:
www.facebook.com/groups/195842203788275
The official magazine of University of Manitoba graduate students.

Le Graffiti
Détenteur: Collège Jean-de-Brebeuf Inc.
3200, ch de la côte Ste-Catherine, Montréal, QC H3T 1C1
Tél: 514-342-9342
ageb@brebeuf.qc.ca

The Grapevine
Owned By: Huron University College
1349 Western Rd., London, ON N6G 1H3
Tel: 519-438-7224
Social Media:
www.facebook.com/pages/Hurons-Grapevine/166794663334282
Frequency: Monthly
The Grapevine Magazine is a student-based publication that circulates monthly on the following campuses in London, Ontario: Huron University College, University of Western Ontario, and Kings College.
Whitney Slightham, Editor-in-Chief

the griff
Owned By: Grant MacEwan College
#7-297C, 10700 - 104 Ave., Edmonton, AB T5J 4S2
Tel: 780-497-4429; Fax: 780-497-5470
online@thegriff.ca
Circulation: 2,500 Frequency: 25 issues per academic year; Weekly; Thursday
the griff is MacEwan University's weekly student newspaper.
Angela Johnston, News Editor

Le Griffonnier
Détenteur: Université du Québec à Chicoutimi
555, boul de l'Université, Chicoutimi, QC G7H 2B1
Tél: 418-545-5011;Téléc: 418-545-5012
journal_griffonnier@uqac.ca
Médias sociaux:
www.facebook.com/ceuc.ca
Le Griffonnier est le journal des étudiants de l'UQAC.
Nancy Desgagné, Rédactrice-en-chef journal

Hebdo Garneau
Détenteur: Cégep François-Xavier-Garneau
1660, boul de l'Entente, Québec, QC G1S 4S3
Tél: 418-688-8310;Téléc: 418-688-1539
communications@cegep-fxg.qc.ca
Fréquence: Hebdomadaire
Sylvie Fortin, Directrice, sfortin@cegep-fxg.qc.ca

L'IdéePhile
Détenteur: Cégep de Chicoutimi
534, rue Jacques-Cartier est, Chicoutimi, QC G7H 1Z6
Tél: 418-549-9520;Téléc: 418-549-1315
info@cchic.ca

Impact Campus
Détenteur: Université Laval
1244, Pavillon Maurice-Pollack, Université Laval, Québec, QC G1V 0A6
Tél: 418-656-5079;Téléc: 418-656-2398
redaction@impact.ulaval.ca
Médias sociaux: www.youtube.com/user/ImpactCampus
twitter.com/ImpactCampus
www.faceboo k.com/impactcampus
Fréquence: Hebdomadaire
Hubert Gaudreau, Rédacteur en chef

L'Inculte
Détenteur: Cégep de Victoriaville
475, rue Notre-Dame est, Victoriaville, QC G6P 4B3
Tél: 819-758-6401;Téléc: 819-758-8126

L'INFO-Cégep
Détenteur: Cégep de Granby-Haute-Yamaska
CP 7000, 235, rue Saint-Jacques, Granby, QC J2G 9H7
Tél: 450-372-6614;Téléc: 450-372-6565
Fréquence: Quotidien, juin-août

L'Infomane
Détenteur: Cégep de Bois-de-Boulogne
10500, av de Bois-de-Boulogne, Montréal, QC H4N 1L4
Tél: 514-332-3000;Téléc: 514-332-5857
infomane@age.bdeb.qc.ca
Médias sociaux:
twitter.com/infomane
www.facebook.com/infomane
Laurence Bissonnet, Coordonatrice Générale

Inter-Anciennement: Suites
Détenteur: Université du Québec à Montréal
Service des communications, CP 8888 Centre-Ville, #WB-5300, Montréal, QC H3C 3P8
Tél: 514-987-3000
magazine.inter@uqam.ca

The Intercamp
Owned By: Grant MacEwan College
City Centre Campus, #297C, 10700 - 104 Ave., Edmonton, AB T5J 4S2
Tel: 780-497-5412
Grant MacEwan College newspaper.
Jenny Feniak, Managing Editor, managing@intercamp.ca

Le Jets
Détenteur: École de technologie supérieure
1100, rue Notre-Dame ouest, Montréal, QC H3C 1K3
Tél: 514-396-8800;Téléc: 514-396-8950
directeur@jets.etsmtl.ca

The Journal
Owned By: Queen's University
Queen's University, 190 University Ave., Kingston, ON K7L 3P4
Tel: 613-533-2800; Fax: 613-533-6728
journal_editors@ams.queensu.ca
Social Media:
twitter.com/queensjournal
www.facebook.com/queensjournal
Frequency: Two issues a week for the first two months and once a week in the last month of each semester, totalling 40 issues.
Queen's University newspaper.
Katherine Fernandez-Blance, Editor-in-Chief

The Journal
Owned By: Saint Mary's University
Student Centre, 923 Robie St., 5th Fl., Halifax, NS B3H 3C3
Tel: 902-266-9731
Social Media:
twitter.com/TheSMUJournal
www.facebook.com/SMUJournal
Saint Mary's University newspaper.
Samuel Hammond, Editor, 902-266-9731, samuelphammond@gmail.com

Journal l'Action
Détenteur: Cégep de Shawinigan
CP 610, Shawinigan, QC G9N 6V8
Tél: 819-539-6401
journal@collegeshawinigan.qc.ca

Journal L'Interêt
Détenteur: Écoles De Hautes Etudes Commerciales Montréal
#RJ718, 3000, ch de la Côte-Sainte-Catherine, Montréal, QC H3T 2A7
Tél: 514-340-6105
redaction.interet@hec.ca
Médias sociaux:
www.facebook.com/journalinteret

Labyrinthe
Détenteur : Cégep de Matane
616, av St-Rédempteur, Matane, QC G4W 1L1
Tél: 418-562-1240;Téléc: 418-566-2115
Ligne sans frais: 800-463-4299
information@cegep-matane.qc.ca

Lambda
Détenteur: Laurentian University of Sudbury
Student Centre, #SCE301, 935 Ramsey Lake Rd., Sudbury, ON P3E 2C6
Tél: 705-673-6548
lambda@laurentian.ca
Médias sociaux:
www.facebook.com/TheLambda
Lambda is Laurentian University's campus newspaper.
Ed Veilleux, News Editor

The Lance
Owned By: University of Windsor
CAW Student Centre, B-91, 401 Sunset Ave., Windsor, ON N9B 3P4
Tel: 519-253-3000; Fax: 519-971-3624
Social Media:
twitter.com/uwindsorlance
www.facebook.com/uwindsorlance
Circulation: 10,000 Frequency: Weekly; Wednesday
University of Windsor newspaper.

The Link
Owned By: Université Concordia
Concordia University Hall Building, Rm H-649, 1455, Maisonneuve Blvd. West, Montréal, QC H3G 1M8
Tel: 514-848-2424; Fax: 514-848-4540
editor@thelinknewspaper.ca
Social Media:
twitter.com/linknewspaper
www.facebook.com/TheLinkNewspaper
Julia Wolfe, Editor-in-chief

The Link
Owned By: BC Institute of Technology
3700 Willingdon Ave., Burnaby, BC V5G 3H2
Tel: 604-432-8600
publications@bcitsa.ca
Social Media:
www.facebook.com/BCITSA
BC Institute of Technology newspaper.
Kevin Willemse, Editor, linkeditor@bcitsa.ca

Lionel
Détenteur: Cégep Lionel-Groulx
100, rue Duquet, Sainte-Thérèse, QC J7E 3G6
Tél: 450-430-3120;Téléc: 450-971-7883
info@clg.qc.ca

MacMedia (McLaughlin College)
Owned By: York University
#004, 4700 Keele St., Toronto, ON M3J 1P3
Tel: 416-736-5128
macmedia@yorku.ca
Social Media:
www.facebook.com/groups/6334572703
York University newspaper.

The Manitoban
Owned By: University of Manitoba
105 University Centre, Winnipeg, MB R3T 2N2
Tel: 204-474-6535; Fax: 204-474-7651
me@themanitoban.com
Social Media:
www.facebook.com/groups/195842203788275
The Manitoban is the official student newspaper of the University of Manitoba.
Ryan Hardy, Editor-in-Chief, 204-474-8293, editor@themanitoban.com

Mars' Hill
Owned By: Trinity Western Seminary
7600 Glover Rd., Langley, BC V2Y 1Y1
Tel: 604-888-6158; Fax: 604-888-5729
marshill@gmail.com.
Trinity Western Seminary newspaper.

The Martlet
Owned By: University of Victoria
PO Box 3035, Student Union Building, Rm. B011, Victoria, BC V8W 3P3
Tel: 250-721-8360; Fax: 250-472-4556
edit@martlet.ca
Circulation: 4,200
The Martlet is an independent weekly student newspaper at the University of Victoria in Victoria, British Columbia, Canada.
Vanessa Annand, Editor-in-Chief, 250-853-3206, edit@martlet.ca

McGill Reporter
Owned By: McGill University
#110, James Administration Bldg., 845, Sherbrooke St. West, Montréal, QC H3A 2T5
Tel: 514-398-1044
Social Media:
twitter.com/mcgillreporter
Frequency: 4 pa
McGill University newspaper.

Le Médiavic
Détenteur: Collège Marie-Victorin
7000, rue Marie-Victorin, Montréal, QC H1G 2J6
Tél: 514-325-0150
promotion@marievictorin.qc.ca
Fréquence: Hebdomadaire

The Medium
Owned By: University of Toronto at Mississauga
#200, 3359 Mississauga Rd., Mississauga, ON L5L 1C6
Tel: 905-828-5260; Fax: 905-569-4301
info@mediumutm.ca
Social Media:
twitter.com/TheMediumUTM
www.facebook.com/groups/293066010726328
The Medium is the print media voice for the students of the University of Toronto Mississauga.
Michael Di Leo, Editor-in-Chief, editor@mediumutm.ca

The Meliorist
Owned By: University of Lethbridge
166 University Dr. West, Lethbridge, AB T1K 3M4
Tel: 403-329-2334; Fax: 403-329-2333
University of Lethbridge newspaper.
Kelti Boissonnault, Editor-in-Chief, 403-329-2334, einc@themeliorist.ca

The Mike
Owned By: St. Michael's College
Elmsley Hall, Main Fl., #2, 81 St. Mary St., Toronto, ON M4S 1J4
Tel: 416-926-7272
editoratlarge@readthemike.com
Social Media:
twitter.com/readthemike
www.facebook.com/readthemike
Circulation: 5,000 Frequency: Bi-weekly
St. Michael's College newspaper
Dan Seljak, Editor-in-Chief, editorinchief@readthemike.com

Le Motdit
Détenteur: Cégep Édouard-Montpetit
#F-045, 945, ch de Chambly, Longueuil, QC J4H 3M6
Tél: 450-679-2631;Téléc: 450-679-5570
Médias sociaux:
twitter.com/collegeedouardm
www.facebook.com/CollegeEdouardM

Mouton Noir
Détenteur: Cégep de Drummondville
#1209, 960, rue St-Georges, Drummondville, QC J2C 6A2
Tél: 819-478-4671;Téléc: 819-478-8823
journal.mnoir@gmail.com

The Muse
Owned By: Memorial University of Newfoundland
PO Box 4200, 230 Elizabeth Ave., St. John's, NL A1C 5S7
Tel: 709-737-8000; Fax: 709-737-4569
chief@themuse.ca
Memorial University of Newfoundland newspaper.

The Navigator
Owned By: Vancouver Island University
Bldg. 193, #217, 900 - 5th St., Nanaimo, BC V9R 5S5
Tel: 250-753-2225; Fax: 250-753-2257
Social Media:
twitter.com/theNav_VIU
www.facebook.com/thenavigatornewspaper
Frequency: Weekly
The Navigator is Vancouver Island University's (formerly Malaspina University-College) student newspaper.
Gareth Boyce, Editor-in-Chief, editor@thenav.ca

Nexus
Owned By: Camosun College
Lansdowne Campus, Richmond House 201, 3100 Foul Bay Rd., Victoria, BC V8P 5J2
Tel: 250-370-3591
nexus@nexusnewspaper.com
Social Media:
www.facebook.com/nexusnewspaper
www.facebook.com/nexusnewspaper
Camosun College newspaper.
Greg Pratt, Editor-in-Chief

NightViews
Owned By: Ryerson University
350 Victoria St., Toronto, ON M5B 2K3
Tel: 416-979-5000
inquire@ryerson.ca
Frequency: Monthly
A monthly newspaper for Ryerson's Continuing Education and Part-time Degree students.

The Nugget
Owned By: The Northern Alberta Institute of Technology
11762 - 106 St., Edmonton, AB T5G 2R1
Tel: 780-423-5834
kerry@playhousepublications.ca
Social Media:
twitter.com/theNAITNugget
www.facebook.com/naitstudents
The Northern Alberta Institute of Technology newspaper.
Celeste Dul, Editor-in-Chief, studenteditor@nait.ca

ô Courant
Détenteur: Cégep régional de Lanaudière
2505, boul des Entreprises, Terrebonne, QC J6X 5S5
Tél: 450-470-0933

The Omega
Owned By: Thompson rivers University
TRU Campus, House 4, PO Box 3010, 900 McGill Rd., Kamloops, BC V2C 0C8
Tel: 250-372-1272
editorofomega@gmail.com
Other information: 250-828-5069
Social Media:
twitter.com/TRU_Omega
www.facebook.com/pages/The-Omega/217031195028151
Frequency: Weekly; Wednesdays
The Omega is Thompson Rivers University's independent student newspaper.
Mike Davies, Editor-in-Chief

L'Original déchainé
Détenteur: Laurentian University of Sudbury
#SCE301, 935 Ramsey Lake Rd., Sudbury, ON P3E 2C6
Tél: 705-673-6548
Médias sociaux:
www.facebook.com/145697498801833
Newspaper which is written for the Francophone Community of Laurentian.

Other Press
Owned By: Douglas College
PO Box 2503, New Westminster, BC V3L 5B2
editor@theotherpress.ca
Social Media:
twitter.com/TheOtherPress
Frequency: weekly during the fall and winter semesters, and monthly during the summer
Douglas College newspaper.
Sharon Miki, Editor-in-Chief

Over the Edge
Owned By: University of Northern British Columbia
3333 University Way, NUSC 6-350, Prince George, BC V2N 4Z9
Tel: 250-960-5633; Fax: 250-960-5407
over-the-edge@unbc.ca
University of Northern British Columbia newspaper.
Shelby Petersen, Editor-in-Chief

La P'tite Antenne
Détenteur: Cégep de Rivière-du-Loup
80, rue Frontenac, Rivière-du-Loup, QC G5R 1R1
Tél: 418-862-6903;Téléc: 418-862-4959

The Papercut
Owned By: Marianopolis College
4873, ave Westmount, Westmount, QC H3Y 1X9
Tel: 514-931-8792; Fax: 514-931-8790
the.marianopolis.papercut@gmail.com
Social Media:
twitter.com/MarianoPapercut
www.facebook.com/the.marianopolis.papercut
Marianopolis College newspaper.

Le Pastiche
Owned By: Cégep de Saint-Laurent
625, av Ste-Croix, Montréal, QC H4L 3X7
Tel: 514-747-6521; Fax: 514-748-1249
info@cegep-st-laurent.qc.ca
Social Media: www.linkedin.com/company/1588262
twitter.com/webcsl
www.facebook.com/1 37132236299536

The Peak
Owned By: Simon Fraser University
#MBC2901, 8888 University Dr., Burnaby, BC V5A 1S6
Tel: 778-782-4560; Fax: 778-782-4343
production@the-peak.ca
Social Media:
twitter.com/peaksfu
www.facebook.com/PeakSFU
Simon Fraser University newspaper.
David Dyck, News Editor, news@the-peak.ca

The Phoenix
Owned By: Okanagan College
3333 University Way, UNC109O, Kelowna, BC V1Y 1V7
Tel: 250-807-9296
Social Media:
twitter.com/ubcophoenix
www.facebook.com/thephoenixnews
Okanagan College newspaper.
Cameron Welch, Editor-in-Chief,
editorinchief@thephoenixnews.com

La Pige
Détenteur: Cégep de Jonquière
#854.2, pavillon Joseph-Angers, Jonquière, QC G7X 7W2
Tél: 418-547-2191
cegep@cjonquiere.qc.ca
Tirage: 5000

La Placote
Détenteur: Cégep de Lévis-Lauzon
205, rue Mgr Bourget, Lévis, QC G6V 6Z9
Tél: 418-833-5110;Téléc: 418-833-8502
Josée Larochelle, V.-p. aux affaires pédagogiques

The Plant
Owned By: Dawson College
3040 Sherbrooke St. West, Montréal, QC H3Z 1A4
Tel: 514-931-8731; Fax: 514-931-5181
Social Media:
twitter.com/issuu
www.facebook.com/issuu
Frequency: Weekly

Le Polyscope
Détenteur: École Polytechnique de Montréal
CP 6079 Centre-ville, Montréal, QC H3C 3A7
Tél: 514-340-4711;Téléc: 514-340-4986
direction@polyscope.qc.ca
Tomasz Drake, Rédacteur en chef, article@polyscope.qc.ca

Portico
Owned By: University of Guelph
University Centre, Level 4, University of Guelph, 50 Stone Rd. East, Guelph, ON N1G 2W1
Tel: 519-824-7962
m.dickieson@exec.uoguelph.ca
Frequency: 3 times a year
The Portico is mailed free to Guelph alumni living around the world.
Mary Dickieson, Editor

Quartier Libre
Détenteur: Université de Montréal
CP 6128 Centre-ville, 3200, rue Jean-Brillant, B-1274-6, Montréal, QC H3T 1N8
Tél: 514-343-7630
Médias sociaux:
twitter.com/quartierlibre
www.facebook.com/QuartierLibre.ca
Marie Roncari, Directrice, directeur@quartierlibre.ca

The Quill
Owned By: Brandon University
270 - 18th St., Brandon, MB R7A 6A9
Tel: 204-727-9667; Fax: 204-571-0029
business.thequill@gmail.com
Social Media:
www.facebook.com/pages/The-Quill/124336617614355
Brandon University newspaper.
Matt Berry, Editor-in-Chief, eic.thequill@gmail.com

The Reflector
Owned By: Mount Royal College
Wyckham House, Mount Royal University, 4825 Mount Royal Gate SW, Calgary, AB T3E 6K6
Tel: 403-440-6268; Fax: 403-440-6762
thereflector@thereflector.ca
Social Media: www.youtube.com/user/SirKrushworth
twitter.com/reflectthis
www.faceboo k.com/TheReflector.ca
Circulation: 10,000 Frequency: Bi-weekly; Sept.-April
Mount Royal College newspaper.
Rachael Frey, Publishing Editor & News Editor,
publishingeditor@thereflector.ca

Réseau - Le magazine de l'Université du Québec
Détenteur: Université du Québec
475, rue du Parvis, Québec, QC G1K 9H7
Tél: 418-657-3551
Fréquence: Fermé

Le Réveil
Détenteur: Collège universitaire de Saint-Boniface
CP 129, 200, av de la Cathédrale, Saint-Boniface, MB R2H 0H7
Tél: 204-237-1818;Téléc: 204-237-3240
mesdiasetudiants@cusb.ca
Le Réveil est un journal francophone par et pour les étudiantes et les étudiants du Collège universitaire de Saint-Boniface (CUSB).
Marie-Christine Bruce, Rédactrice en chef

The Ring
Owned By: University of Victoria
Sedgewick Building, C149, PO Box 1700 CSC, 3800 Finnerty Rd. (Ring Rd.), Victoria, BC V8W 2Y2
Tel: 250-721-7636; Fax: 250-721-8955
ucom@uvic.ca
Social Media: www.youtube.com/uvicring
twitter.com/uvicring
Circulation: 4,200
University of Victoria newspaper.
Bruce Kilpatrick, Director, 250-721-7638, abk@uvic.ca

Rosemont Ici
Détenteur: Cégep de Rosemont
6400, 16e av, Montréal, QC H1X 2S9
Tél: 514-376-1620;Téléc: 514-376-1440
Anne-Marie Lacombe, Éditrice

La Rotonde
Détenteur: University of Ottawa
109, rue Osgoode, Ottawa, ON K1N 6S1
Médias sociaux:
twitter.com/LaRotonde
University of Ottawa newspaper.
Anais Elboujdaïne, Rédactrice en chef, redaction@larotonde.ca

The Runner
Owned By: Kwantlen Unicersity College
Arbutus Bldg., #3710/3720, 12666 72 Ave., Surrey, BC V3W 2M8
Tel: 778-565-3802
production@runnermag.ca
Social Media:
twitter.com/Runnermag
www.facebook.com/runnerpaper
Frequency: 20 issues a year
Kwantlen Polytechnic University newspaper.
Jeff Groat, Editor, 778-565-3803, editor@runnerrag.ca

The Ryerson Free Press
Owned By: Ryerson University
#SCC-301, 55 Gould St., Toronto, ON M5B 1E9
Tel: 416-979-5262
editor@ryersonfreepress.ca
Social Media:
twitter.com/RyeFreePress
Frequency: Monthly
The Ryerson Free Press is the definitive alternative monthly of the Continuing Education Student's Association of Ryerson University (CESAR).
Nora Loreto, Editor-in-Chief, editor@ryersonfreepress.ca

Ryerson Review of Journalism
Owned By: Ryerson University
350 Victoria Street, Toronto, ON M5B 2K3
Tel: 416-979-5319; Fax: 416-979-5216
chair.journalism@ryerson.ca
Social Media:
twitter.com/RyersonReview
www.facebook.com/707355524.2912769015
Frequency: 2 times a year
Produced by final-year students at Ryerson University's School of Journalism in Toronto, Canada.
Sara Harowitz, Editor, sara.harowitz@ryerson.ca

The Ryersonian
Owned By: Ryerson University
350 Victoria Street, Toronto, ON M5B 2K3
sonian@ryerson.ca
Social Media:
twitter.com/TheRyersonian
www.facebook.com/TheRyersonian
Students in Ryerson's School of Journalism's fourth-year undergraduate & second-year graduate program produce The Ryersonian.

Sault College Alumni Magazine
Owned By: Sault College of Applied Arts & Technology
PO Box 60, 443 Northern Ave., Sault Ste Marie, ON P6A 5L3
Toll-Free: - - 0
alumni@saultcollege.ca
Social Media:
twitter.com/SaultCollAlumni
www.facebook.com/pages/Sault-College-Alumni/1274688806274
Sault College of Applied Arts & Technology newspaper.
Meggan Rudnicki, Officer, 705-759-2554 x 2622

Le Savoir
Anciennement: Le Virus
Détenteur: Université du Québec en Outaouais
CP 1250 Hull, #E-2000, 243, boul Alexandre-Taché, Gatineau, QC J8X 3X7
Tél: 819-595-3900;Téléc: 819-595-3830
savoir@uqo.ca
Médias sociaux:
twitter.com/uqo
www.facebook.com/Universite.Quebec.Outaouais
Le Savoir est un bulletin électronique.

The Scanner
Owned By: Saskatchewan Institute of Applied Science and Technology (SIAST)
#119, 1130 Idylwyld Dr. South, Saskatoon, SK S7K 3R5
Tel: 306-659-4421; Fax: 306-933-8220
ssa.scanner@siast.sk.ca
Social Media: www.youtube.com/user/0SIASTSA
twitter.com/ur_ssa
www.facebook.com/SIAS TSSA
Frequency: 2 times a year
The Scanner is the Students' Association's monthly newspaper publication for Saskatchewan Institute of Applied Science and Technology (SIAST).

Le Sentier
Détenteur: Cégep de St-Félicien
CP 7300, Saint-Félicien, QC G8K 2R8
Tél: 418-679-5412;Téléc: 418-679-0238

The Sentinel
Owned By: Selkirk College
301 Frank Bender Way, Castlegar, BC V1N 4L3
The Official News Source for Students at Selkirk College.

The Sheaf
Owned By: University of Saskatchewan
108 Memorial Union Building, 93 Campus Dr., Saskatoon, SK S7N 5B2
Tel: 306-966-8689; Fax: 306-966-8699
editor@thesheaf.com
Social Media:
www.facebook.com/thesheaf1912
University of Saskatchewan newspaper.
Kevin Menz, Editor-in-Chief

The Silhouette
Owned By: McMaster University
McMaster University Student Centre, B110, 1280 Main St. West, Hamilton, ON L8S 4K1
Tel: 905-525-9140; Fax: 905-521-1504
thesil@thesil.ca
Circulation: 10,000 Frequency: Sept-Mar.
McMaster University newspaper.
Sam Colbert, Executive Editor

The Spit
Owned By: Quest University
3200 University Blvd., Squamish, BC V8B 0N8
Tel: 604-898-8000; Fax: 604-815-0829
Toll-Free: 888-783-7808
info@questu.ca
Social Media:
www.facebook.com/QuestU
Quest University's student newspaper.

The Sputnik
Owned By: Wilfrid Laurier University
Grand River Hall, #202, 171 College St., Brantford, ON
Tel: 519-756-8228
allison.leonard@wlusp.com
Social Media:
twitter.com/thesputnikwlusp
www.facebook.com/pages/The-Sputnik/134603623 243364
The official independent newspaper of Laurier Brantford
Kyle Brown, Editor-in-Chief, eic@thesputnik.ca

The Strand
Owned By: Victoria University
63 Charles St. West, Toronto, ON M5S 1K5
Tel: 416-585-4524; Fax: 416-585-4584
editor@thestrand.ca
Circulation: 2,500 Frequency: 14 times a year
Victoria University newspaper.
Fiona Buchanan, Editor-in-Chief
Pauline Holdsworth, Editor-in-Chief

Student Connection
Owned By: Keyano College
8115 Franklin Ave., Fort McMurray, AB T9H 2H7
Tel: 780-791-4800; Fax: 780-791-1555
communicationvp.kcsa@keyano.ca
Frequency: Weekly
Keyano College newspaper.

The Surveyor
Owned By: Holland College of Applied Arts and Technology
140 Weymouth St., Charlottetown, PE C1A 4Z1
Frequency: 10 times a year
Holland College of Applied Arts and Technology newspaper.

The Toike Oike
Owned By: University of Toronto
B740 Sanford Fleming, 10 King's College Rd., Toronto, ON M5S 3G4
Tel: 416-978-2011
toike@skule.ca
Publication by The University of Toronto Engineering Society (EngSoc).
Andrew Jerabek, Editor-in-Chief

The Ubyssey
Owned By: University of British Columbia
Student Union Building, 24 - 6138 SUB Blvd., Vancouver, BC V6T 1Z1
Tel: 604-822-2301; Fax: 604-822-9279
feedback@ubyssey.ca
Social Media: ubyssey.tumblr.com
twitter.com/ubyssey
www.facebook.com/ubyssey
Frequency: every Monday and Thursday during the school year, and every second Tuesday during the summer.
University of British Columbia newspaper.
Jonny Wakefield, Coordinating Editor, coordinating@ubyssey.ca

The Uniter
Owned By: University of Winnipeg
ORM14, University of Winnipeg, 515 Portage Ave., Winnipeg, MB R3B 2E9
Tel: 204-786-9790; Fax: 204-783-7080
uniter@uniter.ca
Social Media:
twitter.com/TheUniter
www.facebook.com/pages/The-Uniter/129195330426257
University of Winnipeg newspaper.
Aaron Epp, Managing Editor, editor@uniter.ca

UQAR-Info
Anciennement : Uquarium
Détenteur: Université du Québec à Rimouski
Service des communications, #E-215, 300, allée des Ursulines, Rimouski, QC G5L 3A1
Tél: 418-723-1986 Ligne sans frais: 800-511-3382
Jean-François Bouchard, Responsable, jean-francois_bouchard@uqar.ca

The Voice
Owned By: Athabasca University
#1213, 10011 - 109th St. NW, Athabasca, AB T5J 3S8
Toll-Free: 800-788-9041
voice@voicemagazine.org
Athabasca University newspaper.
Tamra Ross, Editor—in-Chief

The Voice
Owned By: Langara College
100 West 49th Ave., Vancouver, BC V5Y 2Z6
Tel: 604-323-5511; Fax: 604-323-5555
Social Media: www.youtube.com/user/VoiceLangara
twitter.com/langaravoice
www.face book.com/Langara.Journalism
Frequency: Weekly
Langara College newspaper.

Vox-Populi
Détenteur: Cégep André-Laurendeau
1111, rue Lapierre, Lasalle, QC H8N 2J4
Tél: 514-364-3320;Téléc: 514-364-7130
courrier@claurendeau.qc.ca

The Watch
Owned By: University of King's College
c/o The University of King's College, 6350 Coburg Rd., Halifax, NS B3H 2A1
watcheditors@gmail.com
Social Media:
twitter.com/KingsWatch
University of King's College newspaper.
Ben Harrison, Editor-in-Chief
Rachel Ward, Editor-in-Chief

The Weal
Previous Name: The Emery Weal
Owned By: SAIT
1301 - 16 Ave. NW, Calgary, AB T2M 0L4
Tel: 403-284-8110; Fax: 403-284-7112
Social Media:
twitter.com/theweal
SAIT, Canada's premier technical institute by 2010
Heather Setka, Publications Manager, 403-284-8077, heather.setka@edu.sait.ca

Western News
Owned By: University of Western Ontario
Westminster Hall, #360, 1151 Richmond St., London, ON N6A 5B8
Tel: 519-661-2045; Fax: 519-661-3921
Circulation: 10,000 Frequency: 35 times during the academic year
University of Western Ontario newspaper.
Jason Winders, Editor, newseditor@uwo.ca

The Window
Owned By: New College
40 Willcocks St., Toronto, ON M5S 1C6
Tel: 416-978-2460; Fax: 416-978-0554
Social Media:
www.facebook.com/NewCollegeWindow
New College's official student publication.
Michelle Cramer, Michelle.Cramer@utoronto.ca

Xaverian Weekly
Owned By: St. Francis Xavier University
PO Box 5000, #111, Bloomfield Centre, Antigonish, NS B2G 2W5
Tel: 902-867-5007
xw.eic@stfx.ca
Social Media:
twitter.com/xaverianweekly
www.facebook.com/pages/The-Xaverian-Weekly/154561324597 88
Frequency: Weekly; Thursdays
St. Francis Xavier University newspaper.

YorkU
York University, West Office Bldg., 4700 Keele St., Toronto, ON M3J 1P3
Tel: 416-736-5058; Fax: 416-736-5681
editor@yorku.ca
Social Media:
twitter.com/YorkUnews/york-u-feeds/members
Frequency: 3 times a year
YorkU is the magazine of York University
Berton Woodward, Publications Director

Le Zèle
Détenteur: Cégep Montmorency
475, boul de l'Avenir, Laval, QC H7N 5H9
Tél: 450-975-6209;Téléc: 450-668-8639
journal_zele@hotmail.com
Tirage: 1,500 Fréquence: 5 fois par année

SECTION 14
RELIGION

Broad Faith-Based Associations

Across Boundaries Multifaith Institute
PO Box 437, Stn. A, Toronto ON M5W 1C2
Tel: 416-360-3641
info@acrossboundaries.net
www.acrossboundaries.net
Overview: A small national charitable organization
Chief Officer(s):
Wanda Romer Taylor, Chair, Secretary
Member Profile: Members come from any religious faith.
Description: To strengthen civil society and enhance pluralism in Canada and globally by promoting dialogue and exchange among faith traditions and between secular and religious perspectives.
Publications: Voices Across Boundaries
Frequency: Bi-monthly *Editor:* Bob Chodes
Profile: To promote dialogue and mutual understanding among different religious traditions, and between religious and secular visions of the world
Vox Femininarum
Frequency: Bi-annual *Editor:* Ginny Freeman MacOwan
Profile: Canada's only existing multifaith periodical.

American Academy of Religion (AAR)
#300, 825 Houston Mill Rd., Atlanta GA 30329-4205 USA
Tel: 404-727-3049; *Fax:* 404-727-7959
comment@aarweb.org
www.aarweb.org
www.facebook.com/pages/American-Academy-of-Religion/256288333448
twitter.com/AARWeb
Overview: A medium-sized national charitable organization founded in 1909
Chief Officer(s):
John R. Fitzmier, Executive Director & Treasurer
jfitzmier@aarweb.org
Otto A. Maduro, President
Warren G. Frisina, Secretary
Membership: 10,000+; *Fees:* Schedule available; *Member Profile:* Teachers; Research scholars; *Committees:* Academic Relations; Executive; Finance; Graduate Student; International Connections; Nominations; Program; Publications; Public Understanding of Religion; Regions; Status of Racial & Ethnic Minorities in the Profession; Status of Women in the Profession; Teaching & Learning; Theological Education Steering Committee
Activities: Governance Task Force; Job Placement Task Force; Religion in the Schools Task Force; Sustainability Task Force; Status of Lesbian, Gay, Bisexual, & Transgendered Persons in the Profession; Awards for Excellence in the Study of Religion Book Award Juries; History of Religions Jury; Research Grants Jury; *Speaker Service:* Yes
Description: The American Academy of Religion promotes research, teaching & scholarship in the field of religion.; *Member of:* American Council of Learned Societies
Publications: In the Field
Type: Newsletter
Profile: Calls for papers, grant news, conference announcements, & other opportunities for scholars of religion
Journal of the American Academy of Religion
Type: Journal *Frequency:* Quarterly
Profile: Scholarly articles of world religious traditions & methodologies
Openings: Employment Opportunities for Scholars of Religion
Accepts Advertising

Canadian Association for Spiritual Care (CASC) / Association canadienne de soins spirituels (ACSS)
#27, 1267 Dorval Dr., Oakville ON L6M 3Z4
Tel: 289-837-2272; *Fax:* 289-837-4800
Toll-Free: 866-442-2773
www.spiritualcare.ca
Previous Name: Canadian Association for Pastoral Practice & Education
Overview: A medium-sized national organization founded in 1965
Chief Officer(s):
Tony Sedfawi, Executive Director
office@spiritualcare.ca
Kathy Greig, Office Manager
kathy@spiritualcare.ca
Finances: *Funding Sources:* Membership dues
Fees: $200 associate members, with any amount of CPE or PCE training, & corporate members; $400 certified specialists or teaching supervisors; *Member Profile:* Persons involved in a variety of ministries, in settings such as parishes, prisons & correctional facilities, pastoral counselling centres, health care facilities, & industrial facilities
Activities: Offering educational programs for both clergy & lay persons; Providing certification for supervisors & specialists; Creating networking opportunities
Description: A national multifaith organization which is committed to the professional education, certification and support of people involved in pastoral care and pastoral counselling.
Publications: Canadian Association for Pastoral Practice & Education Handbook
Type: Handbook
Profile: Information about accreditation, certification, & practice
CAPPE [Canadian Association for Pastoral Practice & Education] / ACPEP National E-Newsletter
Type: Newsletter *Price:* Free with membership in the Canadian Association for Pastoral Practice & Education
CAPPE [Canadian Association for Pastoral Practice & Education] / ACPEP Annual Report
Type: Yearbook *Frequency:* Annually *Price:* Free with membership in the Canadian Association for Pastoral Practice & Education

Canadian Society for the Study of Religion (CSSR) / Société canadienne pour l'étude de la religion (SCER)
c/o Dr. Mark D. Chapman, #100, 30 Carrier Dr., Toronto ON M9W 5T7
mchapman@alumni.uwaterloo.ca
www.ccsr.ca/cssr
Overview: A small national organization founded in 1966
Chief Officer(s):
Michel Desjardins, President
mdesjardins@wlu.ca
Mark Chapman, Membership Secretary
mchapman@alumni.uwaterloo.ca
Richard Mann, Treasurer
Richard_mann@carleton.ca
Fees: $50 students; $60 part-time & retired persons; $90 regular; *Member Profile:* Scholars engaged in various academic approaches to the study of religion
Description: To promote research in the study of religion, with particular reference to Canada; To encourage a critical examination of the teaching of the discipline; *Member of:* International Association for the History of Religions (IAHR); Affiliation(s): Canadian Federation for the Humanities & Social Sciences (CFHSS)
Publications: Canadian Society for the Study of Religion Bulletin
Type: Newsletter *Frequency:* Semiannually *Editor:* Mark Chapman *ISSN:* 0708-952X *Price:* Free with CSSR membership
Profile: CSSR activies, member news, departmental news, & conference information
Studies in Religion / Sciences Religieuses
Type: Journal *Price:* Free with CSSR membership

Canadian Theological Society (CTS) / Société théologique canadienne
c/o M. Beavis, St. Thomas More College, 1437 College Dr., Saskatoon SK S7N 0W6
secretary@cts-stc.ca
cts-stc.ca
www.facebook.com/groups/28534722077
Overview: A small national organization founded in 1955
Chief Officer(s):
Doris K. Kieser, President
dkieser@ualberta.ca
Bob McKeon, Treasurer
rmckeon@shaw.ca
Fees: $86 full members; $61 associate members; $45 student, retired, & unwaged members; *Member Profile:* Theologians, clergy, scholars, & students from universities, seminaries, & churches; Lay people
Activities: *Awareness Events:* Annual Student Essay Contest
Description: To promote theological reflection & writing in Canada; *Member of:* Canadian Corporation for the Study of Religion (CCSR); Affiliation(s): Congress of the Humanities & Social Sciences

Canadian Theosophical Society Inc. / Association théosophique canadienne inc.
c/o National Secretary, 3519 Spruce Dr. SW, Calgary AB T3C 3A5
Tel: 403-217-6934
www.theosophical.ca
Overview: A medium-sized national charitable organization founded in 1924
Chief Officer(s):
Medardo Martinez Cruz, President
Elaine Pederzolli, National Secretary
cta.Secretary@rogers.com
Finances: *Annual Operating Budget:* Less than $50,000; *Funding Sources:* Memberships; Donations
Membership: 100-499; *Fees:* $25; *Member Profile:* From all across Canada & all backgrounds
Activities: Promotion of Theosophy or wisdom, whatever the source
Description: To form a nucleus of the Universal Brotherhood of Humanity, without distinction of race, creed, sex, caste, or colour; to encourage the study of comparative religion, philosophy, & science; to investigate unexplained laws of nature & the powers latent in man; *Member of:* Theosophical Society, India; Affiliation(s): 70 other countries
Publications: The Light Bearer
Type: Magazine *Frequency:* Quarterly *Price:* Free with Canadian Theosophical Association membership; $20 Canada non-members

Centre for Faith & the Media
PO Box 5694, Stn. A, Calgary AB T2H 1Y1
Tel: 403-617-0710; *Toll-Free:* 877-210-0077
info@faithandmedia.org
www.faithandmedia.org
Overview: A small national organization
Chief Officer(s):
Jocelyn Burgener, Chair
jocelynburgener@shaw.ca
Description: To inform, advise & help media & the general public achieve a stronger understanding of spiritual history, practices & values in Canadian society

Council on Homosexuality & Religion (CHR) / Conseil de l'homosexualité et la religion
PO Box 1912, Winnipeg MB R3C 3R2
Tel: 204-772-8215; *Fax:* 204-478-1160
Toll-Free: 888-399-0005
cvogel@mts.net
Overview: A small national charitable organization founded in 1976
Chief Officer(s):
Chris Vogel, Sec.-Treas., 204-945-6660
cvogel@nr.gov.mb.ca
A.E. Millward, President
Finances: *Annual Operating Budget:* Less than $50,000; *Funding Sources:* Donations
Staff: 5 volunteer(s)
Membership: 40 individuals + 21 organizations; *Fees:* $10 individual; $20 organization
Activities: Administers the Manitoba Gay & Lesbian Legal Defense Fund & the Victims of Homophobic Violence Memorial; distributes publications; provides referrals for union ceremonies & the like; *Internships:* Yes; *Speaker Service:* Yes *Library:* Yes
Description: To foster the welfare of homosexually-oriented persons & promote the understanding & acceptance of homosexuality within religious institutions; To provide counselling & referral services; To conduct workshops, seminars & lectures; To provide a library & a range of publications on homosexuality & religion; To assist others in the same activities; *Member of:* Association for Manitoba Archives; Manitoba Library Association; Social Planning Council

International Institute of Integral Human Sciences (IIIHS) / Institut international des sciences humaines intégrales
PO Box 1445, Stn. H, Montréal QC H3G 2N3
Tel: 514-937-8359; *Fax:* 514-937-5380
iiihs@iiihs.org
www.iiihs.org
Overview: A medium-sized international organization
Chief Officer(s):
John Rossner
jrossner@iiihs.org
Marilyn Rossner
mrossner@iiihs.org
Membership: 10,000; *Fees:* $15
Activities: Corporate Divisions: SSF-IIIHS National & Regional Chapters; International College of Human Sciences; International Academy for Research & Advanced Studies; International Council of World Religions & Cultures; The Order of the Transfiguration
Description: An interdisciplinary, professional association for scientists, scholars, and spiritual leaders worldwide, who are involved in the sciences of human consciousness & healing, paradigms for the convergence of science, spirituality & humane values in the world, & new insights into the potential of the human spirit.

Multifaith Action Society (MAS)
#5, 305 - 41 Ave. West, Vancouver BC V5Y 2S5
Tel: 604-321-1302; *Fax:* 604-321-1370
admin@multifaithaction.org
www.multifaithaction.org
Previous Name: Canadian Ecumenical Action
Overview: A small national charitable organization founded in 1972
Chief Officer(s):
Derek LaCroix, President

Nancy Chiavario, Executive Director
Finances: *Annual Operating Budget:* Less than $50,000
Staff: 3 staff member(s)
Membership: 200; *Fees:* $25 individual; $40 couple; *Member Profile:* Members come from many religious faiths: Aboriginal, Baha'i, Buddhist, Christian, Hindu, Muslim, Jain, Jewish, Sikh, Unitarian, Zoroastrian; *Committees:* Program; Calendar; Development; Personnel; Advocacy
Activities: Lectures & conferences promoting interreligious dialogue; forums on faith; environmental awareness programs within religious communities; faith centre visits; *Speaker Service:* Yes
Description: MAS is a non-profit organization promote interfaith & multifaith dialogue & understanding. It provides information & resources on world religions to the community & develops community service programs. It is a registered charity, BN: 122214505RR0001.; *Member of:* Affiliation of Multicultural Societies & Service Agencies of BC; Vancouver Multicultural Society

Ontario Consultants on Religious Tolerance (OCRT)
PO Box 27026, Stn. Frontenac, Kingston ON K7M 8W5
Fax: 613-547-9015
ocrt4@religioustolerance.org
www.religioustolerance.org
Overview: A small provincial organization founded in 1995
Chief Officer(s):
B.A. Robinson, Coordinator
Finances: *Annual Operating Budget:* Less than $50,000; *Funding Sources:* Lecture fees; donations; banner ads
Staff: 1 staff member(s); 5 volunteer(s)
Membership: 1-99
Activities: *Speaker Service:* Yes
Description: To promote religious tolerance & expose religious hatred & misinformation

Saint Swithun's Society
427 Lynett Cres., Richmond Hill ON L4C 2V6
Tel: 905-883-0984
norman@stswithunssociety.ca
www.stswithunssociety.ca
Overview: A small local organization founded in 1974
Chief Officer(s):
Norman McMullen, President
Kevin Dark, Vice-President
Elisabeth Stenson, Sec.-Treas.
Finances: *Annual Operating Budget:* Less than $50,000
Staff: 3 staff member(s)
Membership: 300; *Member Profile:* Non-denominational, non-political/sectarian & inclusive
Activities: Annual Celebration; *Library:* Yes (Open to Public)
Description: To promote feelings of goodwill; to encourage the celebration of Saint Swithun's Day (July 15) & to pattern members' lives after the example of our Patron; Affiliation(s): Friends of Winchester Cathedral (England)

Société internationale de sociologie des religions (SISR) / International Society for the Sociology of Religion (ISSR)
Bremveldstraat 16, Herent B-3020 Belgium
sisr@soc.kuleuven.be
www.sisr.org
Aperçu: *Dimension:* petite; *Envergure: internationale; fondée en 1948*
Membre(s) du bureau directeur:
Hilde Van Meerbeek-Cravillon, Secrétaire générale
Finances: *Budget de fonctionnement annuel:* Moins de $50,000; *Fonds:* Cotisations des membres
Personnel: 2 bénévole(s)
Membre: 300; *Montant de la cotisation:* 106 E; *Critères d'admissibilite:* En sciences sociales des religions

Société québécoise pour l'étude de la religion
Université de Montréal, #490, 3333, Chemin Queen Mary, Montréal QC H3V 1A2
Tél: 514-343-6568; *Téléc:* 514-343-5738
sqer.org
Aperçu: *Dimension:* petite; *Envergure: provinciale; fondée en 1989*
Membre(s) du bureau directeur:
Patrice Brodeur, Président
Montant de la cotisation: 50$ régulier; 25$ étudiant
Description: Promouvoir la recherche, l'enseignement et la diffusion des connaissances dans les disciplines ayant pour objet l'étude de la religion

Spiritual Science Fellowship/International Institute of Integral Human Sciences (SSF-IIIHS)
PO Box 1445, Stn. H, 1974, rue de Maisonneuve ouest, Montréal QC H3G 2N3
Tel: 514-937-8359; *Fax:* 514-937-5380
info@iiihs.org
www.iiihs.org
Overview: A small local charitable organization
Chief Officer(s):
Marilyn Z. Rossner
Membership: 10,000; *Fees:* $15; gifts
Activities: *Internships:* Yes; *Speaker Service:* Yes
Description: To provide spiritual services, educational programs, & pastoral ministrations for persons, regardless of religious background, who desire to understand experiences of psyche & spirit, & to dedicate themselves to personal spiritual growth & psychic development, in an atmosphere of informed free-thought & enquiry

World Conference on Religion & Peace (Canada) (WCRP)
#490-1, 333 Queen Mary Rd., Montréal QC H3Z 1A2
Tel: 450-478-3904
www.religionsforpeace.org
Also Known As: Religions for Peace (Canada)
Overview: A medium-sized national organization founded in 1975
Chief Officer(s):
Pascale Frémond, President
pascale.fremond@videotron.ca
Membership: 100-499; *Fees:* $100 institutional; $10 student; $25 individual; $15 senior
Activities: Meetings; occasional conferences; newsletter
Description: To establish peace & justice at the local, national & international levels; to encourage members to work together with like-minded organizations on issues of social & economic justice, human rights, ecological harmony, arms limitation & nuclear disarmament; to aim for world peace through interfaith dialogue & applied ethics; Affiliation(s): World Conference on Religion & Peace (International)

World Council of Churches
PO Box 2100, 150, rte de Ferney, Geneva CH-1211 Switzerland
oikoumene.org
Overview: A medium-sized international organization
Chief Officer(s):
Olav Fykse Tveit, General Secretary
Affiliation(s): International Council of World Religions & Cultures

Specific Faith-Based Associations

Adventist

Adventist Development & Relief Agency Canada (ADRA)
115 Clarence Biesenthal Dr., Oshawa ON L1K 2H5
Tel: 905-433-8004; *Fax:* 905-723-1903
Toll-Free: 888-274-2372
info@adra.ca; donor-relations@adra.ca
www.adra.ca
Social Media: www.youtube.com/adracanada
www.facebook.com/adracanada
twitter.com/adracanada
Also Known As: ADRA Canada
Overview: A medium-sized international charitable organization founded in 1985
Chief Officer(s):
Ronald Kuhn, Executive Director
Finances: *Annual Operating Budget:* $1.5 Million-$3 Million
Staff: 14 staff member(s); 1500 volunteer(s)
Membership: 7,000
Activities: Non-sectarian, humanitarian relief agency; community development projects in 50 countries
Description: To provide community development & disaster relief without regard to political or religious association, age, or ethnicity; *Member of:* Canadian Council for International Cooperation, Canadian Christian Relief and Development Association; Affiliation(s): Canadian Council of Christian Charities
Publications: Global Impact
Type: Newsletter *Frequency:* Quarterly

Adventive Cross Cultural Initiatives (ACCI)
89 Auriga Dr., Nepean ON K2E 7Z2
Tel: 613-298-1546; *Fax:* 613-225-7455
lauren@adventive.ca
www.adventive.ca
www.facebook.com/pages/ACCI/159473104172691
Previous Name: New Life League
Overview: A small national charitable organization founded in 1986
Chief Officer(s):
John Haley, Executive Director
johnhaley@adventive.ca
Lauren Carrion, Canadian National Director
lauren@adventive.ca
Finances: *Annual Operating Budget:* Less than $50,000; *Funding Sources:* Donations
Staff: 4 staff member(s); 1 volunteer(s)
Activities: *Internships:* Yes
Description: To operate as an international, interdenominational Christian missionary organization; To minister through printing & literature, children's homes, national workers, evangelism, & church planting.; *Member of:* Canadian Council of Christian Charities

Canadian Adventist Teachers Network
1148 King St. East, Oshawa ON L1H 1H8
Tel: 905-433-0011; *Fax:* 905-433-0982
dmarshall@sdacc.org
catnet.sdacc.org
Overview: A small national organization
Description: Dedicated to promoting excellence in Christian education by helping facilitate communication and the exchange of ideas among Adventist educators.; Affiliation(s): Seventh-day Adventist Church in Canada

Seventh-day Adventist Church in Canada (SDACC) / Église adventiste du septième jour au Canada
1148 King St. East, Oshawa ON L1H 1H8
Tel: 905-433-0011; *Fax:* 905-433-0982
communications@adventist.ca
www.adventist.ca
Overview: A large national charitable organization founded in 1901
Chief Officer(s):
Mark Johnson, President, 905-433-0011 2086
johnson.mark@adventist.ca
Finances: *Annual Operating Budget:* $3 Million-$5 Million; *Funding Sources:* Donations
Staff: 23 staff member(s)
Membership: 55,000
Activities: Adventist Development & Relief Agency (ADRA); It Is Written Canada; Christian Record Services
Description: To be a significant Christian movement that recognizes the unique role to which Christ has called it & the urgency of the message of salvation & judgment; to lead people to salvation in Jesus; To teach them the biblical faith & discipline of the Christian life; to equip them to serve with their God-given abilities through the leadership of our various administrative & ministry teams; To proclaim Christ; To nurture believers; To serve humanity

Anglicans

The Anglican Church of Canada (ACC) / L'Église anglicane du Canada
80 Hayden St., Toronto ON M4Y 3G2
Tel: 416-924-9192; *Fax:* 416-968-7983
information@national.anglican.ca
www.anglican.ca
Social Media: www.youtube.com/generalsynod;
www.flickr.com/photos/general-synod
www.facebook.com/canadiananglican
twitter.com/generalsynod
Previous Name: Church of England in Canada
Overview: A large national charitable organization founded in 1893
Chief Officer(s):
Fred Hiltz, Primate, Anglican Church of Canada
Michael Thompson, General Secretary
Michèle George, Treasurer
mgeorge@national.anglican.ca
Membership: 800,000 members; 2,346 churches
Activities: *Library:* Yes by appointment
Description: To proclaim & celebrate the gospel of Jesus Christ in worship & action, as a partner in the world-wide Anglican Communion & the universal church; to value our heritage of faith, reason, liturgy, tradition, bishops & synods, & the rich variety of life in community; to acknowledge that God calls us to greater diversity of membership, wider participation in ministry & leadership, better stewardship in God's creation & a strong resolve in challenging attitudes & structures which cause injustice; *Member of:* Canadian Council of Churches

Anglican Foundation of Canada
Anglican Church House, 80 Hayden St., Toronto ON M4V 3G2
Tel: 416-924-9199; *Fax:* 416-924-8672
foundation@anglicanfoundation.org
www.anglicanfoundation.org
Overview: A small national charitable organization founded in 1957
Chief Officer(s):
John Wright, Executive Director
jwright@anglicanfoundation.org
Kavitha Gunaseelan, Executive Assistant
kgunaseelan@anglicanfoundation.org
Activities: *Speaker Service:* Yes
Description: To assist parishes, dioceses & programs of Anglican Church of Canada with low interest loans &/or grants; Affiliation(s): World Council of Churches

Church of the Good Shepherd
116 Queen St. North, Kitchener ON N2H 2H7
Tel: 519-743-3845; *Fax:* 519-743-3375
office@shepherdsway.ca
www.shepherdsway.ca
Also Known As: Swedenborgian Church
Overview: A small local organization
Chief Officer(s):
John Maine, Minister
Membership: 140 individual

Integrity Toronto
PO Box 873, Stn. F, Toronto ON M4Y 2N9
Tel: 416-925-9872
toronto@integritycanada.org
www.toronto.integritycanada.org
Overview: A small local organization founded in 1975
Finances: *Annual Operating Budget:* Less than $50,000; *Funding Sources:* Donations
Staff: 6 volunteer(s)
Membership: 100 individual; *Fees:* $15
Description: International organization of gay & lesbian Anglicans & their friends; to help its members discover & affirm that we can be both Christian & gay/lesbian/bisexual/transgender; Affiliation(s): Integrity Inc. - USA

Integrity Vancouver
PO Box 2797, Stn. Main, Vancouver BC V6B 3X2
Tel: 604-432-1230
vancouver@integritycanada.org
www.vancouver.integritycanada.org
Overview: A small local charitable organization
Finances: *Annual Operating Budget:* Less than $50,000
Staff: 14 volunteer(s)
Membership: 50-100; *Fees:* $20; *Member Profile:* Gay, lesbian, bisexual, transgendered Anglicans
Activities: Monthly services on first Sunday, St. Paul's Anglican Church; monthly potluck dinners at members' homes; *Speaker Service:* Yes
Affiliation(s): Integrity Inc. - USA

Baha'i Faith

Association for Baha'i Studies (ABS) / Association d'études Baha'is
34 Copernicus St., Ottawa ON K1N 7K4
Tel: 613-233-1903; *Fax:* 613-233-3644
www.bahai-studies.ca
www.facebook.com/331784303733
Previous Name: Canadian Association for Studies in the Baha'i Faith
Overview: A medium-sized international charitable organization founded in 1975
Finances: *Annual Operating Budget:* $100,000-$250,000; *Funding Sources:* Grants; Conference & Literature revenue; Membership fees
Staff: 2 staff member(s)
Membership: 2,000; *Fees:* $50 adult; $60 couple; $25 student/senior; $60 institution; $999 life
Activities: *Library:* Yes (Open to Public) by appointment
Description: To foster Baha'i scholarship & to demonstrate the value of this scholarly approach; to promote courses of study on the Baha'i faith; to foster relationships with various leaders of thought & persons of capacity; to publish scholarly materials examining the Baha'i faith, especially on its application to the concerns & needs of humanity; to organize annual meetings & develop chapters of the Association around the world

The Bahá'í Community of Canada / La communauté bahá'íe du Canada
Baha'i National Centre, 7200 Leslie St., Thornhill ON L3T 6L8
Tel: 905-889-8168; *Fax:* 905-889-8184
secretariat@cdnbnc.org
www.ca.bahai.org
Overview: A large national charitable organization founded in 1844
Chief Officer(s):
Susanne Tamas, Director, Government Relations
Koren McKye, Secretary General
Gerald Filson, Director, Public Affairs
externalaffairs@cdnbnc.org
Finances: *Annual Operating Budget:* Greater than $5 Million; *Funding Sources:* Contributions from members
Staff: 30 staff member(s)
Membership: 30,000
Activities: Study circles; Devotional gatherings; Junior youth spiritual empowerment program; Children's classes; *Awareness Events:* Unity in Diversity Week, Nov.; *Speaker Service:* Yes *Library:* Yes (Open to Public) by appointment
Description: An independent religion based on the writings of Baha'u'llah, 1817-1892, teaching the oneness of humanity, the common divine source of all the great religions, equality of the sexes & harmony of science & religion; headquarters in Haifa, Israel; 5-6 million adherents in 214 countries & territories; Canada's 30,000 Baha'is are located in some 1,500 centres, 261 of which elect local governing councils called Spiritual Assemblies; National Spiritual Assembly of Baha'is of Canada incorporated by Act of Parliament in 1949; Affiliation(s): Baha'i International Community

Baptists

Association d'églises baptistes évangéliques au québec
7415, boul Gouin ouest, Montréal QC H4K 1B8
Tél: 514-337-2555; *Téléc:* 514-337-8892
association@aebeq.qc.ca
www.aebeq.qc.ca
Aperçu: *Dimension:* moyenne; *Envergure:* nationale
Membre(s) du bureau directeur:
Michel M. Habbib, Secrétaire général
Membre: 65 000
Activités: Camps de jeunes; retraites; congrès; cohortes; *Stagiaires:* Oui; *Service de conférenciers:* Oui
Description: Aider les églises à: communiquer l'évangile de Jésus-Christ à tous les Québécois; former des disciples et des leaders; devenir plus solides et se reproduire; *Membre de:* Fellowship of Evangelical Baptist Churches in Canada

Canadian Baptist Ministries
7185 Millcreek Dr., Mississauga ON L5N 5R4
Tel: 905-821-3533; *Fax:* 905-826-3441
info@cbmin.org
www.cbmin.org
www.facebook.com/cbmin.org
Merged from: Canadian Baptist International Ministries; Canadian Baptist Federation
Overview: A medium-sized national organization founded in 1912
Chief Officer(s):
Gary V. Nelson, General Secretary
Finances: *Annual Operating Budget:* Greater than $5 Million; *Funding Sources:* Member churches; individuals; CIDA
Staff: 112 staff member(s); 540 volunteer(s)
Membership: 250,000 + 1,000 churches; *Member Profile:* Members of churches affiliated with the four conventions/unions; *Committees:* Public Affairs
Activities: Partners in Mission - 75 missionaries serving in Asia, Africa, Latin America, Europe & Canada; The Sharing Way - relief & development ministries in 13 countries, working in areas of agricultural & community development, community health, etc.; Canadian Baptist Volunteers - short-term ministry opportunities; Canada Caucus - consensus building among the churches in Canada; *Library:* Daniel Global Mission Resource Room
Description: To unite, encourage & enable Canadian Baptist Churches in their national & international endeavor to fulfill the commission of our Lord Jesus Christ, in the power of the Holy Spirit, proclaiming the gospel & sharing the love of God to all people.; *Member of:* Canadian Council of Christian Charities; Affiliation(s): Baptist World Alliance

Canadian Baptists of Ontario and Quebec (CBOQ)
#100, 304 The East Mall, Toronto ON M9B 6E2
Tel: 416-622-8600; *Fax:* 416-622-2308
cboq@baptist.ca
www.baptist.ca
Previous Name: Baptist Convention of Ontario & Québec
Overview: A large local organization founded in 1887
Chief Officer(s):
Tim McCoy, Executive Minister
tmccoy@baptist.ca
Finances: *Annual Operating Budget:* $3 Million-$5 Million; *Funding Sources:* Member churches
Staff: 15 staff member(s)
Membership: 375
Activities: *Internships:* Yes *Library:* Yes (Open to Public)
Description: A family of churches building Christ's kingdom; supports & enables member churches to be healthy, mission congregations as we serve God together; Affiliation(s): Baptist Women of Ontario and Quebec; McMaster Divinity College; Canadian Council of Churches; Evangelical Fellowship of Canada; Canadian Council of Christian Charities

Canadian Baptists of Western Canada (CBWC)
#1100, 550 - 11 Ave. SW, Calgary AB T2R 1M7
Tel: 403-228-9559; *Fax:* 403-228-9048
Toll-Free: 800-820-2479
info@cbwc.ca
www.cbwc.ca
Previous Name: The Baptist Union of Western Canada
Overview: A medium-sized local charitable organization founded in 1908
Chief Officer(s):
Jeremy Bell, Executive Minister
jbell@cbwc.ca
Finances: *Funding Sources:* Church congregations
Staff: 12 staff member(s)
Membership: 178 congregations representing 100,000 worshippers; *Committees:* Western Canada Missions; Evangelism; Finance; Youth
Activities: *Internships:* Yes
Affiliation(s): Baptist World Alliance

Canadian Convention of Southern Baptists (CCSB) / Convention canadienne des baptistes du Sud
100 Convention Way, Cochrane AB T4C 2G2
Fax: 403-932-4937
Toll-Free: 888-442-2272
office@ccsb.ca
www.ccsb.ca
Overview: A medium-sized national charitable organization founded in 1985
Chief Officer(s):
Gérald J. Taillon, Executive Director
gtaillon@cnbc.ca
Alan Braun, President
Finances: *Funding Sources:* Member churches
Staff: 8 staff member(s); 4 volunteer(s)
Membership: 10,189
Activities: *Library:* Resource Centre (Open to Public)
Description: To help churches build the Kingdom of God; a church for every person across Canada & around the world; Affiliation(s): Southern Baptist Convention
Publications: The Baptist Horizon
Type: Journal *Frequency:* Bimonthly *Editor:* Debbie Shelton
ISSN: 1195-4744
Profile: CCSB news

Convention of Atlantic Baptist Churches (CABC) / Convention des Églises Baptistes de l'Atlantique
1655 Manawagonish Rd., Saint John NB E2M 3Y2
Tel: 506-635-1922; *Fax:* 506-635-0366
www.baptist-atlantic.ca
Also Known As: Atlantic Baptist Convention
Previous Name: United Baptist Convention of the Maritime Provinces
Overview: A medium-sized local charitable organization founded in 1905
Chief Officer(s):
Daniel Walton, President
Bruce Fawcett, Associate Executive Minister
Activities: Providing seminars, conferences, stewardship education, & retreats; *Speaker Service:* Yes
Description: To resource pastors, churches, & people; To facilitate a shared mission on behalf of churches; To establish & maintain professional standards & ethics for clergy
Publications: Convention Update
Type: Newsletter *Frequency:* Monthly
Youth & Family Update
Type: Newsletter *Frequency:* Monthly

Brethren

Brethren in Christ
2700 Bristol Circle, Oakville ON L6H 6EH
Tel: 905-339-2335; *Fax:* 905-337-2120
office@canadianbic.ca
www.bic-church.org
www.facebook.com/BrethrenInChristChurch
Overview: A medium-sized international charitable organization founded in 1788
Chief Officer(s):
Brad Fisher, Treasurer
Trish Hogg, Secretary
Darrell Winger, Executive Director
Finances: *Annual Operating Budget:* $500,000-$1.5 Million; *Funding Sources:* Congregational giving
Staff: 8 staff member(s)
Membership: 3,450 + 43 congregations in Canada; *Member Profile:* North American membership is about 20,000 with significant churches in other countries including India, Japan, Zambia, Zimbabwe, Nicaragua, Cuba, Venezuela, Columbia, South Africa
Activities: *Speaker Service:* Yes; *Rents Mailing List:* Yes
Member of: Evangelical Fellowship of Canada; Affiliation(s): Mennonite Central Committee; Canadian Holiness Federation

Christian Brethren Churches of Québec (CBCQ) / Églises de frères chrétiens du Québec (EFCQ)
#101, 1520, rue King ouest, Sherbrooke QC J1J 2G2
Tel: 819-820-1693; *Fax:* 819-821-9287
Also Known As: Plymouth Brethren
Overview: A medium-sized provincial charitable organization founded in 1942
Chief Officer(s):
Richard Strout, Secretary
Finances: *Annual Operating Budget:* Less than $50,000; *Funding Sources:* Dues from local churches
Staff: 2 volunteer(s)
Description: To handle affairs for local affiliated churches regarding government & affairs of civil status

The United Brethren Church in Canada
501 Whitelaw Rd., Guelph ON N1K 1E7
Tel: 519-836-0180; *Fax:* 519-821-8385
www.ubcanada.org
Previous Name: Ontario Conference, Church of the United Brethren in Christ
Overview: A small national charitable organization founded in 1856
Chief Officer(s):
Brian K. Magnus, Bishop
Finances: *Annual Operating Budget:* $50,000-$100,000; *Funding Sources:* Donations
Staff: 1 staff member(s)
Membership: 12 churches; *Fees:* Schedule available; *Member Profile:* Personal knowledge of God through faith in Christ; desire to live a life conforming to biblical principles
Activities: *Library:* At Emmanuel Bible College Library
Description: To organize groups of people into congregations to worship God; to make effective application of principles of righteousness in the Society; *Member of:* Church of the United Brethren in Christ, International; Affiliation(s): Evangelical Fellowship of Canada

Buddhism

Buddhist Association of Canada - Cham Shan Temple
7254 Bayview Ave., Toronto ON L3T 2R6
Tel: 905-886-1522
www.chamshantemple.org/en
Overview: A small national organization founded in 1973
Chief Officer(s):
Dayi Shi, President & Abbot
Activities: Seminars, sutra reading groups, meditation retreats; *Library:* Yes
Description: In addition to the main worship hall & 2 congregation halls, the Buddhist temple also includes a Dharma seminary for the Chinese community to learn Buddhism.

Jodo Shinshu Buddhist Temples of Canada
11786 Fentiman Pl., Richmond BC V7E 6M6
Tel: 604-272-3330; *Fax:* 604-272-6865
jsbtcheadquarters@shaw.ca
www.bcc.ca
Previous Name: Buddhist Churches of Canada
Overview: A medium-sized national charitable organization founded in 1933
Chief Officer(s):
Leslie Kawamura, Director, Living Dharma Centre
Finances: *Annual Operating Budget:* $100,000-$250,000
Staff: 9 staff member(s)
Membership: 2,500; *Fees:* $45
Activities: *Speaker Service:* Yes *Library:* Yes by appointment
Description: Propagation of Buddhism; Affiliation(s): Jodo Shinshu Hongwanji, Kyoto

The Palyul Foundation of Canada
c/o Orgyan Osal Cho Dzong, Buddhist Monastery & Retreat Centre, 1755 Lingham Lake Rd., RR#3, Box 68, Madoc ON K0K 2K0
Tel: 613-967-7432; *Fax:* 416-604-8101
palyul@ca.inter.net
www.palyulcanada.org
Overview: A small local charitable organization founded in 1981
Activities: Classes on Buddhism, meditation, ritual practices; retreats; empowerments; celebration of Buddhist holy days & festivals
Description: Dedicated to the preservation & advancement of the teachings of the Nyingma lineage of Vajrayana Buddhism

Union of Vietnamese Buddhist Churches in Canada
229 Ave. Y South, Saskatoon SK S7M 3J4
Tel: 306-978-0085
www.buddhismcanada.com/sask.html
Previous Name: The General Committee Vietnamese Buddhism in Canada
Overview: A medium-sized national organization founded in 1983
Finances: *Funding Sources:* Membership dues
Staff: 9 staff member(s); 7 volunteer(s)
Activities: *Speaker Service:* Yes *Library:* Bibliothèque Tam Bao Som (Open to Public) by appointment
Description: To preach Buddhism; to preserve traditional culture of the Vietnamese

Catholicism

Alberta Catholic School Trustees Association
#205, 9940 - 106 St., Edmonton AB T5K 2N2
Tel: 780-484-6209; *Fax:* 780-484-6248
admin@acsta.ab.ca
www.acsta.ab.ca
twitter.com/acstanews
Overview: A medium-sized provincial organization
Chief Officer(s):
Stefan Michniewski, Executive Director
Affiliation(s): Canadian Catholic School Trustees Association

Assemblée des évêques catholiques du Québec (AEQ) / Assembly of Québec Catholic Bishops
3331, rue Sherbrooke est, Montréal QC H1W 1C5
Tél: 514-274-4323; *Téléc:* 514-274-4383
aeq@eveques.qc.ca
www.eveques.qc.ca
Nom précédent: Assemblée des Évêques du Québec
Aperçu: *Dimension:* moyenne; *Envergure: provinciale; Organisme sans but lucratif; fondée en 1871*
Membre(s) du bureau directeur:
Pierre Gaudette, Secrétaire général
Finances: *Budget de fonctionnement annuel:* $500,000-$1.5 Million
Personnel: 8 membre(s) du personnel
Membre: 37; *Critères d'admissibilite:* Évêque diocésain; évêque auxiliaire; *Comités:* Éducation; Laicat; Ministères; Missions; Affaires sociales; Théologie; Communications; Prospective; Législation; Administration; Relations interculturelles; Pastorale des Autochtones
Description: Ôtre un lieu d'échange et de concertation où ses membres s'entraident dans la recherche d'actions à entreprendre pour rendre l'Église au Québec toujours plus vivante et engagée dans la société et la culture contemporaines; Affiliation(s): Conférence des évêques catholiques du Canada

Assembly of Catholic Bishops of Ontario / Assemblée des évêques catholiques de l'Ontario
#800, 10 St. Mary St., Toronto ON M4Y 1P9
Tel: 416-923-1423; *Fax:* 416-923-1509
www.acbo.on.ca
Overview: A small provincial organization
Chief Officer(s):
Luciano (Lou) Piovesan, General Secretary
piovesanl@acbo.on.ca
Richard Smith, President, 613-732-7933, *Fax:* 613-732-1697
Description: The association of the Catholic bishops of the Province of Ontario in the service of Catholics of Ontario. Involved in providing information and instruction about the principles and moral positions of the Church on all aspects of life

Association des intervenantes et des intervenants en soins spirituels du Québec (AIISSQ)
CP 59013, 6595, rue St-Hubert, Montréal QC H2S 2M0
Tél: 514-259-9229; *Téléc:* 514-259-3741
secretariat@aiissq.org
www.aiissq.org
Nom précédent: Association québécoise de la pastorale de la santé
Aperçu: *Dimension:* petite; *Envergure: provinciale; Organisme sans but lucratif; fondée en 2005*
Finances: *Budget de fonctionnement annuel:* $50,000-$100,000
Personnel: 1 membre(s) du personnel
Membre: 250; *Montant de la cotisation:* 250$; 50$ par jour; *Critères d'admissibilite:* Animateur(trice) de pastorale dans un établissement de santé; *Comités:* Pastorale pratique; pastorale en santé mentale
Activités: Congrès annuel; colloques; sessions de formation; *Stagiaires:* Oui; *Listes de destinataires:* Oui
Description: Formation professionnelle des membres et promotion de leurs intérêts spirituels et professionnels; représentation des membres auprès d'instances civiles et religieuses reconnues; *Membre de:* Association canadienne des périodiques catholiques; Affiliation(s): Association canadienne pour la pratique et l'éducation pastorale; Association catholique canadienne de la santé; Carrefour Humanisation - Santé

Association des parents catholiques du Québec (APCQ)
5425 - 5e av, Montréal QC H1Y 2S8
Tél: 514-276-8068; *Téléc:* 514-948-2595
apcq406@bellnet.ca
www.apcqc.net
Aperçu: *Dimension:* grande; *Envergure: provinciale; Organisme sans but lucratif; fondée en 1966*
Finances: *Budget de fonctionnement annuel:* $50,000-$100,000
Personnel: 25 bénévole(s)
Membre: 4 000; *Montant de la cotisation:* 12$; *Critères d'admissibilite:* Familles; *Comités:* Éducation de la foi; comité provincial d'enseignement privé; carrefour famille-Québec
Activités: Secrétariat permanent; Périodique; colloques; Conférences; Cours; Congrès parents-jeunes; Pétitions; Rédactions de mémoires; *Service de conférenciers:* Oui
Description: Regroupe des parents catholiques pour promouvoir et défendre leurs droits et leurs intérêts selon les valeurs catholiques en matière d'éducation, de famille et de culture par l'information et la représentation de ses membres auprès de la population et des autorités civiles et religieuses; *Membre de:* Regroupement Inter-Organismes pour une politique familiale au Québec; Affiliation(s): Organisation internationale de l'enseignement catholique (OIEC)

Augustines de la Miséricorde de Jésus
2655, rue Guillaume - Le Pelletier, Québec QC G1C 3X7
Tél: 418-628-8860
secretaire@augustines.org
www.augustines.org
Aperçu: *Dimension:* petite; *Envergure:* locale
Membre(s) du bureau directeur:
Claire Gagnon, Supérieure générale
Description: Les trois dimensions de la vie spirituelle des Augustines d'hier et de demain sont: communion fraternelle; louange et intercession; et miséricorde

Benedictine Sisters of Manitoba (OSB)
225 Masters Ave., Winnipeg MB R4A 2A1
Tel: 204-338-4601; *Fax:* 204-339-8775
stbens@mts.net
www.stbens.ca
Also Known As: Sisters of the Order of St. Benedict
Overview: A small provincial charitable organization founded in 1912
Chief Officer(s):
Virginia Evard, Prioress
Finances: *Funding Sources:* Donations
Staff: 35 staff member(s); 30 volunteer(s)
Membership: 33
Activities: Programs in spirituality, personal growth & a variety of retreats; *Library:* St. Benedict's Monastery Library by appointment
Description: To witness Jesus Christ, through community life & prayer, contemplative living, hospitality, service to the people of God & stewardship of all God's gifts; *Member of:* Federation of St. Gertrude

Calgary Catholic Immigration Society (CCIS)
120 - 17th Ave., 3rd Fl., Calgary AB T2S 2T2
Tel: 403-262-2006; *Fax:* 403-262-2033
contact@ccis-calgary.ab.ca
www.ccis-calgary.ab.ca
Overview: A small international organization
Chief Officer(s):
Fariborz Birjandian, Executive Director

Activities: Pre-employment training & counseling; community outreach for families & seniors; temporary accommodation facility; Integrated Resettlement Program
Description: CCIS is a non-profit organization which provides settlement & integration services to immigrants & refugees in Southern Alberta.

Canadian Catholic Historical Association - English Section (CCHA) / Société canadienne d'histoire de l'église catholique - Section anglaise
c/o St. Michael's College, 81 St. Mary St., Toronto ON M5S 1J4

Tel: 905-893-9754; *Fax:* 416-934-3444
www.umanitoba.ca/colleges/st_pauls/ccha/ccha.html
Overview: A medium-sized national organization founded in 1933
Chief Officer(s):
Peter Meehan, President-General
peter.meehan@senecac.on.ca
Edward Jackman, Secretary-General
revedjackman@rogers.com
Finances: *Annual Operating Budget:* Less than $50,000; *Funding Sources:* Membership fees; donations
Staff: 11 volunteer(s)
Membership: 100-499; *Fees:* $50 Canadian; US$50 American; $30 student; $60 French-English
Activities: Annual scholarly conference at the Canadian Congress
Description: The Association promotes interest & research in the history of the Canadian Catholic Church, its dioceses, religious communities, institutions, parishes, buildings, sites, & personalities. It is divided into English & French sections.

Canadian Catholic School Trustees' Association (CCSTA) / Association canadienne des commissaires d'écoles catholique
Catholic Education Centre, 570 West Hunt Club Rd., Nepean ON K2G 3R4

Tel: 613-224-4455; *Fax:* 613-224-3187
ccsta@ottawacatholicschools.ca
www.ccsta.ca
Overview: A medium-sized national organization founded in 1960
Chief Officer(s):
John Stunt, Executive Director
john.stunt@ocsb.ca
Paula Peroni, President
peronip@scdsb.edu.on.ca
Ted Paszek, Vice-President
tedp@eics.ab.ca
Finances: *Funding Sources:* Sponsorships
Membership: 7 associations; *Member Profile:* Provincial & territorial Catholic school trustees' associations in Canada
Activities: Promoting Catholic education; Providing professional development opportunities for trustees; Collaborating with the Canadian Conference of Catholic Bishops; Liaising with Canadian government agencies & other Catholic education organizations; *Awareness Events:* Catholic Education Week
Description: To protect the right to Catholic education in Canada; To promote excellence in Catholic education across Canada
Publications: Build Bethlehem Everywhere - A Statement on Catholic Education
Type: Book
CCSTA [Canadian Catholic School Trustees' Association] Newsletter
Type: Newsletter
Profile: Includes CCSTA activities, conferences, & provincial reports

Canadian Catholic Students Association (CCSA)

cccmadmin@cccm.ca
www.cccm.ca
www.facebook.com/group.php?gid=2230853889
Overview: A small national charitable organization
Chief Officer(s):
Lori Neale, National Coordinator, 416-506-0183
Victoria Tuason, President & Central Representative
central.rep@cccm.ca
Maureen Callaghan, Atlantic Representative & Contact, Communications
ccsa.communications@cccm.ca
Sharayhah Ulrich, Western Representative & Contact, Social Justice
ccsa.socialjustice@cccm.ca
Finances: *Funding Sources:* Donations
Member Profile: Persons who support the purpose of the association
Activities: Supporting prayerful, pastoral action; *Awareness Events:* Catholic Students' Week, March
Description: To unite Catholic students on Canadian post-secondary campuses; To nurture Christian student leadership; Affiliation(s): Canadian Catholic Campus Ministry; the International Movement of Catholic Students - Canada

Canadian Conference of Catholic Bishops (CCCB) / Conférence des évêques catholiques du Canada (CECC)
2500 Don Reid Dr., Ottawa ON K1H 2J2

Tel: 613-241-9461; *Fax:* 613-241-8117
cecc@cccb.ca
www.cccb.ca
Social Media: www.youtube.com/user/cccbadmin
www.facebook.com/cccbcecc
twitter.com/CCCB_CECC
Previous Name: Canadian Catholic Conference
Overview: A small national charitable organization founded in 1943
Chief Officer(s):
Patrick Powers, P.H., General Secretary, 613-241-9461 209
gensec@cccb.ca
Member Profile: Diocesan bishops in Canada; Coadjutor Bishops; Auxiliary Bishops; Titular Bishops of any rite within the Catholic Church
Activities: Providing aid to developing countries & Christian education; Offering a forum for bishops to share experiences & insights
Description: To exercise pastoral functions for Catholics in Canada
Publications: At Home with the Word
Type: Yearbook *Frequency:* Annually *Price:* $9
Children's Daily Prayer
Type: Yearbook *Frequency:* Annually *ISBN:* 978-1-56854-662-9 *Price:* $18
Daily Prayer
Type: Yearbook *Frequency:* Annually *Price:* $15
A Simple Guide to the Daily Mass Readings
Type: Yearbook *Frequency:* Annually *Price:* $3
Sourcebook for Sundays & Seasons
Type: Yearbook *Frequency:* Annually *ISBN:* 978-1-56854-674-2 *Price:* $18
Workbook for Lectors & Gospel Readers
Type: Yearbook *Frequency:* Annually *ISBN:* 978-0-88997-572-9 *Price:* $15

Canadian Jesuits International (CJI)
70 Saint Mary St., Toronto ON M5S 1J3

Tel: 416-465-1824; *Fax:* 416-967-9097
Toll-Free: 800-448-2148
www.canadianjesuitsinternational.ca
Also Known As: Canadian Jesuit Missions
Overview: A medium-sized national charitable organization founded in 1955
Chief Officer(s):
Jenny Cafiso, Director
Membership: 100-499
Activities: Support projects in Africa, India, Nepal, Jamaica, & Ukraine
Description: Committed to the service of faith & the promotion of justice for the poor of the world; especially dedicated to the educational needs of women, children, elderly & indigenous people at home & abroad
Publications: Mission News
Type: Newsletter *Frequency:* 3 pa
Profile: News & stories about people in developing countries

Canadian Latvian Catholic Association
34 Edenvale Cres., Toronto ON M9A 4A4

Tel: 416-244-4576; *Fax:* 416-244-1513
Overview: A medium-sized national organization founded in 1949
Finances: *Annual Operating Budget:* Less than $50,000
Staff: 10 volunteer(s)
Membership: 3,000 individual; *Fees:* $10 individual

Carrefour des mouvements d'action catholique
435, rue du Roi, Québec QC G1K 2X1

Tél: 418-525-6187; *Téléc:* 418-525-6081
Nom précédent: Comité diosésain d'action catholique
Aperçu: *Dimension:* petite; *Envergure:* locale
Membre(s) du bureau directeur:
Bernadette Dubuc, Contact
Description: Groupe de coordination des associations d'action catholique dans le diocèse de Québec

Catholic Biblical Association of Canada (CBAC)
#1407, 2300 Confederation Pkwy., Mississauga ON L5B 1R5

Tel: 416-406-4398; *Fax:* 416-406-5139
www.cbac.org
Previous Name: Canadian Catholic Biblical Association
Overview: A medium-sized national charitable organization founded in 1974
Chief Officer(s):
Jocelyn Monette, Executive Director
jocelyn@cbac.org
Elizabeth M. Davis, President
Finances: *Annual Operating Budget:* $100,000-$250,000
Fees: $30; *Committees:* Media & Communications; Resource; Program; Finance
Activities: *Rents Mailing List:* Yes *Library:* Resource Centre (Open to Public)
Description: To foster knowledge & love of the Word of God as found in the Scriptures, through provision of a variety of sources, primarily to the Catholic community.; Affiliation(s): World Catholic Biblical Federation

Catholic Biblical Federation (CBF) / Fédération biblique catholique (FBC)
St. Ottilien 86941 Germany

gensec@c-b-f.org
www.c-b-f.org
Overview: A small international charitable organization founded in 1969
Chief Officer(s):
Alexander Schweitzer, General Secretary
Membership: 300+ in 130 countries
Activities: Workshops; Plenary Assembly
Affiliation(s): Catholic Biblical Association of Canada

Catholic Charities of The Archdiocese of Toronto
#400, 1155 Yonge St., Toronto ON M4T 1W2

Tel: 416-934-3401; *Fax:* 416-934-3402
info@catholiccharitiestor.org
www.catholiccharitiestor.org
Previous Name: Council of Catholic Charities
Overview: A medium-sized local licensing charitable organization founded in 1913
Chief Officer(s):
Maryann Burton, Association Administrator
Finances: *Annual Operating Budget:* $250,000-$500,000
Staff: 1 staff member(s); 10 volunteer(s)
Activities: *Speaker Service:* Yes
Description: Catholic Charities of the Archidiocese of Toronto is dedicated to ensuring the provision of health and social sciences and to provide leadership and advocacy on behalf of the member agencies and those in need. The people served live and work throughout the Greater Toronto Area, as well as, in Simcoe, Durham, Peel, and York.; Affiliation(s): Catholic Family Services of Toronto & 26 member agencies

Catholic Children's Aid Society of Hamilton (CCAS)
735 King St. East, Hamilton ON L8M 1A1

Tel: 905-525-2012; *Fax:* 905-525-5606
karen.dolyniuk@hamiltonccas.on.ca
www.hamiltonccas.on.ca
Overview: A small local charitable organization founded in 1954
Chief Officer(s):
Ersilia DiNardo, Executive Director
Anne Niec, President
Finances: *Annual Operating Budget:* Greater than $5 Million; *Funding Sources:* Ontario Ministry of Community & Social Services
Staff: 180 staff member(s); 191 volunteer(s)
Membership: 100-499; *Fees:* $10
Activities: Annual general meeting; *Awareness Events:* Serendipity Auction, Nov.; *Internships:* Yes; *Speaker Service:* Yes
Description: To provide child welfare services to the Roman Catholic population of the City of Hamilton; *Member of:* Ontario Association of Children's Aid Societies; Affiliation(s): Council of Catholic Service Organziations

Catholic Children's Aid Society of Toronto (CCAS)
26 Maitland St., Toronto ON M4Y 1C6

Tel: 416-395-1500; *Fax:* 416-395-1581
pr@ccas.toronto.on.ca
www.ccas.toronto.on.ca
Previous Name: Catholic Children's Aid Society of Metropolitan Toronto
Overview: A medium-sized local organization founded in 1894
Chief Officer(s):
Joseph Fanutti, President
Mary A. McConville, Executive Director
Finances: *Funding Sources:* Provincial government; private donations
Activities: Parental healthcare & child management training; foster care; Central Adoption Centre; *Awareness Events:* Child Abuse Prevention Campaign
Description: CCAS investigates concerns that a child may be abused or neglected, then assesses the risk to the child & develops a plan to keep the child safe. It is mandated to provide protective services to Catholic children at any time. It is a registered charity, BN: 129863577RR0001.; *Member of:* Catholic Charities of the Archdiocese of Toronto

Catholic Community Services Inc. (CCS) / Services communautaires catholiques inc.
1857, boul de Maisonneuve ouest, Montréal QC H3H 1J9
Tel: 514-937-5351; *Fax:* 514-937-5548
info@ccs-montreal.org
www.ccs-montreal.org
Overview: A medium-sized local organization founded in 1974
Chief Officer(s):
Bruno J. Mital, Managing Director
brunom@ccs-montreal.org
Finances: *Annual Operating Budget:* $1.5 Million-$3 Million
Staff: 33 staff member(s); 1104 volunteer(s)
Membership: 65; *Fees:* $10
Activities: Youth groups; home sharing; administrative & support services; community organization & development; family support programs; personal development & support groups; camping services; Almage Senior Centre; Teapot Senior Centre; Good Shepherd Community Centre; Home Support Program; volunteer coordination; Home Day Care Program; *Speaker Service:* Yes
Description: To provide a broad spectrum of social services on behalf of the English-speaking Catholic community of the Diocese of Montréal

Catholic Education Foundation of Ontario (CEFO)
80 Sheppard Ave. East, Toronto ON M2N 6E8
Tel: 416-229-5326; *Fax:* 416-229-5345
Overview: A small provincial charitable organization founded in 1976
Chief Officer(s):
John J. Flynn, Executive Secretary
Description: To foster & promote the principles of Catholic education; to support parents in their role as primary educators; to assist the Church in its pastoral responsibilities to the schools; to encourage the establishment of Catholic schools; to promote equity of educational funding in Ontario

Catholic Family Service of Ottawa (CFS Ottawa) / Service familial catholique d'Ottawa
310 Olmstead St., Ottawa ON K1L 7K3
Tel: 613-233-8478; *Fax:* 613-233-9881
info@cfsottawa.ca
www.cfsottawa.ca
Previous Name: Catholic Family Service of Ottawa-Carleton
Overview: A small local charitable organization founded in 1940
Chief Officer(s):
Normand Levasseur, President
Franca DiDiomete, Executive Director
Finances: *Annual Operating Budget:* $1.5 Million-$3 Million; *Funding Sources:* Provincial/municipal government; United Way; private donations
Staff: 34 staff member(s); 15 volunteer(s)
Membership: 50
Activities: *Internships:* Yes *Library:* Yes (Open to Public)
Description: CFS Ottawa offers a range of social services in English & French to all residents of the Ottawa-Carleton area. Services include counselling, support to the victims or witnesses of family violence or sexual abuse, advocacy, community development. It is a registered charity, BN: 118841105RR0001.; *Member of:* Family Service Canada

Catholic Family Services of Hamilton (CFS)
#201, 447 Main St. East, Hamilton ON L8N 1K1
Tel: 905-527-3823; *Fax:* 905-546-5779
Toll-Free: 877-527-3823
intake@cfshw.com
www.cfshw.com
Previous Name: Catholic Family Services of Hamilton-Wentworth
Overview: A small local organization founded in 1944
Chief Officer(s):
Linda Dayler, Executive Director & Secretary
Teresa Hartnett, Chair
Kathleen Leach, Vice-Chair
Carol James, Treasurer
Paula Forbes, Associate Director
Mary Jefferson, Associate Director
Finances: *Funding Sources:* Government of Canada; Province of Ontario; City of Hamilton; United Way of Burlington & Greater Hamilton; Foundations such as ON Trillium Foundation
Activities: Offering programs, such as the Employee Assistance Program, Debt Management Program, K.I.D.S. (Kids in Divorced / Separated Situations), Men's Anti-Violence & Abuse Program, & the Senior's Intervention & Support Program; Providing mediation services, in areas such as the workplace, credit, estates, & commerce; Offering consumer credit education to the general public; Offering money management coaching
Description: To provide individual, marriage, family, & credit counselling services in the Hamilton & Burlington communities; *Member of:* Ontario Association of Credit Counselling Service; Affiliation(s): Ontario Community Support Association; ONTCHILD; Family Services Ontario; Canadian Association for Community Care; Continuing Gerontological Education Cooperative; Older Persons' Mental Health & Addictions Network; Ontario Association on Developmental Diabilities; Ontario Case Managers Association; Ontario Gerontology Association; Ontario Partnership on Aging Development Disabilities

Catholic Family Services of Peel Dufferin (CFSPD)
Emerald Centre, #400, 10 Kingsbridge Garden Circle, Mississauga ON L5R 3K6
Tel: 905-897-1644; *Fax:* 905-897-2467
Toll-Free: 888-940-0584
info@cfspd.com
www.cfspd.com
Previous Name: Peel Dufferin Catholic Services
Overview: A small local charitable organization founded in 1981
Chief Officer(s):
Andrea Broadley, President
Mark Creedon, Executive Director
Finances: *Annual Operating Budget:* $500,000-$1.5 Million
Staff: 30 staff member(s); 85 volunteer(s)
Activities: Individual, couple & family therapy; support groups; workshops; *Internships:* Yes; *Speaker Service:* Yes
Description: CFSPD is a multi-service counselling agency that supports families coping with difficulties, notably violence, trauma & abuse. Services are available in many languages to help people deal with such problems as depression, anxiety, grief, marital difficulties, parent-child conflict, developmental transitions & cutural adjustments. Offices in Mississauga & Brampton have walk-in clinics. The Society is a registered charity, BN: 119087823RR0001.; *Member of:* Catholic Charities; Archdiocese of Toronto; United Way of Peel Region

Catholic Family Services of Simcoe County (CFSSC)
#5, 20 Bell Farm Rd., Barrie ON L4M 6E4
Tel: 705-726-2503; *Fax:* 705-726-2570
info@cfssc.ca
www.cfssc.ca
Previous Name: Catholic Family Life Centre-Simcoe South; North Simcoe Catholic Family Life Centre
Overview: A small local charitable organization founded in 1979
Chief Officer(s):
Heather Bebb, Executive Director
hbebb@cfssc.ca
Finances: *Annual Operating Budget:* $250,000-$500,000; *Funding Sources:* Charities; United Way
Staff: 20 staff member(s)
Membership: 1-99
Activities: Family, individual & group counselling; family life education
Description: To offer professional social services to all residents of Simcoe South; services will be directed to the treatment of troubled families & individuals, as well as to strengthening & enriching family life & individual functioning in all their dimensions & contexts

Catholic Family Services of Toronto (CFS Toronto) / Services familiaux catholiques de Toronto
Catholic Pastoral Centre, #200, 1155 Yonge St., Toronto ON M4T 1W2
Tel: 416-921-1163; *Fax:* 416-921-1579
info@cfsofto.org
www.cfsofto.org
Previous Name: Catholic Welfare Bureau
Overview: A medium-sized local charitable organization founded in 1922
Chief Officer(s):
Stephen Mills, President
Lucia Furgiuele, Executive Director
Finances: *Annual Operating Budget:* $1.5 Million-$3 Million
Staff: 35 staff member(s); 18 volunteer(s)
Activities: *Library:* Yes
Description: CFS Toronto is a non-profit, counselling agency for individuals, couples, & families. Within the context of Catholic beliefs, it offers a range of specialised programs, as well as a safe environment for women & families who are victims of abuse. It is a registered charity, BN: 100844919RR0001.; *Member of:* Catholic Charities of the Archdiocese of Toronto; Affiliation(s): Family Service Canada; Family Service Ontario

Catholic Family Services of Windsor-Essex County
6038 Empress St., Windsor ON N8T 1B5
Tel: 519-254-5164; *Fax:* 519-254-0611
intake@cfswindsor-essex.com
Previous Name: Windsor Catholic Family Service Bureau
Overview: A small local charitable organization founded in 1947
Chief Officer(s):
Mary Reaume, Executive Assistant
Tim Ellard, Executive Director
Finances: *Annual Operating Budget:* $250,000-$500,000; *Funding Sources:* United Way; government; fees
Staff: 8 staff member(s); 2 volunteer(s)
Activities: *Speaker Service:* Yes
Description: To strengthen the ability of individuals, families & communities to reach their potential within the context of Catholic beliefs, values & teachings, while affirming the cultural, racial & specific differences of people; *Member of:* Family Service Canada; Family Service Ontario

The Catholic Foundation of Manitoba / Fondation catholique du Manitoba
#5, 434 Archibald St., Winnipeg MB R2J 0X5
Tel: 204-233-4268; *Fax:* 204-233-1800
cfmb@mts.net
catholicfoundation.mb.ca
Overview: A medium-sized provincial organization founded in 1964
Chief Officer(s):
Tom Lussier, President
Description: The vision of the Catholic Foundation is to provide for the needy, better the situation of the underprivileged, promote cultural advancement and scientific research, and promote the cultural life of the Catholic community of Manitoba by encouraging the funding of endowments and by providing prudent management of funds and responsible distribution of the derived revenue

Catholic Health Alliance of Canada / Alliance catholique canadienne de la santé
Annex C, Saint-Vincent Hospital, 60 Cambridge St. North, Ottawa ON K1R 7A5
Tel: 613-562-6262; *Fax:* 613-782-2857
challiance@bruyere.org
www.chac.ca
Previous Name: Catholic Health Association of Canada; Catholic Hospital Association of Canada
Overview: A large national charitable organization founded in 1939
Chief Officer(s):
Mike Shea, Chair
James Roche, Executive Director
jroche@bruyere.org
Nuala Kenny, Ethics & Health Policy Advisor
nkenny@eastlink.ca
Finances: *Annual Operating Budget:* $1.5 Million-$3 Million; *Funding Sources:* Membership dues
Membership: 7 provincial associations + 23 sponsors & owners of health care organizations + 96 hospitals, long-term care organizations & health care professionals; *Fees:* Schedule available; *Member Profile:* Sponsor organizations of Catholic health care in Canada.
Description: To strengthen & support the ministry of Catholic health care organizations & providers, through advocacy & governance
Publications: Catholic Health Alliance of Canada Annual Report
Type: Yearbook *Frequency:* Annually
Profile: Financial & executive reports
Facing Death, Discovering Life
Number of Pages: 78 *Author:* James Roche *ISBN:* 9780920705360 *Price:* $10.95
Forming Health Care Leaders: A Guide
Number of Pages: 143 *ISBN:* 9780920705421 *Price:* $12.50
Health Ethics Guide
Number of Pages: 122 *ISBN:* 9780920705018 *Price:* $12.50 members
Lift Up Your Hearts to the Lord
Number of Pages: 104 *ISBN:* 9780920705056 *Price:* $4 members
Living With Hope in Times of Illness
Number of Pages: 30 *Editor:* Barry McGrorry; Greg J. Humbert *ISBN:* 9780920705407 *Price:* $2
Spirituality & Health: What's Good for the Soul Can Be Good for the Body, Too
Number of Pages: 74 *Author:* James Roche *ISBN:* 9780920705247 *Price:* $9.95

Catholic Health Association of British Columbia (CHABC)
9387 Holmes St., Burnaby BC V3N 4C3
Tel: 604-524-3427; *Fax:* 604-524-3428
smhouse@shawlink.ca
chabc.bc.ca
Overview: A medium-sized provincial organization founded in 1940
Chief Officer(s):
Dianne Doyle, President
Membership: 114; *Committees:* Mission Intergration; Pastral Care; Ethics
Description: To witness to the healing ministry and abiding presence of Jesus. Inspired by the Gospel, this Association strives to have a universal concern for health as a condition for full human development.; *Member of:* Catholic Health Association of Canada; Health Employers Association of British

Columbia; Affiliation(s): Euthanasia Prevention Coalition; Canadian Association of Parish Nurse Ministries

Catholic Health Association of Manitoba (CHAM) / Association catholique manitobaine de la santé (ACMS)

SBGH Education Bldg., #N5067, 409 Taché Ave., Winnipeg MB R2H 2A6
Tel: 204-235-3136; *Fax:* 204-235-3811
www.cham.mb.ca

Overview: A medium-sized provincial charitable organization founded in 1943
Chief Officer(s):
Wilmar Chopyk, Executive Director
executivedirector@cham.mb.ca
Daniel Lussier, Chair
Fees: $20 personal members; $100 associate members; *Member Profile:* Organizations; Health care facilities; Individuals
Activities: Promoting collaboration in health care services; Providing education to health care professionals, parish workers, & volunteers; Engaging in advocacy activities for the needs of the vulnerable & disadvantaged; Promoting the dignity & sacredness of each person; *Awareness Events:* CHAC World Day of the Sick
Description: To carry out the healing ministry of the Catholic Church in the delivery of both health & social services in Manitoba; To treat the people of Manitoba with compassion & respect for all; to recognize the spiritual dimension integral to health & healing; Affiliation(s): Bishops of Manitoba; Diocese of Churchill-Hudson Bay, Northwest Territories
Publications: CHAM [Catholic Health Association of Manitoba] Newsletter
Type: Newsletter
Profile: Educational information for members & CHAM activities

Catholic Health Association of Saskatchewan (CHAS)

1702 - 20 St. West, Saskatoon SK S7M 0Z9
Tel: 306-655-5330; *Fax:* 306-655-5333
cath.health@sasktel.net
www.chassk.ca

Overview: A medium-sized provincial charitable organization founded in 1943
Chief Officer(s):
Sandra Kary, Executive Director
sandra.chassk@sasktel.net
Brian Martin, President
Christopher Boychuk, Vice-President
Peter Martens, Secretary-Treasurer
Fees: $25 person members; $75 associations; *Member Profile:* Institutions, groups, & individuals who are interested in Catholic health care & support the work of the association
Activities: Providing education & resources to members; Offering programs, such as the Parish Home Ministry of Care Program & the Catholic Health Leadership Program; Engaging in advocacy activities with government; Providing both provincial & national networking opportunities; *Awareness Events:* Mission Week; World Day of the Sick *Library:* Catholic Health Association of Saskatchewan Resource Library
Description: To provide leadership in mission, ethics, spiritual care, & social justice in Saskatchewan; To promote the sanctity of life & the dignity of all

Catholic Health Corporation of Ontario (CHCO)

PO Box 1879, 712 College Ave. West, Guelph ON N1H 7A1
Tel: 519-767-5600; *Fax:* 519-767-5602
chco@chco.ca
www.chco.ca

Overview: A medium-sized provincial organization
Chief Officer(s):
Don McDermott, President
Sarah Quackenbush, Consultant, Mission & Education
Description: Sponsors member institutions and thereby continues and strengthens Catholic health care in Ontario

Catholic Health of Alberta (ACHC)

9810 - 165 St., Edmonton AB T5P 3S7
Tel: 780-481-9900; *Fax:* 780-455-4150

Previous Name: Alberta Catholic Health Corporation
Overview: A small provincial organization
Chief Officer(s):
Patrick Dumelie, Interim CEO

Catholic Missions in Canada (CMIC) / Missions catholiques au Canada

#201, 1155 Yonge St., Toronto ON M4T 1W2
Tel: 416-934-3424; *Fax:* 416-934-3425
Toll-Free: 866-937-2642
info@cmic.info
www.cmic.info
www.facebook.com/catholicmissionsincanada
twitter.com/canadamissions

Previous Name: Catholic Church Extension Society of Canada
Overview: A large national charitable organization founded in 1908
Chief Officer(s):
Thomas C. Collins, Apostolic Chancellor & Chair, Executive Committee
Philip J. Kennedy, President, president@cmic.info, 416-934-3424, Fax: 416-934-3425
John P. McGrath, Secretary
Finances: *Funding Sources:* Donations; Fundraising
Staff: 11 staff member(s)
Activities: Supporting over 600 missionaries who serve in home mission communities throughout Canada; *Speaker Service:* Yes *Library:* Yes
Description: To keep the Catholic faith in remote & poor communities throughout Canada; *Member of:* Association of Fundraising Professionals (Toronto)
Publications: Catholic Missions in Canada
Type: Magazine
Profile: Information about missionaries who serve in home mission communities across Canada
Catholic Missions in Canada Annual Report
Type: Yearbook *Frequency:* Annually
Profile: Featuring information on CMIC's expenses & distributions

Catholic Organization for Life & Family (COLF) / Organisme catholique pour la vie et la famille (OCVF)

2500 Don Reid Dr., Ottawa ON K1H 2J2
Tel: 613-241-9461; *Fax:* 613-241-9048
info@colf.ca
www.colf.ca

Overview: A small national organization founded in 1996
Chief Officer(s):
Noël Simard, Chair
Michèle Boulva, Director
Peter D. Murphy, Assistant Director
Jocelyne Pagé, Administrative Assistant
Finances: *Funding Sources:* Donations
Staff: 1 staff member(s)
Activities: Promoting the teaching of the Catholic Church in circumstances from conception to natural death; Preparing & providing educational resources; Strengthening the role of the family; Participating in public debate about the family & respect for life; Collaborating with the Canadian Conference of Catholic Bishops & the Knights of Columbus
Description: To build a civilization of love; To promote respect for human life & the important role of the family; Affiliation(s): Canadian Conference of Catholic Bishops (CCCB)
Publications: Catholic Organization for Life & Family Activity Report
Type: Yearbook *Frequency:* Annually
Profile: Details about the organization's activities, projects, & initiatives
Euthanasia & Assisted Suicide — Urgent Questions
Life in the Balance: Workshop on Euthanasia & Assisted Suicide
Type: Guide
Stem Cells: Astonishing Promises . . . But at What Cost?

The Catholic Principals' Council of Ontario (CPCO)

#400, 161 Eglinton Ave. East, Toronto ON M4P 1J5
Tel: 416-483-1556; *Fax:* 416-483-2554
Toll-Free: 888-621-9190
info@cpco.on.ca
www.cpco.on.ca

Overview: A small provincial organization
Chief Officer(s):
Clara Pitoscia, Executive Director
director@cpco.on.ca
Paul Lacalamita, President
president@cpco.on.ca
Finances: *Annual Operating Budget:* $1.5 Million-$3 Million
Staff: 6 staff member(s); 6 volunteer(s)
Membership: 2,000 members who are principals & vice-principals in more than 1,300 elementary & secondary separate schools across Ontario; *Committees:* Communications; Member Security; Professional Development; Finance; Issues in Catholic Education
Activities: Advocacy, professional development; legal services; *Speaker Service:* Yes
Description: CPCO is a voluntary, professional association that serves more than 2,100 principals and vice-principals in twenty-nine Catholic school boards across Ontario

Congrégation de Sainte-Croix - Les Frères de Sainte-Croix / Congregation of Holy Cross

3745, ch Queen Mary, Montréal QC H3V 1A7
Tél: 514-737-6660; *Téléc:* 514-341-0739
saintecroixcsc@yahoo.ca

Aperçu: *Dimension:* petite; *Envergure:* locale
Membre(s) du bureau directeur:
Réjean Charette, Supérieur provincial
Description: Congrégation religieuse catholique qui oeuvre en éducation, en milieu paroissial et dans divers autres secteurs de la société

Congregation of St-Basil (Basilian Fathers) (CSB)

95 St. Joseph St., Toronto ON M5S 3C2
Tel: 416-921-6674; *Fax:* 416-920-3413
contact@basilian.org
www.basilian.org
Social Media: www.youtube.com/user/cavalka124
www.facebook.com/pages/Congregation-of-St-Basil/125825700793462

Also Known As: Basilian Fathers
Overview: A small international organization founded in 1822
Chief Officer(s):
Michael P. Cerretto, Secretary General
Ronald P. Fabbro, Superior General
Finances: *Annual Operating Budget:* Less than $50,000
Staff: 3 volunteer(s)
Membership: 325; *Member Profile:* Priests; students for the priesthood
Activities: *Library:* Yes by appointment
Description: Roman Catholic congregation of priests whose primary apostolate is education, parishes & Hispanic ministry in Canada, USA, Mexico, Colombia, & France; *Member of:* RC Church

Council of Catholic School Superintendents of Alberta

AB
superintendents@ccssa.ab.ca
www.ccssa.ab.ca

Overview: A small provincial organization
Chief Officer(s):
George Zeigner, Executive Director
Membership: 35
Description: Provides a forum for discussion regarding the direction & development of Catholic Education in Alberta

Development & Peace / Développement et paix

1425, boul René-Lévesque ouest, 3e étage, Montréal QC H3G 1T7
Tel: 514-257-8711; *Fax:* 514-257-8497
Toll-Free: 888-234-8533
info@devp.org
www.devp.org
Social Media: www.youtube.com/devpeacetv;
www.flickr.com/photos/devpedu/sets
www.facebook.com/devpeace
twitter.com/DevPeace

Also Known As: Canadian Catholic Organization for Development & Peace
Overview: A large international charitable organization founded in 1967
Chief Officer(s):
Pat Hogan, President
Michael Casey, Executive Director
Finances: *Annual Operating Budget:* Greater than $5 Million; *Funding Sources:* Donations; CIDA (Canadian International Development Agency) provides grants for projects & programs
Staff: 70 staff member(s); 5000 volunteer(s)
Membership: 13,000; *Fees:* 5$
Activities: Financial support of projects in the developing world; emergency relief; advocacy on crises/issues in developing countries
Description: An official, volunteer-driven arm of the Canadian Catholic Church for international development, the organization aims to educate the Canadian population about the causes of poverty. It fosters solidarity, forming alliances with groups in developing countries, & promotes alternatives to unfair social, political & economic structures. Head offices are in Toronto & Montreal. It is a registered charity, BN: 118829902RR0001.; *Member of:* Caritas Internationalis; Conseil canadien pour la coopération internationale/Canadian Council for International Cooperation; Affiliation(s): Coopération internationale pour le développement et la solidarité
Publications: Development & Peace Annual Report
Frequency: Annually
Global Village Voice [a publication of Development & Peace]
Type: Newsletter *Frequency:* 3 pa *ISSN:* 0383-6703

Dignity Canada Dignité

PO Box 2102, Stn. D, Ottawa ON K1P 5W3
Tel: 613-746-7279; *Fax:* 613-746-0353
info@dignitycanada.org
www.dignitycanada.org

Overview: A medium-sized national organization
Chief Officer(s):
Frank Testin, President
Norman Prince, Secretary

Finances: *Funding Sources:* Donations
Activities: Encouraging spiritual development, education, & social involvement
Description: To voice the concerns of Roman Catholic sexual minorities; To promote the development of sexual theology, justice, & acceptance of the lesbian & gay community; To reinforce a sense of dignity & to encourage gay men & lesbian women to become more active members in the Church & society

Dignity Toronto Dignité
175 Windermere Ave., Toronto ON M6S 3J8
Tel: 416-925-9872
toronto@dignitycanada.org
www.dignitycanada.org
Overview: A small local organization founded in 1974
Chief Officer(s):
Frank Testin, President
president@dignitycanada.org
Finances: *Annual Operating Budget:* Less than $50,000
Membership: 20; *Fees:* $30
Activities: Monthly liturgical meeting to support gay & lesbian Roman Catholics; social gatherings
Description: To support & affirm gay & lesbian Roman Catholics through spiritual development, education, social involvement, equity issues, social events; *Member of:* Dignity Canada Dignité

Dignity Vancouver Dignité
PO Box 3016, Stn. Terminal, Vancouver BC V6B 3X5
vancouver@dignitycanada.org
Overview: A small local organization founded in 1977
Chief Officer(s):
Dennis Benoit, President, 604-669-3677
president@dignitycanada.org
Finances: *Annual Operating Budget:* Less than $50,000
Membership: 12; *Fees:* $35 individual; *Member Profile:* Roman Catholic gays, lesbians, friends
Description: The organization works within the Catholic Church & with other Catholic groups to reform the church's theological stance pertaining to sexual minorities. It supports gay & lesbian Catholics & their friends, encouraging participation in educational, spiritual, & social activities.; *Member of:* Dignity Canada Dignité

Dignity Winnipeg Dignité
PO Box 1912, Winnipeg MB R3C 3R2
Tel: 204-779-6446; *Fax:* 204-284-0132
winnipeg@dignitycanada.org
www.dignitycanada.org
Overview: A small provincial organization founded in 1970
Chief Officer(s):
Thomas Novak, National Chaplain, 204-287-8583
Finances: *Annual Operating Budget:* Less than $50,000
Staff: 3 volunteer(s)
Membership: 20; *Fees:* $25 (optional); *Member Profile:* LGBT community; non-gay men & women, encompassing a broad spectrum of professions, political beliefs, ethnic & linguistic backgrounds & economic levels
Activities: Regular liturgies/discussion groups; annual retreat; social events; brochures; *Speaker Service:* Yes
Description: To bring together gay & lesbian Catholics & their friends; To encourage a process of self-understanding & personal integration with respect to issues, including spirituality & sexuality; *Member of:* Dignity Canada Dignité

Diocèse militaire du Canada
USFC (O), Site Uplands, Édifice 469, Ottawa ON K1A 0K2
Tél: 613-990-7824; *Téléc:* 613-991-1056
rc.milord@on.aibn.com
www.missa.org
Aperçu: *Dimension:* petite; *Envergure:* nationale; *Organisme sans but lucratif; fondée en 1987*
Membre(s) du bureau directeur:
A. Asselin, Chancelier
Donald Thériault, Évêque
R. Marchand, Aumônier principal
Activités: *Bibliothèque:* Centre d'entraînement des aumôniers de Borden
Description: Fournir une dimension spirituelle et morale à toutes les activités affectant le moral et le bien-être des membres catholiques des Forces canadiennes, leurs familles et les employés civils du Ministère de la Défense nationale; *Membre de:* La Conférence des évêques catholiques du Canada

Fédération nationale du MFC - Mouvement des Femmes Chrétiennes (MFC)
CP 174, 49, boul Lanaudière, Sainte-Anne-de-la-Pérade QC G0X 2J0
Tél: 418-325-2338; *Téléc:* 418-325-2255
mfcnational@hotmail.com
Aperçu: *Dimension:* grande; *Envergure:* nationale; *Organisme sans but lucratif; fondée en 1962*
Finances: *Budget de fonctionnement annuel:* Moins de $50,000
Personnel: 1 membre(s) du personnel; 700 bénévole(s)
Membre: 8000; *Montant de la cotisation:* 15$; *Critères d'admissibilite:* Femmes de tout âge, condition et culture
Activités: Rencontre mensuelle sur le programme d'action; formation
Description: Un mouvement d'action catholique générale, il forme des femmes efficaces et dynamiques sur le plan familial, paroissial, social, et chrétien afin de transformer le milieu de vie par des projects concrets et en utilisant la méthode de l'action catholique; *Membre de:* Regroupement des Organismes Volontaires d'Éducation Populaire

Foundation of Catholic Community Services Inc (FCCS)
#310, 1857, boul de Maisonneuve ouest, Montréal QC H3H 1J9
Tel: 514-934-1326; *Fax:* 514-934-0453
info@fccsmontreal.org
www.fccsmontreal.org
Overview: A small local organization founded in 1932
Chief Officer(s):
Georges A. Renaud, President
Membership: 100 individual

Frères de Notre-Dame de la Miséricorde / Brothers of Our Lady of Mercy
1149, ch Tour du Lac nord, Lac-Sergent QC G0A 2J0
Tél: 418-875-2792; *Téléc:* 418-875-4829
fndm@cite.net
Aperçu: *Dimension:* petite; *Envergure:* internationale; *Organisme sans but lucratif; fondée en 1839*
Membre(s) du bureau directeur:
Omer Beaulieu, Délégué du Supérieur général
Finances: *Budget de fonctionnement annuel:* Moins de $50,000
Personnel: 1 membre(s) du personnel; 6 bénévole(s)
Membre: 9
Description: Rassembler des personnes en vue d'un travail apostolique auprès des jeunes et particulièrement auprès des personnes éprouvant des difficultés

Holy Childhood Association (HCA)
3329 Danforth Ave., #D, Toronto ON M1L 4T3
Tel: 416-699-7077; *Fax:* 416-699-9019
Toll-Free: 800-897-8865
hca@missionsocieties.ca
www.missionsocieties.ca
Also Known As: Children Helping Children
Overview: A medium-sized international charitable organization founded in 1843
Chief Officer(s):
Mary Jo Mahon-Oakes, National Secretary
hca@missionsocities.ca
Description: To develop mission awareness through a school program for elementary Catholic school children; to provide aid to children in developing countries.; *Member of:* Pontificial Mission Societies

IMCS Pax Romana
7 Impasse Reille, Paris 75014 France
international_secretariat@imcs-miec.org
www.imcs-mierc.org
Également appelé: International Catholic Organization
Nom précédent: International Movement of Catholic Students; International Catholic Movement for Intellectual & Cultural Affairs
Aperçu: *Dimension:* grande; *Envergure:* internationale; *fondée en 1921*
Membre(s) du bureau directeur:
Mehulbhai Kantibhai Dabhi, International President
mdabhi@imcs-miec.org
Activités: Pax Romana has consultative status with the United Nations Economic & Social Council, UNESCO & the European Council, & has accredited representatives to those organisations in New York, Vienna, Paris, Geneve & Strasbourg
Description: Aims, through its various professional & intellectual commitments in society & the Church, to engage in pro-active dialogue between Christian faith & cultures in order to promote the evangelization of cultures & the inculturation of the Gospel for the realization of the Kingdom of God; Affiliation(s): Mouvement d'étudiants chrétiens du Québec; Association of Canadian Catholic Students

Institut Voluntas Dei / Voluntas Dei Institute
7385, boul Parent, Trois-Rivières QC G9A 5E1
Tél: 819-375-7933; *Téléc:* 819-691-1841
ivd.cent@cgocable.ca
www.voluntasdei.org
Média social:
www.youtube.com/voluntasdeis?feature=mhee#p/u/22/
www.facebook.com/voluntasdei
twitter.com/voluntasdei
Également appelé: I.V. Dei
Aperçu: *Dimension:* petite; *Envergure:* internationale; *Organisme sans but lucratif; fondée en 1958*
Finances: *Budget de fonctionnement annuel:* $100,000-$250,000
Personnel: 3 membre(s) du personnel
Membre: 752; *Critères d'admissibilite:* Clerics & laymen who commit their lives to the service of Jesus Christ; married people as associate members who live out the same ideal & same apostolic project as the celibate members
Activités: *Stagiaires:* Oui
Description: To make known & communicate God's love for all to all people; To be present in every milieu; apostolic objective is "to create peace & brotherhood in Jesus Christ"; *Membre de:* Roman Catholic Church

Jesuit Development Office (JDO)
c/o Jesuit in English Canada, Provincial Office, 43 Queen's Park Cres. East, Toronto ON M5S 2C3
Tel: 416-481-9154; *Fax:* 416-920-5799
www.jesuits.ca
Overview: A medium-sized international charitable organization founded in 1940
Chief Officer(s):
Winston Rye, National Director
wrye@jesuits.ca
Barbara DeCarlo, Director, Development & Administration
bdecarlo@jesuits.ca
Membership: under 200
Description: To raise & provide the funds necessary for the support of Jesuit brothers & priests in formation, in ministry & in their senior years; *Member of:* Jesuit Fathers & Brothers of Upper Canada

Jeunes canadiens pour une civilisation chrétienne
CP 6453, Succ. A, Toronto ON M5W 1X3
Tél: 418-683-5222
Aperçu: *Dimension:* petite; *Envergure:* locale; *fondée en 1977*
Membre(s) du bureau directeur:
Sébastien Bolduc
Finances: *Budget de fonctionnement annuel:* Moins de $50,000
Description: Travailler avec la jeunesse pour préserver les principes catholiques et éducatifs

Latin American Mission Program (LAMP)
81 Prince St., Charlottetown PE C1A 4R3
Tel: 902-368-7337; *Fax:* 902-368-7180
www.dioceseofcharlottetown.com
Overview: A small international organization founded in 1967
Finances: *Annual Operating Budget:* $50,000-$100,000; *Funding Sources:* Share Lent collections taken up annually in all parishes
Membership: 20
Activities: Educational events; orientation & support for missionaries
Description: To send out & receive back missionaries; to learn from the dispossessed & oppressed & to stand with them in building a society of justice; to develop & encourage a Faith response based on the life & struggle of dispossessed peoples; to participate in "return mission" by working with groups committed to social justice in Canada & developing education programs in PEI which analyze the causes of exploitation of the poor & which exposes the reality of their lives; Affiliation(s): Diocese of Charlottetown; Les missionnaires du Sacre-Coeur; Scarboro Foreign Mission Society

LAUDEM, L'Association des musiciens liturgiques du Canada
1085, rue de la Cathédrale, Montréal QC H3B 2V3
Tél: 514-866-1661; *Téléc:* 514-767-1168
info@laudem.org
www.laudem.org
Nom précédent: L'Association des organistes liturgiques du Canada
Aperçu: *Dimension:* petite; *Envergure:* nationale; *fondée en 1992*
Membre(s) du bureau directeur:
Hélène Dugal, Présidente
Membre: 117; *Critères d'admissibilite:* Laudem accueille parmi ses membres actifs les organistes professionnels, amateurs et étudiants, titulaires, assistants, ou remplaçants dans les paroisses, sanctuaires, dessertes et communautés religieuses d'expression française de l'Église canadienne; Laudem accueille en outre parmi ses membres donateurs toutes les personnes intéressées à promouvoir les buts pour lesquels l'association a été créé
Description: De réunir les organistes liturgiques pour la promotion et le développement de leur ministère dans l'Église catholique romaine; *Membre de:* Fédération francophone des amis de l'orgue

Little Brothers of the Good Shepherd / Petits Frères du Bon-Pasteur
Good Shepherd Centre, PO Box 1003, 135 Mary St., Hamilton ON L8N 3R1
Tel: 905-528-9109; *Fax:* 905-528-6967
info@goodshepherdcentres.ca
www.goodshepherdcentres.ca
Overview: A small local organization founded in 1964
Chief Officer(s):
Richard MacPhee, Executive Director
Finances: *Annual Operating Budget:* $500,000-$1.5 Million
Activities: Housing for battered women & children; residence for homeless youth; men's hostel; food bank & food line; speakers on topics dealing with violence & abuse; *Speaker Service:* Yes

Messagères de Notre-Dame de l'Assomption (MNDA)
#4, 45, rue de la Sapiniere-dorion, Québec QC G1L 1A3
Tél: 418-626-7492
Aperçu: *Dimension:* petite; *Envergure:* locale; *Organisme sans but lucratif; fondée en 1964*
Membre(s) du bureau directeur:
Lucie Dorval, Présidente
Finances: *Budget de fonctionnement annuel:* $50,000-$100,000
Membre: 100-499

Missionary Sisters of The Precious Blood of North America
St Bernard's Convent, 685 Finch Ave. West, Toronto ON M2R 1P2
Tel: 416-630-3298
vocationscps@gmail.com
www.cpsmissionarysisters.com
Overview: A small international organization founded in 1885
Finances: *Funding Sources:* donations
Staff: 60 staff member(s)
Description: Involved in early childhood education and teaching at the elementary, secondary, and college levels. Also work in health care services as nurses, doctors, administrators, physical and occupational therapists, hospital chaplains, caregivers for the elderly, with AIDs patients and in nutrition education. Serves in social work, parish ministry, domestic work, gardening, religious education, work with the mentally and physically handicapped, retreat work, art, and in ministry to the Hispanic and First Nations people.

Mosaic Counselling & Family Services
400 Queen St. South, Kitchener ON N2G 1W7
Tel: 519-743-6333
info@mosaiconline.ca
www.mosaiconline.ca
Previous Name: Catholic Family Counselling Centre; Catholic Social Services; Catholic Welfare Bureau
Overview: A small local charitable organization founded in 1952
Chief Officer(s):
Cathy Brothers, Executive Director, 519-743-6333 232
Jennifer Berry, Director, Communications, 519-743-6333 303
Megan Conway, Director, Pathways to Education, 519-743-6333 306
Peter Fisher, Director, Clinical Services, 519-743-6333 223
Sandy Hoy, Director, Research & Evaluation, 519-743-6333 267
Nancy Kyle, Director, Community Services, 519-743-6333 229
Kathie Must, Director, Workplace Programs, 519-743-6333 231
Judy Nairn, Director, Business, 519-743-6333 328
Karin Voisin, Director, Volunteers & Community Relations, 519-743-6333 243
Andrew Wilding, Director, Resource Development, 519-743-6333 307
Heather Cudmore, Manager, Credit Counselling Program, 519-743-6333 236
Finances: *Annual Operating Budget:* $3 Million-$5 Million; *Funding Sources:* United Way; Government of Canada; Province of Ontario; Regional Municipality of Waterloo; Foundations, such as Pathways to Education Canada
Activities: Offering individual, group, & credit counselling; Providing workplace & employee assistance programs; Offering community outreach services; *Library:* Mosaic Counselling & Family Services Library
Description: To provide full-service professional counselling services in Kitchener & the surrounding region; *Member of:* Canadian Association of Credit Counselling Services; Ontario Association of Credit Counselling Services; United Way of Kitchener-Waterloo & Area; Family Service Ontario

New Brunswick Catholic Health Association (NBCHA)
1773 Water St., Miramichi NB E1N 1B2
Tel: 506-778-5302; *Fax:* 506-778-5303
nbcha@nb.aibn.com
www.chanb.com/chanb/
Also Known As: Catholic Health Association of New Brunswick
Overview: A small provincial organization founded in 1986
Chief Officer(s):
Robert Stewart, Executive Director
rstewart@health.nb.ca
Membership: 300
Description: The New Brunswick Catholic Health Association is a provincial Christian organization promoting health care in the tradition of the Catholic Church. The Association fosters healing in all its aspects: Physical, psychological, social and spiritual

Newman Foundation of Toronto
89 St. George St., Toronto ON M5S 2E8
Tel: 416-979-2468; *Fax:* 416-596-6920
secretary@newmantoronto.com
www.newmantoronto.com
Overview: A small local charitable organization
Chief Officer(s):
W.F. Morneau, President
Patrick O'Dea, Director
Description: To maintain & support Roman Catholic chaplaincy on University of Toronto campus

Ontario English Catholic Teachers' Association (CLC) (OECTA)
#400, 65 St. Clair Ave. East, Toronto ON M4T 2Y8
Tel: 416-925-2493; *Fax:* 416-925-7764
Toll-Free: 800-268-7230
membership@oecta.on.ca
www.oecta.on.ca
Overview: A large provincial organization founded in 1944
Chief Officer(s):
Kevin O'Dwyer, President
Marshall Jarvis, General Secretary
m.jarvis@oecta.on.ca
Membership: 36,000; *Fees:* $950
Description: To advance Catholic education; To provide professional services, support, protection, & leadership; *Member of:* Canadian Teachers' Federation; Canadian Labour Congress; Ontario Federation of Labour; Affiliation(s): Ontario Teachers' Federation

Orthodox Church in America Archdiocese of Canada (OCA ADOC)
Office of the Bishop, PO Box 179, Spencerville ON K0E 1X0
Tel: 613-925-5226; *Fax:* 613-925-1521
vladyka@archdiocese.ca
www.archdiocese.ca/home.htm
Also Known As: Orthodox Church in Canada
Previous Name: Russian Orthodox Greek Catholic Church (Metropolia)
Overview: A medium-sized international organization founded in 1902
Chief Officer(s):
Seraphim Storheim, Bishop of Ottawa
Dennis Pihach, Chancellor, 514-481-0109
Membership: 10,000+
Description: A component of the Orthodox Church in America, an autocephalous (self-governing) church with territorial jurisdiction in Canada, the USA & Mexico; its doctrine & worship are those of the world-wide One Holy Catholic & Apostolic Church; *Member of:* Canadian Council of Churches; Churches of Manitoba; Orthodox Clergy Association of Québec

Religious of The Sacred Heart / Religieuses du Sacré-Coeur
#811, 325 Dalhousie St., Ottawa ON K1N 7G2
Tel: 613-241-4050; *Fax:* 613-241-3142
sshcph@on.aibn.com
www.sshc.ca
Also Known As: Society of the Sacred Heart
Overview: A small local charitable organization founded in 1800
Chief Officer(s):
Mary Finlayson, Provincial Superior
mfinlayson@on.aibn.com
Membership: 1-99
Activities: *Library:* Provincial Archives (Open to Public) by appointment
Description: To make known the love of Jesus in the world, through educaton & social justice activities

St. John's Cathedral Polish Catholic Church
186 Cowan Ave., Toronto ON M6K 2N6
Tél: 416-532-8249; *Fax:* 416-532-4653
stjohnscathedralcc@sympatico.com
Previous Name: Polish National Catholic Church of Canada
Overview: A small national organization
Chief Officer(s):
Joris Vercammen, Bishop Administrator
Finances: *Annual Operating Budget:* $100,000-$250,000
Membership: 300
Member of: The Canadian Council of Churches

ShareLife
1155 Yonge St., Toronto ON M4T 1W2
Tel: 416-934-3411; *Fax:* 416-934-3412
Toll-Free: 800-263-2595
sharelife@archtoronto.org
www.sharelife.org
Overview: A large international charitable organization founded in 1976
Chief Officer(s):
Arthur Peters, Executive Director
Bill Steinburg, Communications Manager
Finances: *Annual Operating Budget:* $500,000-$1.5 Million
Membership: 34 organizations
Activities: *Awareness Events:* Kickoffs; *Speaker Service:* Yes
Description: ShareLife is the Catholic Community's response to helping the whole community through Catholic agencies by effectively raising & allocating funds; *Member of:* International Catholic Stewardship Council; Affiliation(s): Canadian Centre for Philanthropy

Sisters Adorers of the Precious Blood / Soeurs Adoratrices du Précieux Sang
301 Ramsay Rd., London ON N6G 1N7
Tel: 519-473-2499; *Fax:* 519-473-6590
sremwalsh@pbsisters.on.ca
www.vocations.ca
Overview: A small local charitable organization founded in 1861
Chief Officer(s):
Eileen Mary Walsh, General Superior

Sisters of Charity of Halifax (SC)
215 Seton Rd., Halifax NS B3M 0C9
Tel: 902-406-8077; *Fax:* 902-457-3506
communications@schalifax.ca
www.schalifax.ca
Overview: A small local organization founded in 1849
Chief Officer(s):
Carrie Flemming, Advancement Associate
advancement@schalifax.ca
Ruth Jeppesen, Director, Communications
Membership: 500
Description: To develop a sensitivity to the oppressed through presence, prayer & ministry to others

Sisters of Mary of The Miraculous Medal
81 Lunness Rd., Toronto ON M8W 4M7
Tel: 416-259-2808; *Fax:* 416-259-2808
Overview: A small local charitable organization
Chief Officer(s):
Mirta Rezar, Sr. Superior
Finances: *Annual Operating Budget:* Less than $50,000
Staff: 3 staff member(s)
Membership: 100-499
Activities: Nursing order

Sisters of Saint Joseph of Pembroke (CSJ)
1127 Pembroke St. West, Pembroke ON K8A 5R3
Tel: 613-732-3694
csjadmin@csjpembroke.ca
www.csjpembroke.ca
Overview: A small local organization founded in 1921
Chief Officer(s):
Mary McGuire, General Superior
Membership: 1-99
Description: The Sisters of St. Joseph of Pembroke are a group of fifty Roman Catholic women religious based in eastern Ontario

Sisters of Saint Joseph of Peterborough (CSJ)
PO Box 566, Mount Saint Joseph, Peterborough ON K9J 6Z6
Tel: 705-750-1688; *Fax:* 705-745-1377
csjteamtwo@nexicom.net
Overview: A small local charitable organization founded in 1890
Chief Officer(s):
Helen Russell, Vocation Director
Membership: 90
Description: To respond to the poor & most needy, particularly where the need is not already met

Sisters of Saint Joseph of Sault Ste Marie
2025 Main St. West, North Bay ON P1B 2X6
Tel: 705-474-3800; *Fax:* 705-495-3028
csjnbay@ontera.net
www.csjssm.ca
Overview: A small local organization
Chief Officer(s):
Shirley Anderson, General Superior
csjshrly@ontera.net
Description: Lives and works that all people may be united with God and with one another

Sisters of the Child Jesus (SEJ) / Soeurs de l'Enfant-Jésus
318 Laval St., Coquitlam BC V3K 4W4
Tel: 604-939-7545; *Fax:* 604-939-7549
gpainchaud@shaw.ca
members.shaw.ca/gmlamy
Also Known As: Sisters of Instruction of the Child Jesus
Overview: A small local charitable organization founded in 1667
Chief Officer(s):
Gilberte Painchaud, Provincial Superior
Description: To be a presence of love to the Father & to others for the definite purpose of awakening & deepening the faith; to enable people to grow in the uniqueness of their person as created by God & to liberate themselves from all that prevents their being truly human; to bring hope & direction to contemporaries; to be at the service of the least favoured, the marginalized & those who have no voice in society

Sisters of the Sacred Heart / Suore del Sacro Cuore di Ragusa
1 Edward St., Welland ON L3C 5H2
Tel: 905-732-4542
sacredhe@iaw.com
www.sacredheartsisters.ca
Overview: A small local charitable organization founded in 1889
Membership: 500-999
Activities: Day care, schools, orphanages & retirement homes for the elderly; Parish work; Home visits; Missions; Nursing
Description: To live an apostolic life in the church & society through the works of beneficence among the poor & needy; To instruct & educate youth; To collaborate in parish pastoral work, especially through the teaching of catechism

Société canadienne d'histoire de l'Église Catholique - Section française (SCHEC) / Canadian Catholic Historical Association - French Section
SCHEC, Université du Québec à Trois-Rivières, 3351, boul des Forges, Trois-Rivières QC G9A 5H7
Tél: 819-376-5011; *Téléc:* 819-376-5179
schec.cieq.ca
Aperçu: *Dimension:* moyenne; *Envergure:* nationale; *fondée en 1933*
Membre(s) du bureau directeur:
René Hardy, Président
rene.hardy@uqtr.ca
Finances: *Budget de fonctionnement annuel:* Moins de $50,000
Personnel: 4 bénévole(s)
Membre: 150 individu; 100 institutionnel; *Montant de la cotisation:* 30$ individu; 40$ institutionnel; *Critères d'admissibilité:* La Société compte des membres dans toutes les parties du Canada de même qu'en Europe et aux États-Unis; les membres peuvent être des individus, ou des institutions publiques ou privées, tels des dépôts d'archives, bibliothèques, diocèses, communautés religieuses
Description: Grouper les personnes intéressées à l'histoire de l'Église catholique au Canada; stimuler l'intérêt pour cette histoire dans le grand public; tenir des congrès annuels dans diverses régions du Canada afin de susciter un dialogue entre chercheurs participants et de promouvoir les travaux d'histoire régionale

Société catholique de la Bible (SOCABI) / Catholic Bible Society
#608, 7400, boul St-Laurent, Montréal QC H2R 2Y1
Tél: 514-274-4381; *Téléc:* 514-274-5184
Aperçu: *Dimension:* moyenne; *Envergure:* nationale; *Organisme sans but lucratif; fondée en 1940*
Membre(s) du bureau directeur:
Yvon Forgues, Directeur général
Finances: *Budget de fonctionnement annuel:* $100,000-$250,000
Personnel: 6 membre(s) du personnel; 3 bénévole(s)
Membre: 130; *Montant de la cotisation:* 45$ tous les trois ans; *Critères d'admissibilité:* Implication dans le pastorale biblique; *Comités:* Administration; Financement
Activités: Service de librairie; conférences sur cassettes; cours par correspondance; cours d'initiation et formation; voyage en Israël; retraites; publication d'articles; *Bibliothèque:* Oui (Bibliothèque publique) rendez-vous
Description: Rendre la bible accessible au plus grand nombre de personnes possible, en facilitant la lecture et la compréhension; *Membre de:* Association canadienne des périodiques catholiques; Affiliation(s): World Catholic Federation for the Biblical Apostolate

The Society of St. Peter the Apostle
3329 Danforth Ave., Toronto ON M1L 4T3
Tel: 416-699-7077; *Fax:* 416-699-9019
Toll-Free: 800-897-8865
missions@missionsocieties.ca
www.missionsocieties.ca
Overview: A small national charitable organization founded in 1889
Finances: *Annual Operating Budget:* $500,000-$1.5 Million
Activities: Funds the training of local clergy & religious missions; *Speaker Service:* Yes
Description: To educate local clergy & religious men & women in developing countries

Soeurs Auxiliatrices
1637, rue St-Christophe, Montréal QC H2L 3W7
Tél: 514-522-4452; *Téléc:* 514-524-1448
auxiqc@point-net.com
Aperçu: *Dimension:* petite; *Envergure:* provinciale; *fondée en 1856*
Membre(s) du bureau directeur:
Maria-Paule Lebél
Suzanne Loiselle
Andrée Brosseau

Les Soeurs de Sainte-Anne
#22, 1950, rue Provost, Lachine QC H8S 1P7
Tél: 514-637-3783; *Téléc:* 514-637-5400
accueil@ssacong.org
www.ssacong.org
Aperçu: *Dimension:* petite; *Envergure:* internationale; *Organisme sans but lucratif; fondée en 1850*
Membre(s) du bureau directeur:
Marie Ellen King, Supérieure générale
Madeleine Lanoue, Secrétaire générale
Finances: *Budget de fonctionnement annuel:* $100,000-$250,000
Description: Impliquée dans l'éducation, les soins de santé, l'animation pastorale et sociale en divers milieux

Soeurs de Sainte-Marie de Namur / Sisters of Saint Mary of Namur
156, voul. Lorrain, Gatineau QC J8P 2G2
Tél: 819-663-5736
cdjeunes@comnet.ca
Aperçu: *Dimension:* petite; *Envergure:* internationale; *Organisme sans but lucratif; fondée en 1819*
Membre(s) du bureau directeur:
Réjeanne Roussel, Secrétaire-trésorière
Françoise Sabourin, Supérieure provinciale
Suzanne Martineau, Secrétaire-trésorière, 613-725-3427
ssmnproc@sympatico.ca
Finances: *Budget de fonctionnement annuel:* $250,000-$500,000
Membre: 1-99

Soeurs de Saint-Joseph de Saint-Vallier (SSJ)
860, av Louis-Fréchette, Québec QC G1S 3N3
Tél: 418-683-9653; *Téléc:* 418-681-8781
ssjvallier1903@videotron.ca
Aperçu: *Dimension:* petite; *Envergure:* locale; *fondée en 1683*
Membre(s) du bureau directeur:
Berthe Fortin, Supérieure générale, 418-681-2989
Membre: 165

Soeurs missionnaires Notre-Dame des Anges / Missionary Sisters of Our Lady of the Angels
323, rue Queen, Sherbrooke QC J1M 1K8
Tél: 819-569-9248; *Téléc:* 819-569-9180
mindalen@videotron.ca
Aperçu: *Dimension:* petite; *Envergure:* internationale; *Organisme sans but lucratif; fondée en 1919*
Membre(s) du bureau directeur:
Fernande Leblanc, Contact
Membre: 142
Description: The congregation is exclusively at the service of the missionary Church. Its specific mission is the formation of religious sisters, catechists and committed lay people. In addition, they respond to the needs of the local churches by working in the medical, social and educational fields when it is possible

Sovereign Military Hospitaller Order of St-John of Jerusalem of Rhodes & of Malta - Canadian Association / Ordre souverain militaire hospitalier de St-Jean de Jérusalem, de Rhodes et de Malte - Association canadienne
#302, 1247 Kilborn Pl., Ottawa ON K1H 6K9
Tel: 613-731-8897; *Fax:* 613-731-1312
orderofmaltacanada@gmail.com
www.orderofmaltacanada.org
Previous Name: Association of Canadian Knights of the Sovereign Military Order of Malta
Overview: A medium-sized national charitable organization founded in 1953
Chief Officer(s):
Albert André Morin, President
Finances: *Annual Operating Budget:* $100,000-$250,000; *Funding Sources:* Donations
Staff: 1 staff member(s); 259 volunteer(s)
Membership: 100-499
Description: To act as a Roman Catholic religious, chivalric & charitable organization; To provide assistance for: Good Shepherd Refuge, St. Francis, Second Mile Club, Providence Centre in Toronto, Czech Republic, Safe Motherhood Project, Nigeria, & ambulance brigades, Montréal, Cap-de-la-Madeleine, Ste. Anne de Beaupré; Affiliation(s): Sovereign Military Order of Malta

Spiritans, the Congregation of the Holy Ghost
Laval House, 121 Victoria Park Ave., Toronto ON M4E 3S2
Tel: 416-691-9319; *Fax:* 416-691-8760
communications@spiritans.com
www.spiritans.com
Social Media:
www.youtube.com/profile?user=SpiritansTransCanada
Overview: A medium-sized national organization
Chief Officer(s):
Paul McAuley, Contact
Membership: 3,000+
Description: Roman Catholic religious congregation specializing in education & mission

Union mondiale des organisations féminines catholiques (UMOFC) / World Union of Catholic Women's Organizations (WUCWO)
37, rue Notre-Dame des Champs, Paris F-75006 France
wucwoparis@wanadoo.fr
www.wucwo.org
Aperçu: *Dimension:* grande; *Envergure:* internationale; *fondée en 1910*
Membre(s) du bureau directeur:
Joann C. Hillebrand, Secrétaire générale
denouncer.5@comcast.net
Maria Giovanna Ruggieri, Présidente générale
wucwopregen@gmall.com
Membre: Over 50,000; *Critères d'admissibilité:* Organisation féminine catholique ayant 3 ans d'existance; *Comités:* Commissions Permanentes - Droits Humains; Développement et Coopération; Femmes et Église; Famille; Oecuménisme; Comités permanents - International; Finances; Procédures; Liturgie
Activités: Groupe de travail sur la violence contre les femmes, santé et prises de décisions; éducation; droits humains
Description: Promouvoir l'apport des femmes catholiques à la communauté ecclésiale et humaine; étudier et encourager la participation des femmes dans la mission d'évangélisation de l'Église; promouvoir une action qui rend les femmes capables de mieux remplir leur rôle dans l'Église et dans la société; *Membre de:* Conférence des Organisations Internationales Catholiques (OIC); Affiliation(s): Catholic Women's League of Canada; Ukrainian Catholic Women's League of Canada; Association féminine d'éducation d'action sociale; Mouvement des femmes chrétiennes - Inter-Montréal

Christian

Action des Chrétiens pour l'abolition de la torture (ACAT) / Action by Christians for the Abolition of Torture
#C-246, 2715, ch de la Côte-Sainte-Catherine, Montréal QC H3T 1B6
Tél: 514-890-6169; *Téléc:* 514-890-6484
info@acatcanada.org
www.acatcanada.org
Également appelé: ACAT Canada
Aperçu: *Dimension:* moyenne; *Envergure:* nationale; *Organisme sans but lucratif; fondée en 1984*
Membre(s) du bureau directeur:
Raoul Lincourt, Président
Célene Dupuis, Directeur
Finances: *Budget de fonctionnement annuel:* $50,000-$100,000
Personnel: 2 membre(s) du personnel; 30 bénévole(s)
Membre: 600; *Montant de la cotisation:* 30 $-80 $; *Critères d'admissibilité:* ouvert; *Comités:* Commission des interventions; Financement; Relations publiques; Ressourcement
Activités: Campagne annuelle; *Listes de destinataires:* Oui *Bibliothèque:* Oui rendez-vous
Description: Dans un but d'engagement évangélique, encourager les différentes communautés Chrétiennes du Canada à porter ensemble, par la prière, les souffrances des victimes de la torture; dans un but éducatif, sensibiliser particulièrement les Chrétiens au scandale de la torture (par l'information et la formation aux droits de la personne); dans un but de soulager la misère des victimes de la torture, apporter une aide concrète par l'envoi de lettres et pétitions aux responsables de torture et des lettres d'encouragement aux

victimes; Affiliation(s): Fédération internationale de l'action des Chrétiens pour l'abolition de la torture (FIACAT)

The Antiochan Orthodox Christian Archdiocese of North America

Antiochian Orthodox Christian Archdiocese, PO Box 5238, Englewood NJ 07631-5238 USA
Tel: 201-871-1355; *Fax:* 201-871-7954
archdiocese@antiochian.org
www.antiochian.org

Overview: A small national organization founded in 1875
Chief Officer(s):
Philip Saliba, Archpriest
Membership: 275 parishes, 19 in Canada
Description: The Antiochan Orthodox Community in Canada is under the jurisdiction of the Patriarch of Antioch & all the East, with headquarters in Damascus, Syria. There are five churches in Canada & eight missions. The headquarters for all churches in North America is the Antiochan Orthodox Christian archdiocese, in Englewood, New Jersey, under Archbishop Philip Salica; Affiliation(s): Canadian (Can-Am) Region

Armenian Holy Apostolic Church - Canadian Diocese (AHAC)

615, av Stuart, Outremont QC H2V 3H2
Tel: 514-276-9479; *Fax:* 514-276-9960
adiocese@armenianchurch.ca
www.armenianchurch.ca
Social Media: www.youtube.com/user/CanArmChurch
www.facebook.com/239802236057531

Overview: A medium-sized national charitable organization founded in 1984
Chief Officer(s):
Bagrat V. Galstanian, Primate
Silva Mangassarian, Executive Secretary
Finances: *Annual Operating Budget:* $250,000-$500,000; *Funding Sources:* Donations; parish dues
Staff: 6 staff member(s)
Membership: Over 50,000; *Member Profile:* Baptized in the Armenian faith; *Committees:* Endowment Fund
Activities: Humanitarian Aid to Armenia; *Library:* Yes (Open to Public) by appointment
Description: To preserve & promote Christian & national heritage; humanitarian aid to Armenia; Affiliation(s): Canadian Council of Churches

Association internationale des études patristiques (AIEP) / International Association for Patristic Studies (IAPS)

60 S. Mississippi River Blvd., Saint Paul MN 55105 USA
secaiep@duq.edu
www.aiep-iaps.org

Aperçu: *Dimension:* moyenne; *Envergure: internationale; fondée en 1965*
Finances: *Budget de fonctionnement annuel:* Moins de $50,000
Membre: 740; *Montant de la cotisation:* US$17; *Critères d'admissibilite:* Interessé aux pères de l'Eglise; *Comités:* Executive
Activités: *Listes de destinataires:* Oui
Description: Chercheurs et professeurs qui s'intéressent à l'antiquité chrétienne au général

Association of Christian Churches in Manitoba (ACCM) / Association des églises chrétiennes du Manitoba

151 de la Cathedrale Ave., Winnipeg MB R2H 0H6
Tel: 204-237-9851

Previous Name: Ecumenical Committee of Manitoba
Overview: A medium-sized provincial organization founded in 1990
Finances: *Annual Operating Budget:* Less than $50,000
Description: To bring Christian churches into living encounter with one another; to provide a network of news & events which can help member churches act together in all matters except those in which deep differences compel us to act separately; to act as common Christian voice & media contact on issues of spiritual & social concern in the Province

Association of Christian Schools International (ACSI)

PO Box 65130, 731 Chapel Hills Dr., Colorado Springs CO 80962-5130 USA
Tel: 719-528-6906; *Fax:* 719-531-0631
info@acsi.org
www.acsi.org

Overview: A medium-sized international organization founded in 1978
Chief Officer(s):
Brian S. Simmons, President
Finances: *Funding Sources:* Membership fees
Membership: 5300 schools/colleges in 100 countries; *Fees:* Schedule available; *Member Profile:* Christian school; affirmation of ACSI statement of faith
Activities: Teacher conferences; student leadership conferences; board/administrator conferences; district principals meetings; music events; professional development days; *Speaker Service:* Yes
Description: ACSI is an association of Protestant schools. It strives for school improvement, professional development & a provision of resources to enable Christian educators & schools worldwide to effectively prepare students for life.

The Bible League of Canada / Société canadienne pour la distribution de la Bible

PO Box 5037, Burlington ON L7R 3Y8
Tel: 905-319-9500; *Fax:* 905-319-0484
Toll-Free: 800-363-9673
ministry@bibleleague.ca
www.bibleleague.ca

Previous Name: World Home Bible League
Overview: A large international charitable organization founded in 1949
Chief Officer(s):
John Hessels, Chairman
Paul Richardson, President
Finances: *Annual Operating Budget:* $3 Million-$5 Million; *Funding Sources:* Donations
Staff: 15 staff member(s)
Activities: *Speaker Service:* Yes *Library:* Yes
Description: To introduce people to Jesus Christ; to spread God's Word worldwide; *Member of:* Canadian Council of Christian Charities; International Association of Bible Leagues; Affiliation(s): The Bible League

Bibles & Literature in French Canada (BLF)

256, Marc-Aurele-Fortin, Lachuteg QC J8H 3W7
Tél: 450-562-7859; *Téléc:* 450-562-7859
info@blfcanada.org
www.blfcanada.org

Également appelé: BLF Canada
Aperçu: *Envergure: nationale*
Membre(s) du bureau directeur:
Toe-Blake Roy, Director
toeblake@blfcanada.org
Description: BLF Canada distribue une littérature de qualité afin de permettre de présenter, à ces millions de Canadiens, celui qui seul peut leur apporter la vraie vie.

Bibles for Missions Foundation (BFM)

Head Office, #201, 7491 Vedder Rd., Chilliwack BC V2R 4E7
Tel: 604-858-4980; *Fax:* 604-858-4334
Toll-Free: 855-204-4980
admin@bfmthriftstores.ca
www.bfmthriftstores.ca
www.facebook.com/279261462189925
twitter.com/bfmfred

Overview: A large international charitable organization founded in 1989
Chief Officer(s):
Fred Meyerink, Director, Store Development, 604-799-7215
fred@bfmthriftstores.ca
Finances: *Funding Sources:* Donations
Description: BFM is a volunteer-driven, non-denominational Christian organization that operates thrift stores across Canada.; *Member of:* The Bible League of Canada (TBLC)

British Israel World Federation (Canada) Inc. (BIWF)

313 Sherbourne St., Toronto ON M5A 2S3
Tel: 416-921-5996; *Fax:* 416-921-9511
info@british-israel-world-fed.ca
www.british-israel-world-fed.ca

Overview: A small international charitable organization founded in 1929
Chief Officer(s):
Douglas C. Nesbit, President
Membership: 1,200; *Fees:* $10
Activities: Meetings; *Speaker Service:* Yes
Description: To proclaim the Gospel of the Kingdom of God as contained in the Holy Bible
Publications: The Kingdom Herald
Profile: Magazine, 10 issues published annually

Canadian Bible Society (CBS) / Société biblique canadienne

National Support Office, 10 Carnforth Rd., Toronto ON M4A 2S4
Toll-Free: 800-465-2425
info@biblesociety.ca
www.biblesociety.ca
www.facebook.com/CanadianBibleSociety
twitter.com/CanadianBible

Overview: A large national charitable organization founded in 1904
Chief Officer(s):
Ted Seres, National Director
tseres@biblesociety.ca
Joel Coppieters, Director, Scripture Resources
jcoppieters@biblesociety.ca
Guillaume Duvieusart, Director, National Francophone Services
gduvieusart@societebiblique.ca
Giorgio Gori, Director, Strategic Services
ggori@biblesociety.ca
Nesa Gulasekharam, Director, Finance
ngulasekharam@biblesociety.ca
Dennis Hillis, Director, Operations
dhillis@biblesociety.ca
Meggy Kwok, Director, Human Resources
mkwok@biblesociety.ca
Hart Wiens, Director, Scripture Translation
hwiens@biblesociety.ca
Finances: *Funding Sources:* Donations; Sale of gifts; Fundraising
Activities: Offering various programs to share God's Word, such as Operation Bible for the Canadian military, & welcoming newcomers to Canada with God's message
Description: To translate, publish, & distribute Bibles, New Testaments, & other Scriptures throughout Canada & Bermuda; *Member of:* United Bibles Societies
Publications: Canadian Bible Society Annual Report
Type: Yearbook *Frequency:* Annually

Canadian Church Press (CCP)

8 MacDonald Ave., Hamilton ON L8P 4N5
Tel: 905-521-2240
info@canadianchurchpress.com
www.canadianchurchpress.com
www.facebook.com/CanadianChurchPress

Overview: A small national organization founded in 1957
Chief Officer(s):
Pamela Richardson, President
Ian Adnams, Vice-President
Jim O'Leary, Treasurer
Finances: *Funding Sources:* Sponsorships
Activities: Offering fellowship for members; Supporting members; Conducting professional development workshops
Description: To promote high standards of religious journalism; to encourage a positive Christian influence on contemporary society
Publications: Canadian Church Press Membership Directory
Type: Directory
Profile: Listings of publication members, associate members, & honorary life members

Canadian Council of Christian Charities (CCCC)

#1, 43 Howard Ave., Elmira ON N3B 2C9
Tel: 519-669-5137; *Fax:* 519-669-3291
mail@cccc.org
www.cccc.org

Overview: A medium-sized national licensing charitable organization founded in 1972
Chief Officer(s):
John Pellowe, CEO
Finances: *Annual Operating Budget:* $500,000-$1.5 Million
Staff: 17 staff member(s); 56 volunteer(s)
Membership: 3,200; *Fees:* $195-$520
Activities: Education; training on legal, financial & leadership issues
Description: To encourage the Canadian Christian community to a biblical stewardship of all He has entrusted to us by integrating practical concepts of administration, development & accountability with the spiritual concerns of ministry
Publications: CCCC [Canadian Council of Christian Charities] Bulletin
Type: Newsletter *Frequency:* 5-7 pa *Accepts Advertising Editor:* Heather Hanson *ISSN:* 0838-6803 *Price:* Free with CCCC membership; $45 non-members
Profile: CCCC news & information & legislative developments for executives, administrators, & stewardship representatives of Christian charitiesoperating under Canadian law
Charities Handbook
Price: Free with CCCC membership; $95 non-members

The Canadian Council of Christians & Jews (CCCJ) / Conseil canadien des chrétiens et des juifs

PO Box 17, #515, 4211 Yonge St., Toronto ON M2P 2A9
Tel: 416-597-9693; *Fax:* 416-597-9775
Toll-Free: 800-663-1848
info@cccj.ca

Overview: A medium-sized national charitable organization founded in 1947

Finances: *Annual Operating Budget:* $250,000-$500,000; *Funding Sources:* Private; corporate; government for special projects
Staff: 4 staff member(s)
Membership: 100-499
Activities: Educational workshops/forums; research; public service announcements; *Awareness Events:* Brotherhood/Sisterhood Week, 3rd week of Feb. *Library:* Yes by appointment
Description: Non-sectarian organization that builds on our common heritage in pursuit of our goal to eradicate discrimination, prejudice & bigotry in Canadian society through education, research, communication & community building. The CCCJ promotes religious, racial & cultural equality through programming for young people; Affiliation(s): International Council of Christians & Jews
Publications: The Canadian Council of Christians & Jews Annual Report
Frequency: Annually
The Word [a publication of The Canadian Council of Christians & Jews]
Type: Newsletter

Canadian Foodgrains Bank Association Inc. (CFGB) / Association de la banque canadienne de grains inc.

PO Box 767, #400, 393 Portage Ave., Winnipeg MB R3B 3H6
Tel: 204-944-1993; *Fax:* 204-943-2597
Toll-Free: 800-665-0377
cfgb@foodgrainsbank.ca
www.foodgrainsbank.ca
www.facebook.com/CanadianFoodgrainsBank
twitter.com/FoodgrainsJames
Also Known As: Foodgrains Bank
Overview: A large international charitable organization founded in 1983
Chief Officer(s):
Jim Cornelius, Executive Director
jcornelius@foodgrainsbank.ca
Sol Janzen, Manager, Human Resources & Administration
sjanzen@foodgrainsbank.ca
Finances: *Funding Sources:* Donations; Fundraising
Membership: 15; *Member Profile:* Canadian church agencies
Activities: Improving community development; Protecting & building sustainable economic livelihoods; Encouraging peace-building; Strengthening Canadian & international policy & action towards hunger issues; Increasing public awareness & engagement; Collecting grain & cash donations from donors
Description: To provide a Christian response to hunger; to share resources with & support hungry populations outside Canada to achieve food security; To reduce hunger in developing countries
Publications: Breaking Bread
Type: Newsletter
Canadian Foodgrains Bank Annual Report
Type: Yearbook *Frequency:* Annually
Food Justice Update
Type: Newsletter *Frequency:* 3 pa

Canadian Society of Biblical Studies (CSBS) / Société canadienne des études bibliques (SCEB)

c/o Prof. Robert A. Derrenbacker, Jr., Regent College, 5800 University Blvd., Vancouver BC V6T 2E4
rderrenbacker@regent-college.edu
www.ccsr.ca/csbs
Overview: A small national organization founded in 1933
Chief Officer(s):
Terry Donaldson, President
terry.donaldson@utoronto.ca
Francis Landy, Vice-President
francis.landy@ualberta.ca
Robert A. Derrenbacker, Jr., Treasurer & Membership Secretary
rderrenbacker@regent-college.edu
Richard S. Ascough, Officer, Communications
rsa@queensu.ca
Fees: $35 students & retired & unemployed persons; $72 full membership; *Member Profile:* Individuals interested in all aspects of the academic study of the Bible
Description: To stimulate the critical investigation of the classical biblical literature & related literature
Publications: Canadian Society of Biblical Studies Membership Directory
Type: Directory
The CSBS [Canadian Society of Biblical Studies] / SCÉB [Société canadienne des études bibliques] Bulletin
Type: Yearbook *Frequency:* Annually *Editor:* Richard S. Ascough *Price:* Free withCSBS membership
Profile: CSBS membership news, events, annual general meeting minutes, & financial statements
Studies in Religion / Sciences Religieuses
Type: Journal *Price:* Free with CSBS membership
Profile: Refereed articles

Canadian Society of Church History (CSCH) / Société canadienne d'histoire de l'Église

c/o Robynne R. Healey, Dept. of History, Trinity Western University, 7600 Glover Rd., Langley BC V2Y 1Y1
robynne.healey@twu.ca
www.augustana.ab.ca/csch/
Overview: A small national organization founded in 1960
Chief Officer(s):
Todd Webb, President
Marguerite Van Die, Vice-President & Program Chair
Robynne Rogers Healey, Administrative Secretary
John H. Young, Treasurer
Fees: $36 students; $53 retired academics; $60 individuals; *Member Profile:* Historians of Christianity in Canada & the United States
Description: To encourage research in the history of Christianity, especially the history of Christianity in Canada; *Member of:* Canadian Corporation for Studies in Religion; Congress of Social Sciences & Humanities
Publications: Historical Papers: Canadian Society of Church History
Type: Journal *Frequency:* Annually *Editor:* Robynne Rogers Healey *Price:* Free with CSCH membership
Profile: A selection of papers delivered at the CSCH annual meeting

Canadian Society of Patristic Studies (CSPS) / Association canadienne des études patristiques

c/o Dr. S. Muir, Religious Studies, Concordia University College of AB, 7128 Ada Blvd., Edmonton AB T5B 4E4
www.ccsr.ca/csps
Overview: A small national organization founded in 1975
Chief Officer(s):
Tim Hegedus, President
Lorraine Buck, Vice-President
George Bevan, Secretary
Steven Muir, Treasurer
Fees: $48 studemts & retired members (with subscription); $65 regular members (including subscription); *Committees:* Program; Nominating
Description: To encourage the academic study of the Church Fathers; *Member of:* Canadian Federation for the Humanities & Social Sciences / Fèderation canadienne des sciences humaines
Publications: Canadian Society of Patristic Studies Bulletin
Type: Newsletter *Frequency:* Semiannually *Editor:* Adriana Bara
Profile: Society activities, including information about recent & upcoming conferences, membership updates, research, & other scholarly activities in patristics

Carrefour Humanisation Santé

CP 12, 1431, Fullum, Montréal QC H2K 3M3
Tél: 514-544-4154; *Téléc:* 514-259-0857
carrefour.humanisation@videotron.ca
www.carrefourhumanisationsante.org
Nom précédent: Carrefour des Chrétiens du Québec pour la Santé
Aperçu: *Dimension:* petite; *Envergure:* provinciale
Membre(s) du bureau directeur:
Andrée Chapleau-Lorrain, Co-présidente
Pierre Côté, Co-président
Description: Carrefour Humanisation-Santé est une association sans but lucratif qui vise l'humanisation des milieux de soins et de services de santé, en s'inspirant des valeurs judéo-chrétiennes. Elle met l'accent sur l'harmonisation entre la dimension humaine et spirituelle.

Christ for the Nations (Canada) Inc. (CFNI)

19533 - 64 Ave., Surrey BC V4N 3G6
Tel: 604-514-2364; *Fax:* 604-514-2604
Toll-Free: 888-999-2364
info@cfnc.ca
www.cfni.bc.ca
www.facebook.com/pages/CFN-Bible-College/25228314663
Also Known As: Christ for the Nations Bible College
Overview: A small national charitable organization founded in 1978
Chief Officer(s):
Gerald Nussbaum, President
Ken Deeks, Academic Dean
Membership: 1-99
Description: To prepare spiritually mature servant leaders who are competent in Ministry & who influence their world by living as Jesus did.; *Member of:* The Christ for the Nations Association of Bible Schools; Affiliation(s): Association for Biblical Higher Education

Christian Blind Mission International (CBMI)

PO Box 800, 3844 Stoufville Rd., Stouffville ON L4A 7Z9
Tel: 905-640-6464; *Fax:* 905-640-4332
Toll-Free: 800-567-2264
cbm@cbmcanada.org
www.cbmcanada.org
Overview: A medium-sized international charitable organization founded in 1978
Chief Officer(s):
Ted Dueck, Chair
Ed Epp, Executive Director
Finances: *Annual Operating Budget:* Greater than $5 Million
Staff: 28 staff member(s); 45 volunteer(s)
Activities: Talking Book Library; Craft Store; works with nearly 600 mission agencies, local churches, Christian relief organizations & self-help groups overseas; *Rents Mailing List:* Yes *Library:* Talking Book Library (Open to Public)
Description: With core values based on Christian faith, CBMI serves the blind & disabled in the developing world, irrespective of nationality, race, sex, or religion; prevents & treats blindness & other disabilities through medical care, rehabilitation training & integration programs; helps people to help themselves.; *Member of:* Canadian Council of Christian Charities

Christian Catholic Church Canada (CCRCC) / Église catholique-chrétien Canada

PO Box 2043, Stn. Hull, Gatineau QC J8X 3Z2
Tel: 613-738-2942; *Fax:* 613-738-7835
info@ccrcc.ca
www.ccrcc.ca
Previous Name: Canadian Chapter of the International Council of Community Churches
Overview: A large international charitable organization founded in 1858
Chief Officer(s):
Serge A. Thériault, Bishop Ordinary
Finances: *Annual Operating Budget:* Less than $50,000; *Funding Sources:* Clergy; churches; benefactors
Staff: 15 staff member(s); 25 volunteer(s)
Membership: 1,000-4,999; *Fees:* $200 church; $50 clergy; *Committees:* Order of the Crown of Thorns
Activities: Church Ministry; Seminary Program; counselling & mediation services; *Library:* Archives (Open to Public) by appointment
Description: Advancing the kingdom of God through worship, pastoral work & fellowship. Parishes in Ottawa-Gatineau, North Bay, Montreal; Affiliation(s): International Council of Community Churches (ICCC), ICCC Canada, World Council of Churches

Christian Children's Fund of Canada (CCFC)

1200 Denison St., Markham ON L3R 8G6
Tel: 905-754-1010; *Toll-Free:* 800-263-5437
supporter-relations@ccfcanada.ca
www.ccfcanada.ca
Overview: A large international organization founded in 1960
Chief Officer(s):
Mark Lukowski, Chief Executive Officer
Felicitas Adrian, Vice-President, Marketing & Communications
Jim Carrie, Vice-President, Global Operations
Jeff Hogan, Vice-President, Finance & Administration
Finances: *Funding Sources:* Donations
Staff: 200 volunteer(s)
Membership: 30,000+; *Fees:* $35/month suggested donation
Activities: Working to help those affected by HIV/AIDS; Providng water & sanitation; Offering education; *Internships:* Yes; *Speaker Service:* Yes
Description: To focus upon community development ministry, starting with basic assistance & leading to programs stressing self-help & eventual independence; To work with colleagues & partners in developing countries; To reach out to children & families of all faiths; *Member of:* Canadian Council for International Cooperation; Affiliation(s): Canadian Direct Marketing Association; National Society of Fundraising Executives

Christian Church (Disciples of Christ) in Canada (DISCAN) / Église chrétienne (Disciples du Christ) au Canada

PO Box 1, Springfield ON N0L 2J0
Tel: 519-269-9800
ccinca@eastlink.ca
www.disciplesofchrist.ca
Previous Name: All-Canada Committee of the Christian Church (Disciples of Christ)
Overview: A small national charitable organization founded in 1922
Chief Officer(s):
Janet Fountain, Moderator, 902-354-5988
pjfountain@eastlink.ca
Catherine Hubbard, Regional Minister
Finances: *Annual Operating Budget:* $100,000-$250,000; *Funding Sources:* Donations

Staff: 2 staff member(s)
Membership: 4,000 + 30 churches; *Committees:* Archives; Biennial Convention; Christian Nurture, Service, Witness; Church Development; College; Ministry
Activities: *Internships:* Yes; *Speaker Service:* Yes *Library:* Resource Centre
Member of: The Canadian Council of Churches; Affiliation(s): The Christian Church (Disciples of Christ) in USA

Christian Health Association of Alberta (CHAA)
132 Warwick Rd., Edmonton AB T5X 4P8
Tel: 780-488-8074; *Fax:* 780-475-7968
chaaa@compusmart.ab.ca
www.chaaa.ab.ca
Previous Name: Catholic Health Care Conference of Alberta
Overview: A medium-sized provincial charitable organization founded in 1943
Chief Officer(s):
Glyn J. Smith, Administrator
Finances: *Annual Operating Budget:* $50,000-$100,000
Staff: 1 staff member(s); 13 volunteer(s)
Membership: 22 health facilities + 29 associate + 48 personal + 10 life; *Fees:* $25 individual; $75 associate
Description: Represents the shared vision & values of those seeking to make visible Jesus the Healer; provides support & leadership to members & the community through education, advocacy & collaboration

Christian Medical & Dental Society of Canada (CMDS)
246 Main St., #B, Steinbach MB R5G 1Y8
Tel: 204-326-2523; *Fax:* 204-326-3098
Toll-Free: 888-256-8653
office@cmdscanada.org
www.cmdscanada.org
Overview: A medium-sized provincial organization founded in 1971
Chief Officer(s):
Roger Gingerich, Executive Director
Abraham Ninan, President
Rudy W. Hamm, Treasurer
Sue McLoughlin, Secretary
Finances: *Funding Sources:* Dues; Donations
Fees: $365 Full-time Medical & Dental Practitioners; $180 Part-time Practitioners; $55 Residents; $25 Medical or Dental Students or Missionaries; *Member Profile:* Christian physicians, dentists, & students who wish to integrate faith with professional practice
Activities: Offers workshops & conferences; supports a toll-free helpline for medical & dental trainees; publishes a Members Directory & other literature; offers mission opportunities
Description: To uphold a Christian view of medicine & dentistry; to understand & minister to the spiritual needs of colleagues; to create educational materials about public policy & health; to develop programs that promote a Christian view of medical ethics; & to support local group activities, plan conferences, & locate mentorship & other opportunities.; *Member of:* International Christian Medical & Dental Association

Christian Record Services Inc.
PO Box 31119, #119, 1300 King St. East, Oshawa ON L1H 8N9
Tel: 905-436-6938; *Fax:* 905-436-7102
Toll-Free: 888-899-0006
crs-ncb@hotmail.com
www.crsblindservices.ca
Also Known As: National Camps for the Blind
Previous Name: Christian Record Braille Foundation Inc.
Overview: A medium-sized national charitable organization founded in 1899
Chief Officer(s):
Patricia L. Page, Executive Director
ppage@christianrecordservices.ca
Finances: *Annual Operating Budget:* $500,000-$1.5 Million; *Funding Sources:* Public contribution
Staff: 14 staff member(s)
Activities: Magazines in braille, large print & on audio cassette; full-vision books (a combination of print & braille for blind parents with sighted children); Bible Correspondence School (Bible study guides available in braille, in large print, on audio cassettes & in easy English for the deaf); National Camps for the Blind; personal visitation; glaucoma screenings; deaf services.; *Library:* Lending Library for the Blind (Open to Public)
Description: To enrich the lives of blind, deaf, visually, physically & hearing impaired persons regardless of race, creed, economic status or sex.; *Member of:* Christian Camping International; Canadian Camping Association

Christian Reformed Church in North America (CRCNA)
PO Box 5070, Stn. LCD 1, 3475 Mainway, Burlington ON L7R 3Y8
Tel: 905-336-2920; *Fax:* 905-336-8344
Toll-Free: 800-730-3490
crcna@crcna.org
www.crcna.org
Overview: A large international organization founded in 1857
Chief Officer(s):
Bruce Adema, Director, Canadian Ministries
Finances: *Annual Operating Budget:* Greater than $5 Million; *Funding Sources:* Gifts & donations
Staff: 225 staff member(s)
Membership: In US & Canada: 275,000 members in more than 1,000 congregations; *Committees:* Abuse Prevention; Back to God Hour; Calvin College; Calvin Theological Seminary; CRC Publications; Home Missions; World Missions; World Relief; Chaplaincy Ministries; CRC Loan Fund; Disability Concerns; Fund for Smaller Churches; Pastor-Church Relations; Pensions & Insurance; Race Relations; Historical; Interchurch Relations; Sermons for Reading Services
Activities: *Awareness Events:* Sea to Sea Celebration Rally; *Speaker Service:* Yes
Description: The Denominational Office in Canada coordinates the work of the Church in Canada, overseeing the Committee for Contact with the Government (social justice issues), urban Aboriginal Ministry Centres (Edmonton, Regina, Winnipeg), & ecumenical involvement in KAIROS task forces (KAIROS: Canadian Ecumenical Justice Initiatives); Affiliation(s): National Association of Evangelicals; Reformed Ecumenical Council; World Alliance of Reformed Churches; Canadian Council of Churches; Evangelical Fellowship of Canada

Christian Reformed World Relief Committee (CRWRC)
PO Box 5070, 3475 Mainway, Burlington ON L7R 3Y8
Tel: 905-336-2920; *Toll-Free:* 800-730-3490
crwrc@crcna.ca
www.crwrc.org
Social Media: www.youtube.com/user/CRWRCComm/featured
www.facebook.com/CRWRC
twitter.com/crwrc
Overview: A large international charitable organization founded in 1962
Chief Officer(s):
Ida Mutoigo, Director, 905-336-2920 303
imutoigo@crwrc.org
Wayne de Jong, Director, International Disaster Response, 905-336-2920 240
wdejong@crwrc.org
Iona Buisman, Contact, Missionary Partnerships & Volunteer Opportunities, 905-336-2920 321
ibuisman@crwrc.org
Judy Eising, Contact, Donations & Planned Giving, 905-336-2920 297
jeising@crwrc.org
Renee Scobel, Contact, Church Relations, 905-336-2920 237
rscobel@crwrc.org
Kristen VanderBerg, Contact, Communications, 905-336-2920 305
kvanderberg@crwrc.org
Finances: *Funding Sources:* Christian Reformed Churches; CIDA; Other denominations
Membership: 15,000-49,999
Activities: *Awareness Events:* World Hunger Week, November; *Internships:* Yes; *Speaker Service:* Yes *Library:* CRWRC Development Education Library (Open to Public)
Description: To engage God's people in redeeming resources & developing gifts in collaborative activities of love, mercy, justice, & compassion; *Member of:* Canadian Foodgrains Bank; Canadian Council of Christian Charities; Canadian Council for International Cooperation.; Affiliation(s): Christian Reformed Church in North America

Christian Science / La Première Église du Christ, Scientiste
The First Church of Christ, Scientist, 210 Massachusetts Ave., Boston MA 02115 USA
Tel: 617-450-2000; *Fax:* 617-450-3790
Toll-Free: 800-775-2775
info@churchofchristscientist.org
christianscience.com; www.marybakereddylibrary.org
www.facebook.com/TheMotherChurch
twitter.com/cschurches
Also Known As: The Mother Church
Overview: A large international organization founded in 1879
Chief Officer(s):
Marta Greenwood, President
Russ Gerber, Manager, Committee on Publication
Finances: *Annual Operating Budget:* Greater than $5 Million; *Funding Sources:* Donations
Staff: 850 staff member(s)
Membership: 2,200 churches in over 70 countries; *Fees:* Per capita tax of not less than 1$; *Member Profile:* The Church is open those who are "believer(s) the doctrines of Christian Science textbook: Science & Health with Key to the Scriptures, by Rev. Mary Baker Eddy."
Activities: Sunday worship services, Wednesday testimonial meetings; Sunday School for children; worldwide speakers bureau; retail book stores; Christian Science Reading Rooms; Christian Science programs & Weekly Bible Lessons are broadcast on public media; *Internships:* Yes; *Speaker Service:* Yes *Library:* Mary Baker Eddy Library for the Betterment of Humanity (Open to Public) by appointment
Description: Christian Scientists believe in one God, the Bible & in Christ Jesus as the Messiah. They believe that the application of the laws of God are practical & provable, hence scientific.
Publications: The Christian Science Journal
Type: Magazine *Frequency:* Monthly
Profile: www.spirituality.com/journal
The Christian Science Monitor
Type: Newspaper *Frequency:* Daily

Christian Stewardship Services (CSS)
#214A, 500 Alden Rd., Markham ON L3R 5H5
Tel: 905-947-9262; *Fax:* 905-947-9263
Toll-Free: 800-267-8890
admin@csservices.ca
www.csservices.ca
Overview: A medium-sized national charitable organization founded in 1976
Chief Officer(s):
Henry Eygenraam, Executive Director
Chris Platteel, Administrator, Finance & Systems
Rick DeGraaf, Coordinator, Stewardship Education, 519-620-2242
Finances: *Funding Sources:* Christian charities, including churches & schools; Social service organizations
Activities: Providing advice about will & estate planning; Offering the Growing & Giving program, featuring presentations & workshops
Description: To connect families, faith, & finances for efficient estate & gift planning; To promote Biblical stewardship; *Member of:* Canadian Council of Christian Charities; Affiliation(s): Diaconal Ministries of the Christian Reformed Church
Publications: Advancing Stewardship
Type: Newsletter *Frequency:* Semiannually
Profile: Information about the organization & its work
Christian Stewardship Services Annual Report
Type: Yearbook *Frequency:* Annually

Christos Metropolitan Community Church
Trinity St. Paul's Centre, 427 Bloor St. West, Toronto ON M5S 1X7
Tel: 416-925-7924; *Fax:* 416-922-8587
Also Known As: Christos MCC
Overview: A small local charitable organization founded in 1984
Chief Officer(s):
Deana Dudley, Pastor
Judi Bonner, Secretary
Finances: *Annual Operating Budget:* Less than $50,000
Staff: 1 staff member(s); 8 volunteer(s)
Membership: 30
Activities: Weekly worship services; spirituality-based study groups; social events
Description: Ministry by and for the LGBT community of Toronto.; *Member of:* Universal Fellowship of Metropolitan Community Churches

Church Council on Justice & Corrections (CCJC) / Conseil des églises pour la justice et la criminologie
#303, 200 Isabella St., Ottawa ON K1S 1V7
Tel: 613-563-1688; *Fax:* 613-237-6129
info@ccjc.ca
www.ccjc.ca
Overview: A medium-sized national charitable organization founded in 1972
Chief Officer(s):
Laurent Champagne, President
Lorraine Berzins, Communication Chair of Justice, 613-563-1688 2
lberzins@ccjc.ca
Finances: *Annual Operating Budget:* $250,000-$500,000
Staff: 3 staff member(s)
Membership: 46 directors + 292 supporting; *Fees:* $40 individuals; $200 organizations; *Committees:* Steering
Activities: *Internships:* Yes; *Speaker Service:* Yes *Library:* Yes
Description: To strengthen churches' ministry in fields of crime prevention, justice & corrections; to initiate, encourage & support programs which sensitize congregations & educate volunteer

groups to participate in development of community responses to crime, justice & corrections; to promote a healing justice; to examine & respond to policy concerns with assistance of churches; to call on churches to address issues; to provide resources to churches & other related organizations.; *Member of:* National Associations Active in Criminal Justice; Affiliation(s): The Network - Interaction for Conflict Resolution

The Church Lads' Brigade (CLB)
PO Box 28126, 82 Harvey Rd., St. John's NL A1B 4J8
Tel: 709-722-1737; *Fax:* 709-722-1734
info@theclb.ca
www.theclb.ca

Overview: A medium-sized national organization founded in 1892
Chief Officer(s):
Keith Arns, Chair
Finances: *Annual Operating Budget:* $50,000-$100,000; *Funding Sources:* Donations; building rentals; fundraising
Staff: 1 staff member(s); 200 volunteer(s)
Membership: 800; *Fees:* $20; *Member Profile:* Boys & girls of all religious affiliations
Activities: Youth activities; recreational, educational & social; *Internships:* Yes *Library:* CLB Archives (Open to Public) by appointment
Description: The advancement of Christ's kingdom among youth, the promotion of Christian charity, reverence, discipline, self-respect, respect for others & all that lends towards true Christian character; Affiliation(s): The Church Lads' & Church Girls' Brigade (UK)

Congregational Christian Churches in Canada (CCCC)
442 Grey St., #H, Brantford ON N3S 7N3
Tel: 519-751-0606; *Fax:* 519-751-0852
Toll-Free: 866-868-8702
cccnationaloffice@bellnet.ca
www.cccc.ca

Overview: A small national charitable organization founded in 1821
Chief Officer(s):
David Schrader, National Pastor
nationalpastor@bellnet.ca
Bill MacDougall, Chair
b-pmacdougall@ns.sympatico.ca
Kim Adeniran, Administrative Assistant
ccccnationaloffice@bellnet.ca
Finances: *Annual Operating Budget:* $100,000-$250,000
Staff: 2 staff member(s)
Membership: 8,000 + 100 churches across Canada; *Fees:* $50; *Member Profile:* Churches or individuals in accord with CCCC's Statement of Faith and Founding Principles as set out in our By-Law and Supplementary Letters Patent.
Activities: *Internships:* Yes
Description: To celebrate & serve Jesus Christ in the 21st century through shared concern for others.

CrossTrainers Canada
PO Box 1426, Bradford ON L3Z 2B7
Tel: 416-697-0147; *Fax:* 905-775-0444
ct@ctministries.ca
www.ctministries.ca

Overview: A small local organization
Chief Officer(s):
Jodi Greenstreet, Co-founder
Patti LaRose, Co-founder
Joshua Schrader, Director, The Hub Youth Centre
Finances: *Funding Sources:* Corporate sponsors
Staff: 5 staff member(s)
Activities: Connections Centre with True Vibe program, Playzone, cafe & special events; The Hub Youth Centre with A Hand Up Clothing Room; Mercy House, a women's shelter
Description: The association is a Christian ministry organization with members from several local churches serving the Bradford community. It is a registered charity, BN: 889735023RR0001.

Direction Chrétienne Inc.
#520, 1450, rue City Councillors, Montréal QC H3A 2E6
Tel: 514-878-3035; *Fax:* 514-878-8048
info@direction.ca
www.direction.ca

Also Known As: Christian Direction
Overview: A small provincial charitable organization founded in 1964
Membre(s) du bureau directeur:
Glen Smith, Executive Director
Finances: *Budget de fonctionnement annuel:* $500,000-$1.5 Million
Staff: 13 staff member(s); 3 volunteer(s)
Membership: 1-99
Description: Rendre visite aux communautés chrétiennes locales et particulièrement celles des grands centres urbains afin de se faire connaître et partager son mandat

Edmonton & District Council of Churches (EDCC)
c/o Garneau United Church, #123, 11148 - 84 Ave., Edmonton AB T6G 0V8
Tel: 780-439-2501; *Fax:* 780-439-3067
admin@EDCCunity.org
www.edccunity.org

Overview: A small local organization founded in 1942
Chief Officer(s):
Julien Hammond, President, 780-469-1010 2271, Fax: 780-465-3003
Finances: *Annual Operating Budget:* Less than $50,000
Staff: 1 staff member(s); 7 volunteer(s)
Membership: 22; *Fees:* $60 denominational member; $30 individual member; *Member Profile:* Christian denominations; *Committees:* Ecumenical Coordinators; Week of Prayer for Christian Unity Service Planning Committee; Way of the Cross Planning Committee; No Room in the Inn Planning Committee
Activities: Organization of events; distribution of information; participation in interdenominational projects; *Awareness Events:* Week of Prayer for Christian Unity, Jan.; Good Friday Way of the Cross; No Room in the Inn Fundraising for Low Income Housing, Dec.
Description: To express through fellowship, consultation, cooperation, & service, the essential unity of the Christian church; To maintain open relationships & foster dialogue with other faith groups & inter-faith organizations; To provide support & monitoring for chaplaincy programs; Affiliation(s): Canadian Council of Churches

Focus on the Family Canada
19946 - 80A Ave., Langley BC V2Y 0J8
Tel: 604-539-7900; *Fax:* 604-539-7999
Toll-Free: 800-661-9800
letters@fotf.ca; events@fotf.ca; hr@fotf.ca; volunteers@fotf.ca
www.focusonthefamily.ca
www.facebook.com/fotfcanada
twitter.com/fotfcanada

Overview: A large national charitable organization founded in 1982
Chief Officer(s):
Terence Rolston, President
Finances: *Funding Sources:* Donations
Staff: 250 volunteer(s)
Activities: *Library:* Yes
Description: To strengthen & encourage the Canadian family through education & resources; *Member of:* Canadian Council of Christian Charities

General Church of the New Jerusalem in Canada
c/o Olivet Church of the New Jerusalem, 279 Burnhamthorpe Rd., Toronto ON M9B 1Z6
Tel: 416-239-3054; *Fax:* 416-239-4935
assistant@olivetnewchurch.org
www.newchurch.org/societies/toronto

Overview: A small national organization
Chief Officer(s):
James Cooper, Pastor
Nathan Cole, Assistant Pastor
Member of: General Church of the New Jerusalem

Global Outreach Mission Inc.
PO Box 1210, St Catharines ON L2R 7A7
Tel: 905-684-1401; *Fax:* 905-684-3069
Toll-Free: 866-483-5787
glmiss@on.aibn.com
www.missiongo.org
www.facebook.com/Gomission2012

Previous Name: European Evangelistic Crusade, Inc.
Overview: A small international organization founded in 1943
Chief Officer(s):
Len Lane, Vice-President, Candidates/Personnel
Affiliation(s): Interdenominational Foreign Mission Association

Grace Commuinion International Canada
#101, 5660 - 192 St., Surrey BC V3S 2V7
Tel: 604-575-2705; *Fax:* 604-575-2758
info@gcicanada.ca
www.wcg.ca

Previous Name: Worldwide Church of God Canada
Overview: A small national organization
Chief Officer(s):
Gary Moore, National Director
gmoore@telus.net
Description: To proclaim the gospel of Jesus Christ around the world & to help members grow spiritually

Habitat for Humanity Canada (HFHC) / Habitat pour l'Humanité Canada
40 Albert St., Waterloo ON N2L 3S2
Tel: 519-885-4565; *Fax:* 519-885-5225
Toll-Free: 800-667-5137
habitat@habitat.ca
www.habitat.ca

Overview: A medium-sized national charitable organization founded in 1985
Chief Officer(s):
Stewart Hardacre, President & CEO
Finances: *Annual Operating Budget:* $3 Million-$5 Million; *Funding Sources:* Corporate & individual donations of cash & building materials
Staff: 20 staff member(s); 15 volunteer(s)
Membership: 72 local affiliates
Activities: Ed Schreyer Work Project; All Women Build Project; *Speaker Service:* Yes *Library:* Yes (Open to Public)
Description: To provide affordable & adequate housing for God's people in need by mobilizing local communities, volunteers & material & financial resources in wide-ranging, inclusive partnerships; to support, encourage, facilitate & empower those affiliates to build affordable homes in partnership with needy families.; *Member of:* Habitat for Humanity International

Hamilton & District Christian Churches Association
Redeemer College, 777 Hwy. 53 East, Ancaster ON L9K 1J4
Tel: 905-648-2139; *Fax:* 905-648-2134
www.iciworld.net/churches/hdcca.htm

Overview: A small local organization founded in 1890
Chief Officer(s):
John Johnston, Contact
Membership: 13+; *Fees:* Proportional; *Member Profile:* Mainline denominations in Hamilton
Activities: Pre-ordinating ecumenical work of denominations in Hamilton
Description: To strengthen the work & witness of Jesus Christ by fostering cooperation among Christians of different traditions; *Member of:* The Canadian Council of Churches

Holy Face Association
CP 1000, Succ A, Montréal QC H3C 2W9
Tel: 514-747-0357; *Fax:* 514-747-9147
holyface@holyface.com
www.holyface.org

Overview: A small national charitable organization founded in 1976
Chief Officer(s):
Gordon Deery, Contact
Finances: *Annual Operating Budget:* $250,000-$500,000; *Funding Sources:* Donations
Staff: 20 volunteer(s)
Membership: 15,000-49,999
Activities: *Speaker Service:* Yes *Library:* Yes by appointment
Description: The goal of this apostolate is reparation to God (Father, Son and Holy Spirit) through contemplative devotion to the Holy Face of Jesus

Independent Assemblies of God International - Canada
PO Box 653, Chatham ON N7M 5K8
Tel: 519-352-1743; *Fax:* 519-351-6070
pmcphail@ciaccess.com
www.iaogcan.com

Also Known As: IAOGI Canada
Overview: A small national charitable organization founded in 1918
Chief Officer(s):
Paul McPhail, General Secretary
pmcphail@ciaccess.com
Finances: *Annual Operating Budget:* $100,000-$250,000; *Funding Sources:* Membership fees; offerings
Staff: 2 staff member(s); 12 volunteer(s)
Membership: 500 churches/ministries; *Fees:* $100; *Member Profile:* Must be called by God to preach His Word
Activities: *Awareness Events:* National Convention, May; *Speaker Service:* Yes
Member of: Independent Assemblies of God International
Publications: The Canadian Mantle
Type: Newsletter *Frequency:* 3 pa

Indian Métis Christian Fellowship (IMCF)
3131 Dewdney Ave., Regina SK S4T 0Y5
Tel: 306-359-1096; *Fax:* 306-359-0103
imcfr@sasktel.net
metfel.sasktelwebsite.net

Overview: A small local organization founded in 1978
Chief Officer(s):
Bert Adema, Director
Finances: *Annual Operating Budget:* $100,000-$250,000
Membership: 30 individual

Activities: Drop-in ministry; daily prayer circle; soup & bannock lunch; computer club
Description: IMCF is an urban aboriginal ministry supported by the Christian Reformed Church in North America - Canada. Its mission is to develop a worshipping, working community through serving the spiritual & social needs of aboriginal people in Regina.; Affiliation(s): Canadian Ministry Board; Indian Family Center, Winnipeg; Native Healing Centre, Edmonton

Institut Séculier Pie X (ISPX) / Pius X Secular Institute

CP 87731, Succ. Succ. Charlesbourg, 1645, boul Louis-XIV, Québec QC G1G 5W6
Tél: 418-626-5882; *Téléc:* 418-624-2277
info@ispx.org
www.ispx.org

Aperçu: *Dimension:* petite; *Envergure: internationale; Organisme sans but lucratif; fondée en 1939*
Membre(s) du bureau directeur:
Gérald Cyprien Lacroix, Directeur général
Finances: *Budget de fonctionnement annuel:* $100,000-$250,000
Membre: 17 consacrés + 250 associés
Activités: Apostolat catholique; évangélisation; présence au monde; *Service de conférenciers:* Oui
Description: Évangéliser les milieux populaires par la présence et par des activités apostoliques; *Membre de:* Conférence canadienne des instituts séculiers; Conférence mondiale des instituts séculiers

Intercede International

201 Stanton St., Fort Erie ON L2A 3N8
Tel: 905-871-1773; *Fax:* 905-871-5165
Toll-Free: 800-871-0882
friends@intercedenow.ca
www.intercedenow.ca

Previous Name: Christian Aid Mission
Overview: A medium-sized international charitable organization founded in 1953
Chief Officer(s):
James S. Eagles, President
Finances: *Annual Operating Budget:* $500,000-$1.5 Million; *Funding Sources:* Private donations
Staff: 10 staff member(s); 50 volunteer(s)
Membership: 10; *Committees:* Audit Review
Activities: Sponsorship programs; relief aid; equipment & materials provisions; Missions cafe held in major cities; *Speaker Service:* Yes *Library:* Yes (Open to Public) by appointment
Description: To aid, encourage & strengthen indigenous new testament Christianity, particularly where Christians are impoverished, few, or persecuted; to encourage Christian witness & ministry to the international community in North America; *Member of:* Canadian Council of Christian Churches; Affiliation(s): Evangelical Fellowship of Canada

Inter-Varsity Christian Fellowship (IVCF)

1 International Blvd., Toronto ON M9W 6H3
Tel: 416-443-1170; *Fax:* 416-443-1499
Toll-Free: 800-668-9766
info@ivcf.ca
www.ivcf.ca

Overview: A medium-sized national charitable organization founded in 1929
Chief Officer(s):
Geri Rodman, President
Finances: *Funding Sources:* Donations
Activities: Offering Pioneer Camps across Canada; Providing ministry at university & college campuses; Offering travel opportunities through Inter-Varsity's World Services' Global Partnerships; Participating in the Urbana Student Mission Convention
Description: To help young people live a transformed life in Jesus Christ

Jews for Jesus

#402, 1315 Lawrence Ave. East, Toronto ON M3A 3R3
Tel: 416-444-7020; *Fax:* 416-444-1028
toronto@jewsforjesus.ca
www.jewsforjesus.ca

Overview: A small local charitable organization
Chief Officer(s):
Andrew Barron, Canadian Director
Member of: Canadian Council of Christian Charities; Evangelical Fellowship of Canada; Interdenominational Foreign Mission Association

Lifewater Canada

#194, 307 Euclid Ave., Thunder Bay ON P7E 6G6
Tel: 807-622-4848; *Fax:* 807-577-9798
Toll-Free: 888-543-3426
gehrelji@yahoo.com
www.lifewater.ca

Overview: A small international organization
Chief Officer(s):
Jim Gehrels, President
Member Profile: Hydrogeologists, well drillers, educators, engineers, environmental scientists, businessmen & many other people with diverse skills & training
Description: Christian organization dedicated to ensuring that people everywhere have access to adequate supplies of safe water; to train & equip Nationals with drill rigs & hand pumps so they can solve their own water problems; to place as many technical documents on-line as possible so they can benefit people everywhere, regardless of affiliation

M2/W2 Association - Restorative Christian Ministries (M2/W2)

#208, 2825 Clearbrook Rd., Abbotsford BC V2T 6S3
Tel: 604-859-3215; *Fax:* 604-859-1216
Toll-Free: 800-298-1777
info@m2w2.com
www.m2w2.com

Also Known As: Man-to-Man/Woman-to-Woman
Overview: A small provincial charitable organization founded in 1966
Chief Officer(s):
Wayne Northey, Co-Director
Bernie Martens, Co-Director
Finances: *Annual Operating Budget:* $250,000-$500,000; *Funding Sources:* 65% community fundraising; 35% federal & provincial government contracts
Staff: 11 staff member(s); 400 volunteer(s)
Membership: 190; *Fees:* $10; *Member Profile:* Wide range of people whose common interest is the focus of M2/W2; *Committees:* Finance/Promotion; Program/New Initiatives; Personnel
Activities: Organizing annual promotion dinners; *Speaker Service:* Yes
Description: To mutually transform lives - one relationship at a time; To see individuals & communities in British Columbia safer, transformed, reconciled, & restored through justice, accountability, partnerships, mutual support, mediation, education & prevention; To provide one-to-one volunteers for men & women in British Columbia prisons, combined with pre- & post-release support & resources; To counsel prisoners, ex-prisoners, & their families; To prevent crime through one-to-one support for parents of young children at risk; *Member of:* Canadian Council of Christian Charities

Missionaires de la Royauté du Christ / Missionaries of the Kingship of Christ

5750, boul Rosemont, Montréal QC H1T 2H2
Tél: 514-259-2542; *Téléc:* 514-259-6911
Aperçu: *Dimension:* petite; *Envergure: locale*

Les Missions des Soeurs Missionnaires du Christ-Roi

4730, boul Lévesque ouest, Chomedey QC H7W 2R4
Tél: 450-687-2100
missionsmcr@hotmail.com

Également appelé: Missions MCR
Aperçu: *Dimension:* moyenne; *Envergure: internationale; Organisme sans but lucratif; fondée en 1979*
Membre(s) du bureau directeur:
Maekawa Harumi, Présidente
Finances: *Budget de fonctionnement annuel:* $100,000-$250,000; *Fonds:* Fondations; Subventions
Personnel: 1 membre(s) du personnel
Membre: 213 institutionnel
Activités: *Bibliothèque:* Oui (Bibliothèque publique)
Description: Organiser, administrer, maintenir une oeuvre dont les fins sont la religion, la charité; promouvoir l'éducation et le bien-être, particulièrement en ce qui a trait aux différents buts qu'il s'est fixé; aide internationale

National Christian School Association

PO Box 26005, Saskatoon SK S7K 8C1
Tel: 306-280-9991
lbrunelle@aceministries.com
www.aisca.ab.ca/associations.htm

Also Known As: School of Tomorrow Canada
Previous Name: Canadian National Accelerated Christian Education Association
Overview: A small national organization founded in 1991
Chief Officer(s):
Lou Brunelle, President
Finances: *Annual Operating Budget:* Less than $50,000; *Funding Sources:* Provincial dues
Staff: 24 volunteer(s)
Membership: 100-499
Description: To continue to assure Canadians of the freedom to choose alternative Christian education; Affiliation(s): Federation of Independent Schools in Canada

New Apostolic Church Canada

319 Bridgeport Rd. East, Waterloo ON N2J 2K9
Tel: 519-884-2862; *Toll-Free:* 866-622-7828
info@naccanada.org
www.newapostolicchurch.com

Overview: A medium-sized international organization
Chief Officer(s):
E. Wagner, President
T. Witt, Treasurer
Membership: 4,283,287 internationally
Description: The New Apostolic Church comprises a world-wide community of Christian worshippers that are growing into the future together. We take a balanced approach to our bible-based faith and enjoy life and the many benefits that come from faith, family and friendship.; *Member of:* New Apostolic Church (International)

Les Oblates missionnaires de Marie Immaculée (OMMI) / Oblate Missionaries of Mary Immaculate

#100, 7535, boul Parent, Trois-Rivières QC G9A 5E1
Tél: 819-375-7317; *Téléc:* 819-691-1769
ommi@ommi-is.org
www.ommi-is.org

Aperçu: *Dimension:* petite; *Envergure: internationale; fondée en 1952*
Membre(s) du bureau directeur:
Claire Nantel, Presidente-directrice générale

OMF International - Canada (OMF)

5155 Spectrum Way, Bldg. 21, Mississauga ON L4W 5A1
Tel: 905-568-9971; *Fax:* 905-568-9974
Toll-Free: 888-657-8010
omfcanada@omf.ca
www.ca.omf.org

Also Known As: Overseas Missionary Fellowship
Previous Name: China Inland Mission
Overview: A medium-sized international organization founded in 1865
Chief Officer(s):
Ron Adams, Director, Administration & Finance
Richard J. Konieczny, National Director
Membership: 1,300 missionaries worldwide; *Member Profile:* Four years post-secondary education
Member of: Interdenomination Foreign Mission Association; Affiliation(s): Evangelical Fellowship of Canada

Ontario Alliance of Christian Schools (OACS)

790 Shaver Rd., Ancaster ON L9G 3K9
Tel: 905-648-2100; *Fax:* 905-648-2110
oacs@oacs.org
www.oacs.org

Overview: A medium-sized provincial organization founded in 1952
Chief Officer(s):
Adrian Guldemond, Executive Director
Finances: *Annual Operating Budget:* $500,000-$1.5 Million; *Funding Sources:* Membership dues
Staff: 15 staff member(s); 200 volunteer(s)
Membership: 1-99; *Fees:* Schedule available; *Committees:* Finance; Education; PR; Planning; Government Relations; Personnel
Activities: *Speaker Service:* Yes; *Rents Mailing List:* Yes
Description: To promote independent schools in Ontario; to promote Christian education in Canada; to provide educational services for member schools; to lobby government for educational choice. Canada's largest & oldest independent school organization, representing 79 schools with approximately 14,000 students.; Affiliation(s): Christian Schools International; Christian Schools Canada

Ontario Christian Music Assembly

90 Topcliff Ave., Toronto ON M3N 1L8
Tel: 416-636-9779; *Fax:* 905-775-2230
Overview: A small provincial organization founded in 1961
Chief Officer(s):
Érick De Bellefeuille, Président
Membership: 130 individual
Activities: Spring & Christmas concerts series; annual christian festival concert

Pioneer Clubs Canada Inc.

#100, 3350 South Service Rd., Burlington ON L7N 3M6
Tel: 905-681-2883; *Fax:* 905-681-3256
Toll-Free: 800-465-5437
www.pioneerclubs.org

Also Known As: Pioneer Girls/Pioneer Boys
Overview: A large national licensing charitable organization founded in 1974
Finances: *Annual Operating Budget:* $250,000-$500,000
Staff: 9 staff member(s)
Membership: 216 institutional; 16,000 individual; *Fees:* $12 child

Activities: *Speaker Service:* Yes
Description: To serve God by assisting churches & other ministries in helping children & youth make Christ Lord in every aspect of life; Affiliation(s): Canadian Council of Christian Charities

Prairie Association of Christian Librarians (PACL)
Briercrest College & Seminary, 510 College Dr., Caronport SK S0H 0S0
Tel: 306-756-3262; *Fax:* 306-756-5588
library@briercrest.ca
www.pacl.ca
Overview: A small local organization
Chief Officer(s):
Brad Doerksen, Sec.-Treas.
bdoerksen@briercrest.ca
Finances: *Annual Operating Budget:* Less than $50,000
Membership: 1-99

Prison Fellowship Canada / Fraternite des prisons du Canada
#5700, 100 King St. West, Toronto ON M5X 1C7
Tel: 416-915-4102; *Fax:* 416-915-4103
Toll-Free: 877-858-2891
info@prisonfellowship.ca
www.prisonfellowship.ca
www.facebook.com/pages/Prison-Fellowship-Canada/231865723490994
twitter.com/ServingLifePFC
Overview: A small national organization founded in 1980
Chief Officer(s):
Eleanor Clitheroe, Executive Director/CEO
Judith Laus, Managing Director
Description: To challenge, equip, & serve the body of Christ in its ministry to prisoners, ex-prisoners, their families, & victims; To promote the advancement of restorative justice; *Member of:* Prison Fellowship International

Project Peacemakers
745 Westminster Ave., Winnipeg MB R3G 1A5
Tel: 204-775-8178; *Fax:* 204-784-1339
info@projectpeacemakers.org
www.projectpeacemakers.org
www.facebook.com/pages/project-peacemakers/108617822532248
Overview: A small international charitable organization founded in 1983
Chief Officer(s):
Dianne Cooper, Chair
Finances: *Annual Operating Budget:* Less than $50,000; *Funding Sources:* Member donations; church grants
Staff: 2 staff member(s); 30 volunteer(s)
Membership: 200; *Fees:* $25 one year; $40 two years; $8 low income
Activities: Concerts; film festivals; protests; witness-for-peace delegations; forums; *Speaker Service:* Yes *Library:* Yes (Open to Public)
Description: Project Peacemakers is a group of people working for peace from a faith perspective. Its activities are varied, from peace delegations in war zones to educational forums on such issues as child soldiers & violent video games.; *Member of:* Project Ploughshares; Affiliation(s): Canadian Centre for Arms Control & Disarmament; Manitoba Environmental Network; Mennonite Central Committee; Peace Alliance Winnipeg; Manitoba Japanese-Canadian Citizens Association
Publications: Peace Projections
Type: Newsletter *Frequency:* Quarterly

REHOBOTH Christian Ministries
3920 - 49th Ave., Stony Plain AB T7Z 2J7
Tel: 780-963-4044; *Fax:* 780-963-3075
stonyplain@ rehoboth.ab.ca
rehoboth.ab.ca
Also Known As: Christian Association for the Mentally Handicapped of Alberta
Overview: A medium-sized provincial charitable organization founded in 1976
Chief Officer(s):
Wally Mulder, CEO & Executive Director
wally.mulder@rehoboth.ab.ca
Finances: *Annual Operating Budget:* Greater than $5 Million; *Funding Sources:* Provincial government; membership fees; donations; church offerings
Staff: 535 staff member(s); 950 volunteer(s)
Membership: 4,600; *Fees:* $10; *Member Profile:* Everybody accepting their mission statement; *Committees:* Regional Advisory
Activities: Residential, vocational & recreational support for individuals who live with disabilities; summer camp program; fundraising golf tournament; *Internships:* Yes
Description: To convey God's love to persons with disabilities through support, advocacy & public education, & by providing opportunities for personal growth & meaningful participation in society; *Member of:* Alberta Council of Disability Services; Canadian Centre for Philanthropy; Affiliation(s): Christian Stewardship Services

Religious Freedom Council of Christian Minorities
PO Box 223, Stn. A, Vancouver BC V6C 2M3
Tel: 250-492-3376
Also Known As: Bible Holiness Movement
Overview: A small local organization founded in 1979
Chief Officer(s):
Wesley H. Wakefield, Chair
Finances: *Annual Operating Budget:* Less than $50,000
Staff: 4 volunteer(s)
Activities: *Speaker Service:* Yes *Library:* Bible Holiness Movement by appointment
Description: To act as a sponsored organization of the Bible Holiness Movement

The Salvation Army in Canada
Territorial Headquarters, Canada & Bermuda, 2 Overlea Blvd., Toronto ON M4H 1P4
Tel: 416-425-2111; *Toll-Free:* 800-725-2769
www.salvationarmy.ca
Social Media: www.youtube.com/user/salvationarmy;
flickr.com/photos/salvationarmy
www.facebook.com/salvationarmy
twitter.com/salvationarmy
Overview: A large international charitable organization founded in 1882
Chief Officer(s):
Brian Peddle, Territorial Commander
Gail Cook-Bennett, Chair
Floyd J. Tidd, Chief Secretary
Finances: *Annual Operating Budget:* $3 Million-$5 Million
Staff: 152 staff member(s)
Membership: 343 Corps (congregations); 165 social institutes across Canada
Activities: *Speaker Service:* Yes
Description: To preach the Gospel of Jesus Christ; To supply basic human needs; To provide personal counselling & undertake the spiritual & moral regeneration & physical rehabilitation of all persons in need who come within its sphere of influence regardless of race, colour, creed, sex or age; *Member of:* Evangelical Fellowship of Canada

Samaritan House Ministries Inc.
630 Rosser Ave., Brandon MB R7A 0K7
Tel: 204-726-0758; *Fax:* 204-729-9951
exec@samaritanhouse.net
samaritanhouse.net
Overview: A small local charitable organization founded in 1987
Chief Officer(s):
Marla Somersall, Executive Director
Activities: *Internships:* Yes; *Speaker Service:* Yes
Description: To provide support & services to at-risk populations - the homeless, those living in poverty, people with literacy challenges or persons leaving abusive relationships

Samaritan's Purse Canada
20 Hopewell Way NE, Calgary AB T3J 5H5
Tel: 403-250-6565; *Fax:* 403-250-6567
Toll-Free: 800-663-6500
info@samaritan.org
www.samaritanspurse.ca
Also Known As: Operation Christmas Child
Overview: A large international charitable organization founded in 1973
Chief Officer(s):
Jeff Adams, Communications Director
Franklin Graham, President & CEO
Sean P. Campbell, Executive Director
Finances: *Annual Operating Budget:* Greater than $5 Million; *Funding Sources:* Donations
Staff: 60 staff member(s); 1300 volunteer(s)
Activities: Operation Christmas Child packages; Turn on the Tap access to safe water program; *Internships:* Yes; *Speaker Service:* Yes
Description: A nondenominational evangelical Christian international relief organization with projects around the globe, meeting both physical & spiritual needs of people who are victims of war, poverty, natural disasters, disease & famine. Focus is on emergency relief & development programs, medical projects. International offices in Canada, Australia, Germany, Ireland, the Netherlands, the U.S. & the U.K.; *Member of:* Canadian Council of Christian Charities; Affiliation(s): Samaritan's Purse USA

Society of Christian Schools in British Columbia (SCSBC)
Fosmark Centre, Trinity Western University, 7600 Glover Rd., Langley BC V2Y 1Y1
Tel: 604-888-6366; *Fax:* 604-888-2791
contact@scsbc.ca; scsbc@twu.ca (Library & membership information)
www.scsbc.ca
Previous Name: Southwest British Columbia League of Christian Schools
Overview: A small provincial organization founded in 1976
Chief Officer(s):
Henry Contant, Executive Director, 604-888-6366 104
leadership@scsbc.ca
Joanne Den Boer, Director of Learning, Preschool to Grade 5, 604-888-6366 106
joanne@scsbc.ca
Bill de Jager, Director of Learning, Grades 6 - 13, 604-888-6366 103
bill@scsbc.ca
Karen Bush, Coordinator, Communications & Publications, 604-888-6366 101
karen@scsbc.ca
Membership: 1-99; *Member Profile:* Christian school campuses & societies in British Columbia
Activities: Monitoring government policies & regulations regarding Christian schoools, & advising schools about government relations; Promoting Christian education throughout British Columbia; Offering workshops; Publishing resource handbooks; Assisting new Christian schools & expanding schools; Supporting digital learning; *Library:* Society of Christian Schools in British Columbia Resource Library
Description: To serve Christian schools in British Columbia; To seek support in the provision of Christian education; To develop policies & curriculum outlines & units; Affiliation(s): Christian Schools International (CSI); Christian Schools Canada (CSC); Christian Teachers Association of British Columbia; Christian Principals Association of British Columbia
Publications: eBulletin
Type: Newsletter
Profile: Information, such as Ministry of Education updates, society policies, & forthcoming workshops & courses, sent regularly to member school board members, principals, curriculum coordinators, & preschooldirectors
Educating for Life Today & Tomorrow: Resource Manual for High School Guidance
Type: Manual
Educating toward Wisdom
Type: Booklet
Profile: A resource for curriculum leaders & administrators in Christian schools
Educating with Heart & Mind: Principles for Curriculum in Christian Schools
Type: Booklet
Profile: A collection of biblical perspective statements
For the Love of Your Child
Type: Booklet *Number of Pages:* 20
Profile: Christian education information
Good Teaching Comes from the Inside
Type: Booklet
Profile: Information for school leaders & teachers
International Education Program: Student Coordinator Handbook
Type: Handbook
Profile: Information for schools initiating or restructuring an international student program
La Joie de la langue française
Type: Booklet
Profile: A resource for both elementary & secondary French teachers
Learning Together in the Middle
Type: Booklet
Profile: Renewing middle level education in Christian schools
The Link
Type: Newsletter *Frequency:* Quarterly
Profile: Information for Christian school, staff, & committee members, including new resources & school news & events
Living, Loving, & Learning: A Kindergarten Handbook
Type: Handbook
Profile: A resource for kindergarten teachers in Christian schools
Responding to a School Emergency
Type: Booklet
Profile: School emergency preparedness
SCSBC Administrative Handbook
Type: Handbook
Profile: General guidelines to shape school policy & practice
SCSBC Internal Control Checklist
Type: Booklet
Profile: Internal controls which may be suitable for SCSBC schools & other independent schools

The SCSBC Language Arts Handbook
Type: Handbook
Profile: Fundamental principles for language arts education
The SCSBC Visual Arts Activity Handbook
Type: Booklet
Profile: Direction for visual arts programs in Christian schools
Serving All Children Well
Type: Booklet
Profile: Information for Christian educators

Strathcona Christian Academy Society
1011 Cloverbar Rd., Sherwood Park AB T8A 4V7
Tel: 780-767-4752
Accounting@SCASociety.ca
www.scasociety.ca
Overview: A small local organization founded in 1980
Chief Officer(s):
Vincent Kath, Chair
Finances: *Annual Operating Budget:* $3 Million-$5 Million; *Funding Sources:* Regional Government
Staff: 47 staff member(s); 120 volunteer(s)
Description: To challenge students, through Christ-centred education, to know Jesus Christ as Savior & Lord in order to pursue a life of Godly character, personal & academic excellence & service to others; *Member of:* Elk Island Public Schools

Union of Spiritual Communities of Christ
PO Box 3024, Castlegar BC V1N 3H4
Tel: 250-365-5477
info@iskra.ca
iskra.ca
Overview: A small national organization
Chief Officer(s):
Lisa Poznikoff, Contact
Description: The Union of Spiritual Communities of Christ (USCC) is a registered Canadian charitable society dedicated to the sustainability and enrichment of the Doukhobor Life-Concept based on the Law of God and the Teachings of Jesus Christ

VISION TV
Liberty Market Building, #230, 171 East Liberty St., Toronto ON M6K 3P6
Tel: 416-368-3194; *Fax:* 416-368-9774
TTY: 416-216-6311
visiontv@visiontv.ca
www.visiontv.ca
www.facebook.com/visiontelevision
twitter.com/visiontv
Overview: A medium-sized national charitable organization founded in 1988
Chief Officer(s):
William D. Roberts, Chief Executive Officer
Finances: *Funding Sources:* Sale of airtime; Advertising; Cable fees
Staff: 3 volunteer(s)
Description: To reflect & illuminate the full spectrum of faith & religious belief which make up Canada's diverse society; To build bridges of knowledge & understanding between faiths & cultures; To provide paid access to all eligible religious & faith communities & broadcast ministries; To broadcast non-sectarian programs based on values, ethics, & spirituality on a wide variety of issues & themes; *Member of:* Canadian Association of Broadcasters; North American Interfaith Network; Affiliation(s): North American Broadcasters Association

Women's Inter-Church Council of Canada (WICC) / Conseil oecuménique des chrétiennes du Canada
47 Queen's Park Cres. East, Toronto ON M5S 2C3
Tel: 416-929-5184; *Fax:* 416-929-4064
wicc@wicc.org
www.wicc.org
www.facebook.com/WICCanada
Overview: A medium-sized national organization founded in 1918
Chief Officer(s):
Janet Anstead, President
Patricia Burton-Williams, Executive Director
burton-williams@wicc.org
Finances: *Funding Sources:* World Day of Prayer offerings
Member Profile: Representatives from the Anglican Church of Canada, the Canadian Baptist Ministries, the Christian Church (Disciples of Christ), the Evangelical Lutheran Church in Canada, the Mennonite Central Committee, the Presbyterian Church in Canada, the Religious Society of Friends, the Roman Catholic Church, the Salvation Army, & the United Church of Canada; Membership is by appointment & election; *Committees:* Program; Communications; Membership & Nominating; Finance
Activities: Establishing the Ecumenical Network for Women's Justice; Preparing policy statements on issues such as racial justice & health care; Granting funds for a variety of projects that benefit women & children in Canada & around the world; Coordinating the Fellowship of the Least Coin program in Canada; Providing education, such as theology workshops
Description: To focus on national & international issues affecting women, growth in ecumenism, action for social justice, & the sharing of spirituality & prayer
Publications: WICC News
Type: Newsletter *Frequency:* Semiannually
Profile: Updates on the work of the Women's Inter-Church Council of Canada, including results of project grants & forthcoming events

World-Wide Bible Study Association
PO Box 98590, 873 Jane St., Toronto ON M6N 4C0
Tel: 416-766-1855
richard.kruse@sympatico.ca
www.ibcschool.ca
Also Known As: International Bible Correspondence School
Overview: A small local organization founded in 1968
Chief Officer(s):
Richard Kruse, Director

Wycliffe Bible Translators of Canada, Inc. (WBTC)
4316 - 10th St. NE, Calgary AB T2E 6K3
Tel: 403-250-5411; *Fax:* 403-250-2623
Toll-Free: 800-463-1143
info@wycliffe.ca
www.wycliffe.ca
Social Media: www.youtube.com/wycliffecanada; www.godtube.com/wycliffecanada
www.linkedin.com/WycliffeBibleTranslatorsCanada
www.facebook.com/WycliffeCanada
twitter.com/wycliffe_canada
Also Known As: Wycliffe Canada
Overview: A large national charitable organization founded in 1968
Chief Officer(s):
David Ohlson, Executive Director
Finances: *Annual Operating Budget:* Greater than $5 Million; *Funding Sources:* Charitable donations; CIDA funding for literacy projects
Staff: 146 staff member(s); 50 volunteer(s)
Membership: 501 individual
Activities: Quarterly newsletter on website; *Internships:* Yes; *Speaker Service:* Yes *Library:* Resource Centre (Open to Public)
Description: To serve minority language groups worldwide by fostering an understanding of God's Word through Bible translation, while encouraging literacy, education & stronger communities; *Member of:* Evangelical Fellowship of Canada; Canadian Council of Christian Charities; Affiliation(s): Wycliffe Bible Translators International; Summer Institute of Linguistics; Canada Institute of Linguistics; Wycliffe Associates Canada
Publications: Word Alive [a publication of Wycliffe Bible Translators of Canada Inc.]
Type: Magazine *Frequency:* Quarterly *Editor:* Dwayne Janke
Price: Donation of $16 annually
Profile: Feature stories about the Bible translation movement

Yonge Street Mission (YSM)
306 Gerrard St. East, Toronto ON M5A 2G7
Tel: 416-929-9614; *Fax:* 416-929-7204
Toll-Free: 800-416-5111
info@ysm.ca
www.ysm.ca
www.facebook.com/YongeStreetMission
twitter.com/YSM_TO
Overview: A medium-sized local charitable organization founded in 1896
Chief Officer(s):
Andrew Williams, Mission Program Officer 4222
awilliams@ysm.ca
Ann Barnard Ball, Mission Development Officer 4244
abarnardball@ysm.ca
Paul Davidson, Mission Operations Officer 4246
pdavidson@ysm.ca
Bill Ryan, Director, Staff Care 4231
bryan@ysm.ca
Jon Unger Brandt, Director, Development 4259
jungerbrandt@ysm.ca
Finances: *Annual Operating Budget:* Greater than $5 Million; *Funding Sources:* Donations; churches; individuals; businesses; foundations; grants
Staff: 120 staff member(s); 4000 volunteer(s)
Activities: Recreation; education; social & family events; relief; housing; *Internships:* Yes; *Speaker Service:* Yes
Description: To bring God's peace, love & justice to people living with economic, social & spiritual poverty in Toronto

Youth for Christ - Canada
PO Box 93008, #135, 19705 Fraser Highway, Langley BC V3A 8H2
Tel: 604-595-2498; *Fax:* 604-595-2473
Toll-Free: 800-899-9322
info@yfccanada.com
www.yfccanada.com
Overview: A medium-sized national organization
Chief Officer(s):
Dave Brereton, National Director
Shirley Loewen, Office Manager
Activities: Responsible, effective & culturally sensitive evangelism of youth, communicating & caring in ways that are relevant to this generation
Description: To impact every young person in Canada with the person, work & teachings of Jesus Christ & discipling them into the Church

Yukon Church Heritage Society (YCHS)
PO Box 31461, Whitehorse YT Y1A 6K8
Tel: 867-668-2555; *Fax:* 867-667-6258
logchurch@.klondiker.com
yukonmuseums.ca/museum/oldlog/oldlog.html
Also Known As: Old Log Church Museum
Overview: A small provincial charitable organization founded in 1982
Chief Officer(s):
Susan Twist, Director/Curator
L. Thistle, President
Finances: *Annual Operating Budget:* $50,000-$100,000
Staff: 1 staff member(s); 8 volunteer(s)
Membership: 25; *Fees:* $15 student/senior; $20 adult; $30 family
Activities: Operates Old Log Church Museum; *Library:* Yes (Open to Public) by appointment
Description: To promote & preserve church history in the Yukon; *Member of:* Yukon Historical & Museums Association; Affiliation(s): Canadian Museums Association

Creationist

Creation Science Association of British Columbia
PO Box 39577, White Rock BC V4B 5L6
Tel: 604-535-0019
info@creationbc.org
www.creationbc.org
Overview: A small provincial charitable organization founded in 1968
Chief Officer(s):
George Pearce, President
Finances: *Annual Operating Budget:* Less than $50,000
Staff: 25 volunteer(s)
Membership: 125 individual; *Fees:* $15 individual
Activities: *Speaker Service:* Yes *Library:* Yes by appointment
Description: To compile scientific as well as Biblical evidence which supports creation & contradicts evolution; To communicate this information to schools, churches & the general public

Creation Science of Saskatchewan Inc. (CSSI)
PO Box 26, Kenaston SK S0G 2N0
Tel: 306-252-2842; *Fax:* 306-252-2842
www.creation-science.sk.ca
Overview: A small provincial charitable organization founded in 1978
Chief Officer(s):
Rudi Fast, President
Finances: *Annual Operating Budget:* Less than $50,000; *Funding Sources:* Donations
Staff: 13 volunteer(s)
Membership: 15 institutional + 140 individual; *Fees:* $10 institutional; $10 individual
Activities: Meetings; speakers; book tables; tours; summer camp; *Speaker Service:* Yes *Library:* Yes by appointment
Description: To share scientific & scriptural evidence for special creation & the Creator

Ecumenism

The Canadian Churches' Forum for Global Ministries / Le forum des églises canadiennes pour les ministères globaux
47 Queens Park Cres. East, Toronto ON M5S 2C3
Tel: 416-924-9351; *Fax:* 416-978-7821
www.ccforum.ca
Previous Name: Ecumenical Forum of Canada
Overview: A medium-sized international charitable organization founded in 1921
Chief Officer(s):
Jonathan Schmidt, Co-director
Alice Schuda, Co-director

Finances: *Annual Operating Budget:* $100,000-$250,000; *Funding Sources:* Churches; religious orders; individuals
Staff: 2 staff member(s); 30 volunteer(s)
Membership: 1-99
Activities: Mission Personnel Programs, Jan., July & Sept.; Annual Katherine Hockin Award & Dinner; International Visitor; *Library:* Yes by appointment
Description: To provide ecumenical orientation & re-entry programs for mission personnel; to stimulate ecumenical dialogue on issues of mission, global concerns & social justice; to prepare individuals to serve faithfully in mission in an ever-changing world; *Member of:* International Association for Mission Studies; Forum on International Personnel; Forum on Mutuality in Mission; Affiliation(s): Canadian Council of Churches
Publications: Forum Focus [a publication of the The Canadian Churches' Forum for Global Ministries]
Type: Newsletter *Frequency:* Annually *Editor:* Alice Schuda; Jonathan Schmidt
Profile: Letters from overseas, information about mission personnel programs, book reviews, articles byinternational visitors, articles related to global mission, & updates on Forum staff & board members

The Canadian Council of Churches (CCC) / Le Conseil canadien des églises
Toronto School of Theology Building, 47 Queen's Park Cres. East, 3rd Fl., Toronto ON M5S 2C3
Tel: 416-972-9494; *Fax:* 416-927-0405
Toll-Free: 866-822-7645
info@councilofchurches.ca; delph@councilofchurches.ca
www.councilofchurches.ca
Overview: A large national charitable organization founded in 1944
Chief Officer(s):
Karen A. Hamilton, General Secretary
hamilton@councilofchurches.ca
Mary Marrocco, Associate Secretary, Commission on Faith & Witness, 416-972-9494 23
marrocco@councilofchurches.ca
Peter Noteboom, Associate Secretary, Commission on Justice & Peace, 416-972-9494 26
noteboom@councilofchurches.ca
Lindsay Ann Cox, Officer, Communications, 416-972-9494 42
cox@councilofchurches.ca
Finances: *Funding Sources:* Member churches
Staff: 2 volunteer(s)
Membership: 10 original member churches, 4 affiliates
Activities: Sponsoring of Project Ploughshares; Maintaining dialogue with all faith groups
Description: To engage in ecumenical education & training; To address issues of justice, liberty, peace, & human rights in keeping with principals inherent in the Christian Gospel; To promote understanding among member churches & with other Christian churches & religious organizations in Canada; To provide coordinating services for preparation of statements, programs, activities & resources; To aid in development of ecumenism in Canada; To provide a forum in which members & interested parties can discuss, study, & act on issues of faith & worship; Affiliation(s): Anglican Church of Canada; Baptist Convention of Ontario & Québec; Canadian Conference of Catholic Bishops; British Methodist Episcopal Church; Canadian Diocese of the Armenian Orthodox Church; Christian Church (Disciples of Christ); Christian Reformed Church in North America; Coptic Orthodox Church; Ethiopian Orthodox Church; Greek Orthodox Church; Evangelical Lutheran Church in Canada; Mennonite Church Canada; Orthodox Church in America; Polish National Catholic Church of Canada; Presbyterian Church in Canada; Reformed Church in America; Religious Society of Friends; Salvation Army

The Churches' Council on Theological Education in Canada: an Ecumenical Foundation (CCTE) / Le Conseil des Églises pour l'éducation théologique au Canada: une fondation oecuménique
47 Queen's Park Cres., Toronto ON M5S 2C3
Tel: 416-928-3223; *Fax:* 416-928-3563
director@ccte.ca
www.ccte.ca
Overview: A small national organization founded in 1962
Chief Officer(s):
Robert Faris, Executive Director
Robert Smith, President
Finances: *Annual Operating Budget:* $100,000-$250,000
Staff: 2 staff member(s); 24 volunteer(s)
Membership: 24 individual
Description: To provide for the coordination of consultation, research, & administration of grants awarded by the Council, in order to promote the development of theological education for ministry; Affiliation(s): Association of Theological Schools

Student Christian Movement of Canada (SCM) / Mouvement d'étudiant(e)s chrétien(ne)s
310 Danforth Ave., Toronto ON M4K 1N6
Tel: 416-463-4312; *Fax:* 416-463-9410
Toll-Free: 877-674-3842
info@scmcanada.org
scmcanada.org
www.facebook.com/scmcanada
twitter.com/scmcanada
Overview: A medium-sized national charitable organization founded in 1921
Chief Officer(s):
Jan Braun, Co-General Secretary
Ryan Tristin Chapman, Co-General Secretary
Finances: *Annual Operating Budget:* $50,000-$100,000
Staff: 2 staff member(s)
Membership: 500; *Member Profile:* Groups at Canadian universities
Description: National, ecumenical student organization; to encourage members in theological/social reflection & in actions for social change. Offices in Toronto & Winnipeg; *Member of:* World Student Christian Federation

World Association for Christian Communication (WACC) / Association mondiale pour la communication
308 Main St., Toronto ON M4C 4X7
Tel: 416-691-1999; *Fax:* 416-691-1997
info@waccglobal.org
www.waccglobal.org
Overview: A small international charitable organization founded in 1975
Chief Officer(s):
Karin Achtelstetter, General Secretary
ka@waccglobal.org
Musimbi Kanyoro, President
Young-Cheol Cheon, Treasurer
Membership: 1,000-4,999; *Fees:* US$120 corporate; US$40 personal; US$10 student; *Member Profile:* Individuals, churches, church-related agencies, media producers, educational institutions, secular communication organizations, & persons who share WACC's mission
Activities: *Speaker Service:* Yes *Library:* Yes by appointment
Description: Communication for social change is promoted by WACC through advocacy, education, training, & the creation & sharing of knowledge. Areas of chief concern include media diversity, equal & affordable access to communication & knowledge, media & gender justice, & the relationship between communication & power.; *Member of:* UNESCO; ECOSOC
Publications: Media Development
Type: Journal *Frequency:* Quarterly *Price:* US$40 individual; US$50-US$75 libraries & institutions
Profile: Theory & practice of communication worldwide
No-Nonsense Guides
Number of Pages: 6
Profile: Different aspects of communication for practitioners & activists

Evangelism

Africa Inland Mission International (Canada) (AIM) / Mission à l'intérieur de l'Afrique (Canada)
1641 Victoria Park Ave., Toronto ON M1R 1P8
Tel: 416-751-6077; *Fax:* 416-751-3467
Toll-Free: 877-407-6077
general.can@aimint.net
www.aimint.org
www.facebook.com/aimcanada
Also Known As: AIM Canada
Overview: A medium-sized international charitable organization founded in 1895
Finances: *Annual Operating Budget:* $1.5 Million-$3 Million; *Funding Sources:* Donations from churches & individuals
Staff: 8 staff member(s); 3 volunteer(s)
Membership: 135; *Committees:* Finance; Personnel; Projects
Description: Evangelization of people within Eastern & Central Africa & Islands around India Ocean; To plant & establish churches; To train leadership for those churches; To provide medical, educational & agricultural services; *Member of:* Africa Inland Mission International, Bristol, England; Interdenominational Foreign Mission Association

Associated Gospel Churches (AGC) / Association des églises évangéliques (AEE)
1500 Kerns Rd., Burlington ON L7P 3A7
Tel: 905-634-8184; *Fax:* 905-634-6283
admin@agcofcanada.com
www.agcofcanada.com
Overview: A medium-sized national charitable organization founded in 1925
Chief Officer(s):
Bill Fietje, President
bill@agcofcanada.com
Susan Page, Church Relations Coordinator
sue@agcofcanada.com
Finances: *Annual Operating Budget:* $250,000-$500,000
Staff: 5 staff member(s)
Membership: 21,400 members; 140+ churches; *Fees:* 4% of revenue minus missions support; *Committees:* Doctrine & Credentials; Finance & Administration; Communication; Church Growth; Church Renting
Description: To glorify God by partnering together in obedience to the Great Commandment & the Great Commission; to become a movement of healthy, reproducing churches; Affiliation(s): World Relief; World Team; UFM International; Evangelical Fellowship of Canada

Baptist Foundation, Alberta, Saskatchewan & the Territories, Inc. (B-FAST)
PO Box 159, 14-9988 178 St NW, Edmonton AB T5T 6J6
Tel: 780-451-4878; *Fax:* 780-758-4453
febcast@shaw.ca
www.febcast.ca
Overview: A small local organization founded in 1982
Chief Officer(s):
Nanja Reynolds, Office Manager
Membership: 15 individual
Description: Funding capital projects for Fellowship of Evangelical Baptist Churches in Alberta, Saskatchewan & the Territories

Baptist General Conference of Canada (BGCC)
#205, 15824 - 131 Ave., Edmonton AB T5V 1J4
Tel: 780-438-9127; *Fax:* 780-435-2478
office@bgc.ca
www.bgc.ca
Overview: A large national charitable organization founded in 1981
Chief Officer(s):
Jamey McDonald, Executive Director, 780-438-9127 22
Finances: *Funding Sources:* Churches; individuals; BGC Stewardship Foundation
Staff: 5 staff member(s); 12 volunteer(s)
Membership: 7,000+ individuals + 106 churches; *Member Profile:* Agreement with our Affirmation of Faith, Distinctives & ministry goals; *Committees:* Global Ministries; Equipping Ministries; Women; Youth; Regents - Canadian Baptist Seminary; Finance
Activities: Global Ministries; new church development; leadership training; youth programs; women's ministries; international development consulting; *Library:* BGC Canada Archives by appointment
Description: To unite churches in a fellowship that is scriptual in doctrine, evangelical in character & irenic (peaceful) in spirit, & seeking to fulfil the Great Commission of Christ (Mt.28: 19-20) in Canada & abroad; *Member of:* Evangelical Fellowship of Canada

Billy Graham Evangelistic Association of Canada (BGEAC)
20 Hopewell Ave. NE, Calgary AB T3J 5H5
Tel: 403-219-2300; *Fax:* 403-250-6567
Toll-Free: 800-293-3717
www.billygraham.ca
Overview: A small national charitable organization founded in 1968
Chief Officer(s):
Fred Weiss, Executive Director
Steve Wile, Director, Ministry
Finances: *Funding Sources:* Donations
Staff: 21 staff member(s)
Activities: Television & radio broadcasts; schools of evangelism; evangelistic crusades; teaching seminars
Description: To expose those who are searching to the message of Christ; To help edify the Christian body in Canada; Affiliation(s): Bill Graham Evangelistic Association USA

Canada's National Bible Hour (CNBH)
PO Box 1210, St Catharines ON L2R 7A7
Tel: 905-684-1401
gonow@missiongo.org
www.missiongo.org/biblehour.html
Overview: A small national organization founded in 1925
Chief Officer(s):
Brian Albrecht, President, GOM
Len Lane, Contact
len@missiongo.org
Description: The Hour is a bible-teaching ministry, & Canada's oldest religious broadcast, heard from coast to coast. It is sponsored by Global Outreach Mission (GOM), an organization dedicated to evangelism & missions.; *Member of:* Global Outreach Mission

Child Evangelism Fellowship of Canada
PO Box 165, Stn. Main, 337 Henderson Highway, Winnipeg MB R3C 2G9
Tel: 204-943-2774; *Fax:* 204-943-9967
Toll-Free: 866-943-2774
info@cefcanada.org
www.cefcanada.org
Also Known As: CEF Canada
Overview: A medium-sized national charitable organization founded in 1937
Chief Officer(s):
Jerry Hanson, National Director
jhanson@cefcanada.org
Finances: *Annual Operating Budget:* $500,000-$1.5 Million; *Funding Sources:* Individual, corporate & church donations
Staff: 45 staff member(s); 200 volunteer(s)
Membership: 8
Activities: Children's Ministries Institute; offers courses/programs, materials & training for Christian education among children
Description: CEF Canada is a bible-centred organization of born-again believers whose purpose is to evangelize & disciple children with the gospel of Jesus Christ.; *Member of:* Canadian Council of Christian Charities; Affiliation(s): Child Evangelism Fellowship Inc.; CEF of Nations

The Christian & Missionary Alliance in Canada (C&MA) / L'Alliance chrétienne et missionnaire au Canada
#100, 30 Carrier Dr., Toronto ON M9W 5T7
Tel: 416-674-7878; *Fax:* 416-674-0808
info@cmacan.org
cmalliance.ca
Also Known As: The Alliance Church
Overview: A large national charitable organization founded in 1972
Chief Officer(s):
Franklin Pyles, President
Finances: *Annual Operating Budget:* Greater than $5 Million; *Funding Sources:* Donations
Staff: 1642 staff member(s)
Membership: 430 churches + 300 missionaries + 43,700 baptized + 127,000 inclusive members
Description: To proclaim the truth of God's Word & to disciple people of all nations, particularly where Christ has not been named, emphasizing the Lordship of Jesus Christ & the person & work of the Holy Spirit, & looking for the coming of the Lord; To establish & nurture churches related in fellowship with C&MA around the world, dedicated to evangelism & missions; to establish local churches throughout Canada; To teach & train believers for the work of the ministry of Christ; to provide fellowship for individual believers of kindred spirit with one another without affecting their denominational relations; To encourage the cooperation of such evangelical groups of churches or Christians as may be disposed to send their missionaries through C&MA & contribute their missionary offerings through the general treasury; *Member of:* Alliance World Fellowship; Affiliation(s): Evangelical Fellowship of Canada

Emmanuel International (Canada) (EIC)
PO Box 4050, 3967 Stouffville Rd., Stouffville ON L4A 8B6
Tel: 905-640-2115; *Fax:* 905-640-2186
info@e-i.org
www.e-i.org
www.facebook.com/group.php?gid=239293974881
Overview: A large national charitable organization founded in 1975
Chief Officer(s):
Doug Anderson, International Director
Finances: *Annual Operating Budget:* $1.5 Million-$3 Million; *Funding Sources:* Government; donations
Staff: 14 staff member(s); 3 volunteer(s)
Membership: 1-99
Activities: *Internships:* Yes
Description: To encourage, strengthen & assist churches worldwide to meet the spiritual & physical needs of the poor in accordance with the Holy Scriptures through programs of relief, rehabilitation, community development, evangelism & church planting; *Member of:* Canadian Council of Christian Charities

Evangelical Covenant Church of Canada (ECCC)
PO Box 34025, RPO Fort Richmond, Winnipeg MB R3T 5T5
Tel: 204-269-3437; *Fax:* 204-269-3584
Toll-Free: - - 020
ccc1@mts.net
www.canadacovenantchurch.org
Overview: A medium-sized national charitable organization founded in 1904
Chief Officer(s):
Jeff Anderson, ECCC Conference Superintendent
ccc1@mts.net
Finances: *Funding Sources:* Donations
Member Profile: Evangelical Covenant Churches in Canada
Member of: World Relief Canada; The Evangelical Fellowship of Canada; The Canadian Council of Christian Charities

Evangelical Fellowship of Canada (EFC) / Alliance évangélique du Canada
+, PO Box 3745, Stn. MIP, #300, 600 Alden Rd., Markham ON L3R 0Y4
Tel: 905-479-5885; *Fax:* 905-479-4742
Toll-Free: 866-302-3362
efc@evangelicalfellowship.ca
www.evangelicalfellowship.ca
www.facebook.com/theefc
Overview: A medium-sized national charitable organization founded in 1964
Chief Officer(s):
David Wells, Chair
Bruce J. Clemenger, President
Finances: *Annual Operating Budget:* $1.5 Million-$3 Million; *Funding Sources:* General & corporate donations; member & subscriber fees
Staff: 20 staff member(s); 90 volunteer(s)
Membership: 32 evangelical denominations + 110 organizations + 1,200 churches
Activities: Task forces: Evangelism; Women in Ministry; Aboriginal; Global Mission; Commissions: Education; Religious Liberty; Social Action; *Speaker Service:* Yes
Description: EFC is the national association of evangelical Christians in Canada. Its aims are to be a public advocate of the gospel of Jesus Christ; to provide an evangelical identity which unites Canadian Christians of diverse backgrounds; to express biblical views on current issues; to assist individuals & groups in proclaiming the gospel & advancing Christian values.; *Member of:* World Evangelical Fellowship

Evangelical Medical Aid Society (EMAS)
PO Box 820, Stn. Main, 3967 Stouffville Road, Stouffville ON L4A 7Z9
Tel: 905-642-4661; *Fax:* 905-640-2186
Toll-Free: 866-648-0664
info@emascanada.org
www.emascanada.org
twitter.com/EMASCANADA
Overview: A small international charitable organization founded in 1948
Chief Officer(s):
Hendrik Visser, Chair
Finances: *Annual Operating Budget:* $500,000-$1.5 Million
Staff: 1 staff member(s); 175 volunteer(s)
Membership: 25 individual
Description: To operate as a global medical ministry, revealing Christ's love; To work with national groups to provide assistance in healing & teaching

The Evangelical Order of Certified Pastoral Counsellors of America (EOCPCA)
#210, 3017 St. Clair Ave., Burlington ON L7N 3P5
Tel: 905-639-0137; *Fax:* 905-333-8901
admin@eocpc.com
www.eocpc.com
Previous Name: Order of Certified Pastoral Counsellors of America
Overview: A medium-sized national organization founded in 1982
Chief Officer(s):
Stephen Hambly, Contact
shambly@eocpc.com
Finances: *Annual Operating Budget:* $500,000-$1.5 Million
Staff: 3 staff member(s)
Membership: 1,200 individual; *Fees:* $75-250
Description: To promote a Christian-oriented order; to certify & accredit pastoral counsellors by federal charter; *Member of:* Canadian Christian Counsellors Association; Canadian Christian Clinical Counsellors College; Affiliation(s): California State Christian University

Evangelical Tract Distributors (EDT)
PO Box 146, Stn. Main, 12151 - 67 St. NW, Edmonton AB T5J 2G9
Tel: 780-477-1538; *Fax:* 780-477-3795
etdsupport@evangelicaltract.com
www.evangelicaltract.com
Overview: A small national organization founded in 1935
Chief Officer(s):
John Harder, President/Managing Director
Description: EDT is a non-profit organization that prints & distributes Christian gospel tracts free of charge. It is a registered charity, BN: 130522659RR0001.
Publications: The Evangelist
Type: Newsletter *Frequency:* Monthly

Fellowship of Evangelical Baptist Churches in Canada
PO Box 457, 351 Elizabeth St., Guelph ON N1H 6K9
Tel: 519-821-4830; *Fax:* 519-821-9829
president@fellowship.ca
www.fellowship.ca
Also Known As: The Fellowship
Overview: A large national organization
Chief Officer(s):
Steven Jones, President
sjones@fellowship.ca
Finances: *Annual Operating Budget:* Greater than $5 Million
Staff: 16 staff member(s)
Membership: 501 churches
Activities: *Library:* Archives
Description: To glorify God & to proclaim the good news of Jesus Christ, evangelizing our generation & producing healthy, growing churches in Canada & around the world

Fondation Père-Eusèbe-Ménard
1195, rue Sauvé est, Montréal QC H2C 1Z8
Tél: 514-274-7645; *Téléc:* 514-274-7647
Ligne sans frais: 800-665-7645
info@fondationperemenard.org
www.fondationperemenard.org
Aperçu: *Dimension:* petite; *Envergure: internationale; Organisme sans but lucratif; fondée en 1970*
Membre(s) du bureau directeur:
Nicole Bernard, Directrice générale
Finances: *Budget de fonctionnement annuel:* $1.5 Million-$3 Million
Personnel: 3 membre(s) du personnel; 10 bénévole(s)
Membre: 15 000+
Activités: La Fondation travaille en partenariat avec les Missionnaires de Saints-Apôtres présents dans les pays d'intervention pour assurer la croissance des Églises locales en contribuant particulièrement à la formation de futurs prêtres et agents de pastorale, et pour améliorer les conditions de vie inhumaines de nos frères et soeurs dans ces pays
Description: Encourager les personnes qui le désirent à appuyer les efforts de développement et d'évangélisation des populations défavorisées dans le Tiers-Monde

Foursquare Gospel Church of Canada
#307, 2099 Lougheed Hwy., Port Coquitlam BC V3B 1A8
Tel: 604-941-8414; *Fax:* 604-941-8415
info@foursquare.ca
www.foursquare.ca
Overview: A medium-sized national charitable organization founded in 1981
Chief Officer(s):
Steve Falkiner, President
Finances: *Annual Operating Budget:* $250,000-$500,000
Staff: 3 staff member(s)
Membership: 67 churches
Member of: Evangelical Fellowship of Canada

Full Gospel Business Men's Fellowship in Canada (FGBMFI)
#403, 50 Gervais Dr., Toronto ON M3C 1Z3
Tel: 416-449-7272; *Fax:* 416-449-9743
fgbmfi@allstream.net
www.fgbmfi.ca
Overview: A medium-sized national charitable organization founded in 1964
Finances: *Annual Operating Budget:* $100,000-$250,000
Staff: 2 staff member(s); 2 volunteer(s)
Membership: 1,000-4,999; *Fees:* $60 individual
Activities: National convention; *Internships:* Yes; *Speaker Service:* Yes
Description: To reach men at all levels of our modern society, calling them to God, & releasing them into their respective gifts & talents through the Holy Spirit; *Member of:* Full Gospel Business Men's Fellowship International

Gideons International in Canada / Les Gédéons - L'Association Internationale des Gédéons au Canada
PO Box 3619, 501 Imperial Rd. North, Guelph ON N1H 7A2
Tel: 519-823-1140; *Fax:* 519-767-1913
Toll-Free: 888-482-4253
info@gideons.ca
www.gideons.ca
www.linkedin.com/company/the-gideons-international-in-canada
www.facebook.com/group.php?gid=177253638952857
twitter.com/GideonsCanada
Overview: A medium-sized international charitable organization founded in 1911
Chief Officer(s):
Paul Mercer, Executive Director

Finances: *Annual Operating Budget:* Greater than $5 Million; *Funding Sources:* Membership fees; voluntary donations; funds from other registered charities
Membership: 4,500; *Fees:* $100; *Member Profile:* Christian business & professional people
Activities: Sharing faith; Placing Bibles & New Testaments to the public; Distributing New Testaments to selected groups
Description: The interdenominational lay association communicates/gives away freecopies of God's Word in Canada & around the world.
Publications: The Canadian Gideon: The Official Publication of The Gideons International in Canada
Type: Magazine *Editor:* Neil Bramble *Price:* $15
Profile: Information & resources for Gideon & Auxiliary members
Gideon News
Type: Newsletter

Good News Broadcasting Association of Canada
PO Box 246, Stn. A, abbotsford BC V2T 6Z6
Toll-Free: 800-663-2425
bttb@backtothebible.ca
www.backtothebible.ca
www.facebook.com/BTTBCanada
twitter.com/BTTBC
Also Known As: Back to the Bible Canada
Overview: A small local charitable organization
Chief Officer(s):
Byron Reaume, CFO & Director of Stewardship
Bob Beasley, CEO
Member of: Canadian Council of Christian Charities; Evangelican Fellowship of Canada

Lighthouse Mission
669 Main St., Winnipeg MB R3B 1E3
Tel: 204-943-9669; *Fax:* 204-949-9479
sean@lighthousemission.ca
www.lighthousemission.ca
Overview: A small local organization founded in 1911
Chief Officer(s):
Sean Goulet, Director
Activities: Operates a soup kitchen; distributes clothing to the needy
Description: Provides food and services to the needy in Winnipeg.

Living Bible Explorers (LBE)
600 Burnell St., Winnipeg MB R3G 2B7
Tel: 204-786-8667; *Fax:* 204-775-7525
Toll-Free: 866-786-8667
lbe@mts.net
livingbibleexplorers.com
Overview: A small local charitable organization founded in 1969
Chief Officer(s):
George Hill, General Manager
MaryAnn Funk, Girls Program Coordinator
Michelle MacGibbon, Teen Girls Coordinator
Mark Henkleman, Teen Boys Coordinator
Ben Krocker, Boys Program Coordinator
Diana Cuthbertson, Volunteer Coordinator
Randal Moroskitson, Vehicle Coordinator
Finances: *Annual Operating Budget:* $250,000-$500,000; *Funding Sources:* Individual and cooperate donations; Provincial government; individual churches; foundations
Staff: 9 staff member(s); 200 volunteer(s)
Membership: 700 individual; *Member Profile:* Manitobans who have a tangible interest by working, volunteering or giving to the work; *Committees:* New Bible Camp; Board of Directors
Activities: Boys & Girls Clubs; summer camps; weekend camps; weekly kids church; teens church; food distribution; weekly home visitation; annual banquet, Mar. Currently constructing a New Bible Camp for children in Hadoshville, Manitoba.; *Awareness Events:* Mission Fest - Feb; Annual Fundraising Banquet - Mar; Garage Sale - May; *Internships:* Yes; *Speaker Service:* Yes *Library:* Resource Library (Open to Public)
Description: To develop relationships with children & teens from inner city homes in an effort to evangelize them & to promote discipleship with a view to integrating them into the life & care of Bible-believing churches; *Member of:* Canadian Council of Christian Charities

Society for International Ministries (SIM Canada)
10 Huntingdale Blvd., Toronto ON M1W 2S5
Tel: 416-497-2424; *Fax:* 416-497-2444
Toll-Free: 800-294-6918
info@sim.ca
www.sim.ca
Overview: A small international organization founded in 1893
Chief Officer(s):
Gregg Bryce, Executive Director
Finances: *Annual Operating Budget:* $3 Million-$5 Million
Staff: 30 staff member(s)
Membership: 300
Description: To evangelize the unreached & minister to human need

Solbrekken Evangelistic Association of Canada
PO Box 44220, Stn. Garside, Edmonton AB T5V 1N6
Tel: 780-460-8444
mswm@shaw.ca
www.mswm.org
Also Known As: Max Solbrekken World Mission
Overview: A small national charitable organization founded in 1961
Chief Officer(s):
Max Solbrekken, President
Donna Solbrekken, Secretary
Description: To promote the gospel; Affiliation(s): Europa for Kristus, Oslo, Norway

TEAM of Canada Inc. (TEAM)
2635 - 32 St. SW, Calgary AB T3E 2R8
Tel: 403-248-2344; *Fax:* 403-207-6025
Toll-Free: 800-295-4160
team@teamcanada.org
www.teamcanada.org
Also Known As: The Evangelical Alliance Mission of Canada Inc.
Overview: A medium-sized international charitable organization founded in 1969
Chief Officer(s):
Robert Hodge, Chairman
Jim Couture, Vice Chairman
Finances: *Annual Operating Budget:* $1.5 Million-$3 Million
Staff: 6 staff member(s)
Membership: 1-99
Activities: *Internships:* Yes; *Speaker Service:* Yes *Library:* Resource Centre
Description: To help churches send missionaries to establish reproducing churches among the nations, to the Glory of God; *Member of:* Canadian Council of Christian Charities

Episcopal

Atlantic Episcopal Assembly (AEA) / Assemblée des évêques de l'Atlantique
3 Oakley Ave., halifax ns B3M 3G6
Tel: 902-443-9325
Overview: A small local organization founded in 1967
Chief Officer(s):
Gérald LeBlanc, Secretary-Treasurer
geraldleblanc@eastlink.ca
François Thibodeau, President
Terrence Prendergast
Finances: *Annual Operating Budget:* Less than $50,000
Membership: 12; *Committees:* Exécutif; Affaires sociales
Description: Proposer l'évangile de Jésus Christ dans les diverses situations de la vie ainsi que ses implications pratiques de notre temps; echange d'information pour les évêques

The Christian Episcopal Church of Canada (CECC)
9280 #2 Rd., Richmond BC V6E 3C8
Tel: 604-275-7422
xnec1662@gmail.com
www.xnec.ca
Also Known As: Traditional Anglican Church in Canada
Overview: A small national charitable organization founded in 1991
Chief Officer(s):
Robert D. Redmile
Finances: *Annual Operating Budget:* $100,000-$250,000; *Funding Sources:* Donations
Staff: 12 staff member(s); 40 volunteer(s)
Membership: 450; *Fees:* Free-will offerings; *Member Profile:* Baptised & confirmed Anglican Christians; *Committees:* Parochial Church Council, Assembly & Consistory; Diocesan Synod & Diocesan Council
Activities: Traditional Anglican faith & worship according to the Book of Common Prayer
Member of: Anglican Communion; Affiliation(s): Christian Episcopal Church in the USA

The Reformed Episcopal Church of Canada - Diocese of Central & Eastern Canada (REC)
PO Box 2532, 320 Armstrong St., New Liskeard ON P0J 1P0
Tel: 705-647-4565; *Fax:* 705-647-1340
trinityfed@hotmail.com
recus.org; www.reccec.homestead.com
Overview: A medium-sized provincial charitable organization founded in 1886
Chief Officer(s):
Alison Buffet, Secretary
Michael Fedechko, Bishop Ordinary
Finances: *Annual Operating Budget:* Less than $50,000; *Funding Sources:* Donations
Staff: 4 volunteer(s)
Membership: 210 + 6 churches; *Committees:* Standing; Constitution & Canons; Church Extension
Activities: Synodical Council, 3rd week of Sept.; *Library:* Yes (Open to Public) by appointment
Description: We believe the Bible to be the inspired, the only infallible, inerrant, authoritative Word of God

The Reformed Episcopal Church of Canada - Diocese of Western Canada & Alaska (RECWCAN)
2604 Quadra St., Victoria BC V8T 4E4
Tel: 250-727-3722; *Fax:* 250-727-3722
recwcan@islandnet.com
www.recwcan.ca
Overview: A small national licensing charitable organization founded in 1874
Chief Officer(s):
John Boudewyn, Treasurer, 250-544-0098
Jack Cryderman, Secretary, 250-339-4014
Charles W. Dorrington, Diocesan Bishop, 250-652-8850
Finances: *Annual Operating Budget:* Less than $50,000; *Funding Sources:* Offerings; bequests; church assessments
Staff: 2 staff member(s)
Membership: 300; *Fees:* Church offerings; *Committees:* Council; Vestry; Executive; Standing; Synod
Activities: Douglas House Retirement Home Ministry; Victoria Prayer Counselling; Healing Rooms; *Internships:* Yes; *Speaker Service:* Yes *Library:* Diocesan Office Library by appointment
Description: To reach out to those outside the existing congregation; establish new churches; assist congregations within the Diocese; receive congregations wishing to affiliate with the Reformed Episcopal Church; ordain candidates into the ministry; Affiliation(s): Common Cause Network

Friends

Canadian Friends Service Committee (CFSC) / Secours Quaker Canadien
60 Lowther Ave., Toronto ON M5R 1C7
Tel: 416-920-5213; *Fax:* 416-920-5214
cfsc@quaker.ca
www.cfsc.quaker.ca
Also Known As: Religious Society of Friends (Quakers)
Overview: A medium-sized national charitable organization founded in 1931
Chief Officer(s):
Jane Orion Smith, General Secretary
Svetlana MacDonald, Clerk
Finances: *Annual Operating Budget:* $500,000-$1.5 Million; *Funding Sources:* Individuals; meetings
Staff: 7 staff member(s); 40 volunteer(s)
Activities: Peace & social justice work; *Internships:* Yes; *Speaker Service:* Yes *Library:* Friends House Library (Open to Public)
Description: To unify & expand the concerns of Friends (Quakers); *Member of:* The Canadian Council of Churches; Kairos: Canadian Ecumenical Justice Initiatives; Project Ploughshares; Canadian Council for Refugees; War Resistors Support Campaign
Publications: Quaker Concern
Type: Newsletter *Frequency:* 3 pa *Editor:* M. Egan; J. Preston; G. Broughtone
Profile: CFSC information & feature articles on CFSC concerns

Friends Historical Association (FHA)
Quaker Collection, Haverford College, 370 Lancaster Ave., Haverford PA 19041-1392 USA
Tel: 610-896-1161; *Fax:* 610-896-1102
fha@haverford.edu
www.haverford.edu/library/fha/fha.html
Overview: A medium-sized international charitable organization founded in 1873
Chief Officer(s):
Kenneth Carroll, President
Joelle Bertolet, Office Manager
Finances: *Annual Operating Budget:* Less than $50,000; *Funding Sources:* Membership dues; subscriptions; donations
Staff: 1 staff member(s); 21 volunteer(s)
Membership: 800; *Fees:* $15; *Member Profile:* Friends & interested historians; *Committees:* Membership; Publication; Historical Research; Finance; Curatorial; Development
Activities: Pilgrimages to historic Friends Meetings; lectures; *Rents Mailing List:* Yes
Description: To promote the study, preservation & publication of material relating to the history of the Religious Society of Friends; Affiliation(s): Conference of Quaker Historians & Archivists

Publications: Quaker History
Type: Journal *Frequency:* Semiannually *Editor:* Charles L. Cherry

Friends Historical Society - London (FHS)
c/o Friends House, 173 Euston Rd., London NW1 2BJ United Kingdom

Overview: A small international organization founded in 1903
Finances: *Funding Sources:* Membership fees
Membership: 400
Description: To encourage the study of Quaker history; *Member of:* Association of Denominational Historical Societies & Cognate Libraries

Hare Krishna

International Society for Krishna Consciousness (Toronto Branch) (ISKCON) / Subuddhi Deri Dasi
243 Avenue Rd., Toronto ON M5R 2J6
Tel: 416-922-5415; *Fax:* 416-922-1021
toronto@pamho.net
www.iskcon.com
Also Known As: ISKCON Toronto - Hare Krishna Movement
Overview: A medium-sized local charitable organization founded in 1966
Chief Officer(s):
Subuddhi Dasi, President
Finances: *Annual Operating Budget:* $3 Million-$5 Million; *Funding Sources:* Donations from congregations & festivals
Staff: 10 staff member(s); 20 volunteer(s)
Membership: 700 institutional; 2,000 individual; *Fees:* $1,100
Activities: Distribution of free food; taking care of seniors & youth; *Internships:* Yes *Library:* Yes (Open to Public)
Description: To preach Krishna Consciousness around the world, following in the footsteps of the founder & spiritual master, His Divine Grace A.C. Bhaktivedanta Swami Prabhupada.

Hinduism

Hindu Society of Alberta
14225 - 133 Ave., Edmonton AB T5L 4W3
Tel: 780-451-5130; *Fax:* 780-451-5130
webmaster@hindusociety.ab.ca
www.hindusociety.ab.ca
Overview: A small provincial charitable organization founded in 1967
Chief Officer(s):
Jivan Kayande, President, 780-459-3852
Membership: 500
Activities: Classes in yoga & meditation; language classes; lectures & seminars on history & religion; religious celebrations; music & dance performances; hall rentals; *Library:* library
Description: The Society is a cultural, social & religious institute catering to the needs of those influenced by Hinduism. It is a registered charity, BN: 118958370RR0001.

Yasodhara Ashram Society
PO Box 9, Kootenay Bay BC V0B 1X0
Tel: 250-227-9224; *Fax:* 250-227-9494
Toll-Free: 800-661-8711
yashram@yasodhara.org
www.yasodhara.org
Overview: A small international charitable organization founded in 1963
Finances: *Annual Operating Budget:* $500,000-$1.5 Million
Staff: 15 volunteer(s)
Membership: 125; *Fees:* $25
Activities: *Internships:* Yes; *Speaker Service:* Yes *Library:* Yes by appointment
Description: To maintain a centre for adults engaged in a life of spiritual intent; to provide instruction in & opportunities for religious & spiritual practice

Islam

Ahmadiyya Muslim Centre
525 Kylemore Ave., Winnipeg MB R3L 1B5
Tel: 204-475-2642; *Fax:* 204-452-2455
www.ahmadiyya.ca
Overview: A small local organization founded in 1979
Membership: 1-99
Activities: *Library:* Yes

Ahmadiyya Muslim Jamaat Canada
10610 Jane St., Maple ON L6A 3A2
Tel: 905-832-2669; *Fax:* 905-832-3220
info@ahmadiyya.ca
www.ahmadiyya.ca
Also Known As: Ahmadiyya Muslim Community Canada
Overview: A medium-sized national charitable organization
Chief Officer(s):
Lal Khan Malik, President
Abdul Aziz Khalifa, Vice-President
Aslam Daud, Secretary
Khalid Naeem, Treasurer
Rana Manzoor Ahmed, Librarian, 905-832-2669 2245
Finances: *Annual Operating Budget:* Greater than $5 Million
Staff: 30 staff member(s); 1,00 volunteer(s)
Activities: Offering religious education; *Internships:* Yes; *Speaker Service:* Yes *Library:* Ahmadiyya Muslim Jamaat Canada Library (Open to Public) by appointment
Description: To promote interfaith understanding
Publications: Ahmadiyya Gazette Canada
Type: Magazine *Frequency:* Monthly *Accepts Advertising Editor:* Chaudhary Hadi Ali sahib *Price:* Free
Profile: Educational material about Islam, summaries of sermons or addresses, announcements, & news about the organization

ANNISAA Organization of Canada (ANNISAA)
111 - 7 St Dennis Dr., Toronto ON M3C 1E4
Tel: 647-761-0745
info@annisaa.org
annisaa.org
www.facebook.com/179651935453963
twitter.com/ANNISAAORG
Overview: A medium-sized national organization founded in 2012
Member Profile: Practising Muslim women
Description: ANNISAA aims to promote the best interest of the Muslim women and their families' rights within the Canadian society, providing a voice for the Muslim women. They promote an interest in education, research, sports and recreation, social development, Islamic spiritual advancement and moral values, as well as sponsoring literary, art and other educational and cultural events, festivals, and conventions for the promotion of Islam and Muslims.
Publications: ANNISAA Magazine
Type: Magazine *Frequency:* Quarterly
Profile: Magazine presents various aspects of morality, and of Islamic religion, to be useful both in this life and the Hereafter.

Association des Projets charitables Islamiques (AICP) / Association of Islamic Charitable Projects
6691, av du Parc, Montréal QC H2V 4J1
Tel: 514-274-6194; *Fax:* 514-274-0011
www.aicp.ca
Overview: A small local organization
Membre(s) du bureau directeur:
Bassam Derbas, 514-945-1549
Maher Bissany, 514-892-2295
Description: Dénonce tout acte de terrorisme et promouvoit le support envers la communauté musulmane

Canadian Council of Muslim Women (CCMW) / Conseil canadien des femmes musulmanes
PO Box 154, Gananoque ON K7G 2T7
Tel: 613-383-2847
info@ccmw.com
www.ccmw.com
Overview: A medium-sized national organization founded in 1982
Chief Officer(s):
Razia Jaffer, President
Alia Hogben, Executive Director, 613-382-2847
Najet Hassan, Treasurer
Finances: *Funding Sources:* Fundraising; Public funds
Staff: 20 volunteer(s)
Membership: 100-499; *Fees:* Schedule available; *Member Profile:* Practising Muslim women
Activities: *Speaker Service:* Yes
Description: To assist Muslim women in participating effectively in Canadian society; To promote mutual understanding with women of other faiths
Publications: CCMW [Canadian Council of Muslim Women] National Newsletter
Type: Newsletter

Council on American-Islamic Relations Canada (CAIR-CAN)
PO Box 13219, Ottawa ON K2K 1X4
Tel: 613-254-9704; *Fax:* 613-254-9810
Toll-Free: 866-524-0004
info@caircan.ca
www.caircan.ca
Overview: A small international organization
Chief Officer(s):
Selma Djukic, Acting Chair
Ihsaan Gardee, Executive Director, 613-853-4111
Activities: Seminars & workshops; publication of guides, handbooks & media resource kits
Description: CAIR-CAN is a nonprofit organization promoting the civic engagement of Canadian Muslims, the protection of their human rights, & the education of non-Muslims so they may hold an accurate understanding of Islam. It is active in the areas of media relations, anti-discrimination & political advocacy.

International Development & Relief Foundation (IDRF)
#210, 2 Berkeley St., Toronto ON M5A 4J5
Tel: 416-497-0818; *Fax:* 416-497-0686
Toll-Free: 866-497-4373
office@idrf.ca
www.idrf.ca
www.facebook.com/group.php?gid=16466183244
twitter.com/IDRF
Overview: A small international organization founded in 1985
Chief Officer(s):
Winston Shyam Liaquat Kassim, Chair
Finances: *Annual Operating Budget:* $500,000-$1.5 Million
Staff: 9 staff member(s)
Activities: Providing relief, rehabilitation & development aid to communities in need, both overseas & in Canada; *Speaker Service:* Yes
Description: To empower the disadvantaged peoples of the world, through emergency relief & participatory development programs based on the Islamic principles of human dignity, self-reliance, & social justice; Affiliation(s): Canadian Council for International Cooperation

Islamic Affairs Council of Québec (IACQ)
1830, Thierry, Brossard QC J4W 2M8
Tel: 450-672-8027
naseer@library.mcgill.ca
Overview: A small local organization founded in 1991
Chief Officer(s):
Syed Naseer, President
Finances: *Annual Operating Budget:* Less than $50,000
Staff: 5 volunteer(s)
Description: Seeks effective cooperation among Islamic organizations & Muslims of all nationalities or schools of thought; seeks better understanding of Islam; assists media by open discussion; takes part in multicultural activities

Islamic Association of Nova Scotia (IANS)
42 Leaman Dr., Dartmouth NS B3A 2K9
Tel: 902-469-9490
info@islamnovascotia.ca
www.islamnovascotia.ca
Previous Name: Islamic Association of the Maritimes
Overview: A small local organization
Chief Officer(s):
Mohsin Rashid, President
rashid@eastlink.ca
Mohammed Amin Aliyar, Secretary
Fees: $50 single; $100 family; $25 student

Islamic Association of Saskatchewan (Saskatoon)
222 Copland Cres., Saskatoon SK S7H 2Z5
Tel: 306-665-6424
info@islamiccenter.sk.ca
www.islamiccenter.sk.ca
Overview: A small provincial organization founded in 1968
Chief Officer(s):
Khalil-Ur Rehman, President
president@islamiccenter.sk.ca
Aman Abid, Secretary
Fees: $40 family; $25 single; *Committees:* The Muslim Communications and Outreach Committee (MCOC); The Takaful Fund Committee (TFC); The Strategic Planning Committee (SPC); The Constitution Review Committee (CRC)
Activities: Operates Islamic Centre; represents Muslims; provides activities; responsible for Muslim Cemetery
Affiliation(s): Multi-Faith Group; Saskatchewan Organization for Heritage Language; Saskatchewan Intercultural Association; Saskatchewan Forum for "Racialized" Canadians; Saskatchewan Council for International Cooperation

Islamic Foundation of Toronto
441 Nugget Ave., Toronto ON M1S 5E1
Tel: 416-321-0909; *Fax:* 416-321-1995
info@islamicfoundation.ca
www.islamicfoundation.ca
Also Known As: Nugget Mosque
Overview: A small local charitable organization founded in 1969
Chief Officer(s):
Shakil Akhter, Administrator
Zaib Mirza, Social Services Coordinator
Finances: *Annual Operating Budget:* $3 Million-$5 Million
Staff: 72 staff member(s)
Membership: 1,000-4,999; *Committees:* DAwah; Library; School Board; Social Services
Activities: Full time Islamic school, JK to Grade 10; part-time evening Islamic school; Arabic language centre for adults; Friday & Sunday schools; *Library:* Yes (Open to Public)

Islamic Information Centre (IIC)
312 Lisgar St., Ottawa ON K2P 0E8
Tel: 613-232-0210; *Fax:* 613-232-0210
mail@islamottawa.com
www.islamottawa.com
Also Known As: Daw'ah Centre
Overview: A small national organization founded in 1993
Chief Officer(s):
Sulaiman Khan, Director
Finances: *Annual Operating Budget:* $50,000-$100,000
Staff: 2 staff member(s); 10 volunteer(s)
Membership: 35; *Fees:* $50; *Committees:* Business; Conference; Daw'ah; Membership; Newsletter
Activities: *Speaker Service:* Yes *Library:* Islamic Information (Open to Public)
Member of: Muslim Community Council of Ottawa; Affiliation(s): Islam Care Centre

Islamic Information Foundation (IIF)
8 Laurel Lane, Halifax NS B3M 2P6
Tel: 902-445-2494; *Fax:* 902-445-2494
Overview: A small national charitable organization founded in 1981
Chief Officer(s):
Jamal Badawi, Chairperson
Finances: *Annual Operating Budget:* $100,000-$250,000; *Funding Sources:* Sale of religious material; donations
Staff: 4 volunteer(s)
Membership: 40 individuals
Activities: *Speaker Service:* Yes
Description: To promote better understanding of Islam among Muslims & Christians through information provided in print, audio & video forms & through lecture, seminars & interfaith dialogues

Islamic Propagation Centre International (Canada) (IPCI (Canada))
5761 Coopers Ave., Mississauga ON L4Z 1R9
Tel: 905-507-3323; *Fax:* 905-507-3323
zsyed@ipci-canada.com
www.ipci-canada.com
Also Known As: Jama Masjid Mississauga
Overview: A small local charitable organization founded in 1984
Finances: *Annual Operating Budget:* $50,000-$100,000
Staff: 2 staff member(s); 100 volunteer(s)
Membership: 100 student; 1,000 individual; *Fees:* $200 individual; *Committees:* Fundraising; Eid & Ramadhan; Executive
Activities: Congregation; marriages; family counselling; summer & evening school for kids; *Speaker Service:* Yes *Library:* IPC Office Library (Open to Public) by appointment
Description: The Centre offers a selection of resource material for those interested in learning about Islam. Topics covered include comparative religion, history, culture, lifestyle, politics, law & women in Islam. It is a registered charity, BN: 886810191RR0001.

Manitoba Islamic Association (MIA)
247 Hazelwood Ave., Winnipeg MB R2M 4W1
Tel: 204-256-1347
editorialboard@miaonline.org
www.miaonline.org
www.facebook.com/pages/MIA-2011-2013/210028615746389
Overview: A small provincial organization founded in 1976
Chief Officer(s):
Ismael Mukhtar, President
Khaled Al-Nahar, Office Manager
Fees: $30; *Member Profile:* Muslim persons in Manitoba who abide by the association's rules & regulations; *Committees:* Takaful Fund
Activities: Accepting applications for financial assistance, through the Takaful Fund; Providing funeral services to the Muslim community, through partnership with Cropo Funeral Services; Offering services for marriage; Conducting Sunday Qur'an classes for children & the MIA Al Nur Weekend Islamic School; Sponsoring the Al-Hamd Learning Center, which offers an Arabic & Islamic educational program for preschoolers
Publications: Manitoba Muslim
Type: Newsletter *Accepts Advertising*
Profile: Editorials, reports, articles, announcements, community news, & local events

Muslim Association of Canada (MAC)
#332, 1568 Merivale Rd., Ottawa ON K2G 5Y7
Tel: 613-321-5000; *Fax:* 613-321-5001
mac@macnet.ca
www.macnet.ca
Overview: A medium-sized national organization
Activities: Schools & community centres; educational & other projects; youth projects; outreach
Description: Seeks to promote a balanced, constructive & integrated Islamic presence in Canada; operates in 11 Canadian cities

Muslim Community of Québec (MCQ) / Communauté musulmane du Québec
7445, av Chester, Montréal QC H4V 1M4
Tel: 514-484-2967; *Fax:* 514-484-3802
Also Known As: Mosque of Montréal
Overview: A small local organization founded in 1979
Chief Officer(s):
Mohammed M. Amin, Founder
Finances: *Annual Operating Budget:* $500,000-$1.5 Million
Membership: 500
Activities: *Speaker Service:* Yes
Description: To facilitate Muslim religious life

Muslim Education & Welfare Foundation of Canada (MEWFC)
Southbourne Centre, #101, 6125 Sussex Ave, Burnaby BC V5H 4G1
Tel: 604-715-4096
al.iman.education.metrotown@gmail.com
Also Known As: Al Iman Education
Overview: A medium-sized national charitable organization founded in 1987
Chief Officer(s):
Abdellah Seddiki, Teacher
Activities: *Library:* Jannat Bibi Library
Description: To provide for the educational, religious & welfare needs of the Muslim community

Muslim World League - Canada
#3, 6680 Campobello Rd., Mississauga ON L5N 2L8
Tel: 905-542-1050; *Fax:* 905-542-1054
mwl@mwlcanada.org
www.mwlcanada.org
Overview: A small national organization founded in 1985
Chief Officer(s):
Mohamad Khatib, Director
abusinan@yahoo.com
Member Profile: Muslims
Activities: *Rents Mailing List:* Yes *Library:* Yes (Open to Public)
Description: The League is a non-profit, non-governmental organization that serves the religious needs of Muslims in Canada. It promotes Islam & Islamic teachings among Canadian Muslims & helps non-Muslims grasp an accurate understanding of the religion. It also serves as a resource centre, publishing booklets & flyers on current issues.; Affiliation(s): Muslim World League, Makkah, Saudia Arabia

Ottawa Muslim Community Circle (OMCC)
PO Box 29105, Stn. Barrhaven, Nepean ON K2J 4A9
Tel: 613-825-7059; *Fax:* 613-825-4667
omcc@magma.ca
www.magma.ca/~omcc
Overview: A small local organization founded in 1984
Chief Officer(s):
Mahmood Rasheed, President
Finances: *Annual Operating Budget:* Less than $50,000
Staff: 15 volunteer(s)
Membership: 400
Activities: Social services; seminars & conferences
Description: To foster unity among various Muslims; to promote better understanding of Muslims & Islam among Canadians of other faiths; to maintain cultural identity

Scarborough Muslim Association (SMA)
2665 Lawrence Ave. East, Toronto ON M1P 2S2
Tel: 416-750-2253; *Fax:* 416-750-1616
info@smacanada.ca
www.smacanada.ca
Overview: A small local organization
Chief Officer(s):
Yakub Hatia, President

Windsor Islamic Association (WIA)
c/o Windsor Mosque, 1320 Northwood Dr., Windsor ON N9W 1A4
Tel: 519-966-2355
wia@windsormosque.com
www.wiao.org
www.facebook.com/windsormosque
Overview: A small local organization founded in 1964
Chief Officer(s):
Osman Tarabain, President
Abdallah Shamisa, Vice-President
Majed Mahmoud, Secretary
Description: Serves a population of over 25,000 Muslims in the Windsor locality; Affiliation(s): World Muslim League

Janism

Jain Society of Toronto (JSOT)
48 Rosemeade Ave., Etobicoke ON M8Y 3A5
Tel: 416-251-8112
info@jsotcanada.org
www.jsotcanada.org
www.facebook.com/pages/Jain-Society-of-Toronto-Inc/113683345319551
Overview: A organization founded in 1974
Chief Officer(s):
Arpana Vora, President
arpana7@hotmail.com
Activities: Picnics, cultural dances, ski camps
Description: The objective to provide a forum for Jains to observe and perform various activities related to Jainism, to preserve Jain culture for future generations, and to promote fellowship among all Jains.

Jehovah's Witnesses

Watch Tower Bible & Tract Society of Canada
PO Box 4100, Georgetown ON L7G 4Y4
Tel: 905-873-4100; *Fax:* 905-873-4554
www.watchtower.org
Also Known As: Jehovah's Witnesses
Overview: A medium-sized national organization
Chief Officer(s):
Kenneth Little, President
Description: To serve Jehovah's Witnesses in Canada

Judaism

Canadian Council for Reform Judaism
#301, 3845 Bathurst St., Toronto ON M3H 3N2
Tel: 416-630-0375; *Fax:* 416-630-5089
Toll-Free: 800-560-8242
ccrj@urj.org
urj.org/ccrj/
Previous Name: Canadian Council of Reform Rabbis
Overview: A medium-sized national organization
Chief Officer(s):
Sharon L. Sobel, Executive Director
Description: The CCRJ is the Canadian region of the Union for Reform Judasim Congregations, and serves as the umbrella organization for Reform Judaism in Canada, representing about 10,000 households in 26 affiliated congregations.; *Member of:* Union for Reform Judaism

Chosen People Ministries (Canada)
PO Box 897, Stn. B, Toronto ON M2K 2R1
Tel: 416-250-0177; *Fax:* 416-250-9235
Toll-Free: 888-442-5535
info@chosenpeople.ca
www.chosenpeople.ca
Also Known As: Beth Sar Shalom Mission
Overview: A medium-sized national charitable organization founded in 1894
Chief Officer(s):
Jorge Sedaca, Director
Finances: *Annual Operating Budget:* $500,000-$1.5 Million; *Funding Sources:* Donations
Staff: 14 staff member(s)
Activities: *Speaker Service:* Yes; *Rents Mailing List:* Yes
Description: To share the Good News of Jesus the Messiah and help others do the same

Congregation Beth Israel - British Columbia
4350 Oak St., Vancouver BC V6H 2N4
Tel: 604-731-4161; *Fax:* 604-731-4989
info@bethisrael.ca
www.bethisrael.ca
Overview: A small local organization founded in 1932
Chief Officer(s):
Catherine Epstein, President
Jonathan Infeld, Klei Kodesh
rabbiinfeld@bethisrael.ca
Shannon Etkin, Executive Director
shannon@bethisrael.ca
Activities: Youth programs; Hebrew school; facility rental; Rabbi Wilfred & Phyllis Solomon Museum; *Library:* Moe Cohen Library (Open to Public)
Description: The congregation is dedicated to the strengthening of all aspects of Jewish life, including worship & Torah study, religious, educational & social activities for all ages, & the observance of life cycle events.; *Member of:* United Synagogue of Conservative Judaism

National Council of Jewish Women of Canada
#118, 1588 Main St., Winnipeg MB R2V 1Y3
Tel: 204-339-9700; *Fax:* 204-334-3779
info@ncjwc.org
www.ncjwc.org
Overview: A medium-sized national charitable organization founded in 1897
Description: To further human welfare in the Jewish & general communities; To help fulfill unmet needs & to serve the individual & the community; *Member of:* UNESCO Canadian Subcommission of the Status of Women; Jewish Women Against Domestic Violence; Coalition for Agunot Rights; Affiliation(s): International Council of Jewish Women

Orthodox Rabbinical Council of British Columbia
#401, 1037 West Broadway, Vancouver BC V6H 1E3
Tel: 604-731-1803; *Fax:* 604-731-1804
info@bckosher.org
www.bckosher.org
Also Known As: BC Kosher
Overview: A small provincial charitable organization founded in 1983
Finances: *Annual Operating Budget:* $100,000-$250,000
Staff: 4 staff member(s); 6 volunteer(s)
Membership: 1-99
Activities: Providing information about Kashruth (kosher food - kashruth symbol BCK); *Speaker Service:* Yes

Shaare Zion Congregation
5575 Côte St. Luc Rd., Montréal QC H3X 2C9
Tel: 514-481-7727; *Fax:* 514-481-1219
info@shaarezion.org
www.shaarezion.org
Overview: A small local charitable organization
Chief Officer(s):
David Moscovitch, Executive Director
david.moscovitch@shaarezion.org
Lionel E. Moses, Rabbi
Affiliation(s): United Synagogue of Conservative Judiasm

Toronto Association of Synagogue & Temple Administrators
1445 Eglinton Ave. West, Toronto ON M6C 2E6
Tel: 416-783-6103; *Fax:* 416-783-9923
Overview: A small local organization
Chief Officer(s):
Barbara Berke, President
Finances: *Annual Operating Budget:* Less than $50,000
Membership: 12; *Fees:* $50; *Member Profile:* Executive directors of synagogues & temples

Vaad Harabonim (Orthodox Rabbinical Council)
3600 Bathurst St., Toronto ON M6A 2C9
Tel: 416-787-1631; *Fax:* 416-785-5378
Also Known As: Rabbinical Council of Ontario
Overview: A small provincial organization founded in 1982
Finances: *Annual Operating Budget:* Less than $50,000
Membership: 40
Description: To serve & guide the Jewish community

Lutheran

Canadian Lutheran World Relief (CLWR)
Portage Place Mall, #302, 393 Portage Ave., Winnipeg MB R3B 3H6
Tel: 204-694-5602; *Fax:* 204-694-5460
Toll-Free: 800-661-2597
clwr@clwr.mb.ca
www.clwr.org
Overview: A large national charitable organization founded in 1946
Chief Officer(s):
Robert Granke, Executive Director, 204-631-0113
Tom Brook, Director, Community Relations Team, 204-631-0115

Irma McKenzie, Director, Administration & Human Resources Team, 204-631-0502
Elaine Peters, Director, Program Team, 204-631-0116
Lyn Stienstra, Director, Finance Team, 204-631-0507
Finances: *Funding Sources:* Lutheran churches; Canadian International Development Agency; Province of Saskatchewan
Activities: *Speaker Service:* Yes
Description: To provide development programming in Africa, Asia, Latin America, & the Middle East; To provide emergency relief in case of disaster; To enable sponsorships for refugee resettlement in Canada; To focus on development, peace building, alternative approaches to trade, education, & community building; *Member of:* Canadian Council for International Cooperation; Manitoba Council for International Cooperation; Affiliation(s): Canadian Foodgrains Bank; Inter-Church Action
Publications: Canadian Lutheran World Relief Annual Report
Type: Yearbook *Frequency:* Annually
Profile: Distributed to CLWR donors
Canadian Lutheran World Relief Bulletin of Reports
Type: Yearbook *Frequency:* Annually
Profile: CLWR activities & financial information
CLWR [Canadian Lutheran World Relief] News Briefs
Type: Newsletter *Frequency:* Weekly
Profile: Summary of significant CLWR-related news events in Canada or around the world
CLWR [Canadian Lutheran World Relief] Monthly Briefs
Frequency: Monthly
Profile: Information for constituents about events in the developing world & the response of Canadians
Four Corners [a publication of the Canadian Lutheran World Relief]
Type: Newsletter *Frequency:* Semiannually
Profile: News about alternative trade to create opportunities for artists in the developing world
Partnership Newsletter [a publication of the Canadian Lutheran World Relief]
Type: Newsletter *Frequency:* Quarterly *Editor:* Lorne Kletke
ISSN: 1916-2308
Profile: Inspirational stories about people in the developing world

Estonian Evangelical Lutheran Church Consistory (EELC Consistory)
383 Jarvis St., Toronto ON M5B 2C7
Tel: 416-925-5465; *Fax:* 416-925-5688
e.e.l.k@eelk.ee
www.eelk.ee/eelcabroad.html
Overview: A small national organization founded in 1950
Chief Officer(s):
Udo Petersoo, Archbishop & Dean of Canada
udo.petersoo@eelk.ee
Membership: 7,200 + 13 churches
Description: EELC is an independent, self-governing church which functions on democratic grounds, calls together congregations, ordains pastors, holds services & carries out religious ceremonies according to the Service Book, the Statutes & the established order. The Consistory is the government of the EELC.; Affiliation(s): Lutheran World Federation; World Council of Churches

Evangelical Lutheran Church in Canada (ELCIC)
#302, 393 Portage Ave., Winnipeg MB R3B 3H6
Tel: 204-984-9150; *Fax:* 204-984-9185
Toll-Free: 888-786-6707
www.elcic.ca
Overview: A medium-sized national charitable organization founded in 1986
Chief Officer(s):
Susan Johnson, Bishop
Donald Storch, Secretary
Ken Hartviksen, Treasurer
Finances: *Annual Operating Budget:* $1.5 Million-$3 Million; *Funding Sources:* Donations
Staff: 20 staff member(s)
Membership: 153,000 individuals; 607 congregations; *Member Profile:* Current members in a congregation
Description: The Church shares the gospel of Jesus Christ with people in Canada & around the world through the proclamation of the Word, celebration of the sacraments, & through service in Christ's name. It functions through three major entities: nationally as the ELCIC, regionally as synods, & locally as congregations.; *Member of:* Canadian Council of Churches; Lutheran Council in Canada; Lutheran World Federation; World Council of Churches

Lutheran Association of Missionaries & Pilots (LAMP)
4966 - 92 Ave. NW, Edmonton AB T6B 2V4
Tel: 780-466-8507; *Fax:* 780-466-6733
Toll-Free: 800-307-4036
office@lampministry.org
www.lampministry.org
Social Media: www.youtube.com/user/LAMPMinistry/videos
www.facebook.com/group.php?gid=233505351133
Overview: A small international organization founded in 1970
Chief Officer(s):
Ron Ludke, Executive Director
ron@lampministry.org
Finances: *Annual Operating Budget:* $500,000-$1.5 Million
Staff: 300 volunteer(s)
Activities: *Speaker Service:* Yes *Library:* Yes (Open to Public)
Description: To share Jesus Christ with the people of remote areas of Canada; Affiliation(s): Lutheran Church Canada; Evangelical Lutheran Church in Canada

Lutheran Bible Translators of Canada Inc. (LBTC)
PO Box 934, Kitchener ON N2G 4E3
Tel: 519-742-3361; *Fax:* 519-742-5989
Toll-Free: 866-518-7071
info@lbtc.ca
www.lbtc.ca
Overview: A small international charitable organization founded in 1974
Finances: *Annual Operating Budget:* $250,000-$500,000
Staff: 5 staff member(s)
Membership: 1-99
Activities: *Speaker Service:* Yes
Description: To bring people to faith in Jesus Christ through Bible translations & literacy work; Affiliation(s): Canadian Council of Christian Charities

Mennonites

Calgary Mennonite Centre for Newcomers Society
#125, 920 - 36th St. NE, Calgary AB T2A 6L8
Tel: 403-569-3325; *Fax:* 403-248-5041
newcomer@cmcn.ab.ca
www.centrefornewcomers.ca
Overview: A small local organization founded in 1988
Chief Officer(s):
Dale Taylor, Executive Director, Centre for Newcomers, 403-537-8800
Member Profile: Members beyond the Mennonite constituency is enoucraged.
Activities: Calgary Career Show for immigrant youth; preschool activities for immigrant children; employment preparation courses; anti-bullying workshop; EthniCity Catering Program; ESL classes
Description: The Society is a not-for-profit, registered charity that operates the Centre for Newcomers, assisting refugees & immigrants arriving in Calgary to meet their settlement needs.; Affiliation(s): Canadian Red Cross

Canadian Conference of Mennonite Brethren Churches
1310 Taylor Ave., Winnipeg MB R3M 3Z6
Tel: 204-669-6575; *Fax:* 204-654-1865
Toll-Free: 888-669-6575
www.mbconf.ca
Overview: A medium-sized national organization founded in 1945
Chief Officer(s):
Willy Reimer, Executive Director
Finances: *Funding Sources:* Donations
Staff: 19 staff member(s)
Membership: 31,264; *Committees:* Mennonite Central Committee; Mennonite Disaster Service; Manitoba Missions/Service
Activities: *Library:* Centre for M.B. Studies (Open to Public)
Description: To glorify God, to nurture & equip members to live the Christian life, & to mobilize them for ministry
Publications: Chinese Manitoba Brethren Herald
Frequency: Monthly
Profile: Written in Chinese, the Herald serves the conference's Chinese community
Le Lien
Frequency: Bimonthly
Profile: Written in French, the publication serves the conference's francophone churches in Québec
Mennonite Brethren Herald
Frequency: Monthly
Profile: Feature articles, columns, letters, news, people, & events for the Mennonite Brethren community

Communitas Supportive Care Society
#103, 2776 Bourquin Cres. West, Abbotsford BC V2S 6A4
Tel: 604-850-6608; *Fax:* 604-850-2634
Toll-Free: 800-622-5455
office@communitascare.com
www.communitascare.com
www.linkedin.com/company/communitas-supportive-care-society
www.facebook.com/group.php?gid=121270768851
Previous Name: Mennonite Central Committee Supportive Care Services Society
Overview: A small local organization
Finances: *Annual Operating Budget:* Greater than $5 Million
Activities: *Awareness Events:* Curl for Care, Jan.
Description: Provide various resources to persons living & dealing with mental, physical &/or emotional disabilities.; *Member of:* Association for Community Living; Community Social Services Employers Association; Psychosocial Rehabilitation Canada; BC Association for Child Development & Intervention; Denominational Health Association; Fraser Valley Brain Injury Association; Affiliation(s): Jean Vanier; Henri Nouwen; Copeland Centre for Wellness & Recovery; International Initiative for Mental Health; Living Room; Mental

Health Commission of Canada; STEP Enterprises; Mennonite Central Committee (British Columbia & Canada); Mennonite Disaster Service; Ten Thousand Villages

Evangelical Mennonite Conference (EMC)
440 Main St., Steinbach MB R5G 1Z5
Tel: 204-326-6401; *Fax:* 204-326-1613
www.emconf.ca
www.facebook.com/emconference
Overview: A medium-sized national charitable organization founded in 1812
Chief Officer(s):
Tim Dyck, General Secretary
Finances: *Annual Operating Budget:* $1.5 Million-$3 Million; *Funding Sources:* Donations
Membership: 7,300
Activities: *Library:* Evangelical Mennonite Conference Archives
Description: To encourage local churches to work together on missions in Canada & around the world

MBMS International (MBMSI) / Mennonite Brethren Mission & Service International
International & Western Canada (BC), #302, 32025 George Ferguson Way, Abbotsford BC V2T 2K7
Tel: 604-859-6267; *Fax:* 604-589-6422
Toll-Free: 866-964-7627
mbmsi@mbmsi.org
www.mbmsi.org
Also Known As: Board of Missions & Services of the Mennonite Brethren Churches of North America
Overview: A medium-sized local charitable organization founded in 1900
Chief Officer(s):
Ike Bergen, Chair
Randy Friesen, General Director
randyf@mbmsi.org
John Best, Regional Mobilizer, Western Canada
johnb@mbmsi.org
Finances: *Annual Operating Budget:* Greater than $5 Million; *Funding Sources:* Voluntary contributions; grants
Staff: 2 staff member(s)
Activities: Cross-cultural mission agency of Mennonite Brethren churches in Canada & the US; *Internships:* Yes; *Speaker Service:* Yes
Description: To make disciples & plant churches globally through church planting & envangelism, discipleship & leadership training & social ministry; *Member of:* Evangelical Fellowship of Mission Agencies

Mennonite Church Canada (MC Canada)
600 Shaftesbury Blvd., Winnipeg MB R3P 0M4
Tel: 204-888-6781; *Fax:* 204-831-5675
Toll-Free: 866-888-6785
office@mennonitechurch.ca; resources@mennonitechurch.ca
www.mennonitechurch.ca
Also Known As: Conference of Mennonites in Canada
Overview: A medium-sized national charitable organization founded in 1903
Chief Officer(s):
Willard Metzger, General Secretary
Finances: *Funding Sources:* Donations
Staff: 40 staff member(s)
Membership: 33,000 baptized believers in 225 congregations & 5 area conferences
Activities: *Library:* Resource Centre
Description: To form a people of God; To become a global church; To grow leaders

Mennonite Economic Development Associates Canada
#I-106, 155 Frobisher Dr., Waterloo ON N2V 2E4
Tel: 519-725-1633; *Fax:* 519-725-9083
Toll-Free: 800-665-7026
meda@meda.org
www.meda.org
Also Known As: MEDA Canada
Overview: A medium-sized international charitable organization founded in 1953
Chief Officer(s):
Allan Sauder, President
Finances: *Annual Operating Budget:* $1.5 Million-$3 Million
Membership: 3,000 Canada & US
Activities: *Library:* Yes by appointment
Description: To be committed to the nurture & expression of Christian faith in a business setting; To enable members to integrate biblical values & business principles in their daily lives; To address the needs of the disadvantaged through programs of economic development

Mennonite Foundation of Canada (MFC)
#12, 1325 Markham Rd., Winnipeg MB R3T 4J6
Tel: 204-488-1985; *Fax:* 204-488-1986
Toll-Free: 800-772-3257
contact@mennofoundation.ca
www.mennofoundation.ca
Overview: A medium-sized national charitable organization founded in 1974
Chief Officer(s):
Lloyd Plett, Chair
Darren Pries-Klassen, Executive Director, 905-934-0484 23, Fax: 905-935-0153
dpklassen@mennofoundation.ca
Dori Zerbe Cornelsen, Stewardship Consultant, Winnipeg
mfcwpg@mennofoundation.ca
Finances: *Annual Operating Budget:* $500,000-$1.5 Million
Staff: 12 staff member(s)
Membership: 24; *Member Profile:* Representatives of 7 conferences
Activities: *Speaker Service:* Yes *Library:* Yes (Open to Public)
Description: The Foundation was established to accumulate, manage & distribute financial resources exclusively for charitable purposes, as a means, for example, of supporting the Mennonite Community by providing loans to churches & related organizations. Resources provide stewardship education & service from an Anabaptist perspective. It is a registered charity, BN: 129253308RR0001.; Affiliation(s): Mennonite Church Canada; Evangelical Mennonite Mission Conference; Mennonite Church Eastern Canada; Northwest Mennonite Conference; Evangelical Mennonite Conference; Chortitzer Mennonite Conference; Evangelical Missionary Church of Canada

Northwest Mennonite Conference
PO Box 1316, 2025 - 20 Ave., Didsbury AB T0M 0W0
Tel: 403-337-3283
www.nwmc.ca
Overview: A medium-sized local organization
Chief Officer(s):
Carol Gelleny, Contact
Membership: 14 congregations; *Committees:* Congregational Ministries; Congregational Leadership; Missions & Service; Stewardship
Member of: Mennonite Church North America

Methodists

The Bible Holiness Movement / Mouvement de sainteté biblique
PO Box 223, Stn. A, Vancouver BC V6C 2M3
Tel: 250-492-3376
www.bible-holiness-movement.com
Previous Name: The Bible Holiness Mission
Overview: A medium-sized international charitable organization founded in 1949
Chief Officer(s):
Wesley H. Wakefield, Bishop-General
Finances: *Annual Operating Budget:* $100,000-$250,000; *Funding Sources:* Unsolicited gifts from Christian believers
Staff: 16 staff member(s); 6 volunteer(s)
Membership: 93,658 worldwide in 89 countries; 954 Canadian; *Fees:* None
Activities: *Internships:* Yes; *Speaker Service:* Yes *Library:* Yes by appointment
Description: To emphasize the original Methodist faith of salvation & scriptural holiness, with principles of discipline, non-conformity, & non-resistance, & to administer overseas indigenous missionary centres in West Africa, the Philippines, East Africa & the West Indies; South Korea, India; *Member of:* Christian Holiness Partnership; National Black Evangelical Association; Anti-Slavery International; Affiliation(s): Religious Freedom of Council of Christian Minorities; Christians Concerned for Racial Equality

Free Methodist Church in Canada (FMCIC) / Église méthodiste libre du Canada
4315 Village Centre Ct., Mississauga ON L4Z 1S2
Tel: 905-848-2600; *Fax:* 905-848-2603
ministrycentre@fmc-canada.org
www.fmc-canada.org
www.facebook.com/137599632927885
Overview: A medium-sized national organization founded in 1880
Chief Officer(s):
Daniel Sheffield, Director, Global & Intercultural Ministries
Jared Siebert, Director, Growth Ministries
Mark Molczanski, Director, Administrative Services
Keith A. Elford
Kim Henderson, Director, Personnel
Finances: *Annual Operating Budget:* $1.5 Million-$3 Million
Staff: 11 staff member(s)
Membership: 12,000+ attendees at 144 churches
Activities: *Internships:* Yes; *Speaker Service:* Yes
Description: To make known to people everywhere God's call to wholeness through forgiveness & holiness in Jesus Christ & to invite into membership & to equip for ministry all who respond in faith; to see healthy churches within the reach of all people in Canada & beyond.; *Member of:* Free Methodist World Conference; Affiliation(s): Evangelical Fellowship of Canada; Canadian Council of Christian Charities; World Relief Canada

The Wesleyan Church of Canada - Atlantic District
229 Beulah Rd., Browns Flat NB E5M 2R5
Tel: 506-468-2286; *Fax:* 506-468-2004
office@atlanticdistrict.com
www.atlanticdistrict.com
Overview: A medium-sized local organization
Chief Officer(s):
David W. LeRoy, District Superintendent

The Wesleyan Church of Canada - Central Canada District
17 St. Paul St., Belleville ON K8N 1A4
Tel: 613-966-7527; *Fax:* 613-968-6190
ccd@on.aibn.com
www.ccdwesleyan.com
Also Known As: The Wesleyan Methodist Church of Canada
Overview: A medium-sized national charitable organization founded in 1897
Chief Officer(s):
Donald E. Hodgins, District Superintendent
Finances: *Annual Operating Budget:* $500,000-$1.5 Million; *Funding Sources:* District churches
Staff: 3 staff member(s)
Membership: 1,736; *Member Profile:* Covenant members & community members
Activities: *Internships:* Yes
Description: To create a context that produces healthy churches; Affiliation(s): Tyndale Seminary; World Hope International; World Relief Canada; Bethany Bible College; Outreach Canada; Evangelical Fellowship of Canada

Mormonism

Church of Jesus Christ of Latter-day Saints
c/o Toronto Ontario Temple, 10060 Bramalea Rd., Brampton ON L6R 1A1
Tel: 905-799-1122
www.lds.org
Overview: A medium-sized national organization founded in 1830
Membership: 178,000 members + 324 congregations in Canada
Activities: *Speaker Service:* Yes *Library:* Family History Library by appointment

Community of Christ - Canada East Mission
390 Speedvale Ave. East, Guelph ON N1E 1N5
Tel: 519-822-4150; *Fax:* 519-822-1236
Toll-Free: 888-411-7537
contact@CofChrist.org
www.cofchrist.org
Also Known As: Saints' Church
Previous Name: Reorganized Church of Jesus Christ of Latter Day Saints (Canada)
Overview: A medium-sized local charitable organization founded in 1830
Chief Officer(s):
Ken Barrows, Canada East Mission President
ken@communityofchrist.ca
Jim Poirier, Canadian Bishop & Financial Officer
jim@communityofchrist.ca
Description: To promote communities of joy, hope, love, & peace

Community of Christ - Canada West Mission (CWM)
Stn. General Delivery, Edgerton AB T3G 1B5
Tel: 877-411-2632; *Fax:* 403-239-3542
Toll-Free: 877-411-2632
darrell@communityofchrist.ca
www.communityofchrist.ca/west/west.htm
Overview: A medium-sized local organization
Chief Officer(s):
Greg Goheen, President & CFO, 403-537-2565
greg@communityofchrist.ca
Description: To promote communities of joy, hope, love, & peace
Publications: Family Camps, Youth Camps, Retreats
Type: Directory
Profile: Dates, directors & registrars of upcoming camps & retreats
The Mission Messenger
Type: Newsletter

Profile: Articles & events to inform members & friends of the church

New Thought

Association of Unity Churches Canada
2631 Kingsway Dr., Kitchener ON N2C 1A7
Tel: 519-894-0810
info@unitycanada.org
www.unitycanada.org
Also Known As: Unity
Overview: A small national charitable organization founded in 1978
Chief Officer(s):
Doris Lewis, President
info@unityvictoria.ca
Pat Ball, Exec. Assistant
revpatball@gmail.com
Finances: *Annual Operating Budget:* $50,000-$100,000
Membership: 20 churches
Activities: *Internships:* Yes; *Speaker Service:* Yes
Description: Unity is a Christian association asserting that reunion with God in mind brings certain fulfillment in life. It is a registered charity, BN: 118794544RR0001.; Affiliation(s): Association of Unity Churches USA

Orthodox

The Canadian Orthodox Church (COC) / L'Église Orthodoxe canadienne (EOC)
37323 Hawkins Pickle Rd., Dewdney BC V0M 1H0
Tel: 604-826-9336; *Fax:* 604-820-5247
synaxis@new-ostrog.org
www.orthodoxcanada.org
Overview: A medium-sized national organization founded in 1970
Chief Officer(s):
Lazar Puhalo, Archbishop
Finances: *Funding Sources:* Publications; candle factory sales
Membership: 2,000
Activities: *Speaker Service:* Yes *Library:* Yes (Open to Public) by appointment
Member of: Ukrainian Orthodox Church, Kiev, Ukraine; Affiliation(s): The Nemanjic Institute for Serbo-Byzantine Studies; Centre for Canadian Orthodox Studies

The Coptic Orthodox Church (Canada)
St. Mark's Coptic Orthodox Church, 41 Glendinning Ave., Toronto ON M1W 3E2
Tel: 416-494-4449; *Fax:* 416-494-4196
mail@coptorthodox.ca
www.stmark.toronto.on.coptorthodox.ca
Overview: A small national organization
Chief Officer(s):
M.A. Marcos, Protopriest
Membership: 45,000
Member of: The Canadian Council of Churches; Coptic Orthodox Patriarchate

Greek Orthodox Metropolis of Toronto (Canada)
86 Overlea Blvd., Toronto ON M4H 1C6
Tel: 416-429-5757; *Fax:* 416-429-4588
metropolis@gocanada.org
www.gocanada.org
Previous Name: Greek Orthodox Church (Canada)
Overview: A large national organization
Membership: Over 50,000
Description: There are 76 Greek Orthodox Communities in Canada under the jurisdiction of the Greek Orthodox Metropolis of Toronto (Canada); *Member of:* The Canadian Council of Churches

Romanian Orthodox Deanery of Canada
PO Box 4023, Regina SK S4P 3R9
romanianorthodoxdeanery.org
Overview: A small national organization
Chief Officer(s):
Nathaniel Popp, Archbishop, 517-522-4800
nathaniel@roea.org
Ionel Cudritescu, Dean, Eastern Canada, 416-614-1942
icudritescu5303@rogers.com
Michael Lupu, Dean, Western Canada, 403-203-7033
fatherlupu@shaw.ca
Description: The Romanian Orthodox Episcopate of America is grouped geographically into 7 deaneries & the Deanery of Canada is one of them, with 30 parishes across the country. It is non-profit, registered charity, BN: 888289642RR0001.; *Member of:* Romanian Orthodox Episcopate of America; Orthodox Church in America

Serbian Orthodox Church in the United States of America & Canada - Diocese of Canada
7470 McNiven Rd., RR#3, Campbellville ON L0B 1B0
Tel: 905-878-0043; *Fax:* 905-878-1909
vladika@istocnik.com
www.istocnik.com
Overview: A medium-sized national charitable organization founded in 1983
Chief Officer(s):
Georgije, 905-878-3438
Finances: *Annual Operating Budget:* $500,000-$1.5 Million; *Funding Sources:* Donations; parish taxes; dispensations
Staff: 23 staff member(s)
Membership: 150,000; *Committees:* Diocesan Executive Board; Diocesan Assembly
Activities: *Library:* Holy Transfiguration (Open to Public) by appointment
Description: To serve the Serbian Orthodox community & teach the Orthodox faith & culture

Ukrainian Orthodox Church of Canada
Ecumenical Patriarchate, 9 St. Johns Ave., Winnipeg MB R2W 1G8
Tel: 204-586-3093; *Fax:* 204-582-5241
Toll-Free: 877-586-3093
consistory@uocc.ca
www.uocc.ca
Overview: A large national organization founded in 1918
Chief Officer(s):
John Stinka, Archbishop
Yurij Kalistchuk, Archbishop
Victor Lakusta, Chancellor
Membership: 120,000
Activities: *Speaker Service:* Yes *Library:* Yes (Open to Public) by appointment

World Fellowship of Orthodox Youth - Syndesmos
Syndesmos General Secretariat, PO Box 66051, Holargos 15510 Greece
syndesmos@syndesmos.org
www.syndesmos.org
Also Known As: Syndesmos
Overview: A small international organization founded in 1953
Chief Officer(s):
Christopher D'Aloisio, President
christophedaloisio@hotmail.com
Tony El Soury, Vice-President
telsoury@Tidm.net.lb
Tsimouris Spyros, Secretary General
Finances: *Annual Operating Budget:* $50,000-$100,000; *Funding Sources:* Orthodox churches; Orthodox church organisations; council of Eurpoe; European Christina Diakonia age
Staff: 2 staff member(s); 4 volunteer(s)
Membership: 121 organizations in 42 countries; *Fees:* $500 affiliated; *Member Profile:* Christian Orthodox youth organizations & theological schools; *Committees:* Publications
Activities: Orthodox youth camps, festivals, encounters, seminars, consultations, conferences, training courses, workshops; *Internships:* Yes *Library:* Yes (Open to Public)
Description: To serve as a bond of unity among Orthodox youth movements, organisations & theological schools around the world, promoting a consciousness of the catholicity of the Orthodox faith; to foster relations, coordination & mutal aid among them; to promote among young people a full understanding of the Orthodox faith & the mission of the Church in the contemporary world & an active participation of youth in ecclesial life; to promote a way of life founded in eucharistic communion, in the Gospel & in patristic teaching, for witness & service to the world; to assist & promote Orthodox effocrts for visible Christian unity & for positive relations with people of other faiths; to encourage reflection & action on issues affecting the lives of Orthodox Christians & the local churches; to be an instrument for furthering cooperation & deeper communion between the Orthodox Church & the Oriental Orthodox Churches

Pentecostal

The Apostolic Church in Canada
220 Adelaide St. North, London ON N6B 3H4
Tel: 519-438-7036; *Fax:* 519-438-5800
cheryl@apostolic.ca
www.apostolic.ca
Overview: A small national organization founded in 1934
Chief Officer(s):
D. Karl Thomas, National Leader
Finances: *Annual Operating Budget:* $500,000-$1.5 Million
Staff: 15 staff member(s)
Membership: 500-999
Activities: *Internships:* Yes

Apostolic Church of Pentecost of Canada Inc. (ACOP) / Église apostolique de Pentecôte du Canada inc.
International Office, #119, 2340 Pegasus Way NE, Calgary AB T2E 8M5
Tel: 403-273-5777; *Fax:* 403-273-8102
acop@acop.ca
www.acop.ca
Overview: A small national licensing charitable organization founded in 1921
Chief Officer(s):
Wes Mills, President & National Director
Finances: *Annual Operating Budget:* $1.5 Million-$3 Million; *Funding Sources:* Donations
Staff: 30 staff member(s)
Membership: 155 affiliated churches + 436 members; *Fees:* Varies
Activities: *Internships:* Yes; *Speaker Service:* Yes *Library:* Yes by appointment
Description: To provide fellowship, encouragement & accountability in the proclamation of the Gospel of Jesus Christ by the Power of the Holy Spirit; Affiliation(s): Evangelical Fellowship of Canada

Church of God of Prophecy in Canada
Eastern Canada Head Office, 5145 Tomken Rd., Mississauga ON L4W 1P1
Tel: 905-625-1278; *Fax:* 905-625-1316
info@cogop.ca
www.cogop.ca
Overview: A medium-sized national charitable organization
Finances: *Annual Operating Budget:* $100,000-$250,000
Staff: 3 staff member(s)
Membership: 31 churches
Activities: *Internships:* Yes; *Speaker Service:* Yes
Description: The Church of God of Prophecy has its roots in the Holiness/Pentecostal tradition and has felt a special burden to call attention to the principle of unity in the body of Christ, while faithfully proclaiming the gospel of Jesus Christ before a watching world.

General Conference of the Canadian Assemblies of God / Conférence générale des assemblées de dieu canadiennes
PO Box 37315, Stn. Marquette, 6724 Fabre St., Montréal QC H2E 3B5
Tel: 514-279-1100; *Fax:* 514-279-1131
info@caogonline.org
www.caogonline.org
Previous Name: Italian Pentecostal Church of Canada
Overview: A small national charitable organization founded in 1912
Chief Officer(s):
Dino Cianflone, General Treasurer
Daniel Ippolito, Overseer Emeritus
David Di Staulo, General Superintendent
Raymond Narula, General Secretary
Giulio Gabeli, Overseer
Finances: *Annual Operating Budget:* $100,000-$250,000
Staff: 2 staff member(s); 3 volunteer(s)
Membership: 6,000 + 21 affiliated churches
Activities: Hosting an annual conference; *Internships:* Yes
Description: To provide distinctive ministry to the Italian community, extending to all Canadians, regardless of language, nationality, or race; To proclaim the gospel of Jesus Christ in the power of the Holy Spirit throughout Canada & the world, based on the biblical standard of ministry in the New Testament; *Member of:* The Evangelical Fellowship of Canada; Canadian Council of Christian Charities

Pentecostal Assemblies of Canada (PAOC) / Assemblées de la Pentecôte du Canada
2450 Milltower Ct., Mississauga ON L5N 5Z6
Tel: 905-542-7400; *Fax:* 905-542-7313
info@paoc.org
www.paoc.org
Overview: A large national charitable organization founded in 1919
Chief Officer(s):
David Wells, General Superintendent
David Hazzard, Asst. Superintendent, Fellowship Services
Murray Cornelius, Asst. Superintendent, International Missions
Finances: *Annual Operating Budget:* Greater than $5 Million; *Funding Sources:* Local churches; individuals
Staff: 50 staff member(s)
Membership: 1,100 churches, 3,500 pastors representing 235,000 parishoners; *Committees:* General Executive; Administrative; Overseas Missions
Activities: Task Force; Work Force; Volunteers in Mission; Short-Term Missions; Volunteers in Special Assignment; ERDO

(Emergency Relief & Development Overseas); Child Care Plus; *Library:* The PAOC Archives (Open to Public) by appointment
Description: PAOC makes disciples everywhere by the proclamation & practice of the gospel of Christ in the power of the Holy Spirit with the goal to establish local congregations & to train spiritual leaders.; Affiliation(s): World Pentecost; Pentecostal/Charismatic Churches of North America; Pentecostal World Fellowship; World Assemblies of God Fellowship; Focus on the Family; Canadian Foodgrains Bank; Pentecostal European Mission; Seeds International; VisionLEDD; Canadian Council of Christian Charities; Every Home for Christ; Evangelical Missiological Society; Evangelical Fellowship of Canada; Canadian Children's Ministries Network; Canadian Bible Society; Family Life Ministries; Society of Pentecostal Studies

The Pentecostal Assemblies of Newfoundland & Labrador (PAON)
PO Box 8895, Stn. A, 57 Thorburn Rd., St. John's NL A1B 3T2
Tel: 709-753-6314; *Fax:* 709-753-4945
info@paonl.ca
www.paonl.ca
Overview: A medium-sized provincial charitable organization founded in 1911
Chief Officer(s):
H. Paul Foster, General Superintendent
Finances: *Annual Operating Budget:* $1.5 Million-$3 Million
Membership: 40,000
Activities: *Internships:* Yes; *Speaker Service:* Yes *Library:* Yes by appointment
Description: To promote evangelism, world missions, famine relief, & education; Affiliation(s): Pentecostal Fellowship of North America

Presbyterian

Église Réformée St-Jean
3407A, av du Musee, Montréal QC H4E 4L7
Tél: 514-767-3165
info@erq.qc.ca
www.stjean.erq.qc.ca
Aperçu: *Dimension:* moyenne; *Envergure: provinciale*
Membre(s) du bureau directeur:
Jean Zoellner, Pastor
Description: The majority of our members are French-speaking Québecers practising various occupations in society, blue and white collared workers. People coming from a wide range of cultural, regional and national backgrounds also contribute to a rich diversity. People of all ages can be found amongst us: young children, adolescents, students, the middle-aged and the retired. The dynamic nature of our church can be seen in the presence of many young families. We recognise that the Lord Jesus Christ, head of the Church, has assembled us, with our children in a community which holds one vision, one love, one faith and one hope: to live for His Glory and to serve Him where He has placed us.; Affiliation(s): Christian Reformed Church; Presbyterian Church of North America

Presbyterian Church in Canada (PCC) / Église presbytérienne au Canada
50 Wynford Dr., Toronto ON M3C 1J7
Tel: 416-441-1111; *Fax:* 416-441-2825
Toll-Free: 800-619-7301
www.presbyterian.ca
twitter.com/pcconnect
Overview: A large national organization founded in 1875
Chief Officer(s):
John Vissers, Principal, Presbyterian College
M. Jean Morris, Moderator
Tony Plomp, Deputy Clerk
Sarah Kim, Executive Director, Women's Missionary Society
skim@presbyterian.ca
Margaret McGillvary, WMS President
Donald Muir, Deputy Clerk
S. Kendall, Principal Clerk
Richard Fee, General Secretary, Life & Mission Agency
Stephen Roche, CFO
Dorcas J. Gordon, Principal, Knox College, Toronto
Helen Humphreys, AMS President
Finances: *Funding Sources:* Congregations
Membership: 125,509; *Member Profile:* Presbyteries; congregations; communicants on roll; ministers
Activities: *Library:* Knox College & Presbyterian College Libraries (Open to Public)
Member of: The Canadian Council of Churches; World Alliance of Reformed Churches; World Council of Churches; Action By Churches Together; Ecumenical Advocacy Alliance

Protestants

Grand Orange Lodge of Canada
94 Sheppard Ave. West, Toronto ON M2N 1M5
Tel: 416-223-1690; *Fax:* 416-223-1324
Toll-Free: 800-565-6248
secretary@grandorangelodge.ca
www.grandorangelodge.ca
Also Known As: Loyal Orange Association
Previous Name: The Grand Orange Lodge of British America
Overview: A large national organization founded in 1830
Chief Officer(s):
Roy Dawe, Grand Secretary
Finances: *Annual Operating Budget:* Less than $50,000; *Funding Sources:* Membership dues
Staff: 8 staff member(s)
Membership: 100,000; *Fees:* Schedule available; *Member Profile:* Protestant faith
Activities: *Awareness Events:* Annual Golf Tournament
Description: To encourage its members to actively participate in the Protestant church of their choice; to actively support the Canadian system of government; to anticipate legislation & its impact on the civil & religious liberties of all Canadians; to provide social activities which will enrich the lives of its members; to participate in benevolent activities which will enrich our communities & our country; *Member of:* Imperial Orange Council of the World

Operation Mobilization Canada (OM)
84 West St., Port Colborne ON L3K 4C8
Tel: 905-835-2546; *Fax:* 905-835-2533
Toll-Free: 877-487-7777
info@cdn.om.org
www.omcanada.org
Overview: A small international charitable organization founded in 1966
Chief Officer(s):
Harvey Thiessen, Executive Director
Finances: *Annual Operating Budget:* $1.5 Million-$3 Million
Staff: 25 staff member(s)
Activities: *Speaker Service:* Yes *Library:* Yes
Description: Missionary training movement operating in 80 countries with 6,000 people in program every year; mobilizes & trains young Protestant believers for mission fields.; *Member of:* Evangelical Fellowship of Canada; Canadian Council of Christian Charities

Scientology

Church of Scientology of Toronto
696 Yonge St., Toronto ON M4Y 2A7
Tel: 416-925-2146
toronto@scientology.net
www.scientology.ca
Overview: A medium-sized local organization
Member of: Church of Scientology

Seicho-No-Le

Seicho-No-Ie Toronto Centre
662 Victoria Park Ave., Toronto ON M4C 5H4
Tel: 416-690-8686; *Fax:* 416-690-3917
www.seicho-no-ie.org/eng/center/canada.html
Also Known As: Home of Infinite Growth
Previous Name: Seicho-No-Ie Canada Truth of Life Centre
Overview: A small national organization founded in 1963
Description: Provides a place of worship for those who believe in the Seicho-No-Ie Humanity Enlightenment Movement, which says that all religions emanate from one universal god; *Member of:* Seicho-No-Ie (Canada)

Sikhism

Maritime Sikh Society (MSS)
10 Parkhill Rd., Halifax NS B3P 1R3
Tel: 902-477-0008
www.maritimesikhsociety.com
Overview: A small local organization founded in 1968
Chief Officer(s):
Jagpal S. Tiwana, President, 902-435-3793
Finances: *Annual Operating Budget:* Less than $50,000
Membership: 46; *Fees:* $12
Activities: *Library:* Yes by appointment
Member of: Multicultural Association of Nova Scotia

The Sikh Foundation
#4900, 40 King St. West, Toronto ON M5H 4A2
Tel: 416-777-6697; *Fax:* 416-484-9656
Overview: A small national organization
Description: Distributes literature regarding the Sikh religion to anyone who is interested.

World Sikh Organization of Canada (WSO)
1183 Cecil Ave., Ottawa ON K1H 7Z6
www.worldsikh.org
www.facebook.com/WSOCanada
twitter.com/WorldSikhOrg
Overview: A medium-sized international organization founded in 1984
Chief Officer(s):
Prem Singh Vinning, President
Gurpreet Singh Bal, Senior Vice-President
Ramanjot Kaur Sachdev, Director, Administration
Sandeep Singh Sahota, Director, Finance
Membership: 15,000-49,999; *Fees:* $1,000 institutional; $10 student/associate; $100 individual
Activities: *Library:* Yes (Open to Public) by appointment
Description: To foster understanding & goodwill amongst all nations, creeds & races; To promote & protect the rights of humanity as articulated in UN declarations & covenants; Affiliation(s): World Sikh Organization (International)

Sufism

The Jerrahi Sufi Order of Canada
Canadian Sufi Cultural Centre, 270 Birmingham St., Toronto ON M8V 2E4
jerrahi@jerrahi.ca
www.jerrahi.ca
Overview: A medium-sized local organization
Chief Officer(s):
Louise Koopman, Contact
Description: The Jerrahi Sufi Order of Canada holds weekly gatherings where attendees come to gain knowledge about Islam through participating in discourses and discussions, observing the art of Sufi music and poetry, and celebrating the praises of God through prayer and Zikrullah (Sufi remembrance ceremony).

Taoism

Fung Loy Kok Institute of Taoism
1376 Bathurst St., 2nd Fl., Toronto ON M5R 3J1
Tel: 416-656-2110; *Fax:* 416-654-3937
fungloykok@ttcs.org
Overview: A small international organization

Unitarian

Canadian Unitarian Council (CUC) / Conseil unitarien du Canada
#100, 344 Dupont St, Toronto ON M5R 1V9
Tel: 416-489-4121; *Fax:* 416-489-9010
Toll-Free: 888-568-5723
info@cuc.ca
www.cuc.ca
Also Known As: Unitarian Church
Overview: A medium-sized national charitable organization founded in 1961
Chief Officer(s):
Philip Strapp, Financial Administrator, 416-489-4121
phil@cuc.ca
Gary Groot, President
gary@cuc.ca
Finances: *Annual Operating Budget:* $250,000-$500,000; *Funding Sources:* Donations; membership dues
Staff: 6 staff member(s); 20 volunteer(s)
Membership: 50 institutional + 25 individual; *Fees:* $80 individual; congregations - assessment per member; *Committees:* Lay & Chaplaincy; Social Responsibility
Activities: *Library:* CUC Library by appointment
Description: To enhance, nurture & promote Unitarian & Universalist religion in Canada; to provide support for religious exploration, spiritual growth & social responsibility; Affiliation(s): International Association for Religious Freedom; International Council of Unitarians & Universalists
Publications: The Canadian Unitarian
Frequency: 3 pa *Accepts Advertising ISSN:* 0527-9860 *Price:* Free for members of CUC congregations; $15 non-members
Canadian Unitarian Council National Directory
Type: Directory *Price:* Free for members of CUC congregations

First Unitarian Congregation of Toronto
175 St. Clair Ave. West, Toronto ON M4V 1P7
Tel: 416-924-9654; *Fax:* 416-924-9655
administrator@firstunitariantoronto.org
www.firstunitariantoronto.org
www.facebook.com/223855447667879
Overview: A small national charitable organization founded in 1845
Chief Officer(s):
Shawn Newton, Minister, 416-924-9654 222, Fax: 416-924-9655
Finances: *Annual Operating Budget:* $250,000-$500,000

Staff: 9 staff member(s); 25 volunteer(s)
Membership: 306 individuals
Activities: *Internships:* Yes *Library:* Yes by appointment
Description: To serve the religious needs of those who embrace Unitarian Universalist principles, who respect the free exercise of private judgment in all matters of belief & who live in the Metropolitan Toronto area.; *Member of:* Canadian Unitarian Council

USC Canada
#705, 56 Sparks St., Ottawa ON K1P 5B1
Tel: 613-234-6827; *Fax:* 613-234-6842
Toll-Free: 800-565-6872
info@usc-canada.org
www.usc-canada.org
Social Media: www.youtube.com/user/USCCanada; www.flickr.com/photos/usc-canada
www.facebook.com/78368904729
twitter.com/usccanada
Also Known As: Unitarian Service Committee of Canada
Overview: A medium-sized international charitable organization founded in 1945
Chief Officer(s):
Lise Latrémouille, Director, International Programs
Sheila Petzold, Director, Communications
Francine Longtin, Director, Finance & Administration
Susan Walsh, Executive Director
Finances: *Annual Operating Budget:* Greater than $5 Million; *Funding Sources:* Support from the general public; bequests; foundations & corporations; investment income; government
Staff: 22 staff member(s)
Membership: 1,000; *Member Profile:* Membership is offered to individuals supporting USC through volunteer or financial means; *Committees:* Finance; Executive; Programs
Activities: Communications/Media Program; Development Education Program to raise awareness about development issues & their impact on our lives in Canada; Fundraising & Volunteer Program; Overseas Program to work in partnership with people in the developing world to build self-reliant communities; *Speaker Service:* Yes; *Rents Mailing List:* Yes *Library:* Yes by appointment
Description: Committed to enhancing human development through an international partnership of people linked in the challenge to reduce poverty; *Member of:* Canadian Council for International Cooperation

United Church of Christ

Affirm United / S'affirmer Ensemble
PO Box 57057, Stn. Somerset, Ottawa ON K1R 1A1
affirmunited@affirmunited.ca
www.affirmunited.ca
Overview: A medium-sized national organization founded in 1982
Chief Officer(s):
Read Sherman, Communications Coordinator
Finances: *Annual Operating Budget:* Less than $50,000
Staff: 20 volunteer(s)
Membership: 500 individual; *Fees:* $40 individual/household; $100 institutional
Activities: *Speaker Service:* Yes
Description: To affirm gay, lesbian, bisexual & transgender people & their friends, within The United Church of Canada; to provide a network of supports among affirming ministries & regional groups; to act as a point of contact for individuals; to speak to the church in a united fashion encouraging it to act prophetically & pastorally both within & beyond the church structure.; Affiliation(s): United Church of Canada

Alberta CGIT Association
Percy Page Centre, 11759 Groat Rd., Edmonton AB T5M 3K6
Tel: 780-427-6655; *Fax:* 780-427-8677
cgit@telus.net
Also Known As: Canadian Girls in Training - Alberta
Overview: A small provincial organization

Boys & Girls Clubs of Alberta
J. Percy Page Centre, 11759 Groat Rd., Edmonton AB T5M 3K6
Tel: 780-415-1734; *Fax:* 780-415-1737
www.bgccan.com/clubresults.asp?l=e&location=ab
www.facebook.com/group.php?gid=24403790656
Overview: A medium-sized provincial organization
Chief Officer(s):
Karen McCullagh, Western Region Director
kmccullagh@bgccan.com
Pearl Kapitzke, Regional Services Coordinator
pkapitzke@bgccan.com
Finances: *Annual Operating Budget:* $100,000-$250,000
Staff: 2 staff member(s)
Membership: 15,000-49,999
Activities: Counselling; conflict resolution training; street safety
Description: The Clubs offer educational, recreational & skills development programs & services to children from pre-school to young adulthood. Activities are scheduled after school, evenings & weekends, providinge a safe, supportive place where children & youth can build positive relationships, & develop confidence & skills.; *Member of:* Boys & Girls Clubs of Canada

Boys & Girls Clubs of Manitoba
Central Region, #204, 7100 Woodbine Ave., Markham ON L3R 5J2
Tel: 416-535-9675; *Fax:* 905-477-2056
www.bgccan.com/clubresults.asp?l=e&location=mb
Overview: A medium-sized provincial organization
Chief Officer(s):
Sandra Morris, Central Region Director
smorris@bgccan.com
Brittany Tough, Central Region Coordinator
btough@bgccan.comm
Activities: Counselling; conflict resolution training; street safety
Description: The Clubs offer educational, recreational & skills development programs & services to children from pre-school to young adulthood. Activities are scheduled after school, evenings & weekends, providinge a safe, supportive place where children & youth can build positive relationships, & develop confidence & skills.; *Member of:* Boys & Girls Clubs of Canada

Boys & Girls Clubs of New Brunswick
Maritime Region, c/o #204, 7100 Woodbine Ave., Markham ON L3R 5J2
Tel: 902-469-1550
www.bgccan.com/clubresults.asp?l=e&location=nb
Overview: A medium-sized provincial organization
Chief Officer(s):
Wendy Johnston, Maritime Region Director
wjohnston@bgccan.com
Activities: Counselling; conflict resolution training; street safety
Description: The Clubs offer educational, recreational & skills development programs & services to children from pre-school to young adulthood. Activities are scheduled after school, evenings & weekends, providinge a safe, supportive place where children & youth can build positive relationships, & develop confidence & skills.; *Member of:* Boys & Girls Clubs of Canada

Boys & Girls Clubs of Québec / Clubs garçons et filles du Québec
Region de Québec, c/o #204, 7100 Woodbine Ave., Markham ON L3R 5J2
Tél: 905-477-7272; *Téléc:* 905-477-2056
www.bgccan.com/clubresults.asp?l=e&location=qc
Aperçu: *Dimension:* moyenne; *Envergure:* provinciale
Membre(s) du bureau directeur:
Marlene Deboisbriand, Vice-President, Member Services
mdeboisbriand@bgccan.com
Membre de: Boys & Girls Clubs of Canada

Boys & Girls Clubs of Saskatchewan
J. Percy Page Centre, 11759 Groat Rd., Edmonton AB T5M 3K6
Tel: 780-415-1734; *Fax:* 780-415-1737
Toll-Free: 877-615-1734
www.bgccan.com/clubresults.asp?l=e&location=sk
Overview: A medium-sized provincial organization
Chief Officer(s):
Karen McCullagh, Western Region Director
kmccullagh@bgccan.com
Pearl Kapitzke, Regional Services Coordinator
pkapitzke@bgccan.com
Finances: *Annual Operating Budget:* $100,000-$250,000
Staff: 2 staff member(s)
Activities: Counselling; conflict resolution training; street safety
Description: The Clubs offer educational, recreational & skills development programs & services to children from pre-school to young adulthood. Activities are scheduled after school, evenings & weekends, providinge a safe, supportive place where children & youth can build positive relationships, & develop confidence & skills.; *Member of:* Boys & Girls Clubs of Canada

Boys & Girls Clubs of Yukon
Pacific Region, PO Box 20222, 1434 Graham St., Kelowna BC V1Y 9H2
Tel: 250-762-3914; *Fax:* 250-762-6562
www.bgccan.com/clubresults.asp?l=e&location=yt
Overview: A medium-sized provincial organization
Chief Officer(s):
Carrie Wagner-Miller, Pacific Region Director
cwmiller@bgccan.com
Activities: Counselling; conflict resolution training; street safety
Description: The Clubs offer educational, recreational & skills development programs & services to children from pre-school to young adulthood. Activities are scheduled after school, evenings & weekends, providinge a safe, supportive place where children & youth can build positive relationships, & develop confidence & skills.; *Member of:* Boys & Girls Clubs of Canada

KAIROS: Canadian Ecumenical Justice Initiatives / Initiatives canadiennes oecuméniques pour la justice
#200, 310 Dupont St., Toronto ON M5R 1V9
Tel: 416-463-5312; *Fax:* 416-463-5569
Toll-Free: 877-403-8933
info@kairoscanada.org
www.kairoscanada.org
twitter.com/kairoscanada
Previous Name: Ecumenical Coalition for Economic Justice; GATT-Fly
Overview: A small national organization founded in 1973
Chief Officer(s):
Mary Corkery, Executive Director
Adiat Junaid, Communications Coordinator
Finances: *Annual Operating Budget:* $100,000-$250,000
Staff: 4 staff member(s)
Fees: $100
Activities: *Speaker Service:* Yes
Description: To undertake a program of research & action with churches & popular groups emphasizing coalition-building & social transformation; five churches have participated in the Coalition since its inception: the Anglican Church of Canada, the Canadian Conference of Catholic Bishops, the Evangelical Lutheran Church in Canada, the Presbyterian Church in Canada, the United Church of Canada; *Member of:* Action Canada Network; Affiliation(s): Canadian Council of Churches

Manitoba CGIT Association
PO Box 52073, Winnipeg MB R2M 5P9
Tel: 204-254-2378
cgit@cgitmanitoba.ca
Also Known As: Canadian Girls in Training - Manitoba
Previous Name: National CGIT Association - Manitoba & Northwestern Ontario
Overview: A small local organization

Maritime Regional CGIT Committee
PO Box 383, Pictou NS B0K 1H0
Tel: 902-485-4011
g.cmacdonald@ns.sympatico.ca
Also Known As: Canadian Girls in Training - Maritimes
Previous Name: National CGIT Association - Maritime Regional Committee
Overview: A small local organization
Chief Officer(s):
Chris MacDonald, Contact

Ontario CGIT Association
PO Box 371, Norwich ON N0J 1P0
Tel: 519-863-6760; *Fax:* 519-863-6760
ontario@cgit.ca
www.cgit.ca
Also Known As: Canadian Girls in Training - Ontario
Previous Name: National CGIT Association - Ontario
Overview: A small provincial charitable organization founded in 1915
Finances: *Annual Operating Budget:* Less than $50,000
Staff: 1 staff member(s); 150 volunteer(s)
Membership: 350; *Member Profile:* Teen girls & adult women; *Committees:* Leadership Training; Camps; Publicity & Promotion
Activities: Leadership training weekend; camp council leadership training for senior girls; Red Maple Leaf Program
Affiliation(s): The United Church of Canada; The Presbyterian Church in Canada

Provincial CGIT Board of BC
c/o J. Grinnell, 13780 Hill Rd., Ladysmith BC V9G 1G7
Tel: 250-245-4016
grinncon@nanaimo.ark.com
www.cgit.ca/contactingus.htm
Also Known As: Canadian Girls in Training - BC
Previous Name: National CGIT Association - BC Provincial Board
Overview: A small provincial organization

Saskatchewan CGIT Committee
3624 - 28th Ave., Regina SK S4S 2N6
saskcgit@accesscomm.ca
www.cgit.ca/saskatchewan
Also Known As: Canadian Girls in Training - Saskatchewan
Previous Name: National CGIT Association - Saskatchewan Committee
Overview: A small provincial organization
Chief Officer(s):
Alice Monks, Chair

Wicca

Pagan Federation International - Canada (PFI)
PO Box 986, Tavistock ON N0B 2R0
Nuhyn@paganfederation.org
www.ca.paganfederation.org
Overview: A national organization founded in 1998
Publications: Pagan Dawn
Type: Magazine

Wiccan Church of Canada
The Occult Shop, 1373 Bathurst St., Toronto ON M5R 3J1
info@wcc.on.ca
www.wcc.on.ca
Overview: A national organization founded in 1979
Chief Officer(s):
Richard James, Priest
richard@wcc.on.ca
Description: To assist practicing Wiccans in achieving a spiritual balance that brings them into true harmony with the Gods.

Zoroastrianism

Association Zoroastrianne de Québec (AZQ) / Zoroastrian Associaton of Québec (ZAQ)
4220 Melrose, Montréal QC H4A 2S4
Tel: 514-486-6408
zaq.org
Overview: A small provincial charitable organization founded in 1984
Chief Officer(s):
Faranak Firoozi, President
faranakfiroozi@yahoo.com
Affiliation(s): Federation of North American Zoroastrian Associations

Ontario Zoroastrian Community Foundation (OZCF)
4244 Taffey Cres., mississauga ON L5L 2J2
Tel: 905-271-0366
www.ozcf.com
Overview: A small provincial charitable organization
Chief Officer(s):
Jal Panthaky, President, 905-568-4946
jal_panthaky@yahoo.ca
Fees: $75 family; $25 seniors; $50 single; $20 student; *Member Profile:* Zoroastrians living in Ontario; *Committees:* Communication/IT, Social & Entertainment, Facility Management, Finance, Lectures & Learning, Memebership, Newsletter, Religious, Seniors, Sports, Youth

Zoroastrian Society of Ontario (ZSO)
3590 Bayview Ave., Toronto ON M2M 3S6
Tel: 416-225-7771
info@zso.org
www.zso.org
Overview: A small provincial charitable organization founded in 1971
Chief Officer(s):
Sam M. Vesuna, President
Kevin Mancherjee, Exec. Vice-President
Fram Sethna, Treasurer
Mehroo Chothia, Secretary
Finances: *Annual Operating Budget:* $100,000-$250,000; *Funding Sources:* Membership fees; donations; investment income
Staff: 1 staff member(s); 200 volunteer(s)
Membership: 1,000; *Fees:* $70 family; $40 individual; $20 seniors & students; *Member Profile:* Zoroastrians living in Ontario; *Committees:* 15 sub-committees reporting to elected executive committee
Activities: Religious, cultural, youth, religious classes, seniors activities; sponsors 100th Scout Group; *Library:* ZSO Library by appointment
Description: Meeting the religious & cultural needs of the Zoroastrian community of Ontario; Affiliation(s): Federation of North American Zoroastrian Associations

SECTION 15
SPORTS

Associations & Organizations

Aquatic Sports

ACUC International
PO Box 1179, #3, 101 Nelson St. East, Port Dover, ON N0A 1N0
Tel: 519-583-9798; Fax: 519-583-3247
acuchq@acuc.ca
www.acuc.es
www.facebook.com/acucinternational
Affiliation(s): World Diving Federation; Undersea Hyperbaric Medical Society
Juan Rodriguez, President & Chief Executive Officer
Nancy Cronkwright, Vice-President & Officer Manager
Patricia Molina, Vice-President & Manager, Clinet Service

Aquatic Federation of Canada / Fédération aquatique du Canada
c/o Martin Richard, Director, Communications, Swimming Canada, #B140, 2445 St-Laurent Blvd., Ottawa, ON K1G 6C3
Tel: 613-260-1348; Fax: 613-260-0804
www.aquaticfederation.ca
Affiliation(s): Synchro Canada; Canadian Amateur Diving Association Inc.; Water Polo Canada; Swimming Canada
Bill Hogan, President

Athabasca Landing Pool Association (ALPA)
4705 - 48th Ave., Athabasca, AB T9S 1R3
Tel: 780-675-5656; Fax: 780-675-4700
Jaymie Mullin, Manager
Alan Fisher, President

Canadian Aquafitness Leaders Alliance Inc. (CALA)
125 Lilian Dr., Toronto, ON M1R 3W6
Tel: 416-751-9823; Fax: 416-755-1832
Toll-Free: 888-751-9823
cala_aqua@mac.com
www.calainc.org
www.facebook.com/profile.php?id=100001107894346
Affiliation(s): CanFitPro; BCRPA; Ontario Fitness Council; Go50 (UK); AGEconcern (UK); LEAD (Ger.); Univ. of Stellenbosch (SA); H2Oz (Aus.)
Charlene Kopansky, President

Water Polo Canada (WPC)
#12, 1010 Polytek St., Gloucester, ON K1G 9H9
Tel: 613-748-5682; Fax: 613-748-5777
office@waterpolo.ca
www.waterpolo.ca
www.facebook.com/pages/Water-Polo-Canada/193992167322377
twitter.com/waterpolocanada
Affiliation(s): Aquatic Federation of Canada
Ahmed El-Awadi, Executive Director

Archery

Alberta Bowhunters Association (ABA)
c/o Mike Walliser, #8, 7957 - 49 Ave., Red Deer, AB T4P 2V5
Tel: 403-309-7221
membership@bowhunters.ca
www.bowhunters.ca
Mike Walliser, Director, Membership

Archers Association of Nova Scotia (AANS)
c/o Sport Nova Scotia, 5516 Spring Garden Rd., Halifax, NS B3J 1G6
president@aans.ca
www.aans.ca
Alfred W. O'Quinn, President
William Currie, President

Archery Association of New Brunswick (AANB)
1003 Duckcove Lane, Saint John, NB E2M 3G3
Tel: 506-647-5766
contact@archerynb.ca
www.archerynb.ca
Robert McIntyre, Provincial President

Fédération de tir à l'arc du Québec (FTAQ)
CP 1000, Succ. M, 4545, av Pierre-de Coubertin, Montréal, QC H1V 3R2
Tél: 514-252-3054; Téléc: 514-252-3165
ftaq@ftaq.qc.ca
www.ftaq.qc.ca
Gabriela Cosovan, Directrice technique

Federation of Canadian Archers Inc. (FCA) / Fédération canadienne des archers inc.
#108, 2255 St. Laurent Blvd., Ottawa, ON K1G 4K3
Tel: 613-260-2113
information@archerycanada.ca
www.archerycanada.ca
www.facebook.com/ArcheryCanada
twitter.com/ArcheryCanada
Scott Ogilvie, Executive Director
Publications: Archery Canada Annual Report

International Archery Federation (IAF) / Fédération internationale de tir à l'arc (FITA)
Maison du Sport International, Avenue de Rhodanie 54, Lausanne, 1007, Switzerland
Tel: 41-21-614-3050; Fax: 41-21-614-3055
info@archery.org
www.archery.org
Affiliation(s): Federation of Canadian Archers Inc.
Ugur Erdener, President
Tom Dielen, Secretary General

Ontario Association of Archers Inc. (OAA)
PO Box 45, Stn. Caledon Village, Caledon, ON L7K 3L3
Tel: 519-927-3256; Fax: 519-927-9137
info@oaa-archery.on.ca
www.oaa-archery.on.ca
Adam Thomas, President
Cathy Fischer, Secretary-Treasurer

Saskatchewan Archery Association (SAA)
PO Box 5, RR#2, Site 6, Craven, SK S0G 0W0
Tel: 306-775-0385
rlakeman.coram@sasktel.net
www.saskarchery.com
Robert Lakeman, President

Tir-à-l'arc Moncton Archers Inc.
99 West Lane, Coal Branch, NB E4T 4K1
Tel: 506-785-9806
spencers@nb.sympatico.ca
Affiliation(s): New Brunswick Archery Association; Canadian Archery Association
Charles Spencer, President

Athletics

Alberta Schools' Athletic Association (ASAA)
Percy Page Centre, 11759 Groat Rd., Edmonton, AB T5M 3K6
Tel: 780-427-8182; Fax: 780-415-1833
info@asaa.ca
www.asaa.ca
Affiliation(s): National Federation of State High School Associations
John F. Paton, Executive Director
Joyce Loucks, President

Amateur Athletic Union (AAU)
PO Box 22049, 1910 Hotel Plaza Blvd., Lake Buena Vista, FL 32830, USA
Tel: 407-934-7200; Fax: 407-934-7242
Toll-Free: 800-228-4872
anita@aausports.org
www.aausports.org
www.facebook.com/realaau
twitter.com/therealaau
Louise Stout, President/CEO
Mike Killpack, Director, Sports

Association régionale du sport collégial de l'Ile de Montréal (ARSCIM)
a/s FQSE, CP 1000, Succ. M, 4545, av Pierre-de-Coubertin, Montréal, QC H1V 3R2
Tél: 514-252-3300; Téléc: 514-254-3292
infos@arscim.qc.ca
www.arscim.qc.ca
Robert Dussault, Directeur général

Association régionale du sport étudiant de l'Abitibi-Témiscamingue (ARSEAT)
375, ave. Centrale, Val-d'Or, QC J9P 1P4
Tél: 819-825-2047; Téléc: 819-825-0125
Ligne sans frais: 866-626-2047
mlangelier@ulsat.qc.ca
www.ulsat.qc.ca/lsat/pages/sportetudiant.php
Affiliation(s): Fédération québécoise du sport étudiant
Pierre Boulerice, Président
Serge Hurtubise, Vice-président

Association régionale du sport étudiant de la Côte-Nord (ARSECN)
110, rue Comeau, Sept-Iles, QC G4R 1J4
Tél: 418-968-3731; Téléc: 418-968-4033
sport.etudiant.cn@globetrotter.net
sportetudiantcotenord.qc.ca
Gilles Briand, Président

Association régionale du sport étudiant de la Mauricie (ARSEM)
260, rue Dessureault, Trois-Rivières, QC G8T 9T9
Tél: 819-693-5805; Téléc: 819-693-1189
www.arsem.qc.ca
Micheline Guillemette, Directrice générale

Association régionale du sport étudiant de Laval
#221, 3235, St-Martin Est, Laval, QC H7E 5G8
Tél: 450-664-1917; Téléc: 450-664-7832
info@sportslaval.qc.ca
www.sportslaval.qc.ca
Richard Courteau, Directeur général

Association régionale du sport étudiant de Québec et Chaudière-Appalaches (ARSEQCA)
2450, ch Ste-Foy, Québec, QC G1V 1T2
Tél: 418-657-7678; Téléc: 418-657-1367
mleclerc@sportetudiant.qc.ca
www.sportetudiant.qc.ca
Daniel Veilleux, Directeur général

Association régionale du sport étudiant du Richelieu (ARSER)
École secondaire Gérard-Filion, 1330, boul. Curé-Poirier Ouest, Longueuil, QC J4K 2G8
Tél: 450-463-4055; Téléc: 450-463-4229
sport_etudiant@csmv.qc.ca
www.arser.qc.ca/site/index.html
Sylvie Cornellier, Directrice générale

Association régionale du sport étudiant Lac Saint-Louis
2900, rue Lake, Dollard-des-Ormeaux, QC H9B 2P1
Tél: 514-855-4230; Téléc: 514-685-4643
administration@arselsl.qc.ca
www.arselsl.qc.ca
Serge Bélanger, Directeur général

Association régionale du sport étudiant Laurentides-Lanaudière
430, boul. Arthur-Sauvé, Saint-Eustache, QC J7R 6V6
Tél: 450-419-8786; Téléc: 450-419-8892
ginette.laforest@cssmi.qc.ca
www7.cssmi.qc.ca/sportell
Jacinthe Lussier, Directrice générale

Athletes CAN
#301, 1376 Bank St., Ottawa, ON K1H 7Y3
Tel: 613-526-4025; Fax: 613-526-9735
Toll-Free: 888-832-4222
info@athletescan.com
www.athletescan.com
Erik Petursson, President, Diving
Ahren Cadieux, Vice President, Beach Volleyball

Athletes International
#2702, 3550 Jeanne Mauce, Montréal, QC H2X 3P7
Tel: 514-982-9989; Fax: 514-982-0111
Toll-Free: 800-344-1810
info@athletes-int.com
www.athletes-int.com
Peter Schleicher, President

Athletics Alberta
Percy Page Centre, 11759 Groat Rd., Edmonton, AB T5M 3K6
Tel: 780-427-8792; Fax: 780-427-8899
info@athleticsalberta.com
www.athleticsalberta.com
Peter Ogilvie, Executive Director
Sheryl Mack, Office Manager

Athletics Manitoba
#214, 200 Main St., Winnipeg, MB R3C 4M2
Tel: 204-925-5743; Fax: 204-925-5792
office@athleticsmanitoba.com
www.athleticsmanitoba.com
Rob Guy, Managing Director

Athletics New Brunswick (ANB) / Athlétisme du Nouveau-Brunswick
Tel: 506-457-4122; Fax: 506-325-9420
ncactm@nb.aibn.com
www.anb.ca
Bill MacMackin, President
Germain Landry, Vice-President
Gabriel (Gabe) LeBlanc, Director, Technical
Camilla MacDougall, Registrar

Athletics Nova Scotia
5516 Spring Garden Rd, 4th Fl., Halifax, NS B3J 1G6
Tel: 902-425-5450; Fax: 902-425-5606
athletics@sportnovascotia.ca
www.athleticsnovascotia.ca
Jonathan Brill, Executive-Chair
Dan Bainard, CEO

Athletics Ontario
#211, 3 Concorde Gate, Toronto, ON M3C 3N7
Tel: 416-426-7215; Fax: 416-426-7358
ontrack@eol.ca
www.athleticsontario.ca
John Craig, Managing Director
Michael Brennan, Director, Membership Program
Roman Olszewski, Director, Technical Services
Anthony Biggar, Manager, Communications & Public Relations
Publications: Athletics Magazine

Athletics PEI
55 Villa Ave., Charlottetown, PE C1A 2B2
Tel: 902-566-6861; Fax: 902-368-4548
Barrie Stanfield, Treasurer

Athletics Yukon
4061 - 4th Ave., Whitehorse, YT Y1A 1H1
Tel: 867-668-2545
info@athleticsyukon.ca
www.athleticsyukon.ca
Chris Locke, President

British Columbia Athletics
#120, 3820 Cessna Dr., Richmond, BC V7B 0A2
Tel: 604-333-3550; Fax: 604-333-3551
bcathletics@bcathletics.org
www.bcathletics.org
Brian McCalder, President & CEO

Canadian Wheelchair Basketball Association (CWBA) / Association canadienne de basketball en fauteuil roulant (ACBFR)
#8, 6 Antares Dr., Phase 1, Ottawa, ON K2E 8A9
Tel: 613-260-1296; Fax: 613-260-1456
Toll-Free: 877-843-2922
info@wheelchairbasketball.ca
www.wheelchairbasketball.ca
www.facebook.com/wheelchairbasketball
twitter.com/WCBballCanada
Affiliation(s): Canada Basketball
Wendy Gittens, Executive Director
Steven Bach, President
Publications: Around The Rim [a publication of the Canadian Wheelchair Basketball Association], CWBA [Canadian Wheelchair Basketball Association] Annual Report

Fédération québécoise d'athlétisme (FQA)
CP 1000, Succ. M, 4545, av Pierre-de Coubertin, Montréal, QC H1V 3R2
Tél: 514-252-3041; Téléc: 514-252-3042
fqa@athletisme.qc.ca
www.athletisme.qc.ca
Jean-Paul Baert, Directeur général

Greater Montreal Athletic Association (GMAA) / Association régionale du sport scolaire
#101, 5925, av Monkland, Montréal, QC H4A 1G7
Tel: 514-482-8555; Fax: 514-487-0121
gmaa@gmaa.ca
www.gmaa.ca
Don McEwen, Executive Director

Manitoba High Schools Athletic Association (MHSAA)
145 Pacific Ave., Winnipeg, MB R3B 2Z6
Tel: 204-925-5640; Fax: 204-925-5624
info@mhsaa.ca
www.mhsaa.mb.ca
Morris Glimcher, Executive Director
Scott Kwasnitza, President

National Association of Collegiate Directors of Athletics (NACDA)
PO Box 16428, 24651 Detroit Rd., Westlake, Cleveland, OH 44116, USA
Tel: 440-892-4000; Fax: 440-892-4007
www.nacda.com
Mike Cleary, Executive Director

Newfoundland & Labrador Athletics Association (NLAA)
PO Box 21406, RPO MacDonald Dr., St. John's, NL A1A 5G6
Tel: 709-576-1303; Fax: 709-576-7493
athletics@nlaa.ca
www.nlaa.ca
Affiliation(s): Athletics North-East; Mariners Athletics Club; Nautilus Running Club; New World Running Club; Pearlgate T&F Club; Trappers Running Club; Trinity-Conception Athletics Club; Westerland Track Club
Bob Walsh, President
Alison Walsh, Treasurer
George Stanoev, Technical Director

Nova Scotia School Athletic Federation
5516 Spring Garden Rd., Halifax, NS B3J 3G6
Tel: 902-425-8662; Fax: 902-425-5606
dweston@sportnovascotia.ca
nssaf.ednet.ns.ca
Darrell Dempster, Executive Director
Dianne Weston, Secretary

Ontario Federation of School Athletic Associations (OFSAA) / Fédération des associations du sport scolaire de l'Ontario
#204, 3 Concorde Gate, Toronto, ON M3C 3N7
Tel: 416-426-7391; Fax: 416-426-7317
lindsey@ofsaa.on.ca (Newsletter)
www.ofsaa.on.ca
www.facebook.com/group.php?gid=57198022397
Martin Ritsma, President
Lynn Kelman, Vice-President
Doug Gellatly, Executive Director
Lindsey Evanoff, Coordinator, Marketing & Communications
Publications: Baseball Coaching Manual, Curling Coaching Manual, Football Coaching Manual: Teacher's Instruction Manual, In the Zone, Rugby Coaching Manual, Volleyball Coaching Manual

Saskatchewan Athletics
2020 College Dr., Saskatoon, SK S7N 2W4
Tel: 306-664-6744; Fax: 306-664-6761
athletics@sasktel.net
www.saskathletics.ca
Bob Reindl, Executive Director
Janine Platana, Administrative Assistant

World Masters Athletics
Via Padre Leopoldo da Castel-Nuovo 1, Assenza di Brenzon, I-370 10, Italy
info@world-masters-athletics.org
www.world-masters-athletics.org

Automobile Racing

Motorsport Club of Ottawa (MCO) / Club des sports moteur d'Ottawa
PO Box 65006, RPO Merivale Mall, Nepean, ON K2G 5Y3
Tel: 613-788-0525
registrar@mco.org
www.mco.org
Affiliation(s): ASN Canada FIA; CASC-OR; Rallysport Ontario
Pat McDermott, President

Toronto Autosport Club (TAC)
#1214, 2267 Lakeshore Dr. West, Toronto, ON M8V 3X2
president@torontoautosportclub.ca
www.torontoautosportclub.ca
Dietmar Seelemnayer, President

Aviation

Canada's Aviation Hall of Fame (CAHF)
c/o Reynolds-Alberta Museum, PO Box 6360, Wetaskiwin, AB T9A 2G1
Tel: 780-361-1351; Fax: 780-361-1239
cahf@telusplanet.net
www.cahf.ca
John Holding, Chair
David R. Crone, Curator
Julie Stalker, Administrator

Badminton

Badminton Alberta
c/o Alberta Badminton Centre, 60 Patterson Blvd. SW, Calgary, AB T3H 2E1
Tel: 403-297-2722; Fax: 403-297-2706
Toll-Free: 888-397-2722
tech@badmintonalberta.ca
www.badmintonalberta.ca
www.facebook.com/pages/Badminton-Alberta/17023477970217 6
Jeff Bell, Executive Director

Badminton BC
#252, 3820 Cessna Dr., Richmond, BC V7B 0A2
Tel: 604-333-3595; Fax: 604-333-3594
Toll-Free: 800-483-2473
info@badmintonbc.com
www.badmintonbc.com
Phil Weier, Acting Executive Director
Ken Thiesen, Acting Executive Director

Badminton Canada
#99, 2201 Riverside Dr., Ottawa, ON K1H 8K9
Tel: 613-569-2424; Fax: 613-569-3232
badminton@badminton.ca
www.badminton.ca
Affiliation(s): International Badminton Federation
Sonia Blanchard, Office Administrator
Kyle Hunter, Executive Director

Badminton New Nouveau Brunswick
PO Box 355, Stn. Main, Bathurst, NB E2A 3Z3
Tel: 506-783-4654
badminton@bnnb.ca
www.bnnb.ca
Maurice Boudreau, President
Daryl Beers, Executive Director

Badminton Newfoundland & Labrador Inc.
PO Box 21248, #213, 810 East White Hills Rd., St. John's, NL A1A 5B2
Tel: 709-576-7606; Fax: 709-576-7493
badminton@sportnl.ca
www.sportnl.ca/badminton/index.html
www.facebook.com/group.php?gid=3468211930
Janice Reid Boland, Executive Director

Badminton Québec
4940, rue Hochelaga est, Montréal, QC H1V 1E7
Tél: 514-252-3066; Téléc: 514-252-3175
badmintonquebec@videotron.ca
www.badmintonquebec.com
Chantal Brouillard, Directrice générale
Christian Guibourt, Directeur technique
Alexandre Grosleau, Coordonnateur des services aux membres

Badminton World Federation (BWF)
Amoda Bldg., #17.05, 22 Jalan Imbi, L. 17, Kuala Lumpur, 55100, Malaysia
Tel: 603-2141 7155; Fax: 603-2143 7155
bwf@bwfbadminton.org
www.bwfbadminton.org
www.facebook.com/bwfbadminton
twitter.com/bwfmedia
Kang Young Joong, President

Manitoba Badminton Association (MBA)
#323, 145 Pacific Ave., Winnipeg, MB R3B 2Z6
Tel: 204-925-5679; Fax: 204-925-5703
badminton@shawbiz.ca
www.badminton.mb.ca
Ron Waterman, President
Ryan Giesbrecht, Executive Director

Northwest Territories Badminton Association
c/o Sport North Federation, PO Box 11089, 4908 - 49th St., 3rd Fl., Yellowknife, NT X1A 3X7
Tel: 867-669-8326; Fax: 867-669-8327
Toll-Free: 800-661-0797
www.nwtbadminton.ca
Julie Jeffery, President

Nova Scotia Badminton Association
5516 Spring Garden Rd., Halifax, NS B3J 1G6
Tel: 902-425-5450; Fax: 902-425-5606
nsbadminton@sportnovascotia.ca
www.nsba.ca
Jennifer Petrie, Executive Director
Linda Pride, President

Ontario Badminton Association (OBA)
#209, 3 Concorde Gate, Toronto, ON M3C 3N7
Tel: 416-426-7192; Fax: 416-426-7346
info@ontariobadminton.on.ca
www.ontariobadminton.on.ca
Affiliation(s): Badminton Canada; Badminton World Federation
Val Butler, Executive Director

Prince Edward Island Badminton Association
c/o Sport PEI, PO Box 302, Charlottetown, PE C1A 7K7
Tel: 902-368-4262; Fax: 902-368-4548
Dawna Woodside, President

Saskatchewan Badminton Association (SBA)
3615 Pasqua St., Regina, SK S4S 6W8
Tel: 306-780-9368; Fax: 306-780-9369
saskbadminton@sasktel.net
www.saskbadminton.ca
Frank Gaudet, Executive Director

Yukon Badminton Association
4061 - 4th Ave., Whitehorse, YT Y1A 1H1
Tel: 867-668-4821
bluestone@northwestel.net
Michael Muller, President
Randy Carlson, Vice-President

Ball Hockey

British Columbia Ball Hockey Association (BCBHA)
1302 Cliveden Ave., Delta, BC V3M 6G4
Tel: 604-812-6720; Fax: 604-588-7760
www.bcbha.com
Affiliation(s): Canadian Ball Hockey Association
Wade Traversy, President
Kris Little, Vice-President
Rob Moxness, Secretary
Roger Sidhu, Treasurer

Canadian Ball Hockey Association / Association canadienne de hockey-balle
9107 Norum Rd., Delta, BC V4C 3H9
Tel: 604-638-1480; Fax: 604-998-1410
info@cbha.com
www.cbha.com
George Gortsos, Executive Director
Shelley Callaghan, Vice-President, Women's
Connie Liosis, Vice-President, Men's
Steve Rumsey, Vice-President, Minor's

Manitoba Ball Hockey Association
306-145 Pacific Ave., Winnipeg, MB R3B 2Z6
Tel: 204-925-5602
mbha1@hotmail.com
www.manitobaballhockey.com
www.facebook.com/group.php?gid=50027852199
Affiliation(s): Sport Manitoba
Kelly Huff, Executive League Director

New Brunswick Ball Hockey Association (NBBHA)
16 Reflection Lane, Quispamsis, NB E2E 6E7
Tel: 506-333-7772; Fax: 506-847-8585
sheila@committedtoyourgoals.com
Sheila Elliott, Contact
Publications: New Brunswick Ball Hockey Association Team Handbook

Newfoundland & Labrador Ball Hockey Association (NLBHA)
PO Box 2579, Stn. C, St. John's, NL A1C 6K1
Tel: 709-729-0689
paulbarron@gov.nl.ca
Paul Barron, President

Nova Scotia Ball Hockey Association
100 Auburn Drive, Dartmouth, NS B2W 3S6
Tel: 902-462-5433; Fax: 902-477-0243
Affiliation(s): Canadian Ball Hockey Association; Sport Nova Scotia
Bill Davidson, Contact

Ontario Ball Hockey Association (OBHA)
#5, 56 Pennsylvania Ave., Concord, ON L4K 3V9
Tel: 905-738-3320; Fax: 905-738-3321
www.ontarioballhockey.ca
www.facebook.com/group.php?gid=2374843443
Affiliation(s): Canadian Ball Hockey Association; International Street & Ball Hockey Association; Sport Canada; Canadian Hockey Association
Mauro Cugini, Executive Director

Québec Ball Hockey Association (QBHA)
#203, 5960 Jean-Talon E, St. Leonard, QC H1S 1M2
Tel: 514-251-9346; Fax: 514-251-8285
Tony Iannitto

Wild Rose Ball Hockey Association
7604 - 182 St., Edmonton, AB T5T 1Y9
Tel: 780-970-0637; Fax: 780-484-9957
wrbha@telus.net
www.wrballhockey.com
Connie Liosis, Executive Director

Baseball

Baseball Alberta (BA)
Percy Page Centre, 11759 Groat Rd., Edmonton, AB T5M 3K6
Tel: 780-427-8943; Fax: 780-427-9032
registrar@baseballalberta.com
www.baseballalberta.com
www.facebook.com/pages/Baseball-Alberta/130042917037092
Affiliation(s): Alberta Amateur Baseball Council
Don Paulencu, President

Baseball BC
#310, 15225 - 104th Ave., Surrey, BC V3R 6Y8
Tel: 604-586-3310; Fax: 604-586-3311
info1@baseball.bc.ca
www.baseball.bc.ca
www.facebook.com/pages/Baseball-BC/233202485008
John Berry, President

Baseball Canada / Fédération canadienne de baseball amateur
2212 Gladwin Cres., #A7, Ottawa, ON K1B 5N1
Tel: 613-748-5606; Fax: 613-748-5767
info@baseball.ca
www.baseball.ca
Affiliation(s): Canadian Olympic Association
Ray Carter, President
Jason Dickson, Vice President

Baseball New Brunswick (BNB) / Baseball Nouveau-Brunswick
#13, 900 Hanwell Rd., Fredericton, NB E3B 6A2
Tel: 506-451-1329; Fax: 506-451-1325
director@baseballnb.ca
www.baseballnb.ca
www.facebook.com/pages/Baseball-NB/87671406193
Affiliation(s): Sport New Brunswick; Baseball Atlantic
Brian Richard, Chair

Baseball Nova Scotia (BNS)
5516 Spring Garden Rd., 4th Fl., Halifax, NS B3J 1J
Tel: 902-425-5450; Fax: 902-425-5606
www.baseballnovascotia.com
Brad Lawlor, Executive Director

Baseball Ontario
#3, 131 Sheldon Dr., Cambridge, ON N1R 6S2
Tel: 519-740-3900; Fax: 519-740-6311
baseball@baseballontario.com
www.baseballontario.com
Affiliation(s): Little League Ontario
Mary-Ann Smith, Administrative Director

Fédération du baseball amateur du Québec
CP 1000, Succ. M, 4545, av Pierre-de Coubertin, Montréal, QC H1V 3R2
Tél: 514-252-3075; Téléc: 514-252-3134
info@baseballquebec.qc.ca
www.baseballquebec.qc.ca

Little League Canada / Petite ligue Canada
235 Dale Ave., Ottawa, ON K1G 0H6
Tel: 613-731-3301; Fax: 613-731-2829
canada@littleleague.org
www.littleleague.ca
www.facebook.com/pages/Little-League-Baseball-Canada/137589529592785
twitter.com/LittleLgeCanada
Roy Bergerman, President & Chair
Marthe Dubroy, Secretary
Bruce Campbell, Treasurer

Manitoba Baseball Association
145 Pacific Ave., Winnipeg, MB R3B 2Z6
Tel: 204-925-5763; Fax: 204-925-5928
baseball.morgan@sportmanitoba.ca
www.baseballmanitoba.ca
www.facebook.com/pages/Baseball-Manitoba/171229052909245
twitter.com/BaseballMB
Morgan de Pe¤a, Executive Director

Newfoundland Baseball
83 Ashford Dr., Mount Pearl, NL A1N 3N7
Tel: 709-368-2819; Fax: 709-368-6080
nlbaseball@nl.rogers.com
www.sport.ca/nlbaseball
John Janes, President

Prince Edward Island Amateur Baseball Association
PO Box 302, 40 Enman Cres., Charlottetown, PE C1A 7K7
Tel: 902-569-0583; Fax: 902-368-4548
Toll-Free: 800-247-6712
www.baseballpei.ca
Cheryl Crozier, Executive Director
Don LeClair, President

Saskatchewan Baseball Association (SBA)
1870 Lorne St., Regina, SK S4P 2L7
Tel: 306-780-9237; Fax: 306-352-3669
mramage@sasktel.net
www.saskbaseball.ca
Mike Ramage, Executive Director

Basketball

Basketball Alberta
Percy Page Centre, 11759 Groat Rd., 2nd Fl., Edmonton, AB T5M 3K6
Tel: 780-427-9044; Fax: 780-427-9124
bballab@basketballalberta.ab.ca
www.basketballalberta.ca
www.facebook.com/BasketballAlberta
twitter.com/BasketballAB
Bob Mitchell, President
Paul Sir, Executive Director

Basketball BC
#210, 7888 - 200th St., Langley, BC V2Y 3J4
Tel: 604-718-7852; Fax: 604-888-8323
www.basketball.bc.ca
twitter.com/BasketballBC
Lawrie Johns, Executive Director, Youth Development Manager

Basketball Manitoba
145 Pacific Ave., Winnipeg, MB R3B 2Z6
Tel: 204-925-5775; Fax: 204-925-5929
info@basketball.mb.ca
www.basketball.mb.ca
www.facebook.com/basketballmanitoba
twitter.com/basketballmb
Adam Wedlake, Executive Director

Basketball New Brunswick (BNB) / Basketball Nouveau-Brunswick
#13, 900 Hanwell Rd., Fredericton, NB E2E 6A2
Tel: 506-849-4667; Fax: 506-451-1325
info@basketball.nb.ca
www.basketball.nb.ca
Affiliation(s): New Brunswick Association of Approved Basketball Officials; New Brunswick Interscholastic Athletic Association
Carolyn Peppin, Executive Director
Kim Flemming, Office Administrator

Basketball Nova Scotia
5516 Spring Garden Rd., 4th Fl., Halifax, NS B3J 1G6
Tel: 902-425-5450; Fax: 902-425-5606
bnsadmin@basketball.ns.ca
www.basketball.ns.ca
Affiliation(s): Sport Nova Scotia
Peter Halpin, President
Liam Blanchard, Executive Director

Basketball PEI
PO Box 302, 40 Enman Cres., Charlottetown, PE C1A 7K7
Tel: 902-368-4208; Fax: 902-368-4208
Toll-Free: 800-247-6712
info@basketballpei.ca
www.basketballpei.ca
Stephen Marchbank, Executive Director

Basketball Saskatchewan (BSI)
2205 Victoria Ave., Regina, SK S4P 0S4
Fax: 306-525-4009
basketball@basketballsask.com
www.basketballsask.com
Affiliation(s): Sask Sport
Greg Lucas, Executive Director, glucas@basketballsask.com
Nathan Schellenberg, Director, Basketball Development
Stacey Silzer, Coordinator, Program
Dave Werry, Coordinator, High Performance

Canada Basketball
#11, 1 Westside Dr., Toronto, ON M9C 1B2
Tel: 416-614-8037; Fax: 416-614-9570
info@basketball.ca
www.basketball.ca
Affiliation(s): 10 provincial + 2 territorial associations; Canadian Interuniversity Athletic Union; Canadian Colleges Athletic Association; Canadian School Sports Federation; Toronto Raptors; Canadian Wheelchair Basketball Association; Canadian Association of Basketball Officials; National Association of Basketball Coaches of Canada; Women's Basketball Coaches Association
Wayne Parrish, President & CEO

Fédération de basketball du Québec (FBBQ) / Québec Basketball Federation
CP 1000, Succ. M, 4545, av Pierre-De Coubertin, Montréal, QC H1V 3R2
Tél: 514-252-3057; Téléc: 514-252-3357
Ligne sans frais: 866-557-3057
www.basketball.qc.ca
Daniel Grimard, Directeur général
Francis Jetté, Agent, Communications & marketing

Newfoundland & Labrador Basketball Association
The Didham Building, PO Box 21029, 1296A Kenmount Rd., Paradise, NL A1L 1N3
Tel: 709-576-0247; Fax: 709-576-8787
nlba@sportnf.com
www.nlba.nf.ca
www.facebook.com/nlbasketball
twitter.com/nlbasketball
Bill Murphy, Executive Director
Bas Kavanagh, President

Ontario Basketball
#311, 3 Concorde Gate, Toronto, ON M3C 3N7
Tel: 416-426-7200; Fax: 416-426-7360
info@basketball.on.ca
www.basketball.on.ca
Affiliation(s): Provincial Sports Organizations Council; Canada Basketball; Toronto Raptors Basketball Club; NBA Canada; Coaches Association of Ontario; Canadian Sports Centre; and other provincial basketball organizations
Michele O'Keefe, Executive Director
Ken Urbach, President
Greg Verner, Vice President

Biathlon

Biathlon Alberta
Bob Niven Training Centre, #102, 88 Canada Olympic Rd. SW, Calgary, AB T3B 5R5
Tel: 403-202-6548
info@biathlon.ca
www.biathlon.ca
Ken Davies, President
Andy Holmwood, Executive Director

Biathlon Canada
#111, 2197 Riverside Dr., Ottawa, ON K1H 7X3
Tel: 613-748-5608; Fax: 613-748-5762
information@biathloncanada.ca
www.biathloncanada.ca
Affiliation(s): International Biathlon Union; Canadian Olympic Committee
Joanne Thomson, Executive Director
Chris Lindsay, Director, High Performance
Katie Dobson, Coordinator, Technical Programs

Bicycling

Alberta Bicycle Association (ABA)
Percy Page Centre, 11759 Groat Rd., Edmonton, AB T5M 3K6
Tel: 780-427-6352; Fax: 780-427-6438
Toll-Free: 877-646-2453
info@albertabicycle.ab.ca
www.albertabicycle.ab.ca
Heather Lothian, Executive Director

Bicycle Newfoundland & Labrador
PO Box 2127, Stn. C, St. John's, NL A1C 5R6
Tel: 709-738-2597
admin@bnl.nf.ca
www.bnl.nf.ca
www.facebook.com/pages/Bicycle-NL/144379652267580
Leon Organ, President

Bicycle Nova Scotia (BNS)
5516 Spring Garden Rd., 4th Fl., Halifax, NS B3J 1G6
Tel: 902-425-5454; Fax: 902-425-5606
staff@bicycle.ns.ca
www.bicycle.ns.ca
Tamara Stephen, Office Administrator

Bicycle Trade Association of Canada (BTAC) / Association canadienne de l'industrie du vélo (ACIV)
17 Main St. North, Newmarket, ON L3Y 3Z6
Tel: 905-853-5031; Fax: 905-853-7632
Toll-Free: 866-528-2822
info@btac.org
www.btac.org
Janet O'Connell, Executive Director

Canadian Cycling Association (CCA) / Association cycliste canadienne
#203, 2197 Riverside Dr., Ottawa, ON K1H 7X3
Tel: 613-248-1353; Fax: 613-248-9311
general@canadian-cycling.com
www.canadian-cycling.com
Greg Mathieu, Chief Executive Officer & Secretary General
Jacques Landry, Director, High Performance
Mathieu Boucher, Director, Development
Brett Stewart, Director, Finance & Administration
Publications: Athlete Bios [a publication of the Canadian Cycling Association], Canadian Cycling Association / Association cycliste canadienne Directory, CCA [Canadian Cycling Association] Annual Report, Cycling Long Term Athlete Development Model

Cycling Association of the Yukon
4061, 4th Avenue, Whitehorse, YT Y1A 1H1
Tel: 867-668-4990; Fax: 867-668-8212
sue.richards@gov.yk.ca
Sue Richards, President

Cycling British Columbia (CBC)
#201, 210 West Broadway, Vancouver, BC V5Y 3W2
Tel: 604-737-3034; Fax: 604-737-3141
info@cyclingbc.net
www.cycling.bc.net
Keith Ryan, Chief Executive Officer
Colin Campbell, Director, Race & Business Development
Conan Cooper, Director, Development
Diana Hardie, Director, Finance & Administration
Kevin MacCuish, Director, Road & Technical
Adam Muys, Director, BMX
Richard Wooles, Director, High Performance

Cycling PEI (CPEI)
Sport PEI, PO Box 302, 40 Enman Cresent, Charlottetown, PE C1A 7K7
Tel: 902-368-4985; Fax: 902-368-4548
mconnolly@sportpei.pe.ca
www.cpei.ca
Mike Connolly, Executive Director

Edmonton Bicycle & Touring Club (EBTC)
PO Box 52017, Stn. Garneau, Edmonton, AB T6G 2T5
Tel: 780-424-2453
info@bikeclub.ca
www.bikeclub.ca
www.facebook.com/group.php?gid=21002145481
Affiliation(s): Alberta Bicycle Association
Sid Bennett, President

Fédération québécoise des sports cyclistes (FQSC) / Québec Cycling Sports Federation
4545, av Pierre-de-Coubertin, Montréal, QC H1V 3R2
Tél: 514-252-3071; Téléc: 514-252-3165
reception@fqsc.net
www.fqsc.net
Affiliation(s): Association cycliste canadienne; Union cycliste internationale; Sports-Québec; Regroupement loisir Québec
Simon Thériault, Directeur technique
Louis Barbeau, Directeur général
André Michaud, Président

Ontario Cycling Association (OCA) / Association cycliste ontarienne
#307, 3 Concorde Gate, Toronto, ON M3C 3N7
Tel: 416-426-7416; Fax: 416-426-7349
info@ontariocycling.org; ocamagazine@ontariocycling.org
www.ontariocycling.org
Affiliation(s): Canadian Cycling Association
Duncan Vipond, President
Malcolm Eade, Vice-President, Administration & Finance
Glenn Meeuwisse, Vice-President, High Performance
Matthias Schmidt, Vice-President, Development
Jim Crosscombe, Executive Director
Denise Kelly, Director, Provincial Coaching
Chris Baskys, Coordinator, Membership
Nicky Pearson, Coordinator, BMX Growth & Development
Publications: Cycle Ontario, Ontario Cycling Association Handbook, Young Cyclist's Guide

Saskatchewan Cycling Association
2205 Victoria Ave., Regina, SK S4P 0S4
Tel: 306-780-9299; Fax: 306-525-4009
cycling@accesscomm.ca
www.saskcycling.ca
Wayne Walker, President

Toronto Bicycling Network
PO Box 279, #200, 131 Bloor St. West, Toronto, ON M5S 1R8
Tel: 416-760-4191
info@tbn.ca
www.tbn.ca
Brian Mclean, President

Vélo New Brunswick
536 McAllister Rd., Riverview, NB E1B 4G1
Tel: 506-474-0214
www.velo.nb.ca
www.facebook.com/home.php?sk=group_171814622867730
Affiliation(s): Sport New Brunswick
Kelly Murray, President
Michelle Chase, Vice-President
Sheila Colbourne, Executive Director

Vélo Québec
1251, rue Rachel est, Montréal, QC H2J 2J9
Tél: 514-521-8356; Téléc: 514-521-5711
Ligne sans frais: 800-567-8356
www.velo.qc.ca
www.facebook.com/VeloQuebec
twitter.com/VeloQuebec
Jean-François Pronovost, Directeur général

Blindness

Blind Sailing Association of Canada (BSAC)
45 Brahms Ave., Toronto, ON M2H 1H3
Tel: 416-489-2433; Fax: 416-489-2433
info@blindsailing.ca
www.blindsailing.ca
David Brown, President
Grant Robinson, Vice-President
Randy Nelson, Treasurer

Blind Sports Nova Scotia
c/o CNIB, 6136 Almon St., Halifax, NS B3K 1T8
Tel: 902-453-1480; Fax: 902-454-6570
info@blindsportsnovascotia.ca
www.blindsportsnovascotia.ca
Yvon Clement, President

British Columbia Blind Sports & Recreation Association (BCBSRA)
#330, 5055 Joyce St., Vancouver, BC V5R 6B2
Tel: 604-325-8638; Fax: 604-325-1638
info@bcblindsports.bc.ca
www.bcblindsports.bc.ca
Affiliation(s): International Blind Sports Association; BC Sport & Fitness Council for the Disabled
Brian Cowie, President
Tami Grenon, Vice President

Canadian Blind Sports Association Inc. / Association canadienne des sports pour aveugles inc.
#325, 5055 Joyce St., Vancouver, BC V5R 6B2
Tel: 604-419-0480; Fax: 604-419-0481
Toll-Free: 866-604-0480
jane@canadianblindsports.ca
www.canadianblindsports.ca
Affiliation(s): International Blind Sports Association; Canadian Paralympic Committee; Active Living Alliance
Jane D. Blaine, Executive Director

Manitoba Blind Sport Association
#311, 200 Main St., Winnipeg, MB R3C 4M2
Tel: 204-925-5694; Fax: 204-925-5703
blindsport@shawbiz.ca
www.blindsport.mb.ca
Cathy Drewianchuk, Executive Director

Ontario Blind Sport Association (OBSA)
#104, 3 Concorde Gate, Toronto, ON M3C 3N6
Tel: 416-426-7191; Fax: 416-426-7361
Toll-Free: 888-711-1112
matt@osrc.com
www.blindsports.on.ca
Shirley Shelby, President

Boating

Canadian International Dragon Boat Festival Society
110 Keefer St., Vancouver, BC V6A 1X4
Tel: 604-688-2382; Fax: 604-677-2147
www.adbf.com
Ann Phelps, General Manager

Canadian Power & Sail Squadrons (Canadian Headquarters) (CPS) / Escadrilles canadiennes de plaisance (ECP)
26 Golden Gate Ct., Toronto, ON M1P 3A5
Tel: 416-293-2438; Fax: 416-293-2445
Toll-Free: 888-277-2628
hqg@cps-ecp.ca
www.cps-ecp.ca
www.facebook.com/groups/6654534451
twitter.com/cpsboat
Alain Brière, Executive Director
John Gullick, Manager, Government & Special Programs

Bobsledding & Luge

Alberta Bobsleigh Association
Bob Niven Training Centre, #205, 88 Canada Olympic Rd. SW, Calgary, AB T3B 5R5
Tel: 403-297-2721; Fax: 403-286-7213
slide@albertabobsleigh.com
www.albertabobsleigh.com
www.facebook.com/group.php?gid=68082934483&ref=search
Tim Dyrgas, President

Alberta Luge Association (ALA)
Rm 201, BNTC, 88 Canada Olympic Rd. SW, Calgary, AB T3B 5R5
Tel: 403-202-6570; Fax: 403-247-5497
admin@albertaluge.com
www.albertaluge.com
Affiliation(s): Canadian Luge Association
Darryl Gunn, President

Bobsleigh Canada Skeleton
140 Canada Olympic Rd. SW, Calgary, AB T3B 5R5
Tel: 403-247-5950; Fax: 403-247-5951
ddreher@bobsleigh.ca
www.bobsleigh.ca/
Affiliation(s): Fédération internationale de bobsleigh et de tobogganing
Don Wilson, CEO

Canadian Luge Association / Association canadienne de luge
88 Canada Olympic Rd. SW, Calgary, AB T3B 5R5
Tel: 403-202-6581; Fax: 403-247-8820
hpprchris@comcast.net
www.luge.ca
www.facebook.com/138340422883168
twitter.com/LugeCanada
Tim Farstad, Executive Director

Fédération internationale de bobsleigh et de tobogganing
Via Piranesi, 44/B, Milan, 120137, Italy
Tél: 39-02-7395-1819; Téléc: 39-02-7000-8071
egarde@tin.it
www.fibt.com
Affiliation(s): Canadian Amateur Bobsleigh & Tobogganing Association
Ivo Ferriani, Président
Ermanno Gardella, Secrétaire général

Fédération Internationale de Luge de Course (FIL) / International Luge Federation
Rathausplatz 9, Berchtesgaden, 83471, Germany
Tél: 49-86-526-6960; Téléc: 49-86-526-6969
office@fil-luge.org
www.fil-luge.org
Affiliation(s): Canadian Luge Association
Josef Fendt, Président
Svein Romstad, Secrétaire général

Bowling

Alberta 5 Pin Bowlers' Association (A5-PBA)
Bowling Headquarters, 432 - 14 St. South, Lethbridge, AB T1J 2X7
Tel: 403-320-2695; Fax: 403-320-2676
Toll-Free: 800-762-3075
communications@edmonton5pin.ca
www.alberta5pin.com
Annette Bruneau, President
Julie Kind, Secretary
Don MacIver, Treasurer
Brian Sudbury, Director, Technical

Bowling Federation of Canada / Fédération des quilles du Canada
c/o Administrator, #206, 720 Belfast Rd., Ottawa, ON K1G 0Z5
Tel: 613-744-5090; Fax: 613-744-2217
info@canadabowls.ca
www.canadabowls.ca
Affiliation(s): Bowling Proprietors Association of Canada; Canadian 5-pin Bowlers Association; Canadian Tenpin Federation.
Bryan Sargeant, President
Sheila Carr, Administrator

Bowling Federation of Saskatchewan
#101, 1805 - 8th Ave., Regina, SK S4R 1E8
Tel: 306-780-9412; Fax: 306-780-9455
bowling@sasktel.net
saskbowl.com
Rhonda Sereda, Executive Director

Bowling Proprietors' Association of BC
#209, 332 Columbia St., New Westminster, BC V3L 1A6
Tel: 604-522-2990; Fax: 604-522-2055
bowl4fun@bowlbc.com
www.bowlbc.com
Ken Clarke, President

Bowling Proprietors' Association of Canada (BPAC)
#10A, 250 Shields Ct., Markham, ON L3R 9W7
Tel: 905-479-1560; Fax: 905-479-8613
info@bowlcanada.ca
www.bowlcanada.ca
Mariano Meconi, President
Paul Oliveira, Executive Director

Bowling Proprietors' Association of Ontario (BPAO)
#202, 500 Alden Rd., Markham, ON L3R 5H5
Tel: 905-940-8200; Fax: 905-940-8201
info@bowlontario.ca
www.bowlontario.ca
Affiliation(s): Bowling Proprietors' Association of Canada
Filippo Corradi, President
Melanie Girard, Director, Administration

Canadian 5 Pin Bowlers' Association (C5PBA) / Association canadienne des cinq quilles (AC5Q)
#206, 720 Belfast Rd., Ottawa, ON K1G 0Z5
Tel: 613-744-5090; Fax: 613-744-2217
c5pba@c5pba.ca
www.c5pba.ca
Affiliation(s): Bowling Federation of Canada
Sheila Carr, Executive Director
Mel Osmond, President
Don MacIver, Corporate Sec.-Treas.

Canadian Tenpin Federation, Inc. (CTF) / Fédération canadienne des dix-quilles, inc.
916 - 3 Ave. North, Lethbridge, AB T1H 0H3
Tel: 403-381-2830; Fax: 403-381-6247
www.gotenpinbowling.ca
Affiliation(s): Fédération internationale des quilleurs
Stan May, Executive Director
Gus Badali, Manager, Domestic Team
Publications: CTF Connection

Fédération de pétanque du Québec
CP 1000, Succ. M, 4545, av Pierre-de Coubertin, Montréal, QC H1V 3R2
Tél: 514-252-3077
petanque@loisirquebec.qc.ca
www.petanque.qc.ca
Denise Coutu, Secrétaire administrative

Manitoba Five Pin Bowling Federation, Inc.
#219, 200 Main St., Winnipeg, MB R3C 4M2
Tel: 204-925-5766; Fax: 204-925-5767
Toll-Free: 800-282-8069
www.mfpbf.org
Deanne Zilinsky, Executive Director

New Brunswick Candlepin Bowlers Association
PO Box 4315, 11 Sawyer Rd., Woodstock, NB E7M 6B7
Tel: 506-328-8418

Northwest Territories 5 Pin Bowlers' Association (NWT5PBA)
PO Box 2643, Yellowknife, NT X1A 2P9
Tel: 867-873-8189; Fax: 867-873-8237
www.nwt5pba.ca
Gary Black, President

Ontario 5 Pin Bowlers' Association (O5PBA)
#302, 3 Concorde Gate, Toronto, ON M3C 3N7
Tel: 416-426-7167; Fax: 416-426-7364
o5pba@o5pba.ca
www.o5pba.ca
Johnda Cresswell, President
Heather Dwinnell, Coordinator, Administration
Rhonda Gifford, Coordinator, Program
Jackie Henriques, Coordinator, Finances
Al Hong, Coordinator, Events
Publications: Pinboard

Prince Edward Island Five Pin Bowlers Association Inc.
c/o Sport PEI, PO Box 302, Charlottetown, PE C1A 7K7
Tel: 902-368-4110; Fax: 902-368-4548
Toll-Free: 800-247-6712
sports@sportpei.pe.ca
www.sportpei.pe.ca
Nina Costain, President

Saskatchewan 5 Pin Bowlers' Association
#100, 1805 - 8th Ave., Regina, SK S4R 1E8
Tel: 306-780-9412; Fax: 306-780-9455
bowling@sasktel.net
saskbowl.com
Affiliation(s): Bowling Federation of Saskatchewan
Rhonda Sereda, Executive Director

Youth Bowling Canada (YBC)
c/o Bowl Canada, #10A, 250 Shields Ct., Markham, ON L3R 9W7
Tel: 905-479-1560; Fax: 905-479-8613
info@bowlcanada.ca
www.youthbowling.ca; www.bowlcanada.ca
www.facebook.com/pages/youth-bowling-canada/103402153046873
Mariano Meconi, President, Bowl Canada
Paul Oliveira, Executive Director, Bowl Canada

Boxing

Boxing Alberta
Percy Page Centre, 11759 Groat Rd., Edmonton, AB T5M 3K6
Tel: 780-427-6515; Fax: 780-427-1205
www.boxingalberta.com
Jim Titley, President
Dennis Belair, Executive Director

Boxing BC Association
481 - 23rd St. NE, Salmon Arm, BC V1E 1Y8
Tel: 250-832-7759; Fax: 250-832-7769
boxingbc@telus.net
www.boxing.bc.ca
Affiliation(s): Canadian Amateur Boxing Association
Scotty Jackson, President

Boxing Ontario
#202, 3 Concorde Gate, Toronto, ON M3C 3N7
Tel: 416-426-7250; Fax: 416-426-7367
info@boxingontario.com
www.boxingontario.com

Affiliation(s): Canadian Amateur Boxing Association (CABA); Association International de Boxe Amateur (AIBA); Ontario Ministry of Health Promotion
Tom Hennessey, President
Matt Kennedy, Executive Director

Boxing Saskatchewan
PO Box 4711, Regina, SK S4P 3Y3
Tel: 306-525-6678; Fax: 306-569-3454
skboxing@accesscomm.ca
www.boxingsask.com
Affiliation(s): Canadian Amateur Boxing Association
Frank Fiacco, President
Graham Craig, Executive Director

Calgary Boxing & Wrestling Commission (CBWC)
PO Box 2100, Stn. M #63, Calgary, AB T2P 2M5
Tel: 403-268-5367
Candy S. Schacter, Chair

Canadian Amateur Boxing Association (CABA) / Association canadienne de boxe amateur (ACBA)
888 Belfast Rd., Ottawa, ON K1G 0Z6
Tel: 613-238-7700; Fax: 613-238-1600
caba@boxing.ca
www.boxing.ca
Affiliation(s): International Amateur Boxing Association
Robert G. Crête, Executive Director
Daniel Trépanier, Coordinator, Technical
Michelle Ethier, Registrar & Accountant

Edmonton Combative Sports Commission (ECSC)
10250 - 101 St. NW, 13th Fl., Edmonton, AB T6J 3P4
Tel: 780-495-0382; Fax: 780-429-6976
ecsc.ca
Affiliation(s): Association of Boxing Commissions
Pat Reid, Executive Director

Fédération québécoise de boxe olympique (FQBO)
CP 1000, Succ. M, 4545, av Pierre-de Coubertin, Montréal, QC H1V 3R2
Tél: 514-252-3047; Téléc: 514-254-2144
Ligne sans frais: 866-241-3779
info@fqbo.qc.ca
www.fqbo.qc.ca
Kenneth Piché, Directeur général
Victoria Sullivan-Smith, Adjointe administrative

Manitoba Amateur Boxing Association
#302, 200 Main St., Winnipeg, MB R3C 4M2
Tel: 204-925-5658
Rosemary Broadbent

Manitoba Boxing Commission
#420, 213 Notre Dame Ave., Winnipeg, MB R3B 1N3
Tel: 204-945-1788; Fax: 204-948-3649
www.manitobaboxingcommission.com
Henry Janzen, Chair
Joel Fingard, Executive Director

Broomball

Alberta Broomball Association
Percy Page Centre, 11759 Groat Rd., Edmonton, AB T5M 3K6
Tel: 780-459-7668; Fax: 780-460-0527
neigel@telus.net
Greg Mastervick, President

British Columbia Broomball Society
c/o 5356 Lochside Dr., Victoria, BC V8Y 2G7
www.bcbroomball.ca
Rick Przybysz, President
Bruce MacRae, Sec.-Treas.

Broomball Newfoundland & Labrador
734 Birch St., Labrador City, NL A2V 1C8
Tel: 709-944-5780; Fax: 709-944-5780
clarkep@nf.sympatico.ca
Harold Clarke, President

Canadian Broomball Federation / Fédération canadienne de ballon sur glace
#302, 200 Main St., Winnipeg, MB R3C 4M2
Tel: 204-925-5656; Fax: 204-925-5703
cbfbroomball@shaw.ca
www.broomball.ca

Federation of Broomball Associations of Ontario
515 Gascon St., Russell, ON K4R 1C6
Tel: 613-445-0904; Fax: 613-445-9844
www.ontariobroomball.ca
Gerry Wever, President

Fédération québécoise de ballon sur glace
4545, av Pierre-de Coubertin, Montréal, QC H1V 3R2
Tél: 514-252-3078; Téléc: 888-455-8547
www.fqbg.net
Richard Mimeau, Président

Manitoba Amateur Broomball Association (MABA)
145 Pacific Ave., Winnipeg, MB R3B 2Z6
Tel: 204-925-5668; Fax: 204-925-9792
www.mbbroomball.com
Raymond Massinon, President
Ron Marohn, Vice President

Northwest Territories Broomball Association
529 Range Lake Road, Yellowknife, NT X1A 3Y1
justjan529@theedge.ca
www.nwtbroomball.com
Jan Vallillee, President

Saskatchewan Broomball Association (SBA)
2205 Victoria Ave., Regina, SK S4P 0S4
Tel: 306-780-9215; Fax: 306-525-4009
saskbroomball@sasktel.net
www.saskbroomball.ca
Greg Perreaux, Executive Director

Canoeing & Rafting

Alberta Sprint Racing Canoe Association
11759 Groat Rd., Edmonton, AB T5M 3K6
Tel: 780-203-3987
arsca@shaw.ca
www.albertasprintcanoe.com
Rick Hill, President

Association québécoise de canoë-kayak de vitesse (AQCKV)
CP 1000, Succ. M, 4545, av Pierre-de Coubertin, Montréal, QC H1V 3R2
Tél: 514-252-3086; Téléc: 514-252-3094
directeur.technique@aqckv.qc.ca
www.aqckv.qc.ca
Luc Therrien, Président

Canoe Kayak New Brunswick
c/o Doug Forbes, 42 Third St., Rothesay, NB E2H 1M9
Tel: 506-849-0793
communications@canoekayaknb.org
www.canoekayaknb.org
Tim Humes, President

Canoe Kayak Nova Scotia (CKNS)
5516 Spring Garden Rd., Halifax, NS B3J 1G6
Tel: 902-425-5454; Fax: 902-425-5606
canoens@sportnovascotia.ca
www.ckns.ca

Canoe Newfoundland & Labrador
PO Box 23072, Stn. Churchill Sq., St. John's, NL A1B 4J9
Tel: 709-364-1601; Fax: 709-368-8357
tumblehome.nfld@gmail.com
www.canoenfld.ca
Corey Locke, President

Canoe Ontario
c/o OCSRA, 2078 Lemay Cres., Ottawa, ON K1G 2X4
Tel: 613-618-1715
www.canoeontario.org
Affiliation(s): Ontario Canoe Sprint Racing Affiliation; Ontario Marathon Canoe Racing Association; Whitewater Ontario

CanoeKayak BC
#102A, 11410 Kingston St., Maple Ridge, BC V2X 0Y5
Tel: 604-465-5268; Fax: 604-460-0587
info@canoekayakbc.ca
www.canoekayakbc.ca
www.facebook.com/canoekayakbc
twitter.com/CanoeKayakBC
Mary Jane Abbot, Executive Director

CanoeKayak Canada (CKC)
#700, 2197 Riverside Dr., Ottawa, ON K1H 7X3
Tel: 613-260-1818; Fax: 613-260-5137
www.canoekayak.ca
www.facebook.com/CanoeKayakCAN?ref=profile
twitter.com/CanoeKayakCAN
Lorraine Lafrenière, Director General
John Edwards, Director, Domestic Development
Peter Niedre, Director, Coaching Development & Education
Barney Wainwright, Director, High Performance

CanoeKayak Canada - Atlantic Division
c/o Sport NS, 5516 Spring Garden Rd., 4th Fl., Halifax, NS B3J 3G6
Tel: 902-425-5450; Fax: 902-425-5606
ccaatlantic@sportnovascotia.ca
www.ccaatlantic.ca
Liz Orton, Program Coordinator

Fédération québécoise du canot et du kayak (FQCK)
CP 1000, Succ. M, 4545, av Pierre-de Coubertin, Montréal, QC H1V 3R2
Tél: 514-252-3001; Téléc: 514-252-3091
info@canot-kayak.qc.ca
www.canot-kayak.qc.ca
www.facebook.com/group.php?gid=254842564559812
Pierre Trudel, Directeur général
Bernard Hugonnier, Directeur, Technique
Magalie Bernard, Agente, L'Information et aux communications
Philippe Pelland, Agent, Développement

Ikaluktutiak Paddling Association
PO Box 125, Cambridge Bay, NU X0B 0C0
Tel: 867-983-2068
ipanorth69@gmail.com
Rob Harmer, President

Manitoba Paddling Association Inc. (MPA)
145 Pacific Ave., Winnipeg, MB R3B 2Z6
Tel: 204-925-5681; Fax: 204-925-5792
mpa@sportmanitoba.ca
www.mpa.mb.ca

New Brunswick Competitive Canoe Association
c/o Sport New Brunswick, 181 Kennebecasis River Rd., Hampton, NB E5N 6L1
nbcca_m@hotmail.com
J. Timothy Flood, President

Newfoundland & Labrador Paddling Association (NLPA)
PO Box 181, 27 Lakeview Dr., Goulds, NL A1S 1G4
Tel: 709-745-6482
www.kayakers.nf.ca/nlpa
Affiliation(s): Kayak Newfoundland & Labrador; Tumblehome Recreational Canoe Club
Allan Goodridge, President
Brian Hemeon, Vice-President, Canoeing
Darren MacDonald, Vice-President, Kayaking
Neil Burgess, Secretary
Alex Mcgruer, Treasurer

Paddle Manitoba
PO Box 2663, Winnipeg, MB R3C 4B3
Tel: 204-338-6722
info@paddle.mb.ca
www.paddle.mb.ca
Affiliation(s): Manitoba Paddling Association
Catherine Holmen, President
Publications: The Ripple

Prince Edward Island Canoe Kayak Association
RR#4, Alliston, Montague, PE C0A 1R0
Tel: 902-962-3883; Fax: 902-962-3883
justin.heidi@windsinc.com
www.windsinc.com/canoekayak/canoekayak.htm
Justin Richard Batten, President

Prince Edward Island Recreational Canoeing Association
PO Box 5604, RR#5, Charlottetown, PE C1A 7J8
Tel: 902-368-6355; Fax: 902-368-6186

Recreational Canoeing Association BC (RCABC)
1755 East 7th Ave., Vancouver, BC V5N 1S1
Tel: 604-253-5410; Fax: 604-253-5490
sec@bccanoe.com
www.bccanoe.com
Alan Thomson, President
Jean Chandler, Secretary

Whitewater Kayaking Association of British Columbia (WKABC)
PO Box 91549, Stn. West Vancouver, Vancouver, BC V7V 3P2
Tel: 604-515-6376
admin@whitewater.org
www.whitewater.org
Affiliation(s): Outdoor Recreation Council of BC
Don Butler, President

Whitewater Ontario
411 Carnegie Beach Rd., Port Perry, ON L9L 1B6
Tel: 905-985-4585; Fax: 905-985-5256
Toll-Free: 888-322-2849
info@whitewaterontario.ca
www.whitewaterontario.ca
Claudia Kerkoff, Vice-President

Yukon Canoe & Kayak Club
PO Box 40080, 3 Sitka Cres., Whitehorse, YT Y1A 6M6
Tel: 867-456-4827
current@yckc.ca
www.yckc.ca
Eyvi Smith, President

Cerebral Palsy

Canadian Cerebral Palsy Sports Association (CCPSA) / Association canadienne de sport pour paralytiques cérébraux (ACPSA)
PO Box 41009, 1910 St. Laurent Blvd., Ottawa, ON K1G 5K9
Tel: 613-748-1430; Fax: 613-748-1355
Toll-Free: 866-247-9934
info@ccpsa.ca
www.ccpsa.ca
www.facebook.com/112866075626
Affiliation(s): Canadian Paralympic Committee; Cerebral Palsy International Sport & Recreation Association
Earl Church, Executive Director

Cerebral Palsy Sports Association of British Columbia (CPSABC)
6235A - 136th St., Surrey, BC V3X 1H3
Tel: 604-599-5240; Fax: 604-599-5241
sportinfo@sportabilitybc.ca
www.cpsports.com
Affiliation(s): Sport BC
Terri Moore, Executive Director

Manitoba Cerebral Palsy Sports Association (MCPSA)
145 Pacific Ave., Winnipeg, MB R3B 2Z6
Tel: 204-925-5682; Fax: 204-925-5703

Sport Ability Alberta
Percy Page Centre, 11759 Groat Rd., Edmonton, AB T5M 3K6
Tel: 780-422-2904; Fax: 780-422-2663
Toll-Free: 866-282-4356
brennan@acpsa.ca
www.acpsa.ca
Brennan Hermiston-Nicoll, Provincial Coordinator
Norma Lorincz, Executive Director

Coaching

Coaches Association of British Columbia (CABC)
#200, 3820 Cessna Drive, Richmond, BC V7B 0A2
Tel: 604-333-3600; Fax: 604-333-3450
info@coaches.bc.ca
www.coaches.bc.ca
www.facebook.com/media/set/?set=o.22542167140&ref=mf#!/CoachesBC
twitter.com/CoachesBC
Gordon May, Executive Director

Coaches Association of PEI (CAPEI)
PO Box 302, Charlottetown, PE C1A 7K7
Tel: 902-569-0583; Fax: 902-368-4548
Toll-Free: 800-247-6712
cgcrozier@sportpei.pe.ca
www.coachespei.ca
Cheryl G. Crozier, Executive Director

Coaching Association of Canada (CAC) / Association canadienne des entraîneurs
#300, 141 Laurier Ave. West, Ottawa, ON K1P 5J3
Tel: 613-235-5000; Fax: 613-235-9500
www.coach.ca
www.facebook.com/coach.ca
Affiliation(s): Professional Arm: Canadian Professional Coaches Association
John Bales, Chief Executive Officer
Cyndie Flett, Vice-President, Research & Development
Nancy Spotton, Vice-President, Sales & Marketing
Marc Schryburt, Director, Finance & Administration, International Programs
Julie Parkins-Forget, Manager, Marketing & Communications

Commonwealth Games

The Commonwealth Games Association of Canada Inc. (CGAC) / Association canadienne des jeux du Commonwealth inc.
#120, 2255 St. Laurent Blvd., Ottawa, ON K1G 4K3
Tel: 613-244-6868; Fax: 613-244-6826
info@commonwealthgames.ca
www.commonwealthgames.ca
Affiliation(s): Commonwealth Games Federation - London, England
Kelly Laframboise, Administrative Coordinator
Thomas Jones, CEO

Croquet

Fédération des clubs de croquet du Québec (FCCQ)
CP 1000, Succ. M, 4545, av Pierre-de Coubertin, Montréal, QC H1V 3R2
Tél: 514-252-3032
croquet@fqjr.qc.ca
www.fqjr.qc.ca/croquet.html
Yves Bédard, Président

Curling

Alberta Curling Federation (ACF)
Percy Page Centre, 11759 Groat Rd., 3rd Floor, Edmonton, AB T5M 3K6
Tel: 780-643-0809; Fax: 780-427-8103
www.albertacurling.ab.ca
J.W. (Jim) Pringle, Executive Director
Debi Vion, Programs & Office Administrator

Canadian Curling Association (CCA) / Association canadienne de curling
1660 Vimont Ct., Orleans, ON K4A 4J4
Tel: 613-834-2076; Fax: 613-834-0716
Toll-Free: 800-550-2875
boc@curling.ca (business of curling);
championships@curling.ca
www.curling.ca
www.facebook.com/ccacurling
Affiliation(s): World Curling Federation
Greg Stremlaw, Chief Executive Officer
Pat Ray, Chief Operating Officer
Warren Hansen, Director, Event Operations & Media
Danny Lamoureux, Director, Championship Services & Curling Club Development
Gerry Peckham, Director, High Performance

Curl BC
#293, 3820 Cessna Dr., Richmond, BC V7B 0A2
Tel: 604-737-3040; Fax: 604-737-1476
Toll-Free: 800-667-2875
curling@curlbc.ca
www.curlbc.ca
www.facebook.com/318254030482
twitter.com/curlbc
Scott Braley, Executive Director & CEO
Terry Vandale, President

Curling Québec
CP 1000, Succ. M, 4545, av Pierre-de Coubertin, Montréal, QC H1V 3R2
Tél: 514-252-3088; Téléc: 514-252-3342
Ligne sans frais: 888-292-2875
info@curling-quebec.qc.ca
www.curling-quebec.qc.ca
Marco Berthelot, Directeur général

International Curling Information Network Group (ICING)
73 Appleford Rd., Hamilton, ON L9C 6B5
Tel: 905-389-7781
psmith@icing.org
www.icing.org
Peter M. Smith, Contact

Manitoba Curling Association (MCA)
#309, 145 Pacific Ave., Winnipeg, MB R3B 2Z6
Tel: 204-925-5723; Fax: 204-925-5720
mca@curlmanitoba.org
www.curlmanitoba.org
Affiliation(s): Canadian Curling Association
Shane Ray, Executive Director
Cole Skinner, Event/Media Coordinator
Cindy Maddock, President

New Brunswick Curling Association (NBCA) / Association de Curling du Nouveau-Brunswick (ACNB)
PO Box 812, Moncton, NB E1C 8N6
Tel: 506-854-9143; Fax: 506-388-5708
Toll-Free: 800-592-2875
nbca@nb.sympatico.ca
www.nbcurling.com
Affiliation(s): Curl Atlantic
Marg Maranda, Executive Director
Jerry McCann, President
Catherine MacLean, Treasurer

Newfoundland & Labrador Curling Association
c/o Bob Osborne, 54 Hoyles Ave., St. John's, NL A1B 1E3
Tel: 709-738-3640
www.curlingnl.ca
Bob Osborne, President
Roy Hodder, Vice-President
Baxter House, Secretary
Carl C. Loughlin, Treasurer
Jean Blackie, Coordinator, Technical
Len Kostaszek, Coordinator, Tournament

Northern Alberta Curling Association (NACA)
#110, 9440 - 49 St., Edmonton, AB T6B 2M9
Tel: 780-440-4270; Fax: 780-463-4519
naca@planet.eon.net
northernalbertacurling.com
Marylynn Morris, Executive Director

Northern Ontario Curling Association
PO Box 940, Unit #4, 214 Main St. West, Atikokan, ON P0T 1C0
Tel: 807-597-8730; Fax: 888-622-8884
Toll-Free: 888-597-8730
info@curlnoca.ca
www.curlnoca.ca
www.facebook.com/curlnoca?sk=wall
twitter.com/curlnoca
Leslie Kerr, Executive Director
Al Gemmell, President

Northwest Territories Curling Association
PO Box 11089, Yellowknife, NT X1A 3X7
Tel: 867-669-8339; Fax: 867-669-8327
Toll-Free: 800-661-0797
mnorburn@sportnorth.com
www.nwtcurling.com
www.facebook.com/pages/NWT-Curling/316251248400802
twitter.com/nwt_curling
Maureen Miller, President

Northwestern Ontario Curling Association (NWOCA)
433 Catherine St., Thunder Bay, ON P7E 1K9
Tel: 807-622-8254; Fax: 807-626-9622
www.norontcurl.tripod.com
Colleen Syrja, Sec.-Treas.
Don R. MacLeod, President

Northwestern Québec Curling Association (NWQCA) / Association de curling du Nord-Ouest québécois
281, 3e rue est, Amos, QC J9T 2A7
Tel: 819-732-2089; Fax: 819-732-1617
Claude Noel, Secretary

Ontario Curling Association (OCA)
Office Mall 2, #2B, 1400 Bayly St., Pickering, ON L1W 3R2
Tel: 905-831-1757; Fax: 905-831-1083
Toll-Free: 877-668-2875
doug@ontcurl.com
www.ontcurl.com
Affiliation(s): Curl Ontario
Doug Bakes, Executive Director

Ottawa Valley Curling Association (OVCA)
PO Box 40129, Ottawa, ON K1V 0W8
Tel: 613-521-5822; Fax: 613-521-5344
Toll-Free: 800-385-6621
events@ovca.com
www.ovca.com
Affiliation(s): Curling Quebec
Perry Anderson, President
Lily Ooi, Coordinator, Events

Peace Curling Association (PCA)
PO Box 265, Grande Prairie, AB T8V 3A4
Tel: 780-532-4782; Fax: 780-538-2485
peaccurl@telusplanet.net
www.peacecurl.org
Bob Cooper, President

Prince Edward Island Curling Association (PEICA)
PO Box 302, 40 Enman Cres., Charlottetown, PE C1A 7K7
Tel: 902-368-4208; Fax: 902-368-4548
info@peicurling.com
www.peicurling.com
www.facebook.com/peicurling
twitter.com/peicurling
Affiliation(s): Sports PEI, Curl Atlantic
Amy Duncan, Executive Director

Saskatchewan Curling Association (SCA)
613 Park St., Regina, SK S4N 5N1
Tel: 306-780-9202; Fax: 306-780-9404
Toll-Free: 877-722-2875
saskcurling@sasktel.net
www.saskcurl.com/sca/scahome.htm
Del Jones, President

Southern Alberta Curling Association (SACA)
#720, 3 St. NW, Calgary, AB T2N 1N9
Tel: 403-246-9300; Fax: 403-246-9349
curling@saca.ca
www.saca.ca
Brent Syme, General Manager

World Curling Federation (WCF)
74 Tay St., Perth, PH2 8NP, Scotland
Tel: 44-173-845-1630; Fax: 44-173-845-1641
info@worldcurling.org
www.worldcurling.org
Lester Harrison, President
Kate Caithness, Vice-President
Mike Thomson, Secretary General

Yukon Curling Association (YCA)
4061 - 4th Ave., Whitehorse, YT Y1A 1H1
Tel: 867-668-7121; Fax: 867-667-4237
yca@sportyukon.com
yukoncurling.inthehack.com
Affiliation(s): Watson Lake Curling Club; Mayo Curling Club
Gord Zealand, President

Deafness

Alberta Deaf Sports Association (ADSA)
11404 - 142 St., Edmonton, AB T5M 1V1
www.albertadeafsports.ca
www.facebook.com/AlbertaDeafSports
Arista Haas, President
Calvin Novak, Vice-President
Kimberley Keba, Secretary
Nyla Kurylowich, Treasurer
Publications: Alberta Deaf Sports Newsletter

British Columbia Deaf Sports Federation (BCDSF)
#254, 3820 Cessna Dr., Richmond, BC V7B 0A2
Tel: 604-333-3606; Fax: 604-333-3450; TTY: 604-333-3606
info@bcdeafsports.bc.ca
www.bcdeafsports.bc.ca
www.facebook.com/139556792849947
twitter.com/bcdeafsports
Affiliation(s): BC Sport & Fitness Council for the Disabled
Johnson Leonor, Administrator

Canadian Deaf Ice Hockey Federation (CDIHF)
c/o C. Cooper, #137, 201 Queen Victoria Dr., Hamilton, ON L8W 1W7
cdihf@rogers.com
www.cdihf.deafhockey.com
www.facebook.com/group.php?gid=152070790142
Affiliation(s): Canadian Hockey Association; Ontario Deaf Sports Association, Inc.; Canadian Deaf Sports Association
Danny Daniels, President
Eugene Franciosi, Vice-President
Brenda Stanley, Secretary
Raymond Patterson, Treasurer

Canadian Deaf Sports Association (CDSA) / Association des sports des sourds du Canada (ASSC)
#202A, 10217, boul Pie IX, Montréal, QC H1H 3Z5
Tel: 514-321-8686; TTY: 514-321-2937
info@assc-cdsa.com
www.assc-cdsa.com
www.facebook.com/assc.cdsa
twitter.com/ASSC_CDSA
Affiliation(s): International Committee of Sports for the Deaf
Kimberley D. Rizzi, Executive Director
Ghysline "Gigi" Fiset, Project Coordinator
Mark Kusak, President

International Committee of Sports for the Deaf (ICSD) / Comité international des Sports des Sourds (CISS)
528 Trail Ave., Frederick, MD 21701, USA
Fax: 301-620-2990
info@ciss.org
www.deaflympics.com
Affiliation(s): Canadian Deaf Sports Association
Craig A. Crowley, President

New Brunswick Deaf Sports Association
#902, 656 Brunswick Dr., Saint John, NB E2L 3S5
Tel: 506-642-3903
Eugene Frost, President

Ontario Deaf Sports Association
#303, 3 Concorde Gate, Toronto, ON M3C 3N7
Tel: 416-413-0299
office@ontariodeafsports.on.ca
www.ontariodeafsports.on.ca
Rohan Smith, President

Saskatchewan Deaf Sports Association
1860 Lorne St., Regina, SK S4P 2L7
Toll-Free: 800-855-0511
www.saskdeafsports.ca
Affiliation(s): Regina Deaf Athletic Club; Saskatoon Deaf Athletic Club; Saskatchewan Sport Inc.; Canadian Deaf Sports Assn.
Kenneth Hoffman, President
Dale Birley, Administrator

Diabetes

Diabetes Exercise & Sports Association (DESA)
#604, 310 West Liberty, Louisville, KY 40202, USA
Fax: 502-581-0207
Toll-Free: 800-898-4322
desa@diabetes-exercise.org
www.diabetes-exercise.org
Guy Hornsby, Chair
Doug Dressman, Executive Director

Diving

Alberta Diving
426 Reeves Cres., Edmonton, AB T6R 2A4
Tel: 780-988-5571; Fax: 780-988-7753
www.albertadiving.ca
Cindy Casper, President
Susan Zwaenepoel, Vice-President
Barbara Dauphinais, Executive Director
Jim MacDonald, Secretary
Curtis Yano, Treasurer

British Columbia Diving
#114, 15272 Croydon Dr., Surrey, BC V3S 0Z5
Tel: 604-531-5576; Fax: 604-542-0387
bcdiving.sportbc.com
Jayne McDonald, Executive Director
Beverley Boys, Technical Director

Dive Ontario
216 Gilwood Park Dr., Penetang, ON L9M 1Z6
Tel: 705-355-3483; Fax: 705-355-4663
contactus@diveontario.com
www.diveontario.com
www.facebook.com/groups/7005127562
Affiliation(s): Community & recreation centres around the province
Janice Moore, President

Diving Plongeon Canada (DPC) / Association canadienne du plongeon amateur Inc.
#312, 700 Industrial Ave., Ottawa, ON K1G 0Y9
Tel: 613-736-5238; Fax: 613-736-0409
cada@diving.ca
www.diving.ca
Affiliation(s): Aquatics Federation of Canada; Swimming Natation Canada; Synchronized Swimming; Water Polo Canada
Penny Joyce, Chief Operating Officer
Mitch Geller, Chief Technical Officer
Scott Cranham, Director, High Performance
Jeff Feeney, Manager, Events & Communications

Fédération du plongeon amateur du Québec (FPAQ)
CP 1000, Succ. M, 4545, av Pierre-de-Coubertin, Montréal, QC H1V 0b2
Tél: 514-252-3096; Téléc: 514-252-3094
info@plongeon.qc.ca
www.plongeon.qc.ca
Isabelle Cloutier, Directrice exécutive

Fédération québécoise des activités subaquatiques (FQAS)
CP 1000, Succ. M, 4545, av Pierre-de Coubertin, Montréal, QC H1V 3R2
Tél: 514-252-3009; Téléc: 514-254-1363
Ligne sans frais: 866-391-8835
info@fqas.qc.ca
www.fqas.qc.ca
Affiliation(s): Confédération mondiale des activités subaquatiques
Jean-Sébastien Naud, Directeur général

Manitoba Diving Association
145 Pacific Ave., Winnipeg, MB R3B 2Z6
Tel: 204-925-5654; Fax: 204-925-5703
headcoach@panamdiving.com
www.manitobadiving.com
Jim Lambie, Head Coach

Manitoba Underwater Council (MUC)
PO Box 711, Winnipeg, MB R3C 2K3
Tel: 204-632-8508
info@manunderwater.com
www.manunderwater.com

Ontario Underwater Council (OUC)
#104, 1185 Eglinton Ave. East, Toronto, ON M3C 3C6
Tel: 416-426-7033; Fax: 416-426-7280
ouc@underwatercouncil.com
www.underwatercouncil.com
Raimund Krob, President

Saskatchewan Diving
1870 Lorne St., Regina, SK S4P 2L7
Tel: 306-780-9405; Fax: 306-781-6021
info@divesask.ca
www.saskdiving.ca
www.facebook.com/DIVESASK
twitter.com/divesask
Jaime Valentine, President

Equestrian Sports & Activities

Alberta Equestrian Federation (AEF)
#100, 251 Midpark Blvd. SE, Calgary, AB T2X 1S3
Tel: 403-253-4411; Fax: 403-252-5260
Toll-Free: 877-463-6233
info@albertaequestrian.com
www.albertaequestrian.com
www.facebook.com/group.php?gid=107271125975133
Dixie Crowson, President
Sonia Dantu, Executive Director

Atlantic Canada Trail Riding Association
Sylvia Gillies, #344 Route 875, Belleisle Creek, NB E5P 1C8
Roy Drinnan, Chair

British Columbia Competitive Trail Riders Association (BCCTRA)
c/o 2980 Giovando Road, Nanaimo, BC V9X 1K5
Tel: 250-245-4405
nicole.vaugeois@viu.ca
www.bcctra.ca
Nicole Vagueois, Sec.-Treas.

Canadian Sport Horse Association (CSHA)
PO Box 970, 7904 Franktown Rd., Richmond, ON K0A 2Z0
Tel: 613-686-6161; Fax: 613-686-6170
csha@canadian-sport-horse.org
www.c-s-h-a.org
www.facebook.com/group.php?gid=10649610317
Paul Morgan, President
David Lancaster, Treasurer

Distance Riders of Manitoba Association (DRMA)
PO Box 47, Gr 36, RR#2, Dugald, MB R0E 0K0
Tel: 204-444-2314
www.kucera.mb.ca/drma
Affiliation(s): American Endurance Ride Conference
Myna Cryderman, President
Linda Cruden, Membership Director

Drive Canada
PO Box 2062, Vancouver, BC V6B 3S3
Tel: 604-875-1905; Fax: 604-857-9582
drivecanada@shaw.ca
www.drivecanada.org
Affiliation(s): American Driving Society
Simon Rosenman, President

Endurance Riders Association of British Columbia (ERABC)
c/o 1624 Duncan Dr., Delta, BC V4L 1S2
info@erabc.com
www.erabc.com
Affiliation(s): Endurance Canada
Terre O'Brennan, Ride Manager

Endurance Riders of Alberta (ERA)
c/o President, PO Box 418, Seba Beach, AB T0E 2B0
Tel: 780-797-5404
www.enduranceridersofalberta.com
Affiliation(s): Canadian Long Distance Riding Association
Carol Wadey, Treasurer
Owen Fulcher, President

Equestrian Association for the Disabled
8360 Leeming Rd., RR#3, Mount Hope, ON L0R 1W0
Tel: 905-679-8323; Fax: 905-679-1705
www.tead.on.ca
Jim Sykes, Chair & President
Patrick Warner, Vice-President
Hilary Webb, Executive Director
Gord Hyland, Treasurer
Trish Brakewell, Coordinator
Pat Bullock, Instructor, Riding
Publications: The Rocking Horse Review

Equine Canada (EC) / Canada Hippique
#100, 2685 Queensview Dr., Ottawa, ON K2B 8K2
Tel: 613-248-3433; Fax: 613-248-3484
Toll-Free: 866-282-8395
inquiries@equinecanada.ca
www.equinecanada.ca
www.facebook.com/group.php?gid=385910086067
twitter.com/Equine_Canada
Affiliation(s): Provincial Partners: Horse Council of B.C., Alberta Equestrian Federation, Saskatchewan Horse Federation, Manitoba Horse Council, Ontario Equestrian Federation, Fédération Équestre du Quebec, New Brunswick Equestrian Association, PEI Horse Council, Nova Scotia Equestrian Federation, Newfoundland Equestrian Association, Canadian Pony Club
Mike Gallagher, President
Craig Andreas, Chief Operating Officer
Michael Arbour, CMA, Chief Financial Officer
Publications: Horse Life

Fédération équestre du Québec inc. (FEQ)
CP 1000, Succ. M, 4545, av Pierre-de Coubertin, Montréal, QC H1V 3R2
Tél: 514-252-3053; Téléc: 514-252-3068
Ligne sans frais: 866-575-0515
infocheval@feq.qc.ca
www.feq.qc.ca
www.facebook.com/386728291214
Richard Mongeau, Directeur général

Horse Council British Columbia (HCBC)
27336 Fraser Hwy., Aldergrove, BC V4W 3N5
Tel: 604-856-4304; Fax: 604-856-4302
Toll-Free: 800-345-8055
reception@hcbc.ca; membership@hcbc.ca; education@hcbc.ca
www.hcbc.ca
Lisa Laycock, Executive Director
Orville Smith, President
Carol Cody, Secretary
Carolyn Farris, Treasurer

Horse Trials New Brunswick
c/o Donna Lee Cole, 7515 Rte.102, Browns Flat, NB E5M 2N8
Tel: 506-468-2098
www.htnb.org
Affiliation(s): Horse Trials Canada
Donna Lee Cole, President
Louise McSheffrey, Secretary

Horse Trials Nova Scotia (HTNS)
60 Rockwell Drive, Mount Uniacke, NS B0N 1Z0
Tel: 902-866-3889
www.htns.org
Affiliation(s): Horse Trials Canada; Nova Scotia Equestrian Federation
Kim Elliott-Foster, President

Island Horse Council (IHC)
PO Box 302, Charlottetown, PE C1A 7K7
www.islandhorsecouncil.ca
www.facebook.com/islandhorsecouncil
Affiliation(s): Equine Canada
Wendell Grasse, Chair
Marg Younker, Treasurer
Publications: Business Directory, Island Horse Council Newsletter

Manitoba Horse Council Inc.
145 Pacific Ave., Winnipeg, MB R3B 2Z6
Tel: 204-925-5718; Fax: 204-925-5703
admin@manitobahorsecouncil.ca
www.manitobahorsecouncil.ca
Geri Sweet, President
Bruce Rose, Executive Director

Manitoba Trail Riding Club Inc. (MTRC)
838 Alfred Ave., Winnipeg, MB R2X 0T6
www.mbtrailridingclub.ca
Affiliation(s): Canadian Long Distance Riding Association
Kelli Hayhurst, President
Mary Anne Kirk, Treasurer

New Brunswick Equestrian Association (NBEA)
#13, 900 Hanwell Rd., Fredericton, NB E3B 6A3
Tel: 506-454-2353; Fax: 506-454-2363
www.nbea.ca
Deanna Phelan, President
Bonnie Robertson, Secretary

Newfoundland Equestrian Association (NEA)
PO Box 372, Stn. C, St. John's, NL A1C 5J9
www.horsenewfoundland.com
Katrina Butler, President
Sheila Anstey, Vice-President & Director, Competitions
Katie Murray, Secretary
Cathy Favre, Treasurer

North American Riding for the Handicapped Association (NARHA)
PO Box 33150, Denver, CO 80233, USA
Tel: 303-452-1212; Fax: 303-252-4610
Toll-Free: 800-369-7433
narha@narha.org
www.narha.org
Carol Nickell, CEO

Nova Scotia Distance Riding Association (NSDRA)
RR#3, Site 802, Newport, NS B0N 2A0
Affiliation(s): Canadian Long Distance Riding Association

Nova Scotia Equestrian Federation
5516 Spring Garden Rd., 4th Fl., Halifax, NS B3J 1G6
Tel: 902-425-5450; Fax: 902-425-5606
nsef@sportnovascotia.ca
www.horsenovascotia.ca
Heather Myrer, Executive Director

Ontario Competitive Trail Riding Association Inc. (OCTRA)
R.R.#4, Tottenham, ON L0G 1W0
Tel: 905-936-3362
webmaster@octra.on.ca
www.octra.on.ca
Affiliation(s): Horse Ontario; Ontario Equestrian Federation
Mark Ford, President
Joe Mezenberg, Vice-President
Marg Murray, Secretary
Kelly Corbyn, Treasurer

Ontario Equestrian Federation (OEF)
#203, 9120 Leslie St., Richmond Hill, ON L4B 3J9
Tel: 905-709-6545; Fax: 905-709-1867
Toll-Free: 877-441-7112
horse@horse.on.ca
www.horse.on.ca
Affiliation(s): Equine Guelph; Ontario Trails Council; Ontario Federation of Agriculture
Deborah Thompson, Executive Director
Gary Yaghdjian, President
Kathy Fremes, Secretary

Ontario Horse Trials Association (OHTA)
#186, 3-304 Stone Rd. West, Guelph, ON N1G 4W4
ohta@hotmail.ca
www.horsetrials.on.ca
Glenn McMechan, President
Robin Campbell, Secretary

Ontario Trail Riders Association (OTRA)
PO Box 3038, Elmvale, ON L0L 1P0
www.otra.ca
Affiliation(s): Ontario Trails Council; Ontario Equestrian Federation
Janice Clegg, President

Saskatchewan Horse Federation (SHF)
2205 Victoria Ave., Regina, SK S4P 0S4
Tel: 306-780-9244; Fax: 306-525-4009
sk.horse@sasktel.net
www.saskhorse.ca
Affiliation(s): Sask Sport; Western College Veterinary Medicine; SK Agriculture & Food (SAF)
Mae Smith, Executive Director

Saskatchewan Long Riders
c/o Brian Zwaan, PO Box 41, St. Denis, SK S0K 3W0
Tel: 306-978-1225
www.sasklongriders.com
Affiliation(s): Canadian Long Distance Riding Association
Trisha Dowling, President
Burt Sutherland, Contact

Trail Riding Alberta Conference (TRAC)
738 Wheeler Road, Edmonton, AB T6M 2E8
Tel: 403-486-0957
shanharms@shaw.ca
www.trailriding.ab.ca
Affiliation(s): Canadian Long Distance Riding Association
Brent Seufert, President

Fencing

Alberta Fencing Association (AFA)
Percy Page Centre, 11759 Groat Rd., Edmonton, AB T5M 3K6
Tel: 780-427-9474; Fax: 780-447-5959
info@fencing.ab.ca
www.fencing.ab.ca
Nicolas Allen, Executive Director

British Columbia Fencing Association (BCFA)
c/o #15, 12900 Jack Bell Dr., Richmond, BC V6V 2V8
www.fencing.bc.ca
John French, President

Canadian Fencing Federation (CFF) / Fédération canadienne d'escrime
10 Masterson Dr., St Catharines, ON L2T 3P1
Tel: 647-476-2401; Fax: 647-476-2402
cff@fencing.ca
www.fencing.ca
Affiliation(s): Fédération internationale d'escrime
Stephen Symons, President
Ron Dewar, Vice-President

Fédération d'escrime du Québec
CP 1000, Succ. M, 4545, av Pierre-de-Coubertin, Montréal, QC H1V 3R2
Tél: 514-252-3045; Téléc: 514-254-3451
info@escrimequebec.qc.ca
www.escrimequebec.qc.ca
Maître Dominique Teisseire, Directeur, technique et administratif

Fencing - Escrime New Brunswick (FENB)
c/o Mark Dobson, 20 Branch Cres., Quispamsis, NB E2E 0A9
Tel: 506-847-4204
www.fencingnb.ca
Lee McLean, President
Mark Dobson, Registrar

Fencing Association of Nova Scotia (FANS) / Association d'escrime de la Nouvelle-Écosse
c/o Sport Nova Scotia, 5516 Spring Garden Rd., 4th Fl., Halifax, NS B3J 3G6
Fax: 902-425-5606
www.chebucto.ns.ca/SportFit/Fencing
Diane Buote, President
Michael Barton, Treasurer
Bob Gillis, Registrar
Florian Friedrich, Technical Director
Janessa Green, Administrative Coordinator

Manitoba Fencing Association (MFA)
#308, 145 Pacific Ave., Winnipeg, MB R3B 2Z6
Tel: 204-925-5696; Fax: 204-925-5703
fencingmb@shawbiz.ca
www.fencing.mb.ca
Monica Feist, President
Robert Hornford, Vice-President, Technical
Jane Solomon, Vice-President

Newfoundland & Labrador Fencing Association (N&LFA)
#168, Unit 50 Hamlyn Road Plaza, St. John's, NL A1E 5X7
Fax: 709-368-8830
nlfencing@gmail.com
sites.google.com/site/nlfencing/
Justin So, President

Ontario Fencing Association (OFA) / Association d'escrime de l'Ontario
984 Main St. West, Hamilton, ON L8S 1B2
Tel: 905-525-6693
info@fencingontario.ca
fencingontario.ca/cms
Ranil Sonnadara, President
June McGuire, Executive Director

Prince Edward Island Fencing Association (PEIFA)
c/o Sport PEI, PO Box 302, 40 Enman Cres., Charlottetown, PE C1A 7K7
Tel: 905-368-4110; Fax: 905-386-4548
Toll-Free: 800-247-6712
sports@sportpei.pe.ca
www.upei.ca/~fencing

Saskatchewan Fencing Association (SFA)
510 Cynthia St., Saskatoon, SK S7L 7K7
Tel: 306-975-0823; Fax: 306-242-8007
saskfencing@shaw.ca
saskfencing.com
Affiliation(s): Saskatchewan Sport
Lynn Seguin, Executive Assistant

Field Hockey

Fédération de hockey sur gazon Québec / Québec Field Hockey Federation
CP 1000, Succ. M, 4545, av Pierre-de Coubertin, Montréal, QC H1V 3R2
Tél: 514-426-8405; Téléc: 514-426-9418
vimal.patel2@mail.mcgill.ca
www.hockeysurgazonquebec.com
Affiliation(s): Field Hockey Canada; Sports Canada
Harbir Bhamrah, Président

Field Hockey Alberta (FHA)
#1, 2135 Westmount Rd. NW, Calgary, AB T2N 3N3
Tel: 403-670-0014; Fax: 403-670-0018
Toll-Free: 888-670-0018
info@fieldhockey.ab.ca
fieldhockey.ab.ca
www.facebook.com/group.php?gid=21871703180
Liz Allan, Executive Director

Field Hockey Canada (FHC) / Hockey sur gazon Canada
#240, 1101 Prince of Wales Dr., Ottawa, ON K2C 3W7
Tel: 613-521-8774; Fax: 613-521-0261
fhc@fieldhockey.ca; communications@fieldhockey.ca (media)
www.fieldhockey.ca
www.facebook.com/FHCanada
twitter.com/FieldHockeyCan
Carole Lemire, Lead, Finance & Operations
Dawn Phillips, Manager, High Performance
Amy van Hemmen, Coordinator, Communications

Field Hockey Manitoba (FHM)
145 Pacific Ave., Winnipeg, MB R3B 2Z6
Tel: 204-925-5794; Fax: 204-925-5792
info@fieldhockeymb.org
www.fieldhockeymb.org
www.facebook.com/group.php?gid=7322580942
Kim Knowles, President

Field Hockey Nova Scotia
5516 Spring Garden Rd., 4th Fl., Halifax, NS B3J 1G6
www.fieldhockey.ns.ca
www.facebook.com/group.php?gid=39499666567
Mike Fearon, President

Field Hockey Ontario (FHO)
PO Box 1037, Erin, ON N0B 1T0
Tel: 905-492-1680
fhoboard@gmail.com
www.fieldhockeyontario.netfirms.com
www.facebook.com/group.php?gid=2211466956
Ann Doggett, President

New Brunswick Field Hockey Association (NBFHA)
c/o 2341 Golden Grove Rd., Saint John, NB E2N 1Z8
Tel: 506-634-1241
sara.hayward@nbed.nb.ca
Sara Hayward, President

Saskatchewan Field Hockey Association
1860 Lorne St., Regina, SK S4P 2L7
Tel: 306-780-9256; Fax: 306-781-6021
sfha@sasktel.net
www.saskfieldhockey.ca
Stefanie Sloboda, Technical Director

Football

Alberta Amateur Football Association (AAFA)
Percy Page Centre, 11759 Groat Rd., Edmonton, AB T5M 3K6
Tel: 780-427-8108; Fax: 780-427-0524
bfryer@telus.net
www.footballalberta.ab.ca
Neil Gerritsen, President
Brian Fryer, Executive Director

Canadian Football Hall of Fame & Museum
58 Jackson St. West, Hamilton, ON L8P 1L4
Tel: 905-528-7566; Fax: 905-528-9781
info@cfhof.ca
www.cfhof.ca
twitter.com/cfhof
Steve Howse, Chair
Mark DeNobile, Executive Director
Meghan Sturgeon, Curator

Canadian Football League (CFL) / Ligue canadienne de football (LCF)
50 Wellington St. East, 3rd Fl., Toronto, ON M5E 1C8
Tel: 416-322-9650; Fax: 416-322-9651
www.cfl.ca
www.facebook.com/CFL
twitter.com/CFL
Mark Cohon, Commissioner
Michael Copeland, Chief Operating Officer
Doug Allison, Vice-President, Finance & Business Operations
Matt Maychak, Vice-President, Communications & Broadcast
Kevin McDonald, Vice-President, Football Operations

Canadian Football Officials Association
c/o Ontario Region, 73 Alpaca Dr., Toronto, ON M1J 2Z9
Tel: 416-431-7887
webcommittee@cfoa-acof.ca
www.cfoa-acof.ca
Mike Groleau, President

Canadian Junior Football League (CJFL)
9611 RR#1, Richmond, BC V7E 1R8
Tel: 604-277-8133; Fax: 604-277-8136
www.cjfl.net
www.facebook.com/group.php?gid=109346462416307

Canadian University Football Coaches Association (CUFCA)
c/o Huskies Football, St. Mary's University, Halifax, NS B3H 3C3
Tel: 902-420-5550
Affiliation(s): Canadian Interuniversity Athletic Union
Blake Nill, President

Football BC
#434, 6939 Hastings St., Burnaby, BC V5B 4Z5
Tel: 604-677-1025; Fax: 604-677-1025
communications@playfootball.bc.ca
www.playfootball.bc.ca

Football Canada
#100, 2255 St. Laurent Blvd., Ottawa, ON K1G 4K3
Tel: 613-564-0003; Fax: 613-564-6309
info@footballcanada.com
footballcanada.com
Richard Munro, CEO
Bob Swan, Technical Consultant
Cara Lynch, Manager, Non-Contact Programs
Josh Sacobie, Technical Coordinator
Christine Piché, Administrative Coordinator

Football Nova Scotia Association
#536, 1657 Barrington St., Halifax, NS B3J 2A1
Tel: 902-454-5105; Fax: 902-425-5606
footballns@ns.aliantzinc.ca
www.footballnovascotia.ca
Affiliation(s): Canadian Amateur Football Association
Richard MacLean, President
Rob Manson, Vice-President

Football Québec (FFAQ) / Fédération de football amateur de Québec
CP 1000, Succ. M, 4545, av Pierre-de-Coubertin, Montréal, QC H1V 3R2
Tél: 514-252-3059; Téléc: 514-252-5216
jeancharles@football.qc.ca
www.football-quebec.com
Affiliation(s): National Football Federation of Canada
René Robillard, Président

Ontario Football Alliance
7384 Wellington Rd. 30, Guelph, ON N1H 6J2
Tel: 519-780-0200; Fax: 519-780-0705
otf@on.aibn.com
www.ontariofootballalliance.ca
Tina Turner, Executive Director
Smith Ian, President

Foundations

Dr. James Naismith Basketball Foundation / La fondation de basketball Dr James Naismith
PO Box 1030, 14 Bridge St., Almonte, ON K0A 1A0
Tel: 613-256-0492; Fax: 613-256-7883
info@naismithminorbasketball.ca
www.naismithbasketball.ca
Affiliation(s): Basketball Canada
John Gosset, Executive Director
Kevin Hickey, President

Royal Canadian Golf Association Foundation
#1, 1333 Dorval Dr., Oakville, ON L6M 4X7
Tel: 905-849-9700; Fax: 905-845-7040
Toll-Free: 800-263-0009
info@golfcanada.ca
www.golfcanada.ca
www.facebook.com/TheGolfCanada
twitter.com/TheGolfCanada
Karen Rackel, President

Fundraising

WinSport Canada
88 Canada Olympic Rd. SW, Calgary, AB T3B 5R5
Tel: 403-247-5452; Fax: 403-286-7213
info@coda.ca
www.winsportcanada.ca
Affiliation(s): Canadian Olympic Committee; Canadian Paralympic Committee
Trevor Nakka, Chair

Golf

Alberta Golf Association (AGA)
#22, 11410 - 27 St. SE, Calgary, AB T2Z 3R6
Tel: 403-236-4616; Fax: 403-236-2915
Toll-Free: 888-414-4849
info@albertagolf.org
www.albertagolf.org
www.facebook.com/pages/Alberta-Golf/144026188016
twitter.com/AGinthenews
Brent Ellenton, Executive Director
Jack Lane, Manager, Championships
Eric Rogers, Accountant

Association des golfeurs professionnels du Québec (AGP)
435, boul. Saint-Luc, Saint-Jean-sur-Richelieu, QC J2W 1E7
Tél: 450-349-5525; Téléc: 450-349-6640
agpinfo@agp.qc.ca
www.agp.qc.ca
Jean Trudeau, Directeur général

Association des surintendants de golf du Québec (ASGQ) / Québec Golf Superintendents Association (QSGA)
CP 642, Succ. B, Montréal, QC H3B 3K3
Tél: 514-285-4874; Téléc: 514-282-4292
info@asgq.org
www.asgq.org
Christian Pilon, Président

British Columbia Golf Association (BCGA)
#2110, 13700 Mayfield Pl., Richmond, BC V6V 2E4
Tel: 604-279-2580; Fax: 604-207-9535
Toll-Free: 888-833-2242
info@bcga.org
www.britishcolumbiagolf.org
www.facebook.com/BritishColumbiaGolf
twitter.com/bc_golfer

Affiliation(s): Canadian Golf Foundation; Professional Golf Association of BC; Canadian Ladies Golf Association of BC; Golf Course Superintendents Association of BC; International Association of Golf Administrators; National Golf Foundation; Pacific Coast Golf Association; Pacific Northwest Golf Association
Kris Jonasson, Executive Director
Deborah Pyne, Managing Director, Player Development
Andy Fung, Director, Finance & Administration
Susan White, Director, Rules, Competitions, & Education
Christopher McGrath, Manager, Communications & Marketing
Shirley Simmons-Doyle, Manager, Member Services

British Columbia Golf Superintendents Association (BCGSA)
PO Box 807, 231 Nootka Cres., Lake Cowichan, BC V0R 2G0
Tel: 250-749-6703; Fax: 250-749-6702
admin@bcgsa.com
www.bcgsa.com
Ginny Tromp, Executive Administrator
Rob Wilke, BCGSA President
Jerry Rousseau, Treasurer
Publications: BCGSA Newsletter

Canadian Caribbean Amateur Golfers Association (CCAGA)
#718, 7305 Woodbine Ave, Markham, ON L3R 3V7
Fax: 905-420-8421
info@ccaga.ca
www.ccaga.ca

Canadian Golf Superintendents Association (CGSA) / Association canadienne des surintendants de golf
#205, 5520 Explorer Dr., Mississauga, ON L4W 5L1
Tel: 905-602-8873; Fax: 905-602-1958
Toll-Free: 800-387-1056
cgsa@golfsupers.com
www.golfsupers.com
www.facebook.com/group.php?gid=151227228150
twitter.com/GolfSupers
Kenneth S. Cousineau, Executive Director
Tim Kubash, President
John Mills, Vice-President
Christian Pilon, Secretary-Treasurer
Publications: CGSA [Canadian Golf Superintendents Association] Membership Directory, Environmental Management Resource Manual [a publication of the Canadian Golf Superintendents Association], GreenMaster, Greenmatter E-News [a publication of the Canadian Golf Superintendents Association]

Canadian Professional Golfers' Association (CPGA) / Association canadienne des golfeurs professionnels
13450 Dublin Line, RR#1, Acton, ON L7J 2W7
Tel: 519-853-5450; Fax: 519-853-5449
Toll-Free: 800-782-5764
cpga@cpga.com
www.cpga.com
Gary Bernard, Interim Executive Director

Canadian Society of Club Managers (CSCM) / La Société canadienne des directeurs de club
2943B Bloor St. West, Toronto, ON M8X 1B3
Tel: 416-979-0640; Fax: 416-979-1144
Toll-Free: 877-376-2726
national@cscm.org
www.cscm.org
Elizabeth Di Chiara, Executive Director

Golf Association of Ontario (GAO)
PO Box 970, Uxbridge, ON L9P 1N3
Tel: 905-852-1101; Fax: 905-852-8893
administration@gao.ca
www.gao.ca
www.facebook.com/GAOGolf
twitter.com/GAOGolf
David Mills, Executive Director
Dave Colling, Director, Rules & Competitions
Mike Kelly, Director, Sport Development
Craig Loughryne, Director, Handicapping & Course Rating
Kyle McFarlane, Director, Marketing & Communications
Kate Sheldon, Director, Administration

Golf Manitoba Inc.
420 - 145 Pacific Ave., Winnipeg, MB R3B 2Z6
Tel: 204-925-5730; Fax: 204-925-5731
golfmb@golfmanitoba.mb.ca
golfmanitoba.mb.ca
Rob MacDonald, President
Dave Comaskey, Executive Director

Golf Newfoundland & Labrador (GNL)
PO Box 174, Gander, NL A1V 1W6
Tel: 709-424-3102
golf@hnl.ca
www.golfnewfoundland.ca
Greg Hillier, President

Golf Québec
4545, av Pierre-de-Coubertin, Montréal, QC H1V 3R2
Tél: 514-252-3345; Téléc: 514-252-3346
golfquebec@golfquebec.org
www.golfquebec.org
Jean-Pierre Beaulieu, President
François Roy, Directeur général adjoint
Patrice Clément, Directeur, Développement des joueurs
Éric Couture, Directeur, Tournois
Gladys V. Iodio, Coordonnatrice, Services aux membres

National Golf Course Owners Association Canada (NGCOA)
#105, 955 Green Valley Cres., Ottawa, ON K2C 3V4
Tel: 613-226-3616; Fax: 613-226-4148
Toll-Free: 866-626-4262
ngcoa@ngcoa.ca
www.ngcoa.ca
Jeff Calderwood, CEO
Nathalie Lavallée, COO

New Brunswick Golf Association (NBGA) / Association de golf du nouveau brunswick
PO Box 1555, Stn. A, Fredericton, NB E3B 5G2
Tel: 506-451-1324; Fax: 506-451-1348
nbgolf@nb.aibn.com
www.nbga.nb.ca
Tyson Flinn, Executive Director

Nova Scotia Golf Association (NSGA)
#4, 24 Simmonds Dr., Dartmouth, NS B3B 1R3
Tel: 902-468-8844; Fax: 902-484-5327
www.nsga.ns.ca
www.facebook.com/pages/The-Nova-Scotia-Golf-Association/64019542477
twitter.com/novascotiagolf
Affiliation(s): Royal Canadian Golf Association
David Campbell, Executive Director
Jan Gaudette, Executive Assistant

Prince Edward Island Golf Association
PO Box 51, Charlottetown, PE C1A 7K2
Tel: 902-393-3293; Fax: 902-628-2260
peiga@peiga.ca
www.peiga.ca
Don Chandler, Executive Director
Jean Kelly, President

Professional Golfers' Assocation of British Columbia (PGA of BC)
#3280, 21331 Morgan Creek Way, Richmond, BC V6W 1J9
Tel: 604-303-6766; Fax: 604-303-6765
Toll-Free: 800-667-4653
www.pgabc.org
www.facebook.com/pgabc
twitter.com/pgaofbc
Donald Miyazaki, Interim Executive Director
Troy Peverley, President

Royal Canadian Golf Association (RCGA) / Association royale de golf du Canada
#1, 1333 Dorval Dr., Oakville, ON L6M 4X7
Tel: 905-849-9700; Fax: 905-845-7040
Toll-Free: 800-263-0009
info@golfcanada.ca; members@golfcanada.ca
www.golfcanada.ca
www.facebook.com/group.php?gid=61328126412
Affiliation(s): World Amateur Golf Council
Scott Simmons, Executive Director & CEO
Dave Lafleur, Chief Financial Officer
Larry Thomas, Chief Commercial Officer
Jeff Thompson, Chief Sport Development Officer
Rick Desrochers, Senior Director
Bill Paul, Managing Dir, Professional Championships
Sean Van Kesteren, Managing Dir, Professional Championships
Brent McLaughlin, Director, Rules, Competitions & Amateur Status

Saskatchewan Golf Association Inc.
510 Cynthia St., Saskatoon, SK S7L 7K7
Tel: 306-975-0850; Fax: 306-975-0840
info@saskgolf.ca
www.saskgolf.ca
Brian Lee, Executive Director
Candace Dunham, Manager, Programs & Member Services
Phil Grosse, Manager, Marketing & Sport Development
Dan Ukrainetz, Manager, Tournaments & Player Services

Gymnastics

Alberta Gymnastics Federation (AGF)
#207, 5800 - 2 St. SW, Calgary, AB T2H 0H2
Tel: 403-259-5500; Fax: 403-259-5588
Toll-Free: 800-665-1010
info@abgym.ab.ca
www.abgym.ab.ca
www.facebook.com/AlbertaGymnastics
Scott Hayes, President & CEO

Fédération de gymnastique du Québec (FGQ) / Québec Gymnastics Federation
CP 1000, Succ. M, 4545, av Pierre-de-Coubertin, Montréal, QC H1V 3R2
Tél: 514-252-3043; Téléc: 514-252-3169
info@gymnastique.qc.ca
www.gymnastique.qc.ca
Serge Castonguay, Directeur général
Claude Aubertin, Président
Serge Sabourin, Vice-président

Gymnastics B.C. (GBC)
#230, 3820 Cessna Dr., Richmond, BC V7B 0A2
Tel: 604-333-3496; Fax: 604-333-3499
Toll-Free: 800-556-2242
info@gymnastics.bc.ca
www.gymnastics.bc.ca
www.linkedin.com/groups/Gymnastics-BC-3800514?trk=myg_ugrp_ovr
www.facebook.com/GymnasticsBC
twitter.com/GymnasticsBC
Moira Gooksetter, CEO
Twyla Ryan, President

Gymnastics Canada Gymnastique (GCG)
#120, 1900 City Park Dr., Ottawa, ON K1J 1A3
Tel: 613-748-5637; Fax: 613-748-5691
info@gymcan.org
www.gymcan.org
www.facebook.com/gymcan
twitter.com/GymnasticsCan
Affiliation(s): Fédération internationale de gymnastique
Jean-Paul Caron, President & Chief Executive Officer
Cathy Haines, Chief Technical Officer
Stephan Duchesne, Director, High Performance
Annie Gagnon, Coordinator, Events

Gymnastics Newfoundland & Labrador Inc.
PO Box 21248, Stn. MacDonald Dr., St. John's, NL A1A 5B2
Tel: 709-576-0146; Fax: 709-576-7493
gymnastics@sportnl.ca
www.gymnastics.nl.ca
Bob Godden, President
Carol White, Executive Director

Gymnastics Nova Scotia (GNS)
5516 Spring Garden Rd., 4th Fl., Halifax, NS B3J 1G6
Tel: 902-425-5450; Fax: 902-425-5606
gns@sportnovascotia.ca
www.gymns.ca
Byron Topp, President
Angela Gallant, Executive Director
Vaughn Arthur, Chair, Fair Play & Equity
Nick Lenehan, Chair, Competition
Eleanor Melrose, Chair, Education & Recreation
Cathy Huntington, Secretary
Steve Lowe, Treasurer
Publications: Gymnastics Nova Scotia Newsletter, Gymnastics Nova Scotia Policy Manual

Gymnastics PEI
Sport PEI, PO Box 302, Charlottetown, PE C1A 7K7
Tel: 902-368-4262; Fax: 902-368-4548
gflood@sportpei.pe.ca
www.sportpei.pe.ca
Glen Flood, Executive Director

Gymnastics Saskatchewan
1870 Lorne St., Regina, SK S4P 2L7
Tel: 306-780-9229; Fax: 306-780-9475
info@gymsask.com
www.gymsask.com
Klara Miller, Executive Director

Manitoba Gymnastics Association (MGA)
145 Pacific Ave., Winnipeg, MB R3B 2Z6
Tel: 204-925-5781; Fax: 204-925-5932
mga@sportmanitoba.ca
www.gymnastics.mb.ca
Kathy Stoesz, Executive Director

New Brunswick Gymnastics Association (NBGA) / Association gymnastique du Nouveau-Brunswick (AGNB)
110 Rivercrest Ave., Riverview, NB E1B 1M7
Tel: 506-384-6242; Fax: 506-384-6244
nbga@gym.nb.ca
www.gym.nb.ca
Nathalie Colpitts, Executive Director
Mike Waddell, President

Ontario Gymnastic Federation (OGF)
#214, 3 Concorde Gate, Toronto, ON M3C 3N7
Tel: 416-426-7100; Fax: 416-426-7377
Toll-Free: 866-565-0650
info@ogf.com
www.ogf.com
Affiliation(s): Gymnastics Canada
Ruth Simpson, Chief Executive Officer
Linda Clifford, President
Angel Crossman, Secretary & Director, Policies & Procedures
Sean Holmes, Technical Director, Gymnastics Program Development
Yuliana Korolyova, Coordinator, Education
Colleen O'Hare, Coordinator, Membership Services
Terri Parsons, Coordinator, Administrative Services

Rhythmic Gymnastics Alberta (RGA)
c/o Percy Page Centre, 11759 Groat Rd., 3rd Fl., Edmonton, AB T5M 3K6
Tel: 780-427-8152; Fax: 780-427-8153
Toll-Free: 800-881-2504
rga@rgalberta.com
www.rgalberta.com
www.facebook.com/pages/Rhythmic-Gymnastics-Alberta/298160665303?ref=ts
Joan Jack, President
Odette Lindstrom, Treasurer
Helen Marchak, Vice-President

Yukon Gymnastics Association
4061 - 4th Ave., Whitehorse, YT Y1A 1H1
Tel: 867-456-7896; Fax: 867-668-6922
polarett@internorth.com
yukongymnastic.com
Kelly Mock, Technical Director

Halls of Fame

Alberta Sports Hall of Fame & Museum (ASHFM)
#102-4200 Hwy 2, Red Deer, AB T4N 1E3
Tel: 403-341-8614; Fax: 403-341-8619
info@ashfm.ca
www.ashfm.ca
Donna Hateley, Managing Director

British Columbia Sports Hall of Fame & Museum
Gate A, BC Place Stadium, 777 Pacific Blvd. South, Vancouver, BC V6B 4Y8
Tel: 604-687-5520; Fax: 604-687-5510
sportsinfo@bcsportshalloffame.com
www.bcsportshalloffame.com
Affiliation(s): International Association of Sports Museums & Halls of Fame
Colin Brown, Chair

Canada's Sports Hall of Fame / Temple de la renommée des sports du Canada
Exhibition Place, 115 Princes' Blvd., Toronto, ON M6K 3C3
Tel: 416-260-6789; Fax: 416-260-9347
info@cshof.ca
www.cshof.ca
Sheryn Posen, COO
J. Trevor Eyton, Chair

Canadian Golf Hall of Fame & Museum (CGHF) / Musée et Temple canadien de la renommée du golf
Glen Abbey Golf Club, 1333 Dorval Dr., Oakville, ON L6M 4X7
Tel: 905-849-9700; Fax: 905-845-7040
rdands@golfcanada.ca
www.rcga.org
Scott Simmons, Executive Director, Golf Canada
Meggan Gardner, Curator, Canadian Golf Hall of Fame & Museum
Jason Cheong, Assistant, Canadian Golf Hall of Fame & Museum

Canadian Lacrosse Hall of Fame
302 Royal Ave., New Westminster, BC V3L 1H7
Tel: 604-527-4640; Fax: 604-527-4641
allan@lacrosse.ca
Allan Blair, Curator

Canadian Olympic Hall of Fame / Temple de la renommée olympique du Canada
c/o COC, #1400, 85 Albert St., Ottawa, ON K1P 6A4
Tel: 613-244-2020; Fax: 613-244-0169
www.olympic.ca/en/programs/canadian-olympic-hall-fame

Manitoba Sports Hall of Fame & Museum (MSHF&M)
145 Pacific Ave., Winnipeg, MB R3B 2Z6
Tel: 204-925-5735; Fax: 204-925-5792
halloffame@sportmanitoba.ca
www.halloffame.mb.ca
Affiliation(s): Sport Manitoba
Rick Brownlee, Sport Heritage Manager

New Brunswick Sports Hall of Fame (NBSHF) / Temple de la renommée sportive du N.-B.
503 Queen St., Fredericton, NB E3B 5H1
Tel: 506-453-3747
nbsportshalloffame@gnb.ca
www.nbsportshalloffame.com
www.facebook.com/150319378347024
twitter.com/NBSHF
Affiliation(s): International Sports Heritage Association
Jamie Wolverton, Executive Director

Northwestern Ontario Sports Hall of Fame & Museum
219 May St. South, Thunder Bay, ON P7E 1B5
Tel: 807-622-2852; Fax: 807-622-2736
nwosport@tbaytel.net
www.nwosportshalloffame.com
Kathryn Dwyer, Curator
Diane Imrie, Executive Director

Nova Scotia Sport Heritage Centre
#446, 1800 Argyle Street, Halifax, NS B3J 3N8
Tel: 902-421-1266; Fax: 902-425-1148
Bill Robinson, Executive Director

Ottawa Sports Hall of Fame Inc. (OSHOF) / Temple de la renommée des sports d'Ottawa
Ottawa, ON
Tel: 613-562-6515
frank.lambros@NBPCD.com
www.ottawasportshalloffame.com
Tom Deacon, Chair

Prince Edward Island Sports Hall of Fame & Museum Inc.
PO Box 1523, Summerside, PE C1N 4K4
Tel: 902-436-0423; Fax: 902-436-0960
publicrelations@sportpei.pe.ca
www.peisportshalloffame.ca
Clair Sudsbury, Chair

Saskatchewan Sports Hall of Fame & Museum (SSFHM)
2205 Victoria Ave., Regina, SK S4P 0S4
Tel: 306-780-9232; Fax: 306-780-9427
sshfm@sasktel.net
www.sshfm.com
Sheila Kelly, Executive Director

Handball

Alberta Team Handball Federation (ATHF)
Percy Page Centre, 11759 Groat Rd., Edmonton, AB T5M 3K6
Tel: 780-415-2666; Fax: 780-422-2663
Handballalberta@gmail.com
www.teamhandball.ab.ca
www.facebook.com/pages/Alberta-Team-Handball-Federation/111368133359
twitter.com/handballalberta
Dan Stetic, President & CEO
Mike Rott, Chief Financial Officer

Balle au mur Québec (BAMQ) / Québec Handball Association
CP 1000, Succ. M, 4545, av Pierre-de-Coubertin, Montréal, QC H1V 3R2
Tél: 514-252-3062
info@sports-4murs.qc.ca
www.balleaumur.qc.ca
Affiliation(s): Association canadienned de Balle au mur
Michel Foster, Directeur général
Danny Bell, Président

Canadian Handball Association (CHA) / Fédération de balle au mur du Canada
30 Melwood Ave., Halifax, NS B3N 1E3
Tel: 902-477-2902; Fax: 902-431-3145
handball@cdnhandball.org
www.canadianhandballcourts.ca
Doug Santha, President
Heather Mueller, Treasurer

Canadian Team Handball Federation (CTHF) / Fédération canadienne de handball olympique (FCHO)
453, rue Jacob-Nicol, Sherbrooke, QC J1J 4E5
Tel: 819-563-7937; Fax: 819-563-5352
f.lebeau@videotron.ca
www.handballcanada.ca
Affiliation(s): International Handball Federation; Pan American Team Handball Federation; Commonwealth Handball Federation
François LeBeau, COO
Ward Hrabi, President

Fédération québécoise de handball olympique
CP 1000, Succ. M, 4545, av Pierre-de-Coubertin, Montréal, QC H1V 3R2
Tél: 514-252-3067; Téléc: 514-251-8882
handball@handball.qc.ca
www.handball-elite.com
Michelle Lortie, Directrice

Manitoba Team Handball Federation
#311, 200 Main St., Winnipeg, MB R3C 4M2
Tel: 204-925-5652; Fax: 204-925-5703
www.handballmanitoba.com
Ward Hrabi, Contact

New Brunswick Team Handball Association
585, Pointe des Ferguson, Tracadie-Sheila, NB E1X 1C6
Tél: 506-395-7722; Téléc: 506-395-3809
Adair Losier, President

Newfoundland & Labrador Handball Federation
c/o School of Human Kinetics, Memorial Univ., St. John's, NL A1C 5S7
Tel: 709-737-8684
rwheeler@mun.ca
Ralph Wheeler, Contact

Team Handball Federation of British Columbia
5849 Fleming St., Vancouver, BC V5P 3G4
Tel: 604-871-0824
info@vancouverhandball.ca
www.vancouverhandball.ca
Deborah Magdee, President

Hang Gliding

British Columbia Hang Gliding & Paragliding Association (BCHPA)
www.bchpa.ca
Nance Margit, President

Hang Gliding & Paragliding Association of Atlantic Canada (HPAAC)
General Delivery, Diligent River, NS B0M 1H0
Tel: 902-254-2972
jnewman@eastlink.ca
www.hpaac.ca

Affiliation(s): Hang Gliding & Paragliding Association of Canada
Judith Newman, Contact

Hang Gliding & Paragliding Association of Canada (HPAC) / Association canadienne de vol libre (ACVL)
5 Millennium Dr., Stratford, PE C1B 2H2
Fax: 902-367-3358
Toll-Free: 877-370-2078
admin@hpac.ca
www.hpac.ca
Domagoj Juretic, President
Sam Jeyes, Business Manager

Health

Island Fitness Council
#2, 1216 Sand Cove Rd., Saint John, NB E2M 5V8
Tel: 506-672-1993; Fax: 506-672-8762
Toll-Free: 888-790-1411
membershipservices@fitnessnb.ca
www.fitnessnb.ca
Affiliation(s): National Fitness Leadership Alliance

Physical & Health Education Canada / Éducation physique et santé Canada
#301, 2197 Riverside Dr., Ottawa, ON K1H 7X3
Tel: 613-523-1348; Fax: 613-523-1206
Toll-Free: 800-663-8708
info@phecanada.ca
www.phecanada.ca
Mark Jones, President
Andrea Grantham, Executive Director
Sharon May, Director, Programs
Publications: In Touch Newsletter, Physical & Health Education Journal

Hiking

Federation of Mountain Clubs of British Columbia
PO Box 19673, 130 West Broadway, Vancouver, BC V5T 4E7
Tel: 604-873-6096; Fax: 604-873-6086
fmcbc@mountainclubs.bc.ca
www.mountainclubs.bc.ca
Patrick R. Harrison, President
Ron Ford, Registrar
Brian Jones, Manager
Peter Rothermel, Vice-President

Hockey

British Columbia Amateur Hockey Association (BCAHA) / Association de hockey amateur de la Colombie-Britannique
6671 Oldfield Rd., Saanichton, BC V8M 2A1
Tel: 250-652-2978; Fax: 250-652-4536
info@bchockey.net
www.bchockey.net
Barry Petrachenko, Executive Director
Ed Mayert, President

Canadian Adult Recreational Hockey Association (CARHA)
#610, 1420 Blair Pl., Ottawa, ON K1J 9L8
Tel: 613-244-1989; Fax: 613-244-0451
Toll-Free: 800-267-1854
hockey@carhahockey.ca
www.carhahockey.ca
Michael S. Peski, President
Patti Kenny, Director, Finance
Lori Lopez, Director, Business Operations
Karen Salaj, Manager, Member Services
Laurie Snider, Manager, Service & Administration
Publications: Ice Chips

Canadian Hockey League
#201, 305 Milner Ave., Toronto, ON M1B 3V4
Tel: 416-332-9711; Fax: 416-332-1477
www.chl.ca

Fédération internationale de hockey (FIH) / International Hockey Federation
Résidence du Parc, Rue du Valentin 61, Lausanne, 1004, Switzerland
Tél: 41-21-641-0606; Téléc: 41-21-641-0607
info@fih.ch
www.fih.ch
Affiliation(s): Field Hockey Canada
Leandro Negre, President

Hockey Alberta / Hockey l'Alberta
#1, 7875 - 48 Ave., Red Deer, AB T4P 2K1
Tel: 403-342-6777; Fax: 403-346-4277
www.hockey-alberta.ca
www.facebook.com/group.php?gid=43831380491
twitter.com/HockeyAlberta
Rob Litwinski, General Manager
Mike Olesen, Senior Manager, Systems & Administration
Tim Leer, Senior Manager, Hockey Development

Hockey Canada
#204N, 801 King Edward Ave., Ottawa, ON K1N 6N5
Tel: 613-562-5677; Fax: 613-562-5676
Toll-Free: 877-648-7465
customerservice@store.hockeycanada.ca
www.hockeycanada.ca
www.facebook.com/HockeyCanada
Affiliation(s): International Ice Hockey Federation
Sean Kelly, General Counsel
Glen McCurdie, Vice-President, Member Services

Hockey Development Centre for Ontario (HDCO)
#312, 3 Concorde Gate, Toronto, ON M3C 3N7
Tel: 416-426-7252; Fax: 416-426-7348
Toll-Free: 888-843-4326
hockey@hdco.on.ca
www.hdco.on.ca
Wayne Dillon, Executive Director
Wayne Salatino, Chair

Hockey Manitoba
508 - 145 Pacific Ave., Winnipeg, MB R3B 2Z6
Tel: 204-925-5755; Fax: 204-925-5761
info@hockeymanitoba.mb.ca
www.hockeymanitoba.mb.ca
www.facebook.com/pages/Hockey-Manitoba/296995075852?
Affiliation(s): Hockey Canada
Brian Franklin, President
Peter Woods, Executive Director
Bernie Reichardt, Director, Hockey Development

Hockey New Brunswick (HNB) / Hockey Nouveau-Brunswick
PO Box 456, 861 Woodstock Rd., Fredericton, NB E3B 4Z9
Tel: 506-453-0089; Fax: 506-453-0868
www.hnb.ca
Brian Whitehead, Executive Director
Tom Donovan, President
Pat MacFadzen, Director, Administration

Hockey Newfoundland & Labrador (NLHA) / Association de hockey de Terre-Neuve et Labrador
PO Box 176, 13B High St., Grand Falls-Windsor, NL A2A 2J4
Tel: 709-489-5512; Fax: 709-489-2273
office@hockeynl.ca
www.hockeynl.ca
Craig Tulk, Executive Director
Tamar Hobbs, Administrative Assistant

Hockey North
3506 McDonald Dr., Yellowknife, NT X1A 2H1
Tel: 867-874-6903; Fax: 867-874-4603
ccarriere@northwestel.net
www.hockeynorth.ca
Cheryl Carriere, Executive Director

Hockey Northwestern Ontario (HNO)
#100, 216 Red River Rd., Thunder Bay, ON P7B 1A6
Tel: 807-623-1542; Fax: 807-623-0037
info@hockeyhno.com
www.hockeyhno.com
John Pucci, General Manager
Ron MacKinnon, Development Coorindator

Hockey Nova Scotia
#200, 6300 Lady Hammond Rd., Halifax, NS B3K 2R6
Tel: 902-454-9400; Fax: 902-454-3883
www.hockeynovascotia.ca
www.facebook.com/group.php?gid=2222858784
Darren Cossar, Executive Director

Hockey PEI
PO Box 302, 40 Enman Cres., Charlottetown, PE C1A 7K7
Tel: 902-368-4334; Fax: 902-368-4337
info@hockeypei.com
www.hockeypei.com
Rob Newson, Executive Director

Hockey Québec (FQHG)
#210, 7450, boul. les Galeries d'Anjou, Montréal, QC H1M 3M3
Tél: 514-252-3079; Téléc: 514-252-3158
info@hockey.qc.ca
www.hockey.qc.ca
www.facebook.com/group.php?gid=66611750398
Gérard Bélanger, Président
Sylvain B. Lalonde, Directeur général

International Hockey Hall of Fame & Museum (IHHOF)
PO Box 82, 277 York St., Kingston, ON K7L 4V6
Tel: 613-544-2355; Fax: 613-544-2844
info@ihhof.com
www.ihhof.com
Mark Potter, President

International Hockey Heritage Centre
c/o MacDonnell Group Consulting Ltd., #1100, 1505 Barrington St., Halifax, NS B3J 3K5
Tel: 902-425-3980; Fax: 902-423-7593
info@hockeyland.ca
www.hockeyland.ca
Ralston MacDonnell, Project Manager
Wayne Russell, Chair

International Ice Hockey Federation (IIHF)
Brandschenkestrasse 50, Zurich, CH-8027, Switzerland
Tel: 41-1-562-2200; Fax: 41-1-562-2229
office@iihf.com; media@iihf.com
www.iihf.com
www.facebook.com/group.php?gid=294239820899
twitter.com/IIHFHockey
Affiliation(s): Hockey Canada
Horst Lichtner, General Secretary
René Fasel, President

Minor Hockey Alliance of Ontario
71 Albert St., Stratford, ON N5A 3K2
Tel: 519-273-7209; Fax: 519-273-2114
alliance@alliancehockey.com
www.alliancehockey.com
www.facebook.com/group.php?gid=114981545258512
Tony Martindale, Executive Director

Northern Ontario Hockey Association (NOHA)
108 Lakeshore Dr., North Bay, ON P1A 2A8
Tel: 705-474-8851; Fax: 705-474-6019
noha@NOHA.on.ca
www.noha.on.ca
Affiliation(s): Ontario Hockey Federation
Bryce Kulik, President
Chris May, Executive Director
Publications: NOHA Bulletin, NOHA Managers Manual, Rink Report

Nova Scotia Minor Hockey Council
c/o Hockey Nova Scotia, #17, 7 Mellor Ave., Dartmouth, NS B3B 0E8
Affiliation(s): Nova Scotia Hockey Association
Arnie Farrell, Chair

Ontario Hockey Federation (OHF)
#9, 400 Sheridon Dr., cambridge, ON N1T 2H9
Tel: 226-533-9070; Fax: 519-620-7476
info@ohf.on.ca
www.ohf.on.ca
www.facebook.com/OHFHockey
twitter.com/ohfhockey
Affiliation(s): Minor Hockey Alliance of Ontario; Greater Toronto Hockey League; Northern Ontario Hockey Association; Ontario Minor Hockey Association; Ontario Hockey Association; Ontario Hockey League; Ontario Women's Hockey Association
Phillip McKee, Executive Director
Bill Bowman, President
Publications: OHF Handbook

Ontario Minor Hockey Association (OMHA)
#3, 25 Brodie Dr., Richmond Hill, ON L4B 3K7
Tel: 905-780-6642; Fax: 905-780-0344
omha@omha.net
www.omha.net
twitter.com/HometownHockey
Affiliation(s): Ontario Hockey Federation
Marg Ensoll, President
Richard Ropchan, Executive Director
Kevin Boston, Director, Marketing & Events
Ian Taylor, Director, Development
Bill Rowney, Treasurer
Mark Dickie, Manager, Communications & IT
Publications: Hometown Hockey, OHF & OMHA [Ontario Minor Hockey Association]: Your Memberhip Opportunities & Benefits, OMHA [Ontario Minor Hockey Association] Insider, OMHA

[Ontario Minor Hockey Association] Manual of Operations: By-law, Regulations, & Policies, OMHA [Ontario Minor Hockey Association] Participant Guide

Ontario Women's Hockey Association (OWHA) / Association de hockey féminin de l'Ontario
#3, 5155 Spectrum Way, Mississauga, ON L4W 5A1
Tel: 905-282-9980; Fax: 905-282-0499
info@owha.on.ca; stats@owha.on.ca
www.owha.on.ca
Suzanne Essex, Chair
Fran Rider, President
Mary Ann Blunt, Secretary
Debbie MacDonald, Treasurer

Ottawa & District Hockey Association (ODHA) / Association de hockey du district d'Ottawa
#D 300, 1247 Kilborn Pl., Ottawa, ON K1H 6K9
Tel: 613-224-3589; Fax: 613-224-4625
odmha@odmha.on.ca
www.odmha.on.ca
Richard T. Sennott, Executive Director

Pan American Hockey Federation (PAHF)
46 Barton St., Ottawa, ON K1S 4R7
Tel: 819-956-8023; Fax: 819-956-8019
info@panamhockey.org
www.panamhockey.org
www.facebook.com/group.php?gid=174792322573292
twitter.com/PanAmHockey
Antonio von Ondarza, President
Aaron Sher, Honorary General Secretary
Derek Sandison, Honorary Treasurer

Saskatchewan Hockey Association (SHA) / Association de hockey de la Saskatchewan
#2, 575 Park St., Regina, SK S4N 5B2
Tel: 306-789-5101; Fax: 306-789-6112
carissal@sha.sk.ca
www.sha.sk.ca
Al Hubbs, President
Kelly McClintock, General Manager

Sledge Hockey of Canada (SHOC)
c/o Hockey Canada, #N204, 801 King Edward Ave., Ottawa, ON K1N 6N5
Tel: 613-562-5677; Fax: 613-562-5676
cchampagne@hockeycanada.ca
www.hockeycanada.ca
www.facebook.com/HCSledge
twitter.com/HC_Sledge
Adam Crockatt, Manager

Western Hockey League (WHL)
Father David Bauer Arena, 2424 University Dr. NW, Calgary, AB T2N 3Y9
Tel: 403-693-3030; Fax: 403-693-3031
info@whl.ca
www.whl.ca
www.facebook.com/WHLHockey
twitter.com/theWHL
Ron Robison, Commissioner

Horse Racing

Alberta Horse Trials Association
c/o Joanne Cameron, 21 Greenbrier Cres., St Albert, AB T8N 1A2
Tel: 780-922-3170
mgaglione@xplornet.com
www.albertahorsetrials.com
Affiliation(s): Canadian Equestrian Federation
George Balogh, President

Association Trot & Amble du Québec (ATAQ) / Québec Trotting & Pacing Society
#216, 5375, rue Paré, Montréal, QC H4P 1P7
Tél: 514-731-9484; Téléc: 514-731-7687
Ligne sans frais: 800-731-9484
www.trotetamble.ca
Marc Camirand, Président

Jockey Club of Canada / Jockey Club du Canada
PO Box 66, Stn. B, Toronto, ON M9W 5K9
Tel: 416-675-7756; Fax: 416-675-6378
jockeyclub@bellnet.ca
www.jockeyclubcanada.com
twitter.com/jockeyclubofCAN
Affiliation(s): The Jockey Club (New York)
James Lawson, Chief Steward
Stacie Roberts, Executive Director

Jockeys Benefit Association of Canada (JBAC)
c/o Thoroughbred Race Office, 555 Rexdale Blvd., Toronto, ON M9W 5L2
Tel: 416-798-8715
jbacmanager@mac.com
jbac.ca/trainers/jbac
Chad Hoverson, President
Robert King, Secretary-Manager

Ontario Horse Racing Industry Association (OHRIA)
PO Box 456, Stn. B, Toronto, ON M9W 5L4
Tel: 416-679-0741; Fax: 416-679-9114
ohria@ohria.com
www.ohria.com
Hector Clouthier, Executive Director

Horses

Saskatchewan Standardbred Horsemen's Association
PO Box 4122, Regina, SK S4P 3W5
Tel: 306-737-0667
info@harnessracingssha.com
www.harnessracingssha.com
Glenn Le Drew, President

Kayaking

Canoe Kayak Saskatchewan (CKS)
1870 Lorne St., Regina, SK S4P 2L7
Tel: 306-729-4220; Fax: 306-729-4216
cks@accesscomm.ca
www.saskcanoe.ca
Jan Hanson, Executive Director
Fiona Vincent, President
Jeanette Hamilton, Treasurer
Publications: Stern Word

Fédération québécoise de canoë-kayak d'eau vive
CP 1000, Succ. M, 4545, av Pierre-de Coubertin, Montréal, QC H1V 3R2
Tél: 514-252-3099; Téléc: 514-252-3094
fqckev@kayak.qc.ca
www.kayak.qc.ca
Patrick Lévesque, Coordonnateur

Ontario Recreational Canoeing & Kayaking Association (ORCKA)
#209, 3 Concorde Gate, Toronto, ON M3C 3N7
Tel: 416-426-7016; Fax: 416-426-7363
info@orcka.on.ca
www.orcka.on.ca
www.facebook.com/group.php?gid=228950560506530
Bruce Hawkins, President

Paddle Canada (PC) / Pagaie Canada
PO Box 126, Stn. Main, Kingston, ON K7L 4V6
Tel: 613-547-3196; Fax: 613-547-4880
Toll-Free: 888-252-6292
info@paddlingcanada.com
www.paddlingcanada.com
Affiliation(s): Active Living Alliance for Canadians with a Disability; Canadian Heritage Rivers System; Girl Guides of Canada
Blair Doyle, President & Regional Director
Rick Wise, Vice-President & Chair, Member Services Committee
Corey Locke, Regional Director & Chair, Communications (Marketing & Promotions)

Wilderness Canoe Association (WCA)
PO Box 91068, 2901 Bayview Ave., Toronto, ON M2K 2Y6
Tel: 416-223-4646
info@wildernesscanoe.ca
www.wildernesscanoe.ca
Aleks Gusev, Chair

Labour Unions

Canadian Football League Players' Association (CFLPA) / Association des joueurs de la ligue de football canadienne
#207, 603 Argus Rd., Oakville, ON L6J 6G6
Tel: 905-844-7852; Fax: 905-844-5127
Toll-Free: 800-616-6865
admin@cflpa.com
www.cflpa.com
Stu Laird, President
Mike O'Shea, 1st Vice-President
Jay McNeil, 2nd Vice-President
Sean Fleming, Member-at-Large
Edward Molstad, Legal Counsel
Fred James, Benefits Chairman
Deanne Mitchell, Executive Assistant
Publications: Canadian Football League Players' Association Negotiation Booklet, Canadian Football League Players' Association Salary Survey, CFLPA [Canadian Football League Players' Association] Newsletter

Major League Baseball Players' Association (Ind.) / Association des joueurs de la Ligue majeure de baseball (ind.)
12 East 49th St., 24th Fl., New York, NY 10017, USA
Tel: 212-826-0808; Fax: 212-752-4378
feedback@mlbpa.org
www.mlb.com/pa
Michael Weiner, Executive Director
Martha Child, CAO

Professional Hockey Players' Association (PHPA)
#701, 1 St Paul St., St Catharines, ON L2R 7L2
Tel: 905-682-4800; Fax: 905-682-4822
phpa@phpa.com
www.phpa.com
Larry Landon, Executive Director

Lacrosse

British Columbia Lacrosse Association (BCLA)
4041B Remi Pl., Burnaby, BC V5A 4J8
Tel: 604-421-9755; Fax: 604-421-9775
info@bclacrosse.com
www.bclacrosse.com
Rochelle Winterton, Executive Director

Canadian Lacrosse Association (CLA) / Association canadienne de crosse (ACC)
Gladstone Sports & Health Centre, #101, 18 Louisa St., Ottawa, ON K1R 6Y6
Tel: 613-260-2028; Fax: 613-260-2029
info1@lacrosse.ca
www.lacrosse.ca
www.facebook.com/CanadianLacrosseAssociation
twitter.com/LacrosseCanada
Affiliation(s): International Lacrosse Federation; International Federation of Women's Lacrosse Associations; Fédération internationale d'Inter-crosse; Canadian Lacrosse Foundation; Sport Canada; Coaching Association of Canada
Melissa McKenzie, Executive Director

Fédération de crosse du Québec (FCQ)
CP 1000, Succ. M, 4545, av Pierre-de Coubertin, Montréal, QC H1V 3R2
Tél: 514-252-3058; Téléc: 514-251-8038
crosse@crosse.qc.ca
www.crosse.qc.ca
Affiliation(s): Sports Québec; Regroupement Loisir Québec
Joe Cambria, Président

Lacrosse Nova Scotia
PO Box 3010 South, Halifax, NS B3J 3G6
Tel: 902-233-1783; Fax: 902-425-5606
bill.brydon@rcmp-grc.gc.ca
www3.ns.sympatico.ca/hami/
Affiliation(s): Canadian Lacrosse Association; Sport Nova Scotia
Stephen Brown, Vice-President, Administration
Wayne Finck, Vice-President, Technical Development
Brian Thompson, Vice-President, Finance

Ontario Lacrosse Association
#607, 1185 Eglinton Ave. East, Toronto, ON M3C 3C6
Tel: 416-426-7068; Fax: 416-426-7382
info@ontariolacrosse.com
www.ontariolacrosse.com
Stan Cockerton, Executive Director

Saskatchewan Lacrosse Association
2205 Victoria Ave., Regina, SK S4P 0S4
Tel: 306-780-9216; Fax: 306-525-4009
lacrosse@sasktel.net
www.sasklacrosse.net
Dale Measner, Executive Director

Lawn Bowling

Bowls British Columbia
#501, 1710 Bayshore Dr., Vancouver, BC V6G 3G4
www.bowlsbc.ca
Affiliation(s): World Bowls Board; World Indoor Bowls Board
Jim Aitken, President
Dave Muir, Vice-President
Judith Parkes, Secretary
Pat Cutt, Treasurer
Publications: Bowls British Columbia Newsletter

Bowls Canada Boulingrin (BCB)
#207, 720 Belfast Rd., Ottawa, ON K1G 0Z5
Tel: 613-244-0021; Fax: 613-244-0041
Toll-Free: 800-567-2695
office@bowlscanada.com
www.bowlscanada.com
Affiliation(s): Commonwealth Games Association of Canada
Kevin Penny, Executive Director

Bowls Manitoba
145 Pacific Ave., Winnipeg, MB R3B 2Z6
Tel: 204-925-5694; Fax: 204-925-5703
bowls@shawbiz.ca
www.bowls.mb.ca
Affiliation(s): Bowls Canada Boulingrin; World Bowls Ltd
Cathy Derewianchuk, Executive Director

Bowls Saskatchewan Inc.
#102, 1860 Lorne St., Regina, SK S4P 2L7
Tel: 306-780-9426; Fax: 306-781-6021
bowlsask@sasktel.net
www.bowls.sk.ca
Karen Swanson, Executive Director
Jean Roney, President

Lawn Bowls Association of Alberta
Percy Page Centre, 11759 Groat Rd., 3rd Fl., Edmonton, AB T5M 3K6
Tel: 780-427-8119; Fax: 780-452-5932
lawnbowl@telusplanet.net
www.bowls.ab.ca
Fred Kodnar, President
Gayell Slater, Vice-President
Pete Wilson, Treasurer

New Brunswick Lawn Bowling Association
929A Cloverdale Rd., Riverview, NB E1B 5E6
Tel: 506-386-5568; Fax: 506-386-5567
Ruth Katagi, Secretary

Ontario Lawn Bowls Association
c/o Elaine Stevenson, 23018 Lakeridge Rd., RR#2, Sunderland, ON L0C 1H0
Tel: 705-228-8058
olba@olba.ca
www.olba.ca
Arja Nesbitt, President
Elaine Houtby, Vice-President
Alan Dean, 2nd Vice-President
Bob O'Neil, Executive Director
Edith Pedden, Secretary
Richard Peart, Treasurer
Publications: E-Banter, Ontario Lawn Bowls Association Tournament Listings

Prince Edward Island Lawn Bowling Association
Sport PEI, PO Box 302, Charlottetown, PE C1A 7K7
Tel: 902-368-4110; Fax: 902-368-4548
Toll-Free: 800-247-6712
sports@sportpei.pe.ca
Sharon Renner, President

Québec Lawn Bowling Federation / Fédération de Boulingrin du Québec
#662 Oak Ave., Saint-Lambert, QC J4P 2R6
www.qlbf.org
Debbie Smits, Contact

Libraries

North American Sport Library Network (NASLIN)
c/o University of Calgary Law Library, 2500 University Dr. NW, Calgary, AB T2N 1N4
Tel: 403-220-6097; Fax: 403-282-6837
gghent@ucalgary.ca
www.naslin.org
Affiliation(s): International Association for Sports Information
Gretchen Ghent, Chair

Martial Arts

Association de taekwondo du Québec
CP 1000, Succ. M, 4545, av Pierre-de Coubertin, Montréal, QC H1V 3R2
Tél: 514-252-3198; Téléc: 514-254-7075
Ligne sans frais: 800-762-9565
info@taekwondo-quebec.ca
www.taekwondo-quebec.ca
Jean Faucher, Président
Elise Paradis, Vice-président

Canadian Chito-Ryu Karate-Do Association
89 Curlew Ave., Toronto, ON M3A 2P8
Tel: 416-444-5310
www.canadianchitoryu.ca
David Smith, President
Derek J. Ryan, Vice-President

Canadian Jiu-jitsu Council
PO Box 543, Madoc, ON K0K 2K0
Tel: 613-473-4366
www.jiujitsucouncil.ca
Robert Walthers, President

Canadian Kendo Federation (CKF) / Fédération canadienne de kendo
8013 Hunter St., Burnaby, BC V5A 2B8
Tel: 604-420-0438; Fax: 604-420-1971
hokusa@kendo-canada.com
www.kendo-canada.com
Hiro Okusa, President
Yoshiaki Taguchi, Vice-President
Christian d'Orangeville, 2nd Vice-President
Kim Taylor, Secretary
John Maisonneuve, Treasurer

Judo Alberta
11759 Groat Rd., Edmonton, AB T5M 3K6
Tel: 780-427-8379; Fax: 780-447-1915
Toll-Free: 866-919-5836
judo@judoalberta.com
www.judoalberta.com
Affiliation(s): International Judo Federation
Garry Yamashita, President

Judo British Columbia
PO Box 78049, 3295 Coast Meridian Rd., Port Coquitlam, BC V3B 7H5
Tel: 604-333-3513; Fax: 604-333-3514
info@judobc.ca
www.judobc.ca
Diane St-Denis, Executive Director

Judo Canada
#212, 1725 St. Laurent, Ottawa, ON K1G 3V4
Tel: 613-738-1200; Fax: 613-738-1299
Toll-Free: 877-738-5836
info@judocanada.org
www.judocanada.org
www.facebook.com/judocanada
twitter.com/judocanada
Affiliation(s): International Judo Federation
Yves Régimbald, Director, Operations & Finance
Andrzej Sadej, Director, Sports
Gosselin Nathalie, Coordinator, Eclipse
Francine Latreille, Officer, Administration

Judo Manitoba
c/o Sport Manitoba, #310, 200 Main St., Winnipeg, MB R3C 4M2
Tel: 204-925-5691; Fax: 204-925-5703
judomb@sport.mb.ca
www.judomanitoba.mb.ca
John Wenham, Executive Director
David Minuk, President

Judo New Brunswick / Judo Nouveau Brunswick
#13, 900 Hanwell Rd., Fredericton, NB E3B 6A2
Tel: 506-451-1322; Fax: 506-451-1325
judonb@nb.aibn.com
www.sport.nb.ca/judonb/
Jean Pierre Cantin, Executive Director

Judo Newfoundland
#112, Hamlyn Rd. Plaza, Unit 50, St. John's, NL A1E 5X7
Fax: 709-722-2573
Toll-Free: 877-879-5836
judo@nfld.com
www.judonl.ca
Blair Bradbury, President

Judo Nova Scotia
224 Victoria Rd., Bridgewater, NS B4V 2P1
Tel: 902-543-2836; Fax: 902-527-4847
tim.lohnes@abitibibowater.com
www.judons.ca
www.facebook.com/judons
Gordon Brown, Administrative Manager
Bill Anderson, Chair
Peter Croxall, Co-Chair

Judo Ontario
1185 Eglinton Ave. East, Toronto, ON M3C 3C6
Tel: 416-426-7006; Fax: 416-426-7390
Toll-Free: 866-553-5836
info@judoontario.ca
www.judoontario.ca
Ron Wilson, Executive Director
Charles Formosa, President
Mohamad Hassani, Secretary General

Judo Prince Edward Island
40 Enman Cres., Charlottetown, PE C1E 1E6
Tel: 902-368-4262; Fax: 902-368-4548
gflood@sportpei.pe.ca
sites.townsquare.ca/JudoPEI/index.cfm
John Wilbert, President

Judo Saskatchewan
c/o Registrar, 3130 Parkland Dr., Regina, SK S4V 1W5
Tel: 306-789-7395
abyuen@sasktel.net
www.judosask.ca
Affiliation(s): International Judo Federation
T.V. Taylor, President
Bev Yuen, Registrar

Judo-Québec inc
CP 1000, Succ. M, 4545, av Pierre-de-Coubertin, Montréal, QC H1V 3R2
Tél: 514-252-3040; Téléc: 514-254-5184
info@judo-quebec.qc.ca
www.judo-quebec.qc.ca
Affiliation(s): Fédération internationale de Judo; Union panaméricaine du Judo
Daniel De Angelis, Président
Patrick Esparbès, Directeur général
Patrick Vesin, Coordonnateur technique

Karate BC (KBC)
#225, 3820 Cessna Dr., Richmond, BC V7B 0A2
Tel: 604-333-3610; Fax: 604-333-3612
info@karatebc.org
www.karatebc.org
Affiliation(s): National Karate Association; Sport BC; Sport Canada; Canadian Olympic Association
Dan Wallis, President
Robert G. Tuss, Executive Director
Ken Corrigan, Treasurer

Karate Manitoba
PO Box 2519, 266 Graham Ave., Winnipeg, MB R3C 4A7
Tel: 204-925-5605; Fax: 204-925-5916
info@karatemanitoba.ca
www.karatemanitoba.ca
Daniel Piché, President
Ron Porath, Secretary

Karate New Brunswick
294 Water St., St Andrews, NB E5B 1B7
david.langley@gnb.ca
karatenb.com
Rick MacMichael, Treasurer
Joe Hatfield, Secretary
Paul Oliver, President

Karate Ontario
#8, 531 Atkinson Ave., Thornhill, ON L4J 8L9
Tel: 647-706-4835
info@karate-ontario.com
karate-ontario.com
www.facebook.com/309961174058?ref=mf
twitter.com/KarateOntario
Affiliation(s): World Karate Federation; Sport Alliance of Ontario; Coaches Assocation of Ontario
Dragan Kljenak, President
Publications: Black Belt Journal, Karate Masters

Karaté Québec
CP 1000, Succ. M, 4545, rue Pierre de Coubertin, Montréal, QC H1V 3R2
Tél: 514-252-3161; Téléc: 514-252-3036
info@karatequebec.com
www.karatequebec.com
Jean-Pierre Gendron, Président

Manitoba Tae Kwon-Do Association
145 Pacific Ave., Winnipeg, MB R3B 2Z6
Tel: 204-925-5682; Fax: 204-925-5703
tkd-exec@rainyday.mb.ca
K.S. Cho, President

National Tae Kwon-Do Federation
c/o Whitecroft Hall, #314, 52313 Range Rd. 232, Sherwood Park, AB T8B 1B5
Tel: 780-468-3418
www.ntf.ca
Wilfred Ho, President & Founder

Newfoundland & Labrador WTF (World Taekwondo Federation) Tae Kwon Do Association
PO Box 28083, 48 Kenmount Rd., St. John's, NL A1B 4J8
www.nltkd.ca
Affiliation(s): WTF Canada; Sport Canada; Sport NL; Kukkiwon
Neil Tucker, President
Paul Gosse, Vice-President
Sheila McGrath, Secretary
Lisa Collette, Treasurer

Ontario Taekwondo Association
#5-6, 9078 Leslie St., Richmond Hill, ON L4B 3L8
Tel: 416-245-8582; Fax: 416-245-8582
otatkdinfo@gmail.com
www.taekwondo.on.ca
Hwa Sun Myung, President
Hwan Yong Seong, Secretary General

Police Martial Arts Association
PO Box 7303, Sub. #12, Riverview, NB E1B 4T9
Tel: 506-387-5126
pmaa@nbnet.nb.ca
www.policemartialarts.org
Rannie MacDonald
Foster MacLeod

Prince Edward Island Karate Association (PEIKA)
PO Box 640, Montague, PE C0A 1R0
Tel: 902-892-3640
www.karatepei.ca
Affiliation(s): Sport PEI; National Karate Association
Erick A. Silva, Treasurer
Ken Roper, President
Lori Beck, Secretary

WushuCanada
#22-25B, 2370 Midland Ave., Toronto, ON M1S 5C6
Tel: 416-321-5913; Fax: 416-321-5068
cdnwushu@rogers.com
www.canadawushu.com
www.facebook.com/group.php?gid=41708279391
Alan Tang, National President

Yukon Judo
4061 - 4th Ave., Whitehorse, YT Y1A 1H1
Tel: 867-668-4236; Fax: 867-667-4237
jessup@klondiker.com
Penny Prysnuk, President

Massage Therapy

Canadian Sport Massage Therapists Association (CSMTA) / Association canadienne des massothérapeutes du sport
1030 Burnside Rd. West, Victoria, BC V8Z 1N3
Tel: 250-590-9861; Fax: 250-388-7835
natoffice@csmta.ca
www.csmta.ca
Affiliation(s): Canadian Olympic Committee; Expert Provider Group
Kim Mark-Goldsworthy, President
Roberta Graham, National Office Coordinator
Trish Schiedel, Vice President
Monty Churchman, Secretary

Mediation

Sport Dispute Resolution Centre of Canada (SDRCC)
#950, 1080 Beaver Hall Hill, Montréal, QC H2Z 1S8
Tel: 450-686-1245; Fax: 450-686-1246
Toll-Free: 866-733-7767
info@adrsportred.ca
www.crdsc-sdrcc.ca
Carla Qualtrough, President
Benoit Girardin, Executive Director

Motorcycles

Association des motocyclistes gais du Québec (AMGQ)
CP 36, Succ. C, Montréal, QC H2L 4J7
Tél: 514-247-9564
info@amgq.org
www.amgq.org
www.facebook.com/groups/amgqqc/
Luc Quintal, Président
Tisserand Sébastien, Vice-Président
Luc Tremblay, Vice-Président
Martin Cyr, Trésorerie

Canadian Motorcycle Association (CMA) / Association motocycliste canadienne
PO Box 448, Hamilton, ON L8L 8C4
Tel: 905-522-5705; Fax: 905-522-5716
registration@canmocycle.ca
www.canmocycle.ca
Affiliation(s): Fédération internationale motocycliste; Canadian Olympic Association; North American Motorcycle Union
Marilyn Bastedo, CEO
Joseph Godsall, President

Fédération motocycliste du Québec (FMQ) / Quebec Motorcyclist Federation
#208, 4875, boul Métropolitain est, Montréal, QC H1R 3J2
Tél: 514-252-8121; Téléc: 514-252-7857
fmq@fmq.qc.ca
www.fmq.qc.ca
Jacques Lafontaine, Président

Mountaineering

The Alpine Club of Canada (ACC) / Club alpin du Canada
PO Box 8040, 201, Indian Flats Rd., Canmore, AB T1W 2T8
Tel: 403-678-3200; Fax: 403-678-3224
info@alpineclubofcanada.ca
www.alpineclubofcanada.ca
www.facebook.com/alpineclubofcanada
twitter.com/alpineclubcan
Affiliation(s): International Union of Alpinist Associations
Lawrence White, Executive Director
Peter Muir, President
Toby Harper, Director, Programs
Emma Varga, Manager, Finance

Association of Canadian Mountain Guides (ACMG) / Association des guides de montagne canadiens
PO Box 8341, Canmore, AB T1W 2V1
Tel: 403-678-2885; Fax: 403-609-0070
acmg@acmg.ca
www.acmg.ca
Keith Reid, President
Peter Tucker, Executive Director

British Columbia Mountaineering Club
PO Box 2674, Vancouver, BC V6B 3W8
Tel: 604-268-9502
info@bcmc.ca
www.bcmc.ca
Affiliation(s): Federation of Mountain Clubs of BC
David Scanlon, President

Native Peoples

Aboriginal Sport & Recreation Association of British Columbia (ASRA)
#4, 2475 Mt. Newton X Rd., Saanichton, BC V8M 2B7
Tel: 250-544-8172; Fax: 250-544-8173
asra@asra.ca
www.asra.ca
Alex Nelson, President & CEO
Patrick Chénier, General Manager
Gordon Celesta, Operations Manager
Karen Henry, Program Manager
Linda Bristol, Office Manager

Aboriginal Sport Circle
Roundpoint Memorial Bldg., #7, 34 McCumber Rd., Akwesasne Mohawk Territory, Cornwall Island, ON K6H 5R7
Tel: 613-938-1176; Fax: 613-938-9181
rbrant@aboriginalsportcircle.ca
www.aboriginalsportcircle.ca
Viginia Doucett, Executive Director

Netball

British Columbia Netball Association
3468 Triumph St., Vancouver, BC V5K 1T8
Tel: 604-293-1820; Fax: 604-293-1851
netball_info@bcnetball.net
www.bcnetball.net

Fédération de Netball du Québec / Québec Amateur Netball Federation (QANF)
CP 1000, Succ. M, 4545, av Pierre-de-Coubertin, Montréal, QC H1V 3R2
www.netballquebec.ca
Avice Roberts-Joseph, Présidente
Donna Baker, Secrétaire
Lecita Audain, Trésoriere

Netball Alberta
PO Box 270, 7620 Elbow Dr. SW, Calgary, AB T2V 1K2
Tel: 403-238-8041
info@albertanetball.com
www.netballalberta.com
Affiliation(s): International Federation of Netball Associations
Paula MacWilliam, President

Obesity

Active Healthy Kids Canada / Jeunes en forme Canada
#1804 - 2 Bloor St. E, Toronto, ON M4W 1A8
Tel: 416-913-0238; Fax: 416-913-1541
info@activehealthykids.ca
www.activehealthykids.ca
Michelle Brownrigg, Chief Executive Officer

Olympic Games

Canadian Olympic Committee (COC) / Comité olympique canadien
#900, 21 St Clair Ave. East, Toronto, ON M4T 1L9
Tel: 416-962-0262; Fax: 416-967-4902
www.olympic.ca
twitter.com/CDNOlympicTeam
Chris Rudge, CEO

Vancouver Organizing Committee for the 2010 Olympic & Paralympic Winter Games
#400, 1095 West Pender St., Vancouver, BC V6E 2M6
Tel: 778-328-2010; Fax: 778-328-2011
Toll-Free: 877-408-2010
www.vancouver2010.com
John Furlong, CEO

Orienteering

Alberta Orienteering Association (AOA)
#128, 4307 - 130 Ave. SE, Calgary, AB T2Z 3V8
Tel: 403-697-5750
pascale@orienteeringalberta.ca
www.orienteeringalberta.ca
Don Riddle, President
J.P. Buysschaert, Treasurer
Pascale Levesque, Executive Director

Canadian Orienteering Federation (COF) / Fédération canadienne de course d'orientation
1239 Colgrove Ave. NE, Calgary, AB T2C 5C3
Tel: 403-283-0807; Fax: 403-451-1681
info@orienteering.ca
www.orienteering.ca
www.facebook.com/group.php?gid=64406548384
twitter.com/orienteeringcan
Affiliation(s): International Orienteering Federation
Charlotte MacNaughton, Executive Director
Alex Kerr, Vice-President
Dave Graupner, Secretary-Treasurer
Publications: Legends

Manitoba Orienteering Association Inc. (MOA)
145 Pacific Ave., Winnipeg, MB R3B 2Z6
Tel: 204-925-5706; Fax: 204-925-5792
info@orienteering.mb.ca
www.orienteering.mb.ca
Affiliation(s): Sports Manitoba
Jennifer Hamilton, President
Dave Graupner, Treasurer

Orienteering Association of British Columbia (OABC)
4337 San Cristo Pl., Victoria, BC V8N 5G5
www.orienteeringbc.ca
Affiliation(s): Canadian Orienteering Federation (COF); Coaching Association of Canada
John Rance, President
Alex Kerr, Secretary

Orienteering Association of Nova Scotia (OANS)
c/o Andrew Harding, 5516 Spring Garden Rd., 4th Fl., Halifax, NS B3J 1G6
Tel: 902-446-2295; Fax: 902-425-5606
info@orienteeringns.ca
www.orienteeringns.ca
Andrew Harding, Executive Director
Michael Price, President
Dale Ellis, Vice-President
Ian Folkins, Treasurer

Orienteering New Brunswick (ONB)
34 Fairview Dr., Moncton, NB E1E 3C7
Tel: 506-389-8091
www.orienteering.nb.ca
Affiliation(s): International Orienteering Federation
David Ross, President
Paul Looker, Secretary

Orienteering Ontario Inc.
2163 Third Side Rd., Campbellville, ON L0P 1B0
Tel: 416-284-5580
Toll-Free: 888-810-9990
admin@orienteering.on.ca
www.orienteering.on.ca

Orienteering Québec (OQ) / Fédération québécoise de course d'orientation
QC
Tel: 450-433-3624
orientering_quebec@orienteringquebec.ca
www.orienteringquebec.ca
Michael MacConaill, President
Randall Kemp, Vice-President
Colin Kirk, Treasurer
Publications: OQ Newsletter

Yukon Orienteering Association (YOA)
4061 - 4th Ave., Whitehorse, YT Y1A 1H1
info@yukonorienteering.ca
www.yukonorienteering.ca
Barbara Scheck, President
Jean-François Roldan, Vice-President

Parachuting

Alberta Sport Parachuting Association (ASPA)
#63, 2505 - 42 St., Edmonton, AB T6L 7G8
admin@aspa.ca
www.aspa.ca
Affiliation(s): Canadian Sport Parachuting Association
Henry Komant, Acting President
Tina Connolly, Program Coordinator

Canadian Sport Parachuting Association (CSPA) / Association canadienne du parachutisme sportif (ACPS)
300 Forced Rd., Russell, ON K4R 1A1
Tel: 613-445-1881; Fax: 613-445-2698
office@cspa.ca
www.cspa.ca
David Hodge, President
Christopher Charlesworth, Vice-President
Nicole Demers, Secretary
Publications: Parachutist Information Manuals

Manitoba Sport Parachute Association (MSPA)
#309, 200 Main St., Winnipeg, MB R3C 4M2
Tel: 204-925-5682; Fax: 204-925-5703
president@mspa.mb.ca
www.mspa.mb.ca
Jill Forbes, President

Sport Parachute Association of Saskatchewan
PO Box 37056, Regina, SK S4S 7K3
Tel: 306-934-8528
www.skydive.sk.ca
Craig Skihar, President
Burk Reiman, Vice-President

Pentathlon

Alberta Modern Pentathlon Association
info@albertapentathlon.com
albertapentathlon.com
Joanne Willis, President

Canadian Modern Pentathlon Association (CAMPA) / Association canadienne du pentathlon moderne
70 Como Gardens, Hudson, QC J0P 1H0
Tel: 450-458-7974; Fax: 450-458-1746
president@pentathloncanada.ca
www.pentathloncanada.ca
www.facebook.com/pages/Pentathlon-Canada/168702639822958
Affiliation(s): Union internationale de pentathlon moderne et biathlon
Angela Ives, President
Blaine Dombowsky, Vice-President
Aline Lafrenière, Vi-ce President
Bob Noble, Vice-President & Director, High Performance
Colin Peace, Vice-President & Chair, Technical Committee

Physical Education & Training

Association régionale du sport étudiant de l'Est du Québec (ARSEEQ)
#J-201, 60 rue de L'Evêché ouest, Rimouski, QC G5L 4H6
Tél: 418-723-1880; Téléc: 418-722-0457
marcboud@cegep-rimouski.qc.ca
www.arseeq.net
Affiliation(s): Fédération québécoise du sport étudiant
Marc Boudreau, Directeur

Association régionale du sport étudiant de Montréal (ARSEM)
#200, 7800, boul. Métropolitain Est, Montréal, QC H1K 1A1
Tél: 514-645-6923; Téléc: 514-354-8632
secretariat@arsemontreal.com
www.arsemontreal.com
Jacques Desrochers, Directeur général
Dominique Blanc, Secrétaire

Fédération des éducateurs et éducatrices physiques enseignants du Québec (FEEPEQ)
2500, boul de l'Université, Sherbrooke, QC J1K 2R1
Tél: 819-821-8000; Téléc: 819-821-7970
info@feepeq.com
www.feepeq.com
www.facebook.com/180360724546
twitter.com/feepeq
Affiliation(s): Sports Québec; Fédération québécoise du sport étudiant
Dav Bergeron, Président
Nathalie Morneau, Directrice, Opérations

Ontario Physical & Health Education Association (OPHEA)
#608, 1 Concorde Gate, Toronto, ON M3C 3N6
Tel: 416-426-7120; Fax: 416-426-7373
Toll-Free: 888-446-7432
info@ophea.org
www.ophea.org
Mark Seaton, President
Chris Markham, Executive Director & CEO
Jennifer Cowie Bonne, Director, Marketing & Development
Gwen Slauenwhite, Director, Finance & Administration
Brenda Whitteker, Director, Programs
Publications: e-Connection [a publication of the Ontario Physical & Health Education Association], OPHEA [Ontario Physical & Health Education Association] Annual Report

Saskatchewan Physical Education Association (SPEA)
PO Box 193, Harris, SK S0L 1K0
Tel: 306-656-4423; Fax: 306-656-4405
spea@xplornet.com
www.speaonline.ca
Affiliation(s): Canadian Association for Health, Physical Education, Recreation, & Dance; Saskatchewan Teachers' Federation
Holly Stevens, Executive Director
Darryl Elaschuk, President
Publications: On the Move

Physical Fitness

Alberta Fitness Leadership Certification Association (AFLCA)
Percy Page Bldg., 11759 Groat Rd., 3rd Fl., Edmonton, AB T5M 3K6
Tel: 780-492-4435; Fax: 780-455-2264
Toll-Free: 866-348-8648
general@provincialfitnessunit.ca
www.provincialfitnessunit.ca
Katherine MacKeigan, Executive Director

The Canadian Association of Fitness Professionals / Association canadienne des professionnels en conditionnement physique
#110, 255 Consumers Rd., Toronto, ON M2J 1R4
Tel: 416-493-3515; Fax: 416-493-1756
Toll-Free: 800-667-5622
info@canfitpro.com
www.canfitpro.com
www.facebook.com/group.php?gid=2524100816
Maureen Hagan, Executive Director
Kathy Ash, Contact, Administration

Canadian Fitness & Lifestyle Research Institute (CFLRI) / Institut canadien de la recherche sur la condition physique et le mode de vie
#201, 185 Somerset St. West, Ottawa, ON K2P 0J2
Tel: 613-233-5528; Fax: 613-233-5536
www.cflri.ca
Nancy Dubois, Chair
Christine Cameron, Acting President
Mathilde Costa, Senior Manager, Finance, Administration, & Human Resources
Cora Lynn Craig, Senior Researcher
Publications: Capacity Study, Kids CANPLAY, The Lifestyle Tips, Physical Activity Monitor, The Research File

Canadian Society for Exercise Physiology (CSEP) / Société canadienne de physiologie de l'exercice (SCPE)
#370, 18 Louisa St., Ottawa, ON K1R 6Y6
Tel: 613-234-3755; Fax: 613-234-3565
Toll-Free: 877-651-3755
info@csep.cap
www.csep.ca
www.facebook.com/group.php?gid=291577755198
twitter.com/CSEPdotCA
Affiliation(s): Public Health Agency of Canada - Physical Activity Unit
Earl Noble, President
Brian MacIntosh, Executive Director
Mike Plyley, Vice-President, Research
Panagiota Klentrou, Treasurer
Publications: Active Living During Pregnancy: Physical Activitiy Guidelines for Mother & Baby, Applied Physiology, Nutrition & Metabolism (APNM), Canada's Physical Activity Guide to Healthy Active Living (Adults 20-55): PA Guide Handbook, The Canadian Physical Activity, Fitness & Lifestyle Approach (CPAFLA), Communiqué [a publication of the Canadian Society for Exercise Physiology], CSEP [Canadian Society for Exercise Physiology] Member Directory, The CSEP [Canadian Society for

Exercise Physiology] Certified Exercise Physiologist Certification Guide, CSEP [Canadian Society for Exercise Physiology] Certified Personal Trainer Study Guide, Inclusive Fitness & Lifestyle Services for all (dis)Abilities, Physical Activity Guide for Children (6-9 Years of Age): Family Guide to Physical Activity for Children, Physical Activity Guide for Children (6-9 Years of Age): Teacher's Guide to Physical Activity for Children, Physical Activity Guide for Older Adults (Over 55): PA Guide Handbook for Older Adults, Physical Activity Guide for Youth (10-14 Years of Age): Family Guide to Physical Activity for Youth, Physical Activity Guide for Youth (10-14 Years of Age): Teacher's Guide to Physical Activity for Youth, Professional Fitness & Lifestyle Consultant (PFLC) Resource Manual

Certified Professional Trainers Network (CPTN)
122 D'Arcy St., Toronto, ON M5T 1K3
Tel: 416-979-1654; Fax: 416-979-1466
info@cptn.com
www.cptn.com
Susan Lee, President

National Association of Physical Activity & Health (NAPAH)
Tel: 416-879-2348; Fax: 416-879-1905
Toll-Free: 866-228-3492
info@napah.ca; volunteer@napah.ca
www.napah.ca

Physical Culture Association of Alberta
Percy Page Centre, 11759 Groat Rd., Edmonton, AB T5M 3K6
Tel: 780-415-1744
physicalculture@hotmail.com
www.physicalculture.ca
Lesley McEwan, Executive Director

The Recreation Association / L'Association récréative
2451 Riverside Dr., Ottawa, ON K1H 7X7
Tel: 613-733-5100
racentre@racentre.com
www.racentre.com
Rick Baker, General Manager
Jane Proudfoot, Director, Recreation, Sports & Fitness Services

Polo

Canadian Polo Association (CPA)
PO Box 17, Stn. 9, R.R.2, Okotos, AB T1S 1A2
Tel: 430-995-1987; Fax: 403-938-8205
Toll-Free: 855-995-1987
info@polocanada.ca
www.polocanada.ca
Affiliation(s): Canadian Amateur Athletic Association (RCAAA); Federation of International Polo (FIP); Equine Canada; Ontario Equestrian Federation (OEF); International Olympic Committee (IOC)
Justin R. Fogarty, Chair
Cam Clark, President
Don. B. Pennycook, Vice-President
Ada Pally, Secretary
Dave Offen, Treasurer
Publications: Instructor's Manual

Powerlifting

Canadian Powerlifting Organization (CPO)
PO Box 51180 RPO Beddington, Calgary, AB T3K EV9
Fax: 403-698-2434
powerlifting@gmail.com; info@wpc-canada.com
www.worldpowerlifting.com/cpo
Publications: Maximum Power

Canadian Powerlifting Union (CPU)
c/o Mike Armstrong, 4709 Fordham Cres. SE, Calgary, AB T2A 2A5
www.powerlifting.ca
www.facebook.com/CDNpowerliftingunion
Affiliation(s): International Powerlifting Federation
Ryan Stinn, President
Louis Levesque, Chair, Coaching
Mike Armstrong, Secretary
Barry Antoniow, Treasurer

Nova Scotia Powerlifting Association
Sydney, NS B1P 3W7
Tel: 902-567-0893
johnfraser56@hotmail.com
John Fraser, President

Ontario Powerlifting Association
412 Big Creek Rd., Caledonia, ON N3W 2G9
Tel: 905-765-5345
info@ontariopowerlifting.org
www.ontariopowerlifting.org
Bill Jamison, President

Racquetball

Association québécoise de racquetball (AQR)
CP 1000, Succ. M, 4545, av Pierre-de-Coubertin, Montréal, QC H1V 3R2
Tél: 514-252-3062
info@sports-4murs.qc.ca
www.sports-4murs.qc.ca/racquetball/accueil-AQR.html
Michel Gagnon, Président

British Columbia Racquetball Association (BCRA)
1282 - 7th Ave. West, Vancouver, BC V6H 1B6
Tel: 604-737-1786; Fax: 604-737-1786
bcracquetball@hotmail.com
www.racquetballbc.ca
twitter.com/bcracquetball
Cheryl McKeeman, President, Memberships
Cal Smith, Vice-President, Officiating & Communication
Diana Hambley, Treasurer, Ranking
Publications: Racquetball Matters

Canadian Racquetball Association (CRA) / Association canadienne de racquetball
145 Pacific Ave., Winnipeg, MB R3B 2Z6
Tel: 613-692-5394
ed.rbcanada@sportmanitoba.ca
www.racquetball.ca
Affiliation(s): Canadian Sport Council; Canadian Olympic Association; Coaching Association of Canada
Ron Brown, President
Darrell Davis, Vice-President, High Performance
Manny Gregorio, Vice-President, Marketing & Communications
Jack McBride, Vice-President, Technical
Bob Papineau, Vice-President, Finance
Publications: Canadian Racquetball, Racquetball Canada Newsletter

New Brunswick Racquetball Association (NBRA)
24 Baxter St., Lower Coverdale, NB E1J 1B4
Tel: 506-387-4196
moorbar@rogers.com
Barry Moore, NB Provincial Representative, Racquetball Canada

Newfoundland Racquetball Association
16 Fairhaven Pl., St. John's, NL A1E 4S1
Tel: 709-364-9151; Fax: y09-364-9151
Eric Easton, Vice-President

Racquetball Manitoba
#304, 200 Main St., Winnipeg, MB R3C 4M2
Tel: 204-925-5666; Fax: 204-925-5703
rball@shawbiz.ca
members.shaw.ca/racquetball
Jennifer Saunders, Executive Director

Racquetball Ontario (RO)
5591 McAdam Rd., Mississauga, ON L4Z 1N4
Tel: 519-584-0235
info@racquetballontario.ca
www.racquetballontario.ca
twitter.com/Rball_Ontario
Sue Swaine, Vice-President & Director, Coaching
Peter Fisher, Director, Development
Tanya Hodgin, Director, Memberships
Bob Lickers, Director, Rankings

Racquetball PEI
c/o Sport PEI, PO Box 302, Charlottetown, PE C1A 7K7
Tel: 902-368-4110; Fax: 902-368-4548
postie@vapordragon.ca
Allan Postie, President

Recreation

Canadian Volkssport Federation (CVF) / Fédération canadienne volkssport (FCV)
PO Box 2668, Stn. D, Ottawa, ON K1P 5W7
Tel: 613-234-7333
cvffcv@bellnet.ca
www.walks.ca
Benoît Pinsonneault, President
Publications: Volkssport Canada

Coalition for Active Living
#301, 2197 Riverside Dr., Ottawa, ON K1H 7X3
Tel: 613-277-9979
info@activeliving.ca
www.activeliving.ca
Christa Costas-Bradstreet, Co-Chair
Nancy Dubois, Co-Chair

Fitness New Brunswick (NBCFAL) / Conditionnement physique Noueau-Brunswick (CCPVANB)
#2, 1216 Sand Cove Rd., Saint John, NB E3M 5V8
Tel: 506-672-1993; Fax: 506-672-8762
Toll-Free: 888-790-1411
membershipservices@fitnessnb.ca
www.fitnessnb.ca
Affiliation(s): Atlantic Canadian Society for Exercise Physiology (CSEP) Health & Fitness Program (H&FP); National Fitness Leadership Alliance (NFLA)
Gina Simpson, Executive Director
Lauren Rogers, President
Publications: Fitness New Brunswick Member Handbook, Fitness New Brunswick Monthly Update, Inside Fitness

International Masterathlete Federation (IMAF)
PO Box 185, Richmond Hill, ON L4B 4R5
Tel: 905-473-9714; Fax: 905-473-9715
Toll-Free: 888-883-3315
Liz Roach, President
Iain Douglas, Vice-President

International Orienteering Federation (IOF)
Radiokatu 20, Slu, FI-00093, Finland
Tel: 358-9-3481-3112; Fax: 358-9-3481-3113
iof@orienteering.org
www.orienteering.org
Affiliation(s): Canadian Orienteering Federation
Barbro Rönnberg, Secretary General
Anna Zeelig, Assistant to the Secretary General

ParaSport and Recreation PEI
Royalty Center House Of Sport, PO Box 841, #115, 40 Enman Cres., Charlottetown, PE C1A 7L9
Tel: 902-368-4540; Fax: 902-368-4548
info@parasportpei.ca
www.parasportpei.ca
Affiliation(s): The JoyRiders Therapeutic Riding Association of PEI Inc.; The Canadian Council of the Blind - Prince County and Queensland Chapters; The Abegweit Club of Summerside; G.E.A.R. (Getting Everyone Accessibly Riding)
Tracy Stevenson, Executive Director

Sport Alliance of Ontario
3 Concorde Gate, Toronto, ON M3C 3N7
Tel: 416-426-7000; Fax: 416-426-7381
jjoseph@sportalliance.com
www.sportalliance.com
Jim Bradley, CEO
Larry Rudner, Interim CFO

Rhythmic Sportive Gymnastics

Canadian Rhythmic Sportive Gymnastic Federation (CRSGF) / Fédération canadienne de gymnastique rythmique sportive
c/o 2288 Covington Pl., Victoria, BC V8N 5N6
Tel: 250-472-3322; Fax: 250-472-2659
dfrattaroli@shaw.ca
Danielle Frattaroli, GCG-RG Program Coordinator

Rhythmic Gymnastics Manitoba Inc. (RGM)
145 Pacific Ave., Winnipeg, MB R3B 2Z6
Tel: 201-492-5573
rhythmic@sportmanitoba.ca
www.rgmanitoba.com
Affiliation(s): Sport Manitoba; Rhythmic Gymnastics Canada; Gymnastics Canada; International Gymnastics Federation; Canadian Sport Centre - Manitoba; Coaching Manitoba; Gymnastics Manitoba
Katherine Kwiecien, Executive Director
Raymond Chu, President
Zdravka Tchonkova, Vice-President, Marketing
Susan Yurkiw, Vice-President, Finance
John Matthews, Director, Events

Ringette

British Columbia Ringette Association (BCRA) / Association de ringuette de Colombie-Britannique
#319, 789 West Pender St., Vancouver, BC V6C 1H2
Fax: 604-629-0876
www.bcringette.org
Glen Ritchie, President
Donna Mihalcheon, Vice President

Fédération sportive de ringuette du Québec
CP 1000, Succ. M, 4545, av Pierre-de-Coubertin, Montréal, QC H1V 3R2
Tél: 514-252-3085; Téléc: 514-254-1069
ringuette@ringuette-quebec.qc.ca
www.ringuette-quebec.qc.ca
Florent Gravel, Président

Manitoba Ringette Association (MRA) / Association de ringuette du Manitoba
145 Pacific Ave., Winnipeg, MB R3B 2Z6
Tel: 204-925-5710; Fax: 204-925-5925
ringette.admin@sportmanitoba.ca
www.manitobaringette.ca
twitter.com/MBRingette
Affiliation(s): Sport Manitoba
Laralle Higginson, Executive Director
Melanie Reimer, Technical Director

Northwest Territories Ringette / Association de ringuette des Territoires Nord-Ouest
#2, 496 Range Lake Rd., Yellowknife, NT X1A 3R5
Tel: 867-920-7419; Fax: 867-920-2843
Affiliation(s): Ringette Alberta
Miles Harris, President

Ontario Ringette Association (ORA) / Association de ringuette de l'Ontario
#207, 3 Concorde Gate, Toronto, ON M3C 3N7
Tel: 416-426-7204; Fax: 416-426-7359
www.ontario-ringette.com
Keith Kaiser, President
Michael Beaton, Executive Director
Karla Romphf, Director, Technical
Stephanie Corrado, Coordinator, Administration

Ringette Association of Saskatchewan (RAS) / Association de ringuette de Saskatchewan
1860 Lorne St., Regina, SK S4P 2L7
Tel: 306-780-9432; Fax: 306-780-9460
www.ringettesask.com
Denise Treslan, President
Crystal Gellner, Executive Director
Keith Doering, Director, Technical

Ringette Canada (RC) / Ringuette Canada
#201, 5510 Canotek Rd., Ottawa, ON K1J 9J4
Tel: 613-748-5655; Fax: 613-748-5860
ringette@ringette.ca
www.ringette.ca
David Patterson, Executive Director
Frances Losier, Director, Sport Development
Nathalie Muller, Director, Technical
Monty Aldous, Coordinator, Club Development
Alayne Martel, Contact, Media & Public Relations

Ringette New Brunswick (RNB) / Ringuette Nouveau-Brunswick
c/o Marise Aufrey, Administrative Assistant, 940 Centrale St., Memramcook, NB E4K 3T4
Tel: 506-758-2546
MariseA@rrsb.nb.ca
www.sport.nb.ca/ringette/
Ron Richard, President
Hélène L. Beaulieu, Vice-President

Ringette Nova Scotia
5516 Spring Garden Rd., 4th Fl., Halifax, NS B3J 1G6
Tel: 902-425-5450; Fax: 902-425-5606
ringette@sportnovascotia.ca
www.ringette.ns.ca
Lindsay Bennett, Executive Director
Dennis Barnhart, President

Ringette PEI
PO Box 302, Charlottetown, PE C1A 7K7
Tel: 902-368-4208; Fax: 902-362-4548
www.ringettepei.ca
Kelsey McIntosh, Executive Director
Ian MacIsaac, President
Dan Delaney, Vice-President
Susan McInnis, Treasurer

Rowing

Alberta Rowing Association (ARA)
Percy Page Centre, 11759 Groat Rd., Edmonton, AB T5M 3K6
Tel: 780-427-8154; Fax: 780-422-2663
albertarows@can.rogers.com
www.albertarowing.ca
Carol Hermansen, President

Association québécoise d'aviron (AQA)
CP 1000, Succ. M, 4545, av Pierre-de Coubertin, Montréal, QC H1V 3R2
Tél: 514-252-3191; Téléc: 514-252-3094
info@avironquebec.ca
www.avironquebec.ca
Daniel Aucoin, Président

Ontario Rowing Association (ORA)
#210, 3 Concorde Gate, Toronto, ON M3C 3N7
Tel: 416-426-7002; Fax: 416-426-7309
admin@rowontario.ca
www.rowontario.ca
www.facebook.com/pages/ROWONTARIO/84916401948
twitter.com/ROWONTARIO
Affiliation(s): Ontario Sport Council
Derek Ventor, Executive Director

Rowing Canada Aviron (RCA) / Association canadienne d'aviron amateur
#321, 4371 Interurban Rd., Victoria, BC V9E 2C5
Fax: 250-220-2503
Toll-Free: 877-722-4769
rca@rowingcanada.org
www.rowingcanada.org
www.facebook.com/pages/Rowing-Canada-Aviron/81982893039?ref=ts
twitter.com/rowingcanada
Affiliation(s): Fédération Internationale des Sociétés d'Aviron; Canadian Olympic Association
Donna Atkinson, Executive Director

Rowing Newfoundland
PO Box 50536, SS#3, St. John's, NL A1B 4M2
Tel: 709-753-8515
Adrian Miller, President

Saskatchewan Rowing Association (SRA)
510 Cynthia St., Saskatoon, SK S7L 7K7
Tel: 306-975-0842; Fax: 306-242-8007
saskrowing@sasktel.net
www.saskrowing.ca
Affiliation(s): Rowing Aviron Canada, Saskatchewan Sports Hall of Fame & Museum, Saskatchewan Coaches Association
John Haver, Provincial Head Coach North
Garett Mathiason, Provincial Head Coach South
Russ Hart, President

Rugby

Alberta Rugby Football Union
Percy Page Centre, 11759 Groat Rd., Edmonton, AB T5M 3K6
Tel: 780-415-1773; Fax: 780-422-5558
www.rugbyalberta.com
www.facebook.com/groups/92155233636/
John Seaman, President
Simon Chi, Vice-President
Debby Ashmore, Executive Director
Sandy Nesbitt, Director, Finance & Administration

British Columbia Rugby Union
#203, 210 West Broadway, Vancouver, BC V5Y 3W2
Tel: 604-737-3065; Fax: 604-737-3916
bcrugby@telus.net
www.bcrugby.com
Louise Wheeler, Manager, Member Services
Jeff Sauvé, CEO

Fédération de rugby du Québec (FRQ) / Quebec Rugby Union
CP 1000, Succ. M, 4545, av Pierre-de Coubertin, Montréal, QC H1V 3R2
Tél: 514-252-3189; Téléc: 514-252-3159
info@rugbyquebec.qc.ca
www.rugbyquebec.qc.ca
www.facebook.com/pages/Rugby-Qu%C3%A9bec/98779487768
twitter.com/RugbyQuebec
Nicholas Clapinson, Directeur

Newfoundland & Labrador Rugby Union
349 Old Broad Cove Rd., St. Phillips, NL A1M 3N2
Tel: 709-895-2608; Fax: 709-895-0214
www.rockrugby.ca
Tom Jacobs, Treasurer

Nova Scotia Rugby Football Union
5516 Spring Garden Rd., Halifax, NS B3J 1G6
Tel: 902-425-5450; Fax: 902-425-5606
rugby@sportnovascotia.ca
www.rugbyns.ns.ca
Affiliation(s): International Rugby Board
Marty Williams, CEO

Rugby Ontario
#307, 3 Concorde Gate, Toronto, ON M3C 3N7
Tel: 416-426-7050; Fax: 416-426-7369
www.rugbyontario.com
www.facebook.com/RugbyOntario
twitter.com/rugbyontario
Affiliation(s): Canadian Rugby Union
Andrew Backer, Executive Director
Andrew Hall, Director
Fran Mason, Manager, Member Services

Saskatchewan Rugby Union (SRU)
510 Cynthia St., Saskatoon, SK S7L 7K7
Tel: 306-975-0895; Fax: 306-242-8007
sru@sasktel.net
www.saskrugby.com

Sailing

Alberta Sailing Association (ASA)
4915 Graham Dr. SW, Calgary, AB T3E 4L3
Tel: 403-617-9092
info@albertasailing.com
www.albertasailing.com
Peter MacDougal, Executive Director & Head Coach
Ron Hewitt, President

Association maritime du Québec (AMQ)
#200, 621, rue Stravinski, Brossard, QC J4X 1Y7
Tél: 450-466-1777; Téléc: 450-466-6056
Ligne sans frais: 877-560-1777
info@nautismequebec.com
www.nautismequebec.com
Yves Paquette, Directeur général
Béatrice Launay, Directrice, Québec Stations Nautiques

British Columbia Sailing Association
#223, 3820 Cessna Dr., Richmond, BC V7B 0A2
Tel: 604-333-3628; Fax: 604-333-3626
crew@bcsailing.bc.ca
www.bcsailing.bc.ca
Affiliation(s): Canadian Yachting Association; International Sailing Federation; Sport BC
Tine Moberg-Parker, Executive Director

Canadian Albacore Association (CAA)
PO Box 98093, 970 Queen St. East, Toronto, ON M4M 1J8
info@albacore.ca
www.albacore.ca
Jeff Beitz, Commodore
Mary Free, Treasurer
Publications: Shackles & Cringles

Canadian Yachting Association (CYA) / Association canadienne de yachting
Portsmith Olympic Harbour, 53 Yonge St., Kingston, ON K7M 6G4
Tel: 613-545-3044; Fax: 613-545-3045
Toll-Free: 877-416-4720
sailcanada@sailing.ca
www.sailing.ca
Affiliation(s): International Sailing Federation; International Sailing Schools Association
Gerry Giffin, President

Manitoba Sailing Association Inc. (MSA)
#406, 200 Main St., Winnipeg, MB R3C 4M2
Tel: 204-925-5650; Fax: 204-925-5624
sailing@sport.mb.ca
www.sailmanitoba.com
Ivan McMorris, President
Brigitte Smutny, Executive Director

Ontario Sailing / Association de voile de l'Ontario
65 Guise St. East, Hamilton, ON L8L 8B4
Tel: 905-572-7245; Fax: 905-572-6056
Toll-Free: 888-672-7245
info@ontariosailing.ca
www.ontariosailing.ca
Glenn Lethbridge, Executive Director

S.A.L.T.S. Sail & Life Training Society (SALTS)
PO Box 5014, Stn. B, Victoria, BC V8R 6N3
Tel: 250-383-6811; Fax: 250-383-7781
Toll-Free: 888-383-6811
info@salts.ca
www.salts.ca
www.facebook.com/saltsvictoria?ref=ts
Loren Hagerty, Executive Director

Tanzer 22 Class Association
PO Box 11122, Stn. H, Nepean, ON K2H 7T9
president@tanzer22.com
www.tanzer22.com
Affiliation(s): Canadian Yachting Association; United States Sailing Association

Schools

Prince Edward Island School Athletic Association (PEISAA)
109 Water St., Summerside, PE C1N 1A8
Tel: 902-888-8037; Fax: 902-432-2659
grturtle@gov.pe.ca
www.edu.pe.ca/peisaa
Garth Turtle, Executive Director
Lona Ryan, Game Reporting
Gerald MacCormack, Secretary-Treasurer

School Sports Newfoundland & Labrador (SSNL)
c/o Dennis Lush, President, PO Box 400, Gambo, NL A0G 1T0
Tel: 709-674-5336; Fax: 709-674-4244
www.schoolsportsnl.ca
www.facebook.com/141101766485
Karen Richard, Executive Director
Dennis Lush, President

Senior Citizens

Alberta Senior Citizens Sport & Recreation Association (ASCSRA)
#400, 7015 Macleod Trail., Calgary, AB T2H 2K6
Tel: 403-803-9852; Fax: 403-800-5599
info@alberta55plus.ca
www.alberta55plus.ca
Affiliation(s): Alberta Sport, Recreation, Parks & Wildlife Foundation
Pat Covington, President

Shooting Sports

Alberta Federation of Shooting Sports (AFSS)
Percy Page Centre, 11759 Groat Rd., Edmonton, AB T5M 3K6
Tel: 780-415-1775; Fax: 780-422-2663
afss@abshooters.org
www.abshooters.org
Bernie Harrison, President
Trudie Snider, Office Manager

Alberta Metallic Silhouette Association
2306 - 22nd St. South, Lethbridge, AB T1K 2K2
Tel: 403-327-7552
amsa@albertasilhouetteshooting.ca
www.silhouette-alberta.org
Affiliation(s): Shooting Federation of Canada; Alberta Federation of Shooting Sports
Ralph Oler, President
Kathy Oler, Sec.-Treas.

Atlantic Marksmen Association
PO Box 181, Stn. Dartmouth Main, Dartmouth, NS B2Y 3Y3
Tel: 902-469-2062
boudreau@chebucto.ns.ca
www.atlanticmarksmen.ca
Edward Doane, President

British Columbia Rifle Association (BCRA)
43583 Bracken Dr., Chilliwack, BC V2R 4A3
Tel: 604-793-0300; Fax: 604-793-4385
contact@bcrifle.org
www.bcrifle.org
Affiliation(s): Responsible Firearms Owners Coalition of British Columbia
Robert Pitcairn, Secretary

British Columbia Target Sports Association
PO Box 496, Kamloops, BC V2C 5L2
Tel: 250-374-6705
targetsports@bctsa.bc.ca
www.bctsa.bc.ca

Buckskinners Muzzleloading Association, Limited
PO Box 4127, Stn. Champlain Place, Dieppe, NB E1A 6E8
Tel: 506-576-1959; Fax: 506-859-1249
buckskinnersweb@yahoo.com
buckskinnersweb.weebly.com
Affiliation(s): New Brunswick Wildlife Federation
Shirley Stuart, Contact

Calgary & District Target Shooters Association
612 - 500 Country Hills Blvd. NE, #142, Calgary, AB T3K 5K3
Tel: 403-275-3257; Fax: 403-291-5579
cowboy@cdtsa.org
www.cdtsa.org
Affiliation(s): Alberta Federation of Shooting Sports; Alberta Fish & Game Association; Alberta Black Powder Association; Alberta Metallic Silhouette Association

Canadian Shooting Sports Association
#106, 3 Director Ct., Vaughan, ON L4L 4S5
Tel: 905-265-0692; Fax: 905-265-9794
Toll-Free: 888-873-4339
info@cdnshootingsports.org
www.cdnshootingsports.org
Affiliation(s): Ontario Council of Shooters; Shooting Federation of Canada

Canadian Trapshooting Association (CTA)
RR#1, Penhold, AB T0M 1R0
Tel: 403-886-2600; Fax: 403-886-2600
Bob Brown, President

Dominion of Canada Rifle Association (DCRA) / L'Association de tir dominion du canada
45 Shirley Blvd., Ottawa, ON K2K 2W6
Tel: 613-829-8281; Fax: 613-829-0099
office@dcra.ca
www.dcra.ca
Jim Thompson, Executive Director
Stan E. Frost, Executive Vice-President
T.F. deFaye, President

Fédération québécoise de tir (FQT) / Québec Shooting Federation
CP 1000, Succ. M, 4545, av Pierre-De Coubertin, Montréal, QC H1V 3R2
Tél: 514-252-3056; Téléc: 514-252-3060
fqt@fqtir.qc.ca
www.fqtir.qc.ca
Affiliation(s): Regroupment Loisir Québec; Sports Québec
Yvon Morissette, Directeur exécutif
Gérald Tousignant, Président

Manitoba Provincial Handgun Association (MPHA)
PO Box 314, Stn. Corydon Ave., Winnipeg, MB R3M 3S7
Tel: 204-925-5682; Fax: 204-925-5703
mbhndgn@shaw.ca
www.handgun.mb.ca
Randy Myrdal, President

Manitoba Provincial Rifle Association Inc. (MPRA)
795 Valour Rd., Winnipeg, MB R3G 3B3
Tel: 204-783-0768
www.manitobarifle.ca
Affiliation(s): Sports Manitoba
John C. Chapman, President

Nova Scotia Rifle Association (NSRA)
PO Box 482, Dartmouth, NS B2Y 3Y8
Tel: 902-456-7468
nsrifle@ns.sympatico.ca
www.nsrifle.org
Affiliation(s): Shooting Federation of Canada
A.S. Webber, President
D.G. Beaulieu, Secretary

Ontario Muzzle Loading Association (OMLA)
c/o Irene Wardell, 372 Beattie St., Strathroy, ON N7G 2X6
www.omla.ca
Irene Wardell, President
Russ Moore, Vice-President
Vivian Moore, Secretary
George Wortner, Treasurer

Ontario Provincial Trapshooting Association
c/o 273 Bousfield Cres., Milton, ON L9T 3N5
Tel: 905-878-5669
info@trapshooting.on.ca
www.trapshooting.on.ca
Smokey Smith, President
Gord Kerr, Secretary-Treasurer

Ontario Rifle Association
PO Box 60, Locust Hill, ON L0H 1J0
Tel: 905-294-8266
oraatt@yahoo.ca
www.ontariorifleassociation.org
Affiliation(s): Dominion of Canada Rifle Association
Peter Westlake, Contact, Membership Inquiries

Ontario Skeet Shooting Association (OSSA)
PO Box 96, Hampton, ON L0B 1J0
Tel: 905-263-8174; Fax: 905-263-4870
info@ontarioskeet.com
www.ontarioskeet.com
Bill Marsh, Secretary
Brad McRae, President

Province of Québec Rifle Association (PQRA) / Association de tir de la province de Québec (ATPQ)
PO Box 141, St Augustin de Desmaures, QC G2N 1W5
Tel: 418-878-4195
jacques.denis@globetrotter.net
www.pqra.org
Jacques Denis, President

Saskatchewan Black Powder Association (SBPA)
PO Box 643, Saskatoon, SK S7K 3L7
information@sbpa.ca; president@sbpa.ca
www.sbpa.ca

Saskatchewan Provincial Rifle Association Inc. (SPRA)
PO Box 1838, Kindersley, SK S0L 1S0
Tel: 306-463-4427; Fax: 306-463-1034
fullbore.rifle@saskrifle.ca
www.saskrifle.ca
Keith Skjerdal, Match Director

Shooting Federation of Canada (SFC) / Fédération de tir du Canada (FTC)
45 Shirley Blvd., Nepean, ON K2K 2W6
Tel: 613-727-7483; Fax: 613-727-7487
info@sfc-ftc.ca
www.sfc-ftc.ca
Affiliation(s): Canadian Shooting Sports Association
Asmir Arifovic, President

Shooting Federation of Nova Scotia (SFNS)
PO Box 28023, Dartmouth, NS B2W 6E2
Tel: 902-462-7048; Fax: 902-462-7048
marcom79@ns.sympatico.ca
Ray Fisher, President

Yellowknife Shooting Club (YKSC)
PO Box 2931, Yellowknife, NT X1A 2R2
Tel: 867-873-3212; Fax: 867-873-9008
mail@yellowknifeshootingclub.ca
yellowknifeshootingclub.ca
Affiliation(s): NWT Federation of Shooting Sports; Shooting Federation of Canada; NRA
Barry Taylor, President
Bud Rhyndress, Vice-President

Skating

Alberta Amateur Speed Skating Association (AASSA)
2500 University Dr. NW, Calgary, AB T2N 1N4
Tel: 403-220-7911; Fax: 403-220-9226
aassa@ucalgary.ca
www.albertaspeedskating.ca
Wendy Walker, Office Administrator

British Columbia Speed Skating Association
PO Box 2023, Stn. A, Abbotsford, BC V2T 3T8
Tel: 604-746-4349; Fax: 604-746-4549
lorna@speed-skating.bc.ca
www.speed-skating.bc.ca
Ted Houghton, Executive Director

Fédération de patinage artistique du Québec (FPAQ)
CP 1000, Succ. M, 4545, av Pierre-de-Coubertin, Montréal, QC H1V 3R2
Tél: 514-252-3073; Téléc: 514-252-3170
patinage@patinage.qc.ca
www.patinage.qc.ca
Josée Beauséjour, Directeur exécutif

Fédération de Patinage de Vitesse du Québec
930, av Roland Beaudin, Sainte-Foy, QC G1V 4H8
Tél: 418-651-1973; Téléc: 418-651-1977
fpvq@fpvq.org
www.fpvq.org
Robert Dubreuil, Directeur général

International Skating Union (ISU) / Union Internationale de Patinage
Chemin de Primerose 2, Lausanne, 1007, Switzerland
Tel: 41-21-612-6666; Fax: 41-21-612-6677
info@isu.ch
www.isu.org
Fredi Schmid, General Secretary

Manitoba Speed Skating Association
145 Pacific Ave., Winnipeg, MB R3B 2Z6
Tel: 204-925-5657; Fax: 204-925-5792
Toll-Free: 888-628-9921
office@mbspeedskating.ca
www.mbspeedskating.org
Paul Daeninck, President

Newfoundland & Labrador Speed Skating Association (NLSSA)
81 Birchy Cove Dr., Corner Brook, NL A2H 6W8
Tel: 709-785-1403
rzrenos@gmail.com

Nunavut Speed Skating Association
PO Box 761, Iqaluit, NU X0A 0H0
Tel: 867-979-1226; Fax: 867-975-3384
jtmaurice@northwestel.net
www.nunavutspeedskating.ca
John Maurice, President

NWT Speed Skating Association
PO Box 2664, Yellowknife, NT X1A 2P9
pamela@ssimicro.com
www.nwtspeedskating.ca
Pam Dunbar, President

Ontario Speed Skating Association (OSSA)
PO Box 1179, 2 Queen St., 2nd Fl., Lakefield, ON K0L 2H0
Tel: 705-652-9490; Fax: 705-652-1227
ontariospeedskating.ca
www.facebook.com/OntarioSpeedSkating
twitter.com/OSSA
Jacqueline Deschenes, Executive Director
Sarah Leslie, Manager, Sport

Saskatchewan Amateur Speed Skating Association (SASSA)
2205 Victoria Ave., Regina, SK S4P 0S4
Tel: 306-780-9400; Fax: 306-525-4009
sassa@sasktel.net
www.saskspeedskating.ca
Affiliation(s): Sask Sport Inc.
Shawn MacLennan, Executive Director

Skate Canada / Patinage Canada
865 Shefford Rd., Ottawa, ON K1J 1H9
Tel: 613-747-1007; Fax: 613-748-5718
Toll-Free: 888-747-2372
skatecanada@skatecanada.ca;
memberservices@skatecanada.ca
www.skatecanada.ca
www.facebook.com/group.php?gid=129815677038
William Thompson, Chief Executive Officer
Cheryl McEvoy, Chief Operating Officer
Barbara Draper, Director, Member Services
Barb MacDonald, Director, Corporate Communications
Michael Slipchuk, Director, High Performance
Jackie Stell-Buckingham, Director, Events

Skate Ontario
Tel: 705-472-4835
skateontario@sympatico.ca
www.skateontario.org
www.facebook.com/SkateOntario
twitter.com/SkateOntario
Tracey McCague-McElrea, Executive Director
Wendy St. Denis, President

Speed Skate New Brunswick
246 St. Pierre East Blvd., Caraquet, NB E1E 1B1
Tel: 506-727-6334; Fax: 506-727-6334
speedskatenb@gmail.com
ssnb.homestead.com
Ray Harris, President
Peter Steele, Provincial Coach

Speed Skate Nova Scotia
10 Thistle Dr., North Sydney, NS B2A 3R1
Tel: 902-794-8954
laurolea@ns.sympatico.ca
Terri Dixon, President

Speed Skate PEI
PO Box 383, Charlottetown, PE C1A 7K7
Tel: 902-628-6606
info@speedskatepei.ca
www.speedskatepei.com
Wendy A. Francis, President
Alban Moran, Secretary

Speed Skating Canada (SSC) / Patinage de vitesse Canada
#402, 2781 Lancaster Rd., Ottawa, ON K1B 1A7
Tel: 613-260-3669; Fax: 613-260-3660
ssc@speedskating.ca
www.speedskating.ca
Affiliation(s): International Skating Union
John-Paul Cody-Cox, Chief Executive Officer
Mark Mathies, Executive Director, Sport
Patricia Brennan, Director, Finance & Administration
Douglas Duncan, Director, Leadership Eduation
Phil Legault, Director, Communications
Publications: ING on the Edge Newsletter

Yukon Speed Skating Association
11 Buttercup Pl., Whitehorse, YT Y1A 5V1
Tel: 867-668-4591; Fax: 867-393-8101
Bruce Henry, Branch President

Skiing

Alberta Freestyle Ski Association (AFSA)
88 Canada Olympic Rd. SW, Calgary, AB T3B 5R5
Tel: 403-297-2718; Fax: 403-202-2522
info@abfreestyle.com
www.abfreestyle.com
Affiliation(s): Canadian Feestyle Ski Association
Gord Campbell, Executive Director
Larry Bilton, Chair
Al Ulsifer, Vice-Chair
Neil Orr, Treasurer
Publications: Alberta Freestyle Skiing Association Newsletter

Alpine Canada ALPIN
#153, 401 - 9th Ave. SW, Calgary, AB T2P 3C5
Tel: 403-777-3200; Fax: 403-777-3213
info@alpinecanada.org
alpinecanada.org
Max Gartner, President
Jennifer Duggan, Manager, National Services

Association des stations de ski du Québec (ASSQ)
#100, 7665, rue Larrey, Anjou, QC H1J 2T7
Tél: 514-493-1810; Téléc: 514-493-3975
media@assq.qc.ca
www.quebecskisurf.com
Claude Péloquin, Président-directeur général

British Columbia Alpine Ski Association
#403, 1788 West Broadway, Vancouver, BC V6J 1Y1
Tel: 604-678-3070; Fax: 604-678-8073
info@bcalpine.com
www.bcalpine.com
Bruce Goldsmid, CEO

Canadian Association of Nordic Ski Instructors (CANSI)
c/o Secrétariat, 8 Douglas Rd., Chelsea, QC J9B 1K4
Tel: 819-360-6700; Fax: 819-827-0017
office@cansi.ca; membership@cansi.ca
www.cansi.ca
Jeff Hampshire, President
Françoise Chatenoud, Office Coordinator
Publications: XCitation

Canadian Freestyle Ski Association / Association canadienne de ski acrobatique
808 Pacific St., Vancouver, BC V6Z 1C2
Tel: 604-714-2233; Fax: 604-714-2232
info@freestyleski.com
www.freestyleski.ca
Affiliation(s): Canadian Ski & Snowboard Association
Peter Judge, CEO

Canadian Masters Cross-Country Ski Association (CMCSA) / Association canadienne des maîtres en ski de fond
c/o 2 MacNeil Cres., Stephenville, NL A2N 3E3
www.canadian-masters-xc-ski.ca/en_index.htm
Affiliation(s): World Masters Cross-Country Ski Association; Cross-Country Canada
Bruce Legrow, National Director
Publications: Canadian Masters Cross-Country Ski Association Newsletter

Canadian Ski Council (CSC) / Conseil canadien du ski
21 Fourth St. East, Collingwood, ON L9Y 1T2
Tel: 705-445-9140; Fax: 705-445-0525
info@skicanada.org
www.skicanada.org
www.facebook.com/pages/Canadian-Ski-Council/152259956560
twitter.com/cdnskicouncil
Affiliation(s): Canadian Association for Disabled Skiing; Canadian Association of Nordic Ski Instructors; Canadian Ski Area Operators' Association; Canadian Ski Association; Canadian Ski Instructors' Alliance; Canadian Ski Coaches Federation; Canadian Ski Patrol System; Canadian Association of Snowboard Instructors; National Snow Industries Association

Canadian Ski Instructors' Alliance (CSIA) / Alliance des moniteurs de ski du Canada
#220, 4900, rue Jean Talon ouest, Montréal, QC H4P 1W9
Tel: 514-748-2648; Fax: 514-748-2476
Toll-Free: 800-811-6428
national@snowpro.com
www.snowpro.com/csia/e
www.facebook.com/CSIAAMSC
Affiliation(s): International Ski Instructors Association
Dan Ralph, Managing Director
Lisa Cambise, Director, Shared Services
Martin Jean, Director, Education & Membership Services
Benoit Fournier, Coordinator, National Programs
Publications: CSIA [Canadian Ski Instructors' Alliance] eBLAST, Ski Pro

Canadian Ski Instructors' Alliance (CSIA) / Fédération des entraîneurs de ski du Canada
#220, 4900 Jean Talon ouest, Montréal, QC H4P 1W9
Tel: 514-748-2648; Fax: 514-748-2476
Toll-Free: 800-811-6428
national@snowpro.com
www.snowpro.com/en
Otto Kamstra, Chair

Canadian Ski Marathon (CSM) / Marathon canadien de ski
#200, 81 Jean-Prolux, Gatineau, QC J8Z 1W2
Tel: 819-770-6556; Fax: 819-770-7428
Toll-Free: 877-770-6556
ski@csm-mcs.com
www.csm-mcs.com
Affiliation(s): Tourisme Outaouais; Tourisme Laurentides
Gregory Koegl, President

Canadian Ski Patrol System (CSPS) / Patrouille canadienne de ski (OPCS)
4531 Southclark Pl., Ottawa, ON K1T 3V2
Tel: 613-822-2245; Fax: 613-822-1088
Toll-Free: 900-565-2777
info@skipatrol.ca
www.csps.ca
Renée Scanlon, Office Manager
Brian Low, Chair
John Leu, National President
Publications: SK-E Patrolling News, Sweep

Canadian Snowsports Association (CSA) / L'Association canadienne des sports d'hiver (ACSH)
#202, 1451 West Broadway, Vancouver, BC V6H 1H6
Tel: 604-734-6800; Fax: 604-669-7954
info@canadiansnowsports.com
www.canadiansnowsports.com
Lillian Alderton, Administrator
David Pym, Managing Director

Cross Country Alberta (CCA)
Percy Page Centre, 11759 Groat Rd., Edmonton, AB T5M 3K6
Tel: 780-415-1738; Fax: 780-427-0524
manager@xcountryab.net
www.xcountryab.net
Ken Hewitt, Chair
Michael Neary, Manager, Sport

Cross Country British Columbia
#106, 3003 - 30th St., Vernon, BC V1T 9J5
Tel: 250-545-9600; Fax: 250-545-9614
office@crosscountrybc.ca
www.crosscountrybc.ca

Cross Country Canada (CCC) / Ski de fond Canada (SFC)
c/o Bill Warren Training Centre, #100, 1995 Olympic Way, Canmore, AB T1W 2T6
Tel: 403-678-6791; Fax: 403-678-3644
Toll-Free: 877-609-3215
info@cccski.com
www.cccski.com
www.facebook.com/CrossCountryCanada
twitter.com/cccsk
Affiliation(s): Canadian Ski & Snowboard Association
Jim McCarthy, President
Davin MacIntosh, Executive Director
Cathy Sturgeon, Director, Administration & Communication

Cross Country New Brunswick / Ski de fond Nouveau-Brunswick
1450 Maria St., Bathurst, NB E2A 3G2
Tel: 506-542-2617; Fax: 506-542-2638
skis@nbnet.nb.ca
www.xcski-nb.ca
Dave Moore, Chair
Suzanne Landry, Vice-Chair, Competition & President, High Performance Committee
Carole Daigle, Secretary
Édouard Daigle, Treasurer

Cross Country Ontario (CCO)
738 River St, Thunder Bay, ON P7A 3S8
Tel: 807-768-4617
admin@xco.org
www.xco.org
Don Nixon, Chair
Liz Inkila, Director, Administration
Al White, Director, Technical
Pavlina Sudrich, Ontario Coach, High Performance Committee

Cross Country Saskatchewan (CCS)
1860 Lorne St., Regina, SK S4P 2L7
Tel: 306-780-9240; Fax: 306-780-9462
ccs@sasktel.net
www.crosscountrysask.ca
Dave Martinuk, President
Alana Ottenbreit, Executive Director

Cross Country Ski Association of Manitoba
Sport for Life Centre, 145 Pacific Ave., Winnipeg, MB R3B 2Z6
Tel: 204-925-5639; Fax: 204-231-0297
info@ccski.mb.ca
www.ccski.mb.ca
Affiliation(s): Sport Manitoba
Richard Huybers, Chair
Karin McSherry, Executive Director

Cross Country Ski Nova Scotia (CCSNS)
5516 Spring Garden Rd., 4th Fl., Halifax, NS B3J 1G6
Tel: 902-425-5450; Fax: 902-425-5606
ccsns@sportnovascotia.ca
crosscountryskins.ca
Keith Ayling, President
John Hudec, Vice-President
Derek Estabrook, Secretary
Tim Carroll, Treasurer

Cross Country Yukon (CCY)
4061 - 4th Ave., Whitehorse, YT Y1A 1H1
Tel: 867-334-9220; Fax: 867-667-4237
xcyukon@northwestel.net
www.crosscountryyukon.com
Alain Masson, Coordinator

Fédération québécoise de la montagne et de l'escalade (FQME)
CP 1000, Succ. M, 4545, av Pierre-de-Coubertin, Montréal, QC H1V 3R2
Tél: 514-252-3004; Téléc: 514-252-3201
Ligne sans frais: 866-204-3763
fqme@fqme.qc.ca
www.fqme.qc.ca
Affiliation(s): Union internationale des associations d'alpinisme
André St-Jacques, Directeur des opérations

National Snow Industries Association (NSIA) / Association nationale des industries de la neige
#810, 245, av Victoria, Montréal, QC H3Z 2M6
Tel: 514-939-7370; Fax: 514-939-7371
Toll-Free: 800-263-6742
central.station@nsia.ca
www.nsia.ca
Anna Di Meglio, President
Nicole Garand, Administration & Customer Service
Publications: National Snow Industries Association Directory

Northwest Territories Ski Division
c/o PO Box 682, Yellowknife, NT X1A 2N5
Tel: 867-873-4782
cygnus@theedge.ca
Brenda Hans

Ontario Track 3 Ski Association for the Disabled
PO Box 67, Stn. D, #4, 61 Advance Rd., Toronto, ON M9A 4X1
Tel: 416-233-3872; Fax: 416-233-7862
Toll-Free: 877-308-7225
track3@track3.org
www.track3.org
Steve Jones, President
Darrell Jarvic, Secretary
Tracy Johnston, Treasurer
J. Richard Clarke, Vice-President
Publications: On Track

Ski Hawks Ottawa
522 Hillcrest Ave., Ottawa, ON K2A 2M9
Tel: 613-725-2472
www.cads-ncd.ca/skihawks/Skihawks_home.html
Bruce Meredith, Treasurer
Carolyn Mitrow, President

Ski Québec alpin (SQA)
CP 1000, Succ. M, 4545, av Pierre de Coubertin, Montréal, QC H1V 3R2
Tél: 514-252-3089
www.skiquebec.qc.ca
Daniel Paul Lavallée, Directrice général
Éric Préfontaine, Directeur athlétique
Marie-Pier Jourdain, Coordonnatrice, Développement élite
Sylvie Grenier, Responsable, Services comptables
Anthony Lamour, Responsable, Communications et du service aux partenaires

Snowbound
#1, 733 Ross Ave. East, Timmins, ON P4N 8S8
Tel: 705-264-4700; Fax: 705-268-3585
Toll-Free: 800-575-3210

Union internationale des associations d'alpinisme (UIAA) / International Union of Alpine Associations
c/o International Mountaineering & Climbing Federation, Monbijoustrasse 61/Postfach, 23, Bern, CH-3000, Switzerland
Tel: 41-(0)31-370-18-28; Fax: 41-(0)31-370-18-38
office@uiaa.ch
www.theuiaa.org
Affiliation(s): Alpine Club of Canada; Fédération québecoise de la montagne
Jordi Colomer, Acting President

Snowboarding

Canadian Association of Snowboard Instructors (CASI) / Association canadienne des moniteurs de surf des neiges (ACMS)
60 Canning Cres., cambridge, on N1T 1X2
Tel: 877-976-2274; Fax: 866-471-6594
headoffice@casi-acms.com
www.casi-acms.com
www.facebook.com/CASIACMS
twitter.com/casiacms
Affiliation(s): Canadian Ski Instructors Alliance; Canadian Snowboard Federation
Dan Genge, Executive Director

HeliCat Canada
#102, 810 Waddington Dr., Vernon, BC V1T 8T3
Tel: 250-542-9020; Fax: 250-542-5070
info@helicatcanada.com
www.helicatcanada.com
John Forrest, President

Snowmobiles

Alberta Snowmobile Association (ASA)
11759 Groat Rd., Edmonton, AB T5M 3K6
Tel: 780-427-2695; Fax: 780-415-1779
info@altasnowmobile.ab.ca
www.altasnowmobile.ab.ca
Affiliation(s): Canadian Council of Snowmobile Organizations
Darryl Copithorne, President, president@altasnowmobile.ab.ca
Janet Riopel, Vice-President, mriopel@mcsnet.ca

British Columbia Snowmobile Federation (BCSF)
Stn. 400, 2439 Poulton Ave., Houston, BC V0Y 1Z0
Tel: 250-845-7705; Fax: 250-845-7715
Toll-Free: 877-537-8716
office@bcsf.org
www.bcsf.org
Affiliation(s): International Snowmobile Council; Canadian Council of Snowmobile Organizations
Les Auston, Executive Director

Canadian Council of Snowmobile Organizations (CCSO) / Conseil canadien des organismes de motoneige (CCOM)
PO Box 21059, Thunder Bay, ON P7A 8A7
Tel: 807-345-5299
ccso.ccom@tbaytel.net
www.ccso-ccom.ca
www.facebook.com/group.php?gid=126035004176384
Dennis Burns, Executive Director
Publications: CCSO [Canadian Council of Snowmobile Organizations] / CCOM [Conseil canadien des organismes de motoneige] News Bulletin

Fédération des clubs de motoneigistes du Québec (FCMQ)
CP 1000, Succ. M, 4545, av Pierre-de Coubertin, Montréal, QC H1V 3R2
Tél: 514-252-3076; Téléc: 514-254-2066
info@fcmq.qc.ca
www.fcmq.qc.ca
Dany Quirion, Président

Great Slave Snowmobile Association
4209 - 49A Ave., Yellowknife, NT X1A 1B3
Tel: 867-766-4353
bruceh@sub-arctic.ca
www.yktrailriders.com
Affiliation(s): Canadian Council of Snowmobile Organizations; International Snowmobile Council
Bill Braden, President

Klondike Snowmobile Association
PO Box 9034, 29 Wann Rd., Whitehorse, YT Y1A 4A2
Tel: 867-667-7680
klonsnow@yknet.ca
www.ksa.yk.ca
Affiliation(s): Trans Canada Trail - Yukon

Ontario Federation of Snowmobile Clubs (OFSC)
#9, 501 Welham Rd., Barrie, ON L4N 8Z6
Tel: 705-739-7669; Fax: 705-739-5005
www.ofsc.on.ca
Publications: How to Make Smart Choices: Take It Easy, Ontario Federation of Snowmobile Clubs District Trail Guides, The Right Way: Snowmobile Driver Training Safety Course - Adult Training Kit

Saskatchewan Snowmobile Association (SSA)
PO Box 533, 221 Centre St., Regina Beach, SK S0G 4C0
Tel: 306-729-3500; Fax: 306-729-3505
Toll-Free: 800-499-7533
sasksnow@sasktel.net
www.sasksnowmobiling.sk.ca
www.facebook.com/people/Sask-Snow/100001758383580
twitter.com/sasksnow
Chris Brewer, President & Chief Executive Officer
Chelsie Stuermer, Club Coordinator
Jeannie Brewer, Comptroller

Snowmobilers Association of Nova Scotia (SANS)
5516 Spring Garden Rd., 4th Fl., Halifax, NS B3J 3G6
Tel: 902-425-5450; Fax: 902-425-5606
info@snowmobilersNS.com
www.snowmobilersns.com
John Cameron, General Manager

Snowmobilers of Manitoba Inc.
2121 Henderson Hwy., Winnipeg, MB R2G 1P8
Tel: 204-940-7533; Fax: 204-940-7531
info@snoman.mb.ca
www.snoman.mb.ca

Affiliation(s): Canadian Council of Snowmobile Organizations
Duncan Stokes, Executive Director

Thunder Bay Adventure Trails
PO Box 29190, Thunder Bay, ON P7B 6P9
Tel: 807-939-7533
www.tbat.ca
Marcel Gauthier, Club Executive
Lloyd Chaykowski, Club Executive
Harold Harkonen, Club Executive
Bradley Pollock, Club Executive

Soaring

Aéro-Club des Outardes
1455, de Biencourt, Montréal, QC H4E 1T1
Tél: 514-465-7806
francisco45@gmail.com
aeroclubdesoutardes.iquebec.com
Jacques Fairpault, Président

Air Sailing Club
144 Maple St., Guelph, ON N1G 2G7
Tel: 519-836-7049
stephen.szikora@sympatico.ca
Stephen Szikora

Alberta Soaring Council
PO Box 13, Black Diamond, AB T0L 0H0
Tel: 403-813-6658
asc@stade.ca
www.soaring.ab.ca
Phil Stade, Executive Director

Association de vol à voile Champlain
10, 745 de Martigny, Montréal, QC H2B 2N1
Tél: 450-771-0500
champlain@videotron.ca
www.avvc.qc.ca

Base Borden Soaring
PO Box 286, Borden, ON L0M 1C0
Tel: 705-424-1200
users.csolve.net/~ourplace/
Ray Leiska

Bonnechere Soaring Club
PO Box 1081, Deep River, ON K0J 1P0
Tel: 613-584-4636; Fax: 613-584-4636
Iver Theilmann

Central Alberta Gliding Club
4309 Grandview Blvd., Red Deer, AB T4N 3E7
Tel: 403-340-3506
hammondv@telus.net
www.cagcsoaring.ca
Affiliation(s): Alberta Soaring Council
Drew Hammond, President

Club de vol à voile de Québec
CP 9276, Sainte-Foy, QC G1V 4B1
Tél: 418-337-4905
www.cvvq.net
Richard Noël, Président

Cu Nim Gliding Club
113 Midridge Pl. SW, Calgary, AB T2X 1E4
Tel: 403-630-4332
www.soaring.ab.ca/exec.html
Affiliation(s): Alberta Soaring Council
Danny Russell

Edmonton Soaring Club (ESC)
PO Box 472, Edmonton, AB T5J 2K1
Tel: 780-363-3860
www.edmontonsoaringclub.com
Affiliation(s): Alberta Soaring Council; other soaring clubs
Gary Hill, President
Bob Hagen, Facilities Manager

Gatineau Gliding Club
PO Box 8145, Stn. T, Ottawa, ON K1G 3H6
Tel: 613-673-5386
ggc@gatineauglidingclub.ca
www.gatineauglidingclub.ca

Grande Prairie Soaring Society
PO Box 64, Hythe, AB T0H 2C0
soaring.ab.ca/gpss
Lloyd Sherk, President
Terry Hatfield, Sec.-Treas.

London Soaring Club
130 Holcroft St. West, Ingersoll, ON N5C 2B8
Tel: 519-661-7844
info@londonsoaringclub.ca
www.londonsoaringclub.ca
Cal Gillett, Treasurer

Manitoba Soaring Council
145 Pacific Ave., Winnipeg, MB R3B 2Z6
Tel: 204-925-5682; Fax: 204-925-5703
www.wgc.mb.ca/msc/Manitoba_Soaring_Council_Home_Page.htm

Montréal Soaring Council (MSC) / Club de Vol à Voile MSC
PO Box 1804, Hawkesbury Airfield, Saint-Laurent, QC H4L 4W6
Tel: 613-632-5438
alainlaprade@hotmail.com
www.flymsc.org
Arvind K. Jain, Administration

Ontario Soaring Association
10 Courtwood Pl., Toronto, ON M2K 1Z9
Tel: 416-223-6487
Walter Chmela, Contact

Pemberton Soaring Centre
Pemberton, BC V0N 2L1
Tel: 604-894-5727; Fax: 604-894-5776
Toll-Free: 800-831-2611
info@pembertonsoaring.com
www.pembertonsoaring.com
Rudy Rozsypalek

Prince Albert Gliding & Soaring Club (PAG&SC)
219 Scissons Ct., Saskatoon, SK S7S 1B7
Tel: 306-249-1859
www.soar.sk.ca/pagsc
Affiliation(s): Soaring Association of Saskatchewan; Soaring Association of Canada
Keith Andrews, President
Don Klassen, Treasurer

Regina Gliding & Soaring Club
PO Box 4093, Regina, SK S4P 3W5
Tel: 306-536-4119
fly@soar.regina.sk.ca
www.soar.regina.sk.ca

Saskatoon Soaring Club
510 Cynthia St., Saskatoon, SK S7L 7K7
Tel: 306-975-0844
j.toles@sasktel.net
www.ssc.soar.sk.ca
John Toles, Secretary

Soaring Association of Canada (SAC) / Association canadienne de vol à voile (ACVV)
c/o COPA National Office, 71 Bank St., 7th Fl., Ottawa, ON K1P 5N2
Tel: 613-236-4901; Fax: 613-236-8646
sac@sac.ca
www.sac.ca
Affiliation(s): Aero Club of Canada; International Gliding Commission of the Fédération Aéronautique Internationale
Sylvain Bourque, President
John Mulder, Vice-President & Secretary
Publications: Free Flight

Soaring Nova Scotia
c/o Charles Yeates, #110, 105 Dunbrack St., Halifax, NS B3M 3G7
Tel: 902-443-0094
www.soarns.ca
Larry Bogan, Chair
Charles Yeates, Sec-Treas.

SOSA Gliding Club
PO Box 81, Rockton, ON L0R 1X0
Tel: 519-740-9328
sosa@sosaglidingclub.com
www.sosaglidingclub.com
Dave Springford, President/Treasurer

Toronto Soaring Club
c/o President, 58 River Ridge Rd., Barrie, ON L4N 7E8
Tel: 705-735-4422
dellis@rogers.com
www.toronto-soaring.ca
Dave Ellis, President

Winnipeg Gliding Club (WGC)
PO Box 1255, Winnipeg, MB R3C 2Y4
Tel: 204-735-2868
info@wgc.mb.ca
www.wgc.mb.ca

York Soaring Association
10 Courtwood Pl., Toronto, ON M2K 1Z9
Tel: 416-223-6487; Fax: 416-223-6487
robertocentazzo@yorksoaring.com
www.yorksoaring.com
Walter Chmela, President

Soccer

Alberta Soccer Association
#203, 9440 - 49th St., Edmonton, AB T6B 2M9
Tel: 780-474-2200; Fax: 780-474-6300
Toll-Free: 866-250-2200
www.albertasoccer.com
Richard Adams, Executive Director
Anthony Traficante, Manager, Operations
Carmen Charron, Coordinator, Program
Federico Sanmartin, Coordinator, Technical Operations

British Columbia Soccer Association
#510, 375 Water St., Vancouver, BC V6B 5C6
Tel: 604-299-6401; Fax: 604-299-9610
bcsoccer@gmail.com
www.bcsoccer.net
Bjorn Osieck, Executive Director

Canadian Soccer Association (CSA) / Association canadienne de soccer
Place Soccer Canada, 237 Metcalfe St., Ottawa, ON K2P 1R2
Tel: 613-237-7678; Fax: 613-237-1516
info@soccercan.ca
www.canadasoccer.com
www.facebook.com/canadasoccer
twitter.com/CanadaSoccerEN
Affiliation(s): Féderation Internationale de Football Association, FIFA; Football Confederation; Canadian Olympic Association
Peter Montopoli, General Secretary
Joe Guest, Deputy General Secretary
Sean Hefferman, Chief Financial Officer
Ray Clark, Director, Coaching & Player Development
Cathy Breda, Manager, Administration
Michèle Dion, Manager, Communications

Fédération de soccer du Québec
#210, 955, av Bois-de-Boulogne, Laval, QC H7N 4G1
Tél: 450-975-3355; Téléc: 450-975-1001
www.federation-soccer.qc.ca
Martial Prud'homme, Président
Brigitte Frot, Directrice générale
Edward Witkowskie, Vice-Président
Bruno Bédard, Responsable, Technique
Robert Ganache, Responsable, Finances
Pierre Marchand, Responsable, Compétition

Fraser Valley Soccer Referees' Association (FVSRA)
10945B River Rd, Delta, BC V4C 2R8
Tel: 604-588-3959
www.fraservalleysoccerreferees.com
David Miller, President

Newfoundland & Labrador Soccer Association
39 Churchill Ave., St. John's, NL A1A 0H7
Tel: 709-576-0601; Fax: 709-576-0588
info@nlsa.ca (business); nlsatechnical@sportnl.ca (technical)
www.nlsa.ca
Doug Redmond, President
Dragan Mirkovic, Director, Technical
Rob Comerford, Manager, Business

Northwest Territories Soccer Association (NWTSA)
PO Box 11089, Yellowknife, NT X1A 3X7
Tel: 867-669-8326; Fax: 867-669-8327
Toll-Free: 800-661-0797
www.nwtkicks.ca
Affiliation(s): Sport North Federation
Melanie Kornacki, Sport Consultant
Ryan Fequet, President

Ontario Soccer Association (OSA)
7601 Martin Grove Rd., Vaughan, ON L4L 9E4
Tel: 905-264-9390; Fax: 905-264-9445
TheOSA@soccer.on.ca
www.soccer.on.ca
www.facebook.com/TheOntarioSoccerAssociation
twitter.com/OSA_Tweeter
Ron Smale, President
Lisa Beatty, Executive Director

Prince Edward Island Soccer Association (PEISA)
PO Box 1863, 40 Enman Cres., Charlottetown, PE C1A 7N5
Tel: 902-368-6251; Fax: 902-569-7693
admin@peisoccer.com
www.peisoccer.com
Gerald MacDonald, President
Daphne Andrews, Secretary/Registrat
Colleen Arsenault, Treasurer

Saskatchewan Soccer Association Inc. (SSA)
1870 Lorne St., Regina, SK S4P 2L7
Tel: 306-780-9225; Fax: 306-780-9480
k.sumner@sasksoccer.com
www.sasksoccer.com
www.facebook.com/pages/Saskatchewan-Soccer-Association/83226704916
Bonnie Lee Copeman, Business Administrator

Soccer New Brunswick
#2, 125 Russ Howard Dr., Moncton, NB E1C 0L7
Tel: 506-382-7529; Fax: 506-382-5621
office@soccernb.org
www.soccernb.org
www.facebook.com/group.php?gid=183461681180
Jeff Salvis, Executive Director

Soccer Nova Scotia (SNS)
210 Thomas Raddall Dr., Halifax, NS B3S 1K3
Tel: 902-445-0265; Fax: 902-445-0258
admin@soccerns.ns.ca; programs@soccerns.ns.ca
www.soccerns.ns.ca
George Athanasiou, Chief Executive Officer
Daniel Worthington, Director, High Performance
Carman King, Officer, Referee Development

Yukon Soccer Association
4061 - 4th Ave., Whitehorse, YT Y1A 1H1
Tel: 867-633-4625; Fax: 867-667-4237
yukonsoccer@sportyukon.com
www.yukonsoccer.yk.ca
Kim King, Administrator

Softball

Alberta Amateur Softball Association (AASA)
9860 - 33 Ave., Edmonton, AB T6N 1C6
Tel: 780-461-7735; Fax: 780-461-7757
calie@softballalberta.ca
www.softballalberta.ca
Affiliation(s): Western Canada Softball Association
Michele Patry, Executive Director

British Columbia Amateur Softball Association (BCASA)
PO Box 45570, Stn. Sunnyside Mall, 2201 - 148th St., Surrey, BC V4A 9N3
Tel: 604-531-0044; Fax: 604-531-8831
info@softball.bc.ca
www.softball.bc.ca
Dennis Bidin, President

Ontario Rural Softball Association
RR#1, Innerkip, ON N0J 1M0
Tel: 519-469-3593
www.ontarioruralsoftball.ca/index.php
Carl Littlejohns, Secretary
Dennis Wilson, President

Softball Canada
#212, 223 Colonnade Rd., Ottawa, ON K1H 7X3
Tel: 613-523-3386; Fax: 613-523-5761
info@softball.ca
www.softball.ca
www.facebook.com/pages/Softball-Canada/203017655217
Hugh Mitchener, CEO
Kevin Quinn, President

Softball Manitoba
#321, 145 Pacific Ave., Winnipeg, MB R3B 2Z6
Tel: 204-925-5673; Fax: 204-925-5703
softball@softball.mb.ca
www.softball.mb.ca
Bill Finch, President

Softball NB Inc. (SNB) / Softball Nouveau-Brunswick Inc.
4242 Water St., Miramichi, NB E1N 4L2
Tel: 506-773-3507; Fax: 506-773-5630
softball@softballnb.ca
www.softballnb.ca
Bev Adams, President
Réjean Léger, Sec.-Treas.
Peter McLean, Executive & Technical Director

Softball Newfoundland & Labrador
PO Box 21165, St. John's, NL A1A 5B2
Tel: 709-576-7231; Fax: 709-576-7081
softball@sportnl.ca
www.softball.nf.ca
Lloyd Power, President

Softball Ontario
Sport Alliance Bldg., #305, 1185 Eglinton Ave. East, Toronto, ON M3C 3C6
Tel: 416-426-7150; Fax: 416-426-7368
info@softballontario.ca
www.softballontario.ca
www.facebook.com/SoftballOntario
Affiliation(s): Provincial Women's Softball Association (PWSA); Ontario Amateur Softball Association (OASA); Ontario Rural Softball Association (ORSA); Slo-Pitch Ontario Association (SPOA)
Wendy Cathcart, Executive Director

Softball Québec
CP 1000, Succ. M, 4545, av Pierre-de Coubertin, Montréal, QC H1V 3R2
Tél: 514-252-3061; Téléc: 514-252-3134
www.softballquebec.com
Chantal Gagnon, Directrice générale
Poste vacant, Présidente

Softball Saskatchewan
2205 Victoria Ave., Regina, SK S4P 0S4
Tel: 306-780-9235; Fax: 306-780-9483
info@softball.sk.ca
www.softball.sk.ca
Guy Jacobson, Executive Director

Softball Yukon
18 Stewart Rd., Whitehorse, YT Y1A 3S3
sbyukon@whtvcable.com
www.softballyukon.com
Rob Andison, President

Sport Medicine

Alberta Athletic Therapists Association
PO Box 61115, Kensington RPO, Calgary, AB T2N 4S6
Tel: 403-220-8957
info@aata.ca
www.aata.ca
Breda Lau, President
Sarah Klassen, Secretary

Athletic Therapy Association of British Columbia (ATABC)
c/o Camosun College Interurban Campus, #PISE 306E, 4371 Interurban Rd., Victoria, BC V9E 2C5
mail@athletictherapybc.ca
www.athletictherapybc.ca
Noreen Ortilla, President
Kelly Uniewski, Registrar

Atlantic Provinces Athletic Therapists Association
c/o Memorial University, PO Box 4200, 2300 Elizabeth Ave., St. John's, NL A1C 5S7
Tel: 709-737-3442
contact@apata.ca
www.apata.ca
Shauna Stone, President

Canadian Academy of Sport Medicine (CASM) / Académie canadienne de médecine du sport (ACMS)
#4, 5330 Canotek Rd., Ottawa, ON K1J 9C1
Tel: 613-748-5851; Fax: 613-748-5792
Toll-Free: 877-585-2394
bfalardeau@casm-acms.org
www.casm-acms.org
Affiliation(s): World Federation of Sport Medicine
Dawn Haworth, Executive Director
Publications: Canadian Academy of Sport Medicine Newsletter, Clinical Journal of Sport Medicine

Canadian Athletic Therapists Association (CATA) / Association canadienne des thérapeutes du sport
#402, 1040 - 7th Ave. SW, Calgary, AB T2P 3G9
Tel: 403-509-2282; Fax: 403-509-2280
info@athletictherapy.org
www.athletictherapy.org
Grant Slessor, Executive Director
Publications: Athletic Therapy Today, CATA [Canadian Athletic Therapists Association] Newsletter

Corporation des thérapeutes du sport du Québec (CTSQ)
Concordia University, #SP165.04, 7141, rue Sherbrooke ouest, Montréal, QC H4B 1R6
Tél: 514-848-2424
admin@ctsq.qc.ca
www.ctsq.qc.ca
Christina Grace, President
Diana Berardi, General Manager

Manitoba Athletic Therapists Association Inc. (MATA)
University of Manitoba, 233 Investors Group Athletic Centre, 75 Sidney Smith St., Winnipeg, MB R3T 2N2
Tel: 204-474-6004; Fax: 204-474-7680
mail@mata.mb.ca
www.mata.mb.ca
Mike Hutton, President

Ontario Athletic Therapists Association
283 Danforth Avenue, Toronto, ON M4K 1N2
Tel: 416-845-4993
president@athletictherapist.on.ca
www.athletictherapist.on.ca
Drew Laskoski, President

Saskatchewan Athletic Therapists Association (SATA)
Tel: 306-291-6069
karihiebert@yahoo.ca
www.smscs.ca/sata.htm
Kari Hiebert, President

Sport Medicine & Science Council of Manitoba Inc.
145 Pacific Avenue, Winnipeg, MB R3B 2Z6
Tel: 204-925-5750; Fax: 204-925-5624
sport.med@sportmanitoba.ca
sportmed.mb.ca
Russ Horbal, Presidnet

Sport Medicine Council of Alberta (SMCA)
Percy Page Centre, 11759 Groat Rd., Edmonton, AB T5M 3K6
Tel: 780-415-0812; Fax: 780-422-3093
smca@sportmedab.ca
www.sportmedab.ca
Ray Kardas, President

Sport Medicine Council of British Columbia
1325 Keith Road, North Vancouver, BC V7J 1J3
Tel: 604-903-3880; Fax: 604-929-3877
Toll-Free: 888-755-3375
info@sportmedbc.com
www.sportmedbc.com
Lynda Cannell, President/CEO

Sports Medicine Council of Nova Scotia (SMCNS)
50 West Porters Lake Rd., Porters Lake, NS B3E 1K2
Fax: 902-435-4491
kelliott@smcns.ca
www.smcns.ca
Affiliation(s): Sport Medicine & Science Council of Canada
Kate Elliott, President

Sport Sciences

Canadian Society for Psychomotor Learning & Sport Psychology (CSPLSP) / Société canadienne d'apprentissage psychomoteur et de psychologie du sport (SCAPPS)
c/o Dr. N. Holt, Faculty of Physical Ed. & Rec., University of Alberta, Van Vliet Centre, Edmonton, AB T6G 2H9
nick.holt@ualberta.ca
www.scapps.org
Nick Holt, President
Sean Horton, Secretary-Treasurer

Ontario Association of Sport & Exercise Sciences (OASES)
295 Broadway, Orangeville, ON L9W 1L2
Tel: 519-925-2265; Fax: 519-925-9853
Affiliation(s): Canadian Society for Exercise Physiology
Patricia Clark, Executive Director

Sports

Arctic Winter Games International Committee (AWGIC)
#400, 5201 - 50 Ave., Yellowknife, NT X1A 3S9
Tel: 867-873-7245; Fax: 867-920-6467
www.awg.ca
Lloyd Bentz, Secretary
Gerry Thick, President
Wendell Shiffler, Vice-President
Ian D. Legaree, Technical Director

Association régionale du sport étudiant du Saguenay-Lac St-Jean (ARSESLSJ)
CEGEP de Chicoutimi, 534, rue Jacques Cartier Est, Chicoutimi, QC G7H 1Z6
Tél: 418-543-3532; Téléc: 418-693-0503
arse@arseslsj.qc.ca
www.arseslsj.qc.ca
Éric Benoit, Directeur général

Atlantic University Sport Association (AUSA)
#403, 5657 Spring Garden Rd., Halifax, NS B3J 3R4
Tel: 902-425-4235; Fax: 902-425-7825
feedback@atlanticuniversitysport.com
www.atlanticuniversitysport.com
Philip M. Currie, Executive Director

The Boomerang Association of Canada (BAC)
www.canboom.org
Andy Cross, Contact

British Columbia Games Society
#200, 990 Fort St., Victoria, BC V8V 3K2
Tel: 250-387-1375; Fax: 250-387-4489
info@bcgames.org
www.bcgames.org
Kelly Mann, President & CEO

British Columbia School Sports (BCSS)
PO Box 97, 20800 Lougheed Hwy., Maple Ridge, BC V2X 7E9
Tel: 604-477-1488; Fax: 604-477-1484
info@bcschoolsports.ca
www.bcschoolsports.ca
Affiliation(s): USA National Federation of State High Schools
Sue Keenan, Executive Director
Raj Puri, President

Canada Games Council (CGC) / Conseil des jeux du Canada
#701, 2197 Riverside Dr., Ottawa, ON K1H 7X3
Tel: 613-526-2320; Fax: 613-526-4068
canada.games@canadagames.ca
www.canadagames.ca
www.facebook.com/CanadaGames
twitter.com/CanadaGames
Sue Hylland, President/CEO
Kelly-Ann Paul, Director of Sport

Canadian Centre for Ethics in Sport (CCES) / Centre canadien pour l'éthique dans le sport
#350, 955 Green Valley Cr., Ottawa, ON K2C 3V4
Tel: 613-521-3340; Fax: 613-521-3134
Toll-Free: 800-672-7775
info@cces.ca
www.cces.ca
Affiliation(s): True Sport Foundation
Louise Walker, Chair
Paul Melia, CEO

Canadian Paintball Association
92 Arlington Ave., Oshawa, ON L1G 2N6
admin@canadianpaintball.ca
www.canadianpaintball.ca
Jody L.E. McLeod, Contact

Canadian Sport Tourism Alliance (CSTA)
#600, Lisgar St., Ottawa, ON K2P 0C2
Tel: 613-688-5843; Fax: 613-238-3878
info@canadiansporttourism.com
www.canadiansporttourism.com
Janet Gates, Chair
Rick Traer, CEO

Canadian Ultimate Players Association (CUPA)
4382 Shelbourne St., Vancouver, BC V8N 3G3
Toll-Free: 888-691-1080
info@canadianultimate.com
www.canadianultimate.com
www.facebook.com/UltimateCanada?ref=ts
twitter.com/Ultimate_Canada
Publications: CUPA Connection

Fédération québécoise du sport étudiant (FQSE)
CP 1000, Succ. M, 4545, av Pierre-De Coubertin, Montréal, QC H1V 3R2
Tél: 514-252-3300; Téléc: 514-254-3292
www.fqse.qc.ca; www.sportetudiant.com
Yves Paquette, Président

Ottawa Carleton Ultimate Association (OCUA)
#1, 875 Banks St., Ottawa, ON K1S 3W4
Tel: 613-860-6282; Fax: 866-225-6282
board@ocua.ca
www.ocua.ca
Marci Morris, Executive Director
Axel Garcia, Chair
Publications: OCUA Board of Directors Newsletters, OCUA Summer League Handbook, Ultimate Happenings

Sask Sport Inc.
1870 Lorne St., Regina, SK S4P 2L7
Tel: 306-780-9300; Fax: 306-781-6021
sasksport@sasksport.sk.ca
www.sasksport.sk.ca
Jim Burnett, General Manager

Société des Jeux de l'Acadie inc. (SJA)
#210, 702, rue Principale, Petit-Rocher, NB E8J 1V1
Tél: 506-783-4207; Téléc: 506-783-4209
sja1@nbnet.nb.ca
www.jeuxdelacadie.org
Stéphane Hachey, Président
Mario Doucet, Directeur général

Sport BC
#295, 3820 Cessna Dr., Richmond, BC V7B 0A2
Tel: 604-333-3400; Fax: 604-333-3401
info@sportbc.com
sport.bc.com
www.facebook.com/SportBC
twitter.com/SportBC
Pete Quevillon, Director, KidSport BC

Sport Manitoba
145 Pacific Ave., Winnipeg, MB R3b 2Z6
Tel: 204-925-5600; Fax: 204-925-5916
Toll-Free: 866-774-2220
info@sportmanitoba.ca
www.sportmanitoba.ca
www.facebook.com/sportmb
twitter.com/SportManitoba
Jeff Hnatiuk, President/CEO
Tara Skibo, Communications/Public Relations

Sport New Brunswick / Sport Nouveau-Brunswick
#13, 900 Hanwell Rd., Fredericton, NB E3B 6A2
Tel: 506-451-1320; Fax: 506-451-1325
director@sportnb.com
www.sportnb.com
Jason Dickson, Executive Director

Sport Newfoundland & Labrador
PO Box 8700, St. John's, NL A1B 4J6
Tel: 709-576-4932; Fax: 709-576-7493
sportnl@sportnl.ca
www.sportnl.ca
Troy Croft, Executive Director

Sport North Federation
Don Cooper Building, PO Box 11089, 4908 - 49 St., Yellowknife, NT X1A 3X7
Tel: 867-669-8326; Fax: 867-669-8327
Toll-Free: 800-661-0797
www.sportnorth.com
Doug Rentmeister, Executive Director

Sport Nova Scotia (SNS)
PO Box 3010, Stn. South, 5516 Spring Garden Rd., Halifax, NS B3J 1G6
Tel: 902-425-5450; Fax: 902-425-5606
sportns@sportnovascotia.ca
www.sportnovascotia.ca
Jamie Ferguson, CEO

Sport PEI Inc.
PO Box 302, Charlottetown, PE C1A 7K7
Tel: 902-368-4110; Fax: 902-368-4548
Toll-Free: 800-247-6712
sports@sportpei.pe.ca
www.sportpei.pe.ca
Lyall Huggan, Special Projects
Gemma Koughan, Executive Director
Wendy Reid, President
Nick Murray, Communications
Lisa MacKay, Finance & Administration

Sport Yukon
4061 - 4 Ave., Whitehorse, YT Y1A 1H1
Tel: 867-668-4236; Fax: 867-667-4237
news@sportyukon.com
www.sportyukon.com
George Arcand, President

Sports-Québec
CP 1000, Succ. M, 4545, av Pierre-De Coubertin, Montréal, QC H1V 3R2
Tél: 514-252-3114; Téléc: 514-254-9621
sports@sportsquebec.com
www.sportsquebec.com
Luc Denis, Directeur général
Jean Couvrette, Directeur, Développement des affaires et partenariats
Isabelle Ducharme, Directrice, Programmes
Pierre Bégin, Coordonnateur, Développement sportif
Michelle Gendron, Coordonnatrice, Communications stratégiques

True Sport Foundation / Fondation sport pur
#350, 955 Green Valley Crescent, Ottawa, ON K2C 3V4
Tel: 613-526-6043; Fax: 613-521-3134
Toll-Free: 888-995-8899
info@truesport.ca
www.truesportfoundation.ca
Victor Lachance, Executive Director

World Arm Wrestling Federation
135 - 29th St. East, Prince Albert, SK S6V 1Y5
Tel: 306-763-0899
fred.roy@sasktel.net
waf.homestead.com

Sports for the Disabled

Active Living Alliance for Canadians with a Disability (ALACD) / Alliance de vie active pour les canadiens/canadiennes ayant un handicap
#104, 720 Belfast Rd., Ottawa, ON K1G 0Z5
Tel: 613-244-0052; Fax: 613-244-4857
Toll-Free: 800-771-0663; TTY: 888-771-0663
ala@ala.ca
www.ala.ca
Affiliation(s): Canadian Amputee Sports Association; Canadian Association for Disabled Skiing; Canadian Association for Health, Physical Education, Recreation & Dance; Canadian Blind Sports Association; Canadian Cerebral Palsy Sports Association; Canadian Deaf Sports Association; Canadian Intramural Recreation Association; Canadian National Institute for the Blind; Canadian Paralympic Committee; Canadian Paraplegic Association; Canadian Parks/Recreation Association; Canadian Red Cross Society; Canadian Special Olympics; Learning Disabilities Association of Canada; National Network for Mental Health
Jane Arkell, Director

Alberta Amputee Sports & Recreation Association (AASRA)
PO Box 708, Stn. M, Calgary, AB T2P 2J3
Tel: 403-201-0507; Fax: 403-256-7611
Toll-Free: 800-501-0507
info@aasra.ab.ca
www.aasra.ab.ca
Gwen Davies, Executive Director

Alberta Northern Lights Wheelchair Basketball Society
8944 - 182 St. NW, Edmonton, AB T5T 2E3
Tel: 780-433-4310; Fax: 780-431-1764
Toll-Free: 800-465-2992
programs@albertanorthernlights.com
www.albertanorthernlights.com
www.facebook.com/172864392765380

Alberta Sports & Recreation Association for the Blind (ASRAB)
#007, 15 Colonel Baker Pl. NE, Calgary, AB T2E 4Z3
Tel: 403-262-5332; Fax: 403-265-7221
Toll-Free: 888-882-7722
info@asrab.ab.ca
www.asrab.ab.ca
Marilyn McIntosh, Executive Director
Peter Wettlaufer, President

Association des sports pour aveugles de Montréal (ASAM)
CP 95, Succ. M, Montréal, QC H1V 3L6
Tél: 514-252-3178; Téléc: 514-254-1303
infoasam@sportsaveugles.qc.ca
www.sportsaveugles.qc.ca/asam

Affiliation(s): Association sportive des aveugles du Québec
Gérald Cousineau, Président
Guillaume Thibault, Vice-président

Association québécoise des sports en fauteuil roulants (AQSFR)
CP 1000, Succ. M, 4545, rue Pierre-de-Coubertin, Montréal, QC H1V 3R2
Tél: 514-252-3108; Téléc: 514-254-9793
aqsfr@aqsfr.qc.ca
www.aqsfr.qc.ca
José Malo, Directrice générale

Association sportive des aveugles du Québec inc. (ASAQ)
CP 1000, Succ. M, 4545, av Pierre-de Coubertin, Montréal, QC H1V 3R2
Tél: 514-252-3178; Téléc: 514-254-1303
infoasaq@sportsaveugles.qc.ca
www.sportsaveugles.qc.ca
Nathalie Chartrand, Directrice générale

British Columbia Disability Sports (BCDS)
#217, 12837 - 76th Ave., Surrey, BC V3W 2V3
Tel: 604-598-7890; Fax: 604-598-7892; TTY: 604-598-7890
info@disabilitysport.org
www.disabilitysport.org
Affiliation(s): Sportability BC; Deaf Sports Federation of BC; Disabled Skiers Association of BC; Canadian Amputee Sports Association BC Division; BC Blind Sports & Recreation Association; BC Therapeutic Riding Association; Disabled Sailing Association of BC; BC Sledge Hockey & Ice Picking; Wheeling Eights Square Dance Club; BC Wheelchair Basketball Society
Jane Samletzki, Executive Director

British Columbia Wheelchair Sports Association (BCWSA)
#210 - 3820 Cessna Dr., Richmond, BC V7B 0A2
Tel: 604-333-3520; Fax: 604-333-3450
Toll-Free: 877-737-3090
info@bcwheelchairsports.com
www.bcwheelchairsports.com
Kathy Newman, Executive Director

Canadian Amputee Golf Association (CAGA)
PO Box 6091, Stn. A, Calgary, AB T2H 2L4
canamps@caga.ca
www.caga.ca
Gwen Davies, President

Canadian Amputee Sports Association (CASA) / Association canadienne des sports pour amputés
c/o Dale Murphy, 1126 Millcove Rd., RR#1, Mount Stewart, PE C0A 1T0
www.canadianamputeesports.ca
Affiliation(s): Canadian Paralympic Committee; Hockey Canada
James Reilly, President
Dale Murphy, Secretary
Wayne Epp, Treasurer

Canadian Association for Disabled Skiing (CADS) / Association canadienne pour les skieurs handicapés (ACSH)
91 Nelson St., Barrie, ON L4M 4K4
Tel: 705-725-4845; Fax: 705-725-4804
michelle.bavington@sympatico.ca
www.disabledskiing.ca
David O'Brien, Executive Director
Al Matile, President
Helen Grimm, Secretary
Jeff Laidlaw, Treasurer
Publications: The Perspective: CADS National Newsletter

Canadian Association for Disabled Skiing - Alberta (CADS Alberta)
11759 Groat Rd., Edmonton, AB T5M 3K6
Tel: 780-427-8104; Fax: 780-427-0524
info@cadsalberta.ca
www.cadsalberta.ca
Affiliation(s): Canadian Ski Instructors' Alliance (CSIA), Canadian Association of Snowboard Instructors (CASI)
Mike Low, President
Allyson Szafranski, Executive Coordinator

Canadian Association for Disabled Skiing - Newfoundland & Labrador Division
6 Albany Pl., St. John's, NL A1E 1Y2
Tel: 709-753-3625; Fax: 709-777-4884
margaret.tibbo@easternhealth.ca
Marg Tibbo, Secretary

Canadian Association for Disabled Skiing Nova Scotia
c/o Alpine Ski Nova Scotia, 5516 Spring Garden Rd., Halifax, NS B3J 1G6
Tel: 902-425-5450; Fax: 902-425-5606
alpinens@sportnovascotia.ca
disabledskiing.ca
Linda Scott

Canadian Electric Wheelchair Hockey Association (CEWHA)
#920, 200 Yorkland Blvd., Toronto, ON M2J 5C1
Tel: 416-757-8544; Fax: 416-490-9334
info@cewha.ca
www.cewha.ca
www.facebook.com/group.php?gid=6455375361

Canadian Paralympic Committee (CPC) / Comité paralympique canadien
#310, 225 Metcalfe St., Ottawa, ON K2P 1p9
Tel: 613-569-4333; Fax: 613-569-2777
www.paralympic.ca
www.facebook.com/CDNParalympics?ref=ts
twitter.com/CDNParalympics
Affiliation(s): International Paralympic Committee
Henry Storgaard, CEO & Secretary General
Karen Poapst, Senior Coordinator, Special Events & Project

Canadian Wheelchair Sports Association (CWSA) / Association canadienne des sports en fauteuil roulant (ACSFR)
#108, 2255 St. Laurent Blvd., Ottawa, ON K1G 4K3
Tel: 613-523-0004; Fax: 613-523-0149
info@cwsa.ca
www.cwsa.ca/en/site/
Affiliation(s): International Stoke Mandeville Wheelchair Sports Federation
Cathy Cadieux, Executive Director
Duncan Campbell, Director, National Development
Andy Van Neutegem, Director, High Performance
Don Lane, Manager, Program
Arley McNeney, Coordinator, Communications

Commission de Ski pour Personnes Handicapées du Québec (CSPHQ)
165 Place Lilas, Pincourt, QC J7V 5B6
Tél: 514-425-8894; Téléc: 514-425-8894
hwohler@yahoo.com
Henry Wohler, President

Disabled Sailing Association of BC
#207, 3077 Granville Street, Vancouver, BC V6H 3J9
Tel: 604-668-6464; Fax: 604-688-6463
dsa@disabilityfoundation.org
www.disabilityfoundation.org/dsa
Affiliation(s): BC Sport & Fitness Council for the Disabled
Kirk Duncan, Program Coordinator

Disabled Skiers Association of BC (DSABC)
#220, 3820 Cessna Dr., Richmond, BC V7B 0A2
Tel: 604-333-3630; Fax: 604-333-3450
disabledskiers@telus.net
www.disabledskiingbc.com
Brian Forrester, Executive Director
Kevin ter Kuile, President

Manitoba Amputee Sport & Recreation Association
286 Harvard Ave., Winnipeg, MB R3M 0K8
Tel: 204-489-9278; Fax: 204-488-1094
rootel@shaw.ca
Raquel Godin, Contact

Manitoba Wheelchair Sports Association
145 Pacific Ave., Winnipeg, MB R3B 2Z6
Tel: 204-925-5790; Fax: 204-925-5792
mwsa@sportmanitoba.ca
www.mwsa.ca
Tricia Klassen, Executive Director

National Capital Sports Council of the Disabled Inc. (NCSCD) / Le Conseil des sports des handicapées de la capitale nationale inc. (CSHCN)
#104, 720 Belfast Rd., Ottawa, ON K1G 0Z5
Tel: 613-569-7632; Fax: 613-244-4857
ncscd@ncscd.ca
www.ncscd.ca

Ontario Amputee & Les Autres Sports Association (OALASA)
#102, 1185 Eglinton Ave. East, Toronto, ON M3C 3C6
Tel: 519-659-7452
www.oalasa.org
Rodney Reimer, President
Douglas Walker, Treasurer
Archie Watts, Secretary

Ontario Wheelchair Sports Association (OWSA)
#104, 3 Concordia Gate, Toronto, ON M3C 3N7
Tel: 416-426-7189
info@ontwheelchairsports.org
ontwheelchairsports.org
Affiliation(s): Canadian Wheelchair Sports Association
Barb Montemurro, President
Lynda Charters, Executive Director

Paralympic Sports Association (Alberta) (PSA)
10024 - 79 Ave., Edmonton, AB T6E 1R5
Tel: 780-439-8687; Fax: 780-432-0486
info@parasports.net
www.parasports.net
Affiliation(s): Wheelchair Sports Alberta
Kim McDonald, Executive Director
Suzanne Harrison, Coordinator, Programs

ParaSport Ontario
#104, 3 Concorde Gate, Toronto, ON M3C 3N7
Tel: 416-426-7187; Fax: 416-426-7361
Toll-Free: 800-265-1539
info@parasportontario.ca
www.parasportontario.ca
www.facebook.com/parasportontario
twitter.com/parasport_ont
Affiliation(s): Ontario Amputee & Les Autres Sports Association; Ontario Blind Sports Association; Ontario Cerebral Palsy Sports Association; Ontario Wheelchair Sports Association
Cathy Vincelli, Executive Director

Saskatchewan Blind Sports Association Inc.
510 Cynthia St., Saskatoon, SK S7L 7K7
Tel: 306-975-0888
Toll-Free: 877-772-7798
sbsa.sk@shaw.ca
www.saskblindsports.ca
Tony Badger, Executive Director
Jerry Johnson, President

Saskatchewan Ski Association - Skiing for Disabled (SASKI)
1860 Lorne St., Saskatoon, SK S4P 2L7
Tel: 306-780-9236; Fax: 306-781-6021
sask.ski@sasktel.net
www.saski.ca

Saskatchewan Wheelchair Sports Association (SWSA)
510 Cynthia St., Saskatoon, SK S7L 7K7
Tel: 306-975-0824; Fax: 306-975-0825
info@swsa.ca
www.swsa.ca
Judy Peddle, Executive Director

Special Olympics Alberta (SOA)
Percy Page Centre, 11759 Groat Rd., Edmonton, AB T5M 3K6
Tel: 780-415-0719; Fax: 780-422-2663
Toll-Free: 800-444-2883
info@specialolympics.ab.ca
www.specialolympics.ab.ca
Carmen Wyton, President & CEO

Wheelchair Sports Alberta
Percy Page Center, 11759 Groat Rd., Edmonton, AB T5M 3K6
Tel: 780-427-8699; Fax: 780-427-8723
Toll-Free: 888-453-6770
wsa1@telus.net
www.abwheelchairsport.ca
Mike Sandomirsky, Executive Director

Wheelchair Sports Association of Newfoundland & Labrador (WSANL)
40 Imogene Cr., Paradise, NL A1L 1H5
Tel: 709-782-0487
gpower@cwsa.ca
Gary Power, President

Squash

Squash Alberta
3415 - 3rd Ave. NW, Calgary, AB T2N 0M4
Tel: 403-270-7344; Fax: 403-270-8445
Toll-Free: 877-646-6566
lynn@squashalberta.com
www.squashalberta.com
Lynn Nixon, Executive Director

Squash British Columbia
4867 Ontario St., Vancouver, BC V5H 3H4
Tel: 604-737-3084; Fax: 604-736-3527
info@squashbc.com
www.squashbc.com
Mark Robinson, President

Squash Canada
#401, 2197 Riverside Dr., Ottawa, ON K1H 7X3
Tel: 613-731-7385; Fax: 613-731-6291
info@squash.ca
www.squash.ca
www.facebook.com/squashcanada
twitter.com/squashcanada
Danny Da Costa, Executive Director
Jamie Hickox, Director, Performance
Whitney Fuller, Coordinator, Sport Development
Judith Post, Coordinator, Finance

Squash Manitoba
145 Pacific Ave., Winnipeg, MB R3B 2Z6
Tel: 204-925-5661; Fax: 204-925-5792
squash@sportmanitoba.ca
www.squashmb.org
Lynn Colliou, Executive Director

Squash New Brunswick
276 Parkhurst Dr., Fredericton, NB E3B 2J9
Tel: 506-457-0877; Fax: 506-443-0830
russky@unb.ca
www.squashnb.ca
Liam McGuigan, President

Squash Nova Scotia
PO Box 3010, Stn. Park Lane Centre, #401, 5516 Spring Garden Rd., Halifax, NS B3J 3G6
Tel: 902-425-5450; Fax: 902-425-5606
gcouture@ns.sympatico.ca
www.squashns.ca

Squash Ontario
#308, 3 Concorde Gate, Toronto, ON M3C 3N7
Tel: 416-426-7201; Fax: 416-426-7393
Toll-Free: 888-741-5111
info@squashontario.com
www.squashontario.com
Tom Craig, President
Sherry Funston, Executive Director
Geoffrey Johnson, Program Coordinator
Laura Mauer, Administrative Coordinator
Publications: Policies & Procedures Manual

Squash P.E.I.
C/O Sport PEI, PO Box 302, Stn. Enman Cres., Charlottetown, PE C1A 7K7
Tel: 902-566-0338
meleclair@edu.pe.ca
www.squashpei.org
Steven Banks, President
Nicole Blanchard, Secretary
Des Lecky, Treasurer

Squash Québec
CP 1000, Succ. M, 4545, av Pierre-de Coubertin, Montréal, QC H1V 3R2
Tél: 514-252-3062; Téléc: 514-252-3103
info@sports-4murs.qc.ca
www.squash.qc.ca
Barry Faguy, Président

Squash Yukon
PO Box 31226, Whitehorse, YT Y1A 5P7
Tel: 867-667-7071; Fax: 867-668-6442
squashyukon@yknet.yk.ca
www.squashyukon.yk.ca
Jim Gilpin, President

Swimming

Fédération de natation du Québec
CP 1000, Succ. M, 4545, av Pierre-de-Coubertin, Montréal, QC H1V 3R2
Tél: 514-252-3200; Téléc: 514-252-3232
fnq@fnq.qc.ca
www.fnq.qc.ca
www.facebook.com/group.php?gid=163831313666941
Affiliation(s): Éducation, Loisir et Sport Québec; AQUAM Équipes; Groupe Hospitalité Westmont (Quality et Comfort Inn); Location Sauvageau; Trophies Dubois; Westjet; Financière Manuvie; McAuslan
Chrystian Gauvin, Responsable, Comité provincial des Maîtres

International Amateur Swimming Federation (IASF) / Fédération internationale de natation amateur (FINA)
Av. de l'Avant-Poste 4, Lausanne, 1005, Switzerland
Tel: 41-21-310-4710; Fax: 41-21-312-6610
www.fina.org
www.linkedin.com/company/952149
www.facebook.com/fina1908
Paolo Barelli, Hon. Secretary
Julio C. Maglione, President
Cornel Marculescu, Executive Director

Solo Swims of Ontario Inc. (SSO)
32 Coxwell Cres., Brantford, ON N3P 1Z1
www.soloswims.com
Greg Taylor, President

Swim Alberta
Percy Page Centre, 11759 Groat Rd., Edmonton, AB T5M 3K6
Tel: 780-415-1780; Fax: 780-415-1788
office@swimalberta.ca
www.swimalberta.ca
Doug Bird, President
James Hood, General Manager

Swim BC
#204, 4475 Viewmont Ave., Victoria, BC V8Z 6L8
Tel: 250-479-2069; Fax: 250-479-3021
markschuett@swim.bc.ca
www.swim.bc.ca
Mark Hahto, Executive Director

Swim Manitoba / Natation Manitoba
#224, 200 Main St., Winnipeg, MB R2C 4M2
Tel: 204-925-5778; Fax: 204-925-5792
office@swimmanitoba.mb.ca
www.swimmanitoba.mb.ca
Cathie Pickerl, President
Michael McMullen, Vice-President
Sharra Hinton, Treasurer

Swim Nova Scotia (SNS)
5516 Spring Garden Rd., Halifax, NS B3J 1G6
Tel: 902-425-5450; Fax: 902-425-5606
swimming@sportnovascotia.ca
www.swimnovascotia.com
Lynn Sitland, President
Bette El-Hawary, Executive Director

Swim Ontario
#206, 3 Concorde Gate, Toronto, ON M3C 3N7
Tel: 416-426-7220; Fax: 416-426-7356
info@swimontario.com
www.swimontario.com
www.facebook.com/pages/Swim-Ontario/117335688316744
twitter.com/SwimOntario
John Vadeika, Executive Director

Swim Saskatchewan
2205 Victoria Ave., Regina, SK S4P 0S4
Tel: 306-780-9291; Fax: 306-525-4009
office@swimsask.ca; marjwalton@swimsask.ca
www.swimsask.ca
Marj Walton, Executive Director

Swimming / Natation Canada
#B140, 2445 St-Laurent Blvd., Ottawa, ON K1G 6C3
Tel: 613-260-1348; Fax: 613-260-0804
natloffice@swimming.ca
www.swimming.ca
www.facebook.com/group.php?gid=56320144853
Affiliation(s): Aquatic Federation of Canada
Pierre Lafontaine, Chief Executive Officer & National Coach
Mark Hahto, Chief Operating Officer
Lance Cansdale, Director, Domestic Operation
Ken Radford, Director, High Performance
Martin Richard, Director, Communications
Craig McCord, National Para-swimming Coach
Ken McKinnon, National Junior Coach

Swimming New Brunswick
#13, 900 Hanwell Rd., Fredericton, NB E3B 6A3
Tel: 506-451-1323; Fax: 506-451-1325
swimnb@nb.aibn.com
www.swimnb.ca
David Frise, President

Swimming Newfoundland & Labrador
1296A Kenmount Road, Paradise, NL A1L 1N3
Tel: 709-576-7946; Fax: 709-576-7493
swimnl@sportnl.ca
www.swimnl.nfld.net
Corina Hartley, Executive Director
Eugene Murphy, President

Swimming Prince Edward Island
PO Box 302, 40 Enman Cres., Charlottetown, PE C1A 7K7
Tel: 902-368-6167; Fax: 902-368-4548
SwimPEI@sportpei.pe.ca
www.swimpei.com
Paul Murphy, President

Synchro Alberta
The Percy Page Centre, 11759 Groat Rd., Edmonton, AB T5M 3K6
Tel: 780-415-1789; Fax: 780-415-0056
syncro@synchroalberta.com
www.synchroalberta.com
Chris Hampshire, President

Synchro BC
#301, 1367 West Broadway, Vancouver, BC V6H 4A9
Tel: 604-737-3169; Fax: 604-738-7175
synchrobc@telus.net
www.synchro.bc.ca
Twyla Ryan, Executive Director
Cathy Chapell, Office Coordinator

Synchro Canada / Association canadienne de nage synchronisée amateur
#200, 1010 Polytek St., Unit 14, Gloucester, ON K1J 9H9
Tel: 613-748-5674; Fax: 613-748-5724
catherine@synchro.ca
www.synchro.ca
Kristen Brawley, High Performance Manager

Synchro Manitoba
145 Pacific Ave., Winnipeg, MB R3B 2Z6
Tel: 204-925-5693; Fax: 204-925-5703
execdirector@synchromb.ca
www.synchromb.ca
Affiliation(s): Manitoba Sports Federation
Allison Gervais, Executive Director

Synchro Newfoundland & Labrador
1 Pine Bud Pl., St. John's, NL A1B 1N1
Tel: 709-722-0439
Lorna Proudfoot, Contact

Synchro Ontario
128 Galaxy Boul., Etobicoke, ON M9W 4Y6
Tel: 416-679-9522; Fax: 416-679-9535
www.synchroontario.com
Mary Dwyer, Executive Director

Synchro PEI
PO Box 302, Charlottetown, PE C1A 7K7
Tel: 902-892-1873
lucillecarter@aol.com
www.sportpei.pe.ca
Lucille Carter, President

Synchro Saskatchewan
#209, 1860 Lorne St., Regina, SK S4P 2L7
Tel: 306-780-9227; Fax: 306-780-9445
synchro.sk@sasktel.net
www.synchrosask.com
Kathleen Reynolds, Executive Director

Synchro-Québec
CP 1000, Succ. M, 4545, av Pierre-de Coubertin, Montréal, QC H1V 3R2
Tél: 514-252-3087; Téléc: 514-252-5658
Ligne sans frais: 866-537-3164
fnsq@synchroquebec.qc.ca
www.synchroquebec.com
www.facebook.com/synchro.quebec
twitter.com/synchroquebec
Diane Lachapelle, Directrice générale

Table Soccer

Canadian Table Soccer Federation
8311, rue Ouimet, Brossard, QC J4Y 3B3
Tel: 514-668-2326
secretary@canadafoos.com
Eric Dunn, President
Adam Imanpoor, Secretary

Ontario Table Soccer Association & Tour
Tel: 905-812-9994
Toll-Free: 866-247-7702
info@ontariotablesoccer.com
www.ontariotablesoccer.com
Mario Recupero, Executive Director

Table Tennis

Alberta Table Tennis Association (ATTA)
Percy Page Centre, 11759 Groat Rd., Edmonton, AB T5M 3K6
Tel: 780-427-8588; Fax: 866-273-6708
atta@abtabletennis.com
www.abtabletennis.com
Affiliation(s): International Table Tennis Federation
Joseph Chan, President
Judy Ellefson, Program Coordinator

British Columbia Table Tennis Association
#227 - 3820 Cessna Drive, Richmond, BC V7B 0A2
Tel: 604-333-3655; Fax: 604-333-3450
bctta@hotmail.com
www.bctta.ca
Amelia Ho, President

Canadian Table Tennis Association (CTTA) / Association canadienne de tennis de table
#400, 2211 Riverside Dr., Ottawa, ON K1H 7X5
Tel: 613-733-6272; Fax: 613-733-7279
ctta@ctta.ca
www.ctta.ca
Affiliation(s): Sports Council of Canada
Manali Haridas, Office Administrator
Tony Kiesenhofer, Director General

Fédération de tennis de table du Québec (FTTQ)
CP 1000, Succ. M, 4545, av Pierre-de Coubertin, Montréal, QC H1V 3R2
Tél: 514-252-3064; Téléc: 514-251-8038
www.tennisdetable.ca/
Jacques Plamandon, Directeur général

Manitoba Table Tennis Association (MTTA)
145 Pacific Ave., Winnipeg, MB R3B 2Z6
Tel: 204-925-5690; Fax: 204-925-5916
table.tennis@sportmanitoba.ca
www.mtta.ca
Affiliation(s): International Table Tennis Federation
Ron Edwards, Executive Director
Dan Racicot, President
Ryan Szajkowski, Vice-President, Administration
Greg Chan, Vice-President, Technical

Ontario Table Tennis Association (OTTA)
PO Box 42040, Stn. Conestoga, 550 King St. North, Waterloo, ON N2L 6K5
Toll-Free: 877-396-6601
larry.laughlen@ottacanada.com
www.ottacanada.com
Larry Laughlen, President

Prince Edward Island Table Tennis Association (PEITTA)
3 Hurry Rd., RR#10, Charlottetown, PE C1E 1Z4
Tel: 902-368-2360
nchishti@biovectra.com
Todd Gaudin, Vice-President
Lorne Clow, Secretary
Wade Gregory, Treasurer
Najam Chishti, President

Saskatchewan Table Tennis Association Inc. (STTA)
John V. Remai Centre, 510 Cynthia St., Saskatoon, SK S7N 7K7
Tel: 306-975-0835
info@sasktabletennis.ca
www.sasktabletennis.ca
Dwayne Yachiw, Program Coordinator
Joseph Chan, President
Edward Hung, Vice-President

Teaching

British Columbia Physical Education Provincial Specialist Association
c/o B.C. Teachers' Federation, #100, 550 West 6th Ave., Vancouver, BC V5Z 4P2
Tel: 604-871-2283; Fax: 604-871-2286
www.bctf.bc.ca/pebc
Debbie Keel, President

Tennis

Alberta Tennis Association (ATA)
11759 Groat Rd., Edmonton, AB T5M 3K6
Tel: 780-415-1661; Fax: 780-415-1693
info@tennisalberta.com
www.tennisalberta.com
Ken Rutherford, Executive Director
Jill Groves, Manager, Administration & Programs
Charlie McLean, Coordinator, High Performance
Jeff Spiers, Coordinator, Community Development

International Tennis Federation (ITF)
Bank Lane, Roehampton, London, SW15 5XZ, United Kingdom
Tel: 44-20-8878-6464; Fax: 44-20-8392-4744
www.itftennis.com
Affiliation(s): Tennis Canada
Francesco Ricci Bitti, President
Juan Margets, Executive Vice-President

Nova Scotia Tennis Association
5516 Spring Garden Rd., Halifax, NS B3J 1G6
Tel: 902-425-5454
tennisns@sportnovascotia.ca
www.tennisnovascotia.ca
Andrew Oxner, President
Roger Keating, Executive Director
Paul Richard, Chair, Communications

Ontario Tennis Association (OTA)
#200, 1 Shoreham Dr., Toronto, ON M3N 3A7
Tel: 416-514-1100; Fax: 416-514-1112
Toll-Free: 800-387-5066
ota@tennisontario.com
www.tennisontario.com
Michel Lecavalier, President
Jim Boyce, Executive Director
Simon Bartram, Vice-President
Scott Fraser, Vice-President, Finance & Administration
Glenna Poick, Vice-President, Marketing & Communications
Liz Wood, Vice-President, Membership & Regional Development
Publications: Ontario Tennis, OTA Club Manual, OTA News, OTA Yearbook

Prince Edward Island Tennis Association
PO Box 302, 40 Enman Cres., Charlottetown, PE C1A 7K7
Tel: 902-368-4985; Fax: 902-368-4548
mconnolly@sportpei.pe.ca
www.tennispei.ca
Mike Connolly, Executive Director
Brian Hall, Technical Director

Tennis BC
#204, 210 West Broadway, Vancouver, BC V5Y 3W2
Tel: 604-737-3086; Fax: 604-737-3124
tbc@tennisbc.org
www.tennisbc.org
www.facebook.com/pages/Tennis-BC/189016975927
twitter.com/intent/user?screen_name=TennisBC
Ryan Clark, Chief Executive Officer
Sarah Kadi, Director, Community Development
Lois Ker, Director, Events
Chee Ng, Director, Finance
Lanei Lee, Manager, Member Services & Marketing Communications

Tennis Canada
Rexall Centre, #100, 1 Shoreham Dr., Toronto, ON M3N 3A6
Tel: 416-665-9777; Fax: 416-665-9017
Toll-Free: 877-283-6647
www.lovemeansnothing.ca
www.facebook.com/TennisCanada
twitter.com/Tennis_Canada
Roger Martin, Chair
Michael S. Downey, President & Chief Executive Officer
Derek Strang, Chief Operating Officer
Heather Waldman, Chief Financial Officer & Vice-President, Finance & Administration
Hatem McDadi, Vice-President, Tennis Development
Publications: Tennis Canada Annual Report, Topspin

Tennis Manitoba
#419, 145 Pacific Ave., Winnipeg, MB R3B 2Z6
Tel: 204-925-5660; Fax: 204-925-5703
info@tennismanitoba.com
www.tennismanitoba.com
twitter.com/tennismanitoba
Alexandra Gomez, Chair, Resource Development Committee
Mohamed Ismath, Chair, High Performance Committee
David Scrapneck, Chair, Competitive Structure Committee
Selvi Varathappan, Chair, Community Development Committee

Tennis New Brunswick
PO Box 604, Fredericton, NB E3B 5A6
Tel: 506-444-0885
tnb@tennisnb.net
www.tennisnb.net

Tennis Newfoundland & Labrador
PO Box 728, Stn. C, 114 Newtown Rd., St. John's, NL A1C 5L4
Tel: 709-765-0426; Fax: 709-722-1670
tennis@sportnl.ca
www.tennisnl.ca
Derrick Rowe, President
Ryan Maarschalk, Executive Director

Tennis Northwest Territories
PO Box 671, Yellowknife, NT X1A 2N5
Tel: 867-873-2018
eastarm@ssimicro.com
www.tennisnwt.ca
Fran Hurcomb, President

Tennis Québec (TQ)
285, rue Faillon ouest, Montréal, QC H2R 2W1
Tél: 514-270-6060; Téléc: 514-270-2700
courrier@tennis.qc.ca
www.tennis.qc.ca
Jean François Manibal, Directeur général
Réjean Genois, Président

Tennis Saskatchewan
2205 Victoria Ave., Regina, SK S4P 0S4
Tel: 306-780-9410; Fax: 306-525-4009
tennissask@sasktel.net
www.tennissask.com
Affiliation(s): Sask Sport Incorporated
Rory Park, Executive Director

Therapeutic Riding

Antigonish Therapeutic Riding Association
50 The Heights, Antigonish, NS B2G 1K5
Tel: 902-863-1479
www.nsnet.org/riding/
Claire Reeves, Program Coordinator

British Columbia Therapeutic Riding Association (BCTRA)
25768 - 128th Ave., Maple Ridge, BC V4R 1C4
Tel: 604-462-9884; Fax: 604-462-9597
supremehm@shaw.ca
vcn.bc.ca/bctra
Affiliation(s): Horse Council BC; Sports & Fitness Council for the Disabled
Jane James, President

Canadian Therapeutic Riding Association / Association canadienne d'équitation thérapeutique
#11, 5420 Hwy. 6 North, RR#5, Guelph, ON N1H 6J2
Tel: 519-767-0700; Fax: 519-767-0435
ctra@golden.net
www.cantra.ca
Daphne Davey, President
Donna Naylor, Executive Director
Nanci Picken, Coordinator, Development
Anita LeMaître, Secretary
Neil Mahnke, Treasurer
Publications: CanTRA [Canadian Therapeutic Riding Association] Caller / L'Appel ACET , Communiqué [a publication of the Canadian Therapeutic Riding Association]

Cavalier Riding Club Ltd. (CRC)
c/o Ashton Ridge Equestrian Centre, 711 Pine Glen Rd., Pine Glen, NB E1J 1S1
Tel: 506-386-2596
mgs500@gmail.com
ashton-ridge.com/cavalier.htm
Mark G. Stevens, President

Central Ontario Developmental Riding Program (CODRP)
Pride Stables, 584 Pioneer Tower Rd., Kitchener, ON N2P 2H9
Tel: 519-653-4686; Fax: 519-653-5565
info@pridestables.com
www.codrp.com; www.pridestables.com
Affiliation(s): Ontario Therapeutic Riding Association (ONTRA)
Heather Mackneson, Executive Director

Community Association for Riding for the Disabled (CARD)
4777 Dufferin St., Toronto, ON M3H 5T3
Tel: 416-667-8600; Fax: 416-739-7520
info@card.ca
www.card.ca
twitter.com/CARDTherapy
Affiliation(s): Ontario Therapeutic Riding Association
Penny Smith, Executive Director

Comox Valley Therapeutic Riding Society (CVTRS)
PO Box 3666, Courtenay, BC V9N 7P1
Tel: 250-338-1968; Fax: 250-338-4137
cvtrs@telus.net
www.cvtrs.com
Affiliation(s): North American Handicapped Riding Association
Margaret Hind, Coordinator

Errington Therapeutic Riding Association (ETRA)
Pyramid Stables, PO Box 462, 7581 Harby Rd., Lantzville, Parksville, BC V9P 2G6
etrainfo@shaw.ca
islandpages.com/etra/
Affiliation(s): BC Therapeutic Riding Association; Canadian Therapeutic Riding Association
Tom Roy, President

Halifax Area Leisure & Therapeutic Riding Association
The Stables, 1690 Bell Rd., Halifax, NS B3H 2Z3
Tel: 902-860-0697
haltr@bengallancers.com
www.bengallancers.com/haltr.html
Affiliation(s): Sport Canada; Equine Canada
Sally Murphy, Contact

Lanark County Therapeutic Riding Programme (LCTRP)
103 Judson St., Carleton Place, ON K7C 2S5
Tel: 613-257-7121; Fax: 613-257-2675
Toll-Free: 800-667-2617
info@therapeuticriding.ca
www.therapeuticriding.ca
Susan Cressy, Contact

Lethbridge Handicapped Riding Association
RR#8-24-6, Lethbridge, AB T1J 4P4
Tel: 403-328-2165
lhra@telusplanet.net
Nancy Conan, Contact
Cory Conan, Contact

Little Bits Therapeutic Riding Association
PO Box 29016, Stn. Lendrum, Edmonton, AB T6H 5Z6
Tel: 780-476-1233
info@littlebits.ca
www.littlebits.ca

Manitoba Riding for the Disabled Association Inc. (MRDA)
145 Pacific Ave., Winnipeg, MB R3B 2Z6
Tel: 204-925-5905; Fax: 204-925-5792
exedir@mrda.cc
www.mrda.cc
www.facebook.com/105010909544565
Peter Manastyrsky, Executive Director

Mirabel Morgan Special Riding Centre
1201 - 2nd Line South, RR#1, Bailieboro, ON K0L 1B0
Tel: 705-939-6485
mirabel.ms@sympatico.ca
Colleen Baptist, Contact

Mount View Special Riding Association (MVSRA)
5629 - 49 Ave., Olds, AB T4H 1G5
Tel: 403-556-7247

New Brunswick Therapeutic Riding Association
c/o Stan Cassidy Centre for Rehab, 190 Woodbridge St., Fredericton, NB E3B 4R3
Tel: 506-452-5879; Fax: 506-452-5190
Krista MacMillan, President
Publications: Fredericton Therapeutic Riding

Nova Scotia Riding for the Disabled Association (NSRDA)
608 West Lawrencetown Rd., Lawrencetown, NS B2Z 1S5
Tel: 902-435-9344; Fax: 902-434-0545
salliemurphy@hotmail.com
Affiliation(s): Nova Scotia Equestrian Federation; Recreation Council on Disability in Nova Scotia
Sallie Murphy, Sec.-Treas.

Ontario Therapeutic Riding Association (OnTRA) / Association ontarienne d'équitation thérapeutique
RR#1, 54117 Heritage Line, Straffordville, ON N0J 1Y0
www.ontra.ca
www.facebook.com/group.php?gid=158261594210016
Viki Davidson LaCombe, President

Pacific Riding for Developing Abilities (PRDA)
1088 - 208 St., Langley, BC V2Z 1T4
Tel: 604-530-8717; Fax: 604-530-8617
admin@prda.ca
www.prda.ca
Affiliation(s): Ishtar Transition Housing Society; Burnaby Association for Community Inclusion
Donna Morris, Administration Manager
Michelle Meacher, Program Manager

PARD Therapeutic Riding (PARD)
PO Box 1654, Peterborough, ON K9J 5S4
Tel: 705-742-6441
info@pard.ca
www.pard.ca
Joanna Primavesi, President

Peace Area Riding for the Disabled (PARDS)
PO Box 2, Site 24, RR#1, Grande Prairie, AB T8V 2Z8
Tel: 780-538-3211; Fax: 780-538-3683
pards@telusplanet.net
www.pards.ca
Jennifer Douglas, Executive Director

Quinte Therapeutic Riding Association (QUINTRA)
PO Box 22129, Belleville, ON K8N 5V7
Tel: 613-395-4472
barbara.davis@sympatico.ca
www.quintra.org
Affiliation(s): United Way of Quinte
Barb Davis, Contact

SARI Therapeutic Riding
12659 Medway Rd., RR#1, Arva, ON N0M 1C0
Tel: 519-666-1123; Fax: 519-666-1971
office@sari.ca
www.sari.ca
Affiliation(s): Ontario Therapeutic Riding Association
Diane Blackall, Executive Director

Saskatchewan Therapeutic Riding Association
PO Box 1072, North Battleford, SK S9A 3E6
Tel: 306-398-2889
Ed Gendall, Contact

Sunrise Therapeutic Riding & Learning Centre
6920 Concession 1, RR#2, Puslinch, ON n0B 2J0
Tel: 519-837-0558; Fax: 519-837-1233
info@sunrise-therapeutic.ca
www.sunrise-therapeutic.ca
Affiliation(s): Ontario's Promise
Ann Caine, Executive Director
Suzy Bender, Head Instructor

Therapeutic Ride Algoma
188 Upton Rd., Sault Ste Marie, ON P6A 3W4
Tel: 705-759-2935; Fax: 705-541-5700
Toll-Free: 877-526-4438
slavik@sympatico.ca
www.ridealgoma.com

Victoria Riding for Disabled Association (VRDA)
PO Box 43032, Stn. Victoria North, Victoria, BC V8X 3G2
Tel: 250-658-6272
vrda@shaw.ca
www.members.shaw.ca/vrda
Affiliation(s): B.C. Therapeutic Riding Association; Horse Council of British Columbia

Windsor Essex Therapeutic Riding Association (WETRA) / Association d'équitation thérapeutique Windsor-Essex
4465 Huron Church Line Rd., Windsor, ON N9H 1H3
Tel: 519-969-1261; Fax: 519-969-4016
wetra@on.aibn.com
www.wetra.ca
Affiliation(s): Ontario Therapeutic Riding Association
Sue Klotzer, Program Director

Track & Field Sports

Achilles Canada
199 Snowden Ave., Toronto, ON M4N 2A8
Tel: 416-485-6451; Fax: 416-485-0823
Brian McLean, Contact

Athletics Canada / Athlétisme Canada
#B1-110, 2445 St-Laurent Blvd., Ottawa, ON K1G 6C3
Tel: 613-260-5580; Fax: 613-260-0341
athcan@athletics.ca
www.athletics.ca
www.facebook.com/Canadatrackandfield
twitter.com/athleticscanada
Affiliation(s): International Amateur Athletic Federation
Rob Guy, Chief Executive Officer
Larry Clough, Director, Finance
Mathieu Gentès, Director, Public Relations & Corporate Services
Donna Harris, Director, Coach Development
Scott MacDonald, Director, National Team Programs

Canadian Masters Athletic Association (CMAA)
Tel: 416-380-2503
canadianmasters.ca
Paul Osland, President
Sherry Watts, Membership
Publications: The MASTERpiece

Northwest Territories Track & Field Association
PO Box 11089, Yellowknife, NT X1A 3X7
Fax: 867-669-8327
Toll-Free: 800-661-0797
Joe LeBlanc, President

Ontario Masters Track & Field Association (OMTFA)
1185 Eglinton Ave. East, Toronto, ON M3C 3C6
Tel: 416-426-4427; Fax: 416-426-7358
douglasj.smith@sympatico.ca
www.ontariomasters.ca
Doug Smith, President
Paul Osland, Vice-President

Ontario Roadrunners Association
#158, 2255B Queen St. East, Toronto, ON M4E 1G3
Tel: 416-691-9556
info@ontarioroadrunners.com
www.ontarioroadrunners.com

Triathlon

Alberta Triathlon Association (ATA)
11759 Groat Rd., Edmonton, AB T5M 3K6
Tel: 780-427-8616; Fax: 780-427-8628
Toll-Free: 866-888-7448
psm@triathlon.ab.ca
www.triathlon.ab.ca
Kenneth Sackley, President
Stephen Paiano, Executive Director

Ontario Association of Triathletes (OAT)
#205, 3 Concorde Gate, Toronto, ON M3C 3N7
Tel: 416-426-7025; Fax: 416-426-7303
info@triathlonontario.com
www.triathlonontario.com
Linda Kirk, Executive Director
Steve Harrigan, President

Triathlon Canada
#106, 3 Concorde Gate, Toronto, ON M3C 3N7
Tel: 416-426-7180; Fax: 416-426-7294
info@triathloncanada.com
www.triathloncanada.com
Alan Trivett, Executive Director

Triathlon Newfoundland & Labrador
PO Box 113, 1 Union St., Corner Brook, NL A2H 6C3
Tel: 709-634-9570; Fax: 709-634-9417
triathlon@nf.sympatico.ca
Affiliation(s): International Triathlon Union
Allen Vansen, President

Triathlon Québec
CP 1000, Succ. M, 4545, av Pierre-de-Coubertin, Montréal, QC H1V 3R2
Tél: 514-252-3121; Téléc: 514-252-5328
info@triathlonquebec.org
www.triathlonquebec.org
Affiliation(s): Triathlon Canada
Benoît-Hugo St-Pierre, Directeur

Universities & Colleges

Alberta Colleges Athletic Conference (ACAC)
Percy Page Centre, 11759 Groat Rd., Edmonton, AB T5M 3K6
Tel: 780-427-8068; Fax: 780-427-9289
office@acac.ab.ca
www.acac.ab.ca

Robert D. Day, Executive Director
Wade Kolmel, President
Alan Rogan, Vice-President, Operations
Leigh Goldie, Vice-President, Finance
Laurie de Grace, Coordinator, Marketing & Communications
Publications: ACAC By-laws, ACAC Operating Code, Alberta Colleges Athletic Conference Annual Report, Official's Handbooks, Outlook: The Newsletter of the ACAC

British Columbia Colleges' Athletic Association (BCCAA)
100 West 49th Ave., Vancouver, BC V5X 2X6
Tel: 604-439-9325; Fax: 604-439-9245
www.bccaa.ca
Affiliation(s): Canadian Colleges Athletics Association (CCAA)
Clayton Munro, President
Bruce Hunter, Chair, Discipline
Elise Le Brun, Chair, Eligibility
Publications: Operations Manual

Canadian Colleges Athletic Association / Association canadienne du sport collégial
c/o St. Lawrence College, 2 Belmont St., Cornwall, ON K6H 4Z1
Tel: 613-937-1508; Fax: 613-937-1530
sandra@ccaa.ca
www.ccaa.ca
Affiliation(s): Atlantic Colleges Athletic Association; Fédération québécoise du sport étudiant; Ontario Colleges Athletic Association; Alberta Colleges Athletic Conference; British Columbia Colleges Athletic Association
Sandra Murray-MacDonell, Executive Director

Canadian Council of University Physical Education & Kinesiology Administrators (CCUPEKA) / Conseil canadien des administrateurs universitaires en éducation physique et kinésiologie (CCAUEPK)
c/o Dr. J. Starkes, Department of Kinesiology, McMaster University, Hamilton, ON L8S 4K1
www.ccupeka.ca
Janet Starkes, Coordinator, Accreditation Council

Canadian Interuniversity Sport (CIS) / Sport interuniversitaire canadien (SIC)
#N205, 801 King Edward, Ottawa, ON K1N 6N5
Tel: 613-562-5670; Fax: 613-562-5669
cisoffice@universitysport.ca
www.cis-sic.ca
twitter.com/CIS_SIC
Affiliation(s): Atlantic University Sport; Québec Student Sport Federation; Ontario University Athletics; Canada West Universities Athletic Association
Marg McGregor, CEO

Ontario Colleges Athletic Association (OCAA)
#201m 3 Concorde Gate, Toronto, ON M3C 3N7
Tel: 416-426-7043; Fax: 416-426-7308
admin@ocaa.com
www.ocaa.com

Mark Couch, Sport Services Coordinator
Lindsay Bax, Marketing/Communications
Blair Webster, Executive Director
Ron Fearon, President

Ontario University Athletics (OUA) / Sports universitaires de l'Ontario
#230, 1119 Fennell Ave. East, Hamilton, ON L8T 1S2
Tel: 905-540-5148; Fax: 905-574-2840
info@oua.ca
www.oua.ca

Ward Disle, Executive Director

Volleyball

Alberta Volleyball Association (AVA)
Percy Page Centre, 11759 Groat Rd., Edmonton, AB T5M 3K6
Tel: 780-415-1703; Fax: 780-415-1700
info@albertavolleyball.com
www.albertavolleyball.com
Affiliation(s): Federation of Outdoor Volleyball Associations
Terry Gagnon, Executive Director
Jim Plakas, Director, Technical
Terri Dorfman, Office Manager

Fédération de volleyball du Québec (FVBQ)
CP 1000, Succ. M, 4545, av Pierre-de Coubertin, Montréal, QC H1V 3R2
Tél: 514-252-3065; Téléc: 514-252-3176
info-fvbq@volleyball.qc.ca
www.volleyball.qc.ca
Affiliation(s): Sports Québec; Regroupement loisirs Québec
Alain D'Amboise, Directeur général
Charles H. Cardinal, Président

International Volleyball Association / Fédération Internationale de Volleyball (FIVB)
Edouard-Sandoz 2-4, Lausanne, 1006, Switzerland
Tel: 41-21-345-3535; Fax: 41-21-345-3545
info@fivb.org
www.fivb.ch
Affiliation(s): Canadian Volleyball Association
Jizhong Wei, President

Manitoba Volleyball Association (MVA)
#412, 145 Pacific Ave., Winnipeg, MB R3B 2Z6
Tel: 204-925-5783; Fax: 204-925-5786
volleyball.ed@sportmanitoba.ca
www.volleyballmanitoba.ca
www.facebook.com/pages/Volleyball-Manitoba/150460355015535
Affiliation(s): Volleyball Canada
Ron Betts, Executive Director

Newfoundland & Labrador Volleyball Association (NLVA)
PO Box 21248, St. John's, NL A1A 5B2
Tel: 709-576-0817; Fax: 709-576-7493
nlvaruss@sportnl.ca
www.nlva.net

Russell Jackson, Executive Director
Eric Hiscock, President
Mike Murrran, Elite Development Chair

Northwest Territories Volleyball Association (NWTVA)
c/o Sport North Federation, PO Box 11089, 4909 - 49 St., 3rd Fl., Yellowknife, NT X1A 3X7
Tel: 867-669-8326; Fax: 867-669-8327
Doug Rentmeister, Executive Director, Sport North

Ontario Volleyball Association (OVA)
#304, 3 Concorde Gate, Toronto, ON M3C 3N7
Tel: 416-426-7316; Fax: 416-426-7109
Toll-Free: 800-563-5938
ova@ontariovolleyball.org
www.ontariovolleyball.org
twitter.com/ova_updates

Kristine Drakich, President
Linda Melnick, Secretary & Vice-President, Operations
Gord Ley, Vice-President, Beach
Jos Nederveen, Vice-President, Indoors

Saskatchewan Volleyball Association
1750 McAra St., Regina, SK S4N 6L4
Tel: 306-780-9250; Fax: 306-780-9288
officemanager@saskvolleyball.ca
www.saskvolleyball.ca
www.facebook.com/group.php?gid=121947301797
Dalene Phillips, President
Dan Medford, Executive Director
Tammy Schneider, Office Manager

Volleyball BC
Harry Jerome Sports Centre, 7564 Barnet Hwy., Burnaby, BC V5A 1E7
Tel: 604-291-2007; Fax: 604-291-2602
communications@volleyballbc.ca
www.volleyballbc.ca

Chris Densmore, Executive Director
Chris Berglund, Director, Technical & High Performance
Jenny Graham, Manager, Programs
Brian Hiebert, Manager, Communications

Volleyball Canada (VC)
#202, 5510 Canotek Rd., Gloucester, ON K1J 9J5
Tel: 613-748-5681; Fax: 613-748-5727
info@volleyball.ca
www.volleyball.ca
www.facebook.com/VolleyballCanada?ref=ts
twitter.com/VBallCanada
Affiliation(s): International Volleyball Federation; Canadian Olympic Association; Coaching Association of Canada
Mark Eckert, Executive Director
Hugh Wong, President
Linden Leung, Manager, Finance & Operations
James Sneddon, Director, Domestic Development

Volleyball New Brunswick
#13, 900 Hanwell Rd., Fredericton, NB E3B 6A3
Tel: 506-451-1346; Fax: 506-451-1325
vnb@nb.aibn.com
www.vnb.nb.ca

John Richard, President
Mike Gallagher, Executive Director & Technical Director
Catherine Boudreau, Coordinator, Indoor & Beach Programs

Volleyball Nova Scotia
5516 Spring Garden Rd., 4th Fl., Halifax, NS B3J 1G6
Tel: 902-425-5450; Fax: 902-425-5606
vns@sportnovascotia.ca
www.volleyballnovascotia.ca

Dave Swetnam, President
Al Scott, Executive Director
Brock Pehar, Director, Technical

Volleyball Prince Edward Island
PO Box 302, Charlottetown, PE C1N 7K7
Tel: 902-569-0583; Fax: 902-368-4548
Toll-Free: 800-247-6712
cgcrozier@sportpei.pe.ca
www.volleyballpei.com
Affiliation(s): Sport PEI
Cheryl Crozier, Executive Director
Krista Walsh, President
Harvey Mazerolle, Vice-President

Volleyball Yukon
4061 - 4th Ave., Whitehorse, YT Y1A 1H1
Tel: 867-334-4592; Fax: 867-667-4237
www.volleyballyukon.com
Michael Hanson, President

Water Polo

Alberta Water Polo Association (AWPA)
PO Box 54, 2225 Macleod Trail SE, Calgary, AB T2G 5B6
office@albertawaterpolo.ca
www.albertawaterpolo.ca
www.facebook.com/group.php?gid=143394719017308
Martin Thumwood, President
Dayna Christmas, Executive Director
Sherry Schaefer, Secretary
Nicolas Youngblud, Treasurer

British Columbia Water Polo Association (BCWPA)
#227, 3820 Cessna Dr., Richmond, BC V7B 0A2
Tel: 604-333-3480; Fax: 604-333-3450
bcwaterpolo@telus.net
www.bcwaterpolo.com; www.bcwaterpolo.ca
www.facebook.com/group.php?gid=257337230951081
twitter.com/bcwaterpolo
Dave Soul, Executive Director

Fédération de Water-Polo du Québec (FWPQ) / Water Polo Québec
CP 1000, Succ. M, 4545, Pierre de Coubertin, Montréal, QC H1V 3R2
Tél: 514-252-3098; Téléc: 514-252-5658
waterpolo@waterpolo-quebec.qc.ca
www.waterpolo-quebec.qc.ca

Jean Thomas, Directeur général
Guy Lapointe, Président

Manitoba Water Polo Association Inc.
#304, 200 Main St., Winnipeg, MB R3C 4M2
Tel: 204-925-5777; Fax: 204-925-5730
mwpa@shaw.ca
www.mbwaterpolo.com
Affiliation(s): Sport Manitoba
Bruce Rose, Executive Director
Cindra Leclerc, President
Rhonda Haight, Secretary

Ontario Water Polo Association (OWPA) / L'Association de water polo d'Ontario
#206, 3 Concorde Gate, Toronto, ON M3C 3N7
Tel: 416-426-7028; Fax: 416-426-7356
info@ontariowaterpolo.ca
www.ontariowaterpolo.ca
Ross McDonald, Technical Director

Water Polo Saskatchewan Inc. (WPS)
1860 Lorne St., Regina, SK S4P 2L7
Tel: 306-780-9260; Fax: 306-780-9467
admin@wpsask.ca
www.wpsask.ca
www.facebook.com/waterpolosask?sk=wall
Cyril Dorgigne, Executive Director
Amanda Walton, Office Administrator

Water Skiing

Fédération québécoise de ski nautique (FQSN)
CP 1000, Succ. M, 4545, av Pierre-de Coubertin, Montréal, QC H1V 3R2
Tél: 514-252-3092; Téléc: 514-252-3186
louissimard@skinautiquequebec.qc.ca
www.skinautiquequebec.qc.ca
Louis Simard, Président

Nova Scotia Water Ski Association (NSWSA)
PO Box 783, Dartmouth, NS B2Y 3Z3
nswsa@aol.com
www.nswsa.com
Gary Allen, President

Ontario Water Ski Association (OWSA)
#209-3 Concorde Gate, Toronto, ON M3C 3N7
Tel: 416-426-7092; Fax: 416-426-7378
office@wswo.ca
www.wswo.ca
www.facebook.com/88367451677
twitter.com/wswo
Paul Roberts, President

Water Ski - Wakeboard Manitoba (WSWM)
#415, 145 Pacific Ave., Winnipeg, MB R3B 2Z6
Tel: 204-925-5700; Fax: 204-925-5792
info@wswm.ca
www.wswm.ca
Alanna Boudreau, Executive Director
Kevin Polley, President

Water Ski & Wakeboard Alberta (WSWA)
Percy Page Centre, 11759 Groat Rd., Edmonton, AB T5M 3K6
Tel: 780-415-0088; Fax: 780-422-2663
Toll-Free: 866-258-2754
info@wswa.ca
www.wswa.ca
Affiliation(s): Water Ski Canada; International Water Ski Federation
Dan Velcic, President
Glenn Sommerville, Executive Director

Water Ski & Wakeboard British Columbia (WSWBC)
PO Box 56011, #101, 1497 Admiral's Rd., victoria, BC V9A 2P0
Toll-Free: 888-696-6677
iankellow@wswbc.org
www.wswbc.org
Ian Kellow, President

Water Ski & Wakeboard Canada / Ski nautique et planche Canada
#210, 223 Colonnade Rd. South, Ottawa, ON K2E 7K3
Tel: 613-526-0685; Fax: 613-526-4380
wswc@waterski-wakeboard.ca
www.waterski-wakeboard.ca
Glenn Bowie, President
Dan Wolfenden, Executive Director

Water Ski & Wakeboard Saskatchewan
PO Box 202, Warman, SK S0K 4S0
Tel: 306-931-2901; Fax: 306-249-3062
sheri@wswsask.com
www.wswsask.com
Sheri Seiferling, Executive Director
Berk Summach, President

Women in Sports

Canadian Association for the Advancement of Women & Sport & Physical Activity (CAAWS) / Association canadienne pour l'avancement des femmes du sport et de l'activité physique (ACAFS)
#202N, 801 King Edward Ave., Ottawa, ON K1N 6N5
Tel: 613-562-5667; Fax: 613-562-5668
caaws@caaws.ca
www.caaws.ca
Karin Lofstrom, Executive Director
Sydney Millar, Manager, National Program
Stéphanie Legault, Manager, Marketing & Projects
Jessica Lowe, Administrator & Office Coordinator
Publications: Health Benefits of Physical Activity for Girls & Women, In Her Voice: An Exploration of Young Women's Sport & Physical Activity Experiences, Including Transitioned & Transitioning Athletes in Sport - Issues, Facts, & Perspectives, Making the Most of Your Opportunities: A Media Guide for Athletes & Their Coaches, On the Move, Seeing the Invisible, Speaking about the Unspoken: A Position Paper on Homophobia in Sport, Sex Discrimination in Sport - An Update, Success Stories: Increasing Opportunities for Girls & Women in National & Multi-Sport Organizations, Women on Boards: A Guide to Getting Involved

Field Hockey BC (FHBC) / Hockey sur gazon C-B
#202, 210 Broadway West, Vancouver, BC V5Y 3W2
Tel: 604-737-3046; Fax: 604-737-6488
info@fieldhockeybc.com
www.fieldhockeybc.com
twitter.com/FieldHockeyBC
Mark Saunders, Executive Director

Ladies' Golf Union (LGU)
The Scores, St. Andrews, Fife, KY16 9AT, United Kingdom
Tel: 44-13-34-475811; Fax: 44-13-34-472818
info@lgu.org
www.lgu.org
Affiliation(s): Canadian Ladies' Golf Association
Maureen Lockett, President
Shona Malcolm, CEO

Nova Scotia Curling Association (NSCA)
5516 Spring Garden Rd., 4th Fl., Halifax, NS B3J 1G6
Tel: 902-421-2875; Fax: 902-425-5606
nsca@sportnovascotia.ca
www.nscurl.com
Affiliation(s): Canadian Curling Association
Jeremiah Anderson, Executive Director
Shirley Osborne, President

Wrestling

Alberta Amateur Wrestling Association (AAWA)
Percy Page Centre, 11759 Groat Rd., Edmonton, AB T5M 3K6
Tel: 780-415-0140; Fax: 780-427-0524
aawa@ocii.com
www.albertawrestling.ab.ca
www.facebook.com/group.php?gid=37817165947&ref=ts
Jerry Derewonko, President
Tammie Bradley, Executive Director
Michael Drought, Technical Director

British Columbia Wrestling Association (BCWA)
#335, 2416 Main St., Vancouver, BC V5T 3E2
Tel: 604-737-3092; Fax: 604-737-6043
info@bcwrestling.com
www.bcwrestling.com
Affiliation(s): BC School Sports
MaryAnn DeCorby, Executive Director

Canadian Amateur Wrestling Association (CAWA) / Association canadienne de lutte amateur
#7, 5370 Canotek Rd., Gloucester, ON K1J 9E6
Tel: 613-748-5686; Fax: 613-748-5756
info@wrestling.ca
www.wrestling.ca
Tamara Medwidsky, Executive Director
Doug Cox, President
Clint Kingsbury, Manager, Domestic Development
Dave Mair, Manager, High Performance
Dave McKay, National Coach, Senior Men
Leigh Vierling, National Coach, Senior Women

Lutte NB Wrestling (LNBW)
www.luttenbwrestling.com
Mary Singh, Executive Director
Kevin Scully, President

Manitoba Amateur Wrestling Association (MAWA)
c/o Sport Manitoba, 145 Pacific Ave., Winnipeg, MB R3B 2Z6
Tel: 204-925-5670; Fax: 204-925-5703
mawawrestling@mts.net
www.mawawrestling.ca

Newfoundland & Labrador Amateur Wrestling Association (NLAWA)
1 Wade's Ln., Flatrock, NL A1K 1C3
Fax: 709-643-5103
contact@nlawa.com
www.nlawa.com
Randy Ralph, President

Ontario Amateur Wrestling Association (OAWA)
#213, 3 Concorde Gate, Toronto, ON M3C 3N7
Tel: 416-426-7274; Fax: 416-426-7343
admin@oawa.ca
www.oawa.ca
Affiliation(s): International Amateur Wrestling Association; Canadian Amateur Wrestling Association
Tim MaGarrey, Provincial Director

Saskatchewan Amateur Wrestling Association (SAWA)
510 Cynthia St., Saskatoon, SK S7L 7K7
Tel: 306-975-0822; Fax: 306-242-8007
sk.wrestling@shaw.ca
www.saskwrestling.com
Anna-Beth Zulkoskey, Executive Director

Wrestling Nova Scotia
General Delivery, Bear River, NS B0S 1B0
Tel: 902-857-1761
wrestlingns@canada.com
www.wrestlingnovascotia.ca
Peter Coulthard, President
Scott Aldridge, Vice-President
Debbie MacDonald, Sec.-Treas.

Wrestling PEI
Sport PEI, PO Box 302, 40 Enman Crescent, Charlottetown, PE C1A 7K7
Tel: 902-368-4110; Fax: 902-368-4548
Toll-Free: 800-247-6712
gflood@sportpei.pe.ca; sports@sportpei.pe.ca
www.wrestlingpei.ca
www.facebook.com/group.php?gid=213998623017
Glen Flood, Executive Director

Professional Leagues & Teams

Baseball, Professional: Major League

Major League Baseball/MLB
245 PARK AVENUE
31ST FLOOR
NEW YORK, NY 10167
212-931-7800
866-800-1275
www.mlb.com
Allan Bud H. Selig, Commissioner of Baseball
Bob DuPuy, President & Chief Operating Officer
Jimmie Lee Solomon, Executive Vice President, Baseball Operations
Tim Brosnan, Executive Vice President, Business
Rob Manfred, Executive VP, Labor Relations & Human Resources
John McHale, Jr., Executive VP, Administration & CIO
Joe Torre, Executive VP, Baseball Operations
Nature of Service:
Administrates professional baseball. Established and enforces rules regarding franchise operation. Supervises national radio and television contracts. Handles publicity and marketing of baseball and legal matters pertaining to baseball as an industry. Operates the World Series and All-Star games.
Membership Requirements:
Teams operating in the American or National Leagues.
Year Founded:
1920
Sponsors:
Anheuser-Busch, Bank of America, Bayer (One a Day), DHL, FIA Card Service, NA, Frito Lay, Gatorade, Gillette, General Motors (Chevrolet), InterContinental Hotels Group (Holiday Inn), KPMG, MasterCard International, Nike, Pepsi-Cola, Sharp, State Farm, Taco Bell, XM Satellite Radio.

Teams:

Toronto Blue Jays
ROGERS CENTRE
ONE BLUE JAYS WAY
SUITE 3200
TORONTO, ON M5V 1J1
416-341-1000
888-654-6529
Fax: 416-341-1250
http://toronto.bluejays.mlb.com
Tony Pelley, President, Rogers Media
Paul Beeston, President and CEO of Blue Jays Roger Center
Jay Stenhouse, Vice President Communications
Howard Starkman, Vice President of Special Projects
George Poulis, Head Trainer
Matthew Shuber, Director of Business Affairs & Legal Counsel
Jay Sartori, Assistant General Manager
Perry Minasian, Director, Professional Scouting
Stephen Brooks, Senior VP & Business Operations
Jason Diplock, VP of Ticket Sales & Service
Mario Coutinho, Vice President, Stadium Operations & Security
John Farrell, Team Manager
Honsing Leung, Senior Manager, Business Development
Marnie Starkman, Director, Game Entertainment &

Promotions
Andrew Tinnish,
Phil Lind, Vice Chair, Rogers Communications
Heather Connolly, Admin, Baseball Operations
Stadium:
Rogers Centre, a recently renovated stadium to include an all-new Club 200 VIP.
Stadium Seating Capacity:
50,516
Publications:
Inside Pitch Newsletter

Baseball, Professional Leagues/Teams: Minor

Canadian American Association of Professional Baseball
1415 HIGHWAY 54 WEST
SUITE 210
DURHAM, NC 27707
919-401-8150
Fax: 919-401-8152
info@baseballoffice.com
www.canamleague.com

Miles Wolff, Commissioner
mwolff@canamleague.com
Dan Moushon, President/Chief Operating Officer
dmoushon@canamleague.com
Nature of Service:
Independent Professional Baseball League
Year Founded:
2004
History:
The history of the Can-Am League dates back to 1936 when Brockville, Ogdensburg, Oswego, Ottawa, Perth and Watertown/Massena were part of the Class C. The association continued until the 1942 season, but due to World War II the league folded only to resurrect at the start of the 1946 season featuring teams from the cities of Amsterdam, Gloversville-Johnstown, Oneonta, Pittsfield, Rome, Quebec. Schenectady and Trois Rivieres. The second installment of the Can-Am League ended its run after the 1951 season due to the rise of television and professional football. On October 6, 2004, the Can-Am League was reborn.
Player Eligibility:
Minimum of five first-year players; maximum of four veterans (at least four years of professional service).
Teams:
9

Teams:

Quebec Les Capitales
LE STADE DE QUEBEC
100 RUE DU CARDINAL MAURICE-ROY
QUEBEC CITY G1K8Z1
418-521-2255
Fax: 418-521-2266
baseball@capitalesdequebec.com
www.capitalesdequebec.com
Miles Wolff, Director of Baseball Operations
Michel Laplante, President
Alexandre Harvey, General Manager
Pier-Luc Nappert, Director of Marketing & Communications
Ballpark:
Le Stade de Quebec opened in 1939 with a seating capacity of 4,800.
Team History:
Eastern Canada League - 1923; Quebec-Ontario-Vermont League - 1924; Quebec Provincial League - 1940; Canadian-American League - 1941-42, 1946-50, 2005-present; Provincial League - 1951-55; Eastern League - 1971-77; Northern League - 1999-2002; Northeast League - 2003-04.
Publications:
Le Journal de Quebec; Le Soleil
Media Broadcast:
CHRC 800 AM

Canadian Baseball League/Independent Minor League
1140 WEST PENDER STREET
SUITE 440
VANCOUVER, BC V6E 4G1
604-689-1566
Fax: 604-689-1534
http://www.thecbl.com

Graham Colvin, Commissioner
James Wesley, Co-Commissioner
Charlton Lui, President/Chief Executive Officer
Eric Blatt, Chief Operating Officer
John Briggs, Vice President, Advanced Media
Andrew Laurie, Baseball Operations Coordinator
Michael Connolly, Communications Coordinator
Chris Lang, Community Relations Manager
John Haar, Director of Operations
Raymondy Lee, Special Events Coordinator
Alex Klenman, Director of Communications
Greg Breakell, Director of Broadcasting
Description:
The Canadian Baseball League is made up of 27 teams in two leagues. Farmer's League: Grand Rapids Red Dogs, Moose Jaw Dragons, Regina Pirates, Sask Yellow Jackets, Yellowknife Bluenotes, Calvary Remparts, Cold Lake Mud Cats, Fort mac Roughnecks, Lethbridge Typhoon, St. Paul Pride, Creston Kokanee, Kelonna Okanagans, Victoria Islanders. Fishermen League: Charlottetown Blues, Fredericton Bandits, Halifax Oilers, PEI Agronauts, West Bay Red Skulls, Cazourg Stempeders, Ottawa Milk Men, Port Hope Battery, Quebec Bulldogs, Val d'or Sharks, Guelph Storm, London Mustangs, Owen Sound Crusaders, Toronto Polar Bears

Northwest League (A Level League)
PO BOX 1645
BOISE, ID 83701
208-429-1511
Fax: 208-429-1525
mail@northwestleague.com
www.northwestleague.com

Bob Richmond, President
Todd Rahr, Vice President
League History:
The Northwest League was established in 1955. Including its predecessor leagues, the NWL has existed since 1901. Due to the fact that major-league baseball did not arrive on the west coast until the late 1950's, minor-league baseball prospered in the Northwest.
Number of Teams:
8

Teams:

Vancouver Canadians
4601 ONTARIO ST
VANCOUVER, BC V5V 3H4
604-872-5232
Fax: 604-872-1714
staff@canadiansbaseball.com
www.canadiansbaseball.com
Jake Kerr, Prinicpal Owner/Managing General Partner
Jeff Mooney, Co-Owner/Partner
Andy Dunn, President
Jason Takefman, General Manager
(604)872-5232
jtakefman@canadiansbaseball.com
Graham Wall, Vice President
(604)872-5232
gwall@canadiansbaseball.com
Rob Fai, Director Media/Broadcast
(604)872-5232
rfai@canadiansbaseball.com
JC Fraser, Assistant General Manager/ Ballpark Operations
(604)872-5232
jcfraser@canadiansbaseball.com
Years in League:
1967-71, 1979-present.
Ballpark:
Scotiabank Field at Nat Bailey Stadium.
Ballpark Description:
Opened in 1951. Seating Capacity: 6,500
Media Broadcast:
The TEAM Sports Radio 1040-AM.
MLB Affiliate:
Toronto Blue Jays

Basketball, Leagues and Teams

National Basketball Association/NBA
645 FIFTH AVENUE
NEW YORK, NY 10022
212-407-8000
Fax: 212-832-3861
info@nba.com
www.nba.com

Description:
The premier professional basketball league in North America. Many of the world's best players play in the NBA, and the overall standard of the competition is considerably higher than any other professional competition. The NBA was founded in New York City on June 6, 1946 as the Basketball Association of America (BAA). It adopted the name National Basketball Association in the fall of 1949 after adding several teams from the rival National Basketball League.

Teams:

Toronto Raptors
AIR CANADA CENTER
40 BAY STREET
SUITE 400
TORONTO M5J 2X2
416-815-5600
Fax: 416-359-9332
www.nba.com/raptors
Larry Tanenbaum, Chairman of the Board/NBA Governor
Richard Peddie, President/Chief Executive Officer
Bryan Colangelo, President/General Manager
Tom Anselmi, Executive VP/Chief Operating Officer
Ian Clarke, Executive VP/Chief Financial Officer
Dwane Casey, Head Coach
History:
Founded in 1995 in Toronto.
Arena:
Air Canada Center. Seating Capacity: 19,800

Football, Professional Leagues/Teams

Canadian Football League/CFL
50 WELLINGTON STREET EAST
3RD FLOOR
TORONTO, ON M5E 1C8
416-322-9650
Fax: 416-322-9651
www.cfl.ca

Mark Cohon, Commissioner
Michael Copeland, Chief Operating Officer
Kevin McDonald, Vice President, Football Operations
Matt Maychak, Vice President, Communications & Broadcast
Douglas Allison, Vice President, Finance and Business Operations

Teams:

B.C. Lions
10605- 135TH STREET
SURREY, BC V6B 4Y9
604-930-5466
Fax: 604-583-7882
communityrelations@bclions.com
www.bclions.com
David Braley, Owner
Wally Buono, General Manager, VP of Football Operations
Roy Shivers, Director, Player Personnel
George Chayka, Vice President, Business
Mike Benevides, Head Coach
Dennis Skulsky, President/ CEO
Jamie Taras, Director of Community Relations
Jamie Cartmell, Director, Communications
Carol Longmuir, Finance Administrator
Phil Adams, Director, Corporate Partnerships

Calgary Stampeders
MCMAHON STADIUM
1817 CROWCHILD TRAIL NW
CALGARY, AB T2M 4R6
403-289-0205
Fax: 403-289-7850
stampeder@stampeders.com
www.stampeders.com
John Forzani, Chairman
Lyle Bauer, President, Chief Operating Officer
Doug Mitchell, Governor
Bob Viccars, Executive Member
Stan Schwartz, Executive Vice President
Valerie Pak, Director Marketing
Jamie Seguin, Director of Game Operations
Tanya Mettimano, Director Ticketing & Customer Relations
John Hufnagel, General Manager/Head Coach

Edmonton Eskimos
11000 STADIUM ROAD
EDMONTON, AB T5B 2R7
780-448-1525
Fax: 780-429-3452
comments@esks.com
www.esks.com
Lenn Rhoades, President/Chief Executive Officer
Eric Tillman, General Manager
Kavis Reed, Head Coach
Dan McKinnon, Assistant General Manager
Paul Jones, Director Player Personnel
Dave Jamieson, Vice President of Communication & Broadcast
Greg Treble, Director Business Operations
Cathy Presniak, Vice President of Finance

Montreal Alouettes
4545 PIERRE-DE-COUBERTIN
PO BOX 65, STATION M
MONTREAL, PQ H1V 3L6
514-253-0008
Fax: 514-253-8821
info@montrealalouettes.com
www.montrealalouettes.com
Robert Wetenall, Owner
Larry Smith, President/Chief Executive Officer
Laurie Bennett, VP Business Operations
lbennett@montrealalouettes.com
Olivier Poulin, Director Communications
opoulin@montrealalouettes.com
Jim Popp, VP/GM/Director Football Operations
jpopp@montrealalouettes.com
Claude Rochon, VP Marketing/Communications
crochon@montrealalouettes.com
Marcel Desjardins, Assistant General Manager
Marc Trestman, Head Coach

Toronto Argonauts
212 KING STREET WEST, SUITE 501
TORONTO, ON M5H 1K5
416-341-2700
Fax: 416-341-2714
info@argunauts.on.ca
www.argonauts.ca
David Braley, Owner
Chris Rudge, Executive Chair, Chief Executive Officer
Jason Colero, Manager Community Relations
Lou Ragagnin, President, Chief Operating Officer
David Bedford, Vice President, Marketing & Communications
Carlos Ferreira, Director Marketing/Events
Beth Waldman, Director Communications
Mike Hagen, Director Player Personnel
Scott Milanovich, Head Coach
Jim Backer, General Manager

Winnipeg Blue Bombers
1465 MAROONS ROAD
WINNIPEG, MB R3G 0L6
204-784-2583
Fax: 204-783-5222
bbombers@bluebombers.com
www.bluebombers.com
Jim Bell, Vice President, Chief Operating Officer
Garth Buchko, President, Chief Executive Officer
Bill Watchorn, Board Chairperson
Jerry Maslowsky, Vice President Marketing
Hodgkinson Ross, Director of Football Operations
Shirlee Preteau, Vice President of Event Operations
Darren Cameron, Director of Media Relations
Joe Mack, Vice President & GM of Football Operations
Paul LaPolice, Head Coach

Hockey, Professional Hockey (NHL)

National Hockey League/NHL
1185 AVENUE OF THE AMERICAS
15TH FLOOR
NEW YORK, NY 10036
212-789-2000
Fax: 212-789-2020
www.nhl.com

Gary Bettman, Commissioner
Steve Solomon, Executive Vice President/COO
Craig Harnett, Executive Vice President/CFO
William Daly, EVP/Chief Legal Officer
Keith Ritter, SVP New Business Development
(212)789-2000
Doug Perlman, SVP Television/Media Ventures
(212)789-2000
Jim Haskins, VP Consumer Products/Marketing
Adam Acone, VP Broadcasting/Programming
Scott Carmichael, Vice President Club Marketing
Brain Jennings, Grp VP Consumer Products Marketing
(212)789-2000
Andrew Judelson, Group VP Corporate Marketing
Ken Yaffe, Group VP/Managing Director
Ed Home, President NHL Enterprises
Lisa Schoeck, Director Human Resources
Andy Van Hellemond,
Susan Cohig, SVP Club Consulting & Services
John Collins, Senior Executive Vice President
Edward Horne, Senior Executive Vice President Communications
Year Founded:
1917
Description:
League of professional hockey teams
Membership Requirements:
Approval by NHL Board of Governors
Publications:
NHL Rule Book, annual; NHL Schedule, annual; NHL MEDIA DIRECTORY, annual; NHL Official Guide and Record Book, annual
Additional Offices:
75 International Blvd, Ste 300, Rexdale, Ont, Canada M9W 6L9. 416 798-0809; FAX: 416 798-0819. Montreal Office: 1800 McGill College Ave, Ste 2600, Montreal, P.Q., Canada H3A 3J6. 514 288-9220; FAX: 514 284-0300

Teams:

Calgary Flames
PO BOX 1540
STATION M
CALGARY, AB T2P 3B9
403-777-2177
888-5-FLAMES
Fax: 403-777-2171
www.calgaryflames.com
Murray Edwards, Owner
Alvin Libin, Owner
Allan Markin, Owner
Jeffrey McCaig, Owner
Clayton Riddell, Owner
Byron Seaman, Owner
Ken King, President/Chief Executive Officer
Lyle Edwards, Chairman
Brent Sutter, Head Coach/General Manager
Dave Lowry, Assistant Coach
Troy Ward, Assistant Coach
John Bean, Senior Vice President
Year Founded:
1972
Description:
The Calgary Flames are a National Hockey League team based in Calgary, Alberta
Home Arena:
Pengrowth Saddledome

Edmonton Oilers
11230 110TH STREET
2ND FLOOR
EDMONTON, AB T5G 3H7
780-414-4000
Fax: 780-409-5890
www.oilers.nhl.com
Patrick LaForge, President/Chief Executive Officer
Steve Tambellini, General Manager
Darryl Boessenkool, VP Finance/Chief Financial Officer
Allan Watt, VP Communications/Broadcast
Kevin Lowe, President, Hockey Operations
Steven Katzman, Chief Marketing Officer
Tom Renney, Head Coach
Ralph Krueger, Assistant Coach
Steve Smith, Assistant Coach
Kelly Buchberger, Assistant Coach
Frederic Chabot, Goaltending Coach
Year Founded:
1972
Description:
The Edmonton Oilers are a National Hockey League twam based in Edmontn, Alberta
Home Arena:
Rexall Place

Montreal Canadiens
1275 ST. ANTOINE STREET WEST
MONTREAL H3C 5L2
514-932-2582
Fax: 514-932-8285
www.canadiens.nhl.com
Geoff Molson, President/Owner
Fred Steer, Chief Financial Officer
Pierre Gauthier, Executive Vice President
Jacques Aube, Vice President/ General Manager
Jacques Martin, Head Coach
Perry Pearn, Assistant Coach
Pierre Groulx, Assistant Coach/Goaltending Coach
Year Founded:
1909
Description:
The Montreal Canadiens are the oldest established National Hockey League
Home Arena:
Centre Bell

Ottawa Senators
1000 PALLADIUM DRIVE
KANATA, ON K2V 1A5
613-599-0250
Fax: 613-599-0358
info@ottawasenators.com
www.ottawasenators.com
Eugene Melnyk, Owner/Chairman/Alt Gov
Cyril Leeder, President/ Alternate Governor
Erin Crowe, Chief Financial Officer
Anders Hedberg, Director Player Personnel
Steve Keogh, Director Communications
Bryan Murray, Executive Vice President/ General Manager
Tim Murray, Assistant General Manager
Paul MacLean, Head Coach
Dave Cameron, Assistant Coach
Year Founded:
1992
Description:
The Ottawa Senators are a National Hockey League team based in Ottawa, Ontario Canada
Home Arena:
Scotiabank Place

Toronto Maple Leafs
50 BAY STREET
SUITE 500
TORONTO, ON M5J 2L2
416-815-5400
Fax: 416-359-9331
www.torontomapleleafs.com
Brian Burke, President/General Manager
Ian Clark, EVP/CFO/Business Development
Tom Anselmi, EVP/Chief Operations Officer
Pat Park, Director Media Relations
Ron Wilson, Head Coach
Rob Zettler, Assistant Coach
Scott Gordon, Assistant Coach
Jim Hughes, Director of Player Development
Year Founded:
1917
Description:
The Toronto Maple Leafs are a National Hockey League team based in Toronto, Ontario
Home Arena:
Air Canada Centre

Vancouver Canucks
800 GRIFFITHS WAY
VANCOUVER, BC V6B 6G1
604-899-7400
855-523-6800
Fax: 604-899-7401
info@canucks.com
www.canucks.com
Francesco Aquilini, Chairman/Gov
Mike Gillis, President/ General Manager
Lorne Henning, VP Player Personnel
Laurence Gilman, VP Hockey Operations
Dave Gagner, Director, Player Development
Alain Vigneault, Head Coach
Rick Bowness, Associate Coach
Newell Brown, Assistant Coach
Darryl Williams, Assistant Coach
Roland Melanson, Goaltending Coach
Year Founded:
1970
Description:
The Vancouver Canucks are a National Hockey League team based in Vancouver, British Columbia
Home Arena:
GM Place

Winnipeg Jets
260 HARGRAVE STREET
WINNIPEG, MB R3C 5S5
204-987-7825
Fax: 204-926-5555
www.jets.nhl.com
Jim Ludlow, President/ CEO
Mark Chipman, Chairman
Kevin Cheveldayoff, EVP/ General Manager
Norva Riddell, Senior Vice President Sales & Marketing
Craig Heisinger, Director of Hockey Operations
Claude Noel, Head Coach
Year Founded:
2011
Description:
The Winnipeg Jets are a National Hockey League team based in Winnipeg, Manitoba. The franchise was formerly known as the Atlanta Thrashers until their purchase in 2011.

Home Arena
MTS Centre

Hockey, Professional, Minor Leagues

American Hockey League/AHL
1 MONARCH PLACE
SPRINGFIELD, MA 01144
413-781-2030
Fax: 413-733-4767
info@theahl.com
www.theahl.com

David Andrews, President/CEO
Jim Mill, EVP Hockey Operations
Drew Griffin, Director Finance and Administration
Year Founded:
1936
Description:
Promotes and operates the sport of professional ice hockey
Membership Requirements:
Purchase of a franchise
Publications:
Official guide and record book; Rule book; Schedule; Year End Statistical Package

Teams:

St. John's Icecaps
120 NEW GOWER ST
ST JOHN'S, NL A1C 6K4
709-576-2277
www.stjohnsicecaps.com
Craig Heisinger, General Manager
Keith McCambridge, Head Coach
Home Ice:
Mile One Centre

Toronto Marlies
100 PRINCESS BOULEVARD
TORONTO, ON M6K 3C3
416-263-3900
Fax: 416-263-3901
www.marlies.ca
Peter Church, General Manager
Michael Cosentino, Director Business Operations
Dallas Eakins, Head Coach
Gord Dineen, Assistant Coach
Derek King, Assistant Coach
Brad Lynn, Manager of Hockey Operations & Communications
Home Ice:
Ricoh Coliseum

Ontario Hockey League
305 MILNER AVENUE
SUITE 208
SCARBOROUGH, ON M1B 3V4
416-299-8700
Fax: 416-299-8787
ohl@chl.ca
www.ontariohockeyleague.com

Sherwood Bassin, Chairman
David Branch, Commissioner
Year Founded:
1896

Teams:

Barrie Colts
555 BAYVIEW DRIVE
BARRIE, ON L4N 8Y2
705-722-6587
Fax: 705-721-9709
operations@barriecolts.com
www.barriecolts.com
Jason Ford, General Manager
Jim Payetta, VP of Marketing
Dale Hawerchuk, Head Coach
Jay Wells, Assistant Coach
Todd Miller, Assistant Coach
Howie Campbell, President
Home Ice:
Barrie Molson Centre

Belleville Bulls
265 CANNIFTON ROAD
BELLEVILLE, ON K8N 4V8
613-966-8338
Fax: 705-966-8761
hockey@bellevillebulls.com
www.bellevillebulls.com
Gord Simmonds, President
Robert Vaughan, Founder/Alt Gov
George Burnett, General Manager/Head Coach
Barclay Branch, Assistant General Manager
Jake Grimes, Assistant Coach
David Steenburgh, Director of Business Operations
Home Ice:
Yardmen

Guelph Storm
55 WYNDHAM STREET NORTH
GUELPH, ON N1H 7TB
519-837-9690
Fax: 519-837-9692
info@guelphstorm.com
www.guelphstorm.com
Rick Hoyle, President
Lindsay Pink, Media Relations Manager
Sarah Twigger, Communication Relations
Mike Kelly, Vice President/ General Manager
Scott Walker, Head Coach
Chris Hajt, Assistant Coach
Home Ice:
Guelph Sports Entertainment Centre

Kingston Frontenacs
PO BOX 665
KINGSTON, ON K7I 4X1
613-542-4042
Fax: 613-542-2834
www.kingstonfrontenacs.com
Jeff Stilwell, Director Sales/Marketing
Doug Gilmour, General Manager
Todd Gill, Head Coach
Darren Keily, Assistant Coach
Craig Belfer, Head Trainer
Doug Springer, President/Governor
Home Ice:
Kingston Memorial Centre

Kitchener Rangers
400 EAST AVENUE
KITCHENER, ON N2H 1Z6
519-576-3700
Fax: 519-576-7571
info@kitchenerrangers.com
www.kitchenerrangers.com
Craig Campbell, President
Steve Bienkowski, Chief Operating Officer
Steve Spott, General Manager/Head Coach
Paul Fixter, Assistant Coach
Troy Smith, Assistant Coach
Brandon Merli, Strength Coach
Dan Lebold, Head Trainer
Home Ice:
Kitchener Memorial Auditorium

London Knights
99 DYBDAS STREET
LONDON, ON N6A 6K1
519-681-0800
Fax: 519-668-7291
info@londonknights.com
www.londonknights.com
Trevor Whiffen, Governor
Dale Hunter, President/Head Coach
Geoffrey Hare, Director Marketing
Mark Hunter, Vice President/General Manager
Jim McKellar, Assistant General Manager
Misha Donskov, Assistant Coach
Home Ice:
John Labatt Centre

Mississauga St. Michael's Majors
5500 ROSE CHERRY PLACE
MISSISSAUGA, ON L4Z 4B6
905-502-7788
Fax: 905-502-0169
administration@majors.ca
www.stmichaelsmajors.com
Roger Lajoie, Executive Vice-President
Rick Radovski, Vice-President, Marketing and Sales
James Boyd, General Manager/ Head Coach
Kelly Harper, Assistant General Manager/ Assistant Coach
Brad May, Assistant Coach
Home Ice:
Hershey Centre

Oshawa Generals
99 ATHOL STREET EAST
OSHAWA, ON L1H IJ8
905-433-0900
Fax: 905-433—0868
admin@oshawagenerals.com
www.oshawagenerals.com
Rocco Tullio, President/ Governor
John McMahon, Vice President/ Governor
Chris DePiero, General Manager/ Head Coach
Duncan Stauth, VP of Business Operations
Joe Cirella, Assistant GM/Assistant Head Coach
Mark Fitzgerald, Sports Conditioning Coach
Bryan Boyes, Head Trainer
Home Ice:
Civic Auditorium

Ottawa 67's
LANSDOWNE PARK
1015 BANK STREET
OTTAWA, ON K1S 3W7
613-232-6767
Fax: 613-232-5582
ottawa67s@chl.ca
www.ottawa67s.com
Jeff Hunt, Governor & Team Owner
Patrick Whalen, President/ CEO
Randy Burgress, Vice-President
Chris Byrne, Head Coach/ General Manager
Larry Skinner, Assistant Coach
Bobby Brooks, Assistant Coach
Neil Hoch, Head Trainer
Home Ice:
Ottawa Civic Centre

Owen Sound Attack
1900 THIRD AVENUE EAST
OWEN SOUND N4K 2M6
519-371-7452
Fax: 519-371-7990
attack@bmts.com
www.attackhockey.com
Bob Severs, Owner/President
Dale DeGray, General Manager
Ray McKelvie, Business Manager
Brent Fisher, Director of Marketing and Public Relations
Greg Ireland, Head Coach
Terry Virtue, Assistant Coach
Andy Brown, Head Trainer
Home Ice:
Harry Lumley Bayshore Community Centre

Peterborough Petes
151 LANDSDOWNE STREET WEST
PETERBOROUGH, ON K9J 1Y4
705-743-3681
Fax: 705-743-5497
petes@gopetesgo.com
www.gopetesgo.com
Jim Devlin, President
David Reid, General Manager
Aaron Garfat, Director Marketing/Public Relations
Jeff Twohey, General Manager
(705)743-3681
jtwohey@gopetesgo.com
Pete Dalliday, Ticket Sales Account Executive
Mike Pelino, Head Coach
Jody Hull, Assistant Coach
Brian Miller, Head Trainer
Home Ice:
Peterborough Memorial Centre

Sarina Sting
1455 LONDON ROAD
SARNIA, ON N7S 6K7
519-542-4494
Fax: 519-542-2388
info@sarniasting.com
www.sarniasting.com
Robert Ciccarelli, Governor/ Owner
Larry Ciccarelli, President/ Owner
Bill Abercrombie, VP of Operations
Dean Collver, Director Business Operations
Jacques Beaulie, Head Coach/ General Manager
Trevor Letowski, Associate Coach
Larry Lucas, Goaltending Coach
Chad Oliver, Head Trainer
Home Ice:
Sarnia Sports Entertainment Centre

Sault Ste. Marie Greyhounds
269 QUEEN STREET EAST
SAULT STE. MARIE, ON P6A 1Y9
705-253-5976
Fax: 705-945-9458
info@soogreyhounds.com
www.soogreyhounds.com
Lou Lukenda, President
Gerry Liscumb, Director of Public Relations
Kyle Dubas, General Manager
Mike Stapleton, Head Coach
Nick Warriner, Assistant Coach
Seamus Kotyk, Assistant Coach
Lorne Robinson, Equipment Manager
Home Ice:
Sault Memorial Gardens

Sudbury Wolves
240 ELGIN STREET SOUTH
SUDBURY, ON P3E 3N6
705-675-3941
Fax: 705-675-3944
info@sudburywolves.com
www.sudburywolves.com
Blaine Smith, President/ General Manager
Mark Burgess, Chairman/ CEO
Trent Cull, Head Coach
Ken MacKenzie, Assistant General Manager
Jeff Buekeboom, Assistant Coach
Home Ice:
Sudbury Community Arena

Quebec Major Junior Hockey League

1205 AMPERE
SUITE 101
BOUCHERVILLE, QC J4B 7M6
450-650-0500
Fax: 450-650-0510
hockey@lhjmq.qc.ca
www.lhjmq.qc.ca

Gilles Courteau, Commissioner
Marcel Patenaude, Executive Vice- President
Richard Trottier, Director Officiating
Photi Sotiropoulos, Director Communications
Pierre Leduc, Director Hockey Operations
Description:
Member of Canadian Hockey League.

Teams:

Acadie-Bathurst Titan
850 ST. ANNE STREET
BATHURST, NB E2A 6X2
506-549-3300
Fax: 506-549-3355
letitan@nbnet.nb.ca
www.letitan.com
Earl Dimitroff, Director Marketing
Sylvain Courturier, General Manager
Eric Dubois, Head Coach
Gianni Cantini, Assistant Coach
Nathan Belliveau, Head Trainer
Home Ice:
K.C. Irving Regional Centre

Baie-Comeau Drakkar
70 AVENUE MICHEL-HŠMON
BAIE-COMEAU G4Z 2A5
418-296-2522
Fax: 418-296-0011
drakkar@globetrotter.net
www.le-drakkar.com
Patrice Jean, Owner
Raymond Cote, Owner
Sylvie Fortier, Owner
Michel Beaulieu, Owner/President
Steve Ahern, General Manager
Dennis Francoeur, Assistant General Manager
Mario Pouliot, Head Coach
Mathieu Gravel, Assistant Coach
Home Ice:
Henry Leonard Center

Chicoutimi Sagueneens
643 BEGIN
C.P. 323
CHICOUTIMI, QC G7H 5C2
418-549-9489
Fax: 418-549-1645
sagueneens@videotron.ca
www.sagueneens.com
Marc Fortier, General Manager
Carl Bouchard, Assistant General Manager
Marc-Etienne Hubert, Head Coach
Mario Durocher, Assistant Coach

Drummondville Voltigeurs
300 COCKBURN STREET
DRUMMONDVILLE, PQ J2C 4L6
819-477-9400
Fax: 819-477-0561
info@voltigeurs.ca
www.voltigeurs.ca
Louis Brousseau, Governor
Dominic Ricard, General Manager
Mario Duhamel, Head Coach
Dennis Gauthier, Assistant Coach
Alain Couturier, Head Trainer
Home Ice:
Centre Marcel Dionne

Gatineau Olympiques
STATION HULL
125 CARILLON STREET
PO BOX 1251
GATINEAU, QC J8X 3X7
819-777-0661
Fax: 819-777-6933
hockey@olympiquesdegatineau.ca
www.olympiquesdegatineau.ca
Alain Sear, Governor
Daniel Brunet, Marketing Director
Benoit Groulx, Manager/Head Coach
Guy Lalonde, Assistant Coach
Jonathan Carrier, Assistant Coach
Michel Valliere, Goaltenders Coach
Serge Hache, Head Trainer
Home Ice:
Robert Gatineau Arena

Moncton Wildcats
100 MIDLAND DRIVE
DIEPPE, NB E1A 6X4
506-382-5555
Fax: 506-858-2222
www.moncton-wildcats.com
Jean Brousseau, Governor
Andrew Benson, Marketing Manager
Jeff Rose, General Manager
Danny Flynn, Director of Hockey Operations/Head Coach
Fabien Joseph, Associate Coach
Darryl Seward, Assistant Coach
Home Ice:
Moncton Coliseum

Quebec Remparts
250 WILFRID HAMEL
QUEBEC, QC G1L 5A7
418-525-1212
Fax: 418-525-2242
info@remparts.qc.ca
www.remparts.qc.ca
Julien Gagnon, Governor
Claude Rousseau, President
Lucie Cloutier, Director Communications/Marketing
Myriam Raby, Controller
Louis Painchaud, Vice President Operations
Roy Patrick, General Manager
Martin Laperriere, Assistant Coach
Gabriel Hardy, Head Trainer
Home Ice:
Colisee Pepsi

Rimouski Oceanic
111 2ND STREET WEST
PO BOX 816
RIMOUSKI, QC G5L 7C9
418-723-4444
Fax: 418-725-0944
hockey@oceanic.qc.ca
www.oceanic.qc.ca
Camille Leblanc, Governor
Henri Martin, President
Phillipoe Boucher, General Manager
Andre Jolicoeur, Hockey Operations Manager
Yannick Dumais, Assistant General Manager
Serge Beausoleil, Head Coach
Daniel Renaud, Assistant Coach
Donald Dufresne, Assistant Coach
Francis St-Pierre, Head Trainer
Home Ice:
Rimouski Coliseum

Rouyn-Noranda Huskies
218 MURDOCH AVENUE
ROUYN-NORANDA, QC J9X 1E6
819-797-3022
Fax: 819-797-4311
admin@huskies.qc.ca
www.huskies.qc.ca
Pierre Cloutier, Governor
Jacques Blais, President
Andre Tourigny, General Manager/Head Coach
Connor Cameron, Assistant Coach
Marc Lafleur, Assistant Coach
Mathieu Roussel, Head Trainer
Home Ice:
Dave Keon Arena

Saint John Sea Dogs
99 STATION STREET
SUITE 200
SAINT JOHN, NB E2L 4X4
506-657-3647
Fax: 506-696-0611
info@saintjohnseadogs.com
www.saintjohnseadogs.com
Wayne Long, President
Mike McGraw, Vice President
Scott McCain, Chief Executive Officer
Gerard Gallant, Head Coach
Yvon Vautour, Assistant Coach
Mike Kelly, Director of Hockey Operations
Home Ice:
Harbour Station

Shawinigan Cataractes
855 BROADWAY
SHAWINIGAN, QC G9N 8B8
819-537-6327
Fax: 819-537-3538
www.cataractes.qc.ca
Mario Clermont, Governor
Martin Mondou, General Manager
Louis Caron, President
Roger Shannon, Assistant General Manager
boisvert.michel@cataractes.qc.ca
Eric Veilleux, Head Coach
Alain Petit, Assistant Coach
Patrick Leonard, Head Trainer
Home Ice:
Arena Jacques-Plante

Val D'Or Foreurs
810 6TH AVENUE
VAL-D'OR, QC J9P 1B4
819-824-0093
Fax: 819-824-7602
www.foreurs.qc.ca
Glenn J. Mullan, Governor
Louis Blanchette, President
Stephane Pilotte, Director Hockey Operations
Marc-Andre Dumont, Head Coach
Mario Carriere, General Manager
Joey Bucci, Assistant Coach
Maxime Paquin, Head Trainer
Home Ice:
Palais des Sports

Victoriaville Tigers
400 JUTRAS BOULEVARD EAST
PO BOX 857
VICTORIAVILLE, QC G6P 7W7
819-752-6353
Fax: 819-758-2846
www.tigersvictoriaville.com
Jean Marcotte, Governor
Eric Bernier, President
Patrick Villeneuve, Director Finance
Alain Danault, Director Marketing/Media Relations
(819)752-6353
Jerome Mesonero, General Manager
Yannick Jean, Head Coach
Simon Olivier, Assistant Coach
Patrick Villenueve, Head Trainer
Home Ice:
Colisee des Bois-Francs

Western Hockey League
1 - 3030 SUNRIDGE WAY NE
CALGARY, AB T1Y 7K4
403-693-3030
Fax: 403-693-3031
info@whl.ca
www.whl.ca
Ed Chynoweth, Chairman
Ron Robison, Commissioner
Cory Flett, Director Communications
Yvonne Bergmann, VP Operations
Kevin Muench, Director Officiating
Richard Doerksen, Vice President Hockey
Jim Donlevy, Director, Education Services

Teams:

Brandon Wheat Kings
1175 - 18 STREET
SUITE 2
BRANDON, MB R7A 7C5
204-726-3535
Fax: 204-726-3540
office@wheatkings.com
www.wheatkings.com
Kelly McCrimmon, General Manager/ Governor
Rick Dillabough, Director of Sales and Marketing
Al MacPherson, Director of Player Personnel
Cory Clouston, Head Coach
Darren Ritchie, Assistant Coach
Grant Ammann, Athletic Trainer
Home Ice:
Keystone Arena

Calgary Hitmen
PO BOX 1540
STATION M
CALGARY, AB T2P 3B9
403-571-2200
Fax: 403-571-2211
info@hitmenhockey.com
www.hitmenhockey.com
Ken King, Governor/President/CEO
Kelly Kisio, Director Marketing
Mike Moore, Director of Business Operations
Kelly Kisio, General Manager/ Executive VP/ Alternate Governor
Joel Otto, Assistant Coach
Mike Williamson, Head Coach
Home Ice:
Pengrowth Saddledome

Edmonton Oil Kings
11230- 110 STREET
EDMONTON, AB T5B 1Z7
780-409-3700
Fax: 780-409-3701
www.oilkings.ca
Patrick LaForge, Governor
Darryl Porter, Vice President
Bob Green, General Manager
Jordi Weidman, Director of Business Operations
Derek Laxdal, Head Coach
Home Ice:
Rexall Place

Kamloops Blazers
300 MARK RECCHI WAY
KAMLOOPS, BC V2C 1W1
250-828-1144
Fax: 250-828-7822
info@blazerhockey.com
www.blazerhockey.com
Murray Owen, President
Craig Bonner, General Manager
Matt Recchi, Director Player Personnel
Guy Charron, Head Coach
Dave Hunchak, Associate Coach
Home Ice:
Interior Savings Centre

Kelowna Rockets
#101-1223 WATER STREET
KELOWNA, BC V1Y 9V1
250-860-7825
Fax: 250-860-7880
info@kelownarockets.com
www.kelownarockets.com
Bruce Hamilton, Governor/President/GM
(250)860-7825
info@kelownarockets.com
Anthony Campese, Media Relations/Promotions
(250)860-7825
anthonyc@kelownarockets.com
Lorne Frey, Asst GM/Director Player Personnel
(250)860-7825
lornef@kelownarockets.com
Ryan Huska, Head Coach
Dan Lambert, Assistant Coach
Kim Dillabaugh, Assistant Coach
Scott Hoyer, Strength Coach/Head Trainer
Home Ice:
Prospera Place

Kootenay Ice
#2 - 1777 2ND STREET NORTH
CRANBROOK, BC V1C 7G9
250-417-0322
Fax: 250-417-0323
info@kootenayice.net
www.kootenayice.net
Jeff Chynoweth, President/General Manager
Kris Knoblauch, Head Coach
Todd Johnson, Assistant Coach
Jerry Bancks, Assistant Coach
Tiffany Harris-Johnson, Director of Marketing
Home Ice:
Cranbrook Rec Plex

Lethbridge Hurricanes
ENMAX CENTRE
2510 SCENIC DRIVE S
LETHBRIDGE, AB T1K 7V7
403-328-1986
Fax: 403-329-1622
info@lethbridgehurricanes.com
www.lethbridgehurricanes.com
Herman Elfring, Governor
Don Clark, President
Rick Preston, General Manager/ Head Coach
Brad Robson, Assistant General Manager
Matt Kabayama, Assistant Coach
Home Ice:
Enmax Center

Medicine Hat Tigers
155 ASH AVENUE SE
MEDICINE HAT, AB T1A 7G2
403-526-2666
Fax: 403-526-3072
admin@tigershockey.com
www.tigershockey.com
Darrell Maser, Governor/President
Brent Maser, Vice President
Dave Andjelic, Director of Marketing/Public Relations
Brad McEwen, General Manager
Shaun Clouston, Head Coach
Darren Kruger, Assistant Coach
Home Ice:
The Arena

Prince Albert Raiders
690 - 32ND STREET EAST
PRINCE ALBERT, SK S6V 2W8
306-764-4263
Fax: 306-764-5454
info@raiderhockey.com
www.raiderhockey.com
Dale McFee, President
Bruce Vance, Marketing Director
Bruno Campese, General Manager/ Head Coach
Steve Young, Assistant General Manager/ Assistant Coach
Craig Bedard, Assistant Coach
Home Ice:
Art Hauser Centre

Prince George Cougars
#102 2187 OSPIKA BOULEVARD SOUTH
PRINCE GEORGE, BC V2N 6Z1
250-561-0783
Fax: 250-561-0743
cougars@mag-net.com
www.pgcougars.com
Rick Brodsky, President
rbrodksy@mag-net.com
Brandi Brodsky, Vice President
Wade Klippenstein, Director of Player Personnel
Dean Clark, Head Coach
Brent Arsenault, Assistant Coach
Ramandeep Singh Dhanjal, Head Trainer
Dallas Thompson, General Manager
dallas@mag-net.com
Home Ice:
CN Center

Red Deer Rebels
4847C-19 STREET
RED DEER, AB T4R 2N7
403-341-6000
Fax: 403-341-6009
rebels@telusplanet.net
www.reddeerrebels.com
Brent Sutter, Owner/ President
bsutter@reddeerrebels.com
Jesse Wallin, Vice-President Hockey Operations/ Head Coach
Bryce Thoma, Assistant Coach
Chris Neiszner, Assistant Coach
Dave Horning, Head Trainer
Home Ice:
Enmax Centrium

Saskatoon Blades
201-3515 THATCHER AVENUE
SASKATOON, SK S7R 1C4
306-975-8844
Fax: 306-934-1097
info@saskatoonblades.com
www.saskatoonblades.com
Jack Brodsky, Owner/President/Governor
Mike Jenkins, Director of Business Operation
Lorne Molleken, General Manager/Head Coach
Dave Struch, Associate Coach
Steve Hildebrand, Head Trainer
Home Ice:
Credit Union Centre

Vancouver Giants
100 NORTH RENFREW STREET
VANCOUVER, BC V5K 3N7
604-444-2687
Fax: 604-254-2687
info@vancouvergiants.com
www.vancouvergiants.com
Ron Toigo, Owner
Sultan Thiara, Owner
Pat Quinn, Owner
Gordie Howe, Owner
Colleen Howe, Owner
Jason Ripplinger, Director Player Personnel
Paul Lucrezi, Vice President Marketing/Sales
Scott Bonner, General Manager
Don Hay, Head Coach
Glen Hanlon, Assistant Coach
Ian Gallagher, Strength Coach
Paul Fricker, Goaltending Consultant
Nick Murray, Athletic Trainer
Home Ice:
Pacific Coliseum

Victoria Royals
1925 BLANSHARD STREET
VICTORIA, BC V8T 4J2
250-220-2600
info@vicwhl.com
www.vicwhl.com
Marc Habscheid, General Manager/ Head Coach
Home Ice:
Save-On-Foods Memorial Centre

Lacrosse, Leagues/Teams

National Lacrosse League
53 WEST 36TH STREET
SUITE 406
NEW YORK, NY 10018
212-764-1390
Fax: 917-510-9890
comments@nll.com
www.nll.com
Jim Jennings, Commissioner
Brian Lemon, VP Operations
Matt Miller, Marketing Director
Doug Fritts, VP Communications
George Daniel, Deputy Commissioner/Chief Operating Officer
Description:
Founded 1997. Professional Indoor Lacrosse League.

Teams:

Calgary Roughnecks
555 SADDLEDOME RISE SE
CALGARY, ALBERTA T2G 2W1
403-777-4646
Fax: 403-777-3695
info@calgaryroughnecks.com
www.calgaryroughnecks.com
Ken King, President/CEO
John Bean, Governor/ CFO
Mike Board, General Manager
Dave Pym, Head Coach
Description:
Arena: Pengrowth Saddledome.

Edmonton Rush
137 TURBO DRIVE
SHERWOOD PARK, ALBERTA T8H 2J6
780-732-7874
Fax: 780-467-7854
info@edmontonrush.com
www.edmontonrush.com
Bruce Urban, Owner/Governor
Gord Sawyer, President
Derek Keenan, Head Coach/ General Manager

Toronto Rock
416 NORTH SERVICE ROAD EAST
SUITE 100
OAKVILLE L6H 5R2
416-596-3075
855-665-7625
Fax: 905-339-3473
info@torontorock.com
www.torontorock.com
Jamie Dawick, President
bwatters@torontorock.com
Terri Giberson, Business Manager
Troy Cordingley, Head Coach

Soccer, Leagues/Teams

Canadian Professional Soccer League
5160 EXPLORER DRIVE
MISSISSAUGA, ON L4W 4T7
905-564-2297
888-216-9913
Fax: 905- 671-6450
info@canadiansoccerleague.com
www.canadiansoccerleague.com

Vincent Ursini, Chairman
Pino Jazbec, League Administrator
Stan Adamson, Director of Media
Tony Camacho, Director of Officials

Teams:

Brampton City United
8820 JANE STREET
VAUGHAN, ON L4K 2M9
647-999-8484
Fax: 905-760-2820
www.bramptoncityutd.ca

Brantford Galaxy
245 KING GEORGE ROAD
SUITE 308
BRANTFORD,ON N3R 7N7
519-865-7827
brantfordgalaxy@hotmail.com
www.brantfordgalaxy.com
Bosko Borjan, President
Gerry Crnic, Managing Director
Lazo Dzepina, Head Coach

London City
PO BOX 125
STATION B
LONDON N6A 4V6
519-630-8138
Fax: 519-438-4625
info@londoncity.ca
www.londoncity.ca
Markus Gauss, President
Ryan Gauss, CEO/VP/General Manager
Luka Shaqiri, Head Coach

Montreal Impact Academy
4750 SHERBROOKE EST
MONTREAL, QC H1V 3S8
514-328-3668
Fax: 514-328-1287
info@impactmontreal.com
www.montrealimpact.com
Philippe Eullaffroy, Head Coach
Olivier Brett, Assistant Coach

North York Astros
1589 WESTON ROAD
TORONTO, ON M9N 1T4
416-240-1718
Fax: 416-240-1648
astros@northyorkastros.ca
www.northyorkastros.ca
Bruno Ierullo, General Manager
Jorge Collazo, Director of Football

Sc Toronto
964 THE QUEENSWAY
TORONTO, ON M6H 1A2
416-815-5400
Fax: 416-815-5452
pfcsoccerclub@gmail.com
www.sctoronto.ca
Jimmy Carvalho, General Manager
Carmine Isacco, Head Coach
Patrice Gheisar, Assistant Coach

Serbian White Eagles Fc
30 TITAN ROAD
UNIT #15
TORONTO, ON M8Z 5Y2
416-252-4762
dragan@serbianwhiteeagles.ca
www.serbianwhiteeagles.ca
Dragan Bakoc, President
dragan@serbianwhiteeagles.ca
Mario Ostojic, Sports Director
Dusko Prijic, Head Coach

St Catharines Wolves
125 VANSICKLE ROAD
P.O. Box 26006 Glendale Ave.
ST. CATHERINES, ON L2S 3X5
905-682-7621
Fax: 905-682-8811
Armand Di Fruscio, General Manager
Armand Di Fruscio, General Manager
James McGillivray, Head Coach

Tfc Academy
170 PRINCES' BLVD
TORONTO ONTARIO M6K 3C3
416-815-5400
Fax: 416-815-5452
www.torontofc.ca/academy
Stuart Neely, General Manager/ Head Coach
Anthony Capotosto, Assistant Coach

Toronto Croatia
89 QUEEN STREET S
MISSISSAUGA, ON L5M 2K7
905-812-7868
Fax: 905-828-7753
jzaradic@sympatico.ca
www.torontocroatia.com
Joe Pavicic, President
Ivan Kulis, General Manager
Arapovic Pero, Head Coach
Alen Vukobrad, Assistant Coach

Windsor Stars
700 ERIE ST E
WINDSOR, ON N9A 3Y2
519-818-6696
Fax: 519-252-9202
info@starsprosoccer.com
www.starsprosoccer.com
Filip Rocca, President
Joseph Giorgi, Director of Operations
Mike Mesic, General Manager
Steve Vagnini, Head Coach

Major League Soccer
110 E. 42ND ST, 10TH FLoor
NEW YORK, NY 10017
212-450-1200
Fax: 212-450-1300
feedback@mlssoccer.com
www.mlssocer.com

Don Garber, Commissioner
Mark Abbott, President
Kathy Carter, President, Soccer United Marketing

Teams:

Montreal Impact
STADE SAPUTO
4750 SHERBROOKE EST
MONTREAL, QC H1V 3S8
514-328-3668
Fax: 514-328-1287
info@impactmontreal.com
www.montrealimpact.com
Joey Saputo, President
(514)328-3668
Rochard Legendre, Executive Vice-President
(514)328-3668
John Di Terlizzi, Vice President Corporate Sales
(514)328-3668
Patrick Vallee, Director of Communications
(514)328-3668
Jesse Marsch, Head Coach
Teams:
Pro, U21, U16, U15, U14
Home Field:
Saputo Stadium

Toronto Fc
BMO FIELD
170 PRINCES' BLVD
TORONTO, ON M6K 3C3
416-360-4625
www.torontofc.ca
Paul Beirne, Business Operations Director
Earl Cochrane, Team Operations Director
Aron Winter, Head Coach
Cesar Velasco, Director, Marketing & Communications

Vancouver Whitecaps Fc
375 WATER STREET
SUITE 550
VANCOUVER, BC V6B 5C6
604-669-9283
604-684-5173
info@whitecapsfc.com
www.whitecapsfc.com
Bob Lenarduzzi, President
Paul Barber, CEO
Roberto Cabrone, Director of Sales
Tom Soehn, Director of Soccer Operations
Martin Rennie, Head Coach

United Soccer Leagues
1715 N WESTSHORE BLVD
STE 825
TAMPA, FL 33607
813-963-3909
Fax: 813-963-3807
www.uslsoccer.com

Francisco Marcos, Senior Director
Tim Holt, President
Jay Preble, Director Public Relations

Teams:

Hamilton Avalanche
1185 STONE CHURCH ROAD E
HAMILTON, ON L8W 2C6
905-388-3203
Fax: 905-388-0711
Valdi Greco, CEO
(905)389-5090
valdigreco@hamiltonavalanche.com
Stefan Avramovic, Coach
(905)923-0811
stefan_0707@hotmail.com

Laval Comets
955 AVENUE BOIS-DE-BOULOGNE
LAVAL, QC H7N 4G1
450-945-8639
Fax: 450-975-4977
Philippe Ciarlo, General Manager
Mohamed Hilen, Head Coach
Mohamed Hilen, Head Coach

Lyndon Gryphons
75 GREENBRIER CRESCENT
LONDON ON N6J 3X7
519-473-5880
Fax: 519-681-7050
Aaron Lauterbach, General Manager
atlauterbach@gmail.com

Ottawa Fury
458 MACLAREN STREET
FLOOR 2
OTTAWA ON K1R 5K6
613-235-3879
Fax: 613-567-3879
www.ottawafury.com
John Pugh, Owner/CEO
Melanie Rutherford, Director of Operations
Klaus Linnenbruegger, Head Coach

Quebec City Amiral
1173 BOUL
CHAREST OUEST BUR 350
QUEBEC G1N 2C9
Maxime Barabe, General Manager
mbarabe@admiealdequebec.com
Fabien Cottin, Head Coach
fcottin@admiealdequebec.com

Toronto Lady Lynx
100 WESTMORE DRIVE
SUITE 8
TORONTO, ON M9V 5C3
416-251-4625
Fax: 416-946-1899
lynx@lynxsoccer.com
www.lynxsoccer.com
Danny Stewart, Head Coach

Women's Tackle Football

Independent Women's Football League/IWFL
PO Box 1844
Round Rock, TX 78680
512-215-4238
Fax: 866-482-1342
info@iwflsports.com
www.iwflsports.com

Laurie Frederick, President/CEO
Kezia Disney, Chief Operating Officer
Kim Hampson, Vice President of Administration
Description:
A full tackle women's football league focused on creating a fun, safe and positive atmosphere for the players and fans. It was founded in 2000, and currently has over 51 teams in North America. The IWFL enables its members to function independently while providing a stable organization to draw from and combine resources for the promotion of women's football.

Teams:

Montreal Blitz
MONTREAL
866-612-5489
montrealblitz@gmail.com
www.montrealblitz.ca
Saadia Ashraf, President
Jessee Lebouc, General Manager
Home Field:
Dalbe-Viau, Lachine

Facilities

Arenas & Stadiums

Air Canada Centre
50 BAY STREET
SUITE 500
TORONTO, ON M5J 2X2
416-815-5500
Fax: 416-359-9332
www.theaircanadacentre.com
Beth Robertson, Marketing Vice President
Tom Anselmi, Executive Vice President/ COO
Richard Peddie, President/ CEO
Year Founded:
1999
Seating Capacity:
Basketball-19,800; Hockey-18,800; Concerts-19,800; Theatre-5,200; also 1020 Club Seats, 40 Platinum Lounges, 65 Executive Suites, and 32 Theatre Suites.
Tenant(s):
NBA - Toronto Raptors basketball, NHL - Toronto Maple Leafs hockey, NLL - Toronto Rock lacrosse.

Bc Place Stadium
777 PACIFIC BOULEVARD
VANCOUVER, BC V6B 4Y8
604-669-2300
Fax: 604-661-3412
stadium@bcpavco.com
www.bcplacestadium.com
Crosley Howard, General Manager
Brian Griffin, Director of Construction
Graham Ramsay, Director, Business Development Division
Harvey Repp, Director of Operations
Seating Capacity:
60,000
Description:
Future host of the 2010 Winter olympic Games Opening/Closing Ceremonies.

Bell Centre
1909 AVENUE DES CANADIENS-DE-MONTREAL
MONTREAL, QC H4B 5G0
514-932-2582
800-663-6786
Fax: 514-989-2871
services@bellcentre.ca
www.bellcentre.ca

Tenant(s):
NHL - Montreal Canadiens Hockey, NLL - Montreal Express Lacrosse.
Permanent Seating Capacity:
21,500

Colisee Pepsi De Quebec
250 BOULEVARD WILFRID-HAMEL
QUEBEC G1L 5A7
418-691-7110
888-866-3976
Fax: 418-691-7249
info@expocite.com
www.expocite.com

Bruno St-Onge, Manager, Operations
Mark Sparrow, General Manager
Arena Seating Capacity:
15,399.00
Year Founded:
1950

Commonwealth Stadium
11000 STADIUM ROAD
PO BOX 2359
EDMONTON, AB T5J 2R7
780-944-7561
Fax: 780-944-7545

Evelyn Ehrman, Director
Seating Capacity:
67,606
Taam:
University of Kentucky football.
Playing Field:
Grass
Teams:
Edmonton Eskimos

Edmonton Coliseum
PO BOX 1480
EDMONTON, AB T5J 2N5
780-471-7210
888-800-7275
Fax: 780-471-8176
info@northlands.com
www.northlands.com

Richard Andersen, President
Opal Blackstock, Vice President/Program Development
Sharilee Fossum, Chief Executive Officer
Permanent Seating Capacity:
17,099
Permanent Seating Capacity:
17,099
Facility:
Edmonton Coliseum.
Facility:
Edmonton Coliseum.

Exhibition Place
200 PRINCES' BOULEVARD
TORONTO, ON M6K 3C3
416-263-3600
Fax: 416-263-3029
info@explace.on.ca
www.explace.on.ca

Joe R Pantalone, Chair
Laura Purdy, Director of Sales & Marketing
Stadium Seating Capacity:
55,000
Arena Seating Capacity:
5,777

Frank Clair Stadium In Lansdowne Park
1015 BANK STREET
OTTAWA, ON K1S 3W7
613-580-2429
Fax: 613-564-1619
lansdowne@ottawa.ca
www.lansdownepark.ca

Richard Haycock, General Manager
Mark Hennigar, Facilities Operations Manager
Kay Boland, Event Coordinator
Seating Capacity:
30,927
Playing Surface:
Artificial
Description:
Host of the 92nd Grey Cup and the FIFA U-20 World Cup Soccer.

Harbour Station
99 STATION STREET
SAINT JOHN, NB E2L 4X4
506-632-6103
Fax: 506-632-6121
mail@harbourstation.nb.ca
www.harbourstation.nb.ca

Michael Caddell, General Manager
(506)632-6103
Ewan Cameron, Operations Director
(506)632-6167
Brenda Lee, Box Office Manager
(506)648-4668

Independent Telus Field
1023396 AVENUE NW
EDMONTON, AB T5K 0A5

Sport:
Baseball.
Team:
Edmonton Prospects.
Year Founded:
1995
Capacity:
9,200

John Labatt Centre
99 DUNDAS STREET
LONDON, ON N6A 6K1
519-667-5700
Fax: 519-432-3386
info@johnlabattcentre.com
www.johnlabattcentre.com

Brian Ohl, General Manager
Chris Campbell, Marketing Director
ccampbell@johnlabattcentre.com
Gary Turrell, Operations Director
(519)667-5704
gturrell@johnlabattcentre.com
Arena Seating Capacity:
10,000.00
Year Founded:
2002
Clients:
Harlem Globetrotters, Stars on Ice, US Hot Rod Monster Jam, Sesame Street, Disney on Ice, various concerts.
Nature of Service:
Multi-purpose Sports, Entertainment Facility.

Landsdowne Park
1015 BANK STREET
OTTAWA, ON K1S 3W7
613-580-2429
Fax: 613-564-1619
lansdowne@ottawa.ca
www.lansdownepark.ca

Richard Haycock, General Manager
(613)580-2428
richard.haycock@ottawa.ca

Arena Seating Capacity:
10,000
Stadium Seating Capacity:
30,000

McMahon Stadium
1817 CROWCHILD TRAIL NW
CALGARY, AB T2M 4R6

403-282-2044
Fax: 403-282-2018
mcmahonstadium@shaw.ca
www.mcmahonstadium.ca

John Haverstock, Manager
Year Opened:
1960
Seating Capacity:
36,000 permanent with 10,000 additional seats available.
Description:
Home to the Calgary Stampeders and the University of Calgary Dinos.
Events:
Held the opening and closing ceremonies of the 1988 Olympic Winter Games. Opening ceremonies of the 1997 World Police/Fire Games. CFL Grey Cup Championship games in 1975, 1993, and 2000.

Molson Stadium
475 PINE AVENUE WEST
MONTREAL, QC H2W 1S4

514-398-7000
Fax: 514-398-4901
athletics@mcgill.ca
athletics.mcgill.ca

Phil Quintal, Facilities Manager
(514)398-7000
Eyal Baruch, Assistant Manager - Events
(514)398-7017
Playing Surface:
FieldTurf
Description:
Also known as the Pervical Molson Memorial Stadium

Mosaic Stadium At Taylor Field
1910 PIFFES TAYLOR WAY
REGINA, SK S4P 3E1

306-569-2323
Fax: 306-566-4299
www.saskriders.com

Robert Pletch, Director
Seating Capacity:
30,945
Playing Surface:
Field Turf
Teams:
Saskatchewan Roughriders, Regina Rams High School Football, University of Regina Rams (CIS) and the Regina Thunder (Canadian Junior Football League).

Mts Centre
260 HARGRAVE STREET
WINNIPEG, MB R3C 555

204-987-7825
888-626-6673
Fax: 204-926-5555
info@truenorth.mb.ca
www.mtscentre.ca

Jim Ludlow, President/CEO
Kevin Donnely, VP & General Manager, MTS Centre
Craig Heisinger, General Manager, Manitoba Moose Hockey Club
Seating Capacity:
15,015
Year Founded:
2004
Owned By:
True North Sports & Entertainment Limited
Tenants:
Manitoba Moose Hockey Club (AHL)

Olympic Stadium
4141 PIERRE-DE COUBERTIN AVENUE
MONTREAL, QC H1V 3N7

514-252-4141
Fax: 514-252-4440
rio@rio.gouv.qc.ca
www.rio.gouv.qc.ca

David Heurtel, Chief Executive Officer
Suzanne Audet, President
Stadium Seating Capacity:
66,000
Year Founded:
1976

Ottawa Baseball Stadium
300 COVENTRY ROAD
OTTAWA, ON K1K 4P5

613-749-2020
Fax: 613-747-0003
info@ottawafatcats.com
www.ottawafatcats.com

Brian Carolan, President
Duncan MacDonald, General Manager
Seating Capacity
10,332
Year Founded:
1993
Track Type
Natural grass
Track Size
325 feet LF and RF, 404 feet CF

Pacific Coliseum
2901 E HASTING STREET
VANCOUVER, BC V5K 5J1

604-253-2311
Fax: 604-251-7768
info@pne.ca
www.pne.bc.ca

Michael McDaniel, President/Chief Executive Officer
Peter Male, Sales VP
(604)251-7787
peterm@pne.bc.ca
Shelley Frost, Marketing Vice President
Arena Seating Capacity:
17,300
Clients:
Boys Basketball, Old Timers Hockey, Slam City Jam.
Nature of Service:
Ice Hockey Services, Catering, Event Concessions, Arena Configurations, Video, Scoreboard.
Tenant(s):
Vancouver Giants, Western Hockey League.
Description:
The Official Venue for Short Track Speed Skating and Figure Skating during the 2010 Olympic Winter Games.

Scotiabank Saddledome
555 SADDLEDOME RISE SE
CALGARY, AB T2G 2W1

403-777-4646
Fax: 403-777-3695
saddledome@calgaryflames.com
www.scotiabanksaddledome.com

Libby Raines, Vice-President, Building Operations
Garry McKenzie, Marketing VP
George Greenwood, Operations Manager
John Vidalin, Advertising/Promotions Director
Owned by:
Calgary Flames Ltd. Partnership (20 year lease from Saddledome Foundation, City of Calgary).
Teams:
NHL - Calgary Flames hockey; NLL - Calgary Roughnecks lacrosse; WHL - Calgary Hitmen hockey.
Permanent Seating Capacity:
18,800
Teams:
NHL Calgary Flames, WHL Calgary Hitmen, NLL Calgary Roughnecks

Rexall Place
7424 118TH AVENUE
EDMONTON, AB T5B 4M9

780-471-7210
888-800-7275
Fax: 780-471-8195
www.rexall-place.com

Daryl Katz, Chairman
Seating Capacity:
17,100

Ricoh Coliseum
100 PRINCES BOULEVARD
EXHIBITION PLACE
TORONTO, ON M6K 3C3

416-263-3900
Fax: 416-263-3901
www.ricohcoliseum.com

Vince Bozzo, General Manager
(416)263-5705
vbozzo@mapleleafsports.com
Nathalie Burri, Event Services Manager
(416)263-3916
nburri@mapleleafsports.com
Food & Beverage:
Centerplate Inc.
Management Firm:
O&Y/SMG Canada
Permanent Seating Capacity:
10,000
Tenant(s):
AHL - Toronto Marlies.

General Motors Place
800 GRIFFITHS WAY
VANCOUVER, BC V6B 6G1

604-899-7400
Fax: 604-899-7490
www.rogersarena.com

Harvey Jones, VP/General Manager Arena Operations
(604)899-7459
harvey.jones@canucks.com
Indira Fisher, Event Services Director
(604)899-7544
indira.fisher@canucks.com
Tenant(s):
NHL - Vancouver Canucks
Seating Capacity:
Stadium/Arena: 18,810; Event: 20,000

Rogers Centre
ONE BLUE JAYS WAY
TORONTO, ON M5V 1J1

416-341-3000
Fax: 416-341-3101
guestservices@rogerscentre.com
www.rogerscentre.com

Sylvia A'Ddario, Chief Operating Officer
silvio.daddario@rogerscentre.com
Mario Coutinho, Director Operations
Owned by:
Rogers Communications, Inc
Tenants:
MLB - Toronto Blue Jays baseball, CFL - Toronto Argonauts football.
Permanent Seating Capacity:
53,506 - Football; 51,517 - Baseball.

Sarnia Sports and Entertainment Centre
1455 LONDON ROAD
SARNIA, ON N7S 1P6

519-541-1000
877-364-8232
Fax: 519-541-0303
info@ssec.on.ca
www.ssec.on.ca

Ryan Chamney, Events Manager
Edgar Hunt, Finance Manager
Trevor Sanderson, Operations Manager
Year Opened:
1998
Tenant(s):
OHL - Sarnia Sting hockey.
Permanent Seating Capacity:
5,500

Scotiabank Place
1000 PALLADIUM DRIVE
KANATA, ON K2V 1A5

613-599-0100
Fax: 613-599-0359
feedback@scotiabankplace.com
www.scotiabankplace.com

Conroy Tom, VP/Executive Director
Krista Pogue, Director Media/Marketing
Owned by:
Capital Sports Properties
Tenant(s):
NHL - Ottawa Senators hockey.
Permanent Seating Capacity:
18,500

Stade Municipal De Quebec
100 RUE DU CARDINAL MAURICE-ROY
QUEBEC CITY, QC G1K 8Z1

418-521-2255
877-521-2244
Fax: 418-521-2266
baseball@capitalesdequebec.com
www.capitalesdequebec.com

Jean Tremblay, Proprietor
Michel Laplante, President
Sport:
Baseball
Team:
Capitales de Quebec
Year Founded:
1939

Capacity:
4,800

Race Tracks - Auto

Sanair International Raceway
669 PETIT RANG ST FRANCOIS
CP 222
SAINT-PIE, QC J0H 1W0

450-772-6400
Fax: 450-772-2236
www.sanairracing.com

Description:
Auto race track.

Shannonville Motorsport Park
7047 OLD HIGHWAY #2
PO BOX 259
SHANNONVILLE, ON K0K 3A0

613-969-1906
800-959-8955
Fax: 613-966-6890
info@shannonville.com
www.shannonville.com

Jean Gauthier, Promoter
Description:
Auto Race Track.
Long Track:
4.03km.
Pro Track:
2.47km
Fabi Circuit:
2.23km.

Race Tracks - Equestrian Downs & Parks

Calgary Exhibition & Stampede
1410 OLYMPIC WAY SE
CALGARY, AB T2P-2KB

403-261-0101
800-661-1260
Fax: 403-265-7197
reception3@calgarystampede.com
www.calgarystampede.com

Warren Connell, Chief Operating Officer
Laurie Schild, Vice President Marketing
Gordon Fache, Vice President

Clinton Raceway
147 BEECH STREET
CLINTON, ON N0M 1LO

519-482-5270
Fax: 519-482-1489
info@clintonraceway.com
www.clintonraceway.com

Jessica Carnochan, Marketing Director
Murray Watt, President
Description:
Horse race track.

Stampede Park
1410 OLYMPIC WAY SE
CALGARY, AB T2G 2W1

403-261-0214
Fax: 403-265-7009
kmarrington@calgarystampede.com
www.calgarystampede.com

Patti Hunt, Promotions & Advertising Manager
(403)261-0253
phunt@calgarystampede.com

Sudbury Downs Holdings
2070 OLD BURWASH ROAD
SUDBURY, ON P3E 4Z4

705-855-9001
Fax: 705-855-5434
sudburydowns@gmail.com
www.sudburydowns.com

Patrick H. MacIsaac, President
Ken M. Le Drew, General Manager
Year Founded:
1974
Nature of Sports Service:
Harness horse race track.

Windsor Raceway
5555 OJIBWAY PARKWAY
PO BOX 998
WINDSOR, ON N9A 6P6

519-969-8311 EXT 347
Fax: 519-969-0780
youbet@windsorraceway.com
www.windsorraceway.com

Richard Jacob, VP Operations
Patrick Soulliere, President
Description:
Horse race track.

Woodstock Raceway
875 NELLIS STREET
PO BOX 234
WOODSTOCK, ON N4S 7W8

519-537-5717
Fax: 519-421-7374
wdstock@windsorraceway.com
www.windsorraceway.com

Paul Masters, General Manager

SECTION 16
TRANSPORTATION

Associations

Aerospace Industries Association of Canada (AIAC) / Association des industries aérospatiales du Canada
#7030, 255 Albert St., Ottawa ON K1P 6A9
Tel: 613-232-4297; *Fax:* 613-232-1142
info@aiac.ca
www.aiac.ca
Previous Name: Air Industries Association of Canada
Overview: A large national organization founded in 1962
Membership: 400; *Committees:* Airworthiness; International Exhibition; Technology Council; Defence Procurement Council; Suppliers Council; Space Council
Description: To promote & facilitate the continued success & growth of this strategic industry; To establish & maintain a public policy environment that enables sustained aerospace industry growth; To strengthen the international competitiveness of all aerospace firms in Canada; To strengthen Canadian aerospace SME capabilities & position them as "suppliers of choice"; To represent & involve the full range of aerospace companies that operate in Canada

Air Canada Pilots Association (ACPA) / L'Association des pilotes d'Air Canada
#205, 6299 Airport Rd., Mississauga ON L4V 1N3
Tel: 905-678-9008; *Fax:* 905-678-9016
Toll-Free: 800-634-0944
info@acpa.ca
www.acpa.ca
Overview: A medium-sized national organization founded in 1995
Membership: 3,100
Affiliation(s): Association of Star Alliance Pilots

Air Line Pilots Association, International - Canada (ALPA)
#1715, 360 Albert St., Ottawa ON K1R 7X7
Tel: 613-569-5668; *Fax:* 613-569-5681
www.alpa.org
www.facebook.com/pages/We-Are-ALPA/200676905671
Previous Name: Canadian Air Line Pilots Association
Overview: A large national organization founded in 1931
Finances: *Funding Sources:* Membership dues
Staff: 10 staff member(s); 360 volunteer(s)
Membership: 2,200 + 19 locals in Canada; *Member Profile:* Active airline pilots employed by airlines in Canada; *Committees:* Air Safety; Aeromedical; Insurance
Activities: In Québec call 1-888-337-2033
Description: To promote & represent the interests of the airline pilot profession; To safeguard the rights of individual members; To promote & maintain the highest standards of flight safety; To function as a trade union & professional association
Affiliation(s): International Federation of Air Line Pilots' Associations; Canadian Labour Congress

Air Transport Association of Canada (ATAC) / Association du transport aérien du Canada
#700, 255 Albert St., Ottawa ON K1P 6A9
Tel: 613-233-7727; *Fax:* 613-230-8648
atac@atac.ca
www.atac.ca
Overview: A medium-sized national organization founded in 1934
Membership: 200; *Member Profile:* Operators; Associates; Affiliates
Activities: Engaging in lobbying activities; *Speaker Service:* Yes
Description: To advance the issues that affect members from the commercial aviation & flight training industries as well as avaiation industry suppliers

Airport Management Council of Ontario
10 Geddes Cres., Barrie ON L4N 7B3
Tel: 705-726-2626; *Fax:* 705-739-8520
Toll-Free: 877-636-2626
amco@amco.on.ca
www.amco.on.ca
Overview: A small provincial organization founded in 1985
Membership: 51 airports + 44 businesses
Activities: Workshops, presentations, conventions; *Speaker Service:* Yes *Library:* Resource
Description: AMCO is committed to the sustainability of airports nationally. It monitors the airport industry, lobbies, provides networking opportunities and training to airports & businesses that work to enhance airport operations.

Alberta Construction Trucking Association (ACTA)
#400, 1040 - 7 Ave. SW, Calgary AB T2P 3G9
Tel: 403-244-4487; *Fax:* 403-244-2340
info@myacta.ca
www.myacta.ca
Previous Name: Alberta Gravel Truckers Association
Overview: A medium-sized provincial organization
Description: To develop & promote the business of transporting construction & construction-related material

Alberta Motor Transport Association (AMTA)
#1, 285005 Wrangler Way, Rocky View AB T1X 0K3
Fax: 403-243-4610
Toll-Free: 800-267-1003
amtamsc@amta.ca
www.amta.ca
Merged from: Alberta Trucking Industry Safety Association; Alberta Trucking Association
Overview: A medium-sized provincial organization
Membership: 12,000; *Member Profile:* All sectors of the highway transportation industry; *Committees:* Injury Reduction & Training; Compliance & Regulatory Affairs; Member Services
Description: To take a leadership role in fostering a healthy, vibrant industry; *Member of:* Canadian Council of Motor Transport Administrators

Alberta Pioneer Railway Association
PO Box 70014, Stn. Londonderry, Edmonton AB T5C 3R6
Tel: 780-472-6229; *Fax:* 780-968-0167
www.railwaymuseum.ab.ca
Also Known As: Alberta Railway Museum
Overview: A small provincial charitable organization founded in 1968
Finances: *Annual Operating Budget:* $50,000-$100,000; *Funding Sources:* Grants; donations
Membership: 50; *Fees:* $30 regular; $35 family; $20 senior; $10 associate; *Member Profile:* Railway enthusiasts; retired railway workers
Activities: Operates Alberta Railway Museum; *Library:* John Rechner Memorial Library (Open to Public) by appointment
Description: To collect, preserve, restore, exhibit & interpret artifacts which represent the history & social impact of the railways in Western Canada, with emphasis on Canadian National Railways & Northern Alberta Railways & their predecessors in northern & central Alberta; *Member of:* Alberta Museums Association; Museums Canada
Affiliation(s): Heritage Canada

Amalgamated Transit Union (AFL-CIO/CLC) / Syndicat uni du transport (FAT-COI/CTC)
5025 Wisconsin Ave. NW, Washington DC 20016 USA
Tel: 202-537-1645; *Fax:* 202-244-7824
Toll-Free: 888-240-1196
www.atu.org
www.facebook.com/ATUInternational
twitter.com/ATUComm
Overview: A medium-sized international organization

Association des propriétaires d'autobus du Québec (APAQ)
#107, 225, boul Charest est, Québec QC G1K 3G9
Tél: 418-522-7131; *Téléc:* 418-522-6455
apaq@apaq.qc.ca
www.apaq.qc.ca
Aperçu: *Dimension:* moyenne; *Envergure:* provinciale; Organisme sans but lucratif; fondée en 1926
Membre: 250 sociétés; *Montant de la cotisation:* Barème (entre 240$ et 8 000$); *Critères d'admissibilité:* Transportateurs par autocars; Vendeurs de produits touristiques pour les groupes; *Comités:* Scolaire; Interurbain; Nolise
Description: Défendre les intérêts des enterprises offrant des services de transport collectif de personnes par autobus et autocars; *Membre de:* Association de l'industrie touristique du Canada

Association du camionnage du Québec inc. (ACQ) / Québec Trucking Association Inc.
#200, 6450, rue Notre Dame ouest, Montréal QC H4C 1C4
Tél: 514-932-0377; *Téléc:* 514-932-1358
Ligne sans frais: 800-361-5813
info@carrefour-acq.org
www.carrefour-acq.org
Aperçu: *Dimension:* moyenne; *Envergure:* provinciale; Organisme sans but lucratif; fondée en 1951
Finances: *Budget de fonctionnement annuel:* $500,000-$1.5 Million
Personnel: 13 membre(s) du personnel
Membre: 600 sociétés + 251 associés; *Critères d'admissibilite:* transporteurs et locateurs publics & privés
Activités: *Stagiaires:* Oui
Description: Favoriser l'amélioration des normes de sécurité, d'efficacité et d'éthique dans l'industrie du camionnage; maintenir un contact avec l'autorité gouvernementale, les usagers des services de camionnage et le public en général; soutenir le perfectionnement professionnel; soutenir les entreprises dans la défense de leurs intérêts.
Affiliation(s): Union Internationale des Transports Routiers - Genève; American Trucking Association - Washington, DC

Association du transport écolier du Québec (ATEQ)
#300, 5300, boul des Galeries, Québec QC G2K 2A2
Tél: 418-622-6544; *Téléc:* 418-622-6595
Ligne sans frais: 877-622-6544
courrier@ateq.qc.ca
www.ateq.qc.ca
Aperçu: *Dimension:* moyenne; *Envergure:* provinciale; fondée en 1962
Membre: 700 transporteurs scolaires; *Montant de la cotisation:* Barème

Association du transport urbain du Québec (ATUQ)
#8090, 800, rue de la Gauchetière, Montréal QC H5A 1J6
Tél: 514-280-4640; *Téléc:* 514-280-7053
info@atuq.com
www.atuq.com
Aperçu: *Dimension:* moyenne; *Envergure:* provinciale; fondée en 1983
Description: Organisme de concertation et de représentation politique qui a pour mandat d'assurer la promotion du transport en commun et la défense des intérêts de ses membres auprès des partenaires de l'industrie et des différentes instances gouvernementales

Association nationale des camionneurs artisans inc. (ANCAI)
#235, 670, rue Bouvier, Québec QC G2J 1A7
Tél: 418-623-7923; *Téléc:* 418-623-0448
infos@ancai.com
www.ancai.com
Aperçu: *Dimension:* moyenne; *Envergure:* provinciale; fondée en 1966
Finances: *Budget de fonctionnement annuel:* $500,000-$1.5 Million
Personnel: 15 membre(s) du personnel
Membre: 4500; *Montant de la cotisation:* $200; *Critères d'admissibilite:* Camionneur propriétaire de son véhicule
Activités: Congrès annuel; Tirage camion
Description: Défendre les intérêts des transporteurs en vrac (gravier et forêts) auprès des gouvernements, organismes patronaux et entreprises privées

Association of Canadian Port Authorities (ACPA)
#1502, 85 Albert St., Ottawa ON K1P 6A4
Tel: 613-232-2036; *Fax:* 613-232-9554
leroux@acpa-ports.net
www.acpa-ports.net
Previous Name: Canadian Port & Harbour Association
Overview: A medium-sized national organization founded in 1958
Finances: *Annual Operating Budget:* $50,000-$100,000; *Funding Sources:* Membership fees; seminars
Staff: 1 staff member(s)
Membership: 18 corporate + 17 associate; *Fees:* $750 associate & affiliate; $100 individual; *Committees:* Constitution; Finance & Administration; Marketing; Public Relations; Operations & Environment; Past Presidents; Real Property Management
Activities: Annual conferences where papers are given by experts in the field of port operations & where members inspect the host port's dock & industrial facilities; port-related research; special seminars; *Speaker Service:* Yes
Description: To encourage, mentor & stimulate the development of excellence within Canadian ports
Affiliation(s): American Association of Port Authorities

Association québécoise du transport aérien (AQTA)
Aéroport international Jean-Lesage, 600, 6e av de l'Aéroport, Québec QC G2G 2T5
Tél: 418-871-4635; *Téléc:* 418-871-8189
aqta@aqta.ca
www.aqta.ca
www.linkedin.com/groups?home=&gid=2588987
www.facebook.com/group.php?gid=119190028092054
Aperçu: *Dimension:* moyenne; *Envergure:* provinciale; Organisme sans but lucratif; fondée en 1975
Membre: 155; *Montant de la cotisation:* Barème; *Critères d'admissibilite:* Transporteurs aériens et fournisseurs de produits et services liés à l'aviation
Description: Voué à la défense et la promotion des intérêts de tous les secteurs du transport aérien

Association québécoise du transport et des routes inc. (AQTR)
Bureau de Montréal, #200, 1255, rue University, Montréal QC H3B 3B2
Tél: 514-523-6444; *Téléc:* 514-523-2666
info@aqtr.qc.ca
www.aqtr.qc.ca

Aperçu: *Dimension:* grande; *Envergure:* provinciale; fondée en 1965
Finances: *Budget de fonctionnement annuel:* $500,000-$1.5 Million
Personnel: 7 membre(s) du personnel; 100 bénévole(s)
Membre: 950; *Montant de la cotisation:* 270 $; *Critères d'admissibilite:* Secteur privé - Ingénieur conseils; Entrepreneurs; Fournisseurs et manufacturiers; Laboratoires; Transporteurs; Architectes et urbanistes; Étudiants; Spécialistes en environnement; Secteur public et parapublic - Ministères; Municipalités; Maisons d'enseignement; Sociétés de transport; Autres sociétés, départements et services publics; *Comités:* Directions techniques - Infrastructures de transport; Transport des personnes; Circulation; Sécurité dans les transports; Transport aérien; Recherche et développement; Comités - Transport des marchandises; Environnement; Revue; Congrès; Activités municipales
Activités: Regrouper les personnes impliquées dans les techniques du transport; Encourager les échanges multidisciplinaires et favoriser la collaboration entre différents secteurs; Recommander toute mesure permettant de développer des techniques du transport; *Listes de destinataires:* Oui
Description: Assumer un leadership technique; définir des règles en matière de sécurité et d'environnement; Favoriser l'échange international des expertises; promouvoir la recherche et le développement des expertises et des produits en transport; promouvoir la formation dans le domaine des transports; Assumer la représentativité de l'AQTR par la participation aux principaux forums sur les transports; Contribuer à servir la société par l'éducation et l'information du grand public

Association Sectorielle Transport Entreposage (ASTE)
#301, 6455, boul Jean-Talon est, Montréal QC H1S 3E8
Tél: 514-955-0454; *Téléc:* 514-955-0449
Ligne sans frais: 800-361-8906
info@aste.qc.ca
www.aste.qc.ca

Aperçu: *Dimension:* moyenne; *Envergure:* provinciale; fondée en 1983
Membre: 1-99
Description: L'Association Sectorielle Transport Entreposage est une organisme en prèvention, autonome et paritaire, sans but lucratif, fondé et administré par des reprétants des employeurs et des syndicats.

Atlantic Provinces Trucking Association (APTA)
#400, 725 Champlain St., Dieppe NB E1A 1P6
Tel: 506-855-2782; *Fax:* 506-853-7424
Toll-Free: 866-866-1679
apta@apta.ca
www.apta.ca

Overview: A medium-sized local organization founded in 1950
Membership: 400 corporate & individual; *Member Profile:* Open to anyone having an interest in the trucking industry in Atlantic Canada, including common carriers, owner-operators & private fleets; *Committees:* Accident Review; Associated Trades Council; Broker; Common Carrier; Group Insurance; Marine; Membership; New Brunswick Legislative; Newfoundland Legislative; Nova Scotia Legislative; Prince Edward Island Legislative; Safety Council; Workers Compensation
Activities: Infrastructure improvements; complete twinning of the highway between Halifax & Saint John; elimination of motor carrier plates & fees; simplification of multiple registration & other tax collection systems in North America to allow for "one-stop shipping"; establishment of training programs; Annual Meeting & Convention; Atlantic Truck Show; Spring Maintenance Seminar; *Rents Mailing List:* Yes
Description: To promote an efficient, safe & environmentally sound trucking industry in Atlantic Canada. PUBLICATIONS: Atlantic Trucking Magazine (quaterly); Atlantic Report Newsletter (monthly) (only to members).

British Columbia Aviation Council (BCAC)
PO Box 32366, Stn. YVR Domestic Terminal, Richmond BC V7B 1W2
Tel: 604-278-9330; *Fax:* 604-278-8210
info@bcaviationcouncil.org
www.bcaviationcouncil.org

Overview: A small provincial organization founded in 1936
Finances: *Funding Sources:* Membership fees
Description: A self-sustaining organization with the mission to "promote the safe and orderly development of aviation and aviation services to the province of British Columiba."

British Columbia Ferry & Marine Workers' Union (CLC) (BCFMWU) / Syndicat des travailleurs marins et de bacs de la Colombie-Britannique (CTC)
1511 Stewart Ave., Nanaimo BC V9S 4E3
Tel: 250-716-3454; *Fax:* 250-716-3455
Toll-Free: 800-663-7009
mailroom@bcfmwu.com
www.bcfmwu.com

Also Known As: Ferry Workers' Union
Overview: A medium-sized provincial organization founded in 1977
Finances: *Annual Operating Budget:* $1.5 Million-$3 Million; *Funding Sources:* Union dues
Staff: 9 staff member(s)
Membership: 4,400; *Fees:* $60 initiation fee; 1.5% of gross monthly income
Description: To unite in the Union all workers eligible for membership; to seek the best possible wage standards & improvements in the conditions of employment for these workers & to represent members in protecting & maintaining their rights; to act as the representative of the membership; to establish free child day care for all individuals; to engage in educational, legislative, political, civic, social, welfare, community & other activities to safeguard & promote economic & social benefits & justice for all workers, unionized & non-unionized.
Affiliation(s): BC Federation of Labour; National Union of Public & General Employees (NUPGE)

British Columbia Railway Historical Association (BCRHA)
1148 Balmoral Rd., Victoria BC V8T 1B1
Tel: 250-383-7063
bcrha@shaw.ca
www.trainweb.org/bcrha

Overview: A small provincial charitable organization founded in 1961
Finances: *Annual Operating Budget:* Less than $50,000; *Funding Sources:* Donations; book sales; membership dues
Staff: 30 volunteer(s)
Membership: 5 associate + 1 senior/lifetime + 30 individual; *Fees:* $15 full; $4 associate; *Member Profile:* Interest in BC railway history; *Committees:* Acquisitions; Book Sales; New Book Review; Financial
Activities: Research & publication of books on BC railway history; *Library:* Yes (Open to Public)
Description: To preserve railway exhibits, manuscripts & film of BC railways; *Member of:* Heritage Society of BC

British Columbia Supercargoes' Association
#206, 3711 Delbrook Ave., North Vancouver BC V7N 3Z4
Tel: 604-878-1258; *Fax:* 604-904-6545
admin@supercargoes.bc.ca; president@supercargoes.bc.ca
www.supercargoes.bc.ca

Overview: A medium-sized provincial organization founded in 1952
Finances: *Annual Operating Budget:* $50,000-$100,000; *Funding Sources:* Membership dues
Staff: 8 volunteer(s)
Membership: 12; *Member Profile:* Marine professionals in the shipping industry
Description: To provide expert marine cargo planning & onsite management & supervision of shiploading & discharge of all types of cargoes & vessels on the west coast of North America

British Columbia Trucking Association (BCTA)
#100, 20111 - 93A Ave., Langley BC V1M 4A9
Tel: 604-888-5319
bcta@bctrucking.com
www.bctrucking.com

Previous Name: BC Motor Transport Association
Overview: A large provincial organization founded in 1913
Finances: *Funding Sources:* Membership dues
Membership: 1,000 corporate; *Fees:* $325-$400; *Member Profile:* Trucking company operating in BC; Supplier to trucking industry; *Committees:* Convention; Insurance; International; Labour; Freight Claims & Hazardous Goods; Safety; Truxpo; Vehicle Standards
Activities: *Speaker Service:* Yes; *Rents Mailing List:* Yes *Library:* Yes by appointment
Description: To act as the recognised voice of the commercial road transportation industry in British Columbia, by consulting & communicating with the industry, government, & the public; To promote a prosperous, safe, efficient & responsible road transportation industry; To provide programs & services to members

Bytown Railway Society (BRS)
PO Box 47076, Ottawa ON K1B 5P9
Tel: 613-745-1201; *Fax:* 613-745-1201
info@bytownrailwaysociety.ca
www.bytownrailwaysociety.ca

Overview: A medium-sized national charitable organization founded in 1969
Finances: *Annual Operating Budget:* $100,000-$250,000; *Funding Sources:* Publications sale; memberships
Staff: 60 volunteer(s)
Membership: 20 corporate + 3 senior/lifetime + 1,225 individual; *Fees:* $40/year plus $2.00 GST or $5.20 HST; *Committees:* Publications
Activities: Restoration/preservation of owned railway equipment; *Library:* Yes (Open to Public) by appointment
Description: To promote an interest in railways & railway history, with particular emphasis on Canadian railways. PUBLICATIONS: Canadian Trackside Guide, The Quebec Railway Light and Power Company, Montreal Streetcars- Vol.2. People and Places, Montreal and Southern Counties Railway Co., The Ottawa Streetcar Company, Hamilton's Other Railway.

Canadian Aeronautics & Space Institute (CASI) / Institut aéronautique et spatial du Canada
#104, 350 Terry Fox Dr., Ottawa ON K2K 2W5
Tel: 613-591-8787; *Fax:* 613-591-7291
casi@casi.ca; membership@casi.ca
www.casi.ca

Previous Name: Canadian Aeronautical Institute (CAI)
Merged from: Institute of Aircraft Technicians; Ottawa Aeronautical Society; US Institute of Aeronautical Science
Overview: A medium-sized national licensing organization founded in 1954
Membership: 1,600; *Fees:* $36.75 juniors; $63 seniors; $94.50 associates & individuals
Activities: Facilitating communications among the Canadian aeronautics & space community; Developing members' skills
Description: To advance the art, science, engineering, & applications of aeronautics & associated technologies in Canada; To promote Canadian competence & international competitiveness
Affiliation(s): Canadian Air Cushion Technology Society; Canadian Navigation Society; Canadian Remote Sensing Society

Canadian Airports Council (CAC) / Conseil des aéroports du Canada
#600, 116 Lisgar St., Ottawa ON K2P 0C2
Tel: 613-560-9302; *Fax:* 613-560-6599
www.cacairports.ca

Overview: A medium-sized national organization founded in 1991
Finances: *Funding Sources:* Sponsorships
Membership: 48; *Member Profile:* Canadian airports (CAC members are also members of Airports Council International - North America)
Activities: Preparing submissions to governmental bodies & agencies
Description: To act as the voice for Canadian airports on a great range of important issues; *Member of:* Airports Council International - North America (ACI-NA)
Affiliation(s): Air Transport Association of Canada (ATAC); Canadian International Freight Forwarders Association (CIFFA); Canadian Chamber of Commerce; Canadian Tourism Commission; Tourism Industry Association of Canada (TIAC)

Canadian Association of Movers (CAM) / Association canadienne des déménageurs (ACD)
PO Box 30039, Stn. New Westminster, Thornhill ON L4J 0C6
Tel: 905-848-6579; *Fax:* 905-848-8499
Toll-Free: 866-860-0065
admin@mover.net
www.mover.net

Overview: A small national organization
Membership: 400
Activities: Government & political affairs; membership development; volunteer participation & recognition; van lines; public affairs & publications; research & development; education & training; professional ethics & standards; organizational competency
Description: To further the interests of the owner-managed moving & storage companies by providing for its members leadership, motivation, research, education, programs of mutual benefit, consultation & technical advice
Affiliation(s): American Moving & Storage Association; British Association of Removers; International Association of Movers

Canadian Association of Railway Suppliers / Association canadienne des fournisseurs de chemins de fer
#901, 99 Bank St., Ottawa ON K1P 6B9
Tel: 613-237-3888; *Fax:* 613-237-4888
info@railwaysuppliers.ca
www.railwaysuppliers.ca

Previous Name: Canadian Railway & Transit Manufacturers Association

Overview: A medium-sized national organization
Membership: 18 organizations; *Fees:* Schedule available

Canadian Automobile Association (CAA) / Association canadienne des automobilistes
National Office, #200, 1145 Hunt Club Rd., Ottawa ON K1V 0Y3
Toll-Free: 800-564-6222
www.caa.ca
Social Media: www.youtube.com/TheCAAChannel
twitter.com/CAA
Overview: A large national organization founded in 1913
Finances: *Funding Sources:* Membership dues
Membership: 9 clubs serving 5,000,000+ members
Activities: *Speaker Service:* Yes *Library:* Yes
Description: To promote, develop & implement programs & information related to the rights, responsibilities, & needs of the motorist as a consumer
Affiliation(s): Alliance internationale de tourisme; Fédération internationale de l'automobile; Federacion interamericana de touring y automovil-clubes; Commonwealth Motoring Conference; American Automobile Association

Canadian Aviation Historical Society (CAHS)
PO Box 2700, Stn. D, 156 St. Pierre Rd., Ottawa ON K1P 5W7
www.cahs.com
Overview: A small national charitable organization founded in 1962
Finances: *Funding Sources:* Donations
Membership: *Fees:* CAD$40 Canadian members; $50 USA; $60 overseas; *Member Profile:* Individuals with an interest in the history of aviation
Activities: Supporting research in Canadian aeronautical history
Description: The Society collects & disseminates information about Canada's aviation heritage. It aims to foster public interest in the field. It is a registered charity, BN: 118829589RR0001.

Canadian Aviation Maintenance Council (CAMC) / Conseil canadien de l'entretien des aéronefs (CCEA)
#155, 955 Green Valley Cres., Ottawa ON K2C 3V4
Tel: 613-727-8272; *Fax:* 613-727-7018
Toll-Free: 800-448-9715
secretariat@camc.ca
www.camc.ca
Overview: A medium-sized national organization founded in 1992
Finances: *Annual Operating Budget:* $250,000-$500,000; *Funding Sources:* Aviation maintenance industry; Human Resources Development Canada; federal government
Staff: 5 staff member(s)
Membership: 1,000-4,999; *Fees:* Initial: $84/2 yrs; Renewal $59.50/2 yrs; Certified $89.49/2 yrs
Activities: *Internships:* Yes
Description: To develop occupational training standards & facilitate the implementation of a human resources strategy for the Canadian Aviation Maintenance Industry.

Canadian Bus Association (CBA) / Association canadienne de l'autobus
c/o #2001, 45 O'Connor St., Ottawa ON K1P 1A4
Tel: 613-238-1800; *Fax:* 613-241-4936
mresnick@rothwellgroup.ca
Previous Name: Canadian Motor Coach Association
Overview: A medium-sized national organization founded in 1936
Membership: 100 companies
Description: To act as the national voice of the Canadian bus industry; to act as a national forum for the discussion of bus-related issues & the establishment of positions in relation to industry-wide areas of concern; to function as a technical & operational information gathering & exchange mechanism; to further the objectives of safety, convenience & quality of the motor coach industry.

Canadian Business Aviation Association (CBAA) / Association canadienne de l'aviation d'affaires (ACAA)
#430, 55 Metcalfe St., Ottawa ON K1P 6L5
Tel: 613-236-5611; *Fax:* 613-236-2361
info@cbaa.ca
www.cbaa.ca
Previous Name: Canadian Business Aircraft Association Inc.
Overview: A medium-sized national organization founded in 1962
Finances: *Annual Operating Budget:* $500,000-$1.5 Million; *Funding Sources:* Membership dues; convention/tradeshow
Staff: 9 staff member(s)
Membership: 150 business + 5 commercial + 108 associate + 12 affiliate + 9 affiliated organizations; *Member Profile:* Business: owns or operates a Canadian privately or state registered aircraft as an aid to conduct its business; Commercial: owns or operates Canadian commercially registered aircraft; Associate: businesses primarily concerned with aviation activities, including the manufacture of aircraft; Affiliate: owns or operates aircraft exclusively registered in a nation other than Canada
Activities: Leadership; excellence; collaboration; ethics
Description: CBAA acts as a collective voice for the business aviation community in Canada, assisting its members in all aviation related matters, & promoting the Canadian business community globally.
Affiliation(s): National Business Aviation Association; International Business Aviation Council; European Business Aircraft Association

Canadian Council of Motor Transport Administrators (CCMTA) / Conseil canadien des administrateurs en transport motorisé (CCATM)
2323 St. Laurent Blvd., Ottawa ON K1G 4J8
Tel: 613-736-1003; *Fax:* 613-736-1395
ccmta-secretariat@ccmta.ca (general information & membership)
www.ccmta.ca
Overview: A medium-sized national charitable organization founded in 1940
Finances: *Funding Sources:* Member assessments; Special projects; Membership fees
Membership: 100-499; *Fees:* $433.50 associate; *Member Profile:* Members include representatives of provincial, territorial, & federal governments, & associate members from transportation related organizations.; *Committees:* Drivers & Vehicles; Compliance & Regulatory Affairs; Road Safety Research & Policies
Activities: Developing strategies & programs; Managing a communications network, called the Interprovincial Record Exchange system; *Rents Mailing List:* Yes
Description: To coordinate operational matters dealing with the administration, regulation, & control of motor vehicle transportation & highway safety

Canadian Federation of AME Associations (CFAMEA)
837 Charlotte St., Fredericton NB E3B 1M7
Tel: 506-452-1809; *Fax:* 506-452-8251
www.cfamea.com
Also Known As: Aircraft Maintenance Engineers Association
Overview: A medium-sized national organization
Finances: *Annual Operating Budget:* Less than $50,000; *Funding Sources:* Membership dues
Staff: 6 volunteer(s)
Membership: 1,000-4,999
Activities: Liaison with government concerning aircraft maintenance & AME licensing

Canadian Ferry Operators Association (CFOA) / Association canadienne des opérateurs de traversiers
c/o Anthonie A. de Hoog, CFOA Executive Director, 21 Meredith Dr., Sussex Corner NB E4E 2T8
Tel: 506-433-4810; *Fax:* 506-432-9505
adehoog@cfoa.ca
www.cfoa.ca
Overview: A small national organization founded in 1987
Finances: *Funding Sources:* Sponsorships
Membership: 37; *Member Profile:* Major ferry owners & operators in Canada
Activities: Providing opportunities for discussion of matters of interest to members; Promoting the safety, reliability, & efficiency of Canadian ferry operators; Providing representation at regulatory forums such as CMAC
Description: To establish & maintain a standard of professional & technical excellence in the operation of Canadian ferries; To promote & protect the interests of members of the association

Canadian Flight Instructors Association
579 Kingston Rd., Ajax ON L1S 6M1
Tel: 905-683-8986; *Fax:* 905-683-6977
bill@jsdavidson.ca
Overview: A small national organization

Canadian Heartland Training Railway
PO Box 1174, Camrose AB T4V 1X2
Tel: 780-679-4008; *Fax:* 780-672-4032
www.chtr.ca
Overview: A small national organization
Description: To support the practical training needs of the railway industry in Canada & around the world; *Member of:* Railway Association of Canada; Railway Suppliers Association of Canada

Canadian Industrial Transportation Association (CITA) / Association canadienne de transport industriel (ACTI)
#405, 580 Terry Fox Dr., Ottawa ON K2L 4C2
Tel: 613-599-3283; *Fax:* 613-599-1295
info@cita-acti.ca
www.cita-acti.ca
Overview: A medium-sized national organization
Finances: *Annual Operating Budget:* $250,000-$500,000; *Funding Sources:* Membership dues
Staff: 3 staff member(s)
Membership: 400 major shippers
Activities: Advocacy; education; *Speaker Service:* Yes *Library:* Yes (Open to Public)
Description: CITA-ACTI actively promotes a competitive and cost effective North American transportation system serving Canada and its NAFTA allies. Their vision is to be recognized as the "National Voice" of industrial transportation in Canada through increased membership and member representation in all regions of the county.

Canadian Institute of Traffic & Transportation (CITT) / Institut canadien du trafic et du transport
#400, 10 King St. East, Toronto ON M5C 1C3
Tel: 416-363-5696; *Fax:* 416-363-5698
info@citt.ca
www.citt.ca
www.facebook.com/group.php?gid=148552441716
Overview: A medium-sized national organization founded in 1958
Membership: 2,000; *Fees:* $275; *Member Profile:* Members must complete course of study to hold the designation, CITT
Activities: Offers the CITT Diploma Program
Description: Designation granting body in logistics management.

Canadian International Freight Forwarders Association, Inc. (CIFFA) / Association des transitaires internationaux canadiens, inc. (ATIC)
#480, 170 Attwell Dr., Toronto ON M9W 5Z5
Tel: 416-234-5100; *Fax:* 416-234-5152
Toll-Free: 866-282-4332
ciffa@ciffa.com; membership@ciffa.com
www.ciffa.com
Overview: A large international organization founded in 1948
Finances: *Annual Operating Budget:* $500,000-$1.5 Million; *Funding Sources:* Membership dues; education fees
Staff: 5 staff member(s); 20 volunteer(s)
Membership: 188 regular + 94 associate; *Fees:* Schedule available; *Committees:* AGM; Bylaws; Counsel; Education; Electronic Data Interchange; Ethics/Standards; FIATA; Judicial; Logistics Institute; Membership; Public Relations; Road & Rail; Sea Freight; Ways & Means
Activities: CIFFA Professional Training Program; education courses; dangerous goods courses, topical workshops
Description: To represent & support members of the Canadian international freight forwarding industry in providing the highest level of quality & professional services to their clients; *Member of:* Federation internationale des associations de transitaires et assimiles
Affiliation(s): International Federation of Freight Forwarders Associations

Canadian Marine Pilots' Association (CMPA) / Association des pilotes de la marine canadienne
#1302, 155 Queen St., Ottawa ON K1P 6L1
Tel: 613-232-7777; *Fax:* 613-232-7667
cmpa@tnpa.ca
www.marinepilots.ca
Overview: A small national organization founded in 1966
Membership: 400; *Member Profile:* Marine pilots in Canada
Activities: Upholding a Code of Conduct for Canadian pilots; Contributing to matters of safety & regulatory issues; Collaborating with marine stakeholders to maintain a vibrant marine sector
Description: To represent Canadian marine pilots; To raise awareness of marine pilots' role to protect public safety; To ensure a healthy Canadian marine sector; *Member of:* International Maritime Pilots' Association; Canadian Merchant Service Guild
Affiliation(s): International Maritime Organization

Canadian National Railways Police Association (Ind.) (CNRPA) / Association des policiers des chemins de fer nationaux du Canada (ind.)
6479 Miller's Grove, Mississauga ON L5N 3E5
Tel: 905-824-0856; *Fax:* 905-824-4584
fjmorgan@ica.net
www.cnrpa.ca
Also Known As: CNR Police Association
Overview: A small national organization founded in 1923

Membership: 159 + 7 locals

Canadian Northern Society (CNoS)
PO Box 1174, Camrose AB T4V 1X2
Tel: 780-672-3099
canadiannorthern@telus.net
www.canadiannorthern.ca
Overview: A small local charitable organization founded in 1987
Finances: *Funding Sources:* Donations
Fees: $20 full members; $10 associate; *Committees:* Camrose Railway Station Park & Morgan Railway Garden; Meeting Creek Grain Elevator & Railway Station Heritage Site; Big Valley Railway Station & Roundhouse Interpretive Park; Fundraising; Canora Chronicle; Finance & Audit
Description: To preserve prairie heritage

Canadian Owners & Pilots Association (COPA)
71 Bank St., 7th Fl., Ottawa ON K1P 5N2
Tel: 613-236-4901; *Fax:* 613-236-8646
copa@copanational.org
www.copanational.org
Overview: A medium-sized national charitable organization founded in 1954
Finances: *Annual Operating Budget:* $500,000-$1.5 Million; *Funding Sources:* Membership dues; advertising
Staff: 9 staff member(s); 20 volunteer(s)
Membership: 17,000; *Fees:* $50 individual; $250 corporate; *Member Profile:* Pilots & aircraft owners; corporate members; *Committees:* Air Navigation Services National Advisory Group; Canadian Aviation Regulation Advisory Committee
Activities: COPA Flight Chapters located across Canada; *Library:* Yes (Open to Public)
Description: The recognized voice of general aviation in Canada

Canadian Parking Association (CPA)
#350, 2255 St. Laurent Blvd., Ottawa ON K1G 4K3
Tel: 613-727-0700; *Fax:* 613-727-3183
info@canadianparking.ca
www.canadianparking.ca
Also Known As: Association canadienne du stationnement
Overview: A medium-sized national organization founded in 1983
Membership: 320; *Fees:* $475 full
Description: The Association is the national organization that represents the parking industry & provides a dynamic forum for learning & sharing to enhance member's ability to serve the public & improve the economic vitality of communities.

Canadian Ports Clearance Association
#500, 101 Syndicate Ave. North, Thunder Bay ON P7C 3V4
Tel: 807-623-8491; *Fax:* 807-623-2676
Previous Name: British Columbia Grain Shippers Clearance Association; Lake Shippers Clearance Association
Overview: A small national organization
Description: Shipping agent

Canadian Professional Logistics Institute / Institut canadien des professionnels de la logistique
#200, 160 John St., Toronto ON M5V 2E5
Tel: 416-363-3005; *Fax:* 416-363-5598
Toll-Free: 877-363-3005
loginfo@loginstitute.ca
www.loginstitute.ca
Also Known As: The Logistics Institute
Previous Name: Professional Logistics Institute of Canada
Overview: A medium-sized national organization founded in 1990
Finances: *Annual Operating Budget:* $500,000-$1.5 Million; *Funding Sources:* Membership dues; training tuition
Staff: 4 staff member(s); 5 volunteer(s)
Membership: 1,400 professional + 60 institutional + 50 associate; *Fees:* $395 professional; $99 associate; $875 corporate; *Member Profile:* Members must meet a professional standard developed & maintained by the Institute; *Committees:* Administration; Admissions; Legal; Marketing; Policy Development; Professional Development; R & D; Rules
Activities: *Internships:* Yes; *Speaker Service:* Yes
Description: To establish professional standards, certification & a program of professional development for the Logistics community.
Affiliation(s): Canadian Institute of Traffic & Transportation; Canadian International Freight Forwarders Association

Canadian Railroad Historical Association (CRHA) / Association canadienne d'histoire ferroviaire
110, rue St-Pierre, Saint-Constant QC J5A 1G7
Tel: 450-632-2410; *Fax:* 450-638-1563
info@exporail.org
www.exporail.org
Overview: A medium-sized national charitable organization founded in 1932
Membership: 1,100; *Fees:* $36
Activities: *Library:* Yes (Open to Public) by appointment
Description: To collect, preserve & disseminate information/items relating to the history of railways in Canada

Canadian Seaplane Pilots Association (CSPA)
#1001, 75 Albert St., Ottawa ON K1P 5E7
Tel: 613-236-4901; *Fax:* 613-236-8646
Overview: A medium-sized national organization
Finances: *Annual Operating Budget:* $50,000-$100,000
Staff: 2 staff member(s); 10 volunteer(s)
Membership: 400; *Fees:* US$28
Activities: Fly-ins; safety seminars
Description: To maintain communications among seaplane pilots; to represent them at all levels of government; to help develop regulations conducive to safe & pleasurable flying; to prepare & disseminate educational material; to advance among its members information & knowledge of seaplane flying.
Affiliation(s): Seaplane Pilots Association International

Canadian Shipowners Association (CSA) / Association des armateurs canadiens (AAC)
#705, 350 Sparks St., Ottawa ON K1R 7S8
Tel: 613-232-3539; *Fax:* 613-232-6211
csa@shipowners.ca
www.shipowners.ca
Previous Name: Dominion Marine Association
Overview: A medium-sized national organization founded in 1903
Membership: 8 corporate
Activities: Monitors Canadian & US government legislative/regulatory actions, initiatives by various international marine organizations, political trends, public policy relating to navigation, safety & the Canadian shipping environment; executes strategic communications & public relations campaigns to effectively represent the interests of member companies
Description: To promote an economic & competitive Canadian marine transportation industry; to support a national policy conducive to the development & maintenance of the Canadian flag merchant fleet in the inland, coastal & Arctic waters of Canada & foster the growth of a Canadian flag deep sea merchant fleet.; *Member of:* International Chamber of Shipping; International Shipping Federation; Chamber of Maritime Commerce; Canada Maritime Law Association

Canadian Transport Lawyers Association
c/o S.S.T. Thibault, Heenan Blaikie LLP, #600, 900, rue René-Lévesque ouest, Québec QC G1R 2B5
www.ctla.ca
Overview: A small national organization
Membership: *Fees:* $100 - $195; *Member Profile:* Lawyers engaged in transportation law, regulatory policy, procedure, & related legal interests

Canadian Transport Workers Union (Ind.) (CTWU) / Syndicat canadien des travailleurs du transport (ind.)
c/o Local #213, 73 Misty St., Kitchener ON N2B 3V6
Tel: 519-896-2671
Overview: A small national organization
Membership: 90 + 2 locals

Canadian Transportation Equipment Association (CTEA) / Association d'équipement de transport du canada (AETC)
#3B, 16 Barrie Blvd., St Thomas ON N5P 4B9
Tel: 519-631-0414; *Fax:* 519-631-1333
transportation@ctea.on.ca
www.ctea.ca
Overview: A medium-sized national organization founded in 1963
Membership: 544; *Member Profile:* Commercial vehicle & component manufacturers; Dealers & distributors; Service providers
Activities: Lobbying; Providing access to technical & regulatory information; Offering networking opportunities; Encouraging research
Description: To promote excellence in commercial vehicle manufacturing; to develop standard practices

Canadian Transportation Research Forum (CTRF) / Groupe de recherches sur les transports au Canada
PO Box 23033, Woodstock ON N4T 1R0
Tel: 519-421-9701; *Fax:* 519-421-9319
feedback@ctrf.ca, cawoudsma@ctrf.ca
www.ctrf.ca
Overview: A medium-sized national charitable organization founded in 1967
Finances: *Annual Operating Budget:* Less than $50,000
Staff: 21 volunteer(s)
Membership: 320; *Fees:* $129; *Member Profile:* Open to anyone interested in any aspect of transportation; membership is individual rather than corporate; present membership is drawn from carriers, shippers, consultants & suppliers in the commercial sector, the policy, regulatory, planning & research environments at all levels of government, students & professors at universitites & community colleges
Description: To promote the development of research in transportation & related fields; to publish research papers through media & through national & regional forum meetings.

Canadian Trucking Alliance (CTA) / L'Alliance canadienne du camionnage (ACC)
324 Somerset St. West, Ottawa ON K2P 0J9
Tel: 613-236-9426; *Fax:* 866-823-4076
info@cantruck.ca
www.cantruck.com
Overview: A medium-sized national organization founded in 1937
Membership: *Member Profile:* Motor carriers & associated trades
Activities: *Speaker Service:* Yes
Description: To promote business excellence in trucking; to participate in the development of public policy which supports the economic growth, safety & prosperity of the industry; to provide services, including research, development, products & information to meet the needs of the industry.
PUBLICATIONS: Dangerous Goods: A Trucker's Guide; Crossing International Borders:A Trucker's Guide; National Safety Code: A Trucker's Guide.

Canadian Trucking Human Resources Council (CTHRC) / Conseil canadien des ressources humaines en camionnage
#203, 720 Belfast Rd., Ottawa ON K1G 0Z5
Tel: 613-244-4800; *Fax:* 613-244-4535
info@cthrc.com
www.cthrc.com
Overview: A medium-sized national organization
Activities: Conducting research; Training; Offering advice; Liaising with industry members
Description: To respond to the human resource needs of the trucking industry
Affiliation(s): CCA Truck Driver Training Ltd.; Capilano Truck Driver Training Institute; JVI Provincial Transportation & Safety Academy; Mountain Transport Institute Ltd.; Red Deer College; SK Driver Training Ltd.; Wheels On Ltd. / Training & Driver Training

Canadian Urban Transit Association (CUTA) / Association canadienne du transport urbain (ACTU)
#1401, 55 York St., Toronto ON M5J 1R7
Tel: 416-365-9800; *Fax:* 416-365-1295
www.cutaactu.ca
Overview: A large national organization founded in 1904
Membership: 503; *Member Profile:* Transit systems; Manufacturers & suppliers of transit equipment; Federal, provincial, & municipal government agencies; Consultants; Affiliated individuals & companies; *Committees:* Business Members; Communications & Public Affairs; Human Resources; Technical Services; Transit Board Members
Activities: Conducting research & preparing statistics; Providing technical & operational information; Liaising with government; Partnering with other transportation associations & community development stakeholders; Engaging in advocacy activities; Raising public awareness of transit's contributions to communities; *Library:* Canadian Urban Transit Association Library (Open to Public)
Description: To represent the public transit community throughout Canada; To strengthen the industry

Canadians for Responsible & Safe Highways (CRASH)
PO Box 1042, Stn. B, Ottawa ON K1P 5R1
Tel: 613-860-0529; *Fax:* 613-567-6204
Toll-Free: 800-530-9945
Overview: A small national organization
Description: CRASH strives to ensure that safety, environmental & economic concerns are fully considered by governments when the latter establish & administer regulations pertaining to trucking operations on public highways.

Carefree Society Transportation Service
2832 Queensway St., Prince George BC V2L 4M5
Tel: 250-562-1394; *Fax:* 250-562-1393
carefree_society@telus.net
Also Known As: Carefree Society
Overview: A small local charitable organization founded in 1971
Finances: *Annual Operating Budget:* $250,000-$500,000; *Funding Sources:* Provincial government; regional government
Staff: 12 staff member(s); 10 volunteer(s)
Membership: 15; *Fees:* $6; *Committees:* Accessible Transportation Awareness

Description: To provide transportation services for the disabled in our community
Affiliation(s): BC Transit

Central British Columbia Railway & Forest Industry Museum Society
850 River Rd., Prince George BC V2L 5S8
Tel: 250-563-7351; *Fax:* 250-563-3697
trains@pgrfm.bc.ca
www.pgrfm.bc.ca
Also Known As: Railway & Forestry Museum
Overview: A small local charitable organization founded in 1983
Finances: *Annual Operating Budget:* $50,000-$100,000
Staff: 6 staff member(s); 15 volunteer(s)
Membership: 75; *Fees:* $15-$40
Activities: *Awareness Events:* Steam Day; Forester Day; Family Carnival *Library:* Canfor Library by appointment
Description: Administers Prince George Railway & Forest Industry Museum; *Member of:* Canadian Railway Historical Association; Canadian Museum Association; British Columbia Museum Association; American Railway Museum Association

Chamber of Marine Commerce (CMC) / Chambre du commerce maritime (CCM)
#700, 350 Sparks St., Ottawa ON K1R 7S8
Tel: 613-233-8779; *Fax:* 613-233-3743
email@cmc-ccm.com
www.cmc-ccm.com
Previous Name: Great Lakes Waterways Development Association
Overview: A large national organization founded in 1959
Finances: *Funding Sources:* Membership dues
Membership: 180+ institutional; *Member Profile:* Major Canadian & American shippers, ports & marine service providers, domestic & international shipowners
Activities: *Speaker Service:* Yes
Description: To bring together all sectors of the economy that rely on a cost efficient & safe marine transportation system

Chartered Institute of Logistics & Transport (CILT)
Earlstrees Court, Earlstrees Rd., Corbyn NN17 4Ax United Kingdom
enquiry@ciltuk.org.uk
www.cilt-international.com
Previous Name: Chartered Institute of Transport
Overview: A medium-sized international charitable organization founded in 1919
Finances: *Annual Operating Budget:* Greater than $5 Million; *Funding Sources:* Membership dues
Staff: 21 staff member(s)
Membership: 23,000 in UK; 33,000 worldwide; *Fees:* Schedule available; *Member Profile:* Professionals in transport & logistics; *Committees:* Membership; Education
Activities: Providing education programs, lecture meetings, & training; Presenting transport reports; *Speaker Service:* Yes *Library:* Chartered Institute of Logistics & Transport Library (Open to Public)
Description: To promote, encourage & coordinate the study & advancement of the science & art of transportation in all its branches
Affiliation(s): Integrated in UK with Institute of Logistics UK section now titled Institute of Logistics & Transport

The Chartered Institute of Logistics & Transport in North America (CILT) / Institut agréé de la logistique et des transports Amérique du Nord
#900, 275 Slater St., Ottawa ON K1P 5H9
Tel: 613-688-1438; *Fax:* 613-688-0966
requestinfo@ciltna.com
www.ciltna.com
Also Known As: CILT in North America
Previous Name: Chartered Institute of Transport Canadian Division
Overview: A medium-sized international organization founded in 1919
Finances: *Funding Sources:* Membership fees, conferences, workshop revenue
Staff: 1 staff member(s); 15 volunteer(s)
Membership: 250; *Fees:* Schedule available; *Member Profile:* Individuals with experience, interest & education in the transportation field.; *Committees:* Regional
Activities: *Internships:* Yes *Library:* Yes
Description: To promote, encourage, coordinate study & advancement of science & art of transportation.; *Member of:* Chartered Institute of Transport

Chatham Railroad Museum Society
PO Box 434, 2 McLean St., Chatham ON N7M 5K5
Tel: 519-352-3097
Overview: A small local charitable organization founded in 1989
Membership: 1-99
Description: To present history from a retired CN baggage car

Club de trafic de Québec
CP 72, Saint-Jean-Chrysostome QC G6Z 2L3
Tél: 418-654-5446; *Téléc:* 418-619-1044
jcoulombe@videotron.ca
www.clubtraficqc.org
Aperçu: *Dimension:* moyenne; *Envergure:* provinciale; Organisme sans but lucratif; fondée en 1960
Finances: *Budget de fonctionnement annuel:* $100,000-$250,000
Membre: 235; *Montant de la cotisation:* 75$
Description: Regrouper les représentants oeuvrant dans le domaine du transport de la grande région de Québec

Company of Master Mariners of Canada
c/o R. Wallace, 305 Michigan St., Victoria BC V8V 1R6
www.mastermariners.ca
Overview: A medium-sized national organization founded in 1967
Finances: *Funding Sources:* Membership dues
Membership: 455; *Fees:* $70-$140; *Member Profile:* Master Mariners
Activities: *Speaker Service:* Yes
Description: The Company is a central body of command-level mariners that represents senior officers of the Canadian Merchant Service. It maintains the standard of ability & professional conduct of the officers, & also develops education, training & qualifications for young cadets. It helps liaison between Canada's commercial, governmental & military fleets.
Affiliation(s): Master Mariner organizations in the UK, USA, South Africa, Australia & NZ

Dewdney-Alouette Railway Society (DARS)
22520 - 116 Ave., Maple Ridge BC V2X 0S4
Tel: 604-463-5311; *Fax:* 604-463-5317
mrmuseum@telus.net
Overview: A small local organization founded in 1979
Finances: *Annual Operating Budget:* Less than $50,000
Staff: 25 volunteer(s)
Membership: 2 senior/lifetime + 27 individual; *Fees:* $30; *Member Profile:* 20 hour apprenticeship
Activities: Port Haney diorama; *Library:* Yes
Description: The Society preserves the railway history of Maple Ridge, promotes the craft of model railroading, & offers advice to the public who are engaged in the building & operating of model railroads.
Affiliation(s): National Model Railway Association; Pacific Northwest Region 7th Division Society; BC Heritage Society; Maple Ridge Historical Society; Maple Ridge Museum

Edmonton Radial Railway Society (ERRS)
PO Box 76057, Stn. Southgate, Edmonton AB T6H 5Y7
Tel: 780-437-7721; *Fax:* 780-437-3095
info@edmonton-radial-railway.ab.ca
www.edmonton-radial-railway.ab.ca
Overview: A small national charitable organization founded in 1980
Finances: *Annual Operating Budget:* $50,000-$100,000; *Funding Sources:* Municipal, provincial & federal governments; donations
Staff: 100 volunteer(s)
Membership: 100; *Fees:* $20
Activities: Operating 2 historic street railway lines within Edmonton from May to Oct.; streetcar museum; streetcar chartering service; *Library:* Yes
Description: The Society collects, preserves & restores vintage streetcars, primarily those from 1908-1951.; *Member of:* Canadian Museum Association
Affiliation(s): Association of Railway Museums; Alberta Museums Association

Electric Vehicle Council of Ottawa Inc. (EVCO)
PO Box 4044, Stn. E, Ottawa ON K1S 5B1
info@evco.ca
www.evco.ca
Overview: A small local organization founded in 1980
Finances: *Annual Operating Budget:* Less than $50,000; *Funding Sources:* Memberships
Membership: 80; *Fees:* $5 student; $25 electronic; $30 paper
Description: To provide information about electric road vehicles, in Canada & worldwide

Electric Vehicle Society of Canada (EVS)
21 Burritt Rd., Toronto ON M1R 3S5
Tel: 416-755-4324; *Fax:* 416-755-4324
info@evsociety.ca
www.evsociety.ca
Overview: A medium-sized national organization founded in 1991
Membership: *Fees:* $20 students, spouses, & seniors; $30 adults; $50 families; $100 corporations; *Member Profile:* Engineers; Environmentalists; Enthusiasts for electric energy for propulsion
Activities: Providing a forum for member discussions; Examining modes of electric transportation
Description: To investigate & promote clean transportation technologies

Freight Carriers Association of Canada (FCA)
#3-4, 427 Garrison Rd., Fort Erie ON L2A 6E6
Tel: 905-994-0560; *Fax:* 905-994-0117
Toll-Free: 800-559-7421
info@fca-natc.org
www.fca-natc.org
Previous Name: Canadian Transport Tariff Bureau Association
Overview: A medium-sized national organization founded in 1939
Finances: *Annual Operating Budget:* $1.5 Million-$3 Million; *Funding Sources:* Membership fees; sales of publications & software
Staff: 17 staff member(s)
Membership: 100; *Fees:* Based on revenues; *Member Profile:* For-hire motor carriers; *Committees:* Tariff Advisory; Québec Comité Consultatif
Activities: Carrier meetings; seminars; research; info gathering & dissemination; *Speaker Service:* Yes
Description: To provide quality information, products & services to users, providers & third parties involved in motor carrier transportation. PUBLICATIONS: Fuel Price and Surcharge Information Bulletin (weekly); Currency Exchange Bulletin (2X/month -14th and last day of the month).
Affiliation(s): North American Transportation Council

Hope Air / Vols d'espoir
#207, 124 Merton St., Toronto ON M4S 2Z2
Tel: 416-222-6335; *Fax:* 416-222-6930
Toll-Free: 877-346-4673
mail@hopeair.ca
www.hopeair.ca
www.facebook.com/pages/Hope-Air
http://twitter.com/Hope_Air
Previous Name: Mission Air Transportation Network
Overview: A small national charitable organization founded in 1986
Finances: *Annual Operating Budget:* $250,000-$500,000; *Funding Sources:* Corporate; private donations; government
Staff: 6 staff member(s); 30 volunteer(s)
Membership: 1-99; *Fees:* N/A; *Committees:* Air Coordination; Funding; Finance; Office Administrations; Planning; Public Relations
Activities: *Internships:* Yes; *Speaker Service:* Yes *Library:* Yes (Open to Public) by appointment
Description: To provide free air transportation to Canadians in financial need who must travel between their own communities & recognized facilities for medical care

Huntsville & Lake of Bays Railway Society
88 Brunel Rd., Huntsville ON P1H 1R1
Tel: 705-789-7576; *Fax:* 705-789-6169
nicholls@vianet.ca
www.portageflyer.org
Also Known As: The Portage Railway
Overview: A small local charitable organization founded in 1984
Finances: *Annual Operating Budget:* Less than $50,000; *Funding Sources:* Fundraising; Rotary Club; local industry; donations
Staff: 15 volunteer(s)
Membership: 145; *Fees:* $35 1 yr., $100 3 yr. regular; $45 foreign
Activities: A fully functional operating railway
Description: Maintains & displays original artifacts of the old Huntsville & Lake of Bays Railway, plus vintage railway equipment of the turn of the century
Affiliation(s): Muskoka Heritage Place

Industrial Truck Association (ITA)
#460, 1750 K St. NW, Washington DC 20006 USA
Tel: 202-296-9880; *Fax:* 202-296-9884
www.indtrk.org
Overview: A medium-sized international organization
Finances: *Annual Operating Budget:* $1.5 Million-$3 Million
Staff: 5 staff member(s)
Membership: 100; *Fees:* Varies; *Member Profile:* Manufacturers of forklifts & suppliers
Description: Represents the manufacturers of lift trucks & their suppliers who do business in Canada, the United States or Mexico

INFORM Inc.
5 Hanover Sq., 19th Fl., New York NY 10004 USA
Tel: 212-361-2400; *Fax:* 212-361-2412
ramsey@informinc.org
www.informinc.org
www.facebook.com/199694845376
twitter.com/informinc

Overview: A medium-sized international charitable organization founded in 1974
Finances: *Annual Operating Budget:* $1.5 Million-$3 Million; *Funding Sources:* Individual donors; Foundations; Government; Corporate contributions; Book sales
Staff: 25 staff member(s); 5 volunteer(s)
Membership: 1,000; *Fees:* $35
Activities: Researching strategies to prevent chemical hazards & to develop sustainable products & practices; *Internships:* Yes; *Speaker Service:* Yes
Description: To examine the effects of business practices on the environment & human health; *Member of:* Earthshare

Intermodal Association of North America (IANA)
#1100, 11785 Beltsville Dr., Calverton MD 20705 USA
Tel: 301-982-3400; *Fax:* 301-982-4815
info@intermodal.org
www.intermodal.org
Overview: A medium-sized international organization founded in 1991
Membership: 700; *Committees:* Conference Planning; Education & Training; Electronic Business Solutions; Maintenance & Repair, Operations & P.R.
Description: To represent the combined interests of intermodal freight transportation companies & their suppliers

International Air Transport Association / Association du transport aérien international
PO Box 113, 800, Place Victoria, Montréal QC H4Z 1M1
Tel: 514-874-0202; *Fax:* 514-874-9632
www.iata.org
Overview: A small international organization founded in 1945
Description: To promote safe, regular & economical air transport for the benefit of the peoples of the world; to foster air commerce; to study the problems connected with air transport; to provide a means for collaboration among the air transport enterprises engaged directly or indirectly in international air transport service; to cooperate with the International Civil Aviation Organization & other international organizations; to furnish for governments a forum for developing industry working standards &, as appropriate, coordinating international fares & rates; to simplify the travelling process for the general public
Affiliation(s): International Civil Aviation Organization

International Association of Ports & Harbours (IAPH)
7F South Tower, New Pier Takeshiba, 1-16-1 Kaigan, Minato-Ku, Tokyo 105-0022 Japan
info@iaphworldports.org
www.iaphworldports.org
Overview: A large international organization founded in 1955
Finances: *Annual Operating Budget:* $1.5 Million-$3 Million; *Funding Sources:* Membership fees
Staff: 7 staff member(s)
Membership: 360; *Fees:* Schedule available; *Member Profile:* 90 maritime countries are represented; *Committees:* Finance, Constitution & By-Laws; Long Range Planning/Review; Port Safety, Environment & Marine Operations; Dredging Task Force; Legal Protection; Trade Facilitation; Cargo Operations; Ship Trends; Combined Transport & Distribution; Port Planning & Construction; Trade Policy; Membership; Communication & Networking; Human Resources Development
Activities: *Library:* Yes (Open to Public)
Description: To promote the development of the international port & maritime industry by fostering cooperation among members in order to build a more cohesive partnership among the world's ports & harbors, thereby promoting peace in the world & the welfare of mankind; to ensure that the industry's interests & views are represented before international organizations involved n the regulation of international trade & transportation & incorporated in the regulatory initiatives of these organizations; & to collect, analyse, exchange & distribute information on developing trends in international trade, transportation, ports & the regulations of these industries
Affiliation(s): International Maritime Organization; United Nations Conference on Trade & Development; United Nations Economic & Social Council; Permanent International Association of Navigation Congresses; International Cargo Handling Coordination Association; International Maritime Pilots Association; International Association of Independent Tanker Owners; Baltic & International Martime Council

International Industry Working Group (IIWG)
International Air Transport Association, PO Box 113, 800, Place Victoria, Montréal QC H4Z 1M1
Tel: 514-874-0202; *Fax:* 514-874-9632
obrienm@iata.org
www.iata.org
Overview: A small international organization founded in 1970
Membership: 50; *Member Profile:* Aircraft & aeroengine manufacturers; airlines & airport authorities
Description: To promote & develop an open exchange of information to minimize interface problems through well-informed design, development & operation of both aircraft & airports; to study jointly solutions to major problems which impede the development of the air transport system

International Maritime Organization (IMO) / Organisation maritime internationale
4 Albert Embankment, London SE1 7SR United Kingdom
info@imo.org
www.imo.org
Overview: A large international organization founded in 1948
Finances: *Annual Operating Budget:* Greater than $5 Million; *Funding Sources:* Government
Staff: 300 staff member(s)
Membership: 166 governments; *Fees:* Based on shipping fleet tonnage; *Committees:* Maritime Safety; Marine Environment Protection; Legal; Technical Cooperation; Facilitation
Activities: *Library:* Yes by appointment
Description: To encourage the adoption of high standards in matters concerning maritime safety, security, efficiency of navigation & control of marine pollution from ships

Locomotive & Railway Historical Society of Western Canada
#4104, 2120 Southland Dr. SW, Calgary AB T2V 4W3
Tel: 403-265-9229; *Fax:* 403-261-1057
laniganj@telus.net
Overview: A small local charitable organization founded in 1985
Finances: *Annual Operating Budget:* Less than $50,000
Staff: 9 volunteer(s)
Membership: 9
Activities: Preservation & restoration of important historic Canadian railway equipment; *Speaker Service:* Yes
Description: To promote the preservation of railway equipment integral to the history of Western Canada; to act in a consultative capacity on heritage rail projects; *Member of:* Canadian Council for Railway Heritage

Manitoba Trucking Association (MTA)
25 Bunting St., Winnipeg MB R2X 2P5
Tel: 204-632-6600; *Fax:* 204-694-7134
info@trucking.mb.ca
www.trucking.mb.ca
Overview: A medium-sized provincial organization founded in 1932
Finances: *Funding Sources:* Membership dues & fundraising through services
Staff: 5 staff member(s)
Membership: 350 organizations; *Member Profile:* PSV Carriers; City Transportation; Private Fleet; Household Goods Carriers; Associated Trades; Vehicle Maintenance; *Committees:* Associated Trades (Members, Executive); Vehicle Maintenance Council; Maintenace Council Executive
Activities: *Speaker Service:* Yes *Library:* Yes (Open to Public) by appointment
Description: Develops and maintains a safe and healthy business environment for its members
Affiliation(s): Canadian Trucking Alliance; Canadian Council of Motor Transport Administrators; Canadian Trucking Human Resource Council; Winnipeg Chamber of Commerce; Manitoba Chamber of Commerce; Infrastructure Council of Manitoba; Employers' Task Force on Workers' Compensation; Manitoba Employers' Council

Motorcycle & Moped Industry Council (MMIC) / Le Conseil de l'industrie de la motocyclette et du cyclomoteur (CIMC)
#201, 3000 Steeles Ave. East, Markham ON L3R 4T9
Tel: 416-491-4449; *Fax:* 416-493-1985
Toll-Free: 877-470-6642
info@mmic.ca
www.mmic.ca
Overview: A small national organization founded in 1971
Finances: *Annual Operating Budget:* $500,000-$1.5 Million
Staff: 7 staff member(s); 15 volunteer(s)
Membership: 150 corporate; 500 individual; *Fees:* Schedule available
Description: The Motorcycle and Moped Industry Council (MMIC) is a national, non-profit trade association that represents the manufacturers and distributors of street legal motorcycles and related products and services in Canada.

National Association of Railroad Passengers (NARP)
#308, 900 - 2 St. NE, Washington DC 20002-3557 USA
Tel: 202-408-8362; *Fax:* 202-408-8287
narp@narprail.org
www.narprail.org
Overview: A medium-sized international charitable organization founded in 1967
Finances: *Annual Operating Budget:* $250,000-$500,000; *Funding Sources:* Membership dues
Staff: 4 staff member(s)
Membership: 23,000; *Fees:* $35 individual; $45 family; $25 senior
Activities: *Rents Mailing List:* Yes *Library:* Yes (Open to Public)
Description: To encourage & promote a more balanced US transporation system including promotion of federal & state policies beneficial to all forms of rail service, urban rail transit, rural public transporation & intermodal terminals
Affiliation(s): Transport 2000 Ltd.

National Transportation Brokers Association (NTBA)
PO Box 238, Markham ON L3P 3J7
Tel: 905-568-4400; *Fax:* 905-640-9260
info@ntba-brokers.com
www.ntba-brokers.com
Overview: A medium-sized national organization
Finances: *Funding Sources:* Member fees
Membership: *Member Profile:* Freight brokerage services providers
Description: Promotes & continually improves business relationships among shippers, carriers, government & freight brokers

New Brunswick Potato Shippers Association
8824 Route 2, Grand Falls NB E3Z 1P8
Tel: 506-473-5520; *Fax:* 506-473-6701
tatered@nbnet.nb.ca
Overview: A small provincial organization
Description: The shippers association monitors industry growth

The Ninety-Nines Inc./International Organization of Women Pilots
4300 Amelia Earhart Rd., Oklahoma City OK 73159 USA
Tel: 405-685-7969; *Fax:* 405-685-7985
Toll-Free: 800-994-1929
99s@ninety-nines.org
www.ninety-nines.org
Also Known As: 99's
Overview: A small international charitable organization founded in 1929
Finances: *Annual Operating Budget:* $250,000-$500,000
Staff: 4 staff member(s); 4 volunteer(s)
Membership: 5,400 worldwide; *Fees:* US$65 for US; US$57 Canadian; US$44 other countries; *Member Profile:* Women pilots
Activities: *Speaker Service:* Yes *Library:* 99s Museum of Women Pilots
Description: To promote world fellowship through flight; to provide networking & scholarship opportunities for women & aviation aducation in the community; to preserve the unique history of women in aviation

North America Railway Hall of Fame
RPO Centre, PO Box 20040, St Thomas ON N5P 4H4
Tel: 519-633-2535; *Fax:* 519-633-3087
info@narhf.org
www.narhf.org
Overview: A small national charitable organization founded in 1996
Description: To establish a tribute to those who have made significant contributions relating to the railway industry in North America; To honour railway organizations, related innovations & technical accomplishments; To preserve & display a collection of library materials & railway heritage artifacts related to the Hall of Fame inductees; To educate the public about the impact of railway transportation on history & the development of communities, nations & international relations

Northern Air Transport Association (NATA)
PO Box 2457, Yellowknife NT X1A 2P8
Tel: 867-920-2985; *Fax:* 867-920-2983
nata-yzf@theedge.ca
www.nata-yzf.ca
Overview: A small local organization founded in 1977
Membership: *Member Profile:* Northern air carriers
Activities: Advocating for Northern air transport; Establishing partnerships with governments & within the transportation industry; *Speaker Service:* Yes
Description: To promote safe & effective Northern air transportation

Northwestern Ontario Air Carriers Association (NOACA)
PO Box 4075, 143 Cedar Point Dr., Sioux Lookout ON P8T 1J9
Tel: 807-737-7470; *Fax:* 807-583-2812
Overview: A small local organization

Ontario Community Transit Association (OCTA)
#306, 4141 Yonge St., Toronto ON M2P 2A8
Tel: 416-229-6222; *Fax:* 416-229-6281
www.octa.on.ca
Previous Name: Ontario Urban Transit Association

Overview: A medium-sized provincial organization founded in 1997
Membership: *Fees:* Annual fees for transportation service providers & suppliers based on transportation operating budget or net sales; $160 non-profit organizations; *Member Profile:* Representatives of public transit systems; Health & social service agency transportation providers; Government representatives; Suppliers to the industry; Consultants
Activities: Engaging in advocacy activities; Sharing information
Description: To strengthen & improve public transit services in Ontario; To ensure excellence & sustainability in public transit

Ontario Good Roads Association (OGRA)

#22, 1525 Cornwall Rd., Oakville ON L6J 0B2
Tel: 289-291-6472; *Fax:* 289-291-6477
info@ogra.org
www.ogra.org
ca.linkedin.com/pub/ontario-good-roads-association/43/b08/829
twitter.com/Ont_Good_Roads
Overview: A medium-sized provincial organization founded in 1894
Finances: *Funding Sources:* Membership fees; Sponsorships
Membership: 400+ municipalities; *Member Profile:* Ontario municipalities; First Nations communities; Corporations; Life & honourary members; *Committees:* Executive; Policy; Member Services; Nominating; Combined Conference; Companions Program
Activities: Advocating for the collective interests of municipal transportation & works departments; Analyzing policies; Reviewing legislation; Consulting with stakeholders & partners; Offering education & training opportunities
Description: To represent the transportation & public works-related interests of Ontario's municipalities & First Nation communities; To deliver programs & services that meet the needs of members; To support municipalities in the provision of effective & efficient transportation systems throughout Ontario

Ontario Milk Transport Association (OMTA)

#301, 660 Speedvale Ave. West, Guelph ON N1K 1E5
www.milk.org/Corporate/View.aspx?Content=Students/Transportation
Overview: A medium-sized provincial organization founded in 1967
Membership: 60 companies; *Member Profile:* Transporters of milk, such as producer-owned co-operatives, which collect raw milk from Ontario farms & take it to processing plants in Ontario, Quebec, & Manitoba

Ontario Traffic Conference (OTC)

#2, 6355 Kennedy Rd., Mississauga ON L5T 2L5
Tel: 647-346-4050; *Fax:* 647-346-4060
info@otc.org
www.otc.org
twitter.com/ontariotraffic
Overview: A medium-sized provincial organization
Description: To improve traffic conditions & traffic safety in municipalities of Ontario

Ontario Trucking Association (OTA)

555 Dixon Rd., Toronto ON M9W 1H8
Tel: 416-249-7401; *Fax:* 866-713-4188
publicaffairs@ontruck.org; membership@ontruck.org
www.ontruck.org
Overview: A large provincial organization founded in 1926
Finances: *Funding Sources:* Membership fees
Membership: 1,700 member companies; *Committees:* Axle Weight; Credit; Education; Executive; Social/Labour; Tech./Ops; Convention; Dues; Membership; Insurance; Finance; Environmental Issues
Activities: Offering training courses & seminars; *Speaker Service:* Yes *Library:* Yes
Description: To represent companies & industry suppliers; To provide political advocacy, education, & information services to North American freight transport companies

Ontario Trucking Association Education Foundation Inc.

555 Dixon Rd., Toronto ON M9W 1H8
Tel: 416-249-7401; *Fax:* 416-245-6152
education.foundation@ontruck.org
Overview: A small provincial charitable organization
Finances: *Annual Operating Budget:* Less than $50,000
Staff: 1 staff member(s); 5 volunteer(s)
Membership: 18

Operation Lifesaver (OL) / Opération Gareautrain

#1401, 99 Bank St., Ottawa ON K1P 6B9
Tel: 613-564-8100; *Fax:* 613-567-6726
admin@operationlifesaver.ca
www.operationlifesaver.ca
Overview: A small national organization founded in 1981
Finances: *Annual Operating Budget:* $250,000-$500,000; *Funding Sources:* Transport Canada; Railway Association of Canada
Staff: 2 staff member(s); 150 volunteer(s)
Activities: *Awareness Events:* OL Rail Safety Week, April
Description: To create an awareness by the general public of the potential hazards of rail/highway crossings; to improve drivers' & pedestrians' behaviour at these intersections; to inform the public of the dangers associated with trespassing on railway property; & to reduce the number of accidents resulting in fatalities, injuries & monetary losses

Pharmaceutical & Personal Care Logistics Association (PPCLA) / Association de logistique des soins personnels et pharmaceutiques

PO Box 40568, Stn. Six Points Plaza, Toronto ON M9B 6K8
Tel: 416-232-6817; *Fax:* 416-232-6818
Toll-Free: 866-293-1238
ppcla@ppcla.org
www.ppcla.org
Previous Name: Pharmaceutical & Toilet Preparations Traffic Association
Overview: A medium-sized national organization founded in 1958
Finances: *Annual Operating Budget:* Less than $50,000
Staff: 1 volunteer(s)
Membership: 47 institutional; *Fees:* $350; *Member Profile:* Logistics managers in the pharmaceutical & personal care industries
Description: To develop & promote the interchange of ideas & information concerning traffic & transportation matters of the pharmaceutical & toilet preparations industry; To foster fair dealings & cordial relationships among members & between representatives of the various modes of transportation employed by members

Private Motor Truck Council of Canada (PMTC) / Association canadienne du camionnage d'entreprise (ACCE)

#115, 1660 North Service Rd. East, Oakville ON L6H 7G3
Tel: 905-827-0587; *Fax:* 905-827-8212
Toll-Free: 877-501-7682
info@pmtc.ca
www.pmtc.ca
Overview: A medium-sized national organization founded in 1977
Finances: *Annual Operating Budget:* $250,000-$500,000; *Funding Sources:* Seminars; social events; membership fees
Staff: 4 staff member(s)
Membership: 400; *Member Profile:* Private truck fleets or suppliers to same; private truck fleets operated by companies whose principal business is other than transportation, but use their own truck fleets to further their business
Activities: Seminars; annual conference; benchmarking and best practices survey; National Vehicle Graphics Design Competition
Description: Recognized as the leader of the private trucking community in Canada; represents the varied interests of private fleet operators with integrity & sound business practices.; *Member of:* North American Private Truck Council
Affiliation(s): National Private Truck Council

Railway Association of Canada (RAC) / L'Association des chemins de fer du Canada (ACFC)

#901, 99 Bank St., Ottawa ON K1P 6B9
Tel: 613-567-8591; *Fax:* 613-567-6726
rac@railcan.ca
www.railcan.ca
Overview: A large national organization founded in 1917
Finances: *Annual Operating Budget:* Greater than $5 Million; *Funding Sources:* Members fees
Staff: 23 staff member(s)
Membership: 55 railways & 40 associates; *Fees:* $2,000 minimum; *Member Profile:* Railway companies operating in Canada; *Committees:* Policy; Accounting; Finance; Human Resources; Safety & Operations Management; Taxation
Activities: Operation Lifesaver
Description: To promote the commercial viability & the safe & efficient operation of the Canadian railway industry; to act on behalf of, or work jointly with, member companies to promote public policy & regulation that provides equitable treatment between shipping modes; to provide factual information on the railway industry for the public, government & industry, & to provide the views of the industry on public policy issues.
PUBLICATIONS: Interchange; Canadian Railway Medical Rules Handbook; Locomotive Emissions Monitoring Program 2009; Canada's Railway Lead North America.
Affiliation(s): Association of American Railroads

Recreational Aircraft Association (RAA) / Réseau aéronefs amateur

22 - 4881 Fountain St. North, Breslau ON N0B 1M0
Tel: 519-648-3030; *Toll-Free:* 800-387-1028
raa@raa.ca
www.raa.ca
Previous Name: Experimental Aircraft Association of Canada
Overview: A medium-sized national organization founded in 1983
Finances: *Annual Operating Budget:* $100,000-$250,000; *Funding Sources:* Membership dues
Staff: 1 staff member(s); 150 volunteer(s)
Membership: 2,000; *Fees:* $40; *Committees:* 12 regional
Activities: Fly-ins across Canada; *Speaker Service:* Yes
Description: To be a national leader in the development & advancement of recreational aviation; to promote recreational flying & building of amateur built aircraft, restorations of classic & antique aircraft
Affiliation(s): Recreational Aviation Foundation

Saskatchewan Trucking Association (STA)

1335 Wallace St., Regina SK S4N 3Z5
Tel: 306-569-9696; *Fax:* 306-569-1008
Toll-Free: 800-563-7623
ttoope@sasktrucking.com
www.sasktrucking.com
Overview: A medium-sized provincial licensing organization founded in 1937
Finances: *Annual Operating Budget:* $250,000-$500,000; *Funding Sources:* Membership fees; sponsorship of programs
Staff: 5 staff member(s)
Membership: 300; *Fees:* Schedule available
Activities: Truck Driver Roadeos
Description: Helps the industry fight its battles in everything from deregulation to weights and measures. Represents the industry in discussions with government

The Shipping Federation of Canada / La Fédération maritime du Canada

#326, 300, rue St-Sacrement, Montréal QC H2Y 1X4
Tel: 514-849-2325; *Fax:* 514-849-8774
Toll-Free: 877-534-7367
info@shipfed.ca
www.shipfed.ca
Overview: A medium-sized national organization founded in 1903
Finances: *Funding Sources:* International shipping
Staff: 8 staff member(s)
Membership: 83; *Member Profile:* Direct involvement in steamship business; *Committees:* Customs; Dangerous Goods; EDI; Immigration; Pilotage; Railways; Tanker Safety
Activities: To protect members in all matters affecting the operation of shipping from & to Eastern Canada, the St. Lawrence River, the Great Lakes & Arctic ports; areas of concern include pilotage, pollution, navigation aids, port operations, port charges, & federal government legislation & regulation

Shipyard General Workers' Federation of British Columbia (CLC) / Fédération des ouvriers des chantiers navals de la Colombie-Britannique (CTC)

#130, 111 Victoria Dr., Vancouver BC V5L 4C4
Tel: 604-254-8204; *Fax:* 604-254-7447
office@bcshipyardworkers.com
www.bcshipyardworkers.com
Overview: A medium-sized provincial organization
Membership: 1,100 + 3 locals
Affiliation(s): Machinists, Fitters & Helpers Industrial Union #3, Marine Workers & Boilerworkers' Industrial Union #1, Shipwrights, Joiners & Caulkers' Industrial Union #9

Société des traversiers du Québec (STQ)

250, rue Saint-Paul, Québec QC G1K 9K9
Tél: 418-643-2019; *Téléc:* 418-643-7308
Ligne sans frais: 877-787-7483
stq@traversiers.gouv.qc.ca
www.traversiers.gouv.qc.ca
Aperçu: *Dimension:* petite; *Envergure:* provinciale; fondée en 1971
Finances: *Budget de fonctionnement annuel:* Plus de $5 Million
Membre: 100-499
Description: Contribuer à la mobilité des personnes et des marchandises en assurant des services de transport maritime de qualité, sécuritaires et fiables, favorisant ainsi l'essor social, économique et touristique du Québec

Sydney & Louisburg Railway Historical Society / Le Musée de chemin de fer de Sydney à Louisburg

7330 Main St., Louisbourg NS B1C 1P5
Also Known As: S&L Museum
Overview: A small local organization founded in 1973
Finances: *Annual Operating Budget:* Less than $50,000

Staff: 6 volunteer(s)
Membership: 210; *Fees:* $10
Activities: Annual reunion, Sept.; *Awareness Events:* Samuel B. Morse - Museum Day, July 1 *Library:* Resource Centre (Open to Public) by appointment
Description: To commemorate the history of the S&L Railway by preserving & displaying the artifacts & documents which survive; to commemorate the people who worked for the S&L Railway; to explain the local & commercial history of the area which relates to the S&L Railway; to explain & commemorate the general themes of railway & transportation history & technology; *Member of:* Federation of the Nova Scotian Heritage; Heritage Canada

Teamsters Canada Rail Conference (TCRC) / Conference ferroviaire de Teamsters Canada (CFTC)

#1710, 130 Albert St., Ottawa ON K1P 5G4
Tel: 613-235-1828; *Fax:* 613-235-1069
info@teamstersrail.ca
www.teamstersrail.ca
Previous Name: Brotherhood of Locomotive Engineers
Overview: A medium-sized national organization
Membership: 16,000 in 21 divisions; *Fees:* $15
Activities: *Library:* Yes (Open to Public)

Toronto Transportation Society (TTS)

PO Box 5187, Stn. A, Toronto ON M5W 1N5
ttswebmaster@torontotransportationsociety.org
www.torontotransportationsociety.org
Overview: A small local organization founded in 1973
Finances: *Funding Sources:* Membership dues
Staff: 7 volunteer(s)
Membership: 131; *Fees:* $20; *Committees:* Executive; Trips & Excursions
Activities: *Library:* Yes
Description: To afford persons interested in transportation by land, facilities for discussion & exchange of information

Transport Action Canada

Bronson Centre, PO Box 858, Stn. B, #303, 211 Bronson Ave., Ottawa ON K1P 5P9
Tel: 613-594-3290; *Fax:* 613-594-3271
info@transport-action.ca
www.transport-action.ca
Previous Name: Transport 2000 Canada
Overview: A medium-sized national charitable organization founded in 1976
Finances: *Annual Operating Budget:* $50,000-$100,000; *Funding Sources:* Donations
Staff: 15 volunteer(s)
Membership: 1,500; *Fees:* $35 regular; $30 senior; $50 family; $75 affiliate non-profit; $170corporate
Activities: Research, public education & advocacy, representation of the consumer interests before federal, provincial, municipal public hearings & regulatory bodies, direction of consumer complaints to public carriers; *Speaker Service:* Yes *Library:* Yes (Open to Public)
Description: National federation of environmental & consumer groups concerned about the importance of transportation on our environment & quality of life; to inform Canadians of the need for a coherent national transport policy which recognizes that conservation of resources must be a priority & that access to good public transportation is a right of all Canadians; to work for the improvement & greater use of bus & rail transportation in the interests of public safety, social equity & the protection of the environment; to press for the coordination of all transport services for the benefit of users; to demand more attention to the needs of pedestrians, cyclists & public transport users; to maximize the use of the energy-efficient rail & marine modes for the shipment of freight. PUBLICATIONS: National Transport Newsletter.
Affiliation(s): Transport 2000 International

Transportation Association of Canada (TAC) / Association des transports du Canada (ATC)

2323 St. Laurent Blvd., Ottawa ON K1G 4J8
Tel: 613-736-1350; *Fax:* 613-736-1395
secretariat@tac-atc.ca
www.tac-atc.ca
Previous Name: Roads & Transportation Association of Canada
Overview: A large national organization founded in 1970
Finances: *Annual Operating Budget:* Greater than $5 Million
Staff: 30 staff member(s); 500 volunteer(s)
Membership: 550 corporate; *Fees:* Schedule available; *Committees:* Technical & Research; Editing & Publications; Rules of the Road; Project; Technical Steering; Asphalts Advisory; Operations; Pavements; Structures; Aviation; Conference Technical Program; Geometric Design; Goods Movement; Soils & Materials; Traffic; Transit Planning; Technology
Activities: *Library:* Technical Information Centre by appointment
Description: To promote the provision of safe, efficient, effective & environmentally sustainable transportation services in support of Canada's social & economic goals; To act as a neutral forum for the discussion of transportation issues & matters; to act as a technical focus in the highway transportation area

Truck Training Schools Association of Ontario Inc. (TTSAO)

Fax: 519-858-0920
Toll-Free: 866-475-9436
training@ttsao.com
www.ttsao.com
Overview: A small national licensing organization founded in 1992
Finances: *Annual Operating Budget:* $100,000-$250,000
Staff: 7 staff member(s)
Membership: 75; *Fees:* Schedule available
Activities: *Internships:* Yes
Description: To provide the trucking industry with the highest quality driver training programs for entry level individuals that earn & maintain public confidence, adhering to sound & ethical business practices
Affiliation(s): Ontario Trucking Association; Ministry of Education, Ministry of Transportation

Truckers Association of Nova Scotia (TANS)

PO Box 1527, 184 Arthur St., Truro NS B2N 5V2
Tel: 902-895-7447; *Fax:* 902-897-0487
Toll-Free: 800-232-6631
contact@tans.ca
www.tans.ca
Overview: A medium-sized provincial organization founded in 1968
Description: Promotes all matters aiding the development and improvement of the trucking industry and the allied trades in Nova Scotia, including social, recreational, benevolent, educational and charitable activities. In addition, the Truckers Association of Nova Scotia makes presentations to government and other regulatory bodies in relation to the economic welfare of the trucking industry and is the main proponent in gaining access to the provincial haul rates and beneficial changes to the contract specifications used by the contractors; *Member of:* The Transportation Sector of Voluntary Planning
Affiliation(s): Atlantic Provinces Trucking Association of Nova Scotia

Ultralight Pilots Association of Canada (UPAC) / Association canadienne des pilotes d'avions ultra-légers

907289 Township Rd. 12, RR#4, Bright ON N0J 1B0
Tel: 519-684-7628
www.upac.ca
Overview: A small national organization
Finances: *Annual Operating Budget:* Less than $50,000; *Funding Sources:* Membership fees
Staff: 10 volunteer(s)
Membership: 500+; *Fees:* $40; *Member Profile:* Interest in ultralight aviaton
Activities: Video library for members; *Library:* Video Library (Open to Public)
Description: To promote ultralight aviation in Canada

Union of Canadian Transportation Employees (UCTE) / Union canadienne des employés des transports (UCET)

#702, 233 Gilmour St., Ottawa ON K2P 0P2
Tel: 613-238-4003; *Fax:* 613-236-0379
buschml@psac-afpc.comm
www.ucte.com
Overview: A medium-sized national organization
Membership: 7,500 + 90 locals
Description: The Union represents members working in the public & private sectors of the Canadian transportation industry (ports, airports, NAV Canada, pilotage authorities, transportation companies, canals, the Dept. of Transport, lighthouses, ships and Canadian Coast Guard bases)

United Transportation Union (AFL-CIO/CLC) - Canada

71 Bank St., 7th Fl., Ottawa ON K1P 5N2
Tel: 613-747-7979; *Fax:* 613-747-2815
Overview: A medium-sized national organization
Membership: 8,500 + 79 locals
Member of: United Transportation Union (AFL-CIO/CLC), Cleveland USA

University of Toronto Institute for Aerospace Studies

Faculty of Applied Science & Engineering, 4925 Dufferin St., Toronto ON M3H 5T6
Tel: 416-667-7700; *Fax:* 416-667-7799
www.utias.utoronto.ca
Overview: A medium-sized national organization founded in 1949
Membership: 68
Activities: *Library:* Yes
Description: UTIAS is a graduate studies and research institute, forming part of the faculty of Applied Science and Engineering at the University of Toronto.
Affiliation(s): Canadian Aeronautics & Space Institute; Institute for Space & Terrestrial Science; Canadian Space Agency; Intelligent Sensing for Innovative Structures Canada

Upper Canada Railway Society

PO Box 122, Stn. A, Toronto ON M5W 1A2
Tel: 416-921-4023
ucrs@btinternet.com
Overview: A small national organization founded in 1941
Membership: 600; *Fees:* $29
Description: To work to preserve history & railways of Canada; *Member of:* Community Heritage Project

The Van Horne Institute for International Transportation & Regulatory Affairs

#620 Earth Sciences Bldg., 2500 University Dr. NW, Calgary AB T2N 1N4
Tel: 403-220-8455; *Fax:* 403-282-4663
vanhorne@ucalgary.ca
www.vanhorne.info/
Overview: A small international organization founded in 1991
Finances: *Annual Operating Budget:* Less than $50,000; *Funding Sources:* Private sector
Staff: 4 staff member(s)
Membership: 60; *Member Profile:* Government; industry; education; *Committees:* Centre for Transportation; Centre for Regulatory Affairs; Centre for Innovation & Communication
Activities: Transporation research & education; programs to assist in improving the efficiency & equity of transportation & regulated industries; *Speaker Service:* Yes; *Rents Mailing List:* Yes *Library:* Yes (Open to Public)
Description: To contribute to public policy development & education in the areas of transportation & regulated industries. PUBLICATIONS: On-Trac.
Affiliation(s): University of Calgary; University of Alberta; Southern Alberta Institute of Technology

Vintage Locomotive Society Inc.

PO Box 33021, RPO Polo Park, Winnipeg MB R3G 3N4
Tel: 204-832-5259; *Fax:* 866-751-2348
info@pdcrailway.com
www.pdcrailway.com
Also Known As: Prairie Dog Central Steam Train
Overview: A small local charitable organization founded in 1968
Finances: *Annual Operating Budget:* $250,000-$500,000
Staff: 170 volunteer(s)
Membership: 170 individuals; *Fees:* $25 full; $15 junior; $40 family; *Committees:* Restoration-Locomotive; Restoration-Coaches; Painting; Sign Work; Public Relations; Advertising; Photography; Operations & Maintenance
Activities: *Speaker Service:* Yes
Description: To collect, restore for operation & maintain steam locomotives & rolling stock of early part of twentieth-century; to provide source of historical information relating to origin & past operation of acquired equipment & buildings

West Coast Railway Association (WCRA)

PO Box 2790, Vancouver BC V6B 3X2
Tel: 604-524-1011; *Fax:* 604-876-4104
Toll-Free: 800-722-1233
info@wcra.org
www.wcra.org
Overview: A small local charitable organization founded in 1961
Finances: *Annual Operating Budget:* $500,000-$1.5 Million; *Funding Sources:* Tours; government grants; donations; fundraising; foundation
Staff: 12 staff member(s); 150 volunteer(s)
Membership: 600 individual; *Fees:* Schedule available; *Member Profile:* Interest in railways past & present; *Committees:* Museum; Tours; Collections; Motive Power; Children; Education
Activities: Develops & operates West Coast Railway Heritage Park in Squamish B.C. - collection of over 60 locomotives, freight & passenger cars; operates tour progrm; other community event; Day out with Thoma, June; *Speaker Service:* Yes *Library:* Archives (Open to Public) by appointment
Description: Collects, preserves, restores, operates & exhibits artifacts relating to the history of railways, especially those of BC; the West Coast Railway Heritage Park in Squamish BC develops educational exhibits on railway heritage for all age

groups; the tour program encourages the public to travel today's railways to see Canada; *Member of:* Association of Rail Museums; Tourist Railroad Association

Western Transportation Advisory Council (WESTAC)
#1140, 800 Pender St. West, Vancouver BC V6C 2V6
Tel: 604-687-8691; *Fax:* 604-687-8751
infoservices@westac.com
www.westac.com
Overview: A small local organization founded in 1973
Finances: *Annual Operating Budget:* $500,000-$1.5 Million; *Funding Sources:* Membership fees; project fees; professional services fees
Staff: 4 staff member(s)
Membership: 52 corporate; *Fees:* Revenue-related scale; *Member Profile:* Carriers; shippers; ports & terminals; labour unions; government
Activities: *Library:* Yes by appointment
Description: To advance Western Canadian economy through the improvement of the region's transportation system.

Companies

Airline Companies

ACE Aviation Holdings Inc.
5100 boul de Maisonneuve Ouest, Montréal, QC H4A 3T2
www.aceaviation.com
Profile: Air Canada, Aeroplan, Jazz, and ACTS are subsidiaries of ACE Aviation.
Monte R. Brewer, President & CEO, Air Canada
Duncan Dunne, EVP/CFO
Sydney Isaacs, SVP Corporate Affairs/Cheif Administrative Officier
Greg Cote, SVP Corporate Development/Chief Legal Officer
Jack McLean, Controller

Aer Lingus
#130, 300 Jericho Quadrangle, Jericho, NY 11753
Fax: 516-622-4281
ccu@aerlingus.com
www.flyaerlingus.com

Aerolineas Argentinas
#120, 1000 NW 57th Ct., Miami, FL 33126
Tel: 305-261-0100; Fax: 305-648-4102
Toll-Free: 800-333-0276
reserve@us.aerolineas.aero
www.aerolineas.com.ar
Vilma Castellino, Manager, Rep World

Air Canada
Air Canada Centre 1235, PO Box 14000, Dorval, QC H4Y 1H4
Tel: 514-422-5000; Fax: 514-422-5789
www.aircanada.ca
Ticker Symbol: AC
Profile: Scheduled air transportation; Travel agencies; Arrangement of transportation of freight & cargo
Lise Fournel, Sr. Vice-President, E-Commerce
Joseph D. Randell, President, Air Canada Jazz
Joshua Koshy, CFO & Exec. Vice-President
Duncan Dee, Sr. Vice-President, Corporate Affairs

Air Creebec
PO Box 430, 101, 7th St., Val-d'Or, QC J9P 4P4
Tél: 819-825-8355; Ligne sans frais: 800-567-6567
www.aircreebec.ca
Profile: Air Creebec aims to provide safe, reliable, and efficient air transportation within Eeyou Istchee and beyond.
Albert Diamond, President

Air France
 # 1510, 2000 rue Mansfield, Montreal, QC H3A 3A3
Tel: 514-847-1106; Fax: 514-847-5013
Toll-Free: 800-667-2747
www.airfrance.ca
Jean-Cyril Spinette, Chairman and CEO
Pierre-Henri Gourgeon, President and Chief Operating Officier
Philippe Calavia, CEO
Alain Bassil, EVP- Air France Industries
Francois Brousse, SVP Corporate Communications
Pascal de Izaguirre, EVP Ground Operations
Bruno Matheu, EVP Marketing/Network Management
Bruno Matheu, EVP Marketing/Network Management
Edouard Odier, EVP Information Technology
Gilbert Rovetto, EVP Flight Operations

Air India Ltd.
#218, 5955 Airport Rd., Mississauga, ON L4V 1R9
Tel: 905-405-2160; Fax: 905-405-2169
Toll-Free: 800-625-6424
yyz@airindiacanada.ca
www.airindia.com
V. Thulasidas, Chairman and Managing Director, Air India
M. Kacker, Chief Vigiliance Officer/Offg. Executive Director-Secur
Amod Sharma, Director Finance
K.M. Unni, Director Engineering
V.K. Verma, Director Commercial
Jitender Bhargava, Executive Director-Coordination
S. Ranganathan, Executive Director Ground Services
Deepak Anand, Executive Director Operations
Paul Lakra, Executive Director-Mumbai Airport
I.S. Vhatkar, General Manager Properties/Facilities

Air Nootka
PO Box 19, Gold River, BC V0P 1G0
Tel: 250-283-2255; Toll-Free: 877-795-2255
info@airnootka.com
www.airnootka.com
Profile: Air Nootka is a floatplane operation based out of Gold River, British Columbia. It provides service to all of Vancouver Island, including Victoria, Nanaimo, Comox, Campbell River, & Kyuquot, as well as Vancouver.

Air North Airlines
150 Condor Rd., Whitehorse, YK Y1A 6E6
Tel: 867-668-2228; Fax: 867-393-4601
Toll-Free: 800-661-0407
customerservice@flyairnorth.com
www.flyairnorth.com
Profile: Frequent departures from all supported aiports; Great Value Cargo service at the price of general freight (ground service); Cargo Friendly Cargo can be taken directly to the Airport and quickly processed while you wait.

Air St-Pierre
c/o Air Saint-Pierre, PO Box 1660, 1 Bell Blvd., Enfield, NS B2T 1K2
Tel: 902-873-3566; Fax: 902-873-3567
halifax@airsaintpierre.com
www.airsaintpierre.com

Air Transat
5959 Côte-Vertu Blvd., Montréal, QC H4S 2E6
Tel: 514-636-3630; Toll-Free: 877-872-6728
information@airtransat.com
www.airtransat.com
Profile: Air Transat is a wholly owned subsidiary of Transat A.T. Inc. They specialize in both scheduled and charter flights from Canada to vacation destinations. In the winter months, the majority of flights are between Canada to vacation desintations. In the winter months, the majority of flights are between Canada and the Caribbean/USA and in the summer between Canada and many European countries. Year-round schedule services operate between Europe and Canada. The Air Transat fleet of 15 aircraft serves over 90 destinations in 25 countries.
Pierre Ménard, Vice-President, Operations

Alitalia
#202, 5915 Airport Rd., Mississauga, ON L4V 1T1
Tel: 905-673-2442; Fax: 905-673-6089
Toll-Free: 800-268-9277
atitaliasupport@alicos.net
www.alitalia.ca
Berardino Libonati, Chairman

American Airlines Inc. / AA
www.aa.com
A.W. Pliszka, General Manager, Toronto

Austrian Airlines
c/o Airport Toronto - Pearson Int'l (Lester), Toronto, ON L5P 1A2
Toll-Free: 800-563-5954
www.aua.com
Pierre Doueihi, Manager

Avianca
#100, 8350 NW 52nd Ter., Miami, FL 33166
www.avianca.com

British Airways
c/o British Airways Customer Relations, USA, East Elmhurst, NY 11369-0098
www.britishairways.com
Bernie Herenberg

CanJet Airlines
Parent: IMP Group Ltd.
PO Box 980, Enfield, NS B2T 1R6
Tel: 902-873-7800; Fax: 902-873-6580
Toll-Free: 800-809-7777
www.canjet.com

Central Mountain Air Ltd. / CMA
Formerly: Central Mountain International
PO Box 998, 6431 Airport Rd., Smithers, BC V0J 2N0
Tel: 250-877-5000; Fax: 250-874-3744
info@flycma.com
www.flycma.com
Profile: 300+ employees. Centreal Mountain Air is pleased to offer selected cargo services to a majority of our route network destinations. we endeavor to provide our cusomters with a convenient and economical cargo product. Established in 1987 Central Mountain Air (CMA) is a Western Canadian privately owned and operated company offering scheduled and charter flights to over 17 British Columbia and Alberta communities.

CHC Helicopter Corporation
4740 Agar Dr., Richmond, BC V7B 1A3
Tel: 604-276-7500;
commercial@chc.ca
www.chc.ca
Ticker Symbol: FLY
Profile: Nonscheduled & scheduled air transportation; Airports, flying fields & airport terminal services; Vocational schools
Sylvain A. Allard, CEO
Jo Mark Zurel, CFO & Sr. Vice-President

Cougar Helicopters Inc.
Parent: VIH Aviation Group
St. John's International Airport, PO Box 21300, 40 Craig Dobbins' Way, St. John's, NL A1A 4Y3
Tel: 709-758-4800; Fax: 709-758-4850
info@cougar.ca
www.cougar.ca
Profile: The company's main service is flying oil rig workers to & from their offshore locations, with search & rescue as a secondary service to offshore operators.
Hank Williams, General Manager

Cubana
c/o Canada (GSA CGO) Exp-Air Cargo, #206, 675 King St. West, Toronto, ON M5V 1M9
Tel: 905-673-6750; Fax: 905-673-1899
cubana1@cubanaairlines.ca
www.cubana.cu
Ramon Valdivia

Czech Airlines
#1510, 401 Bay St., Toronto, ON M5H 2Y4
Tel: 416-363-3174; Fax: 416-363-0239
Toll-Free: 800-641-0641
call.centre@csa.cz
www.czechairlines.com
Ladislav Slipka, Regional Director

Discovery Air Innovations / DAI
#102, 2344, boul Alfred-Nobel, Montréal, QC H4S 0A4
Tél: 514-447-3655; Téléc: 514-336-4730
info@da-innovations.com
www.da-innovations.com
Ticker Symbol: DA.A; DA.B. / TSX
Profile: DAI is a specialty aviation company that provides air transport, maintenance, & logistics services for its clients in government & business. It was founded in 2004 & currently has 150 aircraft operated & maintained by 850 employees.
Paul Bouchard, President
Cynthia Ballesteros, Manager, Business Development & Marketing

El Al Israel Airlines
#803, 1000 Finch Ave. West, Toronto, ON M3J 2V5
Tel: 416-967-4222; Fax: 416-967-1643
Toll-Free: 800-361-6174
reservations@elalcanada.com
www.elal.co.il

Fast Air Ltd.
80 Hangar Line Rd., Winnipeg, MB R3J 3Y7
Tel: 204-982-7240; Fax: 204-783-2483
Toll-Free: 888-372-3780
info@flyfastair.com
www.flyfastair.com
Profile: Fast Air operates from a private business-class terminal at the Winnipeg James Armstrong Richardson International Airport, & provides aircraft charter, air ambulance, & aircraft management services.

Finnair G.S.A Canada
c/o Finnair Cargo Sales, New York, NY
Tel: 718-656-7570; Toll-Free: 718-917-6361
cargo.jfk@finnair.com
www.finnair.com
Tommi Mormonen, Managing Director

First Air
20 Cope Dr., Kanata, ON K2M 2V8
Tel: 613-254-6200; Fax: 613-254-6398
www.firstair.ca
Profile: Specializes in travel to Northern Canada. First Air operates a versatile fleet of 17 aircraft for regularly scheduled passenger and air cargo services. The fellt of well-maintained, modern aircraft also provides First Air with the size and flexibility to meet your air charter services requirements. First Air offers scheduled service to 28 destinations in Nunavut, Northwest Territories, Manitoba, Alberta, Yukon, Quebec, and Ontario operating a fleet of 20 aircraft. The Inuit owned airline has over 1,000 employees, of which more than 450 work and live in the north.
Rick Lefebvre, Director Sales, Eastern Region
Mike Olsen, Director Sales, Western Region
Scott Bateman, VP Commercial Operations
Don Orr, VP Flight Operations/Maintenance
Jim Ballingall, VP Marketing/Sales
Jan Traversy, VPVP Finance

Harbour Air Seaplanes
c/o Harbour Air Ltd., Corporate Head Office, 4760 Inglis Dr., Richmond, BC V7B 1W4
Tel: 604-274-1277; Fax: 604-274-1200
Toll-Free: 800-665-0212
www.harbour-air.com

Helijet International
c/o Vancouver International Airport, 5911 Airport Rd. South, Richmond, BC V7B 1B5
Tel: 604-273-4688; Fax: 604-273-5301
passengerServices@helijet.com
www.helijet.com
Profile: Helijet are the first scheduled helicopter service in Canada and since their inception in 1986, they now have a fleet of 10 helicopters and airplanes with a staff of over 100 employees. They also have cargo services which ship time sensitive envelops and packages with speed and reliability.

Icelandair
1900 Crown Colony Dr., Quincy, MA 02169
Toll-Free: 800-223-5500
www.icelandair.com
Jón Karl Ólafsson, CEO/President, The Americas
Andri Ass Grétarsson, SVP Finance/Resource Management
Guðjón Arngr¡msson, VP Corporate Communications
Guðmundur Pálsson, SVP Operations
Gunnar Már Sigurfinnsson, SVP Marketing/Sales
Hjörtur Porgilsson, VP Information Technology
Jens Bjarnason, SVP Technical Services
Una Eypórsdóttir, VP Human Resources

Japan Airlines
c/o Vancouver International Airport, #C3152.0B, Richmond, BC V7B 1X8
Toll-Free: 800-525-3663
www.japanair.com
Haruka Nishimatsu, President/CEO

Jazz
c/o Halifax Stanfield International Airport, 310 Goudey Dr., Enfield, NS B2T 1E4
Tel: 902-873-5000; Fax: 902-873-2098
websupport@flyjazz.ca
Profile: At Jazz, their priorities include safe, efficient, and on-time operations and have over 4,300 employees. They have a fleet of 36 planes.

Keewatin Air LP
1 Allen Dyne Rd., Winnipeg, MB R3H 0Z9
Tel: 204-888-0100; Fax: 204-888-3300
Toll-Free: 877-879-8477
www.kivalliqair.com
Profile: Keewatin Air's primary function is medical air travel, although they also offer charter & scheduled airline services to Nunavut & northern Manitoba.
Wayne McLeod, President & Operations Manager
wmcleod@keewatinair.ca
Denis Lavallee, CFO
dlavalee@keewatinair.ca
Penny Triggs, Vice-President, Air Medical Operations
ptriggs@keewatinair.ca

Kelowna Flightcraft Air Charter Ltd. / KFACL
Parent: Kelowna Flightcraft Ltd.
5655 Airport Way, Kelowna, BC V1V 1S1
Tel: 250-491-5500; Fax: 250-765-1489
kfcharters@flightcraft.ca
www.flightcraft.ca
Profile: Kelowna Flightcraft Air Charter Ltd. is a dedicated carrier for Canada Post & Purolator Courier.
Barry Lapointe, President, Kelowna Flightcraft Ltd.
barryl@flightcraft.ca

KLM Royal Dutch Airlines
Formerly: Northwest/KLM Royal Dutch Airlines
235 King St. East, Kitchener, ON N2G 4N5
Toll-Free: 800-375-8723
www.klm.com

Korean Air
1813 Wilshire Blvd., Los Angeles, CA 90057
Toll-Free: 800-438-5000
www.koreanair.com

LAN Airlines
Formerly: LanChile
#902, 18 King St. East, Toronto, ON M5C 1C4
Tel: 416-862-0807; Fax: 416-862-5453
www.lan.com

LOT Polish Airlines
3111 Convair Dr., Mississauga, ON L5P 1B2
Tel: 416-236-4242; Toll-Free: 212-789-0970
www.lot.com
Wojciech Maciszewski, General Manager

Lufthansa German Airlines
PO Box 939, 31 Adelaide St. E, Toronto, ON M5K 2K3
Tel: 877-234-3449; Fax: 866-325-3044
www.lufthansa.com
Justin Gosling, General Manager, Passenger Sales, Canada

Northern Thunderbird Air Inc.
#101, 4245 Hangar Rd., Prince George, BC V2N 4M6
Tel: 250-963-9611; Fax: 250-963-8422
Toll-Free: 800-963-9611
www.ntair.ca
Bill Hesse, General Manager
Bernice Hesse, Operations Manager
Ed Goodkey, Controller
Shawna Finch, Maintenance Manager

Olympic Air
www.olympicair.com

Pacific Coastal Airlines
c/o Vancouver International Airport, #204, 4440 Cowely Crest., Richmond, BC V7B 1B8
Tel: 604-214-2358; Fax: 604-273-4485
www.pacificcoastal.com
Daryl Smith, CEO/Director

PIA Pakistan International Airlines
#620, 56 Aberfoyle Cres., Toronto, ON M8X 2W4
Tel: 416-972-6480; Fax: 416-926-0507
ytouupk@piac.aero
www.piac.com.pk
Zaffar A. Khan, Chairman

Purolator Courier Ltd.
5995 Avebury Rd., Mississauga, ON L5R 3T8
Toll-Free: 888-529-9777
www.purolator.com
Profile: Air courier services
Robert C. Johnson, President/CEO
Sheldon Bell, Sr. Vice-President & CFO

Royal Jordanian
#1B-1, 2085 Union St., Montréal, QC H3A 2C3
Tel: 514-288-1655; Fax: 514-288-7572
Toll-Free: 800-363-0711
yultbrj@rja.com.jo
www.rj.com
Omar Kamal, Area Manager, Canada

Skyservice Airlines Inc.
6120 Midfield Rd., Mississauga, ON L4W 2P7
Tel: 905-677-3000; Fax: 905-677-2747
Toll-Free: 888-759-3269
toronto@skyservice.com
www.skyservice.com

Swiss International Air Lines
c/o Pierre Elliott Trudeau International Airport, Montréal, ON
Toll-Free: 877-359-7947
www.swiss.com
Olivier Schlegel, General Manager

Trans North Helicopters
PO Box 8, 115 Range Rd., Whitehorse, YK Y1A 5X9
Tel: 867-668-2177; Fax: 867-668-3420
email@tntaheli.com
www.tntaheli.com
Arden Meyer, General Manager
Rob Fletcher, Operations Manager
Charlie Hoeller, Director of Maintenance
Doug Kerley, Chief Pilot
Diane Barnhart, Accountant

Transat A.T. Inc.
Place du Parc, #600, 300, rue Léo-Pariseau, Montréal, QC H2X 4C2
Tel: 514-987-1616;
info@transat.com
www.transat.com
Ticker Symbol: TRZ
Profile: Offices of holding companies; Air transportation, scheduled; Travel agencies; Airports, flying fields, & airport terminal services; Tour operators
Jean-Marc Eustache, President/CEO
Nelson Gentiletti, CFO & Vice-President, Finance & Administration
Jean-Marc Bélisle, Vice-President/Chief Information Officer

United Airlines
Formerly: Continental Airlines
PO Box 66100, Chicago, IL 6066
www.united.com
Profile: Subsidary company: Continental Mirconesia, Inc.
Larry Kellner, Chairman/CEO
Jeffery Smisek, President Continental Airlines
Jim Compton, EVP Marketing
Jeff Misner, EVP/CFO
Mark Moran, EVP Operations
Ron Anderson-Lehman, SVP/CIO
Rebecca Cox, SVP Government Affairs
Dave Hilfman, SVP Sales

VIH Aviation Group
1962 Canso Rd., North Saanich, BC V8L 5V5
Tel: 250-656-3987; Fax: 250-655-6839
Toll-Free: 866-844-4354
vih@vih.com
www.vih.com
Profile: VIH is a helicopter management company, with operations in the following divisions: Cougar Helicopters; VIH Helicopters; VIH Aerospace; YYJ FBO Services; & VIH Execujet. VIH Helicopters Ltd. can be contacted at the Group head office address.
Ken Norie, President/CEO
Charlie Mooney, Senior Vice-President, VFR Operations & General Manager, VIH Helicopters Ltd.

VIH Execujet Inc.
Parent: VIH Aviation Group
Victoria International Airport, #101, 1962 Canso Rd., North Saanich, BC V8L 5V5
Tel: 250-656-6887;
www.yyjfbo.com/vihexecujet.asp
Profile: VIH Execujet operates executive-class jet charter services out of Victoria International Airport. The company has two aircraft available for charter: a Challenger 604, & Hawker 800SP.
Jen Norie, Charter Coordinator
250-869-6980, jnorie@vih.com

WestJet
22 Aerial Pl., N.E., Calgary, AB T2E 3J1
www.westjet.com
Profile: Their fleet is the most modern of any large commercial airline which is comprised of 62 Boeing Next-Generation 737 aircrafts equipped with more legroom, leather seats and live seatback televisions on more than 85% of its fleet.
Sean Durfy, President
Donald Bell, Executive VP of Culture

WestJet Airlines Ltd.
22 Aerial Pl. N.E., Calgary, AB T2E 3J1
Toll-Free: 888-937-8538
investor_relations@westjet.com
www.westjet.com
Ticker Symbol: WJA
Profile: Scheduled air transportation throughout North America

Clive J. Beddoe, President & Chair
Alexander (Sandy) Campbell, CFO/Sr. Vice President, Finance
Russ Hall, Exec. Vice-President, Guest Service & Information Technology

Maritime Shipping

Admiral Marine Inc.
6127 Steeles Ave. West, Toronto, ON M9L 2V1
Tel: 416-792-8955; Fax: 888-635-0247
admiral@admiralmarine.ca
www.admiralmarine.ca
Profile: Canstar Ocean Line through Admiral Marine operate a regular break-bulk/conventional service from North America to Europe with transshipment via Antwerp to Eastern Europe, the Middle East and Africa. Canstar is a full service transportation consulting company that specializes in the shipment of over-dimensional, ro.ro, break-bulk, heavy lift, and project cargoes.

Algoma Central Corporation
#1000, 103 Church St., St Catharines, ON L2R 3C4
www.algonet.com
Ticker Symbol: ALC
Profile: Algoma Central Corporation operates vessels throughout the Great Lakes-St. Lawrence Waterway from the Gulf of St. Lawrence, through all 5 Great Lakes. The corporation owns 19 Canadian-flagged dry-bulk vessels. The operational and commercial activities of the Canadian-flag dry-bulk team are managed by Seaway Marine Transport, a partnership with Upper Great Lakes Shipping Inc., an unrelated company. The Corporation also has an interest in one tug & one barge.
Tim S. Dool, President/CEO
G.D. Wight, Vice-President, Finance
Robert Cook, Director, Information Services
Kevin Reid, Director, Safety

Algoma Central Corporation
Formerly: Seaway Marine Transport
#300, 20 Corporate Park Dr., St. Catharines, ON L2S 3W2
Tel: 905-988-2600; Fax: 905-988-1803
www.seawaymarinetransport.com
Profile: Seaway Marine Transport Manages the largest and most versatile fleet of self-unloading vessels and the largest fleet of gearless bulk carriers operating on the Great Lakes, St. Lawrence River and the waters of eastern Canada. This is comprised of 22 self-unloading vessels and 12 gearless bulk cargo vessels.
Allister Paterson, President & CEO
Dennis McPhee, Director, Marketing

American President Lines Ltd.
APL Canada, #181, 10 Four Seasons Pl., Toronto, ON M9B 6H7
Tel: 416-620-7790; Fax: 416-620-7723
www.apl.com
Profile: APL provides customers around the world with container transportation services through a network combining high-quality intermodal operations with state-of-the-art information technology.
David Goodwin, Vice President, Corporate Affairs
Mike Zampa, Director, Corporate Communications

Anglo-Eastern Group
Formerly: Anglo-Eastern Ship Management Ltd.
#235, 6600 Trans-Canada, Pointe Claire, QC H9R 4S2
Tel: 514-697-3091; Fax: 514-697-3048
www.angloeasterngroup.com
Profile: Currently the Anglo-Eastern Group looks after a varied fleet and crew base trading and operates worldwide.
Peter Cremers, President

Atlantic Towing Limited / ATL
Parent: J.D. Irving, Limited
PO Box 5777, 300 Union St., Saint John, NB E2L 4M3
Tel: 506-648-2750; Fax: 506-648-2752
chartering@atlantow.com
www.atlantictowing.com
Profile: ATL provides marine towing services including harbour, coastal, & offshore.
Mary Keith, Vice-President, Communications, J.D. Irving, Limited
506-632-5122, keith.mary@jdirving.com

Canada Steamship Lines Inc.
759 Victoria Square, Montreal, QC H2Y 2K3
Tel: 514-982-3800; Fax: 514-982-3910
info@cslmtl.com
cslcan.ca
Profile: Since 1945 Canada Steamship Lines and its affiliates have been part of the lifeblood of the Canadian economy. Throughout the years, Canada Steamship lines has consistently fulfilled the needs of its clients by providing the supply lines necessary to ensure the survival and prosperity of many industry sectors. Today, Canada Steamship Lines is considered a visionary pioneer in its field and a commendable success story for Canada.
Gerald Carter, President
Claude Dumais, Vice President, Technical Operations
Kirk Jones, Director, Transportation Services

The CSL Group
759, carré Victoria, 6 étage, Montréal, QC H2Y 2K3
Tél: 514-982-3800; Téléc: 514-982-3801
ships@cslmtl.com
www.csl.ca
Profile: Specializes in bulk transportation & self-loading technology
Meredith (Sam) Hayes, President/CEO
Pierre Richard, Vice-President, Finance & Administration

F.K. Warren Ltd.
Cogswell Tower, #920, 2000 Barrington St., Halifax, NS B3J 3X1
Tel: 902-423-8136; Fax: 902-429-1326
www.fkwarren.ca
Profile: F.K. Warren brings together technological, human, and material resources to ensure we meet our of supplying efficient and quality service to those in the Marine and Offshore industries. Provides a comprehensive range of Marine Agency Services at all porst throughout Atlantic Canada.
Gordon Smith, President
gsmith@fkwarren.ca
Richard Danells, Vice President
rdanells@fkwarren.ca

Fednav Group
Formerly: Fednav Limited
#3500, 1000, rue de la Gauchetière ouest, Montréal, QC H3B 4W5
Tel: 514-878-6500; Fax: 514-878-6642
Toll-Free: 800-678-4842
info@fednav.com
www.fednav.com
Profile: Deep sea foreign transportation of freight; Freight transportation on the Great Lakes-St.Lawrence Seaway; Marine cargo handling
Laurence F. Pathy, President/CEO

Groupe Desgagnés Inc.
21 Marché-Champlain St., Québec, QC G1K 8Z8
Tel: 418-692-1000; Fax: 418-692-6044
info@desgagnes.com
www.groupedesgagnes.com
Profile: Groupe Desgagnés' entire history has been marked by sustained, carefully orchestrated efforts that have helped ensure its growth and maintain its position as a shipping industry leader. Purchasing vessels, creating subsidiaries, forming partnerships - this strategy of diversification and combining strengths has helped keep us growing. The fleet includes 14 vessels and 1 barge; 6 vessels for the transportation of general and dry bulk cargo; 7 tankers and 1 barge for the transportation of liquid bulks; 1 passenger and cargo vessels serving the Middle and Lower North shore.
Louis-Marie Beaulieu, CEO

Holmes Maritime Inc.
1345 Hollis St., Halifax, NS B3J 1T8
Tel: 902-422-0400; Fax: 902-422-9439
info@holmesmaritime.com
www.holmesmaritime.com
Profile: Holmes Maritime Inc. is a privately owned Canadian headquartered in Halifax, Nova Scotia, providing port agency & logistics services to international ship owners & operators throughout eastern Canada & along the Great Lakes.
Louis Homes, President

Kent Line Limited
Parent: J.D. Irving, Limited
PO Box 66, 300 Union St., Saint John, NB E2L 4M3
Tel: 506-632-1660; Fax: 506-634-4278
sales@kentline.com; agency@kentline.com
www.kentline.com
Profile: Kent Line provides maritime shipping services including bulk, project cargo, & agency. The company mainly serves the forest products, steel, fertilizer, grain, & construction industries.
Ahmed Ezzat, Director, Operations
506-632-6010, ezzat.ahmed@kentline.com
Gordon Ferris, Director, Business Development
506-648-3119, ferris.gordon@kentline.com
Kevin Lagos, Manager, Kent Line Limited - Agency
506-648-2718, lagos.kevin@kentline.com

Logistec Corporation
#1500, 360, rue Saint-Jacques, Montréal, QC H2Y 1P5
Tel: 514-844-9381; Fax: 514-843-5217
corp@logistec.com
www.logistec.com
Ticker Symbol: LGT
Profile: Deep sea foreign transportation of freight; Freight transportation on the Great Lakes & the St. Lawrence Seaway; Marine cargo handling; Various water transportation services; Refuse systems
Madeleine Paquin, President/CEO
Jean-Claude Dugas, Assistant Sec./Treasurer & Vice-President, Finance
Nicole Paquin, Vice-President, Information Systems

Marine Atlantic Inc.
Baine Johnston Centre, #302, 10 Fort William Pl., St. John's, NL A1C 1K4
Toll-Free: 800-897-2797
customer_relations@marine-atlantic.ca
www.marine-atlantic.ca
Profile: Deep sea domestic transportation of freight; Ferries; Various water transportation of passengers
Sidney J. Hynes, Chair/CEO
Murray Hupman, Chief Information Officer
Anthony deHoog, Sr. Technical Manager

Montship Inc.
Trealmont Transport Inc., #1000, 360, rue Saint-Jacques, Montreal, QC H2Y 1R2
Tel: 514-286-4646; Fax: 514-286-4650
www.montship.ca
Profile: Montship Maritime Inc.'s objective is to ensure the outgoing competitiveness of Maritime operations, & to continue to provide service for Principals.
Kirk Tyler, General Manager
902-420-9184, ktyler@montship.ca
Dennis Merner, Port Superintendent
902-420-9184, dmerner@montship.ca

N.M. Paterson & Sons Limited
c/o Paterson Grain, 333 Main St., 22nd Fl., Winnipeg, MB R3C 4E2
Tel: 204-956-2090; Fax: 204-947-2386
info@patersongrain.com
www.patersongrain.com
Profile: Freight transportation on the great lakes-st.lawrence seaway; Wholesales-grain and field beans
Andrew B. Paterson, CEO
J.B. Gresham, Treasurer/CFO

Oceanex Inc.
#2550, 630 René-Lévesque Blvd. West, Montreal, QC H3B 1S6
Tel: 514-875-9244; Fax: 514-877-0200
www.oceanex.com
Profile: With our modern fleet, state-of-the-art technology and hands-on experience, Oceanex ensures you of prompt, reliable and cost-effective pick-up, handling and delivery of any of the industry's cargo needs. From full-load or LTL, the Oceanex track record for outstanding intermodal freight service and customer satisfaction remains second to none. To Newfoundland from anywhere in North America and just in time...every time. That's what you can count on from Oceanex, your Newfoundland connection.
Peter Henrico, President & CEO
Daniel Bélisle, Vice President, Finance & Administration
Glenn Etchegary, Vice President, Operations
Peter Grayton, Sales Manager

Rigel Shipping Canada
PO Box 5151, Shediac, NB E4P 8T9
Tel: 506-533-9000; Fax: 506-533-9010
www.rigelcanada.com
Profile: Dedicated to being a quality, technology driven company that provides safe, efficient, environmentally friendly, corteous, and cost-effective marine transportation to our partners and clients.
Brian Ritchie, President
Scott Lewis, General Manager
Shirley Cripps, Human Resources Manager

Upper Lakes Group Inc.
49 Jackes Ave., Toronto, ON M4T 1E2
Tel: 416-920-7610;
inquiries@upperlakes.com
www.upperlakes.com
Profile: Upper Lakes Group Inc. is a client focused full service provider, moving, handling, and storing wet and dry bulk commodoties and dry bulk commodities and containerized cargoes in the Great Lakes, across Canada, and around the world. We manage an integrated group of companies offering

innovative solutions to our customers, and growth, sustainability, and profitability to our shareholders.
Pat Loduca, President & CEO
ploduca@upperlakes.com
Sam Amendola, Vice President & CFO, Finance
samendola@upperlakes.com
Ewa Chudecki, Vice President, Human Resources
eshudecki@upperlakes.com

Railroad Companies

Agence métropolitaine de transport / AMT
500, Place d'Armes, 25e étage, Montréal, QC H2Y 2W2
Tel: 514-287-2464; Fax: 514-287-2460
tram@amt.qc.ca
www.amt.qc.ca
Joël Gauthier, Président/CEO

Alberta Prairie Railway
PO Box 1600, Stettler, AB T0C 2L0
Tel: 403-742-2811; Fax: 403-742-2844
info@absteamtrain.com
www.absteamtrain.com
Don Gillespie

Algoma Central Railway Inc. / ACR
PO Box 130, 129 Bay St., Sault Ste Marie, ON P6A 6Y2
Tel: 705-946-7300; Fax: 705-541-2989
Toll-Free: 800-242-9287
www.agawacanyontourtrain.com
Profile: "Rail service, Sault Ste Marie to Hearst, Ont."

BC Rail Ltd.
#660-221 West Esplanade, North Vancouver, BC V7M 3J3
Tel: 604-678-4735; Fax: 604-678-4736
www.bcrproperties.com/bcrco/
Profile: "Full & intermodal service with CP & CN connections; 1,388 miles of track; 125 locomotives; 10,050 freight cars"
Kevin Mahoney, President/CEO

British Columbia Railway Company
#600, 221 West Esplanade Ave, North Vancouver, BC V7M 3J3
Tel: 604-678-4735; Fax: 604-678-4736
westerhouts@bcrco.com
www.bcrco.com
Profile: Offices of holding companies; Real estate operators of nonresidential buildings; Real estate agents & managers; Railroads, line-haul operating; Marine cargo handling
Kevin Mahoney, President/CEO
Michael Kaye, CFO & Vice-President, Finance

Burlington Northern Sante Fe Railway
PO Box 961056, 2650 Lou Menk Dr., Fort Worth, TX 76161-0056
Toll-Free: 800-795-2673
www.bnsf.com
Profile: "31,000 miles (70 miles in Canada); 200,000 railcars; 4,000 locomotives"
Matthew K. Rose, Chair/President/CEO

Canadian National Railway Company
935, rue de la Gauchetière ouest, Montréal, QC H3B 2M9
Tel: 514-399-0052; Fax: 514-399-5985
Toll-Free: 888-888-5909
contact@cn.ca
www.cn.ca
Ticker Symbol: CNR
Profile: Railroads & line-haul operating; Railroad switching & terminal establishments. Founded in 1919; 21,685 employees.
E. Hunter Harrison, President/CEO
Claude Mongeau, CFO & Exec. Vice-President
Fred Grigsby, Sr. Vice-President & Chief Information Officer
J.V. Raymond Cyr, Chair, Environment, Safety & Security Committee

Canadian Pacific Railway
#500, 401 - 9th Ave. SW, Calgary, AB T2P 4Z4
Tél: 403-319-7000; Téléc: 403-319-7567
Ligne sans frais: 800-716-9132
www.cpr.ca
Fred J. Green, President & CEO

Canadian Pacific Railway Limited
Gulf Canada Square, #500, 401 - 9th Ave. SW, Calgary, AB T2P 4Z4
Tel: 403-319-7000; Toll-Free: 888-333-6370
investor@cpr.ca
www.cpr.ca
Ticker Symbol: CP
Profile: Transcontinental carrier; Rail network operates in Canada & the USA. Founded in 1881; over 15,000 employees
Fred J. Green, CEO
Michael R. Lambert, Exec. Vice-President/CFO
Allen H. Borak, Vice-President, Information Services

Cando Contracting Ltd.
740 Rosser Ave., 4th Fl., Brandon, MB R7A 0K9
Tel: 204-725-2627; Fax: 204-725-4100
info@candoltd.com
www.candoltd.com
Profile: "Operates 4 shortlines: Barrie/Collingwood Railway, Central Manitoba Railway Inc., Athabasca Northern, Orangeville-Brampton"
Gord Peters, President

Cape Breton & Central Nova Scotia Railway
PO Box 2240, 121 King St., Stellarton, NS B0K 1S0
Tel: 902-752-3357; Fax: 902-752-2713
Toll-Free: 800-565-5715
www.railamerica.com/railservices/cbns.aspx
Jim Ryan, General Manager

Central Western Railway
PO Box 2240, 121 King St., Stellarton, NS B0K 1S0
www.railamerica.com
Shawn Smith, General Manager
shawn.smith@railamerica.com

CSX Transportation Inc.
500 Water St., Jacksonville, FL 33202
Tel: 904-359-3200;
www.csx.com
Profile: 166 miles in Canada
Michael J. Ward, Chair/President/CEO

Essex Terminal Railway Co. / ETR
PO Box 24025, 1601 Lincoln Rd., Windsor, ON N8Y 4Y9
Tel: 519-973-8222; Fax: 519-973-7234
www.essexterminalrailway.com
Profile: Freight only; 24 miles of main track (CN CP CSX NS connect); 5 locomotives; 5 cars
B.G. McKeown, President

GO Transit
#600, 20 Bay St., Toronto, ON M5J 2W3
Tel: 416-869-3200;
www.gotransit.com
Gary W. McNeil, Managing Director

Goderich-Exeter Railway Company Ltd. / GEXR
Parent: RailAmerica
101 Shakespeare St., 2nd Fl., Stratford, ON N5A 3W5
www.railamerica.com/railservices/gexr.aspx
Cheryl Ford, General Manager

Kelowna Pacific Railway Ltd. / KPR
2806 - 27 Ave., Vernon, BC V1T 9K4
Kenneth Fitzgerald, Chairman & CEO

New Brunswick Southern Railway Company Limited / NBSR
Parent: J.D. Irving, Limited
11 Gifford Rd., Saint John, NB E2M 4X7
Tel: 506-632-4654; Fax: 506-632-5818
nbsr.marketing@nbsouthern.com
ww.nbsouthern.com
Profile: NBSR is a short railway line specializing in truck/rail reloading for goods such as logs & lumber, wood chips, wood pulp, chemicals, & dry bulk.
Ian Simpson, General Manager

Norfolk Southern Corporation
Three Commercial Place, Norfolk, VA 23510-9241
Tel: 800-635-5768;
www.nscorp.com
Profile: "Operating Subsidiary: Norfolk Southern Railway Co.~Track miles 21,500 (245 miles in Canada); 3,000 locomotives; 19,000 road haul equipment"
Charles Moorman, Chairman/President/CEO

OC Transpo
1500 St. Laurent Blvd., Ottawa, ON K1G 0Z8
Tel: 613-741-6440; Fax: 613-230-6543
www.octranspo.com
Alex Cullen, Chairman

Ontario Northland Transportation Commission
555 Oak St. East, North Bay, ON P1B 8L3
Tel: 705-472-4500; Fax: 705-476-5598
Toll-Free: 800-363-7512
info@ontarionorthland.ca
www.ontarionorthland.ca
Profile: (Owned by Province of Ontario)~700 miles; 26 locomotives; 700 cars
Steve Carmichael, President & CEO

Ontario Southland Railway Inc.
896 Cresthaven Cres., London, ON N6K 4W1
Tel: 519-471-9606; Fax: 519-471-7334
info@osrinc.ca
www.osrinc.ca

Québec North Shore & Labrador Railway Company Chemin de fer QNS&L
PO Box 1000, Labrador City, NL A2V 2L8
Tél: 418-968-7497; Téléc: 418-968-7926
www.ironore.ca
M. Robitaille, General Manager

Québec Railway Corporation
c/o Canadian National Railway Company, PO Box 8100, 935, rue de La Gauchetière Ouest, Montréal, QC H3C 2N4
www.cn.ca
Profile: "Operates the following shortlines: Ottawa Central Railway (OCRR), New Brunswick East Coast Railway (NBEC), Chemin de fer Charlevoix (CFC), Chemin de fer de la Matapédia et du Golfe inc. (CFMG)"
Marc Laliberté, President

Rocky Mountaineer Rail
3#101, 369 Terminal Ave., Vancouver, BC V6A 4C4
Tel: 604-606-7200;
reservations@rockymountaineer.com
www.rockymountaineer.com
Peter Armstrong, President & CEO

South Simcoe Railway
PO Box 186, Tottenham, ON L0G 1W0
Tel: 905-936-5815;
www.southsimcoerailway.ca
Eric Smith, President

Southern Ontario Railway
241 Stuart St. West, Hamilton, ON L8R 3H2
Tel: 905-777-1234;
www.railamerica.com/railservices/sor.aspx
Stuart Thomas, General Manager

Southern Railway of British Columbia Limited
2102 River Dr., New Westminster, BC V3M 6S3
Tel: 604-521-1966;
www.syraillink.com
Profile: (freight only)~75 miles; 19 locomotives; 475 cars
John van der Burch, President

Toronto Terminals Railway Company Ltd.
#402, Union Station, 65 Front St. West, Toronto, ON M4J 1E6
Tel: 416-864-3440
www.ttrly.com
S.L. Spares, Director of Operations

Trillium Railway
Tel: 905-835-2772; Fax: 905-835-8943
Karen.Ettingertrilliumrailway.com
www.trilliumrailway.com
Wayne Ettinger, President & CEO

VIA Rail Canada Inc.
PO Box 8116 A, #500, 3, Place Ville Marie, Montréal, QC H3C 3N3
Toll-Free: 888-842-7245
www.viarail.ca
Profile: Railroads, line-haul operating; Local & suburban transit
Paul Côté, President/CEO
J. Roger Paquette, CFO
Paul Raynor, Director, Corporate Communications
Michael Greenberg, Vice-President, Procurement, Real Estate & Environment

West Coast Express Ltd. / WCE
#295, 601 West Cordova, Vancouver, BC V6B 1G1
Tel: 604-488-8906; Fax: 604-689-3896
wcecustomerservice@translink.ca
www.translink.ca
Doug Kelsey, President & CEO

White Pass & Yukon Route
PO Box 435, 231 Second Ave., Skagway, AK 99840-0435
Tel: 907-983-2214; Fax: 907-983-2734
info@wpyr.com
www.wpyr.com
Profile: Express Co.-None 40 miles; 20 locomotives; 59 cars
Gary C. Danielson, President

Windsor & Hantsport Railway Co.
PO Box 578, 2 Water St., Windsor, NS B0N 2T0
Tel: 902-798-0798; Fax: 902-798-0816
jtaylor@whrail.ca
www.whrail.ca
James Taylor, General Manager

Public Transit Systems

100 Mile House Transit System (Paratransit)
c/o LDN Transportation, 6119 Reita Cres., 100 Mile House, BC V0K 2E0
Tel: 250-395-2834;
lnieson@telus.net
www.transitbc.com/regions/one
Profile: The 100 Mile House Transit System has many routes which offer service to major residential areas of 100 Mile House, 103 Mile and 108 Ranch. It also has several accessible services, including rural transit service, HandyDART and priority seating.

Agence métropolitaine de transport
700, rue De La Gauchetière Ouest, 26e ét, Montréal, QC H3B 5M2
Tél: 514-287-8726; Téléc: 514-276-2460
Ligne sans frais: 888-702-8726
www.amt.qc.ca
Profile: AMT's mission is to improve the efficiency of personal travel in the metropolitan area by promoting the use of public transit. AMT is therefore responsible for the planning, coordination, integration and promotion of public transit services (bus, metro, taxi-bus, commuter trains and adapted transit), as well as for improving the efficiency of roads of metropolitan significance.
Joel Gauthier, Président/CEO

Barrie Transit
24 Maple Ave., Barrie, ON L4N 7W4
Tel: 705-739-4209
Profile: The City of Barrie offers both conventional bus service with Barrie Transit and specialized transit services for people with mobility restrictions with Barrie Accessible Community Transportation Service (BACTS)

BC Transit
520 Gorge Rd. East, Victoria, BC V8W 2P3
Tel: 250-385-2551; Fax: 250-995-5639
transitinfo@bctransit.com
www.bctransit.com
Profile: BC Transit provides planning, marketing, fleet and funding support for all transit services in BC, except for the Greater Vancouver region. BC Transit's fleet of 20 fuel cell buses will be the world's first to be placed in regular transit operation.

Belleville Transit
169 Front St., Belleville, ON K8N 2Y8
Tel: 613-968-6481; Fax: 613-967-3206
Profile: Belleville Transit operates 6 days a week, Monday to Saturday, inclusive with 9 routes servicing the urban area of the city. The fleet consists of 14 coaches travelling approximately 2,300 kilometers per day and carries 3,000 riders daily

Boundary Transit System
202 - 843 Rossland Ave., Trail, BC V1R 4S8
Tel: 250-443-2179;
trish.hallstrom@interiorhealth.ca
www.transitbc.com/regions/bdy
Profile: The Boundary Transit System has many routes within Grand Forks, with trips to and from Greenwood on Fridays. It also has several accessible services, including HandyDART and priority seating.

Brampton Transit
185 Clark Blvd., Brampton, ON L6T 4G6
Tel: 905-874-2750;
transit@brampton.ca
Profile: Brampton Transit provides approximately 583,000 transit service hours per year

Brandon Transportation Services
Tel: 204-729-2300;
brandontransit.ca
Profile: Brandon City Transit offers many services to the community, including Handi-Transit, an environmentally friendly way of traveling, and specialized schedules.
Bob MacDonald, City Transportation Manager

Brantford Transit
64 Darling St., Brantford, ON N3T 6G6
Tel: 519-753-3847; Fax: 519-750-0491
transit@brantford.ca
Profile: Operated by the Engineering Department of the Corporation of the City of Brantford. The fleet consists of 25 buses

British Columbia Ferry Services Inc.
Formerly: British Columbia Ferries Corporation
1010 Canada Pl., Vancouver, BC
Tel: 250-381-1401;
customerservice@bcferries.com
www.bcferries.com
Profile: Ferries
David Hahn, President/CEO

Burlington Transit
3332 Harvester Rd., Burlington, ON L7N 3M8
Tel: 905-639-0550; Fax: 905-335-7878
contactBT@burlington.ca

Calgary Transit
224 - 7 Ave. SW, Calgary, AB
Tel: 403-974-4000;
TPCT043@calgary.ca
www.calgarytransit.com
Profile: Calgary Transit serves a population of 991,759 with the help of 960 vehicles on more than 161 routes
John Hubbell, Director

Campbell River Transit System
1050 - 9 Ave., Campbell River, BC V9W 4C2
Tel: 250-287-7433; Fax: 250-287-7488
crtransit@shaw.ca
www.transitbc.com/regions/cam
Profile: The Campbell River Transit System has several services available to the community, including three types of Accessible Service, including Low Floor Busses, handyDART and the Taxi Saver Program. It has routes to most major destinations in Campbell River, and to Willow Point and Oyster Bay.

Cape Breton Transit
320 Esplanade, Sydney, NS B1P 7B9
Tel: 902-563-5005; Fax: 902-564-0481
cbrm@cbrm.ns.ca
www.cbrm.ns.ca
Profile: Transit Cape Breton offers the community travel within Industrial Cape Breton, including Loonie Days every Saturday, and discounted tickets.

Castlegar Regional Transit System
c/o Trail Transit Services Inc., 8170 Old Waneta Rd., Trail, BC V1R 4W9
Tel: 250-365-3100; Fax: 250-364-2418
dennis.trailtransit@shawlink.ca
www.transitbc.com/regions/cas
Profile: The Castlegar Regional Transit system has routes to Downtown and the College. It also has several accessible services, including rural transit services, HandyDART and priority seating.

Central Fraser Valley Transit System
PO Box 156, Abbotsford, BC V2T 6Z5
Tel: 604-854-3232; Fax: 604-854-3598
Chris.Brown@firstgroup.com
www.transitbc.com/regions/cfv
Profile: The Central Fraser Valley Transit System has several services available to the community, including routes to most major destinations in the City of Abbotsford and the District of Mission, as well as accessible services such as low floor busses, HandyDART and a taxi saver program.

Central Kootenay Transit
Formerly: Kaslo Transit System (Paratransit)
c/o Arrow & Slocan Lakes Community Services, PO Box 100, 205 - 6 Ave. North, Nakusp, BC V0G 1R0
Tel: 250-265-3674; Fax: 250-265-3378
gdavidson@aslcs.com
www.transitbc.com/regions/cko

Chatham Transit
PO Box 640, 315 King St. West, Chatham, ON N7M 5K8
Tel: 519-360-1998; Fax: 519-436-3240
cktransit@chatham-kent.ca

Chilliwack Transit
44580 Yale Rd. West, Chilliwack, BC V2R 4H1
Tel: 604-795-3838; Fax: 604-795-5110
www.bctransit.com/regions/chw
Profile: The Chilliwack Transit System has several routes available to the community, which go to most major destinations in the City of Chilliwack, and to Rosedale, Popkum, Agassiz and Harrison Hot Springs, including service to Minter Gardens, Bridal Falls and Dusty's Dino Town. It also has accessible services including low floor busses, HandyDART, a specializex HandyDART flex route and a taxi saver program.

Clearwater & Area Transit System (Paratransit)
c/o Yellowhead Community Services, 612 Park Dr., Clearwater, BC V0E 1N0
Tel: 250-674-3935;
jack.k@yellowheadcs.ca
www.bctransit.com/regions/clr
Profile: The Clearwater & Area transit system services an area that covers Vavenby, Birch Island, Clearwater and Blackpool. On the last Thursday of every month the bus goes to Kamloops and back to Clearwater. It has several accessible services including door-to-door services and priority seating.

Coast Mountain Bus Company
Parent: Greater Vancouver Transportation Authority (TransLink)
13401 - 108 Ave., Surrey, BC V3T 5T4
Tel: 604-953-3000;
www.coastmountainbus.com
Profile: Coast Mountain Bus Company (CMBC) is a vital link in the Greater Vancouver multi-modal public transportation network. You experience our service when you ride a CMBC bus, or cross Vancouver harbour on SeaBus ferry service. Coast Mountain Bus Company (CMBC) operates conventional buses, smaller community shuttles, SeaBus and, soon, a fleet of state-of-the-art trolley buses in Greater Vancouver, in the largest single transit service area in Canada.

Cobourg Transit
c/o Town of Cobourg, 55 King St. West, Cobourg, ON K9A 2M2
Tel: 905-373-0582
Profile: Cobourg Transit is a fully accessible community transit system that combines a fixed route service with the flexibility of door-to-door service for eligible riders

Codiac Transit Commission
Moncton, NB
Tel: 506-857-2008;
info@moncton.ca
www.moncton.ca
Profile: Transit system for Moncton with express routes, charters and airport routes.

Comox Valley Transit System
1635 Knight Rd., Comox, BC V9N 5N1
Tel: 250-339-5453;
www.bctransit.com/regions/com
Profile: Comox Valley Transit has several routes available to the community, which go to Cumberland, Royston/Buckley Bay, Courtenay, Comox, and BC Ferries and the airport. It has accessible services including low floor busses, HandyDART and a taxi saver program.

Cornwall Transit
863 Second St. West, Cornwall, ON K6J 1H5
Tel: 613-930-2636
Profile: The City operated transit system transports approximately 525,000 passengers annually
Gerry Godard, Senior Supervisor

Cowichan Valley Regional Transit System
#8, 180 Central Rd., Duncan, BC V9L 4X3
Tel: 250-746-9899;
www.transitbc.com/regions/cow
Profile: The Cowichan Valley Regional Transit System has several routes to the Duncan/North Cowichan area, including Quamichan, Mt Prevost and Maple Bay; the Cowichan Lake area, including Youbou and Honeymoon Bay; and the South End communities including Mill Bay, Shawnigan Lake, Cobble Hill and Cowichan Bay. It also has accessible services including low floor busses and priority seating.

Cranbrook Transit System
C/O Gray Line of Victoria, 1229 Crambrook St. North, Cranbrook, BC V1C 3S6
Tel: 250-417-4636; Fax: 250-426-5101
john.darula@suncity.bc.ca
www.bctransit.com/regions/cra
Profile: Cranbrook Transit System has several routes available to the community, and many services, such as low-floor busses, HandyDART, etc. for those who are in need of them.

Creston Valley Transit System
c/o Arrow & Slocan Lakes Community Services, PO Box 100, 205 6th Ave. North, Nakusp, BC V0G 1R0
Tel: 250-428-7750; Fax: 250-265-3378
gdavidson@aslcs.com
www.transitbc.com/regions/cre
Profile: The Creston Valley Transit System has routes that go to most of the major destinations in the area. It also has several

accessible services including door to door service and priority seating.

Dawson Creek Transit System
10404-87th Ave., Fort St. John, BC V1G 3V7
Tel: 250-784-3600; Fax: 250-787-9322
harold@peacetransit.pwt.ca
www.transitbc.com/regions/daw
Profile: Dawson Creek Transit system has several routes available to the community, which go to most of the major destinations in Dawson Creek. It has several low floor busses and priority seating.

Durham Region Transit
110 Westney Rd. South, Whitby, ON L1S 2C8
Fax: 905-427-3473
Toll-Free: 866-247-0055
www.durhamregiontransit.com
Profile: Durham Region Transit (DRT) is an integrated transit system serving all communities in Durham Region. The service area is divided into West, East, Centre and North service sectors. Door to door transit for disabled passengers is provided by Specialized Services

Edmonton Transit System
PO Box 2610 Main, Edmonton, AB T5J 3R5
Tel: 780-496-1611; Fax: 780-496-1670
etransit@edmonton.ca
Profile: Today, Edmonton Transit's fleet encompasses over 847 diesel and trolley buses, and 29 community buses. The system covers more than 150 routes, including a Light Rail Transit (LRT) system with 37 vehicles and 11 stations. ETS also offers transportation to persons with disabilities, called the Disabled Adult Transit Service (DATS)

Fort St. John Transit System
c/o Diversified Transportation Ltd., 10404 - 87 Ave., Fort St John, BC V1J 5K7
Tel: 250-787-7433; Fax: 250-787-9322
harold@peacetransit.pwt.ca
www.transitbc.com/regions/fsj
Profile: The Fort St. John Transit system has many routes available to the community, reaching most of the major destinations in the city. It has low floor busses for easy accessibility, and priority seating.

Fredericton Transit
PO Box 130, 397 Queen St., Fredericton, NB E3B 4Y7
Tel: 506-460-2200; Fax: 506-460-2042
www.fredericton.ca
Profile: The City of Fredericton Transit Division operates 27 buses on eight routes, Monday to Saturday, 6:30 am until 11:00 pm, providing safe, affordable mobility to those in the community who do not have access to or choose not to use a private vehicle. In addition we operate chartered busing to various school, tour, and conference groups in and around Fredericton, and a parallel service , Dial-A-Bus, for persons with a disability.
Alex MacNeill, Contact

GP Transit
City Hall, PO Box 4000, Grande Prairie, AB T8V 6V3
Tel: 780-538-0300; Fax: 780-538-0310
Profile: For over 24 years, GP transit has served the citizens of Grand Prairie, Alberta. Fares range from $1.50 to $2.00 per ride, and children under 12 ride free when accompanied by a paying passenger.

Grand River Transit
250 Strasburg Rd., Kitchener, ON N2E 3M6
Tel: 519-585-7555;
www.grt.ca

Greater Sudbury Transit
c/o City of Sudbury, PO Box 5000 A, Sudbury, ON P3A 5P3
Tel: 705-675-3333; Fax: 705-560-4571
www.greatersudbury.ca/transit
Profile: Operates a fleet of 42 buses
Roger Sauvé, Director
roger.sauve@city.greatersudbury.on.c

Guelph Transit
City Hall, 1 Carden St., Guelph, ON N1H 3A1
Tel: 519-822-1811; Fax: 519-822-1322
transit@guelph.on.ca
guelph.ca/transit
Profile: Guelph Transit has 20 low-floor conventional buses in its fleet and guarantees accessible service on ten of its transit routes

The Hamilton Street Railway Company
2200 Upper James St., Hamilton, ON L0R 1W0
Tel: 905-546-2489
Profile: Operates over 30 bus routes serving Hamilton, Stoney Creek, Dundas, Ancaster and Burlington. Buses run seven days a week on most routes, from around 5:30 a.m. to 1:00 a.m. the next morning
Don Hull, Director

Hazeltons' Regional Transit System
c/o Coastal Bus Lines Ltd., 780 Lahakas Blvd., Kitimat, BC V8C 1T9
Tel: 250-847-2134; Toll-Free: 877-842-2131
phil.malnis@farwestgroup.com
www.bctransit.com/regions/haz
Profile: The Hazeltons' Regional Transit System has routes to most communities within the Hazeltons', as well as major destinations like Wrinch Memorial Hospital, Northwest Community College, First Nations Education Centre and the historic Village of 'Ksan. It also has routes to Moricetown and Smithers on Tuesday and Thursdays. It has accessible services which include door to door service and priority seating.

Kamloops Transit System
c/o FirstCanada ULC, 1550 Ord Rd., Kamloops, BC V2B 7V4
Tel: 250-376-1216; Fax: 250-376-7398
ralph.vanderheide@firstgroup.com
www.transitbc.com/regions/kam
Profile: The Kamloops Transit System has several routes available to the public which go to all regions of Greater Kamloops. It also has several services available, including low floor busses, HandyDART, a Taxi Saver Program and priority seating.

Kelowna Regional Transit System
c/o FirstCanada ULC, 1494 Hardy St., Kelowna, BC V1Y 8H2
Tel: 250-860-8121; Fax: 250-861-7872
mike.docherty@firstgroup.com
www.transitbc.com/regions/kel
Profile: The Kelowna Transit System has several routes available to the public, which go to all regions of Greater Kelowna. It also has many accessible services, including low floor busses, HandyDART, a Taxi Saver program and priority seating.

Kimberley Transit System
260 - 4 Ave., Kimberley, BC V1A 2R6
Tel: 250-427-7400;
carole.rausch@interiorhealth.ca
www.transitbc.com/regions/kim
Profile: The Kimberley Transit System has routes within the City of Kimberley, and makes a round-trip to Cranbrook every 1st and 3rd Monday of the month. It also has several accessible services, including door to door service and priority seating.

Kings Transit Authority
29 Crescent Dr., New Minas, NS B4N 3G7
Tel: 902-678-7310; Fax: 902-678-2545
Toll-Free: 888-546-4442
info@kingstransit.ns.ca
www.kingstransit.ns.ca
Profile: King Transit Authority is a public tranist system that operates in teh Annapolis Country between the towns of Bridgetown, Annapolis Royal and Greenwood. Their service also extends to Cornwallis Park and Upper Clements Park, as well as Digby County to Weymouth.
Andrew A. Paterson, General Manager

Kitimat Transit System
c/o FirstCanada ULC, 780 Lahakas Blvd. South, Kitimat, BC V8C 1T9
Tel: 250-632-4444;
phil.malnis@farwestgroup.com
www.transitbc.com/regions/kit
Profile: The Kitimat Transit System has many routes that go to most of the major destinations in Kitimat. It also has several accessible services, including low floor busses, HandyDART, and priority seating.

Kootenay Boundary Transit System
8170 Old Waneta Rd., Trail, BC V1R 4W9
Tel: 250-364-0261; Fax: 250-364-2418
dennis.trailtransit@shawlink.ca
www.transitbc.com/regions/kob
Profile: The Kootenay Transit System has several routes available to the community that go to most of the major destinations in Trail. It also has many accessible services, including low floor busses, HandyDART, and priority seating.

Lethbridge Transit
619 - 4 Ave. North, Lethbridge, AB T1H 0K4
Tel: 403-320-3885; Fax: 403-380-3876
transit@lethbridge.ca
Profile: Lethbridge Transit's mission is to provide a safe and efficient public transportation system that allows community access to economic, social, educational or leisure opportunities.

London Transit Commission
450 Highbury Ave. North, London, ON N5W 5L2
Tel: 519-451-1347;
www.ltconline.ca
Profile: L.T.C. services 32 routes (19 accessible). Annual ridership reaches 18.3 million
Larry E. Ducharme, General Manager

Medicine Hat Transit
333 - 6 Ave. SE, Medicine Hat, AB T1A 2S6
Tel: 403-529-8214; Fax: 403-527-5844
mhtransit@medicinehat.ca
Profile: The City of Medicine Hat operates a public transportation system, which is available and accessible to all residents of the community. Medicine Hat Transit makes every attempt to be responsive to the needs of residents and other community partners. Efficient use of human and physical resources, customer service and satisfaction, and a leadership role in providing a integrated transit system which meets the needs of our community, are just some of the objectives of our Transit Operations Plan.

Metro Transit
c/o Transit Services, Halifax Regional Municipalit, 200 Ilsley Ave., Dartmouth, NS B3B 1V1
Tel: 709-490-4000;
contactHRM@halifax.ca
www.halifax.ca/metrotransit
Profile: Metro Transit has many services available to the community, including Accessible Low-Floor Buses, Charter Services, FRED (Free Rides Everwhere in Dowtown Halifax) as well as using more environmentally friendly biodiesal fuel.

Metrobus Transit
245 Freshwater Rd., St. John's, NL A1B 1B3
Tel: 709-570-2020; Fax: 866-773-6784
informationservices@metrobus.com
www.metrobus.com
Profile: St. John's Metrobus System has recently been revitalized and is now offering more frequent services, more direct routes, reduced travel times and more express routes.

MiWay
Formerly: Mississauga Transit
975 Central Parkway West, Mississauga, ON L5C 3B1
Tel: 905-615-4287;
www.mississauga.ca/portal/miway
Profile: City operated since 1974 with a fleet of over 300 buses

Moose Jaw Transit System
City Hall, 228 Main St. North, Moose Jaw, SK S6H 3J8
Tel: 306-694-4400; Fax: 306-694-4480
Profile: The City of Moose Jaw Transit System offers bus service to all areas of the community. Routes are designed to provide the most efficient service possible to the citizens of Moose Jaw. Charter Service is also available, as is a Special Needs Service.

Nanaimo Regional Transit System
c/o Transit Manager Regional District of Nanaimo, 6300 Hammond Bay Rd., Nanaimo, BC V9T 6N2
Tel: 250-390-4531; Fax: 250-390-2757
transprt@rdn.bc.ca
www.transitbc.com/regions/nan
Profile: Nanaimo Regional Transit System provides both regular transit and HandyDART custom transit service. Regional Transit is operated by the Regional District of Nanaimo in partnership with BC Transit. We serve the area from Cedar in the south of the Regional District to Qualicum Beach in the north.
Anita Wajouda

Nelson/Slocan Valley Transit
c/o City of Nelson Public Works, #101, 310 Ward St., Nelson, BC V1L 5S4
Tel: 250-352-8201;
rdevuono@nelson.ca
www.bctransit.com/regions/nel
Profile: The Nelson/Slocan Valley Transit System has several routes which go to most of the major destinations in the area, as well as many rural stops in Taghum, Blewett, Beasley, Bonnington, South Slocan, Playmor, Shore Acres, Crescent Valley, Slocan Park, Passmore, Winlaw and Appledale. It also has accessible services including low floor busses, HandyDART and priority seating.

Niagara Transit Commission
4320 Bridge St., Niagara Falls, ON L2E 2R7
Tel: 905-356-1179; Fax: 905-356-5576
www.niagarafalls.ca
Profile: Niagara Transit has supplied public transportation for the City of Niagara Falls since 1960. Presently supplies the city with 10 bus routes

Terry Librock, General Manager

North Bay Transit
190 Wyld St., North Bay, ON P1B 1Z2
Tel: 705-474-0419; Fax: 705-476-5308
Profile: Operates a fleet of 25 buses
Peter Reid, Transit Manager
705-474-0626, peter.reid@cityofnorthbay.ca

Oakville Transit
1225 Trafalgar Rd., Oakville, ON L6H 0H3
Tel: 905-815-2020; Fax: 905-338-4703
transit@oakville.ca
www.oakvilletransit.com
Profile: Oakville Transit has been providing bus service to Oakville since 1972

Osoyoos Transit System
6210 - 97th St., Osoyoos, BC V0H 1V2
Tel: 250-495-8054;
obc@persona.ca
www.transitbc.com/regions/oso
Profile: Osoyoos Transit System operates Monday through Thursday, with Monday catering to destinations between Osoyoos and Kelowna Airport, including Oliver, Okanagan Falls, Penticton, Summerland, Peachland, Westbank and Kelowna, and Tuesday through Thursday servicing all destinations between Osoyoos and Summerland, including Oliver, Okanagan Falls and Penticton. It also has accessible services including handyDART and priority seating.

Penticton & Okanagan-Similkameen Transit System
301 Warren Ave. East, Penticton, BC V2A 3M1
Tel: 250-492-5602;
mattb@berryandsmith.com
www.bctransit.com/regions/pen
Profile: The Penticton Transit System & & Okanagan-Similkameen Transit System have many routes available both in the community and in rural areas. They also have several accessible services, including low floor busses, HandyDART, a taxi saver program and priority seating.

Peterborough Transit
190 Simcoe St., Peterborough, ON K9H 2H7
Tel: 705-745-0525;
transitoperations@peterborough.ca
www.peterborough.ca
Profile: Services the City of Peterborough, Ontario with regular and Handi-Van transit services. All regular Peterborough Transit routes now have fully accessible buses
Jim Kimble, Manager

Port Alberni/Clayoquot Transit
c/o Diversified Transportation Ltd., 3701-4th Ave., Port Alberni, BC V9Y 4H7
Tel: 250-724-1311; Fax: 250-724-1377
phil@patransit.pwt.ca
www.transitbc.com/regions/pta
Profile: The Port Alberni/Clayoquot Transit System has several routes that go to most of the major destinations in the area, as well as many accessible services, including low floor busses, handyDART and priority seating.

Powell River Regional Transit System
c/o Powell River Municipal Transportation, 6910 Duncan St., Powell River, BC V8A 1W2
Tel: 604-485-4287; Fax: 604-485-4219
bprice@cdpr.bc.ca
www.transitbc.com/regions/pow
Profile: The Powell River Transit System has many routes available to the community, which go to most of the major destinations in the area. It also has several accessible services, including a rural transit service, low floor busses, HandyDART and priority seating.

Prince George Transit System
1041 Great St., Prince George, BC V2N 2K8
Tel: 250-563-0011; Fax: 250-564-4901
james@pgtransit.pwt.ca
www.transitbc.com/regions/prg
Profile: The Prince George Transit System has many routes that go to most of the major regions in the area. It also has several accessible services available to the community, including community travel training, low floor busses, HandyDART, a taxi saver program and priority seating.

Prince Rupert/Port Edward Transit
c/o FirstCanada ULC, 225 - 2 Ave. West, Prince Rupert, BC V8J 1G4
Tel: 250-624-3343;
darbara.minhas@firstgroup.com
www.bctransit.com/regions/prr
Profile: The Prince Rupert/Port Edward Transit system has several routes available to the community that go to most of the major destinations in the area, as well as many accessible services, including low floor busses, HandyDART, a taxi saver program and door to door service.

Princeton & Area Transit System
c/o Princeton & District Community Services, PO Box 1960, 47 Harold Ave., Princeton, BC V0X 1W0
Tel: 250-295-6666; Toll-Free: 800-291-0911
mail@pdcss.com
www.transitbc.com/regions/pri
Profile: The Princeton and Area Transit System runs Monday through Friday, with door-to-door trips within Princeto and to and from Penticton, Hedley, Keremeos and Coalmont.
Lynn Pelly, Contact

Quesnel Transit System
c/o Five Five Transport, 98A Pinecrest Rd., Quesnel, BC V2J 5W6
Tel: 250-992-1109; Fax: 250-992-1146
fivefivetransport@telus.net
www.busonline.ca/regions/que
Profile: Quesnel Transit has several routes that go to most of the major destinations in the area, as well as many accessible services, including HandyDART and priority seating.

Red Deer Transit
PO Box 5008, Red Deer, AB T4N 3T4
Tel: 403-342-8225; Fax: 403-314-5837
transit@reddeer.ca
Profile: Red Deer Transit has several services available to the community, including Low Floor Buses, Overload Busses, Charter Bus Services, and a Citizen's Action Bus.

Regina Transit
PO Box 1790, 2476 Victoria Ave., Regina, SK S4P 3C8
Tel: 306-777-7726; Fax: 306-949-7211
Profile: The City of Regina Transit System has several services available to the community, including a charter service, a safebus, night stops, and paratransit.

Réseau de transport de la capitale (RTC-Québec)
720, rue des Rocailles, Québec, QC G2J 1A5
Tél: 418-627-2511;
www.stcuq.qc.ca

Le Réseau de transport de Longueuil
Centre administratif, 1150, boul Marie-Victorin, Longueuil, QC J4G 2M4
Tél: 450-442-8600;
www.rtl-longueuil.qc.ca
Profile: Le Réseau de transport de Longueuil's (RTL) mission is to improve the quality of life of citizens in the territory served by the RTL by meeting their evolving transportation needs through the promotion and cost-effective operation of various quality and environmentally friendly public transportation means."
Pierre Del Fante, Dir.-gén.

Saint John Transit Commission
55 McDonald St., Saint John, NB E2J 0C7
Tel: 506-658-4700; Fax: 506-658-4704
sjtransitcustomerservice@saintjohn.ca
www.saintjohntransit.com
Profile: The Saint John Transit Commission was established in 1979 to provide scheduled transit service to the city. It is the largest public transit system in New Brunswick in terms of both mileage and passengers. Saint John Transit's ridership is approximately 50 percent higher than the average for Canadian cities with a population of between 50,000 and 150,000.

St. Albert Transit
5 St. Anne St., St Albert, AB T8N 3Z9
www.stalbert.ca/transit
Profile: St-Albert Transit (StAT) local routes serve all neighbourhoods within the City of St. Albert, connecting with StAT commuter services to Edmonton destinations at either (or both) the Village Transit Station or St. Albert Centre Exchange. Edmonton destinations include downtown, the University of Alberta, MacEwan, NAIT, Government Centre and West Edmonton Mall.

St Catherines Transit Commission
2012 First St. Louth, RR#3, St Catharines, ON L2S 3V9
Tel: 905-687-5555;
phil@yourbus.com
www.yourbus.com

Sarnia Transit
255 North Christina St., Sarnia, ON N7T 7N2
Tel: 519-336-3271; Fax: 519-336-3361
transit@sarnia.ca
www.sarnia.ca
Profile: Operates and maintains a fleet of 25 buses on the conventional transit system and 6 specialized vehicles on their Care-a-Van service (provided to people with disabilities)
Jim Stevens, Director

Saskatchewan Transportation Company
1717 Saskatchewan Dr., Regina, SK S4P 2E2
Tel: 306-787-3340;
www.stcbus.com
Profile: Saskatchewan Transit has been providing passenger and freight transportation services for over 60 years, and provides passenger transportation and parcel express services throughout Saskatchewan operating main terminals in Regina, Saskatoon and Prince Albert with an additional 206 rural agencies in the Province.

Saskatoon Transit Services
c/o City Hall, 222 - 3rd Ave. North, Saskatoon, SK S7K 0J5
Tel: 306-975-3200
Profile: Saskatoon Transit's mission is to provide cost-effective, safe and affordable public transit services using clean and enviornmentally friendly equipment that enables all residents to access work, education, health care, shopping, social and recreational opportunities.

Sault Ste. Marie Transit
111 Huron St., Sault Ste Marie, ON P6A 5P9
Tel: 705-759-5438; Fax: 705-759-5834
d.scott@cityssm.on.ca
Profile: The Sault Ste. Marie Transit has a fleet of 28 regular Transit vehicles, 7 Para Transit buses, and 1 Community Bus
Don Scott, Transit Manager
d.scott@cityssm.on.ca

SkyTrain
Parent: Greater Vancouver Transportation Authority (TransLink)
6800 - 14 Ave., Burnaby, BC V3N 4S7
Tel: 604-520-3641; Fax: 604-521-2818
www.translink.ca
Profile: The SkyTrain in Vancouver, British Columbia, Canada is an advanced light rapid transit system operating fully automated trains on two lines. Built for the Expo 86 World's Fair, it has since become the world's longest automated light rapid transit system. The system uses the same family of linear induction motor-driven trains as the Scarborough RT line in Toronto, the Putra LRT in Kuala Lumpur, Malaysia, and the JFK AirTrain in New York.

Société de transport de l'Outaouais
111, rue Jean-Proulx, Gatineau, QC J8Z 1T4
Tél: 819-770-3242; Ligne sans frais: 800-855-0511
www.sto.ca
Profile: The mission of the Société de transport de l'Outaouais is to provide residents of the municipalities in its area, which includes the Gatineau urban area as well as Cantley and Chelsea, with a reliable public transit system that meets their needs at a reasonable cost for users, taxpayers and these municipalities. They have 246 busses, 259 shelters, 11 million kilometers travelled each ear, 56 bus routes, comprised of 41 regular, 13 express and 2 interzone routes).

Société de transport de Laval
2250, av Francis-Hughes, Laval, QC H7S 2C3
Tél: 450-688-6520; Téléc: 450-662-5457
www.stl.laval.qc.ca
Profile: The Société de transport de Laval ha 34 bus routes, covering a total distance of 627 km, has approx. 22 hours of daily service on weekdays, and 21 hours on weekends, and covers 13.4 million km in a year. It has 463 drivers, 225 busses, 281 bus shelters and 2300 bus stops.
Pierre Giard, Directeur général

Société de transport de Montréal
800, rue de la Gauchetière ouest, Montréal, QC H5A 1J6
Tél: 514-786-4636;
www.stm.info
Profile: Transport Montreal, or STM, has both a bus, para-transit and metro system. It provides 1.3 million trips on its system every day, with 1503 busses, 89 mini paratransit busses and 759 metro cars.

Société de transport de Sherbrooke
895, rue Cabana, Sherbrooke, QC J1K 2M3
Tél: 819-564-2687;
www.sts.qc.ca

Squamish Transit System
c/o Diversified Transportation Ltd., 38928A Production Way, Whistler, BC V8B 0K4
Tel: 604-892-5559;
ken@squamishtransit.pwt.ca
www.transitbc.com/regions/squ
Profile: The Squamish Transit System has many routes that go to Valleycliffe, Brackendale, Highlands, Downtown, Woodfibre Ferry, Garibaldi Highlands and most major destinations in Squamish. It also has accessible services including low floor busses, HandyDART and priority seating.

Stratford City Transit
60 Corcoran St., Stratford, ON N5A 1V7
Tel: 519-271-0250;
www.stratfordcommunity.ca/transit

Strathcona Transit
2001 Sherwood Dr., Sherwood Park, AB T8A 3W7
Tel: 780-464-7433;
transit@strathcona.ab.ca
Profile: Strathcona's Transit's mission is to provide an effective, efficient and customer-focused transit service that aligns with the County's three pillars of sustainability: environmental, economic and social.

Sunshine Coast Transit System
c/o B. Sagman Manager, Transportation & Facilities, 1975 Field Rd., Sechelt, BC V0N 3A1
Tel: 604-885-6899; Fax: 604-885-7909
brian.sagman@scrd.ca
www.transitbc.com/regions/sun
Profile: The Sunshine Coast Transit System has many routes that go to the most built-up residential neighbourhoods between the Langdale, Gibsons and Sechelt. In addition, there is service to Halfmoon Bay and limited service on Saturday, Sunday and holidays to Secret Cove in the summertime.

Terrace Regional Transit System
c/o FirstCanada ULC, 4904 Hwy. 16 West, Terrace, BC V8G 1L8
Tel: 250-635-2666;
phil.malnis@farwestgroup.com
www.bctransit.com/regions/ter
Profile: The Terrace Regional Transit System has many routes through the City of Terrace and the Regional District of Kitimat-Stikine. It also has several accessible services including low floor busses, Handy-DART and priority seating.

Thunder Bay Transit
PO Box 409, 500 Donald St. East, Thunder Bay, ON P7C 5K4
Tel: 807-625-2230
Profile: Operates with a fleet of 49 buses on 17 routes
Alex Grant, Manager

Timmins Transit
220 Algonquin Blvd. East, Timmins, ON P4N 1B3
Tel: 705-360-2654; Fax: 705-360-2698
transit@timmins.ca
www.timminstransit.ca
Profile: Timmins Transit is a service operated by the City of Timmins. They operate a fleet of over 25 buses, low floor buses, and accessible mini-buses
David Onodera, Transit Superintendent
david.onodera@city.timmins.on.ca

Transit Windsor
3700 North Service Rd. East, Windsor, ON N8W 5X2
Tel: 519-944-4141; Fax: 519-944-5121
tw@city.windsor.on.ca
Profile: Fleet consists of 99 transit coaches, including 49 low floor vehicles

TransLink
#1600, 4720 Kingsway, Burnaby, BC V5H 4N2
Tel: 604-953-3333;
www.translink.ca
Profile: TransLink, the Greater Vancouver Transportation Authority, is a small organization involved with transportation planning, administration of service contracts with subsidiary companies and contractors, the management of capital projects, financial management and planning, public affairs and supporting business functions.

Trius Tours Ltd.
7 Mount Edward Rd., Charlottetown, PE C1A 5R7
Tel: 902-566-5664; Fax: 902-566-3497
trius.tours@pei.aibn.com
www.peisland.com/triustours
Profile: Trius Tours has 2-54 passenger motor coaches, 12-47 passenger motor coaches and 5-15 passenger vans which provide scenic tours of Prince Edward Island.
George M. Brookins, Contact

Vernon Regional Transit System
c/o North Okanagan & Vernon Regional Transit, 4210 - 24 Ave., Vernon, BC V1T 1M2
Tel: 250-545-7221;
vernontransit@shawcable.ca
www.transitbc.com/regions/ver
Profile: The Vernon Regional Transit System has many routes available to the community which go to to most major destinations in the City of Vernon, to the District of Coldstream, and Spallumcheen, Armstrong, Endergy, Lavington, Whitevale and Lumby. It has accessible services including community travel training, a taxi saver program, low floor busses and HandyDART.

Victoria Regional Transit Commission
c/o BC Transit, 520 Gorge Rd. East, Victoria, BC V8W 2P3
Tel: 250-385-2551; Fax: 250-995-5639
www.bctransit.com/regions/vic
Profile: The Victoria Regional Transit System began operation on 22 February 1890 with a fleet of four street cars. The system now serves approximately 312,000 persons and operates in a 400-square-kilometre area. The peak fleet in operation is 178 buses operating on 36 conventional routes, and 40 vans providing custom door-to-door service for people who cannot ride the conventional buses.
Barbara Harris, Contact

WAVE Whistler & Valley Express
8011 Hwy. 99, Whistler, BC V0N 1B8
Tel: 604-932-4020;
operations@whistlertransit.pwt.ca
www.bctransit.com/regions/whi
Profile: The Whistler and Valley Express, or WAVE, runs through Emerald Estates, Alpine Meadows, Spruce Grove, White Gold, Nesters, Tapleys Farm, Blueberry Hill, Whistler Village, the Upper Village, Alta Vista, Nordic Whistler Creek, Tamarisk, Function Junction and Pemberton. It has racks on which you can attach your bicycles or skis, and runs from 5:30 am to 3:00 am, 365 days a year.

Welland Transit
c/o City Hall, 60 East Main St., Welland, ON L3B 3X4
Tel: 905-735-1700; Fax: 905-732-1919
www.welland.ca/transit
Margaret Fortin, Office Coordinator

Whitehorse Transit
2121 2nd Ave., Whitehorse, YT Y1A 1C2
Profile: Whitehorse Transit runs six days a week, with no service on Sundays or holidays. There is also a Handy Bus which provides door-to-door transportation for those who are unable to use regular transit.
Dave Muir, Transit Manager

Winnipeg Transit
311@winnipeg.com
winnipegtransit.com
Profile: Winnipeg Transit has 68 fixed routes throughout the city, including main line routes, express routes and suburban feeders, as well as a 'Handi-Transit' system.

Wood Buffalo Transit
9909 Franklin Ave., Fort McMurray, AB T9H 2K4
Tel: 780-743-4157; Fax: 780-788-4391
pwreception@woodbuffalo.ab.ca
Profile: The Fort McMurray Public Transit System provides efficient bus service on a fixed route, fixed schedule basis. Offering eight regular routes and service five days a week, it carries 900,000 riders annually and links all of Fort McMurray's subdivisions through direct or feeder connections. The service is reduced on weekends and not available on some statutory holidays. It is free for seniors and children under five years of age.

York Region Transit
50 High Tech Rd., 5th Fl., Richmond Hill, ON L4B 4N7
Tel: 905-762-2100;
transitinfo@york.ca
www.yorkregiontransit.com
Profile: YRT offers more than 100 routes including conventional services, GO Shuttles, Express services, community buses and high school, college and university services; VIVA bus rapid transit service is integrated with YRT to provide a seamless, 1-fare transit system across York Region.

Trucking Companies

American Cartage Ltd.
#101-9366 200A St., Langley, BC V1M 4B3
Tel: 604-513-3681; Fax: 604-513-3677
www.americancartage.com
Profile: To ensure prompt, safe delivery of marine containers to and from Vancouver's busy waterfront terminals.
Gloria Vander Schaaf, President

AMJ Campbell Inc.
#830, Milverton Dr., Mississauga, ON L5R 4H1
Tel: 905-795-3785; Fax: 905-670-3787
Toll-Free: 888-265-6683
contact@amjcampbell.com
www.amjcampbell.com
Ticker Symbol: AMJ
Profile: Local trucking with storage; Trucking, except local
Bruce Bowser, President/CEO
Richard Smith, CFO

Canadian Freightways
Toll-Free: 888-868-7923
www.canadianfreightways.com
Profile: North American Coverage: Canadian Freightways provides services to 25,000 points across Canada and the U.S. through an integrated network of regional carriers including sister companies Epic Express and Click Express and strategic partners Averitt Express, New England Motor Freight, Midwest Motor Express and the Connection Company. Regional Expertise: Each partner in their North American network is a regional specialist providing overnight and second day service within their region. Partners operate local Service Centers and are represented by professional drivers and sales teams in key economic communities.
Ralph Wettstein, Vice-President

Can-Truck Inc.
1300 Steeles Ave. East, Brampton, ON L6T 1A2
Tel: 905-595-0408;
dispatch@can-truck.com
www.can-truck.com
Profile: Concentrates mainly on truckload freight including consolation and distribution throughout North America
Don Flesch, President
Frank Cassano, General Manager

Challenger Motor Freight Inc.
300 Maple Grove Rd., Cambridge, ON N3E 1B7
Tel: 519-653-6226; Fax: 519-653-9810
Toll-Free: 800-265-6358
ginfo@challenger.com
www.challenger.com
Profile: Challenger transports goods between Canada and anywhere in North America. Has a full range of transportation, warehousing & logistics services
Dan Einwechter, Chairman & CEO

Contrans Group Inc.
Formerly: Contrans Income Fund
PO Box 1669, 1179 Ridgeway Rd., Woodstock, ON N4S 8P6
Tel: 519-421-4600;
info@contrans.ca
www.contrans.ca
Ticker Symbol: CSS
Profile: Offices of holding companies; Long-distance trucking
Stan G. Dunford, Chair/CEO
Gregory W. Rumble, President/COO
James S. Clark, CFO & Vice-President, Finance
Kim Barnes, Manager, Management Information Systems

CRS-Express Inc.
2100, 95e rue, Saint-Georges, QC G5Y 8J3
Tel: 418-227-7379; Fax: 418-222-5539
Toll-Free: 800-807-7379
www.crs-express.com
Profile: CRS Express is dedicated to excellence in the transportation industry. Pur customers will receive high quality services by a professional and complete transport.

Essen Transport Ltd.
PO Box 2229, 300 Airport Dr., Winkler, MB R6W 4B9
Tel: 204-325-5200; Fax: 204-325-5252
www.essentransport.com
Profile: Their focus on teamwork continues to satisfy new customers with effective supply chain management that consistently delivers on time. Essen Transport's team uses cutting edge logistics to track inbound and outbound shipments for over 100 reputable companies in Canada and the US .

Ghost Transportation Services
715E-46th St. West, Saskatoon, SK S7L 6A1
Tel: 306-249-3515; Fax: 306-249-3335
customerservice@ghosttrans.com
www.ghosttrans.com
Profile: Ghost Transportation Services' diversity and flexibility are the keys. Whether it be warehousing, the shipment of raw materials, transportation or distribution of finished products, our dedication to satisfy our customer's needs and wants provides mutual success.
Clay Dowling, President

GN Transport
163 Bowes Rd., Concord, ON L4K 1H3
Tel: 905-760-2888; Fax: 905-760-2040
Toll-Free: 866-738-6661
info@gntransport.com
www.gntransport.com
Profile: With deregulation firmly in place, GN Transport Ltd. has expanded to serve our customers more effectively and to generate business opportunities within Ontario, and cross border into the United States.

Go Transport Ltd.
57 Braid St., New Westminster, BC
Tel: 604-525-0840; Fax: 604-525-3684
Toll-Free: 888-363-6699
admin@gotransport.ca
www.gotransport.ca
Mark Maarsman, President

Grimshaw Trucking LP
11510-151 St., Edmonton, AB T5M 3N6
Tel: 780-414-2880; Fax: 780-455-7818
Toll-Free: 888-414-2850
GRM-CustServ@gtlp.ca
www.grimshaw-trucking.com
Profile: A highly respected transportation company in Western Canada.
Graham McDonald, Vice President

Group Express Inc.
170 Main St. N., Alexandria, ON K0C 1A0
Tel: 613-525-1275; Fax: 613-525-1278
traffic@groupexpress.ca
www.groupexpress.ca
Profile: Groupex will provide our customers with quality transportation services of the highest value while emphasizing sustainable growth and public safety as measures of corporate strength and security for our employees.
Reynald Blais, President
Jeff ManKinnon, Traffic Manager

Harold Newell & Son Trucking Ltd.
R.R. #1, Barrington, NS B0W 1E0
Tel: 902-637-2243; Fax: 902-637-1563
trucking@ns.sympatico.ca
www.tcfb.com/trucking

International Truck & Engine Corporation Canada
5500 North Service Rd., 4th Fl., Burlington, ON L7L 5H7
Toll-Free: 800-448-7825
www.internationaltrucks.com
Profile: Dealers of trucks, buses, vans: engines, parts, services & financing
James J. Schumacher, President

JDI Logistics
Parent: J.D. Irving, Limited
PO Box 5777, 300 Union St., Saint John, NB E2L 4M3
Tel: 506-633-6767; Fax: 506-648-3082
Toll-Free: 888-675-4888
customerservice@jdilogistics.com
www.jdilogistics.com
Profile: JDI Logistics is a third-party logistics company specializing in pulp & paper, & the food & beverage industry.
Mary Keith, Vice-President, Communications, J.D. Irving, Limited
506-632-5122, keith.mary@jdirving.com

Kindersley Transport Inc.
660 Aldford Ave., Delta, BC V3M 6X1
Tel: 604-522-4002; Fax: 604-525-2955
Toll-Free: 800-667-8556
customerservice@kindersleytransport.com
www.kindersleytransport.com
Profile: One of the largest, most modern fleets based in Western Canada providing truckload and less-than-truckload services through a network of strategically located service centers in Canada and the U.S.
Erwen Siemens, President

Kooi Trucking Inc.
1906 Blue Line Rd., Waterford, ON N0E 1Y0
Tel: 519-443-0668; Fax: 519-443-5074
www.kooitruckinginc.com
Profile: Kooi Trucking Inc. is an experienced freight company, specializing in the transportatoin needs of North American importers and exporters since 1993.
Sue Kooi, President

Lark Transport Inc.
312 Fisher Ave. East, Portage la Prarie, MB R1N 3B9
Tel: 888-444-5257; Fax: 888-246-9365
reynold@larktransport.com
www.larktransport.com
Profile: Lark Transport Inc. is proud to be a Canadian based freight transportation company.
Reynold Plett, Contact, Sales
reynold@larktransport.com
Rene Painchaud, Contact, Dispatch
rene@larktransport.com

Lighthouse Transport Services Ltd.
PO Box 38010, #2-150 Wright Ave., Dartmouth, NS B3B 1X2
Tel: 902-468-3696; Fax: 902-468-5267
Toll-Free: 800-770-5457
colleen@lighthousetransport.com
www.lighthousetransport.com
Profile: Offers FTL and LTL transport, container transport, warehousing and crating, oversized cargo moves, pilot car services, flatbed moves, deconsolidations, in bond warehousing, exclusive deliveries, in bond transport.
Ernest O'Toole, President

Midland Transport Limited
Parent: J.D. Irving, Limited
100 Midland Dr., Dieppe, NB E1A 6X4
Tel: 506-858-5551; Fax: 506-863-6000
Toll-Free: 888-643-5263
customerservice@midlandtransport.com
www.midlandtransport.com; www.midlandcourier.com
Profile: Midland specializes in less-than-truckload & truckload services in eastern Canada & the United States. Divisions include: UniLine, Prime Time, Econo Line, Courier, Coast Line, Dedicated Solutions, Green Line, & Refrigerated Distribution Services.
Scott Newby, Vice-President, Sales

Motrux Inc.
731 Belgrave Way, Delta, BC V3M 5R8
Tel: 604-527-1000; Fax: 604-527-1002
Toll-Free: 800-663-3436
info@motrux.com
www.motrux.com
Profile: Over the years Motrux has evolved from a designated carrier, serving only a few specific customers in Western Canada, to one that now serves many customers across a variety of industries - throughout North America.

Mullen Group Ltd.
Formerly: Mullen Transportation Inc.
PO Box 87, 121A - 31 Southridge Dr., Okotoks, AB T1S 2N3
Tel: 403-995-5200; Fax: 403-995-5296
Toll-Free: 866-995-7711
IR@mullen-group.com
www.mullen-group.com
Ticker Symbol: MTL
Profile: Offices of holding companies; Long-distance trucking; Local trucking with storage; Various oil & gas fields services
Murray K. Mullen, CEO/Chair
Stephen H. Lockwood, President & Co-CEO
David E. Olsen, CFO & Vice-President, Finance

Overland West Freight Lines
Formerly: Overland Freight Courrier
#300-10362 King George Hwy., Surrey, BC V3T 2W5
Tel: 604-580-4600; Fax: 604-580-4601
Toll-Free: 800-698-2111
www.overlandwest.ca
Profile: We are a diverse group of Canadian individuals who try to provide our customers with no surprises LTL-freight-courier service in British Columbia Canada, Alberta Canada, and the Western United States of America.

Pacific Coast Express Ltd.
10299 Grade Rd., Surrey, BC V3V 3VY
Tel: 604-582-3230; Fax: 604-588-7906
dispatch@pcx.ca
www.pcx.ca
Profile: Pacific Coast Express Ltd. is a wholly owned operating unit of Landtran Systems Inc., Western Canada's largest integrated regional distribution company. The primary service offered by the company is expedited LTL/TL, dry van motor freight service between all points in Western Canada and core markets in Arizona, California, Oregon Washington and Mexico. We also provide selected service to points in the Idaho and Utah markets from British Columbia and Alberta, as well as domestic transportation to and from Vancouver Island.
Al Turner, President

Polar Express Transportation Ltd.
#4, 10097-201 St., Langley, BC V1M 3G4
Tel: 604-888-3729; Fax: 604-888-3759
jamie@polarexpresstrans.com
www.polarexpresstrans.com
Profile: Starting January 2000 with one 10 ton and one tractor/trailer we began hauling refrigerated goods to/from Seattle/Tacoma, WA and Vancouver, BC. Using this foundation we have grown to become the West's best choice for handling refrigerated goods moving between the US and Canada.

Premium Trucking Ltd.
PO Box 39, 449 Lower Rd., Arichat, NS B0E 1A0
Tel: 902-226-3474; Fax: 902-226-0026
edgar@premiumseafoods.ns.ca
www.premiumseafoods.ns.ca
Profile: Premium Trucking Ltd. provides world-class transportation services at a fair price. The company owns and operates a fleet of high-quality vehicles, which includes five delivery trucks and two tractor-trailers.
Edgar Sampson, President

Rockman Trucking Inc.
Formerly: Rockman Transport
10765 Cote de Liesse #56, Dorval, QC H9P 1A7
Tel: 514-371-6407;
info@rockman.ca
www.rockman.ca
Profile: A bonded transport company with facilities at Montreal and Ottawa, serving the CL and LCL container deliveries for the major Maritime Companies for over 20 years, Rockman Trucking is equipped with recent and well kept equipment to ensure prompt and timely deliveries. We can deliver any size container; from 20' to 53'. Whether regular, High Cube, Open top or Reefer containers for Imports as well as Exports purposes.

Rolls Right Industry
2864 Norland Ave., Burnaby, BC V5B 3A6
Tel: 604-298-0080; Fax: 604-298-1366
info@rollsright.ca
www.rollsright.ca
Profile: At Rolls Right Industries, we understand that our customers depend on timely deliveries to maintain proper inventory levels, fully-stocked shelves and secure sales. Whether your are a local supplier to the retail sector or a custom broker moving containers, with a wide range of time sensitive freight transportation services, Rolls Right will get you there.

RST Industries
Parent: J.D. Irving, Limited
485 McAllister Dr., Saint John, NB E2L 4H8
Tel: 506-634-8800; Fax: 506-634-4259
Toll-Free: 800-463-8551
sales@rsttransport.com
www.rsttransport.com
Profile: RST specializes in the transportation of petroleum, propane, chemicals, food grade products, & dry bulk, & offers flatbed services as well. The Commodities Division, based in Toronto, provides customers with logistics services.
Mary Keith, Vice-President, Communications, J.D. Irving, Limited
506-632-5122, keith.mary@jdirving.com

Shadow Lines Transportation Group
9818 198B St., Langley, BC V1M 2X5
Tel: 604-888-2928; Fax: 604-888-2794
Toll-Free: 800-663-1421
trucking@shadowlines.com
www.shadowlines.com
Profile: Shadow Lines has over 35 years experience as a service based transportation company. We operate in Canada from British Columbia to Ontario and throughout the 48 states of the continental USA.

Sunbury Transport
Parent: J.D. Irving, Limited
PO Box 905 A, Fredericton, NB E3B 5B4
Tel: 506-453-1133; Fax: 506-458-2542
Toll-Free: 800-786-2879
sunbury@sunbury.ca
www.sunbury.ca
Profile: Sunbury provides transportation by van & flatbed, specializes in dry bulk goods, & also provides logistics & brokerage services.
Mary Keith, Vice-President, Communications, J.D. Irving, Limited
506-632-5122, keith.mary@jdirving.com

Katherine Hayman, Contact
hayman.katherine@sunbury.ca

Swift Dispatch Service Ltd.
#112, 4238 Lozells Ave., Burnaby, BC V5A 0C4
Tel: 604-873-5422; Fax: 604-879-2311
Toll-Free: 888-595-6633
info@swiftdispatch.com

TMT Freight System
14 Cadetta Rd., Brampton, ON L6T 3Z8
Tel: 905-794-9845; Fax: 905-794-9846
Toll-Free: 888-817-4410
info@tmtfreight.com
www.tmtfreight.com
Profile: TMT Freight System was emerged as an innovative company in the year 1993 and over our nearly 13 year history; we have dedicated our efforts to being a container carrier with a strong motto of on time delivery with care and safety.
Bobby Mahal, President
Jasbir Sanghera, Vice Prestident

TransForce Inc.
Formerly: TransForce Income Fund
#500, 8801 Trans-Canada Hwy., Saint-Laurent, QC H4S 1Z6
Tel: 514-331-4000; Fax: 514-337-4200
www.transforcecompany.com
Ticker Symbol: TFI
Profile: Long-distance trucking; Local trucking without storage
Alain Bedard, President/CEO & Chair
Salvatore Vitale, CFO

Trappers Transport Ltd.
2475 Day St., Winnipeg, MB R2C 2Z2
Tel: 204-697-7647; Fax: 204-633-5569
info@trapperstransport.com
www.trapperstransport.com
Profile: We specialize in the transportation of refrigerated LTL or Full Loads throughout North America. Our maintenance shop services or repairs all makes and models of trucks, trailers, heavy equipment and reefer units.
Dan Omeniuk, President & CEO
Pankaj Sharma, Vice President & CFO, Finance

Trimac Corporation
PO Box 3500 M, #1700, 800 - 5th Ave. SW, Calgary, AB T2P 2P9
Tel: 403-298-5100; Fax: 403-298-5258
info@trimac.com
www.trimac.com
Ticker Symbol: TMA.UN
Profile: The company provides services in highway transportation of bulk commodities.
Terry Owen, President/CEO
416-298-5101, Fax: 416-298-5355, tjowen@trimac.com
Ed Malysa, Vice-President/CFO
416-298-5176, Fax: 416-298-5146, emalysa@trimac.com

Vitran Express Canada Inc.
Formerly: Vitran Corporation Inc.
1201 Creditstone Rd., Concord, ON L4K 0C2
Tel: 416-798-4965; Fax: 416-798-4753
Toll-Free: 800-263-9588
ltl.cda.webmaster@vitran.com
www.vitran.com
Ticker Symbol: VTN
Profile: Long-distance trucking; Arrangement of transportation of freight & cargo; General warehousing & storage; Refuse systems
Rick E. Gaetz, President/CEO
Sean P. Washchuk, CFO & Vice-President, Finance

Yanke Group of Companies
1359 Fletcher Rd., Saskatoon, SK S7M 5H5
Tel: 800-667-7988; Fax: 306-955-5663
Toll-Free: 888-692-6534
csr@yanke.ca
www.yanke.ca
Profile: During the last 30 years, our founder has seen Yanke expand from a mere two trucks to a fleet of more than 400, and flourish from 33 employees to over 700. Cancom satellite systems. Instant shipment tracking. National weather monitoring system. Why does Yanke do all of this? We strive to stay ahead of our time to make sure that we are always on time.

Zeena Transport
PO Box 759, Morden, MB R6M 1A7
Tel: 204-822-4915; Fax: 204-822-4687
www.zeenatransport.com
Profile: We are proud to offer our customers the best refrigerated and dry van service possible. We accomplish this by utilizing dependable, up-to-date equipment and well trained, dependable employees.
Henry Giesbrecht, President
Reynold Hildebrand, Operations Manager

Transportation Manufacturers & Services

2Source Manufacturing Inc.
5261 Bradco Blvd., Mississauga, ON L4W 2A6
Tel: 905-361-9998; Fax: 905-282-9924
Toll-Free: 866-361-9997
info@2Source.com
www.2source.com
Profile: 2Source specializes in producing landing gear bushings & similar parts for specific aircraft platforms.
Robert Waslyk, Contact, Aerospace Inquiries
416-500-3595, rwaslyk@2source.com

3 Points Aviation
91 Watts Ave., Charlottetown, PE C1E 2B7
Tel: 902-628-8846; Fax: 902-628-8838
www.vmtechnology.ca
Profile: 3 Points supplies aircraft parts & support, including airframe parts, engines, propellers, & landing gear.
Eric Richard, Contact, Corporate Office
erichard@3pointsaviation.com
Tom Considine, Partner
847-433-0576, Fax: 847-433-0609, tomc@3pointsaviation.com
John Druken, Partner
709-834-6034, Fax: 709-834-6058, johnd@3pointsaviation.com
Leo Druken, Contact, Finance
709-834-6034, Fax: 709-834-6058, leo@3pointsaviation.com

3M Canada Company
300 Tartan Dr., London, ON N5V 4M9
Tel: 888-364-3577; Fax: 800-479-4453
www.3m.com/aerospace
Ticker Symbol: MMM / NYSE
Profile: This division of 3M Canada Company specializes in manufacturing, maintenance, & repair of aircraft, airframes, & engines for both commercial & space flight.
Marc M. Simard, Business Director
905-564-9700, mmsimard@mmm.com

ABB Inc.
#300, 585, boul Charest est, Québec, QC G1K 9H4
Tel: 418-877-2944; Fax: 418-877-2834
www.abb.com/analytical
Ticker Symbol: ABB / NYSE; ABBBN / SIX
Profile: The company specializes in the manufacture of analytical technologies, targeting the industrial processes, defense, & space markets.
Jean-René Roy, Vice-President, ABB Canada
Jean-Rene.Roy@ca.abb.com
Jacques G. Giroux, Contact, Business Development, Space Canada
Jacques.G.Giroux@ca.abb.com

ACS-NAI, Ltd.
Formerly: Aero Consulting Services; Northern Aero Industries
Parent: EMTEQ, Inc.
25 Dunlop Ave., Winnipeg, MB R2X 2V2
Tel: 204-783-5402; Fax: 204-783-5436
www.acs-nai.com
Profile: The company provides engineering, manufacturing, & certification services to the global aviation industry. They have offices in Manitoba & Québec.
Doug Peters, Contact, Aftermarket Engineering & Certification
dpeters@acs-nai.com
Rick Williamson, Contact, Manufacturing & Maintenance
rwilliamson@acs-nai.com
Al Wilson, Contact, Manufacturing & Maintenance
awilson@acs-nai.com
Michelle Woo, Contact, Aftermarket Engineering & Certification
mwoo@acs-nai.com

Action Aero Inc.
34 Belmont St., Charlottetown, PE C1A 5H1
Tel: 902-370-3311; Fax: 902-370-3313
info@actionaero.com
www.actionaero.com
Profile: The company provides overhaul & repair services for fuel, oil, & air related engine accessories.
Dave Trainor, President
dave@actionaero.com
Chad Crockett, Manager, Customer Service
ccrockett@actionaero.com
Larry Wilson, Manager, Quality
lwilson@actionaero.com

Adacel Inc.
#E, 4005, boul Matte, Brossard, QC J4Y 2P4
Tel: 407-567-1560; Fax: 407-567-2080
www.adacel.com
Ticker Symbol: ADA / ASX
Profile: The company creates software & simulation products for the training of air traffic controllers, pilots, & airport vehicle operators.
Bill Lang, Vice-President, Air Traffic Management
514-636-6365
Tom Evers, Director, Marketing & Communications
tom.evers@adacel.com

ADGA Group
Groupe ADGA
#600, 116 Albert St., Ottawa, ON K1P 5G3
Tel: 613-237-3022; Fax: 613-237-3024
services@apsaviation.ca
www.adga.ca
Profile: The Group serves the defense & aerospace sectors through its three companies: ADGA Group Consultants Inc., AEPOS Technologies Corporation, & APS Aviation Inc. Its specialities are: weapons systems management; airframe systems; avionics; armaments; automatic test equipment; maintenance support; instrument & electrical systems; technical documentation; & C4ISR.
Brian Deeks, Corporate Vice-President
bdeeks@adga.ca

Advanced Integration Technology Canada / AIT
Parent: Advanced Integration Technology, Inc.
#100, 3168 - 262nd St., Aldergrove, BC V4W 2Z6
Tel: 604-856-8939; Fax: 604-856-8993
ait@aint.com
www.aint.com
Profile: AIT is an industrial automation & tooling company providing turnkey factory integration & the design, manufacture, & installation of machines & systems for the automated assembly of aerospace structures. Their Aldergrove, BC, facility specializes in fabrication, machining, assembly, & metrology.
Ed Chalupa, President

Advanced Precision
70 Thornhill Dr., Dartmouth, NS B3B 1S3
Tel: 902-468-5653; Fax: 902-468-5737
advancedprecision.ca
Profile: The company provides precision component machining, fabrication, & assembly services to the aerospace, military, & industrial sectors.
Stephen Hilchey, Manager, Business Development
shilchey@advancedprecision.ca
Jason Farris, Manager, Estimation
jfarris@advancedprecision.ca

Aéro Montréal
#8000, 380, rue Saint-Antoine ouest, Montréal, QC H2Y 3X7
Tél: 514-987-9332; Téléc: 514-987-1948
info@aeromontreal.ca
www.aeromontreal.ca
Profile: A think tank designed to bring members of Quebec's aerospace industry together to meet common goals & promote shared interests.
Suzanne M. Benoît, President
suzanne.benoit@aeromontreal.ca

Aero Recip Canada Ltd.
Parent: Gregorash Aviation
540 Marjorie St., Winnipeg, MB R3H 0S9
Tel: 204-788-4765; Fax: 204-786-2775
Toll-Free: 800-561-5544
info@aerorecip.com
www.aerorecip.com
Profile: Aero Recip exchanges, overhauls, & repairs piston engines, & specializes in Pratt & Whitney radial engines.
Wayne Cathers, Contact, Tech Support
wcathers@aerorecip.com
Dave Wakeman, Contact, Sales
dwakeman@aerorecip.com

AeroInfo Systems
Parent: Boeing
#200, 13575 Commerce Pkwy., Richmond, BC V6V 2L1
Tel: 604-232-4200; Fax: 604-232-4201
www.aeroinfo.com
Profile: AeroInfo is a business & technology consulting firm serving commercial aviation, defence, marine, & natural resource & energy sectors.
Bob Cantwell, President/CEO
Terry Tarle, COO
Stig Westerlund, CFO

Aero-safe Technologies Inc.
1799 Pettit Rd., Fort Erie, ON L2A 5N1
Tel: 905-871-1663; Fax: 905-871-7093
sales@aerosafe.ca
www.aerosafe.ca
Profile: The company specializes in high precision CNC manufacturing & assembly for the aerospace & defence industries.

Aerospace BizDev
5057 - 2A Ave., Delta, BC V4M 3M6
Tel: 604-839-5504;
www.aerospacebizdev.com
Profile: A consulting company specializing in business development in the aerospace industry.
Linda Wolstencroft, President
linda@aerospacebizdev.com

Aerospace Welding Inc. / AWI
890, boul Michèle-Bohec, Blainville, QC J7C 5E2
Tél: 450-435-9210; Téléc: 450-435-7851
info@aerospacewelding.com
www.aerospacewelding.com
Profile: The company specializes in fabricating & repairing metallic aircraft & engine parts of all sizes.
Michel Dussault, Vice-President, Business Development
mdussault@aerospacewelding.com
Karen Di Genova, Quality Manager

Aerosystems International Inc. / ASI
3538, rue Ashby, Montréal, QC H4R 2C1
Tél: 514-336-9426; Téléc: 514-336-4383
info@asiiweb.com
www.asiiweb.com
Profile: The company was founded in 1971, & provides services to the aviation industry including wire harness assemblies, ground support equipment, component integration, & logistical support.
Fergie Legge, President/CEO
legge@asiiweb.com

AeroTek Manufacturing Ltd.
1449 Hopkins St., Whitby, ON L1N 2C2
Tel: 905-666-3400; Fax: 905-666-3414
customerservice@aerotekmfg.com
www.aerotekmfg.com
Profile: AeroTek provides processing services such as electroplating, anodizing, chemical conversions, painting, non-destructive testing, & sub-assembly, among others.

Aflare Systems Inc.
37 Edgemont Dr., Brampton, ON L6V 1K9
Tel: 416-843-8807;
info@aflaresystems.com
www.aflaresystems.com
Profile: The company was founded in 2005, & specializes in engineering power systems, sensor suites, software applications, & wireless communication for the automotive, telecommunications, aerospace, & medical industries.
Roman Ronge, President
roman.ronge@aflaresystems.com

AgustaWestland
Parent: Finmeccanica S.p.A.
10 Somerset St. West, Ottawa, ON K2P 0H4
Tel: 613-782-2241; Fax: 613-782-0110
www.agustawestland.com
Profile: AugustaWestland is the manufacturer of the Cormorant helecopter used by the Canadian Forces for search & rescue operations. The company also manufactures a range of rotocraft for civil & military use.
Jeremy Tracy, Head, Canada Region
jeremy.tracy@agustawestland.com

AleniaAermacchi
Parent: Finmeccanica S.p.A.
#1150, 45 O'Connor St., Ottawa, ON K1P 1A4
Tel: 202-292-2622; Fax: 202-293-0677
www.aleniana.com
Profile: The company manufactures the C-27J Spartan search & rescue twin turboprop aircraft, which has been in production since 2001 & is currently used by nine national air forces.
Tiziana Cotugno, Deputy COO
tcotugno@aleniainc.com

Alloy Concepts Inc. Precision CNC Machining
59 Wilkinson Ave., Dartmouth, NS B3B 0H5
Tel: 902-468-1144; Fax: 902-468-7632
advancedprecision.ca
Profile: The company specializes in prototyping, production manufacturing, & programming for sectors including avionics, automotive manufacturing, military, renewable energy, & ocean science, among others.
David Schnare, President
dschnare@alloyconceptscnc.com
Perry MacIsaac, Contact, Sales & Marketing
pmacisaac@alloyconceptscnc.com

Alphacasting Inc.
391, av Sainte Croix, Montréal, QC H4N 2L3
Tél: 514-748-7511; Téléc: 514-748-0237
www.alphacasting.com
Profile: The company manufactures castings from ferrous, non-ferrous, titanium, & exotic alloys for industries such as aerospace, military, & telecommunications.
Frederik-Pierre Centazzo, Vice-President
fcentazzo@alphacasting.com
Steve Goulet, Sales Representative

Altitude Aerospace Inc.
#200, 2705, boul Pitfield, Montréal, QC H4S 1T2
Tél: 514-335-6922; Téléc: 514-335-3356
info@altitudeaero.com
www.altitudeaero.com
Profile: The company aids in the development of new aircraft, as well as providing support for existing fleets, through its work in conceptual design, structural analysis, & certification.
Nancy Venneman, President
nvenneman@altitudeaero.com
Dimitri Gauthier-Arapoglou, Director, Marketing & Business Development
dgarapoglou@altitudeaero.com

Apex Industries Inc.
100 Millennium Blvd., Moncton, NB E1C 8M6
Tel: 506-857-7544; Fax: 506-857-1594
www.apexindustries.com
Profile: The company's Aerospace Division is responsible for manufacturing & integrating structural assemblies, sub-assemblies, kitting, & components for the aerospace industry (commercial & defence).
Keith Donaldson, Director, Sales & Business Development
kmdonaldson@apexindustries.com

Argus Industries
20 Murray Park Rd., Winnipeg, MB R3J 3T9
Tel: 204-837-4660; Fax: 204-896-4250
info@argusindustries.ca
www.argusindustries.ca
Profile: Argus custome manufactures rubber molded products & die cut gasket seals. They have facilities in Manitoba & Ontario.
Ross Roy, Vice-President, Sales & Marketing
ross@argusindustries.ca

Arnprior Aerospace Inc.
107 Baskin Dr. East, Arnprior, ON K7S 3M1
Tel: 613-623-1743; Fax: 613-623-1732
sales@arnprioraerospace.com
www.arnprioraerospace.com
Profile: Originally part of Boeing, the company became independent in 2005 & now operates facilities in Canada & Mexico. Arnprior Aerospace supplies products & services (including design, fabrication, machining, processing, assembly, kitting, & product integration) to the aerospace & defence industries.
George Rick, Vice-President, Business Management
Eric Nelson, Director, Business Development
207-894-5641

ASCO Aerospace Canada Ltd.
Parent: ASCO Industries
8510 River Rd., Delta, BC V4G 1B5
Tel: 604-946-4900; Fax: 604-946-4671
www.asco.be
Profile: The company's specialty is the design & manufacture of very large aluminum structures, as well as titanium & steel components for aircraft.
Kevin Russell, Vice-President & General Manager
krussell@ascoaerospace.ca
Dave Belanger, Vice-President, Commercial
dbelanger@ascoaerospace.ca

Atlantis Systems Corp.
Metropolitan Pl., #1100, 99 Wyse Rd., Dartmouth, NS B3A 4S5
Tel: 902-461-6600; Fax: 902-461-6601
info@atlantissc.com
www.atlantissi.com
Profile: Atlantis provides advanced training services for the military & commercial markets.
David Williams, Chair
Ken Howard, CEO
Bill Bartlett, CFO
Chris Lewis, Senior Vice President, Business Development
905-792-1981 ext: 5120, clewis@atlantissc.com
Alan Forsey, Vice President, Sales & Marketing
902-461-6600 ext: 6263, aforsey@atlantissc.com
Charlie Jamieson, Vice President, Business Development
613-238-2392, charlie.jamieson@atlantissc.com

Avcorp Industries Inc.
10025 River Way, Delta, BC V4G 1M7
Tel: 604-587-4888; Fax: 604-582-2620
info@avcorp.com
www.avcorp.com
Ticker Symbol: AVP / TSX
Profile: Avcorp is a designer & builder of major airframe structures & components, including stabilizers, cargo liners, floor panels, engine nacelles, packboards, & wing components.
Mark van Rooij, President/CEO
mvanrooij@avcorp.com
Paul Wiggum, Contact, Sales & Marketing
604-582-6677, pwiggum@avcorp.com

Aversan Inc.
#203, 885 Progress Ave., Toronto, ON M1H 3G3
Tel: 416-289-1554; Fax: 416-289-1554
info@aversan.com
aversan.com
Profile: Aversan specializes in designing, testing, & integrating embedded systems, system integration labs, & test equipment for the aerospace & defence industries. The company has offices in North America, South East Asia, & India.
Ted Sherlock, B.Sc.CEO
Richard Smith, Director, Business Development
rsmith@aversan.com

Aviya Technologies Inc.
Plaza V, #402, 2000 Argentia Rd., Mississauga, ON L5N 2R7
Tel: 905-812-9995; Fax: 905-812-0933
info@aviyatech.com
www.aviyatech.com
Profile: The company specializes in engineering systems, mechanics, hardware, & software for aerospace & defence applications, as well as providing program management & testing of electronic hardware components.
John Koumoundouros, President
john.koumoundouros@aviyatech.com

BASF Canada
Parent: BASF SE; BASF Corporation
100 Milverton Dr., 5th Fl., Mississauga, ON L5R 4H1
Tel: 289-360-6060; Fax: 289-360-6005
aerospace.basf.com
Profile: BASF's Aerospace Division specializes in cabin interiors, fuel & lubricants, flame retardants & fire protection, & more.
Cindy Gruber, Manager, Business & Market Development
cindy.gruber@basf.com

Bell Helicopter Textron Canada Ltd.
Parent: Bell Helicopter Textron Inc.
12 800, rue de l'Avenir, Mirabel, QC J7J 1R4
Tél: 450-437-3400;
aerospace.basf.com
Profile: Bell Helicopter produces rotary-wing aircraft for the civilian & military sectors, including the Griffin Helicopter fleet flown by the Canadian Forces.
Cynthia Garneau, Director, Corporate Affairs
450-971-6500, Fax: 450-437-2006, cgarneau@bh.com

Bluedrop Performance Learning
18 Prescott St., St. John's, NL A1C 3S4
Tel: 709-739-9000; Fax: 709-739-9003
Toll-Free: 800-563-3638
contact@bluedrop.com
www.bluedrop.com
Ticker Symbol: BPL / TSX-V
Profile: Bluedrop provides advanced training technologies to individuals, corporations, the military, & the public sector. The company operates two Groups: CoursePark Learning Services & Defence & Aerospace.
Emad Rizkalla, President/CEO
Michael O'Rourke, COO, Defence & Aerospace
defenceaerospace@bluedrop.com
Al Dillon, Executive Vice-President, Business Development & Government Relations

Boeing Canada Operations
Parent: Boeing
Central Chambers Bldg., #100, 46 Elgin St., Ottawa, ON K1P 5K6
Tel: 613-745-8111; Fax: 613-745-9779
www.boeing.com
Ticker Symbol: BA
Profile: Boeing manufactures commercial jetliners & military aircraft, as well as rotorcraft, electonic & defence systems,

milliles, satellites, launch vehicles, & information & communication systems.
Eddy Morin, Vice-President, Boeing Canada
eddy.morin@boeing.com

Bombardier Inc.
800, boul René-Lévesque ouest, Montréal, QC H3B 1Y8
Tel: 514-861-9481;
www.bombardier.com
Ticker Symbol: BBD
Profile: Manufacturers of railroad equipment, aircraft, aircraft engines & engine parts, aircraft parts & auxiliary equipment, various transportation equipment; Personal credit institutions; Real estate land subdividers & developers
Laurent Beaudoin, Chair/CEO
Pierre Beaudoin, President/COO, Bombardier Aerospace
Pierre Alary, Sr. Vice-President/CFO

Bradean's Tool & Die Limited
#1B, 46 Anson Ave., Amherst, NS B4H 4R2
Tel: 902-661-0669; Fax: 902-661-1748
bradeans@bradeans.com
www.bradeans.com
Profile: The company, which was established in 2002, manufactures aerospace & related parts, as well as conducting research & development, prototyping, & other experimental projects.
Dean Smith, Co-Founder
Brad Sprague, Co-Founder

Brican Flight Systems Inc.
54 Van Kirk Dr., Brampton, ON L7A 1B1
Tel: 905-846-5175; Fax: 905-846-5946
www.brican.com
Profile: BFS supplies the aerospace & defence industry with mission-ready unmanned aerial vehicles.
Brian McLuckie, Contact
mcluckieb@brican.com

Cadorath Aerospace Inc.
2070 Logan Ave., Winnipeg, MB R2R 0H9
Tel: 204-633-2707; Fax: 204-632-7663
Toll-Free: 800-470-7069
info@cadorath.com
www.cadorath.com
Profile: Cadorath Aerospace provides customers with aeronautical repair, modification, & overhaul services.
Gerry Cadorath, President/CEO
Norm Comeault, CFO
Dave Haines, Senior Vice-President
Roy Hartfiel, General Manager, Cadorath Aerospace
204-227-6349, rhartfiel@cadorath.com

CAE Inc.
8585, boul Côte de Liesse, Montréal, QC H4T 1G6
Tél: 514-734-5788; Téléc: 514-340-5519
Ligne sans frais: 866-999-6223
www.cae.com
Ticker Symbol: CAE / TSX, NYSE
Profile: The company specializes in modelling, simulation, & training for civil & defence aviation sectors.
Marc Parent, President/CEO
Nathalie Bourque, Vice-President, Public Affairs & Global Communications
nathalie.bourque@cae.com

Canadian Centre for Unmanned Vehicle Systems / CCUVS
#4, 49 Viscount Ave. SW, Medicine Hat, AB T1A 5G4
Tel: 403-488-7208; Fax: 403-488-7224
www.ccuvs.com
Profile: The company is a federally registered not-for-profit entity that provides the following services to the unmanned systems sector: systems training; providing facilities for tests & launches; consulting; & promotion of civil & commercial use of unmanned systems.
Spencer Fraser, Chair
Sterling Cripps, COO
sterling@ccuvs.com

Canadian Composites Manufacturing R&D Inc. / CCMRD
c/o Composites Innovation Centre Manitoba Inc., 158 Commerce Dr., Winnipeg, MB R3P 0Z6
Tel: 204-262-3400; Fax: 204-262-3409
www.ccmrd.ca; www.compositesinnovation.ca
Profile: The CCMRD is a national consortium of industry leaders, whose goal is to develop & promote advanced composite manufacturing technologies & techniques in order to increase Canada's global competitiveness in this field.
Gene Manchur, Executive Director
204-262-3400 ext: 202, gmanchur@ccmrd.ca;
gmanchur@compositesinnovation.ca

Canadian Light Source Inc. / CLS
Centre canadien de rayonnement synchrotron
101 Perimeter Rd., Saskatoon, SK S7N 0X4
Tel: 306-657-3500; Fax: 306-657-3535
cls@lightsource.ca
www.lightsource.ca
Profile: The Canadian Light Source centre is one of the most powerful synchrotron facilities in the world, generating intense beams of light that allow researchers to view the microstructures of materials. This technology is useful in the fields of aviation & aerospace.
Josef Hormes, Executive Director
Jeffrey Cutler, Director, Industrial Science
306-657-3530, jeffrey.cutler@lightsource.ca
Royal Hinther, Director, Business Development
royal.hinther@lightsource.ca

Canadian Propeller Ltd.
462 Brooklyn St., Winnipeg, MB R3J 1M7
Tel: 204-832-8679; Fax: 204-888-4696
Toll-Free: 800-773-6853
info@canadianpropeller.com
www.canadianpropeller.com
Profile: The company is an authorized service & repair station for Hartzell & McCauley propellers, among others.
Maurice Wills, President & General Manager
mwills@canadianpropeller.com

CanRep Inc.
Parent: CanRep Group
12900, rue Brault, Mirabel, QC J7J 1P3
Tél: 450-434-9898; Téléc: 450-434-6996
sales@canrep.com
www.canrep.com
Profile: CanRep provides distribution services for aircraft interior components & equipment, engine components, & airborne security & surveillance systems.
Marc Gregory, Executive Vice-President

Carillon Information Security Inc.
356, rue Joseph-Carrier, Vaudreuil-Dorion, QC J7V 5V5
Tél: 514-485-0789; Téléc: 450-424-9559
info@carillon.ca
www.carillon.ca
Profile: The company provides identity management consulting services to clients in the air transport & aerospace industries.
Patrick Patterson, President

CarteNav Solutions Inc.
#708, 1809 Barrington St., Halifax, NS B3J 3K8
Tel: 902-446-4988; Fax: 902-446-4987
Toll-Free: 877-723-8729
www.cartenav.com
Profile: CarteNav produces situational awareness software for maritime, land, & air environments, targeting the defence, security, & industry markets.
Brian K. Penney, Chair
Lynn Mason, CEO

Cascade Aerospace Inc.
1337 Townline Rd., Abbotsford, BC V2T 6E1
Tel: 604-850-7372; Fax: 604-857-2655
info@cascadeaerospace.com
www.cascadeaerospace.com
Profile: Cascade provides clients in the military, government, & commercial aerospace sectors with management, engineering, & support services. The company also designs & manufactures various aircraft systems & kits.
David Schellenberg, CEO

Celestica Inc.
844 Don Mills Rd., Toronto, ON M3C 1V7
Tel: 416-448-5800; Toll-Free: 888-899-9998
contactus@celestica.com
www.celestica.com
Ticker Symbol: CLS / TSX; NYSE
Profile: Celestica provides the aerospace & defence industries with design, engineering, manufacturing, logistics, after-market, & supply chain network services. Its specialties are complex printed circuit assembly, system assembly, system integration, & box build assembly.
Dan Stewart, General Manager, Customer Business Unit
416-448-2804, dstewart@celestica.com

CFN Consultants
#1502, 222 Queen St., Ottawa, ON K1P 5V9
Tel: 613-232-1576; Fax: 613-238-5519
info@cfncon.com
www.cfnconsultants.com
Profile: CFN specializes in defence & security issues, & has worked with the Canadian Forces, departments of the Canadian Government, & NATO, as well as off-shore companies in the defence, IM/IT, & aerospace sectors.
George Macdonald, Senior Partner
gmacdonald@cfncon.com

Ciara Technologies Inc.
9300, rte Transcanadienne, Montréal, QC H4S 1K5
Tél: 514-745-4540; Téléc: 514-745-0937
sales@ciaratech.com
www.ciaratech.com
Profile: Ciara provides technology & software solutions & services from companies ranging from small businesses to educational, & government & defence.
André Lamarre, Executive Vice-President
andre.lamarre@hypertec.com

CLS Lexi-tech
10 Dawson St., Dieppe, MB E1A 6C8
Tel: 506-859-5200; Fax: 506-859-5205
info@lexitech.ca
www.cls-lexitech.ca
Profile: CLS lexi-tech provides writing, editing, translation, proof-reading, TACT, & final formatting services for technical publications & corporate documents.
Robin Ayoub, Vice-President, Business Development & Sales
416-409-8202, rayoub@lexitech.ca
Eric Parisien, Contact, Government Sales & Marketing
613-314-1694, eparisien@lexitech.ca

CMTIGroup Inc.
9404, rue du Saguenay, Montréal, QC H1R 3Z8
Tél: 514-328-2166;
info@cmtigroup.com
www.cmtigroup.com
Profile: The company offers specialty engineering services to clients in the aerospace, defence, space & transportation sectors, including black box developers, subsystem integrators, & government agencies.
Tony Zenga, President

Cobham Avionics
Parent: Cobham Group
4105, rue Cousens, Montréal, QC H4S 1V6
Tél: 514-745-1600; Téléc: 514-745-2711
www.airsatori.com
Profile: Cobham specializes in aerospace & defence technology & systems. The company's clients include Boeing, Airbus, Bombardier, Bell, & Eurocopter. Cobham's Montréal location is dedicated to distributing, repairing, maintaining, & overhauling instrument components & avionics.
Marc Lapasset, General Manager
marc.lapasset@cobham.com
Josée Chiurillo, Regional Customer Support Representative

COM DEV International Ltd.
155 Sheldon Dr., Cambridge, ON N1R 7H6
Tel: 519-622-2300; Fax: 519-622-1691
www.comdev.ca
Ticker Symbol: CDV / TSX
Profile: COM DEV is a major designer & manufacturer of space satellite hardware & other space & defence-related products, including microwave electronics & optics systems & subsystems.

Michael Pley, CEO
Ron Holdway, Vice-President, Government Relations
613-591-777, Fax: 613-591-7789, ronald.holdway@comdev.ca

Composites Atlantic Limited / CAL
Parent: EADS Sogerma
PO Box 1150, 71 Hall St., Lunenburg, NS B0J 2C0
Tel: 902-634-8448; Fax: 902-634-3993
www.compositesatlantic.com
Profile: The company provides structural analysis & manufacturing services to the aeronautics, defence, & space sectors.
Claude Baril, President/CEO
902-634-4475, cbaril@compositesatlantic.com

Convergent Manufacturing Technologies Inc.
#403, 6190 Agronomy Rd., Vancouver, BC V6T 1Z3
Tel: 604-822-9682; Fax: 604-822-9659
inquiries@convergent.ca
www.aeroinfo.com
Profile: Convergent produces composite process modelling software & services, useful in the aerospace industry for the modelling of production hardware. The company was originally part of the University of British Columbia's Composites Group, & although they became separately incorporated in 1998, they continue to hold strong ties to UBC.

CRIAQ
#1515, 740, rue Notre-Dame ouest, Montréal, QC H3C 3X6
Tél: 514-313-7561; Téléc: 514-398-0902
info@criaq.aero
www.criaq.aero
Profile: The Consortium for Research & Innovation in Aerospace in Québec (CRIAQ) seeks to enhance the knowledge base of the aerospace industry in the province through education & student training, with the goal of increasing Québec's competitiveness in the international aerospace market. CRIAQ is a non-profit entity supported by the Québec government.
Clément Fortin, President/CEO
clement.fortin@criaq.aero

Cyclone Manufacturing Inc.
7300 Rapistan Crt., Mississauga, ON L5N 5S1
Tel: 905-567-5601; Fax: 905-567-6911
RFQ@cyclonemfg.com
www.cyclonemfg.com
Profile: Cyclone specializes in manufacturing & assembling medium & large structures for the aerospace industry.
Andrew Sochaj, President
andrew.sochaj@cyclonemfg.com
Robert Sochaj, Executive Vice-President
robert.sochaj@cyclonemfg.com

DECA Aviation Engineering Ltd.
#200, 7050 Telford Way, Mississauga, ON L5S 1V7
Tel: 905-405-1371; Fax: 905-405-1373
inquiry@deca-aviation.com
www.deca-aviation.com
Profile: DECA provides engineering, certification, aircraft modification, program management, & integrated kit supply services to the domestic & international aviation community.

Deep Vision Inc.
Quaker Landing Bldg., #125, 33 Ochterloney St., Dartmouth, NS B2Y 4P5
Tel: 902-461-1615; Fax: 902-463-0139
www.deepvision.ca
Profile: Deep Vision specializes in developing intelligent machine perception technology, useful in sectors such as aerospace & defence, intelligent transportation, robotics, surveillance, & autonomous systems, among others.
Ron L'Esperance, Press Officer
902-471-1003, rlesperance@deepvision.ca

Defense & Aviation Wiring Inc.
695 Sovereign Rd., London, ON N5V 4K8
Tel: 519-451-0888; Fax: 519-451-2052
Toll-Free: 866-828-8057
quotes@davwire.com
www.davwire.com
Profile: DAVWIRE specializes in wire harnesses, electrical panels, & electro-mechanical assemblies for the aviation, defence, medical, & rail markets.
Mark MacKenzie, President/CEO
519-451-0888 ext: 232
Mark Boda, Manager, Sales
226-448-5917, Fax: 519-451-2052, mark.boda@davwire.com

Delastek Inc.
2699, 5e av, Grand-Mère, QC G9T 5K7
Tél: 819-533-5788; Téléc: 819-533-3494
info@delastek.com
www.delastek.com
Profile: The company manufactures composite & interior parts for aircraft, as well as supporting the various phases of product development. They also specialize in electrical & electronic systems for other types of vehicles, as well as bumpers & product integration.
Claude Lessard, President
clessard@delastek.com

DRS Pivotal Power
Parent: DRS Power Solutions
150 Bluewater Rd., Bedford, NS B4B 1G9
Tel: 902-835-7268; Fax: 902-835-6026
info@pivotalpower.com
www.pivotalpower.com
Profile: DRS Pivotal Power, as part of DRS Power Solutions, supplies power generation products to the army, naval, aerospace, vehicle export power, alternative energy, marine, government, & emergency services sectors, among others.
Ken Zurawski, Director, Business Development
203-366-5211 ext: 561, kzurawski@upsi.com
Nancy Preeper, Manager, Business Development
902-832-7357, n.preeper@pivotalpower.com
Heidi Jantzen-Hubert, Manager, Marketing & Communications
703-814-8106

Dynetek Industries Ltd.
4410 - 46 Ave. SE, Calgary, AB T2B 3N7
Tel: 403-720-0262; Fax: 403-720-0263
Toll-Free: 888-396-3835
contactus@dynetek.com
www.dynetek.com
Ticker Symbol: DNK
Profile: Manufacturers of cylinders, fuel cell storage systems
Robb D. Thompson, President/CEO
Karen Y. Minton, Vice-President, Finance & Administration

EADS Canada Inc.
Parent: EADS Group
#530, 360 Albert St., Ottawa, ON K1R 7X7
Tel: 613-230-3902; Fax: 613-230-1442
info@ca.eads.net
www.eads.com
Ticker Symbol: EAD
Profile: EADS is a European-based aviation, aerospace, & defence company that unites four leading companies in these industries: Airbus, Astrium, Cassidian, & Eurocopter.
Pierre Delestrade, President/CEO

EAS Exhibition Services Inc.
827 Primrose Crt., Pickering, ON L1X 2S7
Tel: 905-837-5095; Fax: 905-837-1544
info@easexhibitions.com
www.easexhibitions.com
Profile: The company specializes in exhibit management at international trade shows & conferences, & has long-standing ties with the Aerospace Industries Association of Canada & the Canadian aerospace industry in general.
Derek Staines, President
derek@easexhibitions.com

Les Estampages Stamping Inc. / ISE
20, rte de Windsor, Sherbrooke, QC J1C 0E5
Tél: 819-846-1044; Téléc: 819-846-4268
ventes@ise.qc.ca
www.ise.qc.ca
Profile: The company specializes in the laser cutting, bending, stamping, assembly, welding, zinc plating, & enameling of sheet metal for markets including recreational vehicles, automotive, & aerospace.
Clement Fontaine, Vice-President & General Manager

Esterline CMC Electronics Inc.
Parent: Esterline Corporation
600, boul Dr. Frederik Philips, Montréal, QC H4M 2S9
Tél: 514-748-3113; Téléc: 514-748-3184
www.esterline.com/avionicssystems
Ticker Symbol: ESL / NYSE
Profile: The company designs & manufactures electonics for the military & commercial aviation sectors.
Janka Dvornik, Manager, Communications & PR

Eurocopter Canada Limited / ECL
Parent: Eurocopter
PO Box 250, 1100 Gilmore Rd., Fort Erie, ON L2A 5M9
Tel: 905-871-7772; Fax: 905-871-3320
Toll-Free: 800-267-4999
communications@eurocopter.ca
www.eurocopter.ca
Profile: The company sells aircraft, manufactures composites, & provides engineering solutions, repairs, & overhaul. Canadian customers include the RCMP & the Canadian Coast Guard.
Guy Joannes, President/CEO
guy.joannes@eurocopter.ca
Laura Senecal, Director, Communications & Corporate Affairs
905-994-2980, Fax: 905-871-3320

Explorer Solutions
#205, 1494, rue Montarville, Montréal, QC J3V 3T5
Tél: 450-441-9055; Téléc: 514-375-1388
info@explorersolutions.ca
www.explorersolutions.ca
Profile: The company provides business intelligence, government relations, & senior management coaching to companies in the aerospace industry, as well as economic development agencies & municipalities.
Lionel Léveillé, Senior Partner
lionel.leveille@explorersolutions.ca
Christian Perreault, Senior Partner
christian.perreault@explorersolutions.ca

Field Aviation
Parent: AMAVCO
Hangar 2, 2450 Derry Rd. East, Mississauga, ON L5S 1B2
Tel: 905-676-1540; Fax: 905-676-0977
www.fieldav.com
Profile: Field Aviation provides design, engineering, integration, certification, & aircraft delivery services to clients involved in search & rescue, surveillance, & border protection.
Brian Love, Chief Commercial Officer
busdev@fieldav.com
Chris Cooper-Slipper, Vice-President, Marketing

Fleetway Inc.
Parent: J.D. Irving, Limited
#200, 155 Chain Lake Dr., Halifax, NS B3S 1B3
Tel: 902-494-5700; Fax: 902-494-5792
www.fleetway.ca
Profile: Fleetway provides engineering services to the military & government, shipbuilding, oil & gas, & commercial sectors.
John Keast, Contact
keast.john@fleetway.ca
Peter McMillan, Contact
mcmillan.peter@fleetway.ca

Flexibülb Inc.
PO Box 635, 9000, boul Parent, Trois-Rivières, QC G9A 5J3
Tél: 514-952-5025; Téléc: 819-374-5143
www.flexibulb.com
Profile: The company specializes in designing, developing, manufacturing, & integrating aircraft interior systems, components & ground support equipment for clients in the aerospace, military, & paramilitary sectors.
Pierre P. Tellier, President
819-374-9250, ppt@flexibulb.com
Louis-Martin Tellier, Managing Director

Flightcraft Maintenance Services / FMS
155 West Hangar Rd., Winnipeg, MB R3J 3Z1
Tel: 204-783-2754; Fax: 204-783-2848
info@flightcraftmaintenance.com
www.flightcraftmaintenance.com
Profile: The company provides the following services: repairs & modifications; avionics installations, retrofits & repairs; maintenance & overhauls; & line maintenance services. They also technical & mechanical assistance.

General Dynamics Canada
1941 Robertson Rd., Ottawa, ON K2H 5B7
Tel: 613-596-7657; Fax: 613-596-7775
info@gdcanada.com
www.gdcanada.com
Profile: The company provides information, surveillance, & reconnaissance services for air & sea platforms, & networking & computing solutions for land platforms.
Mike Hornby, Director, Marketing
mike.hornby@gdcanada.com
Deborah Breen, Manager, Integrated Communications & Brand
613-356-4668

General Electric Canada Inc.
Parent: General Electric
#1205, 60 Queen St., Ottawa, ON K1P 5Y7
Tel: 613-235-3421; Fax: 613-235-2481
www.ge.com/ca
Profile: GE-Aviation serves the Canadian military & commercial aviation markets through its two plants in Bromont, QC, & Orillia, ON. GE manufactures, markets, & supports aircraft engines, as well as gas turbines for the Canadian Navy.
Daniel Verreault, Vice-President, Government Relations & Business Development, Canada
daniel.verreault@ge.com

Gladstone Systems Solutions Inc. / GSS
18 Prescott St., St. John's, NL A1C 3V3
Tel: 613-686-5616; Fax: 613-280-1312
www.gladstonesystems.com
Profile: The company develops aerospace systems engineering & training software applications, including systems that aid in the landing of helicopters on offshore drilling platforms.
Keith Gladstone, President/CEO
613-697-6802, Fax: 800-791-2755,
kegladstone@gladstonesystems.com

Green Aviation Research & Development Network / GARDN
PO Box 635, 9000, boul Parent, Trois-Rivières, QC G9A 5J3
Tél: 514-952-5025; Téléc: 819-374-5143
info@gardn.org
www.gardn.org
Profile: GARDN was created in 2009 with the goal of bringing together partners in industry, government, & education to reduce the aerospace industry's environmental footprint.
Claude Lajeunesse, Chair
Sylvain Cofsky, Executive Director
514-983-2061, sylvain.cofsky@gardn.org
Suzanne Frigault, Executive Assistant

Greyhound Canada Transportation Corp.
#700, 1111 International Blvd., Burlington, ON L7L 6W1
Toll-Free: 800-661-8747
canada.info@greyhound.ca
www.greyhound.ca
Profile: Intercity & rural bus transportation; travel agencies; courier services
Dave Leach, Sr. Vice President, Canada

Héroux-Devtek inc
Tour est, #658, 1111, rue St-Charles, Longueuil, QC J4K 5G4
Tel: 450-679-3330;
www.herouxdevtek.com
Ticker Symbol: HRX
Profile: Manufacturers of aircraft parts & auxiliary equipment; Wholesalers of transportation equipment & supplies; Airports, flying fields & airport terminal services
Gilles Labbé, President/CEO
Réal Bélanger, CFO & Exec. Vice-President

Honeywell Canada
Parent: Honeywell International Inc.
3333 Unity Dr., Mississauga, ON L5L 3S6
Tel: 905-608-6000; Fax: 905-608-6057
www.honeywell.com
Ticker Symbol: HON / NYSE
Profile: Honeywell Canada's Aerospace Division deals in the following business lines: electric power; electronic control systems; in-flight communication systems; in-flight data networking solutions; repair & overhaul services; & aftermarket services. The company operates sites in Ontario & Prince Edward Island.
Larry Fitzgerald, Site Leader
Jo-Anne O'Quinn-Kallio, Contact, Communications
905-608-6035

The Ian Martin Group
#202, 3333, boul Côte Vertu, Montréal, QC H4R 2N1
Tél: 514-338-3800; Téléc: 514-338-1492
www.ianmartin.com
Profile: A consulting firm specializing in engineering, telecommunications, & information technology, with past projects involving the development & manufacturing of landing gear, flight controls, & aircraft programs.
Frank Ashworth, Regional Director
ashworth@ianmartin.com
Aditi Tyagi, Account Manager
tyagi@ianmartin.com

IDBLUE
Parent: Cathexis Innovations Inc.
Lower Tower, 100 Signal Hill Rd., St. John's, NL A1A 1B3
Tel: 709-754-7343; Fax: 709-754-7349
Toll-Free: 866-304-7343
info@idblue.com
idblue.com
Profile: The company produces mobile Bluetooth radio frequency identification (RFID) readers (HF & UHF) for smartphones & tablets. These readers are applicable in the aerospace, healthcare, oil & gas, retail, & utilities markets.
Steve Taylor, President
Jeff Brown, Vice-President, Services
Daniel P. Pacheco, Vice-President, Product Development

IMP Group International, INC
2651 Joseph Howe Dr., Halifax, NS B3L 4T1
Tel: 902-453-2400; Toll-Free: 877-244-0878
www.impgroup.com
Profile: IMP Group consists of the following divisions: Aerospace & Defence; Airline; Aviation; Healthcare; Hotels; Information Services; & Properties & Development. Please see the company's website for specific divisional contact information.

Kenneth C. Rowe, Executive Chair
Stephen Plummer, Group President/CEO
David A. Gossen, President, IMP Aerospace & Defence
Kirk A. Rowe, President, Execaire Aviation Group
Stephen K. Rowe, President, CanJet Airlines

Integral Machining Ltd. / IML
#8, 1252 Speers Rd., Oakville, ON L6L 5N9
Tel: 905-847-1565; Fax: 905-847-9518
sales@imach.ca; engineering@imach.ca
www.imach.ca
Profile: IML specializes in micromachining, which is loosely defined as being the machining of any features less than two millimeters in size. The company's main clients are in the aerospace, medical, & photonics industries.
Peter Reypa, President
peter@imach.ca

International Custom Products Inc. / ICP
49 Howden Rd., Toronto, ON M1R 3C7
Tel: 416-285-4311; Fax: 416-285-7329
Toll-Free: 800-268-4482
www.icpinc.com
Profile: The company manufactures parachute components for ordnance delivery & unmanned vehicle systems, as well as meeting unique packaging requirements for defence-related initiatives.
Robert A. Harper, President
bharper@icpinc.com

International Water Guard Industries Inc.
Parent: IWG Technologies, Inc.
#1, 3771 North Fraser Way, Burnaby, BC V5J 5G5
Tel: 604-255-5555; Fax: 604-255-5685
Toll-Free: 800-667-0331
support@water.aero; sales@water.aero
www.water.aero
Ticker Symbol: IWG.V / TSX-V
Profile: IWG provides aircraft water treatment systems & components to corporate, VIP, & military operators.
Bruce Gowan, Chair
Bruce MacCoubrey, Interim President
Gerald Eiers, Vice-President & General Manager
Giles Lapierre, Director, Sales & Marketing

Irving Shipbuilding Inc. / ISI
Parent: J.D. Irving, Limited
3099 Barrington St., Halifax, NS B3K 5M7
Tel: 902-423-9271; Fax: 902-422-5253
marketing@irvingshipbuilding.com
www.irvingshipbuilding.com
Profile: Irving provides services including shipbuilding & repair, drill rig construction & conversion, offshore fabrication, industrial manufacturing, engineering, supply chain management, & technical services.

J.D. Irving, Limited / JDI
PO Box 5777, 300 Union St., Saint John, NB E2L 4M3
Tel: 506-632-7777; Fax: 506-648-2205
info@jdirving.com
www.jdirving.com
Profile: J.D. Irving provides services through the following business units: fForestry & Forest Products; Transportation; Shipbuilding & Industrial Marine; Retail; Industrial Equipment, Construction Services & Building Materials; & Consumer Products. The company was founded in 1882, & now has operations in Eastern Canada & the United States.

Kelowna Flightcraft Ltd. / KF
5655 Airport Way, Kelowna, BC V1V 1S1
Tel: 250-491-5500; Fax: 250-765-1489
mro@flightcraft.ca; media@flightcraft.ca
www.flightcraft.ca
Profile: The company's main operations are conducted in Kelowna, BC, & Hamilton, ON, & include maintenance, flight operations, & military flight training. Kelowna Flightcraft Air Charter Ltd., a subsidiary, is a dedicated carrier for Canada Post, & an air cargo carrier for Purolator Courier.
Barry Lapointe, President
barryl@flightcraft.ca
Mike Udala, Director, Maintenance

KPMG LLP
#200, 160 Elgin St., Ottawa, ON K2P 2P8
Tel: 613-212-3613; Fax: 613-212-2896
www.kpmg.com
Profile: KPMG's Aerospace & Defence (A&D) practice, which is part of the firm's global Diversified Industrials practice, offers Audit, Tax, & Advisory services to clients in the A&D industry. The firm also offers a service called KPMG Enterprise for private A&D companies, which involves growth management, tax planning, & financial business. KPMG A&D operates 150 offices worldwide, with 30 of those in Canada.
Marty Phillips, Global Head, Aerospace & Defence
904-354-5671, diversifiedindustrials@kpmg.com
Grant McDonald, National Leader, Aerospace & Defence
613-747-2458, gmcdonald@kpmg.ca

L-3 Communications
Parent: L-3 Communications Holdings, Inc.
#804, 255 Albert St., Ottawa, ON K1P 6A9
Tel: 613-569-5257; Fax: 613-569-3532
www.l-3com.com
Ticker Symbol: LLL / NYSE
Profile: L-3 Communications is a global company specializing in aerospace & defence. In Canada, L-3 operates the following divisions: L-3 Electronic System Services (L-3 ESS); L-3 MAS; L-3 Targa Systems; & L-3 WESCAM. Through these divisions, the company offers the following services: logistics & support; maintenance of avionics & components; manufacturing advanced systems; aircraft management; solid state memory systems; & surveillance & targeting systems.
Peter Gartenburg, Vice-President, L-3 Canada Operations
peter.gartenburg@l-3com.com
Richard D. Ackerman, Vice-President, Business Development, L-3 ESS
416-249-1231 ext: 5092, richard.ackerman@l-3com.com
Paul Jennison, Vice-President, Business Development, L-3 WESCAM
905-633-4000, sales.wescam@l-3.com
Paul Mercier, Vice-President, Business Development, L-3 MAS
450-476-4719, paul.mercier@l-3com.com
Dave Saunders, General Manager, L-3 Targa Systems
613-727-9876, dave.saunders@l-3com.com

Lear Canada Ltd.
Kitchener, ON
Toll-Free: 800-413-5327
www.lear.com
Profile: Designs, tests & produces automotive interiors
Donald J. Stebbins, President/COO, Americas
David C. Wajsgras, CFO & Sr. Vice-President, Lear Corporation

Linamar Corporation
287 Speedvale Ave. West, Guelph, ON N1H 1C5
Tel: 519-836-7550; Fax: 519-824-8479
investorrelations@linamar.com
www.linamar.com
Ticker Symbol: LNR
Profile: Manufacturers of motor vehicle parts & accessories, fabricated plate work, carburetors, pistons, piston rings, valves, farm machinery equipment, aircraft parts & auxiliary equipment, pumps & pumping equipment; Wholesalers of farm & garden machinery & equipment
Linda Hasenfratz, President/CEO
Csaba Havasi, Group President, Europe
Peggy Mulligan, CFO/ Exec. Vice-President & Treasurer
Mark Stoddart, Chief Technology Development Officer & Vice-President, Marketing

Lockheed Martin Canada Inc.
Parent: Lockheed Martin Corporation
3001 Solandt Rd., Kanata, ON K2K 2M8
Tel: 613-599-3280; Fax: 613-599-3282
lmcanada.busdev@lmco.com
www.lockheedmartin.ca
Ticker Symbol: LMT / NYSE
Profile: Lockheed Martin Canada supplies electronic defence & surveillance systems for naval, airborne, land, & civil operations.
Don McClure, Vice-President, Business Development & Government Relations
don.mcclure@lmco.com

Lynch Dynamics Inc.
1799 Argentia Rd., Mississauga, ON L5N 3A2
Tel: 905-363-2400; Fax: 905-363-1191
Toll-Free: 888-626-4365
sales@lynchdynamics.ca
www.lynchdynamics.ca
Profile: The company designs & manufactures hydraulic motion control systems for the aerospace, military, & medical sectors.
Brian Wilson, Manager, Sales

MacDonald, Dettwiler & Associates Ltd. / MDA
13800 Commerce Pkwy., Richmond, BC V6V 2J3
Tel: 604-278-3411; Fax: 604-231-2773
info@mdacorporation.com
www.mdacorporation.com
Ticker Symbol: MDA.TO / TSX
Profile: MDA, a Canadian company, supports commercial, civil, & military clients in the global surveillance, intelligence, communication, & advanced technology marketplaces. It builds & operates unmanned aerial vehicles & provides clients with aircraft, sensors, training, maintenance, in-service support, system certification, data handling, & exploitation systems.

MacKenzie Atlantic Tool & Die Machining
PO Box 121, #3, 6 Rowling Dr., Musquodoboit Harbour, NS B0J 2L0
Tel: 902-889-3047; Fax: 902-889-3673
info@mackenzieatlantic.com
www.mackenzieatlantic.com
Profile: MacKenzie Atlantic is a full-service tool-making & machining company serving the aerospace, marine, military, & oil & gas sectors.
Matthew MacKenzie, Owner
902-880-2240

Magellan Aerospace Corporation
3160 Derry Rd. East, Mississauga, ON L4T 1A9
Tel: 905-677-1889; Fax: 905-677-5658
info@magellan.aero
www.magellanaerospace.com
Ticker Symbol: MAL
Profile: Manufacturers of aircraft parts & auxiliary equipment, aircraft engines & engine parts
Richard A. Neill, President/CEO
John B. Dekker, Secretary/Vice-President, Finance
Donald C. Lowe, Chair, Risk Management & Environmental Committee

Magna International Inc.
337 Magna Dr., Aurora, ON L4G 7K1
Tel: 905-726-2462;
www.magna.com
Ticker Symbol: MG
Profile: Manufacturers of motor vehicle parts & accessories, automotive stampings, various fabricated metal products, motor vehicles & passenger car bodies, vehicular lighting equipment, various fabricated textile products, public building & related furniture; Wholesalers of motor vehicle supplies & new parts; Racing, including track operation; Various amusement & recreation services
Siegfried Wolf, Co-CEO
Vincent J. Galifi, CFO & Exec. Vice-President, Finance

Marand Engineering Ltd.
105 Watts Ave., Charlottetown, PE C1E 2B7
Tel: 902-368-8954; Fax: 902-368-7041
www.marandeng.com
Profile: The company manufactures precision sheet metal, machined components, assemblies, & automated test equipment & control systems for the light rail & aerospace & defence markets.
Andrew Hall, P.Eng.President
andrew.hall@marandeng.com

MarineNav Ltd.
Panmure Island Wharf, 1466 Panmure Island, Montague, PE C0A 1R0
Tel: 902-838-7011;
info@marinenav.ca; sales@marinenav.ca
www.marinenav.ca
Profile: MarineNav designs & manufactures offshore navigation, multimedia, & vessel monitoring systems.
Kevin Merson, Founder

Marinvent Corporation
#23, 50, ch de la Rabastalière est, Saint-Bruno, QC J3V 2A5
Tél: 450-441-6464; Téléc: 450-441-2411
info@marinvent.com
www.marinvent.com
Profile: Marinvent specializes in aerospace research & development. The company was founded in 1983, & now has operations in Canada, the US, & Russia. It is also a founding partner in Canada's Flight Test Centre of Excellence (FTCE).
John Maris, President
514-895-7075
Phil Cole, Vice-President, Business Development
613-363-5107

Marport Deep Sea Technologies Inc.
50 Harbour Dr., St. John's, NL A1C 6J4
Tel: 709-757-5757; Fax: 709-757-5858
sales@marport.com
www.marport.com
Profile: The company develops & markets Software Defined Sonar technology products for use in the underwater defence, commercial fisheries, offshore energy, & ocean science markets.

Bruce MacRae, Chair
Cyril McKelvie, President/CEO
Oskar Axelsson, Executive Vice-President, Sales

Marsh Metrology
Parent: Marsh Group
#2, 1016C Sutton Dr., Burlington, ON L7L 6B8
Tel: 905-332-1172; Fax: 905-332-1668
Toll-Free: 800-449-2719
ron.bake@marshmetrology.com
www.marshmetrology.com
Profile: The company provides accredited calibration services, including repair & re-manufacture of printed circuit boards, & distribution for test & measurement equipment.
Ron Bake, General Manager
ron.bake@marshmetrology.com

MDS Coating Technologies Corporation / MCT
PO Box 312, 60 Aerospace Blvd., Slemon Park, PE C0B 2A0
Tel: 902-888-3900; Fax: 902-888-3901
pr@mdscoating.com
www.mdscoating.com
Profile: MDS is a developer & manufacturer of coatings for gas turbine engines used in the commercial & aerospace & defence industries, with offices in PEI, Québec, & Washington, DC.
Phil Rodger, President/CEO
phil.rodger@mdscoating.com

Meggitt Training Systems Canada Inc. / MTSC
Parent: Meggitt PLC
#3, 1735 Brier Park Rd. NW, Medicine Hat, AB T1C 1V5
Tel: 403-528-8782; Fax: 403-529-2629
mtscanada@meggitt.com
www.meggittcanada.com
Profile: MTSC offers weapon simulation training packages & programs to military, law enforcement, & security personnel. The company operates two Canadian facilities: the Targets & Unmanned Vehicle Group in Medicine Hat, AB, & the Weapons Training Simulation Group in Montréal, QC.
Spencer Fraser, President & General Manager
spencer.fraser@meggitt.com

Meloche Group Inc.
491, boul des Érables, Salaberry-de-Valleyfield, QC J6T 6G3
Tél: 450-371-4646; Téléc: 450-371-4957
Ligne sans frais: 800-567-4265
mail@melocheinc.com
www.melocheinc.com
Profile: Meloche Group provides engineering, technical support, prototyping, precision machining, painting, & surface treatment services to the aerospace, defence, telecommunications, & medical industries.
Marc Bigras, Vice-President & COO
mbigras@melocheinc.com
Jacques Labrie, Director, Sales & Reproduction

Metal Action Machining Ltd.
Parent: Analytic Systems Ware 1993 Ltd.
#206, 12448 - 82nd Ave., Surrey, BC V3W 3E9
Tel: 604-543-7378; Fax: 604-592-7372
www.metalaction.ca
Profile: The company specializes in precision machining of aluminum alloys, alloy steels, titanium, & stainless steel. Other operations include punching, press break forming, anodizing, painting, plating, engraving, & screen printing, using both in-house & outside services. The company also specializes in aerospace tooling. They mainly serve the aerospace, military, marine, cleantech, & commercial markets.
Ken McArdle, Manager, Sales
604-209-1257, kenm@analyticsystems.com

MicroPilot
PO Box 720, 72067 Rd. 8E, Sturgeon Rd., Stony Mountain, MB R0C 3A0
Tel: 204-344-5558; Fax: 204-344-5706
info@micropilot.com
www.micropilot.com
Profile: The company manufactures small autopilot systems for unmanned aerial vehicles & micro aerial vehicles.
Howard Loewen, President

MilAero Electronics Atlantic Inc.
1 Research Dr., Dartmouth, NS B2Y 4M9
Tel: 902-469-6232; Fax: 902-466-6889
info@mil-aero.com
www.mil-aero.com
Profile: MilAero specializes in cables, wire harnesses, & electro-mechanical enclosures for the defence, aerospace, & industrial sectors.

National Research Council of Canada / NRC
Bldg. M-3, Montréal Rd., Ottawa, ON K1A 0R6
Tel: 613-990-0765; Fax: 613-952-7214
www.nrcaerospace.gc.ca
Profile: NRC Aerospace is Canada's national aerospace laboratory, which conducts research & technology development on aerospace topics such as safety, weight, cost, & the environment.
Jerzy Komorowski, General Manager
Jeff Mackwood, Manager, Marketing
jeff.mackwood@nrc.ca

NAV Canada
PO Box 3411 D, 77, rue Metcalfe, Ottawa, ON K1P 5L6
Tél: 613-563-5588; Téléc: 613-563-3426
Ligne sans frais: 800-876-4693
service@navcanada.ca
www.navcanada.ca
Profile: Provides, maintains & enhances an air navigation service
John W. Crichton, President/CEO
R.A. (Sandy) Morrison, Chair
William G. Fenton, Treasurer/CFO & Vice-President, Finance
John Morris, Director, Communications
Sidney Koslow, Vice-President/Chief Technology Officer

Neptec Design Group Ltd.
#202, 302 Legget Dr., Kanata, ON K2K 1Y5
Tel: 613-599-7602; Fax: 613-599-7604
www.melocheinc.com
Profile: The company manufactures & operates spaceflight sensors, payloads, instruments, & equipment. It has been a NASA contractor since 1995, & has supported over 40 Shuttle missions. It operates facilities in Canada & the US, in Ottawa, ON, & Huston, TX.
Ian Christie, CEO
ichristie@neptec.com

Newmercial Technologies International / NTI
680, rue Sherbrooke ouest, 7e étage, Montréal, QC H3A 2M7
Tél: 514-398-3747; Téléc: 514-398-8454
www.melocheinc.com
Profile: The company specializes in engineering research & development related to in-flight icing certifications for aircraft.
Wagdi Habashi, President
wagdi.habashi@newmerical.com

NeXsys Group Inc.
200 Chisholm Dr., Milton, ON L8T 5E7
Tel: 905-593-1504; Fax: 905-593-1503
www.melocheinc.com
Profile: NeXsys helps companies increase productivity & profit through direct consulting & a software suite comprised of NeXflow, NeXwave, & NeXview. The company's clients are in the aerospace, automotive, pharmaceutical, logistics, & manufacturing industries.
Douglas R. Sutherland, President/CEO
drsutherland@nexsysgroup.ca

NGRAIN (Canada) Corporation
#250, 1818 Cornwall Ave., Vancouver, BC V6J 1C7
Tel: 604-669-9973; Fax: 604-669-9972
Toll-Free: 866-420-1781
sales@ngrain.com; support@ngrain.com
www.melocheinc.com
Profile: NGRAIN serves the defence, civil aviation, nuclear, oil & gas, & medical industries with interactive 3D simulation software for maintenance training & support.
Gabe Batstone, CEO
Sarah Grant, Manager, Public Relations
438-257-1290, sgrant@ngrain.com

Noranco Inc.
710 Rowntree Dairy Rd., Woodbridge, ON L4L 5T7
Tel: 905-264-2050; Fax: 905-264-6921
www.noranco.com
Profile: The company manufactures landing gear, & aircraft structure & engine components & assemblies for the commercial, business, & military aerospace sectors.
David Camilleri, President/CEO
John Nicholson, Director, Business Development
john.nicholson@noranco.com

Northern Centre for Advanced Technology Inc. / NORCAT
1545 Maley Dr., Sudbury, ON P3A 4R7
Tel: 705-521-8324; Fax: 705-521-7359
www.norcat.org
Profile: NORCAT is a non-profit corporation, & its Innovation & Development department specializes in research pertaining to space drilling.
Dale Boucher, Director, Innovation & Development
dboucher@norcat.org

Northstar Aerospace
Formerly: Derlan Industries Ltd.
Milton Plant, 180 Market Dr., Milton, ON L9T 3H5
Tel: 416-364-5852; Fax: 416-362-5334
infomilton@nsaero.com
www.nsaero.com
Ticker Symbol: NAS
Profile: Manufacturers of motor vehicle parts & accessories, aircraft parts & auxiliary equipment, speed changers, industrial high-speed drives, gears, aircraft engines & engine parts; Airports, flying fields & airport terminal services
Mark Emery, President/CEO
Thomas E. Connerty, CFO

Northstar Network Ltd.
Parent: Northstar Electronics Inc.
#9, 1 Duffy Pl., St. John's, NL A1B 4M6
Tel: 709-738-6452; Fax: 709-738-6613
northstar@nnl.ca
www.northstarnetwork.ca
Profile: This network of defence, aerospace, marine, & homeland security partners provides research & development, engineering, training, & manufacturing services, as well as operational support, maintenance, & repair, to those respective sectors. Northstar has around 2,000 personnel at its disposal from across Canada.
Wilson E. Russell, Ph.D.Chair
Howard Nash, President
Terry McLeod, B.Sc.CEO

Paradigm Shift Technologies Inc.
60 Signet Dr., Toronto, ON M9L 2Y4
Tel: 416-748-1779; Fax: 416-748-5889
info@paradigmshift.com
www.paradigmshift.com
Profile: The company seeks to improve the reliability of weapon systems & other platforms (commercial & military) through their coating & engineering services.
Gennady Yumshtyk, CEO

Pathix ASP
Parent: Vector Aerospace Corporation
PO Box 13306 A, 21 Hallett Cres., St. John's, NL A1B 4B7
Fax: 709-724-8545
Toll-Free: 866-724-8500
inquiries@pathix.com
www.pathix.com
Profile: Pathix is an information technology company specializing in networking & platform implementation, as well as being the producer of the Navixa aviation software, meant to aid operating & repair & overhaul companies.
Trevor Lewis, President

Patlon Aircraft & Industries Limited
8130 Fifth Line, Halton Hills, ON L7G 0B8
Tel: 905-864-8706; Fax: 905-864-8728
patlon@patlon.com
www.patlon.com
Profile: Patlon provides its clients in the aerospace, military, transportation, & electronics industries with application development & selling. Its products include aircraft interiors, cables, electrical systems, environmental systems, fuel systems, ground power units, hydraulic systems, painting, sensors, & valves, among other things. It also provides services such as repair, calibration, assembly, & training.
Patrick Mann, President

Policy Insights Inc.
#402, 222 Queen St., Ottawa, ON K1P 5V9
Tel: 613-563-8078; Fax: 613-563-4284
info@policyinsights.com
www.policyinsights.com
Profile: Policy Insights is a government relations firm specializing in the fields of high technology, aerospace, defence, & communications.
Ken Mackay, President

Pratt & Whitney Canada Corp.
1000, boul Marie-Victorin, Longueuil, QC J4G 1A1
Tel: 450-677-9411;
www.pwc.ca
Profile: Manufacturers of aircraft engines & engine parts; Wholesalers of transportation equipment & supplies
Alain M. Bellemare, President
Miguel C. Doyon, Vice-President, Finance
Amal M. Girgis, Chief Information Officer
John Saabas, Exec. Vice-President
Nancy German, Vice-President, Communications
nancy.german@pwc.ca

Prevost Car Inc.
35, boul Gagnon, Sainte-Claire, QC G0R 2V0
Tel: 418-883-3391; Fax: 418-883-4157
prevostcar@volvo.com
www.prevostcar.com
Profile: Manufacturers of intercity coaches & coach shells for motorhomes & specialty conversion
Gaetan Bolduc, President/CEO

Provincial Aerospace Ltd.
St. John's International Airport, PO Box 29030, St. John's, NL A1A 5B5
Tel: 709-576-1800; Fax: 709-576-1709
inquiries@provair.com
www.provincialaerospace.com
Profile: Provincial Aerospace specializes in maritime surveillance, systems integration, aircraft modification, training, integrated logistics support, & mission operations.
Keith Stoodley, Senior Vice-President
Derek Scott, Vice-President

Public Storage Canadian Properties
First Canadian Place, #6600, 100 King St. West, Toronto, ON M5X 1B8
Toll-Free: 800-772-2623
www.publicstoragecanada.com
Ticker Symbol: PUB
Profile: General warehousing & storage
David P. Singelyn, President
Vincent R. Chan, Vice-President/Controller

Rolls-Royce Canada ltée
9500, ch de la Côte-de-Liesse, Montréal, QC H8T 1A2
Tel: 514-636-0964; Fax: 514-636-9969
www.rolls-royce.com
Profile: Airports, flying fields & airport terminal services; Manufacturers of steam, gas, hydraulic turbines & turbine generator units
Pierre Racine, President/CEO
Stephane Guerin, CFO

Samuel, Son & Co., Limited
2360 Dixie Rd., Mississauga, ON L4Y 1Z7
Tel: 613-563-8078; Fax: 613-563-4284
aerospacemetals@samuel.com
www.samuel.com
Profile: The Samuel Aerospace Metals division was formed in 2010, & provides materials including surface machining & plastic coating, & services such as plate sawing, water jet profiling, tube & extrusion cutting, shearing, & kitting.
Paul Sutcliffe, Managing Director

Sanmina-SCI Corporation
500 Palladium Dr., Ottawa, ON K2V 1C2
Tel: 613-886-6102; Fax: 613-886-6001
info@sanmina-sci.com
www.sanmina-sci.com
Profile: The company manufactures micro-electronics, radar sub-systems, microwave radios, & optical communication systems for the aerospace, defence, industrial, medical, & renewable energy markets.
Nat Mani, Senior Vice-President, Optical & Micro-electronics Sales & Marketing
408-223-5960
John Pokinko, Vice-President, Design Engineering
john.pokinko@sanmina-sci.com

Sermatech Power Solutions LP
Parent: Praxair Surface Technologies
10300, av Ryan, Montréal, QC H9P 2T7
Tél: 514-631-2240; Téléc: 514-636-6196
www.praxairsurfacetechnologies.com
Profile: Sermatech provides coating services to the Canadian aerospace industry.
Luis Godin, Plant Manager
luis_godin@praxair.com

Solace Power Inc.
Bruneau Centre, MUN, #3003, St. John's, NL A1C 5S7
Tel: 709-765-3353; Fax: 709-864-2539
www.solace.ca
Profile: The company specializes in wireless power technology applicable to the aerospace & defence, consumer electronics, & firefighting electronics markets.
Kris McNeil, Contact

Sonaca Montréal
Parent: Sonaca Group
13075, rue Brault, Mirabel, QC J7J 1P3
Tél: 450-420-7670; Téléc: 450-434-5658
www.sonacamontreal.com
Profile: The company specializes in manufacturing large aluminum structures for the aerospace industry, particularly wing & empennage structures.
Philippe Hoste, CEO
philippe.hoste@sonacamontreal.com
Paul Stafiej, Director, Programs & Business Development
450-420-7680

Sonovision Canada Inc.
Parent: Sonovision Group Inc.
#400, 85 Albert St., Ottawa, ON K1P 6A4
Tel: 514-344-5008; Fax: 514-344-5004
info@sonovisiongroup.com
www.appendix.ca; www.sonovisiongroup.com
Profile: Sonovision Canada manages, authors, & translates technical publications for aerospace & defence manufacturers with an in-house team of writers, editors, illustrators, compositors, translators, & quality assurance staff.
Rick Temelini, President
613-234-4849
Christian Desjardins, Director, Sales & Marketing
514-944-8787

Southwest United Canada
Parent: Southwest United Industries, Inc.
#9, 8201 Keele St., Concord, ON L4K 1Z4
Tel: 905-738-9225; Fax: 905-738-5970
www.swunitedcanada.com
Profile: The company specializes in metal finishing, & provides services such as stress relief, non-destructive testing, shot peening, anodizing, passivation, plating, HVOF thermal spraying, precision grinding, super finishing, & painting. They are accredited to work on aerospace projects, & have two Canadian facilities located in Brampton & Concord, ON.
Steve Little, Vice-President
slittle@swunitedcanada.com

StandardAero
Parent: Dubai Aerospace Enterprise
#1300, 340 Albert St., Ottawa, ON K1R 7Y6
Tel: 613-699-1369; Fax: 613-566-7003
www.standardaero.com
Profile: The company specializes in aircraft engine maintenance, repair, & overhaul, as well as other "nose-to-tail" services including airframe, interior refurbishing, & painting. Their Canadian operations are located in Montréal, Toronto, Winnipeg, Calgary, & Vancouver.
Jim Miller, Vice-President, Global Business Development
Jason Di Tommaso, Director, Canadian Business Development
613-793-5406, jason.ditommaso@standardaero.com

TDM Technical Services
3924 Chesswood Dr., Toronto, ON M3J 2W6
Tel: 416-777-0007; Fax: 416-777-1117
www.tdm.ca
Profile: TDM's Aerospace Division provides stress analysis, structural design, certification, & systems engineering services to clients in the aerospace industry.
Iain Dainter, Managing Director
iain@tdm.ca

Testori Americas Corp. Canada
Parent: Testori Group
45 Cannon Dr., Summerside, PE C0B 2A0
Tel: 902-888-3200; Fax: 902-436-4456
sales@testoriamericas.com
www.testoriamericas.com
Profile: Testori specializes in the engineering & production of interiors for railcars, ships, & aircraft.
Peter George, CEO

Thales Canada Inc.
2800, av Marie-Curie, Montréal, QC H4S 2C2
Tél: 514-832-0900;
inquiries@ca.thalesgroup.com
www.thalesgroup.com/canada
Profile: Thales Canada provides technology & equipment for the defence & security, aerospace, & transportation markets. The company has offices in Québec, Ontario, & British Columbia.
Conrad Bellehumeur, Vice-President, External Relations
613-723-7000, Fax: 613-723-5600,
conrad.bellehumeur@ca.thalesgroup.com
Cristina Trif, Administrative Assistant, Marketing

ThyssenKrupp Budd Canada Inc.
Formerly: Budd Canada Inc
PO Box 1204, 1011 Homer Watson, Kitchener, ON N2G 4G8
Fax: 519-895-0099
Ticker Symbol: BUD
Profile: Manufacturers of motor vehicle parts & accessories; Wholesalers of motor vehicle supplies & new parts
Micheal Balavich, President
David A. Robinson, CFO & Controller

The Toronto Transit Commission / TTC
1900 Yonge St., Toronto, ON M4S 1Z2
Tel: 416-393-4000;
www.ttc.ca
Profile: Operates & maintains urban transit system: buses, subways, streetcars & trolleys
R. Ducharme, CEO
Mike Roche, CFO
John Cannon, Chief Information Officer

Tronos
PO Box 7, Slemon Park, PE C0B 2A0
Tel: 902-436-5318; Fax: 902-436-5319
www.tronosjet.com

Profile: Tronos is an aviation services provider specializing in aircraft leasing, maintenance, & asset management. The company also has operations in the UK serving Europe, the Middle East, Asia, & Africa.

TrueNorth Avionics, Inc.
1682 Woodward Dr., Ottawa, ON K2C 3R8
Tel: 613-224-3301; Fax: 613-224-0954
Toll-Free: 877-610-0110
info@truenorthavionics.com
www.truenorthavionics.com
Profile: The company provides satellite communication technology to allow executives to communicate via Wi-Fi, voice, fax, e-mail, & mobile divices while on board private business aircraft.
Mark van Berkel, President/CEO
Andrew Nasmith, Director, Strategic Business Solutions
613-795-7469, andrew.nasmith@truenorthavionics.com

Tube-Fab Ltd.
105 Industrial Cres., Summerside, PE C1N 5P8
Tel: 902-436-3229; Fax: 902-436-3219
www.tube-fab.com
Profile: Together with its sister company TFL Technologies Inc., Tube-Fab manufactures & assembles precision tubular & machined components, & complete assemblies for fluid delivery & structural assemblies. They serve clients in the aerospace, defence, marine, medical, drug & food processing, robotics, energy, & oil & gas industries.
John Dalziel, President/COO
902-436-3219
Wesley Eric Foley, Senior Executive Vice-President
416-569-8621, efoley@tube-fab.com
Gary Edwards, Vice-President, Quality & Engineering
gedwards@tube-fab.com

Uniglobe Travel International L.P.
#900, 1199 West Pender St., Vancouver, BC V6E 2R1
info@uniglobetravel.com
www.uniglobetravel.com
Profile: Travel franchise specializing in corporate travel services for small to medium accounts as well as individual travelers.
U. Gary Charlwood, Chair/CEO
Tracy Bartram, CFO & Exec. Vice-President

UTC Aerospace Systems
Formerly: Hamilton Sundstrand; Goodrich Corporation
Parent: United Technologies Corporation
1400 South Service Rd. West, Oakville, ON L6L 5Y7
Tel: 905-827-7777; Fax: 905-825-1583
www.goodrich.com
Profile: UTC Aerospace Systems was created in 2012 by merging Hamilton Sundstrand & Goodrich. UTC Aerospace Systems is comprised of two main divisions: Aircraft Systems; & Power, Controls, & Sensing Systems. Within these are the following subdivisions: Actuation Systems; Aerostructures; Air Management Systems; Electric Systems; Engine Components; Engine & Control Systems; Fire Protection Systems; Interiors; ISR Systems; Landing Gear; Propeller Systems; Sensors & Integrated Systems; Space Systems; & Wheels & Brakes.
Alain Bellemare, President/CEO
Mike Dumais, President, Power, Controls, & Sensing Systems
Curtis Reusser, President, Aircraft Systems

VAC Developments Limited
2270 Bristol Circle, Oakville, ON L6H 5S3
Tel: 905-855-6855; Fax: 905-855-6856
www.vacdev.com
Profile: VAC provides the aerospace industry with precision machining, sheet metal, & welding services.
Bill Hristovski, President
Elaine Hristovski, Contact
elaineh@vacdev.com

Vector Aerospace Corporation
#2100, 2 Bloor St. West, Toronto, ON M4W 3E2
Tel: 416-925-1143; Fax: 416-925-7214
www.vectoraerospace.ca
Ticker Symbol: RNO
Profile: Manufacturers of aircraft parts & auxiliary equipment; Electrical & electronic repair shops; Various repair shops & related services
Donald Jackson, President/CEO
Randal L. Levine, Sr. Vice-President/CFO & Corporate Secretary

Versacold Income Fund
Formerly: Versacold Corporation
2115 Commissioner St., Vancouver, BC V5L 1A6
Tel: 604-255-4656; Toll-Free: 800-563-2653
info@versacold.com
www.versacold.com
Ticker Symbol: ICE
Profile: Refrigerated logistics services: storage & transportation
H. Brent Sugden, Chair/President & CEO
Joel M. Smith, CFO & Exec. Vice-President

Versatile Spray Painting Ltd. / VSP
102 Healey Rd., Bolton, ON L7E 5A9
Tel: 905-857-4915; Fax: 905-857-4924
Toll-Free: 877-857-4915
www.versatilespray.com
Profile: VSP specializes in industrial finishing for military, aerospace, medical sectors, as well as for business machines, & electronic packaging.
Dave Gogo, Manager, Operations & Production
davegogo@versatilespray.com
Chris Heslin, Manager, Customer Relations & Purchasing
chrisheslin@versatilespray.com
Ivan Sandrovcan, Manager, Screening & Graphics
screening@versatilespray.com

VIH Aerospace
Parent: VIH Aviation Group
1962 Canso Rd., North Saanich, BC V8L 5V5
Fax: 250-655-6861
Toll-Free: 866-844-4354
vih@vih.com
www.vih.com/Services/vihaerospace.html
Profile: VIH Aerospace offers helicopter maintenance products & services to the aerospace industry, including maintenance of communication & navigation equipment.

Viking Air Ltd.
1959 de Havilland Way, Sidney, BC V8L 5V5
Tel: 250-656-7227; Fax: 250-656-0673
Toll-Free: 800-663-8444
info@vikingair.com
www.vikingair.com
Profile: Viking manufactures seven aircraft types, & provides support services including spares sales, customer service, technical support, engineering, maintenance, repair, overhaul, & conversions.
David Curtis, President/CEO
Robert Mauracher, Vice-President, Business Development

Virtual Marine Technology / VMT
20 Hallett Cres., St. John's, NL A1B 3N4
Tel: 709-738-6306; Fax: 709-738-5996
inquire@vmtechnology.ca
www.vmtechnology.ca
Profile: The company produces simulators for survival craft, fast response craft, & high-speed electronic navigation training.
Anthony Patterson, President/CEO
Randy Billard, Executive Vice-President/CTO
Tyler Brand, Director, Training Services

Wescast Industries Inc.
150 Savannah Oaks Dr., Brantford, ON N3T 5V7
Tel: 519-750-0000; Fax: 519-720-1629
investor.relations@wescast.com
www.wescast.com
Ticker Symbol: WCS
Profile: Manufacturers of motor vehicle parts & accessories; Wholesalers of motor vehicle supplies & new parts
Edward G. Frackwiak, Chair/CEO
Dave Dean, Vice-President, Finance

Wiebel Aerospace (1995) Inc.
Parent: Testori Group
PO Box 70, 175 Greenwood Dr., Summerside, PE C1N 5X6
Tel: 902-888-2568; Fax: 902-888-2008
customerservice@wiebel.ca
www.wiebel.ca
Profile: Wiebel manufactures custom precision machined parts & speciality components & assemblies.
Peter George, CEO

World Point Terminals Inc.
#2500, 1 Place Ville Marie, Montreal, QC H3B 1R1
Tel: 514-847-4519;
www.wpo.ca
Ticker Symbol: WPO
Profile: Various transportation services; Special warehousing & storage; Manufacturers of petroleum refining
Bruce N. Calvin, President
Steven G. Twele, CFO

Xiphos Systems Corporation
#500, 3981, boul St-Laurent, Montréal, QC H2W 1Y5
Tél: 514-847-9474;
info@xiphos.com
www.xiphos.com
Profile: Xiphos provides customers in the aerospace industry with processors integrated into avionics packages, mainly for the space & unmanned aerial vehicles markets. Customers include the Canadian Space Agency & the United States Air Force.
Stephane Germain, Vice-President

YYJ FBO Services
Parent: VIH Aviation Group
Victoria International Airport, #101, 1962 Canso Rd., North Saanich, BC V8L 5V5
Tel: 250-655-8833; Fax: 250-655-5020
csr@yyjfbo.com
www.yyjfbo.com
Profile: The company is a fixed-base operator (FBO) located at Victoria International Airport, & offering fueling services, passenger, executive & pilot lounges, car & hotel reservations, catering services, flight planning room, & other amenities.
Jen Norie, General Manager
jnorie@vih.com
Martin Childs, Manager, Operations
mchilds@yyjfbo.com

Government Agency Guide

AIRPORTS & AVIATION
See Also: Transportation
Canadian Air Transport Security Authority, 99 Bank St., 13th Fl., Ottawa, ON K1P 6B9
Fax: 613-991-6726, 888-294-2202
Institute for Aerospace Research, 1200 Montreal Rd., Ottawa, K1A 0R6 ON
613-991-5738, Fax: 613-952-7214
Transport Canada, Place de Ville, 330 Sparks St., Tower C, Ottawa, K1A 0N5 ON
613-990-2309, Fax: 613-954-4731, minTC@tc.gc.ca
Transportation Appeal Tribunal of Canada, 333 Laurier Ave. West, 12th Fl., Ottawa, ON K1A 0N5
613-990-6906, Fax: 613-990-9153, info@tatc.gc.ca

Newfoundland & Labrador
Department of Transportation & Works, Confederation Bldg., West Block, 6th Fl., PO Box 8700, St. John's, A1B 4J6 NL
709-729-3679, Fax: 709-729-4285, twminister@gov.nl.ca

Northwest Territories
Airports, YK Centre, 4922 - 28th St., 4th fl., PO Box 1320, Yellowknife, X1A 2L9 NT
867-873-7725, Fax: 867-873-0297
Department of Transportation, Lahm Ridge Bldg., 4501 50 Ave., PO Box 1320, Yellowknife, X1A 2L9 NT
867-920-3460, Fax: 867-873-0363

Nunavut
Department of Community & Government Services, J.G. Brown Bldg., PO Box 1000 700,Iqaluit, X0A 0H0 NU
867-975-5400, Fax: 867-975-5305

Ontario
Ministry of Transportation, Ferguson Block, 77 Wellesley St. West, 3rd Fl., Toronto, M7A 1Z8 ON
416-235-4686, Fax: 416-327-9185, 800-268-4686

Saskatchewan
Saskatchewan Highways & Infrastructure, 1855 Victoria Ave., Regina, S4P 3T2 SK
306-787-4800,

Yukon Territory
Yukon Highways & Public Works, PO Box 2703, Whitehorse, Y1A 2C6 YT
867-393-7193, Fax: 867-393-6218, 800-661-0408, hpw-info@gov.yk.ca

RAIL TRANSPORTATION
See Also: Transportation
Transportation Safety Board of Canada, 200 Promenade du Portage, 4th Fl., Ottawa, K1A 1K8 ON
819-994-3741, Fax: 819-997-2239, 800-387-3557
Via Rail Canada Inc., #500, 3, Place Ville-Marie, Montréal, H3B 2C9 QC
514-871-6000, Fax: 514-871-6768

Manitoba
Manitoba Infrastructure & Transportation, Legislative Building, #203, 450 Broadway Ave., Winnipeg, R3C 0V8 MB
204-945-3723, Fax: 204-945-7610

New Brunswick
Department of Transportation, Kings Pl., 440 KingSt., PO Box 6000, Fredericton, E3B 5H8 NB
506-453-3939, Fax: 506-453-2900, Transportation.Web@gnb.ca

Newfoundland & Labrador
Department of Transportation & Works, Confederation Bldg., West Block, 6th Fl., PO Box 8700, St. John's, A1B 4J6 NL
709-729-3679, Fax: 709-729-4285, twminister@gov.nl.ca

Nova Scotia
Department of Transportation & Infrastructure Renewal, Johnston Bldg., 1672 Granville St., 2nd Fl., PO Box 186, Halifax, B3J 2N2 NS
902-424-2297, Fax: 902-424-0171, 888-432-3233, tpwpaff@gov.ns.ca

Ontario
GO Transit, #600, 20 Bay St., Toronto, ON M5J 2W3
416-869-3600, Fax: 416-869-1755, 888-438-6646

Quebec
Société du port ferroviaire Baie-Comeau-Hauterive, 18, rte Maritime, Baie-Comeau, QC G4Z 2L6
418-296-6785, Fax: 418-296-2377, soport@globetrotter.qc.ca
Ministère des Transports, 700, boul René-Lévesque est, 27e étage, Québec, G1R 5H1 QC
Fax: 514-643-1269, 888-355-0511, communications@mtq.gouv.qc.ca

Saskatchewan
Saskatchewan Highways & Infrastructure, 1855 Victoria Ave., Regina, S4P 3T2 SK
306-787-4800

TRANSPORTATION

Atlantic Pilotage Authority Canada, #910, 2000 Barrington St., Halifax, B3J 3K1 NS
902-426-2550, Fax: 902-426-4004
Canadian Air Transport Security Authority, 99 Bank St., 13th Fl., Ottawa, ON K1P 6B9
Fax: 613-991-6726, 888-294-2202
Canadian Coast Guard, Centennial Towers, #6S018, 200 Kent St., Ottawa, K1A 0E6 ON
613-998-1573, Fax: 613-990-2780
Canadian Transportation Agency, Les Terrasses de la Chaudière, 15, rue Eddy, Gatineau, K1A 0N9 QC
819-997-0344, Fax: 819-997-6727, 888-222-2592, info@otc-cta.gc.ca
Centre for Surface Transportation Technology, 2320 Lester Rd., Ottawa, K1V 1S2 ON
613-998-9639, Fax: 613-957-0831, inquiries.cstt@nrc-cnrc.gc.ca
Federal Bridge Corporation Limited, #1210, 55 Metcalfe St., Ottawa, ON K1P 6L5
613-993-6880, Fax: 613-993-6945, info@federalbridge.ca
Great Lakes Pilotage Authority, 202 Pitt St., 2nd fl., PO Box 95, Cornwall, K6H 5R9 ON
613-933-2991, Fax: 613-932-3793, administration@glpa-apgl.com
Institute for Aerospace Research, 1200 Montreal Rd., Ottawa, K1A 0R6 ON
613-991-5738, Fax: 613-952-7214
Laurentian Pilotage Authority Canada, #1501, 555, boul René-Lévesque ouest, Montréal, H2Z 1B1 QC
514-283-6320, Fax: 514-496-2409, administration@apl.gc.ca
Marine Atlantic Inc., Baine Johnston Centre, #802, 10 Fort William Place, St. John's, A1C 1K4 NL
709-772-8957, Fax: 709-772-8956, 800-341-7981, info@marine-atlantic.ca
Old Port of Montréal Corporation Inc., 333, rue de la Commune ouest, Montréal, H2Y 2E2 QC
514-283-5256, Fax: 514-283-8423
Pacific Pilotage Authority Canada, #1000, 1130 Pender St. West, Vancouver, V6E 4A4 BC
604-666-6771, Fax: 604-666-1647, info@ppa.gc.ca
Parc Downsview Park Inc., #1, 35 Carl Hall Rd., Toronto, M3K 2B6 ON
613-952-2222, Fax: 613-952-2225, info@pdp.ca
St. Lawrence Seaway Management Corporation, 202 Pitt St., Cornwall, K6J 3P7 ON
613-932-5170, Fax: 613-932-7286, marketing@seaway.ca
Transport Canada, Place de Ville, 330 Sparks St., Tower C, Ottawa, K1A 0N5 ON
613-990-2309, Fax: 613-954-4731, minTC@tc.gc.ca
Transportation Appeal Tribunal of Canada, 333 Laurier Ave. West, 12th Fl., Ottawa, ON K1A 0N5
613-990-6906, Fax: 613-990-9153, info@tatc.gc.ca
Transportation Safety Board of Canada, 200 Promenade du Portage, 4th Fl., Ottawa, K1A 1K8 ON
819-994-3741, Fax: 819-997-2239, 800-387-3557
Via Rail Canada Inc., #500, 3, Place Ville-Marie, Montréal, H3B 2C9 QC
514-871-6000, Fax: 514-871-6768

Alberta
Automobile Insurance Rate Board, Terrace Bldg., #200, 9515 - 107 St. NW, Edmonton, AB T5K 2C3
780-427-5428, Fax: 780-644-7771, airb@gov.ab.ca
Alberta Infrastructure & Transportation, Twin Atria Bldg., 4999 - 98 Ave., Edmonton, T6B 2X3 AB
780-427-2731, Fax: 780-466-3166,-310-0000
Transportation Safety Board, Twin Atria Bldg., 4999 - 98 Ave., Edmonton, AB T6B 2X3
780-427-7178, Fax: 780-422-9739

British Columbia
British Columbia Ferry Commission, PO Box 1497, Comox, BC V9M 8A2
250-339-2714, info@bcferrycommission.com
British Columbia Transit, 520 Gorge Rd. East, PO Box 610, Victoria, BC V8W 2P3
250-385-2551, Fax: 250-995-5639
British Columbia Ferry Services Inc., 1112 Fort St., Victoria, V8V 4V2 BC
250-381-1401, 888-223-3779
Passenger Transportation Board, #202, 940 Blanshard St., PO Box 9850 Prov Govt, Victoria, BC V8W 9T5
250-953-3777, Fax: 250-953-3788, ptboard@gov.bc.ca
Ministry of Transportation & Infrastructure, 940 Blanshard St., PO Box 9850 Prov Govt,Victoria, V8W 9T5 BC
250-387-3198, Fax: 250-356-7706, tran.webmaster@gov.bc.ca
Transportation Planning & Policy Department, #5C, 940 Blanshard St., PO Box 9850 Prov Govt,Victoria, V8W 9T5 BC
250-387-5062, Fax: 250-387-6431

Manitoba
Highway Traffic Board/Motor Transport Board, #200, 301 Weston St., Winnipeg, MB R3E 3H4
204-945-8912, Fax: 204-783-6529
Manitoba Infrastructure & Transportation, Legislative Building, #203, 450 Broadway Ave., Winnipeg, R3C 0V8 MB
204-945-3723, Fax: 204-945-7610
License Suspension Appeal Board/Medical Review Committee, #200, 301 Weston St., Winnipeg, MB R3E 3H4
204-945-7350, Fax: 204-948-2682
Taxicab Board, #200, 301 Weston St., Winnipeg, MB R3E 3H4
Fax: 204-948-2315

New Brunswick
New Brunswick Transportation Authority, Kings Place, 440 King St., PO Box 6000, Fredericton, NB E3B 5H1
506-453-3939, Fax: 506-453-2900
Department of Transportation, Kings Pl., 440 KingSt., PO Box 6000, Fredericton, E3B 5H8 NB
506-453-3939, Fax: 506-453-2900, Transportation.Web@gnb.ca

Newfoundland & Labrador
Department of Transportation & Works, Confederation Bldg., West Block, 6th Fl., PO Box 8700, St. John's, A1B 4J6 NL
709-729-3679, Fax: 709-729-4285, twminister@gov.nl.ca

Northwest Territories
Highways, 4510 - 50 Ave., 2nd fl., PO Box 1320, Yellowknife, X1A 2L9 NT
867-920-8771, Fax: 867-873-0288
Department of Transportation, Lahm Ridge Bldg., 4501 50 Ave., PO Box 1320, Yellowknife, X1A 2L9 NT
867-920-3460, Fax: 867-873-0363

Nova Scotia
Department of Transportation & Infrastructure Renewal, Johnston Bldg., 1672 Granville St., 2nd Fl., PO Box 186, Halifax, B3J 2N2 NS
902-424-2297, Fax: 902-424-0171, 888-432-3233, tpwpaff@gov.ns.ca

Nunavut
Department of Community & Government Services, J.G. Brown Bldg., PO Box 1000 700,Iqaluit, X0A 0H0 NU
867-975-5400, Fax: 867-975-5305
Department of Economic Development & Transportation, #1104 Inuksugait Plaza, PO Box 1000 1500,Iqaluit, X0A 0H0 NU
867-975-7800, Fax: 867-975-7870, 888-975-5999, edt@gov.nu.ca

Ontario
GO Transit, #600, 20 Bay St., Toronto, ON M5J 2W3
416-869-3600, Fax: 416-869-1755, 888-438-6646
Licence Appeal Tribunal (LAT), 1 St. Clair Ave. West, 12th Fl., Toronto, ON M4V 1K6
416-314-4260, Fax: 416-314-4270, 800-255-2214
Niagara Falls Bridge Commission, PO Box 395, Niagara Falls, L2E 6T8 ON
905-354-5641, Fax: 905-353-6644
Ontario Highway Transport Board, 151 Bloor St. West, 10th Fl., Toronto, ON M5S 2T5
416-326-6732, Fax: 416-326-6738, ohtb@mto.gov.on.ca
Owen Sound Transportation Company Ltd., RR#5, Hwy 6 & 21, Owen Sound, ON N4K 5N7
519-376-8740
Road User Safety Division, #191, Bldg A, 1201 Wilson Ave., Toronto, M3M 1J8 ON
416-235-2999, Fax: 416-235-4153
Ministry of Transportation, Ferguson Block, 77 Wellesley St. West, 3rd Fl., Toronto, M7A 1Z8 ON
416-235-4686, Fax: 416-327-9185, 800-268-4686

Prince Edward Island
Department of Transportation & Public Works, Jones Bldg., 11 Kent St., PO Box 2000, Charlottetown, C1A 7N8 PE
902-368-5100, Fax: 902-368-5395

Quebec
Abitibi-Témiscamingue-Nord-du-Québec, 80, av Québec, Rouyn-Noranda, J9X 6R1 QC
819-763-3271, Fax: 819-763-3493, datnq@mtq.gouv.qc.ca
Bas-Saint-Laurent-Gaspésie-Iles-de-la-Madeleine, #101, 92, 2e rue ouest, Rimouski, G5L 8E6 QC
418-727-3674, Fax: 418-727-3673, dtbgi@mtq.gouv.qc.ca
Capitale-Nationale, 475, boul de l'Atrium, 2e étage, Québec, G1H 7H9 QC
418-643-1911, Fax: 418-646-0003, dcnat@mtq.gouv.qc.ca
Chaudière-Appalaches, 1156, boul de la Rive-Sud, Saint-Romuald, G6W 5M6 QC
418-839-5581, Fax: 418-834-7338, dtca@mtq.gouv.qc.ca
Commission des transports du Québec, 200, ch Sainte-Foy, 7e étage, Québec, QC G1R 5V5
Fax: 418-644-8034, 888-461-2433, courrier@ctq.gouv.qc.ca
Côte-Nord, #110, 625, boul Laflèche, Baie-Comeau, G5C 1C5 QC
418-295-4765, Fax: 418-295-4766, dtcn@mtq.gouv.qc.ca
Est-de-la-Montérégie, 201, place Charles-Lemoyne, 5e étage, Longueuil, J4K 2T5 QC
450-677-3413, Fax: 450-442-1317, dtem@mtq.gouv.qc.ca
Estrie, #2.02, 200, rue Belvédère nord, Sherbrooke, J1H 4A9 QC
819-820-3280, Fax: 819-820-3118, dte@mtq.gouv.qc.ca
Ile-de-Montréal, 440, boul René-Lévesque ouest, 10e étage, Montréal, H2Z 2A6 QC
514-873-7781, Fax: 514-864-3867, dtim@mtq.gouv.qc.ca
Laurentides-Lanaudière, 222, rue Saint-Georges, 2e étage, Saint-Jérôme, J7Z 4Z9 QC
450-569-3057, Fax: 450-569-3072, dll@mtq.gouv.qc.ca
Laval-Mille-Iles, 1725, boul Le Corbusier, Laval, H7S 2K7 QC
450-680-6330, Fax: 450-973-4959, dtlmi@mtq.gouv.qc.ca
Mauricie-Centre-du-Québec, 100, rue Laviolette, 4e étage, Trois-Rivières, G9A 5S9 QC
819-371-6896, Fax: 819-371-6136, dmcq@mtq.gouv.qc.ca
Ouest-de-la-Montérégie, #200, 180, boulevard d'Anjou, Châteauguay, J6K 1C4 QC
450-698-3400, Fax: 450-698-3452, dtom@mtq.gouv.qc.ca
Outaouais, #5.110, 170, rue de l'Hôtel-de-Ville, Gatineau, J8X 4C2 QC
819-772-3849, Fax: 819-772-3338, dto@mtq.gouv.qc.ca
Saguenay-Lac-Saint-Jean-Chibougamau, 3950, boul Harvey, Jonquière, G7X 8L6 QC
418-695-7916, Fax: 418-695-7926, dt.slsjc@mtq.gouv.qc.ca
Société de l'assurance automobile du Québec, 333, boul Jean-Lesage, CP 19600 Terminus, Québec, QC G1K 8J6
418-643-7620, Fax: 418-644-0339, 800-361-7620, courrier@saaq.gouv.qc.ca
Société des traversiers du Québec, 250, rue Saint-Paul, Québec, QC G1K 9K9
418-643-2019, Fax: 418-643-7308, stq@traversiers.gouv.qc.ca
Société du port ferroviaire Baie-Comeau-Hauterive, 18, rte Maritime, Baie-Comeau, QC G4Z 2L6
418-296-6785, Fax: 418-296-2377, soport@globetrotter.qc.ca
Ministère des Transports, 700, boul René-Lévesque est, 27e étage, Québec, G1R 5H1 QC
Fax: 514-643-1269, 888-355-0511, communications@mtq.gouv.qc.ca

Saskatchewan
Saskatchewan Highways & Infrastructure, 1855 Victoria Ave., Regina, S4P 3T2 SK
306-787-4800
Saskatchewan Highway Traffic Board, 1550 Saskatchewan Dr., Regina, SK S4P 0E4
306-775-6674

Yukon Territory
Yukon Community Services, PO Box 2703, Whitehorse, Y1A 2C6 YT
867-667-5811, Fax: 867-393-6295, 800-661-0408, inquiry@gov.yk.ca

Driver Control Board, 308 Steele St., PO Box 2703, Whitehorse, YT Y1A 2C6
867-667-3774, Fax: 867-393-6483, dcb@gov.yk.ca
Yukon Highways & Public Works, PO Box 2703, Whitehorse, Y1A 2C6 YT
867-393-7193, Fax: 867-393-6218, 800-661-0408, hpw-info@gov.yk.ca
Yukon Motor Transport Board, PO Box 2703, Whitehorse, YT Y1A 2C6
867-667-5782, Fax: 867-393-6408, Laurie.Hrynuik@gov.yk.ca

Port Authorities

Halifax Port Authority / HPA
Formerly: Halifax Port Corporation
PO Box 336, 1215 Marginal Rd., Halifax, NS B3J 2P6
Tel: 902-426-8222; Fax: 902-426-7335
www.portofhalifax.ca
Profile: Cargo: Bulk Cargo (Oil, Fuel, Gypsum) - 8.8 million metric tones Breakbulk Cargo (Iron/Steel, Machinery, Rubber) - 136,000 metric tones Roll-on, Roll-off Cargo (Cars and Trucks) - 216,000 metric tones Containerized Cargo - 4.6 million metric tones

Hamilton Port Authority
605 James St. North, 6th Floor, Hamilton, ON L8L 1K1
Tel: 905-525-4330; Fax: 905-528-6554
Toll-Free: 800-263-2131
cargo@hamiltonport.ca
www.hamiltonport.ca

Montreal Port Authority
Édifice du port de Montréal, #1, 2100, ave Pierre-Dupuy, Montréal, QC H3C 3R5
Tel: 514-283-7011; Fax: 514-283-0829
info@port-montreal.com
www.port-montreal.com
Profile: The Montreal Port Authority's mandate is to facilitate domestic and international trade and thereby contribute to the attainment of local, regional and national socioeconomic objectives

Nanaimo Port Authority / NPA
PO Box 131, 100 Port Dr., Nanaimo, BC V9R 5K4
Tel: 250-753-4146; Fax: 250-753-4899
info@npa.ca
www.npa.ca
Profile: The NPA administers the federal harbour from the Nanaimo Assembly Wharf to the Petro-Canada dock on Newcastle Channel and extending to Newcastle and Protection Islands

Port Alberni Port Authority
2750 Harbour Rd., Port Alberni, BC V9Y 7X2
Tel: 250-723-5312; Fax: 250-723-1114
www.portalberniportauthority.ca
Profile: Committed to the continued waterfront development of the Alberni Inlet and the economic sustainability of the Alberni Valley

Port Metro Vancouver
Formerly: Fraser River Port Authority
100 The Pointe, 999 Canada Place, Vancouver, BC V6C 3T4
Tel: 604-665-9000; Fax: 866-284-4271
info@portmetrovancouver.com
www.portmetrovancouver.com
Profile: The Graser River, North Fraser, and Vancouver Port Authorities united to become Vancouver Fraser Port Authority on January 1, 2008; the Vancouver Fraser Port Authority has since become the Port Metro Vancouver.

Port of Belledune
112 Shannon Dr., Belledune, NB E8G 2W2
Tel: 506-522-1200; Fax: 506-522-0803
info@portofbelledune.ca
www.portofbelledune.ca
Profile: To develop to the fullest, the services and facilities of the port, to enable it to become the anchor of economic development in Northern New Brunswick. Existing infrastructures can handle any product & merchandise, We can handle Bulk, break bulk, containers, trailer, liquid, RoRo, Space and storage available for available for lease, Low storage and rental cost, Customize rate available, Custom Bonded available, Space available for break cargo, Industrial location

Prince Rupert Port Authority
200 - 215 Cow Bay Rd., Prince Rupert, BC V8J 1A2
Tel: 250-627-8899; Fax: 250-627-8980
pcorp@rupertport.com
www.rupertport.com
Profile: Significant changes in world trade patterns have shifted the focus of the Prince Rupert Port Authority (PRPA) and have already resulted in new initiatives, including a cruise and container port. Significant opportunities for industrial development mark the next phase in development potential at the port

Quebec Port Authority
PO Box 80 Haute-Ville, 150 rue Dalhousie, Québec, QC G1R 4M8
Tel: 418-648-3640; Fax: 418-648-4160
marketing@portquebec.ca
www.portquebec.ca
Profile: The mission of the Québec Port Authority is to promote and develop maritime trade, to serve the economic interests of the Quebec area and of Canada and to ensure that it is profitable while respecting both its community and the environment

Saguenay Port Authority
6600, rue Quai-Marcel-Dionne, La Baie, QC G7B 3N9
Tel: 418-697-0250; Fax: 418-697-0243
info@portsaguenay.ca
www.portsaguenay.ca
Profile: The Port of Saguenay is the only public port in the Saguenay-Lac-St-Jean area. It is a port recognized for its strategic importance to the country's trade and economy. This international seaport is also part of the essential infrastructures of the municipality and the region and generates several hundred jobs. The port is the cornerstone of the community of Saguenay-Lac-St-Jean. It is an element of Canada's transportation infrastructure and offers a marine gateway to global markets

Saint John Port Authority
111 Water St., Saint John, NB E2L 0B1
Tel: 506-636-4869; Fax: 506-636-4443
port@sjport.com
www.sjport.com

Sept-Iles Port Authority
1 Quai Mgr-Blanche, Sept-Iles, QC G4R 5P3
Tel: 418-968-1231; Fax: 418-962-4445
www.portsi.com

Toronto Port Authority
60 Harbour St., Toronto, ON M5J 1B7
Tel: 416-863-2000; Fax: 416-863-0495
communications@torontoport.com
www.torontoport.com
Profile: Maintains a paved facility of over 50 acres centrally located, adjacent to downtown Toronto. The yard provides convenience, with excellent access to the railroads, as well as all major highways. This facility is fully bonded and has 24-hour security

Windsor Port Authority
#502, 251 Goyeau St., Windsor, ON N9A 6V2
Tel: 519-258-5741; Fax: 519-258-5905
www.portwindsor.com
Profile: The mission of the Windsor Port Authority is to manage, develop, and promote the Port of Windsor for the benefit of its stakeholders and ensure the general security of the port while remaining sensitive to the need for a high degree of safety and environmental responsibility

SECTION 17
UTILITIES

Associations

Alberta Water & Wastewater Operators Association (AWWOA)
11810 Kingsway Ave., Edmonton AB T5G 0X5
Tel: 780-454-7745; *Fax:* 780-454-7748
Toll-Free: 877-454-7745
awwoa@telus.net
www.awwoa.ab.ca
www.facebook.com/group.php?gid=157981630910194
twitter.com/awwoa
Overview: A small provincial organization founded in 1976
Activities: Providing manuals to operators
Publications: Alberta Utility Operator Newsletter
Type: Newsletter *Frequency:* 3 pa *Editor:* Gayle Sacuta
Profile: Information about Alberta's water & wastewater operations, outstanding service, new technologies, research, regulatory changes, & trainingopportunities

American Council for an Energy-Efficient Economy (ACEEE)
#600, 529 14th Street NW, Washington DC 20045-1000 USA
Tel: 202-507-4000; *Fax:* 202-429-2248
www.aceee.org
www.facebook.com/67449893973
twitter.com/ACEEEdc
Overview: A medium-sized national organization founded in 1980
Activities: *Library:* *Yes*

American Public Works Association (APWA)
#700, 2345 Grand Blvd., Kansas City MO 64108-2625 USA
Tel: 816-472-6100; *Fax:* 816-472-1610
Toll-Free: 800-848-2792
apwa@apwa.net
www.apwa.net
Social Media: www.youtube.com/apwatv
www.facebook.com/AmericanPublicWorksAssociation
twitter.com/apwatweets
Overview: A medium-sized international organization founded in 1938
Chief Officer(s):
Peter King, Executive Director
pking@apwa.net
Cindy Long, Assistant to the Exec. Director, 816-595-5220
clong@apwa.net
Finances: *Annual Operating Budget: Greater than $5 Million; Funding Sources: Membership dues; Federal grants; Products*
Staff: 50 staff member(s); 250 volunteer(s)
Membership: 26,000; *Fees: Schedule available; Member Profile: Public agencies, private sector companies, & individuals engaged in public works services; Committees: Transportation; Solid Waste; Water Resources; Engineering & Technology; Management & Leadership; Emergency Management; Fleet Services; Facilities & Grounds; Utility & Public Right of Way*

Association de l'industrie électrique du Québec (AIEQ)
#320, 2000, rue Mansfield, Montréal QC H3A 2Y9
Tél: 514-281-0615; *Téléc:* 514-281-7965
info@aieq.net
www.aieq.net
Nom précédent: *Club d'électricité du Québec inc.*
Aperçu: *Dimension: moyenne; Envergure: provinciale; Organisme sans but lucratif; fondée en 1916*
Membre(s) du bureau directeur:
Jean-François Samray, Président et directeur général
Finances: *Budget de fonctionnement annuel: $500,000-$1.5 Million*
Personnel: 7 membre(s) du personnel
Membre: 121; *Montant de la cotisation: Selon le nombre d'employés au Québec; Critères d'admissibilite: Membres industriels; Comités: Consultatif; Finances; Services aux membres; Promotion; Débats projects*
Activités: Déjeuners; conférences; activités sociales; *Service de conférenciers: Oui*

Association of Major Power Consumers in Ontario (AMPCO)
Sterling Tower, #1702, 372 Bay St., Toronto ON M5H 2W9
Tel: 416-260-0280; *Fax:* 416-260-0442
info@ampco.org
www.ampco.org
Overview: A large provincial organization founded in 1975
Chief Officer(s):
Adam White, President
awhite@ampco.org
Adam White, President
Fareeda Heeralal, Contact
Finances: *Funding Sources: Membership fees*
Membership: 42; *Fees: Based on electrical energy usage; Member Profile: Companies that are major manufacturers, employers, & power consumers (represents key industries - mining, pulp & paper, automobile manufacturing, petro-chemicals, metals, consumer products, steel, etc.); Committees: Transition Issues; Executive*

Association of Manitoba Hydro Staff & Supervisory Employees (AMHSSE)
PO Box 353, 905 Corydon Ave., Winnipeg MB R3M 3V3
Tel: 204-482-2559
tesmith@hydro.mb.ca
Overview: A small provincial organization
Chief Officer(s):
Gord Kirk, President
gdkirk@hydro.mb.ca
Membership: 415

Association of Power Producers of Ontario (APPrO)
PO Box 1084, Stn. F, #1602, 25 Adelaide St. East, Toronto ON M5C 3A1
Tel: 416-322-6549; *Fax:* 416-481-5785
appro@appro.org; marketing@appro.org
www.appro.org
Previous Name: *Independent Power Producers Society of Ontario (IPPSO)*
Overview: A medium-sized provincial organization founded in 1986
Membership: 100+; *Member Profile: Companies involved in the generation of electricity in Ontario, including suppliers of services & consulting services*
Activities: Advocating for generators; Offering resources to assist business, government, utilities, & researchers; Organizing educational programs
Publications: APPrO [Association of Power Producers of Ontario] Conference Proceedings
Type: Yearbook *Frequency:* Annually *Price:* $40
Canadian Power Directory
Type: Directory
Profile: Contact information for organizations involved in all aspects of electricity generation in Canada, such as developers, equipment & service suppliers, utilities, & resource groups
IPPSO FACTO: Magazine of the Association of Power Producers of Ontario
Type: Magazine *Frequency:* Bimonthly *Accepts Advertising Price:* Free with Association of Power Producers of Ontario membership
Profile: Ontario, national, international, & regulatory news

Association québécoise du gaz naturel (AQGN)
#207, 560, boul. Henri-Bourassa Ouest, Montréal QC H3L 1P4
Tél: 514-339-9399; *Téléc:* 514-339-9353
aqgn@aqgn.com
www.aqgn.com
Aperçu: *Dimension: petite; Envergure: provinciale*
Membre(s) du bureau directeur:
Ginette Gamache, Directrice générale
Montant de la cotisation: *450$ régulier; 2 500$ aviseur*

Atlantic Canada Water & Wastewater Association (ACWWA)
PO Box 41002, Dartmouth NS B2Y 4P7
Tel: 902-434-6002; *Fax:* 902-435-7796
acwwa@hfx.andara.com
www.acwwa.ca
Overview: A medium-sized local organization
Membership: 430+; *Member Profile: Water professionals in Atlantic Canada, from areas such as service provision, contracting, utility management, operations, system design, consulting, & academia; Committees: Education; Membership; Newsletter; Technical Papers; CWWA & CAC; Cross Connection Control; Young Professionals; Water for People; Government Affairs; Conference; Operator Involvement; Volunteers; Website*
Activities: Providing training & information about the water & wastewater industry to members; Enhancing government relations; Offering networking opportunities
Publications: ACWWA [Atlantic Canada Water & Wastewater Association] Newsletter
Type: Newsletter
Profile: Association activities
AWWA Wastewater Operator Field Guide
Type: Booklet *Price:* $55
Profile: Information used daily by wastewater system operators
AWWA Water Operator Field Guide
Type: Booklet *Price:* $55
Profile: Information for water treatment plant operators & water distribution operators
Operator Certification Study Guide [a publication of the Atlantic Canada Water & Wastewater Association]
Type: Booklet *Price:* $75
Profile: Information for water treatment & water distribution operators
Wastewater Operator Certification Study Guide
Type: Booklet *Price:* $75
Profile: Sample questions & answer for wastewater operator certification exams

British Columbia Sustainable Energy Association (BCSEA)
#5, 4217 Glanford Ave., Victoria BC V8Z 4B9
Tel: 250-744-2720
info@bcsea.org
www.bcsea.org
www.facebook.com/BCSEA
Overview: A medium-sized provincial organization founded in 2004
Finances: *Funding Sources: Donations*
Membership: *Fees: Schedule available; Member Profile: Individuals & organizations*
Activities: Providing education through programs & webinars

British Columbia Water & Waste Association (BCWWA)
#221, 8678 Greenall Ave., Burnaby BC V5J 3M6
Tel: 604-433-4389; *Fax:* 604-433-9859
Toll-Free: 877-433-4389
contact@bcwwa.org
www.bcwwa.org
www.facebook.com/group.php?gid=21435804125
Overview: A medium-sized provincial organization founded in 1964
Chief Officer(s):
Daisy Foster, Chief Executive Officer, 604-433-7824
dfoster@bcwwa.org
David Icharia, Director, Operations, 604-433-0093
dicharia@bcwwa.org
Judy Zhang, Manager, Finance, 604-433-6941
jzhang@bcwwa.org
Sarah Vaughan, Manager, Communications, 604-630-0011
svaughan@bcwwa.org
Kimberly Perreault, Coordinator, Member Services, 604-433-4389
kperreault@bcwwa.org
TBA, Coordinator, Education & Technology
Finances: *Funding Sources: Membership fees; Courses; Seminars; Annual conference*
Membership: *Fees: $25 students; $35 operators; $60 full members; Member Profile: British Columbia & Yukon professionals & students in the water & wastewater fields; Committees: Young Professionals; Climate Change; Cross Connection Control; Decentralized Wastewater Management; Drinking Water; Energy Management; Infrastructure Management; Residuals Management; Small Water Systems; SCADA & Information Technology; Vancouver Island; Wastewater Collection; Wastewater Management; Wastewater Source Control; Water Sustainability; Watershed (Stormwater) Management; Yukon; Small Wastewater Systems; Small Water Systems; Wastewater Treatment; Water Distribution; Water Treatment; Awards; Elections; Governance; Nominations; Leadership Council*
Activities: Promoting dialogue & information dissemination on environmental matters; Offering operator education & training opportunities (online training now available); Providing networking opportunities such as our Annual Conference; Certifying backflow assembly testers in British Columbia & Yukon through our Cross Connection Control program; Creating awareness of the value of water through Drinking Water Week, which occurs annually in May.; *Awareness Events: Drinking Water Week, May Library: British Columbia Water & Waste Association Library*
Publications: Watermark
Type: Magazine *Frequency:* Quarterly *Accepts Advertising Editor:* Carol Campbell
Profile: Calendar of events, product listings, new member listings, employment opportunities, informative articles, & reports on the annual conference, technical seminars & symposia

CAMPUT, Canada's Energy & Utility Regulators (CAMPUT)
#646, 200 North Service Rd. West, Oakville ON L6M 2Y1
Tel: 905-827-5139; *Fax:* 905-827-3260
info@camput.org
www.camput.org
Previous Name: *Canadian Association of Members of Public Utility Tribunals / Association canadienne des membres des tribunaux d'utilité publique*
Overview: A small national organization founded in 1976
Chief Officer(s):
Terry Rochefort, Executive Director, 905-827-5139
rochefort@camput.org

Lise Duquette, Chair, 514-873-2452
lise.duquette@regie-energie.qc.ca
Carolyn Dahl Rees, Secretary-Treasurer, 414-592-4534
carolyn.dahlrees@auc.ab.ca
Membership: *Member Profile: Any Canadian tribunal, board, commission, or agency that is responsible for the economic regulation of utilities; Any Canadian energy tribunal, board, commission, or agency that makes binding decisions through adjudicative or quasi-judicial processes; Committees: Regulatory Affairs; Education*
Activities: Educating & training commissioners & staff of public utility tribunals; Communicating with members; Liaising with parallel regulatory organizations

Canada - Newfoundland & Labrador Offshore Petroleum Board (C-NLOPB)
TD Place, 140 Water St., 5th Fl., St. John's NL A1C 6H6
Tel: 709-778-1400; Fax: 709-778-1473
information@cnlopb.nl.ca
www.cnlopb.nl.ca

Chief Officer(s):
Max Ruelokke, P.Emg, Chair, CEO, & Chief Conservation Officer, 709-778-1456
David Wells, Deputy Chief Executive Officer, 709-778-1452
John P. Andrews, Manager, Legal & Land, 709-778-1458
Mike Baker, Manager, Support Services, 709-778-1464
Jeffrey M. Bugden, P.Eng., Manager, Industrial Benefits, 709-778-1448
Dave Burley, Manager, Environmental Affairs, 709-778-1403
Nicholle Carter, P.Geo., Manager, Exploration, 709-778-1428
Daniel B. Chicoyne, MSS, Manager, Safety, 709-778-4262
Sean Kelly, Manager, Public Relations, 709-778-1418, Fax: 709-689-0713
skelly@cnlopb.nl.ca
Jeff O'Keefe, Manager, Resource Management, 709-778-1406
Howard L. Pike, P.Eng., Manager, Operations, 709-778-1412
Activities: Facilitating the exploration for & development of hydrocarbon resources
Publications: Canada - Newfoundland & Labrador Offshore Petroleum Board Annual Report
Type: Yearbook *Frequency:* Annually
Profile: Contents include the board's role, objectives, & financial statements

Canada - Nova Scotia Offshore Petroleum Board (CNSOPB)
TD Centre, 1791 Barrington St., 18th Fl., Halifax NS B3J 3K9
Tel: 902-422-5588; Fax: 902-422-1799
postmaster@cnsopb.ns.ca
www.cnsopb.ns.ca
twitter.com/CNSOPB

Chief Officer(s):
Stuart Pinks, P.Eng., Chief Executive Officer, 902-496-3206
spinks@cnsopb.ns.ca
Steve Bigelow, P.Eng., Chief Conservation Officer & Director, Resources & Rights, 902-429-1816
sbigelow@cnsopb.ns.ca
Keith Landra, Director, Operations, Health, Safety, & Environment, 902-496-0723
klandra@cnsopb.ns.ca
Michael S. McPhee, Director, General Counsel, Secretary, & Mgr., Regulatory Policy, 902-496-0739
mmcphee@cnsopb.ns.ca
Kim Nauss, Director, Industrial Benefits, 902-496-0751
knauss@cnsopb.ns.ca
Troy MacDonald, Director, Information Services, 902-496-0734
tmacdonald@cnsopb.ns.ca
Tanya T. White, Director, Public Relations & Administration, 902-496-0750
twhite@cnsopb.ns.ca
Activities: Issuing licences for offshore exploration & development; Collecting & distributing data
Publications: Canada - Nova Scotia Offshore Petroleum Board Annual Report
Type: Yearbook *Frequency:* Annually
Profile: A summary of offshore activities, healthy & safety initiatives, environmental protection, information services, & financial statements

Canadian Association of Petroleum Land Administration (CAPLA)
#628, 138 - 4th Avenue SE, Calgary AB T2G 4Z6
Tel: 403-452-6497; Fax: 403-452-6627
office@caplacanada.org
www.caplacanada.org

Overview: A small local organization
Membership: 2,500; *Fees: $75 associate; $175 active*

Canadian Association of Petroleum Landmen (CAPL)
#350, 500 - 5 Ave. SW, Calgary AB T2P 3L5
Tel: 403-237-6635; Fax: 403-263-1620
reception@landman.ca
www.landman.ca

Overview: A medium-sized national organization founded in 1948
Membership: 1,500+
Activities: Liaising with government departments & other resource based associations; Communicating with members; Providing professional development opportunities; Offering networking events
Publications: Canadian Association of Petroleum Landmen Membership Directory
Type: Directory *Price:* Free access with membership in the Canadian Association of Petroleum Landmen
CAPL [Canadian Association of Petroleum Landmen] Annual Report
Type: Yearbook *Frequency:* Annually
The Negotiator: The Magazine of the Canadian Association of Petroleum Landmen
Type: Magazine *Frequency:* 10 pa *Accepts Advertising Editor:* K. Rennie, M. Innes, & J. Frese *Price:* Free with membership in the CanadianAssociation of Petroleum Landmen
Profile: Feature articles, CAPL conference information, & CAPL news & events

Canadian Association of Petroleum Producers (CAPP) / Association canadienne des producteurs pétroliers
#2100, 350 - 7 Ave. SW, Calgary AB T2P 3N9
Tel: 403-267-1100; Fax: 403-261-4622
communication@capp.ca; membership@capp.ca;
publications@capp.ca
www.capp.ca
Social Media: www.youtube.com/cappvideos
www.facebook.com/OilGasCanada
twitter.com/oilgascanada

Merged from: Canadian Petroleum Association; Independent Petroleum Association of Canada
Overview: A large national organization founded in 1992
Chief Officer(s):
David Collyer, President
dave.collyer@capp.ca
Janet Annesley, Vice-President, Communications
janet.annesley@capp.ca
Bob Bleaney, Vice-President, External Relations
bob.bleaney@capp.ca
Tom Huffaker, Vice-President, Policy & Environment
tom.huffaker@capp.ca
David Pryce, Vice-President, Operations
pryce@capp.ca
Nick Schultz, Vice-President, Pipeline Regulation
schultz@capp.ca
Greg Stringham, Vice-President, Oil Sands & Markets
stringham@capp.ca
Membership: 100+ producer members + 150 associate members; *Member Profile: Producer members range from two person operations to internationally recognized corporations employing thousands; Associate members provide services, such as drilling, baniking, & computing, for Canada's oil & gas industry*
Activities: Reviewing, analyzing, & recommending industry policy positions; Participating in regulatory change dialogues; Representing the industry on multi-sector international, federal, & provincial consultation bodies; Communicating with governments, regulators, stakeholders, & the public; Offering seminars & workshops; Providing industry trends, statistics, & research information; Informing members of industry standards & guidelines; Monitoring pipeline expansions; Improving coordinated land use planning processes

Canadian Association on Water Quality (CAWQ) / Association canadienne sur la qualité de l'eau (ACQE)
PO Box 5050, 867 Lakeshore Rd., Burlington ON L7R 4A6
Tel: 905-336-4513; Fax: 905-336-6444
www.cawq.ca

Also Known As: Canadian National Committee of the International Association on Water Quality
Previous Name: *Canadian Association on Water Pollution Research & Control*
Overview: A medium-sized national charitable organization founded in 1967
Chief Officer(s):
Clayton Tiedemann, President, 780-412-3830, Fax: 780-412-7679
CTiedema@epcor.ca
Yves Comeau, Secretary, 514-340-4711 3728, Fax: 514-340-5918
yves.comeau@polymtl.ca
Peter Jones, Treasurer, 819-821-8000 62165, Fax: 819-821-7955
peter.jones@usherbrooke.ca
Finances: *Funding Sources: Membership fees; Subscriptions; Grants*
Membership: 10 corporate + 210 individual; *Fees: Schedule available; Member Profile: Joint or individual - engaged in water quality & pollution research & control; Corporate - organizations engaged in water quality & pollution research & control; Sustaining - individuals & organizations interested in support & results of water quality & pollution research & control; Joint or student - students engaged in full-time study on water quality & pollution research & control*
Publications: Canadian Association on Water Quality Annual Report
Frequency: Annually
IWA's Water 21
Type: Newsletter *Frequency:* Bimonthly
Water Quality Research Journal of Canada
Type: Journal *Frequency:* Quarterly *Editor:* Ronnie Gehr *Price:* Free for individual CAWQ members; $250 Canada & USA; $295 International
Profile: Peer-reviewed scholarly & review articles & original research on topics such as the impact of pollutants & contaminants on aquatic ecosystems,aquatic species at risk, water treatment & quality, conservation, & water pollution policies

Canadian Centre for Energy Information / Centre info-énergie
#201, 322 - 11th Ave. SW, Calgary AB T2R 0C5
Tel: 403-263-7722; Fax: 403-237-6286
Toll-Free: 877-606-4636
www.centreforenergy.com

Also Known As: Centre for Energy
Overview: A medium-sized national organization founded in 2002
Activities: Raising awareness & understanding about the Canadian energy system; Providing learning resources for teachers & students; *Speaker Service: Yes*
Publications: Energy Research & Innovation Directory
Type: Directory
Profile: Highlights of energy research projects, developed in partnership with the Department of Foreign Affairs & International Trade

Canadian Clean Power Coalition (CCPC)
64 Chapala Heath, Calgary AB T2X 3P9
Tel: 403-606-0973; Fax: 403-256-0424
www.canadiancleanpowercoalition.com

Overview: A medium-sized national organization
Chief Officer(s):
Don Wharton, Chair
Bob Stobbs, Executive Director, 306-566-3326
bstobbs@saskpower.com
Membership: *Member Profile: Canadian coal & coal-fired electricity producers*
Activities: Addressing environmental issues with governments & stakeholders

Canadian District Energy Association (CDEA) / Association canadienne des réseaux thermiques
PO Box 612, #402, 555 Richmond St. West, Toronto ON M5V 3B1
Tel: 416-365-0765; Fax: 416-365-0650
cdea@canurb.com
www.cdea.ca

Overview: A small national organization founded in 1994
Membership: 66; *Fees: $1,200 owner/operator; $900 goods or service supplier; $300 associate; $90 full time student or professor*

Canadian Electricity Association (CEA) / Association canadienne de l'électricité (ACE)
#1100, 350 Sparks St., Ottawa ON K1R 7S8
Tel: 613-230-9263; Fax: 613-230-9326
info@electricity.ca
www.electricity.ca

Overview: A medium-sized national organization founded in 1891
Chief Officer(s):
Pierre Guimond, President & Chief Executive Officer, 613-230-4762
Francis Bradley, Vice-President, Policy Development, 613-230-5027
Sandra Schwartz, Vice-President, Policy Advocacy, 613-230-9876
Louisa Hood, Director, Communications, 613-688-2954
Angela Macleod, Corporate Secretary, 613-230-7384

Richard Lussier, Controller, 613-688-2065
Membership: *Member Profile: Members generate, transmit, & distribute electrical energy to residential, commercial, institutional, & industrial customers throughout Canada*
Activities: Analyzing national & international business issues; Providing a national forum for the electricity business; Advocating industry views; Helping companies in evolving markets; Communicating findings about concerns such as mercury emissions & electric & magnetic fields
Publications: Annual Service Continuity Report on Distribution System Performance in Electrical Utilities
Type: Yearbook *Frequency:* Annually
Profile: Produced by the Performance Excellence & Benchmarking program of the Canadian Electricity Association, the report containsinformation about industry standard metrics for electricity distribution, including system average interruption frequency index & the system average interruption duration index
The CEA [Canadian Electricity Association] Member Directory
Type: Directory *Frequency:* Annually *Price:* $15 members; $65 non-members
Profile: Contact information for the Canadian electricity industry's major players, in addition to information about the operations of the Canadian ElectricityAssociation's member companies
Electricity Annual
Type: Yearbook *Frequency:* Annually
Profile: The Canadian Electricity Association's yearly industry review
Forced Outage Performance of Transmission Equipment [a publication of the Canadian Electricity Association]
Type: Yearbook *Frequency:* Annually
Profile: Produced by the Performance Excellence & Benchmarking program of the Canadian Electricity Association, thereport addresses the performance of transmission equipment in Canada
Generation Equipment Status [a publication of the Canadian Electricity Association]
Type: Yearbook *Frequency:* Annually
Profile: Produced by the Performance Excellence & Benchmarking program of the Canadian Electricity Association, the report features informationon the performance of electrical generating units in Canada

Canadian Energy Efficiency Alliance (CEEA) / L'Association de l'efficacité énergétique du Canada
#402, 2800 Skymark Ave., Mississauga ON L4W 5A6
Tel: 905-614-1641; Toll-Free: 866-614-1641
alliance@energyefficiency.org
www.energyefficiency.org
Overview: A medium-sized national organization founded in 1995
Finances: *Annual Operating Budget: $250,000-$500,000; Funding Sources: Membership dues & projects*
Staff: 14 volunteer(s)
Membership: 40; *Fees: $1,500 corporate; $15,000 leader; Committees: Codes & Standards; Executive; Government Relations*
Activities: Establishing a National Energy Efficiency Centre to be North America's energy technology showcase; promoting/advocating energy efficiency; breakfast policy updates; annual meeting

Canadian Energy Pipeline Association (CEPA) / Association canadienne de pipelines d'énergie
#200, 505 - 3rd St. SW, Calgary AB T2P 3E6
Tel: 403-221-8777; Fax: 403-221-8760
aboutpipelines@cepa.com
www.cepa.com
Social Media: www.youtube.com/aboutpipelines; www.slideshare.net/aboutpipelines
www.facebook.com/aboutpipelines
twitter.com/aboutpipelines
Overview: A medium-sized national organization founded in 1993
Chief Officer(s):
Brenda Kenny, President & Chief Executive Officer
Kim McCaig, Vice-President & Chief Operating Officer
Philippe Reicher, Vice-President, External Communications
Ziad Saad, Vice-President, Safety & Sustainability
Amanda Affonso, Director, Regulatory & Financial
Thomas Linder, Director, Safety
Vanessa Coates-Humen, Administrator & Work Group Analyst
Sandra Burns, Manager, Communications, 403-221-8764
sburns@cepa.com
Cathy Hay, Manager, Industry Information, Research, & Analysis, 403-221-8762
chay@cepa.com
Donna Menuz, Accountant, 403-221-8775
dmenuz@cepa.com
Carole Brownlees, Secretary
Membership: *Member Profile: Canada's pipeline companies that transport natural gas & crude oil throughout North America; Committees: Damage Prevention Regulations; Emergency Security Management; Environment; Health & Safety; Land Issues Task Force; Pipeline Integrity; Aboriginal Affairs; Climate Change; Corporate Tax; Commodity Tax; Pipeline Abandonment Obligations; Pipeline Economics; Property Tax; Regulatory Accounting; Regulatory Policy*
Activities: Liaising with government regarding industry practices

Canadian Energy Research Institute (CERI)
#150, 3512 - 33 St. NW, Calgary AB T2L 2A6
Tel: 403-282-1231; Fax: 403-284-4181
info@ceri.ca
www.ceri.ca
Overview: A medium-sized national organization founded in 1975
Chief Officer(s):
Peter Howard, President & Chief Executive Officer
David McWhinney, Director, Accounting & Operations
Dinara Millington, Director, Research
Jon Rozhon, Senior Researcher
Thorn Walden, Senior Economist
Membership: 150
Activities: *Speaker Service: Yes Library: I.N. McKinnon Memorial Library*

Canadian Energy Workers' Association (CEWA)
9908 - 106 St., Edmonton AB T5K 1C4
Tel: 780-420-7887; Fax: 780-420-7881
cewa@cewa.ca
www.cewa.ca
Previous Name: *Canadian Utilities & Northland Utilities Employees' Association; Alberta Power Employees' Association*
Overview: A small national organization founded in 1969
Chief Officer(s):
A.B. (Toni) Hawkins, Manager, Business
thawkins@cewa.ca
Laurie L. Pederson, Officer, Labour Relations
lpederson@cewa.ca
Fees: *2 hour's rate of pay each month*
Activities: Engaging in problem solving between members & management; Creating programs for members in the areas of safety, security, & skills development; Seeking opportunities to organize & represent workers; Offering an annual bursary program

Canadian Fluid Power Association (CFPA) / Association canadienne d'énergie fluide
#310, 2175 Sheppard Ave. East, Toronto ON M2J 1W8
Tel: 416-499-1416; Fax: 416-491-1670
info@cfpa.ca
www.cfpa.ca
Overview: A medium-sized national organization founded in 1974
Chief Officer(s):
Carolyne Vigon, Administrator
carolyne@taylorenterprises.com
Mary Lou Murray, Registrar, Events
maryloum@taylorenterprises.com
Finances: *Funding Sources: Membership fees; Sponsorships*
Staff: 10 volunteer(s)
Membership: 80 corporate; *Fees: $588.50 large corporation; $401.25 small corporation; $160.50 individual; Member Profile: Open to manufacturers, distributors, assemblers, educators, consultants & designers of fluid power components, systems & services; Committees: Communications; Membership*
Activities: Representing the fluid power industry on the Canadian advisory committee with regard to the drafting of international standards; Representing the fluid power industry in the formulation of applicable national standards; *Speaker Service: Yes*

Canadian Gas Association (CGA) / Association canadienne du gaz
#809, 350 Sparks St., Ottawa ON K1R 7S8
Tel: 613-748-0057; Fax: 613-748-9078
info@cga.ca
www.cga.ca
twitter.com/GoSmartEnergy
Overview: A large national organization founded in 1907
Chief Officer(s):
Timothy M. Egan, President & Chief Executive Officer, 613-748-0057 300
tegan@cga.ca
Paula Dunlop, Director, Public Affairs & Strategy, 613-748-0057 341
pdunlop@cga.ca
Bryan Gormely, Director, Policy, Economics, & Information, 613-748-0057 315
bgormley@cga.ca
Jim Tweedie, Director, Operations, Safety, & Integrity Management, 613-748-0057 311
jtweedie@cga.ca
Valerie Prokop, Manager, Finance & Corporate Services, 613-748-0057 309
vprokop@cga.ca
Membership: *Member Profile: Equipment manufacturers; Distribution companies; Transmission companies; Service providers*
Activities: Advancing policy positions with federal & provincial decision makers; Developing educational information
Publications: Canadian Gas Association Market Updates
Profile: Topics include natural gas markets pre-heating season, post-heating season, supply, & demographics
Canadian Gas Association Membership Directory
Type: Directory
Profile: Available for current CGA members
Canadian Natural Gas Magazine
Type: Magazine *Frequency:* Semiannually *Accepts Advertising*
Editor: Suzy Richardson
Profile: CGA news, feature articles, & a buyers' guide for the natural gas distribution industry in Canada

Canadian Hydropower Association (CHA) / Association canadienne de l'hydroélectricité
#1300, 340 Albert St., Ottawa ON K1R 7Y9
Tel: 613-751-6655; Fax: 613-751-4465
info@canhydropower.org
www.canhydropower.org
Overview: A small national organization founded in 1998
Membership: 16 generators; 21 industry; 8 associate; *Member Profile: Hydroelectic generation; hydroelectric industry; Associated associations and organizations*

Canadian Institute for Energy Training (CIET) / Institut canadien de formation de l'énergie
#200, 160, rue Saint-Paul, Québec QC G1K 3W1
Tel: 418-692-2592; Fax: 418-692-4899
Toll-Free: 800-461-7618
info@cietcanada.com
www.cietcanada.com
Overview: A medium-sized national organization founded in 1994
Finances: *Funding Sources: Fees for service*

Canadian Institute of Energy (CIE)
#26, 181 Ravine Dr., Port Moody BC V3H 4T3
Tel: 604-949-1346; Fax: 604-469-3717
cienergybc@gmail.com
www.cienergy.org
Overview: A medium-sized national organization founded in 1979
Chief Officer(s):
Penny Cochrane, Chair
Melissa McArthur, Administrator
John Oliver, Treasurer
Finances: *Funding Sources: Membership fees*
Staff: 6 volunteer(s)
Membership: 500; *Fees: $60; Member Profile: Professionally involved in all aspects of energy, whether in exploring for sources, conducting energy research, converting or using energy, or in energy planning*
Activities: *Speaker Service: Yes; Rents Mailing List: Yes*

Canadian Institute of Mining, Metallurgy & Petroleum (CIM) / Institut canadien des mines, de la métallurgie et du pétrole
CIM National Office, #1250, 3500, boul de Maisonneuve ouest, Westmount QC H3Z 3C1
Tel: 514-939-2710; Fax: 514-939-2714
cim@cim.org
www.cim.org
Previous Name: *Canadian Institute of Mining & Metallurgy*
Overview: A large national organization founded in 1898
Chief Officer(s):
Jean Vavrek, Executive Director, 514-939-2710 1301, Fax: 513-939-2714
jvavrek@cim.org
Chuck Edwards, President
chuck.edwards@amec.com
Jean-Marc Demers, Deputy Executive Director
jmdemers@cim.org
Lise Bujold, Director, Conferences & Exhibitions
lbujold@cim.org
Marjolaine Dugas, Director, Membership
mdugas@cim.org
Gérard Hamel, Director, Information Technology
ghamel@cim.org
Angela Hamlyn, Director, Media & Communications
ahamlyn@cim.org
Serge Major, Director, Finance & Admininstration
smajor@cim.org

Deborah Sauvé, Manager, Canadian Mining Metallurgical Foundation
dsauve@cim.org
Membership: 12,000+; *Member Profile: Professionals in the Canadian minerals, metals, materials, & energy sectors, from industry, government, & academia; Committees: Central Publications; Audit; Bulletin; By-Laws; CIM Valuation of Mineral Properties; Education; Estimation Guidelines; Human Resources; International Advisory Liaison; Membership; President Elect Nominating; Public Affairs; Special Volumes*
Activities: Providing technical forums & professional networking opportunities; Offering continuing education; Recognizing excellent programs; *Speaker Service: Yes Library: Canadian Institute of Mining, Metallurgy & Petroleum Library*
Publications: CIM [Canadian Institute of Mining, Metallurgy & Petroleum] Magazine
Type: Magazine *Frequency:* 7 pa *Accepts Advertising ISSN:* 1718-4177 *Price:* Free for members; $160 non-members in Canada
Profile: Editorials, technical information, industry events, & industry information
CIM [Canadian Institute of Mining, Metallurgy & Petroleum] Directory
Type: Directory *Frequency:* Annually
Profile: Listing of individual & corporate CIM members
CIM [Canadian Institute of Mining, Metallurgy & Petroleum] Reporter
Frequency: Annually
Profile: Official publication of the annual CIM Conference & Exhibition, for all registered delegates & visitors

Canadian Oil Heat Association (COHA)
#202, 115 Apple Creek Blvd., Markham ON L3R 6C9
Tel: 905-946-0264; Fax: 905-946-0316
Toll-Free: 800-257-1593
oilheat@coha.ca
www.coha.ca
Overview: A small national organization founded in 1983
Finances: *Annual Operating Budget: $250,000-$500,000*
Staff: 3 staff member(s)
Membership: 400; *Fees: $300 - $18,000; Member Profile: Oil companies; HVAC manufacturers & suppliers; service contractors; Committees: Technical Development & Education; Marketing; Membership; Certification & Training*
Activities: Promoting the benefits of residential fuel oil to the consumer public
Publications: COHA [Canadian Oil Heat Association] Directory
Type: Directory
Profile: Listing of equipment wholesalers & manufacturers, fuel oil suppliers, & service contractors
Today's Oilheat Newsletter
Type: Newsletter

Canadian Petroleum Law Foundation
PO Box 4143, Stn. C, Calgary AB T2T 5M9
Tel: 403-237-2423
lara.h.pella@esso.ca
www.cplf.org
Overview: A small national organization founded in 1963
Chief Officer(s):
Ben Rogers, President
ben.rogers@blakes.com
Miles Pittman, Treasurer
miles.pittman@fmc-law.com

Canadian Petroleum Products Institute (CPPI) / Institut canadien des produits pétroliers (ICPP)
#1000, 275 Slater St., Ottawa ON K1P 5H9
Tel: 613-232-3709; Fax: 613-236-4280
www.cppi.ca
Overview: A large national organization founded in 1989
Membership: 10; *Member Profile: Companies engaged in petroleum refining, marketing & distribution*
Activities: Training & education; news releases, reports & technical documents; Driver Certification Program for petroleum transport drivers

Canadian Propane Association (CPA) / Association canadienne du propane (ACP)
#616, 130 Albert St., Ottawa ON K1P 5G4
Tel: 613-683-2270; Fax: 613-683-2279
info@propane.ca
www.propane.ca
twitter.com/Propanedotca
Merged from: Propane Gas Association of Canada Inc.; Ontario Propane Association
Overview: A medium-sized national licensing organization founded in 2011
Chief Officer(s):
Jim Facette, President & CEO
jimfacette@propane.ca
Steven Sparling, Chair
Allison Mallette, Manager, Research & Communications, 647-340-2208
allisonmallette@propane.ca
Peter Maddox, Regional Manager, Ontario, 416-903-8518
petermaddox@propane.ca
Finances: *Funding Sources: Membership dues*
Staff: 7 staff member(s)
Membership: 400+; *Fees: Schedule available; Member Profile: Producers; Wholesalers; Retailers; Transporters; Manufacturers of appliances, cylinders, & equipment; Associates*
Activities: Providing industry related training & emergency response; Promoting the interests of the industry; Engaging in regulatory relations
Publications: CPA Bulletin
Type: Newsletter *Frequency:* Bimonthly
Profile: For members
CPA Newsletter
Type: Newsletter *Frequency:* Monthly
Profile: For members

Canadian Public Works Association (CPWA) / Association canadienne des travaux publics
797 Somerset St. West, Ottawa ON K1R 6R3
Tel: 202-408-9541; Fax: 202-408-9542
Toll-Free: 800-848-2792
cpwa@cpwa.net
www.cpwa.net
Overview: A medium-sized national organization founded in 1986
Chief Officer(s):
Peter King, Executive Director
pking@apwa.net
Gail Clark, Manager, International Affairs
gclark@apwa.net
Brent Colbert, Consultant, Government Relations
bcolbert@tactix.ca
Laura Bynum, Contact, Media Relations
lbynum@apwa.net
Membership: *Member Profile: Public works employees in Canada who are members of the American Public Works Association; Any person or organization in Canada with an interest in infrastructure & public works issues*
Activities: Engaging in advocacy projects; Producing position statements; Facilitating the exchange of information for public works employees

Canadian Renewable Energy Association (CanREA)
new.canrea.ca/site
Overview: A large national organization
Membership: 16; *Member Profile: Registered and incorporated not-for-profit organizations which actively promote renewable energy policy and implementation and are in good standing under applicable laws*
Activities: Conferences

Canadian Society of Petroleum Geologists (CSPG)
#110, 333 - 5th Ave. SW, Calgary AB T2P 1G7
Tel: 403-264-5610; Fax: 403-264-5898
cspg@cspg.org
www.cspg.org
www.linkedin.com/groups/Canadian-Society-Petroleum-Geologists-4153517
www.facebook.com/CSPGOnline
Previous Name: Alberta Society of Petroleum Geologists
Overview: A medium-sized national organization founded in 1929
Chief Officer(s):
Lis Bjeld, Executive Director, 403-513-1235
lis.bjeld@cspg.org
Finances: *Annual Operating Budget: $250,000-$500,000; Funding Sources: Membership dues; publications; programs; trust fund*
Staff: 3 staff member(s); 300 volunteer(s)
Membership: 3,500; *Fees: $65; $20 students; $500 corporate*
Activities: Education trust fund; member programs
Publications: The Bulletin of Canadian Petroleum Geology
Type: Journal *Frequency:* Quarterly *Accepts Advertising Editor:* Denise Then *ISSN:* 0007-4802 *Price:* $120 Canada; $140USA; $170 International
Profile: Peer-reviewed scientific articles, technical papers, book reviews, & debates of interest to the Canadian petroleum geoscience community
Canadian Society of Petroleum Geologists Calendar
Frequency: Annually
Profile: Photographs & CSPG, CSEG, APEGGA, & CWLS events
Digital Atlas: Geological Atlas of the Western Canada Sedimentary Basin
Profile: Created by CSPG & the Alberta Geologic Survey (AGS)
Reservoir [a publication of the Canadian Society of Petroleum Geologists]
Type: Magazine *Frequency:* 11 pa *Accepts Advertising Editor:* Heather Tyminski *Price:* $60 Canada; $70 USA; $80International
Profile: Industry articles & commentaries, conferences, upcoming events, & awards of interest to CSPG members

Canadian Telecommunications Consultants Association (CTCA)
PO Box 361, St. Davids ON L0S 1P0
Tel: 289-477-1465; Fax: 866-584-2822
Toll-Free: 866-584-2822
admin@ctca.ca; membership@ctca.ca
www.ctca.ca
Overview: A small national organization founded in 1985
Chief Officer(s):
Michael Rozender, President
Finances: *Funding Sources: Membership dues; conference registrations*
Membership: 1-99; *Fees: $378.55 affiliate; $452 associate; $525.45 consultant; $728.85 supplier liaison group - primary representative; Member Profile: Independent telecommunications consultants*
Activities: Providing networking, collaboration, & educational opportunities for members; Promoting integrity, competence, & professionalism among members according to its Code of Ethics & Professional Conduct; *Speaker Service: Yes*

Canadian Water & Wastewater Association (CWWA) / Association canadienne des eaux potables et usées (ACEPU)
#11, 1010 Polytek St., Ottawa ON K1J 9H9
Tel: 613-747-0524; Fax: 613-747-0523
tdellison@cwwa.ca
www.cwwa.ca
Overview: A medium-sized national organization founded in 1986
Chief Officer(s):
Schmidt Thomas, President
Membership: *Member Profile: Utility members are owners or operators of municipal infrastructure or services; Associate members are the private sector & academics; Subscription members are federal, provincial, or territorial government departments or agencies; Committees: Wastewater & Stormwater; National Water Efficiency; Drinking Water Quality; Water Protection Information; Biosolids; Energy*
Activities: Monitoring policies, legislation, & standards; Liaising with federal & interprovincial organizations; Hosting workshops; Facilitating networking opportunities; Increasing & improving public awareness; Cooperating with regional water & wastewater associations
Publications: Canadian Municipal Water News & Review / Journal et faits sur l'eau municipale canadienne
Type: Magazine *Frequency:* Semiannually *Accepts Advertising*
Profile: National & international news & events
Canadian Water & Wastewater Association Conference Proceedings
CWWA [Canadian Water & Wastewater Association] Membership Directory
Type: Directory *Accepts Advertising*
Profile: Directory acts as association information as well as a buyers' guide
CWWA [Canadian Water & Wastewater Association] Bulletin
Type: Newsletter *Frequency:* 10 pa *Accepts Advertising*
Profile: National information on water & wastewater developments, for CWWA members
CWWA Members' Briefing Book: Current National Issues & Topics Concerning Water & Wastewater Management in Canada
Frequency: Quarterly
Profile: Briefing notes on current management topics that are national in nature, to assist managers & operators
Directory of Sources of Contaminants Entering Municipal Sewer Systems
Type: Directory
Profile: Aid in identifying industrial, commercial, & institutional sources of contaminants entering municipal sewage treatment plants
Guideline on Sampling, Handling, Transporting, & Analyzing Legal Wastewater Samples
Meters Made Easy: A Guide to the Economic Appraisal of Alternative Metering Investment Strategies
Type: Guidebook
Profile: A tool to assist system owners & operators determine whether the introduction of meters will produce long-term savings intheir community
Municipal Water & Wastewater Rate Manual
Type: Manual
Profile: New & alternative approaches to traditional & current rate setting methods
Municipal Water & Wastewater Rates Primer
Type: Monograph
Profile: An overview of topics on rate setting

National Water Works Operator Training Manuals
Type: Manual
Survey on Chloramine in Drinking Water Disinfection
Water Safety Plans for Municipal Drinking Water Systems
Profile: Hazard Analysis & Critical Control Points (HACCP) plan for the source, treatment, & distribution of drinking water in Canada
Water Treatment Principles & Applications

Canadian Water Quality Association (CWQA)
#330, 295 The West Mall, Toronto ON M9C 4Z4
Tel: 416-695-3068; *Fax:* 416-695-2945
Toll-Free: 866-383-7617
k.wong@cwqa.com
www.cwqa.com
www.linkedin.com/groups/Canadian-Water-Quality-Association-3948494
Overview: A medium-sized national organization founded in 1967
Chief Officer(s):
Kevin Wong, Executive Director
Membership: 106 dealers/distributors + 16 manufacturers/suppliers + 10 associates; *Fees: $355 associate; Based on volume for dealer/distributor & manufacturer/supplier*
Publications: Canadian Water Quality Association Membership Directory
Type: Directory
Profile: A listing of members by their head office or main facility, for use by Canadian Water Quality Association members only
Communiqué [a publication of the Canadian Water Quality Association]
Frequency: 11 pa

Canadian Wind Energy Association Inc. (CanWEA) / Association canadienne d'énergie éolienne
#810, 170 Laurier Ave. West, Ottawa ON K1P 5V5
Tel: 613-234-8716; *Fax:* 613-234-5642
Toll-Free: 800-922-6932
info@canwea.ca
www.canwea.ca
twitter.com/canwindenergy
Overview: A small national organization founded in 1984
Chief Officer(s):
Robert Hornung, President
Chris Forrest, Vice-President, Communications & Marketing
Sean Whittaker, Vice-President, Policy
Penelope Feather, Director, Finance
Janice Taylor, Director, Conference & Events
Finances: *Funding Sources: Membership fees; Conference & workshop fees*
Membership: 420; *Member Profile: Organizations & individuals who are involved in the development & application of wind energy technology, products, & services in Canada*
Activities: Providing information about wind energy; Offering networking opportunities for all stakeholders; Facilitating research; Forming strategic alliances; *Library: Canadian Wind Energy Association Library by appointment*
Publications: CanWEA Members Directory
Type: Directory
Profile: Contact information & a profile of each CanWEA member
WindLink
Type: Newsletter *Frequency:* Semimonthly
Profile: Issues & events that affect the Canadian wind energy for CanWEA members, policymakers, & the public
WindSight
Type: Magazine *Frequency:* Quarterly
Profile: Detailed articles on Canadian wind energy projects & policy

Clean Energy BC
#354, 409 Granville St., Vancouver BC V6C 1T2
Tel: 604-568-4778; *Fax:* 604-568-4724
Toll-Free: 855-568-4778
www.cleanenergybc.org
twitter.com/CleanEnergyBC
Previous Name: *Independent Power Association of BC*
Overview: A small provincial organization founded in 1992
Chief Officer(s):
Paul Kariya, Executive Director
paul.kariya@cleanenergybc.org
Loch McJannett, Vice-President
loch.mcjannett@cleanenergybc.org
Lisa Bateman, Coordinator, Events
lisa.bateman@cleanenergybc.org
Kristen McIntyre, Contact, Membership Services, Registration, & Administration
kristen.mcintyre@cleanenergybc.org
Activities: Engaging in policy implementation

Coalition for Competitive Telecommunications
#880, 45 O'Connor St., Ottawa ON K1P 1A4
Tel: 613-566-7053; *Fax:* 613-566-2026
stikeman@tactix.ca
Overview: A small national organization founded in 2003

Communications, Energy & Paperworkers Union of Canada (CEP) / Syndicat canadien des communications, de l'énergie et du papier (SCEP)
301 Laurier Ave. West, Ottawa ON K1P 6M6
Tel: 613-230-5200; *Fax:* 613-230-5801
Toll-Free: 877-230-5201
info@cep.ca
www.cep.ca
www.facebook.com/group.php?gid=14453572223
Overview: A large national organization founded in 1992
Chief Officer(s):
Gaétan Ménard, Sec.-Treas.
gmenard@cep.ca
Dave Coles, President
dcoles@cep.ca
Finances: *Annual Operating Budget: Greater than $5 Million; Funding Sources: Membership dues*
Staff: 150 staff member(s)
Membership: 167,470 + 853 locals; *Committees: Health & Safety; Pensions; Women's; Special Committees*
Activities: Education Program; *Library: Yes*

Community Energy Association (cea)
#1400, 333 Seymour St., Vancouver BC V6B 5A6
Tel: 604-628-7076; *Fax:* 778-786-1613
info@communityenergy.bc.ca
www.communityenergy.bc.ca
Overview: A medium-sized provincial charitable organization founded in 1993
Chief Officer(s):
Dale Littlejohn, Executive Director
dlittlejohn@communityenergy.bc.ca
Patricia Bell, Senior Community Energy Planner
pbell@communityenergy.bc.ca
Megan Lohmann, Senior Energy Planner, 250-423-7212
Finances: *Funding Sources: Membership revenues; Fundraising*
Activities: Communicating with elected officials, municipal & regional district staff, & First Nations in British Columbia; Offering advisory services to local governments regarding energy innovations; Promoting energy efficiency & renewable energy for infrastructure; Encouraging local governments to consider energy in land planning & development; Conducting research on energy related topics; *Speaker Service: Yes*
Publications: Community Energy Association Directory
Type: Directory
Profile: Listings of association members
Energy Brief for Elected Officials
Type: Guide
Profile: Information for local government leaders
Heating Our Communities
Type: Guide
Profile: A renewable energy guide produced for local government leaders

Compressed Gas Association, Inc. (CGA)
#103, 14501 George Carter Way, Chantilly VA 20151 USA
Tel: 703-788-2700; *Fax:* 703-961-1831
cga@cganet.com; customerservice@cganet.com
www.cganet.com
Overview: A small international organization founded in 1913
Membership: *Member Profile: Manufacturers, suppliers, distributors, & transporters of gases, cryogenic liquids, & related products in Canada & the United States; Committees: Canadian Cylinder Specification; Canadian Medical, Food, & Beverage Gases & Equipment; Canadian Pressure Vessels & Piping Sys.; Canadian Health, Safety, & Environment; Canadian Transportation; Acetylene; Atmospheric Gases & Equipment; Bulk Distribution Equipment & Standards; Carbon Dioxide; Compressed Gas Emergency Action Plan; Cylinder Specifications; Cylinder Valve; Distribution & Fleet Safety; Environmental; Food Gases; Hazard Comm.; Hazardous Materials Codes; Hydrogen Tech.; HYCO; Industrial Gases Apparatus; Liquefied Petroleum Gas; Medical Equipment; Medical Gases; Security; Safety/Health*
Activities: Working with governmental agencies to produce standards & regulations; Promoting compliance with regulations in the workplace; Providing access to edcuational publications & videos; Offering networking opportunities
Publications: Compressions [a publication of the Compressed Gas Association]
Type: Newsletter *Frequency:* Quarterly *Price:* Free with Compressed Gas Association membership
Profile: Association & industry news

Electricity Distributors Association (EDA)
#1100, 3700 Steeles Ave. West, Vaughan ON L4L 8K8
Tel: 905-265-5300; *Fax:* 905-265-5301
Toll-Free: 800-668-9979
email@eda-on.ca
www.eda-on.ca
Previous Name: *Municipal Electric Association*
Overview: A large provincial organization founded in 1986
Chief Officer(s):
C.C. (Charlie) Macaluso, President & CEO, Administration
Tanya Fobear, Coordinator, Communications & Member Relations
Charlie Macaluso, President & CEO
Finances: *Annual Operating Budget: Greater than $5 Million; Funding Sources: Membership dues*
Staff: 18 staff member(s); 100 volunteer(s)
Membership: 256; *Fees: $750 commercial member; Member Profile: Public & privately owned electricity distributors*

Electricity Sector Council / Conseil sectoriel de l'electricité
#600, 130 Slater Street, Ottawa ON K1P 6E2
Tel: 613-235-5540; *Fax:* 613-235-6922
info@brightfutures.ca
www.brightfutures.ca
Overview: A medium-sized national organization

Electro-Federation Canada Inc. (EFC)
#300, 180 Attwell Dr., Toronto ON M9W 6A9
Tel: 905-602-8877; *Fax:* 905-602-5686
Toll-Free: 866-602-8877
info@electrofed.com
www.electrofed.com
twitter.com/EFC_Tweets
Overview: A medium-sized national organization founded in 1995
Chief Officer(s):
Milos Jancik, President/CEO
mjancik@electrofed.com
Ken Frankum, Chair
Harald Henze, Treasurer
Larry Moore, Vice-President, Consumer Councils
lmoore@electrofed.com
Joseph Neu, Vice-President, Engineering, Codes & Standards
jneu@electrofed.com
Membership: 300 companies; *Member Profile: Companies that manufacture, distribute, & service electrical, electronics, & telecommunications products; Committees: Canadian Appliance Manufacturers Association; Consumer Electronics Marketers of Canada; Electrical Equipment Manufacturers Association of Canada; Supply & Manufacturers' Reps Councils; Installation Maintenance & Repair Sector Council & Trade Association; Electro-Federation Canada Alumni Association*
Activities: Collecting & disseminating market data; Providing networking opportunities; Hosting annual conferences; Researching; Offering educational programs; Communicating with members; Promoting the industry; Conducting surveys

Energy Council of Canada / Conseil canadien de l'énergie
#608, 350 Sparks St., Ottawa ON K1R 7S8
Tel: 613-232-8239; *Fax:* 613-232-1079
krystal.piamonte@energy.ca
www.energy.ca
Previous Name: *World Energy Council - Canadian Member Committee*
Overview: A medium-sized national organization founded in 1924
Chief Officer(s):
Murray J. Stewart, President
murray.stewart@energy.ca
Brigitte Svarich, Director, Operations
brigitte.svarich@energy.ca
Membership: 75+; *Member Profile: Representatives from all facets of Canada's energy sector*
Activities: Providing networking opportunities; Sponsoring forums & conferences; Disseminating current energy reports & information; Contributing to the development of the Canadian energy policy

Energy Probe Research Foundation (EPRF)
225 Brunswick Ave., Toronto ON M5S 2M6
Tel: 416-964-9223; *Fax:* 416-964-8239
webadmin@eprf.ca
www.eprf.ca
Overview: A large national charitable organization founded in 1980
Chief Officer(s):
Patricia Adams, President
Lawrence Solomon, Managing Director
Finances: *Annual Operating Budget: $1.5 Million-$3 Million; Funding Sources: Donations*

Staff: 15 staff member(s); 10 volunteer(s)
Membership: 50,000 supporters
Activities: Policy research & education; *Internships: Yes; Speaker Service: Yes Library: Yes (Open to Public)*

Enform: The Safety Association for the Upstream Oil & Gas Industry
Head Office, 5055 - 11th St. NE, Calgary AB T2E 8N4
Tel: 403-516-8000; Fax: 403-516-8166
Toll-Free: 800-667-5557
customerservice@enform.ca
www.enform.ca
Previous Name: *Petroleum Industry Training Service*
Overview: A large national licensing charitable organization founded in 2005
Chief Officer(s):
Duane Mather, Chair
Wallace E. Baer, President, 403-250-0875
wbaer@enform.ca
L. Harman, Vice President, Operations
R. Ogilvie, Vice President, Corporate Services
Activities: Providing training courses; Offering saftey information; Promoting shared safety practices in the Canadian oil & gas industry; Providing the Small Employers Certificate of Recognition (SECOR), the Certificate of Recognition (COR), & the Petroleum Competency Program

Fondation Hydro-Québec pour l'environnement / Hydro-Québec Foundation for the Environment
740, rue Notre-Dame Ouest, 8e étage, Montréal QC H3C 3X6
Tél: 514-289-5384; Téléc: 514-289-2079
fondation_environnement@hydro.qc.ca
www.hydroquebec.com/fondation_environnement
Aperçu: *Dimension: petite; Envergure: provinciale*

Gas Processing Association Canada (GPAC)
#400, 1040 - 7th Ave. SW, Calgary AB T2P 3G9
Tel: 403-244-4487; Fax: 403-244-2340
info@gpacanada.com
www.gpacanada.com
Previous Name: *Canadian Gas Processors Association*
Overview: A medium-sized national organization founded in 1960
Chief Officer(s):
Josh Carter, President
Jeff McPhail, Director, Safety
Rob Nadalutti, Director, Academic
Erika Rauser, Coordinator, Events
Finances: *Funding Sources: Membership dues*
Staff: 17 volunteer(s)
Membership: 450 individual; *Fees: $75 Regular, $9 Retired; Member Profile: Open to those employed in companies processing gaseous & liquid hydrocarbons; Committees: Safety; Research; Environment; Membership; Publications*
Activities: *Library: Yes*

Independent Power Producers Society of Alberta (IPPSA)
#2600, 144 - 4th Ave. SW, Calgary AB T2P 3N4
Fax: 403-256-8342
www.ippsa.com
Overview: A small provincial organization founded in 1993
Chief Officer(s):
Evan Bahry, Executive Director, 403-282-8811, Fax: 403-256-8342
Evan.Bahry@ippsa.com
Joe Novecosky, Contact, Membership & Events, 403-256-1587, Fax: 403-256-8342
joeno@telusplanet.net
Membership: 100+; *Fees: $10,000 power member; $5,000 junior power member; $1,000 corporate member; $250 associate member; Member Profile: Operators of Alberta's power supply*
Activities: Engaging with Alberta's government & its agencies in policy development; Reviewing legislation, regulations, & market rules; Promoting competition in Alberta's electrical market; Providing news about the industry; Sponsoring a bursary for a student at the University of Calgary's Schulich School of Engineering (Electricity Department)
Publications: IPPSA [Independent Power Producer Society of Alberta] News
Type: Newsletter *Frequency:* 5 pa
Profile: Industry happenings for IPPSA members

Industrial Gas Users Association Inc. (IGUA) / Association des consommateurs industriels de gaz (ACIG)
#502, 350 Sparks St., Ottawa ON K1R 7S8
Tel: 613-236-8021; Fax: 613-230-9531
www.igua.ca
Overview: A medium-sized national organization founded in 1973
Chief Officer(s):
Murray Newton, President
mnewton@igua.ca
Ghislaine Carrière, Manager, Accounting & Office Services
gcarriere@igua.ca
Finances: *Annual Operating Budget: $500,000-$1.5 Million; Funding Sources: Membership dues*
Staff: 3 staff member(s)
Membership: 39 corporate; *Fees: Based on gas consumption, $1,200-$36,099; Member Profile: Open to end users of natural gas*

Infrastructure Health & Safety Association (IHSA)
Centre for Health & Safety Innovation, #400, 5110 Creekbank Rd., Mississauga ON L4W 0A1
Tel: 905-625-0100; Fax: 905-625-8998
Toll-Free: 800-263-5024
info@ihsa.ca
www.ihsa.ca
ca.linkedin.com/pub/ihsa-news/41/986/aa3
twitter.com/IHSAnews
Merged from: CSAO; E&USA; THSAO
Overview: A medium-sized provincial organization founded in 2010
Chief Officer(s):
Al Beattie, Chief Executive Officer & President
Activities: Providing training that meets regulatory requirements & compliance standards
Publications: Infrastructure Health & Safety Association Annual Report
Type: Yearbook *Frequency:* Annually
Profile: Departmental updates & financial statements

Institute of Power Engineers (IPE)
PO Box 878, Burlington ON L7R 3Y7
Tel: 905-333-3348; Fax: 905-333-9328
ipenat@nipe.ca
www.nipe.ca
Overview: A medium-sized national organization founded in 1940
Chief Officer(s):
Jude Rankin, National President
Bruce King, 1st National Vice President
Don Purser, National Secretary
Finances: *Annual Operating Budget: $50,000-$100,000*
Staff: 1400 volunteer(s)
Membership: 1,420; *Fees: $60; Member Profile: Persons holding certificates of qualification as recognized by the Institute; persons enrolled in recognized power engineering courses; persons engaged in any pursuit identified or allied with power engineering*

International Academy of Energy, Minerals, & Materials (AEMM)
Esprit Dr., Ottawa ON K4A 4Z1
Tel: 613-322-1029; Fax: 613-830-8371
info@iaemm.com
Overview: A medium-sized international organization
Publications: Additives & Surfactants
Price: $185
Anode Materials for Lithium Ion Batteries — Patent Review, Market Trends, & Mmore
Price: $350
Hard Metal Process, Application & Analysis
Price: $235
Hydrometallurgy
Price: $225
Ore Analysis, Handling, & Preparation
Price: $225
Physical & Chemical Separation
Price: $225
Plant Optimisation & Control
Price: $225
Pyrometallurgy
Price: $225

International Association for Hydrogen Energy (IAHE)
#303, 5794 40th St. SW, Miami FL 33155 USA
info@iahe.org
www.iahe.org
Overview: A medium-sized international organization
Membership: *Member Profile: Professional persons in fields related to hydrogen energy; Laypersons with an interest in hydrogen energy; IAHE Fellows; Emeritus members; Students*
Publications: International Journal of Hydrogen Energy
Type: Journal *Editor:* Emre A. Veziroglu *ISBN:* 0360-3199
Profile: Ideas in the field of hydrogen energy for environmentalists, chemists, energy researchers, energy companies, & engineering students

International Atomic Energy Agency (IAEA) / Agence internationale de l'énergie atomique
Vienna International Centre, PO Box 100, Wagramer Strasse 5, Vienna A-1400 Austria
official.mail@iaea.org
www.iaea.org
Social Media: www.youtube.com/user/IAEAvideo; www.flickr.com/photos/iaea_imagebank
www.facebook.com/iaeaorg
twitter.com/iaeaorg
Overview: A large international organization founded in 1957
Finances: *Annual Operating Budget: Greater than $5 Million; Funding Sources: Member states contributions*
Staff: 2307 staff member(s)
Membership: 140 sovereign states; *Fees: Percentage of share of regular budget is fixed by UN General Assembly; Member Profile: Intergovernmental organization; Committees: Board of Governors of 35 member states*
Activities: Verification in framework of Nuclear Non-Proliferation Treaty (NPT) that over 1,000 nuclear facilities in over 60 non-nuclear weapon states are used for peaceful purposes only; *Library: Yes by appointment*

International Atomic Energy Agency: Canadian Regional Office
Stn. 20, #1702, 365 Bloor St. East, Toronto ON M4W 3L4
Tel: 416-928-9149; Fax: 416-928-0046
official.mail@iaea.org
www.iaea.org
Overview: A large international organization

International Electrotechnical Commission - Canadian National Committee (IEC-CNC) / Commission Électrotechnique Internationale - Comité National du Canada (CEI-CNC)
#200, 270 Albert St., Ottawa ON K1P 6n7
Tel: 613-238-3222; Fax: 613-569-7808
www.scc.ca/acronyms_glossary/article?classPK=agl-iec
Overview: A medium-sized international organization founded in 1912
Finances: *Funding Sources: Parliamentary appropriation; corporate sponsors; individuals*
Staff: 2 staff member(s); 1000 volunteer(s)
Membership: 16; *Committees: Approx. 100, paralleling the IEC committee structure*

International Energy Foundation (IEF)
Clear Mountain Estates, PO Box 64, Site 8, RR#1, Okotoks AB T1S 1A1
Tel: 403-938-6210; Fax: 403-938-6210
chairman@ief-energy.org
www.ief-energy.org
Overview: A medium-sized international charitable organization founded in 1989
Finances: *Annual Operating Budget: $100,000-$250,000; Funding Sources: Contributions, donations, subventions, aids & grants made by donors & benefactors; fees for membership*
Staff: 50 volunteer(s)
Membership: fellows in 49 countries, committee members in 175 countries; *Member Profile: Open to all professionals, educational institutes, industries, governmental or quasi-governmental bodies operating in the field of energy; Committees: Constitution & Bylaws; External Administrative Centres; External & Internal Meetings; Finance; Goals & Objectives; Membership; Publications & Public Relations*
Activities: Conferences, symposiums, workshops; *Speaker Service: Yes*

International Institute for Energy Conservation (IIEC)
#100, 10005 Leamoore Lane, Vienna VA 22181 USA
Tel: 703-281-7263; Fax: 703-938-5153
iiec@iiec.org
www.iiec.org
Overview: A medium-sized international organization founded in 1984

International Solar Energy Society (ISES)
International Headquarters, Villa Tannheim, Wiesentalstrasse 50, Freiburg 79115 Germany
hq@ises.org
www.ises.org
Overview: A medium-sized international charitable organization founded in 1954
Membership: 4,000; *Fees: Schedule available; Member Profile: Persons engaged in the research development & utilisation of solar energy & persons who have an interest in advancing the purposes of the society*
Activities: All aspects of solar energy, including characteristics, effects & methods of use; international congresses on solar energy
Publications: Solar Energy
Type: Journal *Frequency:* Monthly *Editor:* Dr. D. Yogi Goswami

International Solid Waste Association (ISWA)
Auerspergstrasse 15, Top 41, Vienna 1080 Austria
iswa@iswa.dk
www.iswa.org
www.facebook.com/group.php?gid=123367611068687
Overview: A medium-sized international organization founded in 1931
Finances: *Funding Sources: Sponsorships*
Membership: *Member Profile: Non-profit waste management associations representing the waste management industry in a particular country; Organizations or companies associated with or working in the field of waste management*
Activities: Promoting professionalism; Supporting developing countries
Publications: Global News [a publication of the International Solid Waste Association]
Type: Newsletter
Profile: Contents include news from the association president, conference information, awards, news from around the world, & forthcoming events
International Solid Waste Association Conference Proceedings
Type: Yearbook *Frequency:* Annually
Profile: Information from the International Solid Waste Association Annual Congress, the Beacon Conference, & other conferences organized by the association
International Solid Waste Association Annual Report
Type: Yearbook *Frequency:* Annually
Waste Management & Research
Type: Journal *Frequency:* Monthly *Editor:* Jens Aage Hansen
Profile: The theory & practice of waste management & research
Waste Management World
Type: Magazine *Frequency:* Bimonthly *Accepts Advertising*
Editor: Tom Freyberg
Profile: Incorporates the International Directory of Solid Waste Management, with a listing of ISWA members & waste management companies

International Telecommunications Society (ITS)
Bohdan (Don) Romaniuk, ITS Secretariat, 416 Wilverside Way SE, Calgary AB T2J 1Z7
secretariat@itsworld.org
www.itsworld.org
Overview: A small international organization
Chief Officer(s):
Erik Bohlin, Chair
erik.bohlin@chalmers.se
Stanford Levin, Chair, Membership & Nominations
slevin@siue.edu
Gary Madden, Chair, Publications
maddeng@cbs.curtin.edu.au
Teodosio Pérez Amaral, Chair, Conference & Seminars
teodosio@ccee.ucm.es
Leland W. Schmidt, Chair, Finance
lschmidt@metrocast.net
Membership: 400; *Member Profile: Professionals from the communications, technology, & information sectors; Committees: Strategic Planning; Conference & Seminars; Publications; Membership & Nominations; Finance; Marketing & Promotions; Web Development*
Activities: Organizing courses, seminars, & workshops; Disseminating research results & news to members & the public
Publications: Interconnect [a publication of the International Telecommunications Society]
Type: Newsletter *Editor:* Don Romaniuk
Profile: Member profiles, conference information, committee reports, & society news

Manitoba Water & Wastewater Association (MWWA)
PO Box 1600, #215, 9 Saskatchewan Ave. West, 2nd Fl., Portage la Prairie MB R1N 3P1
Tel: 204-239-6868; Fax: 204-239-6872
Toll-Free: 866-396-2549
mwwa@mts.net
www.mwwa.net
www.facebook.com/group.php?gid=167933616574016
Overview: A small provincial organization founded in 1975
Activities: Exchnaging information & experiences
Publications: Waterways [a publication of the Manitoba Water & Wastewater Association]
Type: Newsletter
Profile: Information for members about upcoming conferences & educational opportunities

The Maritimes Energy Association
Cambridge Tower 1, #305, 202 Brownlow Ave., Dartmouth NS B3B 1T5
Tel: 902-425-4774; Fax: 902-422-2332
info@maritimesenergy.com
www.maritimesenergy.com
twitter.com/MEnergyAssoc
Previous Name: *Offshore / Onshore Technologies Association of Nova Scotia (OTANS)*
Overview: A small provincial organization founded in 1982
Chief Officer(s):
Sue Ritter, Chair
Barbara Pike, Executive Director
barbara@maritimesenergy.com
Sara Colburne, Manager, Events & Sponsorship
sara@maritimesenergy.com
Lori Peddle, Manager, Business & Operations
lori@maritimesenergy.com
Amanda White, Manager, Trade Missions & Member Services
amanda@maritimesenergy.com
Tim Gilfoy, Treasurer
Membership: 300+; *Fees: $42 student membership; $475 companies with 1-10 employees; $712.50 businesses with 11-50 employees; $950 for companies with 51 or more employees; Member Profile: Businesses throughout Atlantic Canada that supply goods & services to the energy sector, including the gas, oil, wind, tidal, & solar industries*
Activities: Collaborating with provincial & federal governments & regulatory authories; Facilitating trade missions to investigate export opportunities; Advocating for the interests of the energy industry; Conducting policy research; Offering industry history & news; Organizing sessions with guest speakers who address current topics of interest in the energy industry; Providing networking opportunities
Publications: The Maritimes Energy Association Annual Report with Financials
Type: Yearbook *Frequency:* Annually
Profile: Contents include messages from the chair, executive committee, & board of directors, as well as industry activity in the maritime region, events, &committees
The Maritimes Energy Association Daily Energy Bulletin
Type: Newsletter *Frequency:* Daily
Profile: Current events of interest to members of the energy industry in Eastern Canada, such as notices of trade shows, association events, news releases from membercompanies, & procurement opportunities
The Maritimes Energy Association Directory
Type: Directory
Profile: A listing of association members with company profiles & contact information

Municipal Engineers Association (MEA)
#2, 6355 Kennedy Rd., Mississauga ON L5T 2L5
Tel: 905-795-2555; Fax: 905-795-2660
info@municipalengineers.on.ca
www.municipalengineers.on.ca
Overview: A medium-sized provincial organization founded in 1974
Chief Officer(s):
Rick A. Kester, President, 905-795-2555, Fax: 905-795-2660
J. David Shantz, Executive Director
Gary Carroll, Vice-President
Trevor D. Lewis, Treasurer
Membership: *Member Profile: Public sector professional engineers in full time employment of municipalities, who perform functions in the field of municipal engineering; Committees: Administrative & Seconded; Municipal Transportation Advisory; MEA/CEO Liaison; Development Engineering; MEA/MNR/CO Liaison; MEA Training; MEA/MOE Liaison; Ontario Works Network; Tri-Committee Board*
Activities: Organizing training events; Advocating for sound municipal engineering; Championing positions on municipal engineering issues; Recognizing achievements of municipal engineers
Publications: Annual Report of the Municipal Engineers Association Administrative & Standing Committees
Type: Yearbook *Frequency:* Annually
Profile: A review of the year's activities
Municipal Engineers Association Members Directory
Type: Directory

Municipal Equipment & Operations Association (Ontario) Inc.
ON
Tel: 519-741-2600; Fax: 519-741-2750
admin@meoa.org; stcc@meoa.org (safety matters)
www.meoa.org
Also Known As: MEOA
Overview: A small provincial organization founded in 1965
Chief Officer(s):
Greg Lancaster, Contact
Finances: *Funding Sources: Annual membership dues*
Membership: 250; *Member Profile: Supervisory employees & management support staff from any government body; Suppliers of equipment & services used by municipal corporate organizations; Honorary members who have been beneficial to the association; Affiliate members who have an interest in the association*
Activities: Offering education & training; Organizing field trips; Facilitating the exchange of information; Providing networking opportunities

National Energy Conservation Association Inc. (NECA) / Association nationale pour la conservation de l'énergie
250 McDermot Ave., Winnipeg MB R3B 0S5
Tel: 204-956-5888; Fax: 204-956-5819
Toll-Free: 800-263-5974
neca@neca.ca
www.neca.ca
Previous Name: *National Insulation & Energy Conservation Contractors Association*
Overview: A medium-sized national organization founded in 1983
Chief Officer(s):
Ryan Dalgleish, Contact, Business Development

National Solid Wastes Management Association (NSWMA)
#300, 4301 Connecticut Ave. NW, Washington DC 20008 USA
Tel: 202-244-4700; Fax: 202-966-4824
Toll-Free: 800-424-2869
www.nswma.org
www.facebook.com/group.php?gid=130041787022156
Overview: A medium-sized international organization founded in 1962
Membership: *Member Profile: For-profit companies in North America that provide solid, hazardous, & medical waste collection, recycling, & disposal services; Companies that provide professional & consulting services to the waste services industry*
Activities: Offering educational & training opportunities; Engaging in research; Facilitating networking; *Library: National Solid Wastes Management Association Library*
Publications: NSWMA [National Solid Wastes Management Association] e-News
Type: Newsletter
Profile: Timely information to help businesses make decisions

Natural Gas Employees' Association (NGEA)
#100, 10612 - 124th St. NW, Edmonton AB T5N 1S4
Tel: 780-483-9330; Fax: 780-469-2504
Toll-Free: 877-912-9330
ngea@shaw.ca
www.ngea.ca
Overview: A small national organization
Chief Officer(s):
Keith Hudson, President, 780-983-6569

NOIA
Atlantic Place, #602, 215 Water St., St. John's NL A1C 6C9
Tel: 709-758-6610; Fax: 709-758-6611
www.noianet.com
Also Known As: Newfoundland & Labrador Oil & Gas Industries Association
Overview: A medium-sized provincial organization founded in 1977
Chief Officer(s):
Robert Cadigan, President & CEO
Finances: *Annual Operating Budget: $500,000-$1.5 Million; Funding Sources: Membership fees; conferences, seminars & special events*
Staff: 10 staff member(s); 100 volunteer(s)
Membership: 450; *Fees: Schedule available; Member Profile: Those who develop, manufacture & market products & services in the oil & gas industry, both offshore & onshore; Committees: Board of Directors; Petroleum Research & Information; Membership Services & Internal Communications; External Relations; Finance & Human Resources; Policy & Positions*
Activities: Promotes development of East Coast Canada's hydrocarbon resources & facilitates its membership's participation in oil & gas industries; *Library: Yes by appointment*

Offshore Energy Research Association of Nova Scotia (OERA)
Bank of Montreal Building, #602, 5151 George St., Halifax NS B3J 1M5
Tel: 902-406-7010; Fax: 902-406-7019
Toll-Free: 888-257-8688
www.oera.ca
Merged from: Offshore Energy Environmental Research (OEER); Offshore Energy Technical Research (OETR)
Overview: A medium-sized provincial organization founded in 2012
Chief Officer(s):
Stephen Dempsey, Executive Director, 902-406-7011, Fax: 902-406-7019
Wanda Barrett, Manager, Operations, 902-406-7010, Fax: 902-406-7019

Jennifer Pinks, Manager, Research, 902-406-7013, Fax: 902-406-7019

Ontario Energy Association (OEA)
#409, 45 Sheppard Ave. East, Toronto ON M2N 5W9
Tel: 416-961-2339; Fax: 416-961-1173
oea@energyontario.ca; committees@energyontario.ca
www.energyontario.ca
www.linkedin.com/company/ontario-energy-association
twitter.com/ontarioenergy

Overview: A small provincial organization
Chief Officer(s):
Elise Herzig, President & Chief Executive Officer
Tina Arvanitis, Vice-President, Communications & Stakeholder Relations, 647-920-3269
tarvanitis@energyontario.ca
Finances: *Funding Sources: Sponsorships*
Membership: 150+ corporate members; *Member Profile: Members of Ontario's energy industry, such as power producers, manufacturers, contractors, service providers, energy retailers, marketers, energy distributors, & energy consultants; Committees: Energy Markets Joint Sector; Environment Joint Sector; Government Relations Joint Sector; Green Energy & Conservation Joint Sector; Marketers & Retailers Sector; Utility Sector*
Activities: Providing education & resources about the energy sector; Engaging in advocacy activities for members; Conducting research into energy matters; *Speaker Service: Yes*

Ontario Municipal Water Association (OMWA)
c/o Doug Parker, 43 Chelsea Cres., Belleville ON K8N 4Z5
Tel: 613-966-1100; Fax: 613-966-3024
Toll-Free: 888-231-1115
www.omwa.org

Overview: A medium-sized provincial organization
Chief Officer(s):
Ed Houghton, President
ehoughton@collus.com
Douglas Parker, Executive Director, 613-966-1100, Fax: 613-966-3024
dparker@omwa.org
Membership: 180+ public drinking water authorities in Ontario; *Fees: Schedule available, based upon population; Member Profile: Ontario's public water supply authorities*
Activities: Reviewing policy, & legislative, & regulatory issues; Liaising with government, agencies, & associations to maintain safe & sustainable water sources; Lobbying to improve conditions; Promoting high standards of treatment, infrastructure, & operations; Offering technical training for operating authorities, operators, & owners of drinking water systems; Encouraging dissemination of information for public education
Publications: Councillors Handbook: Stewardship Responsibilities Under the Safe Drinking Water Act
Type: Handbook
Ontario Municipal Water Association Members' Handbook
Type: Handbook

Ontario Petroleum Institute Inc. (OPI)
#104, 555 Southdale Rd. East, London ON N6E 1A2
Tel: 519-680-1620; Fax: 519-680-1621
www.ontpet.com

Overview: A medium-sized provincial organization founded in 1963
Chief Officer(s):
Hugh Moran, Executive Director
Finances: *Funding Sources: Sponsorships*
Membership: *Member Profile: Geologists in Ontario; Geophysicists; Explorationists; Producers; Contractors; Petroleum engineers; Companies involved in the oil & gas, hydrocarbon storage, & solution mining industries*
Activities: Liaising with government agencies; Disseminating information to members; Increasing public awareness of the importance of the industry in Ontario; *Library: Ontario Oil, Gas, & Salt Resources Library*
Publications: Ontario Oil & Gas
Type: Magazine *Accepts Advertising Editor:* Carly Peters
Profile: Articles about the oil & gas industry & technical features
Ontario Petroleum Institute Conference Proceedings
Frequency: Annually *Price:* $50
Profile: Topics presented by guest speakers from around the world at the Institute's annual conference & trade show
Ontario Petroleum Institute Membership Directory
Type: Directory *Frequency:* Annually *Accepts Advertising*
Profile: Listings & advertising are available to members of the Ontario Petroleum Institute only
OPI [Ontario Petroleum Institute Inc.] Newsletter
Type: Newsletter *Frequency:* Bimonthly *Accepts Advertising*
ISSN: 14802201
Profile: Membership updates, reports, conferences, & legislation information

Ontario Sewer & Watermain Construction Association (OSWCA)
#300, 5045 Orbitor Dr., Unit 12, Mississauga ON L4W 4Y4
Tel: 905-629-7766; Fax: 905-629-0587
info@oswca.org
www.oswca.org

Overview: A small local organization
Chief Officer(s):
Joe Accardi, P.Eng, Executive Director
joe.accardi@oswca.org
Susan McGovern, Assistant Executive Director
susan.mcgovern@oswca.org
Don Del Vecchio, Contact, Member Services
don.delvecchio@oswca.org
Mary Reuse, Contact, Financial Services
mary.reuse@oswca.org
Membership: 700+ companies; *Committees: Young Executives; Government Relations; Members Services; Marketing Initiatives; Education Program; Administration*
Activities: Liaising with the Government of Ontario & its agencies; Increasing public awareness about the maintenance of water & wastewater systems in Ontario; Providing apprenticeship training & upgrading training; Informing members of industry developments
Publications: Ontario Sewer & Watermain Construction Association Membership Directory
Type: Directory *Frequency:* Annually *Accepts Advertising*
Profile: A buyers' guide for products & services used by sewer & watermain construction contractors, municipalities, utilities, & engineers
Undergrounder [a publication of the Ontario Sewer & Watermain Construction Association]
Type: Magazine *Frequency:* 3 pa *Accepts Advertising*
Profile: Association business, industry issues, & regulatory updates available in print or digital editions

Ontario Sustainable Energy Association (OSEA)
#201, 156 Front St. West, Toronto ON M5J 2L6
Tel: 416-977-4441; Fax: 416-977-4441
Toll-Free: 888-840-3447
info@ontario-sea.org; employment@ontario-sea.org
www.ontario-sea.org
www.facebook.com/ontariosea?v=wall#!/ontariosea?sk=info

Overview: A small provincial organization founded in 2002
Finances: *Funding Sources: Sponsorships*
; **Fees:** *$56.50 students; $113 minimum donation, friends; $565 - $1,695 supporters; $2,260 champions; $5,650 enablers*
Activities: Engaging in advocacy activities, capacity building, & non-partisan policy work; Providing public outreach services
Publications: Arts Revision Report: Renewables Without Limits [a publication of the Ontario Sustainable Energy Association]
Type: Report *Price:* $1 + $13.50 shipping & handling, members; $10 +$13.50 S&H, non-members
Profile: A review of Ontario's Renewable Energy Standard Offer Program
Community Power Financing Guidebook
Type: Manual *Price:* $40 + $13.50 shipping & handling,members; $65 + $13.40 S&H, non-members
Profile: Contents include pre-development financing, land acquisition, legal contracting, permits & approvals, resource assessment, & community engagement
The Community Power Guidebook
Type: Guide
Profile: A guide to the development of a community power project, from conception to commissioning
Green Energy ACTion Kit
Type: Kit *Price:* $10 + $13.50 shipping & handling, members; $20 + $13.40 S&H, non-members
Profile: Suggestions to help citizens advocate for green energy in Ontario
Ontario Landowner's Guide to Wind Energy
Type: Guide *Author:* Paul Gipe; James Murphy *Price:* $10 + $13.50 shipping & handling, members; $20 + $13.50 S&H,non-members
Profile: A comprehensive manual for rural landowners & farmers who are interested in wind power
Ontario Sustainable Energy Association E-Bulletin
Type: Newsletter *Price:* Free with Ontario Sustainable Energy Association membership
Profile: Updates about the association & upcoming events
OSEA [Ontario Sustainable Energy Association] Member Directory
Type: Directory
Profile: Contact information for members
Permitting & Approvals Processes for CP Projects [a publication of the Ontario Sustainable Energy Association]
Type: Guide *Price:* $40 + $13.50 shipping & handling, members; $65 + $13.50 S&H, non-members
Profile: An overview of the policy environment for biogas & wind projects in Ontario, of interest to municipal planners,project proponents, & the general public
Powering Ontario Communities: Proposed Policy for Projects up to 10mw
Type: Study
Profile: Options to encourage small or community-owned renewable energy generation in Ontario
Proposal for a Green Energy Act for Ontario
Profile: A proposal for renewable energy sources to protect the environment & to manage climate change
Recommendations for Procuring Sustainable Energy: An Addendum to Renewables Without Limits
Profile: An update to recommendations from the Arts Revision Report: Renewable Without Limits
Solar PV Community Action Manual
Type: Manual
Profile: Information for Canadian residents about residential-scale or small-scale commercial Solar PV installations, as well as related topics such as financing & home assessment
Solar Thermal Community Action Manual
Type: Manual
Profile: Information for Canadians about residential-scale or small-scale commercial solar thermal installations, as well as the establishment of a community based organization

Ontario Telecommunications Association (OTA)
29 Peevers Cres., Newmarket ON L3Y 7T5
Tel: 519-595-3975; Fax: 519-595-3976
ota@ota.on.ca
www.ota.on.ca

Previous Name: *Ontario Telephone Association*
Overview: A small provincial organization
Chief Officer(s):
Ian Stevens, President
Angela Schneider, Vice-President
Amedeo Bernardi, Secretary-Treasurer
Finances: *Funding Sources: Sponsorships*
Membership: 22 Small Incumbent Local Exchange Carriers (SILECs)
Activities: Liaising with government departments & agencies & industry associates, such as Bell Canada; Setting policies & compliance guidelines; Offering a forum to share expertise

Ontario Water Works Association (OWWA)
#00, 1092 Islington Ave., Toronto ON M8Z 4R9
Tel: 416-231-1555; Fax: 416-231-1556
Toll-Free: 866-975-0575
waterinfo@owwa.ca
www.owwa.com

Overview: A medium-sized provincial organization
Membership: 1,100+; *Member Profile: Drinking water professionals in Ontario, such as hydrogeologists, scientists, engineers, chemists, & managers & technicians employed by Ontario's municipal water systems; Committees: Climate Change; C-PAC; Conference Management; Continuing Education; Cross Connection Control; Distribution; Government Affairs; Groundwater; Joint OWWA / OMWA; Management; Membership; OWWA / WEAO Joint Asset Management; Publications; Small Systems; Source Water Protection; Training, Certification, & Safety; Treatment; University Forum; Water Efficiency; Water for People - Canada; Young Professionals; Youth Education*
Activities: Improving technology, science & management; Influencing government policy; Providing education for members; *Library: Ontario Water Works Association Library*
Publications: Consultants' Listing [a publication of the Ontario Water Works Association]
Frequency: 3 pa *Accepts Advertising*
Ontario Pipeline
Type: Magazine *Frequency:* 3 pa *Accepts Advertising*
Profile: A joint publication of the Ontario Water Works Association, the Ontario Municipal Water Association, & the Ontario Water Works Equipment Association

Petroleum Human Resources Council of Canada (PHRCC)
5055 - 11 St. NE, Calgary AB T2E 8N4
Tel: 403-516-8100; Fax: 403-516-8171
info@petrohrsc.ca
www.petrohrsc.ca

Overview: A medium-sized national organization

Petroleum Research Newfoundland & Labrador
Baine Johnston Centre, #802, 10 Fort William Pl., St John's NL A1C 1K4
Tel: 709-738-7916; Fax: 709-738-7922
www.pr-ac.ca

Previous Name: *Petroleum Research Atlantic Canada (PRAC*
Overview: A small local organization founded in 1999
Chief Officer(s):
Doug Cook, Chief Executive Officer, 709-738-7920
doug.cook@petroleumresearch.ca

David Finn, Chief Operating Officer, 709-738-7917
dave.finn@petroleumresearch.ca
Susan Hunt, Program Manager, HSE, 709-738-7904
susan.hunt@petroleumresearch.ca
Lisa A. Hutchens, Manager, Business Services, 709-738-7921
lisa.hutchens@petroleumresearch.ca
Matilda Maddigan, Manager, Office, 709-738-7916
matilda.maddigan@petroleumresearch.ca
Metzi Prince, Manager, Project Delivery, 709-738-7919
metzi.prince@petroleumresearch.ca
Charles E. Smith, Senior Technical Advisor, 709-738-7918
charles.smith@petroleumresearch.ca
Robert Trask, Coordinator, Research Grants, 709-738-7974
robert.trask@petroleumresearch.ca
Membership: *Member Profile: Representatives from the oil & gas industry*

Petroleum Services Association of Canada (PSAC)
#1150, 800 - 6 Ave. SW, Calgary AB T2P 3G3
Tel: 403-264-4195; Fax: 403-263-7174
www.psac.ca
Overview: A large national organization founded in 1981
Chief Officer(s):
Mark Salkeld, President & Chief Executive Officer
msalkeld@psac.ca
Elizabeth Aquin, Senior Vice-President
eaquin@psac.ca
Patrick J. Delaney, Vice-President, Health & Safety
pdelaney@psac.ca
Kelly Morrison, Director, Communications & Stakeholder Relations
kmorrison@psac.ca
Heather Doyle, Manager, Meetings & Events
hdoyle@psac.ca
Membership: 250+ companies; *Member Profile: Petroleum services industry companies; Committees: Corporate Finance; Education Fund; Health & Safety; Human Resources; Special Events; Transportation Issues; Cathodic Protection; Drilling Fluids; Oilwell Perforators' Safety Training & Advisory; Snubbing Services; Well Testing*
Activities: Engaging in lobbying activities; Providing educational opportunities
Publications: Canadian Drilling Activity Forecast
Type: Yearbook *Frequency:* Annually
Profile: Five years of historical data, plus forecasts for the coming year across Canada
FAST-Line [a publication of the Petroleum Services Association of Canada]
Type: Newsletter *Frequency:* Biweekly
Profile: Association news & upcoming events
Petroleum Services Association of Canada Membership Directory
Type: Directory
Profile: Contact information for association members
Petroleum Services Association of Canada Annual Report
Type: Yearbook *Frequency:* Annually
Profile: A review of the association's activities, released at the end of each October in conjunction with the Canadian Drilling Activity Forecast & the Annual GeneralMeeting
Petroleum Services News
Type: Magazine *Frequency:* Quarterly *Accepts Advertising*
Profile: Covering issues of importance to the upstream oil & gas industry
Total Compensation Survey [a publication of the Petroleum Services Association of Canada]
Type: Yearbook *Frequency:* Annually
Profile: An analysis of current salary & benefits practices in the petroleum service, supply, & manufacturing industry
Well Cost Study
Type: Study
Profile: Geological, technical, & financial data on wells drilled across Canada

Petroleum Tank Management Association of Alberta (PTMAA)
#980, 10303 Jasper Ave., Edmonton AB T5J 3N6
Tel: 780-425-8265; Fax: 780-425-4722
Toll-Free: 866-222-8265
ptmaa@ptmaa.ab.ca
www.ptmaa.ab.ca
Overview: A medium-sized provincial licensing charitable organization founded in 1994
Activities: Monitoring new storage tank installations; Inspecting existing storage tank installations; Investigating accidents & incidents

Petroleum Technology Alliance Canada (PTAC)
Chevron Plaza, #400, 500 - 5th Ave. SW, Calgary AB T2P 3L5
Tel: 403-218-7700; Fax: 403-920-0054
info@ptac.org
www.ptac.org
Overview: A medium-sized national organization

Petrolia Discovery
PO Box 1480, 4381 Discovery Line, Petrolia ON N0N 1R0
Tel: 519-882-0897; Fax: 519-882-4209
petdisc@xcelco.on.ca
www.petroliadiscovery.com
Overview: A small national charitable organization founded in 1980
Activities: Maintaining historical displays; Organizing programs for schools

Pipe Line Contractors Association of Canada (PLCAC)
#201, 1075 North Service Rd. West, Oakville ON L6M 2G2
Tel: 905-847-9383; Fax: 905-847-7824
plcac@pipeline.ca
www.pipeline.ca
Overview: A small national organization founded in 1954
Chief Officer(s):
O.J. Kavanaugh, President
Neil G. Lane, Executive Director
Michael J. Gallardo, Assistant Executive Director
Membership: 35 regular members; 66 associate members; 18 honorary members; *Member Profile: Employers engaged in contacting for the construction, installation, & maintenance of piplines; Corporations or individuals engages in manufacturing, supplying, & transporting material for the construction & maintenance of piplines; Committees: Convention Planning; Education & Training; Equipment Rental; Executive; Membership & Promotion; National Labour Relations; Negotiating - Distribution; Negotiating - Mainline; Pipeline Standards; Safety*
Activities: Establishing training courses; Reviewing legislation
Publications: Canadian Pipeliner
Type: Newsletter *Frequency:* 4 pa
Profile: News, industry information, & upcoming events
PLCAC [Pipe Line Contractors Association of Canada] Membership Directory
Type: Directory *Frequency:* Annually
Profile: Featuring membership profiles & contact information

Planetary Association for Clean Energy, Inc. (PACE) / Société planétaire pour l'assainissement de l'énergie
#1001, 100 Bronson Ave., Ottawa ON K1R 6G8
Tel: 613-236-6265; Fax: 613-235-5876
paceincnet@gmail.com
pacenet.homestead.com
Overview: A medium-sized international charitable organization founded in 1975
Chief Officer(s):
Andrew Michrowski, President
Finances: *Annual Operating Budget: $100,000-$250,000; Funding Sources: Membership fees; donations*
Staff: 2 staff member(s); 10 volunteer(s)
Membership: 3,600 in 60 countries; *Fees: $50*
Activities: Electromagnetic bioaffect, analyses & abatement; monitors unclean developments; peer review of new technologies; books, databases & technical reports; *Internships: Yes; Speaker Service: Yes Library: Yes by appointment*

Professional Petroleum Data Management Association (PPDM)
PO Box 22155, Stn. Bankers Hall, #860, 736 - 8th Ave. SW, Calgary AB T2P 4J5
Tel: 403-660-7817; Fax: 403-660-0540
info@ppdm.org
www.ppdm.org
www.linkedin.com/groups?home=&gid=146440
www.facebook.com/group.php?gid=108325212519325
twitter.com/PPDMAssociation
Previous Name: *Public Petroleum Data Model Association*
Overview: A small national organization founded in 1991
Chief Officer(s):
David Hood, Chair
dhood@geologic.com
Chellie Hailes, Secretary
Chellie.hailes@chevron.com
Peter MacDougall, Treasurer
peter.macdougall@ihs.com
Activities: Increasing awareness of the value of data management; Providing training

The Road & Infrastructure Program Canada (TRIP Canada)
#400, 75 Albert St., Ottawa ON K1P 5E7
Tel: 613-236-9455; Fax: 613-236-9526
cca@cca-acc.com
www.tripcanada.org
Overview: A small national organization
Finances: *Annual Operating Budget: $50,000-$100,000*
Staff: 1 staff member(s); 35 volunteer(s)
Membership: 11 associations
Activities: *Speaker Service: Yes*

Saskatchewan Water & Wastewater Association (SWWA)
PO Box 7831, Saskatoon SK S7K 4R5
Tel: 306-761-1278; Fax: 306-761-1279
Toll-Free: 888-668-1278
office@swwa.ca
www.swwa.sk.ca
Overview: A medium-sized provincial organization
Membership: *Fees: $42; Member Profile: People involved in the operation, maintenance & troubleshooting of water & wastewater systems*
Activities: Hosting workshops & training sessions; Providing access to job opportunities; Publishing a newsletter; Providing certification through the Operator Certification Board
Publications: The Pipeline
Type: Newsletter *Frequency:* Quarterly
Profile: Latest association news; events in the province & elsewhere

Small Explorers & Producers Association of Canada (SEPAC)
#1060, 717 - 7th Ave. SW, Calgary AB T2P 0Z3
Tel: 403-269-3454; Fax: 403-269-3636
info@sepac.ca
www.sepac.ca
Overview: A small national organization founded in 1986
Chief Officer(s):
Jim Screaton, Chair
Gary Leach, Executive Director
Membership: 387 corporate; *Fees: $500-$3,335*

The Society of Energy Professionals
#300, 425 Bloor St. East, Toronto ON M4W 3R4
Tel: 416-979-2709; Fax: 416-979-5794
Toll-Free: 866-288-1788
society@society.on.ca
www.thesociety.ca
Overview: A medium-sized provincial organization founded in 1948
Chief Officer(s):
Rodney Sheppard, President
shepparr@thesociety.ca
Leslie Forge, Executive Vice-President, Policy
forgel@thesociety.ca
Dennis Minello, Executive Vice-President, Member Services
minellod@thesociety.ca
Rob Stanley, Executive Vice-President, Finance
stanleyr@thesociety.ca
Joan Florence, Senior Financial Officer
florencej@thesociety.ca
Finances: *Funding Sources: Membership dues*
Membership: *Member Profile: Professional members of the elctricity industry in Ontario, such as scientists, engineers, financial specialists, & supervisors*

Society of Petroleum Engineers (SPE)
PO Box 833836, Richardson TX 75083-3868 USA
Tel: 972-952-9393; Fax: 972-952-9435
Toll-Free: 800-456-6863
spedal@spe.org
www.spe.org
Overview: A large international organization founded in 1957
Chief Officer(s):
Mark A. Rubin, Executive Director
Finances: *Annual Operating Budget: $3 Million-$5 Million*
Staff: 87 staff member(s)
Membership: 79,000+ (active operations in some 50 countries); *Member Profile: Managers, engineers, operating personnel & scientists engaged in the exploration, drilling & production sectors of the global oil & gas industry*
Activities: *Internships: Yes; Speaker Service: Yes Library: Yes (Open to Public)*

Solar & Sustainable Energy Society of Canada Inc. (SESCI) / Societé des énergie solaire et durable du Canada Inc.
c/o Frederic Pouyot, #173, 207 Bank St., Ottawa ON k2P 2N2
Tel: 613-686-4474; Fax: 613-533-6550
bruce@techonfoot.com
www.sesci.ca
Previous Name: *Solar Energy Society of Canada Inc.*
Overview: A medium-sized national charitable organization founded in 1974
Chief Officer(s):
Frederic Pouyot, President
president@sesci.ca
Finances: *Annual Operating Budget: $50,000-$100,000; Funding Sources: Membership fees; Donations*

; **Fees:** *$20 students; $40 seniors; $100 regular members; $200 small organizations; $300 libraries; $500 medium organizations; $2000 large organizations*
Activities: Presenting briefs & position papers to government departments in the environment, energy resource, & finance sectors; Liaising with other solar energy societies & environmental groups; Encouraging the exchange of information
Publications: Canadian Renewable Energy Guide
Type: Guide
Profile: Comprehensive information about the use of renewables throughout Canada
SOL [a publication of the Solar & Sustainable Energy Society of Canada Inc.]
Type: Newsletter *Frequency:* Quarterly *Price:* Free with Solar & Sustainable Energy Society of Canada Inc. membership
Profile: Developments in Canada's renewable energy industry, topical articles, & Solar & Sustainable Energy Society of Canada's forthcoming events &activities

Solid Waste Association of North America (SWANA)
#700, 1100 Wayne Ave., Silver Spring MD 20910 USA
Fax: 301-589-7068
Toll-Free: 800-467-9262
info@swana.org
www.swana.org
www.linkedin.com/groups?home=&gid=45037
www.facebook.com/MySWANA
twitter.com/SWANA
Previous Name: *Government Refuse Collection & Disposal Association*
Overview: A medium-sized international organization founded in 1961
Chief Officer(s):
John Skinner, Executive Director & CEO, 240-494-2254
Finances: *Annual Operating Budget: $3 Million-$5 Million; Funding Sources: Membership dues; publications*
Staff: 22 staff member(s)
Membership: 8,000; *Fees: US$62 student; US$72 retired; US$183 public sector; US$243 small business; US$343 private sector; Committees: Technical; Recycling & Special Waste Management; Communication, Education & Marketing; Collection & Transfer; Landfill; Landfill Gas; Planning & Management; Waste-to-Energy*
Activities: Technical divisions: collection & transfer, waste-to-energy, landfill gas management, landfill management, planning & management, special waste management; waste reduction, recycling & composting, communication, education & marketing; publications; trade shows & conferences; *Internships: Yes Library: Yes (Open to Public)*

Syndicat professionnel des ingénieurs d'Hydro-Québec (ind.) (SPIHQ) / Hydro-Québec Professional Engineers Union (Ind.)
bureau #1400, 1255 rue University, Montréal QC H3B 3X1
Tél: 514-845-4239; Téléc: 514-845-0082
Ligne sans frais: 800-567-1260
spihq@spihq.qc.ca
www.spihq.qc.ca
Aperçu: *Dimension: moyenne; Envergure: provinciale; fondée en 1964*
Membre(s) du bureau directeur:
Carole Leroux, Président
Yvon Filion, Secrétaire
Finances: *Budget de fonctionnement annuel: $500,000-$1.5 Million*
Personnel: 3 membre(s) du personnel
Membre: 1 700

Telecommunications Employees Association of Manitoba (TEAM)
#200, 1 Wesley Ave., Winnipeg MB R3C 4C6
Tel: 204-984-9470; Fax: 204-231-2809
Toll-Free: 877-984-9470
team@teamunion.mb.ca
www.teamunion.mb.ca
twitter.com/teamunion161
Overview: A medium-sized provincial organization founded in 1972
Chief Officer(s):
Misty Hughes-Newman, President
m.hughes-newman@teamunion.mb.ca
Bob Linsdell, Executive Director, 204-984-9471
bob.linsdell@teamunion.mb.ca
Tom Milroy, Officer, Labour Relations, 204-984-9473
tom.milroy@teamunion.mb.ca
Darlene Buan, Secretary
d.buan@teamunion.mb.ca
Roland Pokorny, Treasurer
roland.pokorny@teamunion.mb.ca
Activities: Presenting TEAM scholarships

Telecommunications Workers' Union (CLC) (TWU) / Syndicat des travailleurs en télécommunications (CTC) (STT)
Head Office, 5261 Lane St., Burnaby BC V5H 4A6
Tel: 604-437-8601; Fax: 604-435-7760
twu@twu-stt.ca
www.twu-stt.ca
Overview: A medium-sized national organization founded in 1980
Chief Officer(s):
George Doubt, President
John Carpenter, Vice-President
Betty Carrasco, Vice-President
Michael Thompson, Secretary-Treasurer
Activities: Negotiating collective agreements; Promoting fair wages; Protecting & improving benefits & working conditions

Toronto Renewable Energy Co-operative (TREC)
#405, 401 Richmond St. W., Toronto ON M5V 3A8
Tel: 416-977-5093; Fax: 416-306-6476
Toll-Free: 866-560-9463
info@trec.on.ca
www.trec.on.ca
twitter.com/TRECoop
Overview: A small local organization founded in 1998
Finances: *Funding Sources: Donations*
Activities: Community energy projects; interactive, hands-on education; Green City Bike Tours; Green Collar Career program; Our Power solar initiative; solar home tours; round table discussions; Bruce County wind energy co-operative project

United Utility Workers' Association (UUWA)
1207 - 20 Ave. NW, Calgary AB T2M 1G2
Tel: 403-284-4521; Fax: 403-282-1598
info@uuwac.org
www.uuwac.org
Previous Name: *Calgary Power Employees Association; TransAlta Employees' Association*
Overview: A medium-sized national organization founded in 1943
Chief Officer(s):
Chuck Pozzo, Chief Executive Officer & President
Grace Thostenson, Manager, Business
Paul Drew-Brook, Secretary-Treasurer
Membership: 1,400; *Member Profile: Employees in the energy sector, such as meter readers, power line technicians, designers, & administrators*
Activities: Offering training courses

Utility Contractors Association of Ontario, Inc. (UCA)
PO Box 762, Oakville ON L6K 0A9
Tel: 905-847-7305; Fax: 905-412-0339
www.uca.on.ca
Overview: A medium-sized provincial organization founded in 1968
Chief Officer(s):
Rene Beaudry, President
Barry Brown, Executive Director
Glen Hansen, Treasurer
Membership: 10 contractor members + 34 associate (supplier) members
Activities: Organizing networking events; Recognizing exellence in safety through the presentation of awards
Publications: The Conduit [a publication of the Utility Contractors Association of Ontario]
Type: Newsletter *Frequency:* Semiannually
Profile: Association news, action dates, & industry information

World Energy Council (WEC) / Conseil Mondial de l'Energie (CME)
Regency House, 1-4 Warwick St., 5th Fl., London W1B 5LT United Kingdom
info@worldenergy.org
www.worldenergy.org
Overview: A small international organization founded in 1923
Finances: *Annual Operating Budget: $3 Million-$5 Million*
Staff: 14 staff member(s)
Membership: 92 member countries; *Fees: Variable; Member Profile: Commercial; government; non-government*
Activities: Energy; energy conservation; *Library: Information Services by appointment*

World Petroleum Congress (WPC) / Congrès mondiaux du pétrole
#1, 1 Duchess St., 4th Fl., London W1W 6AN United Kingdom
info@world-petroleum.org
www.world-petroleum.org
Overview: A medium-sized international organization founded in 1933
Chief Officer(s):
Pierce Riemer, Director General
pierce@world-petroleum.org
Randy Gossen, President
Finances: *Funding Sources: Membership dues; royalties; levy on registration*
Staff: 4 staff member(s)
Membership: 57 countries; *Fees: Schedule available; Member Profile: Major oil producing & consuming nations of the world; each country has a National Committee made up of representatives of the oil industry, academic & research institutions, & government departments; Committees: Permanent Council; Executive Board; Scientific Program; Congress Arrangements; Environmental Affairs; Development*

Companies

International

Etrion Corporation
rue du Stand 60-62, Geneva, 1204
info@etrion.com
www.etrion.com
Ticker Symbol: ETX / TSX
Profile: The independent power producer owns & operates solar photovoltaic power plants in Italy.
Marco Anotonio Northland, Chief Executive Officer
Garrett Soden, Chief Financial Officer
Robert Eriksson, Contact, Investor Relations
reriksson@etrion.com

Alberta

AltaGas Ltd.
Prior Name: AltaGas Income Trust
#1700, 355 - 4th Ave. SW, Calgary, AB T2P 0J1
Tel: 403-691-7575; Fax: 403-691-7576
Toll-Free: 888-890-2715
www.altagas.ca
Ticker Symbol: ALA, ALA.PR.A, ALA.R/TSX
Profile: AltaGas is a business involved in power, natural gas, & regulated utilities. It will focus on renewable energy sources.
David W. Cornhill, B.Sc.(Hons), MBAChair/CEO
Richard M. Alexander, BBM, CFA, CMAPresident/COO
David Wright, B.Sc., M.Sc., LLBExec. Vice-President, Strategy & Corporate Development
Deborah S. Stein, CFO & Vice-President, Finance
James (Jim) Bracken, CASr. Vice-President, Major Projects
Gregory A. Aarssen, B.Sc.(Hons), MBA, LLBVice-President, Corporate Affairs
Denis C. Fonteyne, Chair, Environment Occupational Health & Safety Committee

AltaLink Management Ltd.
2811 - 3rd Ave. SE, Calgary, AB T2A 7W7
Tel: 403-267-3400; Toll-Free: 866-451-7817
www.altalink.ca
www.facebook.com/altalinktransmission
twitter.com/Altalink
Profile: AltaLink is a regulated electricity transmission company in Alberta. Electricity is generated from hydro, thermal energy, & wind power & transported through tramsmission lines to substations. Electricity is then deliverd to homes & businesses via distribution lines. The company employs over 600 people.
Leanne Niblock, Manager, Communications
Leanne.Niblock@AltaLink.ca

ATCO Ltd.
ATCO Centre, #1400, 909 - 11th Ave. SW, Calgary, AB T2R 1N6
Tel: 403-292-7500; Fax: 403-292-7623
investorrelations@atco.com; mediarelation
www.atco.ca
Ticker Symbol: ACO / TSX
Profile: ATCO Ltd. employs over 8,800 people. The company delivers business solutions with companies engaged in the following: utilities, including natural gas & electricity transmission & distribution; energy, including power generation & liquids extraction; logistics & structures, included manufacturing & noise abatement; & technologies.
Nancy C. Southern, President & Chief Executive Officer
B.R. (Brian) Bale, Chief Financial Officer & Senior Vice-Presidnent
403-292-7502
S.W. Kiefer, Chief Operating Officer, Energy & Utilities
A.M. Skiffington, Chief Information Officer & Vice-President
C.J. Ackroyd, Vice-President, Marketing & Communications
C.L. Gareau, Vice-President & Treasurer
R.C. Neumann, Vice-President & Controller

Canadian Utilities Limited
Investor Relations, #1500, 909 - 11th Ave. SW, Calgary, AB T2R 1N6

Tel: 403-292-7500; Fax: 403-292-7532
investorrelations@atco.com
www.canadian-utilities.com
Ticker Symbol: CU / TSX

Profile: Part of the ATCO Group of Companies, Canadian Utilities Limited is engaged in natural gas & electricity transmission & distribution, as well as technology, logistics, & energy services. Canadian Utilities Limited employs over 6,700 people.

Nancy C. Southern, President/CEO
Karen M. Watson, Sr. Vice-President/CFO
Siegfried W. Kiefer, Chief Information Officer & Managing Director, Utilities
Susan R. Werth, Sr. Vice-President & Chief Administration Officer

Capital Power Corporation
Corporate Head Office, #1200, 10423 - 101 St. NW, Edmonton, AB T5H 0E9

Tel: 780-392-5100;
info@capitalpower.com
www.capitalpower.com
www.facebook.com/capitalpowercommunity
twitter.com/capitalpowerwww.linkedin.com/company/capital-power-corporation
Ticker Symbol: CPX / TSX

Profile: Capital Power Corporation is a power producer. The company has sixteen facilities throughout North America. Capital Power is also developing wind generation projects in Ontario, Alberta, & British Columbia.

Brian Vaasjo, President & Chief Executive Officer
Stuart Lee, Chief Financial Officer & Senior Vice-President, Finance
Peter Arnold, Senior Vice-President, Human Resources & Health, Safety & the Environment
B. Kathryn Chisholm, Q.C.Senior Vice-President, Legal, Regulatory, Government Affairs
Darcy Trufyn, Senior Vice-President, Construction & Engineering

Allan Danroth, Vice-President, Planning, Business Transformation, & Information Svs.

CU Inc.
Parent: Canadian Utilities Limited
Corporate Head Office, #1600, 909 - 11 Ave. SW, Calgary, AB T2R 1N6

Tel: 403-292-7500; Fax: 403-292-7523
www.canadian-utilities.com
Ticker Symbol: CIU / TSX

Profile: A wholly owned subsidiary of Canadian Utilities Limited, CU Inc. is involved in natural gas & electricity transmission & distribution, as well as power generation. The corporation employs more than 4,300 people.

N.C. Southern, Chair, President & Chief Executive Officer
B.R. (Brian) Bale, Chief Financial Officer & Senior Vice-President
403-292-7502,

Enbridge Income Fund Holdings Inc.
Fifth Avenue Place, #3000, 425 - 1st St. SW, Calgary, AB T2P 3L8

Tel: 403-231-3900; Fax: 403-231-3920
Toll-Free: 866-859-5957
webmaster@enbridgeincomefund.com
www.enbridgeincomefund.com
Ticker Symbol: ENF / TSX

Profile: Through its investment in Enbridge Income Fund, Enbridge Income Fund Holdings Inc. holds energy infrastructure assets. These assets include the following: a 100% interest in the pipelines that comprise the Saskatchewan System; a 50% interest in the Canadian segment of the Alliance Pipeline; & interests in renewable & alternative power generation capacity. The manager of Enbridge Income Fund Holdings Inc. is Enbridge Management Services Inc.

John K. Whelen, President
Colin K. Gruending, Chief Financial Officer
Darren Yaworsky, Treasurer
Debra J. Poon, Corporate Secretary
Teri Majer, Manager, Investor Relations
403-508-3185, teri.majer@enbridge.com
Jennifer Varey, Director, Corporate Communications
403-508-6563, jennifer.varey@enbridge.com

ENMAX Corporation
Prior Name: City of Calgary Electric System
Parent: City of Calgary
141 - 50 Ave. SE, Calgary, AB T2G 4S7

Tel: 403-514-3000; Toll-Free: 877-571-7111
customercare@enmax.com
www.enmax.com

Profile: Through its subsidiaries, ENMAX Corporation provides natural gas, electricity, renewable energy, fibre-optic, & value-added services in Alberta.

Gianna Manes, President & Chief Executive Officer
David Halford, Chief Financial Officer & Executive Vice-President, Finance
Terry G. Tyler, B.Sc., MBAChief Information & Technoloyg Officer & Executive VP, Finance
Helen Bremner, Executive Vice-President, Residential Markets
Robert Hemstock, LL.B., B.Comm.Executive Vice-President, Regulatory & Legal Services
Dale McMaster, Executive Vice-President, Transmission & Distribution Services
Dave Rehn, M.Sc., B.ScExecutive Vice-President, Generation
James McKee, Vice-President, Commercial & Industrial Markets
Ian Todd, Vice-President, Government & Media Relations

Epcor Utilities
Parent: City of Edmonton
#2000, 10423 - 101 St. NW, Edmonton, AB T5H 0E8

Tel: 780-412-3414;
corpafrs@epcor.com
www.epcor.com
www.facebook.com/pages/EPCOR/133184853425907
twitter.com/epcor

Profile: EPCOR is a builder & operator of electrical transmission & distribution networks & water & wastewater treatment facilities in Canada & the United States. Operating companies include EPCOR Water Services Inc., EPCOR Distribution & Transmission Inc., EPCOR Energy Alberta Inc., & EPCOR Technologies.

Don Lowry, President & Chief Executive Officer
Wray Steedsman, Chief Information Officer & Senior Vice-President, Business Services
Mark Wiltzen, Chief Financial Officer & Senior Vice-President
Guy Bridgeman, Senior Vice-President, Strategic Planning & Development
Doreen Cole, Senior Vice-President, Electricity Services
Ron Liteplo, Senior Vice-President, Legal & External Relations
Stephen Stanley, Senior Vice-President, Water Services

FortisAlberta Inc.
Parent: Fortis Inc.
320 - 17th Ave. SW, Calgary, AB T2S 2V1

Tel: 403-514-4000; Fax: 403-514-4001
Toll-Free: 866-717-3113
www.fortisalberta.com

Profile: FortisAlberta delivers electricity to residential, business, & farm customers in Alberta. The company also maintains electrical poles & approximately 115,000 kilometres of power lines.

Karl W. Smith, President & Chief Executive Officer
Phonse Delaney, Executive Vice-President, Operations, Engineering, & Information Technology
Ian Lorimer, Chief Financial Officer & Vice-President, Finance
Cam Aplin, Vice-President, Field Operations
Annette Iwasaki, Vice-President, Human Resources & Corporate Communications
Mike Pashak, Vice-President, Customer Service

Keyera Corp.
West Tower, Sun Life Plaza, #600, 144 - 4 Ave. SW, Calgary, AB T2P 3N4

Tel: 403-205-8300; Fax: 403-205-8318
ir@keyera.com; hr@keyera.com
www.keyera.com
Ticker Symbol: KEY / TSX

Profile: Keyera is engaged in natural gas gathering & processing. The company also transports, stores, & markets natural gas liquids. Activities are conducted in the Western Canada Sedimentary Basin.

Jim V. Bertram, President & Chief Executive Officer
Dean Setoguchi, Chief Financial Officer & Vice-President
Graham Balzun, Vice-President, Engineering & Corporate Responsibility
Ron Daniels, Manager, Manager, Information Technology
403-205-7635
Tanis Fiss, Manager, Financial Communications
Murray Selle, Manager, Health & Safety
Rod Sikora, Manager, Environment
403-205-8335
W. John Cobb, Director, Investor Relations
403-205-7670, Fax: 403-205-7670

MAXIM Power Corp.
#1210, 715 - 5th Ave. SW, Calgary, AB T2P 2X6

Tel: 403-263-3021; Fax: 403-263-9125
maxim@maximpowercorp.com
www.maximpowercorp.com
Ticker Symbol: MXG / TSX

Profile: MAXIM Power Corp. is an independent power producer. The company is involved in the acquisition, development, ownership, & operation of environmentally responsible power projects. Its assets include coal & natural gas powered generators in western Canada, the United States, & France.

John R. Bobenic, President & Chief Executie Officer
403-750-9300
Xavier Embroise, President, COMAX France S.A.S.
Michael R. Mayder, Chief Financial Officer & Vice-President, Finance
403-750-9311
Kim Karran, Vice-President, Corporate Development
Jamie Urquhart, Vice-President, Operations

TransAlta Corporation
PO Box 1900 M, 110 - 12 Ave. SW, Calgary, AB T2P 2M1

Tel: 403-267-7110; Fax: 403-267-2559
Toll-Free: 877-700-9288
www.transalta.com
Ticker Symbol: TA / TSX, MYSE

Profile: TansAlta Corporation is engaged in coal & gas-fired generation. The company carries out its activities in Canada, the United States, Mexico, & Australia.
The company works to limit environmental impact by focusing growth on renewable generation methods. It meets ISO 14001 standards.

Stephen G. Snyder, President/CEO
Brian Burden, Exec. Vice-President/CFO
William D.A. Bridge, Exec. Vice-President, Generation Technology & Procurement
Dawn Farrell, Exec. Vice-President, Commercial Operations & Development
Mike Williams, Exec. Vice-President, Human Resources, Information Technology & Communication
Ken Stickland, Exec. Vice-President, Legal, SD, & Environmental Health & Safety

TransCanada Corporation
450 - 1 St. SW, Calgary, AB T2P 5H1

Tel: 403-920-2000; Fax: 403-920-2200
Toll-Free: 800-661-3805
communications@transcanada.com
www.transcanada.com
twitter.com/transcanada
Ticker Symbol: TRP / TSX

Profile: TransCanada is engaged in the development & operation of energy infrastructure, including natural gas & oil pipelines, power generation, & gas storage facilities in North America. Common shares trade on the Toronto & New York stock exchanges.

Russ Girling, President & Chief Executive Officer
Alexander J. Pourbaix, President, Energy
Russell K. Girling, President, Pipelines
Gregory A. Lohnes, Exec. Vice-President/CFO
Sarah E. Raiss, Exec. Vice-President, Corporate Services
Sean McMaster, General Counsel & Exec. Vice-President, Corporate
Don Wishart, Exec. Vice-President, Operations & Engineering

British Columbia

Alterra Power Corp.
#600, 888 Dunsmuir St., Vancouver, BC V6C 3K4

Tel: 604-669-4999; Fax: 604-682-3727
Toll-Free: 877-669-4999
info@alterrapower.ca
www.alterrapower.ca
twitter.com/#%21/Alterra_Powerwww.linkedin.com/company/alterra-power-corp-
Ticker Symbol: AXY / TSX

Profile: In 2011, Magma Energy Corp. & Plutonic Power Corp. merged to create Alterra Power Corp.. The renewable energy company operates power plants & projects in British Columbia, Nevada, Chile, Peru, Iceland, & Italy. In British Columbia, Alterra Power has a wind farm & run of river hydro facilities.

John Carson, Chief Executive Officer
Catherine Hickson, Chief Geologist & Vice-President, Exploration
Bruce Ripley, Chief Operating Officer
Peter Wong, Chief Financial Officer
Rupert Legge, LL.B.Corporate Secretary & Executive Vice-President, Legal
Asgeir Margeirsson, Vice-President, Geothermal
Paul Rapp, Vice-President, Wind Power
Jay Sutton, Vice-President, Hydro Power

Atlantic Power Corporation
#215, 10451 Shellbridge Way, Richmond, BC V6X 2W8
Tel: 250-586-7788;
www.atlanticpower.com
Ticker Symbol: ATP / TSX
Profile: Atlantic Power Corporation is a power & infrastructure company that trades on the TSX under the symbol ATP, & on the New York Stock Exchange, under the symbol AT. The company's portfolio of assets are located in Canada & the United States. Electricity from Atlantic Power's generation projects are sold to utilities & commercial customers.
In 2011, Atlantic Power acquired Capital Power Income L.P.
Barry Welch, President & Chief Executive Officer
Paul Rapisarda, Executive Vice-President, Commercial Development

Atlantic Power Preferred Equity Ltd.
Prior Name: CPI Preferred Equity Ltd; EPCOR Power Equity Ltd.
Parent: Atlantic Power Corporation
#215, 10451 Shellbridge Way, Richmond, BC V6X 2W8
Tel: 250-586-7788;
info@atlanticpower.com
www.atlanticpower.com
Ticker Symbol: AZP.PR.A
Profile: In 2012, CPI Preferred Equity Ltd., a subsidiary of Atlantic Power Corporation, announced that it had changed its name to Atlantic Power Preferred Equity Ltd.. The corporation is listed on the TSX under the symbols, AZP.PR.A & AZP.PR.B. Atlantic Power Preferred Equity Ltd. is an indirect, wholly-owned subsidiary of Atlantic Power Corporation. The subsidiary operates as a holding company. Atlantic Power Preferred Equity Ltd. directly holds Atlantic Power's business & power generation assets in British Coloumbia, & indirectly holds certain of Atlantic Power's business & power generation assets in the United States.
Barry Welch, President & Chief Executive Officer, Atlantic Power Corporation
Amanda Wagemaker, Contact, Investor Relations
617-977-2700

FortisBC Energy In.
16705 Fraser Hwy., Surrey, BC V4N 0E8
Tel: 604-576-7000; Toll-Free: 800-773-7001
rebates@fortisbc.com; commercialrebates@f
www.fortisbc.com
twitter.com/FortisBCww.linkedin.com/company/91362?trk=tya
Profile: Fortis BC employs approximately 2,300 people who provide electricity, natural gas, propane, & geothermal & district energy across British Columbia. The company owns four hydroelectric generating plants, approximately 7,000 kilometres of transmission & distribution power lines, & approximately 47,000 kilometres of natural gas transmission & distribution pipelines.
In 2011, Terasen Gas & FortisBC started to share the name, FortisBC.
John Walker, President & Chief Executive Officer
Michael Mulcahy, Exeuctive Vice-President, Human Resources & Customer & Corporate Services
Michele Leeners, Chief Financial Officer & Vice-President, Finance
Dwain Bell, Vice-President, Operations
David Bennett, Vice-President, General Counsel, & Corporate Secretary
Roger Dall'Antonia, Vice-President, Strategic Planning, Corporate Dev, & Regulatory Affairs
Cynthia Des Brisay, Vice-President, Energy Supply & Resource Development
Tom Loski, Vice-President, Customer Service
Doyle Sam, Vice-President, Engineering & Generation
Douglas Stout, Vice-President, Energy Solutions & External Relations

FortisBC Inc.
Parent: Fortis Inc., St. John's, NL.
16705 Fraser Hwy., Surrey, BC V4N 0E8
Tel: 604-576-7000; Toll-Free: 800-773-7001
electricity.customerservice@fortisbc.com
www.fortisbc.com
Profile: FortisBC delivers energy to homes, institutions, & businesses in British Columbia. The company employs approximately 2,300 people. In 2011, FortisBC & Terasen Gas began sharing the name, FortisBC.
John Walker, President & Chief Executive Officer
Michele Leeners, Chief Financial Officer & Vice-President, Finance
Michael Mulcahy, Executive Vice-President, Customer & Corporate Services
Roger Dall'Antonia, Vice-President, Strategic Planning, Corp. Dev., & Regulatory Affairs
Doyle Sam, Vice-President, Engineering & Generation
Douglas Stout, Vice-President, Energy Solutions & External Relations

Nevada Geothermal Power Inc. / NGP
840, 1140 West Pender St., Vancouver, BC V6E 4G1
Tel: 604-688-1553; Fax: 604-688-5926
Toll-Free: 866-688-0808
info@nevadageothermal.com
www.nevadageothermal.com
Ticker Symbol: NGP / TSX Venture
Profile: Nevada Geothermal Power Inc. is the operator of the Faulkner 1 geothermal plant in Nevada. The company owns leasehold interests in the following properties: New Truckhaven in California; Crump Geyser, in Oregon; & Pumpernickel Valley, North Valley, Blue Mountain, & Edna Mountain in Nevada.
Brian D. Fairbank, B.A.Sc., P. Eng.President & Chief Executive Officer
Andrew T. Studley, P. Eng, CPA, MBAChief Financial Officer & Secretary
Max Walenciak, P. EngSenior Vice-President, Development & Plant Operations
Stuart D. Johnson, Vice-President, Resource Development
Kim Niggemann, Vice-President, Resource Operations & External Affairs

Primary Energy Recycling Corporation
#202, 2215 So. York Rd., Oak Brook, IL
Tel: 630-230-1313;
investorinfo@primaryenergy.com
www.primaryenergyrecycling.com
Ticker Symbol: PRI / TSX
Profile: Primary Energy Recycling Corporation is involved in capturing & recycling recoverable heat & byproduct fuels from industrial & electric generation processes. Recovered materials are then converted into economical electricity & thermal energy. The company is the indirect owner & operator of four recycled energy projects, & it also has a 50% interest in a pulverized coal facility.
John Prunkl, President & Chief Executive Officer
Mike Alverson, Chief Financial Officer

Western Wind Energy Corp.
HSBC Building, #1326, 885 West Georgia St., Vancouver, BC V6C 3E8
Tel: 604-685-9463; Fax: 604-685-9441
Toll-Free: 866-765-0826
investorrelations@westernwindenergy.com
www.westernwindenergy.com
Ticker Symbol: WND / TSX Venture
Profile: Western Wind Energy Corp. is a renewable energy production company. It directly owns more than 165 MW of wind & solar capacity in production in Arizona & California. The company also owns development assets for wind & solar energy in Arizona, California, Ontario, & the Commonwealth of Puerto Rico.
Western Wind Energy Corp. trades on the TSX Venture Exchange, & also in the United States on the OTCQX under the symbol "WNDEF".
Jeffrey J. Ciachurski, President & Chief Executive Officer
Kevin Craig, CAChief Financial Officer
Steve R. Mendoza, Chief Engineer & Executive Vice-President
T. Alana Steele, Chief Operating Officer & General Counsel

Manitoba

Centra Gas Manitoba Inc.
Parent: Manitoba Hydro Electric Board
Manitoba Hydro Corporate Head Office, PO Box 815 Main, Winnipeg, MB R3C 2P4
Toll-Free: 888-624-9376
customerservice@hydro.mb.ca
www.hydro.mb.ca
Profile: Centra Gas Manitoba Inc. distributes natural gas to residential & commercial customers in Manitoba.

Newfoundland & Labrador

Fortis Inc.
Fortis Building, PO Box 8837, #1201, 139 Water St., St. John's, NL A1B 3T2
Tel: 709-737-2800; Fax: 709-737-5307
investorrelations@fortisinc.com
www.fortisinc.com
Ticker Symbol: FTS / TSX
Profile: Fortis Inc. is an international distribution utility holding company, which serves gas & electricity customers. The company also owns hotels & commercial real estate in Canada.
H. Stanley Marshall, President/CEO
Barry V. Perry, CFO & Vice-President, Finance
Ronald W. McCabe, General Counsel & Corporate Secretary

Newfoundland Power Inc.
PO Box 8910, St. John's, NL A1B 3P6
Tel: 709-737-2802; Fax: 709-737-2903
Toll-Free: 800-663-2802
www.newfoundlandpower.com
twitter.com/NFPower
Profile: Newfoundland Power Inc. is a Fortis Company.
Earl Ludlow, President & Chief Executive Officer
Peter Alteen, Corporate Secretary & Vice-President, Regulation & Planning
Jocelyn Perry, Chief Financial Officer & Vice-President, Finance
Gary Smith, Vice-President, Customer Operations & Engineering

Peter Collins, Manager, Customer Relations & Information Technology

Nova Scotia

Emera Incorporated
1223 Lower Water St., Halifax, NS B3J 3S8
Tel: 902-450-0507; Fax: 902-428-6112
Toll-Free: 888-450-0507
investors@emera.com
www.emera.com
Ticker Symbol: EMA / TSX
Profile: The holding company is involved in the energy sector. Emera Inc.'s investments include Bangor Hydro-Electric Company, Nova Scotia Power Inc., Emera Energy, Emera Utility Services, Bayside Power, Maritimes & Northeast Pipeline, ATlantic Hydrogen Inc., Emera New Brunswick, Emera Newfoundland & Labrador, Barbados Light & Power Co., & Grand Bahama Power Ltd.
Christopher Huskilson, President/CEO
Rob Bennett, President/CEO, Nova Scotia Power Inc.
Robert Hanf, President/COO, Bangor Hydro Electric Company
Robin McAdam, President, Brunswick Pipeline Company Ltd.
Nancy Tower, F.C.A.Chief Financial Officer
902-429-6991, nancy.tower@emera.com
Wayne Crawley,, CAVice-President, Corporate Strategy & Development
James Spurr, General Counsel & Vice-President, Government Relations
Jennifer Nicholson, CADirector, Investor Relations & Strategic Development
902-428-6347, jennifer.nicholson@emera.com

Nova Scotia Power Inc. / NSPI
PO Box 910, Halifax, NS B3J 2W5
Tel: 902-450-0507; Fax: 902-428-6112
Toll-Free: 800-428-6230
investors@emera.com
www.nspower.ca
Ticker Symbol: NSI
Profile: Nova Scotia Power Inc. is engaged in the generation, transmission, & distribution of electric power across Nova Scotia.

Rob Bennett, President & Chief Executive Officer
Robin McAdam, Executive Vice-President, Strategic Business & Custome Services
René Gallant, Vice-President, Regulatory Affairs
Claudette Porter, Vice-President, Finance & Information Technology
Mark Savory, Vice-President, Technical & Construction Services

Nunavut

Ram Power, Corp.
Prior Name: Ram Power, Inc.
#200, 9460 Double R. Blvd., Reno, NV 89521
Tel: 775-398-3700; Fax: 775-828-0904
info@ram-power.com
www.ram-power.com
www.facebook.com/pages/Ram-Power-Corp/365229206828708
www.linkedin.com/company/ram-power-corp.
Ticker Symbol: RPG / TSX
Profile: Ram Power is a renewable energy company that was founded in 2008. The company acquires, explores, develops, & operates geothermal properties. Projects are located in Canada, the United States, & Latin America.
Shuman Moore, President & Chief Executive Officer
Selby F. Little, Chief Financial Officer
Gordon Alter, Vice-President & General Counsel

Ontario

Algonquin Power & Utilities Corp.
2845 Bristol Circle, Oakville, ON L6H 7H7
Tel: 905-465-4500; Fax: 905-465-4514
apif@algonquinpower.com
www.algonquinpower.com
Ticker Symbol: AQN / TSX
Profile: Algonquin Power & Utilities Corp. is a renewable energy & regulated utility company. Its operating subsidiaries are Algonquin Power Company & Liberty Utilities. Through these subsidiaries, Algonquin Power & Utilities Corp. invests in sustainable utility distribution businesses as well as hydroelectric, wind, & solar power facilities.
Ian Robertson, Chief Executive Officer
David Pasieka, President, Liberty Utilities
Mike Snow, President, Algonquin Power Company
David Bronicheski, Chief Financial Officer
Linda Beairsto, General Counsel & Corporate Secretary
Kelly Castledine, Contact, Investor Relations

Atomic Energy of Canada Limited / AECL
Énergie atomique du Canada Ltée
Head Office, Chalk River Laboratories, Chalk River, ON K0J 1J0
Tel: 613-584-3311; Toll-Free: 866-513-2325
librarycr@aecl.ca (library requests)
www.aecl.ca
Profile: Atomic Energy of Canada develops peaceful applications from nuclear technology. Services include research, design, engineering, waste management, & decommissioning. The following offices & laboratories are part of Atomic Energy of Canada: Whiteshell Laboratories in Pinawa, Manitoba; Low-Level Radioactive Waste Management in Ottawa, Ontario; AECL Ottawa; Port Hope Office & Laboratory in Port Hope, Ontario; Port Hope Area Initiative; & Centre for Nuclear Energy Research at the University of New Brunswick in Fredericton.
Robert Walker, President & Chief Executive Officer
Allan A. Hawryluk, Senior Vice-President, Strategic Contracting
Jon Lundy, Senior Vice-President & General Manager
Steve Halpenny, Chief Financial Officer & Vice-President
Randy Lesco, Chief Nuclear Officer & Vice-President, Operations
Richard Fujarczuk, Vice-President, General Counsel, & Corporate Secretary
William Kupferschmidt, Vice-President, Research & Development
Joan Miller, Vice-President, Decommissioning & Waste Management

Brookfield Renewable Energy Partners L.P. / BREP
c/o Brookfield Asset Management, Brookfield Pl., #300, 181 Bay St., Toronto, ON M5J 2T3
Toll-Free: 888-327-2722
enquiries@brookfieldrenewable.com
www.brookfieldrenewable.com
Ticker Symbol: BEP.UN / TSX
Profile: In November 2011, Brookfield Renewable Power Fund merged with Brookfield Asset Management Inc.'s wind & hydro assets in Canada, the United States, & Brazil.
The combined organization, Brookfield Renewable Energy Partners L.P., is concentrated largely in hydro power projects. Wind projects make up the balance. The company also holds development projects. The portfolio is diversified across river systems & power markets in Canada, the United States, & Brazil. Brookfield Asset Management (TSX: BAM.A, NYSE: BAM) owns, directly & indirectly, about 68% of Brookfield Renewable on a fully-exchanged basis.
Richard Legault, Chief Executive Officer
Ben Vaughan, President & Chief Operating Officer
Sachin Shah, Chief Financial Officer
Zev Korman, Director, Investor Relations & Communications
416-359-1955, zev.korman@brookfield.com

China Wind Power International Corp.
Corporate Office, #502, 110 Yonge St., Toronto, ON M5C 1T4
www.chinawindpowerinternational.com
www.facebook.com/ChinaWindPower
twitter.com/chinawindpower
Ticker Symbol: CNW / TSX Venture
Profile: China Wind Power International Corp. is an independent wind power producer, with operations in China. The company indirectly holds rights for wind energy development in Du Mon County, Heilongjiang Province.
Jun Liu, Chief Executive Officer
Wendell Zhang, Chief Financial Officer
416-916-4205, Fax: 416-916-5463,
wzhang@chinawindpowerinternational.com
Zhijie Song, Chief Engineer
Walter Huang, Senior Vice-President

EnerCare Inc.
Prior Name: The Consumers' Waterheater Income Fund
PO Box 4645 A, Toronto, ON M5W 7A3
Tel: 416-649-1890; Fax: 866-521-8882
Toll-Free: 866-449-4423
rentalinfo@enercare.ca; connections.care@
www.enercare.ca
Ticker Symbol: ECI / TSX
Profile: EnerCare Inc. is the owner of approximately 1.2 million installed water heaters & other assets, which are rented mainly to residential customers in Ontario. The company also owns EnerCare Connections, a sub-metering company. EnerCare Connections has metering contracts for apartment & condominium suites, primarily in Ontario & Alberta.
John MacDonald, President & Chief Executive Officer
Evelyn Sutherland, Chief Financial Officer
John Toffoletto, General Counsel, Corporate Secretary, & Senior Vice-President
Tom Cooper, Vice-President, Sales & Marketing

Ensource Corp.
3240 Mavis Rd., Mississauga, ON L5C 3K1
Tel: 905-273-9050; Fax: 905-566-2737
info@enersource.com; account-info@enersou
www.enersource.com
Profile: The energy provider serves both residential & commercial customers in Mississauga, Ontario. Emersource also offers conservation programs.
Craig Fleming, President & Chief Executive Officer
Dan Pastoric, Chief Operating Officer & Executive Vice-President
Norm Wolff, Chief Financial Officer & Executive Vice-President
Raymond Rauber, Vice-President, Engineering & Operations
Karen Ras, Director, Corporate Relations
905-283-4275, Fax: 647-401-3942,
publicaffairs@enersource.com

Just Energy
Parent: Just Energy Group Inc.
First Canadian Place, PO Box 355, #2630, 100 King St. West, Toronto, ON M5X 1E1
Tel: 866-587-8674; Fax: 888-548-7690
Toll-Free: 877-488-7809
www.justenergy.com
www.facebook.com/justenergygroup
twitter.com/JustEnergyGroupwww.linkedin.com/company/just-energy_2
Ticker Symbol: JE / TSX
Profile: The independent energy supplier sells electricity & natural gas to residential & commercial customers throughout Canada & the United States. Through National Home Services, high efficiency & tankless water heaters, furnaces, & air conditioners are sold & rented. Wheat-based ethanol is produced & sold through Terra Grain Fuels.
Green products are offered through Just Energy's JustGreen & JustClean programs. JustGreen products are sourced from renewable sources such as wind, biomass, or run of the river hydro. JustClean products allow some customers to offset their carbon footprint.
Ken Hartwick, CAChief Executive Officer & President
905-795-3557
Beth Summers, CAChief Financial Officer
905-795-4206
Gord Potter, Executive Vice-President, Regulatory & Legal Affairs
905-795-4214, gpotter@justenergy.com

Northland Power Inc.
30 St Clair Ave. West, 17th Fl., Toronto, ON M4V 3A1
Tel: 416-962-6262; Fax: 416-962-6266
investorrelations@northlandpower.ca
www.northlandpower.ca
Ticker Symbol: NPI / TSX
Profile: Northland Power Inc. is engaged in the development of wind, solar, run-of-river hydro projects, & additional power generation opportunities. The company's assets include facilities that produce electricity form natural gas & renewable resources such as biomass, solar, & wind.
John W. Brace, Chief Executive Officer
Paul J. Bradley, Chief Financial Officer
Barb Bokla, Manager, Investor Relations
647-288-1438

Toronto Hydro Corporation
Parent: City of Toronto
14 Carlton St., Toronto, ON M5B 1K5
Tel: 416-542-3100;
www.torontohydro.com
Profile: Toronto Hydro Corporation's wholly owned subsidiaries are Toronto Hydro-Electric System Limited & Toronto Hydro Energy Services Inc.. Toronto Hydro-Electric System distributes electricity & engages in conservation activities, while Toronto Hydro Energy Services provides street lighting services.
Anthony Haines, President & Chief Executive Officer
Jean-Sebastien Couillard, Chief Financial Officer
Ivano Labricciosa, Vice-President, Asset Management
Ben LaPianta, Vice-President, Distribution Grid Management
Ave Lethbridge, Vice-President, Organizational Effectiveness, Environment, Health, & Safety
Blair H. Peberdy, Vice-President, Marketing, Communications, & Public Affairs
Dino Priore, Vice-President, Distribution Services
Paul B. Sommerville, General Counsel & Vice-President, Regulatory Affairs
Chris Tyrrell, Chief Conservation Officer & Vice-President, Customer Care
Robert W.F. Wong, Vice-President, Information Technology & Strategic Management

Prince Edward Island

Maritime Electric Company Ltd.
PO Box 1328, Charlottetown, PE C1A 7N2
Fax: 902-629-3630
Toll-Free: 800-670-1012
customerservice@maritimeelectric.com
www.maritimeelectric.com
Profile: Maritime Electric has delivered electricity on Prince Edward Island since 1918. The public utility is regulated by the Island Regulatory & Appeals Commission under the Renewable Energy Act & the Electric Power Act.
Fred J. O'Brien, President & Chief Executive Officer
Steven D. Loggie, Chief Financial Officer & Vice-President, Finance & Corporate Services
John D. Gaudet, Vice-President, Operations & Engineering
Jacqueline M. Baird, Manager, Customer Service
Kim A. Griffin, Manager, Corporate Communications & Public Affairs
Greg S. MacPhail, Manager, Information Technology
Ron J. LeBlanc, Manager, Production & Energy Supply
Jason C. Roberts, Director Regulatory & Financial Planning

Québec

BCE Inc.
Also Known As: Bell Canada
Building A, 1 Carrefour Alexander-Graham-Bell, Montréal, QC H3B 3B3
Tel: 514-870-4619; Fax: 514-766-5735
Toll-Free: 888-932-6666
bcecomms@bce.ca
www.bce.ca
Ticker Symbol: BCE / TSX
Profile: Formed in 1970, BCE Inc. is a communications company that provides broadband wireless & wireline communication services. Clients include both residents & businesses across Canada.
Bell Media is a multimedia company, with assets in television, radio, & digital media.
George Cope, CEO
Stephen Wetmore, President, National Markets
Siim Vanaselja, CFO
Eugene Roman, Group President, Systems & Technology

Boralex Inc.
36, rue Lajeunesse, Kingsey Falls, QC J0A 1B0
Tel: 819-363-5860; Fax: 819-363-5866
info@boralex.com
www.boralex.com
Ticker Symbol: BLX, BLX.DB / TSX
Profile: Boralex Inc. is a power producer. It focuses on the following power generation types: hydroelectric, thermal, wind, & solar. The company has more than 200 employees.
Patrick Lemaire, President & Chief Executive Officer
Jean-François Thibodeau, Chief Financial Officer & Vice-President
Sylvain Aird, Corporate Secretary & Vice-President, Legal Affairs
Patricia Lemaire, Director, Public Affairs & Communications

Gaz Métro
1717, rue du Havre, Montréal, QC H2K 2X3
Tel: 514-598-3222; Fax: 514-598-3144
Toll-Free: 800-875-6202
info@gazmetro.com
www.gazmetro.com
Profile: Gaz Métro is a natural gas distributor in Québec. The company is also involved in natural gas transportation & storage, the electricity distribution market, & the development of energy projects such a wind power.
In 2010, Gaz Métro Limited Partnership & Valener Inc.

announced the reorganization of Gaz Métro's public ownership structure into a dividend paying publicly listed corporation named Valener Inc.
Sophie Brochu, President & Chief Executive Officer
Pierre Despars, Chief Financial Officer & Executive Vice-President, Corporate Affairs
Partrick Cabana, Vice-Presidemt, Gas Supply, Procurement, & Regulatory Affairs
Caroll Carle, Vice-President, Employees & Culture
Martin Imbleau, Vice-President, Operations & Major Projects
Guylaine Lehoux, Vice-President, Growth

Innergex Renewable Energy Inc.

#1255, 1111, rue Saint-Charles ouest, Longueuil, QC J4K 5G4

Tel: 450-928-2550; Fax: 450-928-2544
info@innergex.com
www.innergex.com
Ticker Symbol: INE / TSX

Profile: Innergex Renewable Energy develops & operates renewable power generating facilities. Operations are carried out in British Columbia, Ontario, Québec, & Idaho, USA. The company focuses upon the wind power, solar power, & hydroelectric sectors.
Michel Letellier, MBAPresident & Chief Executive Officer
Jean Perron, Chief Financial Officer & Vice-President
Michèle Beauchamp, LL.B., LL.M.,Corporate Secretary & Vice-President, Legal Affairs
Guy Dufort, Vice-President, Public Affairs
Peter Grover, Eng.Vice-President, Project Management
Jean Trudel, MBAVice-President, Finance & Investor Relations

Government Agency Guide

CONSERVATION & ECOLOGY

See Also: Heritage Resources; Natural Resources

Canadian Heritage, 15 Eddy St., Gatineau, K1A 0M5 QC
819-997-0055, 866-811-0055
Canadian Polar Commission, Constitution Square, #1710, 360 Albert St., Ottawa, K1R 7X7 ON
613-943-8605, Fax: 613-943-8607, 888-765-2701, mail@polarcom.gc.ca
Environment Canada, 10 Wellington St., Gatineau, K1A 0H3 QC
819-997-2800, Fax: 819-994-1412, 800-668-6767, enviroinfo@ec.gc.ca
Commission for Environmental Cooperation, Secretariat, #200, 393, rue St-Jacques ouest, Montréal, H2Y 1N9 QC
514-350-4300, Fax: 514-350-4314, info@cec.org
Fisheries Resource Conservation Council, PO Box 2001 D, Ottawa, ON K1P 5W3
613-998-0433, Fax: 613-998-1146, info@frcc-ccrh.ca
Natural Resources Canada, 580 Booth St., Ottawa, K1A 0E4 ON
613-995-0947, Fax: 613-992-7211
Parks Canada, 25 Eddy St., Gatineau, K1A 0M5 QC
888-773-8888, information@pc.gc.ca

Alberta

Alberta Environmental Appeal Board, Peace Hills Trust Tower, #306, 10011 - 109 St. NW, Edmonton, AB T5J 3S8
780-427-6207, Fax: 780-427-4693
Alberta Special Areas Board, 212 - 2nd Ave. West, PO Box 820, Hanna, AB T0J 1P0
403-854-5600, Fax: 403-854-5527, specarea@telusplanet.net
Alberta Used Oil Management Association, Scotia One, Scotia Place, #1050, 10060 Jasper Ave., Edmonton, AB T5J 3R8
780-414-1510, Fax: 780-414-1519, reception@usedoilrecycling.ca
Beverage Container Management Board, #1010, 10707 - 100 Ave., Edmonton, AB T5J 3M1
780-424-3193, Fax: 780-428-4620, 888-424-7671, info@bcmb.ab.ca
Clean Air Strategic Alliance, Centre West Bldg, 10035 - 108 St., 10th Fl., Edmonton, AB T5J 3E1
780-427-9793, Fax: 780-422-3127, casa@casahome.org
Alberta Environment, South Tower, Petroleum Plaza, 9915 - 108 St., Main Fl., Edmonton, T5K 2G8 AB
780-427-2700, Fax: 780-422-4086,-310-0000, env.infocent@gov.ab.ca
Natural Resources Conservation Board, Sterling Place, 9940 - 106 St., 4th Fl., Edmonton, AB T5K 2N2
780-422-1977, Fax: 780-427-0607, 866-383-6722

British Columbia

British Columbia Assessment Authority, 1537 Hillside Ave., Victoria, BC V8T 4Y2
250-595-6211, Fax: 250-595-6222, info@bcassessment.ca
Ministry of Environment, PO Box 9339 Prov Govt,Victoria, V8W 9M1 BC
250-387-1161, Fax: 250-387-5669, www.envmail@gov.bc.ca
Environmental Appeal Board, 747 Fort St., 4th Fl., PO Box 9425 Prov Govt, Victoria, BC V8W 9V1
250-387-3464, Fax: 250-356-9923, eabinfo@gov.bc.ca
Environmental Stewardship Division, 2975 Jutland Rd., 5th Fl., PO Box 9339 Prov Govt,Victoria, V8T 5J9 BC
250-356-0121, Fax: 250-953-3414
Forest Practices Board, 1675 Douglas St., 3rd Fl., PO Box 9905 Prov Govt, Victoria, BC V8W 9R1
250-387-7964, Fax: 250-387-7009, 800-994-5899, fpboard@gov.bc.ca
Fraser Basin Council, Central Office, 470 Granville St., 1st Fl., Vancouver, BC V6C 1V5
604-488-5350, Fax: 604-488-5351, info@fraserbasin.bc.ca
Mediation & Arbitration Board, #310, 9900 - 100 Ave., Fort St John, BC V1J 5S7
250-787-3403, Fax: 250-787-3228, mab.office@gov.bc.ca
Northern Interior, 1011 - 4 Ave., 5th Fl., Prince George, V2L 3H9 BC
250-565-6100, Fax: 250-565-6671, www.for.gov.bc.ca/rni

Manitoba

Clean Environment Commission, #305, 155 Carlton St., Winnipeg, MB R3C 3H8
204-945-0594, Fax: 204-945-0090
Manitoba Conservation, 200 Saulteaux Cres., Winnipeg, R3J 3W3 MB
204-945-6784, 800-214-6497, mincon@leg.gov.mb.ca
Ecological Reserves Advisory Committee, c/o Manitoba Conservation, Parks & Natural Areas Branch, 200 Saulteaux Cres., Winnipeg, MB R3J 3W3
204-945-4148, Fax: 204-945-0012, hhernandez@gov.mb.ca
Manitoba Conservation Districts Commission, Secretariat c/o Planning & Coordination Branch, 123 Main St., PO Box 20000, Neepawa, MB R0J 1H0
204-476-7033, Fax: 204-476-7539, whildebran@gov.mb.ca

New Brunswick

Assessment & Planning Appeal Board, #201, 435 King St., PO Box 6000, Fredericton, NB E3B 5H1
506-453-2126, Fax: 506-444-4881,
Department of the Environment, Marysville Place, 20 McGloin St., PO Box 6000, Fredericton, E3B 5H1 NB
506-453-2690, Fax: 506-457-4991

Newfoundland & Labrador

Department of Environment & Conservation, Confederation Bldg., West Block, 4th Fl., PO Box 8700, St. John's, A1B 4J6 NL
709-729-2664, Fax: 709-729-6639, 800-563-6181, info@gov.nl.ca

Northwest Territories

Department of Environment & Natural Resources, PO Box 1320, Yellowknife, X1A 2L9 NT

Nova Scotia

Environmental & Natural Areas Management, PO Box 697, Halifax, B3J 3T8 NS
902-424-3571
Department of Natural Resources, Founder's Square, 1701 Hollis St., 3rd Fl., PO Box 698, Halifax, B3J 2T9 NS
902-424-5935, Fax: 902-424-0594, 800-565-2224

Ontario

Ministry of Environment, 135 St. Clair Ave. West, Toronto, M4V 1P5 ON
416-325-4000, Fax: 416-325-3159, 800-565-4923
Ministry of Natural Resources, Whitney Block, #6630, 99 Wellesley St. West, 6th Fl., Toronto, M7A 1W3 ON
800-667-1940
Niagara Escarpment Commission, 232 Guelph St., Georgetown, L7G 4B1 ON
905-877-5191, Fax: 905-873-7452

Prince Edward Island

Department of Environment, Energy & Forestry, Jones Bldg., 11 Kent St., 4th & 5th Fl., PO Box 2000, Charlottetown, C1A 7N8 PE
902-368-5000, Fax: 902-368-5830
Environmental Advisory Council, 11 Kent St., PO Box 2000, Charlottetown, PE C1A 7N8
Department of Tourism, PO Box 2000, Charlottetown, C1A 7N8 PE
800-463-4734

Quebec

Comité consultatif de l'environnement Kativik, CP 930, Kuujjuaq, QC J0M 1C0
819-964-2961, Fax: 819-964-0694, ndea@krg.ca
Ministère du Développement durable, de l'Environnement et des Parcs, Édifice Marie-Guyart, 675, boul René-Lévesque est, 29e étage, Québec, G1R 5V7 QC
418-521-3830, Fax: 418-646-5974, 800-561-1616, info@mddep.gouv.qc.ca
Fondation de la faune du Québec, Place Iberville II, #420, 1175, av Lavigerie, Québec, QC G1V 4P1
418-644-7926, Fax: 418-643-7655, 877-639-0742, ffq@riq.qc.ca
Société de développement de la Baie James, 110, boul Matagami, CP 970, Matagami, QC J0Y 2A0
819-739-4717, Fax: 819-739-4329
Société québécoise de récupération et de recyclage, Siège social, #200, 420, boul Charest est, Québec, QC G1K 8M4
418-643-0394, Fax: 418-643-6507, 866-523-8290, info@recyc-quebec.gouv.qc.ca

Saskatchewan

Saskatchewan Assessment Management Agency, #200, 2201 - 11 Ave., Regina, S4P 0J8 SK
306-924-8000, Fax: 306-924-8070, 800-667-7262, info.request@sama.sk.ca
Saskatchewan Environment, 3211 Albert St., 2nd Fl., Regina, S4S 5W6 SK
306-953-3750, Fax: 306-787-9544, 800-567-4224, inquiry@serm.gov.sk.ca
Saskatchewan Conservation Data Centre, 3211 Albert St., Regina, SK S4S 5W6
306-787-9038, Fax: 306-787-9544
Saskatchewan Watershed Authority, 111 Fairford St. East, Moose Jaw, SK S6H 7X9
306-694-3900, Fax: 306-694-3465, comm@swa.ca

Yukon Territory

Alsek Renewable Resource Council, PO Box 2077, Haines Junction, YT Y0B 1L0
867-634-2524, Fax: 867-634-2527
Carmacks Renewable Resource Council, PO Box 122, Carmacks, YT Y0B 1C0
867-863-6838, Fax: 867-863-6429, carmacksrrc@lscfn.ca
Dawson District Renewable Resource Council, PO Box 1380, Dawson City, YT Y0B 1G0
867-993-6976, Fax: 867-993-6093, dawsonrrc@yknet.yk.ca
Yukon Environment, PO Box 2703, Whitehorse, Y1A 2C6 YT
867-667-5652, Fax: 867-393-6213, 800-661-0408, environmentyukon@gov.yk.ca
Mayo District Renewable Resources Council, PO Box 249, Mayo, YT Y0B 1M0
867-996-2942, Fax: 867-996-2948, mayorrc@yknet.yk.ca
North Yukon Renewable Resources Council, PO Box 80, Old Crow, YT Y0B 1N0
vgrrc@yknet.yk.ca
Selkirk Renewable Resources Council, PO Box 32, Pelly Crossing, YT Y0B 1P0
867-537-3937, Fax: 867-537-3939, selkirkrre@yknet.yk.ca
Teslin Renewable Resource Council, PO Box 186, Teslin, YT Y0A 1B0
867-390-2323, Fax: 867-390-2919, teslinrrc@yknet.yk.ca
Yukon Land Use Planning Council, #201, 307 Jarvis St., Whitehorse, YT Y1A 2H3
867-667-7397, Fax: 867-667-4624, ylupc@planyukon.ca

ENERGY

See Also: Natural Resources

Atomic Energy of Canada Limited, Head Office, 2251 Speakman Dr., Mississauga, L5K 1B2 ON
905-823-9040, webmaster@aecl.ca
Canadian Nuclear Safety Commission, 280 Slater St., PO Box 1046 B,Ottawa, K1P 5S9 ON
613-995-5894, Fax: 613-995-5086, 800-668-5284, info@cnsc-ccsn.gc.ca
Indian Oil & Gas Canada, #100, 9911 Chula Blvd., Tsuu T'ina (Sarcee), AB T2W 6H6
Fax: 403-292-5618
National Energy Board, 444 - 7 Ave. SW, Calgary, T2P 0X8 AB
403-292-4800, Fax: 403-292-5503, 800-899-1265, info@neb-one.gc.ca

Alberta

Alberta Energy & Utilities Board, 640 - 5 Ave. SW, Calgary, AB T2P 3G4
403-297-8311, Fax: 403-297-7336
Alberta Energy Research Institute, AMEC Place, #2540, 801 - 6 Ave. SW, Calgary, AB T2P 3W2
403-297-8650, Fax: 403-297-3638, aeri@gov.ab.ca
Alberta Energy, North Petroleum Plaza, 9945 - 108 St., 7th Fl., Edmonton, T5K 2G6 AB
780-427-7425, Fax: 780-422-0698, 780-310-0000

British Columbia

Ministry of Energy, Mines & Petroleum Resources, PO Box 9318 Prov Govt,Victoria, V8W 9N3 BC
250-952-0241
British Columbia Hydro, 333 Dunsmuir St., 18th Fl., Vancouver, V6B 5R3 BC
604-224-9376, Fax: 604-623-4467, 800-224-9376

Oil & Gas Commission, #100, 10003 - 110 Ave., Fort St John, BC V1J 6M7
250-261-5700, 800-663-7867
Powerex Corp., #1400, 666 Burrard St., Vancouver, BC V6C 2X8
604-891-5000, Fax: 604-891-6060, 800-220-4907, customer.service@bchydro.com
Powertech Labs Inc., 12388 - 88 Ave., Surrey, BC V8W 7R7
604-590-7500, Fax: 604-590-5347, info@powertechlans.com
British Columbia Utilities Commission, 900 Howe St., 6th Fl., PO Box 250, Vancouver, V6Z 2N3 BC
604-660-4700, Fax: 604-660-1102, 800-663-1385, commission.secretary@bcuc.com

Manitoba

Manitoba Hydro, PO Box 815 Main,Winnipeg, R3C 2P4 MB
204-474-3311, Fax: 204-475-0069, publicaffairs@hydro.mb.ca
Petroleum, #360, 1395 Ellice Ave., Winnipeg, R3G 3P2 MB
204-945-6577, Fax: 204-945-0586
Manitoba Science, Technology, Energy & Mines, #333, 450 Broadway, Winnipeg, R3C 0V8 MB

New Brunswick

Efficiency NB, #101, 33 Charlotte St., Saint John, NB E2L 2H3
506-643-7826, Fax: 506-643-7835, 866-643-8833
Department of Energy, Brunswick Square, #100M, 1 Germain St., PO Box 5001, Saint John, E2L 4Y9 NB
506-658-3180, Fax: 506-658-3191
Department of Natural Resources, PO Box 6000, Fredericton, E3B 5H1 NB
506-453-2510, Fax: 506-444-5839, dnrweb@gnb.ca
New Brunswick Power Group of Companies, 515 King St., PO Box 2000, Fredericton, E3B 4X1 NB
506-458-4444, Fax: 506-458-4000, questions@nbpower.com

Newfoundland & Labrador

Canada-Newfoundland Offshore Petroleum Board, TD Place, 140 Water St., 5th Fl., St. John's, NL A1C 6H6
709-778-1400, Fax: 709-778-1473, postmaster@cnlopb.nl.ca
Churchill Falls (Labrador) Corporation Limited, Hydro Place, 500 Columbus Dr., PO Box 12500, St. John's, A1B 4K7 NL
709-737-1859, Fax: 709-737-1816
Newfoundland & Labrador Hydro, Hydro Place, Columbus Dr., PO Box 12400, St. John's, A1B 4K7 NL
709-737-1400, Fax: 709-737-1800
Newfoundland & Labrador Board of Commissioners of Public Utilities, PO Box 21040, St. John's, A1A 5B2 NL
709-726-8600, Fax: 709-726-9604, 866-782-0006, ito@pub.nf.ca
Twin Falls Power Corporation, PO Box 12500, St. John's, A1B 3T5 NL

Northwest Territories

Department of Environment & Natural Resources, PO Box 1320, Yellowknife, X1A 2L9 NT
Northwest Territories Power Corporation, 4 Capital Dr., Hay River, X0E 1G2 NT
867-874-5200, Fax: 867-874-5229, info@ntpc.com

Nova Scotia

Canada-Nova Scotia Offshore Petroleum Board, TD Centre, 1791 Barrington St., 6th Fl., Halifax, NS B3J 3K9
902-422-5588, Fax: 902-422-1799, postmaster@cnsopb.ns.ca
Department of Energy, Bank of Montreal Bldg., #400, 5151 George St., PO Box 2664, Halifax, B3J 3P7 NS
902-424-4575, Fax: 902-424-0528, energyinfo@gov.ns.ca
Nova Scotia Utility & Review Board, 1601 Lower Water St., 3rd Fl., PO Box 1692 M,Halifax, B3J 3S3 NS
902-424-4448, Fax: 902-424-3919, uarb.board@gov.ns.ca

Ontario

Ministry of Energy and Infrastructure, Hearst Block, 900 Bay St., 4th Fl., Toronto, M7A 2E1 ON
416-327-6758, Fax: 416-327-0033, 888-668-4939
Ministry of Environment, 135 St. Clair Ave. West, Toronto, M4V 1P5 ON
416-325-4000, Fax: 416-325-3159, 800-565-4923
Hydro One Inc., North Tower, 483 Bay St., Toronto, M5G 2P5 ON
416-345-5000, 877-955-1155, webmaster@HydroOne.com
Independent Electricity System Operator, PO Box 4474 A,Toronto, M5W 4E5 ON
905-403-6900, Fax: 905-403-6921, 888-448-7777, customer.relations@ieso.ca
Ontario Energy Board, #2700, 2300 Yonge St., Toronto, ON M4P 1E4
416-481-1967, Fax: 416-440-7656, 888-632-6273
Ontario Power Authority, #1600, 120 Adelaide St. West, Toronto, ON M5H 1T1
416-967-7474, Fax: 416-967-1947, info@powerauthority.on.ca
Ontario Power Generation, 700 University Ave., Toronto, M5G 1X6 ON
416-592-2555, 877-592-2555

Prince Edward Island

Department of Environment, Energy & Forestry, Jones Bldg., 11 Kent St., 4th & 5th Fl., PO Box 2000, Charlottetown, C1A 7N8 PE
902-368-5000, Fax: 902-368-5830
PEI Energy Corporation, Jones Bldg., 11 Kent St., 4th Fl., PO Box 2000, Charlottetown, PE C1A 7N8
902-894-0288, Fax: 902-368-0290

Quebec

Agence de l'efficacité énergétique, #B-405, 5700, 4e av ouest, Québec, QC G1H 6R1
418-627-6379, Fax: 418-643-5828, 877-727-6655, aee@aee.gouv.qc.ca
Hydro-Québec, 75, boul René-Lévesque ouest, 20e étage, Montréal, H2Z 1A4 QC
514-289-2211
Régie de l'énergie, Tour de la Bourse, #255, 800, Place Victoria, CP 1, Montréal, QC H4Z 1A2
514-873-2452, Fax: 514-873-2070, 888-873-2452, secretariat@regie-energie.qc.ca
Société d'énergie de la Baie-James, 888, de Maisonneuve est, 2e étage, Montréal, H2L 5B2 QC
514-286-2020

Saskatchewan

Saskatchewan Energy & Resources, #300, 2103 - 11th Ave., Regina, S4P 3Z8 SK
306-787-2528, Fax: 306-787-8447, 866-727-5427
Saskatchewan Power Corporation (SaskPower), 2025 Victoria Ave., Regina, S4P 0S1 SK
306-566-2121, Fax: 306-566-2330, 800-667-4749
SaskEnergy Incorporated, 1777 Victoria Ave., Regina, S4P 4K5 SK
306-777-9225, Fax: 306-777-9200, 800-567-8899

Yukon Territory

Yukon Energy, Mines & Resources, PO Box 2703, Whitehorse, Y1A 2C6 YT
867-667-5466, Fax: 867-667-8601, 800-661-0408, emr@gov.yk.ca

HYDRO ELECTRIC POWER

National Energy Board, 444 - 7 Ave. SW, Calgary, T2P 0X8 AB
403-292-4800, Fax: 403-292-5503, 800-899-1265, info@neb-one.gc.ca

Alberta

Alberta Energy & Utilities Board, 640 - 5 Ave. SW, Calgary, AB T2P 3G4
403-297-8311, Fax: 403-297-7336
Alberta Utilities Consumer Advocate, TD Tower, 10088 - 102 Ave., Edmonton, T5J 2Z1 AB
780-644-5130, Fax: 780-644-5129, 866-714-4455, UtilitiesConsumerAdvocate@gov.ab.

British Columbia

British Columbia Hydro, 333 Dunsmuir St., 18th Fl., Vancouver, V6B 5R3 BC
604-224-9376, Fax: 604-623-4467, 800-224-9376
Powertech Labs Inc., 12388 - 88 Ave., Surrey, BC V8W 7R7
604-590-7500, Fax: 604-590-5347, info@powertechlans.com

Manitoba

Manitoba Hydro, PO Box 815 Main,Winnipeg, R3C 2P4 MB
204-474-3311, Fax: 204-475-0069, publicaffairs@hydro.mb.ca

New Brunswick

New Brunswick Electric Finance Corporation, #376, 670 King St., PO Box 6000, Fredericton, NB E3B 5H1
506-453-3952, Fax: 506-453-2053
New Brunswick Power Group of Companies, 515 King St., PO Box 2000, Fredericton, E3B 4X1 NB
506-458-4444, Fax: 506-458-4000, questions@nbpower.com

Newfoundland & Labrador

Churchill Falls (Labrador) Corporation Limited, Hydro Place, 500 Columbus Dr., PO Box 12500, St. John's, A1B 4K7 NL
709-737-1859, Fax: 709-737-1816
Newfoundland & Labrador Hydro, Hydro Place, Columbus Dr., PO Box 12400, St. John's, A1B 4K7 NL
709-737-1400, Fax: 709-737-1800
Twin Falls Power Corporation, PO Box 12500, St. John's, A1B 3T5 NL

Northwest Territories

Northwest Territories Power Corporation, 4 Capital Dr., Hay River, X0E 1G2 NT
867-874-5200, Fax: 867-874-5229, info@ntpc.com

Nova Scotia

Nova Scotia Utility & Review Board, 1601 Lower Water St., 3rd Fl., PO Box 1692 M,Halifax, B3J 3S3 NS
902-424-4448, Fax: 902-424-3919, uarb.board@gov.ns.ca

Ontario

Hydro One Inc., North Tower, 483 Bay St., Toronto, M5G 2P5 ON
416-345-5000, 877-955-1155, webmaster@HydroOne.com
Independent Electricity System Operator, PO Box 4474 A,Toronto, M5W 4E5 ON
905-403-6900, Fax: 905-403-6921, 888-448-7777, customer.relations@ieso.ca
Ontario Power Authority, #1600, 120 Adelaide St. West, Toronto, ON M5H 1T1
416-967-7474, Fax: 416-967-1947, info@powerauthority.on.ca
Ontario Power Generation, 700 University Ave., Toronto, M5G 1X6 ON
416-592-2555, 877-592-2555

Quebec

Hydro-Québec, 75, boul René-Lévesque ouest, 20e étage, Montréal, H2Z 1A4 QC
514-289-2211
Société d'énergie de la Baie-James, 888, de Maisonneuve est, 2e étage, Montréal, H2L 5B2 QC
514-286-2020

Saskatchewan

Saskatchewan Power Corporation (SaskPower), 2025 Victoria Ave., Regina, S4P 0S1 SK
306-566-2121, Fax: 306-566-2330, 800-667-4749

OIL & NATURAL GAS RESOURCES

See Also: Energy; Natural Resources

Indian Oil & Gas Canada, #100, 9911 Chula Blvd., Tsuu T'ina (Sarcee), AB T2W 6H6
Fax: 403-292-5618
National Energy Board, 444 - 7 Ave. SW, Calgary, T2P 0X8 AB
403-292-4800, Fax: 403-292-5503, 800-899-1265, info@neb-one.gc.ca

Alberta

Alberta Energy & Utilities Board, 640 - 5 Ave. SW, Calgary, AB T2P 3G4
403-297-8311, Fax: 403-297-7336
Alberta Energy, North Petroleum Plaza, 9945 - 108 St., 7th Fl., Edmonton, T5K 2G6 AB
780-427-7425, Fax: 780-422-0698, 780-310-0000

British Columbia

Ministry of Energy, Mines & Petroleum Resources, PO Box 9318 Prov Govt,Victoria, V8W 9N3 BC
250-952-0241
Oil & Gas Commission, #100, 10003 - 110 Ave., Fort St John, BC V1J 6M7
250-261-5700, 800-663-7867
British Columbia Utilities Commission, 900 Howe St., 6th Fl., PO Box 250, Vancouver, V6Z 2N3 BC
604-660-4700, Fax: 604-660-1102, 800-663-1385, commission.secretary@bcuc.com

Manitoba

Petroleum, #360, 1395 Ellice Ave., Winnipeg, R3G 3P2 MB
204-945-6577, Fax: 204-945-0586
Surface Rights Board, #360, 1395 Ellice Ave., Winnipeg, MB R3G 3P2
204-945-0731, Fax: 204-948-2578, 800-282-8069, bmiskimmin@gov.mb.ca

Newfoundland & Labrador

Canada-Newfoundland Offshore Petroleum Board, TD Place, 140 Water St., 5th Fl., St. John's, NL A1C 6H6
709-778-1400, Fax: 709-778-1473, postmaster@cnlopb.nl.ca

Nova Scotia

Canada-Nova Scotia Offshore Petroleum Board, TD Centre, 1791 Barrington St., 6th Fl., Halifax, NS B3J 3K9
902-422-5588, Fax: 902-422-1799, postmaster@cnsopb.ns.ca
Nova Scotia Utility & Review Board, 1601 Lower Water St., 3rd Fl., PO Box 1692 M,Halifax, B3J 3S3 NS
902-424-4448, Fax: 902-424-3919, uarb.board@gov.ns.ca

Nunavut

Department of Environment, PO Box 1000 1300,Iqaluit, X0A 0H0 NU
867-975-7700, Fax: 867-975-7742, 866-222-9063, environment@gov.nu.ca

Ontario

Ministry of Natural Resources, Whitney Block, #6630, 99 Wellesley St. West, 6th Fl., Toronto, M7A 1W3 ON
800-667-1940

Saskatchewan
SaskEnergy Incorporated, 1777 Victoria Ave., Regina, S4P 4K5 SK
306-777-9225, Fax: 306-777-9200, 800-567-8899,

PUBLIC UTILITIES

Alberta
Alberta Energy & Utilities Board, 640 - 5 Ave. SW, Calgary, AB T2P 3G4
403-297-8311, Fax: 403-297-7336
Alberta Utilities Consumer Advocate, TD Tower, 10088 - 102 Ave., Edmonton, T5J 2Z1 AB
780-644-5130, Fax: 780-644-5129, 866-714-4455, UtilitiesConsumerAdvocate@gov.ab.

British Columbia
British Columbia Hydro, 333 Dunsmuir St., 18th Fl., Vancouver, V6B 5R3 BC
604-224-9376, Fax: 604-623-4467, 800-224-9376
British Columbia Transmission Corporation, Four Bentall Centre, #1100, 1055 Dunsmuir St., PO Box 49260, Vancouver, V7X 1V5 BC
604-699-7300, Fax: 604-699-7333, 866-647-3334, contact.us@bctc.com
British Columbia Utilities Commission, 900 Howe St., 6th Fl., PO Box 250, Vancouver, V6Z 2N3 BC
604-660-4700, Fax: 604-660-1102, 800-663-1385, commission.secretary@bcuc.com

Manitoba
Manitoba Hydro, PO Box 815 Main,Winnipeg, R3C 2P4 MB
204-474-3311, Fax: 204-475-0069, publicaffairs@hydro.mb.ca
Public Utilities Board, #400, 330 Portage Ave., Winnipeg, MB R3C 0C4
204-945-2638, Fax: 204-945-2643, 866-854-3698, publicutilities@gov.mb.ca

New Brunswick
NB Board of Commissioners of Public Utilities, #1400, 15 Market Sq., PO Box 5001, Saint John, NB E2L 4Y9
506-658-2504, Fax: 506-643-7300, 866-766-2782, general@pub.nb.ca
New Brunswick Power Group of Companies, 515 King St., PO Box 2000, Fredericton, E3B 4X1 NB
506-458-4444, Fax: 506-458-4000, questions@nbpower.com

Newfoundland & Labrador
Churchill Falls (Labrador) Corporation Limited, Hydro Place, 500 Columbus Dr., PO Box 12500, St. John's, A1B 4K7 NL
709-737-1859, Fax: 709-737-1816
Newfoundland & Labrador Hydro, Hydro Place, Columbus Dr., PO Box 12400, St. John's, A1B 4K7 NL
709-737-1400, Fax: 709-737-1800
Newfoundland & Labrador Board of Commissioners of Public Utilities, PO Box 21040, St. John's, A1A 5B2 NL
709-726-8600, Fax: 709-726-9604, 866-782-0006, ito@pub.nf.ca

Northwest Territories
Northwest Territories Power Corporation, 4 Capital Dr., Hay River, X0E 1G2 NT
867-874-5200, Fax: 867-874-5229, info@ntpc.com
Northwest Territories Water Board, 5114 - 49th St., PO Box 1326, Yellowknife, X1A 1N9 NT
867-765-0106, Fax: 867-765-0114, info@nwtwb.com

Nova Scotia
Nova Scotia Utility & Review Board, 1601 Lower Water St., 3rd Fl., PO Box 1692 M,Halifax, B3J 3S3 NS
902-424-4448, Fax: 902-424-3919, uarb.board@gov.ns.ca

Ontario
Hydro One Inc., North Tower, 483 Bay St., Toronto, M5G 2P5 ON
416-345-5000, 877-955-1155, webmaster@HydroOne.com
Independent Electricity System Operator, PO Box 4474 A,Toronto, M5W 4E5 ON
905-403-6900, Fax: 905-403-6921, 888-448-7777, customer.relations@ieso.ca
Ontario Power Generation, 700 University Ave., Toronto, M5G 1X6 ON
416-592-2555, 877-592-2555

Prince Edward Island
Island Regulatory & Appeals Commission, National Bank Tower, #501, 134 Kent St., PO Box 577, Charlottetown, C1A 7L1 PE
902-892-3501, Fax: 902-566-4076, 800-501-6268, irac@irac.pe.ca

Quebec
Hydro-Québec, 75, boul René-Lévesque ouest, 20e étage, Montréal, H2Z 1A4 QC
514-289-2211
Régie de l'énergie, Tour de la Bourse, #255, 800, Place Victoria, CP 1, Montréal, QC H4Z 1A2
514-873-2452, Fax: 514-873-2070, 888-873-2452, secretariat@regie-energie.qc.ca

Saskatchewan
Saskatchewan Power Corporation (SaskPower), 2025 Victoria Ave., Regina, S4P 0S1 SK
306-566-2121, Fax: 306-566-2330, 800-667-4749
Saskatchewan Water Corporation (SaskWater), #200, 111 Fairford St. East, Moose Jaw, S6H 1C8 SK
306-694-3098, Fax: 306-694-3207, 888-230-1111, comm@saskwater.com
SaskEnergy Incorporated, 1777 Victoria Ave., Regina, S4P 4K5 SK
306-777-9225, Fax: 306-777-9200, 800-567-8899

Yukon Territory
Yukon Utilities Board, #19, 1114 - 1st Ave., PO Box 31728, Whitehorse, YT Y1A 6L3
867-667-5058

ENTRY NAME INDEX

A

C

D

E

F

G

H

I

J

K

M

N

O

P

Q

R

S

T

U

V

W

X

Y

Z

CANADA'S INFORMATION RESOURCE CENTRE (CIRC)

Access all these great resources Online, all the time, at Canada's Information Resource Centre (CIRC)
http://circ.greyhouse.ca

Canada's Information Resource Centre (CIRC) integrates all of Grey House Canada's award-winning reference content into one easy-to-use online resource. With over 100,000 Canadian organizations, contacts, facts and figures, it is the most comprehensive resource for specialized database content in Canada!

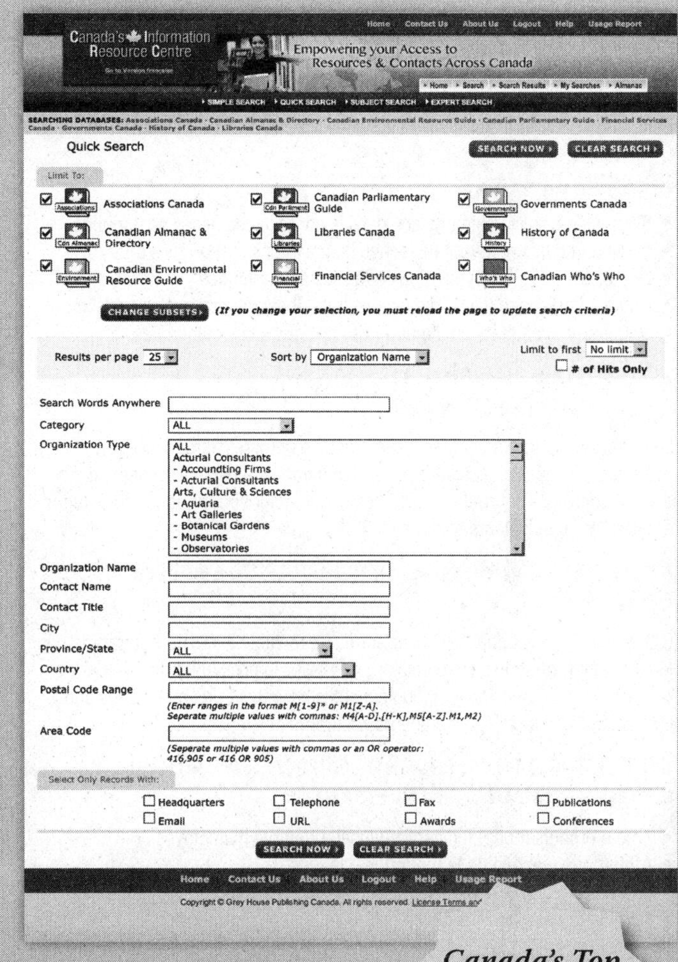

KEY ADVANTAGES OF CIRC:

- seamlessly cross-database search content from select databases
- save search results for future reference
- link directly to websites or email addresses
- clear display of your results make compiling and adding to your research easier than ever before

DESIGN YOUR OWN CUSTOM CONTACT LISTS!

CIRC gives you the option to define and extract your own lists in seconds. Whether you need contact, mail or e-mail lists, CIRC can pull together the information quickly and export it in a variety of formats.

CHOOSE BETWEEN QUICK AND EXPERT SEARCH!

With CIRC, you can choose between Expert and Quick search to pinpoint information. Designed for both novice and advanced researchers, you can conduct simple text searches as well as powerful Boolean searches.

SEARCH THE DATABASE USING COMMON OR UNIQUE FIELDS SUCH AS:

- organization type - area code - number of employees
- affiliations - founding year - language
- category - city - branch name
- contact name - contact title - postal code

ONLY GREY HOUSE DIRECTORIES PROVIDE SPECIAL CONTENT YOU WON'T FIND ANYWHERE ELSE!

Canada's Top Rated Cities soon to be added!

- **Associations Canada:** finances/funding sources, activities, publications, conferences, membership, awards, member profile
- **Canadian Parliamentary Guide:** private and political careers of elected members, complete list of constituencies and representatives
- **Canadian Environmental Resouce Guide:** products/services/areas of expertise, working languages, domestic markets, type of ownership, revenue sources
- **Financial Services:** type of ownership, number of employees, year founded, assets, revenue, ticker symbol
- **Libraries Canada:** staffing, special collections, services, year founded, national library symbol, regional system
- **Governments Canada:** municipal population
- **Canadian Who's Who:** birth city, publications, education (degrees, alma mater), career/occupation and employer

Canada's Top-Rated Cities will soon be added to CIRC! This new database is a highly accessible statistical resource that lets you rank and compare 50 major cities across Canada. With just a few clicks, you can make your own analytical tables with the data provided!

CIRC provides easier searching and faster, more pinpointed results of all of our great resources in Canada, from Associations and Government to Major Companies to Zoos and everything in between. Whether you need fully detailed information on your contact or just an email address, you can customize your search query to meet your needs. Contact us now for a free trial subscription or visit **http://circ.greyhouse.ca**. You'll be amazed at how much data can be right at your fingertips 24/7!

GREY HOUSE PUBLISHING CANADA

For more information please contact Grey House Publishing Canada

Tel.: (866) 433-4739 or (416) 644-6479 Fax: (416) 644-1904 | info@greyhouse.ca | www.greyhouse.ca

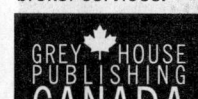

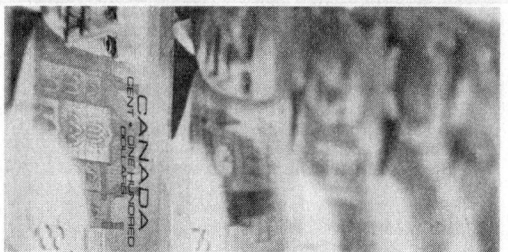

Mailing List Services

As a boutique provider of mailing lists, Grey House Publishing Canada specializes in the areas below to ensure a high level of accuracy. Our clients return to us time and time again because of the reliability of our information and great customer service. We'll work with you to develop a campaign that provides results. No other list services will work as closely as we do to meet your unique needs.

Associations—the most extensive list of Canadian associations available, featuring all professional, trade and business organizations together with not-for-profit groups.

Arts & Culture—the definitive source of key prospects in various Canadian arts and cultural outlets.

Education—the most comprehensive list of educational institutions and organizations in Canada.

Health Care / Hospitals—includes all major medical facilities with chief executives.

Lawyers—key prospects for a number of direct mail offers.

Media—the definitive source of key prospects in various Canadian media outlets, offering the top business managers and/or publishers.

Environmental—a complete profile of the Canadian Environmental scene, constantly revised for the annual Canadian Environmental Resource Guide.

Financial Services—a list of key contacts from the full range of Canada's financial services industry.

Government Key Contacts—a list of key Government contacts, maintained by the Canadian Almanac & Directory, Canada's standard institutional reference for 165 years.

Libraries—the most unique and complete list of government, special and public libraries available.

Major Canadian Companies—listings of Canada's largest private, public and Crown corporations with major key contacts of the top business decision-makers.

AVAILABILITY

Lists are available on CD, labels and via e-mail. They are provided on a one-time use basis or for a one-year lease. For a quotation on tailor-made lists to suit your needs, inquire using the contact information listed below.

For more information please contact Grey House Publishing Canada

Tel.: (866) 433-4739 or (416) 644-6479 Fax: (416) 644-1904 | info@greyhouse.ca | www.greyhouse.ca

Services de liste de distribution

En tant que point de service fournisseur de listes de distribution, Grey House Canada se spécialise dans les domaines ci-dessous pour assurer un degré supérieur de précision. Nos clients nous sont fidèles, car ils souhaitent bénéficier de notre fiabilité et de notre service à la clientèle. Nous collaborerons avec vous pour développer une campagne qui produit des résultats. Aucun autre service de création de listes ne collabore aussi étroitement que nous avec leurs clients pour satisfaire leurs besoins particuliers.

Associations—la liste la plus complète des associations canadiennes qui énumère toutes les associations professionnelles, corporatives et commerciales ainsi que les groupes sans but lucratif.

Arts et culture—la source manifeste des candidats clés des divers vecteurs artistiques et culturels au Canada.

Éducation—la liste la plus complète des établissements et des organismes d'enseignement au Canada.

Soins de santé/hôpitaux—comprend les principaux établissements médicaux et leurs directeurs.

Avocats—les principaux clients potentiels pour nombre d'offres de publipostage direct.

Médias—la source certaine des clients potentiels clés dans divers points de vente de médias canadiens; elle comprend les principaux dirigeants et éditeurs.

Environnement—un profil complet de la scène environnementale canadienne; constamment mis à jour pour le Guide des ressources environnementales canadiennes.

Services financiers—une liste des personnes-ressources clés de tout l'éventail de l'industrie des services financiers du Canada.

Coordonnées gouvernementales clés—une liste des contacts essentiels, entretenue par le Répertoire et almanach canadien, la référence institutionnelle au Canada depuis 165 ans.

Bibliothèques—la liste la plus unique et la plus complète des bibliothèques gouvernementales, spécialisées et publiques disponible.

Principales entreprises canadiennes—une liste des plus grandes sociétés privées, publiques et de la Couronne au Canada, y compris les coordonnées des principaux décideurs du monde des affaires.

DISPONIBILITÉ

Les listes sont offertes sur disque, étiquettes et par courriel. Elles sont fournies sur la base d'une utilisation unique ou d'un abonnement d'un an. Pour obtenir un devis pour une liste personnalisée selon vos besoins, contactez-nous.

Pour obtenir plus d'information, veuillez contacter Grey House Publishing Canada
par tél. : 1 866 433-4739 ou 416 644-6479 par téléc. : 416 644-1904 | info@greyhouse.ca | www.greyhouse.ca

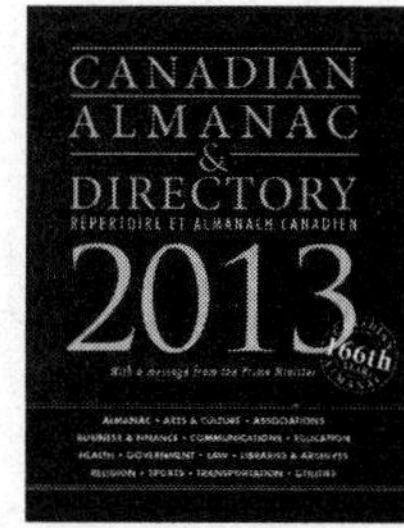

Canadian Almanac & Directory

Grey House Publishing Canada
555 Richmond Street West, Suite 301
Toronto, Ontario M5V 3B1

Fax completed forms to: (416) 644-1904

FREE LISTING & UPDATE
Be sure your organization appears in Canadian Almanac & Directory!

Canadian Almanac & Directory is a comprehensive, carefully updated directory of national information on major institutions, governments, associations, education, health, honours & awards, statistics & almanac data, published every year since 1847.

This listing is **FREE**. To ensure a complete and accurate listing in the upcoming edition, simply fill in the questionnaire and return it by **fax or by mail**. Include any relevant information such as phone, fax or toll free numbers, website and email addresses, and official translations (if applicable).

If you have any questions, please call Tannys Williams at (416) 644-6476 or 1-866-433-4739. You can return this form either by **FAX**: (416) 644-1904, by **mail** to the address above, or **email** info@greyhouse.ca.

Is your organization already listed in this publication? Yes, we're updating existing information______ No, we're new______

Completed by: ____________________Phone:______________Email:____________________

ORGANIZATION

Name: ____________________

Street Address: ____________________

Phone: ____________________

Toll Free: ____________________

Fax: ____________________

Email: ____________________

Website: ____________________

Translated Name: ____________________

Also known as: ____________________

Acronym: ____________________

Founded: ____________________

CHIEF OFFICERS/STAFF

President - ____________________

Secretary - ____________________

Treasurer - ____________________

Vice-President - ____________________

Other Staff: please see following page

Number of staff: ______________; Volunteers: ______________

OTHER STAFF: (attach list if necessary)

Name: ____________________ Title: ____________________
Telephone: ____________________ Email: ____________________

Name: ____________________ Title: ____________________
Telephone: ____________________ Email: ____________________

Name: ____________________ Title: ____________________
Telephone: ____________________ Email: ____________________

MEMBERSHIP

Member of: ____________________

Number of members: ____________________

Membership profile: ____________________

Membership fee: ____________________

ADDITIONAL INFORMATION

SUBJECT FOCUS:

i. ______ ii. ______
iii. ______ iv. ______

SCOPE OF ACTIVITY:

- ❑ International
- ❑ National
- ❑ Provincial/Territorial
- ❑ Local
- ❑ Regional

ORGANIZATION TYPE:

- ❑ Professional
- ❑ Trade/Industry/Business
- ❑ Other (special/common interest)

Please indicate if you are a: ❑ Licensing Body ❑ Registered Charity

MISSION STATEMENT/GOALS/MANDATE:

______

ANNUAL OPERATING BUDGET:

❑ Less than $50,000 ❑ $50,000 - $99,999 ❑ $100,000 - $249,999
❑ $250,000 - $499,999 ❑ $500,000 - $1,499,999 ❑ $1,500,000 - $2,999,999
❑ $3,000,000 - $4,999,999 ❑ Over $5,000,000

DO YOU:

Rent your Mailing Lists? ❑ Yes ❑ No
Have a Speakers Service? ❑ Yes ❑ No
Have an Internship Program? ❑ Yes ❑ No

SERIAL PUBLICATIONS:

Type: (eg. newsletter, journal, magazine) ______ Title: ______

Frequency: ______ Price: ______ Editor:: ______

ISBN: ______ ISSN: ______ Accept advertising? ❑ Yes ❑ No

Description of contents:

______

LIBRARY/RESOURCE CENTRE:

Does your organization have a library, resource centre or documentation centre? ❑ Yes ❑ No

Library/Resource/Documentation Centre Name: ______

Open to the Public: ❑ Yes ❑ No ❑ By Appointment Only

Library Contact Person: ______ Title: ______

Telephone: ______ Fax: ______ Email: ______

CONFERENCE/CONVENTIONS:

Please submit any literature pertaining to future conferences as it becomes available.

2012 2013 2014 2015

Name of Meeting: ______

Location: (City/Province/Country) ______

Facility: ______

Date: ______

Number of Attendees: ______

OTHER:

Awards: Please attach a list

Awareness Events (Please include the date): ______

Activities: ______

Committees: ______

Sources of funding: ______

WE THANK YOU FOR TAKING THE TIME TO PROVIDE YOUR VALUABLE INFORMATION.